VideoHound's® GOLDEN MOVIE RETRIEVER®

Jim Craddock, Editor

Detroit • New York • San Diego • San Francisco • Cleveland • New Haven, Conn. • Waterville, Maine • London • Munich

VideoHound®'s Golden Movie Retriever® 2003

Project Editor
Jim Craddock

Editorial
Carol Schwartz, Christine Tomassini

Editorial Support Services
Wayne Fong

Product Design
Cindy Baldwin

Manufacturing
Rita Wimberley

For more information, contact
The Gale Group, Inc.
27500 Drake Rd.
Farmington Hills, MI 48331-3535
Or you can visit our Internet site at
http://www.gale.com

Most VideoHound books are available at special quantity discounts when purchased in bulk by corporations, organizations, or groups. Customized printings, special imprints, messages, and excerpts can be produced to meet your needs.

For more information, contact:
Inez Torbert
Special Markets Manager,
The Gale Group, Inc.,
27500 Drake Rd.
Farmington Hills MI 48331-3535

ISBN 0-7876-5756-5
ISSN 1095-371X

Printed in the United States of America
10 9 8 7 6 5 4 3 2 1

VideoHound's® GOLDEN MOVIE RETRIEVER®

Also Available from Gale

VideoHound's DVD Guide
Mike Mayo. 730 pages. $19.95.
ISBN: 1-57859-115-5

VideoHound's DVD Guide: Book 2
Mike Mayo. 530 pages. $19.95.
ISBN: 0-7876-5757-3

VideoHound's DVD Guide: Book 3
Mike Mayo. 600 pages. $19.95.
ISBN: 0-7876-5753-3

Credits:
or Who Does What

Project Editor
Jim Craddock

Editorial
Carol Schwartz
Christine Tomassini

Editorial Support Services
Wayne Fong

Product Design
Cindy Baldwin

Manufacturing
Rita Wimberly

Also Starring:

The Big Giant Head:
Peter Gareffa

Review Crew
Martin Craddock
Scott Estes
Beth A. Fhaner
Jeff Hermann
Lynne Konstantin
Hilary White

Titles and Opticals:
Michael Boyd, ATLIS Publishing Services, Inc.

Queen of the Copyright Page:
Tracey Rowens

Makin' Copy:
PJ Butland

Licensing/Special Markets:
Inez Torbert

Contents

Introduction

Everything's been said already. Nothing I write about the post-September world is gonna be news to anyone. Nevertheless, I'm duty-bound to say something about the goings-on since we talked last, so here goes:

First the good news. History was made when Denzel Washington and Halle Berry won Best Actor and Best Actress (respectively) at the Academy Awards for their work in (again, respectively) *Training Day* and *Monster's Ball*, the first time that an African-American won for Best Actress, and the first ever African-American sweep of both awards in one year.

In other good news, Steven Soderbergh made another movie (*Ocean's 11*) and Kevin Costner (the director) didn't. Kevin, however, screwed up his perfect record for the year by starring in *Dragonfly*.

Hollywood, shocked and horrified, vowed to reassess and reprioritize, and some changes were evident, although most were not as long-lasting or far-reaching as had been predicted. At last report, he was still at large and reading scripts.

Other changes were afoot, mostly in the types of movies we watched. Big-bang action gave way to big-budget magic and escapism. Quieter, more intense, emotional, and eerily suspenseful movies, such as *The Others*, *The Man Who Wasn't There*, and *Panic Room* received attention as the din subsided. Filmmakers didn't seem to want to do the same old things, and moviegoers certainly didn't want to see them, anyway. But that seems to have been temporary. The summer movie season has brought the same flash, noise, star power, sequels, and hype we saw last year. If it hadn't, (as everyone seems fond of saying) the terrorists would have won.

Some changes lasted a little longer. The movie biz has seen the money flow slow a bit. Until *Spider-man* swung our way this spring, no one movie seemed to be able to hold the top boxoffice spot for more than one or two weeks at a time, and most of them turned in disappointing numbers. It had many people (prematurely) talking and writing about the end of the "Blockbuster Era." (And no, we aren't talking about the monolithic video store chain!) Spidey even managed to keep the *Star Wars* uber-franchise at bay. The long-awaited duo of *Harry Potter* and *Lord of the Rings* kept the till ringing, and stuck around awhile, but the staying power just wasn't there for the bevy of other short-lived money-making champs. But hey, you don't care how much dough the movies rake in, as long as your hard-earned video movie budget isn't wasted, right? Right.

Never fear, faithful readers! That's why we're here, and staying power is not a problem for us. We've been doing this for 12 years now and we don't know how to stop. And why would we want to? We like what we do, you like what we do (well, most of you anyway), judging by our mail, so we vow to keep at it. Remember, in dog years, we're 84. Where else outside of Gene Shalit's mustache are you gonna find that kind of experience?

Last year we pulled off the incredible feat of getting taller. The green was very slimming, don't you think? Well, this year we've been ravenously gobbling up information on new releases, and old movies that have (finally!) come out on VHS or (more likely) DVD. This, along with our usual appetite for goodies like expanded indexes and new categories, may show in the waistline this time around. We've added more than 70 new categories, some in an effort to break up larger categories into smaller, more digestible bits (Mmmmmm....bits), others because we had movies that fit categories we didn't have, and others because they amused us and we thought they might amuse you, too.

In the interest of fair play, we have decided that writers, composers, and cinematographers have as much right to have their age revealed as actors and directors do. And so, for your dining, dancing, and perusing pleasure, we have added birth and death (where applicable) dates to the Writer, Cinematographer, and Composer Indexes. What can I say? We're givers.

As always, we want to hear from you, but don't feel obligated or anything. Just because we work our fingers (paws?) to the bone for you. We know you have lives of your own, but if you can spare the time, here's how to reach us:

VideoHound's Golden Movie Retriever
27500 Drake Rd.
Farmington Hills, MI 48331-3535

or email at videohound@gale.com or
jim.craddock@gale.com

P.S. The capital of Nepal is Kathmandu.

Using VideoHound

Alphabetization

Titles are arranged on a word-by-word basis, including articles and prepositions. Leading articles (A, An, The) are ignored in English-language titles. The equivalent foreign articles are not ignored, however: *The Abyss* appears under 'A' while *Les Miserables* appears under 'L.' **Other points to keep in mind:**

- Acronyms appear alphabetically as if regular words. For example, *C.H.U.D.* is alphabetized as 'Chud'; *M*A*S*H* as 'Mash.'
- Common abbreviations in titles file as if they were spelled out, so *St. Elmo's Fire* will be found under 'Saint Elmo's Fire' and *Mr. Holland's Opus* will be alphabetized as 'Mister Holland's Opus.'
- Proper names in titles are alphabetized beginning with the individual's first name; for instance, *Monty Python's The Meaning of Life* is under 'M'; *Eddie Murphy: Raw* is under 'E.'
- Titles with numbers (*2001: A Space Odyssey*) are alphabetized as if the number were spelled out under the appropriate letter, in this case 'Two Thousand One.' When numeric titles gather in close proximity to each other (*2000 Year Old Man, 2001, 2069: A Sex Odyssey*), the titles will be arranged in a low (*2000*) to high (*2069*) numeric sequence.

Indexes

Alternate Title Index. A number of videos, particularly older or B-type releases, may have variant titles. Alternate titles are listed alphabetically and refer the reader to the title under which the entry is listed. The alternate titles are also noted within the review.

Category Index. Subject categories ranging from the orthodox to slightly eccentric permit you to video sleuth from broad type to significant themes to signature scenes. The mix, arranged alphabetically by category, includes hundreds of traditional film genres and sub-genres as well as a feast of *VideoHound* exclusives. Integrated into the index are cross references, while preceding the index is a list of definitions. **A tipped triangle (▶) indicates a movie rated three bones or above.**

Kibbles and Series Index. Not your everyday categories, Kibbles span the literary side of movie-making (Adapted from a Play, Books to Film: Ernest Hemingway) and point out key producers and special effects masters. Yearly box-office winners (that are now on video) since 1939 are listed, along with classic movies, four-bone delights, trash films, modern Shakespeare, Disney fare, significant on-screen and director/actor pairings.

The index formerly known as Series, now combined with the Kibbles, provides listings of major movie series, ranging from James Bond to National Lampoon to Indiana Jones. Recurring cinematic collaborations and partnerships of note are also listed, including Hope & Crosby, Abbott & Costello, De Niro & Scorsese, and Rafelson & Nicholson. A complete list of the categories precedes the index. **As in the Category Index, tipped triangles (▶) indicate quality views.**

Awards Index. The Awards Index lists almost 7,000 films honored by national and international award bodies, representing some 90 categories of competition. This information is also contained in the review following the credits. Nominations are once again (thanks to popular demand) included in this index. A star (★) denotes the winner. **Only features available on video and reviewed in the main section are listed in this index; movies not yet released on video are not covered.**

As award-winning and nominated films find their way to video, they will be added to the review section and covered in this index. Awards listed include the American Academy Awards; British Academy of Film and Television Arts; Canadian Genie; Golden Globe; Directors Guild of America; Independent Spirit; Screen Actors Guild; Writers Guild of America; and Golden Raspberries.

Cast/Director Indexes. The Cast Index provides full videographies for all actors and actresses listed in *VideoHound* with more than two movies on their resume. The Director Index lists the works of any director who has made it to video and to *VideoHound*. Although listed in a first name, last name sequence, the names are alphabetized by last name. Film titles, complete with initial year of release, are arranged in chronological order, starting with their most recent. A (V) designation after a film title indicates that the actor lent only vocal talents to that movie, as in animation features. An (N) depicts narration duties. **Birth and death dates (year only) have been added to the citations. While they are not yet complete, they will continue to be updated, with more added to every edition.**

Writer Index. Scriptwriters and script doctors are listed with their vital works. Names are arranged alphabetically by last name. Works are arranged chronologically.

Cinematographer Index. Directors of Photography are listed alphabetically by last name, along with their work, which is arranged chronologically.

Composer Index. Videographies of movie music composers, arrangers, lyricists, and so on are listed. Arranged alphabetically by last name.

The **Video Sources Guide** has changed slightly. Instead of attaching individual titles to specific distributors, *VideoHound* lists a number of mail order and independent video dealers where the videos can be obtained.

Web Site Guide. Lists Internet web sites for studios; general entertainment information; film festivals; and filmmaker resources; as well as sites for gossip, upcoming releases, and trivia.

Sample Review

Each *VideoHound* review contains up to 19 items, ranging from title, to the review, to cast listings, to awards received. The information in these reviews is designed to help you choose a video you'll like, increase your enjoyment of a movie as you watch (especially by answering that nagging question of "What else have I seen that guy in?"), and increase your knowledge of movie trivia.

1 Tainted 2 🦴🦴 **3** *Angry Young Vampires* **4 1998 5 (R) 6** Ever wonder what would happen if the guys from "Clerks" fell in with a bunch of vampires? Well, lucky you. Now you can find out. Video clerks Ryan and J.T. hitch a ride to the midnight movie with their new co-worker Alex, who just happens to be a vampire whose ex is shacking up with the new vamp in town, who wants to taint the city's blood supply with undead blood. Script has many laughs, lots of attitude, and plenty of pop-culture knowledge, but gets a bit windy at times. Sometimes the actors seem to be trying a little too hard, but it doesn't detract from the story. Filmed in Detroit with lots of excellent local product placement. 7 ♫Bottoms Up; Rats!; One More for the Road.

8&9 64m/C 10 VHS, DVD. 11 ***GB*** **12** Brian Evans, Sean Farley, Dusan "Dean" Cechvala, Greg James, Jason Brouwer, Tina Kapousis; **13** ***D:*** Brian Evans; **14** ***W:*** Sean Farley; **15** ***C:*** Brian Evans; **16** ***M:*** Jessie McClear. **17** ***Nar:*** Bela Lugosi. **18** Academy Awards '98: Best Adapted Screenplay; Independent Spirit Awards '99: Best First Feature; Writers Guild of America '98: Best Original Screenplay. **19 VIDEO**

1. Title
2. One- to four-bone rating (or *Woof!*)
3. Alternate Title (we made this up)
4. Year released
5. MPAA rating
6. Description/review
7. Songs (made these up, too)
8. Length (in minutes)
9. Black & White (B) or Color (C)
10. Format (VHS, DVD, CD-I, Widescreen, closed captioned, or 8mm)
11. Country of origin (made up)
12. Cast (***V:*** indicates voiceovers; also includes cameos)
13. Director
14. Writer(s)
15. Cinematographer(s)
16. Composer(s)/Lyricist(s)
17. Narrator (made up)
18. Awards (yet again, made up)
19. Made-for-Television/Cable/Video identification

The movie used in this sample is a real movie, it was filmed in Detroit, released by Troma, and is available from Thomas Video.

Alternate Titles Index

The **Alternate Titles Index** provides variant and foreign titles for movies with more than one name. Titles are listed in alphabetical order, followed by a cross-reference to the appropriate entry in the main video review section. If you don't find a movie you're looking for in the main section, this is the best place to look next.

A-009 Missione Hong Kong *See* Code Name Alpha (1967)

A Bout de Souffle *See* Breathless (1959)

Abar, the First Black Superman *See* In Your Face (1977)

Abbie *See* Steal This Movie! (2000)

Abbott and Costello in the Navy *See* In the Navy (1941)

Abbott and Costello Meet the Ghosts *See* Abbott and Costello Meet Frankenstein (1948)

Abbott and Costello Meet the Killer *See* Abbott and Costello Meet the Killer, Boris Karloff (1949)

ABC Murders *See* The Alphabet Murders (1965)

Abdullah's Harem *See* Abdulla the Great (1956)

Abismos de Pasion *See* Wuthering Heights (1953)

The Abominable Snowman of the Himalayas *See* The Abominable Snowman (1957)

Abraxas *See* Abraxas: Guardian of the Universe (1990)

Abre Los Ojos *See* Open Your Eyes (1997)

Abril Despedacado *See* Behind the Sun (2001)

Absent-Minded *See* The Daydreamer (1975)

Absinthe *See* Madame X (1966)

L'Accompagnatrice *See* The Accompanist (1993)

The Accused *See* The Mark of the Hawk (1957)

Ace *See* The Great Santini (1980)

Ace Ventura Goes to Africa *See* Ace Ventura: When Nature Calls (1995)

Acla *See* Acla's Descent into Floristella (1987)

Across Five Aprils *See* Civil War Diary (1990)

Act of Violence *See* Deadline Assault (1990)

Acts of Love *See* Carried Away (1995)

Adam Wants to Be a Man *See* Adomas Nori Buti Zmogumi (1959)

Addict *See* Born to Win (1971)

Addio, Fratello, Crudele *See* 'Tis a Pity She's a Whore (1973)

Adorable Idiot *See* Ravishing Idiot (1964)

Adorenarin Doraibu *See* Adrenaline Drive (1999)

The Adventure *See* L'Avventura (1960)

Adventure for Two *See* The Demi-Paradise (1943)

The Adventure of Lyle Swan *See* Timerider (1983)

The Adventurer *See* The Rover (1967)

Adventures at Rugby *See* Tom Brown's School Days (1940)

The Adventures of Chatran *See* The Adventures of Milo & Otis (1989)

The Adventures of Galgameth *See* Galgameth (1996)

The Adventures of Hercules *See* Hercules 2 (1985)

The Adventures of Jack London *See* Jack London (1944)

The Adventures of the Great Mouse Detective *See* The Great Mouse Detective (1986)

The Adventuress *See* I See a Dark Stranger (1946)

Aelita: The Revolt of the Robots *See* Aelita: Queen of Mars (1924)

Aerobicide *See* Killer Workout (1986)

An Affair of the Heart *See* Body and Soul (1947)

An Affair of the Heart *See* The Love Affair, or The Case of the Missing Switchboard Operator (1967)

Affairs of the Vampire *See* Curse of the Undead (1959)

AFO *See* Air Force One (1997)

African Fury *See* Cry, the Beloved Country (1951)

After Jenny Died *See* Revenge (1971)

Afula Express *See* Pick a Card (1997)

Afurika Monogatari *See* Green Horizon (1983)

Agaguk: Shadow of the Wolf *See* Shadow of the Wolf (1992)

Against All Enemies *See* The Siege (1998)

Against All Hope *See* One for the Road (1982)

Against All Odds *See* Kiss and Kill (1968)

Agatha Christie's Endless Night *See* Endless Night (1971)

Agatha Christie's Miss Marple: A Murder Is Announced *See* A Murder Is Announced (1987)

Agatha Christie's Miss Marple: A Pocketful of Rye *See* A Pocketful of Rye (1987)

Agatha Christie's Miss Marple: The Body In the Library *See* The Body in the Library (1987)

Agatha Christie's Ten Little Indians *See* Ten Little Indians (1989)

The Age of Beauty *See* Belle Epoque (1992)

Age of Gold *See* L'Age D'Or (1930)

Agent 38-24-36 *See* Ravishing Idiot (1964)

Agent Provocateur *See* Provocateur (1996)

L'Agente Federale Lemmy Caution *See* Your Turn Darling (1963)

The Agitators *See* The Fix (1984)

Agoniya *See* Rasputin (1985)

Agostino di Ippona *See* Augustine of Hippo (1972)

L'Agression *See* Act of Aggression (1973)

Aguirre, der Zorn Gottes *See* Aguirre, the Wrath of God (1972)

Ai No Borei *See* In the Realm of Passion (1980)

Ai No Corrida *See* In the Realm of the Senses (1976)

Aimez-Vous Brahms *See* Goodbye Again (1961)

Aiqing Wansui *See* Vive l'Amour (1994)

Airport '79 *See* The Concorde: Airport '79 (1979)

Akage *See* Red Lion (1969)

Akahige *See* Red Beard (1965)

Akasen Chitai *See* Street of Shame (1956)

Al Di La Della Legge *See* Beyond the Law (1968)

Al-Massir *See* Destiny (1997)

Al-Ris-Alah *See* The Message (1977)

Al 33 di Via Orologio fa Sempre Freddo *See* Shock (1979)

Alas de Mariposa *See* Butterfly Wings (1991)

Alem Da Paixao *See* Happily Ever After (1986)

Alfie Darling *See* Oh, Alfie (1975)

Alfred Hitchcock's Bon Voyage & Aventure Malgache *See* Alfred Hitchcock's Aventure Malgache (1944)

Alfred Hitchcock's Bon Voyage & Aventure Malgache *See* Alfred Hitchcock's Bon Voyage (1944)

Ali Baba et les Quarante Voleurs *See* Ali Baba and the 40 Thieves (1954)

Alias Bulldog Drummond *See* Bulldog Jack (1935)
Alice and Martin *See* Alice et Martin (1998)
Alicja *See* Alice (1986)
Alien 2 *See* Aliens (1986)
Alien P.I. *See* Alien Private Eye (1987)
Alien Terror *See* The Sinister Invasion (1968)
Alien Thunder *See* Dan Candy's Law (1973)
Alien Within *See* Evil Spawn (1987)
The Alien Within *See* Unknown Origin (1995)
Alien Women *See* Zeta One (1969)
The Alien's Return *See* The Return (1980)
Alistair MacLean's Death Train *See* Detonator (1993)
Alistair MacLean's Night Watch *See* Detonator 2: Night Watch (1995)
Alive by Night *See* Evil Spawn (1987)
All for Love *See* Robert Louis Stevenson's St. Ives (1998)
All for One *See* Return to Paradise (1998)
All Forgotten *See* Lover's Prayer (1999)
All Good Citizens *See* All My Good Countrymen (1968)
All in Place *See* All Screwed Up (1974)
All Monsters Attack *See* Destroy All Monsters (1968)
All Night Long *See* Toute Une Nuit (1982)
All Our Fault *See* Nothing Personal (1995)
All That Money Can Buy *See* The Devil & Daniel Webster (1941)
All the Mornings of the World *See* Tous les Matins du Monde (1992)
All the Rage *See* It's the Rage (1999)
All This and Glamour Too *See* Vogues of 1938 (1937)
All Weekend Lovers *See* The Killing Game (1967)
Alla vi barn i Bullerby *See* The Children of Noisy Village (1986)
The Alley of Miracles *See* Midaq Alley (1995)
Alley of Nightmares *See* She-Freak (1967)
Alligators *See* The Great Alligator (1981)
Almok a hazrol *See* 25 Fireman's Street (1973)
Almost Human *See* Shock Waves (1977)
Alone *See* Horton Foote's Alone (1997)
Alone Together *See* Crisscross (1992)
Alphaville, a Strange Case of Lemmy Caution *See* Alphaville (1965)
Alphaville, Une Etrange Aventure de Lemmy Caution *See* Alphaville (1965)
Alter Ego *See* Murder by the Book (1987)
The Alternate *See* Agent of Death (1999)
Amantes *See* Lovers: A True Story (1990)
Amanti d'Oltretomba *See* Nightmare Castle (1965)
Amateur Hour *See* I Was a Teenage TV Terrorist (1987)
Amator *See* Camera Buff (1979)
The Amazing Panda Rescue *See* The Amazing Panda Adventure (1995)
The Amazing Quest of Ernest Bliss *See* Amazing Adventure (1937)
Amazon: Savage Adventure *See* Cut and Run (1985)
Amazon Women *See* Gold of the Amazon Women (1979)
Amazonia: The Catherine Miles Story *See* White Slave (1986)

Ambush in Waco *See* In the Line of Duty: Ambush in Waco (1993)
Amelia and the King of Plants *See* Bed of Roses (1995)
Amelie from Montmartre *See* Amelie (2001)
American Beauty Hostages *See* She Devils in Chains (1976)
An American Daughter *See* Trial by Media (2000)
American Dragons *See* Double Edge (1997)
American Nightmares *See* Combat Shock (1984)
American Rickshaw *See* American Tiger (1989)
American Warrior *See* American Ninja (1985)
The American Way *See* Riders of the Storm (1988)
Amerikaner Shadkhn *See* American Matchmaker (1940)
L'Ami Americain *See* The American Friend (1977)
L'Ami de Mon Ami *See* Boyfriends & Girlfriends (1988)
Amigo/Amado *See* Beloved/Friend (1999)
Amityville 3-D *See* Amityville 3: The Demon (1983)
The Amityville Horror: The Evil Escapes, Part 4 *See* Amityville 4: The Evil Escapes (1989)
Amok *See* Schizo (1977)
Amor Perjudica Seriamente la Salud *See* Love Can Seriously Damage Your Health (1996)
Amore in Citta *See* Love in the City (1953)
The Amorous General *See* Waltz of the Toreadors (1962)
The Amorous Sex *See* Sweet Beat (1962)
Amour de Poche *See* Girl in His Pocket (1957)
L'Amour l'Apres-midi *See* Chloe in the Afternoon (1972)
Amy Fisher: My Story *See* Lethal Lolita—Amy Fisher: My Story (1992)
Amy Foster *See* Swept from the Sea (1997)
Anatomie *See* Anatomy (2000)
And Comes the Dawn...But Colored Red *See* Web of the Spider (1970)
And Life Goes On ... *See* Life and Nothing More ... (1992)
And Once Upon a Love *See* Fantasies (1973)
And Then There Were None *See* Ten Little Indians (1975)
And Woman...Was Created *See* And God Created Woman (1957)
And Your Mother Too *See* Y Tu Mama Tambien (2001)
An Andalusian Dog *See* Un Chien Andalou (1928)
Anders Als du und Ich *See* The Third Sex (1957)
Anderson's Angels *See* Chesty Anderson USN (1976)
Andrews' Raiders *See* The Great Locomotive Chase (1956)
Andy Colby's Incredibly Awesome Adventure *See* Andy and the Airwave Rangers (1989)
Andy Warhol's Flesh *See* Flesh (1968)
Andy Warhol's Heat *See* Heat (1972)
Andy Warhol's Young Dracula *See* Andy Warhol's Dracula (1974)
Angel *See* Danny Boy (1982)
Angel in Red *See* Uncaged (1991)
Angel of Vengeance *See* Ms. 45 (1981)
Angel of Vengeance *See* WarCat (1988)

An Angel Passed Over Brooklyn *See* The Man Who Wagged His Tail (1957)
Angel Sharks *See* Marie Baie des Anges (1997)
Angel Street *See* Gaslight (1940)
Angelos *See* Angel (1982)
Angels for Kicks *See* Wild Riders (1971)
Anglagard *See* House of Angels (1992)
Angst Essen Selle auf *See* Ali: Fear Eats the Soul (1974)
Animal House *See* National Lampoon's Animal House (1978)
Anita—Tanze des Lasters *See* Anita, Dances of Vice (1987)
Anne and Muriel *See* Two English Girls (1972)
Anne of Green Gables: The Sequel *See* Anne of Avonlea (1987)
Annie's Coming Out *See* A Test of Love (1984)
Anno Domini *See* A.D. (1985)
Ansikte mot Ansikte *See* Face to Face (1976)
The Anti-Extortion Woman *See* Minbo—Or the Gentle Art of Japanese Extortion (1992)
The Antichrist *See* The Tempter (1974)
L'Anticristo *See* The Tempter (1974)
Antinea, l'Amante Della Citta Sepolta *See* Journey Beneath the Desert (1961)
Anton der Zauberer *See* Anton, the Magician (1978)
The Anxious Years *See* Dark Journey (1937)
Anyone for Venice? *See* The Honey Pot (1967)
Anything for Love *See* 11 Harrowhouse (1974)
Apa *See* Father (1967)
The Apartment on the 13 Floor *See* Cannibal Man (1971)
Apocalipsis Canibal *See* Hell of the Living Dead (1983)
Apres l'Amour *See* Love After Love (1994)
April One *See* Stand Off (1993)
Apu Sansat *See* The World of Apu (1959)
Apur Sansar *See* The World of Apu (1959)
The Aqua Sex *See* The Mermaids of Tiburon (1962)
Aranyer Din Ratri *See* Days and Nights in the Forest (1970)
Arctic Heat *See* Born American (1986)
Are You Dying Young Man? *See* Beast in the Cellar (1970)
L'Argent de Poche *See* Small Change (1976)
Arizona Ripper *See* Terror at London Bridge (1985)
Armored Attack *See* The North Star (1943)
Armour of God *See* Operation Condor 2: The Armour of the Gods (1986)
Arms and the Woman *See* Mr. Winkle Goes to War (1944)
Army Mystery *See* Criminals Within (1941)
The Arrangement *See* Blood Money (1998)
Arthur the King *See* Merlin and the Sword (1985)
Ascenseur pour L'Echafaud *See* Frantic (1958)
Ascent to Heaven *See* Mexican Bus Ride (1951)
Ashani Sanket *See* Distant Thunder (1973)
Ashanti *See* Ashanti, Land of No Mercy (1979)
The Assassination Team *See* Wardogs (1987)

Assault Force *See* ffolkes (1980)
Assault on Devil's Island *See* Shadow Warriors (1997)
Assault on Paradise *See* Maniac (1977)
Assignment: Istanbul *See* The Castle of Fu Manchu (1968)
Assignment: Kill Castro *See* The Mercenaries (1980)
Assignment: Terror *See* Dracula vs. Frankenstein (1969)
The Astral Factor *See* The Invisible Strangler (1976)
Asylum Erotica *See* Slaughter Hotel (1971)
Asylum of the Insane *See* Flesh and Blood Show (1973)
At First Sight *See* Entre-Nous (1983)
At First Sight *See* Love at First Sight (1976)
At Sachem Farm *See* Uncorked (1998)
At the Villa Rose *See* House of Mystery (1941)
Atame! *See* Tie Me Up! Tie Me Down! (1990)
Atlantic City U.S.A. *See* Atlantic City (1981)
The Atlantis Interceptors *See* Raiders of Atlantis (1983)
Atlas Against the Cyclops *See* Atlas in the Land of the Cyclops (1961)
Atoll K *See* Utopia (1951)
Atomic Monster *See* Man Made Monster (1941)
Atomic Rocketship *See* Flash Gordon: Rocketship (1940)
Ator the Invincible *See* Blade Master (1984)
Atrapadas *See* Condemned to Hell (1984)
Attack of the 5 Ft. 2 Women *See* National Lampoon's Attack of the 5 Ft. 2 Women (1994)
Attack of the Giant Horny Gorilla *See* A*P*E* (1976)
Attack of the Killer Shrews *See* The Killer Shrews (1959)
Attack of the Monsters *See* Gamera vs. Guiron (1969)
Attack of the Normans *See* Conquest of the Normans (1962)
Attack of the Phantoms *See* KISS Meets the Phantom of the Park (1978)
Attack of the Rebel Girls *See* Assault of the Rebel Girls (1959)
Attention! Une Femme Peut en Cacher une Autre *See* My Other Husband (1985)
Au-Dela de la Peur *See* Beyond Fear (1975)
Au-Dela des Grilles *See* The Walls of Malapaga (1949)
L'Auberge Rouge *See* The Red Inn (1951)
Auf der Sonnenseite *See* On the Sunny Side (1962)
Auggie Rose *See* Beyond Suspicion (2000)
Aura *See* The Witch (1966)
Aurora by Night *See* Aurora (1984)
Austerlitz *See* The Battle of Austerlitz (1960)
Austria 1700 *See* Mark of the Devil (1969)
Autopsia de un Fantasma *See* Autopsy of a Ghost (1967)
The Avengers *See* The Day Will Dawn (1942)
Avenging Godfather *See* Avenging Disco Godfather (1976)
L'Aventure Sauvage *See* Trap (1966)
A.W.O.L. *See* Lionheart (1990)
An Axe for the Honeymoon *See* Hatchet for the Honeymoon (1970)

Az en XX. Szazadom *See* My Twentieth Century (1990)

Azucar Amarga *See* Bitter Sugar (1996)

Ba Xian Fan Dian Zhi Ren Rou Cha Shao Bao *See* The Untold Story (1993)

Baba Yaga *See* Kiss Me, Kill Me (1969)

Baba Yaga—Devil Witch *See* Kiss Me, Kill Me (1969)

Babe, the Gallant Pig *See* Babe (1995)

Babes Ahoy *See* Going Overboard (1989)

Babes in Toyland *See* March of the Wooden Soldiers (1934)

Babettes Gaestebud *See* Babette's Feast (1987)

Baby Blood *See* The Evil Within (1994)

Baby Cart 2 *See* Baby Cart at the River Styx (1972)

The Baby Vanishes *See* Broadway Limited (1941)

Bachelor Girl Apartment *See* Any Wednesday (1966)

Bachelor Knight *See* The Bachelor and the Bobby-Soxer (1947)

Back to Even *See* The Debt (1998)

Backwoods Massacre *See* Midnight (1981)

Bad Blood *See* Mauvais Sang (1986)

Bad Boyz *See* Valley Girl (1983)

Bad Girl *See* Teenage Bad Girl (1959)

Bad Girls *See* Delinquent School Girls (1984)

Bad Girls *See* Whore 2 (1994)

Bad Karma *See* Hell's Gate (2001)

Bad Man of Harlem *See* Harlem on the Prairie (1938)

Bad Seed *See* Mauvaise Graine (1933)

Badkonake Sefid *See* The White Balloon (1995)

The Bailiff *See* Sansho the Bailiff (1954)

Baisers Voles *See* Stolen Kisses (1968)

The Bait *See* L'Appat (1994)

The Baited Trap *See* The Trap (1959)

Bakushu *See* Early Summer (1951)

Ballada o Soldate *See* Ballad of a Soldier (1960)

Bamboo Dolls House *See* The Big Doll House (1971)

The Banana Monster *See* Schlock (1973)

Bande a Part *See* Band of Outsiders (1964)

The Bandit *See* Crossfire (1967)

Banditi a Orgosolo *See* Bandits of Orgosolo (1961)

Bang Bang *See* Bang Bang Kid (1967)

Bangiku *See* Late Chrysanthemums (1954)

The Bank Detective *See* The Bank Dick (1940)

Banner in the Sky *See* Third Man on the Mountain (1959)

The Bar Sinister *See* It's a Dog's Life (1955)

Barbados Quest *See* Murder on Approval (1956)

Barbarella, Queen of the Galaxy *See* Barbarella (1968)

The Barbarians and Co. *See* The Barbarians (1987)

The Barbaric Beast of Boggy Creek, Part II *See* Boggy Creek II (1983)

The Bare Breasted Contessa *See* Female Vampire (1973)

Bargain Basement *See* Department Store (1935)

Baron Blood *See* Torture Chamber of Baron Blood (1972)

Baron Munchausen *See* Fabulous Adventures of Baron Munchausen (1961)

Baron of Terror *See* The Brainiac (1961)

Baron Prasil *See* Fabulous Adventures of Baron Munchausen (1961)

Batman: The Animated Movie *See* Batman: Mask of the Phantasm (1993)

Batmen of Africa *See* Darkest Africa (1936)

Battle Beyond the Stars *See* The Green Slime (1968)

The Battle for Anzio *See* Anzio (1968)

Battle of the Astros *See* Godzilla vs. Monster Zero (1968)

The Battle of the Mareth Line *See* Battleforce (1978)

The Battle of the River Plate *See* Pursuit of the Graf Spee (1957)

Battle Stripe *See* The Men (1950)

Battletruck *See* Warlords of the 21st Century (1982)

The Battling Bellhop *See* Kid Galahad (1937)

Battling Hoofer *See* Something to Sing About (1936)

Bawang Bie Ji *See* Farewell My Concubine (1993)

Bay of Blood *See* Twitch of the Death Nerve (1971)

The Bay of Saint Michel *See* Pattern for Plunder (1962)

Bayou *See* Poor White Trash (1957)

Be Beautiful and Shut Up *See* Sois Belle et Tais-Toi (1958)

Be Beautiful but Shut Up *See* Just Another Pretty Face (1958)

Be Beautiful but Shut Up *See* Sois Belle et Tais-Toi (1958)

Be My Valentine, Or Else... *See* Hospital Massacre (1981)

Be Roringen *See* The Touch (1971)

The Beans of Egypt, Maine *See* Forbidden Choices (1994)

The Beast *See* Equinox (1971)

The Beast of War *See* The Beast (1988)

Beasts *See* Twilight People (1972)

The Beating of the Butterfly's Wings *See* Happenstance (2000)

Beatlemania *See* Beatlemania! The Movie (1981)

Beatsville *See* The Rebel Set (1959)

Beaumarchais L'Insolent *See* Beaumarchais the Scoundrel (1996)

Beautiful But Dangerous *See* She Couldn't Say No (1952)

Beautiful But Deadly *See* The Don Is Dead (1973)

A Beautiful Place to Kill *See* Paranoia (1969)

The Beautiful Troublemaker *See* La Belle Noiseuse (1990)

Beethoven's Great Love *See* Beethoven (1936)

Beggars' Opera *See* The Threepenny Opera (1931)

The Beginners *See* The First Time (1969)

The Beginners Three *See* The First Time (1969)

Behind Enemy Lines *See* The P.O.W. Escape (1986)

Behind Locked Doors *See* Human Gorilla (1948)

Behind the Blue *See* L'Enfant d'Eau (1995)

Behind the Forbidden City *See* East Palace, West Palace (1996)

Behind the Iron Mask *See* The Fifth Musketeer (1979)

Believe Me *See* Hollow Reed (1995)

Bells *See* Murder by Phone (1982)

The Beloved *See* Restless (1972)

Below Utopia *See* Body Count (1997)

Berry Gordy's The Last Dragon *See* The Last Dragon (1985)

The Best Way to Walk *See* The Best Way (1976)

Bethune, The Making of a Hero *See* Dr. Bethune (1990)

Betrayal *See* Trahir (1993)

Between Us *See* Entre-Nous (1983)

Betzilo Shel Helem Krav *See* Shell Shock (1963)

Beverly Hills Nightmare *See* Housewife (1972)

Bewitching Scatterbrain *See* Ravishing Idiot (1964)

Beyond Bedlam *See* Nightscare (1993)

Beyond Control *See* The Amy Fisher Story (1993)

Beyond Justice *See* Guardian Angel (1994)

Beyond Obsession *See* Beyond the Door (1975)

Beyond the Door 2 *See* Shock (1979)

Beyond the Fog *See* Tower of Evil (1972)

Beyond the Living *See* Hospital of Terror (1978)

Beyond the Living Dead *See* The Hanging Woman (1972)

Beyond the Rising Moon *See* Star Quest (1989)

Bez Konca *See* No End (1984)

Bez Znieczulenia *See* Without Anesthesia (1978)

Biandan, Guniang *See* So Close to Paradise (1998)

The Big Bang Theory *See* Bang (1995)

The Big Bankroll *See* The King of the Roaring '20s: The Story of Arnold Rothstein (1961)

The Big Boss *See* Fists of Fury (1973)

The Big Day *See* Jour de Fete (1948)

Big Deal at Dodge City *See* A Big Hand for the Little Lady (1966)

Big Duel in the North *See* Godzilla vs. the Sea Monster (1966)

Big Enough and Old Enough *See* Savages from Hell (1968)

The Big Grab *See* Any Number Can Win (1963)

The Big Heart *See* Miracle on 34th Street (1947)

The Big Lobby *See* Rosebud Beach Hotel (1985)

Big Monster on Campus *See* Boltneck (1998)

The Big One: The Great Los Angeles Earthquake *See* The Great Los Angeles Earthquake (1991)

The Big Payoff *See* Win, Place, or Steal (1972)

The Big Search *See* East of Kilimanjaro (1957)

Big Time Operators *See* The Smallest Show on Earth (1957)

Big Town Scandal *See* Underworld Scandal (1947)

The Biggest Fight on Earth *See* Ghidrah the Three Headed Monster (1965)

Biggles: Adventures in Time *See* Biggles (1985)

Bijo to Ekitainigen *See* H-Man (1959)

Bikini Genie *See* Wildest Dreams (1990)

Billy the Kid's Fighting Pals *See* Trigger Men (1941)

Billy the Kid's Law and Order *See* Law and Order (1942)

Billy the Kid's Range War *See* Texas Trouble (1941)

Bio-Force I *See* Mutant Species (1995)

The Bird with the Glass Feathers *See* The Bird with the Crystal Plumage (1970)

Birds of a Feather *See* The Birdcage (1995)

Birds of a Feather *See* La Cage aux Folles (1978)

Birds of Prey *See* Beaks: The Movie (1987)

Birthmark *See* The Omen (1976)

Birumano Tategoto *See* The Burmese Harp (1956)

Bis ans Ende der Welt *See* Until the End of the World (1991)

The Bitch *See* La Chienne (1931)

The Bitter End *See* Love Walked In (1997)

Bittere Ernte *See* Angry Harvest (1985)

Black Angels *See* Black Bikers from Hell (1970)

Black Arrow Strikes *See* Black Arrow (1948)

The Black Book *See* Reign of Terror (1949)

The Black Bounty Killer *See* Boss (1974)

The Black Buccaneer *See* The Black Pirate (1926)

Black Christmas *See* Black Sabbath (1964)

Black Dragon *See* Miracles (1989)

Black Eliminator *See* Kill Factor (1978)

Black Evil *See* Ganja and Hess (1973)

Black Flowers for the Bride *See* Something for Everyone (1970)

Black Forest: Rage in Space *See* Hyper Space (1989)

Black Frankenstein *See* Blackenstein (1973)

Black Gauntlet *See* Black Starlet (1974)

Black Jack *See* Captain Blackjack (1951)

Black Love, White Love *See* Sweet Love, Bitter (1967)

Black Out: The Moment of Terror *See* Ganja and Hess (1973)

Black Rage *See* Sunshine Run (1979)

Black Rider *See* Joshua (1976)

Black River *See* Dean Koontz's Black River (2001)

Black Rose of Harlem *See* Machine Gun Blues (1995)

Black Scorpion 2: Aftershock *See* Black Scorpion 2: Ground Zero (1996)

Black Valor *See* Savage! (1973)

Black Vampire *See* Ganja and Hess (1973)

The Black Velvet Gown *See* Catherine Cookson's The Black Velvet Gown (1992)

Black Vengeance *See* Poor Pretty Eddie (1973)

Black Werewolf *See* The Beast Must Die (1975)

Blackboard Massacre *See* Massacre at Central High (1976)

Blackout *See* Contraband (1940)

Blade of Steel *See* The Far Pavilions (1984)

Blair Witch 2 *See* Book of Shadows: Blair Witch 2 (2000)

Blake Edwards' Son of the Pink Panther *See* Son of the Pink Panther (1993)

Blast-Off *See* Those Fantastic Flying Fools (1967)

Blazing Arrows *See* Fighting Caravans (1931)

Blazing Magnums *See* Strange Shadows in an Empty Room (1976)

Bless 'Em All *See* The Act (1982)

Blind Alley *See* Perfect Strangers (1984)

The Blind Dead *See* Tombs of the Blind Dead (1972)

Blind Man's Bluff *See* Cauldron of Blood (1967)

Blind Terror *See* See No Evil (1971)

Blink of an Eye *See* Blink of an Eye (1992)

Blonde Bombshell *See* Bombshell (1933)

California Man *See* Encino Man (1992)

The Californian *See* The Gentleman from California (1937)

Call Harry Crown *See* 99 & 44/100 Dead (1974)

Call It Love *See* She's So Lovely (1997)

Call It Murder *See* Midnight (1934)

Call of the Savage *See* Savage Fury (1933)

The Call of the Wild: Dog of the Yukon *See* Jack London's The Call of the Wild (1997)

Call the Cops *See* Find the Lady (1975)

The Calling *See* Murder by Phone (1982)

Calling Northside 777 *See* Call Northside 777 (1948)

Campanadas a Medianoche *See* Chimes at Midnight (1967)

Camper John *See* Gentle Savage (1973)

Campsite Massacre *See* The Final Terror (1983)

A Candle for the Devil *See* It Happened at Nightmare Inn (1970)

Canicule *See* Dog Day (1983)

Cannibal Orgy, or the Maddest Story Ever Told *See* Spider Baby (1964)

Cannibals in the City *See* Cannibal Apocalypse (1980)

Cannibals in the Streets *See* Cannibal Apocalypse (1980)

Can't Be Heaven *See* Forever Together (2000)

Capitaine Morgan *See* Morgan the Pirate (1960)

Capitalismo Salvaje *See* Savage Capitalism (1993)

Captain Conan *See* Capitaine Conan (1996)

Captain Mephisto and the Transformation Machine *See* Manhunt of Mystery Island (1945)

Captain Midnight *See* On the Air Live with Captain Midnight (1979)

Captain Yankee *See* Jungle Raiders (1985)

Captive *See* Sex and the Other Man (1995)

Captive Women 3: Sweet Sugar *See* Sweet Sugar (1972)

Captured *See* Agent Red (2000)

Caravan *See* Himalaya (1999)

Caravans West *See* Wagon Wheels (1934)

The Card *See* The Promoter (1952)

Cardigan's Last Case *See* State's Attorney (1931)

Care of the Spitfire Grill *See* The Spitfire Grill (1995)

Caricies *See* Caresses (1997)

Carlo Collodi's Pinocchio *See* The Adventures of Pinocchio (1996)

Carnage *See* Twitch of the Death Nerve (1971)

Carne per Frankenstein *See* Andy Warhol's Frankenstein (1974)

Carne Tremula *See* Live Flesh (1997)

Carnival of Fools *See* Death Wish Club (1983)

Carnival of Thieves *See* Caper of the Golden Bulls (1967)

Carquake *See* Cannonball (1976)

Carrie 2 *See* The Rage: Carrie 2 (1999)

Carry On Follow That Camel *See* Follow That Camel (1967)

Carry On 'Round the Bend *See* Carry On at Your Convenience (1971)

The Cars That Eat People *See* The Cars That Ate Paris (1974)

Cartagine in Fiamme *See* Carthage in Flames (1960)

Cartas del Parque *See* Letters from the Park (1988)

Carter's Army *See* Black Brigade (1969)

Cartes sur Table *See* Attack of the Robots (1966)

Carthage en Flammes *See* Carthage in Flames (1960)

The Case of Jonathan Drew *See* The Lodger (1926)

The Case of the Hillside Stranglers *See* The Hillside Strangler (1989)

Case of the Missing Switchboard Operator *See* The Love Affair, or The Case of the Missing Switchboard Operator (1967)

Cash *See* If I Were Rich (1933)

Cassanova and Co. *See* Sex on the Run (1978)

Castle in the Sky *See* Yidl Mitn Fidl (1936)

Castle of Doom *See* Vampyr (1931)

Castle of Dracula *See* Blood of Dracula's Castle (1969)

Castle of Terror *See* Castle of Blood (1964)

Castle of Terror *See* The Virgin of Nuremberg (1965)

The Castle of the Spider's Web *See* Throne of Blood (1957)

Castle of the Walking Dead *See* The Torture Chamber of Dr. Sadism (1969)

The Cat *See* Le Chat (1975)

The Cat Ate the Parakeet *See* Pot, Parents, and Police (1971)

Cat Murkil and the Silks *See* Cruisin' High (1975)

C.A.T. Squad *See* Stalking Danger (1986)

C.A.T. Squad: Python Wolf *See* Python Wolf (1988)

Catacombs *See* Curse 4: The Ultimate Sacrifice (1990)

Catastrophe 1999 *See* Last Days of Planet Earth (1974)

Catch Me If You Can *See* Deadly Game (1998)

Catchfire *See* Backtrack (1989)

Catholic Boys *See* Heaven Help Us (1985)

Cathy Tippel *See* Katie Tippel (1975)

Cats *See* Night of a Thousand Cats (1972)

Cauchemares *See* Cathy's Curse (1977)

Caught in the Act *See* Cosi (1995)

Cavalleria Commandos *See* Cavalry Command (1963)

The Cave Dwellers *See* One Million B.C. (1940)

Cave Man *See* One Million B.C. (1940)

Cavegirl *See* Cave Girl (1985)

Cell Block Girls *See* Women's Prison Escape (1974)

Celos *See* Jealousy (1999)

Cemetery Girls *See* The Vampire Hookers (1978)

Cemetery Girls *See* The Velvet Vampire (1971)

Cento Dollari D'Odio *See* Uncle Tom's Cabin (1969)

Central Do Brasil *See* Central Station (1998)

Ceremonia Sangrienta *See* The Legend of Blood Castle (1972)

A Certain Mr. Scratch *See* The Devil & Daniel Webster (1941)

Ces Dames Preferent le Mambo *See* Dishonorable Discharge (1957)

C'est Arrive pres de Chez Vous *See* Man Bites Dog (1991)

Cet Obscur Objet du Desir *See* That Obscure Object of Desire (1977)

Ceux Qui M'Aiment Predront le Train *See* Those Who Love Me Can Take the Train (1998)

Chacun Cherche Son Chat *See* When the Cat's Away (1996)

Chained Heat 3 *See* Chained Heat 3: Hell Mountain (1998)

Chained Heat 3: The Horror of Hell Mountain *See* Chained Heat 3: Hell Mountain (1998)

Chaingang Girls *See* Sweet Sugar (1972)

The Challenge *See* It Takes a Thief (1959)

Chamber of Fear *See* The Fear Chamber (1968)

Chamber of Tortures *See* Torture Chamber of Baron Blood (1972)

The Chambermaid *See* The Chambermaid on the Titanic (1997)

Champ d'Honneur *See* Field of Honor (1987)

Changes *See* Danielle Steel's Changes (1991)

Chaos *See* Kaos (1985)

Charades *See* First Degree (1998)

Charles: Mort ou Vif *See* Charles: Dead or Alive (1969)

Charlie's Ghost Story *See* Charlie's Ghost: The Secret of Coronado (1994)

Charterhouse at Parma *See* La Chartreuse de Parme (1948)

Chastnaya Zhizn *See* Private Life (1982)

The Chautauqua *See* The Trouble with Girls (and How to Get into It) (1969)

Che? *See* Diary of Forbidden Dreams (1973)

Cheaters *See* Tricheurs (1984)

Cheeseburger Film Sandwich *See* Amazon Women on the Moon (1987)

Chelovek s Kinoapparatom *See* The Man with the Movie Camera (1929)

Chernobyl: The Final Warning *See* Final Warning (1990)

Cherry Pink *See* Just Looking (1999)

Cheun Gwong Tsa Sit *See* Happy Together (1996)

Cheung Fo *See* The Mission (1999)

Chevy Van *See* The Van (1977)

Chi Sei *See* Beyond the Door (1975)

The Chief Wants No Survivors *See* No Survivors, Please (1963)

Chikamatsu Monogatari *See* The Crucified Lovers (1954)

Chiklo Gouyeung *See* Naked Killer (1992)

Chikyu Boelgun *See* The Mysterians (1958)

Child of Satan *See* To the Devil, a Daughter (1976)

Child of the Night *See* What the Peeper Saw (1972)

Childish Things *See* Confessions of Tom Harris (1972)

The Children of Bullerby Village *See* The Children of Noisy Village (1986)

Children of the Dust *See* A Good Day to Die (1995)

China 9, Liberty 37 *See* Gunfire (1978)

China Ranch *See* Shell Shock (1963)

Chinchero *See* The Last Movie (1971)

Chine, Ma Douleur *See* China, My Sorrow (1989)

Chongqing Senlin *See* Chungking Express (1995)

A Christmas Memory *See* ABC Stage 67: Truman Capote's A Christmas Memory (1966)

Christmas Miracle in Caulfield, U.S.A. *See* The Christmas Coal Mine Miracle (1977)

The Christmas Tree *See* When Wolves Cry (1969)

Christmas Vacation *See* National Lampoon's Christmas Vacation (1989)

Chrome Hearts *See* C.C. & Company (1970)

Chronicle of a Lonely Child *See* Chronicle of a Boy Alone (1964)

Chronos *See* Cronos (1994)

Chuck Norris vs. the Karate Cop *See* Slaughter in San Francisco (1981)

Chungon Satluk Linggei *See* Organized Crime & Triad Bureau (1993)

Ciao! Manhattan *See* Edie in Ciao! Manhattan (1972)

Cica Tomina Koliba *See* Uncle Tom's Cabin (1969)

The Cinder Path *See* Catherine Cookson's The Cinder Path (1994)

The Circle *See* The Vicious Circle (1957)

The Circle *See* Woman in Brown (1948)

Circuitry Man 2 *See* Plughead Rewired: Circuitry Man 2 (1994)

Citadel of Crime *See* Wheel of Fortune (1941)

Citizen's Band *See* FM (1978)

City in Fear *See* A Place Called Today (1972)

The City Jungle *See* The Young Philadelphians (1959)

The City of the Dead *See* Horror Hotel (1960)

City of the Living Dead *See* Gates of Hell (1980)

The Clairvoyant *See* The Evil Mind (1934)

The Clairvoyant *See* Killing Hour (1984)

The Clansman *See* The Birth of a Nation (1915)

Class of '86 *See* National Lampoon's Class of '86 (1986)

Class Reunion *See* National Lampoon's Class Reunion (1982)

Claude *See* The Two of Us (1968)

Claude et Greta *See* Her and She and Him (1969)

Claudine's Return *See* Kiss of Fire (1998)

Clean Slate *See* Coup de Torchon (1981)

The Cleaner *See* The Professional (1994)

Cleo de 5 a 7 *See* Cleo from 5 to 7 (1961)

Clickety Clack *See* Dodes 'ka-den (1970)

Clinton & Nadine *See* Blood Money: The Story of Clinton and Nadine (1988)

Clive Barker's Lord of Illusions *See* Lord of Illusions (1995)

The Cloak *See* The Overcoat (1959)

The Closer You Get *See* American Women (2000)

The Closest of Kin *See* All the Lovin' Kinfolk (1970)

Club Dead *See* Terror at Red Wolf Inn (1972)

Coast of Terror *See* Summer City (1977)

Coastwatcher *See* The Last Warrior (1989)

Cobra Nero *See* The Black Cobra (1987)

Cobweb Castle *See* Throne of Blood (1957)

Code Name: Operation Crossbow *See* Operation Crossbow (1965)

Code Name: Trixie *See* The Crazies (1973)

Code Name: Wolverine *See* Wolverine (1996)

Code 645 *See* G-Men Never Forget (1948)

Codename: The Soldier *See* The Soldier (1982)

Coffin of Terror *See* Castle of Blood (1964)

Colin Nutley's House of Angels *See* House of Angels (1992)

Collision Course *See* The Bamboo Saucer (1968)

Colonel Blimp *See* The Life and Death of Colonel Blimp (1943)

Colorado Ranger *See* Guns of Justice (1950)

Colossus and the Amazons *See* Colossus and the Amazon Queen (1964)

Colour Blind *See* Catherine Cookson's Colour Blind (1998)

Come Back to Me *See* Doll Face (1946)

Come Dance with Me *See* Voulez-Vous Danser avec Moi? (1959)

Come 'n' Get It *See* Lunch Wagon (1981)

Come On Ranger *See* Come on Rangers (1938)

A Comedia de Deus *See* God's Comedy (1995)

Comizi d'Amore *See* Love Meetings (1964)

Comment le Desir Vient aux Filles *See* I Am Frigid...Why? (1972)

Communion *See* Alice Sweet Alice (1976)

Como Agua para Chocolate *See* Like Water for Chocolate (1993)

Como Era Gostoso O Meu Frances *See* How Tasty Was My Little Frenchman (1971)

Como ser Mujer y No Morir en El *See* How to Be a Woman and Not Die in the Attempt (1991)

The Company of Strangers *See* Strangers in Good Company (1991)

Complicity *See* Retribution (1998)

Computer Killers *See* Horror Hospital (1973)

Comrades *See* The Organizer (1964)

Comradeship *See* Kameradschaft (1931)

The Con Man *See* The Con Artists (1980)

Concerto *See* I've Always Loved You (1946)

A Condemned Man Has Escaped *See* A Man Escaped (1957)

Confesion a Laura *See* Confessing to Laura (1990)

Confession *See* Repentance (1987)

The Confession *See* Quick, Let's Get Married (1971)

Confessions of A Peeping John *See* Hi, Mom! (1970)

Confessions of a Prostitute *See* The Immoral One (1980)

Confidential Report *See* Mr. Arkadin (1955)

Conflagration *See* Enjo (1958)

The Conflict *See* Catholics (1973)

Conqueror of the Desert *See* The Conqueror (1956)

The Conquests of Peter the Great *See* Peter the First: Part 2 (1938)

The Conspiracy *See* Le Complot (1973)

Contamination *See* Alien Contamination (1981)

Conte d'Automne *See* Autumn Tale (1998)

Conte d'Ete *See* A Summer's Tale (1996)

Conte D'Hiver *See* A Tale of Winter (1992)

Continuavamo A Chiamarlo Trinita *See* Trinity Is Still My Name (1975)

Contra el Viento *See* Against the Wind (1990)

Convention City *See* Sons of the Desert (1933)

The Cook in Love *See* A Chef in Love (1996)

Coonskin *See* Streetfight (1975)

A Cop for the Killing *See* In the Line of Duty: A Cop for the Killing (1990)

Cop Killers *See* Corrupt (1984)

Cop Tips Waitress $2 Million *See* It Could Happen to You (1994)

Copenhagen's Psychic Loves *See* The Psychic (1968)

Cord *See* Hide and Seek (2000)

A Corps Perdu *See* Straight for the Heart (1988)

The Corpse *See* Crucible of Horror (1969)

A Corpse Hangs in the Web *See* Horrors of Spider Island (1959)

Cosi Dolce...Cosi Perversa *See* Kiss Me, Kill Me (1969)

The Cosmic Man Appears in Tokyo *See* Warning from Space (1956)

Cosmo 2000: Planet Without a Name *See* Cosmos: War of the Planets (1980)

Count Dracula and His Vampire Bride *See* The Satanic Rites of Dracula (1973)

Count Dracula's Great Love *See* Dracula's Great Love (1972)

Country Music *See* Las Vegas Hillbillys (1966)

Country Music Daughter *See* Nashville Girl (1976)

Coup de Foudre *See* Entre-Nous (1983)

Coup de Tete *See* Hothead (1978)

Courage *See* Raw Courage (1984)

The Courage of Kavik, the Wolf Dog *See* Kavik the Wolf Dog (1984)

The Courier *See* Outta Time (2001)

Court Martial *See* Carrington, V.C. (1954)

Courtesan *See* Dangerous Beauty (1998)

The Courtneys of Curzon Street *See* The Courtney Affair (1947)

Covek Nije Tica *See* Man Is Not a Bird (1965)

Cows *See* Vacas (1991)

Coyote Moon *See* Desert Heat (1999)

Crack *See* Strike Force (1975)

Crackerjack 2: Hostage Train *See* Crackerjack 2 (1997)

Cradle of Crime *See* Dead End (1937)

Crash of Silence *See* Mandy (1953)

The Crawling Monster *See* Creeping Terror (1964)

Crazy for You *See* Vision Quest (1985)

Crazy Horse *See* Friends, Lovers & Lunatics (1989)

Crazy House *See* Night of the Laughing Dead (1975)

Crazy Jack and the Boy *See* Silence (1973)

Crazy Joe *See* Dead Center (1994)

Crazy Streets *See* Forever, Lulu (1987)

Crazy World *See* Mondo Cane 2 (1964)

Created to Kill *See* Embryo (1976)

Creature from Galaxy 27 *See* Night of the Blood Beast (1958)

The Creature Wasn't Nice *See* Spaceship (1981)

Creatures *See* From Beyond the Grave (1973)

Creatures of the Devil *See* Dead Men Walk (1943)

Creatures of the Prehistoric Planet *See* Horror of the Blood Monsters (1970)

Creatures of the Red Planet *See* Horror of the Blood Monsters (1970)

The Creature's Revenge *See* Brain of Blood (1971)

The Creeper *See* Dark Side of Midnight (1986)

The Creeper *See* Rituals (1979)

Creepers *See* They Live (1988)

The Creepers *See* Assault (1970)

The Creepers *See* Island of Terror (1966)

The Creeping Unknown *See* The Quatermass Experiment (1956)

Creeps *See* Bloody Birthday (1980)

Creeps *See* Night of the Creeps (1986)

Cria Cuervos *See* Cria (1976)

The Cricket *See* La Cicada (1983)

Crime and Punishment *See* Dostoevsky's Crime and Punishment (1999)

Crime Boss *See* New Mafia Boss (1972)

Crime et Chatiment *See* Crime and Punishment (1935)

Crimes in the Wax Museum *See* Nightmare in Wax (1969)

Crimes, Inc. *See* Gangs, Inc. (1941)

The Crimes of Dr. Mabuse *See* Testament of Dr. Mabuse (1962)

The Criminal *See* The Concrete Jungle (1982)

The Crimson Altar *See* The Crimson Cult (1968)

Crimson Executioner *See* The Bloody Pit of Horror (1965)

The Crimson Ghost *See* Cyclotrode "X" (1946)

Cristo si e fermato a Eboli *See* Christ Stopped at Eboli (1979)

Crocodile *See* Blood Surf (2000)

Cronica de un Nino Solo *See* Chronicle of a Boy Alone (1964)

Crooks in Clover *See* Penthouse (1933)

Crossed Swords *See* The Prince and the Pauper (1978)

Crossing the Line *See* The Big Man: Crossing the Line (1991)

The Crown Caper *See* The Thomas Crown Affair (1968)

Cruel Swamp *See* Swamp Women (1955)

The Cry *See* Il Grido (1957)

Crying Out Loud *See* Cotton Queen (1937)

Crypt of Dark Secrets *See* Mardi Gras Massacre (1978)

Crypt of the Blind Dead *See* Tombs of the Blind Dead (1972)

C.S. Lewis Through the Shadowlands *See* Shadowlands (1985)

Csillagosok, Katonak *See* The Red and the White (1968)

C't'a Ton Tour, Laura Cadieux *See* It's My Turn, Laura Cadieux (1998)

Cuba Crossing *See* The Mercenaries (1980)

Cuban Rebel Girls *See* Assault of the Rebel Girls (1959)

Cult of the Dead *See* The Snake People (1968)

Cumbres Borrascosas *See* Wuthering Heights (1953)

Cupid in the Rough *See* Aggie Appleby, Maker of Men (1933)

Curley and His Gang in the Haunted Mansion *See* Who Killed Doc Robbin? (1948)

Curse of Dark Shadows *See* Night of Dark Shadows (1971)

The Curse of Demon Mountain *See* Shadow of Chikara (1977)

The Curse of Dr. Phibes *See* The Abominable Dr. Phibes (1971)

The Curse of Dracula *See* Return of Dracula (1958)

The Curse of Green Eyes *See* Cave of the Living Dead (1965)

Curse of Melissa *See* The Touch of Satan (1970)

Curse of the Blood-Ghouls *See* The Slaughter of the Vampires (1962)

Curse of the Crimson Altar *See* The Crimson Cult (1968)

The Curse of the Dragon *See* Bruce Lee: Curse of the Dragon (1993)

Curse of the Living Dead *See* Kill, Baby, Kill (1966)

Curse of the Mushroom People *See* Attack of the Mushroom People (1963)

Curses of the Ghouls *See* The Slaughter of the Vampires (1962)

The Cusp *See* Falling Fire (1997)

Cutter and Bone *See* Cutter's Way (1981)

Cybele *See* Sundays & Cybele (1962)

Cyber-Chic *See* Robo-Chic (1989)

Cyberjack *See* Virtual Assassin (1995)

Cyborg 2: Glass Shadow *See* Cyborg 2 (1993)

Cyborg Cop 2 *See* Cyborg Soldier (1994)

Czlowiek z Zelaza *See* Man of Iron (1981)

Da Bancarella a Bancarotta *See* Peddlin' in Society (1947)

Da Zdravstvuyet Meksika *See* Que Viva Mexico (1932)

Daddy *See* Danielle Steel's Daddy (1991)

Daddy Nostalgie *See* Daddy Nostalgia (1990)

Daddy's Deadly Darling *See* Pigs (1973)

Dad's Week Off *See* National Lampoon's Dad's Week Off (1997)

Dagboek Van Een Oude Dwaas *See* Diary of a Mad Old Man (1988)

Dagora *See* Dagora, the Space Monster (1965)

Dai Koesu Yongkari *See* Yongkari Monster of the Deep (1967)

Daibosatsu Toge *See* Sword of Doom (1967)

Daikaiju Baran *See* Varan the Unbelievable (1961)

Daikaiju Gamera *See* Gamera, the Invincible (1966)

Daikaiju Masura *See* Mothra (1962)

Daikyoju Gappa *See* Gappa the Trifibian Monster (1967)

Dairy Queens *See* Drop Dead Gorgeous (1999)

Dakhtaran-e Khorshid *See* Daughters of the Sun (2000)

Dalle Ardenne All'Inferno *See* Dirty Heroes (1971)

Dance Academy *See* Body Beat (1988)

Dance of the Dwarfs *See* Jungle Heat (1984)

Dance of the Vampires *See* The Fearless Vampire Killers (1967)

Dancer *See* Billy Elliot (2000)

Dancing about Architecture *See* Playing by Heart (1998)

Dandelion *See* Tampopo (1986)

Danger Rides the Range *See* Three Texas Steers (1939)

Dangerous Charter *See* Creeping Terror (1964)

Dangerous Female *See* The Maltese Falcon (1931)

A Dangerous Friend *See* The Todd Killings (1971)

Dangerous Kiss *See* True Crime (1995)

Dangerous Love Affairs *See* Dangerous Liaisons (1960)

Danny Travis *See* The Last Word (1980)

Dans la Ville Blanche *See* In the White City (1983)

Dans les Griffes du Maniaque *See* The Diabolical Dr. Z (1965)

Danza Macabra *See* Castle of Blood (1964)

Daoma Zei *See* The Horse Thief (1987)

Dario Argento's Phantom of the Opera *See* The Phantom of the Opera (1998)

Dark Angel *See* I Come in Peace (1990)

The Dark Avenger *See* The Warriors (1955)

Dark Empire *See* Dark City (1997)

Dark Eyes *See* Demon Rage (1982)

Dark Eyes of London *See* Dead Eyes of London (1961)

Dark Eyes of London *See* The Human Monster (1939)

Dark Prince: Intimate Tales of Marquis de Sade *See* Marquis de Sade (1996)

Diabolik *See* Danger: Diabolik (1968)

Diaboliquement Votre *See* Diabolically Yours (1967)

Dial 999 *See* The Way Out (1956)

Dial Rat for Terror *See* Housewife (1972)

Diamond Alley *See* Little Ladies of the Night (1977)

Diamond Earrings *See* The Earrings of Madame De... (1954)

Diamond Skulls *See* Dark Obsession (1990)

Diamond Thieves *See* The Squeeze (1978)

Diamonds and Crime *See* Hi Diddle Diddle (1943)

Dian Zhi Gong Fu Gan Chian Chan *See* Half a Loaf of Kung Fu (1985)

Diario Segreto Di Un Carcere Femminele *See* Women in Cell Block 7 (1977)

Diary of Oharu *See* Life of Oharu (1952)

Dias Contados *See* Running Out of Time (1994)

Dick Tracy Meets Karloff *See* Dick Tracy Meets Gruesome (1947)

Dick Tracy's Amazing Adventure *See* Dick Tracy Meets Gruesome (1947)

Die Abenteuer des Werner Holt *See* The Adventures of Werner Holt (1965)

Die Angst Tormannes beim Elfmeter *See* The Goalie's Anxiety at the Penalty Kick (1971)

Die, Beautiful Marianne *See* Die Screaming, Marianne (1973)

Die Bitteren Traenen der Petra von Kant *See* The Bitter Tears of Petra von Kant (1972)

Die Blechtrommel *See* The Tin Drum (1979)

Die Bleierne Zeit *See* Marianne and Juliane (1982)

Die Brucke *See* The Bridge (1959)

Die Buechse der Pandora *See* Pandora's Box (1928)

Die Dreigroschenoper *See* The Three Penny Opera (1962)

Die Dreigroschenoper *See* The Threepenny Opera (1931)

Die Ehe Der Maria Braun *See* The Marriage of Maria Braun (1979)

Die Erotische Geschichten *See* Tales of Erotica (1993)

Die Flambierte Frau *See* A Woman in Flames (1984)

Die Folterkammer des Dr. Fu Manchu *See* The Castle of Fu Manchu (1968)

Die Freudlosse Gasse *See* Joyless Street (1925)

Die Geschwister Oppermann *See* The Oppermann Family (1982)

Die Hard 3 *See* Die Hard: With a Vengeance (1995)

Die Holle von Macao *See* The Corrupt Ones (1967)

Die Holle von Manitoba *See* A Place Called Glory (1966)

Die Legende von Paul und Paula *See* The Legend of Paul and Paula (1973)

Die Letzte Brucke *See* The Last Bridge (1954)

Die Lustigen Weiber von Windsor *See* The Merry Wives of Windsor (1950)

Die Marquise Von O *See* The Marquise of O (1976)

Die Morder Sind Unter Uns *See* The Murderers Are Among Us (1946)

Die Morder sind Unter Uns *See* The Murderers are Among Us (1946)

Die Nibelungen *See* Kriemhilde's Revenge (1924)

Die Regenschirme von Cherbourg *See* Umbrellas of Cherbourg (1964)

Die Saege des Todes *See* Bloody Moon (1983)

Die Schachnovelle *See* Brainwashed (1960)

Die Schlangengrube und das Pendel *See* The Torture Chamber of Dr. Sadism (1969)

Die Sehns Ucht Der Veronika Voss *See* Veronika Voss (1982)

Die Siebtelbauern *See* The Inheritors (1998)

Die Stille Nach Dem Schuss *See* The Legend of Rita (1999)

Die Tausend Augen des Dr. Mabuse *See* The Thousand Eyes of Dr. Mabuse (1960)

Die Toten Augen von London *See* Dead Eyes of London (1961)

Die Unsichtbaren Krallen des Dr. Mabuse *See* The Invisible Dr. Mabuse (1962)

Die Verlorene Ehre Der Katharina Blum *See* The Lost Honor of Katharina Blum (1975)

Die Vierde Man *See* The 4th Man (1979)

Die Weisse Rose *See* The White Rose (1983)

Die Xue Jie Tou *See* A Bullet in the Head (1990)

Die Xue Shuang Xiong *See* The Killer (1990)

Die Zartlichkeit der Wolfe *See* Tenderness of the Wolves (1973)

Die Zwolfte Stunde *See* Nosferatu (1922)

The Digital Prophet *See* Cyberstalker (1996)

Dillinger 70 *See* Carbon Copy (1969)

Dimensions in Death *See* Castle of Blood (1964)

Dio Mio, Come Sono Caduta in Basso *See* Till Marriage Do Us Part (1974)

A Dirty Knight's Work *See* Choice of Weapons (1976)

Dirty Mary *See* A Very Curious Girl (1969)

Dirty, Mean and Nasty *See* Down & Dirty (1976)

The Disappearance of Nora *See* High Stakes (1993)

Disaster at Valdez *See* Dead Ahead: The Exxon Valdez Disaster (1992)

Disciple of Dracula *See* Dracula, Prince of Darkness (1966)

Disco Godfather *See* Avenging Disco Godfather (1976)

The Discreet *See* La Discrete (1990)

Disney's Blank Check *See* Blank Check (1993)

Dispara *See* Outrage (1993)

Disparen a Matar *See* Shoot to Kill (1990)

Distant Cousins *See* Desperate Motives (1992)

Dites-Lui Que Je L'Aime *See* This Sweet Sickness (1977)

Divertimento *See* La Belle Noiseuse (1990)

Divine Obsession *See* Dangerous Obsession (1988)

Divorzio All'Italiana *See* Divorce—Italian Style (1962)

Django 2: Il Grande Ritorno *See* Django Strikes Again (1987)

Django Spara per Primo *See* Django Shoots First (1974)

Djavulens Oga *See* The Devil's Eye (1960)

Djoflaeyjan *See* Devil's Island (1996)

Do Not Disturb *See* Silent Witness (1999)

Do You Want to Dance with Me? *See* Voulez-Vous Danser avec Moi? (1959)

The Dock Brief *See* Trial & Error (1962)

Docteur Chance *See* Doctor Chance (1997)

Docteur M. *See* Club Extinction (1989)

Docteur Popaul *See* High Heels (1972)

Doctor Beware *See* Teresa Venerdi (1941)

Dr. Black and Mr. White *See* Dr. Black, Mr. Hyde (1976)

Doctor Blood Bath *See* Horror Hospital (1973)

The Doctor from Seven Dials *See* Corridors of Blood (1958)

Doctor Gore *See* The Body Shop (1972)

Dr. Jekyll vs. the Werewolf *See* Dr. Jekyll and the Wolfman (1971)

Dr. Jekyll y el Hombre Lobo *See* Dr. Jekyll and the Wolfman (1971)

Dr. Jekyll's Dungeon of Darkness *See* Dr. Tarr's Torture Dungeon (1975)

Dr. Mabuse, Parts 1 & 2 *See* Dr. Mabuse, The Gambler (1922)

Dr. Maniac *See* The Man Who Lived Again (1936)

Doctor Maniac *See* House of the Living Dead (1973)

Dr. Orloff's Invisible Monster *See* Orloff and the Invisible Man (1970)

Dr. Phibes *See* The Abominable Dr. Phibes (1971)

Dr. Terror's Gallery of Horrors *See* Alien Massacre (1967)

Doctors Wear Scarlet *See* The Bloodsuckers (1970)

A Dog, a Mouse, and a Sputnik *See* Sputnik (1961)

Dog Soldiers *See* Who'll Stop the Rain? (1978)

Dogboys *See* Tracked (1998)

A Dog's Life *See* Mondo Cane (1963)

Dogwater *See* Since You've Been Gone (1997)

Doin' It *See* The First Time (1969)

Doin' It *See* First Time (1982)

Doing Life *See* Truth or Die (1986)

Doing Time *See* Porridge (1991)

Doktor Mabuse der Spieler *See* Dr. Mabuse, The Gambler (1922)

Dolwyn *See* The Last Days of Dolwyn (1949)

Dom Za Vesanje *See* Time of the Gypsies (1990)

Domicile Conjugal *See* Bed and Board (1970)

The Domino Killings *See* The Domino Principle (1977)

Don Juan *See* Private Life of Don Juan (1934)

Don Juan 73 *See* Don Juan (Or If Don Juan Were a Woman) (1973)

Don Juan, Mi Querido Fantasma *See* Don Juan, My Love (1990)

Don Kikhot *See* Don Quixote (1957)

Dona Flor e Seus Dois Maridos *See* Dona Flor and Her Two Husbands (1978)

Dona Herlinda y Su Hijo *See* Dona Herlinda & Her Son (1986)

Donato and Daughter *See* Dead to Rights (1993)

Dong Fang San Xia *See* The Heroic Trio (1993)

Donggong, Xigong *See* East Palace, West Palace (1996)

The Don's Analyst *See* National Lampoon's The Don's Analyst (1997)

Don't Look Now, We've Been Shot At *See* La Grande Vadrouille (1966)

Donzoko *See* The Lower Depths (1957)

Doomed *See* Ikiru (1952)

The Doomsday Machine *See* Escape from Planet Earth (1967)

The Door with Seven Locks *See* Chamber of Horrors (1940)

Dope Addict *See* Reefer Madness (1938)

Doped Youth *See* Reefer Madness (1938)

Doppelganger *See* Journey to the Far Side of the Sun (1969)

Dos Veces Judas *See* Twice a Judas (1969)

The Double *See* Kagemusha (1980)

Double Down *See* Stacy's Knights (1983)

Double Hit *See* The Arab Conspiracy (1976)

Double Possession *See* Ganja and Hess (1973)

Double Trouble *See* No Deposit, No Return (1976)

Douce Violence *See* Sweet Ecstasy (1962)

Doulos—The Finger Man *See* Le Doulos (1961)

Down Went McGinty *See* The Great McGinty (1940)

Dracula *See* Bram Stoker's Dracula (1992)

Dracula *See* The Horror of Dracula (1958)

Dracula and the Seven Golden Vampires *See* The Legend of the 7 Golden Vampires (1973)

Dracula Cerca Sangue di Vergine e...Mori de Sete *See* Andy Warhol's Dracula (1974)

Dracula Contra Frankenstein *See* Dracula vs. Frankenstein (1971)

Dracula in the Castle of Blood *See* Web of the Spider (1970)

Dracula Is Dead and Well and Living in London *See* The Satanic Rites of Dracula (1973)

Dracula Pere et Fils *See* Dracula & Son (1976)

Dracula Pere et Fils *See* Dracula Father and Son (1976)

Dracula Saga *See* The Saga of the Draculas (1972)

Dracula 71 *See* Count Dracula (1971)

Dracula: The Bloodline Continues... *See* The Saga of the Draculas (1972)

Dracula: The Love Story *See* To Die For (1989)

Dracula, the Terror of the Living Dead *See* The Hanging Woman (1972)

Dracula Today *See* Dracula A.D. 1972 (1972)

Dracula vs. Frankenstein *See* The Screaming Dead (1972)

Dracula Vuole Vivere: Cerca Sangue de Vergina *See* Andy Warhol's Dracula (1974)

Dracula's Castle *See* Blood of Dracula's Castle (1969)

Dracula's Dog *See* Zoltan...Hound of Dracula (1978)

Dracula's Virgin Lovers *See* Dracula's Great Love (1972)

The Dragon and the Cobra *See* Fist of Fear, Touch of Death (1980)

Dragon Chow *See* Drachenfutter (1987)

Dragon Forever *See* Dragons Forever (1988)

Dragon Lady *See* G.I. Executioner (1971)

Dragonfly *See* One Summer Love (1976)

Dragon's Food *See* Drachenfutter (1987)

Drawing Blood *See* Sergio Lapel's Drawing Blood (1999)

Draws *See* American Tickler (1976)

The Dreaded Persuasion *See* The Narcotics Story (1958)

Dream Slayer *See* Blood Song (1982)

Dreams *See* Akira Kurosawa's Dreams (1990)

Dreamworld *See* Covergirl (1983)

Dripping Deep Red *See* Deep Red: Hatchet Murders (1975)

Drivers to Hell *See* Wild Ones on Wheels (1962)

Droid Gunner *See* Cyberzone (1995)

Every Home Should Have One *See* Think Dirty (1970)

Every Man For Himself *See* The Ruthless Four (1970)

Every Woman's Man *See* The Prizefighter and the Lady (1933)

Everybody Loves Sunshine *See* B.U.S.T.E.D. (1999)

Everybody's Cheering *See* Take Me Out to the Ball Game (1949)

Evil Angels *See* A Cry in the Dark (1988)

Evil Dead 3 *See* Army of Darkness (1992)

Evil Eden *See* Death in the Garden (1956)

The Evil Eye *See* The Girl Who Knew Too Much (1963)

Evil in the Swamp *See* All the Kind Strangers (1974)

Evil Woman *See* Saving Silverman (2001)

The Evils of Dorian Gray *See* Dorian Gray (1970)

Ewiger Walzer *See* The Eternal Waltz (1954)

Except for Me and Thee *See* Friendly Persuasion (1956)

Exorcismo *See* Exorcism (1974)

Expedition Moon *See* Rocketship X-M (1950)

Exploring the Kinsey Report *See* One Plus One (1961)

Expose *See* Footsteps (1998)

Expose *See* The House on Straw Hill (1976)

Exquisite Tenderness *See* The Surgeon (1994)

Extase *See* Ecstasy (1933)

Extenuating Circumstances *See* Circonstances Attenuantes (1936)

Extreme Close-Up *See* Sex Through a Window (1972)

An Eye for an Eye *See* Psychopath (1973)

An Eye for an Eye *See* Talion (1966)

Eyes of Hell *See* The Mask (1961)

Eyes without a Face *See* The Horror Chamber of Dr. Faustus (1959)

Fabula de la Bella Palomera *See* The Fable of the Beautiful Pigeon Fancier (1988)

The Fabulous Baron Munchausen *See* Fabulous Adventures of Baron Munchausen (1961)

The Fabulous Baron Munchausen *See* The Original Fabulous Adventures of Baron Munchausen (1961)

The Fabulous Destiny of Amelie Poulain *See* Amelie (2001)

Face of a Stranger *See* The Promise (1979)

Face of Fear *See* Peeping Tom (1960)

Face the Music *See* Black Glove (1954)

The Faceless Monsters *See* Nightmare Castle (1965)

Fag Hag *See* Okoge (1993)

Fair Trade *See* Skeleton Coast (1989)

Fairytales *See* Fairy Tales (1976)

Fakebook *See* American Blue Note (1989)

Falcon's Gold *See* Robbers of the Sacred Mountain (1983)

Fall Break *See* The Mutilator (1985)

The Fall Guy *See* What's Up Front (1963)

The Fall of the House of Usher *See* The House of Usher (1988)

The Fall of the House of Usher *See* La Chute de la Maison Usher (1928)

Fallen Knight *See* The Minion (1998)

Falltime *See* Fall Time (1994)

False Face *See* Scalpel (1976)

False Faces *See* Let 'Em Have It (1935)

Falstaff *See* Chimes at Midnight (1967)

The Familiar Stranger *See* My Husband's Double Life (2001)

Family Resemblances *See* Un Air de Famille (1996)

Fanatic *See* Die! Die! My Darling! (1965)

Fanfan the Tulip *See* Fanfan la Tulipe (1951)

Fangelse *See* Devil's Wanton (1949)

Fanny by Gaslight *See* Man of Evil (1948)

Fanny Och Alexander *See* Fanny and Alexander (1983)

Fan's Video *See* Otaku No Video (1991)

The Fantastic Disappearing Man *See* Return of Dracula (1958)

The Far Country *See* Nevil Shute's The Far Country (1985)

Farewell, Friend *See* Honor Among Thieves (1968)

Farewell, My Love *See* Murder, My Sweet (1944)

Farinelli Il Castrato *See* Farinelli (1994)

Farinelli the Castrato *See* Farinelli (1994)

The Farm *See* The Curse (1987)

Farm Girl *See* The Farmer's Other Daughter (1965)

Farm of the Year *See* Miles from Home (1988)

The Farmhouse *See* Eye of the Storm (1998)

Fashion House of Death *See* Blood and Black Lace (1964)

Fashions *See* Fashions of 1934 (1934)

Fast Fortune *See* 11 Harrowhouse (1974)

Fatal Affair *See* Stalker (1998)

Fatal Assassin *See* African Rage (1978)

Fatal Woman *See* Femme Fatale (1990)

The Father *See* Baba (1973)

Father & Son: Dangerous Relations *See* Dangerous Relations (1993)

Father Brown *See* The Detective (1954)

Father Damien: The Leper Priest *See* Damien: The Leper Priest (1980)

Father Goose *See* Fly Away Home (1996)

The Father Kino Story *See* Mission to Glory (1980)

Father Master *See* Padre Padrone (1977)

Father, Son and the Mistress *See* For Richer, for Poorer (1992)

Faust-Eine deutsche Volkssage *See* Faust (1926)

Faustrecht der Freiheit *See* Fox and His Friends (1975)

The FBI Murders *See* In the Line of Duty: The FBI Murders (1988)

Fear *See* Night Creature (1979)

The Fear *See* Gates of Hell (1980)

Fear 2 *See* The Fear: Halloween Night (1999)

Fear Eats the Soul *See* Ali: Fear Eats the Soul (1974)

Fear in the City of the Living Dead *See* Gates of Hell (1980)

Fear in the Night *See* Dynasty of Fear (1972)

Fear: Resurrection *See* The Fear: Halloween Night (1999)

Fearless Little Soldier *See* Fanfan la Tulipe (1951)

Feast of Flesh *See* Blood Feast (1963)

Federico Fellini's 8 1/2 *See* 8 1/2 (1963)

Federico Fellini's Intervista *See* Intervista (1987)

Feel the Heat *See* Catch the Heat (1987)

Felons *See* First Degree (1998)

Female *See* The Violent Years (1956)

The Female Butcher *See* The Legend of Blood Castle (1972)

Female Fiend *See* Theatre of Death (1967)

Femmine Infernali *See* Escape from Hell (1989)

Feng Yue *See* Temptress Moon (1996)

Fengriffen *See* And Now the Screaming Starts (1973)

Festen *See* The Celebration (1998)

A Few Days in the Life of I.I. Oblomov *See* Oblomov (1981)

The Fiend with the Atomic Brain *See* Blood of Ghastly Horror (1972)

The Fiend with the Electronic Brain *See* Blood of Ghastly Horror (1972)

Fiendish Ghouls *See* The Flesh and the Fiends (1960)

Fierce *See* Fighting Mad (1977)

The Fifteen Streets *See* Catherine Cookson's The Fifteen Streets (1990)

The Fifth Chair *See* It's in the Bag (1945)

The Fifth Season *See* Profile for Murder (1996)

50 Violins *See* Music of the Heart (1999)

Figaros Hochzeit *See* The Marriage of Figaro (1949)

The Fighting Phantom *See* The Mysterious Rider (1933)

The Fighting Pimpernel *See* The Elusive Pimpernel (1950)

The Fighting Seventh *See* Little Big Horn (1951)

A Film about Love *See* Love Film (1970)

Film d'Amore et d'Anarchia *See* Love and Anarchy (1973)

Filofax *See* Taking Care of Business (1990)

Fin Aout Debut Septembre *See* Late August, Early September (1998)

The Final Conflict *See* Omen 3: The Final Conflict (1981)

The Final Crash *See* Steelyard Blues (1973)

Finally, Sunday *See* Confidentially Yours (1983)

Fine and Dandy *See* The West Point Story (1950)

Fine Things *See* Danielle Steel's Fine Things (1990)

Fire Festival *See* Himatsuri (1985)

Fire in Eden *See* Tusks (1989)

Fire on the Mountain *See* Volcano: Fire on the Mountain (1997)

The First and the Last *See* 21 Days (1937)

The First Great Train Robbery *See* The Great Train Robbery (1979)

The First Hello *See* High Country (1981)

The First of the Few *See* Spitfire (1942)

The First Rebel *See* Allegheny Uprising (1939)

First Strike *See* Jackie Chan's First Strike (1996)

The First Time *See* The Fighter (1952)

First Woman into Space *See* Space Monster (1964)

A Fist Full of Chopsticks *See* They Call Me Bruce? (1982)

Fist of Fear *See* Fist of Fear, Touch of Death (1980)

Fist of Fury *See* Chinese Connection (1973)

Fist Right of Freedom *See* Fox and His Friends (1975)

Five Angles on Murder *See* The Woman in Question (1950)

The Five at the Funeral *See* House of Terror (1987)

Five Bloody Days to Tombstone *See* Gun Riders (1969)

Five Bloody Graves *See* Gun Riders (1969)

The Five Day Lover *See* Time Out for Love (1961)

Five Days *See* Paid to Kill (1954)

Five Minutes to Live *See* Door to Door Maniac (1961)

Five Women Around Utamaro *See* Utamaro and His Five Women (1946)

Fixing the Shadow *See* Beyond the Law (1992)

The Flame of Torment *See* Enjo (1958)

Flanagan *See* Walls of Glass (1985)

Flash Gordon's Trip to Mars *See* Flash Gordon: Mars Attacks the World (1939)

Flatbed Annie *See* Flatbed Annie and Sweetiepie: Lady Truckers (1979)

The Flesh Creatures *See* Horror of the Blood Monsters (1970)

Flesh Creatures of the Red Planet *See* Horror of the Blood Monsters (1970)

Flesh for Frankenstein *See* Andy Warhol's Frankenstein (1974)

The Flight *See* The Taking of Flight 847: The Uli Derickson Story (1988)

Flight from Fear *See* Justice (1955)

Flight of the Dove *See* The Spy Within (1994)

The Flight of the White Stallions *See* The Miracle of the White Stallions (1963)

Flip Out *See* Get Crazy (1983)

Flipper and the Pirates *See* Flipper's New Adventure (1964)

Floating Weeds *See* Drifting Weeds (1959)

Flood *See* Hard Rain (1997)

Flower of the Arabian Nights *See* Arabian Nights (1974)

Flying Aces *See* The Flying Deuces (1939)

The Flying Dutchman *See* Frozen in Fear (2000)

Flying Wild *See* Fly Away Home (1996)

Fog *See* A Study in Terror (1966)

Folies Bourgeoises *See* Twist (1976)

The Folks at Red Wolf Inn *See* Terror at Red Wolf Inn (1972)

Follow That Bird *See* Sesame Street Presents: Follow That Bird (1985)

Follow the Hunter *See* Fangs of the Wild (1954)

Follow Your Dreams *See* Independence Day (1983)

Fontane Effi Briest *See* Effi Briest (1974)

For a Few Bullets More *See* Any Gun Can Play (1967)

For Better or For Worse *See* Honeymoon Academy (1990)

For Love or Money *See* If I Were Rich (1933)

For Men Only *See* Tall Lie (1953)

For We Too Do Not Forgive *See* Death Is Called Engelchen (1963)

Forbidden Alliance *See* The Barretts of Wimpole Street (1934)

Forbidden Love *See* Freaks (1932)

Forbidden Paradise *See* Hurricane (1979)

Forbidden Passions *See* The Sensuous Teenager (1970)

Forbidden Son *See* Bulldance (1988)

The Forbin Project *See* Colossus: The Forbin Project (1970)

Forbrydelsens Element *See* The Element of Crime (1984)

Ford Fairlane *See* The Adventures of Ford Fairlane (1990)

The Forest Primeval *See* The Final Terror (1983)

Forgotten Prisoners: The Amnesty Files *See* Forgotten Prisoners (1990)

Gnaw: Food of the Gods 2 *See* Food of the Gods: Part 2 (1988)

A Gnome Named Gnorm *See* The Adventures of a Gnome Named Gnorm (1993)

Go and See *See* Come and See (1985)

The Goat *See* La Chevre (1981)

The Goddess *See* Devi (1960)

God's Gift *See* Wend Kuuni (1982)

Godzilla Fights the Giant Moth *See* Godzilla vs. Mothra (1964)

Godzilla Versus the Bionic Monster *See* Godzilla vs. the Cosmic Monster (1974)

Godzilla vs. Gigan *See* Godzilla on Monster Island (1972)

Godzilla vs. Hedora *See* Godzilla vs. the Smog Monster (1972)

Godzilla vs. Mechagodzilla *See* Godzilla vs. the Cosmic Monster (1974)

Godzilla vs. the Giant Moth *See* Godzilla vs. Mothra (1964)

Godzilla vs. the Thing *See* Godzilla vs. Mothra (1964)

Godzilla's Counter Attack *See* Godzilla Raids Again (1959)

Going Ape *See* Where's Poppa? (1970)

Going West in America *See* Switchback (1997)

Gojira *See* Godzilla, King of the Monsters (1956)

Gojira no Musuko *See* Son of Godzilla (1966)

Gojira tai Biorante *See* Godzilla vs. Biollante (1989)

Gojira Tai Hedora *See* Godzilla vs. the Smog Monster (1972)

Gojira tai Megaro *See* Godzilla vs. Megalon (1976)

Gojira Tai Meka-Gojira *See* Godzilla vs. the Cosmic Monster (1974)

Goke, Body Snatcher from Hell *See* Body Snatcher from Hell (1969)

Goke the Vampire *See* Body Snatcher from Hell (1969)

Gokiburi *See* Twilight of the Cockroaches (1990)

Gold Coast *See* Elmore Leonard's Gold Coast (1997)

The Golden Age *See* L'Age D'Or (1930)

Golden Hands of Kurigal *See* Federal Agents vs. Underworld, Inc. (1949)

The Golden Heist *See* Inside Out (1975)

The Golden Hour *See* Pot o' Gold (1941)

Golden Ivory *See* White Huntress (1957)

Golden Marie *See* Casque d'Or (1952)

The Golden Trail *See* Riders of the Whistling Skull (1937)

Golden Virgin *See* The Story of Esther Costello (1957)

Golden Years *See* Stephen King's Golden Years (1991)

Goliat Contra Los Gigantes *See* Goliath Against the Giants (1963)

Goliath and the Giants *See* Goliath Against the Giants (1963)

Goliath and the Golden City *See* Samson and the 7 Miracles of the World (1962)

Goliath Contro I Giganti *See* Goliath Against the Giants (1963)

Goliathon *See* The Mighty Peking Man (1977)

Golpes a Mi Puerta *See* Knocks at My Door (1993)

Gomar the Human Gorilla *See* Night of the Bloody Apes (1968)

The Good Girls *See* Les Bonnes Femmes (1960)

Good Luck, Miss Wyckoff *See* The Shaming (1971)

A Good Marriage *See* Le Beau Mariage (1982)

Good Morning Babilonia *See* Good Morning, Babylon (1987)

Good to Go *See* Short Fuse (1988)

Goodbye Bruce Lee: His Last Game of Death *See* Game of Death (1979)

Goodbye, Children *See* Au Revoir les Enfants (1987)

Goodbye Gemini *See* Twinsanity (1970)

Goodbye to the Hill *See* Paddy (1970)

Gordon il Pirata Nero *See* The Black Pirate (1926)

Gorilla *See* Nabonga (1944)

Gosta Berling's Saga *See* The Atonement of Gosta Berling (1924)

Gotter der Pest *See* Gods of the Plague (1969)

Gouttes d'Eau sur Pierres Brulantes *See* Water Drops on Burning Rocks (1999)

Grace Under Pressure *See* Something to Talk About (1995)

The Grail *See* Lancelot of the Lake (1974)

Gran Amore del Conde Dracula *See* Dracula's Great Love (1972)

The Grand Highway *See* Le Grand Chemin (1987)

The Grand Maneuvers *See* Les Grandes Manoeuvres (1955)

Grandmother's House *See* Grandma's House (1988)

The Grass is Singing *See* Killing Heat (1984)

The Grasshopper *See* The Passing of Evil (1970)

Grave Desires *See* Brides of the Beast (1968)

Grave Robbers from Outer Space *See* Plan 9 from Outer Space (1956)

The Graveside Story *See* The Comedy of Terrors (1964)

Graveyard Tramps *See* Invasion of the Bee Girls (1973)

The Great Adventure *See* The Adventurers (1951)

The Great Balloon Adventure *See* Olly Olly Oxen Free (1978)

The Great Day *See* A Special Day (1977)

Great Freedom No. 7 *See* Die Grosse Freiheit Nr. 7 (1945)

The Great Georgia Bank Hoax *See* Great Bank Hoax (1978)

The Great Hope *See* Submarine Attack (1954)

The Great Lester Boggs *See* Hootch Country Boys (1975)

The Great Manhunt *See* The Doolins of Oklahoma (1949)

Great Moments in Aviation *See* Shades of Fear (1993)

The Great Monster War *See* Godzilla vs. Monster Zero (1968)

Great Monster Yongkari *See* Yongkari Monster of the Deep (1967)

The Great Schnozzle *See* Palooka (1934)

The Great Spy Mission *See* Operation Crossbow (1965)

The Great Wall is a Great Wall *See* A Great Wall (1986)

The Greatest Battle *See* Battleforce (1978)

The Greatest Battle on Earth *See* Ghidrah the Three Headed Monster (1965)

The Greatest Love *See* Europa '51 (1952)

The Greeks Had a Word for Them *See* Three Broadway Girls (1932)

The Green Carnation *See* The Trials of Oscar Wilde (1960)

Green Monkey *See* Blue Monkey (1987)

The Green Ray *See* Summer (1986)

The Greenhouse *See* The Green House (1996)

Greta the Mad Butcher *See* Ilsa, the Wicked Warden (1978)

Grey Matter *See* Mind Warp (1972)

Greystoke 2: Tarzan and Jane *See* Tarzan and the Lost City (1998)

Gridlock *See* Great American Traffic Jam (1980)

Grijpstra and de Gier *See* Fatal Error (1983)

Grimm Brothers' Snow White *See* Snow White: A Tale of Terror (1997)

The Grinch *See* Dr. Seuss' How the Grinch Stole Christmas (2000)

Grine Felder *See* Green Fields (1937)

Gringo *See* Gun Fight at Red Sands (1963)

The Grip of the Strangler *See* The Haunted Strangler (1958)

The Grip of the Vampire *See* Curse of the Undead (1959)

Gritos en la Noche *See* The Awful Dr. Orloff (1962)

The Groove Room *See* A Man with a Maid (1973)

The Grotesque *See* Grave Indiscretions (1996)

Gruner Felder *See* Green Fields (1937)

Gruppo di Famiglia in un Interno *See* Conversation Piece (1975)

Guardian of the Wilderness *See* Mountain Man (1977)

Guilty Assignment *See* Big Town (1947)

Guizi Laile *See* Devils on the Doorstep (2000)

Gun Man from Bodie *See* Gunman from Bodie (1941)

Gun Moll *See* Get Rita (1975)

Gun Moll *See* Jigsaw (1949)

Guney's The Wall *See* The Wall (1983)

Gunpoint *See* At Gunpoint (1955)

Guns in the Afternoon *See* Ride the High Country (1962)

Guns, Sin and Bathtub Gin *See* Lady in Red (1979)

Gwendoline *See* The Perils of Gwendoline (1984)

Gycklarnas Afton *See* Sawdust & Tinsel (1953)

Haakon Haakonsen *See* Shipwrecked (1990)

Hab Og Karlighed *See* Twist & Shout (1984)

Habricha el Hashemesh *See* Escape to the Sun (1972)

Hachigatsu no Kyoshikyoku *See* Rhapsody in August (1991)

Hacks *See* Sink or Swim (1997)

Hadaka No Shima *See* The Island (1961)

Hadduta Misriya *See* An Egyptian Story (1982)

Hail to the Chief *See* Hail (1973)

Hairshirt *See* Too Smooth (1998)

The Hairy Bird *See* All I Wanna Do (1998)

Haishang Hua *See* Flowers of Shanghai (1998)

Hak Hap *See* Black Mask (1996)

Half Slave, Half Free 2 *See* Charlotte Forten's Mission: Experiment in Freedom (1985)

Hallelujah, I'm a Tramp *See* Hallelujah, I'm a Bum (1933)

Halloween 7 *See* Halloween: H20 (1998)

Halloween: H20 (Twenty Years Later) *See* Halloween: H20 (1998)

Halloween: The Origin of Michael Myers *See* Halloween 6: The Curse of Michael Myers (1995)

Hallucination Generation *See* Hallucination (1967)

Ham Ham *See* Jamon, Jamon (1993)

Hamam: Il Bagno Turco *See* Steam: A Turkish Bath (1996)

Ha'Matarah Tiran *See* Sinai Commandos (1968)

The Hammond Mystery *See* The Undying Monster (1942)

Hana-Bi *See* Fireworks (1997)

Hand of Night *See* Beast of Morocco (1966)

Handgun *See* Deep in the Heart (1983)

Handle With Care *See* Citizens Band (1977)

Hands of a Killer *See* Planets Against Us (1961)

Hands of a Strangler *See* The Hands of Orlac (1960)

The Hands of Orlac *See* Mad Love (1935)

Hands of the Strangler *See* The Hands of Orlac (1960)

Hands Off the Loot *See* Grisbi (1953)

Handsome Antonio *See* Il Bell'Antonio (1960)

Handsome Serge *See* Le Beau Serge (1958)

The Hangover *See* The Female Jungle (1956)

Hans Christian Andersen's Thumbelina *See* Thumbelina (1994)

Hao xia *See* Last Hurrah for Chivalry (1978)

Happiness *See* Le Bonheur (1965)

Happiness *See* Le Bonheur Est Dans le Pre (1995)

Happiness Is In the Fields *See* Le Bonheur Est Dans le Pre (1995)

Happy Go Lucky *See* Hallelujah, I'm a Bum (1933)

Happy Mother's Day, Love, George *See* Run, Stranger, Run (1973)

The Happy New Year Caper *See* Happy New Year (1973)

Happy Times *See* The Inspector General (1949)

Hard Driver *See* The Last American Hero (1973)

Hard Stick *See* A Real American Hero (1978)

Hard Times for Vampires *See* Uncle Was a Vampire (1959)

Hard to Die *See* Crime Story (1993)

Hard Way Out *See* Bloodfist 8: Hard Way Out (1996)

Hardball *See* Bounty Hunters 2: Hardball (1997)

The Hardcore Life *See* Hardcore (1979)

Harem Holiday *See* Harum Scarum (1965)

Harlem Hot Shot *See* The Black King (1932)

Harlequin *See* Dark Forces (1983)

Harold Robbins' The Betsy *See* The Betsy (1978)

Harp of Burma *See* The Burmese Harp (1956)

Harrison Bergeron *See* Kurt Vonnegut's Harrison Bergeron (1995)

Harry, A Friend Who Wishes You Well *See* With a Friend Like Harry (2000)

Harry Black *See* Harry Black and the Tiger (1958)

Harry, He's Here to Help *See* With a Friend Like Harry (2000)

Harry Potter and the Philosopher's Stone *See* Harry Potter and the Sorcerer's Stone (2001)

Harry Tracy—Desperado *See* Harry Tracy (1983)

Harry, un Ami Qui Vous Veut du Bien *See* With a Friend Like Harry (2000)

Harry's Game *See* Belfast Assassin (1984)

Harry's Machine *See* Hollywood Harry (1986)

Hasta Clerto Punto *See* Up to a Certain Point (1983)

The Hatchet Murders *See* Deep Red: Hatchet Murders (1975)

Hatred *See* Hate (1995)

The Haunted *See* Curse of the Demon (1957)

The Haunted and the Hunted *See* Dementia 13 (1963)

The Haunted Planet *See* Planet of the Vampires (1965)

The Haunting of Hamilton High *See* Hello Mary Lou: Prom Night 2 (1987)

The Haunting of Hill House *See* The Haunting (1999)

The Haunting of Julia *See* Full Circle (1977)

Haus Der Tausend Freuden *See* The House of 1000 Dolls (1967)

Haut Bas Fragile *See* Up/Down/Fragile (1995)

Haxan *See* Haxan: Witchcraft through the Ages (1922)

He Lived to Kill *See* Night of Terror (1933)

He Loved an Actress *See* Mad About Money (1937)

He or She *See* Glen or Glenda? (1953)

He, She or It *See* The Doll (1962)

Head On *See* Fatal Attraction (1980)

Head Over Heels *See* Chilly Scenes of Winter (1979)

The Head That Wouldn't Die *See* The Brain that Wouldn't Die (1963)

A Heart in Winter *See* Un Coeur en Hiver (1993)

The Heart of New York *See* Hallelujah, I'm a Bum (1933)

Heartbeat *See* Danielle Steel's Heartbeat (1993)

Heartbeat *See* Le Schpountz (1938)

Heartbreak Motel *See* Poor Pretty Eddie (1973)

Hearts and Minds *See* Master Touch (1974)

Heartstone *See* Demonstone (1989)

Heavenly Pursuits *See* The Gospel According to Vic (1987)

Hector Servadac's Ark *See* On the Comet (1968)

Hei Ma *See* A Mongolian Tale (1994)

Heimat-Eine deutsche Chronik *See* Heimat 1 (1984)

The Heir to Genghis Khan *See* Storm over Asia (1928)

Heisser Sommer *See* Hot Summer (1968)

The Heist *See* Carbon Copy (1969)

The Heist *See* Dollars (1971)

The Heist *See* The Squeeze (1978)

Heldorado *See* Helldorado (1946)

Hell Bent for Glory *See* Lafayette Escadrille (1958)

Hell Creatures *See* Invasion of the Saucer Men (1957)

Hell Fire *See* They (1977)

Hell in Normandy *See* Special Forces (1968)

Hell to Macao *See* The Corrupt Ones (1967)

Hellborn *See* The Sinister Urge (1960)

Hellcab *See* Chicago Cab (1998)

Hellcamp *See* Opposing Force (1987)

Hellfire *See* Haunted Symphony (1994)

Hellfire *See* Primal Scream (1987)

Hellfire on Ice, Part 2: Escape from Hell *See* Escape from Hell (1989)

Hello Elephant *See* Pardon My Trunk (1952)

Hellraiser 2 *See* Hellbound: Hellraiser 2 (1988)

Hemoglobin *See* Bleeders (1997)

Henry 2: Portrait of a Serial Killer *See* Henry: Portrait of a Serial Killer 2: Mask of Sanity (1996)

Henry James' The Ghostly Rental *See* The Haunting of Hell House (1999)

Her Bridal Night *See* The Bride Is Much Too Beautiful (1958)

Her Mad Night *See* Held for Murder (1932)

Her Majesty Mrs. Brown *See* Mrs. Brown (1997)

Her Secret Life *See* Code Name: Dancer (1987)

Hercules Against the Sons of the Sun *See* Hercules vs. the Sons of the Sun (1964)

Hercules and the Conquest of Atlantis *See* Hercules and the Captive Women (1963)

Hercules and the Haunted Women *See* Hercules and the Captive Women (1963)

Hercules and the Hydra *See* The Loves of Hercules (1960)

Hercules and the Ten Avengers *See* The Triumph of Hercules (1966)

Hercules Goes Bananas *See* Hercules in New York (1970)

Hercules: The Movie *See* Hercules in New York (1970)

Hercules vs. the Giant Warriors *See* The Triumph of Hercules (1966)

Hercules vs. the Hydra *See* The Loves of Hercules (1960)

Hercules vs. the Moloch *See* Conquest of Mycene (1963)

Here Come the Tigers *See* Manny's Orphans (1978)

Here Is a Man *See* The Devil & Daniel Webster (1941)

Here Lies Love *See* The Second Woman (1951)

Here We Go Again *See* Pride of the Bowery (1941)

The Hero of Pine Ridge *See* Yodelin' Kid from Pine Ridge (1937)

The Heroes *See* The Invincible Six (1968)

Heroes Die Hard *See* Mr. Kingstreet's War (1971)

Herz aus Glas *See* Heart of Glass (1974)

Herzbube *See* King, Queen, Knave (1972)

The Heterosexuals *See* Les Biches (1968)

Hets *See* Torment (1944)

Hex *See* The Shrieking (1973)

Hexen bis aufs Blut Gequaelt *See* Mark of the Devil (1969)

H.G. Wells' New Invisible Man *See* The New Invisible Man (1958)

Hidden Face *See* Jail Bait (1954)

Hidden Power *See* Sabotage (1936)

Hidden Rage *See* Perfect Victims (1987)

The Hidden Room of 1,000 Horrors *See* The Tell-Tale Heart (1962)

Hidden Vision *See* Night Eyes (1990)

Hide and Shriek *See* American Gothic (1988)

Hideous Mutant Freekz *See* Freaked (1993)

Hifazaat *See* In Custody (1994)

High Risk *See* Meltdown (1995)

High Rolling *See* High Rolling in a Hot Corvette (1977)

Higher Love *See* Uncorked (1998)

The Highest Bidder *See* Woman Hunt (1972)

Highlander 2: Renegade Version *See* Highlander 2: The Quickening (1991)

Highlander 3: The Magician *See* Highlander: The Final Dimension (1994)

Highlander 3: The Sorcerer *See* Highlander: The Final Dimension (1994)

Highway to Hell *See* Running Hot (1983)

Hillbillys in a Haunted House *See* Hillbillies in a Haunted House (1967)

Him *See* Only You (1994)

Himalaya - L'Enfance d'un Chef *See* Himalaya (1999)

Himalaya - The Youth of a Chief *See* Himalaya (1999)

The Hindu *See* Sabaka (1955)

His Other Woman *See* Desk Set (1957)

Histoires Extraordinaires *See* Spirits of the Dead (1968)

History is Made at Night *See* Spy Games (1999)

Hit & Run *See* Hot Blooded (1998)

Hitlerjunge Salomon *See* Europa, Europa (1991)

Hitler's Gold *See* Inside Out (1975)

Hitman *See* American Commandos (1984)

HMS Defiant *See* Damn the Defiant (1962)

The Hoary Legends of the Caucasus *See* Ashik Kerib (1988)

Hol Volt, Hol Nem Volt *See* A Hungarian Fairy Tale (1987)

The Hole *See* Le Trou (1959)

Holiday *See* Jour de Fete (1948)

Hollow Point *See* The Wild Pair (1987)

Hollow Triumph *See* The Scar (1948)

Hollyweird *See* Flicks (1985)

Hollywood Cowboy *See* Hearts of the West (1975)

Hollywood Hoodlum *See* Hollywood Mystery (1934)

The Hollywood Strangler *See* Don't Answer the Phone (1980)

Hollywood Stunt Man *See* Movie Stuntmen (1953)

Hollywood Thrillmakers *See* Movie Stuntmen (1953)

Hollywood Vixens *See* Beyond the Valley of the Dolls (1970)

Holocaust 2000 *See* The Chosen (1977)

Holy Terror *See* Alice Sweet Alice (1976)

Hombre Mirando Al Sudeste *See* Man Facing Southeast (1986)

Home Fires Burning *See* The Turning (1992)

Home Front *See* Morgan Stewart's Coming Home (1987)

Home in Oklahoma *See* Big Show (1937)

Home Is Where the Heart Is *See* Where the Heart Is (2000)

Home is Where the Heart Is *See* Square Dance (1987)

Homecoming Night *See* Night of the Creeps (1986)

L'Homme du Minnesota *See* Minnesota Clay (1965)

The Honest Courtesan *See* Dangerous Beauty (1998)

Honeymoon in Bali *See* My Love For Yours (1939)

Honeymoon of Fear *See* Dynasty of Fear (1972)

Hong Kong Express *See* Chungking Express (1995)

Hong Ying Tao *See* Red Cherry (1995)

Hongfen *See* Blush (1995)

Honor Betrayed *See* Fear (1988)

The Honorary Consul *See* Beyond the Limit (1983)

Honour Among Thieves *See* Grisbi (1953)

Hoodlum Girls *See* Youth Aflame (1959)

Hoods *See* Hoodlum (1996)

The Hooker Cult Murders *See* The Pyx (1973)

Hopalong Cassidy Enters *See* Hopalong Cassidy (1935)

The Hopeless Ones *See* The Round Up (1966)

A Hora Da Estrela *See* The Hour of the Star (1985)

Hori, ma panenko *See* The Firemen's Ball (1968)

L'Horloger de Saint-Paul *See* The Clockmaker (1973)

The Horrible House on the Hill *See* Devil Times Five (1974)

The Horrible Mill Women *See* Mill of the Stone Women (1960)

Horror Castle *See* The Virgin of Nuremberg (1965)

Horror Convention *See* Nightmare in Blood (1975)

Horror Creatures of the Prehistoric Planet *See* Horror of the Blood Monsters (1970)

Horror High *See* Twisted Brain (1974)

Horror Hotel Massacre *See* Eaten Alive (1976)

Horror in the Midnight Sun *See* Invasion of the Animal People (1962)

Horror Maniacs *See* The Greed of William Hart (1948)

Horror of the Stone Women *See* Mill of the Stone Women (1960)

Horror on Snape Island *See* Tower of Evil (1972)

Horror Planet *See* Inseminoid (1980)

Horse, My Horse *See* The Horse (1982)

A Horse Named Comanche *See* Tonka (1958)

Horsie *See* Queen for a Day (1951)

Hostage *See* Savage Attraction (1983)

Hostage: Dallas *See* Getting Even (1986)

Hostage: The Christine Maresch Story *See* Savage Attraction (1983)

Hostage Train *See* Crackerjack 2 (1997)

Hostile Force *See* The Heist (1996)

Hostsonaten *See* Autumn Sonata (1978)

Hot and Cold *See* Weekend at Bernie's (1989)

Hot Car Girl *See* Hot Rod Girl (1956)

Hot Lead *See* Run of the Arrow (1956)

The Hot One *See* Corvette Summer (1978)

Hot Seat *See* The Chair (1987)

Hot Spot *See* I Wake Up Screaming (1941)

Hot Sweat *See* Katie Tippel (1975)

Hotaru no Haka *See* Grave of the Fireflies (1988)

Hotel Sorrento *See* Sorrento Beach (1995)

The Houghland Murder Case *See* Murder by Television (1935)

The Hounds of Zaroff *See* The Most Dangerous Game (1932)

Hour of Glory *See* The Small Back Room (1949)

The Hour of the Pig *See* The Advocate (1993)

House 3 *See* The Horror Show (1989)

House by the Lake *See* Death Weekend (1976)

House in Nightmare Park *See* Night of the Laughing Dead (1975)

House of Crazies *See* Asylum (1972)

House of Doom *See* The Black Cat (1934)

House of Evil *See* Dance of Death (1968)

House of Evil *See* The House on Sorority Row (1983)

The House of Exorcism *See* Lisa and the Devil (1975)

House of Fear *See* Fearmaker (1989)

House of Fright *See* Black Sunday (1960)

House of Fright *See* The Two Faces of Dr. Jekyll (1960)

House of Insane Women *See* Exorcism's Daughter (1974)

House of Mortal Sin *See* The Confessional (1975)

House of Mystery *See* Night Monster (1942)

House of Pleasure *See* Le Plaisir (1952)

House of Terror *See* Face of the Screaming Werewolf (1959)

House of Terror *See* The Hanging Woman (1972)

House of the Damned *See* Spectre (1996)

House of the Dark Stairway *See* A Blade in the Dark (1983)

The House of the Screaming Virgins *See* Bloodsucking Freaks (1975)

House of Usher *See* The Fall of the House of Usher (1960)

The House Where Death Lives *See* Delusion (1984)

The House Where Hell Froze Over *See* Keep My Grave Open (1980)

House Without Windows *See* Seven Alone (1975)

How Is It Going? *See* Comment Ca Va? (1976)

How Long Can You Fall? *See* Till Marriage Do Us Part (1974)

How the Grinch Stole Christmas *See* Dr. Seuss' How the Grinch Stole Christmas (2000)

How to Be a Player *See* Def Jam's How to Be a Player (1997)

How to Be a Woman and Not Die Trying *See* How to Be a Woman and Not Die in the Attempt (1991)

How to Irritate People *See* John Cleese on How to Irritate People (1968)

How to Steal a Diamond in Four Easy Lessons *See* The Hot Rock (1970)

How to Steal a Million Dollars and Live Happily Ever After *See* How to Steal a Million (1966)

Howard Beach: Making the Case for Murder *See* Skin (1989)

Howard Stern's Private Parts *See* Private Parts (1996)

Howling 2: Stirba—Werewolf Bitch *See* Howling 2: Your Sister Is a Werewolf (1985)

Howling 7 *See* The Howling: New Moon Rising (1995)

H.P. Lovecraft's The Unnamable Returns *See* The Unnamable 2: The Statement of Randolph Carter (1992)

Hrafninn Flygur *See* Revenge of the Barbarians (1985)

Hsi Yen *See* The Wedding Banquet (1993)

Hua Pi Zhi Yinyang Fawang *See* Painted Skin (1993)

Huang Jia Zhan Shi *See* Royal Warriors (1986)

Huang Tudi *See* Yellow Earth (1989)

Huggers *See* Crazy Moon (1987)

The Human Beast *See* La Bete Humaine (1938)

Human Cargo *See* Escape: Human Cargo (1998)

Human Meat Pies *See* The Untold Story (1993)

The Human Tornado *See* Dolemite 2: Human Tornado (1976)

Hunchback *See* The Hunchback of Notre Dame (1982)

Hungry Pets *See* Please Don't Eat My Mother (1972)

Hungry Wives *See* Season of the Witch (1973)

Hunt to Kill *See* The White Buffalo (1977)

The Hunted *See* Touch Me Not (1974)

Hunter of the Apocalypse *See* The Last Hunter (1980)

Hunters Are For Killing *See* Hard Frame (1970)

Huo Shao Dao *See* The Prisoner (1990)

Huozhe *See* To Live (1994)

Hurricane *See* Hurricane Streets (1996)

Hustler Squad *See* The Doll Squad (1973)

Hydra *See* Attack of the Swamp Creature (1975)

I Accuse *See* J'Accuse (1937)

I Am a Fugitive From the Chain Gang *See* I Am a Fugitive from a Chain Gang (1932)

I Bambini Ci Guardano *See* The Children Are Watching Us (1944)

I Became a Criminal *See* They Made Me a Criminal (1939)

I Became a Criminal *See* They Made Me a Fugitive (1947)

I Call First *See* Who's That Knocking at My Door? (1968)

I Can Make You Love Me: The Stalking of Laura Black *See* Stalking Laura (1993)

I Changed My Sex *See* Glen or Glenda? (1953)

I Cinque Della Vendetta *See* Five Giants from Texas (1966)

I Coltelli Del Vendicatore *See* Knives of the Avenger (1965)

I Compagni *See* The Organizer (1964)

I Corpi Presentano Tracce Di Violenza Carnale *See* Torso (1973)

I Crossed the Line *See* The Black Klansman (1966)

I Fidanzati *See* Fiances (1963)

I Giorni Dell'Inferno *See* Days of Hell (1984)

I Hate Your Guts *See* Shame (1961)

I Have a New Master *See* Passion for Life (1948)

I Have a Stranger's Face *See* Face of Another (1966)

I Have Lived *See* After Midnight (1933)

I Have No Mouth But I Must Scream *See* And Now the Screaming Starts (1973)

I Led Two Lives *See* Glen or Glenda? (1953)

I Love a Man in Uniform *See* A Man in Uniform (1993)

I Love to Kill *See* Impulse (1974)

I Married a Shadow *See* I Married a Dead Man (1982)

I Married Too Young *See* Married Too Young (1962)

I Nuovi Barbari *See* Warriors of the Wasteland (1983)

I Pianeti Contro di Noi *See* Planets Against Us (1961)

I Racconti di Canterbury *See* The Canterbury Tales (1971)

I Remember *See* Amarcord (1974)

I Saw a Dream Like This *See* Akira Kurosawa's Dreams (1990)

I Skiachtra *See* The Enchantress (1985)

I Soliti Ignoti *See* Big Deal on Madonna Street (1958)

I Tre Volti della Paura *See* Black Sabbath (1964)

I Want Her Dead *See* W (1974)

I Was a Teenage Boy *See* Something Special (1986)

I Was a Teenage Teenager *See* Clueless (1995)

I Worship His Shadow *See* Tales from a Parallel Universe: I Worship His Shadow (1997)

I You She He *See* Je Tu Il Elle (1974)

Ich und Er *See* Me and Him (1989)

Ich War Neunzehn *See* I Was Nineteen (1968)

Ich Will Doch Nur, Dass Ihr Mich Liebt *See* I Only Want You to Love Me (1976)

Ici et Ailleurs *See* Here and Elsewhere (197?)

Identificazione di una Donna *See* Identification of a Woman (1982)

Identikit *See* Driver's Seat (1973)

Idi i Smotri *See* Come and See (1985)

The Idiot *See* L'Idiot (1946)

Idioterne *See* The Idiots (1999)

Iedereen Beroemd! *See* Everybody's Famous! (2000)

Ieri, Oggi E Domani *See* Yesterday, Today and Tomorrow (1964)

If He Hollers, Let Him Go *See* Dead Right (1968)

If You Can't Say It, Just See It *See* Whore (1991)

If You Feel Like Singing *See* Summer Stock (1950)

Ike: The War Years *See* Ike (1979)

Il Boia Scarlatto *See* The Bloody Pit of Horror (1965)

Il Buco *See* Le Trou (1959)

Il Buco *See* Night Watch (1972)

Il Castello de Morti Vivi *See* Castle of the Living Dead (1964)

Il Cobra *See* The Cobra (1968)

Il Conformista *See* The Conformist (1971)

Il Conte Dracula *See* Count Dracula (1971)

Il Cristo Proibito *See* The Forbidden Christ (1950)

Il Crudeli *See* Hellbenders (1967)

Il Decameron *See* The Decameron (1970)

Il Deserto dei Tartari *See* The Desert of the Tartars (1976)

Il Deserto Rosso *See* The Red Desert (1964)

Il Diario di una Cameriera *See* Diary of a Chambermaid (1964)

Il Diavolo e i Morti *See* Lisa and the Devil (1975)

Il Diavolo in Corpo *See* Devil in the Flesh (1987)

Il Dio Chiamato a Dorian *See* Dorian Gray (1970)

Il Disprezzo *See* Contempt (1964)

Il Etait une Fois un Pays *See* Underground (1995)

Il Fantasma dell'Opera *See* The Phantom of the Opera (1998)

Il Figlio del Capitano Blood *See* Son of Captain Blood (1962)

Il Fiore delle Mille e Una Notte *See* Arabian Nights (1974)

Il Fiume del Grande Caimano *See* The Great Alligator (1981)

Il Gatto Nero *See* The Black Cat (1981)

Il Generale Della-Rovere *See* Generale Della Rovere (1960)

Il Giardino Del Finzi-Contini *See* The Garden of the Finzi-Continis (1971)

Il Gigante Di Metropolis *See* The Giant of Metropolis (1961)

Il Giorno e L'Ora *See* The Day and the Hour (1963)

Il Gladiatore Di Roma *See* Gladiator of Rome (1963)

Il Gladiatore Invincible *See* The Invincible Gladiator (1963)

Il Ladro Di Bagdad *See* Thief of Baghdad (1961)

Il Ladro di Bambini *See* The Stolen Children (1992)

Il Lago di Satana *See* The She-Beast (1965)

Il Messia *See* The Messiah (1975)

Il Mio Nome e Nessuno *See* My Name Is Nobody (1974)

Il Mondo Di Yor *See* Yor, the Hunter from the Future (1983)

Il Monstro *See* The Monster (1996)

Il Montagna di Dio Cannibale *See* Mountain of the Cannibal God (1979)

Il Mostro e in Tavola...Barone Frankenstein *See* Andy Warhol's Frankenstein (1974)

Il Mulino delle Donne di Pietra *See* Mill of the Stone Women (1960)

Il Natale Che Quasi Non Fu *See* The Christmas That Almost Wasn't (1966)

Il Pianeta Degli Uomini Spenti *See* Battle of the Worlds (1961)

Il Portiere de Notte *See* The Night Porter (1974)

Il Postino *See* The Postman (1994)

Il Processo *See* The Trial (1963)

Il Quartetto Basileus *See* Basileus Quartet (1982)

Il Re Dei Criminali *See* Superargo (1967)

Il Rosso Segmo della Follia *See* Hatchet for the Honeymoon (1970)

Il Sicario *See* The Hit Man (1961)

Il Sigillo de Pechino *See* The Corrupt Ones (1967)

Il Sole Anche di Notte *See* Night Sun (1990)

Il Terror Dei Baraberi *See* Goliath and the Barbarians (1960)

Il Testimone dello Sposo *See* The Best Man (1997)

Il Tigre *See* Tiger and the Pussycat (1967)

Il Treno *See* The Train (1965)

Il Trionfo di Ercole *See* The Triumph of Hercules (1966)

Il Vangelo Secondo Matteo *See* The Gospel According to St. Matthew (1964)

Ill Met By Moonlight *See* Night Ambush (1957)

Illicit Interlude *See* Summer Interlude (1950)

Illuminacja *See* Illumination (1973)

Illumination *See* FairyTale: A True Story (1997)

Ilsa, the Absolute Power *See* Ilsa, the Wicked Warden (1978)

Ilya Mourometz *See* Sword & the Dragon (1956)

Im Lauf der Zeit *See* Kings of the Road—In the Course of Time (1976)

Im Stahlnetz Des Dr. Mabuse *See* The Return of Dr. Mabuse (1961)

Immediate Disaster *See* The Stranger from Venus (1954)

L'Immorale *See* The Immoral One (1980)

The Imp *See* Sorority Babes in the Slimeball Bowl-A-Rama (1987)

The Important Story of Alcoholism *See* One Too Many (1951)

Impossible Object *See* The Story of a Love Story (1973)

In a Year with 13 Moons *See* In a Year of 13 Moons (1978)

In Bed with Madonna *See* Truth or Dare (1991)

In Einem Jahr Mit 13 Monden *See* In a Year of 13 Moons (1978)

In Fashion *See* A la Mode (1994)

In Love *See* Falling in Love Again (1980)

In Old Oklahoma *See* War of the Wildcats (1943)

In Pursuit of Honor *See* G.I. Jane (1997)

In the Bleak Midwinter *See* A Midwinter's Tale (1995)

In the Devil's Garden *See* Assault (1970)

In the Grip of the Spider *See* Web of the Spider (1970)

In the Line of Duty *See* Royal Warriors (1986)

In the Line of Duty: Manhunt in the Dakotas *See* Midnight Murders (1991)

In the Line of Duty: Siege at Marion *See* Children of Fury (1994)

In the Woods *See* Rashomon (1951)

In Weiter Ferne, So Nah! *See* Faraway, So Close! (1993)

Incense for the Damned *See* The Bloodsuckers (1970)

An Inch Over the Horizon *See* Captain Jack (1998)

Incident at Victoria Falls *See* Sherlock Holmes and the Incident at Victoria Falls (1991)

Inconvenienced *See* Held Up (2000)

The Incredible Invasion *See* The Sinister Invasion (1968)

The Incredible Praying Mantis *See* The Deadly Mantis (1957)

The Incredible Torture Show *See* Bloodsucking Freaks (1975)

The Incredibly Strange Creatures *See* Incredibly Strange Creatures Who Stopped Living and Became Mixed-Up Zombies (1963)

Independence *See* Best Men (1998)

An Indian in the City *See* Little Indian, Big City (1995)

Indian Love Call *See* Rose Marie (1936)

Indian Summer *See* Alive and Kicking (1996)

Indiscretion *See* Christmas in Connecticut (1945)

Indiscretion *See* Dangerous Beauty (1998)

Indiscretion *See* Indiscretion of an American Wife (1954)

The Infernal Idol *See* Craze (1974)

Inferno *See* Desert Heat (1999)

Inferno in Diretta *See* Cut and Run (1985)

Infested *See* Ticks (1993)

The Infra Superman *See* Infra-Man (1976)

Inn of the Frightened People *See* Revenge (1971)

Innocence is Bliss *See* Miss Grant Takes Richmond (1949)

The Innocent and the Damned *See* Girls' Town (1959)

Innocents aux Mains Sales *See* Innocents with Dirty Hands (1975)

Insane World *See* Mondo Cane 2 (1964)

The Insect *See* The Insect Woman (1963)

L'Insoumis *See* Fight for Us (1989)

Intensivstation Deutschland *See* Terror 2000 (1992)

Interlude *See* Intermezzo (1936)

Intermezzo: A Love Story *See* Intermezzo (1939)

Intimni Osvetleni *See* Intimate Lighting (1965)

Intramuros *See* The Walls of Hell (1964)

Intruder *See* Intruso (1993)

The Intruder *See* The Innocent (1976)

The Intruder *See* Shame (1961)

The Invader *See* Old Spanish Custom (1936)

The Invaders *See* The Forty-Ninth Parallel (1941)

Invasion Earth 2150 A.D. *See* Daleks—Invasion Earth 2150 A.D. (1966)

Invasion Force *See* Hangar 18 (1980)

Invasion from Inner Earth *See* They (1977)

Invasion of Mars *See* The Angry Red Planet (1959)

Invasion of Planet X *See* Godzilla vs. Monster Zero (1968)

Invasion of the Astro-Monsters *See* Godzilla vs. Monster Zero (1968)

Invasion of the Astros *See* Godzilla vs. Monster Zero (1968)

Invasion of the Flesh Hunters *See* Cannibal Apocalypse (1980)

Invasion of the Flying Saucers *See* Earth vs. the Flying Saucers (1956)

Invasion of the Zombies *See* Horror of Party Beach (1964)

Invasion Siniestra *See* The Sinister Invasion (1968)

An Investigation of Murder *See* The Laughing Policeman (1974)

The Invisible Dead *See* Orloff and the Invisible Man (1970)

The Invisible Horror *See* The Invisible Dr. Mabuse (1962)

The Invisible Killer *See* Curse of the Undead (1959)

An Invited Guest *See* Uninvited Guest (1999)

Io Speriamo Che Me La Cavo *See* Ciao, Professore! (1994)

The Iron Hand *See* Chinese Connection (1973)

The Iron Kiss *See* Naked Kiss (1964)

Iron Monkey: The Young Wong Feihung *See* Iron Monkey (1993)

The Ironman *See* Tetsuo: The Iron Man (1992)

Irving Berlin's Alexander's Ragtime Band *See* Alexander's Ragtime Band (1938)

Irving Berlin's Second Fiddle *See* Second Fiddle (1939)

Iskanderija, Káman oue Kaman *See* Alexandria Again and Forever (1990)

Island of Monte Cristo *See* Sword of Venus (1953)

Island of Shame *See* The Young One (1961)

Island of the Alive *See* It's Alive 3: Island of the Alive (1987)

Island of the Burning Damned *See* Island of the Burning Doomed (1967)

Island of the Fishmen *See* Screamers (1980)

The Island of the Last Zombies *See* Doctor Butcher M.D. (1980)

Island of the Living Dead *See* Zombie (1980)

Island of the Living Horror *See* Brides of the Beast (1968)

Isle of Lost Women *See* 99 Women (1969)

Isle of the Living Dead *See* The Snake People (1968)

Isle of the Snake People *See* The Snake People (1968)

Isn't Life A Bitch? *See* La Chienne (1931)

Istanbul, Keep Your Eyes Open *See* Istanbul (1990)

It Ain't No Sin *See* Belle of the Nineties (1934)

It Comes Up Murder *See* The Honey Pot (1967)

It Fell from the Sky *See* Alien Dead (1979)

It Happened at Lakewood Manor *See* Ants (1977)

It Happened in Paris *See* The Lady in Question (1940)

It Happened One Summer *See* State Fair (1945)

It Hurts Only When I Laugh *See* Only When I Laugh (1981)

It Lives Again *See* It's Alive 2: It Lives Again (1978)

It Lives By Night *See* The Bat People (1974)

It Only Take Five Minutes *See* Five Minutes to Love (1963)

It Runs in the Family *See* My Summer Story (1994)

It Stalked the Ocean Floor *See* Monster from the Ocean Floor (1954)

It! The Vampire from Beyond Space *See* It! The Terror from Beyond Space (1958)

It Won't Rub Off, Baby *See* Sweet Love, Bitter (1967)

The Italian Connection *See* Hired to Kill (1973)

The Italian Connection *See* Manhunt (1973)

Italiensk for Begyndere *See* Italian for Beginners (2001)

It's Hot in Hell *See* Un Singe en Hiver (1962)

It's Hot in Paradise *See* Horrors of Spider Island (1959)

It's My Life *See* My Life to Live (1962)

It's Only Money *See* Double Dynamite (1951)

Ivan Groznyi *See* Ivan the Terrible, Part 1 (1944)

Ivan Groznyi 2 *See* Ivan the Terrible, Part 2 (1946)

Ivan the Terrible, Part 2: The Boyars' Plot *See* Ivan the Terrible, Part 2 (1946)

Ivan's Childhood *See* My Name Is Ivan (1962)

Ja Cuba *See* I Am Cuba (1964)

Jack London's Klondike Fever *See* Klondike Fever (1979)

Jackals *See* American Justice (1986)

Jackie Chan Is the Prisoner *See* The Prisoner (1990)

Jackie Chan's Police Force *See* Police Story (1985)

Jackie Chan's Police Story *See* Police Story (1985)

Jackie Chan's Project A *See* Project A (1983)

Jackie, Ethel, Joan: Women of Camelot *See* Jackie, Ethel, Joan: The Kennedy Women (2001)

Jack's Wife *See* Season of the Witch (1973)

Jacqueline Susann's Once is Not Enough *See* Once Is Not Enough (1975)

Jacquot de Nantes *See* Jacquot (1991)

Jag ar nyfiken-en film i gult *See* I Am Curious (Yellow) (1967)

Jag ar nyfiken-gul *See* I Am Curious (Yellow) (1967)

Jag, en Kvinna *See* I, a Woman (1966)

J'ai Epouse une Ombre *See* I Married a Dead Man (1982)

J'ai Pas Sommeil *See* I Can't Sleep (1993)

Jail Birds *See* Pardon Us (1931)

J'Aimerais pas Crever un Dimache *See* Don't Let Me Die on a Sunday (1998)

Jakob der Lugner *See* Jacob the Liar (1974)

James A. Michener's Texas *See* Texas (1994)

James Clavell's Shogun *See* Shogun (1980)

James Dean: Race with Destiny *See* James Dean: Live Fast, Die Young (1997)

Jana Aranya *See* The Middleman (1976)

Jane Austen's Emma *See* Emma (1997)

Jane Austen's Mafia! *See* Mafia! (1998)

The Janitor *See* Eyewitness (1981)

Japan Sinks *See* Tidal Wave (1975)

Jatszani Kell *See* Lily in Love (1985)

Jaws 3-D *See* Jaws 3 (1983)

Jayne Mansfield: A Symbol of the '50s *See* The Jayne Mansfield Story (1980)

J.C. *See* Iron Horsemen (1971)

Je Suis Frigide...Pourquoi? *See* I Am Frigid...Why? (1972)

Je Vous Salue Marie *See* Hail Mary (1985)

Jealousy *See* L'Enfer (1993)

Jean de Florette 2 *See* Manon of the Spring (1987)

Jeanne et le Garcon Formidable *See* Jeanne and the Perfect Guy (1998)

Jeanne la Pucelle: Les Batailles *See* Jeanne la Pucelle (1994)

Jeanne la Purcelle: Les Prisons *See* Jeanne la Pucelle (1994)

Jeder fur Sich und Gott gegen Alle *See* Every Man for Himself & God Against All (1975)

Jekyll's Inferno *See* The Two Faces of Dr. Jekyll (1960)

Jennie *See* Portrait of Jennie (1948)

Jennifer (The Snake Goddess) *See* Jennifer (1978)

Jenseits der Stille *See* Beyond Silence (1996)

Jerry Springer's Ringmaster *See* Ringmaster (1998)

The Jester *See* Der Purimshpiler (1937)

Jesus de Montreal *See* Jesus of Montreal (1989)

Jette un Sort *See* Rough Magic (1995)

Jeu de Massacre *See* The Killing Game (1967)

Jew Suss *See* Power (1934)

The Jewish Jester *See* Der Purimshpiler (1937)

The Jezebels *See* Switchblade Sisters (1975)

Jian Yu Feng Yun Xu Ji *See* Prison on Fire 2 (1991)

Jiang-Hu: Between Love and Glory *See* The Bride with White Hair (1993)

Jiang-Hu: Between Love and Glory 2 *See* The Bride with White Hair 2 (1993)

Jigokumen *See* Gate of Hell (1954)

Jilly Cooper's Riders *See* Riders (1988)

Jilly Cooper's The Man Who Made Husbands Jealous *See* The Man Who Made Husbands Jealous (1998)

Jim Buck *See* Portrait of a Hitman (1977)

Jim Henson's Jack and the Beanstalk *See* Jack and the Beanstalk: The Real Story (2001)

Jing Wu Men *See* Chinese Connection (1973)

Joan the Maid: The Battles *See* Jeanne la Pucelle (1994)

Joan the Maid: The Prisons *See* Jeanne la Pucelle (1994)

Job Lazadasa *See* The Revolt of Job (1984)

Joe Palooka *See* Palooka (1934)

John Carpenter Presents Body Bags *See* Body Bags (1993)

John Carpenter's Escape from L.A. *See* Escape from L.A. (1996)

John Le Carre's A Perfect Spy *See* A Perfect Spy (1988)

John Travis, Solar Survivor *See* Omega Cop (1990)

Johnnie Mae Gibson: FBI *See* Johnnie Gibson F.B.I. (1987)

Johnny Vagabond *See* Johnny Come Lately (1943)

Johnny Zombie *See* My Boyfriend's Back (1993)

A Joke of Destiny *See* A Joke of Destiny, Lying in Wait Around the Corner Like a Bandit (1984)

Joker's Wild *See* Body Trouble (1992)

Jonas—Qui Aura 25 Ans en l'An 2000 *See* Jonah Who Will Be 25 in the Year 2000 (1976)

Joseph Conrad's Nostromo *See* Nostromo (1996)

Joseph Conrad's The Secret Agent *See* The Secret Agent (1996)

Joshua Tree *See* Woman Undone (1995)

Journey into Autumn *See* Dreams (1955)

Journey of the Hyena *See* Touki Bouki (1973)

Journey to Planet Four *See* The Angry Red Planet (1959)

Journey to the Beginning of the World *See* Voyage to the Beginning of the World (1996)

Joy Girls *See* Story of a Prostitute (1965)

Joyous Laughter *See* Passionate Thief (1960)

J.R. *See* Who's That Knocking at My Door? (1968)

Jude the Obscure *See* Jude (1996)

A Judgement in Stone *See* The Housekeeper (1986)

A Judgment in Stone *See* La Ceremonie (1995)

Jui Kun 2 *See* The Legend of Drunken Master (1994)

Jules et Jim *See* Jules and Jim (1962)

Jules Verne's Rocket to the Moon *See* Those Fantastic Flying Fools (1967)

Julie Darling *See* Daughter of Death (1982)

July Pork Bellies *See* For Pete's Sake (1974)

Jumbo *See* Billy Rose's Jumbo (1962)

Jungfrauenmaschine *See* Virgin Machine (1988)

Jungfrukallan *See* The Virgin Spring (1959)

The Jungle Book *See* Rudyard Kipling's The Jungle Book (1994)

Jungle Book 2 *See* Rudyard Kipling's the Second Jungle Book: Mowgli and Baloo (1997)

Jungle Gold *See* Perils of the Darkest Jungle (1944)

Jungle Woman *See* Nabonga (1944)

Juninatten *See* June Night (1940)

Jurassic Park 2 *See* The Lost World: Jurassic Park 2 (1997)

Jury Duty *See* The Great American Sex Scandal (1994)

Jusqu'au Bout du Monde *See* Until the End of the World (1991)

Just Another Day at the Races *See* Win, Place, or Steal (1972)

Just Ask for Diamond *See* Diamond's Edge (1988)

Just in Time *See* Only You (1994)

Just One of the Girls *See* Anything for Love (1993)

Justice *See* Backlash (1999)

Justice Cain *See* Cain's Cutthroats (1971)

Justice Rides Again *See* Destry Rides Again (1939)

Jutai *See* Traffic Jam (1991)

Kabale und Liebe *See* Intrigue and Love (1959)

Kaiju Daisenso *See* Godzilla vs. Monster Zero (1968)

Kaiju Soshingeki *See* Destroy All Monsters (1968)

Kaitei Daisenso *See* Terror Beneath the Sea (1966)

Kakushi Toride No San Akunin *See* The Hidden Fortress (1958)

Kaleidoscope *See* Danielle Steel's Kaleidoscope (1990)

Kamakazi *See* Attack Squadron (1963)

Kamui No Ken *See* The Dagger of Kamui (1985)

Kansas City Massacre *See* Melvin Purvis: G-Man (1974)

Kanzo Sensei *See* Dr. Akagi (1998)

Karakter *See* Character (1997)

Karamazov *See* The Brothers Karamazov (1958)

Karate Cop *See* Slaughter in San Francisco (1981)

Kat and Allison *See* Lip Service (2000)

Katie's Passion *See* Katie Tippel (1975)

Kavkazsky Plennik *See* Prisoner of the Mountains (1996)

Kayitz Shel Aviya *See* The Summer of Aviya (1988)

Kazoku gaimu *See* The Family Game (1983)

Kazoku Game *See* The Family Game (1983)

Keep the Aspidistra Flying *See* A Merry War (1997)

Keetje Tippel *See* Katie Tippel (1975)

Kenka Ereji *See* Fighting Elegy (1966)

The Kent Chronicles *See* The Bastard (1978)

Kessen Nankai No Daikaiju *See* Yog, Monster from Space (1971)

Kettle Creek *See* Mountain Justice (1930)

The Key *See* Odd Obsession (1960)

Key West Crossing *See* The Mercenaries (1980)

KGOD *See* Pray TV (1980)

Khaneh-Je Doost Kojast? *See* Where Is My Friend's House? (1987)

Kickboxer 5 *See* Redemption: Kickboxer 5 (1995)

The Kidnap of Mary Lou *See* Almost Human (1979)

Kilian's Chronicle *See* The Magic Stone (1995)

Kill and Go Hide *See* The Child (1976)

Kill Castro *See* The Mercenaries (1980)

Kill Two Birds *See* Cry Terror (1974)

Killbots *See* Chopping Mall (1986)

Killer *See* Bulletproof Heart (1995)

Killer! *See* This Man Must Die (1970)

Killer Bait *See* Too Late for Tears (1949)

Killer Bats *See* The Devil Bat (1941)

The Killer Behind the Mask *See* Savage Weekend (1980)

Killer Grizzly *See* Grizzly (1976)

Killer of Killers *See* The Mechanic (1972)

The Killer Whale *See* Orca (1977)

Killer With a Label *See* One Too Many (1951)

The Killers *See* Pigs (1973)

Killers of the Wild *See* Children of the Wild (1937)

The Killing Box *See* The Ghost Brigade (1993)

Killing Cars *See* Blitz (1985)

Killing Mrs. Tingle *See* Teaching Mrs. Tingle (1999)

Kilronan *See* Hush (1998)

Kimono No Kiroku *See* I Live in Fear (1955)

Kin Folk *See* All the Lovin' Kinfolk (1970)

Kinfolk *See* All the Lovin' Kinfolk (1970)

Kinfolks *See* Parental Guidance (1998)

King Cobra *See* Jaws of Satan (1981)

King Gun *See* The Gatling Gun (1972)

King Kong tai Godzilla *See* King Kong vs. Godzilla (1963)

King of Africa *See* One Step to Hell (1968)

The King of Criminals *See* Superargo (1967)

King of the Jungleland *See* Darkest Africa (1936)

King Rikki *See* The Street King (2002)

Kings Ransom *See* Devastator (1985)

KinguKongu tai Gojira *See* King Kong vs. Godzilla (1963)

Kisenga, Man of Africa *See* Men of Two Worlds (1946)

A Kiss from Eddie *See* The Arousers (1970)

Kiss My Butterfly *See* I Love You, Alice B. Toklas! (1968)

Kiss of Evil *See* Kiss of the Vampire (1962)

Kjaerlighetens Kjotere *See* Zero Degrees Kelvin (1995)

KKK *See* The Klansman (1974)

The Knack...and How to Get It *See* The Knack (1965)

The Knock-Out Cop *See* Flatfoot (1978)

Ko Zaprem Oci *See* When I Close My Eyes (1993)

Koks I Kulissen *See* Ladies on the Rocks (1983)

Komissar *See* Commissar (1968)

Kondom des Grauens *See* Killer Condom (1995)

Koneko Monogatari *See* The Adventures of Milo & Otis (1989)

Konjiki Yasha *See* Golden Demon (1953)

Konna Yume Wo Mita *See* Akira Kurosawa's Dreams (1990)

Kootenai Brown *See* Showdown at Williams Creek (1991)

Kopek and Broom *See* Find the Lady (1975)

Koroshi no Rakuin *See* Branded to Kill (1967)

Koukaku Kidoutai *See* Ghost in the Shell (1995)

Krampack *See* Nico and Dani (2000)

Krasnaya Palatka *See* Red Tent (1969)

Kriget ar Slut *See* La Guerre Est Finie (1966)

Krokodillen in Amsterdam *See* Crocodiles in Amsterdam (1989)

Kronos *See* Captain Kronos: Vampire Hunter (1974)

Krug and Company *See* Last House on the Left (1972)

Kumonosujo, Kumonosu-djo *See* Throne of Blood (1957)

Kung Fu Master *See* Le Petit Amour (1987)

Kung Fu: The Head Crusher *See* Tough Guy (1970)

Kunisada Chuji *See* The Gambling Samurai (1960)

Kuroi Ame *See* Black Rain (1988)

Kurotokage *See* Black Lizard (1968)

Kvinn odrom *See* Dreams (1955)

Kvinnorna pa Taket *See* The Women on the Roof (1989)

Kvinnors Vantan *See* Secrets of Women (1952)

Kvish L'Lo Motzah *See* Dead End Street (1983)

Kyoko *See* Because of You (1995)

Kyuketsuki Gokemidoro *See* Body Snatcher from Hell (1969)

La Ardilla Roja *See* The Red Squirrel (1993)

La Banda J.&S. Cronaca Criminale del Far West *See* Sonny and Jed (1973)

La Bataille d'Alger *See* The Battle of Algiers (1966)

La Battaglia di Algeri *See* The Battle of Algiers (1966)

La Beaute du Diable *See* Beauty and the Devil (1950)

La Belle et la Bete *See* Beauty and the Beast (1946)

La Bestia Uccide a Sangue Freddo *See* Slaughter Hotel (1971)

La Bete *See* The Beast (1975)

La Bionda *See* The Blonde (1992)

La Bonne Annee *See* Happy New Year (1973)

La Bride sur le Cou *See* Please Not Now! (1961)

La Cabeza Viviente *See* The Living Head (1959)

La Camara del Terror *See* The Fear Chamber (1968)

La Casa 4 *See* Witchery (1988)

La Casa con la Scala Nel Buio *See* A Blade in the Dark (1983)

La Casa Del Terror *See* Face of the Screaming Werewolf (1959)

La Casa Dell'Exorcismo *See* Lisa and the Devil (1975)

La Casa Embrujada *See* The Curse of the Crying Woman (1961)

La Casa Nel Parco *See* House on the Edge of the Park (1984)

La Case de L'Oncle Tom *See* Uncle Tom's Cabin (1969)

La Caza *See* The Hunt (1965)

La Chambre Ardente *See* The Burning Court (1962)

La Chambre Verte *See* The Green Room (1978)

La Chasse aux Papillons *See* Chasing Butterflies (1994)

La Chiesa *See* The Church (1998)

La Ciociara *See* Two Women (1961)

La Cite des Enfants Perdus *See* The City of Lost Children (1995)

La Citte delle Donne *See* City of Women (1981)

La Ciudad y los Perros *See* The City and the Dogs (1985)

La Commare Secca *See* The Grim Reaper (1962)

La Comtesse Perverse *See* The Perverse Countess (1973)

La Decade Prodigieuse *See* Ten Days Wonder (1972)

La Decima Vittima *See* 10th Victim (1965)

La Dentielliere *See* The Lacemaker (1977)

La Desenchantee *See* The Disenchanted (1990)

La Diagonale du Fou *See* Dangerous Moves (1984)

La Dixieme Victime *See* 10th Victim (1965)

La Donna E Donna *See* A Woman Is a Woman (1960)

La Double Vie de Veronique *See* The Double Life of Veronique (1991)

La Dueda Interna *See* Veronico Cruz (1987)

La Famiglia *See* The Family (1987)

La Femme d'a Cote *See* The Woman Next Door (1981)

La Femme de Chambre du Titanic *See* The Chambermaid on the Titanic (1997)

La Femme de L'Aviateur *See* The Aviator's Wife (1980)

La Femme De Mon Pote *See* My Best Friend's Girl (1984)

La Femme du Boulanger *See* The Baker's Wife (1933)

La Femme Mariee *See* A Married Woman (1965)

La Fiancee du Pirate *See* A Very Curious Girl (1969)

La Figlia di Frankenstein *See* Lady Frankenstein (1972)

La Fille de D'Artagnan *See* Revenge of the Musketeers (1994)

La Fille Du Puisatier *See* Well-Digger's Daughter (1946)

La Fille Seule *See* A Single Girl (1996)

La Flor de My Secreto *See* The Flower of My Secret (1995)

La Folle des Grandeurs *See* Delusions of Grandeur (1976)

La Fortuna di Essere Donna *See* What a Woman! (1956)

La Francaise et L'Amour *See* Love and the Frenchwoman (1960)

La Fuente Amarilla *See* The Yellow Fountain (1999)

La Furia del Hombre Lobo *See* The Fury of the Wolfman (1970)

La Furia Di Ercole *See* The Fury of Hercules (1961)

La Gifle *See* The Slap (1976)

La Gloire de Mon Pere *See* My Father's Glory (1991)

La Grande Guerre *See* The Great War (1959)

La Grande Illusion *See* Grand Illusion (1937)

La Grande Speranza *See* Submarine Attack (1954)

La Grieta *See* Endless Descent (1990)

La Haine *See* Hate (1995)

La Historia Oficial *See* The Official Story (1985)

La Horriplante Bestia Humana *See* Night of the Bloody Apes (1968)

La Illusion Viaja en Tranvia *See* The Illusion Travels by Streetcar (1953)

La Invasion de Los Vampiros *See* Invasion of the Vampires (1961)

La Isla Del Tersoro *See* Treasure Island (1972)

La Joven *See* The Young One (1961)

La Kermesse Heroique *See* Carnival in Flanders (1935)

La Legge *See* Where the Hot Wind Blows (1959)

La Leggenda del Pianista Sull'Oceano *See* The Legend of 1900 (1998)

La Lengua Asesina *See* Killer Tongue (1996)

La Lengua de las Mariposas *See* Butterfly (1998)

La Ley del Deseo *See* Law of Desire (1986)

La Linea Del Cielo *See* Skyline (1984)

La Loi *See* Where the Hot Wind Blows (1959)

La Lune Dans le Caniveau *See* Moon in the Gutter (1983)

La Lunga Notte del '43 *See* That Long Night in '43 (1960)

La Macchina Ammazzacattivi *See* Machine to Kill Bad People (1948)

La Mala Ordina *See* Manhunt (1973)

La Maldicion de a Llorona *See* The Curse of the Crying Woman (1961)

La Maldicion de la Bestia *See* Night of the Howling Beast (1975)

La Maldicion de la Momia Azteca *See* The Curse of the Aztec Mummy (1959)

La Maman et la Putain *See* The Mother and the Whore (1973)

La Marca del Muerto *See* Creature of the Walking Dead (1960)

La Mariee Est Trop Belle *See* The Bride Is Much Too Beautiful (1958)

La Mariee Etait en Noir *See* The Bride Wore Black (1968)

La Maschera del Demonio *See* Black Sunday (1960)

La Matriarca *See* The Libertine (1969)

La Meilleure Facon de Marcher *See* The Best Way (1976)

La Mitad del Cielo *See* Half of Heaven (1986)

La Moglie Vergine *See* You've Got to Have Heart (1977)

La Momia Azteca Contra el Robot Humano *See* The Robot vs. the Aztec Mummy (1959)

La Mort en Ce Jardin *See* Death in the Garden (1956)

La Morte Vestita di Dollar *See* Dog Eat Dog (1964)

La Morte Viene Dalla Spazio *See* The Day the Sky Exploded (1957)

La Morte Vivante *See* The Living Dead Girl (1982)

La Motocyclette *See* The Girl on a Motorcycle (1968)

La Muerte de un Burocrata *See* Death of a Bureaucrat (1966)

La Muerte Viviente *See* The Snake People (1968)

La Nipote del Vampiro *See* Fangs of the Living Dead (1968)

La Noche de la Muerta Ciega *See* Tombs of the Blind Dead (1972)

La Noche de los Mil Gatos *See* Night of a Thousand Cats (1972)

La Noche de Walpurgis *See* The Werewolf vs. the Vampire Woman (1970)

La Noche dell Terror Ciego *See* Tombs of the Blind Dead (1972)

La Noia: L'Ennui Et Sa Diversion, L'Erotisme *See* Empty Canvas (1964)

La Notte Che Evelyn Usca Dalla Tomba *See* The Night Evelyn Came Out of the Grave (1971)

La Notte di San Lorenzo *See* The Night of the Shooting Stars (1982)

La Nouvelle Eve *See* The New Eve (1998)

La Novia Esangrentada *See* The Blood Spattered Bride (1972)

La Nuit Americaine *See* Day for Night (1973)

La Nuit de Generaux *See* Night of the Generals (1967)

La Nuit Des Espions *See* Double Agents (1959)

La Nuit Fantastique *See* The Fantastic Night (1942)

La Orgia de los Muertos *See* The Hanging Woman (1972)

La Padrona e Servita *See* The Boss Is Served (1976)

La Passante du Sans Souci *See* La Passante (1983)

La Passion Beatrice *See* Beatrice (1988)

La Patinoire *See* The Ice Rink (1999)

La Permission *See* The Story of a Three Day Pass (1968)

La Planete Sauvage *See* Fantastic Planet (1973)

La Polizia vuole Giustizia *See* Violent Professionals (1973)

La Poupee *See* The Doll (1962)

La Prise de Pouvoir Par Louis XIV *See* The Rise of Louis XIV (1966)

La Provinciale *See* The Wayward Wife (1952)

La Puppa del Gangster *See* Get Rita (1975)

La Ragazza Che Sapeva Troppo *See* The Girl Who Knew Too Much (1963)

La Ragazza con la Valgia *See* The Girl with a Suitcase (1960)

La Recreation *See* Love Play (1960)

La Regina delle Amazzoni *See* Colossus and the Amazon Queen (1964)

La Reine Margot *See* Queen Margot (1994)

La Romana *See* A Woman of Rome (1956)

La Semana del Asesino *See* Cannibal Man (1971)

La Sindrome di Stendhal *See* The Stendahl Syndrome (1995)

La Sorella de Satan *See* The She-Beast (1965)

La Souffle au Coeur *See* Murmur of the Heart (1971)

La Spada del Cid *See* The Sword of El Cid (1962)

La Spina Dorsale del Diavolo *See* Ride to Glory (1971)

La Strega in Amore *See* The Witch (1966)

La Tatiche de Ercole *See* Hercules (1958)

La Tragedia di un Uomo Ridicolo *See* The Tragedy of a Ridiculous Man (1981)

La Tragedie de la Mine *See* Kameradschaft (1931)

La Tregua *See* The Truce (1996)

La Vallee *See* The Valley Obscured by the Clouds (1972)

La Vendetta di Ercole *See* Goliath and the Dragon (1961)

La Venganza de la Momia *See* The Mummy's Revenge (1973)

La Vergine de Norimberga *See* The Virgin of Nuremberg (1965)

La Veuve de Saint-Pierre *See* The Widow of Saint-Pierre (2000)

La Victoire en Chantant *See* Black and White in Color (1976)

La Vida Segun Muriel *See* Life According to Muriel (1997)

La Vie a L'Envers *See* Life Upside Down (1964)

La Vie de Jesus *See* The Life of Jesus (1996)

La Vie Devant Soi *See* Madame Rosa (1977)

La Vie est Rien d'Autre *See* Life and Nothing But (1989)

La Vie Est Une Longue Fleuve Tranquille *See* Life Is a Long Quiet River (1988)

La Vie Privee *See* A Very Private Affair (1962)

La Vie Revee des Anges *See* The Dreamlife of Angels (1998)

La Vie Sexuelle des Belges *See* The Sexual Life of the Belgians (1994)

La Vieille qui Marchait dans la Mer *See* The Old Lady Who Walked in the Sea (1991)

La Virgen de los Sicarios *See* Our Lady of the Assassins (2001)

La Vita E Bella *See* Life Is Beautiful (1998)

Laberinto de Pasiones *See* Labyrinth of Passion (1982)

Labyrinth *See* A Reflection of Fear (1972)

Ladies Man *See* Your Turn Darling (1963)

Ladies of the Park *See* The Ladies of the Bois de Bologne (1944)

Ladri di Biciclette *See* The Bicycle Thief (1948)

Ladri di Saponette *See* The Icicle Thief (1989)

The Lady and the Outlaw *See* Billy Two Hats (1974)

Lady Beware *See* 13th Guest (1932)

The Lady Dances *See* The Merry Widow (1934)

The Lady Dracula *See* Lemora, Lady Dracula (1973)

Lady Godiva Meets Tom Jones *See* Lady Godiva Rides (1968)

Lady Hamilton *See* That Hamilton Woman (1941)

Lady in the Fog *See* Scotland Yard Inspector (1952)

Lady Jane Grey *See* Nine Days a Queen (1936)

The Lady Killers *See* The Ladykillers (1955)

Lady of Deceit *See* Born to Kill (1947)

Lady of the Shadows *See* The Terror (1963)

Ladykiller *See* Lady Killer (1997)

Laererinden *See* All Things Fair (1995)

L'Aigle a Deux Tetes *See* The Eagle Has Two Heads (1948)

The Lake of the Living Dead *See* Zombie Lake (1980)

L'Albero Degli Zoccoli *See* The Tree of Wooden Clogs (1978)

L'Amant *See* The Lover (1992)

L'Amant de Lady Chatterley *See* Lady Chatterley's Lover (1955)

The Lament of the Path *See* Pather Panchali (1954)

L'Amour en Fuite *See* Love on the Run (1978)

The Lamp *See* The Outing (1987)

Lan Feng Zheng *See* The Blue Kite (1993)

Lancelot and Guinevere *See* Sword of Lancelot (1963)

Lancelot du Lac *See* Lancelot of the Lake (1974)

Landru *See* Bluebeard (1963)

The Lane Frost Story *See* 8 Seconds (1994)

L'Anee Derniere a Marienbad *See* Last Year at Marienbad (1961)

The Langoliers *See* Stephen King's The Langoliers (1995)

Larceny Lane *See* Blonde Crazy (1931)

Large as Life *See* Larger Than Life (1996)

Larsen, Wolf of the Seven Seas *See* The Legend of the Sea Wolf (1958)

Las Cartas de Alou *See* Letters from Alou (1990)

Las Luchadoras Contra la Momia *See* Wrestling Women vs. the Aztec Mummy (1959)

Las Vegas Strip War *See* The Vegas Strip Wars (1984)

Lashou Shentan *See* Hard-Boiled (1992)

Lasky Jedne Plavovlasky *See* Loves of a Blonde (1965)

L'Associe *See* The Associate (1979)

The Last Adventure *See* Les Aventuriers (1977)

The Last Adventurers *See* Down to the Sea in Ships (1922)

The Last Battle *See* Le Dernier Combat (1984)

Last Chance For a Born Loser *See* Stateline Motel (1975)

The Last Days of John Dillinger *See* Dillinger (1991)

The Last Days of Man on Earth *See* The Final Programme (1973)

The Last Days of Sodom and Gomorrah *See* Sodom and Gomorrah (1962)

The Last Elephant *See* Ivory Hunters (1990)

The Last Frontier *See* Savage Wilderness (1955)

The Last Great Treasure *See* Mother Lode (1982)

The Last Horror Film *See* Fanatic (1982)

Last House on the Left, Part 2 *See* Twitch of the Death Nerve (1971)

Last Message From Saigon *See* Operation C.I.A. (1965)

Last of the Cowboys *See* Great Smokey Roadblock (1976)

The Last Outpost *See* Cavalry Charge (1951)

The Last Page *See* Man Bait (1952)

Last Resurrection *See* Haunted Symphony (1994)

Last Rites *See* Dracula's Last Rites (1979)

The Last Shot *See* Carbon Copy (1969)

The Last Victim *See* Forced Entry (1975)

The Last Warrior *See* The Final Executioner (1983)

The Last Will of Dr. Mabuse *See* Crimes of Dr. Mabuse (1932)

The Last Will of Dr. Mabuse *See* Testament of Dr. Mabuse (1962)

The Last Witness *See* Caracara (2000)

The Late Edwina Black *See* The Obsessed (1951)

Latin Love *See* Greek Street (1930)

Latin Quarter *See* Frenzy (1946)

Laughterhouse *See* Singleton's Pluck (1984)

The Law *See* Tilai (1990)

The Law *See* Where the Hot Wind Blows (1959)

Law Breakers *See* Les Assassins de L'Ordre (1971)

Lawnmower Man 2: Jobe's War *See* Lawnmower Man 2: Beyond Cyberspace (1995)

The Lay of the Land *See* The Student Affair (1997)

Lazarus and the Hurricane *See* The Hurricane (1999)

Lazy Bones *See* Hallelujah, I'm a Bum (1933)

Le Battement d'Ailes du Papillon *See* Happenstance (2000)

Le Blonde de Pekin *See* The Peking Blond (1968)

Le Caporal Epingle *See* The Elusive Corporal (1962)

Le Carrosse D'Or *See* The Golden Coach (1952)

Le Cerveau *See* The Brain (1969)

Le Chaland qui Passe *See* L'Atalante (1934)

Le Charme Discret de la Bourgeoisie *See* The Discreet Charm of the Bourgeoisie (1972)

Le Chat et la Souris *See* Cat and Mouse (1978)

Le Chateau de Ma Mere *See* My Mother's Castle (1991)

Le Cheval D'Orgeuil *See* The Horse of Pride (1980)

Le Ciel et le Boue *See* The Sky Above, the Mud Below (1961)

Le Coeur au Poing *See* Street Heart (1998)

Le Comte de Monte Cristo *See* The Count of Monte Cristo (1999)

Le Confessionnal *See* The Confessional (1995)

Le Corniauds *See* The Sucker (1965)

Le Cri du Hibou *See* The Cry of the Owl (1987)

Le Crime de Monsieur Lange *See* The Crime of Monsieur Lange (1936)

Le Danger Vient de l'Escape *See* The Day the Sky Exploded (1957)

Le Declin De L'Empire Americain *See* The Decline of the American Empire (1986)

Le Dejeuner sur l'Herbe *See* Picnic on the Grass (1959)

Le Dernier Metro *See* The Last Metro (1980)

Le Dernier Tango a Paris *See* Last Tango in Paris (1973)

Le Desert des Tartares *See* The Desert of the Tartars (1976)

Le Diable au Corps *See* Devil in the Flesh (1946)

Le Diable, Probablement *See* The Devil, Probably (1977)

Le Diner de Cons *See* The Dinner Game (1998)

Le Distrait *See* The Daydreamer (1975)

Le Docteur Petiot *See* Dr. Petiot (1990)

Le Fabuleux Destin d'Amelie Poulain *See* Amelie (2001)

Le Fantome de la Liberte *See* Phantom of Liberty (1974)

Le Feu Follet *See* The Fire Within (1964)

Le Fille sure le Pont *See* The Girl on the Bridge (1998)

Le Fils du Requin *See* The Son of the Shark (1993)

Le Fils Prefere *See* The Favorite Son (1994)

Le Fruit Defendu *See* Forbidden Fruit (1952)

Le Gai Savoir *See* The Joy of Knowledge (1965)

Le Geant de la Vallee Das Rois *See* Son of Samson (1962)

Le Genou de Claire *See* Claire's Knee (1971)

Le Gentleman d'Epsom *See* Duke of the Derby (1962)

Le Graal *See* Lancelot of the Lake (1974)

Le Grand Bleu *See* The Big Blue (1988)

Le Grand Blond avec une Chassure Noire *See* The Tall Blond Man with One Black Shoe (1972)

Le Grand Meaulnes *See* The Wanderer (1967)

Le Huitieme Jour *See* The Eighth Day (1995)

Le Hussard sur le Toit *See* The Horseman on the Roof (1995)

Le Infedeli *See* The Unfaithfuls (1960)

Le Jardin des Plantes *See* The Green House (1996)

Le Jour et L'Heure *See* The Day and the Hour (1963)

Le Journal du Seducteur *See* Diary of a Seducer (1995)

Le Journal d'un Cure de Campagne *See* Diary of a Country Priest (1950)

Le Journal d'une Femme de Chambre *See* Diary of a Chambermaid (1964)

Le Juge et L'assassin *See* The Judge and the Assassin (1975)

Le Locataire *See* The Tenant (1976)

Le Maitre de Musique *See* The Music Teacher (1988)

Le Mari de la coiffeuse *See* The Hairdresser's Husband (1992)

Le Mepris *See* Contempt (1964)

Le Meraviglie Di Aladino *See* The Wonders of Aladdin (1961)

Le Moine et la Sorciere *See* Sorceress (1988)

Le Monstre *See* The Monster (1996)

Le Mur *See* The Wall (1983)

Le Mura di Malapaga *See* The Walls of Malapaga (1949)

Le Neveu de Beethoven *See* Beethoven's Nephew (1988)

Le Notti Bianche *See* White Nights (1957)

Le Notti de Cabiria *See* Nights of Cabiria (1957)

Le Pacte des Loups *See* Brotherhood of the Wolf (2001)

Le Pays Bleu *See* Blue Country (1977)

Le Peau Douce *See* The Soft Skin (1964)

Le Petit Monde de Don Camillo *See* Little World of Don Camillo (1951)

Le Placard *See* The Closet (2000)

Le Plus Vieux Metier du Monde *See* Oldest Profession (1967)

Le Proces *See* The Trial (1963)

Le Quatrieme Sexe *See* The Fourth Sex (1961)

Le Rayon Vert *See* Summer (1986)

Le Regle du Jeu *See* The Rules of the Game (1939)

Le Retour de Martin Guerre *See* The Return of Martin Guerre (1983)

Le Retour du Grand Blond *See* Return of the Tall Blond Man with One Black Shoe (1974)

Le Roi de Coeur *See* The King of Hearts (1966)

Le Rouble a Deux Faces *See* The Hot Line (1969)

Le Rouge aux Levres *See* Daughters of Darkness (1971)

Le Rouge et le Noir *See* The Red and the Black (1957)

Le Salaire de la Peur *See* Wages of Fear (1955)

Le Sang d'un Poete *See* The Blood of a Poet (1930)

Le Sant de l'Ange *See* Cobra (1971)

Le Sauvage *See* Lovers Like Us (1975)

Le Sirene du Mississippi *See* Mississippi Mermaid (1969)

Le Temps des Loups *See* Carbon Copy (1969)

Le Testament D'Orphee *See* The Testament of Orpheus (1959)

Le Testament du Docteur Cordelier *See* The Testament of Dr. Cordelier (1959)

Le Teur Invisible *See* Curse of the Undead (1959)

Le Tournoi dans la Cite *See* Tournament (1929)

Le Train *See* The Train (1965)

Le Trio Infernal *See* The Infernal Trio (1974)

Le Trou *See* Night Watch (1972)

Le Trou Normand *See* Crazy for Love (1952)

Le Vieil Homme Et L'Enfant *See* The Two of Us (1968)

Le Violon Rouge *See* The Red Violin (1998)

Le Voleur De Bagdad *See* Thief of Baghdad (1961)

Leader of the Pack *See* Unholy Rollers (1972)

The Leather Girls *See* Faster, Pussycat! Kill! Kill! (1965)

The Leatherboys *See* The Leather Boys (1963)

Lebenszeichen *See* Signs of Life (1968)

L'eclisse *See* The Eclipse (1966)

L'Ecole Buissonniere *See* Passion for Life (1948)

Legacy of Blood *See* Blood Legacy (1973)

The Legacy of Maggie Walsh *See* The Legacy (1979)

The Legend *See* James Dean (1976)

Legend in Leotards *See* Return of Captain Invincible (1983)

Legend of Cougar Canyon *See* The Secret of Navajo Cave (1976)

The Legend of Gosta Berling *See* The Atonement of Gosta Berling (1924)

The Legend of Machine Gun Kelly *See* Melvin Purvis: G-Man (1974)

Legend of the Bayou *See* Eaten Alive (1976)

Legend of the Mummy *See* Bram Stoker's The Mummy (1997)

The Legend of the Pianist on the Ocean *See* The Legend of 1900 (1998)

The Legend of the Zaat Monster *See* Attack of the Swamp Creature (1975)

Legend of Witch Hollow *See* The Witchmaker (1969)

Legenda Del Rudio Malese *See* Jungle Raiders (1985)

Legenda Suramskoi Kreposti *See* The Legend of Suram Fortress (1985)

The Legendary Curse of Lemora *See* Lemora, Lady Dracula (1973)

Legion of the Damned *See* Battle of the Commandos (1971)

Lejonsommar *See* Vibration (1968)

Lemon Popsicle V *See* Baby Love (1983)

Lemora: A Child's Tale of the Supernatural *See* Lemora, Lady Dracula (1973)

Len Deighton's Bullet to Beijing *See* Bullet to Beijing (1995)

L'Enfant Sauvage *See* The Wild Child (1970)

Leo Tolstoy's Anna Karenina *See* Leo Tolstoy's Anna Karenina (1996)

Leon *See* The Professional (1994)

Leona Helmsley: The Queen of Mean *See* The Queen of Mean (1990)

Lepa Sela, Lepo Gore *See* Pretty Village, Pretty Flame (1996)

Lepassager de la Pluie *See* Rider on the Rain (1970)

L'Eredita Ferramonti *See* The Inheritance (1976)

Les Amants du Pont-Neuf *See* The Lovers on the Bridge (1991)

Les Amities Particulieres *See* This Special Friendship (1967)

Les Avaleuses *See* Female Vampire (1973)

Les Bas Fonds *See* The Lower Depths (1936)

Les Belles de Nuit *See* Beauties of the Night (1952)

Les Bijoutiers du Clair de Lune *See* The Night Heaven Fell (1957)

Les Boys *See* The Boys (1997)

Les Cent et Une Nuits *See* One Hundred and One Nights (1995)

Les Cent et Une Nuits de Simon Cinema *See* One Hundred and One Nights (1995)

Les Choses De La Vie *See* The Things of Life (1970)

Les Collegiennes *See* The Twilight Girls (1957)

Les Corrompus *See* The Corrupt Ones (1967)

Les Cousins *See* The Cousins (1959)

Les Dames du Bois de Bologne *See* The Ladies of the Bois de Bologne (1944)

Les Demoiselles de Rochefort *See* The Young Girls of Rochefort (1968)

Les Demons *See* The Demons (1974)

Les Deux Anglaises et le Continent *See* Two English Girls (1972)

Les Deux Rivales *See* Time of Indifference (1964)

Les Diabolique *See* Diabolique (1955)

Les Dimanches de Ville d'Arvay *See* Sundays & Cybele (1962)

Les Enfants du Paradis *See* Children of Paradise (1944)

Les Enfants Gates *See* Spoiled Children (1977)

Les Felins *See* Joy House (1964)

Les Feluettes *See* Lilies (1996)

Les Femmes *See* The Women (1969)

Les Fils de Gascogne *See* Son of Gascogne (1995)

Les Gaspards *See* The Holes (1972)

Les Grandes Gueules *See* Jailbird's Vacation (1965)

Les Grandes Personnes *See* Time Out for Love (1961)

Les Griffes du Vampire *See* Curse of the Undead (1959)

Les Innocents aux Mains Sales *See* Dirty Hands (1976)

Les Jeux Interdits *See* Forbidden Games (1952)

Les Liaisons Dangereuses *See* Dangerous Liaisons (1960)

Les Liens de Sang *See* Blood Relatives (1977)

Les Louves *See* Letters to an Unknown Lover (1984)

Les Mille Et Une Nuits *See* The Wonders of Aladdin (1961)

Les Mille et Une Recettes du Cuisinier Amoureux *See* A Chef in Love (1996)

Luci del Varieta *See* Variety Lights (1951)

The Lucifer Project *See* Barracuda (1978)

Lucky Boots *See* Gun Play (1936)

Lucky Break *See* Paperback Romance (1996)

Lucky 13 *See* Running Hot (1983)

Lucky to Be a Woman *See* What a Woman! (1956)

The Lullaby *See* The Sin of Madelon Claudet (1931)

L'Ultimo Uomo Della Terra *See* The Last Man on Earth (1964)

Lulu *See* Pandora's Box (1928)

Lunch on the Grass *See* Picnic on the Grass (1959)

Lunch Wagon Girls *See* Lunch Wagon (1981)

L'Une Chante, l'Autre Pas *See* One Sings, the Other Doesn't (1977)

L'Uomo Dalle Due Ombre *See* Cold Sweat (1971)

L'Uomo di Rio *See* That Man from Rio (1964)

Lust for Evil *See* Purple Noon (1960)

Lust och Fagring Stor *See* All Things Fair (1995)

Lust of the Vampires *See* I Vampiri (1956)

Lycanthropus *See* Werewolf in a Girl's Dormitory (1961)

Lysets Hjerte *See* Heart of Light (1997)

M. Hire *See* Monsieur Hire (1989)

M:I 2 *See* Mission: Impossible 2 (2000)

Ma and Pa Kettle Go to Paris *See* Ma and Pa Kettle on Vacation (1953)

Ma Nuit Chez Maud *See* My Night at Maud's (1969)

Ma Vie Sexuelle...Comment Je Me Suis Dispute *See* My Sex Life...Or How I Got into an Argument (1996)

Maboroshi no Hikari *See* Maborosi (1995)

Macabra *See* Demonoid, Messenger of Death (1981)

Macabre Serenade *See* Dance of Death (1968)

Maccheroni *See* Macaroni (1985)

Maciste Alla Corte Del Gran Khan *See* Samson and the 7 Miracles of the World (1962)

Maciste at the Court of the Great Khan *See* Samson and the 7 Miracles of the World (1962)

Maciste Contro lo Sceicco *See* Samson Against the Sheik (1962)

Maciste la Regina di Samar *See* Hercules against the Moon Men (1964)

Maciste, L'Eroe Piu Grande Del Mondo *See* Goliath and the Sins of Babylon (1964)

Maciste Nella Terra dei Ciclopi *See* Atlas in the Land of the Cyclops (1961)

The Mad Butcher of Vienna *See* The Mad Butcher (1972)

Mad Dog *See* Mad Dog Morgan (1976)

Mad Dog Time *See* Trigger Happy (1996)

Mad Dogs and Englishmen *See* Shameless (1994)

The Mad Hatter *See* Breakfast in Hollywood (1946)

Mad Jake *See* Blood Salvage (1990)

Mad Magazine's Up the Academy *See* Up the Academy (1980)

Mad Max 2 *See* The Road Warrior (1982)

Mad Trapper of the Yukon *See* Challenge To Be Free (1976)

Mad Wednesday *See* The Sin of Harold Diddlebock (1947)

Madagascar Landing *See* Alfred Hitchcock's Aventure Malgache (1944)

Madame De... *See* The Earrings of Madame De... (1954)

Madame Frankenstein *See* Lady Frankenstein (1972)

Mademoiselle France *See* Reunion in France (1942)

Mademoiselle Striptease *See* Plucking the Daisy (1956)

Madmen of Mandoras *See* They Saved Hitler's Brain (1964)

Madonna Truth or Dare *See* Truth or Dare (1991)

Mafia Docks *See* Desperate Crimes (1993)

Mafia Junction *See* Super Bitch (1989)

The Mafu Cage *See* My Sister, My Love (1978)

The Magic Hour *See* Twilight (1998)

The Magnificent One *See* Le Magnifique (1976)

The Magnificent Seven *See* Seven Samurai (1954)

The Magnificent Showman *See* Circus World (1964)

Mahanagar *See* The Big City (1963)

Making It *See* Going Places (1974)

Mako: The Jaws of Death *See* Jaws of Death (1976)

Malenka, the Vampire *See* Fangs of the Living Dead (1968)

Malenkaya Vera *See* Little Vera (1988)

Malibu Hot Summer *See* Sizzle Beach U.S.A. (1974)

Malice in Wonderland *See* The Rumor Mill (1986)

Malizia *See* Malicious (1974)

Malli *See* The Terrorist (1998)

Mamba Snakes *See* Fair Game (1989)

Man against the Mob: The Chinatown Murders *See* The Chinatown Murders: Man against the Mob (1992)

Man and His Mate *See* One Million B.C. (1940)

A Man Betrayed *See* Wheel of Fortune (1941)

Man-Eater *See* Shark! (1968)

A Man Escaped, or the Wind Bloweth Where It Listeth *See* A Man Escaped (1957)

The Man From C.O.T.T.O.N., Purlie Victorious *See* Gone Are the Days (1963)

Man from Music Mountain *See* Texas Legionnaires (1943)

The Man From Nevada *See* The Nevadan (1950)

Man in a Cocked Hat *See* Carlton Browne of the F.O. (1959)

A Man in Mommy's Bed *See* With Six You Get Eggroll (1968)

The Man in Possession *See* Personal Property (1937)

Man in the Middle *See* 48 Hours to Live (1960)

Man Looking Southeast *See* Man Facing Southeast (1986)

Man of Bronze *See* Jim Thorpe: All American (1951)

Man of the Frontier *See* Red River Valley (1936)

Man of the Hour *See* Colonel Effingham's Raid (1945)

Man on the Move *See* Jigsaw (1971)

The Man Who Changed His Mind *See* The Man Who Lived Again (1936)

The Man Who Cried *See* Catherine Cookson's The Man Who Cried (1993)

The Man Who Watched Trains Go By *See* Paris Express (1953)

The Man With The Deadly Lens *See* Wrong Is Right (1982)

The Man with the Green Carnation *See* The Trials of Oscar Wilde (1960)

The Man with the Synthetic Brain *See* Blood of Ghastly Horror (1972)

The Man with the X-Ray Eyes *See* X: The Man with X-Ray Eyes (1963)

The Man with the Yellow Eyes *See* Planets Against Us (1961)

The Man with Thirty Sons *See* The Magnificent Yankee (1950)

Manchester Prep *See* Cruel Intentions 2 (1999)

Manen Pa Taket *See* The Man on the Roof (1976)

Mangiati Vivi dai Cannibali *See* Emerald Jungle (1980)

Manhattan Project: The Deadly Game *See* The Manhattan Project (1986)

Manhunt in the Dakotas *See* Midnight Murders (1991)

Manhunt: The Search for the Night Stalker *See* The Hunt for the Night Stalker (1991)

Mania *See* The Flesh and the Fiends (1960)

The Maniacs Are Loose *See* The Thrill Killers (1965)

Manifesto *See* A Night of Love (1987)

Mannen fran Mallorca *See* Man from Mallorca (1984)

Manon des Sources *See* Manon of the Spring (1987)

Mansion of Madness *See* Dr. Tarr's Torture Dungeon (1975)

The Manster—Half Man, Half Monster *See* The Manster (1959)

Manuela's Loves *See* Le Jupon Rouge (1987)

Marcelino *See* The Miracle of Marcelino (1955)

Marcelino, Pan y Vino *See* The Miracle of Marcelino (1955)

Marching Along *See* Stars and Stripes Forever (1952)

Margaret Bourke-White *See* Double Exposure: The Story of Margaret Bourke-White (1989)

Maria di Mi Corazon *See* Mary, My Dearest (1983)

Maria Marten *See* Murder in the Old Red Barn (1936)

Maria-nap *See* Maria's Day (1984)

Marie Bay of Angels *See* Marie Baie des Anges (1997)

Marie Walewska *See* Conquest (1937)

Marijuana the Devil's Weed *See* She Shoulda Said No (1949)

Marijuana: The Devil's Weed *See* Marihuana (1936)

Marijuana, Weed with Roots in Hell *See* Marihuana (1936)

Marilyn *See* Roadhouse Girl (1953)

Marine Issue *See* Instant Justice (1986)

Mario Puzo's The Last Don *See* The Last Don (1997)

Mario Puzo's The Last Don 2 *See* The Last Don 2 (1998)

Marius et Jeannette: Un Conte de L'Estaque *See* Marius and Jeannette (1997)

Mark of Terror *See* Drums of Jeopardy (1931)

Mark of the Avenger *See* The Mysterious Rider (1938)

Mark of the Beast *See* Curse of the Undead (1959)

Mark of the Claw *See* Dick Tracy's Dilemma (1947)

Mark of the Vampire *See* The Vampire (1957)

Mark of the West *See* Curse of the Undead (1959)

Mark Twain *See* The Adventures of Mark Twain (1985)

Married in Haste *See* Consolation Marriage (1931)

Mars Invades Puerto Rico *See* Frankenstein Meets the Space Monster (1965)

The Marseille Contract *See* The Destructors (1974)

Marshal of Heldorado *See* Blazing Guns (1950)

The Marsupials: Howling 3 *See* Howling 3: The Marsupials (1987)

Marte, Dio Della Guerra *See* Venus Against the Son of Hercules (1962)

Martha, Meet Frank, Daniel and Laurence *See* The Very Thought of You (1998)

Martin Lawrence You So Crazy *See* You So Crazy (1994)

Marusa No Onna *See* A Taxing Woman (1987)

Marusa No Onna II *See* A Taxing Woman's Return (1988)

The Marvelous Visit *See* La Merveilleuse Visite (1974)

The Marx Brothers at the Circus *See* At the Circus (1939)

Marx Brothers Go West *See* Go West (1940)

Mascskajatek *See* Cat's Play (1974)

Masculin Feminin *See* Masculine Feminine (1966)

Mask of Dust *See* Race for Life (1955)

Mask of Fury *See* First Yank into Tokyo (1945)

Mask of Satan *See* Black Sunday (1960)

Massacre at Fort Holman *See* A Reason to Live, a Reason to Die (1973)

Massacre Hill *See* Eureka Stockade (1949)

Massacre Mafia Style *See* The Executioner (1978)

Master of Evil *See* The Demon Lover (1977)

Master of Lassie *See* The Hills of Home (1948)

Mat i Syn *See* Mother and Son (1997)

Matango *See* Attack of the Mushroom People (1963)

Matar al Abuelito *See* Killing Grandpa (1991)

Mater Dolorosa *See* The Torture of Silence (1917)

The Mating of the Sabine Women *See* The Rape of the Sabines (1961)

Matka Joanna Od Aniolow *See* Mother Joan of the Angels (1960)

Matt Riker *See* Mutant Hunt (1987)

A Matter of Life and Death *See* Stairway to Heaven (1946)

Mauri *See* Big Mo (1973)

Mausoleum *See* One Dark Night (1982)

Max, My Love *See* Max, Mon Amour (1986)

Mayerling to Sarajevo *See* De Mayerling a Sarajevo (1940)

The Mayfair Bank Caper *See* The Big Scam (1979)

Mazel Tov Ou le Mariage *See* Marry Me, Marry Me (1969)

McKlusky *See* White Lightning (1973)

The McMasters...Tougher Than the West Itself *See* The McMasters (1970)

M.D.C. Maschera di Cera *See* Wax Mask (1997)

Meachorei Hasoragim *See* Beyond the Walls (1984)

Meat Is Meat *See* The Mad Butcher (1972)

Mecaniques Celestes *See* Celestial Clockwork (1994)

The Medicine Hat Stallion *See* Peter Lundy and the Medicine Hat Stallion (1977)

Murder One *See* Death Sentence (1974)

The Murderer Dmitri Karamazov *See* The Brothers Karamazov (1958)

Muriel, Or the Time of Return *See* Muriel (1963)

Muriel, Ou le Temps d'Un Retour *See* Muriel (1963)

The Murri Affair *See* La Grande Bourgeoise (1974)

Music in Darkness *See* Night Is My Future (1947)

The Music Room *See* Jalsaghar (1958)

Musime si Pomahat *See* Divided We Fall (2000)

Mussolini: The Decline and Fall of Il Duce *See* Mussolini & I (1985)

Mutant *See* Forbidden World (1982)

The Mutation *See* The Freakmaker (1973)

Mutations *See* The Freakmaker (1973)

The Mutilator *See* The Dark (1979)

The Mutineers *See* Pirate Ship (1949)

Mutter Kusters Fahrt Zum Himmel *See* Mother Kusters Goes to Heaven (1976)

Mutter und Sohn *See* Mother and Son (1997)

Mutters Courage *See* My Mother's Courage (1995)

My Brother, the Outlaw *See* My Outlaw Brother (1951)

My Crazy Life *See* Mi Vida Loca (1994)

My Darling Shiksa *See* Over the Brooklyn Bridge (1983)

My Father Is a Hero *See* Jet Li's The Enforcer (1995)

My Father, My Master *See* Padre Padrone (1977)

My Favorite Season *See* Ma Saison Preferee (1993)

My Favourite Year *See* My Favorite Year (1982)

My Forgotten Man *See* Flynn (1996)

My Girlfriend's Boyfriend *See* Boyfriends & Girlfriends (1988)

My Hero *See* A Southern Yankee (1948)

My Life in Pink *See* Ma Vie en Rose (1997)

My Love Letters *See* Love Letters (1983)

My Man *See* Mon Homme (1996)

My Name is John *See* The Legend of Hillbilly John (1973)

My Neighbor's Daughter *See* Angel Blue (1997)

My Night with Maud *See* My Night at Maud's (1969)

My Posse Don't Do Homework *See* Dangerous Minds (1995)

My Son Alone *See* American Empire (1942)

My Teenage Daughter *See* Teenage Bad Girl (1959)

My Uncle *See* Mon Oncle (1958)

My Uncle, Mr. Hulot *See* Mon Oncle (1958)

My World Dies Screaming *See* Terror in the Haunted House (1958)

Mystere Alexina *See* The Mystery of Alexina (1986)

Mysterious Invader *See* The Astounding She-Monster (1958)

The Mysterious Satellite *See* Warning from Space (1956)

The Mystery of Kaspar Hauser *See* Every Man for Himself & God Against All (1975)

The Mystery of Spoon River *See* The Ghost of Spoon River (2000)

Mystery of the Black Jungle *See* The Black Devils of Kali (1955)

The Mystery of the Marie Celeste *See* The Mystery of the Mary Celeste (1937)

Mystique *See* Circle of Power (1983)

Na Komete *See* On the Comet (1968)

Na Samyn Dnie *See* Deep End (1970)

Nachts wenn Dracula Erwacht *See* Count Dracula (1971)

Nagooa *See* Drifting (1982)

The Naked Goddess *See* The Devil's Hand (1961)

Naked Island *See* The Island (1961)

The Naked Night *See* Sawdust & Tinsel (1953)

Naked Space *See* Spaceship (1981)

Naked under Leather *See* The Girl on a Motorcycle (1968)

Naked Warriors *See* The Arena (1973)

The Naked Weekend *See* Circle of Power (1983)

Naked Youth *See* The Cruel Story of Youth (1960)

Nanguo Zaijian, Nanguo *See* Goodbye South, Goodbye (1996)

Nankai No Daikaiju *See* Yog, Monster from Space (1971)

Nankai No Kai Ketto *See* Godzilla vs. the Sea Monster (1966)

Nara Livet *See* Brink of Life (1957)

Narayama-Bushi-Ko *See* The Ballad of Narayama (1983)

Nathaniel Hawthorne's "Twice Told Tales" *See* Twice-Told Tales (1963)

Nattens Engel *See* Angel of the Night (1998)

Nattvardsgaesterna *See* The Winter Light (1962)

Nature's Mistakes *See* Freaks (1932)

Naughty Girl *See* Mam'zelle Pigalle (1958)

Navy Cross *See* G.I. Jane (1997)

Navy Diver *See* Men of Honor (2000)

The Navy Steps Out *See* A Girl, a Guy and a Gob (1941)

Neat and Tidy *See* Adventures Beyond Belief (1987)

Neco Z Alenky *See* Alice (1988)

Necromancy *See* The Witching (1972)

Necronomicon *See* H.P. Lovecraft's Necronomicon: Book of the Dead (1993)

Ned Blessing: The Story of My Life and Times *See* Lone Justice 2 (1993)

Ned Kelly, Outlaw *See* Ned Kelly (1970)

Neil Simon's Biloxi Blues *See* Biloxi Blues (1988)

Neil Simon's Brighton Beach Memoirs *See* Brighton Beach Memoirs (1986)

Neil Simon's Broadway Bound *See* Broadway Bound (1992)

Neil Simon's Lost in Yonkers *See* Lost in Yonkers (1993)

Neil Simon's The Slugger's Wife *See* The Slugger's Wife (1985)

Nella Stretta M Orsa Del Ragno *See* Web of the Spider (1970)

Nelly and Mr. Arnaud *See* Nelly et Monsieur Arnaud (1995)

Nemesis 3: Prey Harder *See* Nemesis 3: Time Lapse (1996)

The Neptune Disaster *See* Neptune Factor (1973)

Neskolko Dnel iz Zhizni I.I. Oblomov *See* Oblomov (1981)

Netforce *See* Tom Clancy's Netforce (1998)

Nettoyage a Sec *See* Dry Cleaning (1997)

Neurosis *See* Revenge in the House of Usher (1982)

Nevada Heat *See* Fake Out (1982)

Never Cry Devil *See* Night Visitor (1989)

The Never Dead *See* Phantasm (1979)

Never Ever *See* Circle of Passion (1997)

Never Give an Inch *See* Sometimes a Great Notion (1971)

The New Adventures of Don Juan *See* Adventures of Don Juan (1949)

New Adventures of Tarzan *See* Tarzan and the Green Goddess (1938)

The New Barbarians *See* Warriors of the Wasteland (1983)

New Girl in Town *See* Nashville Girl (1976)

New Tales of the Taira Clan *See* Shin Heike Monogatari (1955)

New Wave *See* Nouvelle Vague (1990)

New Wine *See* Melody Master (1941)

The Newcomers *See* The Wild Country (1971)

Next! *See* Blade of the Ripper (1970)

The Next Man *See* The Arab Conspiracy (1976)

The Next Victim *See* Blade of the Ripper (1970)

Ngo Hai Sui *See* Jackie Chan's Who Am I (1998)

Nicholas Nickleby *See* The Life and Adventures of Nicholas Nickleby (1981)

Nickel and Dime *See* Larger Than Life (1996)

The Niece of the Vampire *See* Fangs of the Living Dead (1968)

Niewinni Czarodzieje *See* Innocent Sorcerers (1960)

Night Beauties *See* Beauties of the Night (1952)

The Night Caller *See* Night Caller from Outer Space (1966)

Night Comes Too Soon *See* The Ghost of Rashmon Hall (1947)

Night Encounter *See* Double Agents (1959)

The Night Flier *See* Stephen King's The Night Flier (1996)

Night Hair Child *See* What the Peeper Saw (1972)

Night Is the Phantom *See* The Whip and the Body (1963)

Night Legs *See* Fright (1971)

The Night of San Lorenzo *See* The Night of the Shooting Stars (1982)

Night of the Anubis *See* Night of the Living Dead (1968)

Night of the Beast *See* House of the Black Death (1965)

Night of the Big Heat *See* Island of the Burning Doomed (1967)

Night of the Blind Dead *See* Tombs of the Blind Dead (1972)

Night of the Bloodsuckers *See* The Vampire Hookers (1978)

Night of the Claw *See* Island Claw (1980)

Night of the Dark Full Moon *See* Silent Night, Bloody Night (1973)

Night of the Demon *See* Curse of the Demon (1957)

Night of the Demon *See* The Touch of Satan (1970)

Night of the Doomed *See* Nightmare Castle (1965)

Night of the Eagle *See* Burn Witch, Burn! (1962)

Night of the Flesh Eaters *See* Night of the Living Dead (1968)

Night of the Seagulls *See* Night of the Death Cult (1975)

Night of the Silicates *See* Island of Terror (1966)

Night of the Vampire *See* Cave of the Living Dead (1965)

Night of the Wehrmacht Zombies *See* Night of the Zombies (1981)

Night of the Zombies *See* Hell of the Living Dead (1983)

Night of Walpurgis *See* The Werewolf vs. the Vampire Woman (1970)

Night Scare *See* Nightscare (1993)

Night Shadows *See* Mutant (1983)

The Night They Invented Striptease *See* The Night They Raided Minsky's (1969)

Night Train *See* Night Train to Munich (1940)

Night Trap *See* Mardi Gras for the Devil (1993)

Night Walk *See* Deathdream (1972)

Night Watch *See* Detonator 2: Night Watch (1995)

The Night Watch *See* Le Trou (1959)

Nightfall *See* Isaac Asimov's Nightfall (2000)

Nightingale *See* The Young Nurses (1973)

A Nightingale Sang in Berkeley Square *See* The Big Scam (1979)

Nightmare *See* City of the Walking Dead (1983)

Nightmare *See* Nightmare in Badham County (1976)

Nightmare at Shadow Woods *See* Blood Rage (1987)

Nightmare Circus *See* Barn of the Naked Dead (1973)

Nightmare City *See* City of the Walking Dead (1983)

Nightmare Hotel *See* It Happened at Nightmare Inn (1970)

Nightmare House *See* Scream, Baby, Scream (1969)

Nightmare in a Damaged Brain *See* Nightmare (1982)

Nightmare Island *See* The Slayer (1982)

Nightmare Maker *See* Night Warning (1982)

A Nightmare on Elm Street 6: Freddy's Dead *See* Freddy's Dead: The Final Nightmare (1991)

Nightmare on Elm Street 7 *See* Wes Craven's New Nightmare (1994)

Nights in a Harem *See* Son of Sinbad (1955)

The Nights of Dracula *See* Count Dracula (1971)

Nijushi No Hitomi *See* Twenty-Four Eyes (1954)

Nikutai No Mon *See* Gate of Flesh (1964)

9/30/55 *See* September 30, 1955 (1977)

1990 I Guerrieri del Bronx *See* 1990: The Bronx Warriors (1983)

1999—Nen No Natsu Yasumi *See* Summer Vacation: 1999 (1988)

Ningen No Joken *See* The Human Condition: Road to Eternity (1959)

Ninja Dragons *See* Magic Kid (1992)

Nippon Chiubotsu *See* Tidal Wave (1975)

Nippon Konchuki *See* The Insect Woman (1963)

Nizza *See* A Propos de Nice (1929)

No Fear *See* Fear (1996)

No Greater Love *See* The Human Condition: Road to Eternity (1959)

No Hambra mas Penas ni Olvido *See* Funny, Dirty Little War (1983)

No Knife *See* The Frisco Kid (1979)

No Man's Land *See* No Man's Range (1935)

No Place Like Homicide *See* What a Carve-Up! (1962)

The No-Tell Hotel *See* Rosebud Beach Hotel (1985)

No Worries *See* Clueless (1995)

Nobi *See* Fires on the Plain (1959)

Noce In Galilee *See* A Wedding in Galilee (1987)

Nocturna, Granddaughter of Dracula *See* Nocturna (1979)

Non Si Sevizia un Paperino *See* Don't Torture a Duckling (1972)

Norman Rockwell's Breaking Home Ties *See* Breaking Home Ties (1987)

Party Girls *See* Party Incorporated (1989)
Pas de Probleme! *See* No Problem (1975)
Pasazerka *See* Passenger (1961)
Pasqualino Settebellezze *See* Seven Beauties (1976)
Pasqualino: Seven Beauties *See* Seven Beauties (1976)
The Pass *See* Highway Hitcher (1998)
Passages from "Finnegans Wake" *See* Finnegan's Wake (1963)
Passages from James Joyce's "Finnegans Wake" *See* Finnegan's Wake (1963)
The Passerby *See* La Passante (1983)
The Passion Flower Hotel *See* Boarding School (1983)
Passion Play *See* Love Letters (1983)
Passione d'Amore *See* Passion of Love (1982)
Passions *See* The Passing of Evil (1970)
Passport to Shame *See* Room 43 (1958)
The Patsy *See* L'Addition (1985)
Patterns of Power *See* Patterns (1956)
Patton: A Salute to a Rebel *See* Patton (1970)
Patton—Lust for Glory *See* Patton (1970)
Paul Bowles: Halbmond *See* Halfmoon (1995)
Pauline a la Plage *See* Pauline at the Beach (1983)
Paura Nella Citta Dei Morti Viventi *See* Gates of Hell (1980)
P.D. James: A Mind to Murder *See* A Mind to Murder (1996)
P.D. James: Devices & Desires *See* Devices and Desires (1991)
The Peace Game *See* The Gladiators (1970)
Peacemaker *See* The Ambassador (1984)
Peau d'Ane *See* Donkey Skin (1970)
The Peking Medallion *See* The Corrupt Ones (1967)
Penn of Pennsylvania *See* The Courageous Mr. Penn (1941)
Pensionat Oskar *See* Like It Never Was Before (1995)
People Toys *See* Devil Times Five (1974)
People's Enemy *See* Prison Train (1938)
Pepi, Luci, Bom y Otras Chicas del Monton *See* Pepi, Luci, Bom and Other Girls on the Heap (1980)
Perceval Le Gallois *See* Perceval (1978)
Percy's Progress *See* It's Not the Size That Counts (1974)
Perdita Durango *See* Dance with the Devil (1997)
The Perfumed Garden *See* Tales of the Kama Sutra: The Perfumed Garden (1998)
Peril en la Demeure *See* Peril (1985)
Perils from Planet Mongo *See* Flash Gordon: Rocketship (1940)
The Perils of Gwendoline in the Land of the Yik-Yak *See* The Perils of Gwendoline (1984)
Perils of Nyoka *See* Nyoka and the Tigermen (1942)
Persecution *See* The Graveyard (1974)
Perseo l'Invincibile *See* Medusa Against the Son of Hercules (1962)
Perseus the Invincible *See* Medusa Against the Son of Hercules (1962)
Persons Unknown *See* Big Deal on Madonna Street (1958)
Peter Benchley's The Beast *See* The Beast (1996)
Peter Rabbit and Tales of Beatrix Potter *See* Tales of Beatrix Potter (1971)
Petersen *See* Jock Petersen (1974)
Petroleum Girls *See* Legend of Frenchie King (1971)
Phantom Fiend *See* The Return of Dr. Mabuse (1961)
The Phantom of Terror *See* The Bird with the Crystal Plumage (1970)
Phantom of the Air *See* The Phantom Broadcast (1933)
The Phantom Ship *See* The Mystery of the Mary Celeste (1937)
Phar Lap: Heart of a Nation *See* Phar Lap (1984)
Phenomena *See* Creepers (1985)
Philo Vance Returns *See* Infamous Crimes (1947)
Phoebe *See* Zelly & Me (1988)
The Phoenix *See* War of the Wizards (1981)
Phorpa *See* The Cup (1999)
Picking up the Pieces *See* Bloodsucking Pharoahs of Pittsburgh (1990)
Pickup on 101 *See* Where the Eagle Flies (1972)
Pictures of Baby Jane Doe *See* Jane Doe (1996)
Pigsty *See* Porcile (1969)
Pilgrimage to Rome *See* L'Anne Sainte (1978)
The Pill *See* Test Tube Babies (1948)
Pillow of Death *See* Dead Man's Eyes/Pillow of Death (1944)
The Pilot *See* Danger in the Skies (1979)
Pin Down Girl *See* Pin Down Girls (1951)
Pinball Pick-Up *See* Pick-Up Summer (1979)
Pinball Summer *See* Pick-Up Summer (1979)
Pinocchio *See* The Adventures of Pinocchio (1996)
Pioneers *See* Pioneer Woman (1973)
Pippi Langstrump Pa de Sju Haven *See* Pippi in the South Seas (1974)
Piranha 2: Flying Killers *See* Piranha 2: The Spawning (1982)
Pirate's Fiancee *See* A Very Curious Girl (1969)
Pirate's Harbor *See* Haunted Harbor (1944)
Pistol Blues *See* Machine Gun Blues (1995)
Pixote: A Lei do Mais Fraco *See* Pixote (1981)
The Pizza Connection *See* The Sicilian Connection (1985)
The Plains of Heaven *See* Panic Station (1982)
Planet of Blood *See* Planet of the Vampires (1965)
Planet of Horrors *See* Galaxy of Terror (1981)
Planet of Incredible Creatures *See* Fantastic Planet (1973)
The Planet of Junior Brown *See* Junior's Groove (1997)
Planet of Love *See* Galaxies Are Colliding (1992)
Planet of Terror *See* Planet of the Vampires (1965)
Planet of the Damned *See* Planet of the Vampires (1965)
Planet of the Lifeless Men *See* Battle of the Worlds (1961)
The Plants Are Watching *See* The Kirlian Witness (1978)
Players *See* The Club (1981)
Playgirl Gang *See* Switchblade Sisters (1975)
The Playgirls and the Bellboy *See* The Bellboy and the Playgirls (1962)
Playing for Keeps *See* Lily in Love (1985)
Playtime *See* Love Play (1960)
Please! Mr. Balzac *See* Plucking the Daisy (1956)
Plein Soleil *See* Purple Noon (1960)
Plein Sud *See* Heat of Desire (1984)
Pluck of the Irish *See* Great Guy (1936)
Po Dezju *See* Before the Rain (1994)
Pocomania *See* The Devil's Daughter (1939)
Podranki *See* The Orphans (1977)
Poe's Tales of Terror *See* Tales of Terror (1962)
Poisoned by Love: The Kern County Murders *See* Murder So Sweet (1993)
Pokayaniye *See* Repentance (1987)
Poketto Monsutaa: Maboroshi No Pokemon X: Lugia Bakudan *See* Pokemon the Movie 2000: The Power of One (2000)
Pokolenie *See* A Generation (1954)
Police Assassins *See* Royal Warriors (1986)
Police Connection *See* The Mad Bomber (1972)
Police Force *See* Police Story (1985)
Police Story 3, Part 2 *See* Supercop 2 (1993)
Police Story 3: Supercop *See* Supercop (1992)
Police Story 4 *See* Jackie Chan's First Strike (1996)
Pony Express *See* Peter Lundy and the Medicine Hat Stallion (1977)
Pookie *See* The Sterile Cuckoo (1969)
Poopsie *See* Get Rita (1975)
Poor Albert and Little Annie *See* I Dismember Mama (1974)
The Poor Outlaws *See* The Round Up (1966)
The Pope Must Die *See* The Pope Must Diet (1991)
Popiol i Diament *See* Ashes and Diamonds (1958)
Poppies Are Also Flowers *See* The Poppy Is Also a Flower (1966)
Por Que Lo Llaman Amor Cuando Quieren Decir Sexo? *See* Why Do They Call It Love When They Mean Sex? (1992)
Porcherie *See* Porcile (1969)
A Pornographic Liaison *See* An Affair of Love (1999)
Porte Aperte *See* Open Doors (1989)
Portrait of a Woman, Nude *See* Nudo di Donna (1983)
Portrait of Alison *See* Postmark for Danger (1956)
Portrait of Maria *See* Maria Candelaria (1946)
Portraits of Innocence *See* Portraits of a Killer (1995)
Post Coitum *See* After Sex (1997)
Post Coitum, Animal Triste *See* After Sex (1997)
Potemkin *See* The Battleship Potemkin (1925)
Potop *See* The Deluge (1973)
The Powder Keg *See* Cabaret Balkan (1998)
Practice Makes Perfect *See* Le Cavaleur (1978)
Prairie Outlaws *See* Wild West (1946)
Pratidwandi *See* The Adversary (1971)
Pre *See* Without Limits (1997)
Precious *See* Citizen Ruth (1996)
Pred dozhdot *See* Before the Rain (1994)
The Prehistoric Sound *See* Sound of Horror (1964)
Prehistoric World *See* Teenage Caveman (1958)
Prenom: Carmen *See* First Name: Carmen (1983)
Preparez Vous Mouchoirs *See* Get Out Your Handkerchiefs (1978)
Preppies *See* Making the Grade (1984)
The President's Women *See* Foreplay (1975)
Presque Rien *See* Come Undone (2000)
Preston Tylk *See* Bad Seed (2000)
Pret-a-Porter *See* Ready to Wear (1994)
Pride of Kentucky *See* The Story of Seabiscuit (1949)
Prima della Rivoluzione *See* Before the Revolution (1965)
Prince of Jutland *See* Royal Deceit (1994)
Priority Red One *See* Delta Force Commando 2 (1990)
Prison *See* Devil's Wanton (1949)
The Prisoner *See* Cold Room (1984)
Prisoner of the Caucasus *See* Prisoner of the Mountains (1996)
The Private Life of Paul Joseph Goebbels *See* Enemy of Women (1944)
The Private Lives of Elizabeth and Essex *See* Elizabeth, the Queen (1968)
Private Snuffy Smith *See* Snuffy Smith, Yard Bird (1942)
The Private Wore Skirts *See* Never Wave at a WAC (1952)
Pro Urodov i Lyudej *See* Of Freaks and Men (1998)
Profession: Reporter *See* The Passenger (1975)
The Professional *See* Le Professionnel (1981)
The Profile of Terror *See* The Sadist (1963)
Profumo di Donna *See* The Scent of a Woman (1975)
Profundo Carmesi *See* Deep Crimson (1996)
Profundo Rosso *See* Deep Red: Hatchet Murders (1975)
Project Shadowchaser 2 *See* Night Siege Project: Shadowchaser 2 (1994)
Prom Night 2 *See* Hello Mary Lou: Prom Night 2 (1987)
Promenons Nous dans les Bois *See* Deep in the Woods (2000)
The Promise *See* La Promesse (1996)
Promise Her Anything *See* Promises! Promises! (1963)
The Promise of Red Lips *See* Daughters of Darkness (1971)
The Promised Land *See* Legal Deceit (1995)
Prophecies of Nostradamus *See* Last Days of Planet Earth (1974)
A Proposito Luciano *See* Lucky Luciano (1974)
Prorva *See* Moscow Parade (1992)
The Protectors, Book One *See* Angel of H.E.A.T. (1982)
Proud, Damned, and Dead *See* The Proud and the Damned (1972)
Prova d'Orchestra *See* Orchestra Rehearsal (1978)
Przesluchanie *See* The Interrogation (1982)
Psycho a Go Go! *See* Blood of Ghastly Horror (1972)
Psycho-Circus *See* Circus of Fear (1967)
Psycho Killers *See* The Flesh and the Fiends (1960)
Psycho Puppet *See* Delirium (1977)
Psycho Sex Fiend *See* The House that Vanished (1973)
Psycho Sisters *See* The Sibling (1972)
Psychotic *See* Driver's Seat (1973)
Ptang, Yang, Kipperbang *See* Kipperbang (1982)
Public Be Damned *See* The World Gone Mad (1933)
The Public Be Hanged *See* The World Gone Mad (1933)

The Road to Frisco *See* They Drive by Night (1940)

Roaring Timber *See* Come and Get It (1936)

Rob Roy *See* Rob Roy—The Highland Rogue (1953)

Robert A. Heinlein's The Puppet Masters *See* The Puppet Masters (1994)

Robert Louis Stevenson's The Suicide Club *See* Robert Louis Stevenson's The Game of Death (1999)

Robert Ludlum's the Apocalypse Watch *See* The Apocalypse Watch (1997)

Robinson Crusoeland *See* Utopia (1951)

Robo Ninja *See* Cyber Ninja (1994)

Rocco E I Suoi Fratelli *See* Rocco and His Brothers (1960)

Rocco et Ses Freres *See* Rocco and His Brothers (1960)

Rock and Roll Wrestling Women vs. the Aztec Mummy *See* Wrestling Women vs. the Aztec Mummy (1959)

Rocket and Roll *See* Abbott and Costello Go to Mars (1953)

Rocket Man *See* RocketMan (1997)

Rocket to the Moon *See* Cat Women of the Moon (1953)

Rocky Mountain Mystery *See* The Fighting Westerner (1935)

Rodents *See* Ratas, Ratones, Rateros (1999)

Rodgers & Hammerstein's Cinderella *See* Cinderella (1997)

Roger Corman Presents: Black Scorpion *See* Black Scorpion (1995)

Roger Corman Presents Burial of the Rats *See* Burial of the Rats (1995)

Roger Corman Presents: House of the Damned *See* Spectre (1996)

Roger Corman Presents: Humanoids from the Deep *See* Humanoids from the Deep (1996)

Roger Corman Presents Last Exit to Earth *See* Last Exit to Earth (1996)

Roger Corman Presents Subliminal Seduction *See* The Corporation (1996)

Roger Corman Presents: Suspect Device *See* Suspect Device (1995)

Roger Corman Presents: The Alien Within *See* Unknown Origin (1995)

Roger Corman Presents: Vampirella *See* Vampirella (1996)

Roger Corman's Frankenstein Unbound *See* Frankenstein Unbound (1990)

Roma *See* Fellini's Roma (1972)

Roma, Citta Aperta *See* Open City (1945)

Romance and Riches *See* Amazing Adventure (1937)

Romance da Empregada *See* The Story of Fausta (1988)

Romauld et Juliet *See* Mama, There's a Man in Your Bed (1989)

Rome, Open City *See* Open City (1945)

Romeo and Juliet *See* William Shakespeare's Romeo and Juliet (1996)

Romeo in Pyjamas *See* Parlor, Bedroom and Bath (1931)

Romeo, Julia a Tma *See* Sweet Light in a Dark Room (1960)

Romeo, Juliet and Darkness *See* Sweet Light in a Dark Room (1960)

Rommel—Desert Fox *See* The Desert Fox (1951)

Rona Jaffe's Mazes and Monsters *See* Mazes and Monsters (1982)

The Rook *See* Something for Everyone (1970)

Rookies *See* Buck Privates (1941)

Rookies Come Home *See* Buck Privates Come Home (1947)

Rosamunde Pilcher's Coming Home *See* Coming Home (1998)

The Rose and the Sword *See* Flesh and Blood (1985)

Rose Red *See* Stephen King's Rose Red (2002)

Roseanna's Grave *See* For Roseanna (1996)

Rosemary's Killer *See* The Prowler (1981)

The Rotten Apple *See* Five Minutes to Love (1963)

Rouge Baiser *See* Red Kiss (1985)

Rough Company *See* The Violent Men (1955)

Rough Treatment *See* Without Anesthesia (1978)

The Round Tower *See* Catherine Cookson's The Round Tower (1998)

Roveh Huliot *See* The Wooden Gun (1979)

Roxanne: The Prize Pulitzer *See* The Prize Pulitzer (1989)

The Royal Game *See* Brainwashed (1960)

Ruby Cairo *See* Deception (1992)

Rudyard Kipling's Jungle Book *See* The Jungle Book (1942)

Rue Cases Negres *See* Sugar Cane Alley (1983)

Rukajarven Tie *See* Ambush (1999)

Rules of Obsession *See* A Passion to Kill (1994)

Rumpo Kid *See* Carry On Cowboy (1966)

Run for the Money *See* Hard Cash (2001)

Run, Simon, Run *See* Savage Run (1970)

The Runaways *See* South Bronx Heroes (1985)

Russ Meyer's SuperVixens *See* Supervixens (1975)

Russicum *See* Third Solution (1989)

Rustler's Roundup *See* Rustler's Hideout (1944)

The Rutles *See* All You Need Is Cash (1978)

The Saboteur *See* Morituri (1965)

Saboteur: Code Name Morituri *See* Morituri (1965)

The Sabre and the Arrow *See* Last of the Comanches (1952)

The Sabre Tooth Tiger *See* Deep Red: Hatchet Murders (1975)

Sabrina Fair *See* Sabrina (1954)

Sacco e Vanzetti *See* Sacco & Vanzetti (1971)

Sadie & Son *See* Detective Sadie & Son (1984)

Sadko *See* The Magic Voyage of Sinbad (1952)

The Saga of Dracula *See* The Saga of the Draculas (1972)

The Saga of Gosta Berling *See* The Atonement of Gosta Berling (1924)

The Saga of the Road *See* Pather Panchali (1954)

Saikaku Ichidai Onna *See* Life of Oharu (1952)

St. George and the Dragon *See* The Magic Sword (1962)

St. George and the Seven Curses *See* The Magic Sword (1962)

St. Ives *See* Robert Louis Stevenson's St. Ives (1998)

St. Martin's Lane *See* Sidewalks of London (1938)

Sakima and the Masked Marvel *See* The Masked Marvel (1943)

The Salamander *See* La Salamandre (1971)

Salem's Ghost *See* Witchcraft 8: Salem's Ghost (1995)

Salerno Beachhead *See* A Walk in the Sun (1946)

The Salute of the Jugger *See* The Blood of Heroes (1989)

Salvation! Have You Said Your Prayers Today? *See* Salvation! (1987)

Sam Cooper's Gold *See* The Ruthless Four (1970)

Sam Marlowe, Private Eye *See* The Man with Bogart's Face (1980)

Sam's Song *See* The Swap (1971)

The Samurai *See* Le Samourai (1967)

San Fernando *See* San Fernando Valley (1944)

San Michele Aveva un Gallo *See* St. Michael Had a Rooster (1972)

Sanda tai Gailah *See* War of the Gargantuas (1970)

Sandakan House 8 *See* Sandakan No. 8 (1974)

Sandkings *See* The Outer Limits: Sandkings (1995)

Sandokan alla Riscossa *See* The Conqueror & the Empress (1964)

The Sandpit Generals *See* Defiant (1970)

Sandra *See* Sandra of a Thousand Delights (1965)

Sanma No Aji *See* An Autumn Afternoon (1962)

Sans Toit Ni Loi *See* Vagabond (1985)

Sansho Dayu *See* Sansho the Bailiff (1954)

Santa Claus Defeats the Aliens *See* Santa Claus Conquers the Martians (1964)

Santo en el Museo de Cera *See* Samson in the Wax Museum (1963)

Santo in the Wax Museum *See* Samson in the Wax Museum (1963)

Sarajevo *See* De Mayerling a Sarajevo (1940)

Sardonicus *See* Mr. Sardonicus (1961)

Sasom I En Spegel *See* Through a Glass Darkly (1961)

Satan *See* Mark of the Devil (1969)

Satanic Mechanic *See* Perfect Killer (1977)

Satan's Bloody Freaks *See* Dracula vs. Frankenstein (1971)

Satan's Claw *See* The Blood on Satan's Claw (1971)

Satan's Daughters *See* Vampyres (1974)

Satan's Dog *See* Play Dead (1981)

Satan's Mistress *See* Demon Rage (1982)

Satan's Satellites *See* Zombies of the Stratosphere (1952)

Satan's Skin *See* The Blood on Satan's Claw (1971)

Satan's Supper *See* Cataclysm (1981)

Satansbraten *See* Satan's Brew (1976)

Satellite of Blood *See* First Man into Space (1959)

Satin Vengeance *See* Naked Vengeance (1985)

Satsujim-ken *See* The Street Fighter (1974)

Satsujin-ken 2 *See* Return of the Street Fighter (1974)

Saturday Island *See* Island of Desire (1952)

Satyricon *See* Fellini Satyricon (1969)

Saul e David *See* Saul and David (1968)

The Savage *See* Lovers Like Us (1975)

Savage Abduction *See* Cycle Psycho (1972)

Savage Apocalypse *See* Cannibal Apocalypse (1980)

Savage Beasts *See* The Wild Beasts (1985)

Savage Nights *See* Les Nuits Fauves (1992)

The Savage Planet *See* Fantastic Planet (1973)

The Savage State *See* L'Etat Sauvage (1978)

Sayat Nova *See* The Color of Pomegranates (1969)

The Scalper *See* Just the Ticket (1998)

Scaramouche *See* Loves & Times of Scaramouche (1976)

Scared Stiff *See* Treasure of Fear (1945)

The Scaremaker *See* Girls Night Out (1983)

Scarface: The Shame of a Nation *See* Scarface (1931)

Scarlet Buccaneer *See* Swashbuckler (1976)

The Scarlet Buccaneer *See* Swashbuckler (1984)

Scary Movie *See* Scream (1996)

Schatten der Engel *See* Shadow of Angels (1976)

Scherben *See* Shattered (1921)

Schlafes Bruder *See* Brother of Sleep (1995)

Schloss Vogelod *See* The Haunted Castle (1921)

The School That Ate My Brain *See* Zombie High (1987)

Schwestern Oder die Balance des Glucks *See* Sisters, Or the Balance of Happiness (1979)

The Scotland Yard Mystery *See* The Living Dead (1936)

Scoundrel in White *See* High Heels (1972)

Scream *See* The Night God Screamed (198?)

Scream Again *See* Scream 2 (1997)

Scream and Die *See* The House that Vanished (1973)

Scream Bloody Murder *See* House of Terror (1987)

Scream Free! *See* Free Grass (1969)

Screamer *See* Scream and Scream Again (1970)

Screwface *See* Marked for Death (1990)

Scrooge *See* A Christmas Carol (1951)

Scum of the Earth *See* Poor White Trash 2 (1975)

Search for the Mother Lode *See* Mother Lode (1982)

Searchers of the Voodoo Mountain *See* Warriors of the Apocalypse (1985)

Season of Dreams *See* Stacking (1987)

Seated At His Right *See* Black Jesus (1968)

The Second Arrival *See* The Arrival 2 (1998)

Second Chances *See* Probation (1932)

The Second Coming *See* Messiah of Evil (1974)

The Second Jungle Book: Mowgli and Baloo *See* Rudyard Kipling's the Second Jungle Book: Mowgli and Baloo (1997)

The Second Lieutenant *See* The Last Lieutenant (1994)

Secondloitnanten *See* The Last Lieutenant (1994)

Seconds to Live *See* Viva Knievel (1977)

The Secret *See* Catherine Cookson's The Secret (2000)

The Secret Cinema *See* Paul Bartel's The Secret Cinema (1969)

Secret File: Hollywood *See* Secret File of Hollywood (1962)

Secret Honor: A Political Myth *See* Secret Honor (1985)

Secret Honor: The Last Testament of Richard M. Nixon *See* Secret Honor (1985)

The Secret of Dr. Mabuse *See* The Thousand Eyes of Dr. Mabuse (1960)

Solomon Northrup's Odyssey *See* Half Slave, Half Free (1985)

Solyaris *See* Solaris (1972)

Sombra, the Spider Woman *See* The Black Widow (1947)

Some Like It Cool *See* Sex on the Run (1978)

Some Like It Hot *See* Rhythm Romance (1939)

Someone is Killing the Great Chefs of Europe *See* Who Is Killing the Great Chefs of Europe? (1978)

Someone's Killing the World's Greatest Models *See* She's Dressed to Kill (1979)

Something Fishy *See* Pas Tres Catholique (1993)

Something Is Out There *See* Day of the Animals (1977)

Something Like the Truth *See* The Offence (1973)

Something to Hide *See* Shattered (1972)

Something Waits in the Dark *See* Screamers (1980)

Somewhere in France *See* The Foreman Went to France (1942)

Sommarlek *See* Summer Interlude (1950)

Sommarnattens Leende *See* Smiles of a Summer Night (1955)

Son of Blob *See* Beware! The Blob (1972)

Son of Darkness: To Die For 2 *See* To Die For 2: Son of Darkness (1991)

Sondagsengler *See* The Other Side of Sunday (1996)

The Song of the Road *See* Pather Panchali (1954)

Song of the Sierra *See* Springtime in the Sierras (1947)

Sono Otoko, Kyobo ni Tsuki *See* Violent Cop (1989)

Sons and Warriors *See* Some Mother's Son (1996)

Sons of the Legion *See* Sons of the Desert (1933)

Sons of the Musketeers *See* At Sword's Point (1951)

Sophie's Place *See* Crooks & Coronets (1969)

Sotto gli Occhi dell'Assassino *See* Unsane (1982)

Soul *See* Earth (1930)

Soul Man 2 *See* Far Out Man (1989)

Soulmates *See* Evil Lives (1992)

Sound From a Million Years Ago *See* Sound of Horror (1964)

Sound of Fury *See* Try and Get Me (1950)

Soup to Nuts *See* Waitress (1981)

Sous le Sable *See* Under the Sand (2000)

Sous le Soleil de Satan *See* Under Satan's Sun (1987)

Sous les Toits de Paris *See* Under the Roofs of Paris (1929)

South of Panama *See* Panama Menace (1941)

South Pacific *See* Rodgers & Hammerstein's South Pacific (2001)

South Sea Woman *See* Pearl of the South Pacific (1955)

Southwest to Sonora *See* The Appaloosa (1966)

Soy Cuba *See* I Am Cuba (1964)

Space 2074 *See* Star Quest (1989)

Space: 2100 *See* Destination Moonbase Alpha (1975)

The Space Amoeba *See* Yog, Monster from Space (1971)

Space Avenger *See* Alien Space Avenger (1991)

Space Invasion from Lapland *See* Invasion of the Animal People (1962)

Space Invasion of Lapland *See* Invasion of the Animal People (1962)

Space Men *See* Assignment Outer Space (1961)

Space Men Appear in Tokyo *See* Warning from Space (1956)

Space Mission of the Lost Planet *See* Horror of the Blood Monsters (1970)

Space Monster Dagora *See* Dagora, the Space Monster (1965)

Space Mutants *See* Planet of the Vampires (1965)

Space Soldiers *See* Flash Gordon: Rocketship (1940)

Space Travellers *See* Marooned (1969)

The Space Vampires *See* The Astro-Zombies (1967)

Spacemen Saturday Night *See* Invasion of the Saucer Men (1957)

Spaceship to the Unknown *See* Flash Gordon: Rocketship (1940)

Spara Forte, Piu Forte...Non Capisco *See* Shoot Loud, Louder, I Don't Understand! (1966)

Spawn *See* Todd McFarlane's Spawn (1997)

Spawn of the Slithis *See* Slithis (1978)

The Specter of Freedom *See* Phantom of Liberty (1974)

The Spectre *See* The Ghost (1963)

Speed Brent Wins *See* Breed of the Border (1933)

The Spell of Amy Nugent *See* Spellbound (1941)

Spell of the Hypnotist *See* Fright (1956)

Spettri *See* Specters (1987)

The Spider *See* Earth vs. the Spider (1958)

Spider Baby, or the Maddest Story Ever Told *See* Spider Baby (1964)

Spider-Man *See* The Amazing Spider-Man (1977)

Spies-A-Go-Go *See* Nasty Rabbit (1964)

Spies, Lies, and Alibis *See* Code Name: Chaos (1990)

Spinal Tap *See* This Is Spinal Tap (1984)

Spione *See* Spies (1928)

Spirit of Tattoo *See* Irezumi (1983)

Spirit of the Dead *See* The Asphyx (1972)

Spirit of the People *See* Abe Lincoln in Illinois (1940)

The Spiritualist *See* The Amazing Mr. X (1948)

Spivs *See* I Vitelloni (1953)

The Split *See* The Manster (1959)

The Spooky Movie Show *See* The Mask (1961)

Spoorloos *See* The Vanishing (1988)

Spot *See* Dog Pound Shuffle (1975)

Spotswood *See* The Efficiency Expert (1992)

Spring Break USA *See* Lauderdale (1989)

Spring Fever USA *See* Lauderdale (1989)

Spur der Steine *See* Trace of Stones (1966)

Spyder *See* Blackbelt 2: Fatal Force (1993)

Spymaker *See* Spymaker: The Secret Life of Ian Fleming (1990)

Spymaster *See* Goldeneye: The Secret Life of Ian Fleming (1989)

Squadron of Doom *See* Ace Drummond (1936)

Stacey and Her Gangbusters *See* Stacey (1973)

Stadt ohne Mitleid *See* Town without Pity (1961)

Stakeout 2 *See* Another Stakeout (1993)

The Stand *See* Stephen King's The Stand (1994)

Stand and Deliver *See* Bowery Blitzkrieg (1941)

Stand Easy *See* Goon Movie (1953)

Stanno Tutti Bene *See* Everybody's Fine (1990)

Star *See* Danielle Steel's Star (1993)

Star Child *See* Space Raiders (1983)

The Star Man *See* The Star Maker (1995)

Star Wars: Episode 4—A New Hope *See* Star Wars (1977)

Star Wars: Episode 5—The Empire Strikes Back *See* The Empire Strikes Back (1980)

Star Wars: Episode 6—Return of the Jedi *See* Return of the Jedi (1983)

Stardust *See* Mad About Money (1937)

Starflight: the Plane that Couldn't Land *See* Starflight One (1983)

Starknight *See* Star Knight (1985)

Starlight Slaughter *See* Eaten Alive (1976)

The Statutory Affair *See* Lola (1969)

Steiner—Das Eiserne Kreuz *See* Cross of Iron (1976)

Stella Star *See* Star Crash (1978)

Stepfather *See* Beau Pere (1981)

Stephen King's Cat's Eye *See* Cat's Eye (1985)

Stephen King's Graveyard Shift *See* Graveyard Shift (1990)

Stephen King's Silver Bullet *See* Silver Bullet (1985)

Stephen King's Sleepwalkers *See* Sleepwalkers (1992)

Still Smokin' *See* Cheech and Chong: Still Smokin' (1983)

Sto Dnej Do Pri Kaza *See* 100 Days Before the Command (1990)

Stolen Hearts *See* Two If by Sea (1995)

Storia de Ragazzi e di Ragazze *See* The Story of Boys & Girls (1991)

Storm *See* Storm Tracker (1999)

Storm of the Century *See* Stephen King's The Storm of the Century (1999)

Stormy Crossing *See* Black Tide (1958)

Story of a Marriage *See* On Valentine's Day (1986)

The Story of Gosta Berling *See* The Atonement of Gosta Berling (1924)

The Story of Robin Hood *See* The Story of Robin Hood & His Merrie Men (1952)

A Story of the Cruelties of Youth *See* The Cruel Story of Youth (1960)

The Story Without A Name *See* Without Warning (1952)

Straight Jacket *See* Dark Sanity (1982)

Straight on Till Morning *See* Dressed for Death (1974)

Straight to Hell *See* Cut and Run (1985)

Strange Adventure *See* Wayne Murder Case (1938)

The Strange Adventure of David Gray *See* Vampyr (1931)

The Strange Case of Dr. Jekyll and Mr. Hyde *See* Dr. Jekyll and Mr. Hyde (1968)

The Strange Case of Madeleine *See* Madeleine (1950)

Strange Confession *See* Calling Dr. Death/Strange Confession (1943)

Strange Deception *See* The Accused (1948)

Strange Incident *See* The Ox-Bow Incident (1943)

Strange Interval *See* Strange Interlude (1932)

Strange Journey *See* Fantastic Voyage (1966)

The Strange Ones *See* Les Enfants Terrible (1950)

Strange Skirts *See* When Ladies Meet (1941)

The Strange World of Planet X *See* The Cosmic Monsters (1958)

Strangeland *See* Dee Snider's Strangeland (1998)

The Stranger *See* Shame (1961)

A Stranger Came Home *See* Unholy Four (1954)

Stranger in Our House *See* Summer of Fear (1978)

Stranger in the House *See* Black Christmas (1975)

Stranger in the House *See* Cop-Out (1967)

A Stranger Walked In *See* Love from a Stranger (1947)

Strangers *See* Voyage in Italy (1953)

Stranger's Face *See* Face of Another (1966)

Strangest Dreams: Invasion of the Space Preachers *See* Invasion of the Space Preachers (1990)

The Strangler of Vienna *See* The Mad Butcher (1972)

Strangler's Morgue *See* The Crimes of Stephen Hawke (1936)

Stray Dogs *See* U-Turn (1997)

Street Fighter Counterattacks *See* The Street Fighter's Last Revenge (1974)

Street Gang *See* Vigilante (1983)

Street Kill *See* Death Scream (1975)

Street Legal *See* The Last of the Finest (1990)

Street Love *See* Scarred (1984)

Street of Shadows *See* The Shadow Man (1953)

Street of Sorrow *See* Joyless Street (1925)

Streets of Laredo *See* Larry McMurtry's Streets of Laredo (1995)

Streets of New York *See* The Abe Lincoln of Ninth Avenue (1939)

Streetwise *See* Jailbait (1993)

Strictly Confidential *See* Broadway Bill (1934)

Strictly for Pleasure *See* The Perfect Furlough (1959)

Strike! *See* All I Wanna Do (1998)

Striking Back *See* Search and Destroy (1981)

Strip Poker *See* The Big Switch (1970)

Striptease Lady *See* Lady of Burlesque (1943)

Struktura Krysztalu *See* The Structure of Crystals (1969)

Stryker's War *See* Thou Shalt Not Kill...Except (1987)

Student Body *See* Getting In (1994)

Subarashiki Nichiyobi *See* One Wonderful Sunday (1947)

Subida Al Cielo *See* Mexican Bus Ride (1951)

Subliminal Seduction *See* The Corporation (1996)

The Submersion of Japan *See* Tidal Wave (1975)

Subspecies 2 *See* Bloodstone: Subspecies 2 (1992)

Subspecies 3 *See* Bloodlust: Subspecies 3 (1993)

Subspecies 4 *See* Bloodstorm: Subspecies 4 (1998)

Subspecies 4: Bloodstorm—The Master's Revenge *See* Bloodstorm: Subspecies 4 (1998)

Succubus *See* The Devil's Nightmare (1971)

Such Men are Dangerous *See* The Racers (1955)

Sudden Terror *See* Eye Witness (1970)

Thou Shalt Honour Thy Wife *See* Master of the House (1925)

A Thousand and One Nights *See* Arabian Nights (1974)

3x Jugatsu *See* Boiling Point (1990)

Three Bad Men in the Hidden Fortress *See* The Hidden Fortress (1958)

Three Colors: Blue *See* Trois Couleurs: Bleu (1993)

Three Colors: Red *See* Trois Couleurs: Rouge (1994)

Three Colors: White *See* Trois Couleurs: Blanc (1994)

Three Crazy Legionnaires *See* Three Legionnaires (1937)

The Three Faces of Fear *See* Black Sabbath (1964)

The Three Faces of Terror *See* Black Sabbath (1964)

Three For the Money *See* Win, Place, or Steal (1972)

Three Moves to Freedom *See* Brainwashed (1960)

Three Ninjas: Showdown at Mega Mountain *See* 3 Ninjas: High Noon at Mega Mountain (1997)

Three of a Kind *See* Cooking Up Trouble (1944)

Three Rascals in the Hidden Fortress *See* The Hidden Fortress (1958)

Three Steps to the Gallows *See* White Fire (1953)

The Three Stooges Go Around the World in a Daze *See* Around the World in a Daze (1963)

The Threepenny Opera *See* Mack the Knife (1989)

Thriller: Kill Two Birds *See* Cry Terror (1974)

Through the Looking Glass *See* The Velvet Vampire (1971)

Thunder *See* Thunder Warrior (1985)

Thunder County *See* Women's Prison Escape (1974)

Thunder Mountain *See* Shadow of Chikara (1977)

Thunder on the Trail *See* Thundering Trail (1951)

Thunder Point *See* Jack Higgins' Thunder Point (1997)

Thursday the 12th *See* Pandemonium (1982)

Ti Kniver I Hjertet *See* Cross My Heart and Hope to Die (1994)

Tian Yu *See* Xiu Xiu: The Sent Down Girl (1997)

Tianguo Niezi *See* The Day the Sun Turned Cold (1994)

Tidal Wave *See* Portrait of Jennie (1948)

The Tide of Life *See* Catherine Cookson's The Tide of Life (1996)

The Tiger *See* Tiger Warsaw (1987)

Tiger in the Sky *See* The McConnell Story (1955)

Tiger of Bengal *See* Journey to the Lost City (1958)

The Tiger of Eschanapur *See* The Indian Tomb (1921)

The Tiger Woman *See* Perils of the Darkest Jungle (1944)

Tigers Don't Cry *See* African Rage (1978)

Tight Little Island *See* Whiskey Galore (1948)

The Tigress *See* Ilsa, the Tigress of Siberia (1979)

'Til Christmas *See* Breathing Room (1996)

Til Dawn Do Us Part *See* Dressed for Death (1974)

Till Death Us Do Part *See* The Blood Spattered Bride (1972)

Till Gladje *See* To Joy (1950)

Tilly Trotter *See* Catherine Cookson's Tilly Trotter (1999)

Tim Burton's The Nightmare before Christmas *See* The Nightmare before Christmas (1993)

Timber Tramps *See* The Big Push (1975)

Time Flyers *See* The Blue Yonder (1986)

A Time For Caring *See* Generation (1969)

The Time of Return *See* Muriel (1963)

Time of the Beast *See* Mutator (1990)

Time of the Wolves *See* Carbon Copy (1969)

Time Raiders *See* Warriors of the Apocalypse (1985)

Time Trap *See* The Time Travelers (1964)

Time Warp Terror *See* Bloody New Year (1987)

Timecode *See* Time Code (2000)

The Timeshifters *See* Thrill Seekers (1999)

Timeslip *See* The Atomic Man (1956)

Timewarp *See* Day Time Ended (1980)

Tini Zabutykh Predkiv *See* Shadows of Forgotten Ancestors (1964)

Tintorera *See* Tintorera...Tiger Shark (1978)

Tintorera...Bloody Waters *See* Tintorera...Tiger Shark (1978)

Tirez sur le Pianiste *See* Shoot the Piano Player (1962)

Titan Find *See* Creature (1985)

Tito and I *See* Tito and Me (1992)

Tito i Ja *See* Tito and Me (1992)

To Be a Man *See* Cry of Battle (1963)

To Catch a Spy *See* Catch Me a Spy (1971)

To Die For *See* Heaven's a Drag (1994)

To Elvis, With Love *See* Touched by Love (1980)

To Have and to Hold *See* When a Man Loves a Woman (1994)

To Koritsi Me Ta Mavra *See* Girl in Black (1956)

To Live *See* Ikiru (1952)

To Love a Vampire *See* Lust for a Vampire (1971)

To Our Loves *See* A Nos Amours (1984)

To Telefteo Psemma *See* A Matter of Dignity (1957)

To Vlemma Tou Odyssea *See* Ulysses' Gaze (1995)

Toca Para Mi *See* Play for Me (2001)

Today We Live *See* The Day and the Hour (1963)

Todo Sobre Mi Madre *See* All About My Mother (1999)

A Toi de Faire, Mignonne *See* Your Turn Darling (1963)

Tokyo Monogatari *See* Tokyo Story (1953)

Tokyo Nagaremono *See* Tokyo Drifter (1966)

Tomb of the Cat *See* Tomb of Ligeia (1964)

Tomb of the Living Dead *See* Mad Doctor of Blood Island (1969)

Tomb Raider *See* Lara Croft: Tomb Raider (2001)

The Tommyknockers *See* Stephen King's The Tommyknockers (1993)

The Tomorrow Man *See* 984: Prisoner of the Future (1984)

Ton Kero Ton Hellinon *See* When the Greeks (1981)

Tong Nien Wang Shi *See* A Time to Live and a Time to Die (1985)

Too Many Chefs *See* Who Is Killing the Great Chefs of Europe? (1978)

Too Much *See* Wish You Were Here (1987)

Top of the Food Chain *See* Invasion! (1999)

Topio Stin Omichli *See* Landscape in the Mist (1988)

Tora No O Wo Fumu Otokotachi *See* The Men Who Tread on the Tiger's Tail (1945)

Torment *See* L'Enfer (1993)

Torpedo Zone *See* Submarine Attack (1954)

Torture Chamber *See* The Fear Chamber (1968)

Torture Zone *See* The Fear Chamber (1968)

Toto the Hero *See* Toto le Heros (1991)

The Touch of Flesh *See* You've Ruined Me, Eddie (1958)

The Touch of Melissa *See* The Touch of Satan (1970)

Touchez Pas Au Grisbi *See* Grisbi (1953)

Tough Guy *See* Counter Punch (1971)

A Toute Vitesse *See* Full Speed (1996)

Tower of Terror *See* Assault (1970)

Tower of Terror *See* Hard to Die (1990)

A Town Called Bastard *See* A Town Called Hell (1972)

The Town That Cried Terror *See* Maniac (1977)

T.R. Sloane *See* Death Ray 2000 (1981)

Trackers *See* Space Rage (1986)

The Tragedy of Othello: The Moor of Venice *See* Othello (1952)

Trail of the Royal Mounted *See* Mystery Trooper (1932)

Train de Vie *See* Train of Life (1998)

Train of Terror *See* Terror Train (1980)

Train 2419 *See* The Return of Casey Jones (1934)

Traitement de Choc *See* Shock Treatment (1981)

Trance *See* The External (1999)

Trancers *See* Future Cop (1976)

Transport Z Raje *See* Transport from Paradise (1965)

The Transvestite *See* Glen or Glenda? (1953)

Tras el Cristal *See* In a Glass Cage (1986)

Trauma *See* Dario Argento's Trauma (1993)

Trauma *See* The House on Straw Hill (1976)

Travels with Anita *See* Lovers and Liars (1981)

Tre Fratelli *See* Three Brothers (1980)

Tre Passi nel Delirio *See* Spirits of the Dead (1968)

Treasure of the Living Dead *See* Oasis of the Zombies (1982)

Tredowata *See* Leper (1976)

The Tree of Hands *See* Innocent Victim (1990)

Tree of Liberty *See* The Howards of Virginia (1940)

Trial by Combat *See* Choice of Weapons (1976)

Trick of the Eye *See* Primal Secrets (1994)

A Trip with Anita *See* Lovers and Liars (1981)

Triple Trouble *See* Kentucky Kernels (1934)

Tristan and Isolde *See* Lovespell (1979)

Triumph des Willens *See* Triumph of the Will (1934)

Trmavomodry Svet *See* Dark Blue World (2001)

Trois Histoires Extraordinaires d'Edgar Poe *See* Spirits of the Dead (1968)

Trois Hommes et un Couffin *See* Three Men and a Cradle (1985)

Trois Vies et Une Seule Mort *See* Three Lives and Only One Death (1996)

The Trojan War *See* The Trojan Horse (1962)

The Trollenberg Terror *See* The Crawling Eye (1958)

Tromba *See* Tromba, the Tiger Man (1952)

Trop Belle pour Toi *See* Too Beautiful for You (1988)

Trop Jolie pour Etre Honette *See* Too Pretty to Be Honest (1972)

Tropicana *See* The Heat's On (1943)

Trottie True *See* The Gay Lady (1949)

Trouble at 16 *See* Platinum High School (1960)

Trouble Chaser *See* Li'l Abner (1940)

The Trout *See* La Truite (1983)

Truman Capote's A Christmas Memory *See* ABC Stage 67: Truman Capote's A Christmas Memory (1966)

Truman Capote's One Christmas *See* One Christmas (1995)

Truman Capote's The Glass House *See* The Glass House (1972)

Try and Find It *See* Hi Diddle Diddle (1943)

Tsarskaya Nevesta *See* The Tsar's Bride (1966)

Tsubaki Sanjuro *See* Sanjuro (1962)

Tsvet Granata *See* The Color of Pomegranates (1969)

Tudor Rose *See* Nine Days a Queen (1936)

Tueur de Ch Icago *See* Scarface Mob (1962)

Tulitkkutehtaan Tytto *See* The Match Factory Girl (1990)

The Tunnel *See* Transatlantic Tunnel (1935)

Tunnels *See* Criminal Act (1988)

Turkey Shoot *See* Escape 2000 (1981)

Turn Your Pony Around *See* Mortal Danger (1994)

Turtle Beach *See* The Killing Beach (1992)

Tuzolto utca 25 *See* 25 Fireman's Street (1973)

Twelve Miles Out *See* The Second Woman (1951)

Twenty-One Days Together *See* 21 Days (1937)

Twice Bitten *See* The Vampire Hookers (1978)

Twilight of the Dead *See* Gates of Hell (1980)

Twinkle, Twinkle, Killer Kane *See* The Ninth Configuration (1979)

Twinky *See* Lola (1969)

Twins of Dracula *See* Twins of Evil (1971)

Twist of Fate *See* Psychopath (1997)

Twisted *See* Medusa (1974)

The Twisted Road *See* They Live by Night (1949)

2 Cries in the Night *See* Funeral Home (1982)

Two Guys Talkin' About Girls *See* At First Sight (1995)

The Two-Headed Monster *See* The Manster (1959)

Two Minds for Murder *See* Someone Behind the Door (1971)

2002: The Rape of Eden *See* Bounty Hunter 2002 (1994)

Two Weeks in September *See* A Coeur Joie (1967)

Tystnaden *See* The Silence (1963)

U-Boat 29 *See* Spy in Black (1939)

U-238 and the Witch Doctor *See* Jungle Drums of Africa (1953)

Uccellacci e Uccellini *See* The Hawks & the Sparrows (1967)

Uccidero Un Uomo *See* This Man Must Die (1970)

Uchu Daikaiiju Dogora *See* Dagora, the Space Monster (1965)

Uchudai Dogora *See* Dagora, the Space Monster (1965)

Uchujin Tokyo Ni Arawaru *See* Warning from Space (1956)

Ugetsu Monogatari *See* Ugetsu (1953)

Ugly, Dirty and Bad *See* Down & Dirty (1976)

Ukigusa *See* Drifting Weeds (1959)

Ulisse *See* Ulysses (1955)

The Ultimate Chase *See* The Ultimate Thrill (1974)

Ultimate Desires *See* Beyond the Silhouette (1990)

The Ultimate Solution of Grace Quigley *See* Grace Quigley (1984)

Ultimi Giorni di Pompeii *See* The Last Days of Pompeii (1960)

L'Ultimo Tango a Parigi *See* Last Tango in Paris (1973)

Ultra Force *See* Royal Warriors (1986)

Umarete Wa Mita Keredo *See* I Was Born But... (1932)

The Umbrella Woman *See* The Good Wife (1986)

Un Affaire de Gout *See* A Matter of Taste (2000)

Un Amour De Swann *See* Swann in Love (1984)

Un Amour En Allemagne *See* A Love in Germany (1984)

Un Angelo e Sceso a Brooklyn *See* The Man Who Wagged His Tail (1957)

Un Angelo per Satan *See* An Angel for Satan (1966)

Un Arma de Dos Filos *See* Shark! (1968)

Un Autre Homme, Une Autre Chance *See* Another Man, Another Chance (1977)

Un Chapeau de Paille d'Italie *See* Italian Straw Hat (1927)

Un Complicato Intrigo Di Donne, Vicoli E Delitti *See* Camorra: The Naples Connection (1985)

Un Condamne a Mort s'est Echappe, Ou le Vent Souffle ou il Vent *See* A Man Escaped (1957)

Un, Deux, Trois, Quatre! *See* Black Tights (1960)

Un Dimanche a la Campagne *See* A Sunday in the Country (1984)

Un Divan a New York *See* A Couch in New York (1995)

Un Dollar Troue *See* Blood for a Silver Dollar (1966)

Un Elephant a Trompe Enormement *See* Pardon Mon Affaire (1976)

Un Grand Amour de Beethoven *See* Beethoven (1936)

Un Heros Tres Discret *See* A Self-Made Hero (1995)

Un Homme Amoureux *See* A Man in Love (1987)

Un Homme Est Mort *See* The Outside Man (1973)

Un Homme et Un Femme *See* A Man and a Woman (1966)

Un Homme Et Une Femme: Vingt Ans Deja *See* A Man and a Woman: 20 Years Later (1986)

Un Indien dans la Ville *See* Little Indian, Big City (1995)

Un Minuto Per Pregare, Un Istante Per Morire *See* A Minute to Pray, a Second to Die (1967)

Un Paraiso Bajo las Estrellas *See* A Paradise Under the Stars (1999)

Un Partie de Plaisir *See* A Piece of Pleasure (1974)

Un Senor Muy Viejo Con Unas Alas Enormes *See* A Very Old Man with Enormous Wings (1988)

Un Trem Para as Estrelas *See* Subway to the Stars (1987)

Un Uomo da Rispettare *See* Master Touch (1974)

Un Week-end sur Deux *See* Every Other Weekend (1991)

Un Zoo, La Nuit *See* Night Zoo (1987)

Una Bruja Sin Escoba *See* A Witch Without a Broom (1968)

Una Giornata Speciale *See* A Special Day (1977)

Una Hacha para la Luna de Miel *See* Hatchet for the Honeymoon (1970)

Una Pura Formalita *See* A Pure Formality (1994)

Una Ragione Per Vivere e Una Per Morire *See* A Reason to Live, a Reason to Die (1973)

Una Sombra Ya Pronto Seras *See* A Shadow You Soon Will Be (1994)

Unagi *See* The Eel (1996)

Unakrsna Vatra *See* Operation Cross Eagles (1969)

Uncle Harry *See* The Strange Affair of Uncle Harry (1945)

Uncle Silas *See* Inheritance (1947)

Unconventional Linda *See* Holiday (1938)

Under California Skies *See* Under California Stars (1948)

Under Heaven *See* In the Shadows (1998)

Under Solen *See* Under the Sun (1998)

Under the Clock *See* The Clock (1945)

Under the Olive Trees *See* Through the Olive Trees (1994)

Under the Sun of Satan *See* Under Satan's Sun (1987)

Underground *See* The Lower Depths (1936)

An Underwater Odyssey *See* Neptune Factor (1973)

Underworld *See* Transmutations (1985)

Underworld After Dark *See* Big Town After Dark (1947)

Une Affaire de Femmes *See* The Story of Women (1988)

Une Femme a sa Fentre *See* A Woman at Her Window (1977)

Une Femme Douce *See* A Gentle Woman (1969)

Une Femme Est une Femme *See* A Woman Is a Woman (1960)

Une Femme ou Deux *See* One Woman or Two (1985)

Une Histoire Simple *See* A Simple Story (1979)

Une Liaison d'Amour *See* An Affair of Love (1999)

Une Liaison Pornographique *See* An Affair of Love (1999)

Une Partie de Campagne *See* A Day in the Country (1946)

Une Pure Formalite *See* A Pure Formality (1994)

Unknown Satellite Over Tokyo *See* Warning from Space (1956)

The Unnamable Returns *See* The Unnamable 2: The Statement of Randolph Carter (1992)

Untel Pere et Fils *See* Heart of a Nation (1943)

Unterm Birnbaum *See* Under the Pear Tree (1973)

The Untold Story: Human Meat Roast Pork Buns *See* The Untold Story (1993)

The Unvanquished *See* Aparajito (1958)

Uomini Uomini Uomini *See* Men Men Men (1995)

Uomo Dalla Pelle Dura *See* Counter Punch (1971)

L'Uomo delle Stelle *See* The Star Maker (1995)

Up Frankenstein *See* Andy Warhol's Frankenstein (1974)

Up in Smoke *See* Cheech and Chong's Up in Smoke (1979)

Up in the Cellar *See* Three in the Cellar (1970)

Up the Chastity Belt *See* Naughty Knights (1971)

Up to a Point *See* Up to a Certain Point (1983)

The Upstate Murders *See* Savage Weekend (1980)

Urban Justice *See* Under Oath (1997)

Urga *See* Close to Eden (1990)

Ursus *See* Ursus in the Valley of the Lions (1962)

The Usual Unidentified Thieves *See* Big Deal on Madonna Street (1958)

Utamaro O Meguru Gonin No Onna *See* Utamaro and His Five Women (1946)

Utvandrarna *See* The Emigrants (1972)

Uvidet Parizh i Umeret *See* To See Paris and Die (1993)

Vacation *See* National Lampoon's Vacation (1983)

Vagabond Violinist *See* Broken Melody (1934)

Vaghe Stelle Dell'Orsa *See* Sandra of a Thousand Delights (1965)

Valborgmassoafton *See* Walpurgis Night (1941)

The Valdez Horses *See* Chino (1975)

Valdez the Half Breed *See* Chino (1975)

Vale Abraao *See* Abraham's Valley (1993)

Valentine's Day *See* Protector (1997)

Valley of Abraham *See* Abraham's Valley (1993)

Valley of Fear *See* Sherlock Holmes and the Deadly Necklace (1962)

Valley of the Swords *See* The Castilian (1963)

The Vampire *See* Vampyr (1931)

The Vampire and the Robot *See* My Son, the Vampire (1952)

The Vampire-Beast Craves Blood *See* Blood Beast Terror (1967)

Vampire Castle *See* Captain Kronos: Vampire Hunter (1974)

Vampire Men of the Lost Planet *See* Horror of the Blood Monsters (1970)

Vampire Orgy *See* Vampyres (1974)

Vampire Over London *See* My Son, the Vampire (1952)

Vampire Playgirls *See* Dracula's Great Love (1972)

Vampires *See* John Carpenter's Vampires (1997)

The Vampire's Niece *See* Fangs of the Living Dead (1968)

Vampire's Night Orgy *See* Orgy of the Vampires (1973)

Vampires of Prague *See* Mark of the Vampire (1935)

Vampire's Thirst *See* The Body Beneath (1970)

Vampyr, Der Traum des David Gray *See* Vampyr (1931)

Vampyr, Ou l'Etrange Aventure de David Gray *See* Vampyr (1931)

Vampyres, Daughters of Dracula *See* Vampyres (1974)

Van Wilder *See* National Lampoon's Van Wilder (2002)

Vanishing Body *See* The Black Cat (1934)

Vargtimmen *See* Hour of the Wolf (1968)

Variete *See* Variety (1925)

The Varrow Mission *See* Teen Alien (1988)

Vasectomy *See* Vasectomy: A Delicate Matter (1986)

Vaudeville *See* Variety (1925)

The Veil *See* Haunts (1977)

Velocity *See* The Wild Ride (1960)

The Velocity of Gary* (* Not His Real Name) *See* The Velocity of Gary (1998)

Velvet House *See* Crucible of Horror (1969)

Vendetta: Secrets of a Mafia Bride *See* A Family Matter (1991)

A Vendre *See* For Sale (1998)

Vengeance *See* The Brain (1962)

Vengeance: The Demon *See* Pumpkinhead (1988)

Vengeance: The Story of Tony Cimo *See* Vengeance (1989)

The Vengeful Dead *See* Kiss Daddy Goodbye (1981)

Venice *See* Dangerous Beauty (1998)

Venus in Peltz *See* Venus in Furs (1970)

The Venusian *See* The Stranger from Venus (1954)

Vercingetorix *See* Druids (2001)

A Very Big Weekend *See* A Man, a Woman, and a Bank (1979)

A Very Discreet Hero *See* A Self-Made Hero (1995)

Vesnicko Ma Strediskova *See* My Sweet Little Village (1986)

Vessel of Wrath *See* Beachcomber (1938)

The Veteran *See* Deathdream (1972)

Viagem ao Principio do Mundo *See* Voyage to the Beginning of the World (1996)

Viaggio in Italia *See* Voyage in Italy (1953)

The Vicious Circle *See* Woman in Brown (1948)

Victims of the Beyond *See* Sucker Money (1934)

Viehjud Levi *See* Jew-boy Levi (1998)

The Vienna Strangler *See* The Mad Butcher (1972)

Vig *See* Money Kings (1998)

Viking Massacre *See* Knives of the Avenger (1965)

Viktor Vogel: Commercial Artist *See* Advertising Rules! (2001)

Vincent, Francois, Paul et les Autres *See* Vincent, Francois, Paul and the Others (1976)

Vindicator *See* Wheels of Fire (1984)

Violated *See* Party Girls for Sale (1954)

Violence et Passion *See* Conversation Piece (1975)

Violent Journey *See* The Fool Killer (1965)

Violent Midnight *See* Psychomania (1963)

Violent Rage *See* Fearmaker (1989)

Violent Streets *See* Thief (1981)

Violette Nozière *See* Violette (1978)

Virgin Hunters *See* Test Tube Teens from the Year 2000 (1993)

The Virgin Vampires *See* Twins of Evil (1971)

The Virgin Wife *See* You've Got to Have Heart (1977)

The Virtuous Tramps *See* The Devil's Brother (1933)

Virus *See* Cannibal Apocalypse (1980)

Viskingar Och Rop *See* Cries and Whispers (1972)

A Coeur Joie *Two Weeks in September* **1967** Sixties set piece about a gorgeous woman who must choose between her much older lover or her new-found stud. Bardot and U.K. scenery keep this one from sinking entirely. In French with English subtitles. **100m/C VHS.** *FR* Brigitte Bardot, Laurent Terzieff; *D:* Serge Bourguignon.

A. I.: Artificial Intelligence **2001 (PG-13)** Definitely an acquired taste—the uneasy melding of a long-cherished idea by late director Stanley Kubrick and the homage directed by Spielberg. Global warming has submerged the world's coastal cities but advanced humanoid robots, or "mechas," keep things going. Professor Hobby (Hurt) has made a child mecha, David (Osment), designed to be loving and extremely loyal—in this case to his human mother Monica (O'Connor) who eventually abandons him to the cruel wide world. Having heard the Pinocchio story, David (and his mecha bear Teddy) go in search of the Blue Fairy who can make David a "real" boy. Along the way, David meets mecha Gigolo Joe (Law), who profers good advice about the perfidity of human beings. It's long, it's dark, it's confusing, it's sometimes boring, and sometimes touching. Law's role is small but, as usual, Osment carries the picture. Based on the 1969 short story "Supertoys Last All Summer Long" by Brian Aldiss. **145m/C VHS, DVD, Wide.** *US* Haley Joel Osment, Jude Law, Frances O'Connor, Sam Robards, Brendan Gleeson, William Hurt, Jake Thomas, Clara Bellar, Enrico Colantoni, Adrian Grenier, Emmanuelle Chriqui; *D:* Steven Spielberg; *W:* Steven Spielberg; *C:* Janusz Kaminski; *M:* John Williams; *V:* Robin Williams, Chris Rock, Meryl Streep, Jack Angel; *Nar:* Ben Kingsley.

A la Mode ½ *In Fashion* **1994 (R)** It's Paris in the '60s as shy 17-year-old orphan Fausto (Higelin) is apprenticed to fatherly Jewish tailor Mietek (Yanne). But Fausto is transfixed by lovely mechanic Tonie (Darel) and decides what he really wants (besides the girl) is to design women's fashions. Very frothy coming-of-age tale, anchored by Yanne's veteran charm. Based on the novel "Fausto" by Richard Morgieve. French with subtitles. **89m/C VHS.** *FR* Ken Higelin, Jean Yanne, Florence Darel, Francois Hautesserre; *D:* Remy Duchemin; *W:* Remy Duchemin, Richard Morgieve; *M:* Denis Barbier.

A Nos Amours *To Our Loves* **1984 (R)** Craving the attention she is denied at home, a young French girl searches for love and affection from numerous boyfriends in hopes of eradicating her unhappy home. Occasional lapses in quality and slow pacing hamper an otherwise excellent effort. The characterization of the girl Suzanne is especially memorable. In French with English subtitles. **99m/C VHS.** *FR* Sandrine Bonnaire, Dominique Besnehard, Maurice Pialat, Evelyne Ker; *D:* Maurice Pialat; *W:* Arlette Langmann, Maurice Pialat; *C:* Jacques Loiseleux; *M:* Henry Purcell.

A Nous la Liberte *Freedom for Us* **1931** Two tramps encounter industrialization and automation, making one into a wealthy leader, the other into a nature-loving iconoclast. A poignant, fantastical masterpiece by Clair, made before he migrated to Hollywood. Though the view of automation may be dated, it influenced such films as Chaplin's "Modern Times." In French with English subtitles. **87m/B VHS, 8mm.** *FR* Henri Marchand, Raymond Cordy, Rolla France, Paul Olivier, Jacques Shelly, Andre Michaud; *D:* Rene Clair; *W:* Rene Clair; *C:* Georges Perinal; *M:* Georges Auric.

A Propos de Nice *Nizza* **1929** First film by French director Vigo, the silent film parodies French travelogues in a manner that indicates the director's later brilliance. **25m/B VHS.** *FR* *D:* Jean Vigo; *W:* Jean Vigo; *C:* Boris Kaufman.

Aaron Loves Angela **1975 (R)** Puerto Rican girl falls in love with a black teen amidst the harsh realities of the Harlem ghetto. "Romeo and Juliet" meets "West Side Story" in a cliched comedy drama. **99m/C VHS.** Kevin Hooks, Irene Cara, Moses Gunn, Robert Hooks; *Cameos:* Jose Feliciano; *D:* Gordon Parks Jr.; *C:* Richard Kratina; *M:* Jose Feliciano.

Abandon Ship ½ *Seven Waves Away* **1957** A luxury liner hits a derelict mine and sinks within minutes, leaving 27 survivors clinging to one tiny lifeboat. Ship's officer Alex Holmes (Power) knows that the amount of food and water they have is limited, the waters are shark-infested, and the injured stand little chance, so he must decide who will survive. **97m/B VHS.** *GB* Tyrone Power, Mai Zetterling, Lloyd Nolan, Stephen Boyd, Moira Lister, James Hayter, Marie Lohr, Gordon Jackson, Laurence Naismith, John Stratton, Victor Maddern, Eddie Byrne, Noel Willman, Ralph Michael, David Langton, Ferdinand "Ferdy" Mayne, Austin Trevor, Finlay Currie, Jill Melford; *D:* Richard Sale; *W:* Richard Sale; *C:* Wilkie Cooper; *M:* Arthur Bliss.

Abbott and Costello Go to Mars ½ *On to Mars; Rocket and Roll* **1953** Poor parody of sci-fi films finds the frantic duo aboard a rocket ship and accidentally heading off into outer space. They don't land on Mars, but Venus, which is populated by lots of pretty women and no men. Even this duo looks good to the ladies. Cheapie production and uninspired buffoonery. **77m/B VHS.** Bud Abbott, Lou Costello, Mari Blanchard, Robert Paige, Martha Hyer, Horace McMahon, Jack Kruschen, Anita Ekberg, Jean Willes, Joe (Joseph) Kirk, Jackie Loughery, James Flavin; *D:* Charles Lamont; *W:* John Grant, D.D. Beauchamp; *C:* Clifford Stine; *M:* Joseph Gershenson.

Abbott and Costello in Hollywood *Bud Abbott and Lou Costello In Hollywood* **1945** Bud and Lou appear as a barber and porter of a high-class tonsorial parlor in Hollywood. A rather sarcastic look at backstage Hollywood, Abbott & Costello style. Ball makes a guest appearance. **111m/B VHS.** Bud Abbott, Lou Costello, Frances Rafferty, Warner Anderson, Jean Porter, Robert Stanton, Mike Mazurki; *D:* Sylvan Simon; *M:* George Bassman.

Abbott and Costello in the Foreign Legion ½ **1950** Fight promoters Jonesy and Max trail their runaway fighter to Algiers where they're tricked into joining the French Foreign Legion. They have to cope with a sadistic sergeant, a sexy spy, and still find their man. Most amusement comes from Lou's wild desert mirages. **80m/B VHS, DVD.** Bud Abbott, Lou Costello, Walter Slezak, Patricia Medina, Douglass Dumbrille, Leon Belasco, Marc Lawrence, Tor Johnson; *D:* Charles Lamont; *W:* John Grant, Martin Ragaway, Leonard Stern; *C:* George Robinson.

Abbott and Costello Meet Captain Kidd **1952** With pirates led by Captain Kidd on their trail, Abbott and Costello follow a treasure map. Bland A&C swashbuckler spoof with a disinterested Laughton impersonating the Kidd. One of the duo's few color films. **70m/C VHS.** Bud Abbott, Lou Costello, Charles Laughton, Hillary Brooke, Fran Warren, Bill (William) Shirley, Leif Erickson; *D:* Charles Lamont.

Abbott and Costello Meet Dr. Jekyll and Mr. Hyde **1952** Slim (Abbott) and Tubby (Costello) are a couple of cops sent to London, who become involved with crazy Dr. Jekyll (Karloff), who has transformed himself into Mr. Hyde via an experimental serum, and is terrorizing London. Naturally, he goes after the boys. A lame attempt at recapturing the success of "Abbott and Costello Meet Frankenstein" but Karloff is topnotch as always. **77m/B VHS.** Bud Abbott, Lou Costello, Boris Karloff, Craig Stevens, Helen Westcott, Reginald Denny, John Dierkes, Marjorie Bennett, Lucille Lamarr, Patti McKay; *D:* Charles Lamont; *W:* John Grant, Leo Loeb, Howard Dimsdale; *C:* George Robinson.

Abbott and Costello Meet Frankenstein *Abbott and Costello Meet the Ghosts; Meet the Ghosts; The Brain of Frankenstein* **1948** Big-budget A&C classic is one of their best efforts and was rewarded handsomely at the boxoffice. Unsuspecting baggage clerks Chick (Abbott) and Wilbur (Costello) deliver a crate containing the last but not quite dead remains of Dracula (Lugosi) and Dr. Frankenstein's monster (Strange) to a wax museum. When Drac revives, he decides to replace the monster's brain with Wilbur's so he'll be easier to control. Chaney Jr. makes a special wolfish appearance to warn the boys that trouble looms. Last film to use the Universal creature pioneered by Karloff in 1931. **83m/B VHS, DVD.** Bud Abbott, Lou Costello, Lon Chaney Jr., Bela Lugosi, Glenn Strange, Lenore Aubert, Jane Randolph, Frank Ferguson, Charles Bradstreet, Howard Negley, Clarence Straight; *D:* Charles T. Barton; *W:* John Grant, Robert Lees, Frederic Rinaldo; *C:* Charles Van Enger; *M:* Frank Skinner; *V:* Vincent Price. Natl. Film Reg. '01.

Abbott and Costello Meet the Invisible Man 🦴🦴🦴 **1951** Abbott and Costello play newly graduated detectives who take on the murder case of a boxer (Franz) accused of killing his manager. Using a serum that makes people invisible, the boxer helps Costello in a prizefight that will frame the real killers, who killed the manager because the boxer refused to throw a fight. Great special effects and hilarious gags make this one of the best from the crazy duo. **82m/B VHS.** Bud Abbott, Lou Costello, Nancy Guild, Adele Jergens, Sheldon Leonard, William Frawley, Gavin Muir, Arthur Franz, Syd Saylor, Bobby Barber; *D:* Charles Lamont; *W:* Frederic Rinaldo, John Grant, Robert Lees; *C:* George Robinson; *M:* Hans J. Salter.

Abbott and Costello Meet the Keystone Kops 🦴🦴½ **1954** It's 1912 and the boys are bilked into buying a fake movie studio by a clever con man. When they find out they've been tricked, the duo head to Hollywood to track him down and find out the crook is trying to cheat Sennett's film company. Sennett himself trained A&C and the new Keystone Kops in their recreations of his silent screen routines. Good final chase sequence but the earlier work is tired. **79m/B VHS.** Bud Abbott, Lou Costello, Fred Clark, Lynn Bari, Mack Sennett, Maxie "Slapsie" Rosenbloom, Frank Wilcox, Harold Goodwin; *D:* Charles Lamont; *W:* John Grant; *C:* Reggie Lanning; *M:* Joseph Gershenson.

Abbott and Costello Meet the Killer, Boris Karloff 🦴🦴 *Abbott and Costello Meet the Killer* **1949** Unremarkable Abbott and Costello murder mystery. Karloff plays a psychic who tries to frame Lou for murder. Pleasant enough but not one of their best. **84m/B VHS.** Bud Abbott, Lou Costello, Boris Karloff, Lenore Aubert, Gar Moore, Donna (Dona Martel) Martell, Alan Mowbray, James Flavin, Roland Winters, Nicholas Joy, Mikel Conrad, Morgan Farley, Victoria Horne; *D:* Charles T. Barton; *W:* John Grant, Hugh Wedlock Jr., Howard Snyder; *C:* Charles Van Enger; *M:* Milton Schwarzwald.

Abbott and Costello Meet the Mummy 🦴🦴½ **1955** Okay comedy from the duo has them stranded in Egypt with a valuable medallion which will lead to secret treasure and the mummy who guards the tomb. The last of the films the twosome made for Universal. **90m/B VHS, DVD.** Bud Abbott, Lou Costello, Marie Windsor, Michael Ansara, Dan Seymour, Kurt Katch, Richard Deacon, Mel Welles, Edwin Parker, Richard Karlan, George Khoury; *D:* Charles Lamont; *W:* John Grant; *C:* George Robinson; *M:* Joseph Gershenson, Hans J. Salter.

ABC Stage 67: Truman Capote's A Christmas Memory *Truman Capote's A Christmas Memory; A Christmas Memory* **1966** Capote narrates his remembered childhood experience of baking dozens of fruitcakes for friends at Christmas with his elderly distant cousin, Miss Sook Faulk (Page). She is quiet, lovely, and true in this sensitive portrait of why we give and what we have to be thankful for. Adapted from a short story by Capote and Eleanor Perry. **51m/B VHS, 8mm.** Geraldine Page, Donnie Melvin; *D:* Frank Perry; *W:* Truman Capote; *Nar:* Truman Capote. **TV**

Abducted 🦴½ **1986 (PG)** A woman jogger is abducted by a crazed mountain man in the Canadian Rockies. Weird and unbelievably tedious film is nevertheless highlighted by some spectacular wilderness footage of the Vancouver area, a travelogue bonus for those in the mood. **87m/C VHS.** *CA* Dan Haggerty, Roberta Weiss, Lawrence King Phillips; *D:* Boon Collins.

Abducted 2: The Reunion 🦴½ **1994 (R)** Three girlfriends decide to go camping for their reunion trip. Oops—psycho mountain man alert! **91m/C VHS.** Dan Haggerty, Jan-Michael Vincent, Donna Jason, Raquel Bianca, Debbie Rochon, Lawrence King; *D:* Boon Collins; *W:* Boon Collins; *C:* Danny Nowak.

Abduction 🦴½ **1975 (R)** Exploitative account of the Patty Hearst kidnapping, loosely adapted from the Harrison James novel written before the kidnapping. A young woman from a wealthy capitalist family is kidnapped by black radicals and held for an unusual ransom. Oh, and she tangles with lesbians, too. **100m/C VHS.** Judith-Marie Bergan, David Pendleton, Gregory Rozakis, Leif Erickson, Dorothy Malone, Lawrence Tierney; *D:* Joseph Zito.

The Abduction 🦴🦴½ **1996** Fact-based melodrama about Kate Olavsky (Principal) and her abusive marriage to cop Paul (Hays). Afraid to press charges, she finally manages to leave him and get on with her life. But Paul refuses to let Kate go, constantly hounding her, until he takes Kate hostage at gunpoint. **91m/C VHS, DVD.** Victoria Principal, Robert Hays, Christopher Lawford, William Greenblatt; *D:* Larry Peerce; *W:* Marshall Goldberg; *C:* Tony Imi; *M:* Fred Mollin. **CABLE**

The Abduction of Allison Tate 🦴½ **1992 (R)** Rich developer takes land belonging to a group of Native Americans. Three young tribe members retaliate by kidnapping the developer's daughter. But when their plans go awry and one of the trio is killed, Allison finds herself sympathizing more with them than with her father's ambitions. **95m/C VHS.** Leslie Hope, Bernie White; *D:* Paul Leder.

The Abduction of Kari Swenson 🦴½ **1987** An account of the true-life (it really happened) kidnapping of Olympic biathalon hopeful Swensen by a pair of mischievous Montana mountain men with matrimony in mind. The movie details the abduction of Swenson by the scruffy father and son duo and the massive manhunt. As the put-upon Kari, Pollan exceeds script expectations in this exercise in stress avoidance. **100m/C VHS.** Joe Don Baker, M. Emmet Walsh, Ronny Cox, Michael Bowen, Geoffrey Blake, Dorothy Fielding, Tracy Pollan; *D:* Stephen Gyllenhaal. **TV**

Abduction of St. Anne 🦴🦴 **1975** An almost interesting mystical thriller about a detective and a bishop trying to track down a gangster's daughter, who may have nifty supernatural healing powers the Church would be very interested in having documented. **78m/C VHS.** Robert Wagner, E.G. Marshall, William Windom, Lloyd Nolan; *D:* Harry Falk; *M:* George Duning. **TV**

The Abductors 🦴 **1972 (R)** Caffaro's super-agent takes on international white slavery, a worthy target for any exploitation effort. While the novelty is a tough and intelligent on-screen heroine, sufficient sleaze and violence bring it all down to the proper level of swampland video. Sequel to the never-to-be-forgotten "Ginger." **90m/C VHS.** Cheri Caffaro, William Grannel, Richard Smedley, Patrick Wright, Jennifer Brooks, Jeramie Rain; *D:* Don Schain; *W:* Don Schain; *C:* R. Kent Evans; *M:* Robert G. Orpin.

Abdulla the Great 🦴🦴 *Abdullah's Harem* **1956** A dissolute Middle Eastern monarch falls for a model, who spurns him for an army officer. While distracted by these royal shenanigans, the king is blissfully unaware of his subjects' disaffection—until they revolt. Dares to lampoon Egypt's dead King Farouk, going against conventional Hollywood wisdom ("Farouk in film is boxoffice poison"). **89m/C VHS.** *GB* Gregory Ratoff, Kay Kendall, Sydney Chaplin, Alexander D'Arcy; *D:* Gregory Ratoff; *C:* Lee Garmes; *M:* Georges Auric.

Abe Lincoln in Illinois 🦴🦴🦴🦴 *Spirit of the People* **1940** Massey considered this not only his finest film but a part he was "born to play." Correct on both counts, this Hollywood biography follows Lincoln from his log cabin days to his departure for the White House. The Lincoln-Douglass debate scene and Massey's post-presidential election farewell to the citizens of Illinois are nothing short of brilliant. Written by Sherwood from his Pulitzer-Prize winning play. Contrasted with the well-known "Young Mr. Lincoln" (Henry Fonda), its relative anonymity is perplexing. **110m/B VHS.** Raymond Massey, Gene Lockhart, Ruth Gordon, Mary Howard, Dorothy Tree, Harvey Stephens, Minor Watson, Alan Baxter, Howard da Silva, Maurice Murphy, Clem Bevans, Herbert Rudley; *D:* John Cromwell; *W:* Robert Sherwood; *C:* James Wong Howe; *M:* Roy Webb.

The Abe Lincoln of Ninth Avenue 🦴🦴½ *Streets of New York* **1939** All-American tale of a poor young man making good in New York. His role model is Abraham Lincoln. Cooper is exceptional, supported by effective performances by the rest of the cast. **68m/B VHS, 8mm.** Jackie Cooper, Martin Spelling, Marjorie Reynolds, Dick Purcell, George Cleveland, George Irving; *D:* William Nigh.

Aberdeen 🦴🦴 **2000** Ambitious London attorney Kaisa (Headey) gets a call from her terminally ill mother Helen (Rampling), who lives in Aberdeen, Scotland. Helen wants Kaisa to travel to Oslo and retrieve Tomas (Skargard), her alcoholic and estranged father, so Helen and he can have a deathbed reconciliation. Assertive Kaisa tracks the drunk down and makes him come with her on a nightmare trip back. Lead performances are utterly unsentimental. **103m/C VHS, DVD.** *NO GB* Stellan Skarsgard, Lena Headey, Ian Hart, Charlotte Rampling; *D:* Hans Petter Moland; *W:* Hans Petter Moland, Kristin Amundsen; *C:* Philip Ogaard; *M:* Zbigniew Preisner.

Aberration 🦴 **1997 (R)** Amy (Gidley) has traveled to her parents remote cabin and notices a lizard infestation. So she heads to the store for some exterminating equipment and meets biologist Marshall (Bossell), who studies eco-abnormalities. Seems the lizards are vicious mutants who eat Amy's cat and are working their way up the food chain. Doesn't offer many scares. **93m/C VHS.** *AU GB* Pamela Gidley, Simon Bossell, Valery (Valeri Nikolayev) Nikolaev; *D:* Tim Boxell; *W:* Darrin Oura, Scott Lew; *C:* Allen Guilford. **VIDEO**

Abigail's Party 🦴🦴 **1977** Steadman plays the hostess for a very ill-fated dinner party, especially when she realizes her husband has just died on her new carpet. **105m/C VHS.** *GB* Alison Steadman; *D:* Mike Leigh. **TV**

Abilene Town 🦴🦴🦴 **1946** In a post-Civil War Kansas town far from the freeway, Scott is the tough marshal trying to calm the conflict between cattlemen and homesteaders. He also finds time to participate in a romantic triangle with dance hall vixen Dvorak and heart-of-gold Fleming. Snappy pace keeps it interesting. Based on a novel by Ernest Haycox. **90m/B VHS.** Randolph Scott, Ann Dvorak, Edgar Buchanan, Rhonda Fleming, Lloyd Bridges; *D:* Edwin L. Marin; *W:* Harold Shumate; *C:* Archie Stout.

Ablaze 🦴½ **2000 (R)** Greedy developer Wendell Mays (Arnold) arranges for his industrial refinery to be torched and the ensuing fire and explosion taxes both the fire fighters and the hospital that has to deal with the casualties. Wynorski directs under the pseudonym Jay Andrews. **97m/C VHS, DVD.** John H. Bradley, Tom Arnold, Michael Dudikoff, Ice-T, Amanda Pays, Cathy Lee Crosby, Pat Harrington, Edward Albert, Mary Jo Catlett, Richard Biggs; *D:* Jim Wynorski; *W:* Steve Latshaw; *C:* Andrea V. Rossotto; *M:* Neal Acree. **VIDEO**

The Abominable Dr. Phibes 🦴🦴🦴 *Dr. Phibes; The Curse of Dr. Phibes* **1971 (PG)** After being disfigured in a freak car accident that killed his wife, an evil genius decides that the members of a surgical team let his wife die and shall each perish by a different biblical plague. High camp with the veteran cast in top form. **90m/C VHS, DVD, Wide.** *GB* Vincent Price, Joseph Cotten, Hugh Griffith, Terry-Thomas, Virginia North, Susan Travers, Alex Scott, Caroline Munro, Peter Jeffrey, Peter Gilmore, Edward Burnham, Sean Bury, David Hutcheson, Maurice Kaufmann; *D:* Robert Fuest; *W:* William Goldstein, James Whiton; *C:* Norman Warwick; *M:* Basil Kirchin, Jack Nathan.

The Abominable Snowman 🦴🦴 *The Abominable Snowman of the Himalayas* **1957** Corny Hammer horror about adventurer Tom Friend (Tucker), Dr. John Rollason (Cushing), and guide Ed Shelley (Brown) searching for the legandary Yeti. The harsh conditions cause the explorers to lose their grip and, after Shelley shoots a Yeti, Rollason begins to suspect that the creatures practice mind control. **91m/B VHS, DVD, Wide.** *GB* Peter Cushing, Forrest Tucker, Robert Brown, Richard Wattis, Maureen Connell; *D:* Val Guest; *W:* Nigel Kneale; *C:* Arthur Grant; *M:* Humphrey Searle.

The Abomination 🦴 **1988 (R)** After a 5,000-year-old creature possesses him during a nightmare, a boy goes on an eye-gouging frenzy. Only the audience gets hurt. **100m/C VHS.** Van Connery, Victoria Chaney, Gaye Bottoms, Suzy Meyer, Jude Johnson, Blue Thompson, Scott Davis; *D:* Max Raven.

About a Boy 🦴🦴🦴 **2002 (PG-13)** After playing a cad in "Bridget Jones's Diary," Grant continues to take on roles whose charmers are somewhat rancid. This time, he's Will, a 38-year-old bachelor who doesn't work thanks to a legacy from his father and has never made a lasting emotional commitment to anyone. Will's latest dating scheme is to pretend to be a single parent and join support groups so he can hit on the single mums. This is how he meets Marcus (Hoult), the 12-year-old misfit son of the seriously-depressed Fiona (Collette). Will likes Marcus despite himself and becomes his confidante. And he finds a romance with single mum Rachel (Weitz) but that's almost besides the point. Adapted from the novel by Nick Hornby. **100m/C VHS, DVD.** *US GB* Hugh Grant, Rachel Weisz, Toni Collette, Nicholas Hoult, Isabel Brook, Victoria Smurfit; *D:* Chris Weitz, Paul Weitz; *W:* Chris Weitz, Paul Weitz, Peter Hedges; *C:* Remi Adefarasin; *M:* Badly Drawn Boy.

About Adam 🦴🦴 **2000 (R)** Adam (Townsend) is a duplicitous Dublin charmer who worms his way into the Owens family. Waitress Lucy (Hudson) falls in love with Adam and takes him to meet her family and before anyone realizes what's happening, Adam seduces both her sisters, telling each woman exactly what she needs to hear. And no one holds a grudge! **98m/C VHS, DVD, Wide.** *IR GB* Stuart Townsend, Kate Hudson, Frances O'Connor, Charlotte Bradley, Rosaleen Linehan, Brendan F. Dempsey, Alan Maher, Tommy Tiernan, Cathleen Bradley; *D:* Gerard Stembridge; *W:* Gerard Stembridge; *C:* Bruno de Keyzer; *M:* Adrian Johnston.

About Last Night... 🦴🦴🦴 **1986 (R)** Semi-realistic comedy-drama which explores the ups and downs of one couple's (Lowe, Moore) relationship. Mostly quality performances, especially Perkins and Belushi as friends of the young lovers. Based on David Mamet's play "Sexual Perversity in Chicago," but considerably softened so that more people would buy tickets at the boxoffice, the film acts as a historical view of contemporary mating rituals before the onset of the AIDS crisis. **113m/C VHS, DVD.** Rob Lowe, Demi Moore, Elizabeth Perkins, James Belushi, George DiCenzo, Robin Thomas, Michael Alldredge; *D:* Edward Zwick; *W:* Tim Kazurinsky, Denise DeClue; *C:* Andrew Dintenfass; *M:* Miles Goodman.

Above and Beyond 🦴🦴🦴 **1953** Good performance by Taylor as Col. Paul Tibbets, the man who piloted the Enola Gay, which dropped the atomic bomb on Hiroshima. Focuses on the secrecy of the mission and the strain this puts on Tibbets marriage. Exciting action sequences of the mission itself. **122m/B VHS.** Robert Taylor, Eleanor Parker, James Whitmore, Larry Keating, Larry Gates, Robert Burton, Jim Backus, Marilyn Erskine, Steve (Stephen) Dunne, John Pickard, Hayden Rorke, Lawrence (Larry) Dobkin, Jack Raine, Jeff Richards, Barbara Ruick, Harlan Warde, John Close, Frank Gerstle, Dabbs Greer, Ewing Mitchell, Gregory Walcott, John Baer, Jonathon Cott, Dick Simmons, John McKee, G. Pat Collins, John Hedloe, Mack Williams, Dorothy Kennedy; *D:* Melvin Frank, Norman Panama; *W:* Melvin

Frank, Norman Panama, Beirne Lay Jr.; *C:* Ray June; *M:* Hugo Friedhofer.

Above Suspicion 🦴🦴🦴 1943 MacMurray and Crawford are American honeymooners (poor Fred!) asked to assist an international intelligence organization. They engage the Nazis in a tense battle of wits. Well-made and engaging. **91m/B VHS.** Joan Crawford, Fred MacMurray, Conrad Veidt, Basil Rathbone, Reginald Owen, Richard Ainley, Cecil Cunningham; *D:* Richard Thorpe.

Above Suspicion 🦴🦴 1995 (R) Dempsey Cain (Reeve) seems to be the perfect cop, as well as a loving husband and father and a mentor to his younger brother. But when Cain is paralyzed by a drug dealer's bullet, he begins to notice just how close his wife (Cattrall) and brother (Kerr) are. There's adultery, there's murder, and there's the cop who just may be a cold-blooded killer. Unnervingly, Reeve plays a paraplegic in the last movie he made before his own paralyzing riding accident. **92m/C VHS.** Christopher Reeve, Kim Cattrall, Joe Mantegna, Edward Kerr; *D:* Steven Schachter. CABLE

Above Suspicion 🦴🦴 2000 (R) James Stockton (Bakula) seems like the perfect family man but his wife Lisa (Sciorra) starts becoming suspicious of his past—fearing that he's a killer on the lam. **99m/C VHS, DVD.** Scott Bakula, Annabella Sciorra, George Dzundza, Ed Asner, Jack Blessing; *D:* Steven La Rocque.

Above the Law 🦴🦴 1988 (R) In his debut, Seagal does his wooden best to portray a tough Chicago police detective planning an enormous drug bust of one of the biggest felons in the state. Unfortunately, the FBI has ordered him to back off and find another bust. The reasons are almost as complex as Seagal's character, and like most details of the flick, stupid. However, people don't watch these movies for the acting or the plot, but for the fight scenes, which are well-choreographed and violent. Watch it with someone you love. **99m/C VHS, DVD, 8mm.** Steven Seagal, Pam Grier, Henry Silva, Sharon Stone, Ron Dean, Daniel Faraldo, Chelcie Ross, Thalmus Rasulala, Michael Rooker; *D:* Andrew Davis; *W:* Andrew Davis, Steven Pressfield; *C:* Robert Steadman; *M:* David Michael Frank.

Above the Rim 🦴🦴½ 1994 (R) Vulgar, violent hoopster drama about a fiercely competitive inner-city playground game. Kyle-Lee Watson (Martin), a self-involved high school star raised by a saintly single mom (Pinkins), is torn between the lure of the streets and his college recruiting chances. His odds aren't made any easier by homeboy hustler Birdie (Shakur), who wants to improve his chances of making money on the local games by making sure Watson plays for his team. Energetic b-ball sequences, strong performances lose impact amid formulaic melodrama and the usual obscenities. Debut for director Pollack. **97m/C VHS.** Duane Martin, Tupac Shakur, Leon, Marlon Wayans, Tonya Pinkins, Bernie Mac; *D:* Jeff Pollack; *W:* Jeff Pollack, Barry Michael Cooper; *M:* Marcus Miller.

Above Us the Waves 🦴🦴🦴 1956 During WWII, the British navy immobilizes a huge German battleship off the coast of Norway. Effectively dramatizes the British naval preparations for what seemed a suicidal mission: using midget submarines to plant underwater explosives on the hull of the German vessel and detonating them before the Germans could detect the danger. **92m/C VHS.** *GB* John Mills, John Gregson, Donald Sinden, James Robertson Justice, Michael Medwin, James Kenney, O.E. Hasse, Theodore Bikel, Thomas Heathcote, Lee Patterson, Lyndon Brook, Anthony Newley; *D:* Ralph Thomas.

Abraham 🦴🦴½ 1994 Biblical epic chronicling the Old Testament story of humble shepherd Abraham (Harris), who's commanded by God to lead his family into the promised land of Canaan. Among his family's many trials will be God's command that Abraham sacrifice his son Isaac as a test of faith and obedience. Filmed on location in Morocco with a commanding performance by Harris that somewhat redeems the film's dullness. **?m/C VHS.** Richard Harris, Barbara Hershey, Maximilian Schell, Vittorio Gassman, Caroline Rosi, Gottfried John, Kevin McNally; *D:* Joseph Sargent. CABLE

Abraham Lincoln 🦴🦴½ 1930 Griffith's first talking movie takes Abraham Lincoln from his birth through his assassination. This restored version includes the original slavery sequences which were believed to be lost, but obviously were not. Musical score included. **97m/B VHS.** Walter Huston, Una Merkel, Kay Hammond, E. Alyn Warren, Hobart Bosworth, Fred Warren, Henry B. Walthall, Russell Simpson, Ian Keith, Frank Campeau; *D:* D.W. Griffith; *C:* Karl Struss.

Abraham's Valley 🦴🦴 *Vale Abraao; Valley of Abraham* 1993 Beautiful Ema (Silveira) is forced into a wealthy marriage to a friend of her father's and they move to the vineyards of Abraham's Valley where the bride knows no one. Unhappy, Ema refuses to submit to her husband and decides to take a lover of her own. Based on the novel by Augustina Bessa-Luis. Portuguese with subtitles. **180m/C VHS.** *PT* Leonor Silveira, Luis Miguel Cintra, Diogo Doria, Ruy de Carvalho, Luis Lima Barreto; *D:* Manoel de Oliveira; *W:* Manoel de Oliveira; *C:* Mario Barroso.

Abraxas: Guardian of the Universe 🦴½ *Abraxas* 1990 (R) Good space cop versus bad space cop with an ecological twist. Good-guy Abraxas (Ventura) has the task of stopping planets from destroying their environments and fighting senseless wars. His ex-partner Secundas (Ole-Thorsen) has his own mission, seeking an anti-life power which could destroy the universe. They decide to fight it out, using Earth as the battleground. Also available in an edited PG-13 version. **90m/C VHS, DVD.** Jesse Ventura, Sven-Ole Thorsen, Damian Lee, Marjorie Bransfield, Ken Quinn, Marilyn Lightstone, Moses Znaimer, Layne Coleman, Sonja Belliveau, James Belushi; *D:* Damian Lee; *W:* Damian Lee; *C:* Curtis Petersen.

Abroad with Two Yanks 🦴🦴 1944 Two Marine buddies on furlough exhibit slapstick tendencies while competing for the same girl. Along the way a big chase ensues with the two soldiers in drag. Typical wartime shenanigans likely to incite only weak chuckling or inspired snoozing. **81m/B VHS.** William Bendix, Dennis O'Keefe, Helen Walker, John Loder, George Cleveland, Janet Lambert, James Flavin, Arthur Hunnicutt; *D:* Allan Dwan.

Absence of Malice 🦴🦴½ 1981 (PG) High-minded story about the harm that the news media can inflict. Field is the earnest reporter who, after being fed some facts by an unscrupulous federal investigator, writes a story implicating Newman in a murder he didn't commit. Field hides behind journalistic confidentiality privilege to put off the outraged Newman, who loses a friend to suicide during the debacle. Interesting performances by Field and Newman. **116m/C VHS, DVD.** Paul Newman, Sally Field, Bob Balaban, Melinda Dillon, Luther Adler, Barry Primus, Josef Sommer, John Harkins, Don Hood, Wilford Brimley; *D:* Sydney Pollack; *W:* Kurt Luedtke; *C:* Owen Roizman; *M:* Dave Grusin.

Absence of the Good 🦴🦴 1999 (R) Homicide detective Caleb Barnes (Baldwin) is mourning the accidental death of his only child while investigating a series of murders in Salt Lake City. He's under pressure to solve the case, even as his home life is disintegrating, and Caleb's investigation leads to a family's malignant history. **99m/C VHS, DVD.** Stephen Baldwin, Tyne Daly, Allen (Goorwitz) Garfield, Rob Knepper; *D:* John Flynn; *W:* James Reid.

The Absent-Minded Professor 🦴🦴🦴½ 1961 Classic dumb Disney fantasy of the era. A professor accidentally invents an anti-gravity substance called flubber, causing inanimate objects and people to become airborne. Great sequence of the losing school basketball team taking advantage of flubber during a game. MacMurray is convincing as the absent-minded genius in this newly colored version. Followed by "Son of Flubber." **97m/C VHS.** Fred MacMurray, Nancy Olson, Keenan Wynn, Tommy Kirk, Leon Ames, Ed Wynn, Edward Andrews, Wally Brown; *D:* Robert Stevenson; *W:* Bill Walsh; *C:* Edward Colman; *M:* George Bruns.

Absent Without Leave 🦴🦴½ 1995 Ed (McLachlan) marries his pregnant girlfriend Daisy (Hobbs) in 1942 before joining the army. When Daisy miscarries, Ed pledges to take her home even though it means leaving the army wihout permission. As the newleyweds travel across the New Zealand countryside, they struggle with the new demands of their relationship. **104m/C VHS.** *NZ* Craig McLachlan, Katrina Hobbs; *D:* John Laing.

Absolute Beginners 🦴🦴 1986 (PG) Fervently stylish camp musical exploring the lives of British teenagers in the 1950s never quite gets untracked, although MTV video moments fill out a spare plotline. Based on a novel by Colin MacInnes. ♫Absolute Beginners; That's Motivation; Volare; Killer Blow; Have You Ever Been Blue?; Quiet Life; Having It All; Selling Out; Va Va Voom. **107m/C VHS.** *GB* David Bowie, Ray Davies, Mandy Rice-Davies, James Fox, Eddie O'Connell, Patsy Kensit, Anita Morris, Sade Adu, Sandie Shaw; *D:* Julien Temple; *W:* Richard Burridge, Don MacPherson; *C:* Oliver Stapleton.

Absolute Power 🦴🦴½ 1997 (R) Eastwood is "In the Line of Fire," (against the very agents he previously glorified) as an expert thief being pursued by rogue Secret Service men in this fast-paced thriller. While looting a Washington official's place, Luther (Eastwood) inadvertently witnesses a murder committed by none other than U.S. President Richmond (Hackman) and his goons. Immediately, a cover-up is organized by his unbalanced chief-of-staff (Davis) and Luther becomes the prime suspect. Harris gives his usual solid performance as the homicide detective. Eastwood's simple directorial style keeps up the suspense and propels the film steadily forward, alongside a generally solid plot that gets a bit improbable near the end. Based on the novel by David Baldacci. **120m/C VHS, DVD.** Clint Eastwood, Gene Hackman, Ed Harris, Laura Linney, Judy Davis, Scott Glenn, Dennis Haysbert, E.G. Marshall, Melora Hardin; *D:* Clint Eastwood; *W:* William Goldman; *C:* Jack N. Green; *M:* Lennie Niehaus.

Absolutely Fabulous: The Last Shout 🦴🦴½ 1996 The first TV movie from the British comedy series finds Edina (Saunders) selling her fashion PR business after a near-death experience and doing some soul-searching—AbFab style, which involves shopping, travel, and champagne. Naturally, Patsy (Lumley) goes along for the ride. The duo's favorite designer Christian LaCroix even has a cameo. **90m/C VHS.** *GB* Jennifer Saunders, Joanna Lumley; *Cameos:* Marianne Faithfull. TV

Absolution 🦴🦴 1981 (R) Two English boys trapped in a Catholic boarding school conspire to drive a tyrannical priest over the edge of sanity. As a result, bad things (including murder) occur. Burton is interesting in sadistic character study. Not released in the U.S. until 1988 following Burton's death, maybe due to something written in the will. **105m/C VHS.** *GB* Richard Burton, Dominic Guard, Dai Bradley, Andrew Keir, Billy Connolly, Willoughby Gray, Preston Lockwood, James Ottaway, Brook Williams, Jon Plowman, Robin Soans, Trevor Martin; *D:* Anthony Page; *W:* Anthony Shaffer; *C:* John Coquillon; *M:* Stanley Myers.

Abuse 🦴🦴 1982 Fourteen-year-old Tommy (Sbarge) is the victim of child abuse. After a beating causes convulsions, his parents rush him to a New York hospital where the intern on duty phones his student filmmaker friend Larry (Ryder), who's doing a documentary on child abuse as his master thesis. When Tommy learns that Larry is also gay, he agrees to discuss his problems but their continuing contact leads the duo to fall in love and Larry to worry about exploiting Tommy's affections. Interspersed with their story are interviews and photos of child abuse victims and their abusers. Not necessarily for the squeamish. **93m/B VHS.** Richard Ryder, Raphael Sbarge; *D:* Arthur J. Bressan Jr.; *W:* Arthur J. Bressan Jr.; *C:* Douglas Dickinson; *M:* Shawn Phillips.

The Abyss 🦴🦴🦴 *L'Oeuvre au Noir* 1989 (PG-13) Underwater sci-fi adventure about a team of oil-drilling divers pressed into service by the navy to locate and disarm an inoperative nuclear submarine. A high-tech thriller with fab footage underwater and pulsating score. **140m/C VHS, DVD, Wide.** Ed Harris, Mary Elizabeth Mastrantonio, Todd Graff, Michael Biehn, John Bedford Lloyd, J.C. Quinn, Leo Burmester, Kidd Brewer Jr., Kimberly Scott, Adam Nelson, George Robert Kirk, Chris Elliott, Jimmie Ray Weeks; *D:* James Cameron; *W:* James Cameron; *C:* Mikael Salomon; *M:* Alan Silvestri. Oscars '89: Visual FX.

Accatone! 🦴🦴🦴 1961 Accatone (Citti), a failure as a pimp, tries his luck as a thief. Hailed as a return to Italian neorealism, this is a gritty, despairing, and dark look at the lives of the street people of Rome. Pasolini's first outing, adapted by the director from his novel, "A Violent Life." Pasolini served as mentor to Bernardo Bertolucci, listed in the credits as an assistant director. **116m/B VHS.** *IT* Franco Citti, Franca Pasut, Roberto Scaringelli, Silvana Corsini, Paolo Guidi, Adriana Asti; *D:* Pier Paolo Pasolini; *W:* Pier Paolo Pasolini; *C:* Tonino Delli Colli.

Acceptable Risks 🦴½ 1986 (R) Toxic disaster strikes when a plant manager is ordered to cut costs and sacrifice safety at the Citichem plant. Predictable plot stars Dennehy as the plant manager who risks all and fights politicians to reinstate the safety standards. Meanwhile, Tyson is the city manager who tries to warn the town of a possible chemical accident that could have devastating effects on the community. TV drama that shamelessly preys on audience fears. **97m/C VHS.** Brian Dennehy, Cicely Tyson, Kenneth McMillan, Christine Ebersole, Beah Richards, Richard Gilliland; *D:* Rick Wallace. TV

Access Code 🦴 1984 Government agents attempt to uncover a private organization that has gained control of nuclear weapons for the purpose of world domination. A ragged patchwork of disconnected scenes meant to test the virtue of patience. **90m/C VHS.** Martin Landau, Michael Ansara, MacDonald Carey; *D:* Mark Sobel.

Accident 🦴🦴½ 1967 A tangled web of guilt, remorse, humor and thwarted sexuality is unravelled against the background of the English countryside in this complex story of an Oxford love triangle. An inside view of English repression at the university level adapted for the screen by Pinter from the novel by Nicholas Mosley. Long-winded but occasionally engrossing character study with interesting performances. **100m/C VHS, DVD, Wide.** *GB* Dirk Bogarde, Michael York, Stanley Baker, Jacqueline Sassard, Delphine Seyrig, Alexander Knox, Vivien Merchant, Freddie Jones, Harold Pinter; *D:* Joseph Losey; *W:* Harold Pinter; *C:* Gerry Fisher; *M:* John Dankworth. Cannes '67: Grand Jury Prize.

Accident 🦴½ 1983 Skate for your life. A hockey game turns into a nightmare when the roof over the arena collapses under the weight of too much ice and snow. One of the few hockey disaster films. **104m/C VHS.** Terence Kelly, Fiona Reid, Frank Perry; *D:* Donald Brittain.

Accidental Meeting 🦴🦴½ 1993 (R) A female version of "Strangers on a Train." Two women meet because of an auto accident and wind up talking about their lives. The main topic is man trouble and both "jokingly" plot to murder each other's man. Only, one woman does the deed and the other soon finds herself on the murderess' hit list. **91m/C VHS.** Linda Gray, Linda Purl, Leigh McCloskey, David Hayward, Ernie Lively, Kent McCord; *D:* Michael Zinberg; *W:* Pete Best, Christopher Horner.

The Accidental Tourist 🦴🦴🦴½ 1988 (PG) A bittersweet and subtle story, adapted faithfully from Anne Tyler's novel, of an introverted, grieving man who learns to love again after meeting an unconventional woman. After his son's death and subsequent separation from wife Turner, Macon Leary (Hurt) avoids emotional confrontation, burying himself in routines with the aid of his obsessive-compulsive siblings. Kooky dog-trainer Muriel Pritchett (an exuberant Davis) wins his attention, but not without struggle. Hurt effectively uses small gestures to describe Macon's emotional journey, while Davis grabs hearts with her open performance. Outstanding supporting cast. **121m/C VHS, 8mm, Wide.** William Hurt, Geena Davis, Kathleen Turner, Ed Begley Jr., David Ogden Stiers, Bill Pullman, Amy Wright; ***D:*** Lawrence Kasdan; ***W:*** Lawrence Kasdan; ***C:*** John Bailey; ***M:*** John Williams. Oscars '88: Support. Actress (Davis); N.Y. Film Critics '88: Film.

Accidents 🦴½ **1989 (R)** A scientist discovers that his invention has been stolen and is going to be used to cause worldwide havoc. He becomes concerned and spends the remainder of the movie trying to relieve himself of anxiety. **90m/C VHS.** Edward Albert, Leigh Taylor-Young, Jon Cypher; ***D:*** Gideon Amir.

The Accompanist 🦴🦴½ *L'Accompagnatrice* **1993 (PG)** Centers around a Parisian diva Irene's (Safonova) relationship with her talented pianist Sophie (Romane Bohringer), amidst the clamor of WWII Europe. Sophie impresses Irene with her musical abilities, and takes on additional work as her housekeeper. Meanwhile, Charles (Richard Bohringer), Irene's husband, schmoozes with the Nazis to line his own pockets while she helps the war effort by having an affair with a member of the resistance (Labarthe). Unfortunately, Sophie starts to resent living in Irene's shadow. Adapted from the novel by Nina Berberouva. The Bohringers are father and daughter. French with subtitles. **111m/C VHS.** *FR* Elena Safonova, Romane Bohringer, Richard Bohringer, Samuel Labarthe, Nelly Borgeaud, Julien Rassam; ***D:*** Claude Miller; ***W:*** Claude Miller, Luc Beraud, Claude Rich; ***C:*** Yves Angelo; ***M:*** Alain Jomy.

Accomplice 🦴½ **1946** Plodding whodunit with Arlen as a shy, bookish private eye hired by his old flame to locate her missing husband. His investigations uncover several murders and long after the viewers have put 2 + 2 together, the P.I. smells a rat. The missing husband was a ruse to divert him from the real scam-a bank heist. Painfully low-level excitement. **66m/B VHS.** Richard Arlen, Veda Ann Borg, Tom Dugan, Francis Ford; ***D:*** Walter Colmes.

Accused 🦴🦴½ **1936** Married dancers Fairbanks and Del Rio are working in a Parisian revue when the show's sultry leading lady (Desmond) makes a pass at Fairbanks. Though he's turned her down, through a series of misunderstandings Del Rio believes the worst and the two women get into a vicious argument. When the star is found dead guess who gets the blame? Del Rio is lovely, Desmond is spiteful, and Fairbanks serves as a fine object of two women's affections. **83m/B VHS.** *GB* Douglas Fairbanks Jr., Dolores Del Rio, Florence Desmond, Basil Sydney, Athole Stewart, Esme Percy, Googie Withers, Cecil Humphreys; ***D:*** Thornton Freeland.

The Accused 🦴🦴½ *Strange Deception* **1948** Young is cast against character in this story of a college professor who is assaulted by one of her students and kills him in self-defense. A courtroom drama ensues, where Young is defended by the dead man's guardian. Film noir with nice ensemble performance. **101m/B VHS.** Loretta Young, Robert Cummings, Wendell Corey, Sam Jaffe, Douglas Dick, Sara Allgood, Ann Doran; ***D:*** William Dieterle; ***C:*** Milton Krasner.

The Accused 🦴🦴🦴 **1988 (R)** Provocative treatment of a true story involving a young woman gang raped in a bar while onlookers cheer. McGillis is the assistant district attorney who takes on the case and must contend with the victim's questionable past and a powerful lawyer hired by a wealthy defendant's parents. As the victim with a past, Foster gives an Oscar-winning performance that won raves for its strength and complexity. **110m/C VHS, DVD, 8mm, Wide.** Jodie Foster, Kelly McGillis, Bernie Coulson, Leo Rossi, Ann Hearn, Carmen Argenziano, Steve Antin, Tom O'Brien, Peter Van Norden, Woody Brown; ***D:*** Jonathan Kaplan; ***W:*** Tom Topor; ***C:*** Ralf Bode; ***M:*** Brad Fiedel. Oscars '88: Actress (Foster); Golden Globes '89: Actress—Drama (Foster); Natl. Bd. of Review '88: Actress (Foster).

Ace Drummond 🦴🦴 *Squadron of Doom* **1936** The complete 13-chapter serial about a murder organization that tries to stop several countries from forming a worldwide clipper ship air service and government troubleshooter Ace Drummond who's out to stop them. **260m/B VHS.** John "Dusty" King, Jean Rogers, Noah Beery Jr.; ***D:*** Ford Beebe.

Ace High 🦴½ **1968** Spaghetti western about a ruthless outlaw named Cat Stevens trying to save himself from the noose. Patterned after the famous Sergio Leone-Clint Eastwood westerns, with less of a budget and more camp tendencies. **120m/C VHS.** *IT* Eli Wallach, Terence Hill, Bud Spencer, Brock Peters, Kevin McCarthy; ***D:*** Giuseppe Colizzi.

Ace of Aces 🦴🦴 **1933** An American sculptor is reviled, particularly by his girlfriend, when he does not join fellows in enlisting in what becomes WWI. Out to prove he's not lacking testosterone, he becomes a pilot in France, but is embittered by his experiences. Dated but well-acted war melodrama. **77m/B VHS.** Richard Dix, Elizabeth Allan, Theodore Newton, Ralph Bellamy, William Cagney, Frank Conroy; ***D:*** J. Walter Ruben; ***C:*** Henry Cronjager; ***M:*** Max Steiner.

Ace of Hearts 🦴 **1985** A seedy story about a rich guy in the South Pacific who pays heavily to have himself killed. **90m/C VHS.** Mickey Rooney, Chris Robinson, Pilar Velasquez.

Ace Ventura: Pet Detective 🦴🦴 **1993 (PG-13)** Shamelessly silly comedy casts human cartoon Carrey, he of the rubber limbs and spasmodic facial muscles, as Ace, the guy who'll find missing pets, big or small. When the Miami Dolphins' mascot Snowflake is kidnapped, he abandons his search for an albino pigeon to save the lost dolphin just in time for the Super Bowl. This is brain candy, running full throttle with juvenile humor, some charm, and the hyper-energetic Carrey, not to mention Young as the police chief with a secret. Critically trashed boxoffice smash catapulted Carrey into nearly instant stardom after seven seasons as the geeky white guy on "In Living Color." **87m/C VHS, DVD, 8mm.** Jim Carrey, Dan Marino, Courteney Cox Arquette, Sean Young, Tone Loc, Noble Willingham, Troy Evans, Udo Kier; ***D:*** Tom Shadyac; ***W:*** Jim Carrey, Tom Shadyac, Jack Bernstein; ***C:*** Julio Macat; ***M:*** Ira Newborn. Blockbuster '95: Male Newcomer, V. (Carrey), Comedy Actor, V. (Carrey).

Ace Ventura: When Nature Calls 🦴🦴 *Ace Ventura Goes to Africa* **1995 (PG-13)** Ace is back on the case as the pet dick (Carrey) ventures to Africa to restore peace among rival tribes by finding an albino bat that's M.I.A. Plot is secondary, however, to multi-million dollar man Carrey's outrageous brand of physical comedy combined with his unique ability to deliver junior high level lines with pseudo-suave savoir-faire. Contains only a handful of outstanding gags, the best with Ace and a mechanical rhino. Mainly for Carrey aficionados (of which there are many) and original "Ace" fans—the low-brow humor runs a bit thin by the end. **94m/C VHS, DVD.** Jim Carrey, Ian McNeice, Simon Callow, Maynard Eziashi, Bob Gunton, Sophie Okonedo, Tommy Davidson; ***D:*** Steve Oedekerk; ***W:*** Steve Oedekerk; ***C:*** Donald E. Thorin; ***M:*** Robert Folk. MTV Movie Awards '96: Male Perf. (Carrey), Comedic Perf. (Carrey); Blockbuster '96: Comedy Actor, T. (Carrey).

Aces and Eights 🦴🦴½ **1936** Gambler McCoy catches a fellow cardsharp cheating and the marshal runs the varmint out of town. When the cheater is murdered, the lawman suspects McCoy, who sets out to prove his innocence. Title refers to the "death hand" held by Wild Bill Hickok, killed while playing poker. Film opens with a shot of Hickok and a speech about gambler's luck. **62m/B VHS.** Tim McCoy, Jimmy Aubrey, Luana Walters, Wheeler Oakman, Earle Hodgins, Frank Glennon, Rex Lease, Joseph Girard, John Merton; ***D:*** Sam Newfield.

Aces: Iron Eagle 3 🦴🦴 **1992 (R)** Colonel "Chappy" Sinclair returns once again in this air adventure. He's been keeping busy flying in air shows when he stumbles across the nefarious activities of a Peruvian drug baron working out of a remote village. Sinclair recruits a team of maverick air circus pilots and they "borrow" a fleet of WWII vintage aircraft to raid the village, coming up against a fellow Air Force officer who turns out to be another villain. Lots of action and a stalwart cast. **98m/C VHS.** Louis Gossett Jr., Rachel McLish, Paul Freeman, Horst Buchholz, Christopher Cazenove, Sonny Chiba, Fred Dalton Thompson, Mitchell Ryan, Robert Estes, J.E. Freeman; ***D:*** John Glen.

Aces Wild 🦴½ **1937** Another poker title. Outlaws menace an honest newspaper until the lawmen show up and send them on their way. **62m/B VHS.** Harry Carey Sr., Gertrude Messinger, Edward Cassidy, Roger Williams; ***D:*** Harry Fraser.

The Acid Eaters 🦴 **1967** Straight-laced desk jockeys spend their weekends exploring the realm of the senses. Includes nudity. **62m/C VHS.** Buck Kartalian, Pat (Barringer) Barrington; ***D:*** B. Ron Elliott; ***W:*** B. Ron Elliott, Carl Monson; ***M:*** Billy Allen.

The Acid House 🦴🦴½ **1998** Trilogy of tales written by Irving Welsh, author of "Trainspotting," similarly centers on down-on-their-luck Scottish hooligans ravaged by drugs and drink. Its tone, however, makes its predecessor look like a light-hearted romp in the countryside. In "The Granton Star Cause," freeloading loser Boab (McCole) gets turned into a fly by God during a trip to the pub. He proceeds to exact some disgusting revenge on those he feels have wronged him. "A Soft Touch" depicts the twisted relationship between brow-beaten Johnny (McKidd) and kinky wife Catriona (Gomez), who is sleeping with psycho neighbor Larry (McCormack). In the last chapter, "The Acid House," tripped-out rave party boy Coco (Bremner) exchanges personalities with the newborn baby of suburban couple Rory (Clunes) and Jenny (Redgrave). First-time director McGuigan does a good job of translating the material to the screen, but sometimes goes over the top in showing these skanky Scots. Also, be warned that the Scottish accents are so thick that the movie ran with subtitles during its limited U.S. theater run. If you liked "Trainspotting," however, you'll probably like this similar entry in the "if it's Scottish, it's crap!" genre. **118m/C VHS, DVD, Wide.** Stephen McCole, Maurice Roeves, Garry Sweeney, Kevin McKidd, Ewen Bremner, Martin Clunes, Jemma Redgrave, Arlene Cockburn, Jenny McCrindle, Michelle Gomez, Tam Dean Burn, Gary McCormack, Jane Stabler; ***D:*** Paul McGuigan; ***W:*** Irvine Welsh; ***C:*** Alasdair Walker.

Acla's Descent into Floristella 🦴🦴 *Acla* **1987** Twelve-year-old Acla (Cusimano) is sold by his father to work underground in the sulfur mines for eight years. Repeatedly beaten by his owner, Acla runs away, but there are dire consequences for him and his family. Set in 1930s Sicily. Italian with subtitles. **86m/C VHS.** *IT* Francesco Cusimano, Tony Sperandeo; ***D:*** Aurelio Grimaldi; ***W:*** Aurelio Grimaldi; ***C:*** Maurizio Calvesi; ***M:*** Dario Lucantoni.

Acorn People 🦴🦴 **1982** An unemployed teacher takes a summer job at a camp for handicapped children and learns sensitivity. Weeper adapted by Tewkesbury from the book by Ron Jones. **97m/C VHS.** Ted Bessell, Cloris Leachman, LeVar Burton, Dolph Sweet, Cheryl Anderson; ***D:*** Joan Tewkesbury. **TV**

Acqua e Sapone 🦴½ **1983 (PG)** A young innocent model goes to Rome under the watchful eyes of an appointed priest-chaperon, but finds love, fun and other sinful things. Sudsy/romantic comedy. **100m/C VHS.** *IT* Carlo Verdone, Natasha Hovey, Florinda Bolkan, Elena Bolkan; ***D:*** Carlo Verdone.

Across 110th Street 🦴🦴 **1972 (R)** Gritty, violent cop thriller in the blaxploitation genre. Both the Mafia and the cops hunt down three black hoods who, in a display of extremely bad judgment, knocked over a mob-controlled bank while disguised as police. Lots of bullets create buckets of blood. Filmed on location in Harlem. **102m/C VHS, DVD, Wide.** Anthony Quinn, Yaphet Kotto, Anthony (Tony) Franciosa, Paul Benjamin, Ed Bernard, Antonio Fargas, Tim O'Connor, Lewis Gilbert, Richard Ward; ***D:*** Barry Shear; ***W:*** Luther Davis; ***C:*** Jack Priestley.

Across the Bridge 🦴🦴½ **1957** A man on the run from Scotland Yard for stealing a fortune flees to Mexico, in the process killing a man and assuming his identity. An ironic twist and his love for a dog seal his final destiny. Steiger's psychological study as the fugitive is compelling. Based on a novel by Graham Greene. **103m/B VHS.** *GB* Rod Steiger, David Knight, Marla Landi, Noel Willman, Bernard Lee; ***D:*** Ken Annakin; ***M:*** James Bernard.

Across the Great Divide 🦴🦴½ **1976 (G)** Two orphans must cross the rugged snow-covered Rocky Mountains in 1876 in order to claim their inheritance—a 400-acre plot of land in Salem, Oregon. Pleasant coming-of-age tale with majestic scenery. **102m/C VHS.** Robert F. Logan, George "Buck" Flower, Heather Rattray, Mark Hall; ***D:*** Stewart Raffill; ***W:*** Stewart Raffill; ***M:*** Angelo Badalamenti.

Across the Line 🦴🦴½ **2000 (R)** Miranda (Erez) crosses the border from Mexico into the U.S. and immediately witnesses the murder of a tourist and her husband by corrupt Border Patrol officers. A sheriff (Johnson) tries to protect his witness even as he falls in love with her. **97m/C VHS, DVD.** Brad Johnson, Sigal Erez, Brian Bloom, Marshall Teague, Adrienne Barbeau; ***D:*** Martin Spottl; ***W:*** Sigal Erez. **VIDEO**

Across the Moon 🦴🦴 **1994 (R)** A road trip to the desert takes Carmen and Kathy away from their incarcerated boyfriends but into troubles with cowboys and prospectors. **88m/C VHS, DVD.** Elizabeth Pena, Christina Applegate, Tony Fields, Peter Berg, James Remar, Michael McKean, Burgess Meredith, Jack Nance; ***D:*** Lisa Gottlieb; ***W:*** Stephen Schneck; ***C:*** Andrzej Sekula; ***M:*** Christopher Tyng, Exene Cervenka.

Across the Pacific 🦴🦴🦴½ **1942** Classic Bogie/Huston vehicle made on the heels of "The Maltese Falcon." Bogie is an American Army officer booted out of the service on false charges of treason. When no other military will accept him, he sails to China (via the Panama Canal) to offer his services to Chiang Kai-Shek. On board, he meets a variety of seedy characters who plan to blow up the canal. Huston again capitalizes on the counterpoint between the rotundly acerbic Greenstreet, who plays a spy, and stiff-lipped Bogart, who's wooing Astor. Great Bogie moments and fine direction make this an adventure classic. When he departed for the service just prior to filming the final scenes, Huston turned over direction to Vincent Sherman. Also available colorized. **97m/B VHS.** Humphrey Bogart, Mary Astor, Sydney Greenstreet, Charles Halton, Victor Sen Yung, Roland Got, Keye Luke, Richard Loo, Frank Wilcox, Paul Stanton, Lester Matthews, Tom Stevenson, Roland (Walter Goss) Drew, Monte Blue, Rudy Robles, Lee Tung Foo, Chester Gan, Kam Tong, Spencer Chan, Philip Ahn, Frank Faylen, Frank Mayo; ***D:*** John Huston; ***W:*** Richard Macaulay; ***C:*** Arthur Edeson; ***M:*** Adolph Deutsch.

Across the Plains 🦴½ **1939** Predictable oater about two brothers who are raised separately after their parents are murdered by outlaws. One is brought up by Indians, the other by the outlaws responsible for wiping out the folks, who tell the boy that Indians did in his ma and pa. Eventually the brothers meet and fight. Odds favor the good one winning, aided by Indian pals. **59m/B VHS.** Addison "Jack" Randall, Frank Yaconelli, Joyce Bryant, Hal Price, Dennis Moore, Glenn Strange, Bud Osborne; ***D:*** Spencer Gordon Bennet.

Across the Tracks 🦴🦴 **1989 (PG-13)** Two brothers, Billy (Schroder), a juvie-home rebel, and Joe (Pitt), a straight-A jock, are at odds when the black sheep is pressured into selling drugs. In an attempt to save his brother from a life of crime, saintly Joe convinces Billy to join him on the school track team, and the brothers are forced to face off in a big meet. Fairly realistic good guy/bad guy who's really a good guy teen drama. **101m/C VHS.** Rick Schroder, Brad Pitt, Carrie Snodgress; ***D:*** Sandy Tung; ***W:*** Sandy Tung; ***C:*** Michael Delahoussaye; ***M:*** Joel Goldsmith.

Across the Wide Missouri 🦴🦴½ **1951** Pioneer epic stars Gable as a rugged fur trapper who marries an Indian woman (Marques) so he can trap beaver pelts on her people's rich land. On the journey to the Indian territory however, the trapper truly falls in love with his bride. Superior historical drama is marred slightly by the use of narration (provided by Howard Keel). Look for lively performances from Menjou as a French tippler and Naish as the quirky Indian Chief. Beautiful scenery filmed in the spectacular Rocky Mountains. **78m/C VHS.** Clark Gable, Ricardo Montalban, John Hodiak, Adolphe Menjou, Maria Elena Marques, J. Carrol Naish, Jack Holt, Alan Napier; ***D:*** William A. Wellman; ***C:*** William Mellor; ***Nar:*** Howard Keel.

The Act 🦴🦴 *Bless 'Em All* **1982 (R)** A muddled satire about political double dealing and union corruption further muddled by a twangy musical score manufactured by folksy Sebastian. **90m/C VHS.** Jill St. John, Eddie Albert, Pat Hingle, Robert Ginty, Sarah Langenfeld, Nicolas Surovy; ***D:*** Sig Shore; ***M:*** John Sebastian.

Act of Aggression 🦴🦴 *L'Agression* **1973 (R)** When a Parisian man finds his wife and daughter murdered at a summer resort, he takes the law into his own hands, with predictable results. **100m/C VHS.** *FR* Jean-Louis Trintignant, Catherine Deneuve, Claude Brasseur, Milena Vukotic, Jacques Rispal, Philippe Brigaud, Michele Grellier, Robert Charlebois, Franco Fabrizi; ***D:*** Gerard Pires; ***C:*** Silvano Ippoliti.

Act of Passion: The Lost Honor of Kathryn Beck 🦴🦴½ **1983** A woman meets a man at a party and has the proverbial one-night stand. Her privacy is shattered when she discovers that he's a terrorist under surveillance by the police and press. Strong performances by Thomas and Kristofferson help turn this into an interesting American TV remake of the German "Lost Honor of Katharina Blum," based loosely on a novel by Heinrich Boll. **100m/C VHS.** Marlo Thomas, Kris Kristofferson, George Dzundza, Jon (John) DeVries; ***D:*** Simon Langton. **TV**

Act of Piracy 🦴½ **1989 (R)** A bankrupt contractor reunites with his estranged wife to track down the brutal terrorists who have kidnapped their son. **105m/C VHS.** Gary Busey, Belinda Bauer, Ray Sharkey, Nancy Mulford, Dennis Casey Park, Arnold Vosloo, Ken Gampu; ***D:*** John Cardos; ***W:*** Hal Reed; ***C:*** Vincent Cox; ***M:*** Morton Stevens.

Act of Vengeance 🦴🦴 *Rape Squad* **1974 (R)** A group of women band together to hunt down and exact revenge on the man who raped them. Exploitative action-filled thriller. **90m/C VHS.** Jo Ann Harris, Peter Brown, Jennifer Lee, Lisa Moore, Connie Strickland, Pat Estrin; ***D:*** Bob Kelljan.

Act of Vengeance 🦴🦴½ **1986** Drama about Jock Yablonski, a United Mine Workers official who challenged the president, Tony Boyle. Based on fact, showing the events that led up to the murder of Yablonski and his family. Intriguing story lacking cinematic drive. **97m/C VHS.** Charles Bronson, Ellen Burstyn, Wilford Brimley, Hoyt Axton, Robert Schenkkan, Ellen Barkin, Keanu Reeves; ***D:*** John MacKenzie; ***W:*** Scott Spencer. **CABLE**

Act of War 🦴🦴 **1996** Disgraced diplomat/spy Jack Gracey (Scalia) has to stop renegade communists who've taken over a remote nuclear missile site from pressing the button on a missle aimed directly at the White House. Lots of action should hold viewers' interest. **100m/C VHS, DVD.** *CA CZ* Jack Scalia, Ingrid Torrance, Douglas Arthurs; ***D:*** Robert Lee; ***W:*** Michael Bafaro; ***C:*** David Pelletier; ***M:*** Peter Allen. **VIDEO**

Acting on Impulse 🦴🦴 **1993 (R)** Impulsive, troublemaking movie star (Fiorentino) becomes a murder suspect when her producer is killed. This doesn't slow her down. She checks into a hotel with a major party attitude and manages to seduce a conservative businessman (Howell) and his junior exec (Allen) into helping her forget her troubles. And then the businessman's fiancee turns up dead. Any connection? **94m/C VHS.** Linda Fiorentino, C. Thomas Howell, Nancy Allen, Adam Ant, Judith Hoag, Patrick Bauchau, Isaac Hayes, Paul Bartel, Donny Most, Miles O'Keeffe, Dick Sargent, Charles Lane, Mary Woronov, Zelda Rubinstein, Nicholas Sadler, Peter Lupus, Kim McGuire, Cassandra Peterson, Brinke Stevens, Michael Talbot, Robert Alan Golub, Cliff Dorfman, Craig Shoemaker, Scott Thompson Stevens; ***D:*** Sam Irvin; ***W:*** Mark Pittman, Alan Moskowitz; ***C:*** Dean Lent; ***M:*** Daniel Licht. **CABLE**

Action for Slander 🦴🦴½ **1938** A British army officer sporting the typical stiff upper lip is accused of cheating during a card game, and the slander mars his reputation until the case is taken to court. Dryly earnest and honest in its depiction of class differences in pre-war England. Based on a novel by Mary Borden. **84m/B VHS, 8mm.** *GB* Clive Brook, Ann Todd, Margaretta Scott, Ronald Squire, Francis L. Sullivan, Felix Aylmer, Googie Withers; ***D:*** Tim Whelan.

Action in Arabia 🦴🦴 **1944** A newsman uncovers a Nazi plot to turn the Arabs against the Allies while investigating a colleague's murder in Damascus. The desert teems with spies, double agents, and sheiks as suave Sanders goes about his investigative business. Quintessential wartime B-movie. **75m/B VHS.** George Sanders, Virginia Bruce, Lenore Aubert, Gene Lockhart, Robert Armstrong, H.B. Warner, Alan Napier, Michael Ansara; ***D:*** Leonide Moguy.

Action in the North Atlantic 🦴🦴 **1943** Massey and Bogart are the captain and first mate of a Merchant Marine vessel running the lone supply route to the Soviet Union. Eventually they wind up locking horns with a Nazi U-boat. Plenty of action and strenuous flag waving in this propagandorama. Gordon fans won't want to miss her as Massey's wife. Also available colorized. **126m/B VHS.** Humphrey Bogart, Raymond Massey, Alan Hale, Julie (Jacqueline Wells) Bishop, Ruth Gordon, Sam Levene, Dane Clark, Peter Whitney, Minor Watson, J.M. Kerrigan, Dick Hogan, Kane Richmond, Chick Chandler, Donald Douglas, Creighton Hale, Iris Adrian, Elliott Sullivan, Glenn Strange; ***D:*** Lloyd Bacon; ***W:*** A.I. Bezzerides, W.R. Burnett, John Howard Lawson; ***C:*** Ted D. McCord; ***M:*** Adolph Deutsch.

Action Jackson 🦴🦴 **1988 (R)** Power-hungry auto tycoon Nelson tries to frame rebellious black police sergeant Weathers for murder. Being a graduate of Harvard and a tough guy, the cop doesn't go for it. Nelson eats up the screen as the heavy with no redeeming qualities, while Weathers is tongue-in-cheek as the resourceful good guy who keeps running afoul of the law in spite of his best efforts. Lots of action, violence, and a few sexy women help cover the plot's lack of common sense. **96m/C VHS, DVD.** Thomas F. Wilson, Mary Ellen Trainor, Carl Weathers, Vanity, Craig T. Nelson, Sharon Stone; ***D:*** Craig R. Baxley; ***W:*** Robert Reneau; ***C:*** Matthew F. Leonetti; ***M:*** Herbie Hancock, Michael Kamen.

Action U.S.A. 🦴½ **1989** A young woman witnesses the murder of her boyfriend by gangsters, who then pursue her to make sure she will never tell what she saw. Throughout Texas she rambles with the mob sniffing at her heels, grateful for the opportunity to participate in numerous stunts and car crashes. **90m/C VHS.** Barri Murphy, Gregory Scott Cummins, William Knight, William Smith, Cameron Mitchell; ***D:*** John Stewart; ***W:*** David Reskin; ***C:*** Thomas Callaway.

Active Stealth 🦴🦴 **1999 (R)** The Army's most secret weapon, an undetectable fighter jet, is hijacked by terrorists during a training mission. Now, it's up to Jefferson Pike (Baldwin) to lead a team into the Central American jungles to retrieve the military's property. **99m/C VHS, DVD.** Daniel Baldwin, Fred Williamson, Hannes Jaenicke, Chick Vennera, Lisa Vidal; ***D:*** Fred Olen Ray. **VIDEO**

Actor: The Paul Muni Story 🦴🦴 **1978** Musical biography of Paul Muni, from his beginnings as a traveling actor in Hungary to his New York theatre and movie career. **105m/C VHS.** Herschel Bernardi, Georgia Brown, Harold Gould.

Actors and Sin 🦴🦴½ **1952** Two-part film casting a critical eye toward actors and Hollywood. "Actor's Blood" is the melodramatic story of Shakespearean actor Robinson and his unhappy actress daughter. She commits suicide and he sets out to prove it was murder. Heavy going. Lighter and more entertaining is "Woman of Sin," which relates a Hollywood satire involving a theatrical agent and his newest client, a precocious nine-year-old. **82m/B VHS.** Edward G. Robinson, Marsha Hunt, Eddie Albert, Alan Reed, Dan O'Herlihy, Tracey Roberts, Rudolph Anders, Paul Guilfoyle, Alice Key, Douglas Evans, Rick Roman, Jenny Hecht, Jody Gilbert, John Crawford; ***D:*** Lee Garmes, Ben Hecht; ***W:*** Ben Hecht; ***C:*** Lee Garmes; ***M:*** George Antheil.

An Actor's Revenge 🦴🦴 *Yukinojo Henge; Revenge of a Kabuki Actor* **1963** In the early 19th century, a female impersonator in a Kabuki troupe takes revenge on the three men who killed his parents. Fascinating study of opposites—male/female, stage/life, love/hate. In Japanese with English subtitles. **110m/C VHS.** *JP* Kazuo Hasegawa, Fujiko Yamamoto, Ayako Wakao, Ganjiro Nakamura; ***D:*** Kon Ichikawa; ***W:*** Teinosuke Kinugasa, Daisuke Ito, Natto Wada; ***C:*** Setsuo Kobayashi; ***M:*** Yashushi Akutagawa.

A.D. 🦴🦴½ *Anno Domini* **1985** Set shortly after Jesus' death, this rather low-budget miniseries chronicles the life and adventures of Christ's disciples (especially Peter and Paul) and the growing conflicts between Jewish zealots, early Christians, and the power of the Roman empire. Based on the Acts of the Apostles. **540m/C VHS.** Denis Quilley, Philip Sayer, Anthony Andrews, Colleen Dewhurst, Ava Gardner, Richard Kiley, James Mason, David Hedison, John Houseman, John McEnery, Ian McShane, Jennifer O'Neill, Fernando Rey, Richard Roundtree, Ben Vereen, Susan Sarandon, Diane Venora, Anthony Zerbe, Jack Warden, Amanda Pays, Millie Perkins, Michael Wilding Jr.; ***D:*** Stuart Cooper; ***W:*** Anthony Burgess; ***C:*** Ennio Guarnieri; ***M:*** Lalo Schifrin. **TV**

Adam 🦴🦴🦴½ **1983** Docu-drama based on a tragic, true story. John and Reve Williams (Travanti and Williams) desperately search for their six-year-old son abducted during an outing. During their long search and struggle, they lobby Congress for use of the FBI's crime computer. Eventually their efforts led to the creation of the Missing Children's Bureau. Sensitive, compelling performances by Travanti and Williams as the agonized, courageous parents. **100m/C VHS.** Daniel J. Travanti, JoBeth Williams, Martha Scott, Richard Masur, Paul Regina, Mason Adams; ***D:*** Michael Tuchner. **TV**

Adam at 6 a.m. 🦴🦴 **1970 (PG)** Douglas is a young college professor who decides to spend a summer laboring in Missouri, where life, he thinks, is simpler. Of course, he learns that life in the boonies has its own set of problems, but unfortunately it takes him the entire movie before he catches the drift. **100m/C VHS.** Michael Douglas, Lee Purcell, Joe Don Baker, Charles Aidman, Marge Redmond, Louise Latham, Grayson Hall, Dana Elcar, Meg Foster, Richard Derr, Anne Gwynne; ***D:*** Robert Scheerer.

Adam Had Four Sons 🦴🦴½ **1941** Satisfying character study involving the typical turn-of-the-century family nearly consumed by love, jealousy, and hatred. In the early part of the century, a goodly governess (Bergman in her second U.S. film) watches sympathetically over four sons of an American businessman after their mother dies. Economic necessity separates Bergman from the family for several years. Upon her return, she tangles with scheming bride-to-be Hayward, a bad girl intent on dividing and conquering the family before walking down the aisle with one of the sons. Based on a novel by Charles Bonner. **81m/B VHS.** Ingrid Bergman, Warner Baxter, Susan Hayward, Fay Wray, Richard Denning, June Lockhart, Robert Shaw, Johnny Downs; ***D:*** Gregory Ratoff.

Adam's Rib 🦴🦴🦴🦴 **1950** Classic war between the sexes cast Tracy and Hepburn as married attorneys on opposite sides of the courtroom in the trial of blonde bombshell Holliday, charged with attempted murder of the lover of her philandering husband. The battle in the courtroom soon takes its toll at home as the couple is increasingly unable to leave their work at the office. Sharp, snappy dialogue by Gordon and Kanin with superb direction by Cukor. Perhaps the best of the nine movies pairing Tracy and Hepburn. Also available colorized. **101m/B VHS, DVD.** Spencer Tracy, Katharine Hepburn, Judy Holliday, Tom Ewell, David Wayne, Jean Hagen, Hope Emerson, Polly Moran, Marvin Kaplan, Paula Raymond, Tommy Noonan; ***D:*** George Cukor; ***W:*** Garson Kanin, Ruth Gordon; ***C:*** George J. Folsey; ***M:*** Miklos Rozsa. Natl. Film Reg. '92.

The Addams Family 🦴🦴½ **1991 (PG-13)** Everybody's favorite family of ghouls hits the big screen, but something is lost in the translation. An imposter claiming to be long-lost Uncle Fester (Lloyd), who says he was in the Bermuda Triangle for 25 years, shows up at the Addams' home to complete a dastardly deed—raid the family's immense fortune. Although Fester's plan is foiled, a series of plot twists highlight the ghoulish family's eccentricities. Darkly humorous but eventually disappointing: Julia, Huston, and Ricci (as Gomez, Morticia, and Wednesday, respectively) are great in their roles and the sets look good, but the plot is thin. Much closer to the original comic strip by Charles Addams than the popular TV show ever was. **102m/C VHS, DVD, Wide.** Anjelica Huston, Raul Julia, Christopher Lloyd, Dan Hedaya, Elizabeth Wilson, Judith Malina, Carel Struycken, Dana Ivey, Paul Benedict, Christina Ricci, Jimmy Workman, Christopher Hunt, John Franklin; ***Cameos:*** Marc Shaiman; ***D:*** Barry Sonnenfeld; ***W:*** Caroline Thompson, Larry Thompson; ***C:*** Owen Roizman; ***M:*** Marc Shaiman. Golden Raspberries '91: Worst Song ("Addams Groove").

Addams Family Values 🦴🦴½ **1993 (PG-13)** The creepy Addams' are back, but this time they leave the dark confines of the mansion to meet the "real" world. New baby Pubert causes homicidal jealousy in sibs Wednesday and Pugsley, causing Mom and Dad to hire a gold-digging, serial-killing nanny (Cusack) with designs on Uncle Fester to watch over the tot. A step above its predecessor, chock full of black humor, sub-plots, and one-liners. Cusack fits right in with an outrageously over the top performance and Ricci nearly steals the show again as the deadpan Wednesday. **93m/C VHS, DVD, Wide.** Anjelica Huston, Raul Julia, Christopher Lloyd, Joan Cusack, Carol Kane, Christina Ricci, Jimmy Workman, Kaitlyn Hooper, Kristen Hooper, Carel Struycken, David Krumholtz, Christopher Hunt, Dana Ivey, Peter MacNicol, Christine Baranski, Mercedes McNab; ***D:*** Barry Sonnenfeld; ***W:*** Paul Rudnick; ***M:*** Marc Shaiman. Golden Raspberries '93: Worst Song ("WHOOMP! There It Is").

Addicted to Love 🦴🦴½ **1996 (R)** Warning: Do not rent this movie with your significant other if you're thinking about breaking up with them. After they're both dumped, mild-mannered Sam (Broderick) and wild woman Maggie (Ryan) discover they have a lot in common. First of all, their exes Linda (Preston) and Anton (Karyo) are dating each other. Secondly, they're both stalkers! Yep! A romantic comedy about stalking. Sam wants nothing more than to reclaim Linda as his own. Maggie wants nothing less than Anton's head on a plate. Interesting comedy wavers between dark and light moments, aided by the rather murky sets and lighting. Directorial debut for Dunne, who makes his father eat a bug in one scene. **100m/C VHS, DVD.** Meg Ryan, Matthew Broderick, Kelly Preston, Tcheky Karyo, Maureen Stapleton, Remak Ramsay, Nesbitt Blaisdell, Dominick Dunne; ***D:*** Griffin Dunne; ***W:*** Robert Gordon; ***C:*** Andrew Dunn; ***M:*** Rachel Portman.

Addicted to Murder 🦴🦴 **1995** Joel Winter (McCleery) was abused as a child and now takes his anger out on women by killing them. Then he meets vampire Angie (Graham), who decides to transform him since he's already a predator. But Joel develops a conscience and tries to reform, which ticks Angie off and she frames him for a murder he didn't commit. Which ticks Joel off so he becomes a vampire (and a vampire hunter) to get even. **90m/C VHS.** Michael (Mick) McCleery, Sasha Graham, Laura McLaughlin; ***D:*** Kevin J. Lindenmuth; ***W:*** Kevin J. Lindenmuth; ***C:*** Kevin J. Lindenmuth. **VIDEO**

Addicted to Murder 2: Tainted Blood 🦴½ **1997** It's a case of diminishing returns as is usual with sequels in this plotwise mishmash. New York City is the happy hunting grounds for a rogue vamp who's turning others whom Angie (Graham) doesn't considered worthy of getting "The Gift." So she intends to put a stop to it. And just around for more laughs is Joel (McCleery)—the serial killer turned vampire turned vampire hunter. **80m/C VHS.** Sasha Graham, Michael (Mick) McCleery, Sarah K. Lippmann, Robbi Firestone, Ted Grayson, Joe Moretti, Joel D. Wynkoop, Tom NonDorf; ***Cameos:*** Ted V. Mikels; ***D:*** Kevin J. Lindenmuth; ***W:*** Kevin J. Lindenmuth. **VIDEO**

Addicted to Murder 3: Bloodlust 🦴½ **1999** Serial killer Joel Winter (McCleery) continues his quest to eliminate vampires in revenge for his own transformation. One master vamp thinks he has a secure haven but he's very wrong. **85m/C VHS.** Michael (Mick) McCleery, Sarah K. Lippmann, Nick Kostopoulos, Cloud Michaels, Grant Kramer, Frank Lopez, Joe Zaso, Jon Sanborne, Reid Ostrowski; ***D:*** Kevin J. Lindenmuth, Tom Vollmann; ***W:*** Kevin J. Lindenmuth, Tom Vollmann. **VIDEO**

The Addiction 🦴🦴½ **1995 (R)** Ph.D. candidate Kathleen Conklin (Taylor, in a haunting performance) gets bitten by more than the philosophy bug while attending university in Manhattan. When attacked by a female vampire (Sciorra), Kathleen quickly becomes driven by a ferocious blood need, beginning with an attack that parallels drug addiction when she stabs a derelict with a hypodermic needle and injects his blood into her own veins. Bitingly pretentious, themes experiment with the philosophy of Kirkegaard, Nietzsche, and Sartre, and exploitative glimpses of the Holocaust and the My Lai massacre attempt to connect Kathleen's struggle to resist evil to historical atrocities. **82m/B VHS.** Lili Taylor, Christopher Walken, Annabella Sciorra, Edie Falco, Paul Calderon, Fredro Starr, Kathryn Erbe, Michael Imperioli; ***D:*** Abel Ferrara; ***W:*** Nicholas St. John; ***C:*** Ken Kelsch; ***M:*** Joe Delia.

Address Unknown 🦴🦴½ **1996 (PG)** A ten-year-old letter and a priceless stamp provide a teenager with clues to dad's mysterious death. **92m/C VHS.** Kyle Howard, Johna Stewart, Patrick Renna, Corbin Allred, Michael Flynn; ***D:*** Shawn Levy.

Adios Amigo 🦴🦴 **1975 (PG)** Offbeat western comedy has ad-libbing Pryor hustling as a perennially inept con man. Script and direction (both provided by Williamson) are not up to Pryor's level, although excessive violence and vulgarity are avoided in a boring attempt to provide good clean family fare. **87m/C VHS.** Fred Williamson, Richard Pryor, Thalmus Rasulala, James Brown, Robert Philip, Mike Henry; ***D:*** Fred Williamson; ***W:*** Fred Williamson.

Adios, Hombre 🦴 **1968** An innocent man who was imprisoned for murder escapes from prison and seeks revenge. You'll be saying adios as well. **90m/C VHS.** *IT* Craig Hill, Giulia Rubini; ***D:*** Mario Caiano.

The Adjuster 🦴🦴½ **1991 (R)** Critics either loved or hated this strange film. Insurance adjuster Noah Render's clients look to him for all sorts of comfort, so much so that his own identity becomes a blurred reflection of their tragedies. Wife Hera is a film censor who secretly tapes the pornographic videos she watches at work. Their carefully organized lives are invaded by Bubba and Mimi, a wealthy couple who pass themselves off as filmmakers who want to use the Render house as a movie set. They are instead looking to involve the Renders in their latest and most elaborate erotic fantasy. Lots of symbolism, but little substance. **102m/C VHS, DVD, Wide.** *CA* Elias Koteas, Arsinee Khanjian, Maury Chaykin, Gabrielle Rose, David Hemblen, Jennifer Dale, Don McKellar, Raoul Trujillo; ***D:*** Atom Egoyan; ***W:*** Atom Egoyan; ***C:*** Paul Sarossy; ***M:*** Mychael Danna. Toronto-City '91: Canadian Feature Film.

The Admirable Crichton 🦴🦴½ **1957** Social satire about an aristocratic family and their butler who are marooned on a tropical island. Crichton (More), the butler, has a good deal more practical experience and sense than his employers so he's soon in charge of their survival. Filmed in Bermuda and based on the play by James M. Barrie. **93m/C VHS.** *GB* Kenneth More, Cecil Parker, Sally Ann Howes, Diane Cilento, Martita Hunt, Jack Watling, Peter Graves, Gerald Harper; ***D:*** Lewis Gilbert; ***W:*** Vernon Harris; ***C:*** Wilkie Cooper; ***M:*** Douglas Gamley.

The Admiral Was a Lady 🦴🦴 **1950** Four ex-GIs try to get by in life without going to work. Hendrix walks into their lives as a winning ex-Wave gifted with a knack for repartee who is disgusted by their collective lack of ambition. Nevertheless, she is pursued by the zany quartet with predictable results. **87m/B VHS.** Edmond O'Brien, Wanda Hendrix, Rudy Vallee, Steve Brodie; ***D:*** Albert Rogell.

Adomas Nori Buti Zmogumi 🦴🦴 *Adam Wants to Be a Man* **1959** Soviet Lithuanian feature in its original form, with dialogue in Lithuanian. A young worker scrapes together money for a ticket to Buenos Aires, but the money is stolen by the manager of the travel office. **90m/B VHS.** *RU LI* ***D:*** V. Zhalakyavichus.

Adoption 🦴🦴🦴 *Orkobefogadas* **1975** The third of Meszaros's trilogy, involving a middle-aged Hungarian woman who longs for a child and instead forms a deep friendship with a 19-year-old orphan. In Hungarian with English subtitles. **89m/B VHS.** *HU* Kati Berek, Laszlo Szabo, Gyongyver Vigh, Dr. Arpad Perlaky; ***D:*** Marta Meszaros; ***W:*** Marta Meszaros, Gyula Hernadi; ***C:*** Lajos Koltai; ***M:*** Gyorgy Kovacs. Berlin Intl. Film Fest. '75: Golden Berlin Bear.

The Adorable Cheat 🦴🦴 **1928** A low-budget, late-silent melodrama about a young woman who tries to get involved in the family business, despite her father's refusal of her help. Once in the business, she finds love. **76m/B VHS, 8mm.** Lila Lee, Cornelius Keefe, Burr McIntosh; ***D:*** Burton King.

Adorable Julia 🦴🦴 **1962** When an actress takes on a lover many years younger than herself, the laughs begin to fly in this sex comedy based on W. Somerset Maugham's novel. **97m/C VHS.** *FR* Lilli Palmer, Charles Boyer; ***D:*** Alfred Weidenmann.

Adrenalin: Fear the Rush 🦴 **1996 (R)** Dull future thriller in the deadly virus category. In 2007, a plague in Eastern Europe causes those that survive to turn into cannabalistic killers. The U.S. has started quarantine camps, one of which is in Boston, and two cops (Henstridge and Lambert) must track down an infected killer who's escaped. Not worth your time. **77m/C VHS.** Christopher Lambert, Natasha Henstridge, Norbert Weisser, Craig Davis, Elizabeth Barondes, Xavier DeClie; ***D:*** Albert Pyun; ***W:*** Albert Pyun; ***C:*** George Mooradian; ***M:*** Tony Riparetti.

Adrenaline Drive 🦴🦴 *Adorenarin Doraibu* **1999** Sad sack Suzuki (Ando), who's working for a car rental company, accidentally plows a car into the Jaguar of yakuza big guy Kuroiwa (Matushige). Before punishment can be exacted, there's an explosion that lands them in the hospital. There shy nurse Shizuko (Ishida) latches on both to Suzuki and to a yakuza suitcase full of money and drags both on a road trip to freedom. Silly, good-natured comedy. Japanese with subtitles. **111m/C VHS, DVD, Wide.** *JP* Hikari Ishida, Mansanobu Ando, Yataka Matushige, Kazue Tsunogae; ***D:*** Shinobu Yaguchi; ***W:*** Shinobu Yaguchi; ***C:*** Takashi Hamada; ***M:*** Seiichi Yamamoto.

Adrift 🦴🦴½ **1993** Yet another couple-in-terror-from-psychos-on-the-high-seas flick. Katie and Guy Nast (Jackson and Welsh) are on an anniversary sailing adventure intended to shore up their shaky marriage. They discover a boat adrift with two survivors (Greenwood and Rowan) who have a suspicious story but they help them nonetheless. Big mistake. **92m/C VHS.** Kate Jackson, Kenneth Welsh, Bruce Greenwood, Kelly Rowan; ***D:*** Christian Duguay. **TV**

The Adultress 🦴 **1977 (R)** When a husband and wife cannot satisfy their desire to have a family, they hire a young man to help them in this dumb melodrama. **85m/C VHS.** Tyne Daly, Eric (Hans Gudegast) Braeden, Gregory Morton; ***D:*** Norbert Meisel. **TV**

Adventure 🦴🦴 **1945** Gable's first postwar film has him as a roughneck sailor romancing a shy and reserved librarian (Garson). Dull and disappointing—both stars deserve better. However, there is a touching scene of Gable with newborn child that might be of interest to some. Based on the novel by Clyde Brion Davis. **130m/B VHS.** Clark Gable, Greer Garson, Joan Blondell, Thomas Mitchell, Tom Tully, John Qualen, Richard Haydn, Lina Romay; ***D:*** Victor Fleming; ***W:*** Vincent Lawrence, Frederick Hazlitt Brennan; ***C:*** Joseph Ruttenberg.

Adventure Island 🦴½ **1947** En route to Australia, a small ship stops at a remote island for supplies. The crew is greeted by a crazed, tyrannical leader who makes their lives difficult. Dull low-budget remake of 1937's "Ebb Tide." **66m/C VHS.** Rory Calhoun, Rhonda Fleming, Paul Kelly, John Abbott, Alan Napier; ***D:*** Sam Newfield.

Adventure of the Action Hunters 🦴 **1987 (PG)** A dying sailor leaves a tourist couple a message leading to a treasure, and they vie for it along with gangsters, mercenaries and other unsavory types. **81m/C VHS.** Ronald Hunter, Sean Murphy, Joe Cimino; ***D:*** Lee Bonner.

The Adventurer 🦴🦴½ **1917** An escaped convict saves two wealthy women from death. They mistake him for a gallant sportsman and bring him home. Early Chaplin silent with music track. **20m/B VHS.** Charlie Chaplin, Charles Halton; ***D:*** Charlie Chaplin.

The Adventurers 🦴🦴 *Fortune in Diamonds; The Great Adventure* **1951** At the turn of the century, two Boers and an English officer set out to recover stolen jewels hidden in the jungles of South Africa. On the way, greed and anger take their toll a la "The Treasure of Sierra Madre," only on a less convincing scale. **82m/B VHS.** *GB* Dennis Price, Jack Hawkins, Siobhan McKenna, Peter Hammond, Bernard Lee; ***D:*** David MacDonald.

The Adventurers woof! **1970 (R)** Sleazy Harold Robbins novel retains its trashy aura on film. Unfortunately, this turkey is also long and boring. Set in South America, it tells the tale of a rich playboy who uses and destroys everyone who crosses his path. His vileness results from having seen his mother murdered by outlaws, but his obsession is to avenge his father's murder. Blood, gore, revolutions, and exploitive sex follow him everywhere. Watch and be amazed at the big-name stars who signed on for this one. **171m/C VHS.** Candice Bergen, Olivia de Havilland, Bekim Fehmiu, Charles Aznavour, Alan Badel, Ernest Borgnine, Leigh Taylor-Young, Fernando Rey, Thommy Berggren, John Ireland, Sydney Tafler, Rossano Brazzi, Anna Moffo, Christian Roberts, Yorgo Voyagis, Angela Scoular, Yolande Donlan, Ferdinand "Ferdy" Mayne, Jaclyn Smith, Peter Graves, Roberta Haynes; ***D:*** Lewis Gilbert.

Adventures Beyond Belief 🦴 *Neat and Tidy* **1987** An irreverent motorcyclist is chased across Europe for a murder he didn't commit. Firmly within the boundaries of belief. **95m/C VHS.** Elke Sommer, Jill Whitlow, Graham Stark, Stella Stevens, Larry Storch, Thick Wilson, Skyler Cole, Edie Adams, John Astin; ***D:*** Marcus Thompson.

Adventures in Babysitting 🦴🦴½ **1987 (PG-13)** Pleasant comedy has its moments when a babysitter and her charges leave peaceful suburbia for downtown Chicago to rescue a friend in trouble. After a flat tire strands them on the freeway, trouble takes on a new meaning. Shue is charming as the hapless sitter, unexpectedly dateless, who finds herself doing a lot more than just watching the kids. Ludicrous at times, but still fun to watch. **102m/C VHS, DVD, 8mm.** Elisabeth Shue, Keith Coogan, Maia Brewton, Anthony Rapp, Calvin Levels, Vincent D'Onofrio, Penelope Ann Miller, George Newbern, John Ford Noonan, Lolita (David) Davidovich, Albert Collins; ***D:*** Chris Columbus; ***W:*** David Simkins; ***C:*** Ric Waite; ***M:*** Michael Kamen.

Adventures in Dinosaur City 🦴🦴 **1992 (PG)** Expect to see lots of movies riding on the coattails of the dino mania sweeping the land. Some will be good, others will not. "Adventures" falls into the latter category. Modern-day preteen siblings are transported back in time to the stone age. There they meet their favorite TV characters (they're dinosaurs) and help them solve prehistoric crimes. Family film may amuse kids, but adults should stick to "Jurassic Park." **88m/C VHS.** Omri Katz, Shawn Hoffman, Tiffanie Poston, Pete Koch, Megan Hughes, Tony Doyle, Mimi Maynard; ***D:*** Brett Thompson; ***W:*** Willie Baronet, Lisa Morton; ***M:*** Fredric Teetsel.

Adventures in Spying 🦴🦴 **1992 (PG-13)** Brian McNichols is just trying to enjoy his summer vacation when he discovers that a notorious drug lord is living in his neighborhood. After realizing there is a $50,000 reward for his capture, he enlists the help of his friend (Schoelen) to get the man's picture for the police. Action-packed film is geared towards the junior high set, but relies too heavily on coincidence and other plot connivances to compete with espionage flicks directed at an older market. **92m/C VHS.** Jill Schoelen, Bernie Coulson, Seymour Cassel, G. Gordon Liddy, Michael Emil; ***D:*** Hil Covington; ***W:*** Hil Covington; ***M:*** James Stemple.

The Adventures of a Gnome Named Gnorm 🦴🦴½ *A Gnome Named Gnorm* **1993 (PG)** Silly cop caper finds LAPD detective Casey (Hall) stuck with a very strange new partner—a bark-wearing gnome named Gnorm. The two team up to go after a diamond smuggling ring. The special-effects creature may hold the kiddies interest. **86m/C VHS.** Anthony Michael Hall, Jerry Orbach, Claudia Christian; ***D:*** Stan Winston.

Adventures of a Private Eye 🦴 **1987** A self-mocking British detective farce about an inept private eye who takes his time tracking down a beautiful girl's blackmailer, bedding down with all the women he meets along the way. **96m/C VHS.** *GB* Christopher Neil, Suzy Kendall, Irene Handl; ***D:*** Stanley Long.

Adventures of a Taxi Driver woof! **1976** Cabbie finds sex, crime, sex, adventure and sex on the road in this off-duty comedy. **89m/C VHS.** *GB* Barry Evans, Judy Geeson, Adrienne Posta, Diana Dors, Liz Fraser; ***D:*** Stanley Long.

The Adventures of Baron Munchausen 🦴🦴🦴½ **1989 (PG)** From the director of "Time Bandits," "Brazil," and "The Fisher King" comes an ambitious, imaginative, chaotic, and under-appreciated marvel based on the tall (and often confused) tales of the Baron. Munchausen encounters the King of the Moon, Venus, and other odd and fascinating characters during what might be described as a circular narrative in which flashbacks dovetail into the present and place and time are never quite what they seem. Wonderful special effects and visually stunning sets occasionally dwarf the actors and prove what Gilliam can do with a big budget. **126m/C VHS, DVD, 8mm.** *GB GE* John Neville, Eric Idle, Sarah Polley, Valentina Cortese, Oliver Reed, Uma Thurman, Sting, Jonathan Pryce, Bill Paterson, Peter Jeffrey, Alison Steadman, Charles McKeown, Winston Dennis, Jack Purvis, Don Henderson, Ray Cooper, Andrew MacLachlan; ***Cameos:*** Robin Williams; ***D:*** Terry Gilliam; ***W:*** Terry Gilliam, Charles McKeown; ***C:*** Giuseppe Rotunno; ***M:*** Michael Kamen.

The Adventures of Buckaroo Banzai Across the Eighth Dimension 🦴🦴🦴 *Buckaroo Banzai* **1984 (PG)** A man of many talents, Buckaroo Banzai (Weller) travels through the eighth dimension in a jet-propelled Ford Fiesta to battle Planet 10 aliens led by the evil Lithgow. Buckaroo incorporates his vast knowledge of medicine, science, music, racing, and foreign relations to his advantage. Offbeat and often humorous cult sci-fi trip. **100m/C VHS, DVD, Wide.** Peter Weller, Ellen Barkin, Jeff Goldblum, Christopher Lloyd, John Lithgow, Lewis Smith, Rosalind Cash, Robert

Ito, Pepe Serna, Vincent Schiavelli, Dan Hedaya, Yakov Smirnoff, Jamie Lee Curtis, Ronald Lacey, Matt Clark, Clancy Brown, Carl Lumbly, Red Morgan; ***D:*** W.D. Richter; ***W:*** Earl MacRauch; ***C:*** Fred W. Koenekamp; ***M:*** Michael Boddicker.

The Adventures of Bullwhip Griffin 🦴🦴½ **1966** A rowdy, family-oriented comedy-adventure set during the California Gold Rush. Light Disney farce catches Russell at the tail end of his teenage star days. Pleshette and McDowall embark upon an ocean trip from Boston to San Francisco to find her brother, Russell, who's out west digging for gold. Assorted comedic adventures take place. **110m/C VHS.** Roddy McDowall, Suzanne Pleshette, Karl Malden, Harry Guardino, Bryan Russell; ***D:*** James Neilson; ***C:*** Edward Colman; ***M:*** George Bruns.

Adventures of Captain Fabian 🦴½ **1951** When the captain of the "China Sea" learns that a beautiful woman has been falsely imprisoned, he comes to her rescue. Not one of Flynn's better swashbucklers, with typically low-quality Republic production. **100m/B VHS.** Errol Flynn, Vincent Price, Agnes Moorehead, Micheline Presle; ***D:*** William Marshall.

The Adventures of Captain Marvel 🦴🦴½ **1941** A 12-episode cliff-hanging serial based on the comic book character. Details the adventures of klutzy Billy Batson, who transforms into superhero Captain Marvel by speaking the magic word, "Shazam!" **240m/B VHS.** Tom Tyler, Frank "Junior" Coghlan, Louise Currie; ***D:*** William Witney.

Adventures of Don Juan 🦴🦴🦴½ *The New Adventures of Don Juan* **1949** Flynn's last spectacular epic features elegant costuming and loads of action. Don Juan saves Queen Margaret from her evil first minister. He then swashbuckles his way across Spain and England in an effort to win her heart. Grand, large-scale fun and adventure with Flynn at his self-mocking best. **111m/C VHS.** Errol Flynn, Viveca Lindfors, Robert Douglas, Romney Brent, Alan Hale, Raymond Burr, Aubrey Mather, Ann Rutherford; ***D:*** Vincent Sherman; ***M:*** Max Steiner. Oscars '49: Costume Des. (C).

Adventures of Eliza Fraser 🦴½ **1976** A young shipwrecked couple move from bawdy pleasures to cannibalism after being captured by aborigines. **114m/C VHS.** Susannah York, Trevor Howard, Leon Lissek, Abigail, Noel Ferrier, Carole Skinner; ***D:*** Tim Burstall.

The Adventures of Felix 🦴🦴 *Drole de Felix* **1999** Felix (Bouajila) is a gay, HIV-positive Frenchman of Arab descent who decides to go on a road trip to Marseilles after finding some old letters from the father he never knew. Felix has a number of adventures while hitchhiking and makes an impromptu family of those he meets along the way, which leads him to wonder if he really needs to meet his biological dad after all. French with subtitles. **95m/C VHS, DVD.** *FR* Sami Bouajila, Patachou, Ariane Ascaride, Pierre-Loup Rajot, Charly Sergue, Clement Reverend, Maurice Benichou; ***D:*** Olivier Ducastel, Jacques Martineau; ***W:*** Olivier Ducastel, Jacques Martineau; ***C:*** Mathieu Poirot-Delpech.

The Adventures of Ford Fairlane woof! *Ford Fairlane* **1990 (R)** The Diceman plays an unusual detective specializing in rock 'n' roll cases. When a heavy metal singer dies on stage, he takes the case in his own inimitable fashion, pursuing buxom gals, sleazy record executives, and even his ex-wife. Not surprisingly, many of his stand-up bits are worked into the movie. Clay, the ever-so-controversial comic in his first (and likely last) starring role haplessly sneers his way through this rock 'n' roll dud of a comedy thriller. A quick effort to cash in on Clay's fading star. Forget about it. **101m/C VHS, Wide.** Andrew (Dice Clay) Silverstein, Wayne Newton, Priscilla Presley, Morris Day, Lauren Holly, Maddie Corman, Gilbert Gottfried, David Patrick Kelly, Brandon Call, Robert Englund, Ed O'Neill, Sheila E, Kari Wuhrer, Tone Loc; ***D:*** Renny Harlin; ***W:*** David Arnott, Daniel Waters, James Cappe. Golden Raspberries '90: Worst Picture, Worst Actor (Silverstein), Worst Screenplay.

The Adventures of Frank and Jesse James **1948** The bad brothers of the Wild West are trying to make good for rip-offs committed in their names, so they're hoping to hit pay-dirt with a silver mine. A 13-episode serial on two cassettes. **180m/B VHS.** Steve Darrell, Clayton Moore, Noel Neill, Stanley Andrews; ***D:*** Yakima Canutt.

The Adventures of Frontier Fremont 🦴🦴 **1975** A rough and tumble story of a man who leaves the city, grows a beard, and makes the wilderness his home (and the animals his friends). Mountain life, that's the life for me. Almost indistinguishable from Haggerty's "Grizzly Adams," with the usual redeeming panoramic shots of majestic mountains. **95m/C VHS.** Dan Haggerty, Denver Pyle; ***D:*** Richard Friedenberg.

The Adventures of Gallant Bess 🦴🦴 **1948** The time-honored story of a rodeo man torn between his girl and his talented horse (the Bess of the title). **73m/C VHS.** Cameron Mitchell, Audrey Long, Fuzzy Knight, James Millican; ***D:*** Lew (Louis Friedlander) Landers.

The Adventures of Huck Finn 🦴🦴🦴 **1993 (PG)** Decent Disney attempt at adapting an American favorite by Mark Twain. Mischievious Huck and runaway slave Jim travel down the muddy Mississippi, working on life and friendship and getting into all sorts of adventures in the pre-Civil War era. Fast-paced and amusing with good performances by Wood (in the title role) and Broadway trained Vance (as Jim). Racial epithets and minstrel show dialect have been eliminated in this version. Some material, including Jim's close call with a lynch mob and Huck's drunken, brutal father may be too strong for immature children. **108m/C VHS, Wide.** Elijah Wood, Courtney B. Vance, Robbie Coltrane, Jason Robards Jr., Ron Perlman, Dana Ivey, Anne Heche, James Gammon, Paxton Whitehead, Tom Aldredge, Curtis Armstrong, Mary Louise Wilson, Frances Conroy; ***D:*** Stephen Sommers; ***W:*** Stephen Sommers; ***C:*** Janusz Kaminski; ***M:*** Bill Conti.

The Adventures of Huckleberry Finn 🦴🦴🦴 **1939** Mark Twain's classic story about a boy who runs away and travels down the Mississippi on a raft, accompanied by a runaway slave, is done over in MGM-style. Rooney is understated as Huck (quite a feat), while the production occasionally floats aimlessly down the Mississippi. An entertaining follow-up to "The Adventures of Tom Sawyer." **89m/B VHS.** Mickey Rooney, Lynne Carver, Rex Ingram, William Frawley, Walter Connolly; ***D:*** Richard Thorpe.

The Adventures of Huckleberry Finn 🦴🦴½ **1960** A lively adaptation of the Twain saga in which Huck and runaway slave Jim raft down the Mississipi in search of freedom and adventure. Miscasting of Hodges as Huck hampers the proceedings, but Randall shines as the treacherous King. Strong supporting cast includes Keaton as a lion-tamer and boxing champ Moore as Jim. **107m/C VHS.** Tony Randall, Eddie Hodges, Archie Moore, Patty McCormack, Neville Brand, Mickey Shaughnessy, Judy Canova, Andy Devine, Sherry Jackson, Buster Keaton, Finlay Currie, Josephine Hutchinson, Parley Baer, John Carradine, Royal Dano, Sterling Holloway, Harry Dean Stanton; ***D:*** Michael Curtiz.

The Adventures of Huckleberry Finn 🦴🦴 **1978** The classic adventure by Mark Twain of an orphan boy and a runaway slave done again as a TV movie and starring "F-Troop" regulars Tucker and Storch. Lacks the production values of earlier versions. **100m/C VHS.** Forrest Tucker, Larry Storch, Kurt Ida, Mike Mazurki, Brock Peters; ***D:*** Jack B. Hively. **TV**

The Adventures of Huckleberry Finn 🦴🦴½ **1985** An adaptation of the Mark Twain story about the adventures encountered by Huckleberry Finn and a runaway slave as they travel down the Mississippi River. Top-notch cast makes this an entertaining version. Originally made in a much longer version for PBS's "American Playhouse." **121m/C VHS.** Sada Thompson, Lillian Gish, Richard Kiley, Jim Dale, Barnard Hughes, Patrick Day, Frederic Forrest, Geraldine Page, Butterfly McQueen, Samm-Art Williams; ***D:*** Peter H. Hunt. **TV**

The Adventures of Ichabod and Mr. Toad 🦴🦴🦴½ **1949** Disney's wonderfully animated versions of Kenneth Grahame's "The Wind in the Willows" and "The Legend of Sleepy Hollow" by Washington Irving. Rathbone narrates the story of Mr. Toad, who suffers from arrogance and eventually must defend himself in court after being charged with driving a stolen vehicle (Disney did take liberties with the story). Crosby provides all the voices for "Ichabod," which features one of the all-time great animated sequences—Ichabod riding in a frenzy through the forest while being pursued by the headless horseman. A treat for all ages. **68m/C VHS, DVD.** ***D:*** James Nelson Algar, Clyde Geronimi; ***W:*** Winston Hibler, Erdman Penner, Joe Rinaldi, Ted Sears, Homer Brightman, Harry Reeves; ***M:*** Oliver Wallace; ***V:*** Eric Blore, Pat O'Malley, Jack Kinney, Bing Crosby; ***Nar:*** Basil Rathbone.

The Adventures of Marco Polo 🦴🦴½ **1938** Lavish Hollywood production based on the exploits of 13th-century Venetian explorer Marco Polo (Cooper). He becomes the first white man to record his visit to the Eastern court of Kublai Khan, where he falls for a beautiful princess also desired by the evil Rathbone. Lots of action, though its hard to picture the laconic Cooper in the title role. **100m/B VHS.** Gary Cooper, Sigrid Gurie, Basil Rathbone, Ernest Truex, George Barbier, Binnie Barnes, Alan Hale, H.B. Warner; ***D:*** Archie Mayo; ***W:*** Robert Sherwood; ***M:*** Hugo Friedhofer.

The Adventures of Mark Twain 🦴🦴🦴 **1944** March stars as Mark Twain, the nom de plume of Samuel Clemens, the beloved humorist and writer. His travels and adventures along the Mississippi and on to the California gold rush would later result in the books and stories which would make him so well-known. March attains a quiet nobility as he goes from young man to old sage, along with Smith, who plays Olivia, Twain's beloved wife. **130m/B VHS.** Fredric March, Alexis Smith, Donald Crisp, Alan Hale, Sir C. Aubrey Smith, John Carradine, William Henry, Robert Barrat, Walter Hampden, Percy Kilbride; ***D:*** Irving Rapper; ***W:*** Alan LeMay, Harry Chandlee; ***M:*** Max Steiner.

The Adventures of Mark Twain 🦴🦴🦴 *Mark Twain* **1985 (G)** A clay-animated fantasy based on, and radically departing from, the life and work of Mark Twain. Story begins with Twain flying into outer space in a blimp with stowaways Huck Finn, Tom Sawyer and Becky Thatcher and takes off from there. Above average entertainment for kids and their folks. **86m/C VHS.** ***D:*** Will Vinton; ***W:*** Susan Shadburne; ***V:*** James Whitmore, Chris Ritchie, Gary Krug, Michele Mariana.

The Adventures of Milo & Otis 🦴🦴🦴 *Koneko Monogatari; The Adventures of Chatran* **1989 (G)** Delightful Japanese children's film about a farm-dwelling dog and cat and their odyssey after the cat is accidentally swept away on a river. Notable since no humans appear in the film. A record-breaking success in its homeland. Well received by U.S. children. Narrated by Dudley Moore. **76m/C VHS, DVD.** *JP* ***D:*** Masanori Hata; ***W:*** Mark Saltzman; ***C:*** Hideo Fujii, Shinji Tomita; ***M:*** Michael Boddicker; ***Nar:*** Dudley Moore.

The Adventures of Nellie Bly 🦴 **1981** "Classics Illustrated" story of Nellie Bly, a strong-willed female reporter doing her best to expose wrongdoings in the late 19th century. A decent performance by Purl is overshadowed by the general lack of direction. **100m/C VHS.** Linda Purl, Gene Barry, John Randolph, Raymond Buktenica, J.D. Cannon, Elayne Heilveil, Cliff Osmond; ***D:*** Henning Schellerup. **TV**

The Adventures of Picasso 🦴🦴 **1980** A Swedish satire on the life of Picasso, dubbed in English. Don't look for art or facts here, or, for that matter, many laughs. **88m/C VHS.** *SW* Gosta Ekman Jr., Lena Nyman, Hans Alfredson, Margareta Krook, Bernard Cribbins, Wilfrid Brambell; ***D:*** Tage Danielsson.

The Adventures of Pinocchio 🦴🦴½ *Pinocchio; Carlo Collodi's Pinocchio* **1996 (G)** Live-action version of Carlo Collodi's story about woodcarver Gepetto (Landau) who carves himself a puppet son (Thomas) who longs to be a real boy. Story differs from the Disney cartoon version in that it's a little darker and the cat, the fox, and the cricket have larger roles. Jim Henson's Creature Shop provided the animatronic magic to bring Pinocchio to life. His head alone was jammed with wiring and 18 tiny motors to give the "boy" a full range of facial expressions. It took as many as five puppeteers at a time to animate the character. So lifelike was the puppet that some of the crew actually spoke to it as they did the human actors. **88m/C VHS, DVD.** Martin Landau, Jonathan Taylor Thomas, Rob Schneider, Bebe Neuwirth, Udo Kier; ***D:*** Steven Barron; ***W:*** Steven Barron, Tom Benedek, Sherry Mills; ***C:*** Juan Ruiz-Anchia; ***M:*** Rachel Portman.

The Adventures of Pluto Nash **2002 (PG-13)** Pluto Nash (Murphy) has a nightclub on the moon in the year 2087—a club he refuses to sell to the local mob. Not yet reviewed. **?m/C VHS, DVD.** Eddie Murphy, Rosario Dawson, Randy Quaid, Joe Pantoliano, Jay Mohr, John Cleese, Pam Grier, Peter Boyle; ***D:*** Ron Underwood; ***W:*** Neil Cuthbert.

The Adventures of Priscilla, Queen of the Desert 🦴🦴🦴 **1994 (R)** Quirky down-under musical-comedy follows two drag queens and a transsexual across the Australian Outback on their way to a gig in a small resort town. They make the drive in a pink bus nicknamed Priscilla. Along the way they encounter, and perform for, the usual unusual assortment of local characters. Scenes depicting homophobic natives play out as expected. Finest moments occur on the bus or onstage (all hail ABBA). Strong performances, especially by usually macho Stamp as the widowed Bernadette, rise above the cliches in what is basically a bitchy, cross-dressing road movie, celebrating drag as art and the nonconformity of its heroes. Costumes (by Lizzy Gardner and Tim Chappel) are a lark, the photography's surreal, and the soundtrack fittingly campy. **102m/C VHS, DVD, Wide.** *AU* Terence Stamp, Hugo Weaving, Guy Pearce, Bill Hunter, Sarah Chadwick, Mark Holmes, Julia Cortez, Rebel Russell, June Marie Bennett, Alan Dargin, Al Clark, Margaret Pomeranz; ***D:*** Stephan Elliott; ***W:*** Stephan Elliott; ***C:*** Brian J. Breheny; ***M:*** Guy Gross. Oscars '94: Costume Des.; Australian Film Inst. '94: Costume Des.

Adventures of Red Ryder 🦴🦴 **1940** The thrills of the rugged West are presented in this 12-episode serial. Based on the then-famous comic strip character. **240m/B VHS.** Donald (Don "Red") Barry, Noah Beery Sr.; ***D:*** William Witney.

The Adventures of Robin Hood 🦴🦴🦴🦴 **1938** Rollicking Technicolor tale of the legendary outlaw, regarded as the swashbuckler standard-bearer. The justice-minded Saxon knight battles the Normans, outwits evil Prince John, and gallantly romances Maid Marian. Grand castle sets and lush forest photography display ample evidence of the huge (in 1938) budget of $2 million plus. Just entering his prime, Flynn enthusiastically performed most of his own stunts, including intricate sword play and advanced tree and wall climbing. His Robin brims with charm and bravura, the enthusiastic protector of poor Saxons everywhere and the undeclared king of Sherwood forest. The rest of the cast likewise attacks with zest: de Havilland, a cold but eventually sympathetic Maid Marian; Rains' dastardly Prince John (the predecessor to Alan Rickman's over-the-top spin as the Sheriff in Costner's remake); and Rathbone's conniving Sir Guy to Robin's band of very merry men. Based on various Robin Hood legends as well as Sir Walter Scott's "Ivanhoe" and the opera "Robin Hood" by De Koven-Smith. Also available in letterbox format. **102m/C VHS, Wide.** Errol Flynn, Olivia de Havilland, Basil Rathbone, Alan Hale, Una O'Connor, Claude Rains, Patric Knowles, Eugene Pallette, Herbert Mundin, Melville Cooper, Ian Hunter, Montagu Love; *D:* Michael Curtiz; *W:* Seton I. Miller, Norman Reilly Raine; *M:* Erich Wolfgang Korngold. Oscars '38: Film Editing, Orig. Score, Natl. Film Reg. '95.

The Adventures of Rocky & Bullwinkle 🦴🦴½ **2000 (PG)** Flying squirrel and his moose pal, who have been living on residuals since their TV show was cancelled, discover that their old enemies, spies Boris Badenov (Alexander), Natasha Fatale (Russo) and their Fearless Leader (De Niro), have escaped from their two-dimensional existence. Now the trio are headed for Hollywood and a plot to—what else—take over the world. Someone seriously miscalculated in aiming this one at the Pokemon set (the show is 35 years old, and the majority of the jokes were always aimed at adults anyway), but it still provides a few good laughs, and is much more effective back home on the small screen. **88m/C VHS, DVD, Wide.** Robert De Niro, Jason Alexander, Rene Russo, Janeane Garofalo, Randy Quaid, Piper Perabo, Carl Reiner, Jonathan Winters, John Goodman, Kenan Thompson, Kel Mitchell, James Rebhorn, David Alan Grier, Norman Lloyd, Jon Polito, Whoopi Goldberg, Billy Crystal, Don Novello, Harrison Young, Dian Bachar, Paget Brewster; *D:* Des McAnuff; *W:* Kenneth Lonergan; *C:* Thomas Ackerman; *M:* Mark Mothersbaugh; *V:* June Foray, Keith Scott.

The Adventures of Rusty 🦴🦴½ **1945** Forties family film series begins with this classic boy-meets-dog story. Danny's dog dies in an accident and his widowed father has just remarried so the kid's feeling pretty bad. Then he meets neglected German Shepherd Rusty, a former police dog with an undeservedly bad rep. Naturally, boy and dog bond and even capture a couple of escaped convicts (and Danny learns to love his stepmom too). **67m/B VHS.** Ted Donaldson, Margaret Lindsay, Conrad Nagel, Gloria Holden; *D:* Paul Burnford; *W:* Aubrey Wisberg.

The Adventures of Sadie 🦴🦴½ *Our Girl Friday* **1955** Collins is stranded on a desert island with three men, two of whom continuously chase her around. Naturally, she falls for the guy who ignores her. Obvious sex comedy which plays on Collins' scantily clad physical assets. Based on the novel "The Cautious Amorist" by Norman Lindsay. **87m/C VHS.** *GB* Joan Collins, George Cole, Kenneth More, Robertson Hare, Hermione Gingold, Walter Fitzgerald; *D:* Noel Langley; *W:* Noel Langley.

The Adventures of Sebastian Cole 🦴🦴½ **1999 (R)** Sebastian (Grenier) is a misfit highschooler in upstate New York in 1983. Not only does he have to deal with the usual trials of adolescence but there's his unusual family problems. His mother, Joan (Colin), returns to her native England upon learning that Sebastian's stepdad, Hank (Gregg), has decided to become a woman. Sebastian eventually winds up living with Hank, who is now known as Henrietta, and who's still the most stable adult in the teen's fractured world. **99m/C VHS, DVD.** Adrian Grenier, Clark Gregg, Aleksa Palladino, Margaret Colin, John Shea, Joan Copeland, Marni Lustig, Tom Lacy; *D:* Tod Williams; *W:* Tod Williams; *C:* John Foster; *M:* Lynne Geller.

The Adventures of Sherlock Holmes 🦴🦴½ *Sherlock Holmes* **1939** The immortal Sherlock Holmes and his assistant Dr. Watson conflict with Scotland Yard as they both race to stop arch-criminal Professor Moriarty. The Yard is put to shame as Holmes, a mere amateur sleuth, uses his brilliant deductive reasoning to save the damsel in distress and to stop Moriarty from stealing the Crown Jewels. Second in the series. **83m/B VHS.** Basil Rathbone, Nigel Bruce, Ida Lupino, George Zucco, E.E. Clive, Mary Gordon; *D:* Alfred Werker; *W:* Edwin Blum; *C:* Leon Shamroy.

The Adventures of Sherlock Holmes' Smarter Brother 🦴🦴🦴 **1978 (PG)** The unknown brother of the famous Sherlock Holmes takes on some of his brother's more disposable excess cases and makes some hilarious moves. Moments of engaging farce borrowed from the Mel Brooks school of parody (and parts of the Brooks ensemble as well). **91m/C VHS.** Gene Wilder, Madeline Kahn, Marty Feldman, Dom DeLuise, Leo McKern, Roy Kinnear, John Le Mesurier, Douglas Wilmer, Thorley Walters; *D:* Gene Wilder; *W:* Gene Wilder.

Adventures of Smilin' Jack **1943** WWII flying ace Smilin' Jack Martin comes to life in this action-packed serial. Character from the Zack Mosley comic strip about air force fighting over China. **90m/B VHS.** Tom Brown, Sidney Toler; *D:* Ray Taylor.

The Adventures of Tartu 🦴🦴½ *Tartu* **1943** A British secret agent, sent to blow up a Nazi poison gas factory in Czechoslovakia, poses as a Romanian. One of Donat's lesser films, in the style of "The 39 Steps." **103m/C VHS.** *GB* Robert Donat, Valerie Hobson, Glynis Johns; *D:* Harold Bucquet.

The Adventures of Tarzan 🦴🦴 **1921** The screen's first Tarzan in an exciting jungle thriller. Silent. **153m/B VHS.** Elmo Lincoln, Louise Lorraine, Lilian Worth, Frank Whitson, Frank Merrill; *D:* Robert F. "Bob" Hill; *W:* Robert F. "Bob" Hill.

The Adventures of the Wilderness Family 🦴🦴 **1976 (G)** The story of a modern-day pioneer family who becomes bored with the troubles of city life and heads for life in the wilderness. There, they find trouble in paradise. Family-oriented adventure offering pleasant scenery. Followed by "The Wilderness Family, Part 2." **100m/C VHS.** Robert F. Logan, Susan Damante Shaw; *D:* Stewart Raffill; *W:* Stewart Raffill.

The Adventures of Tom Sawyer 🦴🦴🦴 **1938** The vintage Hollywood adaptation of the Mark Twain classic, with art direction by William Cameron Menzies. Not a major effort from the Selznick studio, but quite detailed and the best Tom so far. **91m/C VHS.** Tommy Kelly, Walter Brennan, Victor Jory, May Robson, Victor Kilian, Jackie Moran, Donald Meek, Ann Gillis, Marcia Mae Jones, David Holt, Margaret Hamilton; *D:* Norman Taurog; *C:* James Wong Howe; *M:* Max Steiner.

The Adventures of Tom Sawyer 🦴🦴½ **1973** Tom Sawyer is a mischievous Missouri boy who gets into all kinds of trouble in this white-washed, made for TV adaptation of the Mark Twain classic. **76m/C VHS.** Jane Wyatt, Buddy Ebsen, Vic Morrow, John McGiver, Josh Albee, Jeff Tyler; *D:* James Neilson. **TV**

The Adventures of Werner Holt 🦴🦴 *Die Abenteuer des Werner Holt* **1965** Two teenagers, Werner Holt and Gilbert Wolzow, are taken out of school and conscripted into Hitler's army. Gilbert is a fanatical soldier, while the horrors of the front call Werner's loyalties into question. But when Gilbert is executed by the SS, Werner turns his gun on his own side. Based on the novel by Dieter Noll. German with subtitles. **163m/B VHS.** *GE* Klaus-Peter Thiele, Manfred Karge, Arno Wyzniewski, Gunter Junghans, Peter Reusse, Wolfgang Langhoff; *D:* Joachim Kunert.

The Adventurous Knights woof! **1935** An athlete learns he is the heir to a Transylvanian throne. **60m/B VHS.** David Sharpe, Mary Kornman, Mickey Daniels, Gertrude Messinger; *D:* Edward Roberts.

The Adversary 🦴🦴½ *Pratidwandi* **1971** A young man must quit college because of his father's death. He struggles to find employment in Calcutta but his hardships are magnified by the impersonal society. In Bengali with English subtitles. **110m/C VHS.** *IN* *D:* Satyajit Ray; *W:* Satyajit Ray.

Advertising Rules! 🦴🦴 *Viktor Vogel: Commercial Artist* **2001 (R)** Graphic artist Viktor Vogel actually lands a job after sneaking into an ad agency board meeting. And his luck continues when he meets sexy artist Rosa and helps her with an idea for her debut art exhibition. Then Viktor inadvertantly pitches the same idea for the ad campaign and has to find a way to satisfy both work and Rosa. German with subtitles. **109m/C VHS, DVD, Wide.** *GE* Gudrun Landgrebe, Alexander Scheer, Goetz George, Chulpan Khamatova, Maria Schrader, Vadim Glowna; *D:* Lars Kraume; *W:* Lars Kraume, Tom Schlessinger; *C:* Andreas Daub; *M:* Robert Jan Meyer.

Advise and Consent 🦴🦴🦴 **1962** An interesting political melodrama with a fascinating cast, based upon Allen Drury's novel. The President chooses a candidate for the Secretary of State position which divides the Senate and causes the suicide of a senator. Controversial in its time, though somewhat turgid today. Laughton's last film. **139m/B VHS.** Don Murray, Charles Laughton, Henry Fonda, Walter Pidgeon, Lew Ayres, Burgess Meredith, Gene Tierney, Franchot Tone, Paul Ford, George Grizzard, Betty White, Peter Lawford, Edward Andrews; *D:* Otto Preminger; *W:* Wendell Mayes; *C:* Sam Leavitt. Natl. Bd. of Review '62: Support. Actor (Meredith).

The Advocate 🦴🦴🦴 *The Hour of the Pig* **1993 (R)** Bizarre black comedy about 15th-century Paris lawyer Richard Courtois (Firth) who decides to ply his trade in the country, only to find things stranger than he can imagine. His first case turns out to be defending a pig that's accused of murdering a child. And the pig is owned by beautiful gypsy Samira (Annabi), so the idealistic lawyer can fall in love (or lust). There's religion and superstition, there's power struggles, there's ignorance versus knowledge—things sound very modern indeed. **102m/C VHS.** *GB* Colin Firth, Amina Annabi, Nicol Williamson, Ian Holm, Lysette Anthony, Donald Pleasence, Michael Gough, Harriet Walter, Jim Carter, Dave Atkins; *D:* Leslie Megahey; *W:* Leslie Megahey.

Aelita: Queen of Mars 🦴🦴 *Aelita: The Revolt of the Robots* **1924** Though the title has blockbuster potential, "Aelita" is a little-known silent Soviet sci-fi flick destined to remain little known. After building a rocket to fly to Mars, a Russian engineer finds it's no Martian holiday on the fourth planet from the sun, with the Martians in the midst of a revolution. Silent, with a piano score. **113m/B VHS, DVD.** *RU* Yulia Solntseva, Nikolai Batalov, Igor Illinski, Nikolai Tsereteli, Vera Orlova, Pavel Poi, Konstantin Eggert, Yuri Zavadski, Valentina Kuindzi, N. Tretyakova; *D:* Yakov Protazanov; *W:* Fedor Ozep, Aleksey Fajko; *C:* Yuri Zhelyabuzhsky, Emil Schoenemann.

The Affair 🦴🦴🦴 **1973** Songwriter/polio victim Wood falls in love for the first time with attorney Wagner. Delicate situation handled well by a fine cast. **74m/C VHS, DVD.** Natalie Wood, Robert Wagner, Bruce Davison, Kent Smith, Frances Reid, Pat Harrington; *D:* Gilbert Cates. **TV**

The Affair 🦴🦴½ **1995 (R)** It's 1944 in a small English town, where a troop of black American soldiers are billeted prior to the D-Day invasion. Travis (Vance) falls for the married Maggie (Fox)—whose husband, Edward (Hinds), is supposed to be away at sea—and they begin an affair. Unfortunately, Edward arrives home unexpectedly and accuses Travis of raping his wife. If Maggie denies the accusation, she'll lose her home and family but if she confirms it, Travis, according to Army law, will be condemned to death. **105m/C VHS.** *GB* Courtney B. Vance, Kerry Fox, Ciaran Hinds, Beatie Edney, Leland Gantt, Bill Nunn, Ned Beatty; *D:* Paul Seed; *W:* Pablo F. Fenjves, Bryan Goluboff; *C:* Ivan Strasburg; *M:* Christopher Gunning. **CABLE**

An Affair in Mind 🦴🦴 **1989** A professional writer falls in love with a beautiful woman who tries to convince him to assist her in murdering her husband. **88m/C VHS.** *GB* Amanda Donohoe, Stephen (Dillon) Dillane, Matthew Marsh, Jean-Laurent Cochot; *D:* Michael Baker. **TV**

Affair in Trinidad 🦴🦴 **1952** Fun in the tropics as nightclub singer Hayworth enlists the help of brother-in-law Ford to find her husband's murderer. The trail leads to international thieves and espionage in a romantic thriller that reunites the stars of "Gilda." Hayworth sings (with Jo Ann Greer's voice) "I've Been Kissed Before." **98m/B VHS.** Rita Hayworth, Glenn Ford, Alexander Scourby, Torin Thatcher, Valerie Bettis, Steven Geray; *D:* Vincent Sherman.

An Affair of Love 🦴🦴½ *Une Liaison Pornographique; A Pornographic Liaison; Une Liaison d'Amour* **1999 (R)** French love story sounds like "Last Tango in Paris" but really owes more to "sex, lies and videotape." Elle (Baye) places an ad in a sex magazine and arranges to meet a respondent, Lui (Lopez), for afternoon sexual encounters in a hotel. Virtually all of the physical action takes place behind a closed door. The point is emotional and so, in after-the-fact monologues, they both discuss (separately) what's happened. French with subtitles. **80m/C VHS, DVD, Wide.** *FR BE LU* Nathalie Baye, Sergei Lopez, Paul Pavel; *D:* Frederic Fonteyne; *W:* Philippe Blasband; *C:* Virginie Saint-Martin; *M:* Andre Dziezuk, Marc Mergen, Jeannot Sanavia.

The Affair of the Necklace 🦴½ **2001 (R)** Louis XVI-era history is given a tabloid treatment in this costume drama concerning the vengeful efforts of orphaned Jeanne de la Motte-Valois to restore nobility to her family name. She conspires with a court rogue to hatch a sophisticated scam involving the cardinal of France, Marie Antoinette, German Illuminati, and the fabulous necklace of the title, paving the way for the French Revolution. Excessive narration and flashbacks bog the plot; film offers little other than eye candy in the form of intricate set pieces and fancy dress. Intriguing story potential is mishandled, and Swank is terribly miscast but looks nice in a corset. The remaining actors are underused, except Walken in a scene-chewing role as a Svengali-like mesmerist. **120m/C VHS, DVD.** *US* Hilary Swank, Jonathan Pryce, Simon Baker, Adrien Brody, Brian Cox, Joely Richardson, Christopher Walken, Paul Brooke, Peter Eyre, Simon Kunz, Hayden Panettiere; *D:* Charles Shyer; *W:* John Sweet; *C:* Ashley Rowe; *M:* David Newman.

An Affair to Remember 🦴🦴½ **1957** McCarey remakes his own "Love Affair," with less success. Nightclub singer Kerr and wealthy bachelor Grant discover love on an ocean liner and agree to meet six months later on top of the Empire State Building to see if their feelings are the same. Not as good as the original, but a winner of a fairy tale just the same. Notable for causing many viewers to sob uncontrollably. "Affair" was gathering dust on store shelves until "Sleepless in Seattle" used it as a plot device and rentals skyrocketed. In 1994 real life couple Warren Beatty and Annette Bening attempted a third "Love Affair" remake. **115m/C VHS, DVD, Wide.** Cary Grant, Deborah Kerr, Richard Denning, Cathleen Nesbitt, Neva Patterson, Robert Q. Lewis, Fortunio Bonanova, Matt Moore, Nora Marlowe, Sarah Selby; *D:* Leo McCarey; *W:* Leo McCarey, Delmer Daves, Donald Ogden Stewart; *C:* Milton Krasner; *M:* Hugo Friedhofer.

Affairs of Anatol 🦴🦴 **1921** Philandering playboy Anatol Spencer (Reid) finds no luck with women. He's robbed by one (Ayres), two-timed by another (Hawley), and even madam Satan Synne (Daniels) isn't what she seems. Then Anatol decides to return to his wife, Vivian (Swanson), only to discover that she's being amusing herself with another. Based on a play by Arthur Schnitzler. **117m/B VHS, DVD.** Wallace Reid, Gloria Swanson, Bebe Daniels, Wanda (Petit) Hawley, Agnes Ayres, Monte Blue, Theodore Roberts, Elliott Dexter; *D:* Cecil B. DeMille; *W:* Beulah Marie Dix; *C:* Karl Struss, Alvin Wyckoff.

The Affairs of Annabel 🦴🦴½ **1938** The first of the popular series of Annabel pictures Lucy made in the late 1930s. Appealing adolescent is zoomed to movie stardom by her press agent's stunts. A behind-the-scenes satire on Hollywood, stars, and agents. **68m/B VHS.** Lucille Ball, Jack Oakie, Ruth Donnelly, Fritz Feld, Bradley Page; *D:* Ben Stoloff.

The Affairs of Dobie Gillis 🦴🦴½ **1953** Light musical-comedy about a group of college kids and their carefree antics. Complete with big-band tunes, dance numbers, and plenty of collegiate shenanigans, this '50s classic inspired a hit TV series, "The Many Loves of Dobie Gillis." ♫I'm Through with Love; All I Do Is Dream of You; You Can't Do

Wrong Doing Right; Those Endearing Young Charms. **72m/B VHS.** Debbie Reynolds, Bobby Van, Barbara Ruick, Bob Fosse, Lurene Tuttle, Hans Conried, Charles Lane; ***D:*** Don Weis; ***W:*** Max Shulman; ***C:*** William Mellor.

Affliction 🦴🦴🦴½ **1997 (R)** Nolte, Schrader, and Coburn turn in the finest work of their careers in this bleak tale of one man's battle with the demons of his past and the failures of the present. Nolte is small-town, small-time sheriff Wade Whitehouse, who wants to do the right things, but never does. Damaged beyond repair by his abusive alcoholic father (Coburn), he alienates or scares away anyone who might care for him, including his daughter (Tierney) and his girlfriend (Spacek). When a local businessman dies under mysterious circumstances, Wade sees a chance at redemption, but the investigation turns out to be the catalyst for his final degradation. Schrader has studied the beaten-down male psyche before, but never with this much discipline or implicit knowledge. He adapted the screenplay from Russell Banks' 1989 novel. **113m/C VHS, DVD.** Nick Nolte, James Coburn, Sissy Spacek, Willem Dafoe, Mary Beth Hurt, Jim True, Marian Seldes, Brigid Tierney, Sean McCann, Wayne Robson, Holmes Osborne; ***D:*** Paul Schrader; ***W:*** Paul Schrader; ***C:*** Paul Sarossy; ***M:*** Michael Brook. Oscars '98: Support. Actor (Coburn); N.Y. Film Critics '98: Actor (Nolte); Natl. Soc. Film Critics '98: Actor (Nolte).

Afraid of the Dark 🦴🦴 **1992 (R)** Convoluted psycho-thriller from a child's point of view. Young Lucas is fearful for his blind mother. It seems a vicious slasher has been attacking blind women and Lucas' father, a policeman, has yet to apprehend the criminal. But...Lucas it seems has a problem with reality. With his fantasies and realities mixed, all the people in his life also play entirely different roles. Characters are so detached and unreal that a viewer is prevented from a clear understanding of anything that may, or may not, be going on. Directorial debut of Peploe. **91m/C VHS.** *FR GB* Ben Keyworth, James Fox, Fanny Ardant, Paul McGann, Clare Holman, Robert Stephens; ***D:*** Mark Peploe; ***W:*** Mark Peploe; ***C:*** Bruno de Keyzer.

Africa Screams 🦴🦴½ **1949** Abbott and Costello go on an African safari in possession of a secret map. Unheralded independent A&C film is actually quite good in the stupid vein, with lots of jungle slapstick, generally good production values, and a supporting cast of familiar comedy faces. **79m/B VHS, DVD.** Lou Costello, Bud Abbott, Shemp Howard, Hillary Brooke, Joe Besser, Clyde Beatty, Max Baer Sr.; ***D:*** Charles T. Barton; ***W:*** Earl Baldwin; ***M:*** Walter Schumann.

Africa Texas Style 🦴🦴 **1967** An East African rancher hires an American cowboy and his Navajo sidekick to help run his wild game ranch. Decent family adventure which served as the pilot for the short-lived TV series "Cowboy in Africa." Features lots of wildlife footage and a cameo appearance by Hayley Mills. **109m/C VHS.** Hugh O'Brian, John Mills, Nigel Green, Tom Nardini, Adrienne Corri; ***Cameos:*** Hayley Mills; ***D:*** Andrew Marton; ***M:*** Malcolm Arnold. **TV**

An African Dream 🦴½ **1990 (PG)** A period tale about a black man and a white woman fighting against repression in South Africa. **94m/C VHS.** Kitty Aldridge, John Kani, Dominic Jephcott, John Carson, Richard Haines, Joy Stewart Spence; ***D:*** John Smallcombe.

African Journey **1989** A moving, cross-cultural drama of friendship. A young black American goes to Africa for the summer to be with his divorced father who is working in the diamond mines. There he meets a young black African like himself; they overcome cultural clashes and learn respect for one another. Beautiful scenery, filmed in Africa. Part of the "Wonderworks" series. **174m/C VHS.** Jason Blicker, Pedzisai Sithole.

The African Queen 🦴🦴🦴🦴 **1951** After Bible-thumping spinster Hepburn's missionary brother is killed in WWI Africa, hard-drinking, dissolute steamer captain Bogart offers her safe passage. Not satisfied with sanctuary, she persuades him to destroy a German gunboat blocking the British advance. The two spend most of their time battling aquatic obstacles and each other, rather than the Germans. Time alone on a African river turns mistrust and aversion to love, a transition effectively counterpointed by the continuing suspense of their daring mission. Classic war of the sexes script adapted from C.S. Forester's novel makes wonderful use of natural dialogue and humor. Shot on location in Africa. **105m/C VHS.** *GB* Humphrey Bogart, Katharine Hepburn, Robert Morley, Theodore Bikel, Peter Bull, Walter Gotell, Peter Swanwick, Richard Marner; ***D:*** John Huston; ***W:*** John Huston, James Agee; ***C:*** Jack Cardiff. Oscars '51: Actor (Bogart); AFI '98: Top 100, Natl. Film Reg. '94.

African Rage 🦴🦴 *Tigers Don't Cry; The Long Shot; Target of an Assassin; Fatal Assassin* **1978** Little known release about an aging male nurse (yes, Quinn) who discovers he's dying of an incurable disease. With nothing left to lose, he plans the kidnapping of an African leader, hoping that the ransom will support his family. Meanwhile, another man is plotting the same leader's death. Decent performances help move along the improbable plot. **90m/C VHS.** *SA* Anthony Quinn, John Phillip Law, Simon Sabela, Ken Gampu, Marius Weyers, Sandra Prinsloo; ***D:*** Peter Collinson.

After Dark, My Sweet 🦴🦴🦴 **1990 (R)** A troubled young man in search of a little truth ends up entangled in a kidnapping scheme. Muddled direction is overcome by above average performances and gritty realism. Based on the novel by Jim Thompson. **114m/C VHS, DVD, Wide.** Jason Patric, Rachel Ward, Bruce Dern, George Dickerson, James Cotton, Corey Carrier, Rocky Giordani; ***D:*** James Foley; ***W:*** Robert Redlin, James Foley; ***C:*** Mark Plummer; ***M:*** Maurice Jarre.

After Darkness 🦴 **1985** Slow-moving psycho-suspenser about a man obsessed with trying to remedy his twin brother's schizophrenia. **104m/C VHS.** *SI GB* John Hurt, Julian Sands, Victoria Abril, Pamela Salem; ***D:*** Dominique Othenin-Girard.

After Hours 🦴🦴🦴½ **1985 (R)** An absurd, edgy black comedy that's filled with novel twists and turns and often more disturbing than funny. An isolated uptown New York yuppie (Dunne) takes a late night stroll downtown and meets a sexy woman in an all-night coffee shop. From there he wanders through a series of threatening and surreal misadventures, leading to his pursuit by a vigilante mob stirred by ice cream dealer O'Hara. Something like "Blue Velvet" with more Catholicism and farce. Or similar to "Something Wild" without the high school reunion. Great cameos from the large supporting cast, including Cheech and Chong as burglars. A dark view of a small hell-hole in the Big Apple. **97m/C VHS, Wide.** Griffin Dunne, Rosanna Arquette, John Heard, Teri Garr, Catherine O'Hara, Verna Bloom, Linda Fiorentino, Dick Miller, Bronson Pinchot, Will Patton, Rockets Redglare, Rocco Sisto, Larry Block, Victor Argo; ***Cameos:*** Richard "Cheech" Marin, Thomas Chong, Martin Scorsese; ***D:*** Martin Scorsese; ***W:*** Joe Minion; ***C:*** Michael Ballhaus; ***M:*** Howard Shore. Cannes '86: Director (Scorsese); Ind. Spirit '86: Director (Scorsese), Film.

After Julius 🦴🦴 **1978** Twenty years after Julius Grace's death, his memory still hovers over his wife's and daughters' lives. British soap opera moves with glacier-like speed. Adapted from the book by Elizabeth Jane Howard. **150m/C VHS.** *GB* Faith Brook, John Carson, Cyd Hayman; ***D:*** John Glenister.

After Life 🦴🦴 *Wandafuru Raifu* **1998** A drab office building turns out to be a metaphysical doorway and those who pass through are the recently deceased. Each person is assigned a caseworker and told that they have three days to decide on one particular memory to take with them into the after life. If they cannot chose, they will be forced to remain in the limbo of the processing center until they can do so. Japanese with subtitles. **118m/C VHS, DVD.** *JP* Taketoshi Naito, Susumu Terajima, Arata, Erika Oda, Takashi Naito, Hisako Hara; ***D:*** Hirokazu Kore-eda; ***W:*** Hirokazu Kore-eda; ***C:*** Yutaka Yamazaki, Masayoshi Sukita; ***M:*** Yasuhiro Kasamatsu.

After Midnight 🦴 *I Have Lived* **1933** An aspiring playwright tries to get his work produced, only to meet with dead ends. Eventually, he hooks up with a talented young actress with whom he finds romance and success. **69m/B VHS.** Alan Dinehart, Anita Page, Allen Vincent, Gertrude Astor; ***D:*** Richard Thorpe.

After Midnight 🦴🦴 **1989 (R)** Suspended in a central story about an unorthodox professor who preys upon the deepest fears of his students, a trio of terror tales come to life. From the writers of "The Fly II" and "Nightmare on Elm Street 4." Some chills, few thrills. **90m/C VHS.** Marg Helgenberger, Marc McClure, Alan Rosenberg, Pamela Segall, Nadine Van Der Velde, Ramy Zada, Jillian McWhirter, Billy Ray Sharkey, Judie Aronson, Tracy Wells, Ed Monaghan, Monique Salcido, Penelope Sudrow; ***D:*** Jim Wheat, Ken Wheat; ***W:*** Jim Wheat, Ken Wheat; ***M:*** Marc Donahue.

After Pilkington 🦴🦴 **1988** Thriller about an uptight Oxford professor who runs into his bewitching childhood sweetheart after many years. She persuades him to help search for a missing archaeologist. **100m/C VHS.** *GB* Bob Peck, Miranda Richardson, Barry Foster; ***D:*** Christopher Morahan. **TV**

After Sex 🦴🦴 *Post Coitum, Animal Triste; Post Coitum* **1997** Passion and madness—French style. Confident, middleaged Diane (Rouan) has a successful career and a complacent marriage. Then she meets twentysomething hunk Emilio (Terral) and all bets are off. The twosome have a delirious affair but Diane's passion teeters towards obsession, with reckless disregard for her family. Then the affair ends and Diane falls apart. French with subtitles. **97m/C VHS.** *FR* Brigitte Rouan, Boris Terral, Patrick Chesnais, Nils (Niels) Tavernier, Jean-Louis Richard, Francoise Arnoul; ***D:*** Brigitte Rouan; ***W:*** Santiago Amigorena, Guy Zilberstein, Brigitte Rouan, Jean-Louis Richard; ***C:*** Pierre Dupouey; ***M:*** Michel Musseau, Umberto Tozzi.

After the Fall of New York woof! **1985 (R)** Dim-witted post-apocalyptic tale set in New York after the fall of the "Big Bomb." A man, driven to search for the last normal woman, has reason to believe she is frozen alive and kept in the heart of the city. His mission: locate her, thaw her, engage in extremely limited foreplay with her, and repopulate the planet. A poorly dubbed dating allegory. **95m/C VHS.** *IT FR* Michael Sopkiw, Valentine Monnier, Anna Kanakis, Roman Geer, Edmund Purdom, George Eastman; ***D:*** Sergio Martino.

After the Fox 🦴🦴 *Caccia alla Volpe* **1966** Sellers is a con artist posing as a film director to carry out a bizarre plan to steal gold from Rome. Features occasional backhand slaps at Hollywood, with Mature turning in a memorable performance as the has-been actor starring in Sellers' movie. Though the screenplay was co-written by Neil Simon, the laughs are marginal. **103m/C VHS, DVD, Wide.** *GB IT* Peter Sellers, Victor Mature, Martin Balsam, Britt Ekland; ***D:*** Vittorio De Sica; ***W:*** Neil Simon, Cesare Zavattini; ***C:*** Leonida Barboni; ***M:*** Burt Bacharach.

After the Promise 🦴🦴 **1987** During the Depression, a poor carpenter tries to regain custody of his four sons following the death of his wife. Maudlin melodrama based on a true story. **100m/C VHS.** Mark Harmon, Diana Scarwid, Rosemary Dunsmore, Donnelly Rhodes, Mark Hildreth, Trey Ames, Richard Billingsley; ***D:*** David Greene; ***M:*** Ralph Burns. **TV**

After the Rehearsal 🦴🦴🦴 *Efter Repetitionen* **1984 (R)** Two actresses, one young, the other at the end of her career, challenge their director with love and abuse. Each questions his right to use them on stage and off. A thoughtful discussion of the meaning and reason for art originally made for Swedish TV. Swedish with English subtitles. **72m/C VHS.** *SW* Erland Josephson, Ingrid Thulin, Lena Olin; ***D:*** Ingmar Bergman; ***W:*** Ingmar Bergman; ***C:*** Sven Nykvist. **TV**

After the Revolution 🦴🦴 **1990** A struggling novelist decides to write his next book from the viewpoint of his cat. In Hungarian with English subtitles. **82m/C VHS.** *HU* ***D:*** Andras Szirtes.

After the Shock 🦴🦴 **1990 (PG)** Documentary-like dramatization of the San Francisco-Oakland earthquake of October 1989 and, of course, its aftermath. Incorporates actual footage of the disaster. **92m/C VHS.** Yaphet Kotto, Rue McClanahan, Jack Scalia, Scott Valentine; ***D:*** Gary Sherman; ***W:*** Gary Sherman. **CABLE**

After the Storm 🦴🦴½ **2001 (R)** Beachcomber Arno (Bratt) discovers a sunken yacht but can't salvage the loot, even with the help of girlfriend Coquina (Avital). So he hooks up with Jean-Pierre (Assante) and his wife Janine (Girard), but greed gets the best of everyone. Based on a story by Ernest Hemingway; filmed in Belize. **103m/C VHS, DVD, Wide.** Benjamin Bratt, Armand Assante, Mili Avital, Simone-Elise Girard, Stephen Lang; ***D:*** Guy Ferland; ***W:*** A.E. Hotchner; ***C:*** Gregory Middleton; ***M:*** Bill Wandel. **CABLE**

After the Thin Man 🦴🦴🦴 **1936** Second in a series of six "Thin Man" films, this one finds Nick, Nora and Asta, the lovable terrier, seeking out a murderer from Nora's own blue-blooded relatives. Fast-paced mystery with a witty script and the popular Powell/Loy charm. Sequel to "The Thin Man," followed by "Another Thin Man." **113m/B VHS.** William Powell, Myrna Loy, James Stewart, Elissa Landi, Joseph Calleia, Jessie Ralph, Alan Marshal; ***D:*** Woodbridge S. Van Dyke.

Afterburn 🦴🦴🦴 **1992 (R)** When Ted, her Air Force pilot husband, is killed in a crash of his F-16 fighter, Janet Harduvel learns the official explanation is pilot error. Convinced that something was wrong with his plane, Janet sets out to investigate, and eventually sue, military contractor General Dynamics. Dern turns in a great performance as the tough widow determined to clear her husband's name. Based on a true story. **103m/C VHS.** Laura Dern, Robert Loggia, Vincent Spano, Michael Rooker, Andy Romano; ***D:*** Robert Markowitz; ***W:*** Elizabeth Chandler. **CABLE**

Afterglow 🦴🦴 **1997 (R)** Romantic quadrangle skates by on the performances of its two veterans. Lucky Mann (Nolte) is experiencing marital boredom with his longtime wife Phyllis (the ever-beautiful Christie), a former B-movie actress. Meanwhile twentysomething Marianne Byron (Boyle), who is desperate to have a baby, is sexually frustrated by her workaholic hubby, Jeffrey (Miller). Repairman Lucky happens to come along to work on the Bryon's apartment and Marianne decides to throw herself at him. Then Jeffrey meets the sophisticated Phyllis and soon both couples have uncoupled and re-formed. **113m/C VHS.** Nick Nolte, Julie Christie, Lara Flynn Boyle, Jonny Lee Miller, Jay Underwood, Domini Blythe; ***D:*** Alan Rudolph; ***W:*** Alan Rudolph; ***C:*** Toyomichi Kurita; ***M:*** Mark Isham. Ind. Spirit '98: Actress (Christie); N.Y. Film Critics '97: Actress (Christie); Natl. Soc. Film Critics '97: Actress (Christie).

Aftermath 🦴½ **1985** Three astronauts return to Earth and are shocked to discover that the planet has been ravaged by a nuclear war. Quickly they make new plans. **96m/C VHS.** Steve Barkett, Larry Latham, Lynne Margulies, Sid Haig, Forrest J Ackerman; ***D:*** Ted V. Mikels.

Aftershock 🦴½ **1988 (R)** A beautiful alien and a mysterious stranger battle the Earth's repressive, evil government. **90m/C VHS, DVD.** Jay Roberts Jr., Elizabeth Kaitan, Chris Mitchum, Richard Lynch, John Saxon, Russ Tamblyn, Michael Berryman, Chris De Rose, Chuck Jeffreys; ***D:*** Frank Harris; ***W:*** Michael Standing; ***M:*** Kevin Klinger, Bob Mamet.

Aftershock: Earthquake in New York 🦴½ **1999** Typical TV disaster movie based on the novel by Chuck Scarborough. You're introduced to a bunch of nice people (there's quite a good cast), disaster strikes, death and destruction are everywhere and all it brings out (rather than hysteria, looting, violence and assorted evilness) is good deeds and rescues. Nifty special effects though. **139m/C VHS, DVD.** Tom Skerritt, Sharon Lawrence, Charles S. Dutton, Lisa Nicole Carson, Cicely Tyson, Jennifer Garner, Rachel Ticotin, Frederick Weller, Erika Eleniak, Mitchell Ryan; ***D:*** Mikael Salomon; ***W:*** David Stevens, Paul Eric Meyers, Loren Boothby; ***C:*** Jon Joffin; ***M:*** Irwin Fisch. **TV**

Against a Crooked Sky 🦴🦴 **1975 (G)** A young boy sets out with an elderly trapper to find his sister, who was captured by the Indians. Similiar story to "The Searchers," but no masterpiece. **89m/C VHS.** Richard Boone, Stewart Peterson, Jewel Branch, Geoffrey Land, Henry Wilcoxon; ***D:*** Earl Bellamy.

Against All Flags 🦴🦴🦴 **1952** An enjoyable Flynn swashbuckler about a British soldier slashing his way through the Spanish fleet at the turn of the 18th century. Though the story has been told before, tight direction and good performances win out. O'Hara is a tarty eyeful as a hot-tempered pirate moll. **81m/C VHS.** Errol Flynn, Maureen O'Hara, Anthony Quinn, Mildred Natwick; ***D:*** George Sherman.

Against All Odds 🦴🦴½ **1984 (R)** An interesting love triangle evolves when recently cut quarterback Terry Brogan (Bridges) is asked by his nightclub owning/bookie buddy, Jack (Woods), to travel to Mexico and bring back Jack's sultry girlfriend, Jessie (Ward). Then Terry discovers that Jessie is the daughter of Mrs. Wyler, the football team owner. Contains complicated plot, numerous double crosses, sensual love scenes, and a chase scene along Sunset Boulevard. As the good friend sans conscience, Woods stars. A remake of 1947's "Out of the Past." **122m/C VHS, DVD, 8mm, Wide.** Jeff Bridges, Rachel Ward, James Woods, Alex Karras, Jane Greer, Richard Widmark, Dorian Harewood, Swoosie Kurtz, Bill McKinney, Saul Rubinek; ***D:*** Taylor Hackford; ***W:*** Eric Hughes; ***C:*** Donald E. Thorin; ***M:*** Larry Carlton, Michel Colombier.

Against the Law 🦴½ **1998** Criminal Rex (Grieco) prides himself on his abilities with a gun—leaving a trail of dead cops in his wake. His wants notoriety and, after spotting detective John Shepard (Mancuso) on a news show, decides that TV is the perfect medium to get his 15 minutes of infamy. **85m/C VHS.** Richard Grieco, Nick Mancuso, Nancy Allen, Steven Ford; ***D:*** Jim Wynorski; ***W:*** Steve Mitchell, Bob Sheridan; ***C:*** Andrea V. Rossotto; ***M:*** Kevin Kiner. **VIDEO**

Against the Wall 🦴🦴🦴 **1994** Compelling and tense dramatization of the 1971 Attica, New York prison uprising in which 10 guards were held hostage and state troopers and the National Guard killed 29 prisoners before regaining control. Partially fictionalized version of the story told from the viewpoints of a young prison guard (MacLachlan) and a politicized prisoner (Jackson). Filmed at a prison in Clarksville, Tennessee. **115m/C VHS.** Kyle MacLachlan, Samuel L. Jackson, Clarence Williams III, Frederic Forrest, Harry Dean Stanton, Tom Bower, Philip Bosco, Anne Heche, David Ackroyd; ***D:*** John Frankenheimer; ***W:*** Ron Hutchinson; ***M:*** Gary Chang. **CABLE**

Against the Wind 🦴🦴½ **1948** A motley crew is trained for a mission into Nazi Germany to blow up records and rescue a prisoner. The first half of the film focuses on the group's training, but despite its intensity they win only a pyrrhic victory. A well-done production with solid performances from the cast. **96m/B VHS.** Robert Beatty, Jack Warner, Simone Signoret, Gordon Jackson, Paul Dupuis, Peter Illing; ***D:*** Charles Crichton.

Against the Wind 🦴🦴 *Contra el Viento* **1990** Juan (Banderas) takes refuge in a remote area of Andalusia in an effort to get away from a mutally obsessive love. But his exile is in vain when his lover appears—his sister (Suarez). Spanish with subtitles. **117m/C VHS.** *SP* Antonio Banderas, Emma Suarez; ***D:*** Paco Perinan.

Agatha 🦴🦴½ **1979 (PG)** A speculative period drama about Agatha Christie's still unexplained disappearance in 1926, and a fictional American reporter's efforts to find her. Beautiful but lackluster mystery. Unfortunately, Hoffman and Redgrave generate few sparks. **98m/C VHS.** Dustin Hoffman, Vanessa Redgrave, Timothy Dalton, Helen Morse, Tony Britton, Timothy West, Celia Gregory; ***D:*** Michael Apted.

Agatha Christie's The Pale Horse 🦴🦴½ *The Pale Horse* **1996** When writer Mark Easterbrook is accused of murdering a priest, the only clue to clearing himself is a mysterious list of names. Now he has to figure out the connection between the names if he expects to clear himself. **100m/C VHS.** *GB* Michael Byrne, Ruth Madoc, Leslie Phillips, Jean Marsh; ***D:*** Charles Beeson. **TV**

Age Isn't Everything 🦴 *Life in the Food Chain* **1991 (R)** An appalling clumsy comedy about a recent college graduate who abruptly becomes an old man while retaining his youthful exterior. He looks the same, but walks slowly and talks with a thick Yiddish accent, get it? The cast just marks time until an inexplicable ending. **91m/C VHS.** Jonathan Silverman, Robert Prosky, Rita Moreno, Paul Sorvino, Rita Karin, Robert Cicchini, Brian Williams, Dee Hoty, Dr. Joyce Brothers, Bella Abzug; ***D:*** Douglas Katz; ***W:*** Douglas Katz; ***C:*** Michael Spiller.

The Age of Innocence 🦴🦴🦴 **1993 (PG)** Magnificently lavish adaptation of Edith Wharton's novel of passion thwarted by convention is visually stunning, but don't expect action since these people kill with a word or gesture. In 1870s New York, proper lawyer Newland Archer (Day-Lewis) is engaged to the equally proper May Welland (Ryder). He discovers unexpected romance when May's cousin, the rather scandalous Ellen Olenska (Pfeiffer), returns to the city from Europe but his hesitancy costs them dearly. Woodward's narration of Wharton's observations helps sort out what goes on behind the facades. Although slow, see this one for the beautiful period authenticity, thanks to Scorsese, who obviously labored over the small details. He shows up as a photographer; his parents appear in a scene on a train. **138m/C VHS, DVD, 8mm, Wide.** Martin Scorsese, Daniel Day-Lewis, Michelle Pfeiffer, Winona Ryder, Richard E. Grant, Alec McCowen, Miriam Margolyes, Mary Beth Hurt, Geraldine Chaplin, Stuart Wilson, Michael Gough, Alexis Smith, Jonathan Pryce, Robert Sean Leonard; ***D:*** Martin Scorsese; ***W:*** Martin Scorsese, Jay Cocks; ***C:*** Michael Ballhaus; ***M:*** Elmer Bernstein; ***Nar:*** Joanne Woodward. Oscars '93: Costume Des.; British Acad. '93: Support. Actress (Margolyes); Golden Globes '94: Support. Actress (Ryder); Natl. Bd. of Review '93: Director (Scorsese), Support. Actress (Ryder).

Age Old Friends 🦴🦴🦴½ **1989** Crusty octogenarian Cronyn must choose. His daughter (played by real-life offspring Tandy) wants him to move out of a retirement home and into her house. But he's struggling to keep neighbor and increasingly senile friend Gardenia from slipping into "zombieland." An emotional treat with two fine actors deploying dignity and wit in the battle against old age. Originally adapted for HBO from the Broadway play, "A Month of Sundays" by Bob Larbey. **89m/C VHS.** Vincent Gardenia, Hume Cronyn, Tandy Cronyn, Esther Rolle, Michelle Scarabelli; ***D:*** Allen Kroeker.

The Agency 🦴🦴 *Mind Games* **1981 (R)** An advertising agency attempts to manipulate public behavior and opinion through the use of subliminal advertising. A good premise is bogged down by a dull script and plodding performances by all concerned. Based on a Paul Gottlieb novel. **94m/C VHS.** *CA* Robert Mitchum, Lee Majors, Valerie Perrine, Saul Rubinek, Alexandra Stewart; ***D:*** George Kaczender; ***M:*** Lewis Furey.

Agent of Death 🦴🦴 *The Alternate* **1999 (R)** Philandering President Beck is not Mr. Popularity and there's an election coming up. So his PR head arranges for a fake kidnapping to garner sympathy. But the plans goes wrong and he winds up in the hands of a psycho Secret Service agent (Genesse). And the one man (Roberts) who might be able to rescue the Prez doesn't want the job. **105m/C VHS, DVD.** Ice-T, Eric Roberts, Michael Madsen, Bryan Genesse, John Beck; ***D:*** Sam Firstenberg; ***W:*** Bryan Genesse. **VIDEO**

Agent on Ice 🦴🦴 **1986 (R)** Hockey team is stalked by lawyers. No, wait. An ex-CIA agent is stalked for cover-up purposes by the agency and the mob. One slippery fellow. **96m/C VHS.** Tom Ormeny, Clifford David, Louis Pastore, Matt Craven; ***D:*** Clark Worswick.

Agent Red 🦴½ *Captured* **2000 (R)** Oh so typical story done in a less-than-enthralling manner. Naval Specials Ops Commander Matt Hendricks (Lundgren) is aboard a U.S. sub, escorting a deadly chemical weapon to a safe storage facility. Then the sub is boarded by Russian terrorists who want to unleash the virus on New York City. Naturally, Hendricks must prevent that. **95m/C VHS, DVD, Wide.** Dolph Lundgren, Randolph Mantooth, Meilani Paul, Alexander Kuznitsov, Natalie Radford, Steve Eastin, Tony Becker; ***D:*** Damian Lee; ***W:*** Damian Lee; ***C:*** Ken Blakey; ***M:*** David Wurst, Eric Wurst. **VIDEO**

Aggie Appleby, Maker of Men 🦴½ *Cupid in the Rough* **1933** A wimpy society boy transforms himself into a tough guy, all for the love of a dame. Based on a play by Joseph O. Kesselring. Very slight comedy. **73m/B VHS.** Charles Farrell, Wynne Gibson, William Gargan, ZaSu Pitts, Betty Furness; ***D:*** Mark Sandrich; ***M:*** Max Steiner.

Agnes Browne 🦴🦴½ **1999 (R)** Sentimental, old-fashioned saga concerning recent widow Agnes Browne (Huston), who's trying to cope with her seven children under difficult circumstances in Dublin in 1967. Agnes, who works a market stall, has one personal dream—she wants to see Tom Jones in an upcoming concert. Guess what happens. Director Huston does try to keep the bathos under control. Based on the novel "The Mammy" of Brendan O'Carroll. **91m/C VHS, DVD, Wide.** Anjelica Huston, Ray Winstone, Arno Chevrier, Marion O'Dwyer, Ciaran Owens, Tom Jones; ***D:*** Anjelica Huston; ***W:*** John Goldsmith, Brendan O'Carroll; ***C:*** Anthony B. Richmond; ***M:*** Paddy Moloney.

Agnes of God 🦴🦴 **1985 (PG-13)** Stage to screen translation of John Pielmeier's play loses something in the translation. Coarse chain-smoking psychiatrist Fonda is sent to a convent to investigate whether young nun Tilly is fit to stand trial. Seems that the nun may have given birth to and then strangled her baby, although she denies ever having sexual relations and knows nothing about an infant. Naive Tilly is frightened by probing Fonda, while worldly mother-superior Bancroft is distrusting. Melodramatic stew of Catholicism, religious fervor, and science features generally good performances, although Fonda often seems to be acting (maybe it's the cigarettes). **98m/C VHS, DVD, Wide.** Jane Fonda, Anne Bancroft, Meg Tilly, Anne Pitoniak, Winston Rekert, Gratien Gelinas; ***D:*** Norman Jewison; ***W:*** John Pielmeier; ***C:*** Sven Nykvist; ***M:*** Georges Delerue. Golden Globes '86: Support. Actress (Tilly).

The Agony and the Ecstasy 🦴🦴½ **1965** Big-budget (for 1965 anyway at $12 million) adaptation of the Irving Stone book recounts the conflict between Michelangelo and Pope Julius II after His Holiness directs the artist to paint the Sistine Chapel. Follow the tortured artist through his unpredictable creative process and the hours (it seems literal due to movie length) of painting flat on his back. Heston exudes quiet strength in his sincere interpretation of the genius artist, while Harrison has a fling as the Pope. Slow script is not up to the generally good performances. Disappointing at the boxoffice, but worth a look on the small screen for the sets alone. **136m/C VHS, Wide.** Charlton Heston, Rex Harrison, Harry Andrews, Diane Cilento, Alberto Lupo, Adolfo Celi; ***D:*** Carol Reed; ***W:*** Philip Dunne; ***C:*** Leon Shamroy; ***M:*** Jerry Goldsmith, Alex North. Natl. Bd. of Review '65: Support. Actor (Andrews).

Agony of Love 🦴 **1966** An unhappy homemaker rents a nearby apartment to live out her wildest fantasies and bring some excitment into her otherwise dull life. **?m/C VHS.** Pat (Barringer) Barrington; ***D:*** William Rotsler.

Aguirre, the Wrath of God 🦴🦴🦴½ *Aguirre, der Zorn Gottes* **1972** Herzog at his best, combining brilliant poetic images and an intense narrative dealing with power, irony, and death. Spanish conquistadors in 1590 search for the mythical city of gold in Peru. Instead, they descend into the hell of the jungle. Kinski is fabulous as Aquirre, succumbing to insanity while leading a continually diminishing crew in this compelling, extraordinary drama shot in the jungles of South America. Both English- and German-language versions available. **94m/C VHS, DVD.** *GE* Klaus Kinski, Ruy Guerra, Del Negro, Helena Rojo, Cecilia Rivera, Peter Berling, Danny Ades; ***D:*** Werner Herzog; ***W:*** Werner Herzog; ***C:*** Thomas Mauch; ***M:*** Popul Vuh. Natl. Soc. Film Critics '77: Cinematog.

Ah, Wilderness! 🦴🦴🦴½ **1935** Delightful tale of a teen boy coming of age in small town America. Watch for the hilarious high school graduation scene. Based on the play by Eugene O'Neill. Remade in 1948 as "Summer Holiday," a musical with Mickey Rooney in the lead. **101m/B VHS.** Wallace Beery, Lionel Barrymore, Aline MacMahon, Eric Linden, Cecilia Parker, Spring Byington, Mickey Rooney, Charley Grapewin, Frank Albertson; ***D:*** Clarence Brown; ***C:*** Clyde De Vinna.

Aimee & Jaguar 🦴🦴 **1998** In 1943 Berlin, Jewish Felice (Schrader) is hiding her identity and working for a Nazi newspaper where she can gather information to leak to the resistance. She leads a hedonistic night life with a group of lesbian friends and, one night, encounters Lilly (Koehler), the unfaithful wife of an SS soldier who's away at the Russian front. The odd couple begin a risky affair (the title refers to the nicknames the women gave each other) until the inevitable discovery. Based on a true story from the 1994 book by Erica Fischer. German with subtitles. **125m/C VHS, DVD, Wide.** *GE* Maria Schrader, Juliane Kohler, Johanna Wokalek, Heike Makatsch, Elisabeth Degen, Detlev Buck; ***D:*** Max Farberbock; ***W:*** Rona Munro, Max Farberbock; ***C:*** Tony Imi; ***M:*** Jan A.P. Kaczmarek.

Ain't No Way Back 🦴🦴 **1989** Two hunters stumble upon a feudin' bunch of moonshiners and must leave their city ways behind if they plan to survive. **90m/C VHS.** Campbell Scott, Virginia Lantry, Bernie White, John Durbin, Len Lesser, Joe Mays; ***D:*** Michael Bordon.

Air America 🦴🦴 **1990 (R)** It's the Vietnam War and the CIA is operating a secret drug smuggling operation in Southeast Asia to finance the effort. Flyboys Gibson and Downey drop opium and glib lines all over Laos. Big-budget Gibson vehicle with sufficient action but lacking much of a story, which was adapted from a book by Christopher Robbins. **113m/C VHS, DVD.** Mel Gibson, Robert Downey Jr., Marshall Bell, Nancy Travis, David Marshall Grant, Tim Thomerson, Lane Smith; ***D:*** Roger Spottiswoode; ***W:*** Richard Rush; ***C:*** Roger Deakins; ***M:*** Charles Gross.

Air Bud 🦴🦴½ **1997 (PG)** Buddy's a basketball-playing golden retriever (no relation) who befriends lonely misfit Josh (Zegers) and teaches him the nuances of the layup, fade-away J, and pick-and-roll. It's good to see dog athletes getting to stretch beyond the usual frisbee and stick-fetching roles. Teaming animals (especially canines) with kids usually adds up to success. This one's no exception, especially for the grade school crowd. **92m/C VHS, DVD.** Kevin Zegers, Michael Jeter, Bill Cobbs, Wendy Makkena, Eric Christmas, Brendan Fletcher, Jay Brazeau, Stephen E. Miller, Nicola Cavendish; ***D:*** Charles Martin Smith; ***W:*** Paul Tamasy, Aaron Mendelsohn; ***C:*** Mike Southon; ***M:*** Brahm Wenger.

Air Bud 2: Golden Receiver 🦴🦴 **1998 (G)** Buddy, the canine Michael Jordan of last year's "Air Bud," is back for more organized team sports with small children. His owner, Josh (Zegers) is still mourning the death of his father and isn't ready to deal with his mother's budding romance with the new veterinarian in town (Harrison). Meanwhile, Josh joins the school's football team and finds himself thrust into the spotlight as the team's quarterback when the starter is injured (big surprise!), only to be bailed out by his multi-sport pooch. Actually, Buddy is played by four different Golden Retrievers, as the original died shortly after completing the original. This rehash tries to take itself seriously, with lessons about overcoming tragedy and adjusting to change, but isn't much more than sappy melodrama and cute dog tricks. **90m/C VHS, DVD.** Kevin Zegers, Cynthia Stevenson, Gregory Harrison, Nora Dunn, Robert Costanzo, Tim Conway, Dick Martin, Perry Anzilotti, Suzanne Ristic, Jay Brazeau; ***D:*** Richard Martin; ***W:*** Paul Tamasy, Aaron Mendelsohn; ***C:*** Mike Southon; ***M:*** Brahm Wenger.

Air Bud 3: World Pup 🦴🦴½ **2000 (G)** Buddy went from basketball to football and now to soccer in this third installment. This time he teams up with the U.S. Women's Soccer Team and also becomes a dad. And wouldn't you know—just before the championship game, dad Buddy must rescue one of his pups from a gang of dog-nappers. **83m/C VHS, DVD.** Kevin Zegers, Dale Midkiff, Caitlin Wachs, Martin Ferrero, Duncan Regehr, Brittany Paige Bouck, Briana Scurry, Brandi Chastain, Tisha Venturini; ***D:*** Bill Bannerman. **VIDEO**

Air Bud 4: Seventh Inning Fetch 🦴🦴½ **2002 (G)** Since Josh is off at college, it's his little sis Andrea who needs Buddy's help on her baseball team. But Buddy's got other problems—Rocky the Raccoon has kidnapped Buddy's puppies! **93m/C VHS, DVD.** Richard Karn, Cynthia Stevenson, Kevin Zegers, Caitlin Wachs; ***D:*** Robert Vince. **VIDEO**

Air Force 🦴🦴🦴½ **1943** One of the finest of the WWII movies, Hawks' exciting classic has worn well through the years, in spite of the Japanese propaganda. It follows the hazardous exploits of a Boeing B-17 bomber crew who fight over Pearl Harbor, Manila, and the Coral Sea. Extremely realistic dogfight sequences and powerful, introspective real guy interfacing by the ensemble cast are masterfully combined by Hawks. **124m/B VHS.** John Garfield, John Ridgely, Gig Young, Arthur Kennedy, Charles Drake, Harry Carey Sr., George Tobias, Ray Montgomery, James Brown, Stanley Ridges, Willard Robertson, Moroni Olsen, Edward Brophy, Richard Lane, Faye Emerson, Addison Richards, James Flavin, Ann Doran, Dorothy Peterson, William Forrest, Ward Wood; ***D:*** Howard Hawks; ***W:*** Dudley Nichols, William Faulkner; ***C:*** James Wong Howe, Elmer Dyer, Charles A. Marshall; ***M:*** Franz Waxman. Oscars '43: Film Editing.

Air Force One 🦴🦴🦴 *AFO* **1997 (R)** Ford stars as U.S. President James Marshall, who is not only tough on crime but tough, period. His policy is to not negotiate with terrorists. Then Air Force One, with him, the First Lady and their daughter aboard is hijacked by Russian nationalists, led by ice cold Ivan (Oldman). Close is first woman Veep, Kathryn Bennett, stuck in D.C. coping with the situation. Ford is in fine form as the President who's forced to kick some Commie butt to save the day. Director Petersen ("In The Line of Fire") is becoming a master of building tension in confined places and puts his strong cast to good use. Nail-biting suspense and breath-taking action sequences cap off tour-de-force adventure. **124m/C VHS, DVD, Wide.** Harrison Ford, Gary Oldman, Glenn Close, Dean Stockwell, William H. Macy, Wendy Crewson, Xander Berkeley, Paul Guilfoyle, Liesl Matthews, Bill Smitrovich, Elya Baskin, David Vadim, Tom Everett, Philip Baker Hall, Spencer Garrett, Donna Bullock; ***Cameos:*** Juergen Prochnow; ***D:*** Wolfgang Petersen; ***W:*** Andrew Marlowe; ***C:*** Michael Ballhaus; ***M:*** Jerry Goldsmith.

Air Hawk 🦴 **1984** Australian made for TV release details the adventures of an outback pilot involved with stolen diamonds. **90m/C VHS.** *AU* Eric Oldfield, Louise Howitt, Ellie MacLure, David Robson, David Baker; ***D:*** David Baker. **TV**

Air Rage 🦴🦴 **2001 (R)** General Prescott (Cord) screwed over five Marines, setting them up and sending them to prison in order to advance his career. Now they're out and have just hijacked a 747 with the general on board—they not only want revenge but $100 million as well. Captain Marshall (Ice-T) and his team are sent on a rescue mission but things go wrong and Marshall is left to tackle the bad guys on his own. Familiar but fast-paced. **99m/C VHS, DVD, Wide.** Ice-T, Cyril O'Reilly, Steve Hytner, Gil Gerard, Alex Cord, Kim Oja; ***D:*** Ed Raymond; ***W:*** Sean O'Bannon; ***C:*** Mac Ahlberg. **VIDEO**

Air Raid Wardens 🦴🦴½ **1943** Laurel & Hardy play a couple of small-town failures who become the local air raid wardens during WWII. They even manage to make a mess of this but redeem themselves when they overhear a spy plot and save the town's munitions factory from a German spy ring. A so-so effort from the comic duo. **67m/B VHS.** Stan Laurel, Oliver Hardy, Edgar Kennedy, Jacqueline White, Stephen McNally, Russell Hicks, Howard Freeman, Donald Meek, Henry O'Neill; ***D:*** Edward Sedgwick.

The Air Up There 🦴🦴 **1994 (PG)** Assistant basketball coach Jimmy Dolan (Bacon) heads to the African village of Winabi to recruit talented (and tall) Saleh (Maina) to play b-ball in the U.S. But Saleh is next in line to be the tribe's king and doesn't want to leave. Stupid American in foreign country learning from the natives story is lighthearted, but relies heavily on formula—and borders on the stereotypical, though climatic game is a lot of fun. **108m/C VHS.** Kevin Bacon, Charles Gitona Maina, Sean McCann, Dennis Patrick; ***D:*** Paul Michael Glaser; ***W:*** Max Apple; ***C:*** Elliot Davis; ***M:*** David Newman.

Airborne 🦴½ **1993 (PG)** Cool California rollerblade dude gets transplanted to Cincinnati for a school year, and has to prove himself when those good ol' mid-western boys come after him. Nothing short of a skate vehicle appealing largely, if not solely, to the high school contingent. **91m/C VHS.** Shane McDermott, Seth Green, Brittney Powell, Edie McClurg; ***D:*** Rob Bowman; ***W:*** Bill Apablasa; ***M:*** Stewart Copeland.

Airborne 🦴🦴 **1998 (R)** Members of a covert Special Forces team are targeted for assassination after recovering a biochemical weapon from terrorists. But their leader (Guttenberg) decides to use the virus as bait to find out who wants them dead. Guttenberg tries but can't convince as a tough guy but there's lots of action to make up for this casting quirk. **94m/C VHS, DVD.** Steve Guttenberg, Sean Bean, Colm Feore; ***D:*** Julian Grant. **VIDEO**

Airboss 🦴½ **2000 (R)** A special forces team of FBI agents and the military must track down a hijacked shipment of plutonium before it falls into terrorist hands. When a team member is killed, fighter pilot Frank White (Zagarino) is called in. Lots of machinery, guns, and explosions make up for the lack of believable story. **90m/C VHS, DVD.** Frank Zagarino, John Christian, Kayle Watson, Caroline Strong, Jerry Kokich; ***D:*** J. Christian Ingvordsen. **VIDEO**

Airheads 🦴🦴½ **1994 (PG-13)** "Wayne's World" meets "Dog Day Afternoon." Silly farce has three metal heads (Buscemi, Fraser, Sandler) holding a radio station hostage in order to get their demo tape played. Events snowball and they receive instant fame. Cast and crew rich with subversive comedic talents, including Sandler and Farley from "Saturday Night Live." Soundtrack authenticity supplied by White Zombie and The Galatic Cowboys. **81m/C VHS, DVD, Wide.** Brendan Fraser, Steve Buscemi, Adam Sandler, Chris Farley, Michael McKean, Judd Nelson, Joe Mantegna, Michael Richards, Ernie Hudson, Amy Locane, Nina Siemaszko, John Melendez; ***D:*** Michael Lehmann; ***W:*** Rich Wilkes; ***C:*** John Schwartzman; ***M:*** Carter Burwell.

Airplane! 🦴🦴🦴½ **1980 (PG)** Classic lampoon of disaster flicks is stupid but funny and launched a bevy wanna-be spoofs. Former pilot Ted Striker (Hays), who's lost both his stewardess girlfriend Elaine (Hagerty) and his nerve, takes over the controls of a jet when the crew is hit with food poisoning. The passengers become increasingly crazed and ground support more surreal as our hero struggles to land the plane. Clever, fast-paced, and very funny parody mangles every Hollywood cliche within reach. The gags are so furiously paced that when one bombs it's hardly noticeable. Launched Nielsen's second career as a comic actor. And it ain't over till it's over: don't miss the amusing final credits. Followed by "Airplane 2: The Sequel." **88m/C VHS, DVD, 8mm, Wide.** Jerry Zucker, Jim Abrahams, David Zucker, Robert Hays, Julie Hagerty, Lloyd Bridges, Peter Graves, Robert Stack, Kareem Abdul-Jabbar, Leslie Nielsen, Stephen Stucker, Ethel Merman, Barbara Billingsley, Lorna Patterson, Joyce Bulifant, James Hong, Maureen McGovern, Jimmie Walker; ***D:*** Jerry Zucker, Jim Abrahams, David Zucker; ***W:*** Jerry Zucker, Jim Abrahams, David Zucker; ***C:*** Joseph Biroc; ***M:*** Elmer Bernstein. Writers Guild '80: Adapt. Screenplay.

Airplane 2: The Sequel 🦴🦴 **1982 (PG)** Not a Zucker, Abrahams and Zucker effort, and sorely missing their slapstick and script finesse. The first passenger space shuttle has taken off for the moon and there's a mad bomber on board. Given the number of stars mugging, it's more of a loveboat in space than a fitting sequel to "Airplane." Nonetheless, some funny laughs and gags. **84m/C VHS, DVD, Wide.** Ken Finkleman, Robert Hays, Julie Hagerty, Lloyd Bridges, Raymond Burr, Peter Graves, William Shatner, Sonny Bono, Chuck Connors, Chad Everett, Stephen Stucker, Rip Torn, Kent McCord, Sandahl Bergman, Jack Jones, John Dehner, Richard Jaeckel; ***D:*** Ken Finkleman; ***W:*** Ken Finkleman; ***C:*** Joseph Biroc; ***M:*** Elmer Bernstein.

Airport 🦴🦴🦴 **1970 (G)** Old-fashioned disaster thriller built around an all-star cast, fairly moronic script, and an unavoidable accident during the flight of a passenger airliner. A boxoffice hit that paved the way for many lesser disaster flicks (including its many sequels) detailing the reactions of the passengers and crew as they cope with impending doom. Considered to be the best of the "Airport" series; adapted from the Arthur Hailey novel. **137m/C VHS, DVD.** Dean Martin, Burt Lancaster, Jean Seberg, Jacqueline Bisset, George Kennedy, Helen Hayes, Van Heflin, Maureen Stapleton, Barry Nelson, Lloyd Nolan, Dana Wynter, Barbara Hale, Gary Collins, Jessie Royce Landis; ***D:*** George Seaton; ***W:*** George Seaton; ***C:*** Ernest Laszlo; ***M:*** Alfred Newman. Oscars '70: Support. Actress (Hayes); Golden Globes '71: Support. Actress (Stapleton).

Airport '75 🦴🦴 **1975 (PG)** After a mid-air collision, a jumbo 747 is left pilotless. Airline attendant Black must fly da plane. She does her cross-eyed best in this absurd sequel to "Airport" built around a lesser "all-star cast." Safe on the ground, Heston tries to talk the airline hostess/pilot into landing, while the impatient Kennedy continues to grouse as leader of the foam-ready ground crew. A slick, insincere attempt to find box office magic again (which unfortunately worked, leading to two more sequels). **107m/C VHS, DVD.** Charlton Heston, Karen Black, George Kennedy, Gloria Swanson, Helen Reddy, Sid Caesar, Efrem Zimbalist Jr., Susan Clark, Dana Andrews, Linda Blair, Nancy Olson, Roy Thinnes, Myrna Loy, Ed Nelson, Larry Storch; ***D:*** Jack Smight; ***W:*** Don Ingalls; ***C:*** Philip Lathrop; ***M:*** John Cacavas.

Airport '77 🦴🦴 **1977 (PG)** Billionaire Stewart fills his converted passenger jet with priceless art and sets off to Palm Beach for a museum opening, joined by an uninvited gang of hijackers. Twist to this in-flight disaster is that the bad time in the air occurs underwater, a novel (and some might say, desperate) twist to the old panic in the plane we're all gonna die formula. With a cast of familiar faces, some of them stars and some of them just familiar faces, this is yet another sequel to "Airport" and another boxoffice success, leading to the last of the tired series in 1979. **114m/C VHS, DVD.** Jack Lemmon, James Stewart, Lee Grant, Brenda Vaccaro, Joseph Cotten, Olivia de Havilland, Darren McGavin, Christopher Lee, George Kennedy, Kathleen Quinlan, Monte Markham; ***D:*** Jack Smight.

Akira 🦴🦴 **1989** Secret government experiments on children with ESP go awry, resulting in an cataclysmic explosion on Tokyo. The city in turn builds itself up into a Megalopolis and the experiments continue. Animated; in Japanese with English subtitles or dubbed. **124m/C VHS.** *JP* ***D:*** Katsuhiro Otomo, Sheldon Renan; ***W:*** Katsuhiro Otomo, Izo Hashimoto; ***C:*** Katsuji Misawa; ***M:*** Shoji Yamashiro; ***V:*** Mitsuo Iwata, Nozomu Sasaki, Mami Koyama.

Akira Kurosawa's Dreams 🦴🦴½ *Dreams; Yume; I Saw a Dream Like This; Konna Yume Wo Mita* **1990 (PG)** An anthological lesson regarding the simultaneous loss of humanity and nature that threatens us all from the renowned Japanese director. Although the startling and memorable imagery is still present, Kurosawa's lessons are strangely trite and consequently lack the power that is normally associated with his work. Watch for Scorsese as Van Gogh. With English subtitles. **120m/C VHS, Wide.** *JP* Akira Terao, Mitsuko Baisho, Meiko Harada, Chishu Ryu, Hisashi Igawa, Mitsunori Isaki, Toshihiko Nakano, Yoshitaka Zushi, Toshie Negishi, Martin Scorsese; ***D:*** Akira Kurosawa; ***W:*** Akira Kurosawa; ***C:*** Kazutami Hara, Takao Saito, Masaharu Ueda; ***M:*** Shinichiro Ikebe.

Al Capone 🦴🦴🦴 **1959** Film noir character study of one of the most colorful gangsters of the Roaring '20s. Sort of an underworld "How to Succeed in Business." Steiger chews scenes and bullets as they fly by, providing the performance of his career. Plenty of gangland violence and mayhem and splendid cinematography keep the fast-paced period piece sailing. **104m/C VHS.** Rod Steiger, Fay Spain, Murvyn Vye, Nehemiah Persoff, Martin Balsam, Al Ruscio, Joe De Santis; ***D:*** Richard Wilson.

Alabama's Ghost 🦴½ **1972 (PG)** Musician steals a dead master magician's secrets, incurring the wrath of the paranormal underworld. Far from the best of the "blaxploitation" films of the '70s. **96m/C VHS.** Christopher Brooks, E. Kerrigan Prescott; ***D:*** Fredric Hobbs.

Aladdin 🦴 *Superfantagenio* **1986 (PG)** A comedic Italian modernization of the Aladdin fable. **97m/C VHS.** *IT* Bud Spencer, Luca Venantini, Janet Agren, Julian Voloshin, Umberto Raho; ***D:*** Bruno Corbucci.

Aladdin 🦴🦴🦴½ **1992 (G)** Boy meets princess, loses her, finds her, wins her from evil vizier and nasty parrot, while being aided by big blue genie. Superb animation triumphs over average songs and storyline by capitalizing on Williams' talent for ad-lib with lightning speed genie changes, lots of celebrity spoofs, and even a few pokes at Disney itself. Adults will enjoy the 1,001 impersonations while kids will get a kick out of the big blue genie and the songs, three of which are the late Ashman's legacy. Kane and Salonga are responsible for the singing voices of Aladdin and Jasmine; Gottfried is a riot as the obnoxious parrot sidekick. Be forewarned: small children may be frightened by some of the scarier sequences. ♫A Whole New World; Prince Ali; Friend Like Me; One Jump Ahead; Arabian Nights. **90m/C VHS.** ***D:*** Ron Clements, John Musker; ***W:*** Ron Clements, John Musker, Ted Elliott, Terry Rossio; ***M:*** Alan Menken, Howard Ashman, Tim Rice; ***V:*** Robin Williams, Scott Weinger, Linda Larkin, Jonathan Freeman, Frank Welker, Gilbert Gottfried, Douglas Seale, Brad Kane, Lea Salonga. Oscars '92: Song ("A Whole New World"), Orig. Score; Golden Globes '93: Song ("A Whole New World"), Score; MTV Movie Awards '93: Comedic Perf. (Williams).

Aladdin and His Wonderful Lamp 🦴🦴½ **1984** The story of Aladdin, a young man who finds a magical oil lamp when he is trapped in a tiny cave. From the "Faerie Tale Theatre" series and director of "Beetlejuice" and "Batman" Tim Burton. **60m/C VHS.** Valerie Bertinelli, Robert Carradine, Leonard Nimoy, James Earl Jones; ***D:*** Tim Burton.

Aladdin and the King of Thieves **1996** Second-direct-to-video saga (following "The Return of Jafar") once again features Williams as the voice of the genie (after settling a dispute with Disney). On the eve of Aladdin's marriage to Jasmine, theives try to steal a magic talisman, sending Aladdin on a mission to find the thieves—and his father. Disney had such terrific success with"Return" that it was inevitable they would try again. **82m/C VHS.** ***D:*** Ted Stones; ***W:*** Mark McCorkle, Robert Schooley; ***M:*** Mark Watters; ***V:*** Robin Williams, Scott Weinger, Jerry Orbach, John Rhys-Davies, Gilbert Gottfried, Linda Larkin, CCH Pounder, Frank Welker.

The Alamo 🦴🦴🦴 **1960** Old-fashioned patriotic battle epic recounts the real events of the 1836 fight for independence in Texas. The usual band of diverse and contentious personalities, including Wayne as a coonskin-capped Davy Crockett, defend a small fort against a very big Mexican raiding party outside of San Antonio. Before meeting mythic death, they fight with each other, learn the meaning of life, and ultimately come to respect each other. Just to make it more entertaining, Avalon sings. Big-budget production features an impeccable musical score by Tiomkin and an impressive 7,000 extras for the Mexican army alone. Wayne reportedly received directorial assistance from John Ford, particularly during the big massacre finale. **161m/C VHS, DVD, Wide.** John Wayne, Richard Widmark, Laurence Harvey, Frankie Avalon, Richard Boone, Carlos Arruza, Chill Wills, Veda Ann Borg, Linda Cristal, Patrick Wayne, Joan O'Brien, Joseph Calleia, Ken Curtis, Jester Hairston, Denver Pyle, John Dierkes, Guinn "Big Boy" Williams, Olive Carey, William Henry, Hank Worden, Ruben Padilla, Jack Pennick; ***D:*** John Wayne; ***W:*** James Edward Grant; ***C:*** William Clothier; ***M:*** Dimitri Tiomkin, Paul Francis Webster. Oscars '60: Sound; Golden Globes '61: Score.

Alamo Bay 🦴🦴½ **1985** A slow-moving but sincere tale of contemporary racism. An angry Vietnam veteran and his red-neck buddies feel threatened by Vietnamese refugees who want to go into the fishing business. Set in Texas, filled with Texas-sized characters, and based on a true Texas story, as interpreted by the French Malle. **99m/C VHS.** Ed Harris, Ho Nguyen, Amy Madigan, Donald Moffat, Cynthia Carle, Truyen V. Tran, Rudy Young; ***D:*** Louis Malle; ***W:*** Alice Arlen; ***M:*** Ry Cooder.

The Alamo: Thirteen Days to Glory 🦴🦴 **1987** The legendary Davy Crockett (Keith), Colonel William Travis (Baldwin), and Jim Bowie (Arness) overcome personal differences to unite against the Mexican Army, vowing to hold down the fort or die. It takes a true Texan to fully appreciate the merits of this rather pedestrian retelling of a familiar story, but the battle scenes are pretty heady (although they lose some of their froth on the small screen). If nothing else, the ever-versatile Julia is worth seeing as Santa Anna in this made-for-TV rendering of J. Lon Tinkle's "Thirteen Days to Glory." You may not want to remember the Alamo this way. **180m/C VHS.** James Arness, Lorne Greene, Alec Baldwin, Brian Keith, Raul Julia; ***D:*** Peter Werner; ***M:*** Peter Bernstein.

Alamut Ambush 🦴 **1986** A federal agent is stalked by assassins, and decides to hunt them in return. Sequel to "Cold War Killer." **94m/C VHS.** *GB* Terence Stamp, Michael Culver; ***D:*** Ken Grieve.

Alan & Naomi 🦴🦴½ **1992 (PG)** In 1944, 14-year-old Alan Silverman is more concerned with his Brooklyn stickball team than the war raging across Europe. This changes when his upstairs neighbor offers refuge to a French-Jewish mother and her young daughter and he is asked to befriend the girl. Naomi witnessed the brutal death of her father by the Nazis and retreated into a world of her own. Together the two build a sweet, if unlikely, friendship. Fine performances save this average coming of age tale. Based on the novel by Myron Levoy. **95m/C VHS.** Lukas Haas, Vanessa Zaoui, Michael Gross, Amy Aquino, Kevin Connolly, Zohra Lampert; ***D:*** Sterling Van Wagenen; ***W:*** Jordan Horowitz; ***M:*** Dick Hyman.

An Alan Smithee Film: Burn, Hollywood, Burn 🦴½ *Burn, Hollywood, Burn* **1997 (R)** Follows a British director (Idle), whose given name is Alan Smithee, as he kidnaps the reels of his own picture when he realizes he hates the movie but can't remove his name from it since the Directors Guild of America's official pseudonym for disputed films is "Alan Smithee." O'Neal stars as the boorish producer who drives Smithee to the desperate act. This extended in-joke ran into its own problem when director Arthur Hiller, in what seemed like a publicity stunt, repudiated the version producer/writer Eszterhas recut and had his own name removed from the film, thus making "An Alan Smithee Film" one of the more than 30 Alan Smithee films in as many years. The tedious mockumentary style is relentless in narrating the story to the audience, who is never allowed to just watch what happens. Only interest is the parade of star cameos, including Stallone, Goldberg, and Chan (as themselves), along with writer Eszterhas in a scene with the director who declined credit for the film, Hiller. **86m/C VHS.** Eric Idle, Ryan O'Neal, Coolio, Richard Jeni, Sandra Bernhard, Cherie Lunghi, Harvey Weinstein, M.C. Lyte, Stephen Tobolowsky, Chuck D, Leslie Stefanson, Gavin Polone, Marcello Thedford, Nicole Nagel; ***Cameos:*** Joe Eszterhas, Sylvester Stallone, Whoopi Goldberg, Jackie Chan, Larry King, Billy Bob Thornton, Dominick Dunne, Robert Evans, Shane Black; ***D:*** Arthur Hiller; ***W:*** Joe Eszterhas; ***C:*** Reynaldo Villalobos; ***M:*** Gary G-Wiz. Golden Raspberries '98: Worst Picture, Worst Support. Actor (Eszterhas), Worst Screenplay, Worst Song ("I Wanna Be Mike Ovitz!"), Worst New Star (Eszterhas).

The Alarmist 🦴🦴 *Life During Wartime* **1998** Tommy Hudler (Arquette) is the eager beaver new employee at the L.A. home-security company owned by slick super-salesman Heinrich Grigoris (Tucci). But Tommy's soon shocked to learn that Heinrich makes certain clients continue to need his services by breaking into their homes. Tommy makes his first sale to 40-something widow Gale (Capshaw), who enjoys seducing the boyish innocent, and the two embark on a torrid affair. Then Gale and her teenaged son are murdered after a home break-in and Tommy suspects Heinrich went a little too far. Arquette's amusingly geeky but Tucci steals the film as his sleazy boss. **93m/C VHS, DVD.** Stanley Tucci, David Arquette, Kate Capshaw, Ryan Reynolds, Mary McCormack, Tricia Vessey; ***D:*** Evan Dunsky; ***W:*** Evan Dunsky; ***C:*** Alex Nepomniaschy; ***M:*** Christophe Beck.

Alaska 🦴🦴½ **1996 (PG)** Fourteen-year-old Vincent Barnes (Kartheiser) and his 12-year-old sister Jessie (Birch) try to rescue their bush pilot father Jake (Benedict) whose plane has crashed in the wilderness. They also rescue an orphaned polar bear cub from an evil poacher (Heston) that manages to help them out along the way. See this flick if only to enjoy the lush backdrop of Alaska and British Columbia and, of course, the absolutely adorable polar cub. Director Fraser C. Heston directs dad Charlton, appropriate payback for landing him the role as the infant Moses in "The Ten Commandments." **109m/C VHS.** Thora Birch, Vincent Kartheiser, Dirk Benedict, Charlton Heston; ***D:*** Fraser Heston; ***W:*** Andy Burg, Carol Fuchs; ***C:*** Tony Westman.

Alberto Express 🦴🦴½ **1992** Black comedy explores the debts children owe their parents—literally. Alberto's family has a peculiar tradition. It seems that now he's married and about to become a father, he's expected to pay back every cent spent on his own upbringing. Cash poor (and panicky) Alberto hops a train from Paris to Rome and frantically tries to raise the necessary cash by preying, in a series of increasingly bizarre ways, on his fellow passengers before he faces his father once again. In French and Italian with English subtitles. **90m/C VHS.** *FR* Sergio Castellitto, Nino Manfredi, Marie Trintignant, Jeanne Moreau, Michel Aumont, Dominique Pinon, Marco Messeri, Eugenia Marruzzo; ***D:*** Arthur Joffe; ***W:*** Arthur Joffe.

Albino woof! **1976 (R)** Albino chief leads African terrorists to murder white settlers, one of whom is an ex-policeman's fiancee. So the ex-cop pursues the bad guys, who are fairly easy to identify (just look for the big group hanging with the albino). Danning, Lee, and Howard only briefly show faces and collect checks. **85m/C VHS.** Christopher Lee, Trevor Howard, Sybil Danning, Horst Frank, James Faulkner; ***D:*** Jurgen Goslar.

Albino Alligator 🦴🦴 **1996 (R)** Three small-time crooks bungle a robbery and inadvertently run down a federal officer in Academy Award-winning actor Spacey's directorial debut. The trio, consisting of leader Dova (Dillon), brains Milo (Sinise) and brawn Law (Fichtner) hole up in a seedy bar and grab the occupants as hostages. The police soon surround the dive, and the crooks begin arguing among themselves and with brash barmaid Janet (Dunaway) about their chances and means for escape. All, however, is not as it seems. The claustrophobic setting seems more suitable for the stage than the screen, and the plot twists don't bend very far from predictable. Screenwriter Forte is the son of '60s teen idol Fabian. **94m/C VHS, DVD.** Matt Dillon, Gary Sinise, Faye Dunaway, William Fichtner, Joe Mantegna, Viggo Mortensen, John Spencer, Skeet Ulrich, M. Emmet Walsh; ***D:*** Kevin Spacey; ***W:*** Christian Forte; ***C:*** Mark Plummer; ***M:*** Michael Brook.

The Alchemist woof! **1981 (R)** See humans transformed into murderous zombies! A bewitched man seeks revenge upon the evil magician who placed a curse on him, causing him to live like an animal. Painfully routine, with a few chills along the way. Amonte is an alias for Charles Band. Filmed in 1981 and released four years later. **86m/C VHS.** Robert Ginty, Lucinda Dooling, John Sanderford, Viola Kate Stimpson, Bob Glaudini; ***D:*** Charles Band; ***W:*** Alan J. Adler; ***M:*** Richard Band.

The Alchemists 🦴½ **1999 (PG-13)** The world's leading pharmaceutical company is covering up the fact that their fertility drug has some serious side effects. Employees Show and Gemmell try to expose the corporate conspiracy. Based on the novel by Peter James. **150m/C VHS, DVD.** Grant Show, Ruth Gemmell, Edward Hardwicke; ***D:*** Peter Smith; ***C:*** Peter Middleton; ***M:*** Rick Wentworth.

Aldrich Ames: Traitor Within 🦴🦴½ **1998 (PG)** Hutton stars as Aldrich Ames, a longtime, second-rate CIA employee with an expensive Colombian-born second wife, Rosario (Pena), and a lot of debts. So Ames turns weasel and begins to sell secrets to the Russians in the mid-eighties, which resulted in the deaths of at least 10 agents. Plowright is the CIA analyst in charge of plugging the leak. Both Ames' were arrested and sent to prison in 1994; Rosario was released in 1999 and returned to Bogota. **97m/C VHS.** Timothy Hutton, Joan Plowright, Elizabeth Pena, Eugene Lipinski, C. David Johnson; ***D:*** John MacKenzie; ***W:*** Michael Burton; ***C:*** Walter McGill. **CABLE**

Alex 🦴🦴½ **1992** Inspirational story about 15-year-old New Zealand swimmer Alex Archer (Jackson), who is working towards a spot at the 1960 Rome Olympics. But her goal is threatened by an accident and a new rival and Alex struggles to overcome her obstacles with the help of her boyfriend Andy (Picker). Based on the novel by Tessa Duder. **92m/C VHS.** *AU* Lauren Jackson, Chris Haywood, Josh Picker, Catherine Godbold, Elizabeth Hawthorne; ***D:*** Megan Simpson.

Alex in Wonderland 🦴🦴½ **1970 (R)** A semi-autobiographical and satirical look at Hollywood from the standpoint of a young director who's trying to follow up his recent hit (in real life, "Bob & Carol & Ted & Alice") with a picture of some integrity that will keep the mass audience away. The confused plot provides obvious parallels to Fellini (who appears in a cameo) and some sharp, often bitter insights into the Hollywood of the early '60s. Strong performances by Sutherland and Burstyn compensate somewhat for the patience-trying self-indulgent arty whining of the script. **109m/C VHS.** Donald Sutherland, Ellen Burstyn, Paul Mazursky; ***Cameos:*** Jeanne Moreau, Federico Fellini; ***D:*** Paul Mazursky; ***W:*** Larry Tucker, Paul Mazursky.

Alexander Nevsky 🦴🦴🦴½ **1938** A story of the invasion of Russia in 1241 by the Teutonic Knights of Germany and the defense of the region by good old Prince Nevsky. Eisenstein's first completed project in nearly ten years, it was widely regarded as an artistic disappointment upon release and as pro-war propaganda for the looming conflict with the Nazis. Fabulous Prokofiev score illuminates the classic battle scenes, which used thousands of Russian army regulars. Russian with subtitles. **110m/B VHS, DVD.** *RU* Nikolai Cherkasov, Nikolai P. Okhlopkov, Andrei Abrikosov, Alexandra Danilova, Dmitri Orlov, Vera Ivasheva, Sergei Blinnikov, Lev Fenin, Vladimir Yershov, Nikolai Arsky, Naum Rogozhin, Varvara O. Massalitinova, Vasili Novikov, Ivan Lagutin; ***D:*** Sergei Eisenstein; ***W:*** Sergei Eisenstein, Pyotr Pavlenko; ***C:*** Eduard Tisse; ***M:*** Sergei Prokofiev.

Alexander the Great 🦴🦴½ **1955** A lavish epic about the legendary Greek conqueror of the fourth century B.C., which provides Burton a rare chance at an adventure role. Here we find Alexander is the product of a dysfunctional royal family who hopes to create an idealized world modeled after Greek culture to make up for the love he lacks from daddy. This he does by conquering everything before dying at the age of 33. The great cast helps to overcome the sluggish pacing of the spectacle, while numerous battle scenes featuring loads of spears and arrows are staged effectively. **135m/C VHS, Wide.** Richard Burton, Fredric March, Claire Bloom, Harry Andrews, Peter Cushing, Danielle Darrieux, Helmut Dantine; ***D:*** Robert Rossen; ***C:*** Robert Krasker.

Alexander: The Other Side of Dawn 🦴🦴 **1977** Tired sequel to the television movie "Dawn: Portrait of a Teenage Runaway." A young man turns to prostitution to support himself on the street of Los Angeles. **100m/C VHS.** Leigh McCloskey, Eve Plumb, Earl Holliman, Juliet Mills, Jean Hagen, Lonny (Loni) Chapman; ***D:*** John Erman. **TV**

Alexander's Ragtime Band 🦴🦴🦴 *Irving Berlin's Alexander's Ragtime Band* **1938** Energetic musical that spans 1915 to 1938 and has Power and Ameche battling for Faye's affections. Power is a society nabob who takes up ragtime. He puts together a band, naming the group after a piece of music (hence the title), and finds a singer (Faye). Ameche is a struggling composer who brings a Broadway producer to listen to their performance. Faye gets an offer to star in a show and becomes an overnight success. Over the years the trio win and lose success, marry and divorce, and finally end up happy. Corny but charming. ♫Alexander's Ragtime Band; All Alone; Blue Skies; Easter Parade; Everybody's Doin' It; Everybody Step; For Your Country and My Country; Heat Wave; I Can Always Find a Little Sunshine at the YMCA. **105m/B VHS.** Tyrone Power, Alice Faye, Don Ameche, Ethel Merman, Jack Haley, Jean Hersholt, Helen Westley, John Carradine, Paul Hurst, Joe King, Ruth Terry; ***D:*** Henry King; ***W:*** Kathryn Scola, Lamar Trotti; ***M:*** Irving Berlin. Oscars '38: Score.

Alexandria Again and Forever 🦴🦴 *Iskanderija, Kaman oue Kaman* **1990** Yehia (Chahine) remembers his win as best director at the Berlin Film Festival a decade before for his political film "Alexandria...Why?" and thinks about that film's leading man with whom he fell in love. But when he meets and falls for Nadia, Yehia decides he will launch her career as the star of his new film. The final part of Chahine's Alexandria trilogy, following "Alexandria...Why?" and "An Egyptian Story." Arabic with subtitles. **105m/C VHS, DVD, Wide.** *EG* Youssef Chahine, Zaki Abdel Wahab, Menha Batraoui, Teheya Cariocca, Amr Abdel Guelil, Yousra; ***D:*** Youssef Chahine; ***W:*** Youssef Chahine; ***C:*** Ingy Assolh; ***M:*** Mohammed Nouh.

Alexandria...Why? 🦴🦴 **1978** Schoolboy (director Chahine uses his adolescent recollections) tries to ignore the war in Alexandria in 1942 by escaping into the movies and his dreams of becoming a star. He also witnesses two love affairs—one between a Muslim man and a Jewish woman and the second betweeen an Arab nationalist and an English soldier. Part 1 of Chahine's Alexandria trilogy, followed by "An Egyptian Story" and "Alexandria Again and Forever." Arabic with subtitles. **133m/C VHS, DVD, Wide.** *EG* Gerry Sundquist, Naglaa Fathi, Farid Shawki, Mohsen Mohiedine; ***D:*** Youssef Chahine; ***W:*** Youssef Chahine; ***C:*** Mohsen Nasr; ***M:*** Foad El Zaheri.

Alfie 🦴🦴🦴 **1966 (PG)** What's it all about, Alfie? Caine, in his first starring role, plays the British playboy out of control in mod London. Alfie is a despicable, unscrupulous and vile sort of guy who uses woman after woman to fulfill his basic needs and then casts them aside until...tragedy strikes. Though this box office hit was seen as a sophisticated take on current sexual mores upon release, it now seems a dated but engaging comedy, notable chiefly for its performances. From the play by Bill Naughton. The title song "Alfie," sung by Dionne Warwick, was a top ten hit. **114m/C VHS, DVD, Wide.** *GB* Michael Caine, Shelley Winters, Millicent Martin, Vivien Merchant, Julia Foster, Jane Asher, Shirley Anne Field, Eleanor Bron, Denholm Elliott, Alfie Bass, Graham Stark, Murray Melvin, Sydney Tafler; ***D:*** Lewis Gilbert; ***W:*** Bill Naughton; ***C:*** Otto Heller; ***M:*** Burt Bacharach, Sonny Rollins. Cannes '67: Grand Jury Prize; Golden Globes '67: Foreign Film; Natl. Bd. of Review '66: Support. Actress (Merchant); Natl. Soc. Film Critics '66: Actor (Caine).

Alfred Hitchcock's Aventure Malgache *Madagascar Landing; Alfred Hitchcock's Bon Voyage & Aventure Malgache* **1944** Hitchcock worked with the Moliere Players on this propaganda piece about the French Resistance. He based this story on the experiences of the actor Clarousse. Working for the Resistance in occupied Madagascar, Clarousse is betrayed and sent to prison by the Vichy government. Rescued by the British he returns to resume his work. In French with English subtitles. **31m/B VHS, DVD.** *GB* ***D:*** Alfred Hitchcock; ***C:*** Gunther Krampf.

Alfred Hitchcock's Bon Voyage *Alfred Hitchcock's Bon Voyage & Aventure Malgache* **1944** One of director Hitchcock's short propaganda pieces filmed as a tribute to the French Resistance. In London an RAF pilot is interrogated by the Free French about his escape from France. He was aided by a Polish agent who was actually working for the Gestapo to learn about the Resistance's movements. Flashbacks show the pilot's adventures from the spy's point-of-view. In French with English subtitles. **26m/B VHS, DVD.** *GB* John Blythe; ***D:*** Alfred Hitchcock; ***W:*** J.O.C. Orton; ***C:*** Gunther Krampf.

Alfredo, Alfredo 🦴🦴 **1972 (R)** Hoffman plays a mild-mannered bank clerk who regrets marrying a sexy woman. Lightweight domestic comedy. In Italian with English subtitles (Hoffman's voice was dubbed). **97m/C VHS.** *IT* Dustin Hoffman, Stefania Sandrelli, Carla Gravina, Clara Colosimo, Daniela Patella, Dulio Del Prete; ***D:*** Pietro Germi; ***W:*** Pietro Germi, Leonardo Benvenuti; ***C:*** Aiace Parolini; ***M:*** Carlo Rustichelli.

Algiers 🦴🦴🦴 **1938** Nearly a scene-for-scene Americanized remake of the 1937 French "Pepe Le Moko" about a beautiful rich girl (Lamarr) who meets and falls in love with a notorious thief (Boyer, then a leading sex symbol). Pursued by French police and hiding in the underworld-controlled Casbah, Boyer meets up with Lamarr in a tragically fated romance done in the best tradition of Hollywood. Boyer provides a measured performance as Le Moko, while Lamarr is appropriately sultry in her American film debut (which made her a star). Later remade as the semi-musical "Casbah." **96m/B VHS.** Charles Boyer, Hedy Lamarr, Sigrid Gurie, Gene Lockhart, Joseph Calleia, Alan Hale; ***D:*** John Cromwell; ***C:*** James Wong Howe.

Ali 🦴🦴½ **2001 (R)** Mann, a notorious obsessive, couldn't have picked a more ambitious topic. The herculean task proves too much, yielding a film that lacks focus or insight into its subject. Ali is depicted during a contentious decade (1964-1974), in which he converted to Islam, befriended civil rights icons, refused the draft, was stripped of his title, married three times, and blurred lines between sport, ethics and society. Perhaps it's no coincidence that screenwriter Roth, who previously penned "Forrest Gump," was chosen to chronicle Ali amid such historic happenings. Mann's visual skills are apparent, and Smith gives an inspired performance in and out of the ring. Other noteworthies include Foxx as cornerman "Bundini" Brown, and Voight as verbose sportscaster Cosell. Despite the charisma of its subject (and its lead), film feels distant and subdued. Lands a few clean blows, but certainly not a knockout. **158m/C VHS, DVD, Wide.** *US* Will Smith, Jamie Foxx, Jon Voight, Mario Van Peebles, Ron Silver, Jeffrey Wright, Mykelti Williamson, Jada Pinkett Smith, Michael Michele, Joe Morton, Paul Rodriguez, Nona Gaye, Bruce McGill, Barry (Shabaka) Henley, Giancarlo Esposito, Laurence Mason, LeVar Burton, Albert Hall, David Cubitt, Ted Levine, David Elliott, Michael Bentt, James N. Toney, Charles Shufford, Malick Bowens, Shari Watson, Victoria Dillard, Kim Robillard, Gailard Sartain, Rufus Dorsey, Robert Sale, Damien "Bolo" Wills, Michael Dorn; ***D:*** Michael Mann; ***W:*** Michael Mann, Stephen J. Rivele, Christopher Wilkinson, Eric Roth; ***C:*** Emmanuel Lubezki; ***M:*** Lisa Gerrard, Pieter Bourke.

Ali Baba and the Forty Thieves 🦴🦴½ **1943** Ali Baba and his gang of thieves do battle against Hulagu Khan, leader of the Mongols, to save Baghdad and its citizens from ruin and death. **87m/C VHS.** Jon Hall, Turhan Bey, Maria Montez, Andy Devine, Kurt Katch, Frank Puglia, Fortunio Bonanova, Moroni Olsen, Scotty Beckett; ***D:*** Arthur Lubin; ***W:*** Edmund Hartmann; ***C:*** William Howard Greene.

Ali Baba and the 40 Thieves 🦴🦴🦴 *Ali Baba et les Quarante Voleurs* **1954** French adaptation of the popular novel "A Thousand and One Nights." Servant boy Ali Baba discovers the magic cave holding the stolen treasure of Abdul and his 40 thieves. Shot on location in Morocco. Also available dubbed. **92m/C VHS.** *FR* Samia Gamal, Dieter Borsche, Henri Vilbert; ***D:*** Jacques Becker; ***W:*** Jacques Becker.

Ali: Fear Eats the Soul 🦴🦴🦴 *Fear Eats the Soul; Angst Essen Selle auf* **1974** A widow cleaning woman in her 60s has a love affair with a Moroccan man 30 years her junior. To no one's surprise, both encounter racism and moral hypocrisy in West Germany. Serious melodrama from Fassbinder, who wrote it and appears as the squirmy son-in-law. In German with English subtitles. **68m/C VHS.** *GE* Brigitte Mira, El Hedi Ben Salem, Irm Hermann; ***D:*** Rainer Werner Fassbinder; ***W:*** Rainer Werner Fassbinder; ***C:*** Jurgen Jurges.

Alias Billy the Kid 🦴🦴 **1946** Western adventure with Carson posing as a famous outlaw to find out who's behind the scam involving the Denton City cattle trade. **54m/B VHS.** Sunset Carson, Peggy Stewart, Tom London, Roy Barcroft; ***D:*** Thomas Carr; ***C:*** Bud Thackery.

Alias Jesse James 🦴🦴 **1959 (PG)** Insurance agent Milford Farnsworth (Hope) is an eastern tenderfoot who holds a policy on Jesse James (Corey). So he heads west to make certain the outlaw doesn't get killed. Only Jesse sets Milford up as himself, hoping to collect on his own policy. Fleming's the local beauty. A number of western stars have cameos, coming to Hope's rescue. **92m/C VHS.** Bob Hope, Rhonda Fleming, Wendell Corey, Jim Davis, Gloria Talbott, William Wright, Mary (Marsden) Young, Joseph (Joe) Vitale; ***Cameos:*** Hugh O'Brian, Ward Bond, James Arness, Roy Rogers, Fess Parker, Gail Davis, James Garner, Gene Autry, Jay Silverheels, Bing Crosby, Gary Cooper; ***D:*** Norman Z. McLeod; ***W:*** William Bowers, D.D. Beauchamp; ***C:*** Lionel Lindon.

Alias John Law 🦴 **1935** The Good Guy fights for oil rights against the bad guys. Confused program western with an especially convoluted plot. **54m/B VHS.** Bob Steele; ***D:*** Robert North Bradbury.

Alias John Preston 🦴½ **1956** Yet another one of those pseudo-psychological to sleep perchance to dream movies. Lee plays a man haunted by dreams in which he's a murderer, and soon starts to question whether his dreams might not imitate life. It's been done before, it's been done since, and it's been done better. **66m/B VHS.** *GB* Betta St. John, Alexander Knox, Christopher Lee, Sandra Dorne, Patrick Holt, Betty Ann Davies, John Longden, Bill Fraser, John Stuart; ***D:*** David MacDonald.

Alias, La Gringa 🦴🦴 **1991** Follows the adventures of La Gringa, a likeable criminal capable of escaping from any Peruvian jail. After being aided in his latest escape by a political prisoner, La Gringa decides to return in disguise to pay back the favor. But the prison is rocked by rioting and La Gringa finds himself in a situation out of his control. Spanish with subtitles. **100m/C VHS.** *PV* ***D:*** Alberto Durant.

Alibi 🦴🦴 **1929** Low-budget crime drama from independent producer/director West. Gangster Chick Williams (Morris) reclaims his mob role after being released from prison. But when a cop is killed during a robbery, Williams is suspected of the crime and the detective squad will employ any method to bring him to justice. Noted for its experimental use of sound, its dazzling Art Deco sets, and its eccentric composition. **84m/B VHS.** Chester Morris, Mae Busch, Regis Toomey, Harry Stubbs; ***D:*** Roland West; ***W:*** Roland West, C. Gardner Sullivan; ***C:*** Ray June; ***M:*** Hugo Riesenfeld.

Alice 🦴🦴 *Alicja* **1986** A twist on the "Alice in Wonderland" tale. Alice witnesses an attempted murder, faints, and awakens in a weird, yet strangely familiar environment. Adapted from the stage production. **80m/C VHS.** Sophie Barjae, Susannah York, Jean-Pierre Cassel, Paul Nicholas; ***D:*** Jacek Bromski, Jerzy Gruza.

Alice 🦴🦴🦴½ *Neco Z Alenky* **1988** An acclaimed surreal version of Lewis Carroll's already surreal "Alice in Wonderland," with the emphasis on Carroll's obsessiveness. Utilizing animated puppets and a live actor for Alice, Czech director Svankmajer injects grotesque images and black comedy into Wonderland. Not for the kids. **84m/C VHS, DVD.** *CZ SI GB GE* Kristina Kohoutova; ***D:*** Jan Svankmajer; ***W:*** Jan Svankmajer; ***C:*** Svatopluk Maly.

Alice 🦴🦴🦴 **1990 (PG-13)** Farrow is "Alice," a woman plagued with doubts about her lifestyle, her religion, and her happiness. Her perfect children, husband, and apartment don't prevent her backaches, and she turns to an Oriental "herbalist" for aid. She finds his methods unusual and the results of the treatments surprising. Lightweight fairytale of Yuppiedom gone awry. Fine performances, but superficial and pointed story that may leave the viewer looking for more. (Perhaps that's Allen's point.) Farewell performance from charactor actor Luke, unbilled cameo from Judith Ivey, and first time out for Dylan O'Sullivan Farrow, adopted daughter of Allen and Farrow, as Kate. **106m/C VHS, DVD, Wide.** Mia Farrow, William Hurt, Joe Mantegna, Keye Luke, Alec Baldwin, Cybill Shepherd, Blythe Danner, Gwen Verdon, Bernadette Peters, Judy Davis, Patrick O'Neal, Julie Kavner, Caroline Aaron, Holland Taylor, Robin Bartlett, David Spielberg, Bob Balaban, Dylan O'Sullivan Farrow, Elle Macpherson; ***D:*** Woody Allen; ***W:*** Woody Allen; ***C:*** Carlo Di Palma. Natl. Bd. of Review '90: Actress (Farrow).

Alice Adams 🦴🦴½ **1935** Based on the classic Booth Tarkington novel about a poor girl from a small Midwestern town who falls in love with a man from the upper level of society. She tries desperately to fit in and nearly alienates her family and friends. The sets may be dated, but the insight on human behavior is timeless. **99m/B VHS.** Katharine Hepburn, Fred MacMurray, Evelyn Venable, Fred Stone, Frank Albertson, Ann Shoemaker, Charley Grapewin, Grady Sutton, Hedda Hopper, Hattie McDaniel; ***D:*** George Stevens; ***M:*** Max Steiner.

Alice Doesn't Live Here Anymore 🦴🦴½ **1974 (PG)** Scorsese marries road opera with pseudo-feminist semi-realistic melodrama and produces uneven but interesting results. When Alice's husband dies suddenly, leaving her with their 11-year-old son, she leaves for California, but finds herself stranded in Phoenix, down to her last few bucks. There she lands a job as a waitress in a diner where she meets kindly rancher Kristofferson. Notable for its female point of view, it was also the basis for the once-popular TV show "Alice." Burstyn and Ladd lend key performances, while Kristofferson is typically wooden. **105m/C VHS, Wide.** Ellen Burstyn, Kris Kristofferson, Diane Ladd, Jodie Foster, Harvey Keitel, Vic Tayback, Billy Green Bush; ***D:*** Martin Scorsese; ***W:*** Robert Getchell. Oscars '74: Actress (Burstyn); British Acad. '75: Actress (Burstyn), Film, Screenplay, Support. Actress (Ladd).

Alice et Martin 🦴🦴½ *Alice and Martin* **1998 (R)** Director Andre Techine examines the complexity of relationships through the lives of nervous violinist Alice (Binoche) and psychologically fragile model Martin (Loret). The story opens in Martin's childhood, when he is sent by his free-spirited mother to live with his cold and distant father Victor (Maguelon). Martin flees his father's house after an unrevealed trauma, showing up at the door of his half-brother Benjamin (Amalric), who is Alice's roommate. Despite initial reluctance from Alice, the pair become lovers. During a trip to Spain Alice tells Martin that she's pregnant, and he goes off the deep end, haunted by memories of his father and the fateful event that will continue to affect their lives. Slow-moving but beautifully filmed. **123m/C VHS.** *FR SP* Juliette Binoche, Alexis Loret, Carmen Maura, Pierre Maguelon, Mathieu Almaric; ***D:*** Andre Techine; ***W:*** Andre Techine, Gilles Taurand, Olivier Assayas; ***C:*** Caroline Champetier; ***M:*** Philippe Sarde.

Alice in the Cities 🦴🦴🦴½ **1974** American and German culture are compared and contrasted in this early Wenders road work about a German journalist in the USA on assignment who suddenly finds himself custodian to a worldly nine-year-old girl abandoned by her mother. Together they return to Germany and search for the girl's grandmother. Along the way they learn about each other, with many distinctive and graceful Wenders moments. **110m/B VHS.** Ruediger Vogler, Yella Rottlaender, Elisabeth (Lisa) Kreuzer, Edda Kochi; ***D:*** Wim Wenders; ***W:*** Wim Wenders.

Alice in Wonderland 🦴🦴½ **1950** Another version of the Lewis Carroll classic which combines the usage of Lou Bunin's puppets and live action to tell the story. Released independently to cash in on the success of the Disney version. Takes a more adult approach to the story and is worth viewing on its own merits. **83m/C VHS.** *FR* Carol Marsh, Stephen Murray, Pamela Brown, Felix Aylmer, Ernest Milton; ***D:*** Dallas Bower.

Alice in Wonderland 🦴🦴🦴 **1951 (G)** Classic Disney dream version of Lewis Carroll's famous children's story about a girl who falls down a rabbit hole into a magical world populated by strange creatures. Beautifully animated with some startling images, but served with a strange dispassion warmed by a fine batch of songs. Wynn's Mad Hatter and Holloway's Cheshire Cat are among the treats in store. ♫Alice in Wonderland; I'm Late; A Very Merry Un-Birthday. **75m/C VHS, DVD.** ***D:*** Hamilton Luske, Wilfred Jackson, Clyde Geronimi; ***V:*** Kathryn Beaumont, Ed Wynn, Sterling Holloway, Jerry Colonna.

Alice in Wonderland 🦴🦴½ **1999** Visually elaborate but somewhat tedious version of the popular Lewis Carroll tale filled with scenery chewing by the real actors and the welcome presence of animatronic wonders from the Jim Henson Creature Shop. This time Alice is the poised Majorino, who seems more annoyed by the denizens of Wonderland than amazed at her adventures. **129m/C VHS, DVD.** Tina Majorino, Martin Short, Miranda Richardson, Whoopi Goldberg, Ben Kingsley, Gene Wilder, Christopher Lloyd, Pete Postlethwaite, Peter Ustinov, George Wendt, Robbie Coltrane; ***D:*** Nick Willing; ***W:*** Peter Barnes; ***C:*** Giles Nuttgens; ***M:*** Richard Hartley. **TV**

Alice Sweet Alice 🦴½ *Holy Terror; Communion* **1976 (R)** Mediocre, gory who-killed-her, best remembered as the debut of Shields (in a small role). **112m/C VHS, DVD.** Linda Miller, Paula Sheppard, Mildred Clinton, Niles McMaster, Jane Lowry, Rudolph Willrich, Brooke Shields, Alphonso de Noble, Gary Allen, Tom Signorelli, Lillian Roth; ***D:*** Alfred Sole; ***W:*** Alfred Sole, Rosemary Ritvo; ***C:*** John Friberg, Chuck Hall; ***M:*** Stephen Lawrence.

Alice Through the Looking Glass 1966 Based on Lewis Carroll's classic adventure. Follows the further adventures of young Alice. After a chess piece comes to life, it convinces Alice that excitement and adventure lie through the looking glass. **72m/C VHS.** Judi Rolin, Ricardo Montalban, Nanette Fabray, Robert Coote, Agnes Moorehead, Jack Palance, Jimmy Durante, Tom Smothers, Roy Castle, Richard Denning; ***D:*** Alan Handley.

Alice to Nowhere 1986 Concerns a running argument in the Outback over a fortune in gems unknowingly carried by a young woman. Based on a novel by Evan Green. **210m/C VHS.** *AU* Rosie Jones, Steve Jacobs, John Waters, Ruth Cracknell; ***D:*** John Power. **TV**

Alice's Restaurant ½ 1969 **(PG)** Based on the popular and funny 20-minute Arlo Guthrie song "Alice's Restaurant Massacre" about a Flower Child during the Last Big War who gets hassled for littering, man. Step back in time and study the issues of the hippie era, including avoiding the draft, dropping out of college, and dealing with the local pigs. Sort of a modern movie in the cinematic ambling genre, in that nothing really happens. **111m/C VHS, DVD, Wide.** Arlo Guthrie, James Broderick, Pat Quinn, Geoff Outlaw, Pete Seeger, Lee Hays, Michael McClanathan, Tina Chen, Kathleen Dabney, William Obanhein, Graham Jarvis, M. Emmet Walsh; ***D:*** Arthur Penn; ***W:*** Arthur Penn, Venabel Herndon; ***C:*** Michael Nebbia; ***M:*** Garry Sherman, Arlo Guthrie.

Alien ½ 1979 **(R)** Terse direction, stunning sets and special effects, and a well-seasoned cast save this from being another "Slimy monster from Outerspace" story. Instead it's a grisly rollercoaster of suspense and fear (and a huge boxoffice hit). Intergalactic freighter's crew is invaded by an unstoppable carnivorous alien intent on picking off the crew one by one. While the cast mostly bitches and banters while awaiting the horror of their imminent departure, Weaver is exceptional as Ripley, a self-reliant survivor who goes toe to toe with the Big Ugly. Futuristic, in the belly of the beast visual design creates a vivid sense of claustrophobic doom enhanced further by the ominous score. Oscar-winning special effects include the classic baby alien busting out of the crew guy's chest routine, a rib-splitting ten on the gore meter. Successfully followed by "Aliens" and "Alien 3." **116m/C VHS, DVD.** *GB* Tom Skerritt, Sigourney Weaver, Veronica Cartwright, Yaphet Kotto, Harry Dean Stanton, Ian Holm, John Hurt, Bolaji Badejo; ***D:*** Ridley Scott; ***W:*** Dan O'Bannon; ***C:*** Derek Vanlint; ***M:*** Jerry Goldsmith; ***V:*** Helen Horton. Oscars '79: Visual FX.

Alien 3 1992 **(R)** Picks up where "Aliens" left off as Ripley crash lands on Fiorina 161, a planet that serves as a penal colony for 25 celibate but horny men who smell bad. Ripley is forced to shave her head because of the planet's lice problem, and she sets out to survive on the cold, unfriendly planet until a rescue ship can come for her. Fending off sexual advances from the men, Ripley soon discovers she wasn't the only survivor of the crash—the alien survived too and has somehow implanted her with an alien of her own. Dark and disturbing, filled with religious allegories, and a universe removed from the two earlier Aliens. Intended as the final installment of the series. **135m/C VHS, DVD, Wide.** Sigourney Weaver, Charles S. Dutton, Charles Dance, Paul McGann, Brian Glover, Ralph Brown, Danny Webb, Christopher John Fields, Holt McCallany, Lance Henriksen; ***D:*** David Fincher; ***C:*** Alex Thomson; ***M:*** Elliot Goldenthal.

The Alien Agenda: Endangered Species ½ 1997 Tabloid TV reporter Megan Cross has a too-close encounter with extraterrestrials that frightens her enough to have her join a secret organization that keeps tabs on alien activity. Along with mercenary Cope Ransom and operative Fritz, Megan is sent to infiltrate the mutant wasteland that used to be Florida and see what the aliens are plotting. **102m/C VHS.** Debbie Rochon, Joel D. Wynkoop, Joe Zaso, Candice Meade; ***D:*** Kevin J. Lindenmuth, Ron Ford, Gabriel Campisi, Tim Ritter; ***W:*** Kevin J. Lindenmuth, Ron Ford, Gabriel Campisi, Tim Ritter. **VIDEO**

The Alien Agenda: Out of the Darkness woof! 1996 Cheesy sci-fi with a narrator who ruminates about mysterious aliens who enjoy tormenting humans and can travel through time (and send humans back and forth). You won't care. **80m/C VHS.** Sasha Graham, Michael (Mick) McCleery, Scooter McCrae, John Collins, Marcus Zanders; ***D:*** Michael (Mick) McCleery, Kevin J. Lindenmuth; ***W:*** Michael (Mick) McCleery, Kevin J. Lindenmuth. **VIDEO**

The Alien Agenda: Under the Skin ½ 1997 Scientist Alfred Malone is kidnapped by the mystery guys in black and taken to their hideaway in Puerto Rico, where vicious aliens roam around outside just looking for a tasty earthling snack. Then there's Victor who's a small-time hood who's not only got the cops after him but the new head of Chicago's crime syndicate, who's not exactly what he seems. **75m/C VHS.** Nick Kostopoulos, Arthur Lundquist, Leslie Body, Steven Jon White, Conrad Brooks; ***D:*** Kevin J. Lindenmuth, Mike Legge; ***W:*** Kevin J. Lindenmuth, Mike Legge. **VIDEO**

Alien Cargo 1999 **(PG)** The crew of a Mars transport ship has just awakened from eight months in hypersleep to discover something they're off-course and in big trouble. Standard issue plot makes for boring entertainment. **89m/C VHS.** Jason London, Missy (Melissa) Crider, Simon Westaway, Elizabeth Alexander; ***D:*** Mark Haber. **TV**

Alien Chaser 1996 **(R)** Alien android Zagarino, who crashed in the African desert 5000 years ago, returns to life thanks to the unwitting aid of archeologists Jensen and MacDonald. They literally hold the key to stopping his destruction of mankind. **95m/C VHS, DVD.** Frank Zagarino, Todd Jensen, Jennifer MacDonald, Brian O'Shaughnessy; ***D:*** Mark Roper; ***W:*** B.J. Nelson; ***C:*** Rod Stewart; ***M:*** Robert O. Ragland.

Alien Contamination woof! *Contamination* 1981 **(R)** Tale of two astronauts who return to Earth from an expedition on Mars carrying some deadly bacterial eggs. Controlled by a Martian intent on conquering the world, the eggs squirt a gloppy juice that makes people explode on contact (a special effect). A cheap and sloppy attempt to cash in on the success of "Alien." Dubbed. **90m/C VHS.** *IT* Ian McCulloch, Louise Monroe, Martin Mase, Siegfried Rauch, Lisa Hahn, Louise Marleau, Al Cliver, Carlo de Mejo, Gisela Hahn; ***D:*** Lewis (Luigi Cozzi) Coates; ***W:*** Lewis (Luigi Cozzi) Coates; ***M:*** The Goblins.

Alien Dead *It Fell from the Sky* 1979 **(R)** The teenage victims of a bizarre meteor crash reincarnate as flesh-eating ghouls anxious for a new supply of human food in this extremely low-budget sleep inducer. **75m/C VHS.** Buster Crabbe, Linda Lewis, Ray Roberts, Mike Bonavia, Dennis Underwood; ***D:*** Fred Olen Ray; ***W:*** Fred Olen Ray, Martin Allen Nicholas; ***C:*** Fred Olen Ray.

The Alien Factor ½ 1978 **(PG)** Another low-budget crazed critter from outerspace dispatch, this one featuring multiple aliens, one of whom is good, who have the misfortune of crash landing near Baltimore. The grotesque extraterrestrials jolt a small town out of its sleepy state by wreaking havoc (except for the good one, of course). Decent special effects. **82m/C VHS.** Don Leifert, Tom Griffith, Mary Mertens, Dick Dyszel, Richard Geiwitz, Eleanor Herman, Anne Frith, Christopher Gummer, George Stover, John Walker, Donald M. Dohler; ***D:*** Donald M. Dohler; ***W:*** Donald M. Dohler; ***M:*** Ken Walker.

Alien from L.A. woof! 1987 **(PG)** Awesomely inept comedy about a California girl who unwittingly stumbles onto the famed continent of Atlantis and can't find a yogurt stand. Weakly plotted and acted and filmed. Like, really. **88m/C VHS.** Kathy Ireland, Thom Mathews, Don Michael Paul, Linda Kerridge, William R. Moses, Richard Haines, Janie du Plessis, Russel Savadier, Simon Poland, Locher de Kock, Deep Roy; ***D:*** Albert Pyun; ***W:*** Albert Pyun, Debra Ricci, Regina Davis; ***C:*** Tom Fraser; ***M:*** James Saad.

Alien Fury: Countdown to Invasion 2000 **(PG-13)** Bill Templer (Midkiff) is upset when budget cuts threaten to close his government defense office, which sends probes into space looking for aliens. So he fakes some satellite photos of an alien armada poised to attack Earth from the dark side of the moon. Only, ha ha, the threat turns out to be real. This movie is so lame, you'll hope the aliens do attack and wipe these fools out. **88m/C VHS.** Dale Midkiff, Stephen Tobolowsky, Dondre T. Whitfield, Joanie Laurer, Grace Phillips, Scott Lowell, Paul Schulze, Troy Evans; ***D:*** Rob Hedden; ***W:*** Rob Hedden; ***C:*** John Newby; ***M:*** John Beal, Dennis McCarthy. **TV**

Alien Intruder 1993 **(R)** What happens when an evil demon appears before the soldiers of the future in the guise of a beautiful woman? Futuristic trash B-movie emerges from the depths. **90m/C VHS.** Billy Dee Williams, Tracy Scoggins, Maxwell Caulfield; ***D:*** Ricardo Jacques Gale.

Alien Massacre woof! *Dr. Terror's Gallery of Horrors; Return from the Past; The Blood Suckers; Gallery of Horror* 1967 One of the worst films of all time—five short horror stories about zombies and vampires. Goes by many names—stinks in all of them. **90m/C VHS.** Lon Chaney Jr., John Carradine, Rochelle Hudson, Roger Gentry, Mitch Evans, Joey Benson, Vic McGee; ***D:*** David L. Hewitt; ***W:*** Gary Heacock, David Prentiss; ***C:*** Austin McKinney.

Alien Nation ½ 1988 **(R)** A few hundred thousand alien workers land accidentally on Earth and slowly become part of its society, although widely discriminated against. One of the "newcomers" teams with a surly and bigoted human cop to solve a racially motivated murder. An inconsistent and occasionally transparent script looks at race conflicts and includes some humorous parallels with contemporary American life. Basis for the TV series. Producer Hurd was also the force behind "The Terminator" and "Aliens." **89m/C VHS, DVD, Wide.** James Caan, Mandy Patinkin, Terence Stamp, Kevyn Major Howard, Peter Jason, Jeff Kober, Leslie Bevis; ***D:*** Graham Baker; ***W:*** Rockne S. O'Bannon; ***C:*** Adam Greenberg; ***M:*** Curt Sobel.

Alien Nation: Dark Horizon ½ 1994 **(PG)** The alien Newcomers have successfully adapted to life on Earth but face continuing dangers when a human-supremacy group develops a virus to wipe them out and an alien infiltrator is plotting to return them to slavery on Tencton. Naturally, it's up to detectives Sykes and Francisco to save the day. Based on the TV series. **90m/C VHS.** Gary (Rand) Graham, Eric Pierpont, Scott Patterson, Terri Treas, Michelle Scarabelli, Lee Bryant, Sean Six, Lauren Woodland, Ron Fassler, Jeff Marcus; ***D:*** Kenneth Johnson; ***W:*** Diane Frolov, Andrew Schneider; ***M:*** David Kurtz.

Alien Predators woof! 1980 **(R)** Three friends encounter a malevolent alien in this dull reworking of the plot of "The Andromeda Strain" with laughable special effects tossed in for those outwitted by the script. **92m/C VHS.** Dennis Christopher, Martin Hewitt, Lynn-Holly Johnson, Luis Prendes; ***D:*** Deran Sarafian.

Alien Prey ½ 1983 **(R)** Two lesbians are making love when they are unexpectedly devoured by a hungry and indiscreet alien. No safe sex there. Graphic sex, violence, and cannibalism abound. Interesting twist to the old eat 'em and leave 'em genre. **85m/C VHS.** Barry Stokes, Sally Faulkner; ***D:*** Norman J. Warren.

Alien Private Eye *Alien P.I* 1987 An extraterrestrial detective searches Los Angeles for a missing magic disk while investigating an intergalactic crime ring. **90m/C VHS.** Nikki Fastinetti; ***D:*** Nik Rubenfeld.

Alien: Resurrection 1997 **(R)** Despite her fiery end in the last film, Ripley is brought back, through cloning, by a team of scientist anxious to get their hands on the alien embryo that invaded her. A more buffed and equally strange Ripley (Weaver) results as some of her DNA gets mixed with her alien friend. Injecting new life into the franchise, director Jeunet creates a freaky and macabre journey as the aliens get loose on board the mysterious space craft Auriga and create messy havoc for new alien appetizers including Call (Ryder), who has a personal agenda of her own with Ripley. Ryder may be somewhat out of place, but the humor and energy from the supporting cast, along with the film's dank look raises this one from the bowels of formulaic action/horror. Includes some decent scares with a tense underwater sequence. **108m/C VHS, DVD, Wide.** Sigourney Weaver, Winona Ryder, Ron Perlman, Dominique Pinon, Michael Wincott, Kim Flowers, Leland Orser, Brad Dourif, Dan Hedaya, J.E. Freeman, Raymond Cruz; ***D:*** Jean-Pierre Jeunet; ***W:*** Joss Whedon; ***C:*** Darius Khondji; ***M:*** John (Gianni) Frizzell.

Alien Seed 1989 Aliens kidnap a woman and impregnate her. Estrada is the government scientist hot on her trail. (How far could a woman carrying alien offspring wander?) **88m/C VHS, DVD.** Erik Estrada, Heidi Paine, Steven Blade; ***D:*** Bob James.

Alien Space Avenger ½ *Space Avenger* 1991 A spaceship piloted by four alien convicts crash lands in New York City. Stalked by an intergalatic bounty hunter whose job is to kill them, the aliens attack and hide inside human bodies to avoid discovery. It's a race against time as the preservation of the human race depends on the avenger's ability to seek and destroy the alien invaders. Bland ripoff of "Aliens" is reminiscent of old-time "B" sci-fi flicks, with more gore and violence. Shot with the old 3-strip Technicolor method. **88m/C VHS.** Robert Prichard, Mike McClerie, Charity Staley, Gina Mastrogiacomo, Kick Fairbanks Fogg, Angela Nicholas, Marty Roberts, James Gillis; ***D:*** Richard W. Haines; ***W:*** Richard W. Haines, Linwood Sawyer; ***M:*** Richard Fiocca.

Alien Terminator 1995 **(R)** Scientists experimenting with DNA find themselves creating an organism capable of instant regeneration that also likes to nosh on living flesh. To make matters worse, the scientists are trapped in their lab complex, which happens to be located five miles below Los Alamos. **95m/C VHS.** Maria Ford, Kevin Alber, Rodger Halstead, Cassandra Leigh, Emile Levisetti; ***D:*** Dave Payne.

Alien Visitor *Epsilon* 1995 **(PG-13)** Beautiful alien woman lands on Earth in the Australian outback where she meets a guy and is disappointed in her destination since Earth is considered so backwards. But he manages to show her some things that make Earth life worth living. **92m/C VHS, DVD, Wide.** *AU* Syd Brisbane, Alethea McGrath, Chloe Ferguson, Phoebe Ferguson, Ulli Birve; ***D:*** Rolf de Heer; ***W:*** Rolf de Heer; ***C:*** Tony Clark; ***M:*** Graham Tardiff.

Alien Warrior woof! 1985 **(R)** An extraterrestrial fights a street pimp to save a crime-ridden Earth neighborhood. Low-brain rip-off of Superman. **92m/C VHS.** Brett (Baxter) Clark, Pamela Saunders; ***D:*** Ed(ward) Hunt.

Alienator 1989 **(R)** In the improbable future, an unstoppable android killer is sent after an intergalactic villain. An intentional "Terminator" rip-off. **93m/C VHS.** Jan-Michael Vincent, John Phillip Law, Ross Hagen, Dyana Ortelli, Dawn Wildsmith, P.J. Soles, Teagan Clive, Robert Clarke, Leo Gordon, Robert Quarry, Fox Harris, Hoke Howell, Jay Richardson; ***D:*** Fred Olen Ray.

Aliens ½ *Alien 2* 1986 **(R)** The bitch is back, some 50 years later. Popular sequel to "Alien" amounts to non-stop, ravaging combat in space. Contact with a colony on another planet has mysteriously stopped. Fresh from deep space sleep, Ripley and a slew of pulsar-equipped Marines return to confront the mother alien at her nest, which is also inhabited by a whole bunch of the nasty critters spewing for a fight. Something's gotta give, and the Oscar-winning special effects are especially inventive (and messy) in the alien demise department. Dimension (acting biz talk) is given to our hero Ripley, as she discovers maternal instincts lurking within her space suit while looking after a young girl, the lone survivor of the colony. Tension-filled gore blaster. Followed by "Aliens 3." **138m/C VHS, DVD, Wide.** Sigourney

Weaver, Michael Biehn, Lance Henriksen, Bill Paxton, Paul Reiser, Carrie Henn, Jenette Goldstein, William Hope, Al Matthews, Mark Rolston, Ricco Ross, Colette Hiller; ***D:*** James Cameron; ***W:*** James Cameron, Walter Hill; ***C:*** Adrian Biddle; ***M:*** James Horner. Oscars '86: Sound FX Editing, Visual FX.

Aliens Are Coming 🦴½ **1980** A spaceship crash lands on Earth, and its devious denizens begin invading human bodies. TV movie that's a dull echo of "Invasion of the Body Snatchers." **100m/C VHS.** Tom Mason, Melinda Fee, Max Gail, Eric (Hans Gudegast) Braeden, Matthew Laborteaux; ***D:*** Harvey Hart; ***M:*** William Goldstein.

Aliens from Spaceship Earth 🦴½ **1977** Are strange, celestial forces invading our universe? If they are, is man prepared to defend his planet against threatening aliens of unknown strength? Lame docudrama featuring the Hurdy Gurdy man himself, Donovan. **107m/C VHS.** Donovan, Lynda Day George; ***D:*** Don Como.

Alison's Birthday 🦴🦴 **1979** A teenage girl learns that some of her family and friends are Satan worshipers at a terrifying birthday party. Meanwhile, the ghost of her dad hovers about, asking for more lines. **99m/C VHS.** *AU* Joanne Samuel, Lou Brown, Bunny Brooke; ***D:*** Ian Coughlan.

Alive 🦴🦴½ **1993 (R)** Recounts the true-life survival story of a group of Uruguayan rugby players in 1972. After their plane crashes in the remote, snowy Andes (in a spectacular sequence) they're forced to turn to cannibalism during a 10-week struggle to stay alive. Marshall doesn't focus on the gruesome idea, choosing instead to focus on all aspects of their desperate quest for survival. The special effects are stunning, but other parts of the film are never fully realized, including the final scene. Based on the nonfiction book by Piers Paul Read. **127m/C VHS, Wide.** Ethan Hawke, Vincent Spano, Josh Hamilton, Bruce Ramsay, John Haymes Newton, David Kriegel, Kevin Breznahan, Sam Behrens, Illeana Douglas, Jack Noseworthy, Christian Meoli, Jake Carpenter; ***D:*** Frank Marshall; ***W:*** John Patrick Shanley; ***C:*** Peter James; ***M:*** James Newton Howard; ***Nar:*** John Malkovich.

Alive and Kicking 🦴🦴½ *Indian Summer* **1996 (R)** Tonio (Flemyng) is a handsome, vain ballet dancer with AIDS, who hides his emotions beneath a witty facade and his work. At a club he meets the older, equally driven Jack (Sher), an AIDS counselor, who pursues him. Though they become lovers, Tonio's obsession with his latest (and last) dance role causes a rift between them. Subplot between Tonio and lesbian dancer Millie (Parish) is self-conscious and Tonio's theatrics can become annoying but both Flemyng and Sher do their best in somewhat one-note roles. **100m/C VHS, DVD.** *GB* Jason Flemyng, Anthony Sher, Dorothy Tutin, Anthony (Corlan) Higgins, Diane Parish, Bill Nighy; ***D:*** Nancy Meckler; ***W:*** Martin Sherman; ***C:*** Chris Seager; ***M:*** Peter Salem.

All About Eve 🦴🦴🦴🦴 **1950** One of the wittiest (and most cynical) flicks of all time follows aspiring young actress Eve Harrington (Baxter) as she ingratiates herself with a prominent group of theatre people so she can become a Broadway star without the usual years of work. The not-so-innocent babe becomes secretary to aging star Margo Channing (Davis) and ruthlessly uses everyone in her climb to the top, much to Davis' initial disbelief and eventual displeasure. Satirical, darkly funny view of the theatre world features exceptional work by Davis, Sanders, and Ritter. Based on "The Wisdom of Eve" by Mary Orr. Later staged as the musical "Applause." **138m/B VHS, DVD.** Bette Davis, Anne Baxter, George Sanders, Celeste Holm, Gary Merrill, Thelma Ritter, Marilyn Monroe, Hugh Marlowe, Gregory Ratoff, Eddie Fisher; ***D:*** Joseph L. Mankiewicz; ***W:*** Joseph L. Mankiewicz; ***C:*** Milton Krasner; ***M:*** Alfred Newman. Oscars '50: Costume Des. (B&W), Director (Mankiewicz), Picture, Screenplay, Sound, Support. Actor (Sanders); AFI '98: Top 100; British Acad. '50: Film; Cannes '51: Actress (Davis), Grand Jury Prize; Directors Guild '50: Director (Mankiewicz); Golden Globes '51: Screenplay, Natl. Film Reg. '90;; N.Y. Film Critics '50: Actress (Davis), Director (Mankiewicz), Film.

All About My Mother 🦴🦴🦴 *Todo Sobre Mi Madre* **1999 (R)** Manuela (Roth) is a single mom, emotionally dependent on her 17-year-old son, Esteban (Azorin). After seeing him killed in a car accident, the grief-stricken mom seeks to find Esteban's father—now a transvestite named Lola (Canto)—and meets an old friend, tranvestite prostitute Agrado (San Juan), who offers comfort. Adding to the female roundelay are Huma Rojo (Paredes), Esteban's favorite actress, and Sister Rosa (Cruz), a pregnant nun who runs a shelter. As Manuela encounters each of them, they help give her a renewed sense of hope and the strength to carry on. Spanish with subtitles. **102m/C VHS, DVD, Wide.** *SP* Cecilia (Celia) Roth, Penelope Cruz, Marisa Paredes, Eloy Azorin, Toni Canto, Antonia San Juan, Candela Pena; ***D:*** Pedro Almodovar; ***W:*** Pedro Almodovar; ***C:*** Alfonso Beato; ***M:*** Alberto Iglesias. Oscars '99: Foreign Film; British Acad. '99: Director (Almodovar), Foreign Film; Cannes '99: Director (Almodovar); Cesar '00: Foreign Film; Golden Globes '00: Foreign Film; L.A. Film Critics '99: Foreign Film; N.Y. Film Critics '99: Foreign Film; Broadcast Film Critics '99: Foreign Film.

All About the Benjamins 🦴🦴 **2002 (R)** Cube and Epps re-team (2000's "Next Friday") as bounty hunter Bucum (Ice Cube) and two-bit con Reggie (Epps) who meet mobsters and mayhem in Miami in this hip-hop buddy flick. Bucum, who dreams of opening his own private-eye agency, is sent to track down Reggie, who seeks a lost lottery tickets which gets the mismatched duo mixed up in a diamond heist. As usual, Cube, straight man to Epps' clown, have the usual chemistry and deliver some amusing moments in this light caper comedy, but the director's penchant for gory violence interrupts the otherwise slapstick mood. The two leads would shine if not for being stuck in this nod to "Miami Vice" and Elmore Leonard without the character development and plot. Cube co-wrote with Levy. **98m/C VHS, DVD.** *US* Ice Cube, Mike Epps, Tommy Flanagan, Eva Mendes, Carmen Chaplin, Roger Guenveur Smith, Anthony Michael Hall, Valarie Rae Miller, Lil' Bow Wow; ***D:*** Kevin Bray; ***W:*** Ice Cube, Ronald Lang; ***C:*** Glen McPherson; ***M:*** John Murphy.

All-American Murder 🦴🦴 **1991 (R)** A rebellious young man is enrolled in a typical, all-American college for one last shot at mainstream life. Things start out okay, as he meets an attractive young coed. Hours later, he finds himself accused of her grisly murder. The youth is then given 24 hours to prove his innocence by a canny homicide detective. Average performances highlight this film, which isn't able to rise above the mediocre. **94m/C VHS.** Christopher Walken, Charlie Schlatter, Josie Bissett, Joanna Cassidy, Richard Kind, Woody Watson, J.C. Quinn, Amy Davis; ***D:*** Anson Williams; ***W:*** Barry Sandler.

All Creatures Great and Small 🦴🦴🦴 **1974** Taken from James Herriot's bestselling novels, this is a delightful, quiet drama of a veterinarian's apprentice in rural England. Fine performance by Hopkins. Followed by "All Things Bright and Beautiful" and a popular British TV series. **92m/C VHS, DVD.** *GB* Simon Ward, Anthony Hopkins, Lisa Harrow, Brian Stirner, Freddie Jones, T.P. McKenna; ***D:*** Claude Whatham; ***W:*** Hugh Whitemore; ***C:*** Peter Suschitzsky; ***M:*** Wilfred Josephs.

All Dogs Go to Heaven 🦴🦴 **1989 (G)** Somewhat heavy-handed animated musical (Reynolds sings) about a gangster dog who is killed by his partner in business. On the way to Heaven, he discovers how to get back to Earth to seek his revenge. When he returns to Earth, he is taken in by a little girl and learns about something he missed in life the first time around: Love. Expertly animated, but the plot may not keep the grown-ups engrossed, and the kids may notice its lack of charm. **85m/C VHS, DVD, 8mm.** ***D:*** Don Bluth; ***W:*** Don Bluth, David N. Weiss; ***M:*** Ralph Burns; ***V:*** Burt Reynolds, Judith Barsi, Dom DeLuise, Vic Tayback, Charles Nelson Reilly, Melba Moore, Candy Devine, Loni Anderson.

All Dogs Go to Heaven 2 🦴🦴½ **1995 (G)** Animated musical finds lovable scamp Charlie (Sheen) the dog discovering that the afterlife is not all it's cracked up to be and pining for dysfunction aplenty back on earth. He gets his chance when Gabriel's Horn is stolen and Charlie is assigned to retrieve it. Charlie teams up again with old buddy Itchy (Deluise) as the two come down from Dog Heaven to stop the villainous Carface (Borgnine) and demonic cat Red (Hearn). Along the way, Charlie falls in love with sexy Irish Setter Sasha (Easton), and finds a chance for redemption by helping a little boy in trouble. Animation not outstanding, but should keep the attention of small children. **82m/C VHS, DVD.** ***D:*** Paul Sabella, Larry Leker; ***W:*** Arne Olsen, Kelly Ward, Mark Young; ***M:*** Mark Watters, Barry Mann, Cynthia Weil; ***V:*** Charlie Sheen, Sheena Easton, Ernest Borgnine, Dom DeLuise, George Hearn, Bebe Neuwirth, Hamilton Camp, Wallace Shawn, Bobby DiCicco, Adam Wylie.

All Fall Down 🦴🦴½ **1962** A young man (de Wilde) idolizes his callous older brother (Beatty) until a tragedy forces him to grow up. Saint plays the older woman taken in by the brothers' family, who is seduced and abandoned. When she finds herself pregnant and alone, she commits suicide causing the younger brother, who loved her from afar, to vow to kill his older sibling. A well-acted melodrama. Also available colorized. **111m/B VHS.** Eva Marie Saint, Brandon de Wilde, Warren Beatty, Karl Malden, Angela Lansbury, Constance Ford, Barbara Baxley; ***D:*** John Frankenheimer; ***W:*** William Inge; ***C:*** Lionel Lindon; ***M:*** Alex North.

All God's Children 🦴🦴½ **1980** Drama about the controversial forced busing issue and two families who must face it. Top-notch cast is occasionally mislead by meandering script attempting to stay true to a sensitive issue. **100m/C VHS.** Richard Widmark, Ned Beatty, Ossie Davis, Ruby Dee, Mariclare Costello, George Spell, Trish Van Devere, Ken Swofford; ***D:*** Jerry Thorpe; ***M:*** Billy Goldenberg. **TV**

All I Desire 🦴🦴½ **1953** Estranged wife and mother (Stanwyck) returns to her hometown after fleeing years ago to pursue a stage career. She desires a new beginning with her family, but finds things have changed in her absence. The story examines the will of a strong woman and small town values. Director Sirk disagreed with the happy ending demanded by producers, but the drama is still noteworthy. **80m/B VHS.** Barbara Stanwyck, Richard Carlson, Lyle Bettger, Maureen O'Sullivan; ***D:*** Douglas Sirk; ***W:*** James Gunn, Robert Blees, Carl Guthrie, Gina Kaus; ***M:*** Joseph Gershenson.

All I Wanna Do 🦴🦴½ *The Hairy Bird; Strike!* **1998 (PG-13)** The students of an exclusive, and financially troubled, East Coast girls' school, circa 1963, are vigorously opposed to the merger of their school with a boys' academy. So they decide to stage a protest strike. Rather typical coming of age tale with a notable cast of up-and-comers, Film was briefly released in 1998 at 110 minutes under the title "Strike" and then re-edited and re-released under its current title in 2000. **94m/C VHS, DVD, Wide.** Kirsten Dunst, Gaby Hoffman, Heather Matarazzo, Rachael Leigh Cook, Monica Keena, Merritt Wever, Lynn Redgrave, Vincent Kartheiser, Tom Guiry, Matthew Lawrence, Robert Bockstael; ***D:*** Sarah Kernochan; ***W:*** Sarah Kernochan; ***C:*** Anthony C. "Tony" Jannelli; ***M:*** Graeme Revell.

All I Want for Christmas 🦴🦴 **1991 (G)** Low-budget, sappy holiday tale of a young girl (Birch) who wants to reunite her divorced parents. Determined to fulfill her Christmas wish, Hallie seeks out the Santa Claus at Macy's department store to tell him the one thing she truly wants for Christmas. Birch is charming as are Bacall as her grandmother and Nielsen as Santa but the story is too squishy and bland to be believable. **92m/C VHS.** Thora Birch, Leslie Nielsen, Lauren Bacall, Jamey Sheridan, Harley Jane Kozak, Ethan (Randall) Embry, Kevin Nealon, Andrea Martin; ***D:*** Ron Lieberman; ***W:*** Richard Kramer, Thom Eberhardt, Neal Israel, Gail Parent; ***C:*** Robbie Greenberg; ***M:*** Bruce Broughton.

All in a Night's Work 🦴🦴½ **1961** The founder of a one-man publishing empire is found dead with a smile on his face. His nephew inherits the business and finds himself caught in a series of big and small business misunderstandings. He's also falling in love with the woman he suspects was responsible for his uncle's grin. Nicely paced sex and business comedy with warm performances. **94m/C VHS.** Dean Martin, Shirley MacLaine, Cliff Robertson, Charlie Ruggles; ***D:*** Joseph Anthony; ***W:*** Sidney Sheldon; ***M:*** Andre Previn.

All Mine to Give 🦴🦴½ *The Day They Gave the Babies Away* **1956** Sad saga of a Scottish family of eight who braved frontier hardships, epidemics, and death in the Wisconsin wilderness more than a century ago. Midway through, mom and dad die, leaving the oldest child struggling to keep the family together. A strange, though often effective, combination of pioneer adventures and tearjerking moments that avoids becoming hopelessly soapy due to fine performances. Unless you're pretty weathered, you'll need some hankies. Based on the reminiscences of Dale and Katherine Eunson as detailed in a "Cosmopolitan" magazine article. **102m/C VHS.** Glynis Johns, Cameron Mitchell, Rex Thompson, Patty McCormack, Ernest Truex, Hope Emerson, Alan Hale Jr., Royal Dano, Reta Shaw, Rita Johnson, Ellen Corby, Jon(athan) Provost; ***D:*** Allen Reisner; ***M:*** Max Steiner.

All My Good Countrymen 🦴🦴½ *All Good Citizens* **1968** A lyrical, funny film about the eccentric denizens of a small Moravian village soon after the socialization of Czechoslovakia in 1948. Completed during the Soviet invasion of 1968 and immediately banned. In Czech with English subtitles. **115m/C VHS.** *CZ* Vladimir Mensik, Radoslav Brzobohaty, Pavel Pavlovsky; ***D:*** Vojtech Jasny. Cannes '69: Director (Jasny).

All My Sons 🦴🦴🦴 **1948** Joe Keller (Robinson) is a small-town manufacturer enjoying the profits he made from his WWII contracts. But his family is pulled apart by guilt and shame when son Chris (Lancaster) discovers his father sold defective parts to the military that resulted in loss of life and then covered up the crime. Excellent performances; adapted from the play by Arthur Miller. Remade in 1986 with James Whitmore and Aidan Quinn. **94m/B VHS.** Edward G. Robinson, Burt Lancaster, Mady Christians, Louisa Horton, Howard Duff, Frank Conroy, Arlene Francis, Harry (Henry) Morgan; ***D:*** Irving Reis; ***W:*** Chester Erskine; ***C:*** Russell Metty; ***M:*** Leith Horton.

All My Sons 🦴🦴🦴 **1986** A wealthy family is distraught when their eldest son is listed as missing-in-action during WWII. They must cope with guilt, as well as grief, because the father's business reaped profits from the war. Adapted from the acclaimed Arthur Miller play. **122m/C VHS.** James Whitmore, Aidan Quinn, Joan Allen, Michael Learned; ***D:*** John Power. **TV**

All New Adventures of Laurel and Hardy: For Love or Mummy 🦴🦴½ **1998 (PG)** Stan Laurel (Pinchot) and Oliver Hardy (Sartain) are the equally bumbling nephews of the original comedic duo. The would-be movers are hired to transport an Egyptian mummy to an American museum, where archeologist Leslie (Danford) is the unwitting object of an ancient curse that fortells her marrying the reanimated corpse. **84m/C VHS, DVD.** Bronson Pinchot, Gailard Sartain, F. Murray Abraham, Susan Danford; ***D:*** John R. Cherry III, Larry Harmon.

All Night Long 🦴🦴🦴 **1981 (R)** Offbeat middle-age crisis comedy about a burned-out and recently demoted drugstore executive in L.A. who leaves his wife, takes up with his fourth cousin by marriage, and begins a humorous rebellion, becoming an extremely freelance inventor while joining the drifters, weirdos and thieves of the night. An obscure, sometimes uneven little gem with Hackman in top form and an appealing supporting performance by Streisand. Highlighted by delightful malapropisms and sataric inversion of the usual cliches. **100m/C VHS.**

Gene Hackman, Barbra Streisand, Diane Ladd, Dennis Quaid, Kevin Dobson, William Daniels; *D:* Jean-Claude Tramont; *W:* W.D. Richter; *M:* Ira Newborn.

All of Me ☠☠½ **1984 (PG)** A wealthy woman (Tomlin) dies and her guru accidentally transfers her soul to the right side of her lawyer's body, a modern version of existential hell. Lawyer Martin indulges in some funny slapstick as he discovers that his late client is waging an internal war for control of his body. Flat and cliched at times, but redeemed by the inspired clowning of Martin and witty Martin/Tomlin repartee. Based on the novel "Me Too" by Ed Davis. **93m/C VHS, DVD.** Steve Martin, Lily Tomlin, Victoria Tennant, Madolyn Smith, Richard Libertini, Dana Elcar, Selma Diamond, Jason Bernard, Eric Christmas, Peggy (Margaret) Feury; *D:* Carl Reiner; *W:* Phil Alden Robinson; *C:* Richard H. Kline; *M:* Patrick Williams. N.Y. Film Critics '84: Actor (Martin); Natl. Soc. Film Critics '84: Actor (Martin).

All Over Me ☠☠☠ **1996 (R)** Teen angst/coming of age set in New York's Hell's Kitchen. Ungainly wanna-be guitarist, 15-year-old Claudia-AKA-Claude (Folland), is best friends with flirty blonde Ellen (Subkoff). But their relationship changes when Ellen begins dating the macho older Mark (Hauser) and is soon into sex and drugs, while Claude's sexual quandries lead her to a lesbian bar and an interest in singer Lucy (Hailey). Good performances but a moody and somewhat awkward first feature from Sichel, whose sister wrote the screenplay. **90m/C VHS.** Alison Folland, Tara Subkoff, Cole Hauser, Wilson Cruz, Leisha Hailey, Pat Briggs, Ann Dowd; *D:* Alex Sichel; *W:* Sylvia Sichel; *C:* Joe DeSalvo; *M:* Miki Navazio.

All Over the Guy ☠☠½ **2001 (R)** Writer/director Roos served as executive producer on this film, which re-unites some of the personnel from his hit "The Opposite of Sex." Unfortunately, the quality of that film isn't reproduced here. Eli (writer Bucatinsky adapted from his play) and Tom (Ruccolo) are two gay men who are set up on a blind date by Brett (Goldberg) and Jackie (Alexander). They don't really get along, but they find themselves very attracted to one another. The film then explores the ups and downs of their courtship, as each tries to deal with the baggage from the past which keeps them from succeeding in the present. The problem is it's incredibly unoriginal. There doesn't seem to be any real chemistry between the couple, so whether or not they stay together may become a moot point to some viewers. Some of the performances are good (Goldberg has some good lines), but Ruccolo looks very uncomfortable at times. **95m/C VHS, DVD, Wide.** Dan Bucatinsky, Richard Ruccolo, Adam Goldberg, Sasha Alexander, Doris Roberts, Andrea Martin, Tony Abatemarco, Joanna (Joanna DeVarona) Kerns, Nicolas Surovy, Christina Ricci, Lisa Kudrow; *D:* Julie Davis; *W:* Dan Bucatinsky; *C:* Goran Pavicevic; *M:* Peter Stuart, Andrew Williams.

All Over Town ☠☠½ **1937** Two vaudevillians with a trained seal find themselves involved in a murder when they are kidnapped by a gang of thugs. A lesser Olsen and Johnson comedy with scattered funny moments. **52m/B VHS.** Ole Olsen, Chic Johnson, Mary Howard, Franklin Pangborn, James Finlayson; *D:* James W. Horne; *W:* Jack Townley, Jerome Chodorov.

All Quiet on the Western Front ☠☠☠☠ **1930** Extraordinary and realistic anti-war epic based on the novel by Erich Maria Remarque. Seven patriotic German youths go together from school to the battlefields of WWI. They experience the horrors of war first-hand, stuck in the trenches and facing gradual extermination. Centers on experiences of one of the young men, Paul Baumer, who changes from enthusiastic war endorser to battle-weary veteran in an emotionally exact performance by Ayres. Boasts a gigantic budget (for the time) of $1.25 million, and features more than 2000 extras swarming about battlefields set up on ranchland in California. Relentless anti-war message is emotionally draining and startling with both graphic shots and haunting visual poetry. Extremely controversial in the U.S. and Germany upon release, the original version was 140 minutes long (some versions are available with restored footage) and featured ZaSu Pitts as Ayres mother (later reshot with Mercer replacing her). Remarque, who had fought and been wounded on the Western Front, was eventually forced to leave Germany for the U.S. due to the film's ongoing controversy. **103m/B VHS, DVD.** Lew Ayres, Louis Wolheim, John Wray, Slim Summerville, Russell Gleason, Raymond Griffith, Ben Alexander, Beryl Mercer, Arnold Lucy, William "Billy" Bakewell, Scott Kolk, Owen Davis Jr., Walter Rodgers, Richard Alexander, Harold Goodwin, Pat Collins, Edmund Breese; *D:* Lewis Milestone; *W:* Maxwell Anderson, George Abbott, Del Andrews; *C:* Arthur Edeson, Karl Freund; *M:* David Broeckman. Oscars '30: Director (Milestone), Picture; AFI '98: Top 100, Natl. Film Reg. '90.

All Quiet on the Western Front ☠☠½ **1979** A big-budget TV remake of the 1930 masterpiece starring John Boy. Sensitive German youth Thomas plunges excitedly into WWI and discovers its terror and degradation. Nowhere near the original's quality. **150m/C VHS, DVD.** Richard Thomas, Ernest Borgnine, Donald Pleasence, Patricia Neal; *D:* Delbert Mann; *W:* Paul Monash; *C:* John Coquillon; *M:* Allyn Ferguson. **TV**

All Saint's Day ☠☠ **1998** Tired of his going-nowhere life, Marco (Blatt) recruits four of his screw-up friends to help him rob the Brooklyn fish market where he works. Of course, since they're all losers this doesn't work out as planned. **82m/C VHS, DVD.** Mickey Blatt, Thomas J. La Sorsa, James Patrick McArdle, Mark Love, Christopher Lynn, Anthony Mangano, Ray Garvey, Howard Simon; *D:* Thomas J. La Sorsa; *W:* Thomas J. La Sorsa, Christopher Lynn; *C:* Daniel Marracino.

All Screwed Up ☠☠☠ *All in Place; Nothing in Order* **1974** A group of young immigrants come to Milan and try to adjust to city life; they soon find that everything is in its place, but nothing is in order. Wertmuller in a lighter vein than usual. **104m/C VHS.** *IT* Luigi Diberti, Lina Polito; *D:* Lina Wertmuller; *W:* Lina Wertmuller.

All That Heaven Allows ☠☠☠ **1955** Attractive, wealthy middleaged widow Cary Scott (Wyman) falls for her 15-years-younger gardener, Ron Kirby (Hudson), and becomes the target of small-minded gossips and her disapproving family. Ron's no gigolo or fortune-hunter but societal pressure still gets to Cary and she breaks things off. But loneliness makes her realize what she's missing and she decides to make things up with Ron and forget her critics. Hopeful Sirk romance that still takes some jabs at conformity. **89m/B VHS, DVD, Wide.** Jane Wyman, Rock Hudson, Conrad Nagel, Agnes Moorehead, Virginia Grey, Gloria Talbott, William Reynolds; *D:* Douglas Sirk; *W:* Peggy Fenwick; *C:* Russell Metty; *M:* Frank Skinner, Joseph Gershenson. Natl. Film Reg. '95.

All That Jazz ☠☠☠½ **1979 (R)** Fosse's autobiographical portrait with Scheider fully occupying his best role as the obsessed, pill-popping, chain-smoking choreographer/director dancing simultaneously with love and death. But even while dying, he creates some great dancing. Vivid and imaginative with exact editing, and an eerie footnote to Fosse's similar death almost ten years later. Egocentric and self-indulgent for sure, but that's entertainment. ♫On Broadway; Everything Old is New Again; After You've Gone; There'll Be Some Changes Made; Some of These Days; Bye Bye Love. **120m/C VHS, Wide.** Roy Scheider, Jessica Lange, Ann Reinking, Leland Palmer, Cliff Gorman, Ben Vereen, Erzebet Foldi, John Lithgow, Max Wright, Deborah Geffner, Michael (Lawrence) Tolan, Keith Gordon, David Margulies; *Cameos:* Nicole Fosse; *D:* Bob Fosse; *W:* Bob Fosse, Robert Alan Arthur; *C:* Giuseppe Rotunno; *M:* Ralph Burns. Oscars '79: Art Dir./Set Dec., Costume Des., Film Editing, Orig. Song Score and/or Adapt.; Cannes '80: Film, Natl. Film Reg. '01.

All the Brothers Were Valiant ☠☠½ **1953** Brothers Taylor and Granger are New England whaling captains but Granger decides to treasure hunt instead. He finds a priceless cache of black pearls on an island but angers the locals who regard the gems as sacred. When Taylor rescues him, Granger promptly turns his brother's crew into mutineers in order to return to the island and retrieve his prize. Lots of brawling and there's an incidental love story with Blyth desired by both men (she's married Taylor and just happens to be aboard). Last role for Stone. Based on the novel by Ben Ames Williams. **101m/C VHS.** Robert Taylor, Stewart Granger, Ann Blyth, Betta St. John, Keenan Wynn, James Whitmore, Kurt Kasznar, Lewis Stone, Robert Burton, Peter Whitney, John Lupton, Billie Dove; *D:* Richard Thorpe; *W:* Harry Brown; *C:* George J. Folsey; *M:* Miklos Rozsa.

All the Kind Strangers ☠☠ *Evil in the Swamp* **1974** Traveling photographer Keach picks up a young hitchhiker and takes him to the boy's home. He discovers six other children there who want him as a father, his alternative being death. He and "Mother" Eggar plot their escape from the dangerous orphans. Thriller short on suspense. **72m/C VHS.** Stacy Keach, Robby Benson, John Savage, Samantha Eggar; *D:* Burt Kennedy. **TV**

All the King's Men ☠☠☠☠ **1949** Grim and graphic classic set in the Depression follows the rise of a Louisiana farm-boy from angry and honest political hopeful to powerful but corrupt governor. Loosely based on the life (and death) of Huey Long and told by a newsman who's followed his career (Ireland). Willy Stark (Crawford, in his break-through role) is the politician who, while appearing to improve the state, rules dictatorially, betraying friends and constituents and proving once again that power corrupts. In her first major role, McCambridge delivers a powerful performance as the cunning political aide. Potent morality play based on the Robert Penn Warren book. **109m/B VHS, DVD.** Broderick Crawford, Mercedes McCambridge, John Ireland, Joanne Dru, John Derek, Anne Seymour, Shepperd Strudwick; *D:* Robert Rossen; *W:* Robert Rossen; *C:* Burnett Guffey; *M:* Louis Gruenberg. Oscars '49: Actor (Crawford), Picture, Support. Actress (McCambridge); Golden Globes '50: Actor—Drama (Crawford), Director (Rossen), Film—Drama, Support. Actress (McCambridge), Natl. Film Reg. '01;; N.Y. Film Critics '49: Actor (Crawford), Film.

All the King's Men ☠☠½ **1999** In 1915, Frank Beck (Jason), the manager of the royal estate of Sandringham, trains a company of servants to be volunteer soldiers. Unfortunately, the raw recruits are posted to the disaster of Gallipoli and a battle against the Turks. The true fate of the company was unknown for many years and their disappearance became the stuff of myth (recent discoveries proved much grimmer) but the storyline is muddled and it's not easy to distinguish one youthful character from another (although the veterans do a notable job). Based on the novel by Nigel McCrery. **110m/C VHS.** *GB* David Jason, Maggie Smith, Stuart Bunce, William Ash, James Murray, Sonya Walger, Eamon Boland, David Troughton, Emma Cunniffe, Adam Kotz, Patrick Malahide, Ed Waters, Tom Burke, Ben Crompton, Jo Stone-Fewings, James Hillier, Ian McDiarmid, Phyllis Logan; *D:* Julian Jarrold; *W:* Alma Cullen; *C:* David Odd; *M:* Adrian Johnston. **TV**

All the Little Animals ☠☠½ **1998 (R)** Twenty-four-year old Bobby (Bale) is brain damaged from a childhood accident. After his mother's death, he's left in the less-than-tender care of his malevolent stepfather, De Winter (Benzali), who's only interested in Bobby's inheritance. So Bobby runs away and is taken in by hermit, Mr. Summers (Hurt), who is devoted to burying the remains of animals killed in road accidents. But Bobby's idyll cannot last when his stepfather finds him—and Mr. Summers is also not quite what he seems. Based on the novel by Walker Hamilton. **104m/C VHS.** *GB* John Hurt, Christian Bale, Daniel Benzali, James Faulkner, Amy Robbins; *D:* Jeremy Thomas; *W:* Eski Thomas; *C:* Mike Molloy; *M:* Richard Hartley.

All the Lovin' Kinfolk ☠ *Kin Folk; Kinfolk; The Closest of Kin* **1970 (R)** Two recent Hillbilly High graduates decide to take on the big city, but find themselves in dire situations. For those with time to kill. **80m/C VHS.** Mady Maguire, Jay Scott, Anne Ryan, John Denis, Donna Young, Marland Proctor, Uschi Digart; *D:* John Hayes; *W:* John Hayes.

...All the Marbles ☠☠ *The California Dolls* **1981 (R)** A manager of two beautiful lady wrestlers has dreams of going to the top. Aldrich's last film, and an atypical one, with awkward pacing and a thin veil of sex exploitation. Falk provides needed grace and humor as the seedy manager, with Young contributing his usual competent bit as a hustling promoter dabbling in criminal activity. One of the few tag-team women wrestling pictures, it builds to a rousing finale match in the "Rocky" tradition, although the shift in tone and mounting cliches effectively body slam the intent. **113m/C VHS.** Peter Falk, Burt Young, Vicki Frederick, Richard Jaeckel; *D:* Robert Aldrich; *C:* Joseph Biroc.

All the President's Men ☠☠☠½ **1976 (PG)** True story of the Watergate break-in that led to the political scandal of the decade, based on the best-selling book by Washington Post reporters Bob Woodward and Carl Bernstein. Intriguing, terse thriller is a nail-biter even though the ending is no secret. Expertly paced by Pakula with standout performances by Hoffman and Redford as the reporters who slowly uncover and connect the seemingly isolated facts that ultimately lead to criminal indictments of the Nixon Administration. Deep Throat Holbrook and Robards as executive editor Ben Bradlee lend authenticity to the endeavor, a realistic portrayal of the stop and go of journalistic investigations. **135m/C VHS, DVD, Wide.** Dominic Chianese, David Arkin, Polly Holliday, James Karen, Robert Redford, Dustin Hoffman, Jason Robards Jr., Martin Balsam, Jane Alexander, Hal Holbrook, F. Murray Abraham, Stephen Collins, Lindsay Crouse, Meredith Baxter, Ned Beatty, Penny Fuller; *D:* Alan J. Pakula; *W:* William Goldman; *C:* Gordon Willis; *M:* David Shire. Oscars '76: Adapt. Screenplay, Art Dir./Set Dec., Sound, Support. Actor (Robards); Natl. Bd. of Review '76: Director (Pakula), Support. Actor (Robards); N.Y. Film Critics '76: Director (Pakula), Film, Support. Actor (Robards); Natl. Soc. Film Critics '76: Film, Support. Actor (Robards); Writers Guild '76: Adapt. Screenplay.

All the Pretty Horses ☠☠ **2000 (PG-13)** John Grady Cole (Damon) is a dispossessed Texas cowboy in the late 1940s who, along with his buddy Lacey Rawlins (Thomas) and teen misfit Blevins (Black), crosses the border for, he hopes, a better life in Mexico. What he finds is an ill-fated romance with the beautiful daughter (Cruz) of a possessive rancher (Blades). It's pretty, all right. But thanks to Thornton's uneven pacing and inability to settle on a visual style, the story, and splendor, of the book is lost somewhere along the way. Of the young (and also pretty) cast, Damon and especially Black fare the best. Based on the first book of Cormac McCarthy's Border Trilogy. **117m/C VHS, DVD, Wide.** Matt Damon, Penelope Cruz, Ruben Blades, Lucas Black, Henry Thomas, Robert Patrick, Julio Mechoso, Miriam Colon, Bruce Dern, Sam Shepard; *D:* Billy Bob Thornton; *W:* Ted Tally; *C:* Barry Markowitz; *M:* Marty Stuart. Natl. Bd. of Review '00: Screenplay.

All the Right Moves ☠☠½ **1983 (R)** Cruise is the high school football hero hoping for a scholarship so he can vacate pronto the dying Pennsylvania mill town where he grew up. At least he thinks that's what he wants to do. Further mixing up his own mixed feelings are his pushy, ambitious coach (Nelson, doing what he does best), his understanding dad (Cioffi) and supportive girlfriend (Thompson, in a notable early role). Strong performances push the relatively cliched melodrama into field goal range. Cinematographer Chapman's directorial debut. **90m/C VHS, DVD, Wide.** Tom Cruise, Lea Thompson, Craig T. Nelson, Christopher Penn, Charles Cioffi, Paul Carafotes, Dick Miller; *D:* Michael Chapman; *W:* Michael Kane; *C:* Jan De Bont; *M:* David (Richard) Campbell.

All the Rivers Run **1984** First made-for-cable miniseries. A young Australian girl spends her inheritance on a river boat and becomes the first female river captain in Australian history. Directed by George Miller of "Man from Snowy River" fame. **400m/C VHS.** *AU* Sigrid Thornton, John Waters, Diane Craig, Charles Tingwell, Gus Mercurio; ***D:*** George Miller, Pino Amenta; ***C:*** David Connell. **CABLE**

All the Vermeers in New York 🦴🦴🦴½ **1991** A stressed-out Wall Street broker flees to the soothing recesses of the Metropolitan Museum's Vermeer Room. There he meets a beautiful, manipulative French actress dreaming of success in Manhattan. Amidst the opulent art world of New York, the two pursue their relationship to an ultimately tragic end. Jost offers an inside look at the collision of commerce and art and the corrupt underside of New York in this elegant contemporary film. **87m/C VHS, Wide.** Emmanuelle Chaulet, Stephen Lack, Grace Phillips, Katherine Bean, Laurel Lee Kiefer, Gracie Mansion, Gordon Joseph Weiss, Roger Ruffin; ***D:*** Jon Jost; ***W:*** Jon Jost.

All the Way, Boys 🦴½ **1973 (PG)** Two inept adventurers crash-land a plane in the Andes in the hope of discovering slapstick, but find none. "Trinity" cast up to no good. **105m/C VHS.** *IT* Terence Hill, Bud Spencer, Cyril Cusack, Michel Antoine; ***D:*** Giuseppe Colizzi.

All the Young Men 🦴🦴🦴 **1960** Fairly powerful men-uniting-in-battle story with an interesting cast, highlighted by Poitier in an early role. A tiny marine squadron overrun by the Chinese in the Korean War attempts to resist the numerous attackers. In their spare time, the men confront racial prejudice when a black man (guess who) takes command. **86m/B VHS.** Alan Ladd, Sidney Poitier, James Darren, Glenn Corbett, Mort Sahl, Ana St. Clair, Paul (E.) Richards, Richard (Dick) Davalos, Lee Kinsolving, Joseph (Joe) Gallison, Paul Baxley, Charles Quinlivan, Michael Davis; ***D:*** Hall Bartlett; ***W:*** Hall Bartlett; ***C:*** Daniel F. Fapp; ***M:*** George Duning.

All Things Fair 🦴🦴½ *Lust och Fagring Stor; Love Lessons; Laererinden* **1995** Coming of age story set in neutral Sweden in 1943. Fifteen-year-old Stig (Widerberg, the director's son) has just arrived in Malmo to begin classes at his all-male school—a situation filled with sexual curiosity and repression. Stig is attracted to his beautiful teacher Viola (Lagercrantz), whose marriage to alcoholic traveling salesman Frank (von Bromssen) is less than ideal, and the duo begin an affair. Frank not only seems not to care but befriends his wife's youthful lover, although the situation is ripe for tragedy. Excellent performances, sensual air, though somewhat lacking in logical narrative. Swedish with subtitles. **128m/C VHS.** *DK SW* Johan Widerberg, Marika Lagercrantz, Tomas von Bromssen, Bjorn Kjellman, Charles A. Palmer; ***D:*** Bo Widerberg; ***W:*** Bo Widerberg; ***C:*** Morten Bruus.

All This and Heaven Too 🦴🦴🦴 **1940** When a governess arrives at a Parisian aristocrat's home in the 1840s, she causes jealous tension between the husband and his wife. The wife is soon found murdered. Based on Rachel Field's best-seller. **141m/B VHS.** Charles Boyer, Bette Davis, Barbara O'Neil, Virginia Weidler, Jeffrey Lynn, Helen Westley, Henry Daniell, Harry Davenport, June Lockhart, Montagu Love; ***D:*** Anatole Litvak; ***M:*** Max Steiner.

All Through the Night 🦴🦴🦴 **1942** A very funny spy spoof as well as a thrilling crime story with Bogart playing a gambler who takes on a Nazi spy ring. Features memorable double-talk and a great auction scene that inspired the one with Cary Grant in "North by Northwest." Suspense builds throughout the film as Lorre appears in a sinister role as Pepi and Veidt gives a fine performance as the spymaster. **107m/B VHS.** Humphrey Bogart, Conrad Veidt, Karen Verne, Jane Darwell, Frank McHugh, Peter Lorre, Judith Anderson, William Demarest, Jackie Gleason, Phil Silvers, Barton MacLane, Martin Kosleck, Wallace Ford; ***D:*** Vincent Sherman; ***C:*** Sid Hickox; ***M:*** Adolph Deutsch.

All Tied Up 🦴🦴½ **1992 (R)** Ladies man Brian (Galligan) thinks he's found true love with Linda (Hatcher) but that doesn't mean he's stopped seeing other women. And when Linda finds out, she breaks it off. So Brian goes over to her house to work things out and gets tied up—literally—by Linda and her girlfriends. Talk about teaching a guy a lesson. **90m/C VHS.** Zach Galligan, Teri Hatcher, Tracy Griffith, Lara Harris; ***D:*** John Mark Robinson; ***W:*** Robert Madero, I. Markie Lane; ***M:*** Bernardo Bonazzi.

All You Need Is Cash 🦴🦴🦴 *The Rutles* **1978** "The Rutles" star in this parody of The Beatles' legend, from the early days of the "Pre-Fab Four" in Liverpool to their worldwide success. A marvelous pseudo-documentary, originally shown on NBC-TV and with various SNL alumni, which captures the development of the Beatles and '60s rock with devastating effect. Served as the inspiration for "This Is Spinal Tap." **70m/C VHS.** *GB* Eric Idle, Neil Innes, Ricky Fataar, Dan Aykroyd, Gilda Radner, John Belushi, George Harrison, Paul Simon, Mick Jagger, John Halsey, Michael Palin, Bianca Jagger, Bill Murray, Gwen Taylor, Ron Wood, Jeannette Charles, Al Franken, Lorne Michaels, Tom Davis; ***D:*** Gary Weis, Eric Idle; ***W:*** Eric Idle; ***C:*** Gary Weis; ***M:*** Neil Innes. **TV**

Allan Quatermain and the Lost City of Gold 🦴½ **1986 (PG)** While trying to find his brother, Quatermain discovers a lost African civilization, in this weak adaptation of an H. Rider Haggard adventure. An ostensible sequel to the equally shallow "King Solomon's Mines." **100m/C VHS.** Richard Chamberlain, Sharon Stone, James Earl Jones; ***D:*** Gary Nelson; ***W:*** Gene Quintano, Lee Reynolds; ***C:*** Frederick Elmes.

Allegheny Uprising 🦴🦴½ *The First Rebel* **1939** Set in 1759, the story of a frontiersman who clashes with a British military commander in order to stop the sale of firearms to Indians. The stars of "Stagecoach" are back on board in this lesser effort. Also available colorized. **81m/B VHS.** John Wayne, Claire Trevor, George Sanders, Brian Donlevy, Chill Wills, Moroni Olsen; ***D:*** William A. Seiter.

Allegro Non Troppo 🦴🦴🦴 **1976 (PG)** An energetic and bold collection of animated skits set to classical music in this Italian version of Disney's "Fantasia." Watch for the evolution of life set to Ravel's Bolero, or better yet, watch the whole darn movie. Features Nichetti (often referred to as the Italian Woody Allen, particularly by people in Italy) in the non-animated segments, who went on to write, direct, and star (he may have sold concessions in the lobby as well) in "The Icicle Thief." **75m/C VHS.** *IT* Maurizio Nichetti, Nestor Garay, Maria Giovannini; ***D:*** Bruno Bozzetto; ***W:*** Bruno Bozzetto, Guido Manuli, Maurizio Nichetti; ***C:*** Mario Masini.

Alley Cat 🦴 **1984 (R)** Woman uses martial arts to fight back against a street gang that attacked her. **82m/C VHS.** Karin Mani, Robert Torti, Brit Helfer, Michael Wayne, Jon Greene; ***D:*** Edward Victor.

The Alley Cats 🦴🦴 **1965** Leslie, a part of Berlin's swinging '60s set, is being ignored by fiance Logan in favor of his affair with her friend Agnes. So Leslie decides to retaliate by having an affair with a painter, Christian, but since Leslie just can't stand to be alone, when Christian is called away on business, she succumbs to the charms of socialite Irena. **83m/B VHS, DVD.** Anna Arthur, Sabrina Koch, Karin (Karen) Field, Chaz Hickman, Harold Baerow, Uta Levka; ***D:*** Radley Metzger; ***W:*** Radley Metzger.

Alley Cats Strike 🦴🦴½ **2000** Four teen misfits have an interest in bowling that makes them outcasts among their hipper classmates. But then their skills could win them a major trophy and school glory. **88m/C VHS.** Robert Ri'chard, Kyler Schmid, Kaley Cuoco, Mimi Paley, Daphne Maxwell; ***D:*** Rod Daniel. **CABLE**

Alligator 🦴🦴🦴 **1980 (R)** Dumped down a toilet 12 long years ago, lonely alligator Ramon resides in the city sewers, quietly eating and sleeping. In addition to feasting on the occasional stray human, Ramon devours the animal remains of a chemical plant's experiment involving growth hormones and eventually begins to swell at an enormous rate. Nothing seems to satisfy Ramon's ever-widening appetite: not all the people or all the buildings in the whole town, but he keeps trying, much to the regret of the guilt-ridden cop and lovely scientist who get to know each other while trying to nab the gator. Mediocre special effects are only a distraction in this witty eco-monster take. **94m/C VHS.** Robert Forster, Robin Riker, Jack Carter, Henry Silva, Dean Jagger, Michael V. Gazzo, Perry Lang, Bart Braverman, Angel Tompkins, Sue Lyon, Sydney Lassick, James Ingersoll, John Lisbon Wood, Robert Doyle, Patti Jerome; ***D:*** Lewis Teague; ***W:*** John Sayles, Frank Ray Perilli; ***C:*** Joseph Mangine; ***M:*** Craig Hundley.

Alligator 2: The Mutation 🦴🦴 **1990 (PG-13)** Not a sequel to 1980's surprisingly good "Alligator," but a bland rehash with a decent cast. Once again a toxic alligator grows to enormous size and menaces a community. A Donald-Trump-like villain and pro wrestlers (!) bring this up to date, but it's all on the level of a TV disaster movie; even the PG-13 rating is a bit too harsh. **92m/C VHS.** Steve Railsback, Dee Wallace Stone, Joseph Bologna, Woody Brown, Bill Daily, Brock Peters, Richard Lynch, Holly Gagnier; ***D:*** Jon Hess; ***W:*** Curt Allen; ***C:*** Joseph Mangine.

Alligator Alley 🦴 **1972** When two young divers witness a major drug deal, they become entangled in a web of danger they never expected. **92m/C VHS.** Steve Alaimo, John Davis Chandler, Willie Pastrano, Jeremy Slate, Cece Stone; ***D:*** William Grefe.

Alligator Eyes 🦴🦴½ **1990 (R)** Stranger wearing trouble like a cheap perfume enters the midst of a vacationing trio of New Yorkers. Their vulnerabilities are exposed by a young hitchhiker sporting a slinky polka dot ensemble and way cool sunglasses who insinuates herself into their vacation plans (not to mention their private lives), before the three realize she's blind and full of manipulative and vindictive tricks, thanks to the usual brutal childhood. Psycho-sexo-logical thriller has some fine performances and a promising beginning, before fizzling into celluloid cotton candy. **101m/C VHS.** Annabelle Larsen, Roger Kabler, Mary McLain, Allen McCullough, John MacKay; ***D:*** John Feldman; ***W:*** John Feldman; ***M:*** Sheila Silver.

The Allnighter 🦴 **1987 (PG-13)** A college coed searches through the hyper-sexed beach-party milieu of her senior year for Mr. Right. Bangle Hoffs is directed by her mom, to no avail. **95m/C VHS, DVD.** Susanna Hoffs, John Terlesky, Joan Cusack, Michael Ontkean; ***D:*** Tamar Simon Hoffs; ***W:*** Tamar Simon Hoffs; ***C:*** Joseph D. Urbanczyk; ***M:*** Charles Bernstein.

Allonsanfan 🦴🦴🦴½ **1973** Early Taviani, in which a disillusioned Jacobin aristocrat in 1816, after Napoleon has fallen, struggles with his revolutionary ideals and his accustomed lifestyle. Exciting score. In Italian with English subtitles. **115m/C VHS.** *IT* Marcello Mastroianni, Laura Betti, Renato de Carmine, Lea Massari, Mimsy Farmer, Claudio Cassinelli, Bruno Cirino, Michael Berger; ***D:*** Paolo Taviani, Vittorio Taviani; ***W:*** Paolo Taviani, Vittorio Taviani; ***C:*** Giuseppe Ruzzolini; ***M:*** Ennio Morricone.

All's Fair 🦴 **1989** Silly and predictable comedy about executives who take on their spouses at weekend war games. An unfortunate waste of a good cast. **89m/C VHS.** George Segal, Sally Kellerman, Robert Carradine, Jennifer Edwards, Jane Kaczmarek, John Kapelos, Lou Ferrigno; ***D:*** Rocky Lane; ***C:*** Peter Collister.

Almanac of Fall 🦴🦴 **19??** Set in a claustrophobic apartment, where the occupants reveal all their deepest hostilities, fears, and obsessions. In Hungarian with English subtitles. **119m/C VHS.** *HU* Hedi Temessy, Erika Bodnar, Miklos B. Szekely, Pal Hetenyi, Janos Derzsi; ***D:*** Bela Tarr; ***W:*** Bela Tarr.

...Almost 🦴🦴 *Wendy Cracked a Walnut* **1990 (PG)** Arquette plays a curiously giddy bookworm with a vivid imagination. When her husband disappears on their anniversary, the man of her dreams shows up to sweep her off her feet. Is he real or is he simply another daydream? Almost a good time. **87m/C VHS.** *AU* Rosanna Arquette, Bruce Spence; ***D:*** Michael Pattinson.

Almost an Angel 🦴½ **1990 (PG)** Another in a recent spat of angels and ghosts assigned back to earth by the head office. A life-long criminal (Hogan) commits a heroic act and finds himself a probationary angel returned to earth to gain permanent angel status. He befriends a wheelchair-bound man, falls in love with the guy's sister, and helps her out at a center for potential juvenile delinquents. Melodramatic and hokey in places, relying too much on Hogan's crocodilian charisma. **98m/C VHS.** Paul Hogan, Linda Kozlowski, Elias Koteas, Doreen Lang, Charlton Heston; ***D:*** John Cornell; ***W:*** Paul Hogan; ***C:*** Russell Boyd.

Almost Angels 🦴🦴 **1962** Two boys romp in Austria as members of the Vienna Boys Choir. Lesser sentimental Disney effort that stars the actual members of the Choir; not much of a draw for today's Nintendo-jaded young viewers. **85m/C VHS.** Vincent Winter, Peter Weck, Hans Holt; ***D:*** Steve Previn.

Almost Blue 🦴½ **1993 (R)** A gigantic, slow-moving, movie cliche. Madsen is a sulky, hard-living sax player going off the deep end because of his wife's death. Walden is the good woman who comes along to save him from himself. Tenor saxman Ernie Watts doubles for Madsen. Do yourself a favor—skip the movie and listen to some good jazz instead. **98m/C VHS.** Michael Madsen, Lynette Walden, Garrett Morris, Gale Mayron, Yaphet Kotto; ***D:*** Keoni Waxman.

Almost Dead 🦴🦴½ **1994** Psychiatrist Katherine Roshak's (Doherty) mother committed suicide four years ago and suddenly her corpse is appearing to Katherine. When she visits Mom's grave, Katherine finds an empty coffin. So she teams up with a skeptical cop (Mandylor) to figure out what's going on. Lots of loose ends. Based on the novel "Resurrection" by William Valtos. **92m/C VHS.** Shannen Doherty, Costas Mandylor, John Diehl, William R. Moses; ***D:*** Ruben Preuss; ***W:*** Miguel Tejada-Flores; ***C:*** Zoran Hochstatter.

Almost Famous 🦴🦴🦴 **2000 (R)** Fifteen-year-old budding rock critic William Miller's (Fugit) dream comes true after he bluffs his way into a Rolling Stone writing assignment covering a rising '70s rock band on tour. This ode to the music and youth culture of that decade may lack grit, but its sympathetic treatment of young Miller's coming-of-age amid groupies, drugs, rock and roll, and a worried, undupable mother (McDormand) achieves director Crowe's ends. The film's adoration of the music's energy and emotion appear to be the headliner here, but it never outperforms its devotion to character and relationship. Delicate performances by first-timer Fugit, and by Hudson as the more-than-a-groupie groupie, plus a memorable portrayal of the wise and slightly surly critic Lester Bangs by Hoffman. Based on Crowe's own experiences. **202m/C VHS, DVD, Wide.** Patrick Fugit, Philip Seymour Hoffman, Frances McDormand, Jason Lee, Billy Crudup, Kate Hudson, John Fedevich, Mark Kozelek, Fairuza Balk, Bijou Phillips, Anna Paquin, Noah Taylor, Jimmy Fallon, Zooey Deschanel, Liz Stauber, Eion Bailey, Mark Pellington, Terry Chen, Peter Frampton, Zack (Zach) Ward; ***Cameos:*** Jann Wenner; ***D:*** Cameron Crowe; ***W:*** Cameron Crowe; ***C:*** John Toll; ***M:*** Nancy Wilson. Oscars '00: Orig. Screenplay; Golden Globes '01: Film—Mus./Comedy, Support. Actress (Hudson); L.A. Film Critics '00: Actor (Douglas), Support. Actress (McDormand); Broadcast Film Critics '00: Orig. Screenplay, Support. Actress (McDormand).

Almost Heroes 🦴½ *Edwards & Hunt: The First American Road Trip* **1997 (PG-13)** Farley's last screen appearance teams him with Perry as explorers Edwards and Hunt, who are racing Lewis and Clark to the Pacific Ocean in 1804. Edwards (Perry) is a glory-seeking fop who's totally out of his league, Hunt (Farley) is a slovenly, clumsy tracker with a soft spot for toilet (or would that be outhouse?) humor. Along with a team of misfits and losers, the duo wreaks havok on the American frontier. Perry and Farley show some flashes of comic chemistry, but their left to fend for themselves by a script that's lost in the wilderness, sadly relying too much on Farley's patented self-destructive schtick.

87m/C VHS. Chris Farley, Matthew Perry, Eugene Levy, Bokeem Woodbine, Lisa B(arbuscia), Kevin Dunn, Hamilton Camp, Lewis Arquette; ***D:*** Christopher Guest; ***W:*** Tom Wolfe, Mark Nutter, Boyd Hale; ***C:*** Adam Kimmel, Kenneth Macmillan; ***M:*** C.J. Vanston; ***V:*** Harry Shearer.

Almost Human woof! *The Kidnap of Mary Lou* **1979 (R)** An Italian Mafia gorefest about a second-class don who kidnaps a businessman's daughter, and then has trouble trying to collect a ransom. For aficionados of Italian Mafia gorefests only (check your weapons at the door). **90m/C VHS.** *IT* Henry Silva, Tomas Milian, Laura Belli; ***D:*** Umberto Lenzi; ***M:*** Ennio Morricone.

Almost Partners **1987** Grandpa's ashes are in trouble. His urn and remains have been stolen. Fortunately, his teenage granddaughter and a detective are on the case. From the PBS "Wonderworks" series. **58m/C VHS.** Paul Sorvino, Royana Black, Mary Wickes; ***D:*** Alan Kingsberg. **TV**

An Almost Perfect Affair 🦴🦴 **1979 (PG)** Taxing romantic comedy about an ambitious independent American filmmaker who, after finishing a movie about an executed murderer, travels to the Cannes festival and proceeds to fall in love or lust with the wife of an Italian producer. Numerous inside jokes and capable performances nearly overcome script lethargy. **92m/C VHS.** Keith Carradine, Monica Vitti, Raf Vallone, Christian de Sica, Dick Anthony Williams; ***D:*** Michael Ritchie; ***W:*** Walter Bernstein; ***M:*** Georges Delerue.

Almost Pregnant 🦴🦴½ **1991 (R)** Linda Anderson (Roberts) desperately wants a baby, but her husband, Charlie (Conaway) is unable to get her pregnant. Dead set against artificial insemination, Linda decides to take a lover. Charlie doesn't want to lose her, so he goes along with her idea. Linda falls in love with the new guy; discovers he's had a vasectomy and takes yet another lover while continuing to see the other two guys. Hilarious complications abound in her outrageous quest for a baby. An unrated version containing explicit scenes is also available. **90m/C VHS.** Tanya Roberts, Jeff Conaway, Joan Severance, Dom DeLuise; ***D:*** Michael DeLuise; ***W:*** Fred Stroppel.

Almost Royal Family 🦴 **1984** All kinds of problems arise when a family inherits an island on the St. Lawrence River embargoed by the United States and Canada. **52m/C VHS.** Sarah Jessica Parker, John Femia.

Almost You 🦴🦴 **1985 (R)** Normal marital conflicts and uncertainties grow exponentially when a wealthy New York City 30-something couple hires a lovely young nurse to help care for the wife after a car accident. An unsentimental marital comedy with a good cast that still misses. **91m/C VHS.** Brooke Adams, Griffin Dunne, Karen Young, Marty Watt, Christine Estabrook, Josh Mostel, Laura Dean, Dana Delany, Miguel Pinero, Joe Silver, Suzzy Roche, Spalding Gray; ***D:*** Adam Brooks; ***M:*** Jonathan Elias.

Aloha, Bobby and Rose 🦴🦴½ **1974 (PG)** A mechanic and his girlfriend in L.A. become accidentally involved in an attempted robbery and murder and go on the run for Mexico, of course. Semi-satisfying drama in the surf, with fine location photography. **90m/C VHS, DVD.** Paul LeMat, Dianne Hull, Robert Carradine, Tim McIntire, Noble Willingham, Leigh French; ***D:*** Floyd Mutrux; ***W:*** Floyd Mutrux; ***C:*** William A. Fraker.

Aloha Summer 🦴🦴 **1988 (PG)** Six surfing teenagers of various ethnic backgrounds learn of love and life in 1959 Hawaii while riding the big wave of impending adulthood, with a splash of Kung Fu thrown in for good measure. Sensitive and bland. **97m/C VHS.** Chris Makepeace, Lorie Griffin, Don Michael Paul, Sho Kosugi, Yuji Okumoto, Tia Carrere; ***D:*** Tommy Lee Wallace; ***W:*** Robert Benedetto.

Alone Against Rome 🦴½ **1962** A muscle-bound warrior takes on the forces of Rome to avenge himself against a scornful woman. **100m/B VHS.** *IT* Lang Jeffries, Rossana Podesta, Phillippe LeRoy; ***D:*** Herbert Wise.

Alone in the Dark 🦴🦴 **1982 (R)** Slash and dash horror attempt featuring four escaped patients from a mental hospital who decide that they must kill their doctor because they don't like him. Conveniently, a city-wide blackout provides the opportunity, as the good doctor defends home and family against the aging stars intent on chewing up as much scenery as possible. **92m/C VHS.** Jack Palance, Donald Pleasence, Martin Landau, Dwight Schultz; ***D:*** Jack Sholder; ***W:*** Jack Sholder.

Alone in the Neon Jungle 🦴🦴 **1987** A glamorous big-city police captain is assigned to clean up the most corrupt precinct in town. Pleshette is untypically cast but still manages to make her role believable in a serviceable TV cop drama with more dialogue than action. **90m/C VHS.** Suzanne Pleshette, Danny Aiello, Georg Stanford Brown, Frank Converse, Joe Morton; ***D:*** Georg Stanford Brown.

Alone in the T-Shirt Zone 🦴 **1986** A maniacal T-shirt designer lands in a mental institution. **81m/C VHS.** Michael Barrack, Taylor Gilbert, Bill Barron; ***D:*** Mikel B. Anderson; ***W:*** Mikel B. Anderson.

Alone in the Woods 🦴🦴 **1995 (PG)** Ten-year-old Justin mistakenly gets into the wrong van while on his way to his family's annual mountain vacation. Turns out the duo in the van are would-be kidnappers after Chelsea Stuart, the daughter of a toy magnate and now Justin must escape and rescue Chelsea. **81m/C VHS.** Brady Bluhm, Chick Vennera, Matthias Hues, Laraine Newman, Daniel McVicar, Krystee Clark; ***D:*** John Putch; ***W:*** J. Riley Lagesen; ***C:*** Frank Johnson; ***M:*** David Lawrence. **VIDEO**

Alone with a Stranger 🦴🦴 **1999 (R)** Long lost Evil Twin (Moses) learns that he has a rich brother. Evil Twin and girlfriend (Peeples) plan to kidnap Good Twin, sell his company, and scoot with the loot. But what about Good Twin's wife (Niven) and family? **90m/C DVD.** William R. Moses, Barbara Niven, Priscilla Barnes, Nia Peeples, Mindy Cohn; ***D:*** Peter Paul Liapis; ***W:*** Peter Paul Liapis, Richard Dana Smith; ***C:*** M. David Mullen; ***M:*** Alan Howarth.

Along Came a Spider 🦴🦴 **2001 (R)** Sequel to 1997's "Kiss the Girls" is actually a prequel storywise but Freeman does reprise his character of Detective Alex Cross. This time he must save a U.S. Senator's daughter who's been kidnapped by a serial killer. Freeman is easily the best thing in this convoluted, plot-deficient, murky mess. He makes every "yeah, right" moment (and there are many) palatable. Based on the novel by James Patterson. **103m/C VHS, DVD.** *US* Morgan Freeman, Monica Potter, Michael Wincott, Penelope Ann Miller, Michael Moriarty, Dylan Baker, Billy Burke, Jay O. Sanders, Kim Hawthorne, Mika Boorem; Anton Yelchin; ***D:*** Lee Tamahori; ***W:*** Marc Moss; ***C:*** Matthew F. Leonetti; ***M:*** Jerry Goldsmith.

Along Came Jones 🦴🦴🦴 **1945** Cowboy Cooper, who can't handle a gun and is saddled with grumpy sidekick Demarest, is the victim of mistaken identity as both the good guys and the bad guys pursue him thinking he is a vicious killer. Young is the woman who rides to his defense. Offbeat and charming western parody based on a novel by Alan le May. **93m/B VHS, DVD.** Gary Cooper, Loretta Young, Dan Duryea, William Demarest; ***D:*** Stuart Heisler; ***W:*** Nunnally Johnson; ***C:*** Milton Krasner; ***M:*** Arthur Lange.

Along for the Ride 🦴½ **2000 (R)** Seriously disturbed Lulu (Griffith) checks herself out of the mental hospital and informs old boyfriend Ben (Swayze) that when she was a teen, she gave birth to their son and put him up for adoption. Somehow she manages to persuade him on a cross-country journey to Wisconsin to meet the now-teenaged kid. Naturally, this idea doesn't sit that well with Ben's wife Claire (Miller) who decides to put a stop to the nonsense. Goopy sentiment. **99m/C VHS, DVD.** Melanie Griffith, Patrick Swayze, Penelope Ann Miller, Joseph Gordon-Levitt, Richard Schiff, Annie Corley, Lee Garlington, Michael J. Pollard, Steven Bauer; ***D:*** John Kaye; ***W:*** John Kaye; ***C:*** Dion Beebe; ***M:*** Serge Colbert.

Along the Great Divide 🦴🦴 **1951** A U.S. marshal and his deputy battle pursuing vigilantes and the untamed frontier to bring a falsely accused murderer to trial (and of course, find the real bad guy). Douglas' first western has the usual horse opera cliches supported by excellent cinematography. **88m/B VHS.** Kirk Douglas, John Agar, Walter Brennan, Virginia Mayo; ***D:*** Raoul Walsh.

Along the Navaho Trail 🦴🦴 **1945** A cattle syndicate is threatening the local ranchers and Roy, aided by a band of gypsies, helps thwart the bad guys. **66m/B VHS.** Roy Rogers, Dale Evans, George "Gabby" Hayes, Douglas Fowley; ***D:*** Frank McDonald; ***W:*** Gerald Geraghty; ***C:*** William Bradford.

Along the Sundown Trail 🦴½ **1942** Standard western escapades as cowboy G-men round up the villains. **59m/B VHS.** William Boyd, Art Davis, Lee Powell, Julie Duncan, Kermit Maynard, Charles "Blackie" King; ***D:*** Sam Newfield.

Alpha Beta 🦴🦴½ **1973** A stage production set to film studying the break-up of a marriage, where all the husband and wife have in common is the children. Finney and Roberts efficiently carry the load. **70m/C VHS.** Albert Finney, Rachel Roberts; ***D:*** Anthony Page.

The Alpha Incident 🦴½ **1976 (PG)** Time-worn doomsday drama about an alien organism with the potential to destroy all living things. Government works hard to cover up. **86m/C VHS.** Ralph Meeker, Stafford Morgan, John Goff, Carol Irene Newell, John Alderman; ***D:*** Bill Rebane.

Alphabet City 🦴🦴 **1984 (R)** A drug kingpin who runs New York's Lower East Side has decided to turn over a new leaf, but first he must survive his last night as a criminal while figuring out a way to pay off his large debts. Very stylish and moody, but light on content and plot. **85m/C VHS.** Vincent Spano, Michael Winslow, Kate Vernon, Jami Gertz, Zohra Lampert, Raymond Serra, Ken Marino, Daniel Jordano, Miguel Pinero; ***D:*** Amos Poe; ***W:*** Amos Poe.

The Alphabet Murders 🦴🦴 *ABC Murders* **1965** Picture this: Randall playing Agatha Christie's famous Belgian sleuth, Hercule Poirot, and Rutherford—in a cameo—as Miss Marple. As if that wouldn't be enough to make Dame Agatha roll over in her grave, there's plenty of cloying wisecracking and slapsticking throughout. An adaptation of "The ABC Murders" in which Poirot stalks a literate killer who snuffs out his victims in alphabetical order. Hardly a must-see, unless you're hellbent on viewing the entire Randall opus. **90m/B VHS.** Tony Randall, Anita Ekberg, Robert Morley, Maurice Denham, Guy Rolfe, Sheila Allen, Margaret Rutherford, Julian Glover; ***D:*** Frank Tashlin.

Alphaville 🦴🦴🦴 *Alphaville, a Strange Case of Lemmy Caution; Alphaville, Une Etrange Aventure de Lemmy Caution* **1965** Engaging and inimitable Godard attempt at science fiction mystery. P.I. Lemmy Caution searches for a scientist in a city (Paris as you've never seen it before) run by robots and overseen by a dictator. The futuristic techno-conformist society must be upended so that Caution may save the scientist as well as nonconformists everywhere. In French with subtitles. **100m/B VHS, DVD.** *FR* Eddie Constantine, Anna Karina, Akim Tamiroff, Howard Vernon, Laszlo Szabo, Michel Delahaye, Jean-Pierre Leaud; ***D:*** Jean-Luc Godard; ***W:*** Jean-Luc Godard; ***C:*** Raoul Coutard; ***M:*** Paul Misraki. Berlin Intl. Film Fest. '65: Golden Berlin Bear.

Alpine Fire 🦴🦴½ **1989 (R)** Coming of age story about an adolescent girl and her deaf-mute brother living an isolated life in the Swiss Alps. When life on the mountain overwhelms them, they turn to each other for love. Sharply observed with a naturalistic style, elevating the proceedings above mere voyeurism. **119m/C VHS.** *SI* Thomas Knock, Johanna Lier, Dorothea Moritz, Rolf Illig; ***D:*** Fredi M. Murer.

Alsino and the Condor 🦴🦴🦴 **1982 (R)** An acclaimed Nicaraguan drama about a young boy, caught in war-torn Nicaragua between the Somoza government and the Sandinista rebels, who dreams of flying above the human strife. In Spanish with English subtitles. **89m/C VHS.** *NI* Dean Stockwell, Alan Esquivel; ***D:*** Miguel Littin; ***W:*** Miguel Littin.

Altered States 🦴🦴🦴 **1980 (R)** Obsessed with the task of discovering the inner man, Hurt's ambitious researcher ignores his family while consuming hallucinogenic drugs and floating in an immersion tank. He gets too deep inside, slipping way back through the evolutionary order and becoming a menace in the process. Confusing script based upon Chayefsky's (alias Sidney Aaron) confusing novel is supported by great special effects and the usual self-indulgent and provocative Russell direction. Chayefsky eventually washed his hands of the project after artistic differences with the producers. Others who departed from the film include initial director William Penn and special effects genius John Dykstra (relieved ably by Bran Ferren). Hurt's a solemn hoot in his first starring role. **103m/C VHS, DVD.** William Hurt, Blair Brown, Bob Balaban, Charles Haid, Dori Brenner, Drew Barrymore, Miguel Godreau, Thaao Penghlis, Peter Brandon, Charles White Eagle, Meghan Jeffers, Jack Murdock, John Larroquette; ***D:*** Ken Russell; ***W:*** Paddy Chayefsky, Sidney Aaron; ***C:*** Jordan Cronenweth; ***M:*** John Corigliano.

Alternative 🦴🦴 **1976** A female magazine editor finds herself unmarried and quite pregnant. She is caught in a tug-of-war between the baby's father and her current lover. Dated liberated woman and career snoozer. **90m/C VHS.** Wendy Hughes, Peter Adams, Mary Mackie, Carla Hoogeveen, Tony Bonner.

Alvarez Kelly 🦴🦴½ **1966** Offbeat western with Holden as the Mexican-Irish Kelly who has just sold a herd of cattle to the North during the Civil War. Confederate officer Widmark kidnaps Holden in an effort to have the cattle redirected to the South. Aided by the traditional women in the midst of men intent on double-crossing each other, a fierce hatred develops between the two, erupting into violence. Sleepy performance by Holden is countered by an intensive Widmark. Based on a true Civil War incident, the script occasionally wanders far afield with the cattle, who cleverly heighten the excitement by stampeding. **109m/C VHS, DVD, Wide.** William Holden, Richard Widmark, Janice Rule, Patrick O'Neal, Harry Carey Jr., Victoria Shaw, Roger C. Carmel; ***D:*** Edward Dmytryk; ***W:*** Elliott Arnold, Franklin Coen; ***C:*** Joe MacDonald; ***M:*** Johnny Green.

Alvin Purple 🦴½ **1973 (R)** Pedestrian comedy about a Mr. Purple, an ordinary Aussie who sells waterbeds and is for some reason constantly being pursued by throngs of sexually insatiable women. Fortunately, he too enjoys sex, even though complications abound. Sexual situations, double entendres, and a script that aims for cleverness (but rarely attains it) somehow made the lust romp a hit in its native Australia, while worldwide it helped establish a market for Down Under cinema. Shot in Melbourne, and followed by "Alvin Rides Again." **97m/C VHS.** *AU* Graeme Blundell, George Whaley, Ellie MacLure, Penne Hackforth-Jones; ***D:*** Tim Burstall; ***W:*** Alan Finney, Alan Hopgood, Tim Burstall.

Alvin Rides Again 🦴🦴 **1974** The sexually insatiable Alvin Purple is asked to impersonate an American gangster who was accidentally killed. Another Aussie sex farce from the original writers, who conspire to create a decent sequel to "Alvin Purple," with much of the same cast and crew. **89m/C VHS.** *AU* Graeme Blundell, Alan Finney, Brionny Behets, Frank Thring Jr., Jeff Ashby, Chantal Contouri; ***D:*** David Bilcock, Robin Copping; ***W:*** Tim Burstall, Alan Hopgood, Alan Finney; ***C:*** Robin Copping.

Always 🦴🦴🦴 **1985 (R)** Jaglom fictionally documents his own divorce and reconciliation with Patrice Townsend: set in the director's home and starring his friends and family, the film provides comic insight into the dynamics of married/about-to-be-married/and used-to-be-married relationships. Set at a Fourth of July barbecue, this bittersweet romantic comedy is a veritable feast for Jaglom fans, but not everyone will find the director's free-form narrative to their taste. **105m/C VHS.** Henry Jaglom, Patrice Townsend, Bob Rafelson, Melissa Leo, Andre Gregory, Michael Emil, Joanna Frank, Alan Rachins, Jonathan Kaufer; *D:* Henry Jaglom; *W:* Henry Jaglom; *C:* Hanania Baer.

Always ♂♂½ **1989 (PG)** A hotshot pilot (Dreyfuss) meets a fiery end and finds that his spirit is destined to become a guardian angel to the greenhorn fire-fighting flyboy (Johnson) who steals his girl's heart. Warm remake of "A Guy Named Joe," one of Spielberg's favorite movies. Sparks between Dreyfuss and Hunter eventually ignite, but Goodman delivers the most heat. Hepburn makes an appearance as the angel who guides Dreyfuss. An old-fashioned tree-burner romance that includes actual footage of the 1988 Yellowstone fire. **123m/C VHS, DVD, Wide.** Holly Hunter, Richard Dreyfuss, John Goodman, Audrey Hepburn, Brad Johnson, Marg Helgenberger, Keith David, Roberts Blossom, Dale Dye; *D:* Steven Spielberg; *W:* Jerry Belson; *C:* Mikael Salomon; *M:* John Williams.

Always Outnumbered Always Outgunned ♂♂♂ **1998 (R)** Character study follows ex-con Socrates Fortlow (Fishburne in a dynamic performance). A convicted murderer, he's now trying to lead a non-violent life on the violent streets of L.A.'s Watts, maintain his dignity, and find a job. But none of this is easy. Adapted from the book by Mosley, who wrote the teleplay. **110m/C VHS.** Laurence "Larry" Fishburne, Bill Cobbs, Natalie Cole, Daniel Williams, Laurie Metcalf, Bill Nunn, Cicely Tyson, Isaiah Washington IV; *D:* Michael Apted; *W:* Walter Mosley; *C:* John Bailey; *M:* Michael Franti. **CABLE**

Amadeus ♂♂♂½ **1984 (PG)** Entertaining adaptation by Shaffer of his play about the intense rivalry between 18th century composers Antonio Salieri and Wolfgang Amadeus Mozart. Abraham's Salieri is a man who desires greatness but is tortured by envy and sorrow. His worst attacks of angst occur when he comes into contact with Hulce's Mozart, an immature, boorish genius who, despite his gifts, remains unaffected and delighted by the beauty he creates while irking the hell out of everyone around him. Terrific period piece filmed on location in Prague; excellent musical score, beautiful sets, nifty billowy costumes, and realistic American accents for the 18th century Europeans. ♫Concert No. 27 for Pianoforte and Orchestra in B Flat Major; Ave Verum Corpus; A Quintet For Strings in E Flat; A Concerto for Clarinet and Orchestra in A Major; Number 39 in E Flat Major; Number 40 in G Minor; Number 41 in C Major. **158m/C VHS, DVD.** F. Murray Abraham, Tom Hulce, Elizabeth Berridge, Simon Callow, Roy Dotrice, Christine Ebersole, Jeffrey Jones, Kenny Baker, Cynthia Nixon, Vincent Schiavelli; *D:* Milos Forman; *W:* Peter Shaffer; *C:* Miroslav Ondricek; *M:* John Strauss. Oscars '84: Actor (Abraham), Adapt. Screenplay, Art Dir./Set Dec., Costume Des., Director (Forman), Makeup, Picture, Sound; AFI '98: Top 100; Cesar '85: Foreign Film; Directors Guild '84: Director (Forman); Golden Globes '85: Actor—Drama (Abraham), Director (Forman), Film—Drama, Screenplay; L.A. Film Critics '84: Director (Forman), Film, Screenplay.

Amanda and the Alien ♂½ **1995 (R)** Dumb saga finds flaky Californian Amanda (Eggert) taking care of a sex-starved, shape-changing extraterrestrial (Meneses) while a couple of feds hunt him down. Based on a story by Robert Silverberg. **94m/C VHS.** Richard Speight Jr., Alex Meneses, Nicole Eggert, Michael Dorn, Stacy Keach, Michael C. Bendetti; *D:* Jon Kroll; *W:* Jon Kroll. **CABLE**

Amarcord ♂♂♂½ *I Remember* **1974 (R)** Semi-autobiograpical Fellini fantasy which takes place in the village of Rimini, his birthplace. Focusing on the young Zanin's impressions of his town's colorful slices of life, Fellini takes aim at fascism, family life, and religion in 1930s Italy. Visually ripe, delivering a generous, occasionally uneven mix of satire, burlesque, drama, and tragicomedic lyricism. Considered by people in the know as one of Fellini's best films and the topic of meaningful discussions among art film students everywhere. **124m/C VHS, DVD.** *IT* Magali Noel, Bruno Zanin, Pupella Maggio, Armando Brancia; *D:* Federico Fellini; *W:* Federico Fellini, Tonino Guerra; *C:* Giuseppe Rotunno; *M:* Nino Rota. Oscars '74: Foreign Film; N.Y. Film Critics '74: Director (Fellini), Film.

Amarilly of Clothesline Alley ♂♂½ **1918** Amarilly (Pickford) gets a job as a New York dance hall cigarette girl and is around to help wealthy slumming playboy Gordon Phillips (Kerry) after he gets into a fight. Phillips becomes convinced he loves Amarilly, despite her social inferiority, but Amarilly comes to realize she should stick with those that know her best, including neighborhood beau, Terry (Scott). **77m/B VHS, DVD.** Mary Pickford, William Scott, Norman Kerry, Ida Waterman, Kate Price, Margaret Landis; *D:* Marshall Neilan; *W:* Frances Marion; *C:* Walter Stradling.

The Amateur ♂½ **1982 (R)** Computer technologist for the CIA dives into a plot of international intrigue behind the Iron Curtain when he investigates the death of his girlfriend, murdered by terrorists. Confused and ultimately disappointing spy drama cursed with a wooden script written by Littell, based on his novel. **112m/C VHS.** John Savage, Christopher Plummer, Marthe Keller, Arthur Hill, Ed Lauter; *D:* Charles Jarrott; *W:* Robert Littell.

Amateur ♂♂♂ **1994 (R)** Former nun Huppert, trying to make a living writing pornography, hooks up with an amnesiac (Donovan) who turns out to have a criminal past and a porno actress wife (Lowensohn) who wants him dead. Blackmail plot has oddball characters racing through dark and evocative settings while unfolding a tale loaded with offbeat oppositions and an irresistibly bizarre romantic triangle. Lively and playful without becoming pretentious, Hartley's self-described "action thriller... with one flat tire" evokes his typical deadpan subtle style. **105m/C VHS.** Isabelle Huppert, Martin Donovan, Elina Lowensohn, Damian Young, Chuck Montgomery, David Simonds, Pamela Stewart, Terry Alexander; *D:* Hal Hartley; *W:* Hal Hartley; *C:* Michael Spiller; *M:* Jeff Taylor, Ned Rifle.

Amateur Night ♂ **1985** Sloppy musical comedy about the backstage bickering occuring during the amateur night at a famous nightclub. **91m/C VHS.** Geoffrey Deuel, Dennis Cole, Allen Kirk.

Amazing Adventure ♂♂ *Romance and Riches; The Amazing Quest of Ernest Bliss; Riches and Romance* **1937** A millionaire wins a bet when he rises from a chauffeur's position to the executive board room without using his wealth. Though not particularly amazing, lightweight English comedy has Grant working hard to charm over and above the demands of the dated formula, a performance he undertook during a vacation from Hollywood. Adapted from a novel by E. Phillips Oppenheim. **63m/C VHS.** Cary Grant, Mary Brian, Henry Kendall, Leon M. Lion, Ralph Richardson; *D:* Alfred Zeisler.

The Amazing Colossal Man ♂♂ **1957** A standard '50s sci-fi film about atomic radiation. Colonel Manning is exposed to massive doses of plutonium when an experiment backfires (literally). The former good-guy grows to 70 feet and starts taking out his anger on a helpless Las Vegas. Can anything stop his murderous rampages? Followed by "War of the Colossal Beast." **79m/B VHS.** Glenn Langan, Cathy Downs, William (Bill) Hudson, James Seay, Russ Bender, Lyn Osborn, Frank Jenks, Hank Patterson; *D:* Bert I. Gordon; *W:* Bert I. Gordon, Mark Hanna; *C:* Joseph Biroc; *M:* Albert Glasser.

The Amazing Dobermans ♂♂ **1976 (G)** Family-oriented pooch performance piece featuring Astaire in one of his lesser roles. Ex-con man Astaire and his five trained Dobermans assist an undercover agent in foiling a small-time criminal's gambling and extortion racket. The last in a series that includes "The Daring Dobermans" and "The Doberman Gang." **96m/C VHS.** Fred Astaire, Barbara Eden, James Franciscus, Jack Carter, Billy Barty, Parley Baer; *D:* Byron Ross Chudnow; *M:* Alan Silvestri.

Amazing Dr. Clitterhouse ♂♂♂ **1938** Satirical gangster saga has criminologist Dr. Clitterhouse (Robinson) so fascinated by crime that he commits a few jewel robberies just to test out that bad guy rush. He contacts a fence, luscious Jo Keller (Trevor), who gets Clitterhouse an in with gangster Rocks Valentine (Bogart). Clitterhouse sucessfully masterminds some heists for Valentine—who becomes jealous of Clitterhouse's brain power and things just get more wacky from there (including a farcical trial). This is definitely Robinson's show. **87m/B VHS.** Edward G. Robinson, Claire Trevor, Humphrey Bogart, Gale Page, Donald Crisp, Maxie "Slapsie" Rosenbloom, Thurston Hall, Allen Jenkins, John Litel, Henry O'Neill, Ward Bond, Curt Bois; *D:* Anatole Litvak; *W:* John Huston, John Wexley; *C:* Gaetano Antonio "Tony" Gaudio; *M:* Max Steiner.

Amazing Grace ♂♂ **1974** Some righteous mothers led by Moms Mabley go up against corrupt city politics in this extremely dated comedy that was cast with a sense of the absurd. **99m/C VHS, DVD, Wide.** Moms (Jackie) Mabley, Slappy (Melvin) White, Moses Gunn, Rosalind Cash, Dolph Sweet, Butterfly McQueen, Stepin Fetchit; *D:* Stan Lathan; *W:* Matt Robinson; *C:* Edward R. Brown, Sol Negrin.

Amazing Grace ♂♂ **1992** Eighteen-year-old Jonathan leaves home to share his friend Mickey's apartment. He meets Thomas, who has just returned to Israel after years in New York, and they begin a tentative relationship. But Thomas is hiding the fact that he may be HIV-positive and tries to keep a distance from the eager Jonathan. Hebrew with subtitles. **95m/C VHS.** *IS* Rivka Michaely, Sharon Alexander, Gal Hoyberger, Hina Rozovska; *D:* Amos Guttman.

Amazing Grace & Chuck ♂♂ **1987 (PG)** Perhaps the only anti-war/sports fantasy ever made. After a visit to a Minuteman missile site in Montana, 12-year-old Little Leaguer Chuck learns of the dangers of nuclear arms. He begins a protest by refusing to play until the nations come to a peace agreement. In a sudden surge of social conscience, athletes worldwide put down their equipment and join in droves, starting with pro-basketball star Amazing Grace Smith (Denver Nugget English). Capra-like fantasy has good intentions but ultimately lacks two key elements: coherency and plausibility. **115m/C VHS.** Jamie Lee Curtis, Gregory Peck, William L. Petersen, Joshua Zuehlke, Alex English; *D:* Mike Newell; *C:* Robert Elswit; *M:* Elmer Bernstein.

The Amazing Howard Hughes ♂♂½ **1977** Reveals the full story of the legendary millionaire's life and career, from daring test pilot to inventor to Hollywood film producer to isolated wealthy paranoiac with a germ phobia. Lingers on the rich guy with big problems theme. Big-budget TV drama with a nice performance by Jones. **119m/C VHS.** Tommy Lee Jones, Ed Flanders, James Hampton, Tovah Feldshuh, Lee Purcell; *D:* William A. Graham. **TV**

The Amazing Mrs. Holiday ♂♂½ **1943** Pleasant Durbin outing finds the star playing the daughter of missionaries working in China. Ruth accompanies a group of Chinese orphans aboard a ship bound for San Francisco, aided by steward Timothy (Fitzgerald). She wants the children to stay together, so Timothy passes Ruth off as the wife of a shipping magnate, who's been lost at sea. Ruth admits her deception to the man's grandson Tom (O'Brien) and convinces him that it's okay that she and the children stay in the family mansion. **98m/B VHS.** Deanna Durbin, Edmond O'Brien, Barry Fitzgerald, Arthur Treacher, Harry Davenport, Grant Mitchell, Frieda Inescort, Elisabeth Risdon; *D:* Bruce Manning; *W:* Frank Ryan, John Jacoby; *C:* Elwood "Woody" Bredell; *M:* Frank Skinner, Hans J. Salter.

Amazing Mr. Blunden ♂♂½ **1972 (G)** Solid kidvid about two youngsters aided by a ghost who travel back in time to save the lives of two murdered children. Adapted by Jeffries from Antonia Barber's novel, "The Ghosts." **100m/C VHS.** Laurence Naismith, Lynne Frederick, Garry Miller, Marc Granger, Rosalyn London, Diana Dors; *D:* Lionel Jeffries; *M:* Elmer Bernstein.

The Amazing Mr. X ♂♂½ *The Spiritualist* **1948** When a woman's husband dies, she tries to contact him via a spiritualist. Things are not as they seem however, and the medium may just be part of an intricate scheme to defraud the woman. **79m/B VHS.** Turhan Bey, Lynn Bari, Cathy O'Donnell, Richard Carlson, Donald Curtis, Virginia Gregg; *D:* Bernard Vorhaus; *W:* Ian McLellan Hunter, Muriel Roy Boulton; *C:* John Alton.

The Amazing Panda Adventure ♂♂½ *Little Panda; The Amazing Panda Rescue* **1995 (PG)** Ryan (Slater) is off to China during his spring break to visit dad Michael (Lang), who's working on a project to rescue the dwindling panda population. But there's poacher trouble and Ryan and young translator Ling (Ding) decide to rescue the preserve's panda cub, which has been animal-napped (where's Ace Ventura when you need him). Family fare, with a mixture of totally adorable real and animatronic pandas; filmed in the Sichuan province of China, home to the Wolong Nature Reserve which is famous for its successful breeding of the endangered giant pandas. Slater, in his first starring role, is the younger brother of Christian. **84m/C VHS.** Ryan Slater, Stephen Lang, Yi Ding, Wang Fei; *D:* Christopher Cain; *W:* Laurice Elehwany, Jeff Rothberg; *C:* Jack N. Green; *M:* William Ross.

The Amazing Spider-Man ♂♂ *Spider-Man* **1977** The Marvel Comics superhero's unique powers are put to the test when he comes to the rescue of the government by preventing an evil scientist from blackmailing the government for big bucks. The wall-walking web-slinger has his origins probed (a grad student bit by a radioactive spider develops super-human powers) in his live-action debut, which led to a short-lived TV series. **94m/C VHS.** Nicholas Hammond, David White, Lisa Eilbacher, Michael Pataki; *D:* E.W. Swackhamer. **TV**

Amazing Stories **1985** From the Steven Spielberg produced TV series. "The Mission" sees a WWII turret gunner trapped in an unusual predicament. In "The Wedding Ring," a man gives his wife a strange ring and bizarre situations ensue. **70m/C VHS.** Kevin Costner, Casey Siemaszko, Kiefer Sutherland, Danny DeVito, Rhea Perlman; *D:* Danny DeVito, Steven Spielberg. **TV**

The Amazing Transparent Man **woof! 1960** A mad scientist makes a crook invisible in order to steal the radioactive materials he needs. The crook decides to rob banks instead. Shot at the Texas State Fair for that elusive futuristic look. For Ulmer fans only. **58m/B VHS, DVD, Wide.** Douglas Kennedy, Marguerite Chapman, James Griffith, Ivan Triesault, Red Morgan, Carmel Daniel, Jonathan Ledford, Norman Smith, Patrick Cranshaw, Kevin Kelly; *D:* Edgar G. Ulmer; *W:* Jack Lewis; *C:* Meredith Nicholson; *M:* Darrell Calker.

The Amazing Transplant **woof! 1970** A sleaze-bag psycho has a "love enhancing" transplant, much to the pleasure of his sexual partners. Much to their and our dismay, however, he then kills them and bores us. **90m/C VHS.** Juan Fernandez, Linda Southern, Larry Hunter, Kim Pope; *D:* Doris Wishman; *W:* Doris Wishman; *C:* C. Davis Smith.

Amazon ♂♂ **1990 (R)** An adventure movie filmed in the Brazilian rainforest with an environmental message. A businessman being chased by the police in the Amazon jungle is rescued by a bush pilot who dreams of mining the Amazon's riches. A Brazilian woman enters the picture and persuades the businessman to help save the rainforest. Portions of the proceeds from the sale of this film go to the Rainforest Action Network. **88m/C VHS.** Kari Vaananen, Robert Davi, Rae Dawn Chong; *D:* Mika Kaurismaki.

Amazon Jail ♂ **1985** Scantily clad women go over the wall and promptly get caught by devil worshiping men in the jungle. They should have known better. Redeemed only by lingerie selection. **94m/C VHS.** Elisabeth Hartmann, Mauricio Do Valle, Sondra Graffi; *D:* Oswald De Oliveira.

Amazon Warrior 🦴🦴 **1997** Tara is a mercenary in a future world ruled by violence. The last survivor of her Amazon tribe, she sells her fighting skills to the highest bidder while searching for the leader of the rebel Marauder army, which massacred her people. Tara's well-equipped when that final showdown comes. **85m/C VHS.** J.J. Rodgers, Christine Lydon, Jimmy Jerman, Al Spencer, Raymond Storti; ***D:*** Dennis Devine; ***W:*** Steve Jarvis; ***M:*** David De Palo.

Amazon Women on the Moon 🦴🦴 *Cheeseburger Film Sandwich* **1987 (R)** A plotless, irreverent media spoof, depicting the programming of a slipshod TV station as it crams weird commercials and shorts around a comical '50s science fiction film. Inconsistent, occasionally funny anthology hangs together very loosely. Produced by Landis, with the usual amount of in-joke cameos and allusions to his other works of art. **85m/C VHS, DVD.** Rosanna Arquette, Steve Guttenberg, Steve Allen, B.B. King, Michelle Pfeiffer, Arsenio Hall, Andrew (Dice Clay) Silverstein, Howard Hesseman, Lou Jacobi, Carrie Fisher, Griffin Dunne, Sybil Danning, Henny Youngman, Monique Gabrielle, Paul Bartel, Kelly Preston, Ralph Bellamy, Russ Meyer, Steve Forrest, Joey Travolta, Ed Begley Jr., Forrest J Ackerman, Archie Hahn, Phil Hartman, Peter Horton, Charlie Callas, T.K. Carter, Dick Miller, Roxie Roker; ***D:*** John Landis, Joe Dante, Carl Gottlieb, Robert Weiss, Peter Horton; ***W:*** Michael Barrie, Jim Mulholland; ***C:*** Daniel Pearl; ***M:*** Ira Newborn.

The Amazons 🦴½ **1984** Goofy drama about a beautiful doctor who discovers an underground organization of Amazon-descended women bent on taking over the world or at least making life hard for men while investigating a Congressman's mysterious death. **100m/C VHS.** Tamara Dobson, Jack Scalia, Stella Stevens, Madeleine Stowe, Jennifer Warren; ***D:*** Paul Michael Glaser; ***M:*** Basil Poledouris. **TV**

Amazons 🦴 **1986 (R)** Tall, strong women who occasionally wander around nude search for a magical talisman that will overthrow an evil magician. **76m/C VHS.** Windsor Taylor Randolph, Penelope Reed, Joseph Whipp, Willie Nelson, Danitza Kingsley; ***D:*** Alex Sessa.

The Ambassador 🦴🦴½ *Peacemaker* **1984** An American ambassador (Mitchum) is sent to the Middle East to try to solve the area's deep political problems. He quickly becomes the target of terrorist attacks, and is blamed for the nation's unrest. To make matters worse, his wife is having an affair with a PLO leader. The President ignores him, forcing the ambassador to fend for himself. Talk about your bad days. Hudson's last feature. Based on Elmore Leonard's "52 Pickup," and remade a year later under its own title. **97m/C VHS, DVD.** Robert Mitchum, Ellen Burstyn, Rock Hudson, Fabio Testi, Donald Pleasence; ***D:*** J. Lee Thompson.

Ambassador Bill 🦴🦴 **1931** An Oklahoma rancher is appointed ambassador to a country in revolt. Rogers, of course, saves the day with his rustic witticisms. Based on the story "Ambassador from the United States" by Vincent Sheean. **68m/B VHS.** Will Rogers, Marguerite Churchill, Greta Nissen, Ray Milland, Tad Alexander, Gustav von Seyffertitz; ***D:*** Sam Taylor.

The Ambassador's Daughter 🦴🦴 **1956** The Parisian adventures of an American ambassador's daughter De Havilland and soldier Forsythe, who, unaware of her position, falls in love with her. Faltering comedy is supported by an expert cast (although nearly 40, De Havilland is charming as the young woman) with especially good performances from Menjou and Loy. **102m/C VHS.** Olivia de Havilland, John Forsythe, Myrna Loy, Adolphe Menjou, Edward Arnold, Francis Lederer, Tommy Noonan, Minor Watson; ***D:*** Norman Krasna; ***W:*** Norman Krasna.

Amber Waves 🦴🦴½ **1982** Credible drama about a generation-gap conflict between a Midwestern farmer (Weaver) and an irresponsible male model (Russell) who has coasted through life on con and charm. **98m/C VHS.** Dennis Weaver, Kurt Russell; ***D:*** Joseph Sargent. **TV**

Ambition 🦴½ **1991 (R)** Scriptwriter/star Phillips gets a bone for chutzpah by taking an unsavory lead role; his character torments a paroled psycho so that the killer will kill again and inspire a true-crime bestseller. The plot looks good on paper, but onscreen it's padded and unconvincing. **99m/C VHS.** Lou Diamond Phillips, Clancy Brown, Cecilia Peck, Richard Bradford, Willard Pugh, Grace Zabriskie, Katherine Armstrong, John David (J.D.) Cullum, Haing S. Ngor; ***D:*** Scott Goldstein; ***W:*** Lou Diamond Phillips; ***M:*** Leonard Rosenman.

The Ambulance 🦴🦴½ **1990 (R)** A New York cartoonist witnesses a mysterious ambulance at work and decides to investigate. His probings uncover a plot to sell the bodies of dying diabetics. A surprisingly good no-money feature from low-budget king Cohen. Includes an appearance by Marvel Comics' Stan Lee as himself. **95m/C VHS.** Eric Roberts, James Earl Jones, Megan Gallagher, Richard Bright, Janine Turner, Eric (Hans Gudegast) Braeden, Red Buttons, Laurene Landon, Jill Gatsby, Nicholas Chinlund, James Dixon, Stan Lee; ***D:*** Larry Cohen; ***W:*** Larry Cohen; ***C:*** Jacques Haitkin; ***M:*** Jay Chattaway.

Ambush 🦴🦴🦴 *Rukajarven Tie* **1999** Young lieutenant Eero is serving in the Finnish Army in 1941 pursuing Russian troops along the border. During his mission, Eero is able to briefly spend some time with his lovely fiancee Irina but must soon leave to go on a recon. He receives word that Irina has been killed by Russian soldiers and seeks revenge on any Russians he finds—turning from innocent soldier to dehumanized killer. Co-writer Tuuri adapted from his novel. Finnish with subtitles. **117m/C VHS, DVD, Wide.** *FI* Peter Franzen, Irina Bjorklund, Kari Vaananen, Kari Heiskanen, Taisto Reimalvoto; ***D:*** Olli Saarela; ***W:*** Olli Saarela, Antti Tuuri; ***C:*** Kjell Lagerros; ***M:*** Tuomas Kantelinen.

Ambush at Tomahawk Gap 🦴🦴 **1953** Three released prisoners go in search of hidden loot and tempers rise when the goods don't turn up. Then the Apaches show up. **73m/C VHS.** John Hodiak, John Derek, David Brian, Maria Elena Marques, Ray Teal; ***D:*** Fred F. Sears.

The Ambush Murders 🦴🦴½ **1982** True story of a stalwart white attorney defending a black activist accused of killing two cops. Not the compelling TV drama it could be, but still enjoyable. From Ben Bradlee Jr.'s novel. **100m/C VHS.** James Brolin, Dorian Harewood, Alfre Woodard, Louis Giambalvo, John McLiam, Teddy Wilson, Antonio Fargas, Amy Madigan; ***D:*** Steven Hilliard Stern. **TV**

Ambush Trail 🦴🦴 **1946** Stranger-in-town Steele metes out justice to help local ranchers while sidekick Saylor leaves 'em laughing. **60m/B VHS.** Bob Steele, Syd Saylor, I. Stanford Jolley, Lorraine Miller, Charles "Blackie" King, Kermit Maynard; ***D:*** Harry Fraser.

The Ambushers woof! **1967** Martin's third Matt Helm farce finds him handling a puzzling case involving the first United States spacecraft. When the craft is hijacked with Rule on board, it's Matt to the rescue, regaining control before unfriendly forces can take it back to Earth. Tired formula seems to have worn Martin out while the remainder of the cast goes to camp. Followed by "The Wrecking Crew." **102m/C VHS.** Dean Martin, Janice Rule, James Gregory, Albert Salmi, Senta Berger, Kurt Kasznar, Beverly Adams; ***D:*** Henry Levin; ***W:*** Herbert Baker; ***C:*** Burnett Guffey, Edward Colman; ***M:*** Hugo Montenegro.

Amelia Earhart: The Final Flight 🦴🦴½ **1994** Investigates the mysterious disappearance of pioneering aviatrix Amelia Earhart's 1937 flight to become the first pilot to circumnavigate the globe. Earhart (Keaton) and her navigator Fred Noonan (Hauer) disappeared over the Pacific Ocean and their fate has never been determined. Dern plays Earhart's husband, publisher George B. Putnam, who served as Amelia's manager and publicist. Based on the biography by Doris L. Rich. **95m/C VHS.** Diane Keaton, Rutger Hauer, Bruce Dern, Paul Guilfoyle, Denis Arndt, David Carpenter, Diana Bellamy; ***D:*** Yves Simoneau; ***W:*** Anna Sandor; ***M:*** George S. Clinton. **TV**

Amelie 🦴🦴🦴½ *Amelie from Montmartre; The Fabulous Destiny of Amelie Poulain; Le Fabuleux Destin d'Amelie Poulain* **2001 (R)** Paris waitress Amelie (Tautou) has led a solitary, but not wholly unpleasant, existence. When she finds a box of childhood treasures behind a wall in her apartment, she sets out to return them to their original owner. Accomplishing this, she begins to secretly intervene in the lives of neighbors and coworkers, helping some find romance, others retribution for past wrongs. When her "missions" bring her into contact with a quirky local (Kassovitz), she begins a roundabout courtship involving a treasure hunt instead of approaching him directly. Director Jeunet leaves intact his stunning, and very stylized visual talents, but marshals them in service of a fresh, lighthearted comedy, in contrast to his previous, downcast work. Tautout has no problem carrying the movie and has the look of a budding major star. **120m/C VHS, DVD.** *FR GE* Audrey Tautou, Mathieu Kassovitz, Rufus, Yolanda Moreau, Dominique Pinon, Maurice Benichou, Artus Penguern, Urbain Cancellier, Isabelle Nanty, Claire Maurier, Claude Perron, Clothilde Mollet, Serge Merlin, Jamel Debbouze, Flora Guiet; ***D:*** Jean-Pierre Jeunet; ***W:*** Jean-Pierre Jeunet, Guillaume Laurant; ***C:*** Bruno Delbonnel; ***M:*** Yann Tiersen; ***Nar:*** Andre Dussollier. British Acad. '01: Orig. Screenplay; Cesar '01: Art Dir./Set Dec., Director (Jeunet), Film, Score; Broadcast Film Critics '01: Foreign Film.

America 🦴🦴½ **1924** Young patriot Nathan Holden (Hamilton) is torn between his political beliefs and his love for the daughter of a Virignia Tory (Dempster). Meanwhile, evil redcoat Captain Butler (Barrymore) and his band of murderous Mohawks ruthlessly attack the colonists. **141m/B VHS, DVD.** Neil Hamilton, Carol Dempster, Lionel Barrymore, Erville Alderson, Charles Bennett, Arthur Donaldson, Charles Mack, Frank McGlynn, Henry O'Neill, Ed Roseman, Harry Semels, Louis Wolheim, Hugh Baird, Lee Beggs, Downing Clarke, Sydney Deane, Arthur Dewey, Michael Donavan, Paul Doucet, John Dunton, Riley Hatch, Emil Hoch, Edwin Holland, W.W. Jones, William S. Rising, Frank Walsh; ***D:*** D.W. Griffith; ***W:*** Robert W. Chambers; ***C:*** Marcel Le Picard, Hendrik Sartov, Billy (G.W.) Bitzer.

America 🦴½ **1986 (R)** New York cable station receives worldwide fame when their signal bounces off of the moon. Uninspired piece of fluff from otherwise talented director Downey. **83m/C VHS.** Zack Norman, Tammy Grimes, Michael J. Pollard, Monroe Arnold, Richard Belzer, Liz Torres, Howard Thomashefsky, Laura Ashton, Robert Downey Jr.; ***D:*** Robert Downey.

America at the Movies 🦴🦴½ **1976** Scenes from more than 80 of the finest American motion pictures fly by in an effort to tell the story of the cinema and provide a portrait of America as it has been seen on screen for half a century. Clips from "The Birth of a Nation," "Citizen Kane," "Dr. Strangelove," "East of Eden," "The French Connection," and "From Here to Eternity" are among the many included. Some black-and-white scenes; produced by the American Film Institute. **116m/C VHS.** John Wayne, Orson Welles, Peter Sellers, James Dean, Gene Hackman, Burt Lancaster, Julie Harris, Deborah Kerr, Al Pacino, Robert De Niro; ***M:*** Nelson Riddle; ***Nar:*** Charlton Heston.

America First 🦴½ **1970** A group of seven travelers try to build an "Eden" with the inhabitants of an Appalachian hollow. **90m/C VHS.** Michael Kennedy, Walter Keller, Pat Estrin, Lois McGuire.

America 3000 🦴 **1986 (PG-13)** Hundreds of years in the holocaust-torn future, men rebel against a brutal, overpowering race of women, with predictable results. **94m/C VHS.** Chuck Wagner, Laurene Landon; ***D:*** David Engelbach.

The American 🦴🦴 **2001** Heavy-handed adaptation of Henry James's 1877 novel. Christopher Newman (Modine) makes a fortune in California and heads to Paris in the 1870's where he hopes to acquire both culture and a wife. He meets mysterious widow Claire de Cintre (Sullivan) but his proposal is rejected by her snobby aristocratic family, which is headed by Claire's imperious mother, Madame de Bellegarde (Rigg). Then Newman learns a family secret that could win him Claire's hand. **90m/C VHS.** Matthew Modine, Aisling O'Sullivan, Diana Rigg, Brenda Fricker, Andrew Scott, Eva Birthistle; ***D:*** Paul Unwin; ***W:*** Michael Hastings. **TV**

An American Affair 🦴½ **1999** Washington, D.C., District Attorney Sam Brady (Bernsen) marries Genevieve (D'Abo) even though he's having an affair with her best friend, Barbara (Heitmeyer). But after Genevieve is murdered, her ghost begins to haunt him. And to make things more complicated, a senator seems to have it in for Sam. The two plotlines take too long to intersect, so the story never makes much sense. **90m/C VHS, DVD.** *CA* Corbin Bernsen, Maryam D'Abo, Jayne Heitmeyer, Robert Vaughn; ***D:*** Sebastian Shah. **VIDEO**

The American Angels: Baptism of Blood 🦴 **1989 (R)** Three beautiful young women, each with a personal dream, strive to make it in the world of professional wrestling. Hackneyed plot devices, but those simply watching for the wrestling scenes won't be disappointed. **99m/C VHS.** Jan MacKenzie, Tray Loren, Mimi Lesseos, Trudy Adams, Patricia Cavoti, Susan Sexton, Jean Kirkland, Jeff Lundy, Lee Marshall; ***D:*** Beverly Sebastian, Ferd Sebastian.

American Anthem 🦴 **1986 (PG-13)** A young gymnast must choose between family responsibilities or the parallel bars. Olympic gymnast Gaylord makes his movie debut but doesn't get the gold. Good fare for young tumblers, but that's about it. Followed by two of the films' music videos and tape-ads featuring Max Headroom. **100m/C VHS.** Mitch Gaylord, Janet Jones, Michelle Phillips, Michael Pataki; ***D:*** Albert Magnoli; ***W:*** Evan P. Archerd, Jeff Benjamin; ***M:*** Alan Silvestri.

American Aristocracy 🦴🦴½ **1917** A silent comic romp in which Fairbanks, an old moneyed dandy, wreaks havoc on an island resort whose clientele is composed of the nouveau well-to-do. **52m/B VHS.** Douglas Fairbanks Sr., Jewel Carmen, Albert Parker; ***D:*** Lloyd Ingraham.

American Autobahn 🦴½ **1984** A low-budget independent actioner about a journalist who discovers an underworld weapons ring that hits the highway in pursuit of him. **90m/C VHS.** Jan Jalenak, Michael von der Goltz, Jim Jarmusch; ***D:*** Andre Degas.

American Beauty 🦴🦴🦴½ **1999 (R)** Lester Burnham (Spacey) is dead. This isn't any shock—Lester tells you this himself in his opening narration. It's the time leading up to his death Lester wants to remember. Lester is a middle-aged drone with a brittle, status-conscious wife, Carolyn (Bening), and a sullen teenaged daughter, Jane (Birch). Lester's world is rocked when he meets Jane's Lolita-like friend, Angela (Suvari), and his fantasies find him quitting his job, pumping iron, and smoking dope with Ricky (Bentley), the voyeuristic kid next door who has a thing for videotaping Jane. It's a suburban nightmare writ large with an excellent cast and some unexpected twists. **118m/C VHS, DVD, Wide.** Kevin Spacey, Annette Bening, Mena Suvari, Thora Birch, Wes Bentley, Peter Gallagher, Chris Cooper, Allison Janney, Scott Bakula, Sam Robards; ***D:*** Sam Mendes; ***W:*** Alan Ball; ***C:*** Conrad L. Hall; ***M:*** Thomas Newman. Oscars '99: Actor (Spacey), Cinematog., Director (Mendes), Film, Orig. Screenplay; British Acad. '99: Actor (Spacey), Actress (Bening), Cinematog., Film, Film Editing, Score; Directors Guild '99: Director (Mendes); Golden Globes '00: Director (Mendes), Film—Drama, Screenplay; L.A. Film Critics '99: Director (Mendes); Natl. Bd. of Review '99: Film; Screen Actors Guild '99: Actor (Spacey), Actress (Bening), Cast; Writers Guild '99: Orig. Screenplay; Broadcast Film Critics '99: Director (Mendes), Film, Orig. Screenplay.

American Blue Note 🦴🦴 *Fakebook* **1989 (PG-13)** Loosely plotted, bittersweet account of a struggling jazz quartet in the early 1960s, as its leader (MacNicol) must decide if their fruitless tours of sleazy bars and weddings are still worth it. The debut of director Toporoff. **96m/C VHS.** Peter MacNicol, Carl Capotorto, Tim Guinee, Bill Christopher-Myers, Jonathan Walker, Charlotte d'Amboise, Louis Guss, Zohra Lampert, Trini Alvarado, Sam Behrens; *D:* Ralph Toporoff; *W:* Gilbert Girion, Larry Schanker.

American Born 🦴½ **1989** Murder Inc. returns to the dismay of one idealist who embarks on a battle he doesn't intend to lose. The mob had better look out. **90m/C VHS.** Joey Travolta, Andrew Zeller; *D:* Raymond Martino; *W:* Raymond Martino.

American Boyfriends 🦴🦴 **1989 (PG-13)** An ostensible sequel to "My American Cousin," in which two Canadian girls go to California and discover innocent romance and friendship. **90m/C VHS.** *CA* Margaret Langrick, John Wildman, Jason Blicker, Lisa Repo Martell; *D:* Sandy Wilson; *W:* Sandy Wilson; *C:* Brenton Spencer.

American Buffalo 🦴🦴½ **1995 (R)** Somewhat lackluster but decent screen adaptation of a classic American drama. Franz's junk shop owner Donny plans to steal back a rare Buffalo-head nickel that he feels he was swindled out of, with the help of his protege Bobby (Nelson). Hoffman's ferret-like Teach, one of Donny's card-playing buddies and an arrogant opportunist, tries to weasel in on the plan that never comes to fruition. Set in Corrente's hometown of Pawtucket, the director's reverence for the material is obvious and he plays it too safe. Top-notch performances raise the level. Mamet adapts his play for the screen. **88m/C VHS, DVD, Wide.** Dustin Hoffman, Dennis Franz, Sean Nelson; *D:* Michael Corrente; *W:* David Mamet; *C:* Richard Crudo; *M:* Thomas Newman.

American Chinatown 🦴½ **1996** Orphaned tough guy is taken in by a powerful Chinatown mob family but gets into trouble when he falls for the head man's sister. He has a chance to redeem himself when he learns about a plot to overthrow the triad clan but will he take it? **90m/C VHS.** Henry Lee, Robert Z'Dar, Liat Goodson; *D:* Richard W. Park.

An American Christmas Carol 🦴🦴 **1979** Charles Dickens' classic story is retold with limited charm in a TV effort. This time a greedy American financier (Winkler) learns about the true meaning of Christmas. **98m/C VHS, DVD.** Henry Winkler, David Wayne, Dorian Harewood; *D:* Eric Till; *M:* Hagood Hardy. **TV**

American Commandos 🦴 *Hitman* **1984 (R)** An ex-Green Beret slaughters the junkies who killed his son and raped his wife, and then joins his old buddies for a secret, Rambo-esque mission in Vietnam providing a tired rehash of Vietnam movie cliches. **96m/C VHS, DVD.** Chris Mitchum, John Phillip Law, Franco Guerrero; *D:* Bobby Suarez.

American Cop 🦴½ **1994 (PG-13)** Elmo LaGrange is an ordinary cop taking a vacation, when his layover in the Moscow airport becomes a lesson in mistaken identities. He teams up with the pre-requisite beautiful woman to outwit and outrun the Russian mafia. **91m/C VHS.** Wayne Crawford, Ashley Laurence, Daniel Quinn, William Katt, Olga Vodin, Vladimir Shpoudeiko, Nickolai Nedovodin; *D:* Wayne Crawford; *W:* Carlos Brooks; *C:* Nicholas Josef von Sternberg.

American Cyborg: Steel Warrior 🦴🦴½ **1994 (R)** Basic evil-machine-bent-on-mankind's-destruction movie—with a hero bent on rescuing the world. **95m/C VHS.** Joe Lara, John P. Ryan; *D:* Boaz Davidson; *W:* Bill Crounse.

American Dream 🦴🦴🦴 **1981** A midwestern family leaves the suburbs and moves into a Chicago inner-city neighborhood. Good TV-movie pilot for the short-lived series that was Emmy nominated for direction and writing. **90m/C VHS.** Stephen Macht, Karen Carlson, John Karlen, Andrea Smith, John Malkovich, John McIntire; *D:* Mel Damski; *M:* Artie Butler. **TV**

American Dreamer 🦴🦴 **1984 (PG)** A housewife wins a trip to Paris as a prize from a mystery writing contest. Silly from a blow on the head, she begins living the fictional life of her favorite literary adventure. Sporadic comedy with a good cast wandering about courtesy of a clumsy screenplay. **105m/C VHS.** JoBeth Williams, Tom Conti, Giancarlo Giannini, Coral Browne, James Staley; *D:* Rick Rosenthal; *M:* Lewis Furey.

American Eagle 🦴½ **1990 (R)** A veteran goes crazy and seeks sadistic, bloody revenge on his war buddies. Now his war buddies are the only ones who can stop him. **92m/C VHS.** Asher Brauner, Robert F. Lyons, Vernon Wells, Kai Baker; *D:* Robert J. Smawley.

American Empire 🦴🦴½ *My Son Alone* **1942** Two Civil War heroes struggle to build a cattle empire in Texas and are hampered by rustlers, one of whom was their partner. A fine, veteran cast and a tight script keep things moving, including the cattle. **82m/B VHS.** Preston Foster, Richard Dix, Frances Gifford, Leo Carrillo; *D:* William McGann.

American Fabulous 🦴🦴½ **1992** The posthumously released autobiography of an eccentric homosexual who lived life in the fast lane. Jeffrey Strouth performs his monologue from the back seat of a 1957 Cadillac, where the images of small-town America are seen to contrast sharply with his flamboyant style. His grotesque and candid recollections include his alcoholic Elvis-impersonator father, a stint as a teenage prostitute, drag queen friends, and drug addiction in New York. Strouth puts a comic twist on even the most brutal of his memories. He died of AIDS at the age of 33 in 1992. **105m/C VHS.** Jeffrey Strouth; *D:* Reno Dakota; *W:* Jeffrey Strouth.

American Flyers 🦴🦴½ **1985 (PG-13)** Two competitive brothers train for a grueling three-day bicycle race in Colorado while tangling with personal drama, including the spectre that one of them may have inherited dad's tendency for cerebral aneurisms and is sure to drop dead during a bike race soon. Written by bike movie specialist Tesich ("Breaking Away") with a lot of the usual cliches (the last bike ride, battling bros, eventual understanding), which are gracefully overridden by fine bike-racing photography. Interesting performances, especially Chong as a patient girlfriend and Amos as the trainer. **113m/C VHS, DVD, Wide.** Kevin Costner, David Marshall Grant, Rae Dawn Chong, Alexandra Paul, John Amos, Janice Rule, Robert Townsend, Jennifer Grey, Luca Bercovici; *D:* John Badham; *W:* Steve Tesich; *M:* Lee Ritenour, Greg Mathieson.

The American Friend 🦴🦴🦴½ *Der Amerikanische Freund; L'Ami Americain* **1977** Tribute to the American gangster film helped introduce Wenders to American moviegoers. Young Hamburg picture framer thinks he has a terminal disease and is set up by American expatriate Hopper to become a hired assassin in West Germany. The lure is a promise of quick money that the supposedly dying man can then leave his wife and child. After the first assasination, the two bond. Hopper is the typical Wenders protagonist, a strange man in a strange land looking for a connection. Great, creepy thriller adapted from Patricia Highsmith's novel "Ripley's Game." Fuller and Ray (better known as directors) appear briefly as gangsters. **127m/C VHS.** *FR GE* Bruno Ganz, Dennis Hopper, Elisabeth (Lisa) Kreuzer, Gerard Blain, Jean Eustache, Samuel Fuller, Nicholas Ray, Daniel Schmid, Lou Castel, Rudolf Schuendler, Sandy Whitelaw; *Cameos:* Wim Wenders; *D:* Wim Wenders; *W:* Wim Wenders; *C:* Robby Muller; *M:* Jurgen Knieper.

American Friends 🦴🦴 **1991 (PG)** Genteel story masquerades as high comedy. Palin is a fussy middle-aged Oxford classics tutor. On a holiday he meets American Hartley (Booth) and her adopted daughter, Elinor (Alvarado). Both women are immensely attracted to the don (for reasons that are unclear) and follow him back to Oxford, where he's engaged in a battle of succession with his rival Molina. Dismal screenplay lacks logic and urgency, making it difficult to care about the story or the characters. Script is said to have been inspired by an incident in the life of Palin's great-grandfather. If this sounds like your cup of tea, save your time and watch a Merchant Ivory film instead. **95m/C VHS.** *GB* Michael Palin, Connie Booth, Trini Alvarado, Alfred Molina; *D:* Tristam Powell; *W:* Michael Palin, Tristam Powell; *M:* Georges Delerue.

American Gigolo 🦴🦴 **1979 (R)** A Los Angeles loner who sexually services the rich women of Beverly Hills becomes involved with the wife of a California state senator and is then framed for a murder he did not commit. A highly stylized but empty view of seamy low lives marred by a contrived plot, with decent romp in the hay readiness displayed by Gere. **117m/C VHS, DVD, Wide.** Richard Gere, Lauren Hutton, Hector Elizondo, Nina Van Pallandt, Bill Duke, K. Callan; *Cameos:* Paul Schrader; *D:* Paul Schrader; *W:* Paul Schrader; *C:* John Bailey; *M:* Giorgio Moroder.

American Gothic woof! *Hide and Shriek* **1988 (R)** Three couples headed for a vacation are instead stranded on an island and captured by a demented family headed by Steiger and De Carlo, a scary enough proposition in itself. Even worse, Ma and Pa have three middle-aged moronic offspring who still dress as children and are intent on killing the thwarted vacationers (who are none too bright themselves) one by bloody one. A stultifying career low for all involved. **89m/C VHS.** *CA GB* Rod Steiger, Yvonne De Carlo, Michael J. Pollard, Sarah Torgov, Fiona Hutchinson, William Hootkins, Terry Kelly, Mark Ericksen, Caroline Barclay, Mark Lindsay Chapman; *D:* John Hough; *W:* Michael Vines, Bert Wetanson; *C:* Harvey Harrison; *M:* Alan Parker.

American Graffiti 🦴🦴🦴½ **1973 (PG)** Atmospheric, episodic look at growing up in the innocence of America before the Kennedy assassination and the Vietnam War. It all takes place on one hectic but typical night in the life of a group of recent California high school grads unsure of what the next big step in life is. So they spend their time cruising, listening to Wolfman Jack, and meeting at the drive-in. Slice of '60s life boasts a prudent script, great set design, authentic soundtrack, and consistently fine performances by the young cast. Catapulted Dreyfuss, Ford, and Somers to stardom, branded Lucas a hot directorial commodity with enough leverage to launch "Star Wars," and steered Howard and Williams towards continued age-of-innocence nirvana on "Happy Days." **112m/C VHS, DVD.** Richard Dreyfuss, Ron Howard, Cindy Williams, MacKenzie Phillips, Paul LeMat, Charles Martin Smith, Suzanne Somers, Candy Clark, Harrison Ford, Bo Hopkins, Joe Spano, Kathleen Quinlan, Wolfman Jack; *D:* George Lucas; *W:* George Lucas, Gloria Katz, Willard Huyck; *C:* Jan D'Alquen, Ron Everslage. AFI '98: Top 100; Golden Globes '74: Film—Mus./Comedy, Natl. Film Reg. '95;; N.Y. Film Critics '73: Screenplay; Natl. Soc. Film Critics '73: Screenplay.

American Heart 🦴🦴🦴½ **1992 (R)** Jack (Bridges) is a suspicious ex-con, newly released from prison, with few prospects and little hope. He also has a teenage son, Nick (Furlong), he barely remembers but who desperately wants to have his father back in his life. Jack is reluctantly persuaded to let Nick stay with him in his cheap hotel where Nick befriends fellow resident, Molly (Kaprisky), a teenage hooker, and other castoff street kids. Superb performances by both male leads—Furlong, both yearning and frustrated as he pursues his dream of having a family, and Bridges as the tough parolee, unwilling to open his heart. Hardboiled, poignant, and powerful. **114m/C VHS.** Jeff Bridges, Edward Furlong, Lucinda Jenney, Tracey Kapisky, Don Harvey, Margaret Welsh; *D:* Martin Bell; *W:* Peter Silverman; *C:* James R. Bagdonas; *M:* James Newton Howard. Ind. Spirit '94: Actor (Bridges).

American History X 🦴🦴½ **1998 (R)** Former skinhead Derek (Norton) is released from prison after a three-year stint for killing two black teens. He returns home having renounced his neo-Nazi ideology and lifestyle, only to find his younger brother Danny (Furlong) involved in a skinhead gang. Controversial not only due to its touchy subject matter and startling violence, but also because director Kaye waged a public war with New Line to remove his name from the film, believing his vision had been compromised by the studio. Ultimately, the fuss is much ado about not much, as the film falls short of expectations. The story is predictable and rather simplistic, the script uneven and sometimes preachy, and most of the characters are wafer-thin. Only Norton's mesmerizing, forceful performance and a commendable job by Furlong as the impressionable younger brother lend credibility. **118m/C VHS, DVD.** Edward Norton, Edward Furlong, Fairuza Balk, Beverly D'Angelo, Avery Brooks, Stacy Keach, Jennifer Lien, Elliott Gould, William Russ, Joe Cortese, Ethan Suplee, Guy Torry, Giuseppe Andrews, Jordan Marder, Anne Lambton, Paul LeMat; *D:* Tony Kaye; *W:* David McKenna; *C:* Tony Kaye; *M:* Anne Dudley.

An American in Paris 🦴🦴🦴🦴 **1951** Lavish, imaginative musical features a sweeping score, and knockout choreography by Kelly. Ex-G.I. Kelly stays on in Paris after the war to study painting, supported in his efforts by rich American Foch, who hopes to acquire a little extra attention. But Kelly loves the lovely Caron, unfortunately engaged to an older gent. Highlight is an astonishing 17-minute ballet which holds the record for longest movie dance number—and one of the most expensive, pegged at over half a million for a month of filming. For his efforts, the dance king won a special Oscar citation. While it sure looks like Paris, most of it was filmed in MGM studios. ♫S'Wonderful; I Got Rhythm; Embraceable You; Love Is Here To Stay; Tra-La-La; I'll Build a Stairway to Paradise; Nice Work If You Can Get It; By Strauss; Concerto in F (3rd Movement). **113m/C VHS, DVD, 8mm.** Gene Kelly, Leslie Caron, Oscar Levant, Nina Foch, Georges Guetary; *D:* Vincente Minnelli; *W:* Alan Jay Lerner; *C:* John Alton; *M:* George Gershwin, Ira Gershwin. Oscars '51: Art Dir./Set Dec., Color, Color Cinematog., Costume Des. (C), Picture, Story & Screenplay, Scoring/Musical; AFI '98: Top 100; Golden Globes '52: Film—Mus./Comedy, Natl. Film Reg. '93.

American Justice 🦴🦴 *Jackals* **1986 (R)** Two cops, one of whom looks suspiciously like a Simon of "Simon and Simon," fight political corruption and white slavery near the Mexican border. The chief white slaver bears a full resemblance to the other Simon. Sufficient action but less than original. **96m/C VHS.** Jameson Parker, Gerald McRaney, Wilford Brimley, Jack Lucarelli; *D:* Gary Grillo.

American Kickboxer 1 🦴½ **1991 (R)** Barrett stars as B.J. Quinn, a down on his luck kickboxing champion who spends much of his time onscreen aimlessly wandering (apparently searching for the meaning of his life). Lackluster script and performances will make this one trying—even for kickboxing fans. Barrett is Chuck Norris' former workout partner, but there isn't enough action often enough for him to show off his formidable skills. **93m/C VHS.** John Barrett, Keith Vitali, Brad Morris, Terry Norton, Ted Leplat; *D:* Frans Nel; *W:* Emil Kolbe; *M:* Frank Becker.

American Kickboxer 2: To the Death 🦴½ **1993 (R)** Lillian must find a way to get her cop ex-husband and her kickboxer ex-lover to work together to save her kidnapped daughter's life. **91m/C VHS.** Dale "Apollo" Cook, Evan Lurie, Kathy Shower, Ted Markland; *D:* Jeno Hodi.

American Madness 🦴🦴½ **1932** Benevolent banker Dickson (Huston) has been making loans without sufficient collateral. The bank's board of directors give him a warning and then a robbery causes a run on the bank. The directors are ready to oust Dickson when the small businessmen he's helped rally to his defense. Tedious romantic subplot has Dickson's unhappy wife (Johnson) accusing him of neglect and dallying with unscrupulous bank clerk Cluett (Gordon). **75m/B VHS.** Walter Huston, Pat O'Brien, Kay Johnson, Gavin Gordon, Constance Cummings, Robert Ellis, Walter Walker, Arthur Hoyt; *D:* Frank Capra; *W:* Robert Riskin; *C:* Joseph Walker.

American Matchmaker 🦴🦴½ *Amerikaner Shadkhn* **1940** Nat Silver decides to go into the matchmaking business, after his own marriages fail miserably, hoping to experience happiness vicariously. However, he soon begins to realize that one of his clients is a better match for him than the man he chose for her. In Yiddish with English subtitles. **87m/B VHS.** Leo Fuchs, Judith Abarbanel, Rosetta Bialis, Yudel Dubinsky, Abe Lax; ***D:*** Edgar G. Ulmer; ***W:*** S. (Shirley Ulmer) Castle; ***C:*** Edgar G. Ulmer.

American Me 𝒮𝒮𝒮 **1992 (R)** Violent and brutal depiction of more than 30 years of gang wars and drugs in East Los Angeles. Santana founded a street as a teenager, but has spent the last 18 years in prison, where he's the boss of the so-called Mexican Mafia, which oversees the drugs, scams, murders, and violence that are an everyday fact of prison life. Released from Folsom, Santana goes back to his old neighborhood and attempts to distance himself from his old life but finds his gang ties are stronger than any other alliance. Unsparing and desolate directorial debut from Olmos. **119m/C VHS.** Edward James Olmos, William Forsythe, Pepe Serna, Danny De La Paz, Evelina Fernandez, Sal Lopez, Daniel Villarreal, Cary-Hiroyuki Tagawa; ***D:*** Edward James Olmos; ***W:*** Floyd Mutrux, Desmond Nakano; ***C:*** Reynaldo Villalobos; ***M:*** Dennis Lambert.

American Nightmare 𝒮½ **1981** Young man searches for his missing sister against a background of pornography, drug peddling, and prostitution in the slums of a city. The usual titillating squalid urban drama. **85m/C VHS.** Lawrence S. Day, Lora Staley, Lenore Zann, Michael Ironside, Alexandra Paul; ***D:*** Don McBrearty.

American Nightmare 𝒮½ **2000 (R)** To commemorate the killings of four college students on Halloween the year before, pirate radio show "American Nightmare" is broadcasting all night. The program's host, Caligari (Ryan), has listeners calling in with their worst fears and seven friends take turns calling. Too bad, the killer is also listening and decides to make their nightmares come true. **91m/C VHS, DVD.** Debbie Rochon, Brandy Little, Johnny Sneed, Christopher Ryan, Brinke Stevens; ***D:*** Jon Keeyes; ***W:*** Jon Keeyes; ***C:*** Brad Walker; ***M:*** Peter Gannan, David Rosenblad.

American Ninja 𝒮𝒮 *American Warrior* **1985 (R)** American Dudikoff is G.I. Joe, a martial-arts expert stationed in the Philippines who alienates most everyone around him (he's a rebel). Deadly black-belt war begins with Joe confronting the army which is selling stolen weapons to the South American black market. Aided by one faithful pal, Joe uses his head-kicking martial arts skills to stop hundreds of ninja combatants working for the corrupt arms dealer. In his spare time he romances the base chief's daughter. Efficient rib-crunching chop-socky action wrapped in no-brainer plot and performed by nonactors. Cannon epic mercilessly followed by at least three sequels. **96m/C VHS, DVD, Wide.** Michael Dudikoff, Guich Koock, Judie Aronson, Steve James; ***D:*** Sam Firstenberg; ***W:*** Gideon Amir; ***C:*** Hanania Baer; ***M:*** Michael Linn.

American Ninja 2: The Confrontation 𝒮𝒮 **1987 (R)** Soldiers Dudikoff and James are back again using their martial arts skills (in lieu of any acting) to take on a Caribbean drug-lord. Apparently he has been kidnapping Marines and taking them to his island, where he genetically alters them to become fanatical ninja assassins eager to do his dirty work. The script hardly gets in the way of the rib-crunching action, but is an improvement upon Ninja Number One. **90m/C VHS.** Michael Dudikoff, Steve James, Larry Poindexter, Gary Conway; ***D:*** Sam Firstenberg; ***W:*** Gary Conway, James Booth.

American Ninja 3: Blood Hunt woof! **1989 (R)** Second sequel in the American Ninja series. Bradley replaces Dudikoff as the martial arts good guy fighting the martial arts bad guys on a Caribbean island. He's pursued by ex-evangelist Marjoe, who wants to inject him with a nasty virus before unloading the germs to bad buys worldwide. Less ninjitsu; more uninspired martial arts. **90m/C VHS.** David Bradley, Steve James, Marjoe Gortner, Michele Chan, Calvin Jung; ***D:*** Cedric Sundstrom; ***W:*** Paul DeMielche, Gary Conway; ***M:*** George S. Clinton.

American Ninja 4: The Annihilation woof! **1991 (R)** Dudikoff returns after noticeable absence in last sequel. He should have stayed away from #4—it's a rehash of tired ideas that never gets off the ground. Forget this and see "American Ninja 2: The Confrontation," the best of this series. **99m/C VHS.** Michael Dudikoff, David Bradley, James Booth, Dwayne Alexandre, Robin Stille, Ken Gampu; ***D:*** Cedric Sundstrom; ***W:*** David Geeves; ***M:*** Nicolas Tenbroek.

American Outlaws 𝒮 **2001 (PG-13)** Look kids, it's N'Sync as the James Gang! Remember "Young Guns" (1988)? By the end of this, you'll be begging for Emilio Estevez's constant mugging and Kiefer Sutherland's ridiculous brooding. Jesse (Farrell) and Frank James (Macht), along with cousins Cole (Caan), Bob (McCormack) and Jim Younger (Smith) return from the Civil War to find Ma (Bates) and the family farm threatened by the railroad. So they commence to robbin' banks to help out the poor folk who been done wrong. Along the way Jesse courts purty young filly Zee (Larter). People have been writing the obituary of the Western for a few years now, but "Outlaws" may be the bullet in the genre's back. **95m/C VHS, DVD, Wide.** *US* Colin Farrell, Gabriel Macht, Scott Caan, Gregory Smith, Will McCormack, Timothy Dalton, Kathy Bates, Nathaniel Arcand, Ali Larter, Ronny Cox, Harris Yulin, Terry O'Quinn, Ty O'Neal, Joe Stevens; ***D:*** Les Mayfield; ***W:*** John Rogers, Roderick Taylor; ***C:*** Russell Boyd; ***M:*** Trevor Rabin.

American Pie 𝒮𝒮 *East Great Falls High* **1999 (R)** And you thought you loved dessert! Four high school seniors led by pastry molesting Jim (Biggs) vow to lose their virginity before the Prom. Unfortunately for them, the girls that they're chasing aren't your usual teenage sex comedy tarts. These smart little cookies make sure that the boys' quest is chock full of humiliation. The sensitivity to the female point-of-view is balanced by a heapin' helpin' of crude and disgusting humor for the guys. An absolute must-see for baked goods and the men who love them. **95m/C VHS, DVD, Wide.** Jason Biggs, Thomas Ian Nicholas, Chris Owen, Chris Klein, Natasha Lyonne, Tara Reid, Mena Suvari, Alyson Hannigan, Shannon Elizabeth, Eugene Levy, Seann William Scott, Jennifer Coolidge, Eddie Kaye Thomas, Lawrence Pressman; ***D:*** Chris Weitz, Paul Weitz; ***W:*** Adam Herz; ***C:*** Richard Crudo; ***M:*** David Lawrence.

American Pie 2 𝒮𝒮½ **2001 (R)** No pie is abused in this movie, although everyone (including exec producers Chris and Paul Weitz) is back for a second helping. The story picks up a year later while everyone is on summer vacation from college and sharing a beach house. Jim (Biggs)is nervously anticipating a visit from Nadia, while getting sex tips from band camp geek Michelle (Hannigan). Entertaining sequel shares the original's appealing and effective combination of gross-out situations and sweet silliness, and while it's not quite as good, it doesn't miss by much. They should quit now while they're still ahead. **105m/C VHS, DVD, Wide.** *US* Jason Biggs, Shannon Elizabeth, Alyson Hannigan, Chris Klein, Natasha Lyonne, Thomas Ian Nicholas, Tara Reid, Chris Owen, Seann William Scott, Mena Suvari, Eddie Kaye Thomas, Eugene Levy, Jennifer Coolidge, Christopher Penn, Eli Marienthal, Casey Affleck, Denise Faye, Molly Cheek; ***D:*** James B. Rogers; ***W:*** Adam Herz; ***C:*** Mark Irwin; ***M:*** David Lawrence.

American Pluck 𝒮𝒮 **1925** Before he can inherit anything, a playboy millionaire's son must go out into the world and prove he can make his own way. He meets a beautiful princess, who is pursued by a villainous count. Walsh, as the dashing hero, was the younger brother of director Raoul. Silent with original organ music. **91m/B VHS, 8mm.** George Walsh, Wanda (Petit) Hawley, Frank Leigh, Sidney De Grey; ***D:*** Richard Stanton.

American Pop 𝒮𝒮 **1981 (R)** Animated story of four generations of men told in music. Immigrant Zalmie starts off in vaudeville and winds up involved in the mob, his pianist son Benny gets killed in WWII, Benny's son Tony winds up in the early psychedelic rock scene in Haight-Asbury, and Tony's son Little Pete becomes a rock idol. ♫A Hard Rain's A-Gonna Fall; Don't Think Twice It's All Right; People Are Strange; Purple Haze; Hell is for Children; Free Bird; I'm Waiting for the Man; Night Moves; You Send Me. **95m/C VHS, DVD.** ***D:*** Ralph Bakshi; ***W:*** Ronni Kern; ***M:*** Lee Holdridge; ***V:*** Ron Thompson, Marya Small, Lisa Jane Persky, Roz Kelly, Richard Singer, Jeffrey Lippa.

The American President 𝒮𝒮𝒮 **1995 (PG-13)** Widower president Andrew Shepherd (Douglas) decides it's time to get back into the dating game. But just what woman wants to find her romance in the public eye? Well, it turns out to be feisty environmental lobbyist Sydney Wade (the ever-charming Bening). But the Prez also has to put up with nasty opponent Bob Rumson (Dreyfuss), who's using their courtship as political fodder, approval ratings, and a nosy press. Glossy fairytale material expertly handled by both cast and director. **114m/C VHS, DVD, Wide.** Michael Douglas, Annette Bening, Martin Sheen, Michael J. Fox, David Paymer, Samantha Mathis, John Mahoney, Anna Deavere Smith, Nina Siemaszko, Wendie Malick, Shawna Waldron, Richard Dreyfuss; ***D:*** Rob Reiner; ***W:*** Aaron Sorkin; ***C:*** John Seale; ***M:*** Marc Shaiman.

American Psycho 𝒮𝒮 **1999 (R)** Trimmed-down and (slightly) cleaned-up version of Bret Easton Ellis's widely-hated 1991 novel has Bale as '80s hotshot Wall Street exec and apparent serial-killer Patrick Bateman. Bateman is the poster child for Reagan-era excess and preference for style over substance, a theme with which the film, while shooting for satire, beats you over the head. Like the decade it portrays, "Psycho" is far from subtle, and the characters barely register as two-dimensional, let alone three. They got the look right, but then, that's the point, isn't it? The production drew protests in Toronto, where some scenes were shot, and Leo DiCaprio was rumored to be in line to play the lead for a time. **103m/C VHS, DVD, Wide.** Christian Bale, Willem Dafoe, Jared Leto, Reese Witherspoon, Samantha Mathis, Chloe Sevigny, Justin Theroux, Joshua Lucas, Guinevere Turner, Matt Ross, William Sage, Cara Seymour; ***D:*** Mary Harron; ***W:*** Mary Harron, Guinevere Turner; ***C:*** Andrzej Sekula; ***M:*** John Cale.

American Psycho 2: All American Girl 𝒮𝒮 **2002 (R)** Rachelle Newman (Kunis) is the only victim who managed to escape from serial killer Patrick Bateman. But her ordeal left her obsessed with such killers and when she learns that college prof Robert Strickland was an FBI profiler specializing in the subject, Rachelle is determined to become his teaching assistant. Even if it means killing the competition. **88m/C VHS, DVD.** Mila Kunis, William Shatner, Geraint Wyn Davies, Lindy Booth, Robin Dunne; ***D:*** Morgan J. Freeman; ***W:*** Karen Craig, Alex Sanger; ***C:*** Vanja Cernjul; ***M:*** Norman Orenstein. **VIDEO**

An American Rhapsody 𝒮𝒮𝒮 **2001 (PG-13)** A mother/daughter conflict steeped in history and based on the experiences of writer/director Gardos. Margit (Kinski) and her family flee Hungary during the communist takeover of the 1950s but she is forced to leave her infant daughter behind. While the family settles in L.A., Suzanne is being raised in the country by adoptive parents and knows nothing of her origins. She gets a rude awakening at the age of 6 when her grandmother Helen (Banfalvy) makes arrangements to reunite Suzy with her unknown "real" family. The child grows into a sullen teenager (Johansson) who longs to return to Budapest. Her father finally agrees to a solo trip and Suzanne learns just what her family suffered and where she truly belongs. **106m/C VHS, DVD, Wide.** *US HU* Nastassia Kinski, Scarlett Johansson, Tony Goldwyn, Kelly Endresz-Banlaki, Agnes Banfalvy, Zsuzsi Czinkoczi, Balazs Galko, Zoltan Seress, Mae Whitman, Lisa Jane Persky, Emmy Rossum; ***D:*** Eva Gardos; ***W:*** Eva Gardos; ***C:*** Elemer Ragalyi; ***M:*** Cliff Eidelman.

American Roulette 𝒮 **1988 (R)** Garcia is the exiled president of a Latin American country living in London in this thin political thriller. A plot riddled with weaknesses and poor direction make this potentially interesting film dull and lifeless. **102m/C VHS.** *GB AU* Andy Garcia, Kitty Aldridge, Robert Stephens, Al Matthews, Susannah York; ***D:*** Maurice Hatton; ***M:*** Michael Gibbs.

American Samurai 𝒮½ **1992 (R)** Drew is the adopted son of a Japanese samurai, who gives him the family's sacred sword. This gesture angers his stepbrother who gets involved with Japanese gangsters and illegal live-blade fighting, and who also vows revenge on this American upstart. Lots of sword play to go with the chop-socky action. **89m/C VHS.** David Bradley, Mark Dacascos, John Fujioka, Valarie Trapp; ***D:*** Sam Firstenberg; ***W:*** John Corcoran.

The American Scream 𝒮½ **198?** An innocent family vacationing in the mountains stumbles on to a satanic cult. And that can really ruin a vacation. **85m/C VHS.** Jennifer Darling, Pons Marr, Blackie Cammett, Kimberly Kramer, Jean Sapienza, Kevin Kaye, Matt Borlenghi, James Cooper; ***D:*** Mitchell Linden.

American Shaolin: King of the Kickboxers 2 𝒮½ **1992 (PG-13)** When Drew gets his butt kicked in a karate tournament he decides to head to China and learn some fight-winning moves from a group of warrior monks. **103m/C VHS.** Reese Madigan, Trent Bushy, Daniel Dae Kim, Billy Chang, Cliff Lenderman, Zhang Shi Yen, Kim Chan, Alice Zhang Hung; ***D:*** Lucas Lowe.

The American Soldier 𝒮𝒮½ *Der Amerikanische Soldat* **1970** Fassbinder's homage to the American gangster film tells the story of Ricky, a charismatic hit man. Ricky always wears a gun in a shoulder holster, sports a fedora and a white double-breasted suit, and drinks Scotch straight from the bottle. He also carries out his assigned murders with complete efficiency and no emotion. In German with English subtitles. **80m/C VHS.** *GE* Rainer Werner Fassbinder, Karl Scheydt, Elga Sorbas, Jan George, Ingrid Caven, Ulli Lommel, Kurt Raab; ***D:*** Rainer Werner Fassbinder; ***W:*** Rainer Werner Fassbinder; ***C:*** Dietrich Lohmann; ***M:*** Peer Raben.

An American Story 𝒮𝒮½ **1992 (PG)** Earnest but predictable story based on an actual incident. Six WWII vets return to their small Texas town as heroes. But when they find a corrupt mayor and a brutal sheriff running things they decide to campaign to unseat the local politicos, in spite of some dire warnings. Meade (Johnson), their commanding officer in Europe, is the designated leader in the plan but his ambitious wife and father-in-law want him to align himself with the status quo instead. Hallmark Hall of Fame production is enjoyable and better than most made for TV movies, but fails to reach the heights of many other HHF offerings. **97m/C VHS.** Brad Johnson, Kathleen Quinlan, Tom Sizemore, Josef Sommer, Patricia Clarkson, Lisa Blount, G.W. Bailey, John M. Jackson; ***D:*** John Gray; ***W:*** John Gray; ***C:*** Johnny E. Jensen. **TV**

American Strays 𝒮½ **1996 (R)** Episodic black comedy about various oddballs (most of them violent) who cross paths (usually in Kane's roadside diner) in an isolated desert town. There's a masochist who wants help committing suicide, an unemployed family man on the verge of a breakdown, a serial killer, and more—mostly strange. **97m/C VHS, DVD.** Carol Kane, Jennifer Tilly, Eric Roberts, John Savage, Luke Perry, Joe (Johnny) Viterelli, James Russo, Vonte Sweet, Sam Jones, Brion James, Toni Kalem, Melora Walters; ***D:*** Michael Covert; ***W:*** Michael Covert; ***C:*** Sead Mutarevic; ***M:*** John Graham.

American Streetfighter 𝒮𝒮 **1996** Martial arts expert Jake Tanner gets involved with an illegal streetfighting ring to rescue his brother, Randy, who's the target of a drug courier. But what happens when his next opponent is his sibling? **80m/C VHS, DVD.** Gary Daniels, Ian Jacklin, Tracy Dali; ***D:*** Steve Austin.

American Streetfighter 2: The Full Impact 𝒮½ **1997** Ex-cop becomes a bounty hunter tracking a serial killer who likes to kill his victims with his bare hands. **90m/C VHS, DVD.** Gary Daniels, Graciela Casillas; ***D:*** Marc Messenger. **VIDEO**

An American Summer ♂♂ 1990 A Chicago kid spends a summer with his aunt in beach-rich Los Angeles in this coming-of-age tale filled with '90s teen idols. **100m/C VHS.** Brian Austin Green, Joanna (Joanna DeVarona) Kerns, Michael Landes, Tony Crane, Brian Krause, Wayne Pere, Amber Susa; *D:* James Slocum; *W:* James Slocum; *C:* Bruce Dorfman; *M:* Roger Neill.

An American Tail ♂♂½ **1986 (G)** While emigrating to New York in the 1880s, a young Russian mouse (Fievel) is separated from his family. He matures as he learns to live on the Big Apple's dirty boulevards. The bad guys are of course cats. Excellent animation and a high-minded (though sentimental and stereotypical) plot keep it interesting for adults. Produced by Spielberg and the first big hit for the Bluth factory, a collection of expatriate Disney artists. Knowing better than to let a money-making mouse tale languish, Bluth followed with "An American Tale: Fievel Goes West." **81m/C VHS.** *D:* Don Bluth; *M:* James Horner; *V:* Dom DeLuise, Madeline Kahn, Phillip Glasser, Christopher Plummer, Nehemiah Persoff, Will Ryan, John Finnegan, Cathianne Blore.

An American Tail: Fievel Goes West ♂♂ **1991 (G)** Fievel and the Mousekewitz family continue their pursuit of the American dream by heading West, where the intrepid mouse seeks to become a famous lawman while his sister looks to make it big as a dance hall singer. The score is performed by the London Symphony Orchestra. Unfortunately released at the same time as "Beauty and the Beast," "Fievel Goes West" suffers from comparison. Worthwhile viewing for the whole family, but it won't ever reach the heights of "B&B." The laser edition is letterboxed and features chapter stops. **75m/C VHS, Wide.** *D:* Phil Nibbelink, Simon Wells; *W:* Flint Dille; *M:* James Horner; *V:* John Cleese, Dom DeLuise, Phillip Glasser, Amy Irving, Jon Lovitz, Cathy Cavadini, Nehemiah Persoff, Erica Yohn, James Stewart.

American Tickler *Draws* **1976 (R)** A thigh-slappin' (or is it head-whacking?) series of satirical pastiches in the grand style of "Kentucky Fried Movie," only more sophomoric. A tasteless collection of yearning to be funny sketches about American institutions. **77m/C VHS.** W.P. Dremak, Joan Sumner, Marlow Ferguson, Jeff Alin, Joe Piscopo; *D:* Chuck Vincent.

American Tiger ♂♂ *American Rickshaw* **1989 (R)** The collegiate hero of "American Tiger" is, like so many college students, framed for murder, and he applies himself to clearing his sullied name. Somewhere during this process, he finds himself in the middle of a battle between good and evil on a football field. About what you'd expect from a supernatural kung-fu teen-action drama. **93m/C VHS.** Mitch Gaylord, Donald Pleasence, Daniel Greene, Victoria Prouty; *D:* Sergio Martino.

American Tragedy ♂♂½ **2000 (PG-13)** Remember the O.J. Simpson trial? Well, if you don't, this cable drama is here to remind you as it explores the egos and infighting of Simpson's four defense lawyers: Johnny Cochran (Rhames), Bob Shapiro (Silver), F. Lee Bailey (Plummer), and Barry Scheck (Kirby). Based on the book by Schiller, who also directed. **170m/C VHS, DVD, Wide.** Ving Rhames, Ron Silver, Christopher Plummer, Bruno Kirby, Nicholas Pryor, Robert LuPone, Ruben Santiago-Hudson, Richard Cox, Clyde Kusatsu, Jeff Kober; *D:* Lawrence Schiller; *W:* Norman Mailer; *C:* Bruce Surtees; *M:* Bill Conti. CABLE

American Vampire ♂♂½ **1997 (R)** Teenager Frankie (Lussauer) has been left alone while his parents are on vacation. One night on the beach, he and his friend Bogie (Hitt) meet Moondoggie (Venokur), who promises to help them party the summer away. He soon reappears with two babes (Electra and Xavier) who appear to be undead. Frankie must turn to The Big Kahuna (West) to stop the vampires. Yes, the plot strictly follows the formula, but the effects are not bad for a low-budget production; the photography is better than it needs to be; and the humor is intentional. **99m/C VHS, DVD.** Trevor Lissauer, Danny Hitt, Johnny Venokur, Carmen Electra, Debora Xavier, Adam West, Sydney Lassick; *D:* Luis Esteban; *W:* Rollin Jarrett; *C:* Jurgen Baum, Goran Pavicevic. VIDEO

American Virgin ♂ *Live Virgin* **1998 (R)** Ronny Bartoloti (Loggia) is a successful Hollywood adult film director who has upset his virginal 18-year-old daughter, Katrina (Suvari), with his double-standard attitudes. So she decides to get even by sharing her first sexual experience with millions—by going live on camera on closed-circuit—with the help of Ronny's rival Joey Quinn (Hoskins). But can daddy get his determined little darling to change her mind? Exploitative would-be satire falls flat. **87m/C VHS, DVD.** Mena Suvari, Robert Loggia, Bob Hoskins, Gabriel Mann, Sally Kellerman, Bobbie Phillips, Lamont Johnson, Rick Peters, O-lan Jones, Alexandra Wentworth; *D:* Jean Pierre Marois; *W:* Jean Pierre Marois, Ira Israel; *C:* Eagle Egilsson.

An American Werewolf in London ♂♂♂ **1981 (R)** Strange, darkly humorous version of the classic man-into-wolf horror tale became a cult hit, but never clicked with most American critics. Two American college students, David (Naughton) and Jack (Dunne), are backpacking through England when they're viciously attacked by a werewolf one foggy night. Jack is killed, but keeps appearing (in progressively decomposed form) before the seriously wounded David, warning him of impending werewolfdom when the moon is full; Jack advises suicide. Seat-jumping horror and gore, highlighted by intensive metamorphosis sequences orchestrated by Rick Baker, are offset by wry humor, though the shifts in tone don't always work. Great moon songs permeate the soundtrack, including CCR's "Bad Moon Rising" and Van Morrison's "Moondance." Followed by "An American Werewolf in Paris" (1997). **97m/C VHS, DVD.** *GB* David Naughton, Griffin Dunne, Jenny Agutter, Frank Oz, Brian Glover, Lila Kaye, David Schofield, John Woodvine, Don McKillop, Paul Kember, Colin Fernandes, Rik Mayall, Paddy Ryan; *D:* John Landis; *W:* John Landis; *C:* Robert Paynter; *M:* Elmer Bernstein. Oscars '81: Makeup.

An American Werewolf in Paris ♂♂ **1997 (R)** More of a remake than a sequel, horror-comedy fails to live up to the wit and quirkiness of the original. Andy (Scott) is on a daredevil tour of Europe along with buddies Brad (Vieluf) and Chris (Buckman). As he attempts to bungee jump off of the Eiffel Tower, he spots a French femme attempting to plungee jump nearby. He saves her and immediately falls in love with her. The girl, Serafine (Delpy) warns him to stay away, but he keeps sniffing around. They tail her to a creepy house she shares with a guy named Claude (Cosso), where Andy secures a date and his friends are invited to a dinner party. Claude, however, is top dog in a pack of racist werewolves, and Andy's pals end up as the main course. Bitten himself, Andy learns that he's now a werewolf. Brad and the other victims pop up now and again to remind Andy that they're doomed to walk the earth until the werewolves that killed them are destroyed. Special effects have advanced a long way since the original and it shows, although the computer generated wolves are difficult to tell apart. **100m/C VHS, DVD.** Anthony Waller, Julie Delpy, Tom Everett Scott, Julie Bowen, Pierre Cosso, Thierry Lhermitte, Vince Vieluf, Phil Buckman, Tom Novembre, Isabelle Constantini; *D:* Anthony Waller; *W:* Anthony Waller, Tim Burns, Tom Stern; *C:* Egon Werdin; *M:* Wilbert Hirsch.

American Women ♂♂ *The Closer You Get* **2000 (PG-13)** Poor schlub County Donegal lads, weary of their lack of female companionship, send an ad to the Miami Herald, looking for young, nubile American women to come over and "see what happens." Hoping to see the American lasses in time for the social event of the season, the St. Martha's Day dance, they're disappointed when the day arrives but the girls don't. To make matters worse, the local ladies have brought in some Spanish fishermen to play music at the dance. Old fashioned ethnic comedy tries to cash in on the successes of "The Full Monty" and "Waking Ned Devine," but contains a wee bit too many Irish cliches, and the charm is squeezed out by the patronizing view of what is supposed to be modern-day Ireland. **90m/C VHS.** *IR GB* Ian Hart, Sean McGinley, Niamh Cusack, Ruth McCabe, Ewan Stewart, Maureen O'Brien, Pat Laffan, Britta Smith, Pat Shortt, Cathleen Bradley, Sean McDonagh, Risteard Cooper; *D:* Aileen Ritchie; *W:* William Ivory; *C:* Robert Alazraki; *M:* Rachel Portman.

American Yakuza ♂♂ **1994 (R)** FBI agent Nick Davis (Mortensen) is sent to L.A. to infiltrate the American arm of the Yakuza, Japan's dangerous criminal underworld. He rises through the ranks and is adopted into the powerful Tendo family. Now Davis finds himself caught between the FBI, the Yakuza, and the vengeful American mafia. **95m/C VHS, DVD.** Viggo Mortensen, Michael Nouri, Ryo Ishibashi, Franklin Ajaye; *D:* Frank Cappello; *W:* Max Strom, John Allen Nelson; *C:* Richard Clabaugh; *M:* David Williams.

Americana ♂♂½ **1981 (PG)** A troubled Vietnam vet tries to restore himself by rebuilding a merry-go-round in a small midwestern town, while dealing with opposition from the local residents. Offbeat, often effective post-Nam editorial that was produced and directed in 1973 by Carradine and then shelved. Hershey and Carradine were a couple back then. **90m/C VHS, DVD.** David Carradine, Barbara Hershey, Michael Greene, John Blythe Barrymore Jr.; *D:* David Carradine; *W:* Richard Carr.

The Americanization of Emily ♂♂♂ **1964** A happy-go-lucky American naval officer (Garner) with no appetite for war discovers to his horror that he may be slated to become the first casualty of the Normandy invasion as part of a military PR effort in this black comedy-romance. Meanwhile, he spreads the charisma in an effort to woo and uplift Emily (Andrews), a depressed English woman who has suffered the loss of her husband, father, and brother during the war. A cynical, often funny look at military maneuvers and cultural drift that was adapted by Paddy Chayefsky from William Bradford Huie's novel. Also available colorized. **117m/B VHS, Wide.** James Garner, Julie Andrews, Melvyn Douglas, James Coburn, Joyce Grenfell, Keenan Wynn, Edward Binns, Liz Fraser, William Windom; *D:* Arthur Hiller; *W:* Paddy Chayefsky.

The Americano ♂♂½ **1917** Ever-suave Fairbanks frees a South American politician locked in a dungeon, returns him to political success, and captures the heart of his beautiful daughter. Based on Eugene P. Lyle Jr.'s "Blaze Derringer." **58m/B VHS.** Douglas Fairbanks Sr., Alma Rubens, Spottiswoode Aitken, Lillian Langdon, Carl Stockdale, Tom Wilson; *D:* John Emerson.

Americano ♂♂ **1955** A cowboy travelling to Brazil with a shipment of Brahma bulls discovers the rancher he's delivering them to has been murdered. An odd amalgam of western cliches and a South American setting. **85m/C VHS.** Glenn Ford, Frank Lovejoy, Abbe Lane, Cesar Romero; *D:* William Castle.

America's Deadliest Home Video ♂♂ **1991** Camp spoof about America's obsession with videotaping everything in sight. Video enthusiast Doug is taken hostage by the Clint Dryer gang who want him to tape their crime spree. Every aspect is only seen through the lens of the video camera. **90m/C VHS.** Danny Bonaduce, Mick Wynhoff, Mollena Williams, Melora Walters; *D:* Jack Perez; *W:* Jack Perez.

America's Dream ♂♂♂ **1995 (PG-13)** Trilogy of short stories covering black life from 1938 to 1958. In "Long Black Song," based on a short story by Richard Wright, Alabama farmer Silas (Glover) lives with lonely wife Sarah (Lifford), who succumbs to the charms of white travelling salesman, David (Donovan). "The Boy Who Painted Christ Black" is young Aaron (Golden), who gives the drawing to his teacher, Miss Williams (Calloway). But the portrait causes a great deal of controversy in Aaron's 1948 Georgia school, especially for ambitious principal George Du Vaul (Snipes). Based on a story by John Henrich Clarke. The last story is Maya Angelou's "The Reunion," about Chicago jazz pianist Philomena (Toussaint), who encounters her childhood nemesis, Beth Ann (Thompson), the daughter of the white family who employed her parents as servants. **87m/C VHS.** Danny Glover, Tina Lifford, Tate Donovan, Dan Kamin, Wesley Snipes, Jasmine Guy, Vanessa Bell Calloway, Norman D. Golden II, Timothy Carhart, Yolanda King, Rae'ven (Alyia Larrymore) Kelly, Lorraine Toussaint, Susanna Thompson, Carl Lumbly, Phyllis Cicero; *D:* Bill Duke, Kevin Rodney Sullivan, Paris Barclay; *W:* Ron Stacker Thompson, Ashley Tyler; *C:* Karl Herrmann; *M:* Patrice Rushen.

America's Sweethearts ♂♂ **2001 (PG-13)** This just in: Hollywood is shallow and fake, Julia Roberts is pretty, and entertainment reporters are freeloading numbskulls. These are the themes covered in this disappointing romantic comedy in which America's favorite on- and off-screen couple Eddie (Cusack) and Gwen (Zeta-Jones) pretend to reconcile during a disaster-filled press junket cooked up by desparate publicist Lee (Crystal). Complicating matters are the developing relationship between Gwen's sister and assistant Kiki (Roberts) and Eddie. Roth hasn't directed a film in over 10 years, and it shows here. But beneath the rust, there are some funny moments, mostly including Walken as the crazy director who has taken his own film hostage. **103m/C VHS, DVD, Wide.** *US* Julia Roberts, Catherine Zeta-Jones, John Cusack, Billy Crystal, Hank Azaria, Christopher Walken, Seth Green, Stanley Tucci; *Cameos:* Larry King; *D:* Joe Roth; *W:* Billy Crystal, Peter Tolan; *C:* Phedon Papamichael; *M:* James Newton Howard.

Americathon woof! **1979 (PG)** It is the year 1998 and the United States is almost bankrupt, so President Chet Roosevelt decides to stage a telethon to keep the country from going broke. Interesting satiric premise with a diverse cast, but a poor script and slack pacing spoil all the fun. The soundtrack features music by The Beach Boys and Elvis Costello while the narration is by George Carlin. **85m/C VHS.** Terence McGovern, Allan Arbus, David Opatoshu, John Lone, Cybill Shepherd, Dorothy Stratten, Peter Riegert, John Ritter, Nancy Morgan, Harvey Korman, Fred Willard, Meat Loaf Aday, Elvis Costello, Chief Dan George, Howard Hesseman, Jay Leno; *Cameos:* Tommy Lasorda, Peter Marshall; *D:* Neal Israel; *W:* Monica Johnson, Neal Israel; *M:* Earl Brown Jr.; *Nar:* George Carlin.

Amin: The Rise and Fall woof! **1982** Excessively violent and ultimately pointless dramatization of Idi Amin's eight-year reign of terror in Uganda, which resulted in the deaths of a half million people and the near ruin of a nation. **101m/C VHS.** Joseph Olita, Geoffrey Keen; *D:* Sharad Patel.

Amistad ♂♂♂ **1997 (R)** Spielberg again creates an epic from another historic example of man's inhumanity, although not quite as effectively this time around. In 1839, African captives aboard the slaveship Amistad, led by a Mende tribesman named Cinque (Hounsou), free themselves and take over the ship in a bloody mutiny. Property attorney Robert Baldwin (McConaughey) must prove in lengthy court battles that the Africans were rightfully freed individuals in the eyes of the law. John Quincy Adams (Hopkins) presents the Africans' defense to the Supreme Court. Sequences depicting the horrors of slavery are bogged down with heavy handed musical orchestrations that elicit emotion, but at the price of storytelling. McConaughey seems a bit too Californian to be colonial and Morgan Freeman is reduced to periodic cameos as an abolitionist. Fortunately, thanks to an eye for rich detail and superb acting by dynamic newcomer Hounsou, the film nearly escapes the clutches of melodrama to emerge educational and moving. Film's release was marred by a French author accusing Spielberg and his Dreamworks studio of plagiarism. **152m/C VHS, DVD.** Paul

Guilfoyle, Djimon Hounsou, Anthony Hopkins, Matthew McConaughey, Morgan Freeman, Nigel Hawthorne, David Paymer, Pete Postlethwaite, Stellan Skarsgard, Anna Paquin, Austin Pendleton, Tomas Milian; **D:** Steven Spielberg; **W:** David Franzoni; **C:** Janusz Kaminski; **M:** John Williams. Broadcast Film Critics '97: Support. Actor (Hopkins).

The Amityville Horror 🦴🦴 **1979 (R)** Sometimes a house is not a home. Ineffective chiller that became a boxoffice biggie, based on a supposedly real-life occurrence in Amityville, Long Island. The Lutz family moves into the house of their dreams only to find it full of nightmares. Once the scene of a grisly mass murder, the house takes on a devilish attitude, plunging the family into supernatural terror. Pipes and walls ooze icky stuff, flies manifest in the strangest places, and doors mysteriously slam while exorcist Steiger staggers from room to room in scene-chewing prayer. Based on the Jay Anson book and followed by a number of sequels. **117m/C VHS, DVD, Wide.** James Brolin, Margot Kidder, Rod Steiger, Don Stroud, Murray Hamilton, Helen Shaver, Amy Wright, Val Avery, Natasha Ryan, John Larch, K.C. Martel, Meeno Peluce; **D:** Stuart Rosenberg; **W:** Sandor Stern; **C:** Fred W. Koenekamp; **M:** Lalo Schifrin.

Amityville 2: The Possession woof! **1982 (R)** More of a prequel than a sequel to "The Amityville Horror" (1979). Relates the story of the house's early years as a haven for demonic forces intent on driving a father to beat the kids, a mother to prayer, and a brother to lust after his sister (before he murders them all). Young etc. portray an obnoxious family that you're actually glad to see wasted by the possessed son. A stupid, clumsy attempt to cash in on the success of the first film, which was also stupid and clumsy but could at least claim novelty in the bad housing development genre. Followed by "Amityville 3: The Demon" in 1983. **110m/C VHS.** James Olson, Burt Young, Andrew Prine, Moses Gunn, Rutanya Alda, Jack Magner, Diane Franklin; **D:** Damiano Damiani; **W:** Tommy Lee Wallace; **C:** Franco Di Giacomo; **M:** Howard Blake, Lalo Schifrin.

Amityville 3: The Demon 🦴½ *Amityville 3-D* **1983 (R)** America's worst real-estate value dupes another funky buyer. The infamous Amityville house is once again restless with terror and gore, though supported with even less plot than the usual smidgin. Cynical reporter Roberts moves in while trying to get to the bottom of the story by way of the basement. Courtesy of 3-D technology, monsters sprang at theatre patrons but the video version is strictly two-dimensional, forcing the viewer to press his or her face directly onto the TV screen in order to derive similar effect. **98m/C VHS.** Tony Roberts, Tess Harper, Robert Joy, Candy Clark, John Beal, Leora Dana, John Harkins, Lori Loughlin, Meg Ryan, Rikke Borge, Jack Cardiff; **D:** Richard Fleischer; **W:** William Wales, David Ambrose; **C:** Fred Schuler; **M:** Howard Blake.

Amityville 4: The Evil Escapes 🦴½ *The Amityville Horror: The Evil Escapes, Part 4* **1989 (R)** It's an unusual case of house-to-house transference as the horror from Amityville continues, now lodged in a Californian residence. The usual good-house-gone-bad story has the place creating a lot of unusual creaks and rattles before deciding to use its inherited powers to attack and possess a little girl. Special effects from Richard Stutsman ("The Lost Boys" and "Jaws"). **95m/C VHS.** Patty Duke, Jane Wyatt, Norman Lloyd, Frederic Lehne, Brandy Gold; **D:** Sandor Stern; **W:** Sandor Stern; **M:** Rick Conrad. TV

Amityville: A New Generation 🦴½ **1993 (R)** And the bad sequels just go on and on and on. Terry is a young photographer who's given an old mirror by a crazy homeless man (tell me why he took it). He shares a loft with three friends and all begin experiencing vivid and terrifying dreams of murder. Seems the mirror is tied to Amityville and its evil legacy and Terry is the designated inheritor. **92m/C VHS.** Ross Partridge, Julia Nickson-Soul, David Naughton, Richard Roundtree, Terry O'Quinn; **D:** John Murlowski; **W:** Christopher DeFaria, Antonio Toro.

The Amityville Curse woof! **1990 (R)** The possessed house is yet again purchased by a pathetically uninformed family. The usual ghostly shenanigans occur with low-budget regularity in this fifth film in the series. Never released theatrically, for good reason. **91m/C VHS.** *CA* Kim Coates, Dawna Wightman, Helen Hughes, David Stein, Cassandra Gava, Jan Rubes; **D:** Tom Berry; **W:** Michael Krueger, Norvell Rose.

Amityville Dollhouse 🦴½ **1996 (R)** Family moves into their Victorian dream home in Amityville, which comes complete with a replica dollhouse that charms the daughter. But the Amityville curse inhabits the plaything and soon the poltergeists make their nasty appearance. **97m/C VHS.** Robin Thomas, Starr Andreeff, Allen (Culter) Cutler, Rachel Duncan, Jarrett Lennon, Clayton Murray, Frank Ross, Lenora Kardorf, Lisa Robin Kelly; **D:** Steve White; **W:** Joshua Michael Stern; **C:** Thomas Callaway.

Amityville 1992: It's About Time 🦴🦴 **1992 (R)** Time is of the essence in the sixth installment of the Amityville flicks. A vintage clock (from Amityville, of course), causes creepy goings-on in a family's house. Actually a halfway decent horror film with high-grade special effects, and much, much better than previous Amityville sequels, which isn't saying much. **95m/C VHS.** Stephen Macht, Shawn Weatherly, Megan Ward, Damon Martin, Nita Talbot, Dick Miller; **D:** Tony Randel; **W:** Christopher DeFaria, Antonio Toro.

Amnesia 🦴🦴 **1996 (R)** Minister Paul Keller (Walker) is having an affair with his son's teacher, Veronica Dow (Tomanovich). Paul decides to fake his death, leaving wife Martha (Sheedy) with the insurance money, and allowing him to start a new life with Veronica. Only he has an accident that causes amnesia and runs into more trouble than he can imagine. Has more humor than you might imagine, thanks to its wacky characters, but as usual Kirkland is way over the top as a love-starved motel owner. **92m/C VHS.** Nicholas Walker, Ally Sheedy, Sally Kirkland, John Savage, Dara Tomanovich, Vincent Berry; **D:** Kurt Voss.

Among Giants 🦴🦴 **1998 (R)** Postlethwaite is Ray, the foreman of a crew of painters assigned to slap a new coat on the electrical towers that line the Yorkshire countryside. When a female Australian rock climber (Griffiths) wanders into town, joins the crew, and starts sleeping with Ray, she causes static between him and his best friend (Thornton). Understated to the point of being comatose, nothing much happens with the romance or the dangerous occupation angle. Postlethwaite does a fine job as the unlikely romantic lead, though. **93m/C VHS.** *GB* Pete Postlethwaite, Rachel Griffiths, James Thornton, Lennie James, Andy Serkis, Rob Jarvis; **D:** Sam Miller; **W:** Simon Beaufoy; **C:** Witold Stok; **M:** Tim Atack.

Among the Cinders 🦴🦴 **1983** Sometimes interesting coming of age drama about a 16-year-old New Zealand boy who runs away to his grandfather's farm to forget about his friend's accidental death. At the farm, he meets an older woman and compromises his virtue. **103m/C VHS.** *GE NZ* Paul O'Shea, Derek Hardwick, Rebecca Gibney, Yvonne Lawley, Amanda Jones; **D:** Rolf Haedrich.

Amongst Friends 🦴🦴 **1993 (R)** Three boyhood buddies, Trevor (McGaw), Billy (Lindsey), and Andy (Parlavecchio), from a nice Long Island neighborhood turn to crime out of boredom. Trevor gets busted and goes to prison for two years. Upon getting out, he finds his old cronies still share the taste for crime and general aimlessness but also still want that one big score. Trevor finally agrees to join Andy and Billy in a drug deal but the jealous Billy, who wants Trevor's old girlfriend Laura (Sorvino), plans a double-cross that will affect them all. Filled with cutting attacks on the society that spawns aimless youth. Debut of then 26-year-old writer/director Weiss. **88m/C VHS.** Louis Lombardi, Patrick McGaw, Steve Parlavecchio, Joseph Lindsey, Mira Sorvino, David Stepkin, Michael Artura; **D:** Rob Weiss; **W:** Rob Weiss; **C:** Michael Bonvillain; **M:** Mick Jones.

Amor Bandido 🦴🦴½ **1979** When cab drivers in Rio are turning up dead, a young prostitute is torn between her detective father and her prime suspect boyfriend. Drama based on a true story. In Portuguese with English subtitles. **95m/C VHS.** *BR* Paulo Gracindo, Cristina Ache, Paulo Guarniero; **D:** Bruno Barreto.

Amore 🦴🦴🦴 **1948** Rossellini's tribute to actress Magnani consists of the short films "The Human Voice" and "The Miracle." In "The Human Voice," Magnani is shown alone, speaking to her lover on the telephone. Based on Jean Cocteau's one-act drama. In "The Miracle," she is a simple peasant girl who believes her illegitimate child is acutally the new Messiah. In Italian with English subtitles. **78m/B VHS.** *IT* Anna Magnani; **D:** Roberto Rossellini.

Amore! 🦴🦴½ **1993 (PG-13)** Wealthy investment banker Saul Schwartz (Scalia) hates his job, his wife, and his life. The only way he loses himself is by watching movies starring Italian matinee idol Rudolfo Carbonera (Hamilton). So Saul gets divorced and decides to change his life—by going to Hollywood and becoming an actor like his debonair idol. With the help of some newfound friends he transforms himself into suave leading man material (under the name of Salvatore Guiliano III) but promptly winds up falling for a writer (Ireland), who couldn't care less. **93m/C VHS.** Jack Scalia, Kathy Ireland, Elliott Gould, George Hamilton, Brenda Epperson, James Doohan, Katherine Helmond, Betsy Russell, Norm Crosby, Frank Gorshin; **D:** Lorenzo Doumani; **W:** Lorenzo Doumani.

Amores Perros 🦴🦴🦴 *Love's a Bitch* **2000 (R)** A Mexico City car accident and the fortunes of a dog bring together three stories of love, loss, and redemption in director/producer Gonzalez Inarritu's impressive feature debut. Octavio's love for his brother's wife leads him to enter his dog, Cofi, in a dogfight for elopement money. When Cofi is wounded, it leads to a car chase, and the central accident. A woman, Valeria, is injured and permanently scarred in the accident. This affects her beau, who has just left his family to be with her. A homeless man, a former revolutionary turned hitman, witnesses the crash and rescues the dog, who becomes a part of his search for his estranged daughter. The plot structure invites comparisons to Tarantino, but these characters inhabit a more consequences-and-morality-oriented world than Q's characters ever did. Film came under fire from animal rights activists for the dogfight scenes, although it was made clear from the start that no animals were actually harmed. **153m/C VHS, DVD, Wide.** *MX* Vanessa Bauche, Emilio Echeverria, Gael Garcia Bernal, Goya Toledo, Alvaro Guerrero, Jorge Salinas, Marco Perez, Rodrigo Murray, Humberto Busto, Gerardo Campbell, Rosa Maria Bianchi, Dunia Saldivar, Adriana Barraza; **D:** Alejandro Gonzalez Inarritu; **W:** Guillermo Arriaga; **C:** Rodrigo Prieto; **M:** Gustavo Santaolalla. British Acad. '01: Foreign Film; Natl. Bd. of Review '01: Foreign Film.

The Amorous Adventures of Moll Flanders 🦴🦴 **1965** An amusing romp set in 18th century England focusing on a poor orphan girl who seeks wealth. Moll plots to get ahead through an advantageous series of romances and marriages. Her plan is ruined when she falls in love and he turns out to be a wanted highwayman, landing her in prison. Not surprisingly, love (and money) conquers all. Based on the novel by Daniel Defoe. Novak tries in this female derivative of "Tom Jones," but this period piece isn't her style. **126m/C VHS.** Kim Novak, Richard Johnson, Angela Lansbury, Vittorio De Sica, Leo McKern, George Sanders, Lilli Palmer; **D:** Terence Young; **C:** Ted Moore; **M:** John Addison.

Amos 🦴🦴½ **1985** Douglas is Amos, an aging baseball coach confined most reluctantly to a nursing home. He's disturbed by recent suspicious events there, his concern causing him to take on Montgomery, the staunch head nurse. Well-acted drama produced by Douglas's son Peter, offering an echo of "One Flew Over the Cuckoo's Nest," which Dad starred in on Broadway and son Michael helped produced as a movie classic. **100m/C VHS.** Kirk Douglas, Elizabeth Montgomery, Dorothy McGuire, Noriyuki "Pat" Morita, James Sloyan, Ray Walston; **D:** Michael Tuchner; **M:** Georges Delerue.

Amos and Andrew 🦴½ **1993 (PG-13)** Embarrassing attempt at comedy stops short of endorsing the stereotypes it tries to parody. Prizewinning African-American author Andrew Sterling (Jackson) is seen moving into a house on an island previously reserved for the uptight white, and the neighbors call the cops, assuming he's a thief. Chief of police (Coleman) eagerly gets into the act, then exploits drifter Amos (Cage) in a cover-up attempt when he realizes his mistake. Talented cast can't overcome lame jokes and transparent plot that serves as an opportunity to bring black and white together for a "see how much we have in common" bonding session. **96m/C VHS, DVD.** Nicolas Cage, Samuel L. Jackson, Michael Lerner, Margaret Colin, Giancarlo Esposito, Dabney Coleman, Bob Balaban, Aimee Graham, Brad Dourif, Chelcie Ross, Jodi Long; **D:** E. Max Frye; **W:** E. Max Frye; **M:** Richard Gibbs.

The Amphibian Man 🦴🦴 **1961** What does a scientist do once he's created a young man with gills? Plunge him in the real world of aqua pura to experience life and love, albeit underwater. Trouble is, the protagonist, who's come to be known as the Sea Devil, takes a dive for a young pretty he's snatched from the jaws of death. A '60s Soviet sci-fi romance originally seen on American TV. **93m/C VHS, DVD.** *RU* K. Korieniev, M. Virzinskaya, Mikhail Kozakov, Vladlen Davydov; **D:** Y. Kasancki; **W:** Aleksei Kapler.

The Amsterdam Connection 🦴 **197?** Film company acts as a cover for prostitution and drug smuggling, with the girls acting as international couriers. **90m/C VHS.** *HK* Chen Shing, Kid Sherrif, Yeung Sze, Jason Pai Piu, Fang Mui San; **D:** Fang Mui San, Lo Ke.

The Amsterdam Kill 🦴🦴 **1978 (R)** A washed-up ex-agent of the U.S. Drug Enforcement Agency is hired by a desperate U.S. Drug Enforcement Agency to hunt down the kingpin of a narcotics syndicate in Hong Kong. Tedious pace with occasional spells of violence fails to awaken somnambulent Mitchum. Shot on location in Hong Kong. **93m/C VHS.** *HK* Robert Mitchum, Richard Egan, Keye Luke, Leslie Nielsen, Bradford Dillman; **D:** Robert Clouse; **W:** Robert Clouse.

Amsterdamned 🦴🦴 **1988 (R)** A crime thriller taking place on the canals of Amsterdam featuring a serial skindiver killer who surfaces periodically to slash and splash. A steely detective fishes for clues. Dubbed. **114m/C VHS, Wide.** *NL* Monique Van De Ven, Huub Stapel, Hidde Maas, Serge-Henri Valcke, Wim Zomer, Tatum Dagelet; **D:** Dick Maas; **W:** Dick Maas; **C:** Marc Felperlaan.

Amuck! 🦴🦴½ **1971** Vintage early '70s Euro-sleaze makes a belated debut on home video. Greta (Bouchet) is hired to be a secretary to world-famous author Richard Stuart (Granger). But Stuart's wife Eleanora (Neri) has designs on the young woman, and Greta has secrets of her own. Nostalgic treat for fans of the era. **98m/C DVD.** *IT* Farley Granger, Barbara Bouchet, Rosalba (Sara Bay) Neri, Umberto Raho, Patrizia Viotti, Dino Mele, Petar Martinovic, Nino Segurini; **D:** Silvio Amandio; **W:** Silvio Amandio; **C:** Aldo Giordani; **M:** Teo Usuelli.

Amy 🦴🦴½ **1981 (G)** Set in the early 1900s, the story follows the experiences of a woman after she leaves her well-to-do husband to teach at a school for the deaf and blind. Eventually she organizes a football game between the handicapped kids and the other children in the neighborhood. Good Disney family fare. **100m/C VHS.** Jenny Agutter, Barry Newman, Kathleen Nolan, Margaret O'Brien, Nanette Fabray, Chris Robinson, Louis Fant; **D:** Vincent McEveety; **M:** Robert F. Brunner.

Amy 🦴🦴½ **1998** Quirky to say the least. Nine-year-old Amy (De Roma) has been an elective deaf-mute since witnessing the death of her rock star father Will (Barker), who was electrocuted during a concert. The only way Amy does communiate is through music—something discovered by luckless musician Robert (Mendelsohn). Meanwhile, Amy's bitter mom Tanya (Griffiths) is trying to avoid the welfare authorities who want to take charge of Amy's schooling and treatment. Uneasy mix of genres but the performance by child actress De Roma is remarkable. **103m/C VHS.** *AU* Rachel Griffiths, Alana De Roma, Ben Mendelsohn, Nick Barker, Kerry Armstrong; ***D:*** Nadia Tass; ***W:*** David Parker; ***C:*** David Parker; ***M:*** Phil Judd.

The Amy Fisher Story 🦴🦴 *Beyond Control* **1993** Amy Fisher wishes she looked this good. Perhaps if she did, she could be acting in TV movies like Barrymore instead of providing fodder for them. The ABC account draws from a variety of sources to dramatize the relationship between Amy and her married, ahem, friend, and Amy's subsequent attack on his wife. Although it tries not to take sides, it does include some pretty hot sex scenes which could be why this docudrama garnered the highest ratings of the three network productions released on TV. See also: "Casualties of Love: The 'Long Island Lolita' Story" and "Lethal Lolita—Amy Fisher: My Story." **93m/C VHS, DVD.** Drew Barrymore, Anthony John (Tony) Denison, Harley Jane Kozak, Tom Mason, Laurie Paton, Ken Pogue, Linda Darlow, Garry Davey, Dwight McFee, Gabe Khouth, Philip Granger, Stephen Cooper; ***D:*** Andy Tennant; ***W:*** Janet Brownell; ***C:*** Glen MacPherson; ***M:*** Michael Hoenig. **TV**

Anaconda 🦴🦴½ **1996 (PG-13)** Snakes—lots and lots of snakes. Teeny baby snakes, little snakes, medium-sized snakes, large snakes, and one gigantic 40-foot long snake that likes to swallow people and then vomit them up again (the better to have room to swallow somebody else). Oh yeah, the minimal plot concerns a documentary film crew traveling the Amazon River looking for a legendary Indian tribe. They not only have to contend with the snakes but with crazy, snake-obsessed guide Paul Sarone (Voight). The actors react appropriately to becoming snake food. **90m/C VHS, DVD.** Jon Voight, Jennifer Lopez, Ice Cube, Eric Stoltz, Owen C. Wilson, Kari Wuhrer, Jonathan Hyde, Vincent Castellanos, Danny Trejo; ***D:*** Luis Llosa; ***W:*** Jim Cash, Jack Epps Jr., Hans Bauer; ***C:*** Bill Butler; ***M:*** Randy Edelman.

Analyze This 🦴🦴🦴 **1998 (R)** Robert De Niro stars as anxiety-stricken mob boss Paul Vitti. He begins to see suburban shrink Ben (Crystal), and is so pleased with the results that he strong-arms the doc into seeing him whenever he wants. Unfortunately for Ben and fiance Laura (Kudrow), that usually happens to be when they're trying to get married. Palminteri is a rival gangster with whom Vitti "seeks closure." De Niro expertly winks at the mob genre (which he helped create) without losing the air of menace that surrounds the good fella character. His performance carries the movie despite the somewhat hokey ending. It's De Niro's underworld, Billy's just living in it. **110m/C VHS, DVD.** Robert De Niro, Billy Crystal, Lisa Kudrow, Chazz Palminteri, Joe (Johnny) Viterelli, Bill Macy, Leo Rossi, Rebecca Schull, Molly Shannon, Max Casella, Pat Cooper, Richard C. Castellano, Jimmie Ray Weeks, Elizabeth Bracco, Tony Darrow, Kyle Sabihy, Donnamarie Recco; ***D:*** Harold Ramis; ***W:*** Harold Ramis, Peter Tolan, Kenneth Lonergan; ***C:*** Stuart Dryburgh; ***M:*** Howard Shore.

Anastasia 🦴🦴🦴½ **1956** Bergman won her second Oscar, and deservedly so, for her classic portrayal of the amnesia victim chosen by Russian expatriate Brynner to impersonate Anastasia, the last surviving member of the Romanoff dynasty. As such, she becomes part of a scam to collect millions of rubles deposited in a foreign bank by her supposed father, the now-dead Czar. But is she just impersonating the princess? Brynner as the scheming White General and Hayes as the Grand Duchess who needs to be convinced turn in fine performances as well. Based on Marcelle Maurette's play. **105m/C VHS, Wide.** Ingrid Bergman, Yul Brynner, Helen Hayes, Akim Tamiroff, Martita Hunt, Felix Aylmer, Ivan Desny, Sacha (Sascha) Pitoeff; ***D:*** Anatole Litvak; ***W:*** Arthur Laurents; ***C:*** Jack Hildyard. Oscars '56: Actress (Bergman); Golden Globes '57: Actress—Drama (Bergman); N.Y. Film Critics '56: Actress (Bergman).

Anastasia 🦴🦴½ **1997 (G)** Let's face it, this is a pretty weird story to turn into a cartoon fairy tale. Fox's first entry into the Disney-dominated full-length animated musical fray is the story of Princess Anastasia and the fall of the Romanov empire. She has been missing ever since the evil Rasputin put a curse on the Romanov family and started the Russian Revolution (Lenin must have flunked the screen test. Not "toon" enough). Ten years later, con artist Dimitri and ex-aristocrat Vladimir try to convince orphaned 18-year-old Anya that she's the ex-royal so they can claim a reward from the princess' grandmother. Little do they know that she actually is the lost princess, but they must battle Rasputin and his albino bat henchman to put things right. Among the big names lending their voices are Meg Ryan, John Cusack (Cossack?), and Christopher Lloyd. Now let me tell you how the Katzenjammer Kids started WWII... **90m/C VHS, DVD.** ***D:*** Don Bluth, Gary Goldman; ***W:*** Bruce Graham, Susan Guathier, Bob Tzudiker, Noni White; ***M:*** David Newman; ***V:*** Meg Ryan, John Cusack, Kelsey Grammer, Angela Lansbury, Christopher Lloyd, Hank Azaria, Bernadette Peters, Kirsten Dunst.

Anastasia: The Mystery of Anna 🦴🦴½ **1986** Irving stars as Anna Anderson, a woman who claimed to be the Grand Duchess Anastasia, the sole surviving daughter of Russian Czar Nicholas II. A powerful epic reliving her experience of royalty, flight from execution, and struggle to retain her heritage. The story of Anastasia remains as one of the greatest dramatic mysteries of the 20th century. Adapted from the book "Anastasia: The Riddle of Anna Anderson" by Peter Kurth. **190m/C VHS.** Amy Irving, Olivia de Havilland, Jan Niklas, Nicolas Surovy, Susan Lucci, Elke Sommer, Edward Fox, Claire Bloom, Omar Sharif, Rex Harrison; ***D:*** Marvin J. Chomsky; ***W:*** James Goldman. **CABLE**

Anatomy 🦴🦴🦴 *Anatomie* **2000 (R)** Medical student Paula Henning (Potente) is accepted into a prestigious Heidelberg anatomy class. She's carrying on the family tradition of her grandfather, who's dying in the hospital he built, and her father, with whom she disagrees on almost everything. But when she gets to the new university, she finds that very creepy stuff is going on. Medical horror/thriller is right up there with "Coma." It's inventive, grotesque, and the special effects work very well. Franka Potente shows that the impression she made in "Run, Lola, Run" was no fluke. **100m/C VHS, DVD, Wide.** *GE* Franka Potente, Benno Furmann, Anna Loos, Holger Spechhahn, Sebastian Blomberg; ***D:*** Stefan Ruzowitzky; ***W:*** Stefan Ruzowitzky; ***C:*** Peter von Haller; ***M:*** Marius Ruhland.

Anatomy of a Murder 🦴🦴🦴🦴 **1959** Considered by many to be the best courtroom drama ever made. Small-town lawyer in northern Michigan faces an explosive case as he defends an army officer who has killed a man he suspects was his philandering wife's rapist. Realistic, cynical portrayal of the court system isn't especially concerned with guilt or innocence, focusing instead on the interplay between the various courtroom characters. Classic performance by Stewart as the down home but brilliant defense lawyer who matches wits with Scott, the sophisticated prosecutor; terse and clever direction by Preminger. Though tame by today's standards, the language used in the courtroom was controversial. Filmed in upper Michigan; based on the bestseller by judge Robert Traver. **161m/B VHS, DVD.** James Stewart, George C. Scott, Arthur O'Connell, Ben Gazzara, Lee Remick, Orson Bean, Eve Arden, Duke Ellington, Kathryn Grant, Murray Hamilton, Joseph Welch; ***D:*** Otto Preminger; ***W:*** Wendell Mayes; ***C:*** Sam Leavitt; ***M:*** Duke Ellington. N.Y. Film Critics '59: Actor (Stewart), Screenplay.

Anatomy of a Psycho 🦴 **1961** A man plans to avenge his gas chambered brother by committing mass murder. Very cheaply and poorly produced. **75m/B VHS.** Ronnie Burns, Pamela Lincoln, Darrell Howe, Russ Bender; ***D:*** Brooke L. Peters.

Anatomy of a Seduction 🦴🦴 **1979** TV formula melodrama of a middle-aged divorcee's affair with her son's best friend. Age knows no boundaries when it comes to television lust. **100m/C VHS, 8mm.** Susan Flannery, Jameson Parker, Rita Moreno, Ed Nelson, Michael Le Clair; ***D:*** Steven Hilliard Stern; ***M:*** Hagood Hardy. **TV**

Anatomy of Terror 🦴 *An Echo of Teresa* **1974** Drama about an army vet going bonkers (what? really?) and revealing espionage secrets in his home life. **73m/C VHS.** Paul Burke, Polly Bergen, Dinsdale Landen, Basil Henson, Roger Hume, William Job. **TV**

Anchors Aweigh 🦴🦴🦴 **1945** Snappy big-budget (for then) musical about two horny sailors, one a girl-happy dancer and the other a shy singer. While on leave in Hollywood they return a lost urchin to his sister. The four of them try to infiltrate a movie studio to win an audition for the girl from maestro Iturbi. Kelly's famous dance with Jerry the cartoon Mouse (of "Tom and Jerry" fame) is the second instance of combining live action and animation. The young and handsome Sinatra's easy crooning and Grayson's near operatic soprano are blessed with music and lyrics by Styne and Cahn. Lots of fun, with conductor-pianist Iturbi contributing and Hollywood-style Little Mexico also in the brew. ♫We Hate to Leave; I Fall in Love Too Easily; The Charm of You; The Worry Song; Jalousie; All of a Sudden My Heart Sings; I Begged Her; What Makes the Sun Set?; Waltz Serenade. **139m/C VHS, DVD.** Frank Sinatra, Gene Kelly, Kathryn Grayson, Jose Iturbi, Dean Stockwell, Carlos Ramirez, Pamela Britton, Sharon McManus, Leon Ames; ***D:*** George Sidney; ***M:*** Jule Styne, Sammy Cahn. Oscars '45: Scoring/Musical.

Ancient Evil: Scream of the Mummy 🦴½ **2000 (R)** Six archeology students discover accidentally revive an Aztec mummy and unleash a deadly curse that could destroy mankind. **86m/C VHS, DVD.** Ariauna Albright, Jeff Peterson, Russell Richardson, Christopher Cullen; ***D:*** David DeCoteau. **VIDEO**

And a Nightingale Sang 🦴🦴½ **1991** WWII England is the scene of this sweet romance, a sad and humorous tale of a woman who gives everything for the war effort. Stunning recreation of the final days of the Blitzkreig. Originally produced for Masterpiece Theatre. **90m/C VHS.** *GB* Joan Plowright, Tom Watt, Phyllis Logan, John Woodvine, Pippa Hinchley, Stephen Tompkinson; ***D:*** Robert Knights.

And Baby Makes Six 🦴🦴½ **1979** An unexpected pregnancy creates new challenges for a couple with grown children. Dewhurst is excellent as usual. Followed by "Baby Comes Home." **100m/C VHS, 8mm.** Colleen Dewhurst, Warren Oates, Maggie Cooper, Mildred Dunnock, Timothy Hutton, Allyn Ann McLerie; ***D:*** Waris Hussein; ***W:*** Shelley List. **TV**

And God Created Woman 🦴🦴½ *And Woman...Was Created; Et Dieu Crea la Femme* **1957 (PG)** Launching pad for Bardot's career as a sex siren, as she flits across the screen in a succession of scanty outfits and hangs out at the St. Tropez beach in what is euphemistically known as a swimsuit while turning up the heat for the males always in attendance. The plot concerns an 18-year-old nymphomaniac who is given a home by a local family with three handsome young sons. A cutting-edge sex film in its time that was boffo at the boxoffice. In French with English subtitles. **93m/C VHS, DVD, Wide.** *FR* Brigitte Bardot, Curt Jurgens, Jean-Louis Trintignant, Christian Marquand; ***D:*** Roger Vadim; ***W:*** Roger Vadim, Raoul Levy; ***C:*** Armand Thirard; ***M:*** Paul Misraki.

And God Created Woman 🦴½ **1988 (R)** Loose, dull remake by Vadim of his own 1957 softcore favorite about a free-spirited woman dodging men and the law while yearning for rock and roll stardom. DeMornay is a prisoner who hopes to marry one of the local hunks (Spano) so she can be paroled. They marry, she strips, he frets, while political hopeful Langella smacks his lips in anticipation. Available in an unrated 100-minute version. **98m/C VHS, DVD.** Rebecca DeMornay, Vincent Spano, Frank Langella, Donovan Leitch, Judith Chapman, Thelma Houston; ***D:*** Roger Vadim; ***M:*** Tom Chase, Steve Rucker.

And God Said to Cain 🦴 *E Dio Disse a Caino* **1969** Another Biblically titled western from the prolific Kinski, about a put-upon gunman who must fight for his life. **95m/C VHS.** *IT* Klaus Kinski, Antonio Cantafora, Peter Carsten, Marcella Michelangeli, Luciano Pigozzi, Giuliano Raffaelli; ***D:*** Anthony (Antonio Margheriti) Dawson; ***W:*** Anthony (Antonio Margheriti) Dawson, Giovanni Addessi; ***C:*** Riccardo (Pallton) Pallottini, Luciano Trasatti; ***M:*** Carlo Savina.

...And God Spoke 🦴🦴 **1994 (R)** Low budget spoof takes on both religion and moviemaking with two schlockmeisters filming a biblical epic. Since the duo have no budget and are basic hacks with pretensions, they have to settle...so Sales plays Moses, "The Incredible Hulk" Ferrigno gets cast as Cain, while Plumb ("Jan" on "The Brady Bunch") does Mrs. Noah. Has some lulls but also covers very recognizable territory. Directorial debut of Borman. **82m/C VHS.** Michael Riley, Stephen Rappaport, Soupy Sales, Lou Ferrigno, Eve Plumb, Andy Dick, R.C. Bates, Fred Kaz, Daniel Tisman; ***D:*** Arthur Borman; ***W:*** Gregory S. Malins, Michael Curtis; ***C:*** Lee Daniel.

And Hope to Die 🦴🦴½ **1972** Moody, muddled crime drama with a good cast about a fleeing Frenchman who joins a gang of hardened criminals in Canada. They go ahead with their plans to kidnap a retarded girl even though she is already dead. Standard caper film is enhanced by arty camera work and some unusual directorial touches. **95m/C VHS.** *FR* Robert Ryan, Jean-Louis Trintignant, Aldo Ray, Tisa Farrow, Lea Massari; ***D:*** Rene Clement.

And I Alone Survived 🦴🦴 **1978** True story of a woman who survives a leisure-plane crash in the Sierra Nevadas and her struggle to get to the village below. Brown does her best to elevate the proceedings above the usual I-hope-I-don't-die cliches. **90m/C VHS.** Blair Brown, David Ackroyd, Vera Miles, G.D. Spradlin; ***D:*** William A. Graham; ***C:*** Jordan Cronenweth. **TV**

And Justice for All 🦴🦴½ **1979 (R)** Earnest attorney Pacino questions the law and battles for justice in and out of the courtroom. He's hired to defend a detested judge from a rape charge, while dealing with a lost-soul caseload of eccentric and tragedy-prone clients. Overly melodramatic, an odd mix of satire, cynicism, and seemingly sincere drama that hits with a club when a stick will do. Jewison aims for black surrealism, permitting both Pacino and Warden (as a judge losing his sanity) to veer into histrionics, to the detriment of what is essentially a gripping behind-the-scenes story. Excellent cast creates sparks, including Lahti in her film debut. And Baltimore never looked lovelier. **120m/C VHS, DVD, Wide.** Dominic Chianese, Al Pacino, Jack Warden, Christine Lahti, Thomas G. Waites, Craig T. Nelson, John Forsythe, Lee Strasberg, Jeffrey Tambor; ***D:*** Norman Jewison; ***W:*** Barry Levinson, Valerie Curtin; ***C:*** Victor Kemper; ***M:*** Dave Grusin.

And Nothing But the Truth 🦴🦴½ *Giro City* **1982** A multinational corporation is out to ruin the investigative TV report team trying to do a story on the company. **90m/C VHS.** *GB* Glenda Jackson, Jon Finch, Kenneth Colley, James Donnelly; ***D:*** Karl Francis.

And Now for Something Completely Different 🦴🦴🦴 **1972 (PG)** A compilation of skits from BBC-TV's "Monty Python's Flying Circus" featuring Monty Python's own weird, hilarious brand of humor. Sketches include "The Upper Class Twit of the Year Race," "Hell's Grannies," and "The Townswomen's Guild Reconstruction of Pearl Harbour." A great intro to Python for the uninitiated, or a chance for the converted to see their favorite sketches again. **89m/C VHS, DVD.** *GB* John Cleese, Michael Palin, Eric Idle, Graham Chapman, Terry Gilliam, Terry Jones, Carol Cleveland, Connie Booth; ***D:*** Ian McNaughton, Terry Gilliam; ***W:*** John Cleese, Michael Palin, Eric Idle, Graham Chapman, Terry Gilliam, Terry Jones; ***C:*** David Muir; ***M:*** Douglas Gamley.

And Now Miguel 🦴🦴 **1966** Plodding tale of a young boy who wants to take over as head shepherd of his family's flock. Filmed in New Mexico, but the overlong outdoor shots make it drag a bit in spite of Cardi's competent performance. **95m/C VHS.** Pat Cardi, Michael Ansara, Guy Stockwell, Clu Gulager, Joe De Santis, Pilar Del Rey, Buck Taylor; ***D:*** James B. Clark.

And Now My Love 🦴🦴½ **1974 (PG)** A French couple endeavor to maintain their romance despite interfering socio-economic factors—she's a millionaire and he's an ex-con filmmaker. Keller plays three roles spanning three generations, as Lelouch invests autobiographical details to invent a highly stylized, openly sentimental view of French folks in love with love. Along the way he comments on social mores and changing attitudes through the years. Dubbed in English. **121m/C VHS.** *FR* Marthe Keller, Andre Dussollier, Carla Gravina; ***D:*** Claude Lelouch; ***W:*** Claude Lelouch. L.A. Film Critics '75: Foreign Film.

And Now the Screaming Starts 🦴🦴½ *Bride of Fengriffen; Fengriffen; I Have No Mouth But I Must Scream* **1973 (R)** The young bride-to-be of the lord of a British manor house is greeted by bloody faces at the window, a severed hand, and five corpses. Then Cushing shows up to investigate. Good-looking, sleek production with genuine chills. **91m/C VHS, DVD, Wide.** *GB* Peter Cushing, Herbert Lom, Patrick Magee, Ian Ogilvy, Stephanie Beacham, Rosalie Crutchley, Guy Rolfe, Janet Key, Gillian Lind; ***D:*** Roy Ward Baker; ***W:*** Roger Marshall; ***C:*** Denys Coop; ***M:*** Douglas Gamley.

And Soon the Darkness 🦴🦴 **1970 (PG)** One of two vacationing young nurses disappears in France where a teenager was once murdered and the search is on. Predictable, ineffective suspenser. **94m/C VHS, DVD, Wide.** *GB* Pamela Franklin, Michele Dotrice, Sandor Eles, John Nettleton, Claire Kelly, Hanna-Marie Pravda; ***D:*** Robert Fuest; ***W:*** Terry Nation, Brian Clemens; ***C:*** Ian Wilson; ***M:*** Laurie Johnson.

And the Band Played On 🦴🦴🦴 **1993 (PG-13)** Randy Shilts's monumental, and controversial, 1987 book on the AIDS epidemic comes to TV in an equally controversial cable movie. Details the intricate medical research undertaken by doctors in France and the U.S. who fought to isolate and identify the mystery virus despite governmental neglect, red tape, clashing egos, and lack of funding. Various aspects of gay life are shown objectively, without sensationalizing. Celebrity cameos are somewhat distracting though most acquit themselves well. The script went through numerous rewrites; director Spottiswoode reportedly objected to HBO interference at the editing stage. **140m/C VHS, DVD, Wide.** Matthew Modine, Alan Alda, Ian McKellen, Lily Tomlin, Glenne Headly, Richard Masur, Saul Rubinek, Charles Martin Smith, Patrick Bauchau, Nathalie Baye, Christian Clemenson; ***Cameos:*** Richard Gere, David Clennon, Phil Collins, Alex Courtney, David Dukes, David Marshall Grant, Ronald Guttman, Anjelica Huston, Ken Jenkins, Richard Jenkins, Tcheky Karyo, Swoosie Kurtz, Jack Laufer, Steve Martin, Dakin Matthews, Peter McRobbie, Lawrence Monoson, B.D. Wong, Donal Logue, Jeffrey Nordling, Stephen Spinella; ***D:*** Roger Spottiswoode; ***W:*** Arnold Schulman; ***C:*** Paul Elliott; ***M:*** Carter Burwell. **CABLE**

... And the Earth Did Not Swallow Him 🦴🦴½ *...Y No Se Lo Trago La Tierra* **1994** Family trials of migrant farm workers from the perspective of 12-year-old Marcos, who travels with his parents on their annual (it's 1952) move from Texas throughout the midwest during harvest season. Balances their struggles with the strong family bonds that allow them to endure. Based on the semi-autobiographical novel by Tomas Rivera. **99m/C VHS.** Jose Alcala, Rose Portillo, Marco Rodriguez; ***D:*** Severo Perez; ***W:*** Severo Perez; ***C:*** Virgil Harper; ***M:*** Marcos Loya.

And the Ship Sails On 🦴🦴🦴 *E la Nave Va* **1983 (PG)** On the eve of WWI, a group of devoted opera lovers take a luxury cruise to pay their respects to a recently deceased opera diva. Also on board is a group of fleeing Serbo-Croation freedom fighters. A charming and absurd autumnal homage-to-life by Fellini shot entirely in the studio. **130m/C VHS, DVD.** *IT* Freddie Jones, Barbara Jefford, Janet Suzman, Peter Cellier, Philip Locke, Victor Poletti, Norma West; ***D:*** Federico Fellini; ***W:*** Federico Fellini, Tonino Guerra; ***C:*** Giuseppe Rotunno; ***M:*** Gianfranco Plenizio.

And Then There Were None 🦴🦴🦴½ **1945** An all-star cast makes up the ten colorful guests invited to a secluded estate in England by a mysterious host. What the invitations do not say, however, is the reason they have been specifically chosen to visit—to be murdered, one by one. Cat and mouse classic based on Agatha Christie's book with an entertaining mix of suspense and black comedy. Remade in 1966 and again in 1975 as "Ten Little Indians," but lacking the force and gloss of the original. **97m/B VHS, DVD.** Louis Hayward, Barry Fitzgerald, Walter Huston, Roland Young, Sir C. Aubrey Smith, Judith Anderson, Mischa Auer, June Duprez; ***D:*** Rene Clair; ***W:*** Rene Clair, Dudley Nichols; ***C:*** Lucien N. Andriot; ***M:*** Mario Castelnuovo-Tedesco.

And Then You Die 🦴🦴🦴 **1988 (R)** An intense crime drama about a Canadian drug lord who amasses a fortune from the cocaine and marijuana trade. His empire is threatened as the Mafia, Hell's Angels, and the police try to bring him down. **115m/C VHS.** *CA* Kenneth Welsh, R.H. Thomson, Wayne Robson, Tom Harvey, George Bloomfield, Graeme Campbell; ***D:*** Francis Mankiewicz.

And You Thought Your Parents Were Weird! 🦴🦴½ **1991 (PG)** A pair of introverted, whiz kid brothers invent a lovable robot to provide fatherly guidance as well as companionship for their widowed mother. Surprisingly charming, sentimental film is only slightly hampered by low-budget special effects. **92m/C VHS, DVD.** Marcia Strassman, Joshua John Miller, Edan Gross, John Quade, Sam Behrens, Susan Gibney, Gustav Vintas, Eric Walker; ***D:*** Tony Cookson; ***W:*** Tony Cookson; ***C:*** Paul Elliott; ***M:*** Randy Miller; ***V:*** Alan Thicke, Richard Libertini.

The Anderson Tapes 🦴🦴🦴 **1971 (PG)** Newly released from prison, an ex-con assembles his professional pals and plans the million-dollar robbery of an entire luxury apartment house on NYC's upper east side. Of course, he's unaware that a hoard of law men from federal, state, and local agencies are recording their activities for a wide variety of reasons, though none of the surveillance is coordinated and it has nothing to do with the planned robbery. Based on the novel by Lawrence Sanders, the intricate caper is effectively shaped by Lumet, who skillfully integrates broad satire with suspense. Shot on location in New York City. Walken is The Kid, his first major role. **100m/C VHS.** Sean Connery, Dyan Cannon, Martin Balsam, Christopher Walken, Alan King, Ralph Meeker, Garrett Morris, Margaret Hamilton, Val Avery, Dick Williams, Richard B. Shull, Conrad Bain, Paul Benjamin; ***D:*** Sidney Lumet; ***W:*** Frank Pierson; ***M:*** Quincy Jones.

Andersonville 🦴🦴🦴 **1995** Andersonville was an infamous Confederate prison camp in Georgia that by August, 1864 contained more than 32,000 Union POWs—and was planned to hold 8,000 men. One in four soldiers died in the camp. The story is told through the eyes of Massachusetts Corporal Josiah Day (Emick), who is captured in 1864 and struggles to survive the hellish conditions. The commander of the Andersonville was a deranged German-Swiss captain named Wirz (Triska)—who became the only Civil War soldier to be hanged for war crimes (depicted in "The Andersonville Trial"). The TV miniseries was filmed some 150 miles from the original site. **168m/C VHS.** Thomas F. Wilson, Jarrod Emick, Frederic Forrest, Ted Marcoux, Jan Triska, Cliff DeYoung, Tom Aldredge, Frederick Coffin, Justin Henry, Kris Kamm, William H. Macy, Gabriel Olds, William Sanderson, Bud Davis, Carmen Argenziano, Peter Murnik; ***D:*** John Frankenheimer; ***W:*** David W. Rintels; ***C:*** Ric Waite; ***M:*** Gary Chang.

The Andersonville Trial 🦴🦴🦴½ **1970** Details the atrocities experienced by captured Union soldiers who were held in the Confederacy's notorious Andersonville prison during the American Civil War. Provides an interesting account of the war-crimes trial of the Georgia camp's officials, under whom more than 14,000 prisoners died. Moving, remarkable TV drama based on the book by Pulitzer prize-winner MacKinlay Kantor. **150m/C VHS.** Martin Sheen, William Shatner, Buddy Ebsen, Jack Cassidy, Richard Basehart, Cameron Mitchell; ***D:*** George C. Scott. **TV**

Andre 🦴🦴½ **1994 (PG)** More human-animal interaction from the director of "The Man from Snowy River," telling the true story of an orphaned seal that was adopted by the local Maine harbormaster (Carradine) and his family. As they raise their houseguest, the question arises whether Andre should be returned to the wild. It'll remind you of "Free Willy" with an appealing smaller sea mammal and the equally appealing Majorino, as the youngster who befriends Andre. For those who are sticklers for accuracy, Andre is actually portrayed by a sea lion and not a seal. **94m/C VHS, DVD, Wide.** Keith Carradine, Tina Majorino, Chelsea Field, Keith Szarabajka, Shane Meier, Joshua Jackson; ***D:*** George Miller; ***W:*** Dana Baratta; ***C:*** Thomas Burstyn; ***M:*** Bruce Rowland.

Andrei Rublev 🦴🦴🦴🦴 **1966** A 15th-century Russian icon painter must decide whether to record history or participate in it as Tartar invaders make life miserable. During the black and white portion, he becomes involved in a peasant uprising, killing a man in the process. After a bout of pessimism and a vow of silence, he goes forth to create artistic beauty as the screen correspondingly blazes with color. A brilliant historical drama censored by Soviet authorities until 1971. In Russian with English subtitles. **185m/C VHS, DVD.** *RU* Anatoli (Otto) Solonitzin, Ivan Lapikov, Nikolai Grinko, Nikolai Sergeyev; ***D:*** Andrei Tarkovsky; ***W:*** Andrei Tarkovsky, Andrei Konchalovsky; ***C:*** Vadim Yusov; ***M:*** Vyacheslav Ovchinnikov.

Androcles and the Lion 🦴🦴½ **1952** Stage-bound Hollywood version of the George Bernard Shaw story about a tailor in Imperial Rome who saves Christians from a hungry lion he had previously befriended. Sharp dialogue and a plot that's relatively (within the bounds of Hollywood) faithful help a great play become a semi-satisfying cinematic morsel. Harpo Marx was originally cast as Androcles, but was fired by producer Howard Hughes five weeks into the shooting. **105m/B VHS.** Jean Simmons, Alan Young, Victor Mature, Robert Newton, Maurice Evans, Elsa Lanchester; ***D:*** Chester Erskine; ***C:*** Harry Stradling Sr.

Android 🦴🦴½ **1982 (PG)** When an android who has been assisting a quirky scientist in space learns that he is about to be permanently retired, he starts to take matters into his own synthetic hands. Combines science fiction, suspense and cloned romance. A must for Kinski fans. **80m/C VHS.** Klaus Kinski, Don Opper, Brie Howard, Norbert Weisser, Crofton Hardester, Kendra Kirchner; ***D:*** Aaron Lipstadt; ***W:*** James Reigle, Don Opper; ***C:*** Tim Suhrstedt; ***M:*** Don Preston.

The Android Affair 🦴🦴½ **1995 (PG-13)** Karen Garrett (Kozak) is studying at the Institute for Surgical Research where doctors practice experimental techniques on lifelike androids. Her next patient is William (Dunne), a handsome and charming android with a heart defect, who doesn't want to "die" during Karen's risky surgical procedure. What's worse is Karen finds this 'droid all too humanly appealing and decides to help him escape the Institute. From a story by Isaac Asimov and screenwriter Kletter. **90m/C VHS.** Harley Jane Kozak, Griffin Dunne, Ossie Davis, Saul Rubinek, Peter Outerbridge, Natalie Radford; ***D:*** Richard Kletter; ***W:*** Richard Kletter; ***C:*** Berhard Salzmann; ***M:*** Simon Boswell.

The Andromeda Strain 🦴🦴½ **1971 (G)** A satellite falls back to earth carrying a deadly bacteria that must be identified in time to save the population from extermination. The tension inherent in the bestselling Michael Crichton novel is talked down by a boring cast. Also available in letterbox format. **131m/C VHS, DVD, Wide.** Arthur Hill, David Wayne, James Olson, Kate Reid, Paula Kelly, Ramon Bieri, George Mitchell; ***D:*** Robert Wise; ***W:*** Nelson Gidding; ***C:*** Richard H. Kline; ***M:*** Gil Melle.

Andy and the Airwave Rangers 🦴🦴 *Andy Colby's Incredibly Awesome Adventure* **1989** Andy is whisked into the TV!! He finds adventure and excitement—car chases, intergalactic battles, and cartoons. **75m/C VHS.** Dianne Kay, Vince Edwards, Bo Svenson, Richard Thomas, Erik Estrada, Randy Josselyn, Jessica Puscas, Chuck Kovacic; ***D:*** Deborah Brock.

Andy Hardy Gets Spring Fever 🦴🦴 **1939** Andy falls for a beautiful acting teacher, and then goes into a funk when he finds she's engaged. Judge Hardy and the gang help heal the big wound in his heart. A lesser entry (and the seventh) from the popular series. **88m/B VHS.** Mickey Rooney, Lewis Stone, Ann Rutherford, Fay Holden, Cecilia Parker, Sara Haden, Helen Gilbert; ***D:*** Woodbridge S. Van Dyke.

Andy Hardy Meets Debutante 🦴🦴½ **1940** Seems like there should be an article in that title. Garland's second entry in series, wherein Andy meets and falls foolishly for glamorous debutante Lewis with Betsy's help while family is on visit to New York. Judy/Betsy sings "I'm Nobody's Baby" and "Singing in Rain." **86m/B VHS.** Mickey Rooney, Judy Garland, Lewis Stone, Ann Rutherford, Fay Holden, Sara Haden, Cecilia Parker, Diana Lewis, Tom Neal; ***D:*** George B. Seitz.

Andy Hardy's Double Life 🦴🦴½ **1942** In this entertaining installment from the Andy Hardy series, Andy proposes marriage to two girls at the same time and gets in quite a pickle when they both accept. Williams makes an early screen splash. **91m/B VHS.** Mickey Rooney, Lewis Stone, Ann Rutherford, Fay Holden, Sara Haden, Cecilia Parker, Esther Williams, William Lundigan, Susan Peters, Robert (Bobby) Blake; ***D:*** George B. Seitz; ***C:*** George J. Folsey.

Andy Hardy's Private Secretary 🦴🦴 **1941** After Andy fails his high school finals he gets help from a sympathetic faculty member. As the secretary, Grayson makes a good first impression in one of her early screen appearances. The Hardy series was often used as a training ground for new MGM talent. **101m/B VHS.** Mickey Rooney, Kathryn Grayson, Lewis Stone, Fay Holden, Ian Hunter, Gene Reynolds, Ann Rutherford; ***D:*** George B. Seitz.

Andy Warhol's Bad 🦴🦴🦴 **1977 (R)** In the John Waters' school of "crime is beauty," a Queens housewife struggles to make appointments for both her home electrolysis clinic and her all-female murder-for-hire operation, which specializes in children and pets (who are thrown out of windows and knived, respectively). Her life is further complicated by a boarder (King) who's awaiting the go-ahead for his own assignment, an autistic child unwanted by his mother. One of Warhol's more professional-appearing films, and very funny if your tastes run to the tasteless. **100m/C VHS.** Perry King, Carroll Baker, Susan Tyrrell, Stefania Cassini, Cyrinda Foxe, Lawrence Tierney, Tito Goya; ***D:*** Jed Johnson; ***C:*** Alan Metzger; ***M:*** Michael Bloomfield.

Andy Warhol's Dracula 🦴🦴🦴 *Blood for Dracula; Young Dracula; Dracula Cerca Sangue di Vergine e...Mori de Sete; Dracula Vuole Vivere: Cerca Sangue de Vergina; Andy Warhol's Young Dracula* **1974 (R)** Sex and camp humor, as well as a large dose of blood, highlight Warhol's treatment of the tale. As Dracula can only subsist on the blood of pure, untouched maidens ("were-gins"), gardener Dallesandro rises to the occasion in order to make as many women as he can ineligible for Drac's purposes. Very reminiscent of Warhol's "Frankenstein," but with a bit more spoofery. Look for Roman Polanski in a cameo peek as a pub patron. Available in R and unrated versions. **106m/C VHS, DVD.** *IT FR* Udo Kier, Arno Juerging, Maxine McKendry, Joe Dallesandro, Vittorio De Sica, Milena Vukotic, Dominique Darel, Stefania Casini, Silvia Dionisio; ***Cameos:*** Roman Polanski; ***D:*** Paul Morrissey, Anthony (Antonio Margheriti) Dawson; ***W:*** Paul Morrissey; ***C:*** Luigi Kuveiller; ***M:*** Claudio Gizzi.

Andy Warhol's Frankenstein 🦴🦴½ *Flesh for Frankenstein; The Frankenstein Experiment; Up Frankenstein; The Devil and Dr. Frankenstein; Carne per Frankenstein; Frankenstein; Il Mostro e in Tavola...Barone Frankenstein* **1974 (X)** A most outrageous parody of Frankenstein, featuring plenty of gore, sex, and bad taste in general. Baron von Frankenstein (Kier) derives sexual satisfaction from his corpses (he delivers a particularly thought-provoking philosophy on life as he lustfully fondles a gall bladder); his wife seeks her pleasure from the monster himself (Dallesandro). Originally made in 3-D, this is one of Warhol's campiest outings. Also available on video in an R-rated version. **95m/C VHS, DVD.** *GE FR IT* Udo Kier, Monique Van Vooren, Joe Dallesandro, Dalia di Lazzaro, Arno Juerging, Srdjan Zelenovic, Nicoletta Elmi, Marco Liofredi, Cristina Gajoni, Carla Mancini, Liu Bozizio; ***D:*** Paul Morrissey; ***W:*** Paul Morrissey; ***C:*** Luigi Kuveiller; ***M:*** Claudio Gizzi.

Angel 🦴🦴½ **1937** Melodrama finds Maria Barker (Dietrich) the bored wife of British diplomat Sir Frederick (Marshall). So she heads off to Paris to visit a friend and meets the dashing Anthony Halton (Douglas), with whom she has a fling. Too bad Halton's next stop is jolly old England where he runs into an old military chum (Sir Fred, of course). High gloss but no heart. **91m/B VHS.** Marlene Dietrich, Herbert Marshall, Melvyn Douglas, Edward Everett Horton, Laura Hope Crews; ***D:*** Ernst Lubitsch; ***W:*** Guy Bolton, Samson Raphaelson, Russell Medcroft; ***C:*** Charles B(ryant) Lang Jr.; ***M:*** Frederick "Friedrich" Hollander.

Angel 🦴🦴 *Angelos* **1982** Angel (Maniatis) falls for a sailor (Xanthos) who promises a better life away from his abusive father and the poverty that surrounds him. Instead, Angel winds up on the Athens' streets as a transvestite prostitute, a situation that eventually lead the distraught young man to a shocking act of violence. Explicit but not prurient and based on a true story. Greek with subtitles. **126m/C VHS, DVD.** *GR* Michael Maniatis, Dionyssis Xanthos, Maria Alkeou, Katerina Helmi; ***D:*** George Katakouzinos; ***W:*** George Katakouzinos; ***C:*** Tassos Alexakis; ***M:*** Stamatis Spanoudakis.

Angel 🦴½ **1984 (R)** Low-budget leerer about a 15-year-old honor student who attends an expensive Los Angeles private school during the day and by night becomes Angel, a streetwise prostitute making a living amid the slime and sleaze of Hollywood Boulevard. But wait, all is not perfect. A psycho is following her, looking for an opportunity. **94m/C VHS.** Donna Wilkes, Cliff Gorman, Susan Tyrrell, Dick Shawn, Rory Calhoun, John Diehl, Elaine Giftos, Ross Hagen; ***D:*** Robert Vincent O'Neil; ***W:*** Joseph M. Cala.

Angel 3: The Final Chapter woof! **1988 (R)** Former hooker Angel hits the streets to save her newly discovered sister from a life of prostitution. Trashy sequel with a better cast to tepid "Avenging Angel," which was the inept 1985 follow-up to 1984's tasteless "Angel." **100m/C VHS.** Maud Adams, Mitzi Kapture, Richard Roundtree, Mark Blankfield, Kin Shriner, Tawny (Ellis) Fere, Toni Basil; ***D:*** Tom De Simone; ***M:*** Eric Allaman.

Angel and the Badman 🦴🦴🦴 **1947** When notorious gunslinger Wayne is wounded during a shoot-out, a pacifist family takes him in and nurses him back to health. While he's recuperating, the daughter in the family (Russell) falls for him. She begs him not to return to his previous life. But Wayne, though smitten, thinks that a Duke's gotta do what a Duke's gotta do. And that means finding the dirty outlaw (Cabot) who killed his pa. Predictable but nicely done, with a good cast and script. Wayne provides one of his better performances (and also produced). **100m/B VHS, DVD.** John Wayne, Gail Russell, Irene Rich, Harry Carey Sr., Bruce Cabot; ***D:*** James Edward Grant; ***W:*** James Edward Grant; ***C:*** Archie Stout; ***M:*** Richard Hageman.

An Angel at My Table 🦴🦴🦴🦴 **1989 (R)** New Zealand TV miniseries chronicling the life of Janet Frame, New Zealand's premiere writer/poet. At once whimsical and tragic, the film tells of how a mischievous, free-spirited young girl was wrongly placed in a mental institution for eight years, yet was ultimately able to cultivate her incredible storytelling gifts, achieving success, fame and happiness. Adapted from three of Frame's novels: "To the Is-land," "An Angel at My Table," and "The Envoy From Mirror City." Highly acclaimed the world over, winner of over 20 major international awards. **157m/C VHS.** *NZ* Kerry Fox, Alexia Keogh, Karen Fergusson, Iris Churn, K.J. Wilson, Martyn Sanderson; ***D:*** Jane Campion; ***W:*** Laura Jones; ***C:*** Stuart Dryburgh. Ind. Spirit '92: Foreign Film. **TV**

Angel Baby 🦴🦴½ **1961** A mute girl struggles to re-define her faith when she is cured by preacher, but then sees him fail with others. Fine performances all around, notably Reynolds in his screen debut. Adapted from "Jenny Angel" by Elsie Oaks Barber. **97m/B VHS.** George Hamilton, Salome Jens, Mercedes McCambridge, Joan Blondell, Henry Jones, Burt Reynolds; ***D:*** Paul Wendkos, Hubert Cornfield; ***C:*** Haskell Wexler.

Angel Baby 🦴🦴🦴 **1995 (R)** Psychiatric out patients Kate (McKenzie) and Harry (Lynch) fall in love and move in together despite some misgivings from family and the medical bureaucracy. When Kate becomes pregnant, they decide to stop taking their medication so the baby has a better chance of being born healthy. Kate's doctors believe she's not capable of dealing with a child, although she is equally determined to have her baby, while Harry struggles to make a life for all of them. Strong performances and an assured debut by writer/director Rymer. Film won all seven of the Australian Film Institute Awards for which it was nominated. **101m/C VHS.** *AU* John Lynch, Jacqueline McKenzie, Colin Friels, Deborra-Lee Furness, Robyn Nevin; ***D:*** Michael Rymer; ***W:*** Michael Rymer; ***C:*** Ellery Ryan; ***M:*** John Clifford Ryan. Australian Film Inst. '95: Actor (Lynch), Actress (McKenzie), Cinematog., Director (Rymer), Film, Film Editing, Orig. Screenplay.

Angel Blue 🦴½ *My Neighbor's Daughter* **1997** All-around married nice guy Dennis Cromwell (Bottoms) lives with his wife, Jill (Eichhorn) and newborn child in his California hometown. He befriends newcomer Enrique (Rodriguez) and soon Enrique's daughter Angela (Behrens) is babysitting for the infant Cornwell. David should really know better when his friendship with the teen turns sexual and their secret gets out. **91m/C VHS, DVD.** Karen Black, Sandor Tecsi, Sam Bottoms, Yeniffer Behrens, Lisa Eichhorn, Marco Rodriguez; ***D:*** Steven Kovacs; ***W:*** Steven Kovacs; ***C:*** Mickey Freeman; ***M:*** Joel Lindheimer. **CABLE**

Angel City 🦴🦴½ **1980** A Florida labor camp is the setting for this made-for-TV drama. A family of rural West Virginia migrant workers find themselves trapped inside the camp and exploited by the boss-man. Adapted from Patricia Smith's book. **90m/C VHS.** Ralph Waite, Paul Winfield, Jennifer Warren, Jennifer Jason Leigh, Mitchell Ryan; ***D:*** Philip Leacock; ***W:*** James Lee Barrett.

Angel Dust 🦴🦴 **1996** Nightmare noir about a serial killer who haunts Tokyo's subways. Setsuko (Minami) is a criminal psychologist investigating the murders of several young women, all committed during rush hour at various commuter stops. Each victim has been killed with a poisonous injection. Setsuko learns the first victim was psychologically deprogrammed after leaving a religious cult and contacts her ex-lover, Rei (Wakamatsu), who runs a clinic specializing in such deprogramming. But Rei also becomes the chief suspect when he begins to play sadistic mind games with Setsuko. Is she paranoid or truly in danger? Japanese with subtitles. **116m/C VHS.** *JP* Kaho Minami, Takeshi Wakamatsu; ***D:*** Sogo Ishii; ***W:*** Sogo Ishii, Yorozu Ikuta; ***C:*** Norimichi Kasamatsu; ***M:*** Hiroyuki Nagashima.

Angel Eyes 🦴🦴½ **2001 (R)** Although the film's marketing campaign implied some supernatural elements, there's nothing unworldly about this romantic drama. And despite some capable performances by the leads, the film is utterly predictable as well. Tough Chicago police officer Sharon Pogue (Lopez) is still dealing with the effects of an abusive childhood when she meets another lost soul, Catch (Caviezel), who's grappling with the death of his wife and child. He saves her life, they fall for each other, but things are hardly that simple. They both have emotional issues and a past connection that's all too easy to determine. **104m/C VHS, DVD, Wide.** Jennifer Lopez, James Caviezel, Sonia Braga, Terrence DaShon Howard, Jeremy Sisto, Monet Mazur, Victor Argo, Shirley Knight, Jeremy Ratchford, Peter MacNeill, Stephen Kay; ***D:*** Luis Mandoki; ***W:*** Gerald Di Pego; ***C:*** Piotr Sobocinski; ***M:*** Marco Beltrami.

An Angel for Satan 🦴½ *Un Angelo per Satan* **1966** Steele plays a dual role in her last major, Italian horror film. She gives a strong performance as a woman possessed by the spirit of a statue. In Italian with no subtitles. **90m/B VHS.** *IT* Barbara Steele, Anthony Steffen, Aldo Berti, Mario Brega, Ursula Davis, Claudio Gora; ***D:*** Camillo Mastrocinque; ***W:*** Camillo Mastrocinque; ***M:*** Francesco De Masi.

Angel Heart 🦴🦴½ **1987 (R)** Exotic, controversial look at murder, voodoo cults, and sex in 1955 New Orleans. Bonet defiantly sheds her image as a young innocent (no more Cosby Show for you, young lady). Rourke is slimy as marginal NYC private eye Angel, hired by the devilish De Niro to track a missing big band singer who violated a "contract." His investigation leads him to the bizarre world of the occult in New Orleans, where the blood drips to a different beat. Visually stimulating, with a provocative sex scene between Bonet and Rourke, captured in both R-rated and unrated versions. Adapted by Parker from "Falling Angel" by William Hjortsberg. **112m/C VHS, DVD.** Mickey Rourke, Robert De Niro, Lisa Bonet, Charlotte Rampling, Michael Higgins, Charles Gordone, Kathleen Wilhoite, Stocker Fountelieu, Brownie McGhee, Elizabeth Whitcraft, Eliott Keener, Dann Florek; ***D:*** Alan Parker; ***W:*** Alan Parker; ***C:*** Michael Seresin; ***M:*** Trevor Jones.

Angel in a Taxi 🦴🦴 **1959** A six-year-old boy in an orphanage decides to choose his own mother, a beautiful ballerina he sees in a magazine, when an ugly couple try to adopt him. Italian film dubbed in English. **89m/B VHS, 8mm.** *IT* Wera Cecova, Ettore Manni, Vittorio De Sica, Marietto, Gabriele Ferzetti; ***D:*** Antonio Leonviola.

The Angel Levine 🦴🦴½ **1970 (PG)** Morris (Mostel) is an old Jewish man who has lost his faith in God after a series of personal and professional losses. Alexander Levine (Belafonte) is a black angel who can earn his wings if he can convince Morris that his life does have meaning. As sentimental as it sounds but the leads are pros. Based on a story by Bernard Malamud. **104m/C VHS.** Zero Mostel, Harry Belafonte, Ida Kaminska, Milo O'Shea, Gloria Foster, Eli Wallach, Anne Jackson; ***D:*** Jan Kadar; ***W:*** Bill Gunn, Ronald Ribman; ***C:*** Richard Kratina; ***M:*** William Eaton.

Angel of Death woof! **1986 (R)** A small mercenary band of Nazi hunters attempt to track down Josef Mengele in South America. Stupid entry in the minor "let's find the darn Nazi before he really causes trouble" genre. Director Franco is also known as A. Frank Drew White. **92m/C VHS.** Chris Mitchum, Fernando Rey, Susan Andrews; ***D:*** Jess (Jesus) Franco.

Angel of Destruction 🦴½ **1994 (R)** Undercover cop is assigned to protect controversial rock star from psycho fan. Cop gets killed and cop's sister decides to go after the killer. **80m/C VHS.** Maria Ford, Charlie Spradling; ***D:*** Charles Philip Moore.

Angel of Fury 🦴🦴½ **1993 (R)** Rothrock plays the head of security of a computer corporation who must battle terrorists after the company's top-secret computer. And there's no one she can trust. Lots of martial arts action with the competent Rothrock. **91m/C VHS.** Cynthia Rothrock, Christopher Barnes, Peter O'Brien; ***D:*** Ackyl Anwary.

Angel of H.E.A.T. woof! *The Protectors, Book One* **1982 (R)** Porn-star Chambers is Angel, a female super-agent on a mission to save the world from total destruction. Sex and spies abound with trashy nonchalance. **90m/C VHS.** Marilyn Chambers, Mary Woronov, Steve Johnson; ***D:*** Helen Sanford, Myrl A. Schreibman.

Angel of the Night 🦴🦴 *Nattens Engel* **1998 (R)** Rebecca inherits her grandmother's creepy mansion and invites her best friend and her boyfriend for a visit. While exploring, Rebecca discovers that great-grandpa Rico was a vampire and she inadvertently releases him from his tomb. Dubbed from Danish. **98m/C VHS, DVD, Wide.** *DK* Ulrich Thomsen, Maria Karlsen, Erik Holmey; ***D:*** Shakey Gonzaless; ***W:*** Shakey Gonzaless; ***C:*** Jacob Kusk; ***M:*** Soren Hyldgaard.

Angel on My Shoulder 🦴🦴🦴 **1946** A murdered convict makes a deal with the Devil (Rains) and returns to earth for revenge as a respected judge who's been thinning Hell's waiting list. Occupying the good judge, the murderous Muni has significant problems adjusting. Amusing fantasy with Muni in a rare and successful comic role. Co-written by Segall, who scripted "Here Comes Mr. Jordan," in which Rains played an angel. Remade in 1980. **101m/B VHS, DVD.** Paul Muni, Claude Rains, Anne Baxter, Onslow Stevens; ***D:*** Archie Mayo; ***W:*** Harry Segall; ***C:*** James Van Trees; ***M:*** Dimitri Tiomkin.

Angel on My Shoulder 🦴🦴 **1980** A small-time hood wrongfully executed for murder comes back as district attorney. He owes the devil, but he's finding it tough to be evil enough to repay his debt. O.K. TV remake of the better 1946 film starring Paul Muni. **96m/C VHS.** Peter Strauss, Richard Kiley, Barbara Hershey, Janis Paige; ***D:*** John Berry; ***M:*** Artie Butler. **TV**

Angel Square 🦴🦴 **1992** A Canadian production from the director of the acclaimed "Bye Bye Blues." When the father of a neighborhood boy is brutally attacked, the community bands together to search for the culprit. **106m/C VHS.** *CA* Ned Beatty; ***D:*** Anne Wheeler; ***W:*** James DeFelice.

Angel Town 🦴 **1989 (R)** A foreign exchange student, who happens to be a champion kick-boxer, is forced into combat with LA street gangs. **90m/C VHS, DVD.** Olivier Gruner, Theresa Saldana, Frank Aragon, Tony Valentino, Peter Kwong, Mike Moroff; ***D:*** Eric Karson.

Angel Unchained 🦴½ **1970** Typical biker exploitation flick has bikers and hippies joining together to fend off small-town redneck hostility. **92m/C VHS.** Don Stroud, Tyne Daly, Luke Askew, Larry Bishop, Aldo Ray, Bill McKinney; ***D:*** Lee Madden; ***W:*** Jeffrey Alladin Fiskin.

Angel with the Trumpet 🦴🦴 **1950** Depressing character study of a woman who marries to please her family, rather than herself. When the Gestapo finds out about her Jewish ancestry, she must make the most important decision of her life. **98m/B VHS.** *GB* Eileen Herlie, Basil Sydney, Norman Wooland, Maria Schell, Olga Edwards, Oskar Werner, Anthony Bushell, Wilfrid Hyde-White; ***D:*** Anthony Bushell.

Angela 🦴 **1977** Twisted love story about a young man (Railsback) who jumps the bones of an older woman, unaware that she is the mother he's been separated from for 23 long years. Seems that way back when, the boy was kidnapped by crime boss Huston from mom Loren, an ex-prostitute, who then turned in the boy's dad, who was something of a criminal. Mom thought son was dead, dad vowed revenge from prison, and son went about his unwitting business. It all comes together insipidly, at the expense of the cast and viewer. **91m/C VHS.** *CA* Sophia Loren, Steve Railsback, John Huston, John Vernon; ***D:*** Boris Sagal; ***M:*** Henry Mancini.

Angela 🦴🦴 **1994** Exceedingly mystical film focuses on religiously obsessed 10-year-old Angela (Rhyne), who tells her six-year-old sister Ellie (Blythe) that unless they are very good the Devil will come to take them away. Meanwhile, she tries to cope with volatile family relationships, including their unstable mother. Good performances in a sometimes sluggish and abstract drama. **105m/C VHS.** Miranda Stuart Rhyne, Charlotte Blythe, Anna Thomson, John Ventimiglia, Vincent Gallo; ***D:*** Rebecca Miller; ***W:*** Rebecca Miller; ***C:*** Ellen Kuras; ***M:*** Michael Rohatyn. Sundance '95: Cinematog., Filmmakers Trophy.

Angela's Ashes 🦴🦴½ **1999 (R)** Frank McCourt's devastating memoir covers growing up poverty-stricken in Limerick during the 1930s, with an alcoholic father (Carlyle) and a mother (Watson) struggling to hold the family together while dealing with her own deep depression. The book had the saving graces of lyricism and wit. Unfortunately, the film misses all that and is merely bleak despite the talented cast (including the three actors who play Frank through the years). **145m/C VHS, DVD, Wide.** Emily Watson, Robert Carlyle, Joe Breen, Ciaran Owens, Michael Legge, Ronnie Masterson, Pauline McLynn; ***D:*** Alan Parker; ***W:*** Robert Carlyle, Laura Jones; ***C:*** Michael Seresin; ***M:*** John Williams; ***Nar:*** Andrew Bennett.

Angele 🦴🦴🦴 **1934** A lovely, naive country girl is lured to the city by a cunning pimp who knows that she wants to escape her oppressive father. With her illegitimate baby, she's discovered in a whorehouse and taken in disgrace back home to dad, who promptly locks her in the barn. One special guy, however, appreciates her purity and plots to rescue her. What he lacks in material resources he makes up for in character. An overlong but moving story of lost innocence and intolerence. In French with English subtitles. Based on the novel "Un de Baumugnes" by Jean Giono. **130m/B VHS.** *FR* Orane Demazis, Fernandel, Henri Poupon, Edouard Delmont; ***D:*** Marcel Pagnol.

Angelo My Love 🦴🦴🦴 **1983 (R)** Compassionate docudrama about New York's modern gypsy community. Follows the adventures of 12-year-old Angelo Evans, the streetwise son of a fortune teller, who, with a fresh view, explores the ups and downs of his family's life. Duvall financed the effort and cast non-professional actors in this charming tale of reality and fairy-tale. **91m/C VHS.** Angelo Evans, Michael Evans, Steve "Patalay" Tsiginoff, Cathy Kitchen, Millie Tsiginoff; ***D:*** Robert Duvall; ***M:*** Michael Kamen.

Angels and Insects 🦴🦴🦴 **1995 (R)** Very strange Victorian-era romantic drama is definitely an acquired taste. The mysteries of nature are nothing compared to the mysteries of human life as naturalist William Adamson (Rylance) comes to discover when he takes up a position at the home of amateur insect collector, Sir Harald Alabaster (Kemp). He falls in love and quickly marries blondly beautiful Eugenia (Kensit), whose outward propriety hides a sensual nature and some decadent family secrets. Based on A.S. Byatt's novella "Morpho Eugenia." Take particular note of the costumes by Paul Brown, which mimic the exoticness of insects. **116m/C VHS, DVD, Wide.** *GB* Mark Rylance, Patsy Kensit, Kristin Scott Thomas, Jeremy Kemp, Douglas Henshall, Chris Larkin, Annette Badland, Anna Massey, Saskia Wickham; ***D:*** Philip Haas; ***W:*** Belinda Haas, Philip Haas; ***C:*** Bernard Zitzermann; ***M:*** Alexander Balanescu.

Angel's Brigade 🦴🦴 **1979 (PG)** Seven models get together to stop a big drug operation. Drive-in vigilante movie fare fit for a rainy night. **97m/C VHS.** Jack Palance, Peter Lawford, Jim Backus, Arthur Godfrey; ***D:*** Greydon Clark; ***W:*** Greydon Clark; ***C:*** Dean Cundey.

Angel's Dance 🦴🦴½ **1999 (R)** Tony (Chandler) works for mobster Uncle Vinnie (Polito) and wants to be a hit man. So, Vinnie sends him to L.A. for training with Stevie Rossellini (Belushi) who, despite appearances, is an expert. Part of Tony's education is to choose and kill a victim at random and he selects Angel (Lee). This is Tony's big mistake, since this Angel is turns out to be the avenging kind. Gets a little too goofy but does provide some action. **102m/C VHS, DVD.** James Belushi, Sheryl Lee, Kyle Chandler, Jon Polito, Ned Bellamy, Mac Davis, Frank John Hughes, Mark Carlton; ***D:*** David Corley; ***W:*** David Corley; ***C:*** Michael G. Wojciechowski; ***M:*** Tim Truman.

Angels Die Hard 🦴🦴 **1984 (R)** Novel biker story with the cyclists as the good guys intent on helping a town during a mining disaster. Grizzly Adams makes an early film appearance. **86m/C VHS.** Tom Baker, R.G. Armstrong, Dan Haggerty, William Smith; ***D:*** Richard Compton.

Angels Don't Sleep Here 🦴🦴 **2000** Forensic pathologist Michael Daniels returns to his hometown when his twin brother disappears. He gets involved with district attorney Kate, who was his brother's childhood girlfriend, and whose father is the town's mayor. Michael thinks his brother is stalking him and when the mayor is killed, he believes his brother is the culprit. But local detective Russell Stark thinks Michael is the real criminal. **97m/C VHS, DVD.** Dana Ashbrook, Robert Patrick, Roy Scheider, Susan Allison, Gary Farmer, Kelly Rutherford, Christina Pickles; ***D:*** Paul Cade. **VIDEO**

Angels from Hell 🦴 **1968** Early application in the nutso 'Nam returnee genre. Disillusioned Vietnam veteran forms a massive biker gang for the sole purpose of wreaking havoc upon the Man, the Establishment and anyone else responsible for sending him off to war. The big gang invades a town, with predictably bloody results. Sort of a follow-up to "Hell's Angels on Wheels." **86m/C VHS.** Tom Stern, Arlene Martel, Ted Markland, Stephen Oliver, Paul Bertoya, James Murphy, Jack Starrett, Pepper Martin, Luana Talltree; ***D:*** Bruce Kessler.

Angels Hard As They Come 🦴🦴 **1971 (R)** Opposing Hell's Angels leaders clash in a hippie-populated ghost town. A semi-satiric spoof of the biker genre's cliches features an early Glenn appearance and Busey's film debut. **86m/C VHS, DVD.** Gary Busey, Scott Glenn, James Iglehart, Gary Littlejohn, Charles Dierkop, Larry Tucker, Gilda Texter, Janet Wood, Brendan Kelly; ***D:*** Joe Viola; ***W:*** Jonathan Demme, Joe Viola; ***M:*** Richard Hieronymous.

Angels in the Endzone 🦴🦴½ **1998** TV follow-up to Disney's 1994 "Angels in the Outfield" finds the heavenly troops trying to aid a failing high school football squad, especially the leading players (Gallagher and Lawrence) who are also trying to also handle the death of their father. **85m/C VHS.** Matthew Lawrence, David Gallagher, Paul Dooley, Christopher Lloyd; ***D:*** Gary Nadeau. **TV**

Angels in the Infield 🦴🦴½ **2000** Third in the Disney series finds former baseball player Bob "The Bungler" Bugler (Grier) trying to earn his Guardian Angels wings by looking out for pitcher Eddie Everett (Warburton) who's lost his self-confidence. But with daughter Laurel (Irvin) praying for some heavenly intervention, things are certainly looking up. **93m/C VHS.** David Alan Grier, Patrick Warburton, Kurt Fuller, Rebecca Jenkins, Colin Fox, Peter Keleghan, Duane Davis, Brittney Irvin; ***D:*** Robert King. **TV**

Angels in the Outfield 🦴🦴🦴 **1951** Enjoyable comedy fantasy about the lowly Pittsburgh Pirates who get a little celestial help in their race for the pennant. Naturally, it takes the prayers of young Bridget (Corcoran) to get the angel Gabriel to assist. Oh yeah, only the kid can actually see the angels (no special effects in this movie). Great performances all around, especially Douglas as gruff losing manager Guffy McGovern, with Janet Leigh as the reporter he makes a play for. Based on a story by Richard Conlin. **102m/C VHS.** Paul Douglas, Janet Leigh, Keenan Wynn, Donna Corcoran, Lewis Stone, Spring Byington, Bruce (Herman Brix) Bennett, Marvin Kaplan, Ellen Corby, Jeff Richards; ***D:*** Clarence Brown; ***W:*** Dorothy Kingsley, George Wells; ***C:*** Paul Vogel.

Angels in the Outfield 🦴🦴½ **1994 (PG)** Remake of the 1951 fantasy about a lowly baseball team who, along with some heavenly animated help find themselves on a winning streak. The new lineup includes Glover as manager of the hapless California Angels, Danza as a washed-up pitcher, and Lloyd as captain of the celestial spirits. Gordon-Levitt plays the foster child who believes he'll get his family back together if the Angels win the pennant. Familar ground still yields good, heartfelt family fare. Oakland A's third baseman Carney Lansford served as technical advisor, molding actors into fair semblance of baseball team. **105m/C VHS, DVD, Wide.** Danny Glover, Tony Danza, Christopher Lloyd, Brenda Fricker, Ben Johnson, Joseph Gordon-Levitt, Jay O. Sanders, Dermot Mulroney; ***D:*** William Dear; ***W:*** Holly Goldberg Sloan; ***C:*** Matthew F. Leonetti; ***M:*** Randy Edelman.

Angels of the City 🦴🦴 **1989** What's a girl got to do to join a sorority? A house prank turns vicious when two coeds take a walk on the wild side and accidentally observe a murder, making them the next targets. Credible exploitation effort, if that's not an oxymoron. **90m/C VHS.** Lawrence-Hilton Jacobs, Cynthia Cheston, Kelly Galindo, Sandy Gershman; ***D:*** Lawrence-Hilton Jacobs; ***W:*** Lawrence-Hilton Jacobs, Raymond Martino, Joseph Merhi.

Angels One Five 🦴🦴 **1954** A worm's-eye view of British air power in WWII. What little "excitement" there is, is generated by flashing lights, plotting maps, and status boards. Hawkins and Denison are the only bright spots. **97m/B VHS.** *GB* Jack Hawkins, Michael Denison, Dulcie Gray, John Gregson, Cyril Raymond, Veronica Hurst, Geoffrey Keen, Vida Hope, Andrew Osborn; ***D:*** George More O'Ferrell; ***W:*** Derek Twist; ***C:*** Christopher Challis, Stanley Grant; ***M:*** John Wooldridge.

Angels Over Broadway 🦴🦴🦴 **1940** Slick, fast-paced black comedy about con man Fairbanks, who plans to hustle suicidal thief Qualen during a poker game, but has a change of heart. With the help of call-girl Hayworth and drunken playwright Mitchell, he helps Qualen turn his life around. Ahead of its time with an offbeat morality, but a delight in the '90s. **80m/B VHS.** Douglas Fairbanks Jr., Rita Hayworth, Thomas Mitchell, John Qualen, George Watts; ***D:*** Ben Hecht, Lee Garmes; ***W:*** Ben Hecht; ***C:*** Lee Garmes.

Angels' Wild Women woof! **1972** From the man who brought you "Dracula vs. Frankenstein" comes an amalgamation of hippies, motorcycle dudes, evil desert gurus and precious little plot. **85m/C VHS, DVD.** Kent Taylor, Regina Carrol, Ross Hagen, Maggie Bemby, Vicki Volante; ***D:*** Al Adamson.

Angels with Dirty Faces 🦴🦴🦴🦴 **1938** Rousing classic with memorable Cagney twitches and the famous long walk from the cell to the chair. Two young hoods grow up on NYC's lower East Side with diverse results—one enters the priesthood and the other opts for crime and prison. Upon release from the pen, famed gangster Cagney sets up shop in the old neighborhood, where Father O'Brien tries to keep a group of young toughs (the Dead End Kids) from following in his footsteps. Bogart's his unscrupulous lawyer and Bancroft a crime boss intent on double-crossing Cagney. Reportedly they were blasting real bullets during the big shootout, no doubt helping Cagney's intensity. Adapted from a story by Rowland Brown. **97m/B VHS.** James Cagney, Pat O'Brien, Humphrey Bogart, Ann Sheridan, George Bancroft, Billy Halop, Leo Gorcey, Huntz Hall, Bobby Jordan, Bernard Punsley, Gabriel Dell, Adrian Morris; ***D:*** Michael Curtiz; ***W:*** John Wexley, Warren Duff; ***C:*** Sol Polito; ***M:*** Max Steiner. N.Y. Film Critics '38: Actor (Cagney).

Angi Vera 🦴🦴🦴🦴 **1978** Naive 18-year-old Angi (Papp) is living in 1948 Hungary during the early days of socialism. Sent to a re-education school, she falls in love with her married Party leader but gradually loses her personal integrity to a corrupt system. Hungarian with subtitles. **96m/C VHS.** *HU* Veronika Papp, Erszi Pasztor, Eva Szabo, Tamas Dunai, Laszlo Horvath; ***D:*** Pal Gabor; ***W:*** Pal Gabor; ***C:*** Lajos Koltai; ***M:*** Gyorgy Selmeczi.

Angie 🦴🦴 **1994 (R)** Brassy Angie finds herself pregnant and unmarried. Tired of the advice and criticism she receives from her close knit neighborhood she strikes out of Brooklyn to find a new life for herself. Average "woman's movie" wrought with messages of pregnancy, childbirth, friendship, love, and family has far too much going on and relies too heavily on formula soap. Davis, in what could have been a juicy (read "Oscar") role is strong, but her performance is drowned by all the melodrama. Madonna was originally cast as Angie, but was bounced when the filming of "Snake Eyes" conflicted. Adapted from the book "Angie, I Says" by Avra Wing. **108m/C VHS, Wide.** Geena Davis, Aida Turturro, Stephen Rea, Philip Bosco, James Gandolfini, Jenny O'Hara; ***D:*** Martha Coolidge; ***W:*** Todd Graff.

AngKor: Cambodia Express 🦴 **1981** An American journalist travels back to Vietnam to search for his long lost love. **96m/C VHS.** Robert Walker Jr., Christopher George; ***D:*** Lek Kitiparaporn.

Angry Harvest 🦴🦴🦴 *Bittere Ernte* **1985** During the WWII German occupation of Poland, a gentile farmer shelters a young Jewish woman on the run, and a serious, ultimately interdependent relationship forms. Acclaimed; Holland's first film since her native Poland's martial law imposition made her an exile to Sweden. In German with English subtitles. Contains nudity and violence. **102m/C VHS.** *GE* Armin Mueller-Stahl, Elisabeth Trissenaar, Wojciech (Wojtek Psoniak) Pszoniak, Margit Carstensen, Kurt Raab, Kathe Jaenicke, Hans Beerhenke, Isa Haller; ***D:*** Agnieszka Holland; ***W:*** Agnieszka Holland. Montreal World Film Fest. '85: Actor (Mueller-Stahl).

Angry Joe Bass 🦴 **1976** Contemporary Native American Joe Bass faces government officials who continually usurp his fishing rights. Something like "Billy Jack" without the intelligence. **82m/C VHS.** Henry Bal, Molly Mershon; ***D:*** Thomas G. Reeves.

The Angry Red Planet 🦴 *Invasion of Mars; Journey to Planet Four* **1959** An unintentionally amusing sci-fi adventure about astronauts on Mars fighting off aliens and giant, ship-swallowing amoebas. Filmed using bizarre "Cinemagic" process, which turns almost everything pink. Wild effects have earned the film cult status. **83m/C VHS, DVD.** Gerald Mohr, Les Tremayne, Jack Kruschen, Nora Hayden, Paul Hahn, J. Edward McKinley, Tom Daly, Don Lamond; ***D:*** Ib Melchior; ***W:*** Ib Melchior, Sidney Pink; ***C:*** Stanley Cortez; ***M:*** Paul Dunlap.

Anguish 🦴🦴½ **1988 (R)** Well-done horror thriller about a lunatic who, inspired to duplicate the actions of an eyeball-obsessed killer in a popular film, murders a movie audience as they watch the movie. Violence and gore abound. **89m/C VHS, DVD, Wide.** *SP* Zelda Rubinstein, Michael Lerner, Talia Paul, Clara Pastor; ***D:*** Bigas Luna; ***W:*** Bigas Luna; ***C:*** Josep Civit; ***M:*** J(ose) M(anuel) Pagan.

Angus 🦴🦴 **1995 (PG-13)** Dull teen comedy about self-esteem revolves around the overweight Angus (Talbert), a friendly kid tormented by the usual school bullies. His best bud is twerp Troy (Owen), who tries to help Angus out with his crush on cute blonde Melissa (Ariana). There's even a schmaltzy prom scene. The profanity, though mild, and the boys sexual interests make this questionable for the pre-teen audience that could actually enjoy it. **87m/C VHS.** Charlie Talbert, Kathy Bates, George C. Scott, Chris Owen, Ariana Richards, Lawrence Pressman, Rita Moreno, James Van Der Beek, Anna Thompson; ***D:*** Patrick Read Johnson; ***W:*** Jill Gordon; ***C:*** Alexander Grusynski; ***M:*** David E. Russo.

Anima 🦴🦴 **1998** Sam and Iris have long left their pasts in Nazi Germany behind them for a secluded life in a New England farmhouse. At least until young journalist Bill discovers them while researching an article on taxidermy and mummification and sees their bizarre private world. **88m/C VHS, DVD.** Bray Poor, George Bartenieff, Jacqueline Bertrand; ***D:*** Craig Richardson; ***W:*** Craig Richardson; ***C:*** Randy Drummond; ***M:*** Joel Diamond, Adam Hurst.

The Animal 🦴🦴½ **2001 (PG-13)** Meek clerk Schneider is injured in a serious car accident and is rescued by a mad scientist who surgically replaces his damaged organs with animal parts. These animalistic traits tend to surface at the worst possible time for Schneider, just as he's realizing his dream of becoming a supercop. Haskell (from TV's first "Survivor") is pleasant in her big screen debut as the animal-rights advocate girlfriend, but Schneider is the one who makes this surprisingly enjoyable comedy work with his affable loser persona and willingness to go with the joke. **83m/C VHS, DVD, Wide.** *US* Rob Schneider, Guy Torry, John C. McGinley, Colleen Haskell, Michael Caton, Louis Lombardi, Ed Asner, Michael (Mike) Papajohn; ***D:*** Luke Greenfield; ***W:*** Rob Schneider, Tom Brady; ***C:*** Peter Collister; ***M:*** Teddy Castellucci.

Animal Behavior ☠ **1989 (PG)** An animal researcher and a music professor fall in love on a college campus. Bowen's (she actually released it under the alias Riley H. Anne) comedy was filmed in 1985 and edited/shelved for over four years, with good reason. **79m/C VHS.** Karen Allen, Armand Assante, Holly Hunter, Josh Mostel, Richard Libertini; ***D:*** Jenny (H. Anne Riley) Bowen; ***W:*** Susan Rice; ***C:*** Richard Bowen; ***M:*** Cliff Eidelman.

Animal Called Man ☠ **1987** Two crooked buddies join a big western gang in pillaging a small town and get in too deep. **83m/C VHS.** Vassilli Karis, Craig Hill, Gillian Bray; ***D:*** Robert (Roberto) Mauri.

Animal Crackers ☠☠☠½ **1930 (G)** The second and possibly the funniest of the 13 Marx Brothers films, "Animal Crackers" is a screen classic. Groucho is a guest at the house of wealthy matron Margaret Dumont and he, along with Zeppo, Chico, and Harpo, destroy the tranquility of the estate. Complete with the Harry Ruby music score—including Groucho's "Hooray for Captain Spaulding" with more quotable lines than any other Marx Brothers film: "One morning I shot an elephant in my pajamas. How he got into my pajamas, I'll never know." Based on a play by George S. Kaufman. **98m/B VHS, DVD.** Groucho Marx, Chico Marx, Harpo Marx, Zeppo Marx, Lillian Roth, Margaret Dumont, Louis Sorin, Hal Thompson, Robert Greig, Margaret Irving, Edward Metcalf, Kathryn Reece; ***D:*** Victor Heerman; ***W:*** Morrie Ryskind; ***C:*** George J. Folsey; ***M:*** Bert Kalmar, Harry Ruby.

Animal Factory ☠☠½ **2000 (R)** When first-time felon Ron Decker (Furlong) is sentenced to two years in a decaying prison, he is introduced to a world where violence is a way of life. After witnessing a riot, Ron is taken under the wing of Earl Copen (Dafoe), the main-man on the cellblock, but the younger man soon discovers that life in prison is not about rehabilitation, it's about survival. Bunker wrote the screenplay based on his novel of the same name. **94m/C VHS, DVD, Wide.** Edward (Eddie) Bunker, Willem Dafoe, Edward Furlong, Danny Trejo, John Heard, Mickey Rourke, Tom Arnold, Mark Boone Jr., Steve Buscemi, Seymour Cassel; ***D:*** Steve Buscemi; ***W:*** Edward (Eddie) Bunker, John Steppling; ***C:*** Phil Parmet; ***M:*** John Lurie.

Animal Farm ☠☠☠ **1955** An animated version of George Orwell's classic political satire about a barnyard full of animals who parallel the growth of totalitarian dictatorships. Not entirely successful, but probably best translation of Orwell to film. **73m/C VHS, 8mm.** ***D:*** John Halas, Joy Batchelor; ***V:*** Maurice Denham, Gordon Heath.

Animal Farm ☠½ **1999** Orwell's political satire is given the "Babe" treatment in this live-action version. Drunken farmer Mr. Jones (Postlethwaite) has his power overthrown by his barnyard animals, who in turn are ruled by the farm's pig population. Only porker Napoleon (Stewart) turns out to be as big a tyrant as his human counterpart. Far beyond the scope of children, this retelling is clunky and its propaganda value has certainly come and gone. (Orwell was originally satirizing Stalinist Russia.) **91m/C VHS, DVD.** Pete Postlethwaite; ***D:*** John Stephenson; ***W:*** Martyn Burke, Alan Janes; ***C:*** Mike Brewster; ***M:*** Richard Harvey; ***V:*** Patrick Stewart, Kelsey Grammer, Ian Holm, Julia Ormond, Julia Louis-Dreyfus, Paul Scofield, Peter Ustinov. **CABLE**

Animal Instincts ☠☠ **1992 (R)** A woman takes a prescription drug that makes her a nymphomaniac, and her police officer husband discovers that he's turned on by videotaping her in bed with other men and women. One of the many in her constant stream of lovers is a politician whose campaign is based on shutting down all the town's sex clubs. Another in the string of sexual thrillers riding on the coattails of "Basic Instinct." **94m/C VHS, DVD.** Maxwell Caulfield, Jan-Michael Vincent, Mitch Gaylord, Shannon Whirry, Delia Sheppard, John Saxon, David Carradine; ***D:*** Alexander Gregory (Gregory Dark) Hippolyte; ***W:*** Jon Robert Samsel, Georges des Esseintes; ***C:*** Paul Desatoff; ***M:*** Joseph Smith.

Animal Instincts 2 ☠☠ **1994 (R)** Joanna leaves her overbearing husband and moves into a supposedly quiet community. Neighbor Steve is a security expert—and a voyeur. He's hidden a camera in Joanna's bedroom but she knows he's watching. **92m/C VHS, DVD.** Shannon Whirry, Woody Brown, Elizabeth Sandifer, Al Sapienza; ***D:*** Alexander Gregory (Gregory Dark) Hippolyte.

Animal Instincts 3: The Seductress ☠ **1995 (R)** Joanna (Schumacher) finds a new kind of sexual excitement when she gets involved with rock music promoter Alex (Matthew), whose kicks include feining blindness. The unrated version contains 12 more minutes of footage. **96m/C VHS, DVD.** Wendy Schumacher, James Matthew, Marcus Graham, John Bates, Anthony Lesa; ***D:*** Alexander Gregory (Gregory Dark) Hippolyte; ***W:*** Selwyn Harris; ***C:*** Ernest Paul Roebuck.

The Animal Kingdom ☠☠☠ *The Woman in His House* **1932** A romantic triangle develops when Howard, married to Loy, has an affair with Harding. The problem is Harding acts more like a wife and Loy a mistress. Intelligently written and directed, with a marvelous performance from veteran character actor Gargan. **95m/B VHS.** Ann Harding, Leslie Howard, Myrna Loy, Neil Hamilton, William Gargan, Henry Stephenson, Ilka Chase; ***D:*** Edward H. Griffith; ***W:*** Horace Jackson; ***C:*** George J. Folsey.

Animal Room ☠☠ **1995** When high school student Arnold Mosk (Harris) is caught using drugs, he's place in the school's controversial isolation program that's nicknamed "The Animal Room." There are no rules and Arnold's life is threatened by delinquent thug, Doug (Lillard). But if Arnold expects to survive, he's going to have to learn how to fight. **98m/C VHS, DVD.** Neil Patrick Harris, Matthew Lillard, Gabriel Olds, Catherine Hicks, Brian Vincent; ***D:*** Craig Singer.

Anita, Dances of Vice ☠☠ *Anita—Tanze des Lasters* **1987** German avant-garde film celebrates Anita Berber, the "most scandalous woman in 1920s Berlin." Berber was openly bisexual, used drugs, and danced nude in public. In von Praunheim's film, she rises from the dead and creates yet more scandal. **85m/C VHS.** *GE* Lotti Huber, Ina Blum, Mikhael Honesseau; ***D:*** Rosa von Praunheim.

The Ann Jillian Story ☠½ **1988** Jillian stars as herself in this melodrama recounting her battle with breast cancer. Several musical numbers are included. **96m/C VHS.** Ann Jillian, Tony LoBianco, Viveca Lindfors, Leighton Bewley; ***D:*** Corey Allen. **TV**

Ann Vickers ☠☠½ **1933** A dashing young army captain wins over the heart of a dedicated social worker. Okay adaptation of a Sinclair Lewis novel, with Dunne suffering more than usual. **76m/B VHS.** Irene Dunne, Walter Huston, Bruce Cabot, Conrad Nagel, Edna May Oliver; ***D:*** John Cromwell; ***M:*** Max Steiner.

Anna ☠☠ **1951** Novitiate nun Anna (Mangano) is forced to confront her sordid past (as a nightclub entertainer), and her love for two very different men, when her seriously injured former fiancee is brought to the hospital where she is a nurse. Anna must finally deal with her feelings and decide which path her life will take. Dubbed in English. **111m/B VHS.** *IT* Silvana Mangano, Raf Vallone, Vittorio Gassman; ***D:*** Alberto Lattuada; ***C:*** Otello Martelli; ***M:*** Nino Rota.

Anna ☠☠☠ **1987 (PG-13)** Age, envy, and the theatrical world receive their due in an uneven but engrossing drama about aging Czech film star Anna, making a sad living in New York doing commercials and trying for off-Broadway roles. She takes in Krystyna, a young Czech peasant girl who eventually rockets to model stardom. Modern, strongly acted "All About Eve" with a story partially based on a real Polish actress. Kirkland drew quite a bit of flak for shamelessly self-promoting for the Oscar. She still lost. **101m/C VHS.** Sally Kirkland, Paulina Porizkova, Robert Fields, Stefan Schnabel, Larry Pine, Ruth Maleczech; ***D:*** Yurek Bogayevicz; ***W:*** Yurek Bogayevicz, Agnieszka Holland; ***C:*** Bobby Bukowski; ***M:*** Greg Hawkes. Golden Globes '88: Actress—Drama (Kirkland); Ind. Spirit '88: Actress (Kirkland); L.A. Film Critics '87: Actress (Kirkland).

Anna and the King ☠☠½ **1999 (PG-13)** Based on the story of English widow and schoolteacher Anna Leonowens (Foster) who, in 1862, is hired by the King Mongkut of Siam (Yun-Fat) to introduce his 58 children to the ideas of the West. The film looks stunning (it was filmed in Malaysia) and Yun-Fat is regal and charismatic but Foster is too stiff upper-lipped and remote and there's respect rather than any hint of romance. Previously filmed as 1946's "Anna and the King of Siam" and the 1956 musical "The King and I." **147m/C VHS, DVD, Wide.** Jodie Foster, Chow Yun-Fat, Bai Ling, Tom Felton, Syed Alwi; ***D:*** Andy Tennant; ***W:*** Steve Meerson, Peter Krikes; ***C:*** Caleb Deschanel; ***M:*** George Fenton.

Anna and the King of Siam ☠☠☠½ **1946** Splendid adaptation, from the book by Margaret Landon, about the true life adventures of 33-year-old English widow Anna Leonowens. In 1862 Anna and her son travelled to the exotic kingdom of Siam to educate the harem and children of the king. Dunne is splendid as the strong-willed governess as is Harrison (in his first American film) as the authoritarian eastern ruler. Remade as the musical "The King and I." **128m/B VHS.** Irene Dunne, Rex Harrison, Linda Darnell, Lee J. Cobb, Gale Sondergaard, Mikhail Rasumny, Dennis Hoey, Richard Lyon, John Abbott; ***D:*** John Cromwell; ***W:*** Sally Benson, Talbot Jennings; ***C:*** Arthur C. Miller; ***M:*** Bernard Herrmann. Oscars '46: Art Dir./Set Dec., B&W, B&W Cinematog.

Anna Christie ☠☠☠½ **1923** Silent production of Eugene O'Neill's play that even he liked. A young girl is sent away by her father, a seaman, and finds her way to Chicago, where she becomes a prostitute. Later she visits her father's barge and falls for a sailor. She shares her past life story, hoping they will understand. This film was acclaimed when it was released, and still remains a touching work of art. Remade in 1930. **75m/B VHS.** Blanche Sweet, George F. Marion Sr., William Russell, Eugenie Besserer, Chester Conklin, George Siegmann, Victor Potel, Fred Kohler Sr.; ***D:*** John Wray.

Anna Christie ☠☠½ **1930** Garbo is the ex-prostitute who finds love with sailor Bickford. Bickford is unaware of his lover's tarnished past and she does her best to keep it that way. Garbo's first sound effort was advertised with the slogan "Garbo Talks." Adapted from the classic Eugene O'Neill play, the film is a slow but rewarding romantic drama. **90m/B VHS.** Greta Garbo, Marie Dressler, Charles Bickford, George F. Marion Sr.; ***D:*** Clarence Brown; ***C:*** William H. Daniels.

Anna Karenina ☠☠☠½ **1935** Cinematic Tolstoy with Garbo as sad, moody, married Anna willing to give up everything to be near Vronsky (March), the cavalry officer she's obsessed with. And since it's Russian, expect tragedy. A classic Garbo vehicle with March and Rathbone (as the cuckhold husband) providing excellent support. Interestingly, a remake of the Garbo and John Gilbert silent, "Love." **85m/B VHS.** Greta Garbo, Fredric March, Freddie Bartholomew, Maureen O'Sullivan, May Robson, Basil Rathbone, Reginald Owen, Reginald Denny; ***D:*** Clarence Brown; ***W:*** S.N. Behrman, Clemence Dane, Salka Viertel; ***C:*** William H. Daniels; ***M:*** Herbert Stothart. N.Y. Film Critics '35: Actress (Garbo).

Anna Karenina ☠☠½ **1948** Stiff version of Tolstoy's passionate story of illicit love between a married woman and a military officer. In spite of exquisite costumes, and Leigh and Richardson as leads, still tedious. **123m/C VHS, DVD.** *GB* Vivien Leigh, Ralph Richardson, Kieron Moore, Sally Ann Howes, Niall MacGinnis, Martita Hunt, Michael Gough; ***D:*** Julien Duvivier; ***W:*** Julien Duvivier; ***C:*** Henri Alekan; ***M:*** Constant Lambert.

Anna Karenina ☠☠½ **1985 (PG)** TV version of Tolstoy's novel of betrayal, intrigue, and forbidden love. Anna, defying all social practices of the time, falls into the arms of a dashing count. Features an excellent performance from Paul "A Man for All Seasons" Scofield. **96m/C VHS.** Jacqueline Bisset, Christopher Reeve, Paul Scofield, Ian Ogilvy, Anna Massey, Judi Bowker; ***D:*** Simon Langton. **TV**

Anna Karenina ☠☠½ **2000** Well-done British adaptation of the familiar Tolstoy drama although, frankly, Anna (McCrory) is a pill. Less tragic than headstrong, this willful Russian beauty runs from her passionless marriage to Karenin (Dillane) straight into the arms of dashing seducer Vronsky (McKidd). Of course, once they turn each other's lives to misery, what else is left but a tragic end. This version also includes the secondary love affair of Kitty (Baeza) and Levin (Henshall). **240m/C VHS.** Helen McCrory, Kevin McKidd, Stephen (Dillon) Dillane, Douglas Henshall, Paloma Baeza, Amanda Root, Mark Strong; ***D:*** David Blair; ***W:*** Allan Cubitt; ***C:*** Ryszard Lenczewski; ***M:*** John Keane. **TV**

Anna to the Infinite Power ☠☠½ **1984** Sci fi based on the book of the same name follows a young girl with telepathic powers. When the girl discovers that she has sisters as the result of a strange scientific experiment, she sets out to find them, drawing on her own inner strength. **101m/C VHS.** Dina Merrill, Martha Byrne, Mark Patton; ***D:*** Robert Wiemer.

Annapolis ☠ **1928** Life's in the pink for two guys at the U.S. naval academy until jealousy rears its loathsome head when they fall for the same gal. Just when it's beginning to look like love and honor is an either-or proposition, the lovelorn rivals find that although love transcends all, a guy's gotta do what a guy's gotta do, even if it means sticking up for his romantic nemesis. Lots of sub-par male bonding. **63m/B VHS.** Johnny Mack Brown, Hugh Allan, Hobart Bosworth, William "Billy" Bakewell, Charlotte Walker, Jeanette Loff; ***D:*** Christy Cabanne.

The Annapolis Story ☠½ *Blue and the Gold* **1955** Cliche-ridden WWII drama about two naval cadets romancing the same lucky girl. Low-rent time for director Siegel which wastes a decent cast. **81m/C VHS.** John Derek, Kevin McCarthy, Diana Lynn, Pat Conway, L.Q. (Justus E. McQueen) Jones; ***D:*** Donald Siegel.

Anne of Avonlea ☠☠☠½ *Anne of Green Gables: The Sequel* **1987** Equally excellent miniseries sequel to "Anne of Green Gables" in which the romantic heroine grows up and discovers romance. The same cast returns and Sullivan continues his tradition of lavish filming on Prince Edward Island and beautiful costumes. Based on the characters from L.M. Montgomery's classic novels "Anne of Avonlea," "Anne of the Island," and "Anne of Windy Poplars." CBC, PBS, and Disney worked together on this WonderWorks production. **224m/C VHS.** *CA* Megan Follows, Colleen Dewhurst, Wendy Hiller, Frank Converse, Patricia Hamilton, Schuyler Grant, Jonathan Crombie, Rosemary Dunsmore; ***D:*** Kevin Sullivan; ***W:*** Kevin Sullivan; ***M:*** Hagood Hardy. **TV**

Anne of Green Gables ☠☠☠ **1934** A lonely Canadian couple adopts an orphan who keeps them on their toes with her animated imagination, and wins a permanent place in their hearts. Warm (but loose) adaptation of Lucy Maud Montgomery's popular novel is entertaining although 1985 remake is far superior. Followed by "Anne of Windy Poplars." **79m/B VHS.** Anne Shirley, Tom Brown, O.P. Heggie, Helen Westley, Sara Haden, Charley Grapewin; ***D:*** George Nicholls Jr.; ***M:*** Max Steiner.

Anne of Green Gables ☠☠☠½ **1985** Splendid production of the famous Lucy Maud Montgomery classic about a young orphan girl growing to young adulthood with the help of a crusty brother and sister duo. The characters come to life under Sullivan's direction, and the movie is enhanced by the beautiful Prince Edward Island scenery and wonderful costumes. One of the few instances where an adaptation lives up to (if not exceeds) the quality of the original novel. A WonderWorks presentation that was made with the cooperation of the Disney channel, CBC, and PBS. Followed by "Anne of Avonlea." On two tapes. **197m/C VHS.** *CA* Megan Follows, Colleen Dewhurst, Richard Farnsworth, Patricia Hamilton, Schuyler Grant, Jonathan Crombie, Marilyn Lightstone, Charmion King, Rosemary Radcliffe, Jackie Burroughs, Robert E. Collins, Joachim Hansen, Cedric Smith, Paul Brown, Miranda de Pencier, Jennifer Inch, Wendy Lyon, Christiane Krueger, Trish Nettleton, Morgan Chapman; ***D:*** Kevin Sullivan; ***W:*** Kevin Sullivan, Joe Weisenfeld; ***C:*** Rene Ohashi; ***M:*** Hagood Hardy. **TV**

Anne of Green Gables: The Continuing Story 🦴🦴½ **1999** Anne (Follows) learns that fiance Gilbert (Blythe) has accepted a job in a New York hospital. She takes a job in a publishing house where she meets fast-living journalist Jack Garrison (Daddo). Gilbert and Anne return to Avonlea to marry just before WWI and Gilbert joins the army as a doctor and is sent to France. When he's declared MIA, Anne heads overseas with the Red Cross to search for him and runs into Jack again, who leads Anne into numerous intrigues. This far-fetched story is not based on one of Lucy Maud Montgomery's books but Anne at least retains her spunkiness and determination. **185m/C VHS.** *CA* Megan Follows, Jonathan Crombie, Cameron Daddo, Schuyler Grant, Patricia Hamilton, Rosemary Radcliffe, Miranda de Pencier, Barry Morse, Martha Henry, Janet-Laine Green, Nigel Bennett, Shannon Lawson; ***D:*** Stefan Scaini; ***W:*** Kevin Sullivan, Laurie Pearson; ***C:*** Robert Saad; ***M:*** Peter Breiner. **TV**

Anne of the Thousand Days 🦴🦴🦴½ **1969 (PG)** Lavish re-telling of the life and loves of Henry the VIII. In 1526, Henry tosses aside his current wife for the young and devastatingly beautiful Anne Boleyn (Bujold). But after the birth of Princess Elizabeth, Henry tires of Anne and wishes to marry another. So he decides to rid himself of her presence—permanently. Burton's performance of the amoral king garnered him an Oscar nomination. Based on the 1948 play by Maxwell Anderson. Watch for Elizabeth Taylor as a masked courtesan at the costume ball. **145m/C VHS.** Richard Burton, Genevieve Bujold, Irene Papas, Anthony Quayle, John Colicos, Michael Hordern; ***D:*** Charles Jarrott; ***W:*** Bridget Boland, John Hale; ***M:*** Georges Delerue. Oscars '69: Costume Des.; Directors Guild '70: Director (Jarrott); Golden Globes '70: Actress—Drama (Bujold), Director (Jarrott), Film—Drama, Screenplay.

Annie 🦴🦴 **1982 (PG)** Stagy big-budget adaption of the Broadway musical, which was an adaptation of the comic strip. A major financial disaster upon release, still it's an entertaining enterprise curiously directed by Huston and engagingly acted by Finney and Quinn. ♫Tomorrow; It's the Hard Knock Life; Maybe; I Think I'm Gonna Like It Here; Little Girls; We Got Annie; Let's Go to the Movies; You're Never Fully Dressed Without a Smile; Easy Street. **128m/C VHS, DVD, 8mm, Wide.** Aileen Quinn, Carol Burnett, Albert Finney, Bernadette Peters, Ann Reinking, Tim Curry; ***D:*** John Huston; ***W:*** Thomas Meehan; ***C:*** Richard Moore; ***M:*** Ralph Burns. Golden Raspberries '82: Worst Support. Actress (Quinn).

Annie 🦴🦴🦴 **1999** Lively and amusing adaptation of the smash Broadway musical that will make you forget that dud 1982 movie version. Scrappy urchin Annie (newcomer Morton) is incarcerated in a Depression-era orphange run by despotic Miss Hannigan (Bates) when she's offered the chance to spend the holidays with chilly moneybags Oliver Warbucks (Garber). Naturally, Annie thaws his frosty demeanor. Able support is provided by Warbucks' faithful assistant Grace (McDonald) and Miss Hannigan's wastrel brother Rooster (Cumming) and his floozy Lily (Chenoweth). **120m/C VHS, DVD.** Alicia Morton, Victor Garber, Kathy Bates, Alan Cumming, Audra McDonald, Kristin Chenoweth; ***Cameos:*** Andrea McArdle; ***D:*** Rob Marshall; ***W:*** Irene Mecchi; ***C:*** Ralf Bode; ***M:*** Charles Strouse, Martin Charnin. **TV**

Annie: A Royal Adventure 🦴🦴½ **1995** TV sequel to "Annie" finds the red-haired heroine (Johnson) traveling to England with her Daddy Warbucks (Hearn), who's about to be knighted in London. But the evil Lady Edwina Hogbottom (played to a high-camp hilt by Collins) has a plan to blow up Buckingham Palace and take over as queen. Naturally, it's up to Annie to defeat her and have a happy ending. **92m/C VHS.** Ashley Johnson, George Hearn, Joan Collins, Emily Ann Lloyd, Camilla Bell, Ian McDiarmid.

Annie Get Your Gun 🦴🦴🦴 **1950** A lavish production of Irving Berlin's Broadway hit musical. Sharpshooting Annie Oakley (Hutton) is the queen of Buffalo Bill's Wild West show though her talents leave her loveless. Seems fellow marksman Frank Butler's (Keel) ego can't handle the fact that Annie keeps beating him. Lots of singing, with an enthusiastic lead performance by Hutton. ♫There's No Business Like Show Business; My Defenses Are Down; I'm an Indian Too; Doin' What Comes Natur'lly; Colonel Buffalo Bill; The Girl That I Marry; You Can't Get a Man with a Gun; They Say It's Wonderful; I Got the Sun in the Morning. **107m/C VHS, DVD.** Betty Hutton, Howard Keel, Keenan Wynn, Louis Calhern, J. Carrol Naish, Edward Arnold, Clinton Sundberg; ***D:*** George Sidney; ***W:*** Sidney Sheldon; ***C:*** Charles Rosher; ***M:*** Irving Berlin. Oscars '50: Scoring/Musical.

Annie Hall 🦴🦴🦴🦴 **1977 (PG)** Acclaimed coming-of-cinematic-age film for Allen is based in part on his own life. His love affair with Hall/Keaton is chronicled as an episodic, wistful comedy commenting on family, love, loneliness, communicating, maturity, driving, city life, careers, and various other topics. Abounds with classic scenes, including future star Goldblum and his mantra at a cocktail party; Allen and the lobster pot; and Allen, Keaton, a bathroom, a tennis racket, and a spider. The film operates on many levels, as does Keaton's wardrobe, which started a major fashion trend. Don't blink or you'll miss several future stars in bit parts. Expertly shot by Gordon Willis. **94m/C VHS, DVD, Wide.** Woody Allen, Diane Keaton, Tony Roberts, Carol Kane, Paul Simon, Colleen Dewhurst, Janet Margolin, Shelley Duvall, Christopher Walken, Marshall McLuhan, Dick Cavett, John Glover, Jeff Goldblum, Beverly D'Angelo; ***D:*** Woody Allen; ***W:*** Woody Allen, Marshall Brickman; ***C:*** Gordon Willis. Oscars '77: Actress (Keaton), Director (Allen), Orig. Screenplay, Picture; AFI '98: Top 100; British Acad. '77: Actress (Keaton), Director (Allen), Film, Screenplay; Directors Guild '77: Director (Allen); Golden Globes '78: Actress—Mus./Comedy (Keaton); L.A. Film Critics '77: Screenplay; Natl. Bd. of Review '77: Support. Actress (Keaton), Natl. Film Reg. '92;, N.Y. Film Critics '77: Actress (Keaton), Director (Allen), Film, Screenplay; Natl. Soc. Film Critics '77: Actress (Keaton), Film, Screenplay; Writers Guild '77: Orig. Screenplay.

Annie O 🦴🦴½ **1995 (PG)** 15-year-old Annie Rojas (Yares) runs into problems when she joins the boys' basketball team (since her school doesn't have a girls team). Her teammates are jealous and so are her brother and boyfriend. **93m/C VHS.** Coco Yares, Chad Willet, Robert Stewart; ***D:*** Michael McClary.

Annie Oakley 🦴🦴🦴 **1935** Energetic biographical drama based on the life and legend of sharpshooter Annie Oakley and her on-off relationship with Wild Bill Hickok. Stanwyck makes a great Oakley. Later musicalized as "Annie Get Your Gun." **90m/B VHS.** Barbara Stanwyck, Preston Foster, Melvyn Douglas, Pert Kelton, Andy Clyde, Moroni Olsen, Chief Thundercloud; ***D:*** George Stevens.

The Annihilators woof! **1985 (R)** A group of Vietnam vets band together in an extremely violent manner to protect their small town from a gang of thugs. **87m/C VHS.** Gerrit Graham, Lawrence-Hilton Jacobs, Paul Koslo, Christopher Stone, Andy Wood, Sid Conrad, Dennis Redfield; ***D:*** Charles E. Sellier.

The Anniversary 🦴🦴 **1968** One-eyed monster mom Mrs. Taggart (Bette at her baddest) gives new meaning to the word "possessive." Thoroughly cowing her three grown sons, she manages to get them to come home each year on the wedding anniversary to the husband she despised. Only this time, the trio tell her they're going to live their own lives. Hah—not if mom has anything to do with it. Based on the play by Bill MacIlwraith. **93m/C VHS.** *GB* Bette Davis, Jack Hedley, James Cossins, Christian Roberts, Sheila Hancock, Elaine Taylor; ***D:*** Roy Ward Baker; ***W:*** Jimmy Sangster; ***C:*** Henry Waxman; ***M:*** Philip Martell.

The Anniversary Party 🦴🦴🦴 **2001 (R)** Leigh and Cumming co-write, co-direct and star as the central couple in this impressive ensemble comedy-drama about a group of Hollywood friends celebrating said couple's sixth anniversary. Amid much career and personal angst, drug use, and sometimes nasty air-clearing, most of the characters are fleshed out nicely and the dialogue remains sharp throughout. The air is thick with genuine personal dread and interpersonal tension. Among the uniformly excellent performances, two especially stand out: Leigh as the aging actress on the cusp of career oblivion, and Cates as a former actress who's given up her career to focus on being a wife (to just-beyond-leading-man-status hubby Kline) and mother. Filmed in digital video in 19 days under the Dogme 95 guidelines. **117m/C VHS, DVD, Wide.** *US* Jennifer Jason Leigh, Alan Cumming, Gwyneth Paltrow, Kevin Kline, Phoebe Cates, John C. Reilly, Jane Adams, John Benjamin Hickey, Parker Posey, Denis O'Hare, Jennifer Beals, Mina (Badiyi) Badie, Michael Panes; ***D:*** Jennifer Jason Leigh, Alan Cumming; ***W:*** Jennifer Jason Leigh, Alan Cumming; ***C:*** John Bailey; ***M:*** Michael Penn.

Another Chance 🦴🦴 **1988 (R)** Girl-crazy bachelor is returned from heaven for a second chance and has to choose between a "bad" girl and a "good" girl. What a choice! **99m/C VHS.** Bruce Greenwood, Frank Annese, Jeff East, Anne Ramsey, Barbara (Lee) Edwards; ***D:*** Jerry Vint.

Another Country 🦴🦴½ **1984** Julian Mitchell's adaptation of his play about the true story of two English boarding school friends who wind up as spies for the Soviet Union. Based on the lives of Guy Burgess and Donald MacLean, whose youth is rather fancifully depicted in this loving recreation of 1930s English life. Although the film is inferior to the award-winning play, director Kanievska manages to transform a piece into a solid film, and Everett's performance as Burgess is outstanding. **90m/C VHS.** *GB* Rupert Everett, Colin Firth, Michael Jenn, Robert Addie, Anna Massey, Betsy Brantley, Rupert Wainwright, Cary Elwes, Arthur Howard, Tristan Oliver, Frederick Alexander, Adrian Ross-Magenty, Geoffrey Bateman, Philip Dupuy, Jeffrey Wickham, Gideon Boulting, Ivor Howard, Charles Spencer; ***D:*** Marek Kanievska; ***W:*** Julian Mitchell; ***C:*** Peter Biziou; ***M:*** Michael Storey.

Another Day in Paradise 🦴🦴 **1998 (R)** Tulsa teen junkies Bobbie (Kartheiser) and Rosie (Wagner) team up with older junkie couple Mel (Woods) and Sidney (Griffith) and go from bad to worse. Mel's also a dealer and thief and is glad to add two would-be partners in crime to his and Sidney's traveling road to hell. Woods is all sly confidence while Griffith shows some seductive tough-chick grit and the younger twosome manage to hold their own nicely. Not a pic for the faint of heart or queasy of stomach. Based on the book by Eddie Little. **101m/C VHS, DVD.** James Woods, Melanie Griffith, Vincent Kartheiser, Natasha Gregson Wagner, Paul Hipp, Brent Briscoe, Lou Diamond Phillips; ***D:*** Larry Clark; ***W:*** Christopher Landon, Stephen Chin; ***C:*** Eric Alan Edwards.

Another 48 Hrs. 🦴½ **1990 (R)** Continuing chemistry between Nolte and Murphy is one of the few worthwhile items in this stodgy rehash. Any innovation by Murphy seems lost, the story is redundant of any other cop thriller, and violence and car chases abound. Pointlessly energetic and occasionally fun for only the true devotee. **98m/C VHS, DVD, 8mm.** Eddie Murphy, Nick Nolte, Brion James, Kevin Tighe, Bernie Casey, David Anthony Marshall, Ed O'Ross; ***D:*** Walter Hill; ***W:*** Jeb Stuart; ***C:*** Matthew F. Leonetti; ***M:*** James Horner.

Another Man, Another Chance 🦴🦴 *Un Autre Homme, Une Autre Chance* **1977 (PG)** Remake of Lelouch's "A Man and a Woman," set in the turn-of-the-century American West, pales by comparison to the original. Slow-moving tale casts widow Bujold and widower Caan as lovers. **132m/C VHS.** *FR* James Caan, Genevieve Bujold, Francis Huster, Jennifer Warren, Susan Tyrrell; ***D:*** Claude Lelouch; ***W:*** Claude Lelouch.

Another Man's Poison 🦴🦴½ **1952** Melodramatic crime drama with a showy, if stereotypical role, for Davis. She's mystery writer Janet Frobisher and lives on a secluded Yorkshire farm. Too bad her escaped con husband suddenly shows up (and gets killed by Janet). Her troubles aren't over. Hubby's partner, George Bates (Merrill), comes a-lookin' and agrees to dispose of the body if Janet will let him hide out. She tries to kill Bates as well but her scheming comes to an unexpected conclusion. Adapted from the play "Deadlock" by Leslie Sands. **90m/B VHS, DVD.** *GB* Bette Davis, Gary Merrill, Emlyn Williams, Anthony Steel, Barbara Murray, Reginald Beckwith, Edna Morris; ***D:*** Irving Rapper; ***W:*** Val Guest; ***C:*** Robert Krasker; ***M:*** Paul Sawtell.

Another 9 1/2 Weeks woof! **1996 (R)** Uninteresting sequel finds suicidal John (Rourke) overwhelmed by his kinky memories of Elizabeth, so he flies to Paris determined to find her. Instead, he meets fashion designer Lea (Everhart), who claims to be Elizabeth's friend and who puts the sexual tease on the S/M devotee. Monotony sets in early and there's no real heat generated between the duo. **104m/C VHS, DVD.** Mickey Rourke, Angie Everhart, Steven Berkoff, Agathe de la Fontaine, Dougray Scott; ***D:*** Anne Goursaud; ***W:*** Michael Paul Davis; ***C:*** Robert Alazraki; ***M:*** Stephen Parsons, Francis Haines.

Another Pair of Aces: Three of a Kind 🦴🦴🦴 **1991** Nelson and Kristofferson team up to clear the name of Torn, a Texas Ranger accused of murder. Video contains some scenes deemed too racy for TV. Sequel to "A Pair of Aces." **93m/C VHS.** Willie Nelson, Kris Kristofferson, Joan Severance, Rip Torn, Dan Kamin, Ken Farmer, Richard Jones; ***D:*** Bill Bixby. **TV**

Another Stakeout 🦴🦴½ *Stakeout 2* **1993 (PG-13)** Sequel six years after the original finds Dreyfuss and Estevez partnered again for another stakeout, this time to keep an eye on Moriarty, a reluctant witness against the Mob. The two spying detectives find themselves in an upscale neighborhood where blending in is a hard thing to do. O'Donnell is a breath of fresh air as a wisecracking assistant district attorney. Stowe briefly reprises her role as Dreyfuss' girlfriend. Writer Kouf reportedly had difficulty penning the script, surprising since there isn't much new here. **109m/C VHS.** Richard Dreyfuss, Emilio Estevez, Rosie O'Donnell, Cathy Moriarty, Madeleine Stowe, John Rubinstein, Marcia Strassman, Dennis Farina, Miguel Ferrer; ***D:*** John Badham; ***W:*** Jim Kouf; ***C:*** Roy Wagner.

Another Thin Man 🦴🦴½ **1939** Powell and Loy team up for the third in the delightful "Thin Man" series. Slightly weaker series entry takes its time, but has both Powell and Loy providing stylish performances. Nick Jr. is also introduced as the newest member of the sleuthing team. Sequel to "After the Thin Man"; followed by "Shadow of the Thin Man." **105m/B VHS.** William Powell, Myrna Loy, Virginia Grey, Otto Kruger, Sir C. Aubrey Smith, Ruth Hussey; ***D:*** Woodbridge S. Van Dyke.

Another Time, Another Place 🦴🦴 **1958** Sappy melodrama about an American journalist who suffers an emotional meltdown when her married British lover is killed during WWII. So she heads for Cornwall to console the widow and family. **98m/B VHS.** *GB* Lana Turner, Barry Sullivan, Glynis Johns, Sean Connery, Terence Longdon; ***D:*** Lewis Allen; ***C:*** Jack Hildyard.

Another Time, Another Place 🦴🦴🦴 **1983 (R)** Bored young Scottish housewife married to an older fella falls in love with an Italian prisoner-of-war who works on her farm during WWII. Occasionally quirky, always finely crafted view of wartime Britain and the little-known life of POWs in England. **101m/C VHS.** *GB* Phyllis Logan, Giovanni Mauriello, Gian Luca Favilla, Paul Young, Tom Watson; ***D:*** Michael Radford; ***W:*** Michael Radford; ***C:*** Roger Deakins.

Another Way 🦴🦴🦴 *Olelkezo Tekintetek* **1982** The director of 1971's much-lauded "Love" sets this politically charged love story in Hungary in 1958. Opening with a view of a female corpse, the story flashes backward to look at the woman's journalistic career and her relationship with a women colleague. Candid love scenes between women in Hungary of 1958, considered a cinematic novelty in many places outside Hungary. In Hungarian with English subtitles. **100m/C VHS.** *HU* Jadwiga Jankowska Cieslak, Grazyna Szapolowska, Josef Kroner, Hernadi Judit, Andorai Peter; ***D:*** Karoly Makk. Cannes '82: Actress (Cieslak).

Another Woman 🦴🦴🦴 **1988 (PG)** The study of an intellectual woman whose life is changed when she begins to eavesdrop. What she hears provokes her to examine every relationship in her life, finding things quite different than she had believed. Heavy going, with Rowlands effective as a woman coping with an entirely new vision of herself. Farrow plays the catalyst. Although Allen's comedies are more popular than his dramas, this one deserves a look. **81m/C VHS, DVD, Wide.** Gena Rowlands, Gene Hackman, Mia Farrow, Ian Holm, Betty Buckley, Martha Plimpton, Blythe Danner, Harris Yulin, Sandy Dennis, David Ogden Stiers, John Houseman, Philip Bosco, Frances Conroy, Kenneth Welsh, Michael Kirby; ***D:*** Woody Allen; ***W:*** Woody Allen; ***C:*** Sven Nykvist.

Another Woman's Husband 🦴🦴½ **2000** Traumatized as a child by the drowning death of her brother, Laurel (Rinna) finally decides to get over her fear of water by taking swimming lessons. Susan (O'Grady) is her swimming instructor and they become best friends. Until the women realize they also share the same man (Midkiff), who happens to be Susan's husband. Based on the novel "Swimming Lessons" by Anna Villegas and Lynne Hugo. **91m/C VHS, DVD.** Lisa Rinna, Gail O'Grady, Dale Midkiff, Sally Kirkland, Charlotte Rae; ***D:*** Noel Nosseck; ***W:*** Susan Arnout Smith; ***C:*** Alan Caso; ***M:*** Mark Snow. **CABLE**

Another You 🦴 **1991 (R)** Con man Wilder takes pathological liar Pryor under his care and decides to use his talents to his fullest advantage. Posing as successful businessmen, the duo initiate a scam so complicated that they may end up being double-crossed or worse yet, dead! Can the pair see their plan through without losing their lives? Sad to see how far these two gifted comedians have fallen. Their collaboration is tired and the movie generally dreadful. **98m/C VHS, 8mm.** Richard Pryor, Gene Wilder, Mercedes Ruehl, Vanessa Williams, Stephen Lang, Kevin Pollak; ***D:*** Maurice Phillips.

Antarctica 🦴🦴 **1984** Due to unfortunate circumstances, a group of scientists must leave their pack of huskies behind on a frozen glacier in the Antarctic. The film focuses on the dogs' subsequent struggle for survival. Dubbed. **112m/C VHS.** *JP* Ken Takakura, Masako Natsume, Keiko Oginome; ***D:*** Koreyoshi Kurahara; ***M:*** Vangelis.

Anthony Adverse 🦴🦴½ **1936** March is a young man in the 19th century who searches for manhood across America and Mexico. He grows slowly as he battles foes, struggles against adversity and returns home to find his lover in this romantic swashbuckler. A star-studded cast, lush costuming, and an energetic musical score. Highly acclaimed in its time, but now seems dated. Based on the novel by Hervey Allen. **141m/B VHS.** Fredric March, Olivia de Havilland, Anita Louise, Gale Sondergaard, Claude Rains, Edmund Gwenn, Louis Hayward; ***D:*** Mervyn LeRoy; ***C:*** Gaetano Antonio "Tony" Gaudio; ***M:*** Erich Wolfgang Korngold. Oscars '36: Cinematog., Film Editing, Support. Actress (Sondergaard), Score.

Antitrust 🦴½ **2000 (PG-13)** Supernerd code writer Milo (Phillippe) leaves the garage for a Pacific Northwest software giant only to discover the company's mega-monied leader, Winston (Robbins), may not be on the up and up—in fact, the things he's doing to maintain industry supremacy could be downright evil. Robbins's bespectacled techie villain is spot-on Bill Gates, but the film borrows heavily from its paranoid predecessors and offers little of its own to the field. A mediocre thriller among other mediocre thrillers. **120m/C VHS, DVD, Wide.** Ryan Phillippe, Tim Robbins, Rachael Leigh Cook, Claire Forlani, Douglas McFerran, Richard Roundtree, Yee Jee Tso, Tygh Runyan; ***D:*** Peter Howitt; ***W:*** Howard Franklin; ***C:*** John Bailey; ***M:*** Don Davis.

Antoine et Antoinette 🦴🦴½ **1947** Antoine (Pigaut) is a shop foreman and his wife, Antoinette (Maffei), a clerk, who lead a somewhat tempestuous life in Paris. Then the situation worsens when Antoine loses the couple's winning lottery ticket. The first of Becker's romantic trilogy, followed by "Rendez-vous de Juillet" and "Edward and Caroline." French with subtitles; originally released at 95 minutes. **78m/B VHS.** *FR* Roger Pigaut, Claire Maffei, Noel Roquevert; ***D:*** Jacques Becker; ***W:*** Jacques Becker, Maurice Griffe, Francoise Giroud; ***C:*** Pierre Montazel; ***M:*** Jean Jacques Grunenwald.

Anton, the Magician 🦴🦴 *Anton der Zauberer* **1978** Anton likes to live by his wits. A car mechanic, he marries the boss' daughter, Liesel, and uses his skills to make a pile of illegal dough that he hides at the home of the widowed Sabine, with whom he's also involved. When Anton's schemes catch up with him, he ends up in prison, and Sabine takes off to Switzerland with the cash. But this isn't the end of their story. German with subtitles. **101m/C VHS.** *GE* Ulrich Thein, Barbara Dittus, Anna Dymna, Erwin Geschonneck, Erik S. Klein; ***D:*** Guenther Reisch; ***W:*** Guenther Reisch, Karl-Georg Egel; ***C:*** Gunter Haubold; ***M:*** Wolfram Heicking.

Antonia and Jane 🦴🦴🦴 **1991 (R)** Enjoyable film tells the story of a long-standing, heavily tested friendship between two women. From the very beginning, they are a study in contrasts—Jane as rather plain, frumpy, and insecure; Antonia as glamorous, elegant, and successful. Both believe that each other's lives are more interesting and exciting than their own. Kidron, who directed this smart witty comedy for British TV, offers an honest look into the often complex world of adult friendships. **75m/C VHS.** *GB* Imelda Staunton, Saskia Reeves, Patricia Leventon, Alfred Hoffman, Maria Charles, John Bennett, Richard Hope, Alfred Marks, Lila Kaye, Bill Nighy, Brenda Bruce; ***D:*** Beeban Kidron; ***W:*** Marcy Kahan; ***M:*** Rachel Portman. **TV**

Antonia's Line 🦴🦴½ **1995 (R)** 90-year-old Antonia (Van Ammelrooy) has decided that she is going to die today and so begins a 50-year-long flashback of her nonconformist life in a Dutch village. Her lesbian daughter Danielle (Dottermans) wants a child without bothering about a husband and Antonia obliging arranges a brief interlude that produces child prodigy Therese (Van Overloop), who eventually has her own daughter, Sarah (Ravesteijn). Lots of female bonding (the male characters are mostly on the periphery of the action) and a certain magic realism abound. Dutch with subtitles. **102m/C VHS, DVD.** *NL* Willeke Van Ammelrooy, Els Dottermans, Veerle Van Overloop, Thyrza Ravesteijn, Jan Decleir, Mil Seghers, Jan Steen, Marina De Graaf; ***D:*** Marleen Gorris; ***W:*** Marleen Gorris; ***C:*** Willy Stassen; ***M:*** Ilona Sekacz. Oscars '95: Foreign Film.

Antonio 🦴🦴 **1973** A Texas millionaire on the run from his wife and her divorce lawyer alights in a small Chilean village and turns it upside down. **89m/C VHS.** Larry Hagman, Trini Lopez, Noemi Guerrero, Pedro Becker; ***D:*** Claudio Guzman.

Antonio Das Mortes 🦴🦴½ *O Dragao da Maldade contra o Santo Guerreiro* **1968** Antonio is a savage mercenary hired to kill rebels against the Brazilian government. Belatedly he realizes he sympathizes with the targets and turns his guns the other way for an incredible shootout finale. A visually lavish poltical polemic, espousing revolutionary guerrilla action within the format of a South American western. In Portuguese with English subtitles. **100m/C VHS.** *BR* Mauricio Do Valle, Odete Lara, Jofre Soares, Othon Bastos; ***D:*** Glauce Rocha; ***W:*** Glauce Rocha; ***C:*** Alfonso Beato.

Antony and Cleopatra 🦴🦴 **1973 (PG)** Heston wrote, directed, and starred in this long, dry adaptation of the Shakespeare play that centers on the torrid romance between Mark Antony and Cleopatra. **150m/C VHS.** Charlton Heston, Hildegard(e) Neil, Fernando Rey, Eric Porter, John Castle, Freddie Jones, Warren Clarke, Julian Glover; ***D:*** Charlton Heston.

Ants 🦴½ *Panic at Lakewood Manor; It Happened at Lakewood Manor* **1977** A mad bug parable for our planet-obsessed society. Insecticide-infected ants turn militant and check into a local hotel to vent their chemically induced foul mood on the unsuspecting clientele. The guest register includes a gaggle of celebrities who probably wish they'd signed on the Love Boat instead. Made for TV (an ant farm would probably be just too horrible on the big screen). **100m/C VHS.** Suzanne Somers, Robert Foxworth, Myrna Loy, Lynda Day George, Gerald Gordon, Bernie Casey, Barry Van Dyke, Karen Lamm, Anita Gillette, Moosie Drier, Steve Franken, Brian Dennehy, Bruce French, Stacy Keach Sr., Rene Enriquez, James Storm; ***D:*** Robert Scheerer; ***M:*** Ken Richmond. **TV**

Antz 🦴🦴🦴 **1998 (PG)** Malcontent worker ant, Z (Allen), moans to his therapist about his insignificance and the depressing anonymity of "being born in the middle of five million." But after meeting the colony's princess, Bala (Stone), who is facing her own bleak future thanks to an arranged marriage with the colony's power-hungry General Mandible (Hackman), Z and Princess Bala embark on a dangerous mission to the surface in search of the mythical "Insectopia." Only the second film ever created entirely through computer animation ("Toy Story" being the first), pic is visually amazing. The fact that the ant characters do not resemble their performers' appearances makes the relationship between Z and the princess plausible, and actually adds depth to the characters' personalities. An interesting, rather elaborate storyline, along with excellent voice performances (even Stallone!) make this one fun for all ages. **83m/C VHS, DVD.** ***D:*** Eric Darnell, Tim Johnson; ***W:*** Chris Weitz, Paul Weitz, Todd Alcott; ***M:*** Harry Gregson-Williams, John Powell; ***V:*** Woody Allen, Sharon Stone, Sylvester Stallone, Anne Bancroft, Danny Glover, Christopher Walken, Jane Curtin, Jennifer Lopez, John Mahoney, Dan Aykroyd, Paul Mazursky, Gene Hackman.

Any Given Sunday 🦴🦴🦴 **1999 (R)** Stone sets aside his conspiracy theories on war and politics and effectively shines a spotlight on a different kind of battlefield to come up with the most commerical and entertaining film of his career. Pacino heads an all-star cast as the battered, yet wise and resilient coach of a struggling Miami football team who locks horns with not only young quarterback Foxx, but ruthless, ballbuster team owner Diaz. Epic-like runtime (which sprints along thanks to Stone's potent mix of raw camera work and hip-hop soundtrack) allows much of the cast plenty of room, with comedian Foxx holding his own with the big boys in a star-making performance as the hotdog player with a bad case of ego. With an intelligent script and a perfect cast, Stone creates the most realistic look at pro football since 1979's "North Dallas Forty." **170m/B VHS, DVD, Wide.** Al Pacino, Dennis Quaid, Cameron Diaz, Jamie Foxx, Charlton Heston, James Woods, Matthew Modine, Ann-Margret, Lauren Holly, Lela Rochon, L.L. Cool J., Aaron Eckhart, Jim Brown, Bill Bellamy, Elizabeth Berkley, John C. McGinley; ***D:*** Oliver Stone; ***W:*** Oliver Stone, John Logan; ***C:*** Salvatore Totino; ***M:*** Robbie Robertson.

Any Gun Can Play 🦴 *For a Few Bullets More* **1967** Typical spaghetti western. Three men (banker, thief, and bounty hunter) compete for a treasure of gold while wandering about the Spanish countryside. **103m/C VHS.** *IT SP* Edd Byrnes, Gilbert Roland, George Hilton, Kareen O'Hara, Pedro Sanchez, Gerard Herter; ***D:*** Enzo G. Castellari.

Any Man's Death 🦴🦴 **1990 (R)** Savage is a globe-trotting reporter on the trail of a worldwide conspiracy who accidentally uncovers a Nazi war criminal in Africa. Well-meaning but confused tale. **105m/C VHS.** John Savage, William Hickey, Mia Sara, Ernest Borgnine, Michael Lerner; ***D:*** Tom Clegg.

Any Number Can Play 🦴🦴½ **1949** Fast-moving drama about an ailing gambler who faces a series of crises. Gable gives a commanding performance as the noble dice-roller. Based on the novel by Edward Harris Heath. **102m/B VHS.** Clark Gable, Alexis Smith, Wendell Corey, Audrey Totter, Frank Morgan, Mary Astor, Lewis Stone, Barry Sullivan; ***D:*** Mervyn LeRoy; ***W:*** Richard Brooks.

Any Number Can Win 🦴🦴 *Melodie en Sous-Sol; The Big Grab* **1963** Two ex-convicts, aging Charles (Gabin) and his former cellmate Francis (Delon), risk their lives and freedom for one last major heist: a gambling casino on the French Riviera. French with English subtitles. **118m/B VHS, DVD.** *FR* Claude Cerval, Jean Gabin, Alain Delon, Viviane Romance, Maurice Biraud, Carla Marlier, Jose-Luis De Villalonga, Jean Carmet; ***D:*** Henri Verneuil; ***W:*** Henri Verneuil, Michel Audiard, Albert Simonin; ***C:*** Louis Page; ***M:*** Michel Magne.

Any Place But Home 🦴🦴½ **1997 (PG-13)** Roberta (Keller) and Lucas (Lando) Dempsey find themselves in big trouble when Roberta's sister Carrie Miller (Conway) and her low-life hubby Carl (Midkiff) try to involve them in a plan to kidnap 12-year-old John Danforth (Norris), figuring John's rich dad August (Thicke) will be happy to pay the ransom. Roberta manages to get the kid and the money away from the Millers but she and Lucas discover John is an abused child and terrified of his father. The threesome go on the run with the Millers, August's hired help, and the FBI on their trail. **90m/C VHS.** Joe Lando, Mary Page Keller, Alan Thicke, Dale Midkiff, Cristie Conway, Richard Roundtree; ***D:*** Rob Hedden; ***W:*** Bart Baker. **CABLE**

Any Wednesday 🦴🦴½ *Bachelor Girl Apartment* **1966** Okay sex farce about powerful industrialist Robards' use of his mistress's apartment as a tax write-off. When a young company executive learns of the "company" apartment, he meets Robards' nonchalant wife for a tryst of their own. Based on Muriel Resnik's Broadway play; similar to the 1960 "The Apartment." **110m/C VHS.** Jane Fonda, Jason Robards Jr., Dean Jones, Rosemary Murphy; ***D:*** Robert Ellis Miller; ***W:*** Julius J. Epstein; ***M:*** George Duning.

Any Which Way You Can 🦴🦴 **1980 (PG)** Bad brawler Philo Beddoe and his buddy Clyde, the orangutan, are back again in the sequel to "Every Which Way But Loose." This time Philo is tempted to take part in a big bout for a large cash prize. Clyde steals scenes, brightening up the no-brainer story. **116m/C VHS, DVD, Wide.** Clint Eastwood, Sondra Locke, Ruth Gordon, Harry Guardino, William Smith, Geoffrey Lewis, Barry Corbin; ***D:*** Buddy Van Horn; ***W:*** Stanford Sherman; ***C:*** David Worth.

Anything for a Thrill 🦴 **1937** Two kids save a cameraman's career, make friends with a millionaress, and foil some crooks. **59m/B VHS.** Frankie Darro, Kane Richmond; ***D:*** Leslie Goodwins.

Anything for Love 🦴½ *Just One of the Girls* **1993** Teen musician is the object of a school bully's rage so he decides to dress up as a girl to escape the guy's fists. **90m/C VHS.** *CA* Corey Haim, Nicole Eggert, Cameron Bancroft, Kevin McNulty, Wendy Van Riesen, Lochlyn Munro, Rachel Hayward, Molly Parker; ***D:*** Michael Keusch; ***M:*** Amin Bhatia.

Anywhere But Here 🦴🦴½ **1999 (PG-13)** Just who's the Mom here? It certainly doesn't seem to be flaky Adele (Sarandon), who suddenly uproots teen daughter Ann (Portman) from provincial Wisconsin to relocate in sunny L.A., where Adele wants Ann to become an actress. Ann's definitely the practical one of the duo and she tries to rein in Adele's loopier flights of fantasy. Of course, Ann does have some plans (and dreams) of her own. The leads are both pros and there are enough tear-jerking moments to satisfy in this somewhat stereotypical drama. Based on the 1986 novel by Mona Simpson. **114m/C VHS, DVD.** Susan Sarandon, Natalie Portman, Shawn Hatosy, Hart Bochner, Bonnie Bedelia, Eileen Ryan, Ray Baker, John Diehl, Caroline Aaron, Paul Guilfoyle, Mary Ellen Trainor; ***D:*** Wayne Wang; ***W:*** Alvin Sargent; ***C:*** Roger Deakins; ***M:*** Danny Elfman.

Anzacs: The War Down Under 🦴🦴🦴 **1985** Well-made Australian TV miniseries about the Australian and New Zealand Army Corps during WWI. Follows the men from the time they enlist to the campaigns in Gallipoli and France. **165m/C VHS.** *AU* Paul Hogan, Andrew Clarke, Jon Blake, Megan Williams; ***D:*** George Miller. **TV**

Anzio 🦴🦴 *The Battle for Anzio; Lo Sbarco di Anzio* **1968** The historic Allied invasion of Italy during WWII as seen through the eyes of American war correspondent Mitchum. Fine cast waits endlessly to leave the beach, though big battle scenes are effectively rendered. Based on the book by Wynford Vaughan Thomas. **117m/C VHS, DVD, Wide.** Giancarlo Giannini, Robert Mitchum, Peter Falk, Arthur Kennedy, Robert Ryan, Earl Holliman, Mark Damon, Reni Santoni, Patrick Magee; ***D:*** Edward Dmytryk; ***W:*** H.A.L. Craig, Frank De Felitta; ***C:*** Giuseppe Rotunno; ***M:*** Riz Ortolani.

Apache 🦴🦴½ **1954** Lancaster is the only Indian in Geronimo's outfit who refuses to surrender in this chronicle of a bitter battle between the Indians and the U.S. cavalry in the struggle for the West. First western for Aldrich is a thoughtful piece for its time that had the original tragic ending reshot (against Aldrich's wishes) to make it more happy. Adapted from "Bronco Apache" by Paul I. Wellman. **91m/C VHS.** Burt Lancaster, John McIntire, Jean Peters, Charles Bronson, John Dehner, Paul Guilfoyle; ***D:*** Robert Aldrich; ***C:*** Ernest Laszlo.

Apache Blood 🦴½ *Pursuit* **1975 (R)** An Indian Brave, the lone survivor of an Indian massacre by the U.S. Army, squares off with a cavalry scout in the forbidding desert. **92m/C VHS.** Ray Danton, DeWitt Lee, Troy Neighbors, Diane Taylor, Eva Kovacs, Jason Clark; ***D:*** Thomas Quillen.

Apache Chief 🦴 **1950** Two Apache tribe leaders, one good, the other evil clash. Ultimately, and perhaps predictably, they face each other in hand-to-hand combat and peace prevails. **60m/B VHS.** Alan Curtis, Tom Neal, Russell Hayden, Carol Thurston, Fuzzy Knight; ***D:*** Frank McDonald.

Apache Kid's Escape 🦴 **1930** The Apache Kid leads the cavalry on a wild chase across the plains in this saga of the old west. **60m/B VHS.** Jack Perrin, Fred Church, Josephine Hill, Virginia Ashcroft, Bud Osborne, Henry Roquemore, Buzz Barton; ***D:*** Robert J. Horner.

Apache Rose 🦴🦴 **1947** Gambling boat owner plots to gain control of oil found on Vegas Ranch. Roy and Dale oppose the idea. First of the series in color; the original, unedited version of the film. **75m/B VHS.** Roy Rogers, Dale Evans, Olin Howlin, George Meeker; ***D:*** William Witney.

Apache Uprising 🦴½ **1966** A standard western with Calhoun as the lawman up against gunfighters and stagecoach robbers as well as the usual Indians. **60m/C VHS.** Rory Calhoun, Corinne Calvet, DeForest Kelley, John Russell, Lon Chaney Jr., Gene Evans, Richard Arlen, Robert Harris, Arthur Hunnicutt, Jean Parker, Johnny Mack Brown; ***D:*** R.G. Springsteen.

Apache Woman 🦴½ **1955** Bridges stars as a government agent sent to investigate some crimes committed by a group of Apache Indians. As he tries to calm the townspeople, Bridges discovers that the group is made up of white people led by an educated half-breed. He instigates the help of the half-breed's sister (and also Bridges' love interest) to stop the gang. Some good action, but lots of dull spots. **82m/C VHS.** Lloyd Bridges, Joan Taylor, Lance Fuller, Morgan Jones, Paul Birch, Jonathan Haze, Paul Dubov, Lou Place; ***D:*** Roger Corman.

Apache's Last Battle 🦴🦴 *Old Shatterhand; Shatterhand* **1964** A boundary scout discovers the ward of an Apache chief has been framed for murder by a cavalry officer who wants to start an Indian war in this exciting Euro western. **122m/C VHS.** *GE YU FR IT* Lex Barker, Pierre Brice, Daliah Lavi, Guy Madison, Ralf Wolter, Gustavo Rojo, Rick Battaglia, Bill Ramsey; ***D:*** Hugo Fregonese; ***W:*** Ladislas Fodor, Robert A. Stemmle; ***C:*** Siegfried Hold; ***M:*** Riz Ortolani.

Aparajito 🦴🦴🦴½ *The Unvanquished* **1958** The second of the Apu trilogy, about a boy growing up in India, after "Pather Panchali," and before "The World of Apu." Apu is brought to Benares and his education seriously begins. The work of a master; in Bengali with English subtitles. **108m/B VHS.** *IN* Pinaki Sen Gupta, Karuna Banerjee, Kanu Banerjee, Ramani Sen Gupta; ***D:*** Satyajit Ray; ***W:*** Satyajit Ray; ***C:*** Subrata Mitra; ***M:*** Ravi Shankar. Venice Film Fest. '57: Film.

Apart from Hugh 🦴🦴 **1994** Collin and Hugh have been living together for a year and to celebrate the occasion, Hugh decides to plan an anniversary party. Unfortunately, Collin hasn't told Hugh he's having second thoughts about their relationship. Directorial debut of FitzGerald. **87m/B VHS.** ***D:*** Jon FitzGerald.

The Apartment 🦴🦴🦴½ **1960** Lowly insurance clerk C.C. Baxter (Lemmon) tries to climb the corporate ladder by "loaning" his apartment out to executives having affairs. Problems arise, however, when he unwittingly falls for sweet elevator operator Fran Kubelik (MacLaine), the most recent girlfriend of his unfeeling boss J.D. Sheldrake (MacMurray). Highly acclaimed social satire. **125m/B VHS, DVD, Wide.** Jack Lemmon, Shirley MacLaine, Fred MacMurray, Ray Walston, Jack Kruschen, Joan Shawlee, Edie Adams, Hope Holiday, David Lewis; ***D:*** Billy Wilder; ***W:*** I.A.L. Diamond, Billy Wilder; ***C:*** Joseph LaShelle; ***M:*** Adolph Deutsch. Oscars '60: Art Dir./Set Dec., B&W, Director (Wilder), Film Editing, Picture, Story & Screenplay; AFI '98: Top 100; British Acad. '60: Actor (Lemmon), Actress (MacLaine), Film; Directors Guild '60: Director (Wilder); Golden Globes '61: Actor—Mus./Comedy (Lemmon), Actress—Mus./Comedy (MacLaine), Film—Mus./Comedy, Natl. Film Reg. '94;; N.Y. Film Critics '60: Director (Wilder), Film, Screenplay.

Apartment Complex 🦴🦴½ **1998 (R)** An assortment of Hollywood weirdos occupy Dr. Caligari's Wonder View Apartments where psych grad student Stan Warden (Lowe) has just taken a job as the building manager. There's a hot-to-trot psychic, a paranoid ex-government agent, and a recluse, among others and then Stan discovers the body of the previous super. Strange things begin happening (including the appearance of a giant snake), even as hapless Stan becomes the prime suspect and potential victim. Creepy and comic. **99m/C VHS.** Chad Lowe, Fay Masterson, Obba Babatunde, Patrick Warburton, Ron Canada, Amanda Plummer, Miguel (Michael) Sandoval, Jon Polito, R. Lee Ermey, Charles Martin Smith; ***D:*** Tobe Hooper; ***W:*** Karl Schaefer; ***C:*** Jacques Haitkin; ***M:*** Mark Adler. **CABLE**

Apartment Zero 🦴🦴🦴½ **1988 (R)** A decidedly weird, deranged psychological drama about the parasite/host-type relationship between two roommates in downtown Buenos Aires: one, an obsessive British movie nut, the other, a sexually mesmerizing stud who turns out to be a cold-blooded psycho. **124m/C VHS.** *GB* Hart Bochner,, Colin Firth, Fabrizio Bentivoglio, Liz Smith, Dora Bryan, James Telfer, Mirella D'Angelo, Juan Vitale, Francesca D'Aloja, Miguel Ligero, Elvia Andreoli, Marikeva Monti; ***D:*** Martin Donovan; ***W:*** Martin Donovan, David Koepp; ***C:*** Miguel Rodriguez; ***M:*** Elia Cmiral.

The Ape 🦴🦴 **1940** When his daughter dies of a crippling disease, Karloff becomes fixated with the mission to cure paralysis. Obviously distraught, he begins donning the hide of an escaped circus ape whose spinal fluid is the key to the serum. Hide-bedecked, he slays unknowing townspeople to tap them of their spinal fluid and cure his latest patient. **62m/B VHS, DVD.** Boris Karloff, Maris Wrixon, Henry Hall, Gertrude Hoffman; ***D:*** William Nigh.

A*P*E* woof! *Attack of the Giant Horny Gorilla* **1976 (PG)** A*P*E* is 36 feet tall and ten tons of animal fury who destroys anything that comes between him and the actress he loves. Cheap rip-off of Kong. **87m/C VHS, DVD, Wide.** *KN* Rod Arrants, Joanna (Joanna DeVarona) Kerns, Alex Nicol, Francis Lee; ***D:*** Paul Leder; ***W:*** Paul Leder, Reuben Leder.

The Ape Man 🦴🦴 *Lock Your Doors* **1943** With the aid of a secret potion, a scientist turns himself into a murderous ape. The only way to regain his human side is to ingest human spinal fluid. Undoubtedly inspired by Boris Karloff's 1940 film, "The Ape." **64m/B VHS.** Wallace Ford, Bela Lugosi, Louise Currie; ***D:*** William Beaudine.

A.P.E.X. 🦴🦴 **1994 (R)** Nicholas Sinclair (Keats), a researcher from 2073, time travels back to 1973 to retrieve a faulty robot probe called A.P.E.X. (Advanced Prototype Extermination Unit). Unwittingly he has been infected with a mysterious virus and when he returns it's to a version of his own time where humans are dying from the virus and robots are sent to eradicate the few survivors. It also seems Sinclair is now a guerilla in an anti-robot army. Yes, it sounds like "The Terminator" but the action moves and though the budget is limited the special effects are still impressive. **103m/C VHS.** Richard Keats, Mitchell Cox, Lisa Ann Russell, Marcus Aurelius, Adam Lawson; ***D:*** Phillip J. Roth; ***W:*** Phillip J. Roth, Ronald Schmidt; ***M:*** Jim Goodwin.

The Apocalypse 🦴🦴 **1996 (R)** Space pilot J.T. Wayne (Bernhard) teams up with salvage operator Suarez (McCoy) and his crew to retrieve a cargo ship lost in space for 25 years. But crewman Vendler (Zagarino) hijacks the cargo for himself, with only Wayne and Lennon (Dye) as survivors. But it turn's out the ship is one big booby-trap rigged to crash into earth. Now Wayne and Lennon must not only save themselves but the planet as well. Low-budget, with a confusing plot. **96m/C VHS, DVD.** Sandra Bernhard, Laura San Giacomo, Cameron Dye, Frank Zagarino, Matt McCoy; ***D:*** Hubert de la Bouillerie; ***C:*** Greg Gardiner.

Apocalypse Now 🦴🦴🦴🦴 **1979 (R)** Coppola's $40 million epic vision of the Vietnam War was inspired by Joseph Conrad's novella "Heart of Darkness," and continues to be the subject of debate. Disillusioned Army captain Sheen travels upriver into Cambodia to assassinate overweight renegade colonel Brando. His trip is punctuated by surrealistic battles and a terrifying descent into a land where human rationality seems to have slipped away. Considered by some to be the definitive picture of war in its overall depiction of chaos and primal bloodletting; by others, over-wrought and unrealistic. May not translate as well to the small screen, yet worth seeing if for nothing more than Duvall's ten minutes of scenery chewing as a battle-obsessed major ("I love the smell of napalm in the morning!"), a study in manic machismo. Stunning photography by Vittorio Storaro, awe-inspiring battle scenes, and effective soundtrack montage. Both Sheen and Coppola suffered emotional breakdowns during the prolonged filming, and that's a very young Fishburne in his major film debut. Available in a remastered version in letterbox on VHS with a remixed soundtrack that features Dolby Surround stereo. In 1991 a documentary detailing the making of the film, "Hearts of Darkness: A Filmmaker's Apocalypse," was released. **153m/C VHS, DVD, CD-I, Wide.** Francis Ford Coppola, Marlon Brando, Martin Sheen, Robert Duvall, Frederic Forrest, Sam Bottoms, Scott Glenn, Albert Hall, Laurence "Larry" Fishburne, Harrison Ford, G.D. Spradlin, Dennis Hopper, Cynthia Wood, Colleen Camp, Linda Carpenter, Tom Mason, James Keane, Damien Leake, Jack Thibeau, R. Lee Ermey, Vittorio Storaro; ***D:*** Francis Ford Coppola; ***W:*** Francis Ford Coppola, John Milius, Michael Herr; ***C:*** Vittorio Storaro; ***M:*** Carmine Coppola. Oscars '79: Cinematog., Sound; AFI '98: Top 100; British Acad. '79: Director (Coppola), Support. Actor (Duvall); Cannes '79: Film; Golden Globes '80: Director (Coppola), Support. Actor (Duvall), Score, Natl. Film Reg. '00;; Natl. Soc. Film Critics '79: Support. Actor (Forrest).

The Apocalypse Watch 🦴🦴 *Robert Ludlum's the Apocalypse Watch* **1997** CIA analyst Drew (Bergin) takes over his field agent brother's assignment when the latter is killed. Drew hooks up with his bro's girlfriend/partner (Madsen) and their spying leads to a neo-Nazi organization. Based on the novel by Ludlum. **176m/C VHS, DVD.** Patrick Bergin, Virginia Madsen, John Shea, Benedick Blythe, Christopher Neame, Malcolm Tierney; ***D:*** Kevin Connor; ***W:*** John Goldsmith, Christopher Canaan; ***C:*** Dennis C. Lewiston; ***M:*** Ken Thorne. **TV**

Apollo 13 🦴🦴🦴½ **1995 (PG)** Realistic big-budget reenactment of the 1970 Apollo lunar mission that ran into a "problem" 205,000 miles from home reunites Hanks and Sinese from "F. Gump" and Howard and Hanks from "Splash." And an enjoyable reunion it is. Explosion in one of two oxygen tanks helping power the spacecraft leaves the three astronauts (led by Hanks) tumbling through space. With the electrical system kaput and oxygen running low, the men seek refuge in the Lunar Excursion Module. Since it's based on the real event and the outcome is known, director Howard concentrates on the personalities and the details of the seven-day adventure at Mission Control and in space, in the process delivering the dramatic payload. Weightless shots are the real deal as crew filmed for ten days and made 600 parabolic loops in a KC-135 jet, NASA's "Vomit Comet," the long plunge creating 25 seconds of weightlessness. Special effects (by James Cameron's Digital Domain) and set design do the rest; no NASA footage is used, though original TV footage is used to dramatic effect. Script, with an uncredited rewrite by John Sayles, is based on the 1994 book, "Lost Moon," written by 13's Jim Lovell (who has a cameo as the Navy captain welcoming the astronauts aboard the recovery ship), while Apollo 15 commander David Scott served as a consultant. **140m/C VHS, DVD.** Tom Hanks, Kevin Bacon, Bill Paxton, Gary Sinise, Ed Harris, Kathleen Quinlan, Brett Cullen, Emily Ann Lloyd, Miko Hughes, Max Elliott Slade, Jean Speegle Howard, Tracy Reiner, Michelle Little, David Andrews, Mary Kate Schellhardt; ***D:*** Ron Howard; ***W:*** William Broyles Jr., Al Reinert; ***C:*** Dean Cundey; ***M:*** James Horner. Oscars '95: Film Editing, Sound; Directors Guild '95: Director (Howard); Screen Actors Guild '95: Support. Actor (Harris), Cast; Blockbuster '96: Drama Actor, T. (Hanks).

Apology 🦴🦴 **1986** A psychotic killer stalks Warren, an experimental artist, in Manhattan while a detective stalks the killer. Written by Medoff, author of "Children of a Lesser God." **98m/C VHS.** Lesley Ann Warren, Peter Weller, John Glover, George Loros, Jimmie Ray Weeks, Christopher Noth, Harvey Fierstein; ***D:*** Robert Bierman; ***W:*** Mark Medoff; ***M:*** Maurice Jarre. **CABLE**

The Apostate 🦴🦴 *Michael Angel* **1998 (R)** A young Jesuit priest, whose gay prostitute brother has been murdered by a serial killer, heads home to Puerto Rico and offers his assistance to his police inspector uncle in catching the killer, who seems driven by religious torment. But the priest himself is torn by spiritual doubts about his calling and is plunged into a world of temptation and vengeance. **94m/C VHS, DVD.** Richard Grieco, Dennis Hopper, Kristin Minter, Frank Medrano, Michael Cole, Efrain Figueroa, Bridget Ann White; ***D:*** Bill Gove; ***W:*** Bill Gove; ***C:*** Reinhart Pesche; ***M:*** Thomas Morse. **VIDEO**

The Apostle 🦴🦴🦴 **1997 (PG-13)** No-holds-barred look at one man's search for religious redemption. Eulis Dewey (Duvall) is a devout, middle-aged, Pentecostal preacher in Texas, with a true gift for inspiring his congregation. Unfortunately, he's not so inspiring to his wife Jessie (Fawcett), who's cheating on him with younger minister, Horace (Allen). When Eulis discovers the infidelity, he strikes Horace with a bat, sending the man into a coma. Eulis escapes and winds up in the predominantly black town of Bayou Boutte, Louisiana, having shed his old identity for that of E.F., "The Apostle" of

God. He zealously starts up a new church, seeking salvation, but his past comes back to haunt him. **134m/C VHS, DVD.** Robert Duvall, Miranda Richardson, Farrah Fawcett, John Beasley, Todd Allen, June Carter Cash, Billy Bob Thornton, Rick Dial, Walton Goggins, Billy Joe Shaver; ***D:*** Robert Duvall; ***W:*** Robert Duvall; ***C:*** Barry Markowitz; ***M:*** David Mansfield. Ind. Spirit '98: Actor (Duvall), Director (Duvall), Film; L.A. Film Critics '97: Actor (Duvall); Natl. Soc. Film Critics '97: Actor (Duvall).

The Appaloosa 🦴🦴½ *Southwest to Sonora* **1966** A lamenting loner who decides to begin anew by breeding Appaloosas is ripped off by a desperate woman who steals his horse in order to get away from her abusive amour. Brando falls in love with the girl and the two amazingly survive a wealth of obstacles in their battle against Mexican bandits. **99m/C VHS.** Marlon Brando, Anjanette Comer, John Saxon; ***D:*** Sidney J. Furie; ***W:*** James Bridges; ***C:*** Russell Metty.

Appetite 🦴🦴 **1998 (R)** Try to stick with this slow-moving suspenser because it's got a wicked ending. A group of strangers, staying at the same hotel, play a game of cards where the loser must sleep in the reputedly haunted Room 207. **99m/C VHS, DVD.** Ute Lemper, Trevor Eve, Christien Anholt, Edward Hardwicke; ***D:*** George Milton; ***W:*** Dominik Scherrer; ***C:*** Peter Thwaites.

Applause 🦴🦴🦴 **1929** Morgan plays a down-and-out burlesque star trying to protect her fresh from the convent daughter. Definitely dated, but a marvelous performance by Morgan. Film buffs will appreciate this early talkie. **78m/B VHS.** Helen Morgan, Joan Peers, Fuller Mellish Jr., Henry Wadsworth, Dorothy (Dorothy G. Cummings) Cumming; ***D:*** Rouben Mamoulian; ***C:*** George J. Folsey.

The Apple 🦴½ **1980 (PG)** Futuristic musical filmed in Berlin that features a young, innocent, folk-singing couple who nearly become victims of the evil, glitzy record producer who tries to recruit the couple into a life of sex and drugs. **90m/C VHS.** Catherine Mary Stewart, Alan Love, Grace Kennedy, Joss Ackland; ***D:*** Menahem Golan.

The Apple Dumpling Gang 🦴🦴 **1975 (G)** Three frisky kids strike it rich and trigger the wildest bank robbery in the gold-mad West. Unmistakably Disney, a familial subplot and a wacky duo are provided. Mediocre yet superior to its sequel, "The Apple Dumpling Gang Rides Again." **100m/C VHS.** Bill Bixby, Susan Clark, Don Knotts, Tim Conway, David Wayne, Slim Pickens, Harry (Henry) Morgan; ***D:*** Norman Tokar; ***M:*** Buddy (Norman Dale) Baker.

The Apple Dumpling Gang Rides Again 🦴🦴 **1979 (G)** Two lovable hombres terrorize the West in their bungling attempt to go straight. Fans of Conway or Knotts may appreciate this sequel to Disney's "The Apple Dumpling Gang." **88m/C VHS.** Tim Conway, Don Knotts, Tim Matheson, Kenneth Mars, Harry (Henry) Morgan, Jack Elam; ***D:*** Vincent McEveety; ***M:*** Buddy (Norman Dale) Baker.

The Applegates 🦴🦴½ *Meet the Applegates* **1989 (R)** Ecologically correct Amazonian beetles are more than a little miffed about the slash-and-burn tactics in their home and decide to establish a kinder, gentler habitat. Bug Begley and his brood transform themselves into average Americans, but then don't want to leave their decadent life: even insects aren't immune to the lure of sex, drugs, and cable shopping networks. Imaginative, often quite funny one-joke flick should've been shorter. Fits quite well as a double feature with Lehmann's earlier "Heathers." **90m/C VHS.** Ed Begley Jr., Stockard Channing, Dabney Coleman, Camille (Cami) Cooper, Bobby Jacoby, Glenn Shadix, Susan Barnes, Adam Biesk, Savannah Smith Boucher; ***D:*** Michael Lehmann; ***W:*** Michael Lehmann, Redbeard Simmons; ***C:*** Mitchell Dubin; ***M:*** David Newman.

The Appointment woof! **1982** A supernatural force enters the bodies and minds of people and suddenly everyone begins going crazy. **90m/C VHS, 8mm.** Edward Woodward, Jane Merrow; ***D:*** Lindsey C. Vickers; ***C:*** Carlo Di Palma.

Appointment in Honduras 🦴🦴 **1953** An adventurer goes on a dangerous trek through the Central American jungles to deliver funds to the Honduran President. **79m/C VHS.** Glenn Ford, Ann Sheridan, Zachary Scott; ***D:*** Jacques Tourneur.

Appointment with Crime 🦴🦴½ **1945** After serving a prison sentence, an ex-con sets out to avenge himself against the colleagues who double crossed him. Well done, highlighted by superior characterizations. Based on the story by Michael Leighton. **91m/B VHS.** *GB* William Hartnell, Raymond Lovell, Robert Beatty, Herbert Lom, Joyce Howard, Alan Wheatley, Cyril Smith; ***D:*** John Harlow; ***W:*** John Harlow.

Appointment with Death 🦴½ **1988 (PG)** Disappointing Agatha Christie mystery with Hercule Poirot solving the murder of a shrewish widow in 1937 Palestine. **103m/C VHS.** Peter Ustinov, Lauren Bacall, Carrie Fisher, John Gielgud, Piper Laurie, Hayley Mills, Jenny Seagrove, David Soul; ***D:*** Michael Winner; ***W:*** Anthony Shaffer, Peter Buckman, Michael Winner; ***M:*** Pino Donaggio.

Appointment with Fear 🦴 **1985 (R)** A tough detective investigates a murder and all of the clues lead him mysteriously to a comatose asylum inmate. **95m/C VHS.** Michael Wyle, Michelle Little, Kerry Remsen, Douglas Rowe, Garrick Dowhen, Deborah Voorhees; ***D:*** Alan Smithee, Razmi Thomas; ***W:*** Gideon Davis, Bruce Mead.

Apprentice to Murder 🦴🦴 **1988 (PG-13)** A small Pennsylvania Dutch town is shaken by a series of murders, thought to be associated with a bizarre local mystic and healer. Based on a true story, sort of. **97m/C VHS.** Donald Sutherland, Mia Sara, Chad Lowe, Eddie Jones; ***D:*** Ralph L. (R.L.) Thomas; ***W:*** Allan Scott, Wesley Moore.

The Apprenticeship of Duddy Kravitz 🦴🦴🦴½ **1974 (PG)** Young Jewish man in Montreal circa 1948 is driven by an insatiable need to be the "somebody" everyone has always told him he will be. A series of get-rich-quick schemes backfire in different ways, and he becomes most successful at driving people away. Young Dreyfuss is at his best. Made in Canada with thoughtful detail, and great cameo performances. Script by Richler, from his novel. **121m/C VHS.** *CA* Richard Dreyfuss, Randy Quaid, Denholm Elliott, Jack Warden, Micheline Lanctot, Joe Silver; ***D:*** Ted Kotcheff; ***W:*** Mordecai Richler, Lionel Chetwynd. Berlin Intl. Film Fest. '74: Golden Berlin Bear; Writers Guild '74: Adapt. Screenplay.

April Fool 🦴🦴½ **1926** A man makes a fortune in the umbrella business and then discovers his daughter has fallen in love with the son of a nouveaux riche neighbor, resulting in all sorts of complications. **63m/B VHS.** Alexander Carr, Mary Alden, Raymond Keane, Snitz Edwards; ***D:*** Nat Ross; ***W:*** Zion Myers.

April Fools 🦴🦴 **1969 (PG)** A bored stockbroker falls in love with a beautiful woman who turns out to be married to his boss. **95m/C VHS.** Jack Lemmon, Catherine Deneuve, Sally Kellerman, Peter Lawford, Harvey Korman, Melinda Dillon, Kenneth Mars; ***D:*** Stuart Rosenberg; ***M:*** Marvin Hamlisch.

April Fool's Day 🦴½ **1986 (R)** Rich girl Muffy (Foreman) invites eight college friends to spend the April Fool's weekend with her at her family's isolated island mansion. Everyone is subjected to an endless series of practical jokes when things apparently turn deadly and several of the kids begin disappearing. Twist ending. Lame spoof of "Friday the 13th" and other teenagers-in-peril slasher films. **90m/C VHS.** Deborah Foreman, Jay Baker, Pat Barlow, Lloyd Berry, Deborah Goodrich, Ken Olandt, Griffin O'Neal, Tom Heaton, Mike Nomad, Leah K. Pinsent, Clayton Rohner, Amy Steel, Thomas F. Wilson; ***D:*** Fred Walton; ***W:*** Danilo Bach; ***C:*** Charles Minsky; ***M:*** Charles Bernstein.

April in Paris 🦴🦴 **1952** Dynamite Jackson (Day), a chorus girl accidentally sent by the State Department to perform in Paris, meets S. Winthrop Putnam (Bolger), a timid fellow trapped in an unpleasant marriage. They eventually sing and dance their way to warm feelings as they begin a lifelong romance and live happily ever after. **100m/C VHS.** Doris Day, Ray Bolger, Claude Dauphin, Eve Miller, George Givot, Paul Harvey; ***D:*** David Butler; ***W:*** Jack Rose, Melville Shavelson.

Apt Pupil 🦴🦴 **1997 (R)** In 1984, high school senior Todd Bowden (Renfro) becomes fascinated by the Holocaust during a school project and is able to discern from an old photo that neighbor Kurt Dussander (McKellen) was a Nazi concentration camp commander and is a war criminal. Todd agrees to keep quiet if the old man will tell exactly what he did during the war. But Dussander hasn't stayed quiet all these years to have his secrets revealed by a nosy teen, so Todd gets an up close and personal lesson about the nature of evil. Very creepy adaptation of the Stephen King novella with a standout performance by McKellen. **111m/C VHS, DVD.** Ian McKellen, Brad Renfro, Jan Triska, Bruce Davison, Joe Morton, Elias Koteas, David Schwimmer, Michael Byrne, Heather McComb, Ann Dowd, Joshua Jackson, Michael Artura; ***D:*** Bryan Singer; ***W:*** Brandon Boyce; ***C:*** Newton Thomas (Tom) Sigel; ***M:*** John Ottman.

The Arab Conspiracy 🦴🦴 *The Next Man; Double Hit* **1976 (R)** Sharpe plays a hit-woman conspiring with assassins from all over the world to kill Arab leaders. One problem—she falls in love with Saudi Arabian ambassador Connery as he tries to gain peace with Palestine. **108m/C VHS.** Sean Connery, Cornelia Sharpe, Albert Paulsen, Adolfo Celi, Charles Cioffi; ***D:*** Richard Sarafian; ***W:*** Alan R. Trustman; ***C:*** Michael Chapman; ***M:*** Michael Kamen.

Arabesque 🦴🦴½ **1966** A college professor is drawn into international espionage by a beautiful woman and a plot to assassinate an Arab prince. Stylish and fast moving. From the novel "The Cipher" by Gordon Cotler. **105m/C VHS.** Gregory Peck, Sophia Loren, George Coulouris, Alan Badel, Kieron Moore; ***D:*** Stanley Donen; ***M:*** Henry Mancini.

Arabian Nights 🦴🦴 **1942** Two brothers fight for the throne of Turkey and the affection of the sultry dancing girl Scheherazade. Enchanting costumes and lavish sets augment the fantasy atmosphere. **87m/C VHS.** Jon Hall, Maria Montez, Sabu, Leif Erickson, Edgar Barrier, Richard Lane, Turhan Bey; ***D:*** John Rawlins; ***W:*** Michael Hogan; ***C:*** Milton Krasner.

Arabian Nights 🦴🦴🦴 *Il Fiore delle Mille e Una Notte; Flower of the Arabian Nights; A Thousand and One Nights* **1974** The third of Pasolini's epic, explicit adaptations of classic portmanteau, featuring ten of the old Scheherazade favorites adorned by beautiful photography, explicit sex scenes and homoeroticism. In Italian with English subtitles; available dubbed. **130m/C VHS, DVD, Wide.** *IT* Ninetto Davoli, Franco Merli, Ines Pellegrini, Luigina Rocchi, Franco Citti; ***D:*** Pier Paolo Pasolini; ***W:*** Pier Paolo Pasolini; ***C:*** Giuseppe Ruzzolini; ***M:*** Ennio Morricone.

Arabian Nights 🦴🦴½ **2000** Lavish spectacle and good casting overcomes the somewhat sluggish storytelling that combines a number of familiar tales. Sultan Schahriar's (Scott) grip on reality is slim ever since his greedy brother (Frain) and his first (and now late) wife plotted to assassinate him. Although he agrees to marry lovely Scheherezade (Avital), he also plans to kill her the morning after. But the lady is bright and desperate, she sooths her savage sultan with a number of stories involving genies, flying carpets, 40 thieves, and magic in order to stay alive until his sanity returns. Filmed on location in Turkey and Morocco. **175m/C VHS, DVD.** Mili Avital, Dougray Scott, James Frain, John Leguizamo, Rufus Sewell, Jason Scott Lee, Alan Bates, Tcheky Karyo; ***D:*** Steven Barron; ***W:*** Peter Barnes; ***C:*** Remi Adefarasin; ***M:*** Richard Harvey. **TV**

Arachnid 🦴½ **2001 (R)** Plane carrying a rescue crew on a mission to find a downed pilot crashes on a tropical island that contains a gigantic, carnivorous spider. Nothing that hasn't been seen before. **95m/C VHS, DVD, Wide.** Chris Potter, Neus Asensi, Jose Sancho, Alex Reid; ***D:*** Jack Sholder; ***W:*** Mark Sevi; ***C:*** Carlos Gonzalez; ***M:*** Francesc Gener.

Arachnophobia 🦴🦴½ **1990 (PG-13)** Big-budget big-bug horror story has a few funny moments as lots and lots of spiders wreak havoc in a white picket fence community somewhere off the beaten track. Lethal South American spider makes a trek to sunny California, meets up with local spiders, and rapidly multiplies. Utterly arachnophobic (read: totally scared of spiders) town doctor Daniels pairs with gung-ho exterminator Goodman to try and track down the culprits. The script's a bit yawn-inspiring but the cast and effects will keep you from dozing off. Directorial debut for Marshall, a longtime friend and producer for Spielberg. **109m/C VHS, DVD, Wide.** Jeff Daniels, John Goodman, Harley Jane Kozak, Julian Sands, Roy Brocksmith, Stuart Pankin, Brian McNamara, Mark L. Taylor, Henry Jones, Peter Jason, James Handy; ***D:*** Frank Marshall; ***W:*** Wesley Strick, Don Jakoby; ***C:*** Mikael Salomon; ***M:*** Trevor Jones.

Arcade 🦴½ **1993 (R)** All the kids in town are desperate to play the new virtual reality game Arcade, only the game is just a little too real. Seems it can transport you into another world with its stunning graphics and sound effects but you really put your life on the line. Only Alex (Ward) worries when kids start to disappear and she decides to battle the game for their lives. **85m/C VHS.** Megan Ward, Peter Billingsley, John de Lancie, Sharon Farrell, Seth Green, Humberto Ortiz, Jonathan Fuller, Norbert Weisser; ***D:*** Albert Pyun; ***W:*** David S. Goyer; ***M:*** Alan Howarth.

Arch of Triumph 🦴🦴🦴 **1948** In Paris, an Austrian refugee doctor falls in love just before the Nazis enter the city. Big-budget boxoffice loser featuring fine cast but sluggish pace. Based on the Erich Maria Remarque novel. **120m/B VHS.** Ingrid Bergman, Charles Boyer, Charles Laughton, Louis Calhern, Ruth Warrick; ***D:*** Lewis Milestone; ***W:*** Lewis Milestone, Harry Brown; ***C:*** Russell Metty.

Arch of Triumph 🦴🦴½ **1985** A refugee doctor falls in love with a mystery woman as the Nazis enter Paris. TV remake of the 1948 film. **95m/C VHS.** Anthony Hopkins, Lesley-Anne Down, Donald Pleasence, Frank Finlay; ***D:*** Waris Hussein; ***W:*** Charles Israel; ***M:*** Georges Delerue. **TV**

Archer: The Fugitive from the Empire 🦴 **1981** A young warrior battles the forces of evil. Lots of strange names to learn even if you already know who's going to win the final battle. **97m/C VHS.** Lane Caudell, Belinda Bauer, George Kennedy, Victor Campos, Kabir Bedi, George Innes, Marc Alaimo, Allan Rich, John Hancock, Priscilla Pointer, Sharon Barr; ***D:*** Nicholas J. Corea. **TV**

Archer's Adventure 🦴½ **1985** An Australian family film based on a true story. A horsetrainer's young apprentice delivers a prize racehorse to Melbourne, through 600 miles of tough frontier, devious bush rangers, and disaster. **120m/C VHS.** *AU* Brett Climo, Nicole Kidman; ***D:*** Denny Lawrence.

Archie: Return to Riverdale 🦴🦴½ **1990 (PG)** Archie, Reggie, Betty, Veronica, and Jughead return to Riverdale for their 15-year class reunion. Made for TV; based on the comic book. **85m/C VHS.** Christopher Rich, Lauren Holly, Karen Kopins, Sam Whipple, Gary Kroeger, Matt McCoy, David Doyle, Fran Ryan; ***D:*** Dick Lowry; ***C:*** Frank Byers; ***M:*** Mark Snow. **TV**

Arctic Blue 🦴½ **1993 (R)** Alaskan biologist Walsh gets stuck being the local lawman when he's the only one willing to escort Hauer, a homicidal trapper, to a Fairbanks jail. But nothing's that easy—their plane crashes atop a glacier and the duo must battle each other and the elements to survive, while Hauer's brutal partners hunt Walsh. **95m/C VHS, DVD.** Dylan Walsh, Rutger Hauer, Richard Bradford; ***D:*** Peter Masterson; ***W:*** Ross LaManna; ***C:*** Thomas Burstyn; ***M:*** Peter Melnick.

Are Parents People? 🦴🦴 **1925** Lighthearted silent comedy about a young girl's successful attempts to reunite her feuding parents. It all begins as she runs away and spends the night in the office of a doctor she has grown to like. After a frantic night of searching, her parents are reunited through their love for her. **60m/B**

VHS. Betty Bronson, Adolphe Menjou, Florence Vidor, Andre Beranger, Lawrence Gray, Mary Beth Milford, Emily Fitzroy, William Courtwright; *D:* Malcolm St. Clair; *W:* Frances Agnew, Alice Duer Miller; *C:* Bert Glennon.

Are You in the House Alone? 🦴🦴 1978 Adaptation of Richard Peck's award-winning novel. Story of a high school coed who becomes the target of a terror campaign. **100m/C VHS.** Blythe Danner, Kathleen Beller, Tony Bill, Scott Colomby; *D:* Walter Grauman; *M:* Charles Bernstein. **TV**

Are You Lonesome Tonight 🦴🦴½ 1992 (PG-13) Suspense thriller casts Seymour as a wealthy socialite who discovers her husband is having an affair with a phone-sex girl. His sudden and mysterious disapppearance forces her to hire a private detective (Stevenson) to track him down, with only the taped conversations as clues. Average cable TV fare. **91m/C VHS.** Jane Seymour, Parker Stevenson, Beth Broderick, Joel Brooks, Robert Pine; *D:* E.W. Swackhamer; *W:* Wesley Moore. **CABLE**

The Arena 🦴🦴 *Naked Warriors* 1973 (R) Ancient Romans capture beautiful women from around the world and force them to compete in gladiatorial games. New World exploitation gem featuring mostly Italian cast, including Bay, who starred in the previous year's "Lady Frankenstein." **75m/C VHS, DVD.** Margaret Markov, Pam Grier, Lucretia Love, Paul Muller, Daniel Vargas, Marie Louise, Mary Count, Rosalba (Sara Bay) Neri, Vic Karis, Sid Lawrence, Peter Cester, Anna Melita; *D:* Steve Carver; *W:* John W. Corrington, Joyce H. Corrington; *C:* Joe D'Amato; *M:* Francesco De Masi.

Arena 🦴🦴 1989 (PG-13) Remember old boxing melodramas about good-natured palookas, slimy opponents, gangsters and dames? This puts those cliches in a garish sci-fi setting, with handsome Steve Armstrong battling ETs and the astro-mob to be the first human pugilistic champ in decades. A really cute idea (from the screenwriters of "The Rocketeer"), but it conks out at the halfway point. Worth a look for buffs. **97m/C VHS.** *IT* Paul Satterfield, Claudia Christian, Hamilton Camp, Marc Alaimo, Armin Shimerman, Shari Shattuck, Jack Carter; *D:* Peter Manoogian; *W:* Danny Bilson, Paul DeMeo; *M:* Richard Band.

Aria 🦴🦴 1988 (R) Ten directors were given carte blanche to interpret ten arias from well-known operas. Henry and D'Angelo star in Julian Temple's rendition of Verdi's "Rigoletto." In Fonda's film debut, she and her lover travel to Las Vegas and eventually kill themselves in the bathtub, just like "Romeo & Juliet." Jarman's piece (a highlight) shows an aged operatic star at her last performance remembering an early love affair. "I Pagliacci" is the one aria in which the director took his interpretation in a straightforward manner. **90m/C VHS, DVD.** *GB* Theresa Russell, Anita Morris, Bridget Fonda, Beverly D'Angelo, Buck Henry, John Hurt; *D:* Ken Russell, Charles Sturridge, Robert Altman, Bill Bryden, Jean-Luc Godard, Bruce Beresford, Nicolas Roeg, Franc Roddam, Derek Jarman, Julien Temple; *W:* Ken Russell, Charles Sturridge, Robert Altman, Bill Bryden, Jean-Luc Godard, Bruce Beresford, Nicolas Roeg, Franc Roddam, Derek Jarman, Julien Temple; *C:* Caroline Champetier, Oliver Stapleton, Gale Tattersall.

Ariel 🦴🦴🦴 1989 Refreshing, offbeat Finnish comedy by highly praised newcomer Kaurismaki. Hoping to find work in Southern Finland, an out-of-work miner from Northern Finland (Pajala) jets off in his white Cadillac convertible given to him in a cafe by a friend, who promptly shoots himself. There's no linear progression toward a happy ending, although antiheroic subject does find employment and romances a meter maid. Mostly, though, he's one of those it's hell being me guys who wouldn't have any luck if it weren't for bad luck. Strange slice-of-life sporting film noir tendencies, although essentially antistylistic. **74m/C VHS.** *FI* Susanna Haavisto, Turo Pajala, Matti Pellonpaa; *D:* Aki Kaurismaki; *W:* Aki Kaurismaki; *C:* Timo Salminen; *M:* Dimitri Shostakovich. Natl. Soc. Film Critics '90: Foreign Film.

The Aristocats 🦴🦴🦴 1970 Typically entertaining Disney animated story about pampered pussy Duchess (Gabor) and her three kittens, who are left a fortune in their mistress' will. The fortune goes to the butler if the cats don't survive, so he dumps them in the country hoping they won't find their way home. The cats are aided by tough alley denizen O'Malley (Harris)—it's kind of the feline version of "Lady and the Tramp." Maurice Chevalier sings the title tune. **78m/C VHS, DVD.** *D:* Wolfgang Reitherman; *M:* George Bruns; *V:* Eva Gabor, Phil Harris, Sterling Holloway, Roddy Maude-Roxby, Bill Thompson, Hermione Baddeley, Carol(e) Shelley, Pat Buttram, Nancy Kulp, Paul Winchell.

The Aristocrats 🦴🦴½ 1999 True story of the scandalous 18th-century aristocratic Lennox family, including the four beautiful sisters whose elopements, liaisons, and intrigues provided ample English gossip. Based on the novel by Stella Tillyard. Three cassettes. **255m/C VHS.** *GB* Jodhi May, Geraldine Somerville, Serena Gordon, Anne-Marie Duff, Alun Armstrong, Julian Fellowes, Ben Daniels, Diane Fletcher, Clive Swift, Sian Phillips, Richard Dempsey; *D:* David Caffrey; *W:* Harriet O'Carroll. **TV**

Arizona 🦴🦴½ 1940 Arthur is a hellion in wild 1860 Tucson who falls for the wandering Holden. He's headed for California and she can't keep him in town so Arthur throws herself into business by establishing a freight line. Only warring Apaches try to burn her out and Holden rides in to save the day (with the cavalry and a stampeding cattle herd). Holden's first western is lively but long. **121m/B VHS.** Jean Arthur, William Holden, Warren William, Porter Hall, Paul Harvey, George Chandler, Regis Toomey, Edgar Buchanan; *D:* Wesley Ruggles; *W:* Claude Binyon; *M:* Victor Young.

Arizona 🦴½ 1986 A group of illegal aliens struggle for survival after they cross the border into the harsh desert. **94m/C VHS.** *MX* Roberto "Flaco" Guzman, Juan Valentin.

Arizona Bound 🦴 1941 Mesa City is infested with a villain and our "Rough Rider" trio must rid the town of him. **57m/B VHS.** Buck Jones, Tim McCoy, Raymond Hatton, Dennis Moore, Luana Walters; *D:* Spencer Gordon Bennet.

Arizona Bushwackers 🦴½ 1967 Routine western that has Confederate spy Keel taking job as sheriff in small Arizona town. Once there, he has to straighten out a few bad guys who have been selling weapons to the Apaches. Notable for presence of old western-movie veterans Ireland, Donlevy, Brady, and MacLane. Based on a story by Steve Fisher. **87m/C VHS.** Howard Keel, Yvonne De Carlo, John Ireland, Marilyn Maxwell, Scott Brady, Brian Donlevy, Barton MacLane; *D:* Lesley Selander.

Arizona Cowboy 🦴 1949 An ex-G.I., now the rodeo's big attraction, gets involved in a robbery. **57m/B VHS.** Rex Allen, Gordon Jones, Roy Barcroft; *D:* R.G. Springsteen.

Arizona Days 🦴½ 1937 Cowboys join a minstrel group and rescue the show when a group of toughs try to break it up. **56m/B VHS.** Tex Ritter, Eleanor Stewart, Syd Saylor, Snub Pollard; *D:* John English.

Arizona Dream 🦴🦴 1994 (R) Alex (Depp) is a New York drifter who gets stuck working for his uncle's (Lewis) car dealership in a small Arizona town. He meets an eccentric older woman (Dunaway) with a homemade plane and some dreams of her own. Tends toward the surreal and confusing. **119m/C VHS.** Johnny Depp, Faye Dunaway, Jerry Lewis, Lili Taylor, Paulina Porizkova, Tricia Leigh Fisher, Vincent Gallo; *D:* Emir Kusturica; *W:* Emir Kusturica, David Atkins; *C:* Vilko Filac.

Arizona Gangbusters 🦴 1940 Below-average oater has real-life cowboy McCoy fighting city hall in order to fight other baddies. Newfield directed under the pseudonym "Peter Stewart." **57m/B VHS.** Tim McCoy, Pauline Hadden, Forrest Taylor, Julian Rivero; *D:* Sam Newfield; *C:* Jack Greenhalgh.

Arizona Gunfighter 🦴 1937 A young cowhand seeks revenge against the man who murdered his father in this western. **60m/B VHS.** Bob Steele, Ted Adams, Ernie Adams; *D:* Sam Newfield.

Arizona Heat 🦴🦴 1987 (R) A violent cop is teamed up with a tough, but tender female cop in this all-too-familiar tale of two cops chasing a cop killer. **91m/C VHS.** Michael Parks, Denise Crosby, Hugh Farrington; *D:* John G. Thomas.

Arizona Kid 🦴 1939 Another sagebrush saga featuring Roy in singin' and fightin' action. **54m/B VHS.** Roy Rogers, George "Gabby" Hayes; *D:* Joseph Kane.

Arizona Mahoney 🦴 1936 Weird mixture of circus adventure and serious western doesn't work too well. Confused film with farfetched reasons for having the paths of circus performers and cowboys cross. Based on a Zane Grey novel. **58m/B VHS.** Joe Cook, Robert Cummings, June Martel, Marjorie Gateson, John Miljan; *D:* James Hogan; *W:* Robert Yost, Stuart Anthony.

Arizona Raiders 🦴🦴 1965 Arizona rangers hunt down killers who have been terrorizing the territory. **88m/C VHS.** Audie Murphy, Buster Crabbe, Gloria Talbott; *D:* William Witney.

Arizona Roundup 🦴½ 1942 Good vs. bad amid tumbleweed, bleached-white chaps, bloodless shootouts and happy endings. **54m/B VHS.** Tom (George Duryea) Keene, Sugar Dawn, Jack Ingram; *D:* Robert Emmett Tansey.

Arizona Stagecoach 🦴 1942 The Range Busters set out to bust a notorious, guiltless, devil-may-care outlaw gang. **58m/B VHS.** Ray Corrigan, Max Terhune, Kermit Maynard, Charles "Blackie" King, John "Dusty" King; *D:* S. Roy Luby.

Arizona Terror 🦴½ 1931 Our hero is on a quest for vengeance, seeking the posse that killed his partner. **64m/B VHS.** Ken Maynard, Lena Basquette, Hooper Atchley, Michael Visaroff, Tom London, Jack Natteford; *D:* Phil Rosen; *W:* Jack Natteford; *C:* Arthur Reed.

Arizona Whirlwind 🦴 1944 Our intrepid heroes must battle torrents of gunfire in order to prevent a stage hold-up in this western saga. **59m/B VHS.** Ken Maynard, Hoot Gibson, Bob Steele; *D:* Robert Emmett Tansey.

Ark of the Sun God 🦴 1982 Another adventurer battles the Nazis and nutsies for a 2000-year-old ark buried in the Sahara. **95m/C VHS.** David Warbeck, John Steiner, Susie Sudlow, Alan Collins, Riccardo Palacio; *D:* Anthony (Antonio Margheriti) Dawson.

Arlington Road 🦴🦴½ 1999 (R) The tranquility of surburban life is shattered for college professor Faraday (Bridges) when he suspects the picket fence and overly-friendliness of new neighbor Lang (Robbins) is a cover for his right-wing terrorism. As Faraday slowly uncovers Lang's true identity, it becomes harder for him to convince friends to believe the conspiracy. Impressive nail-biter with an interesting twist has a solid performance from Bridges as the paranoid professor, and an eerie one from the otherwise affable Robbins. Director Pellington, with the aide of Badalamenti's haunting score maintains the film's objective of showing how evil can come from the most unlikely place. **119m/C VHS, DVD.** Jeff Bridges, Tim Robbins, Joan Cusack, Hope Davis, Mason Gamble, Stanley Anderson, Robert Gossett, Spencer (Treat) Clark; *D:* Mark Pellington; *W:* Ehren Kruger; *C:* Bobby Bukowski; *M:* Angelo Badalamenti, Tomandandy.

Armageddon 🦴🦴½ 1998 (PG-13) A Texas-sized asteroid is hurtling towards earth, NASA gets nervous, and it's up to oil driller Harry Stamper (Willis) and his misfit crew to turn astronaut, blast off into space, land on that rock, and blow the sucker to kingdom come. Ya get a little romance as hotshot A.J. Frost (Affleck) smooches with babe Grace (Tyler), who's Harry's nubile daughter. Lots of action (naturally), some humor, and some sappy, heart-tugging moments for perfect put-your-brain-on-hold entertainment. The second "space rock hits earth" movie, following the somber "Deep Impact." **150m/C VHS, DVD, Wide.** Erik Per Sullivan, Bruce Willis, Ben Affleck, Billy Bob Thornton, Steve Buscemi, Liv Tyler, Will Patton, Peter Stormare, Keith David, Owen C. Wilson, William Fichtner, Jessica Steen, Grayson McCouch, Jason Isaacs, Michael Clarke Duncan; *D:* Michael Bay; *W:* Jonathan Hensleigh, J.J. Abrams; *C:* John Schwartzman; *M:* Trevor Rabin. MTV Movie Awards '99: Song ("I Don't Want to Miss a Thing"), Action Seq.; Golden Raspberries '98: Worst Actor (Willis).

Armageddon: The Final Challenge 🦴½ 1994 After a nuclear holocaust, evil forces rule the Earth in the guise of "The Future Bank." They send out Fear-Permutator Clones to keep order and kill undesirables but naturally there's a rebel ready to do battle. **85m/C VHS.** Todd Jensen, Graham Clarke, Tony Caprari, Joanna Rowlands; *D:* Michael Garcia; *W:* George Garcia, Michael Garcia; *M:* Johan Lass.

Armed and Dangerous 🦴🦴 1986 (PG-13) Candy and Levy are incompetent security guards assigned to a do-nothing job. Things get spiced up when a mobster tries to run a crime ring under their nose. Candy catches on and winds up in a full-fledged chase. Not as funny as it sounds, though occasionally has moments of genuine comedy. **88m/C VHS.** John Candy, Eugene Levy, Kenneth McMillan, Brion James, Robert Loggia, Meg Ryan, Don Stroud, Jonathan Banks, Steve Railsback, Bruce Kirby, Tony Burton, Larry Hankin, Judy Landers, David Wohl; *D:* Mark L. Lester; *W:* Harold Ramis, Peter Torokvei, James Keach, Brian Grazer.

Armed for Action 🦴🦴 1992 Routine action thriller casts Estevez as Sgt. Phil Towers who gets more than he bargained for when his prisoner, Mafia hitman David Montel, escapes while en route from New York to Los Angeles. When he finally catches up with them, Towers leads a small army of locals on a brutal assault. **88m/C VHS.** Joe Estevez, Rocky Patterson, Barri Murphy, David Harrod, J. Scott Guy; *D:* Shane Spaulding.

Armed Response 🦴🦴 1986 (R) Carradine leads a group of mercenaries in a battle against Chinatown mobsters. They race to locate a priceless jade statue before it can fall into the wrong hands. **86m/C VHS.** David Carradine, Lee Van Cleef, Mako, Lois Hamilton, Ross Hagen, Brent Huff; *D:* Fred Olen Ray; *C:* Paul Elliott.

Armistead Maupin's More Tales of the City 🦴🦴½ *More Tales of the City* 1997 More risque and odd adventures for the inhabitants of Barbary Lane. Sequel picks up some six weeks after the first adventures. In 1977 San Francisco, Mary Ann (Linney) and Mouse (Hopkins) hunt for romance on a Mexican cruise. Mary Ann falls for handsome amnesiac Burke (Ferguson) and tries to help him regain his memory, while Mouse reunites with ex-lover, Dr. Jon (Campbell). Meanwhile, Mona (Siemszko) searches for her roots, which leads to revelations from Mrs. Madrigal (Dukakis). Brian (Hubley) becomes a voyeur and DeDe (Garrick) awaits the birth of twins—whose father is not her supercilious husband Beauchamp (Gibson). **330m/C VHS, DVD.** Laura Linney, Olympia Dukakis, Colin Ferguson, Billy Campbell, Paul Hopkins, Whip Hubley, Thomas Gibson, Barbara Garrick, Nina Siemaszko, Jackie Burroughs, Swoosie Kurtz, Francoise Robertson; ***Cameos:*** Parker Posey, Ed Asner, Paul Bartel, Brian Bedford, Sheila McCarthy, Scott Thompson; *D:* Pierre Gang; *W:* Nicholas Wright; *C:* Serge Ladouceur; *M:* Richard Gregoire.

Armistead Maupin's Tales of the City 🦴🦴½ *Tales of the City* 1993 Carefree '70s San Francisco is the setting for the interconnected stories of the inhabitants of 28 Barbary Lane. There's mysterious landlady Mrs. Madrigal (Dukakis); free-spirit Mona Ramsey (Webb); her gay roomie, Michael "Mouse" Tolliver (D'Amico); hetero lawyer-turned-waiter Brian (Gross); nerdy, secretive Norman (DeSantis); and the naively sweet Mary Ann Singleton (Linney). Definite time-warp factor in this pre-AIDS depiction of sex and drugs, but also the timeless search for love and happiness. Maupin first wrote the stories as an ongoing serial for the *San Francisco Chronicle* and they were later turned into six novels. Made for British TV. **360m/C VHS.** *GB* Olympia Dukakis, Donald Moffat, Chloe Webb, Laura Linney, Marcus D'Amico, Billy Campbell, Thomas Gibson, Paul Gross, Barbara Garrick, Nina Foch, Edie Adams, Meagen Fay, Lou Liberatore, Country Joe McDonald, Mary Kay Place, Parker Posey, Kevin Sessums, McLean

Stevenson, Stanley DeSantis, Cynda Williams, Karen Black, Michael Jeter, Paul Bartel, Lance Loud, Ian McKellen, Bob Mackie, Marissa Ribisi, Mother Love, Don Novello, Rod Steiger, Janeane Garofalo, Armistead Maupin; *D:* Alastair Reid; *W:* Richard Kramer; *M:* John Keane. **TV**

Armored Car Robbery 🦴🦴 **1950** Talman and his buddies plot to rob an armored car but are foiled by McGraw and his crimefighters. Surprisingly good B-crime drama. **68m/B VHS.** Charles McGraw, Adele Jergens, William Talman, Steve Brodie; *D:* Richard Fleischer.

Armored Command 🦴½ **1961** A beautiful German spy infiltrates an American outpost during the Battle of the Bulge. Tepid WWII fare made too long after the fact. **105m/B VHS.** Burt Reynolds, Tina Louise, Howard Keel, Earl Holliman, Warner Anderson, Carleton Young; *D:* Byron Haskin.

Army Brats 🦴½ **1984** In this Dutch film a military family goes bloodily and comically to war with itself. Even in a welfare state, parents can't control their wee ones. **105m/C VHS.** *NL* Akkemay, Frank Schaafsma, Peter Faber; *D:* Ruud Van Hemert.

Army of Darkness 🦴🦴🦴 *Evil Dead 3; The Medieval Dead* **1992 (R)** Campbell returns for a third "Evil Dead" round as the square-jawed, none too bright hero, Ash in this comic book extravaganza. He finds himself hurled back to the 14th-century through the powers of an evil book. There he romances a babe, fights an army of skeletons, and generally causes all those Dark Age knights a lot of grief, as he tries to get back to his own time. Raimi's technical exuberance is apparent and, as usual, the horror is graphic but still tongue-in-cheek. **77m/C VHS, DVD, Wide.** Bruce Campbell, Embeth Davidtz, Marcus Gilbert, Ian Abercrombie, Richard Grove, Michael Earl Reid, Tim Quill, Bridget Fonda, Patricia Tallman, Theodore (Ted) Raimi, Ivan Raimi, Donald Campbell, William Lustig, Josh Becker; *D:* Sam Raimi; *W:* Sam Raimi, Ivan Raimi; *C:* Bill Pope; *M:* Joseph LoDuca, Danny Elfman.

Army of One 🦴½ **1994 (R)** Santee (Lundgren) and his pal are hauling stolen cars across the desert when a cop pulls them over. Soon there's two dead bodies and Santee's in big trouble. An unrated version is also available. **102m/C VHS, DVD.** Dolph Lundgren, George Segal, Kristian Alfonso, Geoffrey Lewis, Michelle Phillips; *D:* Vic Armstrong; *W:* Steven Pressfield, Joel Goldsmith.

Arnold 🦴🦴½ **1973 (PG)** Outrageous black comedy involving a woman who marries a cadaver to gain his large inheritance. Lots of bizarre and creative deaths in this horror spoof. Unusual wedding scene is a must-see. **96m/C VHS.** Stella Stevens, Roddy McDowall, Elsa Lanchester, Victor Buono, Bernard Fox, Farley Granger, Shani Wallis, Jamie Farr, Patric Knowles, John McGiver, Norman Stuart; *D:* Georg Fenady; *W:* Jameson Brewer, John Fenton Murray; *C:* William B. Jurgensen; *M:* George Duning.

Around the Fire 🦴🦴 **1998 (R)** At boarding school, Simon (Sawa) tries to escape his emotional troubles by getting in with the school druggies, including Andrew (Mabius). He also begins a foray into the neo-hippie world of the Grateful Dead, where he falls for the free-spirited Jennifer (Reid). Simon does wind up in rehab, looking back on his life. **107m/C VHS, DVD, Wide.** Devon Sawa, Eric Mabius, Bill Smitrovich, Tara Reid, Charlaine Woodard, Michael McKeever; *D:* John Jacobsen; *W:* John Comerford, Tommy Rosen; *M:* B.C. Smith. **VIDEO**

Around the World 🦴½ **1943** Kyser leads a USO-like tour to entertain troops. Interesting only in a historical sense. ♫Doodle-Ee-Doo; He's Got a Secret Weapon; Candlelight and Wine; Great News in the Making; They Chopped Down the Old Apple Tree; A Moke from Shamokin. **80m/B VHS.** Kay Kyser, Ish Kabibble, Mischa Auer, Joan Davis, Marcy McGuire; *D:* Allan Dwan.

Around the World in 80 Days 🦴🦴🦴 **1956 (G)** Niven is the unflappable Victorian Englishman who wagers that he can circumnavigate the earth in four-score days. With his faithful manservant Cantinflas they set off on a spectacular journey. A perpetual favorite providing ample entertainment. Star-gazers will particularly enjoy the more than 40 cameo appearances by many of Hollywood's biggest names. Adapted from the novel by Jules Verne. **178m/C VHS.** David Niven, Shirley MacLaine, Cantinflas, Robert Newton, Charles Boyer, Joe E. Brown, Martine Carol, John Carradine, Charles Coburn, Ronald Colman; ***Cameos:*** Melville Cooper, Noel Coward, Andy Devine, Reginald Denny, Fernandel, Marlene Dietrich, Hermione Gingold, Cedric Hardwicke, Trevor Howard, Glynis Johns, Buster Keaton, Evelyn Keyes, Peter Lorre, John Gielgud, Victor McLaglen, John Mills, Robert Morley, Jack Oakie, George Raft, Cesar Romero, Gilbert Roland, Red Skelton, Frank Sinatra, Beatrice Lillie, Ava Gardner; *D:* Michael Anderson Sr.; *W:* James Poe, John Farrow, S.J. Perelman; *C:* Lionel Lindon; *M:* Victor Young. Oscars '56: Adapt. Screenplay, Color Cinematog., Film Editing, Picture, Orig. Dramatic Score; Golden Globes '57: Actor—Mus./Comedy (Cantinflas), Film—Drama; N.Y. Film Critics '56: Film, Screenplay.

Around the World in 80 Days 🦴🦴½ **1989** TV adaptation of the Jules Verne adventure novel that finds Victorian gentleman Phineas Fogg (Brosnan) wagering that he can circle the globe in 80 days. He's pursued by private detective Fix (Ustinov), who suspects him of a daring bank robbery, and faces many trials and much excitement along the way. On two cassettes. **270m/C VHS, DVD.** Pierce Brosnan, Peter Ustinov, Eric Idle, Arielle Dombasle, Henry Gibson, John Hillerman, Jack Klugman, Christopher Lee, Patrick Macnee, Roddy McDowall, Darren McGavin, John Mills, Robert Morley, Lee Remick, Pernell Roberts, James B. Sikking, Jill St. John, Robert Wagner, Julia Nickson-Soul; *D:* Buzz Kulik.

Around the World in 80 Ways 🦴🦴½ **1986 (R)** Sometimes clever, sometimes crude Australian comedy about an aging man rescued from a nursing home and taken on a phony trip around the world by his sons. Odd, but genuinely funny at times. **90m/C VHS.** *AU* Philip Quast, Alan Penney, Diana Davidson, Kelly Dingwall, Gosia Dobrowolska; *D:* Stephen MacLean; *W:* Stephen MacLean, Paul Leadon; *M:* Chris Neal.

Around the World in a Daze 🦴🦴½ *The Three Stooges Go Around the World in a Daze* **1963** The Stooges are servants for Phileas Fogg's great-grandson, who has decided to repeat his ancestor's famous feat. Mayhem ensues when the three help out in their usual efficient, competent way. **93m/B VHS.** Moe Howard, Larry Fine, Joe DeRita, Jay Sheffield; *D:* Norman Maurer.

Around the World Under the Sea 🦴🦴 **1965** Bunch of men and one woman scientist plunge under the ocean in an experiment to predict earthquakes. They plant earthquake detectors along the ocean floor and discover the causes of tidal waves. They have men-women battles. They see big sea critters. **111m/C VHS.** David McCallum, Shirley Eaton, Gary Merrill, Keenan Wynn, Brian Kelly, Lloyd Bridges; *D:* Andrew Marton.

Aroused 🦴 **1966** Hollister is an apparently dedicated policeman who commits a number of blunders in the pursuit of a serial killer, including leaving his wife with the sociopath while he cavorts with the prostitute assigned to his protection. Director Holden's psychothriller was gorily ahead of its time. Includes heart-stopping castration sequence. **78m/B VHS.** Janine Lenon, Steve Hollister, Fleurette Carter, Joanna Mills, Tony Palladino, Ted Gelanza; *D:* Anton Holden.

The Arousers 🦴🦴½ *Sweet Kill; A Kiss from Eddie* **1970 (R)** Cult item starring hunk Hunter as a handsome California psycho. Tab travels the coast searching for a woman he is able to make love to; those who fail to arouse him come to tragic, climactic ends. Definitely underground and moderately interesting. **85m/C VHS.** Tab Hunter, Nadyne Turney, Roberta Collins, Isabel Jewell, John Aprea, Angel Fox, Sandy Kenyon, Cherie Latimer; *D:* Curtis Hanson; *W:* Curtis Hanson; *C:* Daniel Lacambre; *M:* Charles Bernstein.

The Arrangement 🦴½ **1969 (R)** Veteran advertising executive Douglas attempts suicide and then sets out to search for the meaning of life. Along the way he attempts to patch up his "arrangements" with his wife, his mistress and his father. Forced, slow, and self-conscious, though well acted. Adapted by Kazan from the director's own novel. **126m/C VHS.** Kirk Douglas, Faye Dunaway, Deborah Kerr, Richard Boone, Hume Cronyn; *D:* Elia Kazan; *W:* Elia Kazan; *C:* Robert L. Surtees; *M:* David Amram.

The Arrangement 🦴🦴🦴 **1999 (R)** Jake (Keskhemnu) lives in Los Angeles. Luhann (James) is in New York. They're engaged until he admits to a one-night stand and invites her to experiment herself before the wedding. When she accepts, he is not pleased. Low-budget independent production is a bit obvious and slow moving in some respects, much more sophisticated in others. The details of everyday life are well observed and ring true. Editing is zippy and the characters are treated seriously. **90m/C DVD, Wide.** Billie James, Keskhemnu; *D:* H.H. Cooper; *W:* H.H. Cooper; *C:* Douglas W. Shannon; *M:* Michael Bearden.

Arrest Bulldog Drummond 🦴🦴 **1938** Captain Drummond is accused of killing the inventor of a futuristic detonator machine and must track down the real killers. Part of the "Bulldog Drummond" series. **57m/B VHS.** John Howard, Heather Angel, George Zucco, H.B. Warner, E.E. Clive, Reginald Denny, John Sutton; *D:* James Hogan.

The Arrival 🦴 **1990 (R)** An never-seen alien parasite turns an old man into a vampiric young stud after female blood. Plot and characterizations never do arrive. Horror director Stuart Gordon cameos as a hairy biker. **107m/C VHS.** John Saxon, Joseph Culp, Robert Sampson, Michael J. Pollard; ***Cameos:*** David Schmoeller; *D:* David Schmoeller; *W:* David Schmoeller; *M:* Richard Band.

The Arrival 🦴🦴½ *Shockwave* **1996 (PG-13)** Radio astronomer Zane (Sheen) picks up a message from deep space and discovers a planned alien invasion. When he brings evidence of such to his boss Gordian (Silver) he finds himself on the run from both government operatives and morphing aliens. Starts off slow, but an intelligent script and premise makes this a grade above cheesy. The aliens, with their kooky flaps of skin and back bending knees, are fun to watch. Directorial debut for Twohy. **109m/C VHS, DVD.** Charlie Sheen, Ron Silver, Lindsay Crouse, Teri Polo; *D:* David N. Twohy; *W:* David N. Twohy; *C:* Hiro Narita; *M:* Arthur Kempel.

The Arrival 2 🦴🦴 *The Second Arrival* **1998 (R)** Computer programmer Muldoon receives information describing an extra-terrestrial conspiracy against earth. Dull story, dull cast. **101m/C VHS, DVD.** Patrick Muldoon, Michael Sarrazin, Jane Sibbett; *D:* Kevin S. Tenney; *W:* Mark David Perry; *C:* Bruno Philip; *M:* Ned Bouhalassa. **VIDEO**

Arrivederci, Baby! 🦴 **1966** An unfunny sex comedy with Curtis as a modern Bluebeard who weds rich women and kills them for their money. His last mate plans to turn the tables and kill him first. **100m/C VHS.** Tony Curtis, Rosanna Schiaffino, Lionel Jeffries, Zsa Zsa Gabor, Nancy Kwan, Fenella Fielding, Anna Quayle, Warren Mitchell, Mischa Auer; *D:* Ken Hughes; *W:* Ken Hughes.

Arrowhead 🦴🦴½ **1953** A long-running argument between a tough Cavalry scout and an Apache chief pits the cowboys against the Indians in this western fantasy. The personal battles that become all-out wars turn back to fist-fights before the matter is finally settled. **105m/C VHS.** Charlton Heston, Jack Palance, Katy Jurado, Brian Keith, Milburn Stone; *D:* Charles Marquis Warren; *C:* Ray Rennahan.

Arrowsmith 🦴🦴½ **1932** A small-town medical researcher battles his conscience as he juggles his selfish and unselfish motivations for the work he does. He travels to the West Indies to confront the issues of his life and come to terms with himself once and for all. A talented cast takes their time. Based on the classic Sinclair Lewis novel. Two edited versions available (99 and 89 minutes), both of which delete much of Loy. **95m/B VHS.** Ronald Colman, Helen Hayes, Myrna Loy; *D:* John Ford.

Arsenal 🦴🦴🦴 **1929** Classic Russian propagandist drama about strikes affecting the Russian home front during WWI, marking Dovzhenko's first great achievement in the realm of Eisenstein and Pudovkin. Silent. **75m/B VHS.** *RU* Semyon Svashenko, Luciano Albertini; *D:* Alexander Dovzhenko; *W:* Alexander Dovzhenko; *C:* Daniil Demutsky.

The Arsenal Stadium Mystery 🦴🦴½ **1939** Inspector Banks of Scotland Yard tracks down the killer of a football star in this clever but unassuming murder mystery. **85m/B VHS.** *GB* Leslie Banks, Greta Gynt, Ian MacLean, Liane Linden, Anthony Bushell, Esmond Knight; *D:* Thorold Dickinson.

Arsenic and Old Lace 🦴🦴🦴½ **1944** Set-bound but energetic adaptation of the classic Joseph Kesselring play. Easy-going drama critic Mortimer Brewster (Grant) is caught in a sticky situation when he learns of his aunts' favorite pastime. Apparently the kind, sweet, lonely spinsters lure gentlemen to the house and serve them elderberry wine with a touch of arsenic, then they bury the bodies in the cellar—a cellar which also serves as the Panama Canal for Mortimer's cousin (who thinks he's Theodore Roosevelt). Massey, as Brewster cousin Jonathan, and Lorre, as his plastic surgeon, excel in their sinister roles. One of the best madcap comedies of all time—a must-see. Shot in 1941 and released a wee bit later. **118m/B VHS, DVD.** Cary Grant, Josephine Hull, Jean Adair, Raymond Massey, Jack Carson, Priscilla Lane, John Alexander, Edward Everett Horton, Peter Lorre, James Gleason, John Ridgely; *D:* Frank Capra; *W:* Julius J. Epstein, Philip G. Epstein; *C:* Sol Polito; *M:* Max Steiner.

Art for Teachers of Children 🦴🦴 **1995** Autobiographical account of 14-year-old Jennifer (McDonnell) who becomes a model for married photographer John (Hannah), who's also her boarding school dorm advisor. He's well-known for his nude portraits of young women as well as his affairs with his models and Jennifer's both confused and excited by her emerging sexuality as she and John become lovers. Remarkably detached considering the provocative subject matter. **82m/B VHS.** Caitlin Grace McDonnell, Duncan Hannah, Coles Burroughs, Bryan Keane; *D:* Jennifer Montgomery; *W:* Jennifer Montgomery; *C:* Jennifer Montgomery.

Art House 🦴½ **1998 (R)** Ray (O'Donahue) and his irritating pal Weston (irritating Hardwick) aspire to be filmmakers, but the road to success is blocked by rocky relationships, money problems, and lack of talent. The comic elements are fitfully funny but the image is so rough that only the most dedicated fans of low-budget ($200,000 according to the director) independent productions will be willing to stick with it. Those hoping to see a lot of Internet babe Weber will be disappointed. **89m/C DVD.** Dan O'Donahue, Chris Hardwick, Luigi Amodeo, Rebecca McFarland, Adam Carolla, Cheryl Pollack, Amy Weber; *D:* Leigh Slawner; *W:* Dan O'Donahue, Leigh Slawner; *C:* Billy Beaird; *M:* Christopher Lennertz.

The Art of Crime 🦴🦴½ **1975** A gypsy/detective is drawn into a homicide case when one of his fellow antique dealers is charged with murder. Maintains an atmospheric edge over others of the crime art genre. A pilot for a prospective TV series based on the novel "Gypsy in Amber." **72m/C VHS.** Ron Leibman, Jose Ferrer, David Hedison, Jill Clayburgh; *D:* Richard Irving; *W:* Bill Davidson, Martin Smith. **TV**

The Art of Dying 🦴🦴🦴 **1990** A loony videophile decides to start staging productions of his all-time favorite scenes. Trouble is, his idea of a fabulous film moment calls for lots of blood and bile as he lures teenage runaways to his casting couch. Director Hauser stars as the cop who's none too impressed with the cinematic remakes, while cult favorite Pollard is his partner. If you like a little atmosphere and psychological depth in your slashers, you'll find this to be the stuff that populates film noir nightmares. **90m/C VHS.** Wings Hauser, Michael J. Pollard, Sarah Douglas,

Kathleen Kinmont, Sydney Lassick, Mitch Hara, Gary Werntz; *D:* Wings Hauser.

The Art of Murder 🦴🦴 **1999 (R)** Married Elizabeth (Pacula) has a wealthy hubby (Moriarty) and a younger lover (Kesnter) to keep her motor running. But then sleazy Willie (Onorati) threatens to show her husband dirty pictures of the affair and blackmail is just the beginning. **97m/C VHS, DVD.** Joanna Pacula, Michael Moriarty, Boyd Kestner, Peter Onorati; *D:* Ruben Preuss; *W:* Shawn Smith, Anthony Stark; *C:* John Tarver. **VIDEO**

The Art of War 🦴½ **2000 (R)** Disappointingly formulaic thriller has Snipes starring as top-secret U.N. operative Neil Shaw, who is framed for the assassination of a Chinese ambassador (Hong). Also involved is his boss, Eleanor Hooks (Archer), Chinese power broker David Chan (Tagawa), and interpreter Julia (Matiko), whom Shaw kidnaps to help him prove his innocence. Plot is both convoluted and obvious (you can pretty much guess what's coming) and you learn so little about the players that you won't be very interested in what happens to them. **117m/C VHS, DVD, Wide.** Wesley Snipes, Marie Matiko, Cary-Hiroyuki Tagawa, Anne Archer, Maury Chaykin, Michael Biehn, Donald Sutherland, Liliana Komorowska, James Hong; *D:* Christian Duguay; *W:* Wayne Beach, Simon Davis Barry; *C:* Pierre Gill; *M:* Normand Corbeil.

Artemisia 🦴🦴 **1997 (R)** Artemisia (Cervi) is the teenaged daughter of well-known artist Orazio Gentileschi (Serrault), who encourages her artistic pursuits. He bullies the local art academy to admit Artemisia, a no-no in 17th-century Rome, and she even tries the forbidden territory of the male nude. Soon her artistic passion is matched by a sexual passion for fellow artist Agostino Tassi (Manojlovic), but this time her father isn't so understanding and Artemisia becomes the center of a rape trial. The real Artemisia is considered to be the first known female artist. French with subtitles. **95m/C VHS.** *FR* Valentina Cervi, Michel Serrault, Miki (Predrag) Manojlovic, Luca Zingaretti, Brigitte Catillon, Frederic Pierrot, Maurice Garrel, Yahn Tregouet, Jacques Nolot; *D:* Agnes Merlet; *W:* Agnes Merlet; *C:* Benoit Delhomme; *M:* Krishna Levy.

Arthur 🦴🦴🦴 **1981 (PG)** Spoiled, alcoholic billionaire Moore stands to lose everything he owns when he falls in love with a waitress. He must choose between wealth and a planned marriage, or poverty and love. Surprisingly funny, with an Oscar for Gielgud as Moore's valet, and great performance from Minnelli. Arguably the best role Moore's ever had, and he makes the most of it, taking the one-joke premise to a Oscar nomination. ♫Arthur's Theme; Blue Moon; If You Knew Susie; Santa Claus Is Coming to Town. **97m/C VHS, DVD, 8mm.** Dudley Moore, Liza Minnelli, John Gielgud, Geraldine Fitzgerald, Stephen Elliott, Jill Eikenberry, Lou Jacobi, Ted Ross, Barney Martin; *D:* Steve Gordon; *W:* Steve Gordon; *C:* Fred Schuler; *M:* Burt Bacharach, Peter Allen, Peter Allen. Oscars '81: Song ("Arthur's Theme"), Support. Actor (Gielgud); Golden Globes '82: Actor—Mus./Comedy (Moore), Film—Mus./Comedy, Song ("Arthur's Theme"), Support. Actor (Gielgud); L.A. Film Critics '81: Support. Actor (Gielgud); N.Y. Film Critics '81: Support. Actor (Gielgud); Writers Guild '81: Orig. Screenplay.

Arthur 2: On the Rocks 🦴½ **1988 (PG)** When Arthur finally marries his sweetheart, it may not be "happily ever after" because the father of the girl he didn't marry is out for revenge. When Arthur discovers that he is suddenly penniless, a bit of laughter is the cure for the blues and also serves well when the liquor runs out. A disappointing sequel with few laughs. **113m/C VHS, 8mm.** Dudley Moore, Liza Minnelli, John Gielgud, Geraldine Fitzgerald, Stephen Elliott, Ted Ross, Barney Martin, Jack Gilford; *D:* Bud Yorkin; *W:* Andy Breckman; *C:* Stephen Burum; *M:* Burt Bacharach. Golden Raspberries '87: Worst Actress (Minnelli).

Arthur's Hallowed Ground 🦴 **1984** A cricket field caretaker battles the board of directors over the fate of his favorite plot of sod. **75m/C VHS.** Jimmy Jewel, Jean Bolt, Michael Elphick; *D:* Frederick A. (Freddie) Young.

Arthur's Quest 🦴🦴½ **1999 (PG)** In this switcheroo on Mark Twain's "A Connecticut Yankee in King Arthur's Court" a five-year-old Arthur is transported by Merlin from his medieval home to the modern age because the wizard fears for the boy's safety. Merlin doesn't reappear for 10 years, so Arthur has become a typical American teen. Now, how do you convince a 15-year-old that he's really a medieval monarch who must return to save Camelot? **91m/C VHS, DVD.** Kevin Elston, Zach Galligan, Arye Gross, Clint Howard, Brion James, Katie Johnston, Neil Mandt; *D:* Neil Mandt. **VIDEO**

Article 99 🦴🦴 **1992 (R)** Doctors in a Kansas City Veteran's Administration hospital try to heal patients while putting up with bureaucratic red tape and a stingy administrator. When rogue physician Sturgess (Liotta) is dismissed, the patients hold a siege. Sort of son of "M.A.S.H." (Big Daddy Sutherland did Hawkeye) that gets its title from a fictional rule that says veterans can be treated only for conditions related to military service. Erstwhile cast labors to combine comedic and dramatic intentions of script. **100m/C VHS.** Ray Liotta, Kiefer Sutherland, Forest Whitaker, Lea Thompson, John C. McGinley, John Mahoney, Keith David, Kathy Baker, Eli Wallach, Noble Willingham, Julie Bovasso, Troy Evans, Lynne Thigpen, Jeffrey Tambor, Rutanya Alda; *D:* Howard Deutch; *W:* Ron Cutler; *C:* Rick Bota; *M:* Danny Elfman.

Artists and Models 🦴🦴½ **1955** Martin is a struggling comic book artist and Lewis his idiot roommate. The pair become mixed up in both romance and intrigue when Lewis begins talking in his sleep about spys and such. One of the duo's more pleasant cinematic outings. ♫Inamorata; Lucky Song; You Look So Familiar; Why You Pretend. **109m/C VHS.** Dean Martin, Jerry Lewis, Shirley MacLaine, Dorothy Malone, Eddie Mayehoff, Eva Gabor, Anita Ekberg, George Winslow, Jack Elam, Herbert Rudley, Nick Castle; *D:* Frank Tashlin; *W:* Frank Tashlin, Hal Kanter, Herbert Baker; *C:* Daniel F. Fapp.

As Good as Dead 🦴🦴½ **1995 (PG-13)** A young woman allows her sick friend to assume her identity but when her friend is murdered, she realizes the killer was really after her. **88m/C VHS.** Crystal Bernard, Traci Lords, Judge Reinhold; *D:* Larry Cohen; *W:* Larry Cohen.

As Good As It Gets 🦴🦴🦴 *Old Friends* **1997 (PG-13)** Entertaining and enjoyable outing from Brooks racked up an impressive list of Oscar noms (including Best Picture). Obsessive-compulsive romance novelist Melvin Udall (Nicholson) is also the meanest guy in New York, liked by nobody and hating all. The only exception is single-mother/waitress Carol (Hunt), who puts up with his annoying habits at the local restaurant where he dines. Forced to look after gay neighbor Kinnear's fussy-but-cute dog, Udall falls into an improbable quest for love, friendship, and a life as "normal as it gets" in this sort of extended-sitcom universe. Snappy dialogue by Brooks and co-writer Andrus, and an easy-going non-stereotypical performance by Kinnear are highlights, almost overshadowing both Hunt's Jodie Foster-like portrayal, and Nicholson's typical but delightful role (both of which won Oscars). **130m/C VHS, DVD.** Missi Pyle, Jack Nicholson, Helen Hunt, Greg Kinnear, Cuba Gooding Jr., Skeet Ulrich, Shirley Knight, Yeardley Smith, Lupe Ontiveros, Bibi Osterwald, Brian Doyle-Murray, Randall Batinkoff, Shane Black, Tara Subkoff; *Cameos:* Danielle Brisebois, Lawrence Kasdan, Harold Ramis, Jimmy Workman, Todd Solondz, Tom McGowan; *D:* James L. Brooks; *W:* Mark Andrus, James L. Brooks; *C:* John Bailey; *M:* Hans Zimmer. Oscars '97: Actor (Nicholson), Actress (Hunt); Golden Globes '98: Actor—Mus./Comedy (Nicholson), Actress—Mus./Comedy (Hunt), Film—Mus./Comedy; Natl. Bd. of Review '97: Actor (Nicholson), Support. Actor (Kinnear); Screen Actors Guild '97: Actor (Nicholson), Actress (Hunt); Writers Guild '97: Orig. Screenplay; Broadcast Film Critics '97: Actor (Nicholson).

As If It Were Raining 🦴🦴 **1963** Constantine gets involved in an embezzlement scheme in Spain in this espionage thriller. **85m/C VHS.** *FR* Eddie Constantine, Henri Cogan, Elisa Montes, Jose Nieto, Silvia Solar; *D:* Jose Monter.

As Is 🦴½ **1985** Two gay New Yorkers deal with a troubled romance and AIDS. Adapted from the William M. Hoffman play. **86m/C VHS.** Jonathan Hadary, Robert Carradine; *D:* Michael Lindsay-Hogg. **CABLE**

As Summers Die 🦴🦴 **1986** Louisiana attorney Glenn fights in the late 1950s to protect the rights of a black family, against the wishes of a powerful local clan. Glenn finds support in surprising places, though. From Winston Groom's acclaimed novel. **100m/C VHS.** Scott Glenn, Jamie Lee Curtis, Penny Fuller, Bette Davis, John Randolph, Beah Richards, Ron O'Neal, John McIntire; *D:* Jean-Claude Tramont. **CABLE**

As You Desire Me 🦴🦴🦴 **1932** Garbo plays an amnesia victim who returns to a husband she doesn't even remember after an abusive relationship with a novelist. An interesting, if not down-right bizarre movie, due to the pairing of the great Garbo and the intriguing von Stroheim. An adaption of Luigi Pirandello's play. **71m/B VHS.** Greta Garbo, Melvyn Douglas, Erich von Stroheim, Owen Moore, Hedda Hopper; *D:* George Fitzmaurice.

As You Like It 🦴🦴½ **1936** A Duke's banished daughter poses as a man to win the attentions of one of her father's attendants in this highly stylized Shakespearean comedy adapted by J.M. Barrie and Robert Cullen. Early Shakespearean Olivier. **96m/B VHS, DVD.** *GB* Elisabeth Bergner, Laurence Olivier, Henry Ainley, Felix Aylmer; *D:* Paul Czinner; *W:* J.M. Barrie, Robert Cullen; *C:* Jack Cardiff, Harold Rosson; *M:* William Walton.

As You Were 🦴 **1951** A girl with a photographic memory enlists in the Army, becoming both a nuisance and comedic victim to her sergeant. **57m/B VHS.** Joseph (Joe) Sawyer, William Tracy, Sondra Rogers, Joan Vohs.

As Young As You Feel 🦴🦴🦴 **1951** A 65-year-old man is forced to retire from his job. He poses as the head of the conglomerate and convinces them to repeal their retirement policy. He then gains national publicity when he makes a speech about the dignity of man. Watch for Monroe as the boss's secretary. Fine comic performances enhance the script; based on a story by Chayefsky. **77m/C VHS.** Monty Woolley, Thelma Ritter, David Wayne, Jean Peters, Constance Bennett, Marilyn Monroe, Allyn Joslyn, Albert Dekker, Clinton Sundberg, Minor Watson; *D:* Harmon Jones; *W:* Paddy Chayefsky.

The Ascent 🦴🦴🦴 *Voskhozhdeniye* **1976** During WWII, two Soviet partisans leave their comrades in order to obtain supplies from a nearby farm. Only the Germans have gotten there first, forcing the Soviets deeper into occupied territory, which leads to their eventual capture and interrogation. Russian with subtitles. **105m/B VHS.** *RU* Boris Plotnikov, Vladimir Gostyukhin; *D:* Larisa Shepitko; *W:* Larisa Shepitko, Yuri Klepikov; *C:* Pavel Lebeshev, Vladimir Chukhnov; *M:* Alfred Schnittke.

The Ascent 🦴🦴½ **1994 (PG)** Based on the true story of Franco (Spano), a WWII Italian POW who's held in a camp in Africa. The prisoners enjoy making fun of the camp commander (Cross), who consistently fails at his attempts to climb the 15,500 peak of Mt. Kenya. Meanwhile, Franco decides to escape and climb the mountain himself—with the commander right behind. Beware if you suffer from vertigo. **96m/C VHS.** Vincent Spano, Ben Cross, Tony LoBianco, Rachel Ward; *D:* Donald Shebib; *C:* David Connell.

Ash Wednesday 🦴 **1973 (R)** Taylor endures the pain of cosmetic surgery in an effort to rescue her floundering union with Fonda. Another undistinguished performance by Liz. Fonda is especially slimy as the philandering husband, but only appears in the latter stages of the film. **99m/C VHS.** Elizabeth Taylor, Henry Fonda, Helmut Berger, Keith Baxter, Margaret Blye, Maurice Teynac, Monique Van Vooren; *D:* Larry Peerce; *M:* Maurice Jarre.

Ashanti, Land of No Mercy 🦴🦴 *Ashanti* **1979** Caine of the week movie with Michael portraying a doctor acting as a missionary in South Africa who finds himself alone in a battle to rescue his wife from a band of slave traders. The chase spans many Middle Eastern countries and begins to look bleak for our man. Talented cast and promising plot are undone by slow pace. Based on the novel "Ebano" by Alberto Vasquez-Figueroa. **117m/C VHS.** Michael Caine, Omar Sharif, Peter Ustinov, Rex Harrison, William Holden, Beverly Johnson; *D:* Richard Fleischer.

Ashes and Diamonds 🦴🦴🦴½ *Popiol i Diament* **1958** In the closing days of WWII, a Polish resistance fighter assassinates the wrong man, tries to find love with the right women, and questions the meaning of struggle. A seminal Eastern European masterpiece that defined a generation of pre-solidarity Poles. Available in Polish with English subtitles or dubbed into English. The last installment of the trilogy that includes "A Generation" and "Kanal" and based on a novel by Jerzy Andrzewski. **105m/B VHS.** *PL* Zbigniew Cybulski, Eva Krzyzewska, Adam Pawlikowski, Bogumil Kobiela, Waclaw Zastrzezynski; *D:* Andrzej Wajda; *W:* Andrzej Wajda, Jerzy Andrzejewski; *C:* Jerzy Wojcik; *M:* Jan Krenz, Filip Nowak.

Ashes and Embers 🦴🦴 **1982** A black Vietnam vet in Los Angeles has trouble fitting into society, eventually running afoul of the police. Ethiopian-born director Gerima endows vital subject matter with a properly alienated mood. **120m/C VHS.** John Anderson, Evelyn Blackwell; *D:* Haile Gerima.

Ashik Kerib 🦴🦴🦴 *The Lovelorn Minstrel; The Hoary Legends of the Caucasus* **1988** Ashik Kerib is a wandering minstrel who is rejected by a rich merchant as his daughter's suitor. He then journeys for 1,000 days trying to earn enough money to marry his beloved. Along the way he's imprisoned by an evil sultan and rides a flying horse, among other adventures. Wonderful use of exotic makeup and costumes highlight this Arabian Nights tale. Adapted from a story by Mikhail Lermontov. Paradjanov's last film. In Russian with English subtitles. **75m/C VHS, DVD.** *RU* Yiur Mgoyan, Veronkia Metonidze, Levan Natroshvili, Sofiko Chiaureli; *D:* Dodo Abashidze, Sergei Paradjanov; *W:* Giya Badridze; *M:* Djavashir Kuliev.

Ask Any Girl 🦴🦴½ **1959** Lighthearted fluff about a small-town girl who moves to Manhattan. MacLaine plays the bright Meg who gets a job at an ad agency and decides to set her sights on marrying her boss (Young). She asks his older brother's (Niven) help in her quest and the inevitable happens. **101m/C VHS.** Shirley MacLaine, David Niven, Gig Young, Rod Taylor, Jim Backus, Claire Kelly, Elisabeth Fraser; *D:* Charles Walters. British Acad. '59: Actress (MacLaine).

Aspen Extreme 🦴 **1993 (PG-13)** Former Aspen ski instructor writes and directs a movie on (what else?) ski instructors in (where?) Aspen! Long on ski shots and short on plot, this movie never leaves the bunny hill. Two Detroiters leave Motown for Snowtown to pursue a life on the slopes. T.J (Gross) soon has his hands full with two beautiful women (Polo and Hughes) who encourage his dream of becoming a writer. His friend Dexter (Berg), however, acquires a few bad habits, and the whole movie just goes downhill from there. **128m/C VHS.** Paul Gross, Peter Berg, Finola Hughes, Teri Polo, Martin Kemp, Nicolette Scorsese, William Russ; *D:* Patrick Hasburgh; *W:* Patrick Hasburgh; *C:* Steven Fierberg; *M:* Michael Convertino.

The Asphalt Jungle 🦴🦴🦴🦴 **1950** An aging criminal emerges from his forced retirement (prison) and assembles the old gang for one final heist. A very realistic storyline and a superb cast make this one of the best crime films ever made. Highly acclaimed; based on the work of W.R. Burnett. **112m/B VHS.** Sterling Hayden, Louis Calhern, Jean Hagen, James Whitmore, Sam Jaffe, John McIntire, Marc Lawrence, Barry Kelley, Anthony Caruso, Teresa Celli, Marilyn Monroe; *D:* John Huston; *W:* Ben Maddow; *M:* Miklos Rozsa. Natl. Bd. of Review '50: Director (Huston); Venice Film Fest. '50: Actor (Hayden).

The Asphyx ♪♪♪ *Spirit of the Dead* **1972 (PG)** Nineteenth century doctor Stephens is studying death when he discovers The Asphyx, an aura that surrounds a person just before they die. Stephens delves deeper into his research and finds the keys to immortality. However, his irresponsibility in unleashing the obscure supernatural power on the world brings a swarm of unforeseen and irreversible troubles. High-class sci fi. **98m/C VHS, DVD, Wide.** *GB* Robert Stephens, Robert Powell, Jane Lapotaire, Alex Scott, Ralph Arliss, Fiona Walker, John Lawrence, Paul Bacon, Terry Scully; ***D:*** Peter Newbrook; ***W:*** Brian Comfort; ***C:*** Frederick A. (Freddie) Young; ***M:*** Bill McGuffie.

Assassin ♪♪ **1986 (PG-13)** Made for TV drama about a mad scientist who creates a bionic killer for a bizarre plot to take over the world. He programs the cyborg to assassinate the President and other key people to help carry out his plan. A retired CIA operative emerges to stop the scientist by trying to destroy the robot. **94m/C VHS, DVD.** Robert Conrad, Karen Austin, Richard Young, Jonathan Banks, Robert Webber; ***D:*** Sandor Stern; ***W:*** Sandor Stern; ***C:*** Chuck (Charles G.) Arnold; ***M:*** Anthony Guefen. **TV**

Assassin ♪♪ **1989 (R)** Fairly lame thriller about a CIA agent protecting a Senator who falls under suspicion when his charge is shot by an assassin. In investigating the killing the agent discovers the usual governmental conspiracy. **92m/C VHS.** Steve Railsback, Nicholas Guest, Xander Berkeley, Elpidia Carrillo; ***D:*** Jon Hess.

Assassin of Youth ♪½ **1935** Girl is introduced to marijuana and soon becomes involved in "the thrills of wild parties," and the horrors of the "killer weed." Camp diversion. **70m/B VHS, DVD.** Luana Walters, Arthur Gardner, Earl Dwire, Fern Emmett, Dorothy Short; ***D:*** Elmer Clifton.

Assassination ♪ **1987 (R)** A serious threat has been made to First Lady Ireland and no one is taking it lightly. Secret Service agent Bronson has been called as Ireland's personal bodyguard and suddenly they are both the target of terrorist attacks. Strangely though, the attacks seem to be directed from inside the White House. Bronson as you've seen him many times before. **93m/C VHS.** Charles Bronson, Jill Ireland, Stephen Elliott, Michael Ansara; ***D:*** Peter Hunt; ***C:*** Hanania Baer.

The Assassination Bureau ♪♪♪ **1969** Set in Victorian-era London, this amusing farce concerns a society of international assassins led by the charming Reed. Rigg is an intrepid reporter who pays Reed to have his own organization try to kill him. Reed in turn will try to get them first. A cross-European chase ends in a battle aboard a Zeppelin. Tongue-in-cheek whimsey with a fine cast. Based on a short story by Jack London. **106m/C VHS.** *GB* Oliver Reed, Diana Rigg, Telly Savalas, Curt Jurgens, Philippe Noiret, Warren Mitchell, Beryl Reid, Clive Revill, Kenneth Griffith, Vernon Dobtcheff, Annabella Incontrera; ***D:*** Basil Dearden; ***C:*** Geoffrey Unsworth.

The Assassination File ♪♪ **1996 (R)** FBI agent Lauren Jacobs (Fenn) quits the Bureau after the first African-American President (Winfield) is killed on her watch. But two years later, when she encounters former co-workers, there's talk of a conspiracy and things turn even more dangerous. **106m/C VHS.** Sherilyn Fenn, Daniel Butler, Tom Verica, Victor Love, Kevin Corrigan, Paul Winfield, Diedrich Bader; ***D:*** John Harrison; ***W:*** Bruce Miller; ***C:*** Rob Draper.

The Assassination Game ♪ **1992 (R)** Rookie CIA agent teams up with a veteran KGB agent to prevent the assassination of a world leader. **90m/C VHS.** Robert Rusler, Theodore Bikel, Doug Wert, Denise Bixler; ***D:*** Jonathan Winfrey.

Assassination of Trotsky ♪♪ **1972** Middling attempt to dramatize the last days of the Russian Revolutionary leader in Mexico before he's done in with an ice pick. **113m/C VHS.** *FR GB IT* Richard Burton, Alain Delon, Romy Schneider, Valentina Cortese, Jean Desailly; ***D:*** Joseph Losey; ***C:*** Pasqualino De Santis.

The Assassination Run ♪ **1984** A retired British spy is involved against his will in an intricate plot of terrorism, counter-terrorism and espionage. **111m/C VHS.** *GB* Malcolm Stoddard, Mary Tamm; ***D:*** Ken Hannam.

Assassins ♪♪½ **1995 (R)** Stallone gets to play elder statesman in the very deadly rivalry between two contract killers. Robert Rath (Stallone) is the man—number one with a bullet—whose reputation has caught up with him. Hot-headed Miguel Bain (the ever-smoldering Banderas) wants to off Rath and assume the position of top hitman. Caught in the middle of this macho posturing is surveillance expert—and potential murderee—Electra (Moore). It's Stallone to the rescue but his character pays more attention to Pearl, Electra's pampered Persian cat than to the lovely lady herself. But then romance isn't what this film is about—and director Donner does know his action. **132m/C VHS, DVD.** Sylvester Stallone, Antonio Banderas, Julianne Moore, Anatoly Davydov; ***D:*** Richard Donner; ***W:*** Brian Helgeland, Andy Wachowski, Larry Wachowski; ***C:*** Vilmos Zsigmond; ***M:*** Mark Mancina.

Assault ♪½ *In the Devil's Garden; Tower of Terror; The Creepers* **1970** Violent sex murders in a girl's school have the police baffled. The school's pretty art teacher offers to act as bait in order to catch the murderer. **89m/C VHS.** *GB* Suzy Kendall, Frank Finlay, Freddie Jones, James Laurenson, Lesley-Anne Down, Tony Beckley; ***D:*** Sidney Hayers.

The Assault ♪♪♪½ *De Aanslag* **1986 (PG)** Powerful and disturbing drama about a Dutch boy who witnesses the arbitrary murder of his family by Nazis. The memory tortures him and leaves him empty as he matures. Years later he meets other victims and also the perpetrators of the incident, each of them changed forever by it. Thought-provoking consideration of WWII and the horrors of living in Nazi Germany from many points of view. Based on a novel by Harry Mulisch. Dutch language dubbed into English. **149m/C VHS.** *NL* Derek De Lint, Marc Van Uchelen, Monique Van De Ven; ***D:*** Fons Rademakers. Oscars '86: Foreign Film; Golden Globes '87: Foreign Film.

Assault and Matrimony ♪½ **1987** Real-life married people Tucker and Eikenberry play a married couple fighting tooth and nail. Lots of slapstick and general nonsense. Based on James Anderson's novel. **100m/C VHS.** John Hillerman, Michelle Phillips, Joe Cortese, Michael Tucker, Jill Eikenberry; ***D:*** James Frawley; ***C:*** Dick Bush. **TV**

Assault at West Point: The Court-Martial of Johnson Whittaker ♪♪½ **1994 (PG-13)** In 1880, Johnson C. Whittaker, a black West Point cadet, is found beaten, mutilated, and tied to his bed. Instead of seeking his attackers, the Academy sets up a court martial to expel Whittaker, claiming he faked his own attack. Clashes also ignite between Whittaker's defense counsel—white abolitionist lawyer Chamberlain, whose own racism is thinly disguised, and black lawyer Greener, who originally encouraged Whittaker to enroll at the Point. Interesting case but a shallow production. Based on a true story and adapted from the book by John Marszalek. **98m/C VHS.** Seth Gilliam, Samuel L. Jackson, Sam Waterston, John Glover, Al Freeman Jr.; ***D:*** Harry Moses; ***W:*** Harry Moses; ***M:*** Terence Blanchard. **TV**

Assault of the Killer Bimbos ♪½ **1988 (R)** A show girl gets framed for the murder of her boss and takes off for the border with a couple of girlfriends. On the way they get pursued by the expected dumb cops and meet up with horny, clean-cut hunks. In Mexico they encounter the villain and extract comic vengeance. Watchable mainly due to the likable female leads and pleasant, lightly camp execution, although it might prove too tame for most of its target audience. **85m/C VHS, DVD.** Patti Astor, Christina Whitaker, Elizabeth Kaitan, Griffin O'Neal, Nick Cassavetes, Clayton Landey, Eddie Deezen, Arell Blanton, David Marsh, Tammara Souza, Jamie Bozian, Mike Muscat, Jeffrey Orman, John Quern, Jay O. Sanders; ***D:*** Anita Rosenberg; ***W:*** Ted Nicolaou; ***C:*** Thomas Callaway; ***M:*** Fred Lapides, Marc Ellis.

Assault of the Party Nerds ♪ **1989 (R)** Nerds throw a wild party to try and attract new members to their fraternity, while a jock frat plots against them. Sound familiar? Little more than a ripoff of "Revenge of the Nerds" made especially for video. **82m/C VHS, DVD.** Michelle (McClellan) Bauer, Linnea Quigley, Troy Donahue, Richard Gabai, C. Paul Demsey, Marc Silverberg, Robert Mann, Richard Rifkin, Deborah Roush; ***D:*** Richard Gabai. **VIDEO**

Assault of the Party Nerds 2: Heavy Petting Detective ♪ **1995** Detective tries to save a beauty from her scheming husband. **87m/C VHS, DVD.** Linnea Quigley, Richard Gabai, Michelle (McClellan) Bauer, Arte Johnson, Burt Ward; ***D:*** Richard Gabai; ***W:*** Richard Gabai.

Assault of the Rebel Girls ♪½ *Cuban Rebel Girls; Attack of the Rebel Girls* **1959** A reporter gets involved with smuggling in Castro's Cuba. Flynn's last film, saving the worst for last. **66m/B VHS.** Errol Flynn, Beverly Aadland, John McKay, Jackie Jackler, Marie Edmund; ***D:*** Barry Mahon; ***W:*** Errol Flynn.

Assault on a Queen ♪ **1966** Stupid Sinatra vehicle about a group of con men who plot together to rob the Queen Mary on one of her trips. Their attack vessel is a renovated WWII German U-boat. The producers tried to capitalize on the popularity of "Ocean's Eleven," but they didn't even come close. Based on a novel by Jack Finney. **106m/C VHS.** Frank Sinatra, Virna Lisi, Anthony (Tony) Franciosa, Richard Conte, Reginald Denny; ***D:*** Jack Donohue; ***W:*** Rod Serling; ***C:*** William H. Daniels.

Assault on Agathon ♪♪ **1975 (PG)** Amid the scenic Greek isles, an "executed" WWII guerilla leader returns to lead a revolution, and bloodshed and bombings ensue. **95m/C VHS.** *GB IT* Nina Van Pallandt, Marianne Faithfull, John Woodvine, Nico Minardos; ***D:*** Laslo Benedek.

Assault on Precinct 13 ♪♪♪ **1976** Urban horror invades LA. A sleepy police station in Los Angeles is suddenly under siege from a violent youth gang. Paranoia abounds as the police are attacked from all sides and can see no way out. Carpenter's musical score adds much to the setting of this unique police exploitation story that somehow stands as Carpenter's adaptation of Howard Hawks' "Rio Bravo." Semi-acclaimed and very gripping. **91m/C VHS, DVD.** Austin Stoker, Darwin Joston, Martin West, Tony Burton, Nancy Loomis, Kim Richards, Henry (Kleinbach) Brandon, Laurie Zimmer, Charles Cyphers, Peter Bruni; ***D:*** John Carpenter; ***W:*** John Carpenter; ***C:*** Douglas Knapp; ***M:*** John Carpenter.

Assault with a Deadly Weapon ♪ **1982** When the police budget is cutback, crime runs rampant in an unnamed American city. **86m/C VHS.** Sandra Foley, Richard Holliday, Lamont Jackson; ***D:*** Arthur Kennedy.

The Assignment ♪♪ **1978** The assassination of a high-ranking officer in an uneasy Latin American nation spurs violence and political instability. A Swedish diplomat is assigned the tremendous task of restoring peace and stability between the political factions. **92m/C VHS.** *SW* Christopher Plummer, Thomas Hellberg, Carolyn Seymour, Fernando Rey; ***D:*** Mats Arehn.

The Assignment ♪♪½ **1997 (R)** Workmanlike thriller is a case of deadly impersonation. Infamous terrorist Carlos the Jackal (Quinn) is shown plying his trade in Europe under the nose of CIA counterterrorism expert Jack Shaw (Sutherland). Later, in Israel, Mossad agent Amos (Kinglsey) captures a man whom he thinks is Carlos, only it's his double—U.S. Navy officer Annibal Ramirez (Quinn again). So Shaw and Amos decide to turn the seaman into the terrorist, in an elaborate plot to have Carlos' Russian handlers think the terrorist has betrayed them. There's a very long setup for a somewhat lame payoff. **115m/C VHS, DVD.** *CA* Aidan Quinn, Donald Sutherland, Ben Kingsley, Liliana Komorowska, Claudia Ferri, Celine Bonnier, Vlasta Vrana, Von Flores, Al Waxman; ***D:*** Christian Duguay; ***W:*** Don Gordon, Sabi H. Shabtai; ***C:*** David Franco; ***M:*** Normand Corbeil.

Assignment Outer Space ♪ *Space Men* **1961** A giant spaceship with bytes for brains is on a collision course with Earth. A team of astronauts is sent to save the world from certain peril. Seems they take the task lightly, though, and their mission (and hence the plot) revolves more around saving sexy sultress Farinon from certain celibacy. If you're into stultifying Italian space operas with a gratuitous sex sub-plot then look up this assignment, but don't say we didn't warn you. Director Margheriti is also known as Anthony Dawson, not to be confused with the actor of the same name. **79m/B VHS.** *IT* Rik von Nutter, Gabriella Farinon, Archie Savage, Dave Montresor, Alan Dijon; ***D:*** Anthony (Antonio Margheriti) Dawson; ***Nar:*** Jack Wallace.

The Assisi Underground ♪♪ **1984** True but boringly told story of how the Catholic Church helped to save several hundred Italian Jews from being executed by the Nazis during the 1943 German occupation of Italy. Edited from 178 minutes, a good-will gesture from the producers. **115m/C VHS.** James Mason, Ben Cross, Maximilian Schell, Irene Papas; ***D:*** Alexander Ramati; ***M:*** Pino Donaggio.

The Assistant ♪♪ **1997** The Jewish Bober family have escaped the anti-Semitism of their homeland and emigrated to the U.S. where they are struggling to run a small grocery store during the depression. Drifter Frank (Bellows) hooks up with thief Ward (Woolvet) and they rob the store, with Ward attacking Morris Bober (Mueller-Stahl). A guilty Frank later returns and offers to help out. Morris doesn't know Frank was part of the robbery and agrees and Frank soons falls for the Bober's duaghter, Helen (Greenhouse). Then Morris discovers the truth. Based on a novel by Bernard Malamud. **105m/C VHS.** *CA* Gil Bellows, Armin Mueller-Stahl, Joan Plowright, Kate Greenhouse, Jaimz Woolvett; ***D:*** Daniel Petrie; ***W:*** Daniel Petrie; ***C:*** Philip Earnshaw.

The Associate ♪♪ *L'Associe* **1979 (R)** French farce about penniless financial consultant Julien Pardot (Serrault) who invents a fictitious partner, Mr. Davis, in order to get his business rolling. When his clients, his wife, and even his mistress are all more intrigued by the partner than Julien, he becomes so jealous he decides to "murder" his creation. Based on the novel "My Partner, Mr. Davis" by Jenaro Prieto. French with subtitles; remade in 1996 with Whoopi Goldberg. **93m/C VHS.** *FR* Michel Serrault, Claudine Auger, Catherine Alric, Matthieu Carriere; ***D:*** Rene Gainville; ***W:*** Jean-Claude Carriere.

The Associate ♪♪ **1996 (PG-13)** Whoopi drags a 20-minute premise over almost two hours when she invents an elderly, white, male business partner to give her fledgling financial consulting business some prestige. After having all her moneymaking ideas appropriated by male colleagues, Laurel Ayres (Goldberg) starts her own business, only to find that no one wants to hire her. She creates the genius and the money comes rolling in. Everyone clamors to meet the mystery man, so she goes undercover as the elusive Robert S. Cutty. The sight of Goldberg in old white guy garb and makeup is jarring, and the payoff doesn't merit the overlong build up. Based on the French film "L'Associate" and the Jenaro Prieto novel "El Socio." **113m/C VHS, DVD.** Whoopi Goldberg, Timothy Daly, Bebe Neuwirth, Dianne Wiest, Eli Wallach; ***D:*** Donald Petrie; ***W:*** Nick Thiel; ***C:*** Alex Nepomniaschy; ***M:*** Christopher Tyng.

Asteroid ♪♪ **1997** Re-edited version of the NBC TV miniseries emphasises the special effects and action, which should help this routine disaster flick. Astronomer Lily McKee (Sciorra) discovers that several giant asteroids are on a collision course with Kansas City. She contacts FEMA and gets hotshot director Jack Wallach (Biehn) anxious to help out (and not just with the rock problem). Naturally, the citizens freak and one asteroid hits but there's an even bigger one on the way. **120m/C VHS, DVD.** Michael Biehn, Annabella Sciorra, Don Franklin,

Anne-Marie Johnson, Anthony Zerbe, Carlos Gomez, Jensen Daggett; ***D:*** Bradford May; ***C:*** David Hennings, Thomas Del Ruth; ***M:*** Shirley Walker. **TV**

The Astounding She-Monster woof! *Mysterious Invader* **1958** How can you not love a movie with a title like this? A bad script and snail-paced plot are a good start. A geologist wanting only to be left alone with his rocks survives a brush with the kidnappers of a wealthy heiress only to happen upon an alien spacecraft that's crashed nearby. At the helm is a very tall, high-heeled fem-alien in an obligatory skintight space outfit. Excellent, our rock jock thinks, but it seems she kills with the slightest touch. For connoisseurs of truly bad movies. **60m/B VHS, DVD.** Robert Clarke, Kenne Duncan, Marilyn Harvey, Jeanne Tatum, Shirley Kilpatrick, Ewing Miles Brown; ***D:*** Ronnie Ashcroft; ***W:*** Frank Hall; ***C:*** William C. Thompson; ***M:*** Guenther Kauer.

The Astro-Zombies woof! *The Space Vampires* **1967** A contender as one of the worst movies of all time. Carradine plays a mad scientist creating zombies who eat people's guts. Cult favorite Satana stars. Co-written and co-produced by Rogers of "M*A*S*H" fame. **83m/C VHS, DVD, Wide.** Tura Satana, Wendell Corey, John Carradine, Tom Pace, Joan Patrick, Rafael Campos, William Bagdad, Joseph Hoover, Victor Izay, Vincent Barbi, Rod Wilmoth; ***D:*** Ted V. Mikels; ***W:*** Ted V. Mikels, Wayne Rogers; ***C:*** Robert Maxwell; ***M:*** Nico Karaski.

The Astronaut's Wife 🦴½ **1999 (R)** Astronaut Spencer Armacost (Depp) just isn't the same guy after he returns from a nearly fatal space shuttle mission. He and his wife, Jillian (Theron), suddenly move to New York and she definitely notices some behavorial changes (he likes to listen to the test pattern on the TV screen). Oh, and then the little woman discovers she's pregnant and things get very "Rosemary's Baby." Theron's role is also very much like her beleagured wife in "The Devil's Advocate," since everyone seems to think Jillian's nuts. Disappointingly formulaic; Depp's more believable in quirky roles in quirky movies. **109m/C VHS, DVD, Wide.** Johnny Depp, Charlize Theron, Joe Morton, Tom Noonan, Blair Brown, Nick Cassavetes, Clea DuVall, Donna Murphy, Samantha Eggar; ***D:*** Rand Ravich; ***W:*** Rand Ravich; ***C:*** Allen Daviau; ***M:*** George S. Clinton.

Asunder 🦴🦴½ **1999** Slick thriller with a familiar storyline. Michael (Beach) and wife Lauren (Morgan) are at the fairground with best friends Chance (Underwood) and his pregnant wife Roberta (Hicks). Roberta is tragically killed in a fall while riding the Ferris wheel. Michael and Lauren invite Chance to stay with them and the viewer learns that Lauren and Chance once had an extramarital affair. Then Chance decides to wreck her marriage and get Lauren back. **102m/C VHS.** Blair Underwood, Debbi (Deborah) Morgan, Michael Beach, Marva Hicks; ***D:*** Tim Reid; ***W:*** Eric Lee Bowers; ***C:*** Johnny (John W.) Simmons; ***M:*** Lionel Cole.

Asylum 🦴🦴½ *House of Crazies* **1972 (PG)** Four strange and chilling stories weave together in this film. A murderer's victim seeks retribution. A tailor seems to be collecting his bills. A man who makes voodoo dolls...only to become one later on. A woman plagued by a double. A doctor visiting the asylum tells each tale. Horrifying and grotesque, not as humorless as American horror films. **100m/C VHS, DVD.** *GB* Peter Cushing, Herbert Lom, Britt Ekland, Barbara Parkins, Patrick Magee, Barry Morse, Robert Powell, Richard Todd, Charlotte Rampling, Ann(e) Firbank, Sylvia Syms, James Villiers, Geoffrey Bayldon, Megs Jenkins; ***D:*** Roy Ward Baker; ***W:*** Robert Bloch; ***C:*** Denys Coop.

Asylum 🦴½ **1997 (R)** Unstable investigator Nick Tordone (Patrick) looks into his shrink's supposed suicide by become a patient at the doctor's mental hospital. By what he finds is serial killer Sullivan Rane (McDowell) and a doctor (Gibson) doing dangerous mind control experiments. Tension holds up well until the unfortunate finale. **92m/C VHS.** Jason Schombing, Kevin Anthony Cole, Peter Brown, Robert Patrick, Malcolm McDowell, Henry Gibson, Sarah Douglas; ***D:*** James Seale; ***W:*** James Seale; ***C:*** David Rakoczy; ***M:*** Alan Williams.

Asylum of Satan 🦴 **1972** A beautiful concert pianist is savagely tortured by a madman in the Asylum of Satan. Filmed on location in Louisville, Kentucky. **87m/C VHS.** Charles Kissinger, Carla Borelli, Nick Jolly, Sherry Steiner; ***D:*** William Girdler; ***W:*** William Girdler.

At Any Cost 🦴🦴½ **2000 (R)** Ah, the music business. Austin, Texas band Beyond Gravity has a shot at a major recording career in L.A. when they're signed by an indie label. Leader Lance (Mills) vows to wife/bandmember Chelsea (Flannigan) that they won't blow their big chance but problems arise quickly. Seems Lance's brother Mike (Franco) can't control his drug problem and ambitious pal Ben (Quinn) wants to strike out on his own when the band starts to go south. Typical price-of-fame cable drama. **92m/C VHS.** Eddie Mills, James Franco, Glenn Quinn, Maureen Flannigan, Cyia Batten; ***D:*** Charles Winkler; ***W:*** Bruce Taylor, Roderick Taylor; ***C:*** Robert Steadman. **CABLE**

At Close Range 🦴🦴🦴 **1986 (R)** Based on the true story of Bruce Johnston Sr. and Jr. in Brandywine River Valley, Pennsylvania. Father, Walken, tempts his teenaged son, Penn, into pursuing criminal activities with talk of excitement and high living. Penn soon learns that his father is extremely dangerous and a bit unstable, but he's still fascinated by his wealth and power. Sometimes overbearing and depressing, but good acting and fancy camera work. A young cast of stars includes Masterson as the girl Penn tries to impress. Features Madonna's "Live to Tell." **115m/C VHS, DVD, Wide.** Sean Penn, Christopher Walken, Christopher Penn, Mary Stuart Masterson, Crispin Glover, Kiefer Sutherland, Candy Clark, Tracey Walter, Millie Perkins, Alan Autry, David Strathairn, Eileen Ryan; ***D:*** James Foley; ***W:*** Nicholas Kazan; ***C:*** Juan Ruiz-Anchia; ***M:*** Patrick Leonard.

At First Sight 🦴½ *Two Guys Talkin' About Girls* **1995 (R)** Yakky pedestrian comedy about schleppy Lenny (Silverman) and his best friend, macho Joey (Cortese), trying to help each other out with their romantic crises. Lenny meets cute when he picks up Rhonda (Smith) at the planetarium while Joey beds a string of girls, all of whom are named Cindy, in an effort to get over the first Cindy who broke his heart. It's been done before—and better. **90m/C VHS.** Jonathan Silverman, Dan Cortese, Allison Smith, Monte Markham, Kathleen Freeman; ***D:*** Steven Pearl; ***W:*** Ken Copel; ***C:*** Glenn Kershaw; ***M:*** Richard Gibbs.

At First Sight 🦴🦴½ **1998 (PG-13)** Slow-paced romantic drama stars Kilmer as a blind masseuse who falls for high-strung architect Sorvino. She persuades him to have an operation that restores his sight, and he's forced to adapt to a world he has never seen. Excellent supporting performances by McGillis as Kilmer's sister and Lane as the doctor that eases his transition. Kilmer does an outstanding job in making his character neither pitiful nor over-sentimental, which is rare in movies that center on disabilities. Based loosely on a case study by Dr. Oliver Sacks, whose work was also the basis for "Awakenings." **128m/C VHS, DVD.** Val Kilmer, Mira Sorvino, Kelly McGillis, Steven Weber, Bruce Davison, Nathan Lane, Ken Howard; ***D:*** Irwin Winkler; ***W:*** Steve Levitt; ***C:*** John Seale; ***M:*** Mark Isham.

At Gunpoint 🦴🦴 *Gunpoint* **1955** A store owner becomes the town hero when, by accident, he shoots and kills a bank robber. **81m/C VHS.** Fred MacMurray, Dorothy Malone, John Qualen, Walter Brennan; ***D:*** Alfred Werker; ***C:*** Ellsworth Fredericks.

At Gunpoint 🦴½ **1990** A no-account bank robber spends his six year stint in the slammer plotting his revenge. Having gone thoroughly stircrazy, the vengeful criminal stalks the lawman who put him away, like so many vengeful criminals before him. Run of the mill addition to big list of bad-guy-hunting-for-revenge flicks. **90m/C VHS.** Frank Kanig, Tain Bodkin, Scott Claflin; ***D:*** Steven Harris; ***W:*** Steven Harris.

At Home with the Webbers 🦴🦴 **1994 (R)** Gerald, Emma, Johnny, and Miranda Webber win a contest to star in a cable TV series about their lives. What they don't expect is that the series will become a hit or that all the family idosyncrasies will be exaggerated by stardom (the manipulative TV producer doesn't help). Over-the-top comedy requires tolerance but does have some amusing performances. **109m/C VHS.** Jeffrey Tambor, Rita Taggart, Jennifer Tilly, David Arquette, Robby Benson, Brian Bloom, Caroline Goodall; ***D:*** Brad (Sean) Marlowe; ***W:*** Brad (Sean) Marlowe.

At Midnight, I'll Take Your Soul 🦴 *A Meia-Noite Levarei Sua Alma* **1963** Brazilian import about sadistic gravedigger Coffin Joe (alter ego of director Jose Mojica Marins), who wanders the streets of his hometown in order to meet a desirable woman. His mission is to sire a son to continue his legacy and wiggle his lips at screaming women. A study in psycho-sexual horror, this makes "Apocalypse Now" look like a beach party. Coffin Joe, or "Ze do Caixao," is a kind of South American Freddy or Jason; Mojica Marin's movies—which are graphically sadistic—were banned by the Brazilian government. In Portugese with English subtitles. Followed by "Tonight I'll Be Incarnated in Your Corpse." **92m/B VHS.** *BR* Jose Mojica Marins, Magda Mei, Nivaldo de Lima; ***D:*** Jose Mojica Marins; ***W:*** Jose Mojica Marins; ***C:*** Giorgio Atilli.

At Play in the Fields of the Lord 🦴🦴🦴 **1991 (R)** A thoughtful epic that never quite lives up to its own self-importance—or length. Two yankee missionary couples try to evangelize a fearsome tribe of Brazilian rain-forest dwellers. One of the Christian families suffers a crisis of faith that's well-acted but not as powerful as a co-plot regarding a modern American Indian (Berenger) who joins the jungle natives with calamitous results. Based on the novel by Peter Matthiessen. **186m/C VHS.** Tom Berenger, Aidan Quinn, Kathy Bates, John Lithgow, Daryl Hannah, Tom Waits, Stenio Garcia, Nelson Xavier, Jose Dumont, Niilo Kivirinta; ***D:*** Hector Babenco; ***W:*** Hector Babenco, Jean-Claude Carriere; ***M:*** Zbigniew Preisner.

At Sword's Point 🦴🦴 *Sons of the Musketeers* **1951** Adventure tale based on characters from Alexandre Dumas's "The Three Musketeers," although the story is original. The French Queen (Cooper) is disturbed by sinister Duke Lavalle (Douglas) who wishes to marry Princess Henriette (Gates) and gain power to the throne. But the children of the four original musketeers come to her rescue, including swordswoman Claire (O'Hara). **81m/C VHS.** Cornel Wilde, Maureen O'Hara, Robert Douglas, Dan O'Herlihy, Alan Hale Jr., Blanche Yurka, Gladys Cooper, June Clayworth, Nancy Gates; ***D:*** Lewis Allen; ***W:*** Walter Ferris, Joseph Hoffman; ***C:*** Ray Rennahan; ***M:*** Roy Webb.

At the Circus 🦴🦴½ *The Marx Brothers at the Circus* **1939** Marx Brothers invade the circus to save it from bankruptcy and cause their usual comic insanity, though they've done it better before. Beginning of the end for the Marxes, a step down in quality from their classic work, though frequently darn funny. ♫Lydia the Tattooed Lady; Step Up and Take a Bow; Two Blind Loves; Blue Moon. **87m/B VHS.** Groucho Marx, Chico Marx, Harpo Marx, Margaret Dumont, Kenny L. Baker, Florence Rice, Eve Arden, Nat Pendleton, Fritz Feld, James Burke, Barnett Parker; ***D:*** Edward Buzzell; ***W:*** Irving Brecher; ***C:*** Leonard Smith; ***M:*** Harold Arlen.

At the Earth's Core 🦴🦴 **1976 (PG)** A Victorian scientist invents a giant burrowing machine, which he and his crew use to dig deeply into the Earth. To their surprise, they discover a lost world of subhuman creatures and prehistoric monsters. Based on Edgar Rice Burrough's novels. **90m/C VHS, DVD, Wide.** *GB* Doug McClure, Peter Cushing, Caroline Munro, Cy Grant, Godfrey James, Keith Barron; ***D:*** Kevin Connor; ***W:*** Milton Subotsky; ***C:*** Alan Hume; ***M:*** Michael Vickers.

At War with the Army 🦴🦴 **1950** Serviceable comedy from Martin and Lewis in their first starring appearance, as the recruits get mixed up in all kinds of wild situations at their army base. Based on the play by James Allardice. **93m/B VHS, DVD.** Dean Martin, Jerry Lewis, Polly Bergen, Mike Kellin; ***D:*** Hal Walker; ***W:*** Fred Finklehoffe; ***C:*** Stuart Thompson; ***M:*** Jerry Livingston.

Atalia 🦴🦴 **1985** Relates the love between Atalia, a war widow, and the younger man she loves. The problem stems from the fact that she lives in a Kibbutz, and the lifestyle contradicts sharply from that of her beliefs in love, forcing her to eventually make a momentous decision. **90m/C VHS.** Michal Bat-Adam, Yftach Katzur, Dan Toren; ***D:*** Akiva Tevet.

Athena 🦴🦴½ **1954** Two sisters (Powell and Reynolds) from an eccentric, health-faddist family fall in love with their opposites. Purdom is the stuffy Boston lawyer who goes off with Powell and Reynolds entices a TV crooner (Damone). Routine romance with routine songs. Reeves, who would become a star as a movie muscleman, appears in a brief role. ♫Love Can Change the Stars; The Girl Next Door; Imagine; Venezia; Chacun le Sait; I Never Felt Better; Vocalize. **96m/C VHS.** Jane Powell, Debbie Reynolds, Edmund Purdom, Vic Damone, Louis Calhern, Evelyn Varden, Linda Christian, Virginia Gibson, Nancy Kilgas, Dolores Starr, Jane Fischer, Cecile Rogers, Steve Reeves; ***D:*** Richard Thorpe; ***W:*** William Ludwig, Leonard Spigelgass; ***M:*** Hugh Martin, Ralph Blane.

Atlantic City 🦴🦴🦴½ *Atlantic City U.S.A* **1981 (R)** A small-time, aging Mafia hood falls in love with a young clam bar waitress, and they share the spoils of a big score against the backdrop of Atlantic City. Wonderful character study that becomes something more, a piercing declaration about a city's transformation and the effect on the people who live there. Lancaster, in a sterling performance, personifies the city, both of them fading with time. **104m/C VHS, DVD, Wide.** *FR CA* Burt Lancaster, Susan Sarandon, Kate Reid, Michel Piccoli, Hollis McLaren, Robert Joy, Al Waxman; ***D:*** Louis Malle; ***W:*** John Guare; ***C:*** Richard Ciupka; ***M:*** Michel Legrand. British Acad. '81: Actor (Lancaster), Director (Malle); Genie '81: Support. Actress (Reid); L.A. Film Critics '81: Actor (Lancaster), Film, Screenplay; N.Y. Film Critics '81: Actor (Lancaster), Screenplay; Natl. Soc. Film Critics '81: Actor (Lancaster), Director (Malle), Film, Screenplay.

Atlantis, the Lost Continent 🦴 **1961** If anything could sink the fabled lost continent of Atlantis it's this cheap fantasy flick. A greek sailor saves a princess and takes her back to her Atlantis home where he's promptly enslaved by the island's evil ruler. But this hero won't put up with any nonsense so he leads his fellow slaves in a revolt and gains his freedom before sinking both evil ruler and island (using atomic power no less!). **90m/C VHS.** *US* Anthony Hall, Joyce Taylor, John Dall, Bill Smith, Edward Platt, Frank De Kova; ***D:*** George Pal.

Atlantis: The Lost Empire 🦴🦴½ **2001 (PG)** Fast-paced and action-packed animated Disney adventure about inexperienced explorer Milo Thatch (Fox) who uses his grandfather's secret journals to discover the whereabouts of the submerged city of Atlantis. Submarine Captain Rourke (Garner) leads the expedition, but the eccentric and multi-ethnic crew are not entirely who or what they seem to be. Once found, the city holds a love interest (Summer) for Milo, and treasures to tempt the less benevolent members of the crew. The animation is old-fashioned and the plotting is reminiscent of adventure movies such as "Raiders of the Lost Ark" and "20,000 Leagues Under the Sea," but these should be considered merits instead of liabilities, especially if you're under 13 years old. **95m/C VHS, DVD, Wide.** ***D:*** Gary Trousdale, Kirk Wise; ***W:*** Tab Murphy; ***M:*** James Newton Howard; ***V:*** Michael J. Fox, James Garner, Claudia Christian, Cree Summer, John Mahoney, Leonard Nimoy, David Ogden Stiers, Jim Varney, Phil Morris, Don Novello, Florence Stanley, Corey Burton, Jacqueline Obradors.

Atlas 🦴 **1960** The mighty Atlas takes on massive armies, one of which includes director Corman, in a bid to win the hand of a princess. About as cheap as they come, although it is one of the few Sword & Sandal epics that isn't dubbed. **84m/C VHS.** Michael Forest, Frank Wolff, Barboura Morris, Walter Maslow, Christos Exarchos, Miranda Kounelaki, Theodore Dimitriou, Charles B. Griffith, Roger Corman, Dick Miller; ***D:*** Roger Corman; ***W:*** Charles B. Griffith; ***C:*** Basil Maros; ***M:*** Ronald Stein.

Atlas in the Land of the Cyclops woof! *Atlas Against the Cyclops; Maciste Nella Terra dei Ciclopi* **1961** Atlas takes on a hideous one-eyed monster to save a baby from an evil queen. Not a divorce custody drama. **100m/C VHS.** *IT* Mitchell Gordon, Chelo Alonso, Vira (Vera) Silenti; ***D:*** Antonio Leonviola.

Atom Age Vampire woof! *Seddok, l'Erede di Satana* **1961** Mad scientist doing research on Japanese nuclear bomb victims falls in love with a woman disfigured in an auto crash. To remove her scars, he treats her with a formula derived from the glands of freshly killed women. English dubbed. Not among the best of its kind (a low-rent district if ever there was one), but entertaining in a mischievous, boy-is-this-a-stupid-film sort of way. **71m/B VHS.** *IT* Alberto Lupo, Susanne Loret, Sergio Fantoni, Franca Parisi Strahl, Ivo Garrani, Andrea Scotti, Rina Franchetti; ***D:*** Anton Giulio Majano; ***W:*** Anton Giulio Majano, Alberto Bevilacqua, Gino De Santis; ***C:*** Aldo Giordani.

Atom Man vs. Superman **1950** Superman saves Metropolis from the machinations of his deadly foe, Atom Man, in this long-unseen second theatrical serial. Contains all 15 episodes on two tapes. **251m/B VHS.** Kirk Alyn, Lyle Talbot, Noel Neill, Tommy "Butch" Bond, Pierre Watkin; ***D:*** Spencer Gordon Bennet.

Atomic Attack 🦴 **1950** Nuclear bomb is dropped on New York City and a family living 50 miles away must escape. Gentlemen, start your engines. **50m/B VHS.** Walter Matthau.

The Atomic Brain woof! *Monstrosity* **1964** An old woman hires a doctor to transplant her brain into the body of a beautiful young girl. Of the three girls who are abducted, two become homicidal zombies and the third starts to act catty when she is given a feline brain. A must-see for bad-brain movie fans. **72m/B VHS.** Frank Gerstle, Erika Peters, Judy Bamber, Marjorie Eaton, Frank Fowler, Margie Fisco; ***D:*** Joseph Mascelli; ***W:*** Jack Pollexfen, Vivian Russell, Dean Dillman Jr., Sue Bradford.

The Atomic Cafe 🦴🦴🦴 **1982** A chillingly humorous compilation of newsreels and government films of the 1940s and '50s that show America's preoccupation with the A-Bomb. Some sequences are in black and white. Includes the infamous training film "Duck and Cover," which tells us what to do in the event of an actual bombing. **92m/C VHS, DVD.** ***D:*** Kevin Rafferty, Jayne Loader, Pierce Rafferty; ***M:*** Miklos Rozsa.

The Atomic City 🦴🦴½ **1952** Barry plays a nuclear physicist at Los Alamos whose son is kidnapped by terrorists who want his bomb-making formulas. The bad guys hide out in the nearby mountains which at least makes for some pleasant scenery in this average thriller. **84m/B VHS.** Gene Barry, Lee Aaker, Michael Moore, Lydia Clarke, Nancy Gates, Milburn Stone; ***D:*** Jerry Hopper.

Atomic Dog 🦴½ **1998 (PG-13)** The Yates family (Hugh-Kelly and Pickett) move to a new town near a nuclear power plant. Soon, the family dog is having puppies—only the sire turns out to be a radioactive hound who wants his offspring and he's a very determined doggie indeed. **86m/C VHS.** Daniel Hugh-Kelly, Isabella Hofmann, Cindy Pickett, Katie Stuart, Micah Gardner; ***D:*** Brian Trenchard-Smith; ***W:*** Miguel Tejada-Flores; ***C:*** David Lewis; ***M:*** Peter Bernstein. **CABLE**

The Atomic Kid 🦴½ **1954** A man survives an atomic blast because of a peanut butter sandwich he was eating. As a result, he himself becomes radioactive and discovers that he has acquired some strange new powers which get him into what pass for hilarious predicaments. **86m/B VHS.** Mickey Rooney, Robert Strauss, Elaine Davis, Bill Goodwin, Whit Bissell; ***D:*** Leslie Martinson; ***W:*** Blake Edwards; ***M:*** Van Alexander.

The Atomic Man 🦴½ *Timeslip* **1956** Owing to radioactive experimentation, a scientist exists for a short time in the future. Once there, both good and evil forces want to use him for their own purposes. **78m/B VHS.** *GB* Gene Nelson, Faith Domergue, Joseph Tomelty, Peter Arne; ***D:*** Ken Hughes.

Atomic Submarine 🦴🦴 **1959** Futuristic sci fi plots government agents against alien invaders. The battle, however, takes place in the ocean beneath the Arctic and is headed by an atomic-powered submarine clashing with a special alien underwater saucer. We all live on the atomic submarine: fun for devotees. **80m/C VHS, DVD.** Arthur Franz, Dick Foran, Bob Steele, Brett Halsey, Joi Lansing, Tom Conway, Paul Dubov; ***D:*** Spencer Gordon Bennet; ***W:*** Orville H. Hampton; ***C:*** Gilbert Warrenton; ***M:*** Alexander Laszlo.

Atomic Train 🦴½ **1999 (PG-13)** Silly two-part TV mini about a runaway train that's packed with toxic waste and a nuclear bomb, which is headed straight for Denver. Lowe (who makes a surprisingly good action hero) is National Transportation Safety Board investigator John Seger, who must derail the disaster. Meanwhile, the relentless media coverage has brought on widespread panic (those fiends!). **168m/C VHS, DVD.** Rob Lowe, Kristen Davis, Esai Morales, John Finn, Mena Suvari, Sean Smith, Edward Herrmann, Erik King, Blu Mankuma; ***D:*** Dick Lowry, David S. Jackson; ***C:*** Steven Fierberg; ***M:*** Lee Holdridge. **TV**

The Atonement of Gosta Berling 🦴🦴🦴 *Gosta Berling's Saga; The Legend of Gosta Berling; The Story of Gosta Berling; The Saga of Gosta Berling* **1924** A priest, forced to leave the priesthood because of his drinking, falls in love with a young married woman. Garbo shines in the first role which brought her critical acclaim; Hanson's performance also makes this a memorable drama. Adapted from the novel by Selma Lagerlof. **91m/B VHS.** *SW* Lars Hanson, Greta Garbo, Ellen Cederstrom, Mona Martenson, Jenny Hasselquist, Gerda Lundequist; ***D:*** Mauritz Stiller.

Ator the Fighting Eagle woof! **1983 (PG)** Styled after "Conan The Barbarian" this mythical action fantasy stars O'Keeffe as Ator, son of Thorn. Ator must put an end to the tragic Dynasty of the Spiders, thereby fulfilling the legend of his family at the expense of the viewer. Goofy low-budget sword and sandal stuff. D'Amato used the pseudonym David Hills. Followed by "The Blade Master." **98m/C VHS.** *IT* Miles O'Keeffe, Sabrina Siani, Ritza Brown, Edmund Purdom, Laura Gemser; ***D:*** Joe D'Amato.

Attack! 🦴🦴🦴 **1956** Cowardly Captain Cooney (Albert) is order to move one of his platoons into a forward position in 1944 Belgium. They are slowly surrounded by the enemy as platoon leader, Lt. Costa (Palance), calls headquarters for reinforcements. But Cooney won't commit his reserves even as the platoon is decimated. Expert portrayals of men under pressure. **107m/B VHS.** Eddie Albert, Jack Palance, Lee Marvin, Robert Strauss, Richard Jaeckel, Buddy Ebsen, William (Bill) Smithers, Strother Martin; ***D:*** Robert Aldrich; ***W:*** James Poe; ***C:*** Joseph Biroc; ***M:*** Frank DeVol.

Attack Force Z 🦴🦴 **1984** An elite corps of Australian military is Force Z. Volunteers are chosen for a dangerous mission: find the plane that crashed somewhere in the South Pacific and rescue the defecting Japanese government official on board, all before the end of WWII and the feature. Talented cast is effectively directed in low-key adventure featuring young Gibson. **84m/C VHS.** *AU* Sam Neill, Chris Haywood, Mel Gibson, John Phillip Law, John Waters; ***D:*** Tim Burstall.

Attack from Mars 🦴🦴½ *Midnight Movie Massacre* **1988** Retro splatterama has really gross vampire alien land outside a Burbank movie theatre in 1956, and the really weird movie patrons try to terminate it. **86m/C VHS, DVD.** Robert Clarke, Ann (Robin) Robinson; ***D:*** Mark Stock; ***W:*** Mark Stock, David Houston.

Attack of the Beast Creatures woof! **1985** The survivors of a wrecked ocean liner are stranded on a desert island overrun by savage creatures. This makes them anxious. **82m/C VHS.** Robert Nolfi, Robert Langyel, Julia Rust, Lisa Pak; ***D:*** Michael Stanley.

Attack of the 50 Foot Woman 🦴🦴½ **1958** A beautiful, abused housewife has a frightening encounter with a giant alien, causing her to grow to an enormous height. Then she goes looking for hubby. Perhaps the all-time classic '50s sci fi, a truly fun movie highlighted by the sexy, 50-foot Hayes in a giant bikini. Has intriguing psychological depth and social commentary done in a suitably cheezy manner. **72m/B VHS.** Allison Hayes, William (Bill) Hudson, Roy Gordon, Yvette Vickers, George Douglas, Ken Terrell, Michael Ross, Frank Chase, Eileen Stevens, Otto Waldis; ***D:*** Nathan (Hertz) Juran; ***W:*** Mark Hanna; ***C:*** Jacques "Jack" Marquette; ***M:*** Ronald Stein.

Attack of the 50 Ft. Woman 🦴🦴½ **1993** Campy remake of the 1958 sci-fi cult classic features the statuesque Hannah in the title role. Nancy's a put-upon hausfrau with zero self-esteem thanks to her domineering father (Windom) and loutish hubby (Baldwin). They should have been sweet to her because after an encounter with a flying saucer Nancy starts to grow...and grow...and grow. And then she decides to get some revenge. **90m/C VHS.** Daryl Hannah, Daniel Baldwin, William Windom, Frances Fisher, Cristi Conaway, Paul Benedict, Lewis Arquette, Xander Berkeley, Hamilton Camp, Richard Edson, Victoria Haas, O'Neal Compton; ***D:*** Christopher Guest; ***W:*** Joseph Dougherty; ***M:*** Nicholas Pike. **TV**

Attack of the Giant Leeches 🦴 *The Giant Leeches; She Demons of the Swamp; Demons of the Swamp* **1959** Cheapo Corman fare about giant leeches in a murky swamp who suddenly decide to make human flesh their new food supply. Perturbed inn keeper plays along by forcing his wife and lover into the murk. Leeches frolic. Sometimes tedious, sometimes chilling, always low budget and slimy. Although the special effects aren't top notch, this might be a fine choice for a late night scare/laugh. **62m/B VHS, DVD.** Kenneth (Ken) Clark, Yvette Vickers, Gene Roth, Bruno VeSota, Michael Emmet, Tyler McVey, Jan Shepard, George Cisar, Dan(iel) White; ***D:*** Bernard L. Kowalski; ***W:*** Leo Gordon; ***C:*** John M. Nickolaus Jr.; ***M:*** Alexander Laszlo.

Attack of the Killer Refrigerator woof! **1990** Chiller featuring a group of sleazy college students having a wild party. In the process, they abuse a hapless refrigerator. Fed up, the vengeful appliance goes on a rampage of murder and destruction. Certain to make you view kitchen appliances in a new light. Planned sequels in the newfound kitchen-utility horror genre include "Refrigerator II: Brutally Defrosted" and "Bloody, Bloody Coffee Maker." **?m/C VHS.**

Attack of the Killer Tomatoes woof! **1977 (PG)** Candidate for worst film ever made, deliberate category. Horror spoof that defined "low budget" stars several thousand ordinary tomatoes that suddenly turn savage and begin attacking people. No sci-fi cliche remains untouched in this dumb parody. A few musical numbers are performed in lieu of an actual plot. Followed by "Return of the Killer Tomatoes." Originally released at 87 minutes. **87m/C VHS.** George Wilson, Jack Riley, Rock Peace, Eric Christmas, David Miller, Sharon Taylor, Jerry Anderson, Nigel Barber, John DeBello; ***D:*** John DeBello; ***W:*** Costa Dillon, John DeBello; ***C:*** John K. Culley.

Attack of the Mayan Mummy woof! **1963** A greedy doctor gets his patient to channel her former self so that she can show him where to find an ancient tomb that is filled with treasure. Good idea. **77m/B VHS.** *MX* Richard Webb, Nina Knight, Norman Burton, Steve Conte; ***D:*** Jerry Warren.

Attack of the Mushroom People 🦴🦴 *Matango; Fungus of Terror; Curse of the Mushroom People* **1963** Secluded island is the site where people eating mysterious mushrooms have been turning into oversized, killer 'shrooms' themselves. Trouble is, the only witness to this madness has gone insane. Will anyone believe him before it's too late? **70m/B VHS.** *JP* Akira Kubo, Kenji Sahara, Yoshio Tsuchiya, Hiroshi Koizumi, Kumi Mizuno, Miki Yashiro, Eisei Amamoto, Hiroshi Tachikawa; ***D:*** Inoshiro Honda; ***W:*** Takeshi Kimura; ***C:*** Hajime Koizumi.

Attack of the Puppet People 🦴🦴 *Six Inches Tall* **1958** This alternative classic from the prolific Bert I. Gordon, a rival to Ed Wood Jr. in the schlock hall of fame, will not make anyone forget "The Incredible Shrinking Man." The insane dollmaker Dr. Franz (Hoyt) shrinks six people (including our heroes Agar and Kenny) to the size of Ken and Barbie. Can they escape the mad scientist? The dog? The rat? The effects are nostalgically charming. **79m/B DVD.** John Agar, John Hoyt, June Kenney, Sally Reynolds, Susan Gordon; ***D:*** Bert I. Gordon; ***W:*** George Worthing Yates; ***C:*** Ernest Laszlo; ***M:*** Albert Glasser.

Attack of the Robots 🦴½ *Cartes sur Table* **1966** Silly spy spoof about powerful government officials who are being killed off by a mad scientist's robots. Interpol agent Lemmy Caution comes to the rescue. **88m/B VHS.** *FR SP* Eddie Constantine, Fernando Rey; ***D:*** Jess (Jesus) Franco; ***W:*** Jean-Claude Carriere.

Attack of the 60-Foot Centerfold 🦴½ **1995 (R)** Angel Grace wants to be Centerfold of the Year so badly that she gets a doctor to enhance her endowments even more through a mystery formula. Only there's a little complication. Cheesy, with pretty women and no discernable acting (and a spoof of that '58 gem "Attack of the 50 Ft. Woman"). **83m/C VHS, DVD.** J.J. North, Tammy Parks, John Lazar, Russ Tamblyn, Tommy Kirk, Stanley Livingston, Michelle (McClellan) Bauer, George Stover, Forrest J Ackerman, Ted Monte, Jim Wynorski, Raelyn Saalman, Tim Abell, Jay Richardson, Nikki Fritz; ***D:*** Fred Olen Ray; ***W:*** Steve Armogida; ***C:*** Gary Graver, Howard Wexler; ***M:*** Jeff Walton.

Attack of the Swamp Creature woof! *Blood Waters of Dr. Z; Zaat; The Legend of the Zaat Monster; Hydra* **1975** A deranged scientist transforms himself into a swamp critter and terrorizes a small town. **96m/C VHS.** Marshall Grauer, Nancy Lien, Paul Galloway, Wade Popwell, Frank Crowell, David Robertson, Doug Thomas; ***D:*** Don Barton, Arnold Stevens; ***W:*** Lee Larew, Ron Kivett.

Attack Squadron 🦴½ *Kamakazi* **1963** Story of Japan's suicidal WWII pilots. **105m/C VHS.** *JP* Toshiro Mifune.

Attention Shoppers 🦴🦴 **1999 (R)** Latin sitcom heartthrob Carbonell angers his wife and threatens his hunk status during a K-Mart publicity appearance in Houston that's taken over by his rival, soap star Perry. **87m/C VHS, DVD.** Nestor Carbonell, Luke Perry, Martin Mull, Kathy Najimy, Michael Lerner, Cara Buono, Lin Shaye, Casey Affleck; ***D:*** Philip Charles MacKenzie; ***W:*** Nestor Carbonell. **VIDEO**

The Attic 🦴🦴½ **1980 (R)** Psychodrama about an overbearing invalid father and his insecure and unmarried daughter. The girl learns to escape her unhappy life by hiding in the attic. Not horrifying, but a clear analytical look into the game of control. **92m/C VHS.** Carrie Snodgress, Ray Milland, Rosemary Murphy, Ruth Cox, Frances Bay, Marjorie Eaton; ***D:*** George Edwards.

The Attic: The Hiding of Anne Frank 🦴🦴½ **1988** Steenburgen is wonderful in the true story of Miep Gies, the Dutch woman who hid Otto Frank, her employer, and his family from the Nazis. Unusual because it is told from Gies's perspective, rather than from the more familiar Anne Frank story. Based on Gies's book, "Anne Frank Remembered." **95m/C VHS.** Mary Steenburgen, Paul Scofield,

Huub Stapel, Eleanor Bron, Miriam Karlin, Lisa Jacobs, Ronald Pickup; *D:* John Erman; *W:* William Hanley; *M:* Richard Rodney Bennett. TV

Attica 1980 Tense depiction of the infamous Attica prison takeover in 1971 and the subsequent bloodbath as state troops were called in. Although edited due to the searing commentary by Nelson Rockefeller, it remains powerful and thought-provoking. Adapted from the Tom Wicker bestseller "A Time to Die." **97m/C VHS.** George Grizzard, Charles Durning, Anthony Zerbe, Roger E. Mosley; *D:* Marvin J. Chomsky. TV

Attila ½ 2001 Epic miniseries takes on the life of Attila the Hun. Early years of Attila are swiftly dealt with as his family is slaughtered and the boy is raised by his uncle—with his cousin as his rival for leadership. The adult Attila (Butler) is tough, charismatic, and bloodthirsty enough to unite the Hun tribes and challenge the domination of the Roman empire, which leads to the politically savvy Roman general Flavius Aetius (Boothe) being dispatched to get Attila on Rome's side. Lots of big battles as this part of history is treacherous indeed. **177m/C VHS, DVD, Wide.** Gerard Butler, Powers Boothe, Alice Krige, Simmone Jade MacKinnon, Tim Curry, Reg Rogers, Steven Berkoff, Tommy Flanagan, Pauline Lynch, Liam Cunningham, Jolyon Baker, Sian Phillips, Jonathan Hyde; *D:* Dick Lowry; *W:* Robert Cochran; *C:* Steven Fierberg; *M:* Nick Glennie-Smith. CABLE

Au Revoir les Enfants *Goodbye, Children* **1987 (PG)** During the Nazi occupation of France in the 1940s, the headmaster of a Catholic boarding school hides three Jewish boys among the other students by altering their names and identities. Two of the students, Julien (Manesse) and Jean (Fejto), form a friendship that ends tragically when Jean and the other boys are discovered and taken away by the Gestapo. Compelling and emotionally wrenching coming of age tale based on an incident from director Malle's childhood is considered to be his best film to date and quite possibly the best he will ever make. In French with English subtitles. Other 1987 movies with similar themes are "Hope and Glory" and "Empire of the Sun." **104m/C VHS.** *FR GE* Gaspard Manesse, Raphael Fejto, Francine Racette, Stanislas Carre de Malberg, Philippe Morier-Genoud, Francois Berleand, Peter Fitz, Francois Negret, Irene Jacob, Pascal Rivet, Benoit Henriet, Richard Leboeuf, Xavier Legrand, Arnaud Henriet, Jean-Sebastien Chauvin, Luc Etienne; *D:* Louis Malle; *W:* Louis Malle; *C:* Renato Berta. British Acad. '88: Director (Malle); Cesar '88: Art Dir./Set Dec., Cinematog., Director (Malle), Film, Sound, Writing; L.A. Film Critics '87: Foreign Film; Venice Film Fest. '87: Film.

The Audrey Hepburn Story 2000 (PG) When you play a movie icon, expect the critical brickbats to fly. Sweet Hewitt does her best in the title role (Hepburn's her longtime idol) but it's all surface gloss. Bio covers 1935 to 1960 as Hepburn deals with family crises (dad's a two-timing Nazi sympathizer who abandons his family), war years in Nazi-occupied Holland, Hepburn's beginnings as a dancer in England and her first small roles. Then it's onto New York and the world of theater and films. Along the way there's a little romance, a marriage to actor Mel Ferrer (McCormack), and various re-creations of some Hepburn movie roles. **133m/C VHS, DVD, Wide.** Jennifer Love Hewitt, Eric McCormack, Frances Fisher, Peter Giles, Keir Dullea, Gabriel Macht, Marcel Jeannin, Swede Svensson, Michael J. Burg, Ryan Hollyman; *D:* Steve Robman; *W:* Marsha Norman; *C:* Pierre Letarte; *M:* Lawrence Shragge. TV

Audrey Rose 1977 (PG) Parents of a young girl are terrified when their darling daughter is having dreadful dreams. Mysterious friend Hopkins cements their fears when he declares that his dead daughter has been reincarnated in their child. The nightmares continue suggesting that none other than Lucifer could be at work. Good cast is hampered by slow-moving take-off on "The Exorcist" with a weak staged ending. Adapted by DeFelitta from his novel. **113m/C VHS, DVD, Wide.** Marsha Mason, Anthony Hopkins, John Beck, John Hillerman, Susan Swift, Norman Lloyd; *D:* Robert Wise; *W:* Frank De Felitta; *C:* Victor Kemper.

August ½ 1995 (PG) Yet another version of Chekov's "Uncle Vanya," this time transported to 1890s Wales. Hopkins (who makes his directorial debut and composed the score) stars as Ieuan Davies, a bitter drinker who manages the estate of brother-in-law Alexander Blathwaite (Phillips). Blathwaite arrives for his annual summer stay with unhappy, young second wife Helen (Burton), who's the object of desire for both Ieuan and the local doctor, Michael Lloyd (Grainger). It's a perfectedly adequate rendition but offers little that's new except a change of scenery. **93m/C VHS.** *GB* Anthony Hopkins, Kate Burton, Leslie Phillips, Gawn Grainger, Rhian Morgan, Hugh Lloyd, Rhoda Lewis, Menna Tussler; *D:* Anthony Hopkins; *W:* Julian Mitchell; *C:* Robin Vidgeon; *M:* Anthony Hopkins.

Augustin 1995 Very short comedy about aspiring actor Augustin (Sibertin-Blanc), who may just get his break when he hears about a part for a room-service waiter and prepares himself rigorously by actually getting a job in a Paris hotel. Pathetically earnest and dignified, at the actual audition he bewilders actor Lhermitte, when instead of just reading the scene, Augustin proceeds to act it out in detail. Very slight but charming thanks to a deadpan performance by Sibertin-Blanc (who's also director Fontaine's brother). French with subtitles. **61m/C VHS.** *FR* Jean-Chretien Sibertin-Blanc, Thierry Lhermitte, Stephanie Zhang, Nora Habib, Guy Casabonne; *D:* Anne Fontaine; *W:* Anne Fontaine; *C:* Jean-Marie Dreujou.

Augustine of Hippo *Agostino di Ippona* **1972** One of Rossellini's later historical epics, depicting the last years of St. Augustine and how they exemplify the growing conflicts between Church and State, Christian ethic and societal necessity. In Italian with subtitles. **120m/C VHS.** *IT D:* Roberto Rossellini.

Auntie Lee's Meat Pies ½ 1992 (R) Auntie Lee's meat pie business is booming thanks to her five beautiful nieces. They help keep their aunt supplied with the secret ingredient—gorgeous young men! Four Playboy Playmates are featured in this cannibalistic horror comedy. **100m/C VHS.** Karen Black, Noriyuki "Pat" Morita, Pat Paulsen, Huntz Hall, Michael Berryman, David Parry, Stephen Quadros, Ava Fabian, Teri Weigel; *D:* Joseph F. Robertson; *W:* Joseph F. Robertson; *C:* Arledge Armenaki.

Auntie Mame 1958 A young boy is brought up by his only surviving relative—flamboyant and eccentric Auntie Mame. Mame is positive that "life is a banquet and most poor suckers are starving to death." Based on the Patrick Dennis novel about his life with "Auntie Mame." Part of the "A Night at the Movies" series, this tape simulates a 1958 movie evening, with a Road Runner cartoon, "Hook, Line and Stinker," a newsreel and coming attractions for "No Time for Sergeants" and "Chase a Crooked Shadow." **161m/C VHS, Wide.** Rosalind Russell, Patric Knowles, Roger Smith, Peggy Cass, Forrest Tucker, Coral Browne; *D:* Morton DaCosta; *W:* Betty Comden, Adolph Green; *C:* Harry Stradling Sr. Golden Globes '59: Actress—Mus./Comedy (Russell).

Aurora ½ *Aurora by Night; Qualcosa di Biondo* **1984** Single mom Aurora (Loren) will do anything for her blind son Ciro (played by Loren's son Edoardo Ponti). When she discovers that there's a possible operation that could restore his sight, Aurora decides to call up all Ciro's possible fathers and get them to finance the surgery. This plan also reunites Aurora with the one man she truly loved. Made for Italian TV. **91m/C VHS.** *IT* Sophia Loren, Daniel J. Travanti, Ricky Tognazzi, Philippe Noiret, Anna Strasberg, Franco Fabrizi; *D:* Maurizio Ponzi; *M:* Georges Delerue. TV

The Aurora Encounter 1985 (PG) Aliens surreptitiously infiltrate a small town in 1897, and spread benevolence everywhere. Family fare. **90m/C VHS.** Jack Elam, Peter Brown, Carol Bagdasarian, Dottie West, George "Spanky" McFarland; *D:* Jim McCullough.

Austin Powers: International Man of Mystery 1997 (PG-13) Hilarious spoof of '60s spy and babe movies. Groovy '60s spy Austin Powers (Myers) discovers that his arch-enemy, Dr. Evil (Myers again) has frozen himself in order to elude capture, so the swingin' dentally challenged Brit decides to do the same. They awaken 30 years later in the same state: woefully out of touch. Dr. Evil is attempting to blackmail the British government and deal with his Gen-X son, Scott Evil (Green), who wants more quality time and less world conquest. Austin, on the other hand, is trying to "shag" every "groovy bird" he sees. He is teamed with Vanessa (Hurley), the daughter of his former partner, and they try to stop the evil machinations of...well..Evil. A festival of crushed velvet, political incorrectness, and female robots with lethal breasts. Myers revels in playing the fool, and he may step over the line every once in a while, but he gets plenty of mileage out of the one-joke premise. **88m/C VHS, DVD.** Mike Myers, Elizabeth Hurley, Michael York, Seth Green, Mimi Rogers, Robert Wagner, Fabiana Udenio, Paul Dillon, Charles Napier, Will Ferrell, Mindy Sterling; *Cameos:* Tom Arnold, Carrie Fisher; *D:* Jay Roach; *W:* Mike Myers; *C:* Peter Deming; *M:* George S. Clinton. MTV Movie Awards '98: Villain (Myers), Dance Seq. (Mike Myers/Londoners).

Austin Powers 2: The Spy Who Shagged Me 1999 (PG-13) Old snaggle-tooth (Myers) returns and time travels back to 1969 in order to foil his look-alike nemesis, Dr. Evil, who steals Powers' mojo. Myers wisely highlights the not-so-good Dr., along with some hilarious new characters, instead of the periodically wearisome Powers. Again plot takes a back seat to the great dialogue, characters (including Rob Lowe doing a dead-on Robert Wagner and a third Myers incarnation, Fat Bastard), and kitchy eye candy. It all still works because of Myers' winking good nature. **95m/C VHS, DVD.** Muse Watson, Burt Bacharach, Elvis Costello, Mike Myers, Heather Graham, Elizabeth Hurley, Seth Green, Robert Wagner, Rob Lowe, Verne Troyer, Kristen Johnston, Mindy Sterling, Gia Carides, Clint Howard, Michael York, Will Ferrell, Woody Harrelson, Charles Napier, Willie Nelson, Tim Robbins, Jerry Springer, Fred Willard, Rebecca Romijn-Stamos, Jack Kehler; *D:* Jay Roach; *W:* Michael McCullers, Mike Myers; *C:* Ueli Steiger; *M:* George S. Clinton. MTV Movie Awards '00: On-Screen Duo (Mike Myers/Verne Troyer), Villain (Myers).

Austin Powers In Goldmember 2002 Myers takes on numerous roles in this continuing franchise—besides Powers and Dr. Evil, he plays their teen personas in the '50s, reprises Fat Bastard, and adds baddie Goldmember to his repertoire. Also aboard: Troyer as Mini-Me, Caine as Powers' secret agent dad Nigel, Knowles as undercover spy Foxxy Cleopatra (did we mention that Austin time-travels to the '70s?), and Green as Scott Evil. Bond studio MGM raised a stink about the title (too close to "Goldfinger") but finally saw the light and allow the parody to continue. Not yet reviewed. **?m/C VHS, DVD.** Mike Myers, Michael Caine, Seth Green, Beyonce Knowles, Verne Troyer, Michael York; *D:* Jay Roach; *W:* Mike Myers, Michael McCullers.

Author! Author! ½ 1982 (PG) Sweet, likable comedy about playwright Pacino who is about to taste success with his first big hit. Suddenly his wife walks out, leaving him to care for her four children and his own son. His views shift as he begins to worry about, among other things, who will watch the obnoxious kids on opening night. **100m/C VHS.** Al Pacino, Tuesday Weld, Dyan Cannon, Alan King, Andre Gregory; *D:* Arthur Hiller; *W:* Israel Horovitz; *M:* Dave Grusin.

Autobiography of a Princess 1975 A brief character study shot by Merchant-Ivory in six days. An East Indian princess, living in self-enforced exile in London, invites her father's former tutor to tea. They watch old movie footage of royal India together and dream of a happier past. **59m/C VHS.** James Mason, Madhur Jaffrey; *D:* James Ivory; *W:* Ruth Prawer Jhabvala.

The Autobiography of Miss Jane Pittman ½ 1974 The history of blacks in the South is seen through the eyes of a 110-year-old former slave. From the Civil War through the Civil Rights movement, Miss Pittman relates every piece of black history, allowing the viewer to experience the injustices. Tyson is spectacular in moving, highly acclaimed drama. Received nine Emmy awards; adapted by Tracy Keenan Wynn from the novel by Ernest J. Gaines. **110m/C VHS, DVD.** Cicely Tyson, Odetta, Joseph Tremice, Richard Dysart, Michael Murphy, Katherine Helmond; *D:* John Korty; *W:* Tracy Keenan Wynn; *C:* James A. Crabe; *M:* Fred Karlin. TV

Automatic ½ 1994 (R) Renegade RobGen Industries android Gruner saves Ashbrook from the loathsome sexual advances of the boss but kills the scum in the process. So the duo are targeted for death by company head Glover with killers, led by Kober, sent to do the mopping up. **90m/C VHS.** Olivier Gruner, Daphne Ashbrook, John Glover, Jeff Kober, Dennis Lipscomb; *D:* John Murlowski; *W:* Susan Lambert, Patrick Highsmith.

Autopsy ½ 1974 (R) Forensic pathologist Farmer is working at a morgue compiling statistics concerning suicides and murders staged to look like suicides. Farmer begins to go nuts when it seems a stalker is killing people around her using the fake suicide method. Then there's the fact that the pathological pathologist is also sexually repressed and everything and everyone starts to scream sex to her and things get really kinky (and gory). **100m/C VHS, DVD.** *IT* Mimsy Farmer, Barry Primus, Angela Goodwin, Ray Lovelock; *D:* Armando Crispino; *W:* Armando Crispino, Lucio Battistrada; *C:* Carlo Carlini; *M:* Ennio Morricone.

Autopsy 197? A young gold-digger and a millionaire marry, and then cheat on each other, provoking blackmail and murder. **90m/C VHS, DVD.** Fernando Rey, Gloria Grahame, Christian Hay.

Autopsy of a Ghost ½ *Autopsia de un Fantasma* **1967** Comedy/horror film stars Rathbone as a ghost and Mitchell as a mad scientist. Notable as Rathbone's last screen appearance. In Spanish with no subtitles. **110m/C VHS.** *SP* Basil Rathbone, John Carradine, Cameron Mitchell, Amadee Chabot; *D:* Ismael Rodriguez; *W:* Armando Crispino, Lucio Battistrada.

An Autumn Afternoon ½ *Sanma No Aji* **1962** Ozu's final film is a beautiful expression of his talent. In postwar Tokyo, an aging widower loses his only daughter to marriage and begins a life of loneliness. A heart-wrenching tale of relationships and loss. In Japanese with English subtitles. **112m/C VHS.** *JP* Chishu Ryu, Shima Iwashita, Shin-Ichiro Mikami, Mariko Okada, Keiji Sada; *D:* Yasujiro Ozu; *W:* Yasujiro Ozu; *C:* Yushun Atsuta; *M:* Kojun Saito.

Autumn Born ½ 1979 (R) Young heiress is abducted by her guardian and imprisoned while she's taught to obey his will. Ill-fated ex-Playmate Dorothy Stratton's first film. **76m/C VHS.** Dorothy Stratten, Ihor Procak, Dory Jackson, Gisselle Fredette, Nate MacIntosh, Joanna McClelland Glass, Roberta Weiss, Roman Buchok, Sharon Elder; *D:* Lloyd A. Simandl; *W:* Sharon Christensen, Shannon Lee, Ihor Procak; *C:* Lloyd A. Simandl.

Autumn in New York ½ 2000 (PG-13) Start with one clunky love story with no chemistry, then mix in cheesy melodrama and a dash of creepy Freudian undertones and what do you get? This recipe for disaster about a doomed May-December romance. Middle-aged Will Keane (Gere) leads a playboy's life as the owner of one of New York's most fashionable restaurants. He falls for much younger sensitive gal Charlotte (Ryder) after finding out that he dated her mother. Unfortunately, Charlotte is afflicted with a life-threatening disease whose symptoms include saying "Wow!" a lot and fainting at overly dramatic moments. Will's life is changed, and he rushes around trying to find some medical miracle or plot device which might be able to save her. Rent "Love Story" instead. Because love means never having to say you're sorry you wasted two hours of your life on this movie. **104m/C VHS, DVD, Wide.** Richard Gere, Winona Ryder, Anthony LaPaglia, Elaine Stritch, Vera Farmiga, Sherry Stringfield, Jill(ian) Hennessey; ***D:*** Joan Chen; ***W:*** Allison Burnett; ***C:*** Changwei Gu; ***M:*** Gabriel Yared.

Autumn Leaves 🦴🦴½ **1956** Crawford plays a middle-aged typist grasping at her last chance for love. She marries a younger man who's been romancing her, then finds him more and more unstable and violent. Weak story material that could turn melodramatic and tawdry, but doesn't because of Crawford's strength. **108m/B VHS.** Cliff Robertson, Joan Crawford, Vera Miles, Lorne Greene; ***D:*** Robert Aldrich; ***W:*** Robert Blees, Lewis Meltzer, Hugo Butler, Jean Rouverol; ***C:*** Charles B(ryant) Lang Jr. Berlin Intl. Film Fest. '56: Director (Aldrich).

Autumn Marathon 🦴🦴½ *Osenny Marafon* **1979** To say that this is one of the better Russian movies of the past three decades is sort of faint praise, given the state of Soviet cinema. Written by playwright Volodin, it's just another paint-by-number version of the philandering man who's really an OK Joe who loves his kids comedy. In Russian with English subtitles. **100m/C VHS.** *RU* Oleg Basilashvili, Natalia Gundareva, Marina Neyelova; ***D:*** Georgi Daniela; ***W:*** Alexander Volodin.

Autumn Moon 🦴🦴 *Qiuyue* **1992** Young Japanese tourist (Nagase) travels to Hong Kong to enjoy some sexual fun but instead he befriends a 15-year-old girl (Wai), who's afraid of her family's impending emigration to Canada. Not much happens but the Hong Kong setting is eye-catching. English and Cantonese with subtitles. **108m/C VHS.** *HK* Masatoshi Nagase, Li Pui Wai; ***D:*** Clara Law; ***C:*** Tony Leung Siu Hung.

Autumn Sonata 🦴🦴🦴 *Hostsonaten* **1978** Nordic family strife as famed concert pianist Bergman is reunited with a daughter she has not seen in years. Bergman's other daughter suffers from a degenerative nerve disease and had been institutionalized until her sister brought her home. Now the three women settle old scores, and balance the needs of their family. Excellent performance by Bergman in her last feature film. **97m/C VHS, DVD.** *SW* Ingrid Bergman, Liv Ullmann, Halvar Bjork, Lena Nyman, Gunnar Bjornstrand, Erland Josephson; ***D:*** Ingmar Bergman; ***W:*** Ingmar Bergman; ***C:*** Sven Nykvist. Golden Globes '79: Foreign Film; Natl. Bd. of Review '78: Actress (Bergman), Director (Bergman); N.Y. Film Critics '78: Actress (Bergman); Natl. Soc. Film Critics '78: Actress (Bergman).

Autumn Sun 🦴🦴🦴 *Solo de Otono* **1998** This is a love story for appreciative adults. Clara (Aleandro) is a middleaged Buenos Aires accountant whose personal ad for a Jewish gentleman caller is answered by older widower (and non-Jew) Raul Ferraro (Luppi). Still, they're attracted to each other, and since Clara needs a man to pose as her admirer for a visit from her long-absent brother, Raul agrees to the ruse and undergoes a crash course in Jewish customs. This isn't actually played for laughs but as a reflection on expanding one's horizons and taking chances. Spanish with subtitles. **103m/C VHS, DVD.** *AR* Norma Aleandro, Federico Luppi, Jorge Luz, Cecilia Rossetto; ***D:*** Eduardo Mignogna; ***W:*** Eduardo Mignogna, Santiago Carlos Oves; ***C:*** Marcelo Camorino; ***M:*** Edgardo Rudnitzky.

Autumn Tale 🦴🦴½ *Conte d'Automne* **1998 (PG)** Middleaged, widowed winegrower Magali (Romand) is lonely now that her children are grown, so her best friend Isabelle (Riviere) secretly places a personal ad and decides to meet the respondents herself in order to find someone suitable for her friend. Isabelle decides saleman Gerald (Libolt) is a likely prospect and schemes to introduce them. Meanwhile, Rosine (Portal), the live-wire girlfriend of Magali's son Leo (Darmon), thinks that her older philosophy professor (and ex-lover), Etienne (Sandre), might be a match. Magali is simply mortified by the entire situation. The fourth film in Rohmer's "Tales of the Four Seasons." French with subtitles. **110m/C VHS.** *FR* Beatrice Romand, Marie Riviere, Alexia Portal, Alain Libolt, Didier Sandre, Stephane Darmon; ***D:*** Eric Rohmer; ***W:*** Eric Rohmer; ***C:*** Diane Baratier; ***M:*** Claude Marti. Natl. Soc. Film Critics '99: Foreign Film.

Avalanche 🦴½ **1978 (PG)** Disasterama as vacationers at a new winter ski resort find themselves at the mercy of a monster avalanche leaving a so-called path of terror and destruction in its wake. Talented cast is buried by weak material, producing a snow-bound adventure yawn. **91m/C VHS, DVD.** Rock Hudson, Mia Farrow, Robert Forster, Rick Moses; ***D:*** Corey Allen; ***W:*** Corey Allen; ***C:*** Pierre William Glenn; ***M:*** William Kraft.

Avalanche 🦴½ **1999 (PG-13)** Prototypical cheesy disaster flic. Alaskan chopper pilot Neil (Griffith) helps out Lia (Feeney), the widow of an old pal, who works for the EPA. She believes the establishment of an oil company's overland pipeline through the mountains will trigger an avalanche that could destroy the city of Juneau. Naturally, no one believes her until there's an avalanche. (Considering the movie's title, you could have guessed this.) **105m/C VHS.** Thomas Ian Griffith, Caroleen Feeney, R. Lee Ermey, C. Thomas Howell, John Ashton, Hilary Shepard; ***D:*** Steve Kroschel; ***W:*** Steve Kroschel; ***C:*** Steve Kroschel, Richard Pepin; ***M:*** Alex Wilkinson.

Avalanche Express 🦴 **1979 (PG)** Marvin is a CIA agent who uses a defector (Shaw) to lure a scientist (Schell), specializing in biological warfare, aboard a European train. Marvin wants to eliminate Schell but all plans go awry when the snow begins to fall. Ineffective thriller. Director Robson's and actor Shaw's last film—much of Shaw's dialogue was dubbed due to his death before the film's soundtrack was completed. Based on a novel by Colin Forbes. **89m/C VHS.** Lee Marvin, Robert Shaw, Maximilian Schell, Linda Evans, Mike Connors, Joe Namath, Horst Buchholz, David A(lexander) Hess; ***D:*** Mark Robson; ***W:*** Abraham Polonsky; ***C:*** Jack Cardiff.

Avalon 🦴🦴🦴 **1990 (PG)** Powerful but quiet portrait of the break-up of the family unit as seen from the perspective of a Russian family settled in Baltimore at the close of WWII. Initally, the family is unified in their goals, ideologies, and social lives. Gradually, all of this disintegrates; members move to the suburbs and TV replaces conversation at holiday gatherings. Levinson based his film on experiences within his own family of Russian Jewish immigrants. **126m/C VHS, DVD, 8mm, Wide.** Armin Mueller-Stahl, Aidan Quinn, Elizabeth Perkins, Joan Plowright, Lou Jacobi, Leo Fuchs, Eve Gordon, Kevin Pollak, Israel Rubinek, Elijah Wood, Grant Gelt, Bernard Hiller; ***D:*** Barry Levinson; ***W:*** Barry Levinson; ***C:*** Allen Daviau; ***M:*** Randy Newman. Writers Guild '90: Orig. Screenplay.

Avanti! 🦴🦴½ **1972 (R)** Stuffy businessman Wendell Armbruster (Lemmon) heads to Italy to claim his father's body when the old man dies while on vacation. Then he discovers dad has been visiting his mistress lo these many years. While trying to get through mountains of red tape, Wendell finds himself romancing the woman's daughter (Mills). Too long but still amusing. **144m/C VHS.** Jack Lemmon, Juliet Mills, Clive Revill, Edward Andrews, Gianfranco Barra, Franco Angrisano; ***D:*** Billy Wilder; ***W:*** I.A.L. Diamond, Billy Wilder.

Ava's Magical Adventure 🦴🦴½ **1994 (PG)** Ten-year-old Eddie decides to take Ava on a little adventure. Too bad she's a 2-ton elephant he's stolen from the circus. Based on the Mark Twain story "The Stolen White Elephant." **97m/C VHS.** Timothy Bottoms, Georg Stanford Brown, Patrick Dempsey, Priscilla Barnes, David Lander, Kaye Ballard, Remi Ryan; ***D:*** Patrick Dempsey, Rocky Parker; ***W:*** Susan D. Nimm; ***M:*** Mark Holden.

The Avenger 🦴🦴½ **1960** The story of a criminal who cuts off the heads of people and mails them off makes for a shocker. Graphic violence will appeal to those who like a good mail-order gorefest and are not employed by the post office. **102m/B VHS.** *GE* Ingrid van Bergen, Heinz Drache, Ina Duscha, Mario Litto, Klaus Kinski; ***D:*** Karl Anton.

The Avenger 🦴 *The Lost Glory of Troy* **1962** This time muscleman Reeves plays Aeneas and leads the Trojans in battle against the Greeks. It's supposedly an adaptation of "The Aeneid" by Virgil. **108m/C VHS.** *FR IT* Steve Reeves, Giacomo "Jack" Rossi-Stuart, Carla Marlier, Gianni "John" Garko, Liana Orfei; ***D:*** Giorgio Rivalta.

The Avengers 🦴🦴 **1998 (PG-13)** Based on the culty '60s Brit TV series, this unfortunate big screen adaptation fails by choosing style over campy charm. Set in a surreal 1999 London, scientist (and leather-girl) Mrs. Emma Peel (Thurman) teams up with dapper secret agent John Steed (Fiennes) to defeat maximum baddie, Sir August de Wynter (Connery). Seems de Wynter has a machine that can manipulate the world's weather—and he's not intending to do good deeds. It's dull, the leads have no chemistry together (although they have their separate charms), and the creators have chosen to include some lesser aspects of the series, such as the boring character of Mother (Broadbent). Unforgiveably, Laurie Johnson's memorable TV theme is not used for the film's opening—replaced instead by generic music by McNeely. (Johnson's theme is heard later.) Original Steed, Patrick MacNee, does have an amusing cameo. **90m/C VHS, DVD.** Ralph Fiennes, Uma Thurman, Sean Connery, Jim Broadbent, Fiona Shaw, Eileen Atkins, John Wood, Eddie Izzard, Carmen Ejogo, Keeley Hawes; ***Cameos:*** Patrick Macnee; ***D:*** Jeremiah S. Chechik; ***W:*** Don MacPherson; ***C:*** Roger Pratt; ***M:*** Joel McNeely. Golden Raspberries '98: Worst Remake/Sequel.

The Avenging 🦴🦴 **1992 (PG)** Horse comes home from college to run the family ranch but has problems with his two resentful brothers. **100m/C VHS.** Michael Horse, Efrem Zimbalist Jr., Sherry Hursey, Joseph Runningfox, Taylor Lacher; ***D:*** Lyman Dayton; ***W:*** Lyman Dayton.

Avenging Angel woof! **1985 (R)** Law student Molly "Angel" Stewart is back on the streets to retaliate against the men who killed the policeman who saved her from a life of prostitution. Worthless sequel to 1984's "Angel," exploiting the original's exploitative intent. Followed listlessly by "Angel III: The Final Chapter." **94m/C VHS.** Betsy Russell, Rory Calhoun, Susan Tyrrell, Ossie Davis, Barry Pearl, Ross Hagen, Karin Mani, Robert Tessier; ***D:*** Robert Vincent O'Neil; ***W:*** Joseph M. Cala; ***C:*** Peter Collister; ***M:*** Paul Antonelli.

The Avenging Angel 🦴🦴½ **1995** Unusual take on religion and western justice. Brigham Young (Heston) and his Mormon sect have established themselves in Utah—with the aid of some sharpshooting vigilantes, including Miles Utley (Berenger). When an assassination attempt is made on Young's life, Utley finds he's stumbled into an ever-widening church conspiracy that threatens to consume him. Based on the novel by Gary Stewart. **100m/C VHS.** Tom Berenger, Charlton Heston, James Coburn, Kevin Tighe, Jeffrey Jones, Tom Bower, Joanna Miles; ***D:*** Craig R. Baxley; ***W:*** Dennis Nemec; ***C:*** Mark Irwin; ***M:*** Gary Chang.

Avenging Conscience 🦴🦴 *Thou Shall Not Kill* **1914** An early eerie horror film, based on tales of Edgar Allan Poe. D.W. Griffith's first large-scale feature. Silent. **78m/B VHS.** Henry B. Walthall, Blanche Sweet; ***D:*** D.W. Griffith.

Avenging Disco Godfather 🦴½ *Avenging Godfather; Disco Godfather* **1976 (R)** Moore parodies the "Godfather" and martial arts movies. **99m/C VHS, DVD.** Rudy Ray Moore, Carol Speed, Jimmy Lynch, Jeny Jones, Lady Reeds, James H. Hawthorne, Frank Finn, Julius J. Carey III; ***D:*** J. Robert Wagoner; ***W:*** J. Robert Wagoner, Cliff Roquemore; ***C:*** Arledge Armenaki; ***M:*** Ernie Fields Jr.

Avenging Force 🦴🦴 **1986 (R)** Okay actioner about retired CIA agent Dudikoff returning to the force to help colleague James run for political office. A group of right-wing terrorists called "Pentangle" threatens James, so Dudikoff adds his name to their wanted list. Conflict leads to a forest manhunt where the avenging force does its avenging. **104m/C VHS.** Michael Dudikoff, Steve James, John P. Ryan; ***D:*** Sam Firstenberg; ***W:*** Mercer Ellington, James Booth; ***M:*** George S. Clinton.

The Avenging Hand 🦴½ **1943** Leaden suspense story about a hotel filled with thieves all searching for stolen loot. **56m/B VHS.** Noah Beery Jr., Kathleen Kelly, Louis Borell, James Harcourt, Charles Oliver, Reginald Long; ***D:*** Victor Hanbury.

The Average Woman 🦴🦴 **1924** Gritty journalist consults plain Jane for "Modern Woman" story and finds a major rewrite in order when he falls with a thud for Miss Jane. **52m/B VHS.** Pauline Garon, David Powell, Burr McIntosh, Harrison Ford, De Sacia Mooers; ***D:*** Christy Cabanne.

The Aviator 🦴🦴 **1985 (PG)** Pilot Reeve, haunted by the memory of a fatal crash, tries to find a new line of work. Large sums of money persuade him to transport spoiled Arquette to Washington. When the biplane crashes in the mountain wilderness, the two fall in love between scavenging for food and fighting wild animals. From the director of "Man From Snowy River." **98m/C VHS, DVD, Wide.** Christopher Reeve, Rosanna Arquette, Jack Warden, Tyne Daly, Marcia Strassman, Sam Wanamaker, Scott Wilson; ***D:*** George Miller; ***W:*** Marc Norman; ***C:*** David Connell; ***M:*** Dominic Frontiere.

The Aviator's Wife 🦴🦴🦴 *La Femme de L'Aviateur* **1980** The first in Rohmer's Comedies and Proverbs series is a comedy of errors involving a post-office worker (Marlaud) who believes that his older girlfriend (Riviere) is seeing another man, a pilot (Carriere). He enlists the aid of a young girl (Meury) to help him spy on his romantic obsession. French with subtitles. **104m/C VHS, DVD.** *FR* Philippe Marlaud, Marie Riviere, Anne-Laure Meury, Matthieu Carriere; ***D:*** Eric Rohmer; ***W:*** Eric Rohmer; ***C:*** Bernard Lutic; ***M:*** Jean-Louis Valero.

The Awakening 🦴½ **1980 (R)** An archeologist discovers the tomb of a murderous queen, but upon opening the coffin, the mummy's spirit is transferred to his baby daughter, born at that instant. They call that bad luck. **101m/C VHS.** *GB* Charlton Heston, Susannah York, Stephanie Zimbalist, Patrick Drury, Ian McDiarmid, Bruce Myers, Nadim Sawalha, Jill Townsend; ***D:*** Mike Newell; ***W:*** Allan Scott, Chris Bryant, Clive Exton; ***C:*** Jack Cardiff; ***M:*** Claude Bolling.

Awakening of Candra woof! **1981** Based on a real 1975 incident, a young couple honeymooning in the mountains is assaulted by a lunatic fisherman. The psycho kills the husband and rapes the girl, then he brainwashes poor Candra into thinking it was all an accident. Intense subject matter should be horrifying, but falls short of the mark in this flop. **96m/C VHS.** Blanche Baker, Cliff DeYoung, Richard Jaeckel; ***D:*** Paul Wendkos. **TV**

Awakenings 🦴🦴🦴½ **1990 (PG-13)** Marshall's first dramatic effort is based on the true story of Dr. Oliver Sacks, from his book of the same title. It details his experimentation with the drug L-dopa which inspired the "awakening" of a number of catatonic patients, some of whom had been "sleeping" for as long as 30 years. Occasionally over-sentimental, but still providing a poignant look at both the patients—who find themselves confronted with lost opportunities and faded youth—and at Sacks, who must watch their exquisite suffering as they slip away. De Niro's performance as the youngest of the group is heart-rending, while Williams offers a subdued, moving performance as the doctor. **120m/C VHS, DVD, 8mm.** Robin Williams, Robert De Niro, John Heard, Julie Kavner, Penelope Ann Miller, Max von Sydow, Anne Meara; ***D:*** Penny Marshall; ***W:*** Steven Zaillian; ***M:*** Randy Newman. Natl. Bd. of Review '90: Actor (De Niro), Actor (Williams); Natl. Soc. Film Critics '90: Actor (De Niro).

Awakenings of the Beast 🦴 *Ritual Dos Sadicos; Ritual of the Maniacs* **1968** Documents the protracted sufferings of an LSD drug user who is beset with hallucinatory visions and is prone to fits of frenzied violence. Director Jose Mojica Marins (AKA Coffin Joe) steps out of his Ze do Ciaxia character in this disjointed mix of drugs and sex intercut with Mojica Marins himself on trial for his offensive movies, followed by a case study on drugs and sexual behavior. By the end of the movie, there is a point—that drugs aren't the cause of evil behavior—but it's very painful getting there. In Portugese with English subtitles. **93m/B VHS, DVD, Wide.** *BR* Jose Mojica Marins, Sergio Hinst, Andrea Bryan, Mario Lima; ***D:*** Jose Mojica Marins; ***W:*** Jose Mojica Marins, Rubens Francisco Lucchetti; ***C:*** Giorgio Atilli.

Away All Boats 🦴🦴½ **1956** The true story of one Captain Hawks, who led a crew of misfits to victory in WWII Pacific aboard transport USS Belinda. Battle scenes are well done; look for early (and brief) appearance by young Clint Eastwood. **114m/B VHS, DVD.** Jeff Chandler, George Nader, Richard Boone, Julie Adams, Keith Andes, Lex Barker, Clint Eastwood; ***D:*** Joseph Pevney; ***W:*** Ted Sherdeman; ***C:*** William H. Daniels; ***M:*** Frank Skinner.

The Awful Dr. Orloff 🦴 *Gritos en la Noche; The Demon Doctor* **1962** Set in a bygone era, Dr. Orloff (Vernon) is a retired prison physician who needs unblemished skin to remedy the horrible disfigurement of his daughter Melissa (Lorys), ravaged by fire. He abducts promising young women candidates with the help of his blind zombie henchman Morpho (Valle), who simply cannot be trusted with a scalpel. After several surgical mishaps, they kidnap the perfect specimen, a woman who bears an uncanny resemblance to Melissa. Unfortunately, she is engaged to suspicious police Inspector Tanner (San Martin). French version with English subtitles that includes more explicit gore is also available. **86m/B VHS, DVD, Wide.** *SP FR* Howard Vernon, Diana Lorys, Frank Wolff, Riccardo Valle, Conrado San Martin, Perla Cristal, Maria Silva, Mara Laso; ***D:*** Jess (Jesus) Franco; ***W:*** Jess (Jesus) Franco; ***C:*** Godofredo Pacheco; ***M:*** Jose Pagan, Antonio Ramirez Angel.

The Awful Truth 🦴🦴🦴🦴 **1937** Lucy (Dunne) and Jerry (Grant) Warriner are a young couple who discard their marriage made in heaven and go their separate ways in search of happiness. Meticulously sabotaging each others' new relationships, they discover they really were made for each other. Grant is at his most charming with dead-on comic timing while Dunne is brilliant as his needling ex. The scene where Dunne poses as Grant's prodigal fan-dancing sister who pays a surprise cocktail-hour visit to the family of his stuffy, upper-class girlfriend (Lamont) is among the most memorable screwball vignettes of all time. And don't miss the custody battle they have over the family dog (Asta of "The Thin Man" fame). Based on Arthur Richman's 1922 play. Preceded by 1925 and 1929 versions; remade in 1953 as "Let's Do it Again." **92m/B VHS.** Irene Dunne, Cary Grant, Ralph Bellamy, Alexander D'Arcy, Cecil Cunningham, Molly Lamont, Esther Dale, Joyce Compton, Robert "Tex" Allen, Robert Warwick, Mary Forbes; ***D:*** Leo McCarey; ***W:*** Vina Delmar. Oscars '37: Director (McCarey), Natl. Film Reg. '96.

An Awfully Big Adventure 🦴🦴 **1994 (R)** Coming-of-age saga set in postwar Liverpool around a provincial reperatory company. Stage-struck 16-year-old Stella (Cates) gets work as a company apprentice, immediately getting a crush on arch, callous theatre manager Meredith Potter (a deliciously nasty Grant), who enjoys degrading everyone around him. The company's chance for success rests on a production of "Peter Pan," with visiting actor P.L. O'Hara (dashing Rickman), who immediately seduces Stella and has more than a few secrets of his own. Theatrically exaggerated; based on the novel by Beryl Bainbridge. **113m/C VHS.** *GB* Georgina Cates, Hugh Grant, Alan Rickman, Peter Firth, Alun Armstrong, Prunella Scales, Rita Tushingham, Alan Cox, Edward Petherbridge, Nicola Pagett, Carol Drinkwater, Clive Merrison, Gerard McSorley; ***D:*** Mike Newell; ***W:*** Charles Wood; ***C:*** Dick Pope; ***M:*** Richard Hartley.

Axe 🦴½ *Lisa, Lisa; California Axe Massacre* **1974 (R)** After a group of thugs kill a man (on an embarrassingly shoddy set), they flee to the country, where they take over a farmhouse. The only residents of this farmhouse are a young girl, Lisa (Lee), and her invalid grandfather. The criminals force Lisa to cook a chicken dinner (NO!) and then generally terrorize the girl and hhhher grandfather. Eventually, Lisa (who is actively hallucinating throughout this episode) gets the titular axe and seeks her revenge. The film is slow and boring, and the sub-amateur acting doesn't help. The only positive aspect is the suspense that mounts over the course of the movie. Having seen films like this before, and given the fact that nothing else is happening, the audience knows that Lisa is going to strike back at some time. **68m/C DVD.** Leslie Lee, Jack Canon, Frederick Friedel, Frank Jones; ***D:*** Frederick Friedel; ***W:*** Frederick Friedel; ***C:*** Austin McKinney.

Ay, Carmela! 🦴🦴🦴 **1990** During the Spanish Civil War, two vaudevillians with strong anti-Franco views are captured by Franco forces and sentenced to execution. They are reprieved when a theatre-loving Lieutenant offers to spare their lives if they will entertain the troops. Clever and entertaining farce, with poignant undertones. **105m/C VHS.** *SP IT* Carmen Maura, Andres Pajares, Gabino Diego, Maurizio De Razza, Miguel Rellan, Edward Zentara, Jose Sancho, Antonio Fuentes; ***D:*** Carlos Saura; ***W:*** Rafael Azcona; ***C:*** Jose Luis Alcaine.

B. Monkey 🦴🦴 **1997 (R)** B—AKA Beatrice—(Argento) hopes she can escape her world of drugs and crime (she's a thief) with the romantic aid of schoolteacher Alan (Harris). But her past catches up with her when ex-partners Paul (Everett) and Bruno (Rhys Meyers) convince her to do one last job (she misses the rush). Based on the novel by Andrew Davies, this one is mainly cool Brit style over substance. **91m/C VHS, DVD, Wide.** *GB* Asia Argento, Jared Harris, Rupert Everett, Jonathan Rhys Meyers, Tim Woodward, Ian Hart; ***D:*** Michael Radford; ***W:*** Michael Thomas, Chloe King; ***C:*** Ashley Rowe; ***M:*** Jennie Muskett.

Baba 🦴🦴🦴 *The Father* **1973** A poor boatman agrees to be the fall guy in a murder in exchange for the actual murderer supporting his family. But after 24 years in prison, the boatman finds all his sacrificing has been in vain. His daughter has become a prostitute and his son is working as one of the murderer's henchman. In Turkish with English subtitles. **95m/C VHS.** *TU* ***D:*** Yilmaz Guney.

Babar: The Movie 🦴🦴½ **1988 (G)** The lovable Babar, king of the elephants, must devise a plan to outwit an angry hoard of attacking rhinos. Based on the characters of Jean and Laurent de Brunhoff. **75m/C VHS, 8mm.** *CA FR* ***D:*** Alan Bunce; ***W:*** Alan Bunce, John deKlein; ***V:*** Gavin Magrath, Gordon Pinsent, Sarah Polley, Chris Wiggins, Elizabeth Hanna.

Babe! 🦴🦴🦴½ **1975** A fine TV movie about the life of one of America's most famous woman athletes, Babe Didrickson. Adapted by Joanna Lee from Didrickson's autobiography "The Life I've Led." The movie was nominated for Outstanding Special of 1975-76 and Clark won an Emmy for her work. **120m/C VHS.** Susan Clark, Alex Karras, Slim Pickens, Jeanette Nolan, Ellen Geer, Ford Rainey; ***D:*** Buzz Kulik; ***M:*** Jerry Goldsmith. **TV**

The Babe 🦴🦴½ **1992 (PG)** Follows the life of legendary baseball player Babe Ruth, portrayed as a sloppy drunkard whose appetites for food, drink, and sex were as large as he was. Alvarado and McGillis do well as the Babe's first and second wives, but this is Goodman's show from start to finish. He's excellent as Ruth, and looks the part, but his fine performance can't make up for a lackluster script filled with holes. **115m/C VHS.** Michael (Mike) Papajohn, John Goodman, Kelly McGillis, Trini Alvarado, Bruce Boxleitner, Peter Donat, J.C. Quinn, Richard Tyson, James Cromwell, Joe Ragno, Bernard Kates, Michael McGrady, Stephen Caffrey; ***D:*** Arthur Hiller; ***W:*** John Fusco; ***C:*** Haskell Wexler; ***M:*** Elmer Bernstein.

Babe 🦴🦴🦴½ *Babe, the Gallant Pig* **1995 (G)** Totally charming fable has intelligent piglet Babe being raised by matriarch sheepdog Fly, and learning the art of sheep herding along with his new canine brothers. Farmer Hoggett (Cromwell), Babe's owner by virtue of a winning raffle ticket, sees that he's more than just a ham, and enters them in the world sheepdog herding championship. Whimsy that never crosses the line into treacle. Four different special effects houses were used to make the barnyard animals talk and walk. Filmed on location in Australia; based on Dick King-Smith's book "The Sheep-Pig." **91m/C VHS, DVD.** *AU* James Cromwell, Magda Szubanski; ***D:*** Chris Noonan; ***W:*** Chris Noonan, George Miller; ***C:*** Andrew Lesnie; ***M:*** Nigel Westlake; ***V:*** Christine Cavanaugh, Miriam Margolyes, Danny Mann, Hugo Weaving; ***Nar:*** Roscoe Lee Browne. Oscars '95: Visual FX; Golden Globes '96: Film—Mus./Comedy; Natl. Soc. Film Critics '95: Film.

Babe: Pig in the City 🦴🦴½ **1998 (PG)** Miller takes over the director's chair for this trip. And he brings along more money, more effects, more animals, and more unsettling images, including Mickey Rooney in a creepy clown suit, than anyone who saw the original would expect. Babe returns home to a hero's welcome, but the joy doesn't last long. Farmer Hoggett (Cromwell) is injured, and with foreclosure imminent, Babe and Mrs. Hoggett (Szubanski) head out to turn Babe's fame into a little cash. Along the way, they miss their connecting flight in "the city" and are forced to stay at a hotel that caters to animals. There, they meet the aforementioned Rooney and his three chimp partners, along with various dogs and cats. Technically well-done, and sporting an imaginative story, but may be a little dark for the younger kiddies. **96m/C VHS, DVD.** James Cromwell, Magda Szubanski, Mickey Rooney, Mary Stein, Julie Godfrey; ***D:*** George Miller; ***W:*** Judy Morris, Mark Lamprell; ***C:*** Andrew Lesnie; ***M:*** Nigel Westlake; ***V:*** Elizabeth (E.G. Dailey) Daily, Danny Mann, Glenne Headly, Steven Wright, James Cosmo, Stanley Ralph Ross, Russi Taylor, Adam Goldberg, Nathan Kress, Myles Jeffrey; ***Nar:*** Roscoe Lee Browne.

Babe Ruth Story 🦴🦴 **1948** An overly sentimental biography about the famed baseball slugger. Bendix is miscast as the Bambino, but the actual film clips of the Babe are of interest. A movie to be watched during those infrequent bouts of sloppy baseball mysticism. **107m/B VHS.** William Bendix, Claire Trevor, Charles Bickford, William Frawley, Sam Levene, Gertrude Niesen; ***D:*** Roy Del Ruth.

Babes in Arms 🦴½ **1939** The children of several vaudeville performers team up to put on a show to raise money for their financially impoverished parents. Loosely adapted from the Rodgers and Hart Broadway musical of the same name; features some of their songs as well as new additions. ♫Babes in Arms; I Cried for You; Good Morning; You Are My Lucky Star; Broadway Rhythm; Where or When; Daddy Was a Minstrel Man; I'm Just Wild About Harry; God's Country. **91m/B VHS.** Judy Garland, Mickey Rooney, Charles Winninger, Guy Kibbee, June Preisser; ***D:*** Busby Berkeley; ***M:*** George Bassman, Richard Rodgers, Lorenz Hart.

Babes in Toyland 🦴🦴 **1961** A lavish Disney production of Victor Herbert's timeless operetta, with Toyland being menaced by the evil Barnaby and his Bogeymen. Yes, Annette had a life after Mickey Mouse and before the peanut butter commercials. Somewhat charming, although the roles of the lovers seem a stretch for both Funicello and Kirk. But the flick does sport an amusing turn by Wynn. **105m/C VHS.** Annette Funicello, Ray Bolger, Tommy Sands, Ed Wynn, Tommy Kirk; ***D:*** Jack Donohue; ***C:*** Edward Colman; ***M:*** George Bruns.

Babes in Toyland 🦴½ **1986** Young girl must save Toyland from the clutches of the evil Barnaby and his monster minions. Bland TV remake of the classic doesn't approach the original. **96m/C VHS.** Drew Barrymore, Noriyuki "Pat" Morita, Richard Mulligan, Eileen Brennan, Keanu Reeves, Jill Schoelen, Googy Gress; ***D:*** Clive Donner; ***M:*** Leslie Bricusse.

Babes on Broadway 🦴🦴½ **1941** Mickey and Judy put on a show to raise money for a settlement house. Nearly the best of the Garland-Rooney series, with imaginative numbers staged by Berkeley. ♫Babes on Broadway; Anything Can Happen in New York; How About You?; Hoe Down; Chin Up! Cheerio! Carry On!; Mama Yo Quiero; F.D.R. Jones; Waiting for the Robert E. Lee. **118m/B VHS.** Mickey Rooney, Judy Garland, Fay Bainter, Richard Quine, Virginia Weidler, Ray Macdonald, Busby Berkeley; ***D:*** Busby Berkeley; ***M:*** George Bassman.

Babette's Feast 🦴🦴🦴½ *Babettes Gaestebud* **1987** A simple, moving pageant-of-life fable. Philippa (Kjer) and Martina (Federspiel) took over their late father's ministry in a small Danish coastal town. Widowed Frenchwoman Babette (Audran) has spent 14 years in their service and, after winning a lottery prize, decides she will prepare a lavish banquet in honor of their father's 100th birthday. The religiously conservative villagers don't know what to make of such bounty—or the pleasure it brings to their senses. Adapted from a tale by Isak Dinesen. French and Danish with subtitles. **102m/C VHS, DVD, Wide.** *DK FR* Stephane Audran, Bibi Andersson, Bodil Kjer, Birgitte Federspiel, Jean-Philippe LaFont, Ebbe Rode, Jarl Kulle; ***D:*** Gabriel Axel; ***W:*** Gabriel Axel; ***C:*** Henning Kristiansen; ***M:*** Per Norgard; ***Nar:*** Ghita Norby. Oscars '87: Foreign Film; British Acad. '88: Foreign Film.

The Baby 🦴🦴 **1972 (PG)** Bizarre story of a social worker who resorts to swinging an ax to cut the apron strings of "baby," a retarded man-child, from his over-protective and insane (bad combination) mother and sisters. Low-budget production looks and feels like a low-budget production, but any movie featuring a grown man wandering about in diapers can't be all bad. **85m/C VHS, DVD.** Anjanette Comer, Ruth Roman, Marianna Hill, Suzanne Zenor, David Manzy, Michael Pataki, Erin O'Reilly, Virginia Vincent; ***D:*** Ted Post; ***W:*** Abe Polsky; ***C:*** Michael D. Margulies; ***M:*** Gerald Fried.

Baby 🦴🦴 **2000** John (Carradine) and Lily (Fawcett) Malone are unsuccessful in coping with their grief over the death of their infant son and in helping their 12-year-old daughter, Larkin (Pill), to deal with her own pain. Then a baby girl is abandoned on the Malone doorstep and Lily immediately wants to keep the child—much to the others' dismay. Formulaic weepie based on the novel by Patricia MacLachlan. **93m/C VHS.** Farrah Fawcett, Keith Carradine, Jean Stapleton, Alison Pill, Vincent Berry, Ann Dowd; ***D:*** Robert Ackerman; ***W:*** Kerry Kennedy, Patricia MacLachlan, David Manson; ***C:*** Ron Garcia; ***M:*** Jeff Danna; ***Nar:*** Glenn Close. **CABLE**

The Baby and the Battleship 🦴🦴½ **1956** The old baby out of (on the?) water plot. While on liberty in Italy, a sailor, after a series of complications, becomes custodian of a baby and attempts to hide the tyke aboard his battleship (hence the title). More complications ensue. Some funny moments. Great cast. **96m/C VHS.** *GB* John Mills, Richard Attenborough, Andre Morell, Bryan Forbes, Lisa Gastoni, Michael Hordern, Lionel Jeffries, Gordon Jackson, John Le Mesurier; ***D:*** Jay Lewis.

Baby Boom 🦴🦴½ **1987 (PG)** J.C. Wiatt (Keaton) is a hard-charging exec who becomes the reluctant mother to an orphaned baby girl (a gift from a long-lost relative). She adjusts with great difficulty to motherhood and life outside the rat race and New York City when J.C. decides she must make some radical changes to her routine. A fairly harmless collection of cliches bolstered by Keaton's usual nervous performance as a power-suited yuppie ad queen saddled with a noncareer-enhancing baby, who moves from manic career woman to jelly-packing Vermont store-owner/mom. Shepherd serves as her new, down-home, doctor beau. To best appreciate flick, see it with a bevy of five- and six-year-olds (a good age for applauding the havoc that a baby creates). **103m/C VHS, DVD, Wide.** Diane Keaton, Sam Shepard, Harold Ramis, Sam Wanamaker, James Spader, Pat Hingle, Mary Gross, Victoria Jackson, Paxton Whitehead, Annie Golden, Dori Brenner, Robin Bartlett, Christopher Noth, Britt Leach; ***D:*** Charles Shyer; ***W:*** Charles Shyer, Nancy Meyers; ***C:*** William A. Fraker; ***M:*** Bill Conti.

Baby Boy **2001 (R)** Singleton returns to the South Central L.A. neighborhood of his breakthrough "Boyz in the Hood" in this candid look at a culture that fosters and tolerates lack of emotional maturity in young African-American males. Jody (Gibson) is a 20-year-old manchild who still lives with his mother (Johnson), has two children with two different women, no job, and cheats on his current girl, Yvette. Jody's life changes when his mother's boyfriend moves in. Melvin (Rhames), an ex-con who's been down the road Jody is heading, shows no tolerance for his attitude. Jody gets a job, but his idea of earning a living is selling stolen dresses at a beauty parlor. Real trouble starts when Rodney (Snoop Dogg), a street thug and Yvette's ex, is released from prison and refuses to leave her house. Singleton toys with two endings, but finishes the story with the message that the means to fix the problems he's described are within reach. **129m/C VHS, DVD, Wide.** *US* Tyrese Gibson, Omar Gooding, Taraji P. Henson, Adrienne-Joi (AJ) Johnson, Snoop Dogg, Tamara La Seon Bass, Ving Rhames, Angell Conwell; ***D:*** John Singleton; ***W:*** John Singleton; ***C:*** Charles Mills; ***M:*** David Arnold.

Baby Cart 1: Lend a Child...Lend an Arm *Lone Wolf and Cub: Sword of Vengeance* **1972** First in a series of six from the sword-wielding samurai genre. Chronicles the events leading up to a samurai warrior's (Wakayama) expulsion from his native village along with his infant son (Tomikawa). Father's intense rivalry with the evil Shogun whom he was ousted by becomes an epic struggle of good vs. evil. The adorable little "Lone Cub" provides an effective counterpoint for Dad's sideline excursion into a local brothel. In Japanese with English subtitles in a letterbox format. **83m/C VHS.** *JP* Tomisaburo Wakayama, Akihiro Tomikawa; ***D:*** Kenji Misumi.

Baby Cart 4: Heart of a Parent...Heart of a Child **1972** Fourth in a series of six. A man (Wakayama) pushes his son (Tomikawa) across Japan in a baby cart loaded with deadly accessories including built-in guns and switchblades. Copious amounts of bloodshed. In Japanese with English subtitles in a letterbox format. **80m/C VHS.** *JP* Tomisaburo Wakayama, Akihiro Tomikawa; ***D:*** Buichi Sato.

Baby Cart at the River Styx *Lone Wolf and Cub: Baby Cart at the River Styx; Baby Cart 2* **1972** Second of six parts in the "Kozure Ohkami" ("Sword of Vengeance") series about a man who wheels his motherless infant through the Chinese countryside in a baby cart armed with secret weapons, plotting his revenge on the warlord who expelled him. This one features the intro of Sayka and her fellow female assassins. Subtitled in English. **80m/C VHS.** *JP* Tomisaburo Wakayama, Akihiro Tomikawa; ***D:*** Kenji Misumi.

Baby Cart to Hades **1972** The third "Kozure Ohkami" ("Sword of Vengeance") film once again finds samurai Itto Ogami and his son Diagoro embroiled in a power struggle between a regional landlord and a governor in feudal Japan. Subtitled in English. **88m/C VHS, Wide.** *JP* Tomisaburo Wakayama, Akihiro Tomikawa; ***D:*** Kenji Misumi.

The Baby Dance **1998** Well-off, middleaged Hollywood marrieds Rachel (Channing) and Richard (Reigert) Luckman have unsuccessfully tried to have a baby for years. Finally they place an adoption ad and receive a response from poor Louisiana trailer park inhabitants Wanda (Dern) and Art (Lineback) LeFauvre, who have an unwanted fifth child on the way. A meeting between the couples soon points out monetary, religious, and cultural differences that may derail their bargain. The two leading ladies carry the picture, which is based on director Anderson's Off-Broadway play. **95m/C VHS, DVD.** Stockard Channing, Laura Dern, Peter Riegert, Richard Lineback; ***D:*** Jane Anderson; ***W:*** Jane Anderson; ***C:*** Jan Kiesser; ***M:*** Terry Allen. **CABLE**

Baby Doll **1956** Suggestive sex at its best, revolving around the love of cotton in Mississippi. Nubile Baker is married to slow-witted Malden, who runs a cotton gin. His torching of Wallach's cotton gin begins a cycle of sexual innuendo and tension, brought to exhilarating life on screen, without a single filmed kiss. Performers and sets ooze during the steamy exhibition, which was considered highly erotic when released. Excellent performances from entire cast, with expert pacing by director Kazan. Screenplay is based on Tennessee Williams' "27 Wagons Full of Cotton." **115m/B VHS.** Eli Wallach, Carroll Baker, Karl Malden, Mildred Dunnock, Rip Torn; ***D:*** Elia Kazan; ***W:*** Tennessee Williams; ***C:*** Boris Kaufman. Golden Globes '57: Director (Kazan).

The Baby Doll Murders **1992 (R)** Someone in L.A. is killing beautiful young women and then leaving a broken baby doll at the scene of the crime. The gruesome murderer manages to elude everyone, until Detective Benz discovers a link between the victims and a pattern begins to form. He also discovers that his partner's wife is going to be the next victim unless he can stop this ruthless serial killer from striking again. **90m/C VHS.** Jeff Kober, Melanie Smith, John Saxon, Tom (Thomas E.) Hodges, Bobby DiCicco; ***D:*** Paul Leder; ***W:*** Paul Leder.

Baby Face **1933** A small town girl moves to the city when her father dies. There she gets a job at a bank and sleeps her way to the top of the business world, discarding used men left and right. The Hays Office was extremely upset with the then risque material and forced Warner to trim the first cut. **70m/B VHS.** Barbara Stanwyck, George Brent, Donald Cook, John Wayne, Henry Kolker, Margaret Lindsay, Douglass Dumbrille, James Murray; ***D:*** Alfred E. Green; ***W:*** Gene Markey, Kathryn Scola; ***C:*** James Van Trees; ***M:*** Leo F. Forbstein.

Baby Face Morgan **1942** Poor comedy about gangsters who attempt to take advantage of the FBI's preoccupation with saboteurs and spies by muscling in on an insurance firm. **60m/B VHS.** Mary Carlisle, Richard Cromwell, Robert Armstrong, Chick Chandler, Charles (Judel, Judells) Judels, Warren Hymer, Vince Barnett, Ralf Harolde; ***D:*** Arthur Dreifuss.

Baby Face Nelson **1997 (R)** Lame Depression-era gangster flick with George "Baby Face" Nelson (Howell) and his moll Helen Womack (Zane) fighting rival Al Capone (Abraham) in Chicago. Kove comes off well as gangster John Dillinger. **80m/C VHS.** C. Thomas Howell, Lisa Zane, F. Murray Abraham, Doug Wert, Martin Kove; ***D:*** Scott Levy; ***W:*** Joseph Farrugia, Craig J. Nevius; ***C:*** Christopher Baffa; ***M:*** Christopher Lennertz.

Baby Geniuses **1998 (PG)** Steals the most irritating parts of "Look Who's Talking," "Home Alone" and that creepy dancing baby and pastes them onto a lame good kids vs. evil adults plot. Turner and Lloyd are evil scientists attempting to crack the secret language of babies, which they believe holds the secrets of the universe (such as how to enjoy drooling and making in your pants). Standing in their way are nursery school operators Cattrall and MacNichol and an array of babies that spout inane dialogue thanks to an abuse of computer morphing. The effect is more disturbing than cute, and an excellent supporting cast is wasted. More interesting things can be found inside a diaper. **94m/C VHS, DVD.** Kathleen Turner, Christopher Lloyd, Kim Cattrall, Peter MacNicol, Dom DeLuise, Ruby Dee, Kyle Howard, Leo Fitzgerald, Myles Fitzgerald, Gerry Fitzgerald; ***D:*** Bob (Benjamin) Clark; ***W:*** Bob (Benjamin) Clark, Steven Paul, Francisca Matos, Robert Grasmere, Greg Michael; ***C:*** Stephen M. Katz; ***M:*** Paul Zaza.

Baby Girl Scott **1987** Hurt and Lithgow play the parents of an extremely premature infant who is being kept alive by technology. They make a heartrending decision and then must battle doctors and the system to let their daughter die with dignity. **97m/C VHS.** John Lithgow, Mary Beth Hurt, Linda Kelsey; ***D:*** John Korty. **TV**

Baby It's You **1982 (R)** In New Jersey in the '60s, the relationship between a smart, attractive Jewish girl who yearns to be an actress and a street-smart Catholic Italian boy puzzles their family and friends. It all works due to Arquette's strong acting and Sayles' script, which explores adolescent dreams, the transition to adulthood, class differences, and the late 1960s with insight and humor. Interesting period soundtrack (Woolly Bully and, for some reason, Bruce Springsteen) helps propel the film, a commercial job which helped finance Sayles' more independent ventures. **105m/C VHS.** Rosanna Arquette, Vincent Spano, Jack Davidson, Joanna Merlin, Nick Ferrari, Leora Dana, Robert Downey Jr., Tracy Pollan, Matthew Modine; ***D:*** John Sayles; ***W:*** John Sayles; ***C:*** Michael Ballhaus.

Baby Love woof! **1969 (R)** A soft-core fluff-fest about a trollop seducing a doctor's family. The doctor may or may not be her father. Hayden tantalizes the doctor, the doctor's son, and the doctor's wife, as well as the neighbors, leaving only those in adjoining communities untouched. Based on the novel by Tina Chad Christian. **98m/C VHS.** *GB* Ann Lynn, Keith Barron, Linda Hayden, Derek Lamden, Diana Dors, Patience Collier; ***D:*** Alastair Reid.

Baby Love woof! *Lemon Popsicle V* **1983** Nerds get revenge against the freshmen who run the local frat house. **80m/C VHS.** *IS* Dolly Dollar, Bea Fiedler, Jesse Katzur, Yftach Katzur, Dvora Kedar, Renate Langer, Zachi Noy, Jonathan Segall; ***D:*** Dan Wolman; ***C:*** Ilan Rosenberg.

The Baby Maker **1970 (R)** A couple who cannot have children because the wife is sterile decides to hire a woman to have a child for them. However, the relationship between the husband and the surrogate progresses beyond what either of them wanted. Hershey stars as the free-love surrogate mama (just before she underwent the supreme 60s transformation into Barbara Seagull) and Bridges makes his directorial debut. Flick is interesting as a combo critique/exploitation of those wild and groovy 1960s. **109m/C VHS.** Barbara Hershey, Collin Wilcox-Paxton, Sam Groom, Scott Glenn, Jeannie Berlin; ***D:*** James Bridges; ***W:*** James Bridges.

Baby Monitor: Sound of Fear **1997 (R)** Matt (Beghe) makes the mistake of falling in love with nanny Ann (Bissett), which makes his wife Carol (Tyson) go psychotic. She overhears everyhing thanks to that darn baby monitor and decides to have Ann killed in a botched kidnapping attempt. But Ann discovers the evil goings-on (because of the baby monitor, natch) and works to save the good guys. **91m/C VHS.** Josie Bissett, Jason Beghe, Barbara Tyson, Jeffrey Noah, Vincent Gale, Gerard Plunkett; ***D:*** John L. Roman; ***W:*** Edgar van Cossart. **CABLE**

Baby of the Bride **1991** Follow-up to "Children of the Bride," has McClanahan settling into wedded bliss with younger husband Shackleford when she discovers she's pregnant. Not only is she unsure about wanting to be a mom again at her age but then grown—and single—daughter McNichol announces she is also pregnant. The sheer silliness of this TV fare makes it fun to watch. **93m/C VHS.** Rue McClanahan, Ted Shackleford, Kristy McNichol, John Wesley Shipp, Anne Bobby, Conor O'Farrell; ***D:*** Bill Bixby; ***W:*** Bart Baker. **TV**

Baby on Board **1992 (PG)** Kane plays the wife of a Mafia bookkeeper who is accidentally killed in a gangland murder. Out for revenge, she tracks her husband's killer to JFK airport with her four-year-old daughter in tow. Just as she pulls the loaded gun from her purse and takes aim, a pickpocket snatches her purse, accidentally firing the gun. Now she's on the run and she jumps into the first cab she can find, driven by Reinhold. New York City is turned upside down as mother, daughter, and cabbie try to elude the mob in this funny but predictable comedy. **90m/C VHS.** Carol Kane, Judge Reinhold, Geza Kovacs, Errol Slue, Alex Stapley, Holly Stapley; ***D:*** Francis Schaeffer.

Baby ... Secret of the Lost Legend **1985 (PG)** A sportswriter and his paleontologist wife risk their lives to reunite a hatching brontosaurus with its mother in the African jungle. Although this Disney film is not lewd in any sense, beware of several scenes displaying frontal nudity and some violence. **95m/C VHS.** William Katt, Sean Young, Patrick McGoohan, Julian Fellowes; ***D:*** Bill W.L. Norton.

The Baby-Sitters' Club **1995 (PG)** Centering on the summer vacation of seven enterprising Connecticut 13-year-olds and their teen trials with parents, boys, and babysitting, this film is sure to hit home with a crowd that is rarely featured, pre-teen girls. Director Mayron claims, "It's the 'Mystic Pizza' of their age." Young girls and girls young at heart should enjoy this touching look at the fragile years of our youth, leaving baby dolls behind and heading towards dating. Based on the best-selling book series by Ann Martin. Fisk, who plays club leader Kristy, is the daughter of actress Sissy Spacek and director Jack Fisk. **92m/C VHS.** Schuyler Fisk, Bre Blair, Rachael Leigh Cook, Larisa Oleynik, Tricia Joe, Stacey Linn Ramsower, Zelda Harris, Brooke Adams, Peter Horton, Bruce Davison, Ellen Burstyn, Austin O'Brien, Aaron Michael Metchik; ***D:*** Melanie Mayron; ***W:*** Dalene Young; ***C:*** Willy Kurant; ***M:*** David Michael Frank.

Baby, Take a Bow **1934 (PG)** Temple's first starring role. As a cheerful Pollyanna-type she helps her father, falsely accused of theft, by finding the true thief. **76m/B VHS.** Shirley Temple, James Dunn, Claire Trevor, Alan Dinehart; ***D:*** Harry Lachman.

Baby, the Rain Must Fall **1964** A rockabilly singer, paroled from prison after serving time for a knifing, returns home to his wife and daughter, but his outbursts of violence make the reunion difficult. Unsentimental with realistic performances, but script is weak (although written by Foote, based on his play, "The Traveling Lady"). Theme song was a Top 40 hit. **100m/B VHS.** Steve McQueen, Lee Remick, Don Murray; ***D:*** Robert Mulligan; ***W:*** Horton Foote; ***C:*** Ernest Laszlo; ***M:*** Elmer Bernstein.

Babycakes **1989** A marshmellow romance between an overweight mortuary attendant who decides to follow her heart when she falls for a hunky ice skater. Can she make him appreciate her inner beauty instead of just her not-the-normal-beauty-standard outward appearance? (Happy ending guaranteed.) TV remake of the darker German film "Sugarbaby." **94m/C VHS.** Ricki Lake, Craig Sheffer, Paul Benedict, Betty Buckley, John Karlen, Nada Despotovich; ***D:*** Paul Schneider. **TV**

Babyfever **1994 (R)** Women gather at a baby shower and tell stories about motherhood and related topics. May be viewed as a babblefest with video accompaniment or as an overdue cinematic exploration of a fairly important aspect of life (where would we be without mom?). That said, pace of the comedy drama is less than feverish, although director Jaglom captures the essence of the stories without disturbing their flow. Foyt, Jaglom's wife and co-screenwriter, makes her acting debut. **110m/C VHS.** Matt Salinger, Eric Roberts, Frances Fisher, Victoria Foyt, Zack Norman, Dinah Lenney, Elaine Kagan; ***D:*** Henry Jaglom; ***W:*** Victoria Foyt, Henry Jaglom; ***C:*** Hanania Baer.

Baby's Day Out **1994 (PG)** Poor man's "Home Alone" refits tired Hughes formula using little tiny baby for original spin. Adorable Baby Bink crawls his way onto the city streets, much to his frantic mother's dismay, and unwittingly outsmarts his would-be kidnappers. As in "HA I and II," the bad guys fall victim to all sorts of cataclysmic Looney Tunes violence. Small kids will get a kick out of this one. Particular problem for the moviemakers was that the nine-month old Worton twins were past the year mark by the end of the shoot, a world of difference in infantdom. Blue screens and out-of-sequence shooting were used to overcome the developmental gap. **99m/C VHS, DVD, Wide.** Adam Worton, Jacob Worton, Joe Mantegna, Lara

Flynn Boyle, Joe Pantoliano, Fred Dalton Thompson, John Neville, Brian Haley, Matthew Glave; ***D:*** Patrick Read Johnson; ***W:*** John Hughes; ***C:*** Thomas Ackerman; ***M:*** Bruce Broughton.

The Babysitter 🦴🦴 **1980** A family hires the mysterious but ingratiating Johanna (Zimbalist) as live-in help without checking on her references (who'd all checked out). The babysitter is the answer to all their problems—Mom's an alcoholic, Dad's a workaholic, and their daughter's just plain maladjusted—but once Johanna's gained their trust (or, in Dad's case, lust), she sets out to manipulate and exploit the family for her own psychotic purposes. Houseman plays the nosy neighbor who's on to her evil plan. Fair made-for-TV treatment of a common suspense plot. **96m/C VHS.** William Shatner, Patty Duke, Stephanie Zimbalist, Quinn Cummings, John Houseman, David Wallace; ***D:*** Peter Medak.

The Babysitter 🦴🦴½ **1995 (R)** All-American teen Jennifer (Silverstone) becomes the unexpected object of desire for family man Harry (Walsh), whose wife Dolly (Garlington) is fantasizing about having an affair with a neighbor (Segal). But then Jennifer's boyfriend (London) gets caught up in a malicious prank that turns bad for everyone involved. Based on a short story by Robert Coover. **90m/C VHS.** Alicia Silverstone, Jeremy London, J.T. Walsh, Lee Garlington, Nicky Katt, Lois Chiles, George Segal; ***D:*** Guy Ferland; ***W:*** Guy Ferland; ***M:*** Loek Dikker.

The Bacchantes 🦴🦴 **1963** Poorly dubbed account of a ballerina, her life and loves. Based on the play by Euripides. **100m/B VHS.** *IT* Taina Elg, Pierre Brice, Alessandra Panaro, Alberto Lupo, Akim Tamiroff; ***D:*** Giorgio Ferroni.

The Bachelor 🦴🦴🦴 **1993** Beautiful, seductive period drama about a shy and solitary physician who is forced into a new life when a family tragedy changes everything he once took for granted. Richardson and Carradine give brilliant performances in this provocative story of one man's sexual awakening. Based on a novel by Arthur Schnitzler. **105m/C VHS.** Keith Carradine, Miranda Richardson, Mari Torocsik, Max von Sydow, Kristin Scott Thomas, Sarah-Jane Fenton, Franco Diogene; ***D:*** Roberto Faenza; ***W:*** Roberto Faenza, Ennio de Concini, Hugh Fleetwood; ***M:*** Ennio Morricone.

The Bachelor 🦴🦴 **1999 (PG-13)** Exec producer/star Chris O'Donnell's remake of Buster Keaton's 1925 silent comedy "Seven Chances" falls short of bringing the story to a modern audience. Well, an audience that's aware of the discovery of talkies, feminism and plot holes anyway. O'Donnell plays Jimmy, who stands to inherit a fortune from his grandfather (Ustinov) if he marries before the age of 30. Unfortunately, he receives this news immediately after his odious proposal to girlfriend Anne (Zellweger) is rejected...And of course his thirtieth birthday happens to be 27 hours away. Madcap antics allegedly ensue as Jimmy trolls for a wife from the pool of his ex-girlfriends and flees the husband-hunting horde who respond to a front-page ad placed by his pal Marco (Lange). **101m/C VHS, DVD.** Chris O'Donnell, Renee Zellweger, Hal Holbrook, James Cromwell, Artie Lange, Ed Asner, Marley Shelton, Stacy Edwards, Rebecca Cross, Jennifer Esposito, Peter Ustinov, Mariah Carey, Brooke Shields; ***D:*** Gary Sinyor; ***W:*** Steve Cohen; ***C:*** Simon Archer; ***M:*** David A. Hughes, John Murphy.

The Bachelor and the Bobby-Soxer 🦴🦴🦴 *Bachelor Knight* **1947** Playboy Grant is brought before Judge Loy for disturbing the peace and sentenced to court her teenage sister Temple. Cruel and unusual punishment? Maybe, but the wise Judge hopes that the dates will help Temple over her crush on handsome Grant. Instead, Loy and Grant fall for each other. **95m/B VHS.** Cary Grant, Myrna Loy, Shirley Temple, Rudy Vallee, Harry Davenport, Ray Collins, Veda Ann Borg; ***D:*** Irving Reis; ***W:*** Sidney Sheldon. Oscars '47: Orig. Screenplay.

Bachelor Apartment 🦴🦴½ **1931** Once at the leading edge of the bachelor on the loose genre, this one's hopelessly dated. The scandalous womanizing of a wealthy '30s Lothario just doesn't have the same impact on the men just don't understand generation. Nevertheless, as vintage if-the-walls-could-talk fluff, it's good for a giggle. **77m/B VHS.** Lowell Sherman, Irene Dunne, Norman Kerry, Claudia Dell, Noel Francis, Charles Coleman; ***D:*** Lowell Sherman.

Bachelor Bait 🦴½ **1934** A marriage license clerk who's tired of just handing out licenses opens a matrimonial service for men. **75m/B VHS.** Stuart Erwin, Rochelle Hudson, Pert Kelton, Richard "Skeets" Gallagher, Berton Churchill, Grady Sutton, Clarence Wilson; ***D:*** George Stevens; ***W:*** Glenn Tryon; ***C:*** Dave Abel; ***M:*** Max Steiner.

Bachelor in Paradise 🦴🦴½ **1969** Silly tale starring Hope as a writer of books to the lovelorn who decides to do firsthand research on the sexual goings-on of a suburban California community. All the married ladies find him charming (much to their husbands' disgust) and the lone single woman, Turner, isn't single by the end of the movie. **109m/C VHS.** Bob Hope, Lana Turner, Janis Paige, Jim Hutton, Paula Prentiss, Don Porter, Virginia Grey, Agnes Moorehead, John McGiver; ***D:*** Jack Arnold; ***W:*** Hal Kanter, Valentine Davies; ***M:*** Henry Mancini.

Bachelor Mother 🦴🦴🦴 **1939** A single salesgirl causes a scandal when she finds an abandoned baby and is convinced by her boss to adopt the child. Smart, witty comedy with nice performance by Rogers. **82m/B VHS.** Ginger Rogers, David Niven, Charles Coburn; ***D:*** Garson Kanin.

Bachelor of Hearts 🦴½ **1958** Sophomoric British comedy set at Cambridge University, with a German exchange student whose difficulty with English brings him to date several women in one evening. Notable for horror fans as the debut of femme fright fave Barbara Steele. **94m/C VHS.** *GB* Hardy Kruger, Sylvia Syms, Ronald Lewis; ***D:*** Wolf Rilla; ***W:*** Frederic Raphael, Leslie Bricusse.

Bachelor Party 🦴🦴 **1984 (R)** Rick (Hank) is silly, cute, and poor. Debbie (Kitaen) is intelligent, beautiful, and rich. It must be a marriage made in heaven, because no one in their right mind would put these two together. All is basically well, except that her parents hate him and his friends dislike her. Things are calm until right before the big event, when the bride-to-be objects to Rick's traditional pre-nuptial partying and with good reason. Light and semi-entertaining with scattered laughs. **105m/C VHS, DVD, Wide.** Tom Hanks, Tawny Kitaen, Adrian Zmed, George Grizzard, Robert Prescott, William Tepper, Wendie Jo Sperber, Barry Diamond, Michael Dudikoff, Deborah Harmon, John Bloom, Toni Alessandra, Monique Gabrielle, Angela Aames, Rosanne Katon, Bradford Bancroft; ***D:*** Neal Israel; ***W:*** Pat Proft; ***C:*** Hal Trussel; ***M:*** Robert Folk.

Back Door to Heaven 🦴🦴🦴½ **1939** Traces the path of a young boy who is born into a poor family and the reasons for his turning to a life of crime. A grim and powerful drama with many convincing performances. **85m/B VHS.** Wallace Ford, Aline MacMahon, Stuart Erwin, Patricia Ellis, Kent Smith, Van Heflin, Jimmy Lydon; ***D:*** William K. Howard.

Back from Eternity 🦴🦴 **1956** Eleven survivors of a plane crash are stranded in a headhunter region of South America's jungle. Remake of "Five Came Back" (1939), which was also directed by Farrow. **97m/B VHS.** Robert Ryan, Rod Steiger, Anita Ekberg, Phyllis Kirk, Keith Andes, Gene Barry; ***D:*** John Farrow; ***C:*** William Mellor.

Back Home 🦴🦴½ **1990** A family reunion movie with pure Disney sentiment. A 12-year-old English girl, who has been living in America during WWII, is reunited with her family in postwar England. **103m/C VHS.** Hayley Carr, Hayley Mills, Jean Anderson, Rupert Frazer, Brenda Bruce, Adam Stevenson, George Clark; ***D:*** Piers Haggard. **CABLE**

Back in Action 🦴½ **1994 (R)** Veteran LA detective Rossi (Piper) is out to bust the ruthless drug gang who gunned down his partner. But he's got company—martial-arts expert Billy (Blanks) whose young sister has fallen prey to the same gang. So the two action junkies reluctantly team up to cause some major damage. **93m/C VHS.** Roddy Piper, Billy Blanks, Bobbie Phillips, Matt Birman, Nigel Bennett, Damon D'Oliveira, Kai Soremekun; ***D:*** Paul Ziller, Steve DiMarco; ***W:*** Karl Schiffman.

Back in Business 🦴🦴 **1996 (R)** Joe Elkhart's (Bosworth) life is down the drain. After failing to expose a fellow police officer as corrupt, he's kicked off the force, abandoned by his friends, and divorced by his wife. Now working as a mechanic, Joe gets pulled back into the action when his ex-partner, Tony (Torry), goes undercover to bring down a major drug dealer and Joe discovers the corrupt cops that framed him are also behind the current heroin deal. **93m/C VHS.** Brian Bosworth, Joe Torry, Dara Tomanovich, Alan Scarfe, Brion James, Ron Glass; ***D:*** Philippe Mora; ***W:*** Ed Decatur, Ash Staley; ***C:*** Walter Bal.

Back in the Saddle 🦴½ **1941** Autry is a ranch foreman who discovers a nearby copper mine is poisoning his cattle. Gene manages to do a lot of singing in between the fist fights. **71m/B VHS.** Gene Autry, Smiley Burnette, Mary Lee, Edward Norris; ***D:*** Lew (Louis Friedlander) Landers; ***W:*** Richard Murphy, Jesse Lasky Jr.; ***C:*** Ernest Miller.

Back in the USSR 🦴½ **1992 (R)** Danger follows two lovers caught up in the Moscow underworld. When young American touring Russia unwittingly gets involved with a beautiful art thief. Lots of fast-paced action in an otherwise muddled film. The first American film shot entirely on location in Moscow. **87m/C VHS.** Frank Whaley, Natalia (Natalya) Negoda, Roman Polanski, Claudia Robinson, Dey Young, Andrew Divoff, Brian Blessed, Ravil Issyanov; ***D:*** Deran Sarafian; ***C:*** Yuri Neyman.

Back of Beyond 🦴🦴 **1995 (R)** Spectacular setting in the Australian outback can't make up for unfocused plot and characters with little impact. Tom (Mercurio) ran a remote desert gas station with his sister, Susan (Elmalogulou), before she was killed on his motorbike. When Connor's (Friels) car breaks down by the derelict station, he, girlfriend Charlie (Smart), and sidekick Nick (Polson) must wait while Tom tries to fix it. Only Connor is a diamond thief and patience isn't one of his virutes, especially when he notices the unhappy Charlie making friends with Tom. Mystical/supernatural elements involving ghosts and Aboriginal sites only add to the confusion. **85m/C VHS.** *AU* Paul Mercurio, Colin Friels, Dee Smart, John Polson, Rebekah Elmaloglou, Bob Maza, Terry Serio; ***D:*** Michael Robertson; ***W:*** Paul Leadon, A.M. Brooksbank, Richard I. Sawyer; ***C:*** Stephen Dobson; ***M:*** Mark Moffatt, Wayne Goodwin.

Back Roads 🦴🦴 **1981 (R)** Southern hooker meets a down-on-his-luck boxer and both head out for a better life in California, finding love along the way. Ritt road trip lacks any comedic rhythm and survives on Field and Jones working to entertain. **94m/C VHS.** Sally Field, Tommy Lee Jones, David Keith; ***D:*** Martin Ritt; ***W:*** Gary De Vore; ***C:*** John A. Alonzo; ***M:*** Henry Mancini.

Back Street 🦴🦴 **1961** The forbidden affair between a married man and a beautiful fashion designer carries on through many anxious years to a tragic end. The lavish third film version of the Fannie Hurst novel. **107m/C VHS.** Susan Hayward, John Gavin, Vera Miles; ***D:*** David Miller; ***C:*** William H. Daniels.

Back to Back 🦴 **1990 (R)** A beautiful young vigilante embarks on a rampage to clear her family's name and make her town's redneck crooks pay for their crimes. Never released in theatres. **95m/C VHS.** Bill Paxton, Todd Field, Apollonia, Luke Askew, Ben Johnson, David Michael-Standing, Susan Anspach, Sal Landi; ***D:*** John Kincade; ***C:*** James L. Carter.

Back to Back 🦴🦴½ **1996 (R)** Ex-cop Malone (Rooker) must team up with hitman Koji (Ishibashi), who's holding Malone's daughter hostage, to double-cross a corrupt cop and stay alive while being hunted by the Mafia. **95m/C VHS, DVD.** Michael Rooker, Ryo Ishibashi, John Laughlin, Danielle Harris, Bob(cat) Goldthwait, Vincent Schiavelli; ***D:*** Roger Nygard; ***W:*** Lloyd Keith; ***C:*** Mark W. Gray; ***M:*** Walter Werzowa.

Back to Bataan 🦴🦴½ **1945** Colonel forms guerrilla army to raid Japanese in the Philippines and to help Americans landing on Leyte. Also available in a colorized version. **95m/B VHS.** John Wayne, Anthony Quinn, Beulah Bondi, Fely Franquelli, Richard Loo, Philip Ahn, Lawrence Tierney; ***D:*** Edward Dmytryk.

Back to Hannibal: The Return of Tom Sawyer and Huckleberry Finn 🦴🦴½ **1990** Mark Twain's characters Tom Sawyer and Huckleberry Finn are reunited as adults to solve a murder mystery. Tom is a lawyer, Finn a newspaper man, and it's Becky Thatcher's husband who's been murdered. Did a freed slave really commit the crime? **92m/C VHS.** Raphael Sbarge, Mitchell Anderson, Megan Follows, William Windom, Ned Beatty, Paul Winfield; ***D:*** Paul Krasny; ***M:*** Lee Holdridge. **TV**

Back to School 🦴🦴½ **1986 (PG-13)** Dangerfield plays an obnoxious millionaire who enrolls in college to help his wimpy son, Gordon, achieve campus stardom. His motto seems to be "if you can't buy it, it can't be had." At first, his antics embarrass his shy son, but soon everyone is clamoring to be seen with the pair as Gordon develops his own self confidence. **96m/C VHS, DVD, Wide.** Rodney Dangerfield, Keith Gordon, Robert Downey Jr., Sally Kellerman, Burt Young, Paxton Whitehead, Adrienne Barbeau, M. Emmet Walsh, Severn Darden, Ned Beatty, Sam Kinison, Kurt Vonnegut Jr., Robert Picardo, Terry Farrell, Edie McClurg, Jason Hervey, William Zabka; ***D:*** Alan Metter; ***W:*** Will Aldis, Steven Kampmann, Harold Ramis, Peter Torokvei; ***C:*** Thomas Ackerman; ***M:*** Danny Elfman.

Back to the Beach 🦴½ **1987 (PG)** Frankie and Annette return to the beach as self-parodying, middle-aged parents with rebellious kids, and the usual run of sun-bleached, lover's tiff comedy ensues. Plenty of songs and guest appearances from television past. Tries to bring back that surf, sun, and sand feel of the orignal "Beach Party" movies, but fails. ♫Absolute Perfection; California Sun; Catch a Ride; Jamaica Sky; Papa-Oom-Mow-Mow; Sign of Love; Sun, Sun, Sun, Sun, Sun; Surfin' Bird; Wooly Bully. **92m/C VHS.** Frankie Avalon, Annette Funicello, Connie Stevens, Lori Loughlin, Tommy Hinkley, Demian Slade, John Calvin, Joe Holland, David Bowe, Paul (Pee-wee Herman) Reubens, Don Adams, Bob Denver, Alan Hale Jr., Tony Dow, Jerry Mathers, Dick Dale, Stevie Ray Vaughan, Edd Byrnes, Barbara Billingsley; ***D:*** Lyndall Hobbs; ***W:*** James Komack, Bill W.L. Norton; ***C:*** Bruce Surtees; ***M:*** Steve Dorff.

Back to the Future 🦴🦴🦴 **1985 (PG)** When neighborhood mad scientist Doc Brown (Lloyd) constructs a time machine from a DeLorean, his youthful companion Marty (Fox) accidentally transports himself to 1955. There, Marty must do everything he can to bring his high-school age parents together (so he can be born), elude the local bully, and get back...to the future. Solid fast-paced entertainment is even better due to Lloyd's inspired performance as the loony Doc while Fox is perfect as the boy completely out of his element. Soundtrack features Huey Lewis and the News. Followed by two sequels. **116m/C VHS, DVD, Wide.** Michael J. Fox, Christopher Lloyd, Lea Thompson, Crispin Glover, Wendie Jo Sperber, Marc McClure, Thomas F. Wilson, James Tolkan, Casey Siemaszko, Billy Zane, George DiCenzo, Courtney Gains, Claudia Wells, Jason Hervey, Harry Waters Jr., Maia Brewton, J.J. (Jeffrey Jay) Cohen; ***Cameos:*** Huey Lewis; ***D:*** Robert Zemeckis; ***W:*** Robert Zemeckis, Bob Gale; ***C:*** Dean Cundey; ***M:*** Alan Silvestri.

Back to the Future, Part 2 🦴🦴½ **1989 (PG)** Taking up exactly where Part 1 left off, Doc Brown and Marty time-hop into the future (2015 to be exact) to save Marty's kids, then find themselves returning to 1955 to retrieve a sports almanac that causes havoc for the McFly family. Clever editing allows for Marty Part 2 to see Marty Part 1 at the school dance. Most of the cast returns, although Glover appears only in cuts from the original and Shue steps in as girlfriend Jennifer. Not up to the original, but still satisfying. Cliffhanger ending sets up Part 3, which was shot simultaneously with this. **107m/C VHS, Wide.** Michael J. Fox, Christopher Lloyd, Lea Thompson, Thomas F. Wilson, Harry Waters Jr., Charles Fleischer, Joe Flaherty, Elisabeth Shue, James Tolkan, Casey Siemaszko, Jeffrey Weissman, Flea, Billy Zane, J.J. (Jeffrey Jay) Cohen, Darlene Vogel, Jason Scott Lee, Crispin Glover, Ricky Dean Logan; ***D:*** Robert Zemeckis; ***W:*** Robert Zemeckis, Bob Gale; ***C:*** Dean Cundey; ***M:*** Alan Silvestri.

Back to the Future, Part 3 𝒮𝒮𝒮 **1990 (PG)** Picks up where Part 2 climaxed a la cliffhanger. Stuck in 1955, time-traveling hero Marty frantically searches for Doc Part 1 so he can return to 1985. Instead, he finds himself in the Wild West circa 1885, trying to save Doc's life. Plot is related to earlier BTTFs, so first time viewers might be confused. For those who've seen previous incarnations, the clever interconnections are really nifty. Nearly matches the original for excitement and offers some snazzy new special effects. Supposedly the last installment, though don't be surprised if another sequel follows. The complete trilogy is available as a boxed set. **118m/C VHS, Wide.** Michael J. Fox, Christopher Lloyd, Mary Steenburgen, Thomas F. Wilson, Lea Thompson, Elisabeth Shue, Matt Clark, Richard Dysart, Pat Buttram, Harry Carey Jr., Dub Taylor, James Tolkan, Marc McClure, Wendie Jo Sperber, J.J. (Jeffrey Jay) Cohen, Ricky Dean Logan, Jeffrey Weissman; ***D:*** Robert Zemeckis; ***W:*** Robert Zemeckis, Bob Gale; ***C:*** Dean Cundey; ***M:*** Alan Silvestri.

Back to the Secret Garden 𝒮𝒮½ **2001** Well-meaning but dull sequel based on characters from the novel by Frances Hodgson Burnett. It's now the 1940s and sullen Mary has grown into the elegant Lady Mary (Lunghi), the wife of the ambassador to the U.S. Mistlethwaite has turned into a sunny English orphanage that is run by Martha (Plowright). Lady Mary arranges for Brooklyn-born orphan Lizzie (Buelle) to join their little band, and the young girl just happens to be a gardening whiz. Which is a good thing, since Mary's special garden been badly neglected once again. **100m/C VHS, DVD.** Camilla Belle, Cherie Lunghi, Joan Plowright, David Warner, Leigh Lawson, Florence Hoath; ***D:*** Michael Tuchner; ***W:*** Joe Wiesenfeld; ***C:*** Ian Wilson. **CABLE**

Back to the Wall 𝒮𝒮 **1956** Moreau is an adulturous wife whose web of deceit results in a suspenseful tale of murder and blackmail. **94m/B VHS.** *FR* Jeanne Moreau, Gerard Oury, Claire Maurier; ***D:*** Edouard Molinaro.

Backbeat 𝒮𝒮𝒮 **1994 (R)** Backed by the beat of early Beatle tunes as rendered by some of today's top alternative musicians, the debut for director Softley explores the Fab Four's beginnings in Hamburg's underground music scene. Storyline is driven by the complications of a romantic triangle between John Lennon, Astrid Kirchherr (the photographer who came up with the band's signature look) and Stu Sutcliffe, Lennon's best friend and the original bass player for the Beatles. Hart's dead-on as Lennon, playing him a second time (check out "The Hours and Times"). Energetic and enjoyable, particularly when the Was-produced music takes center stage. **100m/C VHS, Wide.** *GB* Stephen Dorff, Sheryl Lee, Ian Hart, Gary Bakewell, Chris O'Neill, Scot Williams, Kai Wiesinger, Jennifer Ehle; ***D:*** Iain Softley; ***W:*** Michael Thomas, Stephen Ward, Iain Softley; ***C:*** Ian Wilson; ***M:*** Don Was.

Backdraft 𝒮𝒮½ **1991 (R)** High action story of Chicago firemen has some of the most stupendous incendiary special effects ever filmed. But then there's that plot, B-movie hokum about a mystery arsonist torching strategic parts of the community with the finesse of an expert and a brother-against-brother conflict. Straightforward performances from most of the cast in spite of the weak storyline. Writer Widen wrote from experience—he used to be a fireman; real-life Chicago firefighters were reportedly very happy with the realistic and intense fire scenes. Forget the plot and just watch the fires. Also available in a letterboxed version. **135m/C VHS, DVD, Wide.** Kurt Russell, William Baldwin, Robert De Niro, Donald Sutherland, Jennifer Jason Leigh, Scott Glenn, Rebecca DeMornay, Jason Gedrick, J.T. Walsh, Tony Mockus Sr., Clint Howard, David Crosby; ***D:*** Ron Howard; ***W:*** Gregory Widen; ***C:*** Mikael Salomon; ***M:*** Hans Zimmer.

Backfield in Motion 𝒮𝒮½ **1991** Silly but harmless comedy about a widowed mom who tries to get closer to her high-schooler son by organizing a mother-son football game. But it's the boys' football coach who really wants to get close—to mom. TV movie debut of both Arnolds (past and present). **95m/C VHS.** Roseanne, Tom Arnold, Colleen Camp, Conchata Ferrell, Johnny Galecki, Kevin Scannell; ***D:*** Richard Michaels. **TV**

Backfire 𝒮𝒮 **1922** If you're gonna rob a bank, you shouldn't let anyone hear you plan it, and if you're not gonna rob a bank, you shouldn't let anyone hear you plan one. This vintage "Lightning" Carson crime western has Carson and friend suspected of bank robbery because someone heard them planning one. The sheriff follows their every footstep as they search for the real perpetrators. **56m/B VHS.** Jack Hoxie, George Sowards, Lew Meehan, Florence Gilbert; ***D:*** Alan James.

Backfire 𝒮𝒮 **1988 (R)** A mysterious stranger enters the lives of a disturbed 'Nam vet and his discontented wife, setting a pattern of murder and double-cross in motion. **90m/C VHS.** Karen Allen, Keith Carradine, Jeff Fahey, Bernie Casey, Dinah Manoff, Dean Paul (Dino Martin Jr.) Martin; ***D:*** Gilbert Cates; ***W:*** Larry Brand; ***M:*** David Shire.

Backfire! 𝒮½ **1994 (PG-13)** Silly spoof finds Jeremy (Mosby) wanting to join New York City's all-female fire brigade who are trying to stop an arsonist from blowing up the city's toilets. Mitchum is the fire marshal and Ireland the mayor's charming assistant. **88m/C VHS.** Josh Mosby, Kathy Ireland, Robert Mitchum, Shelley Winters; ***D:*** A. Dean Bell.

Backflash 𝒮𝒮 **2001 (R)** Ray (Patrick) runs a videostore and needs a little excitement in his life. He picks up pretty hitchhiker Harley (Esposito), who's just out of jail, and gets more than he's bargained for since Harley needs Ray to pretend to be her husband so she can get into a safety deposit box. But just who's conning who? **90m/C VHS, DVD.** Robert Patrick, Jennifer Esposito, Melissa Joan Hart; ***D:*** Philip Jones; ***W:*** Philip Jones, Jennifer Farrell, Lillian Jackson; ***C:*** Maximo Munzi; ***M:*** Valentine Leone, Carl Wurtz.

Background to Danger 𝒮𝒮𝒮 **1943** A suspenseful WWII actioner about American agent Raft who travels to Turkey to receive secret documents from the soon-to-be-murdered Massen. Greenstreet is the Nazi master spy who also wants the documents as do Russian spies, Lorre and Marshall. Somewhat confusing plot but fast-paced. Based on the thriller "Uncommon Danger" by Eric Ambler. This film was Warner Bros.' follow-up to "Casablanca" with Raft in the Bogie role he had turned down in that cinema classic. **80m/B VHS.** George Raft, Sydney Greenstreet, Peter Lorre, Brenda Marshall, Osa Massen, Turhan Bey, Kurt Katch; ***D:*** Raoul Walsh.

Backlash 𝒮𝒮½ **1986 (R)** An aborigine barmaid is raped. When her assailant turns up dead, she's charged with murder and winds up in the custody of two police officers on a trip across the outback. Holes in the plot undermine this interesting, although graphic, drama with racial overtones. **88m/C VHS.** *AU* David Argue, Gia Carides, Lydia Miller, Brian Syron, Anne Smith; ***D:*** Bill Bennett; ***W:*** Bill Bennett; ***M:*** Michael Atkinson, Michael Spicer.

Backlash 𝒮𝒮 *Justice* **1999 (R)** Federal prosecutor Gina Gallagher (Needham) has gotten on the wrong side of the Colombian drug cartel. After her partner is killed, Gina works with veteran homicide detective Moe Ryan (Durning) and uncovers a government conspiracy—so maybe trusting a convict (Belushi) to protect her isn't such a bad idea. **103m/C VHS, DVD.** Tracey Needham, Charles Durning, James Belushi, JoBeth Williams, Patrick Ersgard, Tony Plana, Henry Silva, Warren Berlinger; ***D:*** Joakim (Jack) Ersgard; ***W:*** Patrick Ersgard. **VIDEO**

Backlash: Oblivion 2 𝒮𝒮½ *Oblivion 2* **1995 (PG-13)** Galactic supervillainess Lash stakes her claim to a rare derconium mine on the remote space outpost of Oblivion. Will cave monsters thwart her evil plan before space cowboys come to the town's rescue? **82m/C VHS.** Andrew Divoff, Meg Foster, Isaac Hayes, Julie Newmar, Carel Struycken, George Takei, Musetta Vander, Jimmie F. Skaggs, Irwin Keyes, Maxwell Caulfield; ***D:*** Sam Irvin; ***W:*** Peter David; ***M:*** Pino Donaggio.

Backstab 𝒮𝒮½ **1990 (R)** A spellbinding tale of work, lust, and murder. Architect Brolin finds himself unable to get over the death of his wife, until a seductive and mysterious woman helps him over his grief. They spend the night together, engulfed in passion, but in the morning he wakes to find himself sleeping with the corpse of his boss. Only the first twist in this intriguing thriller. **91m/C VHS.** James Brolin, Meg Foster, Isabelle Truchon; ***D:*** Jim Kaufman.

Backstairs 𝒮𝒮 **1921** An obscure German silent film about urban degradation and familial strife. **44m/B VHS.** *GE* Henny Porten, Fritz Kortner, William Dieterle; ***D:*** Leopold Jessner.

Backstreet Dreams 𝒮𝒮 **1990 (R)** The young parents of an autistic child find themselves torn apart due to their feelings of guilt. The father has an affair with a specialist hired to help the boy, causing further strife. Interesting story possibilities never get far. **104m/C VHS.** Brooke Shields, Jason O'Malley, Sherilyn Fenn, Tony Fields, Burt Young, Anthony (Tony) Franciosa, Nick Cassavetes, Ray "Boom Boom" Mancini; ***D:*** Rupert Hitzig; ***M:*** Bill Conti.

Backstreet Justice 𝒮𝒮½ **1993 (R)** Pittsburgh PI Keri Finnegan (Kozlowski) is investigating a series of murders in her neighborhood when she uncovers ties to police corruption dating back 30 years. This doesn't make her popular since it involves her dead cop father and a number of old friends (and enemies). Kozlowski is appropriately feisty and the plot twists will hold your attention. **91m/C VHS.** Linda Kozlowski, Hector Elizondo, John Shea, Paul Sorvino, Viveca Lindfors, Tammy Grimes; ***D:*** Chris T. McIntyre; ***W:*** Chris T. McIntyre.

Backtrack 𝒮𝒮𝒮 *Catchfire* **1989 (R)** Foster co-stars in this thriller about an artist who accidentally witnesses a mob hit. The mob puts a hitman (Hopper) on her trail, and after studying her background and listening to audio tapes she recorded, he finds himself falling in love. Originally intended for a theatrical release, it hit the European screens in a different cut as "Catchfire"; Hopper restored his original version and it was released on cable TV in the U.S. **102m/C VHS.** Dennis Hopper, Jodie Foster, Dean Stockwell, Vincent Price, John Turturro, Fred Ward, G. Anthony "Tony" Sirico, Julie Adams, Frank Gio, Sy Richardson, Helena Kallianiotes, Bob Dylan; ***Cameos:*** Charlie Sheen, Joe Pesci; ***D:*** Dennis Hopper; ***W:*** Ann Louise Bardach; ***M:*** Michel Colombier.

Backwoods 𝒮 **1987 (R)** Two campers wish they had never encountered a mountain man when he begins to stalk them with murder in mind. **90m/C VHS.** Jack O'Hara, Dick Kreusser, Brad Armacot; ***D:*** Dean Crow.

The Bad and the Beautiful 𝒮𝒮𝒮½ **1952** The rise and fall of a Hollywood producer. Douglas stars as the ruthless, arrogant Jonathan Shields, who alienates actress Georgia (Turner), writer James Lee Bartlow (Powell), and director Fred Amiel (Sullivan) as he pursues his career. Much speculation at the time as to who the real-life models for the insider story actually were. Winner of five Oscars, a splendid drama. **118m/B VHS, DVD.** Kirk Douglas, Lana Turner, Dick Powell, Gloria Grahame, Barry Sullivan, Walter Pidgeon, Gilbert Roland, Leo G. Carroll; ***D:*** Vincente Minnelli; ***W:*** Charles Schnee; ***C:*** Robert L. Surtees; ***M:*** David Raksin. Oscars '52: Art Dir./Set Dec., B&W, B&W Cinematog., Costume Des. (B&W), Screenplay, Support. Actress (Grahame).

Bad Attitude 𝒮𝒮 **1993 (R)** Leon is a narcotics officer on a mission to restore his badge after his careless pistol work gets him booted off the force. The quick-tempered cop relentlessly pursues druglord Finque with the help of an open-minded preacher (De Veaux) and his sexy, streetwise assistant (Lim). **87m/C VHS.** Leon, Gina Lim, Nathaniel DeVeaux, Susan Finque; ***D:*** Bill Cummings.

Bad Behavior 𝒮𝒮½ **1992 (R)** Unscripted character-driven drama. Gerry and Ellie McAllister are an Irish couple living in North London. He's tired of working for the local planning commission, she's bored being just a mum at home, and both are still a little uneasy living in England. When they decide to remodel the family bath, the unexpected problems lead to an emotional shakeup. Don't expect a lot of drama, the film works only if you accept the decency of the characters and the small moments of recognizable daily life. Director Blair wrote a basic script outline and had the actors improvise their dialogue, in character, over a long rehearsal period to develop their roles. **103m/C VHS.** *GB* Stephen Rea, Sinead Cusack, Philip Jackson, Clare Higgins, Phil Daniels, Saira Todd; ***D:*** Les Blair; ***M:*** John Altman.

Bad Blood 𝒮𝒮 **1987** The true story of Stan Graham, who went on a killing spree in the New Zealand bush when his farm was foreclosed and his life ruined. **104m/C VHS.** *NZ* Jack Thompson, Carol Burns, Dennis (Denis) Lill; ***D:*** Mike Newell.

Bad Blood 𝒮½ **1994 (R)** Travis Blackstone (Lamas) will use any methods to protect his brother Franklin, who's targeted for death by a ruthless drug lord. Lots of action and violence. **90m/C VHS.** Lorenzo Lamas, Hank Cheyne, Frankie Thorn, Kimberley Kates, Joe Son; ***D:*** Tibor Takacs; ***W:*** Neil Ruttenberg; ***C:*** Berhard Salzmann.

Bad Boy 𝒮½ *Branded* **1939** A country boy goes to the big city, and succumbs to urban evils and temptations, but is eventually saved by motherly love. **60m/B VHS.** Johnny Downs, Helen MacKellar, Rosalind Keith, Holmes Herbert; ***D:*** Kurt Neumann.

Bad Boy Bubby 𝒮𝒮 **1993** Bizarre black comedy about the extremely maladjusted Bubby (Hope), who becomes a pop culture phenomena. The 35-year-old childlike Bubby has been kept a virtual prisoner by his monstrous mom, who has told him the world outside is filled with poisonous gas. Wondering how his cat survived, Bubby wraps it in plastic wrap and is puzzled when it dies. Still, this gives Bubby an idea—he wraps mom in plastic and escapes outside, where he's soon adopted by a struggling rock band that writes a cult song hit about his experiences. It's even stranger than it sounds. **114m/C VHS.** *IT AU* Nicholas Hope, Claire Benito, Carmel Johnson, Ralph Cotterill, Norman Kaye, Paul Philpot, Graham Duckett, Bridget Walters; ***D:*** Rolf de Heer; ***W:*** Rolf de Heer; ***M:*** Graham Tardiff. Australian Film Inst. '94: Actor (Hope), Director (de Heer), Film Editing, Orig. Screenplay.

Bad Boys 𝒮𝒮𝒮 **1983 (R)** When a gang member's little brother is killed in a rumble, the teen responsible (Penn, who else?) goes to a reformatory, where he quickly (though somewhat reluctantly) takes charge. Meanwhile, on the outside, his rival attacks Penn's girlfriend (Sheedy, in her feature film debut) in retaliation, is incarcerated, and ends up vying with Penn for control of the cell block. Backed into a corner by their mutual hatred and escalating peer pressure, the two are pushed over the brink into a final and shattering confrontation. Not as violent as it could be, to its credit; attempts to communicate a message. **104m/C VHS, DVD, Wide.** Sean Penn, Esai Morales, Reni Santoni, Jim Moody, Eric Gurry, Ally Sheedy, Clancy Brown; ***D:*** Rick Rosenthal; ***W:*** Richard Dilello; ***C:*** Donald E. Thorin; ***M:*** Bill Conti.

Bad Boys 𝒮𝒮½ **1995 (R)** And you thought the old buddy-cop formula was played out. Well, Hollywood sticks with what works, and pairing the two TV personalities definitely works at the minimalist level required. Mike (Smith) and Marcus (Lawrence) are Miami cops who must track down $100 million worth of heroin stolen from their evidence room before internal affairs shuts down the precinct. The case leads them to a vicious thief and a beautiful female witness to his murderous handiwork. Plot lacks depth, but high energy and dazzling action sequences keep things moving. Loud adventure is made louder still by cranking soundtrack. Satisfying addition to the odd-couple cops genre with potential to spawn a "Lethal Weapon"-type franchise. Feature film debut for director Bay. **118m/C VHS, DVD.** Nestor Serrano, Michael Imperioli, Julio Mechoso, Martin Lawrence, Will Smith, Tcheky Karyo, Tea Leoni, Theresa Randle, Marg Helgenberger, Joe Pantoliano, John Salley; ***D:*** Michael Bay; ***W:*** Michael Barrie, Jim Mulholland; ***C:*** Howard Atherton; ***M:*** Mark Mancina. Blockbuster '96: Male Newcomer, T. (Smith).

Bad Bunch 🦴🦴 **1976** A white liberal living in Watts tries to befriend a ruthless black street gang, but is unsuccessful. **82m/C VHS.** Greydon Clark, Tom Johnigam, Pamela Corbett, Jacqulin Cole, Aldo Ray, Jock Mahoney; ***D:*** Greydon Clark.

B.A.D. Cats 🦴 **1980** Two members of a police burglary auto detail team chase after a group of car thieves who are planning a million-dollar gold heist. **74m/C VHS.** Asher Brauner, Michelle Pfeiffer, Vic Morrow, Jimmie Walker, Steve Hanks, LaWanda Page; ***D:*** Bernard L. Kowalski.

Bad Channels 🦴🦴 **1992 (R)** Radio goes awry when female listeners of station KDUL are shrunk and put into speciman jars by a way-out disc jockey and a visiting alien, who plans to take the women back to his planet. Mildly amusing comedy features ex-MTV VJ Quinn and score by Blue Oyster Cult. Also available with Spanish subtitles. **88m/C VHS.** Paul Hipp, Martha Quinn, Aaron Lustig, Ian Patrick Williams, Charlie Spradling, Tim Thomerson, Sonny Carl Davis, Robert Factor, Michael Huddleston; ***D:*** Ted Nicolaou; ***W:*** Jackson Barr; ***C:*** Adolfo Bartoli.

Bad Charleston Charlie woof! **1973 (PG)** Dud of a gangster comedy with terrible acting. A comedy? **91m/C VHS.** Ross Hagen, John Carradine; ***D:*** Ivan Nagy.

Bad Company 🦴🦴🦴½ **1972 (PG)** Thoughtful study of two very different Civil War draft dodgers roaming the Western frontier and eventually turning to a fruitless life of crime. Both the cast and script are wonderful in an entertaining film that hasn't been given the attention it's due. **94m/C VHS, DVD, Wide.** Jeff Bridges, Barry Brown, Jim Davis, John Savage; ***D:*** Robert Benton; ***W:*** Robert Benton, David Newman; ***C:*** Gordon Willis.

Bad Company 🦴🦴 **1994 (R)** Cynical thriller pits the bad against the worst. Vic Grimes (Langella) and Margaret Wells (Barkin) run a company of former secret agents who specialize in corporate dirty work. Nelson Crowe (Fishburne) is an ex-CIA agent who's their latest recruit. But maybe he's not so ex and maybe Margaret doesn't like sharing power and maybe the cold-blooded duo will get together to make some changes. Everything is stylish, including the leads, but there's a definite chill in the air. **118m/C VHS.** Ellen Barkin, Laurence "Larry" Fishburne, Frank Langella, Michael Beach, Gia Carides, David Ogden Stiers, Spalding Gray, James Hong, Daniel Hugh-Kelly; ***D:*** Damian Harris; ***W:*** Ross Thomas; ***C:*** Jack N. Green; ***M:*** Carter Burwell.

Bad Company **2002 (PG-13)** Hustler Rock discovers his twin brother was a CIA operative who has just been murdered. He gets recruited by agency honcho Hopkins to take over his bro's assignment, which involves terrorists, bombs, and New York City. Considering these elements, it's no wonder this one got delayed. Not yet reviewed. **?m/C VHS, DVD.** Chris Rock, Anthony Hopkins, Brooke Smith, Garcelle Beauvais, Kerry Washington; ***D:*** Joel Schumacher; ***W:*** Michael Browning, Jason Richman.

Bad Day at Black Rock 🦴🦴🦴½ **1954** Story of a one-armed man uncovering a secret in a Western town. Wonderful performances from all concerned, especially Borgnine. Fine photography, shot using the new Cinemascope technique. Based on the novel by Howard Breslin. **81m/C VHS, Wide.** Spencer Tracy, Robert Ryan, Anne Francis, Dean Jagger, Walter Brennan, John Ericson, Ernest Borgnine, Lee Marvin; ***D:*** John Sturges; ***C:*** William Mellor; ***M:*** Andre Previn. Cannes '55: Actor (Tracy).

Bad Dreams 🦴½ **1988 (R)** The only surviving member of a suicidal religious cult from the '60s awakens in 1988 from a coma. She is pursued by the living-dead cult leader, who seeks to ensure that she lives up (so to speak) to the cult's pact. Blood begins flowing as her fellow therapy group members begin dying, but the only bad dreams you'd get from this flick would be over the money lost on the video rental. **84m/C VHS.** Bruce Abbott, Jennifer Rubin, Richard Lynch, Harris Yulin, Dean Cameron, Elizabeth (E.G. Dailey) Daily, Susan Ruttan, Charles Fleischer, Sy Richardson; ***D:*** Andrew Fleming; ***W:*** Andrew Fleming, Steven E. de Souza; ***C:*** Alexander Grusynski; ***M:*** Jay Ferguson.

Bad Georgia Road 🦴½ **1977 (R)** A New Yorker inherits a moonshine operation from her uncle, and fights off the syndicate for its profits. **85m/C VHS.** Gary Lockwood, Carol Lynley, Royal Dano, John Wheeler, John Kerry; ***D:*** John Broderick.

Bad Girls 🦴🦴½ **1994 (R)** Latest in the current western craze turns the tables as women take their turns being the gunslingers. Four hooker chums hastily flee town after one kills a nasty customer—only to find the bank where their cash was stashed was robbed by baddies Loggia and Russo. Wearing stylish duds and with each hair perfectly in place the beauties manage to recover their loot. Unexciting script leaves a lot to be desired, but a strong performance from Stowe makes this nearly worthwhile. Lots of off-set drama with original director Tamra Davis fired, and the actresses reportedly having a less-than-bonding experience. **99m/C VHS, Wide.** Andie MacDowell, Madeleine Stowe, Mary Stuart Masterson, Drew Barrymore, James Russo, Dermot Mulroney, Robert Loggia, James LeGros; ***D:*** Jonathan Kaplan; ***W:*** Ken Friedman, Yolande Finch; ***M:*** Jerry Goldsmith.

Bad Girls Do Cry woof! **1954** Unbelievably bad exploitation film. Idiotic plot with long scenes of girls stripping down to their undies. Although an American film, the voice track was dubbed in later. **?m/C VHS.** Bill Page, Misty Ayers, Heather English, Ben Frommer.

Bad Girls Dormitory 🦴🦴 **1984 (R)** At the New York Female Juvenile Reformatory, suicide seems a painless and welcome escape. Utilizes standard genre identifiers, including rape, drugs, soapy showers, bad docs, and desperate young women trapped in a web of frustration and desire. Cheap and mindless titillation. **95m/C VHS.** Carey Zuris, Teresa Farley; ***D:*** Tim Kincaid.

Bad Girls from Mars woof! **1990 (R)** "B" movie sleaze-o-rama in which everyone is murdered, either before, after, or during sex, just like in real life. When the director of the film within this film hires an actress who is, shall we say, popular, to be the heroine of his latest sci-fier, the fun, slim as it is, begins. **86m/C VHS.** Edy Williams, Brinke Stevens, Jay Richardson, Oliver Darrow, Dana Bentley, Jeffrey Culver, Jasae; ***D:*** Fred Olen Ray; ***W:*** Sherman Scott, Mark Thomas McGee; ***C:*** Gary Graver; ***M:*** Chuck Cirino.

Bad Girls Go to Hell woof! **1965** From the sultana of sleaze, Wishman, comes this winning entry into Joe Bob Briggs' "Sleaziest Movies in the History of the World" series. A ditsy-but-sexy housewife accidentally commits murder and what follows is a plethora of perversion involving hirsute men and gender-bending women who are hell-bent on showing her how hot it is where bad girls go. **98m/B VHS, DVD.** Gigi Darlene, George La Rocque, Sam Stewart, Sandee Norman, Alan Yorke, Bernard L. Sankett, Darlene Bennett, Marlene Starr, Harold Key; ***D:*** Doris Wishman; ***W:*** Doris Wishman, Dawn Whitman; ***C:*** C. Davis Smith.

Bad Guys 🦴🦴 **1979** A goulash western about the outlaw days of Hungary in the 1860s. A gang of bandits terrorizes the Transdanubian countryside. In Hungarian with English subtitles. For those seeking the Eastern European Wild West experience. **93m/C VHS.** *HU* Janos Derzsi, Djoko Rosic, Mari Kiss, Gyorgy Dorner, Laszlo Szabo, Miklos Benedek; ***D:*** Gyorgy Szomjas.

Bad Guys 🦴 **1986 (PG)** An inane comedy about two ridiculous policemen who decide to take the wrestling world by storm after being kicked off the police force. Featuring scenes with many of the world's most popular wrestlers. **86m/C VHS.** Adam Baldwin, Mike Jolly, Michelle Nicastro, Ruth Buzzi, James Booth, Gene LeBell, Norman Burton; ***D:*** Joel Silberg; ***C:*** Hanania Baer; ***M:*** William Goldstein.

Bad Influence 🦴½ **1990 (R)** A lackluster effort in the evil-doppelganger school of psychological mystery, where a befuddled young executive (Spader) is led into the seamier side of life by a mysterious stranger (Lowe). **99m/C VHS.** Rob Lowe, James Spader, Lisa Zane, Christian Clemenson, Kathleen Wilhoite; ***D:*** Curtis Hanson; ***C:*** Robert Elswit; ***M:*** Trevor Jones.

Bad Jim 🦴½ **1989 (PG)** A cowpoke buys Billy the Kid's horse and, upon riding it, becomes an incorrigible outlaw himself. First feature film for Hollywood legend Clark Gable's son. **110m/C VHS.** James Brolin, Richard Roundtree, John Clark Gable, Harry Carey Jr., Ty Hardin, Pepe Serna, Rory Calhoun; ***D:*** Clyde Ware.

Bad Lands 🦴🦴½ **1939** A small cowboy posse finds themselves trapped by a band of Apache Indians in the Arizona desert. A remake of "The Lost Patrol." **70m/B VHS.** Robert Barrat, Guinn "Big Boy" Williams, Douglas Walton, Andy Clyde, Addison Richards, Robert Coote, Paul Hurst, Noah Beery Jr.; ***D:*** Lew (Louis Friedlander) Landers.

Bad Lieutenant 🦴🦴🦴 **1992 (NC-17)** Social chaos and degeneration characterize story as well as nameless loner lieutenant Keitel, who is as corrupt as they come. Assigned to a case involving a raped nun, he's confronted by his own lagging Catholic beliefs and the need for saving grace. From cult filmmaker Ferrara ("Ms. 45") and filled with violence, drugs, and grotesque sexual situations. Tense, over-the-top, urban drama is not intended for seekers of the subtle. Rent it with "Reservoir Dogs" and prepare yourself for a long tense evening of top-rated Keitel and screen-splitting violence. "R" rated version is also available at 91 minutes. **98m/C VHS, DVD.** Harvey Keitel, Brian McElroy, Frankie Acciario, Peggy Gormley, Stella Keitel, Victor Argo, Paul Calderon, Leonard Thomas, Frankie Thorn; ***D:*** Abel Ferrara; ***W:*** Zoe Tamerlaine Lund, Abel Ferrara; ***C:*** Ken Kelsch; ***M:*** Joe Delia. Ind. Spirit '93: Actor (Keitel).

Bad Love 🦴🦴½ **1995 (R)** Unlucky Eloise (Gidley) stays true to nature when she falls for loser Lenny (Sizemore), who decides the big score lies with robbing the fading movie star (O'Neill) Eloise works for. Naturally, things go badly. Slick production for anyone who likes fringe romances. **93m/C VHS, DVD.** Tom Sizemore, Pamela Gidley, Debi Mazar, Jennifer O'Neill, Margaux Hemingway, Richard Edson, Seymour Cassel, Joe Dallesandro; ***D:*** Jill Goldman; ***C:*** Gary Tieche; ***M:*** Rick Cox.

Bad Man of Deadwood 🦴 **1941** A man-with-a-past joins a circus as a sharp-shooter, and is threatened with disclosure. **54m/B VHS.** Roy Rogers, George "Gabby" Hayes, Carol Adams, Henry (Kleinbach) Brandon, Herbert Rawlinson, Sally Payne, Wally Wales, Jay Novello, Horace Murphy, Monte Blue; ***D:*** Joseph Kane; ***W:*** James R. Webb; ***C:*** William Nobles; ***M:*** Cy Feuer.

Bad Manners 🦴 **1984 (R)** When an orphan is adopted by a wealthy but entirely selfish couple, a group of his orphan friends try to free him from his new home and lifestyle. **85m/C VHS.** Martin Mull, Karen Black, Anne DeSalvo, Murphy Dunne, Pamela Segall, Edy Williams, Susan Ruttan, Richard Deacon; ***D:*** Bobby Houston; ***C:*** Jan De Bont.

Bad Manners 🦴🦴 **1998 (R)** Pompous musicologist Matt (Rubinek) returns to Boston with his razor-tongued girlfriend Kim (Feeney) to give a lecture and check in on his old girlfriend, brittle unhappy Nancy (Bedelia), and her prissy academic husband Wes (Strathairn). It's a weekend in hell for houseguests and hosts as they play not-so-adult games of truth-or-dare. Based on Gilman's play "Ghost in the Machine." **88m/C VHS, DVD, Wide.** David Strathairn, Bonnie Bedelia, Saul Rubinek, Caroleen Feeney, Julie Harris; ***D:*** Jonathan Kaufer; ***W:*** David Gilman; ***C:*** Denis Maloney; ***M:*** Ira Newborn.

Bad Man's River 🦴🦴 **1972** A Mexican revolutionary leader hires a gang of outlaws to blow up an arsenal used by the Mexican Army. **92m/C VHS, DVD.** *IT SP* Lee Van Cleef, James Mason, Gina Lollobrigida; ***D:*** Eugenio (Gene) Martin; ***W:*** Philip Yordan; ***C:*** Alejandro Ulloa; ***M:*** Waldo de los Rios.

Bad Medicine woof! **1985 (PG-13)** A youth who doesn't want to be a doctor is accepted by a highly questionable Latin American school of medicine. Remember that it was for medical students like these that the U.S. liberated Grenada. **97m/C VHS.** Steve Guttenberg, Alan Arkin, Julie Hagerty, Bill Macy, Curtis Armstrong, Julie Kavner, Joe Grifasi, Robert Romanus, Taylor Negron, Gilbert Gottfried; ***D:*** Harvey Miller; ***W:*** Harvey Miller.

Bad Men of the Border 🦴½ **1945** Routine oater has Kirby posing as a bandit in order to infiltrate an outlaw band passing counterfeit money. He rounds up the bad guys and finds time to romance Armida too. **56m/B VHS.** Kirby Grant, Fuzzy Knight, Armida, John Eldridge, Francis McDonald; ***D:*** Wallace Fox; ***W:*** Adele Buffington.

Bad Moon 🦴½ **1996 (R)** Let's put it this way, the werewolf in this movie is not the only thing that bites. Shortest (mercifully) studio release in recent history is a horror (in more ways than one) film with Pare leading the pack as Ted, a photojournalist who comes back from the Amazon a different, more nocturnally hirsute man. Fleeing from the site of his nightly gore, Ted takes refuge with his loving sister Janet (Hemingway) and her son Brett (Gamble). The real hero (and best actor) is a German shepherd named Thor (Primo) who discovers that Ted's a werewolf. Dog steals the show paws down (naturally). Decent special FX. Adapted from Wayne Smith's novel "Thor." **79m/C VHS, DVD, Wide.** Mariel Hemingway, Michael Pare, Mason Gamble, Ken Pogue; ***D:*** Eric Red; ***W:*** Eric Red; ***C:*** Jan Kiesser; ***M:*** Daniel Licht.

The Bad News Bears 🦴🦴🦴 **1976 (PG)** Family comedy about a misfit Little League team that gets whipped into shape by a cranky, sloppy, beer-drinking coach who recruits a female pitcher. O'Neal and Matthau are top-notch. Spawned two sequels and a TV series. **102m/C VHS, DVD, 8mm, Wide.** Walter Matthau, Tatum O'Neal, Vic Morrow, Joyce Van Patten, Jackie Earle Haley, Chris Barnes, Erin Blunt, Gary Cavagnaro, Alfred Lutter, David Stambaugh, Brandon Cruz, Jaime Escobedo, Scott Firestone, George Gonzales, Brett Marx, David Pollock, Quinn Smith; ***D:*** Michael Ritchie; ***W:*** Bill Lancaster; ***C:*** John A. Alonzo; ***M:*** Jerry Fielding. Writers Guild '76: Orig. Screenplay.

The Bad News Bears Go to Japan 🦴 **1978 (PG)** The second sequel, in which the famed Little League team goes to the Little League World Series in Tokyo. Comic adventure features Curtis as a talent agent out to exploit the team's fame. **92m/C VHS, DVD, Wide.** Tony Curtis, Jackie Earle Haley, Tomisaburo Wakayama, George Wyner, Erin Blunt, George Gonzales, Brett Marx, David Pollock, David Stambaugh, Regis Philbin; ***D:*** John Berry; ***W:*** Bill Lancaster; ***C:*** Gene Polito; ***M:*** Paul Chihara.

The Bad News Bears in Breaking Training 🦴½ **1977 (PG)** With a chance to take on the Houston Toros for a shot at the little league baseball Japanese champs, the Bears devise a way to get to Texas to play at the famed Astrodome. Disappointing sequel to "The Bad News Bears"; followed by "The Bad News Bears Go to Japan" (1978). **99m/C VHS, DVD, Wide.** William Devane, Clifton James, Jackie Earle Haley, Jimmy Baio, Chris Barnes, Erin Blunt, George Gonzales, Jaime Escobedo, Alfred Lutter, Brett Marx, David Pollock, Quinn Smith, David Stambaugh, Dolph Sweet; ***D:*** Michael Pressman; ***W:*** Paul Brickman; ***C:*** Fred W. Koenekamp; ***M:*** Craig Safan.

The Bad Pack 🦴½ **1998 (R)** Soldier of fortune puts together a team when he's hired to defend a town beseiged by a sadistic militia. **93m/C VHS, DVD.** Robert Davi, Ralph (Ralf) Moeller, Roddy Piper, Brent Huff, Larry B. Scott, Patrick Dollaghan, Marshall Teague; ***D:*** Brent Huff. **VIDEO**

Bad Ronald 1974 No, not a political biography of Ronald Reagan... Fascinating thriller about a disturbed teenager who kills a friend after being harassed repeatedly. The plot thickens after the boy's mother dies, and he is forced to hide out in a secret room when an unsuspecting family with three daughters moves into his house. The story is accurately recreated from the novel by John Holbrook Vance. **78m/C VHS.** Scott Jacoby, Pippa Scott, John Larch, Dabney Coleman, Kim Hunter, John Fiedler; ***D:*** Buzz Kulik. **TV**

The Bad Seed ½ 1956 A mother makes the tortuous discovery that her cherubic eight-year-old daughter harbors an innate desire to kill. Based on Maxwell Anderson's powerful Broadway stage play. **129m/B VHS.** Patty McCormack, Nancy Kelly, Eileen Heckart, Henry Jones, Evelyn Varden, Paul Fix, Jesse White, Gage Clark, Joan Croyden, Frank Cady, William Hopper; ***D:*** Mervyn LeRoy; ***W:*** John Lee Mahin; ***C:*** Harold Rosson; ***M:*** Alex North. Golden Globes '57: Support. Actress (Heckart).

The Bad Seed 1985 TV remake of the movie with the same name. Story about a sadistic little child who kills for her own evil purposes. Acting is not up to par with previous version. **100m/C VHS.** Blair Brown, Lynn Redgrave, David Carradine, Richard Kiley, David Ogden Stiers, Carrie Wells, Chad Allen, Christa Denton, Anne Haney, Eve Smith; ***D:*** Paul Wendkos; ***M:*** Paul Chihara. **TV**

Bad Seed *Preston Tylk* **2000 (R)** Mild-mannered Preston (Wilson) storms out of the house when he discovers wife Emily (Avital) is having an affair. He returns home to find her murdered—maybe by her boyfriend Jonathan (Reedus) whom Preston then tries to track down. There's another murder, both men go on the lam, and Preston turns to a hard-luck PI, Dick (Farina), for help. Too bad the film doesn't hang together better since it had the makings of a fine little thriller. **92m/C VHS, DVD, Wide.** Luke Wilson, Norman Reedus, Dennis Farina, Mili Avital, Vincent Kartheiser; ***D:*** Jon Bokenkamp; ***W:*** Jon Bokenkamp; ***C:*** Joey Forsyte; ***M:*** Kurt Kuenne.

The Bad Sleep Well ½ *The Worse You Are, the Better You Sleep; Waru Yatsu Hodo Yoku Nemuru* 1960 Japanese variation of the 1940 Warner Bros. crime dramas. A tale about corruption in the corporate world as seen through the eyes of a rising executive. **135m/B VHS.** *JP* Toshiro Mifune, Masayuki Kato, Masayuki Mori, Takashi Shimura, Akira Nishimura; ***D:*** Akira Kurosawa; ***W:*** Akira Kurosawa, Shinobu Hashimoto, Ryuzo Kikushima, Hideo Oguni; ***C:*** Yuzuru Aizawa; ***M:*** Masaru Sato.

Bad Taste 1988 A definite pleaser for the person who enjoys watching starving aliens devour the average, everyday human being. Alien fast-food manufacturers come to earth in hopes of harvesting all of mankind. The earth's fate lies in the hands of the government who must stop these rampaging creatures before the whole human race is gobbled up. Terrific make-up jobs on the aliens add the final touch to this gory, yet humorous cult horror flick. **90m/C VHS, DVD, Wide.** *NZ* Peter Jackson, Pete O'Herne, Mike Minett, Terry Potter, Craig Smith, Doug Wren, Dean Lawrie, Peter Vere-Jones, Ken Hammon, Michael Gooch; ***D:*** Peter Jackson; ***W:*** Tony Hiles, Peter Jackson, Ken Hammon; ***C:*** Peter Jackson; ***M:*** Michelle Scullion.

Badge of the Assassin 1985 True story of a New York assistant DA who directed a campaign to catch a pair of cop-killers from the '70s. **96m/C VHS.** James Woods, Yaphet Kotto, Alex Rocco, David Harris, Pam Grier, Steven Keats, Richard Bradford, Rae Dawn Chong; ***D:*** Mel Damski. **TV**

Badge 373 ½ **1973 (R)** In the vein of "The French Connection," a New York cop is suspended and decides to battle crime his own way. **116m/C VHS.** Robert Duvall, Verna Bloom, Eddie Egan; ***D:*** Howard W. Koch.

The Badlanders 1958 A western remake of the crime drama "The Asphalt Jungle." Ladd and Borgnine plan a gold robbery against Smith, who cheated them out of their share in a gold mine. Cross and double-cross follow the partners as does romance. **85m/C VHS.** Alan Ladd, Ernest Borgnine, Kent Smith, Katy Jurado, Claire Kelly, Nehemiah Persoff, Adam Williams; ***D:*** Delmer Daves.

Badlands ½ **1974 (PG)** Based loosely on the Charlie Starkweather murders of the 1950s, this impressive debut by director Malick recounts a slow-thinking, unhinged misfit's killing spree across the midwestern plains, accompanied by a starry-eyed 15-year-old schoolgirl. Sheen and Spacek are a disturbingly numb, apathetic, and icy duo. **94m/C VHS, DVD.** Martin Sheen, Sissy Spacek, Warren Oates, Ramon Bieri, Alan Vint, Gary Littlejohn, Charles Fitzpatrick, Howard Ragsdale, John Womack Jr., Dona Baldwin; ***Cameos:*** Terrence Malick; ***D:*** Terrence Malick; ***W:*** Terrence Malick; ***C:*** Tak Fujimoto, Stevan Larner, Brian Probyn; ***M:*** Erik Satie, Carl Orff. Natl. Film Reg. '93.

Badman's Territory 1946 A straight-shooting marshal has to deal with such notorious outlaws as the James and Dalton boys in a territory outside of government control. **79m/B VHS.** Randolph Scott, Ann Richards, George "Gabby" Hayes, Steve Brodie; ***D:*** Tim Whelan.

Badmen of Nevada ½ 1933 Badmen roam Nevada in the early days before law and order. **57m/B VHS.** Kent Taylor, Gail Patrick.

Baffled ½ 1972 Nimoy is a race car driver who has visions of people in danger. He must convince an ESP expert (Hampshire) of the credibility of his vision, and then try to save the lives of the people seen with his sixth sense. **90m/C VHS.** Leonard Nimoy, Susan Hampshire, Vera Miles, Rachel Roberts, Jewel Branch, Christopher Benjamin; ***D:*** Philip Leacock. **TV**

Bagdad 1949 Arabian nights story with the lovely O'Hara starring as Princess Marjan, the daughter of a sheik. She returns from England to find her father murdered and Hassan (Christian), the leader of a suspicious group known as The Black Riders, the main suspect. But then there's Turkish Pasha Al Nadim (Price) lurking sinisterly, as well. **83m/C VHS.** Maureen O'Hara, Paul (Christian) Hubschmid, Vincent Price, John Sutton, Jeff Corey, Frank Puglia, David Wolfe, Fritz Leiber; ***D:*** Charles Lamont; ***C:*** Russell Metty.

Bagdad Cafe *Out of Rosenheim* **1988 (PG)** A large German woman, played by Sagebrecht, finds herself stranded in the Mojave desert after her husband dumps her on the side of the highway. She encounters a rundown cafe where she becomes involved with the offbeat residents. A hilarious story in which the strange people and the absurdity of their situations are treated kindly and not made to seem ridiculous. Spawned a short-lived TV series with Whoopi Goldberg. **91m/C VHS, DVD, Wide.** *GE* Marianne Saegebrecht, CCH Pounder, Jack Palance, Christine Kaufmann, Monica Calhoun, Darron Flagg; ***D:*** Percy Adlon; ***W:*** Percy Adlon, Eleonore Adlon; ***C:*** Bernd Heinl; ***M:*** Bob Telson. Cesar '89: Foreign Film.

Bahama Passage ½ 1942 Trite story of one lady's efforts to win the affection of a macho Bahamas stud. **83m/C VHS.** Madeleine Carroll, Sterling Hayden, Flora Robson, Leo G. Carroll; ***D:*** Edward H. Griffith.

Bail Jumper 1989 A story of love and commitment against incredible odds; some of which happen to be a swarm of locusts, a tornado, and falling meteorites. Joe and Elaine are small-time hoods escaping their dreary lives in Murky Springs Missouri by heading for that great bastion of idyllism and idealism—New York City. But even as the world starts to crumble around them, get the message that love prevails. **96m/C VHS.** Eszter Balint, B.J. Spalding, Tony Askin, Joie Lee; ***D:*** Christian Faber.

Bail Out **1990 (R)** Three bounty hunters, armed to the teeth, run a car-trashing police gauntlet so they may capture a valuable crook. **88m/C VHS.** David Hasselhoff, Linda Blair, John Vernon, Tom Rosales, Charlie Brill; ***D:*** Max Kleven.

Bail Out at 43,000 1957 Movie about the lifestyles and love affairs of your average, everyday parachutist. **80m/B VHS.** John Payne, Karen Steele, Paul Kelly; ***D:*** Francis D. Lyon; ***W:*** Paul Monash.

Baise Moi woof! *Rape Me* 2000 French porn dressed up for the arthouse crowd had critics spinning like tops to justify not calling the film what it is—exploitative trash, even if it is done by women. After Manu (Anderson) gets gang raped, she kills her boyfriend, steals his money, and hooks up with prostitute Nadine (Bach) to go on a sex and murder spree. Very, very graphic sex and violence and the literal translation of the French title is not "rape" but another four-letter word beginning with "f." Based on the novel by co-writer/director Despentes; French with subtitles. **77m/C VHS, DVD.** *FR* Raffaela Anderson, Karen Bach; ***D:*** Virginie Despentes, Coralie Trinh Thi; ***W:*** Virginie Despentes, Coralie Trinh Thi; ***C:*** Benoit Chamaillard; ***M:*** Varou Jan.

Bait **2000 (R)** Bait is what you use to catch bigger fish, and hopefully star Foxx can use his performance in this otherwise by-the-book action-comedy to snag bigger and better roles. Petty thief Alvin (Foxx) winds up in the clink after a botched seafood robbery. His cellmate Jaster (Pastorelli) is the double-crossing partner of prancing archvillain Bristol (Hutchinson), who has stolen $40 million in gold. Unfortunately for Alvin, Jaster winds up in the Big House in the sky before he can tell anyone where the hidden loot is stashed. Head Fed Clenteen (Morse), thinking that Alvin knows where the gold is hidden, has him unwittingly equipped with surveillance devices and springs him from the pokey. Alvin, now followed by Bristol and the feds, tries to find the stashed loot by piecing together the cryptic clues that Jaster has left him. Lots of action on a minimal (for these types of movies) budget. **119m/C VHS, DVD, Wide.** Jamie Foxx, Doug Hutchison, David Morse, Jamie Kennedy, Robert Pastorelli, Kimberly Elise, David Paymer, Tia Texada, Mike Epps, Nestor Serrano, Megan Dodds, Jeffrey Donovan, Kirk Acevedo; ***D:*** Antoine Fuqua; ***W:*** Tom Gilroy, Jeff Nathanson, Adam Scheinman, Andrew Scheinman; ***C:*** Tobias Schliessler; ***M:*** Mark Mancina.

Baja **1995 (R)** Bebe (Ringwald) hides out in Baja with her beau Alex (Logue) after a drug deal goes bad. They hold up in a sleazy motel while Bebe waits for dad, John (Bernsen), to bail her out. But instead, John persuades estranged hubby Michael (Nickles) to track down the runaways and Michael finds out that hitman Tom (Henriksen) is hunting for Alex. Must be the desert heat causing all the ensuing commotion. **92m/C VHS.** Molly Ringwald, Lance Henriksen, Michael A. (M.A.) Nickles, Donal Logue, Corbin Bernsen; ***D:*** Kurt Voss; ***W:*** Kurt Voss; ***C:*** Denis Maloney; ***M:*** Reg Powell.

Baja Oklahoma 1987 A country barmaid has dreams of being a country singer. Songs by Willie Nelson, Emmylou Harris, and Billy Vera. **97m/C VHS.** Lesley Ann Warren, Peter Coyote, Swoosie Kurtz, Willie Nelson, Julia Roberts; ***D:*** Bobby Roth; ***W:*** Bobby Roth; ***C:*** Michael Ballhaus. **CABLE**

Baker's Hawk 1976 A young boy befriends a red-tailed hawk and learns the meaning of family and caring. **98m/C VHS, DVD.** Clint Walker, Diane Baker, Burl Ives, Lee Montgomery, Alan Young, Danny Bonaduce; ***D:*** Lyman Dayton; ***W:*** Dan Greer, Hal Harrison Jr.; ***C:*** Bernie Abramson; ***M:*** Lex de Azevedo.

The Baker's Wife ½ *La Femme du Boulanger* 1933 There's a new baker in town, and he brings with him to the small French village an array of tantalizing breads, as well as a discontented wife. When she runs off with a shepherd, her loyal and naive husband refuses to acknowledge her infidelity; however, in his loneliness, the baker can't bake, so the townspeople scheme to bring his wife back. Panned as overly cute Marcel Pagnol peasant glorification, and hailed as a visual poem full of wit; you decide. In French with subtitles. Also available for French students without subtitles; a French script booklet is also available. **101m/B VHS.** *FR* Raimu, Ginette LeClerc, Charles Moulton, Charpin, Robert Vattier; ***D:*** Marcel Pagnol; ***W:*** Marcel Pagnol; ***C:*** Georges Benoit; ***M:*** Vincent Scotto. N.Y. Film Critics '40: Foreign Film.

Balalaika 1939 Rather dull operetta about the Russian revolution with Eddy playing a Russian prince. Eddy masquerades as a member of the proletariat in order to romance Massey, who was expected to become the next Garbo. Didn't happen, though. Eddy's rendition of "Stille Nacht" ("Silent Night") is highlight of film. Based on the operetta by Eric Maschwitz, George Ponford, and Bernard Gruen. **102m/B VHS.** Nelson Eddy, Ilona Massey, Charlie Ruggles, Frank Morgan, Lionel Atwill, Sir C. Aubrey Smith, Joyce Compton; ***D:*** Reinhold Schunzel; ***W:*** Leon Gordon, Charles Bennett, Jacques Deval; ***C:*** Karl Freund.

Balance of Power ½ **1996 (R)** Martial arts master Matsumoto (Mako) prepares fighter Niko (Blanks) for a death match against a former student who's gone bad. **92m/C VHS.** Billy Blanks, Mako, James Lew; ***D:*** Rick Bennet; ***W:*** Phil Good, Rick Bennet; ***C:*** Gilles Corbeil.

Balboa woof! 1982 Set on sun-baked Balboa Island, this is a melodramatic tale of high-class power, jealousy, and intrigue. Never-aired pilot for a TV miniseries, in the night-time soap tradition (even features Steve Kanaly from TV's "Dallas"). Special appearance by Cassandra Peterson, also known as horror hostess Elvira; and if that interests you, look for Sonny Bono, as well. **92m/C VHS.** Tony Curtis, Carol Lynley, Chuck Connors, Sonny Bono, Steve Kanaly, Jennifer Chase, Lupita Ferrer, Martine Beswick, Henry Jones, Cassandra Peterson; ***D:*** James Polakof. **TV**

The Balcony 1963 A film version of the great Jean Genet play about a surreal brothel, located in an unnamed, revolution-torn city, where its powerful patrons act out their fantasies. Scathing and rude. **87m/B VHS, DVD.** Peter Falk, Shelley Winters, Lee Grant, Kent Smith, Peter Brocco, Ruby Dee, Jeff Corey, Leonard Nimoy, Joyce Jameson; ***D:*** Joseph Strick; ***W:*** Ben Maddow; ***C:*** George J. Folsey.

Ball of Fire 1941 A gang moll hides out with a group of mundane professors, trying to avoid her loathsome boyfriend. The professors are busy compiling an encyclopedia and Stanwyck helps them with their section on slang in the English language. Cooper has his hands full when he falls for this damsel in distress and must fight the gangsters to keep her. Stanwyck takes a personal liking to naive Cooper and resolves to teach him more than just slang. **111m/B VHS, DVD.** Gary Cooper, Barbara Stanwyck, Dana Andrews, Gene Krupa, Oscar Homolka, Dan Duryea, S.Z. Sakall, Henry Travers; ***D:*** Howard Hawks; ***W:*** Billy Wilder, Charles Brackett; ***C:*** Gregg Toland; ***M:*** Alfred Newman.

Ballad in Blue *Blues for Lovers* **1966** Real life story of Ray Charles and a blind child. Tearjerker also includes some of Charles' hit songs. ♫I Got a Woman; What'd I Say?. **89m/B VHS.** *GB* Ray Charles, Tom Bell, Mary Peach, Dawn Addams, Piers Bishop, Betty McDowall; ***D:*** Paul Henreid.

Ballad of a Gunfighter 1964 A feud between two outlaws reaches the boiling point when they both fall in love with the same woman. **84m/C VHS.** Marty Robbins, Bob Barron, Joyce Redd, Nestor Paiva, Laurette Luez; ***D:*** Bill Ward.

Ballad of a Soldier ½ *Ballada o Soldate* 1960 As a reward for demolishing two German tanks, a 19-year-old Russian soldier receives a six-day pass so he can see his mother; however, he meets another woman. Well directed and photographed, while avoiding propaganda. Russian with subtitles. **88m/B VHS, DVD.** *RU* Vladimir Ivashov, Shanna Prokhorenko, Antonina Maximova, Nikolai Kryuchkov; ***D:*** Grigori Chukhraj; ***W:*** Grigori Chukhraj, Valentin Yezhov; ***C:*** Sergei Mukhin; ***M:*** Mikhail Ziv. British Acad. '61: Film.

The Ballad of Andy Crocker ½ 1969 Early TV movie take on vets returning home from Vietnam. Andy (Majors) comes home to find his girlfriend has married someone else, his small business is in ruins, and his friends and family haven't a clue as to what has happened or what to expected from the disillusioned ex-soldier. **80m/C VHS.** Lee Majors, Joey Heatherton, Jimmy Dean, Marvin Gaye, Agnes Moorehead, Pat Hingle, Jill Haworth, Peter Haskell, Bobby Hatfield; ***D:*** George McCowan; ***W:*** Stuart Margolin; ***C:*** Henry Cronjager; ***M:*** Billy May. **TV**

Ballad of Cable Hogue 🦴🦴🦴 **1970 (R)** A prospector, who had been left to die in the desert by his double-crossing partners, finds a waterhole. A surprise awaits his former friends when they visit the remote well. Not the usual violent Peckinpah horse drama, but a tongue-in-cheek comedy romance mixed with tragedy. Obviously offbeat and worth a peek. **122m/C VHS.** Jason Robards Jr., Stella Stevens, David Warner, L.Q. (Justus E. McQueen) Jones, Strother Martin, Slim Pickens; ***D:*** Sam Peckinpah; ***C:*** Lucien Ballard; ***M:*** Jerry Goldsmith.

Ballad of Gregorio Cortez 🦴🦴🦴 **1983 (PG)** Tragic story based on one of the most famous manhunts in Texas history. A Mexican cowhand kills a Texas sheriff in self-defense and tries to elude the law, all because of a misunderstanding of the Spanish language. Olmos turns in a fine performance as Cortez. **105m/C VHS.** Edward James Olmos, James Gammon, Tom Bower, Alan Vint, Barry Corbin, Rosana De Soto, Bruce McGill, Brion James, Pepe Serna, William Sanderson; ***D:*** Robert M. Young; ***W:*** Robert M. Young; ***C:*** Reynaldo Villalobos; ***M:*** Michael W. Lewis.

The Ballad of Little Jo 🦴🦴½ **1993 (R)** Inspired by a true story set during the 1866 gold rush. Easterner Josephine Monaghan is cast out of her wealthy family after she has a baby out of wedlock. Heading west, she passes herself off as a man—Little Jo—in an attempt to forestall harrassment. Solemn and overly earnest attempt by Greenwald to demystify the old west and bring a feminist viewpoint to a familiar saga. **110m/C VHS.** Suzy Amis, Bo Hopkins, Ian McKellen, Carrie Snodgress, David Chung, Rene Auberjonois, Heather Graham, Anthony Heald, Sam Robards, Ruth Maleczech; ***D:*** Maggie Greenwald; ***W:*** Maggie Greenwald; ***C:*** Declan Quinn; ***M:*** David Mansfield.

The Ballad of Narayama 🦴🦴🦴🦴 *Narayama-Bushi-Ko* **1983** Director Imamura's subtle and vastly moving story takes place a vague century ago. In compliance with village law designed to control population among the poverty-stricken peasants, a healthy 70-year-old woman must submit to solitary starvation atop a nearby mountain. We follow her as she sets into motion the final influence she will have in the lives of her children and grandchildren, a situation described with detachment and without imposing a tragic perspective. In Japanese with English subtitles. **129m/C VHS.** *JP* Ken Ogata, Sumiko Sakamota, Takejo Aki, Tonpei Hidari, Shoichi Ozawa; ***D:*** Shohei Imamura; ***W:*** Shohei Imamura; ***C:*** Maseo Tochizawa; ***M:*** Shinichiro Ikebe. Cannes '83: Film.

The Ballad of Paul Bunyan **1972** The good-humored, legendary American giant is pitted against a powerful lumber camp boss who likes to pick on the little guy. **30m/C VHS.** ***D:*** Arthur Rankin Jr., Jules Bass.

The Ballad of the Sad Cafe 🦴🦴½ **1991 (PG-13)** Unusual love story set in a small Southern town during the Depression. The everday lives of its townspeople are suddenly transformed when a distant relation of the town's outcast (Redgrave) unexpectedly shows up. A moving story that tries to portray both sides of love and its power to enhance and destroy simultaneously. Emotion never seems to come to life in a movie that's nice to watch, but is ultimately disappointing. Adapted from the play by Edward Albee, which was based on the critically acclaimed novella by Carson McCullers. A British/U.S. co-production. **100m/C VHS.** *GB* Vanessa Redgrave, Keith Carradine, Cork Hubbert, Rod Steiger, Austin Pendleton, Beth Dixon, Lanny Flaherty, Mert Hatfield, Earl Hindman, Anne Pitoniak; ***D:*** Simon Callow; ***W:*** Michael Hirst; ***C:*** Walter Lassally; ***M:*** Richard Robbins.

Ballbuster 🦴½ **1989** Cops take on gangs in an all-out high-stakes battle to win back the streets. **100m/C VHS.** Ivan Rogers, Bonnie Paine, W. Randolph Galvin, Bill Shirk, Brenda Banet; ***D:*** Eddie Beverly Jr.; ***W:*** Eddie Beverly Jr.

Ballistic 🦴½ **1994 (R)** L.A. cop Jesse Gavin (Holden) gets in trouble when the government witness she's supposed to be protecting gets murdered. So she teams up with her ex-con father and her boyfriend to track the mobster responsible for the hit. **86m/C VHS.** Marjean Holden, Richard Roundtree, Sam Jones, Joel Beeson, Charles Napier; ***D:*** Kim Bass.

Balloon Farm 🦴🦴½ **1997** Harvey Potter (Torn), using some magic, raises a crop of balloons on cornstalks. His drought-stricken fellow farmers see the miraculous crop as symbols of hope but grumpy farmer Wheezle (Blossom) is suspicious. And his suspcions begin to infect the rest of the community, except for spunky young Willow (Wilson). Based on Jerdine Nolen's children's book "Harvey Potter's Balloon Farm." **89m/C VHS.** Rip Torn, Mara Wilson, Roberts Blossom, Laurie Metcalf, Neal McDonough, Frederic Lehne, Adam Wylie; ***D:*** William Dear; ***W:*** Steven M. Karczynski. **TV**

Baltic Deputy 🦴🦴🦴½ **1937** An early forerunner of Soviet historic realism, where an aging intellectual deals with post-revolution Soviet life. In Russian with subtitles. **95m/B VHS.** *RU* Nikolai Cherkasov; ***D:*** Yosif Heifitz.

The Baltimore Bullet 🦴🦴 **1980 (PG)** Two men make their living traveling through the country as pool hustlers, bilking would-be pool sharks. Features ten of the greatest pool players in the world. **103m/C VHS.** James Coburn, Omar Sharif, Bruce Boxleitner, Ronee Blakley, Jack O'Halloran; ***D:*** Robert Ellis Miller; ***W:*** Robert Vincent O'Neil, John F. Brascia.

Balto 🦴🦴½ **1995 (G)** Animated adventure, based on a true story, of a half-husky, half-wolf sled dog, Balto, who faces overwhelming odds to bring life-saving medicine to Nome, Alsaka. It's 1925, there's a diptheria epidemic, and Balto is the lead team dog on the final leg of the race to get the serum to Nome in time. Balto and the rest of the team dogs became instant heroes and even journeyed to Hollywood to star in their own silent film "Balto's Race to Nome." **78m/C VHS.** ***D:*** Simon Wells; ***W:*** Cliff Ruby, Elana Lesser, David Steven Cohen, Roger S.H. Schulman; ***M:*** James Horner; ***V:*** Kevin Bacon, Bob Hoskins, Bridget Fonda, Jim (Jonah) Cummings, Phil Collins, Juliette Brewer, Danny Mann, Miriam Margolyes.

Balzac: A Life of Passion 🦴🦴🦴 **1999** Bio of French writer Honore de Balzac (1799-1850)—a larger-then-life figure played by the larger-than-life Depardieu. He has mom problems (she never loved him) and turns to women who encourage him as his writing consumes him. There are balls and duels and all sorts of high and low society life during the Napoleonic era to enjoy. French with subtitles. **210m/C VHS, DVD.** *FR* Gerard Depardieu, Jeanne Moreau, Fanny Ardant, Virna Lisi, Katja Riemann, Claude Rich; ***D:*** Josee Dayan; ***W:*** Didier Decoin; ***C:*** Willy Stassen; ***M:*** Bruno Coulais. **TV**

Bambi 🦴🦴🦴🦴 **1942 (G)** A true Disney classic, detailing the often harsh education of a newborn deer and his friends in the forest. Proves that Disney animation was—and still is—the best to be found. Thumper still steals the show and the music is delightful, including "Let's Sing a Gay Little Spring Song," "Love is a Song," "Little April Shower," "The Thumper Song," and "Twitterpated." Stands as one of the greatest children's films of all time; a genuine perennial from generation to generation. Based very loosely on the book by Felix Salten. **69m/C VHS.** ***D:*** David Hand; ***W:*** Larry Morey; ***M:*** Frank Churchill, Edward Plumb; ***V:*** Bobby Stewart, Peter Behn, Stan Alexander, Cammie King, Donnie Dunagan, Hardie Albright, John Sutherland, Tim Davis, Sam Edwards, Sterling Holloway, Ann Gillis, Perce Pearce.

The Bamboo Saucer 🦴½ *Collision Course* **1968** Russian and American scientists race to find a U.F.O. in Red China. **103m/C VHS.** Dan Duryea, John Ericson, Lois Nettleton, Nan Leslie; ***D:*** Frank Telford.

Bamboozled 🦴🦴½ **2000 (R)** Spike Lee aims for controversy once again as he criticizes Hollywood's portrayal of African-Americans as well as pointing the finger at the black community's complicity in the process. Fed-up black writer Pierre Delacroix (Wayans) comes up with a series idea for a fledgling TV network as a form of protest—a modern day minstrel show complete with performers in burnt cork blackface. Fully expecting the show to fail, he hires struggling street performers Manray (Glover) and Womack (Davidson), changing their names to Mantan and Sleep 'N Eat (a reference to '30s and '40s black actors Mantan Moreland and Stepin Fetchit). The show becomes a surprise hit but also riles a militant black group, resulting in chaos in the lives of Delacroix and his assistant Sloan (Pinkett). The feel of the movie sways toward melodrama halfway through, but the wry observations of the artistic treatment of AfricanAmericans ring eerily true. Don't say it couldn't happen these days. **135m/C VHS, DVD, Wide.** Damon Wayans, Jada Pinkett Smith, Savion Glover, Tommy Davidson, Michael Rapaport, Thomas Jefferson Byrd, Paul Mooney, Susan Batson, Mos Def, Sarah Jones, Gillian Iliana Waters; ***D:*** Spike Lee; ***W:*** Spike Lee; ***C:*** Ellen Kuras; ***M:*** Terence Blanchard.

Bananas 🦴🦴🦴 **1971 (PG-13)** Intermittently hilarious pre-"Annie Hall" Allen fare is full of the director's signature angst-ridden philosophical comedy. A frustrated product tester from New York runs off to South America, where he volunteers his support to the revolutionary force of a shaky Latin-American dictatorship and winds up the leader. Don't miss an early appearance by Stallone. Witty score contributes much. **82m/C VHS, DVD, Wide.** Woody Allen, Louise Lasser, Carlos Montalban, Howard Cosell, Charlotte Rae, Conrad Bain, Allen (Goorwitz) Garfield, Sylvester Stallone; ***D:*** Woody Allen; ***W:*** Mickey Rose, Woody Allen; ***C:*** Andrew M. Costikyan; ***M:*** Marvin Hamlisch.

Bananas Boat woof! *What Changed Charley Farthing* **1978** A captain takes a man and his daughter away from the collapsing government of their banana republic. The cast and director take a few risks but fail in this would-be comedy. **91m/C VHS.** *GB* Doug McClure, Hayley Mills, Lionel Jeffries, Dilys Hamlett, Warren Mitchell; ***D:*** Sidney Hayers.

Band of Angels 🦴🦴½ **1957** Orphaned Amantha (De Carlo) learns she has African-American blood and since it's the pre-Civil War era she promptly winds up on the auction block. She becomes both the property and the mistress of mysterious New Orleans landowner Hamish Bond (Gable). Then the Civil War comes along bringing threats and revelations. De Carlo looks properly sultry but this is a weak attempt at costume drama. Based on the novel by Robert Penn Warren. **127m/C VHS.** Clark Gable, Yvonne De Carlo, Sidney Poitier, Efrem Zimbalist Jr., Rex Reason, Patric Knowles, Torin Thatcher, Andrea King, Ray Teal; ***D:*** Raoul Walsh; ***W:*** John Twist, Ivan Goff; ***M:*** Max Steiner.

Band of Brothers 🦴🦴🦴½ **2001** Steven Spielberg and Tom Hanks executive produced this excellent adaptation of Stephen Ambrose's epic tale of the 101 Airborne's Easy Company as they made their way from D-Day through Operation Market-Garden, The Battle of the Bulge, and finally, the capture of Hitler's "Eagle's Nest" compound. Although uniformly showing the influence of "Saving Private Ryan," each episode focuses on a separate sub-theme or character while not losing sight of the big-picture depth. Some characters are given short shrift, and sometimes it's hard to tell which characters lived or died during a battle, but that's a minor quibble with such a large and, in most cases, unknown, cast. Although they're young and mostly anonymous, they do give excellent, and in some cases, breakout performances (with the exception of one of the few "name" actors, David Schwimmer). The battle scenes are bracing, harrowing, and well-constructed, and the quiet moments serve to underscore the bond that develops between the men as they become battle tested. **600m/C VHS, DVD.** Eion Bailey, Jamie Bamber, Michael Cudlitz, Dale Dye, Scott Grimes, Frank John Hughes, Ron Livingston, James Madio, Neal McDonough, Rene L. Moreno, David Schwimmer, Donnie Wahlberg, Colin Hanks, Marc Warren, Damian Lewis, Kirk Acevedo, Rick Gomez, Richard Speight Jr., Jimmy Fallon, Ian Virgo, Thomas (Tom) Hardy; ***D:*** David Frankel, Tom Hanks, Richard Loncraine, Phil Alden Robinson, Mikael Salomon, David Nutter, David Leland, Tony To; ***W:*** Tom Hanks, E. Max Frye, Erik Jendresen, Bruce McKenna, Graham Yost, Stephen E. Ambrose, Erik Bork, John Orloff; ***C:*** Remi Adefarasin; ***M:*** Michael Kamen. **CABLE**

Band of Gold 🦴🦴🦴 **1995** Unflinching British miniseries follows the lives of Yorkshire prostitutes Rosie (James), Carol (Tyson), and Gina (Gemmell). They try to survive the streets of Bradford while a serial killer is targeting the local hookers. On six cassettes. **312m/C VHS.** *GB* Geraldine James, Cathy Tyson, Ruth Gemmell, Barbara Dickson, David Schofield, Richard Moore, Rachel Davies, Samantha Morton; ***D:*** Richard Standeven, Richard Laxton; ***W:*** Kay Mellor; ***C:*** Peter Jessop; ***M:*** Hal Lindes.

Band of Outsiders 🦴🦴½ *Bande a Part; The Outsiders* **1964** A woman hires a pair of petty criminals to rip off her aunt; Godard vehicle for expousing self-reflexive comments on modern film culture. In French with English subtitles. **97m/B VHS.** *FR* Sami Frey, Anna Karina, Claude Brasseur, Louisa Colpeyn; ***D:*** Jean-Luc Godard; ***W:*** Jean-Luc Godard; ***C:*** Raoul Coutard; ***M:*** Michel Legrand.

Band of the Hand 🦴 **1986 (R)** A "Miami Vice" type melodrama about five convicts who are trained to become an unstoppable police unit. The first feature film by Glaser, last seen as Starsky in "Starsky & Hutch." **109m/C VHS.** Stephen Lang, Michael Carmine, Lauren Holly, Leon Robinson; ***D:*** Paul Michael Glaser; ***W:*** Jack Baran, Leo Garen.

The Band Wagon 🦴🦴🦴 **1953** A Hollywood song-and-dance man finds trouble when he is persuaded to star in a Broadway musical. Charisse has been called Astaire's most perfect partner, perhaps by those who haven't seen Rogers. ♫That's Entertainment; Dancing in the Dark; By Myself; A Shine On Your Shoes; Something to Remember You By; High and Low; I Love Louisa; New Sun in the Sky; I Guess I'll Have to Change My Plan. **112m/C VHS.** Fred Astaire, Cyd Charisse, Oscar Levant, Nanette Fabray, Jack Buchanan, Bobby Watson; ***D:*** Vincente Minnelli; ***W:*** Betty Comden; ***M:*** Arthur Schwartz, Howard Dietz. Natl. Film Reg. '95.

Bandit King of Texas 🦴🦴½ **1949** A varmint is swindling unsuspecting settlers in a land scheme and then robbing and murdering them when they go to visit their supposed property. Rocky and friends come to the rescue. **60m/B VHS.** Allan "Rocky" Lane, Eddy (Eddie, Ed) Waller, Helene Stanley, Robert Bice, Harry Lauter, Jim Nolan, John Hamilton, Lane Bradford; ***D:*** Fred Brannon; ***W:*** Olive Cooper.

Bandit Queen 🦴½ **1951** Spanish girl forms a band to stop seizure of Spanish possessions by lawless Californians. **71m/B VHS.** Barbara Britton, Willard Parker, Philip Reed, Jack Perrin; ***D:*** William Berke.

Bandit Queen 🦴🦴 **1994** Phoolan Devi (Biswas) is a female Robin Hood in modern-day India. A lower-caste woman, Devi is sold into marriage at 11, brutalized by her husband (and many others throughout the film), and eventually winds up with an equally brutal group of hill bandits. Only this time around, Devi takes action by aiding the group in robbing, kidnapping (and murdering) the rich and higher castes. Devi surrendered to authorities in 1983 and spent 11 years in jail. Based on screenwriter Sen's biography "India's Bandit Queen: The True Story of Phoolan Devi" and Devi's diaries. In Hindi with subtitles. **119m/C VHS, DVD.** *GB IN* Seema Biswas, Nirmal Pandey, Manoj Bajpai, Raghubir Yadav, Rajesh Vivek, Govind Namdeo; ***D:***

Shekhar Kapur; ***W:*** Mala Sen; ***C:*** Ashok Mehta; ***M:*** Nusrat Fateh Ali Khan, Roger White.

Bandits 🦴½ **1973** Three cowboys team up with a band of Mexican outlaws to fight a Mexican traitor. **83m/C VHS.** Robert Conrad, Jan-Michael Vincent, Roy Jenson; ***D:*** Robert Conrad, Alfredo Zacharias.

Bandits 🦴🦴½ **1986** Simon Verini (Yanne), a sophisticated fence, is given the loot from a $10 million Cartier heist to exchange for cash by Mozart (Bruel) the leader of the thieves. But two of Mozart's gang want to keep the jewels instead and kidnap Verini's wife as ransom. She's killed, even after he returns the goods, and Verini is then framed for the theft and spends 10 years in prison. He's sent his daughter Marie-Sophie to a Swiss boarding school and upon his release works to both establish a relationship with her and to find those responsible for his wife's death. Director Lelouch's wife portrays the adult Marie-Sophie. In French with English subtitles. **98m/C VHS.** *FR* Jean Yanne, Marie-Sophie L(elouch), Patrick Bruel, Charles Gerard, Corinne Marchand, Christine Barbelivien; ***D:*** Claude Lelouch; ***W:*** Pierre Uytterhoeven, Claude Lelouch.

Bandits 🦴🦴 **1999 (R)** Talk about your band on the run! Four young women form a prison rock-and-roll band called the Bandits. Their first gig on the outside is the policeman's ball, where they escape. They become folk heroes as they elude the police and a clandestine recording they sent to a music exec zooms up the charts. German with subtitles. **109m/C VHS, DVD, Wide.** *GE* Katja Riemann, Jutta Hoffmann, Jasmin Tabatabai, Nicolette Krebitz, Hannes Jaenicke, Werner Schreyer; ***D:*** Katja von Garnier; ***W:*** Katja von Garnier, Uwe Wilhelm; ***C:*** Torsten Breuer.

Bandits 🦴🦴½ **2001 (PG-13)** Willis and Thornton are Joe and Terry, quirky bank robbers known as the "sleepover bandits" for their unusual but non-violent heists. With Willis as the smirky brawn and Thornton as the neurotic brain, the two play the Butch-and-Sundance act until fate puts bored housewife Kate (Blanchett) in their path. She talks her way into their little gang, but can't decide which of the two she should fall for most. The plot then slams on the brakes, although Levinson adds enough padding to cushion the blow. Blanchett is excellent as the sultry, vulnerable Kate, but Thornton steals the show (and chomps on considerable scenery) as the omniphobic hypochondriac Terry (his fear of antique furniture is actually one of Thornton's well-documented quirks as well). **123m/C VHS, DVD, Wide.** *US* Bruce Willis, Billy Bob Thornton, Cate Blanchett, Troy Garity, Bobby Slayton, Brian F. O'Byrne, Azura Skye, Stacy Travis, William Converse-Roberts, Richard Riehle, Micole Mercurio, January Jones; ***D:*** Barry Levinson; ***W:*** Harley Peyton; ***C:*** Dante Spinotti; ***M:*** Christopher Young. Natl. Bd. of Review '01: Actor (Thornton).

Bandits of Orgosolo 🦴🦴½ *Banditi a Orgosolo* **1961** An acclaimed, patient drama about a Sardinian shepherd who shelters a band of thieves from the police. When one of the cops is killed the shepherd panics and flees into the hills for survival. Dubbed in English. **98m/B VHS.** *IT* Michele Cossu, Peppeddu Cuccu; ***D:*** Vittorio de Seta; ***W:*** Vittorio de Seta, Vera Gherarducci; ***C:*** Vittorio de Seta, Luciano Tovoli; ***M:*** Valentino Bucchi.

Bandolero! 🦴🦴½ **1968 (PG)** In Texas, Stewart and Martin are two fugitive brothers who run into trouble with their Mexican counterparts. **106m/C VHS.** James Stewart, Raquel Welch, Dean Martin, George Kennedy, Will Geer, Harry Carey Jr., Andrew Prine; ***D:*** Andrew V. McLaglen; ***C:*** William Clothier; ***M:*** Jerry Goldsmith.

Bandwagon 🦴🦴 **1995** Four unlikely twentysomething guys decide to form a band in Raleigh, NC. Tony Ridge (Holmes) is the lead singer-songwriter who's so shy he practices in a closet; chatty drummer Charlie Flagg (Hennessey) has the rehearsal space; Wynn Knapp (Corrigan) is the band's perpetually stoned guitarist; and bass player Eric Ellwood's (Parlavecchio) hot temper has him in big trouble with a local loan shark. They finally come up with a name (Circus Monkey), get a gig (a raucous frat party), and are on their way when they acquire Zen-like road manager Linus Tate (MacMillan) and a battered van. Of course, life on the road proves to be a challenge. **99m/C VHS.** Kevin Corrigan, Steve Parlavecchio, Lee Holmes, Matthew Hennessey, Doug MacMillan, Lisa Keller; ***D:*** John Schultz; ***W:*** John Schultz; ***C:*** Shawn Maurer; ***M:*** Greg Kendall.

Bang 🦴🦴 *The Big Bang Theory* **1995** This $20,000 indie concerns a nameless, powerless Asian-American would-be actress (Narita) in L.A. She gets kicked out of her apartment, accosted by a homeless crazy (Greene), and sexually propositioned by a sleazy producer (Graff). Finally, she's accused of causing a public disturbance by a cop (Newland), who'll let her off in exchange for sexual favors. Instead, she grabs his gun, forces him to strip, ties him to a tree, puts on the cop's uniform, and steals his motorcycle. In uniform, she's suddenly viewed with authority and decides to take some time to see what that's like. **98m/C VHS.** Darling Narita, Peter Greene, Michael Newland, David Allen Graff, Eric Schrody, Michael Arturo, James Sharpe, Luis Guizar, Art Cruz, Stanley Herman; ***D:*** Ash; ***W:*** Ash; ***C:*** Dave Gasperik.

Bang Bang Kid 🦴🦴 *Bang Bang* **1967 (G)** A western spoof about a klutzy gunfighter defending a town from outlaws. **78m/C VHS.** Tom Bosley, Guy Madison, Sandra Milo; ***D:*** Stanley Prager.

Bang the Drum Slowly 🦴🦴 **1956** The original TV adaptation of a Mark Harris novel about baseball. A ball player stricken by a terminal illness strikes an unlikely friendship with a teammate. Interesting role for an actor (Newman) who claims to have been driven to acting by running away from the sporting goods business. **60m/B VHS.** Paul Newman, George Peppard, Albert Salmi. **TV**

Bang the Drum Slowly 🦴🦴🦴 **1973 (PG)** The touching story of a major league catcher who discovers that he is dying of Hodgkins disease and wants to play just one more season. De Niro is the weakening baseball player and Moriarty is the friend who helps him see it through. Based on a novel by Mark Harris. **97m/C VHS.** Robert De Niro, Michael Moriarty, Vincent Gardenia, Phil Foster, Ann Wedgeworth, Heather MacRae, Selma Diamond, Danny Aiello; ***D:*** John Hancock. N.Y. Film Critics '73: Support. Actor (De Niro).

The Bank Dick 🦴🦴🦴🦴 *The Bank Detective* **1940** Fields wrote the screenplay (using an alias) and stars in this zany comedy about a man who accidentally trips a bank robber and winds up as a guard. Fields' last major role is a classic, a worthy end to his great career. **73m/B VHS, DVD.** W.C. Fields, Cora Witherspoon, Una Merkel, Evelyn Del Rio, Jack Norton, Jessie Ralph, Franklin Pangborn, Shemp Howard, Grady Sutton, Russell Hicks, Richard Purcell, Reed Hadley; ***D:*** Edward F. (Eddie) Cline; ***W:*** W.C. Fields; ***C:*** Milton Krasner. Natl. Film Reg. '92.

Bank Robber 🦴🦴 **1993 (R)** Billy (Dempsey) is a thief who will retire after one final bank heist, if only he hadn't forgotten to break that surveillance camera. Holed up in a New York hotel he's subjected to extortion schemes and finds himself a new outlaw celebrity to newshounds. Bonet is a sweet hooker who falls in love with him. Satire on crooks and fame is too mild-mannered for its own good but not without charm. Directorial debut of Mead. Unedited NC-17 version also available. **94m/C VHS.** Patrick Dempsey, Lisa Bonet, Olivia D'Abo, James Garde, Forest Whitaker, Judge Reinhold, Michael Jeter, Joe Alaskey, John Chappoulis; ***D:*** Nick Mead; ***W:*** Nick Mead; ***M:*** Stewart Copeland.

Bank Shot 🦴🦴🦴 **1974** Hilarious comedy about a criminal who plans to rob a bank by stealing the entire building. Based on the novel by Donald Westlake, and the sequel to "The Hot Rock." **83m/C VHS.** George C. Scott, Joanna Cassidy, Sorrell Booke, G(eorge) Wood, Clifton James, Bob Balaban, Bibi Osterwald; ***D:*** Gower Champion; ***W:*** Wendell Mayes; ***C:*** Harry Stradling Jr.

The Banker 🦴🦴 **1989 (R)** A cop, played by Forster, suspects a wealthy, highly influential banker of brutal serial killings. **90m/C VHS.** Robert Forster, Jeff Conaway, Leif Garrett, Duncan Regehr, Shanna Reed, Deborah Richter, Richard Roundtree, Teri Weigel, E.J. Peaker, Michael Fairman, Juan Garcia; ***D:*** William Webb; ***C:*** John Huneck; ***M:*** Reg Powell, Sam Winans.

Banzai Runner 🦴🦴 **1986** A cop whose brother was killed in an exclusive desert-highway race decides to avenge by joining the race himself. **88m/C VHS, DVD.** Dean Stockwell, John Shepherd, Charles Dierkop; ***D:*** John G. Thomas; ***W:*** Phil Harnage; ***C:*** Howard Wexler; ***M:*** Joel Goldsmith. **VIDEO**

B.A.P.'s 🦴½ **1997 (PG-13)** Ghetto to riches story about Georgia waitresses Nisi (Berry) and Mickey (Desselle) who dream about opening their own business—a combo restaurant and hair salon. An L.A. audition offering $10,000 gets them to the sunny coast and eventually into the Beverly Hills mansion of Mr. Blakemore (Landau), where Nisi's persuaded to pose as the granddaughter of his lost love by Blakemore's money-grubbing nephew, Isaac (Fried). Everybody bonds and butler Manley (Richardson) instructs the women in taste and etiquette. Good cast is wasted and the comedy's lame when not offensive. **91m/C VHS.** Halle Berry, Natalie Desselle, Martin Landau, Ian Richardson, Troy Beyer, Luigi Amodeo, Jonathan Fried, A.J. (Anthony) Johnson; ***D:*** Robert Townsend; ***W:*** Troy Beyer; ***C:*** Bill Dill; ***M:*** Stanley Clarke.

Bar-B-Q woof! **2000** A pro-ball player turned actor needs a break and heads home to have a Bar-B-Q with his girl and old homies. When word gets out the entire neighborhood shows up for the party. A lot of music and a lot of crude jokes and infantile humor make this poorly made, horribly acted film practically unwatchable. The 102-minute running time includes nearly 15 minutes of credits and what the cast and crew apparently considered humorous outtakes. **102m/C DVD.** Layzie Bone, John West, Chanda Watts, Lea Griggs; ***D:*** Amanda Moss, John West; ***W:*** John West.

Bar Girls 🦴🦴 **1995 (R)** Mating rituals, set in L.A. wateringhole "The Girl Bar," finds usually tough cookie Loretta (Wolfe) spotting new face Rachael (D'Agostino) and deciding she likes what she sees. There's various mind games as they chart a rocky course to true love—with jealousy, possessiveness, and past romance all playing their parts. Hoffman adapted from her play and the staginess remains; film debut for director Giovanni. **95m/C VHS, DVD, Wide.** Nancy Allison Wolfe, Liza D'Agostino, Justine Slater, Paula Sorge, Camila Griggs, Pam Raines; ***D:*** Marita Giovanni; ***W:*** Lauran Hoffman; ***C:*** Michael Ferris; ***M:*** Lenny Meyers.

Barabbas 🦴🦴½ **1962** Barabbas, a thief and murderer, is freed by Pontius Pilate in place of Jesus. He is haunted by this event for the rest of his life. Excellent acting, little melodrama, lavish production make for fine viewing. Based on the novel by Lagerkvist. **144m/C VHS, DVD, Wide.** Anthony Quinn, Silvana Mangano, Arthur Kennedy, Jack Palance, Ernest Borgnine, Katy Jurado, Vittorio Gassman; ***D:*** Richard Fleischer; ***W:*** Diego Fabbri, Christopher Fry, Ivo Perilli, Nigel Balchin; ***C:*** Aldo Tonti; ***M:*** Mario Nascimbene.

Baraka 🦴🦴🦴 **1993** Time-lapse photography transforms a fascinating array of scenic panoramas into a thought-provoking experience. No dialogue, but the captivating visuals, shot in 24 countries, are a feast for the eyes. Points of interest include Iguacu Falls in Argentina, Ayers Rock in Australia, the temples of Angkor Wat in Cambodia, and the Grand Canyon. Also tours Auschwitz and the streets of Calcutta, in an effort to warn the viewer of the planet's fragility. Filmed in 70mm. **96m/C VHS, DVD, Wide.** ***D:*** Ron Fricke; ***W:*** Ron Fricke, Mark Magidson, Bob Green; ***C:*** Ron Fricke; ***M:*** Michael Stearns.

Barb Wire 🦴½ **1996 (R)** "Don't call me babe!" That'll be difficult when the figure in question is Anderson Lee's big-screen take on Dark Horse comic book heroine Barb Wire. Barb runs the sleazy Hammerhead Bar & Grille in Steel Harbor, the only neutral city in an America torn by a second civil war, and reluctantly agrees to aid hunky resistance leader Axel (Morrison) on a dangerous peace mission. Pambo gives Stallone a fight for the action title—fetching in high heels and black leather—with lots of fire power and a take-no-prisoners attitude. Plot's secondary to pulchritude but, unfortunately, the movie's just not a lotta fun. **98m/C VHS, DVD, Wide.** Pamela Anderson, Temuera Morrison, Jack Noseworthy, Victoria Rowell, Xander Berkeley, Udo Kier, Steve Railsback, Clint Howard, Tony Bill; ***D:*** David Hogan; ***W:*** Chuck Pfarrer, Ilene Chaiken; ***C:*** Rick Bota; ***M:*** Michel Colombier. Golden Raspberries '96: Worst New Star (Anderson).

Barbarella 🦴🦴½ *Barbarella, Queen of the Galaxy* **1968 (PG)** Based on the popular French sci-fi comic strip drawn by Jean-Claude Forest, this cult classic details the bizarre adventures of a space nymphette (Fonda) encountering fantastic creatures and super beings. You'll see sides of Fonda you never saw before (not even in the workout videos). Notorious in its day; rather silly, dated camp now. Don't miss the elbow-sex scene. Terry Southern contributed to the script. **98m/C VHS, DVD, Wide.** *FR IT* Jane Fonda, John Phillip Law, David Hemmings, Marcel Marceau, Anita Pallenberg, Milo O'Shea, Ugo Tognazzi, Veronique Vendell, Giancarlo Cobelli, Serge Marquand; ***D:*** Roger Vadim; ***W:*** Roger Vadim, Terry Southern, Vittorio Bonicelli, Claude Brule, Tudor Gates, Clement Biddle Wood, Brian Degas, Jean-Claude Forest; ***C:*** Claude Renoir; ***M:*** Charles Fox.

Barbarian and the Geisha 🦴🦴 **1958** The first US diplomat in Japan undergoes culture shock as well as a passionate love affair with a geisha, circa 1856. **104m/C VHS.** John Wayne, Eiko Ando, Sam Jaffe, So Yamamura; ***D:*** John Huston; ***M:*** Hugo Friedhofer.

Barbarian Queen 🦴 **1985 (R)** Female warriors led by beauteous babe seek revenge for the capture of their men in this sword-and-sorcery epic. Low-budget ripoff "Conan the Barbarian" is laughable. Also available in an unrated version. Followed by "Barbarian Queen 2: The Empress Strikes Back." **71m/C VHS, DVD.** *IT* Lana Clarkson, Frank Zagarino, Katt Shea, Dawn Dunlap, Susana Traverso; ***D:*** Hector Olivera; ***W:*** Howard R. Cohen; ***C:*** Rudy Donovan; ***M:*** Christopher Young.

Barbarian Queen 2: The Empress Strikes Back 🦴 **1989 (R)** Apparently one movie wasn't enough to tell the beautiful Princess Athalia's story. This time she fights her evil brother Ankaris. He throws her in prison, she escapes, joins a band of female rebels, and leads them into battle. No better than the first attempt. **87m/C VHS, DVD.** *IT* Lana Clarkson, Greg Wrangler, Rebecca Wood, Elizabeth Jaegen, Roger Cundy; ***D:*** Joe Finley; ***W:*** Howard R. Cohen; ***C:*** Francisco Bojorquez; ***M:*** Christopher Young.

The Barbarians 🦴 *The Barbarians and Co* **1987 (R)** Two bodybuilder siblings in animal skins battle wizards and warlords in this dumb-but-fun U.S./Italian co-production. **88m/C VHS.** *IT* David Paul, Peter Paul, Richard Lynch, Eva LaRue, Virginia Bryant, Sheeba Alahani, Michael Berryman; ***D:*** Ruggero Deodato; ***M:*** Pino Donaggio.

Barbarians at the Gate 🦴🦴🦴½ **1993 (R)** In the "greed is good" financial climate of the '80s, this movie chronicles the $25 billion battle in 1988 for RJR Nabisco, which at the time was working on developing a "smokeless cigarette." Garner is CEO F. Ross Johnson, who is confident that their "smokeless cigarette" will boost the stock's value—until he gets the test-marketing results. Unwilling to risk the product's failure, Johnson decides to buy the company and is challenged by master dealer Kravis (Pryce). Fascinating social commentary on the nastiest mega-deal in history. Based on the book by Bryan Burrough and John Helyar. **107m/C VHS, DVD.** James Garner, Jonathan Pryce, Peter Riegert, Joanna Cassidy, Fred Dalton Thompson, Leilani Sarelle Ferrer, Matt Clark, Jeffrey DeMunn; ***D:*** Glenn Jordan; ***W:*** Larry Gelbart; ***C:*** Thomas Del Ruth, Nicholas D. Knowland; ***M:*** Richard Gibbs. **CABLE**

Barbarosa 1982 (PG) Offbeat western about an aging, legendary outlaw constantly on the lam who reluctantly befriends a naive farmboy and teaches him survival skills. Nelson and Busey are a great team, solidly directed. Lovely Rio Grande scenery. **90m/C VHS.** Willie Nelson, Gilbert Roland, Gary Busey, Isela Vega; ***D:*** Fred Schepisi; ***C:*** Ian Baker; ***M:*** Bruce Smeaton.

Barbary Coast 1935 A ruthless club owner tries to win the love of a young girl by building her into a star attraction during San Francisco's gold rush days. **90m/B VHS.** Edward G. Robinson, Walter Brennan, Brian Donlevy, Joel McCrea, Donald Meek, David Niven, Miriam Hopkins; ***D:*** Howard Hawks.

The Barbary Coast 1974 A turn-of-the-century detective sleuths the streets of San Francisco in this average TV movie. **100m/C VHS.** William Shatner, Dennis Cole, Lynda Day George, John Vernon, Charles Aidman, Michael Ansara, Neville Brand, Bill Bixby; ***D:*** Bill Bixby. **TV**

The Barber Shop 1933 Fields portrays the bumbling, carefree barber Cornelius O'Hare, purveyor of village gossip and problem solver. Havoc begins when a gangster enters the shop and demands that Cornelius change his appearance. **21m/B VHS.** W.C. Fields, Elise Cavanna, Harry Watson, Dagmar Oakland, Frank Yaconelli; ***D:*** Arthur Ripley.

Barcelona 1994 (PG-13) Old-fashioned talkfest about two neurotic Americans experiencing sibling rivalry in Spain. Serious Ted (Nichols) is an American sales rep, posted to Barcelona, who can't quite get into the city's pleasure-loving rhythm. This is not a problem for Ted's cousin Fred (Eigeman), an obnoxious naval officer, with whom Ted has had a rivalry dating back to their boyhood. Set in the 1980s, the two must also deal with anti-Americanism, which leads both to violence and romantic developments. Tart dialogue, thoughtful performances, and exotic locales prove enticing in low-budget sleeper that effectively mixes drama and dry comedy. Watch for Eigeman in Tom Cruise's uniform from "A Few Good Men." **102m/C VHS, DVD, Wide.** Taylor Nichols, Christopher Eigeman, Tushka Bergen, Mira Sorvino, Pep Munne, Francis Creighton, Thomas Gibson, Jack Gilpin, Nuria Badia, Hellena Schmied; ***D:*** Whit Stillman; ***W:*** Whit Stillman; ***C:*** John Thomas; ***M:*** Tom Judson, Mark Suozzo. Ind. Spirit '95: Cinematog.

The Barcelona Kill ½ 1977 When a journalist and her boyfriend get in too deep with the Barcelona mob, their troubles begin. **86m/C VHS.** Linda Hayden, John Astin, Simon Andrew, Maximo Valverde; ***D:*** Jose Antonio De La Loma.

Bare Essentials 1991 (PG) Made for TV yuppie Club Med nightmare in which a high-strung couple from New York find themselves marooned on a desert isle with only two other inhabitants. With no cellular telephoning ability and an absence of large-ticket consumer goods to purchase, the two turn their reluctant sights on each other, focusing on the bare essentials, as it were. Great soul-searching scenes for the inarticulate. **94m/C VHS.** Gregory Harrison, Lisa Hartman Black, Mark Linn-Baker, Charlotte Lewis; ***D:*** Martha Coolidge. **TV**

Bare Knees 1928 A woman causes a scandal in her family when she arrives at her sister's birthday party with bare knees, cigarettes, and other flapper items. The quintessential flapper movie. **61m/B VHS.** Virginia Lee Corbin, Donald Keith, Jane Winton, Johnnie Walker, Forrest Stanley, Maude Fulton; ***D:*** Erle C. Kenton.

Bare Knuckles 1977 (R) The adventures of a low-rent bounty hunter. **90m/C VHS.** Robert Viharo, Sherry Jackson, Michael Heit, Gloria Hendry, John Daniels; ***D:*** Don Edmonds; ***C:*** Dean Cundey.

The Barefoot Contessa 1954 The story, told in flashback, of a Spanish dancer's rise to Hollywood stardom, as witnessed by a cynical director. Shallow Hollywood self-examination. **128m/C VHS, DVD.** Ava Gardner, Humphrey Bogart, Edmond O'Brien, Valentina Cortese, Rossano Brazzi; ***D:*** Joseph L. Mankiewicz; ***W:*** Joseph L. Mankiewicz; ***C:*** Jack Cardiff. Oscars '54: Support. Actor (O'Brien); Golden Globes '55: Support. Actor (O'Brien).

The Barefoot Executive 1971 A mailroom boy who works for a national TV network finds a chimpanzee that can pick hit shows in this Disney family comedy. **92m/C VHS.** Kurt Russell, John Ritter, Harry (Henry) Morgan, Wally Cox, Heather North, Joe Flynn; ***D:*** Robert Butler; ***M:*** Robert F. Brunner.

Barefoot in Athens 1966 TV presentation from "George Schaefer's Showcase Theatre" chronicles the last years of the philosopher Socrates who, barefoot and unkempt, an embarrassment to his wife, and a dangerous critic to the corrupt Athenian leaders, nevertheless believes that democracy and truth are all-important in his city. **76m/C VHS.** Peter Ustinov, Geraldine Page, Anthony Quayle; ***D:*** George Schaefer. **TV**

Barefoot in the Park 1967 Neil Simon's Broadway hit translates well to screen. A newly wedded bride (Fonda) tries to get her husband (Redford, reprising his Broadway role) to loosen up and be as free-spirited as she is. **106m/C VHS, DVD.** Robert Redford, Jane Fonda, Charles Boyer, Mildred Natwick; ***D:*** Gene Saks; ***W:*** Neil Simon; ***C:*** Joseph LaShelle; ***M:*** Neal Hefti.

Barfly 1987 (R) Bukowski's semi-autobiographical screenplay is the story of a talented writer who chooses to spend his time as a lonely barfly, hiding his literary abilities behind glasses of liquor. Dunaway's character is right on target as the fellow alcoholic. **100m/C VHS, 8mm.** Mickey Rourke, Faye Dunaway, Alice Krige, Frank Stallone, J.C. Quinn, Jack Nance, Charles Bukowski; ***D:*** Barbet Schroeder; ***W:*** Charles Bukowski; ***C:*** Robby Muller; ***M:*** Jack Baran.

The Bargain ½ 1915 Hart's first feature, in which he portrays a bandit desperately trying to go straight. Original titles with musical score. **50m/B VHS.** William S. Hart, J. Frank Burke, J. Barney Sherry, Clara Williams, Joseph J. Dowling, Roy Laidlaw, Herschel Mayall, Charles Swickard, Charles French; ***D:*** Reginald Barker; ***W:*** William H. Clifford, Thomas Ince; ***C:*** Joseph August.

Baritone 1985 Concerned Polish drama about a prominent opera singer who promises to deliver a grand concert upon returning to his small town, only to lose his voice just before the show is to start. Proof positive that the opera ain't over 'til the fat lady sings. **100m/C VHS.** *PL* Zbigniew Zapasiewicz; ***D:*** Janusz Zaorski.

Barjo 1993 In a bland and isolated French suburb lives willful housewife Fanfan (Bouchet) with her older businessman husband Charles (Bohringer) and her eccentric twin brother Barjo (Girardot). Barjo is obsessed with lists and extraterrestrials and his sister's affair with their next-door neighbor, which he likes to spy on. Her husband naturally begins to go crazy. Deadpan satire based on the novel "Confessions of a Crap Artist" by Philip K. Dick. The post-WWII American setting of the novel makes a decidedly uneasy transistion to contemporary French life. In French with English subtitles. **85m/C VHS.** *FR* Anne Brochet, Hippolyte Girardot, Richard Bohringer, Consuelo de Haviland, Renaud Danner, Nathalie Boutefeu; ***D:*** Jerome Boivin; ***W:*** Jerome Boivin, Jacques Audiard; ***M:*** Hugues LeBars.

The Barkleys of Broadway 1949 The famous dancing team's last film together; they play a quarreling husband/wife showbiz team. ♫They Can't Take That Away From Me; The Sabre Dance; Swing Trot; Manhattan Downbeat; A Weekend in the Country; My One and Only Highland Fling; You'd Be Hard to Replace; Bouncin' the Blues; Shoes With Wings On. **109m/C VHS.** Fred Astaire, Ginger Rogers, Gale Robbins, Oscar Levant, Jacques Francois, Billie Burke; ***D:*** Charles Walters; ***W:*** Adolph Green, Betty Comden; ***C:*** Harry Stradling Sr.; ***M:*** Ira Gershwin, Harry Warren.

Barn of the Naked Dead woof! *Nightmare Circus; Terror Circus* 1973 Prine plays a sicko who tortures women while his radioactive monster dad terrorizes the Nevada desert. Rudolph's first film, directed under the pseudonym Gerald Comier. **86m/C VHS.** Andrew Prine, Manuella Thiess, Sherry Alberoni, Gylian Roland, Al Cormier, Jennifer Ashley; ***D:*** Alan Rudolph; ***W:*** Alan Rudolph, Roman Valenti.

Barnaby and Me 1977 Australian star Barnaby the Koala Bear joins an international con-man in this romantic adventure. The mob is chasing the conman when he meets and falls for a lovely young woman and her daughter. **90m/C VHS.** *AU* Sid Caesar, Juliet Mills, Sally Boyden; ***D:*** Norman Panama.

Barney's Great Adventure 1998 (G) First the bad news: that big purple dweebosaur made a movie and your three-year-old is going to make you buy the video. Now the good news: since it's on video you can cue it up for the young-uns and run screaming from the room. You see, they don't care what you think about Barney, who looks a little like a big lug in a purple felt suit, actually. In this extravaganza of not so special effects, Barney and two little girls chase a magical egg around town and encounter a parade, a circus and other allegedly wonderful things, all while trying to convince the older Kyle that Barney is "cool." In a surprise move, the egg hatches to reveal....that new stuffed animal you're going to have to buy! **75m/C VHS, DVD.** George Hearn, Shirley Douglas, Kyla Pratt, Trevor Morgan, Diana Rice, Renee Madeleine Le Guerrier; ***D:*** Steve Gomer; ***W:*** Stephen White; ***C:*** Sandi Sissel; ***V:*** Bob West, Julie Johnson.

Barnum ½ 1986 P.T. Barnum's life is focused upon in this biography about the man who helped to form "The Greatest Show On Earth." **100m/C VHS.** Burt Lancaster, Hanna Schygulla, Jenny Lind, John Roney; ***D:*** Lee Philips.

Barocco 1976 Crook kills his lookalike and takes his place and his girlfriend. Together the duo try blackmail to get the money they need to start a new life. Self-conscious would-be film noir. French with subtitles. **102m/C VHS.** *FR* Gerard Depardieu, Isabelle Adjani, Marie-France Pisier, Jean-Claude Brialy; ***D:*** Andre Techine; ***W:*** Andre Techine, Marilyn Goldin; ***C:*** Bruno Nuytten; ***M:*** Philippe Sarde.

The Baron ½ 1988 Vengeance is the name of the game when an underworld boss gets stiffed on a deal. Fast-paced no-brainer street drama. **88m/C VHS.** Calvin Lockhart, Charles McGregor, Joan Blondell, Richard Lynch, Marlene Clark; ***D:*** Philip Fently.

The Baron and the Kid 1984 A pool shark finds out that his opponent at a charity exhibition game is his long-lost son. Based on Johnny Cash's song. Made for TV. **100m/C VHS.** Johnny Cash, Darren McGavin, June Carter Cash, Richard Roundtree; ***D:*** Gary Nelson; ***M:*** Brad Fiedel. **TV**

Baron Munchausen 1943 The German film studio UFA celebrated its 25th anniversary with this lavish version of the Baron Munchausen legend, starring a cast of top-name German performers at the height of the Third Reich. Filmed in Agfacolor; available in English subtitled or dubbed versions. **120m/C VHS.** *GE* Hans Albers, Kaethe Kaack, Hermann Speelmanns, Leo Slezak; ***D:*** Josef von Baky.

Baron of Arizona 1951 Land office clerk almost succeeds in convincing the U.S. that he owned the state of Arizona. **99m/B VHS.** Vincent Price, Ellen Drew, Beulah Bondi, Reed Hadley, Vladimir Sokoloff; ***D:*** Samuel Fuller; ***W:*** Samuel Fuller; ***C:*** James Wong Howe.

Barracuda woof! *The Lucifer Project* 1978 (R) Lots of innocent swimmers are being eaten by crazed killer barracudas. **90m/C VHS.** Wayne Crawford, Jason Evers, Roberta Leighton; ***D:*** Harry Kerwin.

The Barretts of Wimpole Street *Forbidden Alliance* 1934 The moving, almost disturbing, account of poetess Elizabeth Barrett, an invalid confined to her bed, with only her poetry and her dog to keep her company. She is wooed by poet Robert Browning, in whose arms she finds true happiness and a miraculous recovery. Multi-faceted drama expertly played by all. **110m/B VHS.** Fredric March, Norma Shearer, Charles Laughton, Maureen O'Sullivan, Katherine Alexander, Una O'Connor, Ian Wolfe; ***D:*** Sidney Franklin; ***C:*** William H. Daniels.

Barry Lyndon ½ 1975 (PG) Ravishing adaptation of the classic Thackeray novel about the adventures of an Irish gambler moving from innocence to self-destructive arrogance in the aristocracy of 18th Century England. Visually opulent. Kubrick received excellent performances from all his actors, and a stunning display of history, but the end result still overwhelms. O'Neal has seldom been better. **185m/C VHS, DVD, Wide.** Ryan O'Neal, Marisa Berenson, Patrick Magee, Hardy Kruger, Guy Hamilton; ***D:*** Stanley Kubrick; ***W:*** Stanley Kubrick; ***C:*** John Alcott. Oscars '75: Art Dir./Set Dec., Cinematog., Costume Des., Orig. Song Score and/or Adapt.; British Acad. '75: Director (Kubrick); L.A. Film Critics '75: Cinematog.; Natl. Bd. of Review '75: Director (Kubrick); Natl. Soc. Film Critics '75: Cinematog.

Barry McKenzie Holds His Own 1974 In this sequel to "The Adventures of Barry McKenzie," we find that after a young man's aunt is mistaken for the Queen of England, two emissaries of Count Plasma of Transylvania kidnap her to use as a Plasma tourist attraction. Based on the 'Private Eye' comic strip, this crude Australian film is as disappointing as the first of the Barry McKenzie stories. **93m/C VHS.** *AU* Barry Humphries, Barry Crocker, Donald Pleasence; ***D:*** Bruce Beresford; ***W:*** Barry Humphries, Bruce Beresford.

Bartleby ½ 1970 A new version of the classic Herman Melville short story. McEnery is Bartleby the clerk, who refuses to leave his job even after he's fired; Scofield is his frustrated boss. **79m/C VHS.** Paul Scofield, John McEnery, Colin Jeavons, Thorley Walters; ***D:*** Anthony Friedman; ***W:*** Rodney Carr-Smith.

Barton Fink 1991 (R) This eerie comic nightmare comes laden with awards (including the Palme D'Or from Cannes) but only really works if you care about the time and place. Fink is a trendy New York playwright staying in a seedy Hollywood hotel in the 1940s, straining to write a simple B-movie script. Macabre events, both real and imagined, compound his writer's block. Superb set design from Dennis Gassner complements an unforgettable cast of grotesques. **116m/C VHS.** John Turturro, John Goodman, Judy Davis, Michael Lerner, John Mahoney, Tony Shalhoub, Jon Polito, Steve Buscemi, David Warrilow, Richard Portnow, Christopher Murney; ***D:*** Joel Coen; ***W:*** Joel Coen, Ethan Coen; ***C:*** Roger Deakins; ***M:*** Carter Burwell. Cannes '91: Actor (Turturro), Director (Coen), Film; L.A. Film Critics '91: Cinematog., Support. Actor (Lerner); N.Y. Film Critics '91: Cinematog., Support. Actress (Davis); Natl. Soc. Film Critics '91: Cinematog.

The Base ½ 1999 (R) Army Intelligency officer Major John Murphy (Dacascos) is sent undercover to Fort Tilman to investigate the murder of an army operations officer. Murphy is assigned to a border patrol unit and discovers his fellow soldiers are muscling in on the Mexican/American drug trade. When he discovers who's behind the operation, Murphy's cover is blown and he's in for the fight of his life. **101m/C VHS, DVD.** Mark Dacascos, Tim Abell, Paula Trickey, Noah Blake, Frederick Coffin; ***D:*** Mark L. Lester; ***W:*** Jeff Albert, William Martell; ***C:*** Jacques Haitkin; ***M:*** Paul Zaza. **VIDEO**

Based on an Untrue Story ½ 1993 Campy spoof of popular "true story" TV docudramas in which powerful Satin Chau (Fairchild), a perfume mogul, loses her sense of smell. Satin leaves her mentor Varda (Cannon) to discovery herself but finds that only her two separated-at-birth sisters, Velour (Lake) and Corduroy (Jackson), hold the secrets to the past. It's hard to spoof a genre that's become a cliche but this TV movie does its best. **90m/C VHS.** Morgan Fairchild, Dyan Cannon, Victoria Jackson, Ricki Lake, Harvey Korman, Robert Goulet, Dan Hedaya; ***D:*** Jim Drake.

BASEketball ½ 1998 (R) Dude! Three slacker buddies ("South Park"'s Parker and Stone plus Bachar) invent a new game in their driveway—a combo of basketball with baseball rules—and see it turn into big business. Parkere gets to romance Jenna Reed (Bleeth), a social worker who helps "health-challenged" kids. Stone and Parker's penchant for gross-out humor and having their characters say whatever's on their minds (no matter how offensive) mixes well with Zucker's talent for sight gags and physical humor to create an enjoyably guilty pleasure. Based on a game that Zucker invented with friends. **103m/C VHS, DVD.** Trey Parker, Matt Stone, Yasmine Bleeth, Jenny McCarthy, Ernest Borgnine, Dian Bachar, Robert Vaughn, Bob Costas, Al Michaels, Reggie Jackson, Robert Stack, Steve Garvey, Kareem Abdul-Jabbar; ***D:*** David Zucker; ***W:*** David Zucker, Robert Locash, Jeffrey Wright, Lewis Friedman; ***C:*** Steve Mason; ***M:*** Ira Newborn.

The Bashful Bachelor 🦴🦴 **1942** Yokel joker Abner trades his delivery car for a race horse, hoping to win a big race. **78m/B VHS.** Chester Lauck, Norris Goff, ZaSu Pitts, Grady Sutton, Louise Currie, Irving Bacon, Earle Hodgins, Benny Rubin; ***D:*** Malcolm St. Clair.

Basic Instinct 🦴🦴½ **1992 (R)** Controversial thriller had tongues wagging months before its theatrical release. Burnt-out detective Douglas falls for beautiful, manipulative murder suspect Stone, perfectly cast as a bisexual ice queen who may or may not have done the deed. Noted for highly erotic sex scenes and an expensive (3 million bucks) script; ultimately the predictable plot is disappointing. Gay activists tried to interrupt filming because they objected to the depiction of Stone's character but only succeeded in generating more free publicity. The American release was edited to avoid an "NC-17" rating, but an uncut, unrated video version is also available. **123m/C VHS, DVD.** Michael Douglas, Sharon Stone, George Dzundza, Jeanne Tripplehorn, Denis Arndt, Leilani Sarelle Ferrer, Bruce A. Young, Chelcie Ross, Dorothy Malone, Wayne Knight, Stephen Tobolowsky; ***D:*** Paul Verhoeven; ***W:*** Joe Eszterhas; ***C:*** Jan De Bont; ***M:*** Jerry Goldsmith. MTV Movie Awards '93: Female Perf. (Stone), Most Desirable Female (Stone).

Basic Training woof! **1986 (R)** Three sexy ladies wiggle into the Pentagon in their efforts to clean up the government. **85m/C VHS.** Ann Dusenberry, Rhonda Shear, Angela Aames, Walter Gotell; ***D:*** Andrew Sugarman.

Basil 🦴🦴½ **1998 (R)** Turn of the century English aristocrat Basil (Leto) strives for the approval of his overbearing father (Jacobi) while also trying to please the selfish woman he loves (Forlani). Based on the novel by Wilkie Collins. **113m/C VHS.** Jared Leto, Claire Forlani, Christian Slater, Derek Jacobi; ***D:*** Radha Bharadwaj.

Basileus Quartet 🦴🦴🦴 *Il Quartetto Basileus* **1982** The replacement for a violinist in a well-established quartet creates emotional havoc. Beautiful music, excellent and evocative photography. **118m/C VHS.** *FR IT* Pierre Malet, Hector Alterio, Omero Antonutti, Michel Vitold, Alain Cuny, Gabriele Ferzetti, Elisabeth (Lisa) Kreuzer; ***D:*** Fabio Carpi; ***W:*** Fabio Carpi; ***C:*** Dante Spinotti; ***M:*** Claude Debussy.

The Basket 🦴🦴½ **1999 (PG)** There's a lot going on in a small Washington community, circa 1918. Martin Conlon (Coyote) is the new teacher (he's from Boston) at the one-room schoolhouse who introduces opera and basketball into the curriculum. Then German orphans Helmut (Burke) and Brigitta (Willenborg) come to live with the local doctor and are persecuted for their nationality because of WWI. Mr. Emery (MacDonald) is especially hostile since his son was wounded in the war but Mrs. Emery (Allen) is willing to give the newcomers a chance. Helmut turns out to be a hoops natural and the team has a chance to compete in a national championship—if they can set their differences aside. **104m/C VHS, DVD, Wide.** Karen Allen, Peter Coyote, Robert Karl Burke, Amber Willenborg, Jock MacDonald, Eric Dane, Casey Cowan, Brian Skala, Tony Lincoln, Patrick Treadway, Ellen Travolta; ***D:*** Rich Cowan; ***W:*** Rich Cowan, Frank Swoboda, Tessa Swoboda; ***C:*** Dan Heigh; ***M:*** Don Caron.

Basket Case 🦴🦴🦴 **1982** A gory horror film about a pair of Siamese twins—one normal, the other gruesomely deformed. The pair is surgically separated at birth, and the evil disfigured twin is tossed in the garbage. Fraternal ties being what they are, the normal brother retrieves his twin—essentially a head atop shoulders—and totes him around in a basket (he ain't heavy). Together they begin twisted and deadly revenge, with the brother-in-a-basket in charge. Very entertaining, if you like this sort of thing. Followed by two sequels, if you just can't get enough. **89m/C VHS, DVD.** Kevin Van Hentenryck, Terri Susan Smith, Beverly Bonner, Robert Vogel, Diana Browne, Lloyd Pace, Bill Freeman, Joe Clarke, Ruth Neuman, Richard Pierce, Dorothy Strongin; ***D:*** Frank Henenlotter; ***W:*** Frank Henenlotter; ***C:*** Bruce Torbet; ***M:*** Gus Russo.

Basket Case 2 🦴🦴½ **1990 (R)** Surgically separated teenage mutant brothers Duane and Belial are back! This time they've found happiness in a "special" family—until they're plagued by the paparazzi. Higher production values make this sequel slicker than its low-budget predecessor, but it somehow lacks the same charm. **90m/C VHS.** Kevin Van Hentenryck, Annie Ross, Kathryn Meisle, Heather Rattray, Jason Evers, Ted (Theodore) Sorel, Matt Mitler, Ron Fazio, Leonard Jackson, Beverly Bonner; ***D:*** Frank Henenlotter; ***W:*** Frank Henenlotter; ***C:*** Robert M. "Bob" Baldwin Jr.; ***M:*** Joe Renzetti.

Basket Case 3: The Progeny 🦴🦴½ **1992 (R)** In this sequel to the cult horror hits "Basket Case" and "Basket Case 2," Belial is back and this time he's about to discover the perils of parenthood as the mutant Mrs. Belial delivers a litter of bouncing mini-monsters. Everything is fine until the police kidnap the little creatures and chaos breaks out as Belial goes on a shocking rampage in his newly created mechanical body. Weird special effects make this a cult favorite for fans of the truly outrageous. **90m/C VHS.** Annie Ross, Kevin Van Hentenryck, Gil Roper, Tina Louise Hilbert, Dan Biggers, Jim O'Doherty, Jackson Faw, Jim Grimshaw; ***D:*** Frank Henenlotter; ***W:*** Frank Henenlotter, Robert Martin; ***C:*** Bob Paone; ***M:*** Joe Renzetti.

The Basketball Diaries 🦴🦴 **1994 (R)** Disappointing adaptation of underground writer/musician Jim Carroll's 1978 cult memoirs, with DiCaprio starring as the teen athlete whose life spirals into drug addiction and hustling on the New York streets. Carroll and friends Mickey (Wahlberg), Neutron (McGaw), and Pedro (Madio), form the heart of St. Vitus' hot hoopster team. But the defiant quartet really get their kicks from drugs, dares, and petty crime—leading to an ever-downward turn. The book takes place in the '60s but the film can't make up its mind what the decade is, although DiCaprio (and Wahlberg) are particularly effective in a self-conscious first effort from Kalvert. **102m/C VHS, DVD.** Leonardo DiCaprio, Mark Wahlberg, Patrick McGaw, James Madio, Bruno Kirby, Ernie Hudson, Lorraine Bracco, Juliette Lewis, Josh Mostel, Michael Rapaport, Michael Imperioli, James Dennis (Jim) Carroll; ***D:*** Scott Kalvert; ***W:*** Bryan Goluboff; ***C:*** David Phillips; ***M:*** Graeme Revell.

Basquiat 🦴🦴🦴 *Build a Fort Set It on Fire* **1996 (R)** First-time writer/director and reknowned '80s pop artist Schnabel paints a celluloid portrait of African-American artist Jean Michel Basquiat, who went from grafitti artist to overnight sensation in the mid-1980s before dying of a drug overdose at 27. Schnabel's first-hand knowledge provides details of the painters, the dealers, and the patrons of the whirlwind New York art scene of the time, using an all-star cast (no mean feat on a $3 million budget). Making the move from stage to screen, Wright is an aptly deep and elusive Basquiat and Bowie stands out in a marvelously concevied portrayal of Basquiat's pseudo-mentor, the equally sensational Warhol. Features authentic works of the artists portrayed and some very convincing Basquiat reproductions done by Schnabel. **108m/C VHS.** Jeffrey Wright, David Bowie, Dennis Hopper, Gary Oldman, Christopher Walken, Michael Wincott, Benicio Del Toro, Parker Posey, Elina Lowensohn, Courtney Love, Claire Forlani, Willem Dafoe, Paul Bartel, Tatum O'Neal, Chuck Pfeiffer; ***D:*** Julian Schnabel; ***W:*** Julian Schnabel; ***C:*** Ron Fortunato; ***M:*** John Cale. Ind. Spirit '97: Support. Actor (Del Toro).

The Bastard 🦴🦴½ *The Kent Chronicles* **1978** Dashing (but alas, illegitimate) nobleman roams Europe on futile, "Roots"-like search, then settles for America during the Revolutionary War in this long-winded TV adaptation of John Jakes's equally cumbersome bestseller (part of his popular Bicentennial series). Stevens stars, along with many supporting performers merely keeping active. Followed by "The Rebels" and "The Seekers." **189m/C VHS.** Andrew Stevens, Tom Bosley, Kim Cattrall, Buddy Ebsen, Lorne Greene, Olivia Hussey, Cameron Mitchell, Harry (Henry) Morgan, Patricia Neal, Eleanor Parker, Donald Pleasence, William Shatner, Barry Sullivan, Noah Beery Jr., William Daniels, Keenan Wynn; ***D:*** Lee H. Katzin; ***M:*** John Addison; ***Nar:*** Raymond Burr. **TV**

Bastard out of Carolina 🦴🦴 **1996 (R)** Huston's steeped-in-controversy directorial debut tells the story of young mom Anney (Leigh), who lives a hardscrabble life in Greenville, South Carolina, with an illegitimate daughter nicknamed Bone (Malone). Working as a waitress, Anney's eager to find love and succumbs to the charms of laborer Glen (Eldard), despite his nasty temper. Eleven-year-old Bone and Glen are immediately at odds and he begins to beat her, with Anney unwilling to face the truth, until a final horrific event. Based on the 1992 semiautobiographical novel by Dorothy Allison, the film was originally made for Ted Turner's TNT network but was rejected as unsuitable because of its graphic depiction of child abuse. **97m/C VHS, DVD.** Sonny Shroyer, Jennifer Jason Leigh, Jena Malone, Ron Eldard, Glenne Headly, Lyle Lovett, Dermot Mulroney, Christina Ricci, Michael Rooker, Diana Scarwid, Susan Traylor, Grace Zabriskie; ***D:*** Anjelica Huston; ***W:*** Anne Meredith; ***C:*** Anthony B. Richmond; ***M:*** Van Dyke Parks. **TV**

The Bat 🦴🦴🦴 **1926** A bat-obsessed killer stalks the halls of a spooky mansion in this early film version of the Mary Roberts Rinehart novel. **81m/B VHS.** Andre de Beranger, Charles Herzinger, Emily Fitzroy, Louise Fazenda, Arthur Houseman, Robert McKim, Jack Pickford, Jewel Carmen; ***D:*** Roland West; ***W:*** Roland West.

The Bat 🦴🦴 **1959** A great plot centering around a murderer called the Bat, who kills hapless victims by ripping out their throats when he isn't busy searching for $1 million worth of securities stashed in the old house he is living in. Adapted from the novel by Mary Roberts Rinehart. **80m/B VHS, DVD.** Vincent Price, Agnes Moorehead, Gavin Gordon, John Sutton, Lenita Lane, Darla Hood; ***D:*** Crane Wilbur; ***W:*** Crane Wilbur; ***C:*** Joseph Biroc; ***M:*** Louis Forbes.

The Bat People 🦴 *It Lives By Night* **1974 (R)** Less-than-gripping horror flick in which Dr. John Bech is bitten by a bat while on his honeymoon. He then becomes a sadistic bat creature, compelled to kill anyone who stumbles across his path. The gory special effects make for a great movie if you've ever been bitten by that sort of thing. **95m/C VHS.** Stewart Moss, Marianne McAndrew, Michael Pataki, Paul Carr; ***D:*** Jerry Jameson.

Bat 21 🦴🦴 **1988 (R)** Hackman, an American officer, is stranded in the wilds of Vietnam alone after his plane is shot down. He must rely on himself and Glover, with whom he has radio contact, to get him out. Glover and Hackman give solid performances in this otherwise average film. **112m/C VHS, DVD.** Gene Hackman, Danny Glover, Jerry Reed, David Marshall Grant, Clayton Rohner, Erich Anderson, Joe Dorsey; ***D:*** Peter Markle; ***W:*** Marc Norman, William C. Anderson; ***C:*** Mark Irwin; ***M:*** Christopher Young.

The Bat Whispers 🦴🦴½ **1930** A masked madman is stalking the halls of a creepy mansion; eerie tale that culminates in an appeal to the audience to keep the plot under wraps. Unusually crafted film for its early era. Comic mystery based on the novel and play by Mary Roberts Rinehart and Avery Hopwood. **82m/B VHS, DVD.** Chester Morris, Chance Ward, Richard Tucker, Wilson Benge, DeWitt Jennings, Una Merkel, Spencer Charters; ***D:*** Roland West; ***W:*** Roland West; ***C:*** Ray June, Robert Planck.

Bataan 🦴🦴½ **1943** A rugged wartime combat drama following the true story of a small platoon in the Philippines endeavoring to blow up a pivotal Japanese bridge. Also available in a colorized version. **115m/B VHS, DVD.** Robert Taylor, George Murphy, Thomas Mitchell, Desi Arnaz Sr., Lee Bowman, Lloyd Nolan, Robert Walker, Barry Nelson, Phillip Terry, Tom Dugan, Roque Espiritu, Kenneth Spencer, Alex Havier, Donald Curtis, Lynne Carver, Bud Geary, Dorothy Morris; ***D:*** Tay Garnett; ***W:*** Robert D. (Robert Hardy) Andrews; ***C:*** Sidney Wagner; ***M:*** Bronislau Kaper, Eric Zeisl.

Bathing Beauty 🦴🦴½ **1944** This musical stars Skelton as a pop music composer with the hots for college swim teacher Williams. Rathbone is a music executive who sees the romance as a threat to Skelton's career and to his own profit margin. Full of aquatic ballet, Skelton's shtick, and wonderful original melodies. The first film in which Williams received star billing. ♫I Cried for You; Bim, Bam, Boom; Tico-Tico; I'll Take the High Note; Loch Lomond; By the Waters of Minnetonka; Magic is the Moonlight; Trumpet Blues; Hora Staccato. **101m/C VHS.** Red Skelton, Esther Williams, Basil Rathbone, Bill Goodwin, Jean Porter, Carlos Ramirez, Donald Meek, Ethel Smith, Helen Forrest; ***D:*** George Sidney; ***C:*** Harry Stradling Sr.; ***M:*** Xavier Cugat.

Batman 🦴🦴½ **1966** Holy television camp, Batman! Will the caped crusader win the Bat-tle against the combined forces of the Joker, the Riddler, the Penguin, and Catwoman? Will Batman and Robin save the United World Security Council from dehydration? Will the Bat genius ever figure out that Russian journalist Miss Kitka and Catwoman are one and the same? Biff! Thwack! Socko! Not to be confused with the Michael Keaton version of the Dark Knight, this is the pot-bellied Adam West Batman, teeming with Bat satire and made especially for the big screen. **104m/C VHS, DVD, Wide.** Burt Ward, Adam West, Burgess Meredith, Cesar Romero, Frank Gorshin, Lee Meriwether, Alan Napier, Neil Hamilton, Stafford Repp, Madge Blake, Reginald Denny, Milton Frome; ***D:*** Leslie Martinson; ***W:*** Lorenzo Semple Jr.; ***C:*** Howard Schwartz; ***M:*** Nelson Riddle.

Batman 🦴🦴🦴½ **1989 (PG-13)** The blockbuster fantasy epic that renewed Hollywood's faith in media blitzing. The Caped Crusader (Keaton) is back in Gotham City, where even the criminals are afraid to walk the streets alone. There's a new breed of criminal in Gotham, led by the infamous Joker (Nicholson). Their random attacks via acid-based make-up are just the beginning. Keaton is surprisingly good as the dual personality hero though Nicholson steals the show with his campy performance. Basinger is blonde and feisty as photog Vicki Vale, who falls for mysterious millionaire Bruce Wayne (and the bat). Marvelously designed and shot. Followed by three sequels. **126m/C VHS, DVD, Wide.** Michael Keaton, Jack Nicholson, Kim Basinger, Robert Wuhl, Tracey Walter, Billy Dee Williams, Pat Hingle, Michael Gough, Jack Palance, Jerry Hall; ***D:*** Tim Burton; ***W:*** Sam Hamm, Warren Skaaren; ***C:*** Roger Pratt; ***M:*** Danny Elfman, Prince. Oscars '89: Art Dir./Set Dec.

Batman and Robin 🦴🦴 **1997 (PG-13)** Includes lots of flash but, as usual, not much substance in this fourth adventure, which features a less angst-ridden caped crusader in the charming persona of Clooney. O'Donnell, who apparently knows a good gig when he's got one, returns as Robin. They must battle evil industrialist, Mr. Freeze (an impressively costumed Schwarzenegger), and his partner-with-the-deady-kiss (but what a way to go!), Poison Ivy (Thurman), who have plans to freeze Gotham City. Our heroes have some additional help in the person of Batgirl (Silverstone), who's now butler Alfred's (Gough) ward (she was Commissioner Gordon's daughter in the comics). Story's simplified but the secondary characters still get lost in the crowd. Director Schumacher's already agreed to helm a fifth film although the comic book hero's more fanatic followers keep complaining about the films' camp, high-gloss tone.

125m/C VHS, DVD. George Clooney, Chris O'Donnell, Arnold Schwarzenegger, Uma Thurman, Alicia Silverstone, Michael Gough, Pat Hingle, John Glover, Elle Macpherson, Vivica A. Fox, Vendela Thommessen, Jeep Swenson; ***D:*** Joel Schumacher; ***W:*** Joel Schumacher, Akiva Goldsman; ***C:*** Stephen Goldblatt; ***M:*** Elliot Goldenthal. Golden Raspberries '97: Worst Support. Actress (Silverstone).

Batman Forever 🦴🦴🦴 **1995 (PG-13)** Holy franchise, Batman! Third-time actioner considerably lightens up Tim Burton's dark vision for a more family-oriented Caped Crusader (now played by Kilmer, who fills out lip requirement nicely). The Boy Wonder also makes a first-time appearance in the bulked-up form of O'Donnell, a street-smart Robin with revenge on his mind. Naturally, the villains still steal the show in the personas of maniacal Carrey (the Riddler) and the sartorially splendid Jones as Harvey "Two-Face" Dent. Rounding out this charismatic cast is Kidman's slinky psychologist Chase Meridian, who's eager to find the man inside the bat (and who can blame her). Lots of splashy toys for the boys and awe-inspiring sets to show you where the money went. A Gotham City gas that did $53 million at it's opening weekend boxoffice—breaking the "Jurassic Park" record, testimony to the power of aggressive marketing. **121m/C VHS, DVD.** Val Kilmer, Tommy Lee Jones, Jim Carrey, Chris O'Donnell, Nicole Kidman, Drew Barrymore, Debi Mazar, Michael Gough, Pat Hingle, Jon Favreau, George Wallace, Don "The Dragon" Wilson, Ed Begley Jr., Rene Auberjonois, Joe Grifasi, Jessica Tuck, Kimberly Scott; ***D:*** Joel Schumacher; ***W:*** Janet Scott Batchler, Akiva Goldsman, Lee Batchler; ***C:*** Stephen Goldblatt; ***M:*** Elliot Goldenthal. Blockbuster '96: Action Actress, T. (Kidman).

Batman: Mask of the Phantasm 🦴🦴½ *Batman: The Animated Movie* **1993 (PG)** Based on the Fox TV series with the animated Batman fending off old enemy the Joker, new enemy the Phantasm, and dreaming of his lost first love. Cartoon film noir set in the 1940s but filled with '90s sarcasm. Complicated storyline with a stylish dark look may be lost on the kiddies but adults will stay awake. **77m/C VHS, DVD, Wide.** ***D:*** Eric Radomski, Bruce W. Timm; ***W:*** Michael Reeves, Alan Burnett, Paul Dini, Martin Pako; ***M:*** Shirley Walker; ***V:*** Kevin Conroy, Dana Delany, Mark Hamill, Stacy Keach, Hart Bochner, Abe Vigoda, Efrem Zimbalist Jr., Dick Miller.

Batman Returns 🦴🦴½ **1992 (PG-13)** More of the same from director Burton, with Batman more of a supporting role overshadowed by provocative villains. DeVito is the cruelly misshapen Penguin who seeks to rule over Gotham City; Pfeiffer is the exotic and dangerous Catwoman—who has more than a passing pursonal interest in Batman; Walken is the maniacal tycoon Max Shreck. Pfeiffer fares best in her wickedly sexy role and second-skin costume (complete with bullwhip). Plot is secondary to special effects and nightmarish settings. Despite a big budget, this grandiose sequel is of the love it or leave it variety. **126m/C VHS, DVD.** Michael Keaton, Danny DeVito, Michelle Pfeiffer, Christopher Walken, Michael Gough, Michael Murphy, Cristi Conaway, Pat Hingle, Vincent Schiavelli, Jan Hooks, Paul (Pee-wee Herman) Reubens, Andrew Bryniarski; ***D:*** Tim Burton; ***W:*** Daniel Waters; ***C:*** Stefan Czapsky; ***M:*** Danny Elfman.

Baton Rouge 🦴🦴 **1988** Gigolo Antonio (Banderas) gets together with psychiatrist Anao (Abril) in a scheme to seduce one of her patients, the wealthy Isabel (Maura), who suffers from terrible nightmares. They plan to kill her wealthy ex-husband and accuse her of the crime in order to get her fortune. But there's an elaborate double-cross and things go back for all concerned. The spanish trio, all veterans of director Pedro Almodovar's films, certainly know how to steam up the screen. Spanish with subtitles. **90m/C VHS.** *SP* Antonio Banderas, Victoria Abril, Carmen Maura; ***D:*** Rafael Moleon; ***W:*** Rafael Moleon, Augustin Diaz Yanes; ***C:*** Angel Luis Fernandez.

Bats 🦴½ **1999 (PG-13)** B-grade comedy/thriller proves that people with a warped vision can create something that'll suck the life right out of you. Unfortunately, they use dialogue and plot, and not the winged critters in the title. A mad scientist (Gunton) working for the military genetically engineers some extra-nasty super-intelligent bats. Mad scientists being notoriously bad at cage maintenance, they escape. They then rile up a bunch of normally docile bats, turning them into vicious killers through some type of rodent peer pressure. After several attacks on his small Texas town, Sheriff Kimsey (Phillips) summons the nearest beautiful female bat expert (Meyer) and comic relief sidekick (Leon) so the bats have someone to chase around until the finale. They decide to freeze the bats in their cave, at the risk of trudging through a lot of guano to reach the end. You'll know how they feel. **91m/C VHS, DVD, Wide.** Lou Diamond Phillips, Dina Meyer, Bob Gunton, Leon, Carlos Jacott, Oscar Rowland, David Shawn McConnell, Marcia Dangerfield; ***D:*** Louis Morneau; ***W:*** John Logan; ***C:*** George Mooradian; ***M:*** Graeme Revell.

batteries not included** 🦴🦴½ **1987 (PG)** As a real estate developer fights to demolish a New York tenement, the five remaining residents are aided by tiny metal visitors from outer space in their struggle to save their home. Each resident gains a renewed sense of life in this sentimental, wholesome family film produced by Spielberg. Cronyn and Tandy keep the schmaltz from getting out of hand. Neat little space critters. **107m/C VHS, DVD.** Hume Cronyn, Jessica Tandy, Frank McRae, Michael Carmine, Elizabeth Pena, Dennis Boutsikaris; ***D: Matthew Robbins; ***W:*** Matthew Robbins, Brad Bird, Brent Maddock, S.S. Wilson; ***C:*** John McPherson; ***M:*** James Horner.

Battle Beneath the Earth 🦴🦴 **1968** The commies try to undermine democracy once again when American scientists discover a Chinese plot to invade the U.S. via a series of underground tunnels. Perhaps a tad jingoistic. **112m/C VHS.** *GB* Kerwin Mathews, Peter Arne, Viviane Ventura, Robert Ayres; ***D:*** Montgomery Tully.

Battle Beyond the Stars 🦴🦴½ **1980 (PG)** The planet Akir must be defended against alien rapscallions in this intergalactic Corman creation. Sayles authored the screenplay and co-authored the story on which it was based. **105m/C VHS, DVD, Wide.** Richard Thomas, Robert Vaughn, George Peppard, Sybil Danning, Sam Jaffe, John Saxon, Darlanne Fluegel, Jeff Corey, Morgan Woodward, Marta Kristen, Ron Ross, Eric Morris; ***D:*** Jimmy T. Murakami; ***W:*** John Sayles; ***C:*** Daniel Lacambre; ***M:*** James Horner.

Battle Beyond the Sun 🦴🦴 **1963** Former Russian movie "Nebo Zowet" is Americanized. Everyone is trying to send a mission to Mars. Roger Corman was the producer, director Coppola used the pseudonym Thomas Colchart. **75m/C VHS.** Edd Perry, Arla Powell, Bruce Hunter, Andy Stewart; ***D:*** Francis Ford Coppola; ***W:*** Nicholas Colbert, Edwin Palmer; ***M:*** Les Baxter.

Battle Circus 🦴½ **1953** Sappy drama casts Bogart as a surgeon at a M*A*S*H unit during the Korean War. Allyson is a combat nurse who finds love amongst the harsh reality of a war zone. Bogart was badly miscast and his performance proves it. Weak script and uninspired performances don't help this depressing story. **90m/B VHS.** Humphrey Bogart, June Allyson, Keenan Wynn, Robert Keith, William Campbell, Perry Sheehan, Patricia Tiernan, Adele Longmire, Jonathon Cott, Ann Morrison, Helen Winston, Sarah Selby, Danny Chang, Philip Ahn, Steve Forrest, Jeff Richards, Dick Simmons; ***D:*** Richard Brooks; ***W:*** Richard Brooks; ***C:*** John Alton; ***M:*** Lennie Hayton.

Battle Cry 🦴🦴🦴 **1955** A group of U.S. Marines train, romance, and enter battle in WWII. Based on the novel by Leon Uris. Part of the "A Night at the Movies" series, this tape simulates a 1955 movie evening, with a cartoon, "Speedy Gonzales," a newsreel, and coming attractions for "Mr. Roberts" and "East of Eden." **169m/C VHS, Wide.** Van Heflin, Aldo Ray, Mona Freeman, Tab Hunter, Dorothy Malone, Anne Francis, James Whitmore, Raymond Massey, William Campbell, John Lupton, L.Q. (Justus E. McQueen) Jones, Perry Lopez, Fess Parker, Jonas Applegarth, Tommy Cook, Felix Noriego, Nancy Olson, Susan Morrow, Carleton Young, Rhys Williams, Gregory Walcott, Frank Ferguson, Sarah Selby, Willis Bouchey; ***D:*** Raoul Walsh; ***W:*** Leon Uris; ***C:*** Sid Hickox; ***M:*** Max Steiner.

Battle for the Planet of the Apes 🦴🦴 **1973 (G)** A tribe of human atomic bomb mutations are out to make life miserable for the peaceful ape tribe. The story is told primarily in flashback with the opening and closing sequences taking place in the year A.D. 2670. Final chapter in the five-movie simian saga. **96m/C VHS, DVD, Wide.** Roddy McDowall, Lew Ayres, John Huston, Paul Williams, Claude Akins, Severn Darden, Natalie Trundy, Austin Stoker, Noah Keen, Michael Stearns, John Landis; ***D:*** J. Lee Thompson; ***W:*** John W. Corrington, Joyce H. Corrington; ***C:*** Richard H. Kline; ***M:*** Leonard Rosenman.

Battle Hell 🦴🦴 *Yangtse Incident* **1956** The true story of how a British ship was attacked by the Chinese Peoples Liberation Army on the Yangtze River in 1949. **112m/B VHS.** *GB* Richard Todd, Akim Tamiroff, Keye Luke; ***D:*** Michael Anderson Sr.; ***W:*** Eric Ambler.

Battle Hymn 🦴🦴½ **1957** After accidentally bombing an orphanage as a WWII fighter pilot, Dean Hess (Hudson) becomes a minister. He returns to the Air Force in 1950 to train Korean pilots in Seoul and winds up building a home for the local orphans. True story on which the real Hess served as technical advisor. **109m/C VHS.** Rock Hudson, Dan Duryea, Martha Hyer, Anna Kashfi, Don DeFore, Jock Mahoney, Carl Benton Reid, Alan Hale Jr., Richard Loo, Philip Ahn; ***D:*** Douglas Sirk; ***W:*** Charles Grayson, Vincent B. Evans; ***C:*** Russell Metty; ***M:*** Frank Skinner.

The Battle of Algiers 🦴🦴🦴½ *La Bataille d'Alger; La Battaglia di Algeri* **1966** Famous, powerful, award-winning film depicting the uprisings against French Colonial rule in 1954 Algiers. A seminal documentary-style film which makes most political films seem ineffectual by comparison in its use of non-professional actors, gritty photography, realistic violence, and a boldly propagandistic sense of social outrage. **123m/B VHS.** *AL IT* Yacef Saadi, Jean Martin, Brahim Haggiag, Tommaso Neri, Samia Kerbash, Fawzia el Kader, Michele Kerbash, Mohamed Ben Kassen; ***D:*** Gillo Pontecorvo; ***W:*** Gillo Pontecorvo, Franco Solinas; ***C:*** Marcello Gatti; ***M:*** Gillo Pontecorvo, Ennio Morricone. Venice Film Fest. '66: Film.

The Battle of Austerlitz 🦴🦴 *Austerlitz* **1960 (PG)** Ambitious but numbing costume drama about the events leading up to the epic battle between Napoleon and the overwhelming forces of the Czar and the Austrian Emperor at Austerlitz. Napoleon won. Film has been drastically cut from original 166 minute release. Watch director Gance's silent version, "Napoleon," for a truly epic experience. **123m/C VHS.** *FR IT YU* Claudia Cardinale, Martine Carol, Rossano Brazzi, Vittorio De Sica, Jean Marais, Ettore Manni, Jack Palance, Orson Welles; ***D:*** Abel Gance.

The Battle of Blood Island 🦴 **1960** Two G.I.s, one Christian and one Jewish, face death at the hands of the Japanese during WWII. Still, they bicker incessantly before finally pulling together to save themselves. **64m/B VHS.** Richard Devon, Ron Kennedy; ***D:*** Joel Rapp.

Battle of Britain 🦴🦴½ **1969 (G)** A powerful retelling of the most dramatic aerial combat battle of WWII, showing how the understaffed Royal Air Force held off the might of the German Luftwaffe. **132m/C VHS, Wide.** Harry Andrews, Michael Caine, Laurence Olivier, Trevor Howard, Kenneth More, Christopher Plummer, Robert Shaw, Susannah York, Ralph Richardson, Curt Jurgens, Michael Redgrave, Nigel Patrick, Edward Fox, Ian McShane, Patrick Wymark; ***D:*** Guy Hamilton; ***W:*** James Kennaway, Wilfred Greatorex; ***C:*** Frederick A. (Freddie) Young; ***M:*** Malcolm Arnold, Ronald Goodwin, William Walton.

The Battle of El Alamein 🦴🦴 **1968** Action filled movie about the alliance of Italy and Germany in a war against the British, set in a North African desert in the year 1942. Ferroni used the pseudonym Calvin Jackson Padget. **105m/C VHS.** *IT FR* Frederick Stafford, Ettore Manni, Robert Hossein, Michael Rennie, George Hilton, Ira Furstenberg; ***D:*** Giorgio Ferroni.

Battle of Elderbush Gulch **1913** An ancient pioneering western short famous for innocently employing the now-established cliches of bad guy, good guy, and helpless frontier heroine. One of Gish's first films. **22m/B VHS.** Lillian Gish; ***D:*** D.W. Griffith.

Battle of Neretva 🦴🦴 **1969** During WWII, Yugoslav partisans are facing German and Italian troops and local Chetniks as they battle for freedom. Big budget war film lost continuity with U.S. cut. **106m/C VHS.** *YU* Yul Brynner, Curt Jurgens, Orson Welles, Hardy Kruger, Franco Nero, Sergei Bondarchuk; ***D:*** Veljko Bulajic.

Battle of the Bulge 🦴🦴 **1965** A recreation of the famous offensive by Nazi Panzer troops on the Belgian front during 1944-45, an assault that could have changed the course of WWII. **141m/C VHS, Wide.** Henry Fonda, Robert Shaw, Robert Ryan, Dana Andrews, Telly Savalas, Ty Hardin, Pier Angeli, George Montgomery, Charles Bronson, Barbara Werle, Hans-Christian Blech, James MacArthur, Karl Otto Alberty; ***D:*** Ken Annakin; ***W:*** Philip Yordan, John Melson; ***C:*** Jack Hildyard; ***M:*** Benjamin Frankel.

Battle of the Bullies woof! **1985** An unsalvageable nerd plots a high-tech revenge upon a slew of high school bullies. **45m/C VHS.** Manny Jacobs, Christopher Barnes, Sarah Inglis. **TV**

Battle of the Commandos 🦴 *Legion of the Damned* **1971** A tough Army colonel leads a group of convicts on a dangerous mission to destroy a German-built cannon before it's used against the Allied Forces. **94m/C VHS.** *IT* Jack Palance, Curt Jurgens, Thomas Hunter, Robert Hunter; ***D:*** Umberto Lenzi.

Battle of the Eagles 🦴½ **1981** Follows the true adventures of the "Partisan Squadron," the courageous airmen known as the "Knights of the Sky" during WWII in Yugoslavia. **102m/C VHS.** Bekim Fehmiu, George Taylor, Gloria Samara, Frank Phillips; ***D:*** Tom Raymonth.

The Battle of the Japan Sea 🦴🦴 **1970 (G)** A Japanese epic, dubbed in English, centering around the historic WWII battle between Japan and Russia. **120m/C VHS.** *JP* Toshiro Mifune.

Battle of the Sexes 🦴🦴 **1928** Real estate tycoon Judson (Hersholt) abandons his wife (Bennett) and home for money-hungry flapper Marie (Haver). Based on the novel "The Single Standard" by Daniel Carson Goodman. Griffith's remake of his own 1913 film. **88m/B VHS, DVD.** Jean Hersholt, Phyllis Haver, Belle Bennett, Don Alvarado, William "Billy" Bakewell, Sally O'Neil; ***D:*** D.W. Griffith; ***W:*** Gerrit J. Lloyd; ***C:*** Billy (G.W.) Bitzer, Karl Struss.

The Battle of the Sexes 🦴🦴🦴 **1960** Sophisticated British comedy has mild-mannered Sellers trying to prevent a business takeover by the brash American Cummings. A good supporting cast and the impeccable Sellers make this one unique. Adapted from the James Thurber short story "The Catbird Seat." **88m/B VHS.** *GB* Peter Sellers, Robert Morley, Constance Cummings, Jameson Clark, Ernest Thesiger, Donald Pleasence, Moultrie Kelsall, Alex Mackenzie, Roddy McMillan, Michael Goodliffe, Norman MacOwen, William Mervyn; ***D:*** Charles Crichton; ***W:*** Monja Danischewsky; ***C:*** Freddie Francis; ***M:*** Stanley Black; ***Nar:*** Sam Wanamaker.

Battle of the Worlds 🦴 *Il Pianeta Degli Uomini Spenti; Planet of the Lifeless Men* **1961** Typical low-budget science fiction. A scientist tries to stop an alien planet from destroying the Earth. Even an aging Rains can't help this one. Poorly dubbed in English. **84m/C VHS.** *IT* Claude Rains, Maya Brent, Bill Carter, Marina Orsini, Jacqueline Derval; ***D:*** Anthony (Antonio Margheriti) Dawson.

Battle of Valiant 🦴 **1963** Thundering hordes of invading barbarians trample the splendor of ancient Rome beneath their grimy sandals. **90m/C VHS.** Gordon Mitchell, Ursula Davis, Massimo Serato; ***D:*** John Gentil.

Battle Queen 2020 🦴🦴 **1999 (R)** In a frozen post-apocalyptic future (eternal winter after asteroid crash), Gayle (Strain) leads the downtrodden masses in a revolution against the Elites who live above ground. She's a courtesan by day, freedom fighter by night...or is the other way around? This one is at least as good as "Battlefield Earth." It's certainly shorter and was made by people who were under no illusions about what they were doing. **80m/C DVD.** *CA* Julie Strain, Jeff Wincott; ***D:*** Daniel D'or; ***W:*** Michael B. Druxman, William Hulkower, William D. Bostjancic, Caron Nightengale; ***C:*** Billy Brao; ***M:*** Robert Duncan. **VIDEO**

Battle Shock 🦴½ *A Woman's Devotion; War Shock* **1956** Painter is accused of murdering a cantina waitress while on his honeymoon in Mexico. **88m/C VHS.** Ralph Meeker, Janice Rule, Paul Henreid; ***D:*** Paul Henreid; ***M:*** Les Baxter.

Battlefield Earth woof! **2000 (PG-13)** In the year 3000, the Earth has been decimated by 10-foot tall aliens known as Psychlos who are stripping the planet of its natural resources. Only a few humans survive, including Pepper who becomes the leader of a rebellion. Travolta plays the leader of the bad aliens and is extremely evil-lookng but in a strangely campy way. Based on a 1982 novel by Scientology founder L. Ron Hubbard. Film generated controversy for that reason and supposedly "subliminal" church messages but you'll simply be stunned into submission by how badly it blows. **117m/C VHS, DVD, Wide.** John Travolta, Barry Pepper, Forest Whitaker, Kelly Preston, Kim Coates, Richard Tyson, Sabine Karsenti, Michael Byrne, Sean Hewitt, Michel Perron, Shaun Austin-Olsen, Marie Josee Croze; ***D:*** Roger Christian; ***W:*** J. David Shapiro, Cory Mandell; ***C:*** Giles Nuttgens; ***M:*** Elia Cmiral. Golden Raspberries '00: Worst Picture, Worst Actor (Travolta), Worst Support. Actor (Pepper), Worst Support. Actress (Preston), Worst Director (Christian), Worst Screenplay.

Battleforce 🦴 *The Battle of the Mareth Line; The Greatest Battle* **1978** Exciting battle scenes lose their power in the confusion of this mixed-up WWII film about Rommel's last days. Dubbed sequences, news-reel vignettes and surprise performances by big name stars are incomprehensibly glued together. **97m/C VHS.** *GE YU* Henry Fonda, Stacy Keach, Helmut Berger, Samantha Eggar, Giuliano Gemma, John Huston; ***D:*** Umberto Lenzi; ***Nar:*** Orson Welles.

Battleground 🦴🦴🦴 **1949** A tightly conceived post-WWII character drama, following a platoon of American soldiers through the Battle of the Bulge. Available in a Colorized version. **118m/B VHS.** Van Johnson, John Hodiak, James Whitmore, George Murphy, Ricardo Montalban, Marshall Thompson, Jerome Courtland, Don Taylor, Bruce Cowling, Leon Ames, Douglas Fowley, Richard Jaeckel, Scotty Beckett, Herbert Anderson, Thomas E. Breen, Denise Darcel, James Arness, Brett King; ***D:*** William A. Wellman; ***W:*** Robert Pirosh; ***C:*** Paul Vogel; ***M:*** Lennie Hayton. Oscars '49: B&W Cinematog., Story & Screenplay; Golden Globes '50: Screenplay, Support. Actor (Whitmore).

The Battleship Potemkin 🦴🦴🦴🦴 *Potemkin; Bronenosets Potemkin* **1925** Eisenstein's best work documents mutiny aboard the Russian battleship Potemkin in 1905 which led to a civilian uprising against the Czar in Odessa, and the resulting crackdown by troops loyal to the Czar. Beautiful cinematography, especially the use of montage sequences, changed filmmaking. In particular, a horrifying sequence depicting the slaughter of civilians on an Odessa beach by soldiers coming down the stairs leading to it is exceptional; many movies pay homage to this scene including "The Untouchables" and "Love and Death." Viewers should overlook obvious Marxist overtones and see this film for what it is: a masterpiece. **71m/B VHS, DVD.** *RU* Alexander Antonov, Vladimir Barsky, Grigori Alexandrov, Mikhail Gomorov, Sergei Eisenstein, I. Brobov, Beatrice Vitoldi, N. Poltavseva, Alexandr Levshin, Repnikova, Korobei, Levchenko; ***D:*** Grigori Alexandrov, Sergei Eisenstein; ***W:*** Nina Agadzhanova Shutko, Sergei Eisenstein; ***C:*** Eduard Tisse; ***M:*** Dimitri Shostakovich.

Battlestar Galactica 🦴🦴½ **1978 (PG)** Plot episode of the sci-fi TV series which was later released in the theatres. The crew of the spaceship Galactica must battle their robot enemies in an attempt to reach Earth. Contains special effects designed by John "Star Wars" Dykstra. Individual episodes are also available. **125m/C VHS, DVD.** Lorne Greene, Dirk Benedict, Maren Jensen, Jane Seymour, Patrick Macnee, Terry Carter, John Colicos, Richard A. Colla, Laurette Spang, Richard Hatch; ***D:*** Richard A. Colla; ***W:*** Glen Larson, Richard A. Colla; ***C:*** Ben Colman; ***M:*** Stu Phillips. **TV**

Battling Bunyon 🦴🦴½ **1924** A wily youngster becomes a comedy boxer for profit, and eventually gets fed up and battles the champ. Silent. **71m/B VHS.** Chester Conklin, Wesley Barry, Mollie Malone, Jackie Fields, Paul Hurst, Frank Campeau, Johnny Relasco, Landers Stevens, Harry Mann, Pat Kemp; ***D:*** Paul Hurst.

Battling Butler 🦴🦴½ **1926** Rich young Keaton tries to impress a young lady by impersonating a boxer. All goes well until he has to fight the real thing. Mostly charming if uneven; one of Keaton's more unusual efforts, thought to be somewhat autobiographical. Silent. **70m/B VHS, DVD.** Buster Keaton, Sally O'Neil, Snitz Edwards, Francis McDonald, Mary O'Brien, Tom Wilson, Walter James; ***D:*** Buster Keaton; ***W:*** Al Boasberg, Lex Neal, Charles Henry Smith, Paul Girard Smith; ***C:*** Bert Haines, Devereaux Jennings.

Battling for Baby 🦴🦴 **1992** It's the war of the Grandmas. New mother Katherine decides to return to work and both her mother and mother-in-law want to look after the little tyke. Silly made-for-TV fluff. **93m/C VHS.** Courteney Cox Arquette, Suzanne Pleshette, Debbie Reynolds, John Terlesky, Doug McClure, Leigh Lawson, Mary Jo Catlett; ***D:*** Art Wolff; ***W:*** Walter Lockwood, Nancy Silvers.

Battling Marshal 🦴½ **1948** Fast-moving action western starring Carson. **52m/B VHS.** Sunset Carson, Lee Roberts; ***D:*** Oliver Drake.

Battling Orioles **1924** The once scrappy baseball team is now a bunch of grumpy old men, that is until Glenn whips them into shape. Silent. **58m/B VHS, 8mm.** Glenn Tryon, Blanche Mehaffey, Noah Young; ***D:*** Ted Wilde, Fred Guiol.

Battling Outlaws 🦴½ **194?** Western featuring the American cowboy Bob Steele. **64m/B VHS.** Bob Steele.

Battling with Buffalo Bill **1931** Twelve episodes of the vintage serial concerning the exploits of the legendary Indian fighter. **180m/B VHS.** Tom Tyler, Rex Bell, Franklyn Farnum, Lucille Browne, Francis Ford, William Desmond, Jim Thorpe, Yakima Canutt, Chief Thunderbird, Bud Osborne; ***D:*** Ray Taylor; ***W:*** Ella O'Neill, George Plympton.

The Bawdy Adventures of Tom Jones 🦴½ **1976 (R)** An exploitive extension of the Fielding novel about the philandering English lad, with plenty of soft-core skin and lewdness. **89m/C VHS.** *GB* Joan Collins, Trevor Howard, Terry-Thomas, Arthur Lowe, Murray Melvin; ***D:*** Cliff Owen.

Baxter 🦴🦴½ **1989** A bull terrier lives his life with three different sets of masters. He examines all of humankind's worst faults and the viewer quickly realizes that Baxter's life depends on his refusal to obey like a good dog should. Based on the novel by Ken Greenhall. Funny, sometimes erotic, quirky comedy. In French with English subtitles. **82m/C VHS.** *FR* Lisa (Lise) Delamare, Jean Mercure, Jacques Spiesser, Catherine Ferran, Jean-Paul Roussillon, Sabrina Leurquin; ***D:*** Jerome Boivin; ***W:*** Jerome Boivin, Jacques Audiard; ***C:*** Yves Angelo; ***M:*** Marc Hillman, Patrick Roffe.

The Bay Boy 🦴🦴½ **1985 (R)** Set in the 1930s in Nova Scotia, this period piece captures the coming-of-age of a rural teenage boy. Young Sutherland's adolescent angst becomes a more difficult struggle when he witnesses a murder, and is tormented by the secret. **107m/C VHS.** *CA* Liv Ullmann, Kiefer Sutherland, Peter Donat, Matthieu Carriere, Joe MacPherson, Isabelle Mejias, Alan Scarfe, Chris Wiggins, Leah K. Pinsent; ***D:*** Daniel Petrie; ***M:*** Claude Bolling. Genie '85: Film, Support. Actor (Scarfe).

Bayou Romance 🦴 **1986** Painter inherits a Louisiana plantation, moves in, and falls in love with a young gypsy. **90m/C** Annie Potts, Michael Ansara, Barbara Horan, Paul Rossilli; ***D:*** Alan Myerson.

Baywatch the Movie: Forbidden Paradise 🦴🦴½ **1995 (PG)** The "Baywatch" babes and their fellow lifesaving hunks-in-trunks head off to Hawaii to study the latest search and rescue techniques from the state's premier lifeguard team. **90m/C VHS.** David Hasselhoff, Pamela Anderson, Alexandra Paul, Yasmine Bleeth, David Charvet, Gregory Alan-Williams, Jeremy Jackson; ***D:*** Douglas Schwartz.

Be Yourself 🦴🦴½ **1930** Thin plot contrived for Ziegfeld Follies star Brice, who stars as nightclub entertainer Fanny Field. Fanny falls for a down-and-out-boxer (Armstrong) trying to make a comeback. Brice, who was married to impresario Billy Rose at the time, sings several songs co-written by Rose, including "Cookin' Breakfast for the One I Love." **65m/B VHS.** Fanny Brice, Robert Armstrong, Harry Green, Gertrude Astor, G. Pat Collins, Marjorie "Babe" Kane; ***D:*** Thornton Freeland; ***W:*** Thornton Freeland; ***C:*** Karl Struss, Robert Planck.

The Beach 🦴🦴 **2000 (R)** DiCaprio's follow-up to the blockbuster "Titantic" is an uneven adaptation of the novel by Alex Garland concerning a group of hedonists trying to find paradise and destroying their ideal in the process. Cynical young journalist Richard (DiCaprio) meets the manic Daffy (Carylyle) in a Bangkok dive and is given a map to a supposedly unspoiled island off the Thai coast. Impulsively, Richard asks French acquaintances Francoise (Ledoyen) and Etienne (Canet) to accompany him and they discover an odd settlement of Euro-trash, headed by Sal (Swinton), amidst a marijuana plantation guarded by gun-wielding thugs. Paradise turns out to be less than paradisical. **120m/C VHS, DVD, Wide.** Leonardo DiCaprio, Tilda Swinton, Virginie Ledoyen, Guillaume Canet, Robert Carlyle, Paterson Joseph, Peter Youngblood Hills, Jerry Swindall; ***D:*** Danny Boyle; ***W:*** John Hodge; ***C:*** Darius Khondji; ***M:*** Angelo Badalamenti.

Beach Babes 2: Cave Girl Island 🦴 **1995** The babes crash land on a prehistoric planet populated by horny cavemen. **78m/C VHS.** Sara Bellomo, Stephanie Hudson, Rodrigo Bottero; ***D:*** David DeCoteau. **VIDEO**

Beach Babes from Beyond Infinity 🦴 **1993 (R)** "HOT. TAN. ALIEN." Three words that would send shivers through the body of any red-blooded American boy. And as if alien silicone isn't enough to draw a crowd, this piece of fluff also features the relatives of big name stars hoping to cash in on the family name. Typical Hollywood cheese and sleaze should be fun for those who still can't get this kind of quality entertainment on cable. **78m/C VHS.** Joe Estevez, Don Swayze, Joey Travolta, Burt Ward, Jacqueline Stallone, Linnea Quigley, Sara Bellomo, Tamara Landry, Nicole Posey; ***D:*** David DeCoteau.

Beach Blanket Bingo 🦴🦴🦴 **1965** Fifth entry in the "Beach Party" series (after "Pajama Party") is by far the best and has achieved near-cult status. Both Funicello and Avalon are back, but this time a very young Evans catches Avalon's eye. Throw in a mermaid, some moon-doggies, skydiving, sizzling beach parties, and plenty of nostalgic golly-gee-whiz fun and you have the classic '60s beach movie. Totally implausible, but that's half the fun when the sun-worshipping teens become involved in a kidnapping and occasionally break into song. Followed by "How to Stuff a Wild Bikini." ♫Beach Blanket Bingo; The Cycle Set; Fly Boy; The Good Times; I Am My Ideal; I Think You Think; It Only Hurts When I Cry; New Love; You'll Never Change Him. **96m/C VHS, DVD, Wide.** Frankie Avalon, Annette Funicello, Linda Evans, Don Rickles, Buster Keaton, Paul Lynde, Harvey Lembeck, Deborah Walley, John Ashley, Jody McCrea, Marta Kristen, Timothy Carey, Earl Wilson, Bobbi Shaw, Brian Wilson; ***D:*** William Asher; ***W:*** William Asher, Sher Townsend, Leo Townsend; ***C:*** Floyd Crosby; ***M:*** Les Baxter.

Beach Girls 🦴 **1982 (R)** Three voluptuous coeds intend to re-educate a bookish young man and the owner of a beach house. **91m/C VHS, DVD.** Debra Blee, Val Kline, Jeana Tomasina, Adam Roarke; ***D:*** Patrice Townsend; ***C:*** Michael D. Murphy.

The Beach Girls and the Monster 🦴 *Monster in the Surf; Monster from the Surf* **1965** Here's one on the cutting edge of genre bending: while it meticulously maintains the philosophical depth and production values of '60s beach bimbo fare, it manages to graft successfuly with the heinous critter from the sea genre to produce a hybrid horror with acres o' flesh. **70m/B VHS.** Jon Hall, Sue Casey, Walker Edmiston, Arnold Lessing, Elaine DuPont, Dale Davis; ***D:*** Jon Hall; ***W:*** Joan Gardner; ***C:*** Dale Davis; ***M:*** Frank Sinatra Jr.

Beach House 🦴 **1982** In this boring comedy, adolescents frolic on the beach, get inebriated, and listen to rock 'n' roll. **76m/C VHS.** Kathy McNeil, Richard Duggan, Ileana Seidel, John Cosola, Spence Waugh, Paul Anderson, John A. Gallagher; ***D:*** John A. Gallagher; ***W:*** Marino Amaruso, John A. Gallagher.

Beach Party 🦴🦴 **1963** Started the "Beach Party" series with the classic Funicello/Avalon combo. Scientist Cummings studying the mating habits of teenagers intrudes on a group of surfers, beach bums, and bikers, to his lasting regret. Typical beach party bingo, with sand, swimsuits, singing, dancing, and bare minimum in way of a plot. Followed by "Muscle Beach Party." ♫Beach Party; Don't Stop Now; Promise Me Anything; Secret Surfin' Spot; Surfin' and a-Swingin'; Treat Him Nicely. **101m/C VHS, DVD, Wide.** Frankie Avalon, Annette Funicello, Harvey Lembeck, Robert Cummings, Dorothy Malone, Morey Amsterdam, Jody McCrea, John Ashley, Candy Johnson, Dolores Wells, Yvette Vickers, Eva Six, Brian Wilson, Vincent Price, Peter Falk, Dick Dale; ***D:*** William Asher; ***W:*** Lou Rusoff; ***C:*** Kay Norton; ***M:*** Les Baxter.

Beachcomber 🦴🦴🦴 *Vessel of Wrath* **1938** Comedy set in the Dutch East Indies about a shiftless beachcomber (Laughton) who falls in love with a missionary's prim sister (Lanchester), as she attempts to reform him. The real-life couple of Laughton and Lanchester are their usual pleasure to watch. Remade in 1954. Story by W. Somerset Maugham. **88m/B VHS.** *GB* Charles Laughton, Elsa Lanchester, Robert Newton, Tyrone Guthrie; ***D:*** Erich Pommer.

Beaches 🦴🦴🦴½ **1988 (PG-13)** Based on the novel by Iris Rainer Dart about two girls whose friendship survived the test of time. The friendship is renewed once more when one of the now middle-aged women learns that she is dying slowly of a fatal disease. **123m/C VHS, 8mm.** Bette Midler, Barbara Hershey, John Heard, Spalding Gray, Lainie Kazan, James Read, Mayim Bialik; ***D:*** Garry Marshall; ***W:*** Mary Agnes Donoghue; ***C:*** Dante Spinotti; ***M:*** Georges Delerue.

Beaks: The Movie woof! *Birds of Prey* **1987 (R)** Two TV reporters try to figure out why birds of prey are suddenly attacking humans. Owes nothing to Hitchcock's "The Birds." **86m/C VHS.** Christopher Atkins, Michelle Johnson; ***D:*** Rene Cardona Jr.

Bean 🦴🦴🦴 **1997 (PG-13)** Big screen adaption of rubber-faced Atkinson's Mr. Bean character finds our disaster-magnet hero working as a guard in London's National Gallery. When a famous painting is purchased by a museum in L.A., the Gallery's curators jump at the chance to send Bean along with the painting as an "expert," although he is nearly mute and definitely not qualified. David (MacNicol), the American curator, invites him to stay at his house, much to the dismay of his wife and children. Bean, of course, wrecks the painting, ruins David's marriage and career, and generally makes an ass out of himself. He then resourcefully (and sometimes accidentally) puts things right. Atkinson proves himself a master of the almost lost art of slapstick comedy. **92m/C VHS, DVD.** *GB* Rowan Atkinson, Peter MacNicol, Pamela Reed, Harris Yulin, Burt Reynolds, Larry Drake, Johnny Galecki, Richard Gant, Tom McGowan, Dakin Matthews, Peter Capaldi, Sandra Oh, Tricia Vessey, Peter Egan; ***D:*** Mel Smith; ***W:*** Richard

Curtis, Robin Driscoll; *C:* Francis Kenny; *M:* Howard Goodall.

Beanstalk 🦴🦴½ **1994 (PG)** Modern-day version of the fairytale finds young Jack Taylor (Daniels) scheming to make it big to help his hardworking single mom. He meets up with a wacky scientist (Kidder), who gives Jack some recently discovered seeds that naturally grow into an enormous beanstalk. And what does Jack find when he climbs the beanstalk—why an entire family of silly giants. **80m/C VHS.** J.D. Daniels, Margot Kidder, Richard Moll, Amy Stock-Poynton, Patrick Renna, Richard Paul, David Naughton, Stuart Pankin, Cathy McAuley; *D:* Michael Paul Davis; *W:* Michael Paul Davis; *M:* Kevin Bassinson.

The Bear 🦴🦴🦴 *L'Ours* **1989 (PG)** Breathtaking, effortlessly entertaining family film (from France) about an orphaned bear cub tagging after a grown Kodiak male and dealing with hunters. The narrative is essentially from the cub's point of view, with very little dialogue. A huge money-maker in Europe; shot on location in the Dolomites and the Candian Arctic. Based on the 1917 novel "The Grizzly King" by James Oliver Curwood. **92m/C VHS, DVD, Wide.** *FR* Jack Wallace, Tcheky Karyo, Andre Lacombe; *D:* Jean-Jacques Annaud; *W:* Gerard Brach, Michael Kane; *C:* Philippe Rousselot; *M:* Bill Conti.

Bear Island 🦴½ **1980 (PG)** Group of secret agents cleverly disguising themselves as U.N. weather researchers converge upon Bear Island in search of a Nazi U-Boat. Looks like rain. **118m/C VHS.** Donald Sutherland, Richard Widmark, Barbara Parkins, Vanessa Redgrave, Christopher Lee, Lloyd Bridges; *D:* Don Sharp.

Bear Ye One Another's Burden... 🦴🦴 *Einer Trage des Anderen Last* **1988** In the early 50s, communist police officer Josef Heilinger (Pose) is sent to a private sanitorium for consumptives. He's forced to share a room with a young Protestant curate, Hubertus Koschenz (Mock). Their ill health is the only thing they have in common, and they deliberately seem to annoy each other, but soon their situation has them grudgingly developing a mutual respect and even friendship. German with subtitles. **118m/C VHS.** *GE* Jorg Pose, Manfred Mock, Susanne Luning, Dieter Knaup; *D:* Lothar Warneke; *C:* Peter Ziesche; *M:* Gunther Fischer.

The Bears & I 🦴🦴 **1974 (G)** A young Vietnam vet helps Indians regain their land rights while raising three bear cubs. Beautiful photography in this Disney production. **89m/C VHS, DVD.** Patrick Wayne, Chief Dan George, Andrew Duggan, Michael Ansara; *D:* Bernard McEveety; *W:* Jack Speirs, John Whedon; *C:* Ted D. Landon; *M:* Buddy (Norman Dale) Baker.

The Beast 🦴½ *La Bete* **1975** Long considered taboo due to its erotic subject matter, this 1975 French film from director Borowczyk arrives in its uncensored form for the first time in 2000. Young heiress Lucy Broadhurst (Hummel) arrives at the de l'Esperance chateau, where she is to marry the young Mathurn de l'Esperance (Benedetti). After retiring to her room, Lucy finds herself dreaming of the 18th-century lady of the chateau, Romilda de l'Esperance (Lane), who according to legend, encountered a wild, sexual monster in the forest near the manor. Was this an isolated incident or does the Beast still roam the grounds? The once shocking sex scenes will be considered quite tame by today's audience, and some of them come across as quite silly. **94m/C DVD, Wide.** Sirpa Lane, Lisbeth Hummel, Elizabeth Kaza, Pierre Benedetti, Guy Trejan; *D:* Walerian Borowczyk; *W:* Walerian Borowczyk; *C:* Bernard Daillencourt, Marcel Grignon.

The Beast 🦴🦴½ *The Beast of War* **1988 (R)** Violent and cliche-driven war drama notable for its novel twist: wild Russian tank officer becomes lost in the Afghanistan wilderness while being tracked by Afghan rebels with revenge in mind. Filmed in the Israel desert and adapted by William Mastrosimone from his play. **93m/C VHS, DVD, Wide.** George Dzundza, Jason Patric, Steven Bauer, Stephen Baldwin, Don Harvey, Kabir Bedi, Erik Avari, Haim Gerafi; *D:* Kevin Reynolds; *W:* William Mastrosimone; *C:* Doug Milsome; *M:* Mark Isham.

The Beast 🦴🦴 *Peter Benchley's The Beast* **1996 (PG-13)** Benchley once again terrorizes a small coastal community with a giant sea creature that preys on sailors and divers. When a poacher's attempts to capture the creature result in further disaster, a fishing boat captain, a Coast Guard officer, and a marine biologist set sail to to kill the critter. **116m/C VHS.** William L. Petersen, Karen Sillas, Charles Martin Smith, Ronald Guttman, Missy (Melissa) Crider, Sterling Macer, Denis Arndt, Larry Drake; *D:* Jeff Bleckner; *W:* J.B. White; *C:* Geoff Burton; *M:* Don Davis. **TV**

The Beast from Haunted Cave 🦴🦴 **1960** Gold thieves hiding in a wilderness cabin encounter a spiderlike monster. Surprisingly good performances from Sinatra (Frank's nephew) and Carol. Produced by Gene Corman, Roger's brother. **64m/B VHS, DVD, Wide.** Michael Forest, Sheila Carol, Frank Wolff, Richard Sinatra, Wally Campo; *D:* Monte Hellman; *W:* Charles B. Griffith; *C:* Andrew M. Costikyan.

The Beast from 20,000 Fathoms 🦴🦴½ **1953** Atomic testing defrosts a giant dinosaur in the Arctic; the hungry monster proceeds onwards to its former breeding grounds, now New York City. Oft-imitated saurian-on-the-loose formula is still fun, brought to life by Ray Harryhausen special effects. Based loosely on the Ray Bradbury story "The Foghorn." **80m/B VHS.** Paul (Christian) Hubschmid, Paula Raymond, Cecil Kellaway, Kenneth Tobey, Donald Woods, Lee Van Cleef, Steve Brodie, Mary Hill, Jack Pennick, Ross Elliot; *D:* Eugene Lourie; *W:* Eugene Lourie, Fred Freiberger, Louis Morheim, Robert Smith; *C:* John L. "Jack" Russell; *M:* David Buttolph.

Beast in the Cellar 🦴½ *Are You Dying Young Man?* **1970 (R)** Every family has something to hide, and in the case of two spinster sisters, it's their murderous inhuman brother, whom they keep chained in the cellar. Like all brothers, however, the "beast" rebels against his sisters' bossiness and escapes to terrorize their peaceful English countryside. The sisters' (Reid and Robson) performances aren't bad, but rest of effort is fairly disappointing. **85m/C VHS.** *GB* Beryl Reid, Flora Robson, T.P. McKenna; *D:* James Kelly.

The Beast Must Die 🦴🦴 *Black Werewolf* **1975 (PG)** A millionaire sportsman invites a group of men and women connected with bizarre deaths or the eating of human flesh to spend the cycle of a full moon at his isolated lodge. **93m/C VHS, DVD, Wide.** *GB* Peter Cushing, Calvin Lockhart, Charles Gray, Anton Diffring, Marlene Clark, Ciaran Madden, Tom Chadbon, Michael Gambon; *D:* Paul Annett; *W:* Michael Winder; *C:* Jack Hildyard; *M:* Douglas Gamley.

Beast of Morocco 🦴🦴 *Hand of Night* **1966** Interesting vampire film about a Morrocan vampire princess who sets her sights on seducing a noted archaeologist. Of course his girlfriend ends up being abducted by the vampire's servant. **88m/C VHS.** *GB* William Sylvester, Alizia Gur, Terence de Marney, Diane Clare, Edward Underdown, William Dexter, Sylvia Marriott; *D:* Frederick Goode; *W:* Bruce Stewart; *C:* William Jordan; *M:* John Shakespeare.

Beast of the Yellow Night woof! **1970 (R)** A dying soldier sells his soul to Satan at the close of WWII. Years later, existing without aging, he periodically turns into a cannibal monster. Although the first half is tedious, the monster turns things around when he finally shows up. Decent gore effects. **87m/C VHS.** *PH* John Ashley, Mary Wilcox, Eddie Garcia, Vic Diaz; *D:* Eddie Romero.

The Beast of Yucca Flats woof! **1961** A really cheap, quasi-nuclear protest film. A Russian scientist is chased by communist agents into a nuclear testing area and is caught in an atomic blast. As a result, he turns into a club-weilding monster. Voice over narration is used in lieu of dialogue as that process proved too expensive. **53m/B VHS, DVD.** Tor Johnson, Douglas Mellor, Larry Aten, Barbara Francis, Conrad Brooks, Anthony Cardoza, Bing Stafford, John Morrison; *D:* Coleman Francis; *W:* Coleman Francis; *C:* John Cagle; *M:* Irwin Nafshun, Al Remington.

The Beast That Killed Women 🦴🦴½ **1965** Colonists at a sunny Florida nudist camp have their beach party interrupted by an escaped gorilla. Director Mahon, in his first color effort, stretches this panicky moment into an hour of fleshy fun and games. **60m/C VHS, DVD.** *D:* Barry Mahon; *W:* Barry Mahon; *C:* Barry Mahon.

The Beast with Five Fingers 🦴🦴½ **1946** After a pianist mysteriously dies and leaves his fortune to his private nurse, the occupants of his villa are terrorized by a creature that turns out to be the pianist's hand which was severed by his personal secretary (Lorre). Lorre is also terrorized by hallucinations of the hand, and no matter what he does to stop it (nail it to a desk, throw it in the fire, etc.), nothing can keep the hand from carrying out its mission. A creepy thriller with inventive shots of the severed hand. **88m/B VHS.** Robert Alda, Andrea King, Peter Lorre, Victor Francen, J. Carrol Naish, Charles Dingle; *D:* Robert Florey; *W:* Curt Siodmak; *M:* Max Steiner.

The Beast Within 🦴🦴 **1982 (R)** Young woman has the misfortune of being raped by an unseen creature in a Mississippi swamp. Seventeen years later, her son conceived from that hellish union begins to act quite strange, developing a penchant for shedding his skin before turning into an insect-like critter with a cannibalistic appetite. First film to use the air "bladder" type of prosthetic make-up popularized in later, and generally better, horror films. Contains some choice cuts in photo editing: the juxtaposition of hamburger and human "dead meat" is witty. Based on Edward Levy's 1981 novel. **98m/C VHS, DVD, Wide.** Ronny Cox, Bibi Besch, L.Q. (Justus E. McQueen) Jones, Paul Clemens, Don Gordon, Katherine Moffat, John Dennis Johnston, R.G. Armstrong, Logan Ramsey, Ron Soble, Meshach Taylor; *D:* Philippe Mora; *W:* Tom Holland; *C:* Jack L. Richards; *M:* Les Baxter.

Beastmaster 🦴🦴 **1982 (PG)** Adventure set in a wild and primitive world. The Beastmaster is involved in a life-and-death struggle with overwhelming forces of evil. Campy neanderthal flesh flick. **119m/C VHS, DVD, Wide.** Marc Singer, Tanya Roberts, Rip Torn, John Amos, Josh Milrad, Billy Jacoby, Ben Hammer; *D:* Don A. Coscarelli; *W:* Don A. Coscarelli, Paul Pepperman; *C:* John Alcott; *M:* Lee Holdridge.

Beastmaster 2: Through the Portal of Time 🦴½ **1991 (PG-13)** This time the laughs are intentional as the Beastmaster follows an evil monarch through a dimensional gate to modern-day L.A., where the shopping is better for both trendy clothes and weapons. Fun for genre fans, with a behind-the-scenes featurette on the tape. **107m/C VHS.** Marc Singer, Kari Wuhrer, Sarah Douglas, Wings Hauser, James Avery, Robert Fieldsteel, Arthur Malet, Robert Z'Dar, Michael Berryman; *D:* Sylvio Tabet; *M:* Robert Folk.

Beastmaster 3: The Eye of Braxus 🦴🦴½ **1995 (PG)** Heroic hunk Dar the Beastmaster (Singer) returns to battle evil. Lord Agon (Warner) needs to obtain a jeweled eye that will bring the demon Braxus back to life—and he'll stop at nothing, including kidnapping Dar's brother King Tal (Van Dien), to reach his terrifying goal. But Dar isn't alone—he's got the bewitching sorceress Morgana (Down), tempting warrioress Shada (Hess), and loyal advisor Seth (Todd) to help him out. **92m/C VHS.** Marc Singer, David Warner, Lesley-Anne Down, Tony Todd, Casper Van Dien, Keith Coulouris, Sandra Hess, Patrick Kilpatrick; *D:* Gabrielle Beaumont; *W:* David Wise; *C:* Barbara Claman; *M:* Jan Hammer.

Beasts 🦴 **1983** A young couple's plans for a romantic weekend in the Rockies are slightly changed when the pair are savagely attacked by wild beasts. **92m/C VHS.** Tom Babson, Kathy Christopher, Vern Potter; *D:* Don Hawks.

The Beat 🦴 **1988** Unrealistic film about a bookish new kid who intercedes in the tension between two rival street gangs, changing their lives in his literary way. **101m/C VHS.** John Savage, Kara Glover, Paul Dillon, David Jacobson, William McNamara; *D:* Peter Mones; *W:* Peter Mones; *M:* Carter Burwell.

Beat Girl 🦴🦴 *Wild for Kicks* **1960** Pouty rebellious teen Jennifer (Hill) spends her days in art school and her nights at a London beat hangout. She's jealous when daddy (Farrar) marries sexy French Nichole (Adam) and plots to break them up. When Jennifer discovers Nichole's sordid past she winds up in a burlesque club, attracting the unsavory attentions of owner Kenny (Lee). Then Kenny winds up dead. Singer Adam Faith performs and Reed has a bit as a youthful tough. **85m/B VHS.** *GB* Gillian Hills, David Farrar, Noelle Adam, Christopher Lee, Shirley Anne Field, Oliver Reed, Nada Beall, Adam Faith, Nigel Green, Claire Gordon; *D:* Edmond T. Greville; *W:* Dail Ambler; *C:* Walter Lassally; *M:* John Barry.

Beat Street 🦴🦴½ **1984 (PG)** Intended as a quick cash-in on the break dancing trend, this essentially plotless musical features kids trying to break into local show biz with their rapping and dancing skills. Features the music of Afrika Bambaata and the Soul Sonic Force, Grand Master Melle Mel and the Furious Five, and others. ♫Beat Street Breakdown; Baptize the Beat; Stranger in a Strange Land; Beat Street Strut; Us Girls; This Could Be the Night; Breakers Revenge; Tu Carino (Carmen's Theme); Frantic Situation. **106m/C VHS.** Rae Dawn Chong, Leon Grant, Saundra Santiago, Guy Davis, Jon Chardiet, Duane Jones, Kadeem Hardison; *D:* Stan Lathan; *W:* Andrew Davis.

Beat the Devil 🦴🦴🦴 **1953** Each person on a slow boat to Africa has a scheme to beat the other passengers to the uranium-rich land that they all hope to claim. An unusual black comedy which didn't fare well when released, but over the years has come to be the epitome of spy-spoofs. **89m/C VHS, DVD.** Humphrey Bogart, Gina Lollobrigida, Peter Lorre, Robert Morley, Jennifer Jones, Edward Underdown, Ivor Barnard, Bernard Lee, Marco Tulli; *D:* John Huston; *W:* John Huston, Truman Capote; *C:* Oswald Morris; *M:* Franco Mannino.

Beatlemania! The Movie 🦴 *Beatlemania* **1981** Boring look at the Fab Four. Not the real Beatles, but impersonators who do a very inadequate job. Based on the equally disappointing stage show. **86m/C VHS.** Mitch Weissman, Ralph Castelli, David Leon, Tom Teeley; *D:* Joseph Manduke.

The Beatniks 🦴 **1960** Story about the dark secrets of the beat generation in which a man is promised fame and fortune by an agent, but his dreams are dashed when his friend commits murder. A big waste of time. **78m/B VHS.** Tony Travis, Peter Breck, Karen Kadler, Joyce Terry, Sam Edwards, Bob Wells; *D:* Paul Frees; *W:* Paul Frees; *C:* Murray Deatley; *M:* Stanley Wilson.

Beatrice 🦴🦴🦴½ *La Passion Beatrice* **1988 (R)** In France during the Middle Ages, a barbaric soldier of the Hundred Years' War returns to his estate that his daughter has maintained, only to brutalize and abuse her. In French with English subtitles. **132m/C VHS.** *FR* Julie Delpy, Barnard Pierre Donnadieu, Nils (Niels) Tavernier; *D:* Bertrand Tavernier; *W:* Colo Tavernier O'Hagan; *C:* Bruno de Keyzer; *M:* Lili Boulanger. Cesar '88: Costume Des.

Beau Brummel 🦴🦴½ **1924** The famous silent adaptation of the Clyde Fitch play about an ambitious English dandy's rise and fall. **80m/B VHS.** John Barrymore, Mary Astor, Willard Louis, Irene Rich, Carmel Myers, Alec B. Francis, William Humphreys; *D:* Harry Beaumont.

Beau Brummel 🦴🦴🦴 **1954** Lavish production casts Granger in the role of the rags-to-riches dandy and chief adviser to the Prince of Wales. Born into a life of poverty, George Bryan Brummel uses wit and intelligence to meet the vain Prince and ingratiate himself to the future king (George IV). He also manages to catch the eye of Taylor, who falls in love with him. Outstanding period piece cinematography, sets, and costumes. Shot on location in England's beautiful countryside, many of the interior shots are from a 15th-century mansion, Ockwell Manor, located near Windsor Castle. Remake of the 1924 silent film starring John Barrymore. Based on the play by Clyde Fitch. **113m/C VHS.** Stewart Granger, Elizabeth Taylor, Peter Ustinov, Robert Morley, James Donald, James Hayter, Rosemary Harris, Paul Rogers, Noel Willman, Peter Dyneley, Charles Carson; ***D:*** Curtis Bernhardt; ***W:*** Karl Tunberg; ***C:*** Oswald Morris.

Beau Geste 🦴🦴🦴½ **1939** The classic Hollywood adventure film based on the Percival Christopher Wren novel. To protect aging Lady Patricia (Thatcher), who raised the orphaned brothers, Beau Geste (Cooper) takes the blame for a jewel theft and decides to enlist in the Foreign Legion. He's followed by his brothers John (Milland) and Digby (Preston), and all face desert wars and despicable officers, including the psychotic Sgt. Markoff (Donlevy). A rousing, much-copied epic. **114m/B VHS.** Gary Cooper, Ray Milland, Robert Preston, Brian Donlevy, Donald O'Connor, J. Carrol Naish, Susan Hayward, James Stephenson, Albert Dekker, Broderick Crawford, Charles T. Barton, Heather Thatcher, James Burke, G.P. (Tim) Huntley Jr., Harold Huber, Harvey Stephens, Stanley Andrews, Harry Woods, Arthur Aylesworth, Henry (Kleinbach) Brandon, Nestor Paiva, George Chandler, George Regas; ***D:*** William A. Wellman; ***W:*** Robert Carson; ***C:*** Theodor Sparkuhl, Louis Clyde Stouman, Archie Stout; ***M:*** Alfred Newman.

Beau Pere 🦴🦴🦴 *Stepfather* **1981** Bittersweet satiric romp from Blier about the war zone of modern romance, wherein 14-year-old Besse pursues her 30-year-old irresponsible, widowed stepfather (Dewaere). Sharp-edged and daring. In French with subtitles. **125m/C VHS, DVD.** *FR* Patrick Dewaere, Nathalie Baye, Ariel Besse, Maurice Ronet, Genevieve Mnich, Maurice Risch, Macha Meril, Rose Thiery; ***D:*** Bertrand Blier; ***W:*** Bertrand Blier; ***C:*** Sacha Vierny; ***M:*** Philippe Sarde.

Beau Revel 🦴🦴🦴½ **1921** Critically acclaimed romantic drama of the silent era. A passionate dancing girl played by Vidor, one of the '20s' more prolific romantic leads (and erstwhile wife of director King Vidor) is the object of romantic interest of a father and son, which leaves the threesome lovelorn, suicidal, and emotionally scarred. You might recognize Stone from his later role as Judge Hardy in the MGM "Hardy Family" series. **70m/B VHS.** Lewis Stone, Florence Vidor, Lloyd Hughes, Katherine Kirkham, William Conklin; ***D:*** John Wray.

Beaumarchais the Scoundrel 🦴🦴½ *Beaumarchais L'Insolent* **1996** Adapted from an unpublished play by Sacha Guitry. Beautifully filmed romp of the social-climbing and political-spying gadfly Pierre Augustin Caron de Beaumarchais. Molinaro has simplified the fantastic life of the 18th-century dramatist, courtier, and watchmaker to Louis XV (and author of the comic masterpieces "The Barber of Seville" and "The Marriage of Figaro") but the result is still dizzying. French with subtitles. **100m/C VHS.** *FR* Fabrice Luchini, Jacques Weber, Michel Piccoli, Claire Nebout, Jean-Francois Balmer, Florence Thomassin, Michel Serrault, Dominique Besnehard, Jean-Claude Brialy, Murray Head, Jeff Nuttal, Jean Yanne, Manuel Blanc, Sandrine Kiberlain, Axelle Laffont; ***D:*** Edouard Molinaro; ***W:*** Edouard Molinaro, Jean-Claude Brisville; ***C:*** Michael Epp; ***M:*** Jean-Claude Petit.

The Beautician and the Beast 🦴🦴 **1997 (PG)** Evita meets Lucille Ball when TV's "Nanny" enters Eastern Europe whining to conquer fictional "Slovetzia" royalty. Camp comedy casts Drescher as Joy, a beautician who becomes a local hero after a fire in her beauty class and is subsequently hired by a visiting emissary to tutor the children of despotic dictator Pochenko (Dalton). Overridingly well-known caricatures, loosely based on the fairy tale "Beauty and the Beast," as well as a host of old-time, culture clash movies ("The King and I," "Sound of Music"), where the humble nanny attempts to bring joy (get it?) into the life of a man who carries the weight of the world on his shoulders. Lensed in Prague inside a Gothic, 17th-century castle. Pleasant enough, if not original, timekiller. **105m/C VHS.** Fran Drescher, Timothy Dalton, Ian McNeice, Patrick Malahide, Lisa Jakub, Michael Lerner, Phyllis Newman; ***D:*** Ken Kwapis; ***W:*** Todd Graff; ***C:*** Peter Collister; ***M:*** Cliff Eidelman.

Beauties of the Night 🦴🦴 *Night Beauties; Les Belles de Nuit* **1952** Dreamy fantasy finds a shy music teacher (Philipe) escaping from his boring life into romantic adventures with beautiful women. But his dreams slowly turn nightmarish and he's forced to deal with reality—and real love. French with subtitles. **89m/B VHS.** *FR* Gerard Philipe, Gina Lollobrigida, Martine Carol, Magali Vendeuil, Paolo Stoppa, Raymond Bussieres, Raymond Cordy; ***D:*** Rene Clair; ***W:*** Rene Clair; ***C:*** Armand Thirard; ***M:*** Georges Van Parys.

Beautiful 🦴 **2000 (PG-13)** Field's directorial debut is a cloying beauty pageant satire that wants you to like it. REALLY wants you to like it. Unfortunately, the jokes and characters are U-G-L-Y and they ain't got no alibi. Minnie Driver is Mona, a bright girl from an abusive home who escapes her grim reality by trying to win beauty pageants. She's shown as a little ugly duckling who uses any means necessary to win her way up the escalating ladder of swimsuitability. Finally, she qualifies for the Holy Grail of beauty pageants, the Miss American Miss competition. Along the way, however, she has become a single mother, which automatically disqualifies her as a contestant. She comes up with a plan where her daughter Vanessa (Pepsi prodigy and demon-child Hallie Kate Eisenberg) is passed off as the child of her patient best friend Ruby (Adams). Mona then screeches complaints about the kid's behavior being a distraction to her goal (which is no way to treat your child, even if she is Satan's hand-puppet) while an ambitious reporter (Stefanson) tries to reveal her secret. Overly-padded, and it doesn't even have a nice personality. **112m/C VHS, DVD, Wide.** Minnie Driver, Hallie Kate Eisenberg, Joey Lauren Adams, Kathleen Turner, Leslie Stefanson, Bridgette Wilson, Kathleen Robertson, Michael McKean, Gary Collins, Brent Briscoe; ***D:*** Sally Field; ***W:*** Jon Bernstein; ***C:*** Robert Yeoman; ***M:*** John (Gianni) Frizzell.

Beautiful Beast 🦴🦴 *XX: Utukushiki Gakuen; XX Beautiful Beast* **1995** Mysterious Chinese warrior woman known as Black Orchid arrives in Japan and rubs out mob boss Ishizuka. Fleeing the scene, she hides out with bartender Yoichi Fujinami, who becomes torn between helping his old pal Yaguchi and the mystery girl that he's falling in love with. Foregoes a lot of empty soft-core sex in favor of providing more action. Director Toshiharu Ikeda is no John Woo, but at least Black Orchid's trunk full of high-powered weaponry provides a little fun. **87m/C DVD.** *JP* Kaori Shimamura, Takanori Kikuchi, Hakuryu, Minako Ogawa; ***D:*** Toshiharu Ikeda; ***W:*** Tamiya Takehashi, Hiroshi Takehashi; ***C:*** Seizo Sengen.

The Beautiful Blonde from Bashful Bend 🦴🦴½ **1949** Charming comedy-western gets better with age. Grable is the pistol packing mama mistaken for the new school teacher. Fun performances by all, especially Herbert. **77m/C VHS.** Betty Grable, Cesar Romero, Rudy Vallee, Olga San Juan, Hugh Herbert, Porter Hall, Sterling Holloway, El Brendel; ***D:*** Preston Sturges.

Beautiful Creatures 🦴🦴 **2000 (R)** Fitful comedy/thriller follows the adventures of Petulia (Weisz) and Dorothy (Lynch), two Glasgow lasses with abusive boyfriends. Dorothy escapes a beating from her druggie boyfriend Tony (Glen), only to wind up aiding Petulia, who is being attacked in the street by drunken Brian (Mannion). Unfortunately, Brian dies and the women decides to make it look like he's been kidnapped and ask a ransom from his equally violent brother Ronnie (Roeves) so they can get out of town. Then a crooked detective (Norton) enters the scene and the women's plans turn a little complicated. **88m/C VHS, DVD, Wide.** *GB* Rachel Weisz, Susan Lynch, Alex Norton, Iain Glen, Maurice Roeves, Tom Mannion; ***D:*** Bill Eagles; ***W:*** Simon Donald; ***C:*** James Welland; ***M:*** Murray Gold.

Beautiful Dreamers 🦴½ **1992 (PG-13)** Maurice Bucke is a young Canadian physician who runs the London Insane Asylum. After a chance meeting with poet Walt Whitman, both men discover their mutual outrage for current treatment of the mentally ill. Bucke persuades Whitman to visit his asylum in order to try Whitman's theory of human compassion on the asylum's inmates. However, Bucke runs into opposition from the local townspeople, scandalized by Whitman's radical reputation. Fairly humdrum with a larger-than-life performance by Torn as Whitman. Based on Whitman's visit to Canada in 1880. **108m/C VHS, Wide.** *CA* Rip Torn, Colm Feore, Wendel Meldrum, Sheila McCarthy, Colin Fox; ***D:*** John Kent Harrison; ***W:*** John Kent Harrison.

Beautiful Girls 🦴🦴½ **1996 (R)** Slow but easy-going film highlights the differences between men, women, and relationships. A 10-year high school reunion brings together buddies Tommy (Dillon), Kev (Perlich), Paul (Rapaport), Mo (Emmerich), and Willie (Hutton). They ice-fish, drink, and talk about women (about whom they haven't a clue). All are smitten by Andera (Thurman), the gorgeous visiting cousin of another friend, and Willie becomes intrigued by Marty (Portman), his precociously tantalizing 13-year-old neighbor. The guys whining gets annoying and the women are strictly secondary characters, but O'Donnell's tirade about fake femininity is amusing. The Afghan Whigs are featured as the bar band. **110m/C VHS, DVD.** Matt Dillon, Timothy Hutton, Michael Rapaport, Max Perlich, Noah Emmerich, Lauren Holly, Uma Thurman, Natalie Portman, Mira Sorvino, Martha Plimpton, Rosie O'Donnell, Annabeth Gish, Pruitt Taylor Vince, Sam Robards, David Arquette, Anne Bobby, Richard Bright; ***D:*** Ted (Edward) Demme; ***W:*** Scott Rosenberg; ***C:*** Adam Kimmel; ***M:*** David A. Stewart.

Beautiful Hunter 🦴🦴 *XX Beautiful Hunter* **1994** Shion has been raised since birth to be the perfect assassin and executioner for the Magnificat crime family, a devoutly Catholic gang that do their criminal business in the vestments of priests and nuns. Blind Father Kano fully controls the life of his adopted daughter, until photographer Ito gets photos of her. The lethal yet naive heroine finds herself attracted to Ito, but Father Kano Sister Mitsuko and a squad of killers after them. Kuno looks—well, beautiful, in and out of a series of foxy outfits, but doesn't display any kind of martial arts to convince us of her master assassin status. **91m/C DVD.** *JP* Makiko Kuno, Koji Shimizu; ***D:*** Masaura Konuma.

Beautiful Joe 🦴🦴 **2000 (R)** Joe (Connolly) decides to hit the road for adventure and discovers it in Louisville, Kentucky when he meets Hush (Stone), an ex-stripper turned con artist. Then Joe gets in trouble when he tries to help Hush with her debt to crime boss George the Geek (Holm) and the twosome take off to Vegas with Geek's henchman (Bellows) on their trail. **98m/C VHS, DVD, Wide.** Billy Connolly, Sharon Stone, Gil Bellows, Ian Holm, Dann Florek, Barbara Tyson; ***D:*** Stephen Metcalfe; ***W:*** Stephen Metcalfe; ***C:*** Thomas Ackerman.

A Beautiful Mind 🦴🦴🦴½ **2001 (PG-13)** Loose adaptation of Sylvia Nasar's 1998 bio of Nobel Prize winning mathematician John Forbes Nash Jr. An anti-social genius at Princeton University, Nash wrote his thesis on game theory at 21 and worked for the government in the 1950s before succumbing to paranoid schizophrenia, necessitating his confinement to a mental institution. (The treatment scenes are not for the faint-hearted.) His apparent recovery, after some 30 years, led to sharing a Nobel award in economics in 1994. Director Howard manages to keep the inherent sentimentality and sensationalism generally under control thanks to some powerful performances from Crowe (as Nash), Connelly (as wife Alicia), and Harris (as a sinister government official). The usual controversies swirled about the accuracy of the biopic and what was left out. Ignore the petty carping. **129m/C VHS, DVD.** *US* Russell Crowe, Jennifer Connelly, Ed Harris, Paul Bettany, Christopher Plummer, Judd Hirsch, Adam Goldberg, Joshua Lucas, Anthony Rapp, Austin Pendleton, Vivien Cardone; ***D:*** Ron Howard; ***W:*** Akiva Goldsman; ***C:*** Roger Deakins; ***M:*** James Horner. Oscars '01: Adapt. Screenplay, Director (Howard), Film, Support. Actress (Connelly); British Acad. '01: Actor (Crowe), Support. Actress (Connelly); Directors Guild '01: Director (Howard); Golden Globes '02: Actor—Drama (Crowe), Film—Drama, Screenplay, Support. Actress (Connelly); Screen Actors Guild '01: Actor (Crowe); Writers Guild '01: Adapt. Screenplay; Broadcast Film Critics '01: Actor (Crowe), Director (Howard), Film, Support. Actress (Connelly).

Beautiful People 🦴🦴 **1999 (R)** The war in Bosnia (circa 1993) comes to London when former neighbors-turned-enemies, one a Serbian and the other a Croatian, accidentally meet on a bus and try to kill each other. This chaos leads to a variety of intersecting situations: Portia (Coleman), a doctor and daughter of a snobby Tory MP, falls for a refugee; another doctor (Farrell) counsels a pregnant refugee who wants to abort her baby, who is the product of a rape; a druggy skinhead (Nussbaum) winds up experiencing battle firsthand, and on and on and on. **107m/C VHS, DVD, Wide.** *GB* Charlotte Coleman, Nicholas Farrell, Danny Nussbaum, Edin Dzandzanovic, Charles Kay, Rosalind Ayres, Heather Tobias, Siobhan Redmond, Gilbert Martin, Linda Bassett, Steve Sweeney; ***D:*** Jasmin Dizdar; ***W:*** Jasmin Dizdar; ***C:*** Barry Ackroyd; ***M:*** Gary Bell.

The Beautiful, the Bloody and the Bare 🦴 **1969** Sordid screamer in the Herschell Gordon Lewis tradition. Set in New York City in the '60s, a depraved artist kills the nude models who pose for him. **?m/C VHS.** Adela Rogers St. John, Marlene Denes, Debra Page, Jack Lowe; ***D:*** Sande N. Johnsen; ***W:*** Sande N. Johnsen; ***C:*** Jerry Denby; ***M:*** Steve Karmen.

Beautiful Thing 🦴🦴🦴 **1995 (R)** Sweet, fairytalish, gay coming-of-age story set in a working-class southeast London housing estate. Shy teenager Jamie (Berry) lives with his barmaid mum, Sandra (Henry), and her lover, Tony (Daniels). Next-door is his best mate, the stoic Ste (Neal), who's regularly abused by his father and brother. But when things get too bad, he sleeps over with Jamie. And one night, nature hesitantly takes its course. Their tart-tongued, Mama Cass fanatic, friend Leah (Empson) starts rumors about the twosome that lead to some uneasy (but ultimately conciliatory) confrontations. Fine performances; Harvey adapted from his play. **89m/C VHS.** *GB* Glen Berry, Scott Neal, Linda Henry, Tameka Empson, Ben Daniels; ***D:*** Hettie Macdonald; ***W:*** Jonathan Harvey; ***C:*** Chris Seager.

Beauty and the Beast 🦴🦴🦴🦴 *La Belle et la Bete* **1946** The classic medieval fairy tale is brought to life on the big screen for the first time. Beauty takes the place of her father after he is sentenced to die by the horrible Beast and falls in love with him. Cocteau uses the story's themes and famous set-pieces to create a cohesive and captivating surreal hymn to romantic love that is still the definitive version of B&B. In French with subtitles. **90m/B VHS, DVD.** *FR* Jean Marais, Josette Day, Marcel Andre, Mila Parely, Nane Germon, Michel Auclair; ***D:*** Jean Cocteau; ***W:*** Jean Cocteau; ***C:*** Henri Alekan; ***M:*** Georges Auric.

Beauty and the Beast **1983** From "Faerie Tale Theatre" comes the story of a Beauty who befriends a Beast and learns a lesson about physical appearance and true love. **60m/C VHS.** Susan Sarandon, Anjelica Huston, Klaus Kinski, Stephen Elliott; ***D:*** Roger Vadim. **CABLE**

Beauty and the Beast 🦴🦴🦴🦴 **1991 (G)** Wonderful Disney musical combines superb animation, splendid characters, and lively songs about a beautiful girl, Belle, and the fearsome and disagreeable Beast. Supporting cast includes the castle servants (a delightful bunch of household objects). Notable as the first animated feature to be nominated for the Best Picture Oscar. Destined to become a classic. The deluxe video version features a work-in-progress rough film cut, a compact disc of the soundtrack, a lithograph depicting a scene from the film, and an illustrated book. ♫Beauty and the Beast; Belle; Something There; Be Our Guest. **84m/C VHS, Wide.** ***D:*** Kirk Wise, Gary Trousdale; ***W:*** Linda Woolverton; ***M:*** Alan Menken, Howard Ashman; ***V:*** Paige O'Hara, Robby Benson, Rex Everhart, Richard White, Jesse Corti, Angela Lansbury, Jerry Orbach, David Ogden Stiers, Bradley Michael Pierce, Jo Anne Worley, Kimmy Robertson. Oscars '91: Song ("Beauty and the Beast"), Orig. Score; Golden Globes '92: Film—Mus./Comedy.

Beauty and the Devil ✂✂ *La Beaute du Diable* **1950** Ambitious retelling of the Faust legend finds old Faust (Simon) willing to sell his soul to the Devil, courtesy of his agent Mephistopheles (Philipe), in return for youth and beauty to pursue the beautiful woman he loves. Clair has his actors trade roles midway through as Faust makes his bargain. French with subtitles. **97m/B VHS.** *FR* Michel Simon, Gerard Philipe, Simone Valere, Raymond Cordy, Gaston Modot, Paolo Stoppa, Nicole Besnard; ***D:*** Rene Clair; ***W:*** Rene Clair, Armand Salacrou; ***C:*** Michel Kelber; ***M:*** Roman Vlad.

Beauty for the Asking ✂ **1939** It sounds like a workable Lucille Ball vehicle—a beautician develops a bestselling skin cream—and even the title sounds like something you'd like to love Lucy in. But somehow the numerous plot implausibilities managed to get by the story's five writers, and the idea of a jilted woman making millions while being financed by her ex's wife just doesn't fly (perhaps it was an idea ahead of its time). Die-hard Lucy fans may find this interesting. **68m/B VHS.** Lucille Ball, Patric Knowles, Donald Woods, Frieda Inescort, Frances Mercer; ***D:*** Glenn Tryon.

Beauty on the Beach ✂ **196?** A comedy about a mad psychologist, his bizarre experiments with women, and his eventual descent into insanity. In Italian with English subtitles. **90m/C VHS.** *IT* Valeria Fabrizi.

Beauty School ✂ *Sylvia Kristel's Beauty School* **1993 (R)** The promise of an advertising contract pits the owners of rival beauty schools against each other. **95m/C VHS.** Sylvia Kristel, Kevin Bernhardt, Kimberly Taylor, Jane (Veronica Hart) Hamilton; ***D:*** Ernest G. Sauer; ***W:*** Mike MacDonald, Merrill Friedman; ***M:*** Jonathan Hannah.

Beavis and Butt-Head Do America ✂✂½ **1996 (PG-13)** Moronic MTV metalheads go on the road in search of their stolen TV and are somehow mistaken for criminal masterminds. Okay, enough about plot. If you're thinking of renting this one, you don't care about that stuff anyway. Director/writer/voice of B&B Judge is smart enough not to change our "heroes" just because they're on a bigger screen. They're still stupid, obsessed with chicks, (Yeah! Chicks are cool!) and blissfully unaware of what's happening around them. The opening sequence, a parody of 70s cop shows, is hilarious (and cool). For those who like the show, and for people who just don't admit that they do, the boys' movie debut (he said "but") doesn't suck. **82m/C VHS, DVD.** ***D:*** Mike Judge; ***W:*** Mike Judge, Joe Stillman; ***M:*** John (Gianni) Frizzell; ***V:*** Mike Judge, Robert Stack, Cloris Leachman, Demi Moore, Eric Bogosian, Richard Linklater.

Bebe's Kids ✂✂½ **1992 (PG-13)** When ladies' man Robin falls for the lovely Jamika, he gets some unexpected surprises when he takes her out on a first date to an amusement park—and she brings along four kids. Animated comedy takes some funny pot-shots at both black and white culture and Disneyland. The children are amusing, especially baby PeeWee, a tot with chronically dirty diapers and Tone Loc's gravelly voice. Based on characters created by the late comedian Robin Harris. The video includes the seven-minute animated short "Itsy Bitsy Spider." **74m/C VHS.** ***D:*** Bruce Smith; ***W:*** Reginald (Reggie) Hudlin; ***M:*** John Barnes; ***V:*** Faizon Love, Vanessa Bell Calloway, Wayne Collins, Jonell Green, Marques Houston, Tone Loc, Nell Carter, Myra J.

Because of Him ✂✂½ **1945** Actress Kim Walker (Durbin) fakes a letter of introduction from famous thespian John Sheridan (Laughton) in order to impress Broadway producer Charles Gilbert (Ridges). It works and she's given the lead, much to the dismay of the playwright, Paul Taylor (Tone). Naturally, Kim turns out to be an opening night success and Paul comes around and realizes what a swell gal she is. Laughton is at his best as the hammy veteran performer. **88m/B VHS.** Deanna Durbin, Franchot Tone, Charles Laughton, Stanley Ridges, Helen Broderick, Donald Meek; ***D:*** Richard Wallace; ***W:*** Edmund Beloin; ***C:*** Hal Mohr; ***M:*** Miklos Rozsa.

Because of the Cats ✂½ **1974** Police inspector uncovers an evil cult within his seaside village while investigating a bizarre rape and burglary. **90m/C VHS.** Bryan Marshall, Alexandra Stewart, Alex Van Rooyen, Sylvia Kristel, Sebastian Graham Jones; ***D:*** Fons Rademakers.

Because of You ✂✂½ **1952** Parolee Christine Carroll (Young) marries Steve Kimberly (Chandler) without revealing her sordid past. Then said past bites her in the butt when her criminal associates find and involve her in another crime. Lots of tears. **95m/B VHS.** Loretta Young, Jeff Chandler, Alex Nicol, Frances Dee, Alexander Scourby, Lynne Roberts, Mae Clarke; ***D:*** Joseph Pevney; ***W:*** Ketti Frings; ***C:*** Russell Metty; ***M:*** Frank Skinner.

Because of You ✂✂ *Kyoko* **1995 (R)** Jose (Osorio), a Cuban-American serviceman stationed in Japan, taught the young Kyoko how to do latin dancing. When she's 21, Kyoko (Takaoka) travels to New York to see Jose again. When she does find him, she discovers Jose has AIDS and no longer remembers much of his past, including Kyoko. Terminally ill, his one wish is to be reunited with his family in Miami. Kyoko decides to drive Jose home, hoping somehow he'll come to remember her. **85m/C VHS, DVD.** Saki Takaoka, Carlos Osorio, Scott Whitehurst, Mauricio Bustamante, Oscar Colon, Bradford West, Angel Stephens; ***D:*** Ryu Murakami; ***W:*** Ryu Murakami; ***C:*** Sarah Cawley.

Because Why? ✂✂ **1993** After travelling abroad for five years, Alex (Riley) returns to Montreal with a back pack, a skateboard, and an old girlfriend's address. The address only leads to a demolished building, so Alex finds himself a new home and—longing to belong somewhere—a potentially new family and friends. **104m/C VHS, DVD.** *CA* Michael Riley, Martine Rochon, Doru Bandol, Heather Mathieson; ***D:*** Arto Paragamian; ***W:*** Arto Paragamian; ***C:*** Andre Turpin; ***M:*** Nana Vasconcelos.

Because You're Mine ✂✂ **1952** Lanza plays an opera star who is drafted and falls in love with Morrow, his top sergeant's sister. Plenty of singing—maybe too much at times, but Lanza's fans will enjoy it nonetheless. ♫All the Things You Are; Because You're Mine; Be My Love; Granada; Lee-Ah-Loo; The Lord's Prayer; The Song Angels Sing; You Do Something to Me. **103m/C VHS.** Mario Lanza, James Whitmore, Doretta Morrow, Dean Miller, Rita (Paula) Corday, Jeff Donnell, Spring Byington; ***D:*** Alexander Hall.

Becket ✂✂✂ **1964** Adaptation of Jean Anouilh's play about the tumultuous friendship between Henry II of England and the Archbishop of Canterbury Thomas Becket. Becket views his position in the church of little relation to the sexual and emotional needs of a man, until he becomes archbishop. His growing concern for religion and his shrinking need of Henry as friend and confidant eventually cause the demise of the friendship and the resulting tragedy. Flawless acting from every cast member, and finely detailed artistic direction make up for the occasional slow moment. **148m/C VHS, Wide.** Richard Burton, Peter O'Toole, John Gielgud, Donald Wolfit; ***D:*** Peter Glenville; ***W:*** Edward Anhalt; ***C:*** Geoffrey Unsworth. Oscars '64: Adapt. Screenplay; Golden Globes '65: Actor—Drama (O'Toole), Film—Drama.

Becky Sharp ✂✂½ **1935** This premiere Technicolor film tells the story of Becky Sharp, a wicked woman who finally performs one good deed. **83m/C VHS.** Miriam Hopkins, Frances Dee, Cedric Hardwicke, Billie Burke, Nigel Bruce, Pat Nixon; ***D:*** Rouben Mamoulian; ***C:*** Ray Rennahan.

Becoming Colette ✂✂ **1992 (R)** Tedious flashbacking bio of French writer Colette, from her innocent days in the country to her (bad) marriage to writer/publisher Willy and on and on to her own growing career as a writer. She begins writing stories, using an alter-ego character, Claudine, which detail her sexual escapades. Lots of naked flesh but little passion. A postscript notes that Colette wrote "Gigi" and was the first woman to receive the French Legion of Honor. **97m/C VHS.** Mathilda May, Klaus Maria Brandauer, Virginia Madsen, Paul Rhys, Jean-Pierre Aumont, John van Dreelen, Lucienne Hamon; ***D:*** Danny Huston; ***W:*** Ruth Graham; ***M:*** John Scott.

Bed and Board ✂✂✂ *Domicile Conjugal* **1970** The fourth film in the Antoine Doinel (Leaud) cycle finds him marrying Christine (Jade) and becoming a father. The responsibilities of adulthood upset him so much that Antoine leaves his new family and begins an affair. French with subtitles. **100m/C VHS, DVD.** *FR* Jean-Pierre Leaud, Claude Jade, Barbara Laage, Hiroko Berghauer, Daniel Boulanger, Pierre Maguelon, Jacques Jouanneau, Jacques Rispal, Jacques Robiolles, Pierre Fabre, Billy Kearns, Daniel Ceccaldi, Daniele Girard, Claire Duhamel, Sylvana Blasi, Claude Vega, Christian de Tiliere, Annick Asty, Marianne Piketi, Guy Pierauld, Marie Dedieu, Marie Irakane, Yvon Lec, Ernest Menzer, Christophe Vesque; ***D:*** Francois Truffaut; ***W:*** Francois Truffaut, Bernard Revon, Claude de Givray; ***C:*** Nestor Almendros; ***M:*** Antoine Duhamel.

Bed & Breakfast ✂✂½ **1992 (PG-13)** Three generations of women lead quiet lives while running a failing Nantucket bed and breakfast. When a mystery man washes up on their beach, he charms them all, but it seems that he has a past that could endanger everyone. Lightweight final role for Dewhurst, though she provides some sparks as the strong and loving matriarch. Gentle romantic comedy skims the surface, but is still enjoyable. **97m/C VHS.** Roger Moore, Talia Shire, Colleen Dewhurst, Nina Siemaszko, Ford Rainey, Stephen (Steve) Root, Jamie Walters, Victor Slezak; ***D:*** Robert Ellis Miller; ***W:*** Cindy Myers; ***M:*** David Shire.

Bed and Sofa ✂✂✂½ **1927** Adultery, abortion, and women's rights are brought about by a housing shortage which forces a man to move in with a married friend. Famous, ground-breaking Russian silent. **73m/B VHS.** *RU* Nikolai Batalov, Vladimar Fogel; ***D:*** Abram Room.

Bed of Roses ✂✂½ *Amelia and the King of Plants* **1995 (PG)** Wistful romance finds workaholic investment banker Lisa Walker (Masterson) receiving lavish floral tributes from an unknown admirer. When Lisa tracks her giver down, it turns out to be lovestruck widowed florist Lewis Farrell (Slater), who noticed Lisa crying through her apartment window and sent the flowers to cheer her up. Best friend Kim (Seagal) urges Lisa to go for Lewis but a problematic past has Lisa distrusting her emotions and their romantic path has a few bumps (easily overcome). Appealing leads, lots of cliches. Goldenberg's debut. **88m/C VHS, DVD, Wide.** Christian Slater, Mary Stuart Masterson, Pamela Segall, Josh Brolin, Ally Walker, Debra Monk; ***D:*** Michael Goldenberg; ***W:*** Michael Goldenberg; ***C:*** Adam Kimmel; ***M:*** Michael Convertino.

The Bed You Sleep In ✂✂ **1993** Ray (Blair) is a struggling lumber mill owner, living with his wife Jean (McLaughlin) in a small Oregon town. The couple are torn apart when they receive a letter from their daughter, who's away at college, accusing her father of sexual abuse. The secrets and lies of the family soon echo throughout their community. **117m/C VHS, DVD, Wide.** Tom Blair, Ellen McLaughlin, Kathryn Sannella; ***D:*** Jon Jost; ***W:*** Jon Jost; ***C:*** Jon Jost.

Bedazzled ✂✂✂ **1968 (PG)** Short-order cook Stanley Moon (Moore) is saved from suicide by the devil, here known as George Spiggot (Cook), who makes Stanley an offer: seven wishes in exchange for his soul. What Stanley wants is waitress Margaret (Bron) but each of Stanley's wishes is granted with surprising consequences. Cult comedy is a sometimes uneven, but thoroughly entertaining and funny retelling of the Faustian story. **107m/C VHS, Wide.** *GB* Dudley Moore, Peter Cook, Eleanor Bron, Michael Bates, Raquel Welch, Bernard Spear, Parnell McGarry, Howard Goorney, Daniele Noel, Barry Humphries, Lockwood West, Robert Russell, Michael Trubshawe, Robin Hawdon, Evelyn Moore, Charles Lloyd Pack; ***D:*** Stanley Donen; ***W:*** Dudley Moore, Peter Cook; ***C:*** Austin Dempster; ***M:*** Dudley Moore.

Bedazzled ✂✂½ **2000 (PG-13)** Mortals have been falling for this scam for centuries: seven wishes in exchange for your eternal soul. Once again the Devil finds a taker. Fraser plays Elliot, a nice but hopeless geek who will do anything to improve his lowly stature in life and nab the girl of his dreams (O'Connor). The Devil's (Hurley) misinterpretations of his requests result in Elliot becoming, among other things, a drug lord, an NBA star, and a much too sensitive bore. Will Elliot find a way out of his hellish obligation? Is there a lesson to be learned from his experiences? You probably know the answers. Ramis occasionally misfires, but the hits outnumber the misses. An updated remake of the Dudley Moore/Peter Cook film. **105m/C VHS, DVD, Wide.** Brendan Fraser, Elizabeth Hurley, Frances O'Connor, Rudolf Martin, Orlando Jones, Gabriel Casseus, Miriam Shor, Brian Doyle-Murray; ***D:*** Harold Ramis; ***W:*** Harold Ramis, Larry Gelbart, Peter Tolan; ***C:*** Bill Pope.

Bedford Incident ✂✂½ **1965** The U.S.S. Bedford discovers an unidentified submarine in North Atlantic waters. The Bedford's commander drives his crew to the point of exhaustion as they find themselves the center of a fateful controversy. **102m/B VHS.** Richard Widmark, Sidney Poitier, James MacArthur, Martin Balsam, Wally Cox, Donald Sutherland, Eric Portman; ***D:*** James B. Harris.

Bedknobs and Broomsticks ✂✂½ **1971 (G)** A novice witch and three cockney waifs ride a magic bedstead and stop the Nazis from invading England during WWII. Celebrated for its animated art. **117m/C VHS, DVD, Wide.** Angela Lansbury, Roddy McDowall, David Tomlinson, Bruce Forsyth, Sam Jaffe; ***D:*** Robert Stevenson; ***W:*** Don DaGradi, Bill Walsh; ***C:*** Frank Phillips; ***M:*** Richard M. Sherman, Robert B. Sherman. Oscars '71: Visual FX.

Bedlam ✂✂✂ **1945** Creeper set in the famed asylum in 18th-century London. A woman, wrongfully committed, tries to stop the evil doings of the chief (Karloff) of Bedlam, and endangers herself. Fine horror film co-written by producer Lewton. **79m/B VHS.** Jason Robards Sr., Ian Wolfe, Glenn Vernon, Boris Karloff, Anna Lee, Billy House, Richard Fraser, Elizabeth Russell, Skelton Knaggs, Robert Clarke, Ellen Corby, Leyland Hodgson, Joan Newton; ***D:*** Mark Robson; ***W:*** Mark Robson, Val Lewton; ***C:*** Nicholas Musuraca; ***M:*** Roy Webb.

Bedroom Eyes ✂✂ **1986 (R)** A successful businessman becomes a voyeur by returning nightly to a beautiful woman's window, until she is killed and he is the prime suspect. Part comic, part disappointing thriller. **90m/C VHS.** Kenneth Gilman, Dayle Haddon, Christine Cattall; ***D:*** William Fruet.

Bedroom Eyes 2 ✂✂ **1989 (R)** After discovering his wife has had an affair, a stockbroker takes a lover. When she turns up dead, he and his wife become murder suspects. Provides some suspenseful moments. **85m/C VHS.** Wings Hauser, Kathy Shower, Linda Blair, Jane (Veronica Hart) Hamilton, Jennifer Delora; ***D:*** Chuck Vincent.

The Bedroom Window ✂✂½ **1987 (R)** Guttenberg is having an illicit affair with his boss' wife (Huppert), who witnesses an assault on another woman (McGovern) from the bedroom window. To keep the affair secret Guttenberg reports the crime, but since it is secondhand, the account is flawed and he becomes a suspect. Semi-tight thriller reminiscent of

Hitchcock mysteries isn't always believable, but is otherwise interesting. **113m/C VHS, DVD, Wide.** Steve Guttenberg, Elizabeth McGovern, Isabelle Huppert, Wallace Shawn, Paul Shenar, Carl Lumbly, Frederick Coffin, Brad Greenquist; ***D:*** Curtis Hanson; ***W:*** Curtis Hanson; ***C:*** Gilbert Taylor; ***M:*** Patrick Gleeson, Michael Shrieve, Felix Mendelessohn.

Bedrooms and Hallways 🦴🦴½ **1998** Single gay Leo (McKidd) is urged to join a new agey men's therapy group where, during one of their meetings, he expresses his interest in Brendan (Purefoy), who's breaking up with longtime lover, Sally (Ehle). After Leo and Brendan get together, Leo realizes that Sally is his old high school girlfriend and there's still a certain spark between them. And things just get more complicated. Zippy if glib humor, although the film tends to lose steam at the end. **96m/C VHS, DVD.** *GB* Kevin McKidd, James Purefoy, Jennifer Ehle, Tom Hollander, Hugo Weaving, Simon Callow, Harriet Walter, Christopher Fulford, Julie Graham; ***D:*** Rose Troche; ***W:*** Robert Farrar; ***C:*** Ashley Rowe; ***M:*** Alfredo Troche.

Bedtime for Bonzo 🦴🦴½ **1951** A professor adopts a chimp to prove that environment, not heredity, determines a child's future. Fun, lighthearted comedy that stars a future president. Followed by "Bonzo Goes to College." **83m/B VHS.** Ronald Reagan, Diana Lynn, Walter Slezak, Jesse White, Bonzo the Chimp, Lucille Barkley, Herbert (Hayes) Heyes, Herb Vigran, Harry Tyler, Ed Clark; ***D:*** Fred de Cordova; ***W:*** Lou Breslow, Val Burton; ***C:*** Carl Guthrie; ***M:*** Frank Skinner.

Bedtime Story 🦴🦴 **1963** Two con artists attempt to fleece an apparently wealthy woman and each other on the French Riviera. Re-made in 1988 as "Dirty Rotten Scoundrels." One of Brando's thankfully few forays into comedy. **99m/C VHS.** Marlon Brando, David Niven, Shirley Jones, Dody Goodman, Marie Windsor; ***D:*** Ralph Levy.

Beefcake 🦴🦴 **1999** Campy docudrama set in 1950s L.A. covers the muscle (or men's physique) magazine culture. Doting mama's boy Bob Mizer (MacIvor) found his talents as a still photographer and filmmaker, who also published Physique Pictorial, all of which featured chiseled studs. While Mizer insisted that his models were just clean-cut, all-American boys, he still fell afoul of pornography charges and operating a prostitution ring. The mock style turns harder-edged with Mizer's tribulations. To further confuse things, the film also includes present-day interviews with some of Mizer's one-time models and others familiar with the culture. **93m/C VHS, DVD.** Daniel MacIvor, Josh Peace, Carroll Godsman; ***D:*** Thom Fitzgerald; ***W:*** Thom Fitzgerald; ***C:*** Thomas M. Harting; ***M:*** John Roby.

Beer 🦴 **1985 (R)** A female advertising executive devises a dangerous sexist campaign for a cheap beer, and both the beer and its nickname become nationwide obsessions. Not especially amusing. **83m/C VHS.** Loretta Swit, Rip Torn, Dick Shawn, David Alan Grier, William Russ, Kenneth Mars, Peter Michael Goetz; ***D:*** Patrick Kelly; ***C:*** Bill Butler; ***M:*** Bill Conti.

The Bees woof! **1978 (PG)** Sting of a poor movie is painful. A strain of bees have ransacked South America and are threatening the rest of the world. The buzz is that no one is safe. Cheap rip-off of "The Swarm," which is saying something. **93m/C VHS.** John Saxon, John Carradine, Angel Tompkins, Claudio Brook, Alicia Encinas; ***D:*** Alfredo Zacharias.

Beethoven 🦴🦴 *Beethoven's Great Love; The Life and Loves of Beethoven; Un Grand Amour de Beethoven* **1936** Startling biography of the musical genius, filled with opulent, impressionistic visuals. French with subtitles. **116m/B VHS, DVD.** *FR* Harry Baur, Jean-Louis Barrault, Marcel Dalio; ***D:*** Abel Gance; ***W:*** Abel Gance; ***C:*** Marc Fossard, Robert Lefebvre.

Beethoven 🦴🦴½ **1992 (PG)** Adorable St. Bernard puppy escapes from dognappers and wanders into the home of the Newtons, who, over dad's objections, adopt him. Beethoven grows into a huge, slobbering dog who sorely tries dad's patience. To make matters worse, two sets of villains also wreak havoc on the Newton's lives. Evil veterinarian Dr. Varnick plots to steal Beethoven for lab experiments, and yuppie couple Brad and Brie plot to take over the family business. Enjoyable cast, particularly Grodin as dad and Chris as Beethoven enable this movie to please more than the milk and cookies set. Followed by "Beethoven's 2nd." **89m/C VHS, DVD.** Charles Grodin, Bonnie Hunt, Dean Jones, Oliver Platt, Stanley Tucci, Nicholle Tom, Christopher Castile, Sarah Rose Karr, David Duchovny, Patricia Heaton, Laurel Cronin; ***D:*** Brian Levant; ***W:*** John Hughes, Amy Holden Jones; ***C:*** Victor Kemper; ***M:*** Randy Edelman.

Beethoven Lives Upstairs 🦴🦴½ **1992** In 19th century Vienna 10 year-old Christoph's life is turned upside-down when the family's eccentric new tenant turns out to be composer Ludwig Van Beethoven. In time, Christoph comes to appreciate the beauty of the music and the tragedy of the composer's deafness. Features more than 25 excerpts of Beethoven's works. **52m/C VHS.** Neil Munro, Ilya Woloshyn, Fiona Reid, Paul Soles, Sheila McCarthy, Albert Schultz; ***D:*** David Devine; ***W:*** Heather Conkie.

Beethoven's 2nd 🦴🦴½ **1993 (PG)** Sequel has awwww factor going for it as new daddy Beethoven slobbers over four adorable and appealing St. Bernard pups and his new love Missy. Same basic evil subplot as the first, with wicked kidnappers replacing evil vet. During the upheaval, the Newtons take care of the little yapping troublemakers, providing the backdrop for endless puppy mischief and exasperation on Grodin's part. Silly subplots and too many human moments tend to drag, but the kids will find the laughs (albeit stupid ones). **87m/C VHS, DVD, Wide.** Charles Grodin, Bonnie Hunt, Nicholle Tom, Christopher Castile, Sarah Rose Karr, Debi Mazar, Christopher Penn, Ashley Hamilton; ***D:*** Rod Daniel; ***W:*** Len Blum; ***C:*** Bill Butler; ***M:*** Randy Edelman.

Beethoven's 3rd 🦴🦴½ **2000 (PG)** Dad Richard Newton (Reinhold) wants to take the family on vacation and, naturally, huge St. Bernard Beethoven is coming along. Suddenly, that rented luxury RV doesn't seem very big and dad's idea of fun is lame to the kids. Of course, it's not a typical vacation anyway, seems thieves Tommy (Ciccolini) and Bill (Marsh) need to retrieve a videotape that Richard has rented. Beethoven tries to protect his family while being blamed for every little mishap. A dog's life, indeed! **99m/C VHS, DVD, Wide.** Judge Reinhold, Julia Sweeney, Joe Pichler, Michaela Gallo, Jamie Marsh, Michael Ciccolini, Frank Gorshin, Danielle Wiener; ***D:*** David Mickey Evans; ***W:*** Jeff Schechter; ***C:*** John Aronson; ***M:*** Philip Giffin. VIDEO

Beethoven's Nephew 🦴½ *Le Neveu de Beethoven* **1988** A tepid pseudo-historical farce about Beethoven's strange obsession with his only nephew. Directed by erstwhile Warhol collaborator Morrissey. **103m/C VHS.** *FR* Wolfgang Reichmann, Ditmar Prinz, Jane Birkin, Nathalie Baye; ***D:*** Paul Morrissey; ***W:*** Paul Morrissey, Matthieu Carriere.

Beetlejuice 🦴🦴🦴½ **1988 (PG)** The after-life is confusing for a pair of ultra-nice novice ghosts Adam Maitland (Baldwin) and his wife Barbara (Davis), who are faced with chasing an obnoxious family of post-modern art lovers who move into their house. Then they hear of a poltergeist who promises to rid the house of all trespassers for a price. Things go from bad to impossible when the maniacal Keaton (as the demonic "Betelgeuse") works his magic. The calypso scene is priceless. A cheesy, funny, surreal farce of life after death with inventive set designs popping continual surprises. Ryder is striking as the misunderstood teen with a death complex, while O'Hara is hilarious as the yuppie art poseur. **92m/C VHS, DVD, 8mm, Wide.** Michael Keaton, Geena Davis, Alec Baldwin, Sylvia Sidney, Catherine O'Hara, Winona Ryder, Jeffrey Jones, Dick Cavett, Glenn Shadix, Robert Goulet; ***D:*** Tim Burton; ***W:*** Michael McDowell, Warren Skaaren; ***C:*** Thomas Ackerman; ***M:*** Danny Elfman. Oscars '88: Makeup; Natl. Soc. Film Critics '88: Actor (Keaton).

Before and After 🦴½ **1995 (PG-13)** Disjointed drama depicts well-off suburban couple, Carolyn (Streep) and Ben (Neeson), who are thrown into chaos when their teenaged son Jacob (Furlong) is accused of murdering his girlfriend. Upon notification by the police that his son is the prime suspect and on the lam, Ben finds what seems to be bloody evidence in the family's car, which he destroys. The story loses steam from there. Based on the novel by Rosellen Brown, the focus is on the effect the death has on this picture book Massachusetts family. Neeson and Streep fall short of usually deliverable goods and director Schroeder takes the middle-of-the-road sentimental approach. **107m/C VHS.** Meryl Streep, Liam Neeson, Edward Furlong, Alfred Molina, John Heard, Julia Weldon, Daniel von Bargen, Ann Magnuson, Alison Folland, Kaiulani Lee; ***D:*** Barbet Schroeder; ***W:*** Ted Tally; ***C:*** Luciano Tovoli; ***M:*** Howard Shore.

Before I Hang 🦴🦴🦴 **1940** When a doctor invents a youth serum from the blood of a murderer, he'll stop at nothing to keep his secret. Karloff himself stands the test of time, and is satisfying as the mad scientist, giving this horror flick its appeal. **60m/B VHS.** Boris Karloff, Evelyn Keyes, Bruce (Herman Brix) Bennett, Edward Van Sloan, Ben Taggart, Pedro de Cordoba, Wright Kramer, Bertram Marburgh, Don Beddoe, Robert (Fisk) Fiske; ***D:*** Nick Grinde; ***W:*** Robert D. (Robert Hardy) Andrews; ***C:*** Benjamin (Ben H.) Kline.

Before Morning 🦴½ **1933** Police officer poses as a blackmailer to find out which of the two women in the murder victim's life are guilty. **68m/B VHS.** Leo Carrillo, Lora Baxter, Taylor Holmes, Blaine Cordner, Louise Prussing, Russell Hicks, Louis Jean Heydt, Jules Epailly, Constance Bertrand, Terry Carroll; ***D:*** Arthur Hoerl; ***C:*** Walter Strenge.

Before Night Falls 🦴🦴🦴 **2000 (R)** Director Schnabel takes a quantum leap in skill in his second film (after "Basquiat"). This time his tortured artist is the literally tortured late Cuban poet Reinaldo Arenas (Bardem), who falls victim to Castro's repression against both his writings and his sexuality (he's gay). Arenas gets thrown into prison, eventually gets released after confessing his "crimes," and makes his escape as part of the 1980 Mariel boatlift. Ironically, freedom offers little solace to Arenas either in Miami or his last home in New York. Spanish actor Bardem is outstanding as the poet who only seeks to be true to himself and pays a tragic price. Based on the writer's autobiography. **134m/C VHS, DVD, Wide.** Javier Bardem, Olivier Martinez, Andrea Di Stefano, Johnny Depp, Michael Wincott, Sean Penn, Hector Babenco, Najwa Nimri; ***D:*** Julian Schnabel; ***W:*** Julian Schnabel, Lazaro Gomez Carilles, Cunningham O'Keefe; ***C:*** Xavier Perez Grobet, Guillermo Rosas; ***M:*** Carter Burwell. Ind. Spirit '01: Actor (Bardem); Natl. Bd. of Review '00: Actor (Bardem); Natl. Soc. Film Critics '00: Actor (Bardem).

Before Sunrise 🦴🦴½ **1994 (R)** Light, "getting-to-know-you," romance unfolds as two 20-somethings share an unlikely 14-hour date. Gen-Xer Jesse (Hawke) and French beauty (Delpy) meet on the Eurail and he convinces her to join him in exploring Vienna and their mutual attraction before he heads back to the States in the morning. The two exchange life experiences and philosophies in the typical Linklater conversational fashion, but the film strays from the comical accounts of earlier works "Slacker" and "Dazed and Confused." Cinematographer Daniel captures the Old World with finesse, especially in the inevitable "first kiss" atop the Ferris wheel made famous in Orson Welles' "The Third Man." **101m/C VHS, DVD.** Ethan Hawke, Julie Delpy; ***D:*** Richard Linklater; ***W:*** Richard Linklater, Kim Krizan; ***C:*** Lee Daniel. Berlin Intl. Film Fest. '94: Director (Linklater).

Before the Rain 🦴🦴🦴 *Po Dezju; Pred dozhdot* **1994** War-torn Macedonia is the backdrop for Manchevski's first film (and first made in the newly declared republic of Macedonia). Powerful circular narrative joins three stories about the freedom of love and the pervasiveness of violence. "Words" finds young Macedonian monk Kiril (Colin) distracted from his spiritual duties by young Albanian Muslim Zamira (Mitevska), who takes refuge in his monastery. In "Faces," pregnant picture editor Anne (Cartlidge) is torn between her estranged husband and her lover, Aleksander (Serbedzija), a London-based war photographer who left his native Macedonia years before. "Pictures" finds Aleksandar returning to his old village—now torn by ethnic strife. In Macedonian, Albanian, and English, with subtitles. **120m/C VHS.** *GB FR MA* Rade Serbedzija, Katrin Cartlidge, Gregoire Colin, Labina Mitevska, Phyllida Law; ***D:*** Milcho Manchevski; ***W:*** Milcho Manchevski; ***C:*** Manuel Teran; ***M:*** Anastasia. Ind. Spirit '96: Foreign Film; Venice Film Fest. '94: Golden Lion.

Before the Revolution 🦴🦴 *Prima della Rivoluzione* **1965** One of Bertolucci's first films. Love and politics are mixed when the young Fabrizio, who is dabbling in communism, is also flirting with his young aunt. Striking and powerful film that has yet to lose its effect despite the times. Italian with subtitles. **115m/C VHS.** *IT* Francesco Barilli, Adriana Asti, Alain Midgette, Morando Morandini, Domenico Alpi; ***D:*** Bernardo Bertolucci; ***W:*** Bernardo Bertolucci; ***C:*** Aldo Scavarda; ***M:*** Ennio Morricone, Gino Paoli.

Beggars in Ermine 🦴🦴 **1934** A handicapped, impoverished man organizes all the beggars in the world into a successful corporation. Unusual performance from Atwill. **70m/B VHS.** Lionel Atwill, Henry B. Walthall, Betty Furness, Jameson Thomas, James Bush, Astrid Allwyn, George "Gabby" Hayes; ***D:*** Phil Rosen.

Beginning of the End 🦴½ **1957** Produced the same year as "The Deadly Mantis," Gordon's effort adds to 1957's harvest of bugs on a rampage "B"-graders. Giant, radiation-spawned grasshoppers attack Chicago causing Graves to come to the rescue. Easily the best giant grasshopper movie ever made. **73m/B VHS.** Peggy Castle, Peter Graves, Morris Ankrum, Richard Benedict, James Seay, Thomas B(rowne). Henry, Larry J. Blake, John Close, Frank Wilcox; ***D:*** Bert I. Gordon; ***W:*** Lester Gorn, Fred Freiberger; ***C:*** Jack Marta; ***M:*** Albert Glasser.

The Beguiled 🦴🦴🦴 **1970 (R)** During the Civil War a wounded Union soldier is taken in by the women at a girl's school in the South. He manages to seduce both a student and a teacher, and jealousy and revenge ensue. Decidedly weird psychological melodrama from action vets Siegel and Eastwood. **109m/C VHS, DVD.** Clint Eastwood, Geraldine Page, Elizabeth Hartman, Jo Ann Harris; ***D:*** Donald Siegel; ***W:*** Albert (John B. Sherry) Maltz, Irene (Grimes Grice) Kamp; ***C:*** Bruce Surtees; ***M:*** Lalo Schifrin.

Behave Yourself! 🦴½ **1952** A married couple adopts a dog who may be the key for a million-dollar hijacking setup by a gang of hoodlums. **81m/B VHS.** Shelley Winters, Farley Granger, William Demarest, Lon Chaney Jr., Hans Conried, Elisha Cook Jr., Francis L. Sullivan; ***D:*** George Beck.

Behind Enemy Lines 🦴½ **1985 (R)** Special Forces soldier goes on a special mission to eliminate a possible Nazi spy. **83m/C VHS.** Hal Holbrook, Ray Sharkey, David McCallum, Tom Isbell, Anne Twomey, Robert Patrick; ***D:*** Sheldon Larry. TV

Behind Enemy Lines 🦴🦴 **1996 (R)** Ex-Marine Mike Weston (Griffith) believes he was responsible for the death of his friend Jones (Mulkey) during assignment in Vietnam. When Weston discovers Jones is actually being hostage, he decides on a rescue mission. **89m/C VHS.** Thomas Ian Griffith, Chris Mulkey, Courtney Gains; ***D:*** Mark Griffiths; ***W:*** Andrew Osborne, Dennis Cooley; ***C:*** Blake T. Evans; ***M:*** Arthur Kempel.

Behind Enemy Lines 🦴🦴 **2001 (PG-13)** Balkan civil war is mere scenery, and soldiers only caricatures, in this cartoonish cat-and-mouse chase movie. Ace Navy navigator Lt. Burnett (Wilson), tired of flying peace missions, yearns for some real action. When a routine reconnaissance operation goes awry—his plane shot down over Serbian territory and his pilot ruthlessly executed—Burnett gets his wish. Crusty Admiral Reigart (Hackman) wants to rescue his flyboy, but a pesky international peace agreement gets in the way. First-time director Moore, best known for Sega promos, takes a video game approach to war. Utterly unconvincing suspense, but action sequences do their duty. Despite a clear connection to the ordeal of real-life Air Force captain Scott O'Grady, this is no true story. **106m/C VHS, DVD, Wide.** *US* Owen C. Wilson, Gene Hackman, Joaquim de Almeida, David Keith, Gabriel Macht, Charles Malik Whitfield, Olek Krupa, Vladimir Mashkov, Marko Ogonda; ***D:*** John Moore; ***W:*** David Veloz, Zak Penn; ***C:*** Brendan Galvin; ***M:*** Don Davis.

Behind Locked Doors 🦴🦴½ **1948** A journalist fakes mental illness to have himself committed to an asylum, where he believes a crooked judge is in hiding. A superior "B" mystery/suspense feature, with some tense moments. **61m/B VHS, DVD.** Lucille Bremer, Richard Carlson, Tor Johnson, Douglas Fowley, Herbert (Hayes) Heyes, Ralf Harolde; ***D:*** Budd Boetticher; ***W:*** Eugene Ling, Malvin Wald; ***C:*** Guy Roe; ***M:*** Irving Friedman.

Behind Office Doors 🦴🦴 **1931** Astor stars as the secretarial "power behind the throne" in this look at who really wields power in an office. Her boss takes her for granted until things go wrong. **82m/B VHS, DVD.** Mary Astor, Robert Ames, Ricardo Cortez, Charles Sellon; ***D:*** Melville Brown; ***W:*** Carey Wilson.

Behind Prison Walls 🦴🦴 *Youth Takes a Hand* **1943** A steel tycoon and his son are sent to prison, and the son tries to convert his dad to socialism. A fun, light hearted film, the last for veteran Tully. **64m/B VHS.** Alan Baxter, Gertrude Michael, Tully Marshall, Edwin Maxwell, Jacqueline Dalya, Matt Willis; ***D:*** Steve Sekely.

Behind the Front 🦴🦴½ **1926** Two friends tumble in and out of trouble in this comic Army film. One of the most profitable films of the late '20s. **60m/B VHS.** Wallace Beery, Raymond Hatton, Richard Arlen, Mary Brian, Chester Conklin; ***D:*** Edward Sutherland.

Behind the Lines 🦴🦴 *Regeneration* **1997 (R)** Focuses on the friendship between WWI soldier/poets Siegfried Sassoon (Wilby) and Wilfred Owen (Bunce), who receive a brief reprieve from the war when they're treated for shell shock at Edinburgh's Craiglockhart Hospital in 1917. Another patient is working-class soldier Billy Prior (Miller), made mute from the horrors he's witnessed. But their compassionate doctor, William Rivers (Pryce), is himself becoming increasingly unstable over the ethical concerns his work engenders. If he cures his patients, they go back to the front to fight again. The first book in Pat Barker's war trilogy. **96m/C VHS.** *GB CA* Jonathan Pryce, James Wilby, Jonny Lee Miller, Stuart Bunce, Tanya Allen, John Neville, Dougray Scott, David Hayman, David Robb, Julian Fellowes, Kevin McKidd, Jeremy Child; ***D:*** Gilles Mackinnon; ***W:*** Allan Scott; ***C:*** Glen MacPherson; ***M:*** Mychael Danna.

Behind the Mask 🦴🦴½ **1946** Lamont Cranston, better known as do-gooder "The Shadow," finds himself accused of murdering a blackmailing newspaper reporter. Based on the radio serial. **68m/C VHS.** Kane Richmond, Barbara Read, George Chandler, Dorothea Kent, Robert Shayne, June Clyde; ***D:*** Phil Karlson.

Behind the Planet of the Apes 🦴🦴🦴 **1998** AMC documentary hosted by Roddy McDowall. **120m/C DVD.** ***D:*** Kevin Burns, David Comtois; ***W:*** Kevin Burns, David Comtois, Brian Anthony; ***Nar:*** Roddy McDowall. **CABLE**

Behind the Rising Sun 🦴🦴½ **1943** A Japanese publisher's political views clash with those of his American-educated son in 1930s Japan. Well done despite pre-war propaganda themes. **88m/B VHS.** Tom Neal, J. Carrol Naish, Robert Ryan, Mike Mazurki, Margo, Gloria Holden, Don Douglas; ***D:*** Edward Dmytryk.

Behind the Sun 🦴🦴 *Abril Despedacado; Broken April* **2001 (PG-13)** A blood feud between two families nearly destroys them both in Salles' adaptation of Ismail Kadare's novel, which the director relocated to Brazil in 1910. The Ferreiras and the Breveses are both sugarcane planters determined to protect their honor if nothing else. Tonho Breves (Santoro) is expected to avenge the death of his older brother at the hands of the Ferreiras. Tonho's young brother (Lacerda) can't understand why the pointless violence continues and when Tonho falls in love with traveling circus performer Clara (Antonio), the boy becomes determined to see his brother safe and happy. Portuguese with subtitles. **91m/C VHS, DVD.** *BR FR SI* Jose Dumont, Rita Assemany, Rodrigo Santoro, Ravi Ramos Lacerda, Luiz Carlos Vasconcelos, Othon Bastos, Flavia Marco Antonio; ***D:*** Walter Salles; ***W:*** Walter Salles, Karim Ainouz, Sergio Machado; ***C:*** Walter Carvalho; ***M:*** Antonio Pinto. British Acad. '01: Foreign Film.

Behold a Pale Horse 🦴🦴½ **1964** A Spanish police captain attempts to dupe Peck into believing that his mother is dying and he must visit her on her deathbed. Loyalist Spaniard Peck becomes privy to the plot against him, but goes to Spain anyway in this post Spanish Civil War film. **118m/B VHS.** Gregory Peck, Anthony Quinn, Omar Sharif, Mildred Dunnock; ***D:*** Fred Zinnemann; ***W:*** J(ames) P(inckney) Miller; ***M:*** Maurice Jarre.

The Being 🦴 **1983 (R)** People in Idaho are terrorized by a freak who became abnormal after radiation was disposed in the local dump. Another dull monster-created-by-nuclear-waste non-event. Of limited interest is Buzzi. However, you'd be more entertained (read: amused) by Troma's "The Toxic Avenger," which takes itself much (much!) less seriously. **82m/C VHS.** Ruth Buzzi, Martin Landau, Jose Ferrer; ***D:*** Jackie Kong.

Being at Home with Claude 🦴🦴 **1992** Yves (Dupuis) is a 22-year-old Montreal hustler being interrogated by a nameless inspector (Godin) for the murder of his lover, Claude (Pichette). Yves has admitted his guilt but the inspector wants to reconstruct the event and determine a motive. Lots of black-and-white flashbacks as Yves dwells on his work and his psychologically love-death relationship with Claude. Rather pretentious and long-winded. Based on the play by Rene-Daniel DuBois. In French with English subtitles. **86m/C VHS.** *CA* Roy Dupuis, Jacques Godin, Jean-Francois Pichette, Gaston Lepage; ***D:*** Johanne Boisvert; ***W:*** Jean Boudin. Genie '92: Score.

Being Human 🦴🦴½ **1994 (PG-13)** Ambitious comedy drama promises more than it delivers, and shackles Williams in the process. Hector (Williams) is a regular guy continuously reincarnated throughout the milennia. He plays a caveman, a Roman slave, a Middle Ages nomad, a crew member on a 17th century new world voyage, and a modern New Yorker in separate vignettes that echo and/or extend the main themes of family, identity, and random fate. But he manages to emerge from each sketch as an unassuming everyman who never learns his lesson. One of Williams' periodic chancy ventures away from his comedic roots occasionally strikes gold, but often seems overly restrained. **122m/C VHS, Wide.** Robin Williams, John Turturro, Anna Galiena, Vincent D'Onofrio, Hector Elizondo, Lorraine Bracco, Lindsay Crouse, Kelly Hunter, William H. Macy, Grace Mahlaba, Theresa Russell, Charles Miller, Helen Miller; ***D:*** Bill Forsyth; ***W:*** Bill Forsyth; ***C:*** Michael Coulter; ***M:*** Michael Gibbs.

Being John Malkovich 🦴🦴🦴 **1999 (R)** Very weird comedy is the debut feature for Jonze. High-strung street puppeteer Craig Schwartz (Cusack) is married to frumpy pet-store worker Lotte (an unrecognizable Diaz). Forced to take a job as an office clerk in a building on floor seven-and-a-half, Craig falls for office vixen, Maxine (Keener), but his big discovery is a sealed door that reveals a tunnel leading directly into actor John Malkovich's mind. Craig views the world through the actor's eyes for 15 minutes at a time and decides to profit on his findings. Things just get more surreal when both Lotte and Maxine get involved. **112m/C VHS, DVD, Wide.** John Cusack, Cameron Diaz, Catherine Keener, John Malkovich, Orson Bean, Mary Kay Place, Charlie Sheen; ***D:*** Spike Jonze; ***W:*** Charlie Kaufman; ***C:*** Lance Acord; ***M:*** Carter Burwell. British Acad. '99: Orig. Screenplay; Ind. Spirit '00: First Feature, First Screenplay; L.A. Film Critics '99: Screenplay; MTV Movie Awards '00: New Filmmaker (Jonze); N.Y. Film Critics '99: Support. Actor (Malkovich), Support. Actress (Keener); Natl. Soc. Film Critics '99: Film, Screenplay.

Being There 🦴🦴🦴½ **1979 (PG)** A feeble-minded gardener, whose entire knowledge of life comes from watching TV, is sent out into the real world when his employer dies. Equipped with his prize possession, his remote control unit, the gardener unwittingly enters the world of politics and is welcomed as a mysterious sage. Sellers is wonderful in this satiric treat adapted by Jerzy Kosinski from his novel. **130m/C VHS, DVD, Wide.** Peter Sellers, Shirley MacLaine, Melvyn Douglas, Jack Warden, Richard Dysart, Richard Basehart; ***D:*** Hal Ashby; ***W:*** Jerzy Kosinski; ***C:*** Caleb Deschanel; ***M:*** Johnny Mandel. Oscars '79: Support. Actor (Douglas); Golden Globes '80: Actor—Mus./Comedy (Sellers), Support. Actor (Douglas); L.A. Film Critics '79: Support. Actor (Douglas); Natl. Bd. of Review '79: Actor (Sellers); N.Y. Film Critics '79: Support. Actor (Douglas); Natl. Soc. Film Critics '79: Cinematog.; Writers Guild '79: Adapt. Screenplay.

Being Two Isn't Easy 🦴🦴½ **1962** Director Ichikawa shows the world through the eyes of a two-year-old as a young couple struggle to raise their son. In Japanese with English subtitles. **88m/C VHS.** *JP* Fujiko Yamamoto, Eiji Funakoshi; ***D:*** Kon Ichikawa.

Bela Lugosi Meets a Brooklyn Gorilla woof! *The Boys from Brooklyn; The Monster Meets the Gorilla* **1952** Two men who look like Dean Martin and Jerry Lewis (but aren't) get lost in the jungle, where they meet mad scientist Lugosi. Worse than it sounds. Real Jerry sued for unflattering imitation. **74m/B VHS, DVD.** Bela Lugosi, Duke Mitchell, Sammy Petrillo, Charlita, Martin Garralaga, Al Kikume, Muriel Landers, Milton Newberger; ***D:*** William Beaudine; ***W:*** Tim Ryan; ***C:*** Charles Van Enger; ***M:*** Richard Hazard.

Belfast Assassin 🦴 *Harry's Game* **1984** A British anti-terrorist agent goes undercover in Ireland to find an IRA assassin who shot a British cabinet minister. **130m/C VHS.** Derek Thompson, Ray Lonnen, Gil Brailey, Benjamin Whitrow; ***D:*** Lawrence Gordon Clark.

Believe 🦴🦴½ **1999 (PG-13)** Teen prankster Ben Stiles (Mabe) loves to scare people. In fact, his behavior gets him kicked out of prep school and sent to live with his no-nonsense grandfather (Rubes). But the fright's on him when Ben and his friend Katherine (Cuthbert) decide to turn the abandoned Wickwire House into a haunted mansion and a ghostly figure suddenly starts making appearances. **97m/C VHS, DVD.** Ricky Mabe, Elisha Cuthbert, Jan Rubes, Ben Gazzara, Andrea Martin, Jayne Heitmeyer; ***D:*** Robert Tinnell. **VIDEO**

The Believers 🦴🦴½ **1987 (R)** Tense horror mystery set in New York city about a series of gruesome, unexplained murders. A widowed police psychologist investigating the deaths unwittingly discovers a powerful Santeria cult that believes in the sacrifice of children. Without warning he is drawn into the circle of the "Believers" and must free himself before his own son is the next sacrifice. Gripping (and grim), unrelenting horror. **114m/C VHS.** Martin Sheen, Helen Shaver, Malick Bowens, Harris Yulin, Robert Loggia, Jimmy Smits, Richard Masur, Harley Cross, Elizabeth Wilson, Lee Richardson, Carla Pinza; ***D:*** John Schlesinger; ***W:*** Mark Frost; ***C:*** Robby Muller; ***M:*** J. Peter Robinson.

Belizaire the Cajun 🦴🦴½ **1986 (PG)** 19th-century Louisiana love story. White prejudice against the Cajuns is rampant and violent, but that doesn't stop sexy faith healer Assante from falling in love with the inaccessible Cajun wife (Youngs) of a rich local. Made with care on a tight budget. Worthwhile, though uneven. **103m/C VHS.** Armand Assante, Gail Youngs, Will Patton, Stephen McHattie, Michael Schoeffling, Robert Duvall, Nancy Barrett; ***D:*** Glen Pitre; ***W:*** Glen Pitre; ***C:*** Richard Bowen; ***M:*** Michael Doucet, Howard Shore.

Bell, Book and Candle 🦴🦴½ **1958** Gillian Holroyd (Novak) is a beautiful modern-day witch (from a family of witches) who has made up her mind to refrain from using her powers. That is under Sheperd Henderson (Stewart) moves into her building and she decides to enchant him with a love spell. But spells have a way of backfiring on those who cast them. Lanchester is romantic Aunt Queenie and Lemmon is a standout as Gillian's jazz-loving, bongo-playing brother, Nicky. **106m/C VHS, DVD.** James Stewart, Kim Novak, Jack Lemmon, Elsa Lanchester, Ernie Kovacs, Hermione Gingold; ***D:*** Richard Quine; ***W:*** Daniel Taradash; ***C:*** James Wong Howe; ***M:*** George Duning.

Bell from Hell 🦴🦴 **1974** A tale of insanity and revenge, wherein a young man, institutionalized since his mother's death, plots to kill his aunt and three cousins. **80m/C VHS.** Viveca Lindfors, Renaud Verley, Alfredo Mayo; ***D:*** Claudio Guerin Hill.

The Bell Jar 🦴½ **1979 (R)** Based on poet Sylvia Plath's acclaimed semi-autobiographical novel, this is the story of a young woman who becomes the victim of mental illness. Not for the easily depressed and a disjointed and disappointing adaptation of Plath's work. **113m/C VHS.** Marilyn Hassett, Julie Harris, Barbara Barrie, Anne Bancroft, Robert Klein, Anne Jackson; ***D:*** Larry Peerce.

Bella Mafia 🦴🦴½ **1997 (R)** Over-the-top trash and that's meant in the finest possible way. This lurid melodrama, originally a two-part miniseries, concerns the Sicilian mob family, the Lucianos, who have suffered the loss of father Roberto (Farina) and three sons. Widowed matriarch Graziella (Redgrave) decides to join with her three daughters-in-law, Sophia (Kinski), Teresa (Douglas), and Moyra (Tilly), and avenge their deaths. Oh yes, there's also Sophia's secret son Luca (Marsden), a killer who turns up to insinuates himself into family life. Adapted by La Plante from her novel. **117m/C VHS.** Vanessa Redgrave, Nastassia Kinski, Illeana Douglas, Jennifer Tilly, James Marsden, Peter Bogdanovich, Dennis Farina, Gina Philips; ***D:*** David Greene; ***W:*** Lynda La Plante. **TV**

Bellamy 🦴 **1980** Murderous madman massacres masseuses, and Bellamy is the cop out to get him. **92m/C VHS.** John Stanton, Timothy Elston, Sally Conabere; ***D:*** Colin Eggleston, Pino Amenta.

The Bellboy 🦴🦴½ **1960** Lewis makes his directorial debut in this plotless but clever outing. He also stars as the eponymous character, a bellboy at Miami's Fountainbleau Hotel. Cameos from Berle and Winchell are highlights. **72m/B VHS, Wide.** Jerry Lewis, Alex Gerry, Bob Clayton, Sonny Sands, Bill Richmond, Larry Best, Paul Gerson, Maxie "Slapsie" Rosenbloom; ***Cameos:*** Milton Berle, Walter Winchell; ***D:*** Jerry Lewis; ***W:*** Jerry Lewis; ***C:*** Haskell Boggs; ***M:*** Walter Scharf.

The Bellboy and the Playgirls woof! *The Playgirls and the Bellboy; Mit Eva Fing Die Sunde An* **1962** Early Coppola effort adds new film footage to a 1958 German movie. Stars Playboy playmate June "The Body" Wilkinson, with other centerfolds of the time. **93m/C VHS.** June Wilkinson, Donald Kenney, Karin Dor, Willy Fritsch, Michael Cramer, Louise Lawson, Ann Myers; ***D:*** Francis Ford Coppola; ***W:*** Francis Ford Coppola.

Belle Americaine 🦴🦴 *What a Chassis!* **1961** Title refers to the Cadillac car young Parisian factory worker Dhery buys at a suspiciously bargain price. Naturally, his deal is too good to be true and trouble follows. Dubbed in English. **97m/C VHS.** *FR* Robert Dhery, Louis de Funes, Collette Brosset, Alfred Adam, Bernard Lavelette, Annie Ducaux; ***D:*** Robert Dhery; ***W:*** Robert Dhery, Alfred Adam, Pierre Tchernia; ***C:*** Ghislan Cloquet; ***M:*** Gerard Calvi.

Belle de Jour 🦴🦴🦴½ **1967 (R)** Based on Joseph Kessel's novel, one of director Bunuel's best movies has all his characteristic nuances: the hypocrisy of our society; eroticism; anti-religion. Deneuve plays Severine, a chic, frigid Parisian newlywed, who decides to become a daytime prostitute, unbeknownst to her husband. Bunuel blends reality with fantasy, and the viewer is never sure which is which in this finely crafted movie. French with subtitles. **100m/C VHS, DVD, Wide.** *FR* Catherine Deneuve, Jean Sorel, Genevieve Page, Michel Piccoli, Francesco Rabal, Pierre Clementi, Georges Marchal, Francoise Fabian; ***D:*** Luis Bunuel; *W:* Luis Bunuel, Jean-Claude Carriere; *C:* Sacha Vierny.

Belle Epoque 🦴🦴🦴 *The Age of Beauty* **1992 (R)** Young army deserter Fernando (Sanz) embarks on a personal voyage of discovery when he meets Manolo (Gomez), an eccentric old man, and father to four beautiful daughters. Fernando can't believe his luck—and the sisters share his interest, resulting in an amusing round of musical beds. Bittersweet tale set amidst the anarchy and war of 1930s Spain with a terrific screenplay that tastefully handles the material without stooping to the obvious leering possibilities. In addition to Oscar, won nine Spanish Goyas, including best picture, director, actress (Gil), and screenplay. Title ironically refers to the era at the end of the 19th century before the wars of the 20th century tore Europe apart. Spanish with English subtitles or dubbed. **108m/C VHS.** *SP* Jorge Sanz, Fernando Gomez, Ariadna Gil, Maribel Verdu, Penelope Cruz, Miriam Diaz-Aroca, Mary Carmen Ramirez, Michel Galabru, Gabino Diego; *D:* Fernando Trueba; *W:* Rafael Azcona; *C:* Jose Luis Alcaine; *M:* Antoine Duhamel. Oscars '93: Foreign Film.

The Belle of New York 🦴🦴 **1952** A turn-of-the-century bachelor falls in love with a Salvation Army missionary in this standard musical. ♫Naughty But Nice; Baby Doll; Oops; I Wanna Be a Dancin' Man; Seeing's Believing; Bachelor's Dinner Song; When I'm Out With the Belle of New York; Let a Little Love Come In. **82m/C VHS.** Fred Astaire, Vera-Ellen, Marjorie Main, Keenan Wynn, Alice Pearce, Gale Robbins, Clinton Sundberg; *D:* Charles Walters.

Belle of the Nineties 🦴🦴½ *It Ain't No Sin* **1934** West struts as a 1890s singer who gets involved with a boxer. Her trademark sexual innuendos were already being censored but such lines as "It's better to be looked over than overlooked," done in West style, get the point across. **73m/B VHS, DVD.** Mae West, Roger Pryor, Johnny Mack Brown, John Miljan, Katherine DeMille, Harry Woods, Edward (Ed) Gargan; *D:* Leo McCarey; *W:* Mae West; *C:* Karl Struss; *M:* Arthur Johnston.

Belle Starr 🦴½ **1979** The career of Wild West outlaw Belle Starr is chronicled in this strange western pastiche about lawlessness and sexual agression. Wertmuller directed under the pseudonym Nathan Wich. Dubbed in English. **90m/C VHS.** *IT* Elsa Martinelli, Robert Wood, George Eastman, Dan Harrison; *D:* Lina Wertmuller.

The Belles of St. Trinian's 🦴🦴🦴 **1953** Sim is priceless in a dual role as the eccentric headmistress of a chaotic, bankrupt girls' school and her bookie twin brother who scheme the school into financial security. The first in a series of movies based on a popular British cartoon by Ronald Searles about a girls' school and its mischievous students. Followed by "Blue Murder at St. Trinian's," "The Pure Hell of St. Trinian's," and "The Great St. Trinian's Train Robbery." **86m/B VHS.** *GB* Alastair Sim, Joyce Grenfell, Hermione Baddeley, George Cole, Eric Pohlmann, Renee Houston, Beryl Reid, Balbina, Jill Braidwood, Annabelle Covey, Betty Ann Davies, Diana Day, Jack Doyle, Irene Handl, Arthur Howard, Sidney James, Lloyd Lamble, Jean Langston, Belinda Lee, Vivian Martin, Andree Melly, Mary Merrall, Guy Middleton, Joan Sims, Jerry Verno, Richard Wattis; *D:* Frank Launder; *W:* Frank Launder, Sidney Gilliat, Val Valentine; *C:* Stanley Pavey; *M:* Malcolm Arnold.

Bellissima 🦴🦴🦴 **1951** A woman living in an Italian tenement has unrealistic goals for her plain but endearing daughter when a famous director begins casting a role designed for a child. The mother's maternal fury and collision with reality highlight a poignant film. Italian with subtitles. **130m/B VHS.** *IT* Anna Magnani, Walter Chiari, Alessandro Blasetti, Tina Apicella, Gastone Renzelli; *D:* Luchino Visconti; *W:* Luchino Visconti, Cesare Zavattini, Francesco Rosi, Suso Cecchi D'Amico; *C:* Piero Portalupi, Paul Ronald.

Bellman and True 🦴🦴½ **1988 (R)** Rewarding, but sometimes tedious character study of a mild mannered computer whiz who teams with a gang of bank robbers. Fine performances, especially subtle dangerous gang characters. **112m/C VHS.** *GB* Bernard Hill, Kieran O'Brien, Richard Hope, Frances Tomelty, Derek Newark, John Kavanagh, Ken Bones; *D:* Richard Loncraine; *W:* Desmond Lowden; *C:* Ken Westbury; *M:* Colin Towns.

The Bells 🦴🦴🦴 **1926** The mayor of an Alsatian village kills a wealthy merchant and steals his money. The murderer experiences pangs of guilt which are accentuated when a traveling mesmerist comes to town and claims to be able to discern a person's darkest secrets. Silent with music score. **67m/B VHS, DVD.** Lionel Barrymore, Boris Karloff, Gustav von Seyffertitz; *D:* James Young; *W:* James Young; *C:* L.W. O'Connell.

Bells Are Ringing 🦴🦴🦴 **1960** A girl who works for a telephone answering service can't help but take an interest in the lives of the clients, especially a playwright with an inferiority complex. Based on Adolph Green and Betty Comden's Broadway musical. ♫Just in Time; The Party's Over; It's a Perfect Relationship; Do It Yourself; It's a Simple Little System; Better Than a Dream; I Met a Girl; Drop That Name; I'm Going Back. **126m/C VHS, Wide.** Judy Holliday, Dean Martin, Fred Clark, Eddie Foy Jr., Jean Stapleton; *D:* Vincente Minnelli; *W:* Betty Comden, Adolph Green; *C:* Milton Krasner; *M:* Andre Previn.

Bells of Capistrano 🦴½ **1942** The last film Autry made before serving in the Army finds the singing star wanted as a crowd-drawing attraction for two rival rodeo companies. Gene chooses the one owned by the pretty girl, which causes problems with the competition. ♫In Old Capistrano; Forgive Me; Don't Bite the Hand That's Feeding You; At Sundown. **73m/B VHS.** Gene Autry, Smiley Burnette, Virginia Grey, Lucien Littlefield; *D:* William M. Morgan; *W:* Lawrence Kimple; *C:* Reggie Lanning.

Bells of Coronado 🦴🦴 **1950** Rogers and Evans team up to expose the murderer of the owner of a profitable uranium mine. A gang of smugglers trying to trade the ore to foreign powers is thwarted. The usual thin storyline, but filled with action and riding stunts. **67m/B VHS.** Roy Rogers, Dale Evans, Pat Brady, Grant Withers; *D:* William Witney.

Bells of Death 🦴½ **1990** A young martial arts student infiltrates the gang that killed his family and kidnapped his sister, finishing them off one by one. **91m/C VHS.** Chun Ping, Chang Yi, Chao Hsin Yen; *D:* Yueh Fung.

Bells of Rosarita 🦴🦴½ **1945** Roy helps foil an evil plan to swindle Evans out of the circus she inherited. All-star western cast under the big top. **54m/B VHS.** Roy Rogers, Dale Evans, George "Gabby" Hayes, Sunset Carson, Adele Mara, Grant Withers, Roy Barcroft, Addison Richards; *D:* Frank McDonald.

The Bells of St. Mary's 🦴🦴🦴½ **1945** An easy-going priest finds himself in a subtle battle of wits with the Mother Superior over how the children of St. Mary's school should be raised. It's the sequel to "Going My Way." Songs include the title tune and "Aren't You Glad You're You?" Also available in a colorized version. **126m/B VHS, DVD.** Bing Crosby, Ingrid Bergman, Henry Travers; *D:* Leo McCarey; *W:* Dudley Nichols; *C:* George Barnes; *M:* Robert Emmett Dolan, Johnny Burke, James Van Heusen. Oscars '45: Sound; Golden Globes '46: Actress—Drama (Bergman); N.Y. Film Critics '45: Actress (Bergman).

Bells of San Angelo 🦴 **1947** Roy foils thieves' attempts to steal a girl's inherited ranch. **54m/C VHS.** Roy Rogers, Dale Evans; *D:* William Witney.

Bells of San Fernando 🦴 **1947** An Irish seaman wanders into California during early Spanish rule and confronts a cruel overseer in this lackluster Western drama. Scripted by "Cisco Kid" Renaldo. **75m/B VHS.** Donald Woods, Gloria Warren, Byron Foulger; *D:* Terry Morse; *W:* Jack DeWitt, Duncan Renaldo.

Belly 🦴🦴 **1998 (R)** Inner-city crime tale preaches against crime, violence and drugs while it visually glorifies the opulent benefits of them. Childhood pals Tommy (Simmons) and Sincere (Jones) are successful criminals who head down different paths. Sincere dreams of turning legit and moving his family to Africa. Tommy gets deeper into the drug biz until he is caught by feds and forced to bring down innocent black leader Reverend Saviour (Muhammed). Although the movie ends with a plea for change, it may itself be part of the problem. **95m/C VHS, DVD.** Nas, DMX, Taral Hicks, Tionne "T-Boz" Watkins, Method Man, Tyrin Turner, Hassan Johnson, Power, Louie Rankin, Minister Benjamin F. Muhammed; *D:* Hype Williams; *W:* Nas, Hype Williams, Anthony Bodden; *C:* Malik Hassan Sayeed; *M:* Stephen Cullo.

The Belly of an Architect 🦴🦴🦴½ **1991 (R)** A thespian feast for the larger-than-life Dennehy as blustering American architect whose personal life and health both crumble as he obsesssively readies an exhibition in Rome. A multi-tiered, carefully composed tragicomedy from the ideosyncratic filmmaker Greenaway, probably his most accessible work for general audiences. **119m/C VHS.** *GB IT* Brian Dennehy, Chloe Webb, Lambert Wilson, Sergio Fantoni, Geoffrey Copleston, Marino (Martin) Mase; *D:* Peter Greenaway; *W:* Peter Greenaway; *C:* Sacha Vierny; *M:* Glenn Branca, Wim Mertens.

Bellyfruit 🦴🦴 **1999** Film, which refers to pregnancy, was inspired by the real-life stories of teen mothers in L.A. 14-year-old Shanika is living in a home for troubled girls when she's taken in by the charms of Damon, equally young Christina witnesses her mother (who had Christina when she was a teen) drug and party and decides to follow her example, while 16-year-old Aracely becomes pregnant by her boyfriend Oscar. Although he stands by her, Aracely's traditional Latin father kicks her out of the house. And when they have their babies, the teens lives just get more confused. **95m/C VHS, DVD, Wide.** Kelly Vint, Tamara La Seon Bass, Tonatzin Mondragon, T.E. Russell, Michael Pena, Bonnie Dickenson, Kimberly Scott, James Dumant; *D:* Kerri Green; *W:* Kerri Green, Maria Bernhard, Suzannah Blinkoff, Janet Borrus; *C:* Peter Calvin.

Beloved 🦴🦴½ **1998 (R)** Sethe (Winfrey) is a middle-aged former slave in rural Ohio years after her emancipation from a Kentucky planation. She is haunted (literally) by the painful legacy of slavery in the form of a mud-covered feral child known as Beloved (Newton). Another reminder is Paul D (Glover), a former slave from the same Kentucky plantation, who stokes Sethe's embers. Metaphors abound as we wonder if Beloved really is the child Sethe killed years before. Oprah's pet project (she's owned the film rights for 10 years) is a faithful adaptation of Toni Morrison's Pulitzer Prize-winning novel. Unfortunately, the long-awaited feature can't fulfill the huge expectations. While performances are excellent, pic suffers from a sense of self-indulgence, which is accentuated by the three-hour running time. At times powerful and moving, but also slow and occasionally confusing. **172m/C VHS, DVD.** Oprah Winfrey, Thandie Newton, Danny Glover, Kimberly Elise, Lisa Gay Hamilton, Beah Richards, Irma P. Hall, Albert Hall, Jason Robards Jr., Jude Ciccolella; *D:* Jonathan Demme; *W:* Akosua Busia, Richard LaGravenese, Adam Brooks; *C:* Tak Fujimoto; *M:* Rachel Portman.

Beloved Enemy 🦴🦴🦴 **1936** A romantic tragedy set in Civil War-torn Ireland in the 1920s. A rebel leader and a proper English lady struggle to overcome the war's interference with their burgeoning relationship. **86m/B VHS.** David Niven, Merle Oberon, Brian Aherne, Karen Morley, Donald Crisp; *D:* H.C. Potter; *C:* Gregg Toland.

Beloved/Friend 🦴🦴 *Amigo/Amado* **1999** Everybody wants something (or someone) they can't have. Jaume (Pou) is a middleaged gay college prof who pines for his student David (Selvas), a cold-hearted stud who hustles to pay his tuition. In fact, the only way Jaume can get attention from David is to buy his services (although David has something of a father figure complex). Then, Jaume's best friend Pere (Gas) discovers that David has gotten his daughter, Alba (Montala), pregnant. David seems to be a catalyst for a lot of soul-searching but nothing much gets resolved. Spanish with subtitles. **90m/C VHS.** *SP* Jose Maria Pou, David Selvas, Mario Gas, Irene Montala, Rosa Maria Sarda; *D:* Ventura Pons; *W:* Josep Maria Benet i Jornet; *C:* Jesus Escosa; *M:* Carles Cases.

Beloved Infidel 🦴🦴½ **1959** Sudsy, lavish romancer, based on the book by gossip queen Sheilah Graham, about her brief romance with novelist F. Scott Fitzgerald. Fitzgerald (a badly miscast Peck) was in Hollywood trying to write screenplays when he meets young, English, aspiring writer Graham (an equally miscast Kerr). She becomes his mistress, putting up with Fitzgerald's drinking and insults, while he interferes with her career. Story is slanted towards Graham nobly trying to rescue Fitzgerald from himself (he did actually die from a heart attack while with Graham). **123m/C VHS.** Gregory Peck, Deborah Kerr, Eddie Albert, Philip Ober, Herbert Rudley, John Sutton, Karin Booth; *D:* Henry King; *W:* Sy Bartlett; *C:* Leon Shamroy; *M:* Franz Waxman.

The Beloved Rogue 🦴🦴🦴 **1927** Crosland—who gained a reputation for innovation, having directed "Don Juan" the previous year (noted for the debut of synchronized music), and "The Jazz Singer" the following year (noted for the first talkie bits)—mounted this well-designed and special effect-laden medieval costumer. Barrymore is in high profile as a swashbuckling caricature of French poet Francois Villon, who battles mightily (and verbally) with Louis XI (played by Veidt, in his first US film). Marked by the excesses typical of Barrymore's prestige days, it flouts history, taking generous poetic license when the facts ain't fab enough. In short, it's great entertainment. **110m/B VHS.** John Barrymore, Conrad Veidt, Marceline Day, Henry Victor, Mack Swain, Slim Summerville; *D:* Alan Crosland.

Below the Belt 🦴🦴 **1980 (R)** Almost interesting tale of street-smart woman from New York City who becomes part of the blue-collar "circus" of lady wrestlers. Ex-wrestling champ Burke plays herself. **98m/C VHS.** Regina Baff, Mildred Burke, John C. Becher; *D:* Robert Fowler.

Below the Border 🦴½ **1942** The Rough Riders go undercover to straighten out some cattle rustlers. **57m/B VHS.** Buck Jones, Tim McCoy, Raymond Hatton, Linda Brent, Roy Barcroft, Charles "Blackie" King; *D:* Howard Bretherton.

Below the Deadline 🦴🦴 **1929** A man framed for embezzlement is set free and allowed to clear his name by a sympathetic detective. **79m/B VHS.** Frank Leigh, Barbara Worth, Arthur (L.) Rankin, Walter Merrill; *D:* J(ohn) P(aterson) McGowan.

The Belstone Fox 🦴🦴 **1973** Orphaned fox goes into hiding, and is hunted by the hound he has befriended and his former owner. **103m/C VHS.** Eric Porter, Rachel Roberts, Jeremy Kemp; *D:* James Hill.

Ben 🦴½ **1972 (PG)** Sequel to "Willard" finds police Detective Kirtland still on the hunt for a killer rat pack led by Ben, king of the rodents. Title song by young Michael Jackson hit the top of the charts. **95m/C VHS.** Joseph Campanella, Lee Montgomery, Arthur O'Connell, Rosemary Murphy, Meredith Baxter, Norman Alden, Paul Carr, Kaz Garas, Kenneth Tobey, Richard Van Heet; *D:* Phil Karlson; *W:* Gilbert Ralston; *C:* Russell Metty; *M:* Walter Scharf. Golden Globes '73: Song ("Ben").

Ben-Hur 🦴🦴🦴🦴 **1926** Second film version of the renowned story of Jewish and Christian divisiveness in the time of Jesus. Battle scenes and chariot races still look good, in spite of age. Problems lingered on the set and at a cost of over $4,000,000 it was the most expensive film of its time and took years to finish. A hit at the boxoffice, it still stands as the all-time silent classic. In 1931, a shortened version was released. Based on the novel by Lewis Wallace. **148m/B VHS.** Ramon Novarro, Francis X. Bushman, May McAvoy, Betty Bronson, Claire McDowell, Carmel Myers, Nigel de Brulier, Ferdinand P. Earle; *D:* Fred Niblo; *C:* Clyde De Vinna. Natl. Film Reg. '97.

Ben-Hur 🦴🦴🦴🦴 **1959** The third film version of the Lew Wallace classic stars Heston in the role of a Palestinian Jew battling the Roman empire at the time of

Christ. Won a record 11 Oscars. The breathtaking chariot race is still one of the best screen races today. Perhaps one of the greatest pictures of all time. Also available in letterbox format. **212m/C VHS, DVD, Wide.** Charlton Heston, Jack Hawkins, Stephen Boyd, Haya Harareet, Hugh Griffith, Martha Scott, Sam Jaffe, Cathy O'Donnell, Finlay Currie; ***D:*** William Wyler; ***W:*** Karl Tunberg; ***C:*** Robert L. Surtees; ***M:*** Miklos Rozsa. Oscars '59: Actor (Heston), Art Dir./Set Dec., Color, Color Cinematog., Costume Des. (C), Director (Wyler), Film Editing, Picture, Sound, Support. Actor (Griffith), Orig. Dramatic Score; AFI '98: Top 100; British Acad. '59: Film; Directors Guild '59: Director (Wyler); Golden Globes '60: Director (Wyler), Film—Drama, Support. Actor (Boyd); N.Y. Film Critics '59: Film.

Bend of the River 🦴🦴🦴 *Where the River Bends* **1952** A haunted, hardened guide leads a wagon train through Oregon territory, pitting himself against Indians, the wilderness and a former comrade-turned-hijacker. **91m/C VHS.** James Stewart, Arthur Kennedy, Rock Hudson, Harry (Henry) Morgan, Royal Dano; ***D:*** Anthony Mann.

Beneath the Planet of the Apes 🦴🦴½ **1970 (G)** In the first sequel, another Earth astronaut passes through the same warp and follows the same paths as Taylor, through Ape City and to the ruins of bomb-blasted New York's subway system, where warhead-worshipping human mutants are found. The strain of sequelling shows instantly, and gets worse through the next three films; followed by "Escape from the Planet of the Apes." **108m/C VHS, DVD, Wide.** James Franciscus, Kim Hunter, Maurice Evans, Charlton Heston, James Gregory, Natalie Trundy, Jeff Corey, Linda Harrison, Victor Buono, Paul (E.) Richards, David Watson, Thomas Gomez; ***D:*** Ted Post; ***W:*** Paul Dehn; ***C:*** Milton Krasner; ***M:*** Leonard Rosenman.

Beneath the 12-Mile Reef 🦴🦴 **1953** Two rival groups of divers compete for sponge beds off the Florida coast. Lightweight entertainment notable for underwater photography and early Cinemascope production, as well as Moore in a bathing suit. **102m/C VHS, DVD, Wide.** Robert Wagner, Terry Moore, Gilbert Roland, Richard Boone, Peter Graves, J. Carrol Naish; ***D:*** Robert D. Webb; ***W:*** A.I. Bezzerides; ***C:*** Edward Cronjager; ***M:*** Bernard Herrmann.

Beneath the Valley of the Ultra-Vixens 🦴 **1979** Sex comedy retread directed by the man with an obsession for big. Scripted by Roger Ebert, who also scripted the cult classic "Beyond the Valley of the Dolls." Explicit nudity. **90m/C VHS.** Francesca "Kitten" Natividad, Ann Marie, Ken Kerr, Stuart Lancaster, Steve Tracy, Henry Rowland, DeForest Covan, Aram Katcher, Candy Samples, Robert Pearson; ***D:*** Russ Meyer; ***W:*** Roger Ebert, Russ Meyer; ***C:*** Russ Meyer.

The Beneficiary 🦴🦴 **1997 (R)** Widow Haiduk is the primary suspect in her wealthy husband's death until she gives her inheritance to charity, thus eliminating her motive for murder. But detective Ashby, a friend of the husband, still decides to keep his eye (and maybe more) on the lady. **97m/C VHS.** Suzy Amis, Ron Silver, Linden Ashby, Stacy Haiduk, Robert Davi; ***D:*** Marc Bienstock; ***W:*** Vladimir Nemirovsky; ***C:*** Sead Mutarevic. **CABLE**

Benefit of the Doubt 🦴🦴 **1993 (R)** Ex-con Sutherland, released from prison after 22 years, attempts to repaint his family a la Norman Rockwell. Grown-up daughter Irving, who testified against him in her mother's murder, wants to put a crimp in those plans since daddy's new vision of family fondness frankly makes her stomach turn. Aside from the sexual shenanigans, and the haunting Monument Valley backdrop, an extended chase scene would seem to be the film's only hope of salvation. Unfortunately, it fails to deliver, being both implausible and boring. Based on a story by Michael Lieber. **92m/C VHS.** Donald Sutherland, Amy Irving, Christopher McDonald, Rider Strong, Graham Greene, Theodore Bikel, Gisele Kovach, Ferdinand "Ferdy" Mayne; ***D:*** Jonathan Heap; ***W:*** Jeffrey Polman, Christopher Keyser; ***M:*** Hummie Mann.

The Beniker Gang 🦴🦴½ **1983 (G)** Five orphans, supported by the eldest who writes a syndicated advice column, work together as a family. **87m/C VHS.** Andrew McCarthy, Jennifer (Jennie) Dundas Lowe, Danny Pintauro, Charlie Fields; ***D:*** Ken Kwapis. **TV**

Benji 🦴🦴🦴 **1974 (G)** In the loveable mutt's first feature-length movie, he falls in love with a female named Tiffany, and saves two young children from kidnappers. Kiddie classic that was a boxoffice hit when first released. Followed by "For the Love of Benji." **87m/C VHS, DVD.** Benji, Peter Breck, Christopher Connelly, Patsy Garrett, Deborah Walley, Cynthia Smith; ***D:*** Joe Camp; ***W:*** Joe Camp; ***C:*** Don Reddy; ***M:*** Euel Box. Golden Globes '75: Song ("I Feel Love").

Benji the Hunted 🦴½ **1987 (G)** The heroic canine, shipwrecked off the Oregon coast, discovers a litter of orphaned cougar cubs, and battles terrain and predators to bring them to safety. **89m/C VHS.** Benji, Red Steagall, Frank Inn; ***D:*** Joe Camp; ***W:*** Joe Camp; ***M:*** Euel Box.

Benny & Joon 🦴🦴½ **1993 (PG)** Depending on your tolerance for cute eccentrics and whimsy this will either charm you with sweetness or send you into sugar shock. Masterson is Joon, a mentally disturbed young woman who paints and has a habit of setting fires. She lives with overprotective brother Benny (Quinn). Sam (Depp) is the outsider who charms Joon, a dyslexic loner who impersonates his heroes Charlie Chaplin and Buster Keaton with eery accuracy. Depp is particularly fine with the physical demands of his role, but the film's easy dismissal of Joon's mental illness is a serious flaw. **98m/C VHS, DVD, Wide.** Johnny Depp, Mary Stuart Masterson, Aidan Quinn, Julianne Moore, Oliver Platt, CCH Pounder, Dan Hedaya, Joe Grifasi, William H. Macy, Eileen Ryan; ***D:*** Jeremiah S. Chechik; ***W:*** Barry Berman; ***C:*** Jason Schwartzman; ***M:*** Rachel Portman.

The Benny Goodman Story 🦴🦴 **1955** The life and music of Swing Era bandleader Benny Goodman is recounted in this popular bio-pic. Covering Benny's career from his child prodigy days to his monumental 1938 Carnegie Hall Jazz Concert, the movie's soggy plot machinations are redeemed by a non-stop music track featuring the real Benny and an all-star lineup. ♫Don't Be That Way; Memories of You; Sing, Sing, Sing; Slipped Disc. **116m/C VHS.** Steve Allen, Donna Reed, Gene Krupa, Lionel Hampton, Kid Ory, Ben Pollack, Harry James, Stan Getz, Teddy Wilson, Martha Tilton; ***D:*** Valentine Davies; ***M:*** Henry Mancini.

Bent 🦴🦴 **1997 (NC-17)** Theatre director Mathias makes his film debut with Sherman's adaptation of his 1979 play. Gay playboy Max (Owen) is enjoying the nightlife in decadent Berlin—until the Nazi crackdown. Soon, Max is in a cattle car on his way to Dachau, where he passes himself off as Jewish, thinking he'll be treated better. However Horst (Bluteau), who befriended Max on the train, is openly part of the pink triangle prisoners. Still, Max gets Horst assigned to the same meaningless hard labor and the duo fall in love—without ever being allowed to touch. Good performances (with Jagger notable in a brief role as a drag star) but the lingering staginess is to the film's detriment. An R-rated version is also available. **104m/C VHS.** *GB* Clive Owen, Lothaire Bluteau, Ian McKellen, Brian Webber, Mick Jagger, Nikolaj Coster-Waldau, Paul Bettany; ***Cameos:*** Jude Law, Rupert Graves; ***D:*** Sean Mathias; ***W:*** Martin Sherman; ***C:*** Yorgos Arvanitis; ***M:*** Philip Glass.

Beowulf 🦴½ **1998 (R)** Cheesy retelling of the dark ages Saxon saga that has seemingly time travelled to a vague post-apocalypse time. Wandering knight Beowulf (Lambert) battles beast Grendel, who comes each night to feed on those who live in the Outpost. Cult icon Mitra was one of the models for Lara Croft of "Tomb Raider" game fame. **92m/C VHS, DVD, Wide.** Christopher Lambert, Rhona Mitra, Oliver Cotton, Patricia Velasquez, Goetz Otto, Layla Roberts, Brent J. Lowe; ***D:*** Graham Baker; ***W:*** Mark Leahy, David Chappe; ***C:*** Christopher Faloona; ***M:*** Ben Watkins.

Beretta's Island 🦴🦴 **1992 (R)** When Interpol operative Beretta comes out of retirement to track his friend's killer, the chase leads him back to his homeland of Sardinia, which has been overrun by drugs. **97m/C VHS.** Franco (Columbo) Columbu, Ken Kercheval; ***Cameos:*** Arnold Schwarzenegger.

Bergonzi Hand 🦴 **1970** Drama about two art scoundrels who are astonished when an immigrant admits to painting a forged "Bergonzi." **62m/C VHS.** Keith Mitchell, Gordon Jackson, Martin Miller.

Berkeley Square 🦴🦴½ **1998** In 1902 London, three young women become nannies and grow to be friends. Tough and experienced East Ender Matty (Wilkie) goes to work for the well-bred St. Johns; country-raised Hannah (Smurfit) has an illegitimate child by her previous titled employer's son—a fact she keeps hidden from the neglectful Hutchinsons; and farm girl Lydia (Wady) is hired by the avant-garde Lamson-Scribeners, who believe in education even for servants. Naturally, the threesome become very involved in each other's lives and loves. On five cassettes. **500m/C VHS, DVD.** *GB* Victoria Smurfit, Tabitha Wady, Clare Wilkie, Rosemary Leach, Judy Parfitt; ***D:*** Leslie Manning, Richard Signy, Martin Hutchings, Richard Holthouse. **TV**

The Berlin Affair 🦴🦴 **1985 (R)** A sordid tale from "The Night Porter" director about a Japanese woman seducing various parties in pre-WWII Germany. **97m/C VHS.** *IT GE* Mio Takaki, Gudrun Landgrebe, Kevin McNally; ***D:*** Liliana Cavani; ***M:*** Pino Donaggio.

Berlin Alexanderplatz 🦴🦴🦴½ **1980** Fassbinder's 15 1/2-hour epic follows the life, death, and resurrection of Franz Biberkof, a former transit worker who has just finished a lengthy prison term and must learn to adjust in the harsh social atmosphere of Berlin in the 1920s. Melodramatic parable with biblical overtones considered by some to be a masterpiece. Based on the novel by Alfred Doblin; originally aired as a miniseries on German TV. **930m/C VHS.** *GE* Gunter Lamprecht, Hanna Schygulla, Barbara Sukowa, Gottfried John, Elisabeth Trissenaar, Brigitte Mira, Karin Baal, Ivan Desny, Margit Castensen; ***D:*** Rainer Werner Fassbinder; ***W:*** Rainer Werner Fassbinder; ***C:*** Xaver Schwarzenberger; ***M:*** Peer Raben. **TV**

Berlin Blues **1989 (PG-13)** A nightclub singer is torn between two men. **90m/C VHS.** Julia Migenes-Johnson, Keith Baxter; ***D:*** Ricardo Franco.

The Berlin Conspiracy 🦴🦴 **1991 (R)** Espionage/action potboiler does an imaginative job of setting its action against the fall of the Berlin Wall and the end of the Cold War. A CIA agent forms a shaky alliance with his East German spymaster rival to prevent germ warfare technology from falling into terrorist hands. **83m/C VHS.** Marc Singer, Mary Crosby, Stephen Davies, Richard Leparmentier, Terence Henry; ***D:*** Terence H. Winkless.

Berlin Express 🦴🦴🦴½ **1948** Battle of wits ensues between the Allies and the Nazis who are seeking to keep Germans divided in post-WWII Germany. Espionage and intrigue factor heavily. **86m/B VHS.** Robert Ryan, Merle Oberon, Paul Lukas, Charles Korvin; ***D:*** Jacques Tourneur.

Berlin Tunnel 21 🦴½ **1981** Based on the novel by Donald Lindquist in which five American soldiers attempt a daring Cold War rescue of a beautiful German girl. The plan is to construct a tunnel under the Berlin Wall. Better-than-average. **150m/C VHS.** Richard Thomas, Jose Ferrer, Horst Buchholz; ***D:*** Richard Michaels. **TV**

Bernadette 🦴🦴½ **1990** A French-made version of the legend of St. Bernadette, who endured persecution after claiming to have seen the Virgin Mary. Beautiful in its simplicity, but overly long. **120m/C VHS.** *FR* Sydney Penny, Roland LeSaffre, Michele Simonnet, Bernard Dheran, Arlette Didier; ***D:*** Jean Delannoy.

Bernard and the Genie 🦴🦴½ **199? (G)** It seems Bernard Bottle is not going to have a happy Christmas—he's been fired from his job and his girlfriend has left him. But things take a turn for the better when he discovers an antique lamp and its resident Genie. But with the Genie granting his every wish, Bernard's sudden wealth is causing some suspicions among both his greedy ex-employer and the police. Meanwhile, the Genie discovers the delights of modern-day England and poses as a department store Santa to truly fulfill a child's Christmas wish. Amusing family fare. **70m/C VHS.** *GB* Alan Cumming, Lenny Henry, Rowan Atkinson; ***D:*** Paul Weiland.

Berserk! 🦴½ **1967** A seedy traveling circus is beset by a series of murders. Not heralded as one of Crawford's best pieces. **95m/C VHS.** Joan Crawford, Diana Dors, Judy Geeson, Ty Hardin; ***D:*** James O'Connolly.

Berserker 🦴 **1987 (R)** Six camping college students are attacked by a bloodthirsty psychotic out of a Nordic myth, who takes the shape of a badder-than-the-average bear. **85m/C VHS.** Joseph Alan Johnson, Valerie Sheldon, Greg Dawson; ***D:*** Jefferson (Jeff) Richard.

Bert Rigby, You're a Fool 🦴🦴½ **1989 (R)** A starstruck British coal miner finds his way to Hollywood singing old showtunes, only to be rebuffed by a cynical industry. Available with Spanish subtitles. **94m/C VHS.** Robert Lindsay, Robbie Coltrane, Jackie Gayle, Bruno Kirby, Cathryn Bradshaw, Corbin Bernsen, Anne Bancroft; ***D:*** Carl Reiner; ***W:*** Carl Reiner; ***C:*** Jan De Bont; ***M:*** Ralph Burns.

Beshkempir the Adopted Son 🦴🦴 **1998** In a rural community in the Central Asian nation of Kyrgyzstan, a young teen lives a carefree existence getting into mild mischief with his buddies. Until one day, during an argument, he suddenly discovers he was adopted, which throws his world (at least temporarily) into rebellious turmoil. Kyrgyzstani with subtitles. **81m/B VHS, DVD, Wide.** *RU* Mirlan Abdykalykov; ***D:*** Aktan Abdykalykov; ***W:*** Aktan Abdykalykov, Avtandil Adikulov, Marat Sarulu; ***C:*** Hassan Kidirialev; ***M:*** Nurlan Nishanov.

Besieged 🦴🦴½ **1998 (R)** Fans of Bertolucci will enjoy this airy quasi-love story, but the slow pace and meandering plot will frustrate other viewers. Shandurai (Newton) moves to Rome after her husband becomes a political prisoner in Kenya. In order to put herself through medical school, she takes a job as a maid for an eccentric British musician (Thewlis). He begins to fall for his beautiful housekeeper, but she ignores his advances. To prove his love, he begins selling off his personal belongings so he can bribe officials to release her husband. **94m/C VHS, DVD.** *IT* David Thewlis, Thandie Newton, Claudio Santamaria; ***D:*** Bernardo Bertolucci; ***W:*** Bernardo Bertolucci, Clare Peploe; ***C:*** Fabio Cianchetti; ***M:*** Alessio Vlad.

Best Defense 🦴 **1984 (R)** A U.S. Army tank operator is sent to Kuwait to test a new state-of-the-art tank in a combat situation. Although the cast is popular, the movie as a whole is not funny and the story frequently is hard to follow. **94m/C VHS.** Dudley Moore, Eddie Murphy, Kate Capshaw, George Dzundza, Helen Shaver; ***D:*** Willard Huyck; ***W:*** Willard Huyck, Gloria Katz.

Best Enemies 🦴½ **1986** An English film about a man suffering the trials of the 1960s, including Vietnam, and how it affects his relationships with his friends and wife. **96m/C VHS.** *GB* Sigrid Thornton, Paul Williams, Judy Morris, Brandon Burke; ***D:*** David Baker.

Best Foot Forward 🦴🦴½ **1943** Vintage musical about a movie star who agrees to accompany a young cadet to a military ball. Based on the popular Broadway show. The film debuts of Walker, Allyson, and DeHaven. ♫Buckle Down, Winsocki; The Three B's (Barrelhouse, Boogie Woogie, and the Blues); Alive and Kicking; Two O'Clock Jump; Ev'ry Time; Three Men on a Date; Wish I May; Shady Lady; My First Promise. **95m/C VHS.** Lucille Ball, June Allyson, Tommy Dix, Nancy Walker, Virginia Weidler, Gloria De Haven, William Gaxton, Harry James; ***D:*** Edward Buzzell; ***W:*** Irving Brecher; ***M:*** George Bassman.

Best Friends 🦴🦴 1982 (PG) A pair of screenwriters decide to marry after years of living and working together. Story based on the lives of screenwriters Barry Levinson and Valerie Curtin. **109m/C VHS.** Goldie Hawn, Burt Reynolds, Jessica Tandy, Barnard Hughes, Audra Lindley, Keenan Wynn, Ron Silver; ***D:*** Norman Jewison; ***W:*** Valerie Curtin, Barry Levinson; ***C:*** Jordan Cronenweth.

Best in Show 🦴🦴🦴 2000 (PG-13) Director Christopher Guest follows the successful "Waiting for Guffman" with another faux-documentary mixing improvisation and unique characters. This time, the subject is the snooty world of show dogs and the freaky, neurotic pooch-owners hoping to claim its greatest prize: Best in Show at the Mayflower Kennel Club Dog Show. The quirky dog-lovers include Meg (Posey) and Hamilton (Hitchcock), whose kinky sex life is giving their Weimaraner angst; doting gay Shih-Tzu owners Scott (Higgins) and Stefan (McKean); and seemingly tame suburbanites Gerry (Levy) and Cookie (O'Hara). Fred Willard steals the spotlight as Buck Laughlin, a sports announcer who has no knowledge of the event he's broadcasting. Worth a rental just for the bizarre one-liners fired off by the clueless commentator on such subjects as the dogs' anatomy and edibility. **89m/C VHS, DVD, Wide.** Christopher Guest, Michael McKean, Parker Posey, Eugene Levy, Catherine O'Hara, Fred Willard, Michael Hitchcock, John Michael Higgins, Jennifer Coolidge, Trevor Beckwith, Bob Balaban, Ed Begley Jr., Patrick Cranshaw, Don Lake, Larry Miller; ***D:*** Christopher Guest; ***W:*** Christopher Guest, Eugene Levy; ***C:*** Roberto Schaefer; ***M:*** C.J. Vanston.

The Best Intentions 🦴🦴🦴½ 1992 Ingmar Bergman wrote the screenplay chronicling the early years of the stormy relationship of his parents. Set in Sweden at the turn of the century, the film focuses on the class differences that divide his mother and father, while portrayal of little Bergy is limited to a bundle under his mother's maternity dress. Inspired performances and directing illuminates the emotionally complex relationship, revealing truths about the universal human condition along the way. Six-hour version was shot for TV in Europe and Japan. Director August and actress August met and married during filming. In Swedish with English subtitles. **182m/C VHS.** *SW* Samuel Froler, Pernilla August, Max von Sydow, Ghita Norby, Mona Malm, Lena Endre, Bjorn Kjellman; ***D:*** Bille August; ***W:*** Ingmar Bergman; ***C:*** Jorgen Persson; ***M:*** Stefan Nilsson. Cannes '92: Actress (August), Film.

Best Kept Secrets 🦴🦴½ 1988 A feisty woman discovers corruption and blackmail in the police department where her husband is an officer. **104m/C VHS.** Patty Duke, Frederic Forrest, Peter Coyote; ***D:*** Jerrold Freedman.

Best Laid Plans 🦴🦴 1999 (R) Another contemporary noir where no one and nothing is as it seems (except the overly familiar plot). Nick (Nivola) and his bud, Bryce (Brolin), are bar hopping when Bryce picks up Lissa (Witherspoon). Later, a frantic Bryce calls Nick saying Lissa is underage and accusing him of rape. Nick offers to talk to Lissa and the story flashes back to the beginnings of an elaborate scam leading all concerned to a number of ill-considered decisions. **90m/C VHS, DVD.** Alessandro Nivola, Josh Brolin, Reese Witherspoon, Rocky Carroll, Michael G. (Mike) Hagerty, Jamie Marsh; ***D:*** Mike Barker; ***W:*** Ted Griffin; ***C:*** Ben Seresin; ***M:*** Craig Armstrong.

The Best Little Girl in the World 🦴🦴🦴 1981 Exceptional made-for-TV tale of an apparently perfect teenager (Leigh) suffering from anorexia. Slow starvation is her only cry for help. Fine performances from Durning and Saint. Look for Helen Hunt and Ally Sheedy as classmates. **96m/C VHS.** Charles Durning, Eva Marie Saint, Jennifer Jason Leigh, Melanie Mayron, Viveca Lindfors, Jason Miller, David Spielberg, Lisa Pelikan, Ally Sheedy, Helen Hunt; ***D:*** Sam O'Steen; ***M:*** Billy Goldenberg. **TV**

The Best Little Whorehouse in Texas 🦴🦴 1982 (R) Parton is the buxom owner of The Chicken Ranch, a house of ill-repute that may be closed down unless Sheriff-boyfriend Reynolds can think of a way out. Strong performances don't quite make up for the erratically comic script. Based on the long-running Broadway musical, in turn based on a story by Larry McMurtry. **115m/C VHS, Wide.** Dolly Parton, Burt Reynolds, Dom DeLuise, Charles Durning, Jim Nabors, Lois Nettleton; ***D:*** Colin Higgins.

The Best Man 🦴🦴🦴½ 1964 An incisive, darkly satiric political tract, based on Gore Vidal's play, about two presidential contenders who vie for the endorsement of the aging ex-president, and trample political ethics in the process. **104m/B VHS.** Henry Fonda, Cliff Robertson, Lee Tracy, Margaret Leighton, Edie Adams, Kevin McCarthy, Ann Sothern, Gene Raymond, Shelley Berman, Mahalia Jackson; ***D:*** Franklin J. Schaffner; ***W:*** Gore Vidal; ***C:*** Haskell Wexler.

The Best Man 🦴🦴½ *Il Testimone dello Sposo* 1997 (PG) It's 1899 in a small northern Italian town and beautiful Francesca (Sastre) must marry the lascivious older Edgardo Osti (Cantarelli) in order to solve her father's business problems. Francesca is revolted but does become smitten by the best man—Angelo (Abatantuono), who's returned from America, apparently with a fortune. Marriage or no, Francesca becomes obsessed with getting Angelo. Italian with subtitles. **99m/C VHS.** *IT* Ines Sastre, Diego Abatantuono, Dario Cantarelli, Valeria (Valerie Dobson) D'Obici, Mario Erpichini; ***D:*** Pupi Avati; ***W:*** Pupi Avati; ***C:*** Pasquale Rachini; ***M:*** Riz Ortolani.

The Best Man 🦴🦴🦴 1999 (R) Writer/director Malcolm D. Lee, cousin of co-producer Spike Lee, makes an impressive debut in this ensemble piece that plays like a hipper "Big Chill." Novelist Harper (Diggs) heads to New York to attend the wedding of his best friend Lance (Chestnut) and the beautiful Mia (Calhoun). Unfortunately, his soon-to-be-released first novel is a thinly disguised autobiography which alludes to an affair between Harper and the bride-to-be. As other college buddies and old flames show up for the nuptials, past issues and romantic tensions come bubbling back up to the surface. The cast gives good performances across the board, with Howard as the wisecracking and womanizing Quentin standing out in particular. **120m/C VHS, DVD.** Taye Diggs, Monica Calhoun, Morris Chestnut, Nia Long, Melissa DeSousa, Harold Perrineau Jr., Terrence DaShon Howard, Sanaa Lathan, Victoria Dillard; ***D:*** Malcolm Lee; ***W:*** Malcolm Lee; ***C:*** Frank Prinzi; ***M:*** Stanley Clarke.

Best Men 🦴🦴½ *Independence* 1998 (R) There's a wedding, there's a would-be bank heist, and there's five men caught in the siege at the bank of Independence in this kooky crime comedy/drama. Jesse (Wilson) is heading straight from prison to his wedding to Hope (Barrymore) with his four tuxedo-clad buddies. Billy (Flanery) needs some cash before the big event and persuades the boys to stop at the bank—only his withdrawal is the illegal kind. Soon Billy's dad (Ward), who happens to be the local sheriff, is trying to contain the situation when the feds show up as does the bewildered bride-to-be. **89m/C VHS, DVD, Wide.** Sean Patrick Flanery, Dean Cain, Luke Wilson, Andy Dick, Mitchell Whitfield, Drew Barrymore, Fred Ward, Raymond J. Barry, Brad Dourif, Art Edler Brown, Tracy Fraim; ***D:*** Tamra Davis; ***W:*** Art Edler Brown, Tracy Fraim; ***C:*** James Glennon; ***M:*** Mark Mothersbaugh.

The Best of Everything 🦴🦴🦴 1959 Trashy sexist soap opera about women seeking success and love in the publishing world of N.Y.C. Several stories take place, the best being Crawford's hard-nosed editor who's having an affair with a married man. Look for Evans as a philandering playboy (he went on to become the producer of "Chinatown," among others.) Based on the novel by Rona Jaffe. **121m/C VHS.** Hope Lange, Stephen Boyd, Suzy Parker, Diane Baker, Martha Hyer, Joan Crawford, Brian Aherne, Robert Evans, Louis Jourdan; ***D:*** Jean Negulesco; ***W:*** Edith Sommer, Mann Rubin; ***C:*** William Mellor; ***M:*** Alfred Newman.

Best of the Badmen 🦴🦴½ 1950 A whole bunch of outlaws, although seemingly quite nice, are brought together by an ex-Union general who is being framed. Too much talk, not enough action. **84m/B VHS.** Robert Ryan, Claire Trevor, Jack Buetel, Robert Preston, Walter Brennan, Bruce Cabot, John Archer, Lawrence Tierney; ***D:*** William D. Russell.

Best of the Best 🦴½ 1989 (PG-13) An interracial kick-boxing team strives to win a world championship. **95m/C VHS.** Edward (Eddie) Bunker, Eric Roberts, Sally Kirkland, Christopher Penn, Phillip Rhee, James Earl Jones, John P. Ryan, John Dye, David Agresta, Tom Everett, Louise Fletcher, Simon Rhee; ***D:*** Robert Radler.

Best of the Best 2 🦴½ 1993 (R) The Coliseum is a notorious martial-arts venue owned by the champion fighter Brackus and his manager Weldon. No rules death matches are the norm and when their friend is killed Tommy and Alex set up a grudge match with Brackus. **100m/C VHS, Wide.** Edward (Eddie) Bunker, Eric Roberts, Phillip Rhee, Christopher Penn, Ralph (Ralf) Moeller, Wayne Newton, Edan Gross, Sonny Landham, Meg Foster, Simon Rhee, Claire Stansfield, Betty Carvalho; ***D:*** Robert Radler; ***W:*** John Allen Nelson, Max Strom; ***M:*** David Michael Frank.

Best of the Best 3: No Turning Back 🦴🦴 1995 (R) Asian-American Tommy Lee (Rhee) discovers a band of racist vigilantes are trying to take over the rural community of Liberty, where his sister lives. But with the help of his brother-in-law Jack (McDonald), who's also the sheriff, and school teacher Margo (Gershon), Tommy is going to fight back. **102m/C VHS, DVD.** Phillip Rhee, Gina Gershon, Christopher McDonald, Mark Rolston, Peter Simmons, Dee Wallace Stone; ***D:*** Phillip Rhee; ***W:*** Deborah Scott; ***C:*** Jerry Watson; ***M:*** Barry Goldberg.

Best of the Best: Without Warning 🦴½ 1998 (R) It's Russian mobsters, counterfeit money, and high tech gadgets this time around as LAPD martial arts consultant Tommy Lee (Rhee) goes after the gang who killed his best friend's daughter. **90m/C VHS, DVD.** Phillip Rhee, Ernie Hudson, Tobin Bell, Thure Riefenstein, Chris Lemmon, Jessica Collins; ***D:*** Phillip Rhee; ***C:*** Michael D. Margulies; ***M:*** David Grant. **VIDEO**

The Best of Times 🦴🦴 1986 (PG) Slim story of two grown men who attempt to redress the failures of the past by reenacting a football game they lost in high school due to a single flubbed pass. With this cast, it should have been better. **105m/C VHS, DVD, 8mm.** Robin Williams, Kurt Russell, M. Emmet Walsh, Pamela Reed, Holly Palance, Donald Moffat, Margaret Whitton, Kirk Cameron; ***D:*** Roger Spottiswoode; ***W:*** Ron Shelton; ***C:*** Charles F. Wheeler; ***M:*** Arthur B. Rubinstein.

Best Revenge 🦴🦴 1983 (R) Two aging hippies engage in a Moroccan drug deal in order to free a kidnapped friend from a sleazy gangster. They get caught by the police, but escape, searching for the engineers of the frame-up. **92m/C VHS.** John Heard, Levon Helm, Alberta Watson, John Rhys-Davies, Moses Znaimer; ***D:*** John Trent; ***M:*** Keith Emerson.

Best Seller 🦴🦴🦴 1987 (R) Interesting, subtext-laden thriller about a cop/bestselling author with writer's block, and the strange symbiotic relationship he forms with a slick hired killer, who wants his own story written. Dennehy is convincing as the jaded cop, and is paired well with the psychotic Woods. **112m/C VHS, DVD, Wide.** James Woods, Brian Dennehy, Victoria Tennant, Paul Shenar, Seymour Cassel, Allison Balson, George Coe, Anne Pitoniak; ***D:*** John Flynn; ***W:*** Larry Cohen; ***C:*** Fred Murphy; ***M:*** Jay Ferguson.

The Best Way 🦴🦴½ *The Best Way to Walk; La Meilleure Facon de Marcher* 1976 Two summer camp counselors discover they might be gay and desirous of each other. Miller's first film; in French with English subtitles. **85m/C VHS.** *FR* Patrick Dewaere, Patrick Bouchitey, Christine Pascal, Claude Pieplu; ***D:*** Claude Miller; ***W:*** Luc Beraud, Claude Miller; ***C:*** Bruno Nuytten; ***M:*** Alain Jomy.

The Best Years of Our Lives 🦴🦴🦴🦴 1946 Three WWII vets return home to try to pick up the threads of their lives. A film that represented a large chunk of American society and helped it readjust to the modern postwar ambience is now considered an American classic. Supporting actor Russell, an actual veteran, holds a record for winning two Oscars for a single role. In addition to his Best Supporting Actor award, Russell was given a special Oscar for bringing hope and courage to fellow veterans. Based on the novella by MacKinlay Kantor. Remade for TV as "Returning Home" in 1975. **170m/B VHS, DVD.** Fredric March, Myrna Loy, Teresa Wright, Dana Andrews, Virginia Mayo, Harold Russell, Hoagy Carmichael, Gladys George, Roman Bohnen, Steve Cochran, Charles Halton, Cathy O'Donnell, Ray Collins, Victor Cutler, Minna Gombell, Walter Baldwin, Dorothy Adams, Don Beddoe, Ray Teal, Howland Chamberlain; ***D:*** William Wyler; ***W:*** Robert Sherwood; ***C:*** Gregg Toland; ***M:*** Hugo Friedhofer. Oscars '46: Actor (March), Director (Wyler), Film Editing, Picture, Screenplay, Support. Actor (Russell), Orig. Dramatic Score; AFI '98: Top 100; British Acad. '47: Film; Golden Globes '47: Film—Drama; Natl. Bd. of Review '46: Director (Wyler), Natl. Film Reg. '89;, N.Y. Film Critics '46: Director (Wyler), Film.

Bethune 🦴🦴½ 1977 The life story of a Canadian doctor who started a practice in Communist China. **88m/C VHS.** Donald Sutherland, Kate Nelligan, David Gardner, James Hong; ***D:*** Eric Till.

Betrayal 🦴 1974 Psycho-thriller pits an unhappy widow against her seemingly innocent hired companion. Seems this girl has a boyfriend who has a plan to murder the lonely lady for her money. Routine and predictable. **78m/C VHS.** Amanda Blake, Dick Haymes, Tisha Sterling, Sam Groom; ***D:*** Gordon Hessler; ***M:*** Ernest Gold.

Betrayal 🦴½ 1978 Telefilm based on the book by Lucy Freeman and Julie Roy about a historic malpractice case involving a psychiatrist and one of his female patients. The doctor convinced the female patient that sex with him would serve as therapy. **95m/C VHS.** Lesley Ann Warren, Rip Torn, Ron Silver, Richard Masur, Stephen Elliott, John Hillerman, Peggy Ann Garner; ***D:*** Paul Wendkos.

Betrayal 🦴🦴½ 1983 (R) An unusual adult drama, beginning at the end of a seven-year adulterous affair and working its way back in time to finally end at the start of the betrayal of a husband by his wife and his best friend. Kingsley and Irons make Pinter's adaptation of his own play work. **95m/C VHS.** *GB* Ben Kingsley, Patricia Hodge, Jeremy Irons; ***D:*** David Hugh Jones; ***W:*** Harold Pinter.

Betrayal from the East 🦴🦴 1944 A carnival barker saves the Panama Canal from the vicious Japanese war machine in this rather silly wartime drama. **82m/B VHS.** Lee Tracy, Nancy Kelly, Richard Loo, Abner Biberman, Regis Toomey, Philip Ahn, Addison Richards, Victor Sen Yung, Drew Pearson; ***D:*** William Berke.

Betrayal of the Dove 🦴🦴 1992 (R) Slater stars as a divorced woman set-up on a blind date by best friend Le Brock. Zane is the dashing doctor who sweeps Slater off her feet but things are never quite what they seem. He may not be Mr. Right and the best friend has her own hidden agenda. **93m/C VHS.** Helen Slater, Kelly Le Brock, Billy Zane, Alan Thicke, Harvey Korman, Stuart Pankin, David Lander; ***D:*** Strathford Hamilton; ***W:*** Robby Benson.

Betrayed 🦴🦴🦴 1954 Bombshell Turner and strongman Gable star in this story of WWII intrigue. Suspected of being a Nazi informer, Turner is sent back to Holland for a last chance at redemption. Her cover as a sultry nightclub performer has the Nazis drooling and ogling (can you spell h-o-t?), but her act may be blown by an informant. Can luscious Lana get out of this one intact? **107m/C VHS.** Clark Gable, Lana Turner, Victor Mature, Louis Calhern, O.E. Hasse, Wilfrid Hyde-White, Ian Carmichael, Niall MacGinnis, Nora Swinburne, Roland Culver; ***D:*** Gottfried Reinhardt; ***C:*** Frederick A. (Freddie) Young.

Betrayed 1988 (R) A rabid political film, dealing with an implausible FBI agent infiltrating a white supremacist organization via her love affair with a handsome farmer who turns out to be a murderous racist. Winger is memorable in her role as the FBI agent, despite the film's limitations, and admirers of Costa-Gavras's directorial work and political stances will want to see how the director botched this one. **112m/C VHS, DVD, Wide.** Tom Berenger, Debra Winger, John Mahoney, John Heard, Albert Hall, Jeffrey DeMunn; *D:* Constantin Costa-Gavras; *W:* Joe Eszterhas; *C:* Patrick Blossier.

The Betsy *Harold Robbins' The Betsy* 1978 (R) A story of romance, money, power, and mystery centering around the wealthy Hardeman family and their automobile manufacturing business. Loosely patterned after the life of Henry Ford as portrayed in the Harold Robbins' pulptome. Olivier is the redeeming feature. **132m/C VHS, DVD.** Laurence Olivier, Kathleen Beller, Robert Duvall, Lesley-Anne Down, Edward Herrmann, Tommy Lee Jones, Katharine Ross, Jane Alexander; *D:* Daniel Petrie; *W:* William Bast, Walter Bernstein; *C:* Mario Tosi; *M:* John Barry.

Betsy's Wedding ½ 1990 (R) Betsy wants a simple wedding, but her father has other, grander ideas. Then there's the problem of paying for it, which Dad tries to take care of in a not-so-typical manner. Alda at his hilarious best. **94m/C VHS.** Alan Alda, Joey Bishop, Madeline Kahn, Molly Ringwald, Catherine O'Hara, Joe Pesci, Ally Sheedy, Burt Young, Anthony LaPaglia, Julie Bovasso, Nicolas Coster, Bibi Besch, Dylan Walsh; *D:* Alan Alda; *W:* Alan Alda; *M:* Bruce Broughton.

Better Late Than Never 1979 Fun TV tale of senior citizens in revolt at an old-age home. Fine characters portrayed by some of the best in the business. **100m/C VHS.** Harold Gould, Tyne Daly, Strother Martin, Harry (Henry) Morgan, Victor Buono, George Gobel, Lou Jacobi, Donald Pleasence, Larry Storch; *D:* Richard Crenna; *M:* Charles Fox. **TV**

Better Late Than Never ½ 1983 Two penniless old fools vie for the acceptance of a bratty 10-year-old millionairess, who must choose one as her guardian. Niven's last film. **95m/C VHS.** David Niven, Art Carney, Maggie Smith, Kimberly Partridge, Catherine Hicks, Melissa Prophet; *D:* Bryan Forbes; *M:* Henry Mancini.

Better Off Dead ½ 1985 (PG) A compulsive teenager's girlfriend leaves him and he decides to end it all. After several abortive attempts, he decides instead to out-ski his ex-girlfriend's obnoxious new boyfriend. Uneven but funny. **97m/C VHS.** John Cusack, Curtis Armstrong, Diane Franklin, Kim Darby, David Ogden Stiers, Dan Schneider, Amanda Wyss, Taylor Negron, Vincent Schiavelli, Demian Slade, Scooter Stevens, Elizabeth (E.G. Dailey) Daily; *D:* Steve Holland; *W:* Steve Holland; *C:* Isidore Mankofsky; *M:* Rupert Hine.

Better Off Dead ½ 1994 Preachy, manipulative TV movie redeemed by good performances. Kit (Winningham) is an unrepentant white-trash thief who kills a black police officer and is sentenced to death. Cutter Dubuque (Ferrell) is the ambitious black district attorney who prosecuted the case but comes to doubt the wisdom of the death penalty and slowly begins to try to help Kit. **91m/C VHS.** Mare Winningham, Tyra Ferrell, Kevin Tighe, Don Harvey; *D:* M. Neema Barnette; *W:* Marlane X. Meyer; *C:* Ueli Steiger; *M:* John Barnes.

Better Than Chocolate 1999 (R) Sweetly touching romantic comedy follows college dropout Maggie (Dwyer), who's trying to establish her own identity, which isn't so easy when she hasn't told her flighty mother, Lila (Crewson), that she's a lesbian. But now mom is getting divorced and she and Maggie's brother Paul (Mundy) are temporarily moving in, with Maggie trying to pass off her lover Kim (Cox) as just a roommate. Meanwhile, naive Lila is confiding in Maggie's transseuxual friend, singer Judy (a stellar Outerbridge), and discovering the joys of sex toys. **101m/C VHS, DVD, Wide.** *CA* Karyn Dwyer, Wendy Crewson, Christina Cox, Peter Outerbridge, Ann-Marie MacDonald, Kevin Mundy, Marya Delver, Jay Brazeau, Tony Nappo; *D:* Anne Wheeler; *W:* Peggy Thompson; *C:* Gregory Middleton; *M:* Graeme Coleman.

A Better Tomorrow, Part 1 ½ *Ying Huang Boon Sik; Gangland Boss* 1986 Former hit men (Lung and Fat) team up to bring down the mob boss who double-crossed them and sent one to prison and the other to the streets. One of them also has to protect his younger brother, a cop, from the gang. Considered one of the best of Woo's Hong Kong efforts, there's plenty of his hallmark balletic action and an interesting story. In Cantonese with English subtitles. **95m/C VHS, DVD, Wide.** *CH HK* Chow Yun-Fat, Leslie Cheung, Ti Lung, Emily Chu, Waise Lee, John Woo; *D:* John Woo; *W:* John Woo; *C:* Wing-hang Wong; *M:* Ka-Fai Koo.

A Better Tomorrow, Part 2 ½ *Yinghung Bunsik 2* 1988 A smooth-talking gangster, who was killed in Part I, returns in Part II as the dead man's twin brother (unmentioned in Part I). He teams up with a cop and a reformed gangster to fight the forces of evil. In Cantonese with English subtitles. **100m/C VHS, DVD, Wide.** *HK* Chow Yun-Fat, Leslie Cheung; *D:* John Woo; *W:* John Woo; *M:* Joseph Koo.

A Better Tomorrow, Part 3 *Love and Death in Saigon* 1989 Prequel set in 1974 finds detective Mark Gor (Fat) and his cousin (Leung) seeking to escape from Saigon. Unfortunately, they both fall for the same sultry babe (Mui), who's also a gangster's moll. Mandarin with subtitles. **114m/C VHS, DVD.** *HK* Chow Yun-Fat, Tony Leung Ka-Fai, Anita (Yim-Fong) Mui; *D:* Tsui Hark.

A Better Way to Die 2000 (R) An ex-cop heads home to try to start a new life but is instead mistaken for a government agent who has had a contract put out on his life by a Chicago mob boss. So the cop tries to get the feds to assist him before the wiseguys get to him first. **101m/C VHS, DVD, Wide.** Andre Braugher, Joe Pantoliano, Natasha Henstridge, Lou Diamond Phillips, Wayne Duvall, Scott Wiper; *D:* Scott Wiper; *W:* Scott Wiper. **VIDEO**

Betty 1992 Sulky, drunken Betty (Trintignant) is doing her best to destroy her bourgeois life, escaping from her marriage into adultery and debasement. She meets the concerned middle-aged widow Laure (Audran), who inexplicably takes her to her hotel room, cleans her up, and spends the remainder of the movie as Betty's sounding-board. Betty's passive personality offers little to explain her appeal to either Laure or the viewer. Based on the novel by Georges Simenon. French with subtitles. **103m/C VHS.** *FR* Marie Trintignant, Stephane Audran, Jean-Francoise Garreaud, Yves Lambrecht, Christiane Minazolli, Pierre Vernier; *D:* Claude Chabrol; *W:* Claude Chabrol; *M:* Matthieu Chabrol.

Betty Blue *37.2 le Matin; 37.2 Degrees in the Morning* 1986 (R) A vivid, intensely erotic film about two young French lovers and how their inordinately strong passion for each other destroys them, leading to poverty, violence, and insanity. English subtitles. From the director of "Diva." Based on the novel "37.2 Le Matin" by Philippe Djian. **121m/C VHS.** *FR* Beatrice Dalle, Jean-Hugues Anglade, Gerard Darmon, Consuelo de Haviland, Clementine Celarie, Jacques Mathou, Vincent Lindon; *D:* Jean-Jacques Beineix; *W:* Jean-Jacques Beineix; *C:* Jean-Francois Robin; *M:* Gabriel Yared.

Between Fighting Men ½ 1932 The orphaned daughter of a shepherd is adopted by the cowpoke who caused her father's death. The cowpoke's sons fall in love with, and compete for, the love of the girl. **62m/B VHS.** Ken Maynard, Ruth Hall, Josephine Dunn, Wallace MacDonald; *D:* Forrest Sheldon.

Between Friends ½ 1983 Two women with only their respective divorces in common, meet and become fast friends. The rapport between Burnett and Taylor makes for a touching drama. Adapted from the book "Nobody Makes Me Cry," by Shelley List, one of the producers. **105m/C VHS.** Elizabeth Taylor, Carol Burnett; *D:* Lou Antonio; *M:* James Horner. **CABLE**

Between God, the Devil & a Winchester 1972 Violent western with plenty of shooting and dust. Lots of cowboys are hot on the trail of some stolen loot from a church but apparently God isn't on their side since the majority bite the dust and become a snack for the vultures. **98m/C VHS.** Gilbert Roland, Richard Harrison; *D:* Dario Silvester.

Between Heaven and Earth 1993 Maria (Maura) is an ambitious TV journalist, prone to surreal dreams, who becomes pregnant after a one-night stand. After witnessing a violent protest, Maria becomes convinced that she can communicate with her unborn baby and that the child is unwilling to be born into such a violent world. So Maria must try to convince her baby otherwise. In French with English subtitles. **80m/C VHS.** *BE FR SP* Carmen Maura, Jean-Pierre Cassel, Didier Bezace, Samuel Mussen, Andre Delvaux; *D:* Marion Hansel; *W:* Marion Hansel.

Between Heaven and Hell 1956 Prejudiced Southern gentleman Wagner finds how wrong his misconceptions are, as he attempts to survive WWII on a Pacific Island. Ebsen is exceptional, making this rather simplistic story a meaningful classic. **94m/C VHS.** Robert Wagner, Terry Moore, Broderick Crawford, Buddy Ebsen, Robert Keith, Brad Dexter, Mark Damon, Kenneth (Ken) Clark, Harvey Lembeck, Frank Gorshin, Scatman Crothers; *D:* Richard Fleischer.

Between Men 1935 A father kills a man he believes killed his son and flees. Later in life, the son meets his father. For father and son, this causes some major concern. **59m/B VHS.** Johnny Mack Brown, Beth Marion, William Farnum, Earl Dwire, Lloyd Ingraham, Milburn (Milt) Morante; *D:* Robert North Bradbury.

Between the Lines ½ 1977 (R) A witty, wonderfully realized ensemble comedy about the staff of a radical post-'60s newspaper always on the brink of folding, and its eventual sell-out. **101m/C VHS.** John Heard, Lindsay Crouse, Jeff Goldblum, Jill Eikenberry, Stephen Collins, Lewis J. Stadlen, Michael J. Pollard, Marilu Henner, Bruno Kirby; *D:* Joan Micklin Silver; *W:* Fred Barron; *M:* Michael Kamen.

Between Two Women 1986 A wife's relationship with her bossy mother-in-law is rocky until the latter has a stroke and needs care. Dewhurst won an Emmy for her portrayal of the mother-in-law. **95m/C VHS.** Farrah Fawcett, Michael Nouri, Colleen Dewhurst, Steven Hill, Bridgette Andersen, Danny Corkill; *D:* Jon Avnet. **TV**

Between Wars 1974 Young doctor in Australia's Medical Corps encounters conflict when he tries to introduce Freud's principles into his work. **97m/C VHS.** *AU* Corin Redgrave, Arthur Dignam, Judy Morris, Patricia Leehy, Gunter Meisner; *D:* Michael Thornhill.

Beulah Land ½ 1980 Miniseries about 45 years in the lives of a Southern family, including the Civil War. Based on the novels "Beulah Land" and "Look Away, Beulah Land" by Lonnie Coleman. **267m/C VHS.** Lesley Ann Warren, Michael Sarrazin, Don Johnson, Meredith Baxter, Dorian Harewood, Eddie Albert, Hope Lange, Paul Rudd; *D:* Virgil W. Vogel, Harry Falk. **TV**

The Beverly Hillbillies ½ 1993 (PG) Big-screen transfer of the long-running TV show may appeal to fans. Ozark mountaineer Jed Clampett discovers oil, becomes an instant billionaire, and packs his backwoods clan off to the good life in California. Minimal plot finds dimbulb nephew Jethro and daughter Elly May looking for a bride for Jed. Not that any of it matters. Everyone does fine by their impersonations, particularly Varney as the good-hearted Jed and Leachman as stubborn Granny. Ebsen, the original Jed, reprises another of his TV roles, detective Barnaby Jones. And yes, the familiar strains of the "Ballad of Jed Clampett" by Jerry Scoggins starts this one off, too. **93m/C VHS.** Jim Varney, Erika Eleniak, Diedrich Bader, Cloris Leachman, Dabney Coleman, Lily Tomlin, Lea Thompson, Rob Schneider, Linda Carlson, Penny Fuller, Kevin Connolly; ***Cameos:*** Buddy Ebsen, Zsa Zsa Gabor, Dolly Parton; *D:* Penelope Spheeris; *W:* Larry Konner, Mark Rosenthal, Jim Fisher, Jim Staahl; *C:* Robert Brinkmann; *M:* Lalo Schifrin.

Beverly Hills Bodysnatchers ½ 1989 (R) A mad scientist and a greedy mortician plot to get rich, but their plan backfires when they bring a Mafia godfather back to life and he terrorizes Beverly Hills. **85m/C VHS.** Vic Tayback, Frank Gorshin, Brooke Bundy, Seth Jaffe, Art Metrano, Allison Barron, Rodney Eastman, Warren Selko, Keone Young; *D:* Jonathan Mostow.

Beverly Hills Brats 1989 (PG-13) A spoiled, rich Hollywood brat hires a loser to kidnap him, in order to gain his parents' attention, only to have both of them kidnapped by real crooks. **90m/C VHS.** Martin Sheen, Burt Young, Peter Billingsley, Terry Moore; *D:* Dimitri Sotirakis; *M:* Barry Goldberg.

Beverly Hills Cop ½ 1984 (R) When a close friend of smooth-talking Detroit cop Axle Foley is brutally murdered, he traces the murderer to the posh streets of Beverly Hills. There he must stay on his toes to keep one step ahead of the killer and two steps ahead of the law. Better than average Murphy vehicle. **105m/C VHS, DVD, 8mm, Wide.** Eddie Murphy, Judge Reinhold, John Ashton, Lisa Eilbacher, Ronny Cox, Steven Berkoff, James Russo, Jonathan Banks, Stephen Elliott, Bronson Pinchot, Paul Reiser, Damon Wayans, Rick Overton; *D:* Martin Brest; *W:* Danilo Bach, Dan Petrie Jr.; *C:* Bruce Surtees; *M:* Harold Faltermeyer.

Beverly Hills Cop 2 ½ 1987 (R) The highly successful sequel to the first profitable comedy, with essentially the same plot, this time deals with Foley infiltrating a band of international munitions smugglers. **103m/C VHS, DVD, 8mm, Wide.** Eddie Murphy, Judge Reinhold, Juergen Prochnow, Ronny Cox, John Ashton, Brigitte Nielsen, Allen (Goorwitz) Garfield, Paul Reiser, Dean Stockwell, Chris Rock, Gil Hill, Robert Ridgely, Gilbert Gottfried, Todd Susman, Robert Pastorelli, Tommy (Tiny) Lister, Paul Guilfoyle, Hugh Hefner; *D:* Tony Scott; *W:* Larry Ferguson, Warren Skaaren; *C:* Jeffrey L. Kimball; *M:* Harold Faltermeyer. Golden Raspberries '87: Worst Song ("I Want Your Sex").

Beverly Hills Cop 3 ½ 1994 (R) Yes, Detroit cop Axel Foley (Murphy) just happens to find another case that takes him back to his friends on the Beverly Hills PD. This time he uncovers a criminal network fronting WonderWorld, an amusement park with a squeaky-clean image. Fast-paced action, lots of gunplay, and Eddie wisecracks his way through the slow spots. Reinhold returns as the still impossibly naive Rosewood, with Pinchot briefly reprising his role as Serge of the undeterminable accent. Critically panned boxoffice disappointment relies too heavily on formula and is another disappointing followup. **105m/C VHS, DVD, Wide.** Louis Lombardi, Eddie Murphy, Judge Reinhold, Hector Elizondo, Timothy Carhart, Stephen McHattie, Theresa Randle, John Saxon, Alan Young, Bronson Pinchot, Al Green, Gil Hill; *D:* John Landis; *W:* Steven E. de Souza; *C:* Mac Ahlberg; *M:* Nile Rodgers.

Beverly Hills Family Robinson 1997 Cooking show host Marsha Robinson decides to take her family on a yachting vacation in the South Seas. Naturally, they get hijacked by pirates and shipwrecked and must learn to survive on their not-quite-deserted island. And just how good is Marsha is at campfire cooking? **88m/C VHS.** Dyan Cannon, Martin Mull, Sarah Michelle Gellar, Josh Picker, Nique Needles, Ryan O'Donohue; *D:* Troy Miller. **TV**

Beverly Hills Madam 1986 (PG-13) In this routine plot, a stable of elite call girls struggle with their lifestyle and their madam, played by Dunaway. **97m/C VHS.** Faye Dunaway, Louis Jourdan, Donna Dixon, Robin Givens, Marshall Colt, Melody Anderson, Terry Farrell; *D:* Harvey Hart. **TV**

Beverly Hills Ninja ½ 1996 (PG-13) Farley plays Haru, a pathetically inept adopted son of a ninja, who is, nevertheless, sent to Beverly Hills on a rescue mission to break up an international counterfeiting ring. There, second-time spoof siren Sheridan hires the "great white ninja" to follow her no-good boyfriend and becomes the object of Haru's desire. Farley's extraordinary gift for physical comedy is exploited to the hilt, and the increase in Haru's tripping and stumbling (and in one harrowing scene, stripping) usually coincides with the fumbling of the plot. Rock's talents are squandered on a poorly conceived bellboy character. Farley's first feature sans fellow SNL alumni Spade suffers for his absence. Director Duggan, who also helmed Adam Sandler's "Happy Gilmore," might want to start screening his calls. **88m/C VHS, DVD, Wide.** Chris Farley, Nicolette Sheridan, Robin Shou, Nathaniel Parker, Chris Rock, Soon-Teck Oh, Francois Chau, Keith Cooke Hirabayashi; ***D:*** Dennis Dugan; ***W:*** Mark Feldberg, Mitch Klebenoff; ***C:*** Arthur Albert; ***M:*** George S. Clinton.

Beverly Hills Vamp ꝏꝏ **1988 (R)** A madame and her girls are really female vampires with a penchant for hot-blooded men. **88m/C VHS.** Britt Ekland, Eddie Deezen, Debra Lamb, Michelle (McClellan) Bauer, Brigitte Burdine, Tim Conway Jr., Jillian Kesner, Tom Shell; ***D:*** Fred Olen Ray; ***W:*** Ernest Farino; ***C:*** Stephen Blake; ***M:*** Chuck Cirino.

Beware ꝏ½ **1946** A black singer saves a college from bankruptcy and makes off with the gym teacher. The photography may be a bit harsh, but the all-black cast made this a pioneering but impressive film. **64m/B VHS.** Louis Jordan, Frank Wilson, Emory Richardson, Valerie Black, Milton Woods; ***D:*** Bud Pollard.

Beware! Children at Play woof! **1995 (R)** Cult leader kidnaps kids and introduces them to cannibalism. Bleech! As if this didn't sound grim enough, there's also an unrated version. **90m/C VHS, DVD.** Michael Robinson, Eric Tonken, Jamie Krause, Mik Cribben, Danny McClaughlin; ***D:*** Mik Cribben; ***C:*** Mik Cribben.

Beware, My Lovely ꝏꝏ½ **1952** Taut chiller. Lonely widow Lupino hires a new handy-man. He's great with screen doors and storm windows, but has a problem with sharp tools. Intense and gripping with fine performances. **77m/B VHS.** Ida Lupino, Robert Ryan, Taylor Holmes, O.Z. Whitehead, Barbara Whiting, Dee Pollock; ***D:*** Harry Horner.

Beware of a Holy Whore ꝏꝏ *Warnung Vor Einer Heiligen Nutte* **1970** German film crew sits around a Spanish resort—complaining, drinking, and making love—as they wait for financial support from Bonn. Provocative and self-indulgently honest look at filmmaking. Filmed on location in Sorrento, Italy; German with subtitles. **103m/C VHS.** *GE* Lou Castel, Eddie Constantine, Hanna Schygulla, Marquard Bohm, Ulli Lommel, Margarethe von Trotta, Kurt Raab, Ingrid Caven, Werner Schroeter, Rainer Werner Fassbinder; ***D:*** Rainer Werner Fassbinder; ***W:*** Rainer Werner Fassbinder; ***C:*** Michael Ballhaus; ***M:*** Peer Raben.

Beware of Pity ꝏꝏ½ **1946** A crippled baroness thinks she's found true love with a military officer, but it turns out his marriage proposal grew out of pity for her, not passion. A quality but somber British-made historical drama, based on a novel by Stefan Zweig. **129m/B VHS.** Lilli Palmer, Albert Lieven, Cedric Hardwicke, Gladys Cooper, Ernest Thesiger, Freda Jackson, Linden Travers, Ralph Truman, Peter Cotes, Jenny Laird, Emrys Jones, Gerhard Kempinski, John Salew, Kenneth Warrington; ***D:*** Maurice Elvey; ***W:*** W.P. Lipscomb, Elizabeth Barron, Margaret Steen; ***C:*** Derick Williams.

Beware! The Blob ꝏꝏ *Son of Blob* **1972 (PG)** A scientist brings home a piece of frozen blob from the North Pole; his wife accidentally revives the dormant gray mass. It begins a rampage of terror by digesting nearly everyone within its reach. A host of recognizable faces make for fun viewing. Post-Jeannie, pre-Dallas Hagman directed this exercise in zaniness. **87m/C VHS, DVD.** Robert Walker Jr., Godfrey Cambridge, Carol Lynley, Shelley Berman, Larry Hagman, Burgess Meredith, Gerrit Graham, Dick Van Patten, Gwynne Gilford, Richard Stahl, Richard Webb, Cindy Williams; ***D:*** Larry Hagman; ***W:*** Jack Woods, Anthony Harris; ***C:*** Al Hamm; ***M:*** Mort Garson.

The Beyond ꝏꝏ *Seven Doors of Death; E Tu Vivrai Nel Terrore—L'aldila* **1982 (R)** A young woman inherits a possessed hotel. Meanwhile, hellish zombies try to check out. Chilling Italian horror flick that Fulci directed under the alias "Louis Fuller." **88m/C VHS, DVD, Wide.** *IT* Al Cliver, Katherine (Katriona) MacColl, David Warbeck, Farah Keller, Tony St. John; ***D:*** Lucio Fulci; ***W:*** Lucio Fulci, Dardano Sacchetti, Giorgio Mariuzzo; ***C:*** Sergio Salvati.

Beyond a Reasonable Doubt ꝏꝏ **1956** In order to get a behind-the-scenes glimpse at the judicial system, a man plays the guilty party to a murder. Alas, when he tries to vindicate himself, he is the victim of his own folly. Not as interesting as it sounds on paper. **80m/B VHS.** Dana Andrews, Joan Fontaine, Sidney Blackmer, Philip Bourneuf, Barbara Nichols, Shepperd Strudwick, Arthur Franz, Edward Binns; ***D:*** Fritz Lang; ***W:*** Douglas S. Morrow.

Beyond Atlantis woof! **1973 (PG)** An ancient underwater tribe is discovered when it kidnaps land-lubbin' women with which to mate. **91m/C VHS, DVD.** *PH* John Ashley, Patrick Wayne, George Nader; ***D:*** Eddie Romero; ***W:*** Charles Johnson; ***C:*** Justo Paulino.

Beyond Darkness ꝏ½ **1992 (R)** When Peter and his family move into their New England home they are immediately beset by some unknown terror. With the help of Father George, Peter learns his house was built upon the graves of 20 witches burned for heresy. The witches have decided to seek revenge by kidnapping Peter's young son and sacrificing him to an evil demon. Can Peter destroy the evil spirits before they destroy his son? **111m/C VHS.** Gene Le Brock, David Brandon, Barbara Bingham, Michael Stephenson, Stephen Brown; ***D:*** Clyde (Claudio Fragasso) Anderson.

Beyond Desire ꝏꝏ½ **1994 (R)** Elvis Ray (Forsythe) is released after 14 years in prison and gets picked up by corvette-driving prison groupie and Las Vegas prostitute Rita (Wuhrer) but more than sex is on both their minds. **87m/C VHS.** William Forsythe, Kari Wuhrer, Leo Rossi, Sharon Farrell; ***D:*** Dominique Othenin-Girard; ***W:*** Dale Trevillion; ***M:*** Mark Holden.

Beyond Dream's Door ꝏ **1988** A young, All-American college student's childhood nightmares come back to haunt him, making dreams a horrifying reality. **86m/C VHS.** Nick Baldasare, Rick Kesler, Susan Pinsky, Norm Singer; ***D:*** Jay Woelfel.

Beyond Erotica **1979** After being cut out of his father's will, a sadistic young man takes out his rage on his mother and a peasant girl. **90m/C VHS.** David Hemmings, Alida Valli, Andrea Rau; ***D:*** Jose Maria Forque.

Beyond Evil woof! **1980 (R)** Relatively dim-witted newlywed couple moves into an old island mansion despite rumors that the house is haunted. Sure enough, wife George becomes possessed by the vengeful spirit of a woman murdered 200 years earlier, and a reign of pointless terror begins. Poor rip-off of hybrid Amityville/Exorcist paranormality. **98m/C VHS.** John Saxon, Lynda Day George, Michael Dante, Mario Milano; ***D:*** Herb Freed; ***W:*** Herb Freed; ***M:*** Pino Donaggio.

Beyond Fear ꝏꝏ½ *Au-Dela de la Peur* **1975** Compelling drama about a man forced to aid a gang in robbery while they hold his wife and son captive. **92m/C VHS.** *FR IT* Michael Boquet, Michel Constantin, Marilu Tolo, Paul Crauchet, Michel Creton, Moustache, Jean-Pierre Darras; ***D:*** Yannick Andrei; ***W:*** Yannick Andrei; ***C:*** Pierre Petit; ***M:*** Alain Goraguer.

Beyond Fear ꝏꝏ½ **1993 (R)** Tipper Taylor (Lesseos) is a wilderness tour guide who's also a martial arts expert. This is going to come in handy when her tour group is stalked by two men who are after a videotape innocently filmed by someone in Tipper's group. It seems the tape shows the men committing a murder. **84m/C VHS.** Mimi Lesseos.

Beyond Forgiveness ꝏꝏ½ **1994 (R)** Basic maverick cop goes after his brother's killers and winds up involved in an international black market in transplantable human organs. **95m/C VHS.** Thomas Ian Griffith, Rutger Hauer, John Rhys-Davies; ***D:*** Bob Misiorowski; ***W:*** Charles Cohen.

Beyond Innocence ꝏ **1987** A 17-year-old lusts after a mature married woman. Ostensibly based on Raymond Radiguet's "Devil in the Flesh." **87m/C VHS.** Keith Smith, Katia Caballero, John Morris; ***D:*** Scott Murray; ***C:*** Andrzej Bartkowiak.

Beyond Justice ꝏꝏ **1992 (PG-13)** High action-adventure with the prolific Hauer starring as an ex-CIA agent who is hired to rescue the kidnapped son of a beautiful executive. **113m/C VHS.** *IT* Rutger Hauer, Carol Alt, Omar Sharif, Elliott Gould, Kabir Bedi, David Flosi, Brett Halsey, Peter Sands; ***D:*** Duccio Tessari; ***W:*** Sergio Donati, Luigi Montefiore; ***C:*** Giorgio Di Battista; ***M:*** Ennio Morricone.

Beyond Obsession ꝏꝏ **1982** The strange relationship between a political prisoner, his daughter, and her obsession with a mysterious American is provocatively explored. **116m/C VHS.** *IT* Marcello Mastroianni, Elenora Giorgi, Tom Berenger, Michel Piccoli; ***D:*** Liliana Cavani.

Beyond Rangoon ꝏꝏ½ **1995 (R)** Sisters Laura (Arquette) and Andy (McDormand) Bowman travel to Burma to unwind, only to have political unrest and a repressive regime spoil the holiday. Dr. Laura (yeah, right) loses her passport and must flee from trigger-happy soldiers with a political dissident (Ko, a real-life exiled Burmese activist) who befriends her. The search for her passport soon becomes a imperiled trek of survival and self-discovery. Tense, well-crafted action sequences hint at a potential for excitement and intrigue; too bad Arquette isn't the least bit convincing. Filmed in Malaysia. **100m/C VHS.** Patricia Arquette, Frances McDormand, Spalding Gray, U Aung Ko, Victor Slezak; ***D:*** John Boorman; ***W:*** Alex Lasker, Bill Rubenstein; ***C:*** John Seale; ***M:*** Hans Zimmer.

Beyond Reason ꝏ **1977** A psychologist uses unorthodox methods by treating the criminally insane with dignity and respect. **88m/C VHS.** Telly Savalas, Laura Johnson, Diana Muldaur, Marvin Laird, Priscilla Barnes; ***D:*** Telly Savalas; ***C:*** John A. Alonzo.

Beyond Reasonable Doubt ꝏꝏ½ **1980** Chilling true-life murder mystery which shattered the peaceful quiet of a small New Zealand town and eventually divided the country. An innocent farmer (Hargreaves) was convicted of a grisly double murder based on evidence planted by a local cop (Hemmings, in a superb role). It wasn't until Yallop's book questioned the facts of the case that it was reopened. Yallop also wrote the screenplay. **127m/C VHS.** *NZ* David Hemmings, John Hargreaves, Martyn Sanderson, Grant Tilly, Diana Rowan, Ian Watkin; ***D:*** John Laing; ***W:*** David Yallop.

Beyond Redemption ꝏꝏ **1999 (R)** A serial killer goes after highly respected targets, crucifying his victims, and Detective Smith is in charge of catching the bad guy. It all hinges on faith—and whose is stronger. **97m/C VHS, DVD.** *CA* Andrew McCarthy, Michael Ironside, Jayne Heitmeyer, Suzy Joachim; ***D:*** Chris Angel. **VIDEO**

Beyond Silence ꝏꝏ *Jenseits der Stille* **1996 (PG-13)** Lara (Trieb/Testud), the daughter of deaf parents, has been their guide to the outside world since childhood. When her Aunt Clarissa (Canonica) gives her a clarinet, it opens Lara's life to music and gives her the courage to move beyond the limits of her family. German with subtitles. **109m/C VHS.** *GE* Sylvie Testud, Tatjana Trieb, Howie Seago, Emmanuelle Laborit, Sibylle Canonica; ***D:*** Caroline Link; ***W:*** Caroline Link; ***C:*** Gernot Roll; ***M:*** Niki Reiser.

Beyond Suspicion ꝏ½ *Auggie Rose* **2000** John C. Nolan Jr. (Goldblum) is an insurance bigshot, who stops by the neighborhood liquor store and gets caught up in an armed robbery. The store clerk, Auggie Rose (Coates), gets killed and Nolan feels responsible. He learns Auggie is fresh out of prison and is expecting to meet his prison pen pal, Lucy (Heche). John meets Lucy instead and doesn't correct her assumption that he's Auggie. In fact, John decides to just give up his old life and take up with Lucy. Film's got an intriguing premise that never develops. **108m/C VHS, DVD, Wide.** Jeff Goldblum, Anne Heche, Timothy Olyphant, Nancy Travis, Richard T. Jones, Kim Coates, Joe Santos; ***D:*** Matthew Tabak; ***W:*** Matthew Tabak; ***C:*** Adam Kimmel; ***M:*** Don Harper, Mark Mancina. **VIDEO**

Beyond the Bermuda Triangle ꝏ½ **1975** Unfortunate and flat TV flick. Businessman MacMurray, now retired, doesn't have enough to do. He begins an investigation of the mysterious geometric island area when his friends and fiancee disappear. Silly. **78m/C VHS.** Fred MacMurray, Sam Groom, Donna Mills, Suzanne Reed, Dana Plato, Woody Woodbury; ***D:*** William A. Graham. **TV**

Beyond the Call ꝏꝏ½ **1996 (R)** Connecticut housewife Pam O'Brien (Spacek) learns from the paper that her high-school sweetheart Russell Cates (Strathairn) is on death row in South Carolina for killing a cop and his execution has been scheduled within weeks. Pam writes Russell and then hears from his sister Fran (Wright), who urges Pam to visit her brother and get him to apply for a clemency hearing. Husband Keith (Howard) becomes angry and alarmed as Pam gets more involved with Russell and his case, which hinges on Russell's Vietnam experiences and post-traumatic shock syndrome. **101m/C VHS.** David Strathairn, Sissy Spacek, Arliss Howard, Janet Wright; ***D:*** Tony Bill; ***W:*** Doug Magee; ***C:*** Jean Lepine; ***M:*** George S. Clinton. **CABLE**

Beyond the Call of Duty ꝏ½ **1992 (R)** Renegade U.S. Army Commander Len Jordan (Vincent) is after a particularly deadly Vietcong enemy. Aided by the head of a special forces naval unit he tracks his quarry through the notorious Mekong River Delta. But Jordan's mission may be hindered, both personally and professionally, by a beautiful American journalist after a hot story. **92m/C VHS.** Jan-Michael Vincent, Eb Lottimer, Jillian McWhirter; ***D:*** Cirio H. Santiago.

Beyond the Clouds ꝏꝏ½ *Par-dela les Nuages* **1995** A wandering film director (Malkovich) muses on four stories of life and obsession, including unconsummated relationships, romantic triangles, and even violence. Based on sketches from Antonioni's book "That Bowling Alley on the Tiber." English, French, and Italian with subtitles. **109m/C VHS, DVD, Wide.** *IT GE FR* John Malkovich, Marcello Mastroianni, Sophie Marceau, Fanny Ardant, Vincent Perez, Jean Reno, Jeanne Moreau, Irene Jacob, Peter Weller, Chiara Caselli, Ines Sastre, Kim Rossi-Stuart; ***D:*** Michelangelo Antonioni, Wim Wenders; ***W:*** Michelangelo Antonioni, Wim Wenders, Tonino Guerra; ***C:*** Robby Muller, Alfio Contini; ***M:*** Van Morrison, Lucio Dalla, Laurent Petitgrand.

Beyond the Door woof! *Beyond Obsession; Chi Sei; The Devil within Her* **1975 (R)** San Francisco woman finds herself pregnant with a demonic child. One of the first "Exorcist" ripoffs; skip this one and go right to the sequel, "Beyond the Door 2." In Italian; dubbed. **97m/C VHS.** *IT* Juliet Mills, Richard Johnson, David Colin Jr.; ***D:*** Richard Barrett, Oliver (Ovidio Assonitis) Hellman; ***W:*** Richard Barrett, Oliver (Ovidio Assonitis) Hellman.

Beyond the Door 3 woof! **1991 (R)** Fool American students in Yugoslavia board a hellish locomotive which speeds them toward a satanic ritual. Demonic disaster-movie stuff (with poor miniatures) isn't as effective as the on-location filming; Serbian scenery and crazed peasants impart an eerie pagan aura. What this has to do with earlier "Beyond the Door" movies only the marketing boys can say. Some dialogue in Serbo-Croat with English subtitles. **94m/C VHS.** Mary Kohnert, Sarah Conway Ciminera, William Geiger, Renee Rancourt, Alex Vitale, Victoria Zinny, Savina Gersak, Bo Svenson; ***D:*** Jeff Kwitny.

Beyond the Forest ꝏ½ **1949** Camp diva Davis, in her last role for Warner Bros., really turns on the histrionics as a big-city gal married to a small-town guy (Cotten) and bored out of her mind. Although the most memorable line, "What a dump," has become larger-than-life, the film itself is rather small and muddled (interestingly, Vidor directed "The Fountainhead" the same year.) A trashy melodrama full of ennui, envy, unwanted pregnancy, and murder, it's definitely high on camp and low on art. **96m/B VHS.** Bette Davis, Joseph Cotten, David Brian, Ruth Roman,

Minor Watson, Regis Toomey; ***D:*** King Vidor; ***C:*** Robert Burks; ***M:*** Max Steiner.

Beyond the Law 🦴🦴 *Bloodsilver; Al Di La Della Legge* **1968** Spaghetti western with Van Cleef as the too smart bad guy. He becomes sheriff, picks up the stack of silver at the depot, and disappears. Humorous and clever, with fine location photography. **91m/C VHS.** *IT* Lee Van Cleef, Antonio (Tony) Sabato, Lionel Stander, Bud Spencer, Gordon Mitchell, Ann Smyrner; ***D:*** Giorgio Stegani.

Beyond the Law 🦴½ *Fixing the Shadow* **1992 (R)** Ex-undercover cop Danny Saxon (Sheen) is recruited by the FBI to infiltrate a biker gang involved in drugs and gun smuggling. But Saxon finds himself drawn too close into the unconventional biker lifestyle and into an uneasy friendship with leader Blood (Madsen). Clumsy and exploitative. **101m/C VHS, DVD.** Michael Berry, Charlie Sheen, Michael Madsen, Linda Fiorentino, Courtney B. Vance, Leon Rippy, Rip Torn; ***D:*** Larry Ferguson; ***W:*** Larry Ferguson; ***C:*** Robert Stevens; ***M:*** Cory Lerios, John D'Andrea.

Beyond the Limit 🦴🦴½ *The Honorary Consul* **1983 (R)** The story of an intense and darkly ominous love triangle which takes place in the South American coastal city of Corrientes. Based on Graham Greene's novel "The Honorary Consul." **103m/C VHS.** Michael Caine, Richard Gere, Bob Hoskins, Elpidia Carrillo; ***D:*** John MacKenzie; ***W:*** Christopher Hampton; ***C:*** Phil Meheux.

Beyond the Next Mountain 🦴 **1987 (PG)** A missionary in China attempts to convert all those he meets. Thin plot and marginal acting will likely make viewers fall asleep. **97m/C VHS.** Alberto Isaac, Jon Lormer, Bennett Ohta, Richard Lineback, Edward Ashley, Barry Foster; ***D:*** James F. Collier, Rolf Forsberg.

Beyond the Poseidon Adventure 🦴 **1979 (PG)** A sequel to the 1972 film in which salvage teams and ruthless looting vandals compete for access to the sunken ocean liner. Sinking ships should be abandoned. **115m/C VHS.** Michael Caine, Sally Field, Telly Savalas, Peter Boyle, Jack Warden, Slim Pickens, Shirley Knight, Shirley Jones, Karl Malden, Mark Harmon; ***D:*** Irwin Allen; ***C:*** Joseph Biroc.

Beyond the Rockies 🦴🦴½ **1932** Keene and a group of cowboys battle cattle rustlers in this action-packed sagebrush saga. Solid script with good direction by Allen. **55m/B VHS.** Tom (George Duryea) Keene, Rochelle Hudson, Ernie Adams, Julian Rivero, Hank Bell, Tom London; ***D:*** Fred Allen; ***W:*** John P. McCarthy.

Beyond the Silhouette 🦴 *Ultimate Desires* **1990** It starts out as another sleazy video sex thriller, as the lawyer heroine discovers her sensuality and poses a lot in her underclothes. Then in the third act it become a hyper-paranoid political-conspiracy assassination-o-rama. Pretty weird junk. **90m/C VHS.** *CA* Tracy Scoggins, Marc Singer, Brion James; ***D:*** Lloyd A. Simandl.

Beyond the Stars 🦴 **1989** A sci-fi adventure directed by the author of "Cocoon," wherein a whiz-kid investigates the NASA cover-up of a deadly accident that occurred on the moon during the Apollo 11 landing. Unfortunately, the interesting cast can't make up for the script. **94m/C VHS.** Martin Sheen, Christian Slater, Olivia D'Abo, F. Murray Abraham, Robert Foxworth, Sharon Stone; ***D:*** David Saperstein.

Beyond the Time Barrier 🦴🦴½ **1960** Air Force test pilot gets more than he bargained for when his high speed plane carries him into the future. There he sees the ravages of an upcoming plague, to which he must return. **75m/B VHS.** Robert Clarke, Darlene Tompkins, Arianne Arden, Vladimir Sokoloff; ***D:*** Edgar G. Ulmer.

Beyond the Trail **1926** One of Bill Patton's most entertaining and funny films. In this comedic Western adventure he must face Black Mike and his gang and rescue Mary from their clutches. **50m/C VHS.** Bill(y) (William Patten) Patton, Sheldon Lewis, Stuart Holmes, Eric Wayne, Janet Dawn, Clara Horton, James F. Fulton; ***D:*** Al(bert) Herman.

Beyond the Valley of the Dolls 🦴🦴½ *Hollywood Vixens* **1970 (NC-17)** Sleazy, spirited non-sequel to "Valley of the Dolls." Meyer ("Faster, Pussycat! Kill! Kill!") directed this Hollywood parody ("BVD," as it came to be known) about an all-girl rock combo and their search for stardom. Labeled the first "exploitation horror camp musical"—how can you pass that up? Screenplay by film critic Ebert, from an original story by Ebert and Meyer. Mondo trasho. **109m/C VHS.** Dolly Reed, Cynthia Myers, Marcia McBroom, John Lazar, Michael Blodgett, David Gurian, Erica Gavin, Edy Williams, Phyllis E. Davis, Harrison Page, Duncan McLeod, James Iglehart, Charles Napier, Haji, Pam Grier; ***D:*** Russ Meyer; ***W:*** Roger Ebert; ***C:*** Fred W. Koenekamp; ***M:*** The Strawberry Alarm Clock, Stu Phillips.

Beyond the Walls 🦴🦴½ *Meachorei Hasoragim* **1984 (R)** The opposing factions of a hellish Israeli prison unite to beat the system. Brutal with good characterizations. Available in both subtitled and dubbed versions. **104m/C VHS.** *IS* Arnon Zadok, Muhamad Bakri; ***D:*** Uri Barbash; ***W:*** Benny Barbash. Venice Film Fest. '85: Film.

Beyond Therapy 🦴½ **1986 (R)** A satire on modern psychotherapy, from the play by Christopher Durang, about a confused, crazily neurotic couple and their respective, and not any saner, analysts. Unfortunately, comes off as disjointed and confused. **93m/C VHS.** Jeff Goldblum, Tom Conti, Julie Hagerty, Glenda Jackson, Christopher Guest; ***D:*** Robert Altman; ***W:*** Robert Altman.

Beyond Tomorrow 🦴🦴 **1940** Young romance is guided from the spirit world during the Christmas season, as two "ghosts" come back to help young lovers. **84m/B VHS, DVD.** Richard Carlson, Sir C. Aubrey Smith, Jean Parker, Charles Winninger, Harry Carey Sr., Maria Ouspenskaya, Rod La Rocque; ***D:*** Edward Sutherland; ***W:*** Adele Comandini; ***C:*** Lester White.

Bhaji on the Beach 🦴🦴½ **1994 (R)** Amusing comedy-drama about a group of Indian women who organize a bus outing from Birmingham to the seaside resort town of Blackpool. They range from sari-clad elders to feminist Gen Xers and a couple of teenagers looking for romance. There's bonding and gossiping and secrets galore before the story is tidily wrapped up. **100m/C VHS.** *GB* Kim Vithana, Jimmi Harkishin, Sarita Khajuria, Mo Sesay, Lalita Ahmed, Shaheen Khan, Zohra Segal; ***D:*** Gurinder Chadha; ***W:*** Meera Syal, Gurinder Chadha; ***C:*** John Kenway; ***M:*** John Altman, Craig Preuss.

Bhowani Junction 🦴🦴 **1956** A half-Indian, half-English woman is torn between her country and the British officer she loves in post-colonial India. Great cinematography. Based on a book by John Masters. **110m/C VHS, Wide.** Ava Gardner, Stewart Granger, Bill Travers, Abraham Sofaer, Francis Matthews, Marne Maitland, Peter Illing, Edward Chapman, Freda Jackson, Lionel Jeffries; ***D:*** George Cukor; ***C:*** Frederick A. (Freddie) Young; ***M:*** Miklos Rozsa.

The Bible 🦴 **1966** Bloated, even by religious epic standards, Huston's drama covers the first 22 chapters of Genesis. So you get the Creation, Adam and Eve, Noah and the ark, the flood, the Tower of Babel, and Abraham, among other would-be spectacles. **174m/C VHS, DVD, Wide.** Michael Parks, Ulla Bergryd, Richard Harris, Stephen Boyd, George C. Scott, Ava Gardner, Peter O'Toole, Franco Nero, John Huston; ***D:*** John Huston; ***W:*** Christopher Fry, Vittorio Bonicelli; ***C:*** Giuseppe Rotunno; ***M:*** Toshiro Mayuzumi; ***Nar:*** John Huston.

The Bible and Gun Club 🦴🦴 **1996** Foul-mouthed look at the wasted lives of five middle age traveling salesmen who sell, you guessed it, bibles and guns. There's a turf war between the Anaheim, CA and the Las Vegas branches of the club, there's a sales convention, the salesmen try to sell their goods to the real-life denizens of a poor trailer park, there's a porn shoot. There's a number of shootouts and to say the least, the salesmen are not politically correct—they're racist, sexist losers. It's depressing and disturbing and highlighted by some spot-on acting. Harris' debut feature. **87m/B VHS.** Andy Kallok, Don Yanan, Julian Ott, Al Schuerman, Robert Blumenthal; ***D:*** Daniel J. Harris; ***W:*** Daniel J. Harris; ***C:*** Alex Vendler; ***M:*** Shawn Patterson.

Bicentennial Man 🦴🦴½ **1999 (PG)** Robin Williams is Andrew, a domestic robot of the near-future. When he's purchased by the Martin family, they notice that he's different than most robots. He exhibits compassion, as well as other human qualities. Led by Sir, the father (Niell) they help to further Andrew's growth. As time goes on, Andrew continues to develop past his programming, and eventually seeks his freedom and the pursuit of a more human form. The first hour deals mostly with a very leisurely character development, with some amusing moments. The problems occur when the film turns to the serious questions of immortality, defining humanity, and the rights of artificial entities. Director Columbus opts for sentiment and empty platitudes instead of exploring the questions the film raises. **131m/C VHS, DVD, Wide.** Robin Williams, Embeth Davidtz, Sam Neill, Wendy Crewson, Hallie Kate Eisenberg, Oliver Platt, Stephen (Steve) Root, Lynne Thigpen, Bradley Whitford, Kiersten Warren, John Michael Higgins, George D. Wallace; ***D:*** Chris Columbus; ***W:*** Nicholas Kazan; ***C:*** Phil Meheux; ***M:*** James Horner.

The Bicycle Thief 🦴🦴🦴🦴 *Ladri di Biciclette* **1948** A world classic and indisputable masterpiece about an Italian workman who finds a job, only to have the bike he needs for work stolen; he and his son search Rome for it. A simple story that seems to contain the whole of human experience, and the masterpiece of Italian neo-realism. Based on the book by Luigi Bartolini. In Italian with English subtitles. **90m/B VHS, DVD.** *IT* Lamberto Maggiorani, Lianella Carell, Enzo Staiola, Elena Altieri, Vittorio Antonucci, Gino Saltamerenda, Fausto Guerzoni; ***D:*** Vittorio De Sica; ***W:*** Vittorio De Sica, Cesare Zavattini; ***C:*** Carlo Montuori; ***M:*** Alessandro Cicognini. Oscars '49: Foreign Film; British Acad. '49: Film; Golden Globes '50: Foreign Film; Natl. Bd. of Review '49: Director (De Sica); N.Y. Film Critics '49: Foreign Film.

Big 🦴🦴🦴½ **1988 (PG)** 13-year-old Josh makes a wish at a carnival fortuneteller to be "big." When he wakes up the next morning he finds that he suddenly won't fit into his clothes and his mother doesn't recognize him. Until he finds a cure, he must learn to live in the adult world—complete with job (in a toy firm), Manhattan apartment, and romance. Perkins is wonderful as a cynical fellow employee who warms to the new guy's naivete, while Hanks is totally believable as the little boy inside a man's body. Marshall directs with authority and the whole thing clicks from the beginning. **98m/C VHS, DVD.** Tom Hanks, Elizabeth Perkins, John Heard, Robert Loggia, Jared Rushton, David Moscow, Jon Lovitz, Mercedes Ruehl; ***D:*** Penny Marshall; ***W:*** Gary Ross; ***C:*** Michael Ballhaus; ***M:*** Howard Shore. Golden Globes '89: Actor—Mus./Comedy (Hanks); L.A. Film Critics '88: Actor (Hanks).

Big and Hairy 🦴½ **1998** When Picasso Dewlap and his family move from Chicago to a small town, the kid has trouble making friends (no wonder with that name). Then he joins the school basketball team. However, Picasso sucks. But after he meets a teen bigfoot (nicknamed Ed) who just happens to be a natural at hoops, Picasso and his hairy friend become team heroes. Based on the book by Brian Daly. **94m/C VHS.** Richard Thomas, Donnelly Rhodes, Robert Karl Burke, Trevor Jones, Chilton Crane; ***D:*** Philip Spink; ***C:*** Peter Benison; ***M:*** Daryl Bennett, Jim Guttridge. CABLE

Big Bad John 🦴½ **1990 (PG-13)** Some good ol' boys ride around in trucks as they get into a variety of shootouts. The soundtrack includes music by Willie Nelson, The Charlie Daniels Band, and others. **91m/C VHS.** Jimmy Dean, Ned Beatty, Jack Elam, Bo Hopkins, Romy Windsor, Doug English, John Dennis Johnston, Anne Lockhart, Jeffery Osterhage, Jerry Potter, Red Steagall; ***D:*** Burt Kennedy; ***W:*** Joseph Berry; ***C:*** Ken Lamkin; ***M:*** Ken Sutherland.

Big Bad Mama 🦴🦴½ **1974 (R)** Tough and sexy machine-gun toting mother moves her two nubile daughters out of Texas during the Depression, and they all turn to robbing banks as a means of support while creating sharp testosterone increases among the local men. "Wild Palm" Dickinson has notable nude scene with Captain Kirk. "Big Bad Mama 2" arrived some 13 years later. **83m/C VHS, DVD.** Angie Dickinson, William Shatner, Tom Skerritt, Susan Sennett, Robbie Lee, Sally Kirkland, Noble Willingham, Royal Dano, Dick Miller, Joan Prather, Tom Signorelli; ***D:*** Steve Carver; ***W:*** William W. Norton Sr., Frances Doel; ***C:*** Bruce Logan; ***M:*** David Grisman.

Big Bad Mama 2 🦴½ **1987 (R)** Belated Depression-era sequel to the 1974 Roger Corman gangster film, where the pistol-packin' matriarch battles a crooked politician with the help of her two daughters. **85m/C VHS, DVD.** Angie Dickinson, Robert Culp, Danielle Brisebois, Julie McCullough, Bruce Glover, Jeff Yagher, Jacque Lynn Colton, Ebbe Roe Smith, Charles Cyphers; ***D:*** Jim Wynorski; ***W:*** Jim Wynorski, R.J. Robertson; ***C:*** Robert New; ***M:*** Chuck Cirino.

Big Bear 🦴🦴½ **1998** In the 1880s, Cheif Big Bear (Tootoosis) refuses to surrender Cree ancestral lands to settlers for fear of the many broken promises made by the government. So Canadian army troops surround the Cree in order to starve them into submission. Cree warriors decide to stage an attack against the settlers that only brings the troops down on them. **190m/C VHS, DVD.** *CA* Tantoo Cardinal, Gordon Tootoosis, Ken Charlette; ***D:*** Gil Cardinal. TV

The Big Bet 🦴🦴 **1985 (R)** High school sex comedy about a guy who is challenged by the school bully to get the gorgeous new girl into bed. Energetic romp is for adults. **90m/C VHS.** Sylvia Kristel, Kimberly Evenson, Ron Thomas; ***D:*** Bert I. Gordon.

The Big Bird Cage 🦴🦴 *Women's Penitentiary 2* **1972 (R)** Prison spoof sequel to "The Big Doll House." Horny females incarcerated in a rural jail decide to defy their homosexual guards and plan an escape. They are aided by revolutionaries led by a Brooklynese expatriate and his lover. **93m/C VHS, DVD.** Pam Grier, Sid Haig, Anitra Ford, Candice Roman, Teda Bracci, Carol Speed, Karen McKevic, Vic Diaz; ***D:*** Jack Hill; ***W:*** Jack Hill; ***C:*** F. Sacdalan; ***M:*** William Allen Castleman, William Loose.

The Big Blue 🦴½ *Le Grand Bleu* **1988 (PG)** Vapid, semi-true tale about competing free-divers, who descend deep into the big blue without the aid of any kind of breathing apparatus. Arquette is the ditz who makes them come up for air. **122m/C VHS, DVD, Wide.** Rosanna Arquette, Jean Reno, Jean-Marc Barr, Paul Shenar, Sergio Castellitto, Marc Duret, Griffin Dunne; ***D:*** Luc Besson; ***W:*** Luc Besson; ***C:*** Carlo Varini; ***M:*** Bill Conti. Cesar '89: Sound, Score.

Big Bluff 🦴🦴 *Worthy Deceivers* **1955** Disappointing result from an interesting premise; fatally ill woman finds love, but when she surprisingly recovers, her new husband decides to help her back along the path to death. Uneven and melodramatic. **70m/B VHS.** *SI* John Bromfield, Martha Vickers, Robert Hutton, Rosemary Bowe; ***D:*** W. Lee Wilder.

Big Boss 🦴½ *Mr. Scarface* **1977 (R)** A hoodlum climbs to the top of a crime syndicate. An Italian film previously titled "Mr. Scarface." **90m/C** *IT* Jack Palance, Edmund Purdom, Al Cliver, Harry Baer, Gisela Hahn; ***D:*** Fernando Di Leo.

The Big Brass Ring 🦴🦴½ **1999 (R)** Murky political drama based on an unproduced screenplay by Orson Welles. Ambitious William Blake Pellarin (Hurt) is a candidate for governor of Missouri but his ultimate goal is the presidency. However, an ugly scandal threatens his campaign, thanks to the appearance of Dr. Kimball Mennaker (Hawthorne), who's a little too close to the Pellarin family and knows about some skeletons even William isn't aware of. **104m/C VHS, DVD.** William Hurt, Nigel Hawthorne, Miranda Richardson, Irene Jacob, Jefferson Mays, Ewan Stewart, Ron Livingston, Gregg Henry; ***D:*** George Hickenlooper; ***W:*** George Hickenlooper, F.X. Feeney; ***C:*** Kramer Morgenthau; ***M:*** Thomas Morse.

The Big Brawl ½ 1980 (R) Chicago gangster recruits a martial arts expert to fight in a free-for-all match in Texas. **95m/C VHS.** Jackie Chan, Jose Ferrer, Mako, Rosalind Chao; ***D:*** Robert Clouse; ***W:*** Robert Clouse; ***M:*** Lalo Schifrin.

The Big Broadcast of 1938 ½ 1938 Fields is the owner of an ocean liner which he enters in a race. Supposedly, the ship can convert the electricity from radio broadcasts into power for the propellers. No, it doesn't make sense, as it's just an excuse for various radio stars to show off their routines in the ship's entertainment room. Hope, in his first feature, gets to sing his Oscar-winning signature tune "Thanks for the Memories." **94m/B VHS, DVD.** W.C. Fields, Martha Raye, Dorothy Lamour, Shirley Ross, Russell Hicks, Bob Hope, Ben Blue, Leif Erickson; ***D:*** Mitchell Leisen; ***W:*** Walter DeLeon, Francis Martin; ***C:*** Harry Fischbeck; ***M:*** Boris Morros, Ralph Rainger, Leo Robin. Oscars '38: Song ("Thanks for the Memories").

Big Brother Trouble ½ 2000 (G) Mitch (Suchenek) has always lived in the shadow of his big brother Sean (Hart), who's the star of the soccer team. But it's Mitch to the rescue when Sean is kidnapped to insure that his team loses the City Championship game. **88m/C VHS, DVD.** Michael Suchenek, Shad Hart, Lindsay Brooke, Mario Lopez, Bo Hopkins, Dick Van Patten; ***D:*** Ralph Portillo; ***W:*** Jeff Nimoy, Seth Walther; ***C:*** John Huneck; ***M:*** Steven Stern.

Big Bully 1995 (PG) David Leary (Moranis) is an aspiring novelist who moves back to the town where he was picked on as a kid. His son immediately starts bullying a smaller child, whose father happens to be Roscoe "Fang" Bigger (Arnold), David's former tormentor. The timid hen-pecked Roscoe's sadistic streak is awakened with the reappearance of his old prey, leading to a barrage of wet willies and indian burns. The slapstick quickly escalates to danger before all is tied up in a syrupy sweet ending. With Moranis playing the nerdy bespectacled underdog and Arnold playing the loud obnoxious guy (although that might not be acting), it may be time to call the typecasting cops. Don Knotts (looking very un-Barney-like) makes an appearance as the high school principal. **93m/C VHS, DVD.** Tom Arnold, Rick Moranis, Julianne Phillips, Don Knotts, Carol Kane, Jeffrey Tambor, Curtis Armstrong, Faith Prince, Tony Pierce, Blake Bashoff; ***D:*** Steve Miner; ***W:*** Mark Steven Johnson; ***C:*** Daryn Okada; ***M:*** David Newman. Golden Raspberries '96: Worst Actor (Arnold).

The Big Bus 1976 (PG) The wild adventures of the world's first nuclear-powered bus as it makes its maiden voyage from New York to Denver. Clumsy disaster-movie parody. **88m/C VHS.** Joseph Bologna, Stockard Channing, Ned Beatty, Ruth Gordon, Larry Hagman, John Beck, Jose Ferrer, Lynn Redgrave, Sally Kellerman, Stuart Margolin, Richard Mulligan, Howard Hesseman, Richard B. Shull, Rene Auberjonois, Bob (Robert) Dishy, Vic Tayback, Murphy Dunne; ***D:*** James Frawley; ***W:*** Lawrence J. Cohen, Fred Freeman; ***C:*** Harry Stradling Jr.; ***M:*** David Shire.

Big Business 1988 (PG) Strained high-concept comedy about two sets of identical twins, each played by Tomlin and Midler, mismatched at birth by a near-sighted country nurse. The city set of twins intends to buy out the factory where the country set of twins work. So the country twins march up to the big city to stop the sale and destruction of their beloved home. Both set of twins stay in the Plaza Hotel and zany consequences ensue. Essentially a one-joke outing with some funny moments, but talented comediennes Midler and Tomlin are somewhat wasted. Great technical effects. **98m/C VHS, 8mm.** Bette Midler, Lily Tomlin, Fred Ward, Edward Herrmann, Michele Placido, Barry Primus, Michael Gross, Mary Gross, Daniel Gerroll, Roy Brocksmith; ***D:*** Jim Abrahams; ***C:*** Dean Cundey.

Big Business Girl 1931 Less than remarkable comedy starring Young as a corporate climber who must dodge her boss' advances and save her troubled marriage when her jazz singer husband is called away to perform in Paris. Based on a story by Patricia Reilly and Harold N. Swanson. **72m/B VHS.** Loretta Young, Frank Albertson, Ricardo Cortez, Joan Blondell, Dorothy Christy; ***D:*** William A. Seiter; ***W:*** Robert Lord.

The Big Bust Out woof! 1973 (R) Several female convicts escape from prison only to be sold into slavery and face additional torture. Nothing redeeming about this exploitative film. **75m/C VHS.** Vonetta McGee, Monica Taylor, Linda Fox, Karen Carter, Gordon Mitchell; ***D:*** Karen Carter.

Big Calibre 1935 A rancher is inches away from being lynched for his dad's murder before he is found to be innocent. **59m/B VHS.** Bob Steele, Bill Quinn, Earl Dwire, Peggy Campbell, John Elliott, Georgia O'Dell; ***D:*** Robert North Bradbury.

The Big Cat 1949 Mountain valley in Utah is ravaged by a cougar, while two ranchers fuss and feud. Big cat, bickering, help make okay adventure. **75m/C VHS.** Lon (Bud) McCallister, Peggy Ann Garner, Preston Foster, Forrest Tucker; ***D:*** Phil Karlson; ***C:*** William Howard Greene.

Big Chase 1954 A rookie cop chases down a mob of payroll thieves in this early action film. **60m/B VHS.** Glenn Langan, Adele Jergens, Douglas Kennedy, Jim Davis, Jack Daly, Phil Arnold, Wheaton Chambers, Lon Chaney Jr.; ***D:*** Arthur Hilton; ***W:*** Fred Freiberger.

The Big Chill ½ 1983 (R) Seven former '60s radicals, now coming upon middle age and middle-class affluence, reunite following an eighth friend's suicide and use the occasion to re-examine their past relationships and commitments. A beautifully acted, immensely enjoyable ballad to both the counter-culture and its Yuppie descendants. Great period music. Kevin Costner is the dead man whose scenes never made it to the big screen. **108m/C VHS, DVD, 8mm, Wide.** Tom Berenger, Glenn Close, Jeff Goldblum, William Hurt, Kevin Kline, Mary Kay Place, Meg Tilly, JoBeth Williams; ***D:*** Lawrence Kasdan; ***W:*** Lawrence Kasdan, Barbara Benedek; ***C:*** John Bailey. Writers Guild '83: Orig. Screenplay.

The Big City *Mahanagar* 1963 When debts threaten to overwhelm the Mazumdar family, Arati does the unthinkable and gets a job as a saleswoman. She soon begins to realize she not only likes to work but enjoys the freedom and respect her job brings. Bengali with subtitles. **131m/B VHS.** *IN* Anil Chatterjee, Majhabi Mukherjee, Vicky Redwood, Haren Chatterjee; ***D:*** Satyajit Ray; ***W:*** Satyajit Ray; ***C:*** Subrata Mitra; ***M:*** Satyajit Ray.

Big City Blues 1999 (R) One long night in the lives of hit men Connor (Reynolds) and Hudson (Forsythe) as they get mixed up with the plans of a hooker (Cates). **94m/C VHS, DVD.** Burt Reynolds, William Forsythe, Georgina Cates, Giancarlo Esposito, Roger Floyd, Balthazar Getty, Arye Gross, Donovan Leitch, Roxana Zal, Amy Lyndon, Jad Mager; ***D:*** Clive Fleury; ***W:*** Clive Fleury; ***C:*** David Bridges; ***M:*** Tomas San Miguel.

The Big Clock 1948 George Stroud (Milland) is the editor of the successful Crimeways magazine, owned by tyrannical publisher Earl Janoth (Laughton). Forced to miss a vacation with his wife Georgette (O'Sullivan), George winds up spending time with lovely Pauline (Johnson), whom he inadvertently discovers is the boss' mistress. Pauline's murdered and George is quick to realize all the clues are deliberately pointed in his direction. Classic crime melodrama adapted from Kenneth Fearing's novel. Remade as "No Way Out" (1987). **95m/B VHS.** Ray Milland, Charles Laughton, Maureen O'Sullivan, George Macready, Rita Johnson, Dan Tobin, Elsa Lanchester, Harry (Henry) Morgan; ***D:*** John Farrow; ***W:*** Jonathan Latimer; ***C:*** John Seitz; ***M:*** Victor Young.

Big Combo 1955 A gangster's ex-girlfriend helps a cop to smash a crime syndicate. Focuses on the relationship between Wilde's cop and the gangster Conte in an effective film noir, with some scenes of torture that were ahead of their time. **87m/B VHS, DVD.** Cornel Wilde, Richard Conte, Jean Wallace, Brian Donlevy, Earl Holliman, Lee Van Cleef, Helen Walker; ***D:*** Joseph H. Lewis; ***W:*** Philip Yordan; ***C:*** John Alton; ***M:*** David Raksin.

The Big Country ½ 1958 (R) Ex-sea captain Peck heads west to marry fiance Baker and live on her father's (Bickford) ranch. Peck immediately clashes with ranch foreman Heston and finds out there's a vicious feud with neighbor Ives. Then Peck decides he and Baker aren't meant to be and he falls for schoolmarm Simmons instead. It's too long but if you like sprawling western sagas, this one has its moments. **168m/C VHS, DVD, Wide.** Gregory Peck, Charlton Heston, Burl Ives, Jean Simmons, Carroll Baker, Chuck Connors, Charles Bickford; ***D:*** William Wyler; ***W:*** Jessamyn West, Robert Wyler, James R. Webb, Sy Bartlett, Robert Wilder; ***C:*** Franz Planer; ***M:*** Jerome Moross. Oscars '58: Support. Actor (Ives); Golden Globes '59: Support. Actor (Ives).

The Big Crimewave 1986 A cast of unknowns in a comedy about a loner who takes a bus to Kansas City (Kansas City?) to become a screenwriter, with comic adventures along the way. A feast of jabs at genre films. **80m/C VHS.** *CA* John Paizs, Eva Covacs, Darrel Baran; ***D:*** John Paizs.

Big Daddy 1999 (PG-13) Critic-proof film for Sandler's fans—the rest won't find anything to tempt them. He's 32-year-old slacker law-school grad Sonny Koufax, who's got a big Peter Pan complex, since he's incapable of assuming any adult responsibility. However, he does want to impress women, so he decides to go for the "awww" factor by becoming the guardian of his travelling-in-China roommate Kevin's (Stewart) heretofor unknown son, five-year-old Julian (Sprouse). He teaches the kid a number of disgusting traits and winds up bonding with the tyke (they have the same emotional IQ—how hard can it be?). **95m/C VHS, DVD.** Adam Sandler, Cole Sprouse, Dylan Sprouse, Joey Lauren Adams, Jon Stewart, Leslie Mann, Josh Mostel, Rob Schneider, Kristy Swanson, Joseph Bologna, Steve Buscemi; ***D:*** Dennis Dugan; ***W:*** Steve Franks, Tim Herlihy, Adam Sandler; ***C:*** Theo van de Sande; ***M:*** Teddy Castellucci. MTV Movie Awards '00: Comedic Perf. (Sandler); Golden Raspberries '99: Worst Actor (Sandler).

The Big Day *We Met on the Vineyard* 1999 (R) Sara (Margulies) is supposed to be getting married. She shows up at the church but groom John (Sergel) is a no-show after his knucklehead brother Zack (Rohner) confesses to an indiscretion that leaves John with big doubts about the marriage thing. So the family starts to panic and the wedding party tries to find the groom and it's chaos everywhere you go. **88m/C VHS, DVD.** Julianna Margulies, Ivan Sergei, Clayton Rohner, Dixie Carter, Kevin Tighe, Adrian Pasdar, Kathleen York, Andrew Buckley, Nancy Banks; ***D:*** Ian McCrudden; ***W:*** Andrew Buckley, Nancy Banks; ***C:*** Tony Cucchiari.

Big Deadly Game ½ 1954 A vacationing American gets caught up in a complicated espionage plot by helping a mysterious wartime buddy. **63m/B VHS.** Lloyd Bridges, Simone Silva, Finlay Currie; ***D:*** Daniel Birt.

Big Deal on Madonna Street ½ *The Usual Unidentified Thieves; I Soliti Ignoti; Persons Unknown* 1958 Peppe (Gassman) is a bungling thief who leads a band of equally inept crooks who plan to make themselves very rich when they attempt to rob a jewelry store on Madonna Street. Their elaborate plans cause numerous (and hilarious) disasters. Italian with subtitles. Remade in 1984 as "Crackers." **90m/B VHS, DVD.** *IT* Marcello Mastroianni, Vittorio Gassman, Claudia Cardinale, Renato Salvatori, Memmo Carotenuto, Toto, Rosanna Rory; ***D:*** Mario Monicelli; ***W:*** Mario Monicelli, Furio Scarpelli, Suso Cecchi D'Amico; ***C:*** Gianni Di Venanzo; ***M:*** Pierro Umiliani.

The Big Dis 1989 An interracial comedy about a young black soldier on a weekend pass who's looking for a willing sexual partner. His confidence is shattered when 12 possibilities turn him down. Feature debut of Eriksen and O'Brien. **88m/B VHS.** ***D:*** Gordon Eriksen, John O'Brien.

The Big Doll House *Women's Penitentiary 1; Women in Cages; Bamboo Dolls House* 1971 (R) Roger Corman-produced prison drama about a group of tormented female convicts who decide to break out. Features vintage Grier, and a caliber of women's-prison sleaziness that isn't equalled in today's films. **93m/C VHS, DVD.** Judy Brown, Roberta Collins, Pam Grier, Brooke Mills, Pat(ricia) Woodell, Sid Haig, Christiane Schmidtmer, Kathryn Loder, Jerry Frank, Charles Davis; ***D:*** Jack Hill; ***W:*** Don Spencer; ***C:*** Fred Conde; ***M:*** Les Baxter, Hall Daniels.

The Big Easy ½ 1987 (R) A terrific thriller. Slick New Orleans detective Remy McSwain (Quaid, oozing charm and a cornball accent) uncovers a heroin-based mob war while romancing uptight assistant DA Anne Osborne (Barkin, all banked fire) who's investigating corruption on the police force. An easy, Cajun-flavored mystery, a fast-moving action-comedy, a very sexy romance, and a serious exploration of the dynamics of corruption. **101m/C VHS, DVD.** Dennis Quaid, Ellen Barkin, Ned Beatty, John Goodman, Ebbe Roe Smith, Charles Ludlam, Lisa Jane Persky, Tom O'Brien, Grace Zabriskie, Marc Lawrence; ***D:*** Jim McBride; ***W:*** Dan Petrie Jr.; ***C:*** Alfonso Beato; ***M:*** Brad Fiedel. Ind. Spirit '88: Actor (Quaid).

Big Eden ½ 2000 (PG-13) Sweet-natured gay romance says you can go home again. Henry Hart (Gross) is an artist, living in New York, who returns to the small Montana town of Big Eden when his grandfather Sam (Coe) has a stroke. Henry has never admitted to anyone in his hometown that he's gay although it's pretty clear to his quirky neighbors, including the guys who hang out at the post office/general store, which is run by shy Native American Pike Dexter (Schweig), who will display some hidden talents on Henry's behalf. Henry is thrilled to discover his first crush, Dean (DeKay), is also back in town but he's looking for love in the wrong person. A happy ending is a comforting thing. **118m/C VHS, DVD.** Arye Gross, Eric Schweig, George Coe, Tim DeKay, Louise Fletcher, Nan Martin, O'Neal Compton, Corinne Bohrer, Veanne Cox; ***D:*** Thomas Bezucha; ***W:*** Thomas Bezucha; ***C:*** Rob Sweeney; ***M:*** Joseph Conlan.

The Big Empty 1998 Lloyd Matthews (writer McManus) is a private eye who's burned out on divorce work when he's hired by a suspicious wife (Goldwasser) to find the truth about her too-good-to-be true husband (Bryan). Comparisons to Coppola's "The Conversation" are not out of place. This one's a solid sleeper. **93m/C VHS, DVD.** James McManus, Pablo Bryant, Ellen Goldwasser, H.M. Wynant; ***D:*** Jack Perez; ***W:*** James McManus; ***C:*** Shawn Maurer; ***M:*** Jean-Michael Michenaud.

The Big Fall 1996 (R) L.A. private investigator Blaize Rybeck (Howell) is hired by mystery babe Emma (Ward) to find her brother, Kenny, a pilot. Blaize meets some of Kenny's thrill-seeking friends at the airfield and draws the suspicious interest of FBI agent Wilcox (Applegate). Seems Kenny was mixed up in some shady dealings that get both his sister and her nosy P.I. into trouble. **94m/C VHS.** C. Thomas Howell, Sophie Ward, Jeff Kober, Justin Lazard, Titus Welliver, William Applegate Jr.; ***D:*** C. Thomas Howell; ***W:*** William Applegate Jr.; ***C:*** Jurgen Baum.

Big Fat Liar 2002 (PG) The boy who cried wolf goes to Hollywood in search of Marty Wolf (Giamatti), the unscrupulous movie producer who stole his short story. As nobody believes his far-out tale of being ripped off by Hollywood, notorious liar Jason Shepherd (Muniz) also makes sure to bring along a witness to his pursuit, in the form of his friend Kaylee (Bynes). Pulling an array of inspired pranks, the teens zestfully set about dismantling the sanity of Wolf, to the delight, and sometimes with the aid of, some of his many enemies. Talented small-screen star Muniz and his co-star Bynes make this a likeable, though not especially inspired, broad comedy with Giamatti mugging up a storm. Their romp through Universal Studios, especially, lets you know who's really behind this mostly entertaining movie for the pre-teen set. **87m/C VHS,**

DVD. *US* Frankie Muniz, Paul Giamatti, Amanda Bynes, Amanda Detmer, Donald Adeosun Faison, Lee Majors, Sandra Oh, Russell Hornsby, Christine Tucci, Sean O'Bryan, Amy Hill, Michael Bryan French; ***D:*** Shawn Levy; ***W:*** Dan Schneider; ***C:*** Jonathan Brown.

Big Fella ½ **1937** Musical drama starring Robeson as Joe, a Marseilles dockworker (a familiar film occupation for the actor), who's asked by the police to help find a young boy (Grant) missing from an ocean liner. When Joe locates the boy, he discovers the child ran away from his wealthy family and doesn't want to return. Joe takes the boy to his cafe singer girlfriend, Miranda (Welch), and the two become his surrogate parents. Loose adapatation of the 1929 novel, "Banjo," by Claude McKay. ♫Lazin'; Roll Up Sailorman; You Didn't Ought to Do Such Things; All God's Chillun Got a Robe; My Curly Headed Baby; River Steals My Folks from Me. **73m/B VHS, DVD.** *GB* Paul Robeson, Elisabeth Welch, Eldon Grant; ***D:*** J. Elder Wills; ***W:*** Ingram D'Abbes, Fenn Sherie; ***C:*** Cyril Bristow; ***M:*** Eric Ansell.

The Big Fix **1978 (PG)** Private investigator Moses Wine finds himself in an ironic situation: searching for a fugitive alongside whom he'd protested in the 60s. Based on a Roger Simon novel. **108m/C VHS.** Richard Dreyfuss, Susan Anspach, Bonnie Bedelia, John Lithgow, F. Murray Abraham, Fritz Weaver, Mandy Patinkin; ***D:*** Jeremy Paul Kagan; ***M:*** Bill Conti.

Big Foot woof! **1972** Even genre devotees will be disappointed with this one. Sasquatch, who has procreation on his mind, searches rather half-heartedly for a human mate. A horror flick that forgot to include the horror. **92m/C VHS.** Chris Mitchum, Joi Lansing, John Carradine, John Mitchum; ***D:*** Bob Slatzer.

The Big Gag **1987 (R)** An international group of comedians travel the world and pull gags on people. Lame. **84m/C VHS.** *IS* Yehuda Barkan, Cyril Green, Caroline Langford; ***D:*** Yehuda Barkan.

Big Girls Don't Cry...They Get Even ½ **1992 (PG)** A teenage girl decides to run away from home after she's driven crazy by her eccentric new stepfamily. Comic confusion ensues as various family members set out to find her. Hackneyed script and annoying characters hinder this comedy. **98m/C VHS.** Hillary Wolf, Griffin Dunne, Margaret Whitton, David Strathairn, Ben Savage, Adrienne Shelly, Patricia Kalember; ***D:*** Joan Micklin Silver.

The Big Green ½ **1995 (PG)** British teacher Anna Montgomery (D'Abo) blows into a small Texas town determined to give the deprived kiddies a boost of self-esteem. With help from the town sheriff (Guttenberg), Anna organizes a soccer team that's supposed to give the kids a reason to live. Problems abound when the star player disappears just before the face-off with the biggest, nastiest team in the league. Sound familiar? This is the soccer version of "The Bad News Bears," "The Little Giants," and "The Mighty Ducks." The formula is less successful in this case, but some mildly amusing moments and a few fresh performances from the kids offer minor bright spots in this tired scenario. **100m/C VHS.** Olivia D'Abo, Steve Guttenberg, Jay O. Sanders, John Terry, Chauncey Leopardi, Patrick Renna, Billy L. Sullivan, Yareli Arizmendi, Bug Hall; ***D:*** Holly Goldberg Sloan; ***W:*** Holly Goldberg Sloan; ***C:*** Ralf Bode; ***M:*** Randy Edelman.

A Big Hand for the Little Lady ½ *Big Deal at Dodge City* **1966** Fonda and Woodward, playing two Westheaded country bumpkins, get involved in a card game in Laredo against high rollers Robards and McCarthy. Fonda risks their savings, finds himself stuck with a losing hand, and has a bit of heart trouble; that's where the little lady comes in. Fine performances and a nifty twist ending don't entirely compensate for the overly padded script (which evolved from a 48-minute TV play drafted by Sydney Carroll). **95m/C VHS.** Henry Fonda, Joanne Woodward, Jason Robards Jr., Charles Bickford, Burgess Meredith, Kevin McCarthy; ***D:*** Fielder Cook; ***C:*** Lee Garmes.

The Big Hangover **1950** Odd story about a man whose allergy to alcohol makes him drunk at the most inopportune moments. Johnson stars as the attorney with the peculiar problem and Taylor plays the boss' daughter who helps him overcome the allergy. Good supporting cast can't help this otherwise boring and predictable film. **82m/B VHS.** Van Johnson, Elizabeth Taylor, Percy Waram, Fay Holden, Leon Ames, Edgar Buchanan, Selena Royle, Gene Lockhart; ***D:*** Norman Krasna; ***W:*** Norman Krasna; ***C:*** George J. Folsey.

The Big Heat ½ **1953** When detective Ford's wife (played by Jocelyn Brando, sister of Marlon) is killed in an explosion meant for him, he pursues the gangsters behind it and uncovers a police scandal. His appetite is whetted after this discovery and he pursues the criminals even more vigorously with the help of gangster moll Gloria Grahame. Definitive film noir. **90m/B VHS, DVD.** Glenn Ford, Lee Marvin, Gloria Grahame, Jocelyn Brando, Alexander Scourby, Carolyn Jones; ***D:*** Fritz Lang; ***W:*** Sydney Boehm; ***C:*** Charles B(ryant) Lang Jr.

The Big Hit ½ **1998 (R)** Combustible mixture of extravagent stunts, cartoon violence, hip-hop soundtrack, and a colorful cast serve up an intermittently funny look at organized crime. When not executing their skills as ruthless hitmen, Melvin, Cisco, Vince, and Crunch (Wahlberg, Phillips, Sabato, Jr., and Woodbine) are regular working Joes with regular problems. For Melvin, financial and female problems force him to partner with Cisco in the kidnapping of a Chinese heiress. Said heiress turns out to be the goddaughter of their own crime boss. Much hilarity ensues. Phillips brings gusto to his flamboyant homeboy character and Wahlberg is his equal as the sappy gun for hire with a heart of gold. Big plot holes and fickle storyline, but bigger laughs make you not care so much. American directorial debut of Hong Kong import Che-Kirk Wong. **91m/C VHS, DVD, Wide.** Mark Wahlberg, Lou Diamond Phillips, Bokeem Woodbine, Antonio Sabato Jr., Christina Applegate, Avery Brooks, China Chow, Lainie Kazan, Elliott Gould, Lela Rochon, Sab Shimono; ***D:*** Kirk Wong; ***W:*** Ben Ramsey; ***C:*** Danny Nowak; ***M:*** Graeme Revell.

The Big House **1930** Prison melodrama at its best follows top con Beery as he plans a big breakout—and is betrayed. Life in the pen is depicted as brutal and futile, with sadistic guards and a hapless warden. Spawned numerous imitators. **80m/B VHS.** Wallace Beery, Chester Morris, Robert Montgomery, Lewis Stone, Leila Hyams, George F. Marion Sr., Karl (Daen) Dane, DeWitt Jennings; ***D:*** George Hill; ***W:*** Frances Marion.

The Big Hurt ½ **1987 (R)** A reporter investigating a bizarre double murder discovers a secret government agency involved in torture and mind-control. **90m/C VHS.** *AU* David Bradshaw, Lian Lunson, Simon Chilvers, Nick Waters; ***D:*** Barry Peak.

Big Jake **1971 (PG)** An aging Texas cattle man who has outlived his time swings into action when outlaws kidnap his grandson and wound his son. He returns to his estranged family to help them in the search for Little Jake. O'Hara is once again paired up with Wayne and the chemistry is still there. **90m/C VHS, Wide.** John Agar, John Wayne, Richard Boone, Maureen O'Hara, Patrick Wayne, Chris Mitchum, Bobby Vinton; ***D:*** George Sherman; ***C:*** William Clothier; ***M:*** Elmer Bernstein.

Big Jim McLain **1952** Wayne and Arness are federal agents working on behalf of the House Un-American Activities Committee to eliminate communist terrorism in Hawaii. And there's a suspicious psychiatrist, too: Wayne falls for a babe whose boss is a shrink who doesn't quite seem on the level. Definitely not a highpoint in the Duke's career. **90m/C VHS.** John Wayne, Nancy Olson, James Arness, Veda Ann Borg; ***D:*** Edward Ludwig; ***C:*** Archie Stout.

The Big Kahuna ½ **2000 (R)** Spacey produced and stars as Larry, a loudly cynical industrial lubricants salesman at a convention in Kansas. He's there with Phil (DeVito), his burned-out collegue who's going through a divorce and looking for spirituality; and Bob (Facinelli), a newlywed, devout Christian research engineer who's new to the company. They spend the night in a hospitality suite waiting for a potential client—the Big Kahuna—and discussing how work, religion, ethics, and personal life coexist. Adapted from Rueff's play "Hospitality Suite" and it feels like it. The dialogue and setting is very stagey, but the performances are excellent, especially DeVito's. **90m/C VHS, DVD, Wide.** Kevin Spacey, Danny DeVito, Peter Facinelli; ***D:*** John Swanbeck; ***W:*** Roger Rueff; ***C:*** Anastas Michos; ***M:*** Christopher Young.

The Big Knife **1955** Palance plays a Hollywood superstar who refuses to renew his studio contract, which enrages studio boss Steiger. It seems Steiger knows a very damaging secret about the star and is willing to go to any lengths to have Palance re-sign or wind up destroying himself. A ruthless, emotional look at fame and power, with excellent performances by all. Based on the play by Clifford Odets. **113m/B** Jack Palance, Rod Steiger, Ida Lupino, Shelley Winters, Wendell Corey, Jean Hagen, Ilka Chase, Everett Sloane, Wesley Addy, Paul Langton; ***D:*** Robert Aldrich; ***C:*** Ernest Laszlo.

The Big Lebowski ½ **1997 (R)** Jeff Lebowski (Bridges), a stuck-in-the-'70s stoner who insists on being called "the Dude" and loves to go bowling, is mistaken for a wheelchair-bound millionaire of the same name, and suffers a beating at the hands of thugs who are after money owed by the rich Lebowski's slutty wife. Dude is drawn into kidnapping, the attempted scamming of payoff money, and more bowling. While this may seem like plot-a-plenty, it's mainly a showcase for the Coen brothers' unique texturing of style and quirky-but-deep characters. Goodman is loud and funny as a Vietnam vet who takes any opportunity to pull a gun or explode into DI-like obscenities. Turturro steals his scenes as a pervert rival bowler who loves skintight lilac jumpsuits and polishing his ball. The showpiece is an amazing musical-bowling-fantasy sequence that would've made Busby Berkeley proud. **117m/C VHS, DVD.** Jeff Bridges, John Goodman, Steve Buscemi, Julianne Moore, Peter Stormare, David Huddleston, Philip Seymour Hoffman, Flea, Leon Russom, Sam Elliott, John Turturro, David Thewlis, Ben Gazzara, Tara Reid; ***D:*** Joel Coen; ***W:*** Joel Coen, Ethan Coen; ***C:*** Roger Deakins; ***M:*** Carter Burwell.

The Big Lift ½ **1950** Two G.I.'s assigned to the Berlin airlift ally themselves in counter-intelligence when they discover that their mutual girlfriend is a spy. **119m/B VHS, DVD.** Montgomery Clift, Paul Douglas, Cornell Borchers, Bruni Lobel, O.E. Hasse; ***D:*** George Seaton.

The Big Man: Crossing the Line *Crossing the Line* **1991 (R)** Neeson shines as a down on his luck Scottish miner who loses his job during a union strike. Desperate for cash and unable to resolve his bitterness at being unable to support his family, he's enticed by a Glasgow hood to fight in an illegal bareknuckled boxing match. What follows is an overlong and extremely brutal fight. Good performances from a talented cast overcome a rather preachy script that doesn't disguise its contempt for the Thatcher government, but also allows a glimpse into the tough times that many Brits suffered during the '80s. Based on the novel by William McIlvanney. **93m/C VHS.** *GB* Liam Neeson, Joanne Whalley, Ian Bannen, Billy Connolly, Hugh Grant, Maurice Roeves, Rob Affleck; ***D:*** David Leland; ***W:*** Don MacPherson; ***M:*** Ennio Morricone.

Big Man on Campus **1989 (PG-13)** A modern-day Quasimodo makes his home in an affluent university's belltower. Of course he falls in love with one of the pretty young co-eds and races out of his tower only to be captured by the psychology department. Really, really bad. **102m/C VHS.** Tom Skerritt, Corey Parker, Allan Katz, Cindy Williams, Melora Hardin, Jessica Harper, Gerrit Graham; ***D:*** Jeremy Paul Kagan; ***W:*** Allan Katz; ***C:*** Bojan Bazelli; ***M:*** Joseph Vitarelli.

Big Meat Eater **1985** A musical gore-comedy about extraterrestrials using radioactive butcher's discards for ship fuel. Deliberate camp that is so bad its funny! **81m/C VHS.** *CA* George Dawson, Big Miller, Andrew Gillies, Stephen Dimopoulos, Georgina Hegedos, Ida Carnevali, Sharon Wahl; ***D:*** Chris Windsor; ***W:*** Chris Windsor, Phil Savath, Laurence Keane; ***C:*** Doug McKay.

Big Mo *Mauri* **1973 (G)** True story of the friendship that developed between Cincinnati Royals basketball stars Maurice Stokes and Jack Twyman after a strange paralysis hit Stokes. **110m/C VHS.** Bernie Casey, Bo Svenson, Stephanie Edwards, Janet MacLachlan; ***D:*** Daniel Mann.

Big Momma's House **2000 (PG-13)** FBI agent Lawrence is sent to Georgia to protect single mom Long and her son from her escaped con ex. Since he's a master of disguise, Lawrence passes himself off as her grandma, who's known as "Big Momma." Lawrence, like his pal Eddie Murphy, has plenty of experience with costumes, disquises, and multiple roles. So it's kind of disappointing that this isn't a better movie. Sporadic laughs are too often mined from toilet humor, and the plot doesn't allow for many quiet moments, which Lawrence needs to balance out the slapstick. **98m/C VHS, DVD, Wide.** Martin Lawrence, Nia Long, Paul Giamatti, Terrence DaShon Howard, Anthony Anderson, Carl Wright, Ella Mitchell, Jascha Washington, Starletta DuPois, Cedric the Entertainer; ***D:*** Raja Gosnell; ***W:*** Darryl Quarles, Don Rhymer; ***C:*** Michael D. O'Shea; ***M:*** Richard Gibbs.

Big Mouth **1967** A dopey fisherman gets ahold of a treasure map and is pursued by cops and gangsters. Standard Lewis fare, with the requisite infantile histrionics; must be French to appreciate. **107m/C VHS.** Jerry Lewis, Jeannine Riley, Harold J. Stone, Charlie Callas, Buddy Lester, Susan Bay; ***D:*** Jerry Lewis; ***W:*** Jerry Lewis; ***M:*** Harry Betts.

Big News **1929** Based on the play "For Two Cents" by George S. Brooks, this early talkie uses sound to great advantage. Fired for going after a gangster who's a big advertiser (Hardy), reporter Armstrong nevertheless keeps after the crook. When the intrepid reporter pushes too far, murder enters the picture. **75m/B VHS.** Robert Armstrong, Carole Lombard, Tom Kennedy, Warner Richmond, Wade Boteler, Sam Hardy, Lew Ayres; ***D:*** Gregory La Cava.

Big Night ½ **1995 (R)** Set in '50s New Jersey, film provides an Old World/New World look at Italian brothers Primo (Shalhoub) and Secondo (Tucci) Pilaggi and their elegant but failing restaurant. Primo is the perfectionist chef who hates compromise while Secondo wants to Americanize the place in an effort to make it a success. (He knows the customer is always right even if they can't appreciate Primo's exquisitely authentic Italian dishes). In order to get attention, Secondo arranges a special night in honor of jazz great Louis Prima, with Primo out to cook the feast of a lifetime—if they can pull it off. Another food film guaranteed to make you hungry. **109m/C VHS, DVD.** Tony Shalhoub, Stanley Tucci, Ian Holm, Minnie Driver, Campbell Scott, Isabella Rossellini, Marc Anthony, Allison Janney; ***D:*** Stanley Tucci, Campbell Scott; ***W:*** Stanley Tucci, Joseph Tropiano; ***C:*** Ken Kelsch. Ind. Spirit '97: First Screenplay; Natl. Soc. Film Critics '96: Support. Actor (Shalhoub); Sundance '96: Screenplay.

The Big One **1998 (PG-13)** Moore once again takes his populist, CEO-baiting act on the road in search of corporate evil-doers, this time on Random House's dime. Documentary lovingly follows Moore on his 1996 book promo tour, as he highlights plant closings, verbally spars with Nike boss Phil Knight, plays pranks on his "handlers," and mugs for his adoring fans. His style is still the same as in "Roger & Me," but since he's joined the celebrity ranks, Moore isn't going to sneak up on anybody. To his credit, he doesn't try, but to his discredit, he ends up haranguing the very working people he claims to be standing up for, mostly exasperated receptionists and secretaries. Corporate greed and apathy are still squarely in Moore's crosshairs, but this time his own ego prevents him from getting a clear shot at his target. **90m/C VHS.** ***D:*** Michael Moore; ***Nar:*** Michael Moore.

The Big Parade 🦴🦴🦴🦴 **1925** Wonderful WWI silent, considered to be one of the best war flicks of all time. Gilbert and Adoree are exceptional as lovers torn apart by the conflict. Interesting and thoughtful picture of the trauma and trouble brought to men and their loved ones in wartime. Battle scenes are compelling and intense; Vidor's masterpiece. **141m/B VHS.** John Gilbert, Renee Adoree, Hobart Bosworth, Claire McDowell, Claire Adams, Karl (Daen) Dane, Robert Ober, Tom (Thomas E.) O'Brien, Rosita Marstini; ***D:*** King Vidor; ***W:*** Harry Behn; ***C:*** John Arnold; ***M:*** William Axt, David Mendoza. Natl. Film Reg. '92.

The Big Picture 🦴🦴½ **1989 (PG-13)** A hilarious, overlooked comedy by and starring a variety of Second City/National Lampoon alumni, about a young filmmaker who is contracted by a big studio, only to see his vision trampled by formula-minded producers, crazed agents, hungry starlets, and every other variety of Hollywood predator. **95m/C VHS.** Kevin Bacon, Jennifer Jason Leigh, Martin Short, Michael McKean, Emily Longstreth, J.T. Walsh, Eddie Albert, Richard Belzer, John Cleese, June Lockhart, Stephen Collins, Roddy McDowall, Kim Miyori, Teri Hatcher, Dan Schneider, Jason Gould, Tracy Brooks Swope; ***D:*** Christopher Guest; ***W:*** Michael Varhol, Michael McKean, Christopher Guest; ***M:*** David Nichtern.

The Big Push 🦴½ *Timber Tramps* **1975 (PG)** Motley bunch of Alaskan lumberjacks get together to save a poor widow's logging camp from a pair of greedy mill owners. **98m/C VHS.** Joseph Cotten, Claude Akins, Cesar Romero, Tab Hunter, Roosevelt "Rosie" Grier, Leon Ames, Stubby Kaye, Patricia Medina; ***D:*** Tay Garnett.

Big Red 🦴🦴½ **1962** Set amid the spectacular beauty of Canada's Quebec Province, an orphan boy protects a dog which later saves him from a mountain lion. **89m/C VHS, DVD.** Walter Pidgeon, Gilles Payant; ***D:*** Norman Tokar; ***W:*** Louis Pelletier; ***C:*** Edward Colman; ***M:*** Oliver Wallace, Richard M. Sherman, Robert B. Sherman.

The Big Red One 🦴🦴🦴½ **1980 (PG)** Fuller's harrowing, intense semi-autobiographical account of the U.S. Army's famous First Infantry Division in WWII, the "Big Red One." A rifle squad composed of four very young men, led by the grizzled Marvin, cut a fiery path of conquest from the landing in North Africa to the liberation of the concentration camp at Falkenau, Czechoslovakia. In part a tale of lost innocence, the film scores highest by bringing the raw terror of war down to the individual level. **113m/C VHS, DVD.** Lee Marvin, Robert Carradine, Mark Hamill, Stephane Audran, Bobby DiCicco, Perry Lang, Kelly Ward, Siegfried Rauch, Serge Marquand, Charles Macaulay, Alain Doutey, Maurice Marsac, Colin Gilbert, Joseph Clark, Ken Campbell, Doug Werner, Marthe Villalonga; ***D:*** Samuel Fuller; ***W:*** Samuel Fuller; ***C:*** Adam Greenberg; ***M:*** Dana Kaproff.

The Big Scam 🦴🦴½ *A Nightingale Sang in Berkeley Square; The Mayfair Bank Caper* **1979** Criminal mastermind Niven recruits ex-con Jordan to pull off a massive bank heist. **102m/C VHS.** Richard Jordan, David Niven, Oliver Tobias, Elke Sommer, Gloria Grahame, Hugh Griffith, Richard Johnson; ***D:*** Ralph Thomas.

Big Score 🦴 **1983 (R)** When a policeman is falsely accused and dismissed from the Chicago Police Department, he goes after the men who really stole the money from a drug bust. Script was originally intended to be a Dirty Harry flick; too bad it wasn't. **88m/C VHS.** Fred Williamson, John Saxon, Richard Roundtree, Nancy Wilson, Ed Lauter, Ron Dean, D'Urville Martin, Michael Dante, Joe Spinell; ***D:*** Fred Williamson; ***C:*** Joao Fernandes.

Big Shots 🦴 **1987 (PG-13)** Two kids, one naive and white, the other black and streetwise, search for a stolen watch. **91m/C VHS.** Ricky Busker, Darius McCrary, Robert Joy, Paul Winfield, Robert Prosky, Jerzy Skolimowski; ***D:*** Robert Mandel; ***W:*** Joe Eszterhas; ***M:*** Bruce Broughton.

Big Show 🦴🦴 *Home in Oklahoma* **1937** A western adventure about the making of a western adventure. Autry jangles spurs aplenty in duel role. **54m/B VHS.** Gene Autry, Smiley Burnette; ***D:*** Mack V. Wright.

The Big Sky 🦴🦴🦴 **1952** It's 1830, and a rowdy band of fur trappers embark upon a back breaking expedition up the uncharted Missouri River. Based on the A.B. Guthrie Jr. novel, it's an effortlessly enjoyable and level-headed Hawksian American myth, with a streak of gentle gallows humor. Also available colorized. **122m/C VHS.** Kirk Douglas, Dewey Martin, Arthur Hunnicutt, Elizabeth Threatt, Buddy Baer, Steven Geray, Jim Davis; ***D:*** Howard Hawks.

The Big Sleep 🦴🦴🦴🦴 **1946** Private eye Philip Marlowe, hired to protect a young woman from her own indiscretions, falls in love with her older sister while uncovering murders galore. A dense, chaotic thriller that succeeded in defining and setting a standard for its genre. The very best Raymond Chandler on film combining a witty script with great performances, especially from Bogart and Bacall. **114m/B VHS, DVD.** Humphrey Bogart, Lauren Bacall, John Ridgely, Martha Vickers, Louis Jean Heydt, Regis Toomey, Peggy Knudsen, Dorothy Malone, Bob Steele, Elisha Cook Jr.; ***D:*** Howard Hawks; ***W:*** Jules Furthman, Leigh Brackett, William Faulkner; ***C:*** Sid Hickox; ***M:*** Max Steiner. Natl. Film Reg. '97.

The Big Sleep 🦴🦴 **1978 (R)** A tired remake of the Raymond Chandler potboiler about exhausted Los Angeles private dick Marlowe and his problems in protecting a wild young heiress from her own decadence and mob connections. Mitchum appears to need a rest. **99m/C VHS.** Robert Mitchum, Sarah Miles, Richard Boone, Candy Clark, Edward Fox, Joan Collins, John Mills, James Stewart, Oliver Reed, Harry Andrews, James Donald, Colin Blakely, Richard Todd; ***D:*** Michael Winner; ***W:*** Michael Winner.

The Big Slice 🦴½ **1990 (R)** Two would-be crime novelists want to improve their fiction. One masquerades as a cop, the other as a crook, and they infiltrate the underworld from both ends. Clever comedy premise, but vaudeville-level jokes fall flat. **86m/C VHS.** Casey Siemaszko, Leslie Hope, Justin Louis, Heather Locklear, Kenneth Welsh, Nicholas (Nick) Campbell, Henry Ramer; ***D:*** John Bradshaw; ***W:*** John Bradshaw; ***M:*** Mychael Danna, Jeff Danna.

The Big Sombrero 🦴🦴½ **1949** Autry takes a stand against the marriage between an unsuspecting, wealthy Mexican girl and the fortune-seeking bridegroom who wants her land. **77m/C VHS.** Gene Autry, Elena Verdugo, Steve (Stephen) Dunne, George Lewis; ***D:*** Frank McDonald.

The Big Squeeze 🦴🦴½ **1996 (R)** Married bartender Tanya (Boyle) is displeased to find out her born-again hubby Henry (Bercovici) has been holding out a large wad of cash from an insurance settlement, apparently about to donate it to a local Spanish mission. Enter Benny (Dobson), a cocky con man willing to help Tanya get her share of the dough for his own cut; sweet bartender Jesse (Nucci), who's secretly in love in Tanya; and fellow barmaid Cece (Dispina), who catches Benny's wandering eye. All get caught up in the frantic double-dealing. **100m/C VHS, DVD.** Lara Flynn Boyle, Peter Dobson, Luca Bercovici, Danny Nucci, Teresa Dispina, Sam Vlahos, Valente Rodriguez; ***D:*** Marcus De Leon; ***W:*** Marcus De Leon; ***C:*** Jacques Haitkin; ***M:*** Mark Mothersbaugh.

Big Stakes 🦴 **1922** Extremely rare Western feature that has a Texas cowboy falling for a Mexican senorita. Plenty of action as complications ensue. **?m/B VHS.** H.B. Warner, Elinor Fair, Les Bates; ***D:*** Clifford S. Elfelt; ***W:*** Frank Howard Clark.

The Big Stampede 🦴🦴 **1932** Twenty-five-year-old Wayne stars in this action-packed Western that was a remake of "Land Beyond the Law" from Ken Maynard's silent. Based on a story by Marion Jackson. **63m/B VHS.** John Wayne, Noah Beery Sr., Luis Alberni, Berton Churchill, Paul Hurst, Lafe (Lafayette) McKee, Frank Ellis, Hank Bell; ***D:*** Tenny Wright; ***W:*** Kurt Kempler.

Big Steal 🦴🦴🦴 **1949** An Army officer recovers a missing payroll and captures the thieves after a tumultuous chase through Mexico. **72m/B VHS.** Robert Mitchum, William Bendix, Jane Greer, Ramon Novarro, Patric Knowles; ***D:*** Donald Siegel.

Big Store 🦴🦴½ **1941** Late Marx Brothers in which they are detectives in a large metropolitan department store, foiling a hostile takeover and preventing a murder. Their last MGM effort, with some good moments between the Tony Martin song numbers which include "If It's You" and the immortal "Tenement Symphony." Groucho also leads the "Sing While You Sell" number. **96m/B VHS.** Groucho Marx, Harpo Marx, Chico Marx, Tony Martin, Margaret Dumont, Virginia Grey, Virginia O'Brien, Douglass Dumbrille, Marion Martin, Henry Armetta; ***D:*** Charles Reisner; ***W:*** Hal Fimberg, Ray Golden, Sid Kuller; ***C:*** Charles Lawton Jr.; ***M:*** George Bassman.

Big Street 🦴🦴½ **1942** A timid busboy, in love with a disinterested nightclub singer, gets to prove his devotion when she is crippled in a fall. Based on a Damon Runyon story, "Little Pinks." **88m/B VHS.** Henry Fonda, Lucille Ball, Agnes Moorehead, Louise Beavers, Barton MacLane, Eugene Pallette, Ozzie Nelson; ***D:*** Irving Reis.

The Big Sweat 🦴 **1990** Maybe you've heard this one before: a man who has been framed by the mob escapes from prison and heads for Mexico. But first, he's got to get past the mobsters and police who are hot on his trail. And maybe you've seen some of it before: some of the same stock footage appears in Lommel's "Cold Heat." Not surprisingly, this one bypassed theatres and went straight to video. **85m/C VHS.** Robert Z'Dar, Steve Molone, Kevin McBride, William Roebuck, Cheri Caspari, David Rushing, Joanne Watkins, Ken Letner; ***D:*** Ulli Lommel; ***W:*** Max Bolt; ***M:*** John Massari.

VIDEO

The Big Switch 🦴½ *Strip Poker* **1970 (R)** Gambler is framed for murder and becomes embroiled in a plot to reinstate an old gangster kingpin. **68m/C VHS.** Sebastian Breaks, Virginia Wetherell, Erika Raffael; ***D:*** Pete Walker.

The Big Tease 🦴🦴 **1999 (R)** Gay Glasgow hairdresser Crawford Mackenzie (Ferguson) thinks he's being asked to compete in the prestigious World Freestyle Hairdressing Championship being held in Los Angeles. So he heads to Hollywood and discovers he's just been asked to observe. Blithely self-confident, Crawford simply decides he will not only find a way to enter but he will defeat his snippy Swedish rival, Stig (Rasche). Good-natured, campy fluff. **86m/C VHS, DVD, Wide.** *GB* Kevin Allen, Craig Ferguson, Frances Fisher, Chris Langham, Mary McCormack, Donal Logue, Larry Miller, David Rasche, Charles Napier, David Hasselhoff, Cathy Lee Crosby, Bruce Jenner, Isabella Aitken; ***D:*** Kevin Allen; ***W:*** Craig Ferguson, Sacha Gervasi; ***C:*** Seamus McGarvey; ***M:*** Mark Thomas.

Big Top Pee-wee 🦴🦴 **1988 (PG)** Pee-wee's second feature film following the success of "Pee-wee's Big Adventure." This time Pee-wee owns a farm, has a girlfriend (!) and lives the good life until a weird storm blows a traveling circus onto his property. Cute, but not the manic hilarity the first one was. **86m/C VHS, 8mm.** Paul (Pee-wee Herman) Reubens, Kris Kristofferson, Susan Tyrrell, Penelope Ann Miller; ***D:*** Randal Kleiser; ***W:*** Paul (Pee-wee Herman) Reubens; ***C:*** Steven Poster; ***M:*** Danny Elfman.

Big Town 🦴 *Guilty Assignment* **1947** A newspaper is saved by a new editor who brings integrity to the once scandalous paper. The editor and his reporters also solve a series of murders. Some action, but weak dialogue and direction hold it back. Based on the radio program of the same name. **59m/B VHS.** Philip Reed, Hillary Brooke, Robert Lowery, Byron Barr, Veda Ann Borg, Nana Bryant, Charles Arnt; ***D:*** William C. Thomas.

Big Town 🦴🦴½ **1987 (R)** A farmboy, lucky with dice, hits Chicago to claim his fortune where he meets floozies, criminals, and other streetlife. Standard '50s period underworld drama is elevated by exceptional cast's fine ensemble work. Look for Lane's strip number. **109m/C VHS.** Matt Dillon, Diane Lane, Tommy Lee Jones, Bruce Dern, Tom Skerritt, Lee Grant, Suzy Amis, David Marshall Grant, Don Francks, Del Close, Cherry Jones, David Elliot, Don Lake, Diego Matamoros, Gary Farmer, Sarah Polley, Lolita (David) Davidovich; ***D:*** Ben Bolt, Harold Becker; ***W:*** Robert Roy Pool; ***C:*** Ralf Bode; ***M:*** Michael Melvoin.

Big Town After Dark 🦴🦴 *Underworld After Dark* **1947** Daring journalists search for the bottom-line story on a gang of criminals. They find themselves caught behind the firing lines when the sun goes down. Slightly better than average thriller. **69m/B VHS.** Philip Reed, Hillary Brooke, Richard Travis, Ann Gillis; ***D:*** William C. Thomas.

Big Trail 🦴🦴🦴 **1930** This pioneering effort in widescreen cinematography was Wayne's first feature film. A wagon train on the Oregon trail encounters Indians, buffalo, tough terrain, and romantic problems. **110m/B VHS.** John Wayne, Marguerite Churchill, El Brendel, Tully Marshall, Tyrone Power Sr., Ward Bond, Helen Parrish; ***D:*** Raoul Walsh.

Big Trees 🦴🦴🦴 **1952** A ruthless lumberman attempts a takeover of the California Redwood Timberlands that are owned by a group of peaceful homesteaders. **89m/C VHS.** Kirk Douglas, Patrice Wymore, Eve Miller, Alan Hale Jr., Edgar Buchanan; ***D:*** Felix Feist.

Big Trouble 🦴🦴 **1986 (R)** An insurance broker endeavors to send his three sons to Yale by conspiring with a crazy couple in a fraud scheme that goes awry in every possible manner. Look for the cameo by screenwriter Bergman as Warren Bogle. **93m/C VHS.** Alan Arkin, Peter Falk, Beverly D'Angelo, Charles Durning, Robert Stack, Paul Dooley, Valerie Curtin, Richard Libertini; ***Cameos:*** Andrew Bergman; ***D:*** John Cassavetes; ***W:*** Andrew Bergman; ***C:*** Bill Butler; ***M:*** Bill Conti.

Big Trouble 🦴🦴 **2002 (PG-13)** Fast-paced ensemble comedy based on the novel by Dave Barry packs a metric ton of narrative, not to mention characters, into a mere 84 minutes, most of which involve the clash of various characters tracking down a nuclear bomb in Miami. Suburban Anna (Russo) is trapped in a loveless marriage with unscrupulous businessman Arthur Herk (Tucci) who wants to buy a nuclear bomb, thus getting involved with some undesirable characters, most notably two hit men (Farina and Kehler). The plot kicks off when Matt (Foster), the son of divorced journalist Allen decides to snipe the Herk's daughter Jenny (Deschanel) with a high-powered squirt gun on the same night the hit men visit. Of the strong cast, Allen and Foster are the stand-outs. Cartoony, heavy-handed direction buries satire Barry is known for. **84m/C VHS, DVD.** *US* Tim Allen, Rene Russo, Stanley Tucci, Tom Sizemore, Johnny Knoxville, Dennis Farina, Jack Kehler, Janeane Garofalo, Patrick Warburton, Ben Foster, Zooey Deschanel, Dwight Myers, Omar Epps, Jason Lee, Andy Richter, Sofia Vergara; ***D:*** Barry Sonnenfeld; ***W:*** Robert Ramsey, Matthew Stone; ***C:*** Greg Gardiner; ***M:*** James Newton Howard.

Big Trouble in Little China 🦴🦴½ **1986 (PG-13)** A trucker plunges beneath the streets of San Francisco's Chinatown to battle an army of spirits. An uproarious comic-book-film parody with plenty of action and a keen sense of sophomoric sarcasm. **99m/C VHS, DVD, Wide.** Kurt Russell, Suzee Pai, Dennis Dun, Kim Cattrall, James Hong, Victor Wong, Kate Burton; ***D:*** John Carpenter; ***W:*** David Weinstein, Gary Goldman, W.D. Richter; ***C:*** Dean Cundey; ***M:*** John Carpenter, Alan Howarth.

Big Wednesday 🦴🦴½ *Summer of Innocence* **1978 (PG)** Three California surfers from the early '60s get back together after the Vietnam war to reminisce about the good old days and take on the big wave. **120m/C VHS, Wide.** Jan-Michael Vincent, Gary Busey, William Katt, Lee Purcell, Patti D'Arbanville; ***D:*** John Milius; ***W:*** John Milius; ***M:*** Basil Poledouris.

The Big Wheel 🦴🦴½ **1949** Old story retold fairly well. Rooney is young son determined to travel in his father's tracks as a race car driver, even when dad buys the farm on the oval. Good acting and direction keep this a cut above average. **92m/B VHS, DVD.** Mickey Rooney, Thomas Mitchell, Spring Byington, Mary Hatcher, Allen Jenkins, Michael O'Shea; ***D:*** Edward Ludwig.

Big Zapper 🦴½ **1973** Violent P.I. Marlowe and masochistic assistant Rock work together in this British comic strip film. **94m/C VHS.** *GB* Linda Marlowe, Gary Hope, Sean Hewitt, Richard Monette, Penny Irving; ***D:*** Lindsay Shonteff.

The Bigamist 🦴½ **1953** Have you heard the one about the traveling salesman in this movie? He has one wife in Los Angeles, another in San Francisco, and they inevitably find out about each other. A maudlin soap opera with a do-it-yourself ending, only shows why bigamy was done better as farce in the later "Micki and Maude." **79m/B VHS.** Edmond O'Brien, Joan Fontaine, Ida Lupino, Edmund Gwenn, Jane Darwell, Kenneth Tobey; ***D:*** Ida Lupino.

Bigfoot: The Unforgettable Encounter 🦴🦴½ **1994 (PG)** Young boy heads off into the woods, comes face to face with Bigfoot, and sets off a media frenzy and a band of ruthless bounty hunters determined to capture his hairy friend. **89m/C VHS.** Zachery Ty Bryan, Matt McCoy, Barbara Willis Sweete, Clint Howard, Rance Howard, David Rasche; ***D:*** Corey Michael Eubanks; ***W:*** Corey Michael Eubanks; ***M:*** Shimon Arama.

Biggles 🦴🦴 *Biggles: Adventures in Time* **1985 (PG)** Time-travel fantasy in which a young businessman from present-day New York City is inexplicably transferred into the identity of a 1917 WWI flying ace. He suddenly finds himself aboard a fighter plane over Europe during WWI. **100m/C VHS.** *GB* Neil Dickson, Alex Hyde-White, Peter Cushing; ***D:*** John Hough.

Bikini Beach 🦴🦴½ **1964** Surfing teenagers of the "Beach Party" series follow up "Muscle Beach Party" with a third fling at the beach and welcome a visitor, British recording star "Potato Bug" (Avalon in a campy dual role). But, golly gee, wealthy Wynn wants to turn their sandy, surfin' shores into a retirement community. What to do? Sing a few songs, dance in your bathing suits, and have fun. Classic early '60s nostalgia is better than the first two efforts; followed by "Pajama Party." ♫Because You're You; Love's a Secret Weapon; Bikini Drag. **100m/C VHS, DVD, Wide.** Annette Funicello, Frankie Avalon, Martha Hyer, Harvey Lembeck, Don Rickles, Stevie Wonder, John Ashley, Keenan Wynn, Jody McCrea, Candy Johnson, Danielle Aubry, Meredith MacRae, Dolores Wells, Donna Loren, Timothy Carey, Boris Karloff; ***D:*** William Asher; ***W:*** William Asher, Leo Townsend, Robert Dillon; ***C:*** Floyd Crosby; ***M:*** Les Baxter.

Bikini Bistro 🦴 **1994 (R)** A boring vegetarian cafe gets turned into a gourmet restaurant but, faced with an eviction notice, the female owners decide to increase business by waitressing in bikinis. Also available in an unrated version at 84 minutes. **80m/C VHS, DVD.** Marilyn Chambers, Amy Lynn Baxter, Joan Gerardi, Isabelle Fortea, John Altamura, Joseph Pallister; ***D:*** Ernest G. Sauer; ***W:*** Matt Unger.

The Bikini Car Wash Company woof! *California Hot Wax* **1990 (R)** Babes in bikinis in Los Angeles. A young man is running his uncle's carwash when he meets a business major who persuades him to let her take over the business for a cut of the profits. She decides that a good gimmick would be to dress all the female employees in the tiniest bikinis possible. The story is of course secondary to the amount of flesh on display. Also available in an unrated version. **87m/C VHS, DVD.** Joe Dusic, Neriah Napaul, Suzanne Browne, Kristie Ducati; ***D:*** Ed Hansen.

The Bikini Car Wash Company 2 🦴 **1992 (R)** Entrepreneur Melissa and the other lovely ladies of the Bikini Car Wash Co. find themselves a big success, so much so that a greedy businessman wants to buy them out. In order to get money to fight the takeover, the ladies take to the airwaves of a cable-access station. Their new business adventure involves selling sexy lingerie which means the flesh quotient is as great as ever. An unrated version is also available. **94m/C VHS, DVD.** Kristie Ducati, Suzanne Browne, Neriah Napaul, Rikki Brando, Greg Raye, Larry De Russy; ***D:*** Gary Orona; ***W:*** Bart B. Gustis; ***M:*** Michael Smith.

Bikini Drive-In 🦴½ **1994 (R)** Babe (Rhey) inherits grandad's decrepit drive-in, which is wanted by a mall mogul, but she refuses to sell. So to raise some cash, Rhey stages a B-movie marathon with in-person, bikini-clad scream queens. **85m/C VHS.** Ashlie Rhey, Richard Gabai, Ross Hagen, Sara Bellomo, Steve Barkett, Conrad Brooks; ***D:*** Fred Olen Ray.

Bikini House Calls 🦴 **1996** The students of Bikini Med School love anatomy as much as they love to party. In fact, combining both activities is their idea of a perfect time. **87m/C VHS, DVD.** Thomas Draper, Sean Abbananto, Kim (Kimberly Dawn) Dawson, Tamara Landry; ***D:*** Michael Paul Girard; ***W:*** Michael Paul Girard; ***C:*** Denis Maloney; ***M:*** Miriam Cutler. **VIDEO**

Bikini Island 🦴 **1991 (R)** Beautiful swimsuit models gather on a remote tropical island for a big photo shoot, each vying to be the next cover girl of the hottest swimsuit magazine. Before long, scantily clad lovelies are turning up dead and full out madness ensues. Will the mystery be solved before they run out of models, or will the magazine have no choice but to grace its cover with a bikinied cadaver? Low-budget trash that has few, if any, redeeming qualities. **85m/C VHS.** Holly Floria, Alicia Anne, Jackson Robinson, Shannon Stiles, Cyndi Pass, Sherry Johnson; ***D:*** Anthony Markes; ***W:*** Emerson Bixby; ***M:*** Marc David Decker.

Bikini Med School 🦴 **1998** So how do med students get rid of all that nasty tension? Why they party, of course! And practice playing doctor with all the nubile lovelies they can. **87m/C VHS, DVD.** Kim (Kimberly Dawn) Dawson, Tamara Landry, Thomas Draper, Sean Abbananto; ***D:*** Michael Paul Girard; ***W:*** Michael Paul Girard; ***C:*** Denis Maloney; ***M:*** Miriam Cutler. **VIDEO**

Bikini Summer 🦴½ **1991** Laughs, music, and skin are the order of the day as two nutty guys and a few beautiful girls form an unlikely friendship on the beach. Konop was Julia Robert's "Pretty Woman" body double. Sort of the '90s version of the old '60s Frankie and Annette beach parties. **90m/C VHS.** David Millburn, Melinda Armstrong, Jason Clow, Shelley Michelle, Alex Smith, Kent Lipham, Kelly Konop, Carmen Santa Maria; ***D:*** Robert Veze; ***W:*** Robert Veze, Nick Stone; ***M:*** John Gonzalez.

Bikini Summer 2 🦴 **1992 (R)** An eccentric family decides to stage a bikini contest to raise money to help the homeless. **94m/C VHS.** Jeff Conaway, Jessica Hahn, Melinda Armstrong, Avalon Anders; ***D:*** Jeff Conaway; ***M:*** Jim Halfpenny.

Bikini Summer 3: South Beach Heat 🦴 **1997 (R)** Babes in bikinis frolic on Miami's fashionable South Beach for the chance to become the spokesmodel for Mermaid Body Splash. **84m/C VHS.** Heather-Elizabeth Parkhurst, Tiffany Turner; ***D:*** Ken Blakey.

Bilitis 🦴½ **1977 (R)** A young girl from a private girls' school is initiated into the pleasures of sex and the unexpected demands of love. One of director Hamilton's exploitative meditations on nudity. **95m/C VHS.** *FR* Patti D'Arbanville, Bernard Giraudeau, Mona Kristensen; ***D:*** David Hamilton.

Bill 🦴🦴🦴 **1981** Based on a true story about a mentally retarded man who sets out to live independently after 44 years in an institution. Rooney gives an affecting performance as Bill and Quaid is strong as the filmmaker who befriends him. Awarded Emmys for Rooney's performance and the well written script. Followed by "Bill: On His Own." **97m/C VHS.** Mickey Rooney, Dennis Quaid, Largo Woodruff, Harry Goz; ***D:*** Anthony Page. **TV**

Bill & Ted's Bogus Journey 🦴🦴 **1991 (PG)** Big-budget sequel to B & T's first movie has better special effects but about the same quota of laughs. Slain by lookalike robot duplicates from the future, the airhead heroes pass through heaven and hell before tricking the Grim Reaper into bringing them back for a second duel with their heinous terminators. Most excellent closing-credit montage. Non-fans still won't think much of it. **98m/C VHS, DVD, Wide.** Keanu Reeves, Alex Winter, William Sadler, Joss Ackland, Pam Grier, George Carlin, Amy Stock-Poynton, Hal Landon Jr., Annette Azcuy, Sarah Trigger, Chelcie Ross, Taj Mahal, Roy Brocksmith, William Shatner; ***D:*** Peter Hewitt; ***W:*** Chris Matheson, Edward Solomon; ***C:*** Oliver Wood; ***M:*** David Newman.

Bill & Ted's Excellent Adventure 🦴🦴½ **1989 (PG)** Excellent premise: when the entire future of the world rests on whether or not two '80s dudes pass their history final, Rufus comes to the rescue in his time-travelling telephone booth. Bill and Ted share an adventure through time as they meet and get to know some of history's most important figures. Lightweight but fun. **105m/C VHS, DVD, Wide.** Keanu Reeves, Alex Winter, George Carlin, Bernie Casey, Dan Shor, Robert V. Barron, Amy Stock-Poynton, Ted Steedman, Terry Camillieri, Rod Loomis, Al Leong, Tony Camilieri; ***D:*** Stephen Herek; ***W:*** Chris Matheson, Edward Solomon; ***C:*** Tim Suhrstedt; ***M:*** David Newman.

A Bill of Divorcement 🦴🦴½ **1932** Hepburn's screen debut, as the daughter of a shell-shocked WWI vet, who requires her care after her mother decides to divorce him. Creaky early talker. **76m/B VHS.** John Barrymore, Katharine Hepburn, Billie Burke, Henry Stephenson, David Manners, Paul Cavanagh, Elizabeth Patterson; ***D:*** George Cukor; ***M:*** Max Steiner.

Bill: On His Own 🦴🦴🦴 **1983** Rooney is again exceptional in this sequel to the Emmy-winning TV movie "Bill." After 44 years in an institution, a mentally retarded man copes more and more successfully with the outside world. Fine supporting cast and direction control the melodramatic potential. **100m/C VHS.** Mickey Rooney, Helen Hunt, Teresa Wright, Dennis Quaid, Largo Woodruff, Paul Leiber, Harry Goz; ***D:*** Anthony Page.

Billboard Dad 🦴🦴½ **1998 (G)** The Olsen twins decide it's time for their dad to remarry so they paint a personal ad on a billboard advertising his availability. Eventually, their Dad meets Brooke, who's a winner except for her bratty son who's the girls' rival. But nothing will stop the twins if it means making Dad happy. **90m/C VHS.** Ashley (Fuller) Olsen, Mary-Kate Olsen, Tom Amandes, Jessica Tuck, Sam Selatta, Carl Banks; ***D:*** Alan Metter; ***W:*** Maria Jacquemetton; ***C:*** Mauro Fiore; ***M:*** David Michael Frank. **VIDEO**

Billie 🦴½ **1965** Duke stars as a tomboy athlete who puts the boys' track team to shame. Some amusing but very predictable situations, plus a few songs from Miss Duke. Based on Ronald Alexander's play "Time Out for Ginger." **86m/C VHS, Wide.** Patty Duke, Jim Backus, Jane Greer, Warren Berlinger, Billy DeWolfe, Charles Lane, Dick Sargent, Susan Seaforth Hayes, Ted Bessell, Richard Deacon; ***D:*** Don Weis; ***W:*** Ronald Alexander.

The Billion Dollar Hobo 🦴½ **1978 (G)** Poor, unsuspecting heir of a multimillion dollar fortune must duplicate his benefactor's experience as a hobo during the Depression in order to collect his inheritance. Slow-moving family stuff. **96m/C VHS.** Tim Conway, Will Geer, Eric Weston, Sydney Lassick; ***D:*** Stuart E. McGowan.

A Billion for Boris 🦴🦴½ **1990** Boris' TV gives a sneak preview of the future and Boris plans to make some money off of it. Zany comedy in the vein of "Let It Ride." **89m/C VHS.** Lee Grant, Tim Kazurinsky; ***D:*** Alex Grasshof; ***W:*** Mary Rogers.

Billionaire Boys Club 🦴🦴½ **1987** Chilling look at greed in the '80s. Nelson plays Joe Hunt, who gets together with a group of rich, preppie friends to manipulate investments in the commodities markets. When a slick con man (Silver) gets in their way he's murdered to keep their schemes intact. Based on a true story and adapted from the book by Sue Horton. The video version is considerably pared down from the original TV broadcast. **94m/C VHS.** Judd Nelson, Frederic Lehne, Brian McNamara, Raphael Sbarge, John Stockwell, Barry Tubb, Stan Shaw, Jill Schoelen, Ron Silver, James Sloyan, James Karen, Dale Dye; ***D:*** Marvin J. Chomsky. **TV**

Billy Bathgate 🦴🦴½ **1991 (R)** Uneven but well acted drama set in 1935 New York. A street-wise young man decides getting ahead during the Depression means gaining the attention of mobster Dutch Schultz and joining his gang. As Billy becomes the confidant of the racketeer he learns the criminal life is filled with suspicion and violence; in order to stay alive he must rely on every trick he's learned. Willis has a small role as a rival mobster who gets fitted for cement overshoes. Kidman does well as Dutch's girlfriend with Hill fine as the gang's number man. Based on the novel by E.L. Doctorow. **107m/C VHS, Wide.** Dustin Hoffman, Nicole Kidman, Loren Dean, Bruce Willis, Steven Hill, Steve Buscemi, Stanley Tucci, Tim Jerome, Billy Jaye, Katharine Houghton, Mike Starr, John A. Costelloe, Moira Kelly; ***D:*** Robert Benton; ***W:*** Tom Stoppard; ***C:*** Nestor Almendros; ***M:*** Mark Isham.

Billy Budd 🦴🦴🦴 **1962** The classic Melville good-evil allegory adapted to film, dealing with a British warship in the late 1700s, and its struggle between evil master-at-arms and innocent shipmate. Stamp's screen debut as the naive Billy who is tried for the murder of the sadistic first mate. Well directed and acted. **123m/B VHS.** *GB* Terence Stamp, Peter Ustinov, Robert Ryan, Melvyn Douglas, Paul Rogers, John Neville, Ronald Lewis, David McCallum, John Meillon; ***D:*** Peter Ustinov; ***W:*** Peter Ustinov, Robert Rossen; ***C:*** Robert Krasker.

Billy Elliot 🦴🦴🦴 *Dancer* **2000 (R)** Eleven-year-old Billy (Bell) is trying to survive in a Durham County town during the 1984 miners' strike that is affecting his family. His widowed dad (Lewis) wants Billy to take boxing lessons but the boy is more interested in the ballet class taught at the same gym by hard-living Mrs. Wilkinson (Walters), whose daughter Debbie (Blackwell) taunts Billy into trying to dance. Billy's natural talent is so great that Mrs. Wilkinson encourages him to audition for the Royal Ballet School in London. Of course, when his dad finds out what's been going on, there's trouble. The unfortunate rating is due to language but the film has all-around appeal and some fine performances. Stage director Daldry makes his film debut as does Bell. **111m/C VHS, DVD, Wide.** *GB* Jamie Bell, Julie Walters, Gary Lewis, Jamie Driven, Nicola Blackwell, Jean Heywood, Stuart Wells, Adam Cooper; ***D:*** Stephen Daldry; ***W:*** Lee Hall; ***C:*** Brian Tufano; ***M:*** Stephen Warbeck. British Acad. '00: Actor (Bell), Film, Support. Actress (Walters).

Billy Galvin 🦴🦴½ **1986 (PG)** A bull-headed ironworker tries to straighten out the turbulent relationship he has with his rebellious son. **95m/C VHS.** Karl Malden, Lenny Von Dohlen, Joyce Van Patten, Toni Kalem, Keith Szarabajka, Alan North, Paul Guilfoyle, Barton Heyman; ***D:*** John Gray; ***W:*** John Gray; ***M:*** Joel Rosenbaum.

Billy Jack 🦴🦴 **1971 (PG)** On an Arizona Indian reservation, a half-breed ex-Green Beret with pugnacious martial arts skills (Laughlin) stands between a rural town and a school for runaways. Laughlin stars with his real-life wife Taylor. Features the then-hit song "One Tin Soldier," sung by Coven. The movie and its marketing by Laughlin inspired a "Billy Jack" cult phenomenon. A Spanish-dubbed version of this film is also available. Followed by a sequel in 1974, "Trail of Billy Jack," which bombed. **112m/C VHS, DVD.** Tom Laughlin, Delores Taylor, Clark Howat, Bert Freed, Julie Webb, Victor Izay, Teresa Kelly, Lynn Baker, Stan Rice, Howard Hesseman; ***D:*** Tom Laughlin; ***W:*** Tom Laughlin, Delores Taylor; ***C:*** Fred W. Koenekamp, John Stephens; ***M:*** Mundell Lowe.

Billy Liar 🦴🦴🦴 **1963** A young Englishman dreams of escaping from his working class family and dead-end job as an undertaker's assistant. Parallels James Thurber's story, "The Secret Life of Walter Mitty." **94m/B VHS, DVD, Wide.** *GB* Tom Courtenay, Julie Christie, Finlay Currie; ***D:*** John Schlesinger; ***W:*** Willis Hall, Keith Waterhouse; ***C:*** Denys Coop; ***M:*** Richard Rodney Bennett.

Billy Madison 🦴½ **1994 (PG-13)** Wealthy slacker Billy (Sandler) must prove to Dad he is capable of running the family hotel business by undertaking the obvious challenge of repeating grades 1-12 in six months. Ponder a few bodily function gags, and you'll have exhausted the humor in this lame attempt at creating a feature-length movie out of what would barely pass as a Saturday Night Live sketch. For only the most diehard fans of Sandler's silly shtick. **90m/C VHS, DVD.** Adam Sandler, Darren McGavin, Bridgette Wilson, Bradley Whitford, Josh Mostel, Norm MacDonald, Mark Beltzman, Larry Hankin, Theresa Merritt, Chris Farley, Steve Buscemi; ***D:*** Tamra Davis; ***W:*** Adam Sandler; ***C:*** Victor Hammer; ***M:*** Randy Edelman.

Billy: Portrait of a Street Kid ☆☆ **1977** A ghetto youngster tries to pry himself up and out of his bleak surroundings through education, but complications arise when he gets his girlfriend pregnant. **96m/C VHS.** LeVar Burton, Tina Andrews, Ossie Davis, Michael Constantine; ***D:*** Steven Gethers. **TV**

Billy Rose's Jumbo ☆☆☆ *Jumbo* **1962** Better-than-average update of the circus picture. Durante and Raye are terrific, as are the Rodgers and Hart songs. Fun, with lively production numbers in the inimitable Berkeley style. ♫Over and Over Again; Circus on Parade; Why Can't I?; This Can't Be Love; The Most Beautiful Girl in the World; My Romance; Little Girl Blue; What is a Circus; Sawdust, Spangles and Dreams. **125m/C VHS, Wide.** Doris Day, Stephen Boyd, Jimmy Durante, Martha Raye, Dean Jagger; ***D:*** Charles Walters; ***W:*** Sidney Sheldon.

Billy the Kid ☆☆½ **1941** Billy Bonney joins up with a group of outlaws in a Southwest town where he bumps into his old friend Jim Sherwood, now the marshal. Attempting to change his ways, he falls back into the life of a bandit when an outlaw friend is murdered. Although an entertaining western, the story bears no resemblance to the actual last days of Billy the Kid. Based on a story by Howard Emmett Rogers and Bradbury Foote, suggested by the book "The Saga of Billy the Kid" by Walter Noble Burns. **94m/C VHS.** Robert Taylor, Brian Donlevy, Ian Hunter, Mary Howard, Gene Lockhart, Lon Chaney Jr., Guinn "Big Boy" Williams, Cy Kendall, Henry O'Neill, Ted Adams, Frank Puglia, Mitchell Lewis, Dick Curtis, Grant Withers, Joe Yule, Eddie Dunn, Kermit Maynard, Chill Wills, Olive Blakeney, Carl Pitti; ***D:*** David Miller; ***W:*** Gene Fowler Jr.; ***M:*** David Snell.

Billy the Kid in Texas ☆½ **1940** The famed outlaw takes on trouble and makes sure the Texans never forget that he has been there. **52m/B VHS.** Bob Steele, Al "Fuzzy" St. John, Carleton Young, John Merton; ***D:*** Sam Newfield; ***W:*** Joseph O'Donnell; ***C:*** Jack Greenhalgh; ***M:*** Lew Porter.

Billy the Kid Returns ☆½ **1938** While trying to clean up a town of its criminal element, Rogers is mistaken for the legendary Billy. Complications ensue. **60m/B VHS, DVD.** Roy Rogers, George "Gabby" Hayes, Smiley Burnette, Lynne Roberts; ***D:*** Joseph Kane.

Billy the Kid Trapped ☆½ **1942** Billy and his partner are rescued from hanging by an outlaw band. **59m/B VHS.** Buster Crabbe, Al "Fuzzy" St. John, Bud McTaggart, Anne Jeffreys, Glenn Strange; ***D:*** Sam Newfield.

Billy the Kid Versus Dracula ☆☆ **1966** The title says it all. Dracula travels to the Old West, anxious to put the bite on a pretty lady ranch owner. Her fiance, the legendary outlaw Billy the Kid, steps in to save his girl from becoming a vampire herself. A Carradine camp classic. **95m/C VHS.** Chuck Courtney, John Carradine, Melinda Plowman, Walter Janovitz, Harry Carey Jr., Roy Barcroft, Virginia Christine, Bing Russell, Olive Carey, William Challee, William Forrest; ***D:*** William Beaudine; ***W:*** Carl K. Hittleman; ***C:*** Lothrop Worth; ***M:*** Raoul Kraushaar.

Billy Two Hats ☆☆½ *The Lady and the Outlaw* **1974 (PG)** Grizzled Scottish bandit Deans (Peck) teams up with young half-breed Billy (Arnaz Jr.) to pull off a robbery that results in an accidental death and Billy's capture. Deans is shot while breaking the kid out of jail and must rely on Billy to get them through, while being pursued by the law. It ain't happy. Mainly notable as the first western shot in Israel. **139m/C VHS.** Gregory Peck, Desi Arnaz Jr., Jack Warden, Sian Barbara Allen, David Huddleston; ***D:*** Ted Kotcheff; ***W:*** Alan Sharp; ***C:*** Brian West; ***M:*** John Scott.

Billy's Holiday **1995 (R)** Excessively offbeat Australian musical lacks the highly polished look of Hollywood's best, but given the setting and subject matter, it is probably not meant to have it. The subject is Billy Apples (Cullen), hangdog hardware owner by day, hangdog jazz musician at night. His audiences regularly fall asleep, but Kate (McQuade), owner of the beauty shop down the street, still loves him. Then one night, Billy magically receives the ability to sing just like his idol, Billie Holiday. The main attractions are the likeably middle-aged stars and a soundtrack filled with big band tunes. **92m/C DVD, Wide.** *AU* Max Cullen, Kris McQuade, Tina Bursill, Drew Forsythe, Genevieve Lemon, Richard Roxburgh, Rachel Coopes; ***D:*** Richard Wherrett; ***W:*** Denis Whitburn; ***C:*** Roger Lanser.

Billy's Hollywood Screen Kiss ☆☆½ **1998 (R)** Very gay Billy (Hayes) is an aspiring arts photographer in L.A. who's looking for romance. He thinks he's got a hot prospect in handsome-if-sexually-confused Gabriel (Rowe), a waiter/model. Billy's latest project is recreating great film romantic scenes with drag queens and he hires Gabriel to play the male lover. But it looks as if Billy is going to get his heart broken if he expects Gabriel to carry the role over into real life. Amusing feature debut for director O'Haver and a standout performance from the witty Hayes. **92m/C VHS, DVD.** Sean P. Hayes, Brad Rowe, Richard Ganoung, Meredith Scott Lynn, Paul Bartel, Armando Valdes-Kennedy; ***D:*** Tommy O'Haver; ***W:*** Tommy O'Haver; ***C:*** Mark Mervis; ***M:*** Alan Ari Lazar.

Biloxi Blues ☆☆½ *Neil Simon's Biloxi Blues* **1988 (PG-13)** Eugene Morris Jerome has been drafted and sent to boot camp in Biloxi, Mississippi where he encounters a troubled drill sergeant, hostile recruits, and a skillful prostitute. Walken is the drill sergeant from hell. Some good laughs from the ever-wry Broderick. A sequel to Neil Simon's "Brighton Beach Memoirs" and adapted by Simon from his play. Followed by "Broadway Bound." **105m/C VHS.** Matthew Broderick, Christopher Walken, Casey Siemaszko, Matt Mulhern, Corey Parker, Penelope Ann Miller, Michael Dolan, Park Overall; ***D:*** Mike Nichols; ***W:*** Neil Simon; ***C:*** Bill Butler; ***M:*** Georges Delerue.

Bimini Code ☆ **1984** Two female adventurers accept a dangerous mission where they wind up on Bimini Island in a showdown with the mysterious Madame X. **95m/C VHS.** Vickie Benson, Krista Richardson, Frank Alexander, Rosanna Simanaitis; ***D:*** Barry Clark.

Bingo ☆☆½ **1991 (PG)** Mediocre spoof of hero-dog movies. The heroic title mutt roams from Denver to Green Bay in search of his absent-minded master, with numerous absurd adventures en route. Some cute moments, but sometimes Bingo is just lame-o. Good family fare. **90m/C VHS.** Cindy Williams, David Rasche, Robert J. Steinmiller Jr., David French, Kurt Fuller, Joe Guzaldo, Glenn Shadix; ***D:*** Matthew Robbins; ***W:*** Jim Strain; ***M:*** Richard Gibbs.

Bingo Long Traveling All-Stars & Motor Kings ☆☆☆ **1976 (PG)** Set in 1939, this film follows the comedic adventures of a lively group of black ball players who have defected from the old Negro National League. The All-Stars travel the country challenging local white teams. **111m/C VHS, DVD, Wide.** Billy Dee Williams, James Earl Jones, Richard Pryor, Stan Shaw; ***D:*** John Badham; ***W:*** Matthew Robbins, Hal Barwood; ***C:*** Bill Butler; ***M:*** William Goldstein.

Bio-Dome ☆ **1996 (PG-13)** Pauly Shore in a hermetically sealed environment separated from the rest of society? Great! Where do I sign? Unfortunately, it's only a movie, and a typically useless one, at that. Shore brings his lame schtick to a scientifically created "perfect environment" that he and his college (yeah, right) buddy Doyle (Baldwin) mistake for a mall and eventually destroy. In Bloom's not-too-auspicious directorial debut, bodily function jokes found in Jim Carrey's wastebasket masquerade as a script, while the supporting cast wanders aimlessly, perhaps pondering a switch in agents. **94m/C VHS, DVD, Wide.** Pauly Shore, Stephen Baldwin, William Atherton, Henry Gibson, Joey Lauren Adams, Teresa Hill, Kylie Minogue, Kevin West, Denise Dowse, Dara Tomanovich; ***D:*** Jason Bloom; ***W:*** Kip Koenig, Scott Marcano; ***C:*** Phedon Papamichael; ***M:*** Andrew Gross. Golden Raspberries '96: Worst Actor (Shore).

Bio Hazard ☆ **1985 (R)** A toxic monster needs human flesh to survive and consequently goes on a rampage. **84m/C VHS.** Angelique Pettyjohn, Carroll Borland, Richard Hench, Aldo Ray; ***D:*** Fred Olen Ray.

Biohazard: The Alien Force ☆½ **1995 (R)** Reptilian mutant, the result of a genetic experiment gone awry, must be hunted down before it can reproduce. Sounds like a rip-off of "Species." **88m/C VHS.** Steve Zurk, Chris Mitchum, Susan Fronsoe, Tom Ferguson, Patrick Moran, John Maynard; ***D:*** Steve Latshaw.

The Bionic Woman ☆☆ **1975** Sky-diving accident leaves tennis pro Jaimie Somers crippled and near death. Her bionic buddy, Steve Austin, gets his friends to rebuild her and make her better than she was before. Pilot for the TV series. **96m/C VHS.** Lindsay Wagner, Lee Majors, Richard Anderson, Alan Oppenheimer; ***D:*** Richard (Dick) Moder. **TV**

Biozombie ☆☆½ **1998** Playing as a mixture of "Mallrats" and "Dawn of the Dead," this Hong Kong import is aimed squarely at a Generation-X audience. The film introduces us to Woody (Jordan Chan) and Bee (Sam Lee), two slackers who work at a video store. While on an errand to pick up their boss's car, they hit a strange pedestrian and take him back to the mall. This stranger turns out to be a zombie, and he soon infects several others. With the mall locked up for the night, Woody and Bee must take it upon themselves to protect the few humans remaining...while doing the least amount of work possible. The film turns into a true roller-coaster ride, as we start with the comedic opening, then move into the action-horror, and finally, a very nihilistic ending. **94m/C DVD.** *HK* Jordan Chan, Sam Lee; ***D:*** Wilson (Wai-Shun) Yip.

The Birch Interval ☆☆ **1978 (PG)** A chronicle of a young Amish girl growing up and experiencing adult passions and fears when she visits her kin in their isolated Pennsylvania community. **104m/C VHS.** Eddie Albert, Rip Torn, Ann Wedgeworth; ***D:*** Delbert Mann; ***W:*** Joanna Crawford.

Bird ☆☆☆ **1988 (R)** The richly textured, though sadly one-sided biography of jazz sax great Charlie Parker, from his rise to stardom to his premature death via extended heroin use. A remarkably assured, deeply imagined film from Eastwood that never really shows the Bird's genius of creation. The soundtrack features Parker's own solos re-mastered from original recordings. **160m/C VHS, DVD, Wide.** Forest Whitaker, Diane Venora, Michael Zelniker, Samuel E. Wright, Keith David, Michael McGuire, James Handy, Damon Whitaker, Morgan Nagler, Peter Crook; ***D:*** Clint Eastwood; ***W:*** Joel Oliansky; ***C:*** Jack N. Green; ***M:*** Lennie Niehaus. Oscars '88: Sound; Cannes '88: Actor (Whitaker); Golden Globes '89: Director (Eastwood); N.Y. Film Critics '88: Support. Actress (Venora).

Bird of Paradise ☆☆½ **1932** An exotic South Seas romance in which an adventurer is cast onto a remote Polynesian island when his yacht haphazardly sails into a coral reef. There he becomes enamored of an exotic island girl, and nature seems to disapprove. **80m/B VHS, 8mm.** Joel McCrea, Dolores Del Rio, Lon Chaney Jr.; ***D:*** King Vidor; ***M:*** Max Steiner.

Bird of Prey ☆☆½ **1995 (R)** Nick Milev (Milushev) has just been released from a Bulgarian prison for attacking Jonathan Griffith (Chamberlain), the drugs-and-arms dealer who was responsible for the death of Milev's policeman father. But Milev still wants revenge, though matters get complicated by Kily (Tilly), Griffith's naive daughter, with whom he falls in love. Plot's so-so but characters make up for some of the routiness. Filmed on location in Sofia, Bulgaria. **102m/C VHS.** Boyan Milushev, Jennifer Tilly, Richard Chamberlain, Lenny Von Dohlen, Robert Carradine, Lesley Ann Warren; ***D:*** Temistocles Lopez; ***W:*** Boyan Milushev; ***C:*** David Knaus.

Bird on a Wire ☆☆ **1990 (PG-13)** After suddenly being forced to emerge from a prolonged period under the Witness Protection Program, an ex-hood and his ex-girlfriend are pursued by old enemies. **110m/C VHS, DVD, Wide.** Mel Gibson, Goldie Hawn, David Carradine, Bill Duke, Stephen Tobolowsky; ***D:*** John Badham; ***W:*** David Seltzer; ***C:*** Robert Primes; ***M:*** Hans Zimmer.

The Bird with the Crystal Plumage ☆☆½ *L'Ucello dalle Plume di Cristallo; The Phantom of Terror; The Bird with the Glass Feathers; The Gallery Murders* **1970 (PG)** An American writer living in Rome witnesses a murder. He becomes involved in the mystery when the alleged murderer is cleared because the woman believed to be his next victim is shown to be a psychopathic murderer. Vintage Argento mayhem. **98m/C VHS, DVD.** *IT GE* Tony Musante, Suzy Kendall, Eva Renzi, Enrico Maria Salerno, Mario Adorf, Renato Romano, Reggie Nalder, Werner Peters, Umberto Raho, Dario Argento; ***D:*** Dario Argento; ***W:*** Dario Argento; ***C:*** Vittorio Storaro; ***M:*** Ennio Morricone.

The Birdcage ☆☆☆ *Birds of a Feather* **1995 (R)** Somewhat overlong but well-played remake of "La Cage aux Folles" features Williams suppressing his usual manic schtick to portray Armand, the subdued half of a longtime gay couple living in Miami. His partner is the ever-hysterical-but-loving drag queen Albert (Lane), whose presence provides a distinct challenge when Armand's son Val (Futterman) announces his engagement to the daughter of family values, right-wing senator Kevin Keeley (Hackman). When the Senator and family arrive for dinner, Armand tries to play it straight while Albert opts for a matronly mom impersonation (think Barbara Bush). Highlights include Armand's initial attempts to teach Albert to be butch (walk like John Wayne) and Hackman congoing in drag. **120m/C VHS, DVD.** Robin Williams, Nathan Lane, Gene Hackman, Dianne Wiest, Hank Azaria, Dan Futterman, Christine Baranski, Calista Flockhart, Tom McGowan; ***D:*** Mike Nichols; ***W:*** Elaine May; ***C:*** Emmanuel Lubezki; ***M:*** Mark Mothersbaugh, Jonathan Tunick. Screen Actors Guild '96: Cast.

Birdman of Alcatraz ☆☆☆ **1962** Robert Stroud, convicted of two murders and sentenced to life imprisonment on the Island, becomes an internationally accepted authority on birds. Lovingly told, with stunning performance from Lancaster, and exceptionally fine work from the supporting cast. The confinement of Stroud's prison cell makes the film seem claustrophobic and tedious at times, just as the imprisonment must have been. Ritter played Stroud's mother, who never stops trying to get him out of prison. **143m/B VHS, DVD, Wide.** Burt Lancaster, Karl Malden, Thelma Ritter, Betty Field, Neville Brand, Edmond O'Brien, Hugh Marlowe, Telly Savalas; ***D:*** John Frankenheimer; ***W:*** Guy Trosper; ***C:*** Burnett Guffey, Robert Krasker; ***M:*** Elmer Bernstein. British Acad. '62: Actor (Lancaster).

The Birds ☆☆☆½ **1963 (PG-13)** Hitchcock attempted to top the success of "Psycho" with this terrifying tale of Man versus Nature, in which Nature alights, one by one, on the trees of Bodega Bay to stage a bloody act of revenge upon the civilized world. Only Hitchcock can twist the harmless into the horrific while avoiding the ridiculous; this is perhaps his most brutal film, and one of the cinema's purest, horrifying portraits of apocalypse. Based on a short story by Daphne Du Maurier; screenplay by novelist Evan Hunter (aka Ed McBain). **120m/C VHS, DVD.** Rod Taylor, Tippi Hedren, Jessica Tandy, Veronica Cartwright, Suzanne Pleshette, Ethel Griffies, Charles McGraw, Ruth McDevitt, Lonny (Loni) Chapman, Joe Mantell, Morgan Brittany, Alfred Hitchcock; ***D:*** Alfred Hitchcock; ***W:*** Evan Hunter; ***C:*** Robert Burks; ***M:*** Bernard Herrmann.

The Birds 2: Land's End woof! **1994 (R)** Unfortunate rip-off of the Hitchcock fright classic. Killer seagulls begin attacking the inhabitants of east coast Gull Island. Seems they're tired of being oil slick victims. Hedren's the town shopkeeper in a role that's nothing like the one she played in the original. Definitely for the birds—even the director refuses to acknowledge it by officially using the film industry pseudonym "Alan Smithee." Made for TV. **87m/C VHS.** Brad Johnson, Chelsea Field, Tippi Hedren, James Naughton, Jan Rubes, Megan Gallagher; ***D:*** Rick Rosenthal; ***W:*** Jim Wheat, Ken Wheat. **TV**

Birds & the Bees 𝒮𝒮 **1956** A millionaire falls in love with an alluring card shark, and then calls it all off when he learns of her profession, only to fall in love with her again when she disguises herself. A remake—and poor shade—of Preston Sturge's 1941 classic "The Lady Eve." **94m/C VHS.** Mitzi Gaynor, David Niven, George Gobel, Reginald Gardiner, Hans Conried; ***D:*** Norman Taurog; ***W:*** Sidney Sheldon.

Birds of Prey 𝒮𝒮 **1972** Action film pits an ex-WWII army pilot against a group of kidnapping thieves in an airborne chopper chase. **81m/C VHS.** David Janssen, Ralph Meeker, Elayne Heilveil; ***D:*** William A. Graham; ***C:*** Jordan Cronenweth. **TV**

Birdy 𝒮𝒮𝒮½ **1984 (R)** An adaptation of the William Wharton novel about two Philadelphia youths, one with normal interests, the other obsessed with birds, and their eventual involvement in the Vietnam War, wrecking one physically and the other mentally. A hypnotic, evocative film, with a compelling Peter Gabriel soundtrack. **120m/C VHS, DVD.** Matthew Modine, Nicolas Cage, John Harkins, Sandy Baron, Karen Young, Bruno Kirby; ***D:*** Alan Parker; ***W:*** Jack Behr, Sandy Kroopf; ***M:*** Peter Gabriel. Cannes '85: Grand Jury Prize.

Birgitt Haas Must Be Killed 𝒮𝒮½ **1983** A ruthless secret agent (Noiret) plots to murder a German female terrorist and make it appear that her boyfriend was the killer. Never quite hits the mark, despite novel premise and strong cast. **105m/C VHS.** Philippe Noiret, Jean Rochefort, Elisabeth (Lisa) Kreuzer; ***D:*** Laurent Heynemann.

The Birth of a Nation 𝒮𝒮𝒮𝒮 *The Clansman* **1915** Lavish Civil War epic in which Griffith virtually invented the basics of film grammar. Gish and Walthall have some of the most moving scenes ever filmed and the masterful battle choreography brought the art of cinematography to new heights. Griffith's positive attitude toward the KKK notwithstanding, this was the first feature length silent, and it brought credibility to an entire industry. Based on the play "The Clansman" and the book "The Leopard's Spots" by Thomas Dixon, it is still a rouser, and of great historical interest. Silent with music score. Also available in a 124-minute version. **175m/B VHS, DVD.** Lillian Gish, Mae Marsh, Henry B. Walthall, Ralph Lewis, Robert "Bobbie" Harron, George Siegmann, Joseph Henabery, Spottiswoode Aitken, George Beranger, Mary Alden, Josephine Crowell, Elmer Clifton, Walter Long, Howard Gaye, Miriam Cooper, John Ford, Sam De Grasse, Maxfield Stanley, Donald Crisp, Raoul Walsh, Erich von Stroheim, Eugene Pallette, Wallace Reid; ***D:*** D.W. Griffith; ***W:*** D.W. Griffith, Frank E. Woods; ***C:*** Billy (G.W.) Bitzer; ***M:*** D.W. Griffith. AFI '98: Top 100, Natl. Film Reg. '92.

Birth of the Blues 𝒮𝒮½ **1941** Songman Crosby starts a band in New Orleans in the midst of the jazz boom. Help from partner Martin and real-life trombonist Teagarden, with comic relief from Eddie "Rochester" Anderson, make for a fun-filled story. Plot is riddled with some unbelievable gangster scenes, but the music and laughs will keep you amused. In B&W with color segments. ♫St. Louis Blues; St. James Infirmary; Melancholy Baby; Birth of the Blues. **76m/B VHS.** Bing Crosby, Mary Martin, Brian Donlevy, Eddie Anderson, J. Carrol Naish, Cecil Kellaway, Warren Hymer, Horace McMahon, Carolyn Lee, Jack Teagarden; ***D:*** Victor Schertzinger; ***W:*** Harry Tugend, Walter DeLeon; ***C:*** William Mellor; ***M:*** Robert Emmett Dolan.

Birthday Boy 𝒮𝒮 **1985** A cable comedy about a buffoonish salesman's 30th birthday, on which he takes an ill-fated business trip. Written by Belushi. **33m/C VHS.** James Belushi; ***D:*** Claude Conrad; ***W:*** James Belushi. **CABLE**

Birthday Girl 𝒮𝒮 **2002 (R)** Love story cum actioner stars Chaplin as a timid London bank clerk, John, and Kidman as Nadia, his mysterious and sexy online Russian mail-order bride with a secret. Nadia doesn't speak English, but the two begin to speak the international language anyway. Afraid, intrigued, then tickled with his Soviet missus who brings some color into his dull, drab life, John hardly has time to wallow in his newfound bliss when he's beset by Russian baddies (Frenchmen Kassovitz and Cassel) claiming to be Nadia's relatives, who show up on his doorstep one day. Kidman shows her range, however, and reportedly learned Russian for the film. Decent turn from the Butterworth clan, who also produced the hip debut film "Mojo." **93m/C VHS, DVD.** *US GB* Nicole Kidman, Ben Chaplin, Vincent Cassel, Mathieu Kassovitz, Kate Evans; ***D:*** Jez Butterworth; ***W:*** Jez Butterworth, Tom Butterworth; ***C:*** Oliver Stapleton; ***M:*** Stephen Warbeck.

The Bishop's Wife 𝒮𝒮𝒮 **1947** Episcopalian biship Henry (Niven) is praying to find the money to build a new church but his faith is shaky and his marriage to Julia (Young) even more so. But his prayers are answered (although Henry doesn't know it) in the form of angel Dudley (Grant), who's sent down to earth at Christmas to help work things out. Excellent performances by the cast make this an entertaining outing. Based on the novel by Robert Nathan. **109m/B VHS, DVD.** Cary Grant, Loretta Young, David Niven, Monty Woolley, Elsa Lanchester, James Gleason, Gladys Cooper, Regis Toomey; ***D:*** Henry Koster; ***W:*** Leonardo Bercovici, Robert Sherwood; ***C:*** Gregg Toland; ***M:*** Hugo Friedhofer. Oscars '47: Sound.

The Bitch woof! **1978 (R)** High-camp follies are the rule in this lustful continuation of "The Stud" as it follows the erotic adventures of a beautiful divorcee playing sex games for high stakes on the international playgrounds of high society. A collaborative effort by the sisters Collins: written by Jackie, with sister Joan well cast in the title role. **90m/C VHS.** *GB* Joan Collins, Kenneth Haigh, Michael Coby, Ian Hendry, Carolyn Seymour, Sue Lloyd, John Ratzenberger; ***D:*** Gerry O'Hara.

Bite the Bullet 𝒮𝒮𝒮½ **1975 (PG)** Moralistic western tells of a grueling 600-mile horse race where the participants reluctantly develop respect for one another. Unheralded upon release and shot in convincing epic style by Harry Stradling, Jr. Excellent cast. **131m/C VHS, DVD, Wide.** Gene Hackman, James Coburn, Candice Bergen, Dabney Coleman, Jan-Michael Vincent, Ben Johnson, Ian Bannen, Paul Stewart, Sally Kirkland, Mario Arteaga; ***D:*** Richard Brooks; ***W:*** Richard Brooks; ***C:*** Harry Stradling Jr.; ***M:*** Alex North.

Bitter Harvest 𝒮𝒮𝒮 **1981** Emmy-nominated TV movie concerning a dairy farmer frantically trying to discover what is mysteriously killing off his herd. Howard is excellent as the farmer battling the bureaucracy to find the truth. Based on a true story. **98m/C VHS.** Ron Howard, Art Carney, Tarah Nutter, Richard Dysart, Barry Corbin, Jim Haynie, David Knell; ***D:*** Roger Young. **TV**

Bitter Harvest 𝒮𝒮 **1993 (R)** Rubin and Kensit are the femme fatales who turn their considerable wiles on the innocent Baldwin. He's more than happy to be their lover but does he want to be their victim as well? **98m/C VHS.** Stephen Baldwin, Patsy Kensit, Jennifer Rubin, Adam Baldwin, M. Emmet Walsh; ***D:*** Duane Clark; ***W:*** Randall Fontana; ***C:*** Remi Adefarasin.

Bitter Moon 𝒮𝒮 **1992 (R)** Polanski effort looks promising, but ultimately disappoints. Bored British couple (Grant and Scott Thomas) meet up with sexual deviants (Coyote and Seigner, aka Mrs. Polanski) on a cruise and learn that passion and cruelty often share the same path to destruction. Masquerades as high class art, but whenever substance is lacking expect a silly, kinky sex scene. Needless to say, there isn't much substance, so erotic mischief abounds. Scott Thomas manages to hold her own, but Coyote is almost embarrassingly over the top. Based on the Pascal Bruckner novel "Lunes de Fiel." **139m/C VHS, Wide.** Peter Coyote, Emmanuelle Seigner, Hugh Grant, Kristin Scott Thomas, Stockard Channing, Victor Banerjee, Sophie Patel; ***D:*** Roman Polanski; ***W:*** Roman Polanski, Gerard Brach, John Brownjohn; ***C:*** Tonino Delli Colli; ***M:*** Vangelis.

Bitter Rice 𝒮𝒮𝒮 *Riso Amaro* **1949** Mangano became a star with her sultry performance about survival in postwar Italy. She scrapes by, working in the rice fields of the Po Valley, loved by the down-to-earth Vallone, who provides her with little excitement. Gassman is the rotten-to-the-core thief who meets up with Mangano while he's running from the police. He mistreats her, she steals his money and betrays her friends, and both destroy each other. In Italian with English subtitles. **96m/C VHS.** *IT* Silvana Mangano, Vittorio Gassman, Raf Vallone, Doris Dowling; ***D:*** Guiseppe de Santis; ***W:*** Guiseppe de Santis, Carlo Lizzani, Gianni Puccini; ***C:*** Otello Martelli; ***M:*** Goffredo Petrassi.

Bitter Sugar 𝒮𝒮𝒮 *Azucar Amarga* **1996** Young, idealistic communist Gustavo (Lavan) is a Havana university student who still believes that the Castro regime can make things better. His rock musician brother Bobby (Villanueva) is a radical, defying government policies, and his psychiatrist father Tomas (Gutierrez) makes more money playing piano at a tourist hotel than in his practice. But Gustavo's eyes are opened, not only by his family situtation, but when he falls in love with cynical dancer Yolanda (Vilan), who longs to escape to Miami. Serious politics bolstered by excellent performances and sharp cinematography. Spanish with subtitles. **102m/B VHS.** *CU* Rene Lavan, Mayte Vilan, Miguel Gutierrez, Larry Villanueva; ***D:*** Leon Ichaso; ***W:*** Leon Ichaso, Orestes Matacena; ***C:*** Claudio Chea; ***M:*** Manuel Tejada.

Bitter Sweet 𝒮𝒮½ **1933** Tragic tale of a woman who finally marries the man she loves, only to find that he is a compulsive gambler. Written by Coward, adapted from his operetta. **76m/B VHS.** *GB* Anna Neagle, Fernand Graavey, Esme Percy, Clifford Heatherley, Hugh Williams; ***D:*** Herbert Wilcox; ***W:*** Noel Coward.

Bitter Sweet 𝒮𝒮 **1940** The second version of the Noel Coward operetta, about young romance in 1875 Vienna. Creaky and overrated, but the lush Technicolor and Coward standards help to compensate. ♫Ziguener; I'll See You Again. **94m/C VHS.** Jeanette MacDonald, Nelson Eddy, George Sanders, Felix Bressart, Ian Hunter, Sig Rumann, Herman Bing, Fay Holden, Curt Bois, Edward Ashley; ***D:*** Woodbridge S. Van Dyke; ***W:*** Lesser Samuels, Noel Coward.

Bitter Sweet 𝒮𝒮 **1998 (R)** Everhart spends four years in the big house after being tricked by her boyfriend into participating in a robbery. All she wants when she gets out is to get revenge on the lowlife and she gets the opportunity when approached by cop Russo, who's looking to bring down her ex-beau's gangster boss (Roberts). **96m/C VHS, DVD.** Angie Everhart, James Russo, Eric Roberts, Brian Wimmer; ***D:*** Luca Bercovici. **VIDEO**

The Bitter Tea of General Yen 𝒮𝒮𝒮 **1933** Stanwyck arrives in Shanghai to marry a missionary (Gordon) during the threatening days of China's civil war. Unexpectedly swept into the arms of an infamous warlord (Asher), she becomes fascinated, although his attempts to seduce her fail. She even remains with him while his enemies close in. Exotic and poetic, if melodramatic by today's standards. The interracial aspects were considered very daring for their time. Adapted from the book by Grace Zaring Stone. **89m/B VHS.** Barbara Stanwyck, Nils Asther, Gavin Gordon, Walter Connolly, Lucien Littlefield, Toschia Mori, Richard Loo, Clara Blandick; ***D:*** Frank Capra; ***W:*** Edward Paramore.

The Bitter Tears of Petra von Kant 𝒮𝒮½ *Die Bitteren Traenen der Petra von Kant* **1972** Dark German story of lesbian love, the fashion world, obsession and anger. Claustrophobic settings and slow pace may frustrate some viewers. In German with English subtitles. **124m/C VHS.** *GE* Margit Carstensen, Hanna Schygulla, Irm Hermann, Eva Mattes; ***D:*** Rainer Werner Fassbinder; ***W:*** Rainer Werner Fassbinder; ***C:*** Michael Ballhaus.

Bitter Vengeance 𝒮𝒮 **1994 (R)** Security guard Jack Westford (Greenwood) pulls off a bank heist with his lover Isabella (Hocking) and plans to frame his wife Annie (Madsen) for the crime. Only Annie finds out and sets out to get them before the police get her. **90m/C VHS.** Virginia Madsen, Bruce Greenwood, Kristen Hocking, Eddie Velez, Gordon Jump, Carlos Gomez, Tim Russ; ***D:*** Stuart Cooper; ***W:*** Pablo F. Fenjves; ***M:*** David Michael Frank. **CABLE**

Bittersweet Love 𝒮½ **1976 (PG)** Two young people fall in love and marry, only to have the bride's mother and the groom's father confess a 30-year-old affair, disclosing that the two newlyweds are actually half-siblings. **92m/C VHS.** Lana Turner, Robert Lansing, Celeste Holm, Robert Alda, Meredith Baxter; ***D:*** David Miller.

Bix 𝒮𝒮 **1990** Based on the brief life of legendary Jazz Age cornetist Leon Bix Beiderbecke, who died at age 28. Story unfolds in flashbacks, through friend Joe Venuti memories of the dissipated genius and the music he created with Hoagy Carmichael, Pee Wee Russell, Paul Whiteman, and others. **100m/C VHS.** *IT* Bryant Weeks, Emile Levisetti, Mark Collver, Sally Groth; ***D:*** Pupi Avati; ***W:*** Pupi Avati, Antonio Avati, Lino Patruno.

Bizarre 𝒮 **1987** When a wife escapes her perverse, psychologically threatening marriage, she finds her husband still haunts her literally and figuratively, and plots psychological revenge. Dubbed. **93m/C VHS.** *IT* Florence Guerin, Luciano Bartoli, Robert Egon Spechtenhauser, Stefano Sabelli; ***D:*** Giuliana Gamba.

Bizarre Bizarre 𝒮𝒮𝒮 *Drole de Drama* **1939** A mystery writer is accused of murder and disappears, only to return in disguise to try to clear his name. Along the way, a number of French comedians are introduced with a revue of comedy-farce sketches that include slapstick, burlesque, black humor, and comedy of the absurd. In French with English subtitles. **90m/B VHS.** *FR* Louis Jouvet, Michel Simon, Francoise Rosay, Jean-Pierre Aumont, Nadine Vogel, Henri Guisol, Jenny Burnay; ***D:*** Marcel Carne; ***W:*** Jacques Prevert; ***C:*** Eugene Schufftan; ***M:*** Maurice Jaubert.

The Black Abbot 𝒮𝒮 **1963** A mysterious black-hooded figure is seen entering a ruined Abbey tower that leads to a country house with buried treasure. Based on an Edgar Wallace story. **95m/C VHS.** *GE* Joachim Fuchsberger, Dieter Borsche, Gritt Bottcher, Eva Scholtz, Franz Gottlieb; ***D:*** Franz Gottlieb.

Black and White 𝒮𝒮𝒮 **1999 (R)** Director Toback attempts to investigate white kids' facsination with black hip-hop culture by creating an intriguing combination of pseudo-documentary and urban melodrama, with cameos and performances by professional celebrities alongside professional actors. In the more effective part of the film, Shields is a documentary filmmaker asking rich white kids why they're into hip-hop. This section also includes Robert Downey as her gay husband hitting on Mike Tyson (playing himself in one of the film's strongest scenes). The part that doesn't work as well is the more conventional storyline (which seems added to satisfy studio executives looking for straight narrative) involving an undercover cop (Stiller) bribing college basketball star Dean (Houston) to throw a game in an attempt to get at Dean's best friend Rich (Power), a drug kingpin turned rap mogul. While the parts don't add up to an entirely satisfying whole, the journey is worth the interesting ride. **98m/C VHS, DVD, Wide.** Scott Caan, Robert Downey Jr., Stacy Edwards, Gaby Hoffman, Jared Leto, Marla Maples, Joe Pantoliano, Brooke Shields, Power, Claudia Schiffer, William Lee Scott, Ben Stiller, Eddie Kaye Thomas, Elijah Wood, Mike Tyson, James Toback, Allan Houston, Kidada Jones, Bijou Phillips, Raekwon; ***D:*** James Toback; ***W:*** James Toback; ***C:*** David Ferrara.

Black & White 🦴🦴½ **1999 (R)** Rookie cop Chris O'Brien (Cochrane) is partnered with tough veteran female officer Nora Hugosian (Gershon), who's known for both her sexiness and her ruthless style. The two begin an affair while searching for a serial killer. And then the rookie comes across some evidence that seems to implicate his partner in the crimes. **97m/C VHS, DVD, Wide.** Gina Gershon, Rory Cochrane, Ron Silver, Alison Eastwood, Marshall Bell; ***D:*** Yuri Zeltser; ***W:*** Yuri Zeltser, Leon Zeltser; ***C:*** Phil Parmet.

Black and White As Day and Night 🦴🦴 **1963** A man's talent for the game of chess becomes a destructive obsession. In German with English subtitles. **103m/C VHS.** Bruno Ganz; ***D:*** Wolfgang Petersen.

Black and White in Color 🦴🦴🦴 *La Victoire en Chantant* **1976 (PG)** Award-winning satire about a French soldier at an African outpost, who, upon hearing the news of the beginning of WWI, takes it upon himself to attack a neighboring German fort. Calamity ensues. In French, with English subtitles. **100m/C VHS.** *FR* Jean Carmet, Jacques Dufilho, Catherine Rouvel, Jacques Spiesser, Dora Doll, Jacques Perrin; ***D:*** Jean-Jacques Annaud; ***W:*** George Conchon, Jean-Jacques Annaud; ***M:*** Pierre Bachelet. Oscars '76: Foreign Film.

Black Angel 🦴🦴🦴 **1946** Catherine Bennett (Vincent) tries to clear the name of estranged husband Kirk (Phillips), who's accused of murdering his lover, blackmailing chanteuse Mavis Marlowe (Dowling). Catherine enlists the aid of Mavis' husband, drunken songwriter Martin Blair (Duryea), whom she suspects actually did the deed. Another suspect is sleazy nightclub owner Marko (Lorre), where the duo get a job to check things out. Blair falls for Catherine and goes on another bender when she rejects him, as Kirk's execution day draws ever closer. Atmospheric noir is based on the novel by Cornell Woolrich. **80m/B VHS.** June Vincent, Dan Duryea, Peter Lorre, Broderick Crawford, John Phillips, Constance Dowling, Wallace Ford, Hobart Cavanaugh; ***D:*** Roy William Neill; ***W:*** Roy Chanslor; ***C:*** Paul Ivano; ***M:*** Frank Skinner.

Black Arrow 🦴🦴🦴 *Black Arrow Strikes* **1948** Original adventure film of the famous Robert Louis Stevenson novel. Upon return from 16th century's War of the Roses, a young man must avenge his father's murder by following a trail of clues in the form of black arrows. Well made and fun. **76m/B VHS, DVD.** Louis Hayward, Janet Blair, George Macready, Edgar Buchanan, Paul Cavanagh; ***D:*** Gordon Douglas.

The Black Arrow 🦴🦴 **1984** Exiled bowman returns to England to avenge the injustices of a villainous nobleman. Cable version of the Robert Louis Stevenson medieval romp is not as well done as the 1948 adaptation. **93m/C VHS.** Oliver Reed, Benedict Taylor, Georgia Slowe, Stephan Chase, Donald Pleasence; ***D:*** John Hough. CABLE

Black Beauty 🦴🦴 **1946** In this adaptation of Anna Sewell's familiar novel, a young girl develops a kindred relationship with an extraordinary horse. **74m/B VHS.** Mona Freeman, Richard Denning, Evelyn Ankers; ***D:*** Max Nosseck.

Black Beauty 🦴🦴 **1971 (G)** International remake of the classic horse story by Anna Sewell. **105m/C VHS.** *GB GE SP* Mark Lester, Walter Slezak; ***D:*** James Hill; ***C:*** Chris Menges; ***M:*** Lionel Bart.

Black Beauty 🦴🦴🦴 **1994 (G)** Remake of the classic Anna Sewell children's novel about an oft-sold horse whose life has its shares of ups and downs. Timeless tale still brings children and adults to tears. Six-year-old quarterhorse named Justin gives a nuanced portrayal as the Black Beauty, recalling Olivier in "Hamlet." Directorial debut of "Secret Garden" screenwriter Thompson. **88m/C VHS, DVD.** Andrew Knott, Sean Bean, David Thewlis, Jim Carter, Alun Armstrong, Eleanor Bron, Peter Cook, Peter Davison, John McEnery, Nicholas Jones; ***D:*** Caroline Thompson; ***W:*** Caroline Thompson; ***C:*** Alex Thomson.

Black Belt 🦴 **1992 (R)** A private detective is hired to protect a rock star from a fanatic Vietnam vet. **80m/C VHS.** Don "The Dragon" Wilson, Richard Beymer, Alan Blumenfeld, Matthias Hues; ***D:*** Charles Philip Moore; ***W:*** Charles Philip Moore.

Black Belt Jones 🦴 **1974 (R)** Martial arts expert fights the mob to save a school of self-defense in Los Angeles' Watts district. **87m/C VHS.** Jim Kelly, Gloria Hendry, Scatman Crothers; ***D:*** Robert Clouse.

Black Bikers from Hell 🦴½ *Black Angels* **1970 (R)** Black gang-members infiltrate and wreak havoc on their rivals. Who can stop these brutal young men? Cast with real bikers and biker chicks. **87m/C VHS.** John King III, Des Roberts, Linda Jackson, James Whitworth, James Young-El, Clancy Syrko, Beverly Gardner; ***D:*** Lawrence Merrick; ***W:*** Lawrence Merrick.

Black Bird 🦴🦴 **1975 (PG)** In this satiric "sequel" to "The Maltese Falcon," detective Sam Spade, Jr. searches for the mysterious black falcon statuette that caused his father such trouble. Features appearances by Elisha Cook Jr. and Lee Patrick, who starred in the 1941 classic "The Maltese Falcon" with Humphrey Bogart. **98m/C VHS.** George Segal, Stephane Audran, Lionel Stander, Lee Patrick, Elisha Cook Jr., Connie Kreski; ***D:*** David Giler.

Black Box Affair 🦴½ **1966** An American secret agent must find a black box lost in a B-52 plane crash before it falls into the wrong hands. **95m/C VHS.** *IT SP* Craig Hill, Teresa Gimpera, Luis Martin, Jorge (George) Rigaud; ***D:*** James B. Harris.

Black Brigade 🦴🦴 *Carter's Army* **1969** Pryor and Williams star in this low budget movie as leaders of an all-black outfit assigned to a suicide mission behind Nazi lines during WWII. Their force wreaks havoc and earns them the respect of military higher-ups. Lots of action and climactic finish. **90m/C VHS.** Stephen Boyd, Robert Hooks, Susan Oliver, Roosevelt "Rosie" Grier, Moses Gunn, Richard Pryor, Billy Dee Williams; ***D:*** George McCowan; ***W:*** Aaron Spelling; ***M:*** Fred Steiner.

Black Caesar 🦴🦴 **1973 (R)** A small-time hood climbs the ladder to be the head of a Harlem crime syndicate. Music by James Brown. Followed by the sequel "Hell Up in Harlem." **92m/C VHS, DVD, Wide.** Fred Williamson, Julius W. Harris, Val Avery, Art Lund, Gloria Hendry, James Dixon; ***D:*** Larry Cohen; ***W:*** Larry Cohen; ***C:*** Fenton Hamilton, James Signorelli; ***M:*** James Brown.

The Black Castle 🦴🦴 **1952** MacNally plays an 18th-century Austrian count whose guests tend to disappear after a visit. This happens to two of Greene's friends and he decides to investigate. Uninspired and melodramatic, not enough horror. Karloff doesn't have enough to do. **81m/B VHS.** Richard Greene, Boris Karloff, Stephen McNally, Rita (Paula) Corday, Lon Chaney Jr., John Hoyt; ***D:*** Nathan (Hertz) Juran.

The Black Cat 🦴🦴🦴½ *House of Doom; Vanishing Body* **1934** The first of the Boris and Bela pairings stands up well years after release. Polished and taut, with fine sets and interesting acting. Confrontation between architect and devil worshipper acts as plot, with strange twists. Worth a look. **65m/B VHS.** Boris Karloff, Bela Lugosi, David Manners, Julie (Jacqueline Wells) Bishop, Lucille Lund, Henry Armetta, Egon Brecher, Albert Conti, Harry Cording, John Carradine; ***D:*** Edgar G. Ulmer; ***W:*** Edgar G. Ulmer, Peter Ruric; ***C:*** John Mescall; ***M:*** Heinz Roemheld.

The Black Cat 🦴🦴½ **1941** Wealthy Henrietta Winslow (Loftus) has left her estate to her greedy grandchildren but only after her faithful housekeeper Abigail (Sondergaard) and all her beloved cats die. Naturally, strange and murderous events begin occurring. Not to be confused with the 1934 classic horror film of the same title. **71m/B VHS.** Basil Rathbone, Hugh Herbert, Gale Sondergaard, Broderick Crawford, Bela Lugosi, Gladys Cooper, Anne Gwynne, Cecilia Loftus, Claire Dodd, John Eldridge, Alan Ladd; ***D:*** Albert Rogell; ***W:*** Robert Lees, Frederic Rinaldo, Eric Taylor, Robert Neville; ***C:*** Stanley Cortez.

The Black Cat woof! *Il Gatto Nero* **1981** Spaghetti splatter-meister Fulci, best known for his unabashed ripoffs "Zombie" and "Gates of Hell," tones down the gore this time in a vaguely Poe-ish tale of a medium with some marbles loose (Magee) whose kitty provides the temporary habitat for spirits its master calls up. The dreary English village setting and the downright myopic camera work add up to an oppressive viewing experience. **92m/C VHS, DVD, Wide.** *IT GB* Patrick Magee, Mimsy Farmer, David Warbeck, Al Cliver, Dagmar Lassander, Geoffrey Copleston, Daniela Dorio; ***D:*** Lucio Fulci; ***W:*** Lucio Fulci, Biagio Proietti; ***C:*** Sergio Salvati; ***M:*** Pino Donaggio.

Black Cat 🦴½ **1990** Filmmakers find lots of action in a haunted house. Chock full of references to the works of spaghetti horror dons Mario Bava and Dario Argento. **?m/C VHS.** *IT* Caroline Munro, Brett Halsey; ***D:*** Lewis (Luigi Cozzi) Coates; ***W:*** Lewis (Luigi Cozzi) Coates.

Black Cat Run 🦴🦴 **1998 (R)** Race car driver's girlfriend is abducted and then he gets involved with a psycho deputy. Lots of action. **88m/C VHS, DVD.** Patrick Muldoon, Amelia Heinle, Russell Means, Kevin J. O'Connor, Peter Greene, Jake Busey; ***D:*** D.J. Caruso; ***W:*** Frank Darabont, Douglas Venturelli; ***C:*** Bing Sokolsky; ***M:*** Jeff Rona. CABLE

Black Cat, White Cat 🦴🦴🦴 **1998** Emir Kusturica's rambling tale of scheming Gypsies who live on the banks of the Danube river is a mixture of slapstick humor, folk tales and music. The cheesily dressed and mostly nonprofessional actors light up a plot involving a cargo of fuel, an arranged marriage, and a corpse on ice. Non-political (and much lighter) follow-up to Kusturica's Palme d'Or winning "Underground." Serbo-Croatian and Romany with subtitles. **129m/C VHS.** Bajram Severdzan, Florijan Ajdini, Salija Ibraimova, Branka Katic, Zabit Memedov, Sabri Sulejman, Jasar Destani, Srdan Todorovic, Ljubica Adzovic, Predrag Manojlovic; ***D:*** Emir Kusturica; ***W:*** Gordan Mihic; ***C:*** Thierry Arbogast; ***M:*** D. Nele Karajilic, Vajislav Aralica, Dejo Sparavalo.

The Black Cauldron 🦴🦴½ **1985 (PG)** Disney's 25th full-length animated movie follows the adventures of pig-keeper Taran, who discovers his psychic pig Hen Wen is the key to keeping a magical cauldron out of the hands of the evil Horned King. Based on the "Chronicles of Prydain" novels by Lloyd Alexander. **82m/C VHS, DVD, Wide.** ***D:*** Ted Berman, Richard Rich; ***W:*** Ted Berman, Richard Rich; ***M:*** Elmer Bernstein; ***V:*** Grant Bardsley, Susan Sheridan, John Hurt, Freddie Jones, Nigel Hawthorne, John Byner, Arthur Malet; ***Nar:*** John Huston.

Black Christmas 🦴🦴½ *Silent Night, Evil Night; Stranger in the House* **1975 (R)** A college sorority is besieged by an axe-murderer over the holidays. **98m/C VHS, DVD.** *CA* Andrea Martin, Art Hindle, Olivia Hussey, Keir Dullea, Margot Kidder, John Saxon; ***D:*** Bob (Benjamin) Clark; ***W:*** Roy Moore; ***C:*** Reginald Morris; ***M:*** Carl Zittrer.

Black Circle Boys 🦴½ **1997 (R)** Depressed high schooler Kyle (Bairstow) is still trying to fit in at his new school. He makes the mistake of getting involved with the "Black Circle Boys"—a clique of losers involved with drugs and the occult that's led by Shane (Mabius). The Boys enjoy malicious pranks and Kyle begins to have qualms about his participation but Shane doesn't want to let him go. Murky script gets increasingly silly as pic progresses. **100m/C VHS, DVD.** Scott Bairstow, Eric Mabius, Heath Lourwood, Chad Lindberg, Tara Subkoff, Dee Wallace Stone, Donnie Wahlberg, John Doe; ***D:*** Matthew Carnahan; ***W:*** Matthew Carnahan; ***C:*** Geary McLeod.

Black Cobra woof! **1983 (R)** A lesbian exacts revenge for her lover's snakebite murder by trapping the guilty party with his own snakes. **97m/C VHS.** *IT* Laura Gemser, Jack Palance; ***D:*** Joe D'Amato.

The Black Cobra woof! *Cobra Nero* **1987 (R)** After photographing a psychopath in the process of killing someone, a beautiful photographer seeks the help of a tough police sergeant to protect her. The leader of the Black Cobras gang gives chase. **90m/C VHS, DVD.** *IT* Fred Williamson, Karl Landgren, Eva Grimaldi; ***D:*** Stelvio Massi.

Black Cobra 2 🦴🦴 **1989 (R)** A mismatched team of investigators tracks a notorious terrorist. They find him holding a school full of children as hostage. **95m/C VHS.** Fred Williamson.

Black Cobra 3: The Manila Connection 🦴½ **1990 (R)** Interpol turns to police lieutenant Robert Malone (Williamson) when a team of high-tech weapons thieves threatens the world. Malone attacks like a cyclone on the terrorists' jungle haven. They won't know what hit 'em! **92m/C VHS.** Fred Williamson, Forry Smith, Debra Ward; ***D:*** Don Edwards.

Black Day Blue Night 🦴🦴 **1995 (R)** Rinda (Forbes) and Hallie (Sara) take a road trip from Utah to Phoenix and pick up the handsome Dodge (Bellows). Turns out he's being pursued by cop John Quinn (Walsh) as a suspect in a murder/robbery. Women-in-peril-who-help-themselves type story. **99m/C VHS.** Michelle Forbes, Mia Sara, Gil Bellows, J.T. Walsh, Tim Guinee, John Beck; ***D:*** J.S. Cardone; ***W:*** J.S. Cardone; ***C:*** Michael Cardone; ***M:*** Johnny Lee Schell, Joe Sublett.

Black Devil Doll from Hell 🦴 **1984** This shot-on-video movie deals with a nasty little voodoo doll that likes to kill its owners. **70m/C VHS.** Shirley Jones, Rickey Roach, Marie Sainvilvs; ***D:*** Chester Turner.

The Black Devils of Kali 🦴 *Mystery of the Black Jungle* **1955** Adventurers in the Indian jungle discover a lost race of idol-worshipping primitives. Racist garbage produced near the end of Republic Pictures' existence. Based on a novel by Emillio Salgari. **72m/B VHS.** Lex Barker, Jane Maxwell, Luigi Tosi, Paul Muller; ***D:*** Ralph Murphy.

Black Dog 🦴 **1998 (PG-13)** Not since the '70s heyday of CBs and C.W. McCall have 18-wheelers been so lovingly portrayed. Too bad the rest of the characters weren't given the same attention. Swayze (resurrecting his sensitive butt-kicker persona from "Roadhouse") plays disgraced trucker Jack Crews, recently released from prison after a vehicular manslaughter rap. With no driver's license and an overdue mortgage, he agrees to an "off the books" run for his shady boss (Beckel). The cargo turns out to be guns, which attracts the attention of the FBI, ATF, and a scuzzy band of hijackers led by the Bible-quoting Red (Meatloaf). Of course, the paint-by-numbers plot puts Jack's family in harm's way, and gives him a soulful, country-croonin' ally (Travis). Avoid this mutt like three-day-old roadkill unless you're a big-rig fetishist. **88m/C VHS, DVD.** Patrick Swayze, Randy Travis, Meat Loaf Aday, Gabriel Casseus, Graham Beckel, Stephen Tobolowsky, Charles S. Dutton, Brian Vincent, Brenda Strong, Erin Broderick; ***D:*** Kevin Hooks; ***W:*** William Mickelberry, Dan Vining; ***C:*** Buzz Feitshans IV; ***M:*** George S. Clinton.

The Black Dragons 🦴 **1942** Weird and fairly stupid war drama involving sabotage by the Japanese. Lugosi is the plastic surgeon who deftly cuts and pastes Japanese face parts to permit agents to pass as Americans. Also available colorized. **62m/B VHS.** Bela Lugosi, Joan Barclay, George Pembroke, Clayton Moore; ***D:*** William Nigh.

Black Eagle 🦴🦴 **1988 (R)** Pre-Glasnost, anti-Soviet tale of two high-kicking spies. CIA and KGB agents race to recover innovative equipment in the Mediterranean. **93m/C VHS, DVD.** Bruce Doran, Jean-Claude Van Damme, Sho Kosugi; ***D:*** Eric Karson; ***W:*** Shimon Arama; ***M:*** Terry Plumeri.

Black Eliminator 🦴 **1978** A black cop struggles to stop a maniacal secret agent who plans to destroy the world. **84m/C VHS.** Jim Kelly, George Lazenby, Harold Sakata, Bob Minor, Patch MacKenzie, Aldo Ray; ***D:*** Al Adamson.

Black Eyes 🦴½ **1939** A lowly waiter, working in a Moscow restaurant, manages to overhear a number of stock tips from the wealthy patrons and makes a tidy pile of rubles to improve his daughter's life. The daughter already thinks he's a successful businessman and is disillusioned when she discovers dad's true profession. All comes out right in the end. **72m/B VHS.** *GB* Otto Kruger, Mary Maguire, Walter Rilla, George L. Baxt, Marie Wright; ***D:*** Herbert Brenon.

Black Force 🦴🦴 **1975** Brothers who fight crime with violent actions, are called for assistance in the recovery of an African artifact. Originally known as "Force Four." **82m/C VHS.** Malachi Lee, Warhawk Tanzania, Owen Watson, Judie Soriano; ***D:*** Michael Fink.

Black Force 2 🦴🦴 **1978 (R)** The brothers are back on the scene in another violent, cartilage-shattering adventure. **90m/C VHS.** Terry Carter, James B. Sikking, Gwen Mitchell; ***D:*** Edward Lakso.

Black Fox: Blood Horse 🦴🦴½ **1994** Alan Johnson (Reeve) and Britt (Todd) try to maintain an uneasy peace with the local Kiowas until evil Ralph Holtz (Wiggins) tries to stir things up and have some vigilantes attack the tribe. The second episode in the three-part series. **90m/C VHS.** Christopher Reeve, Raoul Trujillo, Tony Todd, Chris Wiggins; ***D:*** Steven Hilliard Stern; ***C:*** Frank Tidy, Eric N. Robertson.

Black Fox: Good Men and Bad 🦴🦴½ **1994** Britt (Todd) accepts a job as a federal marshall while Alan (Reeve) goes after desperado Carl Glenn (Fox) and his gang. During a stagecoach robbery, the outlaws take Hallie (Rowan) hostage, thinking she's the wife of a tycoon and Alan manages to use her to get to Glenn. The third episode in the sagebrush series. **90m/C VHS.** Christopher Reeve, David Fox, Tony Todd, Kim Coates, Kelly Rowan; ***D:*** Steven Hilliard Stern; ***C:*** Frank Tidy; ***M:*** Eric N. Robertson.

Black Fox: The Price of Peace 🦴🦴½ **1994** Former plantation owner Alan Johnson (Reeve) and childhood friend Britt (Todd), whom he frees from slavery, try to forge a new life in 1860s Texas. But there's trouble when abusive bigot Ralph Holtz (Wiggins) threatens the peace between settlers and Indians when he goes after his wife delores (Holtz) who left him for a Kiowa warrior, Running Dog (Trujillo). Based on the novel by Matt Braun; made for TV. **90m/C VHS.** Christopher Reeve, Raoul Trujillo, Tony Todd, Chris Wiggins, Cyndy Preston; ***D:*** Steven Hilliard Stern; ***C:*** Frank Tidy; ***M:*** Eric N. Robertson. **TV**

Black Friday 🦴🦴½ **1940** Karloff is a surgeon who saves the life of his college professor friend (Ridges) by transplanting part of the brain of a gangster (involved in the same car crash) into the man's body. This results in a Jekyll/Hyde complex with the gangster's evil portion taking over and seeking revenge on rival mobster Lugosi. Horror stars Karloff and Lugosi never have any scenes together. **70m/B VHS.** Boris Karloff, Stanley Ridges, Bela Lugosi, Anne Nagel, Anne Gwynne, Paul Fix, Virginia Brissac, James Craig; ***D:*** Arthur Lubin; ***W:*** Curt Siodmak, Eric Taylor; ***C:*** Elwood "Woody" Bredell.

Black Fury 🦴🦴🦴 **1935** A coal miner's efforts to protest working conditions earn him a beating by the company goons who also kill his friend. He draws national attention to this brutal plight of the workers when he barricades himself inside the mine. Muni's carefully detailed performance adds authenticity to this powerful drama, but it proved too depressing to command a big boxoffice. **95m/B VHS.** Paul Muni, Barton MacLane, Henry O'Neill, John Qualen, J. Carrol Naish; ***D:*** Michael Curtiz.

Black Gestapo woof! **1975 (R)** Black-exploitation film about a vigilante army taking over a Los Angeles ghetto, first to help residents, but later to abuse them. Extremely violent. **89m/C VHS.** Rod Perry, Charles Robinson, Phil Hoover, Ed(ward) Cross, Angela Brent, Wes Bishop, Lee Frost, Charles Howerton, Uschi Digart; ***D:*** Lee Frost; ***W:*** Wes Bishop, Lee Frost; ***C:*** Derek Scott.

Black Glove 🦴 *Face the Music* **1954** A trumpet star defends himself against charges of murdering a Spanish singer by tracking down the real killer. **84m/B VHS.** *GB* Alex Nicol, John Salew, Arthur Lane, Eleanor Summerfield, Paul Carpenter, Geoffrey Keen, Martin Boddey, Fred Johnson; ***D:*** Terence Fisher; ***W:*** Ernest Borneman; ***C:*** Walter J. (Jimmy W.) Harvey.

Black God, White Devil 🦴🦴 *Deus e o Diabo na Terra do Sol* **1964** Another Brazilan socio-political commentary by Rocha, an oft-incendiary filmmaker whose left-leaning works are steeped in mysticism, obscure folklore, and powerful images. An impoverished man transforms from a religious zealot to a bandit, his tale underscored by conflict between poor masses and wealthy landowners. Portuguese with subtitles. **102m/C VHS.** *BR* Yona Magalhaes, Geraldo Del Rey, Othon Bastos, Mauricio De Valle, Lidio Silva; ***D:*** Glauce Rocha; ***W:*** Glauce Rocha; ***C:*** Waldemar Lima.

Black Godfather 🦴 **1974 (R)** The grueling story of a hood clawing his way to the top of a drug-selling mob. Features an all-black cast. **90m/C VHS, DVD.** Rod Perry, Damu King, Don Chastain, Jimmy Witherspoon, Diane Summerfield; ***D:*** John Evans; ***W:*** John Evans; ***C:*** Jack Steely.

Black Gold 🦴🦴 **1936** Oil field suspense thriller by "B" movie king Hopton. **57m/B VHS.** Frankie Darro, Leroy Mason; ***D:*** Russell Hopton.

The Black Hand 🦴🦴🦴 **1950** Kelly plays well against character in this atmospheric turn-of-the-century thriller. The evil society of the Black Hand murders his father, and he seeks revenge. Well-made drama. **93m/B VHS.** Gene Kelly, J. Carrol Naish, Teresa Celli, Marc Lawrence, Frank Puglia; ***D:*** Richard Thorpe; ***C:*** Paul Vogel.

Black Hand 🦴½ **1976** Unemployed Italian immigrant is drawn into a web of murder and betrayal after he is attacked by an Irish gang. **90m/C VHS.** Lionel Stander, Mike Placido.

Black Hawk Down 🦴🦴🦴½ **2001 (R)** Bruckheimer and Scott faithfully and superbly recreate the 1993 Battle of Mogadishu of October, 1993. U.S. Army Rangers and Delta Force units are sent to apprehend Somali warlord Muhammad Farah Aidid's top staff in an Aidid-controlled section of the city. Things go wrong right from the beginning, and when two Black Hawk helicopters are shot down the focus of the mission changes to rescue and defense. The usual introduction and preparation of the troops is dispensed with fairly quickly, in favor of background info on the Somalian situation, and details of the impending operation. This no-frills setup works perfectly with the following action, which is fierce, intense, and nonstop. Once the fighting begins, Scott's brilliance with visuals really kicks in, but nothing that happens, no matter how gruesome, seems forced or exploitative. Fine ensemble cast is nominally led by Hartnett, but no one disappoints. Based on the book by Mark Bowden. **143m/C VHS, DVD, Wide.** *US* Josh Hartnett, Eric Bana, Ewan McGregor, Tom Sizemore, William Fichtner, Sam Shepard, Gabriel Casseus, Kim Coates, Hugh Dancy, Ron Eldard, Ioan Gruffudd, Tom Guiry, Charlie Hofheimer, Danny Hoch, Jason Isaacs, Zeljko Ivanek, Glenn Morshower, Jeremy Piven, Brendan Sexton III, Johnny Strong, Richard Tyson, Brian Van Holt, Steven Ford, Gregory Sporleder, Carmine D. Giovinazzo, Chris Beetem, George Harris, Ewen Bremner, Boyd Kestner, Nikolaj Coster-Waldau, Ian Virgo, Thomas (Tom) Hardy, Tac Fitzgerald, Matthew Marsden, Orlando Bloom, Kent Linville, Enrique Murciano, Michael Roof, Treva Etienne, Ty Burrell; ***D:*** Ridley Scott; ***W:*** Ken Nolan; ***C:*** Slawomir Idziak; ***M:*** Hans Zimmer. Oscars '01: Film Editing, Sound.

Black Hills 🦴 **1948** Dull oater with Dean and his sidekick Ates out to avenge the murder of a struggling ranch owner. **60m/B VHS.** Eddie Dean, Roscoe Ates, Shirley Patterson, Terry Frost, Nina Bara, William "Bill" Fawcett; ***D:*** Ray Taylor.

The Black Hole 🦴½ **1979 (G)** A high-tech, computerized Disney space adventure dealing with a mad genius who attempts to pilot his craft directly into a black hole. Except for the top quality special effects, a pretty creaky vehicle. **97m/C VHS, DVD.** Maximilian Schell, Anthony Perkins, Ernest Borgnine, Yvette Mimieux, Joseph Bottoms, Robert Forster; ***D:*** Gary Nelson; ***W:*** Gerry Day; ***C:*** Frank Phillips; ***M:*** John Barry.

Black Ice 🦴🦴 **1992 (R)** After an affair with a popular politician ends violently, Vanessa (Pacula) realizes her boss set up his death—and she's next in line. She finds the nearest taxi and offers the driver plenty of cash if he can quickly get her out of the country. It's going to be the ride of her life. Also available in an unrated version. **90m/C VHS.** Michael Nouri, Michael Ironside, Joanna Pacula; ***D:*** Neill Fearnley; ***M:*** Amin Bhatia.

Black Jesus 🦴🦴 *Seduta Alla Sua Destra; Seated At His Right* **1968** Lalubi (Strode) is an African leader using passive resistance to save his people from a dictatorial regime that's supported by European colonialism. When he's betrayed by a follower, Lalubi's imprisoned and tortured, along with a thief who gains a greater understanding after contact with the leader. Film is a thinly disguised depiction of Zaire and its history. **?m/C VHS.** *IT* Woody Strode, Jean Servais; ***D:*** Valerio Zurlini.

The Black King 🦴½ *Harlem Hot Shot* **1932** Prejudiced propaganda based on the life of Marcus Garvey, black leader of the '20s, who advocated black superiority and a return to Africa. A black con man takes advantage of fellow blacks by organizing a phony back-to-Africa movement, enriching himself in the process. When one man's girlfriend deserts him for the bogus leader, the jilted one blows the whistle. **70m/B VHS.** A.B. Comethiere, Vivianne Baber, Knolly Mitchell, Dan Michaels, Mike Jackson; ***D:*** Bud Pollard.

The Black Klansman 🦴 *I Crossed the Line* **1966** A black man masquerades as a white extremist in order to infiltrate the KKK and avenge his daughter's murder. In the interest of racial harmony, he seduces the Klan leader's daughter. As bad as it sounds. **88m/B VHS.** Richard Gilden, Rima Kutner, Harry Lovejoy; ***D:*** Ted V. Mikels.

Black Knight 🦴 **2001 (PG-13)** The utterly unoriginal title should be a clue. Another remake of "A Connecticut Yankee in King Arthur's Court," and a particularly bad and formulaic one at that. Lazy, selfish Jamal (Lawrence) is transported from his minimum-wage job at theme park Medieval World to 14th century England, the real medieval world, where some life lessons await. Obvious fish-out-of-water jokes ensue, as Jamal seeks to make sense of his new surroundings, knock boots with Nubian maidens and lead a revolution against an evil king. The film's few decent gags are swallowed by lots of inane humor, a tired script and Lawrence's desperate mugging. Ironically, the story's moral message about giving up selfishness for a cause is lost on its star, who acts as if he's the only person on screen. Ye olde bore. **95m/C VHS, DVD, Wide.** *US* Martin Lawrence, Tom Wilkinson, Vincent Regan, Marsha Thomason, Kevin Conway, Darryl (Chill) Mitchell, Jeannette Weegar, Michael Burgess, Isabell Monk, Helen Carey; ***D:*** Gil Junger; ***W:*** Darryl Quarles, Peter Gaulke, Gerry Swallow; ***C:*** Ueli Steiger; ***M:*** Randy Edelman.

The Black Lash 🦴 **1952** Two lawmen go undercover to break a silver hijacking gang. **55m/B VHS.** Lash LaRue, Al "Fuzzy" St. John, Peggy Stewart, Kermit Maynard; ***D:*** Ron Ormond.

The Black Legion 🦴🦴🦴 **1937** Social drama isn't as dated as we'd like to think. Auto worker Frank Taylor (Bogart) is angry at being passed over for an expected promotion that goes to a Polish immigrant. So he's easy pickings for a Klan-like secret society that practices hatred and Frank gets in deep, eventually losing his family. His best pal, Ed (Foran), tries to get Frank out but only tragedy follows. Very grim and one of Bogart's early unsympathetic starring roles. **83m/B VHS.** Humphrey Bogart, Dick Foran, Erin O'Brien-Moore, Helen Flint, Ann Sheridan, Henry (Kleinbach) Brandon, Robert Barrat, Joseph (Joe) Sawyer, Addison Richards, Samuel S. Hinds, John Litel, Eddie Acuff; ***D:*** Archie Mayo; ***W:*** Abem Finkel, William Wister Haines; ***C:*** George Barnes; ***M:*** Bernhard Kaun.

Black Lemons 🦴 **198?** While in prison, a convict is stalked by the Mafia because of what he knows. He eventually spills the beans to the cops, putting himself in unavoidable jeopardy. **93m/C VHS.** *IT* Peter Carsten, Antonio (Tony) Sabato, Florinda Bolkan; ***D:*** Camillo Bazzoni.

Black Like Me 🦴½ **1964** Based on John Howard Griffin's successful book about how Griffin turned his skin black with a drug and traveled the South to experience prejudice firsthand. Neither the production nor the direction enhance the material. **107m/B VHS, DVD.** James Whitmore, Roscoe Lee Browne, Will Geer, Walter Mason, John Marriott, Clifton James, Dan Priest; ***D:*** Carl Lerner; ***W:*** Carl Lerner, Gerda Lerner; ***C:*** Victor Lukens, Henry Mueller; ***M:*** Meyer Kupferman.

Black Limelight 🦴½ **1938** Massey plays a fugitive from justice and Marion the loyal wife who clears her husband of the murder of his mistress. Distracting lead performance by Marion who insists on shouting her lines. Based on the play by Gordon Sherry. **60m/B VHS.** *GB* Raymond Massey, Joan Marion, Walter Hudd, Henry Oscar, Dan Tobin; ***D:*** Paul Stein; ***W:*** Walter Summers.

Black Lizard 🦴🦴 *Kurotokage* **1968** A camp spectacle set in the Japanese underworld. The Lizard is the glamorous queen of Tokyo crime who plots to steal a famous diamond by first kidnapping the owner's daughter. Complications arise when she falls for a detective. The Lizard is played by female impersonator Maruyama. Mishima, who wrote the original drama and the screenplay, has a cameo as an embalmed corpse. Style is all. In Japanese with English subtitles. **112m/C VHS.** *JP* Akihiro Maruyama, Isao Kimura, Yukio Mishima, Kikko Matsuoka; ***D:*** Kinji Fukasaku; ***W:*** Yukio Mishima.

Black Magic 🦴🦴½ **1949** Cagliostro the magician becomes involved in a plot to supply a double for Marie Antoinette. **105m/B VHS.** Orson Welles, Akim Tamiroff, Nancy Guild, Raymond Burr; ***D:*** Gregory Ratoff; ***W:*** Charles Bennett.

Black Magic 🦴🦴½ **1992 (PG-13)** Insomniac Alex, haunted by the nightly appearances of his dead cousin Ross, goes to Ross's hometown to see if he can find a way to make the apparition disappear. On the way, he runs into his cousin's ex-girlfriend Lilian and falls in love. Problem is, Lilian's a witch, maybe. Lightweight cable fare. **94m/C VHS.** Rachel Ward, Judge Reinhold, Brion James, Anthony LaPaglia; ***D:*** Daniel Taplitz; ***W:*** Daniel Taplitz. **CABLE**

Black Magic Terror 🦴 **1979** Jilted by her lover, the old queen of black magic has everybody under her spell. Trouble starts, however, when she turns her back on one of her subjects. **85m/C VHS.** *JP* Suzanna, W.D. Mochtar, Alan Nuary; ***D:*** L. Sudjio.

Black Magic Woman woof! **1991 (R)** An art gallery owner has an affair with a beautiful and exotic woman but starts to get cold feet when he's plagued by inexplicable phenomena. Seems that black magic woman has put a voodoo spell on him. Listless companion to director Warren's "Blood Spell" that gives away the ending, has a wretched script, and poor acting. **91m/C VHS.** Mark Hamill, Amanda Wyss, Apollonia, Abadah Viera, Larry Hankin, Victor Rivers, Bonnie Ebson; ***D:*** Deryn Warren; ***W:*** Gerry Daly; ***M:*** Randy Miller.

The Black Marble 🦴🦴🦴 **1979 (PG)** A beautiful policewoman is paired with a policeman who drinks too much, is divorced, and is ready to retire. Surrounded by urban craziness and corruption, they eventually fall in love. Based on the Joseph Wambaugh novel. **110m/C VHS.** Paula Prentiss, Harry Dean Stanton, Robert Foxworth, James Woods, Michael Dudikoff, Barbara Babcock, John Hancock, Judy Landers, Anne Ramsey, Christopher Lloyd; ***D:*** Harold Becker; ***M:*** Maurice Jarre.

Black Market Rustlers 🦴½ **1943** The Range Busters are at it again. This time they break up a cattle rustling syndicate. **60m/B VHS.** Ray Corrigan, Dennis Moore, Max Terhune; ***D:*** S. Roy Luby.

Black Mask 🦴🦴½ *Hak Hap* **1996 (R)** Hong Kong action star Jet Li (second only to Jackie Chan in Hong Kong boxoffice success) is Tsui, a mild-mannered librarian who used to be a member of a secret, biogenetically enhanced squad of super soldiers known as the "701 Squad." These commandos, who feel no fear or pain, are out to take over Hong Kong's underworld, and are killing the crime lords in grisly fashion. Tsui, aided by his detective buddy and dressed a lot like Kato from the "Green Hornet," goes into action to stop his ex-mates. Action may be a little bloody for those not used to the Hong Kong style, but Jet Li is an exciting performer who should break out big with this one after his impressive Stateside debut in "Lethal Weapon 4." Re-dubbed from the 1996 Hong Kong release. **95m/C VHS, DVD, Wide.** *HK* Jet Li, Karen Mok, Francoise Yip, Lau Ching Wan; ***D:*** Daniel Lee; ***W:*** Tsui Hark, Teddy Chen; ***C:*** Cheung Tung Leung; ***M:*** Ben Vaughn, Teddy Robin.

Black Moon Rising 🦴½ **1986 (R)** Based on an idea by John Carpenter dealing with the theft of a new jet-powered car and its involvement in an FBI investigation. Solid performances and steady action enhance this routine effort. **100m/C VHS, DVD, Wide.** Tommy Lee Jones, Linda Hamilton, Richard Jaeckel, Robert Vaughn; ***D:*** Harley Cokliss; ***W:*** John Carpenter; ***C:*** Misha (Mikhail) Suslov; ***M:*** Lalo Schifrin.

Black Narcissus 🦴🦴🦴½ **1947** A group of Anglican nuns attempting to found a hospital and school in the Himalayas confront native distrust and human frailties amid beautiful scenery. Adapted from the novel by Rumer Godden. Stunning cinematography. Crucial scenes were cut from the American release by censors. **101m/C VHS, DVD.** *GB* Deborah Kerr, David Farrar, Sabu, Jean Simmons, Kathleen Byron, Flora Robson, Esmond Knight, Jenny Laird, Judith Furse, May Hallitt, Nancy Roberts; ***D:*** Michael Powell, Emeric Pressburger; ***W:*** Michael Powell, Emeric Pressburger; ***C:*** Jack Cardiff; ***M:*** Brian Easdale. Oscars '47: Art Dir./Set Dec., Color, Color Cinematog.; N.Y. Film Critics '47: Actress (Kerr).

Black Oak Conspiracy 🦴🦴 **1977 (R)** Based on a true story, this film deals with a mining company conspiracy discovered by an inquisitive stuntman. **92m/C VHS.** Jesse Vint, Karen Carlson, Albert Salmi, Seymour Cassel, Robert F. Lyons; ***D:*** Bob Kelljan.

Black Orchid 🦴🦴½ **1959** A businessman and a crook's widow fall in love and try to persuade their children it can work out. **96m/B VHS.** Sophia Loren, Anthony Quinn, Ina Balin, Peter Mark Richman, Jimmy Baird; ***D:*** Martin Ritt; ***W:*** Joseph Stefano; ***C:*** Robert Burks.

Black Orpheus 🦴🦴🦴½ *Orfeu Negro* **1958** The legend of Orpheus and Eurydice unfolds against the colorful background of the carnival in Rio de Janeiro. In the black section of the city, Orfeo (Mello) is a street-car conductor and Eurydice (Dawn), a country girl fleeing from a stranger sworn to kill her. The man has followed her to Rio and disguised himself as the figure of Death. Dancing, incredible music, and black magic add to the beauty of this film. Based on the play "Orfeu da Conceica" by De Moraes. In Portuguese with English subtitles or dubbed. **103m/C VHS, DVD.** *BR FR PT* Breno Mello, Marpessa Dawn, Lea Garcia, Fausto Guerzoni, Lourdes De Oliveira, Adhemar Da Silva, Alexandro Constantino, Waldetar De Souza; ***D:*** Marcel Camus; ***W:*** Vinicius De Moraes, Jacques Viot; ***C:*** Jean (Yves, Georges) Bourgoin; ***M:*** Antonio Carlos Jobim, Luis Bonfa. Oscars '59: Foreign Film; Cannes '59: Film; Golden Globes '60: Foreign Film.

Black Out 🦴½ **1996 (R)** John Grey (Bosworth), who's suffering from amnesia after a car crash, becomes desperate to remember his life after his wife (DuBois) is murdered. **98m/C VHS.** Brian Bosworth, Brad Dourif, Claire Yarlett, Marta DuBois; ***D:*** Allan Goldstein.

Black Panther 🦴½ **1977** True story of psycho-killer Donald Neilson, who murdered heiress Lesley Whittle in England in the 1970s. **90m/C VHS.** Donald (Don) Sumpter, Debbie Farrington; ***D:*** Ian Merrick; ***W:*** Michael Armstrong.

The Black Pirate 🦴🦴🦴 *Rage of the Buccaneers; The Black Buccaneer; Gordon il Pirata Nero* **1926** A shipwrecked mariner vows revenge on the pirates who destroyed his father's ship. Quintessential Fairbanks, this film features astounding athletic feats and exciting swordplay. Silent film with music score. Also available in color. **122m/B VHS, DVD.** *IT* Douglas Fairbanks Sr., Donald Crisp, Billie Dove; ***D:*** Albert Parker; ***W:*** Jack Cunningham, Douglas Fairbanks Sr.; ***C:*** Henry Sharp; ***M:*** Mortimer Wilson. Natl. Film Reg. '93.

Black Pit of Dr. M 🦴 *Misterios del Ultratumba* **1947** The ghost of a doctor who has been unjustly executed for murder seeks revenge on employees of an insane asylum. The horror is not just confined to the asylum. **90m/B VHS.** *MX* Gaston Santos, Rafael Bertrand, Mapita Cortes; ***D:*** Fernando Mendez; ***W:*** Ramon Obon.

Black Rain 🦴🦴🦴 *Kuroi Ame* **1988** Erstwhile Ozu assistant Imamura directs this powerful portrait of a post-Hiroshima family five years after the bombing. Tanaka plays a young woman who, having been caught in a shower of black rain (radioactive fallout) on an ill-timed visit to Hiroshima, returns to her village to find herself ostracized by her peers and no longer considered marriage-worthy. Winner of numerous awards (including five Japanese Academy Awards). In Japanese with English subtitles. **123m/B VHS, DVD.** *JP* Kazuo Kitamura, Yoshiko Tanaka, Etsuko Ichihara, Shoichi Ozawa, Norihei Miki, Keisuke Ishida; ***D:*** Shohei Imamura; ***W:*** Shohei Imamura, Toshiro Ishido; ***C:*** Takashi Kawamata; ***M:*** Toru Takemitsu.

Black Rain 🦴🦴½ **1989 (R)** Douglas portrays a ruthless American cop chasing a Japanese murder suspect through gang-controlled Tokyo. Loads of action and stunning visuals from the man who brought you "Blade Runner." **125m/C VHS, DVD, 8mm, Wide.** Stephen (Steve) Root, Michael Douglas, Andy Garcia, Kate Capshaw, Ken Takakura, Yusaku Matsuda, John Spencer, Shigeru Koyama; ***D:*** Ridley Scott; ***W:*** Craig Bolotin, Warren Lewis; ***C:*** Jan De Bont; ***M:*** Hans Zimmer.

Black Rainbow 🦴🦴🦴 **1991 (R)** Surprisingly good thriller that's relatively unknown, haunted by a menacing mood. Robards and Arquette are a father/daughter duo who perform clairvoyance scams at carnival sideshows. Suddenly, without warning, Arquette's former cons become real: she sees murder victims—before their demise. Quirky sleeper filmed on location in North Carolina. **103m/C VHS.** Rosanna Arquette, Jason Robards Jr., Tom Hulce, Ron Rosenthal, John Bennes, Linda Pierce, Mark Joy; ***D:*** Mike Hodges; ***W:*** Mike Hodges.

The Black Raven 🦴½ **1943** An action film that combines several plots into one. The Black Raven is an inn that sees more excitement than any other—not the least of which is murder! **64m/B VHS, DVD.** George Zucco, Wanda McKay, Glenn Strange, I. Stanford Jolley; ***D:*** Sam Newfield; ***W:*** Fred Myton; ***C:*** Robert C. Cline.

Black Robe 🦴🦴🦴½ **1991 (R)** In 1634 young Jesuit priest Father Laforgue (Bluteau) journeys across the North American wilderness to bring the word of God to Canada's Huron Indians. The winter journey is brutal and perilous and he begins to question his mission after seeing the strength of the Indian's native ways. Stunning cinematography, a good script, and fine acting combine to make this superb. Portrays the Indians in a realistic manner, the only flaw being that Beresford portrays the white culture with very few redeeming qualities and as the only reason for the Indian's downfall. Moore adapted his own novel for the screen. **101m/C VHS, DVD, Wide.** *AU CA* Lothaire Bluteau, Aden Young, Sandrine Holt, August Schellenberg, Tantoo Cardinal, Billy Two Rivers, Lawrence Bayne, Harrison Liu, Marthe Tungeon; ***D:*** Bruce Beresford; ***W:*** Brian Moore; ***C:*** Peter James; ***M:*** Georges Delerue. Australian Film Inst. '92: Cinematog.; Genie '91: Director (Beresford), Film.

The Black Room 🦴🦴🦴 **1935** As an evil count lures victims into his castle of terror, the count's twin brother returns to fulfill an ancient prophecy. Karloff is wonderful in his dual role as the twin brothers. **70m/B** Boris Karloff, Marian Marsh, Robert "Tex" Allen, Katherine DeMille, John Buckler, Thurston Hall; ***D:*** Roy William Neill; ***W:*** Henry Myers, Arthur Strawn; ***C:*** Allen Siegler.

The Black Room 🦴 **1982 (R)** Couples are lured to a mysterious mansion where a brother and his sister promise to satisfy their sexual desires. Not much to recommend unless you're a fan of the vampire as psychology test case. **90m/C VHS.** Linnea Quigley, Stephen Knight, Cassandra Gaviola, Jim Stathis; ***D:*** Norman Thaddeus Vane.

Black Roses 🦴 **1988 (R)** A disgusting band of rockers shows up in a small town, and the local kids start turning into monsters. Coincidence? **90m/C VHS.** Carmine Appice, Sal Viviano, Carla Ferrigno, Julie Adams, Ken Swofford, John Martin; ***D:*** John Fasano.

Black Sabbath 🦴🦴🦴 *I Tre Volti della Paura; Black Christmas; The Three Faces of Terror; The Three Faces of Fear; Les Trois Visages de la Peur* **1964** An omnibus horror film with three parts, climaxing with Karloff as a Wurdalak, a vampire who must kill those he loves. **99m/C VHS, DVD, Wide.** *IT FR* Boris Karloff, Jacqueline Pierreux, Michele Mercier, Lidia Alfonsi, Susy Andersen, Mark Damon, Rika Dialina, Glauco Onorato, Massimo Righi; ***D:*** Mario Bava; ***W:*** Mario Bava, Marcello Fondato, Alberto Bevilacqua; ***C:*** Ubaldo Terzano; ***M:*** Les Baxter.

Black Samurai 🦴 **1977 (R)** When his girlfriend is held hostage, a martial arts warrior will stop at nothing to destroy the organization that abducted her. **84m/C VHS, DVD.** Jim Kelly; ***D:*** Al Adamson.

The Black Scorpion 🦴½ **1957** Two geologists in Mexico unearth a nest of giant scorpions living in a dead volcano. Eventually one of the oversized arachnids escapes to wreak havoc on Mexico City. **85m/B VHS.** Richard Denning, Mara Corday, Carlos Rivas; ***D:*** Edward Ludwig; ***W:*** Robert Blees.

Black Scorpion 🦴🦴½ *Roger Corman Presents: Black Scorpion* **1995 (R)** Darcy Walker (Severance) is an ex-cop-turned-superhero (the scorpion is her symbol), who dons a mask and fetching (and tight) black vinyl to fight crime and avenge her dad's death. She's got the prerequisite sidekick—an ex-chop shop operator (Morris)—and a supervillain—the asthmatic Breathtaker (Siemaszko) who threatens to annihilate the city with toxic gas. Campy, schlock fun. **92m/C VHS, DVD.** Joan Severance, Garrett Morris, Casey Siemaszko, Rick Rossovich; ***D:*** Jonathan Winfrey; ***W:*** Craig J. Nevius; ***C:*** Geoffrey George; ***M:*** Kevin Kiner. CABLE

Black Scorpion 2: Ground Zero 🦴🦴 *Black Scorpion 2: Aftershock* **1996 (R)** Fetching crimefighter Darcy Walker (Severance) returns to battle villains Gangster Prankster (Jackson) and After-Shock (Rose), who are set on destroying the City of Angels by earthquake. **85m/C VHS, DVD.** Joan Severance, Whip Hubley, Stoney Jackson, Sherrie Rose, Garrett Morris; ***D:*** Jonathan Winfrey; ***W:*** Craig J. Nevius; ***C:*** Mark Kohl; ***M:*** Kevin Kiner. CABLE

Black Shampoo WOOF! **1976** A black hairdresser on the Sunset Strip fights the mob with a chainsaw. **90m/C VHS.** John Daniels, Tanya Boyd, Joe Ortiz; ***D:*** Greydon Clark.

Black Sheep 🦴½ **1996 (PG-13)** Isn't there a five-day waiting period for remakes? The previously viewed copies of "Tommy Boy" hadn't even hit the sale bin before Spade and Farley went in search of more property to destroy. The twist here? Spade is assigned to keep the oafish brother (not son) of a gubernatorial candidate (not auto parts dealer) out of trouble until after the election (not so he can save the family business). In an effort to provide humor, plot points, and character development, Farley falls out of, off of or onto every prop in sight while Spade smirks. **87m/C VHS.** Chris Farley, David Spade, Tim Matheson, Christine Ebersole, Gary Busey, Grant Heslov, Timothy Carhart, Bruce McGill, Fred Wolf; ***D:*** Penelope Spheeris; ***W:*** Fred Wolf; ***C:*** Daryn Okada; ***M:*** William Ross.

The Black Shield of Falworth 🦴½ **1954** Typically silly '50s Technicolor swashbuckler with Curtis (and his New York accent) as Myles, the son of a disgraced knight, who's out to thwart a conspiracy against King Henry IV (Keith) and win the hand of fair maiden, Lady Anne (Leigh, Curtis' wife at the time). Loosely based on the Howard Pyle novel, "Men of Iron." **98m/C VHS.** Tony Curtis, Janet Leigh, Ian Keith, David Farrar, Barbara Rush, Herbert Marshall, Dan O'Herlihy, Rhys Williams, Torin Thatcher, Patrick O'Neal, Craig Hill; ***D:*** Rudolph Mate; ***W:*** Oscar Brodney; ***C:*** Irving Glassberg; ***M:*** Joseph Gershenson.

Black Sister's Revenge 🦴🦴 *Emma Mae* **1976** Poorly selected video title mars this intelligent drama about a young black woman's struggle to adjust to the big city after growing up in the deep South. **100m/C VHS.** Jerri Hayes, Ernest Williams II, Charles D. Brook III, Eddie Allen; ***D:*** Jamaa Fanaka; ***W:*** Jamaa Fanaka.

The Black Six 🦴 **1974 (R)** Six black Vietnam veterans are out to punish the white gang who killed the brother of one of the black men. **91m/C VHS.** Gene Washington, Carl Eller, Lem Barney, Mercury Morris, Joe "Mean Joe" Greene, Willie Lanier, Rosalind Miles, John Isenbarger, Ben Davidson, Maury Wills, Mikel Angel, Fred Scott; ***D:*** Matt Cimber; ***W:*** George Theakos; ***C:*** William Swenning; ***M:*** David Moscoe.

Black Snow 🦴½ **1993** The mob is off on a violent search for 50 million bucks in cocaine. **90m/C VHS.** Jane Badler, Peter Sherayko, Julia Montgomery, Randy Brooks; ***D:*** Frank Patterson.

The Black Stallion 🦴🦴🦴 **1979 (PG)** A young boy and a wild Arabian Stallion are the only survivors of a shipwreck, and they develop a deep affection for each other. When rescued, they begin training for an important race. Exceptionally beautiful first half. Rooney plays a horse trainer, again. Great for adults and kids. **120m/C VHS, DVD, Wide.** Kelly Reno, Mickey Rooney, Teri Garr, Clarence Muse, Hoyt Axton; ***D:*** Carroll Ballard; ***W:*** William D. Wittliff, Melissa Mathison, Jeanne Rosenberg; ***C:*** Caleb Deschanel; ***M:*** Carmine Coppola. Oscars '79: Sound FX Editing; L.A. Film Critics '79: Cinematog.; Natl. Soc. Film Critics '79: Cinematog.

The Black Stallion Returns 🦴🦴½ **1983 (PG)** Sequel to "The Black Stallion" follows the adventures of young Alec as he travels to the Sahara to search for his beautiful horse, which was stolen by an Arab chieftain. Unfortunately lacks much of the charm that was present in the first film. Adapted from the stories by Walt Farley. **103m/C VHS.** Kelly Reno, Teri Garr, Vincent Spano; ***D:*** Robert Dalva; ***C:*** Carlo Di Palma; ***M:*** Georges Delerue.

Black Starlet 🦴½ *Black Gauntlet* **1974 (R)** A girl from the projects of Chicago travels to Hollywood in search of fame. She winds her way through a world of sleaze and drugs in order to make it to the top. **90m/C VHS.** Juanita Brown, Eric Mason, Rockne Tarkington, Damu King, Diane Holden; ***D:*** Chris Munger.

Black Sunday 🦴🦴🦴 *La Maschera del Demonio; The Demon's Mask; House of Fright; Revenge of the Vampire; Mask of Satan* **1960** In 1630, witch Asa (Steele) who also happens to be a vampire, is executed along with her lover Juvato (Dominici) by her own brother. Two hundred years later, they are accidentally resurrected and in revenge, Asa goes after her descendents, including her look-alike, Katia. A must see for horror fans; firsts for Steele as star and Bava as director. **83m/B VHS, DVD.** *IT* Barbara Steele, John Richardson, Ivo Garrani, Andrea Checchi, Arturo Dominici, Antonio Pierfederici, Tino Bianchi, Clara Bindi, Enrico Oliveri, Germana Dominici; ***D:*** Mario Bava; ***W:*** Mario Bava, Ennio de Concini, Mario Serandrei; ***C:*** Mario Bava, Ubaldo Terzano; ***M:*** Les Baxter.

Black Sunday 🦴🦴½ **1977 (R)** An Arab terrorist group plots to steal the Goodyear Blimp and load it with explosives. Their intent is to explode it over a Miami Super Bowl game to assassinate the U.S. president and to kill all the fans. Based on Thomas Harris' novel. **143m/C VHS.** Robert Shaw, Bruce Dern, Marthe Keller, Fritz Weaver, Steven Keats, Michael V. Gazzo, William Daniels; ***D:*** John Frankenheimer; ***W:*** Ernest Lehman; ***C:*** John A. Alonzo; ***M:*** John Williams.

The Black Swan 1942 Swashbuckling pirate film, based on the novel by Rafael Sabatini, stars Power as James Waring, compatriot of notorious buccaneer Henry Morgan (Cregar). Morgan is pardoned and sent to Jamaica as its new governor—if he can prevent his from associates from continuing their criminal ways. He enlists Waring to help him fight the renegades; meanwhile Waring falls in love with former governor's daughter Margaret (O'Hara). Lots of derring do. **85m/C VHS.** Tyrone Power, Maureen O'Hara, Laird Cregar, Thomas Mitchell, George Sanders, Anthony Quinn, George Zucco, Edward Ashley, Fortunio Bonanova; ***D:*** Henry King; ***W:*** Ben Hecht, Seton I. Miller; ***C:*** Leon Shamroy; ***M:*** Alfred Newman. Oscars '42: Color Cinematog.

Black Terrorist 1985 Terrorists take over a ranch and slay the inhabitants. They keep a young boy alive and the mother tries to rescue him. **81m/C VHS.** Allan Granville, Vera Jones; ***D:*** Neil Hetherington.

Black Thunder ½ 1998 (R) An Air Force stealth jet, nicknamed "Black Thunder," is hijacked by a Libyan agent during testing. A top gun, Vince Connors (Dudikoff), is paired with hotdog pilot Rick Jannick (Hudson) to retrieve the jet. A standard actioner. **85m/C VHS.** Michael Dudikoff, Gary Hudson, Richard Norton, Rob Madrid, Nancy Valen, Michael Cavanaugh, Robert Miranda, Frederic Forrest; ***D:*** Rick Jacobson; ***W:*** William Martell; ***C:*** Michael G. Wojciechowski; ***M:*** Michael Clark. **VIDEO**

Black Tide *Stormy Crossing* 1958 Suspicions arise that a drowning may have actually been a murder. **69m/C VHS.** *GB* John Ireland, Derek Bond, Leslie Dwyer, Maureen Connell, Sheldon Lawrence, Jack Taylor, Joy Webster, Cameron Hall, Arthur Lowe, John Horsley; ***D:*** C.M. Pennington-Richards; ***W:*** Brock Williams; ***C:*** Geoffrey Faithfull; ***M:*** Stanley Black.

Black Tight Killers *Ore Ni Sawaru to Abunaize* 1966 Imagine a Japanese Matt Helm movie with an Elvis impersonator in the lead. That's essentially what's going on in this gonzo adventure/comedy from the mid-'60s. Hondo (Kobayashi) is a combat photographer just back from Vietnam. He and his stewardess girlfriend (Matsubara) become involved with various gangsters in a fast-moving plot filled with such bizarre devices as Ninja chewing gum bullets. **84m/C DVD, Wide.** *JP* Akira Kobayashi, Chieko Matsubara; ***D:*** Yasuharu Hasebe.

Black Tights ½ *Un, Deux, Trois, Quatre!* 1960 Chevalier introduces four stories told in dance by Roland Petit's Ballet de Paris company: "The Diamond Crusher," "Cyrano de Bergerac," "A Merry Mourning," and "Carmen." A keeper for dance fans. Shearer's Roxanne in "Cyrano" was her last performance before retirement. **120m/C VHS, DVD, Wide.** *FR* Cyd Charisse, Zizi Jeanmarie, Moira Shearer, Dirk Sanders, Roland Petit; ***D:*** Terence Young; ***Nar:*** Maurice Chevalier.

Black Tower 1950 An interesting murder mystery telling the story of a desperately impoverished medical student. **54m/B VHS.** Peter Cookson, Warren William, Anne Gwynne, Charles Calvert.

A Black Veil for Lisa 1968 A man attempts to exact revenge upon his unfaithful wife, but things go horribly awry. **87m/C VHS.** *IT GE* John Mills, Luciana Paluzzi, Robert Hoffman; ***D:*** Massimo Dallamano.

Black Venus woof! 1983 (R) A soft-core epic, starring the former Miss Bahamas, Josephine Jacqueline Jones, about the 18th-century French aristocracy. Laughably based upon the stories of Balzac. European film dubbed in English. **80m/C VHS.** *SP* Josephine Jacqueline Jones, Emiliano Redondo, Jose Antonio Ceinos, Monique Gabrielle, Florence Guerin, Helga Line, Mandy Rice-Davies; ***D:*** Claude Mulot; ***W:*** Gregorio Garcia Segura, Harry Alan Towers; ***C:*** Jacques Assuerus, Julio Burgos.

Black Water ½ 1994 Tennessee fishing trip turns into a nightmare for an innocent man accused of murder. Based on the novel "Minnie" by Hans Werner Kettenbach. **105m/C VHS.** Julian Sands, Stacey Dash, Ned Beatty, Ed Lauter, Denise Crosby, William McNamara, Rod Steiger; ***D:*** Nicolas Gessner; ***W:*** Nicolas Gessner, Laird Koenig; ***M:*** Gabriel Yared.

Black Water Gold ½ 1969 TV movie about a search for sunken Spanish gold. **75m/C VHS.** Ricardo Montalban, Keir Dullea, Lana Wood, Bradford Dillman, France Nuyen; ***D:*** Alan Landsburg. **TV**

The Black Widow *Sombra, the Spider Woman* 1947 A fortune-teller plots to steal scientific secrets and take over the world. Serial in 13 episodes. **164m/B VHS.** Bruce Edwards, Carol Forman, Anthony Warde; ***D:*** Spencer Gordon Bennet.

Black Widow 1987 (R) A federal agent pursues a beautiful murderess who marries rich men and then kills them, making the deaths look natural. The agent herself becomes involved in the final seduction. The two women are enticing and the locations picturesque. **101m/C VHS.** Debra Winger, Theresa Russell, Sami Frey, Nicol Williamson, Terry O'Quinn, Dennis Hopper, D.W. Moffett, Lois Smith, Mary Woronov, Rutanya Alda, James Hong, Diane Ladd; ***Cameos:*** David Mamet; ***D:*** Bob Rafelson; ***W:*** Ronald Bass; ***C:*** Conrad L. Hall; ***M:*** Michael Small.

The Black Windmill ½ 1974 (PG) An English spy is caught between his service and the kidnapping of his family by rival spies. **102m/C VHS.** Michael Caine, Donald Pleasence, Delphine Seyrig, Clive Revill, Janet Suzman, John Vernon; ***D:*** Donald Siegel.

Blackbeard the Pirate 1952 The 18th-century buccaneer is given the full-blooded, Hollywood treatment. **99m/C VHS.** Robert Newton, Linda Darnell, Keith Andes, William Bendix, Richard Egan; ***D:*** Raoul Walsh.

Blackbeard's Ghost 1967 Disney comedy in which the famed 18th-century pirate's spirit (Ustinov) is summoned to wreak havoc in order to prevent an old family home from being turned into a casino. **107m/C VHS.** Peter Ustinov, Dean Jones, Suzanne Pleshette, Elsa Lanchester, Richard Deacon; ***D:*** Robert Stevenson; ***C:*** Edward Colman; ***M:*** Robert F. Brunner.

Blackbelt 2: Fatal Force ½ *Spyder* 1993 (R) A man seeks to avenge his brother's murder by going after his killers. **83m/C VHS.** Blake Bahner, Roxanne Baird, Michael Vlastas; ***D:*** Joe Mari Avellana.

Blackboard Jungle ½ 1955 Well-remembered urban drama about an idealistic teacher in a slum area who fights doggedly to connect with his unruly students. Bill Hailey's "Rock Around the Clock" over the opening credits was the first use of rock music in a mainstream feature film. Based on Evan Hunter novel. **101m/B VHS.** Glenn Ford, Anne Francis, Louis Calhern, Sidney Poitier, Vic Morrow, Richard Kiley, Margaret Hayes, John Hoyt, Warner Anderson, Paul Mazursky, Jamie Farr, Richard Deacon, Emile Meyer; ***D:*** Richard Brooks; ***W:*** Richard Brooks; ***C:*** Russell Harlan; ***M:*** Charles Wolcott.

Blackenstein woof! *Black Frankenstein* 1973 (R) Doctor into nouveau experimentation restores a man's arms and legs. But a jealous assistant gives our man a bogus injection, causing him to become "Blackenstein," a large African American with chip on hulking shoulder who enjoys killing people and otherwise causing big trouble. Ripe blaxploitation. **87m/C VHS.** John Hart, Ivory Stone, Andrea King, Liz Renay, Joe DeSue, Roosevelt Jackson, Nick Bolin; ***D:*** William A. Levey; ***W:*** Frank R. Salétri; ***C:*** Robert Caramico; ***M:*** Cardella Demilo, Lou Frohman.

Blackheart 1998 (R) A pair of con artists have their scam down—the seductive Annette (Alonso) picks up wealthy men, then Ray (Grieco) steps in, roughs them up, and takes their cash. Things get messy when they learn of a young woman (Loewi) who has yet to learn of an enormous inheritance, and Ray steps into the role of seducer. Although the film runs out of steam in the last 20 minutes, Grieco and Loewi are likeable in the lead roles. **95m/C VHS, DVD.** Maria Conchita Alonso, Richard Grieco, Fiona Loewi, Christopher Plummer; ***D:*** Dominic Shiach; ***W:*** Brock Simpson, Brad Simpson; ***C:*** Ousama Rawi.

Blackjack 1978 (R) Las Vegas is the scene for action and excitement as the mob puts the hit on tough guy William Smith! **104m/C VHS.** William Smith, Tony Burton, Paris Earl, Damu King, Diane Summerfield, Angela May; ***D:*** John Evans.

Blackjack ½ 1997 (R) Former U.S. Marshal Jack Devlin (Lundgren), who has a pathological fear of the color white, becomes the bodyguard of a young supermodel (Haskin) who's the target of a psycho killer (Mackenzie). To highlight Devlin's phobia, Woo sets one of his big action scenes in a dairy flooded with milk. **113m/C VHS, DVD.** *CA* Dolph Lundgren, Kam Haskin, Saul Rubinek, Fred Williamson, Phillip MacKenzie, Kate Vernon, Padraigin Murphy; ***D:*** John Woo; ***W:*** Peter Lance; ***C:*** Bill Wong; ***M:*** Micky Erbe. **VIDEO**

Blacklight 1998 Clairvoyant Sharon Avery (Welch) tried to help the police with a boy's abduction but it was too late and the child was found dead. In despair, Sharon gets into an auto accident and loses both her sight and, apparently, her gift. She later tries to drown herself, but suddenly sees images of another child kidnapping. Inspector Frank Shumann (Ironside) is reluctant to accept her help until a little girl is found murdered. Now Sharon is on a collison course with a child killer. **91m/C VHS.** Tahnee Welch, Michael Ironside, Currie Graham, Anne Marie Loder, Lori Hallier, Walter Mills, Billy Morton; ***D:*** Michael Storey; ***C:*** Michael Storey; ***M:*** Ken Harrison. **VIDEO**

Blackmail 1929 This first sound film for Great Britain and director Hitchcock features an early visualization of some typical Hitchcockian themes. The story follows the police investigation of a murder, and a detective's attempts to keep his girlfriend from being involved. Look for Hitchcock's screen cameo. Made as a silent, this was reworked to become a talkie. **86m/B VHS.** *GB* Anny Ondra, John Longden, Sara Allgood, Charles Paton, Cyril Ritchard, Donald Calthrop, Hannah Jones, Percy Parsons, Johnny Butt, Harvey Braban, Phyllis Monkman, Alfred Hitchcock; ***D:*** Alfred Hitchcock; ***W:*** Charles Bennett, Benn W. Levy, Garnett Weston, Alfred Hitchcock; ***C:*** Jack Cox.

Blackmail 1991 (R) Familiar story is given new life in this suspenseful movie. Blakely is a lonely woman who succumbs to Midkiff's attentions. She doesn't suspect that he's conning her with the help of his lover, Toussaint. Engaging thriller adapted from a short story by Bill Crenshaw. **87m/C VHS.** Susan Blakely, Dale Midkiff, Beth Toussaint, John Saxon, Mac Davis; ***D:*** Ruben Preuss. **CABLE**

Blackmale ½ 1999 (R) Small-time hustlers Jimmy (Woodbine) and Luther (Pierce) bet everything on a fixed fight and lose big. Now they owe $100,000 to a loan shark. So they decide to blackmail a doctor (Rees) with an incriminating videotape and discover that their would-be mark is more dangerous than they could have imagined. **89m/C VHS, DVD, Wide.** Bokeem Woodbine, Justin Pierce, Roger Rees, Sascha Knopf, Erik Todd Dellums; ***D:*** George Baluzy, Mike Baluzy. **VIDEO**

Blackout ½ 1950 Blind man recovers his sight and finds that the brother of his girlfriend, once thought dead, is actually alive and well and running a smuggling ring. Routine. **73m/B VHS.** *GB* Maxwell Reed, Dinah Sheridan, Patric Doonan, Eric Pohlmann; ***D:*** Robert S. Baker.

Blackout *Murder by Proxy* 1954 A drunken private eye is offered a murder case, and is subsequently framed for the crime. **87m/B VHS.** Dane Clark, Belinda Lee, Betty Ann Davies; ***D:*** Terence Fisher.

Blackout 1978 (R) Four killers terrorize an office building during the 1977 New York electrical blackout. Soon the police enter, confront them, and the fun starts. Comic touches provide some relief from the violence here. **86m/C VHS.** Jim Mitchum, Robert Carradine, Ray Milland, June Allyson, Jean-Pierre Aumont, Belinda J. Montgomery; ***D:*** Eddy Matalon; ***W:*** Joseph Stefano.

Blackout ½ 1985 Cable thriller in which an aging police chief suspects a disfigured amnesiac is responsible for past killings, in spite of the fact that he now leads a subdued family life. **99m/C VHS.** Richard Widmark, Keith Carradine, Kathleen Quinlan, Michael Beck, Gerald Hiken; ***D:*** Douglas Hickox; ***W:*** David Ambrose. **CABLE**

Blackout 1988 (R) Strange memories from childhood come back to her as a woman fights for her life. **91m/C VHS.** Carol Lynley, Gail O'Grady, Michael Keys Hall, Joseph Gian, Joanna Miles; ***D:*** Doug Adams; ***C:*** Arledge Armenaki.

The Blackout 1997 (R) Movie star Matty (Modine) has multiple addictions he indulges on a trip home to Miami. He proposes to pregnant girlfriend Annie (Dalle) but when he learns she's had an abortion, Matty goes on a binge and suffers a blackout. 18 months later in New York, Matty has kicked his addictions and found Susan (Schiffer) but his nightmares compel him back to Miami and the possibility that he committed murder. Sleazy and the symbolism is heavy-handed. **100m/C VHS, DVD, Wide.** Matthew Modine, Beatrice Dalle, Claudia Schiffer, Dennis Hopper, Sarah Lassez; ***D:*** Abel Ferrara; ***W:*** Abel Ferrara, Chris Zois, Marla Hanson; ***C:*** Ken Kelsch; ***M:*** Joe Delia.

Blackrock 1997 Cliched though dramatic saga, inspired by a true story, and adapted by Enright from his play. Uncommunicative teenager Jared (Breuls) throws a bash upon the return to town of his best surfing bud Ricko (Lyndon). The party gets out of control and Jared witnesses a group of his mates beating and raping Tracey (Novakovitch), who's discovered dead the next morning. Her death attracts rabid media attention and divides the community while Jared is filled with guilt for doing nothing to stop the act. But his conflicts increase when he realizes the extent of Ricko's involvement and he tries to decide where his loyalties lie. **100m/C VHS, DVD.** *AU* Laurence Breuls, Simon Lyndon, Linda Cropper, Rebecca Smart, David Field, Chris Haywood, Boyana Novakovitch; ***D:*** Steven Vidler; ***W:*** Nick Enright; ***C:*** Martin McGrath, George Greenough; ***M:*** Steve Kilbey.

Blacksnake! woof! *Sweet Suzy; Dutchess of Doom; Slaves* 1973 (R) Overheated sex and race tale, set in 1835, finds a British lord travelling to a Caribbean island in search of his brother. What he finds is his sadistic sister-in-law and her evil overseer using violence to keep the slaves in line. **83m/C VHS.** Milton McCollin, Anouska (Anoushka) Hempel, David Warbeck, Percy Herbert, David Prowse; ***D:*** Russ Meyer; ***W:*** Russ Meyer, Leonard Neubauer; ***C:*** Arthur Ornitz; ***M:*** William Loose, Al Teeter.

Blackwater Trail 1995 (R) Novelist Matt Curran (Nelson) travels from L.A. to Michelton, Australia, to attend the funeral of his best friend Andy, a cop who supposedly committed suicide. But Andy's sister (and Matt's former lover) Cathy (Smart) thinks he was murdered because of a case involving a serial killer. Matt decides to snoop around and finds out the killer likes to leave behind body parts and biblical quotations. Contrived plotting but some good performances and some spectacular scenery. **100m/C VHS.** *AU* Judd Nelson, Dee Smart, Peter Phelps, Mark Lee, Brett Climo; ***D:*** Ian Barry; ***W:*** Andrew Russell; ***C:*** John Stokes; ***M:*** Stephen Rae.

Blacula 1972 (PG) The African Prince Mamuwalde stalks the streets of Los Angeles trying to satisfy his insatiable desire for blood. Mildly successful melding of blaxploitation and horror that spawned a sequel, "Scream, Blacula, Scream." **92m/C VHS.** William Marshall, Thalmus Rasulala, Denise Nicholas, Vonetta McGee, Gordon Pinsent, Emily Yancy, Charles Macaulay, Ted Harris, Elisha Cook Jr., Lance Taylor; ***D:*** William Crain; ***W:*** Raymond Koenig, Joan Torres; ***C:*** John Stevens; ***M:*** Gene Page.

Blade 1972 (PG) An honest cop challenges a dirty cover-up in killer-stalked New York. **79m/C VHS.** Steve Landesberg, John Schuck, Kathryn Walker; ***D:*** Ernest Pintoff.

Blade 1998 (R) Action-packed gore-fest that provides for high-octane escapist entertainment, with some eye-catching visuals and a pulsting techno soundtrack. Blade (Snipes) is a half-vampire/half-human, who's intent on preventing evil, ambitious Deacon Frost (Dorff) from unleashing a vampire apocalypse upon humanity so he can take over. Helping out Blade are his grizzled mentor, vampire hunter Abraham Whistler (Kristofferson), and Dr. Karen Janson (Wright), who's searching for a cure for vampirism. Adapted from the Marvel comic book character. **91m/C VHS, DVD.** Wesley Snipes, Stephen Dorff, Kris Kristofferson, N'Bushe Wright, Donal Logue, Udo Kier, Traci Lords, Tim Guinee, Arly Jover, Sanaa Lathan; ***D:*** Stephen Norrington; ***W:*** David S. Goyer; ***C:*** Theo van de Sande; ***M:*** Mark Isham. MTV Movie Awards '99: Villain (Dorff).

Blade Boxer 🦴 **1997** Police detectives go undercover to expose an illegal fight ring that has its combatants battling to the death, and equipped with deadly steel talons. **91m/C VHS.** Kevin King, Todd McKee, Andrew Martino, Cass Magda, Dana Plato; ***D:*** Bruce Reisman.

Blade II 🦴🦴 **2002 (R)** Sequel takes the more, more, more approach—more vampires, more battles, more gore. Half-vampire, half-human daywalker Blade (Snipes at his coolest) first rescues mentor Whistler (Kristofferson) from the vamps who have been holding him prisoner. Then, he's offered a truce by vampire overload Damaskinos (Kretschmann) who needs Blade to hunt an even more deadly enemy. The rat-like Reapers feed on both humans and vampires and their bite turns their victims into insatiable bloodsuckers themselves. Of course, as Blade goes a-huntin', he discovers the situation isn't as clear-cut as it seems. **116m/C VHS, DVD.** Wesley Snipes, Kris Kristofferson, Ron Perlman, Leonor Varela, Norman Reedus, Thomas Kretschmann, Luke Goss, Matt Schulze, Donnie Yen, Danny John Jules, Daz Crawford, Karel Roden, Tony Curran, Santiago Segura, Marit Velle Kile; ***D:*** Guillermo del Toro; ***W:*** David S. Goyer; ***C:*** Gabriel Beristain; ***M:*** Marco Beltrami, Danny Saber.

Blade in Hong Kong 🦴🦴½ **1985** Investigator travels to Hong Kong, finds trouble and romance in the underbelly of the city. Pilot for un-sold series. **100m/C VHS.** Terry Lester, Keye Luke, Mike (Michael) Preston, Jean-Marie Hon, Leslie Nielsen, Nancy Kwan, Anthony Newley, Ellen Regan; ***D:*** Reza Badiyi. **TV**

A Blade in the Dark 🦴🦴 *La Casa con la Scala Nel Buio; House of the Dark Stairway* **1983** A young man composing a score for a horror film moves into a secluded villa and is inspired and haunted by the mysterious murder he witnesses. **104m/C VHS, DVD, Wide.** Michele (Michael) Soavi, Fabiola Toledo, Valeria Cavalli, Lara Naszinsky, Andrea Occhipinti, Anny Papa; ***D:*** Lamberto Bava; ***W:*** Dardano Sacchetti; ***C:*** Gianlorenzo Battaglia; ***M:*** Guido de Angelis, Maurizio de Angelis.

Blade Master 🦴½ *Ator the Invincible* **1984 (PG)** In this sequel to "Ator the Fighting Eagle," O'Keeffe as Ator is back as the Blade Master. Ator defends his people and his family name in a battle against the "Geometric Nucleus": a primitive bomb. His quest leads him and his small band of men to the castle of knowledge. D'Amato used the pseudonym David Hills. **92m/C VHS.** Miles O'Keeffe, Lisa Foster; ***D:*** Joe D'Amato.

Blade of the Ripper woof! *The Next Victim; Next!; Lo Strano Vizio della Signora Ward* **1970** A madman armed with a razor slashes his way through the lovelies of the international jet set. **90m/C VHS.** George Hilton, Edwige Fenech, Alberto De Mendoza, Ivan Rassimov; ***D:*** Sergio Martino; ***W:*** Ernesto Gastaldi, Eduardo Brochero.

Blade Runner 🦴🦴🦴½ **1982 (R)** Los Angeles, the 21st century. World-weary cop tracks down a handful of renegade "replicants" (synthetically produced human slaves who, with only days left of life, search madly for some way to extend their prescribed lifetimes). Moody, beautifully photographed, dark thriller with sets from an architect's dream. Based on "Do Androids Dream of Electric Sheep" by Philip K. Dick. Director's cut, released at 117 minutes, removes Ford's narration and the last scene of the film, which Scott considered too "up," and inserts several short scenes, including a dream sequence. **122m/C VHS, DVD, 8mm, Wide.** Harrison Ford, Rutger Hauer, Sean Young, Daryl Hannah, M. Emmet Walsh, Edward James Olmos, Joe Turkel, Brion James, Joanna Cassidy, William Sanderson; ***D:*** Ridley Scott; ***W:*** Hampton Fancher, David Peoples; ***C:*** Jordan Cronenweth; ***M:*** Vangelis. L.A. Film Critics '82: Cinematog., Natl. Film Reg. '93.

Blades 🦴 **1989 (R)** Another junk heap from Troma, dealing with the efforts of three golfers who try to stop a maniacal power mower that's been grinding duffers with regularity. **101m/C VHS.** Robert North, Jeremy Whelan, Victoria Scott, Jon McBride; ***D:*** Thomas R. Rondinella; ***W:*** William R. Pace; ***C:*** James Hayman; ***M:*** John Hodian.

Blades of Courage 🦴🦴 *Skate!* **1988** Biography of Olympic skater Lori Larouche. Choreographed by Debbi Wilkes. **98m/C VHS.** *CA* Lynn Nightingale, Christianne Hirt, Colm Feore, Rosemary Dunsmore; ***D:*** Randy Bradshaw. **TV**

The Blair Witch Project 🦴🦴 **1999 (R)** A Sundance Film Festival favorite, this low-budget horror film turned out to be the most successful indie ever, thanks to heavy (and savvy) market promotion. In 1994, a three-person film crew heads into the Black Hills region of Maryland to document a local legend about a demonic apparition. They vanish, but a year later their film footage is found and this amateurish, black and white footage makes up what the audience sees. Largely improvisational, the film manages a palpable sense of dread and claustrophobia, while being (deliberately) technically crude. However, the herky-jerky camera movements made a number of viewers physically sick and an equal number found the would-be theatrics boring. **87m/C VHS, DVD.** Michael Williams, Heather Donahue, Joshua Leonard; ***D:*** Eduardo Sanchez, Daniel Myrick; ***W:*** Eduardo Sanchez, Daniel Myrick; ***C:*** Neal Fredericks; ***M:*** Tony Cora. Golden Raspberries '99: Worst Actress (Donahue).

Blaise Pascal 🦴🦴🦴½ **1971** Another of Rossellini's later historical portraits, detailing the life and times of the 17th-century philosopher, seen as a man whose scientific ideas conflicted with his own religious beliefs. Italian with subtitles. **131m/C VHS.** *IT* ***D:*** Roberto Rossellini. **TV**

Blake of Scotland Yard **1936** Blake, the former Scotland Yard inspector, battles against a villain who has constructed a murderous death ray. Condensed version of the 15 episode serial (originally at 180 minutes). **70m/B VHS.** Ralph Byrd, Herbert Rawlinson, Joan Barclay, Lloyd Hughes; ***D:*** Robert F. "Bob" Hill.

Blame It on Rio 🦴🦴 **1984 (R)** A middle-aged man has a ridiculous fling with his best friend's daughter while on vacation with them in Rio de Janeiro. Caine and Johnson are amusing, but the script is somewhat weak. Remake of the French film "One Wild Moment." **90m/C VHS, DVD, Wide.** Michael Caine, Joseph Bologna, Demi Moore, Michelle Johnson, Valerie Harper; ***D:*** Stanley Donen; ***W:*** Charlie Peters, Larry Gelbart; ***C:*** Reynaldo Villalobos; ***M:*** Kenneth Wannberg.

Blame It on the Bellboy 🦴🦴½ **1992 (PG-13)** Wild farce set in Venice about a hotel bellboy who confuses three similarly named visitors—sending the wrong ones to meet corporate bigwigs, date women, or even kill. The brisk pace loses it towards the end and devolves into chase scenes. **79m/C VHS.** Dudley Moore, Bryan Brown, Richard Griffiths, Andreas Katsulas, Patsy Kensit, Alison Steadman, Bronson Pinchot, Lindsay Anderson, Penelope Wilton; ***D:*** Mark Herman; ***W:*** Mark Herman; ***M:*** Trevor Jones.

Blame It on the Night 🦴🦴 **1984 (PG-13)** A rock star gets to take care of the military cadet son he never knew after the boy's mother suddenly dies. Mick Jagger helped write the story. Available in VHS and Beta Hi-Fi. **85m/C VHS.** Nick Mancuso, Byron Thames, Leslie Ackerman, Billy Preston, Merry Clayton; ***D:*** Gene Taft.

Blanche Fury 🦴🦴½ **1948** Governess Blanche (Hobson) marries her wealthy widowed cousin but the man she truly desires is the illegitimate Philip Thorn (Granger), who manages the estate for her husband. So Blanche decides to get rid of the man she doesn't love. Based on England's 19th-century Rush murder and adapted from the novel by Joseph Shearing. **95m/C VHS.** *GB* Valerie Hobson, Stewart Granger, Walter Fitzgerald, Michael Gough, Maurice Denham, Sybilla Binder; ***D:*** Marc Allegret; ***W:*** Hugh Mills; ***C:*** Guy Green, Geoffrey Unsworth; ***M:*** Clifton Parker.

Blank Check 🦴 *Disney's Blank Check* **1993 (PG)** Parents may want to verify the whereabouts of their checkbooks after this one. Eleven-year-old Preston receives a blank check from a mobster on the run, cashes it for a million bucks, and goes on a spending orgy under an assumed name. Where are his parents? Apparently they don't have a problem with a shadowy benefactor taking their son under his wing. Sound familiar? And who thought it would be a good idea to have the little twerp mooning after a comely bank teller? Formula aside, this blatant rip-off of "Home Alone" tries to throw in an ending moral but probably won't fool the kids either. **93m/C VHS.** Brian Bonsall, Miguel Ferrer, Michael Lerner, Tone Loc, Ric(k) Ducommun, Karen Duffy; ***D:*** Rupert Wainwright; ***W:*** Colby Carr, Blake Snyder; ***M:*** Nicholas Pike.

Blankman 🦴🦴 **1994 (PG-13)** Self-appointed superhero (Wayans), who makes up in creativity what he lacks in superpowers, fights crime in his underwear and a cape made from his grandmother's bathrobe. Life is simple, until an ambitious TV reporter (Givens) finds out about him. Silly one-joke premise is carried a little too far; didn't similar "Meteor Man" crash? Gifted comedian Wayans tries, but can't make this guy fly. **96m/C VHS, DVD, Wide.** Damon Wayans, Robin Givens, David Alan Grier, Jason Alexander, Jon Polito, Nick(y) Corello; ***D:*** Mike Binder; ***W:*** J.F. Lawton, Damon Wayans; ***C:*** Newton Thomas (Tom) Sigel; ***M:*** Miles Goodman.

Blast 🦴🦴 **1996** Terrorists take a group of spectators hostage at the Atlanta Summer Olympics. **98m/C VHS.** Linden Ashby, Andrew Divoff, Rutger Hauer, Tim Thomerson; ***D:*** Albert Pyun.

Blast from the Past 🦴🦴½ **1998 (PG-13)** Mistaking a plane crash in his yard for an atomic bomb blast, paranoid scientist Calvin (Walken) and his pregnant wife Helen (Spacek) lock themselves in their bomb shelter. Fearful of radioactive fallout, they raise their son Adam (Fraser) in the shelter on a diet of canned goods, Perry Como music and ballroom dancing. After thirty-five years, Adam is sent out for supplies and to find a nice, non-mutant wife. Plot degenerates into by-the-book romantic comedy mush after he meets cute with Eve (Silverstone), a thoroughly modern woman with a low opinion of modern men. **106m/C VHS, DVD.** Brendan Fraser, Alicia Silverstone, Christopher Walken, Sissy Spacek, Dave Foley, Joey Slotnick, Dale Raoul; ***D:*** Hugh Wilson; ***W:*** Hugh Wilson, Bill Kelly; ***C:*** Jose Luis Alcaine; ***M:*** Steve Dorff.

Blast-Off Girls 🦴 **1967** A scuzzball promoter sets out to avenge himself for being blacklisted by the rock 'n' roll industry. He discovers a fresh group, but without corporate backing he can only pay them with groovy clothes and mini-skirted girls. Trouble ensues when they unexpectedly hit the charts and want real money. **83m/C VHS, DVD, Wide.** Ray Sager, Dan Conway, Harland "Colonel" Sanders; ***D:*** Herschell Gordon Lewis; ***W:*** Herschell Gordon Lewis.

Blastfighter woof! **1985 (R)** After local hoodlums kill his daughter, an ex-con cop goes on a spree of violence and revenge. Director Bava uses the pseudonym "John Old, Jr.," as his father Mario Bava occasionally credited himself as John Old. Italian film shot in Atlanta. **93m/C VHS.** *IT* Michael Sopkiw, Valerie Blake, George Eastman; ***D:*** Lamberto Bava.

Blaze 🦴🦴½ **1989 (R)** The true story of Louisiana governor Earl Long who became involved with a stripper, Blaze Starr, causing a political scandal of major proportions. Robust, good-humored bio-pic featuring a fine character turn by Newman. **117m/C VHS.** Paul Newman, Lolita (David) Davidovich, Jerry Hardin, Robert Wuhl, Gailard Sartain, Jeffrey DeMunn, Richard Jenkins, Garland Bunting; ***D:*** Ron Shelton; ***W:*** Ron Shelton; ***C:*** Haskell Wexler.

Blazing Across the Pecos 🦴½ **1948** The Durango Kid (Starrett) is after Pecos Flats mayor Ace Brockaway (Wilson), who's secretly selling guns to the local Indian tribe so they'll attack the supply wagons of his business rivals. **54m/B VHS.** Charles Starrett, Smiley Burnette, Charles C. Wilson, Chief Thundercloud; ***D:*** Ray Nazarro.

Blazing Guns 🦴 *Marshal of Heldorado* **1950** A marshal, masquerading inexplicably as a tenderfoot, enters a lawless town and is immediately hired as a deputy. **54m/B VHS.** James Ellison, Russell Hayden, Raymond Hatton, Fuzzy Knight, Julie Adams; ***D:*** Thomas Carr.

Blazing Saddles 🦴🦴🦴½ **1974 (R)** Wild, wacky spoof by Brooks of every cliche in the western film genre. Little is Black Bart, a convict offered a reprieve if he will become a sheriff and clean up a nasty frontier town; the previous recipients of this honor have all swiftly ended up in shallow graves. A crazy, silly film with a cast full of lovable loonies including comedy greats Wilder, Kahn, and Korman. Watch for the Count Basie Orchestra. A group writing effort, based on an original story by Bergman. Was the most-viewed movie in its first year of release on HBO cable. **90m/C VHS, DVD.** Cleavon Little, Harvey Korman, Madeline Kahn, Gene Wilder, Mel Brooks, John Hillerman, Alex Karras, Dom DeLuise, Liam Dunn, Slim Pickens, David Huddleston, Burton Gilliam, Count Basie; ***D:*** Mel Brooks; ***W:*** Norman Steinberg, Andrew Bergman, Richard Pryor, Alan Uger, Mel Brooks; ***C:*** Joseph Biroc; ***M:*** John Morris. Writers Guild '74: Orig. Screenplay.

Blazing Stewardesses woof! *Texas Layover* **1975 (R)** The Hound salutes the distributor for truth in advertising, as they stamped this as one of the world's worst videos. Lusty, busty stewardesses relax at a western guest ranch under siege from hooded riders and the aging gags of the Ritz Brothers. **95m/C VHS.** Yvonne De Carlo, Robert "Bob" Livingston, Donald (Don "Red") Barry, Regina Carrol, Connie Hoffman; ***Cameos:*** Harry Ritz, Jimmy Ritz; ***D:*** Al Adamson.

Bleak House 🦴🦴½ **1985** Miniseries adaptation of the Charles Dickens tome about an interminable lawsuit and the decadent, criminal ruling class of 19th-century England. **391m/C VHS.** *GB* Denholm Elliott, Diana Rigg, Philip Franks, Peter Vaughan, T.P. McKenna; ***D:*** Ross Devenish; ***M:*** Geoffrey Burgon. **TV**

Bleak Moments 🦴🦴 *Loving Moments* **1971** Bored secretary Sylvia (Raitt) tries to work her flirtatious charms on a repressed teacher (Allan) and an eccentric musician (Bradwell) in order to escape the pressures of caring for a mentally retarded sister. **110m/C VHS.** *GB* Anne Raitt, Eric Allen, Mike Bradwell, Joolia Cappleman; ***D:*** Mike Leigh; ***W:*** Mike Leigh; ***C:*** Bahram Manocheri; ***M:*** Mike Bradwell.

Bleeders woof! *Hemoglobin* **1997 (R)** John Struass (Dupuis), suffering from a hereditary blood disease, travels to a remote Atlantic island to research his ancestors and discovers the descendants are a grotesque clan of incestuous malformed creatures, who only emerge from their catacombs to satisfy their need for human blood and flesh. **89m/C VHS, DVD.** *CA* Rutger Hauer, Roy Dupuis, Jackie Burroughs, Kristen Lehman, Joanna Noyes, John Dunn-Hill; ***D:*** Peter Svatek; ***W:*** Dan O'Bannon, Charles Adair, Ronald Shusett; ***C:*** Barry Gravelle; ***M:*** Alan Reeves. **VIDEO**

Bleeding Hearts 🦴🦴½ **1994** A liberal white professor falls in love with the teenaged black student he's tutoring and then becomes aware of the vast differences between them. Their problems increase when the young woman becomes pregnant. **95m/C VHS.** Gregory Hines, Mark Evan Jacobs, Ranjit (Chaudry) Chowdhry, Elliott Gould, Robert Levine, Peter Riegert, Lorraine Toussaint; ***D:*** Gregory Hines.

Bless the Beasts and Children 🦴🦴½ **1971 (PG)** A group of six teenage boys at a summer camp attempt to save a herd of buffalo from slaughter at a national preserve. Treacly Kramer backwater. Based on the novel by Glendon Swarthout. **109m/C VHS.** Billy Mumy, Barry Robins, Miles Chapin, Darel Glaser, Bob Kramer, Ken Swofford, Jesse White; ***D:*** Stanley Kramer; ***M:*** Perry Botkin.

Bless the Child 🦴 **2000 (R)** Basinger doesn't even attempt to hide her boredom as Maggie, aunt and caretaker to a 6-year-old with supernatural powers. Everyone drops the ball in this failed ripoff of "The ExorOmen's Baby's Sixth Sense." Satanist and self-help guru Stark (Sewell) wants to recruit the gifted tyke to work for the Devil, while Maggie gets an occult-expert FBI agent (Smits, perhaps making a mortgage payment) and a bunch of exposition cameos on her side. This movie's idea of thrills is showing kids getting kidnapped and later turning up dead. Not exactly the feel-good movie of the year. **110m/C VHS, DVD, Wide.** Kim Basinger, Jimmy Smits, Rufus Sewell, Holliston Coleman, Christina Ricci, Michael Gaston, Lumi Cavazos, Angela Bettis, Ian Holm, Eugene Lipinski, Anne Betancourt, Dimitra Arlys; ***D:*** Chuck Russell; ***W:*** Tom Rickman, Clifford Green, Ellen Green; ***C:*** Peter Menzies Jr.; ***M:*** Christopher Young.

Blessed Event 🦴🦴🦴 **1932** Fast-moving, entertaining film about a Broadway gossip columnist with a poison pen. Tracy has the role of a lifetime as a Walter Winchell prototype who thinks no one is exempt from his juicy column. Powell makes film debut as a crooner after a brief career as a band singer. Based on a play by Manuel Seff and Forrest Wilson. **77m/B VHS.** Lee Tracy, Mary Brian, Dick Powell, Allen Jenkins, Ruth Donnelly, Emma Dunn, Walter Miller, Tom Dugan, Isabel Jewell; ***D:*** Roy Del Ruth; ***W:*** Howard J. Green.

Blessing 🦴🦴 **1994** It's an unhappy time down on the Wisconsin dairy farm in this tale of family life. Embittered patriarch Jack (Griffis) can barely make a go of it and takes his frustrations out by beating his cows and climbing to the top of the silo. Despairing wife Arlene (Glynn) enters newspaper lotteries and collects religious statues while daughter Randi (Griffis) keeps delaying leaving the farm because of a nagging sense of responsibility. Claustrophobic atmosphere. **94m/C VHS.** Guy Griffis, Carlin Glynn, Melora Griffis, Gareth Williams, Clovis Siemon; ***D:*** Paul Zehrer; ***W:*** Paul Zehrer; ***C:*** Stephen Kazmierski; ***M:*** Joseph S. DeBeasi.

Blind Ambition 🦴🦴½ **1982** Miniseries docudrama traces the career of John Dean, special counsel to President Richard M. Nixon. Focuses on his fractured personal life and touches on virtually all of the Watergate headlines. **95m/C VHS.** Martin Sheen, Rip Torn. **TV**

Blind Date 🦴½ **1984 (R)** Blind man agrees to have a visual computer implanted in his brain in order to help the police track down a psychopathic killer. Violent scenes may be disturbing to some. **100m/C VHS.** Joseph Bottoms, Kirstie Alley, Keir Dullea, James Daughton, Lana Clarkson, Marina Sirtis; ***D:*** Nico Mastorakis; ***W:*** Nico Mastorakis.

Blind Date 🦴🦴 **1987 (PG-13)** A blind date between a workaholic yuppie and a beautiful blonde starts off well, but when she drinks too much at dinner, things get out of hand. In addition to embarrassing her date and destroying the restaurant, she has a jealous ex-boyfriend who must be dealt with. **95m/C VHS, DVD, Wide.** Kim Basinger, Bruce Willis, John Larroquette, William Daniels, George Coe, Mark Blum, Phil Hartman, Stephanie Faracy, Alice Hirson, Graham Stark; ***D:*** Blake Edwards; ***W:*** Dale Launer; ***C:*** Harry Stradling Jr.; ***M:*** Henry Mancini.

Blind Faith 🦴 **1989 (R)** Action and adventure take a turn for the horrific when several men find themselves in captivity. **?m/C VHS.** Eric Gunn, Kevin Yon, Lynne Browne; ***D:*** Dean Wilson; ***W:*** Dean Wilson.

Blind Faith 🦴🦴½ **1998 (R)** In 1957, John Williams (Vance) is a struggling new lawyer, living with elder sibling Charles (Dutton) and his family in a Bronx neighborhood. The first black NYPD sergeant, Charles has an uneasy relationship with his eldest son, Charlie (Whitt). The family's shocked when Charlie's accused of murdering a white boy during a robbery attempt, especially when he confesses. John thinks the cops beat the confession out of the boy and becomes determined to defend him but he gradually becomes suspicious of the story Charlie is telling him. **122m/C VHS, DVD.** Courtney B. Vance, Charles S. Dutton, Garland Whitt, Kadeem Hardison, Lonette McKee, Karen Glave, Dan Lett; ***D:*** Ernest R. Dickerson; ***W:*** Frank Military; ***C:*** Rodney Charters; ***M:*** Ron Carter. **CABLE**

Blind Fear 🦴½ **1989 (R)** A blind woman is stalked by three killers in an abandoned country inn. **98m/C VHS.** Shelley Hack, Jack Langedijk, Kim Coates, Jan Rubes, Heidi von Palleske; ***D:*** Tom Berry; ***W:*** Sergio D. Altieri.

Blind Fools 🦴½ **1940** A scathing indictment of children neglected by ambitious parents. **66m/B VHS.** Herbert Rawlinson, Claire Whitney, Russell Hicks, Miriam Battista.

Blind Fury 🦴🦴½ **1990 (R)** A blind Vietnam vet enlists the aid of a Zen master and a sharpshooter to tackle the Mafia. Hauer works well in the lead, but unfortunately, the movie doesn't. **86m/C VHS.** Rutger Hauer, Terry O'Quinn, Brandon Call, Lisa Blount, Randall "Tex" Cobb, Noble Willingham, Meg Foster, Sho Kosugi, Nick Cassavetes, Charles Cooper, Rick Overton; ***D:*** Phillip Noyce; ***W:*** Charles Robert Carner; ***C:*** Don Burgess; ***M:*** J. Peter Robinson.

Blind Heat 🦴🦴 **2000 (R)** Unfaithful hubby Jeffrey Scott (Sapienza) takes wife Adriana (Alonso) on a business trip to Mexico where she gets kidnapped. Rather than pay the ransom, Scott hires negotiator Paul Burke (Fahey) to get his wife back by force. Meanwhile, kidnapper Victor (Peck) falls for Adriana and doesn't want to kill her when their plot turns sour. **95m/C VHS, DVD.** Maria Conchita Alonso, Jeff Fahey, J. Eddie Peck, Al Sapienza; ***D:*** Adolfo Martinez Solares; ***W:*** Adolfo Martinez Solares, Jeff O'Brien; ***C:*** Keith Holland. **VIDEO**

Blind Husbands 🦴🦴🦴½ **1919** An Austrian officer is attracted to the pretty wife of a dull surgeon. Controversial in its day, this lurid, sumptuous melodrama instigated many stubborn Hollywood myths, including the stereotype of the brusque, jodhpur-clad Prussian officer. This was von Stroheim's first outing as director. **98m/B VHS.** Erich von Stroheim, Fay Wray; ***D:*** Erich von Stroheim.

Blind Justice 🦴🦴 **1986** An innocent man is identified as a rapist, and the accusation ruins his life. **94m/C VHS.** Tim Matheson, Lisa Eichhorn, Mimi Kuzyk, Philip Charles MacKenzie, Tom Atkins; ***D:*** Rod Holcomb; ***M:*** Miles Goodman. **TV**

Blind Justice 🦴🦴½ **1994 (R)** Gunfighter gets blinded in battle and rides into a small town where he's nursed back to health by an attractive lady doctor. While he recovers, he learns the town is trying to protect a cache of government silver from being stolen by bandits. **85m/C VHS, DVD, Wide.** Armand Assante, Elisabeth Shue, Robert Davi, Adam Baldwin; ***D:*** Richard Spence; ***W:*** Daniel Knauf; ***C:*** Jack Conroy; ***M:*** Richard Gibbs. **CABLE**

Blind Man's Bluff 🦴🦴 **1991 (PG-13)** A blind professor is accused of murdering his neighbor, but as he tries to solve the mystery, evidence points to his ex-girlfriend who may have framed him for the murder. Surprisingly suspenseful cable movie is hampered by a stock Hollywood ending. **86m/C VHS.** Robert Urich, Lisa Eilbacher, Patricia Clarkson, Ken Pogue, Ron Perlman; ***D:*** James Quinn; ***W:*** Joel Gross; ***M:*** Richard Bellis. **CABLE**

Blind Rage 🦴 **1978 (R)** When the United States government transports $15 million to the Philippines, five blind kung fu masters want a piece of the action. **81m/C VHS.** *PH* D'Urville Martin, Leo Fong, Tony Ferrer, Dick Adair, Darnell Garcia, Leila Hermosa, Fred Williamson; ***D:*** Efren C. Pinon.

Blind Side 🦴½ **1993 (R)** DeMornay and Silver are a married couple whose Mexican vacation turns into trouble when they get into a hit-and-run accident which they don't report. Back home, they're frightened by the sudden appearance of Hauer, who's also just back from Mexico. They think he's after blackmail but he's really just a run-of-the-mill psycho intrigued by DeMornay, who at least keeps her character in control. Silver and Hauer have a great time chewing scenery. Also available in a 98-minute unrated version. **92m/C VHS.** Rebecca DeMornay, Ron Silver, Rutger Hauer; ***D:*** Geoff Murphy; ***W:*** John Carlen. **CABLE**

Blind Spot 🦴🦴½ **1993** Okay family drama which works because of the performances and not the script. Woodward stars as Nell Harrington, a take-charge U.S. Representative long married to Simon (Weaver). Her troubled, pregnant daughter Phoebe (Linney) is married to Nell's aide Charlie (Diamond). Charlie is killed and Phoebe injured in a car crash but the real tragedy is when Nell discovers what caused the accident—drugs—and that her daughter is a cocaine addict. Lots of suffering. **99m/C VHS.** Joanne Woodward, Laura Linney, Fritz Weaver, Reed Edward Diamond, Cynthia Martells, Patti Yasutake, Patti D'Arbanville; ***D:*** Michael Toshiyuki Uno; ***W:*** Nina Shengold; ***M:*** Patrick Williams. **TV**

Blind Vengeance 🦴🦴½ **1990 (R)** A man whose son was murdered by white supremacists decides to take his own special revenge when they are acquited by the local jury. But this isn't your usual bloodbath; instead, he plays psychological games with the men, waiting for them to break. **93m/C VHS.** Gerald McRaney, Marg Helgenberger, Thalmus Rasulala, Lane Smith, Don Hood, Grand Bush; ***D:*** Lee Philips; ***W:*** Henri Simoun, Curt Allen. **CABLE**

Blind Vision 🦴½ **1991** Von Dohlen stars as William Dalton, a mail clerk who is in love with his beautiful neighbor Leanne (Shelton). Suffering from extreme shyness, Dalton can only spy on her through a telephoto lens. Things start to get complicated for him when one of Leanne's boyfriends turns up dead outside her apartment. Soon afterwards, their landlady and a local police detective uncover a shocking sexual secret that forces Dalton into a deadly game of obsession and desire. **92m/C VHS.** Lenny Von Dohlen, Deborah Shelton, Ned Beatty, Robert Vaughn, Louise Fletcher; ***D:*** Shuki Levy.

Blind Witness 🦴🦴½ **1989** Routine story about a blind woman who's the only witness to her husband's murder during a robbery. **92m/C VHS.** Victoria Principal, Paul Le-Mat, Stephen Macht, Matt Clark, Tim Choate; ***D:*** Richard A. Colla; ***M:*** Robert Alcivar. **TV**

Blinded by the Light 🦴🦴 **1982** Young woman tries to save her brother from attachment to a quasi-religious cult, The Light of Salvation. Real-life brother and sister McNichol team up in this drama, one of the earlier examinations of cult behavior. **90m/C VHS.** Kristy McNichol, Jimmy (James Vincent) McNichol, Anne Jackson, Michael McGuire; ***D:*** John A. Alonzo. **TV**

Blindfold: Acts of Obsession 🦴🦴 **1994 (R)** Madeline's (Doherty) marriage is boring so she consults therapist Jennings (Nelson). He suggests a number of sexual fantasies Madeline plays out with hubby Woods only to have murder enter the picture. Then Madeline's older sister Chris (Alfonso) is assigned to investigate and lets out lots of family secrets. Shannen in the buff, murder, infidelity, deception, and sex. An unrated version is also available. **93m/C VHS.** Shannen Doherty, Judd Nelson, Michael Woods, Kristian Alfonso, Shell Danielson, Drew Snyder; ***D:*** Lawrence L. Simeone; ***W:*** Lawrence L. Simeone; ***M:*** Shuki Levy.

Blindside 🦴🦴 **1988 (R)** A surveillance hobbyist who owns a motel spies on his tenants until a murder involves him in a big-scale drug war. **98m/C VHS.** Harvey Keitel, Lori Hallier, Lolita (David) Davidovich, Alan Fawcett, Michael Rudder; ***D:*** Paul Lynch.

Blindsided 🦴🦴½ **1993 (PG-13)** A former police officer temporarily loses his sight when he plays the middle man in a bank robbery. Sight improving, he falls for a woman who draws him into another crime. **93m/C VHS.** Jeff Fahey, Mia Sara, Rudy Ramos, Jack Kehler, Ben Gazzara; ***D:*** Tom Donnelly.

Blink 🦴🦴½ **1993 (R)** Recent corneal transplants allow blind musician Emma (Stowe) to regain her sight, but until they "settle" what she sees may not register in her mind immediately, a phenomenon the script dubs "retroactive vision." This poses a problem for Chicago cop Quinn when he falls for Emma—the only one who can recognize a sadistic killer. Average thriller has been done better before, but adds two attractive leads, enough suspense, and a unique twist to the typical woman-in-jeopardy tale to keep things interesting. The distorted images in Stowe's blurry vision were created by computer. Stowe also learned fiddle for her place as the fictional member of the real-life Irish-American band, The Drovers. **106m/C VHS, Wide.** Madeleine Stowe, Aidan Quinn, Laurie Metcalf, James Remar, Bruce A. Young, Peter Friedman, Paul Dillon, Michael Kirkpatrick; ***D:*** Michael Apted; ***W:*** Dana Stevens; ***C:*** Dante Spinotti; ***M:*** Brad Fiedel.

Blink of an Eye 🦴½ *Blink of an Eye* **1992 (R)** Special agent Sam Browning (Pare) must use his psychic powers and military skills against the terrorists who have kidnapped the CIA director's daughter. **90m/C VHS.** Michael Pare, Janis Lee, Uri Gavriel, Amos Lavi, Sasson Gabai, Jack Widerker; ***D:*** Bob Misiorowski; ***W:*** Edward Kovach; ***C:*** David Gurfinkel; ***M:*** Vladimir Horunzhy.

Bliss 🦴🦴🦴½ **1985 (R)** A savage, surreal Australian comedy about an advertising executive who dies suddenly for a few minutes, and upon his awakening he finds the world maniacally, bizarrely changed. Based on the Peter Carey novel, and one of the most inspired absurdist films of the decade. **112m/C VHS.** *AU* Barry Otto, Lynette Curran, Helen Jones; ***D:*** Ray Lawrence; ***W:*** Peter Carey. Australian Film Inst. '85: Film.

Bliss 🦴½ **1996 (R)** Creepy feature-length sex-ed lecture delves deeply into sexual problems in modern society. So deeply, in fact, that it could've been called "Ouch, You're on my Hair." Clueless yuppies Joseph (Sheffer) and Maria's (Lee) sexual dysfunctions lead her to seek aid from unconventional therapist Baltazar (Stamp), who does things like compare women to violins (hint: they're not really the same. Unless you REALLY like wood). Joseph has his doubts, but soon becomes a chanting tantric goofball. Too clinical to be sexy, but too sexy to be used as an Army training film. **103m/C VHS.** Sheryl Lee, Craig Sheffer, Terence Stamp, Casey Siemaszko, Spalding Gray, Leigh Taylor-Young, Lois Chiles, Blu Mankuma; ***D:*** Lance Young; ***W:*** Lance Young; ***C:*** Mike Molloy; ***M:*** Jan A.P. Kaczmarek.

The Bliss of Mrs. Blossom 🦴🦴🦴 **1968** Three's a crowd in this light-hearted romp through the machinations of a brassiere manufacturer (Attenborough) and his neglected wife (MacLaine). Mrs. Blossom finds sewing machine repairman Booth so appetizing that she hides him in the attic of the Blossom home. He reads books and redecorates, until, several plot twists later, Attenborough discovers the truth. Witty and wise, with fine supporting cast and excellent pacing. **93m/C** *GB* Shirley MacLaine, Richard Attenborough, James Booth, Freddie Jones, John Cleese; ***D:*** Joseph McGrath.

Blithe Spirit 🦴🦴🦴½ **1945** Charming and funny adaptation of Coward's famed stage play. A man re-marries and finds his long-dead wife is unhappy enough about it to come back and haunt him. Clever supporting cast, with Rutherford exceptional as the medium. Received Oscar for its Special Effects. **96m/C VHS, DVD.** *GB* Rex Harrison, Constance Cummings, Kay Hammond, Margaret Rutherford, Hugh Wakefield, Joyce Carey, Jacqueline Clarke; ***D:*** David Lean; ***W:*** Noel Coward, Anthony Havelock-Allan; ***C:*** Ronald Neame; ***M:*** Richard Addinsell.

Blitz 🦴½ *Killing Cars* **1985 (R)** A German car designer's pet project, a car that runs without gas, is halted by the influence of an Arab conglomerate. He nevertheless tries to complete it, and is hunted down. **104m/C VHS, DVD.** Juergen Prochnow, Senta Berger, William Conrad, Agnes Soral; ***D:*** Michael Verhoeven; ***W:*** Michael Verhoeven; ***C:*** Jacques Steyn; ***M:*** Michael Landau.

The Blob 🦴🦴½ **1958** Sci-fi thriller about a small town's fight against a slimy jello invader from space. Slightly rebellious McQueen (in his first starring role) redeems himself when he saves the town with quick action. Low-budget, horror/teen-fantasy became a camp classic. Other names considered included "The

Glob," "The Glob that Girdled the Globe," "The Meteorite Monster," "The Molten Meteorite," and "The Night of the Creeping Dead." Followed by a worthless sequel in 1972, "Son of Blob," and a worthwhile remake in 1988. **83m/C VHS, DVD, Wide.** Steve McQueen, Aneta Corsaut, Olin Howlin, Earl Rowe, Steve Chase, John Benson, Vincent Barbi; ***D:*** Irvin S. Yeaworth Jr.; ***W:*** Kate Phillips, Theodore Simonson; ***C:*** Thomas E. Spalding; ***M:*** Burt Bacharach, Hal David, Ralph Carmichael.

The Blob 🦴🦴🦴 **1988 (R)** A hi-tech remake of the 1958 camp classic about a small town beset by a fast-growing, maneating mound of glop shot into space by scientists, irradiated into an unnatural being, and then returned to earth. Well-developed characters make this an excellent tribute to the first film. **92m/C VHS.** Kevin Dillon, Candy Clark, Joe Seneca, Shawnee Smith, Donovan Leitch, Jeffrey DeMunn, Ricky Paull Goldin, Del Close; ***D:*** Chuck Russell; ***W:*** Chuck Russell, Frank Darabont; ***C:*** Mark Irwin.

Block-heads 🦴🦴🦴 **1938** Twenty years after the end of WWI, soldier Stan is found, still in his foxhole, and brought back to America, where he moves in with old pal Ollie. Also includes a 1934 Charley Chase short "I'll Take Vanilla." **75m/B VHS.** Stan Laurel, Oliver Hardy, Billy Gilbert, Patricia Ellis, James Finlayson, Charley Chase; ***D:*** John Blystone.

Blockhouse woof! **1973** Four men are entombed in a subterranean stronghold for six years after the D-Day invasion of Normandy. Encourages claustrophobic feeling in viewer. Based on Jean Paul Cleberts' novel "Le Blockhaus." **88m/C VHS.** *GB* Peter Sellers, Charles Aznavour, Per Oscarsson, Peter Vaughan, Leon Lissek, Alfred Lynch, Jeremy Kemp; ***D:*** Clive Rees.

The Blonde 🦴🦴 *La Bionda* **1992** Tommasso (Rubini) is driving through the Milan streets when he knocks down a young blonde woman (Kinski). She loses her memory (apparently due to shock) and Tommasso agrees to help her—soon falling in love. One day her memory returns and Christina remembers she's involved with a drug dealer and other shady characters. She leaves Tommasso to protect him but he's got other ideas. Italian with subtitles. **100m/C VHS, DVD.** *IT* Sergio Rubini, Nastassia Kinski, Ennio Fantastichini, Umberto Raho, Veronica Lazar, Giacomo Piperno; ***D:*** Sergio Rubini; ***W:*** Sergio Rubini, Filippo Ascione, Umberto Marino; ***C:*** Alessio Gelsini Torresi; ***M:*** Jurgen Knieper.

Blonde Blackmailer 🦴 **1958** Boring story about an innocent man who serves time for the murder of a female blackmailer. When he's released, he searches for the real killer. **69m/B VHS.** *GB* Richard Arlen, Susan Shaw, Vincent Ball, Constance Leigh; ***D:*** Charles Deane; ***W:*** Charles Deane.

Blonde Crazy 🦴🦴½ *Larceny Lane* **1931** A charming grifter hooks up with a gorgeous blonde as he works the territory of a big wheel criminal. Escapist fare, with fun performances from Cagney and Blondell. **81m/B VHS.** James Cagney, Joan Blondell, Louis Calhern, Ray Milland, Nat Pendleton; ***D:*** Roy Del Ruth.

Blonde in Black Leather 🦴½ **1977** A bored Italian housewife takes up with a leather-clad lady biker, and together they cavort about. **88m/C VHS.** Claudia Cardinale, Monica Vitti; ***D:*** Carlo Di Palma.

Blonde Savage 🦴 **1947** Charting African territories, an adventurer encounters a white jungle queen swinging amongst the vines. Essentially a cheap, distaff "Tarzan." **62m/B VHS.** Leif Erickson, Gale Sherwood, Veda Ann Borg, Douglass Dumbrille, Frank Jenks, Matt Willis, Ernest Whitman; ***D:*** Steve Sekely.

Blonde Venus 🦴🦴🦴½ **1932** A German cafe singer marries an Englishman, but their marriage hits the skids when he contracts radiation poisoning and she gets a nightclub job to pay the bills. Sternberg's and Dietrich's fourth film together, and characteristically beautiful, though terribly strange. Dietrich's cabaret number "Hot Voodoo," in a gorilla suit and blonde afro, attains new heights in early Hollywood surrealism. **94m/B VHS.** Marlene Dietrich, Herbert Marshall, Cary Grant, Dickie Moore, Hattie McDaniel, Sidney Toler; ***D:*** Josef von Sternberg.

Blondes Have More Guns 🦴🦴 **1995 (R)** Very dumb detective Harry Bates (McGaharin) is investigating a chainsaw murder and falls for the mysterious Montana (Key), who's possibly a serial killer, or maybe it's her half-sister, Dakota (Lusiak). Spoof of "Basic Instinct" and others of that ilk, done in the usual Troma fashion. **90m/C VHS.** Michael McGahern, Elizabeth Key, Gloria Lusiak, Richard Neil, Bennie Buttner, Romana Lisa, Andre Brazeau; ***D:*** George Merriweather; ***W:*** George Merriweather, Dan Goodman, Mary Guthrie; ***C:*** Maximo Munzi; ***M:*** Joe Renzetti.

Blondie 🦴🦴½ **1938** Chic Young's famous comic strip debuted on the big screen with Singleton in the title role, Lake as the bumbling Dagwood, and Simms as Baby Dumpling (son Alexander, when he grows up). The couple are about to celebrate their 5th wedding anniversary when Dagwood loses his job and Blondie suspects him of infidelity. The series eventually contained 28 films. **68m/B VHS.** Penny Singleton, Arthur Lake, Larry Simms, Gene Lockhart, Ann Doran, Jonathan Hale, Gordon Oliver, Stanley Andrews; ***D:*** Frank Strayer; ***W:*** Richard Flournoy; ***C:*** Henry Freulich.

Blondie Brings Up Baby 🦴🦴 **1939** Baby Dumpling is enrolled in school but on his first day he plays hooky to find Daisy who's been caught by the dogcatcher. But Blondie and Dagwood think the tyke has been kidnapped! **67m/B VHS.** Penny Singleton, Arthur Lake, Larry Simms, Jonathan Hale, Danny Mummert, Fay Helm, Peggy Ann Garner, Irving Bacon; ***D:*** Frank Strayer; ***W:*** Richard Flournoy, Gladys Lehman; ***C:*** Henry Freulich.

Blondie for Victory 🦴½ **1942** As her personal contribution to the war effort, Blondie joins the Housewives of America who perform various home front duties. Only their husbands aren't very happy since they're left home tending to the kids and the household chores. **68m/B VHS.** Penny Singleton, Arthur Lake, Larry Simms, Jonathan Hale, Danny Mummert, Stuart Erwin, Irving Bacon; ***D:*** Frank Strayer; ***W:*** Connie Lee, Karen De Wolf; ***C:*** Henry Freulich.

Blondie Goes Latin 🦴🦴 **1942** Mr. Dithers invites the Bumsteads on a South American cruise and Dagwood winds up the drummer in the shipboard band while Singleton gets to show off her Broadway background in some musical numbers. **70m/B VHS.** Penny Singleton, Arthur Lake, Jonathan Hale, Larry Simms, Ruth Terry, Tito Guizar, Danny Mummert, Irving Bacon; ***D:*** Frank Strayer; ***W:*** Richard Flournoy, Karen De Wolf; ***C:*** Henry Freulich.

Blondie Goes to College 🦴🦴 **1942** Actually both Bumsteads enroll but decide to pass themselves off as single, which leads to complications. Blondie draws the attentions of the school's top athlete while Dagwood's joins the rowing team and turns the head of a pretty coed. **68m/B VHS.** Penny Singleton, Arthur Lake, Larry Simms, Jonathan Hale, Danny Mummert, Janet Blair, Larry Parks, Lloyd Bridges; ***D:*** Frank Strayer; ***W:*** Lou Breslow; ***C:*** Henry Freulich.

Blondie Has Trouble 🦴🦴½ *Blondie Has Servant Trouble* **1940** Mr. Dithers has a property he just can't sell because of rumors that the house is haunted. So he offers to let the Bumsteads stay in it to prove that the rumors are false. The Bumsteads also find the creepy mansion comes complete with two equally creepy servants. 6th film in the series. **70m/B VHS.** Penny Singleton, Arthur Lake, Larry Simms, Danny Mummert, Jonathan Hale, Arthur Hohl, Esther Dale, Irving Bacon; ***D:*** Frank Strayer; ***W:*** Richard Flournoy; ***C:*** Henry Freulich; ***M:*** Leigh Harline.

Blondie Hits the Jackpot 🦴½ **1949** Dagwood is fired for the umpteenth time after he makes a mistake in a construction deal and tries frantically to get his job back. Meanwhile, Blondie wins the big prize on a radio quiz show. The 26th film in the series. **66m/B VHS.** Penny Singleton, Arthur Lake, Larry Simms, Marjorie Kent, Jerome Cowan, Lloyd Corrigan, Danny Mummert, James Flavin; ***D:*** Edward L. Bernds; ***W:*** Jack Henley; ***C:*** Vincent Farrar; ***M:*** Mischa Bakaleinikoff.

Blondie in Society 🦴½ **1941** A weak entry (the ninth) in the comedic series. Dagwood brings home a pedigreed Great Dane and Blondie decides to enter the pooch in the local dog show. Then an important client of Dagwood's decides he wants the dog. **77m/B VHS.** Penny Singleton, Arthur Lake, Larry Simms, William Frawley, Edgar Kennedy, Jonathan Hale, Danny Mummert, Chick Chandler; ***D:*** Frank Strayer; ***W:*** Karen De Wolf; ***C:*** Henry Freulich.

Blondie Knows Best 🦴½ **1946** Dagwood impersonates his boss, Mr. Dithers, and causes all sorts of problems. Howard, one of the Three Stooges, has a cameo as a myopic process-server. The 18th film in the series. **66m/B VHS.** Penny Singleton, Arthur Lake, Larry Simms, Marjorie Kent, Jonathan Hale, Steven Geray, Jerome Cowan, Danny Mummert; ***Cameos:*** Shemp Howard; ***D:*** Abby Berlin; ***W:*** Edward L. Bernds, Al Martin.

Blondie Meets the Boss 🦴🦴 **1939** Dagwood goes on a fishing trip and manages to get into trouble with Blondie when a photograph puts him in a compromising pose with another woman. Then, Blondie winds up at the office doing Dagwood's job (whatever that may be). Second in the series. **75m/B VHS.** Penny Singleton, Arthur Lake, Larry Simms, Jonathan Hale, Dorothy Moore, Don Beddoe, Stanley Brown, Danny Mummert, Irving Bacon; ***D:*** Frank Strayer; ***W:*** Richard Flournoy; ***C:*** Henry Freulich.

Blondie On a Budget 🦴🦴 **1940** Dagwood wins 200 bucks in a contest and enlists the aid of ex-girlfriend Joan (Hayworth) to buy Blondie the fur coat she's been wanting. But Blondie wants to use the money to get Dagwood into a fishing club and misinterprets the situation. **68m/B VHS.** Penny Singleton, Arthur Lake, Larry Simms, Rita Hayworth, Danny Mummert, Don Beddoe, Fay Helm, John Qualen, Irving Bacon; ***D:*** Frank Strayer; ***W:*** Richard Flournoy; ***C:*** Henry Freulich.

Blondie Plays Cupid 🦴🦴 **1940** The Bumsteads are traveling to visit relatives in the country when they happen across a young couple (Ford and Walters) trying to elope. So Blondie decides to help the youngsters out. **68m/B VHS.** Penny Singleton, Arthur Lake, Larry Simms, Jonathan Hale, Glenn Ford, Luana Walters, Danny Mummert, Irving Bacon; ***D:*** Frank Strayer; ***W:*** Richard Flournoy, Karen De Wolf; ***C:*** Henry Freulich.

Blondie Takes a Vacation 🦴🦴½ **1939** Third in the series of fluff films adapted from Chic Young's comic strip. After the Bumstead family is snubbed at a snobby mountain resort they move to a friendlier nearby hotel where they try to help out the owners who are in danger of losing their investment. Baby Dumpling does his bit by unleashing a skunk in the ventilation system of the competing hotel. **68m/B VHS.** Penny Singleton, Arthur Lake, Larry Simms, Danny Mummert, Donald Meek, Donald MacBride, Thomas Ross, Robert Wilcox, Irving Bacon; ***D:*** Frank Strayer; ***W:*** Richard Flournoy; ***C:*** Henry Freulich.

Blondie's Blessed Event 🦴🦴½ **1942** Cookie is born, causing even more chaos in the Bumstead household. Meanwhile, Dagwood gets into trouble at work when he hires a cynical playwright to write an important speech for him. 11th entry in series. **69m/B VHS.** Penny Singleton, Arthur Lake, Larry Simms, Norma Jean Wayne, Jonathan Hale, Danny Mummert, Hans Conried, Irving Bacon, Stanley Brown, Mary Wickes, Paul Harvey, Arthur O'Connell; ***D:*** Frank Strayer; ***W:*** Richard Flournoy, Karen De Wolf, Connie Lee; ***C:*** Henry Freulich.

Blood Alley 🦴🦴 **1955** A seasoned Merchant Marine captain takes on a cargo of refugee Chinese to smuggle through enemy territory. Middling, mid-career Wayne vehicle. **115m/C VHS, Wide.** John Wayne, Lauren Bacall, Paul Fix, Joy Kim, Berry Kroeger, Mike Mazurki, Anita Ekberg; ***D:*** William A. Wellman; ***C:*** William Clothier.

Blood and Black Lace 🦴 *Fashion House of Death; Six Women for the Murderer; Sei Donne per l'Assassino* **1964** Beautiful models are being brutally murdered and an inspector is assigned to the case, but not before more gruesome killings occur. Bava is, as usual, violent and suspenseful. Horror fans will enjoy this flick. **90m/C VHS, DVD, Wide.** *IT FR GE* Cameron Mitchell, Eva Bartok, Mary Arden, Dante DiPaolo, Arianna Gorini, Lea Krugher, Harriet Medin, Giuliano Raffaelli, Thomas Reiner, Frank Ressel, Massimo Righi; ***D:*** Mario Bava; ***W:*** Mario Bava, Marcello Fondato, Joe Barilla; ***C:*** Ubaldo Terzano; ***M:*** Carlo Rustichelli.

Blood & Concrete: A Love Story 🦴🦴 **1990 (R)** Bizarre, violent and stylish film-noir spoof, definitely not for all tastes. The innocent hero gets drawn into a maelstrom of intrigue over a killer aphrodisiac drug. Beals, an addicted punk rocker, gets to perform a few songs. **97m/C VHS, Wide.** Billy Zane, Jennifer Beals, Darren McGavin, James LeGros, Nicholas Worth, Mark Pellegrino, Harry Shearer, Billy Bastiani; ***D:*** Jeff Reiner; ***W:*** Jeff Reiner, Richard LaBrie; ***C:*** Declan Quinn; ***M:*** Vinnie Golia.

Blood & Donuts 🦴🦴 **1995 (R)** Hungry vampire Boya (Currie) is looking for a rat snack when he stumbles across an all-night donut shop where pretty cashier Molly (Clarkson) and friendly cabbie Earl (Louis) seek his help with a local crime boss. Mild horror mixed with comedy and limited gore. **89m/C VHS.** *CA* Gordon Currie, Justin Louis, Helene Clarkson, Fiona Reid, Frank Moore; ***Cameos:*** David Cronenberg; ***D:*** Holly Dale; ***W:*** Andrew Rai Berzins; ***C:*** Paul Sarossy.

Blood and Guns 🦴½ **1979 (R)** Romance, revenge, and action abound in post-revolutionary Mexico. **96m/C VHS.** Orson Welles, Tomas Milian, John Steiner; ***D:*** Giulio Petroni.

Blood and Roses 🦴🦴 *Et Mourir de Plaisir* **1961** A girl who is obsessed with her family's vampire background becomes possessed by a vampire and commits numerous murders. The photography is good, but the plot is hazy and only effective in certain parts. Based on the story "Carmilla" by Sheridan Le Fanu. Later remade as "The Vampire Lovers" and "The Blood-Spattered Bride." **74m/C VHS.** *FR IT* Mel Ferrer, Elsa Martinelli, Annette Vadim, Marc Allegret, Jacques-Rene Chauffard, Serge Marquand, Gabriella Farinon, Alberto Bonucci, Nathalie Le Foret; ***D:*** Roger Vadim; ***W:*** Roger Vadim, Claude Martin, Roger Vailand, Claude Brule; ***C:*** Claude Renoir; ***M:*** Jean Prodromides.

Blood and Sand 🦴🦴🦴½ **1922** Vintage romance based on Vicente Blasco Ibanez's novel about the tragic rise and fall of a matador, and the women in his life. The film that made Valentino a star. Remade in 1941. Silent. **87m/B VHS, DVD.** Rudolph Valentino, Nita Naldi, Lila Lee, Walter Long; ***D:*** Fred Niblo; ***W:*** June Mathis; ***C:*** Alvin Wyckoff.

Blood and Sand 🦴🦴🦴 **1941** Director Mamoulian "painted" this picture in the new technicolor technique, which makes it a veritable explosion of color and spectacle. Power is the matador who becomes famous and then falls when he is torn between two women, forsaking his first love, bullfighting. Based on the novel "Sangre y Arena" by Vicente Blasco Ibanez. This movie catapulted Hayworth to stardom, primarily for her dancing, but also for her sexiness and seductiveness (and of course, her acting). Remake of the 1922 silent classic; remade again in 1989. **123m/C VHS.** Tyrone Power, Linda Darnell, Rita Hayworth, Alla Nazimova, Anthony Quinn, J. Carrol Naish, John Carradine, George Reeves; ***D:*** Rouben Mamoulian; ***W:*** Jo Swerling; ***C:*** Ernest Palmer, Ray Rennahan; ***M:*** Alfred Newman. Oscars '41: Color Cinematog.

Blood and Sand 🦴🦴 **1989 (R)** A bullfighter on the verge of super-stardom risks it all when he falls under the spell of a sexy, seductive woman. Will she destroy his one opportunity for fame? Interesting for people who actually enjoy watching the "sport" of bullfighting. Originally made in 1922 and remade in 1941. **96m/C VHS, DVD.** Christopher Rydell, Sharon Stone, Ana Torrent, Jose-Luis De Villalonga, Simon Andrew; ***D:*** Javier Elorrieta; ***W:*** Rafael Azcona, Ricardo Franco, Thomas Fucci; ***C:*** Antonio Rios; ***M:*** Jesus Gluck.

Blood and Steel **1925** The railroad tycoon's daughter and the construction foreman wind up together on an exciting train ride. Silent. **?m/B VHS, 8mm.** Helen Holmes, William Desmond; ***D:*** J(ohn) P(aterson) McGowan.

Blood & Wine 🦴🦴½ **1996 (R)** Miami wine merchant Alex (Nicholson) gets involved with terminally ill safecracker Victor (Caine) to steal a necklace worth a cool million. Meanwhile he must deal with his crumbling marriage to Suzanne (Davis) and the bitter relationship with his stepson Jason (Dorff), who has eyes for both the necklace and his Cuban mistress (Lopez). Characterizations and strong performances (particularly by Nicholson and Caine) haul the sometimes lumbering plot to its violent conclusion. Promoted as the third part of a "dysfunctional family trilogy" with "Five Easy Pieces" and "The King of Marvin's Gardens." Seventh time Nicholson has worked with director Rafelson. **100m/C VHS.** Jack Nicholson, Michael Caine, Judy Davis, Stephen Dorff, Jennifer Lopez, Harold Perrineau Jr.; ***D:*** Bob Rafelson; ***W:*** Nick Villiars, Allison Cross; ***C:*** Newton Thomas (Tom) Sigel; ***M:*** Stephen Cohen.

Blood at Sundown 🦴½ **1988** Routine oater where man returns home after the Civil War to find his wife kidnapped by a group of Mexican outlaws who have also taken over his village. **92m/C VHS.** Giuliano Gemma, Hally Hamond, Nieves Navarro, Antonio Casas, Fernando (Fernand) Sancho, Pajarito, George Martin; ***D:*** Duccio Tessari.

Blood Beach woof! **1981 (R)** A group of teenagers are devoured by menacing sand, which keeps people from getting to the water by swallowing them whole. Weak parody with some humorous moments; more silly than scary. **92m/C VHS.** David Huffman, Marianna Hill, John Saxon, Burt Young, Otis Young, Pamela McMyler, Bobby Bass, Darrell Fetty, Stefan Gierasch, Harriet Medin, Lynn(e) Marta, Mary Jo Catlett; ***D:*** Jeffrey Bloom; ***W:*** Jeffrey Bloom; ***C:*** Steven Poster; ***M:*** Gil Melle.

Blood Beast Terror 🦴½ *The Vampire-Beast Craves Blood; Deathshead Vampire* **1967** An entomologist transforms his own daughter into a Deathshead Moth and she proceeds to terrorize and drink innocent victims' blood. **81m/C VHS, DVD, Wide.** *GB* Peter Cushing, Robert Flemyng, Wanda Ventham, Vanessa Howard; ***D:*** Vernon Sewell; ***W:*** Peter Bryan; ***C:*** Stanley Long; ***M:*** Paul Ferris.

Blood Bride 🦴½ **19??** A lonely young woman finally finds happiness with her new husband but her world comes crashing about her with soul-mangling ferocity when she discovers he is actually a bloodthirsty maniac. **90m/C VHS.** Ellen Barber, Philip English.

Blood Brothers 🦴🦴 **1974 (R)** A young man who dreams of becoming a lawyer is disturbed when he discovers that his family has mafia ties. **148m/C VHS.** *IT* Claudia Cardinale, Franco Nero, Lina Polito; ***D:*** Pasquale Squitieri.

Blood Brothers 🦴🦴 **1997** Darryl has always looked up to older brother Sylvester. And then one day he witnesses a gang murder and Sylvester is one of the killers. The District Attorney senses Darryl knows more than he's saying and the gang bangers want to shut him up permanently, so each brother must look to his conscience and decide how best to be his brother's keeper. **91m/C VHS.** Clark Johnson, Richard Chevolleau, Mia Korf, Richard Yearwood, Ron White, Amir Williams, Ndehru Roberts, Timothy Stickney, Bill Nunn; ***D:*** Bruce Pittman; ***W:*** Paris Qualles; ***M:*** Harold Wheeler.

Blood Clan 🦴½ **1991 (R)** Based on the true story of Katy Bane, daughter of notorious Scottish cult leader, Sawney Bane, in whose lair were found the remains of over 1000 killed and cannibalized followers. When found, Bane's entire family was sentenced to death with the exception of Katy, who left to make a new start in Canada. When a rash of mysterious deaths break out in Katy's new home, she must defend herself from rumors that her father's murderous cult is resurfacing. **91m/C VHS.** Gordon Pinsent, Michelle Little, Robert Wisden; ***D:*** Charles Wilkinson.

Blood Cult 🦴 **1985 (R)** A bizarre series of murder-mutilations take place on a small midwestern campus. Contains graphic violence that is not for the squeamish. This film was created especially for the home video market. **89m/C VHS, DVD.** Chuck Ellis, Julie Andelman, Jim Vance, Joe Hardt; ***D:*** Christopher Lewis; ***M:*** Rod Slane. **VIDEO**

Blood Debts **1983** A father is out for revenge after he saves his daughter from some hunters who raped her and also killed her boyfriend. **91m/C VHS.** Richard Harrison, Mike Manty, Jim Gaines, Anne Jackson, Anne Milhench; ***D:*** Teddy Page.

Blood Diner woof! **1987** Two spirit-possessed, diner-owning brothers kill countless young girls for demonic rituals, and serve their corpses as gourmet food in their restaurant. Some funny moments mixed in with the requisite gore. Cult potential. **88m/C VHS.** Rick Burks, Carl Crew, Roger Dauer, Lisa Guggenheim, Roxanne Cybelle, Cynthia Baker; ***D:*** Jackie Kong; ***W:*** Michael Sonye; ***C:*** Jurg Walther; ***M:*** Don Preston.

Blood Feast 🦴 *Feast of Flesh* **1963** The first of Lewis' gore-fests, in which a demented caterer butchers hapless young women to splice them together in order to bring back an Egyptian goddess. Dated, campy, and gross; reportedly shot in four days (it shows). **70m/C VHS, DVD.** Connie Mason, Thomas Wood, Mal Arnold, Scott H. Hall, Lyn Bolton, Toni Calvert, Gene Courtier, Ashlyn Martin, Jerome (Jerry Stallion) Eden, David Friedman; ***D:*** Herschell Gordon Lewis; ***W:*** Allison Louise Downe; ***C:*** Herschell Gordon Lewis; ***M:*** Herschell Gordon Lewis.

Blood Feud 🦴🦴 *Revenge* **1979 (R)** In Italy preceding Europe's entry into WWII, a young widow is in mourning over the brutal murder of her husband by the Sicilian Mafia. In the meantime she must contend with the rivalry between Mastroianni as a lawyer and Giannini as a small-time crook both vying for her affections. Dubbed. **112m/C VHS.** *IT* Sophia Loren, Marcello Mastroianni, Giancarlo Giannini; ***D:*** Lina Wertmuller; ***W:*** Lina Wertmuller.

Blood for a Silver Dollar 🦴½ *One Silver Dollar; Un Dollar Troue* **1966** Action-filled western, littered with murder, revenge and romance. **98m/C VHS.** *IT FR* Montgomery Wood, Evelyn Stewart, Pierre (Peter Cross) Cressoy; ***D:*** Giorgio Ferroni; ***M:*** Gianni Ferrio.

Blood for Blood 🦴½ **1995 (R)** Cop must take up the martial arts skills he learned in childhood in order to protect his family from assassination. **93m/C VHS.** Lorenzo Lamas, James Lew, Mako, Eric Pierpont, James Shigeta, James Callahan; ***D:*** John Weidner; ***M:*** Joel Goldsmith.

Blood Freak woof! *Blood Freaks* **1972** An absolutely insane anti-drug, Christian splatter film. A Floridian biker is introduced to drugs by a young woman and eventually turns into a poultry-monster who drinks the blood of junkies. Narrated by a chain smoker who has a coughing fit. Don't miss it. **86m/C VHS.** Steve Hawkes, Dana Cullivan, Randy Grinter Jr., Tina Anderson, Heather Hughes; ***D:*** Brad Grinter, Steve Hawkes.

Blood Frenzy 🦴 **1987** Psychologist's patients take a therapeutic trip to the desert. The sun and heat take their toll, and everyone gets violent. This kind of therapy we don't need, and the movie's a waste, as well. Made for video. Loring was Wednesday on TV's "The Addams Family." **90m/C VHS.** John Montero, Lisa Loring, Hank Garrett, Wendy MacDonald; ***D:*** Hal Freeman. **VIDEO**

Blood from the Mummy's Tomb 🦴🦴½ **1971** The immortal spirit of Tera, Egyptian queen of evil, haunts Margaret (Leon), the daughter of an archaeologist who discovered her tomb. As a long-prophesied conjunction of stars begins to occur, Margaret finds herself enthralled by Tera's power and finds herself becoming possessed by Tera's spirit. This adaptation of Bram Stoker's "The Jewel of Seven Stars" begins well, with a wonderfully mysterious and moody first half, but it loses steam in the somewhat muddled (and tedious) second half. Coulouris (without the old age makeup) looks exactly like his Thatcher character in "Citizen Kane," 30 years earlier, but sadly is given not much to do other than roll his eyes and scream. Leon is a likable heroine but that wig and false eyelashes have got to go! Remade in post-"Omen" fashion as "The Awakening." **94m/C VHS, DVD, Wide.** *GB* Andrew Keir, Valerie Leon, James Villiers, Hugh Burden, George Coulouris, Mark Edwards; ***D:*** Seth Holt; ***W:*** Christopher Wicking; ***C:*** Arthur Grant; ***M:*** Tristram Cary.

Blood Games woof! **1990 (R)** Buxom baseball team bats 1000 against the home team and the winning babes find out just how poor losers can be. Diamonds aren't always a girl's best friend. **90m/C VHS.** Gregory Cummings, Laura Albert, Shelly Abblett, Luke Shay, Ross Hagen; ***D:*** Tanya Rosenberg.

Blood, Guts, Bullets and Octane 🦴🦴 **1999 (R)** Used-car salesmen Sid (Carnahan) and Bob (Leis) are trying to keep their failing business afloat when a broker offers then a quarter million to let a 1963 Pontiac Le Mans convertible (burgundy) stay on their lot for 48 hours. The FBI are after the car and its owners, who've left a bloody cross-country trail. And the motor-mouth duo decide to renege on the deal. Desperate lowlifes and vicious crime winds up looking very familiar. **87m/C VHS, DVD.** Joe Carnahan, Dan Leis, Ken Rudolph, James Salter, Dan Harlan; ***D:*** Joe Carnahan; ***W:*** Joe Carnahan; ***C:*** John A. Jimenez; ***M:*** Mark Priolo, Martin Burke.

Blood Hook 🦴½ **1986** A self-parodying teenage-slasher film about kids running into a backwoods fishing tournament while on vacation, complete with ghouls, cannibalism and grotesquerie. **85m/C VHS.** Mark Jacobs, Lisa Todd, Patrick Danz; ***D:*** James Mallon.

Blood In ... Blood Out: Bound by Honor 🦴½ *Bound by Honor* **1993 (R)** Three-hour epic about Chicano gang culture focuses on three buddies whose lives evolve into a drug-addicted artist, a narc, and a prison regular. Written by acclaimed poet Baca, the film touches on issues such as poverty, racism, drugs, and violence as they pertain to Hispanic life. Unfortunately, the extreme violence (shootings, stabbings, and garrotings) completely overwhelms the rest of the story. Based on a story by Ross Thomas. **180m/C VHS, DVD, Wide.** Thomas F. Wilson, Damian Chapa, Jesse Borrego, Benjamin Bratt, Enrique Castillo, Victor Rivers, Delroy Lindo, Tom Towles; ***D:*** Taylor Hackford; ***W:*** Floyd Mutrux, Jimmy Santiago Baca, Jeremy Iacone; ***C:*** Gabriel Beristain; ***M:*** Bill Conti.

Blood Island 🦴🦴 *The Shuttered Room* **1968** A couple inherits an old house on a remote New England island where the woman grew up. They discover that this old house needs more than a paint job to make it livable; seems there's something evil in them there walls. Based on an H.P. Lovecraft story. Greene, who's best known for later directing "Godspell," and the solid cast fail to animate the inert script. **100m/C VHS.** *GB* Gig Young, Carol Lynley, Oliver Reed, Flora Robson; ***D:*** David Greene.

Blood Legacy 🦴🦴 *Legacy of Blood* **1973 (R)** Four heirs must survive a night in a lonely country estate to collect their money; what do you think happens? Average treatment of the haunted house theme. **77m/C VHS.** John Carradine, John Russell, Faith Domergue, Merry Anders, Richard (Dick) Davalos, Jeff Morrow, Roy Engle; ***D:*** Carl Monson; ***W:*** Eric Norden; ***C:*** Jack Beckett.

Blood Mania 🦴 **1970 (R)** A retired surgeon's daughter decides to murder her father to collect her inheritance prematurely, but soon learns that crime doesn't pay as well as medicine. Low-budget, low-interest flick. **90m/C VHS.** Peter Carpenter, Maria de Aragon, Alex Rocco; ***D:*** Robert Vincent O'Neil.

Blood Money 🦴½ **1980 (PG)** A dying ex-criminal returns to Australia to redeem his name and die with dignity. **64m/C VHS.** *AU* Bryan Brown, John Flaus, Chrissie James; ***D:*** Christopher Fitchett.

Blood Money 🦴🦴 *The Arrangement* **1998 (R)** Five dead bodies, $4 million, and one eye-witness, stripper Candy (Petty), are what remains of a drug deal gone south. Now, Detective Connor (Ironside) must protect his witness from Mob reprisals. **95m/C VHS, DVD.** Michael Ironside, Lori Petty, Currie Graham; ***D:*** Michael Ironside. **VIDEO**

Blood Money 🦴🦴 **1999 (R)** Tony Restrelli (Bloom) is the legit member of a mob family who made his money in the stock market. Now his financial knowledge is needed by his family to fend off would-be interlopers—and he can also avenge his brother's murder. **95m/C VHS.** Brian Bloom, Alan Arkin, Alicia Coppola, Jennifer Gatti, Bruce Kirby, Jonathan Scarfe, Gregory Sierra, Leonard Stone; ***D:*** Aaron Lipstadt. **CABLE**

Blood Money: The Story of Clinton and Nadine 🦴🦴½ *Clinton & Nadine* **1988** A confusing action/thriller with a good cast. Garcia is a small-time exotic bird smuggler whose gun-running brother has been murdered. He uses high-class hooker Barkin to get close to his brother's contacts, who turn out to be running guns to the Nicaraguan contras and involved in a dangerous government conspiracy. **95m/C VHS.** Andy Garcia, Ellen Barkin, Morgan Freeman; ***D:*** Jerry Schatzberg. **CABLE**

The Blood of a Poet *Le Sang d'un Poete* **1930** Cocteau's first film, a practically formless piece of poetic cinema, detailing all manner of surreal events occurring in the instant a chimney falls. In French with English subtitles. **55m/B VHS.** Enrique Rivero, Feral Benga, Jean Desbordes; ***D:*** Jean Cocteau; ***W:*** Jean Cocteau; ***C:*** Georges Perinal; ***M:*** Georges Auric.

Blood of Dracula 🦴½ *Blood Is My Heritage; Blood of the Demon* **1957** They don't make 1950s rock 'n' roll girls' school vampire movies like this anymore, for which we may be grateful. Hypnotism, an amulet, and a greasepaint makeup job turn a shy female student into a bloodsucker. **71m/B VHS.** Sandra Harrison, Louise Lewis, Gail Ganley, Jerry Blaine, Heather Ames, Malcolm Atterbury, Richard Devon, Thomas B(rowne). Henry, Don Devlin, Edna Holland; ***D:*** Herbert L. Strock; ***W:*** Ralph Thornton; ***C:*** Monroe Askins; ***M:*** Paul Dunlap.

Blood of Dracula's Castle 🦴🦴 *Dracula's Castle; Castle of Dracula* **1969** Couple inherits an allegedly deserted castle, but upon moving in discover Mr. and Mrs. Dracula have settled there. The vampires keep young women chained in the dungeon for continual blood supply. Also present are a hunchback and a werewolf. Awesome Adamson production is highlighted by the presence of the gorgeous Volante. Early cinematography effort by the renowned Laszlo Kovacs. **84m/C VHS.** John Carradine, Alexander D'Arcy, Paula Raymond, Ray Young, Vicki Volante, Robert Dix, John Cardos, Ken Osborne; ***D:*** Jean Hewitt, Al Adamson; ***W:*** Rex Carlton; ***C:*** Laszlo Kovacs.

Blood of Ghastly Horror woof! *The Fiend with the Atomic Brain; Psycho a Go Go!; The Love Maniac; The Man with the Synthetic Brain; The Fiend with the Electronic Brain* **1972** A young man thinks he has a new lease on life when he is the happy recipient of a brain transplant, but his dreams are destroyed when he evolves into a rampaging killer. This movie is so awful it hides behind numerous but rather creative aliases. **87m/C VHS, DVD.** John Carradine, Kent Taylor, Tommy Kirk, Regina Carrol, Roy Morton, Tracey Robbins; ***D:*** Al Adamson; ***W:*** Chris Martino, Dick Poston; ***C:*** Vilmos Zsigmond.

The Blood of Heroes 🦴🦴 *The Salute of the Jugger* **1989 (R)** A post-apocalyptic action flick detailing the adventures of a battered team of "juggers," warriors who challenge small village teams to a brutal sport (involving dogs' heads on sticks) that's a cross between jousting and football. **97m/C VHS.** Rutger Hauer, Joan Chen, Vincent D'Onofrio, Anna (Katerina) Katarina; ***D:*** David Peoples; ***W:*** David Peoples; ***C:*** David Eggby; ***M:*** Todd Boekelheide.

Blood of Jesus 🦴🦴 **1941** A sinful husband accidentally shoots his newly baptized wife, causing an uproar in their rural town. Williams later starred as Andy on the "Amos 'n' Andy" TV series. **50m/C VHS.** Spencer Williams Jr., Kathryn Caviness; ***D:*** Spencer Williams Jr.; ***W:*** Spencer Williams Jr. Natl. Film Reg. '91.

The Blood of Others 🦴 **1984** A driveling adaptation of the Simone de Beauvoir novel about a young French woman at the outbreak of WWII torn between her absent boyfriend in the Resistance and a kind, wealthy German. Made for French TV, it stars Jodie Foster and Michael Ontkean as the Gallic pair. **130m/C VHS.** *FR* Jodie Foster, Sam Neill, Michael Ontkean, Stephane Audran, Lambert Wilson, John Vernon, Kate Reid, Jean-Pierre Aumont; ***D:*** Claude Chabrol; ***W:*** Brian Moore. **TV**

Blood of the Hunter 🦴🦴½ **1994 (PG-13)** Psycho-killer holds postman's wife captive in a remote cabin in the Canadian wilderness. Turns out hubby and psycho share a mysterious past. **92m/C VHS.** Michael Biehn, Alexandra Vandernoot, Gabriel Arcand; ***D:*** Gilles Carle.

Blood of the Vampire 🦴½ **1958** A Transylvanian doctor is executed for being a vampire and his hunchbacked assistant brings him back to life. **84m/C VHS.** *GB* Donald Wolfit, Vincent Ball, Barbara Shelley, Victor Maddern; ***D:*** Henry Cass; ***W:*** Jimmy Sangster.

The Blood on Satan's Claw 🦴🦴🦴 *Satan's Skin; Satan's Claw* **1971** Graphic tale centering on the Devil himself. Townspeople in an English village circa 1670 find the spirit of Satan taking over their children, who begin to practice witchcraft. Well made with lots of attention to period details. Not for the faint-hearted. **90m/C VHS.** *GB* Patrick Wymark, Linda Hayden, Barry Andrews, Michele Dotrice, James Hayter, Avice Landon, Simon Williams, Tamara Ustinov; ***D:*** Piers Haggard; ***C:*** Dick Bush.

Blood on the Badge 🦴½ **1992** Illegal arms have been stolen from a military arsenal and fall into the hands of Libyan Nationalists who begin a terrorist campaign. Detective Neal Farrow is assigned to stop them. **92m/C VHS.** Ramon Estevez, David Harrod, Rocky Patterson, Desiree Laforge, Dean Nolen, Melissa Deleon, Todd Everett; ***D:*** Bret McCormick.

Blood on the Moon 🦴🦴½ **1948** Well-acted film about a cowboy's involvement in a friend's underhanded schemes. Based on a Luke Short novel, this dark film revolves around a western land dispute between cattlemen and homesteaders. **88m/B VHS.** Robert Mitchum, Robert Preston, Walter Brennan, Barbara Bel Geddes; ***D:*** Robert Wise.

Blood on the Mountain 🦴 **1988** After escaping from prison, Jim plots revenge against his accomplice, only to kill an innocent man instead. **71m/C VHS.** Stracker Edwards, Tim Jones, Paula Preston, Cliff Turknett, Rich Jury; ***D:*** Donald W. Thompson.

Blood on the Sun 🦴🦴½ **1945** Newspaperman in Japan uncovers plans for world dominance as propaganda, violence, and intrigue combine in this action-adventure. Also available colorized. **98m/B VHS, DVD.** James Cagney, Sylvia Sidney, Robert Armstrong, Wallace Ford; ***D:*** Frank Lloyd; ***W:*** Lester Cole, Nathaniel Curtis, Frank Melford; ***C:*** Theodor Sparkuhl; ***M:*** Miklos Rozsa.

The Blood Oranges 🦴½ **1997 (R)** Pretentious film is set in the anything-goes '70s in a tropical backwater village. Bohemian marrieds Cyril (Dance) and Fiona (Lee) believe in fulfilling every sexual fantasy but their latest exchange of marital partners comes with unexpected complications. Fiona is attracted to photographer Hugh (Lane), who resists her charms for more deviant behavior, while Hugh's wife Catherine (Robins) is easily seduced by Cyril's courtship. Dialogue is laughable and the acting equally overblown. Based on the novel by John Fowles. **93m/C VHS, DVD.** Charles Dance, Sheryl Lee, Colin Lane, Laila Robins, Rachael Bella; ***D:*** Philip Haas; ***W:*** Belinda Haas, Philip Haas; ***C:*** Bernard Zitzermann; ***M:*** Angelo Badalamenti.

Blood Orgy of the She-Devils woof! **1974 (PG)** Exploitative gore nonsense about female demons, beautiful witches, and satanic worship. Some movies waste all their creative efforts on their titles. **73m/C VHS.** Lila Zaborin, Tom Pace, Leslie McRae, Ray Myles, Victor Izay, William Bagdad; ***D:*** Ted V. Mikels; ***W:*** Ted V. Mikels; ***C:*** Anthony Salinas.

Blood Rage woof! *Nightmare at Shadow Woods* **1987 (R)** A maniacal twin goes on a murderous rampage through his brother's neighborhood. AKA "Nightmare at Shadow Woods." Only for die-hard "Mary Hartman" fans. **87m/C VHS.** Louise Lasser, Mike Soper; ***D:*** John Grissmer; ***M:*** Richard Einhorn.

Blood Red 🦴½ **1988 (R)** In 1895 Northern California, an Italian immigrant and his family give bloody battle to a powerful industrialist who wants their land in wine-growing country. Watch for the scenes involving veteran Roberts and his then-newcomer sister, pretty woman Julia. **91m/C VHS, 8mm.** Eric Roberts, Dennis Hopper, Giancarlo Giannini, Burt Young, Carlin Glynn, Lara Harris, Susan Anspach, Julia Roberts, Elias Koteas, Frank Campanella, Aldo Ray, Horton Foote Jr.; ***D:*** Peter Masterson; ***W:*** Ron Cutler.

Blood Relations 🦴½ **1987 (R)** A woman is introduced to her fiance's family only to find out that they, as well as her fiance, are murdering, perverted weirdos competing for an inheritance. **88m/C VHS.** *CA* Jan Rubes, Ray Walston, Lydie Denier, Kevin Hicks, Lynne Adams, Sam Malkin, Steven Saylor, Carrie Leigh; ***D:*** Graeme Campbell.

Blood Relatives 🦴 *Les Liens de Sang* **1977** Langlois admits she saw her brother kill her cousin, with whom he had been carrying on an incestuous relationship. But the discovery of the dead girl's diary by police inspector Sutherland reveals many more layers of intrigue than were initially evident. Based on a novel by Ed McBain. The French actors have been dubbed into English. **94m/C VHS.** *CA* Lisa Langlois, Donald Sutherland, Stephane Audran, David Hemmings, Donald Pleasence, Laurent Malet, Micheline Lanctot, Aude Landry; ***D:*** Claude Chabrol; ***W:*** Claude Chabrol.

Blood Ring 🦴½ **1993** When Sue's boxer husband goes missing she enlists old friend Max to help find him. They uncover a gambling ring run by drug lords where the kickboxing matches are to the death. Naturally, Max decides to use his expert kickboxing skills to get a violent revenge. **90m/C VHS.** Dale "Apollo" Cook, Andrea Lamatsch, Don Nakaya Neilsen, Steve Tartalia; ***D:*** Irvin Johnson; ***W:*** Ron Davies.

Blood Salvage 🦴 *Mad Jake* **1990 (R)** A crazy junkman kidnaps beautiful girls, selling their organs to the highest bidder. He meets his match when a potential target refuses to become a victim in spite of her wheelchair. Interesting plot twists keep this Grade B thriller above average. **90m/C VHS.** Danny Nelson, Lori Birdsong, John Saxon, Ray Walston, Christian Hesler, Ralph Pruitt Vaughn, Laura Whyte, Evander Holyfield; ***D:*** Tucker Johnson; ***W:*** Tucker Johnson, Ken Sanders; ***C:*** Michael Karp.

Blood Screams woof! **1988 (R)** Nosy people drop in on an old town in Mexico and attempt to uncover the secrets hidden there, but bizarre entities throw out the unwelcome mat and terrorize them. Lots of blood and screaming. **75m/C VHS.** Ran Sands, James Garnett, Ralph Navarro, Mario Almada, Alfredo Gutierrez, Stacey Shaffer, Russ Tamblyn, Isela Vega; ***D:*** Glenn Gebhard.

Blood Simple 🦴🦴🦴½ **1985 (R)** A jealous husband hires a sleazy private eye to murder his adulterous wife and her lover. A dark, intricate, morbid morality tale that deviates imaginatively from the standard murder mystery thriller. First film scripted by the Coen brothers. **96m/C VHS, DVD, Wide.** John Getz, M. Emmet Walsh, Dan Hedaya, Frances McDormand, Samm-Art Williams, Van Brooks, Lauren Bivens, Holly Hunter; ***D:*** Joel Coen; ***W:*** Joel Coen, Ethan Coen; ***C:*** Barry Sonnenfeld; ***M:*** Carter Burwell. Ind. Spirit '86: Actor (Walsh), Director (Coen); Sundance '85: Grand Jury Prize.

Blood Sisters woof! **1986 (R)** Sorority babes intend to spend a giggle-strewn night in a haunted house but end up decapitated, butchered, and cannibalized. **85m/C VHS.** Amy Brentano, Marla MacHart, Brigete Cossu, Randy Mooers; ***D:*** Roberta Findlay.

Blood Song 🦴 *Dream Slayer* **1982** A patient (yester-decade teen throb Frankie Avalon) escapes into the night from a mental institution after murdering an attendant. He takes his only possession with him, a carved wooden flute. A young woman sees him burying his latest victim, and now he's on a hunt to play his "blood song" for her. Pretty bad, but fun to see Avalon play a less-than-squeaky-clean role. **90m/C VHS.** Frankie Avalon, Donna Wilkes, Richard Jaeckel, Dane Clark, Antoinette Bower; ***D:*** Alan J. Levi.

The Blood Spattered Bride 🦴 *Blood Castle; La Novia Esangrentada; Bloody Fiance; Till Death Us Do Part* **1972** Newlywed couple honeymoons in a remote castle in southern Spain. They are visited by a mysterious young woman who begins to influence the bride in the ways of lesbian bloodsucking. O.K. '70s Euro-eroti-horror based on Sheridan Le Fanu's "Carmilla." **101m/C VHS, DVD.** *SP* Simon Andreu, Maribel Martin, Alexandra Bastedo, Dean Selmier, Rosa Ma Rodriguez, Montserrat Julio, Angel Lombarte; ***D:*** Vicente Aranda; ***W:*** Vicente Aranda; ***C:*** Fernando Arribas.

Blood Surf 🦴 *Crocodile* **2000 (R)** A filmmaker and her crew travel to Australia to do a documentary on the extreme sport of blood surfing where thrillseekers try to out surf sharks to shore. Only the sharks aren't the problem—a giant salt-water crocodile gets to the participants first. Very silly; your enjoyment will depend on your tolerance for the fake croc. **88m/C VHS, DVD, Wide.** Matt Borlenghi, Duncan Regehr, Kate Fischer, Taryn Reif, Joel West, Dax Miller; ***D:*** James D.R. Hickox; ***W:*** Sam Bernard, Robert L. Levy; ***C:*** Christopher Pearson; ***M:*** Jim Manzie. **VIDEO**

Blood Thirst 🦴🦴 **1965** Obscure horror film about a woman who stays young by indulging in ritual killings and strange experiments. **?m/B VHS, DVD.** *PH* Robert Winston, Yvonne Nielson, Vic Diaz; ***D:*** Newton Arnold.

Blood Tide 🦴 *The Red Tide* **1982 (R)** A disgusting, flesh-eating monster disrupts a couple's vacation in the Greek isles. Beautiful scenery, good cast, bad movie. **82m/C VHS.** James Earl Jones, Jose Ferrer; ***D:*** Richard Jeffries; ***W:*** Nico Mastorakis.

Blood Ties 🦴½ **1987** An American naval engineer in Sicily gets involved with the Mob in order to save his father's life. **98m/C VHS.** *IT* Brad Davis, Tony LoBianco, Vincent Spano, Barbara DeRossi, Maria Conchita Alonso; ***D:*** Giacomo Battiato.

Blood Ties 🦴🦴½ **1992** Reporter Harry Martin belongs to an unusual family—modern-day vampires (who prefer to be known as Carpathian-Americans). But they have an age-old problem with a band of fanatical vampire hunters. This time around you'll root for the bloodsuckers. **90m/C VHS.** Harley Venton, Patrick Bauchau, Kim Johnston-Ulrich, Michelle Johnson, Jason London, Bo Hopkins, Grace Zabriskie, Salvator Xuereb; ***D:*** Jim McBride; ***W:*** Richard Shapiro. **TV**

Blood Tracks 🦴½ **1986** A woman kills her abusive husband, then hides out in the mountains with her kids until they turn into cannibalistic savages. Years later, people show up to shoot a music video. Blood runs in buckets. **82m/C** Jeff Harding, Michael Fitzpatrick, Naomi Kaneda; ***D:*** Mike Jackson.

Blood Vows: The Story of a Mafia Wife 🦴🦴 **1987** TV's Laura Ingalls (Gilbert) leaps from the prairie to modern-day mafia in this warped Cinderella story. She meets the man of her dreams, whom she slowly finds is her worst nightmare as she becomes trapped within the confines of her new-found "family." TV soaper is way over the top in terms of melodrama. **100m/C VHS.** Melissa Gilbert, Joe Penny, Eileen Brennan, Talia Shire, Anthony (Tony) Franciosa; ***D:*** Paul Wendkos; ***M:*** William Goldstein. **TV**

Blood Voyage woof! **1977 (R)** A crewman aboard a pleasure yacht must find out who is killing off his passengers one by one. **80m/C VHS.** Jonathon Lippe, Laurie Rose, Midori, Mara Modair; ***D:*** Frank Mitchell.

Blood Warriors 🦴½ **1993** An ex-Marine finds out a old buddy is leading a private army of mercenaries. When he refuses to join up their friendship turns violent. **93m/C VHS.** David Bradley, Frank Zagarino; ***D:*** Sam Firstenberg; ***W:*** David Bradley.

Blood Wedding 🦴🦴🦴 *Bodas de Sangre* **1981** A wonderfully passionate dance film from Saura and choreographed by Gades, based on the play by famed author Federico Garcia Lorca. A young bride (Hoyos) runs off with her married lover (Gades) on her wedding day and her jilted husband (Jimenez) comes after them. The film is set-up at a dress rehearsal where the dancers, led by Gades, perform upon a bare stage. If you like flamenco, there are two more: "Carmen" and "El Amor Brujo." Spanish with subtitles. **71m/C VHS.** *SP* Antonio Gades, Cristina Hoyos, Marisol, Carmen Villena, Juan Antonio Jimenez; ***D:*** Carlos Saura; ***W:*** Carlos Saura, Antonio Gades; ***C:*** Teodoro Escamilla; ***M:*** Emilio De Diego.

Blood Work **2002** Retired FBI profiler Terry McCaleb (Eastwood) has just had a heart transplant. But, while undergoing checkups, he's brought back to track a serial killer who apparently murdered the woman who became his donor. Based on the novel by Michael Connelly. Not yet reviewed. **?m/C VHS, DVD.** Clint Eastwood, Anjelica Huston, Jeff Daniels, Wanda De Jesus, Paul Rodriguez; ***D:*** Clint Eastwood; ***W:*** Brian Helgeland.

Bloodbath *Sky is Falling* **1976** Drugs, sex and terrorism—Hopper is typecast as an American degenerate who, along with his expatriate friends, is persecuted by local religious cults who need sacrifices. **89m/C VHS.** Dennis Hopper, Carroll Baker, Richard Todd, Faith Brook, Win Wells; ***D:*** Silvio Narizzano.

Bloodbath 🦴 **1998** Detectives Tony Martin and Maggie Donovan are investigating a series of murders whose victims are all starlets. As they dig into the world of underground filmmaking, they find a literal bloodbath involving a group of movie-happy vampires. **90m/C VHS.** Susannah Devereux, Kathryn Cleasby, Anthony Martini, Jan Bryant, Charles Currier, Dana Fredsti; ***D:*** Dan Speaker, Anne Kimberly; ***W:*** Dana Fredsti; ***C:*** Joseph Raymond Garcia. **VIDEO**

Bloodbath at the House of Death 🦴🦴 **1985** Price and his compatriots fight a team of mad scientists in this parody of popular horror films. Fun to see Price spoofing his own genre; die-hard horror camp fans will be satisfied. Best line: "Wanna fork?" **92m/C VHS.** *GB* Kenny Everett, Pamela Stephenson, Vincent Price, Gareth Hunt, Sheila Steafel, John Fortune, Graham Stark, Cleo Rocos; ***D:*** Ray Cameron; ***W:*** Ray Cameron, Barry Cryer; ***C:*** Brian West, Dusty Miller; ***M:*** Mark London, Mike Moran.

Bloodbath in Psycho Town 🦴 **1989 (R)** A film crew is marked for death by a hooded man when it enters a remote little village. **87m/C VHS.** Ron Arragon, Donna Baltron, Dave Elliott; ***D:*** Allessandro DeGaetano; ***W:*** Allessandro DeGaetano.

Bloodbeat 🦴 **1985** A supernatural being terrorizes a family as they gather at their country home to celebrate Christmas. **84m/C VHS.** Helen Benton, Terry Brown, Claudia Peyton; ***D:*** Fabrice A. Zaphiratos.

Bloodbrothers 🦴🦴½ **1978 (R)** Portrayal of working-class Italian men's lives—if that's possible without the benefit of Italian writers, producers, or director. Still, lots of cussing and general intensity, as Gere's character struggles between staying in the family construction business and doing what he wants to do—work with children. Re-cut for TV and re-titled "A Father's Love." **120m/C VHS.** Richard Gere, Paul Sorvino, Tony LoBianco, Kenneth McMillan, Marilu Henner, Danny Aiello, Lelia Goldoni, Yvonne Wilder; ***D:*** Robert Mulligan; ***C:*** Robert L. Surtees; ***M:*** Elmer Bernstein.

Bloodfist 🦴🦴 **1989 (R)** A kickboxer tears through Manila searching for his brother's killer. A Roger Corman production. **85m/C VHS, DVD.** Don "The Dragon" Wilson, Rob Kaman, Billy Blanks, Kris Aguilar, Riley Bowman, Michael Shaner, Joe Mari Avellana, Marilyn Bautista; ***D:*** Terence H. Winkless; ***W:*** Robert King; ***C:*** Ricardo Jacques Gale; ***M:*** Sasha Matson.

Bloodfist 2 🦴🦴½ **1990 (R)** Six of the world's toughest martial artists find themselves kidnapped and forced to do the bidding of the evil Su. The mysterious recluse stages a series of incredible fights between the experts and his own army of drugged warriors. **85m/C VHS, DVD.** Don "The Dragon" Wilson, Maurice Smith, James Warring,

Timothy Baker, Richard (Rick) Hill, Rina Reyes, Kris Aguilar, Joe Mari Avellana; *D:* Andy Blumenthal; *W:* Catherine Cyran; *C:* Bruce Dorfman; *M:* Nigel Holton.

Bloodfist 3: Forced to Fight ½ **1992 (R)** Just as long as nobody's forced to watch, real-life world champion kickboxer Wilson thrashes his way through another showdown-at-the-arena plot. Better-than-average fight choreography. **90m/C VHS, DVD.** Don "The Dragon" Wilson, Richard Roundtree, Laura Stockman, Richard Paul, Rick Dean, Peter "Sugarfoot" Cunningham; *D:* Oley Sassone; *W:* Allison Burnett; *C:* Rick Bota; *M:* Nigel Holton.

Bloodfist 4: Die Trying ½ **1992 (R)** To rescue his daughter, a fighter must do battle with the FBI, the CIA, and an international arms cartel. **86m/C VHS, DVD.** Don "The Dragon" Wilson, Catya (Cat) Sassoon, Amanda Wyss, James Tolkan, Liz Torres; *D:* Paul Ziller.

Bloodfist 5: Human Target ½ **1993 (R)** When undercover FBI agent Jim Roth (Wilson) attempts to unravel an international arms deal he's found out and left for dead. He comes to with no memory only to find himself caught between the arms dealers and the FBI, who think he's turned double-agent. Both sides want Roth dead. **84m/C VHS, DVD.** Don "The Dragon" Wilson, Denice Duff, Yuji Okumoto, Don Stark, Danny Lopez, Steve James, Michael Yama; *D:* Jeff Yonis; *W:* Jeff Yonis; *C:* Michael G. Wojciechowski; *M:* David Wurst, Eric Wurst.

Bloodfist 6: Ground Zero ½ **1994 (R)** Nick Corrigan (Wilson) must battle terrorists who have a nuclear missile aimed at New York City. **86m/C VHS, DVD.** Don "The Dragon" Wilson, Cat Sasson, Steve Garvey; *D:* Rick Jacobson; *W:* Brendan Broderick, Rob Kerchner; *C:* Michael Gallagher; *M:* John Graham.

Bloodfist 7: Manhunt **1995 (R)** Martial arts expert Jim Trudell is accused by corrupt cops of murder and is forced on the run while he tries to prove his innocence. **95m/C VHS, DVD.** Don "The Dragon" Wilson, Jonathan Penner, Jillian McWhirter, Stephen Davies, Cyril O'Reilly, Eb Lottimer, Steven Williams; *D:* Jonathan Winfrey; *W:* Brendan Broderick, Rob Kerchner; *C:* Michael Gallagher; *M:* Elliot Anders, Mike Elliot. **VIDEO**

Bloodfist 8: Hard Way Out *Hard Way Out* **1996 (R)** Widowed teacher Rick Cowan (Wilson) turns out to have a lurid past when he and teen son Chris (White) are targeted for death. Dull dad is ex-CIA and someone is afraid their dirty secrets will get out if he's not eliminated. **78m/C VHS, DVD.** Don "The Dragon" Wilson, John Patrick White, Warren Burton, Richard Farrell; *D:* Barry Samson; *W:* Alex Simon; *C:* John Aronson; *M:* John Faulkner.

Bloodhounds **1996 (R)** Detective Nikki Cruz (Harnos), who's skilled in the martial arts, reluctantly agrees to team up with writer Harrison Coyle (Bernsen), whose specialty is criminal cases, to catch escaped serial killer, Charles Veasey (Baltz). **86m/C VHS.** Corbin Bernsen, Christina Harnos, Kirk Baltz, Gina Mastrogiacomo, James Pickens Jr., Marcus Flanagan; *D:* Michael Katleman; *W:* Pablo F. Fenjves; *C:* Fernando Arguelles. **CABLE**

Bloodhounds 2 **1996 (PG-13)** True-crime writer Harrison Coyle (Bersen) teams up with PI Nikki Cruz (Peeples) to nab serial killer Matthew Standing (Tracey), who hunts down convicted rapists he thinks haven't been punished enough. Turns out the killer is also a fan of Coyle's and begins contacting him about them writing a book together. **89m/C VHS.** Corbin Bernsen, Nia Peeples, Ian Tracey, Amy Yasbeck, Jim Byrnes, Suki Kaiser, Tom Cavanagh; *D:* Stuart Cooper; *W:* Pablo F. Fenjves; *C:* Curtis Petersen; *M:* Charles Bernstein. **CABLE**

Bloodhounds of Broadway ½ **1989 (PG)** A musical tribute to Damon Runyon, detailing the cliched adventures of an assortment of jazz-age crooks, flappers, chanteuses, and losers. **90m/C VHS, Wide.** Madonna, Rutger Hauer, Randy Quaid, Matt Dillon, Jennifer Grey, Julie Hagerty, Esai Morales, Anita Morris, Josef Sommer, William S. Burroughs, Ethan Phillips, Stephen McHattie, Dinah Manoff, Googy Gress, Tony Azito, Tony Longo, Madeleine Potter; *D:* Howard Brookner; *W:* Howard Brookner, Colman DeKay; *C:* Elliot Davis; *M:* Jonathan Sheffer.

Bloodknot **1995 (R)** The Reaves' are devastated when their son Martin is killed in a military accident. So they're an easy target when Kaye (Vernon) shows up, claiming to be Martin's girlfriend. Mom Evelyn (Kidder) and brother Tom (Dempsey) are only too eager to welcome Kaye into the family but it wouldn't be a thriller if devious Kaye didn't have some deadly ulterior motives. **98m/C VHS.** Patrick Dempsey, Kate Vernon, Margot Kidder, Craig Sheffer; *D:* Jorge Montesi; *W:* Randy Kornfield; *C:* Philip Linzey; *M:* Ian Thomas. **CABLE**

Bloodlink ½ **1986 (R)** A well-to-do doctor has a recurring nightmare about killing an elderly woman. This prompts him to explore his past, discovering that he was separated at birth from a twin brother. Naturally, only by searching frantically for his long-lost sibling can the good doctor hope to solve the mystery of the recurring nightmare. A somnolent tale indeed. **98m/C VHS.** Michael Moriarty, Penelope Milford, Geraldine Fitzgerald, Cameron Mitchell, Sarah Langenfeld; *D:* Alberto De Martino.

Bloodlust **1959** More teenagers fall prey to yet another mad scientist, who stores their dead bodies in glass tanks. Low-budget ripoff of "The Most Dangerous Game" and other such films. A must for Mike Brady (Robert Reed) fans though. **89m/B VHS.** Wilton Graff, June Kenney, Robert Reed, Lilyan Chauvin; *D:* Ralph Brooke; *W:* Ralph Brooke.

Bloodlust: Subspecies 3 ½ *Subspecies 3* **1993 (R)** Equally gory followup to "Bloodstone: Subspecies 2." Sadistic vampire Radu is still battling for Michelle's soul, this time against Michelle's sister Becky, aided by his disgusting Mummy and the demonic Subspecies. Castle Vladislas is awash is blood and Becky discovers more than Michelle's fate is at risk. **83m/C VHS.** Anders (Tofting) Hove, Kevin Blair Spirtas, Denice Duff, Pamela Gordon, Ion Haiduc, Michael DellaFemina; *D:* Ted Nicolaou; *W:* Ted Nicolaou.

Bloodmatch **1991 (R)** A whodunit, martial-arts-style: the "sleuth" kidnaps all the suspects in a corruption case and kickboxes each to death until somebody confesses. Not exactly Agatha Christie, and artsy camera moves fail to exploit the fancy footwork. **85m/C VHS.** Thom Mathews, Michel Qissi, Benny "The Jet" Urquidez, Marianne Taylor, Hope Marie Carlton, Dale Jacoby, Thunder Wolf, Vincent Klyn, Peter "Sugarfoot" Cunningham, Hector Pena; *D:* Albert Pyun; *W:* K. Mannah; *M:* Tony Riparetti.

Bloodmoon woof! **1990** The setting is Australia but the sleazy story's all too familiar: an insane killer employs knives and other sharp objects to prevent sex-crazed students from getting past third base. **104m/C VHS.** *AU* Leon Lissek, Christine Amor, Ian Patrick Williams, Helen Thomson, Hazel Howson, Craig Cronin, Anya Molina; *D:* Alec Mills; *W:* Richard Brennan; *M:* Brian May.

Bloodmoon ½ **1997** A New York serial killer is quite a specialist—he only kills fighters, and he kills with his bare hands. So it's up to Ken O'Hara (Daniels), who specializes in tracking murderers, to find this guy before he kills again. A good display of martial arts skills keep this one interesting. **105m/C VHS, DVD.** Gary Daniels, Chuck Jeffreys, Darren Shahlavi, Nina Repeta, Frank Gorshin, Jeffrey Pillars, Joe Hess; *D:* Tony Leung Siu Hung; *W:* Keith W. Strandberg; *C:* Derek M.K. Wan; *M:* Richard Yuen.

Bloodshed **1983 (R)** A psychotic harbors a girl's dead body, and systematically kills anyone who discovers his secret. **88m/C VHS.** Laslo Papas, Beverly Ross; *D:* Richard Cassidy.

Bloodspell **1987 (R)** A student with an evil power unleashes it on those who cross his path. **87m/C VHS.** Anthony Jenkins, Aaron Teich, Alexandra Kennedy, John Reno; *D:* Deryn Warren.

Bloodsport ½ **1988 (R)** American soldier Van Damme endeavors to win the deadly Kumite, an outlawed martial arts competition in Hong Kong. Lots of kickboxing action and the sound of bones cracking. **92m/C VHS.** Jean-Claude Van Damme, Leah Ayres, Roy Chiao, Donald Gibb, Bolo Yeung, Norman Burton, Forest Whitaker; *D:* Newton Arnold; *W:* Christopher Cosby.

Bloodsport 2: The Next Kumite ½ **1995 (R)** Old-fashioned kickfest has Alex (Bernhardt) stealing antiquities in Thailand. He's left to take the fall by his partner in the theft of an ancient sword belonging to powerful businessman Leung (Morita) and is sent to a prison where sadistic head guard Demon (Han) takes an instant dislike to him. Alex learns about a sacred fighting competition, the Kumite, from wise prison sage Sun (Hong) and naturally, once Alex manages to get into the contest, his opponent is—you guessed it—Demon. **87m/C VHS.** Daniel Bernhardt, Ong Soo Han, Noriyuki "Pat" Morita, James Hong; *D:* Alan Mehrez.

Bloodsport 3 ½ **1995** Alex (Bernhardt) must avenge the death of his mentor (Hong) and regain the Kumite sword. **92m/C VHS.** Daniel Bernhardt, John Rhys-Davies, James Hong, Noriyuki "Pat" Morita; *D:* Alan Mehrez; *W:* James Williams; *M:* Steve Edwards.

Bloodstalkers woof! **1976** Two vacationers in Florida meet up with a band of slaughtering, swamp-based lunatics. **91m/C VHS.** Kenny Miller, Celea Ann Cole, Jerry Albert; *D:* Robert W. Morgan.

Bloodstone **1988 (PG-13)** A couple honeymooning in the Middle East unexpectedly become involved in a jewel heist when they discover a valuable ruby amongst their luggage. Non-stop action and humor. **90m/C VHS, DVD.** Charlie Brill, Christopher Neame, Jack Kehler, Brett Stimely, Anna Nicholas; *D:* Dwight Little; *W:* Nico Mastorakis, Curt Allen.

Bloodstone: Subspecies 2 ½ *Subspecies 2* **1992 (R)** A gory sequel to "Subspecies" finds Radu the vampire pursuing the luscious Michelle. Radu gets some help from his ghoulish mother and yucky demonic spawn. Filmed on location in Romania. **107m/C VHS.** Anders (Tofting) Hove, Denice Duff, Kevin Blair Spirtas, Michael Denish, Pamela Gordon, Ion Haiduc; *D:* Ted Nicolaou; *W:* Ted Nicolaou.

Bloodstorm: Subspecies 4 ½ *Subspecies 4; Subspecies 4: Bloodstorm—The Master's Revenge* **1998 (R)** Master vampire Radu Vladislas (Hove) has awakened with an agenda. He wants to reclaim his vast wealth and recapture fledgling vamp, Michelle (Duff). Meanwhile, Radu hangs around with former protege, Ash (Morris), and Michelle is taken in by a creepy doctor (Dinvale) who's after the bloodstone. If you liked the first three, this is just more of the same. **90m/C VHS, DVD.** Anders (Tofting) Hove, Denice Duff, Jonathan Morris, Mihai Dinvale, Floriella Grappini; *D:* Ted Nicolaou; *W:* Ted Nicolaou; *C:* Adolfo Bartoli; *M:* Richard Kosinski. **VIDEO**

The Bloodsuckers *Incense for the Damned; Doctors Wear Scarlet; The Freedom Seekers* **1970** British horror tale set on a Greek Island. An Oxford don is seduced into an ancient vampire cult. Director Michael Burrowes replaces Hartford-Davis in the credits due to a dispute over post-production editing. **90m/C VHS.** *GB* Patrick Macnee, Peter Cushing, Patrick Mower, Edward Woodward, Alex Davion, Imogen Hassall, Madeline Hinde, Johnny Sekka; *D:* Robert Hartford-Davis; *W:* Julian More; *C:* Desmond Dickinson.

Bloodsuckers from Outer Space woof! **1983** Via an alien invasion, Texas farmers becoming bloodsucking zombies. **80m/C VHS.** Thom Meyer, Laura Ellis, Billie Keller, Kim Braden; *D:* Glenn Coburn.

Bloodsucking Freaks woof! *The Incredible Torture Show; The House of the Screaming Virgins* **1975 (R)** Virtually plotless Troma gagfest full of torture, cannibalistic dwarfs, and similar debaucheries, all played out on a Soho Grand Guignol stage (horror shows that allegedly contained real torture and death). Features "The Caged Sexoids," if that tells you anything (a cage of naked cannibal women tended by a dwarf). Not to mention the woman who has her brain sucked out through a straw. Filmed in "Ghoulovision" and originally rated X. Intolerable for most. **89m/C VHS, DVD.** Seamus O'Brian, Niles McMaster, Viju Krim, Alan Dellay, Dan Fauci; *D:* Joel M. Reed; *W:* Joel M. Reed; *C:* Gerry Toll; *M:* Michael Sahl.

Bloodsucking Pharoahs of Pittsburgh woof! *Picking up the Pieces* **1990 (R)** Pittsburgh is plagued by crazed cannibals who think eternal life is in Pennsylvania. Two detectives on the case are mystified. **89m/C VHS.** Jake Dengel, Joe Sharkey, Suzanne Fletcher, Beverly Penberthy, Shawn Elliott, Pat Logan, Jane (Veronica Hart) Hamilton; *D:* Dean Tschetter, Alan Smithee; *W:* Dean Tschetter; *C:* Peter Reniers; *M:* Michael Melvoin.

Bloody Avenger **1980** A trio of detectives search for a murderer in the streets of Philadelphia. **100m/C VHS.** Jack Palance, George Eastman, Jenny Tamburi; *D:* Al (Alfonso Brescia) Bradley.

Bloody Birthday ½ *Creeps* **1980 (R)** Three youngsters, bound together by their eerie birth during an eclipse (you know what that means), kill everyone around them that ever gave them problems. Typical "and the fun continues" ending; standard fare. **92m/C VHS.** Susan Strasberg, Jose Ferrer, Lori Lethin, Melinda Cordell, Joe Penny, Ellen Geer, Julie Brown, Michael Dudikoff, Billy Jacoby, Elizabeth Hoy, Andy Freeman; *D:* Ed(ward) Hunt; *W:* Ed(ward) Hunt, Barry Pearson.

The Bloody Brood woof! **1959** Really bad flick about a drug-dealing beatnik gang who commit nasty crimes, like feeding messenger boys hamburgers filled with ground glass. Yuck. **80m/C VHS.** *CA* Jack Betts, Barbara Lord, Peter Falk, Robert Christie; *D:* Julian Hoffman.

Bloody Mama ½ **1970 (R)** Corman's violent, trashy story of the infamous Barker Gang of the 30s, led by the bloodthirsty and sex-crazed Ma Barker (Winters, can't you just picture it?) and backed by her four perverted sons. De Niro is the space cadet sibling, Walden the homosexual ex-con, Stroud the sadistic mama lover, and Kimbrough the lady killer. They're joined by Walden's prison lover, Dern, who also has a thing for Ma Barker. Winters is a riot in this perverse stew of crime, violence, and, of course, sentimental blood bonding (the family that slays together, stays together). First of the Corman-produced (and sometimes directed) mama movies, followed by "Big Bad Mama" and "Crazy Mama." **90m/C VHS.** Shelley Winters, Robert De Niro, Don Stroud, Pat Hingle, Bruce Dern, Diane Varsi, Robert Walden, Clinton Kimbrough, Scatman Crothers, Pamela Dunlap, Michael Fox, Stacy Harris; *D:* Roger Corman; *W:* Robert Thom; *C:* John A. Alonzo; *M:* Don Randi.

Bloody Moon woof! *Die Saege des Todes* **1983** Tourists are being brutally attacked and murdered during a small Spanish village's Festival of the Moon. **84m/C VHS.** *GE* Olivia Pascal, Christopher Brugger, Ann-Beate Engelke, Antonia Garcia, Nadja Gerganoff, Corinna Gillwald, Jasmin Losensky, Maria Rubio, Alexander Waechter; *D:* Jess (Jesus) Franco; *W:* Jess (Jesus) Franco, Rayo Casablanca; *C:* Juan Soler.

Bloody Murder woof! **1999 (R)** Stupid teen campers in peril from maniac movie. This time the creepoid wears a hockey mask (sound familiar?) and has a chainsaw in place of his left arm. Ick. **90m/C VHS, DVD.** Michael Stone, Jessica Morris, Peter Guillemette, Patrick Cavanaugh, Christelle Ford, Tracy Pacheco, Justin Martin; *D:* Ralph Portillo; *W:* John R. Stevenson; *C:* Keith Holland; *M:* Steven Stern. **VIDEO**

Bloody New Year *Time Warp Terror* **1987 (R)** Corpses stalk the living as a group of teens happen upon an impromptu New Year's Eve party on a deserted island. Auld acquaintance shouldn't be forgot, just this flick. **90m/C VHS.** *D:* Norman J. Warren.

The Bloody Pit of Horror ½ *Crimson Executioner; The Red Hangman; Il Boia Scarlatto* **1965** While wife Jayne Mansfield was in Italy filming "Primitive Love," bodybuilder Hargitay starred in this sado-horror epic. He owns a castle that is visited by a group of models for a special shoot. While in the dungeon, Hargitay becomes possessed by the castle's former owner, a sadist, and begins torturing the models. Supposedly based on the writings of the

Marquis de Sade. **87m/B VHS, DVD, Wide.** *IT* Mickey Hargitay, Louise Barrett, Walter Brandi, Moa Thai, Ralph Zucker, Albert Gordon; ***D:*** Max (Massimo Pupillo) Hunter; ***W:*** Romano Migliorini, Roberto Natale; ***C:*** Luciano Trasatti; ***M:*** Gino Peguri.

Bloody Proof 🦴🦴🦴 **1999** A serial killer is stalking well-to-do women in Mexico. Detective Ibarra (Bauer) is assigned to the case. Rookie tabloid reporter Estela (Arizmendi) finds an important clue. The resolution of the stereotypical premise runs true to form, but the characters are treated seriously and the film is stylishly made with a few moments of abrupt, shocking violence. **99m/C VHS, DVD.** Steven Bauer, Yareli Arizmendi, Olivia Hussey; ***D:*** Gabriel Beristain; ***W:*** M. Francesconi, Tim Hoy; ***C:*** Andres Leon Becker; ***M:*** Eduardo Gamboa.

Bloody Trail 🦴 **1972** A Union soldier who chooses the recently pummeled South as the venue for postwar R-and-R is, for some reason, pursued by Confederates. And his good ol' boy pursuers don't have a sudden change of heart when he teams up with a former slave. Lots of violence and nudity; little plot and entertainment. **91m/C VHS.** Paul Harper, Rance Howard, John Mitchum; ***D:*** Richard Robinson.

Bloody Wednesday 🦴🦴½ **1987** It's sanity check-out time when a hotel caretaker is driven mad by tormentors...or is he driving himself mad? What is it about vacant hotels that make men lose their minds? If you can remove "The Shining" from yours, this flick's worthwhile. **89m/C VHS.** Raymond Elmendorf, Pamela Baker, Navarre Perry; ***D:*** Mark Gilhuis; ***W:*** Philip Yordan; ***M:*** Albert Sendry.

Blossoms in the Dust 🦴🦴 **1941** The true story of Edna Gladney is told as she starts the Texas Children's Home and Aid Society of Fort Worth. Major league Garson tear-jerker. **100m/B VHS.** Greer Garson, Walter Pidgeon, Felix Bressart, Marsha Hunt, Fay Holden, Samuel S. Hinds, Kathleen Howard; ***D:*** Mervyn LeRoy.

The Blot 🦴🦴 **1921** A story about a poorly paid professor and his family, whose lifestyle contrasts with that of an affluent neighbor, a butcher. **55m/B VHS.** Louis Calhern, Claire Windsor; ***D:*** Lois Weber.

Blow 🦴🦴½ **2001 (R)** Memorable, visually stunning, true story of cocaine entrepreneur George Jung features, at its best, stellar performances (especially from Reubens, Cruz, and Depp), and at its worst, a "Goodfellas" meets "Traffic" familiarity. Epic follows Jung (Depp) from his humble New England beginnings through his California surfer-bum days, to his rise and fall as America's biggest cocaine pipeline of the '70's and '80's without judging him or his lifestyle, although it does tend to sympathize with his family issues with mom, dad, and his own child. **124m/C VHS, DVD, Wide.** *US* Johnny Depp, Penelope Cruz, Jordi Molla, Franka Potente, Rachel Griffiths, Ray Liotta, Ethan Suplee, Paul (Pee-wee Herman) Reubens, Max Perlich, Clifford Curtis, Miguel (Michael) Sandoval, Kevin Gage, Jesse James, Dan Ferro, Emma Roberts, Bob(cat) Goldthwait, James King; ***D:*** Ted (Edward) Demme; ***W:*** David McKenna, Nick Cassavetes; ***C:*** Ellen Kuras; ***M:*** Graeme Revell.

Blow Dry 🦴🦴 **2000 (R)** Comedic possibilities and family healing ensue when the National British Hairdressing Championships come to a sleepy English town. An odd assortment of Brits and Yanks populate this familiar tale, and even dependable Rickman can't save the film, whose destination is obvious from even the newspaper ads—take "The Full Monty," replace strippers with hairdressers and, voila: "Blow Dry." Written by Simon Beaufoy, author of (you guessed it) "The Full Monty." Director Breathnach fared better with his previous film, the Irish comedy "I Went Down." **91m/C VHS, DVD, Wide.** *GB US* Alan Rickman, Natasha Richardson, Rachel Griffiths, Rachael Leigh Cook, Josh Hartnett, Bill Nighy, Warren Clarke, Rosemary Harris, Hugh Bonneville, Peter McDonald, Heidi Klum, Michael McElhatton; ***D:*** Paddy Breathnach; ***W:*** Simon Beaufoy; ***C:*** Cian de Buitlear; ***M:*** Patrick Doyle.

Blow Out 🦴🦴🦴 **1981 (R)** When a prominent governor and presidential candidate is killed in a car crash, a sound effects engineer becomes involved in political intrigue as he tries to expose a conspiracy with the evidence he has gathered. An intricate mystery and homage to Antonioni's "Blow-Up." **108m/C VHS, DVD, Wide.** John Travolta, Nancy Allen, John Lithgow, Dennis Franz; ***D:*** Brian DePalma; ***W:*** Brian DePalma; ***C:*** Vilmos Zsigmond; ***M:*** Pino Donaggio.

Blow-Up 🦴🦴🦴½ **1966** A young London photographer takes some pictures of a couple in the park and finds out he may have recorded evidence of a murder. Though marred by badly dated 1960s modishness, this is Antonioni's most accessible film, a sophisticated treatise on perception and the film-consumer-as-voyeur, brilliantly assembled and wrought. **111m/C VHS, Wide.** *GB IT* David Hemmings, Vanessa Redgrave, Sarah Miles, Jane Birkin, Veruschka, Peter Bowles, John Castle, Gillian Hills, Julian Chagrin, Harry Hutchinson, The Yardbirds; ***D:*** Michelangelo Antonioni; ***W:*** Michelangelo Antonioni, Tonino Guerra; ***C:*** Carlo Di Palma; ***M:*** Herbie Hancock. Cannes '67: Film; Natl. Soc. Film Critics '66: Director (Antonioni), Film.

Blowback 🦴🦴 **1999 (R)** Police officer Don Morell (Van Peebles) witnesses the execution of serial killer Claude Whitman (Remar)—or does he? Former jury members are being murdered and Morell finds cryptic bible messages at the scenes—a Whitman hallmark. So has the killer come back from the grave or has someone conspired to keep Whitman alive for their own purposes? **93m/C VHS, DVD.** Mario Van Peebles, James Remar, Stephen Caffrey, David Groh; ***D:*** Mark L. Lester; ***W:*** Jeffrey Goldenberg, Bob Held, Randall Frakes; ***C:*** Jacques Haitkin; ***M:*** Sean Callery. **CABLE**

Blowin' Smoke 🦴🦴 *Freak Talks About Sex* **1999 (R)** Goofball stoner Freak (Zahn) lives his life (in his parents' basement) as the ultimate slacker. His best bud (besides the pot) is the equally unambitious Dave (Hamilton), who does at least have a job. Dave also has an ex-girlfriend who wants to see him again, a sweet high schooler who has a crush on him, and a family who wishes he would do something with his life. Well, at least Dave has Freak to turn to in times of stress. Based on the novel by co-writer Galvin. **88m/C VHS, DVD.** Steve Zahn, Josh Hamilton, Heather McComb, Arabella Field, David Kinney; ***D:*** Paul Todisco; ***W:*** Paul Todisco, Michael M.B. Galvin, Peter Speakman; ***C:*** Douglas W. Shannon; ***M:*** Pete Snell.

Blowing Wild 🦴½ **1954** Filmed in Mexico, this Quinn-Stanwyck-Cooper love triangle, set in the early thirties, speaks of lust and vengeance, rashness and greed. Stanwyck, married to oil tycoon Quinn, lusts after one-time lover wildcatter Cooper. **92m/B VHS.** Gary Cooper, Barbara Stanwyck, Anthony Quinn, Ruth Roman, Ward Bond; ***D:*** Hugo Fregonese; ***W:*** Philip Yordan.

Blown Away 🦴 **1990 (R)** A mafia wife goes up against her husband in order to retrieve her kidnapped child. **92m/C VHS.** Loni Anderson, John Heard, James Naughton; ***D:*** Michael Miller.

Blown Away 🦴½ **1993 (R)** Haim and Feldman are brothers working at a ski resort where Haim falls for rich teenager Eggert. She's a young femme fatale who manages to get Haim all hot and bothered but she's actually using the unsuspecting dupe in a murder plot. Also available in an unrated version at 93 minutes. **91m/C VHS.** *CA* Nicole Eggert, Corey Haim, Corey Feldman, Jean LeClerc, Kathleen Robertson, Gary Farmer; ***D:*** Brenton Spencer; ***W:*** Robert Cooper; ***M:*** Paul Zaza.

Blown Away 🦴🦴 **1994 (R)** Boston Irish bomb-squad cop Jimmy Dove (Bridges) is after former compatriot Ryan Gaerity (Jones), an Irish radical who's taken his bombing expertise onto Jimmy's new turf. Meanwhile, Jimmy wants to keep his unsavory past from unsuspecting wife Amis. Real life dad Lloyd plays Jeff's uncle. While Jones seems adequately obsessed with making things go boom and Bridges significantly concerned that they don't, thriller moves on predictable path toward explosive climax. Special effects create the suspense, as everyday objects become lethal in Gaerity's knowledgeable hands. The final explosion was more than even the special effects coordinator desired—windows were unintentionally blown out in nearby buildings. **121m/C VHS, DVD, Wide.** Jeff Bridges, Tommy Lee Jones, Suzy Amis, Lloyd Bridges, Forest Whitaker; ***D:*** Stephen Hopkins; ***W:*** Joe Batteer, John Rice; ***C:*** Gregory McClatchy; ***M:*** Alan Silvestri.

Blue 🦴 **1968** A dull western about an American boy (Stamp) raised by Mexicans who doesn't trust another living soul until he finds himself face to face with his former gang, led by his adoptive father (Montalban). **113m/C VHS.** Terence Stamp, Joanna Pettet, Karl Malden, Ricardo Montalban, Joe De Santis, Sally Kirkland; ***D:*** Silvio Narizzano; ***W:*** Ronald M. Cohen; ***M:*** Manos Hadjidakis.

Blue 🦴🦴 **1993 (R)** Meditation/memoir of director Jarman's deteriorating AIDS condition consists of narration and a soundtrack set against an unvaried blue screen. Jarman ponders the associations with the color blue (sky, ocean, blindness, heaven, eternity) and his own physical problems, alternately expressed with dreamy vagueness or incendiary contempt. Limited in appeal, depending highly on boredom tolerance and ability to suspend visual expectations. **76m/C VHS.** *GB* ***D:*** Derek Jarman; ***W:*** Derek Jarman; ***M:*** Simon Fisher Turner; ***Nar:*** John Quentin, Nigel Terry, Tilda Swinton, Derek Jarman.

The Blue and the Gray 🦴🦴 **1982** Epic miniseries about love and hate inflamed by the Civil War. Keach plays a Pinkerton's secret service agent in this loosely based historical romance. Available in uncut and 295-minute versions. **381m/C VHS, DVD.** Gregory Peck, Lloyd Bridges, Colleen Dewhurst, Stacy Keach, John Hammond, Sterling Hayden, Warren Oates; ***D:*** Andrew V. McLaglen; ***M:*** Bruce Broughton. **TV**

The Blue Angel 🦴🦴🦴🦴 *Der Blaue Engel* **1930** Tale of a man stripped of his dignity. A film classic filled with sensuality and decay, which made Dietrich a European star and led to her discovery in Hollywood. When a repressed professor (Jannings) goes to a nightclub hoping to catch some of his students in the wrong, he's taken by Lola, the sultry singer portrayed by Dietrich. After spending the night with her, losing his job, and then marrying her, he goes on tour with the troupe, peddling indiscreet photos of his wife. Versions were shot in both German and English, with the German version sporting English subtitles. ♫Falling in Love Again; They Call Me Wicked Lola. **90m/B VHS, DVD, 8mm.** *GE* Marlene Dietrich, Emil Jannings, Kurt Gerron, Rosa Valetti, Hans Albers; ***D:*** Josef von Sternberg; ***W:*** Robert Liebmann, Carl Zuckmayer, Karl Vollmoller; ***C:*** Gunther Rittau; ***M:*** Frederick "Friedrich" Hollander.

The Blue Bird 🦴🦴🦴 **1940 (G)** A weird, dark fantasy about two children who search for the blue bird of happiness in various fantasy lands, but find it eventually at home. Overlooked and impressively fatalistic. **98m/C VHS.** Shirley Temple, Gale Sondergaard, John Russell, Eddie Collins, Nigel Bruce, Jessie Ralph, Spring Byington, Sybil Jason; ***D:*** Walter Lang; ***C:*** Arthur C. Miller.

Blue Blazes Rawden **1918** Hart plays a lumberjack who gains control of a local saloon after shooting its villainous proprietor. **?m/B VHS, 8mm.** William S. Hart, Robert McKim, Maud(e) (Ford) George, Jack Hoxie; ***D:*** William S. Hart.

Blue Blood 🦴 **1973** A demonic butler inflicts nightmares upon a family to gain possession of its mansion. **90m/C VHS.** *GB* Oliver Reed, Derek Jacobi, Fiona Lewis; ***D:*** Andrew Sinclair.

Blue Canadian Rockies 🦴½ **1952** Autry's employer sends him to Canada to discourage his daughter from marrying a fortune hunter. The daughter has turned the place into a dude ranch and wild game preserve. When Autry arrives, he encounters some mysterious killings. **58m/B VHS.** Gene Autry, Pat Buttram, Gail Davis, Ross Ford, Tom London; ***D:*** George Archainbaud.

Blue Chips 🦴🦴½ **1994 (PG-13)** Nolte does Bobby Knight in this saga of Western U basketball coach Pete Bell, suffering through his first losing season. What follows is a tug of war between rich alumni who want to win at any cost and his ethics as he recruits for a new season. Larger than life hoopster O'Neal's film debut. McDonnell and Woodard are merely afterthoughts, but look for cameos from many real life b-ballers, including Dick Vitale and Larry Bird. Average script is bolstered by exciting game footage, shot during real games for authenticity. **108m/C VHS, Wide.** Nick Nolte, Shaquille O'Neal, Mary McDonnell, Ed O'Neill, J.T. Walsh, Alfre Woodard; ***Cameos:*** Larry Bird, Bobby Knight, Rick Pitino; ***D:*** William Friedkin; ***W:*** Ron Shelton; ***M:*** Nile Rodgers, Jeff Beck, Jed Leiber.

Blue City 🦴½ **1986 (R)** A young man returns to his Florida hometown to find his father murdered, and subsequently vows to solve and avenge the matter. Based on a Ross MacDonald thriller. **83m/C VHS.** Judd Nelson, Ally Sheedy, Paul Winfield, Anita Morris, David Caruso, Julie Carmen, Scott Wilson; ***D:*** Michelle Manning; ***W:*** Walter Hill, Lukas Heller; ***M:*** Ry Cooder.

Blue Collar 🦴🦴🦴 **1978 (R)** Funnyman Pryor (in one of his best film roles) offers most of the laughs in this very serious drama of how three Detroit auto assembly workers (Pryor, Kotto, and Keitel), feeling the strain of family life and inflation, hatch a plan to rob their corrupt union office only to stumble into a bigger crime that later costs them dearly. Schrader makes his directorial debut in this searing study of the working class and the robbing of the human spirit, which is made memorable by the strong performances of its three leads. Filmed entirely in Detroit and Kalamazoo, Michigan. **114m/C VHS, DVD.** Richard Pryor, Harvey Keitel, Yaphet Kotto, Ed Begley Jr., Lane Smith, Cliff DeYoung; ***D:*** Paul Schrader; ***W:*** Paul Schrader, Leonard Schrader; ***C:*** Bobby Byrne; ***M:*** Jack Nitzsche.

Blue Country 🦴🦴½ *Le Pays Bleu* **1977 (PG)** A joyful romantic comedy about a pair of free souls who leave their stagnant lives behind to seek out a more idyllic existence. Subtitled in English. **104m/C VHS.** *FR* Brigitte Fossey, Jacques Serres, Ginette Garcin, Armand Meffre, Ginette Mathieu, Roger Crouzet; ***D:*** Jean-Charles Tacchella; ***W:*** Jean-Charles Tacchella; ***C:*** Edmond Sechan; ***M:*** Gerard Anfosso.

Blue Crush **2002 (PG-13)** Surfer girl Anne Marie (Bosworth) moves to Hawaii, determined to win the traditionally all-male Rip Masters competition. Naturally, there's a boy (Davis) who vies with the waves for her attentions. Not yet reviewed. **?m/C VHS, DVD.** Kate (Catherine) Bosworth, Michelle Rodriguez, Matthew Davis, Sanoe Lake, Mika Boorem, Faizon Love; ***D:*** John Stockwell; ***W:*** John Stockwell, Kario Salem, Elizabeth Weiss.

The Blue Dahlia 🦴🦴🦴½ **1946** Classic film noir finds Navy vet Johnny Morrison (Ladd) returning home to discover his wife Helen (Dowling) has been keeping the home fires burning—with Eddie Harwood (Da Silva), owner of the Blue Dahlia nightclub. After a nasty fight, Johnny takes off and is picked up by sultry blonde Joyce (Lake). The next day Johnny discovers he's wanted by the cops for the murder of his wife and decides to hide out until he can find the real killer, with Joyce's help. Very stylish and fast-paced with excellent performances; Chandler's first original screenplay. **100m/B VHS.** Alan Ladd, Veronica Lake, William Bendix, Howard da Silva, Doris Dowling, Tom Powers, Hugh Beaumont, Howard Freeman, Don Costello; ***D:*** George Marshall; ***W:*** Raymond Chandler; ***C:*** Lionel Lindon; ***M:*** Victor Young.

Blue De Ville 🦴🦴 **1986 (PG)** Two young women buy a '59 Cadillac and journey from St. Louis to New Mexico, having adventures on the way. The rambling, free-spirited movie was a pilot for a prospective series that never set sail—but when "Thelma & Louise" hit big this superficially similar item was hauled out on video. **96m/C VHS.** Jennifer Runyon, Kimberly Pistone, Mark Thomas Miller, Alan Autry, Robert Prescott; ***D:*** Jim Johnston. **TV**

Blue Desert 🦴🦴🦴 **1991 (R)** Cox is strong in her performance as Lisa Roberts, a comic book artist who leaves New York City for small town Arizona life after surviving a traumatic rape. Once there, she's befriended by Sheffer and Sweeney, a local cop. Battersby does a good job of keeping the suspense level high (in his directorial debut) as Cox finds that there's danger in small towns, too. Fine performances keep this slightly above average. **98m/C VHS.** D.B. Sweeney, Courteney Cox Arquette, Craig Sheffer, Philip Baker Hall, Sandy Ward; ***D:*** Bradley Battersby; ***W:*** Bradley Battersby, Arthur Collis; ***M:*** Jerry Goldsmith.

Blue Fin 🦴🦴 **1978 (PG)** When their tuna boat is shipwrecked, and the crew disabled, a young boy and his father learn lessons of love and courage as the son tries to save the ship. **93m/C VHS.** *AU* Hardy Kruger, Greg Rowe; ***D:*** Carl Schultz; ***C:*** Geoff Burton.

Blue Fire Lady 🦴🦴 **1978** The heartwarming story of a young girl and her love of horses which endures even her father's disapproval. Good family fare. **96m/C VHS.** *AU* Cathryn Harrison, Mark Holden, Peter Cummins, Marion Edward, Anne Sutherland, Gary Waddell, John Wood, John Ewart; ***D:*** Ross Dimsey; ***C:*** Vincent Monton; ***M:*** Mike Brady.

Blue Flame 🦴🦴 **1993 (R)** Vigilante cop is hired to track down two humanoid aliens who have escaped captivity in futuristic L.A. They evade him by time-traveling through alternate realities, infiltrating the cop's mind, and using his fantasies against him. **88m/C VHS.** Brian Wimmer, Ian Buchanan, Kerri Green, Cecilia Peck, Jad Mager; ***D:*** Cassian Elwes; ***W:*** Cassian Elwes.

Blue Hawaii 🦴🦴 **1962 (PG)** A soldier, returning to his Hawaiian home, defies his parents by taking a job with a tourist agency. Presley sings "Can't Help Falling in Love." For Elvis fans. **101m/C VHS, DVD.** Elvis Presley, Angela Lansbury, Joan Blackman, Roland Winters, Iris Adrian, John Archer, Steve Brodie; ***D:*** Norman Taurog; ***W:*** Hal Kanter.

Blue Heaven 🦴 **1984** A couple struggles through problems with their marriage and alcohol abuse. **100m/C VHS.** Leslie Denniston, James Eckhouse; ***D:*** Kathleen Dowdey.

The Blue Hour 🦴🦴 **1991** Theo is a Berlin hustler whose business is so good he can pick his clients. Marie, his next-door neighbor, lives with her boyfriend Paul until he just walks out one day. Marie is shattered and refuses to leave her apartment until Theo takes an interest in her plight. Just when it seems that the improbable couple could find true love, Paul comes back. In German with English subtitles. **87m/C VHS.** *GE* Andreas Herder, Dina Leipzig, Cyrill Rey-Coquais; ***D:*** Marcel Gisler.

Blue Ice 🦴🦴½ **1992 (R)** Harry Anders (Caine) is an ex-spy with an eye for the ladies and a loyalty to his friends. When his friends start winding up dead, Harry decides to investigate—a very dangerous decision, especially when a mysterious woman (Young) takes an interest. **96m/C VHS.** Michael Caine, Sean Young, Ian Bannen, Bob Hoskins; ***D:*** Russell Mulcahy; ***W:*** Ron Hutchinson; ***M:*** Michael Kamen. **CABLE**

Blue Iguana 🦴🦴 **1988 (R)** An inept bounty hunter travels south of the border to recover millions from a crooked South American bank, and meets up with sexy women, murderous thugs, and corruption. **88m/C VHS.** Dylan McDermott, Jessica Harper, James Russo, Dean Stockwell, Pamela Gidley, Tovah Feldshuh; ***D:*** John Lafia.

Blue in the Face 🦴🦴½ **1995 (R)** Wang and Auster's immediate follow-up to "Smoke," shot in five days, recycles the same Brooklyn cigar shop setting and contains a dozen fast-paced, loosely scripted or wholly improvised scenes that they couldn't cram into "Smoke," led by Reed's deadpan riff on eyewear, New York, and smoking. The action again centers around Auggie (Keitel), the shop manager, who hangs out with the mostly eccentric, and sometimes famous clientele. Jarmusch idly waxes philosophic on smoking technique, while puffing on what he claims is his last. Scenes are woven together with videotaped interviews from actual Brooklyn residents, creating a tribute to life in the borough with a documentary feel. Improv lovers will enjoy watching what sometimes seems more like outtakes than finished performances. **83m/C VHS.** Harvey Keitel, Lou Reed, Michael J. Fox, Roseanne, Jim Jarmusch, Lily Tomlin, Mel Gorham, Jared Harris, Giancarlo Esposito, Victor Argo, Madonna, Keith David, Mira Sorvino, Malik Yoba; ***D:*** Wayne Wang, Paul Auster; ***W:*** Wayne Wang, Paul Auster.

Blue Jeans 🦴🦴½ **1978** A young French boy experiences sexual awakening and humiliation in a British school. In French with English subtitles. **80m/C VHS.** *FR* ***D:*** Hugues des Roziers.

Blue Jeans and Dynamite 🦴🦴 **198?** A stuntman is hired to lift the "Golden Mask of the Duct Tomb" and is followed on land, water, and air. Great chase scenes and action-filled finale. **90m/C VHS.** Robert Vaughn, Simon Andrew, Katia Kristine.

Blue Juice 🦴🦴½ **1995 (R)** Early work from several young actors who've gone on to bigger things. Billed as Britain's first surf picture, this comedy follows the escapades of nearly 30 JC (Pertwee), a local hero of the Cornish surfing community who can't commit to his more practical girlfriend, Chloe (Zeta-Jones). Then some of JC's London buddies, Dean (McGregor), Josh (Mackintosh), and Terry (Gunn), show up for a sort of last hurrah against the boredom of acting like adults. **90m/C VHS, DVD.** *GB* Sean Pertwee, Catherine Zeta-Jones, Ewan McGregor, Steven Mackintosh, Peter Gunn, Heathcote Williams; ***D:*** Carl Prechezer; ***W:*** Carl Prechezer, Peter Salmi; ***C:*** Richard Greatrex; ***M:*** Simon Davison.

The Blue Kite 🦴🦴🦴 *Lan Feng Zheng* **1993** Fifteen years of political and cultural upheaval in China is shown through the eyes of young troublemaker Tietou, who certainly earns his nickname of "Iron Head" after his 1954 birth. Soon his father is sent to a labor reform camp and his mother remarries—only to be faced with more struggles as the years go by. The kite is Tietou's cherished toy, which keeps getting lost or destroyed but is always being rebuilt, offering one token of hope. Chinese with subtitles. **138m/C VHS.** *CH* Lu Liping, Zhang Wenyao, Pu Quanxin; ***D:*** Tian Zhuangzhuang; ***W:*** Xiao Mao; ***C:*** Yong Hou; ***M:*** Yoshihide Otomo.

The Blue Knight 🦴🦴½ **1975** Kennedy brings energy and care to this basically standard story. Policeman waiting for retirement searches for his partner's killer. Unexceptional treatment made palatable by actors. **72m/C VHS.** George Kennedy, Alex Rocco, Glynn Turman, Verna Bloom, Michael Margotta; ***D:*** J. Lee Thompson. **TV**

The Blue Lagoon woof! **1980 (R)** Useless remake of 1949 film of the same name. An adolescent boy and girl marooned on a desert isle discover love (read: sex) without the restraints of society. Not too explicit, but nonetheless intellectually offensive. Gorgeous photography of island paradise is wasted on this Shields vehicle. **105m/C VHS, DVD.** Brooke Shields, Christopher Atkins, Leo McKern, William Daniels; ***D:*** Randal Kleiser; ***W:*** Douglas Day Stewart; ***C:*** Nestor Almendros; ***M:*** Basil Poledouris. Golden Raspberries '80: Worst Actress (Shields).

The Blue Lamp 🦴🦴🦴 **1949** Action-adventure fans familiar with the hoary plot where a cop must avenge the wrongful death of his partner will appreciate this suspenseful British detective effort. It's one of the very first in the genre to explore buddy cop revenge in a very British sort of way. Also sports a concluding chase scene which has stood the test of time. Led to the long-running British TV series "Dixon of Dock Green." **84m/B VHS.** *GB* Dirk Bogarde, Jimmy Hanley, Jack Warner, Bernard Lee, Robert Flemyng, Patric Doonan, Bruce Seton, Frederick Piper, Betty Ann Davies, Peggy Evans; ***D:*** Basil Dearden. British Acad. '50: Film.

The Blue Light 🦴🦴🦴 *Das Blaue Licht* **1932** Fairy-tale love story, based on an Italian fable about a mysterious woman, thought to be a witch, and a painter. Riefenstahl's first film which brought her to the attention of Adolf Hitler, who requested she make films glorifying the Nazi Party. In German with English subtitles. **77m/B VHS.** *GE* Leni Riefenstahl, Matthias Wieman, Max Holsboer; ***D:*** Leni Riefenstahl; ***W:*** Bela Belazs, Leni Riefenstahl; ***C:*** Hans Schneeberger; ***M:*** Giuseppe Becce.

The Blue Lightning 🦴🦴½ **1986** Investigator Elliott travels to Australia to retrieve the priceless Blue Lightening gem. He must fight the crime lord in his Aussie encampment. Nice scenery, but unexceptional TV story. **95m/C VHS.** Sam Elliott, Rebecca Gilling, Robert Culp, John Meillon, Robert Coleby, Max Phipps; ***D:*** Lee Philips. **TV**

The Blue Max 🦴🦴½ **1966** During WWI a young German, fresh out of aviation training school, competes for the coveted "Blue Max" flying award with other members of a squadron of seasoned flyers from aristocratic backgrounds. Based on a novel by Jack D. Hunter. **155m/C VHS, Wide.** George Peppard, James Mason, Ursula Andress, Jeremy Kemp, Karl Michael Vogler, Anton Diffring, Harry Towb, Peter Woodthorpe, Derek Newark, Derren Nesbitt, Loni von Friedl; ***D:*** John Guillermin; ***W:*** Ben Barzman, Basilio Franchina, David Pursall, Jack Seddon, Gerald Hanley; ***C:*** Douglas Slocombe; ***M:*** Jerry Goldsmith.

Blue Money 🦴🦴 **1984** A wild, comedic caper film about a cab-driving nightclub impressionist who absconds with a briefcase packed with cash and is pursued by everyone, even the I.R.A. **82m/C VHS.** *GB* Tim Curry, Dabby Bishop, Billy Connolly, Frances Tomelty; ***D:*** Colin Bucksey. **TV**

Blue Monkey 🦴 *Green Monkey* **1987 (R)** A mysterious alien plant impregnates a man, who gives birth to a huge, man-eating insect larva. It subsequently grows up into a giant bug, and roams around a quarantined hospital looking for patients to eat. What made you think it had anything to do with monkeys? **97m/C VHS.** Steve Railsback, Susan Anspach, Gwynyth Walsh, John Vernon, Joe Flaherty; ***D:*** William Fruet.

Blue Moon 🦴🦴½ **2000 (PG-13)** Marrieds Gazzara and Moreno take a trip to the Catskills and wish on the blue moon which, according to legend, will grant them a wish. Of course, exactly how that wish will come true may not be exactly as the couple would hope. **90m/C VHS, DVD.** Ben Gazzara, Rita Moreno, Alanna Ubach, Brian Vincent, Heather Matarazzo, Vincent Pastore, Burt Young, Victor Argo, Lillo Brancato; ***D:*** John A. Gallagher; ***W:*** John A. Gallagher, Steve Carducci; ***C:*** Craig DiBona; ***M:*** Stephen Endelman, Stephen Endelman.

Blue Movies woof! **1988 (R)** A couple of jerks try their hand at making porn films with predictable results. **92m/C VHS.** Larry Linville, Lucinda Crosby, Steve Levitt, Darien Mathias, Larry Poindexter, Christopher Stone, Don Calfa, Russell Johnson; ***D:*** Paul Koval, Ed Fitzgerald; ***W:*** Paul Koval, Ed Fitzgerald.

Blue Murder at St. Trinian's 🦴🦴🦴 **1956** The second of the madcap British comedy series (based on cartoons by Ronald Searle) about an incredibly ferocious pack of schoolgirls. This time they travel to the European continent and make life miserable for a jewel thief. Highlight: fantasy sequence in ancient Rome showing the girls thrown to the lions—and scaring the lions. **86m/B VHS.** *GB* Joyce Grenfell, Terry-Thomas, George Cole, Alastair Sim, Lionel Jeffries, Thorley Walters; ***D:*** Frank Launder; ***M:*** Malcolm Arnold.

Blue Ridge Fall 🦴🦴 **1999 (R)** In the small town of Jefferson Creek, North Carolina, Danny (Facinelli) is the star high school quarterback who can do no wrong. He's befriended simple-minded Aaron (Eastman), who is driven to violent desperation by his abusive father. Danny enlists his buddies to cover up Aaron's crime but their plans quickly go wrong and things just get more desperate for them all. **99m/C VHS, DVD, Wide.** Peter Facinelli, Rodney Eastman, Will Estes, Jay R. Ferguson, Tom Arnold, Amy Irving, Chris Isaak, Brent Jennings, Heather Stephens, Garvin Funches; ***D:*** James Rowe; ***W:*** James Rowe; ***C:*** Chris Walling; ***M:*** Greg Edmonson.

Blue River 🦴🦴½ **1995 (PG-13)** Flashbacks highlight this saga of a troubled family. Successful doctor Edward Sellers (McDonough) is dismayed when his derelict older brother Lawrence (O'Connell), whom he hasn't seen in 15 years, suddenly appears on his doorstep. A gifted teenager, Lawrence once built his world around science and logic after their father deserted the family but his only purpose turns out to be getting even with everyone he feels has betrayed him. Young Edward (Stahl) tried to be the "good" son, while Mom (Dey) retreated into religion and an affair with self-righteously nasty school principal Henry Howland (Elliott). TV adaptation of the novel by Ethan Canin. **90m/C VHS, DVD.** Jerry O'Connell, Nick Stahl, Susan Dey, Sam Elliott, Neal McDonough, Jean Marie Barnwell, Patrick Renna; ***D:*** Larry Elikann; ***W:*** Maria Nation; ***C:*** Eric Van Haren Noman; ***M:*** Lawrence Shragge.

Blue Skies 🦴🦴🦴 **1946** Former dancer turned radio personality Astaire flashes back to his friendship with singer Crosby and the gal (Caulfield) that came between them. Flimsy plot is just an excuse for some 20 Irving Berlin songs and Astaire's split-screen dance number, "Puttin' on the Ritz." ♫All By Myself; Always; Any Bonds Today?; Blue Skies; A Couple of Song and Dance Men; Everybody Step; Getting Nowhere; Heat Wave; I'll See You in C-U-B-A. **104m/C VHS.** Fred Astaire, Bing Crosby, Joan Caulfield, Billy DeWolfe, Olga San Juan, Frank Faylen; ***D:*** Stuart Heisler; ***W:*** Arthur Sheekman; ***C:*** Charles B(ryant) Lang Jr.

Blue Skies Again 🦴½ **1983 (PG)** Spunky young woman determined to play major league baseball locks horns with the chauvinistic owner and the gruff manager of her favorite team. **91m/C VHS.** Robyn Barto, Harry Hamlin, Mimi Rogers, Kenneth McMillan, Dana Elcar, Andy Garcia; ***D:*** Richard Michaels.

Blue Sky 🦴🦴🦴 **1991 (PG-13)** Carly Marshall (Lange) is an irrepressible beauty, long married to adoring but uptight military scientist Hank (Jones). Things are barely in control when they're stationed in Hawaii but after Hank's transfer to a backwater base in Alabama, Carly's emotional mood swings go wildly out of control. Hell truly breaks loose when Carly attracts the attention of the camp's commander (Boothe), who's only too willing to take advantage. Set in 1962, a nuclear radiation subplot (Hank's new project) proves a minor distraction. Exceptional performance by Lange with Jones providing a quiet counterpoint as a man still deeply in love with his disturbed wife. Director Richardson's final film. Release date was delayed to 1994 due to studio Orion's financial problems. **101m/C VHS, DVD, Wide.** Jessica Lange, Tommy Lee Jones, Powers Boothe, Carrie Snodgress, Amy Locane, Chris O'Donnell, Mitchell Ryan, Dale Dye, Richard Jones; ***D:*** Tony Richardson; ***W:*** Arlene Sarner, Jerry Leichtling, Rama Laurie Stagner; ***C:*** Steve Yaconelli; ***M:*** Jack Nitzsche. Oscars '94: Actress (Lange); Golden Globes '95: Actress—Drama (Lange); L.A. Film Critics '94: Actress (Lange).

Blue Steel 🦴🦴 **1934** A young Wayne saves a town from financial ruin by leading the citizens to a gold strike. **59m/B VHS.** John Wayne, George "Gabby" Hayes; ***D:*** Robert North Bradbury.

Blue Steel 🦴🦴 **1990 (R)** Director Bigelow's much-heralded, proto-feminist cop thriller. A serious female rookie's gun falls into the hands of a Wall Street psycho who begins a killing spree. Action film made silly with over-anxious sub-text and patriarchy-directed rage. **102m/C VHS, 8mm.** Jamie Lee Curtis, Ron Silver, Clancy Brown, Louise Fletcher, Philip Bosco, Elizabeth Pena, Tom Sizemore; ***D:*** Kathryn Bigelow; ***W:*** Kathryn Bigelow, Eric Red; ***M:*** Brad Fiedel.

Blue Streak 🦴🦴 **1999 (PG-13)** Only hardcore Martin Lawrence fans will enjoy this formulaic buddy-cop-with-a-twist action comedy. Lawrence plays jewel thief Miles Logan, who hides a gem from his latest heist at a construction site just before he's caught. Three years later and out of jail, Logan tries to retrieve his diamond only to discover the site is now a police station. While impersonating a detective in order to sneak in and grab the stash, he accidentally catches an escaping felon and is forced to continue the charade. He's saddled with rookie partner Carlson

(Wilson) and begins using his criminal knowledge to catch other crooks, including his old crony Tulley (Chappelle). Lawrence gives a good effort but all of his frantic mugging can't save the lame material he's forced to work with, making this feel like a poor man's "Beverly Hills Cop." **94m/C VHS, DVD, Wide.** Martin Lawrence, Luke Wilson, Peter Greene, Dave Chappelle, William Forsythe, Graham Beckel, Tamala Jones, Nicole Parker, Robert Miranda, Olek Krupa; ***D:*** Les Mayfield; ***W:*** Stephen Carpenter, Michael Berry, John Blumenthal; ***C:*** David Eggby.

Blue Sunshine 🦴🦴½ **1978 (R)** A certain brand of L.S.D. called Blue Sunshine starts to make its victims go insane. **94m/C VHS.** Zalman King, Deborah Winters, Mark Goddard, Robert Walden, Charles Siebert, Ann Cooper, Ray Young, Alice Ghostley, Richard Crystal, Bill Adler, Stefan Gierasch, Brion James; ***D:*** Jeff Lieberman; ***W:*** Jeff Lieberman; ***M:*** Charles Gross.

Blue Thunder 🦴🦴½ **1983 (R)** Police helicopter pilot Scheider is chosen to test an experimental high-tech chopper that can see through walls, record a whisper, and level a city block. Seems anti-terrorist supercopter is needed to ensure security during 1984 Olympics. Bothered by Vietnam flashbacks, Scheider then battles wacky McDowell in the skies over L.A. High-techy police drama with satisfying aerial combat scenes nearly crashes with storyline. **110m/C VHS, DVD, Wide.** Roy Scheider, Daniel Stern, Malcolm McDowell, Candy Clark, Warren Oates; ***D:*** John Badham; ***W:*** Dan O'Bannon, Don Jakoby; ***C:*** John A. Alonzo.

Blue Tiger 🦴🦴 **1994 (R)** Gina Hayes (Madsen) is shopping with her young son when a masked gunman enters the store and opens fire. When Gina realizes her son has been killed she becomes obsessed with finding the assailant. Her one clue—a blue tiger tattoo. **88m/C VHS, DVD.** Virginia Madsen, Toru Nakamura, Harry Dean Stanton, Ryo Ishibashi; ***D:*** Norberto Barba; ***W:*** Joel Soisson.

Blue Tornado 🦴 **1990 (PG-13)** An eerie bright light, emitted from a mountain, makes supersonic jets disappear into thin air. A beautiful researcher and a cocky pilot set out to solve the mystery. Better-than-average aerial sequences don't make up for goofy story and ludicrous dialogue. **96m/C VHS.** Dirk Benedict, Patsy Kensit, Ted McGinley, David Warner; ***D:*** Tony B. Dobb.

Blue Velvet 🦴🦴🦴 **1986 (R)** Disturbing, unique exploration of the dark side of American suburbia, involving an innocent college youth who discovers a severed ear in an empty lot, and is thrust into a turmoil of depravity, murder, and sexual deviance. Brutal, grotesque, and unmistakably Lynch; an immaculately made, fiercely imagined film that is unlike any other. Mood is enhanced by the Badalamenti soundtrack. Graced by splashes of Lynchian humor, most notably the movie's lumber theme. Hopper is riveting as the chief sadistic nutcase and Twin Peaks' MacLachlan is a study in loss of innocence. **121m/C VHS, DVD, Wide.** Kyle MacLachlan, Isabella Rossellini, Dennis Hopper, Laura Dern, Hope Lange, Jack Nance, Dean Stockwell, George Dickerson, Brad Dourif, Priscilla Pointer, Angelo Badalamenti; ***D:*** David Lynch; ***W:*** David Lynch; ***C:*** Frederick Elmes; ***M:*** Angelo Badalamenti. Ind. Spirit '87: Actress (Rossellini); L.A. Film Critics '86: Director (Lynch), Support. Actor (Hopper); Montreal World Film Fest. '86: Support. Actor (Hopper); Natl. Soc. Film Critics '86: Cinematog., Director (Lynch), Film, Support. Actor (Hopper).

The Blue Yonder 🦴½ *Time Flyers* **1986** In this made-for-video feature, a young boy travels back in time to meet the grandfather he never knew, risking historical integrity. **89m/C VHS.** Art Carney, Peter Coyote, Huckleberry Fox; ***D:*** Mark Rosman.

Bluebeard 🦴🦴½ **1944** Tormented painter with a psychopathic urge to strangle his models is the basis for this effective, low-budget film. One of Carradine's best vehicles. **73m/B VHS, DVD.** John Carradine, Jean Parker, Nils Asther; ***D:*** Edgar G. Ulmer; ***W:*** Pierre Gendron; ***C:*** Jock Feindel.

Bluebeard 🦴🦴🦴 *Landru* **1963** French biography of Henri-Desire Landru, who seduced and murdered 11 women and was subsequently beheaded. Dubbed into English. **108m/C VHS.** *FR* Charles Denner, Danielle Darrieux, Michele Morgan, Hildegarde Neff; ***D:*** Claude Chabrol.

Bluebeard 🦴½ **1972 (R)** Lady killer Burton knocks off series of beautiful wives in soporific remake of the infamous story. **128m/C VHS, DVD, Wide.** Richard Burton, Raquel Welch, Joey Heatherton, Nathalie Delon, Virna Lisi, Sybil Danning; ***D:*** Edward Dmytryk; ***W:*** Edward Dmytryk, Ennio de Concini, Maria Pia Fusco; ***C:*** Gabor Pogany; ***M:*** Ennio Morricone.

Bluebeard's Eighth Wife 🦴🦴 **1938** Problematic comedy set on the French Riviera about a spoiled millionaire (Cooper) who's been married seven times and wants to go for eight with Colbert, the daughter of a destitute aristocrat. Good for a few laughs, but Coop seemed out of place in his role. Based on the play by Alfred Savoir, American version by Charlton Andrews. **86m/B VHS.** Claudette Colbert, Gary Cooper, David Niven, Edward Everett Horton, Elizabeth Patterson, Herman Bing, William Hymer, Franklin Pangborn; ***D:*** Ernst Lubitsch; ***W:*** Charles Brackett, Billy Wilder.

Blueberry Hill 🦴½ **1988 (R)** While her mother struggles with the grief over husband's death, a young girl in a small town learns about life, music, and her late father from a jazz singer. Good soundtrack. **93m/C VHS.** Jennifer Rubin, Carrie Snodgress, Margaret Avery; ***D:*** Strathford Hamilton.

The Blues Brothers 🦴🦴🦴 **1980 (R)** As an excuse to run rampant on the city of Chicago, Jake (Belushi) and Elwood (Aykroyd) Blues attempt to raise $5,000 for their childhood orphanage by putting their old band back together. Good music, quotable dialogue, lots of wrecked cars, plenty of cameos. A classic. **133m/C VHS, DVD.** Murphy Dunne, John Belushi, Dan Aykroyd, James Brown, Cab Calloway, Ray Charles, Henry Gibson, Aretha Franklin, Carrie Fisher, John Candy, Kathleen Freeman, Steven Williams, Charles Napier, Stephen Bishop; ***Cameos:*** Frank Oz, Steven Spielberg, Twiggy, Paul (Pee-wee Herman) Reubens, Steve Lawrence, John Lee Hooker, John Landis, Chaka Khan; ***D:*** John Landis; ***W:*** John Landis, Dan Aykroyd; ***C:*** Stephen M. Katz; ***M:*** Ira Newborn, Elmer Bernstein.

Blues Brothers 2000 🦴🦴 **1998 (PG-13)** Eighteen years after the original caper, Landis, Aykroyd, and most of the original cast return to the scene of the crime. Jake's died but Elwood's (Aykroyd) still around. He gets the band back together, recruits a Blues cousin (Goodman), a half-foster-brother (Morton), and an orphan (Bonifant) in need of mentoring, and heads for a battle of the bands between New Orleans and Chicago. The music, performed by the original Blues Brothers Band as well as a rock and blues all-star lineup, is the highlight. As for the rest of the flick, watch the original instead. Did Aykroyd learn nothing from Caddyshack II? **123m/C VHS, DVD.** Paul Shaffer, Murphy Dunne, Dan Aykroyd, John Goodman, Joe Morton, Evan Bonifant, Nia Peeples, Kathleen Freeman, Frank Oz, Steve Lawrence, Aretha Franklin, B.B. King, James Brown, Erykah Badu, Darrell Hammond; ***D:*** John Landis; ***W:*** John Landis, Dan Aykroyd; ***C:*** David Herrington; ***M:*** Paul Shaffer.

Blues Busters 🦴🦴½ **1950** Another entry in the "Bowery Boys" series. When Sach emerges from a tonsillectomy with the velvety voice of a crooner, Slip cashes in by turning Louie's Sweet Shop into a nightclub, the better to showcase his buddy's talents. Sach's singing voice provided by John Lorenz. **68m/B VHS.** Leo Gorcey, Huntz Hall, Adele Jergens, Gabriel Dell, Craig Stevens, Phyllis Coates, Bernard Gorcey, David Gorcey; ***D:*** William Beaudine.

Bluffing It 🦴🦴 **1987** TV movie about an older man who has been disguising his illiteracy for years. **120m/C VHS.** Dennis Weaver, Janet Carroll, Michelle Little, Robert Sean Leonard, Cleavant Derricks, Victoria Wauchope; ***D:*** James Sadwith; ***M:*** Brad Fiedel. **TV**

The Blum Affair 🦴🦴 **1948** In post-WWI Germany, a Jewish man is framed for the murder of an accountant and uncovers in his capture and prosecution a rat's nest of corruption and anti-Semitism. In German with English subtitles. **109m/B VHS.** *GE* Hans-Christian Blech, Gisela Trowe, Kurt Ehrhardt, Paul Bildt, Klaus Becker; ***D:*** Erich Engel.

Blume in Love 🦴🦴🦴 **1973 (R)** An ironic comedy/drama about a man who falls hopelessly in love with his ex-wife who divorced him for cheating on her while they were married. **115m/C VHS.** George Segal, Susan Anspach, Kris Kristofferson, Shelley Winters, Marsha Mason; ***D:*** Paul Mazursky; ***W:*** Paul Mazursky; ***C:*** Bruce Surtees; ***M:*** Bill Conti.

Blush 🦴🦴 *Hongfen* **1995** Shanghai prostitutes and friends Quiyi (Ji) and Xiao (Saifei) are stripped of their vocation by the communist takeover in 1949. Quiyi manages to take refuge with her favorite customer, wealthy Lao Pu (Zhiwen), while Xiao is re-educated and becomes a worker in a silk factory. Eventually thrown out of the house by Lao's disapproving mother, Quiyi learns to make her own way. Xiao meets Lao after his family has lost their money and winds up marrying him, unhappily since Lao continually pines for Quiyi. Based on the novel by Su Tong; Cantonese with subtitles. **119m/C VHS.** *CH* Wang Ji, He Saifei, Wang Zhiwen, Wang Rouli; ***D:*** Li Shaohong; ***W:*** Li Shaohong, Ni Zhen; ***C:*** Zeng Nianping; ***M:*** Guo Wenjing.

BMX Bandits 🦴🦴 **1983** Three adventurous Aussie teens put their BMX skills to the test when they witness a crime and are pursued by the criminals. Much big air. **92m/C VHS.** Nicole Kidman, David Argue, John Ley, Angelo D'Angelo; ***D:*** Brian Trenchard-Smith; ***W:*** Patrick Edgeworth.

Boarding House 🦴 **1983 (R)** Residents of a boardinghouse discover sinister doings in the basement. It does not occur to any of them to move to another house. **90m/C VHS.** Hank Adly, Kalassu, Alexandra Day; ***D:*** John Wintergate.

Boarding School 🦴🦴 *The Passion Flower Hotel* **1983 (R)** Basic teen sex comedy about students at a proper Swiss boarding school for girls who devise a plan to seduce the boys at a nearby school by posing as prostitutes. Kinski stars as the American girl who masterminds the caper. **100m/C VHS.** *GE* Nastassia Kinski; ***D:*** Andre Farwagi.

Boardinghouse Blues 🦴🦴 **1948** A showbiz musical centered around a boarding house with tenant troubles. It's an excuse for popular black entertainers of the day to perform, including Lucky Millinder, Bull Moose Jackson, Una Mae Carlisle, and Stumpy and Stumpy. **90m/C VHS.** Dusty Fletcher, Moms (Jackie) Mabley; ***D:*** Josh Binney.

The Boat Is Full 🦴🦴🦴 *Das Boot Ist Voll* **1981** A group of refugees pose as a family in order to escape from Nazi Germany as they seek asylum in Switzerland. Available in German with English subtitles or dubbed into English. **104m/C VHS.** *SI* Tina Engel, Curt Bois, Renate Steiger, Mathias Gnaedinger, Hans Diehl, Martin Walz, Gerd David; ***D:*** Markus Imhoof; ***W:*** Markus Imhoof; ***C:*** Hans Liechti. Berlin Intl. Film Fest. '81: Director (Imhoof).

The Boatniks 🦴🦴½ **1970 (G)** An accident-prone Coast Guard ensign finds himself in charge of the "Times Square" of waterways: Newport Harbor. Adding to his already "titanic" problems is a gang of ocean-going jewel thieves who won't give up the ship! **99m/C VHS.** Robert Morse, Stefanie Powers, Phil Silvers, Norman Fell, Wally Cox, Don Ameche; ***D:*** Norman Tokar; ***M:*** Robert F. Brunner.

Bob & Carol & Ted & Alice 🦴🦴½ **1969 (R)** Two California couples have attended a trendy therapy session and, in an attempt to be more in touch with sexuality, resort to applauding one another's extramarital affairs and swinging. Wacky and well-written, this is a farce on free love and psycho-speak. Mazursky's directorial debut. **104m/C VHS.** Natalie Wood, Robert Culp, Dyan Cannon, Elliott Gould; ***D:*** Paul Mazursky; ***W:*** Paul Mazursky, Larry Tucker; ***C:*** Charles B(ryant) Lang Jr.; ***M:*** Quincy Jones. N.Y. Film Critics '69: Screenplay, Support. Actress (Cannon); Natl. Soc. Film Critics '69: Screenplay; Writers Guild '69: Orig. Screenplay.

Bob le Flambeur 🦴🦴🦴 *Bob the Gambler* **1955** Aging Bob (Duchesne) is a down-on-his-luck gambler who visits the Deauville Casino with his friend Roger (Garret), who just happens to know croupier Jean (Cerval). Informed that the casino safe is bursting with cash, Bob decides to have a final fling by robbing the casino. Low-budget, bittersweet crime comedy. French with subtitles. **97m/B VHS, DVD.** *FR* Roger Duchesne, Isabel Corey, Daniel Cauchy, Howard Vernon, Gerard Buhr, Guy Decomble; ***D:*** Jean-Pierre Melville; ***W:*** Jean-Pierre Melville, Auguste Le Breton; ***C:*** Henri Decae; ***M:*** Jean Boyer, Eddie Barclay.

Bob Roberts 🦴🦴🦴 **1992 (R)** Pseudo-documentary satire about a 1990 Pennsylvania senatorial race between Robbins' titular right-wing folk singer/entrepreneur versus Brickley Paiste's (Vidal) aging liberal incumbent. Roberts seems like a gee-whiz kinda guy but he'll stop at nothing to get elected and he knows a lot about political dirty tricks and, even more important, manipulating the media to get what he wants. Robbins directorial debut turned out to be very timely in view of the 1992 Clinton/Bush presidential campaign. Features a number of cameos. Line to remember: "Vote first. Ask questions later." **105m/C VHS, DVD.** Tim Robbins, Giancarlo Esposito, Ray Wise, Rebecca Jenkins, Harry J. Lennix, John Ottavino, Robert Stanton, Alan Rickman, Gore Vidal, Brian Doyle-Murray, Anita Gillette, David Strathairn, Susan Sarandon, James Spader, John Cusack, Fred Ward, Pamela Reed; ***D:*** Tim Robbins; ***W:*** Tim Robbins; ***C:*** Jean Lepine; ***M:*** David Robbins.

Bobbie Jo and the Outlaw 🦴½ **1976 (R)** Wonderwoman Carter is a bored carhop who yearns to be a country singer. She becomes involved with Marjoe, who fancies himself as a contemporary Billy the Kid. Together, they do their Bonnie and Clyde thing, to a significantly lesser dramatic effect than the original, though a glut of violence keeps the bodies dropping. **89m/C VHS.** Lynda Carter, Marjoe Gortner, Jesse Vint; ***D:*** Mark L. Lester.

Bobby Deerfield 🦴🦴 **1977 (PG)** Cold-blooded Grand Prix driver comes face to face with death each time he races, but finally learns the meaning of life when he falls in love with a critically ill woman. Even with race cars, soap opera stalls. **124m/C VHS.** Al Pacino, Marthe Keller, Anny (Annie Legras) Duperey, Romolo Valli; ***D:*** Sydney Pollack; ***W:*** Alvin Sargent; ***C:*** Henri Decae; ***M:*** Dave Grusin.

Bobo 🦴½ **1967** Lousy bullfighter tries to lure a gorgeous woman into romance. Filmed in Spain and Italy. **103m/C VHS, Wide.** *GB* Peter Sellers, Britt Ekland, Rossano Brazzi, Adolfo Celi; ***D:*** Robert Parrish.

Boca 🦴🦴 **1994 (R)** American journalist J.J. (Chong) arrives in Rio during Carnival to investigate a story about random killings throughout the Brazilian streets. She gets stonewalled asking questions, until she meets an up-from-poverty crimelord named Boca De Ouro (Meira). Now, our noisy journalist may learn too much to keep her alive. Filmed in Rio de Janiero. **92m/C VHS.** Rae Dawn Chong, Martin Kemp, Tarcisio Meira, Martin Sheen; ***D:*** Sandra Werneck, Walter Avancini; ***W:*** Ed Silverstein.

Boccaccio '70 🦴🦴 **1962** Three short bawdy/comedy/pageant-of-life films inspired by "The Decameron," each pertaining to ironically twisted sexual politics in middle class life. A fourth story, "Renzo and Luciana," by Mario Monicelli, has been cut. Dubbed. **145m/C VHS.** *IT* Anita Ekberg, Romy Schneider, Tomas Milian, Sophia Loren, Peppino de Filippo, Luigi Gillianni; ***D:*** Vittorio De Sica, Luchino Visconti, Federico Fellini; ***W:*** Luchino Visconti, Federico Fellini, Tullio Pinelli, Ennio Flaiano, Cesare Zavattini; ***C:*** Otello Martelli, Giuseppe Rotunno; ***M:*** Nino Rota, Armando Trovajoli.

Bodies, Rest & Motion 🦴🦴 **1993 (R)** Stagnant 20-something movie in which four young people basically do nothing in the sun-baked town of Enfield, Arizona. Similar to the movie "Singles," but without the Seattle grunge scene. The title's reference to Newton is fitting: "A body in rest or motion remains in that state unless acted upon by an outside force."

Appealing cast is wasted in listless film that's content to just drift along. Based on the play by Roger Hedden. **94m/C VHS.** Phoebe Cates, Bridget Fonda, Tim Roth, Eric Stoltz, Scott Frederick, Scott Johnson, Alicia Witt, Rich Wheeler, Peter Fonda; ***D:*** Michael Steinberg; ***W:*** Roger Hedden; ***C:*** Bernd Heinl; ***M:*** Michael Convertino.

Bodily Harm && **1995 (R)** By-the-numbers neo-noir features Fiorentino as Vegas detective Rita Cates, who's investigating the murders of two women with ties to ex-cop Sam McKeon (Baldwin), not incidentally Rita's former lover. She rekindles their lust but then begins to have second thoughts about Sam's innocence. Unconvincing despite the expert cast. **91m/C VHS.** Linda Fiorentino, Daniel Baldwin, Gregg Henry, Bill Smitrovich, Troy Evans, Joe Regalbuto, Millie Perkins, Todd Susman, Shannon Kenny; ***D:*** James (Momel) Lemmo; ***W:*** James (Momel) Lemmo, Joseph Whaley, Ronda Barendse; ***M:*** Robert Sprayberry.

The Body & **2001 (PG-13)** Would-be religious thriller with wooden acting, laughable dialog, and clunky plot. In modern-day Jerusalem, Israeli archeologist Sharon Golban (Williams) checks out a tomb discovered beneath a shop and finds the skeleton of a crucified man. Could it be the remains of Jesus? When word reaches the Vatican, Cardinal Pesci (Wood) dispatches Father Matt Gutierrez (Banderas) to deal with the provocative situation. **108m/C VHS, DVD, Wide.** Antonio Banderas, Olivia Williams, John Wood, John Shrapnel, Derek Jacobi, Jason Flemyng, Makram Khoury, Vernon Dobtcheff, Ian McNeice; ***D:*** Jonas McCord; ***W:*** Jonas McCord; ***C:*** Vilmos Zsigmond; ***M:*** Serge Colbert.

Body and Soul && **1924** The first screen appearance of Robeson has him cast in a dual role as a conniving preacher and his good brother. The preacher preys on the heroine, making her life a misery. Objections by censors to the preacher's character caused him to be redeemed and become worthy of the heroine's love. **102m/B VHS.** Paul Robeson, Julia Theresa Russell, Mercedes Gilbert; ***D:*** Oscar Micheaux.

Body and Soul &&&½ *An Affair of the Heart* **1947** Charlie Davis (Garfield) is a Jewish boxer whose parents want him to quit the ring and get an education. Instead, he rises quickly to the top, thanks in part to gangster "protector" Roberts (Goff). After becoming a champ, Charlie starts the inevitable downward slide. One-time pro-welterweight Lee plays boxing rival Ben. A vintage '40s boxing film that defines the genre. Remade in 1981 with Leon Isaac Kennedy. **104m/B VHS.** John Garfield, Lilli Palmer, Hazel Brooks, Anne Revere, William Conrad, Canada Lee, Joseph Pevney, Lloyd Goff; ***D:*** Robert Rossen; ***W:*** Abraham Polonsky; ***C:*** James Wong Howe; ***M:*** Hugo Friedhofer. Oscars '47: Film Editing.

Body & Soul &&½ **1981 (R)** Interesting remake of 1947 gem about a boxer who loses his perspective in the world of fame, fast cars, and women. **109m/C VHS.** Leon Isaac Kennedy, Jayne Kennedy, Peter Lawford, Muhammad Ali, Perry Lang; ***D:*** George Bowers.

Body & Soul &&& **1993** After spending 16 years as a cloistered nun in a Welsh convent, with vows of poverty, chastity, and obedience, Anna Gibson (Scott Thomas) must return to the outside world. Following her brother's suicide, Anna is forced to deal with his pregnant widow (Redman) and two children and her family's failing Yorkshire mill. Anna suffers a crisis of faith as both the secular and the religious exert their strong influences and she's drawn as well to two very different men—younger Hal (Mavers), the mill's supervisor, and divorced bank manager Daniel Stern (Bowe). Based on the 1991 novel by Marcelle Bernstein; British TV miniseries. **312m/C VHS.** *GB* Kristin Scott Thomas, Amanda Redman, Gary Mavers, Anthony Valentine, Sandra Voe, John Bowe, Dorothy Tutin, Patrick Allen; ***D:*** Moira Armstrong; ***W:*** Paul Hines; ***C:*** Peter Middleton; ***M:*** Jim Parker.

Body and Soul && **1998 (R)** Cliched remake of the familiar boxing saga that finds ambitious boxer Mancini and his manager Chiklis heading for a potential championship bout in Reno. Mancini might still have the boxing moves but he's certainly no amateur and his professionalism is actually a deterrent. **95m/C VHS.** Ray "Boom Boom" Mancini, Michael Chiklis, Rod Steiger, Joe Mantegna, Jennifer Beals, Tahnee Welch; ***D:*** Sam Henry Kass; ***W:*** Sam Henry Kass; ***C:*** Arturo Smith; ***M:*** David Waters. **CABLE**

Body Armor &½ **1996 (R)** Special agent Conway (McColm) is recruited by an ex-girlfriend (Schofield) to find a missing scientist. This leads our hero to nutball virologist Dr. Krago (Perlman) who's using germ warfare for personal gain. For the action junkie (who doesn't mind a little eye candy as well). **95m/C VHS, DVD.** Matt McColm, Ron Perlman, Annabel Schofield, Carol Alt, Clint Howard, Morgan Brittany, Shauna O'Brien; ***D:*** Jack Gill; ***W:*** Jack Gill; ***C:*** Robert Hayes; ***M:*** Mark Holden. **VIDEO**

Body Bags &&½ *John Carpenter Presents Body Bags* **1993 (R)** Three gory, though humorous, stories hosted by horrormeister Carpenter as your friendly local coroner. "The Gas Station" finds the young female overnight attendent menaced by a psycho. "Hair" is about a balding yuppie who'll do anything for a full head of hair. Then he meets the sinister Dr. Lock and his magical new-hair growth treatment. The grisly "Eye" concerns a ballplayer who loses the aforementioned appendage and finds that his transplanted eyeball, taken from an executed serial killer, is subject to ghastly visions. Several fellow horror directors have cameos. **95m/C VHS.** Alex Datcher, Robert Carradine, Stacy Keach, David Warner, Mark Hamill, Twiggy, John Agar, Deborah Harry, Sheena Easton, David Naughton, John Carpenter; ***Cameos:*** Wes Craven, Sam Raimi, Roger Corman, Tobe Hooper; ***D:*** Tobe Hooper, John Carpenter; ***W:*** Billy Brown, Dan Angel; ***M:*** John Carpenter, Jim Lang. **CABLE**

Body Beat && *Dance Academy* **1988 (PG)** Wild jazz and rock dancers are integrated into a previously classical ballet academy. While the students become fast friends, the teachers break off into two rival factions. **90m/C VHS.** Tony Fields, Galyn Gorg, Scott Grossman, Eliska Krupka, Virgil Frye, Steve La Chance, Leonora Leal, Julie Newmar, Paula Nichols, Serge Rodnunsky; ***D:*** Ted Mather; ***W:*** Ted Mather; ***C:*** Dennis Peters; ***M:*** Guido de Angelis, Maurizio de Angelis.

The Body Beneath woof! *Vampire's Thirst* **1970** A living-dead ghoul survives on the blood of innocents and is still preying on victims today. **85m/C VHS, DVD.** Gavin Reed, Jackie Skarvellis, Susan Heard, Colin Gordon; ***D:*** Andy Milligan.

Body Chemistry & **1990 (R)** A married sexual-behavior researcher starts up a passionate affair with his lab partner. When he tries to end the relationship, his female associate becomes psychotic. You've seen it all before in "Fatal Attraction." And you'll see it again in "Body Chemistry 2." **84m/C VHS, DVD.** Marc Singer, Mary Crosby, Lisa Pescia, Joseph Campanella, David Kagen; ***D:*** Kristine Peterson; ***W:*** Jackson Barr, Thom Babbes; ***C:*** Phedon Papamichael; ***M:*** Terry Plumeri.

Body Chemistry 2: Voice of a Stranger &½ **1991 (R)** An ex-cop (Harrison) obsessed with violent sex gets involved with a talk-radio psychologist (Pescia) whose advice could prove deadly in this erotic sequel. **84m/C VHS, DVD.** Gregory Harrison, Lisa Pescia, Morton Downey Jr., Robin Riker, Jeremy Piven, John Landis; ***D:*** Adam Simon; ***W:*** Jackson Barr, Christopher Wooden; ***C:*** Richard Michalak; ***M:*** Nigel Holton.

Body Chemistry 3: Point of Seduction && **1993 (R)** TV producer Alan Clay (Stevens) finds himself caught in a business and sexual triangle when he okays the making of a movie about the life of a TV sex therapist (Shattuck). Seems the lady's lovers have a nasty habit of getting murdered which doesn't prevent Clay from getting personally involved. His actress wife (Fairchild), who wants to star in the movie, is not pleased. Lives up to its title. **90m/C VHS, DVD.** Andrew Stevens, Morgan Fairchild, Shari Shattuck; ***D:*** Jim Wynorski; ***W:*** Jackson Barr; ***C:*** Don E. Fauntleroy; ***M:*** Chuck Cirino.

Body Chemistry 4: Full Exposure &½ **1995 (R)** When sex psychologist Claire Archer (Tweed) is accused of murder she hires Simon Mitchell (Poindexter), the best criminal defense attorney around. But Simon becomes just a little too closely involved with his possibly psycho client and it could cost him not only his career and marriage but his life. Also available unrated. **89m/C VHS, DVD.** Shannon Tweed, Larry Poindexter, Andrew Stevens, Chick Vennera, Larry Manetti, Stella Stevens; ***D:*** Jim Wynorski; ***W:*** Karen Kelly; ***C:*** Zoran Hochstatter; ***M:*** Paul Di Franco.

Body Count &½ *The 11th Commandment* **1987** A weird and wealthy family will stop at nothing, including murder and cannibalism, to enhance their fortune. Rather than bodies, count the minutes 'til the movie's over. **90m/C VHS.** Marilyn Hassett, Dick Sargent, Steven Ford, Greg Mullavey, Thomas Ryan, Bernie White; ***D:*** Paul Leder.

Body Count &½ **1995 (R)** Professional killer Makoto (Chiba) and his partner Sybil (Nielsen) seek revenge on the New Orleans cops who set them up. Opposing them are special crime unit partners, Eddie Cook (Davi) and Vinnie Rizzo (Bauer). Lots of shootouts and macho bravado. **93m/C VHS, DVD.** Sonny Chiba, Brigitte Nielsen, Robert Davi, Steven Bauer, Jan-Michael Vincent, Talun Hsu; ***D:*** Talun Hsu; ***W:*** Henry Madden; ***C:*** Blake T. Evans; ***M:*** Don Peake.

Body Count && **1997 (R)** Fiorentino and Caruso are reteamed (after "Jade") in a crime saga about a heist gone bad. There is no honor among thieves as driver Hobbs (Caruso) learns when he plans a job with some unreliable associates at the Boston Museum of Fine Arts and things go very wrong. The gang decide to drive to Miami in order to sell their ill-gotten gains, squabbling all the way. Then mystery woman Natalie (Fiorentino) comes aboard, to cause more friction between the gun-happy boys. **84m/C VHS.** David Caruso, Linda Fiorentino, John Leguizamo, Ving Rhames, Donnie Wahlberg, Forest Whitaker; ***D:*** Robert Patton-Spruill; ***W:*** Theodore Witcher; ***C:*** Charles Mills; ***M:*** Curt Sobel. **VIDEO**

Body Count && *Below Utopia* **1997 (R)** Daniel (Theroux) takes fiancee Suzanne (Milano) home to meet his wealthy family and they just happen to be out of the line of immediate mayhem when a gang of thieves (led by Ice-T) break in to steal the family art collection. Now, they're playing a very serious game of hide-and-seek in order to stay alive—only the situations isn't as clear as it seems. **88m/C VHS, DVD.** Ice-T, Alyssa Milano, Justin Theroux, Tommy (Tiny) Lister, Jeannette O'Connor, Nicholas Walker, Eric Saiet, Marta Kristen, Ron Harper, Robert Pine, Richard Danielson; ***D:*** Kurt Voss; ***W:*** David Diamond; ***C:*** Denis Maloney; ***M:*** Joseph Williams. **VIDEO**

Body Double &&& **1984 (R)** A voyeuristic unemployed actor peeps on a neighbor's nightly disrobing and sees more than he wants to. A grisly murder leads him into an obsessive quest through the world of pornographic films. **114m/C VHS, DVD, Wide.** Craig Wasson, Melanie Griffith, Gregg Henry, Deborah Shelton, Guy Boyd, Dennis Franz, David Haskell, Rebecca Stanley, Barbara Crampton; ***D:*** Brian DePalma; ***W:*** Brian DePalma, Robert J. Avrech; ***C:*** Stephen Burum; ***M:*** Pino Donaggio. Natl. Soc. Film Critics '84: Support. Actress (Griffith).

Body Heat &&&½ **1981 (R)** During a Florida heat wave, a none-too-bright lawyer becomes involved in a steamy love affair with a mysterious woman and then in a plot to kill her husband. Hurt and Turner (in her film debut) became stars under Kasdan's direction (the three would reunite for "The Accidental Tourist"). Hot love scenes supplement a twisting mystery with a suprise ending. Rourke's arsonist and Danson's soft shoe shouldn't be missed. **113m/C VHS, DVD.** William Hurt, Kathleen Turner, Richard Crenna, Ted Danson, Mickey Rourke, J.A. Preston, Kim Zimmer, Jane Hallaren; ***D:*** Lawrence Kasdan; ***W:*** Lawrence Kasdan; ***C:*** Richard H. Kline; ***M:*** John Barry.

The Body in the Library &½ *Agatha Christie's Miss Marple: The Body In the Library* **1987** A Miss Marple mystery, based on Agatha Christie's 1942 novel, involving the septuagenarian detective investigating the murder of a young woman in a wealthy British mansion. **155m/C VHS.** *GB* Joan Hickson; ***D:*** Silvio Narizzano. **TV**

Body Language && **1992 (R)** A successful businesswoman, with a man problem, hires a super secretary with answers to all life's questions—and a deadly agenda all her own. **93m/C VHS.** Heather Locklear, Linda Purl, Edward Albert, James Acheson; ***D:*** Arthur Seidelman; ***W:*** Dan Gurskis, Brian Ross; ***C:*** Hanania Baer.

Body Language &&½ **1995 (R)** Criminal defense attorney Gavin St. Claire (Berenger) falls for a topless dancer (Schanz), which leads him into all sorts of trouble, including murder. **95m/C VHS.** Tom Berenger, Heidi Schanz, Nancy Travis; ***D:*** George Case.

Body Melt &&½ **1993** When a crazed doctor unleashes an experimental drug on an unsuspecting town, the residents begin to literally melt away. **82m/C VHS.** *AU* Gerard Kennedy, Andrew Daddo, Ian Smith, Vincent (Vince Gill) Gil, Regina Gaigalas; ***D:*** Philip Brophy; ***W:*** Philip Brophy, Rod Bishop; ***M:*** Philip Brophy.

Body Moves && **1990 (PG-13)** Romantic entanglements heat up the competition when two couples enter a steamy dance contest. Not apt to move you. **98m/C VHS.** *IT* Kirk Rivera, Steve Messina, Dianne Granger, Linsley Allen, Philip Spruce, Nicole Kolman, Susan Gardner; ***D:*** Gerry Lively; ***W:*** Daniel Steel.

Body of Evidence woof! **1992 (R)** Bad movie with pretensions takes "Basic Instinct" a step further. Instead of an ice pick and sex, sex itself is used as the weapon in a murder trial featuring Madonna as the defendant, Dafoe as her lawyer, and Mantegna as the prosecutor. The plot is, of course, secondary to the S&M sex scenes with Dafoe which feature hot wax and broken glass. Madonna's lack of performance is the least of the film's problems since everyone seems to have forgotten any acting talent they possess. Director Edel fails to direct—the film even looks bad. "Body" was the subject of another NC-17 ratings flap but this film shouldn't be seen by anybody. An unrated version is also available. **99m/C VHS, Wide.** Madonna, Willem Dafoe, Joe Mantegna, Anne Archer, Michael Forest, Charles Hallahan, Mark Rolston, Richard Riehle, Julianne Moore, Frank Langella, Juergen Prochnow, Stan Shaw; ***D:*** Uli Edel; ***W:*** Brad Mirman; ***C:*** Doug Milsome; ***M:*** Graeme Revell. Golden Raspberries '93: Worst Actress (Madonna).

Body of Influence && **1993 (R)** A Beverly Hills psychiatrist gets overly involved with a beautiful female patient. But she not only wants his love—she wants his life. Also available in an unrated version. **96m/C VHS.** Nick Cassavetes, Shannon Whirry, Sandahl Bergman, Don Swayze, Anna Karin, Catherine Parks, Diana Barton, Richard Roundtree; ***D:*** Andrew Garroni; ***W:*** David Schreiber.

Body of Influence 2 & **1996 (R)** Shrink Dr. Benson (Anderson) finds he's using his couch for more than professional purposes with his latest patient, Leza (Fisher), whose seductive charms prove more than the doc can handle. The unrated version is 94 minutes. **88m/C VHS, DVD.** Daniel Anderson, Jodie Fisher, Steve Poletti, Jonathan Goldstein, Pat Brennan; ***D:*** Brian J. Smith; ***W:*** Brian J. Smith; ***C:*** Azusa Ohno; ***M:*** Ron Sures.

Body Parts & **1990** For fans of the demented dismemberer niche. Body Parts, a sleazy skin club, loses some of its star talent when the strippers start turning up in cameo video appearances. Seems there's a psycho killer on the loose who videotapes the dismemberment of his stripper-victims. The police decide they've got to meet this guy when he sends them a sample of his work. **90m/C VHS.** Teri Lee, Dick Monda, Johnny Mandel.

Body Parts 🦴🦴 **1991 (R)** A crime psychologist loses his arm in an auto accident and receives a transplant from an executed murderer. Does the limb have an evil will of its own? Poorly paced horror goes off the deep end in gore with its third act. Based on the novel "Choice Cuts" by French writers Pierre Boileau and Thomas Narcejac, whose work inspired some of the greatest suspense films. **88m/C VHS, Wide.** Jeff Fahey, Kim Delaney, Lindsay Duncan, Peter Murnik, Brad Dourif, Zakes Mokae, James Kidnie, Paul Ben-Victor; ***D:*** Eric Red; ***W:*** Eric Red, Norman Snider, Patricia Herskovic; ***C:*** Theo van de Sande; ***M:*** Loek Dikker.

Body Rock woof! **1984 (PG-13)** Brooklyn breakdancer Lamas deserts his buddies to work at a chic Manhattan nightclub. Watching Lamas as the emcee/ breakdancing fool is a hoot. ♫Body Rock; Team Work; Why Do You Want to Break My Heart?; One Thing Leads to Another; Let Your Body Rock; Vanishing Point; Sharpshooter; The Jungle; Deliver. **93m/C VHS.** Lorenzo Lamas, Vicki Frederick, Cameron Dye, Michelle Nicastro, Ray Sharkey, Grace Zabriskie, Carole Ita White; ***D:*** Marcelo Epstein.

The Body Shop woof! *Doctor Gore* **1972** Unorthodox love story in which a man decides to patch up his relationship with his dead wife by piecing together her dismembered body. For lovers only. Under "Doctor Gore" title the film includes an intro by horror director Herschell Gordon Lewis. **91m/C VHS.** Pat Patterson, Jenny Driggers, Roy Mehaffey, Linda Faile, Candy Furr; ***D:*** Pat Patterson.

Body Shot 🦴🦴½ **1993 (R)** Celebrity shutterbug Mickey Dane (Patrick) is fingered in the murder of a rock star after it turns out he did a kinky layout for a lookalike. When police find out he had an obsession for the dead woman, he employs his photographic expertise in the search for the real killer. Effective tension-builder with fast-paced chases through the seamy side of Los Angeles. **98m/C VHS, DVD.** Robert Patrick, Michelle Johnson, Ray Wise, Jonathan Banks, Kim Miyori, Kenneth Tobey, Charles Napier; ***D:*** Dimitri Logothetis; ***W:*** Robert Strauss; ***C:*** Nicholas Josef von Sternberg; ***M:*** Cliff Magness.

Body Shots 🦴½ **1999 (R)** An ensemble cast of twentysomethings explores sex and dating while traversing L.A.'s nightlife. Eight friends come to reflect on their hedonistic lifestyles when Sara (Reid) accuses macho football player Michael (O'Connell) of date rape. During the ultimate "he said/she said" battle, waferthin declarations on love in the '90s are made by characters who are as appealing as root canal surgery. **102m/C VHS, DVD, Wide.** Sean Patrick Flanery, Jerry O'Connell, Amanda Peet, Tara Reid, Ron Livingston, Emily (Proctor) Procter, Brad Rowe, Sybil Temchen; ***D:*** Michael Cristofer; ***W:*** David McKenna; ***C:*** Rodrigo Garcia; ***M:*** Mark Isham.

Body Slam 🦴½ **1987 (PG)** A small-time talent monger hits it big with a rock and roll/ professional wrestling tour. Piper's debut; contains some violence and strong language. **100m/C VHS.** Roddy Piper, Captain Lou Albano, Dirk Benedict, Tanya Roberts, Billy Barty, Charles Nelson Reilly, John Astin, Wild Samoan, Tonga Kid, Barry J. Gordon; ***D:*** Hal Needham; ***W:*** Steven H. Burkow; ***M:*** John D'Andrea.

The Body Snatcher 🦴🦴🦴½ **1945** Based on Robert Louis Stevenson's story about a grave robber who supplies corpses to research scientists. Set in Edinburgh in the 19th century, this Lewton production is superior. One of Karloff's best vehicles. **77m/B VHS.** Edith Atwater, Russell Wade, Rita (Paula) Corday, Boris Karloff, Bela Lugosi, Henry Daniell, Sharyn Moffett, Donna Lee; ***D:*** Robert Wise; ***W:*** Philip MacDonald, Val Lewton; ***C:*** Robert De Grasse.

Body Snatcher from Hell 🦴½ *Goke, Body Snatcher from Hell; Goke the Vampire; Kyuketsuki Gokemidoro* **1969** An airliner passes through a mysterious cloud and crashes in a desert. One by one, the passengers are turned into vampires. Some interesting special effects. **84m/C VHS.** *JP* Hideo Ko, Teruo Yoshida, Tomomi Sato, Eizo Kitamura, Masay Takahashi, Cathy Horlan, Kazuo Kato, Yuko Kusunoki; ***D:*** Hajime Sato.

Body Snatchers 🦴🦴 **1993 (R)** Yet another version of "Invasion of the Body Snatchers." An innocent family arrive at an Army base which turns out to be infested with pod people. This time around the heroine is angst-ridden teenager Marti (Anwar) and the pods have something to do with a mysterious toxic spill. The 1978 remake was well done; this so-so version takes advantage of the advances in special effects (particularly in Anwar's bathtub scene) and sound technology but is slow-paced with few jolts of terror. **87m/C VHS, DVD, Wide.** Gabrielle Anwar, Meg Tilly, Terry Kinney, Forest Whitaker, Billy Wirth, R. Lee Ermey, Reilly Murphy; ***D:*** Abel Ferrara; ***W:*** Stuart Gordon, Dennis Paoli, Nicholas St. John; ***C:*** Bojan Bazelli; ***M:*** Joe Delia.

Body Strokes 🦴 *Siren's Kiss* **1995** Blocked artist Leo Kessler (Johnston) is aroused by the wild fantasies of his beautiful models Beth (Knittle) and Claire (Weber). But it's just fantasy and it also helps get Leo's marriage back on track when manager/wife Karen (Beck) gets jealous. Also available unrated. **99m/C VHS, DVD.** Bobby Johnston, Dixie Beck, Kristen Knittle, Catherine Weber; ***D:*** Edward Holzman; ***W:*** April Moskowitz; ***C:*** Kim Haun; ***M:*** Richard Bronskill.

Body Trouble 🦴½ *Joker's Wild* **1992 (R)** After being attacked by sharks while vacationing in the Caribbean, a man washes ashore in Miami and then somehow makes his way to New York City. There he meets Vera Vin Rouge and her friends Cinnamon, Spice, Paprika, and Johnny Zero, a gangster. Zero decides he doesn't like the man, so he chases him back to the Caribbean. Supposedly this all happens in only one day. Hmmm... **98m/C VHS, DVD.** Dick Van Patten, Priscilla Barnes, Frank Gorshin, James Hong, Marty Rackham, Michael Unger, Jonathan Soloman, Brit Helfer, Leigh Clark, Patricia Cardell, Richie Barathy; ***D:*** Bill Milling; ***W:*** Bill Milling.

The Body Vanished 🦴🦴 **1939** Murder mystery featuring a corpse that disappears from the scene of the crime. **?m/C VHS.** *GB* Lewis Wilson, Frances Dubay, Dana Wilson.

Body Waves 🦴½ **1992 (R)** Beach comedy starring Calvert as a teenager who bets his father that he can raise money on his own. In typical teen movie fashion, he invents a sex cream that drives boys and girls wild. Brain candy featuring lots of skimpy bikinis. **80m/C VHS.** Bill Calvert, Leah Lail, Larry Linville, Dick Miller, Jim Wise; ***D:*** P.J. Pesce.

The Bodyguard 🦴½ **1976 (R)** The Yakuza, Japan's mafia, and New York's big crime families face off in this martial arts extravaganza. **89m/C VHS, DVD.** *JP* Sue Shiomi, Sonny Chiba, Aaron Banks, Bill Louie, Judy Lee; ***D:*** Maurice Sarli.

The Bodyguard 🦴🦴 **1992 (R)** Buttoned-down, ex-Secret Service agent turned private bodyguard reluctantly takes on a wildly successful singer/actress as a client. Houston, in her acting debut as the over-indulged diva, doesn't have to stretch too far but acquits herself well. Costner has really bad hair day but easily portrays the tightly wound Frank. Critically trashed, a boxoffice smash, and too long. Originally scripted by producer Kasdan over a decade ago, with Steve McQueen in mind. Predictable romantic melodrama is kept moving by the occasional sharp dialog and a few action pieces. Songs include the smash hit "I Will Always Love You," written and originally performed by Dolly Parton. **130m/C VHS, DVD.** Kevin Costner, Whitney Houston, Gary Kemp, Bill Cobbs, Ralph Waite, Tomas Arana, Michele Lamar Richards, Mike Starr, Christopher Birt, DeVaughn Nixon, Charles Keating, Robert Wuhl; ***Cameos:*** Debbie Reynolds; ***D:*** Mick Jackson; ***W:*** Lawrence Kasdan; ***C:*** Andrew Dunn; ***M:*** Alan Silvestri. MTV Movie Awards '93: Song ("I Will Always Love You").

The Bodyguard from Beijing 🦴🦴½ *The Defender; Zhong Nan Hai Bao Biao* **1994** Beijing bodyguard John Chang (Li) is hired to protect pampered rich girl Michelle (Chung), who's the witness to a murder. And John also has to deal with the revenge plans of an ex-soldier whose brother John has killed. Cantonese with subtitles. **90m/C VHS, DVD.** *HK* Jet Li, Christy Chung, Kent Cheng, Ngai Sing; ***D:*** Corey Yuen; ***W:*** Gordon Chan, Kin-Chung Chan; ***C:*** Tom Lau.

Bodywork 🦴🦴 **1999 (R)** Virgil Guppy (Matheson) buys a second-hand Jaguar that gives him nothing but trouble, especially when he finds a dead prostitute in the trunk of the car. Virgil goes on the run and hides out with a young woman (Coleman) who's a professional car thief. British crime caper finally has too many twists for its own good. The Winslet who plays Virgil's girlfriend is the sister of actress Kate. **93m/C VHS, DVD.** *GB* Hans Matheson, Charlotte Coleman, Clive Russell, Beth Winslet; ***D:*** Gareth Rhys Jones; ***W:*** Gareth Rhys Jones; ***C:*** Thomas Wuthvich; ***M:*** Dusan Kojic, Srdjan Kurpjel.

Boeing Boeing 🦴🦴½ **1965** A dated but still amusing sex farce about a bachelor newspaperman (Curtis) in Paris, his three stewardess girlfriends, and the elaborate plots he resorts to in trying to keep them from finding out about each other. When the new Boeing jet makes air travel faster all Curtis' schemes may come crashing down. Ritter is fun as the exasperated housekeeper and Lewis amazingly subdued as Curtis' business rival. **102m/C VHS.** Tony Curtis, Jerry Lewis, Dany Saval, Christiane Schmidtmer, Suzanna Leigh, Thelma Ritter; ***D:*** John Rich; ***W:*** Edward Anhalt.

Boesman & Lena 🦴🦴½ **2000** Adaptation of the apartheid-era play by Athol Fugard follows the travails of downtrodden couple, Boesman (Glover) and Lena (Bassett). Their shanty town home in Cape Town has been bulldozed by the government so they take to the dusty road with their meager belongings, constantly bickering about their plight. The couple construct a makeshift abode for the night, which attracts the attention of an old man (Jonah) even lower on the economic ladder, whom Lena allows to stay to Boesman's displeasure. Performances are outstanding. Last film for director Berry. **86m/C VHS, DVD, Wide.** *FR* Danny Glover, Angela Bassett, Willie Jonah; ***D:*** John Berry; ***W:*** John Berry; ***C:*** Alain Choquart; ***M:*** Wally Badarou.

Bog 🦴 **1984 (PG)** Boggy beast from the Arctic north awakens to eat people. Scientists mount an anti-monster offensive. **90m/C VHS.** Gloria De Haven, Marshall Thompson, Leo Gordon, Aldo Ray, Glen Voros, Ed Clark, Carol Terry; ***D:*** Don Keeslar; ***W:*** Carl Kitt; ***C:*** Jack Willoughby; ***M:*** Bill Walker.

Boggy Creek II 🦴½ *The Barbaric Beast of Boggy Creek, Part II* **1983 (PG)** The continuing saga of the eight-foot-tall, 300 pound monster from Texarkana. Third in a series of low-budget movies including "The Legend of Boggy Creek" and "Return to Boggy Creek." **93m/C VHS.** Charles B. Pierce, Cindy Butler, Serene Hedin; ***D:*** Charles B. Pierce; ***W:*** Charles B. Pierce.

Bogie: The Last Hero **1980** Biography of Humphrey Bogart, populated by almost-lookalikes who can almost act. **100m/C VHS.** Kevin J. O'Connor, Kathryn Harrold, Ann Wedgeworth, Patricia Barry, Alfred Ryder, Donald May, Richard Dysart, Arthur Franz; ***D:*** Vincent Sherman; ***M:*** Charles Bernstein. **TV**

Bogus 🦴🦴 **1996 (PG)** Aptly named fantasy-comedy has orphan Albert (Osment) sent to foster aunt Harriet (Goldberg) after his magician's assistant mom (Travis) dies in a car accident. He brings along an imaginary friend, the eponymous Bogus (Depardieu) to ease the transition. Harriet is your typical workaholic easterner and isn't too thrilled with the arrangement. Goldberg and Depardieu are fine, but predictability drains most of the magic. **112m/C VHS.** Whoopi Goldberg, Gerard Depardieu, Haley Joel Osment, Nancy Travis, Andrea Martin, Denis Mercier, Ute Lemper, Sheryl Lee Ralph, Al Waxman, Fiona Reid, Don Francks; ***D:*** Norman Jewison; ***W:*** Alvin Sargent; ***C:*** David Watkin; ***M:*** Marc Shaiman.

The Bogus Witch Project 🦴 **2000 (R)** In the long and ignoble history of cheap parodies, this is surely one of the cheapest. It's a series of short films—sketches and blackouts, really—that use the premise of the original "Blair Witch" film to poke fun at the movie biz. Here's the preface to one: "In August 1999, three out-of-work actors disappeared in the woods near Sherman Oaks, CA, while looking for Blair Underwood to give him a script. 24 hours later, their footage was found and turned into a vehicle for shameless self-promotion." The episode starring Pauly Shore is the weakest of the weak. Funnier bits appear between spoofs. **85m/C DVD.** Pauly Shore, Michael Ian Black; ***D:*** Victor Kargan; ***M:*** Carvin Knowles.

Bohemian Girl 🦴🦴🦴 **1936** The last of Laurel and Hardy's comic operettas finds them as guardians of a young orphan (Hood, famous for her roles in the Our Gang comedies), whom no one realizes is actually a kidnapped princess. **74m/B VHS.** Stan Laurel, Oliver Hardy, Mae Busch, Darla Hood, Julie (Jacqueline Wells) Bishop, Thelma Todd, James Finlayson; ***D:*** James W. Horne.

Boiler Room 🦴🦴🦴 **2000 (R)** Basic plot about a greedy naive young man caught up in a situation that's out of his control gets the high testosterone treament. Seth (Ribisi) jumps at the chance to become a trainee at an up-and-coming brokerage firm filled with macho twentysomethings greedy for success. But what Seth eventually discovers is that the firm he's allied himself with runs an illegal stock-trading operation that's under investigation. Well-cast and stylish, with Affleck effective in a small role as the firm's strutting recruiter. **120m/C VHS, DVD, Wide.** Jon Abrahams, Kirk Acevedo, Giovanni Ribisi, Vin Diesel, Nicky Katt, Nia Long, Scott Caan, Ron Rifkin, Jamie Kennedy, Taylor Nichols, Tom Everett Scott, Ben Affleck; ***D:*** Ben Younger; ***W:*** Ben Younger; ***C:*** Enrique Chediak.

Boiling Point 🦴½ **1932** Lawman proves once again that justice always triumphs. **67m/B VHS.** Hoot Gibson, Helen Foster, Wheeler Oakman, Skeeter Bill Robbins, Billy Bletcher, Lafe (Lafayette) McKee, Charles Bailey, George "Gabby" Hayes; ***D:*** George Melford; ***W:*** Donald W. Lee; ***C:*** Tom Galligan, Harry Neumann.

Boiling Point 🦴🦴 *3x Jugatsu* **1990** Masaki (Ono) is a young, inarticulate, misfit, loser gas-station attendent who even lets down his local baseball team when he tries to play ball. Then he makes the mistake of slugging a yakuza member, so he heads to Okinawa to buy a gun to defend himself and meets up with the ultimate Mr. Cool—Uehara (Kitano). Uehara is such a bad ass even the yakuza don't want anything to do with him, so who better than the master to teach Masaki how to survive. The Japanese title refers to a baseball score, which somehow seems more apt. Japanese with subtitles. **98m/C VHS, DVD, Wide.** *JP* Takeshi "Beat" Kitano, Masahiko Ono, Hisashi Igawa; ***D:*** Takeshi "Beat" Kitano; ***C:*** Katsumi Yanagishima.

Boiling Point 🦴🦴½ **1993 (R)** Darkly flavored action drama delves into the personalities of its two main characters before setting up a final confrontation. Treasury agent Jimmy Mercer (Snipes) is trying to solve his partner's murder, relentlessly pursuing the murderers in cold and methodical fashion. Sleazy Red Diamond (Hopper), just out of prison, owes the mob and has one week to pay them back. Lawman and crook both come home to women, (Davidovich and Perrine) graduates of the Hollywood school of female martyrdom, selflessly supportive of their men. Grim but cliched. Adapted from the Gerald Petievich novel "Money Men." **93m/C VHS, DVD, Wide.** Wesley Snipes, Dennis Hopper, Lolita (David) Davidovich, Viggo Mortensen, Dan Hedaya, Valerie Perrine, Seymour Cassel, Jonathan Banks, Tony LoBianco, Christine Elise, James Tolkan, Paul Gleason; ***D:*** James B. Harris; ***W:*** James B. Harris; ***C:*** King Baggot; ***M:*** Cory Lerios, John D'Andrea.

Bojangles 🦴🦴½ **2001** Made-for-cable biopic of Bill "Bojangles" Robinson is strictly a by-the-numbers affair from the beginning at the funeral to the various characters who turn and address the camera to explain what they thought of the contradictory man. Gregory Hines does his usual excellent job in the lead, and the film looks very good. **101m/C VHS, DVD.** Gregory Hines, Peter Riegert, Kimberly Elise, Savion Glover, Maria Ricossa; ***D:*** Joseph Sargent; ***W:*** Richard Wesley, Robert P. Johnson; ***C:*** Donald M. Morgan; ***M:*** Terence Blanchard. **CABLE**

The Bold Caballero 🦴½ *The Bold Cavalier* **1936** Rebel chieftain Zorro overthrows oppressive Spanish rule in the days of early California. **69m/B VHS.** Robert "Bob" Livingston, Heather Angel, Sig Rumann, Robert Warwick; ***D:*** Wells Root.

The Boldest Job in the West 🦴 *El Mas Fabulosi Golpe del Far West* **1971** Italian western about bankrobbers who meet to divide their spoils. Problem is, the guys with the loot don't show. Dubbed in English. **200m/C VHS.** *IT* Mark Edwards, Frank Sancho, Carmen Sevilla; ***D:*** J. Anthony (Jose Antonio de la Loma) Loma.

Bolero 🦴🦴½ **1982** Beginning in 1936, this international epic traces the lives of four families across three continents and five decades, highlighting the music and dance that is central to their lives. **173m/C VHS.** James Caan, Geraldine Chaplin, Robert Hossein, Nicole Garcia, Jacques Villeret; ***D:*** Claude Lelouch; ***W:*** Claude Lelouch.

Bolero woof! *Bolero: An Adventure in Ecstasy* **1984 (R)** What sounds like a wet dream come true is really just a good snooze: Bo Derek plays a beautiful young woman who goes on a trip around the world in hopes of losing her virginity; in Spain, she meets a bullfighter who's willing to oblige. Too bad Bo cannot act as good as she looks. **106m/C VHS.** Bo Derek, George Kennedy, Andrea Occhipinti, Anna (Ana Garcia) Obregon, Olivia D'Abo; ***D:*** John Derek; ***W:*** John Derek; ***M:*** Peter Bernstein, Elmer Bernstein. Golden Raspberries '84: Worst Picture, Worst Actress (Derek), Worst Director (Derek), Worst Screenplay, Worst New Star (D'Abo).

Boltneck 🦴½ *Big Monster on Campus; Teen Monster* **1998** When school outcast Karl becomes the victim of a hazing by jocks, nerdy Frank Stein (get it?) decides to try an experiment in re-animating the dead. But unknown to Frank, the brain he's used (which he stole from his father's lab—how convenient) is that of a mass killer and the new Karl has developed quite an attitude. **92m/C VHS, DVD.** Justin Walker, Ryan Reynolds, Christine Lakin, Bianca Lawson, Kenny Blank, Judge Reinhold, Shelley Duvall, Charles Fleischer, Matthew Lawrence, Richard Moll; ***D:*** Mitch Marcus; ***W:*** Dave Payne; ***M:*** Roger Neill. **VIDEO**

Bomb at 10:10 🦴🦴 **1967** An American pilot escapes from a German POW camp and plots to assassinate a camp commandant. **87m/C VHS.** George Montgomery, Rada Popovic, Peter Banicevic; ***D:*** Charles Damic.

Bombardier 🦴🦴½ **1943** A group of cadet bombardiers discover the realities of war on raids over Japan during WWII. Also available colorized. **99m/B VHS.** Pat O'Brien, Randolph Scott, Robert Ryan, Eddie Albert, Anne Shirley, Barton MacLane; ***D:*** Richard Wallace.

Bombay Talkie 🦴🦴½ **1970 (PG)** A bored British writer (Kendal) heads to India to gather "experiences" and becomes involved with an Indian movie actor (Kapoor). Early clash-of-cultures film from Merchant Ivory has it's dull spots; the behind-the-scenes look at the Indian film industry is more interesting than the romance. **110m/C VHS.** *IN* Jennifer Kendal, Shashi Kapoor, Zia Mohyeddin, Aparna Sen; ***D:*** James Ivory; ***W:*** Ruth Prawer Jhabvala.

Bombs Away! 🦴 **1986** An atomic bomb is mistakenly shipped to a seedy war surplus store in Seattle, and causes much chicanery. **90m/C VHS.** Michael Huddleston, Pat McCormick; ***D:*** Bruce Wilson.

Bombshell 🦴🦴🦴 *Blonde Bombshell* **1933** Wry insightful comedy into the Hollywood of the 1930s. Harlow plays a naive young actress manipulated by her adoring press agent. He thwarts her plans until she finally notices and begins to fall in love with him. Brilliant satire with Harlow turning in perhaps the best performance of her short career. **96m/B VHS.** Jean Harlow, Lee Tracy, Pat O'Brien, Una Merkel, Sir C. Aubrey Smith, Franchot Tone; ***D:*** Victor Fleming.

Bombshell 🦴🦴 **1997 (R)** Scientist Buck Hogan (Thomas) discovers a deadly flaw in the world's first cancer-killing drug, which he publicly reveals, much to the dismay of the manufacturer's head honcho Donald (James). But then Hogan and his girlfriend Angeline (Amick) are abducted by a terrorist group, and Buck's implanted with a device that will kill him unless he does as they say. **95m/C VHS.** Michael Jace, Henry Thomas, Frank Whaley, Madchen Amick, Brion James, Pamela Gidley, Shawnee Smith, Martin Hewitt; ***D:*** Paul Wynne; ***W:*** Paul Wynne.

Bon Voyage! 🦴½ **1962** A family's long-awaited European "dream" vacation turns into a series of comic misadventures in this very Disney, very family, very predictable comedy. **131m/C VHS.** Fred MacMurray, Jane Wyman, Deborah Walley, Michael Callan, Tommy Kirk, Jessie Royce Landis; ***D:*** James Neilson.

Bonanno: A Godfather's Story 🦴🦴 **1999** Old-fashioned storytelling seems to fit the story of an old-fashioned New York mobster—Joseph Bonanno (Landau)—thought to be the inspiration for Mario Puzo's Don Vito Corleone. The elderly Bonanno reflects on his life and how he got into criminal activity back in the Prohibition days, drawing the attention of boss Salvatore Maranzano (Olmos). From there it's just a matter of time as Joe works his way up through the ranks. Based on the autobiography of Joseph Bonanno and the book written by his son Bill. **139m/C VHS.** Martin Landau, Bruce Ramsay, Costas Mandylor, Edward James Olmos, Tony Nardi, Zachary Bennett, Philip Bosco, Claudia Ferri, Robert Loggia, Patti LuPone; ***D:*** Michel Poulette; ***W:*** Thomas Michael Donnelly; ***C:*** Serge Ladouceur; ***M:*** Richard Gregoire. **CABLE**

Bonanza: The Return 🦴½ **1993 (PG)** In 1905, the children of various members of the Cartwright clan work to see the Ponderosa is safe from an unscrupulous businessman. Lame update of the classic family western series. **96m/C VHS.** Michael Landon Jr., Dirk Blocker, Emily Warfield, Alistair MacDougall, Brian Leckner, Dean Stockwell, Ben Johnson, Richard Roundtree, Linda Gray, Jack Elam; ***D:*** Jerry Jameson; ***W:*** Michael McGreevey; ***C:*** Haskell Boggs. **TV**

Bonanza Town 🦴½ **1951** Steve Ramsey (Starrett), aka The Durango Kid, and sidekick Smiley (Burnette) are hired to locate the loot stolen in a Dodge City hold-up. Marked money leads our heroes to Bonanza Town, where the Kid tracks down outlaws and corrupt officials. **56m/B VHS.** Charles Starrett, Smiley Burnette, Myron Healey, Fred F. Sears; ***D:*** Fred F. Sears; ***C:*** Henry Freulich.

The Bone Collector 🦴🦴½ **1999 (R)** Lincoln Rhyme (Washington) is a brilliant NYPD detective and forensics expert who was left a quadriplegic after an on-the-job accident. His suicidal thoughts are distracted by the work of a serial killer with a gruesome MO and the admirable work of hotshot young policewoman, Amelia Donoghy (Jolie). Amelia soon becomes Rhyme's surrogate investigator. The situation comes to a climax in Rhyme's apartment as he lies helpless. Thriller turns out to be predictable but Washington, as usual, turns in a fine performance. Based on the 1997 novel by Jeffrey Deaver. **118m/C VHS, DVD.** Denzel Washington, Angelina Jolie, Queen Latifah, Ed O'Neill, Michael Rooker, Mike McGlone, Leland Orser, Luis Guzman, John Benjamin Hickey, Bobby Cannavale; ***D:*** Phillip Noyce; ***W:*** Jeremy Iacone; ***C:*** Dean Semler; ***M:*** Craig Armstrong.

Bone Daddy 🦴🦴 **1997 (R)** Former chief medical examiner William Palmer (Hauer) turns his experiences into a best-selling novel and excites the rage of a psychopathic killer. The surgical killer, who's nicknamed "Bone Daddy" because he likes to extract the bones of his victims, is busy at work and Palmer teams up with a reluctant detective (Williams) to track the looney down. **90m/C VHS.** Rutger Hauer, Barbara Williams, R.H. Thomson, Joseph Kell, Robin Gammell, Daniel Kash, Christopher Kelk; ***D:*** Mario Azzopardi; ***W:*** Thomas Szollosi; ***C:*** Danny Nowak; ***M:*** Christophe Beck.

The Bone Yard 🦴 **1990 (R)** A weird mortuary is the setting for strange goings on when a murder is investigated. **98m/C VHS, DVD.** Ed Nelson, Deborah Rose, Norman Fell, Jim Eustermann, Denise Young, Willie Stratford Jr., Phyllis Diller; ***D:*** James Cummins; ***W:*** James Cummins; ***C:*** Irl Dixon; ***M:*** Kathleen Ann Porter, John Lee Whitener.

Bones 🦴🦴½ **2001 (R)** Combining the best of blaxploitation and horror elements, Dickerson smartly reveals the story of benevolent pimp Jimmy Bones'(Snoop Dogg) disappearance and subsequent resurrection 22 years later as a vengeful spirit. When an entreprenuerial buppie (Kain) decides to open a dance hall in Jimmy's former digs, walls begin oozing, animals become abundant and mean, and old secrets are revealed, much to the chagrin of the kid's rich father (Davis), and a cop (Weiss). Grier shines as a neighborhood psychic, and Snoop adds miles of style and presence, keeping this one a notch above the standard-issue haunted house fare. **94m/C VHS, DVD, Wide.** Snoop Dogg, Pam Grier, Michael T. Weiss, Clifton Powell, Ricky Harris, Bianca Lawson, Khalil Kain, Katharine Isabelle, Merwin Mondesir, Sean Amsing; ***D:*** Ernest R. Dickerson; ***W:*** Adam Simon; ***C:*** Flavio Labiano; ***M:*** Elia Cmiral.

The Bonfire of the Vanities 🦴½ **1990 (R)** If you liked Tom Wolfe's viciously satirical novel, chances are you won't like this version. If you didn't read the book, you probably still won't like it. Miscast and stripped of the book's gutsy look inside its characters, the film's sole attribute is Vilmos Zsigmond's photography. Hanks is all wrong as wealthy Wall Street trader Sherman McCoy who, lost in the back streets of the Bronx, panics and accidentally kills a young black kid. Willis' drunken journalist/narrator, Griffith's mistress, and Freeman's righteous judge are all awkward and thinly written. If you're still awake, look for F. Murray Abraham's cameo as the Bronx D.A. **126m/C VHS, DVD, 8mm, Wide.** Tom Hanks, Melanie Griffith, Bruce Willis, Morgan Freeman, Alan King, Kim Cattrall, Saul Rubinek, Clifton James, Donald Moffat, Richard Libertini, Andre Gregory, Robert Stephens; ***Cameos:*** F. Murray Abraham; ***D:*** Brian DePalma; ***W:*** Michael Cristofer; ***C:*** Vilmos Zsigmond; ***M:*** Dave Grusin.

Bongwater 🦴🦴 **1998 (R)** David (Wilson) is a Portland pot dealer and aspiring artist who becomes roommates with Serena (Witt), although mixed signals prevents anything closer even if David is definitely lovesick. Thanks to a misunderstanding, Serena heads to New York, a bong ignites the house where David was living—burning it to the ground—and he is forced to rely on the kindness of his fellow pot buddies while Serena has her own problems in the Big Apple. However, you won't really care except Wilson is appealing in a goofy doper sort of way. **98m/C VHS, DVD.** Luke Wilson, Alicia Witt, Amy Locane, Brittany Murphy, Jack Black, Andy Dick, Jeremy Sisto, Jamie Kennedy, Scott Caan, Patricia Wettig; ***D:*** Richard Sears; ***W:*** Nora Macoby, Eric Weiss; ***C:*** Richard Crudo; ***M:*** Mark Mothersbaugh, Josh Mancell.

Bonjour Tristesse 🦴🦴🦴 **1957** An amoral French girl (Seberg) conspires to break up her playboy father's (Niven) upcoming marriage to her stuffy godmother (Kerr) in order to maintain her decadent freedom. Preminger attempted, unsuccessfully, to use this soaper to catapult Seberg to stardom. Based on the novel by Francoise Sagan. **94m/B VHS.** *FR* Deborah Kerr, David Niven, Jean Seberg, Mylene Demongeot, Geoffrey Horne, Walter Chiari, Jean Kent; ***D:*** Otto Preminger; ***W:*** Arthur Laurents; ***C:*** Georges Perinal.

Bonnie & Clyde 🦴🦴🦴½ **1967** Based on the biographies of the violent careers of Bonnie Parker (Dunaway) and Clyde Barrow (Beatty), who roamed the Southwest robbing banks. In the Depression era, when any job, even an illegal one, was cherished, money, greed, and power created an unending cycle of violence and fury. Highly controversial and influential, with pronounced bloodshed (particularly the pairs balletic and bullet-ridden end) that spurred mainstream cinematic proliferation. Established Dunaway as a star; produced by Beatty in one of his best performances. **111m/C VHS, DVD.** Warren Beatty, Faye Dunaway, Michael J. Pollard, Gene Hackman, Estelle Parsons, Denver Pyle, Gene Wilder, Dub Taylor, Evans Evans; ***D:*** Arthur Penn; ***W:*** David Newman, Robert Benton; ***C:*** Burnett Guffey; ***M:*** Charles Strouse. Oscars '67: Cinematog., Support. Actress (Parsons); AFI '98: Top 100, Natl. Film Reg. '92;; N.Y. Film Critics '67: Screenplay; Natl. Soc. Film Critics '67: Screenplay, Support. Actor (Hackman); Writers Guild '67: Orig. Screenplay.

Bonnie Prince Charlie 🦴🦴½ **1948** Historical epic opening in 1745 and romanticizing the title pretender to the British throne, who united Scottish clans in a doomed campaign against King George. Talky and rather slow-moving except for stirring battle scenes. A notorious boxoffice flop in its native Britain, where the original running time was 140 minutes. **114m/C VHS.** *GB* David Niven, Margaret Leighton, Judy Campbell, Jack Hawkins, Morland Graham, Finlay Currie, Elwyn Brook-Jones, John Laurie; ***D:*** Anthony Kimmins.

Bonnie Scotland 🦴🦴½ **1935** Laurel & Hardy accidentally join an India-bound Scottish regiment. Laughs aplenty. **81m/B VHS.** Stan Laurel, Oliver Hardy, James Finlayson, Daphne Pollard, June Lang; ***D:*** James W. Horne.

Bonnie's Kids 🦴½ **1973 (R)** Two sisters become involved in murder, sex, and stolen money. **107m/C VHS.** Tiffany Bolling, Robin Mattson, Scott Brady, Alex Rocco; ***D:*** Arthur Marks.

The Boogey Man 🦴🦴 **1980 (R)** Through the reflection in a mirror, a girl witnesses her brother murder their mother's lover. Twenty years later this memory still haunts her; the mirror is now broken, revealing its special powers. Who will be next? Murder menagerie; see footage from this flick mirrored in "The Boogey Man 2." **93m/C VHS, DVD, Wide.** John Carradine, Suzanna Love, Ron James; ***D:*** Ulli Lommel; ***W:*** Ulli Lommel, Suzanna Love; ***C:*** Jochen Breitenstein, David Sperling; ***M:*** Tim Krog.

Boogey Man 2 woof! **1983** The story continues; same footage, new director but with Lommel, the director of the original "Boogey Man," co-writing the script and appearing in the film. **90m/C VHS.** John Carradine, Suzanna Love, Shannah Hall, Ulli Lommel, Sholto Von Douglas; ***D:*** Bruce Starr.

Boogie Boy 🦴½ **1998 (R)** Recently released from prison, Jesse (Dacascos) gets involved as muscle for a drug deal involving his ex-cellmate, the drug-addicted Larry (Woolvett), in order to get some quick cash. Naturally, the deal goes sour and they wind up on the lam. **110m/C VHS, DVD.** Mark Dacascos, Emily Lloyd, Jaimz Woolvett, Traci Lords, Frederic Forrest, Joan Jett, Ben Browder, James Lew, Linnea Quigley; ***D:*** Craig Hamann; ***W:*** Craig Hamann; ***M:*** Tim Truman.

Boogie Nights 🦴🦴🦴½ **1997 (R)** Epic tale covering the rise and fall of porn star Eddie Adams (Wahlberg). The protege of director Jack Horner (Reynolds), 17-year-old Eddie jumps in a hot tub at an industry bash, christens himself Dirk Diggler, and goes on to become the toast of the adult entertainment industry. Brilliantly spanning the decadent disco-era 70s and the excess of the 80s, 27-year-old writer/director Anderson boldly delves into fresh, albeit dangerous, territory most successfully in this lengthy sophomore outing. What Tarantino did for Travolta, Anderson does here for Reynolds, who plays the past-his-prime but touchingly ambitious auteur with a dream to make a legitimately legendary skin flick. Wahlberg proves himself a serious and seriously good actor in his turn, surrounded by equally fine performances of the ensemble cast. Details such as wardrobe, bits of dialogue, and music are deftly used, avoiding parody. Nonstop disco and early 80s music, often with a message, and energetic camera work make you shake your booty. **155m/C VHS, DVD.** Michael Penn, Mark Wahlberg, Burt Reynolds, Julianne Moore, Don Cheadle, William H. Macy, Heather Graham, John C. Reilly, Luis Guzman, Philip Seymour Hoffman, Alfred Molina, Philip Baker Hall, Robert Ridgely, Joanna Gleason, Thomas Jane, Ricky Jay, Nicole Parker, Melora Walters, Michael Jace, Nina Hartley, John Doe, Laurel Holloman, Robert Downey; ***D:*** Paul Thomas Anderson; ***W:*** Paul Thomas Anderson; ***C:*** Robert Elswit; ***M:*** Michael Penn. Golden Globes '98: Support. Actor (Reynolds); L.A. Film Critics '97: Support. Actor (Reynolds), Support. Actress (Moore); MTV Movie Awards '98: Breakthrough Perf. (Graham); N.Y. Film Critics '97: Support. Actor (Reynolds); Natl. Soc. Film Critics '97: Support. Actor (Reynolds), Support. Actress (Moore).

Book of Love 1991 (PG-13) "Zany" hijinks as a teenager struggles with friendship, girls, and those all-important hormones when he moves to a new neighborhood in the mid-'50s. Average rehash of every '50s movie and TV show cliche in existence. Surprise! There's a classic rock 'n' roll soundtrack. Adapted by Kotzwinkle from his novel "Jack in the Box." **88m/C VHS, 8mm.** Chris Young, Keith Coogan, Aeryk Egan, Josie Bissett, Tricia Leigh Fisher, Danny Nucci, Michael McKean, John Cameron Mitchell, Lewis Arquette; ***D:*** Robert Shaye; ***W:*** William Kotzwinkle; ***M:*** Stanley Clarke.

Book of Shadows: Blair Witch 2 ½ *Blair Witch 2* 2000 (R) Thankfully, they've gotten rid of the shaky-cam (which shook more than a few viewers' stomachs), that's one plus for this sequel that finds five followers of the Blair Witch myth heading back into the woods. Unfortunately, they've also gotten rid of the scares produced by mysterious offscreen witchy shenanigans and replaced them with buckets of fake blood. This group is led by Jeff (Donovan), a townie who's decided to cash in on the Blair Witch craze by organizing tours of the sites made famous in the first movie. Grad students Tristen (Skyler) and Stephen (Turner), practicing Wiccan Erica (Leerhsen) and goth-chick Kim (Director), have fun skewering the movie and its internet movement while partying on the first night. The next day they realize they've lost five hours of their lives. They try to discover what happened, and if it has anything to do with another tour group getting disemboweled. Disappointing fictional debut from documentary director Berlinger, who filmed the truly horrific (and true) "Paradise Lost: The Child Murders at Robin Hood Hills." The townspeople of Burkittsville, Maryland were so fed up with the first film that the second was filmed elsewhere. **90m/C VHS, DVD, Wide.** Jeffrey Donovan, Kim Director, Tristen Skylar, Stephen Barker Turner, Erica Leerhsen; ***D:*** Joe Berlinger; ***W:*** Joe Berlinger, Dick Beebe; ***C:*** Nancy Schreiber; ***M:*** Carter Burwell. Golden Raspberries '00: Worst Remake/Sequel.

The Book of Stars ½ 1999 Penny (Masterson) is the older sister and only support for teenaged Mary (Malone), who suffers from cystic fibrosis. Penny is a jaded, pill-popping hooker while Mary, however, refuses to give up her optomistic outlook on life. With the aid of cantankerous neighbor Professor (Lindo) and a couple of new friends, Mary is determined to change Penny's views as well. Manages to skirt the subject's inherent sentimentality with some winning performances. **98m/C VHS, DVD.** Mary Stuart Masterson, Jena Malone, Karl Geary, D.B. Sweeney, Delroy Lindo; ***D:*** Michael Miner; ***W:*** Tasca Shadix; ***C:*** James Whitaker; ***M:*** Richard Gibbs. VIDEO

Boom! ½ 1968 (PG) Laughable adaptation of the Williams' play "The Milk Train Doesn't Stop Here Anymore" was a Hollywood star disaster. Flora Goforth (Taylor) is a dying millionairess living in isolated glory on an island near Sardinia. Chris Flanders (Burton) is a wandering poet, nicknamed the "Angel of Death," who shows up and becomes Flora's confidante. Does have pretty scenery. **113m/C VHS.** Elizabeth Taylor, Richard Burton, Noel Coward, Joanna Shimkus, Michael Dunn, Romolo Valli; ***D:*** Joseph Losey; ***W:*** Tennessee Williams; ***C:*** Douglas Slocombe; ***M:*** John Barry.

Boom in the Moon woof! *A Modern Bluebeard* 1946 Keaton fares poorly in this sci-fi comedy. He's trapped on a space ship to the moon. Poor production, with uneven direction and acting. **83m/C VHS.** Buster Keaton, Angel Garasa, Virginia Serret, Fernando Soto Mantequilla, Luis Barreiro; ***D:*** Jaime Salvador.

Boom Town ½ 1940 A lively vintage comedy/drama/romance about two oil-drilling buddies competing amid romantic mix-ups and fortunes gained and lost. **120m/B VHS.** Clark Gable, Spencer Tracy, Claudette Colbert, Hedy Lamarr, Frank Morgan, Lionel Atwill, Chill Wills, Curt Bois; ***D:*** Jack Conway.

Boomerang 1947 Film noir based on actual events features the murder of a Connecticut clergyman and the quick arrest of vagrant John Waldron (Kennedy). Prosecuting attorney Henry Harvey (Andrews) is told by his political bosses to get an equally quick conviction to stem public outrage. The evidence seems overwhelming but Harvey begins his own investigation and suddenly switches to the defense to prove Waldron's innocence in dramatic courtroom style. Kazan filmed on location in Bridgeport, CT in a successful semi-documentary style that heightened the tension. **88m/B VHS.** Dana Andrews, Arthur Kennedy, Lee J. Cobb, Jane Wyatt, Cara Williams, Sam Levene, Ed Begley Sr., Karl Malden, Taylor Holmes, Robert Keith; ***D:*** Elia Kazan; ***W:*** Richard Murphy; ***C:*** Norbert Brodine; ***M:*** David Buttolph.

Boomerang ½ 1976 A father rescues his wrongly convicted son from prison. Dubbed. **101m/C VHS.** *IT* Alain Delon, Carla Gravina, Dora Doll; ***D:*** Jose Giovanni.

Boomerang 1992 (R) Successful, womanizing marketing exec for a cosmetics company (Murphy) meets his match when he falls for a colleague (Givens) who is as vain and sexually predatory as he is. She treats him the way he treats women (as a sex object), and he's shocked into the arms of a nice girl (Berry). Although it's refreshing to see this sexual role reversal, the typical Murphy-style humor is in play with sexist jokes and a couple of vulgar female characters. Grier and Lawrence are great as Murphy's best friends. Blaustein and Sheffield are the same guys who wrote Murphy's "Coming to America." **118m/C VHS, Wide.** Eddie Murphy, Halle Berry, Robin Givens, David Alan Grier, Martin Lawrence, Grace Jones, Geoffrey Holder, Eartha Kitt, Chris Rock, Tisha Campbell, John Witherspoon, Melvin Van Peebles; ***D:*** Reginald (Reggie) Hudlin; ***W:*** Barry W. Blaustein, David Sheffield.

Boondock Saints 1999 (R) Two Boston Irish-Catholic brothers, Connor (Flanery) and Murphy (Reedus) McManus, turn into unlikely local heroes after the self-defense killings of some Russian mobsters who were threatening to close down their local pub. They turn vigilante, believing they're doing God's work to rid the world of evil, which leads to more slaughter. Investigating the crimes is gay FBI agent Paul Smecker (Dafoe), who is shown reconstructing the carnage in a series of flashbacks. **110m/C VHS, DVD.** Sean Patrick Flanery, Norman Reedus, Willem Dafoe, David Della Rocco, Carlo Rota, Billy Connolly, David Ferry, Brian Mahoney; ***D:*** Troy Duffy; ***W:*** Troy Duffy; ***C:*** Adam Kane; ***M:*** Jeff Danna.

The Boost ½ 1988 (R) A feverish, messy melodrama about a young couple's spiraling decline from yuppie-ish wealth in a haze of cocaine abuse. **95m/C VHS.** James Woods, Sean Young, John Kapelos, Steven Hill, Kelle Kerr, John Rothman, Amanda Blake, Grace Zabriskie; ***D:*** Harold Becker; ***W:*** Darryl Ponicsan; ***C:*** Howard Atherton.

Boot Hill ½ 1969 (PG) Two guys mess with western baddies and wild women in spaghetti oater. **97m/C VHS.** *IT* Terence Hill, Bud Spencer, Woody Strode, Victor Buono, Lionel Stander; ***D:*** Giuseppe Colizzi.

Boot Hill Bandits ½ 1942 "Crash" Corrigan fights on the side of right in this classic western as he helps corral Wells Fargo bandits. **58m/B VHS.** Ray Corrigan, John "Dusty" King, Max Terhune, Jean Brooks, John Merton, Glenn Strange; ***D:*** S. Roy Luby.

Boothill Brigade 1937 Former footballer Brown rides to the rescue when criminals steal land from homesteaders. **58m/B VHS.** Johnny Mack Brown, Claire Rochelle, Dick Curtis, Horace Murphy, Frank LaRue, Edward Cassidy, Bobby Nelson, Frank Ball, Steve Clark; ***D:*** Sam Newfield.

Bootleg 1989 A detective is on a case that leads to crooked politics and espionage. **82m/C VHS.** Ray Meagher; ***D:*** John Prescott.

Bootmen ½ 2000 (R) Young Sean must make his dance dreams come true despite a bitter, critical father and his working-class Australian surroundings. Director Dein Perry has turned his hit show "Tap Dogs" into a fictionalized and semi-autobiographical tale that combines some of the better qualities of "The Full Monty" and the standard twists and turns of so many other dance films. The "Let's put on a show" plot doesn't provide much sustenance to see the viewer through to some of the excellent choreography. Features several players from the original Tap Dogs company. **95m/C VHS.** *AU* Adam Garcia, Sophie Lee, William Zappa, Sam Worthington, Susie Porter; ***D:*** Dein Perry; ***W:*** Steve Worland; ***C:*** Steve Mason. Australian Film Inst. '00: Cinematog., Costume Des., Score.

Boots & Saddles ½ 1937 A young English lord wants to sell the ranch he has inherited but Autry is determined to make him a real Westerner. **54m/B VHS.** Gene Autry, Judith Allen, Smiley Burnette; ***D:*** Joseph Kane.

Boots Malone ½ 1952 An old down-on-his-luck gambling addict and a young, rich kid fascinated by the sordid atmosphere of the racetrack stumble upon one another and form a symbiotic relationship. All goes well for while, but there'd be no movie unless a collection of obstacles suddenly threatens their success, friendship, and even their lives. A rather melodramatic buddy tale, but Holden and Stewart hold interest. **103m/C VHS.** William Holden, John Stewart, Ed Begley Sr., Harry (Henry) Morgan, Whit Bissell; ***D:*** William Dieterle; ***W:*** Harold Buchman, Milton Holmes; ***M:*** Elmer Bernstein.

Boots of Destiny 1937 Cheap western with Maynard and his sidekick Barnett on the lam and coming to the aid of ranch owner Dell. Based on a story by E. Morton Hough. **59m/B VHS.** Ken Maynard, Claudia Dell, Vince Barnett, Edward Cassidy, Martin Garralaga; ***D:*** Arthur Rosson; ***W:*** Arthur Rosson.

Booty Call ½ 1996 (R) Reserved Rushon (Davidson) and conservative Nikki (Jones) have been dating for a couple of months and Rushon's decided they should consummate their relationship. Nikki's more ambivalent and first sets up a double date with her vivacious best friend Lysterine (Fox) and Rushon's bragging buddy Bunz (Foxx). The duos do pair up but since the "no glove, no love" rule prevails, first the guys have to find some condoms. Raunch rules as might be expected but it's an appealing cast. **120m/C VHS, DVD.** Jamie Foxx, Tommy Davidson, Vivica A. Fox, Tamala Jones, Art Malik, Gedde Watanabe, Scott LaRose, Ammie Sin, Bernie Mac, David Hemblen; ***D:*** Jeff Pollack; ***W:*** Takashi Bufford; ***C:*** Ronald Orieux; ***M:*** Robert Folk.

Bopha! 1993 (PG-13) Father-son strife set against the anti-apartheid movement. In the Senior township police officer Mikah takes pride in his peaceful community, particularly in light of the growing unrest in the other townships. Son Zweli has become an activist and wife Rosie must be the family peacemaker. Then a prominent freedom movement member is arrested and two officers of the secret police make their sinister appearance. Well acted; directorial debut of Freeman. Adapted from the play by Percy Mtwa, although the hopeful ending has been changed in the movie. The title, a Zulu word, stands for arrest or detention. Filmed on location in Zimbabwe. **121m/C VHS.** Danny Glover, Maynard Eziashi, Alfre Woodard, Malcolm McDowell, Marius Weyers, Malick Bowens, Robin Smith, Michael Chinyamurindi, Christopher John Hall, Grace Mahlaba; ***D:*** Morgan Freeman; ***W:*** Brian Bird, John Wierick; ***M:*** James Horner.

Bordello 1979 Western spoof about cowboys and shady ladies. **90m/C VHS.** Chuck Connors, Michael Conrad, John Ireland, Isela Vega, George Rivero. TV

The Border 1982 (R) A border guard faces corruption and violence within his department and tests his own sense of decency when the infant of a poor Mexican girl is kidnapped. Excellent cast, fine cinematography, unusual Nicholson performance. **107m/C VHS.** Jack Nicholson, Harvey Keitel, Valerie Perrine, Warren Oates, Elpidia Carrillo; ***D:*** Tony Richardson; ***W:*** Deric Washburn, Walon Green; ***M:*** Ry Cooder.

Border Badmen ½ 1945 It's just another tired old western, even if it does appropriate the classic mystery-thriller plot; following the reading of a silver baron's will, someone starts killing off the relatives. **59m/B VHS.** Buster Crabbe, Lorraine Miller, Charles "Blackie" King, Ray Bennett, Arch (Archie) Hall Sr., Budd Buster, Bud Osborne; ***D:*** Sam Newfield.

Border Bandits 1946 Plodding oater has Brown going after the bad guys. Not only is it a dirty job, but apparently pretty boring. **57m/B VHS.** Johnny Mack Brown, Raymond Hatton, John Merton, Frank LaRue, Steve Clark, Charles Stevens, Bud Osborne; ***D:*** Lambert Hillyer.

Border Caballero ½ 1936 Western star McCoy and lady cowpoke January shoot out the skies in this lackluster McCoy vehicle. Based on a story by Norman S. Hall. **57m/B VHS.** Tim McCoy, Lois January, Ralph Byrd, Ted Adams; ***D:*** Sam Newfield; ***W:*** Joseph O'Donnell.

Border Devils 1932 A boy is pursued by a ruthless gang of outlaws, until he is saved by the good guys. **60m/B VHS.** Harry Carey Sr., Art Mix, George "Gabby" Hayes; ***D:*** William Nigh.

Border Feud 1947 LaRue endeavors to prevent someone who, by instigating a family feud, will claim large gold mine rights. **54m/B VHS.** Lash LaRue, Al "Fuzzy" St. John, Bob Duncan; ***D:*** Ray Taylor.

Border Law ½ 1931 Jones plays a heroic Texas Ranger who goes undercover to find the man who killed his brother. One of Jones' finest outings and far better than most B westerns. **62m/B VHS.** Buck Jones, Lupita Tovar, James Mason, Frank Rice, Glenn Strange; ***D:*** Louis King; ***W:*** Stuart Anthony.

The Border Legion ½ 1940 Sappy retelling of Grey's novel about an outlaw sacrificing himself for a pair of young lovers. This time Rogers is the outlaw with a heart of gold. Originally filmed in 1930 with Jack Holt, Richard Arlen, and Fay Wray. **58m/B VHS.** Roy Rogers, George "Gabby" Hayes, Carol Hughes, Joseph (Joe) Sawyer, Maude Eburne, Jay Novello; ***D:*** Joseph Kane; ***W:*** Olive Cooper, Louis Stevens.

Border Patrol 1943 Another installment in the Hopalong Cassidy series. This time there's a villainous owner of a silvermine to reckon with. A man so low he's abducting hapless Mexicans as they cross the border, forcing them to work his mines. Hoppy is saddled with the task of persuading him that the town ain't big enough for the both of them. Robert Mitchum makes his perfectly forgettable film debut as one of the bad guys. Not one of the best in the series, but plenty of action. **63m/B VHS.** William Boyd, Andy Clyde, Jay Kirby, Russell Simpson, Claudia Drake, George Reeves, Duncan Renaldo; ***D:*** Lesley Selander.

Border Phantom 1937 Steele (whom you might recognize as Canino in "The Big Sleep"), takes on a suave Chinese businessman who heads a mail order business: seems he's smuggling mail-order brides from Mexico in this vintage "B"-grade horse opera. **60m/B VHS.** Bob Steele, Harley Wood, Don Barclay, Karl Hackett, Horace Murphy, Miki Morita; ***D:*** S. Roy Luby.

Border Radio woof! 1988 A rock singer decides to steal a car and try to outrun some tough thugs hot on his trail. **88m/B VHS.** Chris D, Luana Anders; ***D:*** Allison Anders, Kurt Voss; ***W:*** Allison Anders, Kurt Voss; ***M:*** Dave Alvin.

Border Rangers 1950 A man joins the Rangers in order to avenge the murders of his brother and sister-in-law. **57m/B VHS.** Robert Lowery, Donald (Don "Red") Barry, Lyle Talbot, Pamela Blake; ***D:*** William Berke.

Border Romance ½ 1930 Three Americans have their horses stolen by bandits while riding through Mexico. Trouble with the locals follows in this early sound western. **58m/B VHS.** Don Terry, Armida, Marjorie "Babe" Kane, Victor Potel, Nina Martan, J. Frank Glendon, Harry Von Meter, William Costello; ***D:*** Richard Thorpe; ***W:*** Jack Natteford; ***C:*** Harry Zech; ***M:*** Al Short.

Border Roundup 1941 The "Lone Rider" uncovers a gang of thieving crooks. **57m/B VHS.** George Houston, Al "Fuzzy" St. John, Dennis Moore; ***D:*** Sam Newfield.

Border Saddlemates 1952 U.S. government veterinarian Allen is asked to sub for the local doc in the Canadian border town of Pine Rock. But he learns that a gang is using silver fox pelts to smuggle illegal goods into the U.S. and it's up to Allen and the Rhythm Riders to stop them. **67m/B VHS.** Rex Allen, Mary Ellen Kay, Slim Pickens, Roy Barcroft, Forrest Taylor, Jimmy Moss, Zon Murray, Keith McConnell; ***D:*** William Witney; ***W:*** Albert De Mond; ***C:*** John MacBurnie; ***M:*** Stanley Wilson.

Border Shootout 1990 (PG) A trigger-happy sheriff battles a rich young cattle rustler. **110m/C VHS.** Glenn Ford, Charlene Tilton, Jeff Kaake, Michael Horse, Russell Todd, Cody Glenn, Sergio Calderon, Michael Ansara; ***D:*** Chris T. McIntyre.

Border Vengeance ½ 1935 Reb is a member of a family of outlaws. He aims to improve himself and steer his family to the straight and narrow trail. **45m/B VHS.** Reb Russell, Mary Jane Carey, Kenneth MacDonald, Hank Bell, Glenn Strange, Norman Feusier, Charles "Slim" Whitaker; ***D:*** Ray Heinz.

Border Vigilantes 1941 Hoppy and pals try to rid a town of outlaws that even the vigilantes can't run off. The big surprise comes when they find out who the leader of the outlaws is. **61m/B VHS.** William Boyd, Russell Hayden, Andy Clyde, Victor Jory, Morris Ankrum, Frances Gifford, Ethel Wales, Hal Taliaferro; ***D:*** Derwin Abrahams.

Borderline 1950 MacMurray and Trevor play undercover agents trying to infiltrate a Mexican drug ring. With their real identities hidden, they fall for each other and make a run for the border. Although the leads work well together, they're hindered by an occasionally confusing script. Unfortunately, director Seiter never decides whether the material is of a comedic or dramatic nature. **88m/B VHS, DVD.** Fred MacMurray, Claire Trevor, Raymond Burr, Roy Roberts, Jose Torvay, Morris Ankrum, Charles Lane, Don Diamond, Nacho Galindo, Pepe Hern, Richard Irving; ***D:*** William A. Seiter; ***C:*** Lucien N. Andriot; ***M:*** Hans J. Salter.

Borderline 1980 (PG) Bronson is a border patrol guard in pursuit of a murderer in this action flick. Meanwhile, he gets caught up in trying to help an illegal alien and her young child. **106m/C VHS.** Charles Bronson, Wilford Brimley, Bruno Kirby, Benito Morales, Ed Harris, Kenneth McMillan; ***D:*** Jerrold Freedman.

Bordertown Gunfighters ½ 1943 A cowboy breaks up a vicious lottery racket and falls in love in the process. **56m/B VHS.** Wild Bill Elliott, Anne Jeffreys, George "Gabby" Hayes, Ian Keith, Harry Woods, Edward Earle, Karl Hackett, Roy Barcroft, Bud Geary, Carl Sepulveda; ***D:*** Howard Bretherton; ***W:*** Norman S. Hall; ***C:*** Jack Marta.

Boricua's Bond 2000 (R) First-time director Lik (at 21) debuts with an urban drama about Puerto Rican-born artist Tommy (Negron) who would rather paint than be an active part of the South Bronx street gangs that surround him. Then Anglo single mom Susan (Karp) and son Allen (played by Lik) move into the 'hood, where they are immediately hasseled. Tommy befriends Allen but there's a string of not entirely unexpected tragedies that change everyone's lives. **95m/C VHS.** Val Lik, Frankie Negron, Robyn Karp, Marco Sorisio; ***D:*** Val Lik; ***W:*** Val Lik; ***C:*** Brendan Flynt.

Boris and Natasha: The Movie ½ 1992 (PG) The two inept spies from the classic TV cartoon "The Adventures of Rocky and Bullwinkle" star in this mediocre live-action comedy. These nogoodniks are sent by "Fearless Leader" to America and encounter the usual misadventures. For true fun watch the original animated versions. Never released theatrically; it aired for the first time on cable TV. **88m/C VHS.** Sally Kellerman, Dave Thomas, Paxton Whitehead, Andrea Martin, Alex Rocco, Larry Cedar, Arye Gross, Christopher Neame, Anthony Newley; ***Cameos:*** John Candy, John Travolta, Charles Martin Smith; ***D:*** Charles Martin Smith.

B.O.R.N. ½ 1988 (R) Hagen uncovers an underground network of doctors who kill people and sell the body parts and organs. **90m/C VHS.** Ross Hagen, P.J. Soles, William Smith, Hoke Howell, Russ Tamblyn, Amanda Blake, Clint Howard, Rance Howard, Debra Lamb; ***D:*** Ross Hagen.

Born Again 1978 This is the filmed adaptation of Charles Colson's biography of why he became a born again Christian. **110m/C VHS.** Dean Jones, Anne Francis, Dana Andrews, George Brent; ***D:*** Irving Rapper; ***C:*** Harry Stradling Jr.; ***M:*** Les Baxter.

Born American *Arctic Heat* 1986 (R) Pre-Glasnost flick about teenagers vacationing in Finland who "accidentally" cross the Russian border. There they battle the Red Plague. Melodramatic and heavily politicized. Original release banned in Finland. **95m/C VHS.** Mike Norris, Steve Durham, David Coburn, Thalmus Rasulala, Albert Salmi; ***D:*** Renny Harlin.

Born Bad 1997 (R) Teens bungle a bank robbery and hold up in the bank with hostages. The town sheriff wants to end the standoff calmly but the teens' hot-headed leader won't surrender. **84m/C VHS, DVD.** James Remar, Corey Feldman, Taylor Nichols, Justin Walker, Heidi Noelle Lenhardt; ***D:*** Jeff Yonis. **VIDEO**

Born Beautiful ½ 1982 Made for TV. Beautiful young women come to New York, hoping to strike it rich in the world of modeling. At the same time, a still beautiful, but older and overexposed model comes to grips with a change in her career. Well-told, but sugar-coated. **100m/C VHS.** Erin Gray, Ed Marinaro, Polly Bergen, Lori Singer, Ellen Barber, Judith Barcroft, Michael Higgins; ***D:*** Harvey Hart; ***M:*** Brad Fiedel. **TV**

Born Free 1966 The touching story of a game warden in Kenya and his wife raising Elsa the orphaned lion cub. When the cub reaches maturity, they work to return her to life in the wild. Great family entertainment based on Joy Adamson's book. Theme song became a hit. ♪Born Free. **95m/C VHS.** Virginia McKenna, Bill Travers; ***D:*** James Hill; ***W:*** Lester Cole; ***M:*** John Barry. Oscars '66: Song ("Born Free"), Orig. Score.

Born in America *Dead Aim* 1990 A young orphan is adopted by an undertaker. The boy grows up enveloped by his guardian's business and, when things are slow, works to bring in business himself. **90m/C VHS.** James Westerfield, Glen Lee, Virgil Frye, Venetia Vianello; ***D:*** Jose Antonio Bolanos.

Born in East L.A. 1987 (R) Marin brings his Bruce Springsteen-parody song to life as he plays a mistakenly deported illegal alien who struggles to return to the U.S. Suprisingly resolute effort by the usually self-exploiting Mexican-American. Stern is the American expatriate who helps him get back and Lopez is the love interest who stalls him. **85m/C VHS, DVD.** Richard "Cheech" Marin, Daniel Stern, Paul Rodriguez, Jan-Michael Vincent, Kamala Lopez, Tony Plana, Vic Trevino, A. Martinez; ***D:*** Richard "Cheech" Marin; ***W:*** Richard "Cheech" Marin; ***C:*** Alex Phillips Jr.; ***M:*** Lee Holdridge.

Born Innocent ½ 1974 As if "The Exorcist" weren't bad enough, Blair is back for more abuse-on-film, this time as a 14-year-old runaway from a dysfunctional family who lands in a reform school for girls. There, she must struggle to be as brutal as her peers in order to survive. Fairly tame by today's standards, but controversial at its made-for-TV premiere, chiefly due to a rape scene involving a broom handle. First trip up the river for Blair. **92m/C VHS.** Linda Blair, Joanna Miles, Kim Hunter, Richard Jaeckel, Janit Baldwin, Mitch Vogel; ***D:*** Donald Wrye; ***M:*** Fred Karlin. **TV**

Born Killer ½ 1989 Teenagers in the woods meet up with murderous escaped convicts. **90m/C VHS.** Francine Lapensee, Fritz Matthews, Ted Prior, Adam Tucker; ***D:*** Kimberly Casey.

Born Losers 1967 (PG) The original "Billy Jack" film in which the Indian martial arts expert takes on a group of incorrigible bikers bothering some California babes and runs afoul of the law. Classic drive-in fare. **112m/C VHS.** Tom Laughlin, Elizabeth James, Jeremy Slate, William Wellman Jr., Robert Tessier, Jane Russell, Stuart Lancaster, Edwin Cook, Jeff Cooper; ***D:*** Tom Laughlin; ***W:*** E. James Lloyd, Tom Laughlin; ***C:*** Gregory Sandor.

Born of Fire ½ 1987 (R) A flutist investigating his father's death seeks the Master Musician; his search leads him to the volcanic (and supernatural) mountains of Turkey. **84m/C VHS.** Peter Firth, Susan Crowley, Stephan Kalipha; ***D:*** Jamil Dehlavi; ***M:*** Colin Towns.

Born on the Fourth of July ½ 1989 (R) A riveting meditation on American life affected by the Vietnam War, based on the real-life, best-selling experiences of Ron Kovic, though some facts are subtly changed. The film follows him as he develops from a naive recruit to an angry, wheelchair-bound paraplegic to an active antiwar protestor. Well-acted and generally lauded; Kovic co-wrote the screenplay and appears as a war veteran in the opening parade sequence. **145m/C VHS, DVD, Wide.** Bill Allen, Tom Cruise, Kyra Sedgwick, Raymond J. Barry, Jerry Levine, Tom Berenger, Willem Dafoe, Frank Whaley, John Getz, Caroline Kava, Bryan Larkin, Abbie Hoffman, Stephen Baldwin, Josh Evans, Dale Dye, William Baldwin, Don "The Dragon" Wilson, Vivica A. Fox, Holly Marie Combs, Tom Sizemore, Daniel Baldwin, Ron Kovic; ***Cameos:*** Oliver Stone; ***D:*** Oliver Stone; ***W:*** Oliver Stone; ***C:*** Robert Richardson; ***M:*** John Williams. Oscars '89: Director (Stone), Film Editing; Directors Guild '89: Director (Stone); Golden Globes '90: Actor—Drama (Cruise), Director (Stone), Film—Drama, Screenplay.

Born Reckless ½ 1959 Van Doren plays a singer working the rodeo circuit who falls for aging rider Richards. Not bad enough to be funny, however, Van Doren shows an incredible lack of talent while singing several tunes. ♪Song of the Rodeo; Born Reckless; A Little Longer; Home Type Girl; Separate the Men from the Boys; Something to Dream About; You, Lovable You. **79m/B VHS.** Mamie Van Doren, Jeff Richards, Arthur Hunnicutt, Carol Ohmart, Donald (Don "Red") Barry, Nacho Galindo; ***D:*** Howard W. Koch.

Born Romantic 2000 (R) Six lonely Londoners converge at a salsa club hoping to find a little romance. There's screwy Jocelyn (McCormack), no-nonsense Mo (Horrocks), uptight Eleanor (Williams), would-be Lothario Frank (Ferguson), awkward Eddie (Mistry), and lovelorn Fergus (Morrissey). Cabbie Jimmy (Lester) offers advice. Enjoyable (if predictable) romantic comedy. **97m/C VHS, DVD, Wide.** *GB* Craig Ferguson, Adrian Lester, Catherine McCormack, Jimi Mistry, David Morrissey, Olivia Williams, Jane Horrocks, Hermione Norris, Ian Hart, Kenneth Cranham, John Thompson, Paddy Considine; ***D:*** David Kane; ***W:*** David Kane; ***C:*** Robert Alazraki; ***M:*** Simon Boswell.

Born to Be Bad ½ 1950 Fontaine, an opportunistic woman who was b-b-born to be b-b-bad, attempts to steal a wealthy business man away from his wife while carrying on an affair with a novelist. Ray's direction (he's best known for "Rebel Without a Cause," filmed five years later) prevents the film from succumbing to standard Hollywood formula. **93m/B VHS.** Joan Fontaine, Robert Ryan, Zachary Scott, Joan Leslie, Mel Ferrer; ***D:*** Nicholas Ray.

Born to Be Wild 1938 A pair of truck drivers are commissioned to deliver a shipment of dynamite. The dynamite will be used to destroy a dam, preventing the surrounding land from falling into the hands of unscrupulous land barons. Good action picture thanks to the cast. **66m/B VHS.** Ralph Byrd, Doris Weston, Ward Bond, Robert Emmett Keane, Bentley Hewlett, Charles Williams; ***D:*** Joseph Kane.

Born to Be Wild ½ 1995 (PG) Rebellious teenager Rick (Hornoff) befriends Katie, the three-year-old gorilla his behaviorial scientist mom (Shaver) is studying. When Katie's owner (Boyle) decides she would make a better sideshow attraction than science project, Rick busts her out and they head for the Canadian border. Animal slapstick and bodily function jokes ensue as the chase continues. "Free Willy"-inspired plot and primate hijinks should keep young kids interested, but anyone over the age of nine probably won't be too impressed. **98m/C VHS.** Thomas F. Wilson, Wil Horneff, Helen Shaver, Peter Boyle, Jean Marie Barnwell, John C. McGinley, Marvin J. McIntyre; ***D:*** John Gray; ***W:*** John Bunzel, Paul Young; ***C:*** Donald M. Morgan.

Born to Boogie 1972 A concert, a chronicle, and a tribute, "Born To Boogie" is about Marc Bolan and his band T. Rex. The film, which features concert footage from a 1972 concert at the Wembley Empire Pool in London, chronicles the glitter rock era and the next wave of British rock and roll, and pays tribute to Bolan, who died in 1977 just as he was starting a comeback. Ringo Starr and Elton John join T. Rex in the studio for "Children of the Revolution" and "Tutti-Frutti" as well as a psychadelic soiree where Bolan plays acoustic versions of his hits. This film was never released in the United States. **75m/C VHS.** Marc Bolan, Elton John, Ringo Starr; ***D:*** Ringo Starr.

Born to Dance ½ 1936 A quintessential MGM 1930s dance musical, wherein a beautiful dancer gets a sailor and a big break in a show. Great songs by Cole Porter sung in a less than great manner by a gangly Stewart. Powell's first starring vehicle. ♪Love Me Love My Pekinese; I've Got You Under My Skin; Hey Babe Hey; Easy to Love; Rolling Home; Rap Tap on Wood; Entrance of Lucy James; Swingin' the Jinx Away. **108m/B VHS.** Eleanor Powell, James Stewart, Virginia Bruce, Una Merkel, Frances Langford, Sid Silvers, Raymond Walburn, Reginald Gardiner, Buddy Ebsen; ***D:*** Roy Del Ruth; ***M:*** Cole Porter, Cole Porter.

Born to Kill *Lady of Deceit* 1947 A ruthless killer marries a girl for her money. Minor tough-as-nails film noir exemplifying Tierney's stone-faced human-devil film persona. **92m/B VHS.** Lawrence Tierney, Claire Trevor, Walter Slezak, Elisha Cook Jr.; ***D:*** Robert Wise.

Born to Race 1988 (R) In the world of competitive auto racing, a beautiful engineer is kidnapped for her new controversial engine design. **95m/C VHS.** Joseph Bottoms, George Kennedy, Marc Singer, Marla Heasly; ***D:*** James Fargo.

Born to Ride 1991 (PG) A biker rebel joins the Army prior to WWII in order to escape a prison term after a good ol' boy brush with the law. He shuns Army discipline, but proves himself in action as the leader of a scout troup for the Army's motorcycle cavalry brigade. Available with Spanish subtitles. **88m/C VHS.** John Stamos, John Stockwell, Teri Polo, Kris Kamm; ***D:*** Graham Baker.

Born to Run ½ 1993 Nicky Donatello (Grieco) is a Brooklyn street drag racer who gets mixed up with the mob while trying to rescue his no-account brother. But he still finds time to fall for an uptown model who also happens to be the mobster's girlfriend. **97m/C VHS.** Richard Grieco, Jay Acovone, Shelli Lether, Christian Campbell, Brent Stait, Martin Cummins, Wren Roberts, Joe Cortese; ***D:*** Albert Magnoli; ***W:*** Randall Badat. **TV**

Born to Win ½ *Addict* 1971 (R) A New York hairdresser with an expensive drug habit struggles through life in this well-made comedy drama. Excellent acting from fine cast, and interestingly photographed. Not well received when first released, but worth a look. **90m/C VHS, DVD.** George Segal, Karen Black, Paula Prentiss, Hector Elizondo, Robert De Niro, Jay Fletcher; ***D:*** Ivan Passer; ***W:*** Ivan Passer, David Scott Milton; ***C:*** Jack Priestley; ***M:*** William S. Fisher.

Born Wild ½ 1995 (PG) Documentary filmmaker Christine Shaye (Shields) has just gotten her first important assignment from overbearing boss Dan Walker (Sheen), which is to capture the beauty of Africa. Christine arrives at the South African game preserve of Londolozi where she meets passionate conservationist John Varty (who plays himself). Varty has filmed one leopard family for 12 years but when the mother leopard is killed, he violates his own ethical code when he rescues her two orphaned cubs. **98m/C VHS.** Brooke Shields, Martin Sheen, John Varty, David Keith; ***D:*** Duncan McLachlan; ***W:*** Duncan McLachlan, Andrea Buck.

Born Yesterday 🦴🦴🦴½ **1950** Ambitious junk dealer Harry Brock (Crawford) is in love with smart but uneducated Billie Dawn (Holliday). He hires newspaperman Paul Verrall (Holden) to teach her the finer points of etiquette. During their sessions, they fall in love and Billie realizes how she has been used by Brock. She retaliates against him and gets to deliver that now-famous line: "Do me a favor, drop dead." Holliday is a solid gold charmer as the not-so-dumb blonde, in the role she originated in Garson Kanin's Broadway play. Remade in 1993. **103m/B VHS, DVD.** Judy Holliday, Broderick Crawford, William Holden, Howard St. John, Frank Otto, Larry Oliver, Barbara Brown; ***D:*** George Cukor; ***W:*** Albert Mannheimer; ***C:*** Joseph Walker; ***M:*** Frederick "Friedrich" Hollander. Oscars '50: Actress (Holliday); Golden Globes '51: Actress—Mus./Comedy (Holliday).

Born Yesterday 🦴🦴 **1993 (PG)** Remake of the 1950 classic suffers in comparison, particularly Griffith, who has the thankless task of surpassing (or even meeting) Judy Holliday's Oscar-winning mark as not-so-dumb blonde Billie Dawn. Her intellectual inadequacies are glaring when she hits the political world of D.C. with obnoxious tycoon boyfriend Goodman. To save face, he hooks her up with a journalist (Johnson) willing to coach her in Savvy 101, a la Eliza Doolittle. What worked well in post-WWII America seems sadly outdated today; stick with the original. **102m/C VHS, Wide.** Melanie Griffith, John Goodman, Don Johnson, Edward Herrmann, Max Perlich, Fred Dalton Thompson, Nora Dunn, Benjamin C. Bradlee, Sally Quinn, Michael Ensign, William Frankfather, Celeste Yarnall, Meg Wittner; ***D:*** Luis Mandoki; ***W:*** Douglas McGrath; ***C:*** Lajos Koltai; ***M:*** George Fenton.

The Borrower 🦴🦴 **1989 (R)** An exiled unstable mutant insect alien serial killer (you know the type) must switch heads with human beings regularly to survive. This colorful, garish gorefest has humor and attitude, but never develops behind the basic grossout situation. **97m/C VHS.** Rae Dawn Chong, Don Gordon, Antonio Fargas, Tom Towles; ***D:*** John McNaughton.

The Borrowers 🦴🦴🦴 **1993** Excellent TV adaptation of the May Norton children's classics "The Borrowers" and "The Borrowers Afield." This miniature family (about mouse-size) live beneath the floorboards of an English house and borrow what they need to survive from the normal-sized human inhabitants. Problems come when the teeny family are discovered and must make their way to a new home. Sweet and humorous. **199m/C VHS.** *GB* Ian Holm, Penelope Wilton, Rebecca Callard, Paul Cross, Sian Phillips, Tony Haygarth; ***D:*** John Henderson; ***W:*** Richard Carpenter; ***C:*** Clive Tickner; ***M:*** Howard Goodall. **TV**

The Borrowers 🦴🦴½ **1997 (PG)** Charming big-screen, big-budget tale about the little people who live under the floor. The British, elfin, and about four inch tall Clock family, headed by papa Pod (Broadbent) lives hidden in the walls of the home of the normal-sized American Lenders and exist by "borrowing" objects from their human's household. When an evil lawyer (Goodman), also American, threatens their happiness, the Borrowers bond with young Peter Lender (Pierce) who "discovers" them and volunteers to help them save their way of life. This remake focuses mainly on the impressive special effects, lending a modern look and appeal. Goodman is lovably evil in that wonderfully Snidely Whiplash way. Based on the children's books of Mary Norton. **86m/C VHS, DVD, Wide.** *GB* John Goodman, Hugh Laurie, Jim Broadbent, Mark Williams, Celia Imrie, Bradley Michael Pierce, Raymond Pickard, Aden (John) Gillett, Ruby Wax, Flora Newbigin, Tom Felton, Doon Mackichan; ***D:*** Peter Hewitt; ***W:*** John Camps, Gavin Scott; ***C:*** John Fenner, Trevor Brooker; ***M:*** Harry Gregson-Williams.

Borsalino 🦴🦴🦴 **1970 (R)** Delon and Belmondo are partners in crime in this seriocomic film about gang warfare in 1930s Marseilles. The costumes, settings, and music perfectly capture the mood of the period. Followed by a sequel "Borsalino and Co." Based on "The Bandits of Marseilles" by Eugene Saccomano. **124m/C VHS.** *FR* Jean-Paul Belmondo, Alain Delon, Michel Bouquet, Catherine Rouvel, Francoise Christophe, Corinne Marchand; ***D:*** Jacques Deray; ***W:*** Jacques Deray, Jean Cau, Claude Sautet, Jean-Claude Carriere; ***C:*** Jean-Jacques Tarbes; ***M:*** Claude Bolling.

Boss 🦴½ *The Black Bounty Killer; Boss Nigger* **1974 (PG)** Blaxploitation western parody with Williamson and Martin as a couple of bounty hunters tearing apart a town to find a fugitive. Relatively non-violent. **87m/C VHS.** Fred Williamson, D'Urville Martin, R.G. Armstrong, William Smith, Carmen Hayworth, Barbara Leigh; ***D:*** Jack Arnold; ***W:*** Fred Williamson.

Boss Cowboy 🦴 **1935** A cowboy shows who wears the chaps in his family when he kidnaps his girlfriend to prevent her from moving East. **51m/B VHS.** Buddy Roosevelt, Frances Morris, Sam Pierce, Fay McKenzie, Lafe (Lafayette) McKee; ***D:*** Victor Adamson.

The Boss Is Served 🦴🦴 *La Padrona e Servita* **1976** A mother (Berger) and three daughters, racked with debt, are forced to take in boarders. The lascivious man and teenage son want to be more than just boarders to the lovely Berger. In Italian with English subtitles. **95m/C VHS.** *IT* Senta Berger, Maurizio Arena, Bruno Zanin, Erika Blanc, Pina Cei, Angiolina Quinterno, Patrizia de Clara; ***D:*** Mario Lanfranchi; ***W:*** Mario Lanfranchi, Pupi Avati; ***C:*** Pasquale Fanetti; ***M:*** Stelvio Cipriano.

Boss of Big Town 🦴🦴 **1943** Gangsters try to infiltrate the milk industry in this standard crime drama. **65m/B VHS.** John Litel, Florence Rice, H.B. Warner, Jean Brooks, John Miljan, Mary Gordon, John Maxwell; ***D:*** Arthur Dreifuss.

Boss of Bosses 🦴½ **1999** Yet another in a long line of Mafia portrayals and betrayals but this one is flat and uninspired. Paul Castellano (Palminteri) takes organized crime into the white-collar level from the streets into legit businesses but the world is still violent, plagued by internal feuds and the feds sniffing around. Castellano wound up being the last public Mafia hit (arranged by John Gotti)—outside a New York steak house. **94m/C VHS, DVD, Wide.** Chazz Palminteri, Daniel Benzali, Jay O. Sanders, Clancy Brown, Al Ruscio, Steven Bauer, Angela Alvarado, Sonny Marinelli; ***D:*** Dwight Little; ***W:*** Jere P. Cunningham; ***C:*** Brian Reynolds; ***M:*** John Altman. **CABLE**

Boss of Bullion City 🦴½ **1941** A crooked sheriff is exposed by Brown and sidekick Knight in this sagebrush saga. Based on a story by Arthur St. Claire. **61m/B VHS.** Johnny Mack Brown, Fuzzy Knight, Maria Montez, Earle Hodgins, Harry Woods; ***D:*** Ray Taylor; ***W:*** Victor McLeod, Arthur St. Claire.

Boss of Rawhide 🦴 **1944** The Texas Rangers fight for law and order in the old west despite odds against them. **60m/B VHS.** Dave O'Brien, James Newill, Guy Wilkerson, Nell O'Day, Edward Cassidy, Jack Ingram, Billy Bletcher, Charles "Blackie" King, George Chesebro; ***D:*** Elmer Clifton; ***W:*** Elmer Clifton; ***C:*** Robert C. Cline; ***M:*** Lee Zahler, Oliver Drake, Herbert Myers, Dave O'Brien, James Newill.

Boss' Son 🦴🦴🦴 **1978** Worthwhile coming-of-age tale about a young man who learns more than he bargained for about life when he goes to work for his father in the family carpet business. Dad feels he should work his way up through the ranks and makes him a delivery man. The young man meets reality head on and must deal with the injustices of the world around him. Independently filmed by director/writer Roth. **97m/C VHS.** Rita Moreno, James Darren, Asher Brauner, Rudy Solari, Henry Sanders, Richie Havens, Piper Laurie, Elena Verdugo; ***D:*** Bobby Roth; ***W:*** Bobby Roth; ***C:*** Alfonso Beato.

The Boss' Wife 🦴🦴 **1986 (R)** A young stockbroker attempts to fix what's wrong with his life by maneuvering sexually with the boss' wife, and complications set in. **83m/C VHS.** Daniel Stern, Arielle Dombasle, Christopher Plummer, Martin Mull, Melanie Mayron, Lou Jacobi; ***D:*** Ziggy Steinberg; ***M:*** Bill Conti.

Bossa Nova 🦴🦴½ **1999 (R)** Sexy romantic comedy set to the beat of sultry Brazil. Middleaged American widow Mary (Irivng) teaches English in Rio and catches the romantic eye of Pedro (Fagundes), an attorney who has been dumped by his wife. Meanwhile, Mary's soccer-playing pupil Acacio (Borges) is trying to become a teacher's pet before transferring his affections to Pedro's clerk Sharon (Antonelli), who just happens to be involved with Pedro's half-brother (Cardoso). And the romantic complications just keep building. Soundtrack is filled with the songs of bossa nova composer Antonio Carlos Jobim. Based on the novel "Miss Simpson" by Sergio Sant'Anna. **95m/C VHS, DVD, Wide.** *BR* Amy Irving, Antonio Fagundes, Alexandre Borges, Debora Bloch, Pedro Cardoso, Alberto De Mendoza, Stephen Tobolowsky, Drica Moraes, Giovanna Antonelli, Rogerio Cardoso; ***D:*** Bruno Barreto; ***W:*** Alexandre Machado, Fernanda Young; ***C:*** Pascal Rabaud; ***M:*** Eumir Deodato.

Boston Kickout 🦴🦴 **1995** A quartet of teenaged friends/losers struggle to grow up in a bleak concrete town outside London. There are neglected girlfriends, dysfunctional families, menial jobs, petty crime, emotional disasters—and some faint glimmer of hope for at least a couple of the lads. Title refers to a destructive game the boys play. **105m/C VHS, DVD.** *GB* John Simm, Andrew Lincoln, Richard Hanson, Nathan Valente, Emer McCourt, Marc Warren, Derek Martin, Vincent Phillips, Natalie Davies; ***D:*** Paul Hills; ***W:*** Paul Hills, Diane Whitley, Roberto Troni; ***C:*** Roger Bonnici; ***M:*** Robert Hartshorne.

The Boston Strangler 🦴🦴½ **1968** Based on Gerold Frank's bestselling factual book about the deranged killer who terrorized Boston for about a year and a half. Traces events from first killing to prosecution. Curtis, going against type, is compelling in title role. **116m/C VHS.** Tony Curtis, Henry Fonda, George Kennedy, Murray Hamilton, Mike Kellin, George Voskovec, William Hickey, James Brolin, Hurd Hatfield, William Marshall, Jeff Corey, Sally Kellerman; ***D:*** Richard Fleischer; ***W:*** Edward Anhalt.

The Bostonians 🦴🦴½ **1984 (PG)** A faith healer's daughter is forced to choose between the affections of a militant suffragette and a young lawyer in 19th Century Boston. Based on Henry James' classic novel. **120m/C VHS, DVD.** Christopher Reeve, Vanessa Redgrave, Madeleine Potter, Jessica Tandy, Nancy Marchand, Wesley Addy, Linda Hunt, Wallace Shawn; ***D:*** James Ivory; ***W:*** Ruth Prawer Jhabvala; ***C:*** Walter Lassally. Natl. Soc. Film Critics '84: Actress (Redgrave).

Botany Bay 🦴🦴 **1953** A rousing costumer about a convict ship in the 1700s that, after a trying voyage, lands in Australia, wherein a framed doctor conquers the local plague. From the novel by Charles Nordoff. **99m/C VHS.** Alan Ladd, James Mason, Patricia Medina, Cedric Hardwicke; ***D:*** John Farrow.

Bottle Rocket 🦴🦴½ **1995 (R)** A trio of inexperienced but aspiring criminals attempt to make their mark on the world in suburban Dallas. Newcomers Wilson, who plays the group's ambitious leader Dignan, and Anderson penned this smart ensemble piece first as a 13-minute black and white short. A subsequent showing at the Sundance Film Festival got the attention of producer James L. Brooks ("Broadcast News"). Film got the backing to go feature length with Anderson directing, and deservedly so, with its fresh dialogue and surprising warmth. **91m/C VHS, DVD.** Ned Dowd, Owen C. Wilson, Luke Wilson, Robert Musgrave, Lumi Cavazos, James Caan, Andrew Wilson, Jim Ponds; ***D:*** Wes Anderson; ***W:*** Wes Anderson, Owen C. Wilson; ***C:*** Robert Yeoman; ***M:*** Mark Mothersbaugh. MTV Movie Awards '96: New Filmmaker (Anderson).

Boudu Saved from Drowning 🦴🦴🦴½ *Boudu Sauve des Eaux* **1932** A suicidal tramp completely disrupts the wealthy household of the man that saves him from drowning. A gentle but sardonic farce from the master filmmaker. Remade in 1986 as "Down and Out In Beverly Hills." **87m/B VHS.** *FR* Michel Simon, Charles Granval, Jean Daste, Marcelle Hainia, Severine Lerczinska, Jacques Becker; ***D:*** Jean Renoir; ***W:*** Jean Renoir; ***C:*** Marcel Lucien.

Boulevard 🦴½ **1994 (R)** Jennefer (Wuhrer) is forced to give her baby up for adoption, after escaping from an abusive husband, and make her way on the city's mean streets. She meets prostitute Ola (Chong), who decides to look after the naif and protect Jennefer from violent pimp Hassan (Phillips). But Ola gets into trouble with tough cop Claren (Henriksen) and soon Jennefer must survive on her own—against both Hassan and her vengeful husband. Woman empowerment, complete with standard cliches. **96m/C VHS.** Kari Wuhrer, Rae Dawn Chong, Lou Diamond Phillips, Lance Henriksen, Joel Bissonnette; ***D:*** Penelope Buitenhuis; ***W:*** Rae Dawn Chong; ***M:*** Ian Thomas.

Boulevard Nights 🦴🦴 **1979 (R)** A young Latino man tries to escape his neighborhood's streetgang violence, while his older brother is sucked into it. Music by Schifrin, known for the "Mission: Impossible" theme. **102m/C VHS.** Richard Yniguez, Danny De La Paz, Marta DuBois, Carmen Zapata, Victor Millan; ***D:*** Michael Pressman; ***C:*** John Bailey; ***M:*** Lalo Schifrin.

Boulevard of Broken Dreams 🦴🦴 **1988 (PG-13)** Successful Hollywood screenwriter Tom Garfield (Waters) returns to his native Australia to figure out how his life got so screwed up. His estranged wife is living with someone else and his daughter barely remembers him. Affecting look at personal priorities versus success. **95m/C VHS.** *AU* John Waters, Kim Gyngell, Penelope Stewart; ***D:*** Pino Amenta.

Bounce 🦴🦴½ **2000 (PG-13)** Ad exec Affleck swaps his airline ticket with a stranger who's anxious to get home to his wife. But since no good deed goes unpunished, the plane crashes and the man is killed. The guilt-stricken Affleck visits the stranger's widow (Paltrow) and winds up falling in love with her, only she doesn't know about their unfortunate connection. Okay, the plot is contrived, predictable, and a little schmaltzy, but it somehow avoids maudlin, and takes pains to make the emotions real. In this, director Roos is aided greatly by Affleck, who turns in some of his best work to date, and Paltrow, who seems less actress-y in an understated, smart performance. The two leads were said to be an item during filming. **105m/C VHS, DVD, Wide.** Gwyneth Paltrow, Ben Affleck, Natasha Henstridge, Jennifer Grey, Tony Goldwyn, Joe Morton, David Paymer, Johnny Galecki, Alex D. Linz, Juan Garcia, Sam Robards, Julia Campbell, Michael Laskin, John Levin, David Dorfman; ***D:*** Don Roos; ***W:*** Don Roos; ***C:*** Robert Elswit; ***M:*** Mychael Danna.

Bound 🦴🦴 **1996 (R)** Ex-con Corky (Gershon) is busy fixing up her new apartment after serving five years for robbery. Her next-door neighbors are Caesar (Pantoliano), a neurotic, money-laundering mobster, and his sexy girlfriend, a seemingly dumb brunette named Violet (Tilly). The femme twosome hook up (in and out of bed) and hatch a plan to steal two million freshly laundered dollars from Caesar, who goes ballistic when he discovers the money gone. It's a flashy—but not substantive—thriller. Directorial debut for the brothers Wachowski. **107m/C VHS, DVD.** Gina Gershon, Jennifer Tilly, Joe Pantoliano, John P. Ryan, Barry Kivel, Christopher Meloni, Peter Spellos, Richard Sarafian, Mary Mara, Susie Bright, Ivan Kane, Kevin M. Richardson, Gene Borkan; ***D:*** Andy Wachowski, Larry Wachowski; ***W:*** Andy Wachowski, Larry Wachowski; ***C:*** Bill Pope; ***M:*** Don Davis.

Bound and Gagged: A Love Story 🦴 **1993 (R)** For some reason, Elizabeth (Saltarelli), who is desperate for a husband, thinks that she might increase her chances of finding one if she kidnaps her friend Leslie (Allen) and goes on a weird wild goose chase through Minnesota with the hostage and her hopeless partner-in-crime, Cliff (Denton). Go figure. **96m/C VHS, DVD.** Ginger Lynn Allen, Karen Black, Chris Denton, Elizabeth Saltarelli, Mary Ella Ross, Chris Mulkey; ***D:*** Daniel Appleby; ***W:*** Daniel Appleby; ***C:*** Dean Lent; ***M:*** William Murphy.

Bound for Glory 🦴🦴🦴½ **1976 (PG)** The award-winning biography of American folk singer Woody Guthrie set against the backdrop of the Depression. Superb portrayal of the spirit and feelings of the period featuring many of his songs encased in the incidents that inspired them. Haskell Wexler's award-winning camera work is superbly expressive. **149m/C VHS, DVD.** David Carradine, Ronny Cox, Melinda Dillon, Randy Quaid; ***D:*** Hal Ashby; ***W:*** Robert Getchell; ***C:*** Haskell Wexler. Oscars '76: Cinematog., Orig. Song Score and/or Adapt.; L.A. Film Critics '76: Cinematog.; Natl. Bd. of Review '76: Actor (Carradine); Natl. Soc. Film Critics '76: Cinematog.

The Bounty 🦴🦴½ **1984 (PG)** A new version of "Mutiny on the Bounty," with emphasis on a more realistic relationship between Fletcher Christian and Captain Bligh—and a more sympathetic portrayal of the captain, too. The sensuality of Christian's relationship with a Tahitian beauty also receives greater importance. **130m/C VHS, DVD, Wide.** Mel Gibson, Anthony Hopkins, Laurence Olivier, Edward Fox, Daniel Day-Lewis, Bernard Hill, Philip Davis, Liam Neeson; ***D:*** Roger Donaldson; ***W:*** Robert Bolt; ***C:*** Arthur Ibbetson; ***M:*** Vangelis.

Bounty Hunter 2002 🦴½ *2002: The Rape of Eden* **1994** A rogue virus kills most of the world's population and few of those remaining are completely immune. So slave trading in the capture and sale of immune survivors is a lucrative business and a bounty's hunter's last assignment is to bring in a beautiful but deadly woman. **90m/C VHS.** Phil Nordell, Francine Lapensee, Vernon Wells, Jeff Conaway; ***D:*** Sam Auster; ***W:*** Sam Auster.

Bounty Hunters 🦴🦴 **1989 (R)** A man hunts down his friend's killer. **91m/C VHS.** Robert Ginty, Bo Hopkins, Loeta Waterdown; ***D:*** Robert Ginty.

Bounty Hunters 🦴🦴 **1996 (R)** Rival bounty hunters (and ex-lovers) Jersey Bellini (Dudikoff) and B.B. Mitchell (Howard) join forces to capture bail-jumping, stolen-car king Delmos (Ratner), who's also the target of mob hitmen. Gunplay and car chases. **98m/C VHS, DVD, Wide.** Michael Dudikoff, Lisa Howard, Benjamin Ratner; ***D:*** George Erschbamer; ***W:*** George Erschbamer; ***C:*** A.J. Vesak; ***M:*** Norman Ornstein.

Bounty Hunters 2: Hardball 🦴🦴 *Hardball* **1997 (R)** A bounty hunter and his female partner tick off the mob by foiling a heist and now must fend off hired killers looking for revenge. **97m/C VHS, DVD, Wide.** Michael Dudikoff, Lisa Howard, Steve Bacic, Tony Curtis; ***D:*** George Erschbamer; ***W:*** George Erschbamer, Jeff Barmash, Michael Ellis; ***C:*** Brian Pearson; ***M:*** Leon Aronson. **VIDEO**

The Bounty Man 🦴🦴 **1972** A bounty hunter brings an outlaw in, robbing him of his freedom and his girlfriend. **74m/C VHS.** Clint Walker, Richard Basehart, Margot Kidder, Arthur Hunnicutt, John Ericson, Gene Evans; ***D:*** John Llewellyn Moxey.

Bounty Tracker 🦴½ **1993 (R)** Johnny Damone (Lamas) is a bounty-hunter in pursuit of the killer-for-hire who murdered his brother. This personal vendetta leads to an action-packed martial arts showdown between Johnny and his cold-blooded prey. **90m/C VHS.** Lorenzo Lamas, Matthias Hues, Eugene Glazer, Cyndi Pass, Eric Mansker, Judd Omen, Eddie Frias, George Perez; ***D:*** Kurt Anderson.

Bouquet of Barbed Wire 🦴½ **1976** Overlong soaper revolves around a weathly family and their hidden secrets: incest and infidelity. On three tapes. **330m/C VHS.** Frank Finlay, Susan Penhaligon, Deborah Grant, Sheila Allen, James Aubrey; ***D:*** Tom Wharmby.

The Bourne Identity 🦴🦴🦴 **1988** Chamberlain stars as an amnesiac trying to piece together the fragments of his memory. Is he U.S. espionage agent Jason Bourne or an international terrorist? Aided by Smith (the kidnap victim who falls in love with her captor), the two traverse Europe trying to escape the spy network out to assassinate the mystery man who knows too little. Exciting miniseries adaptation of the Robert Ludlum thriller. **185m/C VHS.** Richard Chamberlain, Jaclyn Smith, Denholm Elliott, Anthony Quayle, Donald Moffat, Yorgo Voyagis; ***D:*** Roger Young; ***W:*** Carol Sobieski. **TV**

The Bourne Identity **2002 (PG-13)** Big-budget, big-screen version of Robert Ludlum's 1981 thriller, previously filmed as a 1988 TV miniseries starring Richard Chamberlain. Jason Bourne (Damon) has amnesia, which is a really bad thing when you appear to be an international assassin with a lot of very bad people chasing you across Europe. Supposedly the first in a planned Jason Bourne trilogy. Not yet reviewed. **?m/C VHS, DVD.** Matt Damon, Franka Potente, Clive Owen, Julia Stiles, Chris Cooper, Brian Cox, Gabriel Mann; ***D:*** Doug Liman; ***W:*** Tony Gilroy, W(illiam) Blake Herron.

Bowery at Midnight 🦴½ **1942** Lugosi plays a man who recycles criminals into zombies that commit crimes for his benefit. Bela and an intense mood can't quite save this pic. **60m/B VHS, DVD.** Bela Lugosi, Tom Neal, Dave O'Brien, Wanda McKay; ***D:*** Wallace Fox; ***W:*** Gerald Schnitzer; ***C:*** Mack Stengler; ***M:*** Edward Kay.

Bowery Blitzkrieg 🦴 *Stand and Deliver* **1941** This lesser "East Side Kids" entry has Gorcey opting to enter the boxing ring rather than turn to crime. Needs more Huntz. **62m/B VHS.** Leo Gorcey, Huntz Hall, Bobby Jordan, Warren Hull, Charlotte Henry, Keye Luke; ***D:*** Wallace Fox.

Bowery Boys Meet the Monsters **1954** The infamous Bowery Boys display their usual hilarious hijinks in this comedy in which they confront a group of transplant-happy scientists. **65m/C VHS.** Leo Gorcey, Huntz Hall, Bernard Gorcey, Bennie Bartlett, Lloyd Corrigan; ***D:*** Edward L. Bernds.

Bowery Buckaroos 🦴🦴 **1947** The Bowery Boys take their act West in search of gold, meeting up with the usual amounts of goofy characters and hilarious misunderstandings. **66m/B VHS.** Leo Gorcey, Huntz Hall, Bobby Jordan, Gabriel Dell, William Benedict, David Gorcey, Julie Briggs, Bernard Gorcey, Chief Yowlachie, Iron Eyes Cody; ***D:*** William Beaudine.

Bowfinger 🦴🦴🦴 *Bowfinger's Big Thing* **1999 (PG-13)** Martin stars as wannabe Hollywood player Bobby Bowfinger, who is desperate to break into the big time. His one hope is to convince action star Kit Ramsey (Murphy) to be in a cheesy sci-fi scare flick entitled "Chubby Rain." But Ramsey and his tyrannical New Age advisor Stricter (Stamp) want nothing to do with the movie. Bowfinger gets a crew together and stalks Ramsey through the streets of L.A., filming his every movement so that the material can be used in the movie. After his tactics send Ramsey to the "relaxation home," Bowfinger hires geeky lookalike Jiff (also Murphy) to take his place. The pairing of Martin and Murphy works well, and Frank Oz is an expert at directing off-beat comedies such as this. **96m/C VHS, DVD.** Steve Martin, Eddie Murphy, Christine Baranski, Heather Graham, Terence Stamp, Jamie Kennedy, Robert Downey Jr., Barry Newman; ***D:*** Frank Oz; ***W:*** Steve Martin; ***C:*** Ueli Steiger; ***M:*** David Newman.

Box of Moonlight 🦴🦴 **1996 (R)** Hardworking, by-the-book electrical systems engineer Al Fountain (Turturo) feels mysteriously compelled to play hookey from his family and career while on an out-of-town business trip. Lost and confused, Al meets up with the Kid, a quirky recluse played with energy and appeal by Rockwell. Through a series of mix-ups, the nice-but-stuffy Al and the wild-but-well-meaning Kid end up spending the fourth of July weekend together. Al's inability to see the point of his journey long after the audience probably has makes the film a bit predictable and stale. DeCillo's third feature was six years in the making and financed by the success of his second feature, Living in Oblivion. **111m/C VHS, DVD.** John Turturro, Sam Rockwell, Catherine Keener, Lisa Blount, Annie Corley, Dermot Mulroney, Alexander Goodwin; ***D:*** Tom DiCillo; ***W:*** Tom DiCillo; ***C:*** Paul Ryan; ***M:*** Jim Farmer.

Boxcar Bertha 🦴🦴½ **1972 (R)** Scorsese's vivid portrayal of the South during the 1930s' Depression casts Hershey as a woman who winds up in cahoots with an anti-establishment train robber. Based on the book "Sister of the Road" by Boxcar Bertha Thomson. **90m/C VHS, DVD, Wide.** Barbara Hershey, David Carradine, John Carradine, Barry Primus, Bernie Casey, Victor Argo, Martin Scorsese, John Stephens; ***D:*** Martin Scorsese; ***W:*** John W. Corrington, Joyce H. Corrington; ***C:*** John Stephens; ***M:*** Gib Guilbeau, Thad Maxwell.

Boxcar Blues 🦴 **1990** Bird (Coufos) is a down and out fighter who decides to fight "The Man" (Ventura), a bare knuckle fighter who enjoys beating his opponents to death. On the way to the fight, in New Orleans, he meets up with his girl Casey (Langrick), along with some other shady characters, including a truck driving preacher. **96m/C VHS.** Paul Coufos, Margaret Langrick, Jesse Ventura, M. Emmet Walsh, Donny Lalonde; ***D:*** Damian Lee.

The Boxer 🦴🦴½ **1997 (R)** Affecting, if predictable, romance set in Ulster, Northern Ireland. Having served 14 years in prison Danny Flynn (Day-Lewis) wants nothing more to do with politics and violence. But his return to his old neighborhood—where he hopes to get back to his boxing career—finds him in the thick of both. Danny manages to persuade his ex-trainer, the alcoholic Ike (Stott), to help him re-open the local gym but resentment is high. Particularly from hard-liner Harry (McSorley), who doesn't like Danny's live-and-let-live attitude and is incensed that he's interested in rekindling his lost-but-never-forgotten love for Maggie (Watson), who's the daughter of local IRA boss Joe (Cox), and the wife of another IRA prisoner. Things quickly turn ugly but the emotionally fragile Danny and Maggie continue to fight to be together against formidable odds. **113m/C VHS, DVD.** *GB IR* Daniel Day-Lewis, Emily Watson, Brian Cox, Gerard McSorley, Ken Stott, Ciaran Fitzgerald, Kenneth Cranham; ***Cameos:*** Tom Bell; ***D:*** Jim Sheridan; ***W:*** Jim Sheridan, Terry George; ***C:*** Chris Menges; ***M:*** Gavin Friday, Maurice Seezer.

The Boxer and Death 🦴🦴🦴 **1963** A new-wave Czech film about a boxer in a Nazi concentration camp who interests the boxing-obsessed commandant in a match. In Czech with subtitles. **120m/B VHS.** Stefan Kvietik; ***D:*** Peter Solan.

Boxing Helena 🦴🦴 **1993 (R)** Highly publicized as the film that cost Basinger almost $9 million in damages, the debut of director/writer Jennifer Lynch (daughter of David) explores the dark side of relationships between men and women. Sands is Dr. Nick Cavanaugh, a surgeon who becomes dangerously obsessed with the beautiful, yet unattainable Helena (Fenn). When she is hit by a car near his home, he performs emergency surgery and amputates her arms and legs, forcing her to be dependent on him. Metaphorically a situation, albeit an extreme one, that mirrors the power struggle in any sexual relationship. Problematic in some aspects, although equally fascinating as it is disturbing. **107m/C VHS, DVD, Wide.** Julian Sands, Sherilyn Fenn, Bill Paxton, Kurtwood Smith, Betsy Clark, Nicolette Scorsese, Art Garfunkel, Meg Register, Bryan Smith; ***D:*** Jennifer Lynch; ***W:*** Jennifer Lynch; ***C:*** Bojan Bazelli; ***M:*** Graeme Revell. Golden Raspberries '93: Worst Director (Lynch).

A Boy and His Dog 🦴🦴½ **1975 (R)** In the post-holocaust world of 2024, a young man (Johnson) and his telepathic canine (McIntire supplies narration of the dog's thoughts) cohort search for food and sex. They happen upon a community that drafts Johnson to repopulate their largely impotent race; Johnson is at first ready, willing, and able, until he discovers the mechanical methods they mean to employ. Based on a short story by Harlan Ellison. The dog was played by the late Tiger of "The Brady Bunch." **87m/C VHS, DVD.** Don Johnson, Susanne Benton, Jason Robards Jr., Charles McGraw, Alvy Moore, Helen Winston, Hal Baylor, L.Q. (Justus E. McQueen) Jones; ***D:*** L.Q. (Justus E. McQueen) Jones; ***W:*** L.Q. (Justus E. McQueen) Jones; ***C:*** John Morrill; ***M:*** Tim McIntire; ***V:*** Tim McIntire.

A Boy Called Hate 🦴🦴 **1995 (R)** Troubled teen Steve (Caan)—whose nickname is "Hate" after his tattoo—lives with his divorced dad in an L.A. suburb. Steve's on a latenight motorcycle ride, taking potshots at billboards with his trusty handgun, when he stumbles onto what he thinks is an attempted rape. So Steve shoots at the rapist, Richard (Gould), and takes off with would-be victim Cindy (Crider). Turns out Richard is the assistant D.A. and he tells the cops he's been robbed, so the teen duo are now on the run. Familiar tale with some good twists and believable performances. Caan is the son of James (seen in a cameo as the dad). Debut for director Marcus. **98m/C VHS.** Scott Caan, Missy (Melissa) Crider, Elliott Gould, Adam Beach; ***Cameos:*** James Caan; ***D:*** Mitch Marcus; ***W:*** Mitch Marcus; ***C:*** Paul Holahan.

Boy, Did I Get a Wrong Number! 🦴 **1966** A real estate agent gets more than he bargained for when he accidentally dials a wrong number. Zany comedy persists as Hope gets entangled in the life of sexy starlet Sommer. **100m/C VHS.** Bob Hope, Phyllis Diller, Marjorie Lord, Elke Sommer, Cesare Danova; ***D:*** George Marshall.

The Boy Friend 🦴🦴🦴 **1971 (G)** Russell pays tribute to the Busby Berkeley Hollywood musical. Lots of charming dance numbers and clever parody of plotlines in this adaptation of Sandy Wilson's stage play. Fun! ♫The Boy Friend; I Could Be Happy; Won't You Charleston With Me?; Fancy Forgetting; Sur La Plage; A Room in Bloomsbury; Safety in Numbers; It's Never Too Late to Fall in Love; Poor Little Pierette. **135m/C VHS.** *GB* Twiggy, Christopher Gable, Moyra Fraser, Max Adrian, Vladek Sheybal, Georgina Hale, Tommy Tune; ***D:*** Ken Russell; ***W:*** Ken Russell; ***C:*** David Watkin. Golden Globes '72: Actress—Mus./Comedy (Twiggy).

Boy in Blue 🦴½ **1986 (R)** A "Rocky"-esque biography of Canadian speed-rower Ned Hanlan, who set aside lackluster pursuits to turn to rowing. **97m/C VHS.** *CA* Nicolas Cage, Christopher Plummer, David Naughton; ***D:*** Charles Jarrott; ***W:*** Douglas Bowie.

The Boy in the Plastic Bubble 🦴🦴½ **1976** Well-made, sensitive drama about a young man born with immunity deficiencies who must grow up in a specially controlled plastic environment. Travolta is endearing as the boy in the bubble. **100m/C VHS, DVD.** John Travolta, Robert Reed, Glynnis O'Connor, Diana Hyland, Ralph Bellamy, Anne Ramsey, Vernee Watson-Johnson, P.J. Soles, John Friedrich; ***D:*** Randal Kleiser; ***W:*** Douglas Day Stewart; ***C:*** Arch R. Dalzell; ***M:*** Paul Williams, Mark Snow. **TV**

Boy Meets Girl 🦴🦴🦴 **1938** Cagney and O'Brien play screenwriters whose every film is a variation on the boy meets girl theme. Trouble is they're running out of ideas and their scripts get increasingly outlandish. A fading cowboy actor is supposed to star in the duo's next film—if they can ever settle down to work. Then they get the idea to feature their friend Wilson's baby in the movie—and guess who becomes a new star. Good satire on moviemaking and movie moguls, which made fine use of the Warner studio back lots, sound stages, and offices. Based on the play by Bella and Samuel Spewack who also wrote the screenplay. **86m/B VHS.** James Cagney, Pat O'Brien, Ralph Bellamy, Dick Foran, Marie Wilson, Frank McHugh, Bruce Lester, Ronald Reagan, Penny Singleton, James Stephenson; ***D:*** Lloyd Bacon; ***W:*** Bella Spewack, Samuel Spewack.

Boy Meets Girl 🦴🦴🦴 **1984** Alex (Lavant), a French Holden Caulfield type character, cruises the seamier side of Paris in this acclaimed film. Carax's directoral debut at age 22. Alex will return in the Carax films "Bad Blood" (1986) and "The Lovers on the Bridge" (1991). French with subtitles. **100m/B VHS, DVD, Wide.** *FR* Denis Lavant, Mireille Perrier, Carroll Brooks, Anna Baldaccini; ***D:*** Leos Carax; ***W:*** Leos Carax; ***C:*** Jean-Yves Escoffier; ***M:*** Jacques Pinault.

Boy of Two Worlds ½ 1970 (G) Because he is of a lineage foreign to his late father's town, a boy is exiled to the life of a junior Robinson Crusoe. **103m/C VHS.** Jimmy Sternman, Edvin Adolphson; ***D:*** Astrid Henning Jensen.

Boy Takes Girl 1983 A little girl finds it hard adjusting to life on a farming cooperative during a summer recess. **93m/C VHS.** Gabi Eldor, Hillel Neeman, Dina Limon; ***D:*** Michal Bat-Adam.

Boy! What a Girl 1945 Moore (in drag) is mistaken for a woman, and is fought over by a couple of suitors. **60m/B VHS.** Tim Moore, Duke Williams, Sheila Guyse, Beth Mays, Elwood Smith; ***D:*** Arthur Leonard.

The Boy Who Could Fly 1986 (PG) After a plane crash kills his parents, a boy withdraws into a fantasy land where he can fly. The young daughter of a troubled family makes friends with him and the fantasy becomes real. A sweet film for children, charming though melancholy for adults, too. Fine cast, including Savage, Dewhurst, and Bedelia keep this from becoming sappy. **120m/C VHS.** Lucy Deakins, Jay Underwood, Bonnie Bedelia, Colleen Dewhurst, Fred Savage, Fred Gwynne, Louise Fletcher, Jason Priestley; ***D:*** Nick Castle; ***W:*** Nick Castle; ***C:*** Steven Poster; ***M:*** Bruce Broughton.

The Boy Who Left Home to Find Out About the Shivers 1981 From "Faerie Tale Theatre" comes this tale about a boy who learns about fear. **60m/C VHS.** Peter MacNicol, Christopher Lee, David Warner, Dana Hill, Frank Zappa; ***D:*** Graeme Clifford; ***V:*** Vincent Price. CABLE

The Boy Who Loved Trolls 1984 Paul's fantastic dreams come true when he meets Ofoeti, a real, live troll. The only problem is Ofeoti only has a day to live, and Paul must find a way to save him. Aired on PBS as part of the "Wonderworks" series. **58m/C VHS.** Sam Waterston, Susan Anton, Matt Dill; ***D:*** Harvey Laidman.

The Boy with the Green Hair 1948 When he hears that his parents were killed in an air raid, a boy's hair turns green. The narrow-minded members of his community suddenly want nothing to do with him and he becomes an outcast. Thought-provoking social commentary. **82m/C VHS.** Pat O'Brien, Robert Ryan, Barbara Hale, Dean Stockwell; ***D:*** Joseph Losey.

Boycott ½ 2002 Superb HBO docudrama recreates the Civil Rights movement's early days, from Rosa Parks' (Little-Thomas) refusal to give up her seat to a white man on a segregated Montgomery, Alabama bus, throught the subsequent boycott of the bus system by the city's black population, to the success of the boycott and the rise to prominence of Dr. Martin Luther King Jr. (Wright) as the movement's most eloquent and popular leader. Through the use and mix of many different visual styles, director Johnson uses artful touches to tell the story without overplaying his hand. Wright is fantastic as King, with other outstanding performances turned in by Howard as Ralph Abernathy and Pounder as boycott organizer Jo Anne Robinson. **112m/C VHS, DVD.** Jeffrey Wright, Terrence DaShon Howard, CCH Pounder, Carmen Ejogo, Reg E. Cathey, Brent Jennings, Shawn Michael Howard, Erik Todd Dellums, Iris Little-Thomas, Whitman Mayo, E. Roger Mitchell, Mike Hodge, Clark Johnson; ***D:*** Clark Johnson; ***W:*** Timothy J. Sexton, Herman Daniel Farrell III; ***C:*** David Hennings; ***M:*** Stephen James Taylor. CABLE

Boyfriends 1996 Gay sexual roundelay that takes place over a weekend spent in the English countryside. Paul (Dreyfus) and Ben (Sands) are on the verge of splitting up after five years, orderly Matt's (Urwin) in love with philandering Owen (Ableson), and social worker Will (Coffey) wants more than a one-nighter with working-class pickup Adam (Petrucci). They all head to James's (McGrath) house and the sexual games begin. Low-budget first feature from Hunter and Hunsinger. **82m/C VHS, DVD.** *GB* James Dreyfus, Mark Sands, Andrew Ableson, Michael Urwin, David Coffey, Darren Petrucci, Michael McGrath, Russell Higgs; ***D:*** Neil Hunter, Tom Hunsinger; ***W:*** Neil Hunter, Tom Hunsinger; ***C:*** Richard Tisdall.

Boyfriends & Girlfriends ½ *My Girlfriend's Boyfriend; L'Ami de Mon Ami* 1988 (PG) Another one of Rohmer's "Comedies and Proverbs," in which two girls with boyfriends fade in and out of interest with each, casually reshuffling their relationships. Typical, endless-talks-at-cafes Rohmer, the most happily consistent of the aging French New Wave. In French with subtitles. **102m/C VHS, DVD.** *FR* Emmanuelle Chaulet, Sophie Renoir, Eric Viellard, Francois-Eric Gendron, Anne-Laure Meury; ***D:*** Eric Rohmer; ***W:*** Eric Rohmer; ***C:*** Bernard Lutic; ***M:*** Jean-Louis Valero.

Boys *The Girl You Want* 1995 (PG-13) Seems like only yesterday we saw Haas as that big-eared, doe-eyed Amish kid from "Witness," but now, in this dry love story, he has grown into a big-eared, doe-eyed teenager lusting after older woman Ryder. John (Haas) saves Patty (Ryder) after a riding accident leaves her unconscious near his New England prep school. Immediately taken by her beauty and mystery, John decides to hide her in his dorm room and a romance blossoms between the unlikely pair. But John isn't the only one hiding something. Patty has a terrible secret from her past (gasp!), but when it's finally revealed, you'll be too bored to care. Based on the short story "Twenty Minutes" by James Salter. **86m/C VHS, DVD.** Winona Ryder, Lukas Haas, John C. Reilly, William Sage, Skeet Ulrich; ***D:*** Stacy Cochran; ***W:*** Stacy Cochran; ***C:*** Robert Elswit; ***M:*** Stewart Copeland.

The Boys ½ *Les Boys* 1997 Popular, simply-plotted French-Canadian comedy about a group of ordinary guys who play in an amateur hockey league. "Les Boys" are sponsored by local tavern-owner Stan (Girard), who's got a gambling jones and is in debt to smalltime mobster, Meo (Lebeau). Meo strikes a deal pitting Stan's ragtag hockey players against his own team of thugs. If Stan's team is defeated, he loses his bar. Dirty tricks abound on both sides. French with subtitles. **107m/C VHS, DVD.** *CA* Remy Girard, Marc Messier, Patrick Huard, Serge Theriault, Yvan Ponton, Dominic Philie, Patrick Labbe, Roc Lafortune, Pierre Lebeau, Paul Houde; ***D:*** Louis Saia; ***W:*** Christian Fournier; ***C:*** Sylvain Brault; ***M:*** Normand Corbeil.

The Boys 1998 (R) After his release from prison on an assault charge, psychopathic Brett (Wenham), heads to the home of his mother Sandra (Curran) and younger brother Stevie (Hayes). His other brother Glenn (Polson) is now married to Jackie (Cronin) who wants him to stay out of trouble. Also greeting Brett is girlfriend Michelle (Collette) but the volatile duo are soon arguing furiously. As Brett gets drunker and more stoned, he also becomes more enraged, leading to a brutal crime. Chilling story with powerful performances; adapted from the 1991 play by Gordon Graham. **84m/C VHS.** *AU* David Wenham, Toni Collette, John Polson, Lynette Curran, Anthony Hayes, Jeanette Cronin, Anna Lise, Pete Smith; ***D:*** Rowan Woods; ***W:*** Stephen Sewell; ***C:*** Tristan Milani. Australian Film Inst. '98: Adapt. Screenplay, Director (Woods), Support. Actor (Polson), Support. Actress (Collette).

Boys and Girls 2000 (PG-13) Nondescript teen romance has lifelong acquaintances and most-time friends Ryan (Prinze Jr.) and Jennifer (Forlani) trying to decide if they love each other after their hormones get the better of them one night. And get this! They're complete opposites! She's carefree and live-for-the-moment. He's button-down, plan-every-second-precise. Biggs and Donahue, as the respective sidekicks, steal the movie from the leads whenever they show up. Sort of a young, poor man's "When Harry Met Sally," without the wit and insight. **94m/C VHS, DVD, Wide.** Freddie Prinze Jr., Claire Forlani, Jason Biggs, Heather Donahue, Alyson Hannigan, Amanda Detmer, Lisa Eichhorn; ***D:*** Robert Iscove; ***W:*** Andrew Lowery, Andrew Miller; ***C:*** Ralf Bode; ***M:*** Stewart Copeland.

The Boys Club 1996 (R) Teens-in-trouble film is given a tough core by first time director Fawcett. Excitement-craving 14-year-olds Kyle (Zamprogna), Eric (Sawa), and Brad (Stone) spend all their free time at an abandoned shack at the outskirts of their small town. Only one day they discover it occupied by gun-pointing criminal Luke Cooper (Penn), who tells the boys he's actually a good cop who's been shot and is on the run from some bad cops. The boys are willing to buy into the story at first but Cooper is quick to show his psycho colors, taking Eric hostage, and precipitating a violent finale. **92m/C VHS, DVD.** *CA* Christopher Penn, Stuart Stone, Devon Sawa, Dominic Zamprogna, Nicholas (Nick) Campbell, Jarred Blanchard; ***D:*** John Fawcett; ***W:*** Peter Wellington; ***C:*** Thom Best; ***M:*** Michael Timmins.

Boys Don't Cry 1999 (R) Falls under the truth is stranger than fiction category. Brandon Teena (heavily-awarded Swank) moves from Lincoln, Nebraska to the small town of Falls City hoping to start over and keep his past a secret. Brandon gets a girlfriend, Lana (Sevigny), and runs afoul of the reckless John (Sarsgaard). And then Brandon's secret is discovered—he is actually a girl and the gender revelation leads to tragic consequences. Based on a true story, which is also the subject of the documentary, "The Brandon Teena Story." Pierce's version, not unexpectedly, was subjected to the charges of dramatic license, but the story is still forceful. **116m/C VHS, DVD.** Hilary Swank, Chloe Sevigny, Peter Sarsgaard, Brendan Sexton III, Alison Folland, Alicia (Lecy) Goranson, Matt McGrath, Rob Campbell, Jeanetta Arnette; ***D:*** Kimberly Peirce; ***W:*** Kimberly Peirce, Andy Bienen; ***C:*** Jim Denault; ***M:*** Nathan Larsen. Oscars '99: Actress (Swank); Golden Globes '00: Actress—Drama (Swank); Ind. Spirit '00: Actress (Swank), Support. Actress (Sevigny); L.A. Film Critics '99: Actress (Swank), Support. Actress (Sevigny); N.Y. Film Critics '99: Actress (Swank); Natl. Soc. Film Critics '99: Support. Actress (Sevigny); Broadcast Film Critics '99: Actress (Swank).

The Boys from Brazil ½ 1978 (R) Based on Ira Levin's novel, a thriller about Dr. Josef Mengele endeavoring to reconstitute the Nazi movement from his Brazilian sanctuary by cloning a brood of boys from Hitler's genes. **123m/C VHS, DVD.** Gregory Peck, James Mason, Laurence Olivier, Uta Hagen, Steve Guttenberg, Denholm Elliott, Lilli Palmer; ***D:*** Franklin J. Schaffner; ***W:*** Heywood Gould; ***C:*** Henri Decae; ***M:*** Jerry Goldsmith. Natl. Bd. of Review '78: Actor (Olivier).

The Boys in Company C 1977 (R) A frank, hard-hitting drama about five naive young men involved in the Vietnam War. **127m/C VHS.** Stan Shaw, Andrew Stevens, James Canning, Michael Lembeck, Craig Wasson, R. Lee Ermey, James Whitmore Jr., Scott Hylands, Noble Willingham, Santos Morales, Claude Wilson, Drew Michaels, Karen Hilger, Peggy O'Neal, Stan Johns; ***Cameos:*** Rick Natkin; ***D:*** Sidney J. Furie; ***W:*** Sidney J. Furie, Rick Natkin; ***C:*** Godfret A. Godar; ***M:*** Jaime Mendoza-Nava.

Boys in Love 1995 Four gay shorts about young men in love. "Death in Venice, CA" finds a repressed academic drawn to his landlady's stepson. The animated "Achilles" features the Greek heros Achilles and Petroclus at the battle of Troy. A young man becomes determined to conquer "My Polish Waiter" and a rejected Latin lover finds love again (with some help from a dog) in "Miguel, Ma Belle." **83m/C VHS.** ***D:*** Barry Purves, P. David Ebersole.

Boys in Love 2 1998 Anthology of six short films: "Boot Camp" finds two men cruising each other in a leather bar and breaking out into a musical comedy number; "Twilight of the Gods" features a jungle romance between a Maori warrior and a European soldier; "Karen Black Like Me" is a homage to "Trilogy of Terror," only this time a man is chased around his apartment by a sex toy; "My Body" is about a neurotic young man trying to deny his sexual orientation; "SPF 2000" spoofs Italian sexploitation films and features a space alien and lecherous sunbathers; and "Dirty Baby Does Fire Island" is an animated tale of a baby doll washed up on shore, who gets involved in Island life. The theatrical release also featured the animated "Achilles," which is not included here. **86m/C VHS.** ***D:*** Patrick McGuinn, Stewart Main, Joel Moffett, David Briggs, John Scott Matthews, Todd Downing.

The Boys in the Band ½ 1970 (R) A group of gay friends get together one night for a birthday party. A simple premise with a compelling depiction of friendship, expectations, and lifestyle. One of the first serious cinematic presentations to deal with the subject of homosexuality. The film was adapted from Mart Crowley's play using the original cast. **120m/C VHS.** Frederick Combs, Cliff Gorman, Laurence Luckinbill, Kenneth Nelson, Leonard Frey; ***D:*** William Friedkin; ***W:*** Matt Crowley.

Boys Life 1994 Three shorts about gay teenagers coming of age. "Pool Days" has 17-year-old Justin (Weinstein) taking a summer job as a lifeguard at a health spa. Still clueless as to his sexual preferences, Justin is flustered when cruised by a charming male swimmer but it does get him to thinking. "A Friend of Dorothy" finds NYU student Winston (O'Connell) seeking freedom in Greenwich Village as he looks for like-minded friends (and a little romance). "The Disco Years" takes place in California during the Nixon era as casually gay-bashing high-schooler Tom (Nolan) gradually realizes his true nature. **90m/C VHS, DVD.** Josh Weinstein, Nick Poletti, Kimberly Flynn, Richard Salamanca, Raoul O'Connell, Kevin McClatchy, Greg Lauren, Anne Zupa, Matt Nolan, Russell Scott Lewis, Gwen Welles, Dennis Christopher; ***D:*** Robert Lee King, Brian Sloan, Raoul O'Connell; ***W:*** Robert Lee King, Brian Sloan, Raoul O'Connell; ***C:*** W. Mott Hupfel III, Jonathan Schell, Greg Gardiner.

The Boys Next Door ½ 1985 (R) Two California lads kill and go nuts during a weekend in Los Angeles. Sheen overacts as a budding psychotic, not an easy thing to do. Apparently is trying to show what a particular lifestyle can lead to. Violent. **90m/C VHS, DVD, Wide.** Maxwell Caulfield, Charlie Sheen, Christopher McDonald, Hank Garrett, Patti D'Arbanville, Moon Zappa; ***D:*** Penelope Spheeris; ***W:*** Glen Morgan, James Wong; ***C:*** Arthur Albert; ***M:*** George S. Clinton.

The Boys Next Door ½ 1996 (PG) Gentle comedy/drama, based on Tom Griffin's play, about four mentally disabled men—Norman (Lane), Barry (Leonard), Arnold (Jeter), and Lucien (Vance)—who share a house under the supervision of too-dedicated social worker Jack (Goldwyn). In fact, Jack's devotion is causing enough problems in his marriage to have him consider changing careers, even as each of "the boys" struggle with their daily lives. TV movie is overly sweet but the performances are very good. **99m/C VHS.** Nathan Lane, Tony Goldwyn, Robert Sean Leonard, Michael Jeter, Courtney B. Vance, Mare Winningham, Jenny Robertson, Elizabeth Wilson, Richard Jenkins, Lynne Thigpen; ***D:*** John Erman; ***W:*** William Blinn; ***C:*** Frank Tidy; ***M:*** John Kander. TV

Boys' Night Out 1962 Amusing comedy about four businessmen who desperately want to escape the suburban doldrums by setting up an apartment equipped with plaything Novak. Little do they know, but Novak is a sociology student studying the American male, and they are merely her guinea pigs in an experiment beyond their control. Blair, Page, and Gabor provide comic relief. Based on a story by Marvin Worth and Arne Sultan. **113m/C VHS.** Kim Novak, James Garner, Tony Randall, Howard Duff, Janet Blair, Patti Page, Jessie Royce Landis, Oscar Homolka, Zsa Zsa Gabor; ***D:*** Michael Gordon; ***W:*** Ira Wallach.

The Boys of St. Vincent 1993 Outstanding, and heartbreaking, story of sexual abuse by Catholic clergy that was inspired by actual events. Divided into two segments, the drama begins in 1975 with 10-year-old Kevin Reevey (Morina) living at the St. Vincent orphanage in an eastern Canadian town. The orphanage is run by charismatic and terrifying Brother Lavin (Czerny), who it turns out has a special fondness for "his boy" Kevin. Nor is Brother Lavin alone—a fact eventually revealed by a police investigation, although the matter is hushed up by both the church and the government. Until 15 years later. In 1990, the case is reopened and Lavin, having married and fathered two sons, is returned to face charges. Now the young men must open wounds that have never truly healed and confront their tormentors in a court of law, amidst a blaze of publicity. Czerny gives a truly inspired performance as the self-loathing monster. The emotional agony is excruciating to watch and be forwarned that the depiction of the sexual abuse is unflinching. Made for Canadian TV; on two cassettes. **186m/C VHS.** *CA* Henry Czerny, Johnny Morina, Sebastian Spence, Brian Dodd, David Hewlett, Jonathan Lewis, Jeremy Keefe, Phillip Dinn, Brian Dooley, Greg Thomey, Michael Wade, Lise Roy, Timothy Webber, Kristine Demers, Ashley Billard, Sam Grana; *D:* John N. Smith; *W:* Sam Grana, John N. Smith, Des Walsh; *C:* Pierre Letarte; *M:* Neil Smolar. **TV**

Boys of the City *The Ghost Creeps* **1940** The East Side Kids run amuck in an eerie mansion while trying to solve the murder of a judge. **63m/B VHS.** Leo Gorcey, Bobby Jordan; *D:* Joseph H. Lewis.

Boys on the Side ½ **1994 (R)** It's "Thelma & Louise" come to "Terms of Endearment" by way of "Philadelphia." Goldberg is Jane, an unemployed lesbian singer, who connects with Ms. Priss real estate agent Robin (Parker) for a road trip to California. The two become a female version of the Odd Couple as Jane tags Robin as "the whitest woman in America." They stop off to pick up addle-brain friend Holly (Barrymore) who has just knocked her drug-crazed abusive beau in the head with a baseball bat. Holly's accident turns fatal and the threesome are on the run from cops. They bond like crazy glue and become a family as they face two huge setbacks—one's pregnant, another has AIDS. Strong performances by the lead actresses and a cool soundtrack may make up for this often trite movie of the week premise. **117m/C VHS, DVD.** James Remar, Anita Gillette, Matthew McConaughey, Whoopi Goldberg, Mary-Louise Parker, Drew Barrymore; *D:* Herbert Ross; *W:* Don Roos; *C:* Donald E. Thorin; *M:* David Newman.

Boy's Reformatory ½ **1939** Brothers are framed. One takes the rap, goes to the title institution, breaks out, and hunts the real bad guys. Creaky and antiquated. **62m/B VHS.** Frankie Darro, Grant Withers, David Durand, Warren McCollum; *D:* Howard Bretherton.

Boys Town ½ **1938** Righteous portrayal of Father Flanagan and the creation of Boys Town, home for juvenile soon-to-be-ex-delinquents. **93m/B VHS.** Spencer Tracy, Mickey Rooney, Henry Hull, Gene Reynolds, Sidney Miller, Frankie Thomas Jr.; *D:* Norman Taurog. Oscars '38: Actor (Tracy), Story.

Boys Will Be Boys ½ **1997 (PG)** With their parents away at a company party, Matt and Robbie are home alone for the first time. Expect chaos when the boys discover that their father's business rival has something nasty in store and the brothers will use anything around to defeat him. **89m/C VHS, DVD.** Randy Travis, Julie Hagerty, Jon Voight, Michael DeLuise, Catherine Oxenberg, Mickey Rooney, Ruth Buzzi, Dom DeLuise, Charles Nelson Reilly, James Williams, Drew Winget; *D:* Dom DeLuise; *W:* Gregory Poppon, Mark Dubas; *C:* Leonard Schway; *M:* Kristopher Carter. **VIDEO**

Boyz N the Hood ½ **1991 (R)** Singleton's debut as a writer and director is an astonishing picture of young black men, four high school students with different backgrounds, aims, and abilities trying to survive L.A. gangs and bigotry. Excellent acting throughout, with special nods to Fishburne and Gooding Jr. Violent outbreaks outside theatres where this ran only proves the urgency of its passionately nonviolent, pro-family message. Hopefully those viewers scared off at the time will give this a chance in the safety of their VCRs. Singleton was the youngest director ever nominated for an Oscar. **112m/C VHS, DVD, Wide.** Laurence "Larry" Fishburne, Ice Cube, Cuba Gooding Jr., Nia Long, Morris Chestnut, Tyra Ferrell, Angela Bassett, Whitman Mayo; *D:* John Singleton; *W:* John Singleton; *C:* Charles Mills; *M:* Stanley Clarke. MTV Movie Awards '92: New Filmmaker (Singleton).

Braddock: Missing in Action 3 **1988 (R)** The battle-scarred, high-kicking 'Nam vet battles his way into the jungles once more, this time to rescue his long-lost Vietnamese family. A family effort, Chuck co-wrote the script; his brother directed. **104m/C VHS.** Chuck Norris, Aki Aleong, Roland Harrah III; *D:* Aaron Norris; *W:* Chuck Norris, James Bruner; *C:* Joao Fernandes.

The Brady Bunch Movie **1995 (PG-13)** Grunge and CDs may be the norm in the '90s, but the Bradys still live in the eight-track world of the '70s, where Davy Jones rocks and every day is a sunshine day. Then greedy developer McKean schemes to cash in on Mike and Carol's financial woes. (Hawaii! The Grand Canyon! What were they thinking?) Great ensemble cast capably fills the white platform shoes of the originals—Cole sounds just like Mr. Brady, Cox hilariously channels Jan's tormented middle child angst, and Taylor's self-absorbed Marcia, Marcia, Marcia is dead-on, right down to the frosty pursed lips. Look for neat-o cameos from some original Bradys and most of the Monkees. Followed by "A Very Brady Sequel." **88m/C VHS.** Shelley Long, Gary Cole, Michael McKean, Jean Smart, Henriette Mantel, Christopher Daniel Barnes, Christine Taylor, Paul Sutera, Jennifer Elise Cox, Jesse Lee, Olivia Hack, David Graf, Jack Noseworthy, Shane Conrad, RuPaul Charles; ***Cameos:*** Ann B. Davis, Florence Henderson, Davy Jones, Barry Williams, Christopher Knight, Michael (Mike) Lookinland, Mickey Dolenz, Peter Tork; *D:* Betty Thomas; *W:* Bonnie Turner, Terry Turner, Laurice Elehwany, Rick Copp; *C:* Mac Ahlberg; *M:* Guy Moon.

Brady's Escape ½ *The Long Ride* **1984** American WWII pilot is shot down in the Hungarian countryside and befriended by Hungarian csikos (cowboys). **92m/C VHS.** *HU* John Savage, Kelly Reno; *D:* Pal Gabor. **CABLE**

The Brain ½ *Vengeance* **1962** A scientist learns that a mind isn't always a terrible thing to waste when he finds himself being manipulated by the brain of a dead man he's trying to keep alive. Remake of "Donovan's Brain" (1953). **83m/B VHS.** *GB GE* Anne Heywood, Peter Van Eyck, Bernard Lee, Cecil Parker, Jack MacGowran; *D:* Freddie Francis.

The Brain *Le Cerveau* **1969 (G)** Run of the mill comedy caper has Niven planning to heist millions from a NATO train. The caper begins when lots of other crooks decide to rob the same train. The cast holds this one together. **100m/C VHS.** *FR* David Niven, Jean-Paul Belmondo, Bourvil, Eli Wallach, Silvia Monti, Fernand Valois; *D:* Gerard Oury; *M:* Georges Delerue.

The Brain ½ **1988 (R)** Dr. Blake, host of a popular TV talk-show, is in league with a power-hungry alien brain. Viewers of his show kill themselves and others in the midst of many special effects. The ratings go down. **94m/C VHS.** Tom Breznahan, Cyndy Preston, David Gale; *D:* Ed(ward) Hunt.

Brain Damage **1988 (R)** A tongue-in-bloody-cheek farce about a brain-sucking parasite. The parasite in question, Aylmer, addicts our dubious hero to the euphoria induced by the blue liquid the parasite injects into his brain, paving the way for the bloody mayhem that follows. Poor shadow of Henenlotter's far-superior "Basket Case." In fact, it even includes an inside-joke cameo by Van Hentenryck, reprising his "Basket Case" character; look for him on the subway. **89m/C VHS, DVD.** Rick Herbst, Gordon MacDonald, Jennifer Lowry, Theo Barnes, Lucille Saint Peter, Kevin Van Hentenryck, Beverly Bonner; *D:* Frank Henenlotter; *W:* Frank Henenlotter; *C:* Bruce Torbet; *M:* Gus Russo, Clutch Reiser; *V:* John Zacherle.

Brain Dead ½ **1989 (R)** Low-budget but brilliantly assembled puzzle-film about a brain surgeon who agrees to perform experimental surgery on a psychotic to retrieve some corporately valuable data—his first mistake, which begins a seemingly endless cycle of nightmares and identity alterations. A mind-blowing sci-fi feast from ex-"Twilight Zone" writer Charles Beaumont. **85m/C VHS, DVD.** Bill Pullman, Bill Paxton, Bud Cort, Patricia Charbonneau, Nicholas Pryor, George Kennedy, Brian Brophy, Lee Arenberg, Andy Wood; *D:* Adam Simon; *W:* Adam Simon, Charles Beaumont; *M:* Peter Rotter.

Brain Donors ½ **1992 (PG)** Goofy, uneven film starring Turturro as a sleazy lawyer trying to take over the Oglethorpe Ballet Company by sweet-talking its aged patronness. He is helped by two eccentric friends, and together the three crack a lot of bad but witty jokes. The film culminates into a hilarious ballet scene featuring someone giving CPR to the ballerina playing the dying swan, an actor in a duck suit, duck hunters, and a pack of hounds. This trio reminds us of second-rate Marx Brothers (or the Three Stooges) but the movie has enough funny moments to be worth a watch. **79m/C VHS, Wide.** John Turturro, Bob Nelson, Mel Smith, Nancy Marchand, John Savident, George de la Pena, Juli Donald, Spike Alexander, Teri Copley; *D:* Dennis Dugan; *W:* Pat Proft; *M:* Ira Newborn.

The Brain Eaters **1958** A strange ship from inside the Earth invades a small town, and hairy monsters promptly attach themselves to people's necks in a daring bid to control the planet. The imaginative story compensates somewhat for the cheap special effects. Watch for Nimoy before he grew pointed ears. **60m/B VHS.** Edwin Nelson, Alan Frost, Jack Hill, Joanna Lee, Jody Fair, Leonard Nimoy; *D:* Bruno VeSota.

The Brain from Planet Arous **1957** Lassie meets Alien when an evil alien brain appropriates the body of a scientist in order to take over planet Earth. His plans are thwarted, however, by a good alien brain that likewise inhabits the body of the scientist's dog. High camp and misdemeanors. **80m/B VHS, DVD.** John Agar, Joyce Meadows, Robert Fuller, Henry Travis, Bill Giorgio, Tim Graham, Thomas B(rowne). Henry, Ken Terrell; *D:* Nathan (Hertz) Juran; *W:* Ray Buffum; *C:* Jacques "Jack" Marquette; *M:* Walter Greene.

Brain of Blood woof! *The Creature's Revenge; Brain Damage* **1971** Deals with a scientist who transplants the brain of a politician into the body of a deformed idiot. The change is minimal. **107m/C VHS.** *PH* Kent Taylor, John Bloom, Regina Carrol, Angelo Rossitto, Grant Williams, Reed Hadley, Vicki Volante, Zandor Vorkov, Richard Smedley; *D:* Al Adamson; *W:* Joe Van Rogers; *C:* Louis Horvath.

Brain Smasher...A Love Story **1993 (PG-13)** A bouncer and a super model become the targets of a gang of killer ninjas who want the mysterious blood-red lotus the model's been given. Of course they do. What's the lovely Hatcher doing in such a stupid movie? **88m/C VHS.** Andrew (Dice Clay) Silverstein, Teri Hatcher; *D:* Albert Pyun.

The Brain that Wouldn't Die ½ *The Head That Wouldn't Die* **1963** Love is a many-splattered thing when a brilliant surgeon keeps the decapitated head of his fiancee alive after an auto accident while he searches for a suitably stacked body onto which to transplant the head. Absurd and satiric (head talks so much that Doc tapes her/its mouth shut) adding up to major entry in trash film genre; much of the gore was slashed for the video, however. **92m/B VHS, DVD.** Herb Evers, Virginia Leith, Adele Lamont, Leslie Daniel, Bruce Brighton, Paula Maurice; *D:* Joseph Green; *W:* Joseph Green; *C:* Stephen Hajinal; *M:* Tony Restaino.

The Brainiac ½ *El Baron del Terror; Baron of Terror* **1961** Sorcerer sentenced for black magic returns to strike dark deeds upon the descendants of those who judged him. He turns himself into a hideous monster, feeding on his victims' brains and blood. Yuck. **75m/B VHS.** *MX* Abel Salazar, Ariadne Welter, Mauricio Garces, Rosa Maria Gallardo, Ruben Rojo, German Robles; *D:* Chano Urueto; *W:* Frederick Curiel, Alfredo Torres Portillo; *C:* Jose Ortiz Ramos; *M:* Gustavo Cesar Carrion.

Brainscan **1994 (R)** Teenage loner takes a trip in virtual reality and finds that murder is the first stop. Furlong ("Terminator 2") is the troubled youth whose voyage is led by Smith as Trickster, the Freddy Krueger meets David Bowie tour guide from virtual hell. Langella turns in a straight performance as a local cop hot on the trail. Hard-core horror fans will be disappointed by the lack of on-screen violence, and special effects buffs won't see anything new. Lame effort tries to appeal to a wide audience and is bland as a result. The end is left wide open, so expect a sequel or two or three. **96m/C VHS.** Edward Furlong, Frank Langella, T. Ryder Smith, David Hemblen, Amy Hargreaves, Jamie Marsh, Victor Ertmanis; *D:* John Flynn; *W:* Andrew Kevin Walker; *M:* George S. Clinton.

Brainstorm ½ **1983 (PG)** Husband-and-wife scientist team invents headphones that can record dreams, thoughts, and fantasies (VCR-style) and then allow other people to experience them by playing back the tape. Their marriage begins to crumble as the husband becomes more and more obsessed with pushing the limits of the technology; things get worse when the government wants to exploit their discovery. Special effects and interesting camera work punctuate this sci-fi flick. Wood's last film; in fact, she died before production was completed. **106m/C VHS, DVD, Wide.** Natalie Wood, Christopher Walken, Cliff Robertson, Louise Fletcher; *D:* Douglas Trumbull; *W:* Bruce Joel Rubin; *C:* Richard Yuricich; *M:* James Horner.

Brainwashed *Die Schachnovelle; The Royal Game; Three Moves to Freedom* **1960** Austrian aristocrat Werner von Basil (Jurgens) is captured by the Nazis and interrogated to uncover military information. In order to keep his sanity, the prisoner concentrates on a chess book he keeps hidden in his cell. Based on the novel by Stefan Zweig. German with subtitles. **127m/C VHS.** *GE* Curt Jurgens, Claire Bloom, Hansjorg Felmy, Mario Adorf, Albert Lieven, Alan Gifford, Karel Stepanek; *D:* Gerd Oswald; *W:* Gerd Oswald, Harold Medford; *C:* Gunther Senftleben; *M:* Hans-Martin Majewski.

Brainwaves **1982 (R)** A young woman has disturbing flashbacks after her brain is electrically revived following a car accident. Curtis is the demented doctor who jump-starts her. **83m/C VHS.** Suzanna Love, Tony Curtis, Keir Dullea, Vera Miles; *D:* Ulli Lommel; *W:* Ulli Lommel.

Bram Stoker's Dracula *Dracula* **1992 (R)** Coppola's highly charged view of the vampire classic is visually stunning, heavy on eroticism and violence, and weak in plot and performance. Oldman, in a number of amazing transformations, portrays the deadly bloodsucker as a lonely soul determined to reunite with his lost love, the innocent Ryder. Hopkins cheerfully chews the scenery as nemesis Van Helsing, newcomer Frost is fetching, Reeves is lightweight, and Ryder goes way over the top. Musician Waits is great as bug-eating madman Renfield. Filmed entirely on soundstages with beautiful costumes and some amazing visual effects and sets. **128m/C VHS, DVD, Wide.** Gary Oldman, Winona Ryder, Anthony Hopkins, Keanu Reeves, Richard E. Grant, Cary Elwes, Billy Campbell, Sadie Frost, Tom Waits; *D:* Francis Ford Coppola; *W:* Jim V. Hart; *C:* Michael Ballhaus. Oscars '92: Costume Des., Makeup, Sound FX Editing.

Bram Stoker's Shadowbuilder *Shadowbuilder* **1998 (R)** Silly update that apparently takes the title of the Bram Stoker short story but not much else. Shadowbuilder (Jackson) is a demonic creature that wants to unleash hell's power upon the unsuspecting town of Grand River. But he needs 12-year-old Chris (Zegers) for your basic satanic ritual, which doesn't go over well with the local priest (Rooker) and sheriff (Thompson). **101m/C VHS, DVD.** Michael Rooker, Leslie Hope, Andrew Jackson, Kevin Zegers, Shawn Thompson, Tony Todd, Richard McMillan; *D:* Jamie Dixon; *W:* Michael Stokes; *C:* David Pelletier; *M:* Eckart Seeber. **VIDEO**

Bram Stoker's The Mummy *The Mummy; Legend of the Mummy* **1997 (R)** Modern retelling of the horror tale focuses on the savage incident that left Egyptologist Abel Trelawny (Bochner) in a coma. Now his daughter, Margaret (Locane), seeks the help of her ex-lover, Robert (Lutes), to uncover the connection between Trewlawny and an Egyptian ritual to raise a queen from her tomb. Based on Stoker's book "The Jewel of the Seven Stars." **100m/C VHS, DVD.** Mary Jo Catlett, Amy Locane, Eric Lutes, Louis Gossett Jr., Victoria Tennant, Lloyd Bochner, Mark Lindsay Chapman, Richard Karn; ***D:*** Jeffrey Obrow; ***W:*** Jeffrey Obrow; ***C:*** Antonio Soriano; ***M:*** Rick Cox. **VIDEO**

The Bramble Bush ½ **1960** Guy (Burton) is a doctor who returns to his New England hometown to care for a dying friend, Larry (Drake). Unfortunately, Guy falls for Larry's wife Mar (Rush) and they have an affair. When Guy pulls the plug on his friend's suffering, suspicious townspeople (who of course know what's going on) wonder just how "merciful" the doctor was really being and he's tried for murder. Tawdry "Peyton Place"-ish soap opera based on the novel by Charles Mergendahl. **104m/C VHS.** Richard Burton, Barbara Rush, Tom Drake, Jack Carson, Angie Dickinson, James Dunn, Henry Jones, Frank Conroy, Carl Benton Reid; ***D:*** Daniel Petrie; ***W:*** Philip Yordan.

Brand New Life **1972** A childless couple in their 40s are unexpectedly confronted by the wife's first pregnancy. Both have careers and well-ordered lives that promise to be disrupted. **74m/C VHS.** Cloris Leachman, Martin Balsam, Wilfrid Hyde-White, Mildred Dunnock; ***D:*** Sam O'Steen; ***M:*** Billy Goldenberg. **TV**

Brand of Fear ½ **1949** Crooning cowpoke Wakely puts down his guitar long enough to chase rustlers off the land of an innocent lady in this average oater. **56m/B VHS.** Jimmy Wakely, Dub Taylor, Gail Davis, Tom London; ***D:*** Oliver Drake; ***W:*** Basil Dickey.

Brand of Hate **1934** A good cowboy rustles up a gang of rustlers. **61m/B VHS.** Bob Steele, George "Gabby" Hayes, Lucille Browne, James Flavin; ***D:*** Lewis D. Collins.

Brand of the Outlaws **1936** A cowboy becomes an unwitting aid to rustlers in this early western. **56m/B VHS.** Bob Steele, Margaret Marquis, Virginia True Boardman, Jack Rockwell; ***D:*** Robert North Bradbury.

Branded ½ **1950** Ladd (pre-"Shane") impersonates the long-gone son of rich rancher Bickford, with unusual results. Nicely balanced action and love scenes makes this old Max Brand story a better-than-average western. Filmed in Technicolor. **95m/C VHS.** Alan Ladd, Mona Freeman, Charles Bickford, Joseph Calleia, Milburn Stone; ***D:*** Rudolph Mate.

Branded a Bandit **1924** Yakima must avoid the sheriff while tracking down the killers of an old miner so that he can clear himself of the crime. **58m/C VHS.** Yakima Canutt; ***D:*** Paul Hurst.

Branded a Coward **1935** A man whose parents were killed seeks revenge via his trusty six-shooters. **56m/B VHS.** Johnny Mack Brown, Billie Seward, Yakima Canutt; ***D:*** Sam Newfield.

Branded Men **1931** A couple of oddballs become mixed up in a number of zany, western-type adventures. **60m/B VHS.** Ken Maynard, June Clyde, Irving Bacon, Billy Bletcher, Charles "Blackie" King, Donald Keith; ***D:*** Phil Rosen.

Branded to Kill *Koroshi no Rakuin* **1967** Visual tricks, including animated graphics, and a blues score highlight this gangster story, which follows No. 3 Killer, who's bungled his last hit. Now he's the target of No. 1 Killer. Japanese with subtitles. **91m/B VHS, DVD.** *JP* Joe Shishido, Mari Annu, Koji Nambara, Isao Tamagawa, Mariko Ogawa; ***D:*** Seijun Suzuki; ***W:*** Hachiro Guryu; ***C:*** Kazue Nagatsuka; ***M:*** Naozumi Yamamoto.

Brannigan ½ **1975 (PG)** The Duke stars in the somewhat unfamiliar role of a rough and tumble Chicago police officer. He travels across the Atlantic to arrest a racketeer who has fled the States rather than face a grand jury indictment. Humor and action abound. **111m/C VHS, DVD, Wide.** John Wayne, John Vernon, Mel Ferrer, Daniel Pilon, James Booth, Ralph Meeker, Lesley-Anne Down, Richard Attenborough; ***D:*** Douglas Hickox; ***W:*** Michael Butler, William W. Norton Sr.; ***C:*** Gerry Fisher; ***M:*** Dominic Frontiere.

Brass ½ **1985 (PG)** First post-Archie Bunker role for O'Connor, who plods through this average police drama at a snail's pace, dragging everything else down with him. Made-for-TV pilot for a series that never aired. **94m/C VHS.** Carroll O'Connor, Lois Nettleton, Jimmy Baio, Paul Shenar, Vincent Gardenia, Anita Gillette; ***D:*** Corey Allen. **TV**

The Brass Bottle ½ **1963** Silly but amusing comedy that served as the inspiration for the TV series "I Dream of Jeannie," although Eden plays the girlfriend in this movie. Ives stars as jovial genie Fakrash, whose antique bottle is bought by architect Harold Ventimore (Randall). Fakrash wants nothing more than to make his new master happy but his efforts cause constant crises for the bewildered man, who'd prefer his life return to normal. Based on the novel by F. Anstey. **90m/C VHS.** Tony Randall, Burl Ives, Barbara Eden, Edward Andrews, Ann Doran, Kamala Devi, Howard Smith, Parley Baer; ***D:*** Harry Keller; ***W:*** Oscar Brodney; ***C:*** Clifford Stine; ***M:*** Bernard Green.

Brass Target ½ **1978 (PG)** Hypothetical thriller about a plot to kill George Patton in the closing days of WWII for the sake of $250 million in Nazi gold stolen by his staff. Interesting cast can't find story. **111m/C VHS.** Sophia Loren, George Kennedy, Max von Sydow, John Cassavetes, Patrick McGoohan, Robert Vaughn, Bruce Davison, Edward Herrmann, Ed Bishop; ***D:*** John Hough; ***W:*** Alvin Boretz.

Brassed Off ½ **1996 (R)** Bittersweet tale of despair and hope in the fictional coal mining town of Grimly in Yorkshire, England. Set in 1992, when sweeping closures of British coal mines devastated the area, the sole respite of these workers is playing in the pit's brass band. Secretly suffering from black lung disease, the band's leader (Postlethwaite) dreams of winning a competition in Albert Hall. Fitzgerald plays the flugelhorn-tooting vixen who returns to the small town, inspiring the music (and virility) of the formerly all male band. She resumes her relationship with former flame MacGregor, but all is on shaky ground with the imminent closure of the mine. Fine performances brighten the generally gloomy proceedings. The band is played by the real-life Grimethorpe Colliery Brass Band. **100m/C VHS, DVD.** *GB* Pete Postlethwaite, Ewan McGregor, Tara Fitzgerald, Jim Carter, Philip Jackson, Peter Martin, Stephen Tompkinson; ***D:*** Mark Herman; ***W:*** Mark Herman; ***C:*** Andy Collins; ***M:*** Trevor Jones. Cesar '98: Foreign Film.

The Bravados **1958** A rough, distressing Western revenge tale, wherein a man is driven to find the four men who murdered his wife. In tracking the perpetrators, Peck realizes that he has been corrupted by his vengeance. **98m/C VHS.** Gregory Peck, Stephen Boyd, Joan Collins, Albert Salmi, Henry Silva, Lee Van Cleef, George Voskovec, Barry Coe; ***D:*** Henry King; ***W:*** Philip Yordan; ***C:*** Leon Shamroy. Natl. Bd. of Review '58: Support. Actor (Salmi).

The Brave Bunch ½ **1970** A courageous Greek soldier tries to save his men and country during WWII. **110m/C VHS.** *GR* Peter Funk, John Miller; ***D:*** Costa Carayiannis.

The Brave One **1956** A love story between a Spanish boy and the bull who saves his life. The animal is later carted off to the bullring. Award-winning screenplay by the then-blacklisted Trumbo, credited as "Robert Rich." **100m/C VHS, DVD.** Michel Ray, Rodolfo Hoyos, Joi Lansing; ***D:*** Irving Rapper; ***W:*** Dalton Trumbo; ***C:*** Jack Cardiff; ***M:*** Victor Young. Oscars '56: Story.

Braveheart **1925** When a Native American adapts to the white man's world, he alienates his own people. He eventually chooses to renounce his love for a white woman, and returns to lead his people. Silent. **62m/B VHS, 8mm.** Rod La Rocque; ***D:*** Alan Hale.

Braveheart ½ **1995 (R)** Producer-director-star Gibson does it all in this bold, ferocious, reasonably accurate epic about the passion and cost of freedom. Charismatic 13th century Scottish folk hero William Wallace leads his desperate and outnumbered clansmen in revolt against British oppression. Sweeping, meticulous battle scenes fit suprisingly well with moments of stirring romance and snappy wit. Among the mostly unknown (in the States, anyway) cast, Marceau and McCormack are elegant as Wallace's lady loves, and McGoohan is positively hateful as King Edward I. Gory and excessively violent (as medieval warfare tends to be) and a bit too long (as historical epics tend to be), but rewarding entertainment for those who stick it out—where else can you see the king's army get mooned en masse? Script was based on 300 pages of rhyming verse attributed to a blind poet known as Blind Harry. Gibson put up $15 million of his own money to complete the film. **178m/C VHS, DVD, Wide.** Mel Gibson, Sophie Marceau, Patrick McGoohan, Catherine McCormack, Brendan Gleeson, James Cosmo, David O'Hara, Angus Macfadyen, Peter Hanly, Ian Bannen, Sean McGinley, Brian Cox, Stephen Billington, Barry McGovern, Alun Armstrong, Tommy Flanagan; ***D:*** Mel Gibson; ***W:*** Randall Wallace; ***C:*** John Toll; ***M:*** James Horner. Oscars '95: Cinematog., Director (Gibson), Makeup, Picture; British Acad. '95: Cinematog.; Golden Globes '96: Director (Gibson); MTV Movie Awards '96: Action Seq.; Writers Guild '95: Orig. Screenplay; Broadcast Film Critics '95: Director (Gibson).

Brazil ½ **1985 (R)** The acclaimed nightmare comedy about an Everyman trying to survive in a surreal paper-choked bureaucratic society. There are copious references to "1984" and "The Trial," fantastic mergings of glorious fantasy and stark reality, and astounding visual design. The DVD version has a 142-minute director's cut as well as a documentary. **131m/C VHS, DVD, Wide.** *GB* Jonathan Pryce, Robert De Niro, Michael Palin, Katherine Helmond, Kim Greist, Bob Hoskins, Ian Holm, Peter Vaughan, Ian Richardson; ***D:*** Terry Gilliam; ***W:*** Charles McKeown, Terry Gilliam, Tom Stoppard; ***C:*** Roger Pratt; ***M:*** Michael Kamen. L.A. Film Critics '85: Director (Gilliam), Film, Screenplay.

Breach of Conduct ½ **1994 (PG-13)** Col. Bill Case (Coyote) is the commander of the Fort Benton, Utah, Army base where Helen Lutz's (Thorne-Smith) husband Tom (Verica) has just been transferred. At first there's a mutual attraction between Helen and Case, but then hubby is assigned a mission off base and, when Helen refuses Case's overtures, things turn very nasty. **93m/C VHS.** Peter Coyote, Courtney Thorne-Smith, Tom Verica, Beth Toussaint; ***D:*** Tim Matheson; ***W:*** Scott Abbott; ***C:*** Gideon Porath. **CABLE**

Breach of Trust ½ **1995 (R)** Smalltime crook Casey (Biehn) winds up in big trouble when he steals a computer disc with access codes to millions in drug cartel money. He goes on the lam and meets Madeline (Ferrer), an undercover cop who thinks that some police are on the cartel's payroll. So the daring duo decide to take on the drug lords and the dirty cops. **96m/C VHS.** Michael Biehn, Matt Craven, Leilani Sarelle Ferrer, Miguel (Michael) Sandoval, Kim Coates, Ed Lauter; ***D:*** Charles Wilkinson; ***W:*** Gordon Basichis, Raul Inglis; ***C:*** Michael Slovis; ***M:*** Graeme Coleman.

Bread and Chocolate *Pane e Cioccolata* **1973** Uneducated Italian immigrant Manfredi works a series of odd jobs in complacently bourgeois Switzerland and tries desperately to fit in and better himself (which he fails utterly to do). Culture clash satire, with an engaging everyman lead. Italian with subtitles. **110m/C VHS, DVD, Wide.** *IT* Nino Manfredi, Anna Karina, Johnny Dorelli, Paolo Turco; ***D:*** Franco Brusati; ***W:*** Nino Manfredi, Franco Brusati, Iaia Fiastri; ***C:*** Luciano Tovoli; ***M:*** Daniele Patrucchi. N.Y. Film Critics '78: Foreign Film.

Bread and Roses **2000 (R)** Typical Loach political polemic—this time about union organizing of janitors (many of them illegals) in Los Angeles. Maya (Padilla) is an illegal immigrant from Mexico who's working for an office cleaning company. She meets union organizer Sam (Brody) who convinces Maya to join with him, even though she not only risks her job but deportation. Things go from bad to worse for Maya but Loach never takes the easy road and his characters are flawed human beings rather than mere symbols. English and Spanish with subtitles. **106m/C VHS, DVD, Wide.** *GB* Adrien Brody, Elpidia Carrillo, Pilar Padilla, George Lopez, Jack McGee, Alonso Chavez; ***D:*** Ken Loach; ***W:*** Paul Laverty; ***C:*** Barry Ackroyd; ***M:*** George Fenton.

Bread and Tulips *Pane e Tulipani* **2001 (PG-13)** Sweet Rosalba (Maglietta) is a much-neglected wife and mother who is accidentally left behind at a rest stop while the family is on vacation. Impulsively, Rosalba doesn't go home but hitches a ride to Venice, a city she has always longed to see. Although, she dutifully lets her husband Mimmo (Catania) know where she is, she delays her return, is befriended by waiter Fernando (Ganz), and finds a job working for a florist. Rosalba's idyll doesn't last as her loyalties pull her back to her old life but events don't work out as expected. Italian with subtitles. **105m/C VHS, DVD, Wide.** *IT SI* Licia Maglietta, Bruno Ganz, Marina Massironi, Guiseppe Battiston, Antonio Catania, Felice Andreasi, Vitalba Andrea; ***D:*** Silvio Soldini; ***W:*** Silvio Soldini, Doriana Leondeff; ***C:*** Luca Bigazzi; ***M:*** Giovanni Venosta.

The Break **1995 (PG-13)** Clumsy teen tennis hopeful Ben (Jorgensen) refuses to give up his dreams even after his bookie dad Robbins (Sheen) hires washed-up player Nick Irons (Van Patten) as a coach to show Ben the error of his game. **104m/C VHS.** Vincent Van Patten, Martin Sheen, Ben Jorgensen, Rae Dawn Chong, Valerie Perrine, Betsy Russell; ***D:*** Lee H. Katzin; ***W:*** Dan Jenkins, Vincent Van Patten.

The Break ½ *A Further Gesture* **1997 (R)** Disillusioned IRA gunman Dowd (Rea) breaks out of prison and escapes to New York to find a new life. Instead, he befriends (and falls in love with one of) a group of Guatemalan refugees who plan to kill the dictator who persecuted them. Appalled by their inability, he agrees to help them. This is definitely Rea's film (it's based on an idea of his), mainly because his is the only character that's really fleshed out. Character study of a man who's lost whatever passion he had for the cause but can't give up the life doesn't delve into specific Irish or Guatemalan politics, and loses some impact as a result. **97m/C VHS.** Stephen Rea, Rosana Pastor, Brendan Gleeson, Pruitt Taylor Vince, Maria Doyle Kennedy, Jorge Sanz, Carolyn Seymour, Sean McGinley, Paul Giamatti; ***D:*** Robert Dornhelm, Alfred Molina; ***W:*** Ronan Bennett; ***C:*** Andrzej Sekula; ***M:*** John Keane.

Break of Dawn ½ **1988** Pedro J. Gonzalez (Chavez) is a veteran of Pancho Villa's army who takes his family and crosses into the U.S. Despite the Depression, he finds work at a radio station in L.A. and soon becomes a popular personality in the Latino community. But Gonzalez never leaves politics very far behind and his radical civil rights views lead to a political witchhunt that sends him to prison. **105m/C VHS, DVD.** Oscar Chavez, Maria Rojo, Tony Plana, Peter Henry Schroeder, Pepe Serna, Kamala Lopez-Dawson; ***D:*** Isaac Artenstein; ***W:*** Isaac Artenstein; ***C:*** Stephen Lighthill; ***M:*** Mark Adler. **TV**

Break of Hearts ½ **1935** Hepburn marries Boyer, who becomes an alcoholic, and then more troubles arise. Very soapy, but well-made. **78m/B VHS.** Katharine Hepburn, Charles Boyer, Jean Hersholt, John Beal, Sam Hardy; ***D:*** Philip Moeller; ***W:*** Victor Heerman; ***M:*** Max Steiner.

The Break Up ½ **1998 (R)** Predictable thriller finds Jimmy Dade (Fonda) awakening in the hospital to discover her abusive husband (Bochner) is dead and she is the prime suspect. **101m/C VHS, DVD.** Bridget Fonda, Kiefer Sutherland, Penelope Ann Miller, Steven Weber, Hart Bochner, Tippi Hedren; ***D:*** Paul Marcus; ***W:*** Anne Amanda Opotowsky.

Breakaway **1995 (R)** Myra (Thompson) decides to get away from her drop-woman job with $300,000 of mob money. Naturally, she's pursued by a hit man (Estevez) and then betrayed by a boyfriend (De Rose), who steals the cash and hides it in the apartment of the other woman he's seeing (Harding). Thompson does fine but to describe Harding's debut performance as wooden is to be very, very kind. **94m/C VHS.** Teri Thompson, Joe Estevez, Chris De Rose, Tonya Harding, Tony Noakes, Rick Beatty, Michael Garganese; *D:* Sean Dash; *W:* Sean Dash, Eric Gardner; *C:* Carlos Montaner; *M:* Robert Wait.

Breakdown ♂ **1953** A boxer is set up by his girlfriend's father to take the rap for a murder. Lackluster effort. **76m/B VHS.** Ann Richards, William Bishop, Anne Gwynne, Sheldon Leonard, Wally Cassell, Richard Benedict; *D:* Edmond Angelo.

Breakdown ♂♂♂ **1996 (R)** Jeff (Russell) and Amy (Quinlan) are high-falootin' Easterners on their way to San Diego when their car breaks down somewhere in the vast Southwest. When a trucker (Walsh) stops and offers to take Amy to the next stop while Jeff guards their yuppie treasure trove, they accept willingly. Inconvenience soon turns to terror when Jeff gets the car started, drives to meet his wife and finds her nowhere in sight. Spotting the truck by the side of the road, he confronts the trucker. with the cops only to have him deny ever having seen them before. Thus begins the frantic hunt. Russell's descent from dismay to panic to resolve is grippingly played. You may know where it's going, but the fun is in getting there. **93m/C VHS, DVD, Wide.** Kurt Russell, Kathleen Quinlan, J.T. Walsh, M.C. Gainey, Jack Noseworthy, Rex Linn, Ritch Brinkley, Kim Robillard; *D:* Jonathan Mostow; *W:* Jonathan Mostow; *C:* Doug Milsome; *M:* Basil Poledouris.

Breaker! Breaker! ♂ **1977 (PG)** Convoy of angry truck drivers launch an assault on the corrupt and sadistic locals of a small Texas town. Goofy entry in "mad or sex-crazed trucker armed with a CB radio" genre. **86m/C VHS, DVD, Wide.** Chuck Norris, George Murdock, Terry O'Connor, Don Gentry, Jack Nance; *D:* Don Hulette; *W:* Terry Chambers; *C:* Mario DiLeo; *M:* Don Hulette.

Breaker Morant ♂♂♂½ **1980 (PG)** In 1901 South Africa, three Australian soldiers are put on trial for avenging the murder of several prisoners. Based on a true story which was then turned into a play by Kenneth Ross, this riveting, popular antiwar statement and courtroom drama heralded Australia's film renaissance. Rich performances by Woodward and Waters. **107m/C VHS, DVD.** *AU* Edward Woodward, Jack Thompson, John Waters, Bryan Brown, Charles Tingwell, Terence Donovan, Vincent Ball, Ray Meagher, Chris Haywood, Lewis Fitz-Gerald, Rod Mullinar, Alan Cassell, Rob Steele; *D:* Bruce Beresford; *W:* Bruce Beresford, Jonathan Hardy, David Stevens; *C:* Donald McAlpine; *M:* Phil Cuneen. Australian Film Inst. '80: Actor (Thompson), Film.

Breakfast at Tiffany's ♂♂♂½ **1961** Truman Capote's amusing story of an endearingly eccentric New York City playgirl and her shaky romance with a young writer. Hepburn lends Holly Golightly just the right combination of naivete and worldly wisdom with a dash of melancholy. A wonderfully offbeat romance. ♫Moon River. **114m/C VHS, DVD, 8mm.** Audrey Hepburn, George Peppard, Patricia Neal, Buddy Ebsen, Mickey Rooney, Martin Balsam, John McGiver; *D:* Blake Edwards; *W:* George Axelrod; *C:* Franz Planer; *M:* Henry Mancini. Oscars '61: Song ("Moon River"), Orig. Dramatic Score.

The Breakfast Club ♂♂♂ **1985 (R)** Five students from different cliques at a Chicago suburban high school spend a day together in detention. Rather well done teenage culture study; these characters delve a little deeper than the standard adult view of adolescent stereotypes. One of John Hughes' best movies. Soundtrack features Simple Minds and Wang Chung. **97m/C VHS, DVD.** Ally Sheedy, Molly Ringwald, Judd Nelson, Emilio Estevez, Anthony Michael Hall, Paul Gleason, John Kapelos; *D:* John Hughes; *W:* John Hughes; *C:* Thomas Del Ruth; *M:* Gary Chang, Keith Forsey.

Breakfast in Hollywood ♂½ *The Mad Hatter* **1946** Movie about the popular morning radio show of the 1940s hosted by Tom Breneman, a coast-to-coast coffee klatch. **93m/B VHS.** Tom Breneman, Bonita Granville, Eddie Ryan, Beulah Bondi, Billie Burke, ZaSu Pitts, Hedda Hopper, Spike Jones; *D:* Harold Schuster.

Breakfast in Paris ♂½ **1981** Two American professionals in Paris, both crushed from past failures in the love department, find each other. **85m/C VHS.** *AU* Rod Mullinar, Barbara Parkins, Jack Lenoir; *D:* John Lamond.

Breakfast of Champions ♂½ **1998 (R)** Messy adaptation of Kurt Vonnegut's 1973 satire on American greed and commercialism. Relentlessly upbeat salesman Dwayne Hoover (Willis) runs the most successful car dealership in middle America's Midland City. A leading citizen, who stars in his own garish TV commercials, Dwayne has alienated his tube-addicted wife, Celia (Hershey), and his aspiring lounge singer son, Bunny (Haas). Dwayne also thinks he's going nuts and his one hope for salvation lies with Kilgore Trout (Finney), an eccentric hack sci fi writer/philosopher. Oh yeah, and Nolte is around as Dwayne's sales manager Harry, who likes to wear women's lacy lingerie beneath his suits. **110m/C VHS, DVD, Wide.** Bruce Willis, Albert Finney, Nick Nolte, Barbara Hershey, Glenne Headly, Lukas Haas, Omar Epps, Buck Henry, Vicki Lewis, Ken Campbell, Will Patton, Chip Zien, Owen C. Wilson, Alison Eastwood, Shawnee Smith, Kurt Vonnegut Jr.; *D:* Alan Rudolph; *W:* Alan Rudolph; *C:* Elliot Davis; *M:* Mark Isham.

Breakheart Pass ♂♂ **1976 (PG)** A governor, his female companion, a band of cavalrymen, and a mysterious man travel on a train through the mountains of Idaho in 1870. The mystery man turns out to be a murderer. Based on a novel by Alistair MacLean. **92m/C VHS, DVD, Wide.** Charles Bronson, Ben Johnson, Richard Crenna, Jill Ireland, Charles Durning, Ed Lauter, Archie Moore, Sally Kirkland; *D:* Tom Gries; *W:* Alistair MacLean; *C:* Lucien Ballard; *M:* Jerry Goldsmith.

Breakin' ♂♂ *Breakdance* **1984 (PG)** Dance phenomenon break dancing along with the hit songs that accompanied the fad. ♫Tibetan Jam; Heart of the Beat; Breakin...There's No Stopping Us; Street People; Showdown; 99 1/2. **87m/C VHS.** Lucinda Dickey, Adolfo "Shabba Doo" Quinones, Michael "Boogaloo Shrimp" Chambers, Ben Lokey, Christopher McDonald, Phineas Newborn III; *D:* Joel Silberg; *W:* Allen N. DeBevoise; *C:* Hanania Baer; *M:* Michael Boyd.

Breakin' 2: Electric Boogaloo ♂ *Breakdance 2: Electric Boogaloo; Electric Boogaloo "Breakin' 2"* **1984 (PG)** Breakdancers hold a benefit concert to preserve an urban community center. ♫Electric Boogaloo; Radiotron; Action; When I.C.U. **94m/C VHS.** Lucinda Dickey, Adolfo "Shabba Doo" Quinones, Michael "Boogaloo Shrimp" Chambers, Susie Bono; *D:* Sam Firstenberg; *C:* Hanania Baer.

Breakin' Through ♂ **1984** The choreographer of a troubled Broadway-bound musical decides to energize his shows with a troupe of street dancers. **73m/C VHS.** Ben Vereen, Donna McKechnie, Reid Shelton; *D:* Peter Medak.

Breaking All the Rules ♂½ **1985 (R)** Comedy about two teenage lovers who find themselves embroiled in a slapdash jewel robbery at an amusement park during the last day of summer break. **91m/C VHS.** *CA* Carolyn Dunn, Carl Marotte, Thor Bishopric, Rachel Hayward; *D:* James Orr; *W:* James Orr, Jim Cruickshank.

Breaking Away ♂♂♂½ **1979 (PG)** A lighthearted coming-of-age drama about a high school graduate's addiction to bicycle racing, whose dreams are tested against the realities of a crucial race. An honest, open look at present Americana with tremendous insight into the minds of average youth; shot on location at Indiana University. Great bike-racing photography. Quaid, Barrie, and Christopher give exceptional performances. Basis for a TV series. **100m/C VHS, DVD, Wide.** Dennis Christopher, Dennis Quaid, Daniel Stern, Jackie Earle Haley, Barbara Barrie, Paul Dooley, Amy Wright; *D:* Peter Yates; *W:* Steve Tesich; *C:* Matthew F. Leonetti; *M:* Patrick Williams. Oscars '79: Orig. Screenplay; Golden Globes '80: Film—Mus./Comedy; Natl. Bd. of Review '79: Support. Actor (Dooley); N.Y. Film Critics '79: Screenplay; Natl. Soc. Film Critics '79: Film, Screenplay; Writers Guild '79: Orig. Screenplay.

Breaking Free ♂♂½ **1995 (PG)** Teenaged loser Rick Chilton (London) forms an unlikely friendship with bitter gymnast Lindsay (Phillips) who's been blinded and forced to give up her dreams. Mostly avoids the stickiness inherent in such stories thanks to some fine performances. **106m/C VHS.** Jeremy London, Gina Philips, Christine Taylor, Megan Gallagher, Nicolas Surovy, Adam Wylie, Brian Krause, Scott Coffey; *D:* David Mackay; *C:* Christopher Faloona; *M:* Steve Dorff.

Breaking Glass ♂♂½ **1980 (PG)** A "New Wave" musical that gives an insight into the punk record business and at the same time tells of the rags-to-riches life of a punk rock star. **94m/C VHS.** *GB* Hazel O'Connor, Phil Daniels, Jon Finch, Jonathan Pryce; *D:* Brian Gibson.

Breaking Home Ties ♂♂½ *Norman Rockwell's Breaking Home Ties* **1987** Norman Rockwell's illustration is the basis for this coming-of-age story set in a small Texas town. A young man is eager to be off to college and lessen his family ties but his mother's serious illness may prevent both. Good performances help overcome the sentimentality. **95m/C VHS.** Jason Robards Jr., Eva Marie Saint, Doug McKeon, Claire Trevor, Erin Gray; *D:* John Wilder; *W:* John Wilder. **TV**

Breaking In ♂♂♂ **1989 (R)** A semi-acclaimed comedy about a professional thief who takes a young amateur under his wing and shows him the ropes. Under-estimated Reynolds is especially charming. Witty and innovative script, with intelligent direction from Forsyth. **95m/C VHS, DVD, Wide.** Burt Reynolds, Casey Siemaszko, Sheila Kelley, Lorraine Toussaint, Albert Salmi, Harry Carey Jr., Maury Chaykin, Stephen Tobolowsky, David Frishberg; *D:* Bill Forsyth; *W:* John Sayles; *C:* Michael Coulter; *M:* Michael Gibbs.

Breaking Loose ♂½ **1990 (R)** A surfer is on the run from a vicious motorcycle gang that kidnapped his girlfriend, but turns to fight eventually, board in hand. **88m/C VHS.** Peter Phelps, Vince Martin, Abigail, David Ngcombujarra; *D:* Rod Hay.

Breaking Point ♂♂½ **1994 (R)** Ex-cop Dwight Meadows (Busey) retired from the force when he was nearly killed by a scalpel-wielding mass murderer known as "The Surgeon." Now the psycho is back and Meadows returns to active duty, paired with relentless officer Dana Preston (Fluegel), who wants the killer caught—at any cost. Vancouver, British Columbia fills in for the Seattle, Washington setting. **95m/C VHS.** Gary Busey, Darlanne Fluegel, Jeff Griggs, Kim Cattrall; *D:* Paul Ziller; *M:* Graeme Coleman.

Breaking the Code ♂♂½ **1995** Alan Turing (Jacobi) is a British mathematical genius whose work leads to the birth of the digital computer and who is instrumental in enabling the allies to crack the German WWII Enigma code. An active homosexual when homosexuality was illegal, Turing's personal behavior was tolerated because of the importance of his war work but after the gay spy scare of the '50s, Turing was regarded as a security risk and his life increasingly restricted. British TV adaptation based on the play by Hugh Whitemore (Jacobi also played the role on stage) and the book "Alan Turing: The Enigma" by Andrew Hodges. **90m/C VHS.** *GB* Derek Jacobi, Amanda Root, Prunella Scales, Harold Pinter, Julian Kerridge, Richard Johnson; *D:* Herbert Wise; *W:* Hugh Whitemore.

Breaking the Ice ♂♂ **1938** Unlikely mixture of Mennonites and a big city ice skating show. Young man leaves the farm to get a job singing at the rink. Musical numbers abound with backing by Victor Young and his Orchestra. **79m/B VHS.** Bobby Breen, Charlie Ruggles, Dolores Costello, Billy Gilbert, Margaret Hamilton, Jonathan Hale; *D:* Edward F. (Eddie) Cline; *W:* Mary C. McCall, Bernard Schubert, Manuel Seff; *C:* Jack MacKenzie; *M:* Victor Young.

Breaking the Rules ♂♂½ **1992 (PG-13)** Predicatable buddy-road movie with a tearjerking premise and comedic overtones. Rob, Gene, and Phil were best buds growing up in Cleveland but young adulthood has separated them. They are reunited by Phil, who is dying of leukemia, and whose last wish is a cross-country road trip to California so he can appear as a contestant on "Jeopardy." Along the way they meet brassy waitress Mary, who impulsively decides to join them and winds up bringing the trio's shaky friendship back together. Potts does well as the big-haired, big-hearted Mary but the actors must work hard to maintain any dignity given the story's melodrama. **100m/C VHS.** Jason Bateman, C. Thomas Howell, Jonathan Silverman, Annie Potts, Kent Bateman, Shawn (Michael) Phelan; *D:* Neal Israel; *W:* Paul Shapiro; *M:* David Kitay.

Breaking the Surface: The Greg Louganis Story ♂♂½ **1996** Trials and tribulations of the gold-medal winning Olympic diver, including his overbearing father, abusive lover, and his own HIV-positive status. Based on Louganis' autobiography; made for TV. **95m/C VHS.** Mario Lopez, Michael Murphy, Jeffrey Meek, Bruce Weitz, Rosemary Dunsmore; *D:* Steven Hilliard Stern; *W:* Alan Hines. **CABLE**

Breaking the Waves ♂♂♂ **1995 (R)** Sacrifical journey of shy, religious Bess (Watson), who's living in an austere northern Scotland coastal village in the '70s. Bess, who regularly talks to God, marries Jan (Skarsgard), an adventurer working on a North Sea oil rig. It must be a case of opposites attracting but the couple are happy until Jan is paralyzed from the neck down in a rig accident. Bess, who blames herself, begins sleeping around, believing her actions can somehow help Jan, and slides ever deeper into mental instability. Powerful story is divided into seven chapters and an epilogue. **152m/C VHS, DVD, Wide.** *DK FR* Emily Watson, Stellan Skarsgard, Katrin Cartlidge, Adrian Rawlins, Jean-Marc Barr, Sandra Voe, Udo Kier, Mikkel Gaup; *D:* Lars von Trier; *W:* Lars von Trier; *C:* Robby Muller; *M:* Joachim Holbek. Cannes '96: Grand Jury Prize; Cesar '97: Foreign Film; N.Y. Film Critics '96: Actress (Watson), Cinematog., Director (von Trier); Natl. Soc. Film Critics '96: Actress (Watson), Cinematog., Director (von Trier), Film.

Breaking Up ♂♂½ **1978** A woman fights to rediscover her personal identity after her 15-year marriage crumbles in this Emmy-nominated movie. **90m/C VHS.** Lee Remick, Granville Van Dusen, David Stambaugh; *D:* Delbert Mann. **TV**

Breaking Up ♂½ **1997 (R)** What steamy sheet action brings together, dreary day to day living easily pulls apart. That is the basic message of this bland romantic comedy that brings nothing new to the tired genre. Typical opposites attract but can't stay together (yet can't stay apart) plot finds photographer Crowe and teacher Hayek madly in lust and impulsively marrying. Hayek had more to work with when she played this role in "Fools Rush In," and Crowe seems uncomfortable as the lackluster boyfriend. Told in a chatty style with frequent asides to the audience by the main characters and a string of flashback sequences, director Greenwald's theatre background is apparent here. Clever camera work and editing are highlights. Adapted from Michael Cristofer's Pulitzer Prize-winning play. **90m/C VHS.** Salma Hayek, Russell Crowe; *D:* Robert Greenwald; *W:* Michael Cristofer; *M:* Mark Mothersbaugh.

Breaking Up Is Hard to Do ♂ **1979** Six men leave their wives and shack up together on Malibu for a summer of partying and introspection. Made for television; edited down from its original 201 minute length. **96m/C VHS.** Billy Crystal, Bonnie Franklin, Ted Bessell, Jeff Conaway, Tony Musante, Robert Conrad, Trish Stewart, David Ogden Stiers, George Gaynes; *D:* Lou Antonio; *M:* Richard Bellis. **TV**

Breakout ♂♂ **1975 (PG)** The wife of a man imprisoned in Mexico hires a Texas bush pilot (Bronson) to help her husband (Duvall) escape. **96m/C VHS, DVD, Wide.** Charles Bronson, Jill Ireland, Robert Duvall, John Huston, Sheree North, Randy Quaid; *D:* Tom Gries; *W:* Howard B. Kreitsek, Marc Norman, Elliott Baker; *C:* Lucien Ballard; *M:* Jerry Goldsmith.

Breakout 🦴🦴 **1998** Zack (Carradine) has invented an environmentally-friendly alternative energy source that makes him the scourge of the oil cartels. So the bad guys decide to kidnap Zack's son Joe (Bonifant) as a bargaining chip, only the kid turns out to be as smart as his old man. **86m/C VHS.** Robert Carradine, Evan Bonifant, James Hong, Chris Chinchilla; ***D:*** John Bradshaw; ***W:*** Naomi Jantzen; ***C:*** Edgar Egger; ***M:*** Gary Koftinoff. **VIDEO**

The Breaks 🦴 **1999 (R)** White Irish kid gets adopted by a black family in South Central L.A. and naturally grows up to think of himself as a homeboy. But his adoptive mom is tired of his shenanigans and gives him one simple task to do—bring home a carton of milk by supper—or else. Why isn't this as easy as it sounds ('cause it certainly is as dumb). **86m/C VHS, DVD.** Mitch Mullany, Carl Anthony Payne II, Paula Jai Parker, Clifton Powell, Loretta Devine; ***D:*** Eric Meza; ***W:*** Mitch Mullany; ***C:*** Carlos Gonzalez; ***M:*** Adam Hirsh. **VIDEO**

Breakthrough 🦴🦴 *Sergeant Steiner* **1978 (PG)** German soldier, broken at the end of WWII, sets out to negotiate with the Allies. Average at best. **96m/C VHS.** Richard Burton, Robert Mitchum, Rod Steiger, Michael Parks, Curt Jurgens; ***D:*** Andrew V. McLaglen.

Breast Men 🦴🦴½ **1997 (R)** A campy fictional look into the lives and careers of the two doctors who invented the silicone breast implant in 1960s Texas. Struggling Kevin Saunders (Schwimmer) is an ambitious geek who works with grumpy plastic surgeon mentor, Dr. William Larson (Cooper), to develop a prosthetic breast, made from Dow-Corning's silicone gel. It's an immediate success and the doctors become rich, successful, and ever more obnoxious. Then come the lawsuits and life is suddenly no longer so sweet. And yes, you will see a lot of naked breasts. **95m/C VHS, DVD.** John Stockwell, Terry O'Quinn, Kathleen Wilhoite, Lisa Marie, David Schwimmer, Chris Cooper, Louise Fletcher, Emily (Proctor) Procter, Matt Frewer; ***D:*** Lawrence O'Neil; ***W:*** John Stockwell; ***C:*** Robert Stevens; ***M:*** Dennis McCarthy. **CABLE**

Breath of Scandal 🦴🦴 **1960** An American diplomat in Vienna rescues a princess when she is thrown off a horse; he falls for her like a ton o' bricks. Viennese politics complicate things. Based on a play by Molnar. **98m/C VHS.** Sophia Loren, John Gavin, Maurice Chevalier, Angela Lansbury; ***D:*** Michael Curtiz.

Breathing Fire 🦴🦴 **1991 (R)** A Vietnamese teenager and his American brother find out their ex-GI father is behind an armed bank robbery and murder. They join together to protect the only eyewitness—a young girl—against the ruthless gang of criminals and their own father. Lots of kickboxing action for martial arts fans. **86m/C VHS.** Bolo Yeung, Jonathan Ke Quan, Jerry Trimble; ***D:*** Lou Kennedy.

Breathing Lessons 🦴🦴🦴 **1994 (PG)** Sweet look at a long-term marriage that renews itself on a road trip. Flighty Maggie and pragmatic Ira have been married for 28 squabbling but loving years. They're driving from their Baltimore home to a funeral in Pennsylvania and the road stops provide some small adventures and a great deal of conversation. Drama rests easily on the capable shoulders of the veteran performers. Based on the novel by Anne Tyler. Made for TV. **98m/C VHS.** James Garner, Joanne Woodward, Paul Winfield, Kathryn Erbe, Joyce Van Patten, Eileen Heckart, Tim Guinee, Henry Jones, Stephi Lineburg, Jean (Louisa) Kelly, John Considine; ***D:*** John Erman; ***W:*** Robert W. Lenski. **TV**

Breathing Room 🦴🦴 *'Til Christmas* **1996 (R)** New Yorker David (Futterman) has trouble with commitment to girlfriend Kathy (Floyd) and the duo break up again at Thanksgiving when he won't tell her he loves her. Kathy decides they need a break and refuses to see David until Christmas. She plays at seeing her boss, both get too much advice from friends and family, they attend the same holiday party—and the inevitable happens. Nothing new here. **90m/C VHS.** Dan Futterman, Susan Floyd, David Thornton; ***D:*** Jon Sherman; ***W:*** Jon Sherman, Tom Hughes; ***C:*** Jim Denault; ***M:*** Pat Irwin.

Breathless 🦴🦴🦴🦴 *A Bout de Souffle* **1959** Godard's first feature catapulted him to the vanguard of French filmmakers. Carefree Parisian crook, Michel (Belmondo), who emulates Humphrey Bogart, falls in love with gamine American student Patricia (Sebring) with tragic results. Wonderful scenes of Parisian life. Established Godard's Brechtian, experimental style. Belmondo's film debut. Mistitled "Breathless" for American release, the film's French title actually means "Out of Breath"; however, the fast-paced, erratic musical score leaves you breathless. French with English subtitles. Remade with Richard Gere in 1983 with far less intensity. **90m/B VHS, DVD.** *FR* Jean-Paul Belmondo, Jean Seberg, Daniel Boulanger, Jean-Pierre Melville, Liliane Robin; ***D:*** Jean-Luc Godard; ***W:*** Jean-Luc Godard; ***C:*** Raoul Coutard; ***M:*** Martial Solal. Berlin Intl. Film Fest. '60: Director (Godard).

Breathless 🦴🦴 **1983 (R)** Car thief turned cop killer has a torrid love affair with a French student studying in Los Angeles as the police slowly close in. Glossy, smarmy remake of the Godard classic that concentrates on the thin plot rather than any attempt at revitalizing the film syntax. **105m/C VHS, DVD.** Richard Gere, Valerie Kaprisky, Art Metrano, John P. Ryan, Lisa Jane Persky; ***D:*** Jim McBride; ***W:*** Jim McBride, L.M. Kit Carson; ***M:*** Jack Nitzsche.

Breathtaking 🦴🦴 **2000** Workaholic Dr. Caroline Henshaw (Whalley) is a psychologist with many mental problems of her own, stemming from her own past sexual abuse. But Caroline has managed to keep it together until she meets a new patient (Maitland)—a self-destructive masseuse who's being battered by her sicko hubby (Foreman). **105m/C VHS.** *GB* Joanne Whalley, Neil Dudgeon, Sandra Maitland, Jamie Foreman; ***D:*** David Green; ***W:*** Nicky Cowan; ***C:*** Gavin Finney; ***M:*** Robert Lane.

The Breed **2001 (R)** Set in a noir-ish anytime, this horror film tells the story of an FBI agent Grant (a very stiff Woodbine), who starts out searching for a serial killer and ends up teamed with Aaron Grey (Paul), who turns out to be a vampire. Seems that the vampires who walk among us are ready to come out of the closet and join society, but a political dissident in the vampire ranks is trying to start a war...or is he? Could there be crosses and double crosses afoot? Grant, a black man, is less than thrilled at being teamed with a vampire, which results in not-too-subtle moral banter about racism and the Nazis to explain the vamps' fear of the humans and condemn the human sense of self preservation. It has moments of promise, but the poor acting and choppy editing and direction make everyone look uncomfortable amid the atmospheric scenery. **91m/C VHS, DVD, Wide.** Adrian Paul, Bai Ling, Bokeem Woodbine, Zen Gesner, Jake Eberle; ***D:*** Michael Oblowitz; ***W:*** Christos N. Gage, Ruth Fletcher. **VIDEO**

A Breed Apart 🦴🦴 **1984 (R)** An on-going battle over a rare eagle's eggs strikes sparks between a reclusive conservationist and a scheming adventurer hired by a billionaire collector. **95m/C VHS.** Kathleen Turner, Rutger Hauer, Powers Boothe, Donald Pleasence, Brion James, John Dennis Johnston; ***D:*** Philippe Mora.

Breed of the Border 🦴 *Speed Brent Wins* **1933** Tough-fisted cowboys must take the law into their own hands. **60m/B VHS.** Bob Steele, Marion Byron, George "Gabby" Hayes, Ernie Adams; ***D:*** Robert North Bradbury.

Breeders woof! **1997 (R)** Alien on a mating mission terrorizes a Boston womens' college. Doesn't deliver on its exploitation premise, so don't bother. **92m/C VHS, DVD.** Todd Jensen, Samantha Janus, Kadamba Simmons, Oliver Tobias; ***D:*** Paul Matthews; ***W:*** Paul Matthews; ***M:*** Ben Heneghan.

Brenda Starr 🦴 **1986 (PG)** Amateurish adaptation of the comic strip by Dale Messick. Shields stars as girl reporter Brenda Starr, who is once again risking her life to get the scoop. She finds herself in the jungles of South America searching for a mad scientist who is creating a rocket fuel that could destroy the world. The most entertaining thing about this film is the costumes designed by Bob Mackie. **94m/C VHS, DVD.** Brooke Shields, Timothy Dalton, Tony Peck, Diana Scarwid, Nestor Serrano, Jeffrey Tambor, June Gable, Charles Durning, Eddie Albert, Henry Gibson, Ed Nelson; ***D:*** Robert Ellis Miller; ***W:*** James David Buchanan; ***C:*** Freddie Francis; ***M:*** Johnny Mandel.

The Bretts 🦴🦴🦴 **1988** Amusing two-part British miniseries follows the egos and eccentricities of the British theatrical dynasty, the Bretts. Part 1 is set in the '20s and introduces the family heads, Charles (Rodway) and Lydia (Murray), who enjoy performing off-stage almost as well as they enjoy performing on. Also introduced are their five children and loyal (if opinionated) servants. Part 2 follows the family into the '30s with son Edwin (Yelland) having become a film star, actress daughter Martha (Lang) falling for a politician, and son Tom (Winter) continuing to write his gloomy social dramas. Each part is on six cassettes. **600m/C VHS.** *GB* Barbara Murray, Norman Rodway, David Yelland, Belinda Lang, George Winter, Janet Maw, Tim Wylton, Bert Parnaby, Lysette Anthony, Clive Francis, Frank Middlemass, John Castle, Hugh Fraser, Patrick Ryecart, Sally Cookson, Billy Boyle; ***W:*** Rosemary Anne Sisson.

Brewster McCloud 🦴🦴🦴½ **1970 (R)** Altman's first picture after M*A*S*H reunites much of the cast and combines fantasy, black comedy, and satire in the story of a young man whose head is in the clouds or at least in the upper reaches of the Houston Astrodome. Brewster (Cort) lives covertly in the Dome and dreams of flying. He also has a guardian angel (Kellerman) who watches over him and may actually be killing people who give him a hard time. Murphy is a cop obsessed with catching the killer. And there's a circus allegory as well. Hard to figure what it all means and offbeat as they come, but for certain tastes, exquisite. **101m/C VHS, Wide.** Bud Cort, Sally Kellerman, Shelley Duvall, Michael Murphy, William Windom, Rene Auberjonois, Stacy Keach, John Schuck, Margaret Hamilton; ***D:*** Robert Altman; ***W:*** Doran William Cannon; ***C:*** Lamar Boren, Jordan Cronenweth; ***M:*** Gene Page.

Brewster's Millions 🦴🦴½ **1945** If Brewster, an ex-GI, can spend $1 million in one year, he will inherit a substantially greater fortune. Originally a 1902 novel, this is the fifth of seven film adaptations. **79m/B VHS.** Dennis O'Keefe, June Havoc, Eddie Anderson, Helen Walker, Gail Patrick, Mischa Auer; ***D:*** Allan Dwan.

Brewster's Millions 🦴½ **1985 (PG)** An aging minor league baseball player must spend $30 million in order to collect an inheritance of $300 million. He may find that money can't buy happiness. Seventh remake of the story. **101m/C VHS, DVD, Wide.** Richard Pryor, John Candy, Lonette McKee, Stephen Collins, Jerry Orbach, Pat Hingle, Tovah Feldshuh, Hume Cronyn, Rick Moranis; ***D:*** Walter Hill; ***W:*** Timothy Harris, Herschel Weingrod; ***C:*** Ric Waite; ***M:*** Ry Cooder.

Brian's Song 🦴🦴🦴🦴 **1971 (G)** The story of the unique relationship between Gale Sayers, the Chicago Bears' star running back, and his teammate Brian Piccolo. The friendship between the Bears' first interracial roommates ended suddenly when Brian Piccolo lost his life to cancer. Incredibly well received in its time. **74m/C VHS, DVD.** James Caan, Billy Dee Williams, Jack Warden, Shelley Fabares, Judy Pace, Bernie Casey; ***D:*** Buzz Kulik; ***W:*** William Blinn; ***C:*** Joseph Biroc; ***M:*** Michel Legrand. **TV**

Brian's Song 🦴🦴 **2001** Unnecessary remake of the 1971 made-for-TV classic dealing with the friendship between Gale Sayers and Brian Piccolo, and Piccolo's fight against cancer heads right for the disease-of-the-week cliches with almost none of the original's charm or depth. Phifer, as Sayers, and Cale, as Joy Piccolo, along with a deeper understanding of the wives' point of view, are the main reasons to check it out. But it still can't compare to the original. **89m/C VHS, DVD.** Mekhi Phifer, Sean Maher, Paula Cale, Elise Neal, Ben Gazzara, Aidan Devine, Dean McDermott; ***D:*** John Gray; ***W:*** John Gray, Allen Clare, William Blinn; ***C:*** James Chressanthis; ***M:*** Rick Marvin.

The Bride 🦴½ **1985 (PG-13)** Re-telling of "The Bride of Frankenstein." Sting's Dr. Frankenstein has much more success in creating his second monster (Beals). She's pretty and intelligent and he may even be falling in love with her. When she begins to gain too much independence, though, the awful truth about her origins comes out. Fans of the two leads will want to see this one, but for a true classic see Elsa Lanchester's bride. **118m/C VHS, DVD, Wide.** *GB* Sting, Jennifer Beals, Anthony (Corlan) Higgins, David Rappaport, Geraldine Page, Clancy Brown, Phil Daniels, Veruschka, Quentin Crisp, Cary Elwes; ***D:*** Franc Roddam; ***W:*** Lloyd Fonvielle; ***C:*** Stephen Burum; ***M:*** Maurice Jarre.

The Bride & the Beast woof! *Queen of the Gorillas* **1958** While on an African safari honeymoon, a big game hunter's new bride is carried off by a gorilla. Ludicrous jungle tale. **78m/B VHS.** Charlotte Austin, Lance Fuller, William Justine, Johnny Roth, Jeanne Gerson, Gilbert Frye, Slick Slavin, Bhogwan Singh; ***D:*** Adrian Weiss; ***W:*** Edward D. Wood Jr.; ***C:*** Roland Price; ***M:*** Les Baxter.

The Bride Came C.O.D. 🦴🦴 **1941** Rough'n'tough pilot Cagney is hired by a rich Texas oil man to prevent his daughter (the one with the Bette Davis eyes) from marrying cheesy bandleader Carson. The payoff: $10 per pound if she's delivered unwed. What a surprise when Cagney faces the timeworn dilemma of having to choose between love and money. A contemporary issue of "Time" magazine trumpeted: "Screen's most talented tough guy rough-houses one of screen's best dramatic actresses." That tells you right there it's a romantic comedy. Cagney and Davis—a likely pairing, you'd think—are essentially fish out of water, bothered and bewildered by a weak script. **92m/B VHS.** Bette Davis, James Cagney, Stuart Erwin, Jack Carson, George Tobias, Eugene Pallette, William Frawley; ***D:*** William Keighley; ***W:*** Julius J. Epstein, Philip G. Epstein; ***M:*** Max Steiner.

The Bride Is Much Too Beautiful 🦴🦴½ *Her Bridal Night; La Mariee Est Trop Belle* **1958** French farm girl Bardot becomes a model with the help of some fashion magazine employees and then winds up posing as the bride in a fake marriage. Dubbed. **90m/C VHS.** *FR* Brigitte Bardot, Louis Jourdan, Micheline Presle, Marcel Amont; ***D:*** Pierre Gaspard-Huit; ***W:*** Odette Joyeux, Philippe Agostini; ***C:*** Louis Page; ***M:*** Norbert Glanzberg.

Bride of Chucky 🦴½ **1998 (R)** Just when you thought you had seen the last of that creepy little doll, "Chucky" returns. This fourth installment in the "Child's Play" franchise finds Chucky back on the lam after being sprung from the pen by the ex-girlfriend of his former human incarnation, serial killer Charles Lee Ray. After killing his ex, Tiffany (Tilly), Chucky transforms her soul into an equally creepy girl doll. Together, they must make their way to the very spot where he was gunned down by police in order to transfer their souls back into human forms. Aside from Chucky and both incarnations of Tiffany, the rest of the characters are undeveloped and rather useless. Fortunately, the filmmakers knew not to take themselves too seriously, and managed a few funny moments. But its really only Tilly's excellent campy-vampy performance and an occasional clever jab from the Chuckster that lift this one above a woof. **89m/C VHS, DVD.** Jennifer Tilly, Katherine Heigl, Nick Stabile, John Ritter, Alexis Arquette, Gordon Michael Woolvett, Lawrence Dane, Michael Johnson, Kathy Najimy; ***D:*** Ronny Yu; ***W:*** Don Mancini; ***C:*** Peter Pau; ***M:*** Graeme Revell; ***V:*** Brad Dourif.

The Bride of Frankenstein 🦴🦴🦴🦴 **1935** The classic sequel to the classic original in which Dr. F. seeks to build a mate for his monster. More humor than the first, but also more pathos, including the monster's famous but short-lived friendship with a blind hermit. Lanchester plays both the bride and Mary Shelley in the opening sequence. **75m/B VHS, DVD.** Boris Karloff, Elsa

Lanchester, Ernest Thesiger, Colin Clive, Una O'Connor, Valerie Hobson, Dwight Frye, John Carradine, E.E. Clive, O.P. Heggie, Gavin Gordon, Douglas Walton, Billy Barty, Walter Brennan; ***D:*** James Whale; ***W:*** John Lloyd Balderston, William Hurlbut; ***C:*** John Mescall; ***M:*** Franz Waxman. Natl. Film Reg. '98.

Bride of Killer Nerd **1991** Harold Kunkel, left over from the original "Killer Nerd," finds his opposite sex nirvana in the person of Thelma, also a nerd in mind, body, and soul. They relentlessly pursue revenge on the rockers who humiliate them at a campus beer bash. **75m/C VHS.** Toby Radloff, Wayne A. Harold, Heidi Lohr; ***D:*** Mark Steven Bosko.

Bride of Re-Animator ½ *Re-Animator 2* **1989** Herbert West is back, and this time he not only re-animates life but creates life—sexy female life—in this sequel to the immensely popular "Re-Animator." High camp and blood curdling gore make this a standout in the sequel parade. Available in a R-rated version as well. **99m/C VHS, DVD, Wide.** Bruce Abbott, Claude Earl Jones, Fabiana Udenio, Jeffrey Combs, Kathleen Kinmont, David Gale, Mel Stewart, Irene Forrest; ***D:*** Brian Yuzna; ***W:*** Brian Yuzna, Rick Fry, Woody Keith; ***C:*** Rick Fichter; ***M:*** Richard Band.

Bride of the Gorilla **1951** Burr travels to the jungle where he finds a wife, a plantation, and a curse in this African twist on the werewolf legend. Chaney is the local policeman on his trail. Burr's physical changes are fun to watch. **76m/B VHS.** Raymond Burr, Barbara Payton, Lon Chaney Jr., Tom Conway, Paul Cavanagh; ***D:*** Curt Siodmak; ***W:*** Curt Siodmak.

Bride of the Monster woof! *Bride of the Atom* **1955** Lugosi stars as a mad scientist trying to create a race of giants. Classic Woodian badness. **68m/B VHS, DVD.** Bela Lugosi, Tor Johnson, Loretta King, Tony McCoy, Harvey B. Dunn, George Becwar, Paul Marco, William Benedict, Dolores Fuller, Don Nagel, Bud Osborne, Conrad Brooks; ***D:*** Edward D. Wood Jr.; ***W:*** Edward D. Wood Jr., Alex Gordon; ***C:*** William C. Thompson; ***M:*** Frank Worth.

Bride of the Wind ½ **2001 (R)** Dull biopic of Alma Mahler (Wynter), a 20th-century femme who put her own musical career aside to marry composer Gustav Mahler (Pryce) in old Vienna. Alma intrigues a number of famous men, including architect Walter Gropius (Verhoeven), artist Oskar Kokoschka (Perez), and others while her marriage to the stoic Gustav suffers. Unfortunately, it's neither titillating nor interesting despite the players. **99m/C VHS, DVD, Wide.** Sarah Wynter, Jonathan Pryce, Vincent Perez, Simon Verhoeven, August Schmolzer, Gregor Seberg, Dagmar Schwarz, Wolfgang Hubsch, Johannes Silberschneider; ***D:*** Bruce Beresford; ***W:*** Marilyn Levy; ***C:*** Peter James; ***M:*** Stephen Endelman.

The Bride Walks Out **1936** Newlywed crisis: a woman with rich taste learns how to adjust to living on her husband's poor salary, but not before she samples the life of the wealthy. Interesting in a sociological sort of way. **81m/B VHS.** Barbara Stanwyck, Gene Raymond, Robert Young, Ned Sparks, Willie Best, Helen Broderick, Hattie McDaniel; ***D:*** Leigh Jason.

The Bride with White Hair *Jiang-Hu: Between Love and Glory* **1993** Operatic martial arts fable based on a novel by Leung Yu-Sang. A young warrior revives a beautiful witch (also a champion warrior) who was killed by jealous Siamese twins. Now the duo, who have fallen in love, must battle the evil twins who rule the corrupt Mo Dynasty. Available dubbed or in Chinese with subtitles. **92m/C VHS, DVD, Wide.** *HK* Leslie Cheung, Brigitte Lin Ching Hsia, Nam Kit-Ying, Frances Ng, Elaine Lui; ***D:*** Ronny Yu; ***W:*** Ronny Yu, David Wu, Lan Kei-Tou, Tseng Pik-Yin; ***C:*** Peter Pau; ***M:*** Richard Yuen.

The Bride with White Hair 2 *Jiang-Hu: Between Love and Glory 2* **1993** The magic saga continues with the massacre of the followers of the Eight Lineages. Powerful and obsessed with vengeance, the Bride can only be stopped by the one man who loves her. Chinese with subtitles or dubbed. **80m/C VHS, DVD, Wide.** *HK* Brigitte Lin Ching Hsia, Leslie Cheung, Christy Chung; ***D:*** David Wu, Ronny Yu; ***W:*** David Wu.

The Bride Wore Black *La Mariee Etait en Noir* **1968** Truffaut's homage to Hitchcock, complete with Bernard Herrmann score. Young bride Julie (Moreau) exacts brutal revenge on the five men who accidentally killed her husband on the steps of the church on their wedding day. Adapted from a novel by Cornell Woolrich. **107m/C VHS, DVD, Wide.** *FR* Jeanne Moreau, Claude Rich, Jean-Claude Brialy, Michel Bouquet, Michael (Michel) Lonsdale, Charles Denner, Daniel Boulanger; ***D:*** Francois Truffaut; ***W:*** Francois Truffaut, Jean-Louis Richard; ***C:*** Raoul Coutard; ***M:*** Bernard Herrmann.

The Bride Wore Red **1937** Crawford stars as a cabaret singer who masquerades as a socialite in an attempt to break into the upper crust. When a wealthy aristocrat invites her to spend two weeks at a posh resort in Tyrol, Crawford plays her part to the hilt, managing to charm both a rich gentleman and the village postman. Typical "love conquers all" melodrama. **103m/B VHS.** Joan Crawford, Franchot Tone, Robert Young, Billie Burke, Reginald Owen, Lynne Carver, George Zucco; ***D:*** Dorothy Arzner; ***C:*** George J. Folsey.

Brides of Christ ½ **1991** Set in the Australian Santo Spirito Convent during the Vatican II upheaval of the 1960s. Explores the tensions between old and new religious ideas by focusing on novices, older nuns, and the Reverend Mother of the convent as they try to cope with a changing world. TV miniseries. **300m/C VHS.** Brenda Fricker, Sandy Gore, Josephine Byrnes, Lisa Hensley, Naomi Watts, Kym Wilson, Melissa Thomas; ***D:*** Ken Cameron; ***W:*** John Alsop, Sue Smith.

The Brides of Dracula ½ **1960** A young French woman unknowingly frees a vampire. He wreaks havoc, sucking blood and creating more of the undead to carry out his evil deeds. One of the better Hammer vampire films. **86m/C VHS.** *GB* Peter Cushing, Martita Hunt, Yvonne Monlaur, Freda Jackson, David Peel, Mona Washbourne, Miles Malleson, Henry Oscar, Michael Ripper, Andree Melly; ***D:*** Terence Fisher; ***W:*** Peter Bryan, Edward Percy, Jimmy Sangster; ***C:*** Jack Asher.

Brides of the Beast woof! *Brides of Blood; Grave Desires; Island of the Living Horror* **1968** Filipino radiation monsters get their jollies by eating beautiful young naked women. Newly arrived research scientist and his bride oppose this custom. First in a series of "Blood Island" horrors. **85m/B VHS.** *PH* John Ashley, Kent Taylor, Beverly (Hills) Powers, Eva Darren, Mario Montenegro; ***D:*** Eddie Romero, Gerardo (Gerry) De Leon; ***W:*** Eddie Romero, Gerardo (Gerry) De Leon.

Brideshead Revisited **1981** The acclaimed British miniseries based on the Evelyn Waugh classic about an Edwardian young man who falls under the spell of a wealthy aristocratic family and struggles to retain his integrity and values. On six tapes. **540m/C VHS, DVD.** *GB* Jeremy Irons, Anthony Andrews, Diana Quick, Laurence Olivier, John Gielgud, Claire Bloom, Stephane Audran, Mona Washbourne, John Le Mesurier, Charles Keating; ***D:*** Charles Sturridge, Michael Lindsay-Hogg; ***M:*** Geoffrey Burgon. **TV**

The Bridge *Die Brucke* **1959** In 1945, two days before the end of WWII, seven German schoolboys are drafted to defend an unimportant bridge from American tanks. Emotional anti-war film based on the autobiographical novel of Manfred Gregor. German with subtitles. **102m/B VHS.** *GE* Fritz Wepper, Volker Bohnet, Franz Glaubrecht, Karl Michael Balzer, Gunther Hoffman, Michael Hinz, Cordula Trantow, Wolfgang Stumpf, Volker Lechtenbrink, Gunter Pfitzmann, Edith Schultze-Westrum, Ruth Hausmeister, Eva Vaitl; ***D:*** Bernhard Wicki; ***W:*** Bernhard Wicki, Michael Mansfield, Karl-Wilhelm Vivier; ***C:*** Gerd Von Bonen; ***M:*** Hans-Martin Majewski.

The Bridge **2000** In 1963, Mira (Bouquet) loves to go to the movies to watch "Jules et Jim" and "West Side Story." She has a 15-year-old son, but that doesn't stop her from entering into an affair with a visiting engineer (Berling) who's in her little town to build a bridge. Director Depardieu plays her husband, a builder who's working on the bridge. It's precisely the sort of material that the French handle so deftly and Depardieu proves that he's a competent craftsman behind the camera. **92m/C DVD, Wide.** *FR* Carole Bouquet, Gerard Depardieu, Charles Berling; ***D:*** Frederic Auburtin, Gerard Depardieu; ***W:*** Francois Bupeyron; ***C:*** Pascal Ridao; ***M:*** Frederic Auburtin.

The Bridge at Remagen ½ **1969 (PG)** Based on the true story of allied attempts to capture a vital bridge before retreating German troops destroy it. For war-film buffs. **115m/C VHS, DVD, Wide.** George Segal, Robert Vaughn, Ben Gazzara, Bradford Dillman, E.G. Marshall; ***D:*** John Guillermin; ***W:*** William Roberts; ***C:*** Stanley Cortez; ***M:*** Elmer Bernstein.

Bridge of Dragons **1999 (R)** Dictator Tagawa, having murdered the kingdom's rightful ruler, plots to marry the country's princess (Shane) to consolidate his power. But when the princess escapes to join the rebel forces, human killing machine Lundgren is sent to retrieve her. Only he decides to fight with her instead. Lots of explosions and high-tech gadgets. **91m/C VHS, DVD.** Dolph Lundgren, Cary-Hiroyuki Tagawa, Gary Hudson, Scott Schwartz, Rachel Shane; ***D:*** Isaac Florentine; ***W:*** Carlton Holder; ***C:*** Yossi Wein; ***M:*** Steve Edwards. **VIDEO**

The Bridge of San Luis Rey **1944** A priest investigates the famous bridge collapse in Lima, Peru that left five people dead. Based upon the novel by Thornton Wilder. **89m/B VHS, DVD.** Lynn Bari, Francis Lederer, Louis Calhern, Akim Tamiroff, Donald Woods, Alla Nazimova, Blanche Yurka; ***D:*** Rowland V. Lee; ***W:*** Howard Estabrook, Herman Weissman; ***C:*** John Boyle; ***M:*** Dimitri Tiomkin.

The Bridge on the River Kwai **1957** Award-winning adaptation of the Pierre Bouelle novel about the battle of wills between a Japanese POW camp commander and a British colonel over the construction of a rail bridge, and the parallel efforts by escaped prisoner Holden to destroy it. Holden's role was originally cast for Cary Grant. Memorable too for whistling "Colonel Bogey March." Because the writers were blacklisted, Bouelle (who spoke no English) was originally credited as the screenwriter. **161m/C VHS, DVD, Wide.** *GB* William Holden, Alec Guinness, Jack Hawkins, Sessue Hayakawa, James Donald, Geoffrey Horne, Andre Morell, Ann Sears, Peter Williams, John Boxer, Percy Herbert, Harold Goodwin, Henry Okawa, Keiichiro Katsumoto, M.R.B. Chakrabandhu; ***D:*** David Lean; ***W:*** Carl Foreman, Michael Wilson; ***C:*** Jack Hildyard; ***M:*** Malcolm Arnold. Oscars '57: Actor (Guinness), Adapt. Screenplay, Cinematog., Director (Lean), Film Editing, Picture, Score; AFI '98: Top 100; British Acad. '57: Actor (Guinness), Film, Screenplay; Directors Guild '57: Director (Lean); Golden Globes '58: Actor—Drama (Guinness), Director (Lean), Film—Drama; Natl. Bd. of Review '57: Actor (Guinness), Director (Lean), Support. Actor (Hayakawa), Natl. Film Reg. '97;; N.Y. Film Critics '57: Actor (Guinness), Director (Lean), Film.

Bridge to Hell ½ **1987** A group of allied P.O.W.s try to make their way to the American front during WWII in Yugoslavia. A heavily guarded bridge occupied by Nazi troops stands between them and freedom. A special introduction by Michael Dudikoff doing martial arts. **94m/C VHS.** Jeff Connors, Francis Ferre, Andy Forrest, Paky Valente; ***D:*** Umberto Lenzi.

The Bridge to Nowhere **1986** Five city kids go hunting and backpacking in the New Zealand wilderness, and are hunted by a maniacal backwoodsman. **82m/C VHS.** *NZ* Bruno Lawrence, Alison Routledge, Margaret Umbers, Philip Gordon; ***D:*** Ian Mune.

Bridge to Silence **1989** A young hearing-impaired mother's life begins to crumble following the death of her husband in a car crash. Her mother tries to get custody of her daughter and a friend applies romantic pressure. Melodrama features Matlin in her first TV speaking role. **95m/C VHS.** Marlee Matlin, Lee Remick, Josef Sommer, Michael O'Keefe, Allison Silva, Candice Brecker; ***D:*** Karen Arthur. **TV**

A Bridge Too Far **1977 (PG)** A meticulous recreation of one of the most disastrous battles of WWII, the Allied defeat at Arnhem in 1944. Misinformation, adverse conditions, and overconfidence combined to prevent the Allies from capturing six bridges that connected Holland to the German border. **175m/C VHS, DVD, Wide.** *GB* Sean Connery, Robert Redford, James Caan, Michael Caine, Elliott Gould, Gene Hackman, Laurence Olivier, Ryan O'Neal, Liv Ullmann, Dirk Bogarde, Hardy Kruger, Arthur Hill, Edward Fox, Anthony Hopkins, Maximilian Schell, Denholm Elliott, Wolfgang Preiss, Nicholas (Nick) Campbell, Christopher Good, John Ratzenberger; ***D:*** Richard Attenborough; ***W:*** William Goldman; ***C:*** Geoffrey Unsworth; ***M:*** John Addison. British Acad. '77: Support. Actor (Fox); Natl. Soc. Film Critics '77: Support. Actor (Fox).

The Bridges at Toko-Ri ½ **1955** Based on the James A. Michener novel, the rousing war-epic about a lawyer being summoned by the Navy to fly bombing missions during the Korean War. A powerful anti-war statement. **103m/C VHS, DVD.** William Holden, Grace Kelly, Fredric March, Mickey Rooney, Robert Strauss, Earl Holliman, Keiko Awaji, Charles McGraw, Richard Shannon, Willis Bouchey; ***D:*** Mark Robson; ***W:*** Valentine Davies; ***C:*** Loyal Griggs; ***M:*** Lyn Murray.

The Bridges of Madison County **1995 (PG-13)** Robert Kincaid (Eastwood) is on assignment in 1965 Iowa to photograph Madison County's scenic covered bridges. Only problem is he gets lost and stops for directions at Francesca Johnson's (Streep) farmhouse. There's an immediate attraction between the repressed Italian war-bride-turned-farm-wife and the charismatic world traveler, which they act on in four short days. Much of the treacle from Robert James Waller's novel has been fortunately abandoned but the mature romance remains. 64-year-old Eastwood exudes low-key sexiness while Streep (with a light Italian accent) is all earthy warmth. Fans of both book and stars should be pleased, though the leisurely paced film takes too long to get started. **135m/C VHS, DVD.** Clint Eastwood, Meryl Streep, Victor Slezak, Annie Corley, Jim Haynie; ***D:*** Clint Eastwood; ***W:*** Richard LaGravenese; ***C:*** Jack N. Green; ***M:*** Lennie Niehaus.

Bridget Jones's Diary **2001 (R)** So you've got this petite, sunny-faced Texan playing a "singleton" Brit who drinks and smokes and consumes too many calories and has man trouble and is the beloved heroine of Helen Fielding's novel. No wonder the English got a little upset—not, as it turns out, for any good reason since Zellweger is fab as Bridget tries to take control of her chaotic life. Of course having a romp with your caddish, clever boss Daniel Cleaver (Grant) and ignoring the handsome but apparently stuffy Mark Darcy (Firth) isn't a good start but Bridget—bless her—does try. The movie is truncated (to the detriment of Bridget's friendships) but it still works. **115m/C VHS, DVD, Wide.** Renee Zellweger, Hugh Grant, Colin Firth, Gemma Jones, Jim Broadbent, Embeth Davidtz, Shirley Henderson, James Callis, Sally Phillips; ***D:*** Sharon Maguire; ***W:*** Richard Curtis, Andrew Davies, Helen Fielding; ***C:*** Stuart Dryburgh; ***M:*** Patrick Doyle.

Brief Encounter **1946** Based on Noel Coward's "Still Life" from "Tonight at 8:30," two middle-aged, middle-class people become involved in a short and bittersweet romance in WWII England. Intensely romantic, underscored with Rachmaninoff's Second Piano Concerto. **86m/B VHS, DVD.** *GB* Celia Johnson, Trevor Howard, Stanley Holloway, Cyril Raymond, Joyce Carey, Everley Gregg, Margaret Barton, Dennis Harkin, Valentine Dyall, Marjorie Mars, Irene Handl; ***D:*** David Lean; ***W:*** Noel Coward, David Lean, Ronald Neame, Anthony Havelock-Allan; ***C:*** Robert Krasker. N.Y. Film Critics '46: Actress (Johnson).

A Brief History of Time **1992 (G)** A stunning documentary about physicist Stephen Hawking, the author of the popular book "Brief History of Time." Crippled by Lou Gehrig's Disease, Hawking narrates the film in the computer-synthesized voice he uses to speak. Interviews with family, friends, and colleagues, bring Hawking's scientific theories to light. **85m/C VHS.** Stephen Hawking; ***D:*** Errol Morris; ***W:***

Stephen Hawking; *C:* John Bailey; *M:* Philip Glass. Sundance '92: Filmmakers Trophy.

The Brig 1964 A film by Jonas Mekas documenting the Living Theatre's infamous performance of Kenneth H. Brown's experimental play. Designed by Julian Beck. **65m/B VHS.** Adolfas Mekas, Jim Anderson, Warren Finnerty, Henry Howard, Tom Lillard, James Tiroff, Gene Lipton; *D:* John Mekas.

Brigadoon 1954 The story of a magical, 18th century Scottish village which awakens once every 100 years and the two modern-day vacationers who stumble upon it. Main highlight is the Lerner and Loewe score. ♫Brigadoon; Almost Like Being in Love; I'll Go Home With Bonnie Jean; Wedding Dance; From This Day On; Heather on the Hill; Waitin' For My Dearie; Once in the Highlands. **108m/C VHS, DVD, Wide.** Gene Kelly, Van Johnson, Cyd Charisse; *D:* Vincente Minnelli; *W:* Alan Jay Lerner; *C:* Joseph Ruttenberg; *M:* Alan Jay Lerner, Frederick Loewe.

Brigham City ½ **2001 (PG-13)** Skillful murder-mystery set in the fictitious Brigham City, Utah. The townspeople mostly know each other and most are also members of the Mormon Church. Sheriff Wes Clayton (Dutcher) and his deputy Terry's (Brown) duties are usually mundane—until they discover the mutiliated body of a young female tourist at an abandoned homestead. Clayton is willing to defer to the FBI but then a second body is discovered and the media vultures descend on the formerly quiet community as their faith is all put to an unexpected test. **115m/C VHS, DVD.** Richard Dutcher, Wilford Brimley, Matthew A. Brown, Carrie Morgan, John Enos, Tayva Patch; *D:* Richard Dutcher; *W:* Richard Dutcher; *C:* Ken Glassing; *M:* Sam Cardon.

Brigham Young: Frontiersman 1940 Somewhat interesting story about the pioneering Mormons and their founding of Salt Lake City. Under the leadership of Brigham Young (Jagger), they set out across the plains, battling hardships and starvation along the way. An emphasis was placed on the historical rather than the religious in an effort not to scare off moviegoers, but the picture failed at the boxoffice anyway. Based on the story by Louis Bromfield. **114m/C VHS.** Tyrone Power, Linda Darnell, Dean Jagger, Brian Donlevy, John Carradine, Jane Darwell, Jean Rogers, Mary Astor, Vincent Price; *D:* Henry Hathaway; *W:* Lamar Trotti; *C:* Arthur C. Miller.

Bright Angel ½ **1991 (R)** Road movie pairs an unconventional team: George wants to visit his aunt to see if she's heard from his mother who ran off with another man; Luey is a free-spirit trying to free her brother from jail. Good performances by Mulroney, Taylor, & Pullman. Ford adapted two of his short stories, "Childern" and "Great Falls" for the gritty and uncompromising script of life in the modern west. **94m/C VHS.** Dermot Mulroney, Lili Taylor, Sam Shepard, Valerie Perrine, Burt Young, Bill Pullman, Benjamin Bratt, Mary Kay Place, Delroy Lindo, Kevin Tighe, Sheila McCarthy; *D:* Michael Fields; *W:* Richard Ford; *M:* Christopher Young.

Bright Eyes **1934 (PG)** Shirley (Temple) lives with her widowed mother Mary (Wilson), who works as a maid for the snobbish Smythe family, where only wealthy, crochety Uncle Ned (Sellon) befriends the cutie. His niece Adele (Allen) is engaged to Shirley's godfather, flyboy Loop Merritt (Dunn), who wants the tyke to live with him when her mom is killed. But Uncle Ned also wants to adopt her and there's a battle over custody. Shirley warbles "On the Good Ship Lollipop" in her usual winsome way. **84m/B VHS, DVD.** Shirley Temple, James Dunn, Lois Wilson, Jane Withers, Judith Allen, Jane Darwell, Charles Sellon; *D:* David Butler; *W:* David Butler, Edwin Burke, William Conselman; *C:* Arthur C. Miller.

Bright Lights, Big City **1988 (R)** Based on Jay McInerney's popular novel, Fox plays a contemporary yuppie working in Manhattan as a magazine journalist. As his world begins to fall apart, he embarks on an endless cycle of drugs and nightlife. Fox is poorly cast, and his character is hard to care for as he becomes more and more dissolute. Although McInerney wrote his own screenplay, the intellectual abstractness of the novel can't be captured on film. **110m/C VHS.** Michael J. Fox, Kiefer Sutherland, Phoebe Cates, Frances Sternhagen, Swoosie Kurtz, Tracy Pollan, Jason Robards Jr., John Houseman, Dianne Wiest, Charlie Schlatter, William Hickey; *D:* James Bridges; *C:* Gordon Willis.

A Bright Shining Lie ½ **1998 (R)** Based on Neil Sheehan's 1988 Pulitzer Prize-winning book, which chronicles the Vietnam War as seen through the eyes of Lt. Col. John Paul Vann (Paxton). The brash Vann arrived as a military adviser to the Vietnamese Army in 1962 and eventually left that post to become part of the State Department's Civilian Aid Program, where he exposed falsified battle reports and other deceptions to newsman Steven Burnett (Logue). The complex and controversial Vann was killed in a chopper crash in 1972. **118m/C VHS, DVD.** Bill Paxton, Donal Logue, Kurtwood Smith, Eric Bogosian, Amy Madigan, Vivian Wu, Robert John Burke, James Rebhorn, Ed Lauter, Harve Presnell; *D:* Terry George; *W:* Terry George; *C:* Jack Conroy; *M:* Gary Chang. CABLE

Brighton Beach Memoirs ½ *Neil Simon's Brighton Beach Memoirs* **1986 (PG-13)** The film adaptation of the popular (and semiautobiographical) Neil Simon play. Poignant comedy/drama about a young Jewish boy's coming of age in Depression-era Brooklyn. Followed by "Biloxi Blues" and "Broadway Bound." **108m/C VHS, DVD.** Blythe Danner, Bob (Robert) Dishy, Judith Ivey, Jonathan Silverman, Brian Drillinger, Stacey Glick, Lisa Waltz, Jason Alexander; *D:* Gene Saks; *W:* Neil Simon; *C:* John Bailey; *M:* Michael Small.

Brighton Rock *Young Scarface* **1947** Sterling performances highlight this seamy look at the British underworld. Attenborough is Pinkie Brown, a small-time hood who ends up committing murder. He manipulates a waitress to get himself off the hook, but things don't go exactly as he plans. Based on the novel by Graham Greene. **92m/B VHS.** *GB* Richard Attenborough, Hermione Baddeley, William Hartnell, Carol Marsh, Nigel Stock, Wylie Watson, Alan Wheatley, George Carney, Reginald Purdell; *D:* John Boulting.

Brighton Strangler **1945** An actor who plays a murderer assumes the role of the strangler after suffering from a concussion. Decent psychodrama. **67m/B VHS.** John Loder, June Duprez, Miles Mander; *D:* Max Nosseck.

Brighty of the Grand Canyon ½ **1967** The spunky donkey Brighty roams across the Grand Canyon in search of adventure. He finds friendship with a gold-digging old prospector who hits pay dirt. **90m/C VHS.** Joseph Cotten, Pat Conway, Dick Foran, Karl Swenson; *D:* Norman Foster.

A Brilliant Disguise ½ **1993 (R)** Sportswriter gets involved with an artist who turns out to have multiple personality disorder and a sinister psychiatrist. Then his friends start to turn up dead but things aren't exactly what they seem. **97m/C VHS.** Lysette Anthony, Anthony John (Tony) Denison, Corbin Bernsen, Gregory McKinney, Robert Shafer; *D:* Nick Vallelonga; *W:* Nick Vallelonga.

Brilliant Lies ½ **1996** Susy Connor (Gia Carides) has brought an official complaint of sexual harassment against former boss Gary Fitzgerald (LaPaglia), who denies the charge. She claims her sister Katie (Zoe Carides) will substantiate her story, which she will, even though Katie knows it's a lie. As a matter of fact, Susy's a consummate liar though, in a way, she also turns out to be telling the truth. Fine performances from the Carides sisters, as well as LaPaglia (who's married to Gia) and Barrett, who plays the self-pitying Connor patriarch. Adapted from the play by David Williamson. **93m/C VHS.** *AU* Gia Carides, Anthony LaPaglia, Zoe Carides, Ray Barrett, Michael Veitch, Neil Melville, Catherine Wilkin, Grant Tilly; *D:* Richard Franklin; *W:* Richard Franklin, Peter Fitzpatrick; *C:* Geoff Burton; *M:* Nerida Tyson-Chew.

Brimstone & Treacle **1982 (R)** Weird, obsessive psychodrama in which a young rogue (who may or may not be an actual agent of the Devil) infiltrates the home of a staid British family caring for their comatose adult daughter. **85m/C VHS.** *GB* Sting, Denholm Elliott, Joan Plowright, Suzanna Hamilton; *D:* Richard Loncraine; *W:* Dennis Potter. Montreal World Film Fest. '82: Film.

Bring It On ½ **2000 (PG-13)** Bring on the guilty pleasure. Equal parts satire, exploitation, and earnest (if not totally successful) teen flick, the film follows cheerleader Torrence (Dunst) as she becomes captain of the Rancho Carne High Toros cheer squad, who soon after discovers her squad's championship moves have been lifted from another school, the East Compton High Clovers. All of this culminates in a showdown between the two squads, while interspersed throughout are standard teenage goings-on. No gem, by any means, but fun if you're in the mood (or spirit). But be advised: probably too raunchy for its intended young adult audience. **98m/C VHS, DVD, Wide.** Kirsten Dunst, Eliza Dushku, Jesse Bradford, Gabrielle Union, Clare Kramer, Nicole Bilderback, Tsianina Joelson, Rini Bell, Ian Roberts, Richard Hillman, Lindsay Sloane, Cody McMains; *D:* Peyton Reed; *W:* Jessica Bendinger; *C:* Shawn Maurer; *M:* Christophe Beck.

Bring Me the Head of Alfredo Garcia **1974 (R)** Peckinpah falters in this poorly paced outing. American piano player on tour in Mexico finds himself entwined with a gang of bloodthirsty bounty hunters. Bloody and confused. **112m/C VHS.** Warren Oates, Isela Vega, Gig Young, Robert Webber, Helmut Dantine, Emilio Fernandez, Kris Kristofferson; *D:* Sam Peckinpah; *W:* Gordon Dawson, Sam Peckinpah; *C:* Alex Phillips Jr.; *M:* Jerry Fielding.

Bringing Out the Dead ½ **1999 (R)** Cage hasn't looked this haggard since his boozehound role in "Leaving Las Vegas" which could be considered a dress rehearsal for this turn as burnt out New York City paramedic Frank Pierce. Aided by Scorsese's kinetic filmmaking style, Schrader's on-tempo script, and revved up performances by Rhames and Sizemore as Pierce's partners, movie successfully convey's the day-to-day stress of emergency units. Unfortunately, Cage's sleepwalking character is a bore, and a lack of chemistry with real-life spouse Arquette as Pierce's singular ray of hope only makes you yearn for Scorsese's similarly-themed masterpiece "Taxi Driver." Based on the novel by Joe Connelly. **120m/C VHS, DVD, Wide.** Jon Abrahams, Nicolas Cage, John Goodman, Tom Sizemore, Ving Rhames, Patricia Arquette, Marc Anthony, Mary Beth Hurt, Clifford Curtis, Nestor Serrano, Aida Turturro, Afemo Omilami, Arthur J. Nascarelli, Cynthia Roman, Cullen Oliver Johnson; *D:* Martin Scorsese; *W:* Paul Schrader; *C:* Robert Richardson; *M:* Elmer Bernstein.

Bringing Up Baby **1938** The quintessential screwball comedy, featuring Hepburn as a giddy socialite with a "baby" leopard, and Grant as the unwitting object of her affections. One ridiculous situation after another adds up to high speed fun. Hepburn looks lovely, the supporting actors are in fine form, and director Hawks manages the perfect balance of control and mayhem. From a story by Hagar Wilde, who helped Nichols with the screenplay. Also available in a colorized version. **103m/B VHS.** Katharine Hepburn, Cary Grant, May Robson, Charlie Ruggles, Walter Catlett, Fritz Feld, Jonathan Hale, Barry Fitzgerald, Ward Bond; *D:* Howard Hawks; *W:* Dudley Nichols; *C:* Russell Metty. AFI '98: Top 100, Natl. Film Reg. '90.

Brink ½ **1998** Andy Brinker leads of group of in-line skaters who are dedicated to the sport. But Andy also needs money to help out his family and when a rival team offers him cash to join them on the circuit, Andy's forced into a hard choice. **88m/C VHS.** Christina Vidal, Erik von Detten, Patrick Levis, Asher Gold, Sam Horrigan; *D:* Greg Beeman. CABLE

Brink of Life ½ *Nara Livet* **1957** Three pregnant women in a hospital maternity ward await the impending births with mixed feelings. Early Bergman; in Swedish with English subtitles. **82m/B VHS.** *SW* Eva Dahlbeck, Bibi Andersson, Ingrid Thulin, Babro Ornas, Max von Sydow, Erland Josephson, Gunnar Sjoberg; *D:* Ingmar Bergman. Cannes '58: Actress (Dahlbeck), Actress (Andersson, Thulin), Director (Bergman).

Brink's Job **1978 (PG)** Recreates the "crime of the century," Tony Pino's heist of $2.7 million from a Brink's truck. The action picks up five days before the statute of limitations is about to run out. **103m/C VHS.** Peter Falk, Peter Boyle, Warren Oates, Gena Rowlands, Paul Sorvino, Sheldon Leonard, Allen (Goorwitz) Garfield; *D:* William Friedkin; *W:* Walon Green; *M:* Richard Rodney Bennett.

Britannia Hospital ½ **1982 (R)** This is a portrait of a hospital at its most chaotic: the staff threatens to strike, demonstrators surround the hospital, a nosey BBC reporter pursues an anxious professor, and the eagerly anticipated royal visit degenerates into a total shambles. **111m/C VHS, DVD, Wide.** *GB* Malcolm McDowell, Leonard Rossiter, Graham Crowden, Joan Plowright, Mark Hamill, Alan Bates, Dave Atkins, Marsha A. Hunt; *D:* Lindsay Anderson; *W:* David Sherwin; *C:* Mike Flash; *M:* Alan Price.

Britannic **1999** The Brittanic, the Titanic's sister ship, was built as a luxury liner but when WWI began the ship was turned into a hospital transport after its launch in 1914. The ship did sink off the Greek coast in 1916 (probably due to a torpedo or mine) but the filmmakers haven't let any other facts of the story stand in the way of this poor man's "Titanic" with its class difference romance and other cliches. **96m/C VHS, DVD.** Edward Atterton, Jacqueline Bisset, John Rhys-Davies, Bruce Payne, Amanda Ryan, Ben Daniels; *D:* Brian Trenchard-Smith; *W:* Brian Trenchard-Smith, Brett Thompson, Dennis A. Pratt; *C:* Ivan Strasburg; *M:* Alan Parker. CABLE

British Intelligence ½ **1940** Silly American-made film about British espionage. Boris Karloff plays a butler (who is also a spy) trapped by an agent who visits the home of a British bureaucrat. Half-baked story that doesn't hold up. **62m/B VHS, DVD.** Boris Karloff, Margaret Lindsay, Maris Wrixon, Holmes Herbert, Leonard Mudie, Bruce Lester; *D:* Terry Morse.

A Brivele der Mamen *A Letter to Mother; A Letter to Mama* **1938** A Jewish mother does her best to hold her fragile family together, in spite of the ravages of war and poverty. Her travails take her and her family from the Polish Ukraine to New York City. In Yiddish with English subtitles. **90m/C VHS.** *PL* Berta Gersten, Lucy Gerhman, Misha Gerhman, Edmund Zayenda; *D:* Joseph Green.

Broadcast Bombshells **1995 (R)** TV station WSEX has a station manager who'll do anything to improve ratings, an ambitious associate producer after the weather girl's job, a sexaholic sportscaster, and lots of chaos involving a mad bomber. The barely there plot is just the excuse for a considerable display of T&A anyway. Also available unrated. **80m/C VHS.** Amy Lynn Baxter, Debbie Rochon, John Richardson, Elizabeth Heyman, Joseph Pallister; *D:* Ernest G. Sauer.

Broadcast News ½ **1987 (R)** The acclaimed, witty analysis of network news shows, dealing with the three-way romance between a driven career-woman producer, an ace nebbish reporter and a brainless, popular on-screen anchorman. Incisive and funny, though often simply idealistic. **132m/C VHS, DVD.** William Hurt, Albert Brooks, Holly Hunter, Jack Nicholson, Joan Cusack, Robert Prosky, Lois Chiles, John Cusack, Gennie James; *D:* James L. Brooks; *W:* James L. Brooks; *C:* Michael Ballhaus; *M:* Bill Conti, Michael Gore. L.A. Film Critics '87: Actress (Hunter); Natl. Bd. of Review '87: Actress (Hunter); N.Y. Film Critics '87: Actress (Hunter), Director (Brooks), Film, Screenplay.

Broadway Bill *Strictly Confidential* **1934** A man decides to abandon his nagging wife and his job in her family's business for the questionable pleasures of owning a racehorse known as Broadway Bill. This racetrack comedy was also remade by Frank Capra in 1951 as "Riding High." **90m/C VHS.** Warner Baxter, Myrna Loy, Walter Connolly, Helen Vinson, Margaret Hamilton, Frankie Darro; ***D:*** Frank Capra.

Broadway Bound 🦴🦴½ *Neil Simon's Broadway Bound* **1992** The final film in Simon's trilogy (preceded by "Brighton Beach Memoirs" and "Biloxi Blues"), this one made for TV. The playwright's alter ego, Eugene Morris Jerome, is ready to leave Brooklyn for good, hoping to make it as a comedy writer for a radio show. Meanwhile, his mother decides what to do about his unfaithful father. **90m/C VHS.** Jonathan Silverman, Anne Bancroft, Jerry Orbach, Corey Parker, Hume Cronyn, Michele Lee; ***D:*** Paul Bogart; ***W:*** Neil Simon. **TV**

Broadway Damage 🦴½ **1998** Amateurish gay comedy whose best asset is the shopaholic (and only female) character played by Hobel, as the typical overweight fag hag roomie of aspiring New York actor Marc (Lucas). Beyond-shallow Marc is looking for a lover and only a perfect 10 will do, which means he gets dumped a lot by narcissistic manipulators. Meanwhile, his plain best friend, Robert (Williams), pines for the twit to notice him in a romantic way. **110m/C VHS, DVD.** Michael Shawn Lucas, Aaron Williams, Mara Hobel, Hugh Panaro; ***D:*** Victor Mignatti; ***W:*** Victor Mignatti; ***C:*** Mike Mayers; ***M:*** Elliot Sokolov.

Broadway Danny Rose 🦴🦴🦴½ **1984 (PG)** One of Woody Allen's best films, a hilarious, heart-rending anecdotal comedy about a third-rate talent agent involved in one of his client's infidelities. The film magically unfolds as show business veterans swap Danny Rose stories at a delicatessen. Allen's Danny Rose is pathetically lovable. **85m/B VHS, DVD, Wide.** Woody Allen, Mia Farrow, Nick Apollo Forte, Sandy Baron, Milton Berle, Howard Cosell; ***D:*** Woody Allen; ***W:*** Woody Allen; ***C:*** Gordon Willis. British Acad. '84: Orig. Screenplay; Writers Guild '84: Orig. Screenplay.

The Broadway Drifter 🦴🦴 **1927** A silent Jazz Age drama about a playboy who repents his decadent ways by opening a girls' health school. Complications ensue. **90m/B VHS, 8mm.** George Walsh, Dorothy Hall, Bigelow Cooper, Arthur Donaldson; ***D:*** Bernard McEveety Sr.

Broadway Limited 🦴🦴 *The Baby Vanishes* **1941** Three aspiring actors head for the Great White Way with a baby to use as a prop. Thinking the baby kidnapped, the police make things tough for the trio. McLaglen was wasted on this one, which was apparently made to show off the considerable assets of Woodworth. **75m/B VHS.** Victor McLaglen, Marjorie Woodworth, Dennis O'Keefe, Patsy Kelly, ZaSu Pitts, Leonid Kinskey, George E. Stone; ***D:*** Gordon Douglas.

Broadway Melody 🦴🦴½ **1929** Early musical in which two sisters hope for fame on Broadway, and encounter a wily song and dance man who traps both their hearts. Dated, but still charming, with a lovely score. Considered the great granddaddy of all MGM musicals; followed by three more melodies in 1935, 1937, and 1940. ♫Broadway Melody; Give My Regards to Broadway; Truthful Parson Brown; The Wedding of the Painted Doll; The Boy Friend; You Were Meant For Me; Love Boat; Broadway Babies. **104m/B VHS.** Bessie Love, Anita Page, Charles King, Jed Prouty, Kenneth Thomson, Edward Dillon, Mary Doran; ***D:*** Harry Beaumont; ***M:*** Nacio Herb Brown, Arthur Freed. Oscars '29: Picture.

Broadway Melody of 1936 🦴🦴🦴 **1935** Exceptional musical comedy with delightful performances from Taylor and Powell. Benny is a headline-hungry columnist who tries to entrap Taylor by using Powell. ♫Broadway Melody; Broadway Rhythm; You Are My Lucky Star; I've Got a Feeling You're Fooling; All I Do Is Dream of You; Sing Before Breakfast; On a Sunday Afternoon. **110m/B VHS.** Jack Benny, Eleanor Powell, Robert Taylor, Una Merkel, Sid Silvers, Buddy Ebsen; ***D:*** Roy Del Ruth; ***C:*** Charles Rosher; ***M:*** Nacio Herb Brown, Arthur Freed.

Broadway Melody of 1938 🦴🦴½ **1937** Third entry in the melody series lacks the sparkle of "Broadway Melody of 1936" despite the all-star cast. Lots of singing and dancing without much charm. Two bright spots: a young Garland singing the now famous "Dear Mr. Gable" and the always lovely Powell's dance numbers. ♫Broadway Rhythm; Dear Mr. Gable (You Made Me Love You); A New Pair of Shoes; Yours and Mine; I'm Feeling Like a Million; Everybody Sing; Follow in My Footsteps; Your Broadway and My Broadway; Sun Showers. **110m/B VHS.** Eleanor Powell, Sophie Tucker, George Murphy, Judy Garland, Robert Taylor, Buddy Ebsen, Binnie Barnes; ***D:*** Roy Del Ruth; ***C:*** William H. Daniels; ***M:*** Nacio Herb Brown, Arthur Freed.

Broadway Melody of 1940 🦴🦴½ **1940** The last entry in the melody series features the only screen teaming of Astaire and Powell. The flimsy plot is just an excuse for a potent series of Cole Porter musical numbers. ♫I Concentrate on You; I've Got My Eye on You; Begin the Beguine; I am the Captain; Please Don't Monkey With Broadway; Between You and Me; Il Bacio. **103m/B VHS.** Fred Astaire, Eleanor Powell, George Murphy, Frank Morgan, Ian Hunter; ***D:*** Norman Taurog.

Broadway Rhythm 🦴🦴½ **1944** A too-long look at Broadway behind-the-scenes. Murphy plays a Broadway producer who hopes to land a Hollywood star for his new show. She rejects his offer in favor of a show being produced by his father. Just a chance to showcase a number of popular vaudeville acts, songs, and the music of Tommy Dorsey and his orchestra. ♫All the Things You Are; That Lucky Fellow; In Other Words; Seventeen; All In Fun; Brazilian Boogie; What Do You Think I Am?; Somebody Loves Me; Milkman Keep Those Bottles Quiet. **111m/C VHS.** George Murphy, Ginny Simms, Charles Winninger, Gloria De Haven, Nancy Walker, Ben Blue, Lena Horne, Eddie Anderson; ***D:*** Roy Del Ruth; ***W:*** Dorothy Kingsley, Harry Clork.

Broadway Serenade 🦴🦴½ **1939** Melodramatic musical in which a songwriter (Ayres) and his wife, singer MacDonald, make career choices that destroy their marriage. ♫Broadway Serenade for the Lonely Heart; High Flyin'; One Look at You; Time Changes Everything; Un Bel Di; No Time to Argue; Italian Street Song; Les Filles de Cadiz; Musical Contract. **114m/B VHS.** Jeanette MacDonald, Lew Ayres, Ian Hunter, Frank Morgan, Wally Vernon, Rita Johnson, Virginia Grey, William Gargan; ***D:*** Robert Z. Leonard; ***W:*** Charles Lederer.

Broadway to Cheyenne 🦴 *From Broadway to Cheyenne* **1932** A group of big city gangsters try to take over a small western town but are opposed by heroic cowboys. **53m/B VHS.** Rex Bell, George "Gabby" Hayes, Marceline Day, Robert Ellis, Alan Bridge, Matthew Betz; ***D:*** Harry Fraser.

Brokedown Palace 🦴🦴½ **1999 (PG-13)** Danes and Beckinsale take a trip to Thailand following their high school graduation and are targeted by a smooth-talking Australian drug dealer. After he invites the pair to Hong Kong, he hides heroin in their luggage and they're busted at the airport. Accused of drug trafficking, they are sentenced to 33 years in a Thai prison. Phillips is an unfriendly DEA official, while Pullman is the expatriate American lawyer who comes to their aid. The story focuses more on the girls' relationship as friends than on their legal nightmare, however. Nevertheless, the government of Thailand was none too pleased by the script, so most of the Thai scenes were actually shot in the Phillipines. **100m/C VHS, DVD.** Claire Danes, Kate Beckinsale, Bill Pullman, Daniel Lapaine, Lou Diamond Phillips, Jacqueline Kim, Tom Amandes, Aimee Graham, John Doe; ***D:*** Jonathan Kaplan; ***W:*** David Arata; ***C:*** Newton Thomas (Tom) Sigel; ***M:*** David Newman.

Broken Angel 🦴½ **1988** Jamie seemed to be such a nice girl, with good looks and great grades—and membership in a notorious street gang. When Jamie disappears, her family discovers her secret activities and dad tries to find his wayward little girl. Melodramatic TV goo. **94m/C VHS.** William Shatner, Susan Blakely, Erika Eleniak, Roxann Biggs-Dawson; ***D:*** Richard T. Heffron. **TV**

Broken Arrow 🦴🦴½ **1950** A U.S. scout befriends Cochise and the Apaches, and helps settlers and Indians live in peace together in the 1870s. Acclaimed as the first Hollywood film to side with the Indians, and for Chandler's portrayal of Cochise. Based on the novel "Blood Brother" by Elliot Arnold. **93m/C VHS.** James Stewart, Jeff Chandler, Will Geer, Debra Paget, Basil Ruysdael, Arthur Hunnicutt, Jay Silverheels; ***D:*** Delmer Daves; ***W:*** Albert (John B. Sherry) Maltz; ***C:*** Ernest Palmer.

Broken Arrow 🦴🦴 **1995 (R)** Air Force pilot Vic Deakins (Travolta) rips off a couple of nuclear weapons during a routine exercise over the Utah desert. Deakins' ex-co-pilot Riley Hale (Slater), with help from spunky park ranger Terry Carmichael (Mathis), sets out to find and retrieve the warheads before the big bang. Hong Kong action king Woo once again tries his hand at the big-budget Hollywood action extravaganza, with mixed results. Triple script whammy of cheesy dialogue, continuity problems, and predictability undercuts, but doesn't obscure, his talent for choreographing mayhem. Travolta plays the All-American Boy as creepily charming psychotic to great effect. **108m/C VHS, DVD.** John Travolta, Christian Slater, Samantha Mathis, Delroy Lindo, Bob Gunton, Frank Whaley, Howie Long; ***D:*** John Woo; ***W:*** Graham Yost; ***C:*** Peter Levy; ***M:*** Hans Zimmer.

Broken Badge 🦴🦴🦴 *The Rape of Richard Beck* **1985** Crenna stars as a macho, chauvinistic cop whose attitude towards rape victims changes dramatically after he himself is raped by a couple of thugs. Excellent TV movie. **100m/C VHS.** Richard Crenna, Meredith Baxter, Pat Hingle, Frances Lee McCain, Cotter Smith, George Dzundza, Joanna (Joanna DeVarona) Kerns; ***D:*** Karen Arthur; ***W:*** James G. Hirsch; ***M:*** Peter Bernstein.

Broken Blossoms 🦴🦴🦴½ **1919** One of Griffith's most widely acclaimed films, about a young Chinaman in London's squalid Limehouse district hoping to spread the peaceful philosophy of his Eastern religion. He befriends a pitiful street waif who is mistreated by her brutal father, resulting in tragedy. Silent. Revised edition contains introduction from Gish and a newly recorded score. **89m/B VHS, DVD.** Lillian Gish, Richard Barthelmess, Donald Crisp; ***D:*** D.W. Griffith; ***W:*** D.W. Griffith; ***C:*** Billy (G.W.) Bitzer; ***M:*** Louis F. Gottschalk. Natl. Film Reg. '96.

The Broken Chain 🦴🦴½ **1993** In the mid 18th-century Joseph Brant (Schweig), a member of the Mohawk tribe, is sent away to be educated by the British. When he returns, his loyalties are divided between his Native American roots and his English mentor, Sir William Johnson (Brosnan). His boyhood friend Lohaheo (White Shirt) disdains Joseph's white man ways, leading to tragic consequences. Historical background features the French and Indian Wars, the splintering of the Iroquois Confederacy, and the coming of the American Revolution. Filmed on location in Virginia. **93m/C VHS.** Eric Schweig, Wes Studi, Buffy Saint Marie, Pierce Brosnan, J.C. White Shirt, Floyd "Red Crow" Westerman, Graham Greene, Elaine Bilstad, Kim Snyder; ***D:*** Lamont Johnson; ***W:*** Earl W. Wallace; ***M:*** Charles Fox. **TV**

Broken English 🦴🦴½ **1996 (NC-17)** Ethnically diverse New Zealand is the setting for this story of young lovers and the parents who don't understand them. Croatian refugee Nina (Vujcic) and Maori cook Eddie (Arahanga) meet in the Chinese restaurant where they both work and quickly fall in love. Nina's menacing father Ivan (Serbedzija) objects to their passion, sometimes with a baseball bat. Film deals honestly with immigration and racial issues. Engaging debut for Vujcic, a Croatian refugee director Nicholas met in a bar. Also available in an R-rated version. **92m/C VHS.** *NZ* Aleksandra Vujcic, Julian (Sonny) Arahanga, Rade Serbedzija, Marton Csokas, Jing Zhao, Yang Li, Madeline McNamara; ***D:*** Gregor Nicholas; ***W:*** Gregor Nicholas, Johanna Pigott, Jim Salter; ***C:*** John Toon.

Broken Glass 🦴🦴½ **1996** Set in Brooklyn in 1938 and adapted from a play by Arthur Miller. Jewish housewife, Sylvia Gellberg (Leicester), has been stricken by a mysterious paralysis and Dr. Harry Hyman (Patinkin) is called in to treat her. Her illness is apparently psychosomatic and Sylvia gradually reveals her anxiety about her unhappy marriage and her obsessive fears with newspaper reports concerning Jewish persecution in Germany. Hyman and his wife Margaret (McGovern) soon find themselves drawn in deeper than could have imagined. Made for TV. **120m/C VHS.** Mandy Patinkin, Margot Leicester, Henry Goodman, Elizabeth McGovern; ***D:*** David Thacker; ***W:*** David Thacker, David Holman. **TV**

Broken Harvest 🦴🦴½ **1994** Jimmy O'Leary remembers his youth in rural 1950s Ireland when a poor wheat harvest led to his family's financial demise and a feud between his father (Lane) and neighbor Josie McCarthy (O'Brien) threatened to destroy their lives. The men fought side by side for Ireland's independence, but the friendship dissolved when they took different sides during the ensuing civil war, and fought over Jimmy's mother. Strong performances and the beautiful West Cork and Wicklow location shots provide a nice balance to the uneven narrative. The black and white scenes were actually filmed in the mid-'80s when the independently financed project was begun. Adapted from O'Callaghan's own story "The Shilling." **101m/C VHS, DVD, Wide.** *IR* Colin Lane, Niall O'Brien, Marian Quinn, Darren McHugh, Joy Florish, Joe Jeffers, Pete O'Reilly, Michael Crowley; ***D:*** Maurice O'Callaghan; ***W:*** Maurice O'Callaghan; ***C:*** Jack Conroy; ***M:*** Patrick Cassidy.

The Broken Hearts Club 🦴🦴🦴 **2000 (R)** Talk can be cheap, but it's also what sustains the relationships in the lives of a group of gay friends in this chatty, likable film set in West Hollywood. Despite their mostly superficial (sex) conversations, the boys suspect there's more to life, and aim, hesitantly, to move beyond this dead-end topic. Witty and confident in his characters, writer/director Berlanti (co-creator of "Dawson's Creek") has put together a film about gay men that thankfully moves beyond the staleness of many of its predecessors. Good cast with notable performances by Cain (Superman in TV's "Lois and Clark") and Mahoney as the fatherly proprietor of the Broken Hearts restaurant. **94m/C VHS, DVD, Wide.** Dean Cain, John Mahoney, Timothy Olyphant, Andrew Keegan, Nia Long, Zach Braff, Matt McGrath, Billy Porter, Justin Theroux, Mary McCormack; ***D:*** Greg Berlanti; ***W:*** Greg Berlanti; ***C:*** Paul Elliott; ***M:*** Christophe Beck.

Broken Hearts of Broadway 🦴🦴 **1923** Stories of heartbreak and success along the Great White Way. **85m/B VHS.** Colleen Moore, John Walker, Alice Lake, Tully Marshall, Creighton Hale; ***D:*** Irving Cummings.

Broken Lance 🦴🦴🦴½ **1954** Western remake of "House of Strangers" that details the dissolution of a despotic cattle baron's family. Beautifully photographed. **96m/C VHS, Wide.** Spencer Tracy, Richard Widmark, Robert Wagner, Jean Peters, Katy Jurado, Earl Holliman, Hugh O'Brian, E.G. Marshall; ***D:*** Edward Dmytryk; ***W:*** Philip Yordan. Oscars '54: Story.

The Broken Mask 🦴🦴 **1928** A doctor performs remarkable plastic surgery on a patient, but when the patient becomes attracted to his sweetheart, he throws the Hippocratic oath to the wind, and his patient's spiffy new look has got to go. A ground-breaker amid plastic surgery-gone-amok pieces. **58m/B VHS.** Cullen Landis, Barbara Bedford, Wheeler Oakman, James A. Marcus; ***D:*** James Hogan.

Broken Melody 🦴½ *Vagabond Violinist* **1934** An opera singer sent to prison by mistake must escape in order to return to the woman of his dreams. **62m/B VHS.** *GB* John Garrick, Margot Grahame, Merle Oberon, Austin Trevor, Charles Carson, Harry Terry; ***D:*** Bernard Vorhaus.

Broken Mirrors 🦴🦴½ *Gebroken Spiegels* **1985** A disturbing film which intertwines two stories of violence against women: prostitutes go about their daily business in Amsterdam, while a twisted serial killer who imprisons, photographs, and ultimately destroys his victims, draws near. An independently made chiller with staunch feminist agenda. **110m/C** *NL* Lineke Rijxman, Henriette Tol, Edda Barends, Eddie Brugman, Coby Stunnenberg; ***D:*** Marleen Gorris; ***W:*** Marleen Gorris.

Broken Strings 🦴 **1940** All-black musical in which a concert violinist must come to terms with himself after an auto accident limits the use of his left hand. **50m/B VHS.** Clarence Muse, Sybil Lewis, William Washington, Matthew "Stymie" Beard; ***D:*** Bernard B. Ray.

Broken Trust 🦴🦴 **1993** Erica inherits her fabulously weathy uncle's estate but she has problems knowing who to trust now that she has all this money. Seems her husband is greedy and her sister resentful but just how far will they go to get what Erica has? **85m/C VHS.** Kimberly Foster, Nick Cassavetes, Kathryn Harris, Don Swayze, Edward Albert, Wendy MacDonald; ***D:*** Rafael Portillo.

Broken Trust 🦴🦴½ **1995** Municipal judge Timothy Nash (Selleck) is recruited for a sting operation, designed to ensnare fellow judges, by two slightly less-than-ethical feds (Atherton and McGovern). When Nash decides he doesn't like what's going on he discovers it's not going to be so easy to get out. Selleck's stoic, McGovern provides attractive ornamentation, and Atherton excels as the smarmy villain. From the novel "Court of Honor" by William P. Wood. **90m/C VHS.** Tom Selleck, Elizabeth McGovern, William Atherton, Fritz Weaver, Marsha Mason, Charles Haid, Stanley DeSantis, Cynthia Martells; ***D:*** Geoffrey Sax; ***W:*** Joan Didion, John Gregory Dunne; ***C:*** Ronald Orieux; ***M:*** Richard Horowitz. **CABLE**

Broken Vessels 🦴🦴🦴 **1998 (R)** Rent this with "Bringing Out the Dead" and you'll have a double feature that will make you take 911 off the speed dial. Both movies were released in the same year, but Scorsese's movie depicts a paramedic demented by caring too much. The ambulance drivers in "Broken Vessels" become unhinged by a cold, drug-induced indifference. Tom (London) is pulled into a downward spiral by his crazed partner Jimmy (Field), who smokes heroin and feels up unconscious girls while on break from saving lives. Clearly, things are not destined to go well for the pair, not to mention those who end up in the back of their meat wagon. Excellent debut from producer-director Scott Ziehl. **90m/C VHS, DVD, Wide.** Todd Field, Jason London, Roxana Zal, Susan Traylor, James Hong, Patrick Cranshaw, William Smith, Dave Baer; ***D:*** Scott Ziehl; ***W:*** Scott Ziehl, Dave Baer, John McMahon; ***C:*** Antonio Calvache.

Broken Vows 🦴🦴½ **1987** Thriller with Jones as ghetto priest Father Joseph, who has doubts about his calling. When he gives last rites to a murder victim, he decides to help the victim's girlfriend find his killers. Based on the novel "Where the Dark Secrets Go" by Dorothy Salisbury Davis. **95m/C VHS.** Tommy Lee Jones, Annette O'Toole, M. Emmet Walsh, Milo O'Shea, David Groh, Madeline Sherwood, Jean De Baer, David Strathairn; ***D:*** Jud Taylor; ***C:*** Thomas Burstyn. **TV**

Bronco Billy 🦴🦴½ **1980 (PG)** Eastwood stars as a New Jersey shoe clerk who decides to fulfill his dream of being a cowboy hero by becoming the proprietor of a rag-tag wild west show. Locke's one-note performance as a spoiled rich girl who joins up is a problem and the film's charm is as ragged as the acts. Good if you want to see Eastwood in something other than a shoot-'em-up. **117m/C VHS, DVD, Wide.** Clint Eastwood, Sondra Locke, Bill McKinney, Scatman Crothers, Sam Bottoms, Geoffrey Lewis, Dan Vadis, Sierra Pecheur; ***D:*** Clint Eastwood; ***W:*** Dennis Hackin; ***C:*** David Worth; ***M:*** Steve Dorff.

Bronson's Revenge 🦴½ **1979 (R)** Two frontier soldiers face constant danger as they attempt to transport death row prisoners, a large quantity of gold, and a stranded woman across the Rocky Mountains territory. **90m/C VHS.** Robert Hundar, Roy Hill, Emma Cohen.

The Brontes of Haworth 🦴🦴½ **1973** The bleak moorlands and the village of Haworth are the setting for a dramatic look at the lives of writers Charlotte, Emily, and Anne Bronte, their wastral brother Branwell, and the tragedies that haunted them all. On 4 cassettes. **270m/C VHS.** *GB* Ann Penfold, Michael Kitchen, Vickery Turner, Rosemary McHale, Alfred Burke; ***D:*** Marc Miller; ***W:*** Christopher Fry. **TV**

The Bronx Executioner 🦴 **1986** Android, robot, and human interests clash in futuristic Manhattan and all martial arts hell breaks loose. Special introduction by martial arts star Michael Dudikoff. **88m/C VHS.** Rob Robinson, Margie Newton, Chuck Valenti, Gabriel Gori; ***D:*** Bob Collins.

A Bronx Tale 🦴🦴🦴 **1993 (R)** Vivid snapshot of a young Italian-American boy growing up in the '60s among neighborhood small-time wiseguys. As a nine-year-old Calogero witnesses mobster Sonny kill a man but doesn't rat to the police, so Sonny takes the kid under his wing. His upright bus-driving father Lorenzo doesn't approve but the kid is drawn to Sonny's apparent glamor and power. At 17, he's gotten both an education in school and on the streets but he needs to make a choice. Good period detail and excellent performances. Palminteri shows both Sonny's charisma and violence and De Niro handles the less-showy father role with finesse. Based on Palminteri's one-man play; De Niro's directorial debut. **122m/C VHS, DVD.** Robert De Niro, Chazz Palminteri, Lillo Brancato, Francis Capra, Taral Hicks, Kathrine Narducci, Clem Caserta, Alfred Sauchelli Jr., Frank Pietrangolare, Joseph D'Onofrio; ***Cameos:*** Joe Pesci; ***D:*** Robert De Niro; ***W:*** Chazz Palminteri; ***C:*** Reynaldo Villalobos; ***M:*** Butch Barbella.

The Bronx War 🦴🦴 **1990 (R)** Rival gangs take to the streets in this film from the director of "Hangin' with the Homeboys." A malicious gang leader tricks his gang into going to war over a girl he wants. Very violent; an unrated version available. **91m/C VHS.** Joseph B. Vasquez, Fabio Urena, Charmaine Cruz, Andre Brown, Marlene Forte, Francis Colon, Miguel Sierra, Kim West; ***D:*** Joseph B. Vasquez.

Bronze Buckaroo 🦴🦴 **1939** Horse opera in which a cowpoke seeks revenge for his pa's death. Commendable performances from the all-black cast and crew. **57m/B VHS.** Herbert Jeffries, Artie Young, Rellie Hardin, Spencer Williams Jr., Clarence Brooks, F.E. (Flourney) Miller; ***D:*** Richard C. Kahn; ***W:*** Richard C. Kahn.

The Brood 🦴🦴½ **1979 (R)** Cronenberg's inimitable biological nightmares, involving an experimentally malformed woman who gives birth to murderous demon-children that kill every time she gets angry. Extremely graphic. Not for all tastes. **92m/C VHS.** *CA* Samantha Eggar, Oliver Reed, Art Hindle, Susan Hogan, Nuala Fitzgerald, Cindy Hinds, Robert A. Silverman, Gary McKeehan; ***D:*** David Cronenberg; ***W:*** David Cronenberg; ***C:*** Mark Irwin; ***M:*** Howard Shore.

A Brooklyn State of Mind 🦴🦴 **1997 (R)** Al (Spano) works for shady real estate developer Frank Parente (Aiello) in Brooklyn. When his Aunt Rose (King) rents a room to beautiful Gabriella (Cucinotta), who says she's working on a documentary about the neighborhood, Al is quick to succumb to her charms. But he's also suspicious—and when he finds a dossier on Frank in Gabriella's room, Al learns her father's murder is tied to his own father's death and both involve Frank. **90m/C VHS.** Vincent Spano, Danny Aiello, Maria Grazia Cucinotta, Tony Danza, Morgana King, Abe Vigoda; ***D:*** Frank Rainone; ***W:*** Frank Rainone, Fred Stroppel; ***C:*** Ken Kelsch; ***M:*** Paul Zaza.

Broth of a Boy 🦴🦴½ **1959** A hungry British producer decides to film a birthday party of the oldest man in the world. The old Irishman wants a portion of the profits. Well made and thought provoking. **77m/B VHS.** *IR* Barry Fitzgerald, Harry Brogan, Tony Wright, June Thorburn, Eddie Golden; ***D:*** George Pollock.

Brother 🦴🦴 *Brat* **1997** Danila (Bodrov Jr.) has just gotten out of the army and needs a job so he decides to visit big brother Viktor (Sukhoroukov) in St. Petersburg. He discovers his bro is a contract killer for the Russian mob and hires on as Viktor's assistant. Danila successfully accomplishes his first assignment—the murder of a mob rival—but then has the other gangsters out for revenge. Fast-paced and gritty, with casual violence and crime the easiest options in a brokendown society. Russian with subtitles. **96m/C VHS.** *RU* Sergei Bodrov Jr., Viktor Sukhoroukov, Svetlana Pismitchenko, Maria Joukova, Yuri Kouznetzov; ***D:*** Alexei Balabanov; ***W:*** Alexei Balabanov; ***C:*** Sergei Astakhov; ***M:*** Viatcheslav Boutoussov.

Brother 🦴🦴🦴 **2000 (R)** Kitano's films are something of an acquired taste. He mixes abrupt graphic (and usually brief) violence with prolonged scenes of introspection, and when it comes to expressing emotion, he seldom does more than twitch or take off his sunglasses. But the man is cool, and to those who accept his measured pace, his work has a hypnotic quality. In his first film set in America, he plays Yamamoto, an exiled Japanese yakuza who partners up with street hustler Denny (Epps) and takes on the local drug gangs. Yes, that's the stuff of hundreds of video premiere action flicks, but he transcends the cliches. English and Japanese dialog with subtitles. **118m/C VHS, DVD, Wide.** *JP* Takeshi "Beat" Kitano, Omar Epps, Kuroudo Maki, Masaya Kato, Susumu Terajima, James Shigeta; ***D:*** Takeshi "Beat" Kitano; ***W:*** Takeshi "Beat" Kitano; ***C:*** Katsumi Yanagishima; ***M:*** Joe Hisaishi.

The Brother from Another Planet 🦴🦴🦴 **1984** A black alien escapes from his home planet and winds up in Harlem, where he's pursued by two alien bounty hunters. Independently made morality fable by John Sayles before he hit the big time; features Sayles in a cameo as an alien bounty hunter. **109m/C VHS.** Joe Morton, Dee Dee Bridgewater, Ren Woods, Steve James, Maggie Renzi, David Strathairn; ***Cameos:*** John Sayles; ***D:*** John Sayles; ***W:*** John Sayles; ***M:*** Mason Daring.

Brother Future **1991** T.J., a black, streetsmart city kid who thinks school and helping others is all a waste of time gets knocked out in a car accident. As he's lying unconscious, he is transported back in time to a slave auction block in the Old South. There the displaced urbanite is forced to work on a cotton plantation, and watch the stirrings of a slave revolt. T.J. sees the light and realizes how much opportunity he's been wasting in his own life. He comes to just a few moments later, but worlds away from who he was before. Part of the "Wonderworks" series. **110m/C VHS.** Phill Lewis, Frank Converse, Carl Lumbly, Vonetta McGee.

Brother John 🦴🦴🦴 **1970 (PG-13)** An early look at racial tensions and labor problems. An angel goes back to his hometown in Alabama to see how things are going. **94m/C VHS.** Sidney Poitier, Will Geer, Bradford Dillman, Beverly Todd, Paul Winfield; ***D:*** James Goldstone; ***M:*** Quincy Jones.

Brother of Sleep 🦴🦴🦴 *Schlafes Bruder* **1995 (R)** Elias (Eisermann), the illegitimate son of the local priest, is discovered to have perfect pitch, a beautiful voice, and a special symbiosis with nature. Which does nothing to endear him to the superstitious inhabitants of his 19th-century Austrian mountain village. Elias doesn't know whether his gift is a blessing or a curse but he'd give it up if he could win the love of his cousin Elspeth (Vavrova). Schneider scripted from his 1992 novel, which has previously been adapted as a ballet and opera. German with subtitles. **133m/C VHS.** *GE* Andre Eisermann, Dana Vavrova, Ben Becker; ***D:*** Joseph Vilsmaier; ***W:*** Robert Schneider; ***C:*** Joseph Vilsmaier; ***M:*** Norbert J. Schneider.

Brother Orchid 🦴🦴🦴 **1940** Mobster puts a henchman in charge of his gang while he vacations in Europe. Upon his return, he is deposed and wounded in an assassination attempt. Hiding out in a monastary, he plots to regain control of the gang, leading to fish outta water episodes and a change in his outlook on life. Fine cast fans through farce intelligently. **87m/B VHS.** Edward G. Robinson, Humphrey Bogart, Ann Sothern, Donald Crisp, Ralph Bellamy, Allen Jenkins, Charles D. Brown, Cecil Kellaway; ***D:*** Lloyd Bacon; ***C:*** Gaetano Antonio "Tony" Gaudio.

Brother Sun, Sister Moon 🦴🦴½ **1973 (PG)** Post-'60s costume epic depicting the trials of St. Francis of Assisi as he evaluates his beliefs in Catholicism. **120m/C VHS.** Graham Faulkner, Judi Bowker, Alec Guinness, Leigh Lawson, Kenneth Cranham, Lee Montague, Valentina Cortese; ***D:*** Franco Zeffirelli; ***M:*** Donovan.

The Brotherhood 🦴🦴½ **1968** Two hot-headed brothers in a Mafia syndicate clash over old vs. new methods and the changing of the Family's guard. **96m/C VHS, DVD, Wide.** Kirk Douglas, Alex Cord, Irene Papas, Luther Adler, Susan Strasberg, Murray Hamilton; ***D:*** Martin Ritt; ***W:*** Lewis John Carlino; ***C:*** Boris Kaufman; ***M:*** Lalo Schifrin.

Brotherhood 2: The Young Warlocks woof! **2001** Luke is a new kid at a private school who decides to recruit a group of fellow outcast kids for a coven he's starting. Laughably bad in all regards except that some of the cast are hotties. **?m/C VHS, DVD.** Sean Faris, Forrest Cochran, Stacey Scowley, Noah Frank, Julie Briggs, Justin Allen, C.J. Thomason; ***D:*** David DeCoteau. **VIDEO**

Brotherhood of Death 🦴½ **1976 (R)** Three black Vietnam veterans return to their southern hometown to get even with the Klansmen who slaughtered all of the townspeople. **85m/C VHS.** Roy Jefferson, Larry Jones, Mike Bass, Le Tari, Haskell V. Anderson; ***D:*** Bill Berry.

Brotherhood of Justice 🦴🦴 **1986** Young men form a secret organization to rid their neighborhood of drug dealers and violence. As their power grows, their propriety weakens, until all are afraid of the "Brotherhood of Justice." **97m/C VHS.** Keanu Reeves, Kiefer Sutherland, Billy Zane, Joe Spano, Darren Dalton, Evan Mirand, Don Michael Paul; ***D:*** Charles Braverman; ***M:*** Brad Fiedel. **TV**

Brotherhood of Murder 🦴🦴 **1999** Based on the book by Thomas Martinez and John Gunther that depicts the rise and fall of the white supremacist group known as "The Order." Martinez (Baldwin) is a struglling family man who falls in with charismatic Bob Mathews (Gallagher) and his hate group—until the shooting starts. **93m/C VHS, DVD.** William Baldwin, Peter Gallagher, Kelly Lynch, Joel S. Keller, Zack (Zach) Ward, Vincent Gale; ***D:*** Martin Bell; ***W:*** Robert J. Avrech; ***C:*** James R. Bagdonas; ***M:*** Laura Karpman. **CABLE**

The Brotherhood of Satan 🦴🦴½ **1971 (PG)** In an isolated southern town, a satanic coven persuades children to join in their devil-may-care attitude. Worthwhile. **92m/C VHS.** Strother Martin, L.Q. (Justus E. McQueen) Jones, Charles Bateman, Ahna Capri, Charles Robinson, Alvy Moore, Geri Reischl; ***D:*** Bernard McEveety; ***W:*** William Welch; ***C:*** John Morrill.

The Brotherhood of the Rose 🦴½ **1989 (PG-13)** Too many twists and turns mar the otherwise mediocre plot of this murky adaption of a book by David (First Blood) Morrell. Strauss and Morse are the C.I.A. agents marked for death and running for their lives after uncovering their boss's (Mitchum) plot of world domination. Though almost every scene takes place in a different country, the movie was in fact filmed entirely in New Zealand. Convoluted and frustratingly difficult to follow. **103m/C VHS.** Robert Mitchum, Peter Strauss, Connie Sellecca, James B. Sikking, David Morse, M. Emmet Walsh, James Hong; ***D:*** Marvin J. Chomsky.

Brotherhood of the Wolf ☙☙ *Le Pacte des Loups* **2001** Based on the French legend about the Beast of Gevaudan, a wolf-like creature that killed more than 100 people in the 1760s. In 1765, in a remote province, a mysterious creature is savagely killing women and children throughout the countryside. Naturalist Gregoire de Fronsac (Le Bihan) and his Iroquis blood brother Mani (Dacascos) are sent by King Louis XV to kill and stuff the beast for posterity. But what they finally discover is quite unexpected. Flamboyantly entertaining adventure. French with subtitles. **143m/C VHS.** *FR* Samuel Le Bihan, Mark Dacascos, Vincent Cassel, Emilie Dequenne, Jean Yanne, Monica Bellucci, Edith Scob, Jeremie Renier, Jean-Francois Stevenin, Hans Meyer; ***D:*** Christophe Gans; ***W:*** Christophe Gans, Stephane Cabel; ***C:*** Dan Laustsen; ***M:*** Joseph LoDuca.

Brotherly Love ☙½ **1985** Good twin/bad twin made-for-TV mystery about an escaped psychopath who's out to get his businessman twin brother (Hirsch in both roles). **94m/C VHS.** Judd Hirsch, Karen Carlson, George Dzundza, Barry Primus, Lori Lethin; ***D:*** Jeff Bleckner.

The Brothers ☙☙☙ **2001 (R)** A chain reaction of male introspection is set off as four successful, young African-American men navigate the tricky waters of serious relationships in modern Los Angeles. All the bases are covered: there is the womanizing lawyer, Brian (Bellamy); the one night stand-weary physician, Jackson (Chestnut); the just-engaged Terry (Shemar); and the unhappily married Derrick (Hughley). Not quite as strong as its female counterpart, the much-praised "Waiting to Exhale," but novelist Hardwick's first film is well managed and funny, and he never lets his capable comic actors veer too far away from the exploration of modern sexual politics. **101m/C VHS, DVD.** Morris Chestnut, D.L. Hughley, Bill Bellamy, Shemar Moore, Gabrielle Union, Tamala Jones, Susan Dalian, Angelle Brooks, Jenifer Lewis, Clifton Powell, Marla Gibbs, Tatyana Ali, Julie Benz; ***D:*** Gary Hardwick; ***W:*** Gary Hardwick; ***C:*** Alexander Grusynski.

Brothers in Arms ☙☙ **1988 (R)** Savage mountainmen have developed a weird religion that requires them to hunt down and mercilessly massacre human prey. **95m/C VHS.** Todd Allen, Jack Starrett, Dedee Pfeiffer; ***D:*** George J. Bloom III.

Brothers in Law ☙☙½ **1957** Wry British humor in this tale of a rookie lawyer up against a veteran judge who forces him to sink or swim. **94m/B VHS.** *GB* Richard Attenborough, Ian Carmichael, Terry-Thomas, Miles Malleson, John Le Mesurier; ***D:*** Roy Boulting; ***W:*** Roy Boulting.

Brothers in Trouble ☙☙ **1995** Illegal Pakistani immigrants occupy a squalid boardinghouse in '60s Yorkshire, including newly arrived Amir (Malhotra). He settles in, befriending young student Sakib (Kumar), and learning the ropes from house leader Hossein Shah (Puri). But Shah brings unexpected problems to the group when his pregnant, white English girlfriend Mary (Ball) comes to stay and his nephew Irshad (Bhatti) arranges a paper marriage with the young woman. Based on the novel "Return Journey" by Abdullah Hussein. **104m/C VHS.** *GB* Om Puri, Pavan Malhotra, Pravesh Kumar, Angeline Ball, Ahsen Bhatti; ***D:*** Udayan Prasad; ***W:*** Robert Buckler; ***C:*** Alan Almond; ***M:*** Stephen Warbeck.

The Brothers Karamazov ☙☙☙ *Karamazov; The Murderer Dmitri Karamazov; Der Morder Dimitri Karamasoff* **1958** Hollywood adaptation of the classic novel by Dostoyevsky, in which four 19th-Century Russian brothers struggle with their desires for the same beautiful woman and with the father who brutalizes them. Incredible performances from every cast member, especially Cobb. Long and extremely intense, with fine direction from Brooks. Marilyn Monroe tried desperately to get Schell's part. **147m/C VHS.** Yul Brynner, Claire Bloom, Lee J. Cobb, William Shatner, Maria Schell, Richard Basehart; ***D:*** Richard Brooks; ***W:*** Richard Brooks; ***C:*** John Alton.

Brother's Keeper ☙☙☙ **1992** Filmmakers Berlinger and Sinofsky document the story of the eccentric and reclusive Ward brothers, four bachelor dairy farmers who shared the same two-room shack for more than 60 years in rural New York. When Bill Ward dies, brother Delbert is accused of murder and goes to trial. The film covers a year's span in preparation for the trial and how the media attention changed the Ward's lives. **104m/C VHS.** ***D:*** Joe Berlinger, Bruce Sinofsky; ***C:*** Douglas Cooper. Directors Guild '92: Feature Doc. (Berlinger), Feature Doc. (Sinofsky); Natl. Bd. of Review '92: Feature Doc.; N.Y. Film Critics '92: Feature Doc.; Sundance '92: Aud. Award.

A Brother's Kiss ☙☙ **1997 (R)** Growing up in an East Harlem neighborhood with an alcoholic mother (Moriarty), two brothers are set on different paths that strain their brotherly love. Lex (Chinlund) is a never-was ex-basketball player with a bad marriage and an even worse drug problem. Mick (Raynor) is a tightly wound, obsessive, and sexually dysfunctional cop. Both of their problems stem from a childhood trauma that neither is able or willing to discuss with the other. Starts out strong but runs out of energy by the second half. Expanded from a one-act play by director Rosenfeld. **92m/C VHS, DVD.** Nicholas Chinlund, Michael Raynor, Justin Pierce, Cathy Moriarty, Rosie Perez, Marisa Tomei, Joshua Danowsky, John Leguizamo, Michael Rapaport, Frank Minucci, Adrian Pasdar; ***D:*** Seth Zvi Rosenfeld; ***W:*** Seth Zvi Rosenfeld; ***C:*** Fortunato Procopio; ***M:*** Frank London.

Brothers Lionheart ☙☙½ **1977 (G)** The Lion brothers fight for life, love and liberty during the Middle Ages. Based on a novel by Astrid Lindgren. **120m/C VHS.** *SW* Staffan Gotestam, Lars Soderdahl, Allan Edwall; ***D:*** Olle Hellbom.

The Brothers McMullen ☙☙☙ **1994 (R)** Slice of life drama finds three Irish-American brothers suddenly living under the same Long Island roof for the first time since childhood. Eldest brother Jack (Mulcahy) is a stolid high-school basketball coach married to teacher Molly (Britton) who's pressing him to have children. Cynical middle brother Barry (Burns), a writer, has just broken up with free-spirited Ann (McKay), and earnest young Patrick (McGlone) is engaged to Jewish girlfriend Susan (Albert). All three find their romantic relationships, as well as their belief in each other, tested. Generally good performances and dialogue, with Burns proving himself a triple threat as actor/writer/director. **98m/C VHS, DVD, Wide.** Edward Burns, Jack Mulcahy, Mike McGlone, Connie Britton, Shari Albert, Elizabeth P. McKay, Maxine Bahns, Jennifer Jostyn, Catharine Bolt, Peter Johansen; ***D:*** Edward Burns; ***W:*** Edward Burns; ***C:*** Dick Fisher; ***M:*** Seamus Egan. Ind. Spirit '96: First Feature; Sundance '95: Grand Jury Prize.

Brothers of the West ☙½ **1937** Cowboy saves his brothers from being lynched by proving the guilt of the real outlaws. **56m/B VHS.** Tom Tyler, Bob Terry, Lois Wilde, Dorothy Short, Lafe (Lafayette) McKee, Dave O'Brien, Roger Williams; ***D:*** Sam Katzman; ***W:*** Basil Dickey; ***C:*** William (Bill) Hyer.

Brothers O'Toole ☙☙ **1973 (G)** The misadventures of a pair of slick drifters who, by chance, ride into a broken-down mining town in the 1890s. **94m/C VHS.** John Astin, Steve Carlson, Pat Carroll, Hans Conried, Lee Meriwether; ***D:*** Richard Erdman.

The Browning Version ☙☙☙½ **1951** A lonely, unemotional classics instructor at a British boarding school realizes his failure as a teacher and as a husband. From the play by Terrence Rattigan. **89m/B VHS.** *GB* Michael Redgrave, Jean Kent, Nigel Patrick, Wilfrid Hyde-White, Bill Travers; ***D:*** Anthony Asquith. Cannes '51: Actor (Redgrave).

The Browning Version ☙☙½ **1994 (R)** Mediocre remake of the Terence Rattigan play, previously filmed in 1951. Austere classics professor (Finney) at prestigious British boys school is disillusioned with both his floundering career and marriage. His emotional chill drives his younger wife (Scacchi) into an affair with a visiting American science teacher (Modine). Unfortunately updated to contemporary times, which can't hide apparent mustiness. Worth seeing for Finney's superb work as the out-of-touch prof. **97m/C VHS.** Albert Finney, Greta Scacchi, Matthew Modine, Michael Gambon, Julian Sands, Ben Silverstone, Maryam D'Abo; ***D:*** Mike Figgis; ***W:*** Ronald Harwood; ***M:*** Mark Isham.

Brown's Requiem ☙☙½ **1998 (R)** Ex-cop and ex-drunk Fritz Brown (Rooker) is a sometime L.A. private eye and repo man. He's hired by the aptly named Freddie "Fat Dog" Baker (Sasso) to check out Solly K (Gould), at whose manse Baker's kid sister Jane (Blair) is living. Solly's involved with ex-cop Cathcart (James), with whom Fritz has a longstanding beef, and the P.I. uncovers various lowlifes and a scam. Based on James Ellroy's Chandleresque detailed and dialogue-heavy first novel, which was published in 1981. **97m/C VHS, DVD.** Michael Rooker, Brion James, Harold Gould, Selma Blair, Kevin Corrigan, Tobin Bell, Jack Conley, Brad Dourif, Will Sasso, Valerie Perrine, Barry Newman; ***D:*** Jason Freedland; ***W:*** Jason Freedland; ***C:*** Sead Mutarevic; ***M:*** Cynthia Millar.

Brubaker ☙☙☙ **1980 (R)** A sanctimonious drama about a reform warden who risks his life to replace brutality and corruption with humanity and integrity in a state prison farm. Powerful prison drama. **131m/C VHS.** Robert Redford, Jane Alexander, Yaphet Kotto, Murray Hamilton, David Keith, Morgan Freeman, Matt Clark, M. Emmet Walsh, Everett McGill; ***D:*** Stuart Rosenberg; ***W:*** W.D. Richter, Arthur Ross; ***M:*** Lalo Schifrin.

The Bruce ☙☙½ **1996** Based on the story of Scottish king, Robert the Bruce (Welch) and the battle at Bannockburn against English King Edward I's (Blessed) forces. Not blessed with the biggest budget and the actors tend to chew the scenery but not a bad bit of history. Robert the Bruce may also be familiar from the film "Braveheart." **110m/C VHS.** *GB* Sandy Welch, Oliver Reed, Brian Blessed, Michael Van Wijk, Pavel Douglas.

Bruce Lee: Curse of the Dragon ☙☙☙ *The Curse of the Dragon* **1993** A behind the scenes look at the continuing mystery surrounding the life and untimely death of the martial arts superstar who died in 1973 at the age of 32. Highlights the spectacular fight sequences from Lee's movies as well as footage from his funeral and an interview with his son Brandon Lee, whose own death in 1993 raised further comment about a Lee family curse. **90m/C VHS.** ***Nar:*** George Takei.

Bruce Lee Fights Back from the Grave ☙ **1976 (R)** Bruce Lee returns from the grave to fight the Black Angel of Death with his feet and to wreak vengeance on the evil ones who brought about his untimely demise. **84m/C VHS, DVD.** Bruce Le, Deborah Chaplin, Anthony Bronson; ***D:*** Umberto Lenzi.

Bruiser ☙½ **2000** First film from horror icon Romero in more than seven years offers a great central premise, but little else. Henry Creedlow (Flemyng) is a nice guy who gets used by everyone around him. His cheating wife, his overbearing boss, and his dishonest stock broker all push Henry around, but he never stands up for himself. That is, until the day that he wakes up to find that his face has been replaced by a blank white mask. Being "faceless" allows Henry to assert himself and get revenge. The film is boring and filled with many unlikable characters, the worst of which is Henry. The last act is simply absurd and one can't help but wonder what has happened to the once great Romero. **99m/C VHS, DVD, Wide.** Jason Flemyng, Peter Stormare, Leslie Hope, Nina Garbiras, Tom Atkins, Jeff Monahan; ***D:*** George A. Romero; ***W:*** George A. Romero; ***C:*** Adam Swica; ***M:*** Donald Rubinstein.

Brutal Fury ☙ **1992** Detective Molly Griffin goes undercover at a local high school and discovers a secret female vigilante group, called the "Fury," which goes after the drug dealers and rapists preying on the school's students. Teenagers with an attitude. **97m/C VHS.** Tom Campitelli, Lisa-Gabrielle Greene, Annette Gerbon, Karen Eppers, Jennifer Winder, Allen Arkus; ***D:*** Frederick P. Watkins.

Brutal Glory ☙☙ **1989** Set in New York City in 1918 and based on the true story of the boxer known as "The Real McCoy." Fascinating and detailed history of a period, a champion, and the man who made it happen. **96m/C VHS.** Robert Vaughn, Timothy Brantley, Leah K. Pinsent; ***D:*** Koos Roets.

The Brutal Truth ☙☙ **1999 (R)** Group of high school friends get together for a 10-year reunion at a secluded mountain cabin for a weekend of fun, but then learn that one of the gang, Emily (Applegate), has committed suicide. This leads to arguments and secrets revealed. **89m/C VHS, DVD.** Christina Applegate, Justin Lazard, Johnathon Schaech, Moon Zappa, Paul Gleason, Molly Ringwald, Leslie Horan; ***D:*** Cameron Thor.

The Brute Man ☙☙ **1946** A young man who had been disfigured by his school mates goes out on a trail of revenge. Hatton is convincing in the title role, as in real life he was afflicted with acromegaly, an ailment that produces an enlargment of the bones in the face, hands, and feet. **62m/B VHS, DVD.** Rondo Hatton, Tom Neal, Jane Adams, Donald McBride, Peter Whitney; ***D:*** Jean Yarbrough; ***W:*** George Bricker, M. Coates Webster; ***C:*** Maury Gertsman; ***M:*** Hans J. Salter.

The Brylcreem Boys ☙☙ **1996 (PG-13)** In September, 1941, Canadian pilot Miles Keogh (Campbell) and his crew are forced to bail out of their plane. They land in neutral southern Ireland, where they're interned in the local POW camp run by Sean O'Brien (Byrne). The camp holds both Allies and Germans—separated by only a thin wire fence. Keogh figures it's his patriotic duty to try to escape as does German officer Rudolph von Stegenbeck (Macfadyen), and problems compound when both soldiers are let out on day-release passes and, naturally, fall for the same lovely local colleen, Mattie (Butler). It's pleasant but unmemorable. **105m/C VHS, DVD.** *GB* Billy Campbell, Angus Macfadyen, William McNamara, Gabriel Byrne, Jean Butler, Joe McGann, Oliver Tobias, Gordon John Sinclair; ***D:*** Terence Ryan; ***W:*** Terence Ryan, Jamie Brown; ***C:*** Gerry Lively; ***M:*** Richard Hartley.

Bubble Boy ☙ **2001 (PG-13)** Disney has finally jumped on the crude and offensive humor bandwagon, with a simplistic storyline involving the journey of Jimmy (Gyllenhaal), a naive guy born with an immune system deficiency that requires him to live in a germ-free environment, as he races across the country to stop his sweetheart (Shelton) from marrying a jerk. Jimmy constructs a mobile bubble and hits the road. Along the way, the alleged jokes manage to offend Christians, Hindus, Jews, Republicans, Latinos, Asians and circus freaks while still wallowing in boner humor. That'd be almost forgivable if the "humor" was actually funny. **84m/C VHS, DVD, Wide.** *US* Jake Gyllenhaal, Swoosie Kurtz, Marley Shelton, Danny Trejo, John Carroll Lynch, Stephen Spinella, Verne Troyer, Dave Sheridan, Brian George, Patrick Cranshaw, Fabio; ***D:*** Blair Hayes; ***W:*** Ken Daurio, Cinco Paul; ***C:*** Jerzy Zielinski; ***M:*** John Ottman.

The Buccaneer ☙☙ **1958** A swashbuckling version of the adventures of pirate Jean LaFitte and his association with President Andrew Jackson during the War of 1812. Remake of Cecille B. DeMille's 1938 production. **121m/C VHS.** Yul Brynner, Charlton Heston, Claire Bloom, Inger Stevens, Charles Boyer, Henry Hull, E.G. Marshall, Lorne Greene; ***D:*** Anthony Quinn; ***C:*** Loyal Griggs; ***M:*** Elmer Bernstein.

The Buccaneers ☙☙☙ **1995** Lavish adaptation of the Edith Wharton novel follows the adventures of four American girls in 1870s society. Nouveaux riche, the young ladies are unable to crack New York snobbery and, after vivacious Brazilian Conchita (Sorvino) manages to snag Lord Richard (Vibert), the others are encouraged by English governess Laura Testvalley (Lunghi) to try their luck in London. There, Virginia (Elliott), sister Nan (Gugino), their friend Lizzy (Kihlstedt), and Conchita all find hope and heartbreak among the English aristocracy. Wharton's novel was unfinished at her death and, though she left story notes, scripter Wadey concedes to changes. Made for TV. **288m/C VHS.** *GB* Carla Gugino, Mira Sorvino, Alison Elliott, Rya Kihlstedt, Cherie Lunghi, Connie Booth, Mark Tandy, Ronan Vibert, Jenny Agutter, Richard Huw, Greg Wise, James Frain, Michael Kitchen, Sheila Hancock, Rosemary Leach, Elizabeth Ashley, Conchata Ferrell, Peter Michael Goetz, James Rebhorn, E. Katherine Kerr; *D:* Philip Saville; *W:* Maggie Wadey; *C:* Maggie Wadey; *M:* Colin Towns. **TV**

Buck and the Magic Bracelet 🦴🦴½ **1997 (PG-13)** In the old west a teen and his dog escape an attack on their prospecting camp. They're aided in bringing the bad guys to justice by a shaman's magic bracelet. **99m/C VHS.** Matt McCoy, Abby Dalton, Felton Perry, Conrad Nichols.

Buck and the Preacher 🦴🦴½ **1972 (PG)** A trail guide and a con man preacher join forces to help a wagon train of former slaves who are seeking to homestead out West. Poitier's debut as a director. **102m/C VHS, DVD.** Sidney Poitier, Harry Belafonte, Ruby Dee, Cameron Mitchell, Denny Miller; *D:* Sidney Poitier.

Buck Privates 🦴🦴½ *Rookies* **1941** Abbott and Costello star as two dim-witted tie salesmen, running from the law, who become buck privates during WWII. The duo's first great success, and the film that established the formula for each subsequent film. **84m/B VHS, DVD.** Bud Abbott, Lou Costello, Shemp Howard, Lee Bowman, Alan Curtis, The Andrews Sisters; *D:* Arthur Lubin; *W:* Arthur T. Horman, John Grant; *C:* Milton Krasner; *M:* Charles Previn.

Buck Privates Come Home 🦴🦴🦴 *Rookies Come Home* **1947** Abbott and Costello return to their "Buck Privates" roles as two soldiers trying to adjust to civilian life after the war. They also try to help a French girl sneak into the United States. Funny antics culminate into a wild chase scene. **77m/B VHS, DVD.** Bud Abbott, Lou Costello, Tom Brown, Joan Shawlee, Nat Pendleton, Beverly Simmons, Don Beddoe, Don Porter, Donald MacBride; *D:* Charles T. Barton; *W:* John Grant, Frederic Rinaldo, Robert Lees; *C:* Charles Van Enger; *M:* Walter Schumann.

Buck Rogers Conquers the Universe 🦴🦴 **1939** The story of Buck Rogers, written by Phil Nolan in 1928, was the first science-fiction story done in the modern superhero space genre. Many of the "inventions" seen in this movie have actually come into existence—spaceships, ray guns (lasers), anti-gravity belts—a testament to Nolan's almost psychic farsightedness. **91m/B VHS.** Buster Crabbe, Constance Moore, Jackie Moran; *D:* Ford Beebe, Saul Goodkind.

Buck Rogers in the 25th Century 🦴🦴 **1979 (PG)** An American astronaut, preserved in space for 500 years, is brought back to life by a passing Draconian flagship. Outer space adventures begin when he is accused of being a spy from Earth. Based on the classic movie serial. TV movie that began the popular series. Additional series episodes are available. **90m/C VHS.** Gil Gerard, Pamela Hensley, Erin Gray, Henry Silva; *D:* Daniel Haller; *V:* Mel Blanc. **TV**

A Bucket of Blood 🦴🦴🦴 **1959** Cult favorite Dick Miller stars as a sculptor with a peculiar "talent" for lifelike artwork. Corman fans will see thematic similarities to his subsequent work, "Little Shop of Horrors" (1960). "Bucket of Blood" was made in just five days, while "Little Shop of Horrors" was made in a record breaking two days. Corman horror/spoof noted for its excellent beatnik atmosphere. **66m/B VHS, DVD.** Dick Miller, Barboura Morris, Antony Carbone, Julian Burton, Ed Nelson, Bert Convy, Judy Bamber, John Brinkley, Myrtle Domerel, John Herman Shaner, Bruno VeSota; *D:* Roger Corman; *W:* Charles B. Griffith; *C:* John Marquette; *M:* Fred Katz.

Buckeye and Blue 🦴½ **1987 (PG)** A hero turned outlaw, his 14 year-old female sidekick, and a gang known as the McCoys are all on the lam from the law in this western adventure. **94m/C VHS.** Robin (Robyn) Lively, Jeffery Osterhage, Rick Gibbs, Will Hannah, Kenneth Jensen, Patrick Johnston, Stuart Rogers, Michael Horse; *D:* J.C. Compton.

Buckskin 🦴½ **1968** Slowmoving western about a marshall protecting townspeople from a greedy, land-grabbing cattle baron. **98m/C VHS.** Barry Sullivan, Wendell Corey, Joan Caulfield, Lon Chaney Jr., John Russell, Barbara Hale, Barton MacLane, Bill Williams; *D:* Michael Moore.

Buckskin Frontier 🦴½ **1943** Story is built around Western railroad construction and cattle empires in the 1860s. Cobb tries to stop the railroad from coming through by hiring Jory to do his dirty work. **75m/B VHS.** Richard Dix, Jane Wyatt, Lee J. Cobb, Albert Dekker, Victor Jory, Lola Lane, Max Baer Sr.; *D:* Lesley Selander.

Bucktown 🦴½ **1975 (R)** A black man who reopens his murdered brother's bar fights off police corruption and racism in a Southern town. **95m/C VHS, DVD, Wide.** Fred Williamson, Pam Grier, Bernie Hamilton, Thalmus Rasulala, Art Lund; *D:* Arthur Marks; *W:* Bob Ellison; *C:* Robert Birchall; *M:* Johnny Pate.

Bud and Lou 🦴½ **1978** Comedy/drama recounts Abbott & Costello's rise in Hollywood. While the story, based on the book by Bob Thomas, is interesting, the two funnymen in the leads can't pull off the old classic skits. **98m/C VHS.** Harvey Korman, Buddy Hackett, Michele Lee, Arte Johnson, Robert Reed; *D:* Robert C. Thompson.

The Buddha of Suburbia 🦴🦴🦴 **1992** Satire set in late '70s suburban London follows the coming of age adventures of Karim (Andrews), the handsome son of an Indian father and English mother. His gleeful father Haroon (Seth) exploits the vogue for eastern philosophies he knows nothing about with lectures to the upper-middle classes while he carries on with devotee Eva (Fleetwood). When his mother finds out, Karim and his father move into central London with Eva, where Karim decides to take up acting in fringe theatre and sex while his friend, Eva's son Charlie (Mackintosh), experiments with the punk music scene. TV miniseries adapted by Kureishi from his novel. **220m/C VHS.** *GB* Naveen Andrews, Roshan Seth, Susan Fleetwood, Steven Mackintosh, Brenda Blethyn, John McEnery, Janet Dale, David Bamber, Donald (Don) Sumpter, Jemma Redgrave, David Bradley; *D:* Roger Michell; *W:* Hanif Kureishi, Roger Michell; *C:* John McGlashan; *M:* David Bowie. **TV**

Buddy 🦴🦴½ **1997 (PG)** Animals run amok in the Lintz household. Mother hen Gertrude Lintz (Russo) raises just about everything from mischievous chimps to impressionable parrots on her estate. A baby gorilla (named Buddy, short for Buddha) becomes part of the family, but as he grows in size, so does the difficulty in caring for him. Amiable tale of one woman's motherly bond with a gorilla includes convincing performances by Russo and an animatronic gorilla courtesy of Jim Henson's Creature Shop. Well-paced and very touching at moments, children will definitely enjoy the zany animal antics, and adults should be moved by the unusual relationship. Based on the book by Lintz. **84m/C VHS, DVD, Wide.** Rene Russo, Robbie Coltrane, Irma P. Hall, Alan Cumming, Paul (Pee-wee Herman) Reubens; *D:* Caroline Thompson; *W:* Caroline Thompson; *C:* Steve Mason; *M:* Elmer Bernstein.

Buddy Buddy 🦴🦴½ **1981 (R)** A professional hitman's well-ordered arrangement to knock off a state's witness keeps being interrupted by the suicide attempts of a man in the next hotel room. **96m/C VHS.** Jack Lemmon, Walter Matthau, Paula Prentiss, Klaus Kinski; *D:* Billy Wilder; *W:* Billy Wilder, I.A.L. Diamond; *C:* Harry Stradling Jr.; *M:* Lalo Schifrin.

The Buddy Holly Story 🦴🦴🦴½ **1978 (PG)** An acclaimed biography of the famed 1950s pop star, spanning the years from his meteoric career's beginnings in Lubbock to his tragic early death in the now famous plane crash of February 3, 1959. Busey performs Holly's hits himself. ♫Rock Around the Ollie Vee; That'll Be the Day; Oh, Boy; It's So Easy; Well All Right; Chantilly Lace; Peggy Sue. **113m/C VHS, DVD.** Gary Busey, Don Stroud, Charles Martin Smith, Conrad Janis, William Jordan, Albert "Poppy" Popwell; *D:* Steve Rash; *W:* Robert Gittler; *C:* Stevan Larner; *M:* Joe Renzetti. Oscars '78: Orig. Song Score and/or Adapt.; Natl. Soc. Film Critics '78: Actor (Busey).

The Buddy System 🦴🦴 **1983 (PG)** A tale of contemporary love and the modern myths that outline the boundaries between lovers and friends. **110m/C VHS.** Richard Dreyfuss, Susan Sarandon, Jean Stapleton, Nancy Allen, Wil Wheaton, Edward Winter, Keene Curtis; *D:* Glenn Jordan; *W:* Mary Agnes Donoghue.

Buddy's Song 🦴🦴 **1991 (R)** A '60s coming of age tale, only in this case it's the father and not the son who needs to grow up. Dad (Daltrey) is more interested in hanging out with his no-account musician friends than in looking after his family. Although he's not above meddling in his teenage son's musical career, which could be the success his father's never was. Based on the novel by Nigel Hinton who also did the screenplay. British teen idol Hawkes (in his film debut) had a top ten hit song from the film with "The One and Only." **106m/C VHS.** *GB* Roger Daltrey, Chesney Hawkes, Sharon Duce, Michael Elphick, Douglas Hodge, Lee Ross, James Aubrey, Liza Walker; *D:* Claude Whatham; *W:* Nigel Hinton; *C:* John Hooper; *M:* John Grover, Roger Daltrey.

Buffalo Bill 🦴🦴 **1944** A light, fictionalized account of the life and career of Bill Cody, from frontier hunter to showman. **89m/C VHS.** Joel McCrea, Maureen O'Hara, Linda Darnell, Thomas Mitchell, Edgar Buchanan, Anthony Quinn, Moroni Olsen, Sidney Blackmer; *D:* William A. Wellman; *C:* Leon Shamroy.

Buffalo Bill & the Indians 🦴🦴🦴 *Sitting Bull's History Lesson* **1976 (PG)** A perennially underrated Robert Altman historical pastiche, portraying the famous Wild West character as a charlatan and shameless exemplar of encroaching imperialism. Great all-star cast amid Altman's signature mise-en-scene chaos. **135m/C VHS, DVD, Wide.** Paul Newman, Geraldine Chaplin, Joel Grey, Will Sampson, Harvey Keitel, Burt Lancaster, Kevin McCarthy; *D:* Robert Altman; *W:* Robert Altman, Alan Rudolph; *M:* Richard Baskin.

Buffalo Bill Rides Again 🦴½ **1947** With an Indian uprising on the horizon, Buffalo Bill is called in. Mr. Bill finds land swindlers pitting natives against ranchers, but there's precious little action or interest here. **68m/C VHS.** Richard Arlen, Jennifer Holt, Edward Cassidy, Edmund Cobb, Charles Stevens; *D:* Bernard B. Ray.

Buffalo Girls 🦴🦴½ **1995** Western saga, set in the 1870s, tells of the lifelong friendship between hard-drinking, hard-living Calamity Jane (Huston—who's not exactly any plain Jane) and buxom, soft-hearted madam Dora DuFran (Griffith). Dora's in love (but refuses to marry) rancher Teddy Blue (Byrne) while Calamity has a daughter by Wild Bill Hickok (Elliott) that she gives up for adoption. There's lots of rambling and commiserating over the changing and civilizing of the west and various man trouble. Based on the novel by Larry McMurty; originally a two-part TV miniseries. **180m/C VHS.** Anjelica Huston, Melanie Griffith, Gabriel Byrne, Peter Coyote, Jack Palance, Sam Elliott, Reba McEntire, Floyd "Red Crow" Westerman, Tracey Walter, Russell Means, Charlaine Woodard, John Diehl, Liev Schreiber, Andrew Bicknell, Paul Lazar; *D:* Rod Hardy; *W:* Cynthia Whitcomb; *C:* David Connell; *M:* Lee Holdridge.

Buffalo Heart: The Pain of Death 🦴½ **1996** Buffalo Heart decides to avenge the rape and murder of his daughter by tracking down her killers. **85m/C VHS.** Daniel Matmor, Alex Wexo, Craig Eisner; *D:* Daniel Matmor; *W:* Daniel Matmor; *C:* Paul DeGruccio.

Buffalo Jump 🦴🦴🦴 *Getting Married in Buffalo Jump* **1990** An independent woman, working as a lounge singer in Toronto, returns to her home in Alberta when her father dies. To her surprise he has left her the family ranch and, to the surprise of everyone else, she decides to stay and run it. She hires a good-looking local man to help her out and they both discover that they want more than a working relationship. However, the fireworks really start when he proposes a marriage of convenience. Engaging performances and beautiful scenery help raise this romantic tale of opposites above the average. **97m/C VHS.** *CA* Wendy Crewson, Paul Gross, Marion Gilsenan, Kyra Harper, Victoria Snow; *D:* Eric Till.

Buffalo Rider 🦴½ **1978** An adventure film depicting the real-life experiences of C.J. "Buffalo" Jones who worked to save the American buffalo from extinction. **90m/C VHS.** Rick Guinn, John Freeman, Pricilla Lauris, George Sager, Rich Scheeland; *D:* George Lauris.

Buffalo 66 🦴🦴🦴 **1997** Billy Brown (Gallo) is a loser of epic proportions. He's named after the Buffalo Bills, notorious losers of Super Bowls. After he loses $10,000 on of those Super Bowls, he turns to a life of crime and promptly lands in prison. He gets out of jail as a man with a mission. Stumbling into a dance studio, Billy kidnaps the nubile Layla (Ricci) and forces her to pose as his wife for a visit to his parents. He had explained his five-year absence to them by saying that he was working for the CIA overseas with his new bride. His father Jimmy (Gazzara), a bitter ex-lounge singer, barely hides his disdain for Billy, and mother Janet (Huston) is so too obsessed with the Bills to interact with him. They both like Layla instantly, and she seems to take unexpected glee in playing her part. Former artist and rock musician Gallo also directed, co-wrote and composed the music for the film. **112m/C VHS, DVD, Wide.** Vincent Gallo, Christina Ricci, Anjelica Huston, Ben Gazzara, Kevin Corrigan, Mickey Rourke, Rosanna Arquette, Jan-Michael Vincent; *D:* Vincent Gallo; *W:* Alison Bagnall, Vincent Gallo; *C:* Lance Acord; *M:* Vincent Gallo. Natl. Bd. of Review '98: Support. Actress (Ricci).

Buffalo Soldiers 🦴🦴🦴 **1997** Post-Civil War western concerns the all-black Cavalry troops, created by Congress in 1866 to patrol the west. They received their nickname from the Indians, who thought the black soldiers on horseback looked like buffalo. A former slave and by-the-book Army man, Sgt. Washington Wyatt (Glover) leads the chase for Apache warrior Victorio (Lowe) across the New Mexico Territory while trying tp deal with the common degradation suffered by his troops at the hands of white officers. Lots of cruelty and explicit violence. **120m/C VHS.** Danny Glover, Carl Lumbly, Bob Gunton, Tom Bower, Harrison Lowe, Glynn Turman, Michael Warren, Mykelti Williamson, Timothy Busfield, Gabriel Casseus; *D:* Charles Haid; *W:* Frank Military, Susan Rhinehart; *C:* William Wages; *M:* Joel McNeely. **CABLE**

Buffalo Stampede 🦴 **1933** Our heroes are involved in a plot to round up buffalo to sell for meat. **60m/B VHS.** Randolph Scott, Buster Crabbe, Harry Carey Sr., Noah Beery Sr., Raymond Hatton, Judith Allen, Blanche Frederici; *D:* Henry Hathaway.

Buffet Froid 🦴🦴🦴½ **1979** Surreal black comedy about a group of bungling murderers. First rate acting and directing makes this film a hilarious treat. From the director of "Menage." In French with English subtitles. **95m/C VHS, DVD.** *FR* Gerard Depardieu, Bernard Blier, Jean Carmet, Genevieve Page, Denise Gence, Carole Bouquet, Jean Benguigui, Michel Serrault; *D:* Bertrand Blier; *W:* Bertrand Blier; *C:* Jean Penzer; *M:* Philippe Sarde. Cesar '80: Writing.

Buffy the Vampire Slayer 🦴🦴🦴 **1992 (PG-13)** Funny, near-camp teen genre spoof. Buffy is a typical mall gal concerned with shopping and cheerleading, until the mysterious Sutherland proclaims it her destiny to slay the vampires who have suddenly infested Los Angeles. Like, really. Buffy requires some convincing, but eventually takes up the challenge, fighting off the vamps and their seductive leader Hauer, aided by perpetual guy-in-distress Perry. "Pee-wee" Reubens is unrecognizable and terribly amusing as the vampire king's sinister henchman, engaging in one of the longer death scenes of film history. Check out Cassandra (Wagner), Natalie Wood's daughter. **98m/C VHS, DVD, Wide.** Stephen

(Steve) Root, Kristy Swanson, Donald Sutherland, Luke Perry, Paul (Pee-wee Herman) Reubens, Rutger Hauer, Michele Abrams, Randall Batinkoff, Hilary Swank, Paris Vaughan, David Arquette, Candy Clark, Natasha Gregson Wagner; *D:* Fran Rubel Kuzui; *W:* Joss Whedon; *C:* James Hayman; *M:* Carter Burwell.

Buford's Beach Bunnies **1992 (R)** Harry Buford has made a fortune selling barbecued rabbit sandwiches served by the sexiest waitresses around. Harry wants to leave the business to his son Jeeter—if Jeeter can overcome his overwhelming fear of women. So three of Harry's waitresses decide to show Jeeter a very good time. Lots of pretty girls in not much clothing. **90m/C VHS.** Jim Hanks, Rikki Brando, Monique Parent, Amy Page, Barrett Cooper, Ina Rogers, Charley Rossman, David Robinson; *D:* Mark Pirro; *W:* Mark Pirro.

Bug woof! *The Bug* **1975 (PG)** The city of Riverside is threatened with destruction after a massive earth tremor unleashes a super-race of ten-inch mega-cockroaches that belch fire, eat raw meat, and are virtually impervious to Raid. Produced by gimmick-king William Castle, who wanted to install windshield wiper-like devices under theatre seats that would brush against the patrons' feet as the cockroaches crawled across the screen; unfortunately, the idea was squashed flat. **100m/C VHS.** Bradford Dillman, Joanna Miles, Richard Gilliland, Jamie Smith-Jackson, Alan Fudge, Jesse Vint, Patty McCormack, Brendan Dillon Jr., Frederic Downs, William Castle; *D:* Jeannot Szwarc; *W:* Thomas Page, William Castle; *C:* Michael Hugo; *M:* Charles Fox.

Bug Buster **1999 (R)** The Griffins, dad (Kopell), mom (Lockhart) and daughter Shannon (Heigl) move to scenic Mountainview to flee the stress of city life. But they didn't bargain for the giant creature "unknown to science" that's attacking people and leaving giant bug larvae in 'em. Mutant insects overrun the town, leaving the survivors one last hope, in the form of ex-military man-turned-uberexterminator General George (Quaid). Plenty of gore and over-the-top acting, plus Scotty and Mr. Sulu, give this one late-night cult potential. **93m/C VHS, DVD.** Randy Quaid, Katherine Heigl, Meredith Salenger, Bernie Kopell, Anne Lockhart, George Takei, James Doohan, Ty O'Neal, Downtown Julie Brown, Brenda Doumani, David Lipper; *D:* Lorenzo Doumani; *W:* Malik Khoury; *C:* Hanania Baer; *M:* Sidney James.

Bugged! **1996 (PG-13)** Flesh-eating insects attack a beautiful homemaker and a group of bumbling exterminators are her only hope. **90m/C VHS.** Ronald K. Armstrong, Priscilla Basque, Jeff Lee, Derek C. Johnson, Billy Graham; *D:* Ronald K. Armstrong; *W:* Ronald K. Armstrong; *C:* S. Torriano Berry; *M:* Boris Elkis.

Bugles in the Afternoon **1952** Life in the army during Custer's last days, with a love triangle, revenge and the Little Big Horn for added spice. **85m/C VHS.** Ray Milland, Hugh Marlowe, Helena Carter, Forrest Tucker, Barton MacLane, George Reeves; *D:* Roy Rowland.

A Bug's Life **1998 (G)** Computer animated feature by Pixar, the makers of "Toy Story," takes a cutesy look into the world of insects. Flik (Foley) is an ant who must help defend his colony after he messes up a tribute to a bullying group of grasshoppers led by Hopper (Spacey). He recruits a crew of misfits from a flea circus, including a male ladybug with gender issues (Leary), a prissy stick bug (Pierce), and an obese caterpillar (Ranft). Together they form a plan to keep the grasshoppers away, but still must confront Hopper in order to ensure lasting peace. Amazing animation, from the blades of grass down to the facial expressions of the bugs, along with dozens of sight gags keep this family feature flying. Competed with fellow computer animated insect feature "Antz" on its release. **94m/C VHS, DVD.** *D:* John Lasseter, Andrew Stanton; *W:* Donald McEnery, Bob Shaw, Andrew Stanton, Joe Ranft; *C:* Sharon Calahan; *M:* Randy Newman; *V:* Dave Foley, Kevin Spacey, Julia Louis-Dreyfus, Phyllis Diller, Richard Kind, David Hyde Pierce, Joe Ranft, Denis Leary, Jonathan Harris, Madeline Kahn, Bonnie Hunt, Michael McShane, John Ratzenberger, Brad Garrett, Roddy McDowall, Edie McClurg, Hayden Panettiere, Alex Rocco, David Ossman.

Bugsy ½ **1991 (R)** Beatty is Benjamin "Bugsy" Siegel, the 40s gangster who built the Flamingo Hotel in Las Vegas when it was still a virtual desert, before it became a gambling mecca. Bening is perfect as Bugsy's moll, Virginia Hill, who inspired him to carry out his dream of building the Flamingo (which was her nickname). Beatty and Bening heat up the screen and their off-screen relationship was no different. Fans anticipated their seemingly imminent marriage almost as much as the release of this movie. Almost nothing mars this film which Toback adapted from a novel by Dean Jennings, "We Only Kill Each Other: The Life and Bad Times of Bugsy Siegel." **135m/C VHS, DVD, 8mm.** Warren Beatty, Annette Bening, Harvey Keitel, Ben Kingsley, Elliott Gould, Joe Mantegna, Richard Sarafian, Bebe Neuwirth, Wendy Phillips, Robert Beltran, Bill Graham, Lewis Van Bergen, Debrah Farentino; *D:* Barry Levinson; *W:* James Toback; *C:* Allen Daviau; *M:* Ennio Morricone. Oscars '91: Art Dir./Set Dec., Costume Des.; Golden Globes '92: Film—Drama; L.A. Film Critics '91: Director (Levinson), Film, Screenplay; Natl. Bd. of Review '91: Actor (Beatty).

Bugsy Malone ½ **1976 (G)** Delightful musical features an all-children's cast highlighting this spoof of 1930s' gangster movies. **94m/C VHS.** *GB* Jodie Foster, Scott Baio, Florrie Augger, John Cassisi, Martin Lev; *D:* Alan Parker; *W:* Alan Parker; *C:* Peter Biziou; *M:* Paul Williams. British Acad. '76: Screenplay.

Bull Durham ½ **1988 (R)** Lovable American romantic comedy, dealing with a very minor minor-league team and three of its current constituents: aging baseball groupie Annie Savoy (Sarandon) who beds one player each season; a cocky, foolish new pitcher, Ebby Calvin "Nuke" LaLoosh (Robbins); and older, weary catcher Crash Davis (Costner), who's brought in to wise the rookie up. The scene in which Annie tries poetry out on the banal rookie (who has more earthly pleasures in mind) is a hoot. Highly acclaimed, the film sears with Sarandon and Costner's love scenes and some clever dialogue. **107m/C VHS, DVD, Wide.** Kevin Costner, Susan Sarandon, Tim Robbins, Trey Wilson, Robert Wuhl, Jenny Robertson; *D:* Ron Shelton; *W:* Ron Shelton; *C:* Bobby Byrne; *M:* Michael Convertino. L.A. Film Critics '88: Screenplay; N.Y. Film Critics '88: Screenplay; Natl. Soc. Film Critics '88: Screenplay; Writers Guild '88: Orig. Screenplay.

Bull of the West ½ **1989** Cattlemen battle for land in the wide open spaces of the old West. **90m/C VHS.** Charles Bronson, Lee J. Cobb, Brian Keith, George Kennedy, DeForest Kelley, Doug McClure, James Drury, Geraldine Brooks, Lois Nettleton, Ben Johnson, Gary Clarke; *D:* Jerry Hopper; *W:* Don Ingalls; *C:* Benjamin (Ben H.) Kline; *M:* Hal Mooney.

Bulldance *Forbidden Son* **1988** At a gymnastic school in Crete, a girl's obsession with Greek mythological ritual leads to murder. **105m/C VHS.** Lauren Hutton, Cliff DeYoung, Renee Estevez; *D:* Zelda Barron.

Bulldog Courage **1935** Young man is out to avenge his father's murder. **66m/B VHS.** Tim McCoy, Lois January, Joan Woodbury, John Elliott; *D:* Sam Newfield.

Bulldog Drummond ½ **1929** The Bulldog Drummond character, created by "Sapper" (Herman Cyril McNeile), underwent a number of different incarnations from 20s silents through the 40s, and even occassionally in the 50s and 60s. A suave ex-British officer (a precursor to the glib shaken-not-stirred gentleman-spy variety), Bulldog has been played by the likes of Colman, Ralph Richardson, and Tom Conway, among others. In this, the first installment in the long-standing series, a WWI vet, bored with civilian life, is enlisted by a beautiful woman to help her father in various adventures. **85m/B VHS.** Ronald Colman, Joan Bennett, Montagu Love, Lilyan Tashman, Lawrence Grant, Wilson Benge, Claud Allister, Adolph Milar, Charles Sellon, Tetsu Komai, Donald Novis; *D:* F. Richard Jones; *W:* Sidney Howard, Wallace Smith; *C:* George Barnes, Gregg Toland.

Bulldog Drummond at Bay **1937** Drummond searches for a group of foreign agents who are trying to steal the plans for a top-secret warplane. Poor British entry to the "Bulldog Drummond" series. **63m/B VHS.** *GB* John Lodge, Dorothy Mackaill, Victor Jory, Claud Allister, Hugh Miller; *D:* Norman Lee.

Bulldog Drummond Comes Back **1937** Drummond, aided by Colonel Nielson, rescues his fiancee from the hands of desperate kidnappers. **119m/B VHS.** John Howard, John Barrymore, Louise Campbell, Reginald Denny, Guy Standing; *D:* Louis King.

Bulldog Drummond Escapes **1937** Drummond, aided by his side-kick and valet, rescues a beautiful girl from spies. He then falls in love with her. **67m/B VHS, DVD.** Ray Milland, Heather Angel, Reginald Denny, Guy Standing, Porter Hall, E.E. Clive; *D:* James Hogan; *W:* Edward T. Lowe; *C:* Victor Milner.

Bulldog Drummond's Bride **1939** Ace detective Bulldog Drummond has to interrupt his honeymoon in order to pursue a gang of bank robbers across France and England. The last of the Bulldog Drummond film series. **69m/B VHS.** John Howard, Heather Angel, H.B. Warner, E.E. Clive, Reginald Denny, Eduardo Cianelli; *D:* James Hogan.

Bulldog Drummond's Peril **1938** Murder and robbery drag the adventurous Drummond away from his wedding and he pursues the villains until they are behind bars. One in the film series. **77m/B VHS.** John Barrymore, John Howard, Louise Campbell, Reginald Denny, E.E. Clive, Porter Hall; *D:* James Hogan.

Bulldog Drummond's Revenge ½ **1937** Bulldog's "Revenge" was made during the series' heyday and was the second to star Howard as Drummond; Barrymore revels in the character of Inspector Neilson of Scotland Yard, and Denny is Algy. In this typically fast-paced installment, suave sleuth Drummond stalks the master criminal responsible for stealing the formula to an explosive. **55m/B VHS.** John Howard, John Barrymore, Reginald Denny, Louise Campbell, Frank Puglia, Nydia Westman, Lucien Littlefield; *D:* Louis King.

Bulldog Drummond's Secret Police **1939** The 15th Drummond film, adapted from Herman Cyril McNeile's famed detective novels featuring a million-pound treasure stashed in the Drummond manor and the murderous endeavors to retrieve it. **54m/B VHS, DVD.** John Howard, Heather Angel, H.B. Warner, Reginald Denny, E.E. Clive, Leo G. Carroll; *D:* James Hogan; *W:* Garnett Weston; *C:* Merritt B. Gerstad.

Bulldog Edition **1936** Two newspapers engage in an all-out feud to be number one in the city, even going so far as to employ gangsters for purposes of sabotage. **57m/B VHS.** Ray Walker, Evalyn Knapp, Regis Toomey, Cy Kendall, William "Billy" Newell, Oscar Apfel, Betty Compson, Robert Warwick; *D:* Charles Lamont.

Bulldog Jack *Alias Bulldog Drummond* **1935** Fine entry in the series has Drummond's colleague battling it out with Richardson, the leader of gang of jewel thieves. **62m/B VHS.** *GB* Fay Wray, Jack Hulbert, Claude Hulbert, Ralph Richardson, Paul Graetz, Gibb McLaughlin; *D:* Walter Forde.

Bullet ½ **1994 (R)** Butch (Rourke) gets released from prison and immediately returns to his old drug and burglary ways on New York's mean streets. And he's got a score to settle with crazy drug kingpin Tank (Shakur). Has little to recommend it, except to those who like violence, with lackluster performances and a dull script. **96m/C VHS.** Mickey Rourke, Tupac Shakur, Ted Levine, Adrien Brody, John Enos; *D:* Julien Temple; *W:* Bruce Rubenstein; *C:* Crescenzo G.P. Notarile.

Bullet Code **1940** It's quick-shooting shenanigans when O'Brien chases a pack of angry rustlers off his neighbor's land. **56m/B VHS.** George O'Brien, Virginia Vale, Howard Hickman, Harry Woods, Charles "Slim" Whitaker; *D:* David Howard; *W:* Doris Schroeder.

Bullet for Sandoval **1970 (PG)** An ex-Confederate renegade loots and pillages the north Mexican countryside on his way to murder the grandfather of the woman he loves. **96m/C VHS.** *SP IT* Ernest Borgnine, George Hilton; *D:* Julio Buchs.

A Bullet for the General *Quien Sabe?* **1968** An American mercenary joins with rebel forces during the Mexican Revolution. **95m/C VHS, DVD, Wide.** *IT* Martine Beswick, Lou Castel, Gian Marie Volonte, Klaus Kinski; *D:* Damiano Damiani; *W:* Salvatore Laurani, Franco Solinas; *C:* Antonio Secchi; *M:* Luis Bacalov.

A Bullet in the Head *Die Xue Jie Tou* **1990** Violent (no surprise there) tale of friendship finds Frank (Cheung), Ben (Leung), and Paul (Lee) heading out of 1967 Hong Kong for Saigon, where they hope to make money selling contraband goods in the city. They wind up on the wrong side of the Vietnamese Army, steal a fortune in gold from a local crime lord, and end up the prisoners of the Viet Cong. There's betrayal and death and a final moral reckoning and—did we mention lots and lots of (over-the-top) violence? Chinese with subtitles. **85m/C VHS, DVD.** *HK* Tony Leung Chiu-Wai, Jacky Cheung, Waise Lee, Simon Yam, Fennie Yuen, Yolinda Yam, John Woo; *D:* John Woo; *W:* Janet Chun, Patrick Leung, John Woo; *C:* Wilson Chan, Ardy Lam, Chai Kittikum Som, Wing-hang Wong; *M:* Romeo Diaz, James Wong.

A Bullet Is Waiting **1954** A diligent sheriff finally catches his man only to be trapped in a blinding snowstorm with the hardened criminal. **83m/C VHS.** Jean Simmons, Rory Calhoun, Stephen McNally, Brian Aherne; *D:* John Farrow.

Bullet to Beijing ½ *Len Deighton's Bullet to Beijing* **1995 (R)** After some 30 years, Caine returns to his role as intelligence agent Harry Palmer. Forced into retirement, Harry finds himself privately recruited by Russian businessman Alex (Gambon) to retrieve a stolen chemical weapon being transported on a train headed for China. Harry gets a little local help from Nicolai and Natasha (Connery and Sara) but treachery is all around. Follows "The Ipcress File," "Funeral in Berlin," and "Billion Dollar Brain"; based on the novel by Len Deighton. **105m/C VHS.** *GB* Michael Caine, Michael Gambon, Jason Connery, Mia Sara, Patrick Allen, Burt Kwouk, Michael Sarrazin, Sue Lloyd; *D:* George Mihalka; *W:* Peter Welbeck; *C:* Terence Cole; *M:* Rick Wakeman.

Bulletproof **1988 (R)** An unstoppable ex-CIA agent battles to retrieve a high-tech nuclear tank from terrorist hands. **93m/C VHS.** Gary Busey, Darlanne Fluegel, Henry Silva, Thalmus Rasulala, L.Q. (Justus E. McQueen) Jones, R.G. Armstrong, Rene Enriquez; *D:* Steve Carver; *W:* Steve Carver.

Bulletproof **1996 (R)** Desperately trying to be a male buddy bonding movie, "Bulletproof" fails miserably in every respect. Keats (Wayans) and Moses (Sandler) are an unlikely pair of car thieves with an equally unlikely bond to each other. Turns out Keats is really undercover cop Jack Carter, who is trying to infiltrate a drug cartel via his pal Moses. When the bust goes bad, Carter must bring Moses in unharmed to testify. Meanwhile the two rejuvenate their tainted relationship amid many homoerotic innuendoes. It's an embarrassment all around, especially for ex-Spike Lee cinematographer Dickerson on his first directing outing. **85m/C VHS, DVD, Wide.** Damon Wayans, Adam Sandler, James Caan, Kristen Wilson, James Farentino, Bill Nunn, Mark Roberts, Xander Berkeley, Allen Covert, Jeep Swenson, Larry McCoy; *D:* Ernest R. Dickerson; *W:* Joe Gayton, Lewis Colick; *C:* Steven Bernstein; *M:* Elmer Bernstein.

Bulletproof Heart *Killer* **1995 (R)** Mick (LaPaglia), a hit man with a severe case of burnout, is assigned to kill Fiona (Rogers), a beautiful socialite who, conveniently, wants to die. Despite being warned by his boss (Boyle) that Fiona has a habit of making men weak, he falls in love and can't bring himself to kill her. First-time director Malone takes great care to establish the noir look and feel, capitalizing on the all-in-one-night timeframe to raise the tension level. LaPaglia and Rogers turn in riveting performances, but can't stop the film from losing momentum when it becomes self-consciously melodramatic near the end. **95m/C VHS.** Anthony LaPaglia, Mimi Rogers, Peter Boyle, Matt Craven, Monika Schnarre, Joseph Maher; ***D:*** Mark Malone; ***W:*** Gordon Melbourne, Mark Malone; ***C:*** Tobias Schliessler; ***M:*** Graeme Coleman.

Bullets or Ballots 🦴🦴🦴 **1938** Tough New York cop goes undercover to join the mob in order to get the goods on them. Old-fashioned danger and intrigue follow, making for some action-packed thrills. **82m/B VHS.** Edward G. Robinson, Humphrey Bogart, Barton MacLane, Joan Blondell, Frank McHugh, Louise Beavers; ***D:*** William Keighley; ***C:*** Hal Mohr.

Bullets over Broadway 🦴🦴🦴½ **1994 (R)** Mediocre playwright David Shayne (Cusack, in the Allen role) talks up the virtues of artistic integrity to his pretentious hothouse contemporaries, then sells out to a gangster who agrees to finance his latest play provided his no-talent, brassy moll (Tilly) gets a part. And it's her hit-man bodyguard's (Palminteri) unexpected artistic touches that redeem Shayne's otherwise lousy work. Wiest as the eccentric diva, Ullman as the aging ingenue, Reiner as the Greenwich Village sage, and Broadbent as the increasingly plump matinee idol lead a collection of delicious, over-the-top performances in this smart and howlingly funny tribute to Jazz Age New York City that showcases Woody at his self-conscious best. **106m/C VHS, DVD.** Dianne Wiest, John Cusack, Jennifer Tilly, Rob Reiner, Chazz Palminteri, Tracey Ullman, Mary-Louise Parker, Joe (Johnny) Viterelli, Jack Warden, Jim Broadbent, Harvey Fierstein, Annie-Joe Edwards; ***D:*** Woody Allen; ***W:*** Woody Allen, Douglas McGrath; ***C:*** Carlo Di Palma. Oscars '94: Support. Actress (Wiest); Golden Globes '95: Support. Actress (Wiest); Ind. Spirit '95: Support. Actor (Palminteri), Support. Actress (Wiest); L.A. Film Critics '94: Support. Actress (Wiest); N.Y. Film Critics '94: Support. Actress (Wiest); Natl. Soc. Film Critics '94: Support. Actress (Wiest); Screen Actors Guild '94: Support. Actress (Wiest).

Bullfighter & the Lady 🦴🦴½ **1950** An American goes to Mexico to learn the fine art of bullfighting in order to impress a beautiful woman. **87m/B VHS.** Robert Stack, Gilbert Roland, Virginia Grey, Katy Jurado; ***D:*** Budd Boetticher.

Bullfighters 🦴🦴 **1945** Stan and Ollie are in hot pursuit of a dangerous criminal which leads them to Mexico where Stan winds up in a bull ring. **61m/B VHS.** Stan Laurel, Oliver Hardy, Margo Woode, Richard Lane; ***D:*** Malcolm St. Clair.

Bullies woof! **1986 (R)** A woodland-transplanted young man decides to fight back against an ornery mountain clan who have raped his mother, tortured his father, and beat up his girlfriend. Brutal and unpalatable. **96m/C VHS.** *CA* Janet-Laine Green, Dehl Berti, Stephen Hunter, Jonathan Crombie, Olivia D'Abo; ***D:*** Paul Lynch.

Bullitt 🦴🦴🦴 **1968 (PG)** A detective assigned to protect a star witness for 48 hours senses danger; his worst fears are confirmed when his charge is murdered. Based on the novel, "Mute Witness" by Robert L. Pike, and featuring one of filmdom's most famous car chases. **105m/C VHS, DVD.** Steve McQueen, Robert Vaughn, Jacqueline Bisset, Don Gordon, Robert Duvall, Norman Fell, Simon Oakland; ***D:*** Peter Yates; ***W:*** Alan R. Trustman; ***C:*** William A. Fraker; ***M:*** Lalo Schifrin. Oscars '68: Film Editing; Natl. Soc. Film Critics '68: Cinematog.

Bullseye! 🦴½ **1990 (PG-13)** Knockabout farce is a letdown considering the talents involved. Shady scientists (Moore and Caine) pursue/are pursued by lookalike con-artists (Caine and Moore), who are pursued in turn by international agents. Full of inside jokes and celebrity cameos, but nothing exceptional. **95m/C VHS.** Michael Caine, Roger Moore, Sally Kirkland, Patsy Kensit, Jenny Seagrove, John Cleese, Lee Patterson, Deborah Maria Moore, Mark Burns, Deborah Leng, Alexandra Pigg; ***Cameos:*** Lynn Nesbitt, Steffanie Pitt; ***D:*** Michael Winner; ***W:*** Michael Winner, Leslie Bricusse; ***M:*** John Du Prez.

Bullshot 🦴🦴½ **1983 (PG)** Zany English satire sends up the legendary Bulldog Drummond. In the face of mad professors, hapless heroines, devilish Huns and deadly enemies, our intrepid hero remains distinctly British. **84m/C VHS.** *GB* Alan Shearman, Diz White, Ron House, Frances Tomelty, Michael Aldridge, Ron Pember, Christopher Good; ***D:*** Dick Clement; ***M:*** John Du Prez.

Bullwhip 🦴🦴 **1958** A man falsely accused of murder saves himself from the hangman's noose by agreeing to a shotgun wedding. **80m/C VHS.** Guy Madison, Rhonda Fleming, James Griffith, Peter Adams; ***D:*** Harmon Jones.

Bully 🦴 **2001** Director Clark continues his cinematic theme (announced in "Kids") of amoral and hedonistic young adults with this adaptation of the true story of a 1993 murder by a group of teens in Florida. Bobby (Stahl) is a dominating scumbag who pushes his best friend Marty (Renfro) around and pressures him into unwanted sexual and narcotic experimentation. When Marty meets and begins dating Lisa (Miner), Bobby forces himself into their sexual encounters. After Bobby rapes Lisa's friend Ali (Phillips), Lisa decides that the only solution is to kill Bobby. Inexperienced in such things, the homicidal posse gets some advice from a hit man (Fitzpatrick) who's barely older than they are. Filling the screen with graphic scenes of drug use and joyless sex, Clark doesn't seem to have any message other than "Look how bad these kids are. Now look at them naked." No psychological depth is given to the characters, although the actors do their best with what they've got. Also available in an R-rated version at 107 minutes. **113m/C VHS, DVD.** *US* Brad Renfro, Nick Stahl, Bijou Phillips, Rachel Miner, Michael Pitt, Kelli Garner, Daniel Franzese, Leo Fitzpatrick; ***Cameos:*** Larry Clark; ***D:*** Larry Clark; ***W:*** Zachary Long, Roger Pullis; ***C:*** Steve Gainer.

Bulworth 🦴🦴🦴 **1998 (R)** No-holds barred look at the political process. Senator John Jay Bulworth (Beatty), bored and disillusioned by the banality of his own political career, hires a hitman to end his misery. During his last days on earth fulfilling re-election duties, and with nothing to loose, he starts spewing the truth about politics and big business, much to the dismay of his constituents and assistants. Morphing into a hip-hop political phrophet, he becomes entranced and invigorated by beautiful South Central resident Nina (Berry). Beatty (in an engaging and funny performance) tackles his fiery subject matter of dwindling racial harmony and corporate deceit with a brazen and winning sense of humor lost in contemporary films. Fine script and enjoyable supporting performances by Platt as Bulworth's panic-stricken aide and Cheadle as an enterprising drug lord. **107m/C VHS, DVD, Wide.** Warren Beatty, Halle Berry, Oliver Platt, Paul Sorvino, Don Cheadle, Jack Warden, Christine Baranski, Isaiah Washington IV, Joshua Malina, Richard Sarafian, Amiri Baraka, Sean Astin, Laurie Metcalf, Wendell Pierce, Michele Morgan, Ariyan Johnson, Graham Beckel, Nora Dunn, Jackie Gayle; ***D:*** Warren Beatty; ***W:*** Jeremy Pikser, Warren Beatty; ***C:*** Vittorio Storaro; ***M:*** Ennio Morricone. L.A. Film Critics '98: Screenplay.

The Bumblebee Flies Anyway 🦴🦴½ **1998 (PG-13)** Amnesiac Barney Snow (Wood) is residing at a facility where all the other youths are terminally ill. As the doctors try to help Barney remember his past, Barney and the other patients go through the usual bonding rituals. Ordinary story at least has some winning performers to get past the maudlin aspects. Based on the novel by Robert Cormier. **95m/C VHS, DVD.** Elijah Wood, Janeane Garofalo, Rachael Leigh Cook, Roger Rees, Joe Perrino, George Gore III, Chris Petrizzo; ***D:*** Martin Duffy; ***W:*** Jennifer Sarja; ***C:*** Stephen Kazmierski; ***M:*** Christopher Tyng.

Bummer woof! **1973 (R)** Rock band's wild party turns into tragedy when the bass player goes too far with two groupies. It's a bad scene, man. **90m/C VHS, DVD, Wide.** Kipp Whitman, Dennis Burkley, Carol Speed, Connie Strickland; ***D:*** William Allen Castleman; ***W:*** Alvin L. Fast.

Bums 🦴🦴 **1993** Sergeant Andrew Holloman is a military officer in search of his long lost brother. It turns out his brother was homeless and is now dead at the hands of a skid row killer. Holloman recruits a platoon of other homeless people to help him track the killer but what he discovers is a multimillion conspiracy behind the murders. **94m/C VHS.** Christopher McDonald, Haskell Phillips, Dawn Evans; ***D:*** Andy Galler; ***W:*** Pat Allee, Ben Hurst.

Bunco 🦴 **1983** Two policemen working for the Los Angeles Police Department's Bunco Squad discover a college for con artists complete with tape-recorded lessons and on-the-job training. **60m/C VHS.** Tom Selleck, Robert Urich, Donna Mills, Will Geer, Arte Johnson, Alan Feinstein, James Hampton, Michael Sacks, Bobby Van; ***D:*** Alexander Singer.

Bundle of Joy 🦴🦴½ **1956** Salesgirl who saves an infant from falling off the steps of a foundling home is mistaken for the child's mother. Remake of 1939's "Bachelor Mother." ♫Bundle of Joy; I Never Felt This Way Before; Lullaby in Blue; Worry About Tomorrow; All About Love; Someday Soon; What's So Good About Morning?; You're Perfect In Every Departmant. **98m/C VHS.** Debbie Reynolds, Eddie Fisher, Adolphe Menjou; ***D:*** Norman Taurog.

A Bunny's Tale 🦴🦴 **1985** The story of Gloria Steinem's undercover journey into the Playboy Club as a fledgling journalist. It is here that she discovered her dedication as a feminist. Based on the book by Steinem. **97m/C VHS.** Kirstie Alley, Cotter Smith, Deborah Van Valkenburgh, Joanna (Joanna DeVarona) Kerns, Delta Burke, Diana Scarwid; ***D:*** Karen Arthur.

Buona Sera, Mrs. Campbell 🦴🦴½ **1968** The lovely Lollobridgida and some fast-paced plot moves are the main highlights of this comedy. Mrs. Campbell convinced her three American WWII lovers that each of them had fathered her daughter. All three have supported mother and child through the years, unbeknowst to each other and their wives. When their 20-year reunion brings them back to Italy, Mrs. Campbell must do some fast-thinking and some quick-stepping to keep everyone happy. **113m/C VHS, Wide.** Gina Lollobrigida, Shelley Winters, Phil Silvers, Peter Lawford, Telly Savalas, Lee Grant, Janet Margolin, Marian Moses; ***D:*** Melvin Frank.

The 'Burbs 🦴½ **1989 (PG)** A tepid satire about suburbanites suspecting their creepy new neighbors of murderous activities. Well-designed and sharp, but light on story. **101m/C VHS, DVD, Wide.** Tom Hanks, Carrie Fisher, Ric(k) Ducommun, Corey Feldman, Brother Theodore, Bruce Dern, Gale Gordon, Courtney Gains; ***D:*** Joe Dante; ***W:*** Dana Olsen; ***C:*** Robert Stevens; ***M:*** Jerry Goldsmith.

Burden of Dreams **1982** The landmark documentary chronicling the berserk circumstances behind the scenes of Werner Herzog's epic "Fitzcarraldo." Stuck in the Peruvian jungles, the film crew was subjected to every disaster imaginable while executing Herzog's vision, including disease, horrendous accident, warring local tribes and the megalomaniacal director himself. Considered better than "Fitzcarraldo," although both films discuss a man's obsession. **94m/C VHS.** Klaus Kinski, Mick Jagger, Jason Robards Jr., Werner Herzog; ***D:*** Les Blank.

Bureau of Missing Persons 🦴🦴½ **1933** Comedy-drama about big-city bureau of missing persons, in which the hardened Stone is in charge. O'Brien plays a tough cop who is transferred to the bureau and Davis stars as the mystery woman with whom he gets involved. Although fast-paced and intriguing, the film is somewhat confusing and never stays in one direction for very long. **75m/B VHS.** Bette Davis, Lewis Stone, Pat O'Brien, Glenda Farrell, Allen Jenkins, Ruth Donnelly, Hugh Herbert; ***D:*** Roy Del Ruth.

Burglar 🦴🦴🦴 *Vzlomschik* **1987** Not to be confused with the Whoopi Goldberg vehicle, this Russian film relates a story no less American than apple pie and teenage angst. Senka and would-be punk star Kostya are two neglected and disaffected brothers whose father is a drunken womanizer best known for absentee paternalism. When Howmuch, a serious heavy metalloid, pressures Kostya to steal a synthesizer, brother Senka steps in to steal the Community Center's property himself. In Russian with English subtitles, the solid performances hold their own against the heavy musical content. **89m/C VHS, DVD.** *RU* Konstantin Kinchev, Oleg Yelykomov; ***D:*** Valery Orgorodnikov.

Burglar 🦴🦴 **1987 (R)** A cat burglar moves to the right side of the law when she tries to solve a murder case. Whoopi's always a treat, but this movie's best forgotten; Goldberg's fans should watch "Jumpin' Jack Flash" again instead. Co-star Goldthwait elevates the comedic level a bit. **103m/C VHS, DVD.** Whoopi Goldberg, Bob(cat) Goldthwait, Lesley Ann Warren, John Goodman, G.W. Bailey, James Handy, Anne DeSalvo; ***D:*** Hugh Wilson; ***W:*** Hugh Wilson; ***C:*** William A. Fraker; ***M:*** Sylvester Levay, Bernard Edwards.

Burial Ground 🦴 **1985** A classically grisly splatter film in which the hungry dead rise and proceed to kill the weekend denizens of an isolated aristocratic mansion. **85m/C VHS.** Karen Well, Peter Bark; ***D:*** Andrea (Andrew White) Bianchi.

Burial of the Rats 🦴½ *Roger Corman Presents Burial of the Rats; Bram Stoker's Burial of the Rats* **1995 (R)** Based on a short story by Bram Stoker, this cable campiness features young Bram (Alber) himself being kidnapped while traveling in Eastern Europe. He's taken to the "Queen of Vermin" (Barbeau), who heads a bloodthirsty cult that hate men, worship rats, and live by violence. Fortunately, the Queen decides to spare Bram so he can write of their exploits and he falls for the fleshy charms of rat-woman Madeleine (Ford). **85m/C VHS.** Adrienne Barbeau, Maria Ford, Kevin Alber; ***D:*** Dan Golden.

Buried Alive 🦴 **1939** A man is sent to prison on trumped up charges. Only the prison nurse believes he is innocent as a crooked politician strives to keep him behind bars. **74m/B** Beverly Roberts, Robert Wilcox, George Pembroke, Ted Osborn, Paul McVey, Alden Chase; ***D:*** Victor Halperin.

Buried Alive 🦴🦴 **1981** Director d'Amato reaps his finest gore-fest to date, incorporating the well-established taxidermist gone loony motif in his repertoire of appalling bad taste. Not for the squeamish, this bloodier-than-thou spaghetti spooker is chock full of necrophilia, cannibalism, and more. **90m/C VHS.** *IT* Kieran Canter, Cinzia Monreale, Franca Stoppi; ***D:*** Joe D'Amato.

Buried Alive 🦴🦴 **1989 (R)** Once Ravenscroft Hall was an asylum for the incurably insane. Now, the isolated mansion is a school for troubled teenage girls, run by a charismatic psychiatrist. Captivated by his charm, a young woman joins the staff. Soon, she is tormented by nightmare visions of the long-dead victims of a nameless killer. When the students begin to disappear, she realizes he still lives...and she may be his next victim. Carradine's last role. **97m/C VHS.** Robert Vaughn, Donald Pleasence, Karen Witter, John Carradine, Ginger Lynn Allen; ***D:*** Gerard Kikoine.

Buried Alive 🦴🦴½ **1990 (PG-13)** One of the many horror flicks entitled "Buried Alive," this one is not bad, injecting a bit of levity into the time-worn genre. Schemestress Leigh and her paramour poison her husband. Or so they think, only to discover that he's not quite dead. **93m/C VHS.** Tim Matheson, Jennifer Jason Leigh, William Atherton, Hoyt Axton; ***D:*** Frank Darabont; ***W:*** Mark Patrick Carducci, Jake Clesi; ***M:*** Michel Colombier. CABLE

Buried Alive 2 🦴🦴½ **1997 (PG-13)** Randy (Caffrey) wants to get rid of rich wife Laura (Sheedy) so he and girlfriend Roxanne (Needham) can enjoy her cash. So he slips some blowfish venom into her wine and buries her. But the venom only simulated death and after clawing her way out of the grave, Laura is one angry gal. Clint Goodman (Matheson), who was buried in the first movie, shows up to help out the wronged wife. **92m/C VHS.** Ally Sheedy, Stephen Caffrey, Tracey Needham, Tim Matheson; ***D:*** Tim Matheson; ***W:*** Walter Klenhard. CABLE

Burke & Wills 🦴🦴½ **1985 (PG-13)** A lush, big-budgeted true story of the two men who first crossed Australia on foot, and explored its central region. Popular

Australian film. **120m/C VHS.** *AU* Jack Thompson, Nigel Havers, Greta Scacchi, Ralph Cotterill, Drew Forsythe, Chris Haywood, Matthew Fargher; ***D:*** Graeme Clifford; ***W:*** Michael Thomas; ***C:*** Russell Boyd; ***M:*** Peter Sculthorpe.

Burlesque on Carmen 🦴🦴 **1916** A silent pastiche of the Bizet opera, with Charlie as Don Schmose. Interesting early work. **30m/B VHS, DVD.** Charlie Chaplin, Ben Turpin, Edna Purviance; ***D:*** Charlie Chaplin; ***W:*** Charlie Chaplin.

The Burmese Harp 🦴🦴🦴🦴 *Harp of Burma; Birumano Tategoto* **1956** At the end of WWII, a Japanese soldier is spiritually traumatized and becomes obsessed with burying the masses of war casualties. A searing, acclaimed anti-war statement, in Japanese with English subtitles. Remade by Ichikawa in 1985. **115m/B VHS.** *JP* Shoji Yasui, Rentaro Mikuni, Tatsuya Mihashi, Tanie Kitabayashi, Yunosuke Ito; ***D:*** Kon Ichikawa; ***W:*** Natto Wada; ***C:*** Minoru Yokoyama; ***M:*** Akira Ifukube.

Burn! 🦴🦴🦴½ *Quemimada!* **1970 (PG)** An Italian-made indictment of imperialist control by guerrilla-filmmaker Pontecorvo, depicting the efforts of a 19th century British ambassador to put down a slave revolt on a Portuguese-run Caribbean island. Great Brando performance. **112m/C VHS, Wide.** *FR IT* Marlon Brando, Evarist Marquez, Renato Salvatori, Norman Hill, Dana Ghia, Giampiero Albertini, Tom Lyons; ***D:*** Gillo Pontecorvo; ***W:*** Giorgio Arlorio, Franco Solinas; ***C:*** Marcello Gatti; ***M:*** Ennio Morricone.

Burn Witch, Burn! 🦴🦴🦴 *Night of the Eagle* **1962** A college professor proudly finds himself rapidly rising in his profession. His pride turns to horror though when he discovers that his success is not due to his own abilities, but to the efforts of his witchcraft practicing wife. Excellent, atmospheric horror with a genuinely suspenseful climax. **87m/B VHS.** *GB* Peter Wyngarde, Janet Blair, Margaret Johnston, Anthony Nicholls, Colin Gordon, Kathleen Byron, Reginald Beckwith, Jessica Dunning, Norman Bird, Judith Scott; ***D:*** Sidney Hayers; ***W:*** Richard Matheson, Charles Beaumont, George L. Baxt; ***C:*** Reg Wyer.

Burndown 🦴 **1989 (R)** Victims of a serial killer in a town with a large nuclear reactor are themselves radioactive, which leads the Police Chief and a beautiful reporter to the truth and the hidden conspiracy. **97m/C VHS.** Cathy Moriarty, Peter Firth; ***D:*** James Allen.

The Burning 🦴 **1982 (R)** Story of macabre revenge set in the dark woods of a seemingly innocent summer camp. **90m/C VHS.** Brian Matthews, Leah Ayres, Brian Backer, Larry Joshua, Jason Alexander, Ned Eisenberg, Garrick Glenn, Carolyn Houlihan, Fisher Stevens, Lou David, Holly Hunter; ***D:*** Tony Maylam; ***W:*** Bob Weinstein, Peter Lawrence; ***C:*** Harvey Harrison; ***M:*** Rick Wakeman.

The Burning Bed 🦴🦴🦴½ **1985** Dramatic expose (based on a true story) about wife-beating. Fawcett garnered accolades for her performance as the battered wife who couldn't take it anymore. Highly acclaimed and Emmy-nominated. **95m/C VHS.** Farrah Fawcett, Paul LeMat, Penelope Milford, Richard Masur; ***D:*** Robert Greenwald. **TV**

The Burning Court 🦴½ *La Chambre Ardente* **1962** Unusual horror film involving occultism, possession, and family curses. Dubbed into English. Based on a story by John Dickson Carr. **102m/C VHS.** *IT FR* Nadja Tiller, Jean-Claude Brialy, Edith Scob, Perette Pradier, Claude Rich; ***D:*** Julien Duvivier.

Burning Daylight 🦴🦴 **1928** Alaskan real estate baron loses everything to a group of San Francisco sharpies. Based on the story by Jack London. **72m/B VHS.** Milton Sills, Arthur Stone, Doris Kenyon, Guinn "Big Boy" Williams; ***D:*** Richard A. Rowland.

The Burning Hills 🦴½ **1956** Unexceptional cow flick based on a Louis L'Amour novel. Hunter hides from cattle thieves in a barn and, eventually, in the arms of a half-breed Mexican girl (Wood). Tedious and unsurprising. **94m/C VHS.** Tab Hunter, Natalie Wood, Skip Homeier, Eduard Franz; ***D:*** Stuart Heisler.

Burning Rage 🦴 **1984** A blazing, abandoned coal mine threatens to wreak havoc in the Appalachians. The government sends geologist Mandrell to help prevent a disaster. **100m/C VHS.** Barbara Mandrell, Tom Wopat, Bert Remsen, John Pleshette, Carol Kane, Eddie Albert; ***D:*** Gilbert Cates. **TV**

The Burning Season 🦴🦴🦴 **1994** In one of his last performances, Julia inspires as Chico Mendes, a socialist union leader who fought to protect the homes and land of Brazilian peasants in the western Amazon rain forest. With Mendes' help the peasants form a union and struggle to prevent the building of a road that will provide easy access to forest land for speculators and cattlemen. Naturally, they are violently opposed by corruption-ridden capitalist powers in the government. Julia provides a haunting portrayal of the heroic figure who was assassinated in 1990. Based in part on the book by Andrew Revkin. Filmed on location in Mexico. **123m/C VHS.** Raul Julia, Edward James Olmos, Sonia Braga, Luis Guzman, Nigel Havers, Kamala Dawson, Tomas Milian, Esai Morales, Tony Plana, Carmen Argenziano; ***D:*** John Frankenheimer; ***W:*** William Mastrosimone, Michael Tolkin, Ron Hutchinson; ***M:*** Gary Chang. **CABLE**

Burning Secret 🦴🦴 *Brennendes Geheimnis* **1989 (PG)** After WWI, a widow in Austria (Dunaway) meets a baron (Brandauer) who has befriended her son. Mutual seduction ensues but the sparks don't fly. Adapted from Stefan Zweig story. **107m/C VHS.** *GB* Faye Dunaway, Klaus Maria Brandauer, Ian Richardson, David Eberts; ***D:*** Andrew Birkin; ***W:*** Andrew Birkin; ***M:*** Hans Zimmer.

Burnt by the Sun 🦴🦴🦴 *Outomlionnye Solntsem* **1994 (R)** Masterful evocation of '30s Stalinist Russia, covering a day in the life of Soviet revolutionary hero Serguei (Mikhalkov) and his family, far from the purges and gulags. Enjoying a country existence with wife Moroussia (Dapkounaite) and daughter Nadia (played by Mikhalkov's daughter), his idyll is disturbed by mystery man Dimitri (Menchikov), and Serguei realizes their fates are bound by the difference between their Communist dreams and reality. Symbolism is a little heavy but film delivers emotionally. Russian with subtitles. **134m/C VHS.** *RU FR* Nikita Mikhalkov, Ingeborga Dapkounaite, Oleg Menshikov, Nadia Mikhalkov, Andre Oumansky, Viatcheslav Tikhonov, Svetlana Kriouchkova, Vladimir Ilyine; ***D:*** Nikita Mikhalkov; ***W:*** Nikita Mikhalkov, Rustam Ibragimbekov; ***C:*** Vilen Kalyuta; ***M:*** Eduard Artemyev. Oscars '94: Foreign Film; Cannes '94: Grand Jury Prize.

Burnt Offerings 🦴🦴 **1976 (PG)** A family rents an old mansion for the summer and they become affected by evil forces that possess the house. Based on the novel by Robert Marasco. **116m/C VHS.** Oliver Reed, Karen Black, Bette Davis, Burgess Meredith; ***D:*** Dan Curtis; ***W:*** Dan Curtis.

Burnzy's Last Call 🦴🦴 **1995** Sal (McCaffrey) tends bar at Eppy's, a Manhattan joint where Burnzy (Gray), a retired newspaperman, is a regular. The film is an ensemble piece that focuses on the various colorful characters who drift in and out of the place. **88m/C VHS, DVD, Wide.** Sam Gray, David Johansen, James McCaffrey, Christopher Noth, Sherry Stringfield, Roger Robinson, Tony Todd; ***D:*** Michael de Avila; ***W:*** George Gilmore; ***C:*** Scott St. John.

Bury Me an Angel 🦴 **1971** A female biker sets out to seek revenge against the men who killed her brother. **85m/C VHS.** Dixie Peabody, Terry Mace, Clyde Ventura, Dan Haggerty, Stephen Whittaker, Gary Littlejohn, Dave Atkins, Marie Denn, Alan DeWitt; ***D:*** Barbara Peeters; ***C:*** Sven Walnum; ***M:*** Richard Hieronymous.

Bury Me Not on the Lone Prairie 🦴🦴 **1941** When his brother is murdered in cold blood by claim jumpers, mining engineer Brown goes to avenge the dead. Based on a story by Sherman Lowe. **57m/B VHS.** Johnny Mack Brown, Fuzzy Knight, Nell O'Day, Frank O'Connor, Kermit Maynard; ***D:*** Ray Taylor; ***W:*** Sherman Lowe, Victor McLeod.

The Bus Is Coming 🦴🦴 **1972** A love story entwined with the problems of blacks in a small town. **95m/C VHS.** Mike Sims, Stephanie Faulkner, Morgan Jones; ***D:*** Horace Jackson.

Bus Stop 🦴🦴🦴 *The Wrong Kind of Girl* **1956** Murray plays a naive cowboy who falls in love with Monroe, a barroom singer, and decides to marry her without her permission. Considered by many to be the finest performance by Marilyn Monroe; she sings "That Old Black Magic" in this one. Very funny with good performances by all. Based on the William Inge play. **96m/C VHS, DVD, Wide.** Marilyn Monroe, Arthur O'Connell, Hope Lange, Don Murray, Betty Field, Max (Casey Adams) Showalter, Hans Conried, Eileen Heckart; ***D:*** Joshua Logan; ***W:*** George Axelrod; ***C:*** Milton Krasner; ***M:*** Cyril Mockridge, Alfred Newman.

Bush Pilot 🦴½ **1947** Red North (Willis) has his own small business as a bush pilot in the Canadian north. Then his vindictive half-brother Paul (La Rue) decides to muscle in and steal Red's routes (and maybe his girl as well). **60m/B VHS.** *CA* Austin Willis, Jack La Rue, Rochelle Hudson; ***D:*** Sterling Campbell; ***W:*** W. Scott Darling.

The Bushbaby 🦴½ **1970** The young Brooks is given a tiny bushbaby while visiting Africa with her father. Because of her pet she misses her ship home and finds herself with former servant Gossett, who agrees to take her to a family friend. Unfortunately, the authorities think he's kidnapped the girl and the two, along with the trouble-causing pet, are pursued by the police. Simple-minded kiddie fare. **100m/C VHS.** Margaret Brooks, Louis Gossett Jr., Donald Houston, Laurence Naismith, Marne Maitland, Geoffrey Bayldon, Jack (Gwyllam) Gwillim; ***D:*** John Trent.

The Busher 🦴½ **1919** All-American pitcher's romance is interrupted by a gratuitous Mr. Moneybags. Minor-league conflict with little real hardball. **54m/B VHS.** Charles Ray, Colleen Moore, John Gilbert, Margaret Livingston; ***D:*** Jerome Storm.

The Bushido Blade 🦴🦴½ *The Bloody Bushido Blade* **1980** An action-packed samurai thriller of adventure and betrayal set in medieval Japan. **92m/C VHS.** *JP* Richard Boone, James Earl Jones, Frank Converse; ***D:*** Tom Kotani.

The Bushwackers 🦴½ *The Rebel* **1952** Ireland plays a veteran of the Confederate army who wishes only to put his violent past behind him. He is forced to reconsider his vow when old-west bullies threaten his family. **70m/B VHS.** Dorothy Malone, John Ireland, Wayne Morris, Lawrence Tierney, Jack Elam, Lon Chaney Sr., Myrna Dell; ***D:*** Rod Amateau.

Bushwhacked 🦴🦴½ *Tenderfoots; The Tenderfoot* **1995 (PG-13)** Crude, rude, dim-witted, kid-hating Max Grabelski (Stern) is falsely accused of murder and forced to become a fugitive. While not to be confused with Harrison Ford, he is mistaken for the leader of a group of Cub Scouts out on their maiden camping trip and soon finds himself in an unlikely partnership with the boys. Together they encounter everything from grizzly bears to whitewater rapids. Light-hearted, goofy comedy continues Stern's tendency toward kid-intensive, family-oriented fare in the "Rookie of the Year" vein. **85m/C VHS.** Daniel Stern, Jon Polito, Brad Sullivan, Ann Dowd, Anthony Heald, Thomas Wood; ***D:*** Greg Beeman; ***W:*** Tommy Swerdlow, Michael Goldberg, John Jordan, Danny Byers; ***M:*** Bill Conti.

A Business Affair 🦴🦴½ *D'Une Femme a L'Autre* **1993 (R)** Kate Swallow (the ravishing Bouquet), the neglected wife of tempermental author Alex Bolton (Pryce), begins an affair with his flamboyant American publisher Vanni Corso (Walken). While the men posture between themselves for her affections, Kate, who has literary aspirations, decides to strike out on her own. Based on the romantic triangle of British writers Barbara Skelton and Cyril Connolly and his publisher George Weidenfeld and taken from Skelton's memoirs "Tears Before Bedtime" and "Weep No More." **102m/C VHS.** Carole Bouquet, Jonathan Pryce, Christopher Walken, Sheila Hancock; ***D:*** Charlotte Brandstrom; ***W:*** William Stadiem; ***C:*** Willy Kurant; ***M:*** Didier Vasseur.

Business As Usual 🦴🦴 **1988 (PG)** A meek boutique manager in Liverpool defends a sexually harassed employee, is fired, fights back, and creates a national furor over her rights as a woman. **89m/C VHS.** Glenda Jackson, Cathy Tyson, John Thaw, Craig Charles, Eamon Boland; ***D:*** Lezli-Ann Barrett; ***W:*** Lezli-Ann Barrett; ***C:*** Ernest Vincze.

Business for Pleasure 🦴½ **1996** Wealthy tycoon orchestrates a sexual triangle between himself, his closest assistant, and a beautiful exec in order to explore the wilder side of sex and fantasy. **97m/C VHS.** Gary Stretch, Joanna Pacula, Jeroen Krabbe, Caron Bernstein; ***D:*** Rafael Eisenman; ***W:*** Zalman King; ***C:*** Eagle Egilsson; ***M:*** George S. Clinton.

The Business of Strangers 🦴🦴 **2001 (R)** Julie Styron (Channing) is a tough, middleaged executive for a software company who is having a bad day at an out-of-town meeting. She worries she's about to be fired and then fires her young assistant Paula (Stiles) for missing the meeting and ruining Julie's presentation. Instead, Julie gets a promotion and decides to rehire Paula after they diss men over drinks at the hotel bar. When Paula spots corporate headhunter Nick (Weller), she tells Julie that he raped a friend of hers and it's payback time. But since the two women have been playing mind games, is this the truth or not? **83m/C VHS, DVD.** *US* Stockard Channing, Julia Stiles, Frederick Weller, Marcus Giamatti; ***D:*** Patrick Stettner; ***W:*** Patrick Stettner; ***C:*** Teodoro Maniaci; ***M:*** Alexander Lasarenko.

B.U.S.T.E.D. 🦴🦴 *Everybody Loves Sunshine* **1999 (R)** Gangmates and cousins Terry (Goldie) and Ray (Goth) are just out of prison. Violent Terry is looking to retake control from efficient Bernie (Bowie), who's been looking after the business. Ray decides he wants to go legit and falls for lovely Clare (Shelley). But Terry wants his coz with him and kidnaps Clare to force Ray's hand—a bad move since Ray decides love is thicker than blood. The leads are caricatures and American audiences will be hampered by the regional Brit slang but Bowie's cool intensity is worth watching. **97m/C VHS, DVD.** *GB* Clint Dyer, Sarah Shackleton, Goldie, Andrew Goth, David Bowie, Rachel Shelley; ***D:*** Andrew Goth; ***W:*** Andrew Goth; ***C:*** Julian Morson; ***M:*** Nicky Matthew.

Busted Up 🦴 **1986 (R)** A young, hard-luck urban street-fighter battles for the sake of his family and neighborhood against local crimelords. **93m/C VHS.** *CA* Irene Cara, Paul Coufos, Tony Rosato, Stan Shaw, Gordon Judges; ***D:*** Conrad Palmisano; ***M:*** Charles P. Barnett.

Buster 🦴🦴½ **1988 (R)** The story of Buster Edwards, the one suspect in the 1963 Great Train Robbery who evaded being captured by police. Collins makes his screen debut as one of Britain's most infamous criminals. Collins also performs on the film's soundtrack, spawning two hit singles, "Two Hearts" and "Groovy Kind of Love." **102m/C VHS.** *GB* Phil Collins, Julie Walters, Larry Lamb, Stephanie Lawrence, Ellen Beaven, Michael Atwell, Ralph Brown, Christopher Ellison, Sheila Hancock, Martin Jarvis, Anthony Quayle; ***D:*** David Green; ***M:*** Anne Dudley.

Buster and Billie 🦴½ **1974 (R)** Tragedy ensues when a popular high school student falls in love with the class tramp in rural Georgia in 1948. Serious, decently appointed period teen drama. **100m/C VHS.** Jan-Michael Vincent, Joan Goodfellow, Clifton James, Pamela Sue Martin, Robert Englund; ***D:*** Daniel Petrie.

Bustin' Loose 🦴🦴🦴 **1981 (R)** A fast-talking ex-con reluctantly drives a bus load of misplaced kids and their keeper cross-country. **94m/C VHS, DVD.** Richard Pryor, Cicely Tyson, Robert Christian, George Coe, Bill Quinn; ***D:*** Oz Scott; ***W:*** Lonnie Elder III, Richard Pryor; ***C:*** Dennis Dalzell; ***M:*** Roberta Flack, Mark Davis.

Busting 🦴🦴½ **1974 (R)** Gould and Blake play a pair of slightly off-the-wall L.A. cops. The pair are forced "to bust" local addicts and prostitutes instead of the real crime bosses because much of the police department is on the take. Plenty of comedy and action as well as highly realistic drama. **92m/C VHS.** Elliott Gould, Robert (Bobby) Blake, Allen (Goorwitz) Garfield, Antonio Fargas, Michael Lerner, Sid Haig, Cornelia Sharpe; ***D:*** Peter Hyams; ***W:*** Peter Hyams; ***M:*** Billy Goldenberg.

But I'm a Cheerleader 🦴🦴 **1999 (R)** Broad satire falls flat. Megan (Lyonne) is a peppy high school cheerleader who is suspected of being a lesbian by her rigid parents, who send her off to a rehabilitation camp designed to turn adolescent homosexuals into straight members of society. Megan (who's naively unaware of her true nature) goes along with the program until she befriends rebellious Graham (DuVall) and discovers that, golly, she really does like girls. **81m/C VHS, DVD.** Natasha Lyonne, Clea DuVall, Cathy Moriarty, RuPaul Charles, Bud Cort, Mink Stole, Julie Delpy, Eddie Cibrian; ***D:*** Jamie Babbit; ***W:*** Jamie Babbit, Brian Wayne Peterson; ***C:*** Jules Labarthe; ***M:*** Pat Irwin.

But Not for Me 🦴🦴½ **1959** Gable stars as a middled-aged entertainment executive who thinks he can forestall maturity by carrying on with his youthful secretary. **105m/B VHS.** Clark Gable, Carroll Baker, Lilli Palmer, Lee J. Cobb, Barry Coe, Thomas Gomez, Charles Lane; ***D:*** Walter Lang; ***W:*** John Michael Hayes; ***C:*** Robert Burks.

But Where Is Daniel Wax? 🦴🦴 **1974** At a class reunion, a doctor and a popular singing star reminisce about their youth and Daniel Wax, their one-time hero. Hebrew with English subtitles. **95m/C VHS.** Lior Yaeni, Michael Lipkin, Esther Zevko; ***D:*** Avram Heffner.

Butch and Sundance: The Early Days 🦴🦴½ **1979 (PG)** Traces the origins of the famous outlaw duo. It contains the requisite shoot-outs, hold-ups, and escapes. A "prequel" to "Butch Cassidy and the Sundance Kid." **111m/C VHS.** Tom Berenger, William Katt, John Schuck, Jeff Corey, Jill Eikenberry, Brian Dennehy, Peter Weller; ***D:*** Richard Lester; ***W:*** Allan Burns.

Butch Cassidy and the Sundance Kid 🦴🦴🦴🦴 **1969 (PG)** Two legendary outlaws at the turn of the century take it on the lam with a beautiful, willing ex-school teacher. With a clever script, humanly fallible characters, and warm, witty dialogue, this film was destined to become a boxoffice classic. Featured the hit song "Raindrops Keep Falling on My Head" and renewed the buddy film industry, as Newman and Redford trade insult for insult. Look for the great scene where Newman takes on giant Ted Cassidy in a fist fight. ♫Raindrops Keep Fallin' on My Head; On a Bicycle Built for Joy. **110m/C VHS, DVD.** Paul Newman, Robert Redford, Katharine Ross, Jeff Corey, Strother Martin, Cloris Leachman, Kenneth Mars, Ted Cassidy, Henry Jones, George Furth, Sam Elliott; ***D:*** George Roy Hill; ***W:*** William Goldman; ***C:*** Conrad L. Hall; ***M:*** Burt Bacharach. Oscars '69: Cinematog., Song ("Raindrops Keep Fallin' on My Head"), Story & Screenplay, Orig. Score; AFI '98: Top 100; British Acad. '70: Actor (Redford), Actress (Ross), Director (Hill), Film, Screenplay; Golden Globes '70: Score; Writers Guild '69: Adapt. Screenplay.

The Butcher Boy 🦴🦴🦴 **1997 (R)** Offbeat, black comedy takes a disturbing look into the madness of 12-year old Francie Brady (Owens) in Ireland in the 1960s. An alcoholic father and a mentally strained mother makes Francie escape into a world populated by voices in his head, comic books, and his one childhood friend. When his homelife becomes unbearable, Frankie's demons catapult him into a climatic and destructively criminal breakdown. Newcomer Owens is electrifying as the red-haired dynamo whose lost childhood turns him into a monster and Stephen Rea (a regular in any Jordan film) provides stern support as Francie's loser father and film's narrator. The rural Irish town is recreated with stunning detail, with light touches of kitsch that may put off some looking for a serious treatment of main character's plight. Still a daring movie, with pop star O'Connor as the Virgin Mary. Based on the novel by Peter McCabe. **105m/C VHS.** Eamon Owens, Stephen Rea, Fiona Shaw, Sinead O'Connor, Aisling O'Sullivan, Alan Boyle, Ian Hart, Andrew Fullerton, Patrick McCabe, Sean McGinley, Brendan Gleeson, Milo O'Shea; ***D:*** Neil Jordan; ***W:*** Neil Jordan, Patrick McCabe; ***C:*** Adrian Biddle; ***M:*** Elliot Goldenthal. L.A. Film Critics '98: Score.

The Butcher's Wife 🦴🦴 **1991 (PG-13)** Charming tale of a young psychic (Moore) who brings romance to a Greenwich Village neighborhood that never quite gets off the ground. Moore stars as the clairvoyant whose mystical powers bring magic into the lives of everyone around her, including the local psychiatrist (Daniels), who falls under her spell. Talented cast is virtually wasted with a script that is lightweight; excepting Steenburgen and Dzundza who shine. **107m/C VHS, DVD, Wide.** Demi Moore, Jeff Daniels, George Dzundza, Frances McDormand, Margaret Colin, Mary Steenburgen, Max Perlich, Miriam Margolyes, Christopher Durang, Diane Salinger; ***D:*** Terry Hughes; ***W:*** Ezra Litwack, Marjorie Schwartz; ***C:*** Frank Tidy; ***M:*** Michael Gore.

Butler's Dilemma 🦴🦴 **1943** A jewel thief and a playboy both claim the identity of a butler who never existed, with humorous results. **75m/B VHS.** *GB* Richard Hearne, Francis L. Sullivan, Hermione Gingold, Ian Fleming, Alf Goddard, Judy Kelly, Henry Kendall, Wally Patch, Frank Pettingell, Andre Randall, Marjorie Rhodes, Ronald Shiner, Ralph Truman; ***D:*** Leslie Hiscott; ***W:*** Michael Barringer; ***C:*** Erwin Hillier.

Butterfield 8 🦴🦴🦴 **1960** A seedy film of the John O'Hara novel about a prostitute that wants to go straight and settle down. Taylor won an Oscar, perhaps because she was ill and had lost in the two previous years in more deserving roles. **108m/C VHS, DVD, Wide.** Elizabeth Taylor, Laurence Harvey, Eddie Fisher, Dina Merrill, Mildred Dunnock, Betty Field, Susan Oliver, Kay Medford; ***D:*** Daniel Mann; ***W:*** John Michael Hayes, Charles Schnee; ***C:*** Joseph Ruttenberg. Oscars '60: Actress (Taylor).

Butterflies Are Free 🦴🦴🦴 **1972 (PG)** Fast-paced humor surrounds the Broadway play brought to the big screen. Blind youth Albert is determined to be self-sufficient. A next-door-neighbor actress helps him gain independence from his over-protective mother (Heckart). **109m/C VHS, DVD, Wide.** Goldie Hawn, Edward Albert, Eileen Heckart, Michael Glaser; ***D:*** Milton Katselas; ***W:*** Mary St. Feint; ***C:*** Charles B(ryant) Lang Jr.; ***M:*** Robert Alcivar. Oscars '72: Support. Actress (Heckart).

Butterfly 🦴½ **1982 (R)** Based on James M. Cain's novel about an amoral young woman (Pia, who'd you think?) who uses her beauty and sensual appetite to manipulate the men in her life, including her father. Set in Nevada of the 1930s, father and daughter are drawn into a daring and forbidden love affair by their lust and desperation. **105m/C VHS.** Pia Zadora, Stacy Keach, Orson Welles, Edward Albert, James Franciscus, Lois Nettleton, Stuart Whitman, June Lockhart, Ed McMahon; ***D:*** Matt Cimber; ***W:*** Matt Cimber; ***M:*** Ennio Morricone. Golden Raspberries '82: Worst Actress (Zadora), Worst Support. Actor (McMahon), Worst New Star (Zadora).

Butterfly 🦴🦴🦴 *La Lengua de las Mariposas; Butterfly's Tongue* **1998 (R)** Young Moncho (Lozano) grows up in 1935 Galicia, Spain and is guided by his leftist teacher Don Gregorio (Gomez). But their lives are soon torn apart by the politics of the Spanish Civil War. This kind of languidly paced coming-of-age story is almost never found in American theatrical releases these days. Europeans tend to treat the material with more seriousness. Director Jose Cuerda's work is solidly in the tradition of Fellini and Truffaut. Based on the stories of Manuel Riva; Spanish with subtitles. **94m/C VHS, DVD, Wide.** *SP* Fernando Fernan-Gomez, Manuel Lozano, Uxia Blanco; ***D:*** Jose Luis Cuerda; ***W:*** Rafael Azcona; ***C:*** Javier Salmones; ***M:*** Alejandro Amenabar.

Butterfly Affair 🦴½ **1971 (PG)** Beautiful singer, involved in a scheme to smuggle $2 million worth of gems, plots to double-cross her partners in crime. **75m/C VHS.** Claudia Cardinale, Henri Charriere, Stanley Baker; ***D:*** Jean Herman.

Butterfly Ball 🦴 **1976** Retelling of the 19th century classic combines the rock music of Roger Glover, live action and animation by Halas and Batchelor. Only for the brain-cell depressed. **85m/C VHS.** *GB* Twiggy, Ian Gillian, David Coverdale; ***D:*** Tony Klinger; ***Nar:*** Vincent Price.

Butterfly Kiss 🦴🦴 **1994** Strange psychodrama/road tale finds drifter Eunice (Plummer) wandering the motorways of northern England. At one service station she meets Miriam (Reeves)—the two, immediately drawn together, make love at Miriam's that night. When Eunice hitches a ride with a trucker next morning, Miriam decides to follow and discovers Eunice with the truck and the driver's dead body. It's soon not the only dead body Miriam encounters as she discovers Eunice is a serial killer—not that this seems to worry Miriam a great deal as she herself gets into the spirit of their crimes. Grim all the way 'round. **90m/C VHS.** *GB* Amanda Plummer, Saskia Reeves, Paul Brown, Des McAleer, Ricky Tomlinson; ***D:*** Michael Winterbottom; ***W:*** Frank Cottrell-Boyce; ***C:*** Seamus McGarvey; ***M:*** John Harle.

Butterfly Wings 🦴🦴 *Alas de Mariposa* **1991** The tragedy of a dysfunctional family. Pregnant Carmen longs for a boy to carry on her husband's name but she's afraid to tell her shy six-year-old daughter Ami about the baby. Maybe with reason, since the child's brith triggers a series of nightmarish events. Spanish with subtitles. **105m/C VHS.** *SP* ***D:*** Juanma Bajo Ulloa.

Buy & Cell 🦴½ **1989 (R)** A stockbroker attempts to set up a business while serving a prison sentence. An assortment of amusing inmates doesn't help matters much. Fans of Malcolm McDowell will enjoy his performance as the shady warden. **95m/C VHS.** Robert Carradine, Michael Winslow, Malcolm McDowell, Ben Vereen, Lise Cutter, Randall "Tex" Cobb, Roddy Piper; ***D:*** Robert Boris.

Buying Time 🦴 **1989 (R)** Two teenagers are arrested when they try to pry their money away from a dishonest bookie, and the police use their connections to solve a drug-related murder. **97m/C VHS.** Dean Stockwell, Jeff Schultz, Michael Rudder, Tony De Santis, Leslie Toth, Laura Cruickshank; ***D:*** Mitchell Gabourie.

Buzzy Rides the Range 🦴🦴 **1940** Average "B" western with a kid saving the day. **60m/C VHS.** Robert "Buzzy" Henry, Dave O'Brien, George Eldredge, Frank Marlo, George Morrell, Claire Rochelle; ***D:*** Richard C. Kahn.

By Dawn's Early Light 🦴🦴 **1989** Thriller about two Air Force pilots who must decide whether or not to drop the bombs that would begin WWIII. **100m/C VHS.** Powers Boothe, Rebecca DeMornay, James Earl Jones, Martin Landau, Rip Torn, Darren McGavin; ***D:*** Jack Sholder; ***M:*** Trevor Jones. **CABLE**

By Dawn's Early Light 🦴🦴½ **2000** Aging Colorado cowboy Ben (Crenna) is pleased when his grandson Mike (Olivero) comes to stay for the summer. Until he realizes that Mike is a sullen teen given to pranks that backfire. After one such episode, Ben decides Mike needs some discipline and decides they should go on an 800-mile trip—by horseback. **105m/C VHS, DVD.** Richard Crenna, Chris Olivero, David Carradine, Stella Stevens, Ben Cardinal; ***D:*** Arthur Allan Seidelman; ***W:*** Jacqueline Feather, David Seidler. **CABLE**

By Design 🦴 **1982 (R)** Two cohabiting women want to have a baby, so they embark on a search for the perfect stud. Not one of Astin's better performances. **90m/C VHS.** *CA* Patty Duke, Sara Botsford; ***D:*** Claude Jutra.

By Love Possessed 🦴🦴½ **1961** Can a seemingly typical, quiet, New England town stay quiet when Lana Turner is your neighbor? Vintage romantic melodrama about an attorney who is drawn into an affair when he realizes his home life is not all it could be. **115m/C VHS.** Lana Turner, Efrem Zimbalist Jr., Jason Robards Jr., George Hamilton, Thomas Mitchell; ***D:*** John Sturges; ***C:*** Russell Metty; ***M:*** Elmer Bernstein.

By the Blood of Others 🦴🦴🦴 **1973** In a small French town, a psycho holds two women hostage in a farmhouse, and the townspeople try to figure out a solution without getting anyone killed. In French with English subtitles. **90m/C VHS.** *FR* Mariangela Melato; ***D:*** Marc Simenon.

By the Light of the Silvery Moon 🦴🦴½ **1953** The equally old-fashioned sequel to "On Moonlight Bay" finds Day engaged to MacRae, who's just returned from Army service in WWI. He wants to postpone their marriage until he gets financially secure and the waiting causes some jealous misunderstandings (naturally resolved by movie's end). Based on Booth Tarkington's "Penrod" stories. ♫By the Light of the Silvery Moon; I'll Forget You; Your Eyes Have Told Me So; Be My Little Baby Bumble Bee; If You Were the Only Girl in the World; Ain't We Got Fun; King Chanticleer. **101m/C VHS.** Doris Day, Gordon MacRae, Leon Ames, Billy Gray, Rosemary DeCamp, Mary Wickes, Russell Arms, Maria Palmer; ***D:*** David Butler; ***W:*** Robert O'Brien, Irving Elinson; ***M:*** Max Steiner.

By the Sword 🦴½ **1993 (R)** Maximilian Suba (Abraham) is a one-time fencing whiz who has spent the last 25 years in prison for the murder of his mentor during a fencing match. Upon his release, Suba heads back to his old fencing grounds to see what's become of the murdered man's now-grown son and discovers Alexander (Roberts) is as ruthless and ambitious as Suba once was. Incoherent plot leaves both actors and viewers in the dark. **91m/C VHS.** F. Murray Abraham, Eric Roberts, Mia Sara, Christopher Rydell; ***D:*** Jeremy Paul Kagan; ***W:*** John McDonald, James Donadio; ***C:*** Arthur Albert; ***M:*** Bill Conti.

By Way of the Stars 🦴🦴½ **1992 (PG)** Young man is pursued by a killer while he searches for his father on the 19th-century Canadian frontier. Made for TV. **150m/C VHS.** *CA* Zachary Bennett, Tantoo Cardinal, Gema Zamprogna, Jan Rubes, Michael Mahonen; ***D:*** Allan King. **TV**

Bye-Bye 🦴🦴 **1996** Ismael (Bouajila), 25, and his 14-year-old brother Mouloud (Embarek) are French-born Arabs whose parents have abruptly returned to their Tunisian homeland after a family tragedy. The brothers have travelled from Paris to stay with their uncle (Ahourari) and his family in the port city of Marseilles. Their cousin Rhida (Mammeri), a petty criminal involved with drugs, takes the innocent Mauloud under his wing and hides him away so the boy won't be sent back to his parents. Ismael desperately roams the city trying to find his brother while he also struggles to make a fresh start amidst much societal hostility. French and Arabic with subtitles. **105m/C VHS.** *FR* Sami Bouajila, Ouassini Embarek, Benhaissa Ahourari, Sofiane Mammeri, Jamila Darwich-Farah, Nozha Khouadra; ***D:*** Karim Dridi; ***W:*** Karim Dridi; ***C:*** John Mathieson; ***M:*** Jimmy Oihid, Steve Shehan.

Bye Bye Baby 🦴 **1988 (R)** Two luscious young women cavort amid lusty Italian men on various Mediterranean beaches. **80m/C VHS.** *IT* Carol Alt, Brigitte Nielsen, Jason Connery, Luca Barbareschi; ***D:*** Enrico Oldoini; ***M:*** Manuel De Sica.

Bye, Bye, Birdie 🦴🦴🦴 **1963** Energized and sweet film version of the Broadway musical about a teen rock and roll idol (Pearson doing Elvis) coming to a small town to see one of his fans before he leaves for the army. The film that made Ann-Margret a star. ♫Bye Bye Birdie; The Telephone Hour; How Lovely to be a Woman; Honestly Sincere; One Boy; Put on a Happy Face; Kids; One Last Kiss; A Lot of Livin' to Do. **112m/C VHS, DVD, Wide.** Dick Van Dyke, Janet Leigh, Ann-Margret, Paul Lynde, Bobby Rydell, Maureen Stapleton, Ed Sullivan, Trudi Ames, Jesse Pearson; ***D:*** George Sidney; ***W:*** Irving Brecher; ***C:*** Joseph Biroc; ***M:*** Johnny Green.

Bye Bye Birdie 🦴🦴½ **1995 (G)** TV adaptation of the Broadway musical (previously filmed in 1963) about an Elvis-like singer, about to be inducted into the Army, who causes havoc when he visits fans in a small town. **135m/C VHS, DVD.** Jason Alexander, Vanessa L(ynne) Williams, Chynna

Phillips, George Wendt, Tyne Daly, Marc Kudisch; *D:* Gene Saks. TV

Bye Bye Blues ☙☙½ 1989 (PG) The lives of the Cooper family are disrupted when the husband is called to service during WWII and is then taken prisoner by the Japanese. In need of money, wife Daisy (Jenkins) joins a local swing band and begins charming all who watch her, especially the band's trombone player (Reilly). A sweet-spirited tale of love, loyalty, and the search for inner strength. Jenkins gives a strong performance as the shy wife who becomes an independent woman during her husband's absence. **110m/C VHS.** *CA* Rebecca Jenkins, Michael Ontkean, Luke Reilly, Stuart Margolin, Robyn Stevan, Kate Reid, Wayne Robson, Shiela Moore, Leon Pownall, Vincent Gale, Susan Sneath; *D:* Anne Wheeler; *W:* Anne Wheeler; *C:* Vic Sarin; *M:* George Blondheim. Genie '90: Actress (Jenkins), Support. Actress (Stevan).

Bye Bye Brazil ☙☙½ 1979 A changing Brazil is seen through the eyes of four wandering gypsy minstrels participating in a tent show traveling throughout the country. Lots of Brazilian charm. In Portuguese with English subtitles. **115m/C VHS.** *BR* Jose Wilker, Betty Faria, Fabio Junior, Zaira Zambello; *D:* Carlos Diegues; *W:* Carlos Diegues; *M:* Chico Buarque.

Bye Bye, Love ☙☙½ 1994 (PG-13) Forty-eight hours in the lives of three divorced buddies starts at the local Mickey D's for the biweekly exchange of their kids. The dads don't offer any surprises: Donny (Reiser) still loves his ex, Vic (Quaid) hates his, and Dave (Modine) loves anything in a skirt. Sometimes witty, but just as often sadly poignant, the plot is as shallow as a TV sitcom, with an easy answer for every difficult question about divorce. The three leads are likeable enough, but Garofalo is the gem in an otherwise dull flick. She looks like she's having a blast, stealing scenes with abandon as Vic's blind date from hell. **107m/C VHS.** Brad Hall, Matthew Modine, Randy Quaid, Paul Reiser, Rob Reiner, Janeane Garofalo, Ed Flanders, Lindsay Crouse, James Whitworth, Maria Pitillo, Amy Brenneman, Ross Malinger, Eliza Dushku, Wendell Pierce, Cameron Boyd, Mae Whitman, Jayne Brook, Dana Wheeler-Nicholson, Amber Benson, Stephen (Steve) Root, Danny Masterson; *D:* Sam Weisman; *W:* Gary David Goldberg, Brad Hall; *M:* J.A.C. Redford.

The C-Man ☙☙ 1949 Customs agent Jagger finds work isn't so dull after all. Murder and theft on an international scale make for a busy week as he follows jewel smugglers from Paris to New York. Docu-style though routine crime story. **75m/B VHS.** Dean Jagger, John Carradine, Harry Landers, Rene Paul; *D:* Joseph Lerner.

Cabaret ☙☙☙½ 1972 (PG) Hitler is rising to power, racism and anti-Semitism are growing, and the best place to hide from it all is the Berlin cabaret. With dancing girls, an androgynous master of ceremonies (Grey), and American expatriate singer Sally Bowles (Minnelli), you can laugh and drink and pretend tomorrow will never come. Sally does just that. Face to face with the increasing horrors of Nazism, she persists in the belief that the "show must go on." Along for the ride is Englishman Brian Roberts (York, in a role based on Christopher Isherwood's own experiences), who serves both as participant and observer. Based on the John Kander's hit Broadway musical (and Isherwood's stories), the film is impressive, with excellent direction and cinematography. ♫Cabaret; Wilkommen; Mein Herr; Maybe This Time; Two Ladies; Money, Money; Hieraten; Tomorrow Belongs to Me; If You Could See Her. **119m/C VHS, DVD.** Liza Minnelli, Joel Grey, Michael York, Marisa Berenson, Helmut Griem, Fritz Wepper, Elisabeth Neumann-Viertel; *D:* Bob Fosse; *W:* Jay Presson Allen; *C:* Geoffrey Unsworth; *M:* Ralph Burns. Oscars '72: Actress (Minnelli), Art Dir./Set Dec., Cinematog., Director (Fosse), Film Editing, Sound, Support. Actor (Grey), Orig. Song Score and/or Adapt.; British Acad. '72: Actress (Minnelli), Director (Fosse), Film; Golden Globes '73: Actress—Mus./Comedy (Minnelli), Film—Mus./Comedy, Support. Actor (Grey); Natl. Bd. of Review '72: Director (Fosse), Support. Actor (Grey), Support. Actress (Berenson), Natl. Film Reg. '95;, Natl. Soc. Film Critics '72: Support. Actor (Grey); Writers Guild '72: Adapt. Screenplay.

Cabaret Balkan ☙☙ *The Powder Keg; Bure Baruta* 1998 (R) Acerbicly cruel and frequently physically brutal comedy is set in Belgrade one winter night and features characters whose stories turn out to be inter-related and are bookended by the comments of sneering nightclub M.C. Boris (Ristanovski). There are betrayals, feuds, random acts of violence, and various absurdities set in a war-torn country where the veneer of civilization has long-since disappeared. Based on the play "Bure Baruta" by Dukovski. Serbo-Croatian with subtitles. **102m/C VHS.** *YU* Miki (Predrag) Manojlovic, Nikola Ristanovski, Nebojsa Glogovac, Marko Urosevic, Bogdan Diklic; *D:* Goran Paskalyevic; *W:* Goran Paskalyevic, Dejan Dukovski; *C:* Milan Spasic; *M:* Zoran Simjanovic.

Cabeza de Vaca ☙☙☙ 1990 (R) In 1528, a Spanish expedition shipwrecks in unknown territory off the Florida coast. Only survivor Cabeza de Vaca is captured by the Iguase Indian tribe and made a slave to their shaman. He's later freed, but leaves with respect for their culture. Spanish soldiers find him and want his help in capturing the natives, but he is outraged by their cruelty and must confront his own people. Strong visual style easily brings the audience deeply into this uncharted world. Based on Cabeza de Vaca's book "Naufragios." Director Echevarria's feature film debut. Spanish and Indian with subtitles. **111m/C VHS, DVD.** *MX SP* Juan Diego, Daniel Gimenez Cacho, Roberto Sosa, Carlos Castanon, Gerardo Villarreal, Roberto Cobo, Jose Flores, Ramon Barragan; *D:* Nicolas Echevarria; *W:* Guillermo Sheridan, Nicolas Echevarria; *C:* Guillermo Navarro; *M:* Mario Lavista.

Cabin Boy woof! 1994 (PG-13) Obnoxious "fancy lad" Elliott mistakenly boards the wrong boat and becomes the new cabin boy for a ridiculous bunch of mean, smelly sailors. Fish out of water saga is so bad it's—bad, a blundering attempt at parody that's just plain stupid. Surprisingly produced by Tim Burton, this effort will disappoint even diehard fans. Look for Chris' real life dad Bob as the lad's dad; good friend Letterman appears briefly as nasty "Old Salt," but uses the alias Earl Hofert in the final credits. As usual, the acerbic Letterman gets the best line, "Man, oh, man do I hate them fancy lads." We know how you feel, Dave. **80m/C VHS.** Andy Richter, Chris Elliott, Ann Magnuson, Ritch Brinkley, James Gammon, Brian Doyle-Murray, Russ Tamblyn, Brion James, Ricki Lake, Bob Elliott; *Cameos:* David Letterman; *D:* Adam Resnick; *W:* Adam Resnick; *C:* Amy Barrett; *M:* Steve Bartek.

Cabin by the Lake ☙☙ 2000 Screenwriter Stanley (Nelson) takes his work a little too seriously when he does research on a story about a serial killer who kidnaps and drowns his female victims. Stanley has his own garden of victims until one young woman escapes and a trap is laid for the killer. **91m/C VHS, DVD.** Judd Nelson, Hedy Burress, Michael Weatherly, Bernie Coulson, Susan Gibney; *D:* Po Chich Leong; *W:* C. David Stephens; *C:* Philip Linzey; *M:* Frankie Blue, Daniel Licht. CABLE

The Cabin in the Cotton ☙☙½ 1932 Davis stars as a rich, ruthless Southern belle in this dated melodrama about sharecroppers. Barthelmess is cast as a poor sharecropper who is almost brought to ruin when he falls for the sexy Southern vamp. Contains Davis's most famous line, "Ah'd love t'kiss you, but ah jes washed mah hair." **77m/B VHS.** Bette Davis, Richard Barthelmess, Dorothy Jordan, Henry B. Walthall, Tully Marshall; *D:* Michael Curtiz; *W:* Paul Green.

Cabin in the Sky ☙☙☙ 1943 A poor woman fights to keep her husband's soul out of the devil's clutches. Based on a Broadway show and featuring an all-Black cast. Lively dance numbers and a musical score with contributions from Duke Ellington. Minnelli's first feature film. ♫Cabin in the Sky; Happiness Is Just a Thing Called Joe; Taking a Chance on Love; Life's Full of Consequence; Li'l Black Sheep; Shine; Honey in the Honeycomb. **99m/C VHS.** Ethel Waters, Eddie Anderson, Lena Horne, Rex Ingram, Louis Armstrong, Duke Ellington; *D:* Vincente Minnelli; *M:* Duke Ellington, Harold Arlen, E.Y. Harburg, George Bassman.

The Cabinet of Dr. Caligari ☙☙☙☙ *Das Cabinet des Dr. Caligari; Das Kabinett des Doktor Caligari* 1919 A pioneering film in the most extreme expressionistic style about a hypnotist in a carnival and a girl-snatching somnambulist. Highly influential in its approach to lighting, composition, design and acting. Much imitated. Silent. **92m/B VHS, DVD.** *GE* Conrad Veidt, Werner Krauss, Lil Dagover, Hans von Twardowski, Rudolf Klein-Rogge, Friedrich Feher, Rudolf Lettinger; *D:* Robert Wiene; *W:* Carl Mayer, Hans Janowitz; *C:* Willy Hameister.

Cabiria ☙☙½ 1914 The pioneering Italian epic about a Roman and a slave girl having a love affair in Rome during the Second Punic War. Immense sets and set-pieces; an important influence on Griffith and DeMille. Silent. **123m/B VHS, DVD, 8mm.** *IT* Lidia Quaranta, Bartolomeo Pagano, Umberto Mozzato; *D:* Giovanni Pastrone; *W:* Giovanni Pastrone, Gabriele D'Annunzio; *C:* Segundo de Chomon.

The Cable Guy ☙☙½ 1996 (PG-13) Carrey's first $20 million paycheck finds cable subscriber Broderick in for a comedic nightmare when he accepts the offer of free movie channels. The overeager installer (Carrey, naturally) turns his life upside down. A little darker humor than Carrey fans may be used to, and don't expect any bodily ventriloquism. Carrey (did we mention he's in it?) gets to act with real life people. Director Stiller does a nice job of reining in his more manic impulses when necessary. Broderick holds his own as the reluctant pal. Original scripter Holtz won a Writer's Guild arbitration for sole writing credit from producer-writer Judd Apatow. **95m/C VHS, DVD, 8mm.** Bob Odenkirk, David Cross, Owen C. Wilson, Joel Murray, Kathy Griffin, Sean M. Whalen, Annabelle Gurwitch, Conrad Janis, Alex D. Linz, Jim Carrey, Matthew Broderick, Leslie Mann, George Segal, Diane Baker, Jack Black, Janeane Garofalo, Andy Dick, Charles Napier, Ben Stiller; *D:* Ben Stiller; *W:* Judd Apatow, Lou Holtz Jr.; *C:* Robert Brinkmann; *M:* John Ottman. MTV Movie Awards '97: Villain (Carrey), Comedic Perf. (Carrey).

Cabo Blanco ☙☙ 1981 (R) A bartender and a variety of other characters, including an ex-Nazi and a French woman searching for her lover, assemble in Peru after WWII. Nazi Robards controls police chief Rey, while American Bronson runs the local watering hole and eyes French woman Sanda. Hey, this sounds familiar. Everyone shares a common interest: finding a missing treasure of gold, lost in a ship wreck. Remaking "Casablanca" via "The Treasure of Sierra Madre" is never easy. **87m/C VHS, DVD.** Charles Bronson, Jason Robards Jr., Dominique Sanda, Fernando Rey, Gilbert Roland, Simon MacCorkindale; *D:* J. Lee Thompson; *W:* Morton S. Fine, Milton S. Gelman; *C:* Alex Phillips Jr.; *M:* Jerry Goldsmith.

Cactus ☙☙½ 1986 Melodrama about a young French woman, separated from her husband, who faces the reality of losing her sight after a car accident. She experiences a growing relationship with a blind man and contemplates the thought of risky surgery which may improve her eyesight or cause complete blindness. Countering all that blindness and tangled romance is a camera that pans lush Australian landscapes and humorously focuses on the small telling details of daily life. **95m/C VHS.** *AU* Isabelle Huppert, Robert Menzies, Monica Maughan, Sheila Florance, Norman Kaye, Banduk Marika; *D:* Paul Cox; *W:* Norman Kaye, Paul Cox, Bob Ellis; *C:* Yuri Sokol; *M:* Giovanni Pergolese, Yannis Markopolous, Elsa Davis.

Cactus Flower ☙☙ 1969 (PG) Good cast doesn't quite suffice to make this adaptation of a Broadway hit work. A middle-aged bachelor dentist gets involved with a kookie mistress, refusing to admit his real love for his prim and proper receptionist. Hawn's big leap to stardom. **103m/C VHS, DVD, Wide.** Walter Matthau, Goldie Hawn, Ingrid Bergman, Jack Weston, Rick Lenz; *D:* Gene Saks; *W:* I.A.L. Diamond; *C:* Charles B(ryant) Lang Jr.; *M:* Quincy Jones. Oscars '69: Support. Actress (Hawn); Golden Globes '70: Support. Actress (Hawn).

Cactus in the Snow ☙½ 1972 A virginal Army private serving during the Vietnam War era tries to find sex on a 72-hour leave and instead discovers love. Some guys have all the luck. Melodrama never grabs where it ought to. **90m/C VHS.** Richard Thomas, Mary Layne, Lucille Benson; *D:* Martin Zweiback.

Caddie ☙☙½ 1976 Based on an autobiographical story of a woman who leaves her unfaithful husband in 1930s Australia. Struggling to raise her two children, she works as a waitress in a bar where she finds romance with one of the regulars. Average script bolstered by Morse's performance. **107m/C VHS.** *AU* Helen Morse, Jack Thompson, Takis Emmanuel, Jacki Weaver; *D:* Donald Crombie; *W:* Joan Long; *C:* Peter James; *M:* Patrick Flynn.

The Caddy ☙☙ 1953 Lewis plays frantic caddy prone to slapstick against Martin's smooth professional golfer with a bent toward singing. Mostly a series of Martin and Lewis sketches that frequently land in the rough. Introduces several songs, including a classic Martin and Lewis rendition of "That's Amore." Look for cameos by a host of professional golfers. **95m/C VHS.** Dean Martin, Jerry Lewis, Donna Reed, Barbara Bates, Joseph Calleia, Marshall Thompson, Fred Clark; *Cameos:* Ben Hogan, Sam Snead, Byron Nelson, Julius Boros, Jimmy Thomson, Harry E. Cooper; *D:* Norman Taurog; *W:* Danny Arnold.

Caddyshack ☙☙☙½ 1980 (R) Inspired performances by Murray and Dangerfield drive this sublimely moronic comedy onto the green. The action takes place at Bushwood Country Club, where caddy Danny (O'Keefe) is bucking to win the club's college scholarship. Characters involved in various sophomoric set pieces include obnoxious club president Judge Smails (Knight), playboy Ty Webb (Chase), who is too laid back to keep his score, loud, vulgar, and extremely rich Al Czernik (Dangerfield), and filthy gopher-hunting groundskeeper Carl (Murray). Occasional dry moments are followed by scenes of pure (and tasteless) anarchy, so watch with someone immature. Does for golf what "Major League" tried to do for baseball. **99m/C VHS, DVD.** Chevy Chase, Rodney Dangerfield, Ted (Edward) Knight, Michael O'Keefe, Bill Murray, Sarah Holcomb, Brian Doyle-Murray, Cindy Morgan, Scott Colomby, Dan Resin, Henry Wilcoxon, Elaine Aiken; *D:* Harold Ramis; *W:* Harold Ramis, Doug Kenney, Brian Doyle-Murray; *C:* Stevan Larner; *M:* Johnny Mandel.

Caddyshack 2 ☙½ 1988 (PG) Obligatory sequel to "Caddyshack," minus Bill Murray who wisely avoided further encroachment of gopher holes and director Ramis who opted for the screenwriting chore. Mason is the star of the show as a crude self-made millionaire who tangles with the snobs at the country club. Although it occasionally earns a side-splitting chuckle, "Shack 2" has significantly fewer guffaws than the original, proving once again that funny guys are always undone by lousy scripts and weak direction. **103m/C VHS, DVD, 8mm.** Jackie Mason, Chevy Chase, Dan Aykroyd, Dyan Cannon, Robert Stack, Dina Merrill, Randy Quaid, Jessica Lundy, Jonathan Silverman, Chynna Phillips; *D:* Allan Arkush; *W:* Harold Ramis, Peter Torokvei; *C:* Harry Stradling Jr.; *M:* Ira Newborn. Golden Raspberries '88: Worst Support. Actor (Aykroyd), Worst Song ("Jack Fresh").

Cadence ☙☙ 1989 (PG-13) The directorial debut of actor Martin Sheen, this fitful melodrama stars son Charlie as an unruly trooper on a 1960s army base. Placed in an all-black stockade for punishment, he bonds with his brother prisoners by defying the hardcase sergeant (played by Sheen the elder). Characters and situations are intriguing but not rendered effectively. Based on the novel "Count a Lonely Cadence" by Gordon Weaver. **97m/C VHS, DVD.** Charlie Sheen, Martin Sheen, Laurence "Larry" Fishburne, Michael Beach, Ramon Estevez; *D:* Martin Sheen; *M:* Georges Delerue.

Cadillac Girls 🦴½ 1993 Page is a self-destructive teenager who is arrested for car theft. To avoid jail, Page is placed in her single mom's custody and moves to her family's straitlaced hometown in Nova Scotia. Mom isn't exactly good at parenting and Page's adolescent anger extends to putting the moves on mom's potential new beau. **99m/C VHS.** Jennifer Dale, Gregory Harrison, Mia Kirshner, Adam Beach; ***D:*** Nicholas (Nick) Kendall. Genie '93: Score.

Cadillac Man 🦴🦴 1990 (R) Williams is the quintessential low-life car salesman in this rather disjointed comedy. A lesser comedic talent might have stalled and been abandoned, but Williams manages to drive away despite the flat script and direction. One storyline follows his attempt to sell 12 cars in 12 days or lose his job, while another follows his confrontation with a gun-toting, mad-as-hell cuckolded husband. Williams and Robbins are often close to being funny in a hyperkinetic way, but the situations are dumb enough to rob most of the scenes of their comedy. Watch for a movie-stealing bit by the spunky waitress at the local Chinese restaurant. **95m/C VHS.** Robin Williams, Tim Robbins, Pamela Reed, Fran Drescher, Zack Norman, Annabella Sciorra, Lori Petty, Paul Guilfoyle, Tristen Skylar; ***D:*** Roger Donaldson; ***W:*** Ken Friedman; ***C:*** David Gribble; ***M:*** J. Peter Robinson.

Cadillac Ranch 🦴🦴½ 1996 (R) CJ (Amis), Frances (Feeney), and Mary Katharine (Humphrey) Crowley are three squabbling Texas sisters who have reunited to celebrate Mary K.'s upcoming marriage. CJ works in a strip club owned by greedy ex-Texas Ranger Wood (Lloyd), who sent their long-gone daddy, Travis (Metzler), to prison for a heist Wood was involved in. When CJ gets fired, the threesome steal a key from Wood that will supposedly access money from the heist and the vengeful Wood goes after them. **104m/C VHS, DVD.** Suzy Amis, Renee Humphrey, Caroleen Feeney, Christopher Lloyd, Jim Metzler, Linden Ashby; ***D:*** Lisa Gottlieb; ***W:*** Jennifer Cecil; ***C:*** Bruce Douglas Johnson; ***M:*** Christopher Tyng.

Caesar and Cleopatra 🦴🦴½ 1946 Based on the classic George Bernard Shaw play. Caesar meets the beautiful Cleopatra in ancient Egypt and helps her gain control of her life. Remains surprisingly true to Shaw's adaptation, unlike many other historical films of the same era. **135m/C VHS, DVD.** *GB* Claude Rains, Vivien Leigh, Stewart Granger, Flora Robson, Francis L. Sullivan, Cecil Parker; ***D:*** Gabriel Pascal; ***C:*** Robert Krasker.

Cafe au Lait 🦴🦴🦴 *Metisse* 1994 Actor/director/writer Kassovitz scores in his debut feature about an interracial menage a trois. Beautiful mulatto Lola (Mauduech) is pregnant but she's not sure by which of her two contrasting lovers (who don't yet know about each other). It could be white, Jewish, easy-going bicycle messenger Felix (Kassovitz) or stuffy, wealthy, black Moslem student Jamal (Kounde). Both men desire the fatherhood role and both move in with Lola to share responsibility. This is not without complications. Generally light and frothy without ignoring racial tensions. French with subtitles. **94m/C VHS.** *FR* Mathieu Kassovitz, Julie Mauduech, Hubert Kounde, Vincent Cassel, Tadek Lokcinski, Jany Holt; ***D:*** Mathieu Kassovitz; ***W:*** Mathieu Kassovitz; ***C:*** Pierre Aim; ***M:*** Marie Daulne, Jean-Louis Daulne.

Cafe Express 🦴🦴½ 1983 A con artist (he sells coffee illegally aboard an Italian train) stays one step ahead of the law as he raises money to help his ailing son. As in "Bread and Chocolate," Manfredi is again the put-upon working class hero comedically attempting to find a better way of life in this bittersweet tale. **90m/C VHS.** *IT* Nino Manfredi, Gigi Reder, Adolfo Celi, Vittorio Mezzogiorno; ***D:*** Nanni Loy.

Cafe Romeo 🦴🦴 1991 (R) Tale of 20-something friendships forged in the neighborhood coffeehouse of a heavily Italian community. Lia (Stewart) is a waitress who dreams of becoming a fashion designer, but her marriage to a small time hood holds her back. Crombie, her cousin by marriage, is a dental student confused about his future, but very much in love with Lia. Quiet movie boasts average script that's helped along by strong performances. Originally broadcast on Canadian TV. **93m/C VHS.** *CA* Catherine Mary Stewart, Jonathan Crombie; ***D:*** Rex Bromfield.

Cafe Society 🦴🦴½ 1997 (R) The fictional nightclub El Casbah is the setting for director De Felitta's debut take on a 1952 New York prostitution scandal. Wealthy young playboy Mickey Jelke (Whaley) prefers to mix with lowlifes rather than high society. Newcomer Jack Kale (Gallagher) is working the scene and turns out to be an undercover cop investigating a prostiution ring operating out of the clubs. Jack befriends both Mickey and his latest girlfriend, in-the-know Patricia Ward (Boyle), who's not above selling her favors. Then patsy Jelke gets indicted as a pimp and all cafe society's tawdriness is exposed. **104m/C VHS.** Peter Gallagher, Frank Whaley, Lara Flynn Boyle, John Spencer, Anna Thomson, David Patrick Kelly, Paul Guilfoyle; ***D:*** Raymond De Felitta; ***W:*** Raymond De Felitta; ***C:*** Mike Mayers; ***M:*** Chris Guardino.

The Cage 🦴 1989 (R) Gangsters enlist a brain-damaged Vietnam vet played by Ferrigno to participate in illegal "cage fights," enclosed wrestling matches fought to the death. Crude and annoying. **101m/C VHS.** Lou Ferrigno, Reb Brown, Michael Dante, Mike Moroff, Marilyn Tokuda, James Shigeta, Al Ruscio; ***D:*** Hugh Kelley.

The Cage 🦴🦴🦴 1990 Sent to prison for murdering his girlfriend, Jive has no idea what the pen has in store for him. The inmates stage a mock trial, the defendant is found guilty and the sentence is too horrible to imagine. From a stage play by the San Quentin Drama Workshop and co-starring Hayes, author of "Midnight Express." **90m/C VHS.** Rick Cluchey, William Hayes; ***D:*** Rick Cluchey; ***W:*** Rick Cluchey.

Cage 2: The Arena of Death 🦴½ 1994 (R) Billy Thomas (Ferrigno) is kidnapped by a vicious mobster and forced to battle martial arts experts in a steel cage battle to the death. But his best friend (Brown) plans to infiltrate the show and put a stop to the carnage. **94m/C VHS.** Lou Ferrigno, Reb Brown; ***D:*** Lang Elliott.

Caged Fear 🦴½ 1992 (R) Young Krissie (Cloke) is mistakenly put behind bars in a brutal, high-security prison for a shootout caused by her outlaw husband Tommy (Keith) during their honeymoon. Tommy comes up with an outrageous scheme to rescue her. Not quite as bad as it sounds, but close. **94m/C VHS.** David Keith, Deborah May, Ray Sharkey, Loretta Devine, Karen Black, Kristen (Kristin) Cloke; ***D:*** Bobby Houston; ***W:*** Bobby Houston.

Caged Fury 🦴 1980 (R) American women being held captive in Southeast Asia are brainwashed into becoming walking time bombs. Yes, that dame's gonna blow. Made in the Philippines with the best of intentions. **90m/C VHS.** *PH* Bernadette Williams, Taaffe O'Connell, Jennifer Laine; ***D:*** Cirio H. Santiago.

Caged Fury 🦴 1990 Two Los Angeles women allegedly commit sexual crimes and are sent to prison. Cheap, exploitive women's prison rehash. **85m/C VHS.** Erik Estrada, Richie Barathy, Roxanna Michaels, Paul Smith, James Hong, Greg Cummins; ***D:*** Bill Milling.

Caged Hearts 🦴 1995 (R) Chicks-behind-bars flick finds Kate (Genzel) and Sharon (McClure) framed for murder by a shady organization called "The Shield." Cliches abound. **87m/C VHS.** Tane McClure, Carrie Genzel, Taylor Leigh, Nick Wilder; ***D:*** Henri Charr.

Caged Heat 🦴🦴 *Renegade Girls; Caged Females* 1974 (R) Low-budget babes-behind-bars film touted as the best sexploitation film of the day. Demme's directorial debut is a genre-altering installment in Roger Corman's formulaic cellblock Cinderella cycle. Recycled plot—innocent woman is put behind bars, where she loses some of her innocence—boasts an updated treatment. These babes may wear hot pants and gratuitously bare their midriffs, but they're not brainless bimbos. They're strong individuals who work together to liberate themselves. Reached cult status. Cult diva Steele returned to the big screen after six years to play the wheelchair-ridden prison warden, written specifically for her. **83m/C VHS, DVD, Wide.** Juanita Brown, Erica Gavin, Roberta Collins, Barbara Steele, Ella Reid, Cheryl "Rainbeaux" Smith, John Aprea, Amy Barrett, Gary Goetzman; ***D:*** Jonathan Demme; ***W:*** Jonathan Demme; ***C:*** Tak Fujimoto; ***M:*** John Cale.

Caged Heat 2: Stripped of Freedom 🦴½ 1994 (R) Women-in-prison formula with a princess thrown into the pen following a political coup. CIA agent is sent undercover as an inmate to bust her out. Usual sadistic guards, rape, and revenge scenes. From Roger Corman's direct-to-video factory. **84m/C VHS.** Jewel Shepard, Chanel Akiko Hirai, Pamella D'Pella, Vic Diaz; ***D:*** Cirio H. Santiago.

Caged Heat 3000 🦴 1995 (R) Yes, it's a sci-fi chicks-in-prison movie! Innocent Kira Murphy (Leigh) is wrongly condemned to an underground prison located 45 lightyears from Earth where there are lots of racial tensions and evil prison officials. Prerequisite shower scenes and sadistic guards also add to the standard exploitation. **84m/C VHS.** Cassandra Leigh, Kena Land, Debra Beatty; ***D:*** Cirio H. Santiago; ***W:*** Paul Ziller.

Caged in Paradiso 🦴½ 1989 (R) A convicted criminal and his wife are dumped onto a remote prisoner's isle to live out their lives. When Cara loses contact with her husband, she must fend for herself. Survival tale boringly told. **90m/C VHS.** Irene Cara; ***D:*** Michael Snyder.

Caged Terror woof! 1972 Two urbanites hit the countryside for a weekend and meet a band of crazy rapists who ravage the wife and set the husband raging with bloodthirsty revenge. Squalid stroll through the ruins. **76m/C VHS.** Percy Harkness, Elizabeth Suzuki, Leon Morenzie; ***D:*** Barry McLean.

Caged Women 🦴 *Women's Penitentiary 4* 1984 (R) Undercover journalist enters a women's prison and gets the usual eyeful. Mattei used the pseudonym Vincent Dawn. **97m/C VHS.** *FR IT* Laura Gemser, Gabriele Tinti, Lorraine (De Sette) De Selle, Maria Romano; ***D:*** Bruno Mattei.

Cahill: United States Marshal 🦴🦴 1973 (PG) The aging Duke in one of his lesser moments, portraying a marshal who comes to the aid of his sons. The boys are mixed up with a gang of outlaws, proving that no matter how good a parent you are, sometimes the kids just lean toward the wayward. Turns out, though, that the boys harbor a grudge against the old man due to years of workaholic neglect. Will Duke see the error of his ways and reconcile with the delinquent boys? Will he catch the outlaw leader? Will he go on to star in other Duke vehicles? **103m/C VHS, Wide.** John Wayne, Gary Grimes, George Kennedy, Neville Brand, Marie Windsor, Harry Carey Jr., Clay O'Brien; ***D:*** Andrew V. McLaglen; ***M:*** Elmer Bernstein.

The Caine Mutiny 🦴🦴🦴🦴 1954 A group of naval officers revolt against a captain they consider mentally unfit. Bogart is masterful as Captain Queeg, obsessed with cleanliness while onboard and later a study in mental meltdown during the court-martial of a crew member who participated in the mutiny. Based on the Pulitzer-winning novel by Herman Wouk, the drama takes a close look at the pressure-filled life aboard ship during WWII. **125m/C VHS, DVD, 8mm.** Humphrey Bogart, Jose Ferrer, Van Johnson, Fred MacMurray, Lee Marvin, Claude Akins, E.G. Marshall, Robert Francis, May Wynn, Tom Tully, Arthur Franz, Warner Anderson, Katherine Warren, Jerry Paris, Steve Brodie, Whit Bissell, Robert Bray, Ted Cooper; ***D:*** Edward Dmytryk; ***W:*** Stanley Roberts, Michael Blankfort; ***C:*** Franz Planer; ***M:*** Max Steiner.

The Caine Mutiny Court Martial 🦴🦴🦴 1988 (PG) A young lieutenant is up for a court-martial after taking control of the USS Caine in the midst of a typhoon. In order to save him, his lawyer must discredit the paranoid Commander Queeg. As the events of the mutiny unfold, it becomes clear that Queeg's obsession with discipline had become a threat to everyone aboard. Good performances, particularly by Bogosian as the lawyer. Based on the novel by Pulitzer prize-winner Herman Wouk. **100m/C VHS.** Jeff Daniels, Eric Bogosian, Brad Davis, Peter Gallagher, Michael Murphy, Kevin J. O'Connor, Daniel H. Jenkins; ***D:*** Robert Altman. **TV**

Cain's Cutthroats 🦴 *Cain's Way; The Blood Seekers; Justice Cain* 1971 (R) A former Confederate army captain and a bounty hunting preacher team up to settle the score with soldiers on a gang-raping, murdering spree. **87m/C VHS.** Scott Brady, John Carradine, Robert Dix, Don Epperson, Adair Jamison, Darwin Joston, Bruce (Kemp) Kimball, Russ McCubbin, Valda Hansen; ***D:*** Kent Osborne; ***W:*** Wilton Denmark; ***C:*** Ralph Waldo; ***M:*** Harley Hatcher.

Cairo 🦴🦴 1942 War correspondent Young lands in Cairo where he is supposed to pass along classified information to a Nazi spy posing as a Brit. He meets and falls in love with American movie queen thought to be enemy agent (MacDonald) and a race across the desert follows when Young is trapped in a pyramid. Catchy tunes can't save this cheesy WWII spy spoof that marked the end of MacDonald's MGM contract. **101m/B VHS.** Jeanette MacDonald, Robert Young, Ethel Waters, Reginald Owen, Grant Mitchell, Lionel Atwill, Eduardo Ciannelli, Mitchell Lewis; ***D:*** Woodbridge S. Van Dyke; ***W:*** John McClain; ***M:*** Herbert Stothart.

Cal 🦴🦴🦴 1984 (R) Cal (Lynch), a young Catholic man, is reluctantly recruited into the Irish Republican Army. He falls in love with the older Marcella (Mirren), the widow of a Protestant policeman whom he helped kill while acting as the get-away driver for his fellow Republicans. Thoughtful and tragic, with excellent performances; set in Northern Ireland. **104m/C VHS.** *IR* Helen Mirren, John Lynch, Donal McCann, Kitty Gibson, Ray McAnally, John Kavanagh; ***D:*** Pat O'Connor; ***W:*** Bernard MacLaverty; ***M:*** Mark Knopfler. Cannes '84: Actress (Mirren).

Calamity Jane 🦴🦴🦴 1953 In one of her best Warner musicals, Day stars as the rip-snortin', gun-totin' Calamity Jane of Western lore, in an on-again, off-again romance with Wild Bill Hickok. ♫Secret Love; Just Blew in From the Windy City; The Black Hills of Dakota; The Deadwood Stage (Whip-Crack-Away!). **101m/C VHS, DVD.** Doris Day, Howard Keel, Allyn Ann McLerie, Dick Wesson; ***D:*** David Butler; ***W:*** James O'Hanlon; ***C:*** Wilfrid M. Cline; ***M:*** Sammy Fain, Paul Francis Webster. Oscars '53: Song ("Secret Love").

Calamity Jane 🦴🦴½ 1982 A biography of the famous lady crack shot. Alexander is cast as the tough-as-nails woman who considered herself on a par with any man. **96m/C VHS.** Jane Alexander, Frederic Forrest, Ken Kercheval, Talia Balsam, David Hemmings; ***D:*** James Goldstone. **TV**

Calendar 🦴🦴🦴 1993 A Canadian photographer (Egoyan) is hired to take pictures of ancient Armenian churches for a calendar. His wife (Egoyan's real-life spouse Khanjian) accompanies him, serving as a translator, and they hire a driver (Adamian) who turns out to be an architectural expert. Told in flashback, the film gradually reveals a romantic triangle—with the photographer becoming so caught up in his work that he fails to realize his wife, increasingly drawn to her ethnic heritage, and their driver are having an affair. This romantic puzzle also includes the photographer, having returned to Canada wifeless and apparently seeking a replacement, having dinner with a series of women he's meet through the personals. In English and Armenian. **73m/C VHS, DVD.** *CA* Atom Egoyan, Arsinee Khanjian, Ashot Adamian; ***D:*** Atom Egoyan; ***W:*** Atom Egoyan; ***C:*** Norayr Kasper.

Calendar Girl 🦴🦴½ 1993 (PG-13) In 1962 three high-school best friends borrow a convertible and travel from their Nevada homes to Hollywood to meet their pinup idol, Marilyn Monroe. Roy's (Priestley) a rebel, Ned's (Olds, in his film debut) sensitive, and Scott's (O'Connell) just a nice guy. They stay with Roy's Uncle Harvey (Pantoliano), an aspiring actor, and work to meet their dream girl. Which they finally do, in a notably weak sequence which fits in with this notably uninspired film. The three actors at least have enough comradery to make realistic buddies—one of the few true touches in the film. **86m/C VHS, 8mm.** Jason Priestley, Gabriel Olds, Jerry O'Connell, Joe Pantoliano, Stephen Tobolowsky, Kurt Fuller, Steve Railsback, Emily Warfield, Stephanie Anderson; ***Cameos:*** Chubby Checker; ***D:*** John Whitesell; ***W:*** Paul Shapiro; ***M:*** Hans Zimmer.

Calendar Girl Murders 🦴🦴½ **1984** Minor mystery about the murder of some girlie magazine pinups. **104m/C VHS.** Robert Culp, Tom Skerritt, Barbara Parkins, Sharon Stone; ***D:*** William A. Graham; ***M:*** Brad Fiedel. **TV**

California Casanova woof! **1989 (R)** Mirthless, semi-musical farce about a nerdy stagehand learning to be a great lover to win a beautiful singer's heart who's being blackmailed by a cruel gangster. Nice cast; nobody's home. **94m/C VHS.** Jerry Orbach, Audrey Landers, Tyrone Power Jr., Bryan Genesse, Ken Kercheval, Ted Davis, Joyce Blair; ***D:*** Nathaniel Christian; ***W:*** Nathaniel Christian.

California Dreaming 🦴🦴 **1979 (R)** Nerdy young man heads west to California where he tries to fit in with the local beach crowd. Reminiscent of the popular beach movies of the '60s. **93m/C VHS.** Dennis Christopher, Tanya Roberts, Glynnis O'Connor, John Calvin, Seymour Cassel; ***D:*** John Hancock.

California Girls 🦴 **1984** Radio station stages a beauty contest and three sexy ladies prove to be tough competition. Features women in little swimsuits, minimal plot, and a soundtrack by the Police, Kool & the Gang, Blondie, Queen, and 10cc. **83m/C VHS.** Al Music, Mary McKinley, Alicia Allen, Lantz Douglas, Barbara Parks; ***D:*** Rick Wallace; ***C:*** Gil Hubbs.

California Gold Rush 🦴🦴 **1981** Hays portrays young aspiring writer, Bret Harte, who, in search of adventure in 1849, arrives in Sutter's Fort and takes on a job at the local sawmill. When gold is found, Sutter's Fort is soon overrun with fortune hunters whose greed, violence, and corruption threaten to tear apart the peaceful community. **100m/C VHS.** Robert Hays, John Dehner, Dan Haggerty, Ken Curtis; ***D:*** Jack B. Hively. **TV**

California Joe 🦴 **1943** California is being eyed by Confederate sympathizers and also by their leader, who wants it for his own plans. Enter California Joe, a Union officer in disguise, who will save the day. Standard western. **55m/B VHS.** Donald (Don "Red") Barry, Lynn Merrick, Helen Talbot, Wally Vernon, Twinkle Watts, Brian O'Hara, Terry Frost, Leroy Mason, Edward Earle, Charles "Blackie" King; ***D:*** Spencer Gordon Bennet; ***W:*** Norman S. Hall; ***C:*** Ernest Miller.

California Straight Ahead 🦴🦴 **1925** Denny—whose niche in the '20s was silent action comedies, and who had teamed with director Pollard earlier in the decade to produce "The Leatherpushers" series—stars in this silent actioner which features a cross-country road trip, zoo animals-on-a-rampage, and a car-racing conclusion (sounds like an action formula ahead of its time). Audiences didn't realize until the talkies that the All-American manly man was in fact played by a Brit. For those who revel in trivia, Denny appeared in the 1961 "Batman." **77m/B VHS.** Reginald Denny, Gertrude (Olmstead) Olmsted, Tom Wilson, Lucille Ward, John Steppling; ***D:*** Harry Pollard.

California Suite 🦴🦴🦴 **1978 (PG)** The posh Beverly Hills Hotel is the setting for four unrelated Neil Simon skits, ranging from a battling husband and wife to feuding friends. Smith is notable as a neurotic English actress in town for the Oscar awards while Caine is effectively low-key in the role of her bisexual husband. Simonized dialogue is crisp and funny. **103m/C VHS, DVD, Wide.** Alan Alda, Michael Caine, Bill Cosby, Jane Fonda, Walter Matthau, Richard Pryor, Maggie Smith, Elaine May; ***D:*** Herbert Ross; ***W:*** Neil Simon; ***C:*** David M. Walsh; ***M:*** Claude Bolling. Oscars '78: Support. Actress (Smith); Golden Globes '79: Actress—Mus./Comedy (Smith).

Caligula woof! **1980** Infamous, expensive, extremely graphic, and sexually explicit adaptation of the life of the mad Roman emperor, Caligula. Scenes of decapitation, necrophilia, rape, bestiality, and sadomasochism abound. Biggest question is why Gielgud, O'Toole, and McDowell lent their talents to this monumentally abhorred film (not to mention Gore Vidal on the writing end, who didn't want the credit). Adult magazine publisher Bob Guccione coproduced and didn't particularly want to release it. Also available in a censored, "R" rated version. **143m/C VHS, DVD.** *IT* Malcolm McDowell, John Gielgud, Peter O'Toole, Helen Mirren, Theresa-Ann Savoy, John Steiner, Paolo Bonacelli, Adriana Asti; ***D:*** Tinto Brass; ***W:*** Gore Vidal; ***C:*** Tinto Brass, Silvano Ippoliti; ***M:*** Paul Clemente.

Call Him Mr. Shatter 🦴 *Shatter* **1974 (R)** A hired killer stalks a tottering Third World president and becomes embroiled in international political intrigue. **90m/C VHS.** *GB* Stuart Whitman, Peter Cushing, Anton Diffring; ***D:*** Michael Carreras.

Call Me 🦴🦴 **1988 (R)** Psycho-drama about a lusty young woman who responds positively to an obscene telephone caller until she witnesses him murder another person. Doubt creeps into the relationship. **98m/C VHS.** Patricia Charbonneau, Patti D'Arbanville, Sam Freed, Boyd Gaines, Stephen McHattie; ***D:*** Sollace Mitchell.

Call Me Bwana 🦴½ **1963** Pure cornpone with Hope as a bumbling explorer sent with CIA agent Adams to track down a lost American space capsule in deepest Africa. Enemy agents Ekberg and Jeffries try to make things difficult. **103m/C VHS.** Bob Hope, Edie Adams, Anita Ekberg, Lionel Jeffries, Percy Herbert, Paul Carpenter, Orlando Martins; ***D:*** Gordon Douglas; ***W:*** Nate Monaster, Johanna Harwood.

Call Me Claus 🦴🦴 **2001** Goldberg mugs her way through her role as a TV shopping network producer with Scrooge-like tendencies. Hawthorne is the good-natured St. Nick who wants to retire and have her replace him at the yuletide gig. Might rate a few chuckles if you've seen all the good Christmas movies twice already. **90m/C VHS, DVD.** Whoopi Goldberg, Nigel Hawthorne, Taylor Negron, Brian Stokes Mitchell, Victor Garber, Gregory Bernstein, Brian Bird; ***D:*** Peter Werner; ***W:*** Sarah Bernstein; ***M:*** Garth Brooks. **TV**

Call Northside 777 🦴🦴🦴½ *Calling Northside 777* **1948** Hard-boiled Chicago reporter McNeal (Stewart) finds himself in the crux of a decade-old murder investigation when he follows up a newspaper ad offering $5,000 for any information leading to the arrest and conviction of a police killer. The cunning reporter discovers police coverups and missing evidence pointing to an imprisoned man's innocence. Powerful performance from Stewart directs this docu-drama based on the real-life story of Chicago's Joe Majczek, unjustly imprisoned for 11 years, and the Pulitzer Prize winning reporter Jim McGuire who, through a clever investigation, found enough evidence to have the case reopened. **111m/B VHS.** James Stewart, Richard Conte, Lee J. Cobb, Helen Walker, Betty Garde, Moroni Olsen, E.G. Marshall, Howard Smith, John McIntire, Paul Harvey, George Tyne, Michael Chapin, Addison Richards, Richard Rober, Eddie Dunn, Charles Lane, Walter Greaza, William Post Jr., George Melford, Charles F. Miller, Lionel Stander, Jonathan Hale; ***D:*** Henry Hathaway; ***W:*** Jerome Cady, Jay Dratler; ***C:*** Joe MacDonald; ***M:*** Alfred Newman.

Call of the Canyon 🦴½ **1942** A crooked agent for a local meat packer won't pay a fair price, so Gene goes off to talk to the head man to set him straight. **71m/B VHS.** Gene Autry, Smiley Burnette, Ruth Terry, Thurston Hall, Pat Brady; ***D:*** Joseph Santley.

Call of the Forest 🦴½ **1949** Bobby makes friends with a beautiful wild black stallion which is captured and tamed by his father. The father has found a goldmine, also desired by an villain, and Bobby and his horse must come to his father's aid. Black Diamond (the horse) has the best role. **74m/B VHS.** Robert Lowery, Ken Curtis, Martha Sherrill, Chief Thundercloud, Charles Hughes; ***D:*** John F. Link.

Call of the Rockies 🦴🦴 **1944** Action-packed oater in which Carson and Burnette ride across country to save Placer City's mine from crooked townsmen. **54m/B VHS.** Sunset Carson, Smiley Burnette; ***D:*** Lesley Selander.

Call of the Wild 🦴🦴 **1972 (PG)** Jack London's famous story about a man whose survival depends upon his knowledge of the Alaskan wilderness almost comes to life. Filmed in Finland. **105m/C VHS, DVD.** Charlton Heston, Michele Mercier, George Eastman; ***D:*** Ken Annakin; ***W:*** Harry Alan Towers, Hubert Frank; ***C:*** John Cabrera; ***M:*** Carlo Rustichelli.

Call of the Wild 🦴🦴½ **1993** Another of Jack London's survival tales is dramatized for TV. John Thornton (Schroder) is a rich greenhorn seeking adventure during the 1897 Klondike gold rush. Buck is a German shepherd, sold as a sled dog, who finds adventures of his own in the frozen North until man and dog are united to search for a legendary gold mine. The book is more exciting but the film is more violent. Filmed on location in British Columbia. **97m/C VHS.** *IT* Rick Schroder, Gordon Tootoosis, Mia Sara, Duncan Fraser, Richard Newman, Brent Stait, Allan Lysell, Tom Heaton, Eric McCormack, Vince Metcalfe; ***D:*** Alan Smithee; Michael Toshiyuki Uno; ***C:*** David Geddes; ***M:*** Lee Holdridge. **TV**

Call Out the Marines 🦴🦴 **1942** A group of army buddies re-enlist to break up a spy ring. Two of the guys fall in love with the same girl, not realizing that she's one of the spies. McLaglen and Lowe's last comedy together. Mediocre outing isn't redeemed by below average musical numbers. ♫Call Out the Marines; Zana Zaranda; The Light of My Life; Beware; Hands Across the Border. **67m/B VHS.** Edmund Lowe, Victor McLaglen, Binnie Barnes, Paul Kelly, Dorothy Lovett, Franklin Pangborn; ***D:*** Frank Ryan, William Hamilton.

Call to Glory 🦴🦴½ **1984** Pilot for the critically praised TV series. An Air Force pilot and his family face turbulent times during the Cuban missile crisis. **96m/C VHS.** Craig T. Nelson, Cindy Pickett, Gabriel Damon, Keenan Wynn, Elisabeth Shue, G.D. Spradlin, David Hollander, Kathleen Lloyd; ***D:*** Thomas Carter. **TV**

A Call to Remember 🦴🦴½ **1997 (R)** Paula Rubinek (Danner) and David Tobias (Mantegna) are concentration camp survivors who both had their spouses and children killed by the Nazis. They've married, moved to America, and are living in the suburbs with their two sons and trying to forget the past, which causes problems for their children. But Paula's quiet world explodes when she receives a phone call notifying her that a son she thought died in the war has in fact survived. Writer Eisenberg based this drama on his parents' history. **105m/C VHS.** Blythe Danner, Joe Mantegna, David Lascher, Kevin Zegers, Joe Spano, Kevin McNulty, Blu Mankuma; ***D:*** Jack Bender; ***W:*** Max Eisenberg; ***C:*** David Geddes. **CABLE**

The Caller 🦴 **1987 (R)** A strange man enters the house of a lone woman and sets off a long night of suspense and an almost longer evening of inept moviemaking. **90m/C VHS.** Malcolm McDowell, Madolyn Smith; ***D:*** Arthur Seidelman; ***M:*** Richard Band.

Callie and Son 🦴🦴 *Rags to Riches* **1981** Details the sordid story of a waitress who works her way up to become a Dallas socialite and her obsessive relationship with her illegitimate son. **97m/C VHS, VHS.** Lindsay Wagner, Dabney Coleman, Jameson Parker, Andrew Prine, James Sloyan, Michelle Pfeiffer; ***D:*** Waris Hussein; ***M:*** Billy Goldenberg.

Calling Dr. Death/Strange Confession *Strange Confession* **1943** In 1943's "Calling Dr. Death," Chaney plays a neurologist with an unfaithful wife who gets herself murdered. Naturally, Chaney's the primary suspect. In 1944's "Strange Confession" idealistic writer Chaney is made a fool of by publishing mogul Naish, who not only distorts his work but steals his wife. So Chaney plans an appropriate revenge. Based on the "The Inner Sanctum Mysteries" radio show. **124m/B VHS.** Lon Chaney Jr., J. Carrol Naish, Brenda Joyce, Patricia Morison, Ramsay Ames, David Bruce, Milburn Stone, Lloyd Bridges; ***D:*** Reginald LeBorg, John Hoffman; ***W:*** Edward Dein, M. Coates Webster.

Calling Paul Temple 🦴½ **1948** The wealthy patients of a nerve doctor have been dying and a detective is called in to investigate. **92m/B VHS.** *GB* John Bentley, Dinah Sheridan, Margaretta Scott, Abraham Sofaer, Celia Lipton, Alan Wheatley, Wally Patch; ***D:*** Maclean Rogers.

Calling Wild Bill Elliott 🦴½ **1943** The crooked territorial governor is exposed by hero Elliott and sidekick Hayes and justice is restored in this typical B-western. Elliott's first film for Republic; he went on to star in 16 Red Ryder films as well as other westerns for the studio. **55m/B VHS.** Wild Bill Elliott, George "Gabby" Hayes, Herbert (Hayes) Heyes, Anne Jeffreys, Fred Kohler Jr., Roy Barcroft, Yakima Canutt; ***D:*** Spencer Gordon Bennet.

Calm at Sunset 🦴🦴½ **1996 (PG)** James Pfeiffer (Facinelli) drops out of college to pursue his dream of becoming a commercial fisherman, much to the dismay of his parents (Moriarty, Nelligan) who already know how rough that life can be. But James gets his chance when he rescues seaman Kelly Dobbs (Conway) and the two become partners. Still, James must deal with secrets, a tragedy, and some hard decisions. TV drama with some solid performances. Based on the novel "Calm at Sunset, Calm at Dawn" by Paul Watkins. **98m/C VHS.** Peter Facinelli, Michael Moriarty, Kate Nelligan, Kevin Conway, Gretchen Mol, Melvin Van Peebles; ***D:*** Daniel Petrie; ***W:*** Pamela Gray, John Kent Harrison, David Young; ***C:*** Glen MacPherson; ***M:*** Ernest Troost. **TV**

Came a Hot Friday 🦴🦴 **1985 (PG)** Two cheap conmen arrive in a 1949 southern New Zealand town, run various scams and pursue women. **101m/C VHS.** *NZ* Peter Bland, Philip Gordon, Billy T. James; ***D:*** Ian Mune; ***C:*** Alun Bollinger.

Camel Boy 🦴½ **1984** True story of a young Arabian boy who befriends a camel and their treacherous trek across the desert. **78m/C VHS.** *AU* ***D:*** Yoram Gross; ***V:*** Michael Pate, Ron Haddrick, John Meillon.

Camelot 🦴🦴 **1967** The long-running Lerner and Loewe Broadway musical about King Arthur, Guinevere, and Lancelot was adapted from T.H. White's book, "The Once and Future King." Redgrave and Nero have chemistry as the illicit lovers, Harris is strong as the king struggling to hold together his dream, but muddled direction undermines the effort. ♫I Wonder What the King is Doing Tonight; The Simple Joys of Maidenhood; Camelot; C'est Moi; The Lusty Month of May; Follow Me; How To Handle a Woman; Then You May Take Me to the Fair; If Ever I Would Leave You. **150m/C VHS, DVD, Wide.** Richard Harris, Vanessa Redgrave, David Hemmings, Franco Nero, Lionel Jeffries; ***D:*** Joshua Logan; ***W:*** Alan Jay Lerner; ***C:*** Richard H. Kline; ***M:*** Frederick Loewe, Alan Jay Lerner. Oscars '67: Adapt. Score, Art Dir./Set Dec., Costume Des.; Golden Globes '68: Actor—Mus./Comedy (Harris), Song ("If Ever I Should Leave You"), Score.

Camera Buff 🦴🦴 *Amator* **1979** Satire on bureaucracy finds a factory worker buying a home-movie camera to film his new baby but becoming obsessed with his new toy. So he begins recording everything he sees—even things the authorities don't want shown. Polish with subtitles. **108m/C VHS.** *PL* Jerzy Stuhr, Malgorzata Zajaczkowska, Ewa Pokas, Krzysztof Zanussi; ***D:*** Krzysztof Kieslowski; ***W:*** Jerzy Stuhr, Krzysztof Kieslowski; ***M:*** Krzysztof Knittel.

The Cameraman 🦴🦴🦴🦴 **1928** After moving to MGM, Keaton made his first feature with a major studio, giving up the artistic control he had enjoyed in his previous films. Spared from the vilification of studio politics (not the case with later Keaton films) "The Cameraman" enjoyed both critical and popular success. Keaton's inept tintype portrait-maker has a heart that pitter-patters for an MGM office girl. He hopes to impress her by joining the ranks of the newsreel photographers. Fortuitously poised to grab a photo scoop on a Chinese tong war, he is forced to return empty-handed when an organ-grinder's monkey absconds with his first-hand footage. Silent with a musical score. **78m/B VHS.** Buster Keaton, Marceline Day, Harold Goodwin, Harry Gribbon, Sidney Bracy, Edward Brophy, Vernon Dent, William Irving; ***D:*** Edward Sedgwick.

Cameron's Closet 🦴½ **1989 (R)** Every child's nightmare comes true. A young boy is convinced that a monster lives in his closet due to his perverse father's psychological tortures. Only this time the monster is real! **86m/C VHS.** Cotter Smith, Mel Harris, Scott Curtis, Chuck McCann, Leigh McCloskey, Kim Lankford, Tab Hunter; ***D:*** Armand Mastroianni; ***W:*** Gary Brandner; ***C:*** Russell Carpenter.

Camila 🦴🦴🦴 **1984** The true story of the tragic romance between an Argentinean socialite and a Jesuit priest in 1847. The two lovers escape to a small provincial village where they live together as man and wife. Eventually they are recognized and condemned to death. Available in Spanish with English subtitles or dubbed into English. **105m/C VHS.** *AR SP* Susu Pecoraro, Imanol Arias, Hector Alterio, Elena Tasisto; ***D:*** Maria-Luisa Bemberg.

Camilla 🦴🦴½ **1994 (PG-13)** Tandy is delightful in her last starring role as a former violinist on the run with frustrated musician Fonda. Oafish son (Chaykin) and insensitive husband (Koteas) just don't understand, so its time to head to Toronto, site of a fondly, if perhaps incorrectly, remembered triumph. Sort of a May-December female-bonding roadtrip with lots of conversation and comic asides. An inevitably poignant pairing of Tandy and real-life husband Cronyn offers the chance to experience one of America's greatest acting teams one last time. Lack of stereotyping and fairly novel twist on the road movie keep this one on the highway. **91m/C VHS.** Jessica Tandy, Bridget Fonda, Hume Cronyn, Elias Koteas, Maury Chaykin, Graham Greene; ***D:*** Deepa Mehta; ***W:*** Paul Quarrington; ***M:*** Daniel Lanois.

Camille 🦴🦴 **1921** Dying courtesan falls in love with innocent young man in the Dumas classic. Valentino in his prime. **55m/B VHS.** Rudolph Valentino, Alla Nazimova; ***D:*** Fred Niblo.

Camille 🦴🦴🦴½ **1936** Marguerite (Garbo) has found success as Parisian courtesan "La Dame aux Camille" but has never found love. Until she unwisely falls for a handsome but innocent, young aristocrat, Armand (Taylor). Still, Camille agrees to give him up, realizing her scandalous past will jeopardize his future. Oh yes, then she contracts TB and fades away beautifully in gowns by Adrian. This classic Alexandre Dumas story somehow manages to escape the cliches and stands as one of the most telling monuments to Garbo's unique magic and presence on film. **108m/B VHS.** Greta Garbo, Robert Taylor, Lionel Barrymore, Henry Daniell, Elizabeth Allan, Rex O'Malley, Lenore Ulric, Laura Hope Crews; ***D:*** George Cukor; ***W:*** Frances Marion, James Hilton, Zoe Akins; ***C:*** William H. Daniels; ***M:*** Herbert Stothart. N.Y. Film Critics '37: Actress (Garbo).

Camille Claudel 🦴🦴🦴 **1989 (R)** A lushly romantic version of the art world in the late 19th century, when art was exploding in new forms and independence for women was unheard of. Young sculptor Claudel's (Adjani) tragic love for art, Auguste Rodin (the larger-than-life Depardieu), and independence clash, costing her sanity and her confinement to an insitution for the last 30 years of her life. Very long, it requires an attentive and thoughtful viewing. In French with English subtitles. **149m/C VHS, DVD, Wide.** *FR* Isabelle Adjani, Gerard Depardieu, Laurent Grevill, Alain Cuny, Madeleine Robinson, Katrine Boorman, Daniele Lebrun; ***D:*** Bruno Nuytten; ***W:*** Bruno Nuytten, Marilyn Goldin; ***C:*** Pierre Lhomme; ***M:*** Gabriel Yared. Cesar '89: Actress (Adjani), Art Dir./Set Dec., Cinematog., Costume Des., Film.

Camille 2000 🦴½ **1969** Dumas meets Debbie Does Rome in this artier than thou mess. Unreasonably well endowed Marguerite (Gaubert) spends much horizontal time with Rome's decadent society denizens while pining pitifully for tru luv Armand (Castelnuovo). She dies a horrible death in the end, but her disease's initials aren't TB. **115m/C VHS, DVD.** Silvana Venturelli, Massimo Serato, Daniele Gaubert, Nino Castelnuovo, Eleanora Rossi-Drago; ***D:*** Radley Metzger; ***W:*** Michael DeForrest; ***C:*** Ennio Guarnieri; ***M:*** Piero Piccioni.

Camorra: The Naples Connection 🦴🦴 *Un Complicato Intrigo Di Donne, Vicoli E Delitti* **1985 (R)** A prostitute and an American drug dealer find themselves embroiled in the murders of Neapolitan Mafia heads. Violent, overblown, minor Wertmuller. **94m/C VHS.** *IT* Harvey Keitel, Angela Molina, Lorraine Bracco, Francesco Rabal; ***D:*** Lina Wertmuller; ***W:*** Lina Wertmuller.

Camouflage 🦴🦴½ **2000 (R)** Dumb, blond but likeable actor Marty Mackenzie (Munro) wants to perfect his tough-guy persona so he decides to apprentice with old-timer PI Jack Potter (Nielsen). But the routine surveillance case that Jack assigns Marty to turns out to be the tip of a deadly iceberg. It's a goof but don't expect "Naked Gun" type humor. **98m/C VHS, DVD.** Leslie Nielsen, Lochlyn Munro, Vanessa Angel, William Forsythe; ***D:*** James Keach; ***W:*** Tom Epperson, Billy Bob Thornton; ***C:*** Glen MacPherson. **VIDEO**

Camp Cucamonga: How I Spent My Summer Vacation 🦴 **1990** Zany antics at summer camp abound when Camp Cucamonga's owner mistakes the new handyman for the camp inspector. Well-known stars from TV's "Cheers," "The Jeffersons," "The Wonder Years," and "The Love Boat" are featured in this silly flick. **100m/C VHS.** John Ratzenberger, Sherman Hemsley, Josh Saviano, Danica McKellar, Chad Allen, Dorothy Lyman, Lauren Tewes, G. Gordon Liddy; ***D:*** Roger Duchowny. **TV**

Camp Nowhere 🦴🦴 **1994 (PG)** Video fodder for the juniors in the household as kids turn tables on parents. Instead of trudging off to summer camp for the umpteenth time, a group of upscale kids create their own with the help of laid-off drama teacher Lloyd, who must first con their parents into believing that Camp Nowhere is legit. What follows is that very special summer camp in the Hollywood tradition with lots of junk food, video games galore, and of course, no rules. Camp beserko formula good for a few laughs. **106m/C VHS.** Christopher Lloyd, Wendy Makkena, M. Emmet Walsh, Peter Scolari, Peter Onorati, Ray Baker, Kate Mulgrew, Jonathan Jackson, Romy Walthall, Maryedith Burrell, Thomas F. Wilson, Nathan Cavaleri, Andrew Keegan, Melody Kay; ***D:*** Jonathan Prince; ***W:*** Andrew Kurtzman, Eliot Wald; ***C:*** Sandi Sissel.

The Campus Corpse 🦴 **1977 (PG)** Young man stumbles into deadly college frat hazing and discovers he and rest of cast are utterly devoid of acting ability. **92m/C VHS.** Charles Martin Smith, Jeff East, Brad Davis; ***D:*** Douglas Curtis.

Campus Knights 🦴 **1929** If you're a serious student of the campus caper film, this is one of the earliest (though not one of the best) of the genre (if such a distinction can be made). The story involves twin brothers—one a tweedy high-browed professor, the other a bon vivant man about town—who wreak fraternal chaos on the quads. **70m/B VHS.** Raymond (Ray) McKee, Shirley Palmer, Marie Quillen, Jean Laverty, Sybil Grove; ***D:*** Albert Kelly.

Campus Man 🦴 **1987 (PG)** An entrepreneurial college student markets a beefcake calendar featuring his best friend, until the calendar's sales threaten his friend's amateur athletic status. **94m/C VHS.** John Dye, Steve Lyon, Kim Delaney, Miles O'Keeffe, Morgan Fairchild, Kathleen Wilhoite; ***D:*** Ron Casden; ***W:*** Geoffrey Baere; ***M:*** James Newton Howard.

Can-Can 🦴🦴 **1960** Lackluster screen adaptation of the Cole Porter musical bears little resemblance to the stage version. MacLaine is a cafe owner who goes to court to try and get the "Can-Can," a dance considered risque in gay Paree at the end of the 19th century, made legal. Love interest Sinatra happens to be a lawyer. ♫C'est Manifique; Let's Do It; I Love Paris; You Do Something to Me; It's All Right With Me; Live and Let Live; Come Along With Me; Just One of Those Things. **131m/C VHS, Wide.** Frank Sinatra, Shirley MacLaine, Maurice Chevalier, Louis Jourdan, Juliet Prowse, Marcel Dalio, Leon Belasco; ***D:*** Walter Lang; ***C:*** William H. Daniels.

Can I Do It...Till I Need Glasses? woof! **1977** More to the point, can you stay awake till the end? Prurient juvenile junk. Brief Williams footage was grafted to this mess during 15 minutes of Mork fame. **72m/C VHS.** Robin Williams, Roger Behr, Debra Klose, Moose Carlson, Walter Olkewicz; ***D:*** I. Robert Levy.

Can of Worms 🦴🦴½ **2000** When young Mike Pillsbury's science project goes wrong, he sends a message into outer space to be rescued from his dismal life on Earth. But he certainly isn't expecting aliens to hear his plea and come to his aid. **88m/C VHS.** Malcolm McDowell, Adam Wylie, Michael Schulman, Erika Christensen, Lee Garlington, Brighton Hertford, Terry David Mulligan; ***D:*** Paul Schneider. **CABLE**

Can She Bake a Cherry Pie? 🦴🦴 **1983** Two offbeat characters meet and fall in love in an odd sort of way. Slow-moving and talky but somewhat rewarding. One of Black's better performances. **90m/C VHS.** Karen Black, Michael Emil, Michael Margotta, Frances Fisher, Martin Frydberg; ***D:*** Henry Jaglom; ***W:*** Henry Jaglom; ***M:*** Karen Black.

Can You Feel Me Dancing? 🦴🦴 **1985** Family-happy lightweight entertainment coproduced by Kent Bateman and starring Bateman progeny Jason and Justine as brother and sister, a novel premise that only a father could love. A blind independence-impaired teenager tries to liberate herself from her overbearing family, and finds the secret to conquering her fears and to standing up for herself when she falls in love. Written by spouse-team Steven and J. Miyoko Hensley. **95m/C VHS.** Jason Bateman, Justine Bateman; ***D:*** Michael Miller; ***W:*** Steven Hensley, J. Miyoko Hensley.

Can You Hear the Laughter? The Story of Freddie Prinze 🦴🦴 **1979** Heartstring tugging biography of the late Puerto Rican comedian whose troubled life lead to suicide in spite of his apparent success. He was most noted for his starring role in "Chico and the Man." **100m/C VHS.** Ira Angustain, Kevin Hooks, Randee Heller, Devon Ericson, Julie Carmen, Stephen Elliott; ***D:*** Burt Brinckerhoff.

Canada's Sweetheart: The Saga of Hal C. Banks 🦴🦴 *Sweetheart!* **1985** True story of Banks, hired by the Canadian government to break up a strike among the communist-led seaman's union which had put a stranglehold on Canadian commerce, and who was eventually convicted of strong-arm tactics. **115m/C VHS.** *CA* Maury Chaykin, Colin Fox, R.H. Thomson, Sean McCann; ***D:*** Donald Brittain; ***W:*** Donald Brittain; ***C:*** Andreas Poulsson; ***M:*** Eldon Rathburn; ***Nar:*** Donald Brittain. Toronto-City '85: Canadian Feature Film.

Canadian Bacon 🦴½ **1994 (PG)** Regrettably amateurish satire (with some sharp observations) serves as the feature film debut for Moore, who irritated many with "Roger & Me." Title refers to the military code name for a campaign to whip up anti-Canadian hysteria and justify a U.S. invasion of its neighbor to the north. Evil political advisor Pollak convinces well-meaning but inept President Alda that it's just the thing to get the presidential popularity up and those defense industries humming. Ugly Americans abound, at expense of polite Canadians, eh? Filmed in Toronto, which is shown to good advantage. Candy in one of last roles is the superpatriotic sheriff of Niagara Falls, New York. **110m/C VHS, DVD, Wide.** Alan Alda, Kevin Pollak, John Candy, Rhea Perlman, Rip Torn, Bill Nunn, Kevin J. O'Connor, Steven Wright, G.D. Spradlin, James Belushi, Wallace Shawn, Dan Aykroyd; ***Cameos:*** Michael Moore; ***D:*** Michael Moore; ***W:*** Michael Moore; ***C:*** Haskell Wexler; ***M:*** Elmer Bernstein, Peter Bernstein.

Cancel My Reservation 🦴 **1972 (G)** New York talk show host Hope sets out for a vacation on an Arizona ranch, but winds up in trouble due to a mysterious corpse, a rich rancher, and an enigmatic mystic. Even more muddled than it sounds. Based on the novel "Broken Gun" by Louis L'Amour, with pointless cameos by Crosby, Wayne, and Wilson. **99m/C VHS.** Bob Hope, Eva Marie Saint, Ralph Bellamy, Anne Archer, Forrest Tucker, Keenan Wynn, Flip Wilson, Noriyuki "Pat" Morita, Chief Dan George; ***Cameos:*** John Wayne, Bing Crosby, Doodles Weaver; ***D:*** Paul Bogart; ***W:*** Arthur Marx; ***C:*** Russell Metty.

The Candidate 🦴🦴🦴 **1972 (PG)** Realistic, satirical look at politics and political campaigning. Bill McKay (Redford) is a telegenic, idealistic lawyer whose father (Douglas) was once governor of California. Uninterested in politics, Bill is eventually persuaded to run for the Senate against bluff incumbent Jarman (Porter). Bill refuses to follow the party line but discovers the lure of political power when he begins to gain in the polls. Director Ritchie also worked with Redford on "Downhill Racer." **105m/C VHS, DVD.** Robert Redford, Peter Boyle, Don Porter, Allen (Goorwitz) Garfield, Karen Carlson, Melvyn Douglas, Michael Lerner; ***D:*** Michael Ritchie; ***W:*** Jeremy Larner; ***C:*** John Korty, Victor Kemper; ***M:*** John Rubinstein. Oscars '72: Story & Screenplay; Writers Guild '72: Orig. Screenplay.

Candles at Nine 🦴½ **1944** An innocent showgirl must spend a month in her late uncle's creepy mansion in order to inherit it, much to the malevolent chagrin of the rest of the family who want the place and the loot for themselves. Uninspired. **84m/B VHS.** *GB* Jessie Matthews, John Stuart, Reginald Purdell; ***D:*** John Harlow.

Candleshoe 🦴🦴 **1978 (G)** A Los Angeles street urchin poses as an English matron's long lost granddaughter in order to steal a fortune hidden in Candleshoe, her country estate, where Niven butlers. Somewhat slapschticky Disney fare. **101m/C VHS, DVD.** Vivian Pickles, Helen Hayes, David Niven, Jodie Foster, Leo McKern; ***D:*** Norman Tokar; ***W:*** Rosemary Anne Sisson, David Swift; ***C:*** Paul Beeson; ***M:*** Ronald Goodwin.

Candy 🦴🦴 **1968 (R)** Sexual satire, based on the book by Terry Southern and Mason Hoffenberg, can't sustain its simple premise. The teenaged nubile, blonde, and naive title character (Aulin) sets out to discover her sexual awakening and gets chased by every kook she meets, including guru Brando, alcohlic poet Burton, gardener Starr, general Matthau, hunchback Aznavour, surgeon Coburn, and even her own dad, Astin. Very much of part of its psychedelic age. **124m/C VHS, DVD, Wide.** *FR IT* Ewa Aulin, Marlon Brando, Charles Aznavour, Richard Burton, Ringo Starr, James Coburn, Walter Matthau, John Huston, John Astin, Elsa Martinelli, Anita Pallenberg, "Sugar Ray" Robinson; ***D:*** Christian Marquand; ***W:*** Buck Henry; ***C:*** Giuseppe Rotunno.

Candy Mountain 🦴🦴 **1987 (R)** Guitar playin' O'Connor roadtrips across America and Canada in search of a legendary guitar maker Yulin. Occasional interest derives from musician cameos from the likes of Buster Poindexter, Dr. John and Redbone. **90m/C VHS.** *FR SI CA* Kevin J. O'Connor, Harris Yulin, Tom Waits, Bulle Ogier, David Johansen, Leon Redbone, Joe Strummer, Roberts Blossom; ***Cameos:*** Rita MacNeil, Laurie Metcalf; ***D:*** Robert Frank; ***W:*** Rudy Wurlitzer.

Candy Stripe Nurses 🦴 *Sweet Candy* **1974 (R)** Even hard-core Roger Corman fans might find his final installment in the nursing comedy pentad to be a lethargic exercise in gratuitous "sexual situations." Bet those uniforms don't meet hospital standards. The previous films in the series are: "The Student Nurses," "Private Duty Nurses," "Night Call Nurses," and "The Young Nurses." **80m/C VHS.** Candice Rialson, Robin Mattson, Maria Rojo, Kimberly Hyde, Dick Miller, Stanley Ralph Ross, Monte Landis, Tom Baker, Don Keefer, Sally Kirkland, Rick Gates; ***D:*** Allan Holleb.

Candy Tangerine Man 1975 Respectable businessman leads a double life as loving father and LA pimp. **88m/C VHS.** John Daniels, Tom Hankerson, Eli Haines, Marva Farmer, George "Buck" Flower; *D:* Matt Cimber.

Candyman 1992 (R) Terrifying tale from horror maven Clive Barker is an effective combination of American gothic, academia, and urban squalor. A search for dissertation material leads graduate student Helen Lyle (Madsen) into gang-infested housing. There she encounters the urban myth of Candyman, the son of a former slave who was lynched and is now back with a hook and a vendetta. Filled with the appropriate amount of yucky stuff, yet successfully employs subtle scare tactics and plausible characters. **98m/C VHS, DVD, 8mm, Wide.** Virginia Madsen, Tony Todd, Xander Berkeley, Kasi Lemmons, Vanessa Williams, DeJuan Guy, Michael Culkin, Gilbert Lewis, Stanley DeSantis; *D:* Bernard Rose; *W:* Bernard Rose; *C:* Anthony B. Richmond; *M:* Philip Glass.

Candyman 2: Farewell to the Flesh 1994 (R) Explains the origins of the urban bogeyman called Candyman—the man, the hook, and the bees. Rehashes the same old scare tactics from previous and better horror movies and uses cheesy special effects. The sensual background of New Orleans during Mardi Gras can't help this stale sequel. Embrace this "Farewell" from a distance. Based on stories by Clive Barker. **99m/C VHS, DVD, Wide.** Tony Todd, Kelly Rowan, Veronica Cartwright, Timothy Carhart, William O'Leary, Bill Nunn, Fay Hauser; *D:* Bill Condon; *W:* Rand Ravich, Mark Kruger; *C:* Tobias Schliessler; *M:* Philip Glass.

Candyman 3: Day of the Dead 1998 (R) The Candyman (Todd) haunts an L.A. descendent (D'Errico), framing her for murder, in the hopes that she will join him. **93m/C VHS, DVD.** Tony Todd, Donna D'Errico, Nick Corri, Lupe Ontiveros; *D:* Turi Meyer; *W:* Turi Meyer, Al Septien; *C:* Michael G. Wojciechowski. **VIDEO**

Cannery Row ½ 1982 (PG) Baseball has-been Nolte lives anonymously among the downtrodden in the seamy part of town and carries on with working girl girlfriend Winger. Based on John Steinbeck's "Cannery Row" and "Sweet Thursday." **120m/C VHS.** Nick Nolte, Debra Winger, Audra Lindley, M. Emmet Walsh, Frank McRae, James Keane, Lloyd "Sunshine" Parker; *D:* David S. Ward; *W:* David S. Ward; *C:* Sven Nykvist; *M:* Jack Nitzsche; *Nar:* John Huston.

Cannes Man 1996 (R) Features legendary Hollywood producer Sy Lerner (Cassel), who vows to make unknown cabbie/screenwriter Frank Rhinoslavsky (Quinn) a star, all while being schmoozed at Cannes by stars who want to be in his latest epic, while he tries to find backers for his unwritten script. **88m/C VHS.** Seymour Cassel, Francesco Quinn, Rebecca Broussand; *D:* Richard Martini.

Cannibal Apocalypse woof! *Cannibals in the Streets; Savage Apocalypse; The Slaughterers; Cannibals in the City; Virus; Invasion of the Flesh Hunters* 1980 Group of tortured Vietnam veterans returns home carrying a cannibalistic curse with them. Smorgasbord of gore and sensationalism is not for discriminating tastes. **96m/C VHS, DVD, Wide.** *IT* John Saxon, Elizabeth Turner, John Morghen, Tony King; *D:* Anthony (Antonio Margheriti) Dawson; *W:* Anthony (Antonio Margheriti) Dawson, Dardano Sacchetti, Jimmy Gould; *C:* Fernando Arribas; *M:* Alexander Blonksteiner.

Cannibal Campout 1988 Crazed orphans with eating disorders make square meal of coed babes getting back to nature. **89m/C VHS.** Carrie Lindell, Richard Marcus, Amy Chludzinski, Jon McBride; *D:* Jon McBride, Tom Fisher.

Cannibal Man *The Apartment on the 13 Floor; La Semana del Asesino; Week of the Killer* 1971 Slaughterhouse worker Marcos (Parra) accidentally kills a man in a fight and then covers up the incident with more killings. Then he's got to get rid of all those dead bodies and what better place than at the butcher's where he works. **98m/C VHS, DVD.** *SP* Vicente Parra, Emma Cohen, Eusebio Poncela; *D:* Eloy De La Iglesia; *W:* Eloy De La Iglesia.

Cannibal! The Musical 1996 (R) Only those wacky people at Troma could offer a horror/musical about a group of 1883 gold miners who get lost in the Colorado Rockies, have some strange adventures, and eventually wind up as dinner to cannibal Alferd Packer (who's telling his version of the story to a female reporter while in prison). Seven rather tedious musical numbers lead up to the gore-splashed finale. From director Trey Parker, who also repulses (and amuses us) with TV's "South Park." **105m/C VHS, DVD.** Ian Hardin, Jason McHugh, Matt Stone, Trey Parker, Juan Schwartz; *D:* Trey Parker; *W:* Trey Parker.

Cannibal Women in the Avocado Jungle of Death ½ 1989 (PG-13) Tongue-in-cheek cult classic features erstwhile playmate Tweed as feminist anthropologist who searches with ditzy student and mucho macho male guide for lost tribe of cannibal women who dine on their mates. Lawton directed under the alias "J.D. Athens." **90m/C VHS, DVD.** Shannon Tweed, Adrienne Barbeau, Karen Mistal, Barry Primus, Bill Maher, Jim MacKrell, Brett Stimely, Paul Ross; *D:* J.F. Lawton, J.D. Athens; *W:* J.F. Lawton, J.D. Athens; *C:* Robert Knouse; *M:* Carl Dante.

Cannonball *Carquake* 1976 (PG) Assorted ruthless people leave patches of rubber across the country competing for grand prize in less than legal auto race. Not top drawer New World but nonetheless a cult fave. Inferior to Bartel's previous cult classic, "Death Race 2000." Most interesting for plethora of cult cameos, including Scorsese, Dante, and grandmaster Corman. **93m/C VHS.** *HK* Martin Scorsese, Roger Corman, Joe Dante, Paul Bartel, David Carradine, Bill McKinney, Veronica Hamel, Gerrit Graham, Robert Carradine, Jonathan Kaplan, Belinda Balaski, Judy Canova, Carl Gottlieb, Archie Hahn, Sylvester Stallone, Dick Miller, Mary Woronov; *D:* Paul Bartel; *W:* Paul Bartel, Donald Stewart; *C:* Tak Fujimoto; *M:* David A. Axelrod.

Cannonball Run ½ 1981 (PG) So many stars, so little plot. Reynolds and sidekick DeLuise disguise themselves as paramedics to foil cops while they compete in cross-country Cannonball race. Shows no sign of having been directed by an ex-stuntman. One of 1981's top grossers—go figure. Followed by equally languid sequel "Cannonball Run II." **95m/C VHS, DVD, Wide.** Burt Reynolds, Farrah Fawcett, Roger Moore, Dom DeLuise, Dean Martin, Sammy Davis Jr., Jack Elam, Adrienne Barbeau, Peter Fonda, Molly Picon, Bert Convy, Jamie Farr; *D:* Hal Needham; *W:* Brock Yates; *C:* Michael C. Butler; *M:* Al Capps.

Cannonball Run 2 1984 (PG) More mindless cross-country wheel spinning with gratuitous star cameos. Director Needham apparently subscribes to the two wrongs make a right school of sequels. **109m/C VHS, DVD.** Burt Reynolds, Dom DeLuise, Jamie Farr, Marilu Henner, Shirley MacLaine, Jim Nabors, Frank Sinatra, Sammy Davis Jr., Dean Martin, Telly Savalas, Susan Anton, Catherine Bach, Jack Elam, Sid Caesar, Ricardo Montalban, Charles Nelson Reilly, Henry Silva, Tim Conway, Don Knotts, Molly Picon, Jackie Chan; *D:* Hal Needham; *W:* Harvey Miller; *C:* Nick McLean; *M:* Steve Dorff.

Can't Buy Me Love ½ 1987 (PG-13) Unpopular high school nerd Dempsey buys a month of dates with teen babe Peterson for $1000 in order to win friends and influence people. Semi-amusing and earnest in a John Hughes Lite kind of way. Previously known as "Boy Rents Girl." **94m/C VHS.** Patrick Dempsey, Amanda Peterson, Dennis Dugan, Courtney Gains, Seth Green, Katrina Caspary, Sharon Farrell, Darcy Demoss, Devin Devasquez, Eric Bruskotter, Gerardo Mejia, Ami Dolenz, Max Perlich; *D:* Steve Rash; *W:* Michael Swerdlick; *C:* Peter Collister; *M:* Robert Folk.

Can't Hardly Wait *The Party* 1998 (PG-13) Writer-directors Kaplan and Elfont attempt to reheat the John Hughes 80s teen-party-and-angst casserole for the kids of the 90s. Unfortunately, it's lost its flavor. All of your favorite high school cardboard cut-ups are here. Jock-jerk Mike (Facinelli) dumps teen queen Amanda (Hewitt) on the eve of a graduation blowout. Shy, sensitive Preston (Embry), who believes himself linked to Amanda by fate and their mutual love of toaster pastry, decides this is his opportunity to finally tell her how he feels. Frolicking in the background are your stereotypical foreign exchange students, stoners, geeks, metal heads, jocks and bimbos herded around by the ever-present Girl Whose Party It Is. Wavers between (unsuccessfully) trying to be thoughtful like "American Graffiti" and thoughtless like "Animal House." **101m/C VHS, DVD.** Ethan (Randall) Embry, Jennifer Love Hewitt, Peter Facinelli, Charlie Korsmo, Seth Green, Jerry O'Connell, Lauren Ambrose, Jenna Elfman, Michelle Brookhurst, Erik Palladino; *D:* Harry Elfont, Deborah Kaplan; *W:* Harry Elfont, Deborah Kaplan; *C:* Lloyd Ahern; *M:* David Kitay, Matthew Sweet.

Can't Help Singing ½ 1945 In 1849, willful heiress Caroline (Durbin) ignores her senator father's (Collins) wishes and heads west to marry her Army sweetheart (Bruce). But on the wagon train she falls for wagon master Lawlor (Paige), who's a better guy anyway. Durbin's first color musical. **90m/C VHS.** Deanna Durbin, Robert Paige, David Bruce, Akim Tamiroff, Leonid Kinskey, Ray Collins, June Vincent, Thomas Gomez; *D:* Frank Ryan; *W:* Frank Ryan, Lewis R. Foster; *C:* Elwood "Woody" Bredell, William Howard Greene; *M:* Hans J. Salter, Jerome Kern, E.Y. Harburg.

Can't Stop the Music woof! 1980 (PG) Retired model invites friends from Greenwich Village to a party to help the career of her roommate, an aspiring composer. Disco inferno that nearly reaches heights of surreal ineptness. Put it in a time capsule and let the people of the future decide what the heck was going on in the '70s. Features two of the top hits by the Village People. ♫Y.M.C.A.; Macho Man; Give Me a Break; The Sound of the City; Samantha; I'm a Singing Juggler; Sophistication; Liberation; I Love You to Death. **120m/C VHS, DVD, Wide.** Valerie Perrine, Bruce Jenner, Steve Guttenberg, Paul Sand, Leigh Taylor-Young, Village People; *D:* Nancy Walker; *W:* Bronte Woodard, Allan Carr; *C:* Bill Butler; *M:* Jacques Morali. Golden Raspberries '80: Worst Picture, Worst Screenplay.

A Canterbury Tale 1944 Writer-director team Powell and Pressburger have loosely modeled a retelling of Chaucer's famous tale of a pilgrimage to the cathedral in Canterbury. Set in Nazi-threatened Britain in 1944, the story follows the pilgrimage of three Brits and an American GI to the eponymous cathedral. Strange, effective, worth looking at. The 95-minute American version, with added footage of Kim Hunter, is inferior to the 124-minute original. **124m/B VHS.** *GB* Eric Portman, Sheila Sim, Dennis Price, Esmond Knight, Charles Hawtrey, Hay Petrie; *D:* Michael Powell, Emeric Pressburger.

The Canterbury Tales *I Racconti di Canterbury* 1971 Four Chaucer tales, most notably "The Merchant's Tale" and "The Wife of Bath," are recounted by travelers, with director Pasolini as the bawdy poet. Deemed obscene by the Italian courts, it's the second entry in Pasolini's medieval "Trilogy of Life," preceded by "The Decameron" and followed by "The Arabian Nights." In Italian with English subtitles. **109m/C VHS, DVD.** *IT* Laura Betti, Ninetto Davoli, Pier Paolo Pasolini, Hugh Griffith, Josephine Chaplin, Michael Balfour, Jenny Runacre; *D:* Pier Paolo Pasolini; *W:* Pier Paolo Pasolini; *C:* Tonino Delli Colli; *M:* Ennio Morricone. Berlin Intl. Film Fest. '72: Golden Berlin Bear.

The Canterville Ghost ½ 1944 Laughton, a 300-year-old ghost with a yellow streak, is sentenced to spook a castle until he proves he's not afraid of his own shadow. American troops stay at the castle during WWII, and, as luck would have it, soldier Young is distantly related to spunky young keeper of the castle O'Brien, ghost Laughton's descendant. Once Young is acquainted with his cowardly ancestor, he begins to fear a congenital yellow streak, and both struggle to be brave despite themselves. Vaguely derived from an Oscar Wilde tale. **95m/B VHS.** Charles Laughton, Robert Young, Margaret O'Brien, William Gargan, Reginald Owen, Rags Ragland, Una O'Connor, Peter Lawford, Mike Mazurki; *D:* Jules Dassin; *W:* Edwin Blum; *M:* George Bassman.

The Canterville Ghost 1991 During a family's vacation in an old English manor, they run into a ghost who is doomed to haunt the place until he can overcome his fears. Problems start when the family tries to scare him away. From the "Wonderworks" family movie series. **58m/C VHS.** Richard Kiley, Mary Wickes, Shelley Fabares; *D:* William Claxton.

The Canterville Ghost ½ 1996 (PG) Stewart is the highlight of this updated TV version of the Oscar Wilde short story. He's the cursed Elizabethan spirit of Sir Simon de Canterville, doomed to haunt the family mansion until a prophecy is fulfilled. But he's not happy with a family of American intruders, until teenager Virginia (Campbell) discovers Sir Simon and realizes she may hold the key to freeing the unhappy ghost. **91m/C VHS, DVD.** Patrick Stewart, Neve Campbell, Ed Wiley, Cherie Lunghi, Donald Sinden, Joan Sims, Leslie Phillips, Ciaran Fitzgerald, Daniel Betts, Raymond Pickard; *D:* Syd Macartney; *W:* Robert Benedetto; *C:* Denis Lewiston; *M:* Ernest Troost.

The Cantor's Son ½ *Dem Khann's Zindl* 1937 Real-life story based on Moishe Oysher's life, vaguely influenced by Jolson's "Jazz Singer." Runaway Oysher joins troupe of performers as a youth, travels to the shores of America, and finds fame once his beautiful voice is discovered. Returning to his mother country to celebrate his parents' golden anniversary, he encounters his childhood sweetheart and falls in love, but another woman is written into the plot to complicate matters. Poorly acted, laughable staging. In Yiddish with English subtitles. **90m/B VHS.** Judith Abarbanel, Florence Weiss, Moishe Oysher, Isadore Cashier; *D:* Ilya Motyleff.

Canvas: The Fine Art of Crime 1992 (R) A ruthless, underhanded art gallery owner recruits a desperate young artist into his art stealing schemes. The artist learns how to steal, but decides he wants out after his burglary partner has a brush with death. The gallery owner, however, wants one last job completed. **94m/C VHS.** Gary Busey, John Rhys-Davies, Vittorio Rossi, Nick Cavaiola, Cary Lawrence; *D:* Alain Zaloum.

Canyon Passage 1946 Rip-roarin' western set in the Oregon Territory in 1856. Stuart (Andrews) is a former scout turned store owner who falls for Lucy (Hayward), who happens to be the fiancee of banker/gambler Camrose (Donlevy). Camrose gets into money troubles, there's a villain named Bragg (Bond), and a pretty spectacular Indian attack. Carmichael serves as the wandering minstrel to the action, singing four songs. Director Tourneur was best known for his horror films. **92m/C VHS.** Dana Andrews, Brian Donlevy, Susan Hayward, Ward Bond, Hoagy Carmichael, Lloyd Bridges, Andy Devine, Patricia Roc; *D:* Jacques Tourneur; *W:* Ernest Pascal; *C:* Edward Cronjager; *M:* Frank Skinner.

Cape Fear ½ 1961 Former prosecutor turned small-town lawyer Peck and his family are plagued by the sadistic attentions of criminal Mitchum, who just finished a six year sabbatical at the state pen courtesy of prosecutor Peck. Taut and creepy; Mitchum's a consummate psychopath. Based on (and far superior to) John MacDonald's "The Executioners." Don't pass this one up in favor of the Scorsese remake. **106m/B VHS, DVD, Wide.** Gregory Peck, Robert Mitchum, Polly Bergen, Martin Balsam, Telly Savalas, Jack Kruschen, Lori Martin; *D:* J. Lee Thompson; *C:* Sam Leavitt; *M:* Bernard Herrmann.

Cape Fear 1991 (R) Scorsese takes on this terrifying tale of brutality and manipulation (previously filmed in 1961) and cranks it up a notch as a paroled convict haunts the lawyer who put him away. Great cast, a rollercoaster of suspense. Note the cameos by Mitchum, Peck, and Balsam, stars of the first version. Original source material was "The Executioners" by John D. MacDonald. Breath-taking rollercoaster of a film. Elmer Bernstein adapted the original score by Bernard Herrmann. **128m/C VHS, DVD, Wide.** Robert Mitchum, Gregory Peck, Martin Balsam, Robert De Niro, Nick Nolte, Jessica Lange, Juliette Lewis, Joe Don Baker, Illeana Douglas, Fred Dalton Thompson; ***D:*** Martin Scorsese; ***W:*** Wesley Strick; ***C:*** Freddie Francis; ***M:*** Bernard Herrmann, Elmer Bernstein.

Caper of the Golden Bulls 🦴 *Carnival of Thieves* **1967** Former bank robber Boyd is blackmailed into joining a group of safecrackers who plan to assault the Royal Bank of Spain during the annual Santa Maria bull run. More like siesta of the golden bulls. **104m/C VHS.** Stephen Boyd, Yvette Mimieux, Giovanna Ralli, Walter Slezak, Vito Scotti; ***D:*** Russell Rouse.

Capitaine Conan 🦴🦴🦴 *Captain Conan* **1996** On the Bulgarian border in 1918, during the last clashes of WWI, Conan (Torreton) is a fearless, impulsive warrior, reserving his respect only for his men. Although armistice is finally declared, the troops stationed in the Balkans are not demobilized and become increasingly fractious. This causes a rift between Conan and his educated friend Norbert (Le Bihan), who's been appointed a military legal representative. They are warily reunited in defense of a soldier (Val) charged with desertion, while still dealing with the ravages of the long conflict. Adapted from the book by Roger Vercel; French with subtitles. **129m/C VHS, DVD, Wide.** *FR* Philippe Torreton, Samuel Le Bihan, Bernard Le Coq, Francois Berleand, Claude Rich, Catherine Rich, Pierre Val; ***D:*** Bertrand Tavernier; ***W:*** Bertrand Tavernier, Jean Cosmos; ***C:*** Alain Choquart; ***M:*** Oswald D'Andrea. Cesar '97: Actor (Torreton), Director (Tavernier), Film.

Capital Punishment 🦴½ **1996** Martial arts expert James Thayer (Daniels) is recruited by the DEA to go undercover and stop Nakata (Yamashita), the supplier of a new illegal drug. His operation turns up a corrupt police chief (Carradine), who frames him for murder, and lots of action. **90m/C VHS.** Gary Daniels, Tadashi Yamashita, David Carradine, Mel Novak, Ian Jacklin, Ava Fabian; ***D:*** David Hue; ***W:*** David Hue; ***C:*** David Swett.

The Capitol Conspiracy 🦴½ **1999 (R)** CIA agents Jarrid Maddox (Wilson) and Vicki Taylor (Keith) uncover evidence that links government officials with illegal mind-control experiments. The duo become targets of a hit squad determined to keep the information secret. Very familiar actioner. **83m/C VHS, DVD.** Don "The Dragon" Wilson, Alexander Keith, Paul Michael Robinson, Arthur Roberts, Barbara Steele; ***D:*** Fred Olen Ray; ***C:*** Gary Graver. **VIDEO**

Capone 🦴🦴½ *The Revenge of Al Capone* **1989 (R)** Story of the gangster after Elliot Ness put him in a Chicago jail. That didn't stop Capone from running his crime empire until a single FBI agent worked to sent the crime boss to Alcatraz, where his power would be useless. Exuberant performances from Sharkey and Carradine. **96m/C VHS.** Ray Sharkey, Keith Carradine, Debrah Farentino, Jayne Atkinson, Bradford English, Marc Figueroa, Neil Giuntoli, Charles Haid, Nicholas Mele, Scott Paulin, Alan Rosenberg; ***D:*** Michael Pressman; ***W:*** Tracy Keenan Wynn; ***C:*** Tim Suhrstedt; ***M:*** Craig Safan. **TV**

Capricorn One 🦴🦴🦴 **1978 (R)** Astronauts Brolin, Simpson and Waterston follow Mission Controller Holbrook's instructions to fake a Mars landing on a soundstage when their ship is discovered to be defective. When they find out they're supposed to expire in outer space so that the NASA scam won't become public knowledge, they flee to the desert, while reporter Gould sniffs out the cover up. Based on a pseudonymous novel by Ken Follett. **123m/C VHS, DVD.** Elliott Gould, James Brolin, Brenda Vaccaro, O.J. Simpson, Hal Holbrook, Sam Waterston, Karen Black, Telly Savalas; ***D:*** Peter Hyams; ***W:*** Peter Hyams; ***C:*** Bill Butler; ***M:*** Jerry Goldsmith.

Captain America *The Return of Captain America* **1944** Captain America battles a mad scientist in this 15-episode serial based on the comic book character. **240m/B VHS.** Dick Purcell, Adrian (Lorna Gray) Booth, Lionel Atwill; ***D:*** John English; ***W:*** Elmer Clifton.

Captain America 🦴½ **1979** Marvel Comic character steps into feature film and flounders. The patriotic superhero son of WWII hero fights bad guy with contraband nuclear weapon. **98m/C VHS.** Reb Brown, Len Birman, Heather Menzies, Steve Forrest, Robin Mattson, Joseph Ruskin, Michael McManus; ***D:*** Rod Holcomb. **TV**

Captain America 🦴½ **1989 (PG-13)** Based on the Marvel Comics superhero. It's 1941 and Steve Rogers has just been recruited to join a top secret experimental government program after flunking his army physical. Injected with a serum, Steve becomes super strong, fast, and smart but is matched in all three by an evil Nazi counterpart, Red Skull. The two battle to a WWII standstill and while Red Skull goes on with his evil plots, the next 40 years finds Captain America fast frozen in the Alaskan tundra. Finally, our hero is thawed in time to do a final battle with his evil nemesis. This one is ridiculous even by comic book standards but it may amuse the kids. **103m/C VHS.** Matt Salinger, Scott Paulin, Ronny Cox, Ned Beatty, Darren McGavin, Melinda Dillon; ***D:*** Albert Pyun; ***W:*** Stephen Tolkin.

Captain America 2: Death Too Soon 🦴 **1979** Terrorists hit America where it hurts, threatening to use age accelerating drug. Sequelized superhero fights chronic crow lines and series dies slow, painful death. **98m/C VHS.** Reb Brown, Connie Sellecca, Len Birman, Christopher Lee, Katherine Justice, Lana Wood, Christopher Carey; ***D:*** Ivan Nagy. **TV**

Captain Apache 🦴 **1971** Union intelligence officer Van Cleef investigates murder of Indian commissioner and discovers fake Indian war landscam. As clever as the title. **95m/C VHS.** Lee Van Cleef, Carroll Baker, Stuart Whitman; ***D:*** Alexander Singer; ***W:*** Philip Yordan.

Captain Blackjack 🦴🦴 *Black Jack* **1951** All-star cast craps out in wanna-be thriller about drug smuggling on the French Riviera. Social butterfly Moorehead directs drug traffic, detective Marshall undercovers as doctor, and Sanders looks bored in a British sort of way. **90m/B VHS.** *FR* George Sanders, Herbert Marshall, Agnes Moorehead, Patricia Roc, Marcel Dalio; ***D:*** Julien Duvivier.

Captain Blood 🦴🦴🦴½ **1935** Sabatini adventure story launched then unknown 26-year-old Flynn and 19-year-old De Havilland to fame in perhaps the best pirate story ever. Exiled into slavery by a tyrannical governor, Irish physician Peter Blood is forced into piracy but ultimately earns a pardon for his swashbuckling ways. Love interest De Havilland would go on to appear in seven more features with Flynn, who took the part Robert Donat declined for health reasons. Cleverly budgeted using ship shots from silents, and miniature sets when possible. First original film score by composer Korngold. Also available colorized. **120m/B VHS.** Errol Flynn, Olivia de Havilland, Basil Rathbone, J. Carrol Naish, Guy Kibbee, Lionel Atwill; ***D:*** Michael Curtiz; ***W:*** Casey Robinson; ***C:*** Hal Mohr; ***M:*** Erich Wolfgang Korngold.

Captain Boycott 🦴🦴½ **1947** In 1880 Ireland, Boycott (Parker) is the despised rent collector for an aristocratic English landlord. When the poor tenant farmers can't pay, he's quick to throw them off the land. The farmers then band together to get rid of Boycott. Granger and Ryan are the prerequisite young lovers. Adapted from the novel by Philip Rooney. **94m/B VHS.** *GB* Cecil Parker, Stewart Granger, Kathleen Ryan, Niall MacGinnis, Robert Donat, Mervyn Johns, Alastair Sim, Noel Purcell, Maurice Denham; ***D:*** Frank Launder; ***W:*** Frank Launder, Wolfgang Wilhelm; ***C:*** Wilkie Cooper, Oswald Morris; ***M:*** William Alwyn.

Captain Caution 🦴🦴 **1940** Young girl throws caution to the wind when dad dies during the War of 1812, assisting young Mature to take over the old man's ship to do battle with the British. Watch for then unknown sailor Ladd. **84m/B VHS.** Victor Mature, Louise Platt, Bruce Cabot, Alan Ladd, Robert Barrat, Vivienne Osborne; ***D:*** Richard Wallace.

Captain Corelli's Mandolin 🦴🦴 **2001 (R)** Based on the novel by Louis de Bernieres, the film is set on the Greek island of Cephallonia during the early days of WWII. After numerous scenes of hearty Greek peasant life, the island is occupied by an aria-singing Italian army troop, led by mandolin strumming Captain Corelli (Cage). He moves into the local doctor's (Hurt) place and quickly falls for his daughter Pelagia (Cruz). The problem is that she's engaged to fisherman Mandras (Bale), a Greek partisan. Cage's over-done accent makes him sound like he's trying to sell you a pizza, but it matches the overwrought tone. Director Madden was signed late in pre-production after scheduled director Roger Michell suffered a heart attack. **127m/C VHS, DVD, Wide.** *GB US* Nicolas Cage, Penelope Cruz, Christian Bale, John Hurt, David Morrissey, Irene Papas, Patrick Malahide; ***D:*** John Madden; ***W:*** Shawn Slovo; ***C:*** John Toll; ***M:*** Stephen Warbeck.

Captain from Castile 🦴🦴🦴 **1947** Exciting saga finds 16th-century Spanish nobleman Pedro De Vargas (Power) forced to flee the wrath of Inquisition chief De Silva (Sutton). He takes peasant girl Cantana (Peters), who's helped him, and joins Cortez's expedition to Mexico and the search for Aztec riches. Lots of adventures and old-fashioned pageantry. Peters' screen debut. **141m/C VHS.** Tyrone Power, Jean Peters, Cesar Romero, Lee J. Cobb, John Sutton, Antonio Moreno, Thomas Gomez, Alan Mowbray; ***D:*** Henry King; ***W:*** Lamar Trotti; ***C:*** Charles Clarke, Arthur E. Arling; ***M:*** Alfred Newman.

The Captain from Koepenick 🦴🦴½ *Der Hauptmann von Koepenick* **1956** Popular true life comedy about a Berlin cobbler in 1906 who rebels against military bureaucracy by impersonating a Prussian officer and wreaking havoc on his town, arresting authorities and capturing soldiers, only to enjoy folk herodom when his ruse is discovered. Remake of Richard Oswald's 1931 classic. In German with subtitles. **93m/B VHS.** *GE* Heinz Ruehmann, Hannelore Schroth, Martin Held, Erich Schellow; ***D:*** Helmut Kaeutner.

Captain Horatio Hornblower 🦴🦴🦴 **1951** A colorful drama about the life and loves of the British sea captain during the Napoleonic wars. Peck is rather out of his element as the courageous, swashbuckling hero (Errol Flynn was originally cast) but there's enough fast-paced derring-do to make this a satisfying saga. Based on the novel by C.S. Forester. **117m/C VHS.** *GB* Gregory Peck, Virginia Mayo, Robert Beatty, Denis O'Dea, Christopher Lee; ***D:*** Raoul Walsh; ***W:*** Ivan Goff; ***C:*** Guy Green.

Captain Jack 🦴🦴½ *An Inch Over the Horizon* **1998** Sentimental, old-fashioned story about eccentric sea captain Jack (Hoskin) who dreams of sailing the same journey as Captain Scoresby made in 1791—from Whitby in northern England to the Arctic. But his misfit crew is a group of novices and his vessel is deemed unseaworthy by authorities. Nevertheless, Jack and his group set sail. **96m/C VHS.** *GB* Bob Hoskins, Peter McDonald, Sadie Frost, Gemma Jones, Anna Massey, Maureen Lipman, Robert Addie, Trevor Bannister; ***D:*** Robert M. Young; ***W:*** Jack Rosenthal; ***C:*** John McGlashan; ***M:*** Richard Harvey.

Captain January 🦴🦴½ **1936 (G)** Crusty old lighthouse keeper rescues little orphan girl with curly hair from drowning and everyone breaks into cutesy song and dance, interrupted only when the authorities try to separate the two. Also available colorized. ♫At the Codfish Ball; Early Bird; The Right Somebody to Love. **81m/B VHS.** Shirley Temple, Guy Kibbee, Buddy Ebsen, Slim Summerville, Jane Darwell, June Lang, George Irving, Si Jenks; ***D:*** David Butler.

Captain Kidd 🦴½ **1945** Laughton huffs and puffs and searches for treasure on the high seas, finds himself held captive with rest of cast in anemic swashbuckler. **83m/B VHS, DVD.** Charles Laughton, John Carradine, Randolph Scott, Reginald Owen, Gilbert Roland, Barbara Britton, John Qualen, Sheldon Leonard; ***D:*** Rowland V. Lee; ***W:*** Norman Reilly Raine; ***C:*** Archie Stout.

Captain Kronos: Vampire Hunter 🦴🦴🦴 *Kronos; Vampire Castle* **1974 (R)** Captain Kronos fences thirsty foes in Hammer horror hybrid. Artsy, atmospheric and atypical, it's written and directed with tongue firmly in cheek by Clemens, who penned many an "Avengers" episode. **91m/C VHS.** *GB* Horst Janson, John Carson, Caroline Munro, Ian Hendry, Shane Briant, Wanda Ventham, John Cater, Lois Daine, William Hobbs, Robert James, Elizabeth Dear; ***D:*** Brian Clemens; ***W:*** Brian Clemens; ***C:*** Ian Wilson; ***M:*** Laurie Johnson.

Captain Newman, M.D. 🦴🦴½ **1963** Three army guys visit stiff shrink Peck during the final months of WWII in VA ward for the mentally disturbed. Much guilt and agonizing, with comic relief courtesy of Curtis. Peck is sub par, the direction flounders and there's something unsettling about quicksilver shifts from pathos to parody. Nonetheless touching with fine performance from Darin as guilt ridden hero. Based on the novel by Leo Rosten. **126m/C VHS.** Gregory Peck, Bobby Darin, Tony Curtis, Angie Dickinson, Eddie Albert, James Gregory, Jane Withers, Larry Storch, Robert Duvall; ***D:*** David Miller.

Captain Nuke and the Bomber Boys 🦴½ *Demolition Day* **1995 (PG)** Three teenagers, who've stumbled across an atomic bomb, decide to use the device to get school called off. Instead, they wind up with the FBI and a couple of crooks after them. **?m/C VHS.** Joe Mantegna, Martin Sheen, Joe Piscopo, Joanna Pacula, Rod Steiger, Kate Mulgrew; ***D:*** Charles Gale.

Captain Ron 🦴½ **1992 (PG-13)** Harried couple Short and Place inherit a large boat and, with their two smart-mouthed kids, go to the Caribbean to sail the boat back to the U.S. Of course they know nothing about sailing, so they hire Captain Ron (Russell), a one-eyed, Long John Silver-talking boat captain. From there, numerous mishaps occur. Amusing sounding premise sinks like a stone. Russell looks great in his teeny-weeny bikini, and the scenery is beautiful, but that's about it. **104m/C VHS.** Kurt Russell, Martin Short, Mary Kay Place, Meadow Sisto, Benjamin Salisbury; ***D:*** Thom Eberhardt; ***W:*** Thom Eberhardt.

Captain Scarlett 🦴½ **1953** Formulaic swashbuckler has nobleman Greene and highway guy Young fighting nasty French Royalists who've been putting the pressure on impecunious peasants. Runaway Spanish damsel in distress courtesy of Amar. Most novel aspect of the production is that the post-Napoleon French terrain has that vaguely south of the border feel. **75m/C VHS.** Richard Greene, Leonora Amar, Isobel Del Puerto, Nedrick Young, Manolo Fabregas; ***D:*** Thomas Carr.

Captain Sinbad 🦴🦴½ **1963** Captain Sinbad must destroy the evil El Kerim, but first he must tackle a many-headed ogre, man-eating fish and crocodiles, a large fist clad in a spiked glove, an invisible monster, and more. To kill the villain, Sinbad must destroy his heart, which is kept in a tower with no entrance. A huge, witty, epic production with lots of special effects. This one is fun. **85m/C VHS.** Guy Williams, Heidi Bruhl, Pedro Armendariz Sr., Abraham Sofaer, Bernie Hamilton, Helmut Schneider; ***D:*** Byron Haskin; ***W:*** Ian McLellan Hunter, Guy Endore.

Captain Swagger 🦴½ **1925** A man on the brink of thievery experiences some changes that keep him on the right side of the law. **50m/B VHS.** Rod La Rocque, Sue Carol, Richard Tucker, Victor Potel, Ullrich Haupt; ***D:*** Edward H. Griffith.

Captains Courageous 🦴🦴🦴 **1937** Rich brat Bartholomew takes a dip sans life jacket while leaning over an ocean liner railing to relieve himself of the half dozen ice cream sodas imprudently consumed at sea. Picked up by a Portugese fishing boat, he at first treats his mandatory three month voyage as an unscheduled cab ride, but eventually, through a deepening friendship with crewman Tracy, develops a hitherto unheralded work ethic. The boy's filial bond with Tracy, of course, requires that the seaman meet with watery disaster. Based on the Rudyard Kipling novel. Director Fleming went on to "Gone With the Wind" and "The Wizard of Oz." **116m/B VHS.** Spencer Tracy, Lionel Barrymore, Freddie Bartholomew, Mickey Rooney, Melvyn Douglas, Charley Grapewin, John Carradine, Bobby Watson, Jack LaRue; *D:* Victor Fleming. Oscars '37: Actor (Tracy).

Captains Courageous 🦴🦴½ **1995** TV adaptation of the 1897 novel by Rudyard Kipling finds pampered rich kid Vadas learning to become a man at the hands of stalwart sea captain Urich. **93m/C VHS.** Robert Urich, Kenny Vadas, Kaj-Erik Eriksen, Robert Wisden, Duncan Fraser; *D:* Michael Anderson Jr.; *W:* John McGreevey; *C:* Glen MacPherson; *M:* Eric N. Robertson, Claude Desjardins.

Captains of the Clouds 🦴🦴½ **1942** Unabashedly patriotic film starring Cagney as a daredevil, independent Canadian bush pilot who makes his own flying rules. When WWII begins he joins the Royal Canadian Air Force but washes out when he can't follow orders. However, he finds a way to prove himself a hero as a civilian pilot ferrying a bomber to England. Cagney's first Technicolor film. **113m/C VHS.** James Cagney, Dennis Morgan, Brenda Marshall, Alan Hale, George Tobias, Reginald Gardiner, Reginald Denny, Russell Arms, Paul Cavanagh, Charles Halton; *D:* Michael Curtiz; *M:* Max Steiner.

Captain's Paradise 🦴🦴🦴 **1953** Golden Fleece captain Guinness chugs between wives in Gibraltar and North Africa, much to the adulation of chief officer Goldner. While Gibraltar's little woman Johnson is homegrown homebody, little woman de Carlo is paint the town red type, allowing Guinness to have cake and eat it too, it seems, except that he's inconveniently positioned in front of a firing squad at movie's start. **89m/B VHS.** *GB* Alec Guinness, Yvonne De Carlo, Celia Johnson, Miles Malleson, Nicholas Phipps, Ferdinand "Ferdy" Mayne, Sebastian Cabot; *D:* Anthony Kimmins; *W:* Alec Coppel, Nicholas Phipps; *C:* Edward Scaife; *M:* Malcolm Arnold.

The Captain's Table 🦴🦴 **1960** Former cargo vessel captain Gregson is given luxury liner to command, and fails to revise his cargo captain style to fit new crew and clientele. British cast saves unremarkable script from mediocrity. **90m/C VHS.** *GB* John Gregson, Peggy Cummins, Donald Sinden, Nadia Gray; *D:* Jack Lee.

Captive 🦴½ **1987 (R)** Spoiled heiress is kidnapped by terrorist trio and brainwashed into anti-establishment Hearst-like creature. **98m/C VHS.** Oliver Reed, Irina Brook, Xavier DeLuc, Hiro Arai; *D:* Paul Mayersberg.

Captive 🦴½ **1997** New bride Samantha Hoffman's (Eleniak) husband is murdered on their wedding night. Blaming herself, Samantha attempts suicide and then voluntarily commits herself to a mental institution at her brother-in-law's suggestion. But Samantha soon discovers she can't leave. What's worse is she finds that she's the pawn in a plot involving her husband's death. **93m/C VHS.** *CA* Erika Eleniak, Michael Ironside, Catherine Colvey, Stewart Bick; *D:* Rodney Gibbons; *W:* Rodney Gibbons, Richard Stanford; *C:* Bruno Philip; *M:* David Findlay. **VIDEO**

Captive Heart 🦴🦴🦴 **1947** Czech soldier Redgrave assumes the identity of a dead British officer in order to evade Nazis in WWII. Captured and imprisoned in camp reserved for British POWs, his stalagmates think they smell a spy, but he manages to convince them he's an OK Joe. Meanwhile, he's been writing letters home to the little missus, which means he's got a little explaining to do when he's released from prison. Especially fine Redgrave performance. **86m/B VHS.** *GB* Michael Redgrave, Basil Radford, Jack Warner, Jimmy Hanley, Rachel Kempson, Mervyn Johns; *D:* Basil Dearden.

Captive Hearts 🦴 **1987 (PG)** Well frayed story holds cast captive in sushi romance. Two American flyers are shot down and taken prisoner in isolated Japanese mountain village, and one is shot by Cupid's arrow. **97m/C VHS.** Noriyuki "Pat" Morita, Michael Sarrazin, Chris Makepeace; *D:* Paul Almond; *M:* David Benoit.

A Captive in the Land 🦴½ **1991 (PG)** Routine survival pic pits two strangers against the frozen Arctic tundra. Potapov is a Soviet airman who's too injured to walk when he's discovered by American meteorologist Waterston. When a rescue seems unlikely, the two are forced to try for a trek to civilization. Based on the novel by James Aldridge. **96m/C VHS.** Sam Waterston, Alexander Potapov; *D:* John Berry; *M:* Bill Conti, Lee Gold.

Captive Planet 🦴 **1978** Bargain basement FX and really atrocious acting hold audience captive in routine earth on the verge of obliteration yarn. **95m/C VHS.** Sharon Baker, Chris Auram, Anthony Newcastle; *D:* Al (Alfonso Brescia) Bradley.

Captive Rage 🦴 **1988 (R)** South American general Reed hijacks planeful of girlies to encourage US to release his son, who's in trouble because he swaps money for white powder. Violence lives up to title, all else disappoints. **99m/C VHS.** Oliver Reed, Robert Vaughn, Claudia Udy; *D:* Cedric Sundstrom.

The Captive: The Longest Drive 2 🦴🦴 *The Quest* **1976 (PG-13)** Matheson and Russell play two recently reunited brothers in search of their sister, whom they believe is still a captive of the Cheyenne Indians who also raised Russell. Along the way the two come to the aid of a pioneer woman and her young son. This western was actually a brief TV series known as "The Quest," and is a continuation of the pilot episode released on video as "The Longest Drive." **80m/C VHS.** Kurt Russell, Tim Matheson; *D:* Lee H. Katzin. **TV**

Captive Wild Woman 🦴🦴½ **1943** Mad scientist Dr. Sigmund Walters (Carradine) transforms an ape into the beautiful Paula Depress (Aquanetta), who promptly joins the circus as a mysterious animal trainer. Unfortunately, she falls in love with fellow trainer Fred (Stone), who already has a gal, bringing back the beast in the pretty Paula. Sequelled by "Jungle Captive" and "Jungle Woman." **61m/B VHS.** Acquanetta, John Carradine, Milburn Stone, Evelyn Ankers, Lloyd Corrigan, Vince Barnett, Paul Fix; *D:* Edward Dmytryk; *W:* Griffin Jay, Henry Sucher.

Captives 🦴🦴½ **1994 (R)** Middle-class dentist Rachel Clifford (Ormond), recently separated from her husband, takes a part-time job at a local prison where she becomes attracted to her patient, Cockney charmer Philip Chaney (Roth). He's coming to the end of a 10-year sentence and the lusty duo manage to consummate their relationship during one of Philip's day-releases. Only problem is fellow con Towler (Salmon) notices what's happening and blackmails and threatens Rachel—leading to a violent confrontation. Roth and Ormond click believably as opposites-attract partners though the script has some weak elements. **100m/C VHS.** *GB* Tim Roth, Julia Ormond, Colin Salmon, Keith Allen, Siobhan Redmond, Peter Capaldi, Richard Hawley, Annette Badland, Jeff Nuttal; *D:* Angela Pope; *W:* Frank Deasy; *C:* Remi Adefarasin; *M:* Colin Towns.

The Capture 🦴🦴🦴 **1950** Above-average story told in flashback has Ayres hiding out in Mexico because he thought he killed an innocent man. He seeks out the widow to question her about him and they wind up marrying. When he finds the real culprit, the man is killed and the evidence points to Ayres. Ayres and Wright are great, as is the native Mexican musical score. **67m/B VHS.** Lew Ayres, Teresa Wright, Victor Jory, Jacqueline White, Jimmy Hunt, Duncan Renaldo, William "Billy" Bakewell; *D:* John Sturges.

The Capture of Bigfoot 🦴 **1979 (PG)** Barefoot monster tracks footprints around town after 25 years of peace, and evil businessman attempts to capture creature for personal gain. **92m/C VHS.** Stafford Morgan, Katherine Hopkins, Richard Kennedy, Otis Young, George "Buck" Flower, John Goff; *D:* Bill Rebane.

The Capture of Grizzly Adams 🦴½ **1982** Framed for murder, Adams and his ever-faithful companion Ben the bear must not only clear his name but outwit a band of outlaws who are holding his young daughter captive. **96m/C VHS.** Dan Haggerty, Chuck Connors, June Lockhart, Kim Darby, Noah Beery Jr., Keenan Wynn, Sydney Penny, G.W. Bailey, Todd Everett; *D:* Don Keeslar. **TV**

Captured 🦴 **1999 (R)** Car thief picks the wrong auto to boost when he gets locked inside a special high-tech Porsche, which is maneuvered by a remote control in the hands of its sadistic owner. Who decides the thief needs to be taught a lesson. **95m/C VHS, DVD.** Andrew Divoff, Nick Mancuso, Linda Hoffman, Michael Mahonen; *D:* Peter Paul Liapis. **VIDEO**

Captured in Chinatown 🦴 **1935** Dog chases bad guys in Chinatown. Bow wow. **53m/B VHS.** Marion Shilling, Charles Delaney, Philo (Philip, P.H., P.M.) McCullough, Robert Ellis; *D:* Elmer Clifton.

The Car 🦴🦴 **1977 (PG)** Driverless black sedan appears out of nowhere to terrorize the residents of a small New Mexico town. And it's up to Sheriff Wade Parent (Brolin) to stop the demonic auto. **96m/C VHS, DVD.** James Brolin, Kathleen Lloyd, John Marley, Ronny Cox, John Rubinstein, R.G. Armstrong, Elizabeth Thompson, Roy Jenson; *D:* Elliot Silverstein; *W:* Dennis Shryack, Michael Butler; *C:* Gerald Hirschfeld; *M:* Leonard Rosenman.

Car Crash 🦴 **19??** Organized crime hits stock car racing head on to produce crashing bore. **103m/C VHS.** Joey Travolta, Anna (Ana Garcia) Obregon, Vittorio Mezzogiorno.

Car 54, Where Are You? 🦴 **1994 (PG-13)** Exceedingly lame remake of the exceedingly lame TV series, which ran for only two seasons, 1961-63. This time, Toody (Johansen) and Muldoon (McGinley) are protecting a mafia stool pigeon (Piven), while vampy Velma Velour (Drescher) sets her sights on Muldoon. Not many laughs and a waste of a talented cast. Sat on the shelf at Orion for three years (with good reason). **89m/C VHS.** David Johansen, Fran Drescher, Rosie O'Donnell, John C. McGinley, Nipsey Russell, Al Lewis, Daniel Baldwin, Jeremy Piven; *D:* Bill Fishman; *W:* Ebbe Roe Smith, Erik Tarloff, Peter McCarthy, Peter Crabbe; *M:* Bernie Worrell, Pray for Rain. Golden Raspberries '94: Worst Support. Actress (O'Donnell).

Car Trouble 🦴🦴½ **1986 (R)** Young English husband buys new Jaguar and wife's not so minor car trouble causes major marital trouble. Funnybone-tickling pairing of Walters and Charleson. **93m/C VHS.** *GB* Julie Walters, Ian Charleson; *D:* David Green; *M:* Meat Loaf Aday.

Car Wash 🦴🦴½ **1976 (PG)** L.A. car-wash provides a soap-opera setting for disjointed comic bits about owners of dirty cars and people who hose them down for a living. Econo budget and lite plot, but serious comic talent. A sort of disco car-wash version of "Grand Hotel." **97m/C VHS, DVD.** Franklin Ajaye, Sully Boyer, Richard Brestoff, George Carlin, Richard Pryor, Melanie Mayron, Ivan Dixon, Antonio Fargas; *D:* Michael A. Schultz; *W:* Joel Schumacher; *C:* Frank Stanley; *M:* Norman Whitfield.

Caracara 🦴🦴 *The Last Witness* **2000 (R)** Ornithologist Rachel Sutherland (Henstridge) agrees to allow the FBI to use her apartment for a stakeout and falls for agent David MacMillan (Schaech). Then she learns she's been duped—her "guests" are actually assassins planning to kill Nelson Mandela. **93m/C VHS, DVD.** Natasha Henstridge, Johnathon Schaech, David McIlwraith, Lauren Hutton; *D:* Graeme Clifford; *W:* Craig Smith; *C:* Bill Wong. **CABLE**

Caravaggio 🦴🦴🦴 **1986** Controversial biography of late Renaissance painter Caravaggio (Terry), famous for his bisexuality, fondness for prostitute models, violence and depravity. The painter divides his time between two street models, Ranuccio (Bean) and his lover Lena (Swinton), the decadent cardinals who commission his religious works, and Caravaggio's young assistant (Leigh), who cares for the artist as he lies dying. Photography by Gabriel Beristain reproduces the artist's visual style. **97m/C VHS.** *GB* Spencer Leigh, Michael Gough, Nigel Davenport, Robbie Coltrane, Jack Birkett, Nigel Terry, Sean Bean, Tilda Swinton; *D:* Derek Jarman; *W:* Derek Jarman; *C:* Gabriel Beristain; *M:* Simon Fisher.

Caravan to Vaccares 🦴 **1974 (PG)** French Duke hires young American to sneak Eastern European scientist into the States, and little suspense ensues. Based on Alistair MacLean novel. **98m/C VHS.** David Birney, Charlotte Rampling; *D:* Geoffrey Reeve.

The Caravan Trail 🦴🦴 **1946** A cowboy becomes marshal in order to bring to justice those who have stolen land and murdered his friend. This was shot in color, which was rare for the 1940s. **53m/C VHS.** Eddie Dean, Lash LaRue, Emmett Lynn, Jean Carlin, Charles "Blackie" King, Bob Barron, Lloyd Ingraham, Bud Osborne; *D:* Robert Emmett Tansey.

Carbon Copy 🦴🦴 *Time of the Wolves; The Last Shot; The Heist; Le Temps des Loups; Dillinger 70* **1969** A criminal with a split personality (Hossein) has renamed himself Dillinger because he patterns his crimes after the legendary gangster. As he and his gang strike, an Inspector (Aznavour) tries to bring him down. Dubbed. **105m/C VHS, Wide.** *FR IT* Robert Hossein, Charles Aznavour, Virna Lisi, Marcel Bozzuffi; *D:* Sergio Gobbi; *W:* Andre Tabet, Sergio Gobbi; *C:* Daniel Diot; *M:* Georges Garvarentz.

Carbon Copy 🦴🦴 **1981 (PG)** Successful white executive has life turned inside out when his 17-year-old illegitimate son, who happens to be black, decides it's time to look up dear old dad. Typical comedy-with-a-moral. **92m/C VHS.** George Segal, Susan St. James, Jack Warden, Paul Winfield, Dick Martin, Vicky Dawson, Tom Poston, Denzel Washington; *D:* Michael A. Schultz; *W:* Stanley Shapiro; *M:* Bill Conti.

Cardiac Arrest 🦴 **1974 (PG)** Lunatic eviscerates victims in trolley town. They left their hearts in San Francisco. **95m/C VHS, DVD.** Garry Goodrow, Mike Chan, Max Gail; *D:* Murray Mintz.

The Cardinal 🦴🦴½ **1963** Priestly young Tryon rises through ecclesiastical ranks to become Cardinal, struggling through a plethora of tests of faith, none so taxing as the test of the audience's patience. Had Preminger excised some 60 minutes of footage, he might have had a compelling portrait of faith under fire, but as it stands, the cleric's life is epic confusion. Fine acting, even from Tryon, who later went on to bookish fame, and from Huston who's normally on the other side of the camera. McNamara's final performance. Based on the Henry Morton Robinson novel. **175m/C VHS, Wide.** Tom Tryon, Carol Lynley, Dorothy Gish, Maggie McNamara, Cecil Kellaway, John Huston, John Saxon, Burgess Meredith; *D:* Otto Preminger; *C:* Leon Shamroy. Golden Globes '64: Film—Drama, Support. Actor (Huston).

Career 🦴🦴½ **1959** An overwrought, depressing drama about the trials and tribulations of an actor trying to make it on Broadway. He'll try anything to succeed. Good direction, but so-so acting. **105m/B VHS.** Dean Martin, Anthony (Tony) Franciosa, Shirley MacLaine, Carolyn Jones, Joan Blackman, Robert Middleton, Donna Douglas; *D:* Joseph Anthony; *C:* Joseph LaShelle. Golden Globes '60: Actor—Drama (Franciosa).

Career Girls 🦴🦴🦴 **1997 (R)** Two young women, the caustic acid-tongued Hannah (Cartlidge) and shy eczema-scarred Annie (Steadman), are introduced in a flashback sequence as they meet and become college roommates. They reunite for a weekend visit six years after they graduate. Both have become career women and have smoothed out their rough edges. In their wanders around London, they coincidentally run into people they knew back in the day, including a smarmy real estate agent (Tucker) who dated them both and a despondent schizophrenic (Benton) who pursued Annie. Excellent performances from a largely unknown cast. **87m/C VHS.** Katrin Cartlidge, Lynda Steadman, Kate Byers, Mark Benton, Andy Serkis, Joe Tucker, Margo Stanley, Michael Healy; *D:* Mike Leigh; *W:* Mike Leigh; *C:* Dick Pope; *M:* Marianne Jean-Baptiste, Tony Remy.

Career Opportunities 🦴½ **1991** **(PG-13)** "Home Alone" clone for teenagers from John Hughes' factory. Whaley is an unsuccessful con-artist who finally gets a job as the night janitor of the local department store. He fools around at company expense until he finds the town's beauty (Connelly) asleep in a dressing room. The pair then play make-believe until its time to thwart some small-time thieves. Unexciting and unrealistic in the worst way; no wonder Candy isn't billed—he probably didn't want to be. **83m/C VHS, DVD.** Frank Whaley, Jennifer Connelly, Dermot Mulroney, Kieran Mulroney, John M. Jackson, Jenny O'Hara, Noble Willingham, Barry Corbin, Denise Galik, William Forsythe, John Candy; *D:* Bryan Gordon; *W:* John Hughes; *C:* Donald McAlpine; *M:* Thomas Newman.

Carefree 🦴🦴🦴 **1938** Dizzy radio singer Rogers can't make up her mind about beau Bellamy, so he sends her to analyst Astaire. Seems she can't even dream a little dream until shrink Astaire prescribes that she ingest some funny food, which causes her to dream she's in love with the Fredman. Au contraire, says he, it's a Freudian thing, and he hypnotically suggests that she really loves Bellamy. The two line up to march down the aisle together, and Fred stops dancing just long enough to realize he's in love with Ginger. A screwball comedy with music. ♫I Used to be Colorblind; The Night is Filled With Music; Change Partners; The Yam. **83m/B VHS.** Fred Astaire, Ginger Rogers, Ralph Bellamy, Jack Carson, Franklin Pangborn, Hattie McDaniel; *D:* Mark Sandrich; *M:* Irving Berlin.

Careful 🦴🦴 **1992** Butler-in-training Neale courts Neville in an alpine mountain village where silence is golden, or at least being quiet will lessen the chance of an avalanche. Dig a little deeper and you find incest, repression and other nasty things. Highly individualistic black comedy parodies German Expressionism and Freudian psychology to the point of absurdity, dealing with snow, sex, sleep, spirits, and obsessive/compulsive personality disorders. Third film from Canadian cult director Maddin is awash in vivid primary colors when it suits the scene's mood and employs between-scenes titles in a homage to cinematic antiquity. **100m/C VHS, DVD.** Kyle McCulloch, Gosia Dobrowolska, Jackie Burroughs, Sarah Neville, Brent Neale, Paul Cox, Victor Cowie, Michael O'Sullivan, Vince Rimmer, Katya Gardner; *D:* Guy Maddin; *W:* Guy Maddin, George Toles; *C:* Guy Maddin; *M:* John McCulloch.

Careful, He Might Hear You 🦴🦴🦴 **1984 (PG)** Abandoned by his father, six-year-old P.S. becomes a pawn between his dead mother's two sisters, one working class and the other wealthy, and his worldview is further overturned by the sudden reappearance of his prodigal father. Set in Depression-era Australia, Schultz's vision is touching and keenly observed, and manages a sort of child's eye sense of proportion. Based on a novel by Sumner Locke Elliott. **113m/C VHS, DVD, Wide.** *AU* Nicholas Gledhill, Wendy Hughes, Robyn Nevin, John Hargreaves; *D:* Carl Schultz; *W:* Michael Jenkins; *C:* John Seale; *M:* Ray Cook. Australian Film Inst. '83: Actress (Hughes), Film.

Caresses 🦴🦴 *Caricies* **1997** Eleven short scenes confront the lack of tenderness in the restless lives of a big city's inhabitants over the course of one night, until the film circles back to where it began—with the domestic argument between a young man and woman who no longer love each other. Adaptation of Belbel's play. Spanish with subtitles. **94m/C VHS, Wide.** *SP* Julieta Serrano, Augustin Gonzalez, Sergei Lopez, David Selvas, Laura Conejero, Montserrat Salvador, Naim Thomas, Merce Pons, Jordi Dauder, Roger Coma, Rosa Maria Sarda; *D:* Ventura Pons; *W:* Ventura Pons, Sergi Belbel; *C:* Jesus Escosa; *M:* Carles Cases.

Caribe 🦴½ **1987** Caribbean travelogue masquerades as spy thriller. Arms smuggling goes awry, and neither voodoo nor bikinied blondes can prevent audience from dozing. Never released theatrically. **96m/C VHS.** John Savage, Kara Glover, Stephen McHattie, Sam Malkin; *D:* Michael Kennedy.

The Cariboo Trail 🦴🦴 **1950** Two prospecting men seek their fortune in British Columbia, the golden West of Canada in the 1890s. But they find themselves opposed by a ruthless rancher and claim-jumpers. Actually filmed in Colorado with excellent cinematography and solid performances from some big names, it's still a run-of-the-mill entry. Made the same year that the Gabby Hayes' show first aired. **80m/C VHS.** Randolph Scott, George "Gabby" Hayes, Bill Williams, Victor Jory; *D:* Edwin L. Marin.

Carla's Song 🦴🦴 **1997** Left-leaning director Loach sets his sometimes gripping, sometimes over-bearing political/love story in war torn Nicaragua in the late 1980s. George (Carlyle) is a Glasgow bus driver who helps out passenger Carla (Cabezas), a Nicaraguan emigre who raises money for the Sandanista cause. George falls in love with Carla and decides that the only way she can get on with her life is to confront her former lover Antonio, who was maimed by the contras and has disappeared. The two lovers go to Nicaragua, where George is totally out of his environment. Shot (with great difficulty) on location in Nicaragua. **127m/C VHS, DVD.** Robert Carlyle, Oyanka Cabezas, Gary Lewis, Scott Glenn, Subash Sing Pall; *D:* Ken Loach; *W:* Paul Laverty; *C:* Barry Ackroyd; *M:* George Fenton.

Carlito's Way 🦴🦴🦴 **1993 (R)** Puerto Rican crime czar Carlito Brigante (Pacino) has just gotten out of jail and wants to go straight. But his drug underworld cohorts don't believe he can do it. Penn (barely recognizable) is great as a sleazy coked-out lawyer who's way out of his league. Remarkably subdued violence given DePalma's previous rep—it's effective without being gratuitous, especially the final shootout set in Grand Central Station. Pacino's performance is equally subdued, with controlled tension and lots of eye contact rather than grandiose emotions. Based on the novels "Carlito's Way" and "After Hours" by Edwin Torres. Pacino and DePalma previously teamed up for "Scarface." **145m/C VHS, DVD, Wide.** Al Pacino, Sean Penn, Penelope Ann Miller, Luis Guzman, John Leguizamo, Ingrid Rogers, James Rebhorn, Viggo Mortensen, Jorge Porcel, Joseph Siravo, Adrian Pasdar; *D:* Brian DePalma; *W:* David Koepp; *C:* Stephen Burum; *M:* Patrick Doyle.

Carlton Browne of the F.O. 🦴🦴½ *Man in a Cocked Hat* **1959** Bumbling Brit diplomat Thomas visits tiny Pacific island of Gallardia, forgotten by the mother country for some 50 years, to insure tenuous international agreement after the island's king dies. Not sterling Sellers but some shining moments. **88m/C VHS.** *GB* Peter Sellers, Terry-Thomas, Luciana Paluzzi, Ian Bannen; *D:* Roy Boulting, Jeffrey Dell; *W:* Roy Boulting; *M:* John Addison.

Carmen 🦴🦴🦴 **1983 (R)** Choreographer casts Carmen and finds life imitates art when he falls under the spell of the hotblooded Latin siren. Bizet's opera lends itself to erotically charged flamenco context. Well acted, impressive scenes including cigarette girls' dance fight and romance between Carmen and Don Jose. In Spanish with English subtitles. **99m/C VHS.** *SP* Antonio Gades, Laura Del Sol, Paco DeLucia, Cristina Hoyos; *D:* Carlos Saura; *W:* Antonio Gades, Carlos Saura; *C:* Teodoro Escamilla. British Acad. '84: Foreign Film.

Carmen, Baby 🦴½ **1966** Metzger's erotic modern update of Bizet's opera "Carmen." Spanish prostitute Carmen (Levka) becomes the object of obsession for a local cop (Ringer) and things wind up badly because of his jealousy. **90m/C VHS, DVD.** Uta Levka, Claus Ringer, Barbara Valentin, Walter Wilz; *D:* Radley Metzger; *W:* Jesse Vogel; *C:* Hans Jura; *M:* Daniel Hart.

Carmen Jones 🦴🦴🦴 **1954** Bizet's tale of fickle femme fatale Carmen heads South with an all black cast and new lyrics by Hammerstein II. Soldier Belafonte falls big time for factory working belle Dandridge during the war, and runs off with miss thang after he kills his C.O. and quits the army. Tired of prettyboy Belafonte, Dandridge's eye wanders upon prize pugilist Escamillo, inspiring ex-soldier beau to wring her throaty little neck. Film debuts of Carroll and Peters. More than a little racist undertone to the direction. Actors' singing is dubbed. ♫Dat's Love; Dere's a Cafe on de Corner; Beat Out Dat Rhythm on a Drum; You Talk Just Like My Maw; Stand Up and Fight; Dis Flower; My Joe. **105m/C VHS, DVD, Wide.** Dorothy Dandridge, Harry Belafonte, Pearl Bailey, Roy Glenn, Diahann Carroll, Brock Peters; *D:* Otto Preminger; *W:* Harry Kleiner; *C:* Sam Leavitt; *M:* Oscar Hammerstein, Georges Bizet. Golden Globes '55: Film—Mus./Comedy, Natl. Film Reg. '92.

Carmilla **1989** An adaptation of the Sheridan Le Fanu lesbian vampire tale. From Shelley Duvall's series "Nightmare Classics." **60m/C VHS.** Meg Tilly, Ione Skye, Roddy McDowall, Roy Dotrice; *D:* Gabrielle Beaumont. **CABLE**

Carnage 🦴 **1984** Hungry house consumes inhabitants. **91m/C VHS.** Leslie Den Dooven, Michael Chiodo, Deeann Veeder; *D:* Andy Milligan.

Carnal Crimes 🦴½ **1991 (R)** Well-acted upscale softcore trash about a sensuous woman, ignored by her middle-aged lawyer husband and drawn to a young stud photographer with a shady past and S&M tendencies. Available in a sexy unrated version also. **103m/C VHS, DVD.** Martin Hewitt, Linda Carol, Rich Crater, Alex Kubik, Yvette Stefens, Paula Trickey; *D:* Alexander Gregory (Gregory Dark) Hippolyte; *W:* Jon Robert Samsel; *C:* Paul Desatoff; *M:* Matthew Ross, Jeff Fishman.

Carnal Knowledge 🦴🦴🦴 **1971 (R)** Carnal knowledge of the me generation. Three decades in the sex-saturated lives of college buddies Nicholson and Garfunkel, chronicled through girlfriends, affairs, and marriages. Controversial upon release, it's not a flattering anatomy of Y-chromosome carriers. Originally written as a play. Kane's debut. **96m/C VHS, DVD, 8mm, Wide.** Jack Nicholson, Candice Bergen, Art Garfunkel, Ann-Margret, Rita Moreno, Carol Kane; *D:* Mike Nichols; *W:* Jules Feiffer; *C:* Giuseppe Rotunno. Golden Globes '72: Support. Actress (Ann-Margret).

Carnegie Hall 🦴🦴½ **1947** Widowed Irish-American Nora (Hunt) gets a job at Carnegie Hall and raises her son Tony to be a talented pianist. But the adult Tony (Prince) develops an interest in jazz and popular music that his ma despises. They have a rift, Tony goes on the road with a band, marries singer Ruth (O'Drsicoll), and becomes a famous jazz pianist. After years pass, Ruth decides it's about time to reunite mother and son and Carnegie Hall plays a big part in her scheme. Schmaltzy story showcases a number of big musical stars of the day. **134m/B VHS, DVD.** Marsha Hunt, William Prince, Martha O'Driscoll, Frank McHugh; *D:* Edgar G. Ulmer; *W:* Karl Kamb; *C:* William J. Miller.

Carnival in Flanders 🦴🦴🦴½ *La Kermesse Heroique* **1935** When Spanish invaders enter a small 17th century Flemish village they discover all the men have disappeared. So it's up to the women to save the town from destruction—and they decide to do it by seducing the invaders. Classic French costume farce with a witty script and fine performances. In French with English subtitles. **90m/B VHS.** *FR* Francoise Rosay, Louis Jouvet, Jean Murat, Andre Alerme, Micheline Cheirel; *D:* Jacques Feyder; *C:* Harry Stradling Sr.; *M:* Louis Beydts. N.Y. Film Critics '36: Foreign Film; Venice Film Fest. '36: Director (Feyder).

Carnival Lady 🦴 **1933** Silver spooner Vincent is scheduled to tie the knot until little lady-to-be discovers he's a bit out of pocket after the stock market takes a wee dip. Jilted and impecunious, he heads for the big top, where he horns in on the high diver's turf, and it's all downhill from there. **66m/B VHS.** Patricia "Boots" Mallory, Allen Vincent, Gertrude Astor, Kit Guard, Donald (Don) Kerr, Rollo Lloyd, Jason Robards Sr.; *D:* Howard Higgin; *W:* Harold Tarshis; *C:* Edward Kull.

Carnival of Blood 🦴 *Death Rides a Carousel* **1971 (PG)** Boring talky scenes punctuated by Coney Island murder mayhem followed by more boring talky scenes. Young's debut, not released for five years. The question's not why they delayed release, but why they bothered at all. A carnival of cliches. **80m/C VHS, DVD.** Earle Edgerton, Judith Resnick, Martin Barlosky, John Harris, Burt Young, Kaly Mills, Gloria Spivak; *D:* Leonard Kirtman; *W:* Leonard Kirtman; *C:* David Howe.

Carnival of Souls 🦴🦴🦴 **1962** Cult-followed zero budget zombie opera has young Hilligoss and girlfriends take wrong turn off bridge into river. Mysteriously unscathed, Hilligoss rents room and takes job as church organist, but she keeps running into dancing dead people, led by director Harvey. Spooky, very spooky. **72m/B VHS, DVD.** Candace Hilligoss, Sidney Berger, Frances Feist, Stan Levitt, Art Ellison, Bill de Jarnette, Steve Boozer, Pamela Ballard, Harold (Herk) Harvey; *D:* Harold (Herk) Harvey; *W:* John Clifford; *C:* Maurice Prather; *M:* Gene Moore.

Carnival Rock 🦴½ **1957** Story of love triangular in seedy nightclub. Club owner Stewart loves chanteuse Cabot who loves card playin' Hutton. Who cares? Maybe hard-core Corman devotees. Good tunes from the Platters, the Blockbusters, Bob Luman, and David Houston. **80m/B VHS.** Susan Cabot, Brian Hutton, David J. Stewart, Dick Miller, Iris Adrian, Jonathan Haze, Ed Nelson, Bob Luman, Frankie Ray, Bruno VeSota; *D:* Roger Corman; *W:* Leo Lieberman; *C:* Floyd Crosby; *M:* Buck Ram.

Carnival Story 🦴½ **1954** Yet another melodramatic cliche about love triangular under the big top. German girl joins American-owned carnival and two guys start acting out unbecoming territorial behavior. Filmed in Germany. **94m/C VHS.** Anne Baxter, Steve Cochran, Lyle Bettger, George Nader; *D:* Kurt Neumann.

Carnosaur 🦴🦴 **1993 (R)** Straight from the Corman film factory, this exploitive quickie about dinosaurs harkens back to '50s-style monster epics. Predictable plot with extremely cheap effects. Genetic scientist Dr. Jane Tiptree (Ladd) is hatching diabolic experiments with chickens when things go awry. The experiments result in a bunch of lethal prehistoric creatures wrecking havoc among the community. **82m/C VHS, DVD.** Diane Ladd, Raphael Sbarge, Jennifer Runyon, Harrison Page, Clint Howard, Ned Bellamy; *D:* Adam Simon; *W:* Adam Simon; *C:* Keith Holland; *M:* Nigel Holton.

Carnosaur 2 🦴½ **1994 (R)** Technicians investigating a power shortage at a secret military mining facility encounter deadly dinos. Entertaining schlock. **90m/C VHS, DVD.** John Savage, Cliff DeYoung, Arabella Holzbog, Ryan Thomas Johnson; *D:* Louis Morneau; *C:* John Aronson; *M:* Ed Tomney, Michael Palmer.

Carnosaur 3: Primal Species 🦴½ **1996** Terrorists get big surprise when the cargo they hijack turns out to be three very hungry dinos who make snacks of them all. Then it's up to commando Valentine, scientist Gunn, and some soldiers to get rid of the beasts. **82m/C VHS, DVD.** Scott Valentine, Janet Gunn, Rick Dean, Rodger Halstead, Tony Peck; *D:* Jonathan Winfrey; *C:* Andrea V. Rossotto; *M:* Kevin Kiner.

Carny 🦴🦴🦴 **1980 (R)** Hothead carnival bozo Busey and peacemaker Robertson experience friendship difficulties when runaway Foster rolls in hay with one and then other. Originally conceived as a documentary by "Derby" filmmaker Kaylor, it's a candid, unsavory, behind-the-scenes anatomy. Co-written by "The Band" member Robertson. **102m/C VHS.** Gary Busey, Robbie Robertson, Jodie Foster, Meg Foster, Kenneth McMillan, Elisha Cook Jr., Craig Wasson; *D:* Robert Kaylor; *W:* Robbie Robertson, Thomas Baum; *C:* Harry Stradling Jr.; *M:* Alex North.

Caro Diario 🦴🦴🦴 *Dear Diary* **1993** Three offbeat chapters from director Moretti's own life. "On My Vespa" has the director taking off on a personal tour of Rome, including its cinemas and their influence on him. In "Islands" Moretti and friend Gerardo travel to a series of island communities, including Salina, dominated by only children to whom their parents defer obsessively. "Doctors" finds Moretti experiencing a misdiagnosed medical crisis. Lots of charm and a certain shameless romanticism. Italian with subtitles. **100m/C VHS.** *IT* Nanni Moretti, Renato Carpentieri; ***D:*** Nanni Moretti; ***W:*** Nanni Moretti; ***C:*** Giuseppe Lanci; ***M:*** Nicola Piovani. Cannes '94: Director (Moretti).

Carolina Skeletons **1992 (R)** As a child in a small southern town, Gossett watched as his brother was accused of a vicious double murder and quickly tried and executed. Thirty years later, the ex-Green Beret returns home to find the real killer and clear his brother's name. But there are those in the town who will do anything to stop their secrets from being revealed. **94m/C VHS, DVD.** Louis Gossett Jr., Bruce Dern, Melissa Leo, Paul Roebling, G.D. Spradlin, Bill Cobbs, Henderson Forsythe, Clifton James; ***D:*** John Erman; ***W:*** Tracy Keenan Wynn; ***C:*** Tony Imi; ***M:*** John Morris.

Caroline? **1990 (PG)** A wealthy young woman is presumed dead in a plane crash. Now 15 years later a stranger appears at the family home claiming to be Caroline—and wanting her inheritance. Is it possible that what she says is true or is it all an elaborate ruse? An especially good performance by Zimbalist. A a "Hallmark Hall of Fame" presentation. Based on the novel "Father's Arcane Daughter" by E.L. Konigsburg. **100m/C VHS.** Stephanie Zimbalist, Pamela Reed, George Grizzard, Dorothy McGuire, Patricia Neal, Shawn (Michael) Phelan, Jenny Jacobs; ***D:*** Joseph Sargent; ***M:*** Charles Bernstein. **TV**

Caroline at Midnight **1993 (R)** After a reporter's former girlfriend, Caroline, dies in a mysterious auto accident he winds up falling for her girlfriend Victoria. Then he discovers both women are connected to drug-dealing cops. Good cast in this atmospheric erotic thriller with plenty of puzzles. **92m/C VHS.** Thomas F. Wilson, Clayton Rohner, Mia Sara, Timothy Daly, Judd Nelson, Virginia Madsen, Zach Galligan; ***D:*** Scott McGinnis.

Carousel **1956** Much-loved Rodgers & Hammerstein musical based on Ferenc Molnar's play "Liliom" (filmed by Fritz Lang in 1935) about a swaggering carnival barker (MacRae) who tries to change his life after he falls in love with a good woman. Killed while attempting to foil a robbery he was supposed to help commit, he begs his heavenly hosts for the chance to return to the mortal realm just long enough to set things straight with his teenage daughter. Now indisputably a classic, the film lost $2 million when it was released. ♫If I Loved You; Soliloquy; You'll Never Walk Alone; What's the Use of Wond'rin; When I Marry Mister Snow; When the Children Are Asleep; A Real Nice Clambake; Carousel Ballet; Carousel Waltz. **128m/C VHS, DVD.** Gordon MacRae, Shirley Jones, Cameron Mitchell, Gene Lockhart, Barbara Ruick, Robert Rounseville, Richard Deacon, Tor Johnson; ***D:*** Henry King; ***W:*** Henry Ephron, Phoebe Ephron; ***C:*** Charles Clarke; ***M:*** Richard Rodgers, Oscar Hammerstein.

The Carpathian Eagle **1981** Police wonder why murdered victims have hearts ripped out while audience wonders what weird title has to do with anything. Routine evisceration fest, part of Elvira's Thriller Video. **60m/C VHS.** Suzanne Danielle, Sian Phillips, Pierce Brosnan, Anthony Valentine; ***D:*** Francis Megahy.

The Carpenter **1989 (R)** Post-nervous breakdown woman receives nightly visits from guy who builds stuff with wood. Very scary stuff. Also available in slightly longer unrated version. **85m/C VHS.** *CA* Wings Hauser, Lynne Adams, Pierce Lenoir, Barbara Ann Jones, Beverly Murray; ***D:*** David Wellington; ***W:*** Doug Taylor; ***C:*** David Franco.

Carpet of Horror **1964** The city of London is terrorized by a small ball emitting poison gas in this schlock horror film. Death results when the ball is rolled into the living rooms of intended victims. **93m/C VHS.** *GE* Joachim Fuchsberger, Carl Lange, Karin Dor; ***D:*** Harald Reinl.

The Carpetbaggers **1964 (PG)** Uncannily Howard Hughesian Peppard wallows in wealth and women in Hollywood in the 1920s and 1930s. Spayed version of the Harold Robbins novel. Ladd's final appearance. Followed by the prequel "Nevada Smith." Introduced by Joan Collins. **150m/C VHS.** George Peppard, Carroll Baker, Alan Ladd, Elizabeth Ashley, Lew Ayres, Martha Hyer, Martin Balsam, Robert Cummings, Archie Moore, Audrey Totter, Leif Erickson, Tom Lowell; ***D:*** Edward Dmytryk; ***W:*** John Michael Hayes; ***C:*** Joe MacDonald; ***M:*** Elmer Bernstein. Natl. Bd. of Review '64: Support. Actor (Balsam).

Carpool **1996 (PG)** Dumb but amiable comedy finds harried dad Daniel Miller stuck driving a minivan filled with kids to school. Too bad he gets sidetracked and hijacked by bumbling would-be bank robber Franklin Laszlo (Arnold) who takes them hostage and on a really wild ride through the streets and shopping malls of Seattle (except it's filmed in Vancouver). **92m/C VHS.** Tom Arnold, David Paymer, Rhea Perlman, Rod Steiger, Kim Coates, Rachael Leigh Cook, Mikey Kovar, Micah Gardener, Blake Warkol; ***D:*** Arthur Hiller; ***W:*** Don Rhymer; ***C:*** David M. Walsh; ***M:*** John Debney. Golden Raspberries '96: Worst Actor (Arnold).

Carrie **1952** In a part turned down by Cary Grant, Olivier plays a married American who self destructs as the woman he loves scales the heights to fame and fortune. The manager of a posh epicurean mecca, Olivier deserts wife Hopkins and steals big bucks from his boss to head east with paramour Jones, a country bumpkin transplanted to Chicago. Once en route to thespian fame in the Big Apple, Jones abandons her erstwhile beau, who crumbles pathetically. Adapted from Theodore Dreiser's "Sister Carrie," it's mega melodrama, but the performances are above reproach. **118m/B VHS.** Laurence Olivier, Jennifer Jones, Miriam Hopkins, Eddie Albert, Basil Ruysdael, Ray Teal, Barry Kelley, Sara Berner, William Reynolds, Mary Murphy, Charles Halton; ***D:*** William Wyler; ***C:*** Victor Milner.

Carrie **1976 (R)** Overprotected by religious fanatic mother Laurie and mocked by the in-crowd, shy, withdrawn high school girl Carrie White is asked to the prom. Realizing she's been made the butt of a joke, she unleashes her considerable telekinetic talents. Travolta, Allen, and Irving are teenagers who get what they deserve. Based on the Stephen King novel. **98m/C VHS, DVD, Wide.** Sissy Spacek, Piper Laurie, John Travolta, William Katt, Amy Irving, Nancy Allen, Edie McClurg, Betty Buckley, P.J. Soles, Sydney Lassick, Stefan Gierasch; ***D:*** Brian DePalma; ***W:*** Lawrence D. Cohen; ***C:*** Mario Tosi; ***M:*** Pino Donaggio. Natl. Soc. Film Critics '76: Actress (Spacek).

Carried Away ½ *Acts of Love* **1995 (R)** Exposing his middle-aged bod, as well as the myth that he can play only psycho toughs, Hopper, as the Midwestern teacher Joseph, is seduced by a 17-year-old student (Locane) in their small conservative town. Based on Harrison's novel "Farmer," it's a sexually active slice of life with the injured Joseph limping through the care of his dying mother, the fate of the small country school where he teaches and his relationship with longtime lover Rosealee (Amy Irving). Hopper's not the only one playing against type, as Irving turns in a fine performance as the widowed schoolmarm. Director Barreto (and Irving's husband) pushes the envelope with full frontal nudity. **107m/C VHS.** Dennis Hopper, Amy Irving, Amy Locane, Gary Busey, Julie Harris, Hal Holbrook, Christopher Pettiet, Priscilla Pointer, Gail Cronauer; ***D:*** Bruno Barreto; ***W:*** Ed Jones; ***C:*** Declan Quinn; ***M:*** Bruce Broughton.

The Carrier **1987 (R)** Smalltown Sleepy Rock is ideal family-raising turf until plague mysteriously blights inhabitants, and townspeople are out to exterminate all potential carriers. Silverman is standout as local spiritual leader; well-orchestrated crowd scenes. Best park your IQ before watching. Filmed on location in Manchester, Michigan. **99m/C VHS.** Gregory Fortescue, Steve Dixon, Paul Silverman, Paul Urbanski, Patrick Butler; ***D:*** Nathan J. White; ***W:*** Nathan J. White; ***C:*** Peter Deming; ***M:*** Joseph LoDuca.

Carrington ½ **1995 (R)** England's artistic Bloomsbury group is examined through the eccentric relationship of artist Dora Carrington (Thompson) and her love for homosexual Lytton Strachey (Pryce), celebrated author of "Eminent Victorians." There's many a menage as the duo live together with Carrington's husband (Waddington), on whom Strachey has a crush, and both their various amours (though Carrington's heart is reserved for Lytton). Film is distractingly divided into titled segments (from 1915 to 1932) and, while Pryce gives a bravura performance, Thompson is merely enigmatic. Based on Michael Holroyd's biography "Lytton Strachey." Hampton's directorial debut. **120m/C VHS, DVD, Wide.** *FR GB* Emma Thompson, Jonathan Pryce, Steven Waddington, Samuel West, Rufus Sewell, Penelope Wilton, Jeremy Northam, Peter Blythe, Janet McTeer, Alex Kingston, Sebastian Harcombe, Richard Clifford; ***D:*** Christopher Hampton; ***W:*** Christopher Hampton; ***C:*** Denis Lenoir; ***M:*** Michael Nyman. Cannes '95: Special Jury Prize, Actor (Pryce); Natl. Bd. of Review '95: Actress (Thompson).

Carrington, V.C. *Court Martial* **1954** British army major Niven is brought up for a court-martial on embezzlement charges because he arranges, without official permission, to be reimbursed for money owed to him. A former war hero, he decides to defend himself in court, and, once an affair comes to light, his vindictive wife joins the opposition. Good cast, superlative Niven performance. **100m/B VHS.** *GB* David Niven, Margaret Leighton, Noelle Middleton, Laurence Naismith; ***D:*** Anthony Asquith.

Carry Me Back ½ **1982** Two brothers carry dead dad back to Australian ranch in order to inherit mucho dinero. **93m/C VHS.** *NZ* Grant Tilly, Kelly Johnson, Dorothy McKegg, Derek Hardwick, Joanne Mildehall, Alex Trousdell, Frank Edwards; ***D:*** John Reid; ***W:*** John Reid, Keith Aberdein, Derek Morton; ***C:*** Graeme Cowley; ***M:*** James Hall.

Carry On Admiral ½ *The Ship was Loaded* **1957** Weak British comedy about two friends who get drunk and decide it would be fun to switch identities. One has an easy job as a public relations exec but the other is supposedly the captain of a ship. His lack of sea knowledge causes wacky catastrophes. Unrelated to the "Carry On" series of comedies. **85m/B VHS.** *GB* David Tomlinson, Brian Reece, Peggy Cummins, Eunice Gayson, A.E. Matthews, Lionel Murton, Joan Sims; ***D:*** Val Guest; ***W:*** Val Guest.

Carry On at Your Convenience ½ *Carry On 'Round the Bend* **1971** Williams, who played in the original ("Carry On Sergeant"), and Carry On regulars (charpei-mugged James and ever-zaftig Jacques) go 'round the bend in yet another installment of the British spoof in and around a toilet factory. **86m/C VHS.** *GB* Sidney James, Kenneth Williams, Charles Hawtrey, Joan Sims, Kenneth Cope, Hattie Jacques; ***D:*** Gerald Thomas.

Carry On Behind **1975** "Carry On" crew heads for archeological dig and find themselves sharing site with holiday caravan. **95m/C VHS.** *GB* Sidney James, Kenneth Williams, Elke Sommer, Joan Sims; ***D:*** Gerald Thomas.

Carry On Camping ½ **1971** Another entry in the silly series finds James and Bresslaw trying to persuade their girlfriends to go on a camping trip to what the men hope is a nudist colony. They don't find nudists but they do find a group of sex-starved schoolgirls. **88m/C VHS.** *GB* Sidney James, Bernard Bresslaw, Kenneth Williams, Joan Sims, Charles Hawtrey, Barbara Windsor; ***D:*** Gerald Thomas; ***W:*** Talbot Rothwell.

Carry On Cleo ½ **1965** "Carry On" spoof of Shakespeare's "Antony and Cleopatra." The film used some of the sets from the budget-busting 1963 disaster "Cleopatra." **91m/C VHS.** *GB* Sidney James, Amanda Barrie, Kenneth Williams, Kenneth Connor, Jim Dale, Charles Hawtrey, Joan Sims; ***D:*** Gerald Thomas.

Carry On Cowboy *Rumpo Kid* **1966** "Carry On" Western parody of "High Noon." **91m/C VHS.** *GB* Sidney James, Kenneth Williams, Jim Dale, Joan Sims, Charles Hawtrey, Angela Douglas, Peter Butterworth, Bernard Bresslaw, Percy Herbert, Davy Kaye; ***D:*** Gerald Thomas; ***W:*** Talbot Rothwell; ***C:*** Alan Hume; ***M:*** Eric Rogers.

Carry On Cruising **1962** "Carry On" gang attacks sailing world with low humor and raunchiness. **89m/C VHS.** Sidney James, Kenneth Williams, Liz Fraser; ***D:*** Gerald Thomas.

Carry On Dick **1975** What made the seemingly endless "Carry On" series of super-low-budget British farces such a hit is a mystery not to be solved. Low production values, scripts that peter out midway, and manifest humor don't normally a classic make; and yet the gang has its following. "Dick," a detective movie spoof, was preceded by some 20-odd carryings on; suffice it to say that the series, which began in 1958 with "Carry on Sergeant," has not improved with age in subsequent incarnations. **95m/C VHS.** *GB* Sidney James, Joan Sims; ***D:*** Gerald Thomas.

Carry On Doctor **1968** British series continues as characters of questionable competence join the medical profession. **95m/C VHS.** *GB* Frankie Howerd, Kenneth Williams, Jim Dale, Barbara Windsor; ***D:*** Gerald Thomas.

Carry On Emmanuelle **1978** Emmanuelle, the wife of the French Ambassador to England, uses bedroom diplomacy to foster international relations. Part of the British "Carry On" series. **104m/C VHS.** *GB* Suzanne Danielle, Kenneth O'Connor, Kenneth Williams, Beryl Reid; ***D:*** Gerald Thomas.

Carry On England **1976** Mercifully, the gang didn't carry on much beyond this entry, in which a WWII anti-aircraft gun battery crew bumbles through the usual pranks and imbroglios. **89m/C VHS.** *GB* Kenneth Connor, Patrick Mower, Judy Geeson; ***D:*** Gerald Thomas.

Carry On Henry VIII ½ **1971** Slapstick sex humor with Henry marrying the French Marie of Normandie and having to deal with both her addiction to garlic and the fact that she's pregnant by her lover. **88m/C VHS.** *GB* Sidney James, Kenneth Williams, Joan Sims, Charles Hawtrey, Barbara Windsor, Kenneth Connor, Julian Holloway; ***D:*** Gerald Thomas; ***W:*** Talbot Rothwell.

Carry On Nurse **1959** Men's ward in a British hospital declares war on nurses and the rest of the hospital. The second of the "Carry On" series. **86m/B VHS.** *GB* Shirley Eaton, Kenneth Connor, Hattie Jacques, Wilfrid Hyde-White; ***D:*** Gerald Thomas.

Carry On Screaming **1966** "Carry On" does horror. A pair of goofy detectives trail monsters suspected in kidnapping. **97m/C VHS.** *GB* Harry H. Corbett, Kenneth Williams, Fenella Fielding, Joan Sims, Charles Hawtrey, Jim Dale, Angela Douglas, Jon Pertwee; ***D:*** Gerald Thomas.

The Cars That Ate Paris *The Cars That Eat People* **1974 (PG)** Parasitic town in the Parisian (Australia) outback preys on car and body parts generated by deliberate accidents inflicted by wreck-driving wreckless youths. Weir's first film released internationally, about a small Australian town that survives economically via deliberately contriving car accidents and selling the wrecks' scrap parts. A broad, bitter black comedy with some horror touches. **91m/C VHS.** *AU* Terry Camilleri, Kevin Miles, John Meillon, Melissa Jaffe; ***D:*** Peter Weir; ***W:*** Peter Weir; ***M:*** Bruce Smeaton.

Carson City Kid ½ **1940** Typical western which has Rogers trying to exact revenge on the man who killed his brother. **54m/B VHS.** Roy Rogers, George "Gabby" Hayes, Bob Steele, Noah Beery Jr., Pauline Moore, Francis McDonald, Wally Wales, Arthur Loft, George Rosener, Chester Gan; ***D:*** Joseph Kane; ***W:*** Gerald Geraghty, Robert Yost; ***C:*** William Nobles; ***M:*** Cy Feuer, Peter Tinturin.

Cartel woof! **1990 (R)** O'Keeffe, "B" actor extraordinaire, plays the wrong man to pick on in this rancid dope opera. Hounded by drug lord Stroud and framed for murder, pilot O'Keeffe decides the syndicate has gone too doggone far when they kill his sister. Exploitive and otherwise very bad. **106m/C VHS, DVD.** Miles O'Keeffe, Don Stroud, Crystal Carson, William Smith; ***D:*** John Stewart; ***W:*** Moshe Hadar; ***C:*** Thomas Callaway; ***M:*** Rick Krizman.

Carthage in Flames *Cartagine in Fiamme; Carthage en Flammes* **1960** A graphic portrayal of the destruction of ancient Carthage in a blood and guts battle for domination of the known world. A tender love story is a welcome aside in this colorful Italian-made epic. **96m/C VHS.** *IT* Anne Heywood, Jose Suarez, Pierre Brasseur; ***D:*** Carmine Gallone.

Cartier Affair **1984** A beautiful TV actress unwittingly falls in love with the man who wants to steal her jewels. Collins designed her own wardrobe. **120m/C VHS.** Joan Collins, David Hasselhoff, Telly Savalas, Ed Lauter, Joe La Due; ***D:*** Rod Holcomb; ***C:*** Hanania Baer. **TV**

Cartouche *Swords of Blood* **1962** A swashbuckling action-comedy set in 18th-century France. Belmondo plays a charming thief who takes over a Paris gang, aided by the lovely Cardinale. When he is captured, she sacrifices her life to save him and Belmondo and his cohorts vow to have their revenge. Based on a French legend and a well-acted combination of tragedy, action, and farce. In French with English subtitles. **115m/C VHS.** *FR IT* Jean-Paul Belmondo, Claudia Cardinale, Odile Versois, Philippe Lemaire; ***D:*** Philippe de Broca; ***W:*** Philippe de Broca; ***M:*** Georges Delerue.

Carve Her Name with Pride ½ **1958** The true story of Violette Szabo who at age 19 became a secret agent with the French Resistance in WWII. **119m/B VHS.** *GB* Virginia McKenna, Paul Scofield, Jack Warner, Denise Grey, Alan Saury, Maurice Ronet, Anne Leon, Nicole Stephane, Sydney Tafler, Avice Landone; ***D:*** Lewis Gilbert; ***W:*** Lewis Gilbert, Vernon Harris; ***C:*** John Wilcox; ***M:*** William Alwyn.

Carver's Gate **1996** Thanks to an environmental disaster, earth is in big trouble and its inhabitants take refuge in a virtual reality game called Afterlife. But when an engineer tries to improve the game by heightening its reality, the game's computer-generated demons get loose and it's up to cybercop Pare to stop them by traveling between virtual reality and the actual world. **97m/C VHS.** Michael Pare, Kevin Stapleton.

Casablanca **1942 (PG)** Can you see George Raft as Rick? Jack Warner did, but producer Hal Wallis wanted Bogart. Considered by many to be the best film ever made and one of the most quoted movies of all time, it rocketed Bogart from gangster roles to romantic leads as he and Bergman (who never looked lovelier) sizzle on screen. Bogart runs a gin joint in Morocco during the Nazi occupation, and meets up with Bergman, an old flame, but romance and politics do not mix, especially in Nazi-occupied French Morocco. Greenstreet, Lorre, and Rains all create memorable characters, as does Wilson, the piano player to whom Bergman says the oft-misquoted, "Play it, Sam." Without a doubt, the best closing scene ever written; it was scripted on the fly during the end of shooting, and actually shot several ways. Written from an unproduced play. See it in the original black and white. 50th Anniversary Edition contains a restored and remastered print, the original 1942 theatrical trailer, a film documentary narrated by Lauren Bacall, and a booklet. **102m/B VHS, DVD, 8mm.** Humphrey Bogart, Ingrid Bergman, Paul Henreid, Claude Rains, Peter Lorre, Sydney Greenstreet, Conrad Veidt, S.Z. Sakall, Dooley Wilson, Marcel Dalio, John Qualen, Helmut Dantine, Madeleine LeBeau, Joy Page, Leonid Kinskey, Curt Bois, Oliver Blake, Monte Blue, Martin Garralaga, Ilka Gruning, Ludwig Stossel, Frank Puglia; ***D:*** Michael Curtiz; ***W:*** Julius J. Epstein, Philip G. Epstein, Howard Koch; ***C:*** Arthur Edeson; ***M:*** Max Steiner. Oscars '43: Director (Curtiz), Picture, Screenplay; AFI '98: Top 100, Natl. Film Reg. '89.

Casablanca Express **1989** Nazi commandos hijack Churchill's train in this action-adventure drama. **90m/C VHS.** Glenn Ford, Donald Pleasence, Jason Connery; ***D:*** Sergio Martino.

Casanova **1987 (PG-13)** A comedic romp through the bedrooms of 18th-century Europe with Chamberlain as the legendary lover. Lots of lovely ladies and hammy performances. **122m/C VHS.** Richard Chamberlain, Faye Dunaway, Sylvia Kristel, Ornella Muti, Hanna Schygulla, Sophie Ward, Frank Finlay, Kenneth Colley; ***D:*** Simon Langton; ***W:*** George MacDonald Fraser; ***C:*** Giuseppe Rotunno. **TV**

Casanova Brown ½ **1944** Lighthearted comedy about a shy English professor (Cooper) who learns that his recent ex-wife (Wright) has had a baby (guess whose). When Cooper learns Wright has decided to give their daughter up for adoption he kidnaps the tyke and attempts fatherhood in a hotel room. When Wright finds out where he is, the twosome (who have really been in love all along) decide to remarry and be a family. Cooper, with baby and surrounded by diapers, makes a comedic sight. Based on the play "The Little Accident" by Floyd Dell and Thomas Mitchell. **94m/B VHS.** Gary Cooper, Teresa Wright, Frank Morgan, Anita Louise, Patricia Collinge, Edmund Breon, Jill Esmond, Emory Parnell, Isobel Elsom, Mary Treen, Halliwell Hobbes; ***D:*** Sam Wood; ***W:*** Nunnally Johnson; ***M:*** Arthur Lange.

Casanova '70 ½ **1965** Mastroianni plays a handsome soldier who has a knack for enticing liberated women in this comic rendition of the much-cinematized legendary yarn. Trouble is, he's in the mood only when he believes that he's in imminent danger. In Italian with English subtitles. **113m/C VHS.** *IT* Marcello Mastroianni, Virna Lisi, Michele Mercier, Guido Alberti, Margaret Lee, Bernard Blier, Liana Orfei; ***D:*** Mario Monicelli; ***W:*** Tonino Guerra.

Casanova's Big Night ½ **1954** Classic slapstick comedy stars Hope masquerading as Casanova to test Fontaine's virtue before her marriage to a duke. The all-star cast provides one hilarious scene after another in this dated film. Price has a cameo as the "real" Casanova. Based on a story by Aubrey Wisberg. **85m/C VHS.** Bob Hope, Joan Fontaine, Audrey Dalton, Basil Rathbone, Hugh Marlowe, Vincent Price, John Carradine, Raymond Burr; ***D:*** Norman Z. McLeod; ***W:*** Hal Kanter, Edmund Hartmann; ***C:*** Lionel Lindon.

Casbah **1948** Fine musical remake of the 1937 French film "Pepe Le Moko" and its American counterpart, 1938's "Algiers." Criminal Pepe (Martin) is safe as long as he hides out in the Casbah—outside lurks patient policeman Slimmane (Lorre), who's determined to capture him. Of course, it's l'amour that trips Pepe up when he falls for tourist Gaby (Toren), who's leaving Algiers. If Pepe had any brains, he would have stuck with hot local number, Inez (De Carlo), instead. **94m/B VHS.** Tony Martin, Peter Lorre, Yvonne De Carlo, Marta Toren, Douglas Dick, Hugo Haas, Thomas Gomez, Katherine Dunham; ***D:*** John Berry; ***W:*** Arnold Manoff; ***C:*** Irving Glassberg; ***M:*** Walter Scharf.

A Case for Murder ½ **1993 (R)** Jack Hammet has just become the youngest full partner ever at his Chicago law firm, with a knack for winning impossible cases. His next one's a beaut. Seems an envious colleague has gotten himself murdered and his estranged wife is the prime suspect. Jack decides to work with newly arrived lawyer Kate Weldon but as the two become personally involved, Kate begins to question Jack's ethics. Seems the evidence is more than a little shady and Jack isn't telling all. **94m/C VHS.** Peter Berg, Jennifer Grey, Belinda Bauer; ***D:*** Duncan Gibbins; ***W:*** Duncan Gibbins, Pablo F. Fenjves.

A Case of Deadly Force **1986** Based on the true story of a black man wrongfully killed by Boston's Tactical Police Force who mistook him for a robber. The police investigation calls it self-defense but the family and the attorney they hire fight to change the verdict. Excellent cast, great dramatic story. **95m/C VHS.** Richard Crenna, John Shea, Lorraine Toussaint, Frank McCarthy, Tom Isbell; ***D:*** Michael Miller. **TV**

A Case of Libel ½ **1983** Dramatization based on attorney Louis Nizer's account of Quentin Reynolds's libel suit against columnist Westbrook Pegler. **90m/C VHS.** Daniel J. Travanti, Ed Asner; ***D:*** Eric Till. **TV**

The Case of the Frightened Lady *The Frightened Lady* **1939** A homicidal family does its collective best to keep its dark past a secret in order to collect some inheritance money. Watch, if you're still awake, for the surprise ending. **80m/B VHS.** *GB* Marius Goring, Helen Haye, Penelope Dudley Ward, Felix Aylmer, Patrick Barr; ***D:*** George King.

The Case of the Lucky Legs ½ **1935** Yes, there was a Perry Mason before Raymond Burr. Erle Stanley Gardner's sleuthing litigator's first appearance was 1934's "The Case of the Howling Dog," which initiated Warner Bros' "A"-grade (but soon-to-be "B"-grade) series. More akin to Nick Charles than to Gardner's character or to his later TV incarnation, the "Lucky Legs" Perry is a high-living, interminably hungover tippler who winces and wisecracks as he unravels the case of the corpse of a crooked con man. William, who left shortly after the series was downgraded to "B" status, plays the esquire; Tobin plays his smart-mouthed secretary, and Ellis is the tomato suspected of murder. **76m/B VHS.** Warren William, Genevieve Tobin, Patricia Ellis, Lyle Talbot, Allen Jenkins, Barton MacLane, Peggy Shannon, Porter Hall; ***D:*** Archie Mayo.

The Case of the Mukkinese Battle Horn **1956** The cast of Britain's "The Goon Show" takes over in a zany, slapdash featurette-length mystery spoof. **27m/C VHS, 8mm.** *GB* Peter Sellers, Spike Milligan, Dick Emery; ***M:*** Edwin Astley.

Casey at the Bat **1985** From Shelley Duvall's "Tall Tales and Legends" series, in which the immortal poem is brought to life. Rousing comedy for the whole family. **52m/C VHS.** Bill Macy, Hamilton Camp, Elliott Gould, Carol Kane, Howard Cosell; ***D:*** David Steinberg. **CABLE**

Casey's Shadow **1978 (PG)** The eight-year-old son of an impoverished horse trainer raises a quarter horse and enters it in the world's richest horse race. **116m/C VHS.** Walter Matthau, Alexis Smith, Robert Webber, Murray Hamilton; ***D:*** Martin Ritt; ***C:*** John A. Alonzo.

Cash McCall ½ **1960** McCall (Garner) is a corporate raider who just loves making money. But problems come in when he falls for the lovely daughter (Wood) of his latest takeover target, failing businessman Jagger. Based on the novel by Cameron Hawley. **116m/C VHS.** James Garner, Natalie Wood, Dean Jagger, Nina Foch, E.G. Marshall, Henry Jones, Otto Kruger, Roland Winters, Parley Baer, Dabbs Greer; ***D:*** Joseph Pevney; ***W:*** Lenore Coffee, Marion Hargrove; ***C:*** George J. Folsey; ***M:*** Max Steiner.

Casino ½ **1980** Thriller about backstabbings and ritzy romance aboard a high-priced gambling liner. **100m/C VHS.** Mike Connors, Lynda Day George, Bo Hopkins, Gary Burghoff, Joseph Cotten, Robert Reed, Barry Sullivan; ***D:*** Don Chaffey. **TV**

Casino **1995 (R)** Final part of the Scorsese underworld crime trilogy that began with "Mean Streets" and continued in "GoodFellas." Casino boss Sam "Ace" Rothstein (De Niro), his ex-hustler wife Ginger (Stone), and his loose-cannon enforcer pal Nicky (Pesci) are the principals in this lengthy, fictionalized account of how the mob lost Las Vegas in a haze of drugs, sex, coincidence, and betrayal. Flashy, intricate, and unflinchingly violent account of mob-run '70s Vegas clicks when exploring the inner workings of a major casino and its hierarchy. Although Stone shines as a hedonistic money chaser, visuals are great and the soundtrack is a killer, storyline suffers from deja vu. Pileggi again adapted the screenplay from his own book. **177m/C VHS, DVD.** Robert De Niro, Joe Pesci, Sharon Stone, James Woods, Don Rickles, Alan King, Kevin Pollak, L.Q. (Justus E. McQueen) Jones, Dick Smothers, John (Joe Bob Briggs) Bloom, Frankie Avalon, Steve Allen, Jayne Meadows, Jerry Vale; ***D:*** Martin Scorsese; ***W:*** Nicholas Pileggi, Martin Scorsese; ***C:*** Robert Richardson. Golden Globes '96: Actress—Drama (Stone).

Casino Royale **1967** The product of five directors, three writers and a mismatched cast of dozens, this virtually plotless spoof of James Bond films can stand as one of the low-water marks for 1960s comedy. And yet, there are some marvelous bits within, scenes of bizarre hilarity. Welles and Sellers literally couldn't stand the sight of one another, and their scenes together were filmed separately, with stand-ins. **130m/C VHS.** David Niven, Woody Allen, Peter Sellers, Ursula Andress, Orson Welles, Jacqueline Bisset, Deborah Kerr, Peter O'Toole, Jean-Paul Belmondo, Charles Boyer, Joanna Pettet, John Huston, William Holden, George Raft; ***D:*** John Huston, Ken Hughes, Robert Parrish, Val Guest, Joseph McGrath; ***C:*** Jack Hildyard; ***M:*** Burt Bacharach.

Casper **1995 (PG)** World's friendliest ghost appears on the big screen with outstanding visual trickery (from Industrial Light and Magic) and a lively, if hokey, story. Evilish Carrigan Crittenden (Moriarty) inherits ghost-infested Whiplash Manor and hires scatterbrained "ghost therapist" Dr. Harvey (Pullman) to get rid of its unwanted occupants. His daughter Kat (Ricci) is soon the object of Casper's friendly attention while the good doc must contend with Casper's mischievous uncles—Stinkie, Fatso, and Stretch. Exec producer Spielberg shows his influence with numerous topical gags and screen references that help amuse the adults while the ghosts work their magic on the kiddies. Silberling's directorial debut; based on the comic-book and TV cartoon character created more than 30 years ago. **95m/C VHS, DVD.** Christina Ricci, Bill Pullman, Cathy Moriarty, Eric Idle, Amy Brenneman, Ben Stein; ***Cameos:*** Don Novello, Rodney Dangerfield, Clint Eastwood, Mel Gibson, Dan Aykroyd; ***D:*** Brad Silberling; ***W:*** Sherri Stoner, Deanna Oliver; ***C:*** Dean Cundey; ***M:*** James Horner; ***V:*** Malachi Pearson, Joe Nipote, Joe Alaskey, Brad Garrett.

Casque d'Or *Golden Marie* **1952** Crime passionnel in turn-of-the-century Paris as an honest carpenter (Reggiani) gets drawn into the netherworld of pimps and thieves. He's finally driven to murder—all for love of gangster's moll Marie (a very sultry Signoret). French with subtitles. **96m/B VHS.** *FR* Serge Reggiani, Simone Signoret, Claude Dauphin, Raymond Bussieres, Gaston Modot; ***D:*** Jacques Becker; ***W:*** Jacques Becker, Jacques Companeez; ***C:*** Robert Lefebvre; ***M:*** Georges Van Parys.

Cass **1978** Disenchanted filmmaker returns home to Australia to experiment with alternative lifestyles. **90m/C VHS.** Michelle Fawden, John Waters, Judy Morris, Peter Carroll.

Cass Timberlane ½ **1947** Scandalous story of a May-December romance set in a small Midwestern town. Tracy stars as Cass Timberlane, a widowed judge who falls for a voluptuous young girl from the wrong side of the tracks (Turner). They marry and experience problems when she is shunned by his snobbish friends. Good performances, especially from the supporting cast, dominate this fairly predictable film. Based on the novel by Sinclair Lewis. **119m/B VHS.** Spencer Tracy, Lana Turner, Zachary Scott, Tom Drake, Mary Astor, Albert Dekker, Margaret Lindsay, John Litel, Mona Barrie, Josephine Hutchinson, Rose Hobart, Selena Royle; ***Cameos:*** Walter Pidgeon; ***D:*** George Sidney; ***W:*** Donald Ogden Stewart.

Cassandra **1987 (R)** A fragile young woman has dreams that foretell the future—specifically, a series of grisly murders. **94m/C VHS.** Shane Briant, Brionny Behets, Tessa Humphries, Kit Taylor, Lee James; ***D:*** Colin Eggleston.

The Cassandra Crossing ½ **1976 (R)** A terrorist with the plague causes havoc on a transcontinental luxury train. Turgid adventure filmed in France and Italy. **129m/C VHS, DVD, Wide.** *GB* Sophia Loren,

Richard Harris, Ava Gardner, Burt Lancaster, Martin Sheen, Ingrid Thulin, Lee Strasberg, John Phillip Law, Lionel Stander, O.J. Simpson, Ann Turkel, Alida Valli; *D:* George P. Cosmatos; *W:* George P. Cosmatos, Tom Mankiewicz; *C:* Ennio Guarnieri; *M:* Jerry Goldsmith.

Cassie 1987 (R) Follows the rise of Cassie, a successful country and western singer, and documents all her trials along the way. **75m/C VHS.** Marilyn Chambers; *D:* Godfrey Daniels.

Cast a Dark Shadow 1955 Bogarde is the charmer who decides to reap his reward by marrying and murdering elderly women for their fortunes. But Bogarde meets his match when he plots against his latest intended (Lockwood). Tidy thriller with effective performances. Based on the play "Murder Mistaken" by Janet Green. **82m/B VHS.** *GB* Dirk Bogarde, Margaret Lockwood, Mona Washbourne, Kay Walsh, Kathleen Harrison, Robert Flemyng, Walter Hudd; *D:* Lewis Gilbert; *W:* John Cresswell.

Cast a Deadly Spell 1991 (R) A bubbly, flavorful witch's brew of private-eye and horror cliches, set in a fantasy version of 1948 Los Angeles where sorcery and voodoo abound, but gumshoe Harry P. Lovecraft uses street smarts instead of magic to track down a stolen Necronomicon—and if you know what that is you'll want to watch. Wild creatures and f/x wizardry complement this cable-TV trick and treat. **93m/C VHS.** Fred Ward, David Warner, Julianne Moore, Clancy Brown, Alexandra Powers; *D:* Martin Campbell; *W:* Joseph Dougherty, Dave Edison. CABLE

Cast a Giant Shadow 1966 Follows the career of Col. David "Mickey" Marcus, an American Jew and WWII hero who helped turn Israel's army into a formidable fighting force during the 1947-48 struggle for independence. **138m/C VHS, DVD, Wide.** Kirk Douglas, Senta Berger, Angie Dickinson, John Wayne, James Donald, Chaim Topol, Frank Sinatra, Yul Brynner; *D:* Melville Shavelson; *W:* Melville Shavelson; *C:* Aldo Tonti; *M:* Elmer Bernstein.

Cast Away ½ 2000 (PG-13) Hanks first gained, and then lost, 40 pounds for his role as FedEx employee Chuck Noland, who gets marooned on a South Pacific island for four years. He does an excellent job of showing Chuck's desperation, isolation, and finally, resignation, and for a good chunk of the movie, does it without saying a single word (although later he does get to "talk" to a volleyball named Wilson). Zemeckis does his part with amazing visuals and a restrained approach to the score, which he uses sparingly. **143m/C VHS, DVD, Wide.** Tom Hanks, Helen Hunt, Nick Searcy, Michael Forest, Viveka Davis, Christopher Noth, Geoffrey Blake, Jenifer Lewis, David Allan Brooks, Nan Martin; *D:* Robert Zemeckis; *W:* William Broyles Jr.; *C:* Don Burgess; *M:* Alan Silvestri.

Cast the First Stone 1989 Made for TV soaper based on the true story of a former nun who becomes a small town schoolteacher. After being raped, Diane Martin discovers she's pregnant and when she decides to keep the baby the school board dismisses her. The plot centers around her fight to regain her job and dignity—while trying to convince everybody that she doesn't deserve to lose her job simply because she is an unwed mother. Eikenberry gives a strong performance, but it can't carry this lackluster film. **94m/C VHS.** Jill Eikenberry, Richard Masur, Joe Spano, Lew Ayres, Holly Palance; *D:* John Korty; *M:* Ira Newborn. TV

Castaway ½ 1987 (R) Based on the factual account by Lucy Irvine. The story of Michael Wilmington, who placed an ad for a young woman to spend a year on a Pacific atoll with him, and the battle of the sexes that followed. **118m/C VHS.** *GB* Oliver Reed, Amanda Donohoe, Tony Rickards, Georgina Hale, Frances Barber, Todd Rippon; *D:* Nicolas Roeg; *W:* Allan Scott; *C:* Harvey Harrison; *M:* Stanley Myers.

The Castaway Cowboy 1974 (G) Shanghaied Texas cowboy Lincoln Constain (Garner) jumps ship in Hawaii and becomes partners with widowed Henrieatta MacAvoy (Miles) when she turns her potato farm into a cattle ranch. That means turning the islanders into cowpokes and dealing with both a local witch doctor and Henrieatta's suitor. **91m/C VHS, DVD.** James Garner, Robert Culp, Vera Miles; *D:* Vincent McEveety; *M:* Robert F. Brunner.

The Castilian ½ *Valley of the Swords* 1963 Some very odd casting in this historical tale of heroism and swordplay about a Spanish nobleman who leads his followers against the invading Moors and their evil king (Crawford). Based on a 13th century poem. **128m/C VHS.** Cesar Romero, Broderick Crawford, Alida Valli, Frankie Avalon, Espartaco (Spartaco) Santoni, Fernando Rey, Jorge (George) Rigaud; *D:* Javier Seto; *W:* Sidney Pink.

The Castle *Das Schloss* 1968 A man is summoned by the seemingly invisible occupants of a castle to their village. All his efforts to meet with those inhabiting the castle are futile and the task gradually becomes his obsession. Both wonderfully acted and shot, this is a well-executed adaptation of Franz Kafka's novel. **90m/C VHS.** *GE SI* Maximilian Schell, Cordula Trantow, Trudik Daniel, Helmut Qualtinger; *D:* Rudolf Noelte.

The Castle 1997 (R) The Kerrigans are a working class clan who happily live directly adjacent to Melbourne's Tullamarine airport. But when the airport decides to expand, their house is subject to a compulsory acquisition order. However, Daryl Kerrigan (Caton) decides to fight and takes their case all the way to the High Court in Canberra. It's a David vs. Goliath comedy with an Aussie disdain for authority figures. Cultural references may not travel overseas but the film was a hit on its home turf. **93m/C VHS, DVD.** *AU* Michael Caton, Charles Tingwell, Sophie Lee, Anne Tenney, Eric Bana, Stephen Curry, Anthony Simcoe, Wayne Hope, Tiriel Mora; *D:* Rob Sitch; *W:* Rob Sitch, Santo Cilauro, Tom Gleisner, Jane Kennedy; *C:* Miriana Marusic; *M:* Craig Harnath. Australian Film Inst. '97: Orig. Screenplay.

Castle Freak 1995 (R) Italian countess leaves her creepy haunted castle to her American nephew and his family. They find an unwelcome surprise lurking in the cellar. **90m/C VHS, DVD.** Jeffrey Combs, Barbara Crampton, Jonathan Fuller, Jessica Dollarhide; *D:* Stuart Gordon; *W:* Dennis Paoli; *C:* Mario Vulpiani; *M:* Richard Band.

Castle in the Desert ½ 1942 Charlie Chan investigates murder and other strange goings-on in a spooky old castle. One of the last in the series. **62m/B VHS.** Sidney Toler, Arleen Whelan, Richard Derr, Douglass Dumbrille, Henry Daniell, Victor Sen Yung; *D:* Harry Lachman.

Castle of Blood *Castle of Terror; Coffin of Terror; Danza Macabra; Dimensions in Death; Terrore* 1964 Staying overnight in a haunted castle, a poet is forced to deal with a number of creepy encounters. Cult favorite Steele enhances this atmospheric chiller. Dubbed in English. **85m/B VHS.** *IT FR* Barbara Steele, George Riviere, Margrete Robsahm, Henry Kruger, Montgomery Glenn, Sylvia Sorente; *D:* Anthony (Antonio Margheriti) Dawson; *W:* Jean (Giovanni Grimaldi) Grimaud; *C:* Riccardo (Pallton) Pallottini; *M:* Riz Ortolani.

The Castle of Cagliostro 1980 An animated Japanese adventure tale featuring a hero named Wolf, who's a thief. Wolf infiltrates the suspicious country of Cagliostro, whose one industry is conterfeiting money, and winds up rescuing a princess. Lots of violence to go with the action. In Japanese with English subtitles. **100m/C VHS, DVD, Wide.** *JP D:* Hayao Miyazaki.

Castle of Evil woof! 1966 Group of heirs gathers on a deserted isle to hear the reading of the will of your basic mad scientist. One by one, they fall victim to a humanoid created by the loony doc in his own image. Inspired moments of unintentional fun. **81m/C VHS.** Scott Brady, Virginia Mayo, Lisa Gaye, David Brian, Hugh Marlowe, William Thourlby, Shelly Morrison; *D:* Francis D. Lyon.

The Castle of Fu Manchu *Assignment: Istanbul; Die Folterkammer des Dr. Fu Manchu* 1968 (PG) The final chapter in a series starring Lee as the wicked doctor. This time, Lee has developed a gadget which will put the earth into a deep freeze, and at his mercy. To fine tune this contraption, he enlists the help of a gifted scientist by abducting him. However, the helper/hostage has a bad ticker, so Lee must abduct a heart surgeon to save his life, and thus, the freezer project. Most critics felt this was the weakest installment in the series. **92m/C VHS.** *GE SP IT GB* Christopher Lee, Richard Greene, Howard Marion-Crawford, Tsai Chin, Gunther Stoll, Rosalba (Sara Bay) Neri, Maria Perschy, Werner Abrolat, Jose Martin; *D:* Jess (Jesus) Franco; *W:* Harry Alan Towers; *C:* Manuel Merino; *M:* Gert Wilden.

Castle of the Creeping Flesh woof! 1968 A surgeon's daughter is brutally murdered. Vowing to bring her back he begins ripping out the organs of innocent people and transplanting them into her body. Has the dubious honor of being one of the few movies to sport actual open heart surgery footage. So bad it's...just bad. **85m/C VHS.** Adrian Hoven, Janine Reynaud, Howard Vernon; *D:* Percy G. Parker.

Castle of the Living Dead *Il Castello de Morti Vivi* 1964 Evil Count Drago's hobbies include mummifying a traveling circus group visiting his castle. Lee is as evil as ever, but be sure to look for Sutherland's screen debut. In a dual role, he plays not only the bumbling inspector, but also a witch, in drag. **90m/B VHS.** *IT FR* Christopher Lee, Gaia Germani, Phillippe LeRoy, Jacques Stanislawsky, Donald Sutherland; *D:* Herbert Wise.

Casual Sex? ½ 1988 (R) Two young women, looking for love and commitment, take a vacation at a posh resort where they are confronted by men with nothing on their minds but sex, be it casual or the more formal black-tie variety. Supposedly an examination of safe sex in a lightly comedic vein, though the comic is too light and the morality too limp. Adapted from the play by Wendy Goldman and Judy Toll. **87m/C VHS, DVD.** Lea Thompson, Victoria Jackson, Stephen Shellen, Jerry Levine, Mary Gross, Andrew (Dice Clay) Silverstein; *D:* Genevieve Robert; *W:* William Goldman, Judy Toll; *C:* Rolf Kestermann; *M:* Van Dyke Parks.

Casualties 1997 (R) Annie's (Goodall) got very unfortunate luck with men. Her abusive husband Bill's (Gries) a cop and she can't safely get away from home. Then she meets a seemingly nice guy, Tommy (Harmon), at her cooking class, who offers to help Annie out. But when Tommy's behavior becomes erratic (turns out he's a hitman), Annie figures she just has to rely on herself. **86m/C VHS.** Mark Harmon, Caroline Goodall, Michael Beach, Jonathan (Jon Francis) Gries, John Diehl; *D:* Alex Graves; *W:* Alex Graves.

Casualties of Love: The "Long Island Lolita" Story 1993 (PG-13) Told from the Buttafuoco's point of view, Amy Fisher was nothing but a wacko fatally attracted teenager who misunderstood Joey's harmless flirtations and deliberately went after his wife with a gun. The Buttafuocos received $300,000 from CBS to tell their side of the story which features Milano, who resembles Amy not in the least, as the lead. One of three competing network TV versions of the sordid story. See also: "The Amy Fisher Story" and "Lethal Lolita—Amy Fisher: My Story." **94m/C VHS.** Jack Scalia, Alyssa Milano, Phyllis Lyons, Jack Kehler, Michael Bowen, J.E. Freeman, Nick(y) Corello, Lawrence Tierney, Peter Van Norden, Anne DeSalvo, Leo Rossi; *D:* John Herzfeld; *W:* John Herzfeld; *C:* Karl Walter Lindenlaub; *M:* David Michael Frank. TV

Casualties of War 1989 (R) A Vietnam war morality play about army private Fox in the bush who refuses to let his fellow soldiers and commanding sergeant (Penn) skirt responsibility for the rape and murder of a native woman. Fox achieves his dramatic breakthrough. Based on the true story by Daniel Lang. **120m/C VHS, DVD, 8mm, Wide.** Sean Penn, Michael J. Fox, Don Harvey, Thuy Thu Le, John Leguizamo, Sam Robards, John C. Reilly, Erik King, Dale Dye; *D:* Brian DePalma; *W:* David Rabe; *C:* Stephen Burum; *M:* Ennio Morricone.

A Casualty of War ½ 1990 (R) Made-for-TV adaptation of Frederick Forsyth's thriller about modern-day arms smuggling (Libya to Ireland) and espionage. Well-acted, with the exception of Hack. **96m/C VHS.** Shelley Hack, David Threlfall, Richard Hope, Alan Howard, Clarke Peters; *D:* Tom Clegg; *W:* Frederick Forsyth.

The Cat 1966 A boy and a tamed mountain lion become friends on the run from a murderous poacher. **95m/C VHS.** Peggy Ann Garner, Roger Perry, Barry Coe; *D:* Ellis Kadison.

Cat and Mouse ½ *Le Chat et la Souris* 1978 (PG) A very unorthodox police inspector is assigned to investigate a millionaire's mysterious death. Who done it? French dialogue with English subtitles. **107m/C VHS.** *FR* Michele Morgan, Serge Reggiani, Jean-Pierre Aumont, Philippe Labro, Philippe Leotard, Valerie Lagrange, Michel Perelon, Christine Laurent; *D:* Claude Lelouch; *W:* Claude Lelouch; *C:* Andre Perlstein; *M:* Francis Lai.

The Cat and the Canary 1927 A group of greedy relatives gather on a stormy night in a creepy mansion for the reading of a 20-year-old will. But before anyone can claim the money, they must spend the night in the manor—and an escaped lunatic is at large! Remade twice, once in 1939 and again in 1979. **81m/B VHS, DVD.** Laura La Plante, Creighton Hale, Tully Marshall, Gertrude Astor, Arthur Edmund Carewe, Lucien Littlefield; *D:* Paul Leni; *W:* Robert F. "Bob" Hill, Alfred A. Cohn; *C:* Gilbert Warrenton.

The Cat and the Canary 1979 (PG) A stormy night, a gloomy mansion, and a mysterious will combine to create an atmosphere for murder. An entertaining remake of the 1927 silent film. **96m/C VHS, DVD.** *GB* Carol Lynley, Michael Callan, Wendy Hiller, Olivia Hussey, Daniel Massey, Honor Blackman, Edward Fox, Wilfrid Hyde-White, Beatrix Lehmmann, Peter McEnery; *D:* Radley Metzger; *W:* Radley Metzger; *C:* Alex Thomson.

The Cat and the Fiddle 1934 Lovely Jerome Kern-Oscar Hammerstein operetta in which Novarro plays a struggling composer who forces his affections on MacDonald. She sings in response to his romantic proposals. The final sequence is in color. ♫The Night Was Made for Love; She Didn't Say 'Yes'; A New Love is Old; Try to Forget; One Moment Alone; Don't Ask Us Not To Sing; I Watch the Love Parade; The Breeze Kissed Your Hair; Impressions in a Harlem Flat. **90m/B VHS.** Ramon Novarro, Jeanette MacDonald, Frank Morgan, Charles Butterworth, Jean Hersholt, Vivienne Segal, Frank Conroy, Henry Armetta, Adrienne D'Ambricourt, Joseph Cawthorn; *D:* William K. Howard; *W:* Bella Spewack, Samuel Spewack, Jerome Kern; *C:* Charles Clarke, Ray Rennahan, Harold Rosson; *M:* Herbert Stothart, Jerome Kern.

Cat Ballou ½ 1965 At the turn of the century, a schoolmarm turns outlaw with the help of a drunken gunman. Marvin played Kid Shelleen and his silver-nosed evil twin Tim Strawn in this cheery spoof of westerns. Cole and Kaye sing the narration in a one of a kind Greek chorus. **96m/C VHS, DVD, Wide.** Jane Fonda, Lee Marvin, Michael Callan, Dwayne Hickman, Reginald Denny, Nat King Cole, Stubby Kaye; *D:* Elliot Silverstein; *W:* Frank Pierson; *C:* Jack Marta; *M:* Frank DeVol. Oscars '65: Actor (Marvin); Berlin Intl. Film Fest. '65: Actor (Marvin); British Acad. '65: Actor (Marvin); Golden Globes '66: Actor—Mus./Comedy (Marvin); Natl. Bd. of Review '65: Actor (Marvin).

Cat Chaser 1990 Weller walks listlessly through the role of an ex-soldier in Miami who has an affair with the wife of an exiled—but still lethal—military dictator. Surpisingly low-key, sometimes effective thriller that saves its energy for sex scenes, also available in a less steamy, 90-minute "R" rated version. Based on an Elmore Leonard novel. **97m/C VHS.** Kelly McGillis, Peter Weller, Charles Durning, Frederic Forrest, Tomas Milian, Juan Fernandez; *D:* Abel Ferrara; *W:* Elmore Leonard, Jim Borrelli; *M:* Chick Corea.

The Cat from Outer Space 1978 (G) An extraterrestrial cat named Jake crashes his spaceship on Earth and leads a group of people on endless escapades. Enjoyable Disney fare. **103m/C VHS, DVD.** Ken Berry, Sandy Duncan, Harry (Henry) Morgan, Roddy McDowall, McLean Stevenson; ***D:*** Norman Tokar; ***W:*** Ted Key; ***C:*** Charles F. Wheeler; ***M:*** Lalo Schifrin.

Cat Girl 🦴 **1957** A young bride on her honeymoon finds she has inherited the family curse—she has a psychic link to a ferocious leopard. Numerous murders ensue. Poor production value and a weak script, despite Shelley's fine acting, make this an unworthwhile film. **69m/B VHS.** Barbara Shelley, Robert Ayres, Kay Callard, Paddy Webster; ***D:*** Alfred Shaughnessy.

Cat in the Cage 🦴½ **1968** A young man finds many things have changed at home while he was in a mental institution. Dad has remarried, the housekeeper is practicing witchcraft, the chauffeur is after his mistress, and the cat is gone. So where'd that cat go? **96m/C VHS.** Colleen Camp, Sybil Danning, Mel Novak, Frank De Kova; ***D:*** Tony Zarin Dast.

The Cat o' Nine Tails 🦴 **1971 (PG)** A blind detective and a newsman team up to find a sadistic killer. A gory murder mystery. **112m/C VHS, DVD, Wide.** *GE FR IT* Karl Malden, James Franciscus, Catherine Spaak, Cinzia de Carolis, Carlo Alighiero; ***D:*** Dario Argento; ***W:*** Dario Argento; ***C:*** Erico Menczer; ***M:*** Ennio Morricone.

Cat on a Hot Tin Roof 🦴🦴🦴½ **1958** Tennessee Williams' powerful play about greed and deception in a patriarchal Southern family. Big Daddy (Ives) is dying. Members of the family greedily attempt to capture his inheritance, tearing the family apart. Taylor is a sensual wonder as Maggie the Cat, though the more controversial elements of the play were toned down for the film version. Intense, believable performances from Ives and Newman. **108m/C VHS, DVD.** Paul Newman, Burl Ives, Elizabeth Taylor, Jack Carson, Judith Anderson; ***D:*** Richard Brooks; ***W:*** Richard Brooks, James Poe; ***C:*** William H. Daniels.

Cat on a Hot Tin Roof 🦴🦴½ **1984** Showtime/PBS co-production of the Tennesse Williams classic about alcoholic ex-jock Brick (Jones) and his sultry wife Maggie (Lange) and their desires. This version uses a script revised by Williams to revive some of the sexual frankness watered down in other productions. **122m/C VHS, DVD.** Tommy Lee Jones, Jessica Lange, Rip Torn, Kim Stanley, David Dukes, Penny Fuller; ***D:*** Jack Hofsiss; ***W:*** Tennessee Williams. **TV**

Cat People 🦴🦴🦴 **1942** Irena (Simon) is an immigrant from the Balkans who believes in a curse that will change her into a deadly panther who must kill to survive. So she won't consummate her marriage to Oliver (Smith). When he confides her troubles to co-worker Alice (Randolph), Irena's jealousy precipitates her transformation as she stalks Alice. A classic among the horror genre with unrelenting terror from beginning to end, especially since the metamophosis only suggested. First horror film from RKO producer Val Lewton. **73m/B VHS.** Simone Simon, Kent Smith, Jane Randolph, Jack Holt, Elizabeth Russell, Alan Napier, Tom Conway; ***D:*** Jacques Tourneur; ***W:*** DeWitt Bodeen; ***C:*** Nicholas Musuraca; ***M:*** Roy Webb. Natl. Film Reg. '93.

Cat People 🦴🦴½ **1982 (R)** A beautiful young woman learns that she has inherited a strange family trait—she turns into a vicious panther when sexually aroused. The only person with whom she can safely mate is her brother, a victim of the same genetic heritage. Kinski is mesmerizing as the innocent, sensual woman. Remake of the 1942 film. **118m/C VHS, DVD, Wide.** Nastassia Kinski, Malcolm McDowell, John Heard, Annette O'Toole, Ruby Dee, Ed Begley Jr., John Larroquette; ***D:*** Paul Schrader; ***W:*** Alan Ormsby; ***C:*** John Bailey; ***M:*** Giorgio Moroder.

Cat Women of the Moon 🦴🦴 *Rocket to the Moon* **1953** Scientists land on the moon and encounter an Amazon-like force of skimpily attired female chauvinists. Remade as "Missile to the Moon." Featuring the Hollywood Cover Girls as various cat women. Available in its original 3-D format. **65m/B VHS, DVD.** Sonny Tufts, Victor Jory, Marie Windsor, Bill Phipps, Douglas Fowley, Carol Brewster, Suzanne Alexander, Susan Morrow, Ellye Marshall, Bette Arlen, Judy W, Roxann Delman; ***D:*** Arthur Hilton; ***W:*** Roy Hamilton; ***C:*** William F. Whitley; ***M:*** Elmer Bernstein.

Cataclysm 🦴🦴½ *Satan's Supper* **1981 (R)** A swell flick about a sadistic demon who spends his time either finding people willing to join him or killing the people who won't. **94m/C VHS.** Cameron Mitchell, Marc Lawrence, Faith Clift, Charles Moll; ***D:*** Tom McGowan, Greg Tallas, Philip Marshak.

Catacombs 🦴 **1989 (R)** An investigative monk and a beautiful photographer stumble across a mysterious, centuries-old evil power. **112m/C VHS.** Timothy Van Patten, Laura Schaefer, Ian Abercrombie, Jeremy West; ***D:*** David Schmoeller; ***W:*** C. Courtney Joyner; ***M:*** Pino Donaggio.

The Catamount Killing 🦴½ **1974 (PG)** The story of a small town bank manager and his lover. They decide to rob the bank and run for greener pastures only to find their escape befuddled at every turn. **82m/C VHS.** *GE* Horst Buchholz, Ann Wedgeworth; ***D:*** Krzysztof Zanussi.

Catch as Catch Can 🦴 *Lo Scatenato* **1968** An Italian male model is comically besieged by animals of every type, making a mess of his life and career. Dubbed. **95m/C VHS.** *IT* Vittorio Gassman, Martha Hyer, Gila Golan; ***D:*** Franco Indovina; ***M:*** Luis Bacalov.

Catch Me a Spy 🦴½ *To Catch a Spy* **1971** A foreign agent attempts to lure an innocent man into becoming part of a swap for an imprisoned Russian spy. **94m/C VHS.** *GB FR* Kirk Douglas, Tom Courtenay, Trevor Howard, Marlene Jobert, Bernard Blier, Patrick Mower, Bernadette LaFont; ***D:*** Dick Clement; ***W:*** Dick Clement, Ian LaFrenais; ***M:*** Claude Bolling.

Catch Me ... If You Can 🦴🦴 **1989 (PG)** High school class president Melissa doesn't want to see the school torn down. To raise fast cash, she teams up with a drag racer and the fun begins. **105m/C VHS.** Matt Lattanzi, Loryn Locklin, M. Emmet Walsh, Geoffrey Lewis; ***D:*** Stephen Sommers.

Catch the Heat 🦴 *Feel the Heat* **1987 (R)** Alexandra is an undercover narcotics agent sent to infiltrate Steiger's South American drug operation. **90m/C VHS.** Tiana Alexandra, David Dukes, Rod Steiger; ***D:*** Joel Silberg; ***W:*** Stirling Silliphant; ***M:*** Tom Chase, Steve Rucker.

Catch-22 🦴🦴🦴 **1970 (R)** Buck Henry's adaptation of Joseph Heller's black comedy about a group of fliers in the Mediterranean during WWII. A biting anti-war satire portraying the insanity of the situation in both a humorous and disturbing manner. Perhaps too literal to the book's masterfully chaotic structure, causing occasional problems in the "are you following along department?" Arkin heads a fine and colorful cast. **121m/C VHS, DVD, Wide.** Alan Arkin, Martin Balsam, Art Garfunkel, Jon Voight, Richard Benjamin, Buck Henry, Bob Newhart, Paula Prentiss, Martin Sheen, Charles Grodin, Anthony Perkins, Orson Welles, Jack Gilford, Bob Balaban, Susanne Benton, Norman Fell, Austin Pendleton, Peter Bonerz, Jon Korkes, Collin Wilcox-Paxton, John Brent; ***D:*** Mike Nichols; ***W:*** Buck Henry; ***C:*** David Watkin.

The Catcher 🦴½ **1998** After being released from an insane asylum, a man returns to the ballfield where he murdered his father and begins hanging around the minor-league stadium in order to finish off various players and managers. **90m/C VHS.** David Heavener, Monique Parent, Joe Estevez, Sean Dillingham; ***D:*** Guy Crawford, Yvette Hoffman. **VIDEO**

The Catered Affair 🦴🦴🦴 *Wedding Breakfast* **1956** Davis, anti-typecast as a Bronx housewife, and Borgnine, as her taxi-driving husband, play the determined parents of soon-to-be-wed Reynolds set on giving her away in a style to which she is not accustomed. Based on Paddy Chayefsky's teleplay, the catered affair turns into a familial trial, sharing the true-to-life poignancy that marked "Marty," the Oscar-winning Chayefsky drama of the previous year. **92m/B VHS.** Bette Davis, Ernest Borgnine, Debbie Reynolds, Barry Fitzgerald, Rod Taylor, Robert F. Simon; ***D:*** Richard Brooks; ***W:*** Gore Vidal; ***C:*** John Alton; ***M:*** Andre Previn.

Catfish in Black Bean Sauce 🦴🦴½ **2000 (PG-13)** While serving in Vietnam, African-American Harold Williams (Winfield) saved the lives of Vietnamese Mai (Tom) and her young brother Dwayne (Lo) and he and wife Dolores (Alice) adopted the duo. Dwayne acts black and has a black girlfriend, Nina (Lathan), but married Mai has never forgotten her roots and announces to the stunned family that she has located her birth mother, Thanh (Chinh), and the woman is coming not only to visit but to live with her. But Thanh turns out to be a critical schemer, unreasonably jealous of the Williams', and determined to reclaim her grown children, no matter what the cost. **111m/C VHS, DVD.** Chi Muoi Lo, Lauren Tom, Kieu Chinh, Paul Winfield, Mary Alice, Sanaa Lathan, Tzi Ma, Tyler Christopher; ***D:*** Chi Muoi Lo; ***W:*** Chi Muoi Lo; ***C:*** Dean Lent; ***M:*** Stanley A. Smith.

Catherine & Co. 🦴½ **1976 (R)** Lonely, penniless girl arrives in Paris and "opens shop" on the streets of Paris. As business booms, she takes a cue from the big corporations and sells stock in herself. **91m/C VHS.** *FR IT* Jane Birkin, Patrick Dewaere, Jean-Pierre Aumont, Jean-Claude Brialy; ***D:*** Michel Boisrond.

Catherine Cookson's Colour Blind 🦴🦴½ *Colour Blind* **1998** In post-WWI England, Bridget McQueen comes to stay with her sprawling, poor family with her new husband and their baby daughter. But Bridget has neglected to tell her family that her husband is black. This not only stirs up a lot of trouble but more tribulations follow as Bridget's mixed-race daughter grows up. On two cassettes. **150m/C VHS.** *GB* Niamh Cusack, Carmen Ejogo, Art Malik, Tony Armatrading. **TV**

Catherine Cookson's The Black Velvet Gown 🦴🦴½ *The Black Velvet Gown* **1992** Riah Millican (McTeer) is a poor miner's widow living in rural 1834 England with her three children. She finds work as a housekeeper to the reclusive Miller (Peck), who agrees to educate her children and even gives Riah the titular gown, which was once his mother's. Now educated out of their working-class, the Millican's lives provide unexpected love and tragedy for all concerned. Based on the novel by Catherine Cookson; made for British TV. **103m/C VHS.** *GB* Janet McTeer, Bob Peck, Geraldine Somerville; ***D:*** Norman Stone. **TV**

Catherine Cookson's The Cinder Path 🦴🦴½ *The Cinder Path* **1994** Coming-of-age story begins in 1913 with unassuming Charlie MacFell (Owen) forced to take over the family farm. Charlie (who needs a spine transplant) also goes along with an arranged marriage to local lovely Victoria (Zeta-Jones), a disaster since she's little more than a well-bred tart and it's her younger sister Nellie (Miles) who's really in love with Charlie anyway. As if Charlie didn't have enough to cope with, he's soon an army soldier as WWI begins and up against vindictive Ginger (Byrne), a former farmhand who resents the monied classes Charlie represents. Based on the novel by Catherine Cookson. **145m/C VHS, DVD.** *GB* Lloyd Owen, Catherine Zeta-Jones, Maria Miles, Antony Byrne, Tom Bell; ***D:*** Simon Langton; ***W:*** Alan Seymour; ***M:*** Barrington Pheloung. **TV**

Catherine Cookson's The Dwelling Place 🦴🦴½ *The Dwelling Place* **199?** Sixteen-year-old Cissie (Whitwell) struggles to hold her family together after the death of their parents in 1830's England. But her situation turns tragic when she's raped and left pregnant but drunken young aristocrat Clive (Rawle-Hicks), eventually giving the baby to be raised by Clive's father (Fox). Based on a novel by Catherine Cookson. **145m/C VHS.** *GB* Tracy Whitwell, James Fox, Edward Rawle-Hicks; ***D:*** Gavin Millar. **TV**

Catherine Cookson's The Fifteen Streets 🦴🦴½ *The Fifteen Streets* **1990** Kind-hearted dock worker John O'Brien (Teale) is the quiet one in a boozing, brawling Irish family living in near poverty in late-Victorian England. He meets well-bred schoolteacher Mary Llewellyn (Holman) and the two fall in love but bigotry, scandal, and tragedy challenge their chances at happiness. Based on a novel by Catherine Cookson. **108m/C VHS.** *GB* Owen Teale, Clare Holman, Sean Bean, Billie Whitelaw, Ian Bannen, Jane Horrocks, Anny Tobin, Leslie Schofield; ***D:*** David Wheatley; ***W:*** Rob Bettinson. **TV**

Catherine Cookson's The Gambling Man 🦴🦴½ *The Gambling Man* **1998** Rent collector Rory O'Connor is ambitious to escape his humble past and his talent at gambling leads him to winning a fortune. But a lie and a tragedy return to haunt him. Based on a book by Catherine Cookson. **150m/C VHS.** *GB* Robson Green, Sylvestria Le Touzel, Bernard Hill, Stephanie Putson, Anne Kent. **TV**

Catherine Cookson's The Girl 🦴🦴½ *The Girl* **1996** Illegitimate Hannah Boyle is simply called "The Girl" by her jealous stepmother, who forces her into a disastrous marriage. But Hannah is willing to fight to regain her freedom and the man she truly loves. TV adaptation of the novel by Catherine Cookson. **148m/C VHS, DVD.** *GB* Sidbhan Flynn, Malcolm Stoddard, Jonathan Cake, Jill Baker, Mark Benton; ***D:*** David Wheatley; ***W:*** Gordon Hann. **TV**

Catherine Cookson's The Glass Virgin 🦴🦴½ *The Glass Virgin* **1995** In 1859, young Annabella Lagrange (Mortimer) discovers that her spendthrift father, Edmund (Haver), has been hiding the secrets surrounding her birth. These revelations force Annabella to find her own way in a new life. Based on a novel by Catherine Cookson. **150m/C VHS.** *GB* Emily Mortimer, Nigel Havers, Brendan Coyle, Christine Kavanagh, Sylvia Syms, Samantha Glenn, Jan Graveson; ***D:*** Sarah Hellings. **TV**

Catherine Cookson's The Man Who Cried 🦴🦴½ *The Man Who Cried* **1993** Abel Mason (Hinds) is an unhappily married man with a vindictive wife (Walsh) and a young son he's desperate to provide for. When an affair with a married woman ends in murder, Mason and his son travel in search of a new life. Desperate for a home, Mason enters into a bigamous marriage with a widow—only to find himself falling in love with her sister. Based on the novel by Catherine Cookson. Set in the years between England's depression and WW2. **156m/C VHS.** *GB* Ciaran Hinds, Amanda Root, Kate Buffery, Angela Walsh, Daniel Massey; ***D:*** Michael Whyte. **TV**

Catherine Cookson's The Moth 🦴🦴½ *The Moth* **1996** Robert Bradley leaves the shipyards to work in his uncle's furniture business but soon finds himself at odds with the old man. So he becomes a servant for the destructive Thormans, and falls for the lady of the house, Sarah. But in 1913 this upstairs/downstairs romance can only lead to disaster. TV movie based on the novel by Catherine Cookson. **150m/C VHS.** *GB* Jack Davenport, Juliet Aubrey, David Bradley, Justine Waddell. **TV**

Catherine Cookson's The Rag Nymph 🦴🦴½ *The Rag Nymph* **1996** Aggie Winkowski finds 10-year-old Millie Forrester abandoned on the streets. Knowing how dangerous the child's life could become, Aggie decides to take Millie in. TV movie based on the novel by Catherine Cookson. **150m/C VHS.** *GB* Honeysuckle Weeks, Val McLane, Alec Newman, Perdita Weeks, Crispin Bonham Carter. **TV**

Catherine Cookson's The Round Tower 🦴🦴½ *The Round Tower* **1998** Post-WWII Britain finds 17-year-old Vanessa Radcliffe pregnant. Her wealthy, socially-conscious parents are appalled, especially when they think the father is the son of their housekeeper, Angus Cotten. He's not but winds up marrying Vanessa anyway—this unlikely circumstance putting Angus on the road to success. On 2 cassettes. **150m/C VHS.** *GB* Emilia Fox, Keith Barron, Jan Harvey, Ben Miles, Denis Lawson; ***D:*** Alan Grint; ***W:*** T.R. Bowen; ***C:*** Robin Vidgeon. **TV**

Catherine Cookson's The Secret 🦴🦴🦴 *The Secret* **2000** Complex historical thriller is based on Catherine Cookson's "The Harrogate Secret." In 19th-century England, Freddie Musgrave (Buchanan) has to work through secrets hidden in his own past as a runner and messenger for criminals. Anonymous letters, diamonds, and the like are involved. **156m/C DVD.** *GB* Colin Buchanan, June Whitfield, Stephen Moyer, Hannah Yelland, Clare Higgins; ***D:*** Alan Grint; ***W:*** T.R. Bowen; ***C:*** Allan Pyrah; ***M:*** Colin Towns. **TV**

Catherine Cookson's The Tide of Life 🦴🦴½ *The Tide of Life* **1996** TV adaptation of Catherine Cookson's novel finds young Emily Kennedy entering service as a maid to the McGilby family and weathering various tragedies, romantic and otherwise. **156m/C VHS.** *GB* Gillian Kearney, Ray Stevenson, John Bowler, James Purefoy, Diana Hardcastle.

Catherine Cookson's The Wingless Bird 🦴🦴½ *The Wingless Bird* **1997** Agnes Conway (Skinner) is the strong-minded daughter of a Newcastle shop-owner in class-conscious England in December, 1913. Managing her unhappy father's store, Claire waits on two members of the wealthy Farrier family and is soon drawn into their lives when the younger Farrier son, Charles (Atterton), falls in love with her, despite their class differences. But the Conway's have their own class problems—Agnes' younger sister Jessie becomes pregnant by a lower-class lad and her father's fury is murderous. Still as Agnes' love for Charlie grows, she must also deal with the outbreak of WWI, which will bring changes for all concerned. **156m/C VHS.** *GB* Claire Skinner, Edward Atterton, Julian Wadham, Frank Grimes, Moira Redmond, Elspet Gray, Dinsdale Landen, Anne Reid; ***D:*** David Wheatley; ***W:*** Alan Seymour; ***M:*** Colin Towns. **TV**

Catherine Cookson's Tilly Trotter 🦴🦴½ *Tilly Trotter* **1999** Tilly lives in rural England in the 1830s where the young woman is envied for her beauty by the local ladies and lusted after because of that same beauty by the local gentlemen. Accused of witchcraft, Tilly is rescued by a married farmer but there's another romance on the horizon as well. **210m/C VHS.** *GB* Carli Norris, Simon Shepherd, Gavin Abbott, Madelaine Newton, Rosemary Leach, Basil Moss, Amelia Bullmore, Richard Dempsey; ***D:*** Alan Grint; ***W:*** Ray Marshall; ***C:*** Robin Vidgeon; ***M:*** Colin Towns. **TV**

Catherine the Great 🦴🦴½ *The Rise of Catherine the Great* **1934** Slow but lavish and engrossing British dramatization of the tortured and doomed love affair between Catherine, Empress of Russia, and her irrational, drunken husband Peter. **88m/B VHS.** *GB* Douglas Fairbanks Jr., Elisabeth Bergner, Flora Robson; ***D:*** Paul Czinner; ***C:*** Georges Perinal.

Catherine the Great 🦴🦴½ **1995** Teenaged German princess Sophia (Zeta-Jones) marries into Russian royalty in 1744 when she weds Peter (Jaenicke), nephew of the Empress Elizabeth (Moreau), and has a name change when she's crowned Catherine II. The marriage is a disaster and with the help of her lover Gregory Orlov (McGann), Catherine eventually gets rid of Peter and is crowned Empress and Czarina of all the Russias as she struggles to drag her medieval empire into the modern world. Typically lavish and simplistic historical retelling. Originally released as a two-part miniseries. **100m/C VHS, DVD.** *GE* Catherine Zeta-Jones, Paul McGann, Ian Richardson, Jeanne Moreau, Mark McGann, Hannes Jaenicke, Mel Ferrer, Omar Sharif, John Rhys-Davies, Brian Blessed; ***D:*** Marvin J. Chomsky; ***W:*** John Goldsmith; ***C:*** Elemer Ragalyi; ***M:*** Laurence Rosenthal. **TV**

Catherine's Grove 🦴½ **1998 (R)** Miami detective Jack Doyle (Fahey) is tracking down a serial killer while moonlighting as a P.I. Along with girlfriend Charley (Alonso), Jack's investigating the disappearance of rich girl Catherine, who may be involved with her creepy Uncle Joe (Madsen). So, do you think Doyle's two cases could possibly be connected? **91m/C VHS.** Michael Madsen, Jeff Fahey, Maria Conchita Alonso, Priscilla Barnes, Jeffrey Donovan; ***D:*** Rick King; ***W:*** Tony DiTocco; ***C:*** Bart Tau; ***M:*** Harry Manfredini. **VIDEO**

Catholics 🦴🦴🦴 *The Conflict* **1973** A sensitive exploration of contemporary mores and changing attitudes within the Roman Catholic church. Sheen is sent by the Pope to Ireland to reform some priests. Based on Brian Moore's short novel. **86m/C VHS.** Martin Sheen, Trevor Howard; ***D:*** Jack Gold; ***M:*** Carl Davis. **TV**

Cathy's Curse 🦴 *Cauchemares* **1977** The spirit of her aunt, who died as a child, possesses a young girl in this Canadian-French collaboration. Tries to capitalize on the popularity of "The Exorcist," but falls seriously short. **90m/C VHS.** *FR CA* Alan Scarfe, Beverly Murray; ***D:*** Eddy Matalon.

Catlow 🦴🦴½ **1971 (PG-13)** A comedic western with Brynner aiming to steal $2 million in gold from under the nose of his friend, lawman Crenna. Based on the novel by Louis L'Amour. **103m/C VHS.** Yul Brynner, Richard Crenna, Leonard Nimoy, JoAnn Pflug, Jeff Corey, Michael Delano, David Ladd, Bessie Love; ***D:*** Sam Wanamaker; ***W:*** Scot (Scott) Finch, J.J. Griffith.

Cats & Dogs 🦴🦴 **2001 (PG)** Mix of live-action and animatronics as the secret war between cats and dogs is exposed in your neighborhood. It seems the latest cat plot is to destroy a vaccine that would prevent all human allergies to dogs and the dogs, of course, must keep that from happening. The human actors are upstaged at every turn (naturally) and the plot showcases some inconsistent pacing, but the kids should enjoy it (unless they like cats) and adults won't hate it until, say, the sixth or seventh viewing. **87m/C VHS, DVD.** *US* Jeff Goldblum, Elizabeth Perkins, Miriam Margolyes, Alexander Pollock; ***D:*** Lawrence (Larry) Guterman; ***W:*** John Requa, Glenn Ficarra; ***C:*** Julio Macat; ***M:*** John Debney; ***V:*** Glenn Ficarra, Tobey Maguire, Sean P. Hayes, Alec Baldwin, Joe Pantoliano, Susan Sarandon, Michael Clarke Duncan, Jon Lovitz, Charlton Heston, Salome Jens.

Cats Don't Dance 🦴🦴 **1997 (G)** Animated musical/comedy finds Danny (Bakula) a hoofer wanna-be trying to break into '30s Hollywood. Only problem is that he's a cat and can't understand why he only gets parts playing animals. He gets into trouble with bratty human star Darla Dimple (Peldon) and nearly sees his chance at a career vanish. Combines "Singin' in the Rain" and "Who Framed Roger Rabbit," with some showbiz cynicism from "The Player" to create a cartoon that will most likely sail over the heads of its target audience. Most of the time, as in the old Warner Bros. classics, that's a good thing. Not in this case, however. **77m/C VHS.** ***D:*** Mark Dindal; ***W:*** Cliff Ruby, Roberts Gannaway, Elana Lesser, Theresa Pettengill; ***M:*** Steve Goldstein, Randy Newman; ***V:*** Scott Bakula, Jasmine Guy, Ashley Peldon, Kathy Najimy, John Rhys-Davies, George Kennedy, Rene Auberjonois, Hal Holbrook, Don Knotts, Frank Welker, David Johansen, Natalie Cole.

Cat's Eye 🦴🦴 *Stephen King's Cat's Eye* **1985 (PG-13)** An anthology of three Stephen King short stories connected by a stray cat who wanders through each tale. **94m/C VHS.** Drew Barrymore, James Woods, Alan King, Robert Hays, Candy Clark, Kenneth McMillan, James Naughton, Charles S. Dutton; ***D:*** Lewis Teague; ***W:*** Stephen King; ***C:*** Jack Cardiff; ***M:*** Alan Silvestri.

The Cat's Meow 🦴🦴½ **2001 (PG-13)** Bogdanovich takes on an old Hollywood scandal in this period drama. In 1924 publishing tycoon William Randolph Hearst (Herrmann) and his much-younger mistress, actress Marion Davies (Dunst), invite a group of partygoers aboard Hearst's yacht for a weekend. Producer/director Thomas Ince (Elwes) dies—but how is in question (heart attack? murder?)—and there's a coverup. Did Hearst mistakenly kill Ince while aiming for guest Charlie Chaplin (Izzard), whom Heatst suspected of carrying on with Davies? Film looks terrific, has a talented cast, and the story shows that little has changed in Hollywood regarding sex, scandal, ambition, and power. **112m/C VHS, DVD.** *GB GE* Edward Herrmann, Kirsten Dunst, Cary Elwes, Eddie Izzard, Joanna Lumley, Jennifer Tilly, Victor Slezak, James Laurenson, Ronan Vibert, Claudia Harrison; ***D:*** Peter Bogdanovich; ***W:*** Steven Peros; ***C:*** Bruno Delbonnel.

Cat's Play 🦴🦴 *Macskajatek* **1974** A widowed music teacher makes a ceremonial occasion of a weekly dinner with an old flame. Then an old friend from her youth suddenly reappears and begins an affair with the gentleman, causing self-destructive passions to explode. In Hungarian with English subtitles. **115m/C VHS.** *HU* Margit Dayka, Margit Makay, Elma Bulla; ***D:*** Karoly Makk.

Cattle Queen of Montana 🦴🦴½ **1954** Reagan stars as an undercover federal agent investigating livestock rustlings and Indian uprisings. **88m/C VHS.** Ronald Reagan, Barbara Stanwyck, Jack Elam, Gene Evans, Lance Fuller, Anthony Caruso; ***D:*** Allan Dwan; ***W:*** Robert Blees.

Caught 🦴🦴🦴 **1949** A woman marries for wealth and security and is desperately unhappy. She runs away and takes a job with a struggling physician, and falls in love with him. Her husband finds her, forcing her to decide between a life of security or love. **90m/B VHS.** James Mason, Barbara Bel Geddes, Robert Ryan, Curt Bois, Natalie Schafer, Art Smith; ***D:*** Max Ophuls; ***C:*** Lee Garmes.

Caught 🦴🦴 **1996 (R)** Homeless Irishman Nick (Verveen) winds up in the New Jersey fish shop run by Joe (Olmos) and his wife Betty (Alonso). Betty takes a liking to the good-looking young man and encourages Joe to offer him a job and even invites Nick to stay with them in departed son Danny's (Schub) old room. Soon, room and board isn't all the spicy Betty is offering and Nick's willing to please, especially since Joe turns a blind eye. Too bad cocaine-addicted Danny, a failed comedian, returns home and immediately becomes jealous of the interloper. He's also too willing to drag secrets out into the open, whatever the cost. Based on Pomerantz's novel "Into It." **109m/C VHS.** Edward James Olmos, Maria Conchita Alonso, Arie Verveen, Steven Schub, Bitty Schram, Shawn Elliot; ***D:*** Robert M. Young; ***W:*** Edward Pomerantz; ***C:*** Michael Barrow; ***M:*** Chris Botti.

Caught in the Act 🦴🦴½ **1993 (PG-13)** Scott McNally (Harrison) is an out-of-work actor who teaches acting classes to make a buck. Into one of his classes walks the sultry Rachel (Hope) and they start a hot affair. Then Rachel calls Scott, claiming to be kidnapped, he suddenly finds $10 million in his bank account, and his landlord is murdered. Scott finds himself the pawn in an embezzlement scheme and framed for murder. But this is one role Scott doesn't want and he intends to work with a new script of his own devise. **93m/C VHS.** Gregory Harrison, Leslie Hope, Patricia Clarkson, Kevin Tighe; ***D:*** Deborah Reinisch; ***W:*** Ken Hixon. **CABLE**

Caught in the Draft 🦴🦴🦴 **1941** Hope's funniest role has him as a Hollywood star trying to evade the draft in WW II, but he ends up accidentally enlisting himself. Lamour plays the daughter of a colonel in the Army whom Hope plans to marry, thinking it will get him out of the service. Very funny military comedy and one of Hope's best. Based on a story by Harry Tugend. **82m/B VHS.** Bob Hope, Dorothy Lamour, Lynne Overman, Eddie Bracken, Clarence (C. William) Kolb, Paul Hurst, Ferike Boros, Irving Bacon; ***D:*** David Butler; ***W:*** Harry Tugend.

Caught Up 🦴🦴 **1998 (R)** Directorial debut for Darin Scott follows the luckless path of ex-con Daryl (Woodbine). After serving five years as an unwitting accomplice to a bank robbery, he meets Vanessa (Williams) who is a dead ringer for his ex-girlfriend. She gets him a job as a limo driver that caters to thugs and gangsters. Unfortunately for Daryl, Vanessa has stolen some diamonds from a Rastafarian named Ahmad (Wallace), and he is tangled in a web of deceit and violence. He is also tangled in a plot that twists and turns a little too much for its own good. Director Scott tries a few too many fancy tricks, although some of them work reasonably well. Cameos from Snoop Doggy Dog and LL Cool J. **95m/C VHS, DVD.** Bokeem Woodbine, Cynda Williams, Snoop Dogg, Joseph Lindsey, Clifton Powell, Basil Wallace, Tony Todd, L.L. Cool J., Jeffrey Combs, Damon Saleem, Shedric Hunter Jr.; ***D:*** Darin Scott; ***W:*** Darin Scott; ***C:*** Thomas Callaway; ***M:*** Marc Bonilla.

Cauldron of Blood 🦴½ *Blind Man's Bluff; El Coleccionista de Cadaveres* **1967 (PG)** Blind sculptor Karloff unwittingly uses human skeletons supplied by his crazed wife Lindfors as the framework of his art pieces. **95m/C VHS.** *SP* Boris Karloff, Viveca Lindfors, Jean-Pierre Aumont, Rosenda Monteros, Ruben Rojo, Dianik Zurakowska; ***D:*** Edward Andrew (Santos Alcocer) Mann; ***W:*** Edward Andrew (Santos Alcocer) Mann.

Cause Celebre 🦴🦴🦴 **1987** Absorbing true crime drama set in Britain during the thirties. Alma Rattenbury (Mirren) is in a dull marriage to an aging and ill husband (Andrews) and is beset by financial and domestic difficulties. Then Alma hires 18-year-old George Bowman (Morrissey) as a family servant/chauffeur and, despite their age difference, the two are soon lovers. When her husband is bludgeoned to death, both Alma and George are swiftly arrested and on trial. But just who committed the crime and who is covering up? **105m/C VHS.** *GB* Helen Mirren, David Morrissey, David Suchet, Harry Andrews, Norma West, Oliver Ford Davies, Geoffrey Bayldon, Gillian Martell; ***D:*** John Gorrie; ***W:*** Kenneth Taylor; ***C:*** Malcolm Harrison, Trevor Vaisey; ***M:*** Richard Harvey. **TV**

Cause for Alarm 🦴🦴½ **1951** A jealous husband recovering from a heart attack begins to lose his mind. He wrongly accuses his wife of having an affair and attempts to frame her for his own murder. A fast-paced thriller with a nifty surprise ending. **74m/B VHS.** Loretta Young, Barry Sullivan, Bruce Cowling, Margalo Gillmore, Irving Bacon, Carl "Alfalfa" Switzer; ***D:*** Tay Garnett; ***M:*** Andre Previn.

Cause of Death 🦴½ **1990 (R)** After the accidental death of his brother, Colombian drug lord Manuel Ramirez is lured to L.A. to collect his millions in blood money. **90m/C VHS, DVD.** Michael Barak, Sydney Coale Phillips, Daniel Martine; ***D:*** Philip Jones.

Cavalcade 🦴🦴🦴 **1933** Traces the lives of the British Marryot family from the death of Queen Victoria, through WWI, the Jazz Age, and the Depression. A wistful adaptation of the hit play by Noel Coward with its touching portrayal of one family trying to weather good times and bad together. **110m/B VHS.** Diana Wynyard, Clive Brook, Herbert Mundin, Una O'Connor, Ursula Jeans, Beryl Mercer, Merle Tottenham, Frank Lawton, John Warburton, Margaret Lindsay, Billy Bevan; ***D:*** Frank Lloyd; ***C:*** Ernest Palmer. Oscars '33: Director (Lloyd), Picture.

Cavalcade of the West 🦴🦴 **1936** Typical western with two brothers, separated by a kidnapping, growing up on opposite sides of the law. Much later they meet, and the question is: will the outlaw be reformed and reunited with his happy family? **70m/B VHS.** Hoot Gibson, Rex Lease, Marion Shilling, Earl Dwire; ***D:*** Harry Fraser.

Cavalier of the West 🦴 **1931** An Army captain is the only negotiating force between the white man and a primitive Indian tribe. **66m/B VHS.** Harry Carey Sr., Kane Richmond, George "Gabby" Hayes; ***D:*** John P. McCarthy.

Cavalry 🦴½ **1936** A Union Army Lieutenant is reunited with his family after the Civil War, bringing them happiness and joy. **60m/B VHS.** Bob Steele, Frances Grant, Karl Hackett, Hal Price; ***D:*** Robert North Bradbury.

Cavalry Charge 🦴🦴½ *The Last Outpost* **1951** Vance Britton (Reagan) is the captain of a brigade of Confederate troops wreaking havoc on Union outposts. His brother Jeb (Bennett) is a Union soldier sent to the western frontier to take care of the Confederate problem. Vance's former fiance Julie (Fleming) is also living in the territories with her new husband. All three converge when the Union fort, where Julie is living and Jeb is defending, is attacked by Apaches. Brother Vance rides to the rescue. Lots of action. **72m/C VHS.** Ronald Reagan, Bruce (Herman Brix) Bennett, Rhonda Fleming, Noah Beery Jr., Bill Williams, Peter Hanson, Hugh Beaumont, John Ridgely, Lloyd Corrigan, James Burke, Richard Crane, Ewing Mitchell; ***D:*** Lewis R. Foster; ***W:*** Geoffrey Homes, George Worthing Yates, Winston Miller; ***C:*** Loyal Griggs.

Cavalry Command 🦴½ *Cavalleria Commandos* **1963** Good will and integrity characterize the U.S. soldiers called into a small village to quiet a guerrilla rebellion. **77m/C VHS.** John Agar, Richard Arlen, Myron Healey, Alicia Vergel, William Phipps, Eddie Infante; ***D:*** Eddie Romero; ***W:*** Eddie Romero.

Cave Girl woof! *Cavegirl* **1985 (R)** After falling through a time-warp during a high-school field trip, a social pariah makes a hit with a pre-historic honey. Sexist teen exploitation film, with few original ideas and a not-so-hot cast. **85m/C VHS, DVD, Wide.** Daniel Roebuck, Cindy Ann Thompson, Saba Moor, Jeff Chayette; ***D:*** David Oliver; ***W:*** David Oliver; ***C:*** David Oliver; ***M:*** Jon St. James.

Cave of the Living Dead woof! *Der Fluch Der Gruenen Augen; Night of the Vampire; The Curse of Green Eyes* **1965** Mad professor with a past is up to something in a cave under castle. Villagers summon Inspector Doren of Interpol to solve a rash of nasty murders that they've blamed on green-eyed, cave-dwelling vampires. A challenge to watch till the end. Filmed in Sepiatone. **87m/B VHS, DVD, Wide.** *GE YU* Adrian Hoven, Erika Remberg, Carl Mohner, Wolfgang Preiss, Karin (Karen) Field, John Kitzmiller, Akos Von Rathony; ***D:*** Akos Von Rathony; ***W:*** C.V. Rock; ***C:*** Hrvoje Saric.

Caveman 🦴🦴 **1981 (PG)** Starr stars in this prehistoric spoof about a group of cavemen banished from different tribes who band together to form a tribe called "The Misfits." **92m/C VHS, DVD, Wide.** Ringo Starr, Barbara Bach, John Matuszak, Dennis Quaid, Jack Gilford, Shelley Long, Cork Hubbert, Avery Schreiber; ***D:*** Carl Gottlieb; ***W:*** Carl Gottlieb, Rudy DeLuca; ***C:*** Alan Hume; ***M:*** Lalo Schifrin.

The Caveman's Valentine 🦴½ **2001 (R)** Jackson plays a homeless schizophrenic who finds a dead body outside his cave in Central Park and must pull his faltering mental faculties together enough to play Sherlock Holmes and solve the whodone-it. Plot points stretch well beyond the bounds of believability and venture into the territory of the ridiculous as the Caveman conveniently infiltrates every realm of society he wishes in order to follow up on his suspicions. Granted, he used to be a master pianist before his mental downfall, but come on. Director Lemmons's second feature film, the first being "Eve's Bayou." Based on the Edgar Award-winning 1994 novel by George Dawes Green. **105m/C VHS, DVD, Wide.** Samuel L. Jackson, Aunjanue Ellis, Colm Feore, Ann Magnuson, Rodney Eastman, Tamara Tunie, Anthony Michael Hall, Jay Rodan; ***D:*** Kasi Lemmons; ***W:*** George Dawes Green; ***C:*** Amelia Vincent; ***M:*** Terence Blanchard.

CB4: The Movie 🦴½ **1993 (R)** Falling somewhere between a serious attempt and parody, CB4 tries to do both and succeeds at neither. Written in the key of "Wayne's World" by "Saturday Night Live's" Rock, it starts out as a "rockumentary" (please refer to "This is Spinal Tap"), but quickly turns into a sitcom after two gangsta rap friends assume the identity of a local club owner when he is in jail. Hartman, also of SNL, appears as a right-wing city councilman. Chock full of violence, sexism, and profanity tucked into a wandering plot. **83m/C VHS, Wide.** Chris Rock, Allen Payne, Deezer D, Phil Hartman, Charlie Murphy, Khandi Alexander, Art Evans, Chris Elliott, Willard Pugh, Theresa Randle; ***D:*** Tamra Davis; ***W:*** Chris Rock, Nelson George, Robert Locash; ***M:*** John Barnes.

C.C. & Company 🦴 *Chrome Hearts* **1970 (R)** Rebel biker rescues a buxom gal from a fate worse than death, than vies for control of the gang. Laughable, with Namath hopeless in his film debut. Redeemed only by Ann-Margret in continual disarray. **91m/C VHS, DVD.** Joe Namath, Ann-Margret, William Smith, Jennifer Billingsley, Teda Bracci, Greg Mullavey, Sid Haig, Bruce Glover; ***D:*** Seymour Robbie; ***W:*** Roger Smith; ***C:*** Charles F. Wheeler; ***M:*** Lenny Stack.

Cease Fire 🦴🦴 **1985 (R)** The story of a troubled Vietnam vet who finds solace in a veterans' therapy group. Adapted from the play by George Fernandez. **97m/C VHS.** Don Johnson, Robert F. Lyons, Lisa Blount; ***D:*** David Nutter; ***M:*** Gary Fry.

Cecil B. Demented 🦴🦴½ **2000 (R)** Waters returns to a more hard-edged satire with this indictment against the studio system. Dorff is Cecil B. Demented, indie auteur who, along with his band of cinema terrorists, wreack havoc on Hollywood. They kidnap A-list actress Honey Whitlock (Griffith) and force her to appear in their film—in doing so, making her the poster child for their cause. Punish bad film! No English-language remakes of foreign film! Death to those who are cinematically incorrect! Will appeal more to fans of Waters's very early work than to those who enjoyed "Serial Mom" or "Hairspray." **88m/C VHS, DVD, Wide.** Stephen Dorff, Melanie Griffith, Jack Noseworthy, Alicia Witt, Larry Gilliard Jr., Adrian Grenier, Patty (Patricia Campbell) Hearst, Ricki Lake, Mink Stole, Maggie Gyllenhaal, Eric M. Barry, Zenzele Uzoma, Erika Lynn Rupli, Harriet Dodge, Eric Roberts; ***D:*** John Waters; ***W:*** John Waters; ***C:*** Robert Stevens; ***M:*** Basil Poledouris, Zoe Poledouris.

Ceiling Zero 🦴🦴🦴 **1935** Cagney is an irrepressible pilot who does as he pleases and loves to aggravate his soft-hearted boss O'Brien. He falls for aviatrix Travis and neglects his duties to woo her, which leads to tragedy. Naturally, this sobers Cagney up and he volunteers for a dangerous test flight. Lots of fast-paced action and Cagney is at his swaggering best. Based on a play by Frank Wead, who also wrote the screenplay. Remade in 1941 as "International Squadron." **95m/B VHS.** James Cagney, Pat O'Brien, June Travis, Stuart Erwin, Henry Wadsworth, Isabel Jewell, Barton MacLane; ***D:*** Howard Hawks; ***W:*** Frank Wead.

The Celebration 🦴🦴 *Festen* **1998 (R)** Danish patriarch Helge (Moritzen) is turning 60 and a black-tie bash is being given to celebrate the event. But the celebration turns into a rancid display when all the family skeletons coming rattling out of their closets. Everyone's got a score to settle and is more than happy to air the family's dirty linen. Danish with subtitles. The film was shot with a hand-held video camera in available light and sound according to the tenets of Dogma 95—a Danish filmmaking collective Vinterberg belongs to. **105m/C VHS, DVD.** *DK* Henning Moritzen, Ulrich Thomsen, Thomas Bo Larsen, Paprika Steen, Lene Laub Olsen, Helle Dolleris, Gbatokai Dakinah; ***D:*** Thomas Vinterberg; ***W:*** Thomas Vinterberg, Mogens Rukov; ***C:*** Anthony Dod Mantle. Ind. Spirit '99: Foreign Film; L.A. Film Critics '98: Foreign Film; N.Y. Film Critics '98: Foreign Film.

Celebrity 🦴½ **1985** A tragic childhood secret must be confronted by three friends when one is charged with murder. Based on the Thomas Thompson novel. **313m/C VHS.** Michael Beck, Ben Masters, Joseph Bottoms; ***D:*** Paul Wendkos. **TV**

Celebrity 🦴🦴🦴 **1998 (R)** Woody examines the phenomenon of celebrity with his usual sarcastic and semi-autobiographical perspective. Lee Simon (Branaugh) is a hack celebrity journalist who attempts to enter the glitz and glam world of the famous people he follows and writes about. In true Allen fashion, bitter irony abounds as Simon loses sight of his pathetic reality while those around him acquire what he so desperately seeks. DiCaprio steals his 15 minutes of screen time playing a hedonistic, hotel-trashing, spoiled young film star with amazing ease and conviction (Coincidence? Perhaps...). The writing is among Allen's best, but watching Branaugh, and Judy Davis as Lee's estranged wife, do their best Woody Allen impressions grates on the nerves. Although it's redundant, nobody plays Woody like Woody. **113m/B VHS, DVD.** J.K. Simmons, Kenneth Branagh, Judy Davis, Hank Azaria, Leonardo DiCaprio, Joe Mantegna, Famke Janssen, Winona Ryder, Melanie Griffith, Michael Lerner, Charlize Theron, Bebe Neuwirth, Dylan Baker, Patti D'Arbanville, Kate Burton, Gretchen Mol, Allison Janney, Aida Turturro, Jeffrey Wright; ***Cameos:*** Greg Mottola, Isaac Mizrahi, Andre Gregory, Donald Trump; ***D:*** Woody Allen; ***W:*** Woody Allen; ***C:*** Sven Nykvist.

Celeste 🦴🦴🦴 **1981** Adlon (who later made the offbeat comedy "Sugarbaby") directed this longish but finely detailed and beautifully photographed biographical look at French writer Marcel (Remembrance of Things Past) Proust. Based on the memoirs of Proust's housekeeper, Celeste Albaret, an uneducated farmgirl, portraying the woman's devoted relationship ('til death did them part) with the middle-aged, homosexual author. It does so with wit, poignancy, and insight, but is not entirely successful in its attempt to render Proust's verbal literary style into a visual medium. In German with English subtitles. **107m/C VHS.** *GE* Eva Mattes, Jurgen Arndt, Norbert Wartha, Wolf Euba; ***D:*** Percy Adlon; ***W:*** Percy Adlon; ***C:*** Jurgen Martin; ***M:*** Cesar Franck.

Celestial Clockwork 🦴🦴½ *Mecaniques Celestes* **1994** Runaway Venezuelan bride Ana (Gil), an aspiring opera singer, takes off for Paris clutching her Maria Callas poster. God must protect the innocent because she meets a friendly cabbie, immediately finds a place to live, and gets the perfect singing teacher, a cranky Russian emigre named Grigorief (Debrane). In fact, the only problem in this Cinderella's life is jealous would-be star Celeste (Dombasle), who wants the same lead theatrical role that Ana is also interested in. French with subtitles. **85m/C VHS.** *FR* Ariadna Gil, Arielle Dombasle, Evelyne Didi, Frederic Longbois, Lluis Homar, Michel Debrane; ***D:*** Fina Torres; ***W:*** Fina Torres; ***C:*** Ricardo Aronovich; ***M:*** Michel Musseau, Francois Farrugia.

Celia: Child of Terror 🦴🦴 **1989** Set in the 1950s, this film deals with the awful results of a young girl's inability to handle disappointment. **110m/C VHS.** *AU* Rebecca Smart, Nicholas Eadie, Victoria Longley, Mary-Anne Fahey; ***D:*** Ann Turner; ***C:*** Geoffrey Simpson.

Celine and Julie Go Boating 🦴🦴 **1974** Strange fantasy follows magician Celine (Berto) and her librarian friend, Julie (Labourier). Celine sometimes works as a governess for a little girl who lives with her widowed father in a possibly haunted house. Two women are in love with the father but he'd promised his wife never to remarry as long as their invalid daughter was still alive. Celine and Julie become worried for the little girl and decide to rescue her. An adaptation of the Henry James story "A Romance of Certain Old Clothes." French with subtitles. **193m/C VHS.** Juliet Berto, Dominique Labourier, Bulle Ogier, Marie-France Pisier, Barbet Schroeder, Philippe Clevenot, Nathalie Asnor; ***D:*** Jacques Rivette; ***W:*** Jacques Rivette, Eduardo Di Gregorio; ***C:*** Jacques Renard; ***M:*** Jean-Marie Senia.

The Cell 🦴🦴½ **2000 (R)** Psychotherapist Catherine (Lopez) is involved in breakthrough research that allows her access into a patient's mind. Desperate FBI agent Novak (Vaughn) asks her to invade the mind of a comatose serial killer (D'Onofrio) in order to save his latest victim. As you'd expect, the mind of a serial killer is not an exactly pleasant place to be, and Catherine (and the audience) encounters some pretty creepy and disturbing stuff. Feature debut of music video director Tarsem (REM's "Losing My Religion") is long on dazzling visual effects, trippy images, and style, but short on real suspense and cohesive plotting. Narrative is not the main focus here, however, so the faint of heart and the plot-dependent are forewarned. **110m/C VHS, DVD, Wide.** Jennifer Lopez, Vince Vaughn, Vincent D'Onofrio, Marianne Jean-Baptiste, Dylan Baker, Jake Weber, Patrick Bauchau, James Gammon, Tara Subkoff, Gareth Williams, Colton James; ***D:*** Tarsem; ***W:*** Mark Protosevich; ***C:*** Paul Laufer; ***M:*** Howard Shore.

The Cellar 🦴½ **1990 (PG-13)** A young boy finds an ancient Comanche monster spirit in the basement of his home. His parents, as usual, don't believe him, so he must battle the monster alone. **90m/C VHS.** Patrick Kilpatrick, Suzanne Savoy, Chris Miller, Ford Rainey; ***D:*** Kevin S. Tenney.

Cellar Dweller woof! **1987** A cartoonist moves into an old house and soon discovers it's haunted by a demonic cartoonist who killed himself 30 years earlier. What a coincidence. Low-budget scare-'em-upper filmed on one set and lit by a floodlamp. **78m/C VHS.** Pamela Bellwood, Deborah Muldowney, Brian Robbins, Vince Edwards, Jeffrey Combs, Yvonne De Carlo; ***D:*** John Carl Buechler.

Cellblock Sisters: Banished Behind Bars 🦴½ **1995 (R)** Biker babe Harris reunites with college girl sis Wood to off their disgusting stepfather who separately sold them to adoptive families after killing their junkie mom. Harris does the crime but Wood does the time—until her guilty sibling deliberately gets thrown behind bars in order to protect her. Has all the standard jail chicks elements. **95m/C VHS.** Gail Harris, Annie Wood, Ace Ross; ***D:*** Henri Charr.

The Celluloid Closet 🦴🦴🦴½ **1995 (R)** Terrific documentary on how Hollywood films have depicted homosexual characters, subliminally and otherwise. Working chronologically and in an historical context, beginning with silent films, there are clips from more than 100 films, along with interviews from writers and actors. (Notable is writer Gore Vidal's comments on the gay subtext in 1959's "Ben-Hur"). Based on Vito Russo's 1981 book. **102m/C VHS, DVD.** ***D:*** Robert Epstein, Jeffrey Friedman; ***W:*** Armistead Maupin; ***C:*** Nancy Schreiber; ***M:*** Carter Burwell; ***Nar:*** Lily Tomlin.

Celtic Pride 🦴🦴 **1996 (PG-13)** Mike O'Hara (Stern) and Jimmy Flaherty (Aykroyd) are the worst kind of crazy. They're sports nuts. They are so consumed with passion for their beloved Celtics that they kidnap foul-mouthed superstar Lewis Scott (Wayans) of the Utah Jazz before game seven of the NBA finals. If this sounds far fetched, well...it is, unless you have an ESPN junkie in your life. There's not as much court action as you would expect, since most of the story revolves around intermittent trash-talking and escape attempts. If you're a Celtic hater, stick around for the end, when the Boston Garden is demolished using special effects. **90m/C VHS.** Damon Wayans, Daniel Stern, Dan Aykroyd, Gail O'Grady, Adam Hendershott, Paul Guilfoyle, Deion Sanders, Christopher McDonald, Gus Williams, Ted Rooney, Vladimir Cuk; ***Cameos:*** Bill Walton, Larry Bird; ***D:*** Tom DeCerchio; ***W:*** Judd Apatow; ***C:*** Oliver Wood; ***M:*** Basil Poledouris.

Cement 🦴🦴½ **1999 (R)** Intense performances in a nasty crime story told via flashbacks. Hollywood vice detectives Holt (Penn) and Nin (Wright) have crossed the line between the cops and the criminals. When violent Holt catches his gal (Fenn) with a local wiseguy (DeSando), he buries him in a cement freeway and the mob is out for revenge. Pasdar's directorial debut. **100m/C VHS, DVD, Wide.** Christopher Penn, Jeffrey Wright, Sherilyn Fenn, Anthony De Sando, Henry Czerny; ***D:*** Adrian Pasdar; ***W:*** Justin Monjo; ***C:*** Geary McLeod; ***M:*** Doug Caldwell.

The Cement Garden 🦴🦴 **1993** Fatherless 15-year-old Jack (Robertson) and 16-year-old sister Julie (Gainsbourg) are afraid that they and their two younger siblings Sue (Coulthard) and Tom (Birkin) will be taken into foster care after their mother dies at home. So to keep their secret, they bury her in the basement and try to assume a normal family life. Not that this works for long—Jack and Julie give into an incestuous fascination and the household slowly sinks into chaotic squalor around them. Gainsbourg is the director's niece and the young Birkin is his son. Based on Ian McEwan's 1978 novel. **105m/C VHS, DVD.** *FR GE GB* Charlotte Gainsbourg, Andrew Robertson, Alice Coulthard, Ned Birkin, Sinead Cusack, Hanns Zischler, Jochen Horst; ***D:*** Andrew Birkin; ***W:*** Andrew Birkin; ***C:*** Stephen Blackman; ***M:*** Ed Shearmur.

The Cemetery Club 🦴🦴½ **1993 (PG-13)** Story of three Jewish widows who make weekly visits to their husband's graves while attempting to cope with their lives. Doris (Dukakis) is loyal to the memory of her husband and acts as the moral conscience of the trio. Lucille (Ladd) is a merry widow who wears clothes more suitable for younger women, but she also harbors a painful secret. Esther (Burstyn) struggles with her loneliness until a widowed cab driver begins to woo her. Commendably, the characters are given more dimension than Hollywood usually grants women of a certain age. Based on the play "The Cemetary Club" by Menchell, who also wrote the screenplay. **114m/C VHS.** Ellen Burstyn, Olympia Dukakis, Diane Ladd, Danny Aiello, Lainie Kazan, Christina Ricci, Bernie Casey, Alan Mason, Sam Schwartz, Jeff Howell, Robert Costanzo, Wallace Shawn, Louis Guss; ***D:*** Bill Duke; ***W:*** Ivan Menchell; ***C:*** Steven Poster; ***M:*** Elmer Bernstein.

Cemetery High **1989** Beautiful high school girls decide to lure the local boys into a trap and kill them. **80m/C VHS.** Debi Thibeault, Karen Nielsen, Lisa Schmidt, Ruth (Coreen) Collins, Simone, Tony Kruk, David Coughlin, Frank Stewart; ***D:*** Gorman Bechard; ***W:*** Gorman Bechard, Carmine Capobianco.

Cemetery Man *Dellamorte Dellamore; Of Death, of Love* **1995 (R)** Grotesque little saga about zombies and necrophilia set in a small Italian cemetery. Thanks to a weird post-death plague the corpses refuse to stay quietly in their graves, forcing watchman Francisco Dellamorte (Everett) and mute gravedigger Gnaghi (Hadji-Lazaro) to split their heads open. But when Francisco's dead sweetheart (Falchi) rises from her grave, he's a little slow to rebury the still-active corpse. Based on the Italian graphic novel "Dellamorte Dellamore," from the "Dylan Dog" series by Tiziano Sclavi. **100m/C VHS.** *IT* Rupert Everett, Anna Falchi, Francois Hadji-Lazaro, Mickey Knox; ***D:*** Michele (Michael) Soavi; ***W:*** Gianni Romoli; ***C:*** Mauro Marchetti; ***M:*** Manuel De Sica.

Centennial **1978** Epic 12-part TV miniseries, based on the 1974 novel by James Michener, about the building of the Rocky Mountain town of Centennial, Colorado, from 1795 to the present. There are trappers and Indians, immigrants and cattlemen, soldiers, conservationists, and politicians all with their own stories to tell. **1258m/C VHS.** Robert Conrad, Richard Chamberlain, Raymond Burr, Sally Kellerman, Barbara Carrera, Michael Ansara, Gregory Harrison, Stephanie Zimbalist, Christina Raines, Stephen McHattie, Kario Salem, Chad Everett, Alex Karras, Mark Harmon, Dennis Weaver, Timothy Dalton, Richard Crenna, Cliff DeYoung, Glynn Turman, Brian Keith, Les Lannom, Rafael Campos, Anthony Zerbe, Doug McKeon, Lynn Redgrave, William Atherton, A. Martinez, Lois Nettleton, David Janssen, Robert Vaughn, Andy Griffith, Sharon Gless; ***D:*** Virgil W. Vogel, Harry Falk, Paul Krasny, Bernard McEveety; ***W:*** John Wilder.

Center of the Web **1992 (R)** John Phillips is a victim of mistaken identity—someone thinks he's a professional hit man. After surviving an apparent mob attempt on his life, Phillips is persuaded by a CIA operative to go along with the deception in order to capture a potential political assassin. At least that's what Phillips is told, but he soon realizes that the deeper he gets into his new role, the deadlier the plot becomes. Davi is one of the best bad guys around and the fast-paced stunts and plot twists make this watchable. **88m/C VHS.** Ted Prior, Robert Davi, Tony Curtis, Charlene Tilton, Bo Hopkins, Charles Napier; ***D:*** David A. Prior.

The Center of the World **2001** Put this one strongly in the love it or hate it category. Richard (Sarsgaard) is a wealthy dot.com geek who offers stripper Florence (Parker) a lot of dough to spend a few days with him in Vegas. She makes some strict rules about what she will and won't do for him—which she promptly breaks. They're both immature and vulnerable and inclined to play humiliating mind games with each other. The sex show turns out to be nothing to get hot and bothered about and the leads give as credible performances as the narrowness of their characters allow. Shot in digital video; the screenwriters used the pseud. "Ellen Benjamin Wong." **86m/C VHS, DVD, Wide.** Peter Sarsgaard, Molly Parker, Carla Gugino, Balthazar Getty, Mel Gorham; ***D:*** Wayne Wang; ***W:*** Wayne Wang; ***C:*** Mauro Fiore.

Center Stage **2000 (PG-13)** How familar does this sound? Newcomers enrolled at the American Ballet Academy vie for places in the professional company. Meanwhile, former dancer/company director Jonathan (Gallagher) has to contend with his insolent star dancer Cooper (Stiefel), whose ambitions are growing by leaps and bounds. There's also the usual love connections to be made (and unmade). The professional dancers in the cast have limited acting ability and aren't served particularly well by most of the choreography. **116m/C VHS, DVD, Wide.** Peter Gallagher, Ethan Stiefel, Amanda Schull, Sascha Radetsky, Susan May Pratt, Ilia Kulik, Donna Murphy, Zoe Saldana, Debra Monk, Julie Kent, Eion Bailey, Shakiem Evans, Victor Anthony, Elizabeth Hubbard, Priscilla Lopez; ***D:*** Nicholas Hytner; ***W:*** Carol Heikkinen; ***C:*** Geoffrey Simpson; ***M:*** George Fenton.

The Centerfold Girls woof! **1974 (R)** Microscopic storyline involves a deranged man who is determined to kill all the voluptuous young women who have posed nude for a centerfold. **93m/C VHS.** Andrew Prine, Tiffany Bolling, Aldo Ray, Jeremy Slate, Ray Danton, Francine York; ***D:*** John Peyser.

Central Station *Central Do Brasil* **1998 (R)** Dora (Montenegro) is a bitter, aging woman who makes a living writing letters for the illiterate at a stand located in Rio de Janeiro's central railway station. One of her customers sends letters to her 9-year-old son Josue's (de Oliveira) father, who lives in northern Brazil and who has never seen the boy. When Josue's mother is killed in an accident, Dora reluctantly takes the homeless boy in and reluctantly decides they must locate his father. Their road trip turns out to have some unexpected consequences. Portuguese with subtitles. **110m/C VHS, DVD.** *BR* Fernanda Montenegro, Vinicius de Oliveira, Marilia Pera, Othon Bastos; ***D:*** Walter Salles; ***W:*** Joao Emmanuel Carneiro, Marcos Bernstein; ***C:*** Walter Carvalho; ***M:*** Antonio Pinto, Jaques Morelembaum. British Acad. '98: Foreign Film; Golden Globes '99: Foreign Film; L.A. Film Critics '98: Actress (Montenegro); Natl. Bd. of Review '98: Actress (Montenegro), Foreign Film.

Century **1994 (R)** Ambitious young doctor Paul Reisner (Owen), the son of a prosperous Jewish father (Stephens), gets a position at a London research hospital headed by the charismatic Professor Mandry (Dance). Paul manages to disgrace himself by provoking Mandry and is dismissed but finds out some disturbing information and is determined to discredit his former mentor. Anti-Semitism lurks as does the change from Victorian mores to the challenging dawn of the 20th century. Complex performances are somewhat undermined by the static direction. **112m/C VHS.** *GB* Clive Owen, Charles Dance, Miranda Richardson, Robert Stephens, Joan Hickson, Lena Headey, Neil Stuke; ***D:*** Stephen Poliakoff; ***W:*** Stephen Poliakoff; ***C:*** Witold Stok; ***M:*** Michael Gibbs.

Certain Fury **1985 (R)** Two timid women go on the lam when they are mistaken for escaped prostitutes who shot up a courthouse. The sooner they get caught, the better. **88m/C VHS.** Tatum O'Neal, Irene Cara, Peter Fonda, Nicholas (Nick) Campbell, Moses Gunn; ***D:*** Stephen Gyllenhaal.

A Certain Justice ½ **1999** Adam Dalgleish's (Marsden) latest case of murder involves barrister Venetia Aldridge (Downie), who is found bizarrely costumed and stabbed to death in her chambers. It turns out a number of people had a reason to dislike Venetia and prying the truth from a group of lawyers proves to be a challenge even for Scotland Yard's eminent Commander. **180m/C VHS.** *GB* Roy Marsden, Penny Downie, Ricci Harnett, Flora Montgomery, Frederick Treves, Matthew Marsh, Ian McNeice, Sarah Winman, Richard Huw, Ken Jones, Britta Smith, Miles Anderson, Philip Stone; ***D:*** Ross Devenish; ***W:*** Michael Russell. **TV**

Certain Sacrifice **1980** Nineteen-year-old Madonna expresses herself in her film debut. Seeking revenge on the man who raped her, she murders him in a strange ritualistic manner underneath the Brooklyn Bridge. Poor is the man whose pleasures depend on the permission of another? **60m/C VHS.** Madonna, Jeremy Pattnosh, Charles Kurtz; ***D:*** Stephen Lewicki.

Cesar **1936** This is the third and most bittersweet part of Pagnol's famed trilogy based on his play depicting the lives and loves of the people of Provence, France. Marius returns after a 20-year absence to his beloved Fanny and his now-grown son, Cesariot. The first two parts of the trilogy are "Marius" and "Fanny" and were directed by Alexander Korda and Marc Allegret respectively. In French with English subtitles. **117m/B VHS.** *FR* Raimu, Pierre Fresnay, Orane Demazis, Charpin, Andre Fouche, Alida Rauffe; ***D:*** Marcel Pagnol; ***W:*** Marcel Pagnol; ***M:*** Vincent Scotto.

Cesar & Rosalie **1972 (PG)** Acclaimed French comedy depicts the love triangle between a beautiful divorcee, her aging live-in companion and a younger man. Engaging portrait of how their relationship evolves over time. In French with English subtitles. **110m/C VHS.** *FR* Romy Schneider, Yves Montand, Sami Frey, Umberto Orsini; ***D:*** Claude Sautet; ***W:*** Jean-Loup Dabadie, Claude Neron, Claude Sautet; ***C:*** Jean Boffety; ***M:*** Philippe Sarde.

Cesare Borgia **1923** Veidt stars in this bloodthirsty saga as the ruthless son of Pope Alexander VI who'll let nothing come between him and his desires. **83m/B VHS.** *GE* Conrad Veidt; ***D:*** Richard Oswald.

Chain Gang Killings **1985** Pair of shackled prisoners, one black, the other white, escape from a truck transporting them to prison. **99m/C VHS.** Ian Yule, Ken Gampu.

Chain Gang Women woof! **1972 (R)** Sordid violence. Two escaped convicts plunder, rob, and rape until a victim's husband comes looking for revenge. **85m/C VHS.** Robert Lott, Barbara Mills, Michael Stearns, Linda York, Wes Bishop, Phil Hoover, Chuck Wells; ***D:*** Lee Frost.

Chain Lightning **1950** Bogart stars as a bomber pilot who falls in love with a Red Cross worker (Parker) while fighting in Europe in 1943. They lose touch after the war until Bogie goes to work as a test pilot for the same shady airplane manufacturer (Massey) where Parker works. He is given the chance to test a new plane, which has already cost the life of one of his friends. Bogart has more success, along with rekindling the flames of romance. Average script but the flying sequences are well-done. **94m/B VHS.** Humphrey Bogart, Eleanor Parker, Raymond Massey, Richard Whorf; ***D:*** Stuart Heisler; ***W:*** Liam O'Brien, Vincent B. Evans.

Chain of Command **1995 (R)** Anti-terrorist agent Merrill Ross (Dudikoff) goes up against hired mercenaries trying to overthrow the government of the oil-rich Republic of Qumir. Then Ross realizes he's being manipulated and it could be by any number of players. **97m/C VHS.** Michael Dudikoff, R. Lee Ermey.

Chain of Command **2000 (R)** Agent Mike Connelly (Muldoon) must protect the President's (Scheider) briefcase-sized computer that holds the nuclear codes. But when one of Connelly's colleagues betrays them, a nuclear winter could be as close as a madman's command. **96m/C VHS, DVD.** Patrick Muldoon, Roy Scheider, Michael Biehn, Maria Conchita Alonso, Ric Young, William R. Moses, Michael Mantell, Pat Skipper; ***D:*** John Terlesky. **VIDEO**

Chain of Desire **1993** Nightclub inside Manhattan's Chrysler Building is the spot for numerous folk to have lot of meaningless sexual encounters and look at the emptiness of their lives. **107m/C VHS.** Linda Fiorentino, Elias Koteas, Malcolm McDowell, Grace Zabriskie, Tim Guinee, Assumpta Serna, Patrick Bauchau, Seymour Cassel, Kevin Conroy, Angel Aviles, Holly Marie Combs, Jamie Harold, Dewey Weber, Suzzanne Douglass; ***D:*** Temistocles Lopez; ***W:*** Temistocles Lopez; ***C:*** Nancy Schreiber; ***M:*** Nathan Birnbaum.

Chain Reaction ½ *Nuclear Run* **1980** When a nuclear scientist is exposed to radiation after an accident at an atomic power plant, he must escape to warn the public of the danger. **87m/C VHS.** Steve Bisley, Ross Thompson; ***D:*** Ian Barry; ***C:*** Russell Boyd.

Chain Reaction ½ *Dead Drop* **1996 (PG-13)** Government/scientific conspiracy chase story finds Chicago lab tech Eddie Kasalivich (Reeves) a member of a research team that's discovered the formula for cheap, pollution-free energy. This doesn't sit well with someone since the team's leader is murdered and the lab destroyed in an explosion. Eddie and scientist Lily Sinclair (Weisz) become prime suspects and are pursued by the feds as they try to find the real culprits. Old pro Freeman, as money man Paul Shannon, is the best reason to watch (as usual). Davis did "The Fugitive," so he knows his tension-filled chases but this is just more same old-same old. **107m/C VHS.** Keanu Reeves, Morgan Freeman, Rachel Weisz, Fred Ward, Brian Cox, Kevin Dunn, Joanna Cassidy, Chelcie Ross, Tzi Ma, Nicholas Rudall, Peter J. D'Noto; ***D:*** Andrew Davis; ***W:*** J.F. Lawton, Michael Bortman; ***C:*** Frank Tidy; ***M:*** Jerry Goldsmith.

Chained ½ **1934** Crawford and Gable star in this love triangle that somehow never sizzles. Crawford, in love with married businessman Kruger, takes a South American cruise to get away from it all, meets Gable, and of course falls in love. Seems simple enough, but wait! Crawford goes back to New York City and marries Kruger (his wife grants him a divorce) and is miserable. But then Gable shows up, further complicating matters. Choices, choices. Predictable script was not helped by half-hearted performances. **73m/B VHS.** Joan Crawford, Clark Gable, Otto Kruger, Stuart Erwin, Una O'Connor; ***D:*** Clarence Brown; ***C:*** George J. Folsey.

Chained for Life woof! **1951** Daisy and Violet Hilton, real life Siamese twins, star in this old-fashioned "freak" show. When a gigolo deserts one twin on their wedding night, the other twin shoots him dead. The twins go on trial and the judge asks the viewer to hand down the verdict. Exploitative and embarrassing to watch. **81m/B VHS.** Daisy Hilton, Violet Hilton, Allen Jenkins, Sheldon Leonard; ***D:*** Harry Fraser; ***W:*** Nat Tanchuck.

Chained Heat **1983 (R)** Seamy tale of the vicious reality of life for women behind bars. Naive Blair is imprisoned again (after another bad jailhouse gig in "Born Innocent") and has usual assortment of negative experiences with domineering prisoners, degenerative guards, and the creepy warden who maintains a prison bachelor pad equipped with hot tub. Needless to say, she grows up in a hurry. Trashifying, archetypal women-in-prison effort that aims to satisfy full range of low-quality audience demands. Sequel to 1982 "Concrete Jungle." **97m/C VHS.** *GE* Linda Blair, Stella Stevens, Sybil Danning, Tamara Dobson, Henry Silva, John Vernon, Nita Talbot, Louisa Moritz, Sharon Hughes, Robert Miano, Kendal Kaldwell; ***D:*** Paul Nicholas; ***W:*** Paul Nicholas, Vincent Mongol; ***C:*** Mac Ahlberg; ***M:*** Joseph Conlan. Golden Raspberries '83: Worst Support. Actress (Danning).

Chained Heat 2 ½ **1992 (R)** Another sordid tale of women behind bars. Nielsen stars as the psychotic stiletto-heeled warden of an infamous prison, complete with sadistic heroin-smuggling guards. This drug ring also deals in prostitution, which results in two imprisoned sisters (innocent, naturally) being separated from one another. One sister is determined to find true justice. **98m/C VHS.** Brigitte Nielsen, Paul Koslo, Kari Whitman, Kimberley Kates; ***D:*** Lloyd A. Simandl; ***W:*** Chris Hyde.

Chained Heat 3: Hell Mountain ½ *Chained Heat 3: The Horror of Hell Mountain; Chained Heat 3* **1998 (R)** Future Earth is a barren wasteland where survivors are forced to work in the mines of overlord Stryker. Each year, young women are taken to the mines on Hell Mountain but this time Kal is determined to save his girlfriend and destroy Stryker. **97m/C VHS, DVD.** Bentley Mitchum, Kate Rodger, Christopher Clarke, Karel Augusta, Noelle Balfour, Jack Scalia, Sarah Douglas; ***D:*** Mike Rohl; ***W:*** Chris Hyde; ***C:*** David Frazee; ***M:*** Peter Allen. **VIDEO**

Chains 🦴🦴 **1989 (R)** A Chicago gangland feud entraps two couples in its web, and the innocents must take care of themselves when the situation goes from bad to worse. **93m/C VHS.** Jimi Jourdan, Michael Dixon, John L. Eves; ***D:*** Roger J. Barski.

Chains of Gold 🦴🦴 **1992 (R)** Kind social worker (Travolta) befriends teen who wants to get out of the crack-dealing gang in which he's involved. He infiltrates the gang and risks his life helping the boy get out. **95m/C VHS, DVD.** John Travolta, Marilu Henner, Bernie Casey, Hector Elizondo, Joey Lawrence; ***D:*** Rod Holcomb; ***M:*** Trevor Jones. **CABLE**

The Chair 🦴🦴 *Hot Seat* **1987 (R)** The penitentiary where an evil superintendent was fried in his own electric chair during an inmate uprising is reopened after two decades. The new warden (Benedict), who used to be a subordinate to the dead man, believes in rigid control of the inmates and locks horns with the big-house shrink (Coco), who on the surface is an intelligent humanitarian, but may have a darker side. This acrimonious dispute takes a back seat, when it appears that the spirit of the late warden has come back to make the inmates pay for his untimely death. **90m/C VHS.** James Coco, Paul Benedict, Stephen Geoffreys, Trini Alvarado, Gary McCleery, Paul Calderon; ***D:*** Waldemar Korzenioswsky; ***C:*** Steven J. Ross.

Chairman of the Board woof! **1997 (PG-13)** Some studio executive decided to take a bad prop comic named after a vegetable and give him a major motion picture. If this movie accomplishes one thing, it may be the abolition of Friday afternoon twelve-martini lunches in Hollywood. Carrot Top plays Edison, a wacky surfer/inventor who befriends an old eccentric man. After the old guy heads for the big wave in the sky, it turns out that he was fabulously wealthy and left his company to Edison. This doesn't sit well with the conniving Bradford (Miller). Courtney Thorne-Smith plays Natalie (although this does not stop Mr. Top from calling her Courtney in one scene) as the standard love interest. Also appearing are Jack Warden, Raquel Welch and M. Emmet Walsh. Why? That's what they're asking their agents. Rent it only if every single video, including the instructional mime section, is already out. **95m/C VHS, DVD.** Carrot Top, Courtney Thorne-Smith, Larry Miller, Raquel Welch, Jack Warden, Estelle Harris, Bill Erwin, M. Emmet Walsh, Jack McGee, Glenn Shadix, Fred Stoller, Mystro Clark, Jack Plotnick; ***D:*** Alex Zamm; ***W:*** Al Septien, Turi Meyer, Alex Zamm; ***C:*** David Lewis; ***M:*** Chris Hajian.

The Chalk Garden 🦴🦴🦴 **1964** A woman with a mysterious past takes on the job of governess for an unruly 14-year-old girl, with unforseen consequences. An excellent adaptation of the Enid Bagnold play although not as suspenseful as the stage production. **106m/C VHS.** *GB* Deborah Kerr, Hayley Mills, Edith Evans, John Mills, Elizabeth Sellars, Felix Aylmer; ***D:*** Ronald Neame; ***W:*** John Michael Hayes; ***M:*** Malcolm Arnold. Natl. Bd. of Review '64: Support. Actress (Evans).

The Challenge 🦴🦴🦴 **1938** Story of the courageous party of explorers who conquered the Matterhorn. Incredible avalanche scenes. **77m/B VHS.** *GB* Luis Trenker, Robert Douglas, Joan Gardner, Mary Clare, Frank Birch, Geoffrey Wardwell, Lyonel (Lionel) Watts, Fred Groves, Lawrence (Laurence) Baskcomb, Ralph Truman; ***D:*** Milton Rosmer, Luis Trenker; ***W:*** Milton Rosmer, Patrick Kirwan; ***C:*** Albert Benitz, Georges Perinal; ***M:*** Allan Gray, Muir Mathieson.

Challenge woof! **1974 (PG)** When his entire family is killed, dad decides to seek revenge with his shotgun. Very bloody and violent and very nearly plotless. **90m/C VHS.** Earl Owensby, William T. Hicks, Katheryn Thompson, Johnny Popwell; ***D:*** Martin Beck.

The Challenge 🦴🦴½ **1982 (R)** A contemporary action spectacle which combines modern swordplay with the mysticism and fantasy of ancient Samurai legends. **108m/C VHS.** Scott Glenn, Toshiro Mifune; ***D:*** John Frankenheimer; ***W:*** John Sayles, Richard Maxwell; ***M:*** Jerry Goldsmith.

A Challenge for Robin Hood 🦴½ **1968** Innocuous and poorly-done children's adventure tale about the daring 12th century nobleman-turned-bandit, Robin Hood (Ingham), and his usual gang in Sherwood Forest. This time Robin has been framed for murder by his evil cousin, Roger (Blythe), and must prove his innocence. **96m/C VHS.** *GB* Barrie Ingham, Peter Blythe, James Hayter, John Arnatt, Leon Greene, Gay Hamilton; ***D:*** C.M. Pennington-Richards; ***W:*** Peter Bryan; ***C:*** Arthur Grant; ***M:*** Gary Hughes.

Challenge of a Lifetime 🦴🦴½ **1985** Marshall stars as a divorcee whose dream is to compete in the Hawaiian Ironman Triathlon. Cult favorite; Woronov has a substantial supporting role. **100m/C VHS.** Penny Marshall, Richard Gilliland, Jonathan Silverman, Mary Woronov, Paul Gleason, Mark Spitz, Cathy Rigby; ***D:*** Russ Mayberry.

Challenge of McKenna 🦴🦴 **1983** Run-of-the-prairie horse opera has drifter Ireland stumble upon danger and intrigue when he enters a mysterious town. **90m/C VHS.** John Ireland, Robert Woods.

Challenge of the Masters 🦴 **1989** A young Kung-Fu artist wins a new tutor in a contest. Soon he's fighting for a friend to protect his family's honor. **97m/C VHS.** Liu Chia Hui, Liu Chia-Yung, Chen Kuan-Tai, Chiang Yang; ***D:*** Liu Chia-Liang.

Challenge To Be Free 🦴🦴 *Mad Trapper of the Yukon* **1976 (G)** Action adventure geared toward a young audience depicting the struggles of a man being pursued by 12 men and 100 dogs across a thousand miles of frozen wilderness. The last film directed by Garnett, who has a cameo as Marshal McGee. Produced in 1972, the release wasn't until 1976. **90m/C VHS.** Mike Mazurki, Jimmy Kane; ***Cameos:*** Tay Garnett; ***D:*** Tay Garnett.

Challenge to Lassie 🦴🦴½ **1949 (G)** When Lassie's Scottish master dies, the faithful pup remains at his grave. An unsympathetic policeman orders Lassie to leave the premises, inspiring a debate among the townsfolk as to the dog's fate. Based on a true story (although the original hero was a Skye Terrier); remade as "Greyfriar's Bobby." **76m/C VHS.** Edmund Gwenn, Donald Crisp, Geraldine Brooks, Reginald Owen, Alan Webb, Henry Stephenson, Alan Napier, Sara Allgood; ***D:*** Richard Thorpe; ***M:*** Andre Previn.

Challenge to White Fang 🦴½ **1986 (PG)** A courageous dog prevents a scheming businessman from taking over an old man's gold mine. **89m/C VHS.** Harry Carey Jr., Franco Nero; ***D:*** Lucio Fulci.

The Challengers 🦴🦴½ **1993** Young Mackie wants to join local rock band The Challengers, only to discover their main rule is no girls. So Mackie disguises herself as her male cousin Mac—getting ever more confused as she tries to juggle her dual identities. Then she gets found out. **97m/C VHS.** Gema Zamprogna, Gwynyth Walsh, Eric Christmas, Eric Till; ***W:*** Clive Endersby.

The Chamber 🦴🦴 **1996 (R)** Dull retelling of yet another John Grisham legal thriller fails to engross. White supremacist Sam Cahall (Hackman) is on Mississippi's death row for killing two Jewish boys in a 1967 bombing. Young Chicago lawyer Adam Hall (O'Donnell), looking to find out more about his family's odious past, volunteers to work on his grandfather's case and win a stay of execution. Sam's an unrepentent racist but there's some question about whether he was the only culprit. Hackman and Dunaway (as his alcoholic daughter) are their usual professional selves while the charming O'Donnell seems out of his depth. Co-screenwriter Robinson used the pen name Chris Reese. **113m/C VHS, DVD.** Gene Hackman, Chris O'Donnell, Faye Dunaway, Lela Rochon, Robert Prosky, Raymond J. Barry, Bo Jackson, David Marshall Grant, Millie Perkins; ***D:*** James Foley; ***W:*** Phil Alden Robinson, William Goldman; ***C:*** Ian Baker; ***M:*** Carter Burwell.

Chamber of Horrors 🦴🦴½ *The Door with Seven Locks* **1940** A family is brought together at an English castle to claim a fortune left by an aristocrat. However, there's a catch—seven keys may open the vault with the fortune, or leave the key turner dead. Based on the work by Edgar Wallace. **80m/B VHS.** *GB* Leslie Banks, Lilli Palmer; ***D:*** Norman Lee.

The Chambermaid on the Titanic 🦴🦴 *La Femme de Chambre du Titanic; The Chambermaid* **1997** French foundry worker Horty (Martinez) wins a strongman contest and his prize is a trip to Southampton to see the launch of the Titanic. There he (platonically) shares a hotel room with maid Maria (Sanchez-Gijon), who says she has a job aboard the ship. After returning home and learning about the Titanic's sinking, Horty regales his friends with stories of his night with Maria—gradually beginning to believe his own lies about his passionate escapade. Based on the novel by Didier Decoin. French with subtitles. **96m/C VHS.** *FR SP* Olivier Martinez, Aitana Sanchez-Gijon, Romane Bohringer, Didier Bezace, Aldo Maccione; ***D:*** Bigas Luna; ***W:*** Bigas Luna, Cuca Canals; ***C:*** Patrick Blossier; ***M:*** Alberto Iglesias.

Chameleon 🦴🦴 **1995 (R)** Undercover agent, and master of disguise, Willie Serling (LaPaglia), had his wife and daughter murdered by drug smuggler Alberto Cortese (Mandola) and he naturally wants revenge. Willie poses as a bank auditor to learn if Cortese is behind a money-laundering scheme and things get increasingly complex. Talky thriller with lots of cliches. **108m/C VHS.** Anthony LaPaglia, Kevin Pollak, Melora Hardin, Wayne Knight, Tony Mandola, Derek McGrath, Andy Romano, Robin Thomas, Richard Brooks; ***D:*** Michael Pavone; ***W:*** Michael Pavone; ***C:*** Ross Berryman; ***M:*** John Debney.

Chameleon 🦴🦴 **1998 (R)** Phillips is a genetically engineered hit woman who can literally blend into any background (hence the title). Her evil creator/employers send her to dispose of a ragtag band of malcontent scientists whose leader has invented a dangerous microchip. But she develops unexpected maternal feelings towards the now-orphaned young son (Lloyd) of the group's leader and vows to protect him. **90m/C VHS.** Bobbie Phillips, Eric Lloyd, Philip Casnoff; ***D:*** Stuart Cooper. **TV**

Chameleon 2: Death Match 🦴🦴 **1999** Kam (Phillips), the genetically-engineered ultimate hunter, returns and her assignment is to infiltrate an exclusive nightclub where a terrorist is holding a bunch of execs hostage. **87m/C VHS.** Bobbie Phillips, Casey Siemaszko, Tasha Smith, Kara Zediker, Simon Westaway, Mark Lee; ***D:*** Russell King; ***W:*** Bennett Cohen; ***C:*** David Connell; ***M:*** Roger Neill. **TV**

Chameleon 3: Dark Angel 🦴🦴 **2000** Genetically-engineered Kam (Phillips), who's working for the International Bureau of Investigation, is called upon to protect a sullen, suspicious young woman who knows how to control an energy matter device that was stolen from a government facility. But Kam's assignment is threatened by her evil counterpart—her own genetically-engineered brother, Kane (Kuzelicki). **87m/C VHS.** Bobbie Phillips, Suzi Dougherty, Alex Kuzelicki, Teal Redmann, Doug Penty; ***D:*** John Lafia; ***W:*** Ronnie Christensen; ***C:*** David Foreman; ***M:*** Joel Goldsmith. **TV**

Chameleon Street 🦴🦴🦴 **1989 (R)** Entertaining fact-based account of William Douglas Street, a Detroit man who successfully impersonated, among others, a Time magazine reporter and a surgeon until he was caught and sent to prison. He escaped and went to Yale, faked his identity as a student, and then returned to Michigan to impersonate a lawyer for the Detroit Human Rights Commission. Harris wrote and directed this insightful look into the man who fooled many people, including the mayor of Detroit, Coleman A. Young, who appears briefly as himself. **95m/C VHS.** Wendell B. Harris Jr., Angela Leslie, Amina Fakir, Paula McGee, Mano Breckenridge, David Kiley, Anthony Ennis; ***Cameos:*** Coleman A. Young; ***D:*** Wendell B. Harris Jr.; ***W:*** Wendell B. Harris Jr.; ***C:*** Daniel S. Noga; ***M:*** Peter S. Moore. Sundance '90: Grand Jury Prize.

The Champ 🦴🦴🦴 **1932** A washed up boxer dreams of making a comeback and receives support from no one but his devoted son. Minor classic most notorious for jerking the tears and soiling the hankies, this was the first of three Beery/Cooper screen teamings. **87m/B VHS.** Wallace Beery, Jackie Cooper, Irene Rich, Roscoe Ates, Edward Brophy, Hale Hamilton, Jesse Scott, Marcia Mae Jones; ***D:*** King Vidor; ***W:*** Frances Marion. Oscars '32: Actor (Beery), Story.

The Champ 🦴½ **1979 (PG)** An ex-fighter with a weakness for gambling and drinking is forced to return to the ring in an attempt to keep custody of his son. Excessive sentiment may cause cringing. Remake of the 1931 classic. **121m/C VHS, Wide.** Jon Voight, Faye Dunaway, Rick Schroder, Jack Warden, Arthur Hill, Strother Martin, Joan Blondell, Elisha Cook Jr.; ***D:*** Franco Zeffirelli; ***C:*** Fred W. Koenekamp; ***M:*** Dave Grusin.

Champagne 🦴🦴 **1928** A socialite's father fakes bankruptcy to teach his irresponsible daughter a lesson. Early, silent endeavor from Hitchcock is brilliantly photographed. **93m/B VHS.** *GB* Betty Balfour, Gordon Harker, Ferdinand von Alten, Clifford Heatherley, Jack Trevor; ***D:*** Alfred Hitchcock; ***W:*** Alfred Hitchcock.

Champagne for Breakfast 🦴 **1935 (R)** Sex comedy follows the fun-filled adventures of "Champagne," a free-spirited beauty living life to the fullest. **69m/B VHS.** Mary Carlisle, Hardie Albright, Joan Marsh, Lila Lee, Sidney Toler, Bradley Page, Emerson Treacy; ***D:*** Melville Brown.

Champagne for Caesar 🦴🦴🦴 **1950** The laughs keep coming in this comedy about a self-proclaimed genius-on-every-subject who goes on a TV quiz show and proceeds to win everything in sight. The program's sponsor, in desperation, hires a femme fatale to distract the contestant before the final program. Wonderful spoof of the game-show industry. **99m/B VHS.** Ronald Colman, Celeste Holm, Vincent Price, Art Linkletter, Barbara Britton; ***D:*** Richard Whorf.

Champion 🦴🦴🦴½ **1949** An ambitious prizefighter alienates the people around him as he desperately fights his way to the top. When he finally reaches his goal, he is forced to question the cost of his success. From a story by Ring Lardner. Certainly one of the best films ever made about boxing, with less sentiment than "Rocky" but concerned with sociological correctness. **99m/B VHS, DVD.** Kirk Douglas, Arthur Kennedy, Marilyn Maxwell, Ruth Roman, Lola Albright, Paul Stewart; ***D:*** Mark Robson; ***W:*** Carl Foreman; ***C:*** Franz Planer; ***M:*** Dimitri Tiomkin. Oscars '49: Film Editing.

Champions 🦴🦴 **1984** Moving but cliched story of Bob Champion, a leading jockey who overcame cancer to win England's Grand National Steeplechase. A true story, no less. **113m/C VHS, DVD.** *GB* John Hurt, Gregory Jones, Mick Dillon, Ann Bell, Jan Francis, Peter Barkworth, Edward Woodward, Ben Johnson, Kirstie Alley, Alison Steadman; ***D:*** John Irvin; ***W:*** Evan Jones; ***M:*** Carl Davis.

Chan Is Missing 🦴🦴🦴 **1982** Two cab drivers try to find the man who stole their life savings. Wry, low-budget comedy filmed in San Francisco's Chinatown was an art-house smash. The first full-length American film produced exclusively by an Asian-American cast and crew. **80m/B VHS.** Wood Moy, Marc Hayashi, Laureen Chew, Judy Mihei, Peter Wang, Presco Tabios, Frankie Allarcon, Virginia Cerenio, Roy Chan, George Woo, Emily Yamasaki, Ellen Yeung; ***D:*** Wayne Wang; ***W:*** Wayne Wang, Terrel Seltzer, Isaac Cronin; ***C:*** Michael G. Chin; ***M:*** Robert Kikuchi-Yngojo. Natl. Film Reg. '95.

Chance 🦴½ **1989** With over $1 million in diamonds missing, Haggerty and Jacobs throw out all the stops to recover them in this action thriller. **90m/C VHS.** Dan Haggerty, Lawrence-Hilton Jacobs, Addison Randall, Roger Rudd, Charles Gries, Pamela Dixon; ***D:*** Addison Randall, Charles Kanganis.

Chances Are 🦴🦴🦴 **1989 (PG)** After her loving husband dies in a chance accident, a pregnant woman remains unmarried, keeping her husband's best friend as her only close male companion. Years later, her now teenage daughter brings a friend home for dinner, but due to an error in heaven, the young man begins to realize that this may not be the first time he and this family have met. A wonderful love-story hampered only minimally by the unbelievable plot. **108m/C VHS, DVD, 8mm.** Cybill Shepherd, Robert Downey Jr., Ryan O'Neal, Mary Stuart Masterson, Josef Sommer, Christopher McDonald, Joe Grifasi, James Noble, Susan Ruttan, Fran Ryan; ***D:*** Emile Ardolino; ***W:*** Randy Howze, Perry Howze; ***C:*** William A. Fraker; ***M:*** Maurice Jarre.

Chandu on the Magic Island 🦴🦴 **1934** Chandu the Magician takes his powers of the occult to the mysterious lost island of Lemuri to battle the evil cult of Ubasti. Sequel to "Chandu the Magician" and just as campy. **67m/B VHS.** Bela Lugosi, Maria Alba, Clara Kimball Young; ***D:*** Ray Taylor.

Chandu the Magician 🦴🦴 **1932** Bad guy searches desperately for the secret of a powerful death ray so he can (surprise!) destroy civilization. Not well received in its day, but makes for great high-camp fun now. One of Lugosi's most melodramatic performances. **70m/B VHS.** Edmund Lowe, Bela Lugosi, Irene Ware, Henry B. Walthall; ***D:*** William Cameron Menzies, Marcel Varnel; ***C:*** James Wong Howe.

Chanel Solitaire 🦴🦴 **1981 (R)** Uninspiring biography follows the fabulous (simply fabulous) career of dress designer Gabrielle "Coco" Chanel. Ah, go sew something. **124m/C VHS.** Marie-France Pisier, Rutger Hauer, Timothy Dalton, Karen Black, Brigitte Fossey; ***D:*** George Kaczender.

Chang: A Drama of the Wilderness 🦴🦴🦴½ **1927** A farmer and his family has settled a small patch of ground on the edge of the jungle and must struggle for survival against numerous wild animals. The climatic elephant stampede is still thrilling. Shot on location in Siam. **67m/B VHS, DVD.** ***D:*** Merian C. Cooper, Ernest B. Schoedsack; ***W:*** Merian C. Cooper, Ernest B. Schoedsack; ***C:*** Ernest B. Schoedsack.

Change of Habit 🦴🦴 **1969 (G)** Three novitiates undertake to learn about the world before becoming full-fledged nuns. While working at a ghetto clinic a young doctor forms a strong, affectionate relationship with one of them. Presley's last feature film. ♫Change of Habit; Let Us Pray; Rubberneckin'. **93m/C VHS.** Richard Carlson, Elvis Presley, Mary Tyler Moore, Barbara McNair, Ed Asner, Ruth McDevitt, Regis Toomey, Jane Elliot, Leora Dana, Robert Emhardt; ***D:*** William A. Graham; ***W:*** Eric Bercovici, John Joseph; ***C:*** Russell Metty; ***M:*** Billy Goldenberg.

Change of Heart 🦴🦴½ **1998** Smart is always good in wronged woman roles and she's got a doozy in this weepie. Elaine Marshall (Smart) thinks she and husband Jim (Terry) are doing okay marriage-wise. They've been together 20 years, have a couple of kids, two good careers, and apparent happiness. Then Elaine realizes Jim's having an affair. The real shocker for Elaine comes when she finds out her husband's lover is another man. **?m/C VHS.** Jean Smart, John Terry, Gretchen Corbett, Phillip Geoffrey Hough, Shawna Waldron, Dorian Harewood; ***D:*** Arvin Brown; ***W:*** Aaron Mendelsohn; ***C:*** John Campbell; ***M:*** Patrick Williams. **CABLE**

A Change of Seasons 🦴🦴 **1980 (R)** One of them so-called sophisticated comedies that look at the contemporary relationships and values of middle-class, middle-aged people who should know better. The wife of a college professor learns of her husband's affair with a seductive student and decides to have a fling with a younger man. The situation reaches absurdity when the couples decide to vacation together. **102m/C VHS.** Shirley MacLaine, Bo Derek, Anthony Hopkins, Michael Brandon, Mary Beth Hurt; ***D:*** Richard Lang; ***W:*** Erich Segal; ***M:*** Henry Mancini.

The Changeling 🦴🦴½ **1980 (R)** A music teacher moves into an old house and discovers that a young boy's ghostly spirit is his housemate. The ghost wants revenge against the being that replaced him upon his death. Scary ghost story with some less than logical leaps of script. **114m/C VHS, DVD, Wide.** *CA* George C. Scott, Trish Van Devere, John Russell, Melvyn Douglas, Jean Marsh, John Colicos, Barry Morse, Roberta Maxwell, James B. Douglas; ***D:*** Peter Medak; ***W:*** William Gray, Diana Maddox; ***C:*** John Coquillon. Genie '80: Film.

Changes 🦴 **1969 (PG)** A young man leaves home and thumbs across the California coast in order to find himself. On the road again. **103m/C VHS.** Kent Lane, Michele Carey, Jack Albertson, Marcia Strassman; ***D:*** Hall Bartlett.

Changing Habits 🦴½ **1996 (R)** Starving artist Soosh (Kelly) moves into a nunnery, in exchange for doing chores, in order to save money. She's so broke, she's taken to stealing art supplies, but salesman Felix (Walsh) is more interested in romancing Soosh than turning her in. Dull, dull, dull, and a waste of a talented cast. **92m/C VHS, DVD.** Moira Kelly, Christopher Lloyd, Teri Garr, Shelley Duvall, Dylan Walsh, Marissa Ribisi, Frances Bay, Bob Gunton, Anne Haney, Eileen Brennan; ***D:*** Lynn Roth; ***W:*** Scott Davis Jones; ***C:*** Mike Mayers; ***M:*** David McHugh.

Changing Lanes 🦴🦴🦴 **2002 (R)** A fender-bender on the FDR pits two harried New Yorkers in an escalating battle of revenge. Banek (Affleck), a privileged Wall Street lawyer, and Gipson (Jackson), a recovering-alcoholic insurance man, both need to get to court on time. Banek to file documents crucial to his firm's success, and Gipson, to prove he's fit to retain joint custody of his two kids. Because of the accident, neither gets quite what he wants. When Gipson finds that he has the the vital document, after having been stranded by Banek (and subsequently late to the custody hearing), he begins the battle. Throughout the back and forth, the plot (and many of its excesses), gives way to a fully realized character study and thoughtful pondering of motivations, corruption, and desperation, powered by dialogue not usually seen in a "revenge" flick. Michell deftly brings out the best in every member of a talented cast. **98m/C VHS, DVD.** *US* Ben Affleck, Samuel L. Jackson, Toni Collette, Sydney Pollack, William Hurt, Amanda Peet, Richard Jenkins, Kim Staunton, John Benjamin Hickey, Jennifer (Jennie) Dundas Lowe, Dylan Baker, Matt Malloy; ***D:*** Roger Michell; ***W:*** Michael Tolkin, Chap Taylor; ***C:*** Salvatore Totino; ***M:*** David Arnold.

The Channeler 🦴 **1989** The traditional dopey students probe an old Colorado mine and encounter black-robed, demon whazzits. A spunky cast and nice scenery didn't stop the Hound from switching channels on this one. **90m/C VHS.** Dan Haggerty, Richard Harrison, Jay Richardson, David Homb, Oliver Darrow, Robin Sims, Charles Solomon; ***D:*** Grant Austin Waldman.

Chantilly Lace 🦴🦴½ **1993 (R)** Ensemble cast tries hard in this story of modern American women and friendship in the '90s. Val (Eikenberry) gathers a group of seven close friends at her new house in Sundance. Turns out trying to "have it all" is causing some emotional crises to surface, which are explored over the course of a year. Actresses improvised their dialogue from basic character information. Lots of weeping and bonding. **102m/C VHS.** Jill Eikenberry, Ally Sheedy, Helen Slater, Lindsay Crouse, JoBeth Williams, Martha Plimpton, Talia Shire; ***D:*** Linda Yellen; ***W:*** Linda Yellen, Rosanne Ehrlich; ***M:*** Patrick Seymour. **CABLE**

Chaos Factor 🦴🦴 **2000 (R)** Jack Poynt (Sabato Jr.) is an Army Intelligence officer working in Cambodia. He discovers evidence linking the death of American soldiers to high-ranking officials and becomes the target of a deadly coverup by the Defense Department. **102m/C VHS, DVD.** Antonio Sabato Jr., Fred Ward, Kelly Rutherford, Sean Kanan, R. Lee Ermey; ***D:*** Terry Cunningham. **VIDEO**

Chapayev 🦴🦴🦴 **1934** Striking propagandist drama dealing with the exploits of a legendary Red Army commander during the 1919 battle with the White Russians. Stunning, and carefully choreographed, battle scenes. Adapted from a biographical novel by Dmitri Furmanov. In Russian with English subtitles. **101m/B VHS.** *RU* Boris Babochkin, Leonid Kmit, Boris Chirkov, Varvara Myasnikova, Illarian Pevzov, Stephan Shkurat, Boris Blinov, Vyacheslav Volkov, Nikolai Simonov, Georgi Zhzhenov; ***D:*** Sergei Vassiliev, Georgy Vassiliev; ***W:*** Sergei Vassiliev, Georgy Vassiliev; ***C:*** Aleksander Sigayev, Alexander Xenofontov; ***M:*** Gavriil Popov.

Chaplin 🦴🦴🦴 **1992 (PG-13)** The life and career of "The Little Tramp" is chronicled by director Attenborough and brilliantly portrayed by Downey, Jr, as Chaplin. A flashback format traces his life from its poverty-stricken Dickensian origins in the London slums through his directing and acting career, to his honorary Oscar in 1972. Slow-moving at parts, but captures Chaplin's devotion to his art and also his penchant towards jailbait. In a clever casting choice, Chaplin's own daughter from his fourth marriage to Oona O'Neill, Geraldine Chaplin, plays her own grandmother who goes mad. **135m/C VHS, DVD, Wide.** *GB* Robert Downey Jr., Dan Aykroyd, Geraldine Chaplin, Kevin Dunn, Anthony Hopkins, Milla Jovovich, Moira Kelly, Kevin Kline, Diane Lane, Penelope Ann Miller, Paul Rhys, John Thaw, Marisa Tomei, Nancy Travis, James Woods, David Duchovny, Deborah Maria Moore, Bill Paterson, John Standing, Robert Stephens, Peter Crook; ***D:*** Richard Attenborough; ***W:*** Bryan Forbes, William Boyd, William Goldman; ***C:*** Sven Nykvist; ***M:*** John Barry. British Acad. '92: Actor (Downey).

The Chaplin Revue **1958** The "Revue," put together by Chaplin in 1958, consists of three of his best shorts: "A Dog's Life" (1918), the WWI comedy "Shoulder Arms" (1918), and "The Pilgrim," in which a convict hides out in a clerical guise (1922). Chaplin added self-composed score, narration, and some documentary on-the-set material. **121m/B VHS.** Charlie Chaplin, Edna Purviance, Sydney Chaplin, Mack Swain; ***D:*** Charlie Chaplin.

Chapter Two 🦴🦴 **1979 (PG)** Loosely based on Neil Simon's marriage to Mason and his Broadway hit of the same name. A writer, grief-stricken over the death of his first wife, meets the woman who will become his second. Witty dialogue in first half deteriorates when guilt strikes. **124m/C VHS.** James Caan, Marsha Mason, Valerie Harper, Joseph Bologna; ***D:*** Robert Moore; ***W:*** Neil Simon.

Character 🦴🦴 *Karakter* **1997 (R)** Based on the 1938 novel by F. Bordewijk, which follows the troubled relationship of young lawyer Jacob Willem Katadreuffe (van Huet) and his overbearing father in 1920s Rotterdam. Dreverhaven (Decleir) is a powerful baliff who has an illegitimate son with his servant, Joba (Schuurman), who turns down his marriage proposal. Still, Dreverhaven is determined to control his son's life, even if it means ruining him first. No wonder the old man gets murdered. Dark and unsentimental. Dutch with subtitles. **114m/C VHS.** *NL* Fredja Van Huet, Jan Decleir, Betty Schuurman, Victor Low, Tamar van den Dop, Hans Kestig; ***D:*** Mike van Diem; ***W:*** Mike van Diem; ***C:*** Rogier Stoffers; ***M:*** Paleis Van Boem. Oscars '97: Foreign Film.

Charade 🦴🦴 **1953** Mason and wife Pamela star in this trilogy of love and violence. "Portrait of a Murderer" has a young artist sketching the picture of the man who—unknown to her—has just murdered her girlfriend. "Duel at Dawn" concerns an 1880s Austrian officer who steals a woman from another officer and is then challenged to a duel. "The Midas Touch" revolves around a successful but dissatisfied man who abandons his riches to find the meaning of life. Mason himself had said he hoped "this curiosity" would disappear. **83m/B VHS, DVD.** James Mason, Pamela Mason, Scott Forbes, Paul Cavanagh, Bruce Lester, Sean McClory, Vince Barnett; ***D:*** Roy Kellino.

Charade 🦴🦴🦴½ **1963** After her husband is murdered, a young woman finds herself on the run from crooks and double agents who want the $250,000 her husband stole during WWII. Hepburn and Grant are charming and sophisticated as usual in this stylish intrigue filmed in Paris. Based on the story "The Unsuspecting Wife" by Marc Behm and Peter Stone. **113m/C VHS, DVD.** Cary Grant, Audrey Hepburn, Walter Matthau, James Coburn, George Kennedy; ***D:*** Stanley Donen; ***W:*** Peter Stone; ***C:*** Charles B(ryant) Lang Jr.; ***M:*** Henry Mancini. British Acad. '64: Actress (Hepburn).

The Charge of the Light Brigade 🦴🦴🦴 **1936 (PG-13)** A British army officer stationed in India deliberately starts the Balaclava charge to even an old score with Surat Khan, who's on the other side. Still an exciting film, though it's hardly historically accurate. De Havilland is along to provide the requisite romance with Flynn. Also available colorized. **115m/B VHS.** Errol Flynn, Olivia de Havilland, David Niven, Nigel Bruce, Patric Knowles, Donald Crisp, C. Henry Gordon, J. Carrol Naish, Henry Stephenson, E.E. Clive, Scotty Beckett, G.P. (Tim) Huntley Jr., Robert Barrat, Spring Byington, George Regas; ***D:*** Michael Curtiz; ***W:*** Michael Jacoby, Rowland Leigh; ***C:*** Sol Polito; ***M:*** Max Steiner.

The Charge of the Light Brigade 🦴🦴½ **1968 (PG-13)** Political indictment of imperialistic England in this revisionist retelling of the notorious British defeat by the Russians at Balaclava. Battle scenes are secondary to this look at the stupidity of war. Fine cast; notable animation sequences by Richard Williams. **130m/C VHS, DVD, Wide.** *GB* Trevor Howard, John Gielgud, David Hemmings, Vanessa Redgrave, Harry Andrews, Jill Bennett, Peter Bowles, Mark Burns, Alan Dobie, T.P. McKenna, Corin Redgrave, Norman Rossington, Rachel Kempson, Donald Wolfit, Howard Marion-Crawford, Mark Dignam, Ben Aris, Peter Woodthorpe, Roger Mutton, Joely Richardson; ***D:*** Tony Richardson; ***W:*** Charles Wood; ***C:*** David Watkin; ***M:*** John Addison.

Charge of the Model T's 🦴½ **1976 (G)** Comedy about a WWI German spy who tries to infiltrate the U.S. army. **90m/C VHS.** Louis Nye, John David Carson, Herb Edelman, Carol Bagdasarian, Arte Johnson; ***D:*** Jim McCullough.

Chariots of Fire 🦴🦴🦴½ **1981 (PG)** A lush telling of the parallel stories of Harold Abraham and Eric Liddell, English runners who competed in the 1924 Paris Olympics. One was compelled by a hatred of anti-Semitism, the other by the love of God. Outstanding performances by the entire cast. **123m/C VHS, DVD.** *GB* Ben Cross, Ian Charleson, Nigel Havers, Ian Holm, Alice Krige, Brad Davis, Dennis Christopher, Patrick Magee, Cheryl Campbell, John Gielgud, Lindsay Anderson, Nigel Davenport; ***D:*** Hugh Hudson; ***W:*** Colin Welland; ***C:*** David Watkin; ***M:*** Vangelis. Oscars '81: Costume Des., Orig. Screenplay, Picture, Orig. Score; British Acad. '81: Film, Support. Actor (Holm); Golden Globes '82: Foreign Film; N.Y. Film Critics '81: Cinematog.

Charlemagne 🦴🦴½ **1995** British miniseries follows the life of the royal conqueror who civilized western Europe and ruled as emperor from 800-814. On five cassettes. **250m/C VHS.** *GB* Christian Brendel, Anny (Annie Legras) Duperey; ***D:*** Clive Donner.

Charles & Diana: A Palace Divided 🦴🦴½ **1993** Trashy scandalous tale of the disintegration of the fairytale romance and marriage of Prince Charles and Princess Diana. Oxenberg stars as Princess Di, a role she played a decade ago in "The Royal Romance of Charles and Diana," and Rees does a fine job playing the conservative Prince Charles. Although the film covers all of the couple's highly publicized troubles, it's such a quick superficial treatment that it's often hard to follow. Nonetheless, it's a flashingly inviting look into the privileged House of Windsor. **92m/C VHS.** Roger Rees, Catherine Oxenberg, Benedict Taylor, Tracy Brabin, Amanda Walker, David Quilter, Jane How; ***D:*** John Power.

Charles: Dead or Alive 🦴🦴 *Charles: Mort ou Vif* **1969** Aging Charles De (Simon) has always lead an ordinary life when he suddenly drops out and re-emerges as a madman, who lives only on his own terms. His family becomes so upset by his bizarre behavior that they commit him to an asylum. First feature film by Tanner. French with subtitles. **93m/B VHS.**

S/ Francois Simon; ***D:*** Alain Tanner; ***W:*** Alain Tanner; ***C:*** Renato Berta.

Charles et Lucie 🦴🦴🦴 **1979** A has-been couple are ripped off, pursued, persecuted, and saddled with very bad luck in the South of France. Essentially a character study; semi-acclaimed. In French with subtitles. **96m/C VHS.** *FR* Daniel Ceccaldi, Ginette Garcin, Jean-Marie Proslier, Samson Fainsilber; ***D:*** Nelly Kaplan.

Charleston 🦴🦴🦴 **1926** Renoir's third film, a simple erotic dance fantasy that caused much controversy in its day. Silent, with jazz score and historical introduction. **30m/B VHS.** Catherine Hessling; ***D:*** Jean Renoir.

Charley and the Angel 🦴🦴½ **1973 (G)** Touching story of a man who changes his cold ways with his family when informed by an angel that he hasn't much time to live. Amusing Disney movie set in the Great Depression. **93m/C VHS.** Fred MacMurray, Cloris Leachman, Harry (Henry) Morgan, Kurt Russell, Vincent Van Patten, Kathleen (Kathy) Cody; ***D:*** Vincent McEveety.

Charley Varrick 🦴🦴🦴 **1973 (PG)** Matthau, a small-town hood, robs a bank only to find out that one of its depositors is the Mob. Baker's the vicious hit-man assigned the job of getting the loot back. A well-paced, on-the-mark thriller. **111m/C VHS.** Walter Matthau, Joe Don Baker, Felicia Farr, John Vernon, Sheree North, Norman Fell, Andrew (Andy) Robinson, Jacqueline Scott, Albert "Poppy" Popwell; ***D:*** Donald Siegel; ***W:*** Dean Riesner; ***M:*** Lalo Schifrin.

Charley's Aunt 🦴🦴½ **1925** Amusing Victorian farce in which two young male students convince an older fellow student to dress up as their female chaperon so they can pitch woo to two local lovelies. Fun performances and well-paced direction by Sidney. Based on the Brandon Thomas farce, the movie was remade in 1930, starring Charles Ruggles, and again in 1941, with Jack Benny. **75m/B VHS.** Sydney Chaplin, Ethel Shannon, Lucien Littlefield, Alec B. Francis, Mary Akin, Priscilla Bonner, Jimmy Harrison, David James, Eulalie Jensen, James E. Page, Phillips Smalley; ***D:*** Scott Sidney; ***W:*** F. McGrew Willis, Joe Farnham; ***C:*** Gus Peterson, Paul Garnett.

Charlie and the Great Balloon Chase 🦴🦴 **1982** When a grandfather takes his grandson on a cross-country balloon trip, they are hotly pursued by the boy's mother, her stuffy fiance (who wants the boy in military school), the FBI, a reporter, and the Mafia. **98m/C VHS.** Jack Albertson, Adrienne Barbeau, Slim Pickens, Moosie Drier; ***D:*** Larry Elikann. **TV**

Charlie Boy 🦴½ **1981** The new owner of an ancient African idol enters the world of the supernatural when he casts a death spell on six people. **60m/C VHS.** Leigh Lawson, Angela Bruce, Marius Goring; ***D:*** Robert M. Young.

Charlie Bravo 🦴 **198? (R)** A commando group is commanded to rescue a captured nurse in Vietnam. Dubbed. **94m/C VHS.** *FR* Bruno Pradal, Karen Verlier, Jean-Francois Poron; ***D:*** Rene Demoulin.

Charlie Chan and the Curse of the Dragon Queen 🦴½ **1981 (PG)** The famed Oriental sleuth confronts his old enemy the Dragon Queen, and reveals the true identity of a killer. **97m/C VHS.** Peter Ustinov, Lee Grant, Angie Dickinson, Richard Hatch, Brian Keith, Roddy McDowall, Michelle Pfeiffer, Rachel Roberts; ***D:*** Clive Donner; ***W:*** David Axelrod, Stanley Burns.

Charlie Chan at the Opera 🦴🦴🦴 **1936** The great detective investigates an amnesiac opera star (Karloff) who may have committed murder. Considered one of the best of the series. Interesting even to those not familiar with Charlie Chan. **66m/B VHS.** Warner Oland, Boris Karloff, Keye Luke, Charlotte Henry, Thomas Beck, Nedda Harrigan, William Demarest; ***D:*** H. Bruce Humberstone.

Charlie Chan at the Wax Museum 🦴½ **1940** Charlie and number one son must find a criminal hiding out in a wax museum. Chills abound when the fugitive heads for the chamber of horrors. **63m/B VHS.** Sidney Toler, Victor Sen Yung, C. Henry Gordon, Marc Lawrence, Joan Valerie, Marguerite Chapman, Ted Osborn, Michael Visaroff; ***D:*** Lynn Shores.

Charlie Chan in Paris 🦴🦴½ **1935** Chan scours the city of lights to track down a trio of counterfeiters. Top-notch plot and plenty of suspense will please all. **72m/B VHS.** Warner Oland, Mary Brian, Thomas Beck, Erik Rhodes, John Miljan, Minor Watson, John Qualen, Keye Luke, Henry Kolker; ***D:*** Lewis Seiler.

Charlie Chan in Rio 🦴🦴 **1941** Local police call on Chan to help solve a double murder. One of the series' weaker entries but with fine setting and music. **60m/B VHS.** Sidney Toler, Mary Beth Hughes, Cobina Wright Jr., Ted North, Victor Jory, Harold Huber, Victor Sen Yung; ***D:*** Harry Lachman.

Charlie Chan in the Secret Service 🦴½ **1944** Toler's Chan is now a government agent who is assigned to find the killer of an inventor. Moreland joins up as Chan's taxi-driving, constantly terrified sidekick. The series moved from 20th-century Fox to low-budget Monogram Pictures with this entry, with an ensuing drop in production quality. **64m/B VHS.** Sidney Toler, Mantan Moreland, Gwen Kenyon, Arthur Loft, Marianne Quon, Lela Tyler, Benson Fong; ***D:*** Phil Rosen.

Charlie Chan's Secret 🦴🦴 **1935** Chan must solve the murder of the heir to a huge fortune. A good, logical script with plenty of suspects to keep you guessing. **72m/B VHS.** Warner Oland, Rosina Lawrence, Charles Quigley, Henrietta Crosman, Edward Trevor, Astrid Allwyn; ***D:*** Gordon Wiles.

Charlie Chaplin: Night at the Show 🦴🦴🦴 **1915** Chaplin plays two different mugs, both out for a night on the town. Mr. Pest, a sharp-dressed uppercruster, clings to his disgusting habits, and Mr. Rowdy is his working-class doppleganger. Both obnoxious Chaplins-in-disguise collaborate to wreak havoc on a local theatre. Contains original organ score. **?m/B VHS.** Charlie Chaplin, Edna Purviance; ***D:*** Charlie Chaplin; ***W:*** Charlie Chaplin.

Charlie Chaplin ... Our Hero! **1915** Two shorts from 1915 written and directed by Chaplin, "Night at the Show" and "In the Park," as well as a 1914 film, "Hot Finish," in which Charlie plays the villain. **58m/B VHS, 8mm.** Charlie Chaplin, Edna Purviance, Lloyd Bacon, Mabel Normand, Chester Conklin, Mack Sennett; ***D:*** Charlie Chaplin.

Charlie Grant's War 🦴🦴 **1980** The true story of a Canadian businessman who hears of Nazi brutality and determines to save European Jews from persecution during the Holocaust. Not among the more distinguished works of its kind. **130m/C VHS.** *GB* Jan Rubes, R.H. Thomson, Joan Orenstein; ***D:*** Martin Lavut.

Charlie, the Lonesome Cougar 🦴🦴 **1967 (G)** Life for a rugged logger will never be the same after he adopts an orphaned cougar. From the Disney factory. **75m/C VHS, DVD.** Linda Wallace, Jim Wilson, Ron Brown, Brian Russell, Clifford Peterson; ***D:*** Winston Hibler; ***W:*** Jack Speirs; ***C:*** William W. Bacon III, Lloyd Beebe; ***M:*** Franklyn Marks; ***Nar:*** Rex Allen.

Charlie's Angels 🦴🦴½ **2000 (PG-13)** Seventies TV jigglefest finally gets a belated big screen treatment that has the trio (Barrymore, Diaz, Liu) saving Charlie (Forsythe reprises his voice role) from assassination and thwarting bad guy Roger Corwin (Curry). Merchant-Ivory it ain't (yay!), but it is everything a summer movie's supposed to be: loud, flashy, and fun. Matt LeBlanc, Tom Green, and Luke Wilson are around as nominal romantic interests but it's the women who run the show. Everyone seems to be having a good time, especially Murray as Bosley and Diaz as "perky" angel, Natalie. **99m/C VHS, DVD, Wide.** Drew Barrymore, Cameron Diaz, Lucy Alexis Liu, Bill Murray, Tim Curry, Sam Rockwell, Kelly Lynch, Crispin Glover, Matt LeBlanc, L.L. Cool J., Tom Green, Luke Wilson, Sean M. Whalen, Alex Trebek, Michael (Mike) Papajohn; ***D:*** McG; ***W:*** John August, Ryan Rowe, Ed Solomon; ***C:*** Russell Carpenter; ***M:*** Ed Shearmur; ***V:*** John Forsythe.

Charlie's Ghost: The Secret of Coronado 🦴🦴½ *Charlie's Ghost Story* **1994 (PG)** Kid who has trouble fitting in is befriended by the ghost of a Spanish conquistador. **92m/C VHS.** Richard "Cheech" Marin, Trenton Knight, Anthony Edwards, Linda Fiorentino, Daphne Zuniga; ***D:*** Anthony Edwards.

Charlotte Forten's Mission: Experiment in Freedom 🦴🦴🦴 *Half Slave, Half Free 2* **1985** Fact-based story, set during the Civil War. A wealthy, educated black woman, determined to prove to President Lincoln that blacks are equal to whites, journeys to a remote island off the coast of Georgia. There she teaches freed slaves to read and write. Part of the "American Playhouse" series on PBS. Preceded by "Solomon Northrup's Odyssey." **120m/C VHS.** Melba Moore, Mary Alice, Ned Beatty, Carla Borelli, Micki Grant, Moses Gunn, Anna Maria Horsford, Bruce McGill, Glynn Turman, Roderick Wimberly; ***D:*** Barry Crane; ***W:*** Samm-Art Williams.

Charlotte Gray 🦴🦴 **2001 (PG-13)** Uninvolving WWII romantic drama based on the 1998 novel by Sebastian Faulks. Scottish Charlotte (Blanchett) is living in London when she meets dashing RAF pilot Peter Gregory (Penry-Jones). After learning that Peter has been shot down over France, Charlotte (who speaks perfect French) volunteers for British Special Operations and is sent to work with the Resistance in Vichy. Charlotte's contacts are Levade (Gambon) and his handsome son Julian (Crudup). Naturally, there are supposed to be sparks between the two but the romance fizzles rather than sizzles as does the film itself. Chameleon Blanchett and gruff Gambon are the main reasons to watch. **118m/C VHS, DVD.** *GB AU* Cate Blanchett, Billy Crudup, Michael Gambon, Rupert Penry-Jones, Anton Lesser, James Fleet, Ron Cook, Jack Shepherd, Nicholas Farrell, Helen McCrory, Abigail Cruttenden, Charlie Condou; ***D:*** Gillian Armstrong; ***W:*** Jeremy Brock; ***C:*** Dion Beebe; ***M:*** Stephen Warbeck.

Charlotte's Web 🦴🦴½ **1973 (G)** E.B. White's classic story of a friendship between a spider and a pig is handled only adequately by Hanna-Barbera studios. Some okay songs. **94m/C VHS, DVD, Wide.** ***D:*** Charles A. Nichols, Iwao Takamoto; ***W:*** Earl Hamner; ***M:*** Irwin Kostal; ***V:*** Pamelyn Ferdin, Danny Bonaduce, Debbie Reynolds, Agnes Moorehead, Paul Lynde, Henry Gibson; ***Nar:*** Rex Allan.

Charly 🦴🦴🦴 **1968** A retarded man becomes intelligent after brain surgery, then romances a kindly caseworker before slipping back into retardation. Moving account is well served by leads Robertson and Bloom. Adapted from the Daniel Keyes novel "Flowers for Algernon." **103m/C VHS.** Cliff Robertson, Claire Bloom, Lilia Skala, Leon Janney, Dick Van Patten, William Dwyer; ***D:*** Ralph Nelson; ***W:*** Stirling Silliphant. Oscars '68: Actor (Robertson); Golden Globes '69: Screenplay; Natl. Bd. of Review '68: Actor (Robertson).

Charm of La Boheme 🦴🦴½ **1936** A vintage German musical based on the Puccini opera. With English subtitles. **90m/B VHS.** *GE* Jan Kiepura, Martha Eggerth, Paul Kemp; ***D:*** Geza von Bolvary.

The Charmer 🦴🦴½ **1987** Havers stars as Ralph Gorse, a charming but amoral con man who uses any means to get what he wants. This includes using the affection (and money) of an older woman, blackmail, and even murder. Set in the late '30s. Made for British TV miniseries. **312m/C VHS.** *GB* Nigel Havers, Rosemary Leach, Bernard Hepton, Fiona Fullerton, Abigail McKern, George Baker, Judy Parfitt; ***D:*** Alan Gibson; ***W:*** Allan Prior. **TV**

Charming Billy 🦴🦴 **1998** Living a life of quiet desperation finally proves to be too much for Billy Starkman (Hayden) and he goes postal—sniping at passersby from the top of a rural water tower. Flashbacks show how Billy got to that desperate point in his life. **80m/C VHS, DVD, Wide.** Michael Hayden, Sally Murphy, Tony Mockus Sr., Chelcie Ross; ***D:*** William R. Pace; ***W:*** William R. Pace; ***C:*** William Newell; ***M:*** David Barkley.

Charro! 🦴 **1969 (G)** Presley in a straight role as a reformed bandit hounded by former gang members. Western fails on nearly all accounts, with Presley hopelessly acting outside the bounds of his talent. Furthermore, he sings only one song. **98m/C VHS.** Elvis Presley, Ina Balin, Victor French, Lynn Kellogg, Barbara Werle, Paul Brinegar, James B. Sikking; ***D:*** Charles Marquis Warren; ***W:*** Charles Marquis Warren; ***M:*** Hugo Montenegro.

Charulata 🦴🦴 *The Lonely Wife* **1964** Charulata is a loyal and dutiful wife taken for granted by her husband. But when his young cousin Amal comes to live with them, Charulata glimpses what true love could be. Adapted from the novella by Rabindranath Tagore. Bengali with subtitles. **117m/B VHS.** *IN* Shailan Mukherjee, Shyamal Ghoshal, Gitali Roy, Bholanath Koyal, Suku Mukherjee, Dilip Bose, Joydeb, Bankim Ghosh, Subrata Sensharma, Majhabi Mukherjee, Soumitra Chatterjee; ***D:*** Satyajit Ray; ***W:*** Satyajit Ray; ***C:*** Subrata Mitra; ***M:*** Satyajit Ray, Rabindranath Tagore.

The Chase 🦴🦴½ **1946** Not realizing that his boss-to-be is a mobster, Cummings takes a job as a chauffeur. Naturally, he falls in love with the gangster's wife (Morgan), and the two plan to elope. Somewhat miffed, the cuckolded mafioso and his bodyguard (Lorre) pursue the elusive couple as they head for Havana. The performances are up to snuff, but the story's as unimaginative as the title, with intermittent bouts of suspense. **86m/B VHS.** Robert Cummings, Michele Morgan, Peter Lorre, Steve Cochran, Lloyd Corrigan, Jack Holt, Don Wilson; ***D:*** Arthur Ripley; ***W:*** Philip Yordan.

The Chase 🦴🦴½ **1966** Southern community is undone when rumors circulate of a former member's prison escape and return home. Excellent cast only partially shines. Brando is outstanding as the beleaguered, honorable sheriff, and Duvall makes a splash in the more showy role of a cuckold who fears the escapee is returning home to avenge a childhood incident. Reliable Dickinson also makes the most of her role as Brando's loving wife. Fonda, however, was not yet capable of fashioning complex characterizations, and Redford is under-utilized as the escapee. Adapted from the play by Horton Foote. Notorious conflicts among producer, director, and writer kept it from being a winner. **135m/C VHS, Wide.** Marlon Brando, Robert Redford, Angie Dickinson, E.G. Marshall, Jane Fonda, James Fox, Janice Rule, Robert Duvall, Miriam Hopkins, Martha Hyer; ***D:*** Arthur Penn; ***W:*** Lillian Hellman, Horton Foote; ***M:*** John Barry.

Chase 🦴½ **1985** A big-city lawyer returns to her small hometown to defend a killer and ends up at odds with the town, including an ex-lover. Routine drama. **104m/C VHS.** Jennifer O'Neill, Robert Woods, Richard Farnsworth, Michael Parks; ***D:*** Rod Holcomb; ***M:*** Charles Bernstein. **TV**

The Chase 🦴🦴 **1991 (PG-13)** Routine actioner in which an ex-con killer leads a ruthless cop and a TV news team on a wild chase. Loosely based on a true story. **93m/C VHS.** Casey Siemaszko, Ben Johnson, Gerry Bamman, Robert Beltran, Barry Corbin, Ricki Lake, Megan Follows, Sheila Kelley; ***D:*** Paul Wendkos. **TV**

The Chase 🦴🦴½ **1993 (PG-13)** Heiress Natalie Voss (Swanson) is in the wrong place at the wrong time when she's carjacked by escaped con Jack Hammond (Sheen) who uses a Butterfinger for his weapon. Frantic chases ensues as it turns out that Daddy Voss is a media hungry millionaire and he's followed by not only the cops but the media as well. One-dimensional characters aren't helped by a one-dimensional script, but slick filmmaking and a little charm helps. Skewers the media hype that surrounds crime, taking on news programs that offer immediate coverage and reality based shows with glee. **87m/C VHS.** Joao Fernandes, Kristy Swanson, Charlie Sheen, Josh Mostel, Ray Wise, Henry Rollins, Flea; ***D:*** Adam Rifkin; ***W:*** Adam Rifkin; ***M:*** Richard Gibbs.

Chasers 🦴🦴 **1994 (R)** Gruff Navy petty officer Rock Reilly (Berenger) and his conniving partner Eddie Devane (McNamara) are stuck escorting maximum security prisoner Toni Johnson (Eleniak) to a Charleston naval base. Imagine their surprise when Toni turns out to be a beautiful blonde whose one purpose is to escape her jail-sentence for going AWOL. Considering how dumb her jailers are this shouldn't be too difficult. Lots of sneering, leering, and macho posturing. **100m/C VHS, DVD, Wide.** Tom Berenger, William McNamara, Erika Eleniak, Gary Busey, Crispin Glover, Dean Stockwell, Seymour Cassel, Frederic Forrest, Marilu Henner, Dennis Hopper; ***D:*** Dennis Hopper; ***W:*** Joe Batteer, John Rice, Dan Gilroy; ***C:*** Ueli Steiger; ***M:*** Dwight Yoakam, Pete Anderson.

Chasing Amy 🦴🦴½ **1997 (R)** Holden (Affleck) and best friend Banky (Lee), New Jersey comic book artists, attend a convention in New York where Holden is immediately attracted to fellow artist Alyssa (Adams). His ego is quickly deflated when Alyssa lets him know she's a lesbian. They try for friendship, head into a rocky romance, and then Holden discovers Alyssa's had a wild (and heterosexual) past, which pushes all his emotional buttons. Writer/director Smith supplies his trademark sharp dialogue, and the leads all contribute fine performances. Jay (Mewes) and Silent Bob (Smith), from Smith's earlier pics, make another appearance and supply the story that gives the film its title. **113m/C VHS, DVD, Wide.** Ben Affleck, Joey Lauren Adams, Jason Lee, Dwight Ewell, Jason Mewes, Kevin Smith, Matt Damon; ***D:*** Kevin Smith; ***W:*** Kevin Smith; ***C:*** David Klein; ***M:*** David Pirner. Ind. Spirit '97: Screenplay, Support. Actor (Lee).

Chasing Butterflies 🦴🦴 *La Chasse aux Papillons* **1994** Society's decline is represented by a once-grand, now-decaying chateau, located in a small French village, and its equally decaying inhabitants. Marie-Agnes, confined to a wheelchair, is attended to by her cousin Solange and sullen maid Valerie. When Marie-Agnes suddenly dies, the greedy relatives descend, as well as untrustworthy antiques dealers, and Japanese businessmen interested in acquiring foreign real estate. The film is also an acquired taste. French with subtitles. **115m/C VHS.** *FR* Thamar Tarasachvili, Narda Blanchet, Pierrette Pompom Bailhache, Alexandre Tcherkassoff; ***D:*** Otar Iosseliani; ***W:*** Otar Iosseliani.

Chasing Destiny 🦴🦴½ **2000 (PG-13)** Once famous as a sixties rock 'n' roller, Jet James (Lloyd) is in debt and has a collector (Van Dien) at his door. But when his pretty daughter (Graham) comes to visit, Jet thinks getting the two young people together could be his way out of financial crisis. **90m/C VHS, DVD.** Christopher Lloyd, Casper Van Dien, Lauren Graham, Roger Daltrey, Justin Henry, Stuart Pankin, Deborah Van Valkenburgh; ***D:*** Tim Boxell. **VIDEO**

Chasing Dreams 🦴½ **1981 (PG)** Sickly melodrama about a farmboy who finds fulfillment as a baseball player. Lame film promoted as Costner baseball vehicle, but the star of "Bull Durham" and "Field of Dreams" appears only briefly in a secondary role. **96m/C VHS.** David G. Brown, John Fife, Jim Shane, Lisa Kingston, Matt Clark, Kevin Costner; ***D:*** Sean Roche, Therese Conte.

Chasing Holden 🦴½ **2001 (R)** Cliched teen angst comedy/drama does refer to Holden Caulfield of "Catcher in the Rye." 19-year-old Neal (Qualls) is back at prep school after a two-year stay in a mental hospital. His English teacher Alex (Kanan) assigns his students an essay on what happened to Holden after the end of the Salinger novel. Neal decides the best way to find out is to visit the reclusive author—accompanied by his one friend, T.J. (Blanchard). **101m/C VHS, DVD.** DJ Qualls, Rachel Blanchard, Sean Kanan; ***D:*** Malcolm Clarke; ***W:*** Sean Kanan. **VIDEO**

Chasing Sleep 🦴🦴 **2000 (R)** College prof. Ed Saxon (Daniels) worries when his wife doesn't return from work. The cops find her car but that's all. Meanwhile, pill-popping insomniac Ed discovers his wife's diary, which reveals she was having an affair with a neighbor. Then he keeps having to deal with strange household plumbing problems. Ed becomes increasinly disoriented, so is he hallucinating the whole thing or has something terrible really happened? Daniels gives an effective off-center performance but the story loses its momentum. **104m/C VHS, DVD, Wide.** Jeff Daniels, Emily Bergl, Gil Bellows, Zach Grenier, Julian McMahon, Ben Shenkman, Molly Price; ***D:*** Michael Walker; ***W:*** Michael Walker; ***C:*** Jim Denault.

Chasing the Deer 🦴🦴 **1994** In 1745, Scotland's Bonnie Prince Charlie (Carrara) has returned from France intent on resurrecting the Jacobite cause and regaining the English throne. Reluctant Alistair Campbell (Zajac) joins the army only to protect his son Euan (Rae), who's supposedly being held prisoner for shooting a Highlander. Euan's actually fallen into the hands of a sympathetic Englishman, Major Elliot (Blessed), advisor to the government's troops. The Jacobites begin their march south until that fateful day on Culloden Moor, which will determine all their futures. **92m/C VHS.** *GB* Brian Blessed, Matthew Zajac, Iain Cuthbertson, Lewis Rae, Dominique Carrara, Fish; ***D:*** Graham Holloway; ***W:*** Jerome Vincent, Bob Carruthers, Steve Gillham; ***C:*** Alan M. Trow; ***M:*** John Wetton.

Chato's Land 🦴🦴½ **1971 (PG)** An Indian is tracked by a posse eager to resolve a lawman's death. Conventional violent Bronson vehicle is bolstered by presence of masterful Palance. **100m/C VHS, DVD, Wide.** Charles Bronson, Jack Palance, Richard Basehart, James Whitmore, Simon Oakland, Richard Jordan, Ralph Waite, Victor French, Lee Patterson; ***D:*** Michael Winner; ***W:*** Gerald Wilson; ***C:*** Robert Paynter; ***M:*** Jerry Fielding.

Chattahoochee 🦴🦴½ **1989** A man suffering from post-combat syndrome lands in a horrifying institution. Strong cast, with Oldman fine in the lead, and Hopper memorable in extended cameo. Fact-based film is, unfortunately, rather conventionally rendered. **97m/C VHS.** Gary Oldman, Dennis Hopper, Frances McDormand, Pamela Reed, Ned Beatty, M. Emmet Walsh, William De Acutis, Lee Wilkof, Matt Craven, Gary Klar; ***D:*** Mick Jackson; ***W:*** James Cresson.

Chattanooga Choo Choo 🦴½ **1984 (PG)** A football team owner must restore the Chattanooga Choo Choo and make a 24-hour run from Chattanooga to New York in order to collect $1 million left to him in a will. The train never leaves the station. **102m/C VHS.** Barbara Eden, George Kennedy, Melissa Sue Anderson, Joe Namath, Bridget Hanley, Christopher McDonald, Clu Gulager, Tony Azito; ***D:*** Bruce Bilson.

Chatterbox 🦴🦴 **1976** A starlet's life and career are severely altered when her sex organs begin speaking. So why didn't they warn her about movies like this? Plenty of B-queen Rialson on view. Good double bill with "Me and Him." **73m/C VHS.** Candice Rialson, Larry Gelman, Jean Kean, Perry Bullington; ***D:*** Tom De Simone.

The Cheap Detective 🦴🦴🦴 **1978 (PG)** Neil Simon's parody of the "Maltese Falcon" gloriously exploits the resourceful Falk in a Bogart-like role. Vast supporting cast—notable Brennan, DeLuise, and Kahn—equally game for fun in this consistently amusing venture. **92m/C VHS, DVD, Wide.** Peter Falk, Ann-Margret, Eileen Brennan, Sid Caesar, Stockard Channing, James Coco, Dom DeLuise, Louise Fletcher, John Houseman, Madeline Kahn, Fernando Lamas, Marsha Mason, Phil Silvers, Vic Tayback, Abe Vigoda, Paul Williams, Nicol Williamson; ***D:*** Robert Moore; ***W:*** Neil Simon; ***C:*** John A. Alonzo.

Cheap Shots 🦴½ **1991 (PG-13)** Cheap best describes this. Two guys running a sleazy New York State resort motel plot to videotape patrons having sex, but capture an apparent mob murder instead. More of a character study than sexploitation, but who needs these characters? Not a stellar writing/directing debut for Ureles and Stoeffhaas. **90m/C VHS.** Louis Zorich, David Patrick Kelly, Mary Louise Wilson, Michael Twaine, Patience Moore; ***D:*** Jeff Ureles; ***W:*** Jeff Ureles, Jerry Stoeffhaas; ***M:*** Jeff Beal.

Cheaper by the Dozen 🦴🦴🦴 **1950** Turn-of-the-century family comedy based on the book by Frank B. Gilbreth Jr., and Ernestine Gilbreth Carey, which chronicled life in the expansive Gilbreth household—12 children, efficiency expert father Frank (Webb), and psychologist mother Lillian (Loy). Stern dad likes to test his theories on the family (and have everything his own way) while nuturing mom easily manages him as well as their large household. There are various family crises (times 12) but it's all very heartwarming. Followed by "Belles on Their Toes." **85m/C VHS.** Clifton Webb, Myrna Loy, Jeanne Crain, Edgar Buchanan, Mildred Natwick, Sara Allgood, Betty Lynn, Barbara Bates, Norman Ollestad; ***D:*** Walter Lang; ***W:*** Lamar Trotti; ***C:*** Leon Shamroy; ***M:*** Cyril Mockridge.

Cheaper to Keep Her woof! **1980 (R)** Alleged comedy about a private detective hired to track likely alimony dodgers. Loathsome, repellent fare, with Davis hopeless in the lead. **92m/C VHS.** Mac Davis, Tovah Feldshuh, Jack Gilford, Rose Marie; ***D:*** Ken Annakin; ***W:*** Herschel Weingrod, Timothy Harris.

The Cheat 🦴🦴🦴 **1915** Ward plays a frivolous socialite heavily indebted to Hayakawa as the Japanese money lender. Hayakawa makes Ward pay with her honor and her flesh by branding her. A dark and captivating drama. Silent with piano score. **55m/B VHS, DVD.** Jack Dean, James Neill, Dana Ong, Hazel Childers, Fannie Ward, Sessue Hayakawa; ***D:*** Cecil B. DeMille; ***W:*** Alvin Wyckoff, Hector Turnbull: Natl. Film Reg. '93.

The Cheaters 🦴 **1976 (R)** A young gambler runs away with his boss's son's girlfriend, and is pursued therein. **91m/C VHS.** *IT* Dayle Haddon, Luc Merenda, Lino Troisi, Enrico Maria Salerno; ***D:*** Sergio Martino.

Cheaters 🦴½ **1984** Two middle class couples are having affairs with each other's spouses. Complications arise when their respective children decide to marry each other. **103m/C VHS.** Peggy Cass, Jack Kruschen.

Cheaters 🦴🦴½ **2000 (R)** Students at Chicago's run-down Steinmetz High School don't have a prayer of winning the state Academic Decathalon championship until they stumble across a copy of the test and decide that winning is everything—encouraged by their teacher/coach Gerald Plecki (Daniels), who helps them cheat, believing his intentions are good. Based on a true story. **106m/C VHS, DVD.** Jeff Daniels, Jena Malone, Paul Sorvino, Luke Edwards, Blake Heron; ***D:*** John Stockwell; ***W:*** John Stockwell; ***C:*** David Hennings; ***M:*** Paul Haslinger. **CABLE**

Cheatin' Hearts 🦴🦴½ **1993 (R)** Kirkland is a woman beset by woe: she's about to lose her house, her philandering husband (Brolin) wanders back to town with his latest bimbo in tow, and her daughter's getting married. This should be a good thing, except hubby makes a fool of himself at the wedding and nearly ruins everything. Well, at least local rancher Kristofferson is around to lift a woman's spirits. And yes, there's a (predictably) happy ending. **88m/C VHS.** Sally Kirkland, James Brolin, Kris Kristofferson, Pamela Gidley, Laura Johnson; ***D:*** Rod McCall.

Check & Double Check 🦴 **1930** Radio's original Amos 'n' Andy (a couple of black-faced white guys) help solve a lover's triangle in this film version of the popular radio series. Interesting only as a novelty. Duke Ellington's band plays "Old Man Blues" and "Three Little Words." **85m/B VHS.** Freeman Gosden, Charles Correll, Duke Ellington; ***D:*** Melville Brown; ***M:*** Max Steiner.

Check Is in the Mail 🦴½ **1985 (R)** Lame comedy about a financier determined to make his home entirely independent from the rat-race of capitalist society. Dependables Dennehy and Archer are wasted. **83m/C VHS.** Brian Dennehy, Anne Archer, Dick Shawn; ***D:*** Joan Darling.

Check Your Guns 🦴🦴 **1948** A crooked judge and a gang of outlaws team up to prey on law-abiding folk and cause headaches for the new sheriff, who's pushing an unsuccessful Old West version of gun control. Nothing really noteworthy here. **55m/B VHS.** Eddie Dean, Roscoe Ates, Nancy Gates, George Chesebro, I. Stanford Jolley, Mikel Conrad, William "Bill" Fawcett; ***D:*** Ray Taylor.

The Checkered Flag 🦴 **1963** Lame auto-racing drama about an aging, millionaire race car driver with an alcoholic wife who would like nothing more than to see him dead. She talks a young rookie into helping her dispose of hubby. Plans go awry—with horrifying results. Racing scenes overshadow incredibly weak script and performances. **110m/C VHS.** Joe Morrison, Evelyn King, Charles G. Martin, Peggy Vendig; ***D:*** William Grefe; ***W:*** William Grefe.

Checking Out 🦴½ **1989 (R)** Black comedy about a manic hypochondriac who is convinced that his demise will soon occur. You'll pray that he's right. Daniels can't make it work, and supporters Mayron and Magnuson also have little chance in poorly conceived roles. **95m/C VHS.** Jeff Daniels, Melanie Mayron, Michael Tucker, Kathleen York, Ann Magnuson, Allen Havey, Jo Harvey Allen, Felton Perry, Alan Wolfe; ***D:*** David Leland; ***W:*** Joe Eszterhas; ***M:*** Carter Burwell.

Cheech and Chong: Still Smokin' 🦴½ *Still Smokin'* **1983 (R)** Not really. More like still trying to make a buck. Veteran marijuana-dazed comedy duo travel to Amsterdam to raise funds for a bankrupt film festival group by hosting a dope-a-thon. Lots of concert footage used in an attempt to hold the slim plot together. Only for serious fans of the dopin' duo. **91m/C VHS, DVD, Wide.** Richard "Cheech" Marin, Thomas Chong; ***D:*** Thomas Chong; ***W:*** Richard "Cheech" Marin, Thomas Chong; ***C:*** Harvey Harrison; ***M:*** George S. Clinton.

Cheech and Chong: Things Are Tough All Over 🦴🦴 **1982 (R)** Stoner comedy team are hired by two rich Arab brothers (also played by Cheech and Chong in acting stretch) and unwittingly drive a car loaded with money from Chicago to Las Vegas. Tired fourth in the series. **87m/C VHS, DVD.** Richard "Cheech" Marin, Thomas Chong, Shelby Fiddis, Rikki Marin, Evelyn Guerrero, Rip Taylor; ***D:*** Tom Avildsen; ***W:*** Richard "Cheech" Marin, Thomas Chong.

Cheech and Chong's Next Movie 🦴🦴 **1980 (R)** A pair of messed-up bumblers adventure into a welfare office, massage parlor, nightclub, and flying saucer, while always living in fear of the cops. Kinda funny, like. Sequel to "Up in Smoke." **95m/C VHS.** Richard "Cheech" Marin, Thomas Chong, Evelyn Guerrero, Edie McClurg, Paul (Pee-wee Herman) Reubens, Phil Hartman; ***D:*** Thomas Chong; ***W:*** Richard "Cheech" Marin, Thomas Chong.

Cheech and Chong's Nice Dreams 🦴🦴 **1981 (R)** The spaced-out duo are selling their own "specially mixed" ice cream to make cash and realize their dreams. Third in the series. **97m/C VHS, DVD, Wide.** Richard "Cheech" Marin, Thomas Chong, Evelyn Guerrero, Stacy Keach, Paul (Pee-wee Herman) Reubens; ***D:*** Timothy Leary, Thomas Chong; ***W:*** Richard "Cheech" Marin, Thomas Chong; ***C:*** Charles Correll; ***M:*** Harry Betts.

Cheech and Chong's The Corsican Brothers woof! **1984 (PG)** Wretched swashbuckler features the minimally talented duo in a variety of worthless roles. Dumas would vomit in his casket if he knew about this. Fifth in the series. **91m/C VHS, DVD, Wide.** Richard "Cheech" Marin, Thomas Chong, Roy Dotrice, Rae Dawn Chong, Shelby Fiddis, Rikki Marin, Edie McClurg; ***D:*** Thomas Chong; ***W:*** Richard "Cheech" Marin, Thomas Chong; ***C:*** Harvey Harrison.

Cheech and Chong's Up in Smoke 🦴🦴½ *Up in Smoke* **1979 (R)** A pair of free-spirited burn-outs team up for a tongue-in-cheek spoof of sex, drugs, and rock and roll. First and probably the best of the dopey duo's cinematic adventures. A boxoffice bonanza when released and still a cult favorite. **87m/C VHS, DVD, Wide.** Richard "Cheech" Marin, Thomas Chong, Stacy Keach, Tom Skerritt, Edie Adams, Strother Martin, Cheryl "Rainbeaux" Smith; ***D:*** Lou Adler; ***W:*** Richard "Cheech" Marin, Thomas Chong; ***C:*** Gene Polito.

The Cheerful Fraud 🦴🦴½ **1927** Denny, who appeared in some two hundred-odd films in his career, masquerades as a butler to be near the girl he loves. A fool for love is a cheerful fraud. A zanily romantic silent comedy. **64m/B VHS.** Reginald Denny, Gertrude (Olmstead) Olmsted, Emily Fitzroy, Gertrude Astor; *D:* William A. Seiter.

Cheering Section woof! **1973 (R)** High school football teams compete for the grand prize—the privilege of ravishing the losing school's cheerleaders. Rah, rah, rah. **84m/C VHS.** Rhonda Foxx, Tom Leindecker, Gregg D'Jah, Patricia Michelle, Jeff Laine; *D:* Harry Kerwin.

Cheerleader Camp woof! *Bloody Pom Poms* **1988 (R)** Nubile gals are stalked by a psychopath while they cavort semi-clad at summer camp. **89m/C VHS.** Betsy Russell, Leif Garrett, Lucinda Dickey, Lorie Griffin, George "Buck" Flower, Teri Weigel, Rebecca Ferratti, Travis McKenna, Kathryn Litton; *D:* John Quinn; *W:* David Lee Fein, R.L. O'Keefe; *C:* Bryan England; *M:* Joel Hamilton, Muriel Hodler-Hamilton.

The Cheerleaders woof! **1972 (R)** Dim-witted exploitation effort has the usual suspects—moronic jocks and lame-brained gals—cavorting exuberantly. Followed by "Revenge of the Cheerleaders." **84m/C VHS.** Stephanie Fondue, Denise Dillaway, Jovita Bush, Debbie Lowe, Sandy Evans; *D:* Paul Glickler.

Cheerleaders' Wild Weekend woof! **1985 (R)** Group of cheerleaders are held captive by a disgruntled former football star. Pom poms wave. **87m/C VHS.** Jason Williams, Kristine DeBell; *D:* Jeff Werner.

Cheers for Miss Bishop ½ **1941** The story of a woman who graduates from college then teaches at the same institution for the next 50 years. Somewhat moving. Based on Bess Streeter Aldrich's novel. **95m/B VHS.** Martha Scott, William Gargan, Edmund Gwenn, Sterling Holloway, Rosemary DeCamp; *D:* Tay Garnett; *M:* Edward Ward.

Cheetah **1989 (G)** Two California kids visiting their parents in Kenya embark on the adventure of their lives when, with the help of a young Masai, they adopt and care for an orphaned cheetah. Usual Disney kids and animals story. **80m/C VHS.** Keith Coogan, Lucy Deakins, Collin Mothupi; *D:* Jeff Blyth; *W:* John Cotter; *C:* Thomas Burstyn.

A Chef in Love *Les Mille et Une Recettes du Cuisinier Amoureux; The Cook in Love* **1996 (PG-13)** In 1920, Parisian Pascal Ishac (Richard) meets Georgian Princess Cecilia (Kirtadze) while travelling and decides to stay and open a French restaurant in the capital of Tbilisi. When the capital is invaded by the Red Army in 1921, communist leader Zigmund (Kahmhadze) forces Cecilia to marry him and shuts down Pascal's eatery. With his great love and his restaurant both gone, Pascal writes a master cookbook and memoir that is later discovered and translated by Cecilia's son Anton (Gautier), who also discovers that Pascal is his father. French, Russian and Georgian with subtitles. **95m/C VHS.** *FR* Pierre Richard, Nino Kirtadze, Temur Kahmhadze, Jean-Yves Gautier, Micheline Presle; *D:* Nana Dzhordzadze; *W:* Irakli Kvirikadze; *C:* Georgi Beridze; *M:* Goran Bregovic.

Chelsea Walls **2001 (R)** Hawke's directorial debut features wife Thurman as one of the would-be artists living at the legendary (and seedy) Chelsea Hotel. There's a variety of struggling writers, musicians, and artists who all have romantic dilemmas and substance abuse problems as well. Lots of chatter and atmosphere but the characters are all walking cliches. **108m/C VHS, DVD.** *US* Kris Kristofferson, Uma Thurman, Vincent D'Onofrio, Natasha Richardson, Tuesday Weld, Rosario Dawson, Mark Webber, Kevin Corrigan, Robert Sean Leonard, Steve Zahn, Frank Whaley; *D:* Ethan Hawke; *W:* Nicole Burdette; *C:* Tom Richmond; *M:* Jeff Tweedy.

Cherish **2002 (R)** Rock fanatic Tunney ends up accused of murder, under house arrest, and in love with her parole officer Blake. Set in the eighties. Not yet reviewed. **99m/C VHS, DVD.** Robin Tunney, Tim Blake Nelson, Jason Priestley, Nora Dunn, Lindsay Crouse, Liz Phair; *D:* Finn Taylor; *W:* Finn Taylor.

The Cherokee Kid ½ **1996 (PG-13)** Western/comedy about a novice gunslinger (Sinbad) avenging his family. There's a corrupt banker (Coburn), a bounty hunter (Hines), a Mexican freedom fighter (Martinez), and a gang of bankrobbing nuns to keep things interesting while the Kid learns his outlaw ways. **?m/C VHS.** Sinbad, James Coburn, Burt Reynolds, Gregory Hines, A. Martinez, Ernie Hudson; *D:* Paris Barclay; *W:* Tim Kazurinsky, Denise DeClue; *M:* Stanley Clarke. **CABLE**

Cherry Falls ½ **2000 (R)** The small town of Cherry Falls is plagued by a serial killer who only kills teenaged virgins, so naturally every teen there is out to do it and save themselves. However Sheriff Marken (Biehn) has no intention of letting daughter Jody (Murphy) go to such extremes. This one is an amusing parody of slasher flicks, teen sex comedies, and suburban nightmares. **100m/C VHS, DVD, Wide.** Jay Mohr, Michael Biehn, Brittany Murphy, Candy Clark, Gabriel Mann, Keram Malicki-Sanchez, Jesse Bradford; *D:* Geoffrey Wright; *W:* Ken Selden; *C:* Anthony B. Richmond; *M:* Walter Werzowa.

Cherry Hill High woof! **1976 (R)** Five teen girls compete for former-virgin status. Pass on this one. **92m/C VHS.** Linda McInerney, Carrie Olsen, Nina Carson, Lynn Hastings, Gloria Upson, Stephanie Lawlor; *D:* Alex E. Goiten.

Cherry 2000 **1988 (PG-13)** Futuristic flick concerns a man who short-circuits his sex-toy robots and embarks on a search for replacement parts across treacherous territory, only to meet a real female—Griffith. Offbeat, occasionally funny. **94m/C VHS, DVD, Wide.** Melanie Griffith, David Andrews, Ben Johnson, Tim Thomerson, Michael C. Gwynne, Pamela Gidley; *D:* Steve DeJarnatt; *W:* Michael Almereyda; *C:* Jacques Haitkin; *M:* Basil Poledouris.

Chesty Anderson USN *Anderson's Angels* **1976** Ultra-lame sexploitation about female naval recruits. Minimal nudity. **90m/C VHS.** Shari Eubank, Dorri Thompson, Rosanne Katon, Marcie Barkin, Scatman Crothers, Frank Campanella, Fred Willard; *D:* Ed Forsyth.

Cheyenne Autumn ½ **1964** The newly restored version of the ambitious, ultimately hit-and-miss western epic about three hundred Cheyenne Indians who migrate from Oklahoma to their Wyoming homeland in 1878. The cavalry, for once, are not the good guys. Widmark is strong in the lead. Stewart is memorable in his comic cameo as Wyatt Earp. Last film from genre master Ford, capturing the usual rugged panoramas. Based on a true story as told in the Mari Sandoz novel. **156m/C VHS.** Richard Widmark, Carroll Baker, Karl Malden, Dolores Del Rio, Sal Mineo, Edward G. Robinson, Ricardo Montalban, Gilbert Roland, Arthur Kennedy, John Carradine, Victor Jory, Mike Mazurki, George O'Brien, John Qualen; ***Cameos:*** James Stewart; *D:* John Ford; *C:* William Clothier; *M:* Alex North.

Cheyenne Kid ½ **1933** Determined bronco buster is up against a gang of bad guys. **40m/B VHS.** Tom (George Duryea) Keene, Mary Mason, Roscoe Ates, Alan Bridge, Otto Hoffman, Anderson Lawler, Alan Roscoe; *D:* Robert F. "Bob" Hill; *W:* Jack Curtis; *C:* Nicholas Musuraca; *M:* Max Steiner.

Cheyenne Rides Again ½ **1938** Cheyenne poses as an outlaw to hunt a gang of rustlers. **60m/B VHS.** Tom Tyler, Lucille Browne, Lon Chaney Jr., Roger Williams, Charles "Slim" Whitaker; *D:* Robert F. "Bob" Hill.

The Cheyenne Social Club **1970 (PG)** Stewart inherits a brothel and Fonda helps him operate it. Kelly directs, sort of. Some laughs, but this effort is beneath this trio. **103m/C VHS.** Henry Fonda, James Stewart, Shirley Jones, Sue Ane Langdon, Elaine Devry; *D:* Gene Kelly; *C:* William Clothier.

Cheyenne Takes Over **1947** Lash sniffs out the bad guy in the case of a murdered ranch heir. **56m/B VHS.** Lash LaRue, Al "Fuzzy" St. John, George Chesebro; *D:* Ray Taylor.

Cheyenne Warrior ½ **1994 (PG)** Pregnant young bride Rebecca heads west with a husband who soons winds up dead, leaving her stranded at an isolated trading post. She takes in a wounded Cheyenne warrior, nurses him back to health, and he tries to convince her to let his tribe care for her. Respectable performances if unexciting. **90m/C VHS, DVD.** Kelly Preston, Pato Hoffmann, Bo Hopkins, Dan Haggerty, Charles Powell, Rick Dean, Clint Howard; *D:* Mark Griffiths; *W:* Michael B. Druxman.

Chicago Cab *Hellcab* **1998 (R)** This checkered sketch piece about a cab driver (Dillon) and the assorted passengers he picks up during a "normal" day never really pulls away from the curb. Despite cameos from actors such as John Cusack, Gillian Anderson and Laurie Metcalf, the passengers are nasty obnoxious stereotypes drawn to prove the point that other people are irritating. Will Kern adapted the screenplay from his original play "Hellcab." **96m/C VHS.** Paul Dillon, Gillian Anderson, John Cusack, Julianne Moore, Michael Ironside, John C. Reilly, Laurie Metcalf, Matt Roth, Shulle Cowen, Philip Van Lear, Michael Shannon; *D:* Mary Cybulski, John Tintori; *W:* Will Kern; *C:* Hubert Taczanowski; *M:* Page Hamilton.

Chicago Joe & the Showgirl **1990 (R)** A London-based GI befriends a loopy showgirl and helps her in various crimes during WWII. Appealing Lloyd overwhelms Sutherland, who shows only limited acting ability here. Kensit and Pigg are fine in smaller roles. **105m/C VHS.** *GB* Emily Lloyd, Kiefer Sutherland, Patsy Kensit, Keith Allen, Liz Fraser, Alexandra Pigg, Ralph Nossek, Colin Bruce; *D:* Bernard Rose; *M:* Hans Zimmer.

The Chicken Chronicles **1977 (PG)** An affluent high school dude longs to get horizontal with his dream girl. Set in the 1960s. First feature film appearance for Guttenberg. **94m/C VHS.** Phil Silvers, Ed Lauter, Steve Guttenberg, Lisa Reeves, Meridith Baer; *D:* Francis Simon.

Chicken Run ½ **2000 (G)** It's a prisoner-of-war escape movie with chickens. This Claymation wonder is a comedy set on a failing 1950s Yorkshire chicken farm, where the hens realize their necks are literally on the chopping block when greedy farm wife, Mrs. Tweedy (Richardson), decides to go into the chicken pie business. So chicken leader, Ginger (Sawalha), tries to find a workable mass escape plan. And then daredevil Yankee rooster Rocky (Gibson) literally drops into the barnyard and Ginger believes he can teach all the hens to fly out. Chickens are just funny and you'll be amazed at what the animators have managed to make them do and how expressive they are. **86m/C VHS, DVD, Wide.** *GB* *D:* Nick Park, Peter Lord; *W:* Karey Kirkpatrick; *M:* John Powell, Harry Gregson-Williams; *V:* Mel Gibson, Julia Sawalha, Miranda Richardson, Jane Horrocks, Tony Haygarth, Timothy Spall, Imelda Staunton, Phil Daniels, Benjamin Whitrow, Lynn Ferguson.

Chiefs **1983** A police chief in a Southern town discovers a series of murders concealed by town big wigs. Made for TV film boasts a surprisingly strong cast, but provides otherwise conventional entertainment. **200m/C VHS.** Charlton Heston, Paul Sorvino, Keith Carradine, Brad Davis, Billy Dee Williams, Wayne Rogers, Stephen Collins, Tess Harper, Victoria Tennant; *D:* Jerry London. **TV**

The Child *Kill and Go Hide* **1976 (R)** Low-budget horror-quickie combining elements of "The Bad Seed," "The Omen," and "Night of the Living Dead," that attempts to cash in on the fright-film craze of the early '70s. What we get is a poorly dubbed film that makes little sense, but does offer some interesting shocks. A young woman returns to her hometown to be the nanny for a disturbed girl, Rosalie (Cole), who has a bad habit of killing neighbors and talking to zombies in the local graveyard, all the way harping on her mother's mysterious death. This is one of those movies where everyone acts very eccentric, but said behavior doesn't add anything to the plot. The finale offers some excitement, but overall the film is more of a curiosity than a "must-see." **95m/C VHS, DVD.** Laurel Barnett, Rosalie Cole, Frank Janson, Richard Hanners, Ruth Ballan; *D:* Robert Voskanian; *W:* Ralph Lucas; *C:* Mori Alavi; *M:* Rob Wallace.

Child Bride of Short Creek ½ **1981** A young Korean war veteran returns to his community where polygamy is allowed, to find that his father intends to marry again, this time to a 15-year-old. Conflict ensues. Based on an actual event that occurred in the 1950s. **100m/C VHS.** Diane Lane, Conrad Bain, Christopher Atkins, Kiel Martin, Helen Hunt; *D:* Robert Lewis. **TV**

Child in the Night **1990 (R)** A shaken eight-year-old boy is a witness to murder in his family, and a psychologist with plenty of her own problems must get him to testify. First film for Wood. Middling TV-movie suspense. **93m/C VHS.** Tom Skerritt, JoBeth Williams, Darren McGavin, Season Hubley, Elijah Wood; *D:* Mike Robe.

A Child Is Waiting **1963** Poignant and provocative story of teachers in an institution for the mentally retarded. Fine performances include Lancaster as the institution's administrator and Garland as a teacher who cares too much for everyone's good. Cassavetes incorporates footage using handicapped children as extras—not entirely seamlessly—providing a sensitive and candid edge. **105m/B VHS.** Burt Lancaster, Judy Garland, Gena Rowlands, Steven Hill, Bruce Ritchey; *D:* John Cassavetes; *W:* Abby Mann; *M:* Ernest Gold.

Child of Darkness, Child of Light ½ **1991 (PG-13)** A priest is sent to investigate two virgin pregnancies and discovers that one child will be a savior and the other the Anti-Christ. Totally mindless brain candy resembling the "Omen" movies and "Rosemary's Baby." Adapted from James Patterson's book "Virgin." **85m/C VHS.** Anthony John (Tony) Denison, Brad Davis, Paxton Whitehead, Claudette Nevins, Sydney Penny, Kristin Dattilo-Hayward, Viveca Lindfors, Sela Ward, Alan Oppenheimer, Eric Christmas; *D:* Marina Sargenti; *W:* Brian Taggert. **CABLE**

Child of Glass **1978 (G)** A young boy's family moves into a huge New Orleans mansion, and soon after encounters a young girl's ghost and lost treasure from the Civil War. A Disney made for TV movie. **93m/C VHS.** Barbara Barrie, Biff McGuire, Anthony Zerbe, Nina Foch, Steve Shaw, Katy Kurtzman, Olivia Barash; *D:* John Erman. **TV**

Child of the Prairie **1918** An early Mix film about a young cowboy and his city-loving wife down on their luck in a western town. Silent with music score. **63m/B VHS, 8mm.** Tom Mix; *D:* Tom Mix; *W:* Tom Mix.

Child Star: The Shirley Temple Story ½ **2001** TV biopic that charts the rise to Depression-era fame of little Shirley Temple (with an entertaining performance by Orr). Shirley's mom Gertrude (Britton) is around to see that big bad studio mogul Darryl Zanuck (Vidler) doesn't take advantage of her little darling. The best parts are the faithful recreations of some of Temple's most famous song-and-dance numbers, including those with Bill (Bojangles) Robinson, here played by Battle. **88m/C VHS, DVD.** Ashley Rose Orr, Connie Britton, Steven Vidler, Colin Friels, Emily Anne Hart, Hinton Battle; *D:* Nadia Tass; *W:* Joe Wiesenfeld; *C:* David Parker; *M:* Bill Elliot. **TV**

The Children woof! **1980 (R)** Familiar nuclear leak leads to monster mutants done to a novel (though extremely low-budget) turn: after a school bus passes through radioactive fog, the kiddies inside assume the ability to incinerate whoever they hug. They also assume a certain zombie-like demeanor and sport black fingernails. None of this is noted by their uncaring and less-than-observant parents, many of whom are enticed into a very warm hug. This may be intended as social satire. Not only are the little microwaves extremely dangerous, the only way to kill them is to chop off their hands, leading to a wild limbless finale. **89m/C VHS.** Martin Shaker, Gale Garnett, Gil Rogers; *D:* Max Kalmanowicz.

The Children ☠☠½ **1990** Kingsley stars as a middle-aged engineer who finds himself caring for seven children in this touching love story from novelist Edith Wharton. Shot on location in Venice, the cinematography is excellent and the cast is superb, but the film lags in places. A remake of "The Marriage Playground." **90m/C VHS.** *GB GE* Ben Kingsley, Kim Novak, Siri Neal, Geraldine Chaplin, Joe Don Baker, Britt Ekland, Donald Sinden, Karen Black, Robert Stephens, Rupert Graves, Rosemary Leach; ***D:*** Tony Palmer.

The Children Are Watching Us ☠☠☠ *The Little Martyr; I Bambini Ci Guardano* **1944** Sobering drama of a family dissolution as seen by a child. A four-year-old boy drifts unloved by his suicidal father and by his mother, who's only interested in her own love affair. Worthy example of Italian neo-realism marks the first collaboration between Zavattini and De Sica. In Italian with subtitles. **92m/B VHS.** *IT* Luciano de Ambrosis, Isa Pola, Emilio Cigoli; ***D:*** Vittorio De Sica; ***W:*** Cesare Zavattini, Vittorio De Sica.

Children in the Crossfire ☠☠½ **1984** When youngsters from war-torn Northern Ireland spend a summer in America with children from the Republic of Ireland, both sides find their nationalistic prejudices falling away. But a great challenge awaits them when they return home from their summer of fun. Nicely done drama. **96m/C VHS.** Charles Haid, Karen Valentine, Julia Duffy, David Hoffman; ***D:*** George Schaefer; ***M:*** Brad Fiedel. **TV**

Children of a Lesser God ☠☠☠½ **1986 (R)** Based upon the play by Mark Medoff, this sensitive, intelligent film deals with an unorthodox speech teacher at a school for the deaf, who falls in love with a beautiful and rebellious ex-student. Inarguably romantic; the original stage production won the Best Play Tony in 1980. Hurt and Matlin reportedly continued their romance off-screen as well. **119m/C VHS, DVD, Wide.** William Hurt, Marlee Matlin, Piper Laurie, Philip Bosco, E. Katherine Kerr; ***D:*** Randa Haines; ***W:*** Hesper Anderson, Mark Medoff; ***C:*** John Seale; ***M:*** Michael Convertino. Oscars '86: Actress (Matlin); Golden Globes '87: Actress—Drama (Matlin).

The Children of An Lac ☠☠½ **1980** Three women attempt to rescue hundreds of Vietnamese orphans before Saigon falls to the communists. The film derives from actress Balin's actual wartime experience. **100m/C VHS.** Shirley Jones, Ina Balin, Beulah Quo, Alan Fudge, Ben Piazza, Lee Paul, Kieu Chinh, Vic Diaz; ***D:*** John Llewellyn Moxey; ***M:*** Paul Chihara. **TV**

Children of Divorce ☠½ **1980** TV drama shows divorce from the children's point of view. Standard fare. **96m/C VHS.** Barbara Feldon, Lance Kerwin, Stacey Nelkin, Billy Dee Williams; ***D:*** Joanna Lee; ***M:*** Minette Alton. **TV**

Children of Fury ☠☠ *In the Line of Duty: Siege at Marion* **1994 (PG-13)** Fact-based TV movie covers the death (at police hands) of self-proclaimed prophet, Utah polygamist John Singer (Weisser), whose wife Vickie (Harper) and children vow revenge. When fundamentalist Addam Swapp (Secor) joins their group, he soon begins intimidating the locals and bombs a building in the town of Marion. Authorities call in the FBI and chief agent Bill Bryant (Franz) sets up a siege of the property. **85m/C VHS.** Kyle Secor, Tess Harper, Dennis Franz, Ed Begley Jr., Paul LeMat, Norbert Weisser, William H. Macy, Rex Linn; ***D:*** Charles Haid; ***W:*** Rich Husky; ***C:*** William Wages; ***M:*** Gary Chang. **TV**

Children of Heaven ☠☠½ **1998 (PG)** When nine-year-old Ali (Hashemian) discovers that his younger sister Zahra's (Seddiqi) shoes have somehow been lost, he keeps the information from his parents who are already desperately struggling to provide for them. They share Ali's tattered sneakers so that both children can still go to school. Then Ali learns of a race where one of the prizes is a pair of running shoes and he becomes determined to win them. Story is simple enough that kids may enjoy watching other kids even in a foreign film. Farsi with subtitles. **88m/C VHS.** *IA* Mir Farrokh Hashemian, Bahareh Seddiqi, Amir Naji; ***D:*** Majid Majidi; ***W:*** Majid Majidi; ***C:*** Parviz Malekzadeh; ***M:*** Keivan Jahan-shahi.

Children of Nature ☠☠½ *Born Natturunnar* **1991** A 78-year-old man unwillingly enters a nursing home where he meets a long-ago sweetheart. The two fall in love again and decide to escape from the home and return to their childhood village. Sweet love story about late-blooming passions laced with fantasy and humor. Iceland's first Academy Award nomination. In Icelandic with English subtitles. **85m/C VHS.** *IC* Gisli Halldorsson, Sigridur Hagalin, Bruno Ganz; ***D:*** Fridrik Thor Fridriksson; ***W:*** Fridrik Thor Fridriksson, Einar Mar Gudmundsson; ***M:*** Hilmar Orn Hilmarsson.

The Children of Noisy Village ☠☠½ *The Children of Bullerby Village; Alla vi barn i Bullerby* **1986** Noisy Village is a small town in the Swedish countryside consisting of three red frame houses. In the town, a group of adventurous children discover a multitude of fantasy lands right in their own backyard—their backyard being the beautiful pastures, ponds, and fields of Sweden. Based on the stories of Astrid "Pippi Longstocking" Lindgren. Dubbed. **88m/C VHS.** *SW* Linda Bergstrom, Anna Sahlin, Ellem Demerus, Harsald Lonnbro; ***D:*** Lasse Hallstrom.

Children of Paradise ☠☠☠☠ *Les Enfants du Paradis* **1944** Considered by many to be the greatest film ever made, certainly one of the most beautiful. In the Parisian theatre district of the 1800s an actor falls in love with a seemingly unattainable woman. Although circumstances keep them apart, their love never dies. Produced in France during WWII right under the noses of Nazi occupiers; many of the talent (including the writer, poet Jacques Prevert) were active resistance fighters. In French with English subtitles. **188m/B VHS, DVD.** *FR* Jean-Louis Barrault, Arletty, Pierre Brasseur, Maria Casares, Albert Remy, Leon Larive, Marcel Herrand, Pierre Renoir, Gaston Modot, Jane (Jeanne) Marken, Louis Salou; ***D:*** Marcel Carne; ***W:*** Jacques Prevert; ***C:*** Roger Hubert; ***M:*** Maurice Thiriet, Joseph Kosma.

Children of Rage ☠☠½ **1975 (PG)** High-minded and long-winded drama dealing with the Israeli/Palestinian war and terrorism from the viewpoint of an Israeli doctor yearning for peace. **106m/C VHS.** *GB IS* Simon Ward, Cyril Cusack, Helmut Griem, Olga Georges-Picot; ***D:*** Arthur Seidelman; ***W:*** Richard Alfieri.

Children of Sanchez ☠☠ **1979 (PG)** Mexican man attempts to provide for his family with very little except faith and love. U.S./Mexican production based on Oscar Lewis' novel. **103m/C VHS.** *MX* Anthony Quinn, Dolores Del Rio, Katy Jurado, Lupita Ferrer; ***D:*** Hall Bartlett; ***W:*** Hall Bartlett; ***M:*** Chuck Mangione.

Children of the Corn ☠½ **1984 (R)** Young couple lands in a small Iowa town where children appease a demon by murderously sacrificing adults. Time to move or dispense with some major spankings. Infrequently scary. Another feeble attempt to translate the horror of a Stephen King book to film. **93m/C VHS, DVD, Wide.** Peter Horton, Linda Hamilton, R.G. Armstrong, John Franklin, Courtney Gains, Robbie Kiger; ***D:*** Fritz Kiersch; ***W:*** George Goldsmith; ***C:*** Raoul Lomas; ***M:*** Jonathan Elias.

Children of the Corn 2: The Final Sacrifice ☠½ **1992 (R)** Reporter working for a tabloid paper gets more than he bargained for when he decides to do a story on the adults murdered in the town of Gatlin, Nebraska. Gatlin's surviving children, who killed their parents in the first film, are now living in a neighboring town and free to kill again. This youthful satanic cult does in authority figures in a number of sacrifical ways, working ever more smartly to create the prime attraction—blood flow. Not based on anything written by Stephen King. **93m/C VHS.** Terence Knox, Paul Scherrer, Rosalind Allen, Christie Clark, Ned Romero, Ryan Bollman, Ted Travelstead; ***D:*** David F. Price; ***W:*** Gilbert Adler, A.L. Katz.

Children of the Corn 3: Urban Harvest ☠☠ **1995 (R)** Joshua (Melendez) and younger brother Eli (Cerny) are adopted by a wealthy couple and transplanted from Nebraska to Chicago's suburbia. But when Eli grows a corn patch that resurrects an evil force, only Joshua can stop his reign of terror. Contrived premise but lots of nifty special effects. **103m/C VHS.** Daniel Cerney, Ron Melendez, Mari Morrow, Duke Stroud, Jim Metzler, Nancy Lee Grahn; ***D:*** James D.R. Hickox; ***W:*** Dode Levenson; ***M:*** Daniel Licht.

Children of the Corn 4: The Gathering ☠ *Deadly Harvest* **1996 (R)** Medical student Grace Rhodes (Watts) seeks to free the children of her Nebraska hometown from a mysterious plague and a shadowy figure. **85m/C VHS, DVD, Wide.** Naomi Watts, Brent Jennings, Jamie Renee Smith, William Windom, Karen Black; ***D:*** Greg Spence; ***W:*** Stephen Berger, Greg Spence; ***C:*** Richard Clabaugh; ***M:*** David Williams.

Children of the Corn 5: Fields of Terror ☠½ **1998 (R)** Alison (Galina), Greg (Arquette), Tyrus (Vaughan), and Kir (Mendez) have traveled to Divinity Falls to bury the cremated remains of Kir's recently deceased boyfriend. That's when they run into the local cult of murderous children and Alison realizes that her long-lost brother, Jacob (Buzzotta), is one of them. She's determined to get him away but the evil force that leads the children has other ideas. **85m/C VHS, DVD, Wide.** Alexis Arquette, Greg Vaughan, Stacy Galina, Eva Mendez, Adam Wylie, Dave Buzzotta, David Carradine, Fred Williamson; ***D:*** Ethan Wiley; ***W:*** Ethan Wiley; ***C:*** David Lewis; ***M:*** Paul Rabjohns. **VIDEO**

Children of the Corn 666: Isaac's Return ☠½ **1999 (R)** Hannah Martin (Ramsey) is traveling to Nebraska in search of her birth mother but when she arrives in the small town of Gatlin, she finds the residents want to keep their secrets. **82m/C VHS, DVD.** Natalie Ramsey, John Franklin, Stacy Keach, Alix Koromzay, Nancy Allen; ***D:*** Keri Skogland. **VIDEO**

Children of the Corn: Revelation ☠☠ **2001** Jamie (Mink) is looking for her missing grandma at the condemned Hampton Arms where the remaining residents are meeting grisly fates. She and detective Armbrister (Cassie) are informed by a mysterious priest (Ironside) that the condos were built on the site of a tent revival fire that killed a number of children. Of course the kids turn out to be the Gatlin killer-kiddie cult and they return to reclaim their land. Some decent shockers in this 7th installment of the series. **81m/C VHS, DVD, Wide.** Claudette Mink, Michael Ironside, Troy Yorke, Sean Smith, Kyle Cassie, Michael Rogers, Taylor Hobbs, Jeff Ballard, Crystal Lowe; ***D:*** Guy Magar. **VIDEO**

Children of the Damned ☠☠ **1963** Six children, who are a sample of what man will evolve to in a million years, are born all around the world with genius IQs, ray-gun eyes, and murderous dispositions. Two investigators bring the children together, and while they are being examined by scientists they escape. The children hide out in a church, but they are doomed because their destiny is to be destroyed to teach a lesson to modern man. A sequel to "Village of the Damned" based loosely on the novel "The Midwich Cuckoos" by John Wyndham. **90m/B VHS.** *GB* Ian Hendry, Alan Badel, Barbara Ferris, Alfred Burke, Sheila Allen, Clive Powell, Frank Summerscales, Mahdu Mathen, Gerald Delsol, Roberta Rex, Franchesca Lee, Harold Goldblatt, Ralph Michael, Martin Miller, Lee Yoke-Moon; ***D:*** Anton Leader; ***W:*** John Briley; ***C:*** David Boulton.

Children of the Full Moon ☠ **1984** A young couple find themselves lost in a forest that is the home of a family of werewolves. Earns praise only for brevity. Even bad movie aficionados will want to skip this howler. **60m/C VHS.** *GB* Christopher Cazenove, Celia Gregory, Diana Dors, Jacof Witken, Robert Urquhart; ***D:*** Tom Clegg.

Children of the Night ☠½ **1992 (R)** Allburg seems like a typically quiet small town far removed from any danger—until a vampire is released from an underground crypt and decides to make the town his bloodthirsty target. When a teacher, whose girlfriend is visiting Allburg, learns of the supernatural goings on he decides to investigate, which may be a deadly mistake. **92m/C VHS.** Peter DeLuise, Karen Black, Ami Dolenz, Maya McLaughlin, Evan Mackenzie, David Sawyer, Garrett Morris; ***D:*** Tony Randel; ***W:*** Nicolas Falacci; ***C:*** Richard Michalak.

Children of the Revolution ☠☠ **1995 (R)** Mockumentary covering 45 years of Australian history and politics, beginning in 1951 when the conservative Prime Minister attempts to ban the Australian Communist Party. Party member (and Stalin admirer) Joan Fraser (Davis) helps to prevent the ban, bringing her to the Russian leader's attention, and she's invited to Moscow. There, Joan winds up in bed with Stalin (Abraham) and comes home pregnant. Eventually, son Joe (Rush) makes an entry into the Australian political scene, resulting in chaos. There's almost too much more for the film to handle, although the actors don't seem to have any problems. **101m/C VHS.** *AU* Judy Davis, Sam Neill, Richard Roxburgh, Rachel Griffiths, Geoffrey Rush, F. Murray Abraham; ***D:*** Peter Duncan; ***W:*** Peter Duncan; ***C:*** Martin McGrath; ***M:*** Nigel Westlake. Australian Film Inst. '96: Actress (Davis), Art Dir./Set Dec., Costume Des.

Children of the Wild ☠☠½ *Killers of the Wild* **1937** Adventure story about a pack of dogs surviving in the Rocky Mountain wilderness. Splendid scenery and some interesting sequences. **65m/B VHS.** Patsy Moran.

The Children of Theatre Street **1977** Absorbing documentary follows three children attending the renowned Kirov Ballet School. A show for all ages that may be especially enjoyed by kids who are interested in ballet. Kelly's last film appearance. **92m/C VHS.** *RU* Angelina Armeiskaya, Alec Timoushin, Lena Voronzova, Michaela Cerna, Galina Messenzeva, Konstantin Zaklinsky; ***D:*** Robert Dornhelm; ***W:*** Beth Gutcheon; ***C:*** Karl Kofler; ***Nar:*** Grace Kelly.

The Children of Times Square ☠☠ **1986** A mother pursues her son who has fled home and joined a gang of drug dealers in N.Y.C.'s seedy Times Square. Ordinary film despite strong casting of Cassidy and Rollins. **95m/C VHS.** Joanna Cassidy, Howard E. Rollins Jr., Brandon Douglas, David Ackroyd, Griffin O'Neal, Danny Nucci, Larry B. Scott; ***D:*** Curtis Hanson; ***M:*** Patrick Gleeson. **TV**

Children Shouldn't Play with Dead Things ☠☠½ *Revenge of the Living Dead* **1972** A band of foolhardy hippie filmmakers on an island cemetary skimp on special effects by using witchcraft to revive the dead. The plan works. Soon the crew has an island full of hungry ghouls to contend with. Film strives for yucks, frequently succeeds. A late night fave, sporting some excellent dead rising from their grave scenes as well as a selection of groovy fashions. Screenwriter/star Ormsby went on to write the remake of "Cat People," while director Clark would eventually helm "Porky's." **85m/C VHS, DVD.** Alan Ormsby, Valerie Mamches, Jeff Gillen, Anya Ormsby, Paul Cronin, Jane Daly, Roy Engelman, Robert Philip, Bruce Solomon, Alecs Baird, Seth Sklarey; ***D:*** Bob (Benjamin) Clark; ***W:*** Bob (Benjamin) Clark, Alan Ormsby; ***C:*** Jack McGowan; ***M:*** Carl Zittrer.

The Children's Hour ☠☠ *The Loudest Whisper* **1961** The teaching careers of two women are ruined when girls begin circulating vicious rumors. Only an occasionally taut drama despite forceful handling of a lesbian theme. Updated version of Lillian Hellman's play (adapted by Hellman) is more explicit, but less suspenseful in spite of excellent performances from the talented cast. Remake of Wyler's own "These Three." **107m/C VHS.** Shirley MacLaine, Audrey Hepburn, James Garner, Miriam Hopkins, Veronica Cartwright, Fay Bainter; ***D:*** William Wyler; ***W:*** John Michael Hayes; ***M:*** Alex North.

Child's Play ☠☠½ **1988 (R)** A boy discovers that his new doll named Chucky is actually the embodiment of a deranged killer. His initially skeptical mom and a police officer come around after various killings. Exciting, if somewhat moronic, fare, with fine special effects. Followed by "Child's Play 2." **95m/C VHS, DVD.** Catherine Hicks, Alex Vincent, Chris Sarandon, Dinah Manoff, Brad Dourif, Tommy Swerdlow, Jack Colvin; ***D:*** Tom Holland; ***W:*** Tom Holland, Don Mancini, John Lafia; ***C:*** Bill Butler; ***M:*** Joe Renzetti.

Child's Play 2 woof! **1990 (R)** Chucky lives. Basic doll-on-a-rampage story, a metaphor for the Reagan years, lives on in the sequel (you remember: somehow guy-doll Chucky made it past the quality control people with a highly inflammable temper). A little dotty from playing with dolls, young Vincent finds himself fostered by two new parents, and plagued by an obnoxious and very animated doll that fosters ill will toward all. What's worse is the doll is transmigratory, craving the boy's body as his next address. Chef d'effects Kevin Yagher's new toy is bad, real bad, and so are the other part two FX. Little Chucky's saga, however grows a tad tiresome. A bad example for small children. **84m/C VHS, DVD.** Alex Vincent, Jenny Agutter, Gerrit Graham, Christine Elise, Grace Zabriskie; ***D:*** John Lafia; ***W:*** Don Mancini; ***C:*** Stefan Czapsky; ***M:*** Graeme Revell; ***V:*** Brad Dourif.

Child's Play 3 **1991 (R)** Possessed doll Chucky returns to life again in search of a new child to control, and luckily finds his old pal (Whalin) at a military school filled with the usual stereotypes. Gory sequel in a mostly awful series. "Don't F— With the Chuck" was its catch phrase; that should indicate the level of this junk. **89m/C VHS.** Justin Whalin, Perrey Reeves, Jeremy Sylvers, Peter Haskell, Dakin Matthews, Travis Fine, Dean Jacobson, Matthew (Matt) Walker, Andrew (Andy) Robinson; ***D:*** Jack Bender; ***W:*** Don Mancini; ***M:*** Cory Lerios, John D'Andrea; ***V:*** Brad Dourif.

Chill Factor **1990 (R)** A TV reporter for an investigative news show uncovers evidence of an international conspiracy. Plot twists abound. **?m/C VHS.** Paul Williams, Patrick Macnee, Andrew Prine, Carrie Snodgress, Patrick Wayne, Gary Crosby; ***D:*** David L. Stanton.

Chill Factor ½ **1999 (R)** Stealing every plot device and cliche in the action thriller genre, this is indeed one unoriginal cold turkey. After accidentally blowing up a platoon of soldiers while testing a chemical weapon codenamed "Elvis" and pinning the blame on cranky general Brynner (Firth), scientist Dr. Long (Paymer) moves to Montana to take up fly-fishing while continuing his research. He befriends diner clerk Tim (Ulrich), but only until the general is released from prison with a grudge to settle. The general has plans to sell the weapon to the highest bidder, but Long manages to get Elvis out of the building. The canister can't get hotter than fifty degrees, or Elvis will become a hunka hunka burnin' Armageddon. Tim hijacks an ice cream truck and its driver Arlo (Gooding), and the pair are chased and shot at until the movie is mercifully over. **102m/C VHS, DVD, Wide.** Skeet Ulrich, Cuba Gooding Jr., Peter Firth, David Paymer, Daniel Hugh-Kelly, Kevin J. O'Connor, Judson Mills, Hudson Leick, Jim Grimshaw; ***D:*** Hugh Johnson; ***W:*** Drew Gitlin, Mike Cheda; ***C:*** David Gribble; ***M:*** Hans Zimmer, John Powell.

Chillers **1988** Travellers waiting for a bus are besieged by carnivorous zombies and voracious vampires. How this is different from the standard bus trip is unclear. **90m/C VHS.** Jesse Emery, Marjorie Fitzsimmons, Laurie Pennington, Jim Wolfe, David Wohl; ***D:*** Daniel Boyd; ***W:*** Daniel Boyd.

The Chilling woof! *Gamma 693* **1989 (R)** Corpses preserved in a deep freeze come alive and plague Kansas City as flesh-chomping zombies. Utterly worthless film doesn't even provide convincing effects. **91m/C VHS.** Linda Blair, Dan Haggerty, Troy Donahue, Jack A. De Rieux, Ron Vincent; ***D:*** Deland Nuse, Jack A. Sunseri.

Chilly Scenes of Winter ½ *Head Over Heels* **1979 (PG)** Quirky comedy with a cult following about a man obsessed with regaining the love of a former girlfriend who is now married. He must also deal with an insane mom and various other problems. Strong, subtle performances from Heard and Riegert. Hurt is somewhat less satisfying as the supposedly fascinating woman. Released with a different, inferior ending as "Head Over Heels." Adapted by Joan Micklin Silver from Ann Beattie's first novel. Watch for Beattie's cameo as a waitress. **96m/C VHS.** John Heard, Mary Beth Hurt, Peter Riegert, Kenneth McMillan, Gloria Grahame, Nora Heflin, Griffin Dunne; ***Cameos:*** Ann Beattie; ***D:*** Joan Micklin Silver; ***W:*** Joan Micklin Silver.

Chimes at Midnight *Falstaff; Campanadas a Medianoche* **1967** Classic tragedy—derived by Welles from five Shakespeare plays—about a corpulent blowhard and his friendship with a prince. Crammed with classic sequences, including a battle that is both realistic and funny. The love scene between massive Welles and a nonetheless willing Moreau also manages to be both sad and amusing. Great performances all around, but Welles understandably dominates. The film's few flaws (due to budget problems) are inconsequential before considerable strengths. This one ranks among Welles', and thus the entire cinema's, very best. **115m/B VHS.** *SP SI* Orson Welles, Jeanne Moreau, Margaret Rutherford, John Gielgud, Marina Vlady, Keith Baxter, Fernando Rey, Norman Rodway; ***D:*** Orson Welles; ***W:*** Orson Welles; ***C:*** Edmond Richard; ***M:*** Angelo Francesco Lavagnino; ***Nar:*** Ralph Richardson.

China ½ **1943** David Jones (Ladd) is an unfeeling profiteer who's making money off the Japanese invading China (it's 1941). But he and buddy Johnny Sparrow (Bendix) have their truck hijacked by a group of Chinese guerrillas, lead by China-born American teacher Carolyn Grant (Young), who need a group of schoolgirls driven to safety through enemy lines. Naturally, Jones has a change of heart (and sides) and battles the Japanese troops. Typically fervent propaganda film. Based on the play by Archibald Forbes. **79m/B VHS.** Alan Ladd, Loretta Young, William Bendix, Philip Ahn, Victor Sen Yung, Marianne Quon, Richard Loo; ***D:*** John Farrow; ***W:*** Frank Butler; ***C:*** Leo Tover.

China Beach **1988** TV movie/pilot launched the acclaimed series about American military women behind the lines during the chaos of the Vietnam War. Nurse McMurphy has only seven days left on her first tour of duty, and in spite of her hate of the brutality of the war, she has mixed feelings about leaving her friends and her work. A USO singer on a one week tour finds her search for men brings the war too close for comfort. Cherry, a new Red Cross volunteer, shows up at the Beach. Skillfully introduces the viewer to all the characters, their problems and joys, without melodrama or redundancy. **95m/C VHS.** Dana Delany, Chloe Webb, Robert Picardo, Nan Woods, Michael Boatman, Marg Helgenberger, Tim Ryan, Concetta Tomei, Jeff Kober, Brian Wimmer; ***D:*** Rod Holcomb; ***W:*** John Sacret Young. **TV**

China Cry ½ **1991 (PG-13)** Based on the true story of Sung Negn Yee who escaped from Communist China to the freedom of Hong Kong in the early '60s. Fine portrayal of the young woman from a privileged background who witnessed some of the atrocities of Mao's government policies. **103m/C VHS.** Julia Nickson-Soul, Russell Wong, James Shigeta, France Nuyen; ***D:*** James F. Collier.

China Gate **1957** A band of multi-national troops follows a French officer against a communist stronghold in Indochina. Conventional fare bolstered considerably by director Fuller's flair for action. Weak male leads, but Dickinson shines. **97m/B VHS.** Gene Barry, Angie Dickinson, Nat King Cole, Paul Dubov, Lee Van Cleef, George Givot, Marcel Dalio, Gerald Milton, Neyle Morrow, Maurice Marsac, Warren Hsieh, Paul Busch, Sasha Hardin, James Hong, Walter Soo Hoo, Weaver Levy; ***D:*** Samuel Fuller; ***W:*** Samuel Fuller; ***C:*** Joseph Biroc; ***M:*** Max Steiner, Victor Young.

China Girl ½ **1987 (R)** An Italian-American boy and a Chinese-American girl romance despite a war between gangs in their respective NYC communities. This often violent drama is enriched by director Ferrara's slick, high-energy approach. **90m/C VHS.** Richard Panebianco, James Russo, Sari Chang, Russell Wong, David Caruso, Joey Chin; ***D:*** Abel Ferrara; ***W:*** Nicholas St. John; ***C:*** Bojan Bazelli; ***M:*** Joe Delia.

The China Lake Murders ½ **1990 (PG-13)** Crazy-cop-on-the-loose fable in which a serial killer disguised as a highway patrolman practices population control on the inhabitants of a small town in the Mojave desert. Meanwhile the local sheriff (Skerritt), unwittingly befriends the killer-patrolman. **100m/C VHS.** Tom Skerritt, Michael Parks, Nancy Everhard, Lauren Tewes, Bill McKinney, Lonny (Loni) Chapman; ***D:*** Alan Metzger; ***W:*** Nevin Schreiner. **CABLE**

China Moon ½ **1991 (R)** Convoluted police thriller, set in Florida, about beautiful Rachel (Stowe), who's married to rich-but-abusive Rupert (Dance). Kyle (Harris) is the lonely homicide detective who's besotted by Rachel and conveniently helps her dispose of her murdered husband's body. Kyle's problems increase when his rookie partner (Del Toro) turns out to be smarter than anyone thinks. Good performances but the suspense is only average. **99m/C VHS, DVD, Wide.** Ed Harris, Madeleine Stowe, Benicio Del Toro, Charles Dance; ***D:*** John Bailey; ***W:*** Roy Carlson; ***C:*** Willy Kurant; ***M:*** George Fenton.

China, My Sorrow ½ *Chine, Ma Douleur* **1989** Thirteen-year-old "Little Four Eyes" is sent to a Chinese re-education camp for the crime of playing a love song to a girl. There he befriends another enemy of the revolution and a Buddhist monk who help him maintain his familial traditions and identity. Tragi-comic look at how freedom's spirit survived the Cultural Revolution. Mandarin with subtitles. **86m/C VHS.** *CH* Guo Yiang Yi, Tieu Quan Nghieu, Vong Han Lai, Chi-Vy Sam, Chang Cheung Siang; ***D:*** Dai Sijie; ***W:*** Dai Sijie, Shan Yuan Zhu; ***M:*** Chen Qi Gang.

China O'Brien ½ **1988 (R)** Gorgeous police officer with martial arts expertise returns home for a little R&R, but finds she has to kick some major butt instead. Violent, dim-witted action drama proves only that cleavage can be macho too. **90m/C VHS, DVD.** Cynthia Rothrock, Richard Norton, Patrick Adamson, David Blackwell, Steven Kerby, Robert Tiller, Lainie Watts, Keith Cooke; ***D:*** Robert Clouse; ***W:*** Robert Clouse; ***C:*** Kent Wakeford; ***M:*** Paul Antonelli.

China O'Brien 2 ½ **1989 (R)** The unbreakable China, now a sheriff, battles the standard-issue Vietnam-vet druglord who invades her little town. Made back-to-back with the first film (note that both pics' bad guys have the same gang of henchman!), and in both films Rothrock is basically invincible, so there's no suspense. **85m/C VHS.** Cynthia Rothrock, Richard Norton, Keith Cooke; ***D:*** Robert Clouse.

China Seas **1935** The captain of a commercial steamship on the China route has to fight off murderous Malay pirates, a spurned woman, and a raging typhoon to reach port safely. Fast-moving romantic action taken from Crosbie Garstin's novel. **89m/B VHS.** Clark Gable, Jean Harlow, Wallace Beery, Rosalind Russell, Lewis Stone, Sir C. Aubrey Smith, Dudley Digges, Robert Benchley; ***D:*** Tay Garnett.

China Sky **1944** An American doctor fights alongside Chinese guerillas against the Japanese during WWII. Drama, to its credit, often opts for character conflict instead of warfare, but this makes it merely dull instead of cliched. Adapted from a Pearl S. Buck novel. **78m/B VHS.** Randolph Scott, Ellen Drew, Ruth Warrick, Anthony Quinn, Carol Thurston, Richard Loo, Philip Ahn; ***D:*** Ray Enright.

The China Syndrome ½ **1979 (PG)** A somewhat unstable executive at a nuclear plant uncovers evidence of a concealed accident, takes drastic steps to publicize the incident. Lemmon is excellent as the anxious exec, while Fonda and Douglas are scarcely less distinguished as a sympathetic TV journalist and camera operator, respectively. Tense, prophetic thriller that ironically preceded the Three Mile Island accident by just a few months. Produced by Douglas. **123m/C VHS, DVD.** Jane Fonda, Jack Lemmon, Michael Douglas, Scott Brady, James Hampton, Peter Donat, Wilford Brimley, James Karen; ***D:*** James Bridges; ***W:*** James Bridges, Mike Gray, T.S. Cook; ***C:*** James A. Crabe. British Acad. '79: Actor (Lemmon), Actress (Fonda); Cannes '79: Actor (Lemmon); Writers Guild '79: Orig. Screenplay.

China White **1991 (R)** Violence erupts in the streets of Paris, Amsterdam, and Bangkok, when international drug cartels battle over the ownership of China White—premium heroin, its sources and its outlets. Rousing, realistic action. **?m/C VHS.** Billy Drago, Russell Wong, Lisa Schrage, Steven Leigh; ***D:*** Ronny Yu.

Chinatown **1974 (R)** Private detective Jake Gittes (Nicholson) finds himself overwhelmed in a scandalous case involving the rich and powerful of Los Angeles. Gripping, atmospheric mystery excels in virtually every aspect, with strong narrative drive and outstanding performances from Nicholson, Dunaway, and Huston. Director Polanski also appears in a suitable unsettling cameo. Fabulous. A sneaky, snaking delight filled with seedy characters and plots-within-plots. Followed more than 15 years later by "The Two Jakes." **131m/C VHS, DVD, 8mm, Wide.** Roman Polanski, Jack Nicholson, Faye Dunaway, John Huston, Diane Ladd, John Hillerman, Burt Young, Perry Lopez, Darrell Zwerling, Joe Mantell; ***D:*** Roman Polanski; ***W:*** Robert Towne; ***C:*** John A. Alonzo; ***M:*** Jerry Goldsmith. Oscars '74: Orig. Screenplay; AFI '98: Top 100; British Acad. '74: Actor (Nicholson), Director (Polanski), Screenplay; Golden Globes '75: Actor—Drama (Nicholson), Director (Polanski), Film—Drama, Screenplay, Natl. Film Reg. '91;; N.Y. Film Critics '74: Actor (Nicholson); Natl. Soc. Film Critics '74: Actor (Nicholson); Writers Guild '74: Orig. Screenplay.

Chinatown After Dark **1931** Ludicrous, inane melodrama about a white girl raised by the Chinese. **50m/B VHS.** Rex Lease, Barbara Kent, Carmel Myers; ***D:*** Stuart Paton.

Chinatown Connection **1990 (R)** For some inexplicable reason, local drug dealers start selling poisoned cocaine. Two renegade cops discover the super-secret organization doing the poisoning, arm themselves heavily, and kill lots of people while putting an end to the poisonings. Violent, foolish film with dull performances. **94m/C VHS.** Bruce Ly, Lee Majors, Pat McCormick, Art Camacho, Susan Frailey, Scott Richards; ***D:*** Jean-Paul Ouellette.

The Chinatown Kid **1978** Tan Tung escapes from Red China on a ship bound for San Francisco. There he becomes involved in a local extortion racket and he'll need all his martial arts skills to overcome the two gangs fighting for power. **115m/C VHS.** Alexander Fu Sheng, Sun Chein, Shirley Yu, Shaw Yin-Yin; ***D:*** Chen Chen.

The Chinatown Murders: Man against the Mob *Man against the Mob: The Chinatown Murders* **1992 (R)** A tough cop is up against the Chinese mafia and his own corrupt police force as he tries to stay alive and find some justice. **96m/C VHS.** George Peppard, Charles Haid, Richard Bradford, Ursula Andress, Jason Beghe, Julia Nickson-Soul, James Pax, Sandy Ward; ***D:*** Michael Pressman; ***C:*** Tim Suhrstedt.

Chinese Box ½ **1997** Hong Kong's return to Chinese rule is the backdrop for Wang's story of a dying British journalist (Irons) and a former bar girl turned nightclub owner (Li). In the months before the 1997 handover, business writer John learns he is dying of leukemia and decides to pursue Vivian, the woman he has secretly loved for some time. He also sets out to discover the "meaning" of Hong Kong itself. This quest is personified by Jean (Cheung), a street hustler with stories to tell. Metaphors abound as Wang tries to convey the everyday chaos and impenetrability of Hong Kong life. Striking visuals provide cues and clues to the not-always-subtle symbolism. Mandarin and English dialogue. **109m/C VHS, DVD.** *FR JP* Jeremy Irons, Gong Li, Maggie Cheung, Ruben Blades, Michael Hui; ***D:*** Wayne Wang; ***W:*** Wayne Wang, Jean-Claude Carriere, Larry Gross, Paul Theroux; ***C:*** Vilko Filac; ***M:*** Graeme Revell.

Chinese Boxes ½ 1984 An American man in Berlin is framed in a murder and becomes caught in an international web of crime and intrigue. Low budget but interesting thriller. **87m/C VHS.** *GE GB* Will Patton, Adelheid Arndt, Robbie Coltrane; ***D:*** Christopher Petit; ***W:*** L.M. Kit Carson.

The Chinese Cat 1944 Poorly scripted formula mystery has the younger Chan smitten with a girl who needs the elder Chan's detective skills in finding her father's killer. **65m/B VHS.** Sidney Toler, Benson Fong, Mantan Moreland, Weldon Heyburn, Joan Woodbury, Ian Keith, Sam Flint; ***D:*** Phil Rosen.

Chinese Connection ½ *Fist of Fury; The Iron Hand; Jing Wu Men* 1973 (R) A martial arts expert tracks sadistic brutes who slew his instructor. Wild action sequences provide a breathtaking view of Lee's skill. Dubbed. **90m/C VHS, DVD, Wide.** *HK* Bruce Lee, James Tien, Robert Baker; ***D:*** Lo Wei; ***W:*** Lo Wei; ***C:*** Chen Ching Chu; ***M:*** Fu-ling Wang.

Chinese Connection 2 1984 A martial-arts expert learns that the school where he trained is now run by an unappealing master. Conflict ensues. Bruce Li is not Bruce Lee, but he is fairly good in action portions of this otherwise dull, sloppy venture. **96m/C VHS, DVD.** Bruce Li.

Chinese Roulette ½ 1986 A host of unappealing characters convene at a country house for sexual shenanigans and a cruel game masterminded by a sadistic crippled girl. Cold effort from German master Fassbinder. In German with English subtitles. **96m/C VHS, Wide.** *GE* Anna Karina, Margit Carstensen, Ulli Lommel, Brigitte Mira, Macha Meril, Andrea Schober, Volker Spengler; ***D:*** Rainer Werner Fassbinder; ***W:*** Rainer Werner Fassbinder; ***C:*** Michael Ballhaus.

Chinese Web 1978 Spiderman adventure in which Spidey becomes entwined in international intrigue and corrupt officials. **95m/C VHS.** Nicholas Hammond, Robert F. Simon, Rosalind Chao, Ted Danson; ***D:*** Donald McDougall.

Chino *Valdez the Half Breed; The Valdez Horses* 1975 (PG) A half-Indian horse rancher struggles to maintain his livelihood in this spaghetti western. Not among Bronson's stronger—that is, more viscerally effective—films. Adapted from Lee Hoffman's novel. **97m/C VHS, DVD.** *IT* Charles Bronson, Jill Ireland, Vincent Van Patten; ***D:*** John Sturges; ***W:*** Massimo De Rita, Clair Huffaker, Arduino (Dino) Maiuri; ***C:*** Armando Nannuzzi; ***M:*** Guido de Angelis, Maurizio de Angelis.

Chips, the War Dog ½ 1990 A WWII Army recruit, who's scared of dogs, is assigned to train a German shepherd for duty. **90m/C VHS.** Brandon Douglas, Ned Vaughn, Paxton Whitehead, Ellie Cornell, Robert Miranda, William Devane; ***D:*** Ed Kaplan. CABLE

The Chisholms ½ 1979 If you're into oaters, here's a high fiber six-hour serial: Chisolm (Preston) leads the family as they head west and find trouble with a capital "T" en route from Virginia to Californ-i-a. Originally a network miniseries, it's now a two-cassette rentable; adapted by Evan Hunter from his novel. **300m/C VHS.** Robert Preston, Rosemary Harris, Brian Keith, Ben Murphy, Charles Frank; ***D:*** Mel Stuart; ***M:*** Elmer Bernstein.

Chisum ½ 1970 (G) Cattle baron faces various conflicts, including a confrontation with Billy the Kid. Lame Wayne vehicle contributes nothing to exhausted western genre. **111m/C VHS, Wide.** John Agar, John Wayne, Forrest Tucker, Geoffrey Deuel, Christopher George, Ben Johnson, Bruce Cabot, Patric Knowles, Richard Jaeckel, Glenn Corbett; ***D:*** Andrew V. McLaglen; ***W:*** Andrew J. Fenady; ***C:*** William Clothier.

Chitty Chitty Bang Bang 1968 (G) An eccentric inventor spruces up an old car and, in fantasy, takes his children to a land where the evil rulers have forbidden children. Poor special effects and forgettable score stall effort. Loosely adapted by Roald Dahl and Hughes from an Ian Fleming story. ♫Chitty Chitty Bang Bang; Hushabye Mountain; Truly Scrumptious; You Two; Toot Sweet; Me Ol' Bamboo; Lovely Lonely Man; Posh; The Roses of Success. **142m/C VHS, DVD.** *GB* Dick Van Dyke, Sally Ann Howes, Lionel Jeffries, Gert Frobe, Anna Quayle, Benny Hill; ***D:*** Ken Hughes; ***W:*** Ken Hughes, Roald Dahl; ***C:*** Christopher Challis; ***M:*** Richard M. Sherman, Robert B. Sherman.

Chloe in the Afternoon *L'Amour l'Apres-midi* 1972 (R) A married man finds himself inexplicably drawn to an ungainly young woman. Sixth of the "Moral Tales" series is typical of director Rohmer's talky approach. Not for all tastes, but rewarding for those who are drawn to this sort of thing. In French with English subtitles. **97m/C VHS, DVD.** *FR* Bernard Verley, Zouzou, Francoise Verley, Daniel Ceccaldi, Malvina Penne, Babette Ferrier, Suze Randall, Marie-Christine Barrault; ***D:*** Eric Rohmer; ***W:*** Eric Rohmer; ***C:*** Nestor Almendros; ***M:*** Arie Dzierlatka.

Chocolat ½ 1988 (PG-13) A woman recalls her childhood spent in French West Africa and the unfulfilled sexual tension between her mother and black servant. Vivid film provides a host of intriguing characters and offers splendid panoramas of rugged desert landscapes. Profound, if somewhat personal filmmaking from novice director Denis: In French with English subtitles. **105m/C VHS.** Mireille Perrier, Emmet Judson Williamson, Cecile Ducasse, Giulia Boschi, Francois Cluzet, Isaach de Bankole, Kenneth Cranham; ***D:*** Claire Denis; ***W:*** Claire Denis, Jean-Pol Fargeau.

Chocolat 2000 (PG-13) Free-spirited Vianne (Binoche) and her young daughter Anouk (Thivisol) are literally blown into the dull French town of Lansquenet in the late 1950s. Before the scandalized eyes of the Comte de Reynaud (Molina), the community's moral arbitrator, the unmarried hussy opens a chocolaterie—during Lent! While the Comte tries to rally the residents to boycott the establishment, Vianne's delicacies are setting the townspeople's pulses racing, as she becomes intrigued by gypsy vagabond Roux (Depp). Sweetly predictable if overly chastising against religion and conventional morality. Binoche is radiant as usual (and have some chocolate handy when you watch). Based on the novel by Joanne Harris. **121m/C VHS, DVD.** *FR* Juliette Binoche, Victorie Thivisol, Johnny Depp, Alfred Molina, Judi Dench, Lena Olin, Peter Stormare, Carrie-Anne Moss, John Wood, Hugh O'Conor, Leslie Caron, Aurelien Parent Koenig; ***D:*** Lasse Hallstrom; ***W:*** Robert Nelson Jacobs; ***C:*** Roger Pratt; ***M:*** Rachel Portman. Screen Actors Guild '00: Support. Actress (Dench).

The Chocolate Soldier 1941 Dull musical in which an opera star tests his wife's fidelity. Lovers of the musical genre will find that this one has too much talking, not enough singing. Lovers of fine films will realize that more singing would hardly improve things. Based loosely on Molnar's play "The Guardsman." **102m/B VHS.** Nelson Eddy, Rise Stevens, Nigel Bruce, Florence Bates, Dorothy Gilmore, Nydia Westman; ***D:*** Roy Del Ruth; ***C:*** Karl Freund.

The Chocolate War 1988 (R) An idealistic student and a hardline headmaster butt heads at a Catholic boys' school over an unofficial candy business in this tense, unsettling drama. Glover is notable in his familiar villain role, and Gordon is effective in his first effort as director. Based on the Robert Cormier novel. **95m/C VHS.** John Glover, Jenny Wright, Wallace (Wally) Langham, Bud Cort, Ilan Mitchell-Smith, Adam Baldwin; ***D:*** Keith Gordon; ***W:*** Keith Gordon.

The Choice 1981 A young woman must make the choice between aborting or keeping her baby in this fairly insipid drama. **96m/C VHS.** Susan Clark, Jennifer Warren, Mitchell Ryan, Largo Woodruff; ***D:*** David Greene. TV

Choice of Arms ½ 1983 A gangster's rural retirement is undone by a dim-witted criminal in this sometimes-gripping drama. Montand and Deneuve are serviceable in undemanding roles of the gangster and his glamorous wife; Depardieu is more impressive as the trouble-making punk. In French with English subtitles. **114m/C VHS.** *FR* Gerard Depardieu, Catherine Deneuve, Yves Montand; ***D:*** Alain Corneau.

Choice of Weapons *A Dirty Knight's Work; Trial by Combat* 1976 Ex-cop trying to solve murders focuses on a curious group of 20th-century men who live within a 12th-century fantasy—jousting for sport and chivalrous honor. Offbeat lance thruster notable for incongruity and all-star cast. **88m/C VHS.** *GB* David Birney, Peter Cushing, Donald Pleasence, Barbara Hershey, John Mills, Margaret Leighton; ***D:*** Kevin Connor; ***W:*** Julian Bond.

Choices ½ 1981 A hearing-impaired athlete suffers alienation when banned from the football squad. What? Controversial covergirl Moore is a supporting player in this, her first film. **90m/C VHS, DVD.** Paul Carafotes, Victor French, Lelia Goldoni, Val Avery, Dennis Patrick, Demi Moore; ***D:*** Rami Alon; ***W:*** Rami Alon; ***C:*** Hanania Baer; ***M:*** Christopher Stone.

Choices ½ 1986 Scott is a 62-year-old man with a lovely second wife (Bisset) and a rebellious grown daughter (Gilbert), who announces she's pregnant and is getting an abortion. Meanwhile, his wife also discovers she's pregnant and wants the child, although Scott is adamantly opposed to raising a second family at his age. Family strife carried by fine performances. **95m/C VHS.** George C. Scott, Jacqueline Bisset, Melissa Gilbert; ***D:*** David Lowell Rich. TV

The Choirboys 1977 (R) Thoroughly mediocre production about overbearing L.A. cops and their off-hours handling of job stress. Few of the strong cast emerge unscathed. Based on the Joseph Wambaugh novel. **120m/C VHS.** Charles Durning, Louis Gossett Jr., Perry King, Clyde Kusatsu, Stephen Macht, Tim McIntire, Randy Quaid, Chuck Sacci, Don Stroud, James Woods, Burt Young, Robert Webber, Barbara Rhoades, Vic Tayback, Blair Brown, Charles Haid, Jim Davis; ***D:*** Robert Aldrich; ***C:*** Joseph Biroc.

Choke ½ 2000 (R) Weak thriller with dumb dialogue. Shady businessman Harry (Hopper) is trying to cover up his daughter's deadly drunken hit-and-run accident when he's threatened by a con man who knows about the crime. Then Harry just makes the situation worse by accepting the help of a killer (Madsen) who knows how to get rid of troublesome bodies. **95m/C VHS, DVD.** Dennis Hopper, Michael Madsen, L.P. Brown III, Chelsy Reynolds, Roy Tate; ***D:*** John Sjogren. VIDEO

Choke Canyon 1986 (PG) An environmentalist thwarts the henchmen of an industrialist eager to coverup a nuclear dump in a picturesque canyon. Good intentions do not necessarily make for a good movie. **95m/C VHS.** Stephen Collins, Bo Svenson, Lance Henriksen; ***D:*** Charles "Chuck" Bail.

C.H.O.M.P.S. ½ 1979 (PG) Comedy in which a youthful inventor and a popular robot guard dog become the target of a business takeover. Harmless but unfunny and unfun. **90m/C VHS.** Jim Backus, Valerie Bertinelli, Wesley Eure, Conrad Bain, Chuck McCann, Red Buttons; ***D:*** Don Chaffey.

Choose Me ½ 1984 (R) Comedy-drama about sad, lonely, and often quirky characters linked to an unlikely L.A. radio sex therapist. Moody, memorable fare features especially strong playing from Bujold as a sexually inexperienced sex therapist and Warren as one of her regular listeners. Typically eccentric fare from director Rudolph. **106m/C VHS, DVD, Wide.** Keith Carradine, Genevieve Bujold, Lesley Ann Warren, Rae Dawn Chong, John Larroquette, John Considine, Patrick Bauchau; ***D:*** Alan Rudolph; ***W:*** Alan Rudolph; ***C:*** Jan Kiesser; ***M:*** Phil Woods.

Chopper ½ 2000 Biopic of famous Aussie criminal Mark "Chopper" Read is highlighted by Bana's extraordinary performance in the title role. Dominik's directorial debut follows Read's career from prison, where he murders one inmate, forces another to cut off his ears, and generally makes hardened criminal fear for their lives, to his old haunts, where he seeks revenge for past wrongs. Full of gore and ultraviolence, it's not for the sqeamish, but it does make its point about society's preoccupation with the "celebrity criminal." Read didn't participate in the production, but it was based on his nine bestsellers, and he did suggest Bana for the lead. **94m/C DVD, Wide.** *AU* Eric Bana, Vince Colosimo, Simon Lyndon, David Field, Daniel Wyllie, Bill Young, Gary Waddell, Kate Beahan, Kenny Graham; ***D:*** Andrew Dominik; ***W:*** Andrew Dominik; ***C:*** Geoffrey Hall; ***M:*** Mick Harvey. Australian Film Inst. '00: Actor (Bana), Director (Dominik), Support. Actor (Lyndon).

Chopper Chicks in Zombietown 1991 (R) Tough but sexy Chopper Chicks show up in that American vacation mecca, Zombietown, for a little rest and relaxation. Little do they know that a mad mortician has designs on turning our hot heroines into mindless zombie slaves. Can the buxom biker babes thwart the evil embalmer before it's too late, or will they abandon their Harleys to shuffle about in search of human flesh? From the Troma Team, featuring Oscar-winner Billy Bob Thornton as "Donny." **86m/C VHS.** Jamie Rose, Catherine Carlen, Lycia Naff, Vicki Frederick, Kristina Loggia, Gretchen Palmer, Whitney Reis, Nina Peterson, Ed Gale, David Knell, Billy Bob Thornton, Don Calfa, Martha Quinn; ***D:*** Dan Hoskins; ***W:*** Dan Hoskins; ***C:*** Tom Fraser; ***M:*** Daniel May.

The Choppers 1961 Naw, not a fable about false teeth. Teen punk Hall operates a car theft ring made up of fellow punksters. Rock'n'roll tunes by the Hallmeister include the much-overlooked "Monkey in my Hatband." **66m/B VHS, DVD.** Arch Hall Jr., Marianne Gaba, Robert Paget, Tom Brown, Rex Holman, Bruno VeSota; ***D:*** Leigh Jason; ***W:*** Arch (Archie) Hall Sr.; ***C:*** Clark Ramsey; ***M:*** Al Pellegrini.

Chopping Mall ½ *Killbots* 1986 (R) A freak electric storm unleashes killer security robots on a band of teens trapped inside the mall. Nobody shops. Premise undone by obscure humor, lack of flair, action, or horror. Updated imitation of the 1973 TV movie "Trapped." **77m/C VHS.** Kelli Maroney, Tony O'Dell, Suzee Slater, Russell Todd, Paul Bartel, Mary Woronov, Dick Miller, Karrie Emerson, Barbara Crampton, Nick Segal, John Terlesky, Gerrit Graham, Mel Welles; ***D:*** Jim Wynorski; ***W:*** Jim Wynorski, Steve Mitchell; ***C:*** Tom Richmond; ***M:*** Chuck Cirino.

A Chorus Line 1985 (PG-13) A range of performers reveal their insecurities and aspirations while auditioning before a hardnosed director in this adaptation of the popular, overblown Broadway musical. Singing and dancing is rarely rousing. Director Attenborough probably wasn't the right choice for this one. ♫Dance 10, Looks 3; What I Did for Love; At the Ballet; I Can Do That; Let Me Dance For You; I Hope I Get It; Nothing; The Music and the Mirror; And. **118m/C VHS, 8mm.** Michael Douglas, Audrey Landers, Gregg Burge, Alyson Reed, Janet Jones, Michael Blevins, Terrence Mann, Cameron English, Vicki Frederick, Nicole Fosse, Michelle Johnson; ***D:*** Richard Attenborough; ***W:*** Arnold Schulman; ***M:*** Marvin Hamlisch, Ralph Burns.

A Chorus of Disapproval ½ 1989 (PG) Adaptation of prolific Alan Ayckbourn's play about a withdrawn, somewhat dim-witted British widower who attempts social interaction by joining community theatre, then finds himself embroiled in romantic shenanigans and theatrical intrigue. Irons is fine in the lead, but Hopkins sparkles in the more spectacular role of the musical production's demanding but beleaguered director. Seagrove is impressive as an amoral sexpot. Sharper focus from director Winner would have improved this one, but the film is fun even when it isn't particularly funny. **105m/C VHS.** *GB* Jeremy Irons, Anthony Hopkins, Jenny Seagrove, Lionel Jeffries, Patsy Kensit, Gareth Hunt, Prunella Scales, Sylvia Syms, Richard Briers, Barbara Ferris; ***D:*** Michael Winner; ***W:*** Michael Winner, Alan Ayckbourn; ***M:*** John Du Prez.

The Chosen woof! *Holocaust 2000* 1977 (R) Executive of a nuclear power facility located in the Sahara Desert realizes that his son is the Anti-Christ bent on the world's destruction. This truly horrible film provides nothing in terms of entertainment. It's rarely even laughably bad. **102m/C VHS.** Kirk Douglas, Simon Ward, Agostina Belli,

Anthony Quayle, Virginia McKenna, Alexander Knox; *D:* Alberto De Martino; *M:* Ennio Morricone.

The Chosen ♪♪♪ **1981** Set in 1940s Brooklyn about the friendship between two teenagers—Benson, the Hassidic son of a rabbi, and Miller, whose father is a Zionist professor. Based on the novel by Chaim Potok. **108m/C VHS.** Robby Benson, Barry Miller, Maximilian Schell, Rod Steiger, Hildy Brooks, Ron Rifkin, Val Avery; *D:* Jeremy Paul Kagan; *M:* Elmer Bernstein.

The Chosen One: Legend of the Raven ♪♪ **1998 (R)** McKenna Ray ("Baywatch" babe Electra) wants payback after her sister is murdered and is transformed into a superheroine avenger (guided by her shaman father) so she can rid the world of scum. Electra has a provocative costume but the nude scenes are courtesy of a body-double. **105m/C VHS, DVD.** Carmen Electra, Michael Stadvec, David Oliver, Shauna Sand; *D:* Lawrence Lanoff; *W:* Sam Rappaport, Khara Bromiley; *C:* Robert New; *M:* Keith Arem.

Christ Stopped at Eboli ♪♪♪♪ *Eboli; Cristo si e fermato a Eboli* **1979** Subdued work about an anti-Fascist writer exiled to rural Italy in the 1930s. Excellent performances from the lead Volonte and supporting players Papas and Cuny. Slow, contemplative film is probably director Rosi's masterpiece. Adapted from Carlo Levi's book. In Italian with English subtitles. **118m/C VHS.** *IT FR* Gian Marie Volonte, Irene Papas, Paolo Bonacelli, Francois Simon, Alain Cuny, Lea Massari; *D:* Francesco Rosi; *W:* Francesco Rosi; *C:* Pasqualino De Santis. British Acad. '82: Foreign Film.

Christabel ♪♪ **1989** Condensed version of the BBC miniseries based on the true-life WWII exploits of Christabel Bielenberg, a British woman who battled to save her German husband from the horrors of the Ravensbruck concentration camp. **148m/C VHS.** *GB* Elizabeth Hurley, Stephen (Dillon) Dillane, Nigel le Vaillant, Geoffrey Palmer, Ann Bell, Ralph Brown, John Burgess, Suzan Crowley, Eileen Maciejewska, Hugh Simon, Nicola Wright; *D:* Adrian Shergold; *W:* Dennis Potter; *C:* Remi Adefarasin; *M:* Stanley Myers. **TV**

Christian the Lion ♪♪½ **1976 (G)** The true story of Christian, a lion cub raised in a London zoo, who is transported to Africa to learn to live with other lions. With the principals from "Born Free." **87m/C VHS.** *GB* Virginia McKenna, Bill Travers, George Adamson, James Hill; *D:* Bill Travers.

Christiane F. ♪♪♪ **1982 (R)** Gripping, visually impressive story of a bored German girl's decline into drug use and prostitution. Based on a West German magazine article. Sobering and dismal look at a milieu in which innocence and youth have run amok. The film's impact is only somewhat undermined by poor dubbing. Bowie appears in a concert sequence. **120m/C VHS.** *GE* Natja Brunkhorst, Thomas Haustein, David Bowie; *D:* Uli Edel; *M:* David Bowie.

Christina ♪♪½ **1974 (PG)** Gloomy suspense fare in which a beautiful woman pays a forlorn fellow $25,000 to marry her, then disappears as he begins to actually fall in love with her. His search takes him to various gothic settings. Intriguing, but not really fulfilling. Parkins, however, is appropriately mysterious in the lead. **95m/C VHS.** *CA* Barbara Parkins, Peter Haskell; *D:* Paul Krasny.

Christine ♪♪½ **1984 (R)** Unassuming teen gains posession of a classic auto equipped with a murderous will. Then it's the car doing the possessing. The car more than returns the care and consideration its owner provides it. Are you listening GMC? Better than average treatment of Stephen King's work features a creepy performance by Gordon. **110m/C VHS, DVD, 8mm, Wide.** Keith Gordon, John Stockwell, Alexandra Paul, Robert Prosky, Harry Dean Stanton, Kelly Preston, Christine Belford, Roberts Blossom, William Ostrander, David Spielberg, Robert Darnell; *D:* John Carpenter; *W:* Bill Phillips; *C:* Donald M. Morgan; *M:* John Carpenter, Alan Howarth.

The Christmas Box ♪♪½ **1995** Tearjerking Christmas drama based on Richard Paul Evans' surprising 1992 bestseller, which started out as a story for the author's children. Richard (Thomas) and Keri (O'Toole) Evans have money troubles so they and their five-year-old daughter Jenna (Mulrooney) move into the mansion of elderly widow Mary Parkin (O'Hara) as caretakers. Richard keeps seeing an angel in a recurring dream and hears a familiar tune—all of which leads to a music box hidden in the attic, a series of love letters, and Mary's unhappy past. **92m/C VHS.** Maureen O'Hara, Richard Thomas, Annette O'Toole, Kelsey Mulrooney; *D:* Marcus Cole; *W:* Greg Taylor; *C:* John Newby.

A Christmas Carol ♪♪♪ **1938** An early version of Dickens' classic tale about miser Scrooge, who is instilled with the Christmas spirit after a grim evening with some ghosts. Good playing from Owen as Scrooge and Lockhart as the hapless Bob Cratchit. Scary graveyard sequence too. **70m/B VHS.** Reginald Owen, Gene Lockhart, Terence (Terry) Kilburn, Leo G. Carroll, Lynne Carver, Ann Rutherford; *D:* Edwin L. Marin.

A Christmas Carol ♪♪♪♪ *Scrooge* **1951** A fine retelling of the classic tale about a penny-pinching holiday hater who learns appreciation of Christmas following a frightful, revealing evening with supernatural visitors. Perhaps the best rendering of the Dickens classic. "And God bless Tiny Tim!" **86m/B VHS, DVD.** *GB* Alastair Sim, Kathleen Harrison, Jack Warner, Michael Hordern, Patrick Macnee, Mervyn Johns, Hermione Baddeley, Clifford Mollison, George Cole, Carol Marsh, Miles Malleson, Ernest Thesiger, Hattie Jacques, Peter Bull, Hugh Dempster; *D:* Brian Desmond Hurst; *W:* Noel Langley; *C:* C.M. Pennington-Richards; *M:* Richard Addinsell.

A Christmas Carol ♪♪ **1954** Musical version of the Dickens' classic about a stingy old man who is visited by three ghosts on Christmas Eve. **54m/B VHS.** Fredric March, Basil Rathbone, Ray Middleton, Bob Sweeney, Christopher Cook; *D:* Ralph Levy; *W:* Maxwell Anderson; *M:* Bernard Herrmann.

A Christmas Carol ♪♪♪ **1984 (PG)** Excellent TV adaptation of the Dickens Christmas classic features a memorable Scott as miserly misanthrope Ebenezer Scrooge, who gets a scary look at his life thanks to a Christmas Eve visit from the ghosts of Christmas Past, Present, and Future. Terrific supporting cast; filmed on location in Shrewsbury, England. **100m/C VHS, DVD.** George C. Scott, Nigel Davenport, Edward Woodward, Frank Finlay, Lucy Gutteridge, Angela Pleasence, Roger Rees, David Warner, Susannah York; *D:* Clive Donner; *W:* Roger O. Hirson; *C:* Tony Imi; *M:* Nick Bicat.

A Christmas Carol ♪♪½ **1999** Oft-told tale does have the advantage of Stewart (who has a one-man stage production of the Dickens saga as well as recording an audiobook) as the miserly Scrooge. It also has a strong supporting cast and special effects that enhance but don't overwhelm. **120m/C VHS, DVD.** Patrick Stewart, Richard E. Grant, Joel Grey, Saskia Reeves, Desmond Barrit, Bernard Lloyd, Tim Potter, Ben Tibber, Dominic West, Trevor Peacock, Liz Smith, Elizabeth Spriggs, Laura Fraser, Celia Imrie; *D:* David Hugh Jones; *W:* Peter Barnes; *C:* Ian Wilson; *M:* Stephen Warbeck. **CABLE**

The Christmas Coal Mine Miracle ♪½ *Christmas Miracle in Caulfield, U.S.A* **1977** Syrupy story about miners struggling for survival in a collapsed mine on Christmas Eve. **98m/C VHS.** Mitchell Ryan, Kurt Russell, Andrew Prine, John Carradine, Barbara Babcock, Melissa Gilbert, Don Porter, Shelby Leverington; *D:* Jud Taylor. **TV**

Christmas Comes to Willow Creek ♪♪ **1987** Mutually antagonistic brothers are enlisted to deliver Christmas gifts to an isolated Alaskan community. Can brotherly love be far off? Two leads played together in the rowdy TV series "Dukes of Hazzard." This is hardly an improvement. **96m/C VHS.** John Schneider, Tom Wopat, Hoyt Axton, Zachary Ansley, Kim Delaney; *D:* Richard Lang; *M:* Charles Fox.

Christmas Evil ♪½ *Terror in Toyland; You Better Watch Out* **1980 (R)** Once again a knife-wielding lunatic dresses as Santa Claus to strike terror and death into the hearts of children. **92m/C VHS, DVD.** Brandon Maggart, Jeffrey DeMunn, Dianne Hull, Scott McKay, Peter Friedman, Joe Jamrog, Rutanya Alda, Raymond J. Barry, Andy Fenwick, Sam Gray, Patricia Richardson; *D:* Lewis Jackson; *W:* Lewis Jackson; *C:* Ricardo Aronovich.

Christmas in Connecticut ♪♪♪ *Indiscretion* **1945** Lightweight comedy about a housekeeping magazine's successful columnist who isn't quite the expert homemaker she presents herself to be. When a war veteran is invited to her home as part of a publicity gimmick, she must master the ways of housekeeping or reveal her incompetence. Stanwyck is winning in the lead role. Also available in a colorized version. **101m/B VHS.** Barbara Stanwyck, Reginald Gardiner, Sydney Greenstreet, Dennis Morgan, S.Z. Sakall, Una O'Connor, Robert Shayne, Joyce Compton; *D:* Peter Godfrey.

Christmas in Connecticut ♪♪ **1992** Cannon hosts a weekly TV show as America's favorite homemaker/hostess. A local forest ranger (Kristofferson) becomes a hero by saving a little boy's life and her network stages a media event by inviting him to her home for a traditional Christmas dinner. There's only one problem: she can't cook. Schwarzenegger's directorial debut lacks challenge in this fluffy remake. See the original instead. **93m/C VHS.** Dyan Cannon, Kris Kristofferson, Tony Curtis, Richard Roundtree, Kelly Cinnante, Gene Lithgow, Vivian Bonnell; *D:* Arnold Schwarzenegger; *W:* Janet Brownell. **CABLE**

Christmas in July ♪♪♪½ **1940** A young man goes on a spending spree when he thinks he's won a sweepstakes. Things take a turn for the worse when he finds out that it was all a practical joke. Powell provides a winning performance in this second film from comic master Sturges. **67m/B VHS.** Dick Powell, Ellen Drew, Raymond Walburn, William Demarest, Franklin Pangborn; *D:* Preston Sturges.

The Christmas Kid ♪½ **1968** A desperado struggles to determine his true identity while stopping in a frontier town. Gunplay ensues. Don't bother with this one. **87m/C VHS.** *SP* Jeffrey Hunter, Louis Hayward, Gustavo Rojo, Perla Cristal, Luis Prendes; *D:* Sidney Pink.

Christmas Lilies of the Field ♪♪½ **1984** Sequel to "Lilies of the Field" follows an ex-soldier who returns to the church he helped build. This time he sets out to build an orphanage. **98m/C VHS.** Billy Dee Williams, Maria Schell, Fay Hauser, Judith Piquet; *D:* Ralph Nelson. **TV**

A Christmas Reunion ♪♪½ **1993 (PG)** Young boy, still trying to adjust to his parents' death, runs away from his grandfather's house. But they're reunited thanks to street corner Santa and an enchanted book. **92m/C VHS.** James Coburn, Edward Woodward, Meredith Edwards; *D:* David Hemmings.

A Christmas Story ♪♪♪♪ **1983 (PG)** Unlikely but winning comedy of Ralphie's (Billingsley) single-minded obsession to acquire a Red Ryder BB-gun for Christmas, and the obstacles that everyday life in 1940s Indiana can throw his way. Particularly great sequence involving an impatient department-store Santa. Fun for everyone. Based on "In God We Trust, All Others Pay Cash," an autobiographical story by Shepherd. Followed by "My Summer Story" in 1994, also from Shepherd's book. **95m/C VHS, DVD.** Zack (Zach) Ward, Leslie (Les) Carlson, Peter Billingsley, Darren McGavin, Melinda Dillon, Ian Petrella; *Cameos:* Jean Shepherd; *D:* Bob (Benjamin) Clark; *W:* Bob (Benjamin) Clark, Leigh Brown, Jean Shepherd; *C:* Reginald Morris; *M:* Paul Zaza, Carl Zittrer; *Nar:* Jean Shepherd. Genie '84: Director (Clark).

The Christmas That Almost Wasn't ♪½ *Il Natale Che Quasi Non Fu* **1966 (G)** Loathsome humbug decides to destroy Christmas forever by removing Santa Claus from the North Pole. Crude Italian-made children's film nonetheless remembered fondly by a generation of kids. ♫The Christmas That Almost Wasn't; Christmas is Coming; Hustle Bustle; I'm Bad; Kids Get All the Breaks; The Name of the Song is Prune; Nothing to do But Wait; Santa Claus; Time For Christmas. **95m/C VHS.** *IT* Rossano Brazzi, Paul Tripp, Lidia Brazzi, Sonny Fox, Mischa Auer; *D:* Rossano Brazzi.

A Christmas to Remember ♪♪½ **1978 (G)** Depression-era Minnesota farmer who has lost his son in WWI brings his city-bred grandson to the farm for a holiday visit. Somber, occasionally poignant film buoyed by Robards presence, and Saint's as well. **96m/C VHS.** Jason Robards Jr., Eva Marie Saint, Joanne Woodward; *D:* George Englund. **TV**

The Christmas Wife ♪♪½ **1988** A lonely man pays a woman to be his holiday companion at a mountain retreat. Sturdy performances by Robards and Harris manage to keep this one from going to the dogs. Based on a story by Helen Norris. **73m/C VHS.** Jason Robards Jr., Julie Harris, Don Francks, Patricia Hamilton, Deborah Grover, James Eckhouse; *D:* David Hugh Jones. **CABLE**

A Christmas Without Snow ♪♪½ **1980** A lonely divorced woman finds communal happiness within a local church choir led by a crusty choir master. **96m/C VHS.** Michael Learned, John Houseman, Ramon Bieri, James Cromwell, Valerie Curtin, Ruth Nelson, Beah Richards, Calvin Levels; *D:* John Korty; *M:* Ed Bogas. **TV**

Christopher Columbus ♪♪½ **1949** Step-by-step biography of the 15th-century explorer, his discovery of America, the fame that first greeted him, and his last days. **103m/C VHS.** *GB* Fredric March, Florence Eldridge, Francis L. Sullivan; *D:* David MacDonald.

Christopher Columbus ♪♪½ **1985** The man who explored the New World is shown in all his flawed complexity in this film that takes a contemporary approach to the discoveries and character of Christopher Columbus. Shot on location in Spain, Malta, and the Dominican Republic, the film features an exact replica of Columbus's flagship, the Santa Maria. Originally aired as a six-hour TV miniseries. **128m/C VHS.** Gabriel Byrne, Faye Dunaway, Oliver Reed, Max von Sydow, Eli Wallach, Nicol Williamson, Jose Ferrer, Virna Lisi, Raf Vallone; *D:* Alberto Lattuada. **TV**

Christopher Columbus: The Discovery ♪ **1992 (PG-13)** The 500th anniversary of Columbus' voyage brought this lame excursion in historical biography to the screen briefly. Columbus is portrayed as a swashbuckling adventurer who finally gets the Queen of Spain to agree to finance his voyage of discovery (which primarily consists of discovering a lot of bare-breasted native women). Story is secondary to the banality of the entire production, including the acting. Brando is briefly seen as Torquemada—another film in which he took his substantial paycheck and ran. **120m/C VHS.** Georges Corraface, Rachel Ward, Tom Selleck, Marlon Brando, Robert Davi, Oliver Cotton, Benicio Del Toro, Catherine Zeta-Jones, Matthieu Carriere, Nigel Terry, Branscombe Richmond; *D:* John Glen; *W:* John Briley, Mario Puzo, Cary Bates; *M:* Cliff Eidelman. Golden Raspberries '92: Worst Support. Actor (Selleck).

Christopher Strong ♪♪½ **1933** Interesting Hepburn turn as a daredevil aviatrix who falls in love with a married British statesman. **77m/B VHS.** Katharine Hepburn, Billie Burke, Colin Clive, Helen Chandler; *D:* Dorothy Arzner; *M:* Max Steiner.

Christy **1994** Pilot movie for the TV series finds 19-year-old Christy Huddleston (Martin) leaving her privileged Southern life to teach school in the Great Smoky Mountains. It's 1912 in Cutter Gap, Tennessee, and her students are literally dirt poor, with ignorance and supersitition the norm. Christy's inspiration in Miss Alice (Daly), a middle-aged Quaker who runs the mission school. And Christy needs encouragement as she struggles to cope with her new life and responsibilities. Based on the novel by Catherine Marshall, which is a fictional biography of her mother. **90m/C VHS.** Kellie Martin, Tyne Daly, Tess Harper, Randall Batinkoff, Annabelle Price, Stewart Finlay-McLennan; *D:* Michael Rhodes; *M:* Ron Ramin. **TV**

Chrome and Hot Leather ♪½ **1971 (PG)** A Green Beret is out for revenge after vicious bikers kill his fiance. Conventional, tasteless genre fare notable only as

Gaye's first film. **91m/C VHS.** William Smith, Tony Young, Michael Haynes, Peter Brown, Marvin Gaye, Michael Stearns, Kathrine Baumann, Wes Bishop, Herbert Jeffries; ***D:*** Lee Frost.

Chrome Soldiers **1992** Five Vietnam veterans come together to avenge a friend's murder in a town controlled by drug dealers. Busey, as the murdered man's brother, leads the "Chrome Soldiers" in their battle to expose the killers and end local corruption. **92m/C VHS.** Gary Busey, Ray Sharkey, William Atherton, Yaphet Kotto, Nicholas Guest, Kim Robillard, Norman Skaggs, D. David Morin; ***D:*** Thomas J. Wright; ***W:*** Nick Randall; ***C:*** Billy Dickson.

Chronicle of a Boy Alone *Chronicle of a Lonely Child; Cronica de un Nino Solo* **1964** Eleven-year-old Polin is abandoned by his family and sent to live in a state-run orphanage where well-meaning administrators succeed in destroying the childrens' lives. Spanish with subtitles. **86m/C VHS.** *AR* Oscar Espindola, Beto Gianola, Victoriano Moreira, Leonardo Favio; ***D:*** Leonardo Favio; ***W:*** Leonardo Favio; ***C:*** Ignacio Souto.

Chronicle of a Disappearance **1996** Born in Nazareth in 1960, Suleiman has been living in New York in self-imposed exile for 12 years. He finally decides to return to the Middle East and explore his roots as a Palestinian and the problems that political instability have caused his people and their identity. Arabic with subtitles. **88m/C VHS.** Elia Suleiman; ***D:*** Elia Suleiman; ***W:*** Elia Suleiman; ***C:*** Marc Andre Batigne.

The Chronicles of Narnia **1989** Exceptional BBC production of the C.S. Lewis fantasy about four brave children who battle evil in a mythical land where the animals talk and strange creatures roam the countryside. In three volumes; aired on PBS as part of the "Wonderworks" family movie series. **180m/C VHS.** *GB* Barbara Kellerman, Jeffery S. (Jeff) Perry, Richard Dempsey, Sophie Cook, Jonathan Scott, Sophie Wilcox, David Thwaites, Tom Baker; ***D:*** Alex Kirby.

Chu Chu & the Philly Flash woof! **1981 (PG)** A has-been baseball player and a lame dance teacher meet while hustling the same corner; he sells hot watches, she's a one-woman band. A briefcase full of government secrets soon involves them with the feds, the mob, and a motley collection of back-alley bums. Insipid comedy is actually worse than its title, with Burnett and Arkin both trying too hard. Supporters Warden, Aiello, and Glover don't help either. **102m/C VHS.** Alan Arkin, Carol Burnett, Jack Warden, Danny Aiello, Ruth Buzzi, Danny Glover, Lou Jacobi; ***D:*** David Lowell Rich; ***W:*** Barbara Dana.

Chuck & Buck ½ **2000 (R)** In the mood for a pseudo-comedy about a stalking homosexual idiot man-child? Buck (White), the childhood friend from hell, attempts to latch back onto former pal Chuck (Chris Weitz) after a reunion at the funeral of Buck's mother. Apparently, Chuck and Buck shared a furtive moment of experimental sexuality as kids, and Buck never advanced emotionally beyond this point. So when Chuck (who, being an adult, prefers being called Charles) and his fiancee Carlyn (Colt) casually invite Buck to their home in L.A., he drops everything in order to rekindle his imagined affair with the poor guy. After Chuck tells him to stay away, Buck writes and produces an uncomfortably transparent play titled "Hank & Frank" about their relationship, hiring a Chuck look-alike (Paul Weitz, brother of the lead) as his love interest. White manages to keep a sense of innocence in portraying Buck, but the overwhelming creepiness of the plot overrides any sense of subtlety in the performances. **99m/C VHS, DVD, Wide.** Mike White, Chris Weitz, Paul Weitz, Lupe Ontiveros, Paul Sand, Beth Colt, Maya Rudolph, Mary Wigmore, Gino Buccola; ***D:*** Miguel Arteta; ***W:*** Mike White; ***C:*** Chuy Chavez; ***M:*** Joey Waronker. Natl. Bd. of Review '00: Support. Actress (Ontiveros).

Chuck Berry: Hail! Hail! Rock 'n' Roll **1987 (PG)** Engaging, energetic portrait of one of rock's founding fathers, via interviews, behind-the-scenes footage and performance clips of Berry at 60. Songs featured: "Johnny B. Goode," "Roll Over Beethoven," "Maybelline," and more. Appearances by Eric Clapton, Etta James, John and Julian Lennon, Roy Orbison, Linda Ronstadt, Bo Diddley and Bruce Springsteen among others. **121m/C VHS.** Chuck Berry, Eric Clapton, Etta James, Robert Cray, Julian Lennon, Keith Richards, Linda Ronstadt, John Lennon, Roy Orbison, Bo Diddley, Jerry Lee Lewis, Bruce Springsteen, Kareem Abdul-Jabbar; ***D:*** Taylor Hackford.

C.H.U.D. woof! **1984 (R)** Cannibalistic Humanoid Underground Dwellers are what it's about. Exposed to toxic wastes, a race of flesh-craving, sewer-dwelling monstrosities goes food shopping on the streets of New York. Don't be fooled by the presence of real actors, this one is inexcusable. Followed by a sequel. **90m/C VHS, DVD, Wide.** John Heard, Daniel Stern, Christopher Curry, Kim Greist, John Goodman, Jay Thomas, Eddie Jones, Sam McMurray, Justin Hall, Cordis Heard, Michael O'Hare, Vic Polizos; ***D:*** Douglas Cheek; ***W:*** Parnell Hall; ***C:*** Peter Stein; ***M:*** David A. Hughes.

C.H.U.D. 2: Bud the Chud woof! **1989 (R)** Asinine teens steal a corpse that is actually a zombie cannibal capable of passing the trait to anyone it bites (but doesn't eat entirely). Graham excels as the kidnapped corpse, but this horror-comedy is consistently repellent. Contains one of Jagger's few film appearances, a situation of no despair. **84m/C VHS.** Brian Robbins, Bill Calvert, Gerrit Graham, Tricia Leigh Fisher, Bianca Jagger, Robert Vaughn, Larry Cedar; ***D:*** David Irving.

Chuka ½ **1967** A gunfighter tries to resolve a conflict between Indians and unlikeable troops while simultaneously romancing the fort's beautiful occupant. Pedestrian western features convincing playing from the always reliable Taylor. **105m/C VHS.** Rod Taylor, Ernest Borgnine, John Mills, Luciana Paluzzi, James Whitmore, Angela Dorian, Louis Hayward, Michael Cole, Hugh Reilly; ***D:*** Gordon Douglas.

A Chump at Oxford ½ **1940** Two street cleaners foil a bank robbery and receive an all-expenses-paid education at Oxford as their reward. This loopy Laurel and Hardy vehicle provides regular amusement in detailing the duo's exploits in Britain. **63m/B VHS.** Stan Laurel, Oliver Hardy, James Finlayson, Wilfrid Lucas, Peter Cushing, Charlie Hall; ***D:*** Alfred Goulding.

Chungking Express *Hong Kong Express; Chongqing Senlin* **1995 (PG-13)** Director Kar-wai presents two quirky tales of loneliness and love, loosely linked by a snack bar in the tourist section of Hong Kong. Cops and drugs are still a part of the storyline, but this is no chop-socky action movie. Both male protagonists are cops, identified only by their badge numbers, who have recently been dumped by their girlfriends. One has a fixation for canned pineapple and expiration dates, the other talks to the inanimate objects in his apartment. The women they eventually fall for are a blonde-wigged heroin dealer and a shy counter girl who bops to "California Dreaming" after breaking in and cleaning the cop's apartment without his knowledge. Shot commando-style in 23 days during the hiatus of Wong's "Ashes of Time" without permits or professional lighting. The high energy is reflected in the pacing and acting performances. Chosen by Quentin Tarantino as the first release of his Miramax-backed Rolling Thunder imprint. **102m/C VHS.** *HK* Brigitte (Lin Chinag-hsia) Lin, Takeshi Kaneshiro, Tony Leung Chiu-Wai, Faye Wang, Valerie Chow, Piggy Chan; ***D:*** Wong Kar-Wai; ***W:*** Wong Kar-Wai; ***C:*** Christopher Doyle, Lau Wai-Keung; ***M:*** Frankie Chan, Roel A. Garcia.

Chunhyang ½ **2000** Romance based on a 13th-century folktale of forbidden love. Chunhyang (Lee) is the educated daughter of a courtesan who is expected to be a plaything for wealthy gentlemen. Instead, she falls in love and secretly marries the higher-caste Mongryong (Cho), who leaves his bride to complete his studies in Seoul. Chunhyang is soon beset by advances from the new governor and, when she refuses, he sentences her to death. Korean with subtitles. **120m/C VHS, DVD, Wide.** *KN* Hyo Jung Lee, Seung Woo Cho, Jung Hun Lee, Sung Nyu Kim; ***D:*** Kwon Taek Im; ***W:*** Myoung Kon Kim; ***C:*** Il Sung Jung; ***M:*** Jung Gil Kim.

The Church *La Chiesa* **1998** Italian thrill-meister Argento scripted and produced this ecclesiastical gorefest. A gargoyle-glutted gothic cathedral which happens to stand on the site of a gruesome mass murder is renovated, and the kirk-cleaning turns into a special-effects loaded demonic epiphany. It'll have you muttering your pater noster. Unrated, it's also available in an R-rated version. **102m/C VHS, DVD, Wide.** *IT* Tomas Arana, Hugh Quarshie, Feodor Chaliapin Jr., Barbara Cupisti, Antonella Vitale, Asia Argento; ***D:*** Michele (Michael) Soavi; ***W:*** Dario Argento, Michele (Michael) Soavi, Franco Ferrini; ***C:*** Renato Tafuri; ***M:*** Keith Emerson.

Churchill and the Generals **1981** The true story of how Winston Churchill led England away from the bleak Dunkirk battle and rallied the Allied generals to a D-Day victory. Based upon Churchill's memoirs. **180m/C VHS.** Timothy West, Joseph Cotten, Arthur Hill, Eric Porter, Richard Dysart; ***D:*** Alan Gibson; ***Nar:*** Eric Sevareid.

Chutney Popcorn ½ **1999** Amusing and touching comedy about family ties and cultural differences. Reena (Ganatra) is a New York photographer from a very traditional East Indian immigrant family. Her mother Meenu (Jaffrey) is already upset because her daughter is a lesbian but Reena has a chance to get in her good graces when she impulsively agrees to act as a surrogate for her married older sister Sarita (Jaffrey), who is infertile. But the plan upsets Reena's girlfriend Lisa (Hennessy) and then Sarita has her own change of heart, even though Reena is now pregnant. **93m/C VHS, DVD.** Nisha Ganatra, Jill(ian) Hennessey, Madhur Jaffrey, Sakina Jaffrey, Nicholas Chinlund, Cara Buono, Ajay Naidu, Priscilla Lopez; ***D:*** Nisha Ganatra; ***W:*** Susan Carnival, Nisha Ganatra; ***C:*** Erin King; ***M:*** Karsh Kale.

C.I.A.: Code Name Alexa ½ **1992 (R)** Alexa is the beautiful and deadly protege of Victor, who heads an international crime ring. A CIA agent decides the best way to stop Victor is to turn Alexa against her boss. Lots of action and violence. **93m/C VHS.** Kathleen Kinmont, Lorenzo Lamas, Alex Cord, O.J. Simpson, Stephen Quadros, Pamela Dixon, Michael Smith; ***D:*** Joseph Merhi.

C.I.A. 2: Target Alexa **1994** When a nuclear guidance system is stolen from a government facility CIA agent Mark Graver (Lamas) reteams with former terrorist Alexa (Kinmont) to retrieve the system from international terrorist Franz Klug (Savage). Complicating things are ex-CIA agent Straker (Ryan), who now heads his own commando army and wants to sell the device to the highest bidder. **90m/C VHS.** Lorenzo Lamas, Kathleen Kinmont, John Savage, John P. Ryan, Pamela Dixon, Larry Manetti; ***D:*** Lorenzo Lamas; ***W:*** Michael January.

Ciao Federico! Fellini Directs Satyricon **1969** A documentary of Frederico Fellini's filming of Petronius' "Satyricon." Portrays the Italian filmmaker's larger-than-life directorial approach and relationship with his actors. In English and Italian, with English subtitles. **60m/C VHS.** Federico Fellini, Martin Potter, Hiram Keller, Roman Polanski, Sharon Tate; ***D:*** Gideon Bachmann.

Ciao, Professore! ½ *Io Speriamo Che Me La Cavo* **1994 (R)** Okay comedy about conventional teacher Marco Sperelli (Villaggio), from northern Italy, who is mistakenly sent to a ramshackle village school in Naples, populated by poor, wily, unruly students. Both, of course, manage to learn from each other. Humor derived from northern vs. southern Italian culture clash may bypass most viewers although the cast of amateur kid actors provide charm. Italian with subtitles. **91m/C VHS.** *IT* Paolo Villaggio, Isa Danieli, Ciro Esposito; ***D:*** Lina Wertmuller; ***W:*** Leonardo Benvenuti, Piero De Bernardi, Alessandro Bencivenni, Domenico Saverni, Lina Wertmuller.

The Cider House Rules **1999 (PG-13)** Homer Wells (Maguire) grows up in the St. Clouds, Maine orphanage, with his mentor, Dr. Larch (Caine), teaching Homer everything about caring for the children, delivering babies, and performing (illegal) abortions (which Homer refuses to do). But, in 1943, when flyboy Wally (Rudd) shows up with girlfriend Candy (Theron), Homer gets his chance to see something of the world. He winds up as an apple picker and, when Wally returns to the war, Candy's new beau. But Homer has a lot of lessons to learn about making—and living by—your own rules. Irving wrote his first screenplay from his novel. Old-fashioned, coming of age story with excellent performances. **125m/C VHS, DVD, Wide.** Evan Dexter Parke, Tobey Maguire, Charlize Theron, Michael Caine, Delroy Lindo, Paul Rudd, Erykah Badu, Kathy Baker, Jane Alexander, Kieran Culkin, Kate Nelligan, K. Todd Freeman, Heavy D, J.K. Simmons, Erik Per Sullivan; ***Cameos:*** John Irving; ***D:*** Lasse Hallstrom; ***W:*** John Irving; ***C:*** Oliver Stapleton; ***M:*** Rachel Portman. Oscars '99: Adapt. Screenplay, Support. Actor (Caine); Screen Actors Guild '99: Support. Actor (Caine).

Cider with Rosie ½ **1999** Adaptation of Laurie Lee's 1959 story about his Cotswolds childhood. Set in 1918, in the Slad Valley, disorganized Annie Lee (Stevenson) has been left to raise nine children on her own. Laurie's childhood consists of school, church, village festivals, eccentric relations and neighbors, and the usual childhood tribulations. Lee himself provided narration before his death at 82 in 1997. **120m/C VHS.** *GB* Juliet Stevenson, Emily Mortimer, Joe Roberts, Dashiell Reece, David Troughton, Robert Lang, Hugh Lloyd; ***D:*** Charles Beeson; ***W:*** John Mortimer; ***M:*** Geoffrey Burgon. **TV**

The Cigarette Girl of Mosselprom ½ **1924** A lowly cigarette girl is thrust into the world of moviemaking in this sharp Russian satire. Silent with orchestral score. **78m/B VHS.** *RU* ***D:*** Yuri Zhelyabuzhsky.

Cimarron **1931** Hopelessly overblown saga of an American frontier family from 1890 to 1915. Hokey, cliched, with only sporadic liveliness. How did this one win an Oscar? An adaptation of Edna Ferber's novel, featuring Dunne in an early major role. Remade in 1960. **130m/B VHS.** Richard Dix, Irene Dunne, Estelle Taylor, Nance O'Neil, William "Buster" Collier Jr., Roscoe Ates, George E. Stone, Stanley Fields, Edna May Oliver, Dennis O'Keefe; ***D:*** Wesley Ruggles; ***M:*** Max Steiner. Oscars '31: Adapt. Screenplay, Picture.

Cimarron ½ **1960** Director Mann's remake of the 1931 Academy Award-winning film about frontier life in Oklahoma. This version features Ford as a carefree survivor of the Old West with an extreme case of wanderlust. Schell plays his civilizing wife. Based on Edna Ferber's novel. **140m/C VHS, Wide.** Glenn Ford, Maria Schell, Anne Baxter, Arthur O'Connell, Russ Tamblyn, Mercedes McCambridge, Vic Morrow, Robert Keith, Charles McGraw; ***D:*** Anthony Mann; ***W:*** Arnold Schulman; ***M:*** Franz Waxman.

The Cincinnati Kid ½ **1965** Gambler "The Cincinnati Kid" (McQueen) is hustling card games in New Orleans when he comes up against the veteran cardshark Lancey Howard (Robinson). During a marathon card game, Kid notices dealer Shooter (Malden) is throwing the game his way but he only wants to win fair and square. Conventional fare, with Ann-Margaret around for some conventional romance, helped along by serviceable performances and some stunning cinematography. **104m/C VHS.** Steve McQueen, Edward G. Robinson, Ann-Margret, Tuesday Weld, Karl Malden, Joan Blondell, Rip Torn, Jack Weston, Cab Calloway; ***D:*** Norman Jewison; ***W:*** Ring Lardner Jr., Terry Southern; ***C:*** Philip Lathrop; ***M:*** Lalo Schifrin. Natl. Bd. of Review '65: Support. Actress (Blondell).

Cinderella ✓✓✓½ **1950** Classic Disney animated fairytale about the slighted beauty who outshines her evil stepsisters at a royal ball, then returns to her grim existence before the handsome prince finds her again. Engaging film, with a wicked stepmother, kindly fairy godmother, and singing mice. ♫Cinderella; Bibbidy-Bobbidi-Boo; So This Is Love; A Dream Is a Wish Your Heart Makes; The Work Song; Oh Sing, Sweet Nightingale. **76m/C VHS.** ***D:*** Wilfred Jackson; ***V:*** Ilene Woods, William Phipps, Verna Felton, James MacDonald. Venice Film Fest. '50: Special Jury Prize.

Cinderella ✓✓½ **1964** Charming musical version of the fairy tale as scored by Rodgers and Hammerstein. Warren is lovely as Cinderella, Damon is a handsome prince, and Holm is a perfect fairy godmother. **83m/C VHS, DVD.** Lesley Ann Warren, Ginger Rogers, Walter Pidgeon, Stuart Damon, Celeste Holm; ***D:*** Charles S. Dubin; ***W:*** Joseph Schrank; ***M:*** Richard Rodgers, Oscar Hammerstein. **TV**

Cinderella **1984** From the "Faerie Tale Theatre" comes the classic tale of a poor girl who goes to a ball to meet the man of her dreams, despite her nasty stepmother and stepsisters. **60m/C VHS.** Jennifer Beals, Jean Stapleton, Matthew Broderick, Eve Arden; ***D:*** Mark Cullingham. **CABLE**

Cinderella ✓✓½ *Rodgers & Hammerstein's Cinderella* **1997** Disney does some multiracial casting in this lavish, latest TV version of the fairytale. Norwood is sweetly sincere in the title role, with Houston as her diva-like Fairy Godmother. Peters' camps as wicked stepmama, Goldberg's the Prince's mother, and the Prince is handsome newcomer Montalban. And Alexander gets the role of comic relief as the princely confidante, Lionel. The Rodgers and Hammerstein score, written for the 1957 TV version, has been augmented with other Richard Rodgers tunes. ♫The Sweetest Sounds; Impossible; Do I Love You Because You're Beautiful?; Falling in Love with Love. **92m/C VHS, DVD.** Brandy Norwood, Whitney Houston, Paolo Montalban, Jason Alexander, Bernadette Peters, Whoopi Goldberg, Victor Garber; ***D:*** Robert Iscove; ***W:*** Robert Freedman; ***M:*** Richard Rodgers, Oscar Hammerstein. **TV**

Cinderella Liberty ✓✓✓ **1973 (R)** Bittersweet romance in which a kindly sailor falls for a brash hooker with a son. Sometimes funny, sometimes moving, with sometimes crude direction overcome by truly compelling performances from Caan and Mason. Story written by Darryl Ponicsan from his novel. **117m/C VHS.** James Caan, Marsha Mason, Eli Wallach, Kirk Calloway, Burt Young, Bruce Kirby, Dabney Coleman, Sally Kirkland; ***D:*** Mark Rydell; ***W:*** Darryl Ponicsan; ***C:*** Vilmos Zsigmond; ***M:*** John Williams. Golden Globes '74: Actress—Drama (Mason).

Cinderella 2000 ✓✓ **1978 (R)** Softcore musical version of the classic fairy tale. It's the year 2047 and sex is outlawed, except by computer. Strains of Sugarman's score, including "Doin' Without" and "We All Need Love," set the stage for Erhardt's Cinderella to meet her Prince Charming at that conventional single prince romance venue, a sex orgy. Trouble is, it wasn't a shoe Cinderella lost before she fled, and the charming one must interface, as it were, with the local pretenders to the throne in order to find his lost princess. Touching. **86m/C VHS.** Catharine Erhardt, Jay B. Larson, Vaughn Armstrong; ***D:*** Al Adamson; ***M:*** Sparky Sugarman.

Cinderfella ✓✓½ **1960** This twist on the classic children's fairy tale features Lewis as the hapless buffoon guided by his fairy godfather. Somewhat overdone, with extended talking sequences and gratuitous musical interludes. Lewis, though, mugs effectively. **88m/C VHS.** Jerry Lewis, Ed Wynn, Judith Anderson, Anna Maria Alberghetti, Henry Silva, Count Basie, Robert Hutton; ***D:*** Frank Tashlin; ***W:*** Frank Tashlin.

Cinema Paradiso ✓✓✓ *Nuovo Cinema Paradiso* **1988** Memoir of a boy's life working at a movie theatre in small-town Italy after WWII. Film aspires to both majestic sweep and stirring poignancy, but only occasionally hits its target. Still manages to move the viewer, and it features a suitably low-key performance by the masterful Noiret. Autobiographically inspired script written by Tornatore. The version shown in America is approximately a half-hour shorter than the original Italian form. **123m/C VHS, DVD, 8mm.** *IT* Philippe Noiret, Jacques Perrin, Salvatore Cascio, Marco Leonardi, Agnes Nano, Leopoldo Trieste; ***D:*** Giuseppe Tornatore; ***W:*** Giuseppe Tornatore; ***C:*** Basco Giurato; ***M:*** Ennio Morricone. Oscars '89: Foreign Film; British Acad. '90: Actor (Noiret), Foreign Film, Orig. Screenplay, Support. Actor (Cascio); Cannes '89: Grand Jury Prize; Golden Globes '90: Foreign Film.

The Circle ✓✓ *Dayereh* **2000** Arezou (Almani) and Nargess (Mamizadeh) have just been released from an Iranian prison. Arezou apparently prostitutes herself (you don't see anything) in order to get the money for Nargess to travel back to her village, only because of Iranian law the girl can't travel without permission from a male. Nargress leads to two other former inmates who suffer because of their female identity and eventually everything circles back to the prison again. The film was banned in Iran because it makes the ceaseless difficulties of being born female in such a society very clear. Farsi with subtitles. **91m/C VHS, DVD, Wide.** *IA* Mariam Palvin Almani, Nargess Mamizadeh, Fereshteh Sadr Orfani, Fatemeh Naghavi, Monir Arab, Elham Saboktakin, Mojhan Faramarzi; ***D:*** Jafar Panahi; ***W:*** Kambozia Partovi; ***C:*** Bahram Badakhshami. Venice Film Fest. '00: Film.

Circle Canyon ✓ **1933** In a remote canyon two opposing outlaw gangs battle to the death. **48m/B VHS.** Buddy Roosevelt, Allen Holbrook, Clyde McClary, Ernest Scott, John Tyke, Bob Williamson; ***D:*** Victor Adamson; ***W:*** Burl R. Tuttle.

Circle Man ✓ **1987** A made-for-video action drama about the underground sporting phenomenon, bare-knuckle fighting. **90m/C VHS.** William Sanderson.

Circle of Death ✓½ **1936** Average formula western about a white boy who is raised as an Indian. Later he falls in love with a white girl and leaves the tribe. **55m/B VHS.** Monte Montana, Yakima Canutt, Henry Hall, Ben (Benny) Corbett; ***D:*** J. Frank Glendon; ***W:*** Roy Claire; ***C:*** James Diamond.

Circle of Deceit ✓✓½ **1994** SAS officer John Neil (Waterman) is called back into service in Belfast two years after his wife and child were killed by terrorists. His assignment is to assume the identity of recently deceased IRA soldier Jackie O'Connell and learn about an arms shipment headed for Northern Ireland. But can his disguise hold against local IRA commander Liam McAuley (Vaughan)? Made for British TV. **103m/C VHS.** *GB* Dennis Waterman, Peter Vaughan, Derek Jacobi, Clare Higgins; ***W:*** Jean-Claude Carriere. **TV**

Circle of Fear ✓½ **1989 (R)** An ex-hitman who worked for the Mob upends the black market for sex and drugs in the Philippines while looking for his daughter who was sold into a sex slave ring. El cheapo exploiter. **90m/C VHS.** *PH* Patrick Dollaghan, Welsey Pfenning, Joey Aresco, Vernon Wells; ***D:*** Clark Henderson.

Circle of Friends ✓✓½ **1994 (PG-13)** Nostalgic Irish coming-of-ager focuses on three friends and the trials and tribulations they face when hearts and hormones conflict with a strict Catholic upbringing. Small-town teenager Benny (Driver), overweight and slightly awkward, reunites with her friends at university in Dublin. Benny begins a romance with gentle, doe-eyed Jack Foley (O'Donnell) and endures the humorous but sometimes painful passage from adolescence to womanhood. Sentimental moments can be too sticky-sweet at times, but humor, disappointment, and small triumphs are convincingly portrayed, offering a universal appeal. Adapted from the Maeve Binchy novel. **96m/C VHS, DVD.** Chris O'Donnell, Minnie Driver, Geraldine O'Rawe, Saffron Burrows, Colin Firth, Alan Cumming, Aidan Gillen; ***D:*** Pat O'Connor; ***W:*** Andrew Davies; ***C:*** Kenneth Macmillan; ***M:*** Michael Kamen.

Circle of Iron ✓✓½ *The Silent Flute* **1978 (R)** Plenty of action and martial arts combat abound in this story of one man's eternal quest for truth. Originally co-written by and intended for Bruce Lee as a rib-crunching vehicle, until he died before production began and was replaced by Kung-Fu Carradine. A cut above most chopsocky actioners. Filmed in Israel. **102m/C VHS.** *GB* Jeff Cooper, David Carradine, Roddy McDowall, Eli Wallach, Christopher Lee; ***D:*** Richard Moore; ***W:*** Bruce Lee, James Coburn, Stirling Silliphant; ***M:*** Bruce Smeaton.

Circle of Love ✓✓ **1964** Episodic melodrama drifts from romance to romance in contemporary Paris. A somewhat pretentious remake of Ophuls classic "La Ronde," which was in turn adapted from Arthur Schnitzler's play. Credible performers are undone by Vadim's strained direction. **110m/C VHS.** *FR* Jane Fonda, Francine Berge, Marie DuBois, Jean-Claude Brialy, Catherine Spaak, Claude Giraud; ***D:*** Roger Vadim; ***W:*** Jean Anouilh.

Circle of Passion ✓✓ *Never Ever* **1997 (R)** Devoted hubby Thomas Murray (Finch) works for his father-in-law at a London bank. But when Thomas is transferred to Paris and his socialite wife (March) refuses to go with him, devotion falls by the wayside when he falls in love with the free-spirited Katherine (Bonnaire). Now Thomas has to choose between money and love. **94m/C VHS.** Charles Finch, Sandrine Bonnaire, Jane March, Julian Sands, James Fox; ***D:*** Charles Finch.

Circle of Power ✓½ *Brainwash; The Naked Weekend; Mystique* **1983 (R)** Mimieux must cure various business men of their problems (homosexuality, alcoholism and the like) to help them become better executives. Intriguing and somewhat disturbing, supposedly based on a true story. **103m/C VHS.** *GB* Yvette Mimieux, John Considine, Terence Knox, Cindy Pickett, Christopher Allport; ***D:*** Bobby Roth; ***W:*** Stephen F. Bello; ***C:*** Alfonso Beato.

Circle of Two ✓✓ **1980 (PG)** A platonic friendship between an aging artist and a young girl is misunderstood by others. Well, of course they do meet in a porno theatre. Pedestrian fare adapted from a story by Marie Therese Baird. **90m/C VHS.** *CA* Richard Burton, Tatum O'Neal, Kate Reid; ***D:*** Jules Dassin.

Circonstances Attenuantes ✓✓½ *Extenuating Circumstances* **1936** French classic about a retired judge who moves to the outskirts of Paris with his wife and attempts to convert the locals from disreputable to law-abiding citizens. Also available dubbed. **90m/B VHS.** *FR* Michel Simon, Arletty; ***D:*** Jean Boyer.

Circuit ✓½ **2002** Sexual hedonism is alive and well in West Hollywood in this would-be cautionary tale of a small town Midwesterner who comes to the big, bad city. John (Drahos) gets introduced to the party circuit of casual gay sex and lots of drugs but vows to keep his distance. This doesn't last and John sinks ever deeper into the self-destructive pursuit of pleasure. **90m/C VHS.** Jonathan Wade Drahos, Daniel Kucan, Andre Khabbazi, Brian Lane Green, Kiersten Warren, William Katt; ***D:*** Dirk Shafer; ***W:*** Dirk Shafer, Gregory Hinton; ***C:*** Joaquin Sedilb; ***M:*** Tony Moran.

Circuit Breaker ✓½ **1996 (R)** Traveling repairman Foster Carver (Bernsen) and his wife (Harris) encounter a broken-down spaceship with a lone survivor (Grieco). Then they discover he's a cyborg trying to create a new breed of humans. It's "Dead Calm" in space without the talent or suspense and with a whiny would-be heroine and some boring action sequences. **88m/C VHS.** Richard Grieco, Corbin Bernsen, Lara Harris, Edie McClurg; ***D:*** Victoria Muspratt; ***W:*** Victoria Muspratt.

Circuitry Man ✓✓½ **1990 (R)** Post-apocolyptic saga of future American life as a woman tries to deliver a briefcase full of computer chips to the underground Big Apple. Along the way she runs into Plughead, a humanoid with electrical outlets that allow him to "plug in" to other people's fantasies. Intelligent retelling of a standard tale with an inspired soundtrack by Deborah Holland. Witty and original. **85m/C VHS, DVD, Wide.** Jim Metzler, Dana Wheeler-Nicholson, Lu Leonard, Vernon Wells, Barbara Alyn Woods, Dennis Christopher; ***D:*** Steven Lovy; ***W:*** Robert Lovy, Steven Lovy; ***C:*** Jamie Thompson; ***M:*** Deborah Holland.

Circumstances Unknown ✓½ **1995 (R)** Paul Kinsey (Nelson) is a serial killer who drowns his victims, including a woman who happens to be the fiance of his friend Tim (Moses). Years later, Tim has married and Paul decides to stalk him and wife Deena (Glasser). Too many loose ends since you never know why Paul kills. Based on the novel by Jonellen Heckler. **91m/C VHS.** Judd Nelson, Isabel Glasser, William R. Moses; ***D:*** Robert Lewis; ***W:*** Thomas Hood, Emily Shoemaker; ***C:*** Bruce Worrall.

Circumstantial Evidence ✓✓ **1935** Newspaper reporter (Chandler) goes to extremes for a story and nearly dies as a result. Chandler sets it up to look like he's murdered a colleague, and he's tried and convicted on, you guessed it, circumstantial evidence. The colleague's then supposed to come forward but there's a problem. **69m/B VHS.** Chick Chandler, Shirley Grey, Dorothy Revier, Arthur Vinton; ***D:*** Charles Lamont; ***W:*** Ewart Adamson.

The Circus ✓✓✓½ **1919** Classic comedy silent details the tramp's exploits as a member of a traveling circus, including a romance with the bareback rider. Hilarious, less sentimental than most of Chaplin's feature films. Chaplin won a special Academy Award for "versatility and genius in writing, acting, directing and producing" for this one. Outrageous final scenes. **105m/B VHS, DVD.** Charlie Chaplin, Merna Kennedy, Allan Garcia; ***D:*** Charlie Chaplin; ***W:*** Charlie Chaplin; ***C:*** Roland H. Totheroh; ***M:*** Charlie Chaplin.

Circus ✓✓ **2000 (R)** British gambler/con man Leo Garfield (Hannah) is being pressured by gang boss Bruno (Conley) to manage his Brighton casino. But Leo and his equally shady American wife Lily (Janssen) have some double-crossing ideas of their own, involving Bruno's brother Caspar (Burfield), his accountant Julius (Stormare), Julius' unfaithful wife Gloria (Donohue), and well, things get even more complicated but the film doesn't have the flair to pull all the plots off. **95m/C VHS, DVD, Wide.** *GB* John Hannah, Famke Janssen, Peter Stormare, Brian Conley, Eddie Izzard, Fred Ward, Amanda Donohoe, Ian Burfield, Tommy (Tiny) Lister, Neil Stuke; ***D:*** Rob Walker; ***W:*** David Logan; ***C:*** Ben Seresin; ***M:*** Simon Boswell.

Circus Angel ✓✓✓ **1965** The renowned director of "The Red Balloon" creates a fantasy about a klutzy burglar transformed by a found nightgown into an angel. He begins to serve the dreams and actions of an odd lot of characters. Subtitled in English. **80m/B VHS.** *FR* Philippe Avron, Mirielle Negre; ***D:*** Albert Lamorisse.

Circus of Fear ✓½ *Psycho-Circus* **1967** A travelling troupe is stalked by a murderer. The unedited version is occasionally scary. **92m/C VHS.** *GB GE* Christopher Lee, Leo Genn, Anthony Newlands, Heinz Drache, Eddi Arent, Klaus Kinski, Margaret Lee, Suzy Kendall; ***D:*** John Llewellyn Moxey.

Circus of Horrors ✓✓½ **1960** Nip 'n' tuck horror about a plastic surgeon who takes over a circus to escape a disfigured patient bent on revenge. The circus is staffed by former patients with new faces who, one by one, fall victim in fine circus style. A bloody one-ring extravaganza. **92m/C VHS, DVD, Wide.** *GB* Donald Pleasence, Anton Diffring, Erika Remberg, Yvonne Monlaur, Jane Hylton, Kenneth Griffith, Colette Wilde, Charla Challoner; ***D:*** Sidney Hayers; ***W:*** George L. Baxt; ***C:*** Douglas Slocombe; ***M:*** Muir Mathieson.

Circus World ✓✓½ *The Magnificent Showman* **1964** A circus boss tries to navigate a reckless, romancing crew through a European tour while searching for aerialist he loved 15 years before and whose daughter he has reared. Too long and too familiar, but nonetheless well done with an excellent finale. **132m/C VHS, Wide.** John Wayne, Rita Hayworth, Claudia Cardinale, Lloyd Nolan, Richard Conte; ***D:*** Henry Hathaway; ***W:***

Ben Hecht, James Edward Grant, Julian Zimet; ***C:*** Jack Hildyard. Golden Globes '65: Song ("Circus World").

The Cisco Kid 🦴🦴½ **1994** The Cisco Kid and his sidekick Pancho went from O. Henry's short story, to silent movies, talkies, a '50s TV series, and now this made for TV movie. Benito Juarez is leading an uprising to overthrow the French-backed Emperor Maximilian in 1867 Mexico. Cisco's (Smits) supplying the rebels with guns while carrying on romantic escapades (watch for the tango). Meanwhile, true-believer Pancho tries to convince his friend to become a revolutionary. Lighthearted with pedestrian action shots. Filmed on location in Mexico. **96m/C VHS.** Jimmy Smits, Richard "Cheech" Marin, Sadie Frost, Tim Thomerson, Bruce Payne; ***D:*** Luis Valdez; ***W:*** Michael Kane, Luis Valdez. **TV**

The Citadel 🦴🦴🦴 **1938** From the A.J. Cronin novel, the intelligent and honest Hollywood drama about a young British doctor who is morally corrupted by his move from a poor mining village to a well-off practice treating wealthy hypochondriacs. Somewhat hokey but still consistently entertaining, with Donat fine in the lead. **114m/C VHS.** *GB* Robert Donat, Rosalind Russell, Rex Harrison, Ralph Richardson, Emlyn Williams, Penelope Dudley Ward; ***D:*** King Vidor; ***C:*** Harry Stradling Sr. N.Y. Film Critics '38: Film.

Citizen Cohn 🦴🦴 **1992 (R)** An appallingly fascinating look at a human monster. Told in hallucinatory flashbacks, as he lays dying from AIDS, Roy Cohn is a lawyer and power broker, probably best-remembered as the malevolent sidekick to Communist-hunting Senator Joseph McCarthy. But his contempt also extended to antisemitism and gay-bashing (though Cohn was both homosexual and Jewish), and his past comes, literally, back to haunt him. Woods does an exceptional job in bringing this sociopathic heel to wretched life. Adapted from the biography by Nicholas von Hoffman. **112m/C VHS, DVD, Wide.** James Woods, Joe Don Baker, Joseph Bologna, Ed Flanders, Frederic Forrest, Lee Grant, Pat Hingle; ***D:*** Frank Pierson; ***W:*** David Franzoni; ***C:*** Paul Elliott. **CABLE**

Citizen Kane 🦴🦴🦴🦴 **1941** Extraordinary film is an American tragedy of a newspaper tycoon (based loosely on William Randolph Hearst) from his humble beginnings to the solitude of his final years. One of the greatest films ever made—a stunning tour-de-force in virtually every aspect, from the fragmented narration to breathtaking, deep-focus cinematography; from a vivid soundtrack to fabulous ensemble acting. Welles was only 25 when he co-wrote, directed, and starred in this masterpiece. Watch for Ladd and O'Connell as reporters. **119m/B VHS, DVD.** Orson Welles, Joseph Cotten, Everett Sloane, Dorothy Comingore, Ruth Warrick, George Coulouris, Ray Collins, William Alland, Paul Stewart, Erskine Sanford, Agnes Moorehead, Alan Ladd, Gus Schilling, Philip Van Zandt, Harry Shannon, Sonny Bupp, Arthur O'Connell; ***D:*** Orson Welles; ***W:*** Orson Welles, Herman J. Mankiewicz; ***C:*** Gregg Toland; ***M:*** Bernard Herrmann. Oscars '41: Orig. Screenplay; AFI '98: Top 100, Natl. Film Reg. '89;; N.Y. Film Critics '41: Film.

Citizen Ruth 🦴🦴½ *Precious; Meet Ruth Stoops* **1996 (R)** Glue-sniffing, pregnant Ruth Stoops (Dern) has already borne four children and been declared an unfit mother. In trouble again, Ruth's quietly told it's in her best interests to get an abortion but a couple (Smith and Place) from the pro-life community bail her out and give her a place to stay, while the group uses her as a propaganda symbol. Added to the commotion is a smarmy televangelist (Reynolds) and tough pro-choice Diane (Kurtz), who manages to get Ruth to stay with her while Ruth ineffectually tries to get some control over her wayward life. Doesn't take sides—both the pro-choice and pro-life camps are tweaked, with neither willing to compromise. **104m/C VHS.** Laura Dern, Swoosie Kurtz, Mary Kay Place, Kurtwood Smith, Kelly Preston, Burt Reynolds, M.C. Gainey, Kenneth Mars, Kathleen Noone, David Graf, Tippi Hedren, Alicia Witt, Diane Ladd; ***D:*** Alexander Payne; ***W:*** Alexander Payne, Jim Taylor; ***C:*** James Glennon; ***M:*** Rolfe Kent. Montreal World Film Fest. '95: Actress (Dern).

Citizen X 🦴🦴🦴 **1995 (R)** Based on the true story of '80s Russian serial killer Andrei Chikatilo (DeMunn) and his 52 victims. Viktor Burakov (Rea) is a beleaguered rural forensics expert who is blatantly told by party officials that the Soviet state does not have serial killers—in spite of a rising body count. His only ally is Col. Fetisov (Sutherland), who's adept at political maneuvering, but it takes the duo eight frustrating years to bring the grisly killer to justice. Fine performances highlight a literate script from Robert Cullen's book "The Killer Department." Filmed on location in Budapest, Hungary. **100m/C VHS, DVD.** Stephen Rea, Donald Sutherland, Jeffrey DeMunn, John Wood, Joss Ackland, Max von Sydow, Ralph Nossek, Imelda Staunton, Radu Amzulrescu, Czeskaw Grocholski, Ion Caramitru, Andras Balint, Tusse Silberg; ***D:*** Chris Gerolmo; ***W:*** Chris Gerolmo; ***C:*** Robert Fraisse; ***M:*** Randy Edelman. **CABLE**

Citizens Band 🦴🦴🦴 *Handle With Care* **1977 (PG)** Episodic, low-key comedy about people united by their CB use in a midwestern community. Notable performance from Clark as a soft-voiced guide for truckers passing through. Demme's first comedy is characteristically idiosyncratic. **98m/C VHS.** Paul LeMat, Candy Clark, Ann Wedgeworth, Roberts Blossom, Charles Napier, Marcia Rodd, Bruce McGill, Ed Begley Jr., Alix Elias; ***D:*** Jonathan Demme; ***W:*** Paul Brickman; ***C:*** Jordan Cronenweth; ***M:*** Bill Conti. Natl. Soc. Film Critics '77: Support. Actress (Wedgeworth).

The City 🦴 **1976** Police desperately search for a psychotic determined to kill a country singer. He shouldn't be too hard to find. **78m/C VHS.** Don Johnson, Robert Forster, Ward (Edward) Costello, Jimmy Dean, Mark Hamill; ***D;*** Harvey Hart. **TV**

The City and the Dogs 🦴🦴🦴 *La Ciudad y los Perros* **1985** A brutal, cynical adaptation of Mario Vargas Llosa's novel. A young military recruit rebels against the authority establishments around him. In Spanish with English subtitles. **135m/C VHS.** *SP* ***D:*** Francisco J. Lombardi Pery.

City Boy 🦴🦴🦴 **1993** At the turn of the century the orphaned Nick makes his way from Chicago to the Pacific Northwest in search of his natural father. He takes a job guarding Limberlost, a valuable old-growth forest, from thieves and is torn between the ideals of two new friends. His mentor Tom sees the forest as timber that will build homes and provide jobs, while Angelica sees the forest as an irreplaceable sanctuary. Filmed on location in Vancouver, British Columbia. Adaptation of "Freckles" by Gene Stratton Porter. **120m/C VHS.** *GB CA* Christian Campbell, James Brolin, Sarah Chalke, Wendel Meldrum, Christopher Bolton; ***D:*** John Kent Harrison; ***W:*** John Kent Harrison.

City for Conquest 🦴🦴🦴 **1940** Two lovers go their separate ways to pursue individual careers. He attempts to become a boxing champ, but is blinded in the ring and ends up selling newspapers. She takes a shot at a dancing career but hooks up with an unscrupulous partner. Will the ill-fated pair find happiness again? **101m/B VHS.** James Cagney, Ann Sheridan, Frank Craven, Donald Crisp, Arthur Kennedy, Frank McHugh, George Tobias, Anthony Quinn, Blanche Yurka, Elia Kazan, Bob Steele; ***D:*** Anatole Litvak; ***C:*** James Wong Howe; ***M:*** Max Steiner.

City Girl 🦴🦴½ *Our Daily Bread* **1930** Friedrich Murnau, who directed the silent vampire classic "Nosferatu," was removed from the director's chair before "City Girl" was completed and it shows. But so do the marks of his inimitable camera direction. The story concerns a Minnesota grain grower who visits the Windy City and returns with a waitress as his wife. Frustratingly inconsistent, leading you to wonder what could have been had Murnau remained behind the camera (he died the following year). Silent. **90m/B VHS.** Charles Farrell, Mary Duncan; ***D:*** F.W. Murnau.

City Hall 🦴🦴🦴 **1995 (R)** Investigating the deaths of a heroic cop, a drug dealer, and six-year old boy in a shootout, idealistic deputy mayor Cusack uncovers a web of corruption and deceit in the Big Apple. Pacino excels as charismatic mayor John Pappas by showing the crafty string-puller behind the glossy image of the modern politico. Supporting cast is also strong, including Aiello as a Rodgers and Hammerstein-loving Brooklyn boss, and Fonda as the police union lawyer and standard issue love interest. Screenplay was conceived by Ken Lipper, who was once deputy mayor under Ed Koch, but the involvement of three other scripters causes confusion over what type of picture it's aiming to be. Cash-strapped New York rented its actual city hall out for filming at a price of $50,000. **111m/C VHS, DVD.** Al Pacino, John Cusack, Bridget Fonda, Danny Aiello, David Paymer, Martin Landau, Anthony (Tony) Franciosa, Lindsay Duncan, Nestor Serrano, Mel Winkler, Richard Schiff; ***D:*** Harold Becker; ***W:*** Paul Schrader, Nicholas Pileggi, Bo Goldman, Ken Lipper; ***C:*** Michael Seresin; ***M:*** Jerry Goldsmith.

City Heat 🦴🦴½ **1984 (PG)** A hard-nosed cop and a plucky private eye berate each other while opposing the mob in this overdone comedy. Both Eastwood and Reynolds spoof their screen personas, but the results are only slightly satisfactory. Good back-up, though, from Alexander and Kahn as the dames. Screenplay written by Blake Edwards under the pseudonym Sam O. Brown. **98m/C VHS.** Clint Eastwood, Burt Reynolds, Jane Alexander, Irene Cara, Madeline Kahn, Richard Roundtree, Rip Torn, Tony LoBianco, William Sanderson; ***D:*** Richard Benjamin; ***W:*** Blake Edwards; ***M:*** Lennie Niehaus.

City in Fear 🦴🦴🦴 **1980** Stellar cast lights up a drama about a tired newspaper columnist (Janssen) who communicates directly with a murdering psychotic (Rourke), as publisher Vaughn applauds and hypes. Rourke's first role, Janssen's last, and Smithee is actually Jud Taylor. **135m/C VHS.** David Janssen, Robert Vaughn, Mickey Rourke, William Daniels, Perry King, Susan Sullivan, William Prince; ***D:*** Alan Smithee. **TV**

City in Panic 🦴 **1986** A detective and radio talk show host try to catch a psychotic mass murderer busy offing homosexuals throughout the city. Violent with no redeeming social qualities. **85m/C VHS.** Dave Adamson, Ed Chester, Leeann Westegard; ***D:*** Robert Bouvier.

City Killer 🦴 **1987** A lunatic tries to blackmail the girl he loves into going out on a few dates by committing huge destructive acts of inner-city terrorism (flowers won't do). **120m/C VHS.** Heather Locklear, Gerald McRaney, Terence Knox, Peter Mark Richman, John Harkins; ***D:*** Robert Lewis. **TV**

City Lights 🦴🦴🦴🦴 **1931** Masterpiece that was Chaplin's last silent film. The "Little Tramp" falls in love with a blind flower seller. A series of lucky accidents permits him to get the money she needs for a sight-restoring surgery. One of the most eloquent movies ever filmed, due to Chaplin's keen balance between comedy and tragedy. **86m/B VHS, DVD.** Charlie Chaplin, Virginia Cherrill, Florence Lee, Hank Mann, Harry C. (Henry) Myers, Henry Bergman, Jean Harlow; ***D:*** Charlie Chaplin; ***W:*** Charlie Chaplin; ***C:*** Roland H. Totheroh, Gordon Pollock; ***M:*** Alfred Newman, Charlie Chaplin. AFI '98: Top 100, Natl. Film Reg. '91.

City Limits 🦴 **1985 (PG-13)** In a post-apocalyptic city, gangs of young people on choppers clash. **85m/C VHS.** John Stockwell, Kim Cattrall, Darrell Larson, Rae Dawn Chong, Robby Benson, James Earl Jones, Jennifer Balgobin; ***D:*** Aaron Lipstadt.

City of Angels 🦴🦴½ **1998 (PG-13)** Weepy American remake of Wim Wenders' "Wings of Desire" finds guardian angel Seth (Cage) falling in love with heart surgeon Maggie (Ryan) and then trying to decide whether he wants to become mortal in order to join her. Subtle, it is not. Cage does his doe-eyed best to convey Seth's longing and innocence to earthly ways, and the chemistry with Ryan really clicks. Overly sappy and sentimental, especially near the end, but that won't stop the intended audience from loving it. Big Hollywood flick that wears its art-house aspirations on its sleeve. **117m/C VHS, DVD.** Nicolas Cage, Meg Ryan, Andre Braugher, Dennis Franz, Colm Feore, Robin Bartlett, Joanna Merlin; ***D:*** Brad Silberling; ***W:*** Dana Stevens; ***C:*** John Seale; ***M:*** Gabriel Yared.

City of Blood 🦴🦴½ **1988 (R)** A South African doctor is embroiled in mystery with racial overtones when prostitutes are being killed with a spiked club. Packaged as a horror film, this movie actually deals with the questions of South African racial tensions in a sophisticated, ultimately tragic manner. **96m/C VHS.** *SA* Joe Stewardson, Ian Yule, Susan Coetzer; ***D:*** Darrell Roodt.

City of Hope 🦴🦴🦴 **1991 (R)** The picture that "Bonfire of the Vanities" wanted to be, an eventful few days in the fictional metropolis of Hudson: an ugly racial incident threatens to snowball, the corrupt mayor pushes a shady real-estate deal, and a botched robbery has profound implications. Some of the subplots resolve too easily, but this cynical, crazy-quilt of urban life is worthy of comparison with "American Graffiti" and "Nashville" as pure Americana. **132m/C VHS, 8mm.** Vincent Spano, Tony LoBianco, Joe Morton, Todd Graff, David Strathairn, Anthony John (Tony) Denison, Barbara Williams, Angela Bassett, Gloria Foster, Lawrence Tierney, John Sayles, Maggie Renzi, Kevin Tighe, Chris Cooper, Jace Alexander, Frankie Faison, Michael Mantell, Josh Mostel, Joe Grifasi, Louis Zorich, Gina Gershon, Rose Gregorio, Bill Raymond, Maeve Kinkead, Ray Aranha; ***D:*** John Sayles; ***W:*** John Sayles; ***C:*** Robert Richardson; ***M:*** Mason Daring. Ind. Spirit '92: Support. Actor (Strathairn).

City of Industry 🦴🦴 **1996 (R)** Efficient contemporary noir that doesn't always live up to its promise. Old pro thief Roy Egan (Keitel), now retired, is drawn into the final jewel heist of his younger brother, Lee (Hutton), who's also vowed to get out of the game. Unfortunately for him, Lee's picked one wrong partner in volatile wheelman Skip Kovich (Ulrich). When the violent Skip decides he doesn't want to share the goods it starts an elaborate cat-and-mouse hunt through the seedier sides of L.A. **97m/C VHS, DVD, Wide.** Harvey Keitel, Stephen Dorff, Famke Janssen, Timothy Hutton, Michael Jai White, Wade Dominguez, Reno Wilson; ***D:*** John Irvin; ***W:*** Ken Solarz; ***C:*** Thomas Burstyn; ***M:*** Stephen Endelman.

City of Joy 🦴🦴 **1992 (PG-13)** Disillusioned American heart surgeon Swayze flees to India after losing a patient. In Calcutta he is beaten by a street gang and loses his money and passport, but finds help from a farmer (Puri) who takes him to a nearby clinic in the City of Joy, one of Calcutta's poorest areas. Collins runs the clinic and recruits the reluctant doctor, who undergoes a life-changing transformation. The squalor of Calcutta is shown, but the city's portrayal as a magical place where problems miraculously disappear is unrealistic. Swayze lacks the emotional range for his part, but Collins and Puri are excellent in their roles. Adapted from the book by Dominique Lapierre. **134m/C VHS, Wide.** *GB FR* Patrick Swayze, Pauline Collins, Om Puri, Shabana Azmi, Art Malik, Ayesha Dharker, Santu Chowdhury, Imran Badsah Khan, Shyamanand Jalan; ***Cameos:*** Sam Wanamaker; ***D:*** Roland Joffe; ***W:*** Mark Medoff; ***C:*** Peter Biziou; ***M:*** Ennio Morricone.

The City of Lost Children 🦴🦴🦴 *La Cite des Enfants Perdus* **1995 (R)** Weird not-for-the-kiddies fairytale finds crazed inventor Krank (Emilfork) getting his evil one-eyed minions, the appropriately named Cyclops, to kidnap local children so that he can steal their dreams (because Krank himself is incapable of dreaming). The latest victim is young Denree (Lucien), the adopted brother of sideshow strongman One (Perlman), who single-mindedly pursues a way to get Denree back—aided by nine-year-old feral child Miette (Vittet) and a band of orphan thieves. Freaks galore with avant-garde designer Jean-Paul Gaultier in charge of costumes. French with subtitles or dubbed. **114m/C VHS, DVD.** *FR* Marc Caro, Ron Perlman, Daniel Emilfork, Joseph Lucien, Judith Vittet, Dominique Pinon, Jean Claude Dreyfus, Odile Mallet, Genevieve Brunet, Mireille Mosse; ***D:*** Jean-Pierre Jeunet, Marc Caro; ***W:*** Jean-Pierre Jeunet, Marc Caro, Gilles Adrien; ***C:*** Darius Khondji; ***M:*** Angelo Badalamenti; ***V:*** Jean-Louis Trintignant. Cesar '96: Art Dir./Set Dec.

City of Shadows 1986 (R)
Twins separated at birth are reunited by a criminal mind with evil intentions. Double trouble? **97m/C VHS.** John P. Ryan, Paul Coufos, Tony Rosato; *D:* David Mitchell; *M:* Tangerine Dream.

City of the Walking Dead
Nightmare City; Nightmare 1983 Eco-misery as a community must contend with prowling, radiation-zapped zombies who enjoy chewing through human flesh. **92m/C VHS.** *IT SP* Mel Ferrer, Hugo Stiglitz, Laura Trotter, Francesco Rabal; *D:* Umberto Lenzi.

City of Women *La Citte delle Donne* 1981 (R) Visually stunning, but otherwise thin fantasy/drama about a man smothered with women. A journalist wanders through a feminist theme park replete with a roller rink and screening room. Some worthwhile adventures are mixed in with rather dull stretches. Not among the best from either Mastroianni, who is under utilized, or Fellini, who here seems incapable of separating good ideas from bad. Plenty of buxom babes, but otherwise undistinguished. In Italian with English subtitles. **140m/C VHS, DVD, Wide.** *IT* Marcello Mastroianni, Ettore Manni, Anna Prucnall, Bernice Stegers; *D:* Federico Fellini; *W:* Federico Fellini; *C:* Giuseppe Rotunno; *M:* Luis Bacalov.

City on Fire woof! 1978 (R) Arguably the worst of Hollywood's disaster epics, this stinker came at the end of the cycle. The plot borrows heavily from such boxoffice heavyweights as "The Towering Inferno" and "The Poseidon Adventure." A cast of second-magnitude stars (with the exception of Henry Fonda) deals with civic corruption, an enraged pyromaniac, political ambitions, blackmail, and assorted hanky-panky. Several stuntmen are set afire, but the titular blaze is handled with unimpressive effects. The rest is choppy editing, cliched situations, and flat characters. **101m/C VHS.** *CA* Barry Newman, Susan Clark, Shelley Winters, Leslie Nielsen, Henry Fonda, Ava Gardner; *D:* Alvin Rakoff.

City Slickers 1991 (PG-13)
Three men with mid-life crises leave New York City for a cattle-ranch vacation that turns into an arduous, character-building stint. Many funny moments supplied by leads Crystal, Stern, and Kirby, but Palance steals the film as a salty, wise cowpoke. Slater is fetching as the lone gal vacationer on the cattle drive. Boxoffice winner notable for a realistic calf birthing scene, one of few in cinema history. From an idea by Crystal, who also produced. Palance stole the show from Oscar ceremonies host Crystal a second time when he accepted his award and suddenly started doing one-arm pushups, startling the audience into laughter. **114m/C VHS, DVD, 8mm, Wide.** Billy Crystal, Daniel Stern, Bruno Kirby, Patricia Wettig, Helen Slater, Jack Palance, Noble Willingham, Tracey Walter, Josh Mostel, David Paymer, Bill Henderson, Jeffrey Tambor, Phill Lewis, Kyle Secor, Yeardley Smith, Jayne Meadows; *D:* Ron Underwood; *W:* Lowell Ganz, Babaloo Mandel; *C:* Dean Semler; *M:* Marc Shaiman. Oscars '91: Support. Actor (Palance); Golden Globes '92: Support. Actor (Palance); MTV Movie Awards '92: Comedic Perf. (Crystal).

City Slickers 2: The Legend of Curly's Gold ½ 1994 (PG-13) Mid-life crisis meets the wild west, part deux. Crystal and his fellow urban dudes discover a treasure map in the hat of departed trail boss Curly and decide to go a-huntin'. Palance is back as Curly's seafarin,' equally cantankerous, twin brother. Lovitz occupies the screen as Crystal's ne'er-do-well brother, replacing sidekick Bruno Kirby. A bit of a rehash, formulaic and occasionally straining for a punchline, it's still pretty darn funny, especially when the boys start to improvise. **116m/C VHS.** Billy Crystal, Daniel Stern, Jon Lovitz, Jack Palance, Patricia Wettig, Pruitt Taylor Vince, Bill McKinney, Lindsay Crystal, Noble Willingham, David Paymer, Josh Mostel; *D:* Paul Weiland; *W:* Billy Crystal, Lowell Ganz, Babaloo Mandel; *M:* Marc Shaiman.

City That Never Sleeps ½
1953 A Chicago cop must decide whether or not to run off with an entertainer, or continue his life with his family. Decisions, decisions. Moody but dated melodrama that's finely acted and indecisively directed, with good use of dim city lights. Nothing new here. **90m/B VHS.** Gig Young, Mala Powers, Edward Arnold, Paula Raymond, Chill Wills, Marie Windsor; *D:* John H. Auer.

City Unplugged *Darkness in Tallinn* 1995 Heist film with some twists. $970 million in gold, in Paris for safekeeping since WWII, has been returned to the treasury in the newly independent Republic of Estonia. The thieves, who belong to the Russian mob, plan to cut all electricity in the capital city of Tallinn, break into the bank, and move the gold to a nearby cigarette factory where it can be melted down and repackaged as cigarettes. The mob's use of local electrician Toivo proves to be their undoing in a comedy of errors. Estonian with subtitles. **99m/C VHS.** Peter Oja, Ivo Uukkivi, Milena Gulbe, Monika Mager; *D:* Ilkka Jarvilaturi; *W:* Paul Kolsby; *C:* Rein Kotov.

City Without Men ½ 1943 Melodramatic story about a boarding house near a prison where the women tenants await the release of their imprisoned men. Little plot, no suspense. **75m/B VHS.** Linda Darnell, Sara Allgood, Michael Duane, Edgar Buchanan, Leslie Brooks, Glenda Farrell, Margaret Hamilton, Sheldon Leonard; *D:* Sidney Salkow.

The City's Edge ½ 1983 A young man becomes involved with the mysterious residents of a boarding house on the edge of the ocean. **86m/C VHS.** *AU* Mark Lee; *D:* Ken Quinnell.

A Civil Action ½ 1998 (PG-13)
Low-key courtroom thriller doesn't contain many thrills. Travolta is Jan Schlichtmann, a flashy lawyer who freely admits that he's an ambulance chasing weasel. When a grieving mother (Quinlan) approaches him with a case accusing two corporate conglomerates of causing an outbreak of leukemia among children, Jan smells a big payoff. As the case drags on (and his firm falls deeper into debt pursuing it), his perspective changes and he begins to seek justice for the lost children. Robert Duvall steals the show as the homespun Harvard lawyer representing one of the companies. Based on a true story. **115m/C VHS, DVD.** James Gandolfini, John Travolta, Robert Duvall, Kathleen Quinlan, Tony Shalhoub, Zeljko Ivanek, John Lithgow, William H. Macy, Bruce Norris, Sydney Pollack, Peter Jacobson; *D:* Steven Zaillian; *W:* Steven Zaillian; *C:* Conrad L. Hall; *M:* Danny Elfman. Screen Actors Guild '98: Support. Actor (Duvall).

Civil War Diary *Across Five Aprils* 1990
Too young to go to war, a young man struggles for the survival of his family amidst harsh winters, the devastation of the Civil War and his own personal nightmares. Winner of the International Heritage Award in 1990. Based on the Newberry Award winning young people's novel "Across Five Aprils." **82m/C VHS.** Miriam Byrd-Nethery, Todd Duffey, Hollis McCarthy; *D:* Kevin Meyer; *W:* Kevin Meyer.

Civilization 1916 A silent epic about the horrors and immorality of war as envisioned by the ground-breaking film pioneer Ince, who was later murdered. Famous scene involves Christ walking through body-ridden battlefields. **80m/B VHS.** Howard Hickman, Enid Markey, Lola May; *D:* Thomas Ince, Reginald Barker, Raymond B. West. Natl. Film Reg. '99.

The Claim ½ 2000 (R) Winterbottom, who already adapted Thomas Hardy's "Jude the Obscure," takes on Hardy's "The Mayor of Casterbridge," transporting the story to California during the gold rush. Miner Dillon (Mullan) sells his wife Elena (Kinski) and baby daughter for gold and uses the money to establish his own town. But his sins come back to haunt him when his dying wife and grown daughter Hope (Polley) arrive, as does railway surveyor Dalglish (Bentley). Now Dillon's very future is threatened. There's more than the winter weather that's chilly about the film, which never reaches the tragic dimensions it should. **120m/C VHS, DVD, Wide.** *GB CA* Peter Mullan, Nastassia Kinski, Sarah Polley, Wes Bentley, Milla Jovovich, Sean McGinley, Julian Richings; *D:* Michael Winterbottom; *W:* Frank Cottrell-Boyce; *C:* Alwin Kuchler; *M:* Michael Nyman.

Claire Dolan 1997 Irish immigrant Claire (Cartlidge), a hooker, decides to relocate after her mother dies and she leaves town owing her pimp, Roland (Meaney), a lot of money. She moves to Newark, gets a job as a beautician, and begins a romance with Elton (D'Onofrio). Then Roland finds her and forces Claire back into business to pay off her debt. Bleak but well-acted. **95m/C VHS.** Katrin Cartlidge, Vincent D'Onofrio, Colm Meaney; *D:* Lodge Kerrigan; *W:* Lodge Kerrigan; *C:* Teodoro Maniaci; *M:* Simon Fisher Turner.

Claire of the Moon 1992
Famous satirist Claire goes to a women writers retreat in the Pacific Northwest where she's assigned a room with Noel, a solemn sex therapist. Noel's recovering from a disasterous love affair while Claire is promiscuous and unwilling to commit. Inspite of their differences, the two women find themselves drawn together. Too many philosophical debates slow the story down but the gentle romance works well. **102m/C VHS, DVD.** Trisha Todd, Karen Trumbo, Faith McDevitt, Damon Craig; *D:* Nicole Conn; *W:* Nicole Conn; *M:* Michael Allen Harrison.

Claire's Knee ½ *Le Genou de Claire* 1971 A grown man about to be married goes on a holiday and develops a fixation on a young girl's knee. Another of Rohmer's Moral Tales exploring sexual and erotic obsessions. Lots of talk, little else. You'll either find it fascinating or fail to watch more than 10 minutes. Most, however, consider it a classic. Sophisticated dialogue, lovely visions of summer on Lake Geneva. In French with English subtitles. **105m/C VHS, DVD.** *FR* Jean-Claude Brialy, Aurora Cornu, Beatrice Romand, Laurence De Monaghan, Gerard Falconetti; *D:* Eric Rohmer; *W:* Eric Rohmer; *C:* Nestor Almendros. Natl. Soc. Film Critics '71: Film.

Clambake 1967 Noxious Elvis vehicle about a rich man's son who wants success on his own terms, so he trades places with a water-skiing teacher. Inane, even in comparison to other Elvis ventures. ♫Clambake; The Girl I Never Loved; Hey, Hey, Hey; Confidence; Who Needs Money?; A House That Has Everything. **98m/C VHS, DVD, Wide.** Elvis Presley, Shelley Fabares, Bill Bixby, James Gregory, Gary Merrill, Will Hutchins, Harold (Hal) Peary, Suzie Kaye, Angelique Pettyjohn; *D:* Arthur Nadel; *W:* Arthur Browne Jr.; *C:* William Margulies; *M:* Jeff Alexander.

The Clan of the Cave Bear ½ 1986 (R) A scrawny cavegirl is taken in by Neanderthals after her own parents are killed. Hannah is lifeless as a primitive gamine, and the film is similarly DOA. Ponderous and only unintentionally funny. Based on the popular novel by Jean M. Auel. **100m/C VHS, DVD, Wide.** Daryl Hannah, James Remar, Pamela Reed, John Doolittle, Thomas G. Waites; *D:* Michael Chapman; *W:* John Sayles; *C:* Jan De Bont; *M:* Alan Silvestri.

Clara's Heart 1988 (PG-13) A Jamaican maid enriches the lives of her insufferable, bourgeois employers and their particularly repellent son. A kinder, gentler waste of film and Goldberg; sentimental clap-trap which occasionally lapses into comedy. **108m/C VHS.** Whoopi Goldberg, Michael Ontkean, Kathleen Quinlan, Neil Patrick Harris, Spalding Gray, Beverly Todd, Hattie Winston; *D:* Robert Mulligan; *W:* Mark Medoff; *M:* Dave Grusin.

Clarence ½ 1991 (G) Clarence, the benevolent angel from the classic "It's a Wonderful Life," is back, risking his wings for a beautiful young woman. **92m/C VHS.** Robert Carradine, Kate Trotter; *D:* Eric Till; *W:* Lorne Cameron. CABLE

Clarence, the Cross-eyed Lion 1965 Follows the many adventures of a cross-eyed lion and his human compatriots. Great family viewing from the creator of "Flipper." **98m/C VHS.** Marshall Thompson, Betsy Drake, Richard Haydn, Cheryl Miller, Rockne Tarkington, Maurice Marsac; *D:* Andrew Marton; *W:* Alan Caillou.

Clark & McCullough ½ 1933
The zany duo, a hit in burlesque and night clubs, transferred some of their crazy antics onto film. Their comedy shorts include "Fits in a Fiddle" (1933), "Love and Kisses" (1934), "Alibi Bye Bye" (1935), and a rehearsal of "Mademoiselle from New Rochelle" from "Strike Up the Band" (with George Gershwin on piano). **53m/B VHS.** Bobby Clark, Paul McCullough, George Gershwin, James Finlayson.

Clash by Night ½ 1952 A wayward woman marries a fisherman, then beds his best friend. Seamy storyline is exploited to the hilt by master filmmaker Lang. An utterly unflinching melodrama. Early Monroe shines in a supporting role too. Based on the Clifford Odets play. **105m/B VHS.** Barbara Stanwyck, Paul Douglas, Marilyn Monroe, Robert Ryan, J. Carrol Naish; *D:* Fritz Lang.

Clash of the Ninja ½ 1986 Evil Occidental ninja runs medical smuggling operation. Interpol ninja sets out to stop him. Wild ninja nonsense includes ninja with rotating head and exploding ninja. Dubbed poorly. **90m/C VHS.** *HK* Paul Torcha, Louis Roth, Eric Neff, Bernie Junker, Joe Redner, Klaus Mutter, Eddie Chan, Max Kwan, Tom Allen, Stanley Tong; *D:* Wallace Chan; *W:* Kurt Spielberg.

Clash of the Titans woof! 1981 (PG) Mind-numbing fantasy derived from Greek legends about heroic Perseus, who slays the snake-haired Medusa and rescues a semi-clad maiden from the monstrous Kraken. Wooden Hamlin plays Perseus and fares better than more accomplished Olivier and Smith, who seem in need of enemas as they lurch about Mt. Olympus. Only Bloom seems truly godlike in a supporting role. Some good, some wretched special effects from pioneer Harryhausen. **118m/C VHS, Wide.** *GB* Laurence Olivier, Maggie Smith, Claire Bloom, Ursula Andress, Burgess Meredith, Harry Hamlin, Sian Phillips, Judi Bowker; *D:* Desmond Davis; *W:* Beverley Cross; *C:* Ted Moore.

Class 1983 (R) A prep school student discovers that his mother is the lover whom his roommate has bragged about. Lowe is serviceable as the stunned son of sexy Bisset, who woos McCarthy, even in an elevator. Too ludicrous to be enjoyed, but you may watch just to see what happens next. **98m/C VHS, DVD, Wide.** Jacqueline Bisset, Rob Lowe, Andrew McCarthy, Cliff Robertson, John Cusack, Stuart Margolin, Casey Siemaszko; *D:* Lewis John Carlino; *W:* Jim Kouf, David Greenwalt; *C:* Ric Waite; *M:* Elmer Bernstein.

Class Act ½ 1991 (PG-13) Rappers Kid 'N' Play team up once again in this role reversal comedy. A straight-laced brain and a partying, macho bully find their school records and identifications switched when they enroll in a new high school. This turns out to be good for the character of both young men, as the egghead learns to loosen up and the bully learns what it feels like to be respected for his ideas rather than a fierce reputation. Comedy is very uneven but the duo are energetic and likable. **98m/C VHS, Wide.** Christopher Reid, Christopher Martin, Meshach Taylor, Karyn Parsons, Doug E. Doug, Ric(k) Ducommun, Lamont Jackson, Rhea Perlman; *D:* Randall Miller; *M:* Vassal Benford.

Class Action 1991 (R)
1960s versus 1990s ethics clash when a father and daughter, both lawyers, wind up on opposing sides of a litigation against an auto manufacturer. Hackman and Mastrantonio give intense, exciting performances, almost surmounting the melodramatic script. **110m/C VHS.** Mary Elizabeth Mastrantonio, Gene Hackman, Joanna Merlin, Colin Friels, Laurence "Larry" Fishburne, Donald Moffat, Jan Rubes, Matt Clark, Fred Dalton Thompson, Jonathan Silverman, Dan Hicks; *D:* Michael Apted; *W:* Samantha Shad, Christopher Ames; *M:* James Horner.

Class of Fear ½ 1991 (R) The new kid in school is having a particularly rough time. He's been framed for murdering a teacher and must prove his innocence before he winds up in prison. **105m/C VHS.** Julianne McNamara, Noah Blake.

Class of '44 🦴½ **1973 (PG)** The sequel to "Summer of '42" finds insufferable boys becoming insufferable men at military school. Worse than its predecessor, and notable only in that it is Candy's film debut. **95m/C VHS.** Gary Grimes, Jerry Houser, Oliver Conant, Deborah Winters, William Atherton, Sam Bottoms, John Candy; ***D:*** Paul Bogart; ***M:*** David Shire.

The Class of Miss MacMichael 🦴🦴 **1978 (R)** A dedicated instructor inherits and ultimately inspires a class of high school misfits and malcontents. Derivative venture is beneath considerable talents of Jackson. Based on a novel by Sandy Hutson. **95m/C VHS.** *GB* Glenda Jackson, Oliver Reed, Michael Murphy, Rosalind Cash; ***D:*** Silvio Narizzano; ***W:*** Judd Bernard.

Class of 1984 woof! **1982 (R)** Teacher King must face a motley crew of teenagers in the classroom. Ring leader and student psychopath Van Patten leads his groupies on a reign of terror through the high school halls, stopping to gang rape King's wife. Teacher attempts revenge. Bloody and thoughtless update of "Blackboard Jungle." Early Fox appearance. Followed by "Class of 1999." **93m/C VHS.** *CA* Perry King, Roddy McDowall, Timothy Van Patten, Michael J. Fox, Merrie Lynn Ross, Stefan Arngrim, Al Waxman, Lisa Langlois; ***D:*** Mark L. Lester; ***W:*** Mark L. Lester, Tom Holland; ***C:*** Albert J. Dunk; ***M:*** Lalo Schifrin.

Class of 1999 🦴 **1990 (R)** Free-wheeling sci-fi set in the near future where teen gangs terrorize seemingly the entire country. A high school principal determines to enforce law and order by installing human-like robots with rocket launchers for arms. Violent, crude entertainment. Class dismissed. Sequel to "Class of 1984" and available in an unrated version. **98m/C VHS.** Bradley Gregg, Traci Lind, Malcolm McDowell, Stacy Keach, Patrick Kilpatrick, Pam Grier, John P. Ryan, Darren E. Burrows, Joshua John Miller; ***D:*** Mark L. Lester; ***W:*** C. Courtney Joyner.

Class of 1999 2: The Substitute 🦴½ **1993 (R)** High school in 1999 is filled with violent gangs who murder at random. Enter substitute teacher John Bolen, who has his own ideas of discipline—leading to an even higher body count. John just doesn't seem human and when a CIA agent starts investigating, school may never be the same. **90m/C VHS.** Sasha Mitchell, Nick Cassavetes, Caitlin Dulany, Jack Knight, Gregory West, Richard (Rick) Hill; ***D:*** Spiro Razatos; ***W:*** Mark Sevi.

Class of Nuke 'Em High 🦴½ **1986 (R)** Team Troma once again experiments with the chemicals, with violent results. Jersey high school becomes a hotbed of mutants and maniacs after a nuclear spill occurs. Good teens Chrissy and Warren succumb, the school blows, life goes on. High camp, low budget, heavy gore. Followed by "Class of Nuke 'Em High Part 2." **84m/C VHS, DVD.** Janelle Brady, Gilbert Brenton, Robert Prichard, R.L. Ryan, Theo Cohan, Diana De Vries, Brad Dunker, Gary Schneider; ***D:*** Richard W. Haines, Lloyd Kaufman; ***W:*** Richard W. Haines, Lloyd Kaufman, Mark Rudnitsky, Stuart Strutin.

Class of Nuke 'Em High 2: Subhumanoid Meltdown 🦴 **1991 (R)** The Troma team brings us back into the world of the strange. In this adventure, the evil Nukamama Corporation holds secret experiments at their "college" and create sub-humanoids as slave labor, swelling unemployment and wrecking the economy. This does not fare too well with the rest of society, including our heroes Roger the reporter, Professor Holt, and the scantily clad sub-humanoid Victoria. **96m/C VHS.** Lisa Gaye, Brick Bronsky, Leesa Rowland, Michael Kurtz, Scott Resnick; ***D:*** Eric Louzil; ***W:*** Eric Louzil, Lloyd Kaufman; ***C:*** Ron Chapman; ***M:*** Bob Mithoff.

Class of Nuke 'Em High 3: The Good, the Bad and the Subhumanoid woof! **1994 (R)** Revisit Tromie the nuclear rodent and the other disaster-prone denizens of Tromaville, USA. Admire the classic good twin vs. evil subhumanoid twin plot as they battle against each other, aided by chicks with guns and tin undergarments. Supposedly inspired by Shakespeare's "Comedy of Errors." Tip: stick to the BBC production for your senior thesis. **95m/C VHS.** Brick Bronsky, Lisa Gaye, Lisa Star, John Tallman, Albert Rear, Phil Rivo; ***D:*** Eric Louzil; ***W:*** Lloyd Kaufman; ***C:*** Ron Chapman; ***M:*** Bob Mithoff.

Class of '61 🦴🦴½ **1992** 1861, that is, as this class of West Point cadets prepares for the outbreak of war. Three close friends find themselves on opposing sides and with romantic entanglements, as well. Illustrated history, complete with voiceover passages from soldiers' letters, tend to slow the action, although the battles scenes are well done. **95m/C VHS.** Dan Futterman, Clive Owen, Joshua Lucas, Sophie Ward, Laura Linney, Andre Braugher, Len Cariou, Dana Ivey, Scott Burkholder, Niall O'Brien, Christien Anholt, Paul Guilfoyle, Beverly Todd, Ed Wiley, Sue-Ann Leeds; ***D:*** Gregory Hoblit; ***W:*** Jonas McCord; ***C:*** Janusz Kaminski. **TV**

Class of '63 🦴🦴 **1973** An unfulfilled woman finally discovers the lover she lost nearly ten years ago at her college reunion. Nearly average. **74m/C VHS.** James Brolin, Joan Hackett, Cliff Gorman, Ed Lauter; ***D:*** John Korty. **TV**

Class Reunion woof! **1987 (X)** Sexual highjinks are the order of the day at a 10-year high school reunion. Insipid softcore effort. It's cheaper just to cut out heads from yearbooks and paste 'em to skin mags torsos. Not to be confused with "National Lampoon's Class Reunion," equally bad but nonetheless distinct. **90m/C VHS.** Marsha Jordan, Renee Bond, Terry Johnson.

Class Reunion Massacre woof! *The Redeemer* **1977 (R)** Typically lame-brained horror about the mysterious deaths of former school jerks who've reconvened for the 10-year reunion. Worthless flick stars someone named Finkbinder. Contains graphic violence that is not for the squeamish. **87m/C VHS.** T.K. Finkbinder, Damien Knight, Nick Carter, Jeanetta Arnette, Christopher Flint; ***D:*** Constantine S. Gochis; ***W:*** William Vernick.

Claudia 🦴🦴 **1985 (R)** A wealthy woman who's part of London's high society falls for a lowly musician while trying to escape her dominating husband. Melodramatic meanderings not likely to move you. **88m/C VHS.** Deborah Raffin, Nicholas Ball; ***D:*** Anwar Kawadri.

The Claw **1927** A young British profligate goes to Africa to prove his manhood to the woman who rejected him. Silent. **?m/B VHS, 8mm.** Claire Windsor, Norman Kerry; ***D:*** Sidney Olcott.

Claws 🦴 **1977 (PG)** A woodsman, a game commissioner, and an Indian band together to stop a grizzly bear who is killing residents of a small Alaskan town. **100m/C VHS.** Leon Ames, Jason Evers, Anthony Caruso, Glenn Sipes, Carla Layton, Myron Healey; ***D:*** Richard Bansbach, R.E. Pierson.

Claws woof! **1985** A lone farmboy is subjected to repeated attacks by feline mutants. Meow, baby. **84m/C VHS.** Jason Roberts, Brian O'Shaughnessy, Sandra Prinsloo; ***D:*** Alan Nathanson.

The Clay Pigeon 🦴🦴½ **1949** Seaman comes to in the hospital after a long coma and discovers he's about to be court-martialed for treason and murder. Effective suspense as he goes after the man who incriminated him. **63m/B VHS.** Bill Williams, Barbara Hale, Richard Loo; ***D:*** Richard Fleischer.

Clay Pigeons 🦴🦴½ **1998 (R)** Bodies are mysteriously piling up in a sleepy Montana town after strange cowboy trucker Lester (Vaughn) shows up. Clay Birdwell (Phoenix) finds himself a prime suspect after a series of bizarre twists stemming from his affair with his best friend's wife. After crossing paths, Clay and Lester quickly become best buddies. When they discover a body while fishing, Clay begins to link unsolved murders elsewhere in the state to his new pal. Problem is, the FBI has just shown up to investigate the disappearance of Clay's best friend and his wife, while Lester has disappeared, leaving Clay to take the heat. Features outstanding performances by Phoenix and Vaughn. Vaughn is given free reign, and goes near, but never over, the top. Second half is slower and less fun than the first half. Still, the original story and clever twists keep it interesting. **104m/C VHS, DVD.** Vince Vaughn, Joaquin Rafael (Leaf) Phoenix, Janeane Garofalo, Scott Wilson, Georgina Cates, Phil Morris, Vince Vieluf, Nikki Arlyn, Monica Moench, Joseph D. Reitman, Gregory Sporleder; ***D:*** David Dobkin; ***W:*** Matthew Healy; ***C:*** Eric Alan Edwards; ***M:*** John Lurie.

Clayton County Line 🦴 **198?** Plucky buddies decide to end a cruel sheriff's reign of terror. Derivative and unredeeming. **80m/C VHS.** Kelly Bradish, Vince Csapos, Michael Heinz, Donald Kenney, Kathy Kenney, Gregg Schultz, Dan Quine, Steve Szilagyi, Dean Wilson; ***D:*** Dean Wilson.

Clean and Sober 🦴🦴🦴½ **1988 (R)** A drug addict hides out at a rehabilitation clinic and actually undergoes treatment. A serious, subtle, and realistic look at the physical/emotional detoxification of an obnoxious, substance-abusing real estate broker; unpredictable and powerful without moralizing. Keaton is fine in unsympathetic lead, with both Baker and Freeman excelling in lesser roles. Not for all tastes, but it's certainly a worthwhile work. Caron, creator of TV's "Moonlighting," debuts here as director. **124m/C VHS, DVD, 8mm, Wide.** Michael Keaton, Kathy Baker, Morgan Freeman, M. Emmet Walsh, Claudia Christian, Pat Quinn, Ben Piazza, Brian Benben, Luca Bercovici, Tate Donovan, Henry Judd Baker, Mary Catherine Martin; ***D:*** Glenn Gordon Caron; ***W:*** Tod Carroll; ***C:*** Jan Kiesser; ***M:*** Gabriel Yared. Natl. Soc. Film Critics '88: Actor (Keaton).

Clean, Shaven 🦴🦴 **1993** Schizophrenic Peter Winter (Greene in a stunning performance) is searching bleak Miscou Island, off the New Brunswick coast, for the young daughter his mother put up for adoption after Peter was institutionalized and his wife died. Peter's being tailed by Detective McNally (Albert), who suspects him of a child's murder, and his tenuous hold on reality slowly disintegrates into torment and self-mutilation. Debut for director/writer Kerrigan. **80m/C VHS, DVD.** Peter Greene, Robert Albert, Jennifer MacDonald, Megan Owen, Molly Castelloe; ***D:*** Lodge Kerrigan; ***W:*** Lodge Kerrigan; ***C:*** Teodoro Maniaci; ***M:*** Hahn Rowe.

Clean Slate 🦴🦴 **1994 (PG-13)** Private-eye Maurice Pogue (Carvey) sustains injuries that cause a rare type of amnesia making every day seem like the first day of his life. As the only witness to a crime, he bumbles through mix-ups with the mob and his job as a bodyguard. Lightweight comedy fare is good for a few yuks but doesn't work as well as the similar "Groundhog Day." Barkley the sight-impaired dog steals nearly every scene he's in. **106m/C VHS.** Bob Odenkirk, Dana Carvey, Valeria Golino, James Earl Jones, Kevin Pollak, Michael Murphy, Michael Gambon, Jayne Brook, Vyto Ruginis, Olivia D'Abo, Peter Crook; ***D:*** Mick Jackson; ***W:*** Robert King; ***M:*** Alan Silvestri.

Clear and Present Danger 🦴🦴½ **1994 (PG-13)** Ford returns for a second go at CIA agent Jack Ryan in the third installment of Tom Clancy's bestselling adventures. With the Cold War over, the U.S. government is the bad guy as Ryan discovers a link between a South American drug cartel and a Presidential advisor. Viewers will also finally get an answer to that nagging question at the end of "Patriot Games:" is it a boy or a girl? Archer's back as Ryan's annoying wife, and Birch and Jones also return. Keep alert for complex plot twists in lieu of tons of action, though there's enough to keep action fans happy. **141m/C VHS, DVD.** Harrison Ford, Anne Archer, James Earl Jones, Willem Dafoe, Thora Birch, Henry Czerny, Harris Yulin, Raymond Cruz, Joaquim de Almeida, Miguel (Michael) Sandoval, Donald Moffat, Theodore (Ted) Raimi, Dean Jones; ***D:*** Phillip Noyce; ***W:*** John Milius, Donald Stewart, Steven Zaillian; ***C:*** Donald McAlpine; ***M:*** James Horner. Blockbuster '95: Action Actor, T. (Ford); Blockbuster '96: Action Actor, V. (Ford).

Clearcut 🦴🦴½ **1992 (R)** Progressive lawyer finds his liberalism and his survival skills tested among modern Canadian Indians, when a militant native resorts to kidnapping the businessman who threatens their land. Well-acted, brutal drama that asks tough questions; it includes what purports to be the first authentic sweat-lodge ceremony ever filmed. **98m/C VHS.** *CA* Graham Greene, Ron Lea, Michael Hogan, Floyd "Red Crow" Westerman, Rebecca Jenkins; ***D:*** Richard Bugajski.

Clearing the Range 🦴½ **1931** Hoot wants the bad guy who knocked off his brother so he poses as a cringing coward in the hopes of uncovering the villain. Eilers is the love interest as well as his real-life wife. **64m/B VHS.** Hoot Gibson, Sally Eilers, Hooper Atchley; ***D:*** Otto Brower.

Cleo from 5 to 7 🦴🦴🦴½ *Cleo de 5 a 7* **1961** A singer strolls through Paris for 90 minutes, and reconsiders her life while awaiting the results of medical tests for cancer. Typical documentary-like effort from innovative filmmaker Varda, who constructed the film in real time. Look for a brief appearance of master director Jean-Luc Godard. In French with English subtitles. **90m/B VHS, DVD, Wide.** *FR* Corinne Marchand, Antoine Bourseillor, Dorothee Blanck, Michel Legrand, Jean-Claude Brialy, Jean-Luc Godard, Anna Karina, Eddie Constantine, Sami Frey; ***D:*** Agnes Varda; ***W:*** Agnes Varda; ***C:*** Jean Rabier; ***M:*** Michel Legrand.

Cleo/Leo 🦴 **1989 (R)** Crude and sexist jerk Leo gets chased into the East River by a gun-toting feminist. Reincarnated, Leo returns as Cleo and endures the same Neanderthal remarks and attitudes that "he" used to dish out. Tasteless, exploitive comedy only cynically explores the sex reversal theme. **94m/C VHS.** Jane (Veronica Hart) Hamilton, Scott Thompson Baker, Kevin Thomas, Alan Naggar, Ginger Lynn Allen; ***D:*** Chuck Vincent.

Cleopatra 🦴🦴 **1934** Early Hollywood DeMille version of the Egyptian temptress's lust for Marc Antony after Julius Caesar's death. Intermittently interesting extravaganza. Colbert seems to be enjoying herself in the lead role in this hokey, overdone epic. Includes the original theatrical trailer on laser-track 2. Remade in 1963. **100m/B VHS.** Claudette Colbert, Henry Wilcoxon, Warren William, Gertrude Michael, Joseph Schildkraut, Sir C. Aubrey Smith; ***D:*** Cecil B. DeMille; ***C:*** Victor Milner. Oscars '34: Cinematog.

Cleopatra 🦴 **1963** And we thought DeMille's version was extravagant. After the death of Julius Caesar, Cleopatra, Queen of Egypt, becomes infatuated with Mark Antony. Costly four-hour epic functions like a blimp-sized, multi-colored sleeping tablet. Historical characters are utterly dwarfed by the film's massive scope, and audiences are benumbed by a spectacle of crowd scenes and opulent, grotesque interiors. Taylor looks and often acts like a sex bomb ruler, while Harrison has some notion of Caesar's majesty. Burton, however, is hopelessly wooden. Hard to believe this came from director Mankiewicz. **246m/C VHS, DVD, Wide.** Elizabeth Taylor, Richard Burton, Rex Harrison, Roddy McDowall, Martin Landau, Pamela Brown, Michael Hordern, Kenneth Haigh, Andrew Keir, Hume Cronyn, Carroll O'Connor; ***D:*** Joseph L. Mankiewicz; ***W:*** Joseph L. Mankiewicz; ***C:*** Leon Shamroy; ***M:*** Alex North. Oscars '63: Art Dir./Set Dec., Color, Color Cinematog., Costume Des. (C), Visual FX; Natl. Bd. of Review '63: Actor (Harrison).

Cleopatra 🦴🦴 **1999** Lavishly trashy TV miniseries about the infamous Egyptian queen and her Roman lovers. Young royal, Cleopatra (Varela), wants to rule Egypt but she needs the power of Rome to make things happen. When Julius Caesar (Dalton) comes to Egypt, she seduces the conqueror to gain a kingdom. But after Caesar's murder, Cleopatra pins her hopes on rash Marc Antony (Zane) and things don't turn out so well. Based on the book by Margaret George. **139m/C VHS, DVD.** Leonor Varela, Timothy Dalton, Billy Zane, Rupert Graves, Art Malik, John Bowe, Nadim Sawalha, Owen Teale, Daragh O'Malley, Sean Pertwee, Bruce Payne, Caroline Langrishe; ***D:*** Franc Roddam; ***W:*** Stephen Harrigan, Anton Diether; ***C:*** David Connell; ***M:*** Trevor Jones. **TV**

Cleopatra Jones 1973 (PG) Lean and lethal government agent with considerable martial arts prowess takes on loathsome drug lords. Dobson is fetching as the lead performer in this fast-paced, violent flick. Followed by "Cleopatra Jones and the Casino of Gold." **89m/C VHS, DVD.** Tamara Dobson, Shelley Winters, Bernie Casey, Brenda Sykes, Albert "Poppy" Popwell; ***D:*** Jack Starrett; ***W:*** Max Julien, Sheldon Keller; ***C:*** David M. Walsh; ***M:*** J.J. Johnson.

Cleopatra Jones & the Casino of Gold 1975 (R) Dobson returns as the lethal, physically imposing federal agent to Hong Kong to take on a powerful druglord in this sequel to "Cleopatra Jones." Watch for sexy Stevens as the Dragon Lady. **96m/C VHS.** Tamara Dobson, Stella Stevens, Norman Fell, Albert "Poppy" Popwell; ***D:*** Charles "Chuck" Bail.

Cleopatra's Second Husband 2000 (R) Let's play master and servant. Whiny, selfish yuppie couple Robert (Hipp) and Hallie (Schram) Marrs go on vacation and need housesitters for their fabulous L.A. pad. They accept a recommendation from friends to employ sexy Zack (Kestner) and Sophie (Mitchell). Some friends—when the Marrs return early, their housesitters ask to stay on a little longer and proceed to take over. Hallie takes off after Robert gets it on with Sophie but the sexual/mind games are just beginning. **92m/C VHS, DVD.** Paul Hipp, Boyd Kestner, Radha Mitchell, Bitty Schram, Alexis Arquette, Jonathan Penner; ***D:*** Jonathan Reiss; ***W:*** Jonathan Reiss; ***C:*** Matt Faw; ***M:*** Cary Berger.

Clerks 1994 (R) "What kind of convenience store do you run here?" Day in the life of a convenience store clerk is an often hilarious lesson in the profane from first time writer/director Smith (who has a cameo as Silent Bob). Twenty-two-year-old Dante Hicks (O'Halloran) is a disaffected New Jersey Quick Stop employee who spends most of his time bored and dealing with borderline crazies. The next-door video store is clerked by his best friend Randal (Anderson), who derives equal delight from tormenting his customers and debating absolutely anything (especially anything sexual). Nothing much actually happens but the very low-budget ($27,575) production has a decidedly scuzzy charm and a cult following. Based on the director's four years of clerking at the Quick Stop and shot on location. **89m/B VHS, DVD.** Brian O'Halloran, Jeff Anderson, Marilyn Ghigliotti, Lisa Spoonhauer, Jason Mewes; ***Cameos:*** Kevin Smith; ***D:*** Kevin Smith; ***W:*** Kevin Smith; ***C:*** David Klein; ***M:*** Scott Angley. Sundance '94: Filmmakers Trophy.

The Client ½ 1994 (PG-13) Another legal thriller from the Grisham factory. Reggie Love (Sarandon) is a troubled attorney hired by 11-year-old Mark (Renfro), who witnessed the suicide of a Mafia attorney and now knows more than he should. Ambitious federal prosecutor Foltrigg's (Jones) willing to risk the boy's life in exchange for career advancement. Lacks the mega-big Hollywood names of "The Firm" and "The Pelican Brief" but gains solid acting in return with Renfro a find in his film debut. No frills, near-faithful adaptation by Schumacher basically travels down the path of least resistance. Filmed on location in Memphis. **121m/C VHS, DVD, 8mm, Wide.** Ron Dean, Susan Sarandon, Tommy Lee Jones, Brad Renfro, Mary-Louise Parker, Anthony LaPaglia, Bradley Whitford, Anthony Edwards, Ossie Davis, Walter Olkewicz, J.T. Walsh, Will Patton, Anthony Heald, William H. Macy; ***D:*** Joel Schumacher; ***W:*** Robert Getchell, Akiva Goldsman; ***C:*** Tony Pierce-Roberts; ***M:*** Howard Shore. British Acad. '94: Actress (Sarandon).

Cliffhanger 1993 (R) Action-packed thriller. Expert climber Gabe Walker (Stallone) faces his greatest challenge when criminal mastermind Lithgow and his henchman appear on the scene. Turner plays fellow climber and love interest. Lithgow makes a particularly convincing, if not downright chilling, murderous thief. Filmed in the Italian Alps with a budget of $70 million-plus; boasts stunning cinematography and breathtaking footage of the Dolomite mountain range. Harlin's expert pacing and direction combine to produce maximum thrills and suspense. The hit Stallone's been waiting for, placing eighth on the list of top 1993 boxoffice grossers. **113m/C VHS, DVD, Wide.** Sylvester Stallone, John Lithgow, Michael Rooker, Janine Turner, Rex Linn, Caroline Goodall, Leon, Paul Winfield, Ralph Waite, Craig Fairbrass, Michelle Joyner, Max Perlich; ***D:*** Renny Harlin; ***W:*** Sylvester Stallone, Michael France; ***C:*** Alex Thomson; ***M:*** Trevor Jones.

Clifford woof! 1992 (PG) Short plays a 10-year-old in an effort delayed by Orion's financial crisis. Creepy little Clifford's uncle Martin (Grodin) rues the day he volunteered to babysit his nephew to prove to his girlfriend (Steenburgen) how much he likes kids. Clifford terrorizes Grodin in surprisingly nasty ways when their plans for visiting Dinosaurworld fall through, although Grodin sees to well-deserved revenge. Not just bad in the conventional sense, but bad in a bizarre sort of alien fashion that raises questions about who was controlling the bodies of the producers. To create the effect of Short really being short, other actors stood on boxes and sets were built slightly larger. **90m/C VHS.** Martin Short, Charles Grodin, Mary Steenburgen, Dabney Coleman, Sonia Jackson; ***D:*** Paul Flaherty; ***W:*** Bobby Von Hayes, Jay Dee Rock, Steven Kampmann, Will Aldis; ***C:*** John A. Alonzo; ***M:*** Richard Gibbs.

A Climate for Killing ½ 1991 (R) Arizona police are baffled when a woman murdered 16 years earlier is again found dead. Case open? Hunks Bauer and Beck are earnest in leads, and Ross and Sara are foxy. Passable entertainment. **104m/C VHS.** Steven Bauer, John Beck, Katharine Ross, Mia Sara, John Diehl, Phil Brock, Dedee Pfeiffer, Lu Leonard, Jack Dodson, Eloy Casados; ***D:*** J.S. Cardone; ***W:*** J.S. Cardone; ***M:*** Robert Folk.

The Climax ½ 1944 Technicolor highlights this horror saga of obsession. House physician for Vienna's Royal Theatre, Dr. Hohner (Karloff) kills opera singer Marcellina (Vincent) when she rejects him. Twenty years later, Hohner hears the beautiful voice of Angela (Foster), a near duplicate of Marcellina's, and hypnotizes her to prevent her singing. Now, it's up to Angela's composer friend Franz (Bey) to overcome the doctor's evil influence. Adapted from a play by Edward Locke. Waggner directed this "The Phantom of the Opera" clone using the same sets as the 1943 "Phantom" remake. **86m/C VHS.** Boris Karloff, Susanna Foster, Turhan Bey, Gale Sondergaard, Thomas Gomez, June Vincent, Jane Farrar, Scotty Beckett; ***D:*** George Waggner; ***W:*** Curt Siodmak, Lynn Starling; ***C:*** Hal Mohr, William Howard Greene; ***M:*** Edward Ward.

The Climb ½ 1987 (PG) German mountain climbers attempt to conquer the Himalayan Nanga Parbat, the world's fifth highest peak. Sometimes compelling film based on 1953 expedition in which only one member succeeded in reaching the summit. **90m/C VHS.** Bruce Greenwood, James Hurdle, Kenneth Welsh; ***D:*** Donald Shebib; ***W:*** Donald Shebib; ***M:*** Peter Jermyn.

The Climb ½ 1997 (PG-13) In late fifties Baltimore, 12-year-old Danny (Smith) is the target of bullies and humiliated by the fact that his dad Earl (Strathairn) is accused of cowardice because he's not a vet. So Danny decides to prove his own courage by climbing the local, soon-to-be-demolished 203-foot radio tower. Danny is unexpected aided by his crochety neighbor, Chuck Langer (Hurt), a hard-drinking grump dying of cancer. But when Danny gets into trouble, it's his dad who comes to the rescue. Nostalgic family fare. **94m/C VHS, DVD.** *FR NZ* Gregory Smith, John Hurt, David Strathairn, Stephen McHattie, Seth Smith, Sarah Buxton; ***D:*** Bob Swaim; ***W:*** Vince McKewin; ***C:*** Allen Guilford; ***M:*** Greco Casadeus.

Clipped Wings ½ 1953 The Bowery Boys are at their best as they inadvertantly join the army while visiting a friend; in the process of their usual bumblings, they uncover a Nazi plot. **62m/B VHS.** Leo Gorcey, Huntz Hall, Bernard Gorcey, David Condon, Bennie Bartlett, June Vincent, Mary Treen, Philip Van Zandt, Elaine Riley, Jeanne Dean, Lyle Talbot; ***D:*** Edward L. Bernds.

Cloak and Dagger 1946 An American physicist joins the secret service during WWII and infiltrates Nazi territory to release a kidnapped scientist who is being forced to build a nuclear bomb. Disappointing spy show with muted anti-nuclear tone. **106m/B VHS.** Gary Cooper, Lilli Palmer, Robert Alda, James Flavin, Vladimir Sokoloff, J. Edward Bromberg, Marc Lawrence, Ludwig Stossel; ***D:*** Fritz Lang; ***W:*** Ring Lardner Jr., Albert (John B. Sherry) Maltz; ***M:*** Max Steiner.

Cloak & Dagger ½ 1984 (PG) A young boy, last seen befriending E.T., depends upon his imaginary super-friend to help him out when some real-life agents are after his video game. Coleman is particularly fun as both dad and fantasy hero in an interesting family adventure. **101m/C VHS.** Dabney Coleman, Henry Thomas, Michael Murphy, John McIntire, Jeanette Nolan; ***D:*** Richard Franklin; ***W:*** Tom Holland; ***M:*** Brian May.

The Clock *Under the Clock* 1945 Appealing romance about an office worker who meets and falls in love with a soldier on two-day leave in NYC. Charismatic Walker and likeable Garland make a fine screen couple, and Wynn is memorable as the drunk. **91m/B VHS.** Judy Garland, Robert Walker, James Gleason, Marshall Thompson, Keenan Wynn; ***D:*** Vincente Minnelli; ***C:*** George J. Folsey; ***M:*** George Bassman.

Clockers 1995 (R) Strike (Phifer), leader of a group of bottom-feeding drug dealers ("clockers"), engages in a power struggle with his boss (Lindo), his do-the-right-thing brother Victor (Washington), and his own conscience. He's also suspected of murder by relentless narcotics cop Rocco Klein (Keitel). Supported by an excellent cast, first-timer Phifer surprises with a fierce and powerful performance. Lindo, in particular, stands out as the paternally evil Rodney. Aggressively edited, with Turturro's performance mostly lost on the cutting room floor. Critically lauded cinematography is marred by the occasional boom shot. Poignant and compelling street drama is based on the Richard Price novel. Lee took over after Scorsese and De Niro dropped out to make "Casino." **128m/C VHS, DVD.** Mekhi Phifer, Harvey Keitel, Delroy Lindo, Isaiah Washington IV, John Turturro, Keith David; ***D:*** Spike Lee; ***W:*** Richard Price, Spike Lee; ***C:*** Malik Hassan Sayeed; ***M:*** Terence Blanchard.

The Clockmaker ½ *L'Horloger de Saint-Paul* 1973 Contemplative drama about a clockmaker whose life is shattered when his son is arrested as a political assassin. Tavernier regular Noiret excels in the lead. In French with English subtitles. **105m/C VHS, DVD, Wide.** *FR* Philippe Noiret, Jean Rochefort, Jacques Denis, William Sabatier, Christine Pascal; ***D:*** Bertrand Tavernier; ***W:*** Bertrand Tavernier, Jean Aurenche, Pierre Bost; ***C:*** Sylvain Rougerie; ***M:*** Philippe Sarde.

Clockstoppers ½ 2002 (PG) Amusing kid fare has heroes Zak (Bradford) and Venezuelan exchange student Francesca (Garces) zipping around in speeded-up "hypertime" to rescue Zak's scientists dad Dr. Gibbs (Thomas) from time-traveling baddies, headed by corporate bigwig Henry Gates (Biehn). It seems the wristwatch/time machine Gibbs invented needs tweaking, so Gibbs and top grad student Dopler (Stewart) are kidnaped to fix the snag by the evil QT corporation, which wants to use the device to, what else, conquer the world. The pre-teen duo must do their rescuing, however, before they all prematurely age in hypertime (one of the snags). No stranger to sci-fi, director Frakes (Riker on "Star Trek: Next Generation") makes the most of the inherent FX. **94m/C VHS, DVD.** *US* Jesse Bradford, French Stewart, Michael Biehn, Paula Garces, Robin Thomas, Julia Sweeney, Linda Kim, Garikayi Mutambirwa; ***D:*** Jonathon Frakes; ***W:*** Rob Hedden, J. David Stem, David N. Weiss; ***C:*** Tim Suhrstedt; ***M:*** Jamshield Sharifi.

Clockwatchers ½ 1997 (PG-13) Decent cast gets wasted in a slice of life story that goes nowhere. Meek temp Iris's (Collette) new assignment is at a big, faceless credit company. Iris is taken in hand by fellow temps Margaret (Posey), Paula (Kudrow), and Jane (Ubach), who like to complain about how badly they're treated by management. Things gets worse when the company makes an announcement about a rash of petty thefts and the temps get blamed. That's it. **105m/C VHS, DVD.** Toni Collette, Parker Posey, Lisa Kudrow, Alanna Ubach, Stanley DeSantis, Jamie Kennedy, David James Elliott, Kevin Cooney, Bob Balaban, Paul Dooley; ***D:*** Jill Sprecher; ***W:*** Jill Sprecher, Karen Sprecher; ***C:*** Jim Denault.

Clockwise ½ 1986 (PG) Monty Python regular Cleese is a teacher preoccupied by punctuality. His neurosis proves his undoing when he falls victim to misadventure while traveling to deliver a speech. Cleese is acceptable, dialogue and story is less so, though sprinkled with a fair amount of humor. **96m/C VHS, DVD, Wide.** *GB* John Cleese, Penelope Wilton, Alison Steadman, Stephen Moore, Sharon Maiden; ***D:*** Christopher Morahan; ***W:*** Michael Frayn; ***C:*** John Coquillon; ***M:*** George Fenton.

A Clockwork Orange 1971 (R) In the Britain of the near future, a sadistic punk leads a gang on nightly rape and murder sprees, then is captured and becomes the subject of a grim experiment to eradicate his violent tendencies in this extraordinary adaptation of Anthony Burgess's controversial novel. The film is an exhilarating experience, with an outstanding performance by McDowell as the funny, fierce psychopath. Many memorable, disturbing sequences, including a rape conducted while assailant McDowell belts "Singing in the Rain." Truly outstanding, provocative work from master filmmaker Kubrick. **137m/C VHS, DVD, Wide.** *GB* Malcolm McDowell, Patrick Magee, Adrienne Corri, Michael Bates, Warren Clarke, Aubrey Morris, James Marcus, Steven Berkoff, David Prowse, John Clive, Carl Duering, Miriam Karlin; ***D:*** Stanley Kubrick; ***W:*** Stanley Kubrick; ***C:*** John Alcott; ***M:*** Walter (Wendy) Carlos. AFI '98: Top 100; N.Y. Film Critics '71: Director (Kubrick), Film.

Clodhopper 1917 A farmboy decides to head out for New York where he achieves fame on Broadway for his dance number, the "Clophooper Glide." He stays true to his hometown girl, however, and returns to save his father's farm from financial ruin. **47m/B VHS.** Charles Ray, Margery Wilson; ***D:*** Victor Schertzinger.

The Clones 1973 (PG) A doctor discovers a government experiment engineered to murder him with a perfect clone. **90m/C VHS.** Michael Greene, Gregory Sierra; ***D:*** Paul Hunt, Lamar Card.

Clones of Bruce Lee 1980 (R) It's a martial arts free-for-all as bold masters from throughout the world duel for supremacy in the realm of self defense. If you like martial arts movies, you'll probably like this one. If you don't know if you like martial arts movies, find out with one of the actual Bruce Lee's flicks. **87m/C VHS.** Dragon Lee, Bruce Le, Bruce Lai, Bruce Thai; ***D:*** Joseph Kong.

The Clonus Horror ½ *Parts: The Clonus Horror* 1979 A scientist discovers a government plot to clone the population by freezing bodies alive and using their parts in surgery. **90m/C VHS.** Tim Donnelly, Keenan Wynn, Peter Graves, Dick Sargent, Paulette Breen; ***D:*** Robert S. Fiveson.

Close Encounters of the Third Kind 1977 (PG) Middle-American strangers become involved in the attempts of benevolent aliens to contact earthlings. Despite the sometimes mundane nature of the characters, this Spielberg epic is a stirring achievement. Studded with classic sequences; the ending is an exhilarating experience of special effects and peace-on-earth feelings. Dreyfuss and Dillon excel as friends who are at once bewildered and obsessed by the alien presence, and French filmmaker Truffaut is also strong as the stern, ultimately kind scientist. **152m/C VHS, DVD, Wide.** Richard Dreyfuss, Teri Garr, Melinda Dillon, Francois Truffaut, Bob Balaban, Cary Guffey, J. Patrick McNamara; ***D:*** Steven Spielberg; ***W:*** Steven Spielberg; ***C:*** Vilmos Zsigmond; ***M:*** John Williams. Oscars '77: Cinematog., Sound FX Editing; AFI '98: Top 100.

Close My Eyes 🦴🦴 **1991 (R)** A hot, steamy summer arouses vibrant passions in a brother and sister, and neither marriage nor blood relation can halt the inevitable. **105m/C VHS.** Alan Rickman, Clive Owen, Saskia Reeves; ***D:*** Stephen Poliakoff.

Close to Eden 🦴🦴 *Urga* **1990 (PG)** A peasant couple living in inner Mongolia with their three children are prevented by strict Chinese law from having a fourth. The husband sets out from his village to obtain birth control from the nearby town. While on his way, the farmer (Bayaertu) saves a Russian truck driver (Gostukhin) after he drives into a lake. Sergei is introduced to another way of life when he's taken home by his rescuer to meet the family and becomes accustomed to the tranquility of farm life in the rural Mongolian steppe. Essentially a story about the changes modern civilization can bring to a rural way of life. Filmed in Mongolia. In Russian with English subtitles. **109m/C VHS.** *RU* Baoyinhexige, Badema, Nikita Mikhalkov; ***D:*** Nikita Mikhalkov; ***W:*** Rustam Ibragimbekov; ***M:*** Eduard Artemyev. Venice Film Fest. '91: Film.

Close to Home 🦴🦴 **1986** A runaway fleeing a home life of abuse and neglect befriends a TV journalist doing a story on similar girls. She turns to him for support after she is arrested and returned home. Merely mediocre. **93m/C VHS.** *CA* Daniel Allman, Jillian Fargey, Anne Petrie; ***D:*** Rick Beairsto.

Closely Watched Trains 🦴🦴🦴½ *Ostre Sledovane Vlaky* **1966** A novice train dispatcher attempts to gain sexual experience in German-occupied Czechoslovakia during WWII. Many funny scenes in this film regarded by some as a classic. Based upon the Czech novel by Bohumil Hrabal. In Czech with English subtitles. **89m/B VHS, DVD.** *CZ* Vaclav Neckar, Jitka Bendova, Vladimir Valenta, Josef Somr; ***D:*** Jiri Menzel; ***W:*** Jiri Menzel; ***C:*** Jaromir Sofr; ***M:*** Jiri Sust. Oscars '67: Foreign Film.

The Closer 🦴🦴½ **1991 (R)** Aiello is "The Closer," a high-powered salesman whose world is falling apart. Somewhere between the money and the power, he's lost touch with his family and the truly important things in life. Is it too late to get them back? **87m/C VHS.** Danny Aiello, Michael Pare, Joe Cortese, Justine Bateman, Diane Baker, James Karen, Rick Aiello, Michael Lerner; ***D:*** Dimitri Logothetis; ***W:*** Robert Keats, Louis LaRusso II; ***M:*** Al Kasha.

Closer and Closer 🦴🦴½ **1996** Cable thriller finds author Kate Sander (Delaney) paralyzed after being stalked by someone resembling the stalker character in her last book "Gargoyle." Kate works with wheelchair-bound personal trainer B.J. Connors (York) to regain her strength, which she'll need as she writes "Gargoyle 2." This time Kate's decided to kill off her stalker/serial killer and soon real murders begin to occur. **93m/C VHS, DVD.** Kim Delaney, John J. York, Peter Outerbridge, Peter MacNeill, Scott Craft, Anthony Sherwood; ***D:*** Fred Gerber; ***W:*** Matt Dorff. **CABLE**

The Closet 🦴🦴½ *Le Placard* **2000 (R)** Francois Pignon (Auteuil) is a dull everyguy accountant who learns he's about to be fired after 20 years (from his job at a condom factory). His new (gay) neighbor Belone (Aumont) makes a unique suggestion—he will send doctored photos, showing Pignon at a gay bar, to Pignon's company and they will be forced to back down or be accused of sexual discrimination. Francois protests he can't pass as gay but he doesn't have to—his bosses and coworkers believe the rumors and make their own assumptions, including the homophobic personnel director Felix (Depardieu) who fears for his own job if he's not especially nice to Francois. Balances neatly between slapstick and sentiment. French with subtitles. **86m/C VHS, DVD, Wide.** *FR* Daniel Auteuil, Gerard Depardieu, Thierry Lhermitte, Michel Aumont, Michele Laroque, Jean Rochefort, Alexandra Vandernoot; ***D:*** Francis Veber; ***W:*** Francis Veber; ***C:*** Luciano Tovoli; ***M:*** Vladimir Cosma.

Closet Land 🦴½ **1990 (R)** Severe, stylized political allegory aims high but fails to convincingly distill totalitarian repression into just two characters—a government inquisitor and his captive, a woman subjected to hideous mental and physical torture. Child-molesting emerges as an ill-advised subtheme. A better video on the same subject: "Interrogation," from Poland. **95m/C VHS.** Madeleine Stowe, Alan Rickman; ***D:*** Radha Bharadwaj; ***W:*** Radha Bharadwaj; ***C:*** Bill Pope; ***M:*** Richard Einhorn.

Cloud Dancer 🦴🦴 **1980 (PG)** A self-absorbed acrobat uses and abuses those around him, including his girlfriend. Carradine and O'Neill fail to distinguish themselves in this mediocre film. **107m/C VHS.** David Carradine, Jennifer O'Neill, Joseph Bottoms, Colleen Camp; ***D:*** Barry Brown; ***W:*** William Goodhart.

Cloud Waltzing 🦴🦴½ **1987** The screen version of a Harlequin romance about a journalist who arrives in France to interview a vintner and finds romance and danger. Melodrama bolstered by the presence of photogenic Beller. **103m/C VHS.** Kathleen Beller, Francois-Eric Gendron, Paul Maxwell, Therese Liotard, Claude Gensac, David Baxt; ***D:*** Gordon Flemyng.

The Clouded Yellow 🦴🦴🦴 **1951** Young, lovely, and a little unstable, Sophie Malraux (Simmons) is accused of murdering the handyman who worked for her guardians (Jones and Dresdel). Ex-British Secret Service agent David Somers (Howard), who's in love with Sophie, helps her escape from jail and the two head for Liverpool and a ship to Mexico. But the police (hoping to find the real killer) are hot on their trail. Romantic suspense with good lead pairing. **95m/B VHS.** *GB* Jean Simmons, Trevor Howard, Sonia Dresdel, Barry Jones, Maxwell Reed, Kenneth More, Andre Morell, Geoffrey Keen; ***D:*** Ralph Thomas; ***W:*** Eric Ambler; ***C:*** Geoffrey Unsworth.

Clouds over Europe 🦴🦴🦴 *Q Planes* **1939** A test pilot and a man from Scotland Yard team up to find out why new bomber planes are disappearing. **82m/B VHS.** Laurence Olivier, Valerie Hobson, Ralph Richardson, George Curzon, George Merritt, Gus McNaughton, David Tree, Sandra Storme, Hay Petrie, Frank Fox, Gordon McLeod, John Longden, Reginald Purdell, John Laurie, Pat Aherne; ***D:*** Tim Whelan; ***W:*** Ian Dalrymple; ***C:*** Harry Stradling Sr.

Clown 🦴🦴½ **1953** A broken-down funny man with a worshipful son obtains one last career opportunity. This "Champ"-derived tearjerker features credible playing from Skelton and Considine as father and son, respectively. **91m/B VHS.** Red Skelton, Jane Greer, Tim Considine, Steve Forrest; ***D:*** Robert Z. Leonard; ***C:*** Paul Vogel.

Clown House 🦴 **1988 (R)** Young brothers are stalked in their home by three demonic clowns. **95m/C VHS.** Nathan Forrest Winters, Brian McHugh, Sam Rockwell, Viletta Skillman, Timothy Enos, Tree; ***D:*** Victor Salva.

Clown Murders 🦴½ **1983** Posh Halloween party is undone when a cruel group fakes a kidnapping to ruin a too-prosperous pal's business deal. Awkward thriller boasts little suspense. Candy plays it straight, mostly, in this one. **94m/C VHS.** John Candy, Al Waxman, Susan Keller, Lawrence Dane; ***D:*** Martyn Burke.

Clowning Around 🦴🦴½ **1992** Simon, who has lived in foster homes all his life, dreams of becoming a famous circus clown. When he's sent to a new home, his new foster parents think his idea is silly, so he runs away and joins the circus. There he meets Anatole, a European clown has-been who can no longer perform because of injuries. Simon believes Anatole can teach him about clowning, so he follows Anatole to Paris to help make his dream come true. Part of the "Wonderworks" series. **165m/C VHS.** *AU* Clayton Williamson, Jean-Michel Dagory, Ernie Dingo; ***D:*** George Whaley.

Clowning Around 2 🦴🦴½ **1993** The continuing story of Sim, whose dream is to become a world-famous clown. Now a member of the Winter Circus in Paris, he is still training with his mentor Anatole. But Sim is dissatisfied and when he befriends Eve, another young clown, he learns an experimental style of clowning which gets them both fired. He first follows Eve to her home in Montreal but then returns to his own home in Australia where he has been left the co-owner of a less-than-successful circus by a former employer. Filmed on location in Paris, France and Perth, Australia. **120m/C VHS.** *AU* Clayton Williamson, Jean-Michel Dagory, Ernie Dingo, Frederique Fouche; ***D:*** George Whaley.

The Clowns 🦴🦴🦴½ **1971 (G)** An idiosyncratic documentary about circus clowns. Director Fellini has fashioned an homage that is sincere, entertaining, and personal. Contains some truly poignant sequences. Made for Italian TV with English subtitles. **90m/C VHS.** *IT* ***D:*** Federico Fellini; ***W:*** Federico Fellini, Barnardino Zapponi; ***C:*** Dario Di Palma; ***M:*** Nino Rota. **TV**

The Club 🦴🦴🦴 *Players* **1981 (PG)** A soccer coach tries to train and motivate a mediocre squad into one worth playing for—and perhaps even winning—the league cup. Conventional sports story is significantly improved by Thompson's rendering of the coach. **99m/C VHS.** *AU* Jack Thompson, Graham Kennedy, John Howard, Alan Cassell; ***D:*** Bruce Beresford; ***W:*** David Williamson.

The Club 🦴 **1994 (R)** Typical teens-in-peril flick finds the high school prom held in a mysterious old castle with ghouls out to get the unfortunate seniors. Visuals are decent but frights are tepid. **88m/C VHS.** Kim Coates, Joel Wyner, Andrea Roth, Rino Romano, Zack (Zach) Ward, Kelli Taylor, Matthew Ferguson; ***D:*** Brenton Spencer; ***W:*** Robert Cooper; ***M:*** Paul Zaza.

Club Extinction 🦴🦴½ *Docteur M* **1989 (R)** A near-future thriller in which Berlin is plagued by a wave of suicides. An investigator suspects a spa representative and a media tycoon of being involved. Features a fine international cast, but the film is a lesser venture from prolific master Chabrol. **105m/C VHS.** *GE* Alan Bates, Andrew McCarthy, Jennifer Beals, Jan Niklas, Hanns Zischler, Benoit Regent, Peter Fitz, Wolfgang Preiss, Isolde Barth; ***D:*** Claude Chabrol.

Club Fed 🦴½ **1990 (PG-13)** A rigid prison warden's plot to impose greater discipline is undone by inmate highjinks. Crude laughs and one-dimensional play from a cast of recognizable names and faces. **93m/C VHS.** Judy Landers, Sherman Hemsley, Karen Black, Burt Young, Rick Schmidt, Allen (Goorwitz) Garfield, Joseph Campanella, Lyle Alzado, Mary Woronov, Debbie Lee Carrington; ***D:*** Nathaniel Christian; ***C:*** Arledge Armenaki.

Club Havana 🦴½ **1946** A benevolent nightclub owner tries to save one of his singers from the depths of despair by reuniting her with her boyfriend. Minor musical with minor musical numbers. ♫Besame Mucho; Tico Tico. **62m/B VHS.** Tom Neal, Margaret Lindsay, Don Douglas, Isabelita, Dorothy Morris, Ernest Truex; ***D:*** Edgar G. Ulmer.

Club Life 🦴 **1986 (R)** A hardened biker finds sex, drugs, and violence on the Hollywood streets. What did he expect? Peace, love, and understanding? **93m/C VHS.** Tony Curtis, Dee Wallace Stone, Tom Parsekian, Michael Parks, Jamie Barrett; ***D:*** Norman Thaddeus Vane.

Club Med 🦴🦴 **1983 (PG)** An insecure comedian and his goofy friend try to make the most of a ski vacation. Perhaps your only chance to see Thicke, Killy, and Coolidge together. **60m/C VHS.** Alan Thicke, Jim Carrey, Jean-Claude Killy, Rita Coolidge, Ronnie Hawkins; ***D:*** David Mitchell, Bob Giraldi; ***M:*** Peter Bernstein.

Club Paradise 🦴🦴½ **1986 (PG-13)** A Chicago fireman flees the big city for a faltering tropical resort and tries to develop some night life. Somewhat disappointing with Williams largely playing the straight man. Most laughs provided by Martin, particularly when she is assaulted by a shower, and Moranis, who gets lost while windsurfing. **96m/C VHS.** Robin Williams, Peter O'Toole, Rick Moranis, Andrea Martin, Jimmy Cliff, Brian Doyle-Murray, Twiggy, Eugene Levy, Adolph Caesar, Joanna Cassidy, Mary Gross, Carey Lowell, Robin Duke, Simon Jones; ***D:*** Harold Ramis; ***W:*** Harold Ramis, Brian Doyle-Murray; ***M:*** David Mansfield, Van Dyke Parks.

Club Vampire 🦴 **1998 (R)** Vampire Zero (Savage) wants to bite stripper Corri (Andreff) but Laura (Frank) gets there first and Corri starts to transform. Vampire leader Aiko (Parris) doesn't want any new converts and sends Zero to kill her. But Zero has other plans. A bore. **77m/C VHS.** John Savage, Starr Andreeff, Diana Frank, Michael J. Anderson, Marriam Parris, Ross Malinger; ***D:*** Andy Ruben; ***W:*** Andy Ruben; ***C:*** Steve Gainer; ***M:*** Michael Elliott. **VIDEO**

Clubhouse Detectives 🦴🦴½ **1996 (PG)** When Billy witnesses a crime at a neighbor's no one believes him—except his friends, so the clubhouse detectives decide to investigate. **85m/C VHS.** Michael Ballem, Michael Galeota, Jimmy Galeota, Suzanne Barnes; ***D:*** Eric Hendershot.

Clue 🦴🦴½ **1985 (PG)** The popular boardgame's characters must unravel a night of murder at a spooky Victorian mansion. The entire cast seems to be subsisting on sugar, with wild eyes and frantic movements the order of the day. Butler Curry best survives the uneven script and direction. Warren is appealing too. The theatrical version played with three alternative endings, and the video version shows all three successively. **96m/C VHS, DVD, Wide.** Lesley Ann Warren, Tim Curry, Martin Mull, Madeline Kahn, Michael McKean, Christopher Lloyd, Eileen Brennan, Howard Hesseman, Lee Ving, Jane Wiedlin, Colleen Camp, Bill Henderson; ***D:*** Jonathan Lynn; ***W:*** John Landis, Jonathan Lynn; ***C:*** Victor Kemper; ***M:*** John Morris.

Clueless 🦴🦴🦴 *I Was a Teenage Teenager; No Worries* **1995 (PG-13)** Watch out "Beverly Hills 90210," here comes Cher. No, not the singer Cher, but ultra-filthy-rich brat Cher, who's out to make over her classmates and teachers, specifically flannel-shirted transfer student Tai (Murphy). Aerosmith vamp Silverstone stars as the teenage manipulator who knows all too well how to spend her trust fund. The only person who can match her wits is disapproving stepbrother Josh (Rudd). (Ah, love.) Loosely based on Jane Austen's "Emma," Heckerling, of "Fast Times at Ridgemont High" fame, knows this territory and directs a bright, surprisingly satirical romp. **113m/C VHS, DVD, Wide.** Alicia Silverstone, Stacey Dash, Paul Rudd, Brittany Murphy, Donald Adeosun Faison, Julie Brown, Jeremy Sisto, Dan Hedaya, Wallace Shawn, Breckin Meyer, Elisa Donovan, Aida Linares; ***D:*** Amy Heckerling; ***W:*** Amy Heckerling; ***C:*** Bill Pope; ***M:*** David Kitay. MTV Movie Awards '96: Female Perf. (Silverstone), Most Desirable Female (Silverstone); Natl. Soc. Film Critics '95: Screenplay; Blockbuster '96: Female Newcomer, T. (Silverstone).

The Clutching Hand 🦴🦴 **1936** The Clutching Hand seeks a formula that will turn metal into gold and detective Craig Kennedy is out to prevent him from doing so. A serial in 15 chapters on three cassettes. **268m/B VHS.** Jack Mulhall, Rex Lease, Mae Busch, William Farnum, Robert Frazer, Reed Howes, Marion Shilling; ***D:*** Al(bert) Herman.

Coach 🦴½ **1978 (PG)** Sexy woman is unintentionally hired to coach a high school basketball team and mold rookies into lusty young champions. Low-grade roundball fever. **100m/C VHS, DVD.** Cathy Lee Crosby, Michael Biehn, Keenan Wynn, Sidney Wicks; ***D:*** Bud Townsend.

Coal Miner's Daughter 🦴🦴🦴 **1980 (PG)** A strong bio of country singer Loretta Lynn, who rose from Appalachian poverty to Nashville riches. Spacek is perfect in the lead, and she even provides acceptable rendering of Lynn's tunes. Band drummer Helm shines as Lynn's father, and Jones is strong as Lynn's down-home husband. Uneven melodrama toward the end, but the film is still a good one. ♫Coal Miner's Daughter; Sweet Dreams of You; I'm a Honky-Tonk Girl; You're Lookin' at Country; One's On the Way; You Ain't Woman Enough to Take My Man; Back in My Baby's Arms. **125m/C VHS.** Sissy Spacek, Tommy Lee Jones, Levon Helm, Beverly D'Angelo; ***D:*** Michael Apted; ***C:*** Ralf Bode. Oscars '80: Actress (Spacek); Golden Globes '81: Actress—Mus./Comedy (Spacek), Film—Mus./Comedy; L.A. Film Critics '80: Actress (Spacek); Natl. Bd. of Review '80: Actress (Spacek); N.Y. Film Critics '80: Actress (Spacek); Natl. Soc. Film Critics '80: Actress (Spacek).

The Coast Patrol 🦴🦴½ **1925** B. Reeves Eason, responsible for the chariot scene in the silent "Ben Hur" and the action scenes in "The Charge of the Light Brigade," directed Fay in one of her earliest parts, eight years before the role that prompted her to say "I didn't realize that King Kong and I were going to be together for the rest of our lives, and longer... " Much Eason-style high action when smugglers meet the coast patrol. **63m/B VHS.** Kenneth McDonald, Claire De Lorez, Fay Wray; ***D:*** Bud Barsky.

Coast to Coast 🦴🦴 **1980 (PG)** A wacky woman escapes from a mental institution and teams with a pugnacious trucker for a cross-country spree. Ostensibly freewheeling comedy is only occasionally worthwhile despite appropriate playing from leads Cannon and Blake, who deserve better. **95m/C VHS.** Dyan Cannon, Robert (Bobby) Blake, Quinn (K.) Redeker, Michael Lerner, Maxine Stuart, William Lucking; ***D:*** Joseph Sargent; ***M:*** Charles Bernstein.

Cobb 🦴🦴🦴 **1994 (R)** Biography of Ty Cobb (Jones), the universally acknowledged "most hated man in baseball" who, near the end of his life, realizes he doesn't want to be remembered in that way. So he hires sportswriter Al Stump (Wuhl) to ghostwrite (read: sugarcoat) his life story. As seen through Stump's eyes, Cobb is an unrelenting, petty, bigoted, hateful, paranoid, drunken, and yet compelling man. They form an uneasy bond as Stump duly records the fiction Cobb is feeding him, secretly deciding to write the truth after the legend's death. Jones is at his scene-chewing, antagonistic best, while Wuhl seems both overwhelmed and overshadowed as the embattled Stump. Shelton has something to say about American hero worship and a celebrity's desire for posterity, but with the focus intent on portraying Cobb's meanness, it's hard to say what. Surprisingly little baseball action for a baseball bio. Based on Stump's "Cobb: A Biography." **128m/C VHS.** Tommy Lee Jones, Robert Wuhl, Lolita (David) Davidovich; ***D:*** Ron Shelton; ***W:*** Ron Shelton; ***C:*** Russell Boyd.

Cobra 🦴 **1925** To pay off the debts incurred by his profligate playboyance, Valentino takes a job with an antique dealer, falls for the dealer's secretary and arranges an assignation with the dealer's wife, who is inconveniently killed at the designated rendezvous. Complications abound as Valentino finds himself Sheik out of luck. Lesser Valentino effort was released a year before the famous heartthrob's untimely death and enjoyed a rather acrid critical reception. Which isn't to say the public didn't flock to see the Italian stallion flare his nostrils. **75m/B VHS, DVD.** Rudolph Valentino, Nita Naldi, Casson Ferguson, Gertrude (Olmstead) Olmsted; ***D:*** Joseph Henabery.

The Cobra 🦴 *Il Cobra; El Cobra* **1968** A tightlipped U.S. agent ogles a voluptuous siren when not fighting opium smugglers from the Middle East. A must for all admirers of Ekberg. **93m/C VHS.** Dana Andrews, Anita Ekberg; ***D:*** Mario Sequi.

Cobra 🦴🦴½ *Le Sant de l'Ange* **1971** A hired killer destroys most of a mob family and becomes the target of revenge for the lone survivor. Moody thriller boasts an international cast. **93m/C VHS.** *FR IT* Sterling Hayden, Senta Berger, Jean Yanne; ***D:*** Yves Boisset.

Cobra 🦴 **1986 (R)** A cold-blooded cop protects a model from a gang of deranged killers. Low-brow, manipulative action fare void of feeling. Truly exploitive, with little expression from the leads. Highlight is the extended chase sequence. Based on the Paula Gosling novel "Fair Game," which was remade under the book's title (and in a more faithful adaptation) in 1995. **87m/C VHS, DVD.** Sylvester Stallone, Reni Santoni, Brigitte Nielsen, Andrew (Andy) Robinson; ***D:*** George P. Cosmatos; ***W:*** Sylvester Stallone; ***C:*** Ric Waite; ***M:*** Sylvester Levay.

The Cobra Strikes 🦴½ **1948** Nosey thief gets more than he bargained for when he works his way through an inventor's studio. Low-budget and unexceptional. **62m/B VHS.** Sheila Ryan, Richard Fraser, Leslie Brooks, Herbert (Hayes) Heyes; ***D:*** Charles Reisner.

Cobra Verde 🦴🦴 *Slave Coast* **1988** Even by Herzog/Kinski standards, their last collaboration was one wild trip. Kinski is a 19th-century Brazilian bandit, known as Cobra Verde, who finds work as a slave overseer on a sugar plantation. When he impregnates all three of the owner's daughters, he's sent on an impossible mission to re-open the slave trade with a mad African king. Discovering he's being cheated, Cobra Verde trains an army of women to overthrow the king, so he can control the slave trade himself. Based on the novel "The Viceroy of Ouidah" by Bruce Chatwin. German with subtitles. **110m/C VHS, DVD, Wide.** *GE* Klaus Kinski, Peter Berling, Jose Lewgoy, Salvatore Basile; ***D:*** Werner Herzog; ***W:*** Werner Herzog; ***C:*** Viktor Ruzicka; ***M:*** Popul Vuh.

Cobra Woman 🦴🦴½ **1944** Technicolor adventure fantasy about the jungle queen (Montez) of a cobra-worshipping cult and her evil twin sister who wants the throne for herself. **70m/C VHS.** Maria Montez, Jon Hall, Sabu, Edgar Barrier, Lois Collier, Lon Chaney Jr., Mary Nash, Samuel S. Hinds, Moroni Olsen; ***D:*** Robert Siodmak; ***W:*** Richard Brooks, Gene Lewis; ***C:*** William Howard Greene; ***M:*** Edward Ward.

The Cobweb 🦴🦴 **1955** Shady goings on are uncovered at a psychiatric ward run by a bunch of neurotic administrators. A strong cast, director and producer do not add much to this dull outing. **125m/C** Lauren Bacall, Richard Widmark, Gloria Grahame, Charles Boyer, Lillian Gish, John Kerr, Susan Strasberg, Oscar Levant, Tommy Rettig, Paul Stewart, Adele Jergens, Bert Freed, Sandy Descher, Fay Wray, Virginia Christine; ***D:*** Vincente Minnelli; ***C:*** George J. Folsey.

The Coca-Cola Kid 🦴🦴🦴½ **1984 (R)** Smug U.S. sales exec Becker (Roberts) treks to Australia to improve regional sales and becomes embroiled in sexual and professional shenanigans. He gets involved with free-spirited secretary Terri (sexy Scacchi) and discovers that a soft drink locally brewed by eccenric McDowall (Kerr) is his determined competition. Roberts is strong in the difficult lead role, and Scacchi is compelling in an awkwardly constructed part. Ambitious satire is somewhat scattershot, with more storylines than it needs. Still, filmmaker Makavejev is usually capable of juggling the entire enterprise. **94m/C VHS, DVD.** *AU* Eric Roberts, Greta Scacchi, Bill Kerr, Chris Haywood, Kris McQuade, Max Gilles; ***D:*** Dusan Makavejev; ***W:*** Frank Moorhouse; ***C:*** Dean Semler; ***M:*** William Motzig.

Cocaine Cowboys 🦴½ **1979 (R)** Lame rockers support themselves between gigs by peddling drugs then find out they've run afoul of the mob. Palance is the only worthwhile aspect of this rambling venture produced at Andy Warhol's home. **90m/C VHS.** Jack Palance, Andy Warhol, Tom Sullivan, Suzanna Love, Richard Young; ***D:*** Ulli Lommel; ***W:*** Ulli Lommel, Victor Bockris, Tom Sullivan; ***C:*** Jochen Breitenstein; ***M:*** Elliot Goldenthal.

Cocaine Fiends 🦴🦴 *The Pace That Kills* **1936** Drug use leads siblings into a squalid life of addiction, crime, prostitution, and eventually suicide. Ostensibly straight morality tale functions better as loopy camp. Features memorable slang. **74m/B VHS, DVD.** Lois January, Noel Madison, Willy Castello, Dean Benton, Lois Lindsay, Sheila (Manors) Mannors; ***D:*** William O'Connor, W.A. O'Connor.

Cocaine: One Man's Seduction 🦴🦴½ **1983** Documents one man's degeneration into drug addiction. Weaver snorts convincingly in lead. **97m/C VHS.** Dennis Weaver, Karen Grassle, Pamela Bellwood, David Ackroyd; ***D:*** Paul Wendkos; ***M:*** Brad Fiedel. **TV**

Cocaine Wars 🦴 **1986 (R)** An undercover U.S. agent kills dozens while trying to rescue his kidnapped girlfriend from an evil South American drug tycoon. Violent, but otherwise unaffecting. **82m/C VHS.** John Schneider, Kathryn Witt, Royal Dano; ***D:*** Hector Olivera.

Cockeyed Cavaliers 🦴🦴 **1934** Wheeler and Woolsey are stockaded for stealing the Duke's horses and carriage. To escape jail they swap clothes with some drunken royalty. **70m/B VHS.** Bert Wheeler, Robert Woolsey, Dorothy Lee, Thelma Todd; ***D:*** Mark Sandrich.

Cockfighter 🦴🦴🦴 *Gamblin' Man; Born to Kill; Wild Drifters* **1974 (R)** A unique, grim portrait of a cockfighting trainer. Oates, in the lead, provides voiceover narrations, but the film otherwise remains silent until the end. Strong support from Stanton. Interesting, violent fare. **84m/C VHS, DVD, Wide.** Warren Oates, Harry Dean Stanton, Richard B. Shull, Troy Donahue, Millie Perkins, Robert Earl Jones, Warren Finnerty, Ed Begley Jr., Charles Willeford; ***D:*** Monte Hellman; ***W:*** Charles Willeford; ***C:*** Nestor Almendros; ***M:*** Michael Franks.

Cocktail 🦴🦴½ **1988 (R)** A smug young man finds fame and fortune as a proficient, flashy bartender, charming the ladies with his bottle and glass juggling act. Slick, superficial film boasts a busy soundtrack and serviceable exchanges between male leads Cruise and Brown. There's less chemistry between Cruise and love interest Shue. Filmed in a high-tech rock video style. **103m/C VHS, 8mm.** Tom Cruise, Bryan Brown, Elisabeth Shue, Lisa Banes, Laurence Luckinbill, Kelly Lynch, Gina Gershon, Ron Dean, Paul Benedict; ***D:*** Roger Donaldson; ***W:*** Heywood Gould; ***C:*** Dean Semler; ***M:*** J. Peter Robinson. Golden Raspberries '88: Worst Picture, Worst Screenplay.

The Cocoanuts 🦴🦴½ **1929** In their film debut, the Marx Brothers create their trademark, indescribable mayhem. Stagey, technically crude comedy nonetheless delights with zany, free-for-all exchanges, antics. Includes famous "viaduct" exchange. **96m/B VHS, DVD.** Groucho Marx, Chico Marx, Harpo Marx, Zeppo Marx, Margaret Dumont, Kay Francis, Oscar Shaw, Mary Eaton, Cyril Ring, Basil Ruysdael; ***D:*** Robert Florey, Joseph Santley; ***W:*** George S. Kaufman, Morrie Ryskind; ***C:*** George J. Folsey; ***M:*** Irving Berlin.

Cocoon 🦴🦴🦴 **1985 (PG-13)** Humanist fantasy in which senior citizens discover their fountain of youth is actually a breeding ground for aliens. Heartwarming, one-of-a kind drama showcases elderly greats Ameche, Brimley, Gilford, Cronyn, and Tandy. A commendable, recommendable venture. Based on David Saperstein's novel and followed by "Cocoon: The Return." **117m/C VHS.** Wilford Brimley, Brian Dennehy, Steve Guttenberg, Don Ameche, Tahnee Welch, Jack Gilford, Hume Cronyn, Jessica Tandy, Gwen Verdon, Maureen Stapleton, Tyrone Power Jr., Barret Oliver, Linda Harrison, Herta Ware, Clint Howard; ***D:*** Ron Howard; ***W:*** Tom Benedek; ***M:*** James Horner. Oscars '85: Support. Actor (Ameche), Visual FX.

Cocoon: The Return 🦴🦴 **1988 (PG)** Old timers who left with aliens in "Cocoon" return to earth and face grave problems. Less compelling sequel misses guiding hand of earlier film's director, Ron Howard. Still, most of cast from the original is on board here, and the film has its moments. **116m/C VHS.** Don Ameche, Wilford Brimley, Steve Guttenberg, Maureen Stapleton, Hume Cronyn, Jessica Tandy, Gwen Verdon, Jack Gilford, Tahnee Welch, Courteney Cox Arquette, Brian Dennehy, Barret Oliver; ***D:*** Daniel Petrie; ***C:*** Tak Fujimoto; ***M:*** James Horner.

C.O.D. 🦴 **1983 (PG)** Bosom buddies must develop advertising campaign for brassiere producer or find their careers are bust. Premise milked for all its worth, so you may want to keep abreast of this one. On the other hand, you may not give a hoot. Oh well, tit for tat. **96m/C VHS.** Chris Lemmon, Olivia Pascal, Jennifer Richards, Corinne Alphen, Teresa Ganzel, Carole (Raphaelle) Davis; ***D:*** Chuck Vincent; ***W:*** R.J. Marx.

Code Name Alpha 🦴🦴 *Red Dragon; A-009 Missione Hong Kong* **1967** You don't have to have a federal case of intelligence to figure out where this FBI story's going and how it's going to get there. Someone's smuggling sophisticated electrical components to the communists, and a team of intelligence agents, including Granger and Schiaffino, hike over to Hong Kong to break up the party. Based on the story "Le Riviere des Trois Jonques" by Georges Godefroy. **89m/C VHS.** *IT GE* Stewart Granger, Rosanna Schiaffino, Harald Juhnke, Paul Klinger, Helga Sommerfeld, Horst Frank; ***D:*** Ernest Hofbauer.

Code Name: Chaos 🦴🦴 *Spies, Lies, and Alibis* **1990 (R)** A political spoof featuring a group of renegade spies trying to come up with a get-rich-quick scheme. It involves inventing a global crisis in a small Asian country but the plan comes under the scrutiny of a CIA agent who's not in on the scheme. **96m/C VHS.** Robert Loggia, Diane Ladd, David Warner, Alice Krige, Brian Kerwin; ***D:*** Antony Thomas.

Code Name: Dancer *Her Secret Life* **1987** A retired spy leaves her peaceful life, husband, and family to take care of business in Cuba. **93m/C VHS.** Kate Capshaw, Jeroen Krabbe, Gregory Sierra, Cliff DeYoung, Valerie Mahaffey, James Sloyan; ***D:*** Buzz Kulik; ***M:*** Georges Delerue. **TV**

Code Name: Diamond Head 🦴 **1977** In Hawaii, a secret agent is assigned to retrieve a deadly chemical that has been hidden by a master of disguises. **78m/C VHS.** Roy Thinnes, France Nuyen, Zulu, Ian McShane; ***D:*** Jeannot Szwarc. **TV**

Code Name: Emerald 🦴 **1985 (PG)** WWII drama in which an American agent must stop an enemy spy with knowledge of impending D-Day invasion. Conventional TV fare boasts a fine performance by von Sydow, but Stolz is hopelessly miscast as an adult. Perhaps the only film featuring both Buchholz and Berger. First feature film by NBC-TV network. **95m/C VHS.** Ed Harris, Max von Sydow, Eric Stoltz, Horst Buchholz, Helmut Berger, Cyrielle Claire, Patrick Stewart, Graham Crowden; ***D:*** Jonathan Sanger; ***W:*** Ronald Bass; ***M:*** John Addison.

Code Name: Zebra 🦴½ **1984** The Zebra Force helps the cops put bad guys away. When the bad guys get out, they want revenge. The result: lots of violence and action. Wasn't released theatrically. **96m/C VHS.** Jim Mitchum, Mike Lane, Tim Brown, Joe Dante, Deana Jurgens, Frank Sinatra Jr.; ***D:*** Joe Tornatore.

Code of Honor 🦴🦴½ *Sweet Revenge* **1984** A young woman vows revenge on the military commanders who caused her brother's demise. Neatly made psychological thriller is surprisingly good for a TV movie. **105m/C VHS.** Kevin Dobson, Wings Hauser, Alec Baldwin, Merritt Butrick, Kelly McGillis, Alfre Woodard, Savannah Smith, Helen Hunt, Dana Elcar; ***D:*** David Green.

Code of Honor 🦴 **1988** Prominent businessman embarks on mission of revenge when police fail to apprehend his wife's rapist. No surprise here. You either enjoy this sort of thing or you lead a reasonably fulfilling life. **90m/C VHS.** Cameron Mitchell, Mark Sabin.

Code of Silence 🦴🦴 **1985 (R)** A police loner must contend with both a gang war and police department corruption. Hectic, violent action-drama with some wild stunts. **100m/C VHS, DVD.** Chuck Norris, Henry Silva, Bert Remsen, Molly Hagan, Nathan Davis, Dennis Farina; ***D:*** Andrew Davis; ***W:*** Michael Butler, Mike Gray.

Code of the Fearless 🦴 **1939** A cowboy wins the heart of a beautiful maiden while bringing evildoers to justice. **56m/B VHS.** Fred Scott, Claire Rochelle, John Merton, Harry Harvey, Walter McGrail, Roger Williams; ***D:*** Raymond K. Johnson.

Codename: Foxfire 🦴🦴 *Slay It Again, Sam* **1985** An attractive secret agent is framed for wrongdoing and must clear her name by tracking the enemy spy lurking within the intelligence network. Always interesting Cassidy is an asset, but this by-the-numbers TV film is otherwise a misappropriation of the term "intelligence" in relation to espionage. **99m/C VHS.** Joanna Cassidy, John McCook, Sheryl Lee Ralph, Henry Jones, Luke Andreas; ***D:*** Corey Allen.

Codename: Icarus 🦴🦴 **1985** A young mathematical genius, enrolled at a special school for accelerated study, uncovers evil government plots to use the students for espionage. **106m/C VHS.** *GB* Barry Angel, Jack Galloway; ***D:*** Marilyn Fox. **TV**

Codename: Jaguar 🦴🦴½ **2000 (R)** Innocent Stuart Dempsey (Nucci) has just moved to New York when he is mistaken for an international assassin by both the CIA and the FBI. The assassin, codenamed Jaguar, is in town to kill the visiting Russian prez. But is innocent Stuart really that innocent after all? **93m/C VHS, DVD.** Danny Nucci, David Carradine, Victoria Sanchez, Jack Langedijk; ***D:*** John Hamilton; ***W:*** Tim Kring; ***C:*** Bert Tougas. **VIDEO**

Codename Kyril 🦴🦴½ **1991 (R)** Woodward plays a British spy pitted against Soviet assassin Kyril (Charleson) who's been sent to England by the KGB to rout out a double agent. Turns out there's more to it than Kyril knows, and nobody loves an assassin. Based on John Trenhaile's "A Man Called Kyril," the script is slow from the gun, but eventually builds something akin to momentum. **115m/C VHS.** Edward Woodward, Ian Charleson, Denholm Elliott, Joss Ackland, Richard E. Grant, Sven-Bertil Taube, Catherine Nielson, John McEnery, Peter Vaughan, James Laurenson; ***D:*** Ian Sharp; ***W:*** John Hopkins. **CABLE**

Codename: Terminate 🦴½ **1990** Title says it all in this tender exploration of the human condition. Jungle-trained mercenaries grab their guns and go after an American pilot shot down behind enemy lines. **84m/C VHS.** Robert Mason, Jim Gaines.

Codename: Vengeance 🦴 **1987 (R)** A macho fellow tries to stop a killer holding the shah's wife and son hostage. Dated. **97m/C VHS.** Robert Ginty, Cameron Mitchell, Shannon Tweed; ***D:*** David Winters.

Codename: Wildgeese 🦴½ *Geheimecode Wildganse* **1984 (R)** The big-name cast of this meandering mercenary macho-rama probably wish they'd been credited under code names; solid histrionics cannot a silly script save. A troop of commandos-for-hire are engaged by the Drug Enforcement Administration to obliterate an opium operation in Asia's infamous Golden Triangle, and much mindless agitation ensues. **101m/C VHS.** *IT GE* Lewis Collins, Lee Van Cleef, Ernest Borgnine, Klaus Kinski, Mimsy Farmer; ***D:*** Anthony (Antonio Margheriti) Dawson.

Cody 🦴 **1967** A former bronco buster wants his son to "take it like a man" when the boy's dog dies. Then a mystical goose arrives to mellow the old man. That's really the plot. **82m/C VHS.** Tony Becker, Terry Evans.

Coffy 🦴🦴 **1973 (R)** A beautiful woman feigns drug addiction to discover and destroy the evil dealers responsible for her sister's death. Grier is everything in this exploitative flick full of violence and nudity. **91m/C VHS, DVD, Wide.** William Elliott, Sid Haig, Pam Grier, Booker Bradshaw, Robert DoQui, Allan Arbus; ***D:*** Jack Hill; ***W:*** Jack Hill; ***C:*** Paul Lohmann; ***M:*** Roy Ayers.

Cohen and Tate 🦴🦴 **1988 (R)** Two antagonistic mob hitmen kidnap a nine-year-old who witnessed his parent's recent murder by the mob. In order to survive, the boy begins to play one psycho off the other. **113m/C VHS.** Roy Scheider, Adam Baldwin, Harley Cross, Cooper Huckabee; ***D:*** Eric Red; ***W:*** Eric Red; ***M:*** Bill Conti.

Cold Around the Heart 🦴🦴 **1997 (R)** Familiar crime/road movie finds sensitive jewel thief Ned (Caruso) partnering up (both in and out of the sack) with tough cookie Jude (Lynch). Only in their latest heist, Jude takes off with the diamonds and Ned's in pursuit across the southwest but, nice guy that Ned is, he stops to help out pregnant, black hitchhiker Bec (Dash). If you don't expect much, you won't be disappointed. **96m/C VHS.** David Caruso, Kelly Lynch, Stacey Dash, Christopher Noth, John Spencer; ***D:*** John Ridley; ***W:*** John Ridley; ***C:*** Malik Hassan Sayeed; ***M:*** Mason Daring.

Cold Blood 🦴½ *Das Amulett des Todes* **1975 (R)** A pair of kidnap victims turn the tables on their captors. **90m/C VHS.** *GE* Rutger Hauer, Vera Tschechowa, Horst Frank, Gunther Stoll; ***D:*** Ralf Gregan, Gunter Vaessen; ***W:*** Gunter Vaessen; ***C:*** Michael Ballhaus; ***M:*** Rolf Bauer.

Cold Blooded 🦴🦴 **2000 (R)** Reporter suspects a cover-up when the police dismiss the death of a young woman as a suicide. He thinks she's another victim of a serial killer who has already killed 12 and isn't done yet. **94m/C VHS, DVD.** Michael Moriarty, Patti LuPone, John Kapelos, Gloria Reuben; ***D:*** Randy Bradshaw; ***W:*** Ian Adams; ***C:*** Dean Bennett; ***M:*** Tim McCauley. **VIDEO**

Cold Comfort 🦴🦴½ **1990 (R)** A father arranges his teen daughter's romance, but finds his plans going awry in this Canadian thriller. Nominated for several Canadian TV awards, including Best Actress, Best Actor, Best Picture and Best Musical Score. **90m/C VHS.** *CA* Margaret Langrick, Maury Chaykin, Paul Gross; ***D:*** Vic Sarin; ***W:*** Richard Beattie, Elliot L. Sims; ***C:*** Vic Sarin. **TV**

Cold Comfort Farm 🦴🦴½ **1971** The original BBC production of Stella Gibbon's satiric novel. Orphaned London sophisticate Flora Poste (Badel) is forced to rely on the kindness of her dotty country cousins, the Starkadders, when she needs somewhere to live. But Flora is determined to set things right with the peculiar clan. **135m/C VHS.** *GB* Sarah Badel, Brian Blessed, Fay Compton, Rosalie Crutchley, Alastair Sim, Peter Egan, Fionnula Flanagan, Freddie Jones, Sharon Gurney; ***D:*** Peter Hammond; ***W:*** David Turner. **TV**

Cold Comfort Farm 🦴🦴🦴 **1994 (PG)** Stella Gibbons classic 1932 comedic novel is brought to life in this TV adaptation, which finds orphaned London lass Flora Poste (Beckinsdale) trying to take charge of the lives of her very odd country cousins, the Starkadders. The rowdy family and their dilapidated farm are putty in practical Flora's hands as she works to make everybody happy (including herself). Terrific ensemble cast, with a fast pace and wicked humor. **104m/C VHS.** *GB* Kate Beckinsale, Eileen Atkins, Ian McKellen, Sheila Burrell, Rufus Sewell, Maria Miles, Freddie Jones, Ivan Kaye, Miriam Margolyes, Joanna Lumley, Stephen Fry, Christopher Bowen; ***D:*** John Schlesinger; ***W:*** Malcolm Bradbury; ***C:*** Chris Seager; ***M:*** Robert Lockhart.

Cold Days 🦴🦴½ **1966** Four men await execution for their part in the WWII massacre of Jews and Serbs. Their reminiscences and justifications, if any, are examined. Stunning cinematography and unusual theme for 1960s Hungarian political climate. **102m/C VHS.** *HU* ***D:*** Andras Kovacs.

Cold Eyes of Fear 🦴 **1970** A man and his girlfriend are besieged by a raving convict whom his uncle, a judge, had put away years before. Shades of "Cape Fear" on a low budget. **88m/C VHS, DVD.** Fernando Rey, Frank Wolfe, Karin Schubert; ***D:*** Enzo G. Castellari; ***W:*** Enzo G. Castellari, Tito Carpi, Leo Anchoriz; ***C:*** Antonio Ballesteros; ***M:*** Ennio Morricone.

Cold Feet 🦴🦴½ **1984 (PG)** Light romantic comedy about a TV director just recovering from a failed marriage and his fall for a lab researcher who just went through a break-up herself. **96m/C VHS.** Griffin Dunne, Marissa Chibas, Blanche Baker, Mark Cronogue; ***D:*** Bruce Van Dusen.

Cold Feet 🦴🦴½ **1989 (R)** Modern-day western in which a trio of loopy desperados smuggle jewels inside a racehorse's stomach. Quirky comedy offers wild performances from Waits and sexbomb Kirkland, but could use a few more laughs. Filmed largely on McGuane's ranch. **94m/C VHS.** Keith Carradine, Tom Waits, Sally Kirkland, Rip Torn, Kathleen York, Bill Pullman, Vincent Schiavelli, Jeff Bridges; ***D:*** Robert Dornhelm; ***W:*** Thomas McGuane, Jim Harrison; ***C:*** Bryan Duggan; ***M:*** Tom Bahler.

Cold Fever 🦴🦴 **1995** Japanese yuppie Atsushi Hirata (Nagase) is expecting to vacation in the tropical paradise of Hawaii not the frozen reaches of Iceland. But instead he must perform a memorial ritual on the remote Icelandic spot where his parents died some time before. He arrives in a blizzard and things just go downhill from there. Some quirky characters but the film loses focus. **85m/C VHS.** *IC* Masatoshi Nagase, Gisli Halldorsson, Lili Taylor, Fisher Stevens; ***D:*** Fridrik Thor Fridriksson; ***W:*** Fridrik Thor Fridriksson, Jim Stark; ***M:*** Hilmar Orn Hilmarsson.

Cold Front 🦴½ **1989 (R)** A hired assassin turned serial killer is hunted by two dedicated cops. **94m/C VHS.** *CA* Martin Sheen, Michael Ontkean, Beverly D'Angelo, Kim Coates; ***D:*** Allan Goldstein; ***C:*** Thomas Burstyn.

Cold Harvest 🦴🦴 **1998 (R)** A comet strikes the earth, killing a great portion of the population and then disaster strikes again when a deadly disease runs unchecked, killing those who become infected. A bounty hunter and his partner seek to find one of the seven people who carry the antibody to the disease. **93m/C VHS, DVD.** Gary Daniels, Barbara Crampton, Bryan Genesse; ***D:*** Isaac Florentine; ***W:*** Frank Dietz; ***C:*** David Varod; ***M:*** Steve Edwards. **VIDEO**

Cold Hearts 🦴🦴½ **1999** Charles is the head of a group of young vampires who take over a small New Jersey town. But best friends Viktoria and Alicia want to escape from Charles' influence and turn to a stranger for help. Low-budget vamp flick is surprisingly professional and watchable. **88m/C VHS.** Marisa Ryan, Amy Jo Johnson, Christopher Wiehl, Robert Floyd; ***D:*** Robert Masciantonio. **VIDEO**

Cold Heat 🦴🦴 **1990** When a custody battle rocks a crime boss' world, he pulls out all the stops in the war against his wife. **85m/C VHS.** John Phillip Law, Britt Ekland, Robert Sacchi, Roy Summerset, Joanne Watkins, Chance Michael Corbitt; ***D:*** Ulli Lommel.

Cold Heaven 🦴½ **1992 (R)** Alex and Marie Davenport are on vacation when an accident occurs and Alex dies—or does he? The next day his body disappears and his unfaithful wife begins to have paranoid delusions that he is returning to exact retribution for her affair. But these aren't her only visions, for during the past year Marie has also had religious visions she believes are part of a personal battle with God. Harmon does what he can with his role as the alleged corpse but Russell is uncharacteristically whiny and bland. Convoluted story of marriage, death, and spirituality; doesn't pan out on any accounts. Based on a novel by Brian Moore. **103m/C VHS.** Theresa Russell, Mark Harmon, James Russo, Talia Shire, Will Patton, Richard Bradford; ***D:*** Nicolas Roeg; ***W:*** Allan Scott.

Cold Justice 🦴🦴 **1989 (R)** An ex-prizefighter (Daltrey) and his friends welcome an English priest into their tough southside Chicago neighborhood. The good father seems too good to be true as he befriends the locals—even raising funds for the children's hospital. When the funds never make it to the hospital and the neighborhood begins to experience a number of violent tragedies, the residents decide to take their own revenge. **106m/C VHS.** Dennis Waterman, Roger Daltrey, Penelope Milford, Ron Dean, Bert Rosario; ***D:*** Terry Green; ***W:*** Terry Green.

Cold Light of Day 🦴🦴 **1995** Police officer Victor Marek (Grant) is hunting a serial killer of young children in the English countryside—and he'll do anything, including using a young girl as bait. Marek seduces single mother Milena (Baxter) to use her young daughter to set a trap for the killer but can he catch the madman before it's too late? **101m/C VHS.** *GB* Richard E. Grant, Lynsey Baxter, Simon Cadell, Perdita Weeks, James Laurenson, Heathcote Williams; ***D:*** Rudolf Van Den Berg; ***W:*** Doug Magee.

Cold River 🦴🦴½ **1981 (PG)** An experienced guide takes his two children on an extended trip through the Adirondacks. For the children, it's a fantasy vacation until their father succumbs to a heart attack in the chilly mountains. "Cold River" is a journey of survival, and an exploration of human relationships. **94m/C VHS.** Pat Petersen, Richard Jaeckel, Suzanne Weber; ***D:*** Fred G. Sullivan.

Cold Room 🦴½ *The Prisoner* **1984** College student on vacation with her father in East Berlin discovers the horrors hidden in an antiquated hotel room next to hers. From the novel by Jeffrey Caine. **95m/C VHS.** George Segal, Renee Soutendijk, Amanda Pays, Warren Clarke, Anthony (Corlan) Higgins; ***D:*** James Dearden; ***M:*** Michael Nyman. **CABLE**

Cold Sassy Tree 🦴🦴🦴½ **1989** Endearing romance of a scandalous May-December marriage as perceived by the younger woman's teenage son. Dunaway and Widmark shine, and small-town pettiness is vividly rendered. Adapted from the books by Olive Ann Burns. A superior made-for-cable production. **95m/C VHS.** Faye Dunaway, Richard Widmark, Neil Patrick Harris, Frances Fisher, Lee Garlington, John M. Jackson; ***D:*** Joan Tewkesbury; ***W:*** Joan Tewkesbury; ***M:*** Brad Fiedel. **CABLE**

Cold Steel 🦴½ **1987 (R)** Standard revenge drama about a hardnosed Los Angeles cop tracking his father's disfigured psycho-killer. Cast includes the always intense Davis, ex-pop star Ant, and screen scorchstress Stone. Still it's predictable, low-grade fare. **91m/C VHS.** Brad Davis, Jonathan Banks, Adam Ant, Sharon Stone; ***D:*** Dorothy Ann Puzo.

Cold Steel for Tortuga 🦴 **1965** An Italian epic about a mercenary rescuing his woman and his gold from an evil governor. Dubbed. **95m/C VHS.** *IT* Guy Madison, Rick Battaglia, Ingeborg (Inge) Schoener; ***D:*** Luigi Capuano.

Cold Sweat 🦴🦴 *L'Uomo Dalle Due Ombre; De la Part des Copains* **1971 (PG)** A brutal drug trader takes his ultra-violent revenge after his wife is captured by a drug boss' moronic henchmen. Typical Bronson flick boasts superior supporting cast of Ullmann and Mason. Writing and direction, however, are mediocre. **94m/C VHS, DVD.** *IT FR* Charles Bronson, Jill Ireland, Liv Ullmann, James Mason; ***D:*** Terence Young; ***W:*** Albert Simonin, Shimon Wincelberg; ***C:*** Jean Rabier; ***M:*** Michel Magne.

Cold Sweat 🦴🦴 **1993 (R)** A professional hit man (Cross) is literally haunted by the ghost of his last victim (who happens to be female and usually appears naked), so he decides his next assignment will be his last. A ruthless businessman suspects his very sexy wife (Tweed) has been unfaithful but she has lots of other secrets to hide. **93m/C VHS.** Ben Cross, Shannon Tweed, Adam Baldwin, Dave Thomas; ***D:*** Gail Harvey; ***W:*** Richard Beattie.

Cold Turkey 🦴🦴🦴 **1971 (PG)** Often witty satire about what happens when an entire town tries to stop smoking for a contest. Van Dyke is fine as the anti-smoking minister; newscasters Bob and Ray are riotous; oldtimer Horton's swansong. Wholesome, somewhat tame fare. **99m/C VHS.** Dick Van Dyke, Pippa Scott, Tom Poston, Bob Newhart, Vincent Gardenia, Barnard Hughes, Jean Stapleton, Graham Jarvis, Edward Everett Horton; ***D:*** Norman Lear; ***W:*** Norman Lear; ***M:*** Randy Newman.

Cold War Killers 🦴½ **1986 (PG)** Soviet and British agents vie for control of prized cargo plane recently retrieved from the sea floor. **85m/C VHS.** *GB* Terence Stamp; ***D:*** William Brayne.

Coldblooded 🦴½ **1994 (R)** Minor mob flunky (and dim bulb) Cosmo (Priestley) is unwillingly promoted to the position of hit man by his mobster boss. He's tutored by the organization's primo professional (Riegert) and finds out he has a real knack for murder. More sophomoric than satiric and a waste of Riegert's talents; Williams is attractive as Priestley's clueless girlfriend. Directorial debut of Wolodarsky. **92m/C VHS.** Jason Priestley, Peter Riegert, Kimberly Williams, Robert Loggia, Janeane Garofalo, Josh Charles, David Anthony Higgens, Doris Grau; ***Cameos:*** Talia Balsam, Michael J. Fox; ***D:*** M. Wallace Wolodarsky; ***W:*** M. Wallace Wolodarsky; ***C:*** Robert Yeoman; ***M:*** Steve Bartek.

Coldfire 🦴½ **1990** Two rookie cops work to undo the havoc unleashed on the streets of LA because of a deadly new drug sought for its powerful high. Not many surprises here. **90m/C VHS.** Wings Hauser, Kamar Reyes, Robert Viharo, Gary Swanson; ***D:*** Wings Hauser.

The Colditz Story 🦴🦴½ **1955** Prisoners of war from the Allied countries join together in an attempt to escape from Colditz, an allegedly escape-proof castle-prison deep within the Third Reich. **93m/B VHS.** John Mills, Eric Portman, Lionel Jeffries, Bryan Forbes, Ian Carmichael, Anton Diffring; ***D:*** Guy Hamilton.

Cole Justice 𝒮𝒮 1989 An older man, haunted by the memory of his girlfriend's rape and murder 35 years earlier, takes to the streets to protect innocent citizens from lowlife criminals. Somewhat unusual revenge pic filmed in and around Tulsa, Oklahoma. **90m/C VHS.** Carl Bartholomew, Keith Andrews, Mike Wiles, Nick Zickefoose; ***D:*** Carl Bartholomew.

Collateral Damage 𝒮𝒮 **2002 (R)** Revenge drama pits Ah-nuld against the Columbian terrorists whose actions caused the death of his wife and child. When investigators come up short, nothing-left-to-lose fireman Gordy Brewer (Schwarzenegger) takes matters into his own hands and sets out to catch "The Wolf," the rebel leader of Columbia's civil war and the one responsible for his family's demise. In Columbia, he meets Selena (Neri) and her son Mauro (Posey) and his instinct to protect and serve them kicks into action, giving him renewed purpose. Highlights are Leguizamo as Felix, the Columbian drug producer, and Turturro as an exiled Canadian working as a mechanic. Mexico subs for Columbia in this unbelievable and formulaic actioner for genre and Arnold fans only. **109m/C VHS, DVD.** *US* Arnold Schwarzenegger, Elias Koteas, Francesca Neri, Clifford Curtis, John Leguizamo, John Turturro, Miguel (Michael) Sandoval, Harry J. Lennix, Lindsay Frost; ***D:*** Andrew Davis; ***W:*** David Griffiths, Peter Griffiths; ***C:*** Adam Greenberg; ***M:*** Graeme Revell.

Collected Stories 𝒮𝒮𝒮 **2002** Fine two-character study based on the 1997 play by Margulies, who adapted for this PBS presentation. Ruth Steiner (Lanvin) is a respected writer and teacher in her mid-50s who lives comfortably in her Greenwich Village apartment. It's there that Ruth agrees that ambitious graduate student and aspiring writer Lisa Morrison (Mathis) will become her assistant. Over six years, their relationship evolves into a friendship, which Lisa betrays when she turns the scandalous details of Ruth's life into a best-selling novel. **120m/C VHS.** Linda Lavin, Samantha Mathis; ***D:*** Gil(bert) Cates; ***W:*** Donald Margulies; ***C:*** Johnny (John W.) Simmons; ***M:*** Charles Fox. **TV**

The Collector 𝒮𝒮𝒮½ 1965 Compelling adaptation of the John Fowles novel about a withdrawn butterfly collector who decides to add to his collection by kidnapping a beautiful girl he admires. He locks her in his cellar hoping she will fall in love with him. Chilling, unsettling drama with Stamp unnerving, yet sympathetic in lead. **119m/C VHS.** *GB* Terence Stamp, Samantha Eggar, Maurice Dallimore, Mona Washbourne; ***D:*** William Wyler; ***W:*** John Kohn, Stanley Mann; ***C:*** Robert Krasker, Robert L. Surtees; ***M:*** Maurice Jarre. Cannes '65: Actor (Stamp), Actress (Eggar); Golden Globes '66: Actress—Drama (Eggar).

The Collectors 𝒮𝒮 **1999 (R)** Mob boss sends hit men Ray (Van Dien) and A.K. (Fox) to collect a big debt that's owed but they would rather take the payoff and get out of New York—preferably alive. **97m/C VHS, DVD, Wide.** Casper Van Dien, Rick Fox, Catherine Oxenberg, Daniel Pilon; ***D:*** Sidney J. Furie. **VIDEO**

Collector's Item 𝒮𝒮𝒮 1989 Two lovers reunite after 16 years and a flurry of memories temporarily rekindles their passion, which comes dangerously close to obsession. Casting of the physically bountiful Antonelli helps this effective erotic drama. **99m/C VHS.** *IT* Tony Musante, Laura Antonelli, Florinda Bolkan; ***D:*** Giuseppe Patroni-Griffi.

College 𝒮𝒮𝒮½ 1927 A high school valedictorian tries out for every sport in college, hoping to win the girl. Vintage Keaton antics, including disaster as a soda jerk, an attempt to be a track star, and the pole vault through a window to rescue the damsel in distress. **60m/B VHS, DVD.** Buster Keaton, Anne Cornwall, Harold Goodwin; ***D:*** James W. Horne; ***W:*** Brian Foy, Carl Harbaugh; ***C:*** Bert Haines; ***M:*** John Muri.

College Swing 𝒮½ *Swing, Teacher, Swing* **1938** Lightweight, lackluster musical about Allen inheriting a small town college which she turns into a hangout for her vaudeville pals. Top cast is basically wasted performing many forgettable songs and familiar routines. Based on an adaptation by Frederick Hazlitt Brennan from a story by Ted Lesser. ♫College Swing; What Did Romeo Say to Juliet?; I Fall In Love With You Every Day; You're a Natural; The Old School Bell; Moments Like This; How D'ja Like to Love Me?; What a Rumba Does to Romance. **86m/B VHS, DVD.** George Burns, Gracie Allen, Martha Raye, Bob Hope, Edward Everett Horton, Ben Blue, Betty Grable, Jackie Coogan, John Payne; ***D:*** Raoul Walsh; ***W:*** Walter DeLeon, Francis Martin; ***C:*** Victor Milner; ***M:*** Boris Morros, Hoagy Carmichael, Burton Lane, Frank Loesser.

Collision Course 𝒮 **1989 (PG)** A wise-cracking cop from Detroit teams up with Japan's best detective to nail a ruthless gang leader. Release was delayed until 1992 due to a lawsuit, but it was resolved in time to coordinate the release with Leno's debut as the host of "The Tonight Show." Pretty marginal, but diehard fans of Leno may appreciate it. Filmed on location in Detroit. **99m/C VHS.** Noriyuki "Pat" Morita, Jay Leno, Chris Sarandon, Al Waxman; ***D:*** Lewis Teague.

The Colombian Connection 𝒮½ 1991 America's best undercover agent battles a powerful cocaine empire deep in the jungles of the Amazon, where slave labor and political corruption abound. **90m/C VHS.** Miles O'Keeffe, Henry Silva; ***D:*** Michael Lemick.

Colonel Chabert 𝒮𝒮 1994 In the 1807 Battle of Eylau, French officer Chabert (Depardieu) is thought dead and stripped of all he possesses. After 10 years of imprisonment, a man shows up in the office of Paris lawyer Derville (Luchini), claiming to be the dead Chabert. His remarried wife (Ardant), now the Countess Ferraud, has used his fortune to bolster the political aspirations of her second husband (Dussolier) and refuses to acknowledge this stranger's claims. Is Chabert a fraud? And what exactly are the motives of all the players? Based on the novel by Honore de Balzac. Directorial debut of Angelo. French with subtitles. **111m/C VHS.** *FR* Gerard Depardieu, Fanny Ardant, Fabrice Luchini, Andre Dussollier; ***D:*** Yves Angelo; ***W:*** Yves Angelo, Jean Cosmos, Veronique Lagrange; ***C:*** Bernard Lutic.

Colonel Effingham's Raid 𝒮𝒮½ *Man of the Hour* **1945** A retired army colonel uses military tactics to keep an old historical courthouse open, while defeating some crooked politicians in the process. **70m/B VHS.** Joan Bennett, Charles Coburn, William Eythe, Donald Meek; ***D:*** Irving Pichel.

Colonel Redl 𝒮𝒮𝒮𝒮 **1984 (R)** Absorbing, intricately rendered psychological study of an ambitious officer's rise and fall in pre-WWI Austria. Brandauer is excellent as the vain, insecure homosexual ultimately undone by his own ambition and his superior officer's smug loathing. Muller-Stahl and Landgrebe are particularly distinguished among the supporting players. The second in the Szabo/Brandauer trilogy, after "Mephisto" and before "Hanussen." In German with English subtitles. **142m/C VHS, DVD.** *GE HU* Klaus Maria Brandauer, Armin Mueller-Stahl, Gudrun Landgrebe, Jan Niklas, Hans-Christian Blech, Laszlo Mensaros, Andras Balint; ***D:*** Laszlo Szabo; ***W:*** Laszlo Szabo, Peter Dobai; ***C:*** Lajos Koltai; ***M:*** Zdenko Tamassy. British Acad. '85: Foreign Film; Cannes '85: Special Jury Prize.

Colonel Wolodyjowski 𝒮𝒮½ **1969** An adaptation of the monumental novels by Henryk Sinkiewicz chronicling the attack on Poland's eastern border by the Turks in 1668. In Polish with English subtitles. **160m/C VHS.** *PL* Tadeusz Loniski, Magdalena Zawadzka, Daniel Olbrychski; ***D:*** Jerzy Hoffman.

The Colony 𝒮𝒮½ **1995 (PG-13)** "The Colony" is a luxurious and exclusive gated community owned by secretive billionaire developer Phillip Denning (Linden). Newest residents, security expert Rick Knowlton (Ritter), wife Leslie (Keller) and their two children, find out things are just too good to be true—and that trying to leave could be the very last thing they'll ever do. **93m/C VHS, DVD.** John Ritter, Hal Linden, Mary Page Keller, Marshall Teague, Frank Bonner, Michelle Scarabelli, June Lockhart, Todd Jeffries, Alexandra Picatto, Cody Dorkin; ***D:*** Rob Hedden; ***W:*** Rob Hedden; ***C:*** David Geddes.

The Colony 𝒮½ **1998 (R)** Aliens planning an earth invasion decide to test humankind by abducting four people and observing their survival skills. **94m/C VHS, DVD.** Isabella Hofmann, Michael Weatherly, Cristi Conaway, Eric Allen Kramer, Jeff Kober, James Avery, Clare Salstrom; ***D:*** Peter Geiger; ***W:*** Peter Geiger, Richard Kletter; ***C:*** Zoltan David; ***M:*** Paul Rabjohns. **CABLE**

Color Me Blood Red woof! *Model Massacre* **1964** Artist decides that the red in his paintings is best rendered with human blood. He even manages to continue his art career—when not busy stabbing and mutilating the unsuspecting citizenry. Short and shoddy. **74m/C VHS, DVD.** Don Joseph, Candi Conder, Elyn Warner, Scott H. Hall, Jerome (Jerry Stallion) Eden, Patricia Lee, James Jackel; ***D:*** Herschell Gordon Lewis; ***W:*** Herschell Gordon Lewis; ***C:*** Herschell Gordon Lewis.

Color Me Dead 𝒮½ **1969 (R)** A victim of an extremely slow-acting poison frantically spends his final days trying to uncover his killer. Another inferior remake of B-thriller "D.O.A." Rent that one instead. **97m/C VHS.** *AU* Tom Tryon, Carolyn Jones, Rick Jason, Patricia Connolly, Tony Ward; ***D:*** Eddie Davis.

Color of a Brisk and Leaping Day 𝒮𝒮 1995 While living in L.A. at the end of WWII, Chinese-American John Lee (Alexander) learns that the Yosemite Valley Railroad is being scrapped and he becomes determined to save it—in part as a homage to his grandfather who emigrated to work as a railroad laborer. A romantic train fanatic himself, Lee arranges financing from wealthy businessman Pinchot (Diehl) but must make the railroad pay within a year—unlikely as the automobile rapidly takes over as preferred transportation. Well-captures a '40s atmosphere but pacing and dialogue are uneven. **87m/B VHS.** Peter Alexander, Jeri Arredondo, Henry Gibson, Michael Stipe, John Diehl, David Chung, Diana Larkin, Bok Yun Chon; ***D:*** Christopher Munch; ***W:*** Christopher Munch; ***C:*** Rob Sweeney. Sundance '96: Cinematog.

The Color of Courage 𝒮𝒮½ **1998 (PG)** Anna Sipes (Hamilton) is pleased to welcome Minnie McGhee (Whitfield) to her Detroit neighborhood in 1944. But not every one feels the same, since the McGhees are black. The community (including Anna's husband) wants to force an eviction but since Anna and Minnie have become friends, they are equally determined that the McGhees will remain where they are. Based on the landmark civil rights case, Sipes vs. McGhee. **92m/C VHS.** Linda Hamilton, Lynn Whitfield, Bruce Greenwood, Roger Guenveur Smith; ***D:*** Lee Rose; ***W:*** Kathleen McGhee-Anderson; ***C:*** Eric Van Haren Noman; ***M:*** Terence Blanchard. **CABLE**

The Color of Evening 𝒮𝒮 **1995** Aging painter Landau tries to regain his youth by pursuing his young model Skye, but it's the older Burstyn who really inspires his imagination. **?m/C VHS.** Martin Landau, Ellen Burstyn, Ione Skye.

Color of Justice 𝒮𝒮 1997 A political circus ensues after a suburban white woman is killed by four black teens. Betty Gainer (Pelikan) is forced to stop behind a stolen car and is killed by the teens in the struggle that follows. Manhattan D.A. Jim Sullivan (Abraham) insists on trying the four as adults, while court-sppointed attorney Sam Lind (Hirsch) blames the cops, and media savvy black minister Walton (Hines) plays the race card. Meanwhile, Gainer's husband Frank (Davison) becomes increasingly frustrated as his wife's death seems to be forgotten. **95m/C VHS.** F. Murray Abraham, Judd Hirsch, Gregory Hines, Bruce Davison, Lisa Pelikan, Saul Rubinek, Mark L. Taylor, Gloria Carlin, Mia Korf, Dule Hill, Eugene Byrd, Malcolm Goodwin; ***D:*** Jeremy Paul Kagan; ***W:*** Lionel Chetwynd; ***C:*** Steven Poster; ***M:*** Michel Colombier. **CABLE**

The Color of Money 𝒮𝒮𝒮½ **1986 (R)** Flashy, gripping drama about former pool hustler Fast Eddie Felsen (Newman) who, after years off the circuit, takes a brilliant but immature pool shark (Cruise) under his wing. Strong performances by Newman as the grizzled veteran, Cruise as the showboating youth, and Mastrantonio and Shaver as the men's worldly girlfriends. Worthy sequel to "The Hustler." **119m/C VHS, DVD.** Paul Newman, Tom Cruise, Mary Elizabeth Mastrantonio, Helen Shaver, John Turturro, Forest Whitaker; ***D:*** Martin Scorsese; ***W:*** Richard Price; ***C:*** Michael Ballhaus; ***M:*** Robbie Robertson. Oscars '86: Actor (Newman); Natl. Bd. of Review '86: Actor (Newman).

Color of Night 𝒮½ **1994 (R)** Psychologist Dr. Bill Capa (Willis) takes over a murdered colleague's therapy group hoping to find out the killer's identity. Then he meets temptress Rose (March) and gets involved in a hot affair, but she's not what she seems—nor is anyone else. Preposterous thriller fails to deliver necessary suspense although the eroticism could spark some interest, particularly in the director's cut, which puts the sex back in the sex scenes between Willis and March (and is 15 minutes longer than the theatrical release). **136m/C VHS, DVD.** Bruce Willis, Jane March, Scott Bakula, Ruben Blades, Lesley Ann Warren, Lance Henriksen, Kevin J. O'Connor, Andrew Lowery, Brad Dourif, Eriq La Salle, Jeff Corey, Shirley Knight, Kathleen Wilhoite; ***D:*** Richard Rush; ***W:*** Matthew Chapman, Billy Ray, Richard Rush; ***C:*** Dietrich Lohmann; ***M:*** Dominic Frontiere. Golden Raspberries '94: Worst Picture.

The Color of Paradise 𝒮𝒮 *Rang-e Khoda* **1999 (PG)** Mohammad is an eight-year-old blind boy who is regarded as a burden by his recently widowed and hardworking father. His father hopes to remarry but thinks his son will be an obstacle and sends him to live with a carpenter, who is also blind, so that the boy can learn a trade. Of course, it is the father who must truly learn to see, since Mohammad already appreciates everything surrounding him. Farsi with subtitles. **90m/C VHS, DVD.** *IA* Mohsen Ramezani, Hossein Mahjoub; ***D:*** Majid Majidi; ***W:*** Majid Majidi; ***C:*** Mohammad Davudi; ***M:*** Alireza Kohandairy.

The Color of Pomegranates 𝒮𝒮𝒮 *Sayat Nova; Tsvet Granata* **1969** Paradjanov's depiction of the life of Armenian poet Arutiun Sayadin, known as Sayat Nova, who rises from carpet weaver to court minstrel to archbishop. Eloquent imagery and symbols are derived from Armenian paintings, poetry and history. In Armenian with English subtitles. Also includes "Hagop Hovnatanian," a 12-minute short on the artist. **80m/C VHS, DVD.** *RU* Sofiko Chiaureli, M. Aleksanian, V. Galstian; ***D:*** Sergei Paradjanov; ***W:*** Sergei Paradjanov; ***C:*** A. Samvelyan.

The Color Purple 𝒮𝒮𝒮½ **1985 (PG-13)** Celie is a poor black girl who fights for her self-esteem when she is separated from her sister and forced into a brutal marriage. Spanning 1909 to 1947 in a small Georgia town, the movie chronicles the joys, pains, and people in her life. Adaptation of Alice Walker's acclaimed book features strong lead from Goldberg (her screen debut), Glover, Avery, and talk-show host Winfrey (also her film debut). It's hard to see director Spielberg as the most suited for this one, but he acquits himself nicely, avoiding the facileness that sometimes flaws his pics. Brilliant photography by Allen Daviau and musical score by Jones (who co-produced) compliment this strong film. **154m/C VHS, DVD, Wide.** Whoopi Goldberg, Danny Glover, Oprah Winfrey, Margaret Avery, Adolph Caesar, Rae Dawn Chong, Willard Pugh, Akosua Busia; ***D:*** Steven Spielberg; ***W:*** Menno Meyjes; ***C:*** Allen Daviau; ***M:*** Chris Boardman, Quincy Jones. Directors Guild '85: Director (Spielberg); Golden Globes '86: Actress—Drama (Goldberg); Natl. Bd. of Review '85: Actress (Goldberg).

Colorado 𝒮½ 1940 Roy tries to find his brother, a Union deserter, during the Civil War. **54m/B VHS.** Roy Rogers, George "Gabby" Hayes, Milburn Stone; ***D:*** Joseph Kane.

Colorado Serenade 1946 Standard oater has Dean, Sharpe and Ates trying to prevent a young outlaw from bullying the local citizenry. Sharpe shows off his athletic prowess, and King provides some laughs. Other than that, it's pretty routine stuff. **68m/C VHS.** Eddie Dean, David Sharpe, Roscoe Ates, Forrest Taylor, Dennis Moore, Warner Richmond, Bob Duncan, Charles "Blackie" King; ***D:*** Robert Emmett Tansey.

Colorado Sundown 1952 A conniving brother and sister attempt to cheat a man out of his inheritance. **67m/B VHS.** Rex Allen, Mary Ellen Kay, Slim Pickens, June Vincent, Koko; ***D:*** William Witney.

Colors ½ 1988 (R) Vivid, realistic cop drama pairs sympathetic veteran Duvall and trigger-tempered rookie Penn on the gang-infested streets of East Los Angeles. Fine play from leads is one of the many assets in this controversial, unsettling depiction of deadly streetlife. Colorful, freewheeling direction from the underrated Hopper. Rattling rap soundtrack too. Additional footage has been added for video release. **120m/C VHS, DVD, Wide.** Glenn Plummer, Sy Richardson, Damon Wayans, Fred Asparagus, Sherman Augustus, R.D. Call, Seymour Cassel, Nick(y) Corello, Virgil Frye, Courtney Gains, Clark Johnson, Leon, Tina Lifford, Micole Mercurio, Jack Nance, Tony Todd, Gerardo Mejia, Sean Penn, Robert Duvall, Maria Conchita Alonso, Trinidad Silva, Randi Brooks, Grand Bush, Don Cheadle, Rudy Ramos; ***D:*** Dennis Hopper; ***W:*** Michael Schiffer; ***C:*** Haskell Wexler; ***M:*** Herbie Hancock.

Colorz of Rage ½ 1997 Story of an interracial relationship between Tony (Resteghini) and Debbie (Richards) covers familiar ground, but the New York locations have a gritty feel that's accentuated by the rough production values. **91m/C DVD.** Dale Resteghini, Nicki Richards, Cheryl "Pepsii" Riley, Don Wallace; ***D:*** Dale Resteghini; ***W:*** Dale Resteghini; ***C:*** Martin Ahlgren; ***M:*** Tony Prendatt.

Colossus and the Amazon Queen ½ *Colossus and the Amazons; La Regina delle Amazzoni* 1964 Idle gladiators are unwillingly recruited for service to Amazons. Doesn't seem like the worst way to make a living. But lead actor Taylor—so notable in comedies, thrillers, and action flicks—is too good for this sort of thing. Dubbed. **94m/C VHS, 8mm.** *IT* Rod Taylor, Dorian Gray, Ed Fury, Gianna Maria Canale; ***D:*** Vittorio Sala.

Colossus of the Arena 1960 In 4th century Rome, Forest plays a mighty gladiator who uncovers a plot to imprison a beautiful princess. Through an incredible series of feats and combats, he exposes an evil duke as a traitor. **?m/C VHS.** Mark Forest, Scilla Gabel.

Colossus: The Forbin Project *The Forbin Project* 1970 A computer designed to manage U.S. defense systems teams instead with its Soviet equal and they attempt world domination. Wire-tight, suspenseful film seems at once dated yet timely. Based on the novel by D.F. Jones. **100m/C VHS.** Eric (Hans Gudegast) Braeden, Susan Clark, Gordon Pinsent, William Schallert, Georg Stanford Brown; ***D:*** Joseph Sargent; ***W:*** James Bridges; ***C:*** Gene Polito; ***M:*** Michel Colombier.

Colt Comrades 1943 A bad guy's monopoly on water rights is jeopardized when Boyd and Clyde strike water while drilling for oil. Nothing really notable here, except for Bob (Robert) Mitchum and George ("Superman") Reeves in minor roles. **67m/B VHS.** William Boyd, Andy Clyde, Jay Kirby, George Reeves, Gayle Lord, Earle Hodgins, Victor Jory, Douglas Fowley, Herbert Rawlinson, Robert Mitchum; ***D:*** Lesley Selander.

Columbo: Murder by the Book ½ 1971 The rumpled, cigar-smoking TV detective investigates the killing of a mystery writer. Scripted by Bochco of "Hill Street Blues" and "L.A. Law" fame. **79m/C VHS.** Peter Falk, Jack Cassidy, Rosemary Forsyth, Martin Milner; ***D:*** Steven Spielberg; ***W:*** Steven Bochco.

Columbo: Prescription Murder 1967 Falk's debut as the raincoat-clad lieutenant who always has just one more question. In the TV series pilot he investigates the death of a psychiatrist's wife. Rich with subplots. Good mystery fare. **99m/C VHS.** Peter Falk, Gene Barry, Katherine Justice, William Windom, Nina Foch, Anthony James, Virginia Gregg; ***D:*** Richard Irving; ***W:*** Richard Levinson, William Link. **TV**

Coma 1978 (PG) A doctor discovers murder and corpse-nabbing at her Boston hospital, defies her male bosses, and determines to find out what's going on before more patients die. Exciting, suspenseful fare, with Bujold impressive in lead. Based on the novel by Robin Cook. **113m/C VHS, DVD.** Genevieve Bujold, Michael Douglas, Elizabeth Ashley, Rip Torn, Richard Widmark, Lois Chiles, Hari Rhodes, Tom Selleck, Ed Harris; ***D:*** Michael Crichton; ***W:*** Michael Crichton; ***C:*** Victor Kemper, Gerald Hirschfeld; ***M:*** Jerry Goldsmith.

Comanche Station ½ 1960 Loner Jefferson Cody (Scott) agrees to rescue Mrs. Lowe (Gates), a senator's wife who's been captured by the Comanches. After Cody achieves her rescue, they fall in with outlaw Ben Lane (Akins) and his two young proteges, who insist on accompanying them back to the Lowe homestead, saying that they'll need additional protection. But Cody soon realizes that Lane is after the reward money and is planning an ambush. **73m/C VHS.** Randolph Scott, Nancy Gates, Claude Akins, Skip Homeier, Richard Rust, Rand Brooks; ***D:*** Budd Boetticher; ***W:*** Burt Kennedy; ***C:*** Charles Lawton Jr.

Comanche Territory 1950 Western frontiersman Jim Bowie travels to Comanche country and helps the Indians save their land from settlers. Routine oater. Based on a story by Meltzer. **76m/C VHS.** Maureen O'Hara, MacDonald Carey, Will Geer, Charles Drake; ***D:*** George Sherman; ***W:*** Oscar Brodney, Lewis Meltzer.

The Comancheros 1961 Texas Ranger Wayne and his prisoner fight with the Comancheros, an outlaw gang who is supplying guns and liquor to the dreaded Comanche Indians. Musical score adds flavor. Last film by Curtiz. **108m/C VHS, Wide.** John Wayne, Ina Balin, Stuart Whitman, Nehemiah Persoff, Lee Marvin, Bruce Cabot; ***D:*** Michael Curtiz; ***C:*** William Clothier; ***M:*** Elmer Bernstein.

Combat Academy 1986 Weak comedy about two goofballs sent to a military academy to straighten out, but instead turn the academy on its ear with their antics. Unremarkable. **96m/C VHS.** Keith Gordon, Jamie Farr, Sherman Hemsley, John Ratzenberger, Bernie Kopell, Charles Moll, George Clooney; ***D:*** Neal Israel.

Combat Killers 1980 A WWII Army captain grabs for individual glory on the battlefield, and jeopardizes the lives of his platoon. **96m/C VHS.** Paul Edwards, Marlene Dauden, Claude Wilson; ***D:*** Ken Loring.

Combat Shock *American Nightmares* 1984 (R) A Vietnam veteran returns home and can't cope with the stresses of modern life, including the lowlifes who have been taking over the streets. So he goes after some scum who have been trying to kill him, succeeds, but things don't end well. Familiar plot handled in a conventional manner. **85m/C VHS, DVD.** Ricky Giovinazzo, Nick Nasta, Veronica Stork, Mitch Maglio, Aspah Livni; ***D:*** Buddy Giovinazzo; ***W:*** Buddy Giovinazzo; ***C:*** Stella Varveris; ***M:*** Ricky Giovinazzo.

Combination Platter ½ 1993 Anxious young immigrant Robert (Lau), newly arrived from Hong Kong, becomes a waiter at the Szechuan Inn in Queens, New York, where he gets a crash course in American culture and romance (as well as tipping). Gentle comedy works best with little details that ring true: overheard customer conversations, staff banter, the kitchen scenes. Lau's earnest, but effort feels like a series of small vignettes rather than a complete story. Still, a worthy first effort for the then 24-year-old Chan, who directed on a $250,000 budget, using his parents restaurant after hours for a set. **84m/C VHS.** Jeff Lau, Coleen O'Brien, Lester Chan, Thomas S. Hsiung, David Chung, Colin Mitchell, Kenneth Lu, Eleonara Khilberg, James DuMont; ***D:*** Tony Chan; ***W:*** Tony Chan, Edwin Baker; ***C:*** Yoshifumi Hosoya; ***M:*** Brian Tibbs. Sundance '93: Screenplay.

Come Along with Me ½ 1984 TV adaptation of Shirley Jackson's unfinished novel about a woman who sells all and leaves her hometown when her husband dies, determined to start a new career as a seer. **60m/C VHS.** Estelle Parsons, Barbara Baxley, Sylvia Sidney; ***D:*** Joanne Woodward. **TV**

Come and Get It *Roaring Timber* 1936 A classic adaptation of the Edna Ferber novel about a lumber king battling against his son for the love of a woman. Farmer's most important Hollywood role. **99m/B VHS, DVD.** Frances Farmer, Edward Arnold, Joel McCrea, Walter Brennan, Andrea Leeds, Charles Halton; ***D:*** William Wyler, Howard Hawks; ***W:*** Jules Furthman, Jane Murfin; ***C:*** Rudolph Mate, Gregg Toland; ***M:*** Alfred Newman. Oscars '36: Support. Actor (Brennan).

Come and See *Idi i Smotri; Go and See* 1985 Harrowing, unnerving epic which depicts the horrors of war as a boy soldier roams the Russian countryside during the Nazi invasion. Some overwhelming sequences, including tracer-bullets flashing across an open field. War has rarely been rendered in such a vivid, utterly grim manner. Outstanding achievement from Soviet director Klimov. In Russian with English subtitles. **137m/C VHS, DVD.** *RU* Alexei Kravchenko, Olga Mironova, Lubomiras Lauciavicus, Vladas Bagdonas, Viktor Lorents, Juris Lumiste, Kazimir Rabetsky, Yevgeni Tilicheyev; ***D:*** Elem Klimov; ***W:*** Elem Klimov, Alex Adamovich; ***C:*** Alexei Rodionov; ***M:*** Oleg Yanchenko.

Come Back, Little Sheba ½ 1952 Unsettling drama about a worn-out housewife, her abusive, alcoholic husband and a comely boarder who causes further marital tension. The title refers to the housewife's despairing search for her lost dog. Booth, Lancaster, and Moore are all excellent. Based on the play by William Inge, this film still packs an emotional wallop. **99m/B VHS.** Burt Lancaster, Shirley Booth, Terry Moore, Richard Jaeckel, Philip Ober, Lisa Golm, Walter Kelley; ***D:*** Daniel Mann; ***C:*** James Wong Howe. Oscars '52: Actress (Booth); Cannes '53: Actress (Booth); Golden Globes '53: Actress—Drama (Booth); N.Y. Film Critics '52: Actress (Booth).

Come Back to the Five & Dime Jimmy Dean, Jimmy Dean 1982 (PG) Five women convene at a run-down Texas drugstore for a 20-year reunion of a local James Dean fan club. The women recall earlier times and make some stunning revelations. Altman's filming of Ed Graczyk's sometimes funny, sometimes wrenching play proves fine vehicle for the actresses. Cher is probably the most impressive, but Dennis and Black are also memorable. **109m/C VHS.** Sandy Dennis, Cher, Karen Black, Kathy Bates, Sudie Bond, Marta Heflin; ***D:*** Robert Altman.

Come Blow Your Horn 1963 Neil Simon's first major Broadway success is a little less successful in its celluloid wrapper, suffering a bit from a familiar script. Sinatra's a playboy who blows his horn all over town, causing his close-knit New York Jewish family to warp a bit. Dad's not keen on his son's pledge of allegiance to the good life, and kid brother Bill would like to be his sibling's understudy in playboyhood. **115m/C VHS.** Frank Sinatra, Lee J. Cobb, Tony Bill, Molly Picon, Barbara Rush, Jill St. John; ***D:*** Bud Yorkin; ***W:*** Norman Lear; ***C:*** William H. Daniels.

Come on, Cowboys ½ 1937 The Three Mesquiteers rescue an old circus friend from certain death. Part of "The Three Mesquiteers" series. **54m/B VHS.** Robert "Bob" Livingston, Ray Corrigan, Max Terhune, Maxine Doyle, Willie Fung, Edward Peil Jr., Horace Murphy; ***D:*** Joseph Kane; ***W:*** Betty Burbridge; ***C:*** Ernest Miller.

Come on Danger! ½ 1932 Keene makes his "B" Western debut, out to avenge the death of his brother and battle an outlaw gang. Haydon is forced into a life of crime in order to save her ranch from villain Ellis and only Texas Ranger Keene can set her free. **60m/B VHS.** Tom (George Duryea) Keene, Julie Haydon, Roscoe Ates, Robert Ellis, Wade Boteler; ***D:*** Robert F. "Bob" Hill; ***W:*** Bennett Cohen.

Come on Rangers *Come On Ranger* 1938 Rogers and his friends go to Texas to avenge the death of a comrade. **54m/B VHS.** Roy Rogers, George "Gabby" Hayes, Lynne Roberts, Raymond Hatton, J. Farrell MacDonald, Purnell Pratt, Harry Woods; ***D:*** Joseph Kane; ***W:*** Gerald Geraghty, Jack Natteford; ***C:*** Al Wilson; ***M:*** Cy Feuer.

Come on Tarzan ½ 1932 Maynard and his trusty horse Tarzan save wild horses from the bad guys who want to turn them into dog food. **60m/B VHS.** Ken Maynard, Merna Kennedy, Niles Welch, Roy Stewart, Kate Campbell, Robert F. (Bob) Kortman, Nelson McDowell, Jack Rockwell; ***D:*** Alan James; ***W:*** Alan James.

Come See the Paradise 1990 (R) Jack McGurn (Quaid) takes a job at a movie theatre in Los Angeles' Little Tokyo and falls for owner's daughter Lily (Tomita). They marry, but after the bombing of Pearl Harbor all Japanese-Americans are interned. Told in flashback, the story offers a candid look at the racism implicit in the relocations and the hypocrisy that often lurks beneath the surface of the pursuit of liberty and justice for all. Sometimes melodramatic script indulges a bit too much in the obvious, but the subject is worthwhile, one that has not yet been cast into the vast bin of Hollywood cliches. The cast, apart from Quaid's misguided attempt at seriousness, is excellent. **135m/C VHS, Wide.** Dennis Quaid, Tamlyn Tomita, Sab Shimono, Shizuko Hoshi, Stan(ford) Egi, Ronald Yamamoto, Akemi Nishino, Naomi Nakano, Brady Tsurutani, Pruitt Taylor Vince, Joe Lisi; ***D:*** Alan Parker; ***W:*** Alan Parker; ***M:*** Randy Edelman.

Come September ½ 1961 American business tycoon Robert Talbot (Hudson) maintains a holiday villa on the Italian Riveria. But the only time he uses the place is the month of September, so when Talbot arrives in July he discovers his enterprising major domo Maurice (Slezak) has been managing the place as a hotel the rest of the year. Talbot finds his home filled with tourists and, to make matters worse, discovers his Italian lover Lisa (Lollobrigida) about to get married. Darin and Dee are the film's romantic ingenues and wound up getting married after filming wrapped; his screen debut. **114m/C VHS.** Rock Hudson, Gina Lollobrigida, Sandra Dee, Bobby Darin, Walter Slezak, Joel Grey, Brenda de Banzie; ***D:*** Robert Mulligan; ***W:*** Stanley Shapiro, Maurice Richlin; ***C:*** William H. Daniels; ***M:*** Hans J. Salter.

Come to the Stable 1949 Warm, delightful story about two French nuns, Young and Holm, who arrive in New England and set about building a children's hospital. Although Catholic in intent, pic demonstrates that faith and tenacity can move mountains. (This film must have been Fox's response to Paramount's "Going My Way" and "The Bells of Saint Mary's.") Based on a story by Clare Boothe Luce. **94m/B VHS.** Loretta Young, Celeste Holm, Hugh Marlowe, Elsa Lanchester, Regis Toomey, Mike Mazurki; ***D:*** Henry Koster; ***W:*** Oscar Millard, Sally Benson; ***C:*** Joseph LaShelle; ***M:*** Cyril Mockridge.

Come Undone *Presque Rien* 2000 A matter of fact coming of age tale about a French teenager, Mathieu (Elkaim), who acknowledges his sexuality when he falls in love with the slightly older Cedric (Rideau). Mathieu and his younger sister Sarah (Legrix) are stuck at their summer house in a coastal resort town with their depressed mother (Reymond) and their aunt (Matheron) who's serving as a nurse/housekeeper. The emotional Mathieu finds sex and solace with the volatile Cedric but their affair doesn't work out as expected. Film is non-linear and the viewer must piece together what has happened from the various scenes, which can be confusing. French with subtitles. **98m/C VHS, DVD.** *FR* Jeremie Elkaim, Stephane Rideau, Marie Matheron, Laetitia Legrix, Dominique Reymond, Nils Ohlund, Rejane Kerdaffrec, Guy Houssier; *D:* Sabastian Lifshitz; *W:* Sabastian Lifshitz, Stephane Bouquet; *C:* Pascal Paoucet; *M:* Perry Blake.

The Comeback *The Day the Screaming Stopped* **1977** A singer attempting a comeback in England finds his wife murdered. **100m/C VHS.** *GB* Jack Jones, Pamela Stephenson, David Doyle, Bill Owen, Sheila Keith, Richard Johnson; *D:* Pete Walker.

Comeback **1983** The story of a disillusioned rock star, played by Eric Burdon (the lead singer of the Animals), who gives up his life in the fast lane and tries to go back to his roots. **105m/C VHS.** Eric Burdon; *D:* Christel Bushmann; *M:* Eric Burdon.

Comeback Kid **1980** An ex-big league baseball player is conned into coaching an urban team of smarmy street youths, and falls for their playground supervisor. **97m/C VHS.** John Ritter, Susan Dey; *D:* Peter Levin. **TV**

The Comedians **1967** Disturbing and powerful drama of political intrigue set against the murderous dictatorship of "Papa Doc" Duvalier. Burton plays the cynical owner of a resort hotel with Taylor as his German mistress. Ustinov is great as he does his usual scene-stealing in his role as a South American ambassador married to Taylor. Excellent cast was somewhat held back by sluggish direction and an uninspired script. Based on the novel of the same name by Graham Greene. **148m/C VHS.** Elizabeth Taylor, Richard Burton, Alec Guinness, Peter Ustinov, Paul Ford, Lillian Gish, Raymond St. Jacques, Zakes Mokae; *D:* Peter Glenville; *W:* Graham Greene. Natl. Bd. of Review '67: Support. Actor (Ford).

The Comedy of Terrors *The Graveside Story* **1964** Comedy in which some deranged undertakers take a hands-on approach to insuring their continued employment. Much fun is supplied by the quartet of Price, Lorre, Karloff, and Rathbone, all veterans of the horror genre. **84m/C VHS.** Vincent Price, Peter Lorre, Boris Karloff, Basil Rathbone, Joe E. Brown, Joyce Jameson, Beverly (Hills) Powers, Buddy Mason; *D:* Jacques Tourneur; *W:* Richard Matheson; *C:* Floyd Crosby; *M:* Les Baxter.

Comes a Horseman **1978 (PG)** Robards is a cattle baron, attempting to gobble up all the oil-rich land his neighbor owns. Neighbor Fonda has the courage to stand up to him, with the help of a WWII veteran and the local old timer Farnsworth, in this slow-moving but intriguing western drama. **119m/C VHS, DVD, Wide.** James Caan, Jane Fonda, Jason Robards Jr., George Grizzard, Richard Farnsworth, Jim Davis, Mark Harmon; *D:* Alan J. Pakula; *W:* Dennis Lynton Clark; *C:* Gordon Willis; *M:* Michael Small. Natl. Bd. of Review '78: Support. Actor (Farnsworth); Natl. Soc. Film Critics '78: Support. Actor (Farnsworth).

Comfort and Joy **1984 (PG)** After his kleptomaniac girlfriend deserts him, a Scottish disc jockey is forced to reevaluate his life. He becomes involved in an underworld battle between two mob-owned local ice cream companies. Another odd comedy gem from Forsyth, who did "Gregory's Girl" and "Local Hero." Music by Dire Straits guitarist Knopfler. **93m/C VHS.** *GB* Bill Paterson, Eleanor David, Clare Grogan, Alex Norton, Patrick Malahide, Rikki Fulton, Roberto Berrardi; *D:* Bill Forsyth; *W:* Bill Forsyth; *C:* Chris Menges; *M:* Mark Knopfler. Natl. Soc. Film Critics '84: Cinematog.

The Comfort of Strangers **1991 (R)** Atmospheric psychological thriller. Mary and Colin (Richardson and Everett), a handsome young British couple, take a Venetian holiday to rediscover the passion in their relationship. Lost in the city, they chance, it seems, upon Robert (Walken), a sort of Virgil in an Italian suit. He later reappears, and, abetted by his wife Caroline (Mirren), gradually leads the couple on an eerie tour of urbane decadence that hints at danger. Psychologically tantalizing and horrifyingly erotic, the movie's based on Ian McEwan's novel. **102m/C VHS.** Christopher Walken, Natasha Richardson, Rupert Everett, Helen Mirren; *D:* Paul Schrader; *W:* Harold Pinter; *C:* Dante Spinotti; *M:* Angelo Badalamenti.

The Comic **1969 (PG)** Van Dyke is terrific as a silent screen comedian (a composite of several real-life screen comics) whose ego destroys his career. Recreations of silent films, and the blend of comedy and pathos, are especially effective. **96m/C VHS.** Dick Van Dyke, Mickey Rooney, Michele Lee, Cornel Wilde, Nina Wayne, Pert Kelton, Jeannine Riley; *D:* Carl Reiner; *W:* Carl Reiner.

The Comic **1985** In a future police state, a young comedian kills the star and takes his place in the show. His future rises, but who cares? **90m/C VHS.** Steve Munroe, Bernard Plant, Jeff Pirie; *D:* Richard Driscoll.

Comic Act **1998** The world of London stand-up comedy is the setting for a surprisingly sexy look at life beyond the microphone. Gus (Schneider) and Jay (Mullarkey) are struggling until Alex (Webster) joins their act. Her combination of intelligence and unembarrassed sexuality makes them a hit with audiences, and with that come all the temptations (and all the cliches) of show business. Yes, the same story has been told countless times, but this version is fresh and energetic. **107m/C VHS, DVD, Wide.** Stephen Moyer, Neil Mullarkey, David Schneider, Suki Webster, Magnus Hastings; *D:* Jack Hazan; *W:* Jack Hazan, David Mingay; *C:* Richard Branczik; *M:* Patrick Gowers.

Comic Book Kids **1982 (G)** Two youngsters enjoy visiting their friend's comic strip studio, since they have the power to project themselves into the cartoon stories. Viewers will be less impressed. **90m/C VHS.** Joseph Campanella, Mike Darnell, Robyn Finn, Jim Engelhardt, Fay De Witt.

Comic Cabby woof! **1987** A day in the life of an introvert cabby seems to last forever. From "New York City Cab Driver's Joke Book" by Jim Pietsch. **59m/C VHS.** Bill McLaughlin, Al Lewis.

Comin' Round the Mountain **1951** The duo are caught in a Kentucky family feud while seeking a fortune in gold. Funniest bit has backwoods witch Hamilton squaring off with Costello when he refuses to pay for the love potion she's made him. **77m/B VHS.** Bud Abbott, Lou Costello, Dorothy Shay, Kirby Grant, Joseph (Joe) Sawyer, Margaret Hamilton, Glenn Strange, Guy Wilkerson; *D:* Charles Lamont; *W:* John Grant, Robert Lees, Frederic Rinaldo.

Coming Apart **1969** Free-love was never really very free as shrink Torn finds when he secretly films his sexual escapades with a variety of women, which lead to his own nervous breakdown. Avant-garde, sexually daring, and over-the-top. **111m/B VHS, DVD, Wide.** Rip Torn, Sally Kirkland, Viveca Lindfors; *D:* Milton Moses Ginsberg; *W:* Milton Moses Ginsberg; *C:* Jack Yager.

Coming Home **1978 (R)** Looks at the effect of the Vietnam War on home front. The wife of a gung-ho Marine officer volunteers as an aide in a Veteran's Hospital, befriends and eventually falls in love with a Vietnam vet, paralyzed from war injuries. His attitudes, pain, and first-hand knowledge of the war force her to re-examine her previously automatic responses. Honest look at the everyday life of disabled veterans, unusual vision of the possibilities of simple friendship between men and women. Fonda and Voight are great; Dern's character suffers from weak scriptwriting late in the film. Critically acclaimed. Compelling score from late '60s music. **130m/C VHS, DVD, Wide.** Jane Fonda, Jon Voight, Bruce Dern, Penelope Milford, Robert Carradine, Robert Ginty, Mary Gregory, Kathleen Miller, Beeson Carroll, Willie Tyler, Charles Cyphers, Olivia Cole, Tresa Hughes, Bruce French, Richard Lawson, Rita Taggart, Pat Corley; *D:* Hal Ashby; *W:* Robert C. Jones; *C:* Haskell Wexler. Oscars '78: Actor (Voight), Actress (Fonda), Orig. Screenplay; Cannes '78: Actor (Voight); Golden Globes '79: Actor—Drama (Voight), Actress—Drama (Fonda); L.A. Film Critics '78: Actor (Voight), Actress (Fonda), Film; N.Y. Film Critics '78: Actor (Voight); Writers Guild '78: Orig. Screenplay.

Coming Home *Rosamunde Pilcher's Coming Home* **1998** It's 1935, and Judith Dunbar is left behind in a British boarding school when her mother and sister travel to Singapore to join Judith's father. A school friendship with Loveday Carey-Lewis introduces Judith to the eccentric world of British aristocracy but the coming of WWII proves to be her coming of age. Based on the book by Rosamunde Pilcher. Made for German TV. **205m/C VHS.** *GE* Peter O'Toole, Joanna Lumley, David McCallum, Emily Mortimer, Katie Ryder Richardson, Paul Bettany, Susan Hampshire, Penelope Keith, Patrick Ryecart, Malcolm Stoddard; *D:* Giles Foster; *W:* John Goldsmith. **TV**

The Coming of Amos **1925** A wonderful send-up of all those Fairbanks-style melodramas, with La Rocque as an Aussie on vacation on the French Riviera falling for and eventually rescuing Goudal, as the Russian princess held captive by the lustful Beery. **60m/B VHS.** Rod La Rocque, Jetta Goudal, Noah Beery Sr., Florence Vidor; *D:* Paul Sloane.

Coming Out **1989** The first film produced by East Germany to deal with homosexuality. Ambivalent Philip (Freihof) is a popular high school educator, who has been involved with another teacher, Tanja (Manzel), who has just learned she's pregnant. But Philip has just admitted to himself that his attraction to the younger Matthias (Kummer) is more erotic than friendly. Philip, however, is an emotional coward—he's worried about prejudice and can't be honest with either lover, leading to a painful confrontation. German with subtitles. **113m/C VHS, DVD, Wide.** *GE* Matthias Freihof, Dagmar Manzel, Dirk Kummer; *D:* Heiner Carow; *W:* Wolfram Witt; *C:* Martin Schlesinger; *M:* Stefan Carow.

Coming Out Alive **1984** Tense thriller about a woman and her hired mercenary who try to rescue her kidnapped son from his estranged father—a radical is involved in an assassination plot. Hylands is especially compelling. **73m/C VHS.** *CA* Helen Shaver, Scott Hylands, Michael Ironside, Monica Parker; *D:* Don McBrearty.

Coming Out of the Ice **1982 (PG)** Engrossing true story of Victor Herman, an outstanding American athlete who worked in Russia in the 1930s. He was imprisoned in Siberia (for 38 years!) for refusing to renounce his American citizenship. **100m/C VHS.** John Savage, Willie Nelson, Ben Cross, Francesca Annis, Peter Vaughan; *D:* Waris Hussein; *M:* Maurice Jarre. **TV**

Coming Soon **1999 (R)** Three Manhattan prep school seniors deal with their sexual coming of age as well as college admission. Nell (Vessey), Stream (Root), and Jenny (Hoffman) discuss orgasms and try to find just the right guy. The unrated version clocks in at 96 minutes. **90m/C VHS, DVD, Wide.** Gaby Hoffman, Tricia Vessey, Ryan Reynolds, Bonnie Root, James Roday, Spalding Gray, Mia Farrow, Ryan O'Neal, Peter Bogdanovich, Leslie Lyles, Yasmine Bleeth; *D:* Colette Burson; *W:* Colette Burson, Kate Robin; *C:* Joaquin Baca-Asay.

Coming Through **1985** Writer D.H. Lawrence meets the married Frieda von Richthofer and begins a scandalous affair which intertwines with his own writings, and the life of a young man in the present day. British TV production lacks passion. **78m/C VHS.** *GB* Kenneth Branagh, Helen Mirren, Alison Steadman, Philip Martin Brown, Norman Rodway; *D:* Peter Barber-Fleming; *W:* Alan Plater. **TV**

Coming to America **1988 (R)** An African prince (Murphy) decides to come to America in search of a suitable bride. He lands in Queens, and quickly finds American women to be more confusing than he imagined. Sometimes overly cute entertainment relieved by clever costume cameos by Murphy and Hall. Later lawsuit resulted in columnist Art Buchwald being given credit for story. **116m/C VHS, DVD, 8mm.** Eddie Murphy, Arsenio Hall, James Earl Jones, John Amos, Madge Sinclair, Shari Headley, Don Ameche, Louie Anderson, Paul Bates, Allison Dean, Eriq La Salle, Calvin Lockhart, Samuel L. Jackson, Cuba Gooding Jr., Vanessa Bell Calloway, Frankie Faison, Vondie Curtis-Hall; *D:* John Landis; *W:* David Sheffield, Barry W. Blaustein; *C:* Woody Omens; *M:* Nile Rodgers.

Coming Up Roses *Rhosyn A Rhith* **1987 (PG)** Pleasant comedy about the residents of a small mining village in the South of Wales who fight to keep their local movie house from being shut down. In Welsh with English subtitles. **95m/C VHS.** *GB* Dafydd Hywel, Iola Gregory, Olive Michael, Mari Emlyn, Bill Paterson; *D:* Stephen Bayly; *W:* Ruth Carter; *M:* Michael Storey.

Command Decision **1948** Upon realizing he must send his men on missions-of-no-return to destroy German jet production, Gable's WWII flight commander becomes tactically at odds with his political superior, Pidgeon (who's not keen to have his precision bombing plans placed in an unflattering light). Based on the stage hit by William Wister Haines, it's a late war pic by Wood, who earlier directed such diverse efforts as "A Night at the Opera," "The Devil and Miss Jones," and "Our Town." Vintage war-is-hell actioner. **112m/B VHS.** Clark Gable, Walter Pidgeon, Van Johnson, Brian Donlevy, Charles Bickford, John Hodiak, Ray Collins, Edward Earle, Sam Flint, Warner Anderson, Don Haggerty, Henry Hall, Alvin Hammer, Holmes Herbert; *D:* Sam Wood; *W:* George Froeschel, William Wister Haines, William R. Laidlaw; *C:* Harold Rosson; *M:* Miklos Rozsa.

Commandments **1996 (R)** When Seth Warner (Quinn) loses his wife (Going), job, and even his dog, he finds no solace in faith and decides to test why God would make a good man suffer by breaking every one of the 10 commandments. Rachel (Cox), his wife's sister, persuades him to move in with her and her jerk husband Harry (LaPaglia), who can't really be bothered by Seth's problems. The three leads certainly have presence but given the ambivalence of the material, the movie doesn't hang together. **92m/C VHS.** Aidan Quinn, Courteney Cox Arquette, Anthony LaPaglia, Louis Zorich, Pat McNamara, Tom Aldredge, Pamela Gray, Alice Drummond, Jack Gilpin; *Cameos:* Joanna Going; *D:* Daniel Taplitz; *W:* Daniel Taplitz; *C:* Slawomir Idziak; *M:* Joseph Vitarelli.

Commando **1985 (R)** An ex-commando leader's daughter is kidnapped in a blackmail scheme to make him depose a South American president. He fights instead, and proceeds to rescue his daughter amid a torrential flow of falling bodies. Violent action spiced with throwaway comic lines. **90m/C VHS, DVD.** Chelsea Field, Bill Paxton, Arnold Schwarzenegger, Rae Dawn Chong, Dan Hedaya, Vernon Wells, James Olson, David Patrick Kelly, Alyssa Milano, Bill Duke; *D:* Mark L. Lester; *W:* Steven E. de Souza; *C:* Matthew F. Leonetti; *M:* James Horner.

Commando Attack **1967** A tough sergeant leads a group of misfit soldiers to blow up a German radio transmitter the day before D-Day. **90m/C VHS.** Michael Rennie, Monica Randall, Bob Sullivan; *D:* Leon Klimovsky.

Commando Invasion **1987** When an army captain is accused of murder, he hunts down the man he knows is responsible for the crime. Jungle revenge mayhem is confusing. Set in Vietnam. **90m/C VHS.** Jim Gaines, Michael James, Gordon Mitchell, Carol Roberts, Pat Vance, Ken(saku) Watanabe; *D:* John Gale.

Commando Squad **1976 (R)** During WWII, soldiers go to battle to prevent the development of a device that reanimates flesh. The script stays dead. **82m/C VHS.** Chuck Alford, Peter Owen, April Adams; *D:* Charles Nizet.

Commando Squad **1987 (R)** Story of drug agents undercover in Mexico, and a female agent who rescues her kidnapped lover. Firepower is wasted, but Shower is a former "Playboy" Playmate of the Year. **90m/C VHS.** Brian Thompson, William Smith, Kathy Shower, Sid Haig, Robert Quarry, Ross Hagen, Mel Welles, Marie Windsor, Russ Tamblyn; *D:* Fred Olen Ray.

Commandos *Sullivan's Marauders* **1973 (PG)** Commando operation against Rommel's forces in North Africa during WWII. Too much said, not enough action. **100m/C VHS, DVD.** *GE IT* Lee Van Cleef, Jack Kelly, Giampiero Albertini, Marilu Tolo; *D:* Armando Crispino; *W:* Armando Crispino, Lucio Battistrada, Dario Argento, Stefano Strucchi; *C:* Benito Frattari; *M:* Mario Nascimbene.

Commandos Strike at Dawn 🦴🦴½ **1943** Norwegian villagers, including Muni, fight the invading Nazis, and eventually help the British Navy battle them over an Arctic supply line. Okay script helped along by veteran actors Muni and Gish. Based on a C.S. Forester story. **100m/B VHS.** Paul Muni, Lillian Gish, Cedric Hardwicke, Anna Lee, Ray Collins, Robert Coote, Alexander Knox, Rosemary DeCamp; *D:* John Farrow; *W:* Irwin Shaw; *C:* William Mellor.

Comment Ca Va? 🦴🦴 *How Is It Going?* **1976** The boss and workers in a Communist publishing house decide to make a simple film about how information is manufactured. But Odette, one of the workers, has some strange ideas about filmmaking. In French with English subtitles. **76m/C VHS.** *FR* Anne-Marie Mieville; *D:* Jean-Luc Godard.

The Commies Are Coming, the Commies Are Coming 🦴🦴 *Red Nightmare* **1957** Cult classic will leave viewers red from laughing in disbelief. Webb narrates this anticommunist movie about the Russians taking over the United States. Filmed in a documentary style, it captures the paranoia of the times. Re-released in 1984, just before the Evil Empire collapsed. **60m/B VHS.** Jack Webb, Jack Kelly, Jeanne Cooper, Peter Brown, Pat(ricia) Woodell, Andrew Duggan, Peter Breck, Robert Conrad; *D:* George Waggner; *W:* Vincent Fotre; *C:* Robert Hoffman; *M:* William Lara.

Commissar 🦴🦴🦴🦴 *Komissar* **1968** Before the Soviet Union ended up in the ashcan of history, this film was labeled as "treason" and shelved in Red Russia. Now, even Americans can view the story of a female Soviet soldier who becomes pregnant during the civil war of 1922. The Soviet military has no policy regarding pregnancy, so the woman is dumped on a family of outcast Jews to complete her pregnancy. This film makes the strong statement that women were just as discriminated against in the U.S.S.R. as were many races or creeds, especially Jews. In Russian with English subtitles. Released in the U.S. in 1988. **105m/B VHS.** *RU* Nonna Mordyukova, Rolan Bykov, Raisa Nedashkovskaya, Vasily Shukshin, Pavlik Levin, Ludmilla Volinskaya; *D:* Alexander Askoldov; *W:* Alexander Askoldov; *C:* Valery Ginsberg; *M:* Alfred Schnittke.

The Commitments 🦴🦴🦴 **1991 (R)** Convinced that they can bring soul music to Dublin, a group of working-class youth form a band. High-energy production paints an interesting, unromanticized picture of modern Ireland and refuses to follow standard showbiz cliches, even though its lack of resolution hurts. Honest, whimsical dialogue laced with poetic obscenities, delivered by a cast of mostly unknowns. Very successful soundtrack features the music of Wilson Pickett, James Brown, Otis Redding, Aretha Franklin, Percy Sledge, and others, and received a Grammy nomination. Based on the book "The Commitments" by Roddy Doyle, part of a trilogy which includes "The Snapper" and "The Van." **116m/C VHS, DVD.** *IR* Andrew Strong, Bronagh Gallagher, Glen Hansard, Michael Aherne, Dick Massey, Ken McCluskey, Robert Arkins, Dave Finnegan, Johnny Murphy, Angeline Ball, Felim Gormley, Maria Doyle Kennedy, Colm Meaney; *D:* Alan Parker; *W:* Dick Clement, Roddy Doyle, Ian LaFrenais; *C:* Gale Tattersall; *M:* Paul Bushnell. British Acad. '91: Adapt. Screenplay, Director (Parker), Film.

Committed 🦴½ **1991 (R)** Schlockmeister Levey's latest directorial effort is a step above his earlier "Slumber Party" and "Happy Hooker Goes to Washington," a statement ringing with the faintest of praise. Thinking she's applying for a job at an asylum, a nurse discovers she has committed herself. Try as she may, not even a committed nurse can snake her way out of the pit of madness they call "The Institute." **93m/C VHS.** Jennifer O'Neill, William Windom, Robert Forster, Ron Palillo, Sydney Lassick; *D:* William A. Levey.

Committed 🦴🦴½ **1999 (R)** Joline (Graham) is the madly devoted wife of Carl (Wilson) who, two years after their marriage, decides he should leave their New York home to take a job in the Southwest—alone. Joline soon decides to track him down and heads out on the usual misadventurous road trip, accompanied by her brother (Affleck) and a handsome neighbor (Visnjic). Of course, when she does find Carl there's quite a lot that needs to be resolved. **98m/C VHS, DVD, Wide.** Heather Graham, Luke Wilson, Casey Affleck, Goran Visnjic, Patricia Velasquez, Alfonso Arau, Mark Ruffalo, Kim Dickens, Clea DuVall; *D:* Lisa Krueger; *W:* Lisa Krueger; *C:* Tom Krueger. Sundance '00: Cinematog.

The Committee 🦴🦴 **1968 (PG)** Comedy film of the seminal comedy troupe "The Committee," specialists in short, punchy satire. Dated, but of interest to comedy buffs. **88m/C VHS.** Wolfman Jack, Howard Hesseman, Barbara Bosson, Peter Bonerz, Garry Goodrow, Carl Gottlieb; *D:* Jack Del.

Common Bonds 🦴🦴½ **1991 (PG)** After being put together in an experimental outreach program, two mismatched partners struggle to break free from a system that threatens to destroy them both. **109m/C VHS.** Rae Dawn Chong, Michael Ironside, Brad Dourif; *D:* Allan Goldstein; *M:* Graeme Coleman.

Common Ground 🦴🦴½ **2000** Three stories dealing with homosexuality in America from the 1950s to the present in the same small town of Homer, Connecticut. Vogel's "A Friend of Dorothy" finds Dorothy (Murphy) returning home after being dishonorably discharged from the Navy after being caught at a gay bar. McNally's "Mr. Roberts" focuses on the 70s and confused high school senior Toby Anderson (Thomas). Toby reaches out for some understanding from his closeted French teacher (Weber), only to be rejected. Fierstein's "Andy and Amos" takes place in 2000, with Amos (Le Gros) having the jitters over his commitment ceremony to lover Andy (Airlie). But it's his conservative dad Ira (Asner) who turns out to be an unexpected booster. **105m/C VHS.** Brittany Murphy, Margot Kidder, Brian Kerwin, Mimi Rogers, Jason Priestley, Joanne Vannicola, Helen Shaver, Jonathan Taylor Thomas, Steven Weber, Dan Lauria, Ed Asner, James LeGros, Andrew Airlie, Harvey Fierstein, Beau Bridges, Eric Stoltz; *D:* Donna Deitch; *W:* Harvey Fierstein, Terrance McNally, Paula Vogel; *C:* Jacek Laskus. **CABLE**

Common Law Wife 🦴 **1963 (R)** Made-for-the-drive-in flick about a man whose common law marriage is threatened by his niece, who wants his money. Murder and mayhem abound when the man's moonshine is poisoned. Cheap and exploitative. **81m/B VHS.** Lacy Kelly, Shugfoot Rainey, Annabelle Lee, Jody Works, Anne MacAdams, George Edgely; *D:* Eric Sayers.

Communion 🦴🦴 **1989 (R)** A serious adaptation of the purportedly nonfictional bestseller by Whitley Strieber about his family's abduction by extraterrestrials. Spacey new age story is overlong and hard to swallow. **103m/C VHS, DVD, Wide.** Christopher Walken, Lindsay Crouse, Frances Sternhagen, Joel Carlson, Andreas Katsulas, Basil Hoffman; *D:* Philippe Mora; *M:* Eric Clapton.

Companeros 🦴🦴½ **1970 (R)** The Mexican revolution. Shoeshine boy Vasco (Milian) kills a federale officer and is made a lieutenant by General Mongo (Bodalo), one of many warring revolutionary warlords. Vasco and Swedish gun salesman Yodlof Pederson (Nero) become unlikely companions when MonMongo sends them to Yuma, to liberate authentic revolutionary Xantos (Rey), a pre-Gandhi preacher of nonviolence imprisoned by American oil interests in the hope of extorting oil leases from him. The conflict is a simple one between virtuous Communists and oppressive generals and capitalists. Director Corbucci's mood is less cynical, and more inclined toward comedy. The comedy direction is broader than broad, and obvious to the point of playing to juveniles. There is plenty of action in the film, guaranteeing a shootout or stunt every few minutes. **118m/C DVD, Wide.** *IT SP GE* Franco Nero, Tomas Milian, Jack Palance, Fernando Rey, Iris Berben, Francisco Bodalo; *D:* Sergio Corbucci; *W:* Sergio Corbucci, Massimo De Rita, Arduino (Dino) Maiuri, Fritz Ebert; *C:* Alejandro Ulloa; *M:* Ennio Morricone.

The Companion 🦴🦴 **1994 (R)** In 2015 romance novelist Gillian Tanner (Harrold) decides to hide out at a remote mountain cabin to get over a broken love affair. For safety's sake, Gillian takes along custom-designed android companion Geoffrey (Greenwood). But then Gillian decides to tinker with Geoffrey's programming, turning him from domestic guardian to devoted lover. Unfortunately, Geoffrey doesn't understand the difference between fantasy and reality (especially since he's getting his ideas from Gillian's romance novels) and becomes lethally obsessed. **94m/C VHS.** Kathryn Harrold, Bruce Greenwood, Talia Balsam, Brion James, Bryan Cranston, Joely Fisher; *D:* Gary Fleder; *W:* Ian Seeberg, Valerie Bennett; *C:* Rick Bota; *M:* David Shire. **VIDEO**

Company Business 🦴½ **1991 (PG-13)** Sam Boyd is a retired CIA agent who's brought back to swap Pyiotr Grushenko (Baryshnikov), a Russian mole in the State Department, for a U-2 pilot being held in Moscow. The swap is to be made in Berlin and also involves $2 million of what turns out be to Colombian drug money. When things inevitably go wrong (both intelligence agencies would like them out of the way permanently) the two men find they must depend on each other if they want to stay alive. An unimaginative plot wastes a stalwart cast in this old-fashioned spy drama. **104m/C VHS.** Gene Hackman, Mikhail Baryshnikov, Kurtwood Smith, Terry O'Quinn; *D:* Nicholas Meyer; *W:* Nicholas Meyer.

Company Man 🦴🦴 **2000 (PG-13)** Goofy satire about the Bay of Pigs invasion co-written and co-directed by McGrath, who also stars as a wimpy grammar teacher who, through some bizarre coincidences, manages, unwittingly, to cause the Cold War debacle. Though the big name cast seems to be having fun, absurdity abounds and eventually topples this romping, madcap throwback. Woody Allen makes an appearance as a CIA veteran in Cuba. **81m/C VHS, DVD, Wide.** Douglas McGrath, Sigourney Weaver, John Turturro, Anthony LaPaglia, Ryan Phillippe, Denis Leary, Alan Cumming, Woody Allen, Heather Matarazzo, Jeffrey Jones; *D:* Douglas McGrath, Peter Askin; *W:* Douglas McGrath, Peter Askin; *C:* Russell Boyd; *M:* David Lawrence.

The Company of Wolves 🦴🦴🦴 **1985 (R)** Thirteen-year-old Rosaleen (Patterson) lives with her parents (Warner, Silberg) on the outskirts of a forbidding forest. The girl, who's on the verge of womanhood, listens to her grandmother (Lansbury) tell fairy tales and dreams of a medieval fantasy world inhabited by men who turn into wolves. An adult "Little Red Riding Hood" that's heavy on dreamy visuals and Freudian symbolism. **95m/C VHS.** Angela Lansbury, David Warner, Stephen Rea, Tusse Silberg, Sarah Patterson, Brian Glover, Danielle Dax, Graham Crowden, Micha Bergese, Kathryn Pogson, Georgia Slowe; *D:* Neil Jordan; *W:* Neil Jordan, Angela Carter; *C:* Bryan Loftus; *M:* George Fenton.

The Competition 🦴🦴🦴 **1980 (PG)** Two virtuoso pianists meet at an international competition and fall in love. Will they stay together if one of them wins? Can they have a performance career and love too? Is he trying to distract her with sex, so he can win? Dreyfuss and Irving are fine (they practiced for four months to look like they were actually playing the pianos), and Remick's character has some interesting insights into the world of art. **125m/C VHS.** Richard Dreyfuss, Amy Irving, Lee Remick, Sam Wanamaker, Joseph Cali, Ty Henderson, Priscilla Pointer, James B. Sikking; *D:* Joel Oliansky; *M:* Lalo Schifrin.

Complex World 🦴½ **1992 (R)** The Heartbreak Hotel is a notorious rock club which may not be around much longer. It seems the young owner's father is an ex-CIA redneck who is running for President and his son's profession is a political liability. Meanwhile, the town's mayor wants to replace the club with a shopping mall. A bomb is planted in the club's basement, terrorists lurk, and a gang of bikers is spoiling for a fight but the crowd at the Heartbreak just rocks on. **81m/C VHS.** Dan Welch, Bob Owczarek, Jay Charbonneau, Tilman Gandy Jr., David P.B. Stephens, Captain Lou Albano, Stanley Matis; *D:* James Wolpaw; *W:* James Wolpaw.

Compromising Positions 🦴🦴 **1985 (R)** A philandering dentist is killed on Long Island, and a bored housewife begins to investigate, uncovering scandal after scandal. Black comedy mixed unevenly with mystery makes for unsatisfying brew. However, Ivey is a standout as Sarandon's best friend. Screenplay was written by Susan Isaacs, based on her novel of the same title. **99m/C VHS.** Susan Sarandon, Raul Julia, Edward Herrmann, Judith Ivey, Mary Beth Hurt, Joe Mantegna, Josh Mostel, Anne DeSalvo; *D:* Frank Perry; *M:* Brad Fiedel.

Compulsion 🦴🦴🦴½ **1959** Artie Strauss (Dillman) is a mother-dominated sadist who, along with submissive friend Judd Steiner (Stockwell), plan and execute a cold-blooded murder. Flamboyant lawyer Jonathan Wilk (brilliantly portrayed by Welles) knows he has no defense so he attacks the system and establishment, seeking to at least save his clients from death. A suspenseful shocker with taut direction and a tight script. Based on the notorious 1924 Leopold and Loeb murder trial, also filmed as "Rope" and "Swoon." **103m/B VHS.** Orson Welles, Bradford Dillman, Dean Stockwell, Diane Varsi, E.G. Marshall, Martin Milner, Richard Anderson, Robert F. Simon, Edward Binns, Robert Burton, Wilton Graff, Gavin MacLeod; *D:* Richard Fleischer; *W:* Richard Murphy; *C:* William Mellor.

Computer Beach Party 🦴 **1988** A couple of surf-head college computer hackers foil their mayor's plans to develop their favorite beach. The title, at least, is original. **97m/C VHS.** Hank Amigo, Stacey Nemour, Andre Chimene; *D:* Gary A. Troy.

Computer Wizard 🦴 **1977 (G)** Boy genius builds a powerful electronic device. His intentions are good, but the invention disrupts the town and lands him in big trouble. Not the "Thomas Edison Story." **91m/C VHS.** Henry Darrow, Kate Woodville, Guy Madison, Marc Gilpin; *D:* John Florea.

The Computer Wore Tennis Shoes 🦴½ **1969 (G)** Disney comedy (strictly for the kids) about a slow-witted college student who turns into a genius after a "shocking" encounter with the campus computer. His new brains give the local gangster headaches. Sequel: "Now You See Him, Now You Don't." **87m/C VHS.** Kurt Russell, Cesar Romero, Joe Flynn, William Schallert, Alan Hewitt, Richard Bakalyan; *D:* Robert Butler; *M:* Robert F. Brunner.

Comrade X 🦴🦴½ **1940** Gable is an American correspondent in Moscow who is blackmailed into marrying die-hard Communist Lamarr in this comedic spinoff of "Ninotchka." The two stars failed to create any sparks as a love duo, although their previous film "Boom Town" was a hit. Based on a story by Walter Reisch. **87m/B VHS.** Clark Gable, Hedy Lamarr, Oscar Homolka, Felix Bressart, Eve Arden, Sig Rumann, Natasha Lytess, Vladimir Sokoloff; *D:* King Vidor; *W:* Ben Hecht, Charles Lederer.

Comrades in Arms 🦴½ **1991 (R)** When an international drug cartel threatens to take over the world, the United States and Russia must set their differences aside and team up to stop them. **91m/C VHS.** Lyle Alzado, Rick Washburne, John Christian, Lance Henriksen; *D:* J. Christian Ingvordsen; *W:* J. Christian Ingvordsen.

The Comrades of Summer 🦴🦴½ **1992 (R)** Mantegna plays big-league baseball coach Sparky Smith, whose fiery temper gets him into big trouble. Out of a job, he discovers the only team willing to take a chance on him happens to be Russian. Sparky finds the players of the Russian National team need a lot of help—and not just with their English. **90m/C VHS.** Joe Mantegna, Natalia (Natalya) Negoda, Mark Rolston, John Fleck, Eric Allen Kramer, Michael Lerner, Ian Tracey; *D:* Tommy

Lee Wallace; *W:* Robert Rodat; *M:* William Olvis. **CABLE**

The Con 🦴🦴½ **1998 (PG-13)** Barbara (De Mornay) is willing to do anything to get the money to pay off her loanshark, including marry small town Mississippi mechanic Bobby Sommersdinger (Macy), who doesn't know he's about to inherit a lot of money. But Bobby isn't quite the dim-wit he first appears to be, even as he succumbs to Barbara's charms. **92m/C VHS.** Rebecca DeMornay, William H. Macy, Frances Sternhagen, Angela Paton, Don Harvey; *D:* Steven Schachter; *W:* William H. Macy, Steven Schachter; *C:* Peter Stein; *M:* Peter Manning Robinson. **CABLE**

Con Air 🦴🦴🦴 **1997 (R)** Producer Bruckheimer flies solo for the first time, and has a very successful flight. Cage re-ups as former Ranger Cameron Poe, jailed for manslaughter, who gets paroled just in time to catch a ride home aboard a plane filled with the worst of America's criminals. Led by Cyrus "The Virus" Grissom (Malkovich), the first-class psycho passengers take over the plane, and Cameron must save the day. Among the snappy one-liners, chases, shoot-outs, and stuff blowin' up real good, comes Federal Marshal Larkin (Cusack) to help Poe from the ground. Cusack can't shake his indie-film, quirky-kid image enough to really pass as an action hero, but he gives it his all. Flick supplies everything you'd expect from a summer blockbuster actioner, but it's best seen on a big-screen with surround sound to get the full effect. **105m/C VHS, DVD.** Nicolas Cage, John Malkovich, John Cusack, Mykelti Williamson, Ving Rhames, Steve Buscemi, Colm Meaney, Rachel Ticotin, Dave Chappelle, M.C. Gainey, Danny Trejo, Nicholas Chinlund, Jesse Borrego, Angela Featherstone, Monica Potter, John Roselius, Renoly, Landry Allbright, Jose Zuniga; *D:* Simon West; *W:* Scott Rosenberg; *C:* David Tattersall; *M:* Mark Mancina, Trevor Rabin.

The Con Artists 🦴½ *The Con Man* **1980** After con man Quinn is sprung from prison, he and his protege set up a sting operation against the beautiful Capucine. Not clever or witty enough for the caper to capture interest. **86m/C VHS, DVD.** *IT* Anthony Quinn, Adriano Celentano, Capucine, Corinne Clery; *D:* Sergio Corbucci.

Con Man 🦴🦴 **1992** Robin Mitchell is a small-time con man on the fringes of London's underworld. He witnesses a brutal mob hit, which means they want him dead, and his girlfriend has decided it's just too dangerous being a part of his life. But Mitchell is convinced his luck will change for the better as he puts together a million-dollar long-shot that could secure him for life—if he survives. **91m/C VHS.** Ian McShane, Gayle Hunnicutt, Keith Barron, Alan Lake, Luan Peters; *D:* Francis Megahy.

Conagher 🦴🦴½ *Louis L'Amour's Conagher* **1991** A lyrical, if poorly plotted Western about a veteran cowboy who takes the whole movie to decide to end up in the arms of the pretty widow lady. Cable adaptation of Louis L'Amour's novel doesn't have much intensity, though Elliott captures his character well. **94m/C VHS.** Sam Elliott, Katharine Ross, Barry Corbin, Buck Taylor, Dub Taylor, Daniel Quinn, Anndi McAfee, Billy Green Bush, Ken Curtis; *D:* Reynaldo Villalobos. **CABLE**

Conan the Barbarian 🦴🦴🦴 **1982 (R)** A fine sword and sorcery tale featuring brutality, excellent production values, and a rousing score. Conan's (Arnie, who else) parents are killed and he's enslaved. But hardship makes him strong, so when he is set free he can avenge their murder and retrieve the sword bequeathed him by his father. Sandahl Bergman is great as The Queen of Thieves, and Schwarzenegger maintains an admirable sense of humor throughout. Jones is dandy, as always, this time as bad guy Thulsa Doom. Based on the character created by Robert E. Howard. Sequel: "Conan the Destroyer." **115m/C VHS, DVD, Wide.** Arnold Schwarzenegger, James Earl Jones, Max von Sydow, Sandahl Bergman, Mako, Ben Davidson, Valerie Quennessen, Cassandra Gaviola, William Smith; *D:* John Milius; *W:* John Milius, Oliver Stone; *C:* Duke Callaghan, John Cabrera; *M:* Basil Poledouris.

Conan the Destroyer 🦴🦴½ **1984 (PG)** Conan is manipulated by Queen Tamaris into searching for a treasure. In return she'll bring Conan's love Valeria back to life. On his trip he meets Jones and Chamberlain, who later give him a hand. Excellent special effects, good humor, camp fun, somewhat silly finale. Sequel to the better "Conan the Barbarian." **101m/C VHS, DVD.** Arnold Schwarzenegger, Grace Jones, Wilt Chamberlain, Sarah Douglas, Mako, Jeff Corey, Olivia D'Abo, Tracey Walter; *D:* Richard Fleischer; *W:* Stanley Mann; *C:* Jack Cardiff; *M:* Basil Poledouris. Golden Raspberries '84: Worst New Star (D'Abo).

Concealed Weapon 🦴½ **1994 (R)** A struggling actor gets the part of a lifetime but then becomes the prime suspect in a brutal crime. **80m/C VHS.** Daryl Haney, Suzanne Wouk, Monica Simpson, Mark Driscoll, Karen Stone; *D:* Dave Payne, Milan Zivkovich.

Conceiving Ada 🦴🦴 **1997** Experimental film is a homage to Lady Ada Lovelace (Swinton), daughter of Lord Byron, a 19th-century mathematician who developed what is now considered the first computer programming language. Ada is regarded by contemporary computer scientist Amy Coer (Faridany) as her spiritual mentor and Amy becomes obsessed with devising a method to actually communicate with the long-deceased Ada, whose life uncannily paralells her own. **85m/C VHS, DVD.** Tilda Swinton, Francesca Faridany, Karen Black, John E. O'Keefe, J.D. Wolfe, Timothy Leary, John Perry Barlow, Owen Murphy; *D:* Lynn Hershman Leeson; *W:* Lynn Hershman Leeson, Eileen Jones; *C:* Hiro Narita.

The Concentratin' Kid 🦴🦴 **1930** An unusual horse opera sans shootouts and fisticuffs. Hoot's fiancee is kidnapped and taken to the range so that the renegade cowpokes can, uh, benefit from a female perspective on home decorating. Despite being outnumbered, Hoot concentrates and sets the rescue in motion, taking on the gang of rustlers without firing a shot. **54m/B VHS.** Hoot Gibson, Kathryn Crawford, Duke Lee, Robert E. Homans, James Mason; *D:* Arthur Rosson.

The Concorde: Airport '79 🦴 *Airport '79* **1979 (PG)** A supersonic film in the "Airport" tradition has the Concorde chased by missiles and fighter aircraft before it crashes in the Alps. Incredibly farfetched nonsense with an all-star cast doesn't fly. **103m/C VHS.** Alain Delon, Susan Blakely, Robert Wagner, Sylvia Kristel, John Davidson, Charo, Sybil Danning, Jimmie Walker, Eddie Albert, Bibi Andersson, Monica Lewis, Andrea Marcovicci, Martha Raye, Cicely Tyson, Mercedes McCambridge, George Kennedy, David Warner; *D:* David Lowell Rich; *W:* Eric Roth; *M:* Lalo Schifrin.

Concrete Angels 🦴 **1987 (R)** A poignant glimpse at the influence of rock music in its infancy. A group of deprived teens in Toronto form a band and audition to open for the Beatles. Lack of nostalgia is refreshing, but too much of this is amateurish. **97m/C VHS.** *CA* Joseph Dimambro, Luke McKeehan, Omie Craden, Dean Bosacki; *D:* Carlo Liconti.

Concrete Beat 🦴½ **1984** A newspaper reporter simultaneously searches for a murderer, tries to win his ex-wife back, and writes front page stories for his editor/ex-father-in-law. Tough assignment. **74m/C VHS.** Kenneth McMillan, John Getz, Darlanne Fluegel, Rhoda Gemignani; *D:* Robert Butler. **TV**

The Concrete Cowboys 🦴½ *Ramblin' Man* **1979** Two bumbling cowboys from Montana come to the metropolis of Nashville and promptly turn detective to foil a blackmail scheme and locate a missing singer. Barbara Mandrell and Roy Acuff play themselves. Silly made-for-TV pilot of short-lived series. **100m/C VHS.** Jerry Reed, Tom Selleck, Morgan Fairchild, Claude Akins, Gene Evans, Roy Acuff, Barbara Mandrell; *D:* Burt Kennedy. **TV**

The Concrete Jungle 🦴🦴 *The Criminal* **1982 (R)** After being set up by her no-good boyfriend, Bregman is sent to a correctional facility for drug smuggling. There she must learn to fend for herself (or else). Typical prison for gals fare with cute babes in revealing outfits, a topless riot, the bad warden, and a concerned social worker. Followed by "Chained Heat." **106m/C VHS.** Tracy Bregman, Jill St. John, Barbara Luna, Peter Brown, Aimee (Amy) Eccles, Nita Talbot, Sondra Currie; *D:* Tom De Simone; *W:* Alan J. Adler.

Condemned to Hell woof! *Atrapadas* **1984** A tough-as-iron street punk gets thrown into a women's prison, where she must fight for her existence. Low-brow violence galore. **97m/C VHS.** *AR* Leonor Benedetto; *D:* Anibal Di Salvo.

Condemned to Live 🦴🦴 **1935** Mild-mannered doctor Ralph Morgan and his fiancee Maxine Doyle seem like your average early 20th Century Middle-European couple...but the doctor's hunchbacked servant Mischa Auer is a tipoff that this is a horror movie of some sort. Like many men, the doctor has suffered from a vampire curse all his life. And, like many men, he is unaware of his blood-sucking habit, thanks to the concealment efforts of his loyal (hunchback) servant. Doyle discovers her fiance's sanguine secret, but not before she finds out she really loves Gleason, anyway. Answers the question: just how do you jilt a vampire? **68m/B VHS.** Ralph Morgan, Maxine Doyle, Russell Gleason, Pedro de Cordoba, Mischa Auer, Lucy Beaumont, Carl Stockdale; *D:* Frank Strayer.

Condition Red 🦴🦴 **1995 (R)** Philadelphia prison guard Dan Capelli's (Russo) illicit involvement with inmate Gidell (Williams) turns into big trouble and double-crosses thanks to her drug-dealing boyfriend Angel (Calderon). **85m/C VHS.** James Russo, Cynda Williams, Paul Calderon; *D:* Mika Kaurismaki; *W:* Andre Degas; *C:* Ken Kelsch; *M:* Mauri Sumen.

Condorman 🦴🦴½ **1981 (PG)** Woody Wilkins, an inventive comic book writer, adopts the identity of his own character, Condorman, in order to help a beautiful Russian spy defect. A Disney film, strictly for the small fry. **90m/C VHS, DVD.** Michael Crawford, Oliver Reed, Barbara Carrera, James Hampton, Jean-Pierre Kalfon, Dana Elcar; *D:* Charles Jarrott; *W:* Glenn Gordon Caron; *C:* Charles F. Wheeler; *M:* Henry Mancini.

Conduct Unbecoming 🦴🦴½ **1975 (PG)** Late 19th-century India is the setting for a trial involving the possible assault of a British officer's wife. Ambitious production based on a British stage play suffers from claustrophobic atmosphere but is greatly redeemed by the first rate cast. **107m/C VHS.** *GB* Michael York, Richard Attenborough, Trevor Howard, Stacy Keach, Christopher Plummer, Susannah York, James Faulkner, Michael Culver, Persis Khambatta; *D:* Michael Anderson Sr.

The Conductor 🦴🦴 *Dyrygent* **1980** A famous Polish-born conductor (Gielgud) returns to his birthplace after 50 years of living in the U.S. A dying man, he decides to work with a struggling provincial orchestra, much to the dismay of their own conductor. But the conductor finds himself being used in government schemes to take advantage of his return. In English and Polish with subtitles. **101m/C VHS.** *PL* John Gielgud, Krystyna Janda, Andrzej Seweryn, Jan Ciercierski, Tadeusz Czechowski; *D:* Andrzej Wajda; *W:* Andrzej Kijowski.

Coneheads 🦴🦴½ **1993 (PG)** Comedy inspired by once popular characters from "Saturday Night Live" coasts in on the coattails of "Wayne's World." Aykroyd and Curtin reprise their roles as Beldar and Prymaat, the couple from the planet Remulak who are just trying to fit in on Earth. Newman, who created the role of teenage daughter Connie, appears as Beldar's sister, while Thomas takes over as Connie (toddler Connie is Aykroyd's daughter, in her film debut). One-joke premise is a decade late and a dime short, though cast of comedy all-stars provides a lift. **86m/C VHS, DVD, Wide.** Dan Aykroyd, Jane Curtin, Laraine Newman, Jason Alexander, Michelle Rene Thomas, Chris Farley, Michael Richards, Lisa Jane Persky, Sinbad, Shishir Kurup, Michael McKean, Phil Hartman, David Spade, Dave Thomas, Jan Hooks, Chris Rock, Adam Sandler, Julia Sweeney, Danielle Aykroyd; *D:* Steven Barron; *W:* Tom Davis, Bonnie Turner, Terry Turner, Dan Aykroyd; *C:* Francis Kenny; *M:* David Newman.

Confessing to Laura 🦴🦴 *Confesion a Laura* **1990** Set in Colombia after the 1948 assassination of liberal leader Jorge Elieser Gaitain, which begets a violent civil war. Two people are trapped at Laura's house by the riots—setting up a night of volatile emotion. Spanish with subtitles. **90m/C VHS.** *CL* *D:* Jaime Osorio Gomez.

The Confession 🦴🦴½ **1920** A priest hears a killer's confession and must protect the oath of confidentiality, even as his own brother is being convicted of the murder. **78m/B VHS.** Henry B. Walthall, Francis McDonald, William H. Clifford, Margaret McWade, Margaret Landis; *D:* Bertram Bracken.

The Confession 🦴🦴½ **1998 (R)** Slick lawyer Roy Bleakie (Baldwin) suffers a crisis of conscience with his latest case—the one he expects will hand him the District Attorney's office. Harry Fertig (Kingsley) has killed the three people he regards as responsible for the death of his young son. He's confessed to the crime and wants to plead guilty and accept responsiblity—for his own ambitions Roy wants Harry to plead temporary insanity. But it turns out there's more to the case than even Roy knows. Good performances in what could be just another courtroom melodrama. **114m/C VHS, DVD.** Alec Baldwin, Ben Kingsley, Amy Irving, Jay O. Sanders, Kevin Conway, Anne Twomey, Christopher Lawford, Boyd Gaines, Christopher Noth; *D:* David Hugh Jones; *W:* David Black; *C:* Mike Fash; *M:* Mychael Danna.

The Confessional 🦴 *House of Mortal Sin* **1975 (R)** A mad priest unleashes a monster from his confessional to wreak havoc upon the world. Pray for your VCR. **108m/C VHS.** *GB* Anthony Sharp, Susan Penhaligon, Stephanie Beacham, Norman Eshley, Sheila Keith; *D:* Pete Walker.

The Confessional 🦴🦴🦴 *Le Confessionnal* **1995** Ambiguous psychological drama that's, in part, a homage to Alfred Hitchcock's 1952 film "I Confess," which was filmed in the same Quebec City locations. Pierre (Bluteau) returns to Quebec in 1989 for his father's funeral and to reunite with his adoptive brother Marc (Goyette). Marc's mother Rachel (who committed suicide shortly after his birth) refused to name his father, thought to be a priest, perhaps at the church where Hitchcock filmed his movie. Flashbacks depict the rotund director (Burrage) and his assistant (Scott Thomas) and their production. Lots of intriguing visuals, thanks to director Lepage's innovative stage background. French with subtitles. **100m/C VHS.** *CA FR GB* Lothaire Bluteau, Patrick Goyette, Jean-Louis Millette, Kristin Scott Thomas, Ron Burrage, Richard Frechette, Francois Papineau, Marie Gignac, Anne-Marie Cadieux, Normand Daneau, Suzanne Clement, Lynda Lepage-Beaulieu; *D:* Robert Lepage; *W:* Robert Lepage; *C:* Alan Dostie; *M:* Sacha Puttnam. Genie '95: Art Dir./Set Dec., Director (Lepage), Film.

Confessions of a Hit Man 🦴🦴 **1994 (R)** Nephew who stole millions from his mobster uncle must amend his sordid past. **93m/C VHS.** James Remar, Michael Wright, Emily Longstreth; *D:* Larry Leahy; *W:* Tony Cinciripini, Larry Leahy; *M:* Billy Talbot.

Confessions of a Police Captain 🦴🦴 **1972 (PG)** A dedicated police captain tries to wipe out the bureaucratic corruption that is infecting his city. Balsam gives a fine performance in a heavy-going tale. **104m/C VHS, DVD.** *IT* Martin Balsam, Franco Nero, Marilu Tolo; *D:* Damiano Damiani; *W:* Damiano Damiani, Salvatore Laurani; *C:* Claudio Ragona; *M:* Riz Ortolani.

Confessions of a Serial Killer 🦴🦴 **1987** True story based on the life of Henry Lee Lucas, one of the nation's most vicious killers. Burns plays Lucas in this grisly account of his most violent murders. Shocking realistic look inside the mind of a serial killer. **85m/C VHS.** Robert Burns, Dennis Hill; *D:* Mark Blair.

Confessions of a Vice Baron 🦴 **1942** Vice Baron Lombardo makes it big as a drug dealer and flesh peddler, then loses it all when he falls in love. Sleazy exploitation. **70m/B VHS.** Willy Castello; ***D:*** John Melville.

Confessions of Sorority Girls 🦴🦴½ **1994 (PG-13)** Sometime in the early '60s, wicked Sabrina (Luner) shows up at college and takes it by storm. Will she steal Rita's (Milano) beau? That's the least of her schemes. The villainy is played strictly for campy laughs and the film is never as trashy as its title suggests. Originally made as part of Showtime's "Rebel Highway" series and a remake of Roger Corman's 1957 "Sorority Girl." **83m/C VHS, DVD.** Jamie Luner, Alyssa Milano, Bette Rae, Brian Bloom, Natalija Nogulich; ***D:*** Uli Edel; ***C:*** Jean De Segonzac. **CABLE**

Confessions of Tom Harris 🦴 *Tale of the Cock; Childish Things* **1972 (PG)** Somewhere between all the prize-fighting, leg-breaking for the mob, and jail terms for rape, Tom Harris finds time for a life-changing encounter with love. Based on true story. **90m/C VHS.** Don Murray, Linda Evans, David Brian, Gary Clarke, Logan Ramsey, Angelique Pettyjohn; ***D:*** John Derek, David Nelson; ***W:*** Don Murray.

Confidential 🦴🦴½ **1935** A G-man goes under cover to infiltrate a crime ring. Well made and full of action, fun array of character actors. Naish particularly good as nasty killer. **67m/B VHS.** Donald Cook, Evalyn Knapp, Warren Hymer, J. Carrol Naish, Herbert Rawlinson, Morgan Wallace, Kane Richmond, Theodore von Eltz, Reed Howes; ***D:*** Edward L. Cahn.

Confidential woof! **1986 (R)** A '40s detective tries to solve a decades-old axe murder, only to disappear himself. Horrible fare from our friends north of the border. **95m/C VHS.** *CA* Neil Munro, August Schellenberg, Chapelle Jaffe, Tom Butler; ***D:*** Bruce Pittman.

Confidentially Yours 🦴🦴🦴 *Vivement Dimanche!; Finally, Sunday* **1983 (PG)** Truffaut's homage to Hitchcock, based on Charles Williams' "The Long Saturday Night." A hapless small-town real estate agent is framed for a rash of murders and his secretary, who is secretly in love with him, tries to clear his name. Truffaut's last film is stylish and entertaining. In French with English subtitles. **110m/B VHS, DVD.** *FR* Fanny Ardant, Jean-Louis Trintignant, Philippe Morier-Genoud, Philippe Laudenbach, Caroline Sihol; ***D:*** Francois Truffaut; ***W:*** Francois Truffaut, Suzanne Schiffman, Jean Aurel; ***C:*** Nestor Almendros; ***M:*** Georges Delerue.

Conflict 🦴🦴🦴 **1945** Bogart falls for his sister-in-law and asks his wife for a divorce. She refuses, he plots her murder, and thinks up the alibi. When the police fail to notify him of her death, Bogart is forced to report his wife missing. But is she dead? Her guilty husband smells her perfume, sees her walking down the street, and discovers the body is missing from the scene of the crime. Suspenseful thriller also features Greenstreet as a psychologist/family friend who suspects Bogart knows more than he's telling. **86m/B VHS.** Humphrey Bogart, Alexis Smith, Sydney Greenstreet, Rose Hobart, Charles Drake, Grant Mitchell; ***D:*** Curtis Bernhardt.

Conflict of Interest 🦴½ **1992 (R)** Gideon (Nelson) is a thug who runs stolen cars, drugs, and women from his heavy-metal club on the wrong side of town. Mickey Flannery (McDonald) is the new cop determined to get Gideon behind bars, especially after Gideon kills Mickey's wife, sets up his son on a phony murder rap, and kidnaps his son's girlfriend. Now it's personal and Mickey will stop at nothing to get his revenge. Over-the-top performance by Nelson will have the viewer hoping he gets it soon and puts the film out of its misery. **88m/C VHS.** Judd Nelson, Christopher McDonald, Alyssa Milano, Dey Young, Gregory Alan Harris; ***D:*** Gary Davis; ***W:*** Gregory Miller, Michael Angeli; ***C:*** Bryan England.

The Conformist 🦴🦴🦴🦴 *Il Conformista* **1971 (R)** Character study of young Italian fascist, plagued by homosexual feelings, who must prove his loyalty by killing his old professor. Decadent and engrossing story is brilliantly acted. Based on the novel by Alberto Moravia. **108m/C VHS.** *IT FR GE* Jean-Louis Trintignant, Stefania Sandrelli, Dominique Sanda, Pierre Clementi, Gastone Moschin, Pasquale Fortunato; ***D:*** Bernardo Bertolucci; ***W:*** Bernardo Bertolucci; ***C:*** Vittorio Storaro; ***M:*** Georges Delerue. Natl. Soc. Film Critics '71: Cinematog. (Storaro), Director (Bertolucci).

Congo 🦴🦴 **1995 (PG-13)** Communications company supervisor jets off to the African jungle along with a primatologist to search for a lost city's priceless diamonds, and to return Amy, a gorilla who communicates with sign language to her natural habitat. Why she would want to return to volcanoes and bloodthirsty mutant gray gorillas is anybody's guess. This appropriately technology-laden adaptation of Michael Crichton's novel delivers all the cliches of the old B-movie jungle flicks, but none of the thrills or fun of other Crichton adaptations. **109m/C VHS, DVD.** Mary Ellen Trainor, Dylan Walsh, Laura Linney, Ernie Hudson, Tim Curry, Grant Heslov, Joe Don Baker; ***D:*** Frank Marshall; ***W:*** John Patrick Shanley; ***C:*** Allen Daviau; ***M:*** Jerry Goldsmith.

Congress Dances 🦴🦴 *Der Kongress Tanzt* **1931** A rare German musical about a romance in old Vienna. Popular in its day, it was subsequently banned by the Nazis in 1937. In German with English subtitles. **92m/B VHS.** *GE* Lilian Harvey, Conrad Veidt, Willy Fritsch; ***D:*** Erik Charell.

A Connecticut Yankee 🦴🦴🦴 **1931** A charming, if somewhat dated, version of the popular Mark Twain story, "A Connecticut Yankee in King Arthur's Court." Rogers is a radio shop owner who dreams his way back to the Knights of the Round Table. Story rewritten to fit Rogers' amiable style and to make then-current wisecracks. Great cast overcomes weak points in the script. **96m/B VHS.** Will Rogers, Myrna Loy, Maureen O'Sullivan, William Farnum, Frank Albertson; ***D:*** David Butler.

A Connecticut Yankee in King Arthur's Court 🦴🦴½ *A Yankee in King Arthur's Court* **1949** A pleasant version of the famous Mark Twain story about a 20th century man transported to Camelot and mistaken for a dangerous wizard. This was the third film version of the classic, which was later remade as "Unidentified Flying Oddball," a TV movie, and an animated feature. ♫Once and For Always; Busy Doin' Nothin'; If You Stub Your Toe on the Moon; When Is Sometime?; Twixt Myself and Me. **108m/C VHS.** Bing Crosby, Rhonda Fleming, William Bendix, Cedric Hardwicke, Henry Wilcoxon, Murvyn Vye, Virginia Field; ***D:*** Tay Garnett; ***C:*** Ray Rennahan.

A Connecticut Yankee in King Arthur's Court 🦴🦴½ **1989** The Mark Twain classic has had a gender switch in this TV version, with Pulliam as the time-travelling heroine who winds up in the royal court. **100m/C VHS.** Keisha Knight Pulliam, Jean Marsh, Rene Auberjonois, Emma Samms, Whip Hubley, Michael Gross; ***D:*** Mel Damski. **TV**

The Connection 🦴🦴🦴½ **1961** The Living Theatre's ground-breaking performance of Jack Gelber's play about heroin addicts waiting for their connection to arrive, while a documentary filmmaker hovers nearby with his camera. **105m/B VHS.** Warren Finnerty, Carl Lee, William Redfield, Roscoe Lee Browne, Garry Goodrow, James Anderson, Jackie McLean; ***D:*** Shirley Clarke.

The Connection 🦴🦴½ **1973** Durning steps in to work a deal between hotel jewel thieves and the insurance company. Complex plot handled deftly by all concerned. **74m/C VHS.** Charles Durning, Ronny Cox, Dennis Cole, Zohra Lampert, Heather MacRae, Dana Wynter; ***D:*** Tom Gries. **TV**

The Conqueror woof! *Conqueror of the Desert* **1956** Wayne in pointed helmet and goatee is convincingly miscast as Genghis Khan in this woeful tale of the warlord's early life and involvement with the kidnapped daughter of a powerful enemy. Rife with stilted, unintentionally funny dialogue, Oriental western was very expensive to make (with backing by Howard Hughes), and is now listed in the "Fifty Worst Films of All Time." No matter; it's surreal enough to enable viewer to approximate an out-of-body experience. Even those on the set suffered; filming took place near a nuclear test site in Utah and many members of the cast and crew eventually developed cancer. **111m/C VHS, DVD.** John Wayne, Susan Hayward, William Conrad, Agnes Moorehead, Lee Van Cleef, Pedro Armendariz Sr., Thomas Gomez, John Hoyt, Ted de Corsia, Leslie Bradley, Peter Mamakos; ***D:*** Dick Powell; ***W:*** Oscar Millard; ***C:*** Joseph LaShelle, William E. Snyder, Leo Tover, Harry Wild; ***M:*** Victor Young.

The Conqueror & the Empress woof! *Sandokan alla Riscossa* **1964** Low-budget tale of English explorers who roust an island prince from his throne, motivating him to engage in inspired blood-letting. **89m/C VHS.** *IT* Guy Madison, Ray Danton, Mario Petri, Alberto (Albert Farley) Farnese; ***D:*** Luigi Capuano; ***W:*** Luigi Capuano.

The Conqueror Worm 🦴🦴🦴 *Witchfinder General; Edgar Allan Poe's Conqueror Worm* **1968** Price turns in a fine performance portraying the sinister Matthew Hopkins, a real-life 17th-century witchhunter. No "ham" in this low-budget, underrated thriller, based on Ronald Bassett's novel. The last of three films from director Reeves, who died from an accidental overdose in 1969. **95m/C VHS.** *GB* Vincent Price, Ian Ogilvy, Hilary Dwyer, Rupert Davies, Robert Russell, Patrick Wymark, Wilfrid Brambell, Nicky Henson, Bernard Kay, Tony Selby; ***D:*** Michael Reeves; ***W:*** Michael Reeves, Louis M. Heyward, Tom Baker; ***C:*** John Coquillon; ***M:*** Paul Ferris.

Conquest 🦴🦴🦴 *Marie Walewska* **1937** Garbo, as the Polish countess Marie Walewska, tries to persuade Napoleon (Boyer) to free her native Poland from the Russian Tsar. Garbo, Boyer, and Ouspenskaya are outstanding, while the beautiful costumes and lavish production help, but the script is occasionally weak. A boxoffice flop in the U.S., which ended up costing MGM more than any movie it had made up until that time. **115m/B VHS.** Greta Garbo, Charles Boyer, Reginald Owen, Alan Marshal, Henry Stephenson, Leif Erickson, May Whitty, Maria Ouspenskaya, Vladimir Sokoloff, Scotty Beckett; ***D:*** Clarence Brown; ***C:*** Karl Freund.

Conquest 🦴½ **1983 (R)** Sword and sorcery tale of two mighty warriors against an evil sorceress who seeks world domination. Excellent score. **92m/C VHS.** *IT SP MX* Jorge (George) Rivero, Andrea Occhipinti, Violeta Cela, Sabrina Siani; ***D:*** Lucio Fulci; ***M:*** Claudio Simonetti.

Conquest 🦴🦴½ **1998** Pincer Bedier moves back to Conquest, the dying prairie town of his childhood, to run the local bank. Most of the town's aging citizens think he's crazy for trying to revitalize its boarded-up businesses. But Pincer's unexpectedly aided in his mission by Daisy MacDonald, a determined English lass who doesn't have the money to repair the car that stranded her in Conquest. She agrees to help out Bedier and they wind up falling in love. And then the town's other residents begin to believe in Bedier's maybe not-so-impossible dream. **90m/C VHS.** *CA GB* Lothaire Bluteau, Tara Fitzgerald, Monique Mercure, David Fox; ***D:*** Piers Haggard; ***W:*** Rob Forsyth; ***C:*** Gerald Packer; ***M:*** Ron Sures. Genie '98: Support. Actress (Mercure).

Conquest of Cochise 🦴🦴 **1953** Mediocre oater about a cavalry officer who must stop the war between the Apache and Comanche tribes and a group of Mexicans in the Southwest of the 1850s. **70m/C VHS.** John Hodiak, Robert Stack, Joy Page; ***D:*** William Castle.

Conquest of Mycene 🦴½ *Ercole Contro Molock; Hercules vs. the Moloch* **1963** The Prince of Mycene (who becomes Hercules thanks to dubbing) battles evil queen Neri and her equally evil son, Moloch. Typical muscleman fodder. **102m/C VHS.** *IT FR* Gordon Scott, Rosalba (Sara Bay) Neri, Jany Clair, Alessandra Panaro, Michel Lemoine; ***D:*** Giorgio Ferroni; ***W:*** Giorgio Ferroni, Remigio del Grosso; ***C:*** Augusto Tiezzi; ***M:*** Carlo Rustichelli.

Conquest of Space 🦴½ **1955** A spaceship sets off to explore Mars in spite of the commander's attempts to sabotage the voyage. He believes the flight is an heretical attempt to reach God. An uneasy mixture of religion and space exploration detracts from the nifty special effects which are the only reason to watch. **81m/C VHS.** Walter Brooke, Eric Fleming, Mickey Shaughnessy, Phil Foster, William Redfield, William Hopper, Benson Fong, Ross Martin; ***D:*** Byron Haskin; ***C:*** Lionel Lindon.

Conquest of the Normans 🦴 *Normanni, I; Attack of the Normans* **1962** During the Norman invasion of England, Oliver is accused of kidnapping the King. To save his life, Oliver must find the true identity of the abductors. With so much plot, there should have been some suspense. **83m/C** *IT* Cameron Mitchell; ***D:*** Giuseppe Vari; ***W:*** Nino Stresa.

Conquest of the Planet of the Apes 🦴🦴½ **1972 (PG)** The apes turn the tables on the human Earth population when they lead a revolt against their cruel masters in the distant year of 1990. Sure, there's plenty of cliches—but the story drags you along. The 4th film in the series. Followed by "Battle for the Planet of the Apes." **87m/C VHS, DVD, Wide.** Roddy McDowall, Don Murray, Ricardo Montalban, Natalie Trundy, Severn Darden, Hari Rhodes, Asa Maynor, Gordon Jump, John Randolph, H.M. Wynant, Lou Wagner; ***D:*** J. Lee Thompson; ***W:*** Paul Dehn; ***C:*** Bruce Surtees; ***M:*** Tom Scott.

Conrack 🦴🦴🦴 **1974 (PG)** The true story of Pat Conroy, who tried to teach a group of illiterate Black children in South Carolina by using common-sense teaching techniques to inspire their interest. Voight is convincing as the earnest teacher. Based on Conroy's novel "The Water Is Wide." **111m/C VHS.** Jon Voight, Paul Winfield, Madge Sinclair, Hume Cronyn, Martin Ritt; ***D:*** Martin Ritt; ***W:*** Harriet Frank Jr., Irving Ravetch; ***C:*** John A. Alonzo; ***M:*** John Williams.

Conseil de Famille 🦴🦴 **1986** Hallyday returns to his family from a five-year prison stint, ready to resume his safe-cracking career. Then he discovers the real talent lies with his son Francois (Martin), whose expertise raises the family to middleclass prosperity. But just as dad decides to affiliate with a bigger crime organization, Francois decides to get a straight job because he's fallen in love. Based on a novel by Francis Ryck. French with subtitles. **111m/C VHS.** *FR* Johnny Hallyday, Remi Martin, Fanny Ardant, Guy Marchand; ***D:*** Constantin Costa-Gavras; ***W:*** Constantin Costa-Gavras; ***C:*** Robert Alazraki; ***M:*** Georges Delerue.

Consenting Adult 🦴🦴½ **1985** A distressed family comes to terms with a favorite son's homosexuality. Restrained exploration of the controversial subject. Based on Laura Z. Hobson's novel. **100m/C VHS.** Marlo Thomas, Martin Sheen, Barry Tubb, Talia Balsam, Ben Piazza, Corinne Michaels; ***D:*** Gilbert Cates; ***W:*** John McGreevey. **TV**

Consenting Adults 🦴🦴 **1992 (R)** Cookie-cutter thriller capitalizes on popular "psycho-destroys-your-normal-life" theme. Average yuppie couple (Kline and Mastrantonio) are startled and then seduced by the couple moving in next door (Spacey and Miller), who conduct a considerably less-restrained lifestyle. Wife-swapping leads to murder and an innocent man is framed. Plot and characters are underdeveloped yet manage to hold interest through decent performances. **100m/C VHS.** Kevin Kline, Mary Elizabeth Mastrantonio, Kevin Spacey, Rebecca Miller, Forest Whitaker, E.G. Marshall, Billie Neal; ***D:*** Alan J. Pakula; ***W:*** Matthew Chapman.

Consolation Marriage 🦴🦴½ *Married in Haste* **1931** A couple meet and marry after being jilted by others, then must make a choice when their old flames return. Dunne and O'Brien make a charming couple in this early talkie. One of Dunne's early starring roles. **82m/B VHS.** Irene Dunne, Pat O'Brien, John Halliday, Matt Moore, Myrna Loy, Lester Vail; ***D:*** Paul Sloane.

Conspiracy 🦴🦴 **1989 (R)** Defense Secretary William Baine is haunted by a past sexual encounter, and a top secret team moves in to avert any hint of what could become a "sex scandal." Based on a true story. **87m/C VHS.** James Wilby, Kate Hardie, Glyn Houston; ***D:*** Christopher Barnard.

Conspiracy 🦴🦴½ **2001 (R)** Another in HBO's long line of excellent movies based on real-life events. This one covers the January, 1942 meeting of high-ranking Nazi SS and civilian government leaders to decide what to do about "the Jewish question." Led by SS Geneal Reinhard

Heydrich (Branagh, in a riveting performance) and set up by SS Col. Adolf Eichmann (Tucci), this conference was conducted like a board meeting, and that's where the power of the movie comes from, because the outcome of the conference was implementation of the "final solution," the attempted extermination of the Jewish population of Europe. While every man in the room is a villain, they aren't the kind of Nazi villain we're used to. They are bureaucrats who offer administrative and logistical objections, but only token moral dissent (which is dispensed with rather quickly and completely). **96m/C VHS, DVD, Wide.** Stanley Tucci, Kenneth Branagh, Colin Firth, Barnaby Kay, Ben Daniels, David Threlfall, Jonathan Coy, Brendan Coyle, Ian McNeice, Owen Teale, Nicholas Woodeson, Ewan Stewart, Kevin McNally, Brian Pettifer; ***D:*** Frank Pierson; ***W:*** Loring Mandel; ***C:*** Stephen Goldblatt. **CABLE**

Conspiracy of Hearts **1960** A convent of nuns hide Jewish children in 1943 Italy despite threats to their personal safety. Suspenseful tale despite the familiar plot. **113m/B VHS.** *GB* Lilli Palmer, Yvonne Mitchell, Sylvia Syms, Ronald Lewis; ***D:*** Ralph Thomas; ***W:*** Robert Presnell.

A Conspiracy of Love **1987** Three generations of a divorce-torn family try to pull itself back together. Sugary domestic tale tries to be uplifting, succeeds in being cliche-ridden. **93m/C VHS.** Robert Young, Drew Barrymore, Glynnis O'Connor, Elizabeth Wilson, Mitchell Laurance, John Fujioka, Alan Fawcett; ***D:*** Noel Black. **TV**

Conspiracy of Terror **1975** Married detectives investigate a series of murders and unearth a grisly cult in a quiet suburb. Standard fare with a few too cute lines concerning the leads' mixed-faith marriage. **78m/C VHS.** Michael Constantine, Barbara Rhoades, Mariclare Costello, Roger Perry, David Opatoshu, Logan Ramsey; ***D:*** John Llewellyn Moxey. **TV**

Conspiracy: The Trial of the Chicago Eight **1987** Courtroom drama focuses on the rambunctious trial of the Chicago Eight radicals, charged with inciting a riot at the Democratic National Convention of 1968. Dramatized footage mixed with interviews with the defendants. Imaginative reconstruction of history. **118m/C VHS, DVD.** Peter Boyle, Elliott Gould, Robert Carradine, Martin Sheen, David Clennon, David Kagen, Michael Lembeck, Robert Loggia; ***D:*** Jeremy Paul Kagan.

Conspiracy Theory **1997 (R)** Whacked-out New York cabbie Jerry Fletcher (Gibson) writes a newsletter on conspiracy theories, which he finds in every possible place and situation. Naturally, he doesn't keep his thoughts to himself and exasperated Justice Department attorney Alice Sutton (Roberts) is stuck listening to the love-struck fool. But as the saying goes just because you're paranoid doesn't mean they're not out to get you. Sure enough, one of Jerry's conspiracies turns out to be true and suddenly he and Alice are being pursued by CIA shrink Dr. Jonas (Stewart), who's not what he seems to be either. Gibson's more geek than hero but appealing regardless, as is heroine Roberts. Another successful, enjoyable, and highly profitable, teaming of Donner, Gibson and producer Joel Silver. **135m/C VHS, DVD.** Terry Alexander, Mel Gibson, Julia Roberts, Patrick Stewart, Cylk Cozart; ***D:*** Richard Donner; ***W:*** Brian Helgeland; ***C:*** John Schwartzman; ***M:*** Carter Burwell.

Conspirator ½ **1949** Somewhat engrossing drama about a beautiful young girl who discovers that her new husband, a British army officer, is working with the Communists. Elizabeth Taylor stars as the naive American wife and Robert Taylor plays her Russkie agent husband. Although madly in love with his wife, he is given orders to kill her. Picture falls apart at end due to weak script. Based on the novel by Humphrey Slater. **85m/B VHS.** *GB* Robert Taylor, Elizabeth Taylor, Robert Flemyng, Harold Warrender, Honor Blackman, Marjorie Fielding, Thora Hird; ***D:*** Victor Saville; ***W:*** Sally Benson, Gerard Fairlie; ***C:*** Frederick A. (Freddie) Young.

Consuming Passions ½ **1988 (R)** A ribald, food-obsessed English comedy about a young idiot who rises within the hierarchy of a chocolate company via murder. You'll never guess what the secret ingredient in his wonderful chocolate is. Based on a play by Michael Palin and Terry Jones (better known as part of the Monty Python troupe), the film is sometimes funny, more often gross, and takes a single joke far beyond its limit. **95m/C VHS.** *GB* Vanessa Redgrave, Jonathan Pryce, Tyler Butterworth, Freddie Jones, Prunella Scales, Sammi Davis, Thora Hird, John Wells, William Rushton, Timothy West; ***D:*** Giles Foster; ***W:*** Michael Palin, Andrew Davies, Paul Zimmerman.

Contact ½ **1997 (PG)** Thought-provoking (if overlong) drama rather than sci-fi spectacular (though it has its fair share of special effects). Radio astronomer Dr. Ellie Arroway (Foster) discovers signals being transmitted from the distant star Vega. When they're deciphered, the signals turn out to be blueprints for a craft that will take its occupant into space and a first meeting with aliens. Ellie fights to become that first spokesperson for Earth's inhabitants. More philosophical than the usual sci-fi alien encounter epic, but the excellent cast, led by Foster, pulls it off nicely. Based on the novel by Carl Sagan. **150m/C VHS, DVD.** Jodie Foster, Matthew McConaughey, James Woods, Tom Skerritt, Angela Bassett, John Hurt, David Morse, Rob Lowe, Jake Busey, William Fichtner, Geoffrey Blake, Jena Malone; ***D:*** Robert Zemeckis; ***W:*** Michael Goldenberg; ***C:*** Don Burgess; ***M:*** Alan Silvestri.

Contagion ½ **1987** Innocent real estate agent meets a reclusive, eccentric millionaire who offers him unlimited wealth and beautiful women, but only if he kills someone. Interesting ethical premise loses its philosophic purity. **90m/C VHS.** *AU* John (Roy Slaven) Doyle, Nicola Bartlett, Roy Barrett, Nathy Gaffney, Pamela Hawksford; ***D:*** Karl Zwicky.

Contagious ½ **1996 (PG-13)** Epidemiologist Hanna (Wagner) discovers that passengers aboard a flight from Latin American have been exposed to cholera and could cause an epidemic. She teams with Detective Lou (Pena), who's tracking an infected drug smuggler, to find the source of the disease. **90m/C VHS.** Lindsay Wagner, Elizabeth Pena, Tom Wopat, Alexandra Purvis, Matt Hill, Brendan Fletcher; ***D:*** Joe Napolitano; ***W:*** Sandy Kroopf; ***C:*** Andreas Poulsson; ***M:*** Stephen Graziano. **CABLE**

The Contaminated Man **2001 (R)** An infectious disease expert (Hurt) loses his family to an unknown disease. Now some years later at an "infectious disease laboratory" in a vaguely defined Russia, disgruntled security guard Muller (Weller) has been infected with a deadly pathogen, where one drop of his blood will now kill a person in matter of seconds. The disease expert is called in to investigate and teams up with an American reporter, as Muller is determined to get home to see his wife and son, even if it means infecting the entire Russian population. TV movie dull beyond belief. Peter Weller getting to do an eccentric Olivier-like turn as the Russian-accented, bald Muller is the only fun in the whole film. **98m/C DVD, Wide.** William Hurt, Natascha (Natasha) McElhone, Peter Weller, Katja Woywood, Michael Brandon; ***D:*** Anthony Hickox; ***W:*** John Penney; ***C:*** Bruce Douglas Johnson; ***M:*** Michael Hoenig. **TV**

Contempt ½ *Le Mepris; Il Disprezzo* **1964** A film about the filming of a new version of "The Odyssey," and the rival visions of how to tell the story. Amusing look at the film business features Fritz Lang playing himself, Godard as his assistant. Bardot is pleasant scenery. Adapted from Moravia's "A Ghost at Noon." **102m/C VHS.** *IT FR* Brigitte Bardot, Jack Palance, Fritz Lang, Georgia Moll, Michel Piccoli, Jean-Luc Godard, Linda Veras; ***D:*** Jean-Luc Godard; ***W:*** Jean-Luc Godard; ***C:*** Raoul Coutard; ***M:*** Georges Delerue.

The Contender ½ **2000 (R)** An excellent cast propels this political potboiler, although the plot contains some hot air. After the sitting Veep dies, downhome Prez Evans (Bridges) nominates Sen. Laine Hanson (Allen) for the post. Although principled and experienced, she also happens to be a woman with a past. Evans's oily conservative rival Runyon (Oldman) takes advantage by digging up photos of the senator being the life of a college fraternity party. Hanson refuses to answer questions about her youthful indiscretions, arguing that her sexual history is nobody's business. As in real politics, much speechifying ensues and not much is accomplished. Allen shines in a role that was written expressly for her. Reports filtered out after the film's release that exec producer Oldman, a conservative himself, was unhappy about the editing and portrayal of his character, who he thought was the hero of the movie. **127m/C VHS, DVD, Wide.** Joan Allen, Gary Oldman, Jeff Bridges, Sam Elliott, Christian Slater, William L. Petersen, Philip Baker Hall, Saul Rubinek; ***D:*** Rod Lurie; ***W:*** Rod Lurie; ***C:*** Denis Maloney; ***M:*** Lawrence Nash Groupe.

Continental Divide **1981 (PG)** A hard-nosed political columnist takes off for the Colorado Rockies on an "easy assignment"—interviewing a reclusive ornithologist, with whom he instantly falls in love. A city slicker, he first alienates her, but she eventually falls for him, too. But it's not exactly a match made in heaven. Story meanders to a conclusion of sorts. Probably the most normal Belushi ever was on screen. **103m/C VHS.** John Belushi, Blair Brown, Allen (Goorwitz) Garfield, Carlin Glynn, Val Avery, Tony Ganios, Tim Kazurinsky; ***D:*** Michael Apted; ***W:*** Lawrence Kasdan; ***C:*** John Bailey.

Contraband ½ *Blackout* **1940** Danish sea captain Andersen (Veidt) and the mysterious Mrs. Sorenson (Hobson) are kidnapped by a cell of Nazi spies operating in London in the early days of WWII. They manage to turn the tables on the bad guys. Story takes place under blackout conditions lending a lot of atmosphere to this early thriller. **88m/B VHS, DVD.** *GB* Conrad Veidt, Valerie Hobson, Esmond Knight, Hay Petrie, Raymond Lovell, Harold Warrender, Charles Victor; ***D:*** Michael Powell; ***W:*** Michael Powell; ***C:*** Frederick A. (Freddie) Young.

Contraband ½ **1986** The leader of a smuggling gang escapes from an ambush in which his brother was murdered. He searches for a haven of safety while his cronies seek brutal revenge. Average crime yarn lacks much excitement. Dubbed into English. **95m/C VHS.** *IT* Fabio Testi, Ivana Monti; ***D:*** Lucio Fulci.

Contract ½ **1980** A marriage ceremony between the children of two important families gets disrupted when the friends and relatives in attendance can't get along, and the bride can't seem to commit. Provides a biting social commentary against dirty politicians and unethical entrepreneurs. Polish with subtitles. **111m/C VHS.** *PL* Maja Komorowska, Tadeusz Lomnicki, Magda Jaroszowna, Leslie Caron, Ignacy Machowski; ***D:*** Krzysztof Zanussi; ***W:*** Krzysztof Zanussi; ***C:*** Slawomir Idziak; ***M:*** Wojciech Kilar.

The Contract **1998 (R)** Former black ops specialist Luc (Imbault) is now making a living as a pro assassin and is teaching the trade to daughter Hannah (Black). When dad gets killed in a set-up, Hannah wants revenge against the man behind the deed. It's Presidential candidate J. Harmon (Williams), who wants his own black ops past to stay hidden—but Hannah has other ideas. **90m/C VHS, DVD.** Billy Dee Williams, Johanna Black, Laurent Imbault; ***D:*** K.C. Bascombe. **VIDEO**

Control ½ **1987** Tedious tale of 15 volunteers for a 20-day fallout shelter habitation experiment who become trapped when a real nuclear emergency occurs. Filmed in Rome. **83m/C VHS.** *IT* Burt Lancaster, Kate Nelligan, Ben Gazzara, Andrea Ferreol, Lavinia Segurini, Andrea Occhipinti, Cyrielle Claire, Jean Benguigui, Kate Reid, Erland Josephson, Ingrid Thulin; ***D:*** Guiliano Montaldo. **CABLE**

The Convent **1995** Idiosyncratic saga of Paris-based American scholar Michael Padovic (Malkovich) and his French wife Helene (Deneuve) who travel to an ancient Portuguese monastery so Michael may do research at their library. The convent's guardian is the charming and sinister Baltar (Cintra), who flirts with neglected Helene, while playing Mephistopheles to Michael's Faust. Lots of mysticism and religious iconography. Portuguese, French, and English dialogue. **90m/C VHS.** *PT FR* John Malkovich, Catherine Deneuve, Luis Miguel Cintra, Leonor Silveira; ***D:*** Manoel de Oliveira; ***W:*** Manoel de Oliveira; ***C:*** Mario Barroso.

The Convent **2000 (R)** In 1960, a young woman enters a church, shoots several nuns and a priest, and then torches the place. Jump ahead to the present, as a group of college kids enter the now-condemned convent to perform a fraternity prank. Elsewhere in the dilapidated convent, amateur Satanists perform a ritual, releasing the evil spirits held captive in the sanctuary. From this point on, the movie becomes a monster mash, as each character is either possessed, killed, or both. The only hope for the trapped youngsters is the now-grown girl who started all of this in the 1960. The film is creatively shot by director Mendez, and the demon makeup is unusual, but the action owes too much to "Night of the Demons 2," "The Church," and the "Goth Talk" skit from "Saturday Night Live." Horror aficionados will feel as if they've seen it all before. **79m/C VHS, DVD, Wide.** Adrienne Barbeau, Coolio, Bill Moseley, Joanna Canton, Megahn Perry, Dax Miller, David Gunn; ***D:*** Mike Mendez; ***W:*** Chaton Anderson; ***C:*** Jason Lowe; ***M:*** Joseph Bishara.

The Conversation ½ **1974 (PG)** Freelance surveillance expert Harry Caul (Hackman) is becoming increasingly uneasy about his current job for a powerful businessman (Duvall). He and assistant Stan (Cazale) are watching a young couple (Williams, Forrest) when Harry begins to suspect that they are murder targets. Powerful statement about privacy, responsibility and guilt. One of the best movies of the '70s. **113m/C VHS, DVD, Wide.** Gene Hackman, John Cazale, Frederic Forrest, Allen (Goorwitz) Garfield, Cindy Williams, Robert Duvall, Teri Garr, Michael Higgins, Elizabeth McRae, Harrison Ford; ***D:*** Francis Ford Coppola; ***W:*** Francis Ford Coppola; ***C:*** Bill Butler; ***M:*** David Shire. Cannes '74: Film; Natl. Bd. of Review '74: Actor (Hackman), Director (Coppola), Natl. Film Reg. '95;; Natl. Soc. Film Critics '74: Director (Coppola).

Conversation Piece *Violence et Passion; Gruppo di Famiglia in un Interno* **1975 (R)** An aging art historian's life is turned upside down when a Countess and her daughters rent out the penthouse in his estate. Sometimes-talky examination of scholarly pretensions. **112m/C VHS.** *IT FR* Burt Lancaster, Silvana Mangano, Helmut Berger, Claudia Cardinale, Claudia Marsani; ***D:*** Luchino Visconti; ***W:*** Luchino Visconti, Suso Cecchi D'Amico, Enrico Medioli; ***C:*** Pasqualino De Santis; ***M:*** Franco Mannino.

Convict Cowboy ½ **1995 (R)** Hardbitten professional rodeo cowboy Ry Weston (Voight) killed a man and now works the Montana prison rodeo circuit. Newcomer greenhorn Clay Treyton (Chandler) wants to get out of kitchen duty and decides Ry is the perfect ridin' and ropin' teacher. Only Ry isn't interested in wasting his time (at first). It's a predictable bonding experience in a melodramatic movie. **106m/C VHS.** Jon Voight, Kyle Chandler, Ben Gazzara, Marcia Gay Harden, Glenn Plummer, Stephen McHattie; ***D:*** Rod Holcomb; ***C:*** James L. Carter. **CABLE**

Convicted ½ **1932** Lean thriller about a woman cleared of a murder charge, but only when a second, identical murder occurs while she is jailed. **57m/B VHS.** Aileen Pringle, Jameson Thomas, Harry C. (Henry) Myers, Dorothy Christy, Richard Tucker; ***D:*** Christy Cabanne.

Convicted ½ **1986** Solid story of innocent man imprisoned for rape, and his wife's determined efforts to free him. Larroquette does well in unexpected role. Based on a true story. **94m/C VHS.** John Larroquette, Carroll O'Connor, Lindsay Wagner; ***D:*** David Lowell Rich; ***M:*** Steve Dorff. **TV**

Convicted: A Mother's Story 🦴 **1987** Jillian embezzles cash from her employer, all for the sake of a bum of a boyfriend, and goes to jail. Odd casting hinders a ho-hum plot. **95m/C VHS.** Ann Jillian, Kiel Martin, Fred Savage, Gloria Loring, Christa Denton; ***D:*** Richard T. Heffron; ***M:*** David Shire. **TV**

Convicts at Large 🦴 **1938** An escaped convict steals the clothes of a inept architect. Left with only prison duds, the architect stumbles into the bad side of town and gets involved with the mob. Inane. **58m/B VHS.** Ralph Forbes, Paula Stone; ***D:*** Scott E. Beal; ***W:*** Scott E. Beal.

Convoy 🦴🦴½ **1940** Life aboard a convoy ship in the North Sea during WWII. The small cruiser is picked on by a German U-Boat. Will a rescuer appear? Noted for technical production values. **95m/B VHS.** Clive Brook, John Clements, Edward Chapman, Judy Campbell, Edward Rigby, Stewart Granger, Michael Wilding, George Benson; ***D:*** Pen Tennyson.

Convoy 🦴🦴 **1978 (R)** A defiant trucker leads an indestructible truck convoy to Mexico to protect high gasoline prices. Lightweight stuff was inspired by the song "Convoy" by C.W. McCall. **106m/C VHS.** Kris Kristofferson, Ali MacGraw, Ernest Borgnine, Burt Young, Madge Sinclair, Franklin Ajaye, Cassie Yates; ***D:*** Sam Peckinpah; ***C:*** Harry Stradling Jr.

Coogan's Bluff 🦴🦴🦴 **1968 (PG)** An Arizona deputy sheriff (Eastwood) travels to New York in order to track down a killer on the loose. First Eastwood/Siegel teaming is tense actioner. The TV series "McCloud" was based on this film. **100m/C VHS.** Clint Eastwood, Lee J. Cobb, Tisha Sterling, Don Stroud, Betty Field, Susan Clark, Tom Tully, Albert "Poppy" Popwell; ***D:*** Donald Siegel; ***W:*** Dean Riesner; ***M:*** Lalo Schifrin.

The Cook, the Thief, His Wife & Her Lover 🦴🦴🦴½ **1990 (R)** An exclusive restaurant houses four disturbing characters. Greenaway's powerful vision of greed, love, and violence may be too strong for some tastes. Available in several different versions: the standard unrated theatrical release, the unrated version in a letterboxed format, and an R-rated cut which runs half an hour shorter. **123m/C VHS, DVD, Wide.** *GB* Richard Bohringer, Michael Gambon, Helen Mirren, Alan Howard, Tim Roth; ***D:*** Peter Greenaway; ***W:*** Peter Greenaway; ***C:*** Sacha Vierny; ***M:*** Michael Nyman.

Cookie 🦴🦴½ **1989 (R)** Light comedy about a Mafia don's daughter trying to smart mouth her way into the mob's good graces. A character-driven vehicle, this plot takes a backseat to casting. Wiest is superb as Falk's moll. **93m/C VHS, 8mm.** Emily Lloyd, Peter Falk, Dianne Wiest, Jerry Lewis, Brenda Vaccaro, Ricki Lake, Lionel Stander, Michael V. Gazzo, Adrian Pasdar, Bob Gunton, Rockets Redglare, G. Anthony "Tony" Sirico; ***D:*** Susan Seidelman; ***W:*** Alice Arlen, Nora Ephron; ***M:*** Thomas Newman.

Cookie's Fortune 🦴🦴🦴½ **1999 (PG-13)** Neal is Jewel Mae "Cookie" Orcutt, the matriarch of a Mississippi family with its share of female eccentrics. When Cookie offs herself to join her deceased husband, her officious, scandal-fearing spinster neice Camille (Close) destroys the suicide note, setting up the family's loyal, good-natured handyman (Dutton) for the fall. At the same time, she's directing practically the whole town in a church performance of "Salome." Excellent script by Rapp allows more characterization than usual for Altman, as well as a pleasantly leisurely pace. Flawless ensemble work (another Altman hallmark) is highlighted by the performances of Neal, Close, and Dutton. **118m/C VHS, DVD.** Charles S. Dutton, Glenn Close, Patricia Neal, Liv Tyler, Chris O'Donnell, Julianne Moore, Ned Beatty, Courtney B. Vance, Donald Moffat, Lyle Lovett, Matt Malloy, Rufus Thomas, Danny Darst, Randle Mell, Niecy Nash, Ruby Wilson, Preston Strobel; ***D:*** Robert Altman; ***W:*** Anne Rapp; ***C:*** Toyomichi Kurita; ***M:*** David A. Stewart. Natl. Bd. of Review '99: Support. Actress (Moore).

Cooking Up Trouble 🦴🦴 *Three of a Kind* **1944** The crazy trio become foster dads in this "Stooge" type comedy. **60m/B VHS.** Shemp Howard, Billy Gilbert, Maxie "Slapsie" Rosenbloom; ***D:*** David Ross Lederman; ***W:*** Earle Snell.

Cool As Ice 🦴 **1991 (PG)** "Rapper" Vanilla Ice makes his feature film debut as a rebel with an eye for the ladies, who motors into a small, conservative town. Several so-so musical segments. For teenage girls only. **92m/C VHS.** Vanilla Ice, Kristin Minter, Michael Gross, Sydney Lassick, Dody Goodman, Naomi Campbell, Candy Clark; ***D:*** David Kellogg; ***C:*** Janusz Kaminski; ***M:*** Stanley Clarke. Golden Raspberries '91: Worst New Star (Vanilla Ice).

Cool Blue 🦴½ **1988 (R)** An unsuccessful painter meets the woman of his dreams, has a brief affair, then tries to locate her in the greater Los Angeles metro area. Good luck. Watch for Penn's cameo. **93m/C VHS.** Woody Harrelson, Hank Azaria, Ely Pouget, John Diehl; ***Cameos:*** Sean Penn; ***D:*** Mark Mullin, Richard Shepard.

A Cool, Dry Place 🦴🦴½ **1998 (PG-13)** Basically a variation on "Kramer vs. Kramer." Russ Durrell (Vaughn) was a hotshot Chicago lawyer with a five-year old son, Calvin (Moat), when wife Kate (Potter) took a hike. So Russ moves to small town Kansas to make a go of single fatherhood in a slower-paced world. Eventually, he begins dating Beth (Adams) and when things start to get serious, guess who turns up and decides she wants back into her son's life? Vaughn does fine as the dad but Potter is stuck with a dopey, inarticulate character. **97m/C VHS.** Vince Vaughn, Monica Potter, Joey Lauren Adams, Bobby Moat, Devon Sawa; ***D:*** John N. Smith; ***W:*** Matthew McDuffie; ***C:*** Jean Lepine; ***M:*** Curt Sobel.

Cool Hand Luke 🦴🦴🦴½ **1967** One of the last great men-in-chains films. A man (Newman) sentenced to sweat out a term on a prison farm refuses to compromise with authority. Martin shines in his supporting role as the oily warden, uttering that now-famous phrase, "What we have here is a failure to communicate." Kennedy's performance as leader of the chain gang won him an Oscar. Based on the novel by Donn Pearce. **126m/C VHS, DVD.** Paul Newman, George Kennedy, J.D. Cannon, Strother Martin, Dennis Hopper, Anthony Zerbe, Lou Antonio, Wayne Rogers, Harry Dean Stanton, Ralph Waite, Joe Don Baker, Richard (Dick) Davalos, Jo Van Fleet, Robert Drivas, Clifton James, Morgan Woodward, Luke Askew, Robert Donner, Warren Finnerty, James Gammon, Rance Howard, Buck Kartalian, John McLiam, Charles Tyner, Donn Pearce, Marc Cavell, Charles Hicks, James Jeter, Robert Luster, John Pearce, Eddie Rosson; ***D:*** Stuart Rosenberg; ***W:*** Frank Pierson, Donn Pearce; ***C:*** Conrad L. Hall; ***M:*** Lalo Schifrin. Oscars '67: Support. Actor (Kennedy).

Cool Mikado 🦴🦴 **1963** A jazzy modernization of the Gilbert-Sullivan operetta, in which an American soldier is kidnapped by the gangster fiance of the Japanese girl he loves. **81m/C VHS.** *GB* Stubby Kaye, Frankie Howerd, Dennis Price; ***D:*** Michael Winner.

Cool Runnings 🦴🦴½ **1993 (PG)** Bright, slapstick comedy based on the true story of the Jamaican bobsled team's quest to enter the 1988 Winter Olympics in Calgary. Candy is recruited to coach four unlikely athletes who don't quite exemplify the spirit of the Games. He accepts the challenge not only because of its inherent difficulty but because he needs to reconcile himself to past failures as a former sledder. When our heroes leave their sunny training ground for Calgary, their mettle is tested by serious sledders from more frigid climes who pursue the competition with a stern sense of mission. An upbeat story which will appeal to children, its target audience. **98m/C VHS, DVD.** Leon, Doug E. Doug, John Candy, Marco Brambilla, Malik Yoba, Rawle Lewis, Raymond J. Barry, Peter Outerbridge, Larry Gilman, Paul Coeur; ***D:*** Jon Turteltaub; ***W:*** Tommy Swerdlow, Lynn Siefert, Michael Goldberg; ***C:*** Phedon Papamichael; ***M:*** Hans Zimmer.

The Cool Surface 🦴🦴 **1992 (R)** Sex and ambition, Hollywood style. Dani, a wannbe actress, and Jarvis, an aspiring screenwriter become lovers. Jarvis turns their hot affair into a sizzling novel and then a script. Dani may have inspired the lead role but that doesn't mean she'll get the part. But it won't be for lack of trying (anything). **88m/C VHS.** Robert Patrick, Teri Hatcher, Matt McCoy, Cyril O'Reilly, Ian Buchanan; ***D:*** Erik Anjou; ***W:*** Erik Anjou; ***M:*** Dave Kopplin.

The Cool World 🦴🦴½ **1963** Tough-talking docudrama, set on the streets of Harlem, focuses on a 15-year-old black youth whose one ambition in life is to own a gun and lead his gang. **107m/B VHS.** Gloria Foster, Hampton Clanton, Carl Lee; ***D:*** Shirley Clarke. Natl. Film Reg. '94.

Cool World 🦴🦴 **1992 (PG-13)** Underground cartoonist Jack Deebs enters his own adult cartoon "Cool World," lured by his sex-kitten character "Holli Would," who needs him to leave her animated world and become human. Holli's plan is opposed by the only other human to occupy Cool World, a slick detective whose main job is to prevent noids (humans) and doodles (cartoons) from having sex and destroying the balance between the two existences. A mixture of live-action and wild animation. Director Bakshi's creations are not intended for children but this is less explicit than usual, which may be one of the problems. Little humor and a flat script leave this film too uninvolving. **101m/C VHS.** Gabriel Byrne, Kim Basinger, Brad Pitt, Michele Abrams, Deirdre O'Connell, Carrie Hamilton, Frank Sinatra Jr., Michael Lally, William Frankfather; ***D:*** Ralph Bakshi; ***W:*** Michael Grais, Mark Victor; ***C:*** John A. Alonzo; ***M:*** Mark Isham.

A Cooler Climate 🦴🦴½ **1999 (R)** Iris (Fields) is a middleaged married woman who divorces her husband (refusing any settlement) after she falls in love with another man. When her lover leaves her, Iris has no money and no job skills except her homemaking abilities. Those allow her to become the live-in housekeeper for the wealthy Tanners. But brittle Paula Tanner (Davis) soon finds herself on the rocky road to divorce and unable to cope while Iris discovers her self-esteem in her independence. The men are strictly cardboard but Fields and Davis are worth a watch. Based on a novel by Zena Collier. **100m/C VHS.** Sally Field, Judy Davis, Winston Rekert, Jerry Wasserman, Jessalyn Gilsig, Gerard Plunkett, Carly Pope, Peter Yunker; ***D:*** Susan Seidelman; ***W:*** Marsha Norman; ***C:*** John Bartley; ***M:*** Patrick Williams. **CABLE**

Cooley High 🦴🦴🦴 **1975 (PG)** Black high school students in Chicago go through the rites of passage in their senior year during the '60s. Film is funny, smart, and much acclaimed. Great soundtrack featuring Motown hits of the era is a highlight. Basis for the TV series "What's Happening." **107m/C VHS, DVD.** Glynn Turman, Lawrence-Hilton Jacobs, Garrett Morris, Cynthia Davis; ***D:*** Michael A. Schultz; ***W:*** Eric Monte.

Cooperstown 🦴🦴½ **1993** Harry (Arkin) is a former major-league pitcher who now works as a baseball scout in Florida. He's been angry for 30 years over giving up a home-run pitch that kept his team (the ficitional Chicago Barons) out of the World Series. Harry's feels this error cost him his chance at induction into the Baseball Hall of Fame in Cooperstown, New York, and he's always blamed ex-friend and former catcher Raymond (Greene), who's just had the gall to be elected. Only Raymond's just died—but his ghostly figure visits Harry and urges him to take a road trip not only to the baseball shrine but into his past. **100m/C VHS.** Alan Arkin, Graham Greene, Hope Lange, Josh Charles, Ed Begley Jr., Maria Pitillo, Ann Wedgeworth, Paul Dooley, Joanna Miles, Charles Haid; ***D:*** Charles Haid; ***W:*** Lee Blessing. **CABLE**

Cop 🦴🦴½ **1988 (R)** Left by his wife and child, a ruthless and work-obsessed detective goes after a twisted serial killer. Woods' exceptional ability to play sympathetic weirdos is diluted by a script—based on James Ellroys's novel "Blood on the Moon"—that warps the feminist theme, is violent, and depends too heavily on coincidence. **110m/C VHS.** James Woods, Lesley Ann Warren, Charles Durning, Charles Haid, Raymond J. Barry, Randi Brooks, Annie McEnroe, Victoria Wauchope; ***D:*** James B. Harris; ***W:*** James B. Harris; ***M:*** Michel Colombier.

Cop and a Half 🦴½ **1993 (PG)** Streetwise eight-year-old (Golden) accidentally witnesses a murder and then bullies police into letting him join the force (for a day) when he withholds key information. Enter his partner for the day—hard-edged detective Reynolds, who claims to hate kids, but who we know will learn to love them. Meanwhile, the outlaw (Sharkey) knows Devon saw him and is trying to silence him permanently. Predictable fantasy may appeal to kids, but will make most adults yawn. One of Sharkey's last roles. **87m/C VHS, DVD, Wide.** Norman D. Golden II, Burt Reynolds, Ruby Dee, Ray Sharkey, Holland Taylor, Frank Sivero, Marc Macaulay, Rocky Giordani, Sammy Hernandez; ***D:*** Henry Winkler; ***W:*** Arne Olsen; ***C:*** Bill Butler; ***M:*** Alan Silvestri. Golden Raspberries '93: Worst Actor (Reynolds).

The Cop & the Girl 🦴 **1986** A cop falls for a teenage runaway, ends up on the lam. Confused story overpowered by camera work. Lots of violence and strong language. Dubbed. **94m/C VHS.** *GE* Juergen Prochnow, Annette Von Klier; ***D:*** Peter Keglevic.

Cop in Blue Jeans 🦴 **1978** Undercover cop goes after a mob kingpin in this violent, badly dubbed crime yarn. **92m/C VHS.** Tomas Milian, Jack Palance, Maria Rosaria Omaggio, Guido Mannari; ***D:*** Bruno Corbucci.

Cop Land 🦴🦴🦴 **1997 (R)** Partially deaf sheriff (Stallone), whose small New Jersey town is home to a number of New York cops, has divided loyalties when a criminal investigation could implicate his department and the cops he idolizes. Stallone wanted to put "actor" back on his resume, and made the ultimate sacrifice of his physique for the role by gaining some 35 pounds and letting his muscles go. Writer-director Mangold, who grew up in an upstate New York town populated by NYC cops and firemen, pairs his earnest morality tale with a Western feel to provide the excellent cast a chance to do what they do best. Welcome departure from the usual summer bombast. **105m/C VHS, DVD.** Sylvester Stallone, Robert De Niro, Annabella Sciorra, Harvey Keitel, Peter Berg, Janeane Garofalo, Michael Rapaport, Ray Liotta, Cathy Moriarty, Robert Patrick, Noah Emmerich, John Spencer, Malik Yoba, Frank Vincent, Arthur J. Nascarelli, Edie Falco, Deborah Harry; ***D:*** James Mangold; ***W:*** James Mangold; ***C:*** Eric Alan Edwards; ***M:*** Howard Shore.

Cop-Out 🦴🦴 *Stranger in the House* **1967** John Sawyer (Mason) is an alcoholic retired attorney who has lived in seclusion since his wife left him. His estranged daughter, Angela (Chaplin), runs with a swinging crowd and her boyfriend, Jo (Bertoya), is accused of killing another member of their group. So daddy comes to the rescue to defend him and expose the real killer. Mason is the only reason to watch this mishmash. Based on the Georges Simenon's novel "Stranger in the House" and previously filmed in 1942. **95m/C VHS.** *GB* James Mason, Geraldine Chaplin, Paul Bertoya, Bobby Darin, Ian Ogilvy, Clive Morton, James Hayter, Moira Lister; ***D:*** Pierre Rouve; ***W:*** Pierre Rouve; ***C:*** Ken Higgins; ***M:*** Patrick John Scott.

Cop-Out 🦴🦴 **1991** A cop is framed. His brother is mad. Teamed up with a sexy lawyer, he exposes the filth that is corrupting the city. Okay melodrama. **102m/C VHS.** David Buff, Kathryn Luster, Dan Ranger, Reggie DeMorton, Lawrence L. Simeone; ***D:*** Lawrence L. Simeone; ***W:*** Lawrence L. Simeone.

Copacabana 🦴🦴 **1947** A shady theatrical agent (Groucho) books a nightclub singer into two shows at the same time at New York's ritzy nightclub. Lots of energy spent trying to enliven a routine script. Also available colorized. ♫Tico Tico; Stranger Things Have Happened; Je Vous Amie; My Heart Was Doing a Bolero; Let's Do the Copacabana; I Haven't Got a Thing to Sell; We've Come to Copa. **91m/B VHS.** Groucho Marx, Carmen Miranda, Steve Cochran, Gloria Jean, Andy Russell, Earl Wilson; ***D:*** Alfred E. Green.

Copkillers woof! **1977 (R)** Two men desperate for an easy way to make money embark on a murderous shooting spree. Mostly blanks. **93m/C VHS.** Jason Williams, Bill Osco.

Copper Canyon 🦴🦴½ **1950** Milland plays a Confederate Army officer who heads West after the Civil War, meets up with Lamarr, and sparks a romance. Good chemistry between the leads in this otherwise standard western. **84m/B VHS.** Ray Milland, Hedy Lamarr, MacDonald Carey, Mona Freeman, Harry Carey Jr., Frank Faylen, Taylor Holmes, Peggy Knudsen; ***D:*** John Farrow.

Copperhead 🦴 **1984 (R)** A group of copperhead snakes attack a family who possess a stolen Incan gold necklace. This one bites. **90m/C VHS.** Jack Renner, Greta Ratliff, David Fritts, Cheryl Nickerson; ***D:*** Leland Payton; ***W:*** Leland Payton.

Cops and Robbers 🦴🦴½ **1973 (PG)** Two cops use a Wall Street parade for returning astronauts as a cover for a multi-million dollar heist. Exceptional caper film thanks to the likable leads and genuine suspense. **89m/C VHS.** Joseph Bologna, Dick Ward, Shepperd Strudwick, John P. Ryan, Ellen Holly, Dolph Sweet, Joe Spinell, Cliff Gorman; ***D:*** Aram Avakian; ***W:*** Donald E. Westlake.

Cops and Robbersons 🦴 **1994 (PG)** Bored, dim-witted dad Chase, a TV cop-show junkie, wishes his life had a little more danger and excitement. How lucky for him when hard-nosed cop Palance sets up a command post in his house to stake out the mobster living next door (Davi). Predictable plot isn't funny and drags Chase's bumbling idiot persona on for too long; Wiest and Davi are two bright spots, but their talents are wasted, while Palance does little more than reincarnate his "City Slickers" character. Poor effort for otherwise notable director Ritchie. **93m/C VHS, DVD.** Chevy Chase, Jack Palance, Dianne Wiest, Robert Davi, Jason James Richter, Fay Masterson, Miko Hughes, Richard Romanus, David Barry Gray; ***D:*** Michael Ritchie; ***W:*** Bernie Somers; ***C:*** Gerry Fisher; ***M:*** William Ross.

Copycat 🦴🦴 **1995 (R)** Crowded serial killer genre yields crooner Connick as southern psychopath stuck on murder. Soon he's in jail, advising the police in their hunt for another serial killer who imitates the murders of other infamous serial killers. Agoraphobic, boozing criminal psychologist Helen Hudson (Weaver), still suffering the after effects of an attack by sicko subject Darryl Lee Cullum (Connick), is enlisted to help detective M.J. Monahan (Hunter) catch the homage specialist. Weaver and Hunter bring sparks to the usually testosterone-laden formula, helping mask the preponderance of serial killer cliches and giant holes in the script. Connick's turn as a nut-job killer won't make you forget Anthony Hopkins, or even Frank Sinatra. Exploitative and imitative, and always faithful to the formula. **124m/C VHS, DVD.** Sigourney Weaver, Holly Hunter, Dermot Mulroney, Harry Connick Jr., William McNamara, Will Patton, John Rothman, David Michael Silverman; ***D:*** Jon Amiel; ***W:*** Ann Biderman, David Madsen; ***C:*** Laszlo Kovacs; ***M:*** Christopher Young.

Coquette 🦴🦴½ **1929** Pickford's first talkie portrays her as a flirtatious flapper from a well-to-do family who falls in love with a poor man her father despises. So much in fact that daddy kills the young man and then commits suicide, leaving his daughter to face the world alone. Pickford and Brown get to share a melodramatic death scene and audiences flocked to hear "America's Sweetheart" speak onscreen. Based on a play by George Abbott and Anne Preston. **75m/B VHS.** Mary Pickford, Johnny Mack Brown, Matt Moore, John St. Polis, Henry Kolker, George Irving, Louise Beavers, William Janney; ***D:*** Sam Taylor; ***C:*** Karl Struss. Oscars '29: Actress (Pickford).

Cora Unashamed 🦴🦴½ **2000** Adaptation of the Langston Hughes short story that finds racism and tragedy in a small Iowa town in the 1930s. Cora Jenkins (Taylor) and her mother (Pounder) are the only blacks in the community. Cora works as a housekeeper for the Studevant family and becomes strongly attached to the family's daughter, Jessie (Graham). This bond is resented by Jessie's mother, selfish and cold Lizbeth (Jones), whose exaggerated sense of propriety brings about disaster. **95m/C VHS.** Regina Taylor, Cherry Jones, CCH Pounder, Michael Gaston, Arlen Dean Snyder, Molly Graham, Ellen Muth, Kohl Sudduth; ***D:*** Deborah Pratt; ***W:*** Ann Peacock; ***C:*** Ernest Holzman; ***M:*** Patrice Rushen. **TV**

Coriolanus, Man without a Country 🦴 **1964** When the Romans begin to abuse their rights, the Plebians call upon the brave and mighty Coriolanus to lead them into battle against their oppressors. Predictable muscle man outing. **96m/C VHS.** *IT* Gordon Scott, Alberto Lupo, Lilla Brignone; ***D:*** Giorgio Ferroni; ***W:*** Remigio del Grosso.

Corky Romano 🦴 **2001 (PG-13)** Remember when ex-SNL cast members made good movies? Yeah, neither do they. Kattan is the title character—a spastic, twitchy veterinary assistant, estranged from his mob family, who's so naive, he thinks his Pops (Falk) is actually a landscaping mogul. He is talked into infiltrating the FBI to retrieve evidence against the family by gruff henchman Leo (Ward), the actual stool pigeon talking to the feds. His frantic bumbling is mistaken for genius by his FBI superior Schuster (Roundtree) and hottie special agent Kate (Shaw). Corky saves the day, and also tries to get his peepers on Kate's mangoes. The plot is just dressing for Kattan's "funny-looking rubbery guy knocks everything over" routine, and he plays it like Jerry Lewis without the subtlety. First "Night at the Roxbury," then "Monkeybone" and now this? Can someone get Kattan a script consultant? Please? **85m/C VHS, DVD, Wide.** *US* Chris Kattan, Vinessa Shaw, Peter Falk, Peter Berg, Christopher Penn, Fred Ward, Richard Roundtree, Matthew Glave, Dave Sheridan, Roger Fan; ***D:*** Rob Pritts; ***W:*** David Garrett, Jason Ward; ***C:*** Steven Bernstein; ***M:*** Randy Edelman.

Corleone 🦴 **1979 (R)** Limp tale about two boyhood friends who grow up to fight the evil landowners who dominate Italy. To accomplish this, one becomes a mobster, the other a politician. **115m/C VHS.** *IT* Claudia Cardinale, Giuliano Gemma; ***D:*** Pasquale Squitieri. Montreal World Film Fest. '79: Actor (Gemma).

The Corn Is Green 🦴🦴🦴 **1945** Touching story of a school teacher in a poor Welsh village who eventually sends her pet student to Oxford. Davis makes a fine teacher, though a little young, while the on-site photography provides atmosphere. Based on the play by Emlyn Williams. Remade in 1979. **115m/B VHS.** Bette Davis, John Dall, Nigel Bruce, Joan Lorring, Arthur Shields, Mildred Dunnock, Rhys Williams, Rosalind Ivan; ***D:*** Irving Rapper; ***M:*** Max Steiner.

Cornbread, Earl & Me 🦴🦴 **1975 (R)** A high school basketball star from the ghetto is mistaken for a murderer by cops and shot, causing a subsequent furor of protest and racial hatred. Superficial melodrama. **95m/C VHS, DVD, Wide.** Moses Gunn, Rosalind Cash, Bernie Casey, Tierre Turner, Madge Sinclair, Keith Wilkes, Antonio Fargas, Laurence "Larry" Fishburne; ***D:*** Joseph Manduke; ***W:*** Leonard Lamensdorf; ***C:*** Jules Brenner; ***M:*** Donald Byrd.

Cornered 🦴 **1932** McCoy is a sheriff, chasing bad guys, whose life is saved by Welch. Basically boring. **62m/B VHS.** Tim McCoy, Niles Welch, Raymond Hatton, Noah Beery Sr., Shirley Grey, Walter Long; ***D:*** B. Reeves Eason.

Cornered 🦴🦴🦴 **1945** Tough Powell plays an airman released from a German prison camp who pursues a Nazi war criminal to avenge the death of his wife and child. **102m/B VHS.** Dick Powell, Walter Slezak, Micheline Cheirel, Luther Adler; ***D:*** Edward Dmytryk.

Coroner Creek 🦴🦴½ **1948** Chris Danning's (Scott) fiancee commits suicide after being held hostage during an Indian attack on her stagecoach and a payroll robbery. Danning sets out to trace the loot and exact his revenge. A superior production, notable for being one of the first westerns with an adult theme. **89m/B VHS.** Randolph Scott, Marguerite Chapman, George Macready, Sally Eilers, Edgar Buchanan, Wallace Ford, Forrest Tucker; ***D:*** Ray Enright.

Corporate Affairs 🦴🦴 **1990 (R)** A ruthless business woman climbing her way to the top literally seduces her boss to death. **92m/C VHS.** Peter Scolari, Mary Crosby, Chris Lemmon, Ken Kercheval; ***D:*** Terence H. Winkless; ***W:*** Terence H. Winkless, Geoffrey Baere.

The Corporate Ladder 🦴 **1997 (R)** Matt Taylor is looking for the perfect executive assistant and his choice is Nicole—she's beautiful, bright, and devoted. It's no wonder that soon Matt and Nicole are having an affair. Too bad that Nicole would much rather run the company than take dictation—and she has a lethal way of implementing her business plan. Unfortunately, everthing about this film is boringly predictable. **112m/C VHS.** Anthony John (Tony) Denison, Kathleen Kinmont, Talisa Soto, Jennifer O'Neill, Ben Cross; ***D:*** Nick Vallelonga; ***W:*** Nick Vallelonga; ***M:*** Jan Hammer.

The Corporation 🦴½ *Subliminal Seduction; Roger Corman Presents Subliminal Seduction* **1996 (R)** Darrin Danver (Ziering), the new exec at a computer game company, discovers the games are controlling their users with powerful, subliminal messages. So he tries to expose his employers' lethal manipulations before they can kill him. Standard-issue made-for-TV movie doesn't bring anything new new to the "evil company" genre. Shot on location in L.A. and Las Vegas. **82m/C VHS.** Ian Ziering, Andrew Stevens, Katherine Kelly Lang, Dee Wallace Stone, Larry Manetti, Kim Morgan Greene, Kin Shriner, Stella Stevens; ***D:*** Andrew Stevens; ***W:*** Karen Kelly; ***C:*** Gary Graver; ***M:*** Terry Plumeri. **VIDEO**

The Corpse Grinders woof! **1971 (R)** Low-budget bad movie classic in which a cardboard corpse-grinding machine makes nasty cat food that makes cats nasty. Sets are cheap, gore effects silly, and cat attacks ridiculous. **73m/C VHS.** Sean Kenney, Monika Kelly, Sandford Mitchell, Byron J. Foster, Warren Ball, Ann Noble; ***D:*** Ted V. Mikels; ***W:*** Ted V. Mikels, Arch Hall Jr., Joseph L. Cranston; ***C:*** Bill Anneman.

The Corpse Vanishes 🦴🦴½ **1942** Lugosi at his chilling best as a diabolical scientist who snatches young brides and drains their blood in an effort to keep his 70-year-old wife eternally youthful. Not for newlyweds! **64m/B VHS, DVD.** Bela Lugosi, Luana Walters, Tristram Coffin, Elizabeth Russell, Vince Barnett, Joan Barclay, Angelo Rossitto; ***D:*** Wallace Fox.

Corregidor 🦴🦴 **1943** A love triangle develops between doctors treating the wounded during the WWII battle. A poor propaganda piece which contains only shaky stock footage for its "action" sequences. **73m/B VHS.** Otto Kruger, Elissa Landi, Donald Woods, Rick Vallin, Frank Jenks, Wanda McKay, Ian Keith; ***D:*** William Nigh.

The Corridor: Death **1989** Two Americans are involved in a car accident in Israel which triggers a debate on the Jewish perspective of death and the afterlife. Filmed on location at Hadassah Hospital on St. Scopus, Jerusalem. The final part of the trilogy preceded by "The Eighth Day: Circumcision" and "The Journey: Bar Mitzvah." **25m/C VHS.**

Corridors of Blood 🦴🦴½ *The Doctor from Seven Dials* **1958** Karloff is a doctor, in search of a viable anesthetic, who accidently becomes addicted to drugs, then turns to grave robbers to support his habit. Karloff plays usual threatening doctor to perfection. **86m/C VHS, DVD.** *GB* Boris Karloff, Betta St. John, Finlay Currie, Christopher Lee, Francis Matthews, Adrienne Corri, Nigel Green; ***D:*** Robert Day; ***W:*** Jean Scott Rogers; ***C:*** Geoffrey Faithfull; ***M:*** Buxton Orr.

Corrina, Corrina 🦴🦴½ **1994 (PG)** Newly widowed jingle-writer Liotta needs someone to care for his withdrawn eight-year-old daughter. Enter Whoopi, as housekeeper and eventual love interest. Sweet, nostalgic romance set in the 1950s. Goldberg also found off-screen romance (again), this time with the film's union organizer Lyle Trachtenberg. Last role for Ameche. **115m/C VHS, DVD.** Whoopi Goldberg, Ray Liotta, Don Ameche, Tina Majorino, Wendy Crewson, Jenifer Lewis, Larry Miller, Erica Yohn, Anita Baker; ***D:*** Jessie Nelson; ***W:*** Jessie Nelson; ***C:*** Bruce Surtees; ***M:*** Rick Cox, Thomas Newman.

Corrupt 🦴🦴🦴 *Order of Death; Cop Killers* **1984 (PG)** Bad narcotics cop goes after murderer, but mysterious Lydon gets in the way. An acquired taste, best if you appreciate Lydon, better known as Johnny Rotten of the Sex Pistols. **99m/C VHS, DVD.** *IT* Harvey Keitel, John (Johnny Rotten) Lydon, Sylvia Sidney, Nicole Garcia, Leonard Mann; ***D:*** Roberto Faenza; ***W:*** Roberto Faenza, Ennio de Concini, Hugh Fleetwood; ***C:*** Guiseppe Pinori; ***M:*** Ennio Morricone.

Corrupt 🦴½ **1999 (R)** Corrupt (Ice-T) is the drug lord who holds the South Bronx but he has would-be competition from some up-and-coming homeboys. However, one ex-gang banger (Silkk the Shocker) wants out of the 'hood to make a new life for himself and his girl. Only Corrupt and his posse stand in the way. **72m/C VHS, DVD.** Ice-T, Ernie Hudson, silkk the Shocker, Karen Dyer; ***D:*** Albert Pyun. **VIDEO**

The Corrupt Ones 🦴🦴½ *Il Sigillo de Pechino; Die Holle von Macao; Les Corrompus; The Peking Medallion; Hell to Macao* **1967** Everyone's after a photographer who has a medallion that will lead to buried treasure in China. Great characters hampered by pedestrian script. **87m/C VHS.** Robert Stack, Elke Sommer, Nancy Kwan, Christian Marquand, Werner Peters; ***D:*** James Hill; ***W:*** Brian Clemens.

The Corruptor 🦴🦴🦴 **1999 (R)** Slick crime thriller starring Wahlberg as Danny, a young Caucasian cop assigned to New York's Chinatown precinct and partnered with shrewd veteran Chen (Chow Yun-Fat). The two men are drawn into a web of deception and betrayal as they try to stop a war between rival underworld factions. Chow finally receives a Hollywood role that showcases the talents that made him an international star in Asia, although the action segments suffer in comparison to his work with John Woo. The plot and performances are excellent, and there's enough shoot-'em-up to satisfy the average appetite for destruction. **110m/C VHS, DVD.** Chow Yun-Fat, Mark Wahlberg, Ric Young, Paul Ben-Victor, Brian Cox, Byron Mann, Kim Chan, Tovah Feldshuh, Jon Kit Lee, Andrew Pang, Elizabeth Lindsey, Bill MacDonald, Susie Trinh; ***D:*** James Foley; ***W:*** Robert Pucci; ***C:*** Juan Ruiz-Anchia; ***M:*** Carter Burwell.

Corsair 🦴🦴 **1931** Actioner about a gorgeous debutante and a handsome gangster who find themselves caught up with a gang of bootlegging pirates. Todd is always worth watching. **73m/B VHS.** Chester Morris, Thelma Todd, Frank McHugh, Ned Sparks, Mayo Methot; ***D:*** Roland West.

The Corsican Brothers 🦴🦴½ **1942** Siamese-twins Mario and Lucien are separated by Dr. Paoli (Warner) shortly before their parents are murdered by evil Colonna (Tamiroff). One boy is sent to Paris and the other grows up in the Corsican mountains. Reunited as adults (and dashingly played by Faribanks Jr.), the twins plot revenge. Entertaining swashbuckler based on a novel by Alexandre Dumas. **111m/B VHS.** Douglas Fairbanks Jr., Akim Tamiroff, Ruth Warrick, J. Carrol Naish, H.B. Warner, Henry Wilcoxon, Veda Ann Borg; ***D:*** Gregory Ratoff; ***W:*** George Bruce; ***C:*** Harry Stradling Sr.; ***M:*** Dimitri Tiomkin.

Corvette Summer 🦴 *The Hot One* **1978 (PG)** After spending a semester restoring a Corvette in his high school shop class, an L.A. student must journey to Las Vegas to recover the car when it is stolen. There he meets a prostitute, falls in love, and steps into the "real world" for the first time. Potts intriguing as the low-life love interest, but she can't save this one. **104m/C VHS.** Mark Hamill, Annie Potts, Eugene Roche, Kim Milford, Richard McKenzie, William Bryant; ***D:*** Matthew Robbins; ***W:*** Matthew Robbins, Hal Barwood.

Cosh Boy woof! *The Slasher* **1961** Vicious male youths stalk women on the streets of London in this low-budget Jack the Ripper rip-off. **90m/B VHS.** Joan Collins, James Kennedy, Hermione Baddeley; ***D:*** Lewis Gilbert; ***W:*** Lewis Gilbert.

Cosi *Caught in the Act* **1995 (R)** Amiable Lewis (Mendelsohn) is hired to help with drama therapy at the local Sydney mental institution. Pressured by long-term patient Roy (Otto), Lewis finds himself agreeing to stage a production of Mozart's opera "Cosi Fan Tutte" though none of the patients can speak Italian or sing. Rehearsals prove a challenge, there are numerous setbacks, and then it's show time. Fine ensemble cast delivers; adapted from Nowra's play. Friels stepped into the role of security guard Errol when Bruno Lawrence died before filming was completed; pic is dedicated to Lawrence. **100m/C VHS.** *AU* Ben Mendelsohn, Barry Otto, Aden Young, Toni Collette, Rachel Griffiths, Colin Friels, Paul Chubb, Pamela Rabe, Jacki Weaver, David Wenham, Colin Hay, Tony Llewellyn-Jones, Kerry Walker; ***Cameos:*** Greta Scacchi, Paul Mercurio; ***D:*** Mark Joffe; ***W:*** Louis Nowra; ***C:*** Ellery Ryan; ***M:*** Stephen Endelman. Australian Film Inst. '96: Adapt. Screenplay, Support. Actress (Collette).

The Cosmic Eye **1971** Animated tale of three musicians from outer space who come to earth to spread the message of worldwide peace and harmony. A variety of cultural perspectives about the origins and destiny of the Earth are offered. Rather moralizing but the animation is impressive. **71m/C VHS.** ***D:*** Faith Hubley; ***V:*** Dizzy Gillespie, Maureen Stapleton, Benny Carter.

The Cosmic Man ½ **1959** An alien arrives on Earth with a message of peace and restraint. He is regarded with suspicion by us nasty Earthlings. Essentially "The Day the Earth Stood Still" without the budget, but interesting nonetheless. **72m/B VHS, DVD.** Bruce (Herman Brix) Bennett, John Carradine, Angela Greene, Paul Langton, Scotty Morrow; ***D:*** Herbert Greene; ***W:*** Arthur C. Pierce; ***C:*** John F. Warren; ***M:*** Paul Sawtell, Bert Shefter.

The Cosmic Monsters ½ *The Strange World of Planet X* **1958** Scientist accidentally pops a hole in the ionosphere during a magnetism experiment. Then huge, mean insects arrive to plague mankind. Coincidence? You figure it out. **75m/B VHS.** Forrest Tucker, Gaby Andre, Alec Mango, Hugh Latimer, Martin Benson; ***D:*** Gilbert Gunn.

Cosmic Slop **1994 (R)** Three-part anthology. "Space Traders," based on a story by Derrick Bell, finds a fleet of aliens offering to solve all of U.S. society's most pressing social ills if they can have the entire black population in return (for what purpose is never explained). "The First Commandment" features a Catholic priest in a Latino parish who comes up against his parishoners pagan beliefs in Santeria. "Tang," based on a story by Chester Himes, finds a poor, desperately unhappy married couple dreaming about what they'll do with the rifle mysteriously delivered in a flower carton to their door. **87m/C VHS.** Robert Guillaume, Jason Bernard, Nicholas Turturro, Richard Herd, Paula Jai Parker, Chi McBride; ***D:*** Reginald (Reggie) Hudlin, Warrington Hudlin, Kevin Sullivan; ***W:*** Warrington Hudlin, Trey Ellis, Kyle Baker; ***C:*** Peter Deming.

Cosmos: War of the Planets woof! *Cosmo 2000: Planet Without a Name; War of the Planets* **1980 (PG)** The ultimate battle for survival is fought in outer space, though not very well and on a small budget. Special effects especially laughable. **90m/C VHS.** *IT* Katia Christine, West Buchanan, John Richardson, Yanti Somer; ***D:*** Al (Alfonso Brescia) Bradley.

Cottage to Let ½ *Bombsight Stolen* **1941** Propaganda thriller about a Nazi plot to kidnap the inventor of a new bombsight. Focused cast struggles with lackluster script. **90m/B VHS.** *GB* Leslie Banks, Alastair Sim, John Mills, Jeanne de Casalis, Carla Lehmann, George Cole, Michael Wilding, Frank Cellier, Wally Patch, Catherine Lacey; ***D:*** Anthony Asquith.

Cotter **1972** A Native American rodeo clown feels responsible for a cowboy's death, returns home to reflect on his life. Fair story, best at the small town feeling. **94m/C VHS.** Don Murray, Carol Lynley, Rip Torn, Sherry Jackson; ***D:*** Paul Stanley.

Cotton Candy **1982** Follows the faintly interesting trials and tribulations of a high school senior who tries to form a rock band. At first he meets failure, but is ultimately successful with the band and romance. Joint script-writing venture by brothers Clint and Ron Howard. **97m/C VHS.** Charles Martin Smith, Clint Howard, Leslie King; ***D:*** Ron Howard; ***W:*** Clint Howard, Ron Howard. **TV**

The Cotton Club **1984 (R)** With $50 million in his pocket, Francis reaches for an epic and delivers: handsome production, lots of dance, bit of singing, confused plot, uneven performances, tad too long. A musician playing at The Cotton Club falls in love with gangster Dutch Schultz's girlfriend. A black tap dancer falls in love with a member of the chorus line who can pass for white. These two love stories are told against a background of mob violence and music. Excellent performances by Hoskins and Gwynne. ♫Minnie the Moocher; Ill Wind; The Mooch; Ring Dem Bells; Drop Me Off in Harlem; Cotton Club Stomp; Truckin; Mood Indigo; Copper Colored Gal. **121m/C VHS, DVD, Wide.** Diane Lane, Richard Gere, Gregory Hines, Lonette McKee, Bob Hoskins, Fred Gwynne, James Remar, Nicolas Cage, Lisa Jane Persky, Allen (Goorwitz) Garfield, Gwen Verdon, Joe Dallesandro, Jennifer Grey, Tom Waits, Diane Venora; ***D:*** Francis Ford Coppola; ***W:*** William Kennedy, Mario Puzo, Francis Ford Coppola; ***C:*** Stephen Goldblatt; ***M:*** John Barry.

Cotton Comes to Harlem **1970 (R)** Cambridge and St. Jacques star as Harlem plainclothes detectives Grave Digger Jones and Coffin Ed Johnson in this successful mix of crime and comedy. They're investigating a suspicious preacher's back-to-Africa scheme which they suspect is a swindle. Directorial debut of Davis. Filmed on location in Harlem, New York. Based on the novel by Chester Himes. Followed by a weak sequel, "Come Back, Charleston Blue." **97m/C VHS, DVD.** Godfrey Cambridge, Raymond St. Jacques, Calvin Lockhart, Judy Pace, Redd Foxx, John Anderson, Emily Yancy, J.D. Cannon, Teddy Wilson, Eugene Roche, Cleavon Little, Lou Jacobi; ***D:*** Ossie Davis; ***W:*** Ossie Davis; ***C:*** Gerald Hirschfeld; ***M:*** Galt MacDermot.

Cotton Mary **1999 (R)** Lily (Scacchi) is the lonely wife of reporter John (Wilby), living in India in 1954. She cannot nurse her newborn daughter and turns to the ministrations of bossy Anglo-Indian nurse Mary (Jaffrey), who is soon living in their household and having the child fed by her own sister, Blossom (Gupta). Meanwhile, the philandering John eyes Mary's niece, Rosie (Sakina Jaffrey), while Lily sinks into depression, and an increasingly mad Mary ruthlessly takes over their home. **124m/C VHS, DVD, Wide.** *GB* Madhur Jaffrey, Greta Scacchi, James Wilby, Neena Gupta, Sakina Jaffrey, Gemma Jones, Sarah Badel, Joanna David, Riyu Bajaj, Prayag Raj; ***D:*** Ismail Merchant; ***W:*** Alexandra Viets; ***C:*** Pierre Lhomme; ***M:*** Richard Robbins.

Cotton Queen ½ *Crying Out Loud* **1937** Romance and light intrigue plague the children of two rival textile mill owners. **80m/B VHS, 8mm.** Will Fyffe, Stanley Holloway; ***D:*** Bernard Vorhaus.

A Couch in New York *Un Divan a New York* **1995 (R)** Limp romantic comedy features that old standby—opposites attracting. French dancer Beatrice (Binoche) responds to an ad for a temporary Paris-New York apartment switch placed by a stuffy psychoanalyst, Henry Harriston (Hurt). Henry's patients presume Beatrice is his replacement (he works at home) and the free-spirit begins giving them ad hoc advice. Meanwhile in Paris, Henry's plagued by all Beatrice's heartsick boyfriends and decides to come back early. When he arrives unannounced, she assumes he's a new patient and he's intrigued enough to go along. Lots of yakking, not too many sparks, and a strained artificiality make for a dull mix. **104m/C VHS, DVD, Wide.** *FR BE GE* William Hurt, Juliette Binoche, Paul Guilfoyle, Stephanie Buttle, Richard Jenkins, Kent Broadhurst, Henry Bean, Barbara Garrick; ***D:*** Chantal Akerman; ***W:*** Chantal Akerman, Jean-Louis Benoit; ***C:*** Dietrich Lohmann; ***M:*** Paolo Conte, Sonia Atherton.

The Couch Trip ½ **1987 (R)** Aykroyd is an escapee from a mental institution who passes himself off as a radio psychologist and becomes a media sensation. There are a few laughs and some funny characters but for the most part this one falls flat. **98m/C VHS.** Dan Aykroyd, Walter Matthau, Charles Grodin, Donna Dixon, Richard Romanus, Arye Gross, David Clennon, Mary Gross; ***D:*** Michael Ritchie; ***W:*** Will Aldis, Steven Kampmann; ***M:*** Michel Colombier.

Could It Happen Here? **198?** A lurid Italian spectacle about a metropolis thrown into a state of chaotic martial law by terrorism. Dubbed. **90m/C VHS.** *IT* Luc Merenda, Marcella Michelangeli; ***D:*** Massimo Pirri.

The Count ½ **1916** Chaplin pretends to be the secretary of his boss, who in turn is posing as a count. Silent with musical soundtrack added. **20m/B VHS.** Charlie Chaplin; ***D:*** Charlie Chaplin.

Count Dracula ½ *Bram Stoker's Count Dracula; Il Conte Dracula; Dracula 71; Nachts wenn Dracula Erwacht; The Nights of Dracula* **1971 (R)** Passable version of the Dracula legend (based on the novel by Bram Stoker) has Lee as the thirsty count on the prowl for fresh blood. Starts out as one of the most faithful adaptations, but loses momentum because Franco was running out of money. **90m/C VHS.** *SP GE IT* Christopher Lee, Herbert Lom, Klaus Kinski, Frederick Williams, Maria Rohm, Soledad Miranda, Paul Mueller; ***D:*** Jess (Jesus) Franco; ***W:*** Jess (Jesus) Franco, Augusto Finochi, Peter Welbeck, Milo G. Cuccia, Carlo Fadda; ***C:*** Manuel Merino.

The Count of Monte Cristo ½ **1912** One of the first full-length features starring popular stage stars of the day. The first truly American feature, it was based on the classic tale of revenge by Alexander Dumas. Silent. Remade many times. Lead actor O'Neill was the father of famed American playwright, Eugene O'Neill, who covered his father's success in this role in his own family drama "Long Day's Journey Into Night." **90m/B VHS.** James O'Neill; ***D:*** Edwin S. Porter.

The Count of Monte Cristo **1934** A true swashbuckling revenge tale about Edmond Dantes (Donat), who unjustly spends years in prison. After escaping and retrieving a pirate treasure from the island of Monte Cristo, he gains ever so sweet and served quite cold revenge. Adaptation of the Alexandre Dumas classic. **114m/B VHS.** Robert Donat, Elissa Landi, Louis Calhern, Sidney Blackmer, Irene Hervey, Raymond Walburn, O.P. Heggie; ***D:*** Rowland V. Lee; ***W:*** Rowland V. Lee, Philip Dunne; ***C:*** J. Peverell Marley; ***M:*** Alfred Newman.

The Count of Monte Cristo ½ **1974** The Alexander Dumas classic about an innocent man (Chamberlain) who is imprisoned, escapes, and finds the treasure of Monte Cristo, which he uses to bring down those who wronged him. Good version of the historical costumer. Originally shown in theatres in Europe, but broadcast on TV in the U.S. **104m/C VHS.** *GB* Richard Chamberlain, Kate Nelligan, Donald Pleasence, Alessio Orano, Tony Curtis, Louis Jourdan, Trevor Howard, Taryn Power; ***D:*** David Greene.

The Count of Monte Cristo ½ *Le Comte de Monte Cristo* **1999** It seems only fitting that French TV produced this zestful miniseries version of the 1844 novel by Dumas pere. Depardieu obviously is enjoying himself in the lead role of Edmond Dantes, who is unjustly imprisoned for 20 years. After his escape, he discovers a fortune and uses it to get revenge as he adopts a fictional identity as the Count of Monte Cristo. Overwrought, over-the-top and lots of fun. Depardieu's daughter Julie and son Guillaume both have roles. French with subtitles. **480m/C VHS, DVD.** *FR* Gerard Depardieu, Ornella Muti, Sergio Rubini, Guillaume Depardieu, Pierre Arditti, Jean Rochefort, Florence Darel, Julie Depardieu, Naike Rivelli, Jean-Claude Brialy, Ines Sastre, Helene Vincent, Christopher Thompson, Stanislas Merhar, Constanze Engelbrecht, Georges Moustaki; ***D:*** Josee Dayan; ***W:*** Didier Decoin; ***C:*** Willy Stassen; ***M:*** Bruno Coulais. **TV**

The Count of Monte Cristo ½ **2002 (PG-13)** Yet another remake of the Dumas classic revenge tale with some beautiful cinematography by Dunn to distinguish it. Hero Edmond Dantes (Caviezel) is betrayed by best friend Fernand Mondego (Pearce), who wants his girlfriend Mercedes (Dominczyk) among other things, and unjustly imprisoned. Dantes learns of a great treasure from fellow inmate Abbe Faria (Harris), eventually escapes, finds said treasure, and seeks his revenge under the disguise of—well, you know. Pearce has fun as the foppish villain and Caviezel is suitably heroic. **131m/C VHS, DVD.** *US* James Caviezel, Guy Pearce, Richard Harris, Dagmara Dominczyk, Luis Guzman, James Frain, Albie Woodington, Henry Cavill, Michael Wincott, Alex Norton, Freddie Jones; ***D:*** Kevin Reynolds; ***W:*** Jay Wolpert; ***C:*** Andrew Dunn; ***M:*** Ed Shearmur.

The Count of the Old Town *Munkbrogreven* **1934** Feisty townsfolk settle the score after a gang of booze smugglers trick them out of their money. Bergman's film debut as a maid swept off her feet by a mysterious young stranger. Adapted from the play "Greven fran Gamla Sta'n" by Arthur and Sigfried Fischer. In Swedish with English subtitles. **90m/B VHS.** *SW* Edvin Adolphson, Ingrid Bergman, Sigurd Wallen, Valdemar Dahlquist; ***D:*** Edvin Adolphson, Sigurd Wallen; ***W:*** Gosta Stevens.

Count Yorga, Vampire ½ *The Loves of Count Yorga, Vampire* **1970 (PG-13)** The vampire Count Yorga is practicing his trade in Los Angeles, setting up a coven and conducting seances. Good update of the traditional character, with Quarry suitably solemn and menacing. Followed by "The Return of Count Yorga." **93m/C VHS, DVD, Wide.** Robert Quarry, Roger Perry, Michael Murphy, Michael Macready, Donna Anders, Judith Lang, Marsha Jordan, Julie Conners, Paul Hansen; ***D:*** Bob Kelljan; ***W:*** Bob Kelljan; ***C:*** Arch Archambault; ***M:*** Bill Marx.

Countdown ½ **1968** Documentary-type fictional look at the first moon mission and its toll on the astronauts and their families. Timely because the U.S. was trying to send a man to the moon in 1968. Interesting as a look at the developing Altman style. **102m/C VHS.** James Caan, Robert Duvall, Michael Murphy, Ted (Edward) Knight, Joanna Moore, Barbara Baxley, Charles Aidman, Steve Ihnat, Robert Altman; ***D:*** Robert Altman.

Counter Attack ½ **1984** Story of murder and insurance fraud takes place on the back lots of the Hong Kong film industry. As good as these get. **105m/C VHS.** Bruce Li, Dan Inosanto, John Ladalski, Young Kong; ***D:*** Bruce Li.

Counter Measures **198?** A helicopter pilot stumbles on to a bizarre chain of crimes and disasters. **98m/C VHS.** Monte Markham; ***D:*** Gerban Ceth.

Counter Punch ½ *Ripped Off; The Boxer; Uomo Dalla Pelle Dura; Murder in the Ring; Tough Guy* **1971 (R)** Blake is a boxer framed for the murder of his manager who sets out to clear his name by finding the killers. Fair rendition of a familiar plot. **72m/C VHS.** *IT* Robert (Bobby) Blake, Ernest Borgnine, Gabriele Ferzetti, Catherine Spaak, Tomas Milian; ***D:*** Franco Prosperi.

Counterblast *The Devil's Plot* **1948** A Nazi spy assumes the role of a British scientist in order to gain classified information for the Fatherland. The trouble begins when he refuses to carry out an order to execute a pretty young assistant. Appealing performances distract from the somewhat confusing plot. **99m/B VHS.** *GB* Robert Beatty, Mervyn Johns, Nova Pilbeam, Margaretta Scott, Sybilla Binder, Marie Lohr, Karel Stepanek, Alan Wheatley; ***D:*** Paul Stein.

The Counterfeit Traitor ½ **1962** Suspense thriller with Holden playing a double agent in Europe during WWII. Based on the true adventures of Eric Erickson, the top Allied spy of WW II, who was captured by the Gestapo but escaped. **140m/C VHS.** William Holden, Lilli Palmer, Hugh Griffith, Werner Peters, Eva Dahlbeck; ***D:*** George Seaton; ***W:*** George Seaton; ***C:*** Jean (Yves, Georges) Bourgoin.

Counterforce 🦴 *Escuadron* 1987 (R) A rough group of mercenaries is hired to guard a Mideastern leader being chased by his country's ruling despot. Mild action with predictable story. **98m/C VHS.** Jorge (George) Rivero, George Kennedy, Andrew Stevens, Isaac Hayes, Louis Jourdan, Kevin Bernhardt, Hugo Stiglitz, Robert Foster, Susana Dosamantes; *D:* J. Anthony (Jose Antonio de la Loma) Loma.

A Countess from Hong Kong 🦴 1967 (G) Very bad romantic comedy features impoverished Russian countess Natasha (would you believe Loren is Russian?) stowing away in the luxury liner suite of stuffy American diplomat Ogden Mears (equally miscast Brando). The ship is sailing from Hong Kong to Honolulu and Natasha has until then to persuade Ogden to assist her. Chaplin's final film. **108m/C VHS.** Marlon Brando, Sophia Loren, Sydney Chaplin, Tippi Hedren, Patrick Cargill, Michael Medwin, Oliver Johnston, Margaret Rutherford; *D:* Charlie Chaplin; *W:* Charlie Chaplin; *C:* Arthur Ibbetson; *M:* Charlie Chaplin.

Country 🦴🦴🦴 1984 (PG) Strong story of a farm family in crisis when the government attempts to foreclose on their land. Good performances all around and an excellent portrayal of the wife by Lange. "The River" and "Places in the Heart," both released in 1984, also dramatized the plight of many American farm families in the early 1980s. **109m/C VHS.** Jessica Lange, Sam Shepard, Wilford Brimley, Matt Clark, Therese Graham, Levi L. Knebel; *D:* Richard Pearce; *W:* William D. Wittliff.

Country Gentlemen 🦴🦴 1936 Vaudeville team, Olsen and Johnson, play fast-talking conmen who sell shares in a worthless oil field to a bunch of WWI veterans. What a surprise when oil is actually found there. Not one of the duo's better performances. **54m/B VHS.** Ole Olsen, Chic Johnson, Joyce Compton, Lila Lee, Ray Corrigan, Donald Kirke, Pierre Watkin; *D:* Ralph Staub.

Country Girl 🦴🦴🦴½ 1954 In the role that completely de-glamorized her (and won her an Oscar), Kelly plays the wife of alcoholic singer Crosby who tries to make a comeback with the help of director Holden. One of Crosby's four dramatic parts, undoubtedly one of his best. Seaton won an Oscar for his adaptation of the Clifford Odets play. Remade in 1982. ♫The Search is Through; Dissertation on the State of Bliss; It's Mine, It's Yours; The Land Around Us. **104m/B VHS.** Bing Crosby, Grace Kelly, William Holden, Gene Reynolds, Anthony Ross; *D:* George Seaton; *W:* George Seaton. Oscars '54: Actress (Kelly), Screenplay; Golden Globes '55: Actress—Drama (Kelly); Natl. Bd. of Review '54: Actress (Kelly); N.Y. Film Critics '54: Actress (Kelly).

Country Girl 🦴 1982 Aging, alcoholic actor is desperate for a comeback. His director blames his fiercely loving wife for the downfall. Poor cable TV remake of 1954 version with Bing Crosby. **137m/C VHS.** Dick Van Dyke, Faye Dunaway, Ken Howard; *D:* Gary Halvorson. **CABLE**

The Country Kid 🦴🦴🦴 1923 A freckle-faced teenager and his two brothers are beset by a wicked uncle out to steal their inheritance. One of Barry's best-remembered films. **60m/B VHS.** Wesley Barry, "Spec" (Walter) O'Donnell, Bruce Guerin, Kate Toncray, Helen Jerome Eddy, George Nicholls Jr.; *D:* William Beaudine.

Country Life 🦴🦴 1995 (PG-13) Down Under adaptation of Chekov's "Uncle Vanya," has Blakemore returning to Aussie farm roots after 22-year stint as unsuccessful London theatre critic. His bored young wife (Scacchi) upsets the business-as-usual life of her husband's brother-in-law (Hargreaves) and abandoned daughter, Sally (Fox), who is also jealous of the attention paid the beautiful Deborah by both her uncle and longtime crush, Dr. Askey (Neill). Exchanges Chekov's emotional exploration for a light comedy of manners and a message of Australian independence from England. **107m/C VHS.** *AU* Sam Neill, Greta Scacchi, Kerry Fox, John Hargreaves, Googie Withers, Patricia Kennedy, Michael Blakemore; *D:* Michael Blakemore; *W:* Michael Blakemore; *C:* Stephen Windon; *M:* Peter Best.

Countryman 🦴🦴 1983 (R) A dope-smuggling woman crashes her plane in Jamaica and is rescued by Countryman, a rasta super hero. Not very good, but at least there's great music by Bob Marley and others. **103m/C VHS.** Hiram Keller, Kristine Sinclair; *D:* Dickie Jobson.

County Fair 🦴🦴 1920 This early silent film is an adaptation of Neil Burgess' play about life in New England. **60m/B VHS.** Helen Jerome Eddy, David Butler; *D:* Edmund Mortimer, Maurice Tourneur; *W:* J. Grubb Alexander.

Coup de Grace 🦴🦴½ 1978 Engaging political satire about a wealthy aristocratic woman in Latvia during the 1919-20 Civil War, and how she attempts to maintain her lifestyle as German soldiers are housed on her estate. Her unrequited love for a German officer adds to her troubles. In German with English subtitles. Co-written by von Trotta and based on the novel by Marguerite Yourcenar. **96m/B** *GE FR* Margarethe von Trotta, Matthias Habich, Rudiger Kirschstein, Matthieu Carriere; *D:* Volker Schlondorff; *W:* Margarethe von Trotta.

Coup de Torchon 🦴🦴🦴 *Clean Slate* 1981 Set in 1938 French West Africa, Noiret plays corrupt police chief Lucien Cordier who is consistently harrassed by his community, particularly by the town pimp. He usually overlooks the pimp's crimes, but when Cordier catches him and a friend shooting at plague victims' bodies floating down the river he decides to murder them in cold blood. Based on the novel "POP 1280" by Jim Thompson. In French with English subtitles. **128m/C VHS, DVD, Wide.** *FR* Philippe Noiret, Isabelle Huppert, Guy Marchand, Stephane Audran, Eddy Mitchell, Jean-Pierre Marielle, Irene Skobline; *D:* Bertrand Tavernier; *W:* Bertrand Tavernier; *C:* Pierre William Glenn; *M:* Philippe Sarde.

Coupe de Ville 🦴🦴½ 1990 (PG-13) Three brothers are forced by their father to drive mom's birthday present from Detroit to Florida in the summer of '63. Period concerns and music keep it interesting. **98m/C VHS.** Patrick Dempsey, Daniel Stern, Arye Gross, Joseph Bologna, Alan Arkin, Annabeth Gish, Rita Taggart, James Gammon; *D:* Joe Roth; *W:* Mike Binder; *M:* James Newton Howard.

Courage 🦴🦴🦴 1986 Based on fact, about a Hispanic mother in NYC who, motivated by her drug-troubled children, goes undercover and exposes a multimillion-dollar drug ring. Loren is great in a decidedly non-glamorous role. **141m/C VHS.** Sophia Loren, Billy Dee Williams, Hector Elizondo, Val Avery, Dan Hedaya, Ron Rifkin, Jose Perez; *D:* Jeremy Paul Kagan. **TV**

Courage Mountain 🦴 1989 (PG) If you're looking for a good sequel to Johanna Spyri's classic "Heidi" this isn't it. Europe is on the brink of WWI when teenage Heidi leaves her beloved mountain for an exclusive boarding school in Italy. Not surprisingly in a war zone, the military takes over and the kids are sent to an orphanage run by nasties (see also "Oliver!"). The girls escape to the mountains and are saved by none other than Sheen as Heidi's pal Peter (who cast the 20-something Sheen as a teenager? Bad mistake.) Ridiculous sequel to the classic tale will appeal to kids despite what the critics say. **92m/C VHS.** Juliette Caton, Joanna Clarke, Nicola Stapleton, Charlie Sheen, Jan Rubes, Leslie Caron, Jade Magri, Kathryn Ludlow, Yorgo Voyagis, Laura Betti; *D:* Christopher Leitch; *W:* Weaver Webb; *M:* Sylvester Levay.

Courage of Black Beauty 🦴½ 1957 Another version of the perennial heart warmer about a boy and his horse. **80m/C VHS.** Johnny Crawford, Mimi Gibson, John Bryant, Diane Brewster, J. Pat O'Malley; *D:* Harold Schuster.

Courage of Lassie 🦴🦴½ *Blue Sierra* 1946 (G) Fourteen-year-old Taylor is the heroine in this girl loves dog tale. In this case, the dog is actually called Bill, not Lassie, in spite of the film's title. Bill is found wounded by Taylor and she nurses him back to health. He proves to be loving, loyal, and useful, so much so that, through a complicated plotline, he winds up in the Army's K-9 division and returns home with the doggie version of shell-shock. Taylor's still there to nurse him back to his old kind self again. **93m/C VHS.** Elizabeth Taylor, Frank Morgan, Tom Drake, Selena Royle, Harry Davenport; *D:* Fred M. Wilcox.

Courage of Rin Tin Tin 🦴🦴 1983 Rusty and his faithful dog Rin Tin Tin help the cavalry soldiers of Fort Apache keep law and order in a small Arizona town. The perennial kid-pleasing German Shepherd comes through again. **90m/C VHS.** James Brown, Lee Aaker.

Courage of the North 🦴½ 1935 The Mounties break up a fur-stealing ring with the help of Captain Dog and Dynamite Horse. Bound to set your hair on end. **55m/B VHS.** John Preston, June Love, William Desmond, Tom London, Jimmy Aubrey; *D:* Robert Emmett Tansey; *W:* Robert Emmett Tansey.

Courage Under Fire 🦴🦴🦴 1996 (R) Army Lt. Col. Nat Serling (Washington) is unexpectedly assigned to review the candidacy of Capt. Karen Emma Walden (Ryan, seen only in flashbacks) to receive the posthumous Medal of Honor for bravery in combat. A Gulf War Medevac pilot, Walden would be the first woman awarded the honor if Serling can figure out the truth from her surviving crew's wildly conflicting reports. Ironically, Serling's dealing with a guilt complex since four members of his tank unit died in the war under friendly fire. Stellar performances, including a frightening one by Phillips. Based on the novel by Duncan, who also did the screenplay; Washington and director Zwick previously worked together on "Glory." **120m/C VHS, DVD, Wide.** Denzel Washington, Meg Ryan, Matt Damon, Lou Diamond Phillips, Michael Moriarty, Scott Glenn, Bronson Pinchot, Seth Gilliam, Sean Astin, Regina Taylor, Tim Guinee, Ken Jenkins, Kathleen Widdoes, Zeljko Ivanek, Tim Ransom, Ned Vaughn; *D:* Edward Zwick; *W:* Patrick Sheane Duncan; *C:* Roger Deakins; *M:* James Horner.

Courageous Avenger 🦴 1935 A sheriff brings a treacherous ore mine foreman to justice. **59m/B VHS.** Johnny Mack Brown; *D:* Robert North Bradbury; *W:* Charles Francis Royal.

Courageous Dr. Christian 🦴🦴 1940 Dr. Christian is faced with an epidemic of meningitis among the inhabitants of a shanty town. Typical entry in the "Dr. Christian" series. **66m/B VHS.** Jean Hersholt, Dorothy Lovett, Tom Neal, Robert Baldwin, Maude Eburne; *D:* Bernard Vorhaus; *C:* John Alton.

The Courageous Mr. Penn 🦴🦴 *Penn of Pennsylvania* 1941 Slow-moving British film, outlining the achievements of William Penn, the Quaker founder of Pennsylvania. **79m/B VHS.** *GB* Clifford Evans, Deborah Kerr, Dennis Arundell, Aubrey Mallalieu, D.J. Williams, O.B. Clarence, Charles Carson, Henry Oscar, J.H. Roberts; *D:* Lance Comfort.

The Courier 🦴🦴 1988 (R) A former drug addict seeks revenge on the dealers who killed his friend. Only thing that saves it are the songs by U2, The Pogues, and Hothouse Flowers. Musical score by Elvis Costello. **85m/C VHS.** *IR* Gabriel Byrne, Ian Bannen, Padraig O'Loingsigh, Cait O'Riordan, Patrick Bergin; *D:* Frank Deasy, Joe Lee; *M:* Elvis Costello.

Courier of Death 🦴 1984 A courier is embroiled in a mob war/struggle over a locked briefcase with mysterious contents. **77m/C VHS.** Joey Johnson, Barbara Garrison; *D:* Tom Shaw.

Court Jester 🦴🦴🦴½ 1956 Swashbuckling comedy stars Danny Kaye as a former circus clown who teams up with a band of outlaws trying to dethrone a tyrant king. Kaye poses as the court jester so he can learn of the evil king's intentions. Filled with more color, more song, and more truly funny lines than any three comedies put together, this is Kaye's best performance. ♫They'll Never Outfox the Fox; Baby, Let Me Take You Dreaming; My Heart Knows a Lovely Song; The Maladjusted Jester. **101m/C VHS, DVD.** Danny Kaye, Glynis Johns, Basil Rathbone, Angela Lansbury, Cecil Parker, John Carradine, Mildred Natwick, Robert Middleton; *D:* Melvin Frank, Norman Panama; *W:* Norman Panama; *C:* Ray June; *M:* Sammy Cahn, Sylvia Fine, Vic Schoen.

The Court Martial of Billy Mitchell 🦴🦴🦴 *One-Man Mutiny* 1955 Terrific courtroom drama depicts the secret trial of Billy Mitchell, head of the Army Air Service in the 1920s, who predicted the role of airpower in subsequent warfare and the danger of war with Japan. Mitchell incurred the wrath of the military by publicly faulting the lack of U.S. preparedness for invasion. Steiger is outstanding as the attorney; Cooper is great as Mitchell. Debut for Montgomery. **100m/C VHS, Wide.** Gary Cooper, Charles Bickford, Ralph Bellamy, Rod Steiger, Elizabeth Montgomery, Fred Clark, James Daly, Jack Lord, Peter Graves, Darren McGavin, Robert F. Simon, Jack Perrin, Charles Dingle; *D:* Otto Preminger; *C:* Sam Leavitt.

The Court Martial of Jackie Robinson 🦴🦴🦴½ 1990 (R) True story of a little-known chapter in the life of the famous athlete. During his stint in the Army, Robinson refused to take a back seat on a bus and subsequently faced the possibility of court martial. **94m/C VHS.** Andre Braugher, Daniel Stern, Ruby Dee, Stan Shaw, Paul Dooley, Bruce Dern, Dale Dye; *D:* Larry Peerce; *W:* Dennis Lynton Clark; *C:* Don Burgess. **CABLE**

The Courtesans of Bombay 🦴🦴🦴 1985 Gritty docudrama, set in Pavanpul, the poverty-stricken brothel section of Bombay, looks at how the impoverished women support themselves through a combination of prostitution and performing. **74m/C VHS.** *GB* Kareem Samar, Zohra Segal, Saeed Jaffrey; *D:* Ismail Merchant, James Ivory, Ruth Prawer Jhabvala. **TV**

Courtin' Wildcats 🦴½ 1929 Early Gibson programmer in which he plays a frail eastern college boy who was sent west by his father to toughen up. Once there, he meets Gilbert and ends up marrying her. **56m/B VHS.** Hoot Gibson, Eugenia Gilbert, Monte Montague; *D:* Jerome Storm.

The Courtney Affair 🦴🦴½ *The Courtneys of Curzon Street* 1947 An aristocratic young Britisher causes a stir when he marries an Irish maid. As a result, the couple must face terrific social ostracism. Classy soap opera family saga was a big money maker in England. **112m/B VHS.** *GB* Anna Neagle, Michael Wilding, Gladys Young, Michael Medwin, Coral Browne, Jack Watling, Bernard Lee; *D:* Herbert Wilcox.

Courtship 🦴🦴🦴 1987 From renowned playwright Horton Foote comes this touching story about a sheltered, upper-crust young girl who shocks her family and friends by eloping with a traveling salesman. **84m/C VHS.** Hallie Foote, William Converse-Roberts, Amanda Plummer, Rochelle Oliver, Michael Higgins; *D:* Howard Cummings. **TV**

The Courtship of Eddie's Father 🦴🦴🦴 1962 A clever nine-year-old boy plays matchmaker for his widowed dad in this rewarding family comedy-drama (the inspiration for the TV series). Some plot elements are outdated, but young Howard's performance is terrific; he would later excel at direction. Based on the novel by Mark Toby. **117m/C VHS.** Glenn Ford, Shirley Jones, Stella Stevens, Dina Merrill, Ron Howard, Jerry Van Dyke; *D:* Vincente Minnelli; *W:* John Gay; *C:* Milton Krasner.

The Courtyard 🦴🦴 1995 (R) Jonathan Hoffman (McCarthy) seems to have the perfect life—a great job, great girl, great California apartment. But then his apartment complex is bedeviled by a series of sinister crimes and Jonathan becomes the prime suspect. **103m/C VHS.** Andrew McCarthy, Madchen Amick, Richard "Cheech" Marin, Vincent Schiavelli; *D:* Fred Walton; *W:* Christopher Hawthorne.

Cousin Bette 🦴🦴½ 1997 (R) Lange plays a mean game of Old Maid in this adaptation of Honore Balzac's novel, set in 1840s Paris. Always outshone by her more beautiful cousin Adeline (Chaplin), Bette is considered plain and not very bright by her aristocratic family. When Adeline's husband Hector (Laurie) asks her to become his housekeeper instead of his wife after Adeline dies, there is no doubt what she means when she hisses she will "take care of everyone." She uses her family's own baser instincts to bring about their downfall. Lange's performance as the cold and manipulative Bette is worth the price of a rental by itself. Big screen debut for theatrical director McAnuff. **112m/C VHS, DVD, Wide.** Jessica Lange, Elisabeth Shue, Aden Young, Bob Hoskins, Kelly Macdonald, Hugh Laurie, Geraldine Chaplin, Toby Stephens, John Sessions; ***D:*** Des McAnuff; ***W:*** Lynn Siefert, Susan Tarr; ***C:*** Andrzej Sekula; ***M:*** Simon Boswell.

Cousin, Cousine 🦴🦴🦴½ **1976 (R)** Pleasant French comedy about distant cousins who meet at a round of family parties, funerals, and weddings and become friends, but their relationship soon becomes more than platonic. Remade in the U.S. in 1989 as "Cousins." In French with English subtitles. **95m/C VHS.** *FR* Marie-Christine Barrault, Marie-France Pisier, Victor Lanoux, Guy Marchand, Ginette Garcin, Sybil Maas; ***D:*** Jean-Charles Tacchella; ***W:*** Jean-Charles Tacchella; ***C:*** Georges Lendi; ***M:*** Gerard Anfosso. Cesar '76: Support. Actress (Pisier).

The Cousins 🦴🦴🦴 *Les Cousins* **1959** Set against the backdrop of Parisian student life, two very different cousins (one twisted, the other saintly) vie for the hand of Mayniel. This country mouse, city mouse adult fable ultimately depicts the survival of the fittest. Chabrol's lovely but sad second directorial effort. **112m/B VHS.** *FR* Jean-Claude Brialy, Gerard Blain, Juliette Mayniel, Claude Cerval, Genevieve Cluny; ***D:*** Claude Chabrol; ***W:*** Claude Chabrol.

Cousins 🦴🦴🦴½ **1989 (PG-13)** An American remake of "Cousin, Cousine," in which two distant cousins-by-marriage meet at a wedding and, due to their respective spouses' infidelities, fall into each other's arms. A gentle love story with a humorous and biting look at the foibles of extended families. **110m/C VHS, DVD, Wide.** Isabella Rossellini, Sean Young, Ted Danson, William L. Petersen, Norma Aleandro, Lloyd Bridges, Keith Coogan; ***D:*** Joel Schumacher; ***W:*** Stephen Metcalfe; ***C:*** Ralf Bode; ***M:*** Angelo Badalamenti.

Cover Girl 🦴🦴🦴 **1944** A vintage wartime musical about a girl who must decide between a nightclub career and a future as a cover model. Hayworth is beautiful, Kelly dances like a dream, and Silvers and Arden are hilarious. ♫Cover Girl; Sure Thing; Make Way For Tomorrow; Put Me to the Test; Long Ago and Far Away; That's the Best of All; The Show Must Go On; Who's Complaining?; Poor John. **107m/C VHS.** Rita Hayworth, Gene Kelly, Phil Silvers, Otto Kruger, Lee Bowman, Jinx Falkenberg, Eve Arden, Edward Brophy, Anita Colby; ***D:*** Charles Vidor; ***C:*** Rudolph Mate; ***M:*** Ira Gershwin, Jerome Kern. Oscars '44: Orig. Dramatic Score.

Cover Girl Models 🦴 **1975** An action-packed '70s adventure in which beautiful models are forced to fight for survival. **82m/C VHS.** Lindsay Bloom, Pat Anderson, John Kramer, Rhonda Leigh Hopkins, Mary Woronov; ***D:*** Cirio H. Santiago.

The Cover Girl Murders 🦴🦴½ **1993 (PG-13)** Six beautiful models have been brought together on a remote island to shoot a magazine's popular swimsuit issue. Each one wants to be the cover model—but someone is willing to kill to get the job. **87m/C VHS.** Lee Majors, Jennifer O'Neill, Adrian Paul, Beverly Johnson, Vanessa Angel; ***D:*** James A. Contner; ***W:*** Douglas Barr, Bernard Maybeck; ***M:*** Rick Marotta.

Cover Me 🦴🦴 **1995 (R)** When beautiful models turn up dead, L.A. detectives Bobby Colter (Rossovich) and J.J. Davis (Sorvino) discover they were all on the cover of L.A. Erotica magazine. So detective Holly Jacobsen, Colter's girlfriend, (Taylor) goes undercover at the magazine and learns more about the seamy sex underworld than the killer wants her to know. **94m/C VHS.** Courtney Taylor, Rick Rossovich, Paul Sorvino, Elliott Gould, Corbin Bernsen; ***D:*** Michael Schroeder; ***W:*** Steve Johnson.

Cover Story 🦴½ **1993** Journalist Matt McKendree falls in love with a mystery woman whose story he's investigating. Too bad she's dead—or is she. **93m/C VHS.** William Wallace, Tuesday Knight, Robert Forster, Christopher McDonald; ***D:*** J. Grubb Alexander; ***W:*** J. Grubb Alexander.

Cover-Up 🦴½ **1991 (R)** Terrorist attacks on U.S. military bases in Israel are just a smokescreen for a greater threat. The below-par actioner stands out only for the hokey religious symbolism in its Good Friday climax. **89m/C VHS.** Dolph Lundgren, Louis Gossett Jr., John Finn; ***D:*** Manny Coto.

The Covered Wagon 🦴🦴½ **1923** Prototypical silent Western began the genre. Wagon train moves cross-country, battling weather and wild Indians. By today's standards, somewhat bucolic and uneventful, but the location photography holds up quite well. Big budget film in its day, and enormously popular. **98m/B VHS.** Warren Kerigan, Lois Wilson, Alan Hale, Ernest Torrence; ***D:*** James Cruze.

Covered Wagon Days 🦴🦴 **1940** The Three Mesquiteers set out after silver smugglers who have framed Rico's brother for murder. **54m/B VHS.** Robert "Bob" Livingston, Raymond Hatton, Duncan Renaldo, John Merton, Reed Howes; ***D:*** George Sherman.

Covered Wagon Trails 🦴 **1940** Substandard Western has good guy Randall dealing with the shifty cattleman's association and making the West safe for the hardworking locals. Future Frankenstein monster Strange plays the hired muscle. **52m/B VHS.** Addison "Jack" Randall, Sally Cairns, David Sharpe, Lafe (Lafayette) McKee, Budd Buster, Glenn Strange; ***D:*** Raymond K. Johnson; ***W:*** Tom Gibson.

Covergirl 🦴½ *Dreamworld* **1983 (R)** Wealthy man decides to relieve his boredom by molding a young woman into a supermodel. She finds the glamorous life isn't always what it's cracked up to be. TV-type melodrama. **98m/C VHS.** *CA* Jeff Conaway, Irena Ferris, Cathie Shirriff, Roberta Leighton, Deborah Wakeham; ***D:*** Jean-Claude Lord.

Covert Action 🦴½ **1988** A drug kingpin who desires to protect his business tries to frame a captain for a crime he did not commit. **85m/C VHS.** Rick Washburne, John Christian, Stuart Garrison Day, Amanda Zinsser, Johnny Stumper; ***D:*** J. Christian Ingvordsen.

Covert Assassin 🦴🦴 **1994 (R)** Anti-terrorist specialist is hired by wealthy widow to avenge her husband's murder. Adapted from the novel "Wild Justice" by Wilbur Smith. **114m/C VHS.** Roy Scheider, Sam Wanamaker, Ted McGinley, Christopher Buchholz; ***D:*** Tony Wharmby.

Cow Town 🦴🦴 **1950** A range war results when ranchers begin fencing in their land to prevent cattle rustling. Autry's 72nd film has some good songs and a dependable cast. **70m/B VHS.** Gene Autry, Gail Davis, Jock Mahoney, Harry Shannon; ***D:*** John English.

The Coward 🦴🦴 **1962** A schoolteacher and his wife are living in a remote Slovak village during the last days of WWII. The wife supports the anti-Nazi partisans while her husband collaborates with the Germans that occupy the village. Eventually, he finds the courage to save some innocent victims of the Nazi purge. Czech with subtitles. **113m/C VHS.** *CZ* ***D:*** Jiri Weiss.

Coward of the County 🦴🦴½ **1981** A devout pacifist is put to the test when his girlfriend is raped. Good performances by all concerned. Based on the lyrics of Kenny Rogers's hit song of the same name. **115m/C VHS.** Kenny Rogers, Frederic Lehne, Largo Woodruff, Mariclare Costello, Ana Alicia, Noble Willingham; ***D:*** Dick Lowry. **TV**

Cowboy 🦴🦴🦴 **1958** Western round-up based on the memoirs of tenderfoot-turned-cowpoke Frank Harris. Harris (Lemmon) is a Chicago hotel clerk who meets cattle boss Tom Reece (Ford) who's in the city on business. Losing his money in a poker game, Reece reluctantly accepts a loan from Harris in exchange for a piece of his cattle business. So Harris and Reece hit the dusty trail on a cattle drive that takes them into Mexico where Harris falls in love with Maria (Kashfi), the daughter of a wealthy rancher, and gradually turns from city slicker into hardened trail boss. Good cast, no fuss. From the book "Reminiscences As a Cowboy" by Harris. **92m/C VHS, DVD.** Jack Lemmon, Glenn Ford, Anna Kashfi, Brian Donlevy, Dick York, Victor Manuel Mendoza, Richard Jaeckel, King Donovan; ***D:*** Delmer Daves; ***W:*** Edmund H. North; ***C:*** Charles Lawton Jr.; ***M:*** George Duning.

The Cowboy & the Ballerina 🦴🦴 **1984** An aging rodeo star falls in love with a petite ballerina defecting from a Russian Dance Company. Good cast makes it watchable. **96m/C VHS.** Lee Majors, Leslie Wing, Christopher Lloyd, Anjelica Huston, George de la Pena; ***D:*** Jerry Jameson; ***M:*** Bruce Broughton. **TV**

Cowboy & the Bandit 🦴 **1935** A cowboy comes to the aid of a widow being victimized by outlaws. **58m/B VHS.** Rex Lease, Bobby Nelson, William Desmond; ***D:*** Al(bert) Herman.

The Cowboy and the Lady 🦴🦴½ **1938** Oberon plays a madcap heiress who is deposited by her politician father on their Florida estate to keep her out of trouble while he seeks the Presidential nomination. She is bored and decides to go to a local rodeo where she meets cowboy Cooper. Both are instantly smitten and marry on impulse. Cooper doesn't know about her wealth and when her father finds out about the marriage he's appalled that his daughter has married beneath her. Since this is a comedy all comes out right in the end. Good cast, weak story. **91m/B VHS.** Gary Cooper, Merle Oberon, Patsy Kelly, Walter Brennan, Fuzzy Knight, Mabel Todd, Henry Kolker, Harry Davenport; ***D:*** H.C. Potter; ***C:*** Gregg Toland. Oscars '38: Sound.

Cowboy & the Senorita 🦴🦴 **1944** A cowboy solves the mystery of a missing girl and wins her lovely cousin. The first film that paired Rogers and Evans, who went on to become a winning team, on and offscreen. **56m/B VHS.** Roy Rogers, John Hubbard, Dale Evans; ***D:*** Joseph Kane; ***W:*** Gordon Kahn.

Cowboy Commandos 🦴½ **1943** Improbable plot has cowboys riding out after Nazi spies, who want to steal valuable ore. **53m/B VHS.** Ray Corrigan, Dennis Moore, Max Terhune, Budd Buster, John Merton; ***D:*** S. Roy Luby.

Cowboy Counselor 🦴 **1933** Cowboy Hoot Gibson helps an enchanting girl clear her innocent brother's name. **60m/B VHS.** Hoot Gibson, Sheila (Manors) Mannors, Skeeter Bill Robbins, Alan Bridge, Bobby Nelson, Merrill McCormick; ***D:*** George Melford; ***W:*** Jack Natteford.

Cowboy Millionaire 🦴🦴½ **1935** An Englishwoman comes to an American dude ranch and falls in love with one of the ranch hands. Entertaining Western comedy. **65m/B VHS.** George O'Brien, Evalyn Bostock, Edgar Kennedy, Alden Chase; ***D:*** Edward F. (Eddie) Cline.

The Cowboy Way 🦴½ **1994 (PG-13)** A mess from start to finish made somewhat watchable by cowpoke charm of the leads and one good horse chase. Two rodeo stars (Harrelson and Sutherland) from New Mexico ride into New York City to avenge a buddy's death, with Hudson as a mounted NYC cop who always yearned to be a cowboy. Great premise is overcome by tasteless humor and a patched-up plot shot full of holes. Good for a gander is the 90-foot Times Square billboard of Harrelson's character as a Calvin Klein underwear model, which stopped traffic even in jaded New York. **106m/C VHS, DVD.** Woody Harrelson, Kiefer Sutherland, Dylan McDermott, Ernie Hudson, Cara Buono, Marg Helgenberger, Tomas Milian, Joaquin Martinez; ***Cameos:*** Travis Tritt; ***D:*** Gregg Champion; ***W:*** William D. Wittliff, Rob Thompson; ***C:*** Dean Semler; ***M:*** David Newman.

The Cowboys 🦴🦴🦴 **1972 (PG)** Wayne stars as a cattle rancher who is forced to hire 11 schoolboys to help him drive his cattle 400 miles to market. Clever script makes this one of Wayne's better Westerns. Carradine's film debut. Inspired the TV series. **128m/C VHS, DVD, Wide.** John Wayne, Roscoe Lee Browne, A. Martinez, Bruce Dern, Colleen Dewhurst, Slim Pickens, Robert Carradine, Clay O'Brien, Nicolas Beauvy; ***D:*** Mark Rydell; ***W:*** Harriet Frank Jr., Irving Ravetch; ***C:*** Robert L. Surtees; ***M:*** John Williams.

Cowboys Don't Cry 🦴🦴 **1988** When a modern cowboy's wife is killed in an automobile accident, he must change his immature ways and build a solid future with his teenage son or perish in loneliness. **96m/C VHS.** Rebecca Jenkins, Ron White, Janet-Laine Green; ***D:*** Anne Wheeler.

Cowboys from Texas 🦴½ **1939** The Three Mesquiteers bring about a peaceful settlement to a fight between cattlemen and homesteaders. Part of "The Three Mesquiteers" series. **54m/B VHS.** Robert "Bob" Livingston, Raymond Hatton, Duncan Renaldo, Carole Landis; ***D:*** George Sherman; ***W:*** Oliver Drake; ***C:*** Ernest Miller.

Coyote Trails 🦴½ **1935** Standard western adventure has cowboy Tyler helping a damsel in distress. **68m/B VHS.** Tom Tyler, Ben (Benny) Corbett; ***D:*** Bernard B. Ray; ***W:*** Rose Gordon.

Coyote Ugly 🦴½ **2000 (PG-13)** Producer Bruckheimer revisits the "Flashdance" formula for this tale of a young innocent songwriter (Perabo) who ends up slingin' drinks and barin' her navel in the eponymous bar while seeking fame and fortune in New York. The plot is as naive and wide-eyed as the main character, leaving no room for surprise twists, but allowing for a movie-saving performance by John Goodman as the concerned dad and a discovery in Aussie Garcia as the love interest. The rest of the cast consists of jiggly window dressing, but the PG-13 rating guarentees disappointment for a large segment of the audience. It's bad, but not in a career-destroying, "Showgirls" kind of way. **94m/C VHS, DVD, Wide.** Piper Perabo, Maria Bello, Tyra Banks, John Goodman, Melanie Lynskey, Ellen Cleghorne, Bud Cort, Izabella Miko, Bridget Moynahan, Adam Garcia, Del Pentacost, Michael Weston; ***D:*** David McNally; ***W:*** Todd Graff, Kevin Smith, Gina Wendkos; ***C:*** Amir M. Mokri; ***M:*** Trevor Horn.

Crack House 🦴🦴 **1989 (R)** A man seeks revenge for the murder of a relative by drug dealers. Average exploitation flick. **91m/C VHS.** Jim Brown, Richard Roundtree, Anthony Geary, Angel Tompkins, Greg Gomez Thomsen, Clyde Jones, Cheryl Kay; ***D:*** Michael Fischa; ***C:*** Arledge Armenaki.

A Crack in the Floor 🦴½ **2000 (R)** Three couples go on a weekend hiking trip in the mountains and run into the deranged local folk. But their nightmare really begins when they make camp in a seemingly abandoned cabin that's not so empty after all. **90m/C VHS, DVD.** Gary Busey, David Naughton, Mario Lopez, Tracy Scoggins, Bo Hopkins, Rance Howard, Justine Priestley; ***D:*** Sean Stanek, Corbin Timbrook; ***W:*** Sean Stanek. **VIDEO**

Crack Shadow Boxers 🦴 **197?** Through a series of misadventures, Wu Lung and Chu San battle to protect the inhabitants of a small village from the onslaught of relentless bandits. **91m/C VHS, DVD.** *HK* Ku Feng, Chou Li Lung, Han Guo Gai; ***D:*** Weng Yao Hai.

Crack-Up 🦴🦴½ **1946** Largely ignored at the time of its release, this tense tale is now regarded as a minor classic of film noir. An art expert suffers a blackout while investigating a possible forgery and must piece together the missing hours to uncover a criminal conspiracy. **70m/B VHS.** Pat O'Brien, Claire Trevor, Herbert Marshall, Ray Collins, Wallace Ford, Damian O'Flynn, Erskine Sanford; ***D:*** Irving Reis.

Crack Up 🦴🦴 **1997** Three buddies hit a losing streak and decide they can improve their lives by ripping off a drug house. They wind up with more than half a million in cash without the dealers having a clue as to who committed the crime. That is, until two newscasters decide to focus on the story—each tidbit of information leading the drug dealers closer to the guys' hideout and a deadly confrontation. **90m/C VHS.** John Sayre, Mike Terner, Steven Saucedo, Guilanno Bele, Gregg Madsen, Jenny Royar; ***D:*** Jeff Leroy; ***W:*** Jeff Leroy, Marc Lutz; ***M:*** Jeffrey Alan Jones. **VIDEO**

Cracker: Brotherly Love 🦴🦴🦴 **1995** Everyone carries lots of emotional baggage in this entry of the British series. Detective Jane Penhaligon (Somerville) is still suffering from the aftereffects of rape, which she believes was by colleague Jimmy Beck (Cranitch), who's just returned to duty following a breakdown. Meanwhile, Fitz's (Coltrane) mother has died bringing him into contact with his stodgy brother Danny (Russell). And yes, there are murders to investigate—a killer who likes prostitutes to dress up as little girls. **150m/C VHS.** *GB* Robbie Coltrane, Geraldine Somerville, Lorcan Cranitch, Ricky Tomlinson, Barbara Flynn, Clive Russell, Kieran O'Brien, Tess Thompson, Brid Brennan, David Calder, Mark Lambert; ***D:*** Roy Battersby; ***W:*** Jimmy McGovern. **TV**

The Cracker Factory 🦴🦴½ **1979** Wood is impressive as a woman committed to a mental institution who attempts to charm her way out of treatment. **90m/C VHS.** Natalie Wood, Perry King, Shelley Long, Vivian Blaine, Juliet Mills, Peter Haskell; ***D:*** Burt Brinckerhoff; ***M:*** Billy Goldenberg. **TV**

Cracker: Men Should Weep 🦴🦴½ **1994** Fitz's skills are called into play when he must deal with a serial rapist (Aggrey). However, things become personal when Detective Jane Penhaligon (Somerville) is raped. **150m/C VHS.** *GB* Robbie Coltrane, Geraldine Somerville, Lorcan Cranitch, Graham Aggrey; ***D:*** Jean Stewart; ***W:*** Jimmy McGovern. **TV**

Cracker: The Big Crunch 🦴🦴½ **1994** The leader of a Christian fundamentalist sect has an affair with a schoolgirl and then plots her murder to avoid a scandal. But what he can't avoid is Fitz (Coltrane). **150m/C VHS.** *GB* Robbie Coltrane, Jim Carter, Samantha Morton, James Fleet, Cherith Mellor; ***D:*** Julian Jarrold; ***W:*** Jimmy McGovern, Ted Whitehead. **TV**

Cracker: To Be a Somebody 🦴🦴 **1994** The murder of an Asian shopkeeper first prompts the Manchester police to look for their suspect in the violent world of skinheads. But when the professor helping to profile the killer is murdered, the cops are forced to call in irascible forensic psychologist "Fitz" Fitzgerald (Coltrane) to aid in their investigation. Made for TV. **150m/C VHS.** *GB* Robbie Coltrane, Robert Carlyle, Barbara Flynn, Christopher Eccleston, Geraldine Somerville, Lorcan Cranitch; ***D:*** Tim Fywell; ***W:*** Jimmy McGovern. **TV**

Crackerjack 🦴🦴 **1994 (R)** Chicago cop Jack Wild (Griffith) agrees to join his brother's family at a vacation resort in the Rocky Mountains. Coincidentally, a team of mercenaries are determined to hijack $50 million in diamonds from the resort and it's up to Jack to stop them. **96m/C VHS.** Thomas Ian Griffith, Nastassia Kinski, Christopher Plummer; ***D:*** Michael Mazo; ***W:*** Jonas Quastel, Michael Bafaro; ***C:*** Danny Nowak; ***M:*** Peter Allen.

Crackerjack 2 🦴½ *Hostage Train; Crackerjack 2: Hostage Train* **1997 (R)** Cop Jack Wild (Reinhold) discovers that the train carrying his girlfriend, financial analyst Dana Townsend (Alt), and several of her wealthy clients has been hijacked by terrorists. The train is trapped by an explosion in a tunnel in the Rockies and Jack must rescue the passengers before the rest of the terrorists' plan goes into motion. **98m/C VHS.** Karel Roden, Judge Reinhold, Carol Alt, Michael Sarrazin; ***D:*** Robert Lee; ***W:*** Chris Hyde; ***C:*** John Herzog; ***M:*** Peter Allen.

Crackerjack 3 🦴🦴 **2000 (PG-13)** Jack Thorn (Svenson) is an ex-Navy S.E.A.L. and the current director of the CIA's covert ops. He's planning to retire when he discovers his would-be replacement, Marcus Clay (Gruner), wants to cause a worldwide economic catastrophe. So Jack gathers together some fellow oldtimers and tries to cope with high tech in order to save the world. **97m/C VHS, DVD.** Bo Svenson, Olivier Gruner, Leo Rossi, Amy Weber; ***D:*** Lloyd A. Simandl; ***M:*** Peter Allen. **VIDEO**

Crackers 🦴🦴 **1984 (PG)** The offbeat story of two bumbling thieves who round up a gang of equally inept neighbors and go on the wildest crime spree you have ever seen. A would-be comic remake of "Big Deal on Madonna Street." **92m/C VHS.** Donald Sutherland, Jack Warden, Sean Penn, Wallace Shawn, Larry Riley, Trinidad Silva, Christine Baranski, Charlaine Woodard, Tasia Valenza; ***D:*** Louis Malle.

Cracking Up 🦴½ *Smorgasbord* **1983 (PG)** Accident-prone misfit's mishaps on the road to recovery create chaos for everyone he meets. Lewis plays a dozen characters in this overboard comedy with few laughs. **91m/C VHS.** Jerry Lewis, Herb Edelman, Foster Brooks, Milton Berle, Sammy Davis Jr., Zane Buzby, Dick Butkus, Buddy Lester; ***D:*** Jerry Lewis.

The Crackler 🦴🦴 **1984** During the '20s, a husband-and-wife private investigation team (Tommy and Tuppence) set out to find a gang of forgers operating in high society circles. Based on a story by Agatha Christie. Made for British TV. **60m/C VHS.** *GB* James Warwick, Francesca Annis. **TV**

The Cradle Will Fall woof! **1983** Adaptation of the pulpy bestselling mystery by Mary Higgins Clark about a woman who cannot convince anyone she witnessed a murder. The cast of "The Guiding Light" appear. Poor script and poor direction do not a thriller make. **103m/C VHS.** Lauren Hutton, Ben Murphy, James Farentino, Charita Bauer, Peter Simon; ***D:*** John Llewellyn Moxey. **TV**

The Cradle Will Rock 🦴🦴½ **1999 (R)** An exuberant if not always successful attempt by Robbins to capture the artistic/political fervor of New York in the thirties. Theatrical collaborators Orson Welles (Macfadyen) and John Houseman (Elwes) agree to produce Marc Blitzstein's (Azaria) new political musical "The Cradle Will Rock" for their Federal Theater company in 1937. Right-wing political interference closes the theater on opening night but Welles leads his company to another venue in Manhattan where the actors (because of their union) must perform the piece from the audience—the dramatic circumstances offering a unique success and a place in theater history. **133m/C VHS, DVD, Wide.** Angus Macfadyen, Cary Elwes, Hank Azaria, Cherry Jones, Ruben Blades, Joan Cusack, John Cusack, Philip Baker Hall, Bill Murray, Vanessa Redgrave, Susan Sarandon, Jamey Sheridan, John Turturro, Emily Watson, Bob Balaban, Paul Giamatti, Barnard Hughes, Barbara Sukowa, John Carpenter, Gretchen Mol, Harris Yulin, Dominic Chianese; ***D:*** Tim Robbins; ***W:*** Tim Robbins; ***C:*** Jean-Yves Escoffier; ***M:*** David Robbins.

The Craft 🦴🦴½ **1996 (R)** Call it "Heathers" with hexes. Troubled 17-year-old Sarah (Tunney) moves to L.A. and begins her senior year at St. Benedict's Academy. She takes up with three rebels—Nancy (Balk), Bonnie (Campbell), and Rochelle (True)—who like to dabble in witchcraft. Now, with the addition of would-be witch Sarah, these black magic women start slinging spells at their uppity classmates. Works best when concentrating on the girls and their problems, but degenerates into a special effects barrage toward the end. Alas, no one is turned into a newt. **100m/C VHS, DVD, 8mm.** Robin Tunney, Fairuza Balk, Neve Campbell, Rachel True, Skeet Ulrich, Helen Shaver, Cliff DeYoung, Christine Taylor, Assumpta Serna; ***D:*** Andrew Fleming; ***W:*** Andrew Fleming, Peter Filardi; ***C:*** Alexander Grusynski; ***M:*** Graeme Revell. MTV Movie Awards '97: Fight (Fairuza Balk/Robin Tunney).

Craig's Wife 🦴🦴🦴 **1936** A classic soap opera about a pitiful woman driven to total ruin by her desire for social acceptance and material wealth. Russell makes her surprisingly sympathetic. Based on a Pulitzer Prize-winning George Kelly play. Remake of a silent film, was also remade as "Harriet Craig." **75m/B VHS.** Rosalind Russell, John Boles, Alma Kruger, Jane Darwell, Billie Burke; ***D:*** Dorothy Arzner.

Crainquebille 🦴🦴🦴 **1923** The classic satire based on the Anatole France story about a street merchant in Paris unfairly imprisoned and eventually surviving peacefully as a tramp. Silent. **50m/B VHS.** *FR* Maurice Feraudy; ***D:*** Jacques Feyder.

The Cranes Are Flying 🦴🦴🦴½ *Letyat Zhuravit* **1957** When her lover goes off to fight during WWII, a girl is seduced by his cousin. Touching love story is free of politics. Filmed in Russia; English subtitles. **91m/B VHS, DVD, Wide.** *RU* Tatyana Samoilova, Alexei Batalov, Vasily Merkuryev, A. Shvorin; ***D:*** Mikhail Kalatozov; ***W:*** Viktor Rozov; ***C:*** Sergei Urusevsky; ***M:*** Moisej Vajnberg. Cannes '58: Film.

Crash 🦴🦴 **1995 (NC-17)** You can always expect surreal kinkiness from Cronenberg and this film, awarded a Special Jury Prize at Cannes for "daring, originality, and audacity," won't prove the exception. It's "auto" erotica taken to the max, with car crashes and bodily injury turned into fetishes. James (Spader) lands in the hospital after an accident, which injured Helen (Hunter), a passenger in the other car. Helen and James' shared experience soon leads to a sexual relationship, which doesn't bother James' wife, Catherine (Unger). Then there's Vaughan (Koteas) and his group, who like to reenact famous auto crashes (like those of James Dean and Jayne Mansfield). Oh yes, there's lots more sex (in various combinations). Based on J.G. Ballard's 1973 cult novel. An R-rated version clocks in at 90 minutes. **98m/C VHS, DVD.** *CA* James Spader, Holly Hunter, Elias Koteas, Deborah Kara Unger, Rosanna Arquette, Peter MacNeill; ***D:*** David Cronenberg; ***W:*** David Cronenberg; ***C:*** Peter Suschitzsky; ***M:*** Howard Shore. Cannes '96: Special Jury Prize; Genie '96: Adapt. Screenplay, Cinematog., Director (Cronenberg), Film Editing.

Crash and Burn 🦴½ **1990 (R)** Rebels in a repressive future police state reactivate a huge, long-dormant robot to battle the establishment's army of powerful androids. Special effects by David Allen make the mayhem interesting. **85m/C VHS, DVD.** Ralph Waite, Paul Ganus, Eva LaRue, Bill Moseley, Jack McGee; ***D:*** Charles Band; ***W:*** J.S. Cardone; ***M:*** Richard Band.

Crash & Byrnes 🦴🦴½ **1999** Jack "Crash" Riley (Larson) is a retired CIA agent who is reluctantly called back into service to bring down a bioterrorist. A by-the-book kinda guy, Crash is, of course, paired with loose cannon DEA agent Roman Byrnes (Ellis). If the two can ever figure out a way to work together, they may just accomplish their mission. Standard fare in the wannabe "Lethal Weapon" mold. **92m/C VHS, DVD.** *CA* Wolf Larson, Greg Ellis, Joanna Pacula, Steven Williams, Sandra Lindquist, Terry Chen, Melanie Angel; ***D:*** Jon Hess; ***W:*** Wolf Larson; ***C:*** Anthony C. Metchie; ***M:*** Ken Williams.

Crash Course 🦴🦴½ *A Mother's Fight for Justice* **2000** Terry Stone's (Baxter) college student son Terry (Lively) is critically injured in a car crash and suffers from severe brain trauma. Since the accident was caused by a drunk driver, Terry seeks justice while Andrew struggles to regain his life. Based on a true story. **91m/C VHS.** Meredith Baxter, Alan Rosenberg, Eric Lively; ***D:*** Tom Rickman. **CABLE**

Crash Dive 🦴🦴½ **1943** WWII glory film provides comic relief in the form of romance. Second-in-command Power falls hopelessly in love with school teacher Baxter, only to find out later that she is Lt. Commander Andrews' fiance. Once this little tidbit of information is disclosed, the two officers embark on a mission to destroy a Nazi U-Boat responsible for laying mines in the North Atlantic. Fantastic special effects and sound. Based on the story by W.R. Burnett. **105m/B VHS.** Tyrone Power, Anne Baxter, Dana Andrews, James Gleason, May Whitty, Harry (Henry) Morgan, Ben Carter, Frank Conroy, Florence Lake, John Archer, Minor Watson, Kathleen Howard, Stanley Andrews, Thurston Hall, Trudy Marshall, Charles Tannen, Chester Gan; ***D:*** Archie Mayo; ***W:*** Jo Swerling; ***C:*** Leon Shamroy; ***M:*** David Buttolph.

Crash Dive 🦴🦴 **1996 (R)** An atomic submarine is taken hostage by Richter (Schone) and his band of terrorists, who demand $1 billion in gold or Washington D.C. will become a nuclear disaster. Naturally, there's one hero—sub designer James Carter (Dudikoff)—who manages to sneak aboard and plots to save the day. Fast pace and top special effects make this one watchable. **90m/C VHS.** Michael Dudikoff, Reiner Schone, Frederic Forrest, Jay Acovone; ***D:*** Andrew Stevens; ***W:*** William Martell; ***C:*** Michael Slovis; ***M:*** Eric Wurst, David Wurst. **VIDEO**

The Crash of Flight 401 🦴½ **1978** A plane, full of recognizable TV stars, crashes in the Florida Everglades. "Airport" for a smaller screen. Based on a real event. **97m/C VHS.** William Shatner, Adrienne Barbeau, Eddie Albert, Brooke Bundy, Christopher Connelly, Lorraine Gary, Ron Glass, Sharon Gless, Brett Halsey, George Maharis, Gerald S. O'Loughlin; ***D:*** Barry Shear. **TV**

Crashout 🦴🦴½ **1955** Six men break out of prison in this entertaining melodrama. Bendix plays the gang's leader to nasty perfection. **88m/B VHS.** William Bendix, Gene Evans, Arthur Kennedy, Luther Adler, William Talman, Marshall Thompson, Beverly Michaels, Gloria Talbot, Adam Williams, Percy Helton, Melinda Markey, Morris Ankrum; ***D:*** Lewis R. Foster; ***W:*** Hal E. Chester; ***C:*** Russell Metty; ***M:*** Leith Stevens.

The Crater Lake Monster woof! **1977 (PG)** The dormant egg of a prehistoric creature hatches after a meteor rudely awakens the dozing dino. He's understandably miffed and begins a revenge campaign. Prehistoric yawner. **85m/C VHS, DVD.** Richard Cardella, Glenn Roberts, Mark Siegel, Bob Hyman, Kacey Cobb; ***D:*** William R. Stromberg; ***W:*** Richard Cardella; ***C:*** Paul Gentry.

The Craving 🦴 *Return of the Wolfman; El Retorno del Hombre-Lobo* **1980 (R)** Naschy (AKA Jacinto Molina) returns as El Hombre Lobo for the umpteenth time and once again battles a female vampire (see "Werewolf vs. the Vampire Woman"). Although continental Europe's biggest horror star, this film was such a boxoffice disaster that Naschy went bankrupt. He was then forced to turn to Japan for financing (see "The Human Beasts"). Naschy/Molina directed under the pseudonym "Jack" Molina. **93m/C VHS.** *SP* Paul (Jacinto Molina) Naschy, Jacinto (Jack) Molina, Julie Saly, Silvia Aquilar, Azucena Hernandez, Beatriz Elorietta, Pilar Alcon; ***D:*** Jacinto (Jack) Molina.

The Crawlers 🦴 **1993 (R)** Illegal radioactive dumping has caused a living, lethal organism to invade in a small western town. Seems the local sheriff and the nuclear plant manager were partners in a toxic dumping scheme that went awry and two teenagers are the only ones willing to expose the truth. More to the point—scary monster attacks woman with artistically enhanced cleavage. Laurenti used the pseudonym Martin Newlin. **94m/C VHS.** Jason Saucier, Mary Sellers; ***D:*** Fabrizio Laurenti; ***W:*** Dan Price, Fabrizio Laurenti.

The Crawling Eye 🦴🦴 *The Trollenberg Terror* **1958** Hidden in a radioactive fog on a mountaintop, the crawling eye decapitates its victims and returns these humans to Earth to threaten mankind. Average acting, but particularly awful special effects. Based on a British TV series. **87m/B VHS, DVD, Wide.** *GB* Forrest Tucker, Laurence Payne, Janet Munro, Jennifer Jayne, Warren Mitchell; ***D:*** Quentin Lawrence; ***W:*** Jimmy Sangster; ***M:*** Stanley Black.

The Crawling Hand woof! **1963** An astronaut's hand takes off without him on an unearthly spree of stranglings. Silly stuff is a hands-down loser. **98m/B VHS, DVD.** Kent Taylor, Peter Breck, Rod Lauren, Sirry Steffen, Alan Hale Jr., Richard Arlen, Allison Hayes, Arline Judge; ***D:*** Herbert L. Strock; ***W:*** Herbert L. Strock; ***C:*** Willard Van der Veer.

Crawlspace 🦴 **1986 (R)** Beautiful girls lease rooms from a murdering, perverted doctor who spies on them, then kills. You may find Kinski amusing but not terrifying. **86m/C VHS.** Klaus Kinski, Talia Balsam, Joyce Van Patten, Sally Brown, Barbara Whinnery; ***D:*** David Schmoeller; ***W:*** David Schmoeller; ***M:*** Pino Donaggio.

Craze 🦴🦴 *The Infernal Idol; Demon Master* **1974 (R)** Toungue-in-cheek tale of a crazed antique dealer who slays a number of women as sacrifices to an African idol named Chuku. **96m/C VHS.** Jack Palance, Diana Dors, Julie Ege, Suzy Kendall, Michael Jayston, Edith Evans, Hugh Griffith, Trevor Howard; ***D:*** Freddie Francis.

Crazed woof! **1982** Dull plodder about a psychopath who keeps a dead girl's body in his boarding house and kills all intruders to keep his secret. **88m/C VHS.**

Laslo Papas, Belle Mitchell, Beverly Ross; ***D:*** Richard Cassidy.

Crazed Cop 🦴 *One Way Out* **1988** A man's mind snaps when his wife is found raped and murdered, and nothing will stop him on his quest for revenge. Low budget and violent. **85m/C VHS.** Ivan Rogers, Sandy Brooke, Rich Sutherlin, Doug Irk, Abdulah the Great; ***D:*** Paul Kyriazi.

The Crazies 🦴🦴 *Code Name: Trixie* **1973 (R)** A poisoned water supply makes the residents of a small town go on a chaotic, murderous rampage. When the army is called into to quell the anarchy, a small war breaks out. Message film about the military is muddled and derivative. **103m/C VHS.** Lane Carroll, W.G. McMillan, Harold W. Jones, Lloyd Hollar, Lynn Lowry, Richard France, Richard Liberty, Will Disney, Harry Spillman; ***D:*** George A. Romero; ***W:*** George A. Romero; ***C:*** Bill (William Heinzman) Hinzman; ***M:*** Bruce Roberts.

crazy/beautiful 🦴🦴½ **2001 (PG-13)** Cultural clash and teen relationship troubles all set in the affluent neighborhood of Pacific Palisades. Latino Carlos (Hernandez), from the wrong-side-of-the tracks in East L.A., is going to the rich high school in order to better himself. Nicole (Dunst) is the self-destructive wealthy chick (and congressman's daughter) who shows him that money doesn't buy happiness because she's got troubles, man. Familiar teen flick redeemed somewhat by the lead performances with handsome newcomer Hernandez appealing as a decent guy who's intrigued by willful, misunderstood hottie Dunst. **99m/C VHS, DVD, Wide.** *US* Kirsten Dunst, Jay Hernandez, Taryn Manning, Rolando Molina, Bruce Davison, Lucinda Jenney, Soledad St. Hilaire; ***D:*** John Stockwell; ***W:*** Phil Hay, Matt Manfredi; ***C:*** Shane Hurlbut; ***M:*** Paul Haslinger.

Crazy Fat Ethel II woof! **1985** A fat, hungry, homicidal female psychopath gets released from the asylum and goes on a cannabilistic rampage. Offensive junk. Sequel to "Criminally Insane." **90m/C VHS.** Priscilla Alden, Michael Flood, Jane Lambert, Robert Copple; ***D:*** Nick (Steve Millard) Phillips.

Crazy for Love 🦴🦴½ *Le Trou Normand* **1952** A village idiot stands to inherit the town inn if he can get a diploma within a year. With English subtitles. **80m/B VHS.** *FR* Brigitte Bardot, Bourvil, Jane (Jeanne) Marken, Nadine Basile; ***D:*** Jean Boyer; ***W:*** Arlette De Pitray; ***M:*** Paul Misraki.

Crazy from the Heart 🦴🦴🦴 **1991** Sweet cable romance finds Charlotte Bain (Lahti), the straitlaced high school principal in a small South Texas town, changing her ways. Charlotte surprises herself by agreeing to a date with the school's new janitor, Ernesto (Blades), and what's even more shocking to them both is how much they enjoy each other's company over one wild weekend. Strong, nuanced performances from Lahti and Blades make this chestnut of a story work beautifully, with able help from supporting actors. **104m/C VHS.** Christine Lahti, Ruben Blades, Mary Kay Place, Brent Spiner, William Russ, Louise Latham, Tommy Muntz, Robin (Robyn) Lively, Bibi Besch, Kamala Lopez; ***D:*** Thomas Schlamme; ***W:*** Linda Voorhees. **CABLE**

Crazy Horse 🦴🦴🦴 **1996** TV bio of the Oglala Sioux warrior (Greyeyes) whose home in the Black Hills of South Dakota was threatened by western expansion and the constant breaking of government treaties. As war chief, Crazy Horse, along with Teton Sioux leader Sitting Bull (Schellenberg), lead the Cheyenne and Sioux against Custer (Horton) at the battle of Little Bighorn. They elude capture but constant harassment by troops lead to Crazy Horse's surrender and death in 1877, betrayed by both the whites and some of his own people. Gripping story with a fine cast. **120m/C VHS.** Michael Greyeyes, Jimmy Herman, Wes Studi, Irene Bedard, Peter Horton, John Finn, Steve Reevis, Gordon Tootoosis, August Schellenberg, Sheldon Peters Wolfchild, Ned Beatty; ***D:*** John Irvin; ***W:*** Robert Schenkkan; ***C:*** Thomas Burstyn; ***M:*** Lennie Niehaus.

Crazy Horse and Custer: "The Untold Story" 🦴 **1990 (R)** Long before Little Big Horn, two legendary enemies find themselves trapped together in deadly Blackfoot territory. George Armstrong Custer and Crazy Horse are forced to form a volatile alliance in their life-or-death struggle against the murderous Blackfoot Tribe. History takes a back seat to Hollywood scriptwriting. **120m/C VHS, DVD.** Slim Pickens, Wayne Maunder, Mary Ann Mobley, Michael Dante.

Crazy in Alabama 🦴½ **1999 (PG-13)** If they greenlighted this southern fried mess, they're crazy in Hollywood, too. Lucille (Griffith) is an unbalanced aging southern belle who decapitates her husband and heads off to fulfill her dream of becoming a Hollywood star. She also takes his severed noggin with her, although it is a little talkative. Woven through this bizarre storyline is another that focuses on Lucille's nephew Peejoe back home in Alabama as he stands up to a bigoted sheriff, helps protest for civil rights and meets Martin Luther King. Banderas' directoral debut is fine technically, but veers wildly all over the road as far as content goes. **111m/C VHS, DVD, Wide.** Melanie Griffith, David Morse, Lucas Black, Cathy Moriarty, Meat Loaf Aday, Rod Steiger, Richard Schiff, John Beasley, Robert Wagner, Noah Emmerich, Sandra Seacat, Paul Ben-Victor, Brad Beyer, Fannie Flagg, Elizabeth Perkins, Linda Hart, Paul Mazursky, William Converse-Roberts, Holmes Osborne, David Speck; ***D:*** Antonio Banderas; ***W:*** Mark Childress; ***C:*** Julio Macat; ***M:*** Mark Snow.

Crazy in Love 🦴🦴½ **1992** Three generations of women live on an island in the home that has been in their family for years. Hunter is wildly in love with her husband, but misses (and doesn't quite trust) him when he is away on business. Enter Sands, who showers her with affection and fills the void in her life. The supporting cast fleshes out the story nicely and illustrates the reasons behind Hunter's insecurity. Enjoyable romantic comedy doesn't throw out anything heavy. Adapted from the novel by Luanne Rice. **93m/C VHS.** Holly Hunter, Gena Rowlands, Bill Pullman, Julian Sands, Frances McDormand, Herta Ware, Joanne Baron; ***D:*** Martha Coolidge; ***W:*** Gerald Ayres. **TV**

Crazy Mama 🦴🦴½ **1975 (PG)** Three women go on a crime spree from California to Arkansas, picking up men and having a hoot. Crime and comedy in a campy romp. Set in the 1950s and loaded with period kitsch. **81m/C VHS.** Cloris Leachman, Stuart Whitman, Ann Sothern, Jim Backus, Linda Purl, Donny Most, Sally Kirkland, Dick Miller, Bill Paxton; ***D:*** Jonathan Demme; ***W:*** Robert Thom; ***C:*** Bruce Logan.

Crazy Moon 🦴🦴½ *Huggers* **1987 (PG-13)** A rich high school nerd falls in love with a deaf girl, and must struggle against his domineering father's and older brother's prejudices. The viewer must struggle against the romantic cliches and heavy-handed message to enjoy a basically tender tale of romance. **89m/C VHS.** Kiefer Sutherland, Vanessa Vaughan, Peter Spence, Ken Pogue, Eve Napier; ***D:*** Allan Eastman; ***W:*** Tom Berry, Stefan Wodoslowsky; ***M:*** Lou Forestieri.

Crazy People 🦴½ **1990 (R)** Advertising exec Emory Leeston (Moore) writes commercials that describe products with complete honesty, and is committed to a mental hospital as a result. He meets a variety of characters at the hospital, including Hannah, with whom he falls in love. Tepid boxoffice blunder sounds funnier than it is. We give half a bone for the ad slogans, the funniest part of the movie. Our favorite: "Most of our passengers arrive alive" for an airline. **91m/C VHS.** Dudley Moore, Daryl Hannah, Paul Reiser, Mercedes Ruehl, J.T. Walsh, Ben Hammer, Dick Cusack, Alan North, David Paymer, Danton Stone, Doug Yasuda, Bill Smitrovich, Paul Bates, Floyd Vivino; ***D:*** Tony Bill; ***W:*** Mitch Markowitz; ***M:*** Cliff Eidelman.

The Crazy Ray 🦴🦴🦴 *Paris Qui Dort* **1922** The classic silent fantasy about a mad scientist who endeavors to put the whole population of Paris in a trance. Vintage Clair nonsense. **60m/B VHS.** *FR* Henri Rollan, Albert Prejean, Marcel Vallee, Madeleine Rodrigue; ***D:*** Rene Clair.

Crazy Six 🦴½ **1998 (R)** In a futuristic Europe, organized crime families vie for control of the underground arms trade and the black market. **?m/C VHS, DVD.** Rob Lowe, Burt Reynolds, Ice-T, Mario Van Peebles; ***D:*** Albert Pyun.

The Crazy Stranger 🦴🦴 *Gadjo Dilo* **1998** The third film in director Gatlif's Gypsy trilogy following "Latcho Drom" and "Mondo." In order to honor his late father, Parisian Stephane (Duris) travels to Romania to track down and record the music of his father's favorite Gypsy singer. He's taken in by village headman, Isidor (Serban), whose own son has just been sent to prison. Isidor and the villagers make their living as musicians and Stephane is drawn ever deeper into their lives until tragedy forces him to make a choice. In French and Romany with subtitles. **97m/C VHS.** *FR* Romain Duris, Isidor Serban, Rona Hartner, Florin Moldovan; ***D:*** Tony Gatlif; ***W:*** Tony Gatlif; ***C:*** Eric Guichard; ***M:*** Tony Gatlif.

The Crazysitter 🦴🦴½ **1994 (PG-13)** Edie (D'Angelo), a petty thief recently released from jail, is hired as a sitter to the twins-from-hell. So, she decides to sell the little monsters. **92m/C VHS, DVD.** Beverly D'Angelo, Ed Begley Jr., Carol Kane, Phil Hartman, Brady Bluhm, Rachel Duncan, Nell Carter, Steve Landesberg; ***D:*** Michael James McDonald; ***W:*** Michael James McDonald; ***C:*** Christopher Baffa; ***M:*** David Wurst, Eric Wurst.

Creation of Adam 🦴🦴 **1993** Weirdly mystical Russian drama finds Andrey's marriage in trouble because his wife thinks he's gay. She may be right because during a business meeting, Andrey is drawn to the charasmatic Philip, who, it turns out, is some sort of angelic messenger whose mission seems to be to give Andrey confidence in love. Good performances although the plot lacks coherence and is not helped by the poor subtitling. Russian with subtitles. **93m/C VHS.** *RU* Alexander Strizhenov, Anzhelika Nevolina, Saulus Balandis, Serghei Vinogradov, Irina Metlitshkaya; ***D:*** Yuri Pavlov.

The Creation of the Humanoids woof! **1962** Set in the familiar post-holocaust future, this is a tale of humans outnumbered by androids and the resulting struggle for survival. Slow and silly low-budget sets. For some reason, Andy Warhol was reported to love this film. **84m/C VHS.** Don Megowan, Frances McCann, Erica Elliot, Don Doolittle, Dudley Manlove; ***D:*** Wesley Barry.

Creator 🦴🦴 **1985 (R)** A Frankenstein-like scientist plans to clone a being based on his wife, who died 30 years ago. As his experiments begin to show positive results, his romantic attention turns towards his beautiful lab assistant. O'Toole as the deranged scientist almost saves this one. Based on a novel by Jeremy Leven. **108m/C VHS, DVD.** Peter O'Toole, Mariel Hemingway, Vincent Spano, Virginia Madsen, David Ogden Stiers, John Dehner, Karen Kopins, Jeff Corey; ***D:*** Ivan Passer; ***W:*** Jeremy Leven; ***C:*** Robbie Greenberg; ***M:*** Sylvester Levay.

Creature 🦴 *Titan Find* **1985 (R)** A two thousand-year-old alien life form is killing off astronauts exploring the planet Titan. "Alien" rip-off has its moments, but not enough of them. Kinski provides some laughs. **97m/C VHS.** Klaus Kinski, Stan Ivar, Wendy Schaal, Lyman Ward, Annette McCarthy, Diane Salinger; ***D:*** William Malone; ***M:*** Tom Chase, Steve Rucker.

Creature from Black Lake 🦴 **1976 (PG)** Two anthropology students from Chicago travel to the Louisiana swamps searching for the creature from Black Lake. Predictably, they find him. McClenny, incidentally, is Morgan Fairchild's sister. **95m/C VHS.** Jack Elam, Dub Taylor, Dennis Fimple, John David Carson, Bill (Billy) Thurman, Catherine McClenny; ***D:*** Joy Houck Jr.

Creature from the Black Lagoon 🦴🦴🦴 **1954** An anthropological expedition in the Amazon stumbles upon the Gill-Man, a prehistoric humanoid fish monster who takes a fancy to fetching Adams, a coed majoring in "science," but the humans will have none of it. Originally filmed in 3-D, this was one of the first movies to sport top-of-the-line underwater photography and remains one of the most enjoyable monster movies ever made. Sequels: "Revenge of the Creature" and "The Creature Walks Among Us." **79m/B VHS, DVD.** Richard Carlson, Julie Adams, Richard Denning, Antonio Moreno, Whit Bissell, Nestor Paiva, Ricou Browning, Ben Chapman, Bernie Gozier; ***D:*** Jack Arnold; ***W:*** Arthur Ross, Harry Essex; ***C:*** William E. Snyder, Charles S. Welbourne; ***M:*** Hans J. Salter, Henry Mancini.

Creature from the Haunted Sea 🦴🦴 **1960** Monster movie satire set in Cuba shortly after the revolution and centering around an elaborate plan to loot the Treasury and put the blame on a strange sea monster. Corman comedy is predictably low budget but entertaining. "Wain" is really Robert Towne, winner of an Oscar for screenwriting. Remake of "Naked Paradise." **76m/B VHS.** Antony Carbone, Betsy Jones-Moreland, Beach Dickerson, Edward (Robert Towne) Wain, Edmundo Rivera Alvarez, Robert Bean, Sonya Noemi Gonzalez; ***Cameos:*** Roger Corman; ***D:*** Roger Corman, Monte Hellman; ***W:*** Charles B. Griffith; ***C:*** Jacques "Jack" Marquette; ***M:*** Fred Katz.

Creature of Destruction 🦴 **1967** A beautiful young woman is hypnotized and inadvertently reverted to her past life as a hideous sea monster. Buchanan's remake of his own 1956 production, "The She Creature." **80m/B VHS.** Les Tremayne, Aron Kincaid, Pat Delaney, Neil Fletcher, Ann McAdams, Scott McKay; ***D:*** Larry Buchanan; ***C:*** Robert C. Jessup.

Creature of the Walking Dead 🦴½ *La Marca del Muerto* **1960** Scientist brings his grandfather back to life with horrifying results for the cast and the audience. Made cheaply and quickly in Mexico in 1960, then released with added footage directed by Warren. **74m/B VHS.** *MX* Rock Madison, Ann Wells, George Todd, Willard Gross, Bruno VeSota, Rosa Maria Gallardo, Katherine Victor; ***D:*** Fernando Cortes, Jerry Warren; ***W:*** Fernando Cortes, Alfredo Varela; ***C:*** Jose Ortiz Ramos.

The Creature Walks among Us 🦴½ **1956** Sequel to "Revenge of the Creature" has the Gill-Man once again being captured by scientists for studying purposes. Through an accidental lab fire, the creature's gills are burned off and he undergoes surgery in an attempt to live out of water. Final entry in the Creature series has little magic of the original. Also shot in 3-D. **79m/B VHS.** Jeff Morrow, Rex Reason, Leigh Snowden, Gregg (Hunter) Palmer, Ricou Browning, Don Megowan, Maurice Manson, Frank Chase, Larry Hudson, Paul Fierro; ***D:*** John Sherwood; ***W:*** Arthur Ross; ***C:*** Maury Gertsman; ***M:*** Henry Mancini, Joseph Gershenson.

Creature with the Blue Hand 🦴🦴 **1970** A German horror film based on a passable Edgar Wallace story about a man unjustly convicted of murders actually committed by a lunatic. Dubbed. **92m/C VHS.** *GE* Klaus Kinski, Harald Leopold, Hermann Leschau, Diana Kerner, Carl Lange, Ilse Page; ***D:*** Alfred Vohrer.

Creatures the World Forgot woof! **1970** A British-made bomb about two tribes of cavemen warring over power and a cavewoman. No special effects, dinosaurs, or dialogue. **96m/C VHS.** Julie Ege, Robert John, Tony Bonner, Rosalie Crutchley, Sue Wilson; ***D:*** Don Chaffey; ***W:*** Michael Carreras.

The Creeper 🦴🦴 **1948** After experimenting with a variety of serums, a doctor turns into a murderous monster with feline paws. **65m/B VHS.** Eduardo Ciannelli, Onslow Stevens, June Vincent, Ralph Morgan; ***D:*** Jean Yarbrough.

Creepers 🦴🦴½ *Phenomena* **1985 (R)** A young girl talks to bugs and gets them to follow her instructions, which comes in handy when she battles the lunatic who is killing her school chums. Argento weirdness—and graphic gore—may not be for all tastes. **82m/C VHS, DVD, Wide.** *IT* Jennifer Connelly, Donald Pleasence, Daria Nicolodi, Elenora Giorgi, Dalia di Lazzaro, Patrick Bauchau, Fiore Argento, Federica Mastroianni, Michele (Michael) Soavi, Gavin Friday; ***D:*** Dario Argento; ***W:*** Dario Argento, Franco Ferrini; ***C:*** Romano Albani; ***M:*** Simon Boswell.

The Creeping Flesh 🦴🦴½ **1972 (PG)** A scientist decides he can cure evil by injecting his patients with a serum derived from the blood of an ancient corpse. Some truly chilling moments will get your flesh creeping. **89m/C VHS.** *GB* Peter Cushing, Christopher Lee, Lorna Heilbron, George Benson, Kenneth J. Warren, Duncan Lamont, Harry Locke, Hedger Wallace, Michael Ripper, Jenny Runacre; ***D:*** Freddie Francis; ***W:*** Peter Spenceley, Jonathan Rumbold; ***C:*** Norman Warwick.

Creeping Terror woof! *The Crawling Monster; Dangerous Charter* **1964** Gigantic alien carpet monster (look for the tennis shoes sticking out underneath) devours slow-moving teenagers. Partially narrated because some of the original soundtrack was lost, with lots of bad acting, a worse script, laughable sets, and a ridiculous monster. Beware of the thermometer scene. **81m/B VHS.** Vic Savage, Shannon O'Neal, William Thourlby, Louise Lawson, Robin James, Byrd Holland, Jack King, Art J. Nelson; ***D:*** Art J. Nelson; ***W:*** Robert Silliphant; ***C:*** Andrew Janczak.

Creepozoids 🦴 **1987** In the near future, a monster at an abandoned science complex stalks army deserters hiding out there. Violent nonsense done better by others. **72m/C** Linnea Quigley, Ken Abraham, Michael Aranda; ***D:*** David DeCoteau.

The Creeps 🦴🦴 **1997 (PG-13)** A horror-film obsessed scientist, Dr. Winston Berber, steals the original manuscript of Mary Shelley's "Frankenstein" and librarian Anna (Griffin) hires detective David Rawley (Lauer) to get it back. Then Berber returns to steal Bram Stoker's original "Dracula" and kidnaps Anna to use in his wacky experiment as well. He decides to reanimate his four favorite movie monsters but when David rescues Anna before the experiment is complete, Dracula (Fondacaro), the Mummy (Smith), the Wolfman (Simanton), and Frankenstein's Monster (Wellington) wind up only three feet tall. Not pleased by their diminutive size, the creeps work to restore themselves to the proper height (and cause a little mayhem as well). **80m/C VHS, DVD.** Phil Fondacaro, Rhonda Griffin, Justin Lauer, Bill Moynihan, Kristin Norton, Jon Simanton, Joe Smith, Thomas Wellington; ***D:*** Charles Band; ***W:*** Benjamin Carr; ***C:*** Adolfo Bartoli; ***M:*** Carl Dante. VIDEO

Creepshow 🦴🦴½ **1982 (R)** Stephen King's tribute to E.C. Comics, those pulp horror comic books of the 1950s that delighted in grisly, grotesque, and morbid humor. The film tells five horror tales, and features King himself in one segment, as a none-too-bright farmer who unknowingly cultivates a strange, alien-origin moss. With despicable heroes and gory monsters, this is sure to delight all fans of the horror vein. Those easily repulsed by cockroaches beware! **120m/C VHS, DVD.** Hal Holbrook, Adrienne Barbeau, Viveca Lindfors, E.G. Marshall, Stephen King, Leslie Nielsen, Carrie Nye, Fritz Weaver, Ted Danson, Ed Harris, John Amplas, Tom Savini; ***D:*** George A. Romero; ***W:*** Stephen King; ***C:*** Michael Gornick; ***M:*** John Harrison.

Creepshow 2 🦴½ **1987 (R)** Romero adapted three Stephen King stories for this horror anthology which presents gruesome looks at a hit-and-run driver, a wooden Indian, and a vacation gone wrong. Gory and childish stuff from two masters of the genre. Look for King as a truck driver. **92m/C VHS, DVD, Wide.** Lois Chiles, George Kennedy, Dorothy Lamour, Tom Savini, Domenick John, Frank S. Salsedo, Holt McCallany, David Holbrook, Page Hannah, Daniel Beer, Stephen King, Paul Satterfield, Jeremy Green, Tom Wright; ***D:*** Michael Gornick; ***W:*** George A. Romero; ***C:*** Richard Hart, Tom Hurwitz; ***M:*** Les Reed, Rick Wakeman.

Cremains 🦴🦴🦴 **2000** Anthology centers on a mortician (Chester Delacruz) who is being investigated for cremating two bodies at once. As he is questioned by an unseen panel of inquisitors, he relates three stories. In the first, a young woman (Plimmer) makes the mistake of driving through a small town famous for its ritual sacrifices. In the next story, a serial killer (Williams) captures a hitchhiker and then the mind-games begin. The third story features a woman (Cole) who seeks out the help of a horror author (Smith), as she's convinced that a female vampire is after her. The final segment returns to the mortician and the macabre results of his double-cremation. The stories are good; while they aren't incredibly original, they all have that "urban legend" feel, which makes them accessible. Howeverm the film is way too long, and all of the segments feel padded. Not perfect, but actually better than some studio horror films released lately. **107m/C DVD, Wide.** Chester Delacruz, Wanda Plimmer, Chris(topher) Williams, Kimberly Lynn Cole, R.W. Smith; ***D:*** Steve Sessions; ***W:*** Steve Sessions. VIDEO

The Cremators woof! **1972** A meteorite carrying an alien lands at a seaside resort and everyone begins bursting into flames. Low budget effort from the scripter of "It Came from Outer Space." **90m/C VHS.** Marvin Howard, Maria de Aragon; ***D:*** Harry Essex.

The Crew 🦴🦴 **1995 (R)** Sometimes it doesn't pay to be a good samaritan—as a boatload of pleasure cruisers discover when they rescue two psychopaths from a burning boat in the Bahamas. **99m/C VHS.** Viggo Mortensen, Jeremy Sisto, Pamela Gidley, Donal Logue, Laura Del Sol, Grace Zabriskie, John Philbin; ***D:*** Carl Colpaert; ***W:*** Carl Colpaert.

The Crew 🦴🦴 **2000 (PG-13)** Dreyfuss, Hedaya, Reynolds, and Cassel are a quartet of retired wiseguys who hatch a plan to save their South Beach Miami retirement home with a fake mob hit. Complications arise when the body turns out to be a South American druglord's missing father. Occasionally funny but overly plotted script was written by former "Golden Girls" writer Fanaro, and the sitcom lineage is obvious. **88m/C VHS, DVD, Wide.** Richard Dreyfuss, Burt Reynolds, Dan Hedaya, Seymour Cassel, Carrie-Anne Moss, Jennifer Tilly, Lainie Kazan, Miguel (Michael) Sandoval, Jeremy Piven, Casey Siemaszko, Matt Borlenghi, Jeremy Ratchford, Mike Moroff, Billy Jayne Young, Jose Zuniga, Louis Lombardi; ***D:*** Michael Dinner; ***W:*** Barry Fanaro; ***C:*** Juan Ruiz-Anchia; ***M:*** Steve Bartek.

Cria 🦴🦴🦴 *Cria Cuervos; Raise Ravens* **1976 (PG)** The award-winning story of a nine-year-old girl's struggle for maturity in a hostile adult world. In Spanish with English subtitles. **115m/C VHS, Wide.** *SP* Geraldine Chaplin, Ana Torrent, Conchita Perez, Maite Sanchez; ***D:*** Carlos Saura; ***W:*** Carlos Saura; ***C:*** Teodoro Escamilla; ***M:*** Federico Mompoll. Cannes '76: Grand Jury Prize.

Cricket on the Hearth 🦴🦴 **1923** An adaptation of Charles Dickens' short story about a mail carrier and his bride, who find the symbol of good luck, a cricket on the hearth, when they enter their new home. Silent with organ score. **68m/B VHS.** Paul Gerson, Virginia Brown Faire, Paul Moore, Joan Standing, Lorimer Johnston; ***D:*** Lorimer Johnston; ***W:*** Caroline Francis Cooke.

Cries and Whispers 🦴🦴🦴 *Viskingar Och Rop* **1972 (R)** As a woman dies slowly of tuberculosis, three women care for her: her two sisters, one sexually repressed, the other promiscuous, and her servant. The sisters remember family love and closeness, but are too afraid to look death in the face to aid their sister. Only the servant can touch her in her dying and only the servant believes in God and his will. Beautiful imagery, focused through a nervous camera, which lingers on the meaningless and whisks away from the meaningful. Absolute mastery of cinematic art by Bergman. **91m/C VHS, DVD, Wide.** *SW* Harriet Andersson, Ingrid Thulin, Liv Ullmann, Kary Sylway, Erland Josephson, Henning Moritzen; ***D:*** Ingmar Bergman; ***W:*** Ingmar Bergman; ***C:*** Sven Nykvist. Oscars '73: Cinematog.; Natl. Bd. of Review '73: Director (Bergman); N.Y. Film Critics '72: Actress (Ullmann), Director (Bergman), Film, Screenplay; Natl. Soc. Film Critics '72: Cinematog., Screenplay.

Cries of Silence 🦴🦴 **1997** In 1969 a teenaged girl (Buchanan) is found along a remote Mississippi island shore in the aftermath of Hurricane Camille. Young doctor Dorrie Walsh (York) brings the girl to her mother's (Black) home after the locals swear they don't know who she is and the girl herself is mute from trauma. Dorrie calls her Camille and struggles to communicate with her in the face of community opposition. It seems learning Camille's identity could reveal the truth behind more than one local secret. **109m/C VHS.** Kathleen York, Karen Black, Erin Buchanan, Ed Nelson, Ellen Crawford, Guy Boyd; ***D:*** Avery Crounse; ***W:*** Avery Crounse; ***C:*** Michael Barnard; ***M:*** Nigel Holton.

Crime & Passion 🦴½ **1975 (R)** Two scheming lovers plan to get rich by having the woman marry a multimillionaire and sue for a quick divorce. The multimillionaire is no patsy, however, and seeks a deadly revenge. Three scripts by six writers were combined to create this story. That explains the many problems. **92m/C VHS, DVD.** Omar Sharif, Karen Black, Joseph Bottoms, Bernhard Wicki; ***D:*** Ivan Passer.

Crime and Punishment 🦴🦴🦴 **1935** Pared down but well-executed version of the Dostoyevski novel. Lorre is superb as Raskolnikov, who robs and murders an elderly pawnbroker. Believing he has committed the perfect murder, he accepts the invitation of police inspector Porfiry (Arnold) to observe the investigation. Gradually Raskolnikov's conscience begins to overwhelm him as Porfiry slowly works to wring a confession from the killer. Von Sternberg's subdued directorial approach worked well to explore the psychological aspects of guilt, although the melodramatic French film version (released at the same time) scored better with the critics. **88m/B VHS.** Peter Lorre, Edward Arnold, Marian Marsh, Tala Birell, Elisabeth Risdon, Robert "Tex" Allen, Douglass Dumbrille, Gene Lockhart; ***D:*** Josef von Sternberg; ***W:*** S.K. Lauren, Joseph Anthony.

Crime and Punishment 🦴🦴🦴🦴 *Crime et Chatiment* **1935** Original French production (preceding the American version by just one week) of Dostoyevski's novel, the tale of a young murderer, his crime, and ultimately, his confession. Generally considered better than the American version, the French throw out all that is not dramatic, keeping the psychology and suspense. Remade in 1958. French with subtitles. **110m/B VHS.** Harry Baur, Pierre Blanchar, Madeleine Ozeray, Marcelle Geniat, Lucienne Lemarchand; ***D:*** Pierre Chenal; ***W:*** Marcel Ayme, Chenal, Christian Stengel, Wladimir Strijewski; ***M:*** Arthur Honegger.

Crime and Punishment 🦴🦴 **1970** Ponderous, excruciatingly long adaptation of the Dostoyevski classic involving a haunted murderer and the relentless policeman who seeks to prove him guilty. In Russian with English subtitles. **200m/B VHS.** *RU* Georgi Taratorkin, Victoria Fyodorova; ***D:*** Lev Kulijanov; ***W:*** Lev Kulijanov.

Crime and Punishment in Suburbia 🦴½ **2000 (R)** Dostoyevsky heads to the mall in this suburban gloomfest very loosely based on the classic Russian novel. Roseanne (Keena) is a pretty, popular teen whose family life is screwed up beyond repair. Her father Fred (Ironside) is an abusive monster and her mother Maggie (Barkin) is a drunken floozy. She hopes that she can endure the situation until she graduates, but Fred's reaction to an affair by Maggie causes her to contemplate killing her father. With the help of her boyfriend Jimmy (DeBello), Roseanne murders her old man. When her mother is arrested for the crime and she becomes an outcast at school, she turns to mysterious classmate Vincent (Kartheiser) for solace, not knowing he's been lurking in the shadows and observing everything. The themes explored in this grim view of suburbia were better served up in "American Beauty." **98m/C VHS, DVD, Wide.** Monica Keena, Vincent Kartheiser, Ellen Barkin, Michael Ironside, Jeffrey Wright, James DeBello, Conchata Ferrell, Marshall Teague, Brad Greenquist, Lucinda Jenney; ***D:*** Rob Schmidt; ***W:*** Larry Gross; ***C:*** Bobby Bukowski; ***M:*** Michael Brook.

Crime Broker 🦴🦴 **1994** A respected judge (Bisset) decides to experience life on the other side of the bench for a change. So she hooks up with a handsome partner to execute a series of high-profile robberies of bank vaults and museums. Implied sex so don't look for this under erotic thrillers. **93m/C VHS, DVD.** Jacqueline Bisset, Masaya Kato, Gary Day; ***D:*** Ian Barry; ***W:*** Tony Morphett; ***C:*** Dan Burstall; ***M:*** Roger Mason.

Crime Busters 🦴½ **1978 (PG)** Two guys attempt to pull off a bank heist but accidentally join the Miami police force instead. Hill and Spencer are enjoyable as usual but the film suffers from poor dubbing. Remake of "Two Supercops." **114m/C VHS.** *IT* Terence Hill, Bud Spencer, Laura Gemser, Luciana Catenacci, David Huddleston; ***D:*** E.B. (Enzo Barboni) Clucher.

Crime Killer 🦴 **1985** Confusing shenanigans about an explosive ex-CIA agent enlisted by the FBI to battle a brutal crime syndicate shipping guns to nasty Arabs. **90m/C VHS.** George Pan-Andreas, Leo Morrell, Althan Karras; ***D:*** George Pan-Andreas; ***C:*** Arledge Armenaki.

Crime Lords 🦴🦴 **1991 (R)** When a pair of cops are suspended from the force for committing a blunder, they travel to Hong Kong to continue their investigation. Little do they know their sleuthing has drawn then into a confrontation with one of largest crime syndicates in the world. Lots of action, beautiful women, and exotic locations keep this basic buddy plot moving well. **96m/C VHS.** Wayne Crawford, Martin Hewitt, Susan Byun, Mel Castelo, James Hong; ***D:*** Wayne Crawford.

The Crime of Dr. Crespi 🦴🦴 **1935** A doctor takes his revenge on a man who is after his girlfriend by injecting him with suspended animation serum. Extremely campy performance from von Stroheim; Frye's biggest role in terms of screen time. **64m/B VHS.** Erich von Stroheim, Dwight Frye, Paul Guilfoyle, Harriett Russell, John Bohn; ***D:*** John H. Auer.

Crime of Honor 🦴 **1985** A European executive goes public with his company's corruption, and his family suffers predictable ruin as a result. Based on a true story. **95m/C VHS.** Maria Schneider, David Suchet; ***D:*** John Goldschmidt.

The Crime of Monsieur Lange 🦴🦴🦴 *Le Crime de Monsieur Lange* **1936** Charming French socialist fantasy where workers at a publishing company turn the business into a thriving cooperative while their evil boss is gone. When he returns, worker Lefevre plots to kill him. Rather talky, but humorous. In French with subtitles. French script booklet also available. **90m/B VHS.** *FR* Rene Lefevre, Jules Berry, Florelle, Sylvia Bataille, Jean Daste, Nadia Sibirskaia, Henri Guisol; ***D:*** Jean Renoir; ***W:*** Jean Renoir, Jacques Prevert; ***C:*** Jean Bachelet; ***M:*** Jean Wiener, Joseph Kosma.

Crime of Passion 🦴🦴½ **1957** Stanwyck plays a femme fatale whose ambitions for detective hubby lead to murder. Good performances from Stanwyck, Hayden, and Burr make this an above-average, although outlandish, crime-drama. **85m/B VHS.** Barbara Stanwyck, Sterling Hayden, Raymond Burr, Fay Wray, Royal Dano, Virginia Grey, Dennis Cross, Robert E. (Bob) Griffin, Jay Adler, Malcolm Atterbury, S. John Launer, Brad Trumbull, Skipper McNally, Jean Howell, Peg La Centra, Nancy Reynolds, Marjorie Owens, Robert Quarry, Joe Conley, Stuart Whitman; ***D:*** Gerd Oswald; ***W:*** Jo Eisinger; ***C:*** Joseph LaShelle; ***M:*** Paul Dunlap.

Crime of the Century 🦴🦴½ **1996 (PG-13)** Another look at the 1932 kidnapping and death of Charles Lindbergh's 18-month-old son. Based on the 1985 book "The Airman and the Carpenter" by Ludovic Kennedy, it's clear the author regards Bruno Richard Hauptmann (Rea), who was executed in 1936, as an innocent scapegoat essentially railroaded thanks to media and political pressures. **116m/C VHS.** Stephen Rea, J.T. Walsh, David Paymer, John Harkins, Michael Moriarty, Isabella Rossellini, Bert Remsen, Allen (Goorwitz) Garfield, Don Harvey, Gerald S. O'Loughlin, Barry Primus; ***D:*** Mark Rydell; ***W:*** William Nicholson; ***C:*** Toyomichi Kurita; ***M:*** John (Gianni) Frizzell. CABLE

Crime Story 🦴🦴 *Hard to Die* **1993 (R)** Police Inspector Eddie Chan (Chan) tries to crack a kidnapping case and discovers his partner, Detective Hung (Cheng), is not on the up-and-up. Usual arobatic stunts from Chan and company. Cantonese with subtitles. **104m/C VHS, DVD, Wide.** *HK* Jackie Chan, Kent Cheng, Law Hang Kang, Christine Ng; *D:* Kirk Wong; *C:* Arthur Wong, Ardy Lam.

Crime Zone 🦴🦴½ **1988 (R)** In a totalitarian, repressive, future society, two young lovers try to beat the system and make it on their own. A well-made, if occasionally muddled, low-budget film shot in Peru, of all places. **96m/C VHS.** David Carradine, Peter Nelson, Sherilyn Fenn, Orlando Sacha, Don Manor, Michael Shaner; *D:* Luis Llosa; *W:* Daryl Haney; *M:* Rick Conrad.

Crimebusters 🦴½ **1979 (PG)** A man exacts revenge against a government conspiracy that kidnapped his loved ones. **90m/C VHS.** Henry Silva, Antonio (Tony) Sabato; *D:* Michael Tarantini.

Crimes & Misdemeanors 🦴🦴🦴 **1989 (PG-13)** One of Allen's most mature films, exploring a whole range of moral ambiguities through the parallel and eventually interlocking stories of a nebbish filmmaker—who agrees to make a profile of a smug Hollywood TV comic and then sabotages it—and an esteemed ophthalmologist who is being threatened with exposure by his neurotic mistress. Intriguing mix of drama and comedy few directors could pull off. Look for Daryl Hannah in an unbilled cameo. **104m/C VHS, DVD, Wide.** Martin Landau, Woody Allen, Alan Alda, Mia Farrow, Joanna Gleason, Anjelica Huston, Jerry Orbach, Sam Waterston, Claire Bloom, Jenny Nichols, Caroline Aaron, Daryl Hannah, Nora Ephron, Jerry Zaks; *D:* Woody Allen; *W:* Woody Allen; *C:* Sven Nykvist. Natl. Bd. of Review '89: Support. Actor (Alda); N.Y. Film Critics '89: Support. Actor (Alda); Writers Guild '89: Orig. Screenplay.

Crimes at the Dark House 🦴🦴🦴 **1939** In this campy, melodramatic adaptation of Wilkie Collins's novel "The Woman in White," a man kills his rich wife and puts a disguised mental patient in her place. Later remade using the book's title. **69m/B VHS.** *GB* Tod Slaughter, Hilary Eaves, Sylvia Marriott, Hay Petrie, Geoffrey Wardwell; *D:* George King.

Crimes of Dr. Mabuse 🦴🦴🦴½ *The Testament of Dr. Mabuse; The Last Will of Dr. Mabuse* **1932** Supernatural horror classic about the evil Dr. Mabuse controlling an underworld empire while confined to an insane asylum. The third, and only sound, Mabuse film by Lang. German with subtitles. **120m/B VHS.** *GE* Rudolf Klein-Rogge, Otto Wernicke, Gustav Diesl, Karl Meixner; *D:* Fritz Lang.

Crimes of Passion 🦴🦴🦴 **1984** Vintage whacked-out Russell, not intended for the kiddies. A business-like fashion designer becomes a kinky prostitute at night. A disturbed street preacher makes her the heroine of his erotic fantasies. A dark terrifying vision of the underground sex world and moral hypocrisy. Sexually explicit and violent, with an extremely black comedic center. Turner's portrayal is honest and believable, Perkins overacts until he nearly gets a nosebleed, but it's all for good effect. Cut for "R" rating to get it in the theatres; this version restores some excised footage. Also available in rated version. **101m/C VHS, DVD.** Kathleen Turner, Anthony Perkins, Annie Potts, John Laughlin, Bruce Davison, Norman Burton; *D:* Ken Russell; *W:* Barry Sandler; *C:* Dick Bush; *M:* Rick Wakeman. L.A. Film Critics '84: Actress (Turner).

The Crimes of Stephen Hawke 🦴🦴 *Strangler's Morgue* **1936** The world knows Stephen Hawke as a big-hearted money lender. What they don't know is his favorite hobby is breaking peoples' spines. An entertaining thriller set in the 1800s. **65m/B VHS.** *GB* Tod Slaughter, Marjorie Taylor, D.J. Williams, Eric Portman, Ben Soutten; *D:* George King.

Crimes of the Heart 🦴🦴½ **1986 (PG-13)** Based on Beth Henley's acclaimed play. A few days in the lives of three very strange Southern sisters, one of whom has just been arrested for calmly shooting her husband after he chased her black lover out of town. Spacek as the suicidal sister is a lark. A tart, black comedy that works better as a play than a film. **105m/C VHS.** Sissy Spacek, Diane Keaton, Jessica Lange, Sam Shepard, Tess Harper, Hurd Hatfield; *D:* Bruce Beresford; *W:* Beth Henley; *C:* Dante Spinotti; *M:* Georges Delerue. Golden Globes '87: Actress—Mus./Comedy (Spacek); N.Y. Film Critics '86: Actress (Spacek).

Crimetime 🦴½ **1996 (R)** Silly thriller has actor Bobby (Baldwin) finding unexpected success portraying a serial killer in a crime re-enactment TV show called "Crimetime." Meanwhile, Sydney (Postlethwaite), who's the real killer Bobby's character is based on, becomes seduced by the media frenzy surrounding the crimes and seeing them re-enacted on television. He goes on killing, so the show can literally go on. **118m/C VHS.** Stephen Baldwin, Pete Postlethwaite, Sadie Frost, Geraldine Chaplin, Karen Black, James Faulkner; *Cameos:* Marianne Faithfull; *D:* George Sluizer; *W:* Brendan Somers; *C:* Jules Van Den Steenhoven.

Crimewave 🦴🦴 *The XYZ Murders; Broken Hearts and Noses* **1985 (PG-13)** Zany spoof about serial killers set in Detroit (director Raimi's hometown). A rhapsody to comic book style, short on plot and long on style. With such credentials you expect more. **83m/C VHS.** Louise Lasser, Paul Smith, Brion James, Bruce Campbell, Reed Birney, Sheree J. Wilson, Edward R. Pressman, Julius W. Harris, Antonio Fargas, Sean Farley, Frances McDormand, Theodore (Ted) Raimi; *D:* Sam Raimi; *W:* Ethan Coen, Joel Coen, Sam Raimi; *C:* Robert Primes; *M:* Joseph LoDuca, Arlon Ober.

Criminal Act 🦴½ *Tunnels* **1988** A newspaper editor hits the street to prove she's still a tough reporter, but uncovers a dangerous scandal in the process. **94m/C VHS, DVD.** Catherine Bach, Charlene Dallas, Nicholas Guest, John Saxon, Vic Tayback; *D:* Mark Byers.

Criminal Code 🦴🦴½ **1931** Aging melodrama about a young man who's jailed for killing in self-defense. His life worsens at the hands of a prison warden when the head guy's daughter falls for him. Remade as "Penitentiary" and "Convicted." **98m/B VHS.** Walter Huston, Phillips Holmes, Boris Karloff, Constance Cummings, Mary Doran, DeWitt Jennings, John Sheehan; *D:* Howard Hawks.

Criminal Court 🦴🦴 **1946** A man accused of murdering his blackmailer hires the real killer as his attorney. Hard to follow, with an interesting premise that turns flat. **63m/B VHS.** Tom Conway, Martha O'Driscoll, Robert Armstrong, Addison Richards, June Clayworth, Pat Gleason, Steve Brodie; *D:* Robert Wise.

Criminal Hearts 🦴🦴 **1995 (R)** Keli (Locane) is driving to Phoenix when she picks up the hitchhiking Rafe (Dillon), who's just robbed a gas station. Turns out the stations are laundering mob drug money and when the store owners are killed, Rafe gets the blame for the murders as well. The killers are actually corrupt FBI agents Martin (Walsh) and Tierney (McDonald) who are soon of the trail of the twosome. **92m/C VHS.** Kevin Dillon, Amy Locane, Morgan Fairchild, M. Emmet Walsh, Michael James McDonald, Don Stroud; *D:* Dave Payne; *W:* Dave Payne; *C:* Christopher Baffa.

Criminal Justice 🦴🦴🦴 **1990 (R)** A black man is accused of a crime by a woman with whom he was involved. Is it justice or revenge? Strong cast in important story. **92m/C VHS.** Forest Whitaker, Jennifer Grey, Rosie Perez, Anthony LaPaglia, Tony Todd; *D:* Andy Wolk; *W:* Andy Wolk; *C:* Steven Fierberg. **CABLE**

Criminal Law 🦴🦴 **1989 (R)** An ambitious young Boston lawyer gets a man acquitted for murder, only to find out after the trial that the man is guilty and renewing his killing spree. Realizing he's the only one privy to the killer's trust, the lawyer decides to stop him himself. A white-knuckled thriller burdened by a weak script. **113m/C VHS.** Kevin Bacon, Gary Oldman, Karen Young, Joe Don Baker, Tess Harper; *D:* Martin Campbell; *W:* Mark Kasden; *C:* Phil Meheux; *M:* Jerry Goldsmith.

The Criminal Life of Archibaldo de la Cruz 🦴🦴🦴 *Ensayo de un Crimen; Rehearsal for a Crime* **1955** Seeing the death of his governess has a lasting effect on a boy. He grows up to be a demented cretin whose failure with women leads him to conspire to kill every one he meets, a task at which he also fails. Hilarious, bitter Bunuelian diatribe. In Spanish with English subtitles. **95m/B VHS.** *MX SP* Ernesto Alonso, Ariadne Welter, Rita Macedo, Rodolfo Landa, Andrea Palma, Miroslava Stern; *D:* Luis Bunuel; *W:* Luis Bunuel; *C:* Augustin Jimenez; *M:* Jorge Perez.

The Criminal Mind 🦴🦴 **1993 (R)** L.A. District Attorney Nick August (Rossi) reunites with his long-lost brother (Cross), whom he discovers is very familiar with the other side of the law. Tied up with the mob, Cross forces his bro to watch a hit and then Rossi winds up the next target for a group of assassins and some corrupt cops. **93m/C VHS.** Ben Cross, Frank Rossi, Tahnee Welch, Lance Henriksen, Joseph Ruskin, Lynn-Holly Johnson; *D:* Joseph Vittorie; *W:* Sam A. Scribner.

Criminally Insane 🦴 **1975** Authorities release 250 pounds of cleaver-wielding maniacal fury from the loony bin. She seeks food and human blood. They should have known better. Followed by "Crazy Fat Ethel II." **61m/C VHS.** Priscilla Alden, Michael Flood; *D:* Nick (Steve Millard) Phillips.

Criminals Within 🦴 *Army Mystery* **1941** A scientist working on a top secret formula is murdered and a detective tries to nail the spy ring responsible. Very confusing, poor usage of some fine female cast members. **67m/B VHS.** Eric Linden, Ann Doran, Constance Worth, Donald Curtis, Weldon Heyburn, Ben Alexander; *D:* Joseph H. Lewis.

The Crimson Code 🦴½ **1999 (R)** FBI agents Chandler (Muldoon) and Dobson (Moriarty) discover a serial killer who goes after other serial killers. Then Chandler is offered a chance to circumvent that pesky legal thing by joining a covert ops that takes retribution as it sees fit. Just one cliche after another. **90m/C VHS, DVD.** Patrick Muldoon, Cathy Moriarty, C. Thomas Howell, Fred Ward, Tim Thomerson; *D:* Jeremy Haft; *W:* Alex Metcalf; *C:* Ian Elkin; *M:* Ken Williams. **VIDEO**

The Crimson Cult 🦴 *The Crimson Altar; Curse of the Crimson Altar* **1968 (PG)** Eden and his girlfriend are invited to a mysterious mansion. They discover that Lee is out to enact revenge as his ancestor was burned for witchcraft by Eden's. An all-star horror disaster. Karloff was 80 and confined to a wheelchair. Despite ads claiming this as his last film, he made four more in Mexico. Highlights include the scantily clad Steele in sado-masochistic sequences and a psychedelic party with strippers and body painters. **87m/C VHS.** *GB* Boris Karloff, Christopher Lee, Mark Eden, Barbara Steele, Virginia Wetherell, Michael Gough, Rupert Davies; *D:* Vernon Sewell.

Crimson Pirate 🦴🦴🦴½ **1952** An 18th-century buccaneer pits his wits and brawn against the might of a ruthless Spanish nobleman. Considered by many to be one of the best swashbucklers, laced with humor and enthusiastically paced. Showcase for Lancaster and Cravat's acrobatic talents. **104m/C VHS.** *GB* Burt Lancaster, Eva Bartok, Torin Thatcher, Christopher Lee, Nick Cravat; *D:* Robert Siodmak.

The Crimson Rivers 🦴🦴 *Les Rivieres Pourpres* **2001 (R)** Audacious and gruesome thriller set in the French Alps. A librarian from the local private university is found horribly mutilated on a mountain slope and Parisian investigator Pierre Niemans (Reno) is called in. Before long, there's more than one victim, all of whom have ties to the university, and Niemans has a young, aggressive partner in provincial policeman Max Kerkerian (Cassel). French with subtitles or dubbed. **105m/C VHS, DVD, Wide.** *FR* Jean Reno, Vincent Cassel, Nadia Fares, Dominique Sanda, Laurent Avare, Jean-Pierre Cassel, Didier Flamand; *D:* Mathieu Kassovitz; *W:* Mathieu Kassovitz, Jean-Christophe Grange; *C:* Thierry Arbogast; *M:* Bruno Coulais.

Crimson Romance 🦴🦴 **1934** Two unemployed American pilots in Europe decide to join the German airforce for want of anything better to do. Conflicts revolve around a warmongering Commandant and his pilot. **70m/B VHS, 8mm.** Ben Lyon, Sari Maritza, James Bush, Erich von Stroheim, Jason Robards Sr., Herman Bing, Vince Barnett; *D:* David Howard.

Crimson Tide 🦴🦴🦴 **1995 (R)** Mutiny erupts aboard the submarine USS Alabama as Captain Ramsey (Hackman) and his Executive Officer Hunter (Washington) clash over the validity of orders to launch the sub's missiles. Ramsey, who wants to fire the missiles, and Hunter, who refuses to comply until the message is verified, battle for control of the sub. Suspenseful and well-paced thriller lets Hackman and Washington show off their considerable screen presence, while Bruckheimer, Simpson, and Scott show that they haven't lost any of their trademark big-budget, testosterone-laden flash. Original screenplay went under the knife of a number of script doctors, most notably Quentin Tarantino. **116m/C VHS, DVD.** Gene Hackman, Denzel Washington, George Dzundza, Viggo Mortensen, James Gandolfini, Matt Craven, Lillo Brancato, Danny Nucci, Steve Zahn, Rick Schroder, Vanessa Bell Calloway, Rocky Carroll; *Cameos:* Jason Robards Jr.; *D:* Tony Scott; *W:* Michael Schiffer, Richard P. Henrick; *C:* Darius Wolski; *M:* Hans Zimmer.

The Crimson Trail 🦴🦴½ **1935** Buck believes his uncle may be involved in cattle rustling. Lots of action, minimal plot. **56m/B VHS.** Buck Jones, Polly Ann Young, Carl Stockdale, Charles French, Ward Bond, Robert F. (Bob) Kortman, Bud Osborne, Charles Brinley, Robert Walker; *D:* Al Raboch; *W:* Jack Natteford.

The Crippled Masters 🦴🦴 **1982 (R)** After Li Ho's (Shum) arms are cut off by an evil warlord, he wanders the countryside facing ridicule until he teams up with disfigured Dax Oh Jen (Conn). Helped by an elderly yoga master, the duo unite to seek revenge. Features kung-fu masters with real-life disabilities. **90m/C VHS.** Frankie Shum, Jack Conn; *D:* Joe Law.

Crisis at Central High 🦴🦴🦴 **1980** A dramatic re-creation of the events leading up to the 1957 integration of Central High in Little Rock, Arkansas. Based on teacher Elizabeth Huckaby's journal. Emmy-nominated performance by Woodward as Huckaby. **120m/C VHS.** Joanne Woodward, Charles Durning, William Ross, Henderson Forsythe; *D:* Lamont Johnson; *M:* Billy Goldenberg. **TV**

Criss Cross 🦴🦴🦴 **1948** A classic grade-B film noir, in which an armored car driver is suckered into a burglary by his ex-wife and her hoodlum husband. Multiple back-stabbings and double-crossings ensue. **98m/B VHS.** Burt Lancaster, Yvonne De Carlo, Dan Duryea, Stephen McNally, Richard Long, Tony Curtis; *D:* Robert Siodmak; *W:* Daniel Fuchs; *M:* Miklos Rozsa.

Crisscross 🦴🦴½ *Alone Together* **1992 (R)** It's 1969 and Tracy Cross is a divorced mom whose ex-husband is a traumatized Vietnam vet who has left her alone to raise their 12 year-old son Chris during some hard times. She works two jobs, as a waitress and, unbeknownst to her son, as a stripper in a local club. When Chris sneaks into the club and sees her act he takes drastic measures to help out—by selling drugs. Film is sluggish and relies too much on voice-overs to explain thoughts but Hawn gives a convincing and restrained performance as the mother. **107m/C VHS.** Goldie Hawn, David Arnott, Arliss Howard, James Gammon, Keith Carradine, J.C. Quinn, Steve Buscemi, Paul Calderon; *D:* Chris Menges; *M:* Trevor Jones.

Critical Care 🦴½ **1997 (R)** Spader is a doctor in a high-tech intensive care unit dealing with the ethics of modern health care, such as insurance scams, euthanasia, and a drunken administrator (Brooks) whose only concern is the hospital's profits. Two sisters (Sedgwick and Martindale) fight over the fate of their terminally ill, near-vegetable father. Spader finds his career on the line after bedding Sedgwick and backing her attempts to pull the plug. Given the meatiness of the subject, director Lumet could have made a much more scathing satire. Schwartz's script is lame even for a first-time effort, and the usually interesting Shawn falls horribly flat with an embarrassing bit of dialogue. Occasional laughs (this was supposed to be a dark comedy) and good performances from Brooks and Mirren can't keep this one from flatlining. Watch an episode of "ER" instead. **105m/C VHS, DVD, Wide.** James Spader, Albert Brooks, Kyra Sedgwick, Helen Mirren, Margo Martindale, Jeffrey Wright, Wallace Shawn, Anne Bancroft, Philip Bosco, Edward Herrmann, Colm Feore, James Lally, Al Waxman, Harvey Atkin; ***D:*** Sidney Lumet; ***W:*** Steven S. Schwartz; ***C:*** David Watkin; ***M:*** Michael Convertino.

Critical Choices ½ **1997 (R)** The Women's Health Clinic in Milwaukee, Wisconsin, provides safe and legal abortions. Run by Dr. Margaret Ludlow (Buckley) and her pro-choice supporter, Diana Johnson (Scarwid), the clinic becomes the focal point for right-wing evangelist Bobby Ray Flood (Kerwin) and his supporters, including Arlene Dickens (Reed). Tensions mount and violence erupts as everyone believes they're doing the right thing. **88m/C VHS.** Betty Buckley, Pamela Reed, Diana Scarwid, Terry Kinney, Brian Kerwin; ***D:*** Claudia Weill; ***W:*** Susan Cuscuna, Robin Green, Mitchell Burgess; ***M:*** Patrick Seymour. **CABLE**

Critical Condition **1986 (R)** During a blackout, a criminal masquerades as a doctor in a city hospital. Limp comedy embarrassing for Pryor. **99m/C VHS.** Richard Pryor, Rachel Ticotin, Ruben Blades, Joe Mantegna; ***D:*** Michael Apted; ***C:*** Ralf Bode; ***M:*** Alan Silvestri.

Critters ½ **1986 (PG-13)** A gang of furry, razor-toothed aliens escapes from its prison ship to Earth with their bounty hunters right behind them. They make it to a small town in Kansas where they begin to attack anything that moves. Not just a thrill-kill epic, but a sarcastic other-worldly thrill-kill epic. **86m/C VHS.** Dee Wallace Stone, M. Emmet Walsh, Billy Green Bush, Scott Grimes, Nadine Van Der Velde, Terrence Mann, Billy Zane, Don Opper; ***D:*** Stephen Herek; ***W:*** Stephen Herek, Dominic Muir; ***C:*** Tim Suhrstedt; ***M:*** David Newman.

Critters 2: The Main Course **1988 (PG-13)** Sequel to the hit horror-comedy, wherein the voracious alien furballs return in full force to Grovers Bend, Kansas, from eggs planted two years before. Occasionally inspired "Gremlins" rip. **93m/C VHS.** Scott Grimes, Liane (Alexandra) Curtis, Don Opper, Barry Corbin, Terrence Mann; ***D:*** Mick Garris; ***W:*** Mick Garris, David N. Twohy; ***C:*** Russell Carpenter.

Critters 3 **1991 (PG-13)** The not-so-loveable critters are back, terrorizing the occupants of a tenement building. **86m/C VHS.** Frances Bay, Aimee Brooks, Leonardo DiCaprio, Don Opper; ***D:*** Kristine Peterson; ***W:*** David J. Schow.

Critters 4 **1991 (PG-13)** The ghoulish critters are back, and this time a strain of genetically engineered mutant critters (what's the difference?) wants to take over the universe. **94m/C VHS.** Don Opper, Paul Whitthorne, Angela Bassett, Brad Dourif, Terrence Mann; ***D:*** Rupert Harvey; ***W:*** David J. Schow.

Crocodile woof! **1981 (R)** Giant crocodile attacks a beach town, killing and devouring dozens of people. The locals sit around trying to figure a way to stop the critter. Special effects include rear-projected croc. Lots of blood but lacking humor of "Alligator." Filmed in Thailand and Korea. **95m/C VHS.** *KN* Nat Puvanai, Tany Tim, Angela Wells, Kirk Warren; ***D:*** Sompote Sands.

Crocodile ½ **2000 (R)** Cheesy special effects doom this low-budget horror. College students spend spring break on a houseboat and are terrorized by a giant crocodile who regards them as a new snack food. **94m/C VHS, DVD, Wide.** Chris Solari, Mark McLaughlin, Caitlin Martin, Julie Mintz, Sommer Knight; ***D:*** Tobe Hooper; ***W:*** Michael D. Weiss, Adam Gierasch, Jace Anderson; ***C:*** Eliot Rockett. **VIDEO**

Crocodile Dundee ½ **1986 (PG-13)** New York reporter Sue Charlton (Kozlowski) is assigned to the Outback to interview living legend Mike Dundee (Hogan). When she finally locates the man, she is so taken with him that she brings him back to New York with her. There, the naive Aussie wanders about, amazed at the wonders of the city and unwittingly charming everyone he comes in contact with, from high-society transvestites to street hookers. One of the surprise hits of 1986. **98m/C VHS, DVD, 8mm.** *AU* Paul Hogan, Linda Kozlowski, John Meillon, David Gulpilil, Mark Blum; ***D:*** Peter Faiman; ***W:*** John Cornell, Paul Hogan; ***C:*** Russell Boyd; ***M:*** Peter Best. Golden Globes '87: Actor—Mus./Comedy (Hogan).

Crocodile Dundee 2 ½ **1988 (PG)** In this sequel Mike Dundee, the loveable rube, returns to his native Australia looking for new adventure, having "conquered" New York City. He finds trouble when Colombian drug lords kidnap his woman (Kozlowski again) and later track the couple to the Australian Outback. Lacks the charm and freshness of the first film. **110m/C VHS, DVD, Wide.** Stephen (Steve) Root, Jace Alexander, Luis Guzman, Colin Quinn, Paul Hogan, Linda Kozlowski, Kenneth Welsh, John Meillon, Ernie Dingo, Juan Fernandez, Charles S. Dutton; ***D:*** John Cornell; ***W:*** Paul Hogan; ***C:*** Russell Boyd; ***M:*** Peter Best.

Crocodile Dundee in Los Angeles ½ **2001 (PG)** Mick is back, for no good reason other than Hogan and Kozlowski probably needed the dough. The happy couple return to the States so Sue (Kozlowski) can investigate a movie studio that may be involved in a smuggling ring and, even worse, keeps cranking out dumb sequels. Where DO they come up with these ideas? Meanwhile, Dundee introduces their son (Cockburn) to life in the big city while working as an extra on the suspicious studio lot. It looks and feels like a real movie, but something's missing. What is it? Hmmmmm......Oh, yeah! A point! Unless the previous two installments left too many unanswered questions, you can probably skip this one. **95m/C VHS, DVD, Wide.** Paul Hogan, Linda Kozlowski, Jere Burns, Jonathan Banks, Paul Rodriguez, Alec Wilson, Serge Cockburn, Aida Turturro, Kaitlin Hopkins; ***Cameos:*** Mike Tyson; ***D:*** Simon Wincer; ***W:*** Matthew Berry, Eric Abrams; ***C:*** David Burr; ***M:*** Basil Poledouris.

The Crocodile Hunter: Collision Course **2002 (PG)** Crazy Aussie Steve Irwin takes his "The Crocodile Hunter" TV shtick to the big screen. Croc Graham swallows a top secret U.S. satellite beacon and Irwin thinks the agents who are sent to recover it are actually poachers. Not yet reviewed. **?m/C VHS.** Steve Irwin, Terri Irwin, Magda Szubanski, David Wenham; ***D:*** John Stainton; ***W:*** Holly Goldberg Sloan.

Crocodile Tears **1998** Gay art teacher Simon (Sod) makes a devil's bargain (literally) when he learns he's HIV-positive. Sinister Mr. Cheseboro (Salyers) offers the gift of health if Simon will become a straight stand-up comic who specializes in racist, sexist, and homophobic humor. Simon becomes a huge success but can he live with the consequences? Outrageous if heavy-handed. **84m/C VHS.** Ted Sod, William Salyers, Dan Savage, Jeanne L. Klein; ***D:*** Ann Coppel; ***W:*** Ted Sod.

Crocodiles in Amsterdam *Krokodillen in Amsterdam* **1989** Lunatic girl-meets-girl movie about flighty Gino and would-be terrorist Nina who team up to rob Gino's rich uncle. Dutch with subtitles. **88m/C VHS.** *NL* Joan Nederlof, Yolanda Entius; ***D:*** Annette Apon; ***W:*** Yolanda Entius, Annette Apon.

Cromwell ½ **1970 (G)** A lavish British-made spectacle about the conflict between Oliver Cromwell and Charles I, and the British Civil War. History is twisted as Cromwell becomes the liberator of the oppressed. Harris gives a commanding performance and the battle scenes are stunners. **139m/C VHS.** *GB* Richard Harris, Alec Guinness, Robert Morley, Frank Finlay, Patrick Magee, Timothy Dalton; ***D:*** Ken Hughes; ***W:*** Ken Hughes; ***C:*** Geoffrey Unsworth. Oscars '70: Costume Des.

Cronos *Chronos* **1994 (R)** Stylish Mexican variation of the vampire tale. Aged antiques dealer Jesus Gris (Luppi) comes across the mysterious title object—a 14th century golden egg possessing magical powers to grant eternal life. But can its possessor stand the consequences, which include a developing taste for blood? Another problem is Gris isn't the only one to know about the device. First feature for writer/director del Toro. Spanish with subtitles. **92m/C VHS, DVD.** *MX* Federico Luppi, Ron Perlman, Claudio Brook, Tamara Shanath, Margarita Isabel; ***D:*** Guillermo del Toro; ***W:*** Guillermo del Toro; ***C:*** Guillermo Navarro; ***M:*** Javier Alvarez.

The Crooked Circle ½ **1932** More comedy than mystery as slapstick policeman Gleason goes under cover as a swami. Not helped at all by a weak script and poor photography. **68m/B VHS.** Ben Lyon, ZaSu Pitts, James Gleason, C. Henry Gordon, Raymond Hatton, Roscoe Karns; ***D:*** H. Bruce Humberstone.

Crooked Hearts **1991 (R)** Dysfunctional family drama means well but lays it on too thick, as a father/son rivalry threatens to sunder the tight-knit Warrens. Based on a novel by Robert Boswell. **113m/C VHS.** Peter Coyote, Jennifer Jason Leigh, Peter Berg, Cindy Pickett, Vincent D'Onofrio, Noah Wyle, Juliette Lewis, Wendy Gazelle, Marg Helgenberger; ***D:*** Michael Bortman; ***W:*** Michael Bortman; ***C:*** Tak Fujimoto; ***M:*** Mark Isham.

Crooked Trail **1936** A lawman and bad guy become friends. **58m/B VHS.** Johnny Mack Brown, John Merton, Lucille Browne; ***D:*** S. Roy Luby; ***W:*** George Plympton.

Crooklyn **1994 (PG-13)** Director Lee turns from the life of Malcolm X to the early lives of Generation X in this profile of an African-American middle-class family growing up in 1970s Brooklyn. Lee's least politically charged film to date is a joint effort between him and sibs Joie and Cinque, and profiles the only girl in a family of five children coming of age. Tender and real performances from all, especially newcomer Harris, propel the sometimes messy, music-laden trip to nostalgia land. **112m/C VHS, DVD, Wide.** Alfre Woodard, Delroy Lindo, Zelda Harris, David Patrick Kelly, Carlton Williams, Sharif Rashed, Tse-March Washington, Christopher Knowings, Jose Zuniga, Isaiah Washington IV, Ivelka Reyes, N. Jeremi Duru, Frances Foster, Norman Matlock, Patriece Nelson, Joie Lee, Vondie Curtis-Hall, Tiasha Reyes, Spike Lee; ***D:*** Spike Lee; ***W:*** Joie Lee, Cinque Lee; ***C:*** Arthur Jaffa; ***M:*** Terence Blanchard.

Crooks & Coronets ½ *Sophie's Place* **1969 (PG)** Two-bit crooks plot to rob the country estate of an eccentric British dowager. **106m/C VHS.** *GB* Cesar Romero, Telly Savalas, Warren Oates, Edith Evans; ***D:*** James O'Connolly.

The Cross & the Switchblade ½ **1972 (PG)** An idealistic priest tries to bring the message of religion to the members of a vicious street gang. They don't wanna listen. Spanish language version available. **105m/C VHS.** Pat Boone, Erik Estrada, Jackie Giroux, Jo-Ann Robinson; ***D:*** Don Murray.

Cross Country ½ **1983 (R)** Action revolves around the brutal murder of a call girl, with initial suspicion falling on a TV advertising director involved with the woman. The story twists and turns from the suspect to investigating detective Ironside without becoming particularly interesting. **95m/C VHS.** *CA* Richard Beymer, Nina Axelrod, Michael Ironside; ***D:*** Paul Lynch; ***W:*** Logan N. Danforth.

Cross Creek ½ **1983 (PG)** Based on the life of Marjorie Kinnan Rawlings, author of "The Yearling," who, after 10 years as a frustrated reporter/writer, moves to the remote and untamed Everglades. There she meets colorful local characters and receives the inspiration to write numerous bestsellers. Well acted though overtly sentimental at times. **120m/C VHS, DVD, Wide.** Mary Steenburgen, Rip Torn, Peter Coyote, Dana Hill, Alfre Woodard, Malcolm McDowell; ***D:*** Martin Ritt; ***W:*** Dalene Young; ***C:*** John A. Alonzo; ***M:*** Leonard Rosenman.

Cross Examination ½ **1932** A boy is charged with his father's murder, and a defense attorney struggles to acquit him. **61m/B VHS.** H.B. Warner, Sally Blane, Sarah Padden; ***D:*** Richard Thorpe; ***W:*** Arthur Hoerl; ***C:*** M.A. Anderson.

Cross Mission **1989 (R)** Predictable actioner about a photographer and a soldier who are captured by the enemy. Packed with a bit of ninja, ammo, and occult. **90m/C VHS.** Richard Randall; ***D:*** Al (Alfonso Brescia) Bradley.

Cross My Heart **1988 (R)** Light comedy about two single people with complicated, post-divorce lives who go on a date and suffer accordingly. Will true love prevail? **91m/C VHS.** Martin Short, Annette O'Toole, Paul Reiser, Joanna (Joanna DeVarona) Kerns; ***D:*** Armyan Bernstein; ***W:*** Armyan Bernstein; ***M:*** Bruce Broughton.

Cross My Heart **1991** A group of school children conspire to hide the death of one of the group's mothers. This will prevent his placement in the state orphanage. Interesting premise is blandly treated by Fansten. Child actors don't seem realistic, photography is without flair. In French with English subtitles. **?m/C VHS.** *FR* Sylvain Copans; ***D:*** Jacques Fansten.

Cross My Heart and Hope to Die *Ti Kniver I Hjertet* **1994** Young Otto (Garfalk) is an average misfit kid until he comes to the attention of the mischief-making Frank (Kornstad), who is the catalyst for Otto to get into all kinds of trouble. Based on the novel by Lars Saaby Christensen. Norwegian with subtitles. **96m/C VHS, DVD, Wide.** *NO* Martin Dahl Garfalk, Jan Devo Kornstad; ***D:*** Marius Holst; ***W:*** Marius Holst; ***C:*** Philip Ogaard; ***M:*** Kjetil Bjerkestrand, Magne Furuholmen.

Cross of Iron ½ *Steiner—Das Eiserne Kreuz* **1976 (R)** During WWII, two antagonistic German officers clash over personal ideals as well as strategy in combatting the relentless Russian attack. Followed by "Breakthrough." **120m/C VHS, DVD.** *GB GE* James Coburn, Maximilian Schell, James Mason, David Warner, Senta Berger, Klaus Lowitsch, Vadim Glowna, Roger Fritz, Dieter Schidor, Burkhard Driest, Fred Stillkrauth, Michael Nowka, Veronique Vendell, Arthur Brauss; ***D:*** Sam Peckinpah; ***W:*** Julius J. Epstein, Walter Kelley, James Hamilton; ***C:*** John Coquillon; ***M:*** Ernest Gold.

Crossbar **1979** Aaron Kornylo is determined to reach Olympic qualifications in the high jump despite having only one leg. Inspired by a true story, this program dramatically shows how far determination and work can take a person. **77m/C VHS.** John Ireland, Brent Carver, Kate Reid; ***D:*** John Trent.

Crosscut **1995 (R)** Mob hitman Martin Niconi (Mandylor) makes a mistake that could cost him his life when a barroom brawl leads him to shooting the son of a Mafia don. He escapes to a small California logging town, changes his identity, and falls for single mom Anna (Gallagher) but the mob manages to track him down. Big shootout. **90m/C VHS.** Costas Mandylor, Megan Gallagher, Casey Sander, Allen (Cutter) Cutler, Zack Norman, George Murdock; ***D:*** Paul Raimondi; ***W:*** Paul Raimondi, David Masiel, Scott Phillips; ***C:*** David Bridges; ***M:*** Christopher Tyng.

Crossfire ½ **1947** A Jewish hotel guest is murdered and three soldiers just back from Europe are suspected of the crime. The first Hollywood film that explored racial bigotry. Due to the radical nature of its plot, the director and the producer were eventually black-listed for promoting "un-American" themes. Loosely based on Richard Brooks' "The Brick Foxhole." **86m/B VHS.** Robert Young, Robert Mitchum, Robert Ryan, Gloria Grahame, Paul Kelly; ***D:*** Edward Dmytryk.

Crossfire *The Bandit* **1967 (PG)** Two bandits are almost hung in the midst of the Mexican revolution. Released in the U.S. in 1979. **82m/C VHS.** *MX* Robert Conrad, Jan-Michael Vincent, Manuel Lopez Ochoa, Roy Jenson; ***D:*** Robert Conrad, Alfredo Zacharias.

Crossfire **1989 (R)** A rescue team heads to Vietnam to pick up their MIA comrades. With no help from the government and the enemy at every turn, can they possibly succeed? **99m/C VHS.** Richard Norton, Michael Meyer, Daniel Dietrich, Don Pemrick, Eric Hahn, Wren Brown, Steve Young; ***D:*** Anthony Maharaj; ***W:*** Noah Blough.

Crossfire Trail **2001** Cowboy Rafe Covington (Selleck) promises his dying friend that he will look out for the man's wife, Ann (Madsen), and their Wyoming spread. Rafe heads to town with his sidekicks (Brimley, O'Hara, Kane) and discovers the widow is already being courted by ruthless Bruce Barkow (Harmon), who wants the ranch since there's oil on the land. Naturally, Barkow has a hired gun (Johnson) and the sheriff (Corbin) in his pocket. Accomplished cast, straight forward direction, lush scenery (it's Calgary, Alberta), and a little humor. Based on Louis L'Amour's 1954 novel. **100m/C VHS, DVD, Wide.** Tom Selleck, Virginia Madsen, Mark Harmon, Wilford Brimley, David O'Hara, Christian Kane, Barry Corbin, Brad Johnson, William Sanderson, Joanna Miles, Ken Pogue, Rex Linn; *D:* Simon Wincer; *W:* Charles Robert Carner; *C:* David Eggby; *M:* Eric Colvin. CABLE

The Crossing **1992 (R)** Powerful coming-of-age story in which Meg, a sheltered young woman, falls in love with an ambitious artist named Sam. When he decides to leave their small town to pursue his career, she turns to his best friend for comfort and companionship. However, when Sam unexpectedly returns, Meg is forced to make a choice that could drastically change all of their lives. **92m/C VHS.** *AU* Russell Crowe, Danielle Spencer, Robert Mammone; *D:* George Ogilvie; *W:* Ranald Allan; *C:* Jeff Darling; *M:* Martin Armiger.

The Crossing ½ **2000** No, General George Washington did not cross the Delaware river standing in his boat as Emanuel Leutze's famous painting shows. But this historical story is still pretty darn exciting. On Christmas Day in 1776, it seems the American Revolution is destined for failure. Washington (Daniels) has only 2000 troops left and the Continental Army has continually been defeated by the British. But Washington wants to make a final push—a surprise attack on the Hessian garrison at Trenton. Adapted by Howard Fast from his novel. **100m/C VHS.** Jeff Daniels, Roger Rees, Sebastien Roche, Steven McCarthy, John Henry Canavan, Ned Vukovic; *D:* Robert Harmon; *W:* Howard Fast. CABLE

Crossing Delancey **1988 (PG)** Jewish woman (Bozyk), in old world style, plays matchmaker to her independent 30-something granddaughter. Charming modern-day New York City fairy tale deftly manipulates cliches and stereotypes. Lovely performance from Irving as the woman whose heart surprises her. Riegert is swell playing the gentle but never wimpy suitor. Perfectly cast Bozyk was a star on the Yiddish vaudeville stage; this is her film debut. Appealing music by the Roches, with Suzzy Roche giving a credible performance as Irving's friend. Adapted for the big screen by Sandler from her play of the same name. **97m/C VHS, 8mm.** Amy Irving, Reizl Bozyk, Peter Riegert, Jeroen Krabbe, Sylvia Miles, Suzzy Roche, George Martin, John Bedford Lloyd, Rosemary Harris, Amy Wright, Claudia Silver, David Hyde Pierce; *D:* Joan Micklin Silver; *W:* Susan Sandler.

The Crossing Guard **1994 (R)** Nicholson headlines as Freddy Gale, a revenge-minded father who hunts down a drunk driver (Morse), who killed his daughter five years previous. Story focuses on dual emotions of the two men: Gale seeks an end to his grief and rage; Booth attempts to deal with guilt and regret. Writer Penn pairs one-time lovers Nicholson and Huston (playing exspouses here) in his sophomore directorial effort with explosive results. Focus is, accordingly, on emotional performances while narrative and directorial finesse take a back seat. Dedicated to the late chronicler of the curbside, Charles Bukowski. **111m/C VHS, DVD.** Jack Nicholson, Anjelica Huston, David Morse, Robin Wright Penn, Robbie Robertson, Piper Laurie, Richard Bradford, John Savage, Priscilla Barnes, Kari Wuhrer, Jennifer Leigh Warren, Richard Sarafian, Jeff Morris, Joe (Johnny) Viterelli, Eileen Ryan, Ryo Ishibashi, Michael Ryan, Nicky Blair, Gene Kirkwood, Jason Kristofer, Hadda Brooks; *D:* Sean Penn; *W:* Sean Penn; *C:* Vilmos Zsigmond; *M:* Jack Nitzsche.

Crossing the Bridge **1992 (R)** An after high-school tale of three buddies and their restless lives as they take their uncertain steps towards adulthood. It's 1975 in Detroit and Mort, Danny, and Tim cling to high-school memories as they pass time on petty jobs, drinking, and cruising across the Ambassador Bridge to check out the Canadian strip joints. Their big moment—for better or worse—comes when they are offered the chance to make a lot of quick cash if they'll smuggle hash from Toronto to Detroit. Directorial debut of Binder. **105m/C VHS.** Josh Charles, Jason Gedrick, Stephen Baldwin, Cheryl Pollak, Jeffrey Tambor; *D:* Mike Binder; *W:* Mike Binder.

Crossing the Line **1990 (R)** Two motocross racers battle it out for the championship. **90m/C VHS.** Jon Stafford, Rick Hearst, Paul Smith, Cameron Mitchell, Vernon Wells, Colleen Morris, John Saxon; *D:* Gary Graver.

Crossover ½ **1982 (R)** A devoted male nurse works the graveyard shift in the psychiatric ward and neglects his personal life. **96m/C VHS.** James Coburn, Kate Nelligan; *D:* John Guillermin.

Crossover Dreams ½ **1985** Actor and musician Blades moves this old story along. Sure that he has at last made the international Big Time, a salsa artist becomes a self-important back-stabber after cutting an album. Great music. Blades's first film. ♫Good For Baby; Liz's Theme; Sin Fe; Todos Vuelven; Libra Timbero; Elegua; Merecumbe; Judy, Part 2; Yiri Yiri Bon. **86m/C VHS.** Ruben Blades, Shawn Elliott, Elizabeth Pena, Virgilio Marti, Tom Signorelli, Frank Robles, Joel Diamond, Amanda Barber, John Hammil; *D:* Leon Ichaso; *W:* Ruben Blades, Leon Ichaso, Manuel Arce; *M:* Mauricio Smith.

Crossroads ½ **1986 (R)** A blues-loving young white man, classically trained at Juilliard, befriends an aging black blues-master. After helping the old man escape from the nursing home, the two hop trains to the South where it's literally a duel with the devil. Fine performances by Macchio, Gertz, Seneca, and Morton. Wonderful score by Ry Cooder, with some help from Steve Vai in the final showdown. **100m/C VHS.** Ralph Macchio, Joe Seneca, Jami Gertz, Joe Morton, Robert Judd, Harry Carey Jr., Steve Vai; *D:* Walter Hill; *W:* John Fusco; *C:* John Bailey; *M:* Steve Vai, Ry Cooder.

Crossroads ½ **2002 (PG-13)** Underwhelming teen buddy road pic has pop tart Spears debut as Lucy, a virginal, small-town high school senior who hits the road to L.A. with childhood buds Kit (Saldana) and Mimi (Manning), with depressing results. Lucy's searching for her real mom (Cattrall); Kit, a no-good boyfriend; and Mimi trying to get to an open audition as a singer. Convenient cute love interest for Lucy is driver Ben (Mount), who may harbor a dangerous secret. Most laughable scene features Lucy scribbling "poetry" (actually lyrics to one of her soundtrack songs) while Ben "composes" the music for it. Spears is likeable and harmless while Manning is the real stand-out. One notch up from "Glitter," quality competed with quantity (of wardrobe) as lowest priority. **94m/C VHS, DVD.** *US* Britney Spears, Taryn Manning, Zoe Saldana, Anson Mount, Kim Cattrall, Dan Aykroyd, Justin Long, Beverly Johnson, Kool Moe Dee; *D:* Tamra Davis; *W:* Shonda Rhimes; *C:* Eric Alan Edwards; *M:* Trevor Jones.

Crossworlds **1996 (PG-13)** All dimensions of the universe collide in the mystical valley of Crossworlds. When alien night riders attack Joe Talbolt (Charles), he escapes with girlfriend Laura (Roth) and they meet up with mercenary A.T. (Hauer). Turns out the crystal pendant Joe's father left him is one of the keys that unlock the boundaries between the worlds. Along with a scepter, they give the owner unlimited power. So the trio enter Crossworlds to fight a battle between good and evil. **91m/C VHS, DVD.** Rutger Hauer, Josh Charles, Andrea Roth, Stuart Wilson; *D:* Krishna Rao; *W:* Raman Rao, Krishna Rao; *C:* Chris Walling; *M:* Christophe Beck. CABLE

Crouching Tiger, Hidden Dragon ½ **2000** Two veteran Wudan fighters (Yun-Fat and Yeoh) in 19th-century China recognize their passion for each other while tracking down a vengeful master criminal (Pei-Pei) and her protege (the exciting Ziyi). A martial arts love story that satisfies on both accounts. The emotional impact of the romance is as real and true as the choreographed fight scenes are spectacular and graceful. The film's overt feminism flies (literally) in the face of its patriarchal setting, yet doesn't seem a bit out of place. The extraordinary battle scenes were choreographed by Yuen Wo-Ping, who performed the same duties for "The Matrix." Mandarin with subtitles. **120m/C VHS, DVD, Wide.** Chow Yun-Fat, Michelle Yeoh, Zhang Ziyi, Chang Chen, Cheng Pei-Pei, Sihung Lung; *D:* Ang Lee; *W:* James Schamus, Wang Hui Ling, Tsai Kuo Jung; *C:* Peter Pau; *M:* Tan Dun. Oscars '00: Art Dir./Set Dec., Cinematog., Foreign Film, Orig. Score; Australian Film Inst. '01: Foreign Film; British Acad. '00: Director (Lee), Foreign Film, Score; Directors Guild '00: Director (Lee); Golden Globes '01: Director (Lee), Foreign Film; Ind. Spirit '01: Director (Lee), Film, Support. Actress (Ziyi); L.A. Film Critics '00: Cinematog., Film, Score; Natl. Bd. of Review '00: Foreign Film; N.Y. Film Critics '00: Cinematog.; Broadcast Film Critics '00: Foreign Film.

Croupier **1997** Director Hodges scored a hit with the 1971 British crime thriller "Get Carter." And after some rocky followups, he scores another with this cool casino neo-noir. A cynical South African, now living in London, Jack Manfred (Owen) is trying to escape the reach of his con man dad. The would-be writer (his detective character Jake does the film's narrative) takes a job as a casino dealer where he can observe life at his preferred distance—that is until a fellow South African, sulty gambling beauty Jani (Kingston), talks him into a shady scheme that provides fodder for Jack's writing. Owen is especially watchable in the title role. **91m/C VHS, DVD, Wide.** *GB* Clive Owen, Alex Kingston, Kate Hardie, Gina McKee, Nicholas Ball, Nick Reding; *D:* Mike Hodges; *W:* Paul Mayersberg; *C:* Mike Garfath; *M:* Simon Fisher Turner.

The Crow ½ **1993 (R)** Revenge-fantasy finds Eric Draven (Lee) resurrected on Devil's Night, a year after his death, in order to avenge his own murder and that of his girlfriend. 90% of the scenes are at night, in the rain, or both, and it's not easy to tell what's going on (a blessing considering the violence level). Very dark, but with good performances, particularly from Lee, in his last role before an unfortunate on set accident caused his death. That footage has been destroyed, but use of a stunt double and camera trickery allowed for the movie's completion. Film was dedicated to Lee and his fiance Eliza. Based on the comic strip by James O'Barr. The video release includes Brandon Lee's final interview. **100m/C VHS, DVD.** Brandon Lee, Ernie Hudson, Michael Wincott, David Patrick Kelly, Rochelle Davis, Angel David, Michael Massee, Bai Ling, Laurence Mason, Bill Raymond, Marco Rodriguez, Anna Thomson, Sofia Shinas, Jon Polito, Tony Todd; *D:* Alex Proyas; *W:* David J. Schow, John Shirley; *C:* Darius Wolski; *M:* Graeme Revell. MTV Movie Awards '95: Song ("Big Empty").

The Crow 2: City of Angels **1996 (R)** James O'Barr's cult graphic-novel "hero" returns in a new incarnation. It's eight years later (in film time) and the setting's changed from Detroit to L.A. but the horror remains. Ashe (Perez) and his young son witness a murder and are killed themselves by scumbags working for drug lord Judah (Brooks). So the Crow brings back Ashe to get revenge. Also involved is Sarah (Kirshner), who retains her role as story narrator but is now a grown-up tattoo artist who falls in love with Ashe. Lots of kink and flash—no substance—and confusing as well. The eerie sepia-toned look is created with sodium lighting. **93m/C VHS, DVD.** Vincent Perez, Mia Kirshner, Iggy Pop, Richard Brooks, Ian Dury, Thuy Trang, Thomas Jane, Vincent Castellanos, Tracey Ellis; *D:* Tim Pope; *W:* David S. Goyer; *C:* Jean-Yves Escoffier; *M:* Graeme Revell.

Crow Hollow **1952** A Victorian mansion inhabited by three whacko sisters is the site of a murder committed in an attempt to cash in on an inheritance. When a young woman investigates, eyebrows are raised. **69m/B VHS.** *GB* Donald Houston, Nastasha Parry, Nora Nicholson, Esma Cannon, Melissa Stribling; *D:* Michael McCarthy.

The Crow: Salvation **2000 (R)** Third in the series of films based on James O'Barr's comic book finds Alex Corvis (Mabius) wrongly convicted of murdering girlfriend Lauren Randall (O'Keefe). He's executed on his 21st birthday but returns as the Crow to seek revenge on those who wronged him. Alex convinces Erin (Dunst), Lauren's teenaged sister, of his innocence and they team up. Rather than revitalizing the franchise, this one basically got dumped by the studio, although the performances and the production are worth your time. **102m/C VHS, DVD, Wide.** Eric Mabius, Kirsten Dunst, Fred Ward, Jodi Lyn O'Keefe, William Atherton, Dale Midkiff, Grant Shaud; *D:* Bharat Nalluri; *W:* Chip Johannessen; *C:* Carolyn Chen; *M:* Marco Beltrami.

The Crowd **1928** A look at the day-to-day trials of a working-class family set against the backdrop of wealthy society. True-to-life, it's peppered with some happy moments, too. One of the best silent films. **104m/B VHS.** Eleanor Boardman, James Murray, Bert Roach, Daniel G. Tomlinson, Dell Henderson, Lucy Beaumont; *D:* King Vidor. Natl. Film Reg. '89.

Crows *Wrony* **1994** Emotionally neglected by her single mother, a nine-year-old nameless girl, known scornfully as The Crow (Ostrozna), desperately wants a family of her own. So she kidnaps a three-year-old to serve as her make-believe daughter and convinces the young child that they are going on a fairytale adventure to the end of the world. Polish with subtitles. **66m/C VHS.** *PL* Karolina Ostrozna, Kasia Szczepanik, Malgorzata Hajewska; *D:* Dorota Kedzierzawska; *W:* Dorota Kedzierzawska; *C:* Arthur Reinhart; *M:* Wlodek Pawlik.

Crows and Sparrows *Wuya Yu Maque* **1949** Poor tenants of a Shanghai boardinghouse are about to lose their home when their greedy landlord decides to sell and move to Taiwan. But the advancing Red Army causes a change in plans and they're saved! Sounds politically turgid but isn't, thanks to naturalistic acting and dialog. Completed just before the revolution, the film was censored by the Nationalist Kuomintang government but cuts were restored when the Communists came to power. Mandarin with subtitles. **108m/B VHS.** *CH* Zhao Dan, Wu Yin, Wei Heling, Sun Dao-Lin, Li Tianji, Ouyang Yunzhu; *D:* Zheng Junli; *W:* Zhao Dan, Zheng Junli; *C:* Miao Zhenhua, Hu Zhenhua; *M:* Wang Yunjie.

The Crucible *The Witches of Salem; Les Sorcieres de Salem* **1957** Signoret is outstanding in this version of Arthur Miller's play about the Salem witch trials in 17th-century New England. Miller's depiction of witch hunts was written as a searing commentary on McCarthyism and the anti-communist panic that swept America in the 1950s. Film was made in France because Miller was blacklisted in America and blackballed by Hollywood at the time. In French with English subtitles. **135m/B VHS.** *FR* Raymond Rouleau, Simone Signoret, Yves Montand, Mylene Demongeot, Jean Debucourt, Jean Gaven, Jeanne Fusier-Gir; *D:* Raymond Rouleau; *W:* Jean-Paul Sartre; *C:* Claude Renoir; *M:* Georges Auric.

The Crucible **1996 (PG-13)** Mass hysteria reigns in 17th century Salem, Mass., when a group of teenaged girls, caught performing heathen rituals in the woods, concoct an elaborate story to exonerate themselves by whipping the town into a witch-hunting frenzy. Chief liar is Abigail Williams (Ryder), who was cast aside by married farmer John Proctor (Day-Lewis), for whom she still lusts. The deranged lass puts her dubious talents into getting Proctor's wife (Allen) out of the picture. Director Hytner demanded authentic period reproduction, down to the finest detail. Impressive cast does justice to the story, especially Scofield's delightfully odious Judge Danforth. Based on Miller's 1953 play which, not so coincidently, opened during the communist witch hunts of the early 1950s. Screenwriter Miller willingly slashed dialogue from his original work for cinematic purposes. Filmed at the remote wildlife sanctuary of Hog Island,

Massachusetts. **123m/C VHS.** Daniel Day-Lewis, Winona Ryder, Paul Scofield, Joan Allen, Bruce Davison, Jeffrey Jones, Rob Campbell, Peter Vaughan, Karron Graves, Charlaine Woodard, Frances Conroy, Elizabeth Lawrence, George Gaynes; ***D:*** Nicholas Hytner; ***W:*** Arthur Miller; ***C:*** Andrew Dunn; ***M:*** George Fenton. British Acad. '96: Support. Actor (Scofield); Broadcast Film Critics '96: Support. Actress (Allen).

Crucible of Horror 🦴🦴 *Velvet House; The Corpse* **1969** Chilling story of a terrorized wife, who, along with her daughter, plots to murder her sadistic husband to end his abusive treatment of them. However, he isn't yet ready to die and comes back to drive them mad. **91m/C VHS.** *GB* Michael Gough, Yvonne Mitchell, Sharon Gurney, David Butler, Simon Gough, Nicholas Jones, Olaf Pooley, Mary Hignett; ***D:*** Viktors Ritelis; ***W:*** Olaf Pooley; ***C:*** John Mackey.

Crucible of Terror woof! **1972** Mad sculptor covers beautiful models with hot wax, then imprisons them in a mold of bronze. **95m/C VHS, DVD.** *GB* Mike Raven, Mary Maude, James Bolam, John Arnatt, Ronald Lacey, Judy Matheson, Me Me Lay, Melissa Stribling, Beth Morris; ***D:*** Ted Hooker; ***W:*** Ted Hooker, Tom Parkinson; ***C:*** Peter Newbrook.

The Crucifer of Blood 🦴½ **1991** A disappointing Sherlock Holmes yarn. Heston is adequate as the Baker Street sleuth, but the mystery—about two retired British soldiers who share an accursed secret and a vengeful comrade—unreels clumsily in the form of flashbacks that give away most of the puzzle from the start. Interesting only in that Dr. Watson has a love affair, more or less. Adapted from a play (and looking like it) by Paul Giovanni, inspired by Arthur Conan Doyle's "The Sign of Four." **105m/C VHS.** Charlton Heston, Richard Johnson, Susannah Harker, John Castle, Clive Wood, Simon Callow, Edward Fox; ***D:*** Fraser Heston. **CABLE**

The Crucified Lovers 🦴🦴🦴½ *Chikamatsu Monogatari* **1954** A shy scrollmaker falls in love with his master's wife. Excellent Japanese tragedy with fine performances all around. **100m/B VHS.** *JP* Kazuo Hasegawa, Kyoko Kagawa, Yoko Minamida, Eitaro Shindo, Shigehiro (Sakae) Ozawa; ***D:*** Kenji Mizoguchi.

The Crude Oasis 🦴🦴½ **1995 (R)** Shot in 14 days on a $25,000 budget, producer/writer/director Graves' debut is an aggressively moody suspenser. Karen (Taylor) is a neglected, suicidal Kansas housewife who is haunted by dreams of a mystery man. He turns up in the form of Shields, the pump jockey at a local gas station. Obsessed by the stranger, Karen begins following him, leading to situations paralleling her dream. Adept at setting up an atmosphere of small-town menace and constructing a plot with surprising twists and turns, Graves can't quite deliver the payoff required. **82m/C VHS.** Jennifer Taylor, Aaron Shields, Robert Peterson, Mussef Sibay, Lynn Bieler, Roberta Eaton; ***D:*** Alex Graves; ***W:*** Alex Graves; ***C:*** Steven Quale.

Cruel and Unusual 🦴🦴 *Watchtower* **2001 (R)** Adam Turrell (Berenger) comes to stay in a quiet Oregon fishing town, introducing himself as an English professor working on a first novel. He befriends sister and brother Kate (Hayward) and Mike (Runyan) O'Connor whose father has recently died. But their friendship takes a terrifying turn since Adam isn't at all what he seems. **100m/C VHS, DVD, Wide.** Tom Berenger, Rachel Hayward, Tygh Runyan, Mitchell Kosterman; ***D:*** George Mihalka; ***W:*** Robert Geoffrion, Rod Browning, Dan Witt; ***C:*** Peter Benison; ***M:*** Michel Cusson. **VIDEO**

Cruel Intentions 🦴🦴½ **1998 (R)** Fourth film adaptation of Choderlos de Loclos's 1782 novel "Les Liaisons Dangereuses" takes the tale of seduction and intrigue from the 18th century French court to a modern Manhattan prep school. Think "I Know Who You Did Last Summer." Gellar plays teen vamp Kathryn, who bets her step-brother Sebastian (Phillipe) a night of passion against his car that he can't deflower the virginal Annette (Witherspoon). The overall effect is like the characters' lives: full of guilty pleasures. **95m/C VHS, DVD.** Sarah Michelle Gellar, Ryan Phillippe, Reese Witherspoon, Selma Blair, Joshua Jackson, Eric Mabius, Louise Fletcher, Swoosie Kurtz, Christine Baranski, Sean Patrick Thomas; ***D:*** Roger Kumble; ***W:*** Roger Kumble; ***C:*** Theo van de Sande; ***M:*** Ed Shearmur. MTV Movie Awards '00: Female Perf. (Gellar), Kiss (Sarah Michelle Gellar/Selma Blair).

Cruel Intentions 2 🦴🦴 *Manchester Prep* **1999 (R)** A prequel to the 1998 release finds a rather precocious 16-year-old Sebastian deciding to become a one-woman guy—in this case to naive Danielle, the high school headmaster's daughter. However, his new stepsister Katherine has other adventures in mind. This was intended as the pilot to a TV series (based on the film) that was cancelled before it aired. **87m/C VHS, DVD, Wide.** Amy Adams, Mimi Rogers, Robin Dunne, Sarah Thompson, Keri Lynn Pratt, David McIlwraith; ***D:*** Roger Kumble; ***W:*** Roger Kumble; ***C:*** James R. Bagdonas. **TV**

The Cruel Sea 🦴🦴🦴 **1953** Well-made documentary-like account of a Royal Navy corvette on convoy duty in the Atlantic during WWII. **121m/B VHS.** *GB* Jack Hawkins, Stanley Baker, Denholm Elliott, Virginia McKenna; ***D:*** Charles Frend; ***W:*** Eric Ambler.

The Cruel Story of Youth 🦴🦴🦴 *Seishun Zanoku Monogatari; Naked Youth; A Story of the Cruelties of Youth* **1960** A teenage girl and her criminal boyfriend use sex to get money out of rich, middle-aged men in this controversial look at the disillusionment of youth and the breaking of old values and traditions in Japan after WWII. In Japanese with English subtitles. **96m/C VHS.** *JP* Yusuke Kawazu, Miyuki Kuwano, Yoshiko Kuga; ***D:*** Nagisa Oshima; ***W:*** Nagisa Oshima.

Cruise into Terror woof! **1978** A sarcophagus brought aboard a pleasure cruise ship unleashes an evil force that slowly starts to kill off the ship's passengers, most of whom likely thought they were on the Love Boat. **100m/C VHS.** Ray Milland, Hugh O'Brian, John Forsythe, Christopher George, Dirk Benedict, Frank Converse, Lynda Day George, Stella Stevens; ***D:*** Bruce Kessler. **TV**

Cruise Missile 🦴 **1978** Unique task force is on a mission to keep the world from nuclear holocaust. **100m/C VHS.** Peter Graves, Curt Jurgens, Michael Dante; ***D:*** Ted V. Mikels.

Cruisin' High 🦴 *Cat Murkil and the Silks* **1975 (R)** Two city street gangs battle it out. **109m/C VHS.** David Kyle, Kelly Yaegermann, Rhodes Reason; ***D:*** John Bushelman; ***W:*** William C. Thomas.

Cruising 🦴🦴 **1980 (R)** Rookie cop Pacino is deep undercover investigating the bizarre murders of homosexuals in New York's West Village. Sexually explicit but less than suspenseful mystery. Release was sensationalized, with many gay rights groups voicing loud disapproval of the sordid gay characterization, while others feared copy-cat crimes. Excellent NYC cinematography. **102m/C VHS.** Al Pacino, Paul Sorvino, Karen Allen, Powers Boothe; ***D:*** William Friedkin; ***W:*** William Friedkin; ***M:*** Jack Nitzsche.

Crumb **1994 (R)** Countercultural documentary looking at the life of underground cartoonist Robert Crumb—'60s satirist and social misfit who created such drug and sex characters as Fritz the Cat and Mr. Natural. Crumb's extraordinarily dysfunctional family play a significant role, with his mother and two brothers, elder brother Charles and younger brother Max, also interviewed as well as Crumb's friends and current and former wives. The dead abusive father also plays a part. Director Zwigoff spent six years filming his material, and gained wider distribution for his work after taking the Grand Jury prize at Sundance. **119m/C VHS, DVD.** Robert Crumb; ***D:*** Terry Zwigoff; ***C:*** Maryse Alberti. Directors Guild '95: Feature Doc. (Zwigoff); Natl. Soc. Film Critics '95: Feature Doc.; Sundance '95: Cinematog., Grand Jury Prize.

The Crusades 🦴🦴½ **1935** Typical DeMille extravaganza, loosely based on the Third Crusade, which finds Richard the Lionheart (Wilcoxon) and the armies of Europe battling Saladin and the Mahammedan horde in order to reclaim Jerusalem. Meanwhile, Richard marries by proxy in order to gain supplies for his men—something that enrages his bride Berengaria (Young). Once he realizes how beautiful she is, Richard tries to win her love. Obviously, not historically accurate and it's all secondary to the battle scenes, anyway. Based on the Harold Lamb book "The Crusade: Iron Men and Saints." **126m/B VHS.** Henry Wilcoxon, Loretta Young, Sir C. Aubrey Smith, Ian Keith, Katherine DeMille, Joseph Schildkraut, Alan Hale, C. Henry Gordon, George Barbier, Lumsden Hare, William Farnum, Hobart Bosworth, Montagu Love, Pedro de Cordoba, Mischa Auer; ***D:*** Cecil B. DeMille; ***W:*** Waldemar Young, Dudley Nichols, Harold Lamb; ***C:*** Victor Milner; ***M:*** Rudolph Kopp.

Crush 🦴🦴 **1993** Christina is a local New Zealand literary critic on her way to interview Colin, a reclusive novelist. Along for the ride is her seductive American friend Lane who manages to crash the car but walk away with hardly a scratch. Christina appears to be dead and Lane abandons her, finding her way to the home Colin shares with his teenage daughter Angela. Lane promptly sets out to seduce Colin, making Angela jealous, (oh, and Christina's not dead after all). Poor script finds the characters actions baffling and why Lane is so wildly attractive is never apparent. **97m/C VHS.** *NZ* Marcia Gay Harden, Donough Rees, William Zappa, Caitlin Bossley; ***D:*** Alison Maclean; ***W:*** Alison Maclean, Anne Kennedy; ***C:*** Dion Beebe.

The Crush 🦴½ **1993 (R)** Wealthy 14-year-old temptress Silverstone (in her debut) develops an obsessive crush on handsome 28-year-old Elwes, who rents her family's guest house. In an attempt to win his heart, she rewrites his poorly composed magazine articles. This doesn't convince him they should mate for life, so she sabotages his apartment to vent her rage. Sound familiar? The plot's lifted right out of "Fatal Attraction" and Shapiro doesn't offer viewers anything inventively different. He does manage to substitute new methods for the spurned lover to snare her prey. Limp plot would have been exciting if we hadn't seen it so many times before. **89m/C VHS, DVD, Wide.** Cary Elwes, Alicia Silverstone, Jennifer Rubin, Kurtwood Smith, Gwynyth Walsh, Amber Benson; ***D:*** Alan Shapiro; ***W:*** Alan Shapiro; ***C:*** Bruce Surtees; ***M:*** Graeme Revell. MTV Movie Awards '94: Breakthrough Perf. (Silverstone), Villain (Silverstone).

Crush 🦴🦴 **2002 (R)** A "with friends like these, who needs enemies" movie that leaves a sour aftertaste. Kate (MacDowell), Janine (Staunton), and Molly (Chancellor) are three professional women in their forties who live in a small English town and meet weekly to drink and commiserate about their lousy love lives. That is, until sexily repressed American headmistress Kate sets off sparks with hottie 20-something Jed (Doughty), an organist and former pupil. Her friends are outraged and turn distinctly nasty trying to break up the happy twosome. Maybe they're jealous that Kate is having great sex and they're not. **115m/C VHS, DVD.** *GB* Andie MacDowell, Imelda Staunton, Anna Chancellor, Kenny Doughty, Bill Paterson; ***D:*** John McKay; ***W:*** John McKay; ***C:*** Henry Braham; ***M:*** Kevin Sargent.

Crusoe 🦴🦴½ **1989 (PG-13)** A lushly photographed version of the Daniel Defoe classic. Crusoe is an arrogant slave trader stranded on a desert island populated by unfriendly natives. Themes of prejudice, fear, and choice appear in this never-padded, thoughtful film. Quinn gives an excellent performance as the stranded slave-trader. **94m/C VHS.** Aidan Quinn, Ade Sapara, Jimmy Nail, Timothy Spall, Colin Bruce, Michael Higgins, Shane Rimmer, Hepburn Grahame; ***D:*** Caleb Deschanel; ***W:*** Walon Green, Christopher Logue; ***M:*** Michael Kamen.

Cry-Baby 🦴🦴🦴 **1990 (PG-13)** An homage and spoof of '50s teen-rock melodramas by the doyen of cinematic Bad Taste, involving a terminal bad-boy high schooler who goes with a square blond and starts an inter-class rumble. Musical numbers, throwaway gags and plenty of knee-bending to Elvis, with a weak story supported by offbeat celeb appearances. **85m/C VHS.** Johnny Depp, Amy Locane, Polly Bergen, Traci Lords, Ricki Lake, Iggy Pop, Susan Tyrrell, Patty (Patricia Campbell) Hearst, Kim McGuire, Darren E. Burrows, Troy Donahue, Willem Dafoe, David Nelson, Mink Stole, Joe Dallesandro, Joey Heatherton, Robert Walsh, Mary Vivian Pearce; ***D:*** John Waters; ***W:*** John Waters; ***C:*** David Insley; ***M:*** Patrick Williams.

Cry Blood, Apache 🦴🦴 **1970 (R)** An old man (Joel McCrae) remembers when, as a young man (Jody McCrae), he and his sadistic friends massacred a group of Apaches and were hunted by the husband of one of their victims. It's violent but not as sadistic as some. **90m/C DVD.** Joel McCrae, Jody McCrae, Robert Tessier, Marie Gahva, Don Henley; ***D:*** Jack Starrett; ***W:*** Sean McGregor; ***C:*** Bruce Scott; ***M:*** Elliot Kaplan.

Cry Danger 🦴🦴🦴 **1951** A falsely imprisoned man is released from jail, and he searches for those who framed him. **80m/B VHS.** Dick Powell, Rhonda Fleming, William Conrad, Richard Erdman; ***D:*** Robert Parrish; ***C:*** Joseph Biroc.

A Cry for Love 🦴🦴 **1980** An amphetamine addict and an alcoholic meet, fall in love, and help each other recover. Based on the best seller by Jill Schary Robinson, "Bedtime Story." **96m/C VHS.** Susan Blakely, Powers Boothe, Gene Barry, Charles Siebert, Herb Edelman, Fern Fitzgerald, Lainie Kazan; ***D:*** Paul Wendkos.

Cry Freedom 🦴🦴½ **1987 (PG)** A romantic look at the short life of South African activist Steven Biko, and his friendship with the white news editor, Donald Woods. The film focuses on Woods' escape from Africa while struggling to bring Biko's message to the world. Based on a true story. **157m/C VHS, DVD.** Kevin Kline, Denzel Washington, Penelope Wilton, Kevin McNally, John Thaw, Timothy West, John Hargreaves, Alec McCowen, Zakes Mokae, Ian Richardson, Juanita Waterman; ***D:*** Richard Attenborough; ***W:*** John Briley; ***C:*** Ronnie Taylor; ***M:*** George Fenton, Jonas Gwangwa.

A Cry from the Mountain 🦴 **1985 (PG)** Heavily religious film about a father and son who go on a kayak trip through Alaska's wilderness so the father can break the news of his impending divorce. A series of events occurs that change their lives, and they meet a mysterious mountain man who relies on his faith in God to get by in the wilderness. Features an appearance by Rev. Billy Graham. **78m/C VHS.** James Cavan, Wes Parker, Rita Walter, Chris Kidd, Coleen Gray, Jerry Ballew, Allison Argo, Glen Alsworth, Myrna Kidd; ***D:*** James F. Collier.

A Cry from the Streets 🦴🦴 **1957** Drama about the plight of orphan children and dedicated social workers in England. **100m/C VHS.** *GB* Max Bygraves, Barbara Murray, Kathleen Harrison, Colin Petersen; ***D:*** Lewis Gilbert; ***M:*** Larry Adler.

A Cry in the Dark 🦴🦴🦴½ *Evil Angels* **1988 (PG-13)** Tight film story of the infamous Australian murder trial of Lindy Chamberlain (Streep), who was accused of killing her own baby, mostly because of the intensely adverse public opinion, aroused by vicious press, that surrounded the case. Chamberlain blamed the death on a wild dingo dog, which dragged off the baby from where the family was camped. Near-documentary style, with Streep excellent as the religious, unknowable mother. Based on the book "Evil Angels" by John Bryson. This case was also detailed in the film "Who Killed Baby Azaria?" **120m/C VHS, DVD, 8mm.** *AU* Meryl Streep, Sam Neill, Bruce Myles, Charles Tingwell, Nick (Nicholas) Tate, Neil Fitzpatrick, Maurice Fields, Lewis Fitz-Gerald, Tony Martin; ***D:*** Fred Schepisi; ***W:*** Fred Schepisi, Robert Caswell; ***C:*** Ian Baker; ***M:*** Bruce Smeaton. Australian Film Inst. '89: Actor (Neill), Actress (Streep), Film; Cannes '89: Actress (Streep); N.Y. Film Critics '88: Actress (Streep).

A Cry in the Night 🦴🦴½ **1993 (PG-13)** After Jenny (Higgins Clark) marries an internationally acclaimed artist, she thinks her life is complete. However, once she and her two daughters move into his country estate, her life takes a tragic turn as she's haunted by the mysterious deaths of her ex-husband and newborn child. King plays the new husband who turns out to have a few psychological quirks of his own. Actress Higgins Clark is the daughter of bestselling novelist Mary

Higgins Clark, upon whose work the story is based. **99m/C VHS.** Perry King, Carol Higgins Clark; ***D:*** Robin Spry; ***W:*** Robin Spry. **TV**

A Cry in the Wild 🦴🦴🦴 **1990 (PG)** A 14-year-old boy must find his way back to civilization when he's the lone survivor of an airplane crash. Strong acting from Rushton, excellent nature photography make this well used story work again. **93m/C VHS, DVD.** Jared Rushton, Ned Beatty, Pamela Sue Martin, Stephen Meadows; ***D:*** Mark Griffiths; ***W:*** Catherine Cyran; ***C:*** Gregg Heschong; ***M:*** Arthur Kempel.

Cry of a Prostitute: Love Kills 🦴 **1972 (R)** Former prostitute joins with a professional assassin in an effort to pacify rival gangsters in Italy. **86m/C VHS.** Henry Silva, Barbara Bouchet; ***D:*** Andrea (Andrew White) Bianchi.

Cry of Battle 🦴🦴½ *To Be a Man* **1963** Anxious for the challenges of manhood, a well-heeled young man joins a guerrilla militia in the Philippines. **99m/B VHS.** Van Heflin, Rita Moreno, James MacArthur; ***D:*** Irving Lerner.

Cry of the Banshee 🦴🦴½ **1970 (PG)** Witch-hunter Price and family are tormented by Satanic powers seeking revenge. Superior horror period piece. **87m/C VHS.** *GB* Vincent Price, Elisabeth Bergner, Essy Persson, Hugh Griffith, Hilary Dwyer, Sally Geeson, Patrick Mower, Marshall Jones, Michael Elphick, Pamela Fairbrother, Robert Hutton; ***D:*** Gordon Hessler; ***W:*** Christopher Wicking, Tim Kelly; ***C:*** John Coquillon; ***M:*** Les Baxter.

Cry of the Innocent 🦴🦴🦴 **1980** An action-packed thriller about a Vietnam veteran who is out to find a group of Irish terrorists that killed his family. **93m/C VHS.** Cyril Cusack, Alexander Knox, Rod Taylor, Joanna Pettet, Nigel Davenport; ***D:*** Michael O'Herlihy.

The Cry of the Owl 🦴🦴 *Le Cri du Hibou* **1987** Robert (Malavoy) has divorced the dreadful Veronique (Thevenet) and struck up a friendship with Juliette (May). He admires the way her life seems so satisfied and orderly but Juliette decides she doesn't like this idea of herself and impulsively drops her swinish fiance Patrick (Penot) and pursues Robert instead. But Robert is only interested in friendship, leading to some very twisted revenge plots. Suspenseful look at what obsessions can drive people to do. Adapted from the novel by Patricia Highsmith. In French with English subtitles. **102m/C VHS, DVD, Wide.** *FR IT* Christophe MaLavoy, Mathilda May, Virginie Thevenet, Jacques Penot, Jean-Pierre Kalfon, Patrice Kerbrat; ***D:*** Claude Chabrol; ***W:*** Claude Chabrol, Odile Barski; ***C:*** Jean Rabier; ***M:*** Matthieu Chabrol.

Cry of the Penguins 🦴🦴½ *Mr. Forbush and the Penguins* **1971** Womanizing biologist Forbush (Hurt) heads off on an Antartic expedition to study penguins when his would-be romance with Tara (Mills) comes to naught. Beautiful photography, shallow story. Adapted from the novel "Mr. Forbush and the Penguins" by Graham Billing. Note the similarities with "Never Cry Wolf." **105m/C VHS.** *GB* John Hurt, Hayley Mills, Dudley Sutton, Tony Britton, Thorley Walters, Judy Campbell, Joss Ackland, Nicholas Pennell; ***D:*** Albert T. Viola; ***W:*** Anthony Shaffer; ***M:*** John Addison.

Cry of the Werewolf 🦴🦴 **1944** A beautiful New Orleans gypsy protects her mother's mummified remains by periodically turning into a werewolf and killing people. **63m/B VHS.** Nina Foch, Stephen Crane, Osa Massen, Blanche Yurka, Barton MacLane, Ivan Triesault, John Abbott, Fritz Leiber; ***D:*** Henry Levin; ***W:*** Charles "Blackie" O'Neal.

Cry Panic 🦴🦴 **1974** A man is thrown into a strange series of events after accidentally running down a man on a highway. **74m/C VHS.** John Forsythe, Anne Francis, Earl Holliman, Claudia McNeil, Ralph Meeker; ***D:*** James Goldstone. **TV**

Cry Terror 🦴🦴 *Kill Two Birds; Thriller: Kill Two Birds* **1974** Two escaped convicts take two beautiful women hostage hoping to gain their own freedom. Only a quick-thinking undercover police officer can save the girls. **71m/C VHS.** *GB* Bob Hoskins, Susan Hampshire, Gabrielle Drake. **TV**

Cry, the Beloved Country 🦴🦴🦴½ *African Fury* **1951** A black country minister travels to Johannesberg to be with his son after the youth is accused of killing a white man. Through the events of the trial, the horror, oppression, and destruction of South Africa's apartheid system are exposed. Startling and moving, the first entertainment feature set against the backdrop of apartheid. Still trenchant; based on the novel by Alan Paton. **111m/B VHS.** *GB* Canada Lee, Charles Carson, Sidney Poitier, Joyce Carey, Geoffrey Keen; ***D:*** Zoltan Korda; ***W:*** John Howard Lawson, Alan Paton; ***C:*** Robert Krasker.

Cry, the Beloved Country 🦴🦴🦴 **1995 (PG-13)** Alan Paton's classic South African apartheid novel (first filmed in 1951) depicts a Zulu Christian pastor and a wealthy white farmer finding common ground through personal loss—both of their sons were killed in regional violence. Rural black minister Stephen Kumalo (Jones), travels to Johannesburg only to discover his sister (Kente) is a prostitute, his younger brother John (Dutton) no longer believes in Christianity and his son is in prison for the murder of a white man. That man turns out to be the son of rich farmer James Jarvis (Harris), from Kumalo's own village. Both Jones and Harris turn in wonderfully understated performances in this hopeful tale of potential racial harmony. **120m/C VHS.** *SA* James Earl Jones, Richard Harris, Charles S. Dutton, Leleti Khumalo, Dambisa Kente, Vusi Kunene, Eric Miyeni, Ian Robers; ***D:*** Darrell Roodt; ***W:*** Ronald Atwood; ***C:*** Paul Gilpin; ***M:*** John Barry.

Cry Uncle 🦴½ **1971 (R)** Comic account of a private eye who investigates a blackmailing case involving a film of orgies in which, much to his chagrin, he participated. **85m/C VHS, DVD, Wide.** Allen (Goorwitz) Garfield, Paul Sorvino, Devin Goldenberg, Madeleine Le Roux; ***D:*** John G. Avildsen; ***W:*** David Odell; ***C:*** John G. Avildsen; ***M:*** Harper Mckay.

Cry Vengeance 🦴🦴½ **1954** A falsely imprisoned detective gets out of jail and searches for the people who framed him and killed his family. **83m/B VHS.** Mark Stevens, Joan Vohs, Martha Hyer, Skip Homeier; ***D:*** Mark Stevens.

Cry Wolf 🦴🦴 **1947** Weak mystery thriller places Stanwyck in creepy environs when she goes to claim her inheritance from her late husband's estate. Based on the novel by Marjorie Carleton. **83m/B VHS.** Errol Flynn, Barbara Stanwyck, Richard Basehart, Geraldine Brooks, Jerome Cowan, John Ridgely, Patricia Barry; ***D:*** Peter Godfrey; ***W:*** Catherine Turney.

The Crying Child 🦴½ **1996 (PG-13)** Madeline Jeffreys (Hemingway) and her husband Ran (DelHoyo) retreat to their 19th-century island vacation cottage after the stillbirth of their first child. Madeline begins to hear a child crying in the house and sees a ghostly apparition—now she has to discover what the spirit wants (and convince everyone she's not just going crazy). TV movie based on the novel by Barbara Michaels. **93m/C VHS.** Mariel Hemingway, George DelHoyo, Finola Hughes, Kin Shriner, Collin Wilcox-Paxton; ***D:*** Robert Lewis; ***W:*** Rob Gilmer; ***C:*** Stephen Lighthill; ***M:*** Shirley Walker.

The Crying Game 🦴🦴🦴½ **1992 (R)** PR lesson in how to launch a small movie into the hypersphere and ensure critical silence on salient characterization. Jordan's gritty drama is on par with his best, a complex blend of violence, love, betrayal, guilt, and redemption and is not about what it seems to be about much of the time. Wonderful performances by all, including Rea as the appealing, conscience-stricken Fergus; Richardson as the cold, violent IRA moll Jude; and Davidson, in a film debut, as the needy, charismatic Dil. Whitaker is terrific in his 15 minutes of intense screen time. Filled with definite surprises and unexpected pleasures. Title is taken from a top-5 British hit of 1964, three versions of which are heard. **112m/C VHS, DVD, Wide.** *IR* Stephen Rea, Jaye Davidson, Miranda Richardson, Forest Whitaker, Adrian Dunbar, Jim Broadbent, Ralph Brown, Breffini McKenna, Joe Savino, Birdy Sweeney, Andre Bernard; ***D:*** Neil Jordan; ***W:*** Neil Jordan; ***C:*** Ian Wilson; ***M:*** Anne Dudley. Oscars '92: Orig. Screenplay; Australian Film Inst. '93: Foreign Film; Ind. Spirit '93: Foreign Film; L.A. Film Critics '92: Foreign Film; N.Y. Film Critics '92: Screenplay, Support. Actress (Richardson); Natl. Soc. Film Critics '92: Actor (Rea); Writers Guild '92: Orig. Screenplay.

Crypt of Dark Secrets 🦴 **1976 (R)** Vietnam veteran recovering from wounds in the Louisiana swamps encounters a friendly Indian spirit who saves him from death. **100m/C VHS.** Maureen Chan, Ronald Tanet, Wayne Mack, Herbert G. Jahncke; ***D:*** Jack Weis.

Crypt of the Living Dead woof! **1973 (PG)** An undead woman from the 13th century makes life miserable for visitors on Vampire Island. **75m/C VHS.** Andrew Prine, Mark Damon, Teresa Gimpera, Patty (Patti) Shepard, Francisco (Frank) Brana; ***D:*** Ray Danton.

Crystal Heart 🦴 **1987 (R)** A medically isolated songwriter with an incurable disease falls in love with a lovely rock singer. **103m/C VHS.** Lee Curreri, Tawny Kitaen, Lloyd Bochner; ***D:*** Gil Bettman; ***M:*** Joel Goldsmith.

Crystal's Diary 🦴 **1999** Small town Emmanuel Crystal moves to Hollywood and winds up sharing a place with free-spirited Tabetha. The twosome make their cash lap dancing until Emmanuel makes the mistake of falling for a client and things just go downhill from there. **90m/C VHS.** Shelly Gurvitz, Monique Albers, David Alan, Vincent Bilancio, John Sayre; ***D:*** Jeff Leroy; ***W:*** Jeff Leroy; ***M:*** Larry Washington. **VIDEO**

Crystalstone 🦴🦴 **1988 (PG)** A wooden cross leads a pair of orphans on a dangerous search for the legendary Crystalstone. **103m/C VHS.** Frank Grimes, Kamlesh Gupta, Laura Jane Goodwin, Sydney Bromley; ***D:*** Antonio Pelaez.

Cthulhu Mansion woof! **1991 (R)** The oldest-looking juvenile delinquents you've ever seen release evil spirits when they take over a magician's estate. Not very special effects and abominable dialogue; it claims to be based on H.P. Lovecraft stories, but that's a load of dung. **95m/C VHS.** Frank Finlay, Marcia Layton, Brad Fisher, Melanie Shatner, Luis Fernando Alves, Kaethe Cherney, Paul Birchard, Francisco (Frank) Brana; ***D:*** J(uan) Piquer Simon; ***W:*** J(uan) Piquer Simon.

Cuba 🦴🦴🦴 **1979 (R)** Cynical, satirical adventure/love story. Mercenary soldier rekindles an old affair during the Castro revolution. Charismatic cast and good direction make for an entertaining, if overlooked, Connery vehicle. **121m/C VHS, DVD, Wide.** Sean Connery, Brooke Adams, Jack Weston, Hector Elizondo, Denholm Elliott, Chris Sarandon, Lonette McKee; ***D:*** Richard Lester; ***W:*** Charles Wood; ***C:*** David Watkin; ***M:*** Patrick Williams.

Cube 🦴½ **1998 (R)** Claustrophobic sci-fi thriller about six people who inexplicably wake up chained together in a bare room attached to other bare rooms that are fiendishly booby-trapped. They are forced to work together in order to escape. The fact that the bizarro force holding these people hostage is never explained may escape you; since your senses will be dulled by the bad acting and lack of plot. Not as much fun as spending an hour and a half in a refrigerator box. **90m/C VHS, DVD.** *CA* Maurice Dean Wint, Nikki DeBoer, David Hewlett, Wayne Robson, Andrew Miller, Nicky Guadagni, Julian Richings; ***D:*** Vincenzo Natali; ***W:*** Graeme Manson, Vincenzo Natali, Andre Bijelic; ***C:*** Derek Rogers; ***M:*** Mark Korven.

Cujo 🦴🦴 **1983 (R)** Bad doggie!! A rabid St. Bernard goes berserk and attacks mom Donna (Wallace Stone) and her five-year-old son Tad (Pintauro), who are trapped inside a broken-down Pinto. Frighteningly realistic film is based on Stephen King's bestseller. **94m/C VHS, DVD.** Dee Wallace Stone, Daniel Hugh-Kelly, Danny Pintauro, Ed Lauter, Christopher Stone, Kaiulani Lee, Mills Watson, Jerry Hardin, Billy Jacoby, Sandy Ward; ***D:*** Lewis Teague; ***W:*** Lauren Currier, Don Carlos Dunaway; ***C:*** Jan De Bont; ***M:*** Charles Bernstein.

Cul de Sac 🦴🦴🦴 **1966** A macabre, psychological thriller set in a dreary castle on a small island off the British coast. Pleasence is an eccentric, middle-aged hermit living acrimoniously with his young, nympho wife (Dorleac) when their home is invaded by two wounded gangsters (Stander and MacGowran), who proceed to hold the couple hostage. MacGowran soon dies of his wounds, leaving Stander and Pleasence to fight it out, encouraged by the luscious Dorleac, who finds her fun where she can. A bleak, sinister film considered one of Polanski's best. **111m/C VHS.** *GB* Donald Pleasence, Francoise Dorleac, Lionel Stander, Jack MacGowran, Jacqueline Bisset; ***D:*** Roman Polanski; ***W:*** Roman Polanski, Gerard Brach.

Culpepper Cattle Co. 🦴🦴½ **1972 (PG)** A young, starry-eyed yokel wants to be a cowboy and gets himself enlisted in a cattle drive, where he learns the harsh reality of the West. **92m/C VHS.** Gary Grimes, Billy Green Bush, Bo Hopkins, Charles Martin Smith, Geoffrey Lewis; ***D:*** Dick Richards; ***M:*** Jerry Goldsmith.

Cult of the Cobra 🦴🦴 **1955** Mysterious horror film that became minor camp classic. It seems ex-servicemen are being killed by exotic snake-lady Domergue. Cheesy film that can be fun. Based on a story by Jerry Davis. **75m/B VHS.** Faith Domergue, Richard Long, Marshall Thompson, William Reynolds, Jack Kelly, Kathleen Hughes; ***D:*** Francis D. Lyon; ***W:*** Jerry Davis.

The Cup 🦴🦴½ *Phorpa* **1999 (G)** Tibetan teenager Orgyen arrives at a monastery in the Himalayan foothills where he is to join the religious life. But Orgyen is soccer-mad and obsessed with the World Cup (he wears a soccer shirt under his robes) and sneaks out to watch the games. Eventually, the monastery's abbott agrees to allow the monks to have a satellite dish to watch the finals—if they can raise the money to obtain it. Bhutanese with subtitles. **94m/C VHS.** *AU* Jamyang Lodro, Orgyen Tobgyal, Lama Chonjor; ***D:*** Khyentse Norbu; ***W:*** Khyentse Norbu; ***C:*** Paul Warren; ***M:*** Douglas Mills.

Cup Final 🦴🦴 *G'mar Giviya* **1992** The similarities and contradictions in war and sports, where passions and competition run high, are depicted in this emotional drama. Set in 1982 during Israel's invasion of Lebanon. Cohen is an Israeli soldier passionately interested in the World Cup soccer tournament. When he is taken prisoner by the PLO he discovers his captor Ziad shares his interest in the Italian national team. This common interest brings the two antagonists reluctantly together. In Hebrew and Arabic with English subtitles. **107m/C VHS.** *IS* Moshe Ivgi, Muhamad Bacri, Suheil Haddad; ***D:*** Eran Riklis; ***W:*** Eyal Halfon; ***M:*** Raviv Gazil.

Cupid 🦴½ **1996 (R)** Eric (Galligan) develops a deadly obsession for beautiful Jennifer (Laurence), who discovers that Jack and his equally crazy sister Dana (Crosby) have a nasty habit of killing the women that don't measure up to Jack's fantasies. **94m/C VHS.** Zach Galligan, Ashley Laurence, Mary Crosby, Joseph Kell, Michael Bowen; ***D:*** Doug Campbell; ***W:*** David Benullo; ***C:*** M. David Mullen.

Cupid & Cate 🦴🦴½ **2000** Cate De Angelo (Parker) is the quirky owner of a failing D.C. vintage clothing store. The youngest in a large Italian/Irish American family, Cate is still trying to deal with her alcoholic mother's death and an ongoing feud with her overbearing father, Dominic (Bosco). She has a reliable relationship with dull Philip (Lansbury) but doesn't realize the passion she's been missing until she meets handsome Harry (Gallagher) the lawyer. Stereotypes abound as do too many subplots but the leads are endearing. Based on Christina Bartolomeo's novel "Cupid and Diana." **95m/C VHS.** Mary-Louise Parker, Peter Gallagher, Philip Bosco, David Lansbury, Bebe Neuwirth, Joanna Going, Brenda Fricker, Kurt McKinney, Rebecca Luker; ***D:*** Brent Shields; ***W:*** Jennifer Miller, Ron Raley; ***C:*** Kees Van Oostrum; ***M:*** Mark Adler. **TV**

Curdled 🦴🦴½ 1995 (R) And you thought your job sucked. Tarantino-funded dark comedy arouses interest with that tag line alone. Gore-obsessed Gabriela (Jones) gets her dream job cleaning up blood and guts with the Post-Forensic Cleaning Service and becomes obsessed with serial killer to the rich Paul (Baldwin), who is keeping her company hopping with one beheading after another. Cultishly violent pic culminates in a tango by the gruesome twosome around a murder scene. Tarantino spotted Jones, starring in Braddock's original student short, while touring with "Reservoir Dogs" and borrowed her for "Pulp Fiction," only to return the favor by exec producing this interesting feature debut. Soundtrack adds spice to the formaldehyde flavor. **87m/C VHS.** Angela Jones, William Baldwin, Mel Gorham, Barry Corbin, Bruce Ramsey, Daisy Fuentes, Lois Chiles, Carmen Lopez; ***D:*** Reb Braddock; ***W:*** John Maass, Reb Braddock; ***C:*** Steven Bernstein; ***M:*** Joseph Julian Gonzalez.

The Cure 1917 Chaplin arrives at a spa to take a rest cure, accompanied by a trunk full of liquor that somehow gets dumped into the water at the resort. Silent with music track. **20m/B VHS, DVD.** Charlie Chaplin, Edna Purviance, Eric Campbell, Albert Austin; ***D:*** Charlie Chaplin.

The Cure 🦴🦴½ 1995 (PG-13) Erik (Renfro), the neighborhood bad kid, befriends Dexter (Mazzello), a boy with AIDS. As Dexter's health weakens, Erik decides they must go on a quest for a cure, Huck Finn style, by floating along the Mississippi River to New Orleans. Despite film's preposterous plot, the performances of the two young leads do inspire a level of sentiment. **99m/C VHS.** Renee Humphrey, Brad Renfro, Joseph Mazzello, Annabella Sciorra, Diana Scarwid, Bruce Davison; ***D:*** Peter Horton; ***W:*** Robert Kuhn; ***C:*** Andrew Dintenfass; ***M:*** Dave Grusin.

Curfew 🦴🦴 1988 (R) A young woman rushes home so she doesn't break her curfew, only to find two killers with time on their hands waiting for her. Violent. **86m/C VHS.** John Putch, Kyle Richards, William Wellman Jr., Bert Remsen; ***D:*** Gary Winick.

The Curfew Breakers 🦴 1957 Dim teen-exploitation/message-movie finds a pair of community workers investigating the murder of a gas station attendent by a drug-crazed youth. **78m/B VHS.** Regis Toomey, Paul Kelly, Cathy Downs, Marilyn Madison, Sheila Urban; ***D:*** Alex Wells.

Curiosity Kills 🦴½ 1990 (R) Young people find more than they bargained for when they begin to investigate the death of a fellow tenant. Tense made-for-cable thriller. **86m/C VHS.** Rae Dawn Chong, C. Thomas Howell, Courteney Cox Arquette, Paul Guilfoyle, Jeff Fahey; ***D:*** Colin Bucksey; ***W:*** Joe Batteer, John Rice; ***C:*** Bojan Bazelli. CABLE

The Curious Dr. Humpp 🦴 1970 A mad scientist (Barbero) kidnaps exotic dancers and extracts their libidos to preserve his youth. Under the guise of research, he encourages his victims to engage in trysts so that their carnal energies will increase. Everything is hunky dory until a reporter (Bauleo) starts snooping around the laboratory, discovering Dr. Humpp observing multiple couplings via closed-circuit TV. Boldly exploitative, the American distributor added about 10 minutes of raunchy hard-core footage of exotic dance routines. **87m/B VHS, DVD.** *AR* Gloria Prat, Susan Beltran, Ricardo Bauleo, Aldo Barbero; ***D:*** Emilio Vieyra; ***W:*** Emilio Vieyra, Raul Zorrilla; ***C:*** Anibal Gonzalez Paz; ***M:*** Victor Buchino.

Curley 🦴🦴 1947 High-spirited youngsters play pranks on their schoolteacher. A part of the Hal Roach Comedy Carnival. **53m/C VHS.** Larry Olsen, Frances Rafferty, Eilene Janssen, Walter Abel; ***D:*** Bernard Carr.

Curly Sue 🦴🦴 1991 (PG) Adorable, homeless waif Porter and her scheming, adoptive father Belushi plot to rip off single, career-minded female attorney Lynch in order to take in some extra cash. Trouble is, all three heartstrings are tugged, and the trio develop a warm, caring relationship. A throwback to the Depression era's Shirley Temple formula films met with mixed reviews. Undiscriminating younger audiences should have a good time, though. **102m/C VHS, 8mm.** James Belushi, Kelly Lynch, Alison Porter, John Getz, Fred Dalton Thompson; ***D:*** John Hughes; ***W:*** John Hughes; ***M:*** Georges Delerue.

Curly Top 🦴🦴½ 1935 (G) Orphan Temple helps land a husband for her beautiful sister. Along the way, she sings "Animal Crackers in My Soup." Remake of the silent "Daddy Long Legs," which was remade again in 1955. **74m/B VHS.** Shirley Temple, John Boles, Rochelle Hudson, Jane Darwell, Esther Dale, Arthur Treacher, Rafaela (Rafael, Raphaella) Ottiano; ***D:*** Irving Cummings.

The Curse 🦴 *The Farm* 1987 (R) After a meteorite lands near a small farming community and contaminates the area, a young boy tries to prevent residents from turning into slime-oozing mutants. Remake of "Die, Monster, Die." **92m/C VHS.** Wil Wheaton, Claude Akins, Malcolm Danare, Cooper Huckabee, John Schneider, David Keith, Amy Wheaton, David Chaskin, Kathleen Jordan Gregory; ***D:*** David Keith; ***W:*** David Chaskin; ***C:*** Robert D. Forges.

Curse 2: The Bite 🦴 1988 (R) Radiation affected snakes are transformed into deadly vipers whose bites change their unsuspecting victims into horrible creatures. **97m/C VHS.** Jill Schoelen, J. Eddie Peck, Jamie Farr, Savina Gersak, Bo Svenson, Sydney Lassick, Marianne Muellerleile, Terrence Evans; ***D:*** Fred Goodwin; ***W:*** Fred Goodwin, Susan Zelouf; ***C:*** Roberto D'Ettorre Piazzoli.

Curse 3: Blood Sacrifice *Panga* 1990 (R) An African sugar cane plantation becomes host to a horrible nightmare when a voodoo curse is placed on the owners. The monstrous God of the Sea is summoned to avenge the accidental death of a baby, and the hellish journey into insanity begins. **91m/C VHS.** Christopher Lee, Jenilee Harrison, Henry Cele; ***D:*** Sean Barton.

Curse 4: The Ultimate Sacrifice 🦴½ *Catacombs* 1990 (R) Beneath the monastery at San Pietro lies buried the beast of the Apocalypse. For 400 years the secret has been kept and then an American priest and a lovely school teacher unwittingly break the seal and unleash the cursed beast upon an unsuspecting world. **84m/C VHS.** Timothy Van Patten, Laura Schaefer, Jeremy West, Ian Abercrombie; ***D:*** David Schmoeller.

The Curse of Frankenstein 🦴🦴½ 1957 Young Victor Frankenstein reenacts his father's experiments with creating life from the dead resulting in a terrifying, hideous creature. The first in Hammer's Frankenstein series and followed by "Revenge of Frankenstein." From the Shelley story. Make-up by Jack Pierce, who also created the famous make-up for Universal's Frankenstein monster. **83m/C VHS.** *GB* Peter Cushing, Christopher Lee, Hazel Court, Robert Urquhart, Valerie Gaunt, Noel Hood; ***D:*** Terence Fisher; ***W:*** Jimmy Sangster; ***C:*** Jack Asher; ***M:*** James Bernard.

The Curse of Inferno 🦴½ 1996 (R) Dumb-as-posts bankrobbers Shore and Perlich get mixed up in a sting operation to flush out the head of a money-laundering operation. **87m/C VHS.** Pauly Shore, Max Perlich, Janine Turner, Ned Beatty, John Pleshette, Stephen Tobolowsky, Edward "Blue" Deckert; ***D:*** John Warren; ***W:*** John Warren; ***C:*** Nancy Schreiber.

The Curse of King Tut's Tomb 🦴½ 1980 In 1922, archaeologists have just opened Tutankhamen's tomb. The curse of the boy king is unleashed as tragic events bring the adventurers uncommon gloom. Oh boy. **98m/C VHS.** Robin Ellis, Harry Andrews, Eva Marie Saint, Raymond Burr, Wendy Hiller; ***D:*** Philip Leacock; ***Nar:*** Paul Scofield. TV

The Curse of the Aztec Mummy woof! *La Maldicion de la Momia Azteca* 1959 A mad scientist schemes to rob a Mayan pyramid of its treasure but the resident mummy will have none of it. Sequel to "Robot vs. the Aztec Mummy" and followed by "Wrestling Women vs. the Aztec Mummy." **65m/B VHS.** *MX* Ramon Gay, Rosita (Rosa) Arenas, Crox Alvarado; ***D:*** Rafael Portillo.

Curse of the Black Widow 🦴🦴 *Love Trap* 1977 An investigator follows a trail of brutal murders to the lair of a supernatural gigantic spider in the middle of Los Angeles. **100m/C VHS.** Patty Duke, Anthony (Tony) Franciosa, Donna Mills, June Lockhart, Sid Caesar, Vic Morrow, June Allyson, Roz Kelly, Jeff Corey; ***D:*** Dan Curtis. TV

Curse of the Blue Lights woof! 1988 (R) Mysterious lights begin appearing at the local romantic spot. Little do the young lovers know, it hails the arrival of a ghoul, intent on raising the dead. Also available in an unedited version. Unfortunately, nothing can resurrect this film. **93m/C VHS.** Brent Ritter, Bettina Julius, Kent E. Fritzell, Willard Hall; ***D:*** John H. Johnson; ***W:*** John H. Johnson.

Curse of the Cat People 🦴🦴🦴 1944 A young sensitive girl is guided by the vision of her dead mother. Sequel to "Cat People." Available in a colorized version. **70m/B VHS.** Simone Simon, Kent Smith, Jane Randolph, Elizabeth Russell, Ann Carter; ***D:*** Robert Wise, Gunther Von Fritsch.

The Curse of the Crying Woman 🦴½ *La Maldicion de a Llorona; La Casa Embrujada* 1961 Unknowing descendant of a witch is lured to her aunt's home to perform the act that will revive the monstrous crying woman and renew a reign of evil. **74m/B VHS.** *MX* Rosita (Rosa) Arenas, Abel Salazar, Rita Macedo; ***D:*** Rafael Baledon Sr.; ***W:*** Rafael Baledon Sr., Fernando Galiana; ***C:*** Jose Ortiz Ramos.

Curse of the Crystal Eye 🦴🦴 1993 (PG-13) A gunrunner tries to get the treasure of Ali Baba aided by the requisite lovely lady and opposed by your usual bad guys. **90m/C VHS.** Jameson Parker, Cynthia Rhodes, Mike Lane, David Sherwood, Andre Jacobs; ***D:*** Joe Tornatore.

Curse of the Demon 🦴🦴🦴½ *Night of the Demon; The Haunted* 1957 A famous psychologist investigates a colleague's mysterious death and enters a world of demonology and the occult, climaxing in a confrontation with a cult's patron demon. Superb thriller based upon the story "Casting the Runes" by M.R. James. **81m/B VHS.** *GB* Dana Andrews, Peggy Cummins, Niall MacGinnis, Maurice Denham, Athene Seyler, Liam Redmond, Reginald Beckwith, Ewan Roberts, Peter Elliott, Brian Wilde, Rosamund Greenwood; ***D:*** Jacques Tourneur; ***W:*** Charles Bennett, Hal E. Chester; ***C:*** Edward Scaife; ***M:*** Clifton Parker.

Curse of the Devil 🦴½ *El Retorno de la Walpurgis* 1973 (R) This time Naschy is turned into a werewolf by annoyed gypsies whose ancestors were slain by his. **73m/C VHS.** *MX SP* Paul (Jacinto Molina) Naschy, Jacinto (Jack) Molina, Maria Silva, Patty (Patti) Shepard, Fay Falcon, Fabiola Falcon, Antonio Molina, Ines Morales; ***D:*** Carlos Aured; ***W:*** Jacinto (Jack) Molina; ***C:*** Francisco Sanchez.

Curse of the Headless Horseman 1972 The headless horseman rides again, bringing terror to all who cross his path! **80m/C VHS, DVD.** Don Carrara, Claudia Dean, B.G. Fisher, Margo Dean, Lee Byers, Joe Cody; ***D:*** John Kirkland.

The Curse of the Jade Scorpion 🦴🦴½ 2001 (PG-13) Where can a 65-year-old guy who looks like Woody Allen bag a babe like Helen Hunt? In a Woody Allen movie, that's where. Hunt plays efficiency expert Betty Ann Fitzgerald, who's hired to update the offices of a Manhattan insurance agency where C.W. Briggs (Allen) is the chief investigator, so he and "Fitz" develop an immediate mutual dislike. After several increasingly tedious games of verbal darts, the two are mesmerized by nightclub hypnotist Voltan (Stiers) into believing that they're in love. He also uses hypnotic cues to have C.W. unknowingly pull off jewel heists of his own clients. After a mystery woman (Theron) shows up, C.W. begins to question where he's been and who he's been with late at night and enlists the help of the Coopersmith Brothers (Mulheren and Linari) to help crack the case. Lighter and shallower than most of Allen's work, it's still mostly fun to watch. Soundtrack is chock full of Allen's beloved 40s era jazz and Big Band tunes. **103m/C VHS, DVD, Wide.** *US* Woody Allen, Helen Hunt, Dan Aykroyd, Elizabeth Berkley, Charlize Theron, Wallace Shawn, David Ogden Stiers, John Schuck, Brian Markinson, Michael Mulheren, Peter Linari, Prof. Irwin Corey, Peter Gerety; ***D:*** Woody Allen; ***W:*** Woody Allen; ***C:*** Zhao Fei.

Curse of the Living Corpse 🦴 1964 A millionaire comes back to rotting life to kill his negligent relatives. Scheider's first film. **84m/C VHS.** Candace Hilligoss, Roy Scheider, Helen Warren, Margot Hartman; ***D:*** Del Tenney.

Curse of the Pink Panther 🦴🦴 1983 (PG) Clifton Sleigh, an inept New York City detective played by Wass, is assigned to find the missing Inspector Clouseau. His efforts are complicated by an assortment of gangsters and aristocrats who cross paths with the detective. So-so attempt to keep popular series going after Seller's death. Niven's last film. **110m/C VHS.** Ed Parker, Ted Wass, David Niven, Robert Wagner, Herbert Lom, Joanna Lumley, Capucine, Robert Loggia, Harvey Korman, Leslie Ash, Denise Crosby; ***D:*** Blake Edwards; ***W:*** Blake Edwards; ***C:*** Dick Bush; ***M:*** Henry Mancini.

Curse of the Puppet Master: The Human Experiment 🦴½ 1998 (R) The little guys have been taking a break since 1994's "Puppet Master 5" but they're baaaack. This time they're trying to prevent their new master, evil Dr. Magrew, from transforming more victims into living dolls. The director, "Victoria Sloan," is actually DeCoteau. **90m/C VHS, DVD.** George Peck, Emily Harrison, Michael Guerin, Robert Donovan; ***D:*** David DeCoteau; ***W:*** Benjamin Carr; ***C:*** Howard Wexler; ***M:*** Richard Band. VIDEO

Curse of the Queerwolf 🦴🦴 1987 A man is bitten on the butt by gay werewolf and transforms into the title character. Filmed in Santa Barbara in 8mm; some funny moments. From the director of "A Polish Vampire in Burbank." **90m/C VHS.** Michael Palazzolo, Kent Butler, Taylor Whitney, Darwyn Carson, Sergio Bandera, Mark Pirro, Forrest J Ackerman, Conrad Brooks; ***D:*** Mark Pirro; ***W:*** Mark Pirro; ***M:*** Gregg Gross.

Curse of the Starving Class 🦴🦴 1994 (R) Ineffective adaptation of Sam Shepard's 1977 play exploring family disintegration. Weston (Woods) is the alcoholic, irresponsible patriarch of a decaying farm. His unhappy wife, Ella (Bates), wants to sell out to land speculator Taylor (Quaid) and move to Paris while rebellious teenager Emma (Fiorella) plans to run off to Mexico and sullen older brother Wesley (Thomas) desires to stay and make a go of things. One-dimensional characterizations don't translate well from stage to screen. **102m/C VHS.** James Woods, Kathy Bates, Henry Thomas, Kristin Fiorella, Randy Quaid, Louis Gossett Jr.; ***D:*** Michael McClary; ***W:*** Bruce Beresford; ***C:*** Dick Quinlan.

Curse of the Stone Hand woof! 1964 A pair of stone hands causes folks to do suicidal things. A mutation of a Mexican and a Chilean horror film, each purchased and monster-mashed into one by Warren. **72m/B VHS.** *MX* John Carradine, Ernest Walch, Sheila Bon, Katherine Victor, Lloyd Nelson; ***D:*** Jerry Warren.

Curse of the Swamp Creature 🦴 1966 A mad scientist in the Everglades attempts to create half human/half alligator monsters. In turn, a geologic expeditionary force attempts to stop his experimentation. Low budget thrills courtesy of Larry Buchanan. **80m/C VHS.** John Agar, Francine York, Shirley McLine, Bill (Billy) Thurman, Jeff Alexander; ***D:*** Larry Buchanan.

Curse of the Undead 🦴½ *Affairs of the Vampire; Mark of the West; Mark of the Beast; The Invisible Killer; Le Teur Invisible; Les Griffes du Vampire; The Grip of the Vampire* 1959 Mediocre vampire western finds a small town suffering from the deaths of several young women—all with small wounds in the neck. Suspicions fall on gunslinger Drake Robey (Pate) and it's up to preacher Dan Young (Fleming) to take care of the blood-sucking miscreant. **89m/B VHS.** Eric Fleming, Michael Pate, Kathleen Crowley, John Hoyt, Bruce Gordon, Edward Binns, Jimmy Murphy, Jay Adler; ***D:*** Edward Dein; ***W:*** Edward

Dein, Mildred Dein; ***C:*** Ellis W. Carter; ***M:*** Irving Gertz.

The Curse of the Werewolf 🦴🦴½ 1961 Horror film about a 19th-century European werewolf that is renowned for its ferocious departure from the stereotypical portrait of the beast. **91m/C VHS.** *GB* Oliver Reed, Clifford Evans, Yvonne Romain, Catherine Feller, Anthony Dawson, Michael Ripper, Peter Sallis; ***D:*** Terence Fisher; ***W:*** John (Anthony Hinds) Elder; ***C:*** Arthur Grant.

Curse of the Yellow Snake 🦴🦴 1963 Voluminous yarn features a running battle over an ancient Chinese artifact, with crazed Chinese cultists running through foggy London streets. **98m/C VHS.** *GE* Joachim Fuchsberger, Werner Peters; ***D:*** Franz Gottlieb.

The Cursed Mountain Mystery 🦴½ 1993 (R) Two petty thieves steal a legendary precious gem rumored to cursed. The immortal warrior supposed to guard the gem lures the crooks to Sher Mountain, where he intends to eliminate them and return the stone to its keeper. **87m/C VHS.** Phillip Avalon, Tom Richards, Joe Bugner; ***D:*** Vince Martin; ***W:*** Denis Whitburn.

Curtain Call 🦴🦴 1997 (PG-13) Publishing exec Stevenson Lowe (Spader) movies into a brownstone that is haunted by the ghosts of bickering theatrical marrieds Max (Caine) and Lily (Smith). Unfortunately for him, Stevenson is the only one who can see the duo, so his girlfriend Julia (Walker) thinks he's nuts. She has a problem with her commitment-phobe beau anyway and it's up to Max and Lily to see the duo stay together. **94m/C VHS, DVD.** James Spader, Polly Walker, Michael Caine, Maggie Smith, Buck Henry, Sam Shepard, Todd Alcott, Susan Berman, Marcia Gay Harden, Valerie Perrine, Frances Sternhagen, Frank Whaley; ***D:*** Peter Yates; ***W:*** Todd Alcott; ***C:*** Sven Nykvist; ***M:*** Richard Hartley. **VIDEO**

Curtain Up 🦴🦴 1953 "Little theatre" dramatics and the exasperating temperaments of amateur theatricals are exposed in this adaptation of the play "On Monday Next," by Philip King. **82m/C VHS.** *GB* Robert Morley, Margaret Rutherford, Olive Sloane; ***D:*** Ralph Smart; ***W:*** Jack Davies; ***M:*** Malcolm Arnold.

Curtains woof! 1983 (R) Director has a clash of wills with a film star that spells "Curtains" for a group of aspiring actresses gathered together at a haunted house for an audition. Hamfest with no thrills, chills, gore, or gratuitous skin. No wonder why director Richard Ciupka hides behind pseudonym Stryker. **90m/C VHS.** *CA* John Vernon, Samantha Eggar; ***D:*** Jonathan Stryker; ***W:*** Robert Guza Jr.

Curtis's Charm 🦴½ 1996 Thanks to his drug paranoia, crack addict Curtis (Wint) believes his wife Cookie (Crawford) and mother-in-law (Barnes-Hopkins) have put a voodoo spell on him. His friend Jim (Callum Rennie), a former addict, tries to help Curtis by coming up with some magic of his own, intended to convince the addled druggie that it will protect him. Lots of narration does little to make the character's friendship convincing. Based on a short story by Jim Carroll. **74m/B VHS.** *CA* Maurice Dean Wint, Callum Keith Rennie, Rachael Crawford, Barbara Barnes-Hopkins; ***D:*** John L'Ecuyer; ***W:*** James Dennis (Jim) Carroll, John L'Ecuyer; ***C:*** Harald Bachmann; ***M:*** Mark Korven. Genie '96: Score.

The Curve 🦴🦴 *Dead Man's Curve* 1997 (R) Think "Dead Man on Campus" since you've got basically the same premise. College roomies Tim (Lillard), Rand (Batinkoff), and Chris (Vartan) learn that student myth is true at their small university. Should a roomie commit suicide, the survivors receive an automatic 4.0 for the semester. So Tim offs Rand and has Chris help him cover things up. Naturally this doesn't work out entirely as expected. Not nearly as clever as it tries to be. **90m/C VHS, DVD, Wide.** Matthew Lillard, Michael Vartan, Randall Batinkoff, Keri Russell, Dana Delany, Tamara Craig Thomas, Anthony Griffin, Bo Dietle, Kevin Huff, Henry Stozier; ***D:*** Dan Rosen; ***W:*** Dan Rosen; ***C:*** Joey Forsyte.

Custer's Last Fight 🦴½ 1912 Contains the earliest surviving film of Custer's last stand. This 1925 re-release version of the original 1912 Thomas Ince production, filmed on location at the original battlefield, hosts a cast of real American Indians who claim to have taken part in the actual battle. Provides an authentic recreation of the original battle. Comes with a copy of the original production pamphlet. **50m/B VHS.** ***D:*** Francis Ford.

Custer's Last Stand 🦴½ 1936 Feature-length version of the Mascot serial recounting the last days of the famous General. **70m/B VHS.** Frank McGlynn, Rex Lease, Nancy Caseell, Lona Andre, William Farnum, Reed Howes, Jack Mulhall, Josef Swickard, Ruth Mix; ***D:*** Elmer Clifton.

The Custodian 🦴🦴 1994 (R) Honest cop must battle corruption of Australian police precinct while dealing with numerous personal problems. Good cast goes a long way in routine story. **110m/C VHS.** *AU* Anthony LaPaglia, Hugo Weaving, Barry Otto, Bill Hunter, Kelly Dingwall, Gosia Dobrowolska, Naomi Watts; ***D:*** John Dingwall.

Cut 🦴🦴 2000 (R) In this instance the title can be taken literally since a killer is knocking off those involved in a low-budget horror film. It seems that a group of film students want to finish a film that was shut down 15 years earlier after it's female director (Minogue) was murdered on the set. The students manage to get Vanessa (Ringwald), the star of the original, to reprise her role but is the film cursed or is someone giving their efforts a critical thumbs down? **82m/C VHS, DVD, Wide.** *AU* Molly Ringwald, Jessica Napier, Simon Bossell, Sarah Kants, Stephen Curry, Geoff Revell, Frank Roberts, Sam Lewis; ***Cameos:*** Kylie Minogue; ***D:*** Kimble Rendall; ***W:*** Dave Warner; ***C:*** David Foreman; ***M:*** Guy Gross. **VIDEO**

Cut and Run 🦴 *Inferno in Diretta; Amazon: Savage Adventure; Straight to Hell* 1985 (R) Two journalists follow a lead to the former South American home of Jim Jones, and are instantly captured by local guerrillas. **91m/C VHS, DVD, Wide.** *IT* Lisa Blount, Leonard Mann, Willie Aames, Richard Lynch, Michael Berryman, Karen Black, Eriq La Salle; ***D:*** Ruggero Deodato; ***W:*** Cesare Frugoni; ***C:*** Alberto Spagnoli; ***M:*** Claudio Simonetti.

The Cut Throats 🦴 *She Devils of the S.S* 1969 (R) Americans stumble upon an isolated Nazi outpost stocked with gold and beautiful women. Exploitation at its worst. **80m/C VHS.** Jay Scott, Joanne Douglas, Jeff Letham, Pat Michaels, Barbara Lane; ***D:*** John Hayes; ***W:*** John Hayes.

Cutaway 🦴½ 2000 (R) Vic Cooper (Baldwin) is a customs agent who goes undercover to infiltrate a group of drug dealers who deliver their goods via skydiving. He discovers the sport gives him a bigger adrenaline rush than his job, so which one will he choose? **104m/C VHS, DVD, Wide.** Tom Berenger, Stephen Baldwin, Dennis Rodman, Maxine Bahns, Casper Van Dien, Ron Silver; ***D:*** Guy Manos; ***W:*** Guy Manos, Greg Manos; ***C:*** Gerry Lively. **VIDEO**

Cutter's Way 🦴🦴½ *Cutter and Bone* 1981 (R) An embittered and alcoholic disabled Vietnam vet and his small-time crook/gigolo friend wrestle with justice and morality when the drifter uncovers a murder but declines to get involved. An unusually cynical mystery from the novel by Newton Thorburg. **105m/C VHS, DVD, Wide.** Jeff Bridges, John Heard, Lisa Eichhorn, Ann Dusenberry, Stephen Elliott, Nina Van Pallandt, George Dickerson; ***D:*** Ivan Passer; ***W:*** Jeffrey Alladin Fiskin; ***C:*** Jordan Cronenweth; ***M:*** Jack Nitzsche.

Cutthroat Island 🦴🦴½ 1995 (PG-13) Big-budget swashbuckling adventure—long on action and short on plot and character. Female pirate captain Morgan Adams (Davis) is left part of a treasure map by her father and "persuades" educated slave/thief William Shaw (Modine), who has lots of charm and no morals, to assist her. Her scurvy Uncle Dawg (despically well-played by Langella) also has a portion of the map and is willing to let Morgan find the treasure—on Cutthroat Island—before taking it for himself. Director Harlin likes lots of big, noisy explosions (when he doesn't know what else to do) but Davis' exuberance for her pirate queen role is appealing. **123m/C VHS, DVD.** Geena Davis, Matthew Modine, Frank Langella, Patrick Malahide, Stan Shaw, Maury Chaykin, Harris Yulin, George Murcell; ***D:*** Renny Harlin; ***W:*** Robert King, Marc Norman; ***C:*** Peter Levy; ***M:*** John Debney.

Cutting Class 🦴🦴 1989 (R) Murders proliferate in a high school, where a student with a history of mental illness is number one on the suspect list. Tongue-in-cheek mayhem. **91m/C VHS.** Jill Schoelen, Roddy McDowall, Donovan Leitch, Martin Mull, Brad Pitt; ***D:*** Rospo Pallenberg.

The Cutting Edge 🦴🦴½ 1992 (PG) Spoiled figure skater's lifelong quest for Olympic gold is seriously hampered by her inability to be nice to her partners. In a final effort to snag the medal she teams up with a cocky guy who thinks the only sport on ice is hockey, but whose own dreams of NHL stardom were cut short by an injury. Saddled with a predictable and thin plot, it sometimes looks and feels like a TV movie. So why bother? Because the chemistry between photogenic leads Kelly and Sweeney is terrific. Add half a bone for the flying sparks and snappy dialogue, sit back, and enjoy. **101m/C VHS, DVD, Wide.** D.B. Sweeney, Moira Kelly, Roy Dotrice, Terry O'Quinn, Dwier Brown, Rachelle Ottley, Jo Jo Starbuck; ***D:*** Paul Michael Glaser; ***W:*** Tony Gilroy; ***C:*** Elliot Davis; ***M:*** Patrick Williams.

Cyber Bandits 🦴½ 1994 (R) In a future society, navigator Jack Morris (Kemp) has just sailed a pleasure craft to the island city of Pacifica. His passengers included wealthy Morgan Wells (Hays), whose scientists have developed a deadly virtual reality weapon, and Wells' mistress Rebecca (Paul). Rebecca steals the plans for the weapon and seduces Jack into having the data digitally transferred onto his back in the form of a tattoo. Then Rebecca disappears and Jack finds himself in big trouble. **86m/C VHS.** Martin Kemp, Alexandra Paul, Robert Hays, Adam Ant, Grace Jones; ***D:*** Erik Fleming; ***W:*** James Robinson, Winston Beard; ***M:*** Steve Hunter.

Cyber Ninja 🦴🦴½ *Mirai Ninja; Future Ninja; Robo Ninja* 1994 Warrior princess Saki is captured by the Dark Overlord, who plans to sacrifice her. It's up to a mercenary to come to her rescue. Lightweight, action-oriented Japanese mix of samurais and science fiction. Dubbed. **80m/C VHS.** *JP* Hanbel Kawai, Hiroki Ida; ***D:*** Keito Amamiya; ***W:*** Keito Amamiya.

Cyber-Tracker 🦴½ 1993 (R) In the judicial system of the future androids hunt down vicious criminals and execute them immediately. When secret service agent Eric Phillips is framed for murder, he's also marked for death. His only chance is to link up with rebels fighting the mechanized monsters. **91m/C VHS, DVD.** Don "The Dragon" Wilson, Richard Norton, Joseph Ruskin, Abby Dalton, John Aprea; ***D:*** Richard Pepin; ***W:*** Jacobsen Hart; ***C:*** Ken Blakey; ***M:*** Bill Montei, Lisa Popeil.

Cyber-Tracker 2 🦴½ 1995 (R) An international weapons dealer has gotten control of the cybertracker technology and created cyborg lookalikes of secret agent Eric Phillips (Wilson) and his newscaster wife Connie (Foster). When the cyborgs commit murder on live TV, the human duo become fugitives who must expose the real killers. **97m/C VHS.** Don "The Dragon" Wilson, Stacie Foster, Steve (Stephen) Burton; ***D:*** Richard Pepin; ***W:*** Richard Preston Jr.

Cybercity 🦴½ 1999 (R) When mercenary Howell's family is murdered by virtual prophet Piper, who's trying to take over the world, Howell tries for revenge with the aid of assassin von Palleske. **86m/C VHS, DVD.** C. Thomas Howell, Roddy Piper, Heidi von Palleske, David Carradine; ***D:*** Peter Hayman; ***W:*** Nehu Ghiran; ***C:*** Graeme Mears; ***M:*** Donald Quan. **VIDEO**

Cyberstalker 🦴½ *The Digital Prophet* 1996 Detective twosome must track down a serial killer who uses the Internet to select his victims. **96m/C VHS.** Blake Bahner, Jeffrey Combs, Annie Biggs, Schnele Wilson; ***D:*** Christopher Romero; ***W:*** Tony Brownrigg, Annie Biggs.

Cyberzone 🦴½ *Droid Gunner* 1995 (R) Intergalactic investigator pursues four dangerous androids who are hiding on earth. **95m/C VHS.** Marc Singer, Matthias Hues, Rochelle Swanson, Robin Clarke, Kin Shriner, Brinke Stevens; ***D:*** Fred Olen Ray; ***W:*** William Martell.

Cyborg 🦴 1989 (R) In a deathly, dirty, post-holocaust urban world, an able cyborg battles a horde of evil mutant thugs. Poorly made action flick. **85m/C VHS, DVD, Wide.** Jean-Claude Van Damme, Deborah Richter, Vincent Klyn, Dayle Haddon, Alex Daniels, Terrie Batson, Janice Graser, Jackson "Rock" Pinckney; ***D:*** Albert Pyun; ***W:*** Kitty Chalmers; ***C:*** Philip Alan Waters; ***M:*** Kevin Bassinson.

Cyborg 2 🦴🦴 *Cyborg 2: Glass Shadow* 1993 (R) In the year 2074 cyborgs have replaced humans at all levels. A devious company which manufactures cyborgs decides to get rid of its chief competition by literally killing them off. They plan to inject cyborg Cash Reese (Jolie) with a liquid explosive that will detonate her and everything else in sight. Tech-master Mercy (Palance) clues Cash in and she escapes with the help of the human Colton (Koteas) but they've become prey to a group of ruthless hunters. **99m/C VHS, DVD.** Angelina Jolie, Elias Koteas, Jack Palance, Billy Drago; ***D:*** Michael Schroeder; ***W:*** Michael Schroeder, Mark Geldman, Ron Yanover; ***C:*** Jamie Thompson; ***M:*** Peter Allen.

Cyborg 3: The Recycler 🦴🦴 1995 (R) Female cyborg has been programmed to become a creator—essentially making mankind useless. **90m/C VHS.** Khrystyne Haje, Zach Galligan, Andrew Bryniarski, Richard Lynch, Malcolm McDowell; ***D:*** Michael Schroeder; ***W:*** Barry Victor, Troy Bolotnick.

Cyborg Cop 🦴½ 1993 (R) DEA agent Phillip (Jenson) is captured during a foreign drug raid and is turned into a half-man, half-machine by mad scientist Kessel (Rhys-Davies), who wants to sell his cyborgs as unstoppable hitmen. Phillip's brother Jack (Bradley) tries to come to his rescue. Lots of stunts and car chases and even a minor romantic subplot with Jack and a tough reporter (Shaw). **97m/C VHS.** David Bradley, John Rhys-Davies, Todd Jensen, Alonna Shaw; ***D:*** Sam Firstenberg; ***W:*** Glenn A. Bruce, Greg Latter; ***C:*** Yossi Wein.

Cyborg Soldier 🦴🦴½ *Cyborg Cop 2* 1994 (R) Loose cannon cop Jack Ryan (Bradley) is up against psycho killer Starkraven (Hunter) who gets turned into a new-model cyborg by your basic suspicious government agency. But when the cyborg decides to go on an unplanned human killing spree, Ryan gets to break out the heavy artillery to mow him down. Also available in an unrated version. **96m/C VHS.** David Bradley, Morgan Hunter, Jill Pierce; ***D:*** Sam Firstenberg; ***W:*** Jon Stevens.

Cycle Psycho woof! *Numbered Days; Savage Abduction* 1972 (R) Serial killer blackmails the businessman whose wife he was contracted to kill into bringing him young girls to slaughter. The businessman hires out the job to sleazy motorcycle gang. **80m/C VHS.** Joe Turkel, Tom Drake, Stephen Oliver; ***D:*** John Lawrence; ***W:*** John Lawrence.

Cycle Vixens woof! *The Young Cycle Girls* 1979 (R) Three girls jump on their hogs and head from Colorado to California. Much leather, motor revving and other obligatory motorcycle-trash trimmings. **90m/C VHS.** Loraine Ferris, Daphne Lawrence, Deborah Marcus, Lonnie Pense, Kevin O'Neill, Bee Lechat, Billy Bullet; ***D:*** Peter Perry.

Cyclo 🦴🦴 *Xich Lo* 1995 An orphaned 18-year-old (Van Loc), known only by by his profession of cyclo (pedal-taxi) driver, struggles on the streets of Ho Chi Minh City. When his vehicle is stolen, he's forced by his boss to repay its value and takes small-time jobs from local crime boss, The Poet (Leung), who, unbeknownst to the cyclo, is also his sister's (Yen-Khe) pimp. The deeper the young man gets into the criminal world, the closer he also gets to tragedy. Vietnamese with subtitles. **123m/C VHS.** *VT* Le Van Loc, Tran Nu Yen-Khe, Tony Leung Chiu-Wai, Nguyen Nhu Quynh; ***D:*** Tran Anh Hung; ***W:*** Tran Anh Hung; ***C:*** Benoit Delhomme; ***M:*** Ton That Tiet.

Cyclone 1987 (R) The girlfriend of a murdered scientist must deliver a secretly devised motorcycle into righteous government hands, much to the dismay of evil agents and corrupt officials. Good fun, sparked by a stellar "B" cast. **89m/C VHS.** Heather Thomas, Jeffrey Combs, Ashley Ferrare, Dar Robinson, Martine Beswick, Robert Quarry, Martin Landau, Huntz Hall, Troy Donahue, Michael Reagan, Dawn Wildsmith, Bruce Fairbairn, Russ Tamblyn; ***D:*** Fred Olen Ray; ***C:*** Paul Elliott.

Cyclone Cavalier 1925 A dauntless hero travels through Central America on an adventurous spree. **58m/B VHS.** Reed Howes; ***D:*** Albert Rogell.

Cyclone of the Saddle 1935 Typical Western about a range war. **53m/B VHS.** Rex Lease, Bobby Nelson, William Desmond, Yakima Canutt; ***D:*** Elmer Clifton.

Cyclops 1956 When an expedition party searches throughout Mexico for a woman's long lost fiance, they are shocked when they find out that radiation has turned him into a one-eyed monster. **72m/B VHS.** Tom Drake, Gloria Talbott, Lon Chaney Jr., James Craig; ***D:*** Bert I. Gordon.

Cyclotrode "X" *The Crimson Ghost* 1946 The Crimson Ghost attempts to kidnap the inventor of the title machine, which would enable him to rule the world. Moore (The Lone Ranger) plays a bad guy. Serial in 12 episodes. Also available in a 93-minute colorized edition. **100m/B VHS.** Charles Quigley, Linda Stirling, I. Stanford Jolley, Clayton Moore, Kenne Duncan; ***D:*** William Witney, Fred Brannon.

Cypress Edge 1999 (R) The murder of Louisiana Senator Woodrow McCammon's (Steiger) daughter brings her estranged family back together. The motive is clear—an $18 million estate—and the benefactors are the usual suspects. **?m/C VHS, DVD.** Rod Steiger, Damian Chapa, Brad Dourif, Ashley Laurence, Charles Napier; ***D:*** Serge Rodnunsky; ***W:*** Serge Rodnunsky; ***M:*** Carl Dante.

Cyrano de Bergerac 1925 Silent version of Edmond Rostand's novel about romantic Cyrano who fears to reveal his love to Roxanne because he feels his enormous nose makes him unattractive. So, he serves as a surrogate lover by encouraging another man's attentions to her. Color-tinted. **114m/C VHS, DVD.** *IT FR* Pierre Magnier, Linda Moglia, Angelo Ferrari; ***D:*** Augusto Genina; ***M:*** Carlo Moser.

Cyrano de Bergerac 1950 Edmund Rostand's famous story of a large-nosed yet poetic cavalier, who finds himself too ugly to be loved. He bears the pain of his devotion to Roxanne from afar, and helps the handsome but tongue-tied Christian to romance her. Ferrer became famous for this role, which won him an Oscar. Based on Brian Hooke's translation of the play. Also available colorized. **113m/B VHS, DVD.** Jose Ferrer, Mala Powers, William Prince, Elena Verdugo, Morris Carnovsky; ***D:*** Michael Gordon; ***W:*** Carl Foreman; ***C:*** Franz Planer; ***M:*** Dimitri Tiomkin. Oscars '50: Actor (Ferrer); Golden Globes '51: Actor—Drama (Ferrer).

Cyrano de Bergerac 1985 Edmond Rostand's gallant poet and swordsman, with the extraordinary nose, is well-portrayed by Jacobi in this Royal Shakespeare Company production. Translated and adapted by Anthony Burgess. **177m/C VHS.** *GB* Derek Jacobi, Sinead Cusack; ***D:*** Michael A. Simpson, Terry Hands; ***W:*** Anthony Burgess.

Cyrano de Bergerac 1990 (PG) Depardieu brings to exhilarating life Rostand's well-loved play about the brilliant but grotesque-looking swordsman/poet, afraid of nothing—except declaring his love to the beautiful Roxanne (Brochet). But Cyrano expresses his own feelings by helping handsome (but tongue-tied) fellow soldier Christian (Perez) woo Roxanne instead. One of France's costliest modern productions, a multi-award winner for its cast, costumes, music and sets. English subtitles (by Anthony Burgess) are designed to capture the intricate rhymes of the original French dialogue. **135m/C VHS.** *FR* Gerard Depardieu, Jacques Weber, Anne Brochet, Vincent Perez, Roland Bertin, Josiane Stoleru, Phillipe Volter, Philippe Morier-Genoud, Pierre Maguelon; ***D:*** Jean-Paul Rappeneau; ***W:*** Jean-Claude Carriere, Jean-Paul Rappeneau; ***C:*** Pierre Lhomme; ***M:*** Jean-Claude Petit. Oscars '90: Costume Des.; Cannes '90: Actor (Depardieu); Cesar '91: Actor (Depardieu), Art Dir./Set Dec., Cinematog., Costume Des., Director (Rappeneau), Film, Sound, Support. Actor (Weber), Score; Golden Globes '91: Foreign Film.

D-Day on Mars 1945 Alien invader the Purple Monster is bent on taking over Earth. Originally a 15-part Republic serial titled "The Purple Monster Strikes." **100m/B VHS.** Dennis Moore, Linda Stirling, Roy Barcroft, James Craven, Bud Geary, Mary Moore; ***D:*** Spencer Gordon Bennet, Fred Brannon.

D-Day, the Sixth of June *The Sixth of June* 1956 An American soldier has an affair with a Englishwoman weeks before D-Day, where he unhappily finds himself fighting side by side with her husband. Based on the novel by Lionel Shapiro. **106m/C VHS.** Richard Todd, Dana Wynter, Robert Taylor, Edmond O'Brien, John Williams, Jerry Paris, Richard Stapley; ***D:*** Henry Koster; ***C:*** Lee Garmes.

Da 1988 (PG) A middle-aged man returns to Ireland for his father's funeral. As he sorts out his father's belongings, his father returns as a ghostly presence to chat with him about life, death, and their own relationship. Based on the Hugh Leonard play with Hughes recreating his Tony-award winning role. **102m/C VHS.** Barnard Hughes, Martin Sheen, William Hickey, Hugh O'Conor; ***D:*** Matt Clark; ***W:*** Hugh Leonard; ***M:*** Elmer Bernstein.

Da Hip Hop Witch 2000 (R) Not so much a parody of "Blair Witch Project" as a collection of rap artists' unscripted monologues about a woman who is doing terrible things to them. It also marks the return to the screen of Vanilla Ice, last seen in the abominable "Cool As Ice." **93m/C VHS, DVD.** Stacii Jae Johnson, Dale Resteghini, Pras, Killah Priest, Spliff Star, Mobb Deep, (Marshall Mathers) Eminem, Rock, Colleen (Ann) (Vitamin C) Fitzpatrick; ***D:*** Dale Resteghini; ***W:*** Dale Resteghini.

Dad 1989 (PG) Hoping to make up for lost time, a busy executive rushes home to take care of his father who has just had a heart attack. What could have easily become sappy is made bittersweet by the convincing performances of Lemmon and Danson. Based on the novel by William Wharton. **117m/C VHS.** Jack Lemmon, Ted Danson, Ethan Hawke, Olympia Dukakis, Kathy Baker, Zakes Mokae, J.T. Walsh, Kevin Spacey, Chris Lemmon; ***D:*** Gary David Goldberg; ***W:*** Gary David Goldberg; ***M:*** James Horner.

Dad Savage 1997 (R) Strange British crime pic told in flashbacks. Dad Savage (Stewart) is an East Anglia gangster who grows tulips and has a fondness for country music and dressing like a cowboy. His son Sav (Wood) works for him and his right-hand man is H (McKidd). H tells fellow criminals Vic (Warren) and Bob (McFadden) that Dad has a stash of cash buried in a deserted house in the nearby woods. Dad finds out his workers are double-crossing him and there's hell to pay for everyone concerned. **104m/C VHS.** *GB* Patrick Stewart, Kevin McKidd, Joseph McFadden, Jake Wood, Marc Warren, Helen McCrory; ***D:*** Betsan Morris Evans; ***W:*** Steven Williams; ***C:*** Gavin Finney; ***M:*** Simon Boswell.

Daddy Long Legs 1919 Judy (Pickford), the eldest inhabitant of a dreary orphanage, comes to the attention of a mysterious benefactor who sends her to college. She eventually discovers the identity of her guardian, falls in love, and marries him. Based on a play by Jean Webster. **94m/B VHS, DVD.** Mary Pickford, Milla Davenport, Mahlon Hamilton, Lillian Langdon, Marshall Neilan; ***D:*** Marshall Neilan; ***W:*** Agnes Christine Johnston; ***C:*** Charles Rosher, Henry Cronjager.

Daddy Long Legs 1955 Far from the great musicals, but enjoyable. An eccentric millionaire glimpses a French orphan and becomes her anonymous benefactor. Her musing over his identity spawns some surreal (often inexplicable) dance numbers, but love conquers all, even lesser Johnny Mercer songs. From a story by Jean Webster, also done in 1919 with Mary Pickford, 1931 with Janet Gaynor and 1935 with Shirley Temple as "Curly Top." ♫Daddy Long Legs; Something's Got To Give; Sluefoot; Dream; History of the Beat; C-A-T Spells Cat; Welcome Egghead. **126m/C VHS, Wide.** Fred Astaire, Leslie Caron, Terry Moore, Thelma Ritter, Fred Clark, Charlotte Austin, Larry Keating; ***D:*** Jean Negulesco; ***C:*** Leon Shamroy; ***M:*** Alex North.

Daddy Nostalgia *These Foolish Things; Daddy Nostalgie* 1990 Birkin plays the estranged daughter of Bogarde, who rushes from her home in England to France to be with her seriously ill father. She must come to terms with her feelings for him just as Bogarde must deal with his own mortality. Wonderful performances, with Bogarde a charming and dominating presence. In French with English subtitles. **105m/C VHS.** *FR* Dirk Bogarde, Jane Birkin, Odette Laure; ***D:*** Bertrand Tavernier; ***W:*** Colo Tavernier O'Hagan; ***C:*** Denis Lenoir; ***M:*** Antoine Duhamel.

Daddy-O *Out on Probation* 1959 Drag racer Daddy-O traps the killers of his best friend and lands the blonde bombshell Jana. It might seem bad since it's dated, but, hey, it may have been bad in 1959, too! **74m/B VHS.** Dick Contino, Sandra Giles; ***D:*** Lou Place; ***W:*** David Moessinger.

Daddy's Boys 1987 (R) Since farming during the Depression is a rather low-paying endeavor, this family turns to thieving instead. But all-for-one and one-for-all is not the credo for one of the sons who decides to branch out on his own. Produced by Roger Corman. **90m/C VHS.** Daryl Haney, Laura Burkett, Raymond J. Barry, Dan Shor, Robert V. Barron; ***D:*** Joe Minion; ***W:*** Daryl Haney; ***C:*** David G. Stump; ***M:*** Sasha Matson.

Daddy's Dyin'...Who's Got the Will? 1990 (PG-13) Based on the critically acclaimed play, this bittersweet comedy stars Bridges and D'Angelo as two members of the spiteful Turnover clan. When Daddy is on his deathbed, the entire family uses the opportunity to stab each other in the back. Non-stop humor and deep-hearted honesty carries this delightful adaptation quickly from beginning to end. **95m/C VHS.** Beau Bridges, Beverly D'Angelo, Tess Harper, Judge Reinhold, Amy Wright, Keith Carradine, Patrika Darbo, Molly McClure, Bert Remsen; ***D:*** Jack Fisk; ***W:*** Del Shores; ***C:*** Paul Elliott; ***M:*** David McHugh.

Daddy's Girl 1996 (R) When adopted Jody's new family is threatened she'll stop at nothing to protect herself and them. **95m/C VHS.** William Katt, Michele Greene, Roxana Zal, Mimi (Meyer) Craven, Whip Hubley, Gabrielle Boni; ***D:*** Martin Kitrosser; ***W:*** Steve Pesce.

Daddy's Gone A-Hunting 1969 (PG) It's an eye for an eye, a baby for a baby in this well-done psychological thriller. A happily married woman is stalked by her deranged ex-boyfriend, whose baby she aborted years before. Now he wants the life of her child as just compensation for the loss of his. **108m/C VHS.** Carol White, Paul Burke, Scott Hylands, Rachel Ames, Mala Powers, James B. Sikking; ***D:*** Mark Robson; ***W:*** Larry Cohen; ***C:*** Ernest Laszlo; ***M:*** John Williams.

Daens 1992 Looks at the disparity between rich and poor at the turn of the century. Daens, a priest, returns home to Flanders to find desperate poverty among the Flemish-speaking workers of the local textile mill. The French-speaking mill owners are supported by the local Catholic church while Daens believes in the rights of the workers. Decleir makes his priest a complex and troubled man, who must choose between his conscience and social reform and the dictates of his church. Marred by somewhat cardboard villains and a complex political/social situation that isn't adequately explained. Based on the novel by Louis Paul Boon. Flemish and French with English subtitles. **134m/C VHS.** *FR BE NL* Jan Decleir, Gerard Desarthe, Antje De Boeck, Michael Pas, Johan Leysen, Idwig Stephane, Linda Van Dijck, Wim Meuwissen; ***D:*** Stijn Coninx; ***W:*** Francois Chevallier, Stijn Coninx; ***M:*** Dirk Brosse.

Dagger Eyes 198? A political assassin at work is inadvertently captured on film by a photographer. The assassin's mob employers will go to any lengths to destroy the film. Say cheeeeeese! **84m/C VHS.** Carole Bouquet, Philip Coccioletti, John Steiner; ***D:*** Carlo Vanzina.

The Dagger of Kamui *Kamui No Ken; Revenge of the Ninja Warrior* 1985 The only family Jiro has ever known is killed and he is accused of the crime. The evil Tenkai promises to take him to the real killer, but Jiro does not realize until later how cruelly he has been tricked. Then Jiro goes on a quest to find his past, all the while being manipulated by a vast and complex political machine. Watching this and Jiro's reactions make this anime more than a simple adventure or coming of age story. Whatever their motivations, Jiro's travels take him as far as America and into the paths of some characters as familiar to Western viewers as the historical figures in his homeland are to anyone knowledgeable of Japanese history. Based on the novels by Tetsu Yano. **132m/C VHS.** *JP* Michio Hazama; ***D:*** Taro Rin.

Dagora, the Space Monster woof! *Dagora; Space Monster Dagora; Uchudai Dogora; Uchu Daikaiju Dogora* 1965 Giant, slimy, pulsating mass from space lands on Earth and begins eating everything in sight. Scientists join together in a massive effort to destroy the creature. Believe it or not, it's sillier than most of the Japanese sci-fi genre. **80m/C VHS.** *JP* Yosuke Natsuki, Yoko Fujiyama, Akiko Wakabayashi, Hiroshi Koizumi; ***D:*** Inoshiro Honda; ***W:*** Shinichi Sekizawa; ***C:*** Hajime Koizumi.

The Dain Curse *Dashiell Hammett's The Dain Curse* 1978 In 1928, private eye Hamilton Nash must recover stolen diamonds, solve a millionaire's suicide, avoid being murdered, and end a family curse. Miniseries based on the novel by Dashiell Hammett. **138m/C VHS.** James Coburn, Jason Miller, Jean Simmons, Beatrice Straight, Hector Elizondo, Nancy Addison; ***D:*** E.W. Swackhamer. **TV**

Daisy Miller 1974 (G) Shepherd portrays the title character in this adaptation of the Henry James novella about a naive young American woman travelling through Europe and getting a taste of the Continent during the late 19th century. Though it is intelligently written and has a good supporting cast, the film seems strangely flat, due in large part to Shepherd's hollow performance. **93m/C VHS.** Cybill Shepherd, Eileen Brennan, Cloris Leachman, Mildred Natwick; ***D:*** Peter Bogdanovich; ***W:*** Frederic Raphael.

Dakota 1945 Fine cast becomes embroiled in railroad land dispute. In the meantime, love strikes The Duke. Standard Wayne western saga never quite gets on track. **82m/B VHS.** John Wayne, Vera (Hruba) Ralston, Walter Brennan, Ward Bond, Ona Munson; ***D:*** Joseph Kane.

Dakota 1988 (PG) A troubled half-breed teenager works for a rancher, romances his daughter, and befriends his crippled 12-year-old son. A well-meaning, but predictable drama. **96m/C VHS, DVD, Wide.** Lou Diamond Phillips, Dee Dee Norton, Eli Cummins, Herta Ware, Jordan Burton; ***D:*** Fred Holmes; ***C:*** James W. Wrenn.

Dakota Incident 1956 Decent western about stagecoach passengers travelling through Dakota Territory who must defend themselves against an Indian attack. **88m/C VHS.** Dale Robertson, Ward Bond, Linda Darnell, John Lund; ***D:*** Lewis R. Foster.

Daleks—Invasion Earth 2150 A.D. *Invasion Earth 2150 A.D* 1966 A sequel to "Dr. Who and the Daleks," wherein the popular British character endeavors to save the Earth from a robotic threat. **81m/C VHS.** *GB* Peter Cushing, Andrew Keir, Jill Curzon, Ray Brooks; ***D:*** Gordon Flemyng.

The Dallas Connection 1994 (R) Three of the four scientists working on a satellite weapons system are assassinated by a trio of sexy but lethal females. Now the remaining scientist is under federal protection in Dallas while he continues his work. Lots of T&A. **90m/C VHS.**

Julie Strain, Samantha (Sam) Phillips, Julie K. Smith, Wendy Hamilton; ***D:*** Andy Sidaris.

Dalva 🦴½ **1995** Dull TV movie finds restless Dalva Northridge (Fawccett) deciding to search for the son she was forced to give up for adoption some 20 years before. But she gets sidetracked juggling two love affairs—with Sam Creekmouth (Boothe), whose Indian heritage is tied to Dalva's family, and alcoholic university professor Michael (Coyote) who wants the Northridge family diaries for his research on the Great Plains. Based on the novel by Jim Harrison. **?m/C VHS.** Farrah Fawcett, Powers Boothe, Peter Coyote, Rod Steiger, Carroll Baker; ***D:*** Ken Cameron; ***W:*** Jim Harrison; ***C:*** Tony Imi.

Dam Busters 🦴🦴🦴½ **1955** Well-done and exciting film details the efforts of British scientists trying to devise a method of destroying a strategic dam in Nazi Germany during WWII. Definitely one of the better in the war movie genre. **119m/B VHS.** *GB* Michael Redgrave, Richard Todd, Ursula Jeans, Basil Sydney; ***D:*** Michael Anderson Sr.

Damage 🦴🦴🦴 **1992 (R)** The elegant Irons portrays Stephen, a middle-aged, married British politican who has always been completely in control of his life, especially where his feelings are concerned. Then he meets Anna (Binoche), his son's less-than-innocent fiance, and immediately begins an obsessive, wildly sexual affair with her. Stephen should have listened to Anna's warning about herself "Damaged people are dangerous, they know they can survive," because their passion leads to betrayal and tragedy. Binoche is more icon than human being but the film still hypnotizes as an exploration of passion. Based on the novel by Josephine Hart. An unrated version is also available. **111m/C VHS, DVD, Wide.** *GB FR* Jeremy Irons, Juliette Binoche, Rupert Graves, Miranda Richardson, Ian Bannen, Leslie Caron, Peter Stormare, Gemma Clark, Julian Fellowes; ***D:*** Louis Malle; ***W:*** David Hare; ***C:*** Peter Biziou; ***M:*** Zbigniew Preisner. British Acad. '92: Support. Actress (Richardson); L.A. Film Critics '92: Score.

Dames 🦴🦴🦴 **1934** A millionaire with fanatically religious beliefs tries to stop the opening of a Broadway show. In the last of the grand budget-breaking spectacles before the "production code" came into being, distinguished choreographer Busby Berkeley took his imagination to the limit: watch for the dancing clothes on an ironing board and dancing girls with puzzle pieces on their backs which form the real Keeler. ♫Dames; I Only Have Eyes For You; When You Were a Smile on Your Mother's Lips and a Twinkle in Your Father's Eye; Try To See It My Way; The Girl at the Ironing Board. **95m/B VHS.** Dick Powell, Joan Blondell, Ruby Keeler, ZaSu Pitts, Guy Kibbee, Busby Berkeley; ***D:*** Ray Enright; ***W:*** Delmer Daves; ***C:*** George Barnes.

Dames Ahoy 🦴 **1930** Three sailors on shore leave try to find the blonde who tricked one of them out of his pay. This is the original silent version with a piano score. **52m/B VHS.** Glenn Tryon, Otis Harlan, Eddie Gribbon, Helen Wright, Gertrude Astor; ***D:*** William James Craft.

Damien: Omen 2 🦴🦴 **1978 (R)** Sequel to "The Omen" about Damien, a young boy possessed with mysterious demonic powers, who kills those people who anger him. Followed by "The Final Conflict." **110m/C VHS, DVD, Wide.** William Holden, Lee Grant, Lew Ayres, Robert Foxworth, Sylvia Sidney, Lance Henriksen, Jonathan Scott-Taylor, Nicholas Pryor, Allan Arbus, Meshach Taylor; ***D:*** Don Taylor; ***W:*** Mike Hodges; ***C:*** Bill Butler; ***M:*** Jerry Goldsmith.

Damien: The Leper Priest 🦴🦴 *Father Damien: The Leper Priest* **1980** True story of a Roman Catholic priest who doomed himself by voluntarily serving on a leper colony 100 years ago. Somewhat disappointing considering the dramatic material. Originally a vehicle for David Janssen, who died prior to filming. **100m/C VHS.** Ken Howard, Mike Farrell, Wilfrid Hyde-White, William Daniels, David Ogden Stiers; ***D:*** Steven Gethers. **TV**

Damn the Defiant 🦴🦴🦴 *HMS Defiant* **1962** Adventure abounds when Guinness, as captain of the HMS Defiant during the Napoleonic wars, finds himself up against not only the French but his cruel second-in-command (Bogarde) and a mutinous crew as well. In the end, both a fleet-wide mutiny and a French invasion of England are avoided. Much attention is paid to period detail in this well-crafted film. **101m/C VHS, DVD, Wide.** *GB* Alec Guinness, Dirk Bogarde, Maurice Denham, Anthony Quayle; ***D:*** Lewis Gilbert; ***W:*** Nigel Kneale, Edmund H. North; ***C:*** Christopher Challis; ***M:*** Clifton Parker.

Damn Yankees 🦴🦴🦴 *What Lola Wants* **1958** Musical feature adapted from the Broadway hit. A baseball fan frustrated by his team's lack of success makes a pact with the devil to become the team's new star. Verdon is dynamite as the devil's accomplice. Great Bob Fosse choreography. ♫Whatever Lola Wants; (You Gotta Have) Heart; Shoeless Joe From Hannibal Mo; Goodbye, Old Girl; A Little Brains, a Little Talent; Who's Got the Pain; Two Lost Souls; There's Something About an Empty Chair; Those Were the Good Old Days. **110m/C VHS.** Gwen Verdon, Ray Walston, Tab Hunter, Jean Stapleton, Russ Brown; ***D:*** George Abbott, Stanley Donen.

Damnation Alley 🦴½ **1977 (PG)** A warrior, an artist, and a biker jump in tank and set off in search of civilization after Armageddon. They go to Albany instead. So-so attempt to revive the post-nuclear holocaust genre which was more successfully accomplished by the "Mad Max" series. Adapted from Roger Zelazny's novel. **87m/C VHS.** George Peppard, Jan-Michael Vincent, Paul Winfield, Dominique Sanda, Jackie Earle Haley; ***D:*** Jack Smight; ***W:*** Alan Sharp, Lukas Heller; ***C:*** Harry Stradling Jr.; ***M:*** Jerry Goldsmith.

The Damned 🦴🦴½ **1969 (R)** Depicts the Nazi takeover of a German industrialist family and their descent into greed, lust, and madness. Comes in dubbed or subtitled formats. **146m/C VHS.** *IT GE* Dirk Bogarde, Ingrid Thulin, Helmut Griem, Charlotte Rampling, Helmut Berger; ***D:*** Luchino Visconti; ***M:*** Maurice Jarre.

Damned River 🦴½ **1989 (R)** Four friends take a guided tour down Zimbabwe's Zambezi River, only to find midway down that their guide is a murderous psycho. Survival becomes a priority. **93m/C VHS.** Stephen Shellen, Lisa Aliff, John Terlesky, Marc Poppel, Bradford Bancroft; ***D:*** Michael Schroeder; ***W:*** John Crowther.

A Damsel in Distress 🦴🦴🦴 **1937** Astaire falls for an upper-class British girl, whose family wants her to have nothing to do with him. Features memorable songs from the Gershwins. ♫A Foggy Day in Londontown; Nice Work If You Can Get It; Stiff Upper Lip; Put Me to the Test; I Can't Be Bothered Now; The Jolly Tar and the Milkmaid; Things Are Looking Up; Sing of Spring; Ah Che a Voi Perdoni Iddio. **101m/B VHS.** Fred Astaire, Joan Fontaine, George Burns, Gracie Allen, Ray Noble, Montagu Love, Reginald Gardiner; ***D:*** George Stevens; ***M:*** George Gershwin, George Bassman, Ira Gershwin.

Dan Candy's Law 🦴½ *Alien Thunder* **1973** A Canadian mountie becomes a driven hunter, and then desperate prey, when he tries to track down the Indian who killed his partner. **90m/C VHS.** *CA* Donald Sutherland, Gordon Tootoosis, Chief Dan George, Kevin McCarthy; ***D:*** Claude Fournier; ***M:*** Georges Delerue.

Dance 🦴½ **1990** Two ballet dancers struggle to find love amidst the backstage treacheries and demanding schedules of their profession. **90m/C VHS.** John Revall, Ellen Troy, Carlton Wilborn, Charlene Campbell; ***D:*** Robin Murray.

Dance Fools Dance 🦴🦴🦴 **1931** Fast-paced drama has Crawford and Bakewell as a pair of spoiled rich kids who are forced to face poverty when the stock market crashes. He meets up with Gable, who's producing liquor illegally, while she gets a job at a newspaper. When Gable arranges something akin to the St. Valentine's Day Massacre, Bakewell's investigative reporting of the situation produces fatal results. The Hays Office had a problem with Crawford and friends appearing in their underwear. Cast notes: Gable was just starting out at MGM, which is why he was billed sixth; the William Holden here is not THE William Holden, and Edwards went on to provide the voice of Jiminy Cricket in "Pinocchio." **82m/B VHS.** Joan Crawford, Lester Vail, Cliff Edwards, William "Billy" Bakewell, Clark Gable; ***D:*** Harry Beaumont; ***C:*** Charles Rosher.

Dance, Girl, Dance 🦴🦴 **1940** The private lives and romances of a wartime nightclub dance troupe. Standard Hollywood potpourri of dance, drama, comedy. ♫Mother, What Do I Do Now?; Jitterbug Bite; Morning Star. **88m/B VHS.** Maureen O'Hara, Louis Hayward, Lucille Ball, Virginia Field, Ralph Bellamy, Maria Ouspenskaya, Mary Carlisle, Katherine Alexander, Edward Brophy, Walter Abel, Harold Huber; ***D:*** Dorothy Arzner; ***W:*** Frank Davis, Tess Slesinger; ***C:*** Russell Metty; ***M:*** Edward Ward.

The Dance Goes On 🦴🦴 **1992** After the death of an uncle, Keach and his estranged son Almond reunite at the old Quebec family farm left to them. The father is country-bred and appreciates the property but his Los Angeles-reared son wants to sell for a quick profit. Director Almond cast his own son in the starring role as well as ex-wife Bujold, who plays the ambitious showbiz mother. **104m/C VHS.** James Keach, Matt Almond, Genevieve Bujold, Cary Lawrence; ***D:*** Paul Almond; ***W:*** Paul Almond.

Dance Hall 🦴½ **1941** A Pennsylvania dance hall owner is propelled into romantic confusion with the introduction of a sultry blond dancer into his club. **73m/B VHS.** Cesar Romero, Carole Landis, William Henry, June Storey, Charles Halton; ***D:*** Irving Pichel.

Dance Hall Racket 🦴🦴 **1958** A sleazy, stilted expose of dance hall vice featuring a brief appearance by Bruce and his wife, Harlow. **60m/B VHS.** Lenny Bruce, Honey Harlow; ***D:*** Phil Tucker.

Dance Macabre 🦴 **1991 (R)** Englund takes on a dual role as a man with a split personality—one of whom is deadly. Jessica, an American ballerina, enrolls in a Russian dance academy and meets mesmerizing choreographer, Anthony. Unfortunately for Jessica she happens to look exactly like Anthony's long-dead lover and he becomes obsessed with her. Also, her fellow dancers are being brutally murdered. Are the events connected? **97m/C VHS.** Robert Englund, Michelle Zeitlin, Marianna Moen, Julene Renee, Alexander Sergeyev; ***D:*** Greydon Clark; ***W:*** Greydon Clark.

Dance Me Outside 🦴🦴½ **1995 (R)** Native Canadian teens look for some excitement on their Northern Ontario reservation and find themselves cut off from their tradition-bound parents in this slice of life drama. Friends Silas and Blackie plot revenge against a white who murdered a native girl while Silas' sister Illianna comes to visit from Toronto, with her Yuppie lawyer husband, just as her ex-boyfriend returns from a prison stint. Based on the novel by W.P. Kinsella. **91m/C VHS.** *CA* Ryan Black, Adam Beach, Michael Greyeyes, Lisa Lacroix; ***D:*** Bruce McDonald; ***W:*** Bruce McDonald, Don McKellar, John Frizzell. Genie '95: Film Editing.

Dance Me to My Song 🦴🦴 **1998** Very difficult movie to watch provides its own rewards thanks to the skills of filmmaker de Heer and lead Rose. Julia (Rose) suffers from severe cerebral palsy, is wheelchair-bound, and can only speak through a voice synthesizer. Although she lives alone, she is dependent on the daily caregivers supplied by the health department. Her latest is the short-tempered Madelaine (Kennedy), who is neglectful and ill-suited to her demanding work. What makes the situation more difficult is Julia's amible friend Eddie (Brumpton), whom Madelaine jealously decides is the ideal man. **103m/C VHS.** *AU* Heather Rose, Joey Kennedy, John Brumpton, Rena Owen; ***D:*** Rolf de Heer; ***W:*** Rolf de Heer, Frederick Stahl, Heather Rose; ***C:*** Tony Clark; ***M:*** Graham Tardiff.

Dance of Death woof! *House of Evil; Macabre Serenade* **1968** Just before his death, Karloff agreed to appear in footage for four Mexican cheapies that were practically thrown together (Karloff actually filmed his scenes in Los Angeles). If they had mixed the footage instead of matched it, the flicks couldn't be any worse. This one concerns a lunatic toy-maker whose toys kill and maim his heirs. **89m/C VHS.** *MX* Boris Karloff, Julissa, Andres Garcia, Jack Hill; ***D:*** Juan Ibanez.

Dance of Life 🦴🦴½ **1929** A look at the backstage goings-on at a burlesque theatre. A successful entertainer's life goes down the tubes when he hits the bottle. His wife leaves him because of his philandering, but returns when she sees how much he really needs her. One scene of the Ziegfeld Follies uses two-tone Technicolor technology. This was re-made twice: as "Swing High, Swing Low" in 1937 and as "When My Baby Smiles at Me" in 1948. Carroll replaced the stage lead, who was said to have no "name recognition"—Barbara Stanwyck. ♫True Blue Lou; King of Jazzmania; Cuddlesome Baby; Flippity Flop; Ladies of the Dance; The Mightiest Matador; Sweet Rosie O'Grady; In the Gloaming; Sam, the Accordion Man. **115m/B VHS.** Nancy Carroll, Hal Skelly, Ralph Theadore, Charles D. Brown, Dorothy Revier, Al "Fuzzy" St. John, Oscar Levant; ***D:*** John Cromwell.

Dance of the Damned 🦴🦴 **1988 (R)** A case where low-budget isn't synonymous with bomb. Fascinating noir-ish plot concerning a vampire who wants to learn more about the life of his next victim, a deep-thinking stripper, who has lost the will to live it. Surprisingly well-done and acted; above-par for this genre. **83m/C VHS.** Cyril O'Reilly, Starr Andreeff, Deborah Ann Nassar, Maria Ford; ***D:*** Katt Shea; ***W:*** Katt Shea, Andy Ruben; ***C:*** Phedon Papamichael; ***M:*** Gary Stockdale.

Dance or Die 🦴 **1987** Just goes to show that in Las Vegas you can't have your dance and drugs too, because if the Mob doesn't get you, the Feds will. Made for video (though maybe it shouldn't have been made at all). In HiFi Stereo. **90m/C VHS.** Ray Kieffer, Rebecca Barrington; ***D:*** Richard W. Munchkin. **VIDEO**

Dance with a Stranger 🦴🦴🦴½ **1985 (R)** The engrossing and factual story of Ruth Ellis (Richardson) who gained notoriety as the last woman hanged in Great Britain in 1955. This emotional and sometimes violent film mirrors the sensationalism and class conflicts of 1950s British society. The film follows single mom Ellis's pre-trial life as a tawdry nighclub hostess, struggling to maintain her independence, while becoming obsessively involved with immature cas/upper-class playboy David Blakely (Everett) whom she murders when he finally rejects her. **101m/C VHS, DVD, Wide.** *GB* Miranda Richardson, Rupert Everett, Ian Holm, Joanne Whalley, Matthew Carroll, Tom Chadbon, Jane Bertish, David Troughton, Paul Mooney, Stratford Johns, Susan Kyd, Leslie Manville, Sallie-Anne Field, Martin Murphy, Michael Jenn, Daniel Massey; ***D:*** Mike Newell; ***W:*** Shelagh Delaney; ***C:*** Peter Hannan; ***M:*** Richard Hartley. Cannes '85: Film.

Dance with Death 🦴 **1991 (R)** When strippers turn up brutally murdered, a young journalist goes undercover to solve the case. **90m/C VHS.** Maxwell Caulfield, Barbara Alyn Jones, Martin Mull, Drew Snyder, Catya (Cat) Sassoon; ***D:*** Charles Philip Moore.

Dance with Me 🦴🦴½ *Shut Up and Dance* **1998 (PG)** Cuban emigre Rafael (Chayanne) winds up in Houston, teaching at the fading Excelsior Dance Studio, which is owned by a friend of his late mother's, John Burnett (Kristofferson). Instructor (and single mom) Ruby (Williams) is looking for a partner who can help her enter the competitive ballroom dance world but she's not looking for love. But at the World Open Dance Championships in Las Vegas, she may find both. Hot salsa music and dancing, as well as the charm of the two leads, make this one worth watching for any dancer fever fan. **126m/C VHS, DVD.** Vanessa L(ynne) Williams, Chayanne,

Kris Kristofferson, Joan Plowright, Jane Krakowski, Beth Grant; **D:** Randa Haines; **W:** Daryl Matthews; **C:** Fred Murphy; **M:** Michael Convertino.

Dance with Me, Henry ½
1956 When Lou becomes involved with Bud's gambling debts and the local district attorney turns up dead, Lou's not only wanted by the law, but by the mafia as well. This was the great comedy duo's last picture together and it's clear the pair are not happy about working with each other, even on this mediocre effort. **90m/B VHS.** Bud Abbott, Lou Costello, Gigi Perreau, Rusty Hamer, Mary Wickes, Ted de Corsia; **D:** Charles T. Barton.

Dance with the Devil *Perdita Durango* **1997 (R)** Prostitute Perdita (Perez) and witch doctor/drug dealer Romeo (Bardem) meet at the Mexican border and soon become lovers and criminal partners. They get a kinky job hijacking human fetuses for a Vegas mob boss and, since Romeo believes in human sacrifice before starting a new endeavor, they kidnap a cute teen couple as the victims. Then Romeo discovers his ex-partner, Shorty (Segura), isn't so ex—and there's lots more that's very weird and bloody. Based on the novel "59 and Raining: The Story of Perdita Durango" by Barry Gifford. **126m/C VHS, DVD, Wide.** *MX SP* Rosie Perez, Javier Bardem, Harley Cross, Aimee Graham, Don Stroud, James Gandolfini, Santiago Segura, Screamin' Jay Hawkins, Alex Cox, Carlos Bardem; **D:** Alex de la Iglesia; **W:** Alex de la Iglesia, Barry Gifford, Jorge Guerricaechevarria, David Trueba; **C:** Flavio Martinez Labiano; **M:** Simon Boswell.

Dancer in the Dark **1999 (R)** A love it or hate it production from Danish provocateur Von Trier. Czech immigrant Selma (Bjork) is a single mom working in a small factory, where her best friend is another immigrant, Kathy (Deneuve). Selma is also close to her landlords Bill and Jean (Morse, Seymour) but tells no one that she's going blind, a fate her son will also suffer unless he gets an expensive operation. Then the money Selma has been saving is stolen and she accuses the bankrupt Bill, leading to tragedy. It sounds clear enough but mixed up in the story is Selma's participation in an amateur production of "The Sound of Music" and her numerous musical fantasies. Exteriors were filmed in Sweden and interiors in a Danish studio, although it's set in rural America. **141m/C VHS, DVD, Wide.** *DK SW FR* Bjork, Catherine Deneuve, David Morse, Peter Stormare, Cara Seymour, Joel Grey, Vincent Paterson, Vladica Kostic, Jean-Marc Barr, Udo Kier, Zeljko Ivanek; **D:** Lars von Trier; **W:** Lars von Trier; **C:** Robby Muller; **M:** Bjork. Cannes '00: Actress (Bjork), Film; Ind. Spirit '01: Foreign Film.

Dancer, Texas—Pop. 81
1998 (PG) Four buddies have to decide if they're going to fulfill the pact they made when they were 11 to leave the eponymous town upon graduating from high school. Each one has a reason to consider sticking around: Keller (Meyer) tkaes care of his widowed grandfather; Terrell Lee (Facinelli) is expected to join the family's failing oil business; Squirrel (Embry) thinks he should care for his alcoholic father; and John (Mills) is a natural at cattle ranching. Coming-of-age comedy deals in honest emotion and humor, and doesn't resort to syrupy sentiment or small-town stereotyping. Texas-born writer-director McCanlies' feature debut. **95m/C VHS, DVD.** Breckin Meyer, Peter Facinelli, Eddie Mills, Ethan (Randall) Embry, Ashley Johnson, Patricia Wettig, Michael O'Neill, Eddie Jones, Alexandra Holden; **D:** Tim McCanlies; **W:** Tim McCanlies; **C:** Andrew Dintenfass; **M:** Steve Dorff.

Dancers ½ **1987 (PG)** During the filming of the ballet "Giselle" in Italy, a famous, almost-over-the-hill dancer (Baryshnikov, ten years after his role in "The Turning Point") coaches a young, inexperienced starlet. He hopes to revitalize his life and his dancing. Features dancers from the Baryshnikov-led American Ballet Theatre. **99m/C VHS.** Mikhail Baryshnikov, Leslie Browne, Julie Kent, Mariangela Melato, Alessandra Ferri, Lynn Seymour, Victor Barbee, Tommy (Thomas) Rall; **D:** Herbert Ross; **M:** Pino Donaggio.

Dances with Wolves ½
1990 (PG-13) The story of a U.S. Army soldier, circa 1870, whose heroism in battle allows him his pick of posts. His choice, to see the West before it disappears, changes his life. He meets, understands and eventually becomes a member of a Lakota Sioux tribe in the Dakotas. Costner's first directorial attempt proves him a talent of vision and intelligence. This sometimes too objective movie lacks a sense of definitive character, undermining its gorgeous scenery and interesting perspective on the plight of Native Americans. Lovely music and epic proportions. Adapted by Blake from his novel. **181m/C VHS, DVD, Wide.** Kevin Costner, Mary McDonnell, Graham Greene, Rodney A. Grant, Floyd "Red Crow" Westerman, Tantoo Cardinal, Robert Pastorelli, Charles Rocket, Maury Chaykin, Jimmy Herman, Nathan Lee Chasing His Horse, Wes Studi; **D:** Kevin Costner; **W:** Michael Blake; **C:** Dean Semler; **M:** John Barry. Oscars '90: Adapt. Screenplay, Cinematog., Director (Costner), Film Editing, Picture, Sound, Orig. Score; AFI '98: Top 100; Directors Guild '90: Director (Costner); Golden Globes '91: Director (Costner), Film—Drama, Screenplay; Natl. Bd. of Review '90: Director (Costner); Writers Guild '90: Adapt. Screenplay.

Dancing at Lughnasa
1998 (PG-13) Kate (Streep) is the eldest of five lonely unwed sisters living together on a farm in 1930s Ireland. Their brother Father Jack (Gambon) returns home, fresh from a stint as a missionary in Africa, and Gerry (Ifans), who fathered a son with sister Christina, turns up as well. The reunion and resulting emotions are the main elements in this anecdotal tale, but unfortunately most of the episodes are lacking energy and fun. Streep gives her usual impeccably accented performance, McCormack is sensual as Christina, but it's Ifans who delivers the only gusto as he readies to go to war in Spain. Adapted from the Tony Award-winning stage play by Brian Friels. Title refers to a pagan ritual the town engages in annually, and one would think just the dance alone should have led to a more energetic outing. **92m/C VHS, DVD.** *IR GB* Meryl Streep, Michael Gambon, Catherine McCormack, Rhys Ifans, Brid Brennan, Kathy Burke, Sophie Thompson, Lorcan Cranitch, Darrell Johnston, Peter Gowen, Dawn Bradfield, Marie Mullen; **D:** Pat O'Connor; **W:** Frank McGuinness; **C:** Kenneth Macmillan; **M:** Bill Whelan.

Dancing at the Blue Iguana ½ **2000 (R)** These "dancers" are strippers at the titular San Fernando Valley club and their interwoven stories comprise the plot. Stormy (Kelley) is the tough veteran with the questionable past; Angel (Hannah) is sweet but dumb; Jo (Tilly) must deal with an unplanned pregnancy; Jasmine (Oh) is an aspiring poet; and Jesse (Ayanna) is an over-eager newcomer. Eddie (Wisdom) presides over the establishment and has his own demons. Much of the film was improvised in workshops and rehearsals. **123m/C VHS, DVD, Wide.** Sheila Kelley, Daryl Hannah, Sandra Oh, Jennifer Tilly, Charlotte Ayanna, Robert Wisdom, Elias Koteas, Vladimir Mashkov, W. Earl Brown, Chris Hogan, Rodney Rowland, Kristin Bauer; **D:** Michael Radford; **W:** David Linter, Michael Radford; **C:** Ericson Core; **M:** Tal Bergman, Renato Neto.

Dancing in September ½
2000 (R) Black writer Tomasina "Tommy" Crawford (Parker) has just lost her job on a sitcom so she has nothing to lose by pitching a black issues comedy to George (Washington), a slick exec looking to make a name for himself at a startup network. Tommy also discovers the show's lead—former gangbanger and single dad James (Shannon). The three gain success but come under fire from the black community for being sellouts as they re-evaluate their personal and professional aspirations. **106m/C VHS, DVD.** Nicole Ari Parker, Isaiah Washington IV, Vicellous Reon Shannon, Malinda Williams, Jay Underwood, Michael Cavanaugh, Chi McBride, James Avery, LeVar Burton, Peter Onorati, Kadeem Hardison, Jenifer Lewis, Anna Maria Horsford; **D:** Reggie Rock Bythewood; **W:** Reggie Rock Bythewood; **C:** Bill Dill. **CABLE**

Dancing in the Dark ½
1986 (PG-13) An interesting but slow-moving Canadian film about the perfect housewife who learns that after 20 years of devotion to him, her spouse has been unfaithful. Realizing how her life has been wasted she murders her husband and, in the end, suffers a mental breakdown. **93m/C VHS, DVD.** *CA* Martha Henry, Neil Munro, Rosemary Dunsmore, Richard Monette; **D:** Leon Marr; **W:** Leon Marr; **M:** Erik Satie. Genie '87: Actress (Henry).

Dancing Lady ½ **1933** Rarely seen film is MGM's answer to "42nd Street," with Crawford as a small-time hoofer trying to break into Broadway. The screen debuts of Astaire and Eddy. Look for none other than the Three Stooges as stage hands. ♫Everything I Have Is Yours; Heigh-Ho! The Gang's All Here; Hold Your Man; That's the Rhythm of the Day; My Dancing Lady; Let's Go Bavarian; Hey Young Fella. **93m/B VHS.** Clark Gable, Joan Crawford, Fred Astaire, Franchot Tone, Nelson Eddy, Ted Healy, Moe Howard, Curly Howard, Larry Fine, May Robson, Robert Benchley, Eve Arden; **D:** Robert Z. Leonard; **W:** P.J. Wolfson, Allen Rivkin, Zelda Sears; **C:** Oliver Marsh; **M:** Richard Rodgers, Burton Lane, Jimmy McHugh.

Dancing Man ½ **1933** A gigolo romances both mother and daughter and winds up implicated in murder as a result. Dismissable. **65m/B VHS, 8mm.** Judith Allen, Reginald Denny, Natalie Moorhead; **D:** Albert Ray.

Dancing Mothers ½ **1926** A fast-living woman becomes involved with her mother's roguish boyfriend in this silent film with accompanying musical score. **85m/B VHS.** Clara Bow, Alice Joyce, Conway Tearle, Donald Keith; **D:** Herbert Brenon.

Dancing Pirate **1936** A Boston dance instructor is kidnapped by pirates and jumps ship in Mexico, where he romances a mayor's daughter. The silly story boasts some Rodgers and Hart tunes, plus the early use of Technicolor, exploited here for all it was worth and then some. ♫Are You My Love?; When You're Dancing the Waltz. **83m/C VHS.** Charles Collins, Frank Morgan, Steffi Duna, Luis Alberni, Victor Varconi, Jack LaRue; **D:** Lloyd Corrigan.

The Dancing Princesses **1984** When five naughty princesses wear the soles of their slippers out every night, their father the King must foot the bill. He soon tires of this expense and offers a reward to the person who can discover how this happens. A handsome prince becomes invisible to follow the lovely ladies and discover their secret. From the "Faerie Tale Theatre" series. **60m/C VHS.** Lesley Ann Warren, Peter Weller, Sachi (MacLaine) Parker, Roy Dotrice; **D:** Peter Medak. **CABLE**

Dancing with Danger ½
1993 (PG-13) A private investigator is hired to find out why a taxi dancer's customers all end up dead. Soon the PI's employer is the next victim of a serial killer whose ultimate target is the dancer herself. **90m/C VHS.** Cheryl Ladd, Ed Marinaro, Miguel (Michael) Sandoval, Pat Skipper; **D:** Stuart Cooper; **W:** Elisa Bell. **TV**

Dandelions **1974** German softcore flick starring Hauer in an early role as a man jilted by his wife. To make himself feel better he decides to explore the sleazier side of life. Meaningless film evokes no sympathy but some may appreciate the titillation. Dubbed. **92m/C VHS.** *GE* Rutger Hauer, Dagmar Lassander; **D:** Adrian Hoven.

Dandy in Aspic ½ **1968 (R)** A double-agent is assigned to kill himself in this hard to follow British spy drama. The film is based on Derek Marlowe's novel. Mann died midway through shooting and Harvey finished direction. **107m/C VHS, Wide.** *GB* Laurence Harvey, Tom Courtenay, Lionel Stander, Mia Farrow, Harry Andrews, Peter Cook, Per Oscarsson; **D:** Anthony Mann; **M:** Quincy Jones.

Danger Ahead **1940** Newill stars again as Renfrew of the Mounties—this time he tries to rid the north woods of the baddies who are trying to take over. **57m/B VHS.** James Newill, Dorothea Kent, Guy Usher, Dave O'Brien, Bob Terry; **D:** Ralph Staub.

Danger Beneath the Sea
2002 What appears to be a made-for-TV adventure trots out every known submarine movie cliche. The massively jawed Van Dien is Capt. Sheffield, who's been given command of the Lansing, much to the dismay of many of the boat's officers. A nuclear incident occurs while the sub is in the China Sea, and he must deal with uncertainties about a possible war and a mutinous crew. The pace moves along nicely and production values are on the high side. **93m/C VHS, DVD.** Casper Van Dien, Gerald McRaney, Shane Daly, Stewart Bick; **D:** Jon Cassar; **W:** Lucien K. Truscott IV; **C:** Derick Underschultz; **M:** Norman Orenstein.

Danger: Diabolik *Diabolik* **1968 (PG-13)** A superthief called Diabolik (Law) continuously evades the law while performing his criminal antics. **99m/C VHS.** *IT* John Phillip Law, Marisa Mell, Michel Piccoli, Terry-Thomas, Adolfo Celi; **D:** Mario Bava; **W:** Mario Bava, Arduino (Dino) Maiuri, Adriano Barracio, Brian Degas, Tudor Gates; **C:** Antonio Rinaldi; **M:** Ennio Morricone.

Danger in the Skies ½ *The Pilot* **1979 (PG)** An alcoholic airline pilot tries to straighten out his life when he nearly loses everything while drinking on the job. **99m/C VHS.** Cliff Robertson, Diane Baker, Dana Andrews, Gordon MacRae, Milo O'Shea, Frank Converse, Edward Binns; **D:** Cliff Robertson; **C:** Walter Lassally. **CABLE**

Danger Lights ½ **1930** Depicts the railroads and the railroad men's dedication to each other and their trains. **73m/B VHS.** Jean Arthur, Louis Wolheim, Robert Armstrong; **D:** George B. Seitz.

Danger of Love ½ **1995 (R)** Married teacher Michael Carlin (Penny) has an affair with seductive colleague Carolyn Warmus (Robertson) but when he's about to end it, his wife is murdered. The detective (Bologna) thinks Michael is guilty but it's Carolyn who's hiding all the secrets. Based on a true story; made for TV. **95m/C VHS.** Joe Penny, Jenny Robertson, Joseph Bologna, Richard Lewis, Fairuza Balk, Deborah Benson, Sydney Walsh; **D:** Joyce Chopra. **TV**

Danger on the Air **1938** A radio program sponsor—a much-despised misogynist—is murdered, and the sound engineer attempts to solve the mystery. Features Cobb in one of his earliest roles; Garrett also directed "Lady in the Morgue" that year. **70m/B VHS.** Donald Woods, Nan Grey, Berton Churchill, Jed Prouty, William Lundigan, Richard "Skeets" Gallagher, Edward Van Sloan, George Meeker, Lee J. Cobb, Johnny Arthur, Linda Hayes, Louise Stanley; **D:** Otis Garrett.

Danger Trails ½ **1935** Rehashed western programmer. Features the hero who must save the rancher's honor as well as the ranch, while fighting detestable hombres with the traditional fare as an arsenal. **55m/B VHS.** Guinn "Big Boy" Williams, Marjorie Gordon, Wally Wales, John Elliott, Ace Cain, Edmund Cobb; **D:** Robert F. "Bob" Hill.

Danger UXB ½ **1981** During the 1940 London blitz, "Danger UXB" was scrawled wherever there was—or thought to be—an unexploded German bomb. This miniseries covers the exploits of the Royal Engineers whose job it was, with little training and lots of nerve, to defuse the bombs. Based on the memoirs of Major A.B. Hartley of the Royal Engineers. **660m/C VHS.** *GB* Anthony Andrews, Judy Geeson, Maurice Roeves, Kenneth Cranham, Jeremy Sinden, Iain Cuthbertson, George Innes, Norman Chappell, Kenneth Farrington, Gordon Kane, Ken Kitson, Robert Longden, Robert Pugh, Deborah Watling; **D:** Roy Ward Baker, Douglas Camfield, Ferdinand Fairfax, Henry Herbert, Simon Langton, Jeremy Summers. **TV**

Danger Zone **1951** A man is hired to bid for a saxophone at an auction and then has the instrument stolen from him. He discovers it contained stolen jewelry and tries to recover it. **56m/B VHS.** Hugh Beaumont, Tom Neal, Richard Travis, Virginia Dale; **D:** William Burke; **W:** Julian Harmon; **C:** Jack Greenhalgh.

Danger Zone woof! **1987 (R)** A low-budget, low-brow flick about an all-female rock band whose bus breaks down in the middle of the desert, leaving the girls to defend themselves against a merciless motorcycle gang. You'll wish this one was a mirage. **90m/C VHS.** Robert Canada, Jason Williams, Kriss Braxton, Dana Dowell, Jamie Ferreira; ***D:*** Henry Vernon.

Danger Zone 🦴🦴 **1995 (R)** American mining expert Rick Morgan (Zane) uncovers a worldwide nuclear plot when he's lured to East Africa to supposedly contain a toxic spill. Instead, he's being used to recover a load of plutonium. **92m/C VHS.** Billy Zane, Ron Silver, Robert Downey Jr., Cary-Hiroyuki Tagawa; ***D:*** Allan Eastman; ***W:*** Jeff Albert; ***C:*** Yossi Wein.

Danger Zone 2 🦴 **1989 (R)** A pernicious biker is released from prison on a technicality and decides to pay a social call to the undercover cop who set him up. **95m/C VHS.** Jason Williams, Robert Random; ***D:*** Geoffrey G. Bowers; ***W:*** Dulany Ross Clements.

Danger Zone 3: Steel Horse War 🦴 **1990 (R)** The "Danger Zone" dude is back and this time he's taken on a bevy of biker-types in a most gruesome battle to make our deserts safe. **91m/C VHS.** Jason Williams, Robert Random, Barne Suboski, Juanita Ranney, Rusty Cooper, Giles Ashford; ***D:*** Douglas Bronco.

Dangerous 🦴🦴½ **1935** Davis won her first Oscar for her rather overdone portrayal of a has-been alcoholic actress reformed by a smitten architect who recognizes her from her days as a star. **72m/B VHS.** Bette Davis, Franchot Tone, Margaret Lindsay, Alison Skipworth, John Eldridge, Dick Foran; ***D:*** Alfred E. Green. Oscars '35: Actress (Davis).

The Dangerous 🦴½ **1995 (R)** New Orleans' seamy underworld is the setting for a hot-headed cop (Pare), a mystery man (Davi), and the beauty (Barbieri) they're both interested in. Also available unrated. **96m/C VHS.** Robert Davi, Michael Pare, Paula Barbieri, Elliott Gould, John Savage, Joel Grey; ***D:*** Maria Dante, Rod Hewitt; ***W:*** Rod Hewitt.

A Dangerous Age 🦴½ **1957** A young girl, hoping to marry her lover, runs away from boarding school. **70m/C VHS.** Ben Piazza, Ann Pearson; ***D:*** Sidney J. Furie; ***W:*** Sidney J. Furie; ***C:*** Herbert S. Alpert.

Dangerous Appointment 🦴🦴 **1934** Story of an innocent store clerk accused of theft and attempted murder. **?m/C VHS.** Charles Starrett, Dorothy Wilson.

Dangerous Beauty 🦴🦴🦴 *The Honest Courtesan; Indiscretion; Venice; Courtesan* **1998 (R)** In 16th-century Venice, poor but beautiful Veronica (McCormack) gains wealth and power by becoming a sought after courtesan. The bewigged, bewitched and bewildered heads of state fall as hard for the comely courtesan as victims to the plague that strikes Venice later in the film. The one man she wants, however, Marco Venier (Sewell), comes from a wealthy family that looks down on the common Veronica. Director Herskovitz mixes the strong feminist messages with humor and a modern sensibility that sometimes make you forget you're watching a period film. Based on the biography of the real Veronica Franco by Margaret Rosenthal. **112m/C VHS, DVD.** Catherine McCormack, Rufus Sewell, Moira Kelly, Jacqueline Bisset, Oliver Platt, Fred Ward, Naomi Watts, Jeroen Krabbe, Joanna Cassidy, Daniel Lapaine, Jake Weber, Simon Dutton, Michael Culkin, Peter Eyre; ***D:*** Marshall Herskovitz; ***W:*** Jeannine Dominy; ***C:*** Bojan Bazelli; ***M:*** George Fenton.

Dangerous Charter 🦴½ **1962** A group of fishermen discover a deserted yacht and man its helm. But their good fortune takes a decided turn for the worst as they become caught in mob-propelled danger. **76m/C VHS.** Chris Warfield, Sally Fraser, Richard Foote, Peter Foster, Wright King; ***D:*** Robert Gottschalk.

Dangerous Curves 🦴½ **1988 (PG)** Two friends are assigned to deliver a new Porsche to a billionaire's daughter—one of them talks the other into taking a little detour, and the trouble begins. **93m/C VHS.** Robert Stack, Tate Donovan, Danielle von Zerneck, Robert Klein, Elizabeth Ashley, Leslie Nielsen; ***D:*** David Lewis. **VIDEO**

Dangerous Evidence: The Lori Jackson Story 🦴🦴½ **1999** Whitfield stars in this true story as Lori Jackson, a 1980's civil rights activist who takes on the case of Marine Corporal Lindsay Scott (Yearwood), the only black in the battalion, who is falsely accused of raping a white officer's wife. When he is convicted on circumstantial evidence, Jackson secures a new trial, which exacts a high price on her own life. Based on the book "Dangerous Evidence" by Ellis A. Cohen. **90m/C VHS, DVD.** Lynn Whitfield, Richard Lineback, Richard Yearwood, Peter MacNeill, Erica Luttrell, Barbara Mamabolo, Geordie Johnson, Bruce Gray; ***D:*** Sturla Gunnarsson; ***W:*** Sterling Anderson; ***M:*** Jonathan Goldsmith. **CABLE**

Dangerous Game 🦴½ **1990 (R)** A computer hacker leads his friends through a department store's security system, only to find they can't get out until morning. They soon discover they are not alone when one of the group turns up dead. **102m/C VHS.** Miles Buchanan, Sandy Lillingston, Kathryn Walker, John Polson; ***D:*** Stephen Hopkins.

Dangerous Game 🦴🦴 *Snake Eyes* **1993 (R)** Abrasive filmmaker Eddie Israel's (Keitel) new movie is about a couple's disintegrating marriage turning violent. Stars Sarah (Madonna) and Francis (Russo) find the on-camera violence spilling over into their tangled private lives while Eddie finds his personal traumas intruding more and more into the fictional material. Very raw movie within a movie features volatile Keitel (who also worked with Ferrera on "Bad Lieutenant") and suitably histrionic Russo; Madonna manages to hold her own in the least showy role, a cinematic first. Eddie's betrayed and bewildered wife is sympathetically portrayed by Ferrara, director Abel's wife. Also available in an unrated version. **107m/C VHS.** Harvey Keitel, James Russo, Madonna, Nancy Ferrara; ***D:*** Abel Ferrara; ***W:*** Nicholas St. John.

Dangerous Ground 🦴🦴 **1996 (R)** Hackneyed thriller has expatriate South African Vusi (Cube) returning to his homeland to find his younger brother Steven, who has double-crossed the head of a drug cartel. Since Vusi's departure 12 years ago, apartheid's been replaced by gangs and drugs, and while combing the dangerous streets of Johannesburg, the graduate student implausibly turns into a gun-wielding hero. Rhames's sinister drug lord Muki is pic's best character. Lead Cube shows just how limited his acting ability is while Hurley displays the picture's clearly limited wardrobe budget. Interracial relationships are glossed over, while South Africa's sociological problems are used as plot devices and then ignored. Filmed on location in South Africa, this shoot-em-up's locale could easily be Anytown, USA. **92m/C VHS, DVD.** Ice Cube, Elizabeth Hurley, Ving Rhames, Eric Miyeni, Sechaba Morojele; ***D:*** Darrell Roodt; ***W:*** Darrell Roodt, Greg Latter; ***C:*** Paul Gilpin; ***M:*** Stanley Clarke.

Dangerous Heart 🦴🦴 **1993 (R)** A crooked undercover cop steals a bundle from a drug dealer and gets himself killed for his troubles. Only the dealer doesn't know where the money is. So he decides to befriend the cop's widow, get romantically involved, and see what she knows. **93m/C VHS.** Timothy Daly, Lauren Holly, Jeffrey Nordling, Alice Carter, Joe Pantoliano; ***D:*** Michael Scott; ***W:*** Patrick Cirillo.

Dangerous Holiday 🦴🦴 **1937** A young violin prodigy would rather be just "one of the boys" than be forced to practice all the time. He decides to run away but has everyone in an uproar thinking he's been kidnapped. **54m/B VHS.** Hedda Hopper, Guinn "Big Boy" Williams, Jack LaRue, Franklin Pangborn, Grady Sutton; ***D:*** Nicholas T. Barrows; ***W:*** Nicholas T. Barrows; ***C:*** William Nobles; ***M:*** Alberto Colombo.

Dangerous Hours 🦴🦴 **1919** An anti-communist propaganda film with Hughes as the innocent young college boy who gets duped by the evil Marxists until he realizes the truth of his all-American upbringing. Silent with original organ score. **88m/B VHS, 8mm.** Lloyd Hughes; ***D:*** Fred Niblo; ***C:*** George Barnes.

Dangerous Indiscretion 🦴🦴 **1994 (R)** Ad exec finds his girlfriend is actually a woman married to a very powerful man, who's not going to be happy to find out about their liaison. **81m/C VHS.** Joan Severance, C. Thomas Howell, Malcolm McDowell; ***D:*** Richard Kletter; ***W:*** Richard Kletter, Jack Tarpon; ***M:*** Richard Gibbs.

Dangerous Liaisons 🦴🦴 *Les Liaisons Dangereuses; Dangerous Love Affairs* **1960** A couple take each other to the brink of destruction via their insatiable desire for extra-marital affairs. Vadim attempted to repeat his success with Brigitte Bardot by featuring wife Annette as a new sex goddess, but lightning didn't strike twice. **111m/B VHS.** *FR IT* Gerard Philipe, Jeanne Moreau, Jeanne Valeri, Annette Vadim, Simone Renant, Jean-Louis Trintignant, Nikolas Vogel; ***D:*** Roger Vadim; ***W:*** Roger Vadim; ***C:*** Marcel Grignon.

Dangerous Liaisons 🦴🦴🦴 **1988 (R)** Stylish and absorbing, this adaptation of the Laclos novel and the Christopher Hampton play centers around the relationship of two decadent members of 18th-century French nobility. The Marquise de Merteuil (Close) and the Vicomte de Valmont (Malkovich) spend their time testing and manipulating the loves of others. Merteuil wishes Valmont to deflower teenager Cecile (Thurman) while Valmont himself is after the virtuous married Madame de Tourvel (Pfeiffer). They find love often has a will of its own. Interesting to comparison-view with director Milos Forman's version of this story, 1989's "Valmont." **120m/C VHS, DVD, Wide.** John Malkovich, Glenn Close, Michelle Pfeiffer, Uma Thurman, Keanu Reeves, Swoosie Kurtz, Mildred Natwick, Peter Capaldi; ***D:*** Stephen Frears; ***W:*** Christopher Hampton; ***C:*** Philippe Rousselot; ***M:*** George Fenton. Oscars '88: Adapt. Screenplay, Art Dir./Set Dec., Costume Des.; British Acad. '89: Adapt. Screenplay, Support. Actress (Pfeiffer); Cesar '90: Foreign Film; Writers Guild '88: Adapt. Screenplay.

Dangerous Life 🦴🦴 **1989** Explosive drama brings to the screen the story of the Philippine uprising. It shows the horrible events that lead to the fall of Marcos and permitted the rise of Corazon Aquino. **163m/C VHS.** Gary Busey, Ruben Rustia, Cris Vertido; ***D:*** Robert Markowitz; ***W:*** David Williamson.

The Dangerous Lives of Altar Boys **2002 (R)** Catholic schoolboys Hirsch and Culkin channel their boredom into a sacrilegious comic book called "The Atomic Trinity," which gets them into trouble with no-nonsense nun Foster and hard-drinking priest D'Onofrio. Based on the 1994 novel by Chris Fuhrman. Not yet reviewed. **?m/C VHS, DVD.** Kieran Culkin, Emile Hirsch, Jena Malone, Jodie Foster, Vincent D'Onofrio, Jake Richardson; ***D:*** Peter Care; ***W:*** Jeff Stockwell, Michael Petroni.

Dangerous Love woof! **1987** Advice to the lovelorn: Avoid this one. Female members of a video dating service are being filmed in a death scene—their own. **87m/C VHS.** Lawrence Monoson, Brenda Bakke, Peter Marc, Elliott Gould, Anthony Geary; ***D:*** Marty Ollstein.

A Dangerous Man: Lawrence after Arabia 🦴🦴🦴 **1991** At the 1919 Paris Peace Conference, T.E. Lawrence serves as the liaison to the Hashemite delegation in an effort to have the Allies agree to Arab independence. He finds the diplomatic fields more treacherous than anything he encountered during WWI. Fiennes does well in the difficult role of the reluctant, ambivalent hero. **104m/C VHS.** *GB* Ralph Fiennes, Denis Quilley, Alexander Siddig, Nicholas Jones, Roger Hammond, Peter Copley, Paul Freeman, Polly Walker; ***D:*** Christopher Menaul; ***W:*** Tim Rose Price. **TV**

Dangerous Minds 🦴🦴½ *My Posse Don't Do Homework* **1995 (R)** Based on the autobiography of LouAnne Johnson (Pfeiffer), a 10-year Marine turned inspirational inner-city high school English teacher. Naturally, Johnson has to take on the establishment educational system to fight for her kids. If you can buy Pfeiffer as an ex-jarhead, a tough teacher should be no problem. A subplot romance involving Pfeiffer and Andy Garcia was cut from the film to focus on the teacher/student byplay (which seems a real shame); Elaine May did a uncredited script rewrite. Kinda squishy and surprisingly successful. **99m/C VHS, DVD.** Michelle Pfeiffer, George Dzundza, Courtney B. Vance, Robin Bartlett, Renoly Santiago, Lorraine Toussaint, John Neville; ***D:*** John N. Smith; ***W:*** Ronald Bass; ***C:*** Pierre Letarte. Blockbuster '96: Drama Actress, T. (Pfeiffer).

Dangerous Mission 🦴½ **1954** A young woman witnesses a mob murder in New York and flees to the Midwest, pursued by killers and the police. Good cast couldn't do much with this one. **75m/B VHS.** Victor Mature, Piper Laurie, Vincent Price, William Bendix; ***D:*** Louis King; ***W:*** W.R. Burnett, Charles Bennett.

Dangerous Moonlight 🦴🦴🦴 *Suicide Squadron* **1941** Polish concert pianist becomes a bomber pilot for the British in WWII, though his wife wants him to stay at the piano. Great battle and music sequences; the piece "Warsaw Concerto" became a soundtrack hit. **97m/B VHS.** *GB* Anton Walbrook, Sally Gray, Derrick DeMarney, Cecil Parker, Percy Parsons, Kenneth Kent, Guy Middleton, John Laurie, Frederick Valk; ***D:*** Brian Desmond Hurst.

Dangerous Moves 🦴🦴🦴 *La Diagonale du Fou* **1984 (PG)** A drama built around the World Chess championship competition between a renowned Russian master and a young, rebellious dissident. The chess game serves as both metaphor and background for the social and political tensions it produces. With English subtitles. **96m/C VHS.** *SI* Liv Ullmann, Michel Piccoli, Leslie Caron, Alexandre Arbatt; ***D:*** Richard Dembo; ***W:*** Richard Dembo; ***C:*** Raoul Coutard. Oscars '84: Foreign Film.

Dangerous Obsession 🦴 *Divine Obsession; Mortal Sins* **1988 (R)** A woman kidnaps the doctor she blames for her boyfriend's death and instead of exacting revenge, she makes him her personal sex slave. In the case of this flick, it's really a fate worse than death. **81m/C VHS.** *IT* Corinne Clery, Brett Halsey; ***D:*** Lucio Fulci; ***M:*** Simon Boswell.

Dangerous Orphans 🦴½ **1986 (R)** Not completely awful tale of three brothers, orphaned as boys when their father is murdered before their very eyes, and the vendetta they have against the killer. **90m/C VHS.** *NZ* Peter Stevens, Peter Bland, Ian Mune, Ross Girven, Jennifer Ward-Lealand; ***D:*** John Laing.

Dangerous Passage 🦴🦴 **1944** A ne'er-do-well inherits 200 grand but gets in trouble before he can collect it. He ends up falling in with assorted misfits aboard a tramp steamer. **60m/B VHS, 8mm.** Robert Lowery, Phyllis Brooks, Jack LaRue, Victor Kilian; ***D:*** William Berke.

Dangerous Passion 🦴½ **1995** Ruthless Lou (Williams) kills an intruder and tries to force his mechanic, Kyle (Weathers), to take the fall for him. But instead Kyle escapes with Lou's mistreated wife (and Kyle's lover) Meg (McKee), with Lou's henchman Frank (Boswell) on their tail. **94m/C VHS.** Billy Dee Williams, Carl Weathers, Lonette McKee, Charles Boswell, Elpidia Carrillo, Tony DiBenedetto, Dan Ziskie; ***D:*** Michael Miller; ***W:*** Brian Taggert; ***C:*** Steve Shaw; ***M:*** Rob Mounsey.

A Dangerous Place 🦴🦴½ **1994 (R)** Teenaged Ethan (Roberts) joins a karate team to prove his older brother's death was not a suicide. But the Scorpion's leader (Feldman) has a definite mean streak. **97m/C VHS.** Ted Jan Roberts, Corey Feldman, Mako, Erin Gray, Dick Van Patten; ***D:*** Jerry P. Jacobs.

Dangerous Prey 🦴½ **1995 (R)** Young woman, looking for adventure while vacationing in Europe, gets more than she bargained for when she gets mixed up with a high-tech training school for female mercenaries. **93m/C VHS.** Shannon Whirry, Ciara Hunter; ***D:*** Lloyd A. Simandl; ***M:*** Peter Allen.

Dangerous Pursuit 🦴🦴 **1989** A woman discovers that a man she slept with years ago is an assassin. Knowing too much, she finds herself next on his hit list. Decent psycho-thriller that was never released theatrically. **95m/C VHS.** Gregory Harrison, Alexandra Powers, Scott Valentine, Brian Wimmer, Elena Stiteler; ***D:*** Sandor Stern.

Dangerous Relations &&½ *Father & Son: Dangerous Relations* **1993 (PG-13)** Made-for-TV drama with Gossett as a tough convict at the end of 15-year prison sentence whose authority is challenged by young punk prisoner Underwood. Imagine his surprise when the old con realizes the punk is the son he hasn't seen since he started his time behind bars. Things don't improve (well, not at first) when they are paroled into each other's custody. **93m/C VHS.** Louis Gossett Jr., Blair Underwood, Rae Dawn Chong, Clarence Williams III, Rigg Kennedy; ***D:*** Georg Stanford Brown; ***W:*** Walter Halsey Davis; ***C:*** James Chressanthis. **TV**

Dangerous Summer && *The Burning Man* **1982** In Australia, an American businessman building a resort is the victim of elaborate arson/murder insurance schemes. **100m/C VHS, DVD, Wide.** *AU* Tom Skerritt, James Mason, Ian Gilmour, Wendy Hughes; ***D:*** Quentin Masters; ***W:*** David Ambrose; ***C:*** Peter Hannan.

Dangerous Touch &½ **1994 (R)** A very charming sociopath seduces a radio host/therapist into a willing, if kinky, sexual relationship. But everything she values is put at risk when he threatens to show an incriminating video tape if she doesn't continue to do as he demands. An unrated version is also available. **101m/C VHS, DVD.** Lou Diamond Phillips, Kate Vernon; ***D:*** Lou Diamond Phillips.

Dangerous When Wet && **1953** A typical Williams water-musical. A farm girl dreams of fame by swimming the English Channel. One famous number pairs Williams with cartoon characters Tom & Jerry in an underwater frolic. ♫I Got Out of Bed on the Right Side; Ain't Nature Grand; I Like Men; Fifi; In My Wildest Dreams. **96m/C VHS.** Esther Williams, Fernando Lamas, Charlotte Greenwood, William Demarest, Jack Carson; ***D:*** Charles Walters; ***M:*** Arthur Schwartz, Johnny Mercer.

A Dangerous Woman && **1993 (R)** No, this isn't the femme fatale romance the word "dangerous" suggests. Instead, the eponymous character is a mildly retarded woman, Martha (Winger), whose simplistic view on life places her in ethically compromising positions. When a hunky Irish handyman (Byrne) comes on the scene and seduces both her and the aunt with whom she lives (Hershey), Martha awakens to feelings she has never experienced. Winger's performance is both sensitive and provocative, but is wasted in a film filled with two-dimensional characters, and really, not too much of a point. Adapted from a novel by Mary McGarry Morris. Screenplay by Foner, wife of director Gyllenhaal. **101m/C VHS.** Debra Winger, Barbara Hershey, Gabriel Byrne, David Strathairn, Chloe Webb, John Terry, Jan Hooks, Paul Dooley, Viveka Davis, Richard Riehle, Laurie Metcalf; ***D:*** Stephen Gyllenhaal; ***W:*** Naomi Foner; ***C:*** Robert Elswit; ***M:*** Carter Burwell.

Dangerous Youth & *These Dangerous Years* **1958** Would-be Liverpool rocker Vaughan is drafted into the army where he becomes a man. He gets into trouble, goes AWOL, but manages to set things right. The Brit version of the troubled-teen exploitation flick. **97m/B VHS.** *GB* Frankie Vaughan, George Baker, Carole Lesley, Jackie Lane, Eddie Byrne, Thora Hird; ***D:*** Herbert Wilcox; ***W:*** Jack Trevor Story.

Dangerously Close &½ **1986 (R)** A group of anti-crime high school students organize a hall monitoring gang that becomes a group of neo-fascist disciplinarian elite. **96m/C VHS.** John Stockwell, Carey Lowell, J. Eddie Peck; ***D:*** Albert Pyun; ***C:*** Walt Lloyd.

Daniel &&½ **1983 (R)** The children of a couple who were executed for espionage (patterned after the Rosenbergs) struggle with their past in the dissident 1960s. So-so adaptation of E.L. Doctorow's "The Book of Daniel." **130m/C VHS.** Timothy Hutton, Amanda Plummer, Mandy Patinkin, Lindsay Crouse, Ed Asner, Ellen Barkin; ***D:*** Sidney Lumet; ***C:*** Andrzej Bartkowiak.

Daniel Boone &&½ **1934** Daniel Boone guides a party of settlers from North Carolina to the fertile valleys of Kentucky, facing Indians, food shortages and bad weather along the way. O'Brien turns in a fine performance as the early American frontier hero. **75m/B VHS.** George O'Brien, Heather Angel, John Carradine; ***D:*** David Howard.

Daniel Boone: Trail Blazer &&½ **1956** Low-budget, though surprisingly well-acted rendition of the frontiersman's heroics, filmed in Mexico. **75m/B VHS, DVD.** Bruce (Herman Brix) Bennett, Lon Chaney Jr., Faron Young, Damian O'Flynn, Fred Kohler Jr., Claudio Brook, Kem Dibbs; ***D:*** Ismael Rodriguez, Albert C. Gannaway; ***W:*** Tom Hubbard, John Patrick; ***C:*** Jack Draper; ***M:*** Raul Lavista.

Daniel Takes a Train && *Szerencses Daniel* **1983** Daniel (Rudolf) and his friend Gyuri (Zsoter) take a train to a small town on the Austrian border, seeking to escape Hungary after the 1956 uprising. Gyuri is a soldier who has deserted and is anxious to get away, but Daniel refuses to leave his missing girlfriend Mariann (Szerb) behind. Hungarian with subtitles. **92m/C VHS.** *HU* Mari Torocsik, Peter Rudolf, Sandor Zsoter, Kati Szerb, Dezso Garas; ***D:*** Pal Sandor; ***W:*** Zsuzsa Toth; ***C:*** Elemer Ragalyi; ***M:*** Gyorgy Selmeczi.

Daniella by Night && **1961** French model Daniella (Sommer) gets a contract to work for an Italian fashion house in Rome and she's soon attracting a lot of attention, including some that involves a spy plot. This leads to a chase through a Paris cabaret and a nude scene of Sommer, so how much does the story really matter, anyway. French with subtitles. **83m/B VHS, DVD.** *FR* Elke Sommer, Ivan Desny; ***D:*** Max Pecas; ***W:*** Grisha Dabat, Wolfgang Steinhardt; ***C:*** Andre Germain; ***M:*** Charles Aznavour, Georges Garvarentz.

Danielle Steel's Changes &&½ *Changes* **1991** Ladd is a successful, divorced New York TV anchorwoman who turns her life upside-down when she marries an equally successful, widowed Los Angeles surgeon (Nouri). Can they overcome their bicoastal careers to make things work? What do you think? **96m/C VHS.** Cheryl Ladd, Michael Nouri, Christopher Gartin, Randee Heller, Charles Frank, James Sloyan, Cynthia Bain; ***D:*** Charles Jarrott. **TV**

Danielle Steel's Daddy &&½ *Daddy* **1991** Ad exec Oliver Watson (Duffy) is happily married to Sarah (Mulgrew) and living the good life with their three kids—or so he thinks. Then Sarah announces she's leaving and Oliver's left to cope with family crisis as a single parent. A move to a new job in LA finds Oliver falling for an actress (Carter) and wondering if his family can ever be put back together again. **95m/C VHS.** Patrick Duffy, Lynda Carter, Kate Mulgrew; ***D:*** Michael Miller. **TV**

Danielle Steel's Fine Things &&½ *Fine Things* **1990** Bernie Fine thinks everything will be dandy now that he has a beautiful new bride and a cute stepdaughter. Then his wife dies and his stepdaughter's unreliable father wants sole custody. What's a nice guy to do? Based on the novel by Danielle Steel. **145m/C VHS.** D.W. Moffett, Tracy Pollan, Judith Hoag, Cloris Leachman, Noley Thornton; ***D:*** Tom (Thomas R.) Moore; ***W:*** Peter Lefcourt. **TV**

Danielle Steel's Heartbeat &&½ *Heartbeat* **1993** Shameless soap opera with Draper as Adrian Townsend, an L.A. TV-news producer with a self-involved ad-exec hubby (Kilner) who never wants children because of his own lousy childhood. When Adrian gets preggers the louse dumps her and she's left to weep prettily. That is until lovable divorced dad Bill Grant (Ritter) comes along to dry her eyes. Predictable and glossy adaptation of the Steel best-seller. **95m/C VHS.** Polly Draper, John Ritter, Kevin Kilner, Michael Lembeck, Nancy Morgan, Victor Dimattia, Christian Cousins; ***D:*** Michael Miller; ***W:*** Jan Worthington. **TV**

Danielle Steel's Kaleidoscope &&½ *Kaleidoscope* **1990** Three sisters are separated in childhood, after the mysterious deaths of their parents. Then a detective is hired to reunite the adult siblings. But Hilary, the eldest, has secrets she doesn't want her sisters to share. **96m/C VHS.** Jaclyn Smith, Perry King, Colleen Dewhurst, Donald Moffat; ***D:*** Jud Taylor. **TV**

Danielle Steel's Palomino &&½ *Palomino* **1991** Bittersweet romance with Frost as an ambitious photojournalist who gets involved with a headstrong cowboy (Horsley). Their differences drive them apart and tragedy strikes when Frost becomes a paraplegic after a horse-riding accident. This leads her to new goals and the eventual return of her old flame. Between the palomino's blond mane and the equally impressive blond locks of Frost, there's a lot of streaming in the wind hair shots. Horsley's merely tall, dark, and handsome. **90m/C VHS.** Lindsay Frost, Lee Horsley, Eva Marie Saint, Rod Taylor, Michele Greene, Beau Gravitte; ***D:*** Michael Miller; ***W:*** Karol Ann Hoeffner; ***C:*** Lloyd Ahern II; ***M:*** Dominic Frontiere. **TV**

Danielle Steel's Star &½ *Star* **1993** Garth is the country girl with big dreams of a singing career but an unhappy love life. She falls for an idealist lawyer (Bierko) but their romance is put on hold by career ambitions. She goes to Hollywood and gets discovered, becoming a singing/acting sensation who's under the thumb of her increasingly obsessed manager, Wass. Meanwhile, Bierko's trapped in a miserable marriage to the wealthy, influential Farrell. Do the true lovers get together? (Take a guess.) Although the story spans 15 years and lots of tribulations the young Garth never ages a day. **90m/C VHS.** Jennie Garth, Craig Bierko, Ted Wass, Terry Farrell, Penny Fuller, Mitchell Ryan, Jim Haynie; ***D:*** Michael Miller; ***W:*** Claire Labine. **TV**

Danny &&½ **1979 (G)** Charming story of a lonely young girl who receives an injured horse that was no longer fit for the spoiled daughter of the rich owners. **90m/C VHS.** Rebecca Page, Janet Zarish, Barbara Jean Earhardt, Gloria Maddox, George Luce; ***D:*** Gene Feldman.

Danny Boy &½ **1946** Veteran dog, returning from the war, has difficulty adjusting to life back home. Things get worse for him and his young master when Danny Boy is assumed to be shell-shocked and dangerous. One of the few shell-shocked dog stories ever filmed. **67m/B VHS.** Robert "Buzzy" Henry, Ralph Lewis, Sybil Merritt; ***D:*** Terry Morse; ***W:*** Raymond L. Schrock; ***C:*** Jack Greenhalgh; ***M:*** Walter Greene.

Danny Boy &&& *Angel* **1982 (R)** Takes place in Ireland where a young saxaphonist witnesses a murder and, in an effort to understand it, sets out to find the killer. Thought-provoking film is meant to highlight the continuing struggles in Ireland. **92m/C VHS.** *IR* Stephen Rea, Veronica Quilligan, Honor Heffernan, Alan Devlin, Peter Caffrey, Ray McAnally; ***D:*** Neil Jordan; ***W:*** Neil Jordan; ***C:*** Chris Menges.

Dante's Inferno &&& **1924** Abandon all hope you who watch this film. A one-time friend sends his ruthless capitalist nemesis a copy of Dante's "Inferno," and the man reads the book and dreams he's gone to hell (would that be the dress circle?) A silent film that was controversial in its day: the body-stockinged actors were believed to be nude (which would have made it the first nudie Comedy). **54m/B VHS.** Lawson Butt, Howard Gaye, Ralph Lewis, Pauline Starke, Josef Swickard; ***D:*** Henry Otto.

Dante's Inferno: Life of Dante Gabriel Rossetti && **1969** The flamboyant life of mid-19th century English Pre-Raphaelite artist/poet Dante Gabriel Rossetti is depicted with the usual Russell flair. The drunken, drug-taking, womanizing Rossetti was part of the leading intellectual group of his age, which included Swinburne, Morris, Ruskin, and Rossetti's sister, the poet Christina Rossetti. **90m/B VHS.** *GB* Oliver Reed; ***D:*** Ken Russell.

Dante's Peak &&½ **1997 (PG-13)** Northwest volcano serves up a smorgasbord of molten disaster in the second most desirable town in the U.S.—the titular Dante's Peak. Brosnan is the intuitive scientist who comes to Washington to match wits with the conical adversary and joins forces with the town's tres femme mayor Wando (Hamilton). Ashes fall like snow in January, computer generated lava flows profusely, poisonous gases leak out and water turns to acid, all with desired nail-biting effect. Wando's two kids, dog and grandma lend folksy charm and the requisite loved-ones-in-grave-danger, but this heated disaster flick is not exactly for the whole family. Cliched and predictable, flick runs the Disaster Movie Playbook page by page as plot takes a backseat to nonstop action. **112m/C VHS, DVD.** Pierce Brosnan, Linda Hamilton, Charles Hallahan, Grant Heslov, Elizabeth Hoffman, Jamie Renee Smith, Arabella Field, Tzi Ma, Jeremy Foley, Brian Reddy, Kirk Trutner; ***D:*** Roger Donaldson; ***W:*** Leslie Bohem; ***C:*** Andrzej Bartkowiak; ***M:*** John (Gianni) Frizzell.

Danton &&&& **1982 (PG)** A sweeping account of the reign of terror following the French Revolution. Focuses on the title character (wonderfully portrayed by Depardieu) and is directed with searching parallels to modern-day Poland by that country's premier filmmaker, Andrzej Wajda. Well-done period sets round out a memorable film. In French with English subtitles. **136m/C VHS.** *PL FR* Gerard Depardieu, Wojciech (Wojtek Psoniak) Pszoniak, Patrice Chereau, Angela Winkler, Boguslaw Linda; ***D:*** Andrzej Wajda; ***W:*** Jean-Claude Carriere, Agnieszka Holland, Boleslaw Michalek, Jacek Gasiorowski, Andrzej Wajda. British Acad. '83: Foreign Film; Cesar '83: Director (Wajda); Montreal World Film Fest. '83: Actor (Depardieu).

Danzon &&&½ **1991 (PG)** Julia (Rojo), a single, working-class mom escapes the drudgery of her simple existence by going to a Mexico City dance hall every Wednesday. There she loses herself to the movement of the danzon, a dance with Haitian roots, popular in Mexico for over 100 years. When her partner of six years, Carmelo (Rergis), doesn't show up one night, her life is turned upside down. So begins a search for Carmelo—and herself. Quiet and restrained, like the ballroom-style danzon at the center of the plot. Applauded at Cannes. In Spanish with English subtitles. **103m/C VHS.** *SP* Maria Rojo, Carmen Salinas, Blanca Guerra, Tito Vasconcelos, Victor Carpinteiro, Victor Vasconcelos; ***D:*** Maria Novaro; ***W:*** Maria Novaro, Betriz Novaro.

Darby O'Gill & the Little People &&&½ **1959 (G)** Set in Ireland, roguish old story teller Darby O'Gill (Sharpe), whose also the caretaker of a large estate, tumbles into a well and visits the land of leprechauns who give him three wishes in order to rearrange his life. When he tries to tell his friends what happened, they think that it is only another one of his stories. Connery plays the youhg man who takes Darby's job and courts his daughter (Munro) as well. A wonderful Disney production (despite its disappointing boxoffice performance) with wit, charm and an ounce or two of terror. **93m/C VHS.** Albert Sharpe, Janet Munro, Sean Connery, Estelle Winwood, Kieron Moore, Jimmy O'Dea; ***D:*** Robert Stevenson; ***W:*** Lawrence Edward Watkin; ***C:*** Winton C. Hoch.

Darby's Rangers &&½ *Young Invaders* **1958** WWII pot-boiler with Garner as the leader of a commando team put together for covert operations in North Africa and Italy. Successful battle sequences combine with slow-paced romantic scenes as the soldiers chase women when not chasing the enemy. **122m/B VHS.** James Garner, Jack Warden, Edd Byrnes, Peter Brown, Stuart Whitman, David Janssen, Etchika Choureau, Venetia Stevenson, Torin Thatcher, Joan Elan, Corey Allen, Murray Hamilton; ***D:*** William A. Wellman; ***W:*** Guy Trosper; ***C:*** William Clothier; ***M:*** Max Steiner.

Daredevils of the Red Circle **1938** Three young men set out to free a man held prisoner by an escaped convict. A serial in 12 chapters. **195m/B VHS.** Charles Quigley, Bruce (Herman Brix) Bennett, Carole Landis; ***D:*** John English, William Witney.

Daring Danger &½ **1932** McCoy is nearly killed in a fight with the villainous Alexander. When he recovers he finds Alexander has joined forces with a rustler (Ellis), so McCoy battles both of them—while his horse goes for help. **58m/B VHS.** Tim McCoy, Richard Alexander, Robert Ellis, Alberta Vaughn, Wallace MacDonald, Murdock

McQuarrie, Max Davidson; *D:* David Ross Lederman.

Daring Dobermans ✗✗ 1973 (PG) In this sequel to "The Doberman Gang," the barking bank-robbers have a new set of crime-planning masters. A young Indian boy who loves the dogs enters the picture and may thwart their perfect crime. **88m/C VHS.** Charles Robinson, Tim Considine, David Moses, Claudio Martinez, Joan Caulfield; *D:* Byron Ross Chudnow.

Daring Game ✗✗ 1968 A group of scuba divers nicknamed the Flying Fish attempt to rescue a woman's husband and daughter from an island dictatorship. Failed series pilot by producer Ivan Tors, better known for "Sea Hunt" and "Flipper." **100m/C VHS.** Lloyd Bridges, Brock Peters, Michael Ansara, Joan Blackman; *D:* Laslo Benedek; *M:* George Bruns. **TV**

Dario Argento's Trauma ✗✗ *Trauma* 1993 (R) When a teenage girl's parents are decapitated, she and an artist friend start following the clues to a psychotic killer known as "The Headhunter." Trademark horror work for Italian cult director Argento with high suspense quotient and equally high gore. An unrated version is also available. **106m/C VHS.** Christopher Rydell, Asia Argento, Laura Johnson, James Russo, Brad Dourif, Frederic Forrest, Piper Laurie; *D:* Dario Argento; *W:* T.E.D. Klein, Dario Argento.

The Dark ✗½ *The Mutilator* 1979 (R) A supernatural beast commits a string of gruesome murders. **92m/C VHS.** William Devane, Cathy Lee Crosby, Richard Jaeckel, Keenan Wynn, Vivian Blaine, Biff (Elliott) Elliot, Warren Kemmerling, Casey Kasem, John Bloom; *D:* John Cardos; *W:* Stanford Whitmore; *C:* John Morrill.

The Dark ✗½ 1994 (R) Cop and scientist seek a mysterious graveyard creature who holds both the power to heal and destroy. One man wants to kill it, one man wants to save it, and they race to be the first to find it. **90m/C VHS.** Brion James, Jaimz Woolvett, Cynthia Belliveau, Stephen McHattie, Dennis O'Connor, Neve Campbell, Christopher Bondy, William Lynn; *D:* Craig Pryce; *W:* Robert Cooper.

A Dark Adapted Eye ✗✗✗ 1993 Sinister TV mystery adapted from the psychological thriller by Ruth Rendell (writing as Barbara Vine). In 1951 Vera Hillyard (Imrie) is hung for murdering her younger sister Eden (Ward)—an act that has profound effects on the family, including young niece Faith (Bonham Carter). Long haunted by the "why" of the crime, Faith later begins an investigation into her family's past—and discovers very dark and disturbing secrets dating back to WWII. Title refers to a vision problem caused by remaining in darkness too long. **150m/C VHS.** *GB* Helena Bonham Carter, Celia Imrie, Sophie Ward, Robin Ellis, Ciaran Hinds, Pip Torrens, William Gaminara, Polly Adams, Bernice Stegers, Steven Mackintosh, Jason Durr; *D:* Tim Fywell; *W:* Sandy Welch; *M:* David Ferguson.

Dark Age ✗✗½ 1988 (R) An Australian conservationist must track down a rampaging, giant, semi-mythical alligator before it is killed by bounty hunters. Based on the novel (and Aboriginal legend) "Numunwari." **90m/C VHS.** *AU* John Jarratt, David Gulpilil, Max Phipps, Ray Meagher, Nikki Coghill, Burnam Burnam; *D:* Arch Nicholson.

The Dark Angel ✗✗✗ 1991 Maud is the young and innocent heiress to a fortune in this gothic mystery of creeping unease. She is intrigued by the romantic portrait of her youthful and unknown Uncle Silas. But her mysterious uncle is no longer the Byronic hero. What secret wickedness does his ravaged face hide? And what about Maud's drug-addicted governess and the brutish young man in the cemetary? Does Uncle Silas just want Maud's fortune or Maud herself? Excellent performances by O'Toole as the decadent uncle and Edney as the innocent-but-not-stupid Maud. Based on the novel "Uncle Silas" by Sheridan Le Fanu. Made for British TV. **150m/C VHS.** *GB* Peter O'Toole, Beatie Edney, Jane Lapotaire, Tim Woodward, Alan MacNaughton, Barbara Shelley, Guy Rolfe; *D:* Peter Hammond. **TV**

Dark Angel: The Ascent ✗½ 1994 (R) She-devil gets tired of hell and decides to get a look at the world upstairs. She also decides to turn vigilante and dispatch some bad guy souls to her former home. **80m/C VHS.** Charlotte Stewart, Daniel Markel, Michael C. Mahon, Nicholas Worth, Milton James, Angela Featherstone; *D:* Linda Hassani; *W:* Matthew Bright; *M:* Fuzzbee Morse.

Dark Asylum ✗✗ 2001 (R) Shrink Maggie Bleham (Porizkova) is called on to examined a serial killer (Drake) who's so dangerous that authorities have brought him to an abandoned asylum to be evaluated. Naturally, the nutball gets loose and kills his guards with the doc next on his list. Only she's got other ideas. **96m/C VHS, DVD, Wide.** Paulina Porizkova, Larry Drake, Judd Nelson, Juergen Prochnow; *D:* Gregory Gieras; *W:* Gregory Gieras; *C:* Viorel Sergovici Jr. **VIDEO**

Dark August ✗✗ 1976 (PG) A New Yorker drops out and transplants to rural Vermont, where he accidentally kills a young girl and then suffers numerous horrors as a result of a curse put on him by the girl's grandfather. **87m/C VHS.** J.J. Barry, Carole Shelyne, Kim Hunter, William Robertson; *D:* Martin Goldman.

The Dark Backward ✗½ 1991 (R) A dark, subversive comedy about a garbage man who dreams of making it big in show biz as a stand-up comedian. He's terrible until a third arm starts growing out of his back and the sheer grotesqueness of his situation makes him a temporary star. Caan and Newton are interestingly cast, but young, first-time director Rifkin's foray into David Lynch territory was not well received by critics. **97m/C VHS, Wide.** Judd Nelson, Bill Paxton, Wayne Newton, Lara Flynn Boyle, James Caan, Rob Lowe, Claudia Christian, King Moody, Adam Rifkin; *D:* Adam Rifkin; *W:* Adam Rifkin; *C:* Joey Forsyte; *M:* Marc David Decker.

Dark Before Dawn ✗½ 1989 (R) American farmers and Vietnam veterans team up against corrupt government officials and ruthless businessmen in this violent film about the plight of the underdog. **95m/C VHS.** Doug McClure, Sonny Gibson, Ben Johnson, Billy Drago, Rance Howard, Morgan Woodward, Buck Henry, Jeffery Osterhage, Red Steagall, John Martin, Gary Cooper; *D:* Robert Totten.

Dark Blue World ✗✗½ *Trmavomodry Svet* 2001 (R) Told in flashbacks, this is an old-fashioned WWII epic about heroism and romance. In 1950 in Czechoslovakia, Franta (Vetchy) is imprisoned by the Communists who fear the war hero's previous contacts with democracy. After the Nazis invaded his country in 1939, Franta fled to England, where he joins the RAF and befriends younger Czech pilot Karel (Hadek). But the duo have a falling out over a local woman, Susan (Fizgerald), who favors the mature Franta. Czech, German, and English dialogue. **115m/C VHS, DVD, Wide.** *CZ GB* Ondrej Vetchy, Tara Fitzgerald, Krystof Hadek, Oldrich Kaiser, Charles Dance, Linda Rybova, Hans-Jorg Assmann, Anna Massey; *D:* Jan Sverak; *W:* Zdenek Sverak; *C:* Vladimir Smutny; *M:* Ondrej Soukup.

Dark Breed ✗✗ 1996 (R) Ewww, yuck, it's sci-fi infestation time once again as Nick Saxon (Scalia) is assigned to find the bodies of six astronauts whose top secret space craft has mysteriously crashed. He discovers that the bodies are playing host to reptilian parasites with designs on world domination. **104m/C VHS.** Jack Scalia, Jonathan Banks, Robin Curtis, Donna W. Scott; *D:* Richard Pepin.

Dark City ✗✗ *Dark Empire; Dark World* 1997 (R) Brooding city of gloom floats in a sunless world, with skylines nightmarishly changing as its residents sleep. The city seems to belong to no era, looking at times like a neo-goth music video and at others like a work of German expressionism. Sometimes it just looks like '60s Cleveland. Director Proyas seems to have wanted to make a futuristic film noir like "Blade Runner," but gets lost somewhere along the way. He does however, keep the style. Disfigured Dr. Schreber (Sutherland) is forced by a dying race of pasty-faced long-coated aliens to use humans as guinea pigs in an attempt to find out what makes them tick. John Murdoch (Sewell) wakes up in a hotel room with a dead body and no memory of his life. Searching for his past, he wanders through one incredible set after another, but is it real or is it hypodermically injected? Hurt is a detective who only wants to stop the grisly murders. Garbled story rewards persistence at the end. **103m/C VHS, DVD.** Kiefer Sutherland, William Hurt, Rufus Sewell, Richard O'Brien, Jennifer Connelly, Ian Richardson, Colin Friels, Frank Gallacher, Bruce Spence, John Bluthal, Mitchell Butel, Melissa George; *D:* Alex Proyas; *W:* Alex Proyas, Lem Dobbs, David S. Goyer; *C:* Darius Wolski; *M:* Trevor Jones.

Dark Command ✗✗✗ 1940 The story of Quantrell's Raiders who terrorized the Kansas territory during the Civil War until one man came along to put a stop to it. Colorful and talented cast add depth to the script. Also available colorized. **95m/B VHS, DVD.** John Wayne, Walter Pidgeon, Claire Trevor, Roy Rogers, Marjorie Main, George "Gabby" Hayes; *D:* Raoul Walsh.

Dark Corner ✗✗✗ 1946 Private detective Bradford Galt (Stevens) is framed and suspects his ex-partner Jardine (Kreuger) is the culprit. But then Jardine winds up dead. Then there's a guy in a white suit (Bendix) who keeps dogging him and sinister wealthy art dealer Hardy Cathcart (Webb) seems to be pulling everyone's strings. It's a good thing Galt's loyal secretary Kathleen (Ball) believes in the lug. Gripping, intricate film noir. **99m/B VHS.** Mark Stevens, Clifton Webb, William Bendix, Lucille Ball, Cathy Downs, Reed Hadley, Constance Collier, Kurt Kreuger; *D:* Henry Hathaway.

The Dark Crystal ✗✗✗ 1982 (PG) Jen and Kira, two of the last surviving Gelflings, attempt to return a crystal shard (discovered with the help of a sorceress) to the castle where the Dark Crystal lies, guarded by the cruel and evil Skeksis. Designed by Brian Froud. From the creators of the Muppets. **93m/C VHS, DVD, Wide.** *D:* Jim Henson, Frank Oz; *W:* David Odell; *C:* Oswald Morris; *M:* Trevor Jones; *V:* Jim Henson, Frank Oz, Kathryn Mullen, Dave Goetz.

The Dark Dancer ✗½ 1995 (R) Psychology prof Maggie (Tweed), who authors books on feminine sexual behavior, gets her experience first-hand by working in a strip club. Now, she's also the target of a police investigation. Also available unrated. **98m/C VHS.** Shannon Tweed, Jason Carter, Lisa Pescia, Francesco Quinn; *D:* Robert Burge; *W:* Robert Burge, Terry Chambers; *C:* Eric Scott; *M:* David Connor.

The Dark Dealer ✗✗ 1995 Three terror tales find the Devil's assistant dealing a deadly game of blackjack to a trio in limbo, with the cards propelling each man into a horrific adventure. Provides some real scares along with effective (if low-budget) special effects. **85m/C VHS.** Mark Fickert, Richard Hull, Vincent Gaskins, Rocky Patterson, Gordon Fox; *D:* Tom Alexander.

Dark Eyes ✗✗✗½ *Les Yeux Noirs; Oci Ciornie* 1987 An acclaimed Italian film based on a several short stories by Anton Chekov. Mastroianni is a weak-willed Italian, trapped in a marriage of convenience, who falls in love with a mysterious, also married, Russian beauty he meets in a health spa. He embarks on a journey to find her and, perhaps, his lost ideals. Hailed as Mastroianni's consummate performance. In Italian with English subtitles. **118m/C VHS.** *IT* Marcello Mastroianni, Silvana Mangano, Elena Sofonova, Marthe Keller; *D:* Nikita Mikhalkov; *C:* Franco Di Giacomo. Cannes '87: Actor (Mastroianni).

Dark Forces ✗✗ *Harlequin* 1983 (PG) A faith-healer promises to help a senator's dying son and finds the politician's wife also desires his assistance. This Australian film is uneven and predictable. Though rated "PG," beware of two rather brief, but explicit, nudity scenes. **96m/C VHS.** *AU* Robert Powell, David Hemmings, Broderick Crawford, Carmen Duncan; *D:* Simon Wincer.

Dark Habits ✗✗½ *Entre Tinieblas* 1984 An early Almodovar farce about already-demented nuns in a failing convent trying to raise funds with the help of a nightclub singer who is on the run. Although certainly irreverant, it doesn't quite have the zing of his later work. In Spanish with subtitles. **116m/C VHS, Wide.** *SP* Carmen Maura, Christina Pascual, Julieta Serrano, Marisa Paredes; *D:* Pedro Almodovar; *W:* Pedro Almodovar; *C:* Angel Luis Fernandez.

The Dark Half ✗✗ 1991 (R) Flawed chiller based on a Stephen King novel. Thad Beaumont's serious novels have been failures, but writing as George Stark, he's had phenomenal success with grisly horror stories. In a publicity stunt Thad kills off and publicly buries George (who doesn't want to stay dead). Soon everyone who's crossed Thad is brutally murdered. Hutton acquits himself well in a change of pace dual role. Otherwise, the psychological thrills are few and the gore is plentiful. Pittsburgh serves as location double for King's usual New England territory. Film's release was delayed due to Orion's bankruptcy problems. **122m/C VHS, DVD.** Timothy Hutton, Amy Madigan, Michael Rooker, Julie Harris, Robert Joy, Kent Broadhurst, Beth Grant, Rutanya Alda, Tom Mardirosian, Chelsea Field, Royal Dano; *D:* George A. Romero; *W:* George A. Romero; *C:* Tony Pierce-Roberts; *M:* Christopher Young.

Dark Harbor ✗✗ 1998 (R) A wealthy married couple, traveling to their vacation home off the coast of Maine, stop to help an injured young man. A series of coincidences leads the threesome to spend the weekend together in the couple's isolated retreat, where sexual attraction makes the situation very volatile. **89m/C VHS, DVD.** Alan Rickman, Polly Walker, Norman Reedus; *D:* Adam Coleman Howard; *W:* Adam Coleman Howard, Justin Lazard; *C:* Walt Lloyd; *M:* David Mansfield.

Dark Horse ✗✗½ 1992 (PG) Meyers is a young woman distraught over the death of her mother. She gets into trouble and is assigned to do community service work at a horse farm where she finds herself caring for a prize-winning horse. **98m/C VHS.** Ari Meyers, Mimi Rogers, Ed Begley Jr., Donovan Leitch, Samantha Eggar; *D:* David Hemmings.

The Dark Hour ✗½ 1936 Two detectives team up to solve a murder in which multiple suspects are involved. Based on Sinclair Gluck's "The Last Trap." **72m/B VHS.** Ray Walker, Irene Ware, Berton Churchill, Hedda Hopper, Hobart Bosworth, E.E. Clive; *D:* Charles Lamont.

Dark Journey ✗✗✗ *The Anxious Years* 1937 WWI Stockholm is the setting for a love story between a double agent and the head of German Intelligence. Clever, sophisticated production; Leigh is stunning. **82m/B VHS.** *GB* Vivien Leigh, Conrad Veidt, Joan Gardner, Anthony Bushell, Ursula Jeans; *D:* Victor Saville.

Dark Justice ✗✗½ 1991 Judge by day, avenger by night, in this actioner created from three episodes of the late-night TV series. Judge Nicholas Marshall is disgusted by the criminals sprung on legal loopholes and backroom deals, so he decides to take justice into his own hands. **99m/C VHS.** Ramy Zada, Dick O'Neill, Clayton Prince, Begona Plaza. **TV**

Dark Mirror ✗✗✗ 1946 A psychologist and a detective struggle to determine which twin sister murdered a prominent physician. Good and evil siblings finely acted by de Havilland. **85m/B VHS.** Olivia de Havilland, Lew Ayres, Thomas Mitchell, Garry Owen; *D:* Robert Siodmak; *C:* Milton Krasner.

Dark Mountain ✗½ 1944 A forest ranger rescues his gal from the clutches of a hardened criminal. **56m/B VHS.** Robert Lowery, Ellen Drew, Regis Toomey, Eddie Quillan, Elisha Cook Jr.; *D:* William Berke, William C. Thomas.

Dark Night of the Scarecrow ✗✗½ 1981 Thriller with a moral. Prejudiced townspeople execute a retarded man who was innocently befriended by a young girl. After his death unusual things begin to happen. Slow to start but effective. **100m/C VHS.** Charles Durning, Tanya Crowe, Larry Drake; *D:* Frank De Felitta. **TV**

Dark Obsession 🦴🦴 *Diamond Skulls* **1990 (R)** Byrne portrays a husband who lives out his dark erotic fantasies with his wife (Donohoe), and is involved in a hit-and-run accident. Driven by guilt, madness slowly begins to take him. Ugly and depressing. Based on a true scandal. Available in an "NC-17" rated version. **87m/C VHS.** Peter Allen, Gabriel Byrne, Amanda Donohoe, Michael Hordern, Judy Parfitt, Douglas Hodge, Sadie Frost, Ian Carmichael; ***D:*** Nick Broomfield; ***W:*** Tim Rose Price; ***C:*** Michael Coulter; ***M:*** Hans Zimmer.

Dark Odyssey 🦴🦴 **1957** Metzger's first feature tells the tragic tale of a young Greek seaman who jumps ship in New York in order to avenge his sister's rape. He finds himself conflicted between his masculine sense of family honor and love when he falls for a Greek-American woman. Director's cut includes the original theatrical trailer. **85m/B VHS, DVD.** David Hooks, Edward Brazier, Jeanne Jerrems; ***D:*** William Kyriakis, Radley Metzger; ***W:*** William Kyriakis, Radley Metzger; ***C:*** Peter Erik Winkler; ***M:*** Laurence Rosenthal.

Dark of the Night 🦴🦴½ *Mr. Wrong* **1985** A young woman, new to the city, purchases a used Jaguar and finds she must share it with the car's former owner—a woman murdered inside the Jag. Decent psycho-thriller with some suspenseful and amusing moments. **88m/C VHS.** *NZ* Heather Bolton, David Letch, Gary Stalker, Michael Haigh, Danny Mulheron, Kate Harcourt; ***D:*** Gaylene Preston; ***W:*** Gaylene Preston, Geoff Murphy, Graham Tetley; ***C:*** Thomas Burstyn; ***M:*** Jonathan Crayford.

Dark of the Sun 🦴🦴½ *The Mercenaries* **1968 (PG)** Lots of action; routine plot. Taylor is a tough mercenary hired to retrieve a supply of uncut diamonds from a beseiged town in the Congo during the 1950s rebellion. Oh, and if he can help out the town's inhabitants, that's okay too. Based on the novel by Wilbur A. Smith. **101m/C VHS.** *GB* Rod Taylor, Jim Brown, Yvette Mimieux, Kenneth More, Peter Carsten, Calvin Lockhart, Andre Morell; ***D:*** Jack Cardiff; ***W:*** Quentin Werty, Adrian Spies; ***M:*** Jacques Loussier.

Dark Passage 🦴🦴½ **1947** Bogart plays a convict who escapes from San Quentin to prove he was framed for the murder of his wife. He undergoes plastic surgery and is hidden and aided by Bacall as he tries to find the real killer. Stars can't quite compensate for a far-fetched script and so-so direction. **107m/B VHS.** Humphrey Bogart, Lauren Bacall, Agnes Moorehead, Bruce (Herman Brix) Bennett, Tom D'Andrea; ***D:*** Delmer Daves.

The Dark Past 🦴🦴🦴 **1949** A crazy, escaped convict holds a psychologist and his family hostage, and the two men engage in psychological cat-and-mouse combat. An underrated thriller with offbeat casting. **75m/B VHS.** William Holden, Lee J. Cobb, Nina Foch, Adele Jergens; ***D:*** Rudolph Mate; ***M:*** George Duning.

Dark Places 🦴🦴 **1973 (PG)** Masquerading as a hospital administrator, a former mental patient inherits the ruined mansion of a man who had killed his wife and children and died insane. As he lives in the house, the spirit of its former owner seems to overcome him with a need to repeat the crime. Meanwhile, Lee, Collins, and Lom think the nut is hiding money they would like to get their collective hands on. Low-budget but fairly effective. **91m/C VHS.** *GB* Joan Collins, Christopher Lee, Robert Hardy; ***D:*** Don Sharp.

Dark Planet 🦴🦴 **1997 (R)** In the year 2636 Earth is in the middle of WW6 and it's up to rebel commander Hawke (Mercurio) to search for the Dark Planet and complete a secret assignment that is humanity's last hope. **99m/C VHS, DVD.** Paul Mercurio, Harley Jane Kozak, Michael York, Maria Ford, Ed O'Ross; ***D:*** Albert Magnoli; ***W:*** S.O. Lee; ***C:*** William MacCollum.

The Dark Power 🦴 **1985** Ex-cowboy LaRue and his trusty whip provide this flick with its only excitement. As sheriff, he must deal with the dead Mexican warriors who rise to wreak havoc when a house is built on their burial ground. **87m/C VHS.** Lash LaRue, Anna Lane Tatum; ***D:*** Phil Smoot.

The Dark Ride 🦴½ **1984** Lunatic picks up women with the intention of raping and killing them. Ugly thriller based on the evil deeds of serial murderer Ted Bundy. **83m/C VHS.** James Luisi, Susan Sullivan, Martin Speer; ***D:*** Jeremy Hoenack.

Dark Rider **1991** Dark Rider is a mysterious, motorcycle riding hero who comes to the rescue of a small town. Besieged by a gangster who buys up all their land, the townspeople must abandon their homes and indeed, their very dreams. That is until Dark Rider rolls into to town to enact his own unique brand of vengeance. **94m/C VHS.** Joe Estevez, Doug Shanklin, Alicia Kowalski, David Shark, Chuck Williams; ***D:*** Bob Ivy; ***W:*** Bob Ivy, Chuck Williams; ***C:*** Mark W. Gray; ***M:*** Brad Scott Gish.

Dark River: A Father's Revenge 🦴🦴 **1990** When his daughter is killed in a toxic waste dump accident, a man begins revenge on the company and its managers. Tense, with important message. **95m/C VHS.** Helen Hunt, Mike Farrell, Tess Harper, Philip Baker Hall; ***D:*** Michael Pressman. **TV**

Dark Sanity woof! *Straight Jacket* **1982** Uninvolving attempt at horror has a recently de-institutionalized woman envisioning death and destruction (something you'll wish the film would do) while everyone else just thinks she's losing her marbles. Problem is we don't really care. **89m/C VHS.** Aldo Ray, Kory Clark, Andy Gwyn, Bobby Holt; ***D:*** Martin Greene.

The Dark Secret of Harvest Home 🦴🦴½ **1978** An urban couple confront a pagan cult in the New England town into which they've moved. Based upon the Thomas Tryon novel. **118m/C VHS.** Bette Davis, Rosanna Arquette, David Ackroyd, Rene Auberjonois, Michael O'Keefe, Joanna Miles; ***D:*** Leo Penn; ***W:*** Jennifer Miller, Jack Guss; ***Nar:*** Donald Pleasence. **TV**

Dark Secrets 🦴 **1995 (R)** Reporter Claire (Parent) wants to get a hot story on sex club mogul Justin DeVille (Carroll) and winds up falling prey to his charms. But Justin's not the trusting kind and sets up some loyalty tests for Claire. The unrated version is 99 minutes. **90m/C VHS, DVD.** Monique Parent, Julie Strain, Justin Carroll; ***D:*** John Bowen; ***W:*** Steve Tymon; ***C:*** Keith Holland; ***M:*** Efrem Bergman.

Dark Side of Genius 🦴🦴 **1994 (R)** Jennifer Cole (Hughes), a reporter for an L.A. arts weekly, tries to get the story on artist Julian Jons (Fraser), who's just been paroled after being imprisoned for the murder of his model. Now his lurid new paintings of a sultry nude model hint at some obsessive behavior and Jennifer's reporter instincts may be the death of her. **86m/C VHS.** Finola Hughes, Brendan Fraser, Glenn Shadix, Moon Zappa, Patrick Richwood, Seymour Cassel; ***D:*** Phedon Papamichael; ***W:*** Fred Stroppel; ***C:*** Phedon Papamichael; ***M:*** Tom Hiel.

The Dark Side of Love 🦴½ **1979** A young girl gets involved with the rougher side of New Orleans society, gets pregnant, and realizes how she's been degraded. **94m/C VHS.** James Stacy, Glynnis O'Connor, Jan Sterling, Mickey Rooney; ***D:*** Sam Wanamaker; ***C:*** Michael D. Margulies. **TV**

Dark Side of Midnight 🦴½ *The Creeper* **1986 (R)** A super-detective tracks down a psychopathic killer. **108m/C VHS.** James Moore, Wes Olsen, Sandy Schemmel, Dave Bowling; ***D:*** Wes Olsen; ***W:*** Wes Olsen; ***C:*** Wes Olsen.

The Dark Side of the Heart 🦴🦴 *El Lado Oscuro del Corazon* **1992** Magic realism features in this story of struggling Buenos Aires poet Oliverio (Grandinetti) who falls in love with prostitute Ana (Ballesteros). She wants to keep things businesslike but when a man finds a woman whose lovemaking causes them to actually levitate, he's not about to make things easy. Spanish with subtitles. **127m/C VHS.** *CA AR* Dario Grandinetti, Sandra Ballesteros, Nacha Guevara; ***D:*** Eliseo Subiela; ***W:*** Eliseo Subiela; ***C:*** Hugo Colace; ***M:*** Osvaldo Montes. Montreal World Film Fest. '92: Film.

Dark Side of the Moon 🦴🦴 **1990 (R)** Members of a space ship sent on a routine mission to the far side of the moon, discover an unknown force that feeds on human emotion and consumes the soul. Lukewarm science fiction/horror. **96m/C VHS.** William Bledsoe, Alan Blumenfeld, John Diehl, Robert Sampson, Wendy MacDonald, Camilla More, Joe Turkel; ***D:*** D.J. Webster.

Dark Star 🦴🦴🦴 **1974 (G)** John Carpenter's directorial debut is a low-budget, sci-fi satire which focuses on a group of scientists whose mission is to destroy unstable planets. During their journey, they battle their alien mascot (who closely resembles a walking beach ball), as well as a "sensitive" and intelligent bombing device which starts to question the meaning of its existence. Enjoyable early feature from John "Halloween" Carpenter and Dan "Aliens" O'Bannon. Fun, weird, and unpredictable. **95m/C VHS, DVD, Wide.** Dan O'Bannon, Brian Narelle, Dre Pahich, Cal Duniholm; ***D:*** John Carpenter; ***W:*** John Carpenter, Dan O'Bannon; ***C:*** Douglas Knapp; ***M:*** John Carpenter.

Dark Tide 🦴🦴 **1993 (R)** Erotic action thriller about a pair of deep sea divers whose love life is disturbed when their boat captain becomes sexually fixated on the woman. Also available in an uncut, unrated version. **92m/C VHS.** Brigitte Bako, Richard Tyson, Chris Sarandon; ***D:*** Luca Bercovici.

Dark Tower 🦴 **1987 (R)** Decent cast is wasted in yet another inept attempt at horror. An architect is dismayed to learn that an evil force is inhabiting her building and it might just be the ghost of her dearly departed husband. **91m/C VHS.** Michael Moriarty, Jenny Agutter, Theodore Bikel, Carol Lynley, Anne Lockhart, Kevin McCarthy; ***D:*** Ken Barnett, Freddie Francis, Ken Wiederhorn; ***W:*** Robert J. Avrech, Kenneth G. Blackwell.

Dark Universe 🦴½ **1993 (R)** An alien terror wants to conquer the Earth and make its inhabitants their new food source. **83m/C VHS.** Blake Pickett, Cherie Scott, Bently Tittle, John Maynard, Paul Austin Saunders, Tom Ferguson, Steve Barkett, Joe Estevez, Patrick Moran; ***D:*** Steve Latshaw; ***W:*** Patrick Moran.

Dark Victory 🦴🦴🦴½ **1939** A spoiled young heiress discovers she is dying from a brain tumor. She attempts to pack a lifetime of parties into a few months, but is rescued by her doctor, with whom she falls in love. Classic final scene with Davis at the top of her form. Bogart plays an Irish stable hand, but not especially well. Also available in a colorized version. **106m/B VHS, DVD.** Bette Davis, George Brent, Geraldine Fitzgerald, Humphrey Bogart, Ronald Reagan, Henry Travers; ***D:*** Edmund Goulding; ***W:*** Casey Robinson; ***C:*** Ernest Haller; ***M:*** Max Steiner.

Dark Waters 🦴🦴 **1944** The drowning death of her parents has left a young woman mentally unstable. She returns to her family home in the backwaters of Louisiana with her peculiar aunt and uncle to serve as guardians. It eventually becomes apparent that someone is trying to drive her insane. This one tends to be rather murky and it's not simply due to the plentiful scenes of misty swampland. **93m/B VHS, DVD.** Merle Oberon, Franchot Tone, Thomas Mitchell, Fay Bainter, Elisha Cook Jr., John Qualen, Rex Ingram; ***D:*** Andre de Toth; ***W:*** Joan Harrison, Marian Cockrell; ***C:*** Archie Stout, John Mescall; ***M:*** Miklos Rozsa.

The Dark Wind 🦴½ **1991 (R)** The first of Tony Hillerman's popular Native American mysteries comes to the screen in a lame adaptation. Phillips stars as the Navaho cop investigating a murder on a New Mexico Indian reservation. Since the Navaho believe a "dark wind" enters a man's soul when he does evil, expect some "spirited" goings-on as well. **111m/C VHS.** Lou Diamond Phillips; ***D:*** Errol Morris; ***W:*** Eric Bergren.

Darkdrive 🦴🦴½ **1998 (R)** In the near future, the Zircon Corporation has created a virtual prison where the minds of criminals are held in isolation. Naturally, something's gone wrong and it's up to special operations officer Steven Falcon (Olandt) to risk his mind and solve the problem. **100m/C VHS, DVD.** Ken Olandt, Julie Benz, Claire Stansfield, Carlo Scandiuzzi; ***D:*** Phillip J. Roth; ***W:*** Alec Carlin; ***C:*** Andres Garreton; ***M:*** Jim Goodwin. **VIDEO**

Darker than Amber 🦴🦴 **1970 (R)** John D. MacDonald's houseboat-dwelling detective Travis McGee (Taylor) rescues a girl (Kendall) he's fallen for, and soon discovers that the mugs who thugged her were part of a collection racket. A violent action melodrama upgraded from its original "R" rating. **96m/C VHS.** Rod Taylor, Suzy Kendall, Theodore Bikel, Jane Russell, James Booth, Janet MacLachlan, William Smith, Ahna Capri, Chris Robinson; ***D:*** Robert Clouse.

Darkest Africa *Batmen of Africa; King of the Jungleland* **1936** Legendary animal trainer Beatty is the hero of this 15 episode cliffhanger serial as he vies with beasts—both animal and human. **270m/B** Clyde Beatty, Manuel King, Elaine Shepard; ***D:*** Joseph Kane, B. Reeves Eason.

Darkman 🦴🦴🦴 **1990 (R)** Raimi's disfigured-man-seeks-revenge suspenser is comicbook kitsch cross-pollinated with a strain of gothic horror. Neeson plays a scientist who's on the verge of discovering the key to cloning body parts; brutally attacked by the henchmen of a crooked politico, his lab is destroyed and he's left for dead. Turns out he's not dead—just horribly disfigured and a wee bit chafed—and he stalks his deserving victims from the shadows, using his lab know-how to disguise his rugged bad looks. Exquisitely violent. Montage by Pablo Ferro. **96m/C VHS, DVD.** Liam Neeson, Frances McDormand, Larry Drake, Colin Friels, Nelson Mashita, Jenny Agutter, Rafael H. Robledo, Nicholas Worth, Theodore (Ted) Raimi, John Landis, William Lustig, Scott Spiegel, Bruce Campbell; ***D:*** Sam Raimi; ***W:*** Sam Raimi, Ivan Raimi, Daniel Goldin, Joshua Goldin, Chuck Pfarrer; ***C:*** Bill Pope; ***M:*** Danny Elfman.

Darkman 2: The Return of Durant 🦴🦴½ **1994 (R)** The first in a series of direct-to-video adventures about disfigured scientist Peyton "Darkman" Westlake (now played by Vosloo), who's continuing his liquid skin research in the hopes of transforming his grotesque appearance. He finds an ally in scientist David Brinkman but Westlake's nemesis, crime boss Robert G. Durant (Drake), wants the property where Brinkman's lab is located. And what Durant wants, he takes. Sam Raimi, who directed the original film, is one of the series producers. **93m/C VHS, DVD, Wide.** Arnold Vosloo, Larry Drake, Kim Delaney, Renee O'Connor, Rod Wilson; ***D:*** Bradford May; ***W:*** Steven McKay, Chuck Pfarrer; ***C:*** Bradford May; ***M:*** Randy Miller. **VIDEO**

Darkman 3: Die Darkman Die 🦴🦴½ **1995 (R)** The second direct-to-video Darkman saga finds Dr. Peyton Westlake (Vosloo) disrupting the drug-dealing activities of underworld boss Peter Rooker (Fahey). The obsessed Rooker is determined to figure out the secret to Darkman's enormous strength, employing the feminine wiles of his mistress, Dr. Bridget Thorne (Fluegel). Then Westlake/Darkman finds himself drawn to Rooker's neglected wife and young daughter. Our hero suffers a lot (as usual) and there's lots of action (as usual). **87m/C VHS, Wide.** Arnold Vosloo, Jeff Fahey, Darlanne Fluegel, Nigel Bennett, Roxann Biggs-Dawson; ***D:*** Bradford May; ***W:*** Mike Werb, Michael Colleary; ***C:*** Bradford May; ***M:*** Randy Miller.

Darkness Falls 🦴🦴 **1998 (R)** John Barrett (Winstone) is looking for revenge. His adulterous wife Jane (McCaffrey) was critically injured in a car crash from which her lover escaped. So John goes to the Driscoll home and decides to terrorize Jane's boyfriend Mark (Dutton) and his unsuspecting wife Sally (Fenn). Filmed on the Isle of Man, which may be the most interesting thing about this routine thriller. **91m/C VHS, DVD.** Sherilyn Fenn, Ray Winstone, Tim Dutton, Robin McCaffrey, Oliver Tobias, Michael Praed; ***D:*** Gerry Lively; ***W:*** John Howlett; ***C:*** Adam Santelli; ***M:*** Guy Farley.

Darkroom 🦴½ **1990** An unstable young man devises a scheme to photograph his father in bed with his mistress, and then use the pics to blackmail dear ol' dad. **90m/C VHS, DVD.** Jill Pierce, Jeffrey Allen Arbaugh, Sara Lee Wade, Aaron Teich; ***D:*** Terrence O'Hara. **VIDEO**

The Darkside 🦴½ **1987 (R)** In this frightening drama, a young prostitute and an innocent cabbie attempt to escape the clutches of a maniacal film producer with a secret he won't let them reveal. **95m/C VHS.** Tony Galati, Cyndy Preston; ***D:*** Constantino Magnatta.

Darktown Strutters 🦴 *Get Down and Boogie* **1974 (PG)** Effort to satirize racial stereotypes is humorless and ineffective. Black female motorcycle gang searches for the kidnapped mother of one of the members. **85m/C VHS.** Trina Parks, Roger E. Mosley, Shirley Washington; ***D:*** William Witney.

Darling 🦴🦴🦴½ **1965** Amoral young model Diana Scott (Christie) tries to hold boredom at bay by having a number of love affairs. She moves from intellectual Robert (Bogarde) to playboy Miles (Harvey) and eventually joins the international jet set and manages to reach the top of European society by marrying a prince. Diana then learns what an empty life she has. Christie won an Oscar for her portrayal of the disillusioned, cynical young woman. **122m/B VHS.** *GB* Julie Christie, Dirk Bogarde, Laurence Harvey, Jose-Luis De Villalonga, Roland Curram; ***D:*** John Schlesinger; ***W:*** Frederic Raphael; ***C:*** Ken Higgins; ***M:*** John Dankworth. Oscars '65: Actress (Christie), Costume Des. (B&W), Story & Screenplay; British Acad. '65: Actor (Bogarde), Actress (Christie), Screenplay; Golden Globes '66: Foreign Film; Natl. Bd. of Review '65: Actress (Christie), Director (Schlesinger); N.Y. Film Critics '65: Actress (Christie), Director (Schlesinger), Film.

Darling Lili 🦴🦴½ **1970** Big-budget WWI spy comedy/musical with Andrews as a German agent posing as an English music hall performer, who falls in love with squadron leader Hudson and finds she can't betray him. A critical flop when first released, film has its charms though director Edwards did much better for Andrews in "Victor/Victoria." ♫Whistling Away the Dark; The Girl In No Man's Land; Smile Away Each Rainy Day; I'll Give You Three Guesses; Your Good Will Ambassador; Darling Lili; The Little Birds. **136m/C VHS.** Julie Andrews, Rock Hudson, Jeremy Kemp, Jacques Marin, Michael Witney, Vernon Dobtcheff; ***D:*** Blake Edwards; ***W:*** Blake Edwards, William Peter Blatty; ***M:*** Henry Mancini, Johnny Mercer. Golden Globes '71: Song ("Whistling Away the Dark").

Darlings of the Gods 🦴🦴½ **1990** The glittering marriage of actors Sir Laurence Olivier and Vivien Leigh is just as dramatic as anything on stage or screen as Olivier's devotion to work and Leigh's fragile mental and physical health put their relationship on a star-crossed path. **180m/C VHS.** *GB* Anthony (Corlan) Higgins, Mel Martin, Jerome Ehlers, Rhys McConnochie, Lindy Davies, Shane Briant, Anthony Hawkins, Jackie Kelleher; ***D:*** Catherine Miller; ***W:*** Roger Simpson, Graeme Farmer; ***M:*** Brian May. **TV**

D.A.R.Y.L. 🦴🦴 **1985 (PG)** The little boy found by the side of the road is too polite, too honest and too smart. His friend explains to him the necessity of imperfection (If you don't want the grown-ups to bother you too much) and he begins to become more like a real little boy. But the American military has a top-secret interest in this child, since he is in fact the combination of a cloned body and a computer brain. More interesting when it's involved with the human beings and less so when it focuses on science. **100m/C VHS.** Mary Beth Hurt, Michael McKean, Barret Oliver, Colleen Camp, Danny Corkill; ***D:*** Simon Wincer; ***W:*** David Ambrose, Allan Scott; ***M:*** Marvin Hamlisch.

Das Boot 🦴🦴🦴🦴 *The Boat* **1981 (R)** Superb detailing of life in a German U-boat during WWII. Intense, claustrophobic atmosphere complemented by nail-biting action provides a realistic portrait of the stressful conditions that were endured on these submarines. Excellent performances, especially from Prochnow. In German with subtitles. From the novel by Lothar-Guenther Buccheim. Originally a six-hour special made for German TV. **210m/C VHS, DVD.** *GE* Juergen Prochnow, Herbert Gronemeyer, Klaus Wennemann, Hubertus Bengsch, Martin Semmelrogge, Bernd Tauber, Erwin Leder, Martin May, Heinz Honig, Uwe Ochsenknecht, Claude-Oliver Rudolph, Jan Fedder, Ralph Richer, Joachim Bernhard, Oliver Stritzel, Konrad Becker, Lutz Schnell, Martin Hemme, Rita Cadillac; ***D:*** Wolfgang Petersen; ***W:*** Wolfgang Petersen; ***C:*** Jost Vacano; ***M:*** Klaus Doldinger. **TV**

Dash and Lilly 🦴🦴½ **1999** Depicts the 30-year love affair between hard-drinking, promiscuous writers Dashiell Hammett (Shepard) and Lillian Hellman (Davis). Meeting in the 1930s, the successful Hammett becomes the up-and-coming Hellman's mentor. Though both are married, they also begin an affair. Eventually, their positions are reversed as Hammett's career declines and, after serving in WWII, he becomes increasingly plagued by ill health. Meanwhile, playwright Hellman has her own trials when she's blacklisted in the '50s during the Red Scare. **?m/C VHS.** Sam Shepard, Judy Davis, David Paymer, Bebe Neuwirth, Laurence Luckinbill, Zeljko Ivanek, Ned Eisenberg, Mark Zimmerman; ***D:*** Kathy Bates; ***W:*** Jerry Ludwig; ***C:*** Bruce Surtees; ***M:*** Laura Karpman. **CABLE**

Date Bait 🦴 **1960** When a teen couple decides—much to their parents' chagrin—to elope, they find themselves on a date with danger when their post-nuptuals are plagued by pushers and assorted other bad guys. **71m/B VHS.** Gary Clarke, Marlo Ryan, Richard Gering, Danny Logan; ***D:*** O'Dale Ireland.

Date with an Angel 🦴½ **1987 (PG)** When aspiring musician Knight fishes a beautiful angel out of the swimming pool, he is just trying to rescue her. But the beauty of the angel overwhelms him and he finds himself questioning his upcoming wedding to Cates, a cosmetic mogul's daughter. Sickeningly cute and way too sentimental, though Beart's beauty is other-wordly. **105m/C VHS, DVD, Wide.** Charles Lane, Emmanuelle Beart, Michael E. Knight, Phoebe Cates, David Dukes, Bibi Besch, Albert Macklin, David Hunt, Michael Goodwin; ***D:*** Tom McLoughlin; ***W:*** Tom McLoughlin; ***C:*** Alex Thomson; ***M:*** Randy Kerber.

A Date with Judy 🦴🦴 **1948** Standard post-war musical dealing with teenage mix-ups in and around a big high school dance. Choreography by Stanley Donen. ♫Cuanto La Gusto; Strictly on the Corny Side; It's a Most Unusual Day; Judaline; I've Got a Date with Judy; I'm Gonna Meet My Mary; Temptation; Mulligatawny. **114m/C VHS.** Jane Powell, Elizabeth Taylor, Carmen Miranda, Wallace Beery, Robert Stack, Xavier Cugat, Selena Royle, Leon Ames; ***D:*** Richard Thorpe; ***C:*** Robert L. Surtees.

Dating the Enemy 🦴🦴 **1995** War between the sexes comedy about two instantaneous lovers who have nothing in common. Tash (Karvan) is a serious journalist who falls for easy-going Brett (Pearce), the host of a musicvideo program. After a year of togetherness, Tash wishes macho Brett could understand what it's like to be a woman. Surprise! The duo mysteriously switch bodies and find their new sexual (and job) roles aren't easy. **104m/C VHS.** *AU* Claudia Karvan, Guy Pearce, Matt(hew) Day, Lisa Hensley, Pippa Grandison, John Howard; ***D:*** Megan Simpson; ***W:*** Megan Simpson; ***C:*** Steve Arnold; ***M:*** David Hirschfelder.

Daughter of Darkness 🦴🦴½ **1989 (R)** A young woman goes to Hungary in search of her family tree, only to discover vampires nestled there. **93m/C VHS.** Mia Sara, Anthony Perkins, Robert Reynolds, Jack Coleman; ***D:*** Stuart Gordon.

Daughter of Death 🦴 *Julie Darling* **1982 (R)** A little mentally off-center since she witnessed the gruesome rape and murder of her mother, a teenage girl doesn't bond well with her new mom when dad remarries. **100m/C VHS.** *CA GE* Anthony (Tony) Franciosa, Isabelle Mejias, Sybil Danning, Cindy Gurling, Paul Hubbard, Benjamin Schmoll; ***D:*** Paul Nicholas.

The Daughter of Dr. Jekyll 🦴½ **1957** The doc's daughter believes she may have inherited her father's evil curse when several of the locals are found dead. Originally released in theaters on a double bill with "Dr. Cyclops." **71m/B VHS, DVD, Wide.** John Agar, Arthur Shields, John Dierkes, Gloria Talbott; ***D:*** Edgar G. Ulmer; ***W:*** Jack Pollexfen; ***C:*** John F. Warren; ***M:*** Melvyn Lenard.

Daughter of Don Q 🦴🦴½ **1946** Delores' father is very rich with a huge real estate empire and she is his only heir. Greedy cousin Carlos would like to change that—by killing Delores. Delores must dodge speeding cars, hurling harpoons, and more to escape Carlos' evil plot. Part of "The Cliffhanger Serials" series. **166m/B VHS.** Adrian (Lorna Gray) Booth, Kirk Alyn, Leroy Mason; ***D:*** Fred Brannon, Spencer Gordon Bennet; ***W:*** Albert De Mond, Basil Dickey, Jesse Duffy, Lynn Perkins.

Daughter of Horror 🦴🦴 *Dementia* **1955** A young woman finds herself involved with a porcine mobster who resembles her abusive father. Trouble is, Dad's dead, and daughter dearest abetted his departure. Obscure venture into expressionism that was initially banned by the New York State Board of Censors. Shot on a low budget (how low was it? So low that McMahon narrated because shooting with sound was too expensive). The 55 minutes tend to lag, although the film should be intriguing to genre enthusiasts and to fans of things pseudo-Freudian. **60m/B VHS, DVD.** Adrienne Barrett, Ben Roseman, Richard Barron, Ed Hinkle, Lucille Howland, Angelo Rossitto, Bruno VeSota; ***D:*** John Parker; ***W:*** John Parker; ***C:*** William C. Thompson; ***M:*** George Antheil; ***V:*** Marni Nixon; ***Nar:*** Ed McMahon.

Daughter of the Dragon 🦴🦴 **1931** Fu Manchu is again on the prowl, this time sending his daughter to murder Fletcher to avenge the death of his wife and son during China's Boxer Rebellion. Based on a Sax Rohmer story. **70m/B VHS.** Anna May Wong, Warner Oland, Sessue Hayakawa, Bramwell Fletcher, Holmes Herbert; ***D:*** Lloyd Corrigan.

Daughter of the Tong 🦴 **1939** FBI agent gets tong twisted when he tries to put a lid on a smuggling ring headed by a woman (who's beautiful, of course). Something that resembles acting is wasted in a mess of a movie. **56m/B VHS.** Evelyn Brent, Grant Withers, Dorothy Short, Dave O'Brien; ***D:*** Raymond K. Johnson.

Daughters of Darkness 🦴🦴🦴 *Le Rouge aux Levres; Blut an den Lippen; Erzebeth; The Promise of Red Lips; The Red Lips* **1971 (R)** Newlyweds on their way to England stop at a posh French hotel. There they meet a beautiful woman whom the hotel owner swears had been there 40 years ago, even though she hasn't aged a bit. When she introduces herself as Countess of Bathory (the woman who bathed in the blood of virgins to stay young) folks begin to wonder. A really superb erotic vampire film charged with sensuality and a sense of dread. **87m/C VHS, DVD.** *BE GE IT FR* Delphine Seyrig, John Karlen, Daniele Ouimet, Andrea Rau, Paul Esser, Georges Jamin, Joris Collet, Fons Rademakers; ***D:*** Harry Kumel; ***W:*** Harry Kumel, Pierre Drouot, Jean Ferry; ***C:*** Eddy van der Enden; ***M:*** Francois de Roubaix.

Daughters of Satan 🦴🦴 **1972 (R)** Selleck, in an early role as a virile museum buyer, antagonizes a coven of witches when he purchases a painting. His wife, played by Grant, becomes a target of the witches' revenge and salacious shenanigans ensue. **96m/C VHS.** Tom Selleck, Barra Grant, Paraluman, Tani Phelps Guthrie; ***D:*** Hollingsworth Morse.

Daughters of the Dust 🦴🦴🦴½ **1991** Five women of a Gullah family living on the Sea Islands off the Georgia coast in 1902 contemplate moving to the mainland in this emotional tale of change. The Gullah are descendants of West African slaves and their isolation has kept their superstitions and native dialect (a mixture of Western African, Creole, and English) intact. Family bonds and memories are celebrated with a quiet narrative and beautiful cinematography in Dash's feature-film directorial debut. **113m/C VHS, DVD, Wide.** Cora Lee Day, Barbara O, Alva Rogers, Kaycee Moore, Cheryl Lynn Bruce, Adisa Anderson, Eartha D. Robinson, Bahni Turpin, Tommy Redmond Hicks, Malik Farrakhan, Cornell (Kofi) Royal, Vertamae Crosvenor, Umar Abdurrahman, Sherry Jackson, Rev. Ervin Green; ***D:*** Julie Dash; ***W:*** Julie Dash; ***C:*** A. Jafa Fielder; ***M:*** John Barnes. Sundance '91: Cinematog.

Daughters of the Sun 🦴🦴 *Dakhtaran-e Khorshid* **2000** Amanagol (Taghani) is the eldest of six daughters from a poor rural family. In order to get money to support them and help her ill mother, Amanagol's father cuts her hair and disguises her as a boy named Aman, sending her to a distant village as an apprentice weaver. But her employer is dishonest—keeping her earnings instead of sending them to Aman's family. Then Aman learns her mother has died because of her employer's deception. Persian with subtitles. **92m/C VHS.** *IA* Altinay Ghelich Taghani; ***D:*** Mariam Shahriar; ***W:*** Mariam Shahriar; ***C:*** Homayun Payvar; ***M:*** Hosein Ali-Zadeh.

Dave 🦴🦴🦴 **1993 (PG-13)** Regular guy Dave Kovic (Kline) is a dead ringer for the President, launching him into the White House after the prez suffers a stroke in embarrassing circumstances. Seamless comedy prompts lots of hearty laughs and the feel-good faith that despite the overwhelming odds, everything will turn out just fine. Political cameos abound: look for real-life Senators Alan Simpson, Paul Simon, Howard Metzenbaum, Tom Harkin, and Christopher Dodd as well as the commentators from TV's "The McLaughlin Group," and Stone, poking fun at himself on "Larry King Live," as he tries to convince the public there's a conspiracy going on. **110m/C VHS, DVD, Wide.** Stephen (Steve) Root, Kevin Kline, Sigourney Weaver, Frank Langella, Kevin Dunn, Ving Rhames, Ben Kingsley, Charles Grodin, Faith Prince, Laura Linney, Bonnie Hunt, Parley Baer, Stefan Gierasch, Anna Deavere Smith, Bonnie Bartlett, Ben Stein; ***Cameos:*** Jay Leno, Larry King, Oliver Stone, Arnold Schwarzenegger; ***D:*** Ivan Reitman; ***W:*** Gary Ross; ***C:*** Adam Greenberg; ***M:*** James Newton Howard.

David 🦴🦴🦴½ **1979** A haunting portrait of the survival of a Jewish teenager in Berlin during the Nazi reign of terror, based on the novel by Joel Koenig. Universally acclaimed, this was the first film about the Holocaust made in Germany by a German Jew. In German with English subtitles. **106m/C VHS.** *GE* Mario Fischel, Walter Taub, Irene Vrkijan, Torsten Hentes, Eva Mattes; ***D:*** Peter Lilienthal. Berlin Intl. Film Fest. '79: Golden Berlin Bear.

David 🦴🦴½ **1997** TNT's Old Testament biblical series continues with the story of shepherd boy David (Turner) who succeeds Saul (Pryce) to become king over the tribes of Israel. When King David (Parker) becomes smitten with the married Bathsheba (Lee), he sends her husband into battle, soon leaving her a comely widow (although not for long). And there's also subplots involving three of David's children: Absalom (Rowan), Amnon (Hall), and Tamar (Bellar). Lots of action. **?m/C VHS.** Nathaniel Parker, Sheryl Lee, Jonathan Pryce, Leonard Nimoy, Dominic Rowan, Edward Hall, Clara Bellar, Marco Leonardi, Franco Nero, Ben Daniels, Maurice Roeves, Gina Bellman, Gideon Turner; ***D:*** Robert Markowitz; ***W:*** Larry Gross; ***C:*** Raffaele Mertes; ***M:*** Carlo Siliotto.

David and Bathsheba 🦴🦴🦴 **1951** The Bible story comes alive in this lush and colorful Fox production. Peck and Hayward are great together and Peck is properly concerned about the wrath of God over his transgressions. Terrific costumes and special effects, lovely music and a fine supporting cast keep this a notch above other Biblical epics. **116m/C VHS.** Gregory Peck, Susan Hayward, Raymond Massey, Kieron Moore, James Robertson Justice, Jayne Meadows, John Sutton, Dennis Hoey, Francis X. Bushman, George Zucco; ***D:*** Henry King; ***W:*** Philip Dunne; ***C:*** Leon Shamroy.

David and Lisa 🦴🦴🦴 **1962** Director Perry was given an Oscar for this sensitive independently produced film. Adapted from Theodore Isaac Rubin's true case history novel concerning a young man and woman who fall in love while institutionalized for mental illness. Dullea and Margolin are excellent in the title roles of this sleeper. **94m/B VHS, DVD.** Keir Dullea, Janet Margolin, Howard da Silva, Neva Patterson, Clifton James; ***D:*** Frank Perry; ***W:*** Eleanor Perry; ***C:*** Leonard Hirschfield; ***M:*** Mark Laurence.

David Copperfield 🦴🦴🦴🦴 **1935** Superior adaptation of Charles Dickens' great novel. An orphan grows to manhood in Victorian England with a wide variety of help and harm. Terrific acting by Bartholomew, Fields, Rathbone, and all the rest. Lavish production, lovingly filmed. **132m/B VHS.** Lionel Barrymore, W.C. Fields, Freddie Bartholomew, Maureen O'Sullivan, Basil Rathbone, Lewis Stone, Frank Lawton, Madge Evans, Roland Young, Edna May Oliver, Lennox Pawle, Elsa Lanchester, Una O'Connor, Arthur Treacher; ***D:*** George Cukor; ***W:*** Howard Estabrook, Hugh Walpole; ***M:*** Herbert Stothart.

David Copperfield 🦴🦴½ **1970** This British made-for-TV production is more faithful to the Dickens classic than any of its predecessors. The added material, however, fails to highlight any one character as had the successful 1935 MGM version. Still, the exceptional (and largely stage-trained) cast do much to redeem the production. **118m/C VHS.** Richard Attenborough, Cyril Cusack, Edith Evans, Pamela Franklin, Susan Hampshire, Wendy Hiller, Ron Moody, Laurence Olivier, Robin Phillips; ***D:*** Delbert Mann; ***M:*** Malcolm Arnold. **TV**

David Copperfield 🦴🦴½ **1999** Lavish and traditional retelling of the Dickens saga, which concerns the hard-knock life, from birth to maturity, of the title character. Hoskins' Mr. Micawber and Smith's Aunt Betsey Trotwood are particular standouts in a large cast. **210m/C VHS.** Daniel Radcliffe, Ciaran McMenamin, Bob Hoskins, Maggie Smith, Ian McKellen, Nicholas Lyndhurst, Pauline Quirke, Emilia Fox, Trevor Eve, Zoe Wanamaker, Alun Armstrong, Imelda Staunton, Amanda Ryan, Ian McNeice, Joanna Page; ***D:*** Simon Curtis; ***W:*** Adrian Hodges; ***C:*** Andy Collins; ***M:*** Robert Lane; ***Nar:*** Tom Wilkinson. **TV**

David Holzman's Diary 🦴🦴🦴 **1967** Director McBride helmed this fake underground movie, a legendary put-on focusing on film student pretensions. Holzman is a sincere geek who seeks the meaning of life by filming his own existence in oh-so-chic grainy black-and-white verite. He learns reality is more important than film. Drolly captures the state of the art in late '60s America. **71m/B VHS.** L.M. Kit Carson; ***D:*** Jim McBride; ***W:*** L.M. Kit Carson, Jim McBride. Natl. Film Reg. '91.

David Searching 🦴🦴 **1997** Aspiring documentary filmmaker David (Rapp) is broke and boyfriendless in his two-bedroom apartment. He needs a roomie to help with the rent and comes up with newly separated Gwen (Mannheim). She's equally in search of romance (or sex, as the case may be). Oh, and David stills needs to find that elusive job. Series of vignettes do feature some talented actors but the film never goes anywhere. **103m/C VHS.** Anthony Rapp, Camryn Manheim, Joseph Fuqua, Julie Halston, Stephen Spinella, John Cameron Mitchell, David Drake, Kathleen Chalfant, David Courier; ***D:*** Leslie L. Smith; ***W:*** Leslie L. Smith; ***C:*** John P. Scholz.

DaVinci's War 🦴🦴 **1992 (R)** Frank DaVinci's sister is murdered and he wants revenge. So he hooks up with a professional killer and a bunch of Vietnam vets and gets the firepower he needs to blow the bad guys away. **94m/C VHS, DVD.** Joey Travolta, Michael Nouri, Vanity, Richard Foronjy, Branscombe Richmond, Sam Jones, Jack Bannon, Brian Robbins, James Russo; ***D:*** Raymond Martino; ***W:*** Raymond Martino; ***M:*** Jeff Lass.

Davy Crockett and the River Pirates 🦴🦴½ **1956 (G)** Another Disney splice and dice of two episodes from the TV series, chronicling the further adventures of our frontier hero. Davy meets up with Mike Fink, the King of the Ohio River, and the two engage in a furious keelboat race, and then unite to track down a group of thieves masquerading as Indians and threatening the peace. **81m/C VHS.** Fess Parker, Buddy Ebsen, Jeff York; ***D:*** Norman Foster; ***M:*** George Bruns.

Davy Crockett, King of the Wild Frontier 🦴🦴🦴 **1955 (PG)** Three episodes of the popular Disney TV series are blended together here to present the life and some of the adventures of Davy Crockett, including his days as an Indian fighter and his gallant stand in defense of the Alamo. Well-done by a splendid cast, the film helped to spread Davy-mania among the children of the 1950s. **93m/C VHS, DVD.** Fess Parker, Buddy Ebsen, Hans Conried, Ray Whiteside, Pat Hogan, William "Billy" Bakewell, Basil Ruysdael, Kenneth Tobey; ***D:*** Norman Foster; ***M:*** George Bruns. **TV**

Dawn! 🦴🦴 **1983** True story of Dawn Fraser, an Olympic champion swimmer and an unfulfilled woman willing to fight for her happiness. **114m/C VHS.** Bronwyn MacKay-Payne, Tom Richards, Bunny Brooke, Ron Haddrick; ***D:*** Ken Hannam; ***W:*** Joy Cavill; ***C:*** Russell Boyd.

Dawn Express 🦴½ **1942** Nazi spies infiltrate the U.S. in search of a secret formula designed to enhance the power of gasoline. Another film made to contribute to the war effort that doesn't make much sense. **63m/B VHS.** Michael Whalen, Anne Nagel, William "Billy" Bakewell, Constance Worth, Hans von Twardowski, Jack Mulhall, George Pembroke, Kenneth Harlan, Robert Frazer; ***D:*** Al(bert) Herman.

Dawn of the Dead 🦴🦴🦴½ *Zombi; Zombie; Zombies* **1978** Romero's gruesome sequel to his "Night of the Living Dead." A mysterious plague causes the recently dead to rise from their graves and scour the countryside for living flesh. Very violent, gory, graphic, and shocking, yet not without humor. Gives interesting consideration to the violence created by the living humans in their efforts to save themselves. **126m/C VHS, DVD, Wide.** David Emge, Ken Foree, Gaylen Ross, Scott H. Reiniger, David Crawford, David Early, Daniel Dietrich, Richard France, Tom Savini, Howard K. Smith, George A. Romero; ***D:*** George A. Romero; ***W:*** George A. Romero; ***C:*** Michael Gornick; ***M:*** Dario Argento, The Goblins.

Dawn of the Mummy woof! **1982** Lousy plot and bad acting—not to mention gore galore—do this one in. A photographer and a bevy of young fashion models travel to Egypt for a special shoot. They unwittingly stumble upon an ancient tomb, teeming with vengeance-minded mummies. **93m/C VHS.** Brenda King, Barry Sattels, George Peck, Joan Levy; ***D:*** Frank Agrama.

Dawn on the Great Divide 🦴🦴½ **1942** Jones' last film before his tragic and untimely death trying to save people from a fire at the Coconut Grove in Boston. Wagon train has to battle not only Indians, but bad guys as well. Plot provides more depth than the usual western fare. **57m/B VHS.** Buck Jones, Tim McCoy, Raymond Hatton, Mona Barrie, Robert Lowery, Betty Blythe, Jan Wiley, Harry Woods, Roy Barcroft; ***D:*** Howard Bretherton.

Dawn Patrol 🦴🦴🦴 **1938** Flynn plays a flight commander whose nerves are shot in this story of the British Royal Flying Corps during WWI. The focus is on the effects that the pressures and deaths have on all those concerned. Fine performances from all in this well-done remake of the 1930 film. **103m/B VHS.** Errol Flynn, David Niven, Basil Rathbone, Donald Crisp, Barry Fitzgerald, Melville Cooper, Carl Esmond, Peter Willes, Morton Lowry, Michael Brooke, James Burke, Stuart Hall; ***D:*** Edmund Goulding; ***W:*** Seton I. Miller, Dan Totheroh; ***C:*** Gaetano Antonio "Tony" Gaudio; ***M:*** Max Steiner.

Dawn Rider 🦴🦴 **1935** Formula western has all the right ingredients: Wayne as a cowboy out to get revenge on the gang that murdered his father. Features stuntman Canutt in rare acting role. **60m/B VHS, DVD.** John Wayne, Marion Burns, Yakima Canutt; ***D:*** Robert North Bradbury.

The Dawning 🦴🦴½ **1988** An Irish revolutionary in the 1920s draws a young woman into his dangerous world of romance, intrigue, and death. Howard's last film. Based on the novel "Old Jest" by Jennifer Johnston. **97m/C VHS.** *GB* Anthony Hopkins, Jean Simmons, Trevor Howard, Rebecca Pidgeon, Hugh Grant, Tara MacGowran; ***D:*** Robert Knights.

The Dawson Patrol 🦴½ **1978** Royal Canadian Mountie dog-sled race turns into a dramatic battle for survival. **75m/C VHS.** George R. Robinson, Tim Henry, Neil Dainaro, James B. Douglas; ***D:*** Peter Kelly.

The Day After 🦴🦴🦴 **1983** Powerful drama graphically depicts the nuclear bombing of a midwestern city and its aftereffects on the survivors. Made for TV, and very controversial when first shown, gathering huge ratings and vast media coverage. **122m/C VHS.** Jason Robards Jr., JoBeth Williams, John Lithgow, Steve Guttenberg, John Cullum; ***D:*** Nicholas Meyer. **TV**

The Day and the Hour 🦴🦴½ *Today We Live; Le Jour et L'Heure; Il Giorno e L'Ora; Viviamo Oggi* **1963** A woman becomes accidentally involved in the resistance movement during the Nazi occupation of France in WWII. **110m/C VHS.** *FR JP IT* Simone Signoret, Stuart Whitman, Genevieve Page, Michel Piccoli, Reggie Nalder, Pierre Dux, Billy Kearns; ***D:*** Rene Clement; ***M:*** Claude Bolling.

Day at the Beach 🦴🦴½ **1998** Jimmy (Veronis) works in a mob-fronted New York ravioli factory while trying to make a film—a gangster movie that features his fellow pasta workers. But when one of his buddies, John (Fitzgerald), tosses a briefcase over a river bridge for a scene, the heavy case accidently kills a passing fisherman. Now Jimmy's got a guilt-racked John to deal with and numerous other problems—all eventually leading to the palatial home of wealthy (and connected) Antonio Gintolini (Ragno). **93m/C VHS, DVD.** Nick Veronis, Patrick Fitzgerald, Neal Jones, Robert Maisonett, Catherine Kellner, Jane Adams, Joe Ragno, Ed Setrakian; ***D:*** Nick Veronis; ***W:*** Nick Veronis; ***C:*** Nils Kenaston; ***M:*** Tony Saracene.

A Day at the Races 🦴🦴🦴½ **1937** Though it seems labored at times, the brilliance of the brothers Marx still comes through in this rather weak tale of a patient in a sanitorium who convinces horse doctor Groucho to take on running the place. ♫A Message from the Man in the Moon; On Blue Venetian Waters; Tomorrow Is Another Day; All God's Chillun Got Rhythm. **111m/B VHS.** Groucho Marx, Harpo Marx, Chico Marx, Sig Rumann, Douglass Dumbrille, Margaret Dumont, Allan Jones, Maureen O'Sullivan, Leonard Ceeley, Esther Muir; ***D:*** Sam Wood; ***W:*** Robert Pirosh, George Seaton, George Oppenheimer; ***C:*** Joseph Ruttenberg; ***M:*** George Bassman, Bronislau Kaper, Walter Jurmann.

Day for Night 🦴🦴🦴🦴 *La Nuit Americaine* **1973 (PG)** Director Ferrand (Truffaut) is working on a mediocre romantic melodrama with sullen actor Alphonse (Leaud) who falls for his married co-star Julie (Bissset) in just one of the off-screen stories that's more interesting than what's being filmed. A wryly affectionate look at the profession of moviemaking—its craft, character, and the personalities that interact against the performances commanded by the camera. In French with English subtitles. **116m/C VHS.** *FR* Francois Truffaut, Jean-Pierre Leaud, Jacqueline Bisset, Jean-Pierre Aumont, Valentina Cortese, Alexandra Stewart, Dani, Nathalie Baye; ***D:*** Francois Truffaut; ***W:*** Suzanne Schiffman, Jean-Louis Richard, Francois Truffaut; ***C:*** Pierre William Glenn; ***M:*** Georges Delerue. Oscars '73: Foreign Film; British Acad. '73: Director (Truffaut), Film, Support. Actress (Cortese); N.Y. Film Critics '73: Director (Truffaut), Film, Support. Actress (Cortese); Natl. Soc. Film Critics '73: Director (Truffaut), Film, Support. Actress (Cortese).

A Day for Thanks on Walton's Mountain 🦴🦴 **1982** Many of the original television-show cast members returned for this sentimental Thanksgiving reunion on Walton's Mountain. **97m/C VHS.** Ralph Waite, Ellen Corby, Judy Norton-Taylor, Eric Scott, Jon Walmsley, Robert Wightman, Mary (Elizabeth) McDonough, David W. Harper, Kami Cotler, Joe Conley, Ronnie Clair Edwards, Richard Gilliland, Melinda Naud; ***D:*** Harry Harris; ***Nar:*** Earl Hamner. **TV**

A Day in October 🦴🦴½ **1992 (PG-13)** 1943, Copenhagen, Denmark. There are signs the Jewish population is in danger from occupying Nazi officials and the resistance movement is active. Wounded resistance fighter Sweeney is rescued by the Jewish Sara (Wolf), and their relationship deepens as the realities of WWII change their lives. Based on historical fact, but there's little explanation of the politics or the fierce nationalism and intense loyalty most Danes felt towards their fellow countrymen, a loyalty that ultimately saved most of the Danish Jews from the Holocaust. Good performances, particularly Benzali as Sara's father, help overcome the script weaknesses. Filmed on location in Denmark. **96m/C VHS.** D.B. Sweeney, Kelly Wolf, Tovah Feldshuh, Daniel Benzali, Ole Lemmeke, Kim Romer, Anders Peter Bro, Lars Oluf Larsen; ***D:*** Kenneth Madsen; ***W:*** Damian F. Slattery; ***M:*** Jens Lysdal.

A Day in the Country 🦴🦴🦴½ *Une Partie de Campagne* **1946** The son of the famed painter gives us the moving tale of a young woman's sudden and intense love for a man she meets while on a picnic with her family. Beautifully adapted from a story by Guy de Maupassant. Renowned photographer Henri Cartier-Bresson contributed to the wonderful cinematography. Subtitled. **40m/B VHS.** *FR* Sylvia Bataille, Georges Darnoux, Jane (Jeanne) Marken, Paul Temps; ***D:*** Jean Renoir; ***C:*** Henri Cartier-Bresson.

A Day in the Death of Joe Egg 🦴🦴🦴 **1971 (R)** Based on the Peter Nichols play, an unlikely black comedy about a British couple trying to care for their retarded/autistic child, nearly destroying their marriage in the process. They begin to contemplate euthanasia as a solution. Well-acted, but potentially offensive to some. **106m/C VHS.** *GB* Alan Bates, Janet Suzman, Elizabeth Robillard, Peter Bowles, Joan Hickson, Sheila Gish; ***D:*** Peter Medak; ***W:*** David Deutsch.

The Day It Came to Earth woof! **1977 (PG)** Completely silly and unbelievable sci-fi flick has meteor crashing into the watery grave of a mobster. The decomposed corpse is revived by the radiation and plots to take revenge on those who fitted him with cement shoes. **89m/C VHS.** Roger Manning, Wink Roberts, Bob Ginnaven, Rita Wilson, Delight de Bruine; ***D:*** Harry Z. Thomason.

The Day My Parents Ran Away 🦴🦴½ **1993 (PG)** Rebellious 16-year-old gets a tough lesson in responsibility when his parents get tired of his antics and decide to leave home in search of a new life. He finds out things aren't so easy on your own. **95m/C VHS.** Matt Frewer, Bobby Jacoby, Brigid Conley Walsh, Blair Brown, Martin Mull; ***D:*** Martin Nicholson; ***W:*** Handel Glassberg; ***M:*** J. Peter Robinson.

Day of Atonement 🦴🦴½ **1993 (R)** It's a war for power between rival druglords when Hanin is released from prison and finds out his son and cousin are battling over turf. Then Walken is dragged into the fracas. Beals is the government agent trying to regain some control of the dangerous situation. **127m/C VHS.** *FR* Christopher Walken, Jennifer Beals, Jill Clayburgh, Roger Hanin, Richard Berry; ***D:*** Alexandre Arcady; ***W:*** Alexandre Arcady, Daniel Saint Hamont; ***C:*** Willy Kurant.

Day of Judgment 🦴½ **1981** A mysterious stranger arrives in a town to slaughter those people who violate the Ten Commandments. **101m/C VHS.** William T. Hicks, Harris Bloodworth, Brownlee Davis; ***D:*** C.D.H. Reynolds.

Day of the Animals 🦴 *Something Is Out There* **1977 (PG)** Nature gone wild. It seems a depleted ozone layer has exposed the animals to the sun's radiation, turning Bambi and Bugs into brutal killers. A group of backpackers trek in the Sierras, unaware of the transformation. Farfetched and silly (we hope). **95m/C VHS, DVD.** Christopher George, Leslie Nielsen, Lynda Day George, Richard Jaeckel, Michael Ansara, Ruth Roman, Jon Cedar, Susan Backlinie, Andrew Stevens, Gil Lamb; ***D:*** William Girdler; ***W:*** William W. Norton Sr.; ***C:*** Robert Sorrentino; ***M:*** Lalo Schifrin.

Day of the Assassin 🦴 **1981** A Mideast shah's yacht explodes, sending a huge fortune to the bottom of a murky bay. This sets off a rampage of treasure hunting by a variety of ruthless mercenaries. **94m/C VHS.** Glenn Ford, Chuck Connors, Richard Roundtree, Henry Silva, Jorge (George) Rivero; ***D:*** Brian Trenchard-Smith.

The Day of the Beast 🦴🦴 **1995 (R)** Lurid horror/melodrama concerns Father Angel (Angula), whose study of the Apocrypha has convinced him that the Antichrist will be born in Madrid on Christmas, which is only a few hours away. He enlists a couple of unlikely companions in his search for the infant. There's a lot of mayhem for all involved. Spanish with subtitles. **104m/C VHS.** *SP* Alex Angulo, Armando de Razza, Santiago Segura, Terele Pavez, Maria Grazia Cucinotta, Nathalie Sesena; ***D:*** Alex de la Iglesia; ***W:*** Jorge Guerricaechevarria, Alex de la Iglesia; ***C:*** Flavio Martinez Labiano; ***M:*** Battista Lena.

Day of the Cobra 🦴½ **1984** A corrupt narcotics bureau official hires an ex-cop to find a heroin kingpin on the back streets of Genoa, Italy. **95m/C VHS.** *IT* Franco Nero, Sybil Danning, Mario Maranzana, Licinia Lentini, William Berger; ***D:*** Enzo G. Castellari.

Day of the Dead 🦴½ **1985** The third in Romero's trilogy of films about flesh-eating zombies taking over the world. Romero hasn't thought up anything new for the ghouls to do, and the humans are too nasty to care about this time around. For adult audiences. **91m/C VHS, DVD.** Lori Cardille, Terry Alexander, Joe Pilato, Jarlath Conroy, Richard Liberty; ***D:*** George A. Romero; ***W:*** George A. Romero; ***C:*** Michael Gornick; ***M:*** John Harrison.

The Day of the Dolphin 🦴🦴 **1973 (PG)** Research scientist, after successfully working out a means of teaching dolphins to talk, finds his animals kidnapped; espionage and assassination are involved. Dolphin voices by Henry, who also wrote the screenplay. **104m/C VHS.** George C. Scott, Trish Van Devere, Paul Sorvino, Fritz Weaver, Jon Korkes, John Dehner, Edward Herrmann, Severn Darden; ***D:*** Mike Nichols; ***W:*** Buck Henry; ***M:*** Georges Delerue; ***V:*** Buck Henry.

The Day of the Jackal 🦴🦴🦴½ **1973 (PG)** Frederick Forsyth's best-selling novel of political intrigue is splendidly brought to the screen by Zinnemann. A brilliant and ruthless assassin hired to kill Charles de Gaulle skirts the international intelligence pool, while intuitive police work try to stop him. Tense, suspenseful, beautiful location photography. Excellent acting by Fox, Cusack and Britton. **142m/C VHS, DVD, Wide.** Edward Fox, Alan Badel, Tony Britton, Derek Jacobi, Cyril Cusack, Olga Georges-Picot; ***D:*** Fred Zinnemann; ***W:*** Kenneth Ross; ***M:*** Georges Delerue.

The Day of the Locust 🦴🦴🦴½ **1975 (R)** Compelling adaptation of Nathaniel West's novel concerning the dark side of 1930s' Hollywood. A no-talent amoral actress's affair with a meek accountant leads to tragedy and destruction. Told from the view of a cynical art director wise to the ways of Hollywood. **140m/C VHS.** Donald Sutherland, Karen Black, Burgess Meredith, William Atherton, Billy Barty, Bo Hopkins, Richard Dysart, Geraldine Page; ***D:*** John Schlesinger; ***C:*** Conrad L. Hall; ***M:*** John Barry.

Day of the Maniac 🦴½ **1977 (R)** Psychotic drug addict will stop at nothing to support his growing habit. **89m/C VHS.** George Hilton, Susan Scott; ***D:*** Sergio Martino.

Day of the Panther 🦴½ **1988** The Panthers—the world's most formidable martial artists—are mighty torqued when panther-Linda is pithed, and they're not known to turn the other cheek. Much chop-socky kicking and shrilling. **86m/C VHS.** John Stanton, Eddie Stazak; ***D:*** Brian Trenchard-Smith.

Day of the Triffids 🦴🦴🦴 **1963** The majority of Earth's population is blinded by a meteor shower which also causes plant spores to mutate into giant carnivores. Well-done adaptation of John Wyndham's science fiction classic; Philip Yordan acknowledged "fronting" for blacklisted screenwriter Gordon, who finally received credit in 1996. **94m/C VHS, Wide.** *GB* Howard Keel, Janette Scott, Nicole Maurey, Kieron Moore, Mervyn Johns, Alison Leggatt, Ewan Roberts, Janina Faye, Gilgi Hauser, Carol Ann Ford; ***D:*** Steve Sekely, Freddie Francis; ***W:*** Bernard Gordon, Philip Yordan; ***C:*** Ted Moore.

Day of the Warrior 🦴🦴 **1996 (R)** Babes who belong to a paramilitary law-and-order group infiltrate crime lord, the Warrior's, smuggling operations, strip joints and porn palaces. **96m/C VHS.** Julie Strain, Marcus Bagwell; ***D:*** Andy Sidaris; ***W:*** Andy Sidaris.

Day of Triumph **1954** A dynamic version of the life of Christ as seen through the eyes of the apostles Andrew and Zadok, the leaders of the Zealot underground. **110m/C VHS.** Lee J. Cobb, Robert Wilson, Ralph Freud; ***D:*** Irving Pichel.

Day of Wrath 🦴🦴🦴🦴 *Vredens Dag* **1943** An involving psychological thriller based on records of witch trials from the early 1600s. Young Anne (Movin) is married to the much older and puritannical widower, Absalon (Roose) but falls in love with his son Martin (Lerdorff). She wishes aloud for her husband's death and when he does dies, Anne is accused of witchcraft. Grim and unrelentingly pessimistic, moving from one horrific scene to another, director Dreyer creates a masterpiece of terror. Based on a play by Hans Wiers Jenssen. In Danish with English subtitles. **110m/B VHS, DVD.** *DK* Thorkild Roose, Sigrid Neiiendam, Lisbeth Movin, Preben Lerdorff, Anna Svierker; ***D:*** Carl Theodor Dreyer; ***W:*** Carl Theodor Dreyer; ***C:*** Karl Andersson; ***M:*** Poul Schierbeck.

Day One 🦴🦴🦴 **1989** Vivid re-creation of one of the most turbulent periods of American history—the WWII race to build the atomic bomb. Chronicles the two year top-secret efforts of the Manhattan Project, with General Leslie Groves (Dennehy) having to supervise the project and contain the scientific rivalries. Outstanding cast, with Strathairn notable as physicist J. Robert Oppenheimer. Adapted from "Day One: Before Hiroshima and After" by Peter Wyden. **141m/C VHS.** Brian Dennehy, David Strathairn, Michael Tucker, Hume Cronyn, Richard Dysart, Barnard Hughes, Hal Holbrook, David Ogden Stiers, John McMartin; ***D:*** Joseph Sargent; ***W:*** David W. Rintels; ***M:*** Mason Daring. **TV**

The Day Silence Died 🦴🦴 *El Dia Que Murio el Silencio* **1998** Into the sleepy, provincial town of Villaserena, Bolivia, comes Abelardo. This charismatic stranger calls himself a "radio operator" and he installs four public loudspeakers in the town square where he plays music and broadcasts the news. He also offers to sell airtime to the local residents, which results in the airing of much private and dirty laundry, causing a good deal of turmoil within the community. And just who are they going to blame? Spanish with subtitles. **108m/C VHS.** Dario Grandinetti, Gustavo Angarita, Elias Serrano, Guillermo Granda, Maria Laura Garcia, Blanca Morisson; ***D:*** Paolo Agazzi; ***W:*** Paolo Agazzi, Guillermo Aguirre; ***C:*** Livio Delgado, Guillermo Medrano.

The Day That Shook the World 🦴🦴 **1978 (R)** Slow-moving but intriguing account of events surrounding the assassination of Archduke Ferdinand of Austria that triggered WWI. Garnered an R-rating due to some disturbingly graphic scenes. **111m/C VHS.** Christopher Plummer, Florinda Bolkan, Maximilian Schell; ***D:*** Veljko Bulajic.

Day the Bookies Wept 🦴🦴 **1939** Decent yarn about cabbies tricked into buying a "racehorse." Turns out she's old as the hills and hooked on alcohol to boot, but they enter her in the big race anyway. **50m/B VHS.** Betty Grable, Joe Penner, Tom Kennedy, Richard Lane; ***D:*** Leslie Goodwins.

The Day the Earth Caught Fire 🦴🦴🦴½ **1961** The earth is knocked out of orbit and sent hurtling toward the sun when nuclear testing is done simultaneously at both the North and South Poles. Realistic and suspenseful, this is one of the best of the sci-fi genre. **95m/B VHS, DVD, Wide.** Janet Munro, Edward Judd, Leo McKern; ***D:*** Val Guest; ***W:*** Wolf Mankowitz, Val Guest; ***C:*** Harry Waxman; ***M:*** Stanley Black. British Acad. '61: Screenplay.

The Day the Earth Froze 🦴🦴 **1959** Witch steals the sun because she couldn't have a magical mill that produced grain, salt, and gold. Everything on Earth freezes. Based on a Finnish epic poem. **67m/B VHS.** *FI RU* Nina Anderson, Jon Powers, Ingrid Elhardt, Paul Sorenson; ***D:*** Gregg Sebelious; ***Nar:*** Marvin Miller.

The Day the Earth Stood Still 🦴🦴🦴½ **1951** A gentle alien lands on Earth to deliver a message of peace and a warning against experimenting with nuclear power. He finds his views echoed by a majority of the population, but not the ones who are in control. In this account based loosely on the story of Christ, Rennie is the visitor backed by the mighty robot Gort. One of the greatest science fiction films of all time. **92m/B VHS.** Michael Rennie, Patricia Neal, Hugh Marlowe, Sam Jaffe, Frances Bavier, Lock Martin, Billy Gray, Edith Evanson, Frank Conroy, Drew Pearson; ***D:*** Robert Wise; ***W:*** Edmund H. North; ***C:*** Leo Tover; ***M:*** Bernard Herrmann. Natl. Film Reg. '95.

The Day the Sky Exploded 🦴½ *Death From Outer Space; La Morte Viene Dalla Spazio; Le Danger Vient de l'Escape* **1957** Sci-fi disaster drama doesn't live up to the grandiose title, as a runaway rocket ship hits the sun, unleashing an asteroid shower that threatens Earth with tidal waves, earthquakes, heat waves and terrible dialogue. The highlight of this Franco-Italian effort is the cinematography by horror director Mario Bava. **80m/B VHS.** *FR IT* Paul (Christian) Hubschmid, Madeleine Fischer, Fiorella Mari, Ivo Garrani, Dario Michaelis; ***D:*** Richard Benson; ***C:*** Mario Bava.

The Day the Sun Turned Cold 🦴🦴🦴 *Tianguo Niezi* **1994** In an apparent crisis of conscience a young man (Zhong Hua) enters a police station and tries to convince a weary captain (Hu) that his mother (Gowa) murdered his cruel father (Jingwu) 10 years before in order to marry another man. The detective eventually concludes he should investigate the supposed crime, which happened in a remote village, but Zhong Hua's accusations naturally stir up a great deal of resentment and anger. There's lots of questions about guilt, innocence, and motives—on everybody's part. Mandarin with subtitles. **99m/C VHS.** *HK* Siqin Gowa, Tuo Zhong Hua, Wai Zhi, Ma Jingwu, Li Hu; ***D:*** Yim Ho; ***W:*** Yim Ho; ***C:*** Hou Yong; ***M:*** Yoshihide Otomo.

The Day the Women Got Even 🦴½ **1980** Four suburban homemakers take up the life of vigilantes to save unsuspecting actresses from a talent agent's blackmail scheme. **98m/C VHS.** JoAnn Pflug, Tina Louise, Georgia Engel, Barbara Rhoades, Julie Hagerty, Ed O'Neill; ***D:*** Burt Brinckerhoff; ***M:*** Brad Fiedel. **TV**

Day the World Ended 🦴 **1955** The first science-fiction film of exploitation director Roger Corman. Five survivors of nuclear holocaust discover a desert ranch house fortress owned by a survivalist (Birch) and his daughter (Nelson). With relatively abundant supplies, they fatuously wallow in false misery until a disfigured visitor, wasting away from radiation, stumbles into their paradise. His mutation into an alien being confronts them with the horror that lurks outside. **79m/B VHS, Wide.** Paul Birch, Lori Nelson, Adele Jergens, Raymond Hatton, Paul Dubov, Richard Denning, Mike Connors, Paul Blaisdell, Jonathan Haze; ***D:*** Roger Corman; ***W:*** Lou Rusoff; ***C:*** Jockey A. Feindel; ***M:*** Ronald Stein.

Day Time Ended 🦴🦴 *Vortex; Timewarp* **1980** A pair of glowing UFO's streaking across the sky and an alien mechanical device with long menacing appendages are only two of the bizarre phenomena witnessed from a lone house in the desert. Good special effects. Also released as "Time Warp" (1978). **80m/C VHS.** Chris Mitchum, Jim Davis, Dorothy Malone; ***D:*** John Cardos; ***W:*** David Schmoeller, J. Larry Carroll; ***M:*** Richard Band.

The Day Will Dawn 🦴🦴🦴 *The Avengers* **1942** Suspenseful British-made WWII thriller about a reporter and a young Norwegian girl who plot to sabotage a secret Nazi U-boat base near the girl's town. **100m/B VHS, 8mm.** *GB* Deborah Kerr, Hugh Williams, Niall MacGinnis, Ralph Richardson, Francis L. Sullivan, Roland Culver, Finlay Currie, Patricia Medina; ***D:*** Harold French; ***W:*** Terence Rattigan.

Daybreak 🦴🦴½ **1993 (R)** In the near future America has been decimated by a nameless, sexually transmitted disease (read AIDS parable) and public policy is to quarantine the infected in concentration camp-like prisons. This leads to a quasi-official group of green-shirted thugs roaming the streets and imprisoning or killing anyone they suspect has the disease. A small resistance movement is lead by Torch (Gooding Jr.), who happens to fall in love with Blue (Kelly), the sister of one of the fascist leaders. Based on Alan Bowne's play "Beirut, Daybreak." **91m/C VHS.** Cuba Gooding Jr., Moira Kelly, Omar Epps, Martha Plimpton, Alice Drummond, David Eigenberg, John Savage; ***Cameos:*** Phil Hartman; ***D:*** Stephen Tolkin; ***W:*** Stephen Tolkin. **CABLE**

Daybreak 🦴🦴½ **2001 (R)** A throwback to the cheesy disaster flicks of the seventies, which isn't necessarily a bad thing. An L.A. subway train is stuck in a tunnel after an earthquake and it's up to subway supervisor Dillan Johansen (McGinley) to find a way to save himself and the passengers from fire, water, and toxic chemicals. **93m/C VHS, DVD.** Ted McGinley, Roy Scheider, Adam Wylie, Ursula Brooks, Jaime Bergman; ***D:*** Jean Pellerin. **VIDEO**

The Daydreamer 🦴🦴½ *Absent-Minded; Le Distrait* **1975** Actor/director/writer Richard stars as a bumbling fool let loose in the French corporate world with comical results. In French with subtitles. **90m/C VHS.** *FR* Pierre Richard, Bernard Blier, Maria Pacome, Marie-Christine Barrault; ***D:*** Pierre Richard; ***W:*** Pierre Richard; ***M:*** Vladimir Cosma.

Daylight 🦴🦴 **1996 (PG-13)** After a massive explosion seals both ends of New York's Holland Tunnel (The Tunneling Inferno?), a small band of stock disaster flick survivors are trapped under the waters of the Hudson River. Fortunately, a cab driver with a really square jaw who, conveniently, is an ex-emergency rescue worker AND who knows the entire layout of the tunnel happens to be driving toward the tunnel at the exact moment of the disaster. Coincidence? Nope, just Hollywood. Kit Latura (Stallone) leads the survivors through cave-ins, floods, fire, rats, and poison gas (The Poison-Hiding Adventure!) only to discover to their dismay that they have emerged in New Jersey. Long on special effects but short on character development, this nod to the catastrophe movies of the '70s is still enjoyable for those who like to watch things go boom. **109m/C VHS, DVD.** Sylvester Stallone, Viggo Mortensen, Amy Brenneman, Stan Shaw, Claire Bloom, Renoly Santiago, Sage Stallone, Dan Hedaya, Jay O. Sanders, Karen Young, Vanessa Bell Calloway, Colin Fox, Danielle Harris, Jo Anderson, Mark Rolston, Rosemary Forsyth, Barry Newman; ***D:*** Rob Cohen; ***W:*** Leslie Bohem; ***C:*** David Eggby; ***M:*** Randy Edelman.

Days and Nights in the Forest 🦴🦴½ *Aranyer Din Ratri* **1970** Four men living in Calcutta decide to leave the city for a brief vacation. Each has a different emotional experience which will change him forever, including a brief love affair and finding true romance. In Bengali with English subtitles. **120m/C VHS.** *IN* Soumitra Chatterjee, Sharmila Tagore, Shubhendu Chatterjee, Samit Bhanja; ***D:*** Satyajit Ray; ***W:*** Satyajit Ray; ***C:*** Soumendu Roy; ***M:*** Satyajit Ray.

Days of Glory 🦴🦴½ **1943** Peck's screen debut finds him as a Russian peasant bravely fighting the Nazi blitzkrieg almost single-handedly. **86m/B VHS.** Tamara Toumanova, Gregory Peck, Alan Reed, Maria Palmer, Lowell Gilmore, Hugo Haas; ***D:*** Jacques Tourneur; ***C:*** Gaetano Antonio "Tony" Gaudio.

Days of Heaven 🦴🦴🦴½ **1978 (PG)** Drifter Gere, his younger sister, and a woman he claims is his sister become involved with a Texas sharecropper. Told through the eyes of the younger girl, this is a sweeping vision of the U.S. before WWI. Loss and loneliness, deception, frustration, and anger haunt these people as they struggle to make the land their own. Deservedly awarded an Oscar for breathtaking cinematography. **95m/C VHS, DVD.** Richard Gere, Brooke Adams, Sam Shepard, Linda Manz, Stuart Margolin; ***D:*** Terrence Malick; ***W:*** Terrence Malick; ***C:*** Nestor Almendros; ***M:*** Ennio Morricone. Oscars '78: Cinematog.; Cannes '79:

Director (Malick); L.A. Film Critics '78: Cinematog.; N.Y. Film Critics '78: Director (Malick); Natl. Soc. Film Critics '78: Cinematog., Director (Malick), Film.

Days of Hell ♂ *I Giorni Dell'Inferno* **1984** Forgettable tale of four mercenaries who are hired to rescue a doctor and his daughter held captive by guerrillas somewhere in Afghanistan only to find out they're pawns in an even bigger scheme. **90m/C VHS.** Conrad Nichols, Richard Raymond, Stephen Elliott, Kinako Harada; *D:* Anthony Richmond.

Days of Jesse James ♂♂ **1939** Roy is a member of a detective agency who joins the James gang incognito in order to prove that they didn't rob the Northfield bank. Roy figures out that bank officials actually planned the whole scheme. **63m/B VHS.** Roy Rogers, George "Gabby" Hayes, Donald (Don "Red") Barry, Harry Woods, Pauline Moore, Mike Worth, Glenn Strange; *D:* Joseph Kane; *W:* Earle Snell; *C:* Reggie Lanning.

Days of Thrills and Laughter ♂♂♂½ **1961** Delightful compilation of clips from the era of silent films, showcasing the talents of the great comics as well as daring stuntman. **93m/B VHS.** Buster Keaton, Charlie Chaplin, Harold Lloyd, Stan Laurel, Oliver Hardy, Douglas Fairbanks Sr.; *D:* Robert Youngson.

Days of Thunder ♂♂ **1990 (PG-13)** "Top Gun" in race cars! Cruise follows the same formula he has followed for several years now (with the notable exception of "Born on the Fourth of July.") Cruise and Towne co-wrote the screenplay concerning a young kid bursting with talent and raw energy who must learn to deal with his mentor, his girlfriend, and eventually the bad guy. First film that featured cameras that were actually on the race cars. If you like Cruise or race cars then this is the movie for you. **108m/C VHS, DVD, Wide.** Tom Cruise, Robert Duvall, Randy Quaid, Nicole Kidman, Cary Elwes, Michael Rooker, Fred Dalton Thompson, John C. Reilly; *D:* Tony Scott; *W:* Tom Cruise, Robert Towne; *C:* Ward Russell; *M:* Hans Zimmer.

Days of Wine and Roses ♂♂½ **1958** The original "Playhouse 90" TV version of J.P. Miller's story which was adapted for the big screen in 1962. An executive on the fast track and his young wife, initially only social drinkers, find themselves degenerating into alcoholism. A well-acted, stirring drama. **89m/B VHS.** Cliff Robertson, Piper Laurie; *D:* John Frankenheimer. **TV**

Days of Wine and Roses ♂♂♂½ **1962** A harrowing tale of an alcoholic advertising man who gradually drags his wife down with him into a life of booze. Big screen adaptation of the play originally shown on TV. ♫Days of Wine and Roses. **138m/B VHS.** Jack Lemmon, Lee Remick, Charles Bickford, Jack Klugman, Jack Albertson; *D:* Blake Edwards; *W:* J(ames) P(inckney) Miller; *M:* Henry Mancini, Johnny Mercer. Oscars '62: Song ("Days of Wine and Roses").

Dayton's Devils ♂♂ **1968** Nielsen is the leader of a motley crew of losers who plan to rob a military base bank in this action-packed heist flick. **107m/C VHS.** Rory Calhoun, Leslie Nielsen, Lainie Kazan, Eric (Hans Gudegast) Braeden, Georg Stanford Brown, Rigg Kennedy; *D:* Jack Shea.

The Daytrippers ♂♂½ **1996** Happily married Eliza D'Amico is living on Long Island while husband Louis (Tucci) goes to work in Manhattan. That is she's happy until she finds what appears to be a love letter addressed to her husband. Frantic, Eliza runs to aggressive mom Rita (Meara), who decides that her daughter should immediately confront her possibly erring husband at his office. So Eliza, her mom and dad (McNamara), sarcastic younger sister Jo (Posey), and Jo's pretentious boyfriend Carl (Schreiber) all pile into the family station wagon and head into the city. Only Louis isn't at his office and they scour Manhattan to track him down. **88m/C VHS, DVD.** Hope Davis, Anne Meara, Parker Posey, Liev Schreiber, Pat McNamara, Stanley Tucci, Campbell Scott, Marcia Gay Harden, Andy Brown; *D:* Greg Mottola; *W:* Greg Mottola; *C:* John Inwood.

Dazed and Confused ♂♂♂ **1993 (R)** A day in the life of a bunch of high schoolers should prove to be a trip back in time for those coming of age in the '70s. Eight seniors facing life after high school have one last year long hurrah, as they search for Aerosmith tickets and haze the incoming freshmen. Keen characterization by writer/director Linklater captures the spirit of a generation shaped by Watergate, the Vietnam War, feminism, and marijuana. Groovy soundtrack features Alice Cooper, Deep Purple, KISS, and Foghat. **97m/C VHS, DVD, Wide.** Jason London, Rory Cochrane, Sasha Jenson, Wiley Wiggins, Michelle Rene Thomas, Adam Goldberg, Anthony Rapp, Marissa Ribisi, Parker Posey, Joey Lauren Adams, Ben Affleck, Milla Jovovich, Cole Hauser, Matthew McConaughey, Kristin Hinojosa; *D:* Richard Linklater; *W:* Richard Linklater; *C:* Lee Daniel.

D.C. Cab ♂♂½ **1984 (R)** A rag-tag group of Washington, D.C. cabbies learn a lesson in self-respect in this endearing comedy. Though not without flaws, it's charming all the same. **100m/C VHS.** Mr. T, Leif Erickson, Adam Baldwin, Charlie Barnett, Irene Cara, Anne DeSalvo, Max Gail, Gloria Gifford, Gary Busey, Jill Schoelen, Marsha Warfield; *D:* Joel Schumacher; *W:* Joel Schumacher, Topper Carew; *C:* Dean Cundey.

De Mayerling a Sarajevo ♂♂½ *Mayerling to Sarajevo; Sarajevo* **1940** Looks at the romance and marriage, as well as royal pomp and circumstance, of the Countess Sophie (Feuillere) and the Archduke Franz-Ferdinand (Lodge). The assassination of these innocuous rulers at Sarajevo would lead to the outbreak of WWI. French with subtitles. **89m/B VHS.** *FR* Edwige Feuillere, John Lodge, Aime Clariond, Gabrielle Dorziat; *D:* Max Ophuls; *W:* Kurt Alexander; *C:* Curt Courant, Otto Heller; *M:* Oscar Straus.

Deacon Brodie ♂♂ **1998** William Deacon Brodie (Connolly) is one of Edinburgh's most respected citizens in 1788. So his trial and conviction for defrauding the city is doubly shocking—until his secret life of gambling, drinking, and wenching is exposed. **90m/C VHS, DVD.** *GB* Billy Connolly, Patrick Malahide, Catherine McCormack, Lorcan Cranitch; *D:* Philip Saville; *W:* Simon Donald; *C:* Ivan Strasburg; *M:* Simon Boswell. **TV**

The Dead ♂♂♂½ **1987 (PG)** The poignant final film by Huston, based on James Joyce's short story from "Dubliners." At a Christmas dinner party in 1904 Dublin, Gabriel Conroy (McCann) discovers how little he knows about his wife Gretta (Angelica Huston) when a song reminds her of a cherished lost love. Beautifully captures the spirit of the story while providing Huston an opportunity to create a last lament on the fickle nature of time and life. **82m/C VHS.** *GB* Anjelica Huston, Donal McCann, Marie Kean, Donal Donnelly, Dan O'Herlihy, Helen Carroll, Frank Patterson; *D:* John Huston; *W:* Tony (Walter Anthony) Huston; *C:* Fred Murphy; *M:* Alex North. Ind. Spirit '88: Director (Huston), Support. Actress (Huston); Natl. Soc. Film Critics '87: Film.

Dead Again ♂♂♂½ **1991 (R)** Branagh's first film since his brilliant debut as the director/star of "Henry V" again proves him a visionary force on and off camera. Smart, cynical L.A. detective Mike Church (Branagh) is hired to discover the identity of a beautiful but mute woman (Thompson) whom he calls Grace. With the help of hypnotist Franklyn Madson (Jacobi) Mike finds that he's apparently trapped in a nightmarish cycle of murder begun years before, involving a jealous conductor and his concert pianist wife. Literate, lovely to look at, suspenseful, with a sense of humor to match its high style. **107m/C VHS, DVD, Wide.** Kenneth Branagh, Emma Thompson, Andy Garcia, Lois Hall, Richard Easton, Derek Jacobi, Hanna Schygulla, Campbell Scott, Wayne Knight, Christine Ebersole; *Cameos:* Robin Williams; *D:* Kenneth Branagh; *W:* Scott Frank; *C:* Matthew F. Leonetti; *M:* Patrick Doyle.

Dead Ahead ♂♂ **1996 (PG-13)** Skilled archer Maura Loch (Zimbalist) is enjoying a camping trip with her family until four bankrobbers on the lam stumble across them and take Maura's son hostage. Armed with her bow, Maura tracks the criminals to save her child. **92m/C VHS.** Stephanie Zimbalist, Sarah Chalke, Tom Butler, Brendan Fletcher, Peter Onorati, John Tench, Michael Tayles, Douglas Arthurs; *D:* Stuart Cooper; *W:* David Alexander; *C:* Curtis Petersen; *M:* Charles Bernstein. **CABLE**

Dead Ahead: The Exxon Valdez Disaster ♂♂♂ *Disaster at Valdez* **1992 (PG-13)** Focuses on the first crucial days after the March 24, 1989, oil spill when the Exxon Valdez ran aground off Alaska in Prince William Sound. Portrays the inadequate precautions, incompetence, greed, and petty bureaucracy that made an appalling situation even worse. Lloyd stars as Exxon official Frank Iarossi, in charge of the official cleanup, caught between onsite confusion and corporate bungling while Heard is outraged environmentalist Dan Lawn. News and home videotapes of the actual spill are used to enhance the dramatization. Filmed in Vancouver, British Columbia. **90m/C VHS.** Christopher Lloyd, John Heard, Rip Torn, Michael Murphy, Don S. Davies, Ken Walsh, Bob Gunton, Mark Metcalf, Paul Guilfoyle, David Morse, Jackson Davies; *D:* Paul Seed; *W:* Michael Baker; *M:* David Ferguson. **CABLE**

Dead Aim woof! **1987 (R)** A dud about Soviet spies who introduce even more drugs into New York City, ostensibly to bring about the downfall of the U.S. Obviously a completely far-fetched plot. **91m/C VHS.** Ed Marinaro, Isaac Hayes, Corbin Bernsen; *D:* William Vanderkloot.

Dead Air ♂♂ **1994 (PG-13)** Atmospheric murder mystery finds radio deejay Hines getting calls from a mystery woman who says she knows him well and has kidnapped his new girlfriend. Meanwhile, a woman claiming to be a reporter wants to interview him and things around the radio station start looking decidedly sinister. **91m/C VHS.** Gregory Hines, Debrah Farentino, Gloria Reuben, Beau Starr, Laura Harrington, Michael (M.K.) Harris, W. Earl Brown, Veronica Cartwright; *D:* Fred Walton; *W:* David Amann; *M:* Dana Kaproff.

Dead Alive ♂♂ *Braindead* **1993** This outrageously over-the-top horror flick from New Zealand is a gore aficionado's delight (think "Evil Dead" movies for comparison). Set in 1957 and satirizing the bland times, the "plot" has the mom of a nerdy son getting bitten by an exotic monkey, which promptly turns her into a particularly nasty ghoul. This condition is apparently contagious (except for her son who tries to hide the fact mom is literally a monster) and calls for lots of spurting blood and body parts which take on lives of their own. For those with strong stomachs and senses of humor. Also available in an 85-minute R-rated version. **97m/C VHS, DVD, Wide.** *NZ* Timothy Balme, Elizabeth Moody, Diana Penalver, Ian Watkin, Breanda Kendall, Stuart Devenie, Peter Jackson, Forrest J Ackerman; *D:* Peter Jackson; *W:* Frances Walsh, Stephen Sinclair, Peter Jackson; *C:* Murray Milne; *M:* Peter Dasent.

Dead and Buried ♂♂½ **1981 (R)** Farentino is the sheriff who can't understand why the victims of some pretty grisly murders seem to be coming back to life. Eerily suspenseful. **95m/C VHS, DVD, Wide.** James Farentino, Jack Albertson, Melody Anderson, Lisa Blount, Bill Quinn, Michael Pataki, Robert Englund, Barry Corbin, Lisa Marie; *D:* Gary Sherman; *W:* Dan O'Bannon, Ronald Shusett; *C:* Steven Poster; *M:* Joe Renzetti.

Dead Are Alive ♂♂½ **1972** Alcoholic archaeologist Jason (Cord) has come to Italy to search for Etruscan ruins near the home of orchestral conductor Nicos (John Marley) and his wife Myra (Samantha Eggar), Jason's ex-lover. Soon after he opens an Etruscan tomb, a series of violent murders begin. The above-average giallo shocker and is much better than director Crispino's more popular "Autopsy." **103m/C DVD, Wide.** *IT* Alex Cord, Samantha Eggar, John Marley, Nadja Tiller, Horst Frank, Enzo Tarascio; *D:* Armando Crispino; *W:* Armando Crispino, Lucio Battistrada; *C:* Erico Menczer; *M:* Riz Ortolani.

Dead As a Doorman ♂½ **1985** A young writer takes a part-time post as a doorman and becomes the target of a murderous lunatic. **83m/C VHS.** Bradley Whitford, Sharon Schlarth, Bruce Taylor; *D:* Gary Youngman.

Dead Badge ♂♂½ **1994 (R)** An honest cop is reassigned to a corrupt precinct and becomes targeted for death. **95m/C VHS.** Brian Wimmer, Olympia Dukakis, Yaphet Kotto, M. Emmet Walsh, James B. Sikking, Marta DuBois; *D:* Douglas Barr; *W:* Douglas Barr; *M:* Mark Snow.

Dead Bang ♂♂½ **1989 (R)** A frustrated cop uncovers a murderous white supremacist conspiracy in L.A. Frankenheimer's deft directorial hand shapes a somewhat conventional cop plot into an effective vehicle for Johnson. **102m/C VHS, DVD, 8mm.** Don Johnson, Bob Balaban, William Forsythe, Penelope Ann Miller, Tim Reid, Frank Military, Michael Higgins, Michael Jeter, Evans Evans, Tate Donovan; *D:* John Frankenheimer; *W:* Robert Foster; *C:* Gerry Fisher; *M:* Gary Chang, Michael Kamen.

Dead Beat ♂♂½ **1994 (R)** Teen love and lust—and murder—all set in Albuquerque, New Mexico, circa 1965. Womanizer Kit (Ramsey) will use any tale to score with his dates—and is happy to pass on tips to adoring disciple Rudy (Getty). When Kit meets up with rebellious rich girl Kirsten (Wagner), she demands proof of his love and he confides he once murdered a girl. Kirsten tries to tighten her stranglehold on Kit with this info and force Rudy from his life but Kit's dark side doesn't stay hidden either. **94m/C VHS.** Bruce Ramsay, Natasha Gregson Wagner, Balthazar Getty, Meredith Salenger, Sara Gilbert, Deborah Harry, Max Perlich, Alex Cox; *D:* Adam Dubov; *W:* Adam Dubov.

Dead Boyz Can't Fly ♂♂ **1993 (R)** Disturbing look at urban violence. Dysfunctional punk leads his equally amoral cohorts on a looting spree in a near-empty highrise in revenge against a patronizing businessman. The unrated version contains 10 more minutes of violence. **92m/C VHS.** Delia Sheppard, Sheila Kennedy, Ruth (Coreen) Collins, Mark McCulley, Brad Friedman; *D:* Howard Winters.

Dead Calm ♂♂♂ **1989 (R)** A taut Australian thriller based on a novel by Charles Williams. A young married couple is yachting on the open seas when they happen upon the lone survivor of a sinking ship. They take him on board only to discover he's a homicidal maniac. Makes for some pretty suspenseful moments that somewhat make up for the weak ending. **97m/C VHS, DVD, Wide.** *AU* Sam Neill, Billy Zane, Nicole Kidman, Rod Mullinar; *D:* Phillip Noyce; *W:* Terry Hayes; *C:* Dean Semler; *M:* Graeme Revell.

Dead Center ♂♂ *Crazy Joe* **1994 (R)** Street punk gets trained as assassin by secret government agency that frames him for the murder of a U.S. senator. So now he has to stay alive long enough to prove his innocence. **90m/C VHS.** Justin Lazard, Eb Lottimer, Rachel York; *D:* Steve Carver.

Dead Certain ♂ **1992 (R)** A "Silence of the Lambs" rip-off. Dourif (again specializing in weirdos) is the jailed serial killer providing tantalizing clues to the identity of a new killer on the loose. **93m/C VHS.** Brad Dourif, Francesco Quinn, Karen Russell, Joel Kaiser; *D:* Anders Palm; *W:* Anders Palm.

Dead Cold ♂♂½ **1996 (R)** Screenwriter Eric Thornsen (Mulkey) decides he and wife Alicia (Anthony) need a second honeymoon at a remote cabin. But their privacy is disturbed by homicidal fugitive Kale (Dobson), who drugs and dumps Eric's body down a ravine. Turns out Alicia wants hubby's insurance money and she and the disgusting Kale are very intimate friends. But of course Eric's not really dead. Decent thriller is slow to start but picks up speed in the second half. **91m/C VHS.** Lysette Anthony, Chris Mulkey, Peter Dobson, Alina Thompson, Michael Champion; *D:* Kurt Anderson; *W:* Richard Brandes; *C:* M. David Mullen.

Dead Connection ♂♂ **1994 (R)** Beautiful reporter Bonet is in cahoots with cop Madsen to see justice brought the "phone sex killer" who is terrorizing Los Angeles. **93m/C VHS.** Michael Madsen, Lisa Bonet, Gary Stretch; *D:* Nigel Dick; *W:* Larry Grolin; *M:* Rolfe Kent.

Dead Creatures ☆ **2001** A close-knit group of British twentysomething women travels around the dingy areas outside of London satiating their need for human flesh with saran-wrapped body parts they carry in their luggage. The girls are all suffering from a kind of zombie-disease that is inflicted by a bite and eventually results in the victim's literal decomposition. The dreary tone of the film echoes that of lower-class British TV dramas: heavy grainy images, squalid locations with minimal lighting and makeup. Parkinson directs this low-key horror drama without the usual female nudity prevalent in today's micro-budgeted horror films, but the lack of a thriller element or traditional genre structure works against it. Without anywhere to go with the story, this one peters out around the halfway mark. The gore effects, though used minimally, are repugnant and truly nauseating. **89m/C DVD, Wide.** Beverly Wilson, Antonia Beamish, Brendan Gregory; ***D:*** Andrew Parkinson; ***W:*** Andrew Parkinson; ***C:*** Jack Shepherd; ***M:*** Andrew Parkinson.

The Dead Don't Die ☆ **1975** Unbelievable plot set in the 1930s has Hamilton as a detective trying to prove his brother was wrongly executed for murder. He ultimately clashes with the madman who wants to rule the world with an army of zombies. Perhaps if they had cast Hamilton as Master of the Zombies. **74m/C VHS.** George Hamilton, Ray Milland, Linda Cristal, Ralph Meeker, Joan Blondell, James McEachin; ***D:*** Curtis Harrington. **TV**

Dead Easy ☆☆ **1982** Livin' ain't easy for a Sydney sleaze-club owner, his working-girl girlfriend, and a slandered cop when they're caught between machete-wielding enemy gangs (it seems somebody made the crime boss REALLY mad). The three flee in that quintessential escape vehicle—a two-ton truck—to qualify the effort as an Australian contender for greatest chase scene ever (heavy chassis category). **92m/C VHS.** *AU* Scott Burgess, Rosemary Paul; ***D:*** Bert Deling.

Dead End ☆☆☆½ *Cradle of Crime* **1937** Sidney Kingsley play, adapted for the big screen by Lillian Hellman, traces the lives of various inhabitants of the slums on New York's Lower East Side as they try to overcome their surroundings. Gritty drama saved from melodrama status by some genuinely funny moments. Film launched the Dead End Kids. **92m/B VHS.** Sylvia Sidney, Joel McCrea, Humphrey Bogart, Wendy Barrie, Claire Trevor, Allen Jenkins, Marjorie Main, Billy Halop, Huntz Hall, Bobby Jordan, Gabriel Dell, Leo Gorcey, Charles Halton, Bernard Punsley, Minor Watson, James Burke; ***D:*** William Wyler; ***W:*** Lillian Hellman; ***C:*** Gregg Toland; ***M:*** Alfred Newman.

Dead End ☆☆½ **1998 (R)** Police sargeant Henry Smolenski (Roberts) gains custody of his troubled 16-year-old son Adam (Tierney) after his ex-wife's death. Then he learns that the death is being investigated as a murder and Adam is the primary suspect. When Adam takes off, Henry searches for him and winds up becoming a suspect himself. Soon the estranged father and son are teaming up to discover who's out to frame them. Roberts gets to play a likable, caring character for a change of pace. **93m/C VHS, DVD.** *CA* Eric Roberts, Jacob Tierney, Jayne Heitmeyer, Eliza Roberts, Jack Langedijk, Frank Schorpion; ***D:*** Douglas Jackson; ***W:*** Karl Schiffman; ***C:*** Georges Archambault; ***M:*** Milan Kymlicka. **VIDEO**

Dead End City ☆½ **1988** Streetwise resident of L.A. organizes fellow citizens into a vigilante force to fight the gangs for control of the city. **88m/C VHS.** Dennis Cole, Gregory Scott Cummins, Christine Lunde, Robert Z'Dar, Darrell Nelson, Alena Downs; ***D:*** Peter Yuval; ***W:*** Michael Bogert.

Dead End Drive-In ☆☆ **1986 (R)** In a surreal, grim future a man is trapped at a drive-in theatre-cum-government-run concentration camp, where those considered to be less than desirable members of society are incarcerated. **92m/C VHS.** *AU* Ned Manning, Natalie McCurry, Peter Whitford; ***D:*** Brian Trenchard-Smith.

Dead End Street ☆½ *Kvish L'Lo Motzah* **1983** Young prostitute attempts to change her self-destructive lifestyle. It's not easy. **86m/C VHS.** *IS* Anat Atzmon, Yehoram Gaon; ***D:*** Yaky Yosha; ***W:*** Yaky Yosha, Eli Tavor.

Dead Eyes of London ☆☆½ *Dark Eyes of London; Die Toten Augen von London* **1961** Blind old German men are dying to lower their premiums in this geriatric thriller: someone (perhaps the director of the home for the blind?) is killing off the clientele for their insurance money, and a Scotland Yard inspector aims to expose the scam. Relatively early vintage Kinski, it's a remake of the eerie 1939 Lugosi vehicle, "The Human Monster" (originally titled "Dark Eyes of London"), adapted from Edgar Wallace's "The Testament of Gordon Stuart." **95m/B VHS.** *GE* Joachim Fuchsberger, Karin Baal, Dieter Borsche, Ady Berber, Klaus Kinski, Eddi Arent, Wolfgang Lukschy; ***D:*** Alfred Vohrer.

Dead Fire ☆☆ **1998** A space substation has been in orbit around earth for the past 50 years trying to regenerate the planet's poisoned atmosphere. But now a shipboard traitor is trying to destroy the operation. **105m/C VHS.** Matt Frewer, C. Thomas Howell, Monika Schnarre; ***D:*** Robert Lee; ***M:*** Peter Allen. **VIDEO**

Dead for a Dollar ☆½ *T'ammazzo! Raccomandati a Dio* **1970** A Colonel, a con man, and a mysterious woman team up in the Old West to search for the $200,000 they stole from a local bank. **92m/C VHS.** John Ireland, George Hilton, Piero Vida, Sandra Milo; ***D:*** Osvaldo Civirani.

Dead Funny ☆☆ **1994 (R)** Vivian (Pena) returns to her Manhattan walk-up to find boyfriend Reggie (McCarthy) dead on her kitchen table, skewered by a Samurai sword. Instead of calling the police, Viv gets gal pal Louise (Turco) to come over to figure out who did Reg in. Instead, they get drunk and discuss Reggie's (who seen in flashbacks) immaturity and penchent for practical jokes. Good performances, twist ending, but situation runs out of steam. **91m/C VHS.** Elizabeth Pena, Andrew McCarthy, Paige Turco, Blanche Baker, Lisa Jane Persky, Michael Mantell; ***D:*** John Feldman; ***W:*** John Feldman; ***M:*** Sheila Silver.

Dead Girls ☆ **1990 (R)** A rock group whose lyrics focus on suicide goes on vacation. The members find themselves stalked by a serial killer who decides to take matters out of the musicians' hands and into his own. Graphic violence. **105m/C VHS.** Diana Karanikas, Angela Eads; ***D:*** Dennis Devine; ***W:*** Steve Jarvis; ***C:*** Aaron Schneider.

Dead Heart ☆☆☆ **1996** Culture clash story set in the 1930s is highlighted by a terrific lead performance by Brown. He's cop Ray Lorkin, whose territory is the tiny community of Wala Wala in Australia's outback. This remote spot just happens to be a focal point for the local aboriginals, who regard the area as a spiritual place. Trouble erupts when an aboriginal prisoner (Pederson), who just happened to be having an affair with the schoolteacher's white wife (Mikkiken) is found hanged in his cell. Tradition demands revenge—from there every other situation in the community just gets worse. First-timer Parsons directs from his stage play. **106m/C VHS, DVD.** *AU* Bryan Brown, Ernie Dingo, Angie Millikken, Aasron Pedersen, Lewis Fitz-Gerald, John Jarratt, Anne Tenney, Gnarnayarrahe Waitaire, Lafe Charlton; ***D:*** Nick Parsons; ***W:*** Nick Parsons; ***C:*** James Bartle; ***M:*** Stephen Rae.

Dead Heat ☆½ **1988 (R)** Some acting talent and a few funny moments unfortunately don't add up to a fine film, though they do save it from being a complete woofer. In this one even the cops are zombies when one of them is resurrected from the dead to help his partner solve his murder and rid the city of the rest of the undead. **86m/C VHS.** Joe Piscopo, Treat Williams, Lindsay Frost, Darren McGavin, Vincent Price, Keye Luke, Clare Kirkconnell; ***D:*** Mark Goldblatt; ***W:*** Terry Black; ***C:*** Robert Yeoman; ***M:*** Ernest Troost.

Dead Heat on a Merry-Go-Round ☆☆☆ **1966 (R)** Coburn turns in a great performance as the ex-con who masterminds the heist of an airport safe. Intricately woven plot provides suspense and surprises. The film is also notable for the debut of Ford in a bit part (he has one line as a hotel messenger). **108m/C VHS.** James Coburn, Camilla Sparv, Aldo Ray, Nina Wayne, Robert Webber, Rose Marie, Todd Armstrong, Marian Moses, Severn Darden, Harrison Ford; ***D:*** Bernard Girard; ***C:*** Lionel Lindon.

Dead Husbands ☆☆ **1998 (PG-13)** Alex (Sheridan) is the beautiful wife of slick Dr. Carter Elston (Ritter), the best-selling author of relationship books. When Carter decides he wants to give everything up for smalltown life, horrified pampered spouse Alex meets a group of wives who offer her a unique solution (much more permanent than divorce). You see, the wives have a list of husbands to be gotten rid of—Alex kills the hubby at the top of the list and then adds Carter's name. Eventually, a fellow member will return the favor and off her annoying mate. But what happen when Dr. Elston finds the list? **90m/C VHS.** Nicolette Sheridan, John Ritter, Amy Yasbeck, Donna Pescow, Wendie Malick; ***D:*** Paul Shapiro. **CABLE**

Dead in the Water ☆½ **1991 (PG-13)** Brown is Charlie Deegan, a big-time lawyer with a rich wife that he'd rather see dead. Charlie and his mistress plot the perfect murder to dispose of his spouse and collect her money. When plans go awry, he ends up as a suspect for the wrong murder in this story of infidelity and greed. **90m/C VHS.** Bryan Brown, Teri Hatcher, Anne DeSalvo, Veronica Cartwright; ***D:*** Bill Condon; ***W:*** Eleanor Gaver, Robert Seidenberg, Walter Klenhard.

Dead in the Water ☆☆ **2001 (R)** Wealthy hot babe Gloria (Swain) takes her boyfriend (Bairstow), their buddy (Thomas), and Marcos, the son of her father's business partner on the family cabin cruiser for a day of fun. Only tensions rise and violence erupts when Gloria gets too involved with the wrong guy. **89m/C VHS, DVD, Wide.** Dominique Swain, Henry Thomas, Scott Bairstow, Renata Fronzi, Sebastian DeVincente; ***D:*** Gustavo Lipzstein. **VIDEO**

Dead Letter Office ☆☆½ **1998** Lonely Alice (Otto) gets a job at the dead letter office of the postal system. Her boss is Frank (DelHoyo), a political refugee from Chile, who lost his family to the junta. Frank and Alice seem destined to hit it off but not before a few obstacles get in their path. Otto's father Barry has a brief scene as Alice's irresponsible dad. More distinctive than the story might indicate, thanks to the performances and tart comedy. **95m/C VHS.** *AU* Miranda Otto, George DelHoyo, Nicholas Bell, Syd Brisbane, Georgina Naidu, Vanessa Steele, Barry Otto; ***D:*** John Ruane; ***W:*** Deb Cox; ***C:*** Ellery Ryan; ***M:*** Roger Mason.

Dead Lucky ☆½ **1960** A novice tries gambling and wins a fortune, but his luck leads him into an entanglement with an assassin, a scam artist, and a beautiful woman. Based on the novel "Lake of Darkness." **91m/B VHS.** *GB* Vincent Ball, Betty McDowall, John Le Mesurier, Alfred Burke, Michael Ripper; ***D:*** Montgomery Tully.

Dead Man ☆☆ **1995 (R)** Depp wanders throughs the 19th-century American west as William Blake, an Ohio accountant who runs afoul of the law. Hooking up with a Native American named Nobody (Farmer), who envisions Blake as the famous English poet, the two try to stay one step ahead of the hired guns and lawmen out to get them. Action is sporadic and pace is all over the road in this offbeat and long-winded western, while Farmer's performance and Jarmusch's polished visuals are high points. **121m/B VHS, DVD, Wide.** Johnny Depp, Gary Farmer, Lance Henriksen, Michael Wincott, Mili Avital, Crispin Glover, Gabriel Byrne, Iggy Pop, Billy Bob Thornton, Jared Harris, Jimmie Ray Weeks, Mark Bringleson, John Hurt, Alfred Molina, Robert Mitchum; ***D:*** Jim Jarmusch; ***W:*** Jim Jarmusch; ***C:*** Robby Muller; ***M:*** Neil Young. N.Y. Film Critics '96: Cinematog.; Natl. Soc. Film Critics '96: Cinematog.

Dead Man on Campus ☆☆ **1997 (R)** Failing college freshmen Scott and Gosselaar learn that if your roomie commits suicide, you get a straight-A average for the year. So they decide to find a new roommate who's on the edge and make certain to push him over. Anyone who's ever done time in the dorms has heard this rumor, so it was only a matter of time before someone turned it into a screenplay. The wait wasn't long enough. One-joke premise can't sustain a whole movie, and Gosselaar goes a long way toward duplicating "Saved By the Bell" co-star Elizabeth Berkley's "Showgirls" um, success. **94m/C VHS, DVD.** Tom Everett Scott, Mark Paul Gosselaar, Alyson Hannigan, Poppy Montgomery, Lochlyn Munro, Randy Pearlstein, Mari Morrow; ***D:*** Alan Cohn; ***W:*** Michael Traeger, Mike White; ***C:*** John Thomas; ***M:*** Mark Mothersbaugh.

Dead Man Out ☆☆☆ **1989** Both Glover and Blades turn in exceptional performances in this thought-provoking drama. A convict on Death Row (Blades) goes insane and therefore cannot be executed. The state calls in a psychiatrist (Glover) to review the case and determine whether he can be cured so that the sentence can be carried out. Powerful and riveting morality check. **87m/C VHS.** Danny Glover, Ruben Blades, Tom Atkins, Larry Block, Sam Jackson, Maria Ricossa; ***D:*** Richard Pearce; ***M:*** Cliff Eidelman.

Dead Man Walking ☆☆ **1988 (R)** In a post-holocaust future, half the population has been stricken with a deadly plague. Hauser is a mercenary, dying from the disease, who is hired to rescue a young woman who was kidnapped and is being held in the plague zone. **90m/C VHS.** Wings Hauser, Brion James, Pamela Ludwig, Sy Richardson, Leland Crooke, Jeffrey Combs; ***D:*** Gregory (Gregory Dark) Brown; ***W:*** R.J. Marx.

Dead Man Walking ☆☆☆½ **1995 (R)** True story of a nun whose anti-death penalty beliefs put her in moral crisis with grieving victims when she becomes the spiritual advisor to a death-row murderer. Based on the book by Sister Helen Prejean, Sarandon stars as the nun who develops a relationship of understanding with inmate Poncelet (Penn), unwavering in her Christian beliefs even though Penn's character shows little or no remorse for the two young lovers he was accused of murdering. Penn offers one of the best performances (but worst hair-dos) of his career, while writer/director Robbins presents both sides of the death-penalty issue mingled with simple human compassion. **122m/C VHS, DVD, Wide.** Jon Abrahams, Susan Sarandon, Sean Penn, Robert Prosky, Raymond J. Barry, R. Lee Ermey, Celia Weston, Lois Smith, Scott Wilson, Roberta Maxwell, Margo Martindale, Barton Heyman, Larry Pine; ***D:*** Tim Robbins; ***W:*** Tim Robbins; ***C:*** Roger Deakins; ***M:*** David Robbins. Oscars '95: Actress (Sarandon); Ind. Spirit '96: Actor (Penn); Screen Actors Guild '95: Actress (Sarandon).

Dead Man's Eyes/Pillow of Death *Pillow of Death* **1944** In 1944's "Dead Man's Eyes" artist Chaney is accidentally blinded but may get a second chance through an eye operation. His father-in-law offers his own eyes after he dies—and then he's murdered. In 1945's "Pillow of Death" attorney Chaney is accused of smothering various family members to death. Based on radio's "The Inner Sanctum Mysteries." **130m/B VHS.** Acquanetta, J. Edward Bromberg, Rosalind Ivan, Wilton Graff, Bernard B. Thomas, Lon Chaney Jr., Brenda Joyce, George Cleveland, Clara Blandick, Paul Kelly, Jean Parker, George Meeker; ***D:*** Wallace Fox, Reginald LeBorg; ***W:*** George Bricker, Dwight V. Babcock.

Dead Man's Revenge ☆☆½ **1993 (PG-13)** Ruthless railroad mogul Payton McCay (Dern) doesn't let anyone stand in his way—even if it means framing innocent homesteader Hatcher (Ironside) in order to get his land. Hatcher escapes from jail and goes after McCay, trailed by bounty hunter Bodeen (Couloris). But Bodeen's not what he seems and has his own plans on getting even with the villainous McCay. **92m/C VHS.** Bruce Dern, Michael Ironside, Keith Coulouris, Randy Travis; ***D:*** Alan J. Levi; ***W:*** Jim Byrnes, David Chisholm.

Dead Mate ☆ **1988** A woman marries a mortician after a whirlwind romance only to discover that, to her husband, being an undertaker is not just a job, it's a way of life. **93m/C VHS.** Elizabeth Mannino, David Gregory, Lawrence Bockus, Adam Wahl; ***D:*** Straw Weisman.

Dead Men Can't Dance **1997 (R)** CIA agent Victoria Ellis (York) gets sent to South Korea to train with a women-only group of Army Rangers. Meanwhile, Vic's boyfriend Hart (Biehn) and his buddy Shooter (Paul) are in the demilitertized zone where Hart learns Shooter is out to steal nuclear detonators on behalf of crazy Senator Fowler (Ermey), who wants to revive the Cold War. Things go bad and the women are forced to take things into their own more than capable hands. Lots of action. **97m/C VHS.** Kathleen York, Michael Biehn, Adrian Paul, R. Lee Ermey, Grace Zabriskie; ***D:*** Steve (Stephen M.) Anderson; ***W:*** Mark Sevi, Bill Kerby, Paul Sinor; ***C:*** Levie Isaacks; ***M:*** Rick Marvin.

Dead Men Don't Die **1991 (PG-13)** An anchorman is slain by criminals but resurrected as a shambling voodoo zombie. Few viewers notice the difference in this inoffensive but repetitious farce. The living-dead Gould appears to be having a lot of fun. **94m/C VHS.** Elliott Gould, Melissa Anderson, Mark Moses, Philip Bruns, Jack Betts, Mabel King; ***D:*** Malcolm Marmorstein; ***W:*** Malcolm Marmorstein.

Dead Men Don't Wear Plaid **1982 (PG)** Martin is hilarious as a private detective who encounters a bizarre assortment of suspects while trying to find out the truth about a scientist's death. Ingeniously interspliced with clips from old Warner Bros. films. Features Humphrey Bogart, Bette Davis, Alan Ladd, Burt Lancaster, Ava Gardner, Barbara Stanwyck, Ray Milland, and others. Its only flaw is that the joke loses momentum by the end of the film. **89m/B VHS, DVD, Wide.** Steve Martin, Rachel Ward, Reni Santoni, George Gaynes, Frank McCarthy, Carl Reiner; ***D:*** Carl Reiner; ***W:*** Steve Martin, Carl Reiner; ***C:*** Michael Chapman; ***M:*** Miklos Rozsa.

Dead Men Walk *Creatures of the Devil* **1943** A decent, albeit low budget, chiller about twin brothers (Zucco in a dual role); one a nice, well-adjusted member of society, the other a vampire who wants to suck his bro's blood. Sibling rivalry with a bite. **65m/B VHS, DVD.** George Zucco, Mary Carlisle, Dwight Frye, Nedrick Young, Al "Fuzzy" St. John, Fern Emmett, Robert Strange; ***D:*** Sam Newfield; ***W:*** Fred Myton; ***C:*** Jack Greenhalgh; ***M:*** Leo Erdody.

The Dead Next Door **1989** Eerily reminiscent of "Night of the Living Dead." A scientist manufactures a virus which inhabits corpses and multiplies while replacing the former cells with its own. But the newly living corpses need human flesh to survive. In response, the government creates "The Zombie Squad" who do heroic battle with the stiffs. When a bizarre cult whose goal is the eradication of the human race befriend the dead, the battle gets ugly. **84m/C VHS, DVD.** Pete Ferry, Bogdan Pecic, Michael Grossi, Len Kowalewich, Jolie Jackunas, Robert Kokai, Scott Spiegel, J.R. Bookwalter; ***D:*** J.R. Bookwalter; ***W:*** J.R. Bookwalter; ***M:*** J.R. Bookwalter.

Dead of Night **1945** The template for episodic horror films, this suspense classic, set in a remote country house, follows the individual nightmares of five houseguests. Redgrave turns in a chillingly convincing performance as a ventriloquist terrorized by a demonic dummy. Not recommended for light-sleepers. Truly spine-tingling. **102m/B VHS.** *GB* Michael Redgrave, Mervyn Johns, Sally Ann Howes, Basil Radford, Naunton Wayne, Roland Culver, Googie Withers, Frederick Valk, Antony Baird, Judy Kelly, Miles Malleson, Ralph Michael, Mary Merrall, Renee Gadd, Michael Allan, Robert Wyndham, Esme Percy, Peggy Bryan, Hartley Power, Elisabeth Welch, Magda Kun, Garry Marsh; ***D:*** Alberto Cavalcanti, Charles Crichton, Basil Dearden, Robert Hamer; ***W:*** T.E.B. Clarke, John Baines, Angus MacPhail; ***C:*** Stanley Pavey, Douglas Slocombe; ***M:*** Georges Auric.

Dead of Night **1977** This trilogy features Richard Matheson's tales of the Supernatural: "Second Chance," "Bobby," and "No Such Thing As a Vampire," all served up by your hostess, Elvira. **76m/C VHS.** Joan Hackett, Ed Begley Jr., Patrick Macnee, Anjanette Comer; ***D:*** Dan Curtis.

Dead of Night *Lighthouse* **1999 (R)** Leo Rook (Adamson) is a psycho who collects the severed heads of his victims as trophies. He's aboard the prison ship Hyperion, which is transporting criminals to a remote island off the northern English coast. Leo steals a lifeboat and escapes to desolate Gehenna Rocks just before the ship runs aground. Then the few survivors are subjected to Leo's stalking and slashing. Crude and gory. **95m/C VHS, DVD.** *GB* Chris(topher) Adamson, James Purefoy, Rachel Shelley, Paul Brooke, Don Warrington, Chris Dunne, Bob Goody, Pat Kelman; ***D:*** Simon Hunter; ***W:*** Simon Hunter; ***C:*** Tony Imi; ***M:*** Debbie Wiseman.

Dead of Winter **1987 (R)** A young actress is suckered into a private screen test for a crippled old director, only to find she is actually being remodeled in the guise of a murdered woman. Edge-of-your-seat suspense as the plot twists. **100m/C VHS.** Mary Steenburgen, Roddy McDowall, Jan Rubes, Ken Pogue, William Russ; ***D:*** Arthur Penn; ***W:*** Mark Shmuger, Mark Malone; ***M:*** Richard Einhorn.

Dead On **1993 (R)** Illicit lovers want to get rid of their inconvenient spouses so they can be together always. But their perfect plan doesn't work out as expected. Also available in an unrated version. **87m/C VHS.** Matt McCoy, Shari Shattuck, David Ackroyd, Tracy Scoggins, Thomas Wagner; ***D:*** Ralph Hemecker; ***W:*** April Wayne.

Dead on Sight **1994 (R)** A college student dreams of a masked man, a knife, a bound woman, and other terrors. Too bad her nightmares match the actions of a serial killer. **96m/C VHS.** Jennifer Beals, Daniel Baldwin, Kurtwood Smith, William H. Macy; ***D:*** Ruben Preuss; ***W:*** Lewis Green; ***M:*** Harry Manfredini.

Dead on the Money **1991** Adequate made for TV suspenser about a woman who believes her lover plots a dire fate for her cousin. But nothing is what it seems here. Confusing, droopy in spots, but fun. **92m/C VHS.** Corbin Bernsen, Amanda Pays, John Glover, Eleanor Parker, Kevin McCarthy; ***D:*** Mark Cullingham; ***W:*** Gavin Lambert. **TV**

Dead or Alive **1944** Tex and the Texas Rangers pretend to be outlaws in order to join a gang terrorizing a town. **54m/B VHS.** Tex Ritter, Dave O'Brien, Guy Wilkerson, Charles "Blackie" King, Bud Osborne, Reed Howes; ***D:*** Elmer Clifton.

Dead Pigeon on Beethoven Street **1972 (PG)** Sandy (Corbett) is a detective whose partner gets murdered while investigating blackmailers who take compromising pictures of international big-wigs. So Sandy goes undercover and joins the gang. Cheeky paranoia from Fuller. **92m/C VHS.** Glenn Corbett, Christa Lang, Anton Diffring, Alexander D'Arcy; ***D:*** Samuel Fuller; ***W:*** Samuel Fuller.

Dead Pit woof! **1989 (R)** Leave this one in the pit it crawled out of. Twenty years ago a mad scientist was killed as a result of horrible experiments he was conducting on mentally ill patients at an asylum. A young woman stumbles across his experiments, awakening him from the dead. **90m/C VHS.** Jeremy Slate, Steffen Gregory Foster; ***D:*** Brett Leonard.

Dead Poets Society **1989 (PG)** An idealistic English teacher inspires a group of boys in a 1950s' prep school to pursue individuality and creative endeavor, resulting in clashes with school and parental authorities. Williams shows he can master the serious roles as well as the comic with his portrayal of the unorthodox educator. Big boxoffice hit occasionally scripted with a heavy hand in order to elevate the message. The ensemble cast is excellent. **128m/C VHS, DVD, 8mm.** Robin Williams, Ethan Hawke, Robert Sean Leonard, Josh Charles, Gale Hansen, Kurtwood Smith, James Waterson, Dylan Kussman, Lara Flynn Boyle, Melora Hardin, Alexandra Powers; ***D:*** Peter Weir; ***W:*** Tom Schulman; ***C:*** John Seale; ***M:*** Maurice Jarre. Oscars '89: Orig. Screenplay; British Acad. '89: Film; Cesar '91: Foreign Film.

The Dead Pool **1988 (R)** Dirty Harry Number Five features a new twist on the sports pool: a list of celebrities is distributed and bets are placed on who will be first to cross the finish line, literally. Unfortunately someone seems to be hedging their bet by offing the celebs themselves. When Harry's name appears on the list, he decides to throw the game. **92m/C VHS, DVD, Wide.** Clint Eastwood, Liam Neeson, Patricia Clarkson, Evan C. Kim, David Hunt, Michael Currie, Michael Goodwin, Jim Carrey; ***D:*** Buddy Van Horn; ***M:*** Lalo Schifrin.

Dead Presidents **1995 (R)** Sophomore release for the Hughes brothers falls short of impact of "Menace II Society," but not for lack of ambition. Combination coming of age tale, war story, period piece and caper film follows Anthony ("Menace" veteran Tate) from his Bronx neighborhood in 1968 to Vietnam (for "Platoon" adventures in the wilds of Florida) and then back to the 'hood, where his life continues to spiral downward. Desperate to escape, he becomes involved in an armoured car heist to grab some cash (the "dead presidents"). Supported by hard-edged and effective acting, the Hughes continue to develop their control of cinematic imagery, displaying genius for staging violent, confrontational scenes. But the script, based on a story by the brothers, fails to live up to the vision, with characterization and dialogue lagging. Pounding period soundtrack with contributions by Curtis Mayfield, James Brown, and Marvin Gaye keeps things humming. **120m/C VHS, DVD.** Larenz Tate, Keith David, Chris Tucker, Freddy Rodriguez, N'Bushe Wright, Bokeem Woodbine, Rose Jackson, Clifton Powell; ***D:*** Albert Hughes, Allen Hughes; ***W:*** Michael Henry Brown; ***C:*** Lisa Rinzler; ***M:*** Danny Elfman.

Dead Reckoning **1947** Bogart and Prince are two WWII veterans en route to Washington when Prince disappears. Bogart trails Prince to his Southern hometown and discovers he's been murdered. Blackmail and more murders follow as Bogie tries to uncover the truth. Suspenseful with good performances from all, especially Bogart. **100m/B VHS.** Humphrey Bogart, Lizabeth Scott, Morris Carnovsky, Charles Cane, Wallace Ford, William Prince, Marvin Miller; ***D:*** John Cromwell.

Dead Reckoning **1989 (R)** A plastic surgeon and his lovely wife embark on a cruise aboard his new luxury yacht. The intrigue begins with a storm, an isolated island, and the discovery that the captain is the wife's former lover. **95m/C VHS.** Cliff Robertson, Susan Blakely, Rick Springfield; ***D:*** Robert Lewis.

Dead Right *If He Hollers, Let Him Go* **1968** A black man is unjustly put into prison in the Deep South. He manages to escape in order to try and prove his innocence. **111m/C VHS.** Raymond St. Jacques, Dana Wynter, Kevin McCarthy, Barbara McNair; ***D:*** Charles Martin; ***W:*** Charles Martin.

Dead Ringers **1988 (R)** A stunning, unsettling chiller, based loosely on a real case and the bestseller by Bari Wood and Jack Geasland. Irons, in an excellent dual role, is effectively disturbing as the twin gynecologists who descend into madness when they can no longer handle the fame, fortune, drugs, and women in their lives. Bujold is the actress/patient bedded by both brothers but jealouly loved by Beverly. Acutely upsetting film made all the more so due to its graphic images and basis in fact. **117m/C VHS, DVD.** *CA* Jeremy Irons, Genevieve Bujold, Heidi von Palleske, Barbara Gordon, Shirley Douglas, Stephen Lack, Nick Nichols; ***D:*** David Cronenberg; ***W:*** David Cronenberg, Norman Snider; ***C:*** Peter Suschitzsky; ***M:*** Howard Shore. Genie '89: Actor (Irons), Director (Cronenberg), Film; L.A. Film Critics '88: Director (Cronenberg), Support. Actress (Bujold); N.Y. Film Critics '88: Actor (Irons).

Dead Sexy **2001 (R)** Detective Kate McBain (Tweed) is investigating the murders of four L.A. high-price hookers. Of course, she becomes more than a little interested in one of her suspects, charming Blue (Enos), but is Kate willing to die to find out the truth? **89m/C VHS, DVD.** Shannon Tweed, John Enos, Kenneth White, Sam Jones, Eric Keith; ***D:*** Robert Angelo; ***W:*** Anthony Laurence Greene, Elroy Canton; ***C:*** Kazuo Minami; ***M:*** Nicholas Rivera. **VIDEO**

Dead Silence **1990 (R)** Screenwriter Cliff Morgan has written a classic film noir screenplay... with the money, it seems all Cliff's problems are solved... or are they? **92m/C VHS.** Clete Keith, Doris Anne Soyka, Joseph Scott, Craig Fleming; ***D:*** Harrison Ellenshaw.

Dead Silence **1996 (R)** Three escaped convicts, including ruthless Ted Handy (Coates), have hijacked a busload of deaf children and their teacher (Matlin) and are holding them hostage in an abandoned slaughterhouse. Veteran FBI agent John Cooper (Garner) is called in but he not only has to deal with a tense and possibly tragic situation but with a grandstanding politician (Smith) who's criticizing his every action and the last-minute arrival of another hostage negotiator (Davidovich). Based on the novel "A Maiden's Grave" by Jeffery Deaver. **105m/C VHS.** Gary Basaraba, Vanessa Vaughan, Blu Mankuma, Mimi Kuzyk, Scott Speedman, John Bourgeois, Barry Pepper, James Garner, Kim Coates, Marlee Matlin, Charles Martin Smith, Lolita (David) Davidovich, Kenneth Welsh, James Villemaire; ***D:*** Dan Petrie Jr.; ***W:*** Donald Stewart; ***C:*** Thomas Burstyn; ***M:*** Jonathan Goldsmith. **CABLE**

Dead Silence *Wilbur Falls* **1998** Renata (Edwards) decides on a simple plan of revenge against Jeff (Newmark) who humiliated her at their junior-high prom five years before. Only her plans backfire and he accidentally dies. That should be the plot but it's surrounded by so many other storylines that it gets lost in the telling, which is a shame since Edwards does a good job. **95m/C VHS, DVD.** Shanee Edwards, Danny Aiello, Sally Kirkland, Suzanne Cryer, Charles Newmark; ***Cameos:*** Maureen Stapleton; ***D:*** Juliane Glantz; ***W:*** Juliane Glantz; ***C:*** Kurt Brabbee; ***M:*** Jim Halfpenny.

Dead Silent **1999 (R)** Doctor Julia Kerrbridge (Stewart) must care for her traumatized young niece whose parents were killed by the mob. But the girl, who has become mute, also has information that the bad guys will do anything to keep secret. Then there's Julia's new neighbor Kevin Finney (Lowe)—is he really a nice guy? Or a potential killer? **95m/C VHS, DVD.** Catherine Mary Stewart, Rob Lowe, Peter Colvey, Larry Day, Sean Devine, Allen Altman, Mark Camacho; ***D:*** Roger Cardinal; ***W:*** Ed Fitzgerald, Paul Koval; ***C:*** Bruno Philip; ***M:*** David Findlay. **VIDEO**

Dead Simple *Viva Las Nowhere* **2001 (R)** Frank Jacobs (Stern) and his nagging wife Helen (Richardson) owe a failing motel in dusty nowhere Kansas. Frank dreams of being a C&W singer and he hooks up with lounge performer Julie (Kohl), who has an abusive manager, has-been Roy Baker (Caan). Then there's Helen's twin sister Wanda (Richardson again), barmaid Marguerite (Stringfield), and the motel's garden, which gets a lot of unexpected fertilizer. Black comedy can't sustain its edge. **98m/C VHS, DVD, Wide.** Daniel Stern, James Caan, Patricia Richardson, Sherry Stringfield, Lacey Kohl, Tim Abell; ***D:*** Jason Bloom; ***W:*** Richard Uhlig, Steve Seitz; ***C:*** James Glennon; ***M:*** Andrew Gross.

Dead Sleep **1991 (R)** A nurse discovers that comatose patients at a private clinic have been used as guinea pigs by an overzealous doctor. This minor-league chiller from Down Under is said to have been inspired by an actual medical scandal. **95m/C VHS.** Linda Blair, Tony Bonner; ***D:*** Alec Mills.

Dead Solid Perfect **1988** Quaid stars as a golf pro whose life on the PGA tour is handicapped by his taste for scotch and his eye for the ladies. Based on the book by Dan Jenkins. **97m/C VHS.** Randy Quaid, Kathryn Harrold, Jack Warden, Larry Riley, Brett Cullen, Corinne Bohrer; ***D:*** Bobby Roth; ***W:*** Dan Jenkins, Bobby Roth.

Dead Space **1990 (R)** Dead space lay between the ears of whoever thought we needed this remake of 1982's "Forbidden World." At a lab on a hostile planet an experimental vaccine mutates into a prickly puppet monster who menaces the medicos. Needed: a vaccine against cheapo "Alien" ripoffs. **72m/C VHS.** Marc Singer, Laura Tate, Bryan Cranston, Judith Chapman; ***D:*** Fred Gallo.

Dead Tides 🦴🦴 **1997 (R)** Former Navy SEAL Mick (Piper) is hired by Nola (Kitaen) to pilot a sailboat from California to Mexico. But Mick soon realizes that Nola's the wife of a powerful drug dealer and he's in more trouble than he can imagine. **100m/C VHS.** Roddy Piper, Tawny Kitaen, Trevor Goddard, Miles O'Keeffe, Juan Fernandez; ***D:*** Serge Rodnunsky; ***W:*** Serge Rodnunsky. VIDEO

Dead to Rights 🦴🦴½ *Donato and Daughter* **1993 (R)** TV movie finds veteran LAPD cop Donato (Bronson) on the trail of a serial killer along with his new partner—who's not only his daughter but his superior officer. Based on the novel by Jack Early. **90m/C VHS.** Charles Bronson, Dana Delany, Xander Berkeley, Bonnie Bartlett, Jenette Goldstein, Louis Giambalvo; ***D:*** Rod Holcomb; ***W:*** Robert Roy Pool; ***C:*** Thomas Del Ruth; ***M:*** Sylvester Levay.

Dead Waters 🦴🦴 *Dark Waters* **1994** Elizabeth (Salter) travels to a remote Russian island to visit her sister, Theresa (Phipps), who resides at the convent there. But Theresa is murdered after witnessing an occult ritual and Elizabeth finds strange references to "The Beast" in the convent library and realizes the nuns are trying to raise the demonic creature. **94m/C VHS, DVD.** *IT RU GB* Louise Salter, Venera Simmons, Maria Kapnist, Anna Rose Phipps; ***D:*** Mariano Baino; ***W:*** Mariano Baino, Andrew Bark; ***C:*** Alex Howe; ***M:*** Igor Clark.

Dead Weekend 🦴🦴 **1995 (R)** Lt. Weed (Baldwin) is given the task of finding and destroying a seductively dangerous female alien. Turns out she has the ability to physically change into a number of different women—all of whom attract the willing-and-eager soldier. **82m/C VHS.** Richard Speight Jr., Stephen Baldwin, David Rasche, Alexis Arquette, Bai Ling, Tom Kenny, Jennifer MacDonald, Barbara Alyn Woods; ***D:*** Amos Poe; ***W:*** Joel Rose; ***C:*** Gary Tieche; ***M:*** Steve Hunter. CABLE

Dead Women in Lingerie woof! **1990 (R)** When beautiful models are turning up dead, a detective is called in to solve the mystery. Perhaps they committed suicide to avoid being in this picture any longer than necessary. Title sounds like the next episode of "Geraldo." **87m/C VHS.** June Lockhart, Lyle Waggoner, John Romo, Jerry Orbach, Maura Tierney; ***D:*** Erika Fox.

Dead Wrong 🦴½ **1983** Undercover agent falls in love with the drug smuggler she's supposed to bring to justice. **93m/C VHS.** Britt Ekland, Winston Rekert, Jackson Davies; ***D:*** Len Kowalewich; ***W:*** Len Kowalewich.

Dead Zone 🦴🦴🦴 **1983 (R)** Diffident teacher Johnny Smith (Walken) gains extraordinary psychic powers following a near-fatal car accident and a five-year coma. He has developed the ability to foresee a person's future by touching their hands—and when he shakes the hand of presidential candidate Greg Stillson (Sheen), he foresees a holocaust. So Johnny decides to use his "gift" to save mankind from impending evil. A good adaptation of the Stephen King thriller. **104m/C VHS, DVD, Wide.** Christopher Walken, Brooke Adams, Tom Skerritt, Martin Sheen, Herbert Lom, Anthony Zerbe, Colleen Dewhurst; ***D:*** David Cronenberg; ***W:*** Jeffrey Boam; ***C:*** Mark Irwin; ***M:*** Michael Kamen.

Deadbolt 🦴🦴 **1992 (R)** Divorced med student Marty Hiller (Bateman) desperately needs a roommate and Alec Danz (Baldwin) seems perfect. Soon they're sharing more than the rent, until Danz kills her friends and imprisons her in the apartment (equipped of course with soundproof walls and bulletproof glass—one wonders why she doesn't bang on the floor to gain attention.) Predictable and silly would-be thriller attempts to capitalize on the roommate-from-hell theme that started with "Single White Female," but isn't nearly as effective. Went straight to video and showed up on network TV several months later. **95m/C VHS.** Justine Bateman, Adam Baldwin, Michelle Scarabelli, Chris Mulkey, Cyndi Pass, Isabelle Truchon; ***D:*** Douglas Jackson. VIDEO

Deadfall 🦴🦴½ **1993 (R)** Father/son grifters plan an elaborate scam that goes wrong when son Joe (Biehn) inadvertently kills dear old dad (Coburn). When Joe is going through his father's effects he finds out about an unknown twin uncle, who also turns out to be a racketeer. Along with Uncle Lou's mistrustful henchman Eddie (Cage), they plan another con but swindles and vendettas abound. **99m/C VHS, DVD.** Michael Biehn, Sarah Trigger, Nicolas Cage, James Coburn, Charlie Sheen, Peter Fonda; ***D:*** Christopher Coppola; ***W:*** Christopher Coppola, David Peoples; ***C:*** Maryse Alberti; ***M:*** Jim Fox.

Deadline 🦴½ **1981** Journalist must find out the truth behind a minor earthquake in Australia. **94m/C VHS.** Barry Newman, Trisha Noble, Bill Kerr; ***D:*** Arch Nicholson; ***W:*** Walter Halsey Davis.

Deadline 🦴🦴 **1982** Eerie tale of horror writer's life as it begins to reflect his latest story in this play on the "truth is stranger than fiction" adage. **85m/C VHS.** Stephen Young, Sharon Masters, Cindy Hinds, Phillip Leonard; ***D:*** Mario Azzopardi.

Deadline 🦴🦴 **1987 (R)** Walken is a cynical American journalist assigned to cover the warring factions in Beirut. He finds himself becoming more and more involved in the events he's supposed to report when he falls in love with a German nurse who is aiding the rebel forces. Tense, though sometimes murky drama. **110m/C VHS.** *GE* Christopher Walken, Hywel Bennett, Marita Marschall; ***D:*** Nathaniel Gutman.

Deadline 🦴🦴 **2000 (R)** The publisher of a leading Chicago newspaper is murdered following his hostile takeover of said paper and the leading suspect is the paper's editor (but he's the wrong guy). Formulaic thriller. **94m/C VHS, DVD.** Patrick Bergin, Bruce Dinsmore, Annie Dufresne, Alex Ivanovic, Edward Yankie; ***D:*** Robbie Ditchburn; ***W:*** Ron Base, Michael Stokes; ***C:*** Daniel Valdilleneuve. VIDEO

Deadline Assault 🦴½ *Act of Violence* **1990 (R)** Kate McSweeny is a beautiful young reporter who is brutally attacked and raped by a gang of savage youths. Kate must now face the unsettling facts; they're still on the streets and they may be stalking her again. **90m/C VHS.** Elizabeth Montgomery, James Sloyan, Sean Frye, Biff McGuire, Michael Goodwin, Linden Chiles; ***D:*** Paul Wendkos.

Deadline at Dawn 🦴🦴 **1946** Hayward is an aspiring actress who tries to help a sailor (Williams) prove that he is innocent of murder. Based on a novel by Cornell Woolrich. **82m/B VHS.** Bill Williams, Susan Hayward, Lola Lane, Paul Lukas, Joseph Calleia; ***D:*** Harold Clurman; ***W:*** Clifford Odets.

Deadline Auto Theft 🦴 **1983** A fun lovin' guy drives fast cars and meets beautiful women. Nudge, nudge, wink, wink. **90m/C VHS.** H.B. Halicki, Hoyt Axton, Marion Busia, George Cole, Judi Gibbs, Lang Jeffries Jr.; ***D:*** H.B. Halicki.

Deadlock 🦴🦴½ **1991 (R)** Hauer and Rogers star as inmates in a prison of the future. This prison has no walls, no fences and no guards—and no one EVER escapes. Each prisoner wears an explosive collar that is tuned to the same frequency as one of the other prisoner's. Should the two separate by more than 100 yards, the collars explode. When Rogers convinces Hauer that they are on the same frequency, the two escape. Trouble is, they are being pursued not only by the police, but by Hauer's former partners in crime as well. Can the two find the freedom they are looking for—without losing their heads? **103m/C VHS, DVD.** Rutger Hauer, Mimi Rogers, Joan Chen, James Remar, Stephen Tobolowsky, Basil Wallace; ***D:*** Lewis Teague. CABLE

Deadlock 2 🦴🦴 *Deadlocked: Escape from Zone 14* **1994 (R)** Same basic plot as in the first TV movie. Tony Archer (Morales) and Allie Thompson (Peeples), two strangers who have been set up by the same corrupt businessman, are being held in a violent correctional facility. Inmates wear electronic collars programmed to explode if they venture too far apart. But Tony figures a way around this trap only to discover he and Allie are caught in another. **120m/C VHS.** Esai Morales, Nia Peeples, Stephen McHattie, Jon Cuthbert; ***D:*** Graeme Campbell.

Deadlocked 🦴🦴 **2000** Demond Doyle (Jonz) is convicted of rape and murder and prosecutor Ned Stark (Caruso) wants the death penalty. Demond's father, Jacob (Dutton), is convinced that his son is innocent, so he takes the jury hostage. He tells Stark that he has 24 hours to find the evidence that will clear his son or the captives start dying. Compelling leads in a contrived story. **100m/C VHS.** David Caruso, Charles S. Dutton, John Finn, Jo D. Jonz, Malcolm Stewart, Tom Butler, Diego Wallraff, Michael Tomlinson; ***D:*** Michael Watkins; ***W:*** David Rosenfelt, Erik Jendresen; ***C:*** Thomas Burstyn; ***M:*** B.C. Smith. CABLE

Deadly Advice 🦴🦴 **1993 (R)** Meek bookseller Jodie (Horrocks) and her sister are constantly humiliated by their overbearing mother (Fricker), who also objects to Jodie's romance with the local doctor (Pryce). As life becomes increasingly unbearable, Jodie discovers a book on infamous killers and is visited by their ghosts, including Jack the Ripper, who is happy to suggest ways to get rid of mom. **91m/C VHS.** Jane Horrocks, Imelda Staunton, Brenda Fricker, Jonathan Pryce; ***D:*** Mandie Fletcher.

Deadly Alliance 🦴 **1978** Two impecunious filmmakers (who happen to be hunks) and a babe (for good measure) poke their noses in where they're not wanted (in the shady business of an international oil cartel). "Deadly Dull" would be a more appropriate moniker. **90m/C VHS.** Kathleen Arc, Tony de Fonte, Michele Marsh, Walter Prince; ***D:*** Paul S. Parco.

The Deadly and the Beautiful 🦴 *Wonder Women* **1973 (PG)** Dr. Tsu sends her "deadly but beautiful" task force to kidnap the world's prime male athletes for use in her private business enterprise. **82m/C VHS.** *PH* Nancy Kwan, Ross Hagen, Maria de Aragon, Roberta Collins, Tony Lorea, Sid Haig, Vic Diaz, Shirley Washington, Gale Hansen; ***D:*** Robert Vincent O'Neil.

Deadly Bet 🦴½ **1991 (R)** A made-for-video saga of a kickboxer who loses his money and his girl when he loses the big match. Lots of fight sequences as he works to regain his career. **93m/C VHS.** Jeff Wincott, Charlene Tilton, Steven Leigh; ***D:*** Richard W. Munchkin.

Deadly Blessing 🦴🦴 **1981 (R)** A young, recently widowed woman is visited in her rural Pennsylvania home by some friends from the city. Something's not quite right about this country life and they become especially suspicious after meeting their friend's very religious in-laws. **104m/C VHS.** Maren Jensen, Susan Buckner, Sharon Stone, Ernest Borgnine, Jeff East, Lisa Hartman Black, Lois Nettleton, Colleen Riley, Douglas Barr, Michael Berryman; ***D:*** Wes Craven; ***W:*** Wes Craven, Glenn Benest, Matthew F. Barr; ***C:*** Robert C. Jessup; ***M:*** James Horner.

Deadly Breed 🦴½ **1989** Beware your friendly neighborhood cop. A band of white supremacists has infiltrated the local police force, intent on causing violence, not keeping the peace. **90m/C VHS.** William Smith, Addison Randall, Blake Bahner, Joe Vance; ***D:*** Charles Kanganis.

Deadly Business 🦴🦴🦴 **1986** The true story of a man who turned from crime to become a government informant. As a garbage man, he works to stop the illegal dumping of chemicals in New Jersey. An interesting made-for-televison drama. **100m/C VHS.** Alan Arkin, Armand Assante, Michael Learned, Jon Polito, George Morfogen, James Rebhorn; ***D:*** John Korty.

Deadly Business 🦴½ **19??** Hard-nosed collection man for a lethal loan shark finds he is the one with the debt to pay as he's stalked through the city street by hit men. **95m/C VHS.** David Peterson, John Lazarus, Leo Gabrowski.

Deadly Companions 🦴🦴½ **1961** Keith is an ex-gunslinger who agrees to escort O'Hara through Apache territory in order to make up for inadvertenly killing her son. Director Peckinpah's first feature film. **90m/C VHS.** Maureen O'Hara, Brian Keith, Chill Wills, Steve Cochran; ***D:*** Sam Peckinpah; ***C:*** William Clothier.

Deadly Conspiracy 🦴🦴 **1991 (R)** Saxon plays a corrupt businessman who kills an employee about to blow the whistle on his shady dealings. Hauser is the good cop, with the bad personal life, who makes it his mission to bring Saxon to justice. The prolific Hauser brings some fast-paced action to this routine story. **92m/C VHS.** Wings Hauser, John Saxon, Frances Fisher, Patti D'Arbanville, Margaux Hemingway, Greg Mullavey; ***D:*** Paul Leder.

Deadly Currents 🦴🦴 **1993 (R)** Scott plays a former sea captain who owns a bar on the island of Curacao and enjoys regaling his patrons with his seagoing tales. Petersen is the exiled CIA agent stuck as the security officer of the American consulate. The dangerous pasts of both men catch them up and find them caught in a web of international intrigue. Based on the novel "The Prince of Malta" by James David Buchanan. **93m/C VHS.** George C. Scott, William L. Petersen, Julie Carmen, Alexei Sayle, Trish Van Devere, Philip Anglim, Maria Ellingsen; ***D:*** Carl Schultz; ***W:*** James David Buchanan.

Deadly Dancer 🦴½ **1990** It's up to a lone cop to find out who's been offing the hoofers in L.A. **88m/C VHS.** Adolfo "Shabba Doo" Quinones, Smith Wordes, Walter W. Cox, Steve Jonson; ***D:*** Kimberly Casey; ***W:*** David A. Prior.

Deadly Daphne's Revenge 🦴½ **1993** Gory story of rape and revenge from the Troma Team. Hitchhiker Cindy is beaten and raped by Charlie Johnson. When she seeks justice via the local police, Johnson makes plans to have her snuffed out. Meantime, another of his victims escapes from the asylum she's been in and comes looking for him with murder on her mind. **98m/C VHS.** Anthony Holt, Laurie Tait Partridge, John Suttle, Alan Levy, Richard Harding Gardner; ***D:*** Richard Harding Gardner; ***W:*** Tim Bennett, Richard Harding Gardner; ***C:*** Vern Virlene; ***M:*** John Banning.

Deadly Darling woof! **1985** Muddled, completely awful tale centering on two different rapes with no discernible attempt made to link the two or establish a plot. **91m/C VHS.** Fonda Lynn, Warren Chan, Bernard Tsui, Cherry Kwok; ***D:*** Karen Young.

Deadly Desire 🦴🦴 **1991 (R)** Seduced by the beautiful Harrold, security guard Scalia finds himself putting his life on the line when Harrold asks him to help cheat her husband out of millions in an insurance scam. Trouble ensues when they try to outsmart Harrold's powerful entrepreneurial husband. **93m/C VHS.** Jack Scalia, Kathryn Harrold, Will Patton, Joe Santos; ***D:*** Charles Correll.

Deadly Diamonds 🦴½ **1991** Cop is on the trail of diamond smugglers who leave a trail of death in their wake. **90m/C VHS.** Dan Haggerty, Troy Donahue, Eli Rich, Kathleen Kane, Kenna Grob, Nicholas Mercer; ***D:*** Thomas Atcheson; ***W:*** Ron Herbst.

Deadly Dreams 🦴🦴 **1988 (R)** A young boy's parents are killed by a maniac who then commits suicide. Years later, he dreams that he is being stalked anew by the same killer. Nightmares turn into reality in this decent horror/suspense flick. **79m/C VHS.** Mitchell Anderson, Xander Berkeley, Thom Babbes, Juliette Cummins; ***D:*** Kristine Peterson; ***W:*** Thom Babbes.

Deadly Embrace woof! **1988 (R)** Sordid tale of wealthy man (Vincent) who wants to get rid of his wife—permanantly. He enlists the aid of a beautiful young coed. Soft-core sleaze with nary a redeemable quality. **82m/C VHS.** Jan-Michael Vincent, Jack Carter, Ty Randolph, Linnea Quigley, Michelle (McClellan) Bauer, Ken Abraham; ***D:*** David DeCoteau.

Deadly Encounter 🦴🦴🦴 **1972** Thrilling actioner in which Hagman portrays a helicopter pilot—a former war ace—who allows an old flame to talk him into helping her escape from the mobsters on her trail. Terrific edge-of-your-seat aerial action. **90m/C VHS.** Larry Hagman, Susan Anspach, Michael C. Goetz, James Gammon; ***D:*** William A. Graham.

Deadly Encounter woof! **1978 (R)** Lacking any redeemable qualities, this film shows just how low some people go. Merrill hosts a dinner to garner financial support for a budding playwright, but what we get is a look at the lifestyles of the rich and perverse. **90m/C VHS.** Dina Merrill, Carl Betz, Leon Ames, Vicki Powers, Mark Rasmussen, Susan Logan; ***D:*** R. John Hugh.

Deadly Exposure 🦴🦴 **1993 (R)** Benson stars as a burned-out journalist doing his own investigation of the right-wing extremist group that killed his father. Aspiring reporter Johnson helps out and turns up a conspiracy between the extremists, the government, and a plot to assassinate a U.S. senator. Also available in an unrated version. **100m/C VHS.** Robby Benson, Laura Johnson, Paul Hampton, Andrew Prine, Bentley Mitchum, Isaac Hayes; ***D:*** Lawrence Mortorff; ***W:*** Asher Brauner.

Deadly Eyes 🦴½ *The Rats* **1982 (R)** After eating grain laced with steroids a group of rats grows to mammoth proportions (dachshunds in rat drag were used). Their appetites grow accordingly—now they crave humans. Amid the nibbling by the giant rat-dogs, romance blooms. Silly adaptation by Charles Eglee of Frank Herbert's "The Rats." **93m/C VHS.** Sam Groom, Sara Botsford, Scatman Crothers, Lisa Langlois, Cec Linder; ***D:*** Robert Clouse.

Deadly Fieldtrip 🦴½ **1974** Four female students and their teacher are abducted by a biker gang and held hostage on a deserted farm. **91m/C VHS.** Zalman King, Brenda Fogarty, Robert Porter; ***D:*** Earl Barton.

Deadly Force 🦴½ **1983 (R)** Ex-cop turned private detective stalks a killer in Los Angeles who has left an "X" carved in the forehead of each of his 17 victims. If he had just signed his name, things could have been tidied up much earlier. **95m/C VHS.** Wings Hauser, Joyce Ingalls, Paul Shenar, Al Ruscio, Arlen Dean Snyder, Lincoln Kilpatrick; ***D:*** Paul Aaron; ***W:*** Robert Vincent O'Neil, Barry Schneider.

Deadly Friend 🦴🦴 **1986 (R)** A well-meaning horror flick? That's what Wes Craven has tried to provide for us. When the girlfriend of a lonely teenage genius is accidentally killed, he decides to insert his robot's "brain" in her body, though the results aren't entirely successful. The same can be said for the film which was based on Diana Henstell's more effective novel "Friend." **91m/C VHS.** Matthew Laborteaux, Kristy Swanson, Michael Sharrett, Anne Twomey, Richard Marcus, Anne Ramsey; ***D:*** Wes Craven; ***W:*** Bruce Joel Rubin; ***C:*** Philip Lathrop; ***M:*** Charles Bernstein.

Deadly Game 🦴🦴 **1982 (R)** A reunion at a remote hotel leads to an ordeal of psychological terror and murderous intrigue. **108m/C VHS.** George Segal, Robert Morley, Trevor Howard, Emlyn Williams, Alan Webb; ***D:*** George Schaefer.

Deadly Game 🦴½ **1983** Much-maligned and preyed-upon witness is protected by a weary cop, who speaks with the use of English subtitles. **90m/C VHS.** *GE* Mel Ferrer, Helmut Berger, Barbara Sukowa; ***D:*** Karoly Makk, Dieter Geissler.

The Deadly Game 🦴🦴 **198?** East-West intrigue prior to the fall of the Berlin Wall finds a Western operative returning from a dangerous mission, only to walk into a trap set by his own side. **104m/C VHS.** *GB* David Hemmings.

Deadly Game 🦴½ **1991 (R)** Horribly burned, a vengeful millionaire invites seven people he believes have wronged him to spend the weekend on his isolated island. He has promised them each a reward for their good deeds, but instead plans to have a big-game hunt with his "guests" as the prey. **93m/C VHS.** Roddy McDowall, Jenny Seagrove, Marc Singer, Michael Beck; ***D:*** Thomas J. Wright; ***W:*** Wes Claridge.

Deadly Game 🦴🦴 *Catch Me If You Can* **1998** Nathan is a 12-year-old runaway with an attitude who witnesses some mob business and winds up stealing a lot of mob cash. He decides to live it up on his ill-gotten gains until a down-on-his-luck cop (Matheson) catches up with Nathan and tries to protect him from the goons' revenge. **120m/C VHS, DVD.** Tim Matheson, Carol Alt, William Katt, Ryan DeBoer, Catherine Oxenberg, Ed Marinaro, Eddie Mekka; ***D:*** Jeff Reiner; ***W:*** Lorne Cameron, David Hoselton; ***C:*** Jonathan Freeman; ***M:*** Christopher Brady. **TV**

Deadly Games 🦴½ **1980** Ineffective plot involving a series of murders in a small town is seemingly played out by the principal characters in a horror board game. Film is saved from being a complete waste by Groom's good performance as the local cop. **94m/C VHS.** Sam Groom, Jo Ann Harris, Steve Railsback, Dick Butkus, June Lockhart, Colleen Camp; ***D:*** Scott Mansfield.

Deadly Harvest 🦴 **1972 (PG)** Scientists' worst fears have been realized—due to ecological abuse and over-development of the land, food has become extremely scarce. This in turn has caused people to become a bit savage. They are particularly nasty to a farmer and his family. Not a bad plot, but a poorly acted film. **86m/C VHS.** Clint Walker, Nehemiah Persoff, Kim Cattrall, David G. Brown, Gary Davies; ***D:*** Timothy Bond.

Deadly Hero 🦴🦴🦴 **1975 (R)** Gripping tale of a young woman who becomes the prey of a New York City cop after questioning the brutal methods he employed while saving her from being assaulted, ultimately killing her attacker. Williams makes film debut in this chilling suspenser. **102m/C VHS.** Don Murray, James Earl Jones, Diahn Williams, Lilia Skala, Conchata Ferrell, George S. Irving, Treat Williams, Josh Mostel; ***D:*** Ivan Nagy; ***C:*** Andrzej Bartkowiak; ***M:*** Brad Fiedel.

Deadly Heroes 🦴🦴 **1996 (R)** Terrorists highjack an American plane at Athens International Airport with the demand that their leader, Carlos (Drago), who's jailed in Miami, be delivered to them. CIA agent and ex-Navy SEAL, Captain Cody Grant (Vincent), is forced to take Carlos to Athens but having captured Carlos once, Grant is determined that the terrorist and his associates won't be free for long. **104m/C VHS.** Jan-Michael Vincent, Billy Drago, Michael Pare, Claudette Mink; ***D:*** Menahem Golan; ***W:*** Damian Lee, Gregory Lee. **VIDEO**

Deadly Illusion 🦴🦴 *Love You to Death* **1987 (R)** Williams is a private detective who manages to get himself tangled in a complex web of intrigue and winds up framed for murder. Decent outing for all. **95m/C VHS.** Billy Dee Williams, Morgan Fairchild, Vanity, John Beck, Joe Cortese; ***D:*** William Tannen, Larry Cohen; ***W:*** Larry Cohen; ***M:*** Patrick Gleeson.

Deadly Impact 🦴½ **1984** Las Vegas casinos are targeted for rip-off by means of a computer. Svenson and Williamson give good performances, but that's not enough to save this one. De Angelis used the pseudonym Larry Ludman. **90m/C VHS.** *IT* Bo Svenson, Fred Williamson, Marcia Clingan, John Morghen, Vincent Conti; ***D:*** Fabrizio de Angelis.

Deadly Innocence 🦴½ **1988 (R)** A shy, lonely girl works at an isolated gas station. After her father's death, she takes in a boarder—a mysterious woman being chased by her past. **90m/C VHS.** Mary Crosby, Andrew Stevens, Amanda Wyss; ***D:*** John D. Patterson, Hugh Parks.

Deadly Intent 🦴🦴 **1988** The widow of a murdered archeologist becomes the target of fortune hunters when they try to get their hands on the priceless jewel her husband brought back from a dig. **83m/C VHS.** Lisa Eilbacher, Steve Railsback, Maud Adams, Lance Henriksen, Fred Williamson, Persis Khambatta; ***D:*** Nigel Dick.

Deadly Intruder 🦴½ **1984** Quiet vacation spot is being terrorized by an escapee from a mental institution. So much for a little R and R. **86m/C VHS.** Chris Holder, Molly Creek, Tony Crupi; ***D:*** John McCauley; ***W:*** Tony Crupi.

Deadly Lessons 🦴🦴 **1994** Misfit Ann gets shunned by the college "in" crowd but then a childhood friend comes to her aid and decides to take revenge on the nasty students. **90m/C VHS.** Andrea Gall, Mat McGinnis, Dana Wise; ***D:*** Leslie Delano.

The Deadly Mantis 🦴½ *The Incredible Praying Mantis* **1957** A gigantic praying mantis lies in a million-year-old sleep in the frozen reaches of the Arctic. Then a volcanic eruption releases the critter and the flying beastie does it's destructive best on Washington, D.C., and New York City until the military can gas it into oblivion. Typically silly '50s sci-fi with decent special effects. **79m/B VHS.** Craig Stevens, William Hopper, Alix Talton, Pat Conway, Donald Randolph; ***D:*** Nathan (Hertz) Juran; ***W:*** Martin Berkeley.

Deadly Mission 🦴½ *Quel Maledetto Treno Blindato* **1978 (R)** Five soldiers in WWII France are convicted of crimes against the Army, only to escape from lock-up and become focal points in a decisive battle. **99m/C VHS.** *IT* Bo Svenson, Peter Hooten, Fred Williamson; ***D:*** Enzo G. Castellari; ***W:*** Alessandro Continenza, Sergio Grieco, Romano Migliorini, Laura Toscano, Franco Marotta.

Deadly Neighbor 🦴🦴 **1991** New neighbor moves in, dead neighborhood housewives move out. Another neighbor becomes suspicious and investigates. **90m/C VHS.** Don Leifert, George Stover, Lydia Laurans; ***D:*** Donald M. Dohler.

Deadly Obsession 🦴½ **1988 (R)** A disfigured lunatic stalks a young co-ed hoping to extort $1 million from the wealthy dean of the school. **93m/C VHS.** Jeffrey R. Iorio; ***D:*** Jeno Hodi; ***W:*** Brian Cox.

Deadly Outbreak 🦴🦴 **1996 (R)** A chemical weapons facility is taken over by a renegade colonel who threatens to unleash a deadly plague. Now it's up to one man (Speakman) to free the hostage scientist who knows the formula for the antidote. **94m/C VHS.** Jeff Speakman, Ron Silver, Rochelle Swanson, Jonathan Sagalle; ***D:*** Rick Avery; ***M:*** Harvey W. Mason.

Deadly Passion 🦴½ **1985 (R)** A James Cain-like thriller about a private eye getting carnally involved with a beautiful and treacherous woman who is manipulating her late husband's estate through murder and double-crossing. **100m/C VHS.** *SA* Brent Huff, Ingrid Boulting, Harrison Coburn, Lynn Maree; ***D:*** Larry Larson.

Deadly Past 🦴½ **1995 (R)** Predictable story finds dumb ex-con bartender (Marquette) making the mistake of getting involved with a femme fatale (Alt) from his past. Also available in an unrated version. **90m/C VHS.** Ron Marquette, Carol Alt, Dedee Pfeiffer, Mark Dacascos; ***D:*** Tibor Takacs; ***W:*** Steven Iyama; ***C:*** Berhard Salzmann; ***M:*** Alex Wilkinson.

Deadly Possession 🦴🦴 **1988** A college student plays amateur detective when she tries to clear her ex-husband's name after he is accused of the horrible murder of a fellow student. **99m/C VHS.** *AU* Penny Cook, Anna-Maria Winchester, Liddy Clark, Olivia Hamnett; ***D:*** Craig Lahiff.

Deadly Prey woof! **1987 (R)** Prior is up against a fully outfitted army of bloodthirsty mercenaries who are using innocent people as "live targets" at their secret bootcamp. Plot lifted from "The Most Dangerous Game" has more than its share of gruesome violence. **87m/C VHS.** Cameron Mitchell, Troy Donahue, Ted Prior, Fritz Matthews; ***D:*** David A. Prior; ***W:*** David A. Prior.

Deadly Reactor 🦴🦴 **1989** In a post-nuclear future a lone preacher turns into an armed vigilante to protect the people of a town being terrorized by a vicious motorcycle gang. **88m/C VHS.** David Heavener, Stuart Whitman, Darwyn Swalve, Allyson Davis; ***D:*** David Heavener.

Deadly Recruits 🦴½ **1986** The Russians did it! The Russians did it! Stamp is convinced that the downfall of several top students at Oxford, amid scandal and rumor, is due to a KGB conspiracy. **92m/C VHS.** *GB* Terence Stamp, Michael Culver, Carmen (De Sautoy) Du Sautoy, Robin Sachs; ***D:*** Roger Tucker.

Deadly Revenge 🦴 **1983 (R)** Action-adventure pic with not much adventure and even less action. Small-town reporter finds himself up against a mob boss when he takes over the nightclub business of a friend killed by the mobsters. Dubbed. **90m/C VHS.** *IT* Rodolfo Ranni, Julio de Grazia, Silvia Montanari, Fred Commoner; ***D:*** Juan Carlos Sesanzo.

Deadly Rivals 🦴🦴 **1992 (R)** Stevens plays a laser specialist in Miami for a top-secret weapons conference. A beauty takes a interest in him but then she's first accused of being a spy and then mistaken for a courier in the pay of a ruthless crime boss. Can Stevens find the truth? **93m/C VHS.** Andrew Stevens, Cela Wise, Joseph Bologna, Margaux Hemingway, Richard Roundtree, Francesco Quinn, Randi Ingerman; ***D:*** James Dodson; ***W:*** Redge Mahaffey; ***M:*** Ashley Irwin.

Deadly Sanctuary woof! **1968** Censors stopped production of this film several times. The Marquis de Sade's writings provided the inspiration (though there's nothing inspired about it) for this tale of two recently orphaned young women who get caught up in prostitution, an S&M club, and murder. **92m/C VHS.** Jack Palance, Mercedes McCambridge, Sylva Koscina, Klaus Kinski, Akim Tamiroff, Romina Power; ***D:*** Jess (Jesus) Franco.

The Deadly Secret 🦴🦴 **1994** Randall Parks is a successful real estate agent with a past he has managed to hide for 20 years. When he is blackmailed, he decides to take matters into his own hands and track down his accusers. **98m/C VHS.** Joe Estevez, Tracy Spaulding, Reggie Cale, Douglas Stalgren; ***D:*** Jason Hammond; ***W:*** Douglas Stalgren; ***M:*** Erik Hansen.

Deadly Sins 🦴🦴½ **1995 (R)** Deputy sheriff Jack Gates (Keith) hooks up with P.I. Christina Herrera (Milano) to investigate a murder in a Catholic girls school. Christina poses as a student and uncovers sinister secrets. **98m/C VHS.** David Keith, Alyssa Milano, Terry David Mulligan, Corrie Clark; ***D:*** Michael Robison; ***W:*** John Langley, Malcolm Barbour.

Deadly Spygames **1989** A special agent for the United States Special Operations Bureau finds himself in deep trouble. **?m/C VHS.** Troy Donahue, Tippi Hedren; ***D:*** Jack M. Sell; ***W:*** Jack M. Sell.

Deadly Sting 🦴½ **1982** Silva devises an intricate scheme to gain revenge on the men who cheated him out of his share of a gold bullion heist. **90m/C VHS.** *FR* Henry Silva, Philip Clay, Andre Pousse; ***D:*** Jean-Claude Roy.

Deadly Stranger 🦴 *Border Heat* **1988** Fluegel's talents could have been put to much better use than as the selfish mistress of a plantation owner who is taking advantage of the migrant workers toiling on his land. Moore is a drifter and hired hand who rallies the workers to stand up to the owner. **93m/C VHS.** Darlanne Fluegel, Michael J. Moore, John Vernon, Ted White; ***D:*** Max Kleven.

Deadly Strangers 🦴🦴 **1982** Two people meet up on the road and decide to share a ride. We discover that one of them is an insane killer who's escaped from a mental institution. Suspense builds nicely, but the ending is flawed. **89m/C VHS.** *GB* Hayley Mills, Simon Ward, Sterling Hayden, Ken Hutchison; ***D:*** Sidney Hayers.

Deadly Sunday 🦴½ **1982** A family's weekly Sunday drive turns terrifying when desperate jewel thieves detour them and hold them hostage. **85m/C VHS.** Dennis Ely, Henry Sanders, Gylian Roland, Douglas Alexander; ***D:*** Donald M. Jones.

Deadly Surveillance 🦴🦴 **1991 (R)** Two tough policemen investigate a series of drug-related murders and stake out a possible suspect—a beautiful woman who's the lover of one of the lawmen. Tension in this Canadian-made cop opera evaporates in the third act for a standard buddy-buddy action finale. **92m/C VHS.** Michael Ironside, Christopher Bondy, Susan Almgren, Vlasta Vrana, David Carradine; ***D:*** Paul Ziller. **TV**

Deadly Target 🦴½ **1994 (R)** Detective Charles Prince (Daniels) is sent to L.A. to return a notorious Chinese gangster to Hong Kong for trial. But Prince finds out his would-be prisoner's escaped and soon he's involved in martial arts mayhem. **90m/C VHS.** Gary Daniels, Kenneth McLeod, Max Gail, Susan Byun; ***D:*** Charla Driver; ***W:*** Michael January, James Adelstein; ***C:*** Richard Pepin; ***M:*** Michael Lewis.

Deadly Thief *Shalimar* **1978** A former jewel thief comes out of retirement to challenge those who are now tops in the profession to try and steal the world's most precious ruby from him. Of course all they have to lose is their lives. What could have been an exciting adventure is made curiously boring. **90m/C VHS.** *IN* Rex Harrison, John Saxon, Sylvia Miles, Dharmendra, Zenat Aman, Shammi Kapoor; ***D:*** Krishna Shah.

The Deadly Trackers **1973 (PG)** If gorey oaters are your thing, this one's definitely for you; if not, make tracks. Harris plays a spiteful sheriff who heads south of the border to get his pound of flesh from the outlaws who slew his family in a bank robbery. Overlong revenge-o-rama based on Samuel Fuller's short story, "Riata"; might have been bearable if Fuller hadn't been bumped from the director's chair (as it is, he and other contributors refused to be listed in the credits). **104m/C VHS.** Richard Harris, Rod Taylor, Al Lettieri, Neville Brand, William Smith, Paul Benjamin, Pedro Armendariz Jr.; ***D:*** Barry Shear.

The Deadly Trap *Death Scream* **1971 (PG)** Confusing thriller that couldn't. Dunaway is the mentally unstable wife of an ex-spy. His former employers have targeted him with plans to use her and her fragile state-of-mind to their advantage. **96m/C VHS.** *FR IT* Faye Dunaway, Frank Langella, Barbara Parkins, Maurice Ronet; ***D:*** Rene Clement.

Deadly Twins woof! **1985** After being beaten and gang-raped, twin sister singers are out to get revenge. Nothing new here; don't waste your time. **87m/C VHS.** Audrey Landers, Judy Landers, Ellie Russell, Wayne Allison; ***D:*** Joe Oaks.

Deadly Vengeance **1981** It's strictly low budget as the mob kills Jones's boyfriend, forcing her to mount a vengeful but inexpensive offensive against the crime syndicate's bigwigs. **84m/C VHS.** Grace Jones, Alan Marlowe, Arthur Roberts; ***D:*** Amin Q. Chaudhri.

Deadly Voyage ½ **1996 (R)** In 1992, nine Ghanaian dockworkers are discovered hiding aboard a Ukrainian freighter bound for New York. Since each stowaway would cost the shipping company a hefty fine, sadistic first officer Ion (Pertwee) orders them killed. Only one, Kingsley (Epps), manages to survive and reveal the truth. **92m/C VHS.** Omar Epps, Sean Pertwee, Joss Ackland, David Suchet, Jean LaMarre, Andrew Divoff; ***D:*** John MacKenzie; ***C:*** Stuart Urban; ***M:*** John Scott. **CABLE**

Deadly Weapon **1988 (PG-13)** It's a bit of nerdish wish fulfillment when 15-year-old geek Eastman finds a secret anti-matter weapon conveniently lost by the military in an Arizona stream. You won't like the kid any more than you'll like the story of this low rent boy-gets-back-at-bullies sci fi fiasco. **89m/C VHS.** Rodney Eastman, Gary Frank, Michael Horse, Ed Nelson, Kim Walker; ***D:*** Michael Miner; ***W:*** Michael Miner; ***C:*** James L. Carter.

Deadly Weapons **1970 (R)** Chesty Morgan, she of the 73-inch bustline, takes on the mob using only her Godgiven abilities. One of Joe Bob Brigg's "Sleaziest Movies in the History of the World" series, and he is welcome to it. **90m/C VHS, DVD.** Chesty Morgan, Harry (Herbert Streicher) Reems, Greg Reynolds, Saul Meth, Phillip Stahl, Mitchell Fredericks, Denise Purcell, John McMohon; ***D:*** Doris Wishman; ***W:*** J.J. Kendall; ***C:*** Juan Fernandez.

Deadman's Curve **1978** Decent bio pic detailing the lives of Jan Berry and Dean Torrence who, as Jan and Dean, started the surf music wave only to wipe out after an almost-fatal car wreck. Shows how they deal with and recover from the tragedy. **100m/C VHS.** Richard Hatch, Bruce Davison, Pamela Bellwood, Susan Sullivan, Dick Clark, Wolfman Jack; ***D:*** Richard Compton. **TV**

Deadtime Stories ½ **1986** Mother Goose it's not. Fairy tales "Little Red Riding Hood" and "Goldilocks and the Three Bears," among others, are presented like you've never before seen them—as low-budget horror tales. **93m/C VHS.** Michael Mesner, Brian DePersia, Scott Valentine, Phyllis Craig, Melissa Leo, Nicole Picard; ***D:*** Jeffrey Delman.

Deadwood ½ **1965** In the untamed West, a young cowboy is mistaken for the notorious Billy the Kid. **100m/C VHS.** Arch Hall Jr., Jack Lester, Melissa Morgan, Robert Dix; ***D:*** James Landis; ***C:*** Vilmos Zsigmond.

Deadwood Pass **1933** Below-standard fare has Tyler rescuing Monti more times than seems reasonable. Monti was once an all-around helper to W.C. Fields. **62m/B VHS.** Tom Tyler, Alice Dahl, Wally Wales, Buffalo Bill Jr., Lafe (Lafayette) McKee, Bud Osborne, Charles "Slim" Whitaker, Charlotte (Carlotta) Monti; ***D:*** J(ohn) P(aterson) McGowan.

Deal of a Lifetime **1999 (PG)** It's a deal that's too good to be true, of course. Loser teen Henry (Goorjian) is tempted to sell his soul to the Devil's agent, Jerry (Pollak), in order to get a date with the school's most popular babe (Appleby). **95m/C VHS, DVD.** Kevin Pollak, Michael Goorjian, Shiri Appleby, Jennifer Rubin; ***D:*** Paul Levine; ***W:*** Katharine R. Sloan; ***C:*** Denise Brassard; ***M:*** Amotz Plessner. **VIDEO**

Deal of the Century **1983 (PG)** A first-rate hustler and his cohorts sell second-rate weapons to third-world nations; unfortunately, their latest deal threatens to blow up in their faces—literally. **99m/C VHS.** Chevy Chase, Sigourney Weaver, Gregory Hines, Richard Libertini, Wallace Shawn; ***D:*** William Friedkin; ***W:*** Paul Brickman.

Dealers ½ **1989 (R)** Two money-hungry stock traders mix business and pleasure, then set their sights on one final all or nothing score. **92m/C VHS.** *GB* Paul Guilfoyle, Rebecca DeMornay, Paul McGann, Derrick O'Connor; ***D:*** Colin Bucksey; ***W:*** Andrew Maclear; ***C:*** Peter Sinclair.

Dean Koontz's Black River *Black River* **2001 (PG)** Novelist/screenwriter Bo Aikens (Mohr) is in need of a little creative inspiration and leaves Hollywood for the bucolic friendliness of the small town of Black River. Then Bo discovers the town is monitored by video cameras and he begins to get weird phone calls and notices an SUV tailing him. He can't escape unless he figures out the community's sinister secrets (which unfortunately turn out to be lame-o). **87m/C VHS, DVD.** Jay Mohr, Lisa Edelstein, Ann Cusack, Ron Canada, Stephen Tobolowsky; ***D:*** Jeff Bleckner; ***W:*** Daniel Taplitz; ***C:*** John Bartley. **TV**

Dean Koontz's Mr. Murder *Mr. Murder* **1998 (R)** Marty Stillwater (Baldwin) is a successful mystery writer and family man who discovers that he has a killer clone. Seems industrialist Drew Oslett Jr. (Church) managed to screwup in the biotech lab and now there's a bloodthirsty Marty lookalike named Alfie, who decides he wants Marty's life. Meanwhile, everyone thinks Marty is going crazy. **132m/C VHS, DVD.** Stephen Baldwin, Thomas Haden Church, Julie Warner, Bill Smitrovich, James Coburn, Don Hood, Dan Lauria; ***D:*** Dick Lowry; ***W:*** Stephen Tolkin; ***C:*** Greg Gardiner; ***M:*** Louis Febre. **TV**

Dear Boys **1980** A stylized film of sexual fantasies and romance between a moody writer and a carefree young man who relentlessly pursues excitement. Based on the novel by Gerald Reve. **90m/C VHS.** *NL* Hugo Netsers, Hans Dagelet, Bill Van Dijk, Albert Mol; ***D:*** Paul de Lussanet.

Dear Brigitte **1965** A young American kid ("Lost in Space" tyke Mumy) writes a love letter to Brigitte Bardot and travels to Paris to meet her in person. Based on the novel "Erasmus with Freckles" by John Haase. **100m/C VHS.** James Stewart, Billy Mumy, Glynis Johns, Fabian, Cindy Carol, John Williams, Jack Kruschen, Brigitte Bardot, Ed Wynn, Alice Pearce; ***D:*** Henry Koster; ***W:*** Hal Kanter.

Dear Dead Delilah ½ **1972** Moorehead is Delilah, the matriarch of a southern family, who is on her deathbed. Her heirs are fighting to the bitter—and bloody—end to be the first to find Delilah's money, buried somewhere on her land. **90m/C VHS.** Agnes Moorehead, Will Geer, Michael Ansara, Patricia Carmichael, Dennis Patrick; ***D:*** John Farris.

Dear Detective *Dear Inspector; Tendre Poulet* **1977** Comedy/thriller/romance finds female police inspector (Girandot) investigating a murder while romancing a somewhat pompous professor of Greek (Noiret). French with subtitles. **105m/C VHS.** *FR* Annie Girardot, Philippe Noiret, Catherine Alric, Guy Marchand, Simone Renant; ***D:*** Philippe de Broca; ***W:*** Philippe de Broca, Michel Audiard; ***M:*** Georges Delerue.

Dear Detective **1978** Vaccaro is the head of the police homicide unit who is trying to track down the killer of several politicians. In the midst of her investigation, she falls for an old friend, a professor of Greek language. Based on a French TV series. **90m/C VHS.** Brenda Vaccaro, Arlen Dean Snyder, Michael MacRae, John Dennis Johnston, Jack Ging, Stephen McNally, M. Emmet Walsh, Constance Forslund, R.G. Armstrong; ***D:*** Dean Hargrove; ***M:*** Georges Delerue. **TV**

Dear God **1996 (PG)** TV vets Marshall (director) and Kinnear team up for a sappy and predictable "Miracle on Melrose," a little piece of Capra-corn that feels like it lodged in your tooth. Cynical con man Tom (Kinnear) goes to work for the post office and gets stuck with a group of misfits at the Dead Letter Office, sorting mail for the likes of Elvis, Santa, and God. Even though he's merely working the ultimate angle for easy cash, the oddball team of postal workers think he's on a mission from the Lord and joins him in aiding the needy. Most unbelievable is the premise that single mom and love interest Gloria (Pitillo) can give the hardened criminal an instant psychological makeover. Broadly characterized supporting cast, including Conway and Metcalf, suffer at the hands of script. Strictly a star vehicle for Kinnear's budding movie career, it won't help. It also won't do anything for Marshall's downward-spiraling reputation. Ironic cameo from Christopher Darden as a reporter outside the courtroom, and Marshall himself as Postmaster General. **112m/C VHS.** Greg Kinnear, Laurie Metcalf, Maria Pitillo, Hector Elizondo, Tim Conway, Roscoe Lee Browne, Jon Seda, Anna Maria Horsford, Donal Logue, Nancy Marchand, Larry Miller, Rue McClanahan, Toby Huss, Jack Klugman; ***Cameos:*** Garry Marshall; ***D:*** Garry Marshall; ***W:*** Ed Kaplan, Warren Leight; ***C:*** Charles Minsky.

Dear Murderer **1947** A husband suspects his wife of having an affair, and devises an ingenious, if complicated, trap for her. Inspired performances from the leads, but the plot is grim and confusing. **94m/B VHS.** *GB* Eric Portman, Greta Gynt, Dennis Price, Jack Warner, Maxwell Reed, Hazel Court, Andrew Crawford, Jane Hylton; ***D:*** Arthur Crabtree.

Dear Wife ½ **1949** Comedy about those ties that bind. Even though her father is runnning for reelection to the State Senate, Freeman wants her brother-in-law (Holden) to run against him. Sequel to "Dear Ruth." **88m/B VHS.** William Holden, Joan Caulfield, Edward Arnold, Billy DeWolfe, Mona Freeman; ***D:*** Richard Haydn.

Death and Desire **1997 (R)** Fashion photographer Jeff Reed isn't tempted by the beautiful models he shoots because he's happily married. But when his wife is killed in an accident, the vulnerable Jeff becomes the target of fashion mag editor, Lynn, who desperately wants to offer him comfort. Too desperately. Soon Lynn's obsessed and Jeff's fighting for his life. Unrated version runs 88 minutes. **84m/C VHS.** Tane McClure, Tim Abell, Jennifer Burton. **VIDEO**

Death and the Maiden **1994 (R)** Former political prisoner and torture victim (Weaver) turns the tables on the man she believes was her tormentor 15 years before. Pressing her civil rights lawyer husband (Wilson) into duty as defense attorney, she becomes prosecutor, judge, and jury. The accused (Kingsley) learns the dangers of picking up stranded motorists, as he is bound, gagged, and roughed up by the now empowered and vengeful Paulina. Tense, claustrophobic political thriller features a talented ensemble both on screen and behind the scenes. From the Ariel Dorfman play. **103m/C VHS.** Sigourney Weaver, Ben Kingsley, Stuart Wilson; ***D:*** Roman Polanski; ***W:*** Rafael Yglesias, Ariel Dorfman; ***C:*** Tonino Delli Colli; ***M:*** Wojciech Kilar.

The Death Artist ½ **1995 (R)** Struggling busboy and would-be artist Walter Paisley (Hall) finds fame creating sculptures from dead bodies. Gruesome plot is a remake of Corman's 1960 "A Bucket of Blood" but the same premise was done much better with Vincent Price in 1953's "House of Wax." **79m/C VHS.** Anthony Michael Hall, Darcy Demoss, Shadoe Stevens, Paul Bartel, Mink Stole; ***D:*** Michael James McDonald; ***W:*** Michael James McDonald, Brendan Broderick; ***C:*** Christopher Baffa; ***M:*** David Wurst, Eric Wurst.

Death at Love House ½ **1975** A screenwriter becomes obsessed when he is hired to write the life story of a long dead silent movie queen. Filmed at the Harold Lloyd estate. **74m/C VHS.** Robert Wagner, Kate Jackson, Sylvia Sidney, Joan Blondell, John Carradine; ***D:*** E.W. Swackhamer. **TV**

Death Be Not Proud **1975** Based on the book by John Gunther detailing the valiant battle fought by his son against the brain tumor that took his life at the age of 17. Wonderfully acted by the three principals, especially Alexander, this film leaves us feeling hopeful despite its subject. **74m/C VHS.** Arthur Hill, Robby Benson, Jane Alexander, Linden Chiles, Wendy Phillips; ***D:*** Donald Wrye. **TV**

Death Becomes Her **1992 (PG-13)** Aging actress Streep will do anything to stay young and beautiful, especially when childhood rival Hawn shows up, 200 pounds lighter and out to revenge the loss of her fiance, Streep's henpecked hubby. Doing anything arrives in the form of a potion that stops the aging process (and keeps her alive forever). Watch for the hilarious party filled with dead celebrities who all look as good as the day they died. Great special effects and fun performances by Streep and Hawn playing their glamour-girl roles to the hilt add merit to this biting commentary on Hollywood's obsession with beauty and youth. **105m/C VHS, DVD, Wide.** Mary Ellen Trainor, Meryl Streep, Bruce Willis, Goldie Hawn, Isabella Rossellini, Sydney Pollack, Michael Caine, Ian Ogilvy, Adam Storke, Nancy Fish, Alaina Reed Hall, Michelle Johnson, Mimi Kennedy, Jonathan Silverman; ***Cameos:*** Fabio Lanzoni; ***D:*** Robert Zemeckis; ***W:*** Martin Donovan, David Koepp; ***C:*** Dean Cundey; ***M:*** Alan Silvestri. Oscars '92: Visual FX.

Death Before Dishonor ½ **1987 (R)** Formula actioner stars Dryer as a tough Marine sergeant who battles ruthless Middle Eastern terrorists after they slaughter his men and kidnap his commanding officer (Keith). **95m/C VHS, DVD, Wide.** Fred (John F.) Dryer, Brian Keith, Joanna Pacula, Paul Winfield; ***D:*** Terry J. Leonard; ***W:*** John Gatliff; ***C:*** Don Burgess; ***M:*** Brian May.

Death Benefit ½ **1996 (PG-13)** Corporate attorney Steven Keeney (Horton) takes on the case of Lou Anne Wilkins (Ruscio), who's having trouble getting her insurance company to cover the funeral expenses for her teenaged daughter Melissa, who died in a fall. The more Steven investigates, the more suspicious Melissa's death becomes—and he discovers money is the root of all evil. Based on the book "Death Benefit" by David Heilbroner. **89m/C VHS.** Peter Horton, Carrie Snodgress, Wendy Makkena, Elizabeth Ruscio, Belita Morena, Lee DeBroux; ***D:*** Mark Piznarski; ***W:*** Philip Rosenberg; ***C:*** Christopher Taylor. **CABLE**

Death Blow ½ **1987 (R)** The victims of a violent rapist team together to stop the criminal after he repeatedly skirts conviction. **90m/C VHS.** Martin Landau, Frank Stallone, Jerry Van Dyke, Terry Moore, Henry Darrow, Jack Carter, Peter Lapis, Don Swayze, Donna Denton; ***D:*** Raphael Nussbaum.

Death by Dialogue **1988 (R)** Muddled story of some teenagers who discover an old film script from a project never produced because it was haunted by tragic accidents. **90m/C VHS.** Laura Albert, Ken Sagoes; ***D:*** Tom Dewier.

Death by Prescription 🦴½ 198? After adjusting his patients' wills to benefit himself, an evil physician sees to their mysterious deaths. **75m/C VHS.** Timothy West, Nigel Davenport.

Death Challenge 🦴½ **1980** Gangs battle without weapons, motive or discretion in this kung fu extravaganza. **94m/C VHS.** Steve Leving, Susan Wong.

Death Chase 🦴½ **1987** An average Joe, just jogging down the street, is thrown into a desperate game of cat-and-mouse when a body lands at his feet. **86m/C VHS.** William Zipp, Paul Smith, Jack Starrett, Bainbridge Scott; ***D:*** David A. Prior.

Death Collector 🦴½ **1989 (R)** In the future when insurance companies run the world, if you don't pay your premium, you die. **90m/C VHS.** Daniel Chapman, Ruth (Coreen) Collins; ***D:*** Tom Gniazdowski.

Death Cruise 🦴½ **1974** The six winners of a free cruise find that there is a fatal catch to the prize in this made-for-TV movie. **74m/C VHS.** Kate Jackson, Celeste Holm, Tom Bosley, Edward Albert, Polly Bergen, Michael Constantine, Richard Long; ***D:*** Ralph Senensky.

The Death Curse of Tartu woof! **1966** Another aspiring cult classic. (Read: A low-budget flick so bad it's funny). Students accidentally disturb the burial ground of an Indian medicine man who comes to zombie-like life with a deadly prescription. **84m/C VHS, DVD.** Fred Pinero, Doug Hobart, Babette Sherrill, Mayra Christine, Bill Marcos, Sherman Hayes, Gary Holtz, Frank Weed; ***D:*** William Grefe; ***W:*** William Grefe; ***C:*** Julio Chavez; ***M:*** Al Greene, Al Jacobs.

Death Dreams 🦴🦴 **1992** Crista thinks she has a perfect life with her wealth, beautiful daughter Jennie, and handsome new husband George. Then Jennie tragically drowns. It appears to be an accident until Jennie contacts her mother from beyond the grave to tell what really happened. Is the tragedy turning Crista's mind or is there truly something sinister going on—something that involves George? Based on the novel by William Katz. **94m/C VHS.** Marg Helgenberger, Christopher Reeve, Fionnula Flanagan; ***D:*** Martin Donovan; ***W:*** Robert Glass. **CABLE**

Death Driver 🦴½ **1978** In order to make a comeback, a stuntman attempts to do a stunt that was responsible for ending his career ten years earlier. Obviously brave but none too smart. **93m/C VHS.** Earl Owensby, Mike Allen, Patty Shaw, Mary Ann Hearn; ***D:*** Jimmy Huston.

Death Drug 🦴½ **1983** Cliched alarmist film about a talented musician ruining his career by becoming addicted to the drug angel dust. **73m/C VHS.** Philip Michael Thomas, Vernee Watson-Johnson, Rosalind Cash; ***D:*** Oscar Williams.

Death Feud **1989** A man tries to save the woman he loves from the man who would destroy her and her former pimp. **98m/C VHS.** Karen Mayo Chandler, Chris Mitchum, Frank Stallone; ***D:*** Carl Monson.

Death Force 🦴½ **1978 (R)** When a Vietnam veteran comes to New York City, he becomes a hitman for the Mafia. **90m/C VHS.** Jayne Kennedy, Leon Isaac Kennedy, James Iglehart, Carmen Argenziano; ***D:*** Cirio H. Santiago.

Death from a Distance 🦴½ **1936** A reporter and a detective put the moves on a group of astronomers who may be responsible for a murder. **73m/B VHS.** Russell Hopton, Lola Lane, George F. Marion Sr., John St. Polis, Lee Kohlmar, Lew Kelly, Wheeler Oakman, Robert Frazer, Cornelius Keefe; ***D:*** Frank Strayer.

Death Games 🦴½ **1982** Two young men shooting a documentary about an influential music promoter ask too many wrong questions, causing the powers-that-be to want them out of the picture for good. **78m/C VHS.** Lou Brown, David Clendenning, Jennifer Cluff.

Death Goes to School 🦴🦴 **1953** A strangler is loose in a girl's school, and the music teacher has a hunch as to who it is. **65m/B VHS.** *GB* Barbara Murray, Gordon Jackson, Pamela Allan, Jane Aird, Beatrice Varley; ***D:*** Stephen Clarkson.

Death House 🦴½ **1988** Derek Keillor is on Death Row at Townsend State Prison when he discovers a plot to use inmates for scientific experiments in biological warfare. He decides the best way to get out is to volunteer, which means convincing the man who put him in prison that they're now on the same side. **92m/C VHS.** Dennis Cole, Anthony (Tony) Franciosa, Michael Pataki, John Saxon; ***D:*** John Saxon.

Death Hunt 🦴🦴 **1981 (R)** A man unjustly accused of murder pits his knowledge of the wilderness against the superior numbers of his pursuers. **98m/C VHS.** Charles Bronson, Lee Marvin, Ed Lauter, Andrew Stevens, Carl Weathers, Angie Dickinson; ***D:*** Peter Hunt; ***W:*** Mark Victor, Michael Grais.

Death in Brunswick 🦴🦴 *Nothing to Lose* **1990 (R)** Carl Fitzgerald (Neill) seems to be one of life's born losers—his wife's left him, his mother nags him, his house is falling apart, and he's unemployed. At least until he gets a job as a chef in a sleazy rock 'n' roll club and finds Sophie (Carides), the lovely barmaid, who just happens to be engaged to the club's owner. Of course, with Carl's luck, things go from bad to downright dangerous. Based on the novel by Boyd Oxlade. **106m/C VHS.** *AU* Sam Neill, Zoe Carides, Yvonne Lawley, Boris Brkic, John Clarke; ***D:*** John Ruane; ***W:*** John Ruane, Boyd Oxlade; ***C:*** Ellery Ryan.

Death in Deep Water 🦴🦴 **1974** A sensuous woman lures a man into a plot to kill her incredibly rich husband. **71m/C VHS.** Bradford Dillman, Suzan Farmer; ***D:*** James Ormerod; ***W:*** Brian Clemens. **TV**

A Death in the Family 🦴🦴½ **2002** Adaptation of James Agee's Pulitzer Prize-winning novel, set in Knoxville in 1915. Title tells you the tragedy that's about the befall the loving family of May (Gish) and Jay (Slattery) Follet when Jay is killed in an auto accident. It's up to the grieving May to cope and to tell their 7-year-old son Rufus (Wolff) that his father is dead. **90m/C VHS.** Annabeth Gish, John Slattery, James Cromwell, Austin Wolff, Kathleen Chalfant, Bill Raymond, David Alford, Christopher Strand; ***D:*** Gil(bert) Cates; ***W:*** Robert W. Lenski; ***C:*** Stephen M. Katz; ***M:*** Charles Fox. **TV**

Death in the Garden 🦴🦴 *La Mort en Ce Jardin; Evil Eden* **1956** Surreal film, filled with symbolism, about a group of French people, living in a South American settlement, who must flee a riot between soldiers and striking miners. Local adventurer, Chark (Marchal), agrees to lead them to safety but their trek through the jungle is fraught with peril (and not just from the animal life). French with subtitles. **90m/C VHS.** *MX FR* Georges Marchal, Simone Signoret, Charles Vanel, Michele Girardon, Michel Piccoli, Tito Junco; ***D:*** Luis Bunuel; ***W:*** Luis Bunuel, Luis Alcoriza, Raymond Queneau; ***C:*** Jorge Stahl Jr.; ***M:*** Paul Misraki.

Death in Venice 🦴🦴🦴½ *Morte a Venezia* **1971 (PG)** A lush, decadent adaptation of the Thomas Mann novella about a aging, jaded, and dying composer Gustav von Aschenbach (Bogarde)—here suggested to be Gustav Mahler—who is plagued by fears that he can no longer feel anything. Instead, he becomes tragically obsessed with ideal beauty as personified in the young boy, Tadzio (Andresen). Visconti uses Mahler's 3rd and 5th symphonies to haunting effect. **124m/C VHS.** *IT* Dirk Bogarde, Mark Burns, Bjorn Andresen, Marisa Berenson, Silvana Mangano; ***D:*** Luchino Visconti; ***W:*** Luchino Visconti, Nicola Badalucco; ***C:*** Pasqualino De Santis; ***M:*** Gustav Mahler.

Death Is Called Engelchen 🦴🦴🦴½ *For We Too Do Not Forgive* **1963** An influential, important work of the Czech new wave. A survivor of WWII remembers his experiences with the SS leader Engelchen in a series of flashbacks. In Czech with subtitles. **111m/B VHS.** *CZ* ***D:*** Jan Kadar, Elmar Klos.

Death Journey 🦴½ **1976 (R)** Producer and director Williamson portrays private eye Jesse Crowder, hired by the New York D.A. to escort a key witness cross-country. A regular Williamsonfest. **90m/C VHS.** Fred Williamson, D'Urville Martin, Bernie Kuby, Heidi Dobbs, Stephanie Faulkner; ***D:*** Fred Williamson.

The Death Kiss 🦴🦴½ **1933** Creepy thriller about eerie doings at a major Hollywood film studio where a sinister killer does away with his victims while a cast-of-thousands movie spectacular is in production. **72m/B VHS, 8mm.** Bela Lugosi, David Manners, Adrienne Ames, Edward Van Sloan, Vince Barnett; ***D:*** Edwin L. Marin.

Death Kiss 🦴½ **1977 (R)** When a man hires a psychopath to murder his wife, his plan doesn't proceed exactly as expected. **90m/C VHS.** Larry Daniels, Dorothy Moore.

Death Machine 🦴½ **1995 (R)** New company exec Hayden Cale (Pouget) uncovers questionable scientific project at weapons technology company and scientist in charge Jack Dante (Dourif) decides to get even by testing his death machine, which works by sensing fear, in corporate headquarters. **99m/C VHS, DVD.** Brad Dourif, Ely Pouget, William Hootkins; ***D:*** Stephen Norrington; ***W:*** Stephen Norrington; ***C:*** John de Borman.

Death Machines 🦴½ **1976 (R)** Young karate student must face the "Death Machines," a team of deadly assassins who are trained to kill on command. **93m/C VHS.** Ron Marchini, Michael Chong, Joshua Johnson; ***D:*** Paul Kyriazi.

Death Magic 🦴½ **1992** A group of five ceremonial magicians performs a spell to bring someone back from the dead, but the man they bring back, a soldier from the Civil War, decides to go on a vicious murdering spree to kill the descendants of the people who convicted him of murder in 1875. A suspensful first entry from director Clinco. **93m/C VHS.** Anne Coffrey, Keith DeGreen, Jack Dunlap, Danielle Frons, Norman Stone; ***D:*** Paul E. Clinco; ***W:*** Paul E. Clinco.

Death Mask 🦴🦴½ **1998** Screenwriter, executive producer, and star James Best plays Wilbur Johnson, a vengeful carnival worker who was abused and disfigured as a child. He becomes friends with Angel (Linnea Quigley), a sideshow dancer. After hearing Wilbur's story, she takes him to the swamp, where he meets a witch (Brigitte Hill), who gives him the titular "Death Mask." It causes violent and painful death to Wilbur's enemies when he dons the mask, so Wilbur goes on a killing spree. Then it's up to Angel to convince him to stop. Best hams it up in every scene and Quigley proves that she's still willing to take her clothes off whenever necessary. The film doesn't aim to be anything more than campy fun, and on that point, it delivers. **97m/C DVD.** James Best, Linnea Quigley, Brigitte Hill; ***D:*** Steve Latshaw; ***W:*** James Best.

Death Match 🦴 **1994 (R)** John Larson gives up kickboxing after a tragedy but when his friend disappears, John is forced into a fighting bout with no rules and only one outcome. **90m/C VHS.** Matthias Hues, Martin Kove, Ian Jacklin, Nick (Nicholas, Niko) Hill, Renee Ammann; ***D:*** Joe Coppoletta.

The Death Merchant 🦴 **1991** Foundering attempt at a nuclear thriller. A modern mad man hopes to sell a computer chip to third world countries but is thwarted by a secret agent. Confusing, illogical plot highlighted by mediocre performances. **90m/C VHS.** Lawrence Tierney, Martina Castle, Melody Munyan, Monika Schnarre; ***D:*** James R. Winburn; ***W:*** Kari Holman.

Death Nurse 🦴🦴 **1987** Fresh from "Crazy Fat Ethel II," aspiring Queen of Camp Alden takes takes up residence in a health care establishment, much to the dismay of the patients who give up their lives in exchange for their money. **80m/C VHS.** Priscilla Alden, Michael Flood; ***D:*** Nick (Steve Millard) Phillips.

Death of a Bureaucrat 🦴🦴🦴 *La Muerte de un Burocrata* **1966** A Cuban hero dies, and in tribute, the Communist government buries him with his union card. His widow, however, needs the card in order to collect a pension, and she enlists her nephew's help to retrieve it. The nephew soon finds himself buried in red tape, and digs himself in ever-deeper as he seeks to disinter his late uncle. A wry satire of the communist bureaucracy in Cuba, brimming with comedic tributes to Harold Lloyd, Buster Keaton and Laurel & Hardy. Alea's film was only briefly released in 1966 and was promptly banned, eventually finding its way to the U.S. in 1979. In Spanish with English subtitles. **87m/B VHS.** *CU* Salvador Wood, Silvia Planas, Manuel Estanillo, Gaspar de Santelices, Carlos Ruiz de la Tejera, Omar Alfonso, Ricardo Suarez, Luis Romay, Elsa Montero; ***D:*** Tomas Gutierrez Alea; ***W:*** Tomas Gutierrez Alea, Ramon Suarez; ***C:*** Ramon Suarez; ***M:*** Leo Brower.

Death of a Centerfold 🦴🦴 **1981** Drama based on the life and tragic death of Playboy model and actress Dorothy Stratten. More effectively handled in Bob Fosse's "Star 80." **96m/C VHS.** Jamie Lee Curtis, Bruce Weitz, Robert Reed, Mitchell Ryan, Bibi Besch; ***D:*** Gabrielle Beaumont.

Death of a Gunfighter 🦴🦴 **1969 (PG)** A western town courting eastern investors and bankers seeks a way to kill their ex-gunslinger sheriff. **94m/C VHS.** Richard Widmark, Lena Horne, Carroll O'Connor, John Saxon, Larry Gates; ***D:*** Donald Siegel; ***W:*** Robert Totten.

Death of a Salesman 🦴🦴🦴½ **1986** A powerful adaptation of the famous Arthur Miller play. Hoffman won an Emmy (as did Malkovich) for his stirring portrayal of Willy Loman, the aging salesman who realizes he's past his prime and tries to come to grips with the life he's wasted and the family he's neglected. Reid also turns in a fine performance as his long-suffering wife. **135m/C VHS.** Dustin Hoffman, John Malkovich, Charles Durning, Stephen Lang, Kate Reid, Louis Zorich; ***D:*** Volker Schlondorff; ***C:*** Michael Ballhaus; ***M:*** Alex North. **TV**

Death of a Scoundrel 🦴🦴½ *Loves of a Scoundrel* **1956** A womanizing entrepreneur is murdered and the culprit could be any one of his many jealous romantic conquests. **119m/B VHS.** George Sanders, Zsa Zsa Gabor, Yvonne De Carlo, Victor Jory; ***D:*** Charles Martin; ***M:*** Max Steiner.

Death of a Soldier 🦴🦴 **1985 (R)** During WWII, the uneasy U.S.-Australian alliance explodes when a psychotic American soldier murders three Melbourne women. The lawyer hired to defend him has to fight political as well as legal influences. Based on a true story. **93m/C VHS.** *AU* James Coburn, Reb Brown, Maurie Field, Belinda Darey; ***D:*** Philippe Mora.

The Death of Adolf Hitler 🦴🦴½ **1984** Depicts Hitler's last ten days in an underground bunker. Drug-addled, suicidal, and Eva Braun-haunted, he receives the news of the fall of the Third Reich. While the film avoids cliche, it lacks emotional depth. **107m/C VHS.** *GB* Frank Finlay, Caroline Mortimer; ***D:*** Rex Firlin. **TV**

Death of an Angel 🦴½ **1986** When her crippled daughter runs away to join a cult in Mexico, a recently ordained priest (Bedelia) follows her, only to become caught up herself with the leader of the group. **95m/C VHS.** Bonnie Bedelia, Nick Mancuso, Pamela Ludwig, Alex Colon; ***D:*** Petru Popescu.

The Death of Richie 🦴🦴 *Richie* **1976** Gazzara does a fine job as a father driven to kill his drug-addicted teenage son, portrayed by Benson. Occasionally lapses into melodrama, but all-in-all a decent adaptation of Thomas Thompson's book "Richie," which was based on a true story. **97m/C VHS.** Ben Gazzara, Robby Benson, Eileen Brennan, Clint Howard; ***D:*** Paul Wendkos. **TV**

Death of the Incredible Hulk 🦴½ **1990** Scientist David Banner's new job just may provide the clues for stopping his transformation into the monstrous Incredible Hulk. But first there are terrorists after the Hulk who need to be defeated and Banner's new romance to contend with. **96m/C VHS.** Bill Bixby, Lou Ferrigno, Elizabeth (Ward) Gracen, Philip Sterling; ***D:*** Bill Bixby. **TV**

Death on the Nile 🦴🦴½ **1978 (PG)** Agatha Christie's fictional detective, Hercule Poirot, is called upon to interrupt his vacation to uncover who killed an heiress aboard a steamer cruising down the Nile. Ustinov's first stint as the Belgian sleuth. Anthony Powell's costume design won an Oscar. **135m/C VHS, DVD, Wide.** *GB* Peter Ustinov, Jane Birkin, Lois Chiles, Bette Davis, Mia Farrow, David Niven, Olivia Hussey, Angela Lansbury, Jack Warden, Maggie Smith, George Kennedy, Simon MacCorkindale, Harry Andrews, Jon Finch; ***D:*** John Guillermin; ***W:*** Anthony Shaffer; ***C:*** Jack Cardiff; ***M:*** Nino Rota. Oscars '78: Costume Des.; Natl. Bd. of Review '78: Support. Actress (Lansbury).

Death Promise 🦴 **1978 (R)** Ho-hum excuse for a horror flick has murderous landlord trying to evict his tenants using whatever means are necessary. **90m/C VHS.** Charles Bonet; ***D:*** Robert Warmflash; ***W:*** Norbert Albertson Jr.

Death Race 2000 🦴🦴½ **1975 (R)** In the 21st century, five racing car contenders challenge the national champion of a cross country race in which drivers score points by killing pedestrians. Gory fun. Based on the 1956 story by Ib Melchior, and followed by "Deathsport." **80m/C VHS, DVD.** David Carradine, Simone Griffeth, Sylvester Stallone, Mary Woronov, Roberta Collins, Martin Kove, Louisa Moritz, John Landis, Don Steele; ***D:*** Paul Bartel; ***W:*** Charles B. Griffith, Robert Thom; ***C:*** Tak Fujimoto; ***M:*** Paul Chihara. **TV**

Death Rage 🦴½ **1977 (R)** A hitman comes out of retirement to handle the toughest assignment he has ever faced: search for and kill the man who murdered his brother. He finds out he's the victim of a Mafia doublecross. **92m/C VHS.** *IT* Yul Brynner, Martin Balsam; ***D:*** Anthony (Antonio Margheriti) Dawson.

Death Ray woof! **19??** It's a race to the finish as terrorists threaten to unleash the world's most powerful weapon. A very poor James Bond rip-off. Baldanello used the pseudonym Frank G. Carroll. **93m/C VHS.** Gordon Scott; ***D:*** Gianfranco Baldanello.

Death Ray 2000 🦴½ *T.R. Sloane* **1981** Bondian superspy T.R. Sloane must search out the whereabouts of a stolen military device that could kill all life on Earth. TV pilot for the series "A Man Called Sloane." **100m/C VHS.** Robert F. Logan, Ann Turkel, Maggie Cooper, Dan O'Herlihy; ***D:*** Lee H. Katzin. **TV**

Death Rides the Plains 🦴🦴 **1944** Western with a twist. A man lures prospective buyers to his ranch, kills them, and steals their money. It's up to our heroes to ride to the rescue. **53m/B VHS.** Robert "Bob" Livingston, Al "Fuzzy" St. John, Nica Doret, Ray Bennett; ***D:*** Sam Newfield.

Death Rides the Range 🦴½ **1940** Russian spies start a range war as a cover for an operation to pipe helium off a ranch and over the border. Maynard, an undercover FBI agent posing as a cowboy, is out to stop them. **58m/B VHS.** Ken Maynard, Fay McKenzie, Ralph Peters, Julian Rivero, Charles "Blackie" King, John Elliott, Bud Osborne; ***D:*** Sam Newfield.

Death Ring 🦴 **1993 (R)** Basic action/martial arts tale about three men who must battle the bad guys to ensure their own survival. **91m/C VHS.** Mike Norris, Chad McQueen, Don Swayze, Billy Drago, Isabel Glasser; ***D:*** Robert J. Kizer; ***W:*** George T. LeBrun.

Death Row Diner 🦴½ **1988** A movie mogul, executed for a crime he didn't commit, is brought back to life by a freak electrical storm. Nothing will stop him from exacting revenge. **90m/C VHS.** Jay Richardson, Michelle (McClellan) Bauer, John Content, Tom Schell, Dennis Mooney, Frank Sarcinello Sr., Dana Mason; ***D:*** B. Dennis Wood.

Death Scream 🦴🦴 *Street Kill* **1975** Drama based on the New York murder of Kitty Genovese, whose cries for help while being assaulted went ignored by her neighbors. Good casting but the pacing deteriorates. **100m/C VHS.** Raul Julia, John P. Ryan, Lucie Arnaz, Ed Asner, Art Carney, Diahann Carroll, Kate Jackson, Cloris Leachman, Tina Louise, Nancy Walker, Eric (Hans Gudegast) Braeden, Allyn Ann McLerie, Tony Dow, Sally Kirkland, Helen Hunt; ***D:*** Richard T. Heffron; ***W:*** Stirling Silliphant. **TV**

Death Screams 🦴 **1983 (R)** Attractive college coeds have a party and get hacked to pieces for their troubles by a machete-wielding maniac. **88m/C VHS.** Susan Kiger, Jennifer Chase, Jody Kay, William T. Hicks, Martin Tucker; ***D:*** David Nelson; ***W:*** Paul Elliot; ***M:*** Dee Barton.

Death Sentence 🦴½ *Murder One* **1974** When a woman juror on a murder case finds out that the wrong man is on trial, she is stalked by the real killer. **74m/C VHS, DVD.** Cloris Leachman, Laurence Luckinbill, Nick Nolte, William Schallert; ***D:*** E.W. Swackhamer; ***M:*** Laurence Rosenthal. **TV**

Death Ship 🦴 **1980 (R)** A luxury liner is destroyed by an ancient, mysterious freighter on open seas, leaving the survivors to confront the ghost ship's inherent evil in this slow-going horror flick. **91m/C VHS.** *GB CA* George Kennedy, Richard Crenna, Nick Mancuso, Sally Ann Howes, Saul Rubinek, Kate Reid, Victoria Burgoyne, Danny Higham, Jennifer McKinney; ***D:*** Alvin Rakoff; ***W:*** John Robins; ***C:*** Rene Verzier.

Death Shot 🦴 **1973** Two plainclothes detectives (who seem just as sleazy as the criminals they're trying to bust) try to break up a drug ring and find that, with a little coercion, their best sources of information are the pimps and junkies they want to stop. Senseless attempt to make an action pic. **90m/C VHS.** Richard C. Watt, Frank Himes; ***D:*** Mitch Brown.

Death Spa woof! **1987 (R)** A health club is possessed by the spirit of a vengeful woman. The fitness craze takes on a campy new twist. **87m/C VHS.** William Bumiller, Brenda Bakke, Merritt Butrick; ***D:*** Michael Fischa.

Death Sport 🦴🦴 **1978 (R)** In this sequel to the cult hit "Death Race 2000," a group of humans play a game of death in the year 3000. The object is to race cars and kill as many competitors as possible. Not as good as the original, but still watchable. **83m/C VHS, DVD.** David Carradine, Claudia Jennings, Richard Lynch, William (Bill) Smithers, Will Walker, David McLean, Jesse Vint; ***D:*** Henry (Nicholas Niciphor) Suso, Allan Arkush, Nicholas Niciphor; ***W:*** Henry (Nicholas Niciphor) Suso, Donald Stewart, Nicholas Niciphor; ***C:*** Gary Graver; ***M:*** Andrew Stein.

The Death Squad 🦴½ **1973** A police commissioner hires an ex-cop to find a group of vigilante cops who are behind a series of gangland-style executions. Good cast, though that's about all this flick has got going for it. **74m/C VHS.** Robert Forster, Melvyn Douglas, Michelle Phillips, Mark Goddard, Bert Remsen, Claude Akins; ***D:*** Harry Falk. **TV**

Death Stalk 🦴½ **1974** Dream vacation turns nightmarish for two couples when the wives are taken hostage by several escaped convicts. **90m/C VHS.** Vince Edwards, Vic Morrow, Anjanette Comer, Robert Webber, Carol Lynley, Neville Brand, Norman Fell; ***D:*** Robert Day. **TV**

Death Takes a Holiday 🦴🦴🦴 **1934** Death (March) is bored and wonders why humans fear him so much. He takes on human form, pretending to be the handsome Prince Sirki, and becomes a guest of Italian nobleman, Duke Lambert (Standing). He bewilders most, except the lovely Grazia (Venable), who falls in love with him. And when she does, nothing dies because Death is also in love and not attending to business. But Death is also afraid to reveal his true self for fear of repelling her. Based on Alberto Casella's play and the inspiration for the bloated "Meet Joe Black." **79m/B VHS.** Fredric March, Evelyn Venable, Guy Standing, Katherine Alexander, Gail Patrick, Helen Westley, Kent Taylor, Edward Van Sloan; ***D:*** Mitchell Leisen; ***W:*** Maxwell Anderson, Gladys Lehman, Walter Ferris; ***C:*** Charles B(ryant) Lang Jr.

Death Target 🦴½ **1983** Three former mercenaries team up for one last mission that gets sidetracked when one of the soldiers-of-fortune falls for a worker with a habit. **72m/C VHS.** Jorge Montesi, Elaine Lakeman; ***D:*** Peter Hyams.

Death Tide 🦴🦴 **1958** Hoodlums pirate a ship full of diamonds in this story of death and crime on the high seas. **?m/C VHS.** Frank Silvera.

Death to Smoochy 🦴 **2002 (R)** DeVito-directed dark comedy follows a clash of the clowns: one good and one evil. Rainbow Randolph (Williams), is the corrupt, alcoholic star of a kiddie show fired over a bribery scandal and replaced by his polar opposite: Barney-esque purple rhino good-guy, Smoochy (Norton). Keener is the ruthless Kidsnet exec who takes orders from her fetid network boss (Stewart). Director DeVito doubles as a loathsome agent. Although Norton is proficient as the cloying, wide-eyed kiddie magnet and Williams clearly revels in ranting, this over-the-top to the point of ugliness revenge comedy's one note joke wears thin and behind the scenes kiddie show satire is way less subtle than it needs to be. **109m/C VHS, DVD.** *US* Robin Williams, Edward Norton, Catherine Keener, Danny DeVito, Jon Stewart, Harvey Fierstein, Michael Rispoli, Pam Ferris, Danny Woodburn, Vincent Schiavelli; ***D:*** Danny DeVito; ***W:*** Adam Resnick; ***C:*** Anastas Michos; ***M:*** David Newman.

Death Train 🦴½ **1979** Dead man seems to have been struck by a train, but clueless investigator can't figure out where the train came from. **96m/C VHS.** Hugh Keays-Byrne, Ingrid Mason, Max Meldrum; ***D:*** Igor Auzins.

Death Valley 🦴½ **1946** Greed turns gold prospectors in Death Valley against each other. **70m/C VHS.** Robert Lowery, Helen Gilbert, Sterling Holloway; ***D:*** Lew (Louis Friedlander) Landers.

Death Valley 🦴½ **1981 (R)** Good cast, lousy plot. Youngster (Billingsley) gets caught up with a psycho cowpoke while visiting mom in Arizona. **90m/C VHS.** Paul LeMat, Catherine Hicks, Peter Billingsley, Wilford Brimley, Edward Herrmann, Stephen McHattie; ***D:*** Dick Richards; ***C:*** Stephen Burum.

Death Valley Manhunt 🦴🦴 **1943** A marshal hired to protect a man's oil wells discovers that the company manager is keeping the profits for himself. **55m/B VHS.** Wild Bill Elliott, George "Gabby" Hayes, Anne Jeffreys; ***D:*** John English.

Death Valley Rangers 🦴½ **1944** The hero pretends to be an outlaw to expose a gang robbing gold-laden stagecoaches. **59m/B VHS.** Ken Maynard, Hoot Gibson, Bob Steele, Linda Brent, Kenneth Harlan; ***D:*** Robert Emmett Tansey.

Death Warmed Up 🦴½ **1985** A crazed brain surgeon turns ordinary people into bloodthirsty mutants, and a small group of young people travel to his secluded island to stop him. **83m/C VHS.** Michael Hurst, Margaret Umbers, David Letch; ***D:*** David Blyth.

Death Warrant 🦴🦴 **1990 (R)** Van Damme whams and bams a little less than usual in this cop-undercover-in-prison testosterone fest. As a Royal Canadian Mountie undercover in prison—where inmates are perishing under mysterious circumstances—the pectoral-perfect Muscles from Brussels is on the brink of adding two plus two when an inmate transferee threatens his cover. Contains the requisite gratuitous violence, prison bromide, and miscellaneous other Van Dammages. **111m/C VHS, DVD, Wide.** Jean-Claude Van Damme, Robert Guillaume, Cynthia Gibb, George Dickerson, Patrick Kilpatrick; ***D:*** Deran Sarafian; ***W:*** David S. Goyer; ***C:*** Russell Carpenter; ***M:*** Gary Chang.

Death Watch 🦴🦴🦴 **1980 (R)** In the future, media abuse is taken to an all time high as a terminally ill woman's last days are secretly filmed by a man with a camera in his head. Intelligent, adult science fiction with an excellent cast. **128m/C VHS.** *FR GE* Romy Schneider, Harvey Keitel, Harry Dean Stanton, Max von Sydow; ***D:*** Bertrand Tavernier; ***W:*** Bertrand Tavernier, David Rayfiel.

Death Weekend 🦴½ *House by the Lake* **1976** A woman is stalked by a trio of murderous, drunken hoodlums who seek to spoil her weekend. **89m/C VHS.** *CA* Brenda Vaccaro, Don Stroud, Chuck Shamata, Richard Ayres, Kyle Edwards; ***D:*** William Fruet.

Death Wish 🦴🦴½ **1974 (R)** Paul Kersey (Bronson) is a middle-aged businessman who turns vigilante after his wife and daughter are raped and left for dead by a gang of hoodlums (one is Goldblum in his film debut). He stalks the streets of New York seeking revenge on other muggers, pimps, and crooks, making the neighborhood safer for those less macho. Brosnan's his usual stoic self and the violence could be deemed excessive—certainly Brian Garfield, whose novel the film is based on, thought so. **93m/C VHS, DVD, Wide.** Charles Bronson, Vincent Gardenia, William Redfield, Hope Lange, Jeff Goldblum, Stuart Margolin, Olympia Dukakis; ***D:*** Michael Winner; ***W:*** Wendell Mayes; ***C:*** Arthur Ornitz; ***M:*** Herbie Hancock.

Death Wish 2 woof! **1982 (R)** Bronson recreates the role of Paul Kersey, an architect who takes the law into his own hands when his family is victimized once again. Extremely violent sequel to the successful 1974 movie. Followed by "Death Wish 3" (1985) and 4 (1987) in which Bronson continues to torture the street scum and the viewers as well. **89m/C VHS.** J.D. Cannon, Charles Bronson, Jill Ireland, Vincent Gardenia, Anthony (Tony) Franciosa; ***D:*** Michael Winner; ***M:*** Jimmy Page.

Death Wish 3 🦴½ **1985 (R)** Once again, Charles Bronson blows away the low lifes who have killed those who were dear to him and were spared in the first two films. **100m/C VHS.** Charles Bronson, Martin Balsam, Deborah Raffin, Ed Lauter, Alex Winter, Marina Sirtis; ***D:*** Michael Winner; ***M:*** Jimmy Page.

Death Wish 4: The Crackdown 🦴 **1987 (R)** The four-times-weary urban vigilante hits crack dealers this time, hard. **100m/C VHS.** Charles Bronson, John P. Ryan, Kay Lenz; ***D:*** J. Lee Thompson.

Death Wish 5: The Face of Death woof! **1994 (R)** Paul Kersey (Bronson) returns to vigilantism when his clothing manufacturer fiancee Olivia (Downs) has her business threatened by mobsters, one of whom turns out to be her sadistic ex (Parks). Bronson looks bored with the rehashed material. Lots of explicit and grisly violence. **95m/C VHS, DVD.** Charles Bronson, Lesley-Anne Down, Michael Parks, Kenneth Welsh; ***D:*** Allan Goldstein; ***W:*** Allan Goldstein; ***C:*** Curtis Petersen; ***M:*** Terry Plumeri.

Death Wish Club 🦴½ *Carnival of Fools* **1983** Young woman gets involved in a club with an unusual mission—suicide. **93m/C VHS.** Meridith Haze, Rick Barns, J. Martin Sellers, Ann Fairchild; ***D:*** John Carr.

Deathcheaters 🦴½ **1976 (G)** Australian Secret Service offers two stuntmen a top secret mission in the Philippines. **96m/C VHS.** John Hargreaves, Grant Page, Noel Ferrer; ***D:*** Brian Trenchard-Smith; ***W:*** Michael Cove.

Deathdream 🦴🦴½ *Dead of Night; Night Walk; The Veteran* **1972** In this reworking of the "Monkey's Paw" tale, a mother wishes her dead son would return from Vietnam. He does, but he's not quite the person he used to be. Gripping plot gives new meaning to the saying, "Be careful what you wish for—it might come true." **98m/C VHS.** *CA* John Marley, Richard Backus, Lynn Carlin; ***D:*** Bob (Benjamin) Clark; ***W:*** Alan Ormsby.

Deathfight 🦴½ **1993 (R)** Let's face it, no one watches these movies because they have a plot. This is a fast-paced B-grade martial arts flick with numerous butts getting kicked. Oh, all right, if you insist on a plot—Norton's evil half-brother (Guerrero) is trying to turn their legitimate family business into a criminal front by framing Norton for murder. **92m/C VHS.** Richard Norton, Franco Guerrero, Karen Moncrieff, Chuck Jeffreys, Ron Vreeken, Tetchie Agbayani, Joe Mari Avellana; ***D:*** Anthony Maharaj; ***W:*** Tom Huckabee.

Deathhead Virgin 🦴½ **1974 (R)** An evil virgin spirit is waiting to possess one of two men eager to find a sunken fortune. The fate of the fortunate one is only death! **94m/C VHS.** Jock Gaynor, Larry Ward, Diane McBain, Vic Diaz.

Deathmask 🦴🦴 **1969** A four-year-old boy's corpse is found buried in a cardboard box, and a medical examiner—whose daughter met a similar fate—investigates the murder. Could've been done more tastefully. **102m/C VHS.** Farley Granger, Ruth Warrick, Danny Aiello; ***D:*** Richard S. Friedman.

Deathmoon 🦴½ **1978** A businessman plagued by recurring werewolf nightmares goes on a Hawaiian vacation to try to forget his troubles. Made for television.

90m/C VHS. Robert Foxworth, Joe Penny, Debralee Scott, Dolph Sweet, Charles Haid; *D:* Bruce Kessler. TV

Deathrow Gameshow 🦴½ 1988 Condemned criminals can either win their freedom or die in front of millions on a new TV show that doesn't win the host many friends. 78m/C VHS. John McCafferty, Robin Bluthe, Beano, Mark Lasky; *D:* Mark Pirro; *W:* Mark Pirro.

Deathstalker woof! *El Cazador de la Muerte* 1983 (R) Deathstalker sets his sights on seizing the evil wizard Munkar's magic amulet so he can take over Munkar's castle. The only excuse for making such an idiotic film seems to have been to fill it with half-naked women. Filmed in Argentina and followed by two sequels that were an improvement. 80m/C VHS, DVD. Richard (Rick) Hill, Barbi Benton, Richard Brooker, Victor Bo, Lana Clarkson; *D:* John Watson; *W:* Howard R. Cohen; *C:* Leonardo Solis; *M:* Oscar Cardozo Ocampo.

Deathstalker 2: Duel of the Titans 🦴🦴 1987 (R) Campy fantasy comically pits the lead character against an evil wizard. Sword-and-sorcery spoof doesn't take itself too seriously. 85m/C VHS, DVD. John Terlesky, Monique Gabrielle, John Lazar, Toni Naples, Maria Socas, Queen Kong; *D:* Jim Wynorski; *W:* Jim Wynorski; *C:* Leonardo Solis; *M:* Chuck Cirino.

Deathstalker 3 🦴½ *Deathstalker 3: The Warriors From Hell* 1989 (R) Another humorous entry in the Deathstalker saga. This time there's action, romance, magic and the Warriors From Hell. 85m/C VHS. John Allen Nelson, Carla Herd, Terri Treas, Thom Christopher; *D:* Alfonso Corona; *W:* Howard R. Cohen.

Deathstalker 4: Match of Titans 🦴 1992 (R) The sword and sorcery epic continues, with our hero revealing yet more musculature in his efforts to defeat an evil queen and her legion of stone warriors. 85m/C VHS. Richard (Rick) Hill, Maria Ford, Michelle Moffett, Brett (Baxter) Clark; *D:* Howard R. Cohen.

Deathtrap 🦴🦴 1982 (PG) A creatively blocked playwright, his ailing rich wife, and a former student who has written a surefire hit worth killing for, are the principals in this compelling comedy-mystery. Cross and double-cross are explored in this film based on the Broadway hit by Ira Levin. 118m/C VHS, DVD. Henry Jones, Michael Caine, Christopher Reeve, Dyan Cannon, Irene Worth; *D:* Sidney Lumet; *W:* Jay Presson Allen; *C:* Andrzej Bartkowiak; *M:* Johnny Mandel.

The Debt 🦴🦴 *Back to Even* 1998 (R) Printing press operator Mitch's (Lamas) gambling problems get him deeply in debt to local wiseguy Danny Boyle (Pare) who gets Mitch to help him in a counterfeiting operation. Usual gangster cliches but the action moves along. 92m/C VHS, DVD. Lorenzo Lamas, Michael Pare, Heidi Thomas, Angela Jones, Herb Mitchell; *D:* Rod Hewitt; *W:* Rod Hewitt; *C:* Garrett Fisher. VIDEO

The Decalogue 🦴🦴🦴½ 1988 Originally produced for Polish TV, Kieslowski's 10-hour epic offers moments from the lives of residents of a late-Communist era Warsaw apartment complex. Each of the segments is a modern retelling of the Ten Commandments as the individuals confront morality, ethics, betrayal, and a variety of human frailities and crises. Polish with subtitles. 584m/C VHS, DVD. *PL* Krystyna Janda, Aleksander Bardini, Maja Komorowska, Daniel Olbrychski, Janusz Gajos, Maria Pakulnis, Jerzy Stuhr, Zbigniew Zamachowski, Boguslaw Linda, Artur Barcis, Henryk Baranowski; *D:* Krzysztof Kieslowski; *W:* Krzysztof Kieslowski, Krzysztof Piesiewicz; *C:* Wieslaw Zdort, Edward Klosinski, Krysztof Pakulski, Slawomir Idziak, Witold Adamek, Dariusz Kuc, Andrzej Jaroszewicz, Piotr Sobocinski, Jacek Blawut; *M:* Zbigniew Preisner. TV

The Decameron 🦴🦴🦴½ *Il Decameron* 1970 (R) Pasolini's first epic pageant in his "Trilogy of Life" series. An acclaimed, sexually explicit adaptation of a handful of the Boccaccio tales. In Italian with English subtitles. 111m/C VHS, DVD, Wide. *FR IT GE* Franco Citti, Ninetto Davoli, Angela Luce, Patrizia Capparelli, Jovan Jovanovich, Silvana Mangano, Pier Paolo Pasolini; *D:* Pier Paolo Pasolini; *W:* Pier Paolo Pasolini; *C:* Tonino Delli Colli; *M:* Ennio Morricone. Berlin Intl. Film Fest. '71: Silver Prize.

Decameron Nights 🦴🦴½ 1953 Story of Boccaccio's pursuit of a recently widowed young women is interwoven amongst the three of the 14th century Italian writer's bawdy tales. 87m/C VHS. *GB* Louis Jourdan, Joan Fontaine, Binnie Barnes, Joan Collins, Marjorie Rhodes; *D:* Hugo Fregonese.

Deceit 🦴🦴 1993 (R) A sci-fi sex comedy with an environmental premise. Bailey and Brick are two aliens working for their planet's Environmental Protection Agency, whose idea of protection is to vaporize polluter planets. Guess which planet is next on their hit list. But before they get down to business, our two alien studs want to do the horizontal bop with two of the local lovelies, who decide that isn't how they want to spend their last moments on earth. It has a happy ending. 92m/C VHS. Scott Paulin, Norbert Weisser, Samantha (Sam) Phillips; *D:* Albert Pyun; *W:* Kitty Chalmers.

Deceived 🦴🦴½ 1991 (PG-13) A successful career woman with a passionate husband and a young daughter feels she has it all until her husband is apparently killed in a bizarre tragedy. But just how well did she know the man she married? Who was he really and what secrets are hidden in his past? As she struggles to solve these mysteries, her own life becomes endangered in this psychological thriller. 115m/C VHS. Goldie Hawn, John Heard, Ashley Peldon, Jan Rubes, Amy Wright, Maia Filar, Robin Bartlett, Tom Irwin, Beatrice Straight, Kate Reid; *D:* Damian Harris; *W:* Mary Agnes Donoghue, Derek Saunders; *C:* Jack N. Green; *M:* Thomas Newman.

Deceiver 🦴🦴 *Liar* 1997 (R) Contrived psychological thriller starts out with the requisite dead prostitute (Zellwegger, in a questionable career move) and the rounding up of the usual suspects, settling on disturbed but brainy Princeton grad Wayland (indie film icon Roth). Wayland uses his superior I.Q. and penchant for mind games to send head detectives Kennesaw and Braxton (Rooker and Penn) into a tailspin of deceit and lies, turning the investigation around on the gritty cops. Flashy camera work only adds to the tangled mayhem. Fine performances from talented cast bring this up a notch. Twin directors Jonas and Joshua Pate's convoluted spin on a noirish murder mystery follows up their 1996 debut, "Grave." 102m/C VHS, DVD, Wide. Renee Zellweger, Tim Roth, Christopher Penn, Michael Rooker, Ellen Burstyn, Rosanna Arquette; *D:* Jonas Pate, Josh Pate; *W:* Jonas Pate, Josh Pate; *C:* Bill Butler; *M:* Harry Gregson-Williams.

The Deceivers 🦴🦴 1988 (PG-13) Brosnan stars as a British officer sent on a dangerous unercover mission in 1820s India. He's to infiltrate the notorious Thuggee cult, known for robbing and murdering unwary travelers. Interesting premise falters due to slow pacing and Brosnan's lack of believability. 112m/C VHS. *IN GB* Pierce Brosnan, Saeed Jaffrey, Shashi Kapoor, Keith Michell; *D:* Nicholas Meyer; *C:* Walter Lassally.

December 🦴🦴 1991 (PG) Four prep-school students in New Hampshire must confront the reality of war when the Japanese bomb Pearl Harbor. A touching story of courage and friendship that takes place in one night during the suprise-attack. 92m/C VHS. Wil Wheaton, Chris Young, Brian Krause, Balthazar Getty, Jason London; *D:* Gabe Torres; *W:* Gabe Torres.

December Bride 🦴🦴½ 1991 Determined young woman (Reeves) becomes the housekeeper to two taciturn Irish farmer/brothers (Hinds and McCann) and proceeds to bully them into prosperity in early 20th century rural Ireland. She also scandalizes the community by sleeping with both men and refusing to marry either—even after she becomes pregnant. Based on the novel by Sam Hanna Bell. 88m/C VHS. *IR* Saskia Reeves, Ciaran Hinds, Donal McCann, Patrick Malahide, Brenda Bruce; *D:* Thaddeus O'Sullivan; *W:* David Rudkin; *C:* Bruno de Keyzer; *M:* Jurgen Knieper.

December Flower 🦴🦴½ 19?? A young woman arrives at her aunt's estate so she can nurse her back to health, but she finds her aunt a bit down in the mouth: seems someone is trying to kill her, and she could be next in line. 65m/C VHS. Jean Simmons, Mona Washbourne, Bryan Forbes.

December 7th: The Movie 🦴🦴½ 1991 Banned for 50 years by the U.S. Government, this planned Hollywood explanation to wartime audiences of the Pearl Harbor debacle offers such "offensive" images as blacks fighting heroically alongside whites, loyal Japanese-Americans, and Uncle Sam asleep on the morning of the attack. The Chief of Naval Operations confiscated the original film, claiming it demeaned the Navy. The battle scenes were so realistic they fooled even documentarians. This isn't the most incisive video on the event—just an unforgettable snapshot. 82m/B VHS, DVD. Walter Huston, Harry Davenport; *D:* John Ford; *C:* Gregg Toland; *M:* Alfred Newman.

Deception 🦴🦴🦴 1946 Davis is a pianist torn between two loves: her intensely jealous sponsor (Rains) and her cellist boyfriend (Henreid). Plot in danger of going over the melodramatic edge is saved by the very effective performances of the stars. 112m/B VHS. Bette Davis, Paul Henreid, Claude Rains, John Abbott, Benson Fong; *D:* Irving Rapper.

Deception 🦴½ *Ruby Cairo* 1992 (PG-13) Talented cast is wasted in an old-fashioned mystery that lacks a coherent script. MacDowell is married to Mortensen, the owner of an aircraft salvage company. He's supposedly killed in a plane crash but she thinks he's just pulled a fast one and sets off to find him. Tracking her hubby's secret bank accounts takes her all over the world, and finally to Cairo, Egypt where she meets Neeson. Together they discover Mortensen's scam involves smuggling poison gas and the duo then try to outwit the hoods on their trail. Film was originally released at 110 minutes. 90m/C VHS. Andie MacDowell, Liam Neeson, Viggo Mortensen, Jack Thompson, Jeff Corey, Miriam Reed, Luis Cortes, Paco Mauri; *D:* Graeme Clifford; *W:* Robert Dillon, Michael Thomas; *M:* John Barry.

Deceptions 🦴🦴 1990 (R) A risque, semi-erotic thriller about a wealthy society woman (Sheridan) who kills her husband. Sheridan claims that she acted in self-defense, but macho cop Hamlin has a different view. He interrogates her, grows increasingly attracted, and is drawn into her web of seduction. 105m/C VHS. Harry Hamlin, Nicolette Sheridan; *D:* Ruben Preuss; *W:* Richard G. Taylor.

Deceptions 2: Edge of Deception 🦴½ 1994 (R) Voyeur detective becomes obsessed with his comely neighbor, leading to unpleasant consequences. 100m/C VHS. Mariel Hemingway, Jennifer Rubin, Stephen Shellen; *D:* George Mihalka.

The Decline of the American Empire 🦴🦴🦴½ *Le Declin De L'Empire Americain* 1986 (R) The critically acclaimed French-Canadian film about eight academic intellectuals who spend a weekend shedding their sophistication and engaging in intertwining sexual affairs. Examines the differing attitudes of men and women in regards to sex and sexuality. In French with English subtitles. 102m/C VHS. *CA* Dominique Michel, Dorothee Berryman, Louise Portal, Genevieve Rioux; *D:* Denys Arcand; *W:* Denys Arcand. Genie '87: Director (Arcand), Film, Support. Actor (Arcand), Support. Actress (Portal); N.Y. Film Critics '86: Foreign Film; Toronto-City '86: Canadian Feature Film.

Decline of Western Civilization 1 🦴🦴🦴 1981 The L.A. hard core punk scene. Music by X, Circle Jerks, Black Flag, Fear and more. 100m/C VHS. *D:* Penelope Spheeris.

Decline of Western Civilization 2: The Metal Years 1988 (R) Following Spheeris's first documentary about hardcore punk, she in turn delves into the world of heavy metal rock. We are given a look at some of the early rockers, as well as some of the smaller bands still playing L.A. clubs. Features appearances by Alice Cooper, Ozzy Osbourne, Poison, Gene Simmons, and Megadeth. 90m/C VHS. Alice Cooper, Ozzy Osbourne, Gene Simmons, Lizzie Borden; *D:* Penelope Spheeris.

Deconstructing Harry 🦴🦴½ 1997 (R) Interesting idea has Allen as a successful author, Harry Block, whose thinly-veiled autobiographical fiction spills the beans on his ex-wives, lovers, friends, and family, thereby pissing them all off. Toggles back and forth between Harry's "real" life and scenes from his books, giving characters and situations two versions: one slanted to suit Harry and one more real than Harry wants or knows how to deal with. Infidelity, divorce, and art all get their usual treatment. Another not bad, but not great project by Allen that may be too self-absorbed for most. Features an elaborate, star-studded cast, mostly delegated to minor roles. 96m/C VHS, DVD, Wide. Woody Allen, Billy Crystal, Judy Davis, Elisabeth Shue, Kirstie Alley, Caroline Aaron, Bob Balaban, Richard Benjamin, Eric Bogosian, Mariel Hemingway, Amy Irving, Julie Kavner, Eric Lloyd, Julia Louis-Dreyfus, Tobey Maguire, Demi Moore, Stanley Tucci, Robin Williams, Philip Bosco, Gene Saks, Hazelle Goodman; *D:* Woody Allen; *W:* Woody Allen; *C:* Carlo Di Palma.

Deconstructing Sarah 🦴🦴 1994 (R) Sarah Vincent (Ticotin) is a high-powered but bored ad exec who assumes an alter-ego, Ruth, when she heads for the wrong side of the tracks in her pursuit of casual sex. Her secret life is discovered when Sarah is murdered and best friend Elizabeth (Kelley) begins to turn up some likely suspects. Fast-paced whodunnit with good cast work. 120m/C VHS. Rachel Ticotin, Sheila Kelley, A. Martinez, David Andrews, John Vickery, Jenifer Lewis, Dwier Brown, Peter Jason; *D:* Craig R. Baxley; *W:* Lee Rose; *C:* Joao Fernandes; *M:* Tom Scott. CABLE

Decoration Day 🦴🦴🦴 1990 (PG) Garner plays reclusive retired Southern judge Albert Sidney Finch who aids an angry black childhood friend, Gee (Cobbs), who has refused to accept his long-overdue Medal of Honor. Investigating the past leads to a decades-old mystery and a tragic secret that has repercussions for everyone involved. Based on the novel by John William Corrington. A Hallmark Hall of Fame presentation. 99m/C VHS. James Garner, Bill Cobbs, Judith Ivey, Ruby Dee, Laurence "Larry" Fishburne, Jo Anderson; *D:* Robert Markowitz; *W:* Robert W. Lenski. TV

Decoy 🦴🦴½ 1995 (R) Two ex-government operatives, Baxter (Weller) and Travis (Patrick), are hired by their former commanding officer, Wellington (Breck), to protect his daughter Diana (Vogel) from business rival Jensen (Hylands) who's got a grudge against dad. But then it turns out the job's a set up, and Wellington and Jensen have their own deadly agenda. 98m/C VHS. Peter Weller, Robert Patrick, Darlene Vogel, Charlotte Lewis, Peter Breck, Scott Hylands; *D:* Victor Rambaldi; *W:* Robert Sarno; *C:* Jon Kranhouse; *M:* Mark Adler.

Dedee d'Anvers 🦴🦴½ *Dedee; Woman of Antwerp* 1949 A gritty dockside melodrama about a drunken prostitute abused by her pimp. A sailor and a local barkeep don't like it. In French with subtitles. 95m/B VHS. Simone Signoret, Marcel Dalio, Bernard Blier, Marcel Pagliero, Jane (Jeanne) Marken; *D:* Yves Allegret; *C:* Jean (Yves, Georges) Bourgoin.

A Dedicated Man 1986 A lonely woman agrees to act as a wife for a businessman to lend him credibility. A British "Romance Theater" presentation. 60m/C VHS. *GB* Alec McCowen, Joan Plowright; *D:* Robert Knights.

Dee Snider's Strangeland woof! *Strangeland* 1998 (R) Former Twisted Sister singer Dee Snider proves that he can fail at movie-making worse than he can fail as a musician. He wrote, produced and starred in this dud that proves it's possible to be stupid, disgusting and boring at the same time. Snider plays Captain Howdy, an internet chat room sicko who lures young girls into a dungeon and tortures them by involuntarily piercing them and trying to act in front of them. Gage plays the dim detective trying to find the hair-sculpting madman. Only proves that Snider with a movie camera is more dangerous than the internet. **90m/C VHS, DVD.** Dee Snider, Kevin Gage, Brett Harrelson, Elizabeth Pena, Robert Englund, Amy Smart, Linda Cardellini; ***D:*** John Pieplow; ***W:*** Dee Snider; ***C:*** Goran Pavicevic; ***M:*** Anton Sanko.

The Deep 🦴🦴 **1977 (PG)** An innocent couple get involved in an underwater search for a shipwreck, and they quickly find themselves in over their heads. Gorgeous photography manages to keep this slow mover afloat. Famous for Bisset's wet T-shirt scene. Based on the novel by Peter Benchley. **123m/C VHS, DVD, Wide.** Nick Nolte, Jacqueline Bisset, Robert Shaw, Louis Gossett Jr., Eli Wallach; ***D:*** Peter Yates; ***W:*** Peter Benchley, Tracy Keenan Wynn; ***C:*** Christopher Challis; ***M:*** John Barry.

Deep Blue Sea 🦴½ **1999 (R)** It's no longer safe to go back in the water. Marine biologist Susan McAlester (Burrows) is obsessed with finding a cure for Alzheimer's and has genetically enhanced the brains of a group of test sharks at a floating research facility off the Baja coast. Oh, and she didn't bother to tell anyone else in her group about these smarter-than-the-average sharks. But they soon learn, when the research facility suffers several accidents, begins to flood, and the sharks get loose—and looking for snacks. It's not a bomb but it's also nothing that you haven't seen before. And the fake sharks look, well, fake (and hokey). **105m/C VHS, DVD, Wide.** Saffron Burrows, Samuel L. Jackson, Thomas Jane, L.L. Cool J., Jacqueline McKenzie, Michael Rapaport, Stellan Skarsgard, Aida Turturro; ***D:*** Renny Harlin; ***W:*** Duncan Kennedy, Donna Powers, Wayne Powers; ***C:*** Stephen Windon; ***M:*** Trevor Rabin.

Deep Core 🦴🦴 **2000 (PG-13)** A rupture deep in the Earth's core causes a chain of natural disasters and could destroy the planet unless scientist Brian Goodman (Sheffer) can find a way to stop the geological threat. **90m/C VHS, DVD.** Craig Sheffer, James Russo, Terry Farrell, James Lew, Wil Wheaton, Bruce McGill; ***D:*** Rodney McDonald; ***W:*** Martin Lazarus; ***C:*** Richard Clabaugh. **VIDEO**

Deep Cover 🦴½ **1988 (R)** A man dares to go beyond the walls of a mysterious English manor in order to expose the secrets that lie within the manor. **81m/C VHS.** Tom Conti, Donald Pleasence, Denholm Elliott, Kika Markham, Phoebe Nicholls; ***D:*** Richard Loncraine.

Deep Cover 🦴🦴½ **1992 (R)** Fishburne plays Russell Stevens Jr., a straight-arrow cop who goes undercover to infiltrate a Latin American cocaine cartel. While undercover, he becomes partners with drug dealer David Jason (Goldblum), and undergoes an inner transformation until he realizes he is betraying his cause. Confusing and commercial, yet marked with a moral rage. **107m/C VHS, DVD, Wide.** Laurence "Larry" Fishburne, Jeff Goldblum, Victoria Dillard, Charles Martin Smith, Sydney Lassick, Clarence Williams III, Gregory Sierra, Roger Guenveur Smith, Cory Curtis, Glynn Turman, Def Jef; ***D:*** Bill Duke; ***W:*** Michael Tolkin, Henry Bean; ***C:*** Bojan Bazelli; ***M:*** Michel Colombier.

Deep Crimson 🦴🦴 *Profundo Carmesi* **1996** In 1949 Mexico, overweight nurse and willful romantic, Coral (Orozco), impulsively answers a lonely hearts ad placed by Nicolas (Gimenez Cacho), who turns out to be a seedy con man. Coral, however, is certain she's found her true love and is obsessive in her devotion. So much so that she decides to help him with his swindling of vulnerable widows. But Coral's uncontrolled jealousy leads to murder. Based on the same true crime story that inspired the 1969 film, "The Honeymoon Killers." Spanish with subtitles. **109m/C VHS.** *MX SP* Regina Orozco, Daniel Gimenez Cacho, Marisa Paredes; ***D:*** Arturo Ripstein; ***W:*** Paz Alicia Garciadiego; ***C:*** Guillermo Granillo; ***M:*** David Mansfield.

Deep Down 🦴½ **1994 (R)** When young Andy (Young) moves into a new apartment, he discovers his neighbor (Roberts) is a gorgeous married woman just looking for a little fun on the side. Too bad her husband (Segal) is a violent psychopath, totally suspicious of his wife's fidelity. Just how far will everyone go to get what they want? Also available in an unrated version. **86m/C VHS.** Tanya Roberts, Chris Young, George Segal; ***D:*** John Travers; ***W:*** John Travers, Alice Horrigan.

Deep End 🦴🦴🦴 *Na Samyn Dnie* **1970** A 15-year-old boy working as an attendant in a bath house falls in love with a 20-year-old woman in this tragic tale of a young man obsessed. Good British cast and music by Cat Stevens. **88m/C VHS.** *GB GE* Jane Asher, John Moulder-Brown, Diana Dors, Karl Michael Vogler, Christopher Sandord; ***D:*** Jerzy Skolimowski; ***W:*** Jerzy Skolimowski, Jerry Gruza, Bloeslav Sulik; ***C:*** Charly Steinberger; ***M:*** Cat Stevens.

The Deep End 🦴🦴🦴 **2001 (R)** Moms are used to cleaning up their kids' messes and Margaret Hall (Swinton) is no different, even if her situation is. Margaret lives with her three kids and cranky father-in-law in a quiet Lake Tahoe community. Her naval husband is away, which means when Margaret learns that teenaged son Beau (Tucker) is gay and involved with sleazy older bar owner, Darby (Lucas), she has no one to turn to. Things get tricky when Darby turns up dead on the beach and mom thinks son did the deed. She gets rid of the body but is soon being blackmailed by slick stranger Alek (Visnjic). Swinton is amazing as the woman who has no limits when it comes to maternal care. Based on Elizabeth Sanxay Holding's 1947 novel "The Blank Wall," which was previously filmed by Max Ophuls in 1949 as "The Reckless Moment." **99m/C VHS, DVD, Wide.** *US* Tilda Swinton, Goran Visnjic, Jonathan Tucker, Raymond J. Barry, Joshua Lucas, Peter Donat, Tamara Hope, Jordan Dorrance; ***D:*** Scott McGehee, David Siegel; ***W:*** Scott McGehee, David Siegel; ***C:*** Giles Nuttgens; ***M:*** Peter Nashel. Sundance '01: Cinematog. (Nuttgens).

The Deep End of the Ocean 🦴🦴 **1998 (PG-13)** Beth (Pfeiffer) and husband Pat (Williams) live the ideal life in the suburbs, with a nice home and three beautiful kids. All of that is shattered when three-year-old Ben is abducted while Beth is distracted at a hotel. Shows the tortuous road of depression that Beth travels, and the effect it has on her family. Suddenly, nine years later Ben shows up at her doorstep, now named Sam, and offers to cut the lawn. Beth and detective Candy (Goldberg) determine that he is the lost boy, and painful choices must be made by all. Glosses over the story behind the child's abduction and wraps everything up a bit too easily. **105m/C VHS, DVD.** Michelle Pfeiffer, Treat Williams, John Kapelos, Jonathan Jackson, Ryan Merriman, Whoopi Goldberg, Michael McGrady, Brenda Strong; ***D:*** Ulu Grosbard; ***W:*** Stephen Schiff; ***C:*** Stephen Goldblatt; ***M:*** Elmer Bernstein.

Deep Impact 🦴🦴½ **1998 (PG-13)** Poor Morgan Freeman. He gets a chance to play the President of the United States only to have his term shortened by a dastardly comet the size of the Grand Canyon. Although his presidency would have been more interesting, the destruction's the star of this show, as well as the touchy-feely interaction of various two-dimensional characters. There's the astronauts (led by Duvall) sent into space to nuke the thing; ordinary teenager Leo (Wood) who initially discovered the rock; and career-conscious news anchor (Leoni), who first breaks the story. The all-star cast is underused, but lend the film a sense of gravity by their presence. The remaining stick figure characters evoke more yawns than tears. Good thing the comet comes along to, ironically, inject a little life into the flick. The special effects are the best in recent film history, and worth the long, laborious wait. **120m/C VHS, DVD, Wide.** Morgan Freeman, Robert Duvall, Tea Leoni, Elijah Wood, Vanessa Redgrave, Maximilian Schell, James Cromwell, Blair Underwood, Ron Eldard, Jon Favreau, Leelee Sobieski, Mary McCormack, Dougray Scott, Alexander Baluyev, Charles Martin Smith, Richard Schiff, Gary Werntz, Bruce Weitz, Betsy Brantley, O'Neal Compton, Rya Kihlstedt, Denise Crosby, Laura Innes; ***D:*** Mimi Leder; ***W:*** Michael Tolkin, Bruce Joel Rubin; ***C:*** Dietrich Lohmann; ***M:*** James Horner.

Deep in My Heart 🦴🦴½ **1954** A musical biography of the life and times of composer Sigmund Romberg, with guest appearances by many MGM stars. ♫Leg of Mutton; You Will Remember Vienna; Softly, as in a Morning Sunrise; Mr. & Mrs.; I Love to Go Swimmin' with Wimmin; The Road to Paradise; Will You Remember; It; Serenade. **132m/C VHS.** Jose Ferrer, Merle Oberon, Paul Henreid, Walter Pidgeon, Helen Traubel, Rosemary Clooney, Jane Powell, Howard Keel, Cyd Charisse, Gene Kelly, Ann Miller; ***D:*** Stanley Donen; ***C:*** George J. Folsey.

Deep in the Heart 🦴🦴 *Handgun* **1983 (R)** When a young teacher is raped at gunpoint on a second date, she takes the law into her own hands. Just-off-the-target film tries to take a stand against the proliferation of guns in the U.S. Thought-provoking all the same. **99m/C VHS.** *GB* Karen Young, Clayton Day, Ben Jones, Suzie Humphreys; ***D:*** Tony Garnett; ***W:*** Tony Garnett.

Deep in the Heart (of Texas) 🦴🦴 **1998** Two British documentary filmmakers, Robert (Cranham) and his wife Kate (Root), take an assignment for British TV to interview Texans. They choose the capital of Austin and the eccentric locals provide the requisite color but the couple are undergoing their own personal crisis that keeps interfering with their work. **90m/C VHS, DVD, Wide.** Kenneth Cranham, Amanda Root; ***D:*** Stephen Purvis; ***W:*** Tom Huckabee, Stephen Purvis, Jesse Sublett; ***C:*** Thomas Flores Alcala; ***M:*** Joe Ellen Doering, George Doering.

Deep in the Woods 🦴🦴 *Promenons Nous dans les Bois* **2000 (R)** Isolated castle, mute little boy, and a psycho-rapist on the loose as five actors are hired to give a performance of "Little Red Riding Hood." Then they begin to die at the paws of someone wearing the wolf costume. Gruesome creeper; French with subtitles. **88m/C VHS, DVD, Wide.** *FR* Clotilde Courau, Clement Sibony, Vincent Lecoeur, Alexia Stresi, Maud Buquet; ***D:*** Lionel Delplanque; ***W:*** Annabelle Perrichon; ***C:*** Denis Rouden; ***M:*** Jerome Coullet.

Deep Red 🦴🦴 **1994 (R)** When a young girl has an encounter with an extraterrestrial spacecraft her blood chemistry is mysteriously altered. Now the proteins her body manufactures can lead to immortality and ruthless scientist Newmeyer wants to take advantage of the fact—any way he can. **85m/C VHS.** Michael Biehn, Joanna Pacula, John de Lancie; ***D:*** Craig R. Baxley; ***W:*** D. Brent Mote.

Deep Red: Hatchet Murders 🦴🦴½ *The Hatchet Murders; Profundo Rosso; Dripping Deep Red; The Sabre Tooth Tiger; Deep Red* **1975** A stylish but gruesome rock music-driven tale of a composer who reads a book on the occult which happens to relate to the sadistic, sangfroid murder of his neighbor. When he visits the book's author, he discovers that she has been horribly murdered as well. **100m/C VHS, DVD.** *IT* David Hemmings, Daria Nicolodi, Gabriele Lavia, Macha Meril, Eros Pagni, Guiliana Calandra, Erykah Badu, Clara Calamai, Nicoletta Elmi, Glauco Mauri; ***D:*** Dario Argento; ***W:*** Dario Argento, Barnardino Zapponi; ***C:*** Luigi Kuveiller; ***M:*** Girogio Gaslini, The Goblins.

Deep Rising 🦴🦴½ **1998 (R)** Huge sea serpents cause massive destruction to the cruise ship Argonautica and put major dinks in the plans of mercenaries, led by Finnegan (Williams), who board the ship for greedy motives. Sticks to a reliable action-horror formula with the good sense to not take its characters or slimy creatures too seriously. Sea critters have inventive ways of disposing of extraneous cast members, resulting in gore aplenty. Slacker humor provided by Finnegan's sidekick Pantucci (Kevin J. O'Connor) injects the film with a certain goofiness. Typical B-movie fare that leans more toward guilty pleasure than quality entertainment. **106m/C VHS, DVD.** Treat Williams, Famke Janssen, Anthony Heald, Kevin J. O'Connor, Wes Studi, Derrick O'Connor, Jason Flemyng, Djimon Hounsou; ***D:*** Stephen Sommers; ***W:*** Stephen Sommers; ***C:*** Howard Atherton; ***M:*** Jerry Goldsmith.

Deep Six 🦴🦴½ **1958** A WWII drama that examines the conflict between pacifism and loyalty. A staunch Quaker is called to active duty as a lieutenant in the U.S. Navy, where his beliefs put him into disfavor with shipmates. **110m/C VHS.** Alan Ladd, William Bendix, James Whitmore, Keenan Wynn, Efrem Zimbalist Jr., Joey Bishop; ***D:*** Rudolph Mate.

Deep Space 🦴½ **1987** A flesh-eating alien lands on earth and, after devouring a cop, is stalked by his partner. An "Alien" rip-off. Some humorous moments keep us from thinking too hard about how much the monster resembles our friend from "Alien." **90m/C VHS.** Charles Napier, Ann Turkel, Ron Glass, Bo Svenson, Julie Newmar; ***D:*** Fred Olen Ray.

Deep Trouble 🦴½ **2001** It's strictly amateur hour in this hip-hip urban drama. New York drug kingpin Perry (Stovall) decides that the world of organized crime simply isn't enough, and decides to overtake the business of Star (Scarborough), an entertainment manager who represents up-and-coming actress Diana (Horsford), as well as several stand-up comics. Star and Diana decide that they aren't going to be pushed around by this bully, so they take a stand and the "trouble" begins. Filled with bad acting and amateurish special effects (several characters get shot in the head, which is represented by a simple trickle of blood). The film is very poorly paced, having more scenes of pointless dialogue than action. **102m/C DVD.** Count Stovall, Janel C. Scarborough, Alyah Horsford; ***D:*** Juney Smith; ***W:*** Juney Smith.

Deeply 🦴🦴½ **1999** Fiona McKay (Watson) takes her teenaged daughter Claire (Dunst) to her childhood home on an island off the coast of Nova Scotia. Claire's been traumatized by the sudden death of her boyfriend and is susceptible to the stories told by elderly neighbor, Claire (Redgrave), who has some dark secrets. **102m/C VHS, DVD.** *CA* Alberta Watson, Lynn Redgrave, Kirsten Dunst, Julia Brendler, Brent Carver; ***D:*** Sheri Elwood; ***W:*** Sheri Elwood; ***M:*** Micki Meuser.

Deepstar Six 🦴½ **1989 (R)** When futuristic scientists try to set up an undersea research and missile lab, a group of subterranean monsters get in the way. **97m/C VHS, DVD.** Taurean Blacque, Nancy Everhard, Greg Evigan, Miguel Ferrer, Matt McCoy, Nia Peeples, Cindy Pickett, Marius Weyers, Thom Bray, Elya Baskin; ***D:*** Sean S. Cunningham; ***W:*** Lewis Abernathy, Geof Miller; ***C:*** Mac Ahlberg; ***M:*** Harry Manfredini.

The Deer Hunter 🦴🦴🦴🦴 **1978 (R)** A powerful and vivid portrait of Middle America with three steel-working friends who leave home to face the Vietnam War. Controversial, brutal sequences in Vietnam are among the most wrenching ever filmed; the rhythms and rituals of home are just as purely captured. Neither pronor anti-war, but rather the perfect evocation of how totally and forever altered these people are by the war. Emotionally shattering; not to be missed. **183m/C VHS, DVD, Wide.** Robert De Niro, Christopher Walken, Meryl Streep, John Savage, George Dzundza, John Cazale, Chuck Aspegren, Rutanya Alda, Shirley Stoler, Amy Wright, Mady Kaplan, Mary Ann Haenel, Richard Kuss, Pierre Segui, Joe Grifasi, Christopher Colombi Jr., Joe Strnad, Paul D'Amato; ***D:*** Michael Cimino; ***W:*** Michael Cimino, Deric Washburn, Louis Garfinkle; ***C:*** Vilmos Zsigmond; ***M:*** John Williams, Stanley Myers. Oscars '78: Director (Cimino), Film Editing, Picture, Sound, Support. Actor (Walken); AFI '98: Top 100; Directors Guild '78: Director (Cimino); Golden Globes '79: Director (Cimino); L.A. Film Critics '78: Director (Cimino), Natl. Film Reg. '96;; N.Y. Film Critics '78: Film, Support. Actor (Walken); Natl. Soc. Film Critics '78: Support. Actress (Streep).

The Deerslayer 🦴½ **1978** Low-budget snoozer based on the classic novel by James Fenimore Cooper. Frontiersman Hawkeye and his Indian companion Chingachgook set out to rescue a beautiful Indian maiden and must fight bands of hostile Indians and Frenchmen along the way. **98m/C VHS.** Steve Forrest, Ned Romero, John Anderson, Joan Prather; ***D:*** Richard Friedenberg; ***M:*** Andrew Belling.

Def by Temptation 1990 (R) A potent horror fantasy about a young black theology student who travels to New York in search of an old friend. There he meets an evil woman who is determined to seduce him and force him to give in to temptation. Great soundtrack. **95m/C VHS, DVD.** James Bond III, Kadeem Hardison, Bill Nunn, Samuel L. Jackson, Minnie Gentry, Rony Clanton, Cynthia Bond, John Canada Terrell; ***D:*** James Bond III; ***W:*** James Bond III; ***C:*** Ernest R. Dickerson; ***M:*** Paul Lawrence.

Def-Con 4 1985 (R) Three marooned space travelers return to a holocaust-shaken Earth to try to start again, but some heavy-duty slimeballs are in charge and they don't want to give it up. Good special effects bolster a weak script. **85m/C VHS.** Maury Chaykin, Kate Lynch, Tim Choate; ***D:*** Paul Donovan.

Def Jam's How to Be a Player *How to Be a Player* 1997 (R) Dray (Bellamy) thinks that monogamy is a wood used to build furniture. Although he has steady girlfriend Lisa (Voorhies), he also has several other ladies in waiting. He is, in fact, a player. He even teaches others to play. What he needs, however, is a screenplay. His sister Jenny (Desselle), who has been hurt in love, cracks the numerical code to his organizer, and invites all of Dray's harem to one party. The result of this booty intervention is Dray's abandonment of his promiscuous ways. The stand-up comedy roots of much of the cast translate into clunky performances, and the direction is pretty played out, too. **93m/C VHS, DVD.** Bill Bellamy, Natalie Desselle, Mari Morrow, Jermaine "Huggy" Hopkins, A.J. (Anthony) Johnson, Max Julien, Beverly Johnson, Gilbert Gottfried, Bernie Mac, Elise Neal, Amber Smith, Lark Voorhies; ***D:*** Lionel C. Martin; ***W:*** Mark Brown, Demetria Johnson; ***M:*** Darren Floyd.

Defenders of the Law 1931 Early action talkie concerned with gang warfare and law enforcement. **64m/B VHS.** John Holland, Mae Busch, Alan Cooke, Joseph Girard, Edmund Breese, Catherine Dale Owen, Robert Gleckler; ***D:*** Joseph Levering.

The Defenders: Payback 1997 (R) E.G. Marshall returns to the lawyer role of Lawrence Preston that he played in the CBS series from 1961-1965. This time around, Preston has his granddaughter, M.J. (Plimpton), joining the family firm along with son Don (Bridges). Their first case together is a doozy—unrepentent Michael Lane (Laroquette) has confessed to killing the recently paroled man who had gone to prison for raping Lane's young daughter. **95m/C VHS.** E.G. Marshall, Beau Bridges, Martha Plimpton, John Larroquette, Yaphet Kotto, Roma Maffia, Rachael Leigh Cook, Mimi Kuzyk, Clea DuVall, Nicholas Kilbertus; ***D:*** Andy Wolk; ***W:*** Andy Wolk, Peter Wolk; ***C:*** John Newby; ***M:*** Mark Isham. CABLE

The Defenders: Taking the First 1998 (R) Don (Bridges) and M.J. (Plimpton) defend a student accused of beating a Latino to death. Their client claims he was incited by white supremist leader, John Walker (Casnoff), and agrees to a plea bargain. This enrages the victim's brother, who files a wrongful death suit against Walker and chooses Don to represent the case. Now the team must try to prove Walker's culpability without disputing his First Amendment rights to free speech. **96m/C VHS.** Beau Bridges, Martha Plimpton, Philip Casnoff, Jeremy London; ***D:*** Andy Wolk; ***W:*** Andy Wolk, Peter Wolk; ***C:*** John Newby; ***M:*** Mark Isham. CABLE

Defending Your Life 1991 (PG) Brooks' cock-eyed way of looking at the world travels to the afterlife in this uneven comedy/romance. In Judgment City, where everyone goes after death, past lives are examined and judged. If you were a good enough person you get to stay in heaven (where you wear funny robes and eat all you want without getting fat). If not, it's back to earth for another go-round. Brooks plays an L.A. advertising executive who crashes his new BMW and finds himself defending his life. When he meets and falls in love with Streep, his interest in staying in heaven multiplies. Occasionally charming, seldom out-right hilarious. **112m/C VHS, DVD, 8mm, Wide.** Albert Brooks, Meryl Streep, Rip Torn, Lee Grant, Buck Henry, George D. Wallace, Lillian Lehman, Peter Schuck, Susan Walters; ***D:*** Albert Brooks; ***W:*** Albert Brooks; ***C:*** Allen Daviau; ***M:*** Michael Gore.

Defense of the Realm 1985 (PG) A British politician is accused of selling secrets to the KGB through his mistress and only a pair of dedicated newspapermen believe he is innocent. In the course of finding the answers they discover a national cover-up conspiracy. An acclaimed, taut thriller. **96m/C VHS.** *GB* Gabriel Byrne, Greta Scacchi, Denholm Elliott, Ian Bannen, Bill Paterson, Fulton Mackay, Robbie Coltrane; ***D:*** David Drury; ***C:*** Roger Deakins. British Acad. '85: Support. Actor (Elliott).

Defense Play 1988 (PG) Two teenagers are unwittingly stuck in the middle of a Soviet plot to steal the plans that created a technologically advanced helicopter. **95m/C VHS.** David Oliver, Susan Ursitti, Monte Markham, William Frankfather, Patch MacKenzie; ***D:*** Monte Markham.

Defenseless 1991 (R) Hershey tries hard in an unplayable part as a giddy attorney who finds herself trapped in a love-affair/legal case that turns murderous. Good cast and interesting twists contend with a sexist sub-text, which proves a woman can't "have it all." **106m/C VHS.** Barbara Hershey, Sam Shepard, Mary Beth Hurt, J.T. Walsh, Sheree North; ***D:*** Martin Campbell; ***W:*** James Cresson; ***M:*** Trevor Jones.

Defiance 1979 (PG) A former merchant seaman moves into a tenement in a run-down area of New York City. When a local street gang begins terrorizing the neighborhood, he decides to take a stand. Familiar plotline handled well in this thoughtful film. **101m/C VHS.** Jan-Michael Vincent, Art Carney, Theresa Saldana, Danny Aiello; ***D:*** John Flynn; ***W:*** Tom Donnelly; ***M:*** John Beal, Basil Poledouris.

Defiant *The Wild Pack; The Sandpit Generals* 1970 Two rival street gangs clash when one admits a young orphan girl. **93m/C VHS.** Kent Lane, John Rubinstein, Tisha Sterling; ***D:*** Hall Bartlett.

The Defiant Ones 1958 Thought-provoking story about racism revolves around two escaped prisoners (one black, one white) from a chain gang in the rural South. Their societal conditioning to hate each other dissolves as they face constant peril together. Critically acclaimed. **97m/B VHS, DVD, Wide.** Tony Curtis, Sidney Poitier, Theodore Bikel, Lon Chaney Jr., Charles McGraw, Cara Williams; ***D:*** Stanley Kramer; ***W:*** Nedrick Young, Harold Jacob Smith; ***C:*** Sam Leavitt; ***M:*** Steve Dorff. Oscars '58: B&W Cinematog., Story & Screenplay; British Acad. '58: Actor (Poitier); Golden Globes '59: Film—Drama; N.Y. Film Critics '58: Director (Kramer), Film, Screenplay.

The Defilers 1965 (R) Disturbing, low-budget J.D. movie in which two thugs imprison a young girl in a basement and force her to be their love slave. **69m/B VHS, DVD.** Byron Mabe, Jerome (Jerry Stallion) Eden, Mae Johnson; ***D:*** David Friedman.

Defying Gravity 1999 Frat boy John Griffiths (Chilson) is hiding a secret from his fellow brothers—he's gay and even has a boyfriend, Pete (Handfield), who's sick of John's lying. Pete is gay-bashed and John agonizes over going to the cops with information if it means his off-campus activities could get out. Good intentions but director/writer Keitel's inexperience (this is his first film) shows in a slow pace and amateurishness. **101m/C VHS, DVD.** Daniel Chilson, Niklaus Lange, Don Handfield, Linna Carter, Seabass Diamond, Lesley Tesh; ***D:*** John Keitel; ***W:*** John Keitel; ***C:*** Thomas M. Harting; ***M:*** Tim Westergren.

Deja Vu 1984 (R) A lame romantic thriller about the tragic deaths of two lovers and their supposed reincarnation 50 years later. **95m/C VHS.** *GB* Jaclyn Smith, Nigel Terry, Claire Bloom, Shelley Winters; ***D:*** Anthony Richmond; ***W:*** Ezra D. Rappaport; ***M:*** Pino Donaggio.

Deja Vu 1989 Thriller set in 1925 and moving between Chicago and Odessa. A Chicago hitman is hired by the mob to kill a traitor who has fled to Odessa. Niczypur, the traitor, has been using the newly opened Chicago-Constantinople-Odessa shipping line for his own smuggling operation. Filled with shootouts, brawls, and chases. In English, Russian, and Polish with English subtitles. **108m/C VHS.** *PL* Jerzy Stuhr, Galina Pietrowa, Nikolai Karaczencow, Wladimir Golowin; ***D:*** Juliusz Machulski.

Deja Vu 1998 (PG-13) After Dana (Foyt) has an encounter with a mysterious woman in Israel, she is led on a roundabout way to England's White Cliffs of Dover. There she meets Sean (Dillane), and they quickly fall in love, since they have so much in common, such as being married to other people. This proves to be no problem, for destiny, coincidence and director/screenwriter Jaglom conspire to have the two couples share a house for the weekend. Unfortunately, it's hard to detect the true love, since the two leads have as much chemistry as remedial science class. Vanessa Redgrave and her mother Rachel Kempson appear together for the first time as the sister and mother of the host, played by '60s pop singer Neil Harrison. **115m/C VHS.** Victoria Foyt, Stephen (Dillon) Dillane, Vanessa Redgrave, Glynis Barber, Michael Brandon, Vernon Dobtcheff, Noel Harrison, Rachel Kempson, Anna Massey; ***D:*** Henry Jaglom; ***W:*** Henry Jaglom, Victoria Foyt; ***C:*** Hanania Baer; ***M:*** Gaili Schoen.

The Deli 1997 Johnny Amico (Starr) runs a New York deli, has a bad gambling habit and a big debt to mobster Tommy Tomatoes (Vincent), an outspoken Mama (Malina), and a colorful clientele. Not much happens, the budget is small, but the actors charm. **98m/C VHS.** Mike Starr, Judith Malina, Matt Keeslar, Frank Vincent, Ice-T, Heather Matarazzo, Iman, Jerry Stiller; ***D:*** John A. Gallagher; ***W:*** John A. Gallagher, John Dorrian; ***C:*** Robert Lechterman; ***M:*** Ernie Mannix.

Deliberate Intent 2001 Well-done fact-based drama follows the case of a triple murder-for-hire and the First Amendment issues the case raised. When Lawrence Horn (McDaniel) hires a man (Johnson) to kill his family, it's discovered that said killer used a book called "Hot Man: A Technical Manual for Independent Contractors" to plan the crime. Lawyer Siegel (Rifkin) brings in First Amendment expert Rod Smolla (Hutton) to sue the publisher for abetting the murder. **120m/C VHS, DVD.** Timothy Hutton, Ron Rifkin, James McDaniel, Clark Johnson, Penny Johnson, Cliff DeYoung, Ken Walsh; ***D:*** Andy Wolk; ***C:*** Ron Garcia. CABLE

The Deliberate Stranger 1986 Harmon is engrossing as charismatic serial killer Ted Bundy, sentenced to death for several Florida murders and suspected in the killings of a least 25 women in several states. After eluding police for five years Bundy was finally arrested in Florida in 1979. His case became a cause celebre on capital punishment as it dragged on for nine years. Bundy was finally executed in 1989. Based on the book "Bundy: The Deliberate Stranger" by Richard W. Larsen. **188m/C VHS.** Mark Harmon, M. Emmet Walsh, Frederic Forrest, John Ashton, George Grizzard, Ben Masters, Glynnis O'Connor, Bonnie Bartlett, Billy Green Bush, Lawrence Pressman; ***D:*** Marvin J. Chomsky. TV

The Delicate Delinquent 1956 Lewis's first movie without Dean Martin finds him in the role of delinquent who manages to become a policeman with just the right amount of slapstick. **101m/B VHS.** Jerry Lewis, Darren McGavin, Martha Hyer, Robert Ivers, Horace McMahon; ***D:*** Don McGuire; ***W:*** Don McGuire.

Delicatessen 1992 (R) Set in 21st-century Paris, this hilarious debut from directors Jeunet and Caro focuses on the lives of the oddball tenants of an apartment building over a butcher shop. Although there is a famine, the butcher shop is always stocked with fresh meat—made from the building's tenants. Part comedy, part horror, part romance, this film merges a cacophony of sights and sounds with intriguing results. Watch for the scene involving a symphony of creaking bed springs, a squeaky bicycle pump, a cello, and clicking knitting needles. In French with English subtitles. **95m/C VHS.** *FR* Marie-Laure Dougnac, Dominique Pinon, Karin Viard, Jean Claude Dreyfus, Ticky Holgado, Anne Marie Pisani, Edith Ker, Patrick Paroux, Jean-Luc Caron; ***D:*** Jean-Pierre Jeunet, Marc Caro; ***W:*** Gilles Adrien, Jean-Pierre Jeunet, Marc Caro; ***C:*** Darius Khondji; ***M:*** Carlos D'Alessi. Cesar '92: Art Dir./Set Dec., Writing.

Delightfully Dangerous 1945 Often Deadly Dull. A farfetched musical rooted in yesteryear about mismatched sisters, one a 15-year-old farm girl, the other a New York burlesque dancer, in competition on Broadway. ♫I'm Only Teasin'; In a Shower of Stars; Mynah Bird; Through Your Eyes to Your Heart; Delightfully Dangerous; Once Upon a Song. **92m/B VHS.** Jane Powell, Ralph Bellamy, Constance Moore, Arthur Treacher, Louise Beavers; ***D:*** Arthur Lubin.

Delinquent Daughters 1944 Slow-paced drama about a high school girl who commits suicide and the cop and reporter who try to find out why so darn many kids are getting into trouble. **71m/B VHS.** June Carlson, Fifi d'Orsay, Teala Loring; ***D:*** Al(bert) Herman.

Delinquent Parents 1938 A wayward girl gives up her baby for adoption. She turns her life around and becomes a juvenile court judge. Years later, who should come up before her for misdeeds but her long-lost daughter. The Hound cannot improve on a contemporary critic who renamed this "Delinquent Producers." **62m/B VHS.** Doris Weston, Maurice Murphy, Helen MacKellar, Terry Walker, Richard Tucker, Morgan Wallace; ***D:*** Nick Grinde.

Delinquent School Girls woof! *Bad Girls* 1984 (R) Three escapees from an asylum get more than they bargained for when they visit a Female Correctional Institute to fulfill their sexual fantasies. Buys into just about every conceivable stereotype. **89m/C VHS.** Michael Pataki, Bob Minos, Stephen Stucker; ***D:*** Gregory Corarito.

Delirious 1991 (PG) A writer for a TV soap opera wakes from a bash on the head to find himself inside the story where murder and mayhem are brewing. Can he write himself back to safety, and find romance along the way? Somehow Candy just isn't believeable as a romantic lead and the film has few laughs. **96m/C VHS, 8mm.** John Candy, Mariel Hemingway, Emma Samms, Raymond Burr, David Rasche, Dylan Baker, Charles Rocket, Jerry Orbach, Renee Taylor, Robert Wagner; ***D:*** Tom Mankiewicz; ***W:*** Lawrence J. Cohen; ***M:*** Cliff Eidelman.

Delirium woof! *Psycho Puppet* 1977 Homicidal maniac goes on a killing spree and has just one thing in mind—women. Angry group of citizens inadvertently includes the demonic villain in their vigilante club. Nothing redeeming here. **94m/C VHS.** Turk Cekovsky, Debi Shanley, Terry Ten Broeck; ***D:*** Peter Maris.

Deliverance 1972 (R) Terrifying exploration of the primal nature of man and his alienation from nature, based on the novel by James Dickey, which he adapted for the film (he also makes an appearance as a sheriff). Four urban professionals, hoping to get away from it all for the weekend, canoe down a southern river, encounter crazed backwoodsmen, and end up battling for survival. Excellent performances all around, especially by Voight. Debuts for Beatty and Cox. Watch for O'Neill as a sheriff, and director Boorman's son Charley as Voight's son. "Dueling Banjos" scene and tune are memorable as is scene where the backwoods boys promise to make the fellows squeal like pigs. **109m/C VHS, DVD, Wide.** Jon Voight, Burt Reynolds, Ronny Cox, Ned Beatty, James Dickey, Bill McKinney, Ed O'Neill, Charley Boorman; ***D:*** John Boorman; ***W:*** James Dickey; ***C:*** Vilmos Zsigmond; ***M:*** Eric Weissburg.

Delivered *Death by Pizza* 1998 (R) Pizza deliveryman Will Sherman (Strickland) is the unfortunate witness to a murder by serial killer Reed (Eldard). When

Reed realizes Will saw him, he goes after him but the cops have come to the conclusion that it's Will who's the killer—so he has to evade the cops and Reed as well. It's all played for laughs. **90m/C VHS, DVD, Wide.** David Strickland, Ron Eldard, Leslie Stefanson, Scott Bairstow, Nicky Katt, Jillian Armenante, Bob Morrisey, Mark Berry; ***D:*** Guy Ferland; ***W:*** Andrew Liotta, Lawrence Trilling; ***C:*** Shane Kelly; ***M:*** Nicholas Pike.

The Delivery 🦴🦴 **1999 (R)** Euro-thriller finds buddies Guy (Douglas) and Alfred (van Huet) so desperate for money that they agree to do a job for a crime boss. Seems he needs them to deliver a large shipment of Ecstasy from Barcelona to Amsterdam. Added into the mix is the prerequisite tough babe—in this case, Loulou (Meriel). Drugs, chases, sex, and violence. **100m/C VHS, DVD, Wide.** *NL BE* Fredja Van Huet, Freddy Douglas, Auriele Meriel, Rik Launspach, Esmee De La Bretoniere, Jonathan Harvey, Hidde Maas, Christopher Simon; ***D:*** Roel Reine; ***W:*** David Hilton; ***C:*** Jan van den Nieuwenhuyzen.

Delivery Boys 🦴½ **1984 (R)** The "Delivery Boys," three breakdancers aiming to win the $10,000 New York City Break-Off, find unusual perils that may keep them from competing. **94m/C VHS.** Joss Marcano, Tom Sierchio, Jim Soriero, Mario Van Peebles, Samantha Fox; ***D:*** Ken Handley.

Delos Adventure 🦴 **1986 (R)** A geological expedition in South America stumbles upon covert Russian activities and must battle to survive in this overly violent actioner. **98m/C VHS.** Roger Kern, Jenny Neumann, Kevin Brophy; ***D:*** Joseph Purcell.

The Delta 🦴🦴 **1997** White, middleclass Memphis teenager Lincoln Bloom (Gray) is leading a double life. He parties with his girlfriend Monica (Huss) and macho buddies but also sneaks off to cruise the city's gay pick-up spots. Which is where he meets the older John (Chan), an Amerasian immigrant from Vietnam, whose unknown father was a black soldier. The two have a brief romantic idyll but while the openly gay John is desperate for love, Lincoln is still uncertain about his sexual identity and the disparity between their lives. Feature debut for both Sachs and his two lead actors. **85m/C VHS.** Shayne Gray, Thang Chan, Rachel Zan Huss, Ricky Little; ***D:*** Ira Sachs; ***W:*** Ira Sachs; ***C:*** Benjamin P. Speth; ***M:*** Michael Rohatyn.

Delta Force 🦴🦴 **1986 (R)** Based on the true hijacking of a TWA plane in June 1985. Arab terrorists take over an airliner; the Delta Force, led by Lee Marvin and featuring Norris as its best fighter, rescue the passengers in ways that cater directly to our nationalistic revenge fantasies. Average thriller, exciting and tense at times, with fine work from Marvin, Norris, and Forster. **125m/C VHS, DVD.** Lee Marvin, Chuck Norris, Shelley Winters, Martin Balsam, George Kennedy, Hanna Schygulla, Susan Strasberg, Bo Svenson, Joey Bishop, Lainie Kazan, Robert Forster, Robert Vaughn, Kim Delaney; ***D:*** Menahem Golan; ***W:*** James Bruner; ***C:*** David Gurfinkel; ***M:*** Alan Silvestri.

Delta Force 2: Operation Stranglehold 🦴½ **1990 (R)** Delta Force is back with martial artist and military technician Norris at the helm. Action-packed and tense. **110m/C VHS, DVD.** John P. Ryan, Chuck Norris, Billy Drago, Richard Jaeckel, Paul Perri; ***D:*** Aaron Norris; ***W:*** Lee Reynolds; ***C:*** Joao Fernandes; ***M:*** Frederic Talgorn.

Delta Force 3: The Killing Game 🦴½ *Young Commandos* **1991 (R)** A terrorist mastermind plants an atomic bomb in an American city, and the President has only one choice...call in the Delta Force. The leading men in this lackluster thriller are the sons of some of Hollywood's biggest stars. **97m/C VHS.** Nick Cassavetes, Eric Douglas, Mike Norris, Matthew Penn, John P. Ryan, Sandy Ward; ***D:*** Sam Firstenberg; ***W:*** Boaz Davidson.

Delta Force Commando 🦴½ **1987 (R)** Two U.S. Fighter pilots fight against terrorism in the deadly Nicaraguan jungle. **90m/C VHS.** *IT* Fred Williamson, Bo Svenson; ***D:*** Frank (Pierluigi Ciriaci) Valenti.

Delta Force Commando 2 🦴 *Priority Red One* **1990 (R)** The celluloid was hardly dry on the first "Delta Force Commando" before the resourceful Italians began grinding out this follow-up, with the lead commando getting the Force entangled in a deadly international conspiracy. **100m/C VHS.** *IT* Richard Hatch, Fred Williamson, Giannina Facio, Van Johnson; ***D:*** Frank (Pierluigi Ciriaci) Valenti.

Delta Fox 🦴🦴 **1977** Delta Fox is carrying $1 million for the mob, but the mob is carrying a grudge and the chase is on. **90m/C VHS.** Priscilla Barnes, Richard Lynch, Stuart Whitman, John Ireland; ***D:*** Beverly Sebastian, Ferd Sebastian.

Delta Heat 🦴🦴 **1992 (R)** A new designer drug hits L.A. and detective Mike Bishop (Edwards) follows his partner to the drug's source in Louisiana. When Bishop arrives he discovers his partner has been tortured and murdered in order to keep the drug lord's foes in line. Bishop must then save himself and find justice in the steamy streets of New Orleans. Routine lone guy vs. bad guys actioner. **91m/C VHS.** Anthony Edwards, Lance Henriksen, Betsy Russell, Linda Dona, Rod Masterson, John McConnell, Clyde Jones; ***D:*** Michael Fischa.

Delta of Venus 🦴½ **1995 (R)** Paris, 1940—beautiful young American Elena (England), an aspiring author, falls for handsome Lawrence (Mandylor), a writer of dirty books. But she finds out Lawrence isn't faithful and winds up supporting herself as a nude model and writing her own erotic tales. Lots of sex scenes and an equal amount of pretensions. Based on the erotic novel "Delta of Venus" by Anais Nin. Prague substitutes for Paris as the film location. Also availble unrated; the theatrical version came out as NC-17. **100m/C VHS.** Audie England, Costas Mandylor, Erick Da Silva, Raven Snow; ***D:*** Zalman King; ***W:*** Patricia Louisianna Knop, Elisa Rothstein; ***C:*** Eagle Egilsson; ***M:*** George S. Clinton.

Deluge 🦴🦴 **1933** Tidal waves causd by earthquakes have destroyed most of New York (though some may think this is no great loss) in this early sci-fi pic. **72m/B VHS.** Edward Van Sloan, Peggy Shannon, Sidney Blackmer, Fred Kohler Sr., Matt Moore, Samuel S. Hinds, Lane Chandler; ***D:*** Felix Feist.

The Deluge 🦴🦴 *Potop* **1973** Romance woven around the Polish-Swedish war in the 17th century. Adapted from the 1886 novel by Nobel prize-winning author Henryk Sienkiewicz, and filmed largely on location in authentic castles of the era. Polish with subtitles. **185m/C VHS.** *PL* Daniel Olbrychski, Malgorzata Braunek, Wladyslaw Hancza, Leszek Herdegen, Andrzej Lapicki; ***D:*** Jerzy Hoffman; ***C:*** Jerzy Wojcik; ***M:*** Kazimierz Serocki.

Delusion 🦴½ *The House Where Death Lives* **1984 (R)** Gothic thriller in which invalid Cotten and family are harassed by a possibly supernatural killer as told by Cotten's nurse. Filmed in 1980. Ending is a letdown. **93m/C VHS.** Patricia Pearcy, David Hayward, John Dukakis, Joseph Cotten, Simone Griffeth; ***D:*** Alan Beattie.

Delusion 🦴🦴½ **1991 (R)** A yuppie with an embezzled fortune is held up in the Nevada desert by a psycho hood with a showgirl lover. But who's really in charge here? The snappy, hip, film-noir thriller takes a few unlikely twists and has an open Lady-or-the-Tiger finale that may infuriate. **100m/C VHS, Wide.** Jim Metzler, Jennifer Rubin, Kyle Secor, Robert Costanzo, Tracey Walter, Jerry Orbach; ***D:*** Carl Colpaert; ***W:*** Carl Colpaert, Kurt Voss; ***C:*** Geza Sinkovics; ***M:*** Barry Adamson.

Delusions of Grandeur 🦴🦴½ *La Folle des Grandeurs* **1976** A French comedy of court intrigue set in 17th-century Spain. In French with English subtitles. Based loosely on Victor Hugo's "Ruy Blas." **85m/C VHS.** *FR* Yves Montand, Louis de Funes, Alice Sapritch, Karin Schubert, Gabriele Tinti; ***D:*** Gerard Oury.

Demented 🦴 **1980 (R)** Beautiful and talented woman is brutally gang-raped by four men, but her revenge is sweet and deadly as she entices each to bed and gives them a big dose of their own medicine. All-too-familiar plot offers nothing new. **92m/C VHS.** Sallee Elyse, Bruce Gilchrist; ***D:*** Arthur Jeffreys, Alex Rebar; ***W:*** Alex Rebar.

Dementia 🦴🦴½ **1998** Wild-eyed sexual thriller owes a bit to "Diabolique." Recovering from a breakdown, wealthy Kathrine (Bursel) becomes friendly with her outpatient nurse Luisa (Sanchez). Then Luisa's smarmy ex-husband Sonny (Schulze) shows up and things get twisty. Production values are not top drawer and the cast is not well known, but director Keith keeps things moving nicely. **85m/C DVD, Wide.** Marisol Padilla Sanchez, Patricia Bursiel, Matt Schulze, Azura Skye, Matthew Sullivan, Jesus Nebot, Susan Davis; ***D:*** Woody Keith; ***W:*** Woody Keith, R.G. Fry; ***C:*** David Trulli; ***M:*** Karl Preusser.

Dementia 13 🦴🦴½ *The Haunted and the Hunted* **1963** This eerie thriller, set in a creepy castle, is an early Coppola film about the members of an Irish family who are being offed by an axe murderer one by one. **75m/B VHS, DVD.** William Campbell, Luana Anders, Bart Patton, Patrick Magee, Barbara Dowling, Ethne Dunn, Mary Mitchell, Karl Schanzer; ***D:*** Francis Ford Coppola; ***W:*** Francis Ford Coppola; ***C:*** Charles Hannawalt; ***M:*** Ronald Stein.

Demetrius and the Gladiators 🦴🦴½ **1954** A sequel to "The Robe," wherein the holy-robe-carrying slave is enlisted as one of Caligula's gladiators and mixes with the trampy empress Messalina. **101m/C VHS, DVD, Wide.** Victor Mature, Susan Hayward, Michael Rennie, Debra Paget, Anne Bancroft, Jay Robinson, Barry Jones, Richard Egan, William Marshall, Ernest Borgnine; ***D:*** Delmer Daves; ***W:*** Philip Dunne; ***C:*** Milton Krasner.

The Demi-Paradise 🦴🦴🦴 *Adventure for Two* **1943** Tongue-in-cheek look at people's perceptions of foreigners has Olivier as a Russian inventor (?!) who comes to England with some trepidation. Though the Brits are plenty quirky, he manages to find romance with Ward in this charming look at British life. **110m/B VHS.** *GB* Laurence Olivier, Penelope Dudley Ward, Margaret Rutherford, Marjorie Fielding, Felix Aylmer, Guy Middleton, Michael Shepley; ***D:*** Anthony Asquith.

Demolition 🦴½ **1977** Ex-international courier finds that the "simple" task he has consented to do for his old employers is deceptively hazardous. **90m/C VHS.** John Waters, Belinda Giblin, Fred Steele, Vincent Ball; ***D:*** Kevin James Dobson.

Demolition High 🦴🦴½ **1995 (R)** Standard actioner finds New York kid Lenny (Haim) having problems adjusting to his new California high school, where he's labeled a troublemaker. But real trouble comes along when a group of terrorists, fleeing police after a robbery, take over the school and hold the teachers and students as hostages. Fortunately, Lenny is able to lead a secret counterattact. **85m/C VHS.** Corey Haim, Alan Thicke, Jeff Kober, Dick Van Patten; ***D:*** Jim Wynorski; ***W:*** Steve Jankowski; ***C:*** Zoran Hochstatter; ***M:*** Kevin Kiner.

Demolition Man 🦴🦴 **1993 (R)** Nobrain sci-fier rests on the action skills of Stallone and Snipes. Psychovillain Snipes (sporting a Dennis Rodman 'do) is pursued by equally violent cop Stallone in the late 1990s. Then they're cryogenically frozen, defrosted in 2032, and back to their old tricks. One problem. This is not a fun future: virtual reality sex is the only kind allowed and puritan ethics and political correctness are enforced to the max. Cop and bad guy get to show this highly orderly society some really violent times. Implausible plot and minimal acting, but lots of action and violence for fans. **115m/C VHS, DVD, 8mm, Wide.** Sylvester Stallone, Wesley Snipes, Sandra Bullock, Nigel Hawthorne, Benjamin Bratt, Bob Gunton, Glenn Shadix, Denis Leary; ***D:*** Marco Brambilla; ***W:*** Daniel Waters, Robert Reneau, Peter M. Lenkov; ***C:*** Alex Thomson; ***M:*** Elliot Goldenthal.

The Demolitionist 🦴🦴 **1995 (R)** Tough undercover cop Alyssa Lloyd (Eggert) is killed by crimelord Mad Dog Burne (Grieco) and then resurrected by scientist Jack Crowley (Abbott) as a hard-hitting futuristic superheroine who's out to save Metro City from evil. **100m/C VHS, DVD.** Nicole Eggert, Richard Grieco, Bruce Abbott, Susan Tyrrell, Peter Jason, Sarah Douglas, Andras Jones, Heather Langenkamp, David Anthony Marshall, Jack Nance, Tom Savini; ***D:*** Robert Kurtzman; ***W:*** Brian DiMuccio, Dino Vindeni; ***C:*** Marcus Hahn; ***M:*** Shawn Patterson.

The Demon 🦴½ **1981 (R)** A small town may be doomed to extinction, courtesy of a monster's thirst for the blood of its inhabitants. **94m/C VHS, DVD.** *SA* Cameron Mitchell, Jennifer Holmes; ***D:*** Percival Rubens; ***W:*** Percival Rubens; ***C:*** Vincent Cox.

Demon Barber of Fleet Street 🦴🦴½ *Sweeney Todd: The Demon Barber of Fleet Street* **1936** Loosely based on an actual event, this film inspired the 1978 smash play "Sweeney Todd." Slaughter stars as a mad barber who doesn't just cut his client's hair. He happens to have a deal cooked up with the baker to provide him with some nice 'juicy' filling for his meat pies. Manages to be creepy and funny at the same time. **68m/B VHS.** *GB* Tod Slaughter, Eve Lister, Bruce Seton; ***D:*** George King.

Demon for Trouble 🦴 **1934** Outlaws are murdering land buyers in this routine western. **58m/B VHS.** Bob Steele, Don Alvarado, Gloria Shea, Nick Stuart; ***D:*** Robert F. "Bob" Hill; ***W:*** Jack Natteford; ***C:*** William C. Thompson.

Demon Hunter 🦴½ **1988** Terror reigns while a deranged killer stalks his next victim. **90m/C VHS.** George Ellis, Erin Fleming, Marrianne Gordon; ***D:*** Massey Cramer; ***W:*** Bob Corley.

A Demon in My View 🦴🦴½ **1992 (R)** In a role similar to his infamous Norman Bates in "Psycho," Perkins stars as a man who hides a terrible secret—he is a former serial killer. When a fellow tenant in his apartment house accidentally destroys his doll, Perkins' tenuous sanity is shaken and he begins killing again. A smart thriller. Perkins last big-screen role. **98m/C VHS.** Anthony Perkins, Sophie Ward, Stratford Johns; ***D:*** Petra Haffter; ***W:*** Petra Haffter.

The Demon Lover woof! *Devil Master; Master of Evil* **1977 (R)** Leader of a satanic cult calls forth the devil when he doesn't get his way. Poorly acted and badly produced. Features comic book artists Val "Howard the Duck" Mayerick and Gunnar "Leatherface" Hansen. **87m/C VHS.** Christmas Robbins, Val Mayerick, Gunnar Hansen, Tom Hutton, David Howard; ***D:*** Donald G. Jackson, Jerry Younkins; ***W:*** Donald G. Jackson, Jerry Younkins.

Demon Lust 🦴🦴 **2001** "The Sopranos" meet "Dracula" in this ultra low-budget New Jersey independent production. Nick (Teller) and Tony (Vincent) owe $5,000 to a mobster who has sent a thug (Savini) to collect. After some allegedly comic bits, the two guys find themselves hooked up with Amanda (Stevens), a beautiful babe who's really a monster. Most of the lead roles are well acted. **??m/C DVD.** Edward Lee Vincent, Zander Teller, Brinke Stevens, Tom Savini; ***D:*** David A. Goldberg; ***W:*** Coven Balfour; ***C:*** Joseph Robert Jobe; ***M:*** Coven Balfour.

Demon of Paradise woof! **1987 (R)** Dynamite fishing off the coast of Hawaii unearths an ancient, man-eating lizard-man. Unveven, unexciting horror attempt. **84m/C VHS.** Kathryn Witt, William (Bill) Steis, Leslie Huntly, Laura Banks, Frederick Bailey; ***D:*** Cirio H. Santiago; ***W:*** Frederick Bailey; ***C:*** Ricardo Remias.

Demon Possessed 🦴½ **1993 (R)** When Tom is critically injured in a snowmobile race in a remote woods, he and his friends find shelter in a deserted children's camp. It turns out the camp was run by a secret religious cult that practiced occult murder and the demon that haunted the place has never left. When Tom dies this satanic spirit finds the perfect host to return to human form and continue its bloody work. **97m/C VHS.** Dawn Laurrie, Aaron Kjenass, David Fields, Eve Montgomery; ***D:*** Christopher Webster; ***W:*** Julian Weaver; ***M:*** John Tatgenhorst.

Demon Queen 🦴 **1980** A vampirish woman seduces, then murders, many men. **70m/C VHS.** Mary Fanaro, Dennis Stewart, Cliff Dance; ***D:*** Donald Farmer.

Demon Rage 🦴½ *Satan's Mistress; Fury of the Succubus; Dark Eyes* **1982 (R)** Neglected housewife drifts under the spell of a phantom lover. **98m/C VHS.** Britt Ekland, Lana Wood, Kabir Bedi, Don Galloway, John Carradine, Sherry Scott; ***D:*** James Polakof.

Demon Seed 🦴🦴🦴 **1977 (R)** When a scientist (Weaver) and his wife (Christie) separate so he can work on "Proteus," a somewhat biological supercomputer, the terminal within his computer-controlled home allows Proteus to infiltrate, taking over the house and his wife. Proteus' intent? To procreate. Bizarre and taut; based on a Dean Koontz novel. **97m/C VHS.** Julie Christie, Fritz Weaver, Gerrit Graham, Berry Kroeger, Ron Hays, Lisa Lu, Larry J. Blake; ***D:*** Donald Cammell; ***W:*** Robert Jaffe, Roger O. Hirson; ***C:*** Bill Butler; ***V:*** Robert Vaughn.

Demon Wind 🦴½ **1990 (R)** A gateway to Hell opens up on a secluded farm and various heroic types try to close it. Meanwhile, demons attempt to possess those humans in their midst. Zombies abound in this near-woof. **97m/C VHS.** Eric Larson, Francine Lapensee, Rufus Norris; ***D:*** Charles Philip Moore.

Demon with a Glass Hand 🦴½ **1964** In the vein of "The Terminator," a man goes back two hundred years in time to escape the evil race that rules the planet. **63m/B VHS.** Robert Culp, Arlene Martel, Abraham Sofaer.

Demonia woof! **1990** Archaeologists digging in Sicily uncover a sealed convent where five nuns were crucified in the 15th century. This discovery unleashes an ancient evil and bizarre murders begin to take place. Unfortunately, that's about it as far as the plot goes. Even by Fulci's standards, "Demonia" is slow and pondering, with many scenes taking place twice, once in reality and then again in a dream (nightmare?). Fulci's trademark gore is scant and the special effects are laughable. Even die-hard Fulci fans will be disappointed. **90m/C DVD, Wide.** *IT* Brett Halsey, Meg Register, Carla Cassola, Al Cliver, Lucio Fulci; ***D:*** Lucio Fulci; ***W:*** Lucio Fulci, Piero Regnoli; ***C:*** Luis Ciccarese.

Demonic Toys 🦴½ **1990 (R)** The possessed play-things attack a bunch of unfortunates in a warehouse, and pumped-up lady cop Scoggins deserves an award for keeping a straight face. Skimpily scripted gore from the horror assembly-line at Full Moon Productions. Far more entertaining are the multiple behind-the-scenes featurettes on the tape. **86m/C VHS.** Richard Speight Jr., Tracy Scoggins, Bentley Mitchum, Michael Russo, Jeff Weston, Daniel Cerney, Pete Schrum; ***D:*** Peter Manoogian.

Demonoid, Messenger of Death 🦴 *Macabra* **1981 (R)** Discovery of an ancient temple of Satan worship drastically changes the lives of a young couple when the husband becomes possessed by the Demonoid, which initially takes on the form of a severed hand. Poor script needs hand, producing a number of unintentionally laughable moments. **85m/C VHS.** Samantha Eggar, Stuart Whitman, Roy Cameron Jenson; ***D:*** Alfredo Zacharias.

The Demons 🦴 *Les Demons; Los Demonios* **1974 (R)** As she slips into death, a tortured woman curses her torturers. **116m/C VHS.** *FR PT* Anne Libert, Britt Nichols, Doris Thomas, Howard Vernon, Karin (Karen) Field, Luis Barboo; ***D:*** Jess (Jesus) Franco, Clifford Brown; ***W:*** Jess (Jesus) Franco.

Demons 🦴½ *Demoni* **1986 (R)** A horror film in a Berlin theatre is so involving that its viewers become the demons they are seeing. The new monsters turn on the other audience members. Virtually plotless, very explicit. Rock soundtrack by Accept, Go West, Motley Crue, and others. Revered in some circles, blasted in others. Followed by "Demons 2." **89m/C VHS, DVD.** *IT* Urbano Barberini, Natasha Hovey, Paolo Cozza, Karl Zinny, Fiore Argento, Fabiola Toledo, Nicoletta Elmi, Michele (Michael) Soavi; ***D:*** Lamberto Bava; ***W:*** Lamberto Bava, Dario Argento, Franco Ferrini, Dardano Sacchetti; ***C:*** Gianlorenzo Battaglia; ***M:*** Claudio Simonetti.

Demons 2 🦴½ **1987 (R)** Inferior sequel to "Demons." The son of horror-meister Mario Bava, Lamberto collaborated with Italian auteur Argento (who co-wrote and produced) to create an improbable sequel (storywise) which seems to have been edited by some kind of crazed cutting room slasher with equally hackneyed dubbing. Residents of a chi-chi high rise watching a documentary about the events of "Demons"—a sort of high-tech play-within-a-play ploy—when a demon emerges from the TV, spreads his creepy cooties, and causes the tenants to sprout fangs and claws and nasty tempers. Lots of blood drips from ceilings, plumbing fixtures, and various body parts. **88m/C VHS, DVD.** *IT* David Edwin Knight, Nancy Brill, Coralina Cataldi Tassoni, Bobby Rhodes, Asia Argento, Virginia Bryant; ***D:*** Lamberto Bava; ***W:*** Dario Argento, Lamberto Bava; ***C:*** Gianlorenzo Battaglia; ***M:*** Simon Boswell.

Demons in the Garden 🦴🦴🦴 *Demonios En El Jardin* **1982 (R)** Centers on the disintegration of a family after the end of the Spanish Civil War, due to sibling rivalries and a variety of indiscretions. Problems mount as two brothers become involved with their stepsister. Story takes on poignancy in its narration by a young boy. Beautiful cinematography. In Spanish with English subtitles. **100m/C VHS.** *SP* Angela Molina, Ana Belen, Encarna Paso, Imanol Arias; ***D:*** Manuel Gutierrez Aragon; ***C:*** Jose Luis Alcaine.

Demons of Ludlow 🦴 **1975** Demons attend a small town's bicentennial celebration intent on raising a little hell of their own. **83m/C VHS.** Paul von Hauser, Stephanie Cushna, James Robinson, Carol Perry; ***D:*** Steven Kuether.

Demons of the Mind 🦴🦴 *Blood Evil; Blood Will Have Blood* **1972 (R)** A sordid psychological horror film about a baron in 19th century Austria who imprisons his children, fearing that mental illness is a family trait. **85m/C VHS.** *GB* Michael Hordern, Patrick Magee, Yvonne Mitchell, Robert Hardy, Gillian Hills, Virginia Wetherell, Shane Briant, Paul Jones, Thomas Heathcote, Kenneth J. Warren; ***D:*** Peter Sykes; ***W:*** Christopher Wicking; ***C:*** Arthur Grant.

Demonstone 🦴 *Heartstone* **1989 (R)** A TV reporter becomes possessed by a Filipino demon and carries out an ancient curse against the family of a corrupt government official. **90m/C VHS.** R. Lee Ermey, Jan-Michael Vincent, Nancy Everhard; ***D:*** Andrew Prowse.

Demonstrator 🦴🦴½ **1971** A father and son are at odds when dad heads an Asian military coalition and junior protests. Notable for being one of the first major Australian films to use an entirely native cast. **82m/C VHS.** *AU* Joe James, Irene Inescort, Gerard Maguire, Wendy Lingham, Harold Hopkins; ***D:*** Warwick Freeman.

Demonwarp woof! **1987** A vengeance-minded hunter journeys into an evil, primeval forest to kill the monsters that abducted his daughter. **91m/C VHS.** George Kennedy, Pamela Gilbert; ***D:*** Emmett Alston; ***W:*** Bruce Akiyama.

Dempsey 🦴🦴 **1983** In this film, based on Jack Dempsey's autobiography, Williams plays the role of the famed world heavyweight champ. His rise through the boxing ranks as well as his personal life are chronicled. A bit slow-moving considering the pounding fists and other action. **110m/C VHS.** Treat Williams, Sam Waterston, Sally Kellerman, Victoria Tennant, Peter Mark Richman, Jesse Vint, Bonnie Bartlett, James Noble; ***D:*** Gus Trikonis; ***M:*** Billy Goldenberg. **TV**

Denial: The Dark Side of Passion 🦴🦴 **1991 (R)** A strong-willed woman tries to put a destructive love affair behind her—but if she succeeded there'd be no movie. Torrid stuff with a watchable cast. **103m/C VHS.** Robin Wright Penn, Jason Patric, Barry Primus, Christina Harnos, Rae Dawn Chong; ***D:*** Erin Dignam; ***W:*** Erin Dignam.

Denise Calls Up 🦴🦴½ **1995 (PG-13)** Comedy about futility and complications of urban relationships among overworked professionals. A group of six work-at-home city friends socialize, romance, and date entirely via phone, fax, and computer without ever meeting or leaving their homes, even for a close friend's funeral (who dies, oddly enough, while on the phone). Subplot involves title character, Denise (Ubach) tracking down sperm donor Martin (Gunther) and eventually giving birth, with the help of her cellular coaches. Funny premise is executed well, but doesn't hold up over a (barely) feature length film. **79m/C VHS.** Timothy Daly, Dana Wheeler-Nicholson, Caroleen Feeney, Liev Schreiber, Dan Gunther, Aida Turturro, Alanna Ubach, Sylvia Miles; ***D:*** Hal Salwen; ***W:*** Hal Salwen; ***C:*** Mike Mayers; ***M:*** Lynne Geller.

Dennis the Menace 🦴🦴½ **1993 (PG)** Straight from the Hughes kiddie farm comes Kevin McAllister—oops!—Dennis Mitchell (newcomer Gamble), curious, crafty, and blond five-year-old. He dreams and schemes, but everything he does manages to be a threat to the physical and mental well being of hot-head neighbor Mr. Wilson (Matthau, perfectly cast as the grump). Lloyd is very nasty as protagonist Switchblade Sam; Plowright, Thompson, and Stanton round out the cast as Mrs. Wilson and the Mitchell parents, respectively. Sure to please young kids, but parents may be less enthralled with this adaptation of the popular '50s comic strip and subsequent TV series. **96m/C VHS, 8mm, Wide.** Walter Matthau, Mason Gamble, Joan Plowright, Christopher Lloyd, Lea Thompson, Robert Stanton, Billie Bird, Paul Winfield, Amy Sakasitz, Kellen Hathaway, Arnold Stang; ***D:*** Nick Castle; ***W:*** John Hughes; ***C:*** Thomas Ackerman; ***M:*** Jerry Goldsmith.

Dennis the Menace: Dinosaur Hunter 🦴🦴½ **1993 (G)** Another version of Hank Ketchum's mischievous cartoon character brought to life to have adventures and disturb his neighbor Mr. Wilson. This time Dennis discovers a huge, primitive bone in his backyard and when an archaeologist declares it's a dinosaur bone, news crews, tourists, and scientists are suddenly everywhere. This badly disturbs Mr. Wilson's retirement and Dennis and his friends must save the day (and their neighborhood). **118m/C VHS.** Victor Dimattia, William Windom, Pat Estrin, Jim Jansen, Patsy Garrett; ***D:*** Doug Rogers.

Dennis the Menace Strikes Again 🦴🦴½ **1998 (G)** Direct-to-video sequel finds hyperactive Dennis (Cooper) trying to save curmudgeonly Mr. Wilson (Rickles) from a pair of con men. **75m/C VHS.** Justin Cooper, Don Rickles, George Kennedy, Betty White, Brian Doyle-Murray, Carrot Top; ***D:*** Charles Kanganis; ***W:*** Tim McCanlies; ***C:*** Christopher Faloona; ***M:*** Graeme Revell. **VIDEO**

The Dentist 🦴🦴🦴½ **1932** Fields treats several oddball patients in his office. After watching the infamous tooth-pulling scene, viewers will be sure to brush regularly. **22m/B VHS.** W.C. Fields, Elise Cavanna, Marjorie "Babe" Kane, Bud Jamison, Zedna Farley, Dorothy Granger, Arnold Gray; ***D:*** Leslie Pearce, Monte Brice; ***W:*** W.C. Fields.

The Dentist 🦴½ **1996 (R)** After seeing this movie, you may never want to sit in that dental chair again. When his marriage falls apart, L.A. dental specialist Dr. Alan Feinstone (Bernsen) takes to pill popping and psychotic behavior, including demonic drilling and particularly bloody oral surgery. **93m/C VHS, DVD.** Corbin Bernsen, Ken Foree, Linda Hoffman, Michael Stadvec; ***D:*** Brian Yuzna; ***W:*** Charles Finch, Stuart Gordon, Dennis Paoli; ***C:*** Levie Isaacks; ***M:*** Alan Howarth.

The Dentist 2: Brace Yourself 🦴 **1998 (R)** Allan Feinstone (Bernsen) has escaped from the asylum to which he was sent in the first film. He's settled in a rural community and set up another practice. This is one guy who doesn't claim to be painless. **99m/C VHS, DVD.** Corbin Bernsen, Jillian McWhirter, Linda Hoffman; ***D:*** Richard Smith; ***W:*** Richard Smith; ***C:*** Jurgen Baum; ***M:*** Alan Howarth. **VIDEO**

Dentist In the Chair 🦴½ **1960** Dumb Brit comedy about dental students David (Monkhouse) and Brian (Stevens) who inadvertently get involved with small-time crook Sam Field (Connor) who gives them a load of expensive dental equipment. But they have to get rid of the goods before they're accused of theft. **87m/B VHS.** *GB* Bob Monkhouse, Ronnie Stevens, Kenneth Connor, Peggy Cummins, Eric Barker, Stuart Saunders; ***D:*** Don Chaffey; ***W:*** Val Guest, Bob Monkhouse; ***C:*** Reg Wyer; ***M:*** Kenneth V. Jones.

The Denver & Rio Grande 🦴🦴½ **1951** Action-packed western about two rival railroads competing to be the first to complete a line through the Royal Gorge. Plot is predictable, but the scene featuring two trains crashing into each other is worth it (Haskin used actual trains for this stunt). **89m/C VHS.** Edmond O'Brien, Sterling Hayden, Dean Jagger, ZaSu Pitts, J. Carrol Naish; ***D:*** Byron Haskin.

Department Store 🦴 *Bargain Basement* **1935** Confusing crime-drama involving a store manager who mistakes an ex-convict for his employer's heir. Based on a story by H. F. Maltby. **65m/B VHS.** *GB* Garry Marsh, Eve Gray, Sebastian Shaw, Geraldine Fitzgerald, Jack Melford; ***D:*** Leslie Hiscott.

Depraved 🦴½ **1998** Opella and Dan spice up their sex lives by acting out their fantasies. But they start to go too far for Dan and he has a fight with his fiance, who storms out. Only the next morning Dan discovers Opella's dead body. Naturally, instead of calling the cops, Dan calls his brother, and they decide to dispose of the body and come up with an alibi. Can you spell trouble? **90m/C VHS.** Seidy Lopez, Antonio Garcia Guzman, Mario Lopez, Barbara Niven; ***D:*** Rogelio Lobato. **VIDEO**

The Deputy Drummer 🦴½ **1935** Second-rate early British musical, notable as a later vehicle for silent-era star Lane. He plays a penniless composer who impersonates an aristocrat to attend a party, and catches jewel robbers in the act. **71m/B VHS.** *GB* Lupino Lane, Jean Denis, Kathleen Kelly, Wallace Lupino, Margaret Yarde, Syd Crossley; ***D:*** Henry W. George; ***W:*** Reginald Long.

Deputy Marshal 🦴½ **1950** Hall trails a pair of bankrobbers, fights off land-grabbers, and finds romance as well. **75m/B VHS.** Jon Hall, Frances Langford, Dick Foran; ***D:*** William Berke; ***W:*** William Berke.

Der Purimshpiler 🦴🦴½ *The Purim Player; The Jester; The Jewish Jester* **1937** A drifter embarks on a quest for happiness, which takes him to various small towns. In one, he meets and falls in love with a shoemaker's daughter. In Yiddish with English subtitles. **90m/B VHS.** *PL* Miriam Kressyn, Zygmund Turkow, Hymie Jacobsen; ***D:*** Joseph Green.

Deranged 🦴🦴🦴 **1974 (R)** Of the numerous movies based on the cannibalistic exploits of Ed Gein ("Psycho," "The Texas Chainsaw Massacre," etc.), this is the most accurate. A dead-on performance by Blossom and a twisted sense of humor help move things along nicely. The two directors, Gillen and Ormsby, previously worked together on the classic "Children Shouldn't Play with Dead Things." An added attraction is the early special effect work of gore wizard Tom Savini. **82m/C VHS.** *CA* Roberts Blossom, Cosette Lee, Robert Warner, Marcia Diamond, Brian Sneagle, Leslie (Les) Carlson, Marian Waldman, Micki Moore, Pat Orr, Robert McHeady; ***D:*** Jeff Gillen, Alan Ormsby; ***W:*** Jeff Gillen, Alan Ormsby; ***C:*** Jack McGowan; ***M:*** Carl Zittrer.

Deranged 🦴½ **1987 (R)** A mentally unstable, pregnant woman is attacked in her apartment after her husband leaves town. She spends the rest of the movie engaged in psychotic encounters, real and imagined. Technically not bad, but extremely violent and grim. Not to be confused with 1974 movie of the same name. **85m/C VHS.** Jane (Veronica Hart) Hamilton, Paul Siederman, Jennifer Delora, James Gillis, Jill Cumer, Gary Goldman; ***D:*** Chuck Vincent.

Derby 🦴🦴🦴 **1971 (R)** The documentary story of the rise to fame of roller-derby stars on the big rink. **91m/C VHS.** Charlie O'Connell, Lydia Gray, Janet Earp, Ann Colvello, Mike Snell; ***D:*** Robert Kaylor.

Dersu Uzala 🦴🦴🦴½ **1975** An acclaimed, photographically breathtaking film about a Russian surveyor in Siberia who befriends a crusty, resourceful Mongolian. They begin to teach each other about their respective worlds. Produced in Russia; one of Kurosawa's stranger films. **140m/C VHS, DVD, Wide.** *JP RU* Yuri Solomin,

Maxim Munzuk; ***D:*** Akira Kurosawa; ***W:*** Akira Kurosawa, Yuri Nagibin; ***C:*** Asakazu Nakai, Yuri Gantman, Fyodor Dobronravov; ***M:*** Isaak Shvartz. Oscars '75: Foreign Film.

Descending Angel 🦴🦴🦴 **1990 (R)** The premise is familiar: a swastika-friendly collaborator is forced out of the closet. But the cast and scripting make this cable there's-a-Nazi-in the-woodwork suspenser better than average, despite its flawed finale. Scott plays a well-respected Romanian refugee—active in the community, in the church, and in Romanian-American activities—whose daughter's fiance (Roberts) suspects him of Nazi collusion. **96m/C VHS.** George C. Scott, Diane Lane, Eric Roberts, Mark Margolis, Vyto Ruginis, Amy Aquino, Richard Jenkins, Jan Rubes; ***D:*** George C. Scott, Jeremy Paul Kagan; ***W:*** George C. Scott. **CABLE**

Desert Bloom 🦴🦴🦴 **1986 (PG)** On the eve of a nearby nuclear bomb test, a beleaguered alcoholic veteran and his family struggle through tensions brought on by a promiscuous visiting aunt and the chaotic, rapidly changing world. Gish shines as the teenage daughter through whose eyes the story unfolds. From a story by Corr and Linda Ramy. **103m/C VHS.** Jon Voight, JoBeth Williams, Ellen Barkin, Annabeth Gish, Allen (Goorwitz) Garfield, Jay Underwood; ***D:*** Eugene Corr; ***W:*** Eugene Corr; ***C:*** Reynaldo Villalobos; ***M:*** Brad Fiedel.

Desert Blue 🦴🦴 **1998 (R)** Baxter, California is a tiny (pop. 87) desert town whose one claim to fame is a towering re-creation of an ice cream cone that has drawn the attention of pop culture prof Lance (Heard). Lance has come to Baxter with his snooty teen TV star daughter, Skye (Hudson), and the duo are trapped in town when it's quarantined by a toxic spill. Skye eventually connects to the town's disaffected teens, including Blue (Sexton), Pete (Affleck), and Ely (Ricci). **87m/C VHS, DVD.** Brendan Sexton III, Kate Hudson, John Heard, Christina Ricci, Casey Affleck, Sara Gilbert, Ethan Suplee, Lucinda Jenney; ***D:*** Morgan J. Freeman; ***W:*** Morgan J. Freeman; ***C:*** Enrique Chediak; ***M:*** Vytas Nagisetty.

Desert Commandos 🦴🦴 **1967** When the Allies appear to be winning WWII, the Nazis devise a plan to eliminate all of the opposing forces' leaders at once. **96m/C VHS.** *IT GE FR* Kenneth (Ken) Clark, Horst Frank, Jeanne Valeri, Carlo Hinterman, Gianni Rizzo; ***D:*** Umberto Lenzi; ***W:*** Umberto Lenzi.

The Desert Fox 🦴🦴🦴 *Rommel—Desert Fox* **1951** Big-budgeted portrait of German Army Field Marshal Rommel, played by Mason, focuses on the soldier's defeat in Africa during WWII and his subsequent, disillusioned return to Hitler's Germany. Mason played Rommel again in 1953's "Desert Rats." **87m/B VHS.** James Mason, Cedric Hardwicke, Jessica Tandy, Luther Adler; ***D:*** Henry Hathaway.

Desert Gold 🦴½ **1936** A fierce Indian chief battles a horde of greedy white men over his tribe's gold mine. Based on a novel by Zane Grey. **58m/B VHS.** Buster Crabbe, Robert Cummings, Marsha Hunt, Tom (George Duryea) Keene, Raymond Hatton, Monte Blue, Leif Erickson; ***D:*** Charles T. Barton.

Desert Hearts 🦴🦴🦴 **1986 (R)** An upstanding professional woman travels to Reno, Nevada in 1959 to obtain a quick divorce, and slowly becomes involved in a lesbian relationship with a free-spirited casino waitress. **93m/C VHS, DVD, Wide.** Helen Shaver, Audra Lindley, Patricia Charbonneau, Andra Akers, Dean Butler, Jeffrey Tambor, Denise Crosby, Gwen Welles; ***D:*** Donna Deitch; ***W:*** Natalie Cooper; ***C:*** Robert Elswit.

Desert Heat 🦴🦴 *Inferno; Coyote Moon* **1999 (R)** Loner Eddie Lomax (Van Damme) is left for dead at an abandoned highway stop in the Mojave Desert after a gang steals his motorcycle. An unexpected rescue by an old friend leaves Eddie with one thought—revenge. **95m/C VHS, DVD.** Jean-Claude Van Damme, Noriyuki "Pat" Morita, Danny Trejo, Gabrielle Fitzpatrick, Larry Drake, Vincent Schiavelli; ***D:*** Danny Mulroon; ***W:*** Tom O'Rourke; ***C:*** Ross A. Maehl; ***M:*** Bill Conti. **VIDEO**

Desert Kickboxer 🦴🦴 **1992 (R)** A border guard takes on a cocaine dealer and his henchmen, fighting for gold and, of course, a beautiful woman. Lots of kick-boxing action. **86m/C VHS.** John Haymes Newton, Judie Aronson, Sam DeFrancisco, Paul Smith; ***D:*** Isaac Florentine.

Desert of the Lost 🦴🦴½ **1927** Wales flees to Mexico after shooting a man in self-defense. He's aided by Montgomery and, in turn, helps save her from a forced marriage. **58m/B VHS.** Wally Wales, Peggy Montgomery, William J. Dyer, Edward Cecil, Richard Neill, Kelly Cafford, Ray Murro, George Magrill, Charles "Slim" Whitaker; ***D:*** Richard Thorpe.

The Desert of the Tartars 🦴 *Le Desert des Tartares; Il Deserto dei Tartari* **1976 (PG)** Story of a young soldier who dreams of war and discovers that the real battle for him is with time. **140m/C VHS.** *FR IT IA* Vittorio Gassman, Giuliano Gemma, Helmut Griem, Philippe Noiret, Jacques Perrin, Fernando Rey, Jean-Louis Trintignant, Max von Sydow; ***D:*** Valerio Zurlini; ***W:*** Jean-Louis Bertucelli, Andre G. Brunelin; ***C:*** Luciano Tovoli; ***M:*** Ennio Morricone.

Desert Phantom 🦴½ **1936** Villains threaten to rob a woman of her ranch until a stranger rescues her. **66m/B VHS.** Johnny Mack Brown, Sheila (Manors) Mannors, Charles "Blackie" King, Ted Adams, Hal Price, Nelson McDowell; ***D:*** S. Roy Luby.

The Desert Rats 🦴🦴🦴 **1953** A crusty British captain (Burton) takes charge of an Australian division during WWII. Thinking they are inferior to his own British troops, he is stiff and uncaring to the Aussies until a kind-hearted drunk and the courage of the division win him over. Crack direction from Wise and Newton's performance (as the wag) simply steal the movie. Mason reprises his role as Germany Army Field Marshal Rommel from "The Desert Fox." **88m/B VHS.** Richard Burton, Robert Newton, Robert Douglas, Torin Thatcher, Chips Rafferty, Charles Tingwell, James Mason; ***D:*** Robert Wise.

Desert Snow 🦴🦴 **1989 (R)** Here's a non-formulaic dope opera oater: cowboys 'n' drug runners battle it out for an out-of-the-way, underpopulated western town. About as clever as the title. **90m/C VHS.** Frank Capizzi, Flint Carney, Shelley Hinkle, Sam Incorvia, Carolyn Jacobs; ***D:*** Paul de Cruccio.

The Desert Song 🦴🦴½ **1953** MacRae secretly leads a band of do-gooders against the evil forces of a dastardly sheik. Grayson is the general's daughter who falls in love with our disguised hero. Third filmed version of the Sigmund Romberg operetta creaks along with the talents of MacRae and Grayson rising about the hackneyed plot. ♫The Desert Song; Gay Parisienne; Long Live the Night; One Alone; One Flower; The Riff Song; Romance. **96m/C VHS.** Gordon MacRae, Kathryn Grayson, Raymond Massey, Steve Cochran, Dick Wesson, Allyn Ann McLerie, Ray Collins, William Conrad; ***D:*** H. Bruce Humberstone; ***W:*** Roland Kibbee; ***C:*** Robert Burks; ***M:*** Max Steiner.

Desert Steel 🦴½ **1994 (PG)** Rival racers risk their lives in the big off-road race. **89m/C VHS.** David Naughton, Brian Skinner, Amanda Wyss, Russ Tamblyn; ***D:*** Glenn Gebhard.

Desert Thunder 🦴🦴 **1999 (R)** Lee Miller (Baldwin) is a retired Air Force pilot who rejoins the action when he's called to lead a commando mission to defeat an Iraqi terrorist threat. Low-budget still boasts some good explosions and aerial scenes. **88m/C VHS, DVD.** Daniel Baldwin, Richard Tyson, Richard Portnow, Stacy Haiduk; ***D:*** Jim Wynorski; ***W:*** Lenny Juliano. **VIDEO**

Desert Trail 🦴½ **1935** Wayne is a championship rodeo rider accused of bank robbery. **57m/B VHS, DVD.** John Wayne, Paul Fix, Mary Kornman; ***D:*** Robert North Bradbury; ***W:*** Lindsley Parsons; ***C:*** Archie Stout.

Desert Warrior 🦴 **1988 (PG-13)** Earth becomes a waste site after a nuclear war. Ferrigno stars as a post-nuke hero in this low-budget action film. Very bad acting. **89m/C VHS.** Lou Ferrigno, Shari Shattuck, Kenneth Peer, Anthony East; ***D:*** Jim Goldman; ***W:*** Frederick Bailey.

Desert Winds 🦴🦴 **1995** Weird little fantastical romance finds Jackie (Graham), who lives near the New Mexican desert, regularly communing with nature on a rocky plateau. Lonely Jackie once heard the voice of Eugene (Nickles), who lives 500 miles away in Arizona, thanks to a rare phenomenon known as a wind tunnel, but it takes seven years before she hears his voice again. **97m/C VHS, DVD.** Heather Graham, Michael A. (M.A.) Nickles, Grace Zabriskie, Jack Kehler, Adam Ant; ***D:*** Michael A. (M.A.) Nickles; ***W:*** Michael A. (M.A.) Nickles; ***C:*** Denis Maloney; ***M:*** James McVay.

The Deserters 🦴½ **1983** Sergeant Hawley, a Vietnam-era hawk, hunts deserters and draft-dodgers in Canada. There, he confronts issues of war and peace head-on. **110m/C VHS.** *CA* Alan Scarfe, Dermot Hennelly, Jon Bryden, Barbara March; ***D:*** Jack Darcus; ***W:*** Jack Darcus; ***C:*** Tony Westman; ***M:*** Michael Conway Baker.

The Designated Mourner 🦴½ **1997 (R)** Adapted from the play by Wallace Shawn, this pointy-headed inaction movie laments the passing of the class of people who "appreciate the poetry of John Donne" and other forms of high art. It's probably the same class that would like this movie. Set in an unnamed politically repressive country that resembles a large table, Nichols plays the eponymous mourner Jack, a journalist who once ran with a literary crowd but betrayed their ideals for survival. Richardson plays his wife Judy, the daughter of final talking head Howard (de Keyser), who is a humanist poet who doesn't like people. If you need a lecture on culture written by a man who was in "Mom and Dad Save the World" and played the geeky social studies teacher in "Clueless," then this is your movie. To quote Shawn: "Inconceivable!" **94m/C VHS, DVD.** *GB* Mike Nichols, Miranda Richardson, David de Keyser; ***D:*** David Hare; ***W:*** Wallace Shawn; ***C:*** Oliver Stapleton; ***M:*** Richard Hartley.

Designing Woman 🦴🦴🦴 **1957** Bacall and Peck star in this mismatched tale of romance. She's a chic high-fashion designer, he's a rumpled sports writer. The fun begins when they try to adjust to married life together. Neither likes the other's friends or lifestyle. Things get even crazier when Bacall has to work with her ex-lover Helmore on a fashion show and Peck's former love Gray shows up as well. And as if that weren't enough, Peck is being hunted by the mob because of a boxing story he's written. It's a fun, quick, witty tale that is all entertainment and no message. Bacall's performance is of note because Bogart was dying of cancer at the time. **118m/C VHS, DVD, Wide.** Gregory Peck, Lauren Bacall, Dolores Gray, Sam Levene, Tom Helmore, Mickey Shaughnessy, Jesse White, Chuck Connors, Edward Platt, Alvy Moore, Jack Cole; ***D:*** Vincente Minnelli; ***W:*** George Wells; ***C:*** John Alton; ***M:*** Andre Previn. Oscars '57: Story & Screenplay.

Desire 🦴🦴🦴 **1936** Jewel thief Madeleine (Dietrich) manages to involve innocent tourist Tom (Cooper) into carrying her ill-gotten goods across the Spanish border. Then she entices him into joining her at the country estate of her partner-in-crime. By this time Tom is in love—and so is Madeleine but she doesn't think she's good enough for him. Lots of lying until the twosome can figure out what to do. Cooper manages to hold his own with the sophisticated Dietrich in their second film together (after "Morocco"). **96m/B VHS.** Marlene Dietrich, Gary Cooper, John Halliday, William Frawley, Ernest Cossart, Akim Tamiroff, Alan Mowbray; ***D:*** Frank Borzage; ***W:*** Edwin Justus Mayer, Waldemar Young; ***M:*** Frederick "Friedrich" Hollander.

Desire 🦴🦴 **1993 (R)** A free-spirited woman finds herself attracted to a local fisherman. Hardly her intellectual equal but then what she really wants is his body. **108m/C VHS.** Greta Scacchi, Vincent D'Onofrio; ***D:*** Andrew Birkin.

Desire 🦴🦴 **1995 (R)** Security consultant Lauren Allen (Hodge) is working for a perfume manufacturer whose fragrance, Desire, is the fave of a Beverly Hills serial killer who likes to douse his victims in the scent. The prime suspect is scent expert Gordon Lewis (Kemp) and naturally Lauren falls for him. Standard erotic thriller fare. **90m/C VHS.** Kate Hodge, Martin Kemp, Deborah Shelton, Robert Miranda; ***D:*** Rodney MacDonald; ***W:*** Rodney MacDonald.

Desire and Hell at Sunset Motel 🦴½ **1992 (PG-13)** Low-budget thriller takes place at the Sunset Motel in 1950s Anaheim. Fenn is the bombshell wife of a toy salesman who's in town for a sales meeting, while she just wants to visit Disneyland. She's soon fooling around with another guy and her husband hires a psychotic criminal to spy on her as her new lover plots to kill hubby. Very confusing plot isn't worth figuring out. Film's only redeeming quality is the imaginative and creative work used in the visuals. Castle's directorial debut. **90m/C VHS.** Sherilyn Fenn, Whip Hubley, David Hewlett, David Johansen, Paul Bartel, Kenneth Tobey; ***D:*** Alien Castle; ***W:*** Alien Castle; ***C:*** Jamie Thompson.

Desire Under the Elms 🦴🦴½ **1958** Ives, the patriarch of an 1840s New England farming family, takes a young wife (Loren) who promptly has an affair with her stepson. Loren's American film debut. Based on the play by Eugene O'Neill. **114m/B VHS.** Sophia Loren, Anthony Perkins, Burl Ives, Frank Overton; ***D:*** Delbert Mann; ***C:*** Daniel F. Fapp; ***M:*** Elmer Bernstein.

Desiree 🦴🦴½ **1954** A romanticized historical epic about Napoleon and his 17-year-old mistress, Desiree. Based on the novel by Annemarie Selinko. Slightly better than average historical fiction piece. **110m/C Wide.** Marlon Brando, Jean Simmons, Merle Oberon, Michael Rennie, Cameron Mitchell, Elizabeth Sellars, Cathleen Nesbitt; ***D:*** Henry Koster; ***W:*** Daniel Taradash; ***C:*** Milton Krasner; ***M:*** Alex North.

Desk Set 🦴🦴🦴 *His Other Woman* **1957** One of the later and less dynamic Tracy/Hepburn comedies, about an efficiency expert who installs a giant computer in an effort to update a TV network's female-run reference department. Still, the duo sparkle as they bicker, battle, and give in to love. Based on William Marchant's play. **103m/C VHS.** Spencer Tracy, Katharine Hepburn, Joan Blondell, Gig Young, Dina Merrill, Neva Patterson; ***D:*** Walter Lang; ***C:*** Leon Shamroy.

Desolation Angels 🦴🦴 **1995** Nick Adams (Rodrick) returns to New York after a month spent unhappily visiting his mother and discovers his girlfriend Mary (Thomas) has been raped by his best friend Sid (Bassett). At least that's how Nick interprets the situation after an unwilling Mary admits they had sex. Nick goes after Sid, gets beaten up, hires a couple of thugs who botch a retaliation, and just gets increasingly enraged over his inability to settle the situation. The focus is on Nick and Rodrick is more than up to the director McCann's demands. **90m/C VHS, DVD.** Michael Rodrick, Peter Bassett, Jennifer Thomas; ***D:*** Tim McCann; ***W:*** Tim McCann; ***C:*** Matt Howe.

Despair 🦴🦴🦴 *Eine Reise ins Licht* **1978** A chilling and comic study of a victimized chocolate factory owner's descent into madness, set against the backdrop of the Nazi rise to power in the 1930s. Adapted from the Nabokov novel by Tom Stoppard. **120m/C VHS.** *GE* Dirk Bogarde, Andrea Ferreol, Volker Spengler, Klaus Lowitsch; ***D:*** Rainer Werner Fassbinder; ***W:*** Tom Stoppard; ***C:*** Michael Ballhaus; ***M:*** Peer Raben.

Desperado 🦴🦴🦴 *El Mariachi 2* **1995 (R)** Rodriguez's nameless guitar player-turned-gunman returns—this time in the persona of heartthrob Banderas. The director also has a studio budget to play with (a sizable increase over the $7000 for "El Mariachi"), so the action's on a bigger, more violent scale (you'll quickly lose count of flying bodies and bullets) as El Mariachi tracks infamous drug lord Bucho (de Almeida). Gringo Buscemi provides assistance, beautiful bookstore owner Carolina (Hayek) offers solace, and Tarantino meets his well-deserved cameo demise. You'll also find original Mariachi, Gallardo, in a cameo role as a musician/gunslinger amigo of the hero. Filmed in Mexico. **103m/C VHS, DVD, 8mm.** Antonio

Banderas, Salma Hayek, Joaquim de Almeida, Steve Buscemi, Richard "Cheech" Marin, Carlos Gomez; ***Cameos:*** Quentin Tarantino, Carlos Gallardo; ***D:*** Robert Rodriguez; ***W:*** Robert Rodriguez; ***C:*** Guillermo Navarro; ***M:*** Los Lobos.

The Desperadoes ✂✂½ **1943** Sheriff Steve Upton (Scott) has a peaceful little Utah town but things change when his old friend, outlaw Cheyenne Rodgers (Ford), comes to visit. Claiming to have gone straight, Rodgers falls for the lovely Allison (Keyes) but is soon accused of robbing the local bank. However, Sheriff Upton believes in his old friend's innocence, helps him escape jail, and together they go after the real criminals. Based on a story by Max Brand. **85m/C VHS.** Randolph Scott, Glenn Ford, Evelyn Keyes, Claire Trevor, Edgar Buchanan, Raymond Walburn, Porter Hall, Guinn "Big Boy" Williams; ***D:*** Charles Vidor; ***W:*** Robert Carson.

Desperados ✂✂½ **1969 (PG)** After the Civil War, a murderous renegade and two of his sons go on a looting rampage, eventually kidnapping the child of the third son who just wants to live in peace. Made in Spain. **90m/C VHS.** *SP* Jack Palance, Vince Edwards, Christian Roberts, George Maharis, Neville Brand, Sylvia Syms; ***D:*** Henry Levin; ***W:*** Walter Brough; ***C:*** Sam Leavitt.

The Desperados ✂½ **198?** When a young woman is raped by outlaws robbing her stagecoach, a bevy of western heroes band together to avenge her. **86m/C VHS.** Keenan Wynn, Henry Silva, Michele Carey, John Anderson, Joe Turkel; ***D:*** Ron Joy.

Desperate ✂✂½ **1947** An honest truck driver witnesses a mob crime and must escape with his wife in this minor film noir. Eventually, the law is on his tail, too. **73m/B VHS.** Steve Brodie, Audrey Long, Raymond Burr, Jason Robards Sr., Douglas Fowley, William Challee, Ilka Gruning, Nan Leslie; ***D:*** Anthony Mann.

Desperate Cargo ✂½ **1941** Two showgirls stranded in a Latin American town manage to get aboard a clipper ship with hoodlums who are trying to steal the vessel's cargo. **69m/B VHS.** Ralph Byrd, Carol Hughes, Jack Mulhall; ***D:*** William Beaudine; ***W:*** Morgan Cox, John T. Coyle; ***C:*** Jack Greenhalgh.

Desperate Characters ✂✂✂ **1971 (R)** A slice-of-city-life story about a middle-class couple living in a once-fashionable section of Brooklyn, New York, who watch their neighborhood disintegrate around them. Their marriage on remote control, the two find their lives a series of small disappointments, routine work, uncertain friendships, and pervasive violence. Excellent performances, especially by MacLaine as the harried wife, but the film's depressing nature made it a complete boxoffice flop. **87m/C VHS.** Shirley MacLaine, Kenneth Mars, Gerald S. O'Loughlin, Sada Thompson, Michael Higgins, Rose Gregorio, Jack Somack, Chris Gampel, Mary Alan Hokanson, Patrick McVey, Carol Kane; ***D:*** Frank D. Gilroy; ***W:*** Frank D. Gilroy.

Desperate Crimes ✂✂ *Mafia Docks* **1993** Two rival mobs battle over the prostitution and drug trade. When an innocent woman is murdered her brother looks for revenge with the help of a beautiful prostitute. **92m/C VHS, DVD.** Traci Lords, Denise Crosby, Franco (Columbo) Columbu, Van Quattro, Rena Niehaus, Nicoletta Boris, Elizabeth Kaitan, Randi Ingerman; ***D:*** Andreas Marfori; ***W:*** Andreas Marfori; ***C:*** Marco Isoli.

Desperate Hours ✂✂✂ **1955** A tough, gritty thriller about three escaped convicts taking over a suburban home and holding the family hostage. Plenty of suspense and fine acting. Based on the novel and play by Joseph Hayes. **112m/B VHS.** Humphrey Bogart, Fredric March, Martha Scott, Arthur Kennedy, Gig Young, Dewey Martin, Mary Murphy, Robert Middleton, Richard Eyer, Ray Collins, Beverly Garland; ***D:*** William Wyler; ***C:*** Lee Garmes. Natl. Bd. of Review '55: Director (Wyler).

Desperate Hours ✂✂ **1990 (R)** An escaped prisoner holes up in a suburban couple's home, waiting for his lawyer/accomplice to take him to Mexico. Tensions heighten between the separated couple and the increasingly nerve-wracked criminals. Terrific, if not downright horrifying, performance by Rourke in an overall tepid remake of the 1955 thriller. **105m/C VHS, DVD, Wide.** Mickey Rourke, Anthony Hopkins, Mimi Rogers, Kelly Lynch, Lindsay Crouse, Elias Koteas, David Morse, Shawnee Smith, Danny Gerard, Matt McGrath; ***D:*** Michael Cimino; ***W:*** Mark Rosenthal, Larry Konner, Joseph Hayes; ***C:*** Doug Milsome; ***M:*** David Mansfield.

Desperate Journey ✂✂½ **1942** Flynn and Reagan are two of five Allied fighters shot down over Nazi occupied Poland. They go through various tight squeezes such as stealing Goering's car in Berlin, and eliminating a few Nazis at a chemical factory to get back to the safety of England. All the while they are hunted by Massey as Nazi Major Otto Baumester, who of course bumbles and fumbles the whole affair. Strictly propaganda intended to keep up morale on the homefront. Flynn was not pleased about having Reagan as his co-star, seeing as he was usually paired with female leads. **108m/B VHS.** Errol Flynn, Ronald Reagan, Raymond Massey, Nancy Coleman, Alan Hale, Arthur Kennedy, Helmut Dantine; ***D:*** Raoul Walsh; ***M:*** Max Steiner.

Desperate Lives ✂✂ **1982** High school siblings come into contact with drugs and join their guidance counselor in the war against dope. Average made for TV fare. **100m/C VHS.** Diana Scarwid, Doug McKeon, Helen Hunt, William Windom, Art Hindle, Tom Atkins, Sam Bottoms, Diane Ladd, Dr. Joyce Brothers; ***D:*** Robert Lewis; ***M:*** Bruce Broughton. **TV**

Desperate Living ✂✂½ **1977** Typical John Waters trash. A mental patient (Stole) is released and becomes paranoid that her family may be out to kill her. After aiding in the murder of her husband (the hefty maid, Hill, suffocates him by sitting on him), Stole and Hill escape to Mortville, a town populated by outcasts such as transsexuals, murderers, and the woefully disfigured. **90m/C VHS, DVD.** Mink Stole, Jean Hill, Edith Massey, Liz Renay, Mary Vivian Pearce, Cookie Mueller, Susan Lowe, Ed Peranio, Pat Moran, George Stover, Turkey Joe, Channing Wilroy; ***D:*** John Waters; ***W:*** John Waters; ***C:*** Thomas Loizeaux.

Desperate Measures ✂½ **1998 (R)** Police officer Frank Connor (Garcia) desperately searches for a bone marrow donor for his dying son. Turns out the perfect match is vicious murderer and prison inmate Pete McCabe (Keaton). McCabe seizes the opportunity to unleash an elaborate and violent prison escape in a San Francisco hospital. Keaton, as a poor man's Hannibal Lecter, offers this movie's only entertainment. If not for the dying child to propel its already ludicrious story along, it would be a great source for slapstick comedy. Film was held back for several months before its final release and you'll find out why the studio wanted to hide this one. **100m/C VHS, DVD.** Andy Garcia, Michael Keaton, Marcia Gay Harden, Brian Cox, Efrain Figueroa, Joseph Cross, Richard Riehle; ***D:*** Barbet Schroeder; ***W:*** Henry Bean, Neal Jimenez, David Klass; ***C:*** Luciano Tovoli; ***M:*** Trevor Jones.

Desperate Motives ✂✂ *Distant Cousins* **1992 (R)** Keith and his fiancee Helgenberger are a charming couple who arrive to stay with Keith's distant cousin (Katt) and his family. Only what the family doesn't realize is that the duo have escaped from an asylum for the criminally insane and want to take over their lives. **92m/C VHS.** Edward (Eddie) Bunker, David Keith, Marg Helgenberger, William Katt, Mel Harris, Mary Crosby, Brian Bonsall, Cyndi Pass; ***D:*** Andrew Lane; ***W:*** C. Courtney Joyner.

Desperate Moves ✂✂ **1986** An Oregon-transplanted geek in San Francisco sets out to make himself over in order to win his dream girl. Sometimes effective, often sappy treatment of his coming to terms with the big city. **90m/C VHS.** Isabel Sanford, Steve Tracy, Paul Benedict, Christopher Lee, Eddie Deezen; ***D:*** Oliver (Ovidio Assonitis) Hellman.

Desperate Prey ✂½ *Redheads* **1994 (R)** Lucy (Karvan) videotapes herself having sex with lawyer Brewster (Hembrow) and then accidentally films his murder. So she's stalked by the killer. **102m/C VHS.** *AU* Claudia Karvan, Catherine McClements, Mark Hembrow; ***D:*** Danny Vendramini; ***W:*** Danny Vendramini.

Desperate Remedies ✂✂ **1993 (R)** Enjoyment will rest on the viewer's appreciation of campy melodrama. In a Victorian-era New Zealand town, regal shop owner Dorothea Brook (Ward-Lealand) is trying to find a husband for her difficult younger sister Rose (Mills)—who happens to be pregnant and a drug addict. She spots handsome sailor Lawrence (Smith) and decides he'll do but Lawrence is instantly smitten with Dorothea (who's also having heart palpitations over the hunk). Unfortunately, her current lover is Anne (Chappell) and Dorothea has also decided on a marriage of convenience with ambitious politician William (Hurst). It's all very operatic. **92m/C VHS.** *NZ* Jennifer Ward-Lealand, Kevin Smith, Lisa Chappell, Michael Hurst, Kiri Mills, Clifford Curtis; ***D:*** Stewart Main, Peter Wells; ***W:*** Stewart Main, Peter Wells; ***C:*** Leon Narbey; ***M:*** Peter Scholes.

Desperate Target ✂½ **1980** Courageous people fight against all odds to survive. **90m/C VHS.** Chris Mitchum.

The Desperate Trail ✂✂½ **1994 (R)** Prostitute, convicted of killing an abusive client, manages to escape from the marshal who's escorting her to her hanging. She teams up with a con man in a plot to rob a bank while the marshal enlists a posse to track her down. Strong performances augmented by blazing guns, hobbled by weak writing. **93m/C VHS.** Sam Elliott, Linda Fiorentino, Craig Sheffer, Frank Whaley; ***D:*** P.J. Pesce; ***W:*** P.J. Pesce, Tom Abrams; ***C:*** Michael Bonvillain; ***M:*** Stephen Endelman. **CABLE**

Desperate Women ✂½ **1978** Western about three unjustly accused female convicts rescued en route to prison by an ex-hired gun. **98m/C VHS.** Susan St. James, Dan Haggerty, Ronee Blakley, Ann Dusenberry, Susan Myers; ***D:*** Earl Bellamy. **TV**

Desperately Seeking Susan ✂✂ **1985 (PG-13)** Roberta (Arquette) is a bored New Jersey housewife who gets her kicks reading the personals. When she becomes obsessed with a relationship between two lovers who arrange their meetings through the columns, Roberta decides to find out for herself who they are. But after an accident, Robert loses her memory and thinks she is Susan, the free-spirited woman in the personals. Unfortunately, Susan (Madonna) is in a lot of trouble with all sorts of unsavory folk and our innocent housewife finds herself caught in the middle. Terrific characters, with special appeal generated by Arquette and Madonna. Quinn winningly plays Roberta's bewildered romantic interest, Dez. **104m/C VHS, DVD, Wide.** Rosanna Arquette, Madonna, Aidan Quinn, Mark Blum, Robert Joy, Laurie Metcalf, Steven Wright, John Turturro, Will Patton, Richard Hell, Annie Golden, Ann Magnuson, Richard Edson; ***D:*** Susan Seidelman; ***W:*** Leora Barish; ***C:*** Edward Lachman; ***M:*** Thomas Newman. British Acad. '85: Support. Actress (Arquette); Natl. Bd. of Review '85: Support. Actress (Arquette).

Destination Moon ✂✂½ **1950** Story of man's first lunar voyage contains Chesley Bonstell's astronomical artwork and a famous Woody Woodpecker cartoon. Includes previews of coming attractions from classic science fiction films. **91m/C VHS, DVD.** Warner Anderson, Tom Powers, Dick Wesson, Erin O'Brien-Moore; ***D:*** Irving Pichel; ***W:*** Rip Van Ronkel, Robert Heinlein, James O'Hanlon; ***C:*** Lionel Lindon; ***M:*** Leith Stevens.

Destination Moonbase Alpha ✂✂ *Space: 2100* **1975** In the 21st century, an explosion has destroyed half the moon, causing it to break away from the Earth's orbit. The moon is cast far away, but the 311 people manning Alpha, a research station on the moon, must continue their search for other life forms in outer space. A thankless task. Pilot for the TV series "Space: 1999." **93m/C VHS.** *GB* Martin Landau, Barbara Bain, Barry Morse, Nick (Nicholas) Tate; ***D:*** Tom Clegg; ***W:*** Terence Feely; ***M:*** Derek Wadsworth. **TV**

Destination Saturn ✂✂ *Buck Rogers* **1939** Buck Rogers awakens from suspended animation in the 25th century. **90m/B VHS, DVD.** Buster Crabbe, Constance Moore; ***D:*** Ford Beebe.

Destination Tokyo ✂✂ **1943** A weathered WWII submarine actioner, dealing with the search-and-destroy mission of a U.S. sub sent into Tokyo harbor. Available in a colorized version. **135m/B VHS.** Cary Grant, John Garfield, Alan Hale, Dane Clark, John Ridgely, Warner Anderson, William Prince, Robert Hutton, Tom Tully, Peter Whitney, Faye Emerson, John Forsythe; ***D:*** Delmer Daves.

Destination Vegas ✂✂ **1995 (R)** Attorney Sommerfield is on the lam, driving across the Mojave trying to elude hitmen sent to prevent her testimony in a murder trial. She hooks up with drifter Duhamel, who just happens to be an ex-getaway driver, and it's put the pedal to the metal time. Low-budget familiar story with some saving humor. **78m/C VHS, DVD.** Jennifer Sommerfield, Claude Duhamel, Stephen Polk, Richard Lynch; ***D:*** Paul Wynne; ***W:*** Paul Wynne; ***C:*** William H. Molina; ***M:*** Peter Tomashek. **VIDEO**

Destiny ✂✂✂ *Der Mude Tod* **1921** Fritz Lang's silent fantasy is a version of the myth of Orpheus. Death takes a young man on the eve of his wedding, but agrees to return him if his fiancee can save three lives. In terms of style, it's really closer to Dreyer's "Vampyr" than to Lang's own "M." **99m/B VHS, DVD.** *GE* Lil Dagover, Rudolf Klein-Rogge, Bernhard Goetzke, Walther Jansson, Eduard von Winterstein, Paul Biensfeldt; ***D:*** Fritz Lang; ***W:*** Thea von Harbou; ***C:*** Fritz Arno Wagner, Erich Nitzschmann, Hermann Saalfrank.

Destiny ✂✂ *Al-Massir* **1997** Averroes (el-Cherif) is a 12th century Arab humanist philosopher living in Andalusia, Spain. When one of his disciples is burned at the stake for heresy, the man's son Youssef (Rahouma), following his father's wishes, travels to Andalusia to study with Averroes. Youssef finds that the ruling Caliph (Memida) supports Averroes but a fundamentalist Muslim cult hopes to overthrow the Caliph and destroy Averroes and his students. Arabic with subtitles. **135m/C VHS.** *EG* Nour (el-Sherif) el-Cherif, Fares Rahouma, Mahmoud Hemeida, Khaled el-Nabaoui, Laila Eloui; ***D:*** Youssef Cahine; ***W:*** Youssef Cahine, Khaled Youssef.

The Destiny of Marty Fine ✂ **1996** Lame low-budget drama about washed-up boxer Marty Fine (Gelfant), who witnesses the murder of mob boss Capelli (Ironside). He promises old-time gangster Daryl (Fell) he'll keep quiet but Daryl orders a hit anyway. So lowlife Marty tries to get out of L.A. **85m/B VHS.** Mark Ruffalo, Alan Gelfant, Norman Fell, James LeGros, Catherine Keener, Michael Ironside, Glenn Plummer, John Diehl, Sandra Seacat; ***D:*** Michael Hacker; ***W:*** Mark Ruffalo, Michael Hacker; ***C:*** Melinda Sue Gordon.

Destiny Turns on the Radio ✂✂ **1995 (R)** Mystic figure Johnny Destiny (Tarantino) dabbles in the lives of various stock characters in Las Vegas after emerging from a glowing swimming pool. Three years after this grand entrance, he enlists escaped con Julian and partner Thoreau (McDermott and Le Gros, respectively) to help him return to his place of origin. Julian has other plans, which involve getting his ex, Lucille (Travis), back from sleazy casino owner Tuerto (Belushi). Aggressively cheezy, dime novel dialogue and threadbare, convoluted plot wastes talents of interesting cast. Too much time and energy spent trying to be hip. Sadly, Tarantino's only participation was in front of the camera. **101m/C VHS.** Dylan McDermott, Nancy Travis, James LeGros, Quentin Tarantino, Allen (Goorwitz) Garfield, James Belushi, Tracey Walter, Bob(cat) Goldthwait, Richard Edson; ***D:*** Jack Baran; ***W:*** Robert Ramsey, Matthew Stone; ***C:*** James L. Carter; ***M:*** Steven Soles.

Destroy All Monsters ✂✂½ *Kaiju Soshingeki; All Monsters Attack; Operation Monsterland* **1968 (G)** When alien babes take control of Godzilla and his monstrous colleagues, it looks like all is lost for Earth. Adding insult to injury, Ghidra is sent in to take care of the loose ends. Can the planet possibly survive this madness? Classic Toho monster slugfest also features Mothra, Rodan, Son of Godzilla, Angila, Varan, Baragon, Spigas and others. **88m/C VHS, DVD.** *JP* Akira Kubo, Jun Tazaki, Yoshio Tsuchiya, Kyoko Ai, Yukiko Kobayashi, Kenji Sahara, Andrew Hughes, Yoshifumi Tajima, Nadao Kirino, Susumu Kurobe, Hisaya Ito; ***D:*** Inoshiro Honda; ***W:*** Inoshiro Honda, Takeshi Kimura; ***C:*** Taiichi Kankura; ***M:*** Akira Ifukube.

Destroy All Planets *Gamera Tai Viras; Gamera Tai Uchukaiju Bairasu; Gamera Vs. Viras; Gamera Vs. Outer Space Monster Viras* **1968** Aliens whose spaceships turn into giant flying squids are attacking Earth. It's up to Gammera, the flying, fire-breathing turtle to save the day. **?m/C VHS.** *JP* Peter Williams, Kojiro Hongo, Toru Takatsuka; ***D:*** Noriaki Yuasa.

Destroyer **1943** Trials and tribulations aboard a WWII destroyer result in tensions, but when the time comes for action, the men get the job done. **99m/B VHS.** Edward G. Robinson, Glenn Ford, Marguerite Chapman, Edgar Buchanan, Leo Gorcey, Regis Toomey, Edward Brophy, Larry Parks; ***D:*** William A. Seiter.

Destroyer **1988 (R)** Small-budget film crew goes to an empty prison to shoot, and are stalked by the ghost/zombie remains of a huge serial killer given the electric chair 18 months before. **94m/C VHS.** Anthony Perkins, Deborah Foreman, Lyle Alzado; ***D:*** Robert Kirk.

The Destructors *The Marseille Contract* **1974 (PG)** An American narcotics enforcement officer in Paris seeks the help of a hitman in order to catch a druglord. **89m/C VHS.** *GB* Anthony Quinn, Michael Caine, James Mason, Maureen Kerwin, Alexandra Stewart; ***D:*** Robert Parrish; ***W:*** Judd Bernard.

Destry Rides Again *Justice Rides Again* **1939** An uncontrollably lawless western town is whipped into shape by a peaceful, unarmed sheriff. A vintage Hollywood potpourri with Dietrich's finest post-Sternberg moment; standing on the bar singing "See What the Boys in the Back Room Will Have." The second of three versions of this Max Brand story. First was released in 1932; the third in 1954. **94m/B VHS.** James Stewart, Marlene Dietrich, Brian Donlevy, Charles Winninger, Mischa Auer, Irene Hervey, Una Merkel, Billy Gilbert, Jack Carson, Samuel S. Hinds, Allen Jenkins; ***D:*** George Marshall; ***W:*** Gertrude Purcell, Felix Jackson, Henry Myers; ***C:*** Hal Mohr; ***M:*** Frank Skinner. Natl. Film Reg. '96.

Details of a Duel: A Question of Honor ½ **1989** A butcher and a teacher collide in this comedy, and prodded by the church, militia and town officals, must duel before the entire town. In Spanish with English subtitles. **97m/C VHS.** *SP* ***D:*** Sergio Cabrera.

The Detective *Father Brown* **1954** Based on G.K. Chesterton's "Father Brown" detective stories, a slick, funny English mystery in which the famous priest tracks down a notorious, endlessly crafty antique thief. **91m/B VHS.** *GB* Alec Guinness, Peter Finch, Joan Greenwood, Cecil Parker, Bernard Lee; ***D:*** Robert Hamer; ***W:*** Maurice Rapf; ***M:*** Jerry Goldsmith.

The Detective **1968** A New York detective investigating the mutilation murder of a homosexual finds political and police department corruption. Fine, gritty performances prevail in this suspense thriller. Based on the novel by Roderick Thorpe. **114m/C VHS, Wide.** Frank Sinatra, Lee Remick, Ralph Meeker, Jacqueline Bisset, William Windom, Robert Duvall, Tony Musante, Jack Klugman, Al Freeman Jr.; ***D:*** Gordon Douglas; ***W:*** Abby Mann; ***C:*** Joseph Biroc.

Detective **1985** Style over substance as Godard has various characters/suspects investigating a murder committed in a Paris hotel two years previously. However, Godard seems more interested in the look than the plot. French with subtitles. **95m/C VHS.** *FR* Nathalie Baye, Claude Brasseur, Jean-Pierre Leaud, Johnny Hallyday, Laurent Terzieff, Alain Cuny; ***D:*** Jean-Luc Godard; ***W:*** Phillip Setbon, Alain Sarde; ***C:*** Bruno Nuytten.

Detective Sadie & Son *Sadie & Son* **1984** An elderly detective and her young son crack a case. **96m/C VHS.** Debbie Reynolds, Sam Wanamaker, Brian McNamara; ***D:*** John Llewellyn Moxey. **TV**

Detective School Dropouts *Dumb Dicks* **1985 (PG)** Since they couldn't pass detective school, are they smart enough to outwit a kidnapper? Find out and get a few laughs at the same time. **92m/C VHS.** Lorin Dreyfuss, David Landsberg, Christian de Sica, George Eastman; ***D:*** Filippo Ottoni.

Detective Story ½ **1951** Intense drama about a New York City police precinct with a wide array of characters led by a disillusioned and bitter detective (Douglas). Excellent casting is the strong point, as the film can be a bit dated. Based on Sydney Kingsley's Broadway play. **103m/B VHS.** Kirk Douglas, Eleanor Parker, Lee Grant, Horace McMahon, William Bendix, Craig Hill, Cathy O'Donnell, Bert Freed, George Macready, Joseph Wiseman, Gladys George, Frank Faylen, Warner Anderson, Gerald Mohr; ***D:*** William Wyler; ***W:*** Philip Yordan, Robert Wyler; ***C:*** Lee Garmes. Cannes '52: Actress (Grant).

Deterrence **2000 (R)** Stagy one-room thriller set during the presidential campaign of 2008. Veep Walter Emerson (Pollak) became prez when the incumbant died—now he's campaigning for re-election. He's at a Colorado primary when a blizzard forces Emerson and his aides (as well as a TV crew) to take shelter in a small town diner. The diner's cable TV hookup reports an international crisis—Iraq forces have invaded Kuwait and slaughtered American peacekeepers. So Emerson decides the thing to do is nuke Baghdad. Lots of pontificating. **101m/C VHS, DVD, Wide.** Kevin Pollak, Timothy Hutton, Sheryl Lee Ralph, Sean Astin, Clotilde Courau, Badja (Medu) Djola, Mark Thompson; ***D:*** Rod Lurie; ***W:*** Rod Lurie; ***C:*** Frank Perl; ***M:*** Lawrence Nash Groupe.

Detonator *Alistair MacLean's Death Train; Death Train* **1993 (R)** A renegade Russian general has stolen a nuclear bomb and is transporting it from Germany to Iraq via a hijacked train commandeered by his hired band of mercenaries. Stewart is the U.N. troubleshooter delegated to stop the plot, aided by a commando team featuring Brosnan and Paul. Based on the novel "Death Train" by Alistair MacLean. **98m/C VHS.** Pierce Brosnan, Patrick Stewart, Ted Levine, Alexandra Paul, Christopher Lee; ***D:*** David S. Jackson; ***W:*** David S. Jackson. **CABLE**

Detonator 2: Night Watch ½ *Alistair MacLean's Night Watch; Night Watch* **1995 (R)** Brosnan and Paul return as operatives for the secret United Nations Anti-Crime Organization (UNACO). Mike Graham and Sabrina Carver are teamed by their boss Nick Caldwell (Devane) when it's discovered that Rembrandt's "Night Watch" has been replaced by a forgery. This takes our intrepid duo to Hong Kong, a shady computer expert/art collector (Shannon), and a suspicious satellite about to be launched by North Korea. Based on a story by Alistair MacLean. **99m/C VHS.** Pierce Brosnan, Alexandra Paul, William Devane, Michael J. Shannon, Lim Kay Siu, Irene Ng; ***D:*** David S. Jackson; ***W:*** David S. Jackson; ***M:*** John Scott. **CABLE**

Detour **1946** Considered to be the creme de la creme of "B" movies, a largely unacknowledged but cult-followed noir downer. Well-designed, stylish, and compelling, if a bit contrived and sometimes annoyingly shrill. Shot in only six days with six indoor sets. Down-on-his-luck pianist Neal hitches cross-country to rejoin his fiancee. His first wrong turn involves the accidental death of the man who picked him up, then he's en route to Destiny with a capital "D" when he picks up fatal femme Savage, as vicious a vixen as ever ruined a good man. Told in flashback, it's also been called the most despairing of all "B"-pictures. As noir as they get. **67m/B VHS, DVD.** Tom Neal, Ann Savage, Claudia Drake, Edmund MacDonald, Tim Ryan, Esther Howard, Don Brodie, Pat Gleason; ***D:*** Edgar G. Ulmer; ***W:*** Martin Goldsmith; ***C:*** Benjamin (Ben H.) Kline; ***M:*** Leo Erdody. Natl. Film Reg. '92.

Detour **1992 (R)** Remake of the 1945 noir classic even features Neal Jr. in the role that his dad made famous. He's the nightclub musician, hitching his way to Hollywood, who falls into big trouble thanks to fatale dame, Vera (Lavish). Not a patch on the original but not a complete waste of time either. **91m/B VHS.** Tom Neal Jr., Lea Lavish, Susanna Foster, Erin McGrane; ***D:*** Wade Williams; ***W:*** Wade Williams; ***M:*** Bill Crain. **VIDEO**

Detour **1999 (R)** Danny's (Fahey) in trouble with the mob when a $1 million robbery goes sour. So he high tails it to his rural hometown where one of his old friends (Madsen) is now the sheriff. But Danny still can't escape from his ex-partner (Russo) or the rest of the bad guys. Lots of action in a routine plot. **93m/C VHS.** Jeff Fahey, Michael Madsen, James Russo, Gary Busey; ***D:*** Joey Travolta. **VIDEO**

Detour to Danger woof! **1945** Two young men set out on a fishing expedition and run into crooks and damsels in distress. Unintentionally hilarious "acting" by the no-name cast make this a grade-Z "B" movie. Of interest only because it was filmed in the three-color Kodachrome process used primarily in documentaries. **56m/C VHS, 8mm.** Britt Wood, John Day, Nancy Brinckman; ***D:*** Richard Talmadge.

Detroit 9000 ½ *Detroit Heat* **1973 (R)** A pair of Detroit policemen investigate a robbery that occurred at a black congressman's fundraising banquet. **106m/C VHS, DVD, Wide.** Alex Rocco, Scatman Crothers, Hari Rhodes, Lonette McKee, Herbert Jefferson Jr.; ***D:*** Arthur Marks; ***W:*** Orville H. Hampton; ***C:*** Harry J. May; ***M:*** Luchi De Jesus.

Detroit Rock City **1999 (R)** It's 1978, and a group of dim Kiss fans will do anything to get into a sold-out Detroit concert. And non-Kiss fans should do anything to get out of watching this movie. Manages to be tasteless and humorless even when it's not obviously annoying. Co-producer Gene Simmons and the boys only perform the title song, so Kiss fans will be left searching their neighborhood for an Old Folks Kabuki Theater for a fix of the elderly in makeup. Director Rifkin recreated the 1978 Kiss Love Gun Show with the band performing in that haven of heavy metal: Hamilton, Ontario? **95m/C VHS, DVD.** Edward Furlong, Sam Huntington, Giuseppe Andrews, Lin Shaye, James De Bello, Natasha Lyonne, Gene Simmons, Paul Stanley, Ace Frehley, Peter Criss; ***D:*** Adam Rifkin; ***W:*** Carl DuPre; ***C:*** John R. Leonetti; ***M:*** J. Peter Robinson.

Deuce Bigalow: Male Gigolo **1999 (R)** Schneider tries to enter the low-brow leading man territory now occupied by Adam Sandler (who exec produced) as Deuce Bigelow, a hapless tropical fish caretaker turned hapless gigolo. When Deuce is asked to nurse a stereotypically ethnic gigolo's fish to health, he proceeds to practically destroy his house and subsequently take over his "business" to pay for the repairs. With the help of pimp T.J. (Griffin), Deuce finds a clientele and the secret that the women want compassion, not sex. The gags (mostly of the tasteless, toilet humor variety) are very hit and miss, but they should play well to the intended audience of adolescent boys. **86m/C VHS, DVD, Wide.** Rob Schneider, William Forsythe, Eddie Griffin, Oded Fehr, Gail O'Grady, Richard Riehle, Jacqueline Obradors; ***D:*** Mike Mitchell; ***W:*** Rob Schneider, Harris Goldberg; ***C:*** Peter Collister; ***M:*** Teddy Castellucci.

Deuces Wild ½ **2002 (R)** Cliche piles upon cliche in this story of Brooklyn street gangs in the late fifties. The Deuces, led by Leon (Dorff) and his hotheaded younger brother Bobby (Renfro), and their rivals the Vipers, go to war over turf when Vipers leader Marco (Redus) is released from prison. Drug-dealing Marco was responsible for the heroin death of their older brother Sal and the brothers want to keep their streets clean, which also puts them in conflict with local mobster Fritzy (Dillon) and his thugs. There's even a star-crossed romance since Bobby loves Vipers girl Annie (Balk). Director Kalvert did better with teens and drugs and violence in "The Basketball Diaries." **97m/C VHS, DVD.** *US* Stephen Dorff, Brad Renfro, Norman Reedus, Fairuza Balk, Max Perlich, Matt Dillon, Drea De Matteo, Frankie Muniz, Vincent Pastore, Balthazar Getty, James Franco, Louis Lombardi, Deborah Harry, Johnny Knoxville; ***D:*** Scott Kalvert; ***W:*** Paul Kimatian, Christopher Gambale; ***C:*** John A. Alonzo; ***M:*** Stewart Copeland.

Deutschland im Jahre Null ½ **1947** The acclaimed, unsettling vision of post-war Germany as seen through the eyes of a disturbed boy who eventually kills himself. Lyrical and grim, in German with subtitles. **75m/B VHS.** *GE* Franz Gruber; ***D:*** Roberto Rossellini.

Devastator *Kings Ransom; The Destroyers* **1985 (R)** A Vietnam vet exacts violent revenge on the murderer of an old army buddy. **79m/C VHS.** Richard (Rick) Hill, Katt Shea, Crofton Hardester; ***D:*** Cirio H. Santiago.

Devi ½ *The Goddess* **1960** A minor film in the Ray canon, it is, nonetheless, a strange and compelling tale of religious superstition. An Indian farmer becomes convinced that his beautiful daughter-in-law is the reincarnation of the goddess Kali. The girl is then pressured into accepting a worship that eventually drives her mad. In Bengali with English subtitles. **93m/B VHS.** *IN* Chhabi Biswas, Sharmila Tagore, Soumitra Chatterjee; ***D:*** Satyajit Ray; ***W:*** Satyajit Ray; ***C:*** Subrata Mitra; ***M:*** Ali Akbar Khan.

Devices and Desires *P.D. James: Devices & Desires* **1991** Typically complicated mystery adapted from the novel by P.D. James. Scotland Yard Commander Adam Dalgliesh (Marsden) is on holiday on the east coast of England where, of course, there's blackmail, murder, suicide, and trouble at a nearby nuclear power station for him to contend with. Made for TV; on six cassettes. **312m/C VHS.** *GB* Roy Marsden, Susannah York, Gemma Jones, James Faulkner, Tony Haygarth, Tom Georgeson, Tom Chadbon, Nicola Cowper, Suzan Crowley, Robert Hines, Harry Burton, Helena Michell; ***D:*** John Davies; ***W:*** Thomas Ellice. **TV**

The Devil & Daniel Webster ½ *All That Money Can Buy; Here Is a Man; A Certain Mr. Scratch* **1941** In 1840s New Hampshire, a young farmer, who sells his soul to the devil, is saved from a trip to Hell when Daniel Webster steps in to defend him. This classic fantasy is visually striking and contains wonderful performances. Adapted from the story by Stephen Vincent Benet who based it on Goethe's Faust. **106m/B VHS.** James Craig, Edward Arnold, Walter Huston, Simone Simon, Gene Lockhart, Jane Darwell, Anne Shirley, John Qualen, H.B. Warner; ***D:*** William Dieterle; ***M:*** Bernard Herrmann. Oscars '41: Orig. Dramatic Score.

Devil & Leroy Basset **1973 (PG)** Keema Gregwolf kills a deputy, breaks from jail with the Basset brothers, hijacks a church bus, kidnaps a family, and gets into other troublesome situations while on a posse-eluding cross-country adventure. **85m/C VHS.** Cody Bearpaw, John Goff, George "Buck" Flower; ***D:*** Robert E. Pearso; ***M:*** Les Baxter.

The Devil & Max Devlin ½ **1981 (PG)** Good cast wanders aimlessly in Disney family fantasy. The recently deceased Max Devlin strikes a bargain with the devil. He will be restored to life if he can convince three mortals to sell their souls. **95m/C VHS, DVD, Wide.** Sonny Shroyer, Elliott Gould, Bill Cosby, Susan Anspach, Adam Rich, Julie Budd; ***D:*** Steven Hilliard Stern; ***W:*** Jimmy Sangster; ***C:*** Howard Schwartz; ***M:*** Marvin Hamlisch, Buddy (Norman Dale) Baker.

The Devil & Miss Jones ½ **1941** Engaging romantic comedy finds a big business boss posing as an ordinary salesclerk to weed out union organizers. He doesn't expect to encounter the wicked management or his beautiful co-worker, however. **90m/B VHS.** Jean Arthur, Robert Cummings, Charles Coburn, Edmund Gwenn, Spring Byington, William Demarest, S.Z. Sakall; ***D:*** Sam Wood; ***C:*** Harry Stradling Sr.

The Devil at 4 O'Clock ½ **1961** An alcoholic missionary and three convicts work to save a colony of leper children from a South Seas volcano. Quality cast barely compensates for mediocre script. **126m/B VHS.** Spencer Tracy, Frank Sinatra, Kerwin Mathews, Jean-Pierre Aumont; *D:* Mervyn LeRoy; *C:* Joseph Biroc; *M:* George Duning.

The Devil Bat *Killer Bats* **1941** Madman Lugosi trains a swarm of monstrous blood-sucking bats to attack whenever they smell perfume. Followed by the sequel "Devil Bat's Daughter." DVD release is paired with the Lugosi vehicle "Scared to Death" (1946). **67m/B VHS, DVD.** Bela Lugosi, Dave O'Brien, Suzanne Kaaren, Yolande Donlan; *D:* Jean Yarbrough; *W:* John Thomas Neville; *C:* Arthur Martinelli.

The Devil Bat's Daughter ½ **1946** A young woman, hoping to avoid becoming insane like her batty father, consults a psychiatrist when she starts to have violent nightmares. Unsuccessful sequel to "The Devil Bat." **66m/B VHS, DVD.** Rosemary La Planche, Michael Hale, John James, Molly Lamont; *D:* Frank Wisbar; *W:* Griffin Jay; *C:* James S. Brown Jr.

Devil Diamond **1937** Mystery-suspense yarn about two amateur detectives who find themselves facing danger after tracking down a gang of evil jewel thieves. **?m/C VHS.** Kane Richmond, Frankie Darro.

Devil Dog: The Hound of Hell **1978** A family has trouble with man's best friend when they adopt a dog that is the son of the "Hound of Hell." **95m/C VHS.** Richard Crenna, Yvette Mimieux, Kim Richards, Victor Jory; *D:* Curtis Harrington.

Devil Dogs of the Air ½ **1935** Cagney and O'Brien team up in another air drama with Cagney once again the cocky pilot who, this time, joins the Marine Air Corp. O'Brien plays his flying idol (and later rival). Cagney finds all his wisecracking and luck are no match for knowledge and experience but he learns. Good stunt flying; shot on location at the San Diego naval air base. **85m/B VHS.** James Cagney, Pat O'Brien, Margaret Lindsay, Frank McHugh, Robert Barrat, Russell Hicks, Ward Bond; *D:* Lloyd Bacon.

Devil Doll **1936** An escaped convict uses a mad scientist's human-shrinking formula to evil ends—he sends out miniature assassins in the guise of store-bought dolls. Rarely seen horror oldie. **80m/B VHS.** Lionel Barrymore, Maureen O'Sullivan, Frank Lawton, Rafaela (Rafael, Raphaella) Ottiano, Henry B. Walthall, Arthur Hohl, Grace Ford; *D:* Tod Browning; *W:* Tod Browning, Erich von Stroheim, Guy Endore, Garrett Fort; *C:* Leonard Smith.

Devil Doll **1964** Ventriloquist's dummy, which contains the soul of a former performer, eyes a beautiful victim in the crowd. Newspaper guy senses trouble. Cut above the usual talking, stalking dummy story. **80m/B VHS.** *GB* Bryant Holiday, William Sylvester, Yvonne Romain, Sandra Dorne, Karel Stepanek, Francis De Wolff; *D:* Lindsay Shonteff; *W:* Lance Z. Hargreaves, George Barclay; *C:* Gerald Gibbs.

Devil Girl from Mars ½ **1954** Sexy female from Mars and her very large robot arrive at a small Scottish inn to announce that a Martian feminist revolution has occurred. The distaff aliens then undertake a search of healthy Earth males for breeding purposes. Believe it or not, the humans don't want to go and therein lies the rub. A somewhat enjoyable space farce. **76m/B VHS, DVD.** *GB* Hugh McDermott, Hazel Court, Patricia Laffan, Peter Reynolds, Adrienne Corri, Joseph Tomelty, Sophie Stewart, John Laurie, Anthony Richmond; *D:* David MacDonald; *W:* John C. Mather, James Eastwood; *C:* Jack Cox; *M:* Edwin Astley.

Devil Horse **1932** A boy's devotion to a wild horse marked for destruction as a killer leads him into trouble. A serial in 12 chapters of 13 minutes each. **156m/B VHS.** Frankie Darro, Harry Carey Sr., Noah Beery Sr.; *D:* Otto Brower, Richard Talmadge.

Devil in a Blue Dress **1995 (R)** Down-on-his-luck Easy Rawlins (Washington) is an out of work aircraft worker in 1948 LA. He's hired to find mystery woman Daphne (Beals) by a shady businessman (Sizemore). What he finds are the usual noir staples: government corruption backed by thugs who want him to mind his own business. Easy and Daphne's torrid romance featured in the Walter Mosley novel is missing but the racism and violence are intact. Realism and accuracy in period detail enhance solid performance by Washington, though the deliberate, literary pace is at times lulling. Cheadle takes over whenever he shows up as Mouse, Rawlins' loyal friend and muscle. **102m/C VHS, DVD.** Nick(y) Corello, Denzel Washington, Jennifer Beals, Don Cheadle, Tom Sizemore, Maury Chaykin, Terry Kinney, Mel Winkler, Albert Hall, Renee Humphrey, Lisa Nicole Carson, John Roselius, Beau Starr; *D:* Carl Franklin; *W:* Carl Franklin; *C:* Tak Fujimoto; *M:* Elmer Bernstein. L.A. Film Critics '95: Support. Actor (Cheadle); Natl. Soc. Film Critics '95: Cinematog., Support. Actor (Cheadle).

The Devil in Silk ½ **1956** A composer marries a woman, not knowing that she is psychotically jealous. After she commits suicide, he must prove to the police that he did not kill her. Original dialogue in German. **102m/B VHS.** *GE* Lilli Palmer, Curt Jurgens, Winnie Markus; *D:* Rolf Hansen.

Devil in the Flesh *Le Diable au Corps* **1946** Acclaimed drama about a French soldier's wife having a passionate affair with a high school student while her husband is away fighting in WWI. From the novel by Raymond Radiguet. Dubbed. Updated and remade in 1987. **112m/B VHS.** *FR* Gerard Philipe, Micheline Presle, Denise Grey; *D:* Claude Autant-Lara; *W:* Jean Aurenche, Pierre Bost; *C:* Michel Kelber; *M:* Rene Cloerec.

Devil in the Flesh *Il Diavolo in Corpo* **1987 (R)** A angst-ridden, semi-pretentious Italian drama about an obsessive older woman carrying on an affair with a schoolboy, despite her terrorist boyfriend and the objections of the lad's psychiatrist father, who had treated her. Famous for a graphic sex scene, available in the unrated version. Updated remake of the 1946 French film. Italian with subtitles. **110m/C VHS.** *IT* Riccardo De Torrebruna, Maruschka Detmers, Federico Pitzalis; *D:* Marco Bellocchio; *W:* Ennio de Concini, Enrico Palandri, Marco Bellocchio; *C:* Giuseppe Lanci; *M:* Carlo Crivelli.

Devil in the Flesh ½ *Dearly Devoted* **1998 (R)** Troubled Debbie Strand (McGowan) has a crush on teacher Peter Rinaldi (McArthur) and no one is going to stop her getting what (or who) she wants. She tries blackmailing him when he doesn't respond and McArthur learns McGowan has a very deadly past. **92m/C VHS, DVD.** Rose McGowan, Alex McArthur, Sherrie Rose, Phil Morris, Robert Silver; *D:* Steve Cohen. **VIDEO**

Devil in the Flesh 2 ½ *Teacher's Pet* **2000 (R)** In this sequel to the '98 flick, disturbed Debbie (O'Keefe) escapes from the looney bin and causes the accidental death of the college coed who offers her a ride, so she assumes her identity. Passing herself off as wealthy Sydney Hollings, Debbie becomes infatuated with her writing prof Sam (Garcia), who's flattered by the attention. Except that anyone who gets in Debbie's way is permanently disposed of. Sly humor and O'Keefe is remarkably appealing considering she plays a psychopath. **90m/C VHS.** Jodi Lyn O'Keefe, Katherine Kendall, Jsu Garcia, Jeanette Brox, Bill Gratton, Todd McKee, Christiana Frank, Todd Robert Anderson; *D:* Marcus Spiegel; *W:* Richard Brandes; *C:* M. David Mullen. **VIDEO**

The Devil Is a Woman **1935** Dietrich vamps as money-hungry beauty Concha Perez, who soon has best friends and fellow military officers Pasqual (Atwill) and Antonio (Romero) dueling for her dubious affections. Turns out the man she desires may not be the man she truly needs. Flashbacks show how Concha seductively destroyed Pasquel some years earlier and how his jealousy lingered on. Based on the novel "The Woman and the Puppet" by Pierre Louys. After protests by the Spanish government over the depiction of the Spanish military, Paramount agreed to supress the film and few prints survived. **79m/B VHS.** Marlene Dietrich, Lionel Atwill, Cesar Romero, Edward Everett Horton, Alison Skipworth; *D:* Josef von Sternberg; *W:* John Dos Passos, S.K. Winston; *C:* Josef von Sternberg, Lucien Ballard.

Devil Monster **1946** A world-weary traveler searches for a girl's fiance in the South Pacific, and is attacked by a large manta. **65m/B VHS.** Barry Norton, Blanche Mehaffey; *D:* S. Edwin Graham.

Devil of the Desert Against the Son of Hercules ½ **1962** The grandson of Zeus ventures into the wasteland to take on a feisty foe. **?m/C VHS.** *IT* Kirk Morris, Michele Girardon; *D:* Riccardo (Robert Hampton) Freda.

Devil on Horseback **1954** A miner's son journeys to London to become a jockey in this comedy/drama. As he tries to bully his way into the racing circuit, he succeeds, but not in the way he anticipated. **88m/B VHS, 8mm.** *GB* Googie Withers, John McCallum, Jeremy Spenser, Liam Redmond; *D:* Cyril Frankel; *M:* Malcolm Arnold.

The Devil on Wheels **1947** Inspired by his dad's reckless driving, a teenager becomes a hot rodder and causes a family tragedy. A rusty melodrama that can't be described as high-performance. **67m/B VHS.** James B. Cardwell, Noreen Nash, Darryl Hickman, Jan Ford, Damian O'Flynn, Lenita Love; *D:* Crane Wilbur; *W:* Crane Wilbur.

The Devil, Probably *Le Diable, Probablement* **1977** Ennui among Parisian youth, lost in their polluted, consumer society. Charles (Monnier) spins deeper into depression, despite the efforts of his friends, and finally makes a bargain with a junkie to shoot him in Pere Lachaise cemetery. French with subtitles. **95m/C VHS.** *FR* Antoine Monnier, Tina Irissari, Henri De Maublanc; *D:* Robert Bresson; *W:* Robert Bresson; *C:* Pasqualino De Santis; *M:* Philippe Sarde.

Devil Riders ½ **1944** Unspectacular horse opera has a crooked lawyer trying to get his grubby hands on some choice land. Enter Crabbe to set things straight. **56m/B VHS.** Buster Crabbe, Al "Fuzzy" St. John, Patti McCarty, Charles "Blackie" King, John Merton, Kermit Maynard, Frank LaRue, Jack Ingram, George Chesebro, Edward Cassidy; *D:* Sam Newfield.

The Devil Rides Out ½ *The Devil's Bride* **1968** Considered by many to be Hammer's finest achievement, though several other of the studio's films rate serious consideration. This one's a solid witchcraft tale written by Richard Matheson. In 1925, the Duc de Richleau (Lee), a "good" warlock, and the evil Mocata battle each other over De Richleau's friend Simon (Mower). Some of the effects are a little dated now, but director Terence Fisher builds suspense through a stately pace. Production values are highlighted by the usual excellent sets and a fleet of vintage cars. Lee's performance is one of his strongest in a conventionally heroic role. **95m/C DVD, Wide.** *GB* Christopher Lee, Charles Gray, Nike Arrighi, Leon Greene, Patrick Mower, Gwen Ffrangcon Davies, Sarah Lawson, Paul Eddington; *D:* Terence Fisher; *W:* Richard Matheson; *C:* Arthur Grant; *M:* James Bernard.

The Devil Thumbs a Ride **1947** A naive traveller picks up a hitchhiker, not knowing he's wanted for murder. Will history repeat itself in this interesting noir? **63m/B VHS.** Ted North, Lawrence Tierney, Nan Leslie; *D:* Felix Feist.

Devil Times Five ½ *People Toys; The Horrible House on the Hill* **1974 (R)** To take revenge for being incarcerated in a mental hospital, five children methodically murder the adults who befriend them. **87m/C VHS.** Gene Evans, Sorrell Booke, Shelly Morrison; *D:* Sean McGregor.

Devil Wears White **1986 (R)** A student's vacation is disrupted when he becomes involved in a war with an insane arms dealer who wants to take over a Latin American Republic. **92m/C VHS.** Robert Livesy, Jane Higginson, Guy Ecker, Anthony Cordova; *D:* Steven A. Hull.

Devil Woman woof! **1976 (R)** A Filipino Gorgon-woman seeks reptillian revenge on the farmers who killed her family. Bad news. **79m/C VHS.** *PH* Rosemarie Gil; *D:* Albert Yu, Felix Vilars.

Devilfish **1984** A small seaside community is ravaged by berserk manta rays in this soggy saga. **92m/C VHS.** *IT* *D:* Lamberto Bava.

The Devils *The Devils of Loudun* **1971 (R)** In 1631 France, a priest is accused of commerce with the devil and sexual misconduct with nuns. Since he is also a political threat, the accusation is used to denounce and eventually execute him. Based on Aldous Huxley's "The Devils of Loudun," the movie features masturbating nuns and other excesses—shocking scenes typical of film director Russell. Supposedly this was Russell's attempt to wake the public to their desensitization of modern horrors of war. Controversial and flamboyant. **109m/C VHS.** *GB* Vanessa Redgrave, Oliver Reed, Dudley Sutton, Max Adrian, Gemma Jones, Murray Melvin, Michael Gothard, Georgina Hale, Christopher Logue, Andrew Faulds; *D:* Ken Russell; *W:* Ken Russell; *C:* David Watkin; *M:* Peter Maxwell Davies. Natl. Bd. of Review '71: Director (Russell).

The Devil's Advocate ½ **1997 (R)** Forget the actors, this film belongs to cinematographer Bartkowiak and production designer Bruno Rubeo, who offer a lush, rich look that's very enticing. And it's all about enticement—young Florida lawyer Kevin Lomax (Reeves) is seduced by the power and money of a position at an influential New York law firm run by the mysterious John Milton (Pacino). But soon Kevin's beautiful wife Mary Ann (Theron) is having a breakdown, his religious mother (Ivey) is prophesizing doom, and Kevin learns the boss is Satan—literally. Reeves is earnest, Pacino relishes his showy role, and the visual effects provide some much needed jolts. Based on the novel by Andrew Neiderman. **144m/C VHS, DVD, Wide.** Al Pacino, Keanu Reeves, Charlize Theron, Judith Ivey, Craig T. Nelson, Jeffrey Jones, Connie Nielsen, Ruben Santiago-Hudson, Debra Monk, Tamara Tunie, Vyto Ruginis, Laura Harrington, Pamela Gray, Heather Matarazzo, Delroy Lindo; *D:* Taylor Hackford; *W:* Tony Gilroy, Jonathan Lemkin; *C:* Andrzej Bartkowiak; *M:* James Newton Howard.

Devil's Angels **1967** A motorcycle gang clashes with a small-town sheriff. Cheap 'n' sleazy fare. **84m/C VHS.** John Cassavetes, Beverly Adams, Mimsy Farmer, Salli Sachse, Nai Bonet, Leo Gordon; *D:* Daniel Haller; *W:* Charles B. Griffith.

The Devil's Arithmetic ½ **1999** Modern teen Hannah Stern (Dunst) is indifferent to her Jewish faith and reluctant to attend her Aunt Eva's (Fletcher) Passover seder. After getting drunk, she passes out and is mysteriously transported to Poland in 1941, where she and her cousin Rivkah (Murphy) are imprisoned in a concentration camp and Hannah gets a first-hand look at faith and oppression. Pic doesn't play down the Nazi horrors and may not be suitable for the very young. Adapted from Jane Yolen's novel. **101m/C VHS.** Kirsten Dunst, Brittany Murphy, Louise Fletcher, Paul Freeman, Mimi Rogers; *D:* Donna Deitch; *W:* Robert J. Avrech; *C:* Jacek Laskus; *M:* Frederic Talgorn. **CABLE**

The Devil's Backbone *El Espinazo del Diablo* **2001 (R)** In the final days of the Spanish Civil War, staff and children at a remote orphanage run by loyalists Casares (Luppi) and Carmen (Paredes) prepare for an uncertain fate. Carlos (Tielve) is a new arrival who quickly learns that there are many secrets, including the (possible) ghost of schoolboy Santi. Sinister janitor Jacinto (Noriega) also thinks there's gold hidden somewhere and is determined to find it. Uneasy combination of history and the supernatural. Spanish with subtitles. **106m/C VHS, DVD.** *SP MX* Marisa Paredes, Federico Luppi, Eduardo Noriega, Fernando Tielve, Inigo Garces, Irene Visedo, Berta Ojea; *D:* Guillermo del Toro; *W:* Guillermo del Toro, Antonio Trashorras, David Munoz; *C:* Guillermo Navarro; *M:* Javier Navarrete.

The Devil's Brigade **1968** "Dirty Dozen" style film with Holden as the leader of special commando brigade consisting of the usual misfits and oddballs. The team is trained to take on the Nazis in Scandanavia but has their assignment cancelled. Instead, they take them on in the Italian Alps, making for some perilous adventures. Non-acting notables include former football great Hornung and former boxing champ Gene Fullmer. **130m/C VHS, DVD, Wide.** William Holden, Cliff Robertson, Vince Edwards, Andrew Prine, Claude Akins, Michael Rennie, Dana Andrews, Gretchen Wyler, Carroll O'Connor, Richard Jaeckel, Jack Watson, Paul Hornung, Jeremy Slate, Don Megowan, Patric Knowles, James Craig, Richard Dawson, Tom Stern, Luke Askew, Harry Carey Jr., Tom Troupe, Norman Alden, David Pritchard; ***D:*** Andrew V. McLaglen; ***W:*** William Roberts; ***C:*** William Clothier; ***M:*** Alex North.

The Devil's Brother 🦴🦴 *Fra Diavolo; Bogus Bandits; The Virtuous Tramps* **1933** In one of their lesser efforts, Laurel and Hardy star as bumbling bandits in this comic operetta based on the 1830 opera by Daniel F. Auber. **88m/B VHS.** Stan Laurel, Oliver Hardy, Dennis King, Thelma Todd, James Finlayson, Lucille Browne; ***D:*** Charles R. Rogers, Hal Roach.

Devil's Canyon 🦴🦴 **1953** An ex-lawman, serving time in an Arizona prison, is beset by a jailed killer seeking vengeance for his own incarceration. Filmed in 3-D. **92m/B VHS.** Dale Robertson, Virginia Mayo, Stephen McNally, Arthur Hunnicutt, Robert Keith, Jay C. Flippen, Whit Bissell; ***D:*** Alfred Werker.

The Devil's Cargo 🦴½ **1948** When a man is accused of killing a racetrack operator, he calls in the Falcon to clear his name. The master detective finds this to be a most difficult task however, especially when the accused is found poisoned in his cell. One of the final three "Falcon" films, in which Calvert replaced Tom Conway. **61m/B VHS.** John Calvert, Rochelle Hudson, Roscoe Karns, Lyle Talbot, Tom Kennedy; ***D:*** John F. Link.

Devil's Crude 🦴 **1971** Adventurous sailor and a young oil heir uncover a conspiracy within a giant corporation. **85m/C VHS.** *IT* Franco Nero, Francesco Rabal; ***D:*** Tommaso Dazzi.

The Devil's Daughter 🦴½ *Pocomania* **1939** A sister's hatred and voodoo ceremonies play an important part in this all-black drama. **60m/B VHS.** Nina Mae McKinney, Jack Carter, Ida James, Hamtree Harrington; ***D:*** Arthur Leonard; ***C:*** Jay Rescher.

The Devil's Daughter **1991 (R)** Satan, in a desperate bid to take over the planet, orders his minions to flood the earth with horrific evil. Only one woman can prevent the HellMaster from succeeding, and she may be too late! **112m/C VHS.** *IT* Kelly Curtis, Herbert Lom, Maria Angela Giordano, Michel Hans Adatte, Carla Cassola, Angelika Maria Boeck, Tomas Arana; ***D:*** Michele (Michael) Soavi; ***W:*** Dario Argento; ***M:*** Pino Donaggio.

The Devil's Disciple 🦴🦴🦴 **1959** Entertaining adaptation of a minor George Bernard Shaw play set during the American Revolution. British Gen. Burgoyne (Olivier) and his troops are stuck in a northeastern village in 1777 awaiting orders and dealing with rebels. This includes troublemaking Richard Dudgeon (Douglas), whose father has been hanged by the Brits, and pastor Anthony Anderson (Lancaster), working in secret with the rebels. There's also a modest romantic triangle between the two men and Anderson's wife Judith (Scott). Film suffers from choppy direction, but the excellent cast more than makes up for it. **82m/B VHS.** *GB* Burt Lancaster, Kirk Douglas, Laurence Olivier, Janet Scott, Eva LeGallienne, Harry Andrews, Basil Sydney, George Rose; ***D:*** Guy Hamilton; ***W:*** John Dighton, Roland Kibbee; ***C:*** Jack Hildyard; ***M:*** Richard Rodney Bennett.

The Devil's Eye 🦴🦴 *Djavulens Oga* **1960** The devil dispatches Don Juan to tempt and seduce a young virgin bride-to-be, a reverend's daughter, no less. Based on the Danish radio play "Don Juan Returns." **90m/B VHS.** *SW* Stig Jarrel, Bibi Andersson, Jarl Kulle; ***D:*** Ingmar Bergman; ***W:*** Ingmar Bergman; ***C:*** Gunnar Fischer; ***M:*** Erik Nordgren, Domenico Scarletti.

Devil's Gift woof! **1984** A young boy's toy is possessed by a demon and havoc ensues. **112m/C VHS.** Bob Mendlesolin, Vicki Saputo, Steven Robertson; ***D:*** Kenneth Berton.

The Devil's Hand 🦴 *Devil's Doll; The Naked Goddess; Live to Love* **1961** When Alda finds a doll that represents his ideal woman in a curio shop, the shop's owner (Hamilton, aka Commissioner Gordon), tells him the dream girl who modeled for the doll lives nearby. Trouble is, she's part of a voodoo cult, and guess who's head voodoo-man. Big trouble for Alda; big snooze for you. **71m/B VHS.** Linda Christian, Robert Alda, Neil Hamilton, Ariadne Welter; ***D:*** William Hole Jr.

Devil's Island 🦴🦴 *Djoflaeyjan* **1996** An abandoned military base is being used to house poor families outside Reykjavik in the '50s. The trash-filled landscape offers little to those who live there, including four generations of one eccentric no-hope family. The usual family dysfunction is all played for exaggerated caricature. Icelandic with subtitles. **103m/C VHS, DVD.** *IC* Gisli Halldorsson, Baltasar Kormakur, Sveinn Geirsson, Sigurveig Jonsdottir; ***D:*** Fridrik Thor Fridriksson; ***W:*** Einar Karason; ***C:*** Ari Kristinsson; ***M:*** Hilmar Orn Jilmarsson.

The Devil's Mistress 🦴½ **1968** A gang of criminals on a pillaging spree murder a man and rape his Indian wife, only to find out she's a she-demon who won't let bygones be bygones. Lame. **66m/C VHS.** Joan Stapleton, Robert Gregory, Forrest Westmoreland, Douglas Warren, Oren Williams, Arthur Resley; ***D:*** Orville Wanzer; ***W:*** Orville Wanzer.

The Devil's Nightmare 🦴½ *Succubus; The Devil Walks at Midnight* **1971 (R)** A woman leads seven tourists (representing the seven deadly sins) on a tour of a medieval European castle. There they experience demonic tortures. Lots of creepy moments. Euro-horror/sex star Blanc is fantastic in this otherwise mediocre production. **88m/C VHS, DVD.** *BE IT* Erika Blanc, Jean Servais, Daniel Emilfork, Lucien Raimbourg, Jacques Monseau, Colette Emmanuelle, Ivana Novak, Shirley Corrigan, Frederique Hender; ***D:*** Jean Brismee; ***W:*** Patrice Rhomm, Vertunnio De Angelis, Charles Lecocq; ***C:*** Andre Goeffers; ***M:*** Alessandro Alessandroni.

Devils on the Doorstep 🦴🦴 *Guizi Laile* **2000** Chinese film needs some sharp editing before this black comedy about a tiny village's survival during WWII could be anything more than frustrating. Local peasant Ma Dasan is surprised when the Chinese Army dump two prisoners in their remote village—a Japanese POW and his Chinese interpreter. When no one comes for the prisoners after six months, the fearful villagers decide they should be executed and Ma is sent to hire an assassin. When this doesn't work out, the villagers try to return them to nearby Japanese troops. This idea isn't any better and by now the movie's exhausted a viewer's patience. Japanese and Mandarin with subtitles. **162m/B VHS.** *CH* Jiang Wen, Kagawa Teruyuki, Jiang Hongbo, Chen Qiang, Sawada Kenya, Yuan Ding; ***D:*** Jiang Wen; ***W:*** Jiang Wen; ***C:*** Gu Changwei. Cannes '00: Grand Jury Prize.

The Devil's Own 🦴🦴🦴 **1996 (R)** Irish-American New York cop Tom O'Meara (Ford) and wife Sheila (Colin) take charming Irish emigre Rory Devaney (Pitt) into their home and make him part of the family. But Rory, AKA Frankie McGuire, turns out to be an IRA terrorist who has hustled out of trouble in Belfast and now has a bloody purpose for coming to America. When Tom discovers just what it is, he tries to stop Rory before he destroys any more lives—including his own. More a low-key character study than a slam-bang actioner, with Pitt cooly charismatic as the troubled gunman while Ford does his usual professional work as a good cop caught up in a bad situation. **110m/C VHS, DVD.** Harrison Ford, Brad Pitt, Margaret Colin, Ruben Blades, Treat Williams, George Hearn, Natascha (Natasha) McElhone, Mitchell Ryan, Simon Jones, Paul Ronan; ***D:*** Alan J. Pakula; ***W:*** Kevin Jarre, David Aaron Cohen, Vincent Patrick; ***C:*** Gordon Willis; ***M:*** James Horner.

The Devil's Partner 🦴½ **1958** Yet another uninspired devil yarn in which an old-timer trades in his senior citizenship by dying and coming back in the form of his younger self. Young again, he takes a new wife and indulges in multiple ritual sacrifices. Noteworthy only by virtue of the cast's later TV notoriety—Buchanan and Foulger would later appear on "Petticoat Junction," Nelson played Dr. Rossi on "Peyton Place," and Crane beached a role on "Hawaiian Eye." **75m/B VHS.** Ed Nelson, Jean Allison, Edgar Buchanan, Richard Crane, Spencer Carlisle, Byron Foulger, Claire Carleton; ***D:*** Charles R. Rondeau.

Devil's Party 🦴🦴 **1938** A tenement boy's reunion party turns into a night of horror when one of the guests is killed. As a result, the childhood friends band together to uncover the murderer's identity. **65m/B VHS.** Victor McLaglen, Paul Kelly, William Gargan, Samuel S. Hinds, Scotty Beckett; ***D:*** Ray McCarey.

The Devil's Playground 🦴🦴🦴 **1976** Sexual tension rises in a Catholic seminary, distracting the boys from their theological studies. The attentions of the priests only further their sexual confusion. **107m/C VHS.** *AU* Arthur Dignam, Nick (Nicholas) Tate, Simon Burke, Charles Frawley, Jonathan Hardy, Gerry Dugan, Thomas Keneally; ***D:*** Fred Schepisi; ***W:*** Fred Schepisi; ***C:*** Ian Baker; ***M:*** Bruce Smeaton. Australian Film Inst. '76: Actor (Tate), Actor (Burke), Cinematog., Director (Schepisi), Film, Screenplay.

The Devil's Possessed 🦴½ **1974** A Middle Ages despot tortures and maims the peasants in his region until they rise up and enact an unspeakable revenge. **90m/C VHS.** *AR SP* Paul (Jacinto Molina) Naschy, Jacinto (Jack) Molina; ***D:*** Leon Klimovsky.

The Devil's Prey 🦴🦴 **2001 (R)** Partyers attending a rave discover it's a front for satanic cult leader Minister Seth (Bergin) to obtain the young flesh he needs for his blood sacrifies. But Susan (Jones) is willing to fight for her life against the masked cult members. Fast-paced horror. **91m/C VHS, DVD.** Patrick Bergin, Ashley Jones, Charlie O'Connell, Bryan Kirkwood, Tim Thomerson; ***D:*** Bradford May. **VIDEO**

Devil's Rain 🦴½ **1975 (PG)** The rituals and practices of devil worship, possession, and satanism are gruesomely related. Interesting cast. **85m/C VHS, DVD.** Ernest Borgnine, Ida Lupino, William Shatner, Eddie Albert, Keenan Wynn, Tom Skerritt, Joan Prather, Claudio Brook, John Travolta, Anton La Vey; ***D:*** Robert Fuest; ***W:*** James Ashton, Gabe Essoe, Gerald Hopman; ***C:*** Alex Phillips Jr.; ***M:*** Al De Lory.

The Devil's Sleep 🦴 **1951** When a crusading woman sets out to break up a teen narcotics ring, the threatened thugs attempt to draw her daughter into their sleazy affairs, thus assuring the mother's silence. **81m/B VHS.** Lita Grey Chaplin, Timothy Farrell, John Mitchum, William Thomason, Tracy Lynn; ***D:*** W. Merle Connell.

Devil's Son-in-Law woof! **1977 (R)** A black stand-up comic makes a deal with a devil. **95m/C VHS.** Rudy Ray Moore; ***D:*** Cliff Roguemore.

The Devil's Undead 🦴🦴½ **1975 (PG)** When a Scottish orphanage is besieged by a rash of cold-blooded murders, the detectives Lee and Cushing are summoned to investigate. Interesting spin on that old possessed by demons theme. **90m/C VHS.** *GB* Christopher Lee, Peter Cushing; ***D:*** Peter Sasdy.

Devil's Wanton 🦴🦴½ *Fangelse; Prison* **1949** A young girl tries to forget an unhappy relationship by beginning a new romance with an equally frustrated beau. Gloomy, but hopeful. **80m/B VHS.** *SW* Doris Svedlund, Eva Henning, Hasse (Hans) Ekman; ***D:*** Ingmar Bergman; ***W:*** Ingmar Bergman.

The Devil's Web 🦴½ **1974 (PG)** A demonic nurse infiltrates, manipulates, and corrupts three beautiful sisters. **73m/C VHS.** Diana Dors, Andrea Marcovicci, Ed Bishop, Cec Linder, Michael Culver. **TV**

Devil's Wedding Night woof! *El Returno de la Drequessa Dracula; The Return of the Duchess Dracula; Full Moon of the Virgins* **1973 (R)** An archaeologist and his twin brother fight over a ring that lures virgins into Count Dracula's Transylvanian castle. Vampire queen Bay seduces the dimwit twins and strips at every chance she gets. **85m/C VHS.** Mark Damon, Rosalba (Sara Bay) Neri, Frances Davis; ***D:*** Luigi (Paolo Solvay) Batzella.

Devlin 🦴🦴 **1992 (R)** Devlin is a tough cop with an alcohol problem and a bad marriage. His father-in-law, Brennan, is a powerful local political boss. When Brennan's son is murdered, Devlin is the fall guy. Seeking to clear himself, he discovers a conspiracy going back 30 years. **110m/C VHS.** Bryan Brown, Roma Downey, Lloyd Bridges; ***D:*** Rick Rosenthal; ***M:*** Minette Alton. **CABLE**

Devonsville Terror 🦴🦴 **1983 (R)** Strange things begin to happen when a new school teacher arrives in Devonsville, a town that has a history of torture, murder, and witchcraft. The hysterical townspeople react by beginning a 20th-century witchhunt. **97m/C VHS, DVD.** Suzanna Love, Donald Pleasence, Deanna Haas, Mary Walden, Robert Walker Jr., Paul Willson; ***D:*** Ulli Lommel; ***W:*** Ulli Lommel; ***C:*** Ulli Lommel; ***M:*** Ray Colcord.

Devotion 🦴🦴½ **1931** A lovesick British miss disguises herself as a governess so she can be near the object of her affection, a London barrister. **80m/B VHS.** Ann Harding, Leslie Howard, Robert Williams, O.P. Heggie, Louise Closser Hale, Dudley Digges; ***D:*** Robert Milton.

D.I. 🦴🦴 **1957** A tough drill sergeant is faced with an unbreakable rebellious recruit, threatening his record and his platoon's status. Webb's film features performances by actual soldiers. **106m/B VHS.** Jack Webb, Don Dubbins, Jackie Loughery, Lin McCarthy, Virginia Gregg; ***D:*** Jack Webb.

The Diabolical Dr. Z 🦴🦴 *Miss Muerte; Dans les Griffes du Maniaque* **1965** When dad dies of cardiac arrest after the medical council won't let him make the world a kinder gentler place with his personality-altering technique, his dutiful daughter—convinced the council brought on dad's demise—is out to change some personalities in a big way. **86m/B VHS.** *SP FR* Mabel Karr, Fernando Montes, Estella Blain, Antonio J. Escribano, Howard Vernon, Jess (Jesus) Franco, Jose Maria Prada, Guy Mairesse; ***D:*** Jess (Jesus) Franco; ***W:*** Jean-Claude Carriere, Jess (Jesus) Franco; ***C:*** Alejandro Ulloa; ***M:*** Jess (Jesus) Franco.

Diabolically Yours 🦴🦴½ *Diabo-liquement Votre* **1967** A French thriller about an amnesiac who struggles to discover his lost identity. Tensions mount when his pretty spouse and friends begin to wonder if it's all a game. Dubbed. **94m/C VHS.** *FR* Alain Delon, Senta Berger; ***D:*** Julien Duvivier.

Diabolique 🦴🦴🦴½ *Les Diabolique* **1955** Sadistic boarding school master Michel (Meurisse) has a wealthy, neurotic wife, Christina (Clouzet, the director's wife), and a cold-blooded mistress, Nicole (Signoret), who conspire to poison and then drown him in the school's swimming pool. But after the plot is carried out, Christina becomes convinced that Michel is still alive. Plot twists and double-crosses abound. Based on the novel "Celle Qui N'Etait Pas" by Pierre Boileau and Thomas Narcejac. French with subtitles. Remade for TV in 1974 as "Reflections of Murder." **107m/B VHS, DVD.** *FR* Simone Signoret, Vera Clouzot, Paul Meurisse, Charles Vanel, Michel Serrault, Georges Chamarat, Robert Dalban, Therese Dorny, Camille Guerini; ***D:*** Henri-Georges Clouzot; ***W:*** Henri-Georges Clouzot, Frederic Grendel, Jerome Geronimi, Rene Masson; ***C:*** Armand Thirard; ***M:*** Georges Van Parys. N.Y. Film Critics '55: Foreign Film.

Diabolique 🦴½ **1996 (R)** Remake of the 1955 French noir classic, updated for '90s sensibilities, finds timid teacher Mia (Adjani) married to overbearing school head Guy (Palminteri), who's having an affair with fellow teacher Nicole (Stone). The two women, who loathe the Guy equally, plot to kill him. But when a P.I. (Bates) investigates, it seems possible that Guy isn't dead after all. If you're having trouble accessorizing with leopard skin, watch Stone. Otherwise, watch the far superior original. The usually publicity hungry Stone refused to have anything to do with this picture after its release due to a spat with director Chechik. **105m/C VHS, DVD, Wide.** Sharon Stone, Isabelle Adjani, Chazz Palminteri, Kathy Bates, Spalding Gray, Shirley

Knight, Adam Hann-Byrd, Allen (Goorwitz) Garfield; *D:* Jeremiah S. Chechik; *W:* Don Roos; *C:* Peter James; *M:* Randy Edelman.

Dial Help 🦴½ *Ragno Gelido; Minaccia d'Amore* **1988 (R)** A lame Italian-made suspenser about a model plagued by ghostly phone calls. **94m/C VHS.** *IT* Charlotte Lewis, Marcello Modugno, Mattia Sbragia, Victor Cavallo, William Berger, Carlo Monni, Carola Stagnaro; *D:* Ruggero Deodato; *C:* Renato Tafuri.

Dial "M" for Murder 🦴🦴🦴 **1954** Unfaithful playboy Tony's (Milland) cash is all thanks to his marriage to heiress Margot (Kelly) and he fears losing her to writer Mark (Cummings). So Tony devises an elaborate plan to murder his wife for her money, but when she accidentally stabs the killer-to-be, with scissors no less, it's Tony who comes under the suspicious eye of Chief Inspector Hubbard (Williams). Filmed in 3-D. Based on the play by Frederick Knotts. Loosely remade in 1998 as "A Perfect Murder" starring Michael Douglas and Gwenyth Paltrow. **123m/C VHS.** Ray Milland, Grace Kelly, Robert Cummings, John Williams, Anthony Dawson; *D:* Alfred Hitchcock; *W:* Frederick Knott; *C:* Robert Burks; *M:* Dimitri Tiomkin.

Diamond Fleece 🦴🦴½ **1992** Rick (Cross) is a convicted diamond thief who's given a parole just so he can guard the world's largest uncut gemstone. But Inspector Outlaw (Dennehy) figures Rick will never be able to resist stealing the gem himself and the law can finally lock Rick away for good. Oh, and Holly, she thinks a maybe-ex-diamond thief will bring a little romance to her life. **93m/C VHS.** Ben Cross, Brian Dennehy, Kate Nelligan; *D:* Al Waxman; *W:* Michael Norell.

Diamond Head 🦴🦴½ **1962** A Hawaiian landowner brings destruction and misery to his family via his stubbornness. Based on the Peter Gilman novel. **107m/C VHS.** Charlton Heston, Yvette Mimieux, George Chakiris, France Nuyen, James Darren; *D:* Guy Green; *C:* Sam Leavitt; *M:* John Williams.

The Diamond of Jeru 🦴🦴½ **2001** Helen (Jefferson) and John (Carradine) travel to Borneo in search of adventure (and diamonds) in an effort to put some spice back into their marriage. Too bad Helen is very attracted to their guide, Mike (Zane). John gets jealous and decides he and the missus should head out on their own while Mike pursues them through the jungle in an effort to rescue them from certain doom. Based on the story "Off the Mangrove Coast" by Louis L'Amour. **89m/C VHS, DVD.** Billy Zane, Keith Carradine, Paris Jefferson, Jackson Raine, Khoa Do; *D:* Ian Barry, Dick Lowry; *W:* Beau L'Amour; *C:* Stephen Windon; *M:* Christopher Tyng. VIDEO

Diamond Run 🦴½ **1990 (R)** A streetwise American expatriate frantically searches for his girlfriend after unwittingly involving her in an assassination plot. **89m/C VHS.** William Bell Sullivan, Ava Lazar, Ayu Azhari, David Thornton, Peter Fox; *D:* Robert Chappell.

Diamond Trail 🦴½ **1933** East Coast jewel thieves bring their operation to the West, trailed by a New York reporter. **58m/B VHS.** Rex Bell, Frances Rich, Bud Osborne, Lloyd Whitlock, Norman Feusier; *D:* Harry Fraser.

The Diamond Trap 🦴🦴 **1991 (PG)** A Manhatten detective finds himself in the middle of a diamond heist and involved with a con artist. **93m/C VHS.** Howard Hesseman, Brooke Shields, Ed Marinaro, Twiggy; *D:* Don Taylor; *W:* David Peckinpah. TV

Diamondbacks 🦴½ **1999** Militia group, led by O'Keefe, takes over a remote NASA station in order to reprogram a government weapons satellite for evil. And it's up to engineer Lottimer to stop them. Lots of action in a no-brainer adventure. **90m/C VHS, DVD.** Miles O'Keeffe, Chris Mitchum, Timothy Bottoms, Eb Lottimer; *D:* Bernard Salzman. VIDEO

Diamonds 🦴🦴 **1972 (PG)** A tense film in which the Israel Diamond Exchange is looted by a motley array of criminal heisters. Shaw plays a dual role as twin brothers. **108m/C VHS.** *IS* Robert Shaw, Richard Roundtree, Barbara Hershey, Shelley Winters; *D:* Menahem Golan.

Diamonds 🦴🦴½ **1999 (PG-13)** Douglas lends both dignity and humor to his first screen role since recovering from a stroke. Harry Agrensky (Douglas) is a one-time boxing champ (recovering from a stroke) who wants to live as independently as possible. He claims to have a fortune in diamonds, given to him by a mobster, hidden away in Reno and bullies his estranged son, Lance (Aykroyd), and his grandson Michael (Allred) to go on a road trip and retrieve them. There are various adventures and bonding moments and Douglas is re-united with Bacall (as a Nevada madam), with whom he worked in 1950's "Young Man with a Horn." **90m/C VHS, DVD, Wide.** Kirk Douglas, Dan Aykroyd, Corbin Allred, Lauren Bacall, Kurt Fuller, Jenny McCarthy, John Landis, Mariah O'Brien; *D:* John Mallory Asher; *W:* Allan Aaron Katz; *C:* Paul Elliott; *M:* Joel Goldsmith.

Diamonds Are Forever 🦴🦴🦴½ **1971 (PG)** 007 once again battles his nemesis Blofeld, this time in Las Vegas. Bond must prevent the implementation of a plot to destroy Washington through the use of a space-orbiting laser. Fabulous stunts include Bond's wild drive through the streets of Vegas in a '71 Mach 1. Connery returned to play Bond in this film after being offered the then record-setting salary of $1 million. **120m/C VHS, DVD, Wide.** *GB* Sean Connery, Jill St. John, Charles Gray, Bruce Cabot, Jimmy Dean, Lana Wood, Bruce Glover, Putter Smith, Norman Burton, Joseph Furst, Bernard Lee, Desmond Llewelyn, Laurence Naismith, Leonard Barr, Lois Maxwell, Margaret Lacey, Joe Robinson, Donna Garrat, Trina Parks; *D:* Guy Hamilton; *W:* Tom Mankiewicz; *C:* Ted Moore; *M:* John Barry.

Diamond's Edge 🦴🦴 *Just Ask for Diamond* **1988 (PG)** An adolescent private eye and his juvenescent brother snoop into the affairs of the Fat Man, and find out that the opera ain't over until they find out what's in the Fat Man's mysterious box of bon-bons. A genre-parodying kid mystery, written by Horowitz, based on his novel, "The Falcon's Malteser." **83m/C VHS.** Susannah York, Peter Eyre, Patricia Hodge, Nickolas Grace; *D:* Stephen Bayly; *W:* Anthony Horowitz; *M:* Trevor Jones.

Diamonds of the Night 🦴🦴🦴🦴 *Demanty Noci* **1964** A breakthrough masterpiece of the Czech new wave, about two young men escaping from a transport train to Auschwitz and scrambling for survival in the countryside. Surreal, powerfully expressionistic film, one of the most important of its time. In Czech with English subtitles. Accompanied by Nemec's short "A Loaf of Bread." **71m/B VHS.** *CZ* Ladislav Jansky, Antonin Kumbera, Ilse Bischofova; *D:* Jan Nemec; *W:* Arnost Lustig, Jan Nemec.

Diana: Her True Story 🦴🦴½ **1993** Britain's royals are held up to scandalous review in this made for tv adaptaion of Andrew Morton's sympathetic bio of the Princess of Wales. Taking Diana from her lonely childhood to her "fairytale" nuptials and subsequent disillusionment with being a royal, including her bulimia and half-hearted suicide attempts. Charles is portrayed as an arrogant, emotional cold fish, only interested in farming and continuing his liaison with Camilla Parker-Bowles. Handsome production with appropriate inpersonations by the cast. **180m/C VHS.** Serena Scott Thomas, David Threlfall, Elizabeth Garvie, Jemma Redgrave, Tracy Hardwick, Anne Stallybrass, Jeffrey Harmer, Donald Douglas; *D:* Kevin Connor; *W:* Stephen Zito. TV

Diane 🦴🦴 **1955** Overstuffed medieval drama featuring Turner as Diane de Poitier, the mistress of a 16th century French King. Moore plays the king in his Hollywood debut. Gorgeous sets and costumes couldn't boost this film at the boxoffice, which had disappointing figures in spite of the expense bestowed upon it. Based on the novel "Diane de Poitier" by John Erskine. **110m/C VHS, Wide.** Lana Turner, Pedro Armendariz Sr., Roger Moore, Marisa Pavan, Cedric Hardwicke, Torin Thatcher, Taina Elg, John Lupton, Henry Daniell, Sean McClory, Michael Ansara; *D:* David Miller; *W:* Christopher Isherwood; *M:* Miklos Rozsa.

Diary of a Chambermaid 🦴🦴🦴 **1946** A chambermaid wants to marry a rich man and finds herself the object of desire of a poor servant willing to commit murder for her. Excellent comic drama, but very stylized in direction and set design. Produced during Renoir's years in Hollywood. Adapted from a story by Octave Mirbeau, later turned into a play. Remade in 1964 by Luis Bumel. **86m/B VHS.** Paulette Goddard, Burgess Meredith, Hurd Hatfield, Francis Lederer, Judith Anderson, Florence Bates, Almira Sessions, Reginald Owen; *D:* Jean Renoir.

Diary of a Chambermaid 🦴🦴🦴½ *Le Journal d'une Femme de Chambre; Il Diario di una Cameriera* **1964** Vintage Bunuelian social satire about a young girl taking a servant's job in a provincial French family, and easing into an atmosphere of sexual hypocrisy and decadence. In French with English subtitles. Remake of the 1946 Jean Renoir film. **97m/C VHS, DVD, Wide.** *FR* Jeanne Moreau, Michel Piccoli, Georges Geret, Francoise Lugagne, Daniel Ivernel; *D:* Luis Bunuel; *W:* Luis Bunuel, Jean-Claude Carriere; *C:* Roger Fellous.

Diary of a Country Priest 🦴🦴🦴½ *Le Journal d'un Cure de Campagne* **1950** With "Balthazar" and "Mouchette," this is one of Bresson's greatest, subtlest films, treating the story of an alienated, unrewarded young priest with his characteristic austerity and Catholic humanism. In French and English subtitles. **120m/B VHS.** *FR* Nicole Maurey, Antonine Balpetre, Claude Layou, Jean Riveyre, Nicole Ladmiral; *D:* Robert Bresson; *W:* Robert Bresson; *C:* Leonce-Henri Burel; *M:* Jean Jacques Grunenwald.

Diary of a Hitman 🦴🦴½ **1991 (R)** A hitman is hired to knock off the wife and child of a commodities broker who claims his wife is a drug addict and the infant is a crack baby and not his. The hired killer wants out of the business, but needs to pull off one more job for a down payment on his apartment. Beset by doubts, he breaks conduct by conversing with the victim and discovers the broker lied. Based on the play "Insider's Price" by Pressman. **90m/C VHS.** Forest Whitaker, James Belushi, Sherilyn Fenn, Sharon Stone, Seymour Cassel, Lewis Smith, Lois Chiles, John Bedford-Lloyd; *D:* Roy London; *W:* Kenneth Pressman; *M:* Michel Colombier.

Diary of a Lost Girl 🦴🦴🦴½ *Das tagebuch einer verlorenen* **1929** The second Louise Brooks/G.W. Pabst collaboration (after "Pandora's Box") in which a frail but mesmerizing German girl plummets into a life of hopeless degradation. Dark and gloomy, the film chronicles the difficulties she faces, from rape to an unwanted pregnancy and prostitution. Based on the popular book by Margarete Boehme. Silent. Made after flapper Brooks left Hollywood to pursue greater opportunities and more challenging roles under Pabst's guidance. **116m/B VHS, DVD.** *GE* Louise Brooks, Fritz Rasp, Josef Rovensky, Sybille Schmitz; *D:* G.W. Pabst; *W:* Rudolf Leonhard; *C:* Sepp Allgeier, Fritz Arno Wagner; *M:* Timothy Brock.

Diary of a Mad Housewife 🦴🦴🦴 **1970 (R)** Despairing of her miserable family life, a housewife has an affair with a writer only to find him to be even more selfish and egotistical than her no-good husband. Snodgress plays her character perfectly, hearing the insensitive absurdity of her husband and her lover over and over again, enjoying her martyrdom even as it drives her crazy. **94m/C VHS.** Carrie Snodgress, Richard Benjamin, Frank Langella; *D:* Frank Perry. Golden Globes '71: Actress—Mus./Comedy (Snodgress); Natl. Bd. of Review '70: Support. Actor (Langella).

Diary of a Mad Old Man 🦴🦴 *Dagboek Van Een Oude Dwaas* **1988 (PG-13)** A wistful drama about an old man who's lost everything except his desire for his daughter-in-law, which sends him into fits of nostalgia. **93m/C VHS.** *BE FR NL* Derek De Lint, Ralph Michael, Beatie Edney; *D:* Lili Rademakers; *W:* Hugo Claus; *C:* Paul van den Bos; *M:* Egisto Macchi.

Diary of a Madman 🦴🦴 **1963** Price is once again possessed by an evil force in this gothic thriller. Fairly average Price vehicle, based on Guy de Maupassant's story. **96m/C VHS.** Vincent Price, Nancy Kovack, Chris Warfield, Ian Wolfe, Nelson Olmstead, Elaine Devry, Stephen Roberts; *D:* Reginald LeBorg; *W:* Robert Kent; *C:* Ellis W. Carter.

Diary of a Rebel 🦴 **1984** A fictional account of the rise of Cuban rebel leader Che Guevara. **89m/C VHS.** John Ireland, Francesco Rabal.

Diary of a Seducer 🦴🦴 *Le Journal du Seducteur; The Seducer's Diary* **1995** Claire's (Mastroianni) a bored 20-year-old Parisian whose ennui is lifted when she meets philosophy student Gregoire (Poupaud), who lends her a rare copy of Soren Kierkegaard's "Diary of a Seducer." The volume apparently has seductive powers and manages to affect everyone within Claire's orbit. French with subtitles. **98m/C VHS, Wide.** *FR* Danielle Dubroux, Chiara Mastroianni, Melvil Poupaud, Mathieu Amalric, Micheline Presle, Hubert Saint Macary, Jean-Pierre Leaud; *D:* Danielle Dubroux; *W:* Danielle Dubroux; *C:* Laurent Machuel; *M:* Jean-Marie Senia.

Diary of a Serial Killer 🦴🦴 **1997 (R)** Down-on-his-luck journalist Nelson Keece (Busey) witnesses a murder and then is invited by the killer, Stefan (Vosloo), to conduct an exclusive interview. Stefan keeps killing and Nelson keeps writing, but the cops begin to think that Keece is the killer. Then Stefan decides to target Keece's girlfriend Juliette (Campbell) as his next victim. **92m/C VHS, DVD.** Gary Busey, Arnold Vosloo, Michael Madsen, Julia Campbell; *D:* Alan Jacobs; *W:* Jennifer Badham-Stewart; *C:* Keith L. Smith; *M:* Steve Edwards. VIDEO

Diary of a Teenage Hitchhiker 🦴 **1982** Teen girl ignores family restrictions and police warnings about a homicidal rapist stalking the area and continues to thumb rides to her job at a beach resort. One night she's picked up for ride she'll never forget. **96m/C VHS.** Charlene Tilton, Dick Van Patten; *D:* Ted Post.

Diary of a Young Comic 🦴🦴 **1979** New York comedian searches for the meaning of lunacy. He finds it after Improvisation in Los Angeles. **74m/C VHS.** Stacy Keach, Dom DeLuise, Richard Lewis, Bill Macy, George Jessel, Gary Muledeer, Nina Van Pallandt; *D:* Gary Weis.

The Diary of Anne Frank 🦴🦴🦴½ **1959** In June 1945, a liberated Jewish refugee returns to the hidden third floor of an Amsterdam factory where he finds the diary kept by his youngest daughter, Anne. The document recounts their years in hiding from the Nazis. Based on the actual diary of 13-year-old Anne Frank, killed in a death camp during WWII. **150m/B VHS, Wide.** Millie Perkins, Joseph Schildkraut, Shelley Winters, Richard Beymer, Gusti Huber, Ed Wynn, Lou Jacobi, Diane Baker; *D:* George Stevens; *C:* William Mellor. Oscars '59: Art Dir./Set Dec., B&W, B&W Cinematog., Support. Actress (Winters).

Diary of Forbidden Dreams 🦴🦴🦴 *What?; Che?* **1973 (R)** A beautiful young girl finds herself drawn into bizarre incidents at an eccentric millionaire's mansion that cause her to go insane. Set on the Italian Riviera, it's the most offbeat rendition of "Alice in Wonderland" you're apt to find. Unfortunately, the convoluted plot lessens its appeal. Unedited version, under the original title "What!," released at 113 minutes, is also available. **94m/C VHS, Wide.** *IT* Marcello Mastroianni, Hugh Griffith, Sydne Rome, Roman Polanski; *D:* Roman Polanski; *W:* Roman Polanski, Gerard Brach.

Diary of the Dead 🦴 **198? (PG)** A newlywed kills his aggravating mother-in-law, only to have her repeatedly return from the grave. **93m/C VHS.** Hector Elizondo, Geraldine Fitzgerald, Salome Jens; *D:* Arvin Brown.

Dick 🦴🦴🦴 **1999 (PG-13)** If you think Hollywood is done making fun of Nixon, then you don't know "Dick." Satire puts forth the theory that two dizzy teenage girls (Dunst and Williams) caused the downfall of Richard Nixon (Heydaya). They bump into all the major Watergate players, including Liddy (Shearer), Haldemann (Foley) and Dean (Brener). The girls are blissfully blind to Tricky Dick's indiscretions, and one of them even develops a hilarious crush on him. When they overhear him abusing the presidential pup, however, they turn on him. Flouting the Constitution is one thing, but being mean to dogs is clearly icky behavior. They decide to become the famed Deep Throat for bickering reporters Woodward (Ferrell) and Bernstein (McCulloch). Rent this with "All the President's Men" and "Nixon," because this is the movie that Oliver Stone would've made if he had a sense of humor instead of flashbacks. **95m/C VHS, DVD, Wide.** Kirsten Dunst, Michelle Williams, Dan Hedaya, Will Ferrell, Dave Foley, Harry Shearer, Jim Breuer, Bruce McCulloch, Devon Gummersall, Ted McGinley, Ryan Reynolds, Saul Rubinek, Teri Garr, G.D. Spradlin, Ana Gasteyer; ***D:*** Andrew Fleming; ***W:*** Andrew Fleming, Sheryl Longin; ***C:*** Alexander Grusynski; ***M:*** John Debney.

Dick Barton, Special Agent **1948** Dick Barton is called in when a mad scientist threatens to attack London with germ-carrying bombs. The first film production for Hammer Studios, later to be known for its horror classics. **70m/B VHS.** *GB* Don Stannard, Geoffrey Ford, Jack Shaw; ***D:*** Alfred Goulding.

Dick Barton Strikes Back ½ **1948** "Mr. French" Cabot has a nuclear weapon and is willing to use it; that is, until Dick Barton arrives to put the Frenchman out of commission. Generally considered the best of the Dick Barton film series. **73m/B VHS.** *GB* Don Stannard, Sebastian Cabot, Jean Lodge; ***D:*** Godfrey Grayson.

Dick Tracy **1937** Serial, based on the comic-strip character, in 15 chapters. Tracy tries to find his kidnapped brother as he faces the fiend "Spider." The first chapter is 30 minutes and each additional chapter is 20 minutes. **290m/B VHS, DVD.** Ralph Byrd, Smiley Burnette, Irving Pichel, Jennifer Jones; ***D:*** John English, Alan James, Ray Taylor.

Dick Tracy ½ **1990 (PG)** Beatty wears the caps of producer, director, and star, performing admirably on all fronts. One minor complaint: his Tracy is somewhat flat in comparison to the outstanding performances and makeup of the unique villains, especially Pacino. Stylistically superior, shot in only seven colors, the timeless sets capture the essence rather than the reality of the city, successfully bringing the comic strip to life. Madonna is fine as the seductive Breathless Mahoney, belting out Stephen Sondheim like she was born to do it. People expecting the gothic technology of "Batman" may be disappointed, but moviegoers searching for a memory made real will be thrilled. ♫Sooner or Later. **105m/C VHS, DVD, Wide.** Warren Beatty, Madonna, Charlie Korsmo, Glenne Headly, Al Pacino, Dustin Hoffman, James Caan, Mandy Patinkin, Paul Sorvino, Charles Durning, Dick Van Dyke, R.G. Armstrong, Catherine O'Hara, Estelle Parsons, Seymour Cassel, Michael J. Pollard, William Forsythe, Kathy Bates, James Tolkan; ***D:*** Warren Beatty; ***W:*** Jim Cash, Jack Epps Jr.; ***C:*** Vittorio Storaro; ***M:*** Danny Elfman, Stephen Sondheim. Oscars '90: Art Dir./Set Dec., Makeup, Song ("Sooner or Later").

Dick Tracy, Detective **1945** The first Dick Tracy feature film, in which Splitface is on the loose, a schoolteacher is murdered, the Mayor is threatened, and a nutty professor uses a crystal ball to give Tracy the clues needed to connect the crimes. **62m/B VHS, DVD.** Morgan Conway, Anne Jeffreys, Mike Mazurki, Jane Greer, Lyle Latell; ***D:*** William Berke; ***W:*** Eric Taylor; ***C:*** Frank Redman; ***M:*** Roy Webb.

Dick Tracy Meets Gruesome *Dick Tracy's Amazing Adventure; Dick Tracy Meets Karloff* **1947** Gruesome and his partner in crime, Melody, stage a bank robbery using the secret formula of Dr. A. Tomic. Tracy has to solve the case before word gets out and people rush to withdraw their savings, destroying civilization as we know it. **66m/B VHS, DVD.** Boris Karloff, Ralph Byrd, Lyle Latell, Anne Gwynne, Edward Ashley, June Clayworth, Tony Barrett, Skelton Knaggs; ***D:*** John Rawlins; ***W:*** Eric Taylor, Robertson White; ***C:*** Frank Redman; ***M:*** Paul Sawtell.

Dick Tracy Returns **1938** 15-chapter serial. Public Enemy Paw Stark and his gang set out on a wave of crime that brings them face to face with dapper Dick. **100m/B VHS.** Ralph Byrd, Charles Middleton; ***D:*** William Witney.

Dick Tracy vs. Crime Inc. **1941** Dick Tracy encounters many difficulties when he tries to track down a criminal who can make himself invisible. A serial in 15 chapters. **100m/B VHS.** Ralph Byrd, Ralph Morgan, Michael Owen; ***D:*** William Witney; ***W:*** John English.

Dick Tracy vs. Cueball **1946** Dick Tracy has his work cut out for him when the evil gangster Cueball appears on the scene. Based on Chester Gould's comic strip. **62m/B VHS, DVD.** Morgan Conway, Anne Jeffreys, Lyle Latell, Rita (Paula) Corday, Ian Keith, Dick Wessel, Skelton Knaggs; ***D:*** Gordon Douglas; ***W:*** Robert E. Kent, Dane Lussier; ***C:*** George E. Diskant; ***M:*** C. Bakaleinikoff, Phil Ohman.

Dick Tracy's Dilemma *Mark of the Claw* **1947** The renowned police detective Dick Tracy tries to solve a case involving the Claw. Based on the Chester Gould comic strip. **60m/B VHS, DVD.** Ralph Byrd, Lyle Latell, Kay Christopher, Jack Lambert, Ian Keith, Jimmy Conlin; ***D:*** John Rawlins; ***W:*** Robert Stephen Brode; ***C:*** Frank Redman; ***M:*** Paul Sawtell.

Dick Turpin ½ **1925** In this rare film, Mix plays the famed English highwayman who seeks adventure in historical Britain. **60m/B VHS.** Tom Mix, Alan Hale; ***D:*** John Blystone.

Didn't You Hear? **1983 (PG)** An alienated college student discovers that dreams have a life of their own when he becomes immersed in his own fantasy world. **94m/C VHS.** Dennis Christopher, Gary Busey, Cheryl Waters, John Kauffman; ***D:*** Skip Sherwood.

Die! Die! My Darling! ½ *Fanatic* **1965** A young widow visits her mad ex-mother-in-law in a remote English village, and is imprisoned by the mourning woman as revenge for her son's death. Bankhead's last role. Based on Anne Blaisdell's novel. **97m/C VHS, Wide.** *GB* Tallulah Bankhead, Stefanie Powers, Peter Vaughan, Maurice Kaufmann, Donald Sutherland, Gwendolyn Watts, Yootha Joyce, Winifred Dennis; ***D:*** Silvio Narizzano; ***W:*** Richard Matheson; ***C:*** Arthur Ibbetson; ***M:*** Wilfred Josephs.

Die Grosse Freiheit Nr. 7 ½ *Great Freedom No. 7* **1945** A man tries to stop his niece's love affair with a sailor. Nazi propaganda minister Goebbels banned this film in Germany, since it showed German soldiers getting drunk and also had Hildebrand cast as a prostitute. After the war, however, it enjoyed great popularity throughout Germany. Albers sings the classic "Auf der Reeperbahn." In German with no English translation. **100m/C VHS.** *GE* Hans Albers, Hilde Hildebrand, Ilse Werner, Hans Sohnker, Helmut Kautner; ***D:*** Helmut Kautner; ***W:*** Helmut Kautner; ***C:*** Werner Krien; ***M:*** Werner Eisbrenner.

Die Hard **1988 (R)** It's Christmas Eve and NYC cop John McClane (Willis) has arrived in L.A. to spend the holiday with his estranged wife Holly (Bedelia) and their kids. Unfortunately, Holly is one of the hostages being held by a band of ruthless high-stakes terrorists in the Century City high-rise headquarters of a Japanese corporation. Soon it's the loner cop against the intruders, who are led by Eurotrash villain Hugo Gruber (a marvelous performance by Rickman). A high-voltage action thriller that's just as unbelievable as it sounds, but you'll love it anyway. Based on the novel "Nothing Lasts Forever" by Roderick Thorp. **114m/C VHS, DVD, Wide.** Bruce Willis, Bonnie Bedelia, Alan Rickman, Alexander Godunov, Paul Gleason, William Atherton, Reginald Vel Johnson, Hart Bochner, James Shigeta, Mary Ellen Trainor, De'voreaux White, Robert Davi, Ric(k) Ducommun; ***D:*** John McTiernan; ***W:*** Jeb Stuart, Steven E. de Souza; ***C:*** Jan De Bont; ***M:*** Michael Kamen.

Die Hard 2: Die Harder **1990 (R)** Fast, well-done sequel brings another impossible situation before the wise-cracking, tough-cookie cop. Our hero tangles with a group of terrorists at an airport under siege, while his wife remains in a plane circling above as its fuel dwindles. Obviously a repeat of the plot and action of the first "Die Hard," with references to the former in the script. While the bad guys lack the fiendishness of their predecessors, this installment features energetic and finely acted performances. Fairly gory, especially the icicle-in-the-eyeball scene. Adapted from the novel "58 Minutes" by Walter Wager and characters created by Roderick Thorp. **124m/C VHS, DVD, Wide.** Bruce Willis, William Atherton, Franco Nero, Bonnie Bedelia, John Amos, Reginald Vel Johnson, Dennis Franz, Art Evans, Fred Dalton Thompson, William Sadler, Sheila McCarthy, Robert Patrick, John Leguizamo, Robert Costanzo, Tom Verica, Don Harvey, Tony Ganios, Vondie Curtis-Hall, Colm Meaney; ***D:*** Renny Harlin; ***W:*** Doug Richardson, Steven E. de Souza; ***C:*** Oliver Wood; ***M:*** Michael Kamen.

Die Hard: With a Vengeance ½ *Die Hard 3* **1995 (R)** Third time is not a charm in the "Die Hard" series. McClane (Willis) is back home in the Big Apple and having another bad day. More Eurotrash terrorists, led by the brilliant and vengeful Simon (Irons), are out to blow things up, snag some gold, and make life miserable for McClane and his reluctant partner, Zeus Carver (Jackson). The claustrophobic settings of the first two outings have been replaced by the exhausting expanse of New York City, to good effect, but frenetic action scenes and good chemistry between Willis and Jackson don't quite compensate for a lackluster script and more cartoony feel. Jackson brings a fresh perspective and vitality to what will probably be the last ride of John McClane. **131m/C VHS, DVD, Wide.** Bruce Willis, Samuel L. Jackson, Jeremy Irons, Graham Greene, Colleen Camp, Larry Bryggman, Tony Peck, Nick Wyman, Sam (Leslie) Phillips; ***D:*** John McTiernan; ***W:*** Jonathan Hensleigh; ***C:*** Peter Menzies Jr.; ***M:*** Michael Kamen.

Die Laughing woof! **1980 (PG)** A cab driver unwittingly becomes involved in murder, intrigue, and the kidnapping of a monkey that has memorized a scientific formula that can destroy the world. Writer/actor/composer Benson might consider renaming it "Die from Embarassment." **108m/C VHS.** Robby Benson, Charles Durning, Bud Cort, Elsa Lanchester, Peter Coyote; ***D:*** Jeff Werner; ***W:*** Robby Benson, Scott Parker; ***M:*** Robby Benson.

Die, Monster, Die! *Monster of Terror* **1965** A reclusive scientist experiments with a radioactive meteorite and gains bizarre powers. Karloff is great in this adaptation of H.P. Lovecraft's "The Color Out of Space." **80m/C VHS, DVD, Wide.** *GB* Boris Karloff, Nick Adams, Suzan Farmer, Patrick Magee, Freda Jackson, Terence de Marney, Leslie Dwyer, Paul Farrell; ***D:*** Daniel Haller; ***W:*** Jerry Sohl; ***C:*** Paul Beeson; ***M:*** Don Banks.

Die Screaming, Marianne *Die, Beautiful Marianne* **1973** A girl is on the run from her father, a crooked judge, who wants to kill her before her 21st birthday, when she will inherit evidence that will put him away for life. **81m/C VHS, DVD.** *GB* Michael Rennie, Susan George, Karin Dor, Leo Genn; ***D:*** Pete Walker; ***W:*** Murray Smith; ***C:*** Norman G. Langley; ***M:*** Cyril Ornadel.

Die Sister, Die! **1974** Thriller about a gothic mansion with an eerie secret in the basement features a battle between a senile, reclusive sister and her disturbed, tormenting brother. **88m/C VHS.** Jack Ging, Edith Atwater, Antoinette Bower, Kent Smith, Robert Emhardt; ***D:*** Randall Hood.

Die Watching ½ **1993 (R)** Sleazy erotic thriller about a video director (Atkins) who not only likes to film some hot Hollywood babes but may also like to kill them as well. His latest discovery just could be the next victim. **92m/C VHS, DVD.** Christopher Atkins, Vali Ashton, Tim Thomerson, Carlos Palomino, Mike Jacobs Jr.; ***D:*** Charles Davis; ***W:*** Kenneth J. Hall; ***C:*** Howard Wexler; ***M:*** Scott Roewe.

Different for Girls **1996 (R)** Boyish motorcycle dispatch rider Paul Prentice (Graves) nearly gets run over by a London taxi whose passenger Kim Foyle (Mackintosh) seems strangely familiar. Then Paul discovers Kim used to be his boyhood school chum Karl. After a shaky start, the duo discover a genuine attraction but when they get into an argument that leads to a police call and Paul gets thrown in jail, Kim's first instincts are to retreat to her sister's (Reeves) family and back into her quiet life. Director Spence refrains from camping up the situation and some fine performances, especially from the engaging Graves, make this quirky film well worth a watch. **101m/C VHS, DVD.** *GB* Rupert Graves, Steven Mackintosh, Miriam Margolyes, Saskia Reeves, Neil Dudgeon, Charlotte Coleman; ***D:*** Richard Spence; ***W:*** Tony Merchant; ***C:*** Sean Van Hales; ***M:*** Stephen Warbeck. Montreal World Film Fest. '95: Film.

Different Story ½ **1978 (PG)** Romance develops when a lesbian real estate agent offers a homosexual chauffeur a job with her firm. Resorts to stereotypes when the characters decide to marry. **107m/C VHS.** Perry King, Meg Foster, Valerie Curtin, Peter Donat, Richard Bull; ***D:*** Paul Aaron.

Digby, the Biggest Dog in the World **1973 (G)** Poor comedy-fantasy about Digby, a sheepdog, who wanders around a scientific laboratory, drinks an experimental fluid, and grows and grows and grows. **88m/C VHS.** *GB* Jim Dale, Angela Douglas, Spike Milligan, Dinsdale Landen; ***D:*** Joseph McGrath; ***M:*** Edwin Astley.

Digger ½ **1994 (PG)** Digger (Hann-Byrd) arrives at a Pacific Northwest island to stay with relatives, including his Grandma (Dukakis) who's being romanced by the fun-loving Arthur (Nielsen). He makes friends with another youth who turns out to have a terminal heart ailment. **92m/C VHS.** Adam Hann-Byrd, Olympia Dukakis, Leslie Nielsen, Joshua Jackson, Barbara Williams, Timothy Bottoms; ***D:*** Robert Turner; ***W:*** Rodney Gibbons; ***M:*** Todd Boekelheide.

Digging to China ½ **1998 (PG)** Directorial debut of Hutton is the sentimental story of a sweet friendship between misfits—precocious 10-year-old Harriet (Wood) and mentally-handicapped 30-year-old Ricky (Bacon). Harriet's alcoholic mom (Moriarty) runs a motel in rural New Hampshire (film is set in the mid-'60s) with Harriet's slutty older sister Gwen (Masterson). Ricky winds up at the motel with his dying mother Leah (Seldes), who was taking him to an institution when her car breaks down. Harriet thinks Ricky is a terrific playmate but after some shocking news, the young girl and her new friend decide to run away—causing a lot of trouble. **98m/C VHS, DVD.** Evan Rachel Wood, Kevin Bacon, Mary Stuart Masterson, Cathy Moriarty, Marian Seldes; ***D:*** Timothy Hutton; ***W:*** Karen Janszen; ***C:*** Jorgen Persson; ***M:*** Cynthia Millar.

Digging Up Business woof! **1991 (PG)** Johnson tries to save the family funeral home business from financial ruin with some unique interment services. This film needs a decent burial. **89m/C VHS.** Lynn-Holly Johnson, Billy Barty, Ruth Buzzi, Murray Langston, Yvonne Craig, Gary Owens; ***D:*** Mark Byers.

Diggstown ½ **1992 (R)** Lightweight, good-natured sports comedy about a boxing scam. Con man Gabriel Caine (Woods), fresh out of prison, heads for Diggstown and the unregulated boxing matches arranged by town boss, John Gillon (Dern). The bet is that Caine's one boxer can beat any 10 boxers, chosen by Gillon, in a 24-hour period. So Caine decides to hook up with an old friend, former prizefighter "Honey" Roy Palmer (Gossett Jr.), to run the scam of his life. Dern is sufficiently nasty and Woods his usual nervy self but it's Gossett Jr. who manages to hold everything together as the aging boxer. Based on the novel "The Diggstown Ringers" by Leonard Wise. **97m/C VHS, DVD.** James Woods, Louis Gossett Jr., Bruce Dern, Oliver Platt, Heather Graham, Randall "Tex" Cobb, Thomas Wilson Brown, Duane Davis, Willie Green, George D. Wallace; ***D:*** Michael Ritchie; ***W:*** Steven McKay; ***M:*** James Newton Howard.

Digital Man 🦴½ 1994 (R) High-tech military super-soldier prototype has his programming sabotaged and a team of human and robotic commmandoes must prevent him from starting WWIII. **95m/C VHS.** Ken Olandt, Adam Baldwin, Ed Lauter, Matthias Hues, Kristen Dalton, Paul Gleason; ***D:*** Phillip J. Roth; ***W:*** Phillip J. Roth, Ronald Schmidt.

Dilemma 🦴🦴½ 1997 On Death Row, Rudy Salazar (Trejo) volunteers to be a bone-marrow donor to a sick child. LAPD detective Quin (Howell) realizes that it's a set-up for an escape and he's right. Then the cops have to catch Salazar again, but they can't kill him without sacrificing the kid. Similar material was handled much more effectively in the underrated "Desperate Measures." **87m/C DVD.** C. Thomas Howell, Danny Trejo, Sofia Shinas; ***D:*** Erik Larsen; ***W:*** Ira Israel, Chuck Conaway; ***C:*** Mark Melville; ***M:*** Albritton McClain.

Dillinger 🦴🦴🦴 1945 John Dillinger's notorious career, from street punk to public enemy number one, receives a thrilling fast-paced treatment. Tierney turns in a fine performance in this interesting account of the criminal life. **70m/C VHS.** Lawrence Tierney, Edmund Lowe, Anne Jeffreys, Elisha Cook Jr.; ***D:*** Max Nosseck; ***W:*** Philip Yordan.

Dillinger 🦴🦴½ 1973 (R) The most colorful period of criminality in America is brought to life in this story of bank-robber John Dillinger, "Baby Face" Nelson, and the notorious "Lady in Red." **106m/C VHS, DVD, Wide.** Warren Oates, Michelle Phillips, Richard Dreyfuss, Cloris Leachman, Ben Johnson, Harry Dean Stanton; ***D:*** John Milius; ***W:*** John Milius; ***C:*** Jules Brenner; ***M:*** Barry DeVorzon.

Dillinger 🦴🦴½ *The Last Days of John Dillinger* 1991 Harmon stars as the Depression-era bank robber, who became public enemy number one, in this TV gangster story. Fenn's girlfriend Billy Frenchette, with Patton particularly beady-eyed as G-man Melvin Purvis. **95m/C VHS.** Mark Harmon, Sherilyn Fenn, Will Patton, Patricia Arquette, Vince Edwards, Bruce Abbott; ***D:*** Rupert Wainwright; ***C:*** Donald M. Morgan.

Dillinger and Capone 🦴🦴½ 1995 (R) Supposedly the FBI has killed the wrong Dillinger and the gangster (Sheen) decides to make a new life. But his old friend Al Capone (Abraham), newly released from prison, is holding Dillinger's wife (Hicks) and son hostage as insurance that first he'll retrieve $15 million from a mob-owned Chicago bank. **95m/C VHS, DVD.** Martin Sheen, F. Murray Abraham, Catherine Hicks, Stephen Davies, Don Stroud, Clint Howard, Joe Estevez; ***D:*** Jon Purdy; ***W:*** Michael B. Druxman; ***C:*** John Aronson; ***M:*** David Wurst, Eric Wurst.

Dim Sum: A Little Bit of Heart 🦴🦴🦴 1985 (PG) The second independent film from the director of "Chan Is Missing." A Chinese-American mother and daughter living in San Francisco's Chinatown confront the conflict between traditional Eastern ways and modern American life. Gentle, fragile picture made with humor and care. In English and Chinese with subtitles. **88m/C VHS.** Laureen Chew, Kim Chew, Victor Wong, Ida F.O. Chong, Cora Miao, John Nishio, Joan Chen; ***D:*** Wayne Wang; ***W:*** Terrel Seltzer; ***M:*** Todd Boekelheide.

Dimples 🦴🦴½ 1936 (PG) When Shirley's pickpocket grandfather is caught redhanded, she steps in, takes the blame, and somehow ends up in show business. Re-issued version is rated. Also available colorized. ♫Hey, What Did the Bluebird Say?; He Was a Dandy; Picture Me Without You; Oh Mister Man Up in the Moon; Dixie-Anna; Get On Board; Swing Low Sweet Chariot. **78m/B VHS, DVD.** Shirley Temple, John Carradine, Frank Morgan, Helen Westley, Berton Churchill, Robert Kent, Delma Byron; ***D:*** William A. Seiter; ***W:*** Nat Perrin, Arthur Sheekman; ***C:*** Bert Glennon; ***M:*** Louis Silvers.

Diner 🦴🦴🦴½ 1982 (R) A group of old high school friends meet at "their" Baltimore diner to find that more has changed than the menu. A bittersweet look at the experiences of a group of Baltimore twentysomethings, circa 1959, who find adulthood hard to face. Particularly notable was Levinson's casting of "unknowns" who have since become household names. Features many humorous moments and fine performances. **110m/C VHS, DVD, Wide.** Steve Guttenberg, Daniel Stern, Mickey Rourke, Kevin Bacon, Ellen Barkin, Timothy Daly, Paul Reiser, Michael Tucker, Jessica James, Kathryn Dowling, Colette Blonigan; ***D:*** Barry Levinson; ***W:*** Barry Levinson; ***C:*** Peter Sova; ***M:*** Bruce Brody, Ivan Kral. Natl. Soc. Film Critics '82: Support. Actor (Rourke).

Dingaka 🦴🦴½ 1965 A controversial drama from the writer and director of "The Gods Must Be Crazy" about a South African tribesman who avenges his daughter's murder by tribal laws, and is then tried by white man's laws. A crusading white attorney struggles to acquit him. **96m/C VHS.** Stanley Baker, Juliet Prowse, Ken Gampu; ***D:*** Jamie Uys.

Dingo 🦴🦴½ 1990 In Davis' only film appearance he's, what else, a famous jazz trumpeter. Paris-based Billy Cross (Davis) and his combo are on tour in 1969 and momentarily stuck at a remote Australian airstrip. They give an impromptu concert heard by John "Dingo" Anderson (Friels), who instantly decides that music is the life for him. Over the years Dingo keeps in touch with his idol as he works outback bars and secretly saves to go to Paris and check out the scene—even if it means sacrificing his wife and family. **108m/C VHS.** *FR AU* Colin Friels, Miles Davis, Helen Buday, Bernadette LaFont; ***D:*** Rolf de Heer; ***W:*** Marc Rosenberg; ***C:*** Denis Lenoir; ***M:*** Miles Davis, Michel Legrand.

The Dining Room 🦴🦴½ 1986 Six performers play more than 50 roles in this adaptation of A.R. Gurney Jr.'s play set in a dining room, where people live out dramatic and comic moments in their lives. From the "American Playhouse" series. **90m/C VHS.** Remak Ramsay, Pippa Perthree, John Shea, Frances Sternhagen; ***D:*** Allan Goldstein.

Dinner at Eight 🦴🦴🦴🦴 1933 Social-climbing Mrs. Jordan (Burke) and her husband Oliver (Lionel Barrymore) throw a dinner party for various members of the New York elite. During the course of the evening, all of the guests reveal too much. Special performances all around, especially John Barrymore in a parody of his drunken career, Dressler as a grande dame sliding down the social ladder, and Harlow as a gold-digging hussy. Superb comedic direction by Cukor. Adapted from the play by Edna Ferber and George Kaufman. **110m/C VHS, 8mm.** John Barrymore, Lionel Barrymore, Wallace Beery, Madge Evans, Jean Harlow, Billie Burke, Marie Dressler, Phillips Holmes, Jean Hersholt, Lee Tracy, Edmund Lowe, Karen Morley, May Robson; ***D:*** George Cukor; ***W:*** Herman J. Mankiewicz, Frances Marion, Donald Ogden Stewart; ***C:*** William H. Daniels; ***M:*** William Axt.

Dinner at Eight 🦴🦴 1989 A social-climbing romance novelist throws an elegant dinner party. TV remake of the 1933 film does not compare well. **100m/C VHS.** Lauren Bacall, Charles Durning, Ellen Greene, Harry Hamlin, John Mahoney, Marsha Mason, Tim Kazurinsky; ***D:*** Ron Lagomarsino. TV

Dinner at the Ritz 🦴🦴½ 1937 Daughter of a murdered Parisian banker vows to find his killer with help from her fiance. **78m/B VHS.** *GB* David Niven, Annabella, Paul Lukas, Patricia Medina; ***D:*** Harold Schuster.

The Dinner Game 🦴🦴 *Le Diner de Cons* 1998 (PG-13) Smug publisher Pierre (Lhermitte) dines weekly with equally smug friends, their entertainment being to see who can bring the biggest fool as a dinner guest. This nasty joke gets the turnabout it deserves when Pierre intends to bring bumbling Francois (Villeret) to the party, only to have the man proceed to wreck Pierre's life before they even get there—all while Francois maintains his own sweet dignity. French with subtitles. **82m/C VHS, DVD, Wide.** *FR* Thierry Lhermitte, Jacques Villeret, Alexandra Vandernoot, Catherine Frot, Francis Huster, Daniel Prevost; ***D:*** Francis Veber; ***W:*** Francis Veber; ***C:*** Luciano Tovoli; ***M:*** Vladimir Cosma. Cesar '99: Actor (Villeret), Support. Actor (Prevost), Writing.

Dinner with Friends 🦴🦴½ 2001 The main course is a look at the meaning of love, marriage, and friendship, with a heaping side of mid-life angst. Happily married couple Gabe (Quaid) and Karen (MacDowell) deal with the fallout of the breakup of their friends' marriage. Beth (Collette) shows up at their door after husband Tom (Kinnear) leaves her for another woman. When Gabe and Karen try to help (read: offer their advice), they're met with a less than enthusiastic response. **95m/C VHS, DVD.** Dennis Quaid, Andie MacDowell, Greg Kinnear, Toni Collette; ***D:*** Norman Jewison; ***W:*** Donald Margulies. CABLE

Dino 🦴½ 1957 Social worker joins a young woman in helping a 17-year-old delinquent re-enter society. **96m/B VHS.** Sal Mineo, Brian Keith, Susan Kohner; ***D:*** Thomas Carr.

Dinosaur 🦴🦴½ 2000 (PG) Young iguanodon Aladar is separated from his parents and raised by lemurs on an isolated island. Aladar must discover his heritage just as a meteor crash threatens to destroy his world. Raises the bar on animated adventures by having the impossibly realistic critters superimposed onto actual jungle footage. Pic represents the next step in animation evolution, but the amazing visuals are somewhat undercut by the script, which has a pieced-together feel at times. May be too scary for the wee ones since everything does look so lifelike. **82m/C VHS, DVD, Wide.** ***D:*** Ralph Zondag, Eric Leighton; ***W:*** John Harrison, Robert Nelson Jacobs; ***M:*** James Newton Howard; ***V:*** Julianna Margulies, Alfre Woodard, D.B. Sweeney, Ossie Davis, Della Reese, Max Casella, Samuel E. Wright, Joan Plowright, Hayden Panettiere, Peter Siragusa.

Dinosaur Island 🦴 1993 (R) Five military men survive a plane crash and discover an island where scantily clad (leather bikinis being the fashion choice) lascivious ladies live. Will the awesome power of testosterone overcome the fierce dinosaurs which stand between the men and their objects of desire? **85m/C VHS.** Ross Hagen, Richard Gabai, Antonia Dorian, Peter Spellos, Tom Shell, Griffin (Griffen) Drew, Steve Barkett, Toni Naples, Michelle (McClellan) Bauer; ***D:*** Jim Wynorski, Fred Olen Ray; ***W:*** Bob Sheridan, Christopher Wooden; ***C:*** Gary Graver; ***M:*** Chuck Cirino.

Dinosaur Valley Girls 🦴½ 1996 Hollywood action hero Tony Markham comes into posession of a magic stone that hurls him backwards through time into a prehistoric world. That just happens to be populated by fierce, beautiful babes in animal-print bikinis. A PG version is also available. **94m/C VHS, DVD.** Karen Black, William D. Russell, Ron Jeffries, Jeff Rector, Griffin (Griffen) Drew, Ed Fury; ***D:*** Don Glut; ***W:*** Don Glut.

Dinosaurus! 🦴 1960 Large sadistic dinosaurs appear in the modern world. They eat, burn, and pillage their way through this film. Also includes a romance between a Neanderthal and a modern-age woman. **85m/C VHS, DVD, Wide.** Ward Ramsey, Kristina Hanson, Paul Lukather, Fred Engelberg; ***D:*** Irvin S. Yeaworth Jr.; ***W:*** Dan E. Weisburd, Jean Yeaworth; ***C:*** Stanley Cortez; ***M:*** Ronald Stein.

Dinotopia 🦴🦴½ 2002 TV miniseries based on two books by author/illustrator James Gurney about a fantasy island paradise where humans and talking dinos coexist peacefully. Teenaged half-brothers Karl (Leitso) and David (Miller) survive a plane crash and wind up on Dinotopia where they are befriended by young princess Marion (Carr). But the island has problems—rogue carnivorous dinosaurs and sinister human Cyrus Crabb (Thewlis) as well as some magical sunstones that are losing their power. Fanciful storytelling with some fun special effects. **?m/C VHS, DVD.** Tyron Leitso, Wentworth Miller, Katie Carr, David Thewlis, Jim Carter, Alice Krige, Colin Salmon, Hannah Yelland, Stuart Wilson, Anna McGuire; ***D:*** Marco Brambilla; ***W:*** Simon Moore; ***C:*** Tony Pierce-Roberts; ***M:*** Trevor Jones; ***V:*** Lee Evans. TV

Diplomaniacs 🦴🦴½ 1933 Wheeler and Woolsey, official barbers on an Indian reservation, are sent to the Geneva peace conference to represent the interests of their tribe. Slim plot nevertheless provides quite a few laughs. Fun musical numbers. **62m/B VHS.** Bert Wheeler, Robert Woolsey, Marjorie White, Hugh Herbert; ***D:*** William A. Seiter; ***W:*** Joseph L. Mankiewicz, Henry Myers; ***M:*** Max Steiner.

Diplomatic Courier 🦴🦴🦴 1952 Cold-war espionage saga has secret agent Power attempting to re-steal sensitive documents from the hands of Soviet agents. Involved and exciting thriller. Michael Ansara, Charles Bronson and Lee Marvin made brief appearanes. **97m/B VHS.** Tyrone Power, Patricia Neal, Stephen McNally, Hildegarde Neff, Karl Malden; ***D:*** Henry Hathaway; ***C:*** Lucien Ballard.

Diplomatic Immunity 🦴½ 1991 (R) Vicious killer gets off scot-free due to his diplomatic immunity. That is, until the victim's ex-soldier father follows this lowlife to the jungles of Paraguay to exact revenge. A heap o' action. **95m/C VHS.** Bruce Boxleitner, Billy Drago, Meg Foster, Robert Forster; ***D:*** Peter Maris.

Diplomatic Siege 🦴🦴 *Enemy of My Enemy* 1999 (R) The U.S. Embassy is taken over by Serbian terrorists who demand that foreign forces clear out of Bosnia or they'll kill their hostages. But General Buck Swain (Berenger) decides to get rid of the Serbs instead. And just to keep things interesting, CIA ops Steve Parker (Weller) and Erica Long (Hannah) are in the embassy basement trying to defuse a bomb. **94m/C VHS, DVD, Wide.** Tom Berenger, Daryl Hannah, Peter Weller; ***D:*** Gustavo Graef-Marino; ***W:*** Robert Boris, Kevin Bernhardt, Sam Bernard, Mark Amin; ***C:*** Steven Wacks; ***M:*** Terry Plumeri. VIDEO

Direct Hit 🦴🦴½ 1993 (R) A CIA assassin discovers retiring is not an option. John Hatch (Forsythe) decides he wants out, particularly when his next kill, Savannah (Champa), turns out to be an innocent pawn. So Hatch turns protector and decides to best the agency at its own deadly game. **91m/C VHS.** William Forsythe, Richard Norton, Jo Champa, John Aprea, Juliet Landau, George Segal; ***D:*** Joseph Merhi; ***W:*** Jacobsen Hart.

Dirkham Detective Agency 🦴½ 1983 Three children team up to form the Dirkham Detective Agency and are hired by a veterinarian to recover two dognapped poodles. **60m/C VHS.** Sally Kellerman, Stan Shaw, John Quade, Gordon Jump, Randy Morton.

Dirt Bike Kid 🦴½ 1986 (PG) A precocious brat is stuck with a used motorbike that has a mind of its own. Shenanigans follow in utterly predictable fashion as he battles bankers and bikers with his bad bike. **91m/C VHS, 8mm.** Peter Billingsley, Anne Bloom, Stuart Pankin, Patrick Collins, Sage Parker, Chad Sheets; ***D:*** Hoite C. Caston; ***W:*** Lewis Colick, David Brandes.

Dirt Gang 🦴 1971 (R) A motorcycle gang terrorizes the members of a film crew on location in the desert. **89m/C VHS.** Paul Carr, Michael Pataki, Michael Forest; ***D:*** Jerry Jameson.

Dirty Dancing 🦴🦴🦴 1987 (PG-13) An innocent 17-year-old (Grey) is vacationing with her parents in the Catskills in 1963. Bored with the program at the hotel, she finds the real fun at the staff dances. Falling for the sexy dance instructor (Swayze), she discovers love, sex, and rock and roll dancing. An old story, with little to save it, but Grey and Swayze are appealing, the dance sequences fun, and the music great. Swayze, classically trained in ballet, also performs one of the sound-track songs. ♫(I've Had) the Time of My Life; Be My Baby; Big Girls Don't Cry; Cry to Me; Do You Love Me?; Hey Baby; Hungry Eyes; In the Still of the Nite; Love is Strange. **97m/C VHS, DVD.** Patrick Swayze, Jennifer Grey, Cynthia Rhodes, Jerry Orbach, Jack Weston, Jane Brucker, Kelly Bishop, Lonny Price, Charles "Honi" Coles, Bruce Morrow; ***D:*** Emile Ardolino; ***W:*** Eleanor Bergstein; ***C:*** Jeffrey Jur; ***M:*** John Morris. Oscars '87: Song ("(I've Had) the Time of My Life"); Golden Globes '88: Song ("(I've Had) the Time of My Life"); Ind. Spirit '88: First Feature.

Dirty Dishes 🦴🦴🦴 1982 (R) A French film sardonically examining the fruitless life of the average housewife as she confronts a series of bizarre but pointless experiences during the day. Dubbed and subtitled versions available. The director is the American daughter-in-law of the late Luis Bunuel. **99m/C VHS.** *FR* Carol Laurie, Pierre Santini; ***D:*** Joyce Bunuel.

The Dirty Dozen 🦴🦴🦴 **1967 (PG)** A tough Army major is assigned to train and command 12 hardened convicts offered absolution if they participate in a suicidal mission into Nazi Germany in 1944. Well-made movie is a standout in its genre. Rough and gruff Marvin is good as the group leader. Three made-for-TV sequels followed in the '80s. **149m/C VHS, DVD, Wide.** Lee Marvin, Ernest Borgnine, Charles Bronson, Jim Brown, George Kennedy, John Cassavetes, Clint Walker, Donald Sutherland, Telly Savalas, Robert Ryan, Ralph Meeker, Richard Jaeckel, Trini Lopez, Robert Webber, Stuart Cooper, Robert Phillips, Al Mancini; ***D:*** Robert Aldrich; ***W:*** Nunnally Johnson, Lukas Heller; ***C:*** Edward Scaife; ***M:*** Frank DeVol. Oscars '67: Sound FX Editing.

The Dirty Dozen: The Deadly Mission 🦴🦴½ **1987** A second made-for-TV sequel to the '67 movie finds Borgnine ordering another suicide mission. Savalas (killed in the original, he's playing a new character) must pick 12 convicted army prisoners for an assault on a Nazi-held French monastery. Their mission is to rescue six scientists who are working on a deadly new nerve gas. Followed by "The Dirty Dozen: The Fatal Mission." **96m/C VHS.** Ernest Borgnine, Telly Savalas, Vince Edwards, Gary (Rand) Graham, James Van Patten, Vincent Van Patten, Bo Svenson; ***D:*** Lee H. Katzin.

The Dirty Dozen: The Fatal Mission 🦴🦴½ **1988** This third TV sequel has Borgnine learning of a plan to bring a group of high-ranking Nazis to Instanbul via the Orient Express. Naturally, he assigns Savalas the task of getting his motley gang together to thwart the Nazi schemes. To add intrigue, a female has joined the ranks of the Dirty Dozen and a spy may also have infiltrated the group. **91m/C VHS.** Ernest Borgnine, Telly Savalas, Hunt Block, Jeff Conaway, Erik Estrada, Ray "Boom Boom" Mancini, Heather Thomas, Alex Cord; ***D:*** Lee H. Katzin.

The Dirty Dozen: The Next Mission 🦴½ **1985** Disappointing TV sequel to the 1967 hit, with Marvin reprising his role as the leader of the motley pack. In this installment, the rag-tag toughs are sent on yet another suicide mission inside Nazi Germany, this time to thwart an assassination attempt of Hitler. Followed by two more sequels. **97m/C VHS.** Lee Marvin, Ernest Borgnine, Richard Jaeckel, Ken Wahl, Larry Wilcox, Sonny Landham, Ricco Ross; ***D:*** Andrew V. McLaglen. **TV**

Dirty Games 🦴½ **1993** Nicola Kendra is part of a team sent to Africa to inspect a nuclear waste site. Once there, the scientists discover terrorists are plotting to blow up the nuclear complex unless Nicola and her new allies can prevent it. **97m/C VHS.** Jan-Michael Vincent, Valentina Vargas, Ronald France, Michael McGovern; ***D:*** Gray Hofmeyr.

Dirty Gertie from Harlem U.S.A. 🦴🦴 **1946** All-black cast performs a variation of W. Somerset Maugham's "Rain." Gertie goes to Trinidad to hide out from her jilted boyfriend. **60m/B VHS.** Francine Everett, Katherine Moore, Spencer Williams Jr., Alfred Hawkins; ***D:*** Spencer Williams Jr.

The Dirty Girls 🦴½ **1964** Typical Metzger sexcapades featuring two stories about prostitute Garance, who works in Paris, and Monique, who plies her trade in Munich. **82m/B VHS, DVD.** Reine Rohan, Denise Roland, Marlene Sherter, Peter Parten, Lionel Bernier; ***D:*** Radley Metzger; ***W:*** Peter Fernandez.

Dirty Hands 🦴🦴 *Les Innocents aux Mains Sales* **1976** A woman and her lover conspire to murder her husband. A must for fans of the sexy Schneider. Cinematography provides moments that are both interesting and eerie. **102m/C VHS.** *FR* Rod Steiger, Romy Schneider, Paul(o) Giusti, Jean Rochefort, Hans-Christian Blech; ***D:*** Claude Chabrol.

Dirty Harry 🦴🦴🦴½ **1971 (R)** Rock-hard cop Harry Callahan attempts to track down a psychopathic rooftop killer before a kidnapped girl dies. Harry abuses the murderer's civil rights, however, forcing the police to return the criminal to the streets, where he hijacks a school bus and Harry is called on once again. The only answer to stop this vicious killer seems to be death in cold blood, and Harry is just the man to do it. Taut, suspenseful direction by Siegel, who thoroughly understands Eastwood's on-screen character. Features Callahan's famous "Do you feel lucky?" line, the precursor to his "Go ahead, make my day." **103m/C VHS, DVD, 8mm, Wide.** Clint Eastwood, Harry Guardino, John Larch, Andrew (Andy) Robinson, Reni Santoni, John Vernon, Albert "Poppy" Popwell; ***D:*** Donald Siegel; ***W:*** Dean Riesner, Harry Julian Fink, Rita M. Fink; ***C:*** Bruce Surtees; ***M:*** Lalo Schifrin.

Dirty Heroes 🦴🦴 *Dalle Ardenne All'Inferno* **1971 (R)** A band of escaped WWII POWs battle the Nazis for a precious treasure in the war's final days. **117m/C VHS.** John Ireland, Curt Jurgens, Adolfo Celi, Daniela Bianchi, Michael Constantine; ***D:*** Alberto De Martino; ***M:*** Ennio Morricone.

Dirty Laundry woof! **1987 (PG-13)** Insipid wreck of a comedy about a klutz who accidentally gets his laundry mixed up with $1 million in drug money. Features Olympians Lewis and Louganis. Never released theatrically. **81m/C VHS.** Leigh McCloskey, Jeanne O'Brien, Frankie Valli, Sonny Bono, Carl Lewis, Greg Louganis, Nicholas Worth; ***D:*** William Webb. **VIDEO**

Dirty Little Secret 🦴🦴½ **1998 (R)** Sarah Weatley (Gold) hires some hoods to kidnap the adopted 10-year-old son of a wealthy, hot-tempered sheriff (Wagner). But there's more to this than meets the eye—both Sarah and the sheriff share a nasty secret and, after 10 years of keeping silent, what Sarah really wants is revenge. **92m/C VHS.** Tracey Gold, Jack Wagner, Mary Page Keller; ***D:*** Robert M. Fresco; ***W:*** Robert M. Fresco. **CABLE**

Dirty Mary Crazy Larry 🦴🦴🦴 **1974 (PG)** A racecar driver, his mechanic, and a sexy girl hightail it from the law after pulling off a heist. Great action, great fun, and an infamous surprise ending. **93m/C VHS.** Peter Fonda, Susan George, Adam Roarke, Vic Morrow, Roddy McDowall; ***D:*** John Hough; ***W:*** Leigh Chapman.

Dirty Pictures 🦴🦴 **2000 (R)** Dull telepic on controversial subject that features real-life interviews, which only serve to cut the story's momentum. Dennis Barrie (Woods) is the director of the Cincinnati Contemporary Arts Center who decides to book an exhibition of Robert Mapplethorpe photographs in 1990. He gets indicted on obscenity charges and decides on a court fight based on First Amendment rights though it costs him personally. **104m/C VHS, DVD.** James Woods, Diana Scarwid, Craig T. Nelson, Leon Pownall, David Huband, Judah Katz, R.D. Reid, Matt North; ***D:*** Frank Pierson; ***W:*** Ilene Chaiken; ***C:*** Hiro Narita; ***M:*** Mark Snow. **CABLE**

Dirty Rotten Scoundrels 🦴🦴🦴 **1988 (PG)** A remake of the 1964 "Bedtime Story," in which two confidence tricksters on the Riviera endeavor to rip off a suddenly rich American woman, and each other. Caine and Martin are terrific, Martin has some of his best physical comedy ever, and Headly is charming as the prey who's always one step ahead of them. Fine direction from Oz, the man who brought us the voice of Yoda in "The Empire Strikes Back." **112m/C VHS, DVD, Wide.** Steve Martin, Michael Caine, Glenne Headly, Anton Rodgers, Barbara Harris, Dana Ivey; ***D:*** Frank Oz; ***W:*** Stanley Shapiro, Paul Henning, Dale Launer; ***C:*** Michael Ballhaus; ***M:*** Miles Goodman.

Dirty Tricks 🦴½ **1981 (PG)** History professor Gould fights with bad guys for a letter written by George Washington. Thoroughly forgettable comedy lacking in laughs. **91m/C VHS.** *CA* Elliott Gould, Kate Jackson, Arthur Hill, Rich Little; ***D:*** Alvin Rakoff; ***W:*** William W. Norton Sr.; ***M:*** Hagood Hardy.

Dirty Work 🦴🦴 **1992 (R)** A drug-dealing bail bondsman (Ashton) steals counterfeit money from the mob and then sets up his partner (Dobson) as the fall guy. Can Dobson survive long enough to set things straight? **88m/C VHS.** John Ashton, Kevin Dobson, Roxann Biggs-Dawson, Donnelly Rhodes, Jim Byrnes, Mitchell Ryan; ***D:*** John McPherson; ***W:*** Aaron Julien.

Dirty Work 🦴½ **1997 (PG-13)** You'll notice that star and ex-Saturday Night Live newsguy MacDonald isn't even trying to act, he's just doing his deadpan wise guy routine with a different name. His delivery and attitude, however, are about the only funny things in this tale of Mitch (MacDonald) and Sam (Lange), two losers who can't keep a job but have a talent for petty revenge. When Sam's father (Warden) has a heart attack, the boys decide to open a business specializing in dirty deeds done dirt cheap to pay for a heart transplant. Although the premise is good, the tricks are mostly of the junior high variety and don't seem quite dirty enough. Several unbilled cameos, including Adam Sandler, John Goodman and the late Chris Farley. **81m/C VHS, DVD.** Fred Wolf, Norm MacDonald, Artie Lange, Chevy Chase, Don Rickles, Jack Warden, Traylor Howard, Christopher McDonald, Chris Farley, Gary Coleman, Ken Norton, John Goodman, Adam Sandler; ***D:*** Bob Saget; ***W:*** Fred Wolf; ***C:*** Arthur Albert; ***M:*** Richard Gibbs.

Disappearance 🦴🦴 **1981 (R)** A hired assassin discovers an ironic link between his new target and his missing wife. **80m/C VHS.** *CA* Donald Sutherland, David Hemmings, John Hurt, Christopher Plummer, David Warner, Virginia McKenna; ***D:*** Stuart Cooper.

The Disappearance of Aimee 🦴🦴🦴 **1976** Dramatic re-creation of events surrounding the 1926 disappearance of evangelist Aimee Semple McPherson. She claimed she was abducted, but her mother insisted she ran away to have an affair. Excellent TV movie with an exceptional cast. Originally was to star Ann-Margret. **110m/C VHS.** Faye Dunaway, Bette Davis, James Sloyan, James Woods, John Lehne, Lelia Goldoni, Barry Brown, Severn Darden; ***D:*** Anthony Harvey; ***W:*** John McGreevey; ***C:*** James A. Crabe. **TV**

The Disappearance of Christina 🦴🦴½ **1993 (PG-13)** Successful entrepreneur Joe Seldon (Stamos) is married to heiress Christina (Yarlett) and they seem to be the perfect couple. But when Christina mysteriously vanishes during a sailing trip, was it really an accident? Detective Nora Davis (Pounder) doesn't think so and naturally, Joe is suspect numero uno. **93m/C VHS.** John Stamos, Kim Delaney, Robert Carradine, Claire Yarlett, CCH Pounder; ***D:*** Karen Arthur; ***W:*** Camille Thomasson.

The Disappearance of Garcia Lorca 🦴🦴½ *Death in Granada; Lorca* **1996 (R)** In 1954, Spanish-born journalist Ricardo Fernandez (Morales) returns to Granada to look into the death of his idol, poet/playwright Gabriel Garcia Lorca (Garcia). Ricardo's family fled Spain for Puerto Rico in 1936, at the start of the Spanish Civil War, when anti-fascist Lorca was executed. Ricardo wants to find out just who Lorca's killers were but Franco's Spain is a country eager to bury its past. Based on two books by Ian Gibson. **114m/C VHS.** *SP* Esai Morales, Andy Garcia, Edward James Olmos, Jeroen Krabbe, Miguel Ferrer, Giancarlo Giannini, Marcela Wallerstein, Jose Coronado; ***D:*** Marcos Zurinaga; ***W:*** Marcos Zurinaga, Neil Cohen, Juan Antonio Ramos; ***C:*** Juan Ruiz-Anchia; ***M:*** Mark McKenzie.

The Disappearance of Kevin Johnson 🦴🦴½ **1995 (R)** Mockumentary about a British TV crew, doing a film about successful Brits in Hollywood, stumbling across the disappearance of wanna-be producer and wealthy Englishman, Kevin Johnson. So they begin asking questions of the agents, executives, stars, business associates, and women in Johnson's life. So just who is—or was—Kevin Johnson? **105m/C VHS.** Michael Brandon, Bridget Baiss, Keely Sims, Rick Peters, Kari Wuhrer, John Hillard, Heather Stephens, Richard Beymer, Richard Neil, Michael Laskin, Ian Ogilvy, Stoney Jackson; ***Cameos:*** Pierce Brosnan, James Coburn, Dudley Moore; ***D:*** Francis Megahy; ***W:*** Francis Megahy; ***C:*** John Newby; ***M:*** John Coda; ***Nar:*** Francis Megahy.

Disappearing Acts 🦴🦴½ **2000 (R)** Zora Banks (Lathan) is a college-educated music teacher with dreams of becoming a singer. She meets high school dropout Franklin (Snipes), who's doing construction work and wants to become a contractor. Neither wants a relationship but opposites still attract and they get involved. But not without trouble. Based on the 1989 novel by Terry McMillan. **115m/C VHS, DVD.** Sanaa Lathan, Wesley Snipes, Regina Hall, Clark Johnson, John Amos, CCH Pounder, Aunjanue Ellis, Lisa Arrindell Anderson, Kamaal Fareed, Michael Imperioli; ***D:*** Gina Prince-Bythewood; ***W:*** Lisa Jones; ***C:*** Tami Reiker. **CABLE**

Disaster at Silo 7 🦴🦴 **1988** When the engine of a Titan missile goes on the fritz, the Air Force tries to prevent a nuclear disaster. Based on an actual Titan II missile incident near Little Rock, Arkansas. **92m/C VHS.** Peter Boyle, Patricia Charbonneau, Perry King, Michael O'Keefe, Joe Spano, Dennis Weaver; ***D:*** Larry Elikann; ***W:*** Douglas Lloyd McIntosh; ***C:*** Roy Wagner. **TV**

The Disciple 🦴½ **1915** Vintage silent western wherein Hart's unsmiling good-bad guy tries to clean up a lawless town and win back his wife, who has shamelessly fallen in with a corrupt saloon-keeper. **80m/B VHS, 8mm.** William S. Hart, Dorothy Dalton, Robert McKim, Jean Hersholt; ***D:*** William S. Hart; ***W:*** Thomas Ince.

Disciple of Death 🦴 **1972 (R)** Raven plays "The Stranger," a ghoul who sacrifices virgins to the Devil. **82m/C VHS.** *GB* Mike Raven, Ronald Lacey, Stephen Bradley, Virginia Wetherell; ***D:*** Tom Parkinson.

Disclosure 🦴🦴 **1994 (R)** Likable, responsible executive and family man (Douglas) finds himself sexually harassed by his ex-lover turned dragon-lady boss (Moore). But when he rejects her lusty come-on, she points the finger at him. One-dimensional characters and hollow material turn sexual harassment into a trivial issue. High-tech saga of corporate politics, while flashy, is nothing we haven't seen before. Douglas just can't pass up these "Regular Joe meets beautiful, horny babe, bad things happen" roles, can he? Based on the Michael Crichton novel. **129m/C VHS, DVD.** Michael Douglas, Demi Moore, Donald Sutherland, Caroline Goodall, Dylan Baker, Dennis Miller, Rosemary Forsyth, Roma Maffia; ***D:*** Barry Levinson; ***W:*** Paul Attanasio; ***C:*** Tony Pierce-Roberts; ***M:*** Ennio Morricone. Blockbuster '95: Drama Actress, T. (Moore); Blockbuster '96: Drama Actress, V. (Moore).

Disconnected 🦴½ **1987** "Sorry, Wrong Number" is updated, with more than ample doses of sex and violence. **81m/C VHS.** Mark Walker, Frances Raines; ***D:*** Gorman Bechard; ***W:*** Gorman Bechard; ***C:*** Gorman Bechard.

Discontent 🦴½ **1916** An early silent film by Lois Weber in which a cantankerous old vet goes to live with his wealthy nephew. The harmonious family life is disrupted by his meddling ways. **30m/B VHS.** ***D:*** Lois Weber.

The Discovery Program 🦴🦴½ **1989** Four award-winning short films on one video: "Ray's Male Heterosexual Dance Hall," "Greasy Lake," "The Open Window," and "Hearts of Stone." The subjects range from humorous and offbeat to tragic and deadly serious. **106m/C VHS.** Tim Choate, Boyd Gaines, John Achorn, Eric Stoltz; ***D:*** Bryan Gordon, Steven E. Anderson, Damian Harris, Rupert Wainwright; ***W:*** Bryan Gordon.

The Discreet Charm of the Bourgeoisie 🦴🦴🦴🦴 *Le Charme Discret de la Bourgeoisie* **1972 (R)** Bunuel in top form, satirizing modern society. These six characters are forever sitting down to dinner, yet they never eat. Dreams and reality, actual or contrived, prevent their feast. **100m/C VHS, DVD, Wide.** *FR* Milena Vukotic, Fernando Rey, Delphine Seyrig, Jean-Pierre Cassel, Bulle Ogier, Michel Piccoli, Stephane Audran, Luis Bunuel; ***D:*** Luis Bunuel; ***W:*** Luis Bunuel, Jean-Claude Carriere; ***C:*** Edmond Richard. Oscars '72: Foreign Film; British Acad. '73: Actress (Seyrig), Screenplay; Natl. Soc. Film Critics '72: Director (Bunuel), Film.

Discretion Assured 🦴🦴½ **1993 (R)** Successful businessman Trevor McCabe (York) finds himself in a romantic quandry with three women, leading to his involvement in embezzlement and murder. **97m/C VHS.** Michael York, Jennifer O'Neill, Dee Wallace Stone, Elizabeth (Ward) Gracen; ***D:*** Odorico Mendes.

The Disenchanted 🦴🦴½ *La Desenchantee* **1990** Seventeen-year-old Beth (Godreche) is having a rough time growing up. She's forced to look after her bedridden mother and younger brother and their survival depends on the generosity of her mother's ex-lover, who's now taking a more personal interest in the beautiful teenager. Meanwhile, Beth's arrogant boyfriend decides Beth should prove her love for him by sleeping with the ugliest man she can find. French with subtitles. **78m/C VHS, DVD, Wide.** *FR* Judith Godreche, Ivan Desny, Therese Liotard, Malcolm Conrath, Marcel Bozonnet; ***D:*** Benoit Jacquot; ***W:*** Benoit Jacquot; ***C:*** Caroline Champetier; ***M:*** Jorge Arriagada.

The Dish 🦴🦴🦴 **2000 (PG-13)** Tells the true story of a NASA official (Neill) and his group of local Aussie technicians as they manned the satellite dish responsible for bringing to TV sets around the world man's first footsteps on the moon in 1969. Originally only a backup plan, the Australian dish was called into action when the receiver in California became useless after a change in Apollo 11's flight path. Treats the central, spectacular event itself with dignity and appropriate awe, but also squeezes humor and emotion out of all that leads up to it. **104m/C VHS, DVD, Wide.** *AU* Sam Neill, Patrick Warburton, Tom Long, Kevin Harrington, Bille Brown, John McMartin, Tayler Kane, Eliza Szonert, Carl Snell; ***D:*** Rob Sitch; ***W:*** Rob Sitch, Santo Cilauro, Tom Gleisner, Jane Kennedy; ***C:*** Graeme Wood; ***M:*** Edmund Choi.

Dish Dogs 🦴🦴½ **1998 (R)** Morgan (Astin) and Jason (Lillard) are a couple of bachelor best friends who cruise SoCal in their old Chevy looking for the best surfing and work as dishwashers to make ends meets. But the slacker duo are beset by love (Ward, Elizabeth) and cracks surface in their buddyhood. **96m/C VHS, DVD, Wide.** Matthew Lillard, Sean Astin, Shannon Elizabeth, Maitland Ward, Brian Dennehy, Richard Moll; ***D:*** Bob (Robert) Kubilos; ***W:*** Ashley Scott Meyers, Nathan Ives; ***C:*** Mark Vicente; ***M:*** Herman Beeftink.

Dishonorable Discharge 🦴🦴 *Ces Dames Preferent le Mambo; Women Prefer the Mambo* **1957** American sailor Burt Brickford (Constantine) gets mixed up with dames, drugs, crooks, and treasure hunters—all in a seedy European coastal town. Loosely based on Ernest Hemingway's "To Have and Have Not." Dubbed. **105m/B VHS.** *FR* Eddie Constantine, Jacques Castelot, Jean Murat, Pascale Roberts, Joelle Bernard, Robert Berri, Lisa Bourdin, Rene Harvard; ***D:*** Bernard Borderie; ***W:*** Bernard Borderie; ***C:*** Jacques Lemare; ***M:*** Charles Aznavour.

Dishonored 🦴🦴½ **1931** Dated spy drama has Dietrich playing secret agent X-27 in WWI and masquerading on the side as a peasant girl. Although not one of the more famous Dietrich-Sternberg productions, its camp plot and Dietrich's lavish performance make it worth watching. Based on the infamous spy Mata Hari, who was shot by the French in 1917 for espionage. **91m/B VHS.** Marlene Dietrich, Victor McLaglen, Lew Cody, Gustav von Seyffertitz, Warner Oland, Barry Norton, Davison Clark, Wilfrid Lucas; ***D:*** Josef von Sternberg; ***W:*** Josef von Sternberg, Daniel N. Rubin; ***C:*** Lee Garmes.

Dishonored Lady 🦴½ **1947** After her ex-boyfriend is murdered, a female art director finds that she's the number one suspect. When put on trial for the dastardly deed, she takes the fifth in this mediocre melodrama. **85m/B VHS.** Hedy Lamarr, Dennis O'Keefe, William Lundigan, John Loder; ***D:*** Robert Stevenson.

Disney's The Kid 🦴🦴 **2000 (PG)** Cynical 40-year-old Willis comes face-to-face with his 8-year-old self (Breslin), who wants to know how he grew up to become such a jerk. It's Disney, so their are Important Lessons to be learned, and dramatic changes in behavior to be witnessed, but Breslin, Willis, and Tomlin as his assistant, make the schmaltz bearable with excellent performances. Wells' sophisticated, funny script helps smooth out Turteltaub's heavy-handed direction. **104m/C VHS, DVD, Wide.** Bruce Willis, Emily Mortimer, Jean Smart, Spencer Breslin, Chi McBride, Lily Tomlin, Dana Ivey, Daniel von Bargen; ***D:*** Jon Turteltaub; ***W:*** Audrey Wells; ***C:*** Peter Menzies Jr.; ***M:*** Jerry Goldsmith.

Disorderlies 🦴 **1987 (PG)** Members of the popular rap group cavort as incompetent hospital orderlies assigned to care for a cranky millionaire. Fat jokes abound with performances by the Fat Boys. **86m/C VHS.** The Fat Boys, Ralph Bellamy; ***D:*** Michael A. Schultz; ***M:*** Anne Dudley.

Disorderly Orderly 🦴½ **1964** When Jerry Lewis gets hired as a hospital orderly, nothing stands upright long with him around. Vintage slapstick Lewis running amuck in a nursing home. **90m/C VHS.** Jerry Lewis, Glenda Farrell, Everett Sloane, Kathleen Freeman, Susan Oliver; ***D:*** Frank Tashlin.

Disorganized Crime 🦴🦴 **1989 (R)** On the lam from the law, Bernsen attempts to organize a group of his ex-con buddies to pull off the perfect heist. Before the boys can organize, however, the cops are hot on Bernsen's trail, and he must vacate the meeting place. Good cast attempts to lift this movie beyond script. **101m/C VHS.** Lou Diamond Phillips, Fred Gwynne, Corbin Bernsen, Ruben Blades, Hoyt Axton, Ed O'Neill, Daniel Roebuck, William Russ; ***D:*** Jim Kouf; ***M:*** David Newman.

Disraeli 🦴🦴🦴 **1930** Arliss deservedly won the Best Actor Oscar for his title role as the famed British prime minister to Queen Victoria. This particular slice of the cunning statesman's life depicts his efforts to secure the Suez Canal for England against the Russians. Arliss' wife also played his screen spouse. One of Warner's earliest and best biographical pictures. Based on a play by Louis Napoleon Parker. **87m/B VHS.** George Arliss, Joan Bennett, Florence Arliss, Anthony Bushell, David Torrence, Doris Lloyd, Ivan Simpson, Gwendolyn Logan; ***D:*** Alfred E. Green; ***C:*** Lee Garmes. Oscars '30: Actor (Arliss).

Disraeli 🦴🦴🦴 **1979** Flamboyant, irreverant, a dandy, and a womanizer, Benjamin Disraeli (McShane) was also England's first Jewish Prime Minister and one of its greatest. This British miniseries examines the controversial figure and the Victorian era his life and career spanned. **208m/C VHS.** *GB* Ian McShane, Mary Peach, Mark Dignam, Leigh Lawson, Rosemary Leach, Anton Rodgers, Margaret Whiting; ***D:*** Claude Whatham; ***W:*** David Butler.

Distant Drums 🦴🦴 **1951** A small band of adventurers tries to stop the Seminole War in the Florida Everglades. **101m/C VHS.** Gary Cooper, Mari Aldon, Robert Barrat, Richard Webb, Ray Teal, Arthur Hunnicutt; ***D:*** Raoul Walsh; ***M:*** Max Steiner.

Distant Justice 🦴½ **1992 (R)** Tokyo police inspector Rio (Sugawara) is vacationing in Boston with his wife and daughter, where he can also visit old friend, Chief Bradfield (Kennedy). But Rio's wife is murdered and his daughter kidnapped by vicious drug dealer Roy Pennola (Carradine) and Bradfield assigns young officer Charlie Givens (Lutes) to see that Rio doesn't get himself killed as well. **91m/C VHS.** Bunta Sugawara, George Kennedy, David Carradine, Eric Lutes; ***D:*** Toru Murakawa.

Distant Thunder 🦴🦴🦴½ *Ashani Sanket* **1973** A bitter, unrelenting portrait of a small Bengali neighborhood as the severe famines of 1942, brought about by the "distant thunder" of WWII, take their toll. A mature achievement from Ray; in Bengali with English subtitles. **92m/C VHS.** *IN* Soumitra Chatterjee, Sandhya Roy, Babita, Gobinda Chakravarty, Romesh Mukerji; ***D:*** Satyajit Ray; ***W:*** Satyajit Ray; ***C:*** Soumendu Roy; ***M:*** Satyajit Ray. Berlin Intl. Film Fest. '73: Golden Berlin Bear.

Distant Thunder 🦴🦴 **1988 (R)** A scarred Vietnam vet, who has become a recluse, and his estranged son reunite in the Washington State wilderness, causing him to reflect on his isolation. Strong premise and cast watered down by weak script. **114m/C VHS.** *CA* John Lithgow, Ralph Macchio, Kerrie Keane, Janet Margolin, Rick Rosenthal; ***D:*** Rick Rosenberg; ***C:*** Ralf Bode; ***M:*** Maurice Jarre.

Distant Voices, Still Lives 🦴🦴🦴 **1988** A profoundly executed, disturbing film chronicling a British middle-class family through the maturation of the three children, under the dark shadow of their abusive, malevolent father. An evocative, heartbreaking portrait of British life from WWII on, and of the rhythms of dysfunctional families. A film festival favorite. **87m/C VHS.** *GB* Freda Dowie, Pete Postlethwaite, Angela Walsh, Dean Williams, Lorraine Ashbourne; ***D:*** Terence Davies; ***W:*** Terence Davies; ***C:*** Patrick Duval. L.A. Film Critics '89: Foreign Film.

The Distinguished Gentleman 🦴🦴 **1992 (R)** A small-time con man (Murphy) manages to scam his way into a political career and winds up in Congress. The other characters serve mostly as foils for Murphy's comedic talent. Viewers will laugh despite the story's predictablity. **122m/C VHS, DVD.** Eddie Murphy, Lane Smith, Sheryl Lee Ralph, Joe Don Baker, Victoria Rowell, Grant Shaud, Kevin McCarthy, Charles S. Dutton, James Garner; ***D:*** Jonathan Lynn; ***W:*** Marty Kaplan; ***C:*** Gabriel Beristain; ***M:*** Randy Edelman.

Distortions 🦴🦴 **1987 (PG)** Hussey is a widow whose evil aunt (Laurie) is holding her hostage. What the film lacks in suspense throughout most of the movie is made up for in the end. **90m/C VHS.** Piper Laurie, Steve Railsback, Olivia Hussey, Edward Albert, Rita Gam, Terence Knox; ***D:*** Armand Mastroianni.

Disturbance 🦴½ **1989** The two personas of a young schizophrenic get him entangled in a mysterious string of murders. **81m/C VHS.** Timothy Greeson, Lisa Geoffreion; ***D:*** Cliff Guest.

Disturbed 🦴 **1990 (R)** Lusty mental hospital director McDowell meets sex starved and suicidal Gidley in this less-than-stellar erotic creeper. Redeemed only by McDowell's performance and more evidence that the droog's career hasn't been just peachy since "Clockwork Orange." **96m/C VHS.** Malcolm McDowell, Geoffrey Lewis, Priscilla Pointer, Pamela Gidley, Clint Howard; ***D:*** Charles Winkler; ***W:*** Emerson Bixby, Charles Winkler.

Disturbing Behavior 🦴🦴½ **1998 (R)** Gavin (Stahl) welcomes new kid in town Steve (Marsden) by pointing out the social castes at Cradle Bay High School. The Uber-group is the goody-goody Blue Ribbons, an excessively straitlaced and perky group of athletes and cheerleaders. Along with fellow outcasts Rachel (Holmes) and U.V. (Donella), they joke about a possible conspiracy, but when Gavin shows up with a crewcut and an inordinate love of pep rallies and bake sales, his friends know something is up. They discover that parents have allowed the school shrink (Greenwood) to use drugs to tinker with the brains of the Blue Ribbons. They also discover that the Stepford Teens' vanilla lives are topped with sprinkles of homicidal fury. Director Nutter creates just the right creepy and paranoid mood in his feature debut. **84m/C VHS, DVD.** James Marsden, Nick Stahl, Katie Holmes, Bruce Greenwood, William Sadler, Chad E. Donella, Ethan (Randall) Embry, Steve Railsback; ***D:*** David Nutter; ***W:*** Scott Rosenberg; ***C:*** John Bartley; ***M:*** Mark Snow. MTV Movie Awards '99: Breakthrough Perf. (Holmes).

Diva 🦴🦴🦴½ **1982 (R)** While at a concert given by his favorite star, a young French courier secretly tapes a soprano who has refused to record. The film follows the young man through Paris as he flees from two Japanese recording pirates, and a couple of crooked undercover police who are trying to cover-up for the chief who not only has a mistress, but runs a prostitution ring. Brilliant and dazzling photography compliment the eclectic soundtrack. **123m/C VHS, DVD, Wide.** *FR* Frederic Andrei, Roland Bertin, Richard Bohringer, Gerard Darmon, Jacques Fabbri, Wilhelmenia Wiggins Fernandez, Dominique Pinon; ***D:*** Jean-Jacques Beineix; ***W:*** Jean-Jacques Beineix; ***C:*** Philippe Rousselot; ***M:*** Vladimir Cosma. Cesar '82: Cinematog., Sound, Score; Natl. Soc. Film Critics '82: Cinematog.

The Dive 🦴🦴 **1989 (PG-13)** Two North Sea oil-rig workers are trapped far below the waves when the lifeline to their diving bell snaps in rough seas. **90m/C VHS.** Bjorn Sundquist, Frank Grimes, Einride Eidsvold, Michael Kitchen; ***D:*** Tristan De Vere Cole.

Dive Bomber 🦴🦴🦴 **1941** Exciting aviation film that focuses on medical problems related to flying. Flynn stars as an aviator-doctor who conducts experiments to eliminate pilot-blackout. MacMurray, Toomey, and Heydt perform well as three flyboys stationed in Hawaii. Great flying sequences filmed at San Diego's naval base with extra scenes shot at Pensacola. Warner Bros. released this film just months before the Japanese attacked Pearl Harbor. Based on the story "Beyond the Blue Sky" by Frank Wead. **130m/B VHS.** Errol Flynn, Fred MacMurray, Ralph Bellamy, Alexis Smith, Regis Toomey, Robert Armstrong, Allen Jenkins, Craig Stevens, Herbert Anderson, Moroni Olsen, Dennie Moore, Louis Jean Heydt, Cliff Nazarro, Tod Andrews, Ann Doran, Charles Drake, Alan Hale Jr., William Forrest, Creighton Hale, Howard Hickman, Russell Hicks, George Meeker, Richard Travis, Addison Richards; ***D:*** Michael Curtiz; ***W:*** Frank Wead, Robert Buckner; ***C:*** Bert Glennon, Winton C. Hoch; ***M:*** Max Steiner.

Divided by Hate 🦴🦴 **1996 (PG-13)** In 1984, struggling farmer Louis Gibbs (Walsh), wife Carol (Roth), and their children fall under the spell of charismatic preacher Steve Riordan (Skerritt) whose anti-government sentiments lead to the forming of a local militia. Naturally, the FBI gets involved and there's a struggle between the feds and the militia, with the family caught in the middle. If it sounds familiar that's because it's based on the 1995 Branch Davidian incident. **92m/C VHS.** Dylan Walsh, Andrea Roth, Tom Skerritt; ***D:*** Tom Skerritt; ***W:*** Leonard Gross.

Divided We Fall 🦴🦴½ *Musime si Pomahat* **2000 (PG-13)** In 1943, the inhabitants of an unnamed Czechoslovakian town are existing under the Nazi occupation. Josef (Polivka) recognizes his former employer David (Kassai), a Jew who has escaped the camps. Josef and his wife Marie (Siskova) agree to hide David in their home although they are under the scrutiny of Nazi collaborator Horst (Dusek), who keeps making passes at Marie. Although they are childless, Marie claims to be pregnant to get Horst to leave her alone. Which leads Josef to ask a delicate favor of David so they can make good on Marie's lie. Czech with subtitles. **123m/C VHS, DVD, Wide.** *CZ* Boleslav Polivka, Anna Siskova, Csongor Kassai, Jaroslav Dusek, Jiri Pecha, Simona Stasova, Marin Huba, Vladimir Marek, Jiri Kodet, Richard Tesarik; ***D:*** Jan Hrebejk; ***W:*** Petr Jarchovsky; ***C:*** Jan Malir; ***M:*** Ales Brezina.

Divided We Stand 🦴🦴 **2000 (R)** Naive college coed Lisa joins the Black Student Coalition and soon accuses fellow member Robey of rape. However, BSC member and law student Jarrod, who knows what really happened, is hesitant to get involved. **81m/C VHS, DVD, Wide.** Andrea Lisa, Crayton Robey, J.R. Jarrod; ***D:*** J.R. Jarrod; ***W:*** J.R. Jarrod; ***C:*** Joan Crawford; ***M:*** Charles D. Jackson, Sherwood Seward, Derek Seward.

Divine 🦴🦴½ **1990** Two Divine flicks from Waters. First, Divine plays a naughty girl who, not surprisingly, since this one is titled "The Diane Linkletter Story," ends up a successful suicide. "The Neon Woman" is a rare live performance, with Divine a woman who owns a strip joint and has a slew of problems you won't read about in Dear Abby. **110m/C VHS.** Divine; ***D:*** John Waters.

The Divine Enforcer 🦴½ **1991** A monsignor in a crime-ridden L.A. neighborhood reaches his wit's end in trying to stave off perpetrators of injustice. Fortunately, help arrives in the form of a mysterious priest who is equally handy with his fists, nunchakus, and guns. From then on it's no more mister nice guy, and the criminals haven't a prayer. **90m/C VHS.** Jan-Michael Vincent, Erik Estrada, Jim Brown, Judy Landers, Don Stroud, Robert Z'Dar, Michael Foley, Carrie Chambers, Hiroko; ***D:*** Robert Rundle.

Divine Nymph 🦴½ **1971 (R)** Charts the erotic adventures of the beautiful and young Manuela, who is dangerously pursued by two cousins. **100m/C VHS.** *IT* Laura Antonelli, Marcello Mastroianni, Terence Stamp; ***D:*** Giuseppe Patroni-Griffi; ***M:*** Ennio Morricone.

Divine Secrets of the Ya-Ya Sisterhood **2002 (PG-13)** Southern dramedy about a group of girlfriends (Smith, Flanagan, Knight) who stage an intervention to help about to be married, New York-based playwright Sidda Lee (Bullock) discover the truth about her eccentric, alcoholic Southern mama Vivi (Burstyn). Based on the novels "Divine Secrets of the Ya-Ya Sisterhood" and "Little Altars Everywhere" by Rebecca Wells. Not yet reviewed. **116m/C VHS, DVD.** *US* Ashley Judd, Sandra Bullock, Ellen Burstyn, Maggie Smith, James Garner, Fionnula Flanagan, Shirley Knight, Cherry Jones, Angus Macfadyen, Jacqueline McKenzie, Katy Selverstone, Kiersten Warren, Gina McKee, Matthew Settle, David Rasche, Fred Koehler, Leslie Silva, Ron Dortoh, David Lee Smith; ***D:*** Callie Khouri; ***W:*** Callie Khouri, Mark Andrus; ***C:*** John Bailey; ***M:*** T Bone Burnett.

Diving In 🦴🦴 **1990 (PG-13)** Have you heard the one about the acrophobic diver? It seems a paralyzing fear of heights is the only thing between a young diver and Olympic gold. Much splashing about and heartstring-tugging. **92m/C VHS.** Burt Young, Matt Adler, Kristy Swanson, Matt Lattanzi, Richard Johnson, Carey Scott, Yolanda Jilot; ***D:*** Strathford Hamilton; ***C:*** Hanania Baer; ***M:*** Guy Moon, Paul Buckmaster.

Divorce American Style 🦴🦴½ **1967** Dated but still amusing look at love, marriage, and the big D. Richard (Van Dyke) and Barbara (Reynolds) Harmon find their longtime marriage in a tailspin as they spend all their time arguing. They split but find single life and the dating game have their own pitfalls. **103m/C VHS.** Dick Van Dyke, Debbie Reynolds, Jason Robards Jr., Jean Simmons, Van Johnson, Lee Grant, Joe Flynn, Shelley Berman, Martin Gabel, Tom Bosley, Dick Gautier, Eileen Brennan; ***D:*** Bud Yorkin; ***W:*** Norman Lear; ***C:*** Conrad L. Hall; ***M:*** Dave Grusin.

Divorce His, Divorce Hers 🦴🦴 **1972** The first half of this drama shows the crumbling of a marriage through the husband's eyes. The second half offers the wife's perspective. **144m/C VHS, DVD.** Richard Burton, Elizabeth Taylor; ***D:*** Waris Hussein. **TV**

Divorce—Italian Style 🦴🦴🦴½ *Divorzio All'Italiana* **1962** A middle-aged baron bored with his wife begins directing his amorous attentions to a teenage cousin. Since divorce in Italy is impossible, the only way out of his marriage is murder—and the baron finds a little-known law that excuses a man from murdering his wife if she is having an affair (since he would merely be defending his honor). A hilarious comedy with a twist ending. Available in Italian with English subtitles or dubbed in English. **104m/B VHS.** *IT* Marcello Mastroianni, Daniela Rocca, Leopoldo Trieste, Stefania Sandrelli; ***D:*** Pietro Germi; ***W:*** Pietro Germi, Ennio de Concini, Alfredo Giannetti; ***C:*** Carlo Di Palma, Leonida Barboni; ***M:*** Carlo Rustichelli. Oscars '62: Story & Screenplay; British Acad. '63: Actor (Mastroianni); Golden Globes '63: Actor—Mus./Comedy (Mastroianni), Foreign Film.

The Divorce of Lady X 🦴🦴½ **1938** A spoiled British debutante, in the guise of "Lady X," makes a woman-hating divorce lawyer eat his words through romance and marriage. Based on the play by Gilbert Wakefield. **92m/C VHS.** *GB* Merle Oberon, Laurence Olivier, Ralph Richardson, Binnie Barnes; ***D:*** Tim Whelan; ***C:*** Harry Stradling Sr.; ***M:*** Miklos Rozsa.

The Divorcee 🦴🦴½ **1930** Early Leonard film (he'd later direct "The Great Ziegfield" and "Pride and Prejudice") casts Shearer as a woman out to beat her husband at philandering. Married to a journalist, she cavorts with her husband's best friend and a discarded old flame as only a pre-production code gal could. Shearer—who Lillian Hellman described as having "a face unclouded by thought"—grabbed an Oscar. Based on the novel "Ex-Wife" by Ursula Parrott. **83m/B VHS.** Norma Shearer, Chester Morris, Conrad Nagel, Robert Montgomery, Mary Doran, Tyler Brooke, George Irving, Helen Johnson; ***D:*** Robert Z. Leonard. Oscars '30: Actress (Shearer).

Dixiana 🦴½ **1930** A Southern millionaire falls for a circus performer shortly before the start of the Civil War. Part color. ♫Dixiana; Here's to the Old Days; A Tear, a Kiss, a Smile; My One Ambition is You; A Lady Loved a Soldier; Mr. & Mrs. Sippi; Guiding Star. **99m/B VHS, DVD.** Bebe Daniels, Bert Wheeler, Robert Woolsey, Dorothy Lamour, Bill Robinson; ***D:*** Luther Reed; ***M:*** Max Steiner.

Dixie: Changing Habits 🦴🦴🦴 **1985** A New Orleans madam and a Mother Superior go head to head in this amusing TV movie. In the end all benefit as the nuns discover business sense and pay off a debt, while the former bordello owner cleans up her act. Above-average scripting and directing for the medium. **100m/C VHS.** Suzanne Pleshette, Cloris Leachman, Kenneth McMillan, John Considine, Geraldine Fitzgerald, Judith Ivey; ***D:*** George Englund. **TV**

Dixie Dynamite 🦴 **1976 (PG)** The two daughters of a Georgia moonshiner set out to avenge the murder of their father. The music is performed by Duane Eddy and Dorsey Burnette. **88m/C VHS, DVD.** Warren Oates, Christopher George, Jane Anne Johnstone, Kathy McHaley, R.G. Armstrong, Wes Bishop; ***D:*** Lee Frost; ***W:*** Lee Frost, Wes Bishop.

Dixie Jamboree 🦴 **1944** Low-budget musical has gangster on the lam using an unusual method to escape from St. Louis—the last Mississippi Showboat. ♫Dixie Showboat; No, No, No; If It's a Dream; You Ain't Right with the Lord; Big Stuff. **69m/B VHS.** Guy Kibbee, Frances Langford, Louise Beavers, Charles Butterworth; ***D:*** Christy Cabanne.

Dixie Lanes 🦴 **1988** A relentlessly nostalgic comedy set in a small town at the end of WWII. A woman, troubled by her nephew's restless antics, puts him to work. Unfortunately she adds to his plight, as her business involves the Black Market. **92m/C VHS.** Hoyt Axton, Karen Black, Art Hindle, John Vernon, Ruth Buzzi, Tina Louise, Pamela Springsteen, Nina Foch; ***D:*** Don Cato.

Django 🦴½ **1968 (PG)** Django is a stranger who arrives in a Mexican-border town (dragging a coffin behind him) to settle a dispute between a small band of Americans and Mexicans. **90m/C VHS, DVD.** Franco Nero, Loredana Nusciak, Angel Alvarez, Jose Bodalo, Eduardo Fajardo, Simon Arriaga, Ivan Scratuglia; ***D:*** Sergio Corbucci; ***W:*** Sergio Corbucci, Bruno Corbucci, Jose Maesso, Piero Vivarelli, Franco (Fred Gardner) Rossetti; ***C:*** Enzo Barboni; ***M:*** Luis Bacalov.

Django Shoots First 🦴½ *Django Spara per Primo* **1974** Spaghetti western with usual amount of action and plot twists. **96m/C VHS.** *IT* Glen Saxson, Evelyn Stewart, Alberto Lupo; ***D:*** Alberto De Martino; ***W:*** Alberto De Martino.

Django Strikes Again 🦴🦴 *Django 2: Il Grande Ritorno* **1987** Django (Nero) has abandoned his former life of violence in favor of the peaceful life of a monk. That is, until his daughter is kidnapped. Then he manages to find that old coffin and go after the dastardly dogs. **96m/C VHS, DVD.** *SP* Franco Nero, Donald Pleasence, Rodrigo Obregon, Christopher Connelly, William Berger; ***D:*** Nello (Ted Archer) Rossati; ***W:*** Nello (Ted Archer) Rossati; ***M:*** Gianfranco Plenizio.

DNA 🦴½ **1997 (R)** Idealistic doctor Ash Mattley (Dacascos) mistakenly reveals his radical DNA theories to creepy scientist Wessinger (Prochnow), who uses the knowledge in mutant experiments. One mutant, an insect-like creature with super powers, lurks in the rain forest, waiting for prey, while Mattley sets out to destroy it. **94m/C VHS.** Mark Dacascos, Juergen Prochnow, Robin McKee; ***D:*** William Mesa; ***W:*** Nick Davis; ***C:*** Gerry Lively; ***M:*** Christopher Stone.

Do or Die 🦴½ **1991 (R)** Former "Playboy" centerfolds Speir and Vasquez team up as a couple of federal agent babes who take on international crime boss Morita. But the crimelord is ready for our scantily clad heroines with a sick game of revenge—and the stakes are their very lives! **97m/C VHS.** Erik Estrada, Dona Speir, Roberta Vasquez, Noriyuki "Pat" Morita, Bruce Penhall, Carolyn Liu, Stephanie Schick; ***D:*** Andy Sidaris; ***W:*** Andy Sidaris.

Do the Right Thing 🦴🦴🦴½ **1989 (R)** An uncompromising, brutal comedy about the racial tensions surrounding a white-owned pizzeria in the Bed-Stuy section of Brooklyn on the hottest day of the summer, and the violence that eventually erupts. Ambivalent and, for the most part, hilarious; Lee's coming-of-age. **120m/C VHS, DVD, Wide.** Spike Lee, Danny Aiello, Richard Edson, Ruby Dee, Ossie Davis, Giancarlo Esposito, Bill Nunn, John Turturro, John Savage, Rosie Perez, Frankie Faison; ***D:*** Spike Lee; ***W:*** Spike Lee; ***C:*** Ernest R. Dickerson; ***M:*** Bill Lee. L.A. Film Critics '89: Director (Lee), Film, Support. Actor (Aiello), Natl. Film Reg. '99;; N.Y. Film Critics '89: Cinematog.

D.O.A. 🦴🦴🦴½ **1949** A man is given a lethal, slow-acting poison. As his time runs out, he frantically seeks to learn who is responsible and why he was targeted for death. Dark film noir remade in 1969 as "Color Me Dead" and in 1988 with Dennis Quaid and Meg Ryan. Also available colorized. **83m/B VHS, DVD.** Edmond O'Brien, Pamela Britton, Luther Adler, Neville Brand, Beverly Garland, Lynne Baggett, William Ching, Henry Hart, Laurette Luez, Virginia Lee, Jess Kirkpatrick, Cay Forrester, Michael Ross; ***D:*** Rudolph Mate; ***W:*** Russell Rouse, Clarence Green; ***C:*** Ernest Laszlo; ***M:*** Dimitri Tiomkin.

D.O.A. 🦴🦴½ **1988 (R)** Well-done remake of the 1949 thriller with Quaid portraying a college professor who is poisoned and has only 24 hours to identify his killer. His search for the suspect is further complicated by the fact that he is being sought by the police on phony charges of murder. Directed by the same people who brought "Max Headroom" to TV screens. **98m/C VHS.** Dennis Quaid, Meg Ryan, Charlotte Rampling, Daniel Stern, Jane Kaczmarek, Christopher Neame, Jay Patterson; ***D:*** Rocky Morton, Annabel Jankel; ***W:*** Charles Edward Pogue; ***M:*** Chaz Jankel.

The Doberman Gang 🦴🦴 **1972 (PG)** Clever thieves train a gang of Dobermans in the fine art of bank robbery. Sequelled by "The Daring Dobermans." **85m/C VHS.** Byron Mabe, Hal Reed, Julie Parrish, Simmy Bow, JoJo D'Amore; ***D:*** Byron Ross Chudnow; ***W:*** Frank Ray Perilli.

Doc Hollywood 🦴🦴½ **1991 (PG-13)** A hotshot young physician on his way to a lucrative California practice gets stranded in a small Southern town. Will the wacky woodsy inhabitants persuade the city doctor to stay? There aren't many surprises in this fish-out-of-water comedy, but the cast injects it with considerable charm. Adapted from Neil B. Shulman's book "What?...Dead Again?" **104m/C VHS, DVD, 8mm, Wide.** Michael J. Fox, Julie Warner, Woody Harrelson, Barnard Hughes, David Ogden Stiers, Frances Sternhagen, Bridget Fonda, George Hamilton, Roberts Blossom, Helen Martin, Macon McCalman, Barry Sobel; ***D:*** Michael Caton-Jones; ***W:*** Daniel Pyne, Jeffrey Price, Peter S. Seaman; ***C:*** Michael Chapman; ***M:*** Carter Burwell.

Doc Savage 🦴🦴½ **1975 (PG)** Doc and "The Amazing Five" fight a murderous villain who plans to take over the world. Based on the novels of Kenneth Robeson. **100m/C VHS.** Ron Ely, Pamela Hensley, Paul Gleason, Paul Wexler, William Lucking; ***D:*** Michael Anderson Sr.; ***W:*** George Pal, Joe Morhaim; ***C:*** Fred W. Koenekamp.

Docks of New York 🦴🦴🦴 **1928** Von Sternberg made his mark in Hollywood with this silent drama about two dockside losers finding love amid the squalor. A rarely seen, early masterpiece. **60m/B VHS.** George Bancroft, Betty Compson, Olga Baclanova; ***D:*** Josef von Sternberg; ***M:*** Gaylord Carter. Natl. Film Reg. '99.

The Doctor 🦴🦴½ **1991 (PG-13)** A hotshot doctor develops throat cancer and gets treated at his own hospital, an ordeal that teaches him a respect and compassion for patients that he formerly lacked. Potential melodrama is saved by fine acting and strong direction. Based on the autobiographical book "A Taste of My Own Medicine" by Dr. Edward Rosenbaum. **125m/C VHS, Wide.** William Hurt, Elizabeth Perkins, Christine Lahti, Mandy Patinkin, Wendy Crewson, Charlie Korsmo, Adam Arkin, Bill Macy; ***D:*** Randa Haines; ***W:*** Robert Caswell; ***C:*** John Seale; ***M:*** Michael Convertino.

Dr. Akagi 🦴🦴 *Kanzo Sensei* **1998** In 1945, the dedicated Dr. Akagi (Emoto) is more worried about a hepatitis epidemic in his seaside village that the Japanese wartime defeat. He becomes obsessed with finding a cure and assembles a ragtag group of compatriots to assist him, including a teenaged prostitute and an escaped Dutch prisoner of war. Based on the novel "Dr. Liver" by Ango Sakaguchi. Japanese with subtitles. **128m/C VHS.** *JP* Akira (Tsukamoto) Emoto, Jacques Gamblin, Kumiko Aso, Masanori Sera, Jyuro Kara, Keiko Matzuzaka; ***D:*** Shohei Imamura; ***W:*** Shohei Imamura, Daisuke Tengan; ***C:*** Shigeru Komatsubara; ***M:*** Yosuke Yamashita.

Dr. Alien 🦴 **1988 (R)** Alien poses as beautiful scientist and turns a college freshman into a sex-addicted satyr. Likewise, the cast turns this flick into a dog. **90m/C VHS.** Billy Jacoby, Olivia Barash, Stuart Fratkin, Troy Donahue, Arlene Golonka, Judy Landers; ***D:*** David DeCoteau.

The Doctor and the Devils 🦴🦴½ **1985 (R)** Based on an old screenplay by Dylan Thomas, this is a semi-Gothic tale about two criminals who supply a physician with corpses to study, either digging them up or killing them fresh. **93m/C VHS.** *GB* Timothy Dalton, Julian Sands, Jonathan Pryce, Twiggy, Stephen Rea, Beryl Reid, Sian Phillips, Patrick Stewart, Phyllis Logan, T.P. McKenna; ***D:*** Freddie Francis; ***W:*** Ronald Harwood; ***M:*** John Morris.

Doctor at Large 🦴🦴½ **1957** A fledgling doctor seeks to become a surgeon at a hospital for the rich. Humorous antics follow. The third of the "Doctor" series. **98m/C VHS.** *GB* Dirk Bogarde, Muriel Pavlow, James Robertson Justice, Shirley Eaton, Donald Sinden, Anne Heywood; ***D:*** Ralph Thomas.

Doctor at Sea 🦴🦴½ **1956** To escape a troublesome romantic entanglement and the stresses of his career, a London physician signs on a cargo boat as a ship's doctor and becomes involved with French bombshell Bardot. The second of the "Doctor" series. **93m/C VHS.** *GB* James Robertson Justice, Dirk Bogarde, Brigitte Bardot; ***D:*** Ralph Thomas; ***W:*** Jack Davies.

Dr. Bethune 🦴🦴🦴 *Bethune, The Making of a Hero* **1990** Canadian surgeon Norman Bethune was a larger-than-life hero with equally great flaws. A crusader for socialized medicine and an outspoken opponent of Fascism (as well as an alcoholic womanizer), he worked for the Loyalist forces in the Spanish Civil War and was instrumental in developing mobile medical units for treating battlefield wounded. He's also credited with bringing modern medical care to China, where he attended to Mao's revolutionary forces. Sutherland's strong performance shows the intensity and vision of a complicated man; he previously played the doctor in 1977's "Bethune." Awkward jumps in time and place rob the story of narrative drive. **115m/C VHS.** *CA FR* Donald Sutherland, Helen Mirren, Helen Shaver, Colm Feore, Anouk Aimee, Ronald Pickup, Harrison Liu; ***D:*** Phillip Borsos; ***W:*** Ted Allan; ***C:*** Raoul Coutard; ***M:*** Alan Reeves.

Dr. Black, Mr. Hyde 🦴 *Dr. Black and Mr. White; The Watts Monster* **1976 (R)** Not-so-horrifying tale of a black Jekyll who metamorphoses into a white monster with the help of the special potion. Unintended laughs lessen suspense. **88m/C VHS.** Rosalind Cash, Stu Gilliam, Bernie Casey, Marie O'Henry; ***D:*** William Crain.

Doctor Blood's Coffin 🦴🦴½ **1962** The aptly named doctor performs hideous experiments on the unsuspecting denizens of a lonely village. Good cast in this effective chiller. **92m/C VHS.** *GB* Kieron Moore, Hazel Court, Ian Hunter; ***D:*** Sidney J. Furie.

Doctor Butcher M.D. woof! *Queen of the Cannibals; Zombie Holocaust; The Island of the Last Zombies* **1980 (R)** Mad doctor's deranged dream of creating "perfect people" by taking parts of one person and interchanging them with another backfires as his monstrosities develop strange side effects. The M.D., by the way, stands for "Medical Deviate." Dubbed. **81m/C VHS.** *IT* Ian McCulloch, Alexandra Cole, Peter O'Neal,

Donald O'Brien, Sherry Buchanan, Walter Patriarca; *D:* Frank Martin, Mariano Laurenti; *W:* Fabrizio de Angelis, Romano Scandariato; *M:* Nico Fidenco, Walter Sear.

Dr. Caligari **1989 (R)** The granddaughter of the original Dr. Caligari promotes "better living through chemistry" in her insane asylum while using her patients as guinea pigs in her bizarre sexual experiments. Nothing outstanding here in terms of story or performance, but "Dick Tracy" has nothing on the visually compelling set designs and make-up. **80m/C VHS.** Madeleine Reynal, Fox Harris, Laura Albert, Jennifer Balgobin, John Durbin, Gene Zerna, David Parry, Barry Phillips; *D:* Stephen Sayadian; *W:* Stephen Sayadian, Jerry Stahl; *C:* Stephen Sayadian.

Doctor Chance *Docteur Chance* **1997** Frustrated Angstel (Hestnes) decides it's time to make a big change in his life. He heads to a nightclub and buys the favors (with counterfeit cash) of dancer Ancetta (Elvire) but events get out of hand. Soon the duo are heading out of the city with a car trunk full of weapons and adventure on their minds. French with subtitles. **97m/C VHS.** *FR* Pedro Hestnes, Elvire, Marisa Paredes, Stephane Ferrara, Joe Strummer, Feodor Atkine; *D:* F.J. Ossang; *W:* F.J. Ossang; *C:* Remy Chevrin.

Dr. Christian Meets the Women ½ **1940** This entry in the "Dr. Christian" series of films has the small-town physician once again exposing a con man trying to filch the townspeople. **63m/B VHS, 8mm.** Jean Hersholt, Edgar Kennedy, Rod La Rocque, Dorothy Lovett, Veda Ann Borg; *D:* William McGann.

Dr. Cyclops ½ **1940** The famous early Technicolor fantasia about a mad scientist miniaturizing a group of explorers who happen upon his jungle lab. Landmark F/X and a slow-moving story. **76m/C VHS.** Albert Dekker, Janice Logan, Victor Kilian, Thomas Coley, Charles Halton, Frank Yaconelli, Paul Fix, Frank Reicher; *D:* Ernest B. Schoedsack; *W:* Tom Kilpatrick; *C:* Winton C. Hoch, Henry Sharp; *M:* Gerard Carbonara, Albert Hay Malotte, Ernst Toch.

Dr. Death, Seeker of Souls **1973 (R)** Evil doctor discovers a process for transmigrating his soul into the bodies of people he murdered 1000 years ago. Now he seeks to revive his wife. Final role for 77-year-old "Stooge" Moe Howard. **93m/C VHS.** John Considine, Barry Coe, Cheryl Miller, Stewart Moss, Leon Askin, Jo Morrow, Florence Marly, Sivi Aberg, Athena Lorde, Moe Howard; *D:* Eddie Saeta.

Doctor Detroit **1983 (R)** Aykroyd is funny in thin film, portraying a meek college professor who gets involved with prostitutes and the mob, under the alias "Dr. Detroit." Aykroyd later married actress Donna Dixon, whom he worked with on this film. Features music by Devo, James Brown, and Pattie Brooks. **91m/C VHS.** Dan Aykroyd, Howard Hesseman, Donna Dixon, T.K. Carter, Lynn Whitfield, Lydia Lei, Fran Drescher, Kate Murtagh, George Furth, Andrew Duggan, James Brown, Glenne Headly; *D:* Michael Pressman; *W:* Carl Gottlieb, Robert Boris; *M:* Lalo Schifrin.

Doctor Dolittle **1967** An adventure about a 19th century English doctor who dreams of teaching animals to speak to him. Realistic premise suffers from poor script. Based on Hugh Lofting's acclaimed stories. ♫Doctor Dolittle; My Friend the Doctor; Talk to the Animals; I've Never Seen Anything Like It; Beautiful Things; When I Look in Your Eyes; After Today; Fabulous Places; Where Are the Words?. **151m/C VHS, DVD, Wide.** Rex Harrison, Samantha Eggar, Anthony Newley, Richard Attenborough, Geoffrey Holder, Peter Bull; *D:* Richard Fleischer; *W:* Leslie Bricusse; *C:* Robert L. Surtees; *M:* Leslie Bricusse. Oscars '67: Song ("Talk to the Animals"), Visual FX; Golden Globes '68: Support. Actor (Attenborough).

Dr. Dolittle ½ **1998 (PG-13)** Loose non-musical adaption of the 1967 movie has Eddie Murphy playing straight man to a group of furry friends voiced by the likes of Chris Rock, Garry Shandling and Albert Brooks. He is reduced to reacting lamely, and is upstaged throughout by the wisecracking critters created by Jim Henson's Creature Shop. Fellow humans Dr. Weller (Platt) and Calloway (Boyle) are shallow villains created to prop up a shaky plot involving the corporate takeover of Dolittle's vet clinic. May contain a bit too much bathroom humor for some family tastes. No animals were harmed during the making of this movie, but there was probably cruel and unusual treatment of the interns involving pooper-scoopers. **85m/C VHS, DVD.** Eddie Murphy, Oliver Platt, Peter Boyle, Jeffrey Tambor, Ossie Davis, Richard Schiff, Kyla Pratt, Raven-Symone, Steven Gilborn; *D:* Betty Thomas; *W:* Nat Mauldin, Larry Levin; *C:* Russell Boyd; *M:* Richard Gibbs; *V:* Julie Kavner, Albert Brooks, Chris Rock, John Leguizamo, Garry Shandling, Norm MacDonald, Reni Santoni, Paul (Pee-wee Herman) Reubens, Gilbert Gottfried.

Dr. Dolittle 2 **2001 (PG)** The good doctor (Murphy) returns, along with his furry talking friends, who persuade him to save their forest from human developers. The vet must also find a mate for an endangered Pacific Western bear, but the only candidate is Archie (Zahn), a circus performer who has to be taught how to survive in the wilderness. Gastrointestinal and other bodily functions dominate the humor, and a subplot involving Dolittle's moody teenage daughter (Raven-Symone) nearly undoes the charm, but it's passable entertainment. Add half a bone if you're under 12 years old for this flatulence-obsessed outing. **87m/C VHS, DVD, Wide.** *US* Eddie Murphy, Jeffrey Jones, Kevin Pollak, Raven-Symone, Kyla Pratt, Kristen Wilson, Zane R. (Li'l' Zane) Copeland Jr., Andy Richter; *D:* Steve Carr; *W:* Larry Levin; *C:* Daryn Okada; *M:* David Newman; *V:* Norm MacDonald, Lisa Kudrow, Steve Zahn, Mike Epps, Michael Rapaport, Jacob Vargas, Isaac Hayes, Andy Dick, Joey Lauren Adams, Richard Sarafian.

Doctor Faustus ½ **1968** A stilted, stagy, but well-meaning adaptation of the Christopher Marlowe classic about Faust, who sold his soul to the devil for youth and the love of Helen of Troy. **93m/C VHS.** Richard Burton, Andreas Teuber, Elizabeth Taylor, Ian Marter; *D:* Richard Burton, Nevill Coghill.

Dr. Frankenstein's Castle of Freaks **1974 (PG)** Dr. Frankenstein and his dwarf assistant reanimate a few Neanderthals that are terrorizing a nearby Rumanian village. **90m/C VHS, DVD.** *IT* Rossano Brazzi, Michael Dunn, Edmund Purdom, Christiane Royce, Simone Blondell; *D:* Robert (Dick Randall) Oliver; *W:* William Rose, Mark Smith, Robert Spano; *C:* Mario Mancini.

Dr. Giggles **1992 (R)** Drake plays the psycho-genius Dr. Giggles, an escaped mental patient who sets out to avenge the death of his psycho-genius father (dementia runs in the family). He returns to his family home to procure the necessary medical instruments, most notably a hypodermic needle, and starts killing people—on screen with the tools and in the audience with remarkably stupid one-liners. Opening scenes are especially mired in gore. **96m/C VHS, DVD, Wide.** Larry Drake, Holly Marie Combs, Glenn Quinn, Keith Diamond, Cliff DeYoung; *D:* Manny Coto; *W:* Manny Coto, Graeme Whifler; *C:* Rob Draper; *M:* Brian May.

Dr. Goldfoot and the Bikini Machine **1966** A mad scientist employs gorgeous female robots to seduce the wealthy and powerful, thereby allowing him to take over the world. Title song by the Supremes. **90m/C VHS, DVD, Wide.** Vincent Price, Frankie Avalon, Dwayne Hickman, Annette Funicello, Susan Hart, Kay Elkhardt, Fred Clark, Deanna Lund, Deborah Walley; *D:* Norman Taurog; *M:* Les Baxter.

Dr. Hackenstein ½ **1988 (R)** A doctor tries to revive his wife by "borrowing" parts from unexpected (and unsuspecting) guests. **88m/C VHS.** David Muir, Stacy Travis, Catherine Davis Cox, Dyanne DiRosario, Anne Ramsey, Logan Ramsey; *D:* Richard Clark.

Dr. Heckyl and Mr. Hype **1980 (R)** A naughty, comical version of the Jekyll and Hyde story. Exuberantly wicked performances from Reed and Coogan; stellar cast of "B" veterans. **100m/C VHS.** Oliver Reed, Sunny Johnson, Maia Danzinger, Mel Welles, Virgil Frye, Kedrick Wolfe, Jackie Coogan, Corinne Calvet, Dick Miller, Lucretia Love; *D:* Charles B. Griffith; *W:* Charles B. Griffith; *M:* Richard Band.

Doctor in Distress ½ **1963** Aging chief surgeon falls in love for the first time. His assistant tries to further the romance as well as his own love life. Comedic fourth in the six-film "Doctor" series. **102m/C VHS.** *GB* Dirk Bogarde, James Robertson Justice, Leo McKern, Samantha Eggar; *D:* Ralph Thomas.

Doctor in the House ½ **1953** Four medical student/roommates seek only to examine lovely women and make lots of cash. In the process, they are also tempted by the evils of drink, but rally to make their grades. A riotous British comedy with marvelous performances all around. Led to six sequels and a TV series. **92m/C VHS.** *GB* Dirk Bogarde, Muriel Pavlow, Kenneth More, Donald Sinden, Kay Kendall, James Robertson Justice, Donald Houston, Geoffrey Keen, George Coulouris, Shirley Eaton, Joan Hickson, Richard Wattis; *D:* Ralph Thomas. British Acad. '54: Actor (More).

Dr. Jekyll and Ms. Hyde ½ **1995 (PG-13)** Chemist Richard Jacks (Daly) stumbles across the secret formula of great-grandad Dr. Jekyll and, after trying to improve the potion, he finds himself transformed into wicked woman Helen Hyde (Young). Cheap cross-gender gags abound. **89m/C VHS.** Timothy Daly, Sean Young, Lysette Anthony, Stephen Tobolowsky, Harvey Fierstein, Polly Bergen, Stephen Shellen; *D:* David F. Price; *W:* William Davies, William Osborne, Tim John, Oliver Butcher; *C:* Tom Priestley; *M:* Mark McKenzie.

Dr. Jekyll and Mr. Hyde **1920** The first American film version of Robert Louis Stevenson's horror tale about a doctor's experiments that lead to his developing good and evil sides to his personality. Silent. Kino Video's edition also contains the rarely seen 1911 version of the film, as well as scenes from a different 1920 version. **96m/B VHS, DVD.** John Barrymore, Martha Mansfield, Brandon Hurst, Charles Lane, J. Malcolm Dunn, Nita Naldi, Louis Wolheim; *D:* John S. Robertson; *W:* Clara Beranger; *C:* Karl Struss, Roy F. Overbaugh.

Dr. Jekyll and Mr. Hyde **1932** The hallucinatory, feverish classic version of the Robert Louis Stevenson story, in which the good doctor becomes addicted to the formula that turns him into a sadistic beast. Upright Dr. Jekyll (March) has a genteel fiance, Muriel (Hobart), while twisted alter-ego Hyde delights in torturing barmaid Ivy (Hopkins)—the bond between violence and sexuality in these scenes is highly charged. Possibly Mamoulian's and March's best work, and a masterpiece of subversive, pseudo-Freudian creepiness. Eighteen minutes from the original version, lost until recently, have been restored, including the infamous whipping scene. **96m/B VHS.** Fredric March, Miriam Hopkins, Halliwell Hobbes, Rose Hobart, Holmes Herbert, Edgar Norton; *D:* Rouben Mamoulian; *W:* Samuel Hoffenstein, Percy Heath; *C:* Karl Struss. Oscars '32: Actor (March); Venice Film Fest. '31: Actor (March).

Dr. Jekyll and Mr. Hyde **1941** Strangely cast adaptation of the Robert Louis Stevenson story about a doctor's experiment on himself to separate good and evil. **113m/B VHS.** Spencer Tracy, Ingrid Bergman, Lana Turner, Donald Crisp, Ian Hunter, Barton MacLane, Sara Allgood, Billy Bevan; *D:* Victor Fleming; *W:* John Lee Mahin; *C:* Joseph Ruttenberg; *M:* Franz Waxman.

Dr. Jekyll and Mr. Hyde *The Strange Case of Dr. Jekyll and Mr. Hyde* **1968** Yet another production of Robert Louis Stevenson's classic story of a split-personality. **90m/C VHS.** Jack Palance, Denholm Elliott, Tessie O'Shea, Oscar Homolka, Torin Thatcher; *D:* Charles Jarrott. **TV**

Dr. Jekyll and Mr. Hyde **1973** Dr. Jekyll discovers a potion that turns him into the sinister Mr. Hyde. Based on the classic story by Robert Louis Stevenson. **90m/C VHS.** Kirk Douglas, Michael Redgrave, Susan George, Donald Pleasence; *D:* David Winters.

Dr. Jekyll & Mr. Hyde **1999 (R)** Henry Jekyll (Baldwin) is a successful surgeon who is traveling to Hong Kong on his honeymoon. But shortly after his arrival, both he and his bride are killed in an explosion during a gang war. However, Henry is resurrected by Chinese healer Dr. Chau, although the potion he must take alters him physically and mentally. Henry only seeks revenge but he learns that his arrival was predestined and his fate is to become the legendary fighter known as the White Dragon. Obviously has little or nothing to do with the Robert Louis Stevenson story. **96m/C VHS, DVD.** *CA AU* Adam Baldwin, Steve Bastoni, Chang Tseng, Jason Chong, Richard Chong, Kira Clavel, Karen Cliche; *D:* Colin Budds; *W:* Peter M. Lenkov; *C:* Mark Wareham; *M:* Garry McDonald. **VIDEO**

Dr. Jekyll and Sister Hyde ½ **1971 (R)** A tongue-in-cheek variation on the split-personality theme, which has the good doctor transforming himself into a sultry, knife-wielding woman who kills prostitutes. **94m/C VHS, DVD, Wide.** *GB* Ralph Bates, Martine Beswick, Gerald Sim; *D:* Roy Ward Baker; *W:* Brian Clemens; *C:* Norman Warwick; *M:* Philip Martell, David Whitaker.

Dr. Jekyll and the Wolfman *Dr. Jekyll y el Hombre Lobo; Dr. Jekyll vs. the Werewolf* **1971 (R)** Naschy's sixth stint as El Hombre Lobo. This time he visits a mysterious doctor in search of a cure but ends up turning into Mr. Hyde, a man who likes to torture women. **85m/C VHS.** *SP* Paul (Jacinto Molina) Naschy, Shirley Corrigan, Jack Taylor, Barta Barry, Luis Induni, Mirta Miller, Jacinto (Jack) Molina; *D:* Leon Klimovsky; *W:* Jacinto (Jack) Molina; *C:* Francisco Fraile.

Dr. Jekyll's Dungeon of Death **1982 (R)** Dr. Jekyll and his lobotomized sister, Hilda, scour the streets of San Francisco looking for human blood to recreate his great-grandfather's secret serum. **90m/C VHS.** James Mathers, Dawn Carver Kelly, John Kearney, Jake Pearson; *D:* James Wood.

Dr. Kildare's Strange Case **1940** Dr. Kildare administers a daring treatment to a man suffering from a mental disorder of a dangerous nature. One in the film series. **76m/B VHS.** Lew Ayres, Lionel Barrymore, Laraine Day; *D:* Harold Bucquet.

Dr. Mabuse, The Gambler ½ *Doktor Mabuse der Spieler; Dr. Mabuse, Parts 1 & 2* **1922** The massive, two-part crime melodrama, introducing the raving mastermind/extortionist/villain to the world. The film follows Dr. Mabuse (Klein-Rogge) through his life of crime until he finally goes mad. Highly influential and inventive. Lang meant this to be a criticism of morally bankrupt post-WWI Germany. Lang also directed "The Crimes of Dr. Mabuse" (1932) and "The Thousand Eyes of Dr. Mabuse" (1960). **242m/B VHS, DVD.** *GE* Rudolf Klein-Rogge, Aud Egede Nissen, Alfred Abel, Gertrude Welcker, Lil Dagover, Paul Richter, Bernhard Goetzke; *D:* Fritz Lang; *W:* Fritz Lang, Thea von Harbou; *C:* Carl Hoffmann.

Dr. Mabuse vs. Scotland Yard ½ **1964** A sequel to the Fritz Lang classics, this film features the arch-criminal attempting to take over the world with a mind-controlling camera. **90m/B VHS.** *GE* Sabine Bethmann, Peter Van Eyck; *D:* Paul May.

Doctor Mordrid: Master of the Unknown **1990 (R)** Two immensely powerful sorcerers from the 4th dimension cross over into present time with two very different missions—one wants to destroy the Earth, one wants to save it. **102m/C VHS.** Jeffrey Combs, Yvette Nipar, Jay Acovone, Brian Thompson; *D:* Albert Band, Charles Band; *M:* Richard Band.

Dr. No **1962 (PG)** The world is introduced to British secret agent 007, James Bond, when it is discovered that mad scientist Dr. No (Wiseman) is sabotaging rocket launchings from his hideout in Jamaica. The first 007 film is far less glitzy than any of its successors but boasts the sexiest "Bond girl" of them all in Andress as Honey Ryder who walks out of the surf in a white bikini, and promptly made stars of her and Connery. **111m/C VHS, DVD, Wide.** *GB* Sean Connery, Ursula Andress, Joseph Wiseman, Jack Lord, Zena Marshall, Eunice Gayson, Margaret LeWars, John Kitzmiller, Lois Maxwell, Bernard Lee, Anthony Dawson; ***D:*** Terence Young; ***W:*** Johanna Harwood, Richard Maibaum, Berkely Mather; ***C:*** Ted Moore; ***M:*** John Barry.

Doctor of Doom woof! *Wrestling Women vs. the Aztec Ape* **1962** An unclassifiable epic wherein female wrestlers battle a mad doctor and his Aztec robot gorilla. Dubbed badly, of course. Much anticipated follow-up to "Wrestling Women vs. the Aztec Mummy." **111m/C VHS, DVD.** *MX* Elizabeth Campbell, Lorena Velazquez, Armando Silvestre, Roberto Canedo, Chucho Salinas, Sonia Infante; ***D:*** Rene Cardona Sr.; ***W:*** Alfredo Salazar; ***C:*** Enrique Wallace; ***M:*** Antonio Diaz Conde.

Dr. Orloff's Invisible Horror 🦴½ **1972** In this horror film, Dr. Orloff creates an invisible ape-monster that escapes and goes on a rampage. **?m/C VHS.** *FR SP* Howard Vernon; ***D:*** Pierre Chevalier; ***W:*** Pierre Chevalier.

Dr. Orloff's Monster woof! **1964** As if "The Awful Dr. Orloff" wasn't awful enough, the doctor is back, this time eliminating his enemies with his trusty killer robot. Awful awful. **88m/B VHS, DVD, Wide.** *SP* Jose Rubio, Agnes Spaak; ***D:*** Jess (Jesus) Franco; ***C:*** Alfonso Nieva.

Dr. Otto & the Riddle of the Gloom Beam 🦴½ **1986 (PG)** Ernest is in your face again. Fresh from the TV commercials featuring "Ernest" comes Varney playing a villain out to wreck the global economy. He also plays all the other characters, too. Way bizarre, "Know whut I mean?" **92m/C VHS.** Jim Varney; ***D:*** John R. Cherry III.

Dr. Petiot 🦴🦴 *Le Docteur Petiot* **1990** Based on the true life story of a French WWII doctor who promised to smuggle Jews to freedom but instead killed them for their money and possessions. He was executed in 1946—accused of 60 murders and convicted of 27. The gruesome details are left to the imagination rather than shown. In French with subtitles. **102m/C VHS.** *FR* Michel Serrault, Berangere Bonvoisin, Aurore Prieto, Nita Klein, Dominique Marcas, Andre Lacombe, Pierre Romans, Zbigniew Horoks, Claude Degliame, Martine Montgermont, Nini Crepon, Andre Julien, Andre Chaumeau, Axel Bogousslavsky, Maxime Collion, Nadege Boscher, Jean Dautremay, Michel Hart; ***D:*** Christian de Chalonge; ***W:*** Christian de Chalonge, Dominique Garnier; ***C:*** Patrick Blossier; ***M:*** Michel Portal.

Doctor Phibes Rises Again 🦴🦴½ **1972 (PG)** The despicable doctor contines his quest to revive his beloved wife. Fun, superior sequel to "The Abominable Dr. Phibes." **89m/C VHS, DVD, Wide.** *GB* Vincent Price, Robert Quarry, Peter Cushing, Beryl Reid, Hugh Griffith, Terry-Thomas, Valli Kemp, Peter Jeffrey, Fiona Lewis, Caroline Munro; ***D:*** Robert Fuest; ***W:*** Robert Fuest, Robert Blees; ***C:*** Alex Thomson; ***M:*** John Gale.

Doctor Satan's Robot 🦴🦴½ **1940** Indestructible robot is battled by insane Dr. Satan in reedited serial, "Mysterious Dr. Satan." **100m/B VHS.** Eduardo Ciannelli, Robert Wilcox, William "Billy" Newell, Ella Neal; ***D:*** William Witney, John English.

Dr. Seuss' How the Grinch Stole Christmas 🦴🦴½ *How the Grinch Stole Christmas; The Grinch* **2000 (PG)** If you've seen the cartoon, then you know it was padded. Just think of the stuff that Ron Howard added!/A new plot line here, an embellishment there, all Carreyed by a big star in green skin and hair./Crass Whos are shown doing frantic Yule shopping, and decoration-envy keeps each neighbor hopping./This anti-shop message is curiously told, considering the junk that this film clearly sold./ Cindy Lou Who loses her Christmastime zest, and starts to research the town's Yuletide pest./In a flashback it's shown why the Grinch is so mean, and a love interest is added from when he's a teen./He's elected Cheermeister of the holiday season; but again leaves bitter, and with good Grinchy reason./Mayor May Who, his rival for Martha May's hand, repeats an insult about too-active glands./The stage is now set for his Grinchy attacks, assisted by his trusty reindeer/dog Max./Though he gave back Christmas for all the Whos' sakes, the Grinch got away with huge box office takes./Young tots may think that this Grinch is too scary, but big kids will like the antics of Carrey./Fair holiday flick, even though the plot thins. Narrated by Sir Anthony Hopkins. **102m/C VHS, DVD.** Jim Carrey, Jeffrey Tambor, Christine Baranski, Taylor Momsen, Molly Shannon, Josh Ryan Evans, Clint Howard, Bill Irwin; ***D:*** Ron Howard; ***W:*** Jeffrey Price, Peter S. Seaman; ***C:*** Don Peterman; ***M:*** James Horner; ***Nar:*** Anthony Hopkins.

Dr. Strange 🦴½ **1978** TV pilot based upon the Marvel Comics character who, with the help of a sorcerer, practices witchcraft in order to fight evil. **94m/C VHS.** Peter Hooten, Clyde Kusatsu, Jessica Walter, Eddie Benton, John Mills; ***D:*** Philip DeGuere. **TV**

Dr. Strangelove, or: How I Learned to Stop Worrying and Love the Bomb 🦴🦴🦴🦴 **1964** Sellers plays a tour-de-force triple role in Kubrick's classic black anti-war comedy. While a U.S. President (Sellers) deals with the Russian situation, a crazed general (Hayden) implements a plan to drop the A-bomb on the Soviets. Famous for Pickens' wild ride on the bomb, Hayden's character's "purity of essence" philosophy, Scott's gumchewing militarist, a soft-drink vending machine dispute, and countless other scenes. Based on the novel "Red Alert" by Peter George. **93m/B VHS, DVD, Wide.** *GB* Peter Sellers, George C. Scott, Sterling Hayden, Keenan Wynn, Slim Pickens, James Earl Jones, Peter Bull, Tracy Reed, Shane Rimmer, Glenn Beck, Gordon Tanner, Frank Berry, Jack Creley; ***D:*** Stanley Kubrick; ***W:*** Stanley Kubrick, Terry Southern, Peter George; ***C:*** Gilbert Taylor; ***M:*** Laurie Johnson. AFI '98: Top 100; British Acad. '64: Film, Natl. Film Reg. '89;; N.Y. Film Critics '64: Director (Kubrick).

Dr. Syn 🦴🦴 **1937** The story of a seemingly respectable vicar of Dymchurch who is really a former pirate. The last film of George Arliss. **90m/B VHS.** *GB* George Arliss, Margaret Lockwood, John Loder; ***D:*** Roy William Neill.

Dr. Syn, Alias the Scarecrow 🦴🦴½ **1964 (G)** A mild-mannered minister is, in reality, a smuggler and pirate avenging King George III's injustices upon the English people. Originally broadcast in three parts on the Disney TV show. **129m/C VHS.** Patrick McGoohan, George Cole, Tony Britton, Michael Hordern, Geoffrey Keen, Kay Cole; ***D:*** James Neilson. **TV**

Dr. T & the Women 🦴🦴🦴 **2000 (R)** Gere stars as Dr. Sullivan Travis, a charming and sensitive gynecologist to the affluent women of Dallas, Texas. Yet despite his respect for and adoration of the women in his life, Dr. T, as he is known, cannot truly fathom their complexity. And none are more baffling to him than those closest to him—his wife (Fawcett), who is slowly descending into mental illness, and his daughters (Hudson and Reid). Director Altman has set his sights on ordinary human weaknesses and shortcomings here, staying away from the social commentary and cynicism of some of his earlier films, and often hits his target with a sweet and humorous note. Gere's charm and mannerisms fit the doctor to a "T," while Dern, Hunt, and Long put in good performances as well. Screenwriter Ann Rapp also collaborated with Altman on his previous film, "Cookie's Fortune." **122m/C VHS, DVD, Wide.** Richard Gere, Farrah Fawcett, Kate Hudson, Helen Hunt, Lee Grant, Liv Tyler, Shelley Long, Laura Dern, Tara Reid, Andy Richter, Matt Malloy, Robert Hays, Janine Turner; ***D:*** Robert Altman; ***W:*** Anne Rapp; ***C:*** Jan Kiesser; ***M:*** Lyle Lovett.

Doctor Takes a Wife 🦴🦴🦴 **1940** A fast, fun screwball comedy wherein two ill-matched career people are forced via a publicity mix-up to fake being married. **89m/B VHS.** Ray Milland, Loretta Young, Reginald Gardiner, Gail Patrick, Edmund Gwenn, George Metaxa, Charles Halton; ***D:*** Alexander Hall; ***W:*** George Seaton.

Dr. Tarr's Torture Dungeon woof! *Dr. Jekyll's Dungeon of Darkness; Mansion of Madness* **1975 (R)** A mysterious man is sent to the forest to investigate the bizarre behavior of Dr. Tarr who runs a torture asylum. **90m/C VHS.** *MX* Claudio Brook, Ellen Sherman, Robert Dumont; ***D:*** Juan Lopez Moctezuma; ***W:*** Carlos Illescas.

Dr. Terror's House of Horrors 🦴🦴½ *The Blood Suckers* **1965** On a train, six traveling companions have their fortunes told by a mysterious doctor. Little do they realize that their final destination has changed. Creepy and suspenseful, especially the severed-hand chase sequence. Amazingly, Christopher Lee and Peter Cushing manage to appear in the movie but not the vampire story. **92m/C VHS.** *GB* Christopher Lee, Peter Cushing, Donald Sutherland, Roy Castle, Neil McCallum, Max Adrian, Ann Bell, Michael Gough; ***D:*** Freddie Francis; ***W:*** Milton Subotsky; ***C:*** Alan Hume; ***M:*** Elisabeth Lutyens.

Doctor Who 🦴🦴½ **1996** The late British sci-fi series, which ended in 1989, has been resurrected in this TV movie. The TARDIS is forced down in 1999 San Francisco and renegade Time Lord The Master's sluglike remains escape from the Doctor (McCoy) and into a temporary host body (Roberts). Meanwhile, the Doctor's been hospitalized and a botched operation by Dr. Grace Holloway (Ashbrook) leaves him clinically dead—until he manages to regenerate once again (as McGann). With Grace's help, the Doctor tries to stop his enemy from destroying the world on New Year's Eve in a plot that will also give the Master the Doctor's body as his new home. Production design and special effects are lavish (particularly in relation to the cheesiness of the series). **?m/C VHS.** *GB CA* Paul McGann, Eric Roberts, Daphne Ashbrook, Yee Jee Tso, Sylvester McCoy; ***D:*** Geoffrey Sax; ***W:*** Matthew Jacobs; ***C:*** Glen MacPherson; ***M:*** John Debney.

Doctor X 🦴🦴½ **1932** An armless mad scientist uses a formula for "synthetic flesh" to grow temporary limbs and commit murder. A classic, rarely seen horror oldie, famous for its very early use of two-color Technicolor. **77m/C VHS.** Lionel Atwill, Fay Wray, Lee Tracy, Preston Foster, Arthur Edmund Carewe, Leila Bennett, Mae Busch; ***D:*** Michael Curtiz; ***W:*** Earl Baldwin, Robert Tasker; ***C:*** Ray Rennahan, Richard Towers.

Doctor Zhivago 🦴🦴🦴 **1965 (PG-13)** Sweeping adaptation of the Nobel Prize-winning Boris Pasternak novel. An innocent Russian poet-intellectual is caught in the furor and chaos of the Bolshevik Revolution. Essentially a poignant love story filmed as a historical epic. Panoramic film popularized the song "Lara's Theme." Overlong, with often disappointing performances, but gorgeous scenery. Lean was more successful in "Lawrence of Arabia," where there was less need for ensemble acting. **197m/C VHS, DVD, Wide.** Omar Sharif, Julie Christie, Geraldine Chaplin, Rod Steiger, Alec Guinness, Klaus Kinski, Ralph Richardson, Rita Tushingham, Siobhan McKenna, Tom Courtenay, Bernard Kay, Gerard Tichy, Noel Willman, Geoffrey Keen, Adrienne Corri, Jack MacGowran, Mark Eden, Erik Chitty, Peter Madden, Jose Maria Caffarell, Jeffrey Rockland, Wolf Frees, Lucy Westmore; ***D:*** David Lean; ***W:*** Robert Bolt; ***C:*** Frederick A. (Freddie) Young; ***M:*** Maurice Jarre. Oscars '65: Adapt. Screenplay, Art Dir./Set Dec., Color, Color Cinematog., Costume Des. (C), Orig. Score; AFI '98: Top 100; Golden Globes '66: Actor—Drama (Sharif), Director (Lean), Film—Drama, Screenplay, Score; Natl. Bd. of Review '65: Actress (Christie).

Doctors and Nurses 🦴🦴 **1982** A children's satire of soap operas wherein the adults play the children and vice-versa. **90m/C VHS.** Rebecca Rigg, Drew Forsythe, Graeme Blundell; ***D:*** Maurice Murphy.

Doctors' Wives 🦴½ **1970 (R)** An adaptation of the Frank Slaughter potboiler about a large city hospital's doctors, nurses, and their respective spouses, with plenty of affairs, medical traumas, and betrayals. **102m/C VHS.** Dyan Cannon, Richard Crenna, Gene Hackman, Carroll O'Connor, Rachel Roberts, Janice Rule, Diana Sands, Ralph Bellamy, John Colicos; ***D:*** George Schaefer; ***W:*** Daniel Taradash; ***C:*** Charles B(ryant) Lang Jr.; ***M:*** Elmer Bernstein.

Dodes 'ka-den 🦴🦴🦴½ *Clickety Clack* **1970** In this departure from his samurai-genre films, Kurosawa depicts a throng of fringe-dwelling Tokyo slum inhabitants in a semi-surreal manner. Fascinating presentation and content. **140m/C VHS.** *JP* Yoshitaka Zushi, Junzaburo Ban, Kiyoko Tange; ***D:*** Akira Kurosawa; ***W:*** Shinobu Hashimoto, Hideo Oguni, Akira Kurosawa; ***C:*** Takao Saito, Yasumichi Fukuzawa; ***M:*** Toru Takemitsu.

Dodge City 🦴🦴🦴 **1939** Flynn stars as Wade Hutton, a roving cattleman who becomes the sheriff of Dodge City. His job: to run a ruthless outlaw and his gang out of town. De Havilland serves as Flynn's love interest, as she did in many previous films. A broad and colorful shoot-em-up! **104m/C VHS.** Errol Flynn, Olivia de Havilland, Bruce Cabot, Ann Sheridan, Alan Hale, Frank McHugh, Victor Jory, Henry Travers, Charles Halton; ***D:*** Michael Curtiz; ***M:*** Max Steiner.

Dodsworth 🦴🦴🦴½ **1936** The lives of a self-made American tycoon and his wife are drastically changed when they take a tour of Europe. The success of their marriage seems questionable as they re-evaluate their lives. Huston excels as does the rest of the cast in this film, based upon the Sinclair Lewis novel. **101m/B VHS, DVD.** Walter Huston, David Niven, Paul Lukas, John Payne, Mary Astor, Ruth Chatterton, Maria Ouspenskaya, Charles Halton; ***D:*** William Wyler; ***W:*** Sidney Howard; ***C:*** Rudolph Mate; ***M:*** Alfred Newman. Natl. Film Reg. '90;; N.Y. Film Critics '36: Actor (Huston).

Does This Mean We're Married? 🦴🦴 **1990 (PG-13)** A stand-up comedian is trying to find success in the comedy clubs of Paris but without her green card she may soon be deported. She finds a sleazy marriage broker who fixes her up with a womanizing songwriter who needs money. As usual, immigration officials suspect that the marriage is a fake and the mismatched couple must live together to prove them wrong. **93m/C VHS.** Patsy Kensit, Stephane Freiss; ***D:*** Carol Wiseman.

Dog Day 🦴🦴½ *Canicule* **1983** An American traitor, who is on the lam from the government, and his cronies, takes refuge on a small farm. A surprise awaits him when the farmers come up with an unusual plan to bargain for his life. **101m/C VHS.** *FR* Lee Marvin, Miou-Miou, Victor Lanoux; ***D:*** Yves Boisset.

Dog Day Afternoon 🦴🦴🦴½ **1975 (R)** Based on a true story, this taut, yet fantastic thriller centers on a bi-sexual and his slow-witted buddy who rob a bank to obtain money to fund a sex change operation for the ringleader's lover. Pacino is breathtaking in his role as the frustrated robber, caught in a trap of his own devising. Very controversial for its language and subject matter when released, it nevertheless became a huge success. Director Lumet keeps up the pace, fills the screen with pathos without gross sentiment. **124m/C VHS, DVD, Wide.** Dominic Chianese, Al Pacino, John Cazale, Charles Durning, James Broderick, Chris Sarandon, Carol Kane, Lance Henriksen, Dick Williams; ***D:*** Sidney Lumet; ***W:*** Frank Pierson; ***C:*** Victor Kemper. Oscars '75: Orig. Screenplay; British Acad. '75: Actor (Pacino); Natl. Bd. of Review '75: Support. Actor (Durning); Writers Guild '75: Orig. Screenplay.

Dog Eat Dog 🦴 *Einer Frisst den Anderen; La Morte Vestita di Dollar* **1964** Centering on a heist scheme by Mitchell, this one has nothing to offer except Mansfield's attributes. **86m/B VHS, 8mm.** Cameron Mitchell, Jayne Mansfield, Isa Miranda; ***D:*** Ray Nazarro.

A Dog of Flanders 🦴🦴½ **1959** A young Dutch boy and his grandfather find a severely beaten dog and restore it to health. **96m/C VHS.** David Ladd, Donald Crisp, Theodore Bikel, Max Croiset, Monique Ahrens; ***D:*** James B. Clark.

A Dog of Flanders 🦴🦴 **1999 (PG)** Fifth screen version of Marie Louise de la Ramee's 1872 children's story is put to sleep by slow pacing and murky settings. Orphan Nello (Kissner) and his grandfather Jehan (Warden) find an abused dog and nurse it back to health. The boy and his dog team up to support the household as Jehan's health begins to fade. Nello is noticed sketching in the town square by artist Michel (Voight), who then befriends and encourages the boy. As his artistic gifts flower, he attempts to win his childhood sweetheart Aloise (Monet) over the protests of her father. The rather depressing climax of the original story is replaced by a brighter ending in an attempt to make the movie more child-friendly, but the uneven acting and accents won't even fool the kiddies. **100m/C VHS, DVD.** Jack Warden, Jon Voight, Jeremy James Kissner, Jesse James, Cheryl Ladd, Bruce McGill, Steven Hartley, Dirk Lavrysen, Andrew Bicknell, Antje De Boeck; ***D:*** Kevin Brodie; ***W:*** Robert Singer, Kevin Brodie; ***C:*** Walther Vanden Ende; ***M:*** Richard S. Friedman.

Dog Park 🦴🦴 **1998 (R)** Andy (Wilson) and Lorna (Henstridge) have only their doggy companions to keep them warm after their respective lovers take a hike. At least until they find each other while walking their pups. Not that the course of true love (or even dating) will run smoothly. Pleasant enough romantic comedy but Henstridge seems out of her element. **91m/C VHS.** *CA* Luke Wilson, Natasha Henstridge, Janeane Garofalo, Bruce McCulloch, Kathleen Robertson, Kristen Lehman, Mark McKinney, Gordon Currie, Amie Carey, Harland Williams; ***D:*** Bruce McCulloch; ***W:*** Bruce McCulloch; ***C:*** David Makin; ***M:*** Craig Northey. Genie '99: Support. Actor (McKinney).

Dog Pound Shuffle 🦴🦴🦴 *Spot* **1975 (PG)** Two drifters form a new song-and-dance act in order to raise the funds necessary to win their dog's freedom from the pound. Charming Canadian production. **98m/C VHS.** *CA* Ron Moody, David Soul; ***D:*** Jeffrey Bloom; ***W:*** Jeffrey Bloom.

Dog Star Man 🦴🦴🦴 **1964** The silent epic by the dean of experimental American film depicts man's spiritual and physical conflicts through Brakhage's characteristically freeform collage techniques. **78m/C VHS.** ***D:*** Stan Brakhage. Natl. Film Reg. '92.

The Dog Who Stopped the War 🦴🦴 **1984 (G)** A Canadian children's film about a dog who puts a halt to an escalating snowball fight between rival gangs. **90m/C VHS.** *CA* ***D:*** Andre Melancon.

Dogfight 🦴🦴🦴 **1991 (R)** It's 1963 and a baby-faced Marine and his buddies are spending their last night in San Francisco before leaving the U.S. for a tour of duty in Vietnam. They agree to throw a "dogfight," a competition to see who can bring the ugliest date to a party. Birdlace (Phoenix) chooses Taylor, a shy, average-looking waitress who dreams of becoming a folk singer and realizes too late that she doesn't deserve the treatment he's about to subject her to. This quiet film didn't see a wide release, but is worth renting due to an above average script which is held up by the splendid performances of Phoenix and Taylor. **94m/C VHS, 8mm.** River Phoenix, Lili Taylor, Richard Panebianco, Anthony Clark, Mitchell Whitfield, Elizabeth (E.G. Dailey) Daily, Holly Near, Brendan Fraser, Peg Phillips; ***D:*** Nancy Savoca; ***W:*** Bob Comfort.

The Dogfighters 🦴🦴 **1995 (R)** Ex-Air Force pilot Rowdy Wells (Davi) is blackmailed into trying to destroy a plutonium plant in an eastern European country. That is, if Rowdy can survive an air battle with nemisis Lothar Krasna (Godunov). Small budget is reflected in the mediocre aerial sequences. **96m/C VHS.** Robert Davi, Alexander Godunov, Ben Gazzara, Lara Harris; ***D:*** Barry Zetlin; ***W:*** Sean Smith, Anthony Stark; ***C:*** Levie Isaacks; ***M:*** Jimmie Haskell.

Dogma 🦴🦴½ **1999 (R)** Smith packs a lot into his brave, controversial comedy on Catholicism and, as a Catholic himself, illustrates that he has some issues about his religion. He vents with a film that's both devilishly funny and agonizingly boring. A great cast does his dirty work, including Affleck and Damon as two cast out angels with a plan to re-enter heaven. Rock plays an angry apostle, Hayek is a muse turned stripper, and Rickman is the voice of God informing an abortion worker (Fiorentino) that she's to stop the angels. Rounding out the motley crew is Carlin as a cardinal. The first half is loaded with on-target jokes, but laughs are hard to find in the second hour, which falls victim to excessive religious yakety-schmakety. Smith's a talented screenwriter, unfortunately this time out, it's his directing that's really a sin. **125m/C VHS, DVD, Wide.** Ben Affleck, Matt Damon, Linda Fiorentino, Chris Rock, Salma Hayek, Jason Lee, George Carlin, Alan Rickman, Jason Mewes, Janeane Garofalo, Kevin Smith, Alanis Morissette, Bud Cort, Jeff Anderson, Guinevere Turner; ***D:*** Kevin Smith; ***W:*** Kevin Smith; ***C:*** Robert Yeoman; ***M:*** Howard Shore.

Dogs in Space 🦴🦴 **1987** A low-budget Australian film about a clique of aimless Melbourne rock kids in 1978, caught somewhere between post-hippiedom and punk, free love and heroin addiction. Acclaimed. Includes music by Hutchence, Brian Eno, Iggy Pop, and others. **109m/C VHS.** *AU* Michael Hutchence, Saskia Post, Nique Needles, Tony Helou, Deanna Bond; ***D:*** Richard Lowenstein; ***W:*** Richard Lowenstein.

Dogs of Hell 🦴½ **1983 (R)** The sheriff of an idyllic resort community must stop a pack of killer dogs from terrorizing the residents. **90m/C VHS.** Earl Owensby, Bill Gribble, Jerry Rushing; ***D:*** Worth Keeter.

The Dogs of War 🦴🦴½ **1981 (R)** A graphic depiction of a group of professional mercenaries, driven by nothing but their quest for wealth and power, hired to overthrow the dictator of a new West African nation. Has some weak moments which break up the continuity of the movie. Based on the novel by Frederick Forsyth. **102m/C VHS, DVD, Wide.** *GB* Christopher Walken, Tom Berenger, Colin Blakely, Paul Freeman, Hugh Millais, Victoria Tennant, JoBeth Williams; ***D:*** John Irvin; ***W:*** Gary De Vore; ***C:*** Jack Cardiff; ***M:*** Geoffrey Burgon.

Dogs: The Rise and Fall of an All-Girl Bookie Joint 🦴🦴 **1996** On the surface, this is a story about some twentysomething women who are bad at relationships and can't pay the rent. To solve one of their problems they turn their apartment into a bookie joint. However, underneath there is the story of the girl who has just lost her mother and needs money to pay for her funeral. The thread that weaves it all together is the drive to survive and rise above what life has given you, or sometimes what you give yourself. This is an indie, low-budget film and the acting and lighting reflect its limitations, but overall it is a good story with competent acting. **88m/C DVD.** Pam Columbus, Pam Gray, Eve Annenberg, Toby Huss, Leo Marks, Amedo D'Adamo; ***D:*** Eve Annenberg; ***W:*** Eve Annenberg; ***C:*** Wolfgang Held.

Dogtown 🦴🦴 **1997** Former beauty queen/cheerleader Dorothy Sternen feels trapped in her small town of Cuba, Missouri. Her longtime boyfriend Ezra Good is a bitter ex-athlete stuck in a dull job who sometimes gets violent. Then high school classmate Philip returns to town. Although he's a struggling actor, Philip is treated like a celebrity, and Dorothy starts giving him the eye. Tensions arise as they all realize how dissatisfied each of them are. **99m/C VHS, DVD.** Mary Stuart Masterson, Trevor St. John, Jon Favreau, Rory Cochrane, Karen Black, Natasha Gregson Wagner, Maureen McCormick, Harold Russell, John Livingston, Shawnee Smith; ***D:*** George Hickenlooper; ***W:*** George Hickenlooper; ***C:*** Kramer Morgenthau; ***M:*** Steve Stevens.

Dogwatch 🦴🦴 **1997 (R)** San Francisco police detective Charlie Falon (Elliott) tries to avenge his partner's murder but kills the wrong man. Then he learns dirty cops are behind the crime. Thriller takes the easy road by solving everything with violence. **100m/C VHS.** Sam Elliott, Esai Morales, Paul Sorvino, Dan Lauria, Richard Gilliland, Jessica Steen, Mimi (Meyer) Craven; ***D:*** John Langley; ***W:*** Martin Zurla; ***C:*** Robert Yeoman; ***M:*** Lennie Niehaus. **CABLE**

Doin' Time 🦴 **1985 (R)** At the John Dillinger Memorial Penitentiary, the inmates take over the prison under the supervision of warden "Mongo." Silliness prevails. **80m/C VHS.** Jeff Altman, Dey Young, Richard Mulligan, John Vernon, Colleen Camp, Melanie Chartoff, Graham Jarvis, Pat McCormick, Eddie Velez, Jimmie Walker, Judy Landers, Nicholas Worth, Mike Mazurki, Muhammad Ali, Melinda Fee, Francesca "Kitten" Natividad, Ron Palillo; ***D:*** George Mendeluk; ***W:*** George Mendeluk, Dee Caruso, Ron Zwang, Franelle Silver; ***M:*** Charles Fox.

Doin' Time on Planet Earth 🦴🦴½ **1988 (PG-13)** A young boy feels out of place with his family and is convinced by two strange people (aliens themselves?) that he is really an extraterrestrial. Amusing, aimless fun directed by the son of Walter Matthau. **83m/C VHS.** Adam West, Candice Azzara, Hugh O'Brian, Matt Adler, Timothy Patrick Murphy, Roddy McDowall, Maureen Stapleton, Andrea Thompson; ***D:*** Charles Matthau.

Doing Time for Patsy Cline 🦴🦴🦴 **1997** Humor and charm highlight this country music/road/jailhouse comedy. Hitchhiking, country music-loving teenager Ralph (Day) has a ticket for his dream trip to Nashville when he's picked up in a stolen Jag by drug-runner Boyd (Roxburgh) and the beautiful Patsy (Otto), who tells Ralph she was named for Patsy Cline. When the cops pull them over, Patsy gets away and Boyd lays all their crimes on the innocent Ralph. While the pair are in lockup, Ralph befriends three brothers who are equally interested in country tunes. This fractured fairytale does manage to come together and, of course, has a happy ending. **93m/C VHS.** *AU* Matt(hew) Day, Richard Roxburgh, Miranda Otto, Tom Long, Tony Barry, Kiri Paramore, Laurence Coy, Annie Byron, Roy Billing; ***D:*** Chris Kennedy; ***W:*** Chris Kennedy; ***C:*** Andrew Lennie; ***M:*** Peter Best. Australian Film Inst. '97: Actor (Roxburgh), Cinematog., Costume Des.

Dolemite 🦴½ **1975 (R)** An ex-con attempts to settle the score with some of his former inmates. He forms a band of kung-fu savvy ladies. Strange combination of action and comedy. **88m/C VHS, DVD.** Rudy Ray Moore, Jerry Jones, D'Urville Martin, Lady Reeds; ***D:*** D'Urville Martin; ***W:*** Jerry Jones; ***C:*** Nicholas Josef von Sternberg; ***M:*** Arthur Wright.

Dolemite 2: Human Tornado 🦴½ *The Human Tornado* **1976 (R)** Nobody ever said Moore was for everybody's taste. But, hey, when blaxploitation movies were the rage, Rudy the standup comic was out there rapping through a series of trashy movies that, when viewed today, have survived the test of time. This one's just as vile, violent, and sexist as the day it was released. When Rudy is surprised in bed with a white sheriff's wife, he flees and meets up with a madam and a house of kung-fu-skilled girls who are embroiled in a fight with a local mobster. **98m/C VHS, DVD.** Rudy Ray Moore, Lady Reeds, Ernie Hudson, Howard Jackson, Herb Graham, Jerry Jones, Jimmy Lynch; ***D:*** Cliff Roguemore; ***W:*** Jerry Jones; ***C:*** Fred Conde, Bob Wilson; ***M:*** Arthur Wright.

The Doll 🦴🦴 *La Poupee; He, She or It* **1962** A lonely night watchman happens upon two burglars and, in the chase, the thieves knock over a mannequin. The watchman reports the mannequin stolen, brings it home and begins to have conversations with it. Soon, the doll's needs cause him to steal jewelry and clothes, until his brutish neighbor discovers his secrets. In Swedish with English subtitles. **96m/B VHS.** *SW* Per Oscarsson, Gio Petre, Tor Isedal, Elsa Prawitz; ***D:*** Arne Mattson.

Doll Face 🦴🦴½ *Come Back to Me* **1946** Story of a stripper who wants to go legit and make it on Broadway. Film was adapted from the play "The Naked Genius" by tease queen Gypsy Rose Lee. ♫Dig You Later; Here Comes Heaven Again; Chico-Chico; Somebody's Walkin' In My Dreams; Red Hot and Beautiful. **80m/B VHS.** Vivian Blaine, Dennis O'Keefe, Perry Como, Carmen Miranda, Reed Hadley; ***D:*** Lewis Seiler.

The Doll Squad 🦴 *Hustler Squad* **1973 (PG)** Three voluptuous special agents fight an ex-CIA agent out to rule the world. **93m/C VHS, DVD, Wide.** Michael Ansara, Francine York, Anthony Eisley, John N. Carter, Rafael Campos, William Bagdad, Lisa Todd, Lillian Garrett, Herb Robbins, Tura Satana; ***D:*** Ted V. Mikels; ***W:*** Ted V. Mikels, Jack Pichesin, Pam Eddy; ***C:*** Anthony Salinas; ***M:*** Nicholas Carras.

Dollar 🦴🦴 **1938** The actress wife of an industrialist, convinced that he is having an affair, follows him to a ski lodge in attempt to catch him in the act. In Swedish with English subtitles. **74m/B VHS.** *SW* Georg Rydeberg, Ingrid Bergman, Kotti Chave, Tutta Rolf, Hakan Westergren, Elsa Burnett, Edvin Adolphson, Gosta Cederlund, Eric Rosen; ***D:*** Gustaf Molander.

Dollars 🦴🦴🦴 *The Heist* **1971 (R)** A bank employee and his dizzy call-girl assistant plan to steal the German facility's assets while installing its new security system. Lighthearted fun. **119m/C VHS.** Warren Beatty, Goldie Hawn, Gert Frobe, Scott Brady, Robert Webber; ***D:*** Richard Brooks; ***W:*** Richard Brooks; ***M:*** Quincy Jones.

The Dollmaker 🦴🦴½ **1984** Excellent adaptation of Harriette Arnow's novel. A strong-willed Kentucky mother of five helps move her family to Detroit in the 1940s. Petrie's direction moves the story along and creates a lovely period vision. **140m/C VHS.** Jane Fonda, Levon Helm, Geraldine Page, Amanda Plummer, Susan Kingsley; ***D:*** Daniel Petrie. **TV**

Dollman 🦴½ **1990 (R)** An ultra-tough cop from an Earth-like planet (even swear words are the same) crashes in the South Bronx—and on this world he's only 13 inches tall. The filmmakers squander a great premise and cast with bloody shootouts and a sequel-ready non-ending. **86m/C VHS.** Tim Thomerson, Jackie Earle Haley, Kamala Lopez, Humberto Ortiz, Nicholas Guest, Michael Halsey, Eugene Glazer, Judd Omen, Frank Collison, Vincent Klyn; ***D:*** Albert Pyun.

Dollman vs Demonic Toys 🦴🦴 **1993 (R)** Let's combine elements from three separate films and make one disgusting sequel: "Dollman," the 13-inch cop from the planet Arturus; his new girlfriend, Dollchick, who was shrunk to a diminutive 10 inches in "Bad Channels"; and tough cop Judith Grey, who's once again battling those loathsome playthings from "Demonic Toys." If you feel the need for a plot—Dollchick is kidnapped by Baby Doll and needs to be rescued. **84m/C VHS.** Tim Thomerson, Tracy Scoggins, Melissa Behr, Phil Brock, Phil Fondacaro; ***D:*** Charles Band; ***W:*** Craig Hamann; ***M:*** Richard Band.

The Dolls woof! **1983** A tropically located photographer recruits an area beauty into the fashion world with his winning smile and macho charm, only to learn native traditions forbid her to follow him. **96m/C VHS.** Tetchie Agbayani, Max Thayer, Carina Schally, Richard Seward; ***D:*** Hubert Frank.

Dolls 🦴🦴½ **1987 (R)** A group of people is stranded during a storm in an old, creepy mansion. As the night wears on, they are attacked by hundreds of antique dolls. Tongue-in-cheek. **77m/C VHS.** Ian Patrick Williams, Carolyn Purdy-Gordon, Carrie Lorraine, Stephen Lee, Guy Rolfe, Bunty Bailey, Cassie Stuart, Hilary Mason; ***D:*** Stuart Gordon; ***W:*** Ed Naha; ***M:*** Richard Band.

A Doll's House 🦴🦴½ **1959** An all-star cast is featured in this original TV production of Henrik Ibsen's classic play about an independent woman's quest for freedom in 19th-century Norway. **89m/B VHS.** Julie Harris, Christopher Plummer, Jason Robards Jr., Hume Cronyn, Eileen Heckart, Richard Thomas; ***D:*** George Schaefer. **TV**

A Doll's House 🦴🦴½ **1973 (G)** Fonda plays Nora, a subjugated 19th-century housewife who breaks free to establish herself as an individual. Based on Henrik Ibsen's classic play; some controversy regarding Fonda's interpretation of her role. **98m/C** Jane Fonda, Edward Fox, Trevor Howard, David Warner, Delphine Seyrig; ***D:*** Joseph Losey; ***W:*** Christopher Hampton; ***M:*** John Barry.

A Doll's House 🦴🦴🦴 **1989 (G)** A Canadian production of the Henrik Ibsen play about a Norwegian woman's search for independence. **96m/C VHS.** *CA* Claire Bloom, Anthony Hopkins, Ralph Richardson, Denholm Elliott, Anna Massey, Edith Evans; ***D:*** Patrick Garland.

Dolly Dearest 🦴½ **1992 (R)** Strange things start happening after an American family takes over a run-down Mexican doll factory. They create a new doll called "Dolly Dearest" with deadly results. In the same tradition as the "Chucky" series. **94m/C VHS.** Rip Torn, Sam Bottoms, Denise Crosby; ***D:*** Maria Lease.

The Dolly Sisters 🦴🦴½ **1946** Competent musical about sisters Jenny (Grable) and Rosie (Haver), who become turn-of-the-century vaudeville stars and also find romance. Good songs, extravagent costuming, fine support work, and the charms of the two leading actresses provide simple enjoyment. ♫I Can't Begin to Tell You; I'm Always Chasing Rainbows; Powder, Lipstick and Rouge; Give Me the Moonlight; On the Mississippi; We Have Been Around; Carolina In the Morning; Arrah Go On, I'm Gonna Go Back to Oregon; The Darktown Strutter's Ball. **114m/C VHS.** Betty Grable, June Haver, John Payne, Frank Latimore, S.Z. Sakall, Reginald Gardiner, Gene Sheldon, Sig Rumann; ***D:*** Irving Cummings; ***W:*** Marian Spitzer, John Larkin; ***C:*** Ernest Palmer.

Dolores Claiborne 🦴🦴🦴 **1994 (R)** Stephen King gets the Hollywood treatment again (the check cleared, King approved), with better results than previous outings (remember "Needful Things"?). Successful but neurotic New York journalist Selena (Leigh) confronts her troubled past when coarse, hard-talking mom Dolores (Bates) is accused of murdering her wealthy employer (Parfitt). Plummer is vengeful detective John Mackey who, like everyone else on the fictitious Maine island, believes Dolores murdered her husband 15 years before. Top-notch performances by Bates and Leigh highlight this sometimes manipulative tale. Straithairn is wonderfully despicable as the stereotypically deadbeat dad. **132m/C VHS, DVD.** Kathy Bates, Jennifer Jason Leigh, Christopher Plummer, Judy Parfitt, David Strathairn, John C. Reilly; ***D:*** Taylor Hackford; ***W:*** Tony Gilroy; ***C:*** Gabriel Beristain; ***M:*** Danny Elfman.

The Dolphin 🦴🦴½ **1987** A dolphin visits a Brazilian fishing village each full moon, turns himself into a man, and casts a spell of seduction over the women. Villagers are both enchanted and angered by the dolphin-man, since his presence creates desire in local women but scares fish from the waters. In Portuguese with English subtitles. **95m/C VHS.** *BR* Carlos Alberto Riccelli, Cassia Kiss, Ney Latorraca; ***D:*** Walter Lima Jr.; ***W:*** Walter Lima Jr.

Domestic Disturbance 🦴🦴 **2001 (PG-13)** Lame entry in the "evil step-parent" genre features Travolta as Frank, a hard-working boat builder who shares custody of his son Danny (O'Leary) with ex-wife Susan (Polo). Danny starts acting out by getting in trouble and lying after Susan gets involved with suave local businessman Rick (Vaughn). Although Danny is clued into Rick's dark side from the start, it takes the appearance of Ray (Buscemi), a sleazy hood from Rick's shady past, to awaken Frank's suspicion. When Danny hides in Rick's van and witnesses Ray's murder, nobody believes him except his dad. The stage is set for the "good dad" versus "bad dad" showdown, which is handled as clumsily and unbelievably as possible. Most of the performances seem listless, with the exception of Vaughn as the oily villain and O'Leary as the terrorized kid. **89m/C VHS, DVD, Wide.** *US* John Travolta, Vince Vaughn, Teri Polo, Matt O'Leary, Ruben Santiago-Hudson, Susan Floyd, Steve Buscemi, Angelica Torn; ***D:*** Harold Becker; ***W:*** Lewis Colick; ***C:*** Michael Seresin; ***M:*** Mark Mancina.

Dominick & Eugene 🦴🦴🦴 **1988 (PG-13)** Dominick is a little slow, but he makes a fair living as a garbageman—good enough to put his brother through medical school. Both men struggle with the other's faults and weaknesses, as they learn the meaning of family and friendship. Well-acted, especially by Hulce, never melodramatic or weak. **96m/C VHS, DVD, Wide.** Ray Liotta, Tom Hulce, Jamie Lee Curtis, Todd Graff, Bill Cobbs, David Strathairn; ***D:*** Robert M. Young; ***W:*** Alvin Sargent, Corey Blechman; ***C:*** Curtis Clark; ***M:*** Trevor Jones.

Dominion 🦴🦴½ **1994 (R)** Six buddies take off for a weekend hunting trip that turns deadly when a murderous hunter believes they've trespassed on his territory and begins stalking them. **98m/C VHS.** Michael (Mike) Papajohn, Brad Johnson, Brion James, Tim Thomerson, Woody Brown, Glenn Morshower, Richard Riehle, Geoffrey Blake; ***D:*** Michael Kehoe; ***W:*** Woody Brown, Michael Kehoe.

Dominique Is Dead 🦴🦴 **1979 (PG)** A woman is driven to suicide by her greedy husband; now someone is trying to drive him mad. A.K.A. "Dominique" and "Avenging Spirit." **95m/C VHS.** Cliff Robertson, Jean Simmons, Jenny Agutter, Simon Ward, Ron Moody; ***D:*** Michael Anderson Sr.

Domino 🦴 **1988 (R)** A beautiful woman and a mysterious guy link up for sex, murder and double-crosses. Dubbed. Tries to be arty and avant-garde, but only succeeds in being a piece of soft-core fluff. **95m/C VHS.** *IT* Brigitte Nielsen, Tomas Arana, Daniela Alzone; ***D:*** Ivana Massetti.

The Domino Principle 🦴½ *The Domino Killings* **1977 (R)** It's got nothing to do with pizza. Viet vet Hackman is a doltish convict sprung from the joint by a government organization to do some dirty work: working as a political assassin. Heavy-handed direction and lack of suspense make it less than it should be. **97m/C VHS.** Gene Hackman, Candice Bergen, Richard Widmark, Mickey Rooney, Edward Albert, Eli Wallach; ***D:*** Stanley Kramer; ***C:*** Fred W. Koenekamp; ***M:*** Billy Goldenberg.

Don Daredevil Rides Again 🦴 **1951** A greedy political boss tries to take over homesteaders' claims for their mineral rights. One settler adopts the identity of an ancestor (Don Daredevil), and a black mask, and becomes a frontier avenger. A 12-episode serial. **180m/B VHS.** Ken Curtis, Aline Towne, Roy Barcroft; ***D:*** Fred Brannon.

The Don Is Dead 🦴½ *Beautiful But Deadly* **1973 (R)** A violent Mafia saga wherein a love triangle interferes with Family business, resulting in gang wars. **96m/C VHS.** Anthony Quinn, Frederic Forrest, Robert Forster, Al Lettieri, Ina Balin, Angel Tompkins, Charles Cioffi; ***D:*** Richard Fleischer; ***W:*** Michael Butler; ***M:*** Jerry Goldsmith.

Don Juan 🦴🦴🦴½ **1926** Barrymore stars as the swashbuckling Italian duke with Spanish blood who seduces a castleful of women in the 1500s before falling in love with innocent Astor. Many exciting action sequences, including classic sword fights in which Barrymore eschewed a stunt double. Great attention is also paid to the detail of the costumes and settings of the Spanish-Moor period. Noted for employing fledgling movie sound effects and as the first film with a synchronized musical score from the Vitaphone Company, which, ironically, were responsible for eclipsing the movie's reputation. Watch for Loy as an Asian vamp and Oland as a pre-Charlie Chan Cesare Borgia. **90m/B VHS.** John Barrymore, Mary Astor, Willard Louis, Estelle Taylor, Helene Costello, Myrna Loy, June Marlowe, Warner Oland, Montagu Love, Hedda Hopper, Gustav von Seyffertitz; ***D:*** Alan Crosland; ***W:*** Bess Meredyth; ***C:*** Byron Haskin; ***M:*** William Axt.

Don Juan DeMarco 🦴🦴½ **1994 (PG-13)** Burned-out clinical psychiatrist Dr. Jack Meckler (Brando) is romantically inspired by a cape-wearing, suicidal manchild from Queens (Depp), who thinks he's legendary lover Don Juan. Delusional Depp recounts, in a convincing Castilian accent, thousands of conquests as the sympathetic shrink decides it's time to bring some spice to his own ho-hum life and marriage (to Dunaway). Depp turns in a sincere, engaging performance that avoids the huge potential for melodrama and compensates for inconsistent pacing. Brando and Dunaway make a charmingly quirky couple. Watch for slain Tejano queen Selena in a musical interlude. **92m/C VHS, DVD.** Marlon Brando, Johnny Depp, Faye Dunaway, Geraldine Pailhas, Rachel Ticotin, Bob (Robert) Dishy, Talisa Soto; ***D:*** Jeremy Leven; ***W:*** Jeremy Leven; ***C:*** Ralf Bode; ***M:*** Michael Kamen.

Don Juan, My Love 🦴🦴🦴 *Don Juan, Mi Querido Fantasma* **1990** Sexy comedy finds the ghost of Don Juan given a chance, after 450 years in Purgatory, to perform a good deed and free his soul. In Spanish with English subtitles. **96m/C VHS.** *SP* Juan Luis Galiardo, Rossy de Palma, Maria Barranco, Loles Leon; ***D:*** Antonio Mercero; ***M:*** Bernardo Bonazzi.

Don Juan (Or If Don Juan Were a Woman) 🦴 *Don Juan 73; Ms. Don Juan; Si Don Juan Etait une Femme* **1973** Offers unintentional amusement with Bardot in the title role. Jeanne specializes in humiliation and seduction of, among others, her cousin the priest, a poltician, and a businessman. French with subtitles. **94m/C VHS, DVD, Wide.** *FR* Brigitte Bardot, Jane Birkin, Matthieu Carriere, Robert Hossein, Maurice Ronet, Michele Sand; ***D:*** Roger Vadim; ***W:*** Jean Cau; ***C:*** Henri Decae.

Don King: Only in America 🦴🦴½ **1997 (R)** Rhames reigns in this bio of flamboyant, notorious boxing promoter Don King. King starts off as a Cleveland numbers runner at ease with violence, which eventually sends him to a four-year prison term for manslaughter. Released in 1971, King uses his friendship with R&B singer Lloyd Price (Curtis-Hall) to meet Muhammed Ali (McCrary), leading to his set-up of the 1974 Ali-Foreman fight in Zaire. From there it's just more self-promotion. **112m/C VHS.** Gabriel Casseus, Ving Rhames, Vondie Curtis-Hall, Jeremy Piven, Darius McCrary, Keith David, Bernie Mac, Loretta Devine, Lou Rawls, Ron Leibman; ***D:*** John Herzfeld; ***W:*** Kario Salem; ***C:*** Bill Butler; ***M:*** Anthony Marinelli. **CABLE**

Don Q., Son of Zorro 🦴🦴 **1925** Zorro's son takes up his father's fight against evil and injustice. Silent sequel to the 1920 classic. **111m/B VHS, DVD.** Douglas Fairbanks Sr., Mary Astor, Donald Crisp; ***D:*** Donald Crisp; ***W:*** Jack Cunningham; ***C:*** Henry Sharp.

Don Quixote 🦴🦴🦴🦴 **1935** Miguel de Cervantes' tale of the romantic who would rather be a knight in shining armor than shining armor at night. Chaliapin stars as the knight-errant on his nightly errands, tilting at windmills and charging flocks of sheep. Certain scenes were adapted to fit the pre-WWII atmosphere, as it was filmed during the same time that the Nazis were burning books. **73m/B VHS.** Feodor Chaliapin Sr., George Robey, Sidney (Sydney) Fox, Miles Mander, Oscar Asche, Emily Fitzroy, Wally Patch; ***D:*** G.W. Pabst; ***W:*** Paul Morand, Alexandre Arnoux; ***M:*** Jacques Ibert.

Don Quixote 🦴🦴🦴½ *Don Kikhot* **1957** The lauded, visually ravishing adaptation of the Cervantes classic, with a formal integrity inherited from Eisenstein and Dovshenko. In Russian with English subtitles. **110m/B VHS.** *SP RU* Nikolai Cherkasov, Yuri Tobubeyev; ***D:*** Grigori Kozintsev; ***W:*** Yevgeni Schwarz; ***C:*** Appolinari Dudko, Andrei Moskvin; ***M:*** Kara Karayev.

Don Quixote 🦴🦴 **2000** Spanish nobleman Alonso Quijano of La Mancha (Lithgow) decides to dedicate himself to chivalry. With his sanity in question, he dubs himself a knight errant—becoming Don Quixote—picks up sidekick Sancho Panza (Hoskins), and finds his lady fair—washerwoman Dulcinea (Williams). Episodic retelling has a number of familiar touches (including windmill-tilting) but doesn't add up to much, although the Spanish scenery is a plus. Based on Miguel de Cervantes' 1605 novel. **150m/C VHS.** John Lithgow, Bob Hoskins, Vanessa L(ynne) Williams, Isabella Rossellini, James Purefoy, Lambert Wilson, Tony Haygarth, Peter Eyre; ***D:*** Peter Yates; ***W:*** John Mortimer; ***C:*** David Connell; ***M:*** Richard Hartley. **CABLE**

Don Segundo Sombra 🦴🦴½ **1969** An interesting film seen through the eyes of an old gaucho, who is the mentor of a young boy growing to manhood. Based on the novel by Ricardo Guiraldes. In Spanish with English subtitles. **110m/C VHS.** *SP* Juan Carballido, Juan Carlos Gene, Soledad Silveyra, Alejandra Boero; ***D:*** Manuel Antin.

Don Winslow of the Coast Guard **1943** Serial in 13 episodes features comic-strip character Winslow as he strives to keep the waters of America safe for democracy. **234m/B VHS.** Don Terry, Elyse Knox; ***D:*** Ford Beebe, Ray Taylor.

Don Winslow of the Navy **1943** Thirteen episodes centered around the evil Scorpion, who plots to attack the Pacific Coast, but is thwarted by comic-strip hero Winslow. **234m/B VHS.** Don Terry, Walter Sande, Anne Nagel; ***D:*** Ford Beebe, Ray Taylor.

Dona Flor and Her Two Husbands 🦴🦴🦴 *Dona Flor e Seus Dois Maridos* **1978** Dona Flor (Braga) is widowed when her philandering husband Vadhino (Wilker) finally expires from drink, gambling, and ladies. She remarries, but her new husband Teodoro (Mendonca) is so boring and proper that she begins fantasizing spouse number one's return. But is he only in her imagination? Based on the novel by Jorge Amado. Portuguese with subtitles. Remade as "Kiss Me Goodbye." **106m/C VHS.** *BR* Sonia Braga, Jose Wilker, Mauro Mendonca; ***D:*** Bruno Barreto; ***W:*** Bruno Barreto; ***C:*** Maurilo Salles; ***M:*** Chico Buarque.

Dona Herlinda & Her Son 🦴🦴 *Dona Herlinda y Su Hijo* **1986** A Mexican sex comedy about a mother who manipulates her bisexual son's two lovers (one male, one female), until all four fit together into a seamless unit. In Spanish with English subtitles. Slow, but amusing. **90m/C VHS, DVD.** *MX* Guadalupe Del Toro, Arturo Meza, Marco Antonio Trevino, Leticia Lupersio; ***D:*** Jaime Humberto Hermosillo; ***W:*** Jaime Humberto Hermosillo; ***C:*** Miguel Ehrenberg.

Donkey Skin 🦴🦴🦴 *Peau d'Ane* **1970** A charming, all-star version of the medieval French fairy tale about a king searching for a suitable wife in a magical realm after his queen dies. In his quest for the most beautiful spouse, he learns that his daughter is that woman. She prefers Prince Charming, however. In French with English subtitles. **89m/C VHS.** *FR* Catherine Deneuve, Jean Marais, Delphine Seyrig, Jacques Perrin; ***D:*** Jacques Demy; ***C:*** Ghislan Cloquet; ***M:*** Michel Legrand.

Donner Pass: The Road to Survival 🦴🦴 **1984** Tame retelling of the western wagon-train pioneers who were forced to resort to cannibalism during a brutal snowstorm in the Rockies. The tragedy is lightly implied, keeping the film suitable for family viewing. **98m/C VHS.** Robert Fuller, Diane McBain, Andrew Prine, John Anderson, Michael Callan; ***D:*** James L. Conway.

Donnie Brasco 🦴🦴🦴 **1996 (R)** Excellent look at the unglamourous working end of the mob and an undercover operation. In the late '70s, FBI agent Joe Pistone (Depp) infiltrates the New York Bonanno crime family, under the alias of Donnie Brasco, where he's mentored by aging low-level hood Lefty (Pacino). As Joe/Donnie gets deeper into the wiseguy life, Lefty takes a fatherly pride in his protege and the agent also becomes ensnared by his new identity—to the possible detriment of both feds and family. Terrific lead performances. Based on a true story and adapted from the book by Pistone and Richard Woodley. **126m/C VHS, DVD, Wide.** Johnny Depp, Al Pacino, Anne Heche, Michael Madsen, Bruno Kirby, James Russo, Zeljko Ivanek, Gerry Becker, Zach Grenier, Robert Miano; ***D:*** Mike Newell; ***W:*** Paul Attanasio; ***C:*** Peter Sova; ***M:*** Patrick Doyle. Natl. Bd. of Review '97: Support. Actress (Heche).

Donnie Darko 🦴🦴🦴 **2001 (R)** Stylish, exciting debut by writer/director Kelly that, like "Mulholland Drive," leaves much unexplained as dark doings occur in an idyllic suburb, circa 1988. Aptly named Darko family is full of complex characters, including the gifted but schizophrenic Donny, a teenager able to see the future with the aid of a life-size, doomsday-spewing rabbit named Frank. Donny's psychiatrist (Ross) discovers he's sleepwalking on Frank's orders, which actually saves his life when a jet engine falls from a plane, landing squarely in the teen's bedroom. Even more mysteriously, no plane has reported a missing engine, which turns out to be just one of the many eerie events that may be real or imagined. McDonnel and Osborne are both fine as Donny's upper- middle class Republican parents. Like "Harvey" on anti-psychotic meds, this challenging and complex film is worth the effort. **113m/C VHS, DVD, Wide.** *US* Jake Gyllenhaal, Jena Malone, Drew Barrymore, Mary McDonnell, James Duval, Maggie Gyllenhaal, Holmes Osborne, Katharine Ross, Patrick Swayze, Noah Wyle, Arthur Taxier, Stuart Stone; ***D:*** Richard

Kelly; *W:* Richard Kelly; *C:* Steven Poster; *M:* Michael Andrews.

The Donor 🦴½ **1994 (R)** Cartel stalks victims and kills them for a human organ black market. **94m/C VHS.** Jeff Wincott, Michelle Johnson, Gordon Thomson; *D:* Damian Lee; *W:* Neal Dobrofsky, Tippi Dobrofsky.

Donor Unknown 🦴🦴 **1995 (R)** Driven businessman Nicholas Stillman (Onorati) has always put work before his family—and both wife Alice (Krige) and teenaged daughter Danielle (Herbst) have suffered from his attitude. When Nick is hit by a massive heart attack and gets a transplant, he insists on knowing everything about the donor. What he uncovers is a black market in organ procurement and Nash Creed (Brown), who'll do anything to stop Nick from exposing his lucrative business. Based on the novel "Corazon" by William H. Mooney. **93m/C VHS.** Peter Onorati, Alice Krige, Clancy Brown, Becky Herbst, Sam Robards, Richard Portnow, T.J. Castranovo, Leo Garcia, John Dorman; *D:* John Harrison; *W:* John Harrison; *C:* Zoltan David; *M:* David Bergeaud.

Donovan's Brain 🦴🦴🦴 **1953** Dedicated scientist Dr. Cory (Ayres) has succeeded in keeping a dismembered monkey's brain alive and gets his chance to experiment on a human when the victim of a plane crash is brought to his lab. Over the objections of his wife Janice (Davis) and assistant Frank (Evans), Cory keeps the brain alive in a tank. Too bad for him, since the organ belongs to a ruthless, vicious businessman (the titular Donovan) who begins to influence Cory in horrible ways. Based on the novel by Curt Siodmak, and also filmed as "The Lady and the Monster" (1944), "Vengeance" (1963), and "The Brain" (1965). **85m/B VHS, DVD.** Lew Ayres, Gene Evans, Nancy Davis, Steve Brodie; *D:* Felix Feist; *W:* Felix Feist, Hugh Brooke; *C:* Joseph Biroc; *M:* Eddie Dunstedter.

Donovan's Reef 🦴🦴🦴 **1963** Two WWII buddies meet every year on a Pacific atoll to engage in a perpetual bar-brawl, until a stuck-up Bostonian maiden appears to find her dad, a man who has fathered a brood of lovable half-casts. A rollicking, good-natured film from Ford. **109m/C VHS, DVD, Wide.** John Wayne, Lee Marvin, Jack Warden, Elizabeth Allen, Dorothy Lamour, Mike Mazurki, Cesar Romero; *D:* John Ford; *W:* James Edward Grant, Frank Nugent; *C:* William Clothier; *M:* Cyril Mockridge.

Don's Party 🦴🦴🦴 **1976** A rather dark comedy focusing on Australian Yuppie-types who decide to watch the election results on TV as a group. A lot more goes on at this party, however, than talk of the returns. Sexual themes surface. Cast members turn fine performances, aided by top-notch script and direction. **90m/C VHS, DVD.** *AU* Pat Bishop, Graham Kennedy, Candy (Candida) Raymond, Veronica Lang, John Hargreaves, Ray Barrett, Claire Binney, Graeme Blundell, Jeanie Drynan; *D:* Bruce Beresford; *W:* David Williamson; *C:* Donald McAlpine; *M:* Leos Janacek. Australian Film Inst. '77: Actress (Bishop).

Don't Answer the Phone 🦴 *The Hollywood Strangler* **1980 (R)** Deeply troubled photographer stalks and attacks the patients of a beautiful psychologist talk-show hostess. **94m/C VHS, DVD.** James Westmoreland, Flo Gerrish, Ben Frank; *D:* Robert Hammer; *W:* Robert Hammer, Michael Castle; *C:* James L. Carter; *M:* Byron Allred.

Don't Be a Menace to South Central While Drinking Your Juice in the Hood 🦴🦴 **1995 (R)** Parody of "life in the hood" movies pokes fun at the attitudes and characters that are quickly becoming cliches in the genre. Shawn Wayans plays G-next-door Ashtray, sent by his mother to discover "what it is to be a man" from his father in South Central L.A. He hooks up with his homey Loc Dog (Marlon Wayans), a gun-crazed beer-swilling gangsta who packs a nuclear warhead. As the title implies, almost every major black film in recent memory is given the Wayans' drive-by treatment, with a majority of the plot lifted from "Boyz N the Hood." Fans of the TV series "In Living Color" will love this twisted look at ghetto life, but others may be offended. **88m/C VHS, DVD.** Shawn Wayans, Marlon Wayans, Tracey Cherelle Jones, Chris Spencer, Suli McCullough, Darrell Heath, Helen Martin, Isaiah Barnes, Lahmard Tate; ***Cameos:*** Keenen Ivory Wayans; *D:* Paris Barclay; *W:* Shawn Wayans, Marlon Wayans, Phil Beauman; *C:* Russ Brandt; *M:* John Barnes.

Don't Be Afraid of the Dark 🦴🦴½ **1973** A young couple move into their dream house only to find that demonic little critters are residing in their basement and they want more than shelter. Made for TV with creepy scenes and eerie makeup for the monsters. **74m/C VHS.** Kim Darby, Jim Hutton, Barbara Anderson, William Demarest, Pedro Armendariz Jr., Felix Silla, Patty Maloney, Tamara DeTreaux; *D:* John Newland; *W:* Nigel McKeand; *C:* Andrew Jackson; *M:* Billy Goldenberg. **TV**

Don't Bother to Knock 🦴🦴½ **1952** As a mentally unstable hotel babysitter, Monroe meets a pilot (Widmark) and has a brief rendezvous with him. When the little girl she is babysitting interrupts, Monroe is furious, and later tries to murder the girl. This is one of Monroe's best dramatic roles. Bancroft's film debut as the Widmark's girlfriend. **76m/B VHS, DVD.** Richard Widmark, Marilyn Monroe, Anne Bancroft, Elisha Cook Jr., Jim Backus, Lurene Tuttle, Jeanne Cagney, Donna Corcoran; *D:* Roy Ward Baker; *W:* Daniel Taradash; *C:* Lucien Ballard; *M:* Lionel Newman.

Don't Change My World 🦴½ **1983 (G)** To preserve the natural beauty of the north woods, a wildlife photographer must fight a villainous land developer and a reckless poacher. Eco-correct. **89m/C VHS.** Roy Tatum, Ben Jones, Edie Kramer, George Macrenais, Paul Newmark, David Eidson; *D:* Robert Rector.

Don't Cry, It's Only Thunder 🦴🦴½ **1982 (PG)** A young army medic who works in a mortuary in Saigon becomes involved with a group of Vietnamese orphans and a dedicated army doctor. Based on a true story. **108m/C VHS.** Dennis Christopher, Susan St. James, Roger Aaron Brown, Li Lu, Thu Thuy, James Whitmore; *D:* Peter Werner; *M:* Maurice Jarre.

Don't Do It 🦴🦴½ **1994 (PG-13)** Three 20-something couples, attempting to find love, all wind up in the same cafe and try to tell the truth about how they feel and whom they desire. **90m/C VHS, DVD.** James Marshall, James LeGros, Sheryl Lee, Esai Morales, Alexis Arquette, Balthazar Getty, Sarah Trigger, Heather Graham; *D:* Eugene Hess; *W:* Eugene Hess; *C:* Ian Fox.

Don't Drink the Water 🦴🦴½ **1969 (G)** Based on Woody Allen's hit play, this film places an average Newark, New Jersey, family behind the Iron Curtain, where their vacation photo-taking gets them accused of spying. **100m/C VHS.** Jackie Gleason, Estelle Parsons, Joan Delaney, Ted Bessell, Michael Constantine; *D:* Howard Morris.

Don't Fence Me In 🦴🦴 **1945** Evans is a magazine photographer who heads west to do a story on a legendary character named Wildcat Kelly, who's supposedly dead. She meets rancher Rogers and sidekick Hayes and, of course, discovers that Rogers is the man she's looking for. **71m/B VHS.** Roy Rogers, Dale Evans, George "Gabby" Hayes, Robert "Bob" Livingston; *D:* John English; *W:* Dorrell McGowan, Stuart E. McGowan; *C:* William Bradford.

Don't Go in the House 🦴 **1980 (R)** Long-dormant psychosis is brought to life by the death of a young man's mother. **90m/C VHS, DVD.** Dan Grimaldi, Robert Osth, Ruth Dardick; *D:* Joseph Ellison; *W:* Joseph Ellison, Ellen Hammill; *C:* Oliver Wood; *M:* Richard Einhorn.

Don't Go in the Woods woof! **1981 (R)** Routine exercise in "don't do that" terror genre (includes warnings about going into houses, answering phones, looking into basements, opening windows, etc.). This time, four young campers are stalked by a crazed killer armed with prerequisite ax. **88m/C VHS.** Angie Brown, James Hayden, Mary Gail Artz, Jack McClelland; *D:* James Bryan.

Don't Go Near the Water 🦴🦴 **1957** Somewhat amusing comedy about the happenings at a Naval installation on a South Pacific tropical paradise. Clark outshines the others in his role as a frustrated officer. Based on the novel by William Brinkley. **107m/C VHS.** Glenn Ford, Gia Scala, Earl Holliman, Anne Francis, Keenan Wynn, Fred Clark, Eva Gabor, Russ Tamblyn; *D:* Charles Walters; *W:* Dorothy Kingsley, George Wells.

Don't Go to Sleep 🦴🦴 **1982** After a fatal car crash, a young girl misses mom and dad so much she returns from the grave to take them where they can be one big happy family again. Better than most made-for-TV junk-food fright-fests, written by Keenan Wynn's son, Ned. **93m/C VHS.** Dennis Weaver, Valerie Harper, Robin Ignico, Kristin Cummings, Ruth Gordon, Robert Webber; *D:* Richard Lang; *W:* Ned Wynn. **TV**

Don't Hang Up 🦴🦴½ *Separation* **1990** Handicapped New York actress Sarah (Arquette) wants to do a production of agoraphobic London writer Joe's (Suchet) play. So she calls him up to get his permission and the two begin a phone relationship that develops from business to romance. **84m/C VHS.** *GB* Rosanna Arquette, David Suchet; *D:* Barry Davis; *W:* Tom Kempinski. **TV**

Don't Let Me Die on a Sunday 🦴🦴½ *J'Aimerais pas Crever un Dimache* **1998** Bizarre, disturbing wallow in Parisian depravity begins in a morgue. That's where attendant Ben (Barr) meets Teresa (Bouchez). The details of that first encounter will not be recounted, but the two begin a downward spiral into joyless sex, angst, alienation, and despair. Not for the fainthearted. French with subtitles. **86m/C VHS, DVD, Wide.** *FR* Elodie Bouchez, Jean-Marc Barr, Martin Petitguyot, Patrick Catalifo, Gerard Loussine, Jeanne Casilas, Florence Darel; *D:* Didier Le Pecheur; *W:* Didier Le Pecheur; *C:* Denis Rouden; *M:* Philippe Cohen-Solal.

Don't Let Your Meat Loaf 🦴½ **1995** Three struggling comedians take their act on the road, including subway stations and street corners, in order to get the money to open their own comedy club. **82m/C VHS.** Leander Sales, Dana S. Hubbard, Brad Albright; *D:* Leander Sales.

Don't Look Back 🦴🦴🦴 **1996 (R)** Musician and heroin addict Jesse Parish (Stoltz) stumbles across a suitcase full of cash after witnessing a drug deal gone bad. He heads back to family and friends in Texas so he can kick his habit, but is marked for death by the dealers who want their money back. Strong script and performances. **91m/C VHS.** Eric Stoltz, John Corbett, Josh Hamilton, Annabeth Gish, Dwight Yoakam, Amanda Plummer; *D:* Geoff Murphy; *W:* Billy Bob Thornton, Tom Epperson. **CABLE**

Don't Look Back: The Story of Leroy "Satchel" Paige 🦴🦴½ **1981** Drama of the legendary baseball pitcher who helped break down racial barriers, based on his autobiography. Made-for-TV fare. Gossett hits a home run in the lead, but the overall effort is a ground-rule double. **98m/C VHS.** Louis Gossett Jr., Beverly Todd, Cleavon Little, Clifton Davis, John Beradino, Jim Davis, Ossie Davis, Hal Williams; *D:* George C. Scott, Richard A. Colla.

Don't Look in the Attic woof! **1981** A couple finds a haunted house with cows in the attic. **90m/C VHS.** Beba Loncar, Jean-Pierre Aumont; *D:* Carl Ausino.

Don't Look in the Basement 🦴½ **1973 (R)** Things get out of hand at an isolated asylum and a pretty young nurse is caught in the middle. Straight-jacketed by a low budget. **95m/C VHS, DVD.** Rosie Holotik, Anne MacAdams, William Bill McGhee, Rhea MacAdams, Gene Ross, Betty Chandler, Camilla Carr, Robert Dracup, Jessie Kirby, Hugh Feagin, Harryete Warren, Jessie Lee Fulton, Michael Harvey; *D:* S.F. Brownrigg; *W:* Tim Pope, Tom Pope; *M:* Robert Farrar.

Don't Look Now 🦴🦴🦴 **1973 (R)** A psychological creepfest with a chilling climax, based on the novel by Daphne Du Maurier. John (Sutherland) and Laura (Christie) Baxter travel to a dank, off-season Venice in an attempt to put the drowning death of their young daughter behind them. But while working on a church restoration, John begins to have psychic visions which are encouraged by a pair of strange sisters (Matania, Mason). There's a steamy love scene between Sutherland and Christie that became the object of much gossip. **110m/C VHS.** *GB IT* Donald Sutherland, Julie Christie, Hilary Mason, Clelia Matania, Massimo Serato, Leopoldo Trieste, Adelina Porrio; *D:* Nicolas Roeg; *W:* Chris Bryant, Allan Scott; *C:* Anthony B. Richmond; *M:* Pino Donaggio.

Don't Mess with My Sister! 🦴🦴½ **1985** A married, New York junkyard worker falls in love with a belly dancer he meets at a party. The affair leads to murder and subsequently, revenge. An interesting, offbeat film from the director of "I Spit on Your Grave." **90m/C VHS, DVD, Wide.** Joe Perce, Jeannine Lemay, Jack Gurci, Peter Sapienza, Laura Lanfranchi; *D:* Mier Zarchi.

Don't Open the Door! woof! **1974 (PG)** A young woman is terrorized by a killer located inside her house. **90m/C VHS.** Susan Bracken, Gene Ross, Jim Harrell; *D:* S.F. Brownrigg.

Don't Open Till Christmas woof! **1984** A weirdo murders various Santa Clauses in assorted gory ways. Best to take this one back to the department store. **86m/C VHS.** *GB* Edmund Purdom, Caroline Munro, Alan Lake, Belinda Mayne, Gerry Sundquist, Mark Jones; *D:* Edmund Purdom.

Don't Raise the Bridge, Lower the River 🦴🦴 **1968 (G)** After his wife leaves him, an American with crazy, get-rich-quick schemes turns his wife's ancestral English home into a Chinese discotheque. Domestic farce that comes and goes; if mad for Lewis, rent "The Nutty Professor." **99m/C VHS.** Jerry Lewis, Terry-Thomas, Jacqueline Pearce; *D:* Jerry Paris.

Don't Say a Word 🦴🦴½ **2001 (R)** Douglas plays the stable family man pushed to the brink once again in this chilly kidnaping thriller. Dr. Nathan Conrad (Douglas) is a psychiatrist whose idyllic life is shattered when his eight-year-old daughter Jessie (Bartusiak) is kidnaped by a gang of thieves. They threaten to kill his little girl unless he can retrieve a six-digit number locked in the brain of Nathan's new patient Elisabeth (Murphy), a raving lunatic who slashed an orderly to death. Meanwhile, the bad guys have rigged surveillance equipment in his apartment and are menacing his wife Aggie (Janssen), as cop Esposito stumbles across the plot, inadvertently threatening Nathan's efforts. All the plot threads are conveniently tied up in a standard final showdown scene. **112m/C VHS, DVD, Wide.** *US* Michael Douglas, Sean Bean, Brittany Murphy, Skye McCole Bartusiak, Famke Janssen, Guy Torry, Jennifer Esposito, Shawn Doyle, Victor Argo, Oliver Platt, Conrad Goode, Paul Schulze, Lance Reddick; *D:* Gary Fleder; *W:* Patrick Smith Kelly, Anthony Peckham; *C:* Amir M. Mokri; *M:* Mark Isham.

Don't Talk to Strangers 🦴🦴½ **1994 (R)** Formula thriller has Brosnan marrying divorcee Reed and becoming instant father to her nine-year-old son. But someone appears to be a whacko—is it the kid's real dad (Quinn) or is Brosnan just too good to be true? **94m/C VHS.** Pierce Brosnan, Shanna Reed, Terry O'Quinn; *D:* Robert Lewis; *W:* Neill D. Hicks, Jon George, Nevin Schreiner.

Don't Tell Her It's Me 🦴 *The Boyfriend School* **1990 (PG-13)** Guttenberg is determined to win the heart of an attractive writer. With the assistance of his sister, he works to become a dream man. Clever premise, promising cast, lame comedy. From the novel by Sarah Bird. **101m/C VHS.** Steve Guttenberg, Jami Gertz, Shelley Long, Kyle MacLachlan, Madchen Amick; *D:* Malcolm Mowbray; *W:* Sarah Bird; *M:* Michael Gore.

Don't Tell Mom the Babysitter's Dead 🦴½ **1991 (PG-13)** Their mother traveling abroad, the title situation leaves a houseful of teenagers with the whole summer to themselves. Eldest daughter Applegate cons her way into the high-powered business world while the metalhead son parties hardy. Many tepid comic situations, not adding up to very much. **105m/C VHS, DVD, 8mm, Wide.** Christina Applegate, Keith Coogan, Joanna Cassidy, John Getz, Josh Charles, Concetta Tomei, Eda Reiss Merin; ***D:*** Stephen Herek; ***W:*** Neil Landau, Tara Ison; ***C:*** Tim Suhrstedt; ***M:*** David Newman.

Don't Torture a Duckling 🦴🦴 *Non Si Sevizia un Paperino* **1972** Newspaperman Andrea Martelli (Milian) investigates the deaths of several young boys in the Sicily village where his father was born. The suspicious villagers take their revenge on a couple of outcast locals but Martelli teams up with seductive Patrizia (Bouchet) to uncover the real killer. Creepy rather a gorefest, although Fulci recycled one of the more violent scenes for his later film, "The Psychic." **102m/C VHS, DVD, Wide.** *IT* Tomas Milian, Barbara Bouchet, Irene Papas, Florinda Bolkan, Marc Porel; ***D:*** Lucio Fulci; ***W:*** Lucio Fulci, Robert Gianviti; ***C:*** Sergio d'Offizi; ***M:*** Riz Ortolani.

The Doolins of Oklahoma 🦴🦴½ *The Great Manhunt* **1949** Scott is the leader of the last of the southwestern outlaw gangs, pursued by lawmen and changing times with the onset of the modern age. Fast-paced and intelligent. **90m/B VHS.** Randolph Scott, George Macready, Louise Allbritton, John Ireland, Virginia Huston, Charles Kemper, Noah Beery Jr.; ***D:*** Gordon Douglas; ***M:*** George Duning.

Doom Asylum woof! **1988 (R)** Several sex kittens wander into a deserted sanatorium and meet up with the grisly beast wielding autopsy instruments. The people involved with this spoof should have been (more) committed. **77m/C VHS.** Patty Mullen, Ruth (Coreen) Collins, Kristen Davis, William Hay, Kenny L. Price, Harrison White, Dawn Alvan, Michael Rogan; ***D:*** Richard S. Friedman.

The Doom Generation 🦴🦴🦴 **1995 (R)** Alienated trio on the road trip to hell (doubling as L.A.). Beautiful 17-year-old druggie Amy Blue (McGowan), her sweetly dim boyfriend Jordan White (Duval), and hot-tempered stud/drifter Xavier Red (Schaech) flee after Red kills a store clerk. They're basically from nowhere, going nowhere, and finding sex and (lots of gruesomely depicted) violence along the way. The subtitle, "A Heterosexual Movie by Gregg Araki," may be technically accurate but the homoerotic subtext is very clear. Terrific performances. Second film in Araki's teen trilogy, following "Totally F***ked Up," and preceding "Nowhere." An unrated version is also available. **84m/C VHS, DVD.** Parker Posey, Lauren Tewes, Christopher Knight, Margaret Cho, Skinny Puppy, Heidi Fleiss, Rose McGowan, James Duval, Johnathon Schaech; ***D:*** Gregg Araki; ***W:*** Gregg Araki; ***C:*** Jim Fealy; ***M:*** Don Gallo.

Doom Runners 🦴🦴 **1997** Ah, yes—another dark and dangerous postapocalyptic world. Evil ruler Dr. Kao (Curry) uses "mindwiping" to erase the memories of his victims and maintains order with an army of "Doom Troopers." Teen Jada (Moreno) finds a map that will lead her to New Eden, the only free society left. And she's determined to make it, despite Kao's threats. **87m/C VHS.** Tim Curry, Lea Moreno, Bradley Michael Pierce, Nathan Jones. **CABLE**

Doomed at Sundown 🦴🦴½ **1937** Decent Steele vehicle has the tough cowpoke as a sheriff's son known for playing practical jokes. When his father gets knifed, it's no laughing matter and he takes off after the killers. Based on a story by Fred Myton. **55m/B VHS.** Bob Steele, Laraine Day, Warner Richmond, Harold Daniels, David Sharpe; ***D:*** Sam Newfield; ***W:*** George Plympton.

Doomed Caravan 🦴🦴🦴 **1941** Hoppy and his pals lend a hand when some villains try to monopolize the wagon train business. Location shooting was done in the valleys of central California. **60m/B VHS.** William Boyd, Russell Hayden, Andy Clyde, Minna Gombell, Morris Ankrum, Georgia Hawkins, Trevor Bardette, Pat O'Brien; ***D:*** Lesley Selander.

Doomed Love 🦴🦴½ **1983** Love is hell, especially when the object of your affection happens to be deceased. A professor of literature in the throes of unrequited love decides to reunite himself with his lost love. Won awards when released in Berlin. **75m/C VHS.** Bill Rice; ***D:*** Andrew Horn.

Doomed to Die 🦴🦴 **1940** Cargo of stolen bonds leads to a tong war and the murder of a shipping millionaire. Part of Mr. Wong series. Worth a look if only for Karloff's performance. **67m/B VHS.** Boris Karloff, Marjorie Reynolds, Grant Withers; ***D:*** William Nigh.

Doomsday 🦴🦴½ **1928** Vidor marries for wealth instead of love and, in classic fashion, finds that money doesn't buy happiness. **73m/B VHS.** Florence Vidor, Gary Cooper, Lawrence Grant; ***D:*** Rowland V. Lee.

The Doomsday Flight 🦴🦴 **1966** Uneven thriller in which O'Brien plants an altitude-triggered bomb on a jet in an effort to blackmail the airline. Search for the bomb provides some suspenseful and well-acted moments. **100m/C VHS.** Jack Lord, Edmond O'Brien, Van Johnson, John Saxon, Katherine Crawford, Michael Sarrazin, Ed Asner, Greg Morris, Richard Carlson, Don Stewart; ***D:*** William A. Graham; ***W:*** Rod Serling. **TV**

Doomsday Gun 🦴🦴½ **1994** Fact-based thriller about arms manufacturer Gerald Bull (Langella), who dreams of building the world's biggest gun—a behemoth with a range of 1000 miles. Only problem is Bull's willingness to sell the weapon to the highest bidder, who happens to be Saddam Hussein. This doesn't sit well with Israeli Mossad agent Yossi (Arkin). **110m/C VHS.** Frank Langella, Alan Arkin, Kevin Spacey, Tony Goldwyn, James Fox, Michael Kitchen, Francesca Annis, Marianne (Cuau) Denicourt; ***D:*** Robert M. Young; ***W:*** Lionel Chetwynd, Walter Bernstein; ***C:*** Ian Wilson. **CABLE**

Doomsdayer 🦴½ **1999 (R)** Okay, see how familiar this sounds. Jack Logan (Lara) works for a covert agency. His assignment is to prevent a new explosive from falling into terrorists' hands. This Doomsdayer device is currently held by a ruthless billionaire weapons dealer (Kier) and his equally nasty wife (Nielsen), who have their own island. Logan and his team run into trouble before they save the day. Now you won't have to actually watch the video. **93m/C VHS, DVD.** Joe Lara, Udo Kier, Brigitte Nielsen, Sandra Gomez, January Isaac, T.J. Storm, Paige Rowland, Ravil Issyanov; ***D:*** Michael J. Sarna; ***W:*** Bob Couttie; ***C:*** David Rakoczy. **VIDEO**

Doomwatch 🦴🦴½ **1972** A scientist discovers a chemical company is dumping poison into local waters, deforming the inhabitants of an isolated island when they eat the catch of the day. Unsurprising. **89m/C VHS, DVD.** *GB* Ian Bannen, Judy Geeson, John Paul, Simon Oates, George Sanders; ***D:*** Peter Sasdy; ***W:*** Clive Exton; ***C:*** Ken Talbot.

Door to Door 🦴🦴 **1984** Comedy about two door-to-door salesmen who race to stay one step ahead of the law and their own company. Fairly lightweight, but it has its moments. **93m/C VHS.** Ron Leibman, Jane Kaczmarek, Arliss Howard, Alan Austin; ***D:*** Patrick Bailey. **CABLE**

Door to Door Maniac 🦴½ *Five Minutes to Live* **1961** Criminals hold a bank president's wife hostage, unaware that the husband was looking to get rid of her in favor of another woman. Cash's screen debut. Aside from the strange cast ensemble, not particularly worth seeing. **80m/B VHS.** Johnny Cash, Ron Howard, Vic Tayback, Donald Woods, Cay Forrester, Pamela Mason; ***D:*** Bill Karn.

Door with the Seven Locks 🦴🦴½ **1962** Bizarre Edgar Wallace story of man who leaves seven keys to a treasure vault in his will. Remake of "Chamber of Horrors." **96m/C VHS.** *GE* Eddi Arent, Heinz Drache, Klaus Kinski, Ady Berber; ***D:*** Alfred Vohrer.

The Doorbell Rang: A Nero Wolfe Mystery 🦴🦴½ **2001** Detective Nero Wolfe (Chaykin) and his investigator Archie Goodwin (Hutton) get involved in the case of an eccentric woman who comes to Wolfe with a tale of FBI harassment that leads to murder. Based on the mystery by Rex Stout. **100m/C VHS.** Timothy Hutton, Maury Chaykin, Saul Rubinek, Debra Monk, Colin Fox; ***W:*** Timothy Hutton, Michael Jaffe. **CABLE**

The Doors 🦴🦴½ **1991 (R)** Stone approached Jim Morrison with an early incarnation of this docudrama, but it's hard to believe even the Lizard King could play himself with any more convincing abandon than Kilmer, in a great performance. Trouble is, the story—one of drugs, abuse, and abject self-indulgence—grows tiresome, and the audience, with the exception of die-hard fans, may lose sight of any sympathy they might have had. Ryan is forgettable as Morrison's hippie-chick wife, MacLachlan sports a funny wig and dabbles on the keyboards as Ray Manszarek, and Quinlan is atypically cast as a sado-masochistic journalist paramour. Based on "Riders on the Storm" by John Densmore. **138m/C VHS, DVD, 8mm, Wide.** Kelly Hu, Val Kilmer, Meg Ryan, Kevin Dillon, Kyle MacLachlan, Frank Whaley, Michael Madsen, Kathleen Quinlan, Crispin Glover, Josh Evans, John Densmore, William Jordan, Mimi Rogers, Paul Williams, Bill Graham, Billy Vera, William Kunstler, Wes Studi, Costas Mandylor, Billy Idol, Michael Wincott, Dennis Burkley; ***D:*** Oliver Stone; ***W:*** Oliver Stone, Ralph Thomas, Randy Johnson, J. Randall Johnson; ***C:*** Robert Richardson.

The Doorway 🦴½ **2000 (R)** Four college students are fixing up a house that they discover is built over a doorway to hell—and they've just opened it up. So they ask the local expert on the paranormal (Scheider, whose role is very limited) for help. **91m/C VHS, DVD.** Roy Scheider, Lauren Woodland, Suzanne Bridgham, Teresa De Priest, Christian Harmony, Don Maloney; ***D:*** Michael B. Druxman; ***W:*** Michael B. Druxman; ***C:*** Yoram Astrakhan. **VIDEO**

Dope Case Pending 🦴 **2000** Extremely low-budget urban action picture revolves around Devon King (Prime Time), who's got a bright future in athletics ahead of him until the cops are called to a party at his house and he's arrested for drug possession. It's a downward spiral from there on. Everything about the film is substandard. Semi-professional writing, acting, and directing. **91m/C DVD.** Prime Time, Thinline, Kid Frost, Coolio, Sean Levert, Tony Dorian; ***D:*** Patrick McKnight, Jeff Williams; ***W:*** Patrick McKnight; ***C:*** Steve Van Dyne; ***M:*** Prime Time.

Doppelganger: The Evil Within 🦴🦴 **1990 (R)** Holly Gooding (Barrymore) seems like such a nice girl—until the police suspect her of the brutal murder of her mother. Her new friend Patrick (Newbern) begins to see another side to the vulnerable Holly—a seductress capable of doing anything to get what she wants. **105m/C VHS.** Drew Barrymore, George Newbern, Dennis Christopher, Sally Kellerman, Leslie Hope; ***D:*** Avi Nesher; ***W:*** Avi Nesher.

Dorian Gray 🦴½ *The Secret of Dorian Gray; Il Dio Chiamato a Dorian; Das Bildness des Dorian Gray; The Evils of Dorian Gray* **1970 (R)** Modern-day version of the famous tale by Oscar Wilde about an ageless young man whose portrait reflects the ravages of time and a life of debauchery. More sex, less acting with Berger in lead. Not nearly as good as the original version, "The Picture of Dorian Gray." **92m/C VHS.** *GE IT* Richard Todd, Helmut Berger, Herbert Lom, Marie Liljedahl, Margaret Lee, Maria Rohm, Beryl Cunningham, Isa Miranda, Eleanora Rossi-Drago, Renato Romano; ***D:*** Massimo Dallamano; ***W:*** Massimo Dallamano, Marcello Costa; ***C:*** Otello Spila.

Dorm That Dripped Blood woof! **1982 (R)** Five college students volunteer to close the dorm during their Christmas vacation. A series of grisly and barbaric incidents eliminates the youngsters one by one. As the terror mounts, the remaining students slowly realize that they are up against a terrifyingly real psychopathic killer. Merry Christmas. **84m/C VHS.** Laura Lopinski, Stephen Sachs, Pamela Holland; ***D:*** Stephen Carpenter, Jeffrey Obrow; ***W:*** Stephen Carpenter.

Dostoevsky's Crime and Punishment 🦴🦴 *Crime and Punishment* **1999 (PG-13)** Muddled TV adaptation of the 1866 Dostoevsky novel is anchored by Dempsey's lead performance as impoverished student Rodya Raskolnikov. He murders the local pawnbroker in a "perfect crime" only to be consumed by guilt. Then he falls under the suspicious eyes of unrelenting inspector Porfiri (Kingsley), who waits for Rodya to make a mistake. **89m/C VHS.** Patrick Dempsey, Ben Kingsley, Julie Delpy, Eddie Marsan, Richard Bremmer, Lili Horvath, Carole Nimmons, Penny Downie, Michael Mehlmann, Sara Toth; ***D:*** Joseph Sargent; ***W:*** David Stevens; ***C:*** Elemer Ragalyi. **TV**

Double Agent 73 🦴 **1980 (R)** The title refers to star Chesty Morgan's amazing bust size. Here, she's a secret agent who has a camera/bomb implanted in her oh, never mind. The result is more curiosity than exploitation. Director Doris Wishman doesn't care about the plot and neither should you. **73m/C DVD.** Chesty Morgan, Frank Silvano, Saul Meth, Jill Harris, Louis Burdi, Peter Petrillo, Cooper Kent; ***D:*** Doris Wishman; ***W:*** Doris Wishman, Judy J. Kushner; ***C:*** Yuri Haviv.

Double Agents 🦴 *La Nuit Des Espions; Night Encounter* **1959** Two double agents are sent on a rendezvous to exchange vital government secrets. Dubbed in English. **81m/B VHS.** *FR* Marina Vlady, Robert Hossein.

Double Cross 🦴🦴 **1992 (R)** Tank Polling (Connery), a British journalist, uses the secrets of an ex-hooker (Donohoe) to get back at a corrupt politician who ruined Polling's life five years earlier. Lots of action and a few graphic murders in this thriller. **96m/C VHS.** Amanda Donohoe, Peter Wyngarde, Jason Connery; ***D:*** James A. Marcus.

Double Cross 🦴🦴 **1994 (R)** Man has what seems to be a chance erotic encounter with a beautiful blonde. But this wouldn't be a thriller if it ended there, so there's blackmail and murder to contend with as well. **95m/C VHS.** Patrick Bergin, Jennifer Tilly, Kelly Preston, Matt Craven, Kevin Tighe.

Double-Crossed 🦴🦴½ **1991** In 1984 Barry Seal agrees to inform on Colombia's Medellin Cartel and its links to the Sandanista government of Nicaragua in exchange for leniency on drug-smuggling charges. Little does he know that the personal consequences will turn deadly when his cover is blown and the government double-crosses him. Hopper's hyped-up performance as drug smuggler turned DEA informant Seal showcases this true-crime tale. **111m/C VHS.** Dennis Hopper, Robert Carradine, G.W. Bailey, Adrienne Barbeau; ***C:*** Donald M. Morgan; ***M:*** Richard Bellis.

Double Deal 🦴🦴 **1939** An honest man and a gangster are rivals in love. The gangster robs a jewelry store and tries to pin the crime on the good guy. This is a movie with a moral so don't expect him to get away with it. **60m/C VHS.** Monte Hawley, Jeni Le Gon, Edward Thompson, Florence O'Brien; ***D:*** Arthur Dreifuss.

Double Deal 🦴½ **1950** Murder, mayhem, and industrial espionage come into play as parties fight over an oil field. **65m/B VHS.** Marie Windsor, Richard Denning, Taylor Holmes; ***D:*** Abby Berlin.

Double Deal 🦴½ **1984** Unfaithful woman and her lover plot to steal priceless opal from hubby. Lifeless and silly. **90m/C VHS.** Louis Jourdan, Angela Punch McGregor; ***D:*** Brian Kavanagh.

Double Double Toil and Trouble 🦴🦴½ **1994** The twins come to the financial rescue of their family when Dad's business gets into trouble and their home is threatened. But first they need to get a magic moonstone from their wicked Aunt Agatha (Leachman) and rescue kind Aunt Sophia, all before midnight on Halloween. Made for TV. **93m/C VHS.** Ashley (Fuller) Olsen, Mary-Kate Olsen, Cloris Leachman, Meshach Taylor; ***D:*** Jeff Franklin; ***W:*** Jeff Franklin. **TV**

Double Down 🦴½ *Zigs* **2001 (R)** Five buddies, for whom gambling is a career, owe a lot of moolah to the local L.A. bookies. Naturally, they decide that one last bet will get them out of debt and on their way to their dream of owning a sports bar. Low-budget feature with lots of hanging around. **93m/C VHS, DVD, Wide.** Peter Dobson, Jason Priestley, Orien Richman, Kane Picoy, Richard Portnow, Luca Palanca, Alicia Coppola, Alexandra Powers, David Proval; ***D:*** Mars Callahan; ***W:*** Mars Callahan; ***C:*** Christopher Pearson. **VIDEO**

Double Dragon 🦴🦴½ **1994 (PG-13)** Generally harmless brain candy, based on the videogame, finds orphaned brothers Jimmy (Dacascos) and Billy (Wolf) living in the rubble of post earthquake L.A., circa 2007. They have half of a mystical dragon amulet and obsessed mogul Koga Shuko (Patrick), who possesses the other half, after them. Seems he needs the entire amulet in order to control its vast power. Non-stop action should keep the kiddies amused. **96m/C VHS, DVD.** Scott Wolf, Mark Dacascos, Robert Patrick, Alyssa Milano, Kristina Malandro Wagner, Julia Nickson-Soul; ***D:*** Jim Yukich; ***W:*** Michael Paul Davis, Peter Gould; ***C:*** Gary B. Kibbe; ***M:*** Jay Ferguson.

Double Dynamite 🦴½ *It's Only Money* **1951** A bank teller is at a loss when his racetrack winnings are confused with the cash lifted from his bank during a robbery. Forgettable, forgotten shambles. Originally filmed in 1948. **80m/B VHS.** Frank Sinatra, Jane Russell, Groucho Marx, Don McGuire, Howard Freeman, Harry Hayden, Nestor Paiva, Lou Nova, Joe Devlin; ***D:*** Irving Cummings; ***W:*** Melville Shavelson.

Double Edge 🦴🦴 **1992 (PG-13)** The Palestinian-Israeli conflict is the focus of this drama about an ambitious reporter (Dunaway). On her first foreign assignment, New Yorker Faye Milano finds herself way out of her depth when she covers a colleague's beat in Jerusalem. Unable to remain a detached observer, Faye instead becomes an active participant, alternating between her affair with an Israeli reserves officer and her friendship with a family of Palestinian intifada leaders. Dunaway and Kollek are unfortunately stiff in their performances but the location (Israel and the West Bank) is interesting and the story surprisingly balanced. **85m/C VHS.** *IS* Faye Dunaway, Amos Kollek, Muhamad Bakri, Shmuel Shilo, Makram Khouri, Michael Schneider, Anat Atzmon, Ann Belkin; ***D:*** Amos Kollek; ***W:*** Amos Kollek.

Double Edge 🦴½ *American Dragons* **1997 (R)** Obsessed NYC cop Tony Luca (Biehn) tries to bring down crimelord Rocco (Stark) but things go badly and instead he's taken off the case. His new assignment is investigating yakuza murders in Little Tokyo, which has also drawn the unwanted attention of South Korean detective Kim (Park), who recognizes the killer's MO. But when mobsters also start dying it turns out the bad guy is trying to get rid of the mob and the yakuza and take over. **95m/C VHS.** Michael Biehn, Joong-Hoon Park, Cary-Hiroyuki Tagawa, Don Stark, Byron Mann; ***D:*** Ralph Hemecker; ***W:*** Erik Saltzgaber; ***C:*** Ernest Holzman; ***M:*** Joel Goldsmith, Alex Wilkinson. **VIDEO**

Double Exposure 🦴🦴 **1982 (R)** A young photographer's violent nightmares become the next day's headlines. Unsurprising vision. **95m/C VHS.** Michael Callan, James Stacy, Joanna Pettet, Cleavon Little, Pamela Hensley, Seymour Cassel, David Young, Misty Rowe, Don Potter; ***D:*** William B. Hillman.

Double Exposure 🦴½ **1993 (R)** A possessive husband discovers his wife's infidelity and decides to get revenge, only his plan doesn't work out as he intends. **93m/C VHS.** Ron Perlman, Ian Buchanan, Jennifer Gatti, William R. Moses, James McEachin, Dedee Pfeiffer; ***D:*** Claudia Hoover; ***W:*** Christine Colfer, Bridget Hoffman, Claudia Hoover.

Double Exposure: The Story of Margaret Bourke-White 🦴🦴½ *Margaret Bourke-White* **1989** Beautifully shot but slow biography of a woman who became a well-known professional photographer for "Life" magazine during the 1930s and 1940s, as well as the first official female photojournalist of WWII. **105m/C VHS.** Farrah Fawcett, Frederic Forrest, Mitchell Ryan, David Huddleston, Jay Patterson, Ken Marshall; ***D:*** Lawrence Schiller; ***C:*** Robert Elswit. **CABLE**

Double Face 🦴½ **1970** A wealthy industrialist kills his lesbian wife with a car bomb, but she seems to haunt him through pornographic films. **84m/C VHS.** Klaus Kinski, Annabella Incontrera.

Double Happiness 🦴🦴🦴 **1994 (PG-13)** Slice of life comedy-drama finds 20-something Chinese-Canadian Jade Li (Oh) struggling to balance her would-be acting career and new world romance with her family's traditional values. Jade wants to please her old world father (Chang) so she endures his arranged dates and puts on a pleasant demeanor for family friends. But Jade must decide who she wants to be when she gets involved with non-Asian college student Mark (Rennie). Fine performances and assured direction from Shum in her feature film debut. **87m/C VHS.** *CA* Sandra Oh, Stephen Chang, Alannah Ong, Frances You, Johnny Mah, Callum Keith Rennie; ***D:*** Mina Shum; ***W:*** Mina Shum; ***C:*** Peter Wunstorf. Genie '94: Actress (Oh), Film Editing.

Double Identity 🦴🦴½ **1989 (PG-13)** Former college professor turned criminal Mancuso moves to a corn patch called New Hope in hopes of returning to the straight and narrow. He finds a good woman to stand by him, but, alas, crime, like smoking, is easier to start than to quit. Much intrigue and deceit. **95m/C VHS.** *CA FR* Nick Mancuso, Leah K. Pinsent, Patrick Bauchau, Anne LeTourneau, Jacques Godin; ***D:*** Yves Boisset.

Double Impact 🦴½ **1991 (R)** Van Damme plays twins re-united in Hong Kong to avenge their parents' murder by local bad guys, but this lunkhead kick-em-up doesn't even take advantage of that gimmick; the basic story would have been exactly the same with just one Jean-Claude. Lots of profane dialogue and some gratuitous nudity for the kiddies. **107m/C VHS, DVD, Wide.** Jean-Claude Van Damme, Cory Everson, Geoffrey Lewis; ***D:*** Sheldon Lettich; ***W:*** Jean-Claude Van Damme, Sheldon Lettich; ***C:*** Richard H. Kline; ***M:*** Arthur Kempel.

Double Indemnity 🦴🦴🦴🦴 **1944** The classic seedy story of insurance agent Walter Neff (MacMurray), who's seduced by deadly blonde Phyllis Dietrichson (Stanwyck) into killing her husband (Powers) so they can collect together from his company. But the husband's "accident" invites suspicions from claims adjustor Keyes (Robinson) and Walter and Phyllis begin to turn on each other. Terrific, influential film noir, the best of its kind. Based on the James M. Cain novel. **107m/B VHS, DVD.** Fred MacMurray, Barbara Stanwyck, Edward G. Robinson, Tom Powers, Porter Hall, Jean Heather, Byron Barr, Fortunio Bonanova; ***D:*** Billy Wilder; ***W:*** Raymond Chandler, Billy Wilder; ***C:*** John Seitz; ***M:*** Miklos Rozsa. AFI '98: Top 100, Natl. Film Reg. '92.

Double Jeopardy 🦴🦴 **1992 (R)** Boxleitner stars as a married man who risks his family and life when his sexy ex-lover returns to town. She easily involves him in deception—and murder. A cake-walk for Ward as the femme fatale. **101m/C VHS.** Bruce Boxleitner, Rachel Ward, Sela Ward, Sally Kirkland; ***D:*** Lawrence Schiller; ***M:*** Eduard Artemyev. **CABLE**

Double Jeopardy 🦴🦴½ **1999 (R)** This film really doesn't make much sense. But it certainly struck a nerve, as well as box-office gold, as an entertaining thriller, probably because it doesn't give you much time to catch your breathe or think about plot holes. Libby (Judd) does time for murdering hubby Nick (Greenwood) after she's set up by the sleaze. Once she's released, she decides since she can't be tried for the same crime twice (this is actually faulty logic), she might as well get rid of the lowlife for real. Wisecracking parole officer Travis Lehman (Jones) winds up getting deeply involved ferreting out the truth of the messy situation. **105m/C VHS, DVD, Wide.** Ashley Judd, Tommy Lee Jones, Bruce Greenwood, Annabeth Gish, Roma Maffia, Jay Brazeau, Gillian Barber, Davenia McFadden, Spencer (Treat) Clark; ***D:*** Bruce Beresford; ***W:*** David Weisberg, Douglas S. Cook; ***C:*** Peter James; ***M:*** Normand Corbeil.

A Double Life 🦴🦴🦴 **1947** Colman plays a Shakespearean actor in trouble when the characters he plays begin to seep into his personal life and take over. Things begin to look really bad when he is cast in the role of the cursed Othello. Colman won an Oscar for this difficult role, and the moody musical score garnered another for Rosza. **107m/B VHS.** Ronald Colman, Shelley Winters, Signe Hasso, Edmond O'Brien, Ray Collins, Millard Mitchell; ***D:*** George Cukor; ***W:*** Ruth Gordon, Garson Kanin; ***C:*** Milton Krasner; ***M:*** Miklos Rozsa. Oscars '47: Actor (Colman), Orig. Dramatic Score; Golden Globes '48: Actor—Drama (Colman).

The Double Life of Veronique 🦴🦴 *La Double Vie de Veronique* **1991 (R)** They say everyone has a twin, but this is ridiculous. Two women—Polish Veronika and French Veronique—are born on the same day in different countries, share a singing talent, a cardiac ailment, and, although the two never meet, a strange awareness of each other. Jacob is unforgettable as the two women, and director Krzysztof creates some spell-binding scenes but the viewer has to be willing to forgo plot for atmosphere. **96m/C VHS.** *FR PL* Irene Jacob, Phillipe Volter, Sandrine Dumas, Aleksander Bardini, Louis Ducreux, Claude Duneton, Halina Gryglaszewska, Kalina Jedrusik; ***D:*** Krzysztof Kieslowski; ***W:*** Krzysztof Kieslowski, Krzysztof Piesiewicz; ***C:*** Slawomir Idziak; ***M:*** Zbigniew Preisner. Cannes '91: Actress (Jacob); Natl. Soc. Film Critics '91: Foreign Film.

The Double McGuffin 🦴🦴 **1979 (PG)** A plot of international intrigue is uncovered by teenagers—a la the Hardy Boys—when a prime minister and her security guard pay a visit to a small Virginia community. They're not believed, though. Action-packed from the makers of Benji. Dogs do not figure prominently here. **100m/C VHS.** Ernest Borgnine, George Kennedy, Elke Sommer, Ed "Too Tall" Jones, Lisa Whelchel, Vincent Spano; ***D:*** Joe Camp; ***M:*** Euel Box; ***V:*** Orson Welles.

The Double Negative 🦴½ *Deadly Companion* **1980** A photojournalist pursues his wife's killer in a confusing story. Based on Ross MacDonald's "The Three Roads." **96m/C VHS.** *CA* Michael Sarrazin, Susan Clark, Anthony Perkins, Howard Duff, Kate Reid, Al Waxman, Elizabeth Shepherd, John Candy; ***D:*** George Bloomfield; ***W:*** Janis Allen.

The Double O Kid 🦴🦴½ **1992 (PG-13)** Lance is a 17-year-old video game master who's interning at the Agency, a covert spy organization. Ordered to rush a package to Los Angeles, Lance discovers that a madman computer virus designer and his henchwoman desperately want what he's carrying. Aided by the prerequisite pretty girl, Lance must avoid all the hazards sent his way. **95m/C VHS.** Corey Haim, Wallace Shawn, Brigitte Nielsen, Nicole Eggert, John Rhys-Davies, Basil Hoffman, Karen Black; ***Cameos:*** Anne Francis; ***D:*** Duncan McLachlan; ***W:*** Andrea Buck, Duncan McLachlan.

Double Obsession 🦴½ **1993 (R)** College roommates Heather (Hemingway) and Claire (d'Abo) are inseparable friends—until Claire falls in love. Heather becomes possessive and, though the years pass, her obsession with Claire only grows. When Heather's affections turn deadly, can Claire stop her? **88m/C VHS.** Margaux Hemingway, Maryam D'Abo, Frederic Forrest, Scott Valentine; ***D:*** Eduardo Montes; ***W:*** Jeffrey Delman, R.J. Marx, Eduardo Montes.

Double Parked 🦴🦴½ **2000** Meter maid Rita (Thorne) is divorced from an alcoholic abuser and finally has a steady job. Which she needs to support her teenaged son Matt (Read) who suffers from cystic fibrosis and bad judgement since his best friend is a delinquent (Fleiss). Rita's been taken care of business while putting her personal needs on hold but that's about to change. Fine performances. **98m/C VHS, DVD, Wide.** Callie (Calliope) Thorne, Rufus Read, Noah Fleiss, William Sage, Anthony De Sando, Eileen Galindro, Michelle Hurd, P.J. Brown; ***D:*** Stephen Kinsella; ***W:*** Stephen Kinsella, Paul Solberg; ***C:*** Jim Denault; ***M:*** Craig Hazen, David Wolfert.

Double Platinum 🦴🦴½ **1999 (PG)** Baby diva Brandy squares off against mega-diva Ross—the mommy who abandoned her for a fabulous career. Eighteen years later Brandy decides to pursue a singing career herself and meets Ross—not knowing about their relationship. But when she finds out, there are a lot of abandonment issues to deal with and this teen is determined to get even by besting mommy dearest at her own game. You go, girl! **91m/C VHS, DVD.** Diana Ross, Brandy, Harvey Fierstein, Roger Rees, Brian Stokes Mitchell, Christine Ebersole, Tony Payne; ***D:*** Robert Ackerman; ***W:*** Nina Shengold, Katie Ford, Renee Longstreet. **TV**

Double Play 🦴🦴½ **1996 (PG)** Updated version of "The Prince and the Pauper" finds teenaged computer genius Rudy (Jackson) inheriting his dad's successful computer company. But his evil Uncle Mike (Shatner), who's not the boy's guardian, wants the company for himself and hires some thugs to kidnap the kid and force him to sign over control of the business. But Rudy just happens to have a double—a high school baseball star who's in town for the championship game—and confusion rules when he takes his place. Jackson's brother, Richard Lee Jackson, plays his cousin in the movie. **101m/C VHS.** Jonathan Jackson, William Shatner, Richard Lee Jackson, Jay Brazeau; ***D:*** Stefan Scaini; ***W:*** Richard Clark; ***C:*** Maris Jansons; ***M:*** John Welsman.

Double Revenge 🦴½ **1989** Two men feel they have a score to settle after a bank heist gone sour leaves two people dead. **90m/C VHS.** Bobby DiCicco, Joe Dallesandro, Nancy Everhard, Leigh McCloskey, Richard Rust, Theresa Saldana; ***D:*** Armand Mastroianni.

Double Standard 🦴½ **1988** You'll be less concerned with the plot—a community discovers that a prominent judge has maintained two marriages for nearly 20 years—than with the possibility that such dim-witted myopes might actually have existed in the real world. This made-for-TV slice of bigamy is for fans of the oops-I-forgot-I'm-married genre only. **95m/C VHS.** Robert Foxworth, Michele Greene, Pamela Bellwood, James Kee; ***D:*** Louis Rudolph.

Double Suicide 🦴🦴🦴 *Shinju Ten No Amijima* **1969** From a play by Monzarmon Chikamatsu, a tragic drama about a poor salesman in 18th century Japan who falls in love with a geisha and ruins his family and himself trying to requite the hopeless passion. Stylish with Iwashita turning in a wonderful dual performance. In Japanese with subtitles. **105m/B VHS, DVD.** *JP* Kichiemon Nakamura, Shima Iwashita, Yusuke Takita, Hosei Komatsu; ***D:*** Masahiro Shinoda; ***W:*** Masahiro Shinoda, Toru Takemitsu, Taeko Tomioka; ***C:*** Toichiro Narushima; ***M:*** Toru Takemitsu.

Double Take 🦴🦴 **1997 (R)** Writer Connor McEwen (Sheffer) witnesses a murder and identifies the suspect from a police line-up. But when he sees a dead ringer for the alleged murderer, he becomes convinced the police have arrested the wrong guy. **86m/C VHS.** Craig Sheffer, Costas Mandylor, Brigitte Bako, Torri Higginson, Maurice Godin; ***D:*** Mark L. Lester; ***W:*** Ed Rugoff, Ralph Rugoff; ***M:*** Paul Zaza.

Double Take 🦴 **2001 (PG-13)** Businessman Daryl Chase (Jones) is framed as a money-launderer for a drug cartel and assumes the identity of street hustler Freddy (Griffin) in order to clear his name. Fans of "Mad TV" and "Malcolm and Eddie" (Jones and Griffin's TV ventures, respectively) will probably be sorely disappointed with this action-comedy attempt. While the two stars trade zingers and dodge gunfire, you're left to wonder why you didn't rent "Midnight Run," or even "Beverly Hills Cop 3." **88m/C VHS, DVD.** *US* Orlando Jones, Eddie Griffin, Gary Grubbs, Daniel Roebuck, Sterling Macer, Garcelle Beauvais, Edward Herrmann, Benny Nieves, Shawn Elliott, Brent Briscoe, Carlos Carrasco; ***D:*** George Gallo; ***W:*** George Gallo; ***C:*** Theo van de Sande; ***M:*** Graeme Revell.

Double Team 🦴🦴 **1997 (R)** Counter-terrorist expert Jack Quinn (Van Damme) teams with weapons specialist Yaz (Rodman, in his film debut) to take down international terrorist Stavros (Roarke). After Jack kills Stavros's son, he is sent to a high-security superspy retirement village. When his wife and newborn son are kidnapped, Jack escapes, with Yaz's help, to finish the job and try to save his family. Van Damme teams with his third famous Hong Kong action director, Tsui Hark (the other two are John Woo and Ringo Lam) to create yet another disappointment. He's slightly more charismatic than usual (not saying much), but Rodman easily steals the flick as he gets most of the good lines, and delivers them with relish. **93m/C VHS, DVD.** Jean-Claude Van Damme, Dennis Rodman, Mickey Rourke, Natasha Lindinger, Paul Freeman, Valeria Cavalli, Jay Benedict; ***D:*** Tsui Hark; ***W:*** Paul Mones, Don Jakoby; ***C:*** Peter Pau; ***M:*** Gary Chang. Golden Raspberries '97: Worst Support. Actor (Rodman), Worst New Star (Rodman).

Double Threat 🦴🦴 **1992 (R)** An aging sex star makes her return to the screen opposite a younger actor with whom she is having an affair. When the director wants to include nude sex scenes in the film she agrees to use a younger body-double. Then the actress discovers her lover is involved in off-screen action with the double as well. This does not please her and she decides to take a deadly revenge. An unrated version is also available. **94m/C VHS.** Sally Kirkland, Andrew Stevens, Lisa Shane, Richard Lynch, Anthony (Tony) Franciosa, Sherrie Rose, Chick Vennera; ***D:*** David A. Prior.

Double Trouble 🦴🦴½ **1941** Langdon and Rogers are hired to work in a canning factory and accidentally package a valuable necklace in a can of beans. The rest is a mad chase to get the necklace back. Langdon was best known as a silent-screen comedian but he hadn't lost his farcical touch. **62m/B VHS.** Harry Langdon, Charles "Buddy" Rogers, Dave O'Brien, Wheeler Oakman, Catherine Lewis, Mira McKinney; ***D:*** William West; ***W:*** Jack Natteford; ***C:*** Arthur Martinelli; ***M:*** Ross DiMaggio.

Double Trouble 🦴🦴 **1967** When rock star Presley falls in love with an English heiress, he winds up involved in an attempted murder. The king belts out "Long Legged Girl" while evading cops, criminals, and crying women. A B-side. Based on a story by Marc Brandell. **92m/C VHS.** Elvis Presley, Annette Day, John Williams, Yvonne Romain, Michael Murphy, Chips Rafferty; ***D:*** Norman Taurog; ***W:*** Jo Heims.

Double Trouble 🦴 **1991 (R)** Twin brothers—one a cop, one a jewel thief—team up to crack the case of an international jewel smuggling ring headed by a wealthy and politically well-connected businessman and his righthand man. **87m/C VHS.** David Paul, Peter Paul, James Doohan, Roddy McDowall, Steve Kanaly, A.J. (Anthony) Johnson, David Carradine; ***D:*** John Paragon.

Double Vision 🦴🦴 **1992 (PG-13)** Suspense thriller starring Cattrall as Caroline, a medical student who goes to London to check out the strange disappearance of her twin sister, Lisa. Assuming her identity, Caroline gets deeply involved in a kinky lifestyle that may result in murder. Based on a short story by Mary Higgins Clark. **92m/C VHS.** Kim Cattrall, Gale Hansen, Christopher Lee; ***D:*** Robert Knights.

Double Wedding 🦴🦴🦴 **1937** Madcap comedy starring Powell as a wacky painter who doesn't believe in working and Loy as a workaholic dress designer. Loy has chosen a fiance for her younger sister, Irene, to marry, but Irene has plans of her own. When Irene and her beau meet bohemian Powell, the fun really begins. Script suffers slightly from too much slapstick and not enough wit, although the stars (in their seventh outing as a duo) play it well. Based on the play "Great Love" by Ferenc Molnar. **86m/B VHS.** William Powell, Myrna Loy, Florence Rice, John Beal, Jessie Ralph, Edgar Kennedy, Sidney Toler, Mary Gordon; ***D:*** Richard Thorpe; ***W:*** Jo Swerling.

Doubting Thomas 🦴🦴½ **1935** Rogers' last film, which was in theatres when he was killed in a plane crash. Silly story of a husband and his doubts about his wife and her amateur-acting career. The show goes on in spite of his doubts, her forgotten lines, and wardrobe goofs. Remake of 1922's silent film "The Torch Bearers." **78m/B VHS.** Will Rogers, Billie Burke, Alison Skipworth, Sterling Holloway; ***D:*** David Butler.

Doughboys 🦴🦴½ *Forward March* **1930** Keaton's second talkie is a so-so comedy about a rich man who mistakenly enlists in the Army during WWI. He manages to bumble his way through basic training and win the heart of a pretty girl. There are a few bright moments, particularly a musical number between Keaton and "Ukulele Ike" Edwards. **80m/B VHS.** Buster Keaton, Cliff Edwards, Edward Brophy, Sally Eilers, Victor Potel, Arnold Korff, Frank Mayo; ***D:*** Edward Sedgwick.

Doughnuts & Society 🦴½ **1936** Two elderly ladies who run a coffee shop suddenly strike it rich and find that life among the bluebloods is not all it's cracked up to be. No sprinkles. **70m/B VHS.** Louise Fazenda, Maude Eburne, Eddie Nugent, Ann Rutherford, Hedda Hopper, Franklin Pangborn.

Doug's 1st Movie 🦴🦴🦴 **1999 (G)** Feature-length version of the children's animated series assumes sequels according to the title, but has problem stretching the storyline over an hour. However, kids who like the series will enjoy the adventures of 12-year-old Doug Funnie and his pal Skeeter as they try to hide the lake monster Herman Melville (so named because he tries to eat a copy of "Moby Dick") from the clutches of polluting bad guy Mr. Bluff. He also has to impress Patti before the big Valentine's Day Dance. Not overly preachy, but the animation will not impress children used to the glossy Disney style. **77m/C VHS.** ***D:*** Maurice Joyce; ***W:*** Ken Scarborough; ***M:*** Mark Watters; ***V:*** Guy Hadley, Eddie Korbich, Thomas McHugh, Fred Newman, Chris Phillips, Constance Shulman, Frank Welker, Alice Playten, Doris Belack, Doug Preis.

The Dove 🦴🦴½ **1974 (PG-13)** The true story of a 16-year-old's adventures as he sails around the world in a 23-foot sloop. The trip took him five years and along the way he falls in love with a girl who follows him to exotic locales. Photography and scenery are magnificent. **105m/C VHS.** Joseph Bottoms, Deborah Raffin, Dabney Coleman, Peter Gwynne; ***D:*** Charles Jarrott; ***W:*** Peter S. Beagle; ***C:*** Sven Nykvist.

Down Among the Z Men 🦴🦴 **1952** Enlisted man helps a girl save an atomic formula from spies. Funny in spots but weighed down by musical numbers from a female entourage. From the pre-Monty Python comedy troupe "The Goons." **71m/B VHS.** *GB* Peter Sellers, Spike Milligan, Harry Secombe, Michael Bentine, Carole Carr; ***D:*** Maclean Rogers.

Down & Dirty 🦴🦴🦴 *Brutti, Sporchi, e Cattivi; Ugly, Dirty and Bad; Dirty, Mean and Nasty* **1976** A scathing Italian satire about a modern Roman family steeped in petty crime, incest, murder, adultery, drugs, and arson. In Italian with English subtitles. **115m/C VHS.** *IT* Nino Manfredi, Francesco Anniballi, Maria Bosco; ***D:*** Ettore Scola; ***W:*** Ruggero Maccari, Ettore Scola; ***C:*** Dario Di Palma; ***M:*** Armando Trovajoli. Cannes '76: Director (Scola).

Down and Out in Beverly Hills 🦴🦴½ **1986 (R)** A modern retelling of Jean Renoir's classic "Boudu Saved from Drowning" with some nice star turns. Neurotic and wealthy Beverly Hills married Dave (Dreyfuss) and Barbara (Midler) find their lives turned upside down when they prevent suicidal bum Jerry Baskin (Nolte) from drowning in their pool. Jerry takes over the household—bedding Barbara, her daughter Jenny (Nelson), and their sultry maid Carmen (Pena)—offering encouragement to a frustrated Dave and his son Max (Richards)—and even solving family dog Matisse's identity crisis. Naturally, Jerry learns there's more to life than being a bum. **103m/C VHS.** Nick Nolte, Bette Midler, Richard Dreyfuss, Little Richard, Tracy Nelson, Elizabeth Pena, Evan Richards, Valerie Curtin, Barry Primus, Dorothy Tristan, Alexis Arquette; ***D:*** Paul Mazursky; ***W:*** Paul Mazursky, Leon Capetanos; ***C:*** Donald McAlpine; ***M:*** Andy Summers.

Down Argentine Way 🦴🦴🦴 **1940** A lovely young woman falls in love with a suave Argentinian horse breeder. First-rate Fox musical made a star of Grable and was Miranda's first American film. ♫South American Way; Down Argentina Way; Two Dreams Met; Mama Yo Quiero; Sing to Your Senorita. **90m/C VHS.** Don Ameche, Betty Grable, Carmen Miranda, Charlotte Greenwood, J. Carrol Naish, Henry Stephenson, Leonid Kinskey; ***D:*** Irving Cummings; ***C:*** Leon Shamroy.

Down by Law 🦴🦴🦴 **1986 (R)** In Jarmusch's follow-up to his successful "Stranger than Paradise," he introduces us to three men: a pimp, an out-of-work disc jockey, and an Italian tourist. When the three break out of prison, they wander through the Louisiana swampland with some regrets about their new-found freedom. Slow-moving at times, beautifully shot throughout. Poignant and hilarious, the film is true to Jarmusch form: some will love the film's offbeat flair, and others will find it bothersome. **107m/B VHS.** John Lurie, Tom Waits, Roberto Benigni, Ellen Barkin, Billie Neal, Rockets Redglare, Vernel Bagneris, Nicoletta Braschi; ***D:*** Jim Jarmusch; ***W:*** Jim Jarmusch; ***C:*** Robby Muller; ***M:*** John Lurie, Tom Waits.

Down Came a Blackbird 🦴🦴½ **1994 (R)** Anna Lenka (Redgrave), a Holocaust survivor, runs a clinic for healing both the physical and psychological wounds of torture victims. Journalist Helen McNulty (Dern), herself a survivor, decides to write about the clinic but Anna believes Helen's covering up the pain she's never dealt with. Also at the clinic is Tomas Ramirez (Julia), a former college professor with a terrible secret, with whom Helen discovers a special rapport. Conventional script with some fine performances; Julia died shortly after principal photography was completed on the TV film, which is dedicated to his memory. **112m/C VHS.** Vanessa Redgrave, Laura Dern, Raul Julia, Jay O. Sanders, Cliff Gorman, Sarita Choudhury, L. Scott Caldwell, Jeffrey DeMunn; ***D:*** Jonathan Sanger; ***W:*** Kevin Droney; ***C:*** Kees Van Oostrum; ***M:*** Graeme Revell.

Down Dakota Way 🦴½ **1949** Strange coincidence between a recent murder and a fatal cow epidemic. Rogers helps some locals bring the link to light. **67m/C VHS.** Roy Rogers, Dale Evans, Pat Brady, Monte Montana, Elisabeth Risdon, Byron Barr, James B. Cardwell, Roy Barcroft, Emmett Vogan; ***D:*** William Witney.

Down in the Delta 🦴🦴🦴 **1998 (PG-13)** Chicago matriarch Rosa Lynn (Alice) tries to prevent her jobless, single-mom daughter Loretta (Woodard) from succumbing to drugs, alcohol, and the other destructive forces that are a part of her rough neighborhood. She sends her Loretta and her two grandchildren (including an autistic boy) to her brother's home in the Mississippi delta, hoping that they'll reconnect to their roots. Though reluctant at first, Loretta finds herself slowly changing her ways as she works in Uncle Earl's restaurant; she is moved by his love of family, particularly his Alzheimer-ridden wife (Rolle). Poet-novelist Maya Angelou's first outing as a director skillfully demonstrates the importance of connecting to one's heritage. Woodard shines energetically as the strung-out mom and Freeman is nearly perfect as the elegant and tender Uncle Earl. **111m/C VHS, DVD.** Alfre Woodard, Al Freeman Jr., Mary Alice, Wesley Snipes, Esther Rolle, Loretta Devine, Anne-Marie Johnson, Mpho Koaho, Kulani Hassen, Richard Blackburn; ***D:*** Maya Angelou; ***W:*** Myron Goble; ***C:*** William Wages; ***M:*** Stanley Clarke. **CABLE**

Down Mexico Way 🦴🦴 **1941** Two cowboys come to the aid of a Mexican town whose residents have been hoodwinked by a phony movie company. Very exciting chase on horseback, motorcycle, and in automobiles. **78m/B VHS.** Gene Autry, Smiley Burnette, Fay McKenzie, Duncan Renaldo; ***D:*** Joseph Santley.

Down, Out and Dangerous 🦴🦴 **1995 (R)** Expectant couple Brad (Davison) and Monica (Ettinger) Harrington find out that Tim (Thomas), the charming homeless man they've befriended, is really a psycho killer. **90m/C VHS.** Richard Thomas, Bruce Davison, Cynthia Ettinger, Steve Hytner, Christine Cavanaugh, George DiCenzo, Jason Bernard, Melinda Culea, Stuart Pankin; ***D:*** Noel Nosseck; ***W:*** Carey Hayes, Chad Hayes; ***C:*** Paul Maibaum; ***M:*** Mark Snow.

Down Periscope 🦴🦴½ **1996 (PG-13)** Tom Dodge (Grammer) dreams of commanding a nuclear sub, but gets stuck with an out-of-mothballs, rusting WWII vintage tub with the usual goof-off crew. In order for Dodge to get his dream assignment, he and his losers must beat the nuclear subs of generic mean authority figure Admiral Graham (Dern), in a war game. Predictable comedy is kept afloat by amusing cast, especially Schneider as the weaselly Executive Officer Pascal. Many jokes revolve around Dodge's tattoo, which is on a body part that is normally private first-class. Denied cooperation from the U.S. Navy, the shipyard scenes were filmed on three barges tied together in the San Francisco Bay area, with empty discarded frigates and destroyers belonging to the U.S. Department of Transportation playing the fleet. **92m/C VHS.** Kelsey Grammer, Lauren Holly, Bruce Dern, Rob Schneider, Rip Torn, Harry Dean Stanton, William H. Macy, Ken Campbell, Toby Huss, Duane Martin, Jonathan Penner, Bradford Tatum, Harland Williams; ***D:*** David S. Ward; ***W:*** Hugh Wilson, Andrew Kurtzman, Eliot Wald; ***C:*** Victor Hammer; ***M:*** Randy Edelman.

Down Texas Way 🦴🦴 **1942** One of the "Rough Riders" series. When one of the boys is accused of murdering his best friend, his two companions search for the real killer. **57m/B VHS.** Buck Jones, Tim McCoy, Raymond Hatton; ***D:*** Howard Bretherton.

Down the Drain 🦴🦴 **1989 (R)** A broad-as-a-city-block farce about an unscrupulous criminal lawyer and his assortment of crazy clients. A fine first half but someone pulls the plug in the middle of the bath. **90m/C VHS.** Andrew Stevens, John Matuszak, Teri Copley, Joseph Campanella, Don Stroud, Stella Stevens, Jerry Mathers, Benny "The Jet" Urquidez; ***D:*** Robert C. Hughes.

Down the Wyoming Trail 🦴 **1939** Western hero Ritter battles some rustlers who are terrorizing farmers during the winter, while still managing to find time to warble some tunes. **52m/B VHS.** Tex Ritter, Horace Murphy, Mary Brodel, Bobby Lawson, Charles "Blackie" King, Bob Terry; ***D:*** Al(bert) Herman; ***W:*** Peter Dixon, Roger Merton.

Down to Earth 🦴🦴🦴 **1917** Ever-gallant lover Fairbanks overruns a mental hospital to save his sweetheart. Once inside, he's determined to show the patients that their illness is illusion, and reality's the cure. A quixotic gem from Fairbanks' pre-swashbuckling social comic days. Director Emerson's wife was the scenarist, and Victor Fleming, who went on to direct "The Wizard of Oz" and "Gone with the Wind" (to name a few), was the man behind the camera. **68m/B VHS.** Douglas Fairbanks Sr., Eileen (Elaine Persey) Percy, Gustav von Seyffertitz, Charles P. McHugh, Charles Gerrard, William H. Keith, Ruth Allen, Fred Goodwine; ***D:*** John Emerson.

Down to Earth 🦴🦴 **1947** A lackluster musical and boxoffice flop with an impressive cast. Hayworth is the Greek goddess of dance sent to Earth on a mission to straighten out Broadway producer Parks and his play that ridicules the Greek gods. Anita Ellis dubs the singing of Hayworth. A parody of "Here Comes Mr. Jordan," remade in 1980 as "Xanadu." **101m/C VHS.** Rita Hayworth, Larry Parks, Marc Platt, Roland Culver, James Gleason, Edward Everett Horton, Adele Jergens, George Macready, William Frawley, James Burke, Fred F. Sears, Lynn Merrick, Myron Healey; ***D:*** Alexander Hall; ***W:*** Edwin Blum; ***M:*** George Duning.

Down to Earth 🦴🦴 **2001 (PG-13)** Rock is called to heaven before his time by angel Levy but the only body available to send him back in is that of a 60-ish white businessman. Rock's presence and comic sensibility saves what could've been a lame time-waster but he's the only reason to see it and if you don't like Rock, don't bother. Remake of "Heaven Can Wait," which was a remake of "Here Comes Mr. Jordan." **87m/C VHS, DVD, Wide.**

US Chris Rock, Regina King, Chazz Palminteri, Eugene Levy, Frankie Faison, Mark Addy, Greg Germann, Jennifer Coolidge; ***D:*** Chris Weitz, Paul Weitz; ***W:*** Chris Rock, Lance Crouther, Ali LeRoi, Louis CK; ***C:*** Richard Crudo; ***M:*** Jamshield Sharifi.

Down to the Sea in Ships 🦴🦴½ *The Last Adventurers* **1922** Bow made her movie debut in this drama about the whalers of 19th-century Massachusetts. Highlighted by exciting action scenes of an actual whale hunt. Silent with music score and original tinted footage. **83m/B VHS, DVD.** Marguerite Courtot, Raymond (Ray) McKee, Clara Bow; ***D:*** Elmer Clifton; ***W:*** John L.E. Pell; ***C:*** Alexander Penrod.

Down to You 🦴🦴½ **2000 (PG-13)** Light romantic comedy has appealing leads and a predictable plot (and references to about a gazillion similar movies). Aspiring chef Al (Prinze Jr.) and artist Imogen (Stiles) are immediately smitten when they meet at the campus dive. The relationship develops at headlong speed but then they both realize neither of them is ready for a lifelong commitment. So, do they just split or try being friends or slow things down or what? **92m/C VHS, DVD, Wide.** Freddie Prinze Jr., Julia Stiles, Selma Blair, Shawn Hatosy, Zak Orth, Rosario Dawson, Henry Winkler, Ashton Kutcher, Lucie Arnaz; ***D:*** Kris Isacsson; ***W:*** Kris Isacsson; ***C:*** Robert Yeoman; ***M:*** Edmund Choi.

Down Twisted 🦴 **1989 (R)** A young woman gets involved with a thief on the run in Mexico in this "Romancing the Stone" derivative. The muddled plot deserves such a confusing title. **89m/C VHS.** Carey Lowell, Charles Rocket, Trudi Dochtermann, Thom Mathews, Linda Kerridge, Courteney Cox Arquette; ***D:*** Albert Pyun; ***W:*** Albert Pyun; ***C:*** Walt Lloyd; ***M:*** Eric Allaman.

Down Under 🦴 **1986** Two gold-hungry beach boys go to Australia looking for riches, and document their adventures on film. Essentially a crudely shot, tongue-in-cheek travelogue narrated by Patrick Macnee. **90m/C VHS.** Don Atkinson, Donn Dunlop, Patrick Macnee.

Downdraft 🦴🦴 **1996 (R)** A special forces unit has six hours to penetrate a subterranean bunker, which protects a supercomputer that's about to launch a nuclear attack. Assaulted by a variety of sophisticated weapons, the unit must also outwit the computer's android defender. **101m/C VHS.** Vincent Spano, Kate Vernon, Paul Koslo.

Downhill Racer 🦴🦴½ **1969 (PG)** An undisciplined American skier locks skitips with his coach and his new-found love while on his way to becoming an Olympic superstar. Character study on film. Beautiful ski and mountain photography keep it from sliding downhill. **102m/C VHS.** Robert Redford, Camilla Sparv, Gene Hackman, Dabney Coleman; ***D:*** Michael Ritchie.

Downhill Willie 🦴½ **1996 (PG)** Willie (Coogan) isn't the brightest guy around—except on skies. Now he wants to enter the Kamikaze Run, which takes place on an extreme race course, and win the half-million top prize as well as the prettiest snow bunny (Keanan) on the slopes. **90m/C VHS, DVD.** Keith Coogan, Staci Keanan, Lochlan Monroe, Estelle Harris, Fred Stoller, Lee Reherman; ***D:*** David Mitchell; ***W:*** Stephanie Cedar; ***C:*** David Pelletier; ***M:*** Norman Orenstein.

Downtown 🦴½ **1989 (R)** Urban comedy about a naive white suburban cop who gets demoted to the roughest precinct in Philadelphia, and gains a streetwise black partner. Runs a routine beat. **96m/C VHS.** Anthony Edwards, Forest Whitaker, Joe Pantoliano, Penelope Ann Miller; ***D:*** Richard Benjamin; ***M:*** Alan Silvestri.

D.P. **1985** A black orphan attaches to the only other black in post-WWII Germany. From a story by Kurt Vonnegut Jr. **60m/C VHS.** Stan Shaw, Rosemary Leach, Julius Gordon. **TV**

Drachenfutter 🦴🦴🦴 *Dragon's Food; Dragon Chow* **1987** Powerful story dealing with a Pakistani immigrant's attempts to enter the Western world. Themes of alienation and helplessness are emphasized. Dialogues occur in 12 languages, predominantly German and Mandarin Chinese; subtitled in English. **75m/B VHS.** *GE SI* Bhasker, Ric Young, Buddy Uzzaman; ***D:*** Jan Schutte; ***W:*** Thomas Strittmatter; ***M:*** Claus Bantzer.

Dracula (Spanish Version) 🦴🦴½ **1931** Filmed at the same time as the Bela Lugosi version of "Dracula," using the same sets and the same scripts, only in Spanish. Thought to be more visually appealing and more terrifying than the English-language counterpart. The only thing it's missing is a presence like Lugosi. Based on the novel by Bram Stoker. **104m/B VHS.** Carlos Villarias, Lupita Tovar, Eduardo Arozamena, Pablo Alvarez Rubio, Barry Norton, Carmen Guerrero; ***D:*** George Melford; ***W:*** Garrett Fort.

Dracula 🦴🦴🦴 **1931** Lugosi, in his most famous role, plays a vampire who terrorizes the countryside in his search for human blood. From Bram Stoker's novel. Although short of a masterpiece due to slow second half, deservedly rated a film classic. What would Halloween be like without this movie? Sequelled by "Dracula's Daughter." The 1999 re-release was re-scored by Philip Glass and performed by the Kronos Quartet. **75m/B VHS, DVD.** Bela Lugosi, David Manners, Dwight Frye, Helen Chandler, Edward Van Sloan, Frances Dade, Herbert Bunston; ***D:*** Tod Browning; ***W:*** Garrett Fort; ***C:*** Karl Freund. Natl. Film Reg. '00.

Dracula 🦴🦴½ *Bram Stoker's Dracula* **1973** Count on squinty-eyed Palance to shine as the Transylvanian vampire who must quench his thirst for human blood. Adaptation of the Bram Stoker novel that really flies. **105m/C VHS, DVD.** Jack Palance, Simon Ward, Fiona Lewis, Nigel Davenport, Pamela Brown, Penelope Horner, Murray Brown, Virginia Wetherell, Sarah Douglas, Barbara Lindley; ***D:*** Dan Curtis; ***W:*** Richard Matheson; ***C:*** Oswald Morris; ***M:*** Wojciech Kilar. **TV**

Dracula 🦴🦴½ **1979 (R)** Langella recreates his Broadway role as the count who needs human blood for nourishment. Notable for its portrayal of Dracula as a romantic and tragic figure in history. Overlooked since the vampire spoof "Love at First Bite" came out at the same time. **109m/C VHS, DVD, Wide.** Frank Langella, Laurence Olivier, Kate Nelligan, Donald Pleasence, Janine Duvitsky, Trevor Eve, Tony Haygarth; ***D:*** John Badham; ***W:*** W.D. Richter; ***C:*** Gilbert Taylor; ***M:*** John Williams.

Dracula A.D. 1972 🦴🦴 *Dracula Today* **1972** Lee returned to England for his sixth (and by most accounts, worst) go-round as Dracula for Hammer Films, where the creative juices seemed to be drying up. The decision was made to turn Dracula loose in the modern world. The movie actually opens in 1872 with a scene that is one of the highlights of the entire production—an action scene that features Dracula battling his nemesis Van Helsing (Cushing) atop a speeding stagecoach. When the coach is wrecked, Dracula is impaled on a wheel spoke and dies. From that point, the scene immediately jumps ahead one century. A Satanist named Johnny Alucard and a group of naive hippie teenagers revive the long-dead vampire in an abandoned church building in England. The teens and Dracula are opposed by Van Helsing's grandson (Cushing again) and his granddaughter Jessica (Beacham). Hammer's unwillingness to pay Lee to speak more than a few lines, together with a sterile plot that had Dracula essentially paralyzed by the modern world, forced the teenagers to carry the story. It appears that the idea for *Dracula A.D. 1972* came from the Count Yorga movies, which had some success in placing an Old World vampire in modern Los Angeles. However, the Yorga movies were only moderately successful and this Hammer copy did not even do that well. *Dracula A.D. 1972* was the sequel to *The Scars of Dracula* (1971) and was followed by *The Satanic Rites of Dracula* (1973). **95m/C VHS.** *GB* Christopher Lee, Peter Cushing, Christopher Neame, Stephanie Beacham, Michael Coles, Caroline Munro, Marsha A. Hunt, Philip Miller, Janet Key, William Ellis; ***D:*** Alan Gibson; ***W:*** Don Houghton; ***C:*** Dick Bush; ***M:*** Michael Vickers.

Dracula & Son 🦴 *Dracula Pere et Fils* **1976 (PG)** Dracula spoof in which the count fathers a son who prefers girls and football to blood. Poor English dubbing and choppy ending drive a stake through the heart. **88m/C VHS.** *FR* Christopher Lee, Bernard Menez, Marie Breillat; ***D:*** Edouard Molinaro; ***M:*** Vladimir Cosma.

Dracula Blows His Cool 🦴 **1982 (R)** Three voluptuous models and their photographer restore an ancient castle and open a disco in it. The vampire lurking about the castle welcomes the party with his fangs. **91m/C VHS.** John Garco, Betty Verges; ***D:*** Carlo Ombra; ***W:*** Carlo Ombra.

Dracula: Dead and Loving It woof! **1995 (PG-13)** King of the spoofs Nielsen takes on the title role as the ever-loving, if clumsy, Count who still enjoys necking—particularly with luscious damsels in distress, Lucy (Anthony) and Mina (Yasbeck). And he's still got his bug-eating minion Renfield (MacNichol) and egomaniacal vampire-hunter Van Helsing (Brooks) around. As usual, Brooks throws everything possible on the screen, hoping some schtick will stick (not very much does). **90m/C VHS.** Leslie Nielsen, Mel Brooks, Peter MacNicol, Lysette Anthony, Amy Yasbeck, Steven Weber, Harvey Korman, Anne Bancroft; ***D:*** Mel Brooks; ***W:*** Mel Brooks, Rudy DeLuca, Steve Haberman; ***C:*** Michael D. O'Shea; ***M:*** Hummie Mann.

Dracula Father and Son 🦴½ *Dracula Pere et Fils* **1976** Badly-dubbed French satire finds the elegant Count (Lee) deciding that beautiful Hermaine (Marie-Helene Breillat) would be the perfect vampire mommy. Thus Dracula's son Ferdinand is born. Some 300 years later, Ferdinand (Menez) is proving to be a trial to his father, since he has yet to drink anyone's blood. Driven from their castle, the Count winds up in London and becomes a star in vampire films, while Ferdinand lives in Paris. When the two reunite, it's to feud over the beautiful Nicole (Catherine Breillat), who happens to be a dead ringer for Hermaine. Based on the novel "Paris Vampire" by Claude Klotz. **70m/C VHS.** *FR* Christopher Lee, Bernard Menez, Catherine Breillat, Marie Breillat; ***D:*** Edouard Molinaro; ***W:*** Edouard Molinaro.

Dracula/Garden of Eden 🦴🦴 **1928** The abridged version of the chilling vampire film "Nosferatu" is coupled with "The Garden of Eden," in which Tini Le Brun meets her Prince Charming while vacationing with her Baroness friend. Silent. **52m/B VHS.** Max Schreck, Alexander Granach, Corine Griffith, Charles Ray, Louise Dresser.

Dracula Has Risen from the Grave 🦴🦴½ **1968 (G)** Lee's Dracula is foiled by the local priest before he can drain the blood from innocent villagers. Effectively gory. One of the Hammer series of Dracula films followed by "Taste the Blood of Dracula." **92m/C VHS.** *GB* Christopher Lee, Rupert Davies, Veronica Carlson, Barbara Ewing, Barry Andrews, Michael Ripper, Ewan Hooper, Marion Mathie; ***D:*** Freddie Francis; ***W:*** John (Anthony Hinds) Elder; ***C:*** Arthur Grant; ***M:*** James Bernard.

Dracula, Prince of Darkness 🦴🦴 *The Bloody Scream of Dracula; Disciple of Dracula; Revenge of Dracula* **1966** Sequel to 1958's "Horror of Dracula" finds the Count (Lee) extending his hospitality at Castle Dracula to four unwary tourists, one of whom is immediately killed for his blood. Then Dracula takes the dead man's wife (Shelley) and turns her into a vampire and the gruesome twosome go after the remaining couple. Standard Hammer horror. **90m/C VHS, DVD.** *GB* Christopher Lee, Barbara Shelley, Andrew Keir, Francis Matthews, Suzan Farmer, Charles Tingwell, Thorley Walters, Philip Latham; ***D:*** Terence Fisher; ***W:*** John Sansom, John (Anthony Hinds) Elder; ***C:*** Michael Reed; ***M:*** James Bernard.

Dracula Rising 🦴🦴½ **1993 (R)** A modern-day art historian (Travis) turns out to have been a witch, burned at the stake, in a past life. She was also the blood-drinking Count's lost love. Now Dracula's a monk and when he sees this reincarnated beauty is he going to be able to keep his hands—er, fangs—off her? **?m/C VHS.** Christopher Atkins, Stacy Travis, Doug Wert, Zahari Vatahov; ***D:*** Fred Gallo.

Dracula Sucks 🦴 **1979 (R)** A softcore edit of a hardcore sex parody about Dracula snacking on the usual bevy of screaming quasi-virgins. **90m/C VHS.** James Gillis, Reggie Nalder, Annette Haven, Kay Parker, Serena, Seka, John Leslie; ***D:*** Philip Marshak.

Dracula: The Dark Prince 🦴🦴½ *Dark Prince: The True Story of Dracula* **2001 (R)** Costume bio on the life of Vlad the Impalder AKA Vlad Dracula (Martin). In the 15th century, Vlad and his brother are captured by the Turkish sultan who rules over their native Romania. During their captivity, the boys' father (the country's regent) is killed and when Vlad returns home years later he seeks to expel the Turks and rule himself. But his dreams of a unified country are undermined by tragedy and his own brutality. **89m/C VHS, DVD.** Rudolf Martin, Jane March, Peter Weller, Roger Daltrey, Michael Sutton, Christopher Brand; ***D:*** Joe Chappelle; ***W:*** Thomas Baum; ***C:*** Dermott Downs; ***M:*** Frankie Blue. **CABLE**

Dracula 2000 🦴 *Wes Craven Presents: Dracula 2000* **2000 (R)** Dracula finds his way to New Orleans to terrorize the modern world in this adaptation of the classic vampire tale that borrows freewheelingly from many supernatural legends. Butler plays Dracula well enough, but doesn't add anything memorable to a character that's been done, redone, and overdone so many times, while Plummer struggles to make the most of a bad situation. Horror fans will no doubt enjoy the gore, but the overall clumsiness is hard to take by anyone's standards. Presented by Wes Craven, but directed by Patrick Lussier, Craven's editor on many films, including the "Scream" trilogy. **98m/C VHS, DVD, Wide.** Jonny Lee Miller, Justine Waddell, Gerard Butler, Colleen (Ann) (Vitamin C) Fitzpatrick, Jennifer Esposito, Danny Masterson, Jeri Ryan, Lochlyn Munro, Sean Patrick Thomas, Omar Epps, Christopher Plummer; ***D:*** Patrick Lussier; ***W:*** Joel Soisson; ***C:*** Peter Pay; ***M:*** Marco Beltrami.

Dracula: Up in Harlem woof! **1983** When the Prince of Darkness gets together with the people of the night, the Pentagon rolls out the heavy metal. This may suck your brain out. **90m/C VHS.**

Dracula vs. Frankenstein 🦴 *Assignment: Terror* **1969** An alien reanimates Earth's most infamous monsters in a bid to take over the planet. Rennie's last role. **91m/C VHS.** *IT GE SP* Michael Rennie, Paul (Jacinto Molina) Naschy, Jacinto (Jack) Molina, Karin Dor, Patty (Patti) Shepard, Craig Hill; ***D:*** Hugo Fregonese, Tulio Demicheli; ***W:*** Jacinto (Jack) Molina.

Dracula vs. Frankenstein woof! *Blood of Frankenstein; They're Coming to Get You; Dracula Contra Frankenstein; The Revenge of Dracula; Satan's Bloody Freaks* **1971 (PG)** The Count makes a deal with a shady doctor to keep him in blood. Vampire spoof that's very bad but fun. Last film for both Chaney and Naish. Features a cameo by genre maven Forrest J. Ackerman. **90m/C VHS, DVD.** *SP* J. Carrol Naish, Lon Chaney Jr., Regina Carrol, Russ Tamblyn, Jim Davis, Anthony Eisley, Zandor Vorkov, John Bloom, Angelo Rossitto, Forrest J Ackerman; ***D:*** Al Adamson; ***W:*** William Pugsley, Sam M. Sherman; ***C:*** Paul Glickman, Gary Graver; ***M:*** William Lava.

Dracula's Daughter 🦴🦴🦴 **1936** Count Dracula's daughter, Countess Marya Zaleska, heads to London supposedly to find the cure to a mysterious illness. Instead she finds she has a taste for human blood, especially female blood. She also finds a man, falls in love, and tries to keep him by casting a spell on him. A good script and cast keep this sequel to Bela Lugosi's "Dracula" entertaining. **71m/B VHS, DVD.** Gloria Holden, Otto Kruger, Marguerite Churchill, Irving Pichel, Edward Van Sloan, Nan Grey, Hedda Hopper; ***D:*** Lambert Hillyer; ***W:*** Garrett Fort; ***C:*** George Robinson.

Dracula's Great Love woof! *Gran Amore del Conde Dracula; Count Dracula's Great Love; Dracula's Virgin Lovers; Vampire Playgirls* **1972 (R)** Four travellers end up in Dracula's castle for the night, where the horny Count takes a liking to one of the women. Left out in the sun too long. **96m/C VHS.** *SP*

Paul (Jacinto Molina) Naschy, Jacinto (Jack) Molina, Charo Soriano, Haydee Politoff, Rossana Yanni, Ingrid Garbo, Mirta Miller; *D:* Javier Aguirre; *W:* Javier Aguirre, Jacinto (Jack) Molina.

Dracula's Last Rites woof! *Last Rites* **1979 (R)** Blood-curdling tale of a sheriff and a mortician in a small town who are up to no good. Technically inept: film equipment can be spotted throughout. Don't stick your neck out for this one. **86m/C VHS.** Patricia Lee Hammond, Gerald Fielding, Victor Jorge; *D:* Domonic Paris.

Dracula's Widow 🦴🦴 **1988 (R)** Countess Dracula, missing her hubby and desperately in need of a substitute, picks innocent Raymond as her victim. His girlfriend and a cynical cop fight to save his soul from the Countess' damnation. Directed by the nephew of Frances Ford Coppola. **85m/C VHS.** Sylvia Kristel, Josef Sommer, Lenny Von Dohlen, George Stover; *D:* Christopher Coppola.

Dragnet 🦴🦴½ **1954** Sgt. Joe Friday and Officer Frank Smith try to solve a mob slaying but have a rough time. Alexander plays the sidekick in "Dragnet" pre-Morgan days. Just the facts: feature version of the TV show that's suspenseful and well-acted. **88m/C VHS.** Jack Webb, Ben Alexander, Richard Boone, Ann (Robin) Robinson; *D:* Jack Webb.

Dragnet 🦴🦴 **1987 (PG-13)** Semi-parody of the vintage '60s TV cop show. Sgt. Joe Friday's straitlaced nephew and his sloppy partner take on the seamy crime life of Los Angeles. Neither Aykroyd nor Hanks can save this big-budget but lack-luster spoof that's full of holes. **106m/C VHS, DVD.** Dan Aykroyd, Tom Hanks, Christopher Plummer, Harry (Henry) Morgan, Elizabeth Ashley, Dabney Coleman, Alexandra Paul, Kathleen Freeman, Jack O'Halloran; *D:* Tom Mankiewicz; *W:* Tom Mankiewicz, Alan Zweibel, Dan Aykroyd; *C:* Matthew F. Leonetti; *M:* Ira Newborn.

Dragon Fury 🦴½ **1995** Evil dictator tries to conquer what remains of America in the year 2099—a world peopled by barbarians and victims of a deadly plague. Naturally, there's a martial arts hero around to stop him. **80m/C VHS.** Robert Chapin, Richard Lynch, Chona Jason, Deborah Stamble; *D:* David Heavener.

Dragon Fury 2 🦴½ **1996** Futuristic action finds a heroic female struggling alone against a violent gang who want to rule the world (with the help of a computer chip). But a scientist unthaws an ancient warrior to help her out. Of course, things don't go exactly as expected. **90m/C VHS.** Mike Norris, Robert Chapin, Cathleen Ann Gardner, Cole Andersen, Walter O'Neill, Kayla Murphy; *D:* Bryan Michael Stoller; *W:* Parker Bostwick.

Dragon Lord 🦴 **1982** Young kung-fu hero (Chan) defends his village against greedy outlaws. Comic interludes tend to slow the action. **90m/C VHS, DVD.** Jackie Chan.

Dragon Seed 🦴🦴½ **1944** The lives of the residents of a small Chinese village are turned upside down when the Japanese invade it. Based on the Pearl S. Buck novel. Lengthy and occasionally tedious, though generally well-made with heart-felt attempts to create Oriental characters, without having Asians in the cast. **145m/B VHS.** Katharine Hepburn, Walter Huston, Agnes Moorehead, Akim Tamiroff, Hurd Hatfield, J. Carrol Naish, Henry Travers, Turhan Bey, Aline MacMahon; *D:* Jack Conway.

Dragon: The Bruce Lee Story 🦴🦴🦴 **1993 (PG-13)** Entertaining, inspiring account of the life of Chinese-American martial-arts legend Bruce Lee. Jason Scott Lee (no relation) is great as the talented artist, exuding his joy of life and gentle spirit, before his mysterious brain disorder death at the age of 32. Ironically, this release coincided with son Brandon's accidental death on a movie set. The martial arts sequences in "Dragon" are extraordinary, but there's also romance as Lee meets and marries his wife (Holly, who acquits herself well). Based on the book "Bruce Lee: The Man Only I Knew" by his widow, Linda Lee Caldwell. **121m/C VHS, DVD, Wide.** Jason Scott Lee, Lauren Holly, Robert Wagner, Michael Learned, Nancy Kwan, Kay Tong Lim, Sterling Macer, Ric Young, Sven Ole-Thorsen; *D:* Rob Cohen; *W:* Edward Khmara, John Raffo, Rob Cohen; *C:* David Eggby; *M:* Randy Edelman.

Dragonard 🦴½ **1988 (R)** Slaves on a West Indies island rebel against their cruel masters. **93m/C VHS.** Eartha Kitt, Oliver Reed, Annabel Schofield, Patrick Warburton; *D:* Gerard Kikoine; *W:* R.J. Marx.

Dragonfight 🦴½ **1992 (R)** Corporations rule the world and vie for supremacy through gladiator combat in this action-adventure saga set in the near future. Fights are to the death and when the current champ refuses a new challenger the corporate honchos decide to provoke him into battle by having the challenger mow down innocent bystanders. Several execs also decide the slaughter has to stop but they may be the next targets. **84m/C VHS.** Robert Z'Dar, Michael Pare, Paul Coufos, Charles Napier, James Hong, Alexa Hamilton, Fawna MacLaren.

Dragonfly 🦴½ **2002 (PG-13)** I see dead performances. Cheesy, self-gratifying supernatural snorer has Costner as Chicago's dour ER doctor Joe Darrow, righteously widowed when his doctor wife bites the dust tending to the poor in Venezuela, while pregnant, no less. Unable to accept her death, Darrow is convinced she's trying to contact him from Beyond as he receives a series of cryptic messages, some from the children in his wife's pediatric oncology ward. Darrow's talking parrot provides some of the sillier scenes in this slow-paced, must-miss melodrama. Bates as the neighbor manages to liven up her scenes, anyway. Director Shadyac ("Patch Adams") certainly didn't want his lead here displaying any of his other doctor's kid-loving antics, and glum and glummer Costner is a dutiful downer as he pumps the kids in the ward for info about his dead wife. **103m/C VHS, DVD.** *US* Kevin Costner, Joe Morton, Susanna Thompson, Ron Rifkin, Linda Hunt, Kathy Bates, Jay Thomas, Matt Craven, Robert Bailey Jr., Lisa Banes, Jacob Smith; *D:* Tom Shadyac; *W:* David Seltzer, Brandon Camp, Mike Thompson; *C:* Dean Semler; *M:* John Debney.

Dragonfly Squadron 🦴🦴 **1954** Korean war drama about pilots and their romantic problems. Never gets off the ground. **82m/C VHS.** John Hodiak, Barbara Britton, Bruce (Herman Brix) Bennett, Jess Barker; *D:* Lesley Selander.

Dragonheart 🦴🦴½ **1996 (PG-13)** Okay, get past the fact that Connery's Scottish burr is coming out of the teeth-filled mouth of an 18 ft. tall, 43 ft. long dragon and you'll be well on your way to enjoying this 10th-century fantasy. Knightly Bowen (Quaid) is the one-time mentor of evil-hearted King Einon (Thewlis) and it's up to him, Draco the dragon, feisty Kara (Meyer), and some fearful peasants to band together and free themselves from the king's tyranny. There's some slow spots but Bowen and Draco make for an amusing pairing and the dragon does seem, well, real. Work on Draco took more than a year of Industrial Light & Magic's expertise. **103m/C VHS, DVD.** Dennis Quaid, David Thewlis, Pete Postlethwaite, Dina Meyer, Julie Christie, Jason Isaacs, Brian Thompson, Wolf Christian, Terry O'Neill; *D:* Rob Cohen; *W:* Charles Edward Pogue; *C:* David Eggby; *M:* Randy Edelman; *V:* Sean Connery, John Gielgud.

Dragonheart: A New Beginning **2000 (PG)** Geoff (Masteron) is a monastery stableboy who wants to become a knight. Then he discovers Friar Peter (Woodnutt) has secretly been raising a young dragon called Drake (voiced by Benson). When the evil Lord Osric (Van Gorkum) learns of the beast's existence, he wants to claim its powers for himself. But Geoff, who's aided by two mysterious warriors from the east, is determined to save both Drake and the kingdom. **85m/C VHS, DVD.** Christopher K. Masterson, Henry O, Harry Van Gorkum, John Woodnutt, Rona Figueroa, Ken Shorter; *D:* Doug Lefler; *W:* Shari Goodhartz; *C:* Buzz Feitshans IV; *V:* Robby Benson. **VIDEO**

Dragons Forever 🦴½ *Dragon Forever* **1988** A big time lawyer is persuaded to work against a chemical plant who wants to take over a site used by local fisherman. Complications arise when he falls for the beautiful cousin of the fishery's owner. A comic king-fu battle between Chan, Hung, and Biao is the rousing finale. In Cantonese with English subtitles. **88m/C VHS, DVD.** *CH* Jackie Chan, Yuen Biao, Sammo Hung, Pauline Yeung, Yuen Wah; *D:* Sammo Hung, Corey Yuen; *W:* Roy Szeto, Gordon Chan.

Dragonslayer 🦴🦴🦴 **1981 (PG)** A sorcerer's apprentice suddenly finds himself the only person who can save the kingdom from a horrible, fire-breathing dragon. Extreme violence but wonderful special effects, smart writing, and a funny performance by Richardson. **110m/C VHS.** Peter MacNicol, Caitlin Clarke, Ralph Richardson, John Hallam, Albert Salmi, Chloe Salaman; *D:* Matthew Robbins; *W:* Matthew Robbins, Hal Barwood; *M:* Alex North.

Dragonworld 🦴🦴½ **1994 (PG)** Five-year-old Johnny McGowan is sent to Scotland to live with his grandfather. A wish for a friend has Johnny mysteriously awakening a baby dragon he names Yowler. Years later, the financially strapped adult Johnny agrees to loan Yowler to an amusement park only to find out the park's owner never intends to give Yowler back. Both baby dragon and young Johnny are unbearably cute. **86m/C VHS.** Sam Mackenzie, Courtland Mead, Brittney Powell, John Calvin, Andrew Keir, Lila Kaye, John Woodvine; *D:* Ted Nicolaou; *W:* Ted Nicolaou, Suzanne Glazener Naha; *M:* Richard Band.

Dragstrip Girl 🦴🦴 **1957** An 18-year-old girl comes of age while burning rubber at the dragstrip—the world of boys, hot rods, and horsepower. A definite "B" movie that may seem dated. **70m/B VHS.** Fay Spain, Steven Terrell, John Ashley, Frank Gorshin; *D:* Edward L. Cahn.

Dragstrip Girl 🦴🦴½ **1994** Remake of the 1857 "B" movie; a part of Showtime's Rebel Highway series. Latino Johnny (Dacasos) works as a valet during the day and goes drag racing at night. He's got big plans that may be derailed by rich white girl Laura (Wagner) who likes taking a walk on the wild side. **82m/C VHS, DVD.** Mark Dacascos, Natasha Gregson Wagner, Raymond Cruz, Traci Lords; *D:* Mary Lambert; *W:* Jerome Gary; *C:* Sandi Sissel. **CABLE**

The Drake Case 🦴🦴 **1929** A slight courtroom drama made during the waning days of the silent era. You'll probably recognize Brit Lloyd from her later career. **56m/B VHS.** Robert Frazer, Doris Lloyd, Gladys Brockwell.

The Draughtsman's Contract 🦴🦴🦴 **1982 (R)** A beguiling mystery begins when a wealthy woman hires an artist to make drawings of her home. Their contract is quite unusual, as is their relationship. Everything is going along at an even pace until murder is suspected, and things spiral down to darker levels. A simple story turned into a bizarre puzzle. Intense enough for any thriller fan. **103m/C VHS, DVD.** *GB* Anthony (Corlan) Higgins, Janet Suzman, Anne Louise Lambert, Hugh Fraser; *D:* Peter Greenaway; *W:* Peter Greenaway; *C:* Sacha Vierny; *M:* Michael Nyman.

Draw! 🦴🦴 **1981** Two has-been outlaws warm up their pistols again in this old-fashioned Western. Star power and some smart moments make it worthwhile. Made for TV. **98m/C VHS.** Kirk Douglas, James Coburn, Alexandra Bastedo, Graham Jarvis; *D:* Steven Hilliard Stern.

Dream a Little Dream 🦴🦴 **1989 (PG-13)** Strange teen transformation drama about an old man and his wife trying mystically to regain their youth. When they collide bikes with the teenagers down the street, their minds are exchanged and the older couple with the now young minds are transported to a permanent dream-like state. Same old switcheroo made bearable by cast. **114m/C VHS.** Corey Feldman, Corey Haim, Meredith Salenger, Jason Robards Jr., Piper Laurie, Harry Dean Stanton, Victoria Jackson, Alex Rocco, William McNamara; *D:* Marc Rocco; *W:* Marc Rocco.

Dream a Little Dream 2 🦴½ **1994 (PG-13)** Friends Dinger Holefield (Haim) and Bobby Keller (Feldman) receive a mysterious package containing two pairs of sunglasses, which they discover have magic powers. The wearer of one pair is driven to do the bidding of the wearer of the second pair of specs—whether for good or evil. Naturally, there are evildoers who want the glasses as well. **91m/C VHS.** Corey Haim, Corey Feldman, Stacie Randall, Michael Nicolosi; *D:* James (Momel) Lemmo; *W:* David Weissman, Susan Forman.

Dream Chasers 🦴 **1984 (PG)** A bankrupt old codger and an 11-year-old boy stricken with cancer run away together during the Great Depression. **97m/C VHS.** Harold Gould, Justin Dana.

Dream Date 🦴🦴½ **1993 (PG-13)** Lovely teenager is wooed by hip, playful suitor until trouble ensues when goofball sidekick enters the picture. Family entertainment. **96m/C VHS.** Tempestt Bledsoe, Clifton Davis, Kadeem Hardison, Anne-Marie Johnson, Pauly Shore, Richard Moll; *D:* Anson Williams.

Dream Demon 🦴 **1988** The appearance of Wilhoite, a visiting American, disrupts the status quo at a spooky British manor where the charming Redgrave debates her impending marriage to wealthy rogue Greenstreet. Aside from a terrific opening dream sequence, most of the scary bits have been done before. **89m/C VHS.** *GB* Jemma Redgrave, Kathleen Wilhoite, Timothy Spall, Jimmy Nail, Mark Greenstreet; *D:* Harley Cokliss.

Dream for an Insomniac 🦴½ **1996 (R)** Irritating characters put the kibosh on this attempt at 20-something romantic comedy. Whiny would-be actress Frankie (Skye) works at her Uncle Leo's (Cassel) cafe and hangs out with assorted, equally whiny friends. Frankie seems more interested in finding the "perfect" boyfriend than a career anyway and her interest is sparked by new guy David (a sweet Astin). Lots of overacting. Debut for writer/director DeBartolo. **108m/C VHS.** Ione Skye, MacKenzie Astin, Jennifer Aniston, Seymour Cassel, Michael Landes, Robert Kelker-Kelly; *D:* Tiffanie DeBartolo; *W:* Tiffanie DeBartolo; *C:* Guillermo Navarro; *M:* John Laraio.

A Dream for Christmas 🦴🦴🦴 **1973** Earl Hamner Jr. (best known for writing the "The Waltons") wrote this moving story of a black minister whose church in Los Angeles is scheduled to be demolished. **100m/C VHS.** Hari Rhodes, Beah Richards, George Spell, Juanita Moore, Joel Fluellen, Robert DoQui, Clarence Muse; *D:* Ralph Senensky. **TV**

Dream House 🦴🦴 **1998 (R)** This dream house of the future turns out to be a nightmare for its new owners. The supercomputer that runs everything has been misprogrammed and regards these humans as interlopers who must be killed. Tedious horror. **90m/C VHS.** *CA* Timothy Busfield, Jennifer Dale, Lisa Jakub; *D:* Graeme Campbell. **TV**

Dream Lover 🦴🦴 **1985 (R)** Terrifying nightmares after an assault lead McNichol to dream therapy. Treatment causes her tortured unconscious desires to take over her waking behavior, and she becomes a violent schizophrenic. Slow, heavy, and not very thrilling. **105m/C VHS.** Kristy McNichol, Ben Masters, Paul Shenar, Justin Deas, Joseph Culp, Gayle Hunnicutt, John McMartin; *D:* Alan J. Pakula; *W:* Jon Boorstin; *C:* Sven Nykvist.

Dream Lover 🦴🦴 **1993 (R)** Divorced architect Ray (Spader) meets and marries Lena (Amick), beautiful and seemingly perfect, who nonetheless warns him that she's just your average mixed-up gal. Suspense is supposed to come into play as Ray suspects Lena's been lying to him about her past. Visually appealing (considerably helped by the attractive leads) but good looks don't make up for the lack of substance and the minimal number of surprises expected in a thriller. Directorial debut of Kazan. Also available in an unrated version. **103m/C VHS, DVD.** James Spader, Madchen Amick, Frederic Lehne, Bess Armstrong, Larry Miller, Kathleen York, Blair Tefkin, Scott Coffey, William Shockley, Clyde Kusatsu; *D:* Nicholas Kazan; *W:* Nicholas Kazan; *C:* Jean-Yves Escoffier; *M:* Christopher Young.

Dream Lovers *Meng zhong ren* **1986** A supernatural love story which moves back and forth from contemporary Hong Kong to the mysterious Qin dynasty. When an orchestra conductor and the daughter of a noted architect meet at an exhibit featuring the famed terracotta army, an affair from the past is resurrected. In Cantonese with English subtitles. **95m/C VHS, DVD.** *CH* Chow Yun-Fat, Brigitte (Lin Chinag-hsia) Lin, Cher Yeung; ***D:*** Tony Au; ***W:*** Yau Da Ah-Pin, Manfred Wong; ***C:*** Bill Wong.

Dream Machine 🦴½ **1991 (PG)** A childish teen comedy, based on that old urban legend of the lucky kid given a free Porshe by the vengeful wife of a wealthy philanderer. The gimmick is that the husband's body is in the trunk; the murderer is in pursuit. The tape includes an anti-drug commerical—but nothing against reckless driving, which the picture glorifies. **88m/C VHS.** Corey Haim, Evan Richards, Jeremy Slate, Randall England, Tracy Fraim, Brittney Lewis, Susan Seaforth Hayes; ***D:*** Lyman Dayton.

Dream Man 🦴🦴½ **1994 (R)** Kris Anderson (Kensit) is a Seattle cop with the clairvoyant ability to see crimes as they're committed. But that doesn't stop her from getting involved with the handsome murder suspect (McCarthy) she's supposed to be investigating. **94m/C VHS.** Patsy Kensit, Andrew McCarthy, Bruce Greenwood; ***D:*** Rene Bonniere; ***W:*** Michael Alexander Miller; ***M:*** Graeme Coleman.

Dream No Evil 🦴½ **1975** A mentally disturbed woman is forced to commit bizarre murders to protect her warped fantasy world. **93m/C VHS.** Edmond O'Brien, Brooke Mills, Marc Lawrence, Arthur Franz; ***D:*** John Hayes.

A Dream of Kings 🦴🦴🦴 **1969 (R)** Quinn is exceptional in this Petrakis story of an immigrant working to get his dying son home to Greece. Last film appearance for Stevens before committing suicide at age 36. **107m/C VHS.** Anthony Quinn, Irene Papas, Inger Stevens, Sam Levene, Val Avery; ***D:*** Daniel Mann; ***M:*** Alex North.

A Dream of Passion 🦴½ **1978 (R)** A woman imprisoned in Greece for murdering her children becomes the object of a publicity stunt for a production of "Medea," and she and the lead actress begin to exchange personalities. Artificial gobbledygook. **105m/C VHS.** *GR SI* Ellen Burstyn, Melina Mercouri, Andreas Voutsinas; ***D:*** Jules Dassin; ***W:*** Jules Dassin; ***C:*** Yorgos Arvanitis.

Dream Street 🦴🦴 **1921** A weak morality tale of London's lower classes. Two brothers, both in love with the same dancing girl, woo her in their own way, while a Chinese gambler plans to take her by force. Silent with music score. Based on Thomas Burke's "Limehouse Nights." **138m/B VHS.** Tyrone Power Sr., Carol Dempster, Ralph Graves, Charles Mack; ***D:*** D.W. Griffith.

The Dream Team 🦴🦴½ **1989 (PG-13)** On their way to a ball game, four patients from a mental hospital find themselves lost in New York City after their doctor is knocked out by murderers. Some fine moments from a cast of dependable comics. Watch for numerous nods to "One Flew Over the Cuckoo's Nest," another Lloyd feature. Keaton fans won't want to miss this one. **113m/C VHS.** Michael Keaton, Christopher Lloyd, Peter Boyle, Stephen Furst, Lorraine Bracco, Milo O'Shea, Dennis Boutsikaris, Philip Bosco, James Remar, Cynthia Belliveau; ***D:*** Howard Zieff; ***W:*** Jon Connolly, David Loucka; ***M:*** David McHugh.

D.R.E.A.M. Team 🦴🦴 **1999 (R)** Garrison (Sheen) heads a secret United Nations agency that has uncovered terrorist activities in Puerto Rico involving a bomb laced with anthrax. He turns to CIA agent Zack (Kaake) to form a team of agents to stop the madness. Their cover just happens to be as models working on a fashion shoot, which means Zack gets to choose three babes to kick butt. **81m/C VHS, DVD.** Jeff Kaake, Angie Everhart, Traci Lords, Traci Bingham, Martin Sheen, Roger Moore, Ian McShane, James Remar; ***D:*** Dean Hamilton; ***W:*** Michael Snyder; ***M:*** Matthias Weber. **TV**

Dream to Believe 🦴🦴 **1985** Slice of the life of your typical high school coed—mom's dying, stepdad's from hell, sports injury hurts, and, oh yeah, championship gymnastic competitions loom. Designed to make you feel oh-so-good in that MTV kind of way. Reeves is most excellent as the girl's blushing beau. **96m/C VHS.** Rita Tushingham, Keanu Reeves, Olivia D'Abo, Jessica Steen; ***D:*** Paul Lynch.

Dream Trap 🦴½ **1990** A young man is obsessed with a girl in his dreams. When he meets a girl who really exists, fantasy louses up every opportunity for the real thing. **90m/C VHS.** Kristy Swanson, Sasha Jenson, Jeanie Moore; ***D:*** Tom Logan, Hugh Parks; ***W:*** Tom Logan.

Dream with the Fishes 🦴🦴½ **1997 (R)** Suicidal voyeur Terry (Arquette) is about to jump from a bridge when terminally ill thief Nick (Adams) strikes a strange deal with him. In exchange for funding a few of Nick's fantasies, he will kill Terry in a less messy way. After various strange escapades (including an unplanned robbery and nude bowling), the pair arrive in Nick's hometown, where he attempts to resolve old issues with an ex-girlfriend and his abusive father. As Nick's health fades, Terry reexamines his wish to die. As the story develops, the cliches of both the buddy and road movie genres fall away, letting you actually care about both of these guys. In an homage to the independent spirit of movies of the early 70s, the film stock copies their grainy look, gradually dissolving over the course of the movie to a clearer look. Debut for director Finn Taylor. **97m/C VHS.** David Arquette, Brad Hunt, Kathryn Erbe, Cathy Moriarty, Allyce Beasley, Patrick McGaw, J.E. Freeman; ***D:*** Finn Taylor; ***W:*** Finn Taylor; ***C:*** Barry Stone; ***M:*** Tito Larriva.

Dreamchild 🦴🦴🦴 **1985 (PG)** A poignant story of the autumn years of Alice Hargreaves, the model for Lewis Carroll's "Alice in Wonderland." Film follows her on a visit to New York in the 1930s, with fantasy sequences including Wonderland characters created by Jim Henson's Creature Shop invoking the obsessive Reverend Dodgson (a.k.a. Carroll). **94m/C VHS.** *GB* Coral Browne, Ian Holm, Peter Gallagher, Jane Asher, Nicola Cowper, Amelia Shankley, Caris Corfman, Shane Rimmer, James Wilby; ***D:*** Gavin Millar; ***W:*** Dennis Potter; ***C:*** Billy Williams; ***M:*** Max Harris, Stanley Myers.

Dreamer 🦴🦴 **1979 (PG)** The excitement of bowling is exploited for all it's worth in this "strike or die" extravaganza. One of a kind. **86m/C VHS.** Tim Matheson, Susan Blakely, Jack Warden, Richard B. Shull; ***D:*** Noel Nosseck; ***W:*** Larry Bischof; ***M:*** Bill Conti.

Dreaming Lips 🦴🦴½ **1937** An orchestra conductor's wife falls in love with her husband's violinist friend. Tragedy befalls the couple. Bergner outstanding in a familiar script. **70m/B VHS.** *GB* Raymond Massey, Elisabeth Bergner, Romney Brent, Joyce Bland, Charles Carson, Felix Aylmer; ***D:*** Lee Garmes, Paul Czinner; ***C:*** Lee Garmes.

Dreaming of Joseph Lees 🦴🦴 **1999 (R)** Eva (Morton) has long had fantasies about her worldly older cousin Joseph Lees (Graves), but he's retreated from society after a terrible accident and lives in Italy. Meanwhile, lonely Eva is stuck in boring rural England in 1958. So she's willing to respond to the romantic gestures of working-class Harry Flyte (Ross) and, shockingly, decides to move in with him. Then Eva re-meets Joseph at a family wedding and, perversely, her desire for him only increases, which leads Harry to desperate measures. Strained symbolism pushes the plot but the accomplished performances take up the slack. **92m/C VHS.** *GB* Rupert Graves, Samantha Morton, Lee Ross, Miriam Margolyes, Frank Finlay, Nicholas Woodeson, Holly Aird; ***D:*** Eric Styles; ***W:*** Catherine Linstrum; ***C:*** Jimmy Dibling; ***M:*** Zbigniew Preisner.

Dreaming of Rita 🦴🦴 **1994** Bob (Oscarsson) named his daughter Rita after long-lost love Sabine's resemblance to Hollywood goddess, Rita Hayworth. Now an elderly widower, Bob suddenly decides to try and find Sabine, taking off across the Swedish countryside. The unhappily married Rita (Lagercrantz), leaving husband and children behind, goes after him—and meets sympathetic hitchhiker Erik (Ersgard), who's happy to offer a little romance. Swedish with subtitles. **108m/C VHS.** *SW* Per Oscarsson, Marika Lagercrantz, Patrick Ersgard, Philip Zanden; ***D:*** Jon Lindstrom; ***W:*** Jon Lindstrom, Rita Holst; ***C:*** Kjell Lagerros.

Dreaming Out Loud 🦴🦴 **1940** Screen debut of popular radio team Lum 'n Abner. The boys get involved in several capers to bring progress to their small Arkansas town. Rural wisecracks make for pleasant outing. First in film series for the duo. **65m/B VHS.** Frances Langford, Phil Harris, Clara Blandick, Robert Wilcox, Chester Lauck, Norris Goff, Frank Craven, Bobs Watson, Irving Bacon; ***D:*** Harold Young.

The Dreamlife of Angels 🦴🦴🦴 *La Vie Revee des Anges* **1998** Deceptively simple debut from director Zouca follows the friendship of two opportunistic working class French women, Marie (Regnier) and Isa (Bouchez). Tensions between the two arise when Marie becomes involved with brutal nightclub owner Chriss (Cohn). Zouca had his female leads live together during filming to create the realistic bickering scenes. French with subtitles. **113m/C VHS, DVD.** *FR* Elodie Bouchez, Natacha Regnier, Gregoire Colin, Jo Prestia, Patrick Mercado; ***D:*** Erick Zonca; ***W:*** Erick Zonca, Roger Bohbot; ***C:*** Agnes Godard; ***M:*** Yann Thiersen. Cesar '99: Actress (Bouchez), Film.

Dreams 🦴🦴 *Kvinn odrom; Journey into Autumn* **1955** Unfocused film about the lives and loves of two successful women. Subtitled. **86m/B VHS.** *SW* Harriet Andersson, Gunnar Bjornstrand, Eva Dahlbeck, Ulf Palme; ***D:*** Ingmar Bergman; ***W:*** Ingmar Bergman; ***C:*** Hilding Bladh; ***M:*** Stuart Gorling.

Dreams Come True 🦴 **1984 (R)** Silly young comedy-romance about two young lovers who discover the trick of out-of-body travel, and have various forms of spiritual contact while their bodies are sleeping. **95m/C VHS.** Michael Sanville, Stephanie Shuford; ***D:*** Max Kalmanowicz.

Dreams Lost, Dreams Found 🦴½ **1987** A young widow journeys from the U.S. to Scotland in search of her heritage. The third "Harlequin Romance Movie." **102m/C VHS.** Kathleen Quinlan, Betsy Brantley, Charles Gray; ***D:*** Willi Patterson. **CABLE**

Dreamscape 🦴🦴½ **1984 (PG-13)** When a doctor teaches a young psychic how to enter into other people's dreams in order to end their nightmares, somebody else wants to use this psychic for evil purposes. The special effects are far more convincing than the one man-saves-the-country-with-his-psychic-powers plot. **99m/C VHS, DVD.** Dennis Quaid, Max von Sydow, Christopher Plummer, Eddie Albert, Kate Capshaw, David Patrick Kelly, George Wendt, Jana Taylor; ***D:*** Joseph Ruben; ***W:*** Chuck Russell; ***C:*** Brian Tufano; ***M:*** Maurice Jarre.

The Dress 🦴🦴 **1996** The title character turns out to be a very malevolent object indeed, in this Dutch absurdist comedy. The bright blue dress with the striking leaf design first causes havoc for the fabric designer, who's nearly fired, while the garment manufacturers get into a fight over the pattern. The dress goes from wearer to wearer, causing havoc for them all, until it is finally destroyed. Dutch with subtitles. **103m/C VHS.** *NL* Henri Garcin, Ariane Schluter, Alex Van Warmerdam; ***D:*** Alex Van Warmerdam; ***W:*** Alex Van Warmerdam; ***C:*** Marc Felperlaan; ***M:*** Vincent van Warmerdam.

The Dress Code 🦴🦴 *Bruno* **1999 (PG-13)** Eight-year-old Bruno is the kind of meek kid who gets picked on by schoolyard bullies and is a disappointment to his dad. So his grandma comes up with a plan to toughen the kid up. **108m/C VHS, DVD.** Alex D. Linz, Gary Sinise, Jennifer Tilly, Kathy Bates, Joey Lauren Adams, Shirley MacLaine, Brett Butler, Gwen Verdon, Stacey Halprin, Kiami Davael; ***D:*** Shirley MacLaine; ***W:*** David Ciminello; ***C:*** Jan Kiesser; ***M:*** Chris Boardman.

Dress Gray 🦴🦴🦴 **1986** Fine, exciting adaptation of the Lucian K. Truscott IV novel about a coverup at an Eastern military academy. Baldwin is cadet Slaight, an upperclassman who finds more secrets than he can handle when a younger cadet (Cassidy), with whom he had an adversarial relationship, is murdered. He's torn between investigating the death or keeping quiet—for the sake of his career if not his life. **192m/C VHS.** Alec Baldwin, Hal Holbrook, Eddie Albert, Lloyd Bridges, Susan Hess, Timothy Van Patten, Patrick Cassidy, Alexis Smith, James B. Sikking, Lane Smith; ***D:*** Glenn Jordan; ***W:*** Gore Vidal; ***M:*** Billy Goldenberg. **TV**

Dressed for Death 🦴½ *Straight on Till Morning; Til Dawn Do Us Part* **1974 (R)** A tale of true love gone bad as a woman is chased and murdered in her castle by the psychopath she loves. **121m/C VHS.** *GB* Rita Tushingham, Shane Briant, Tom Bell, Annie Ross, Katya Wyeth, James Bolam, Claire Kelly; ***D:*** Peter Collinson.

Dressed to Kill 🦴🦴½ **1946** Sherlock Holmes finds that a series of music boxes holds the key to plates stolen from the Bank of England. The plot's a bit thin, but Rathbone/Bruce, in their final Holmes adventure, are always a delight. **72m/B VHS, DVD.** Basil Rathbone, Nigel Bruce, Patricia Morison, Edmund Breon, Tom Dillon; ***D:*** Roy William Neill; ***W:*** Frank Gruber, Leonard Lee; ***C:*** Maury Gertsman; ***M:*** Hans J. Salter.

Dressed to Kill 🦴🦴½ **1980 (R)** Contemporary thriller merges bombastic DePalma with a tense Hitchcockian flare. Sexually unsatisfied Kate (Dickinson) is told to have an affair by her sympathetic shrink Dr. Elliott (Caine) and ends up in bed with a man who catches her eye in a museum. Then Kate's found brutally murdered by prostitute Liz (Allen). Kate's son Peter (Gordon) teams up with Liz to track and lure the killer into their trap. Suspenseful and fast paced. Dickinson's museum scene is wonderfully photographed and edited. DePalma was repeatedly criticized for using a stand-in during the Dickinson shower scene; he titled his next film "Body Double" as a rebuttal. **105m/C VHS, DVD, Wide.** Angie Dickinson, Michael Caine, Nancy Allen, Keith Gordon, Dennis Franz, David Margulies, Brandon Maggart; ***D:*** Brian DePalma; ***W:*** Brian DePalma; ***C:*** Ralf Bode; ***M:*** Pino Donaggio.

The Dresser 🦴🦴🦴½ **1983 (PG)** Film adaptation of Harwood's play (he also wrote the screen version) about an aging English actor/manager (Finney), his dresser (Courtenay), and their theatre company touring England during WWII. Marvelous showbiz tale is lovingly told, superbly acted. **119m/C VHS.** Albert Finney, Tom Courtenay, Edward Fox, Michael Gough, Zena Walker, Eileen Atkins, Cathryn Harrison; ***D:*** Peter Yates; ***W:*** Ronald Harwood; ***M:*** James Horner. Golden Globes '84: Actor—Drama (Courtenay).

Dressmaker 🦴🦴½ **1956** French comedian Fernandel stars as a man's tailor who designs dresses in secret so as not to compete with his dressmaker wife. Lightweight but entertaining. English subtitled. **95m/B VHS.** *FR* Fernandel, Francoise Fabian; ***D:*** Jean Boyer.

The Dressmaker 🦴🦴½ **1989** Two sisters in WWII Liverpool must deal with their young niece's romantic involvement with an American soldier. Plowright and Whitelaw turn in fine performances as the two siblings with very different outlooks on life. **90m/C VHS.** *GB* Joan Plowright, Billie Whitelaw, Pete Postlethwaite, Jane Horrocks, Tim Ransom; ***D:*** Jim O'Brien; ***C:*** Michael Coulter; ***M:*** George Fenton.

Drift 🦴🦴 **2000** Angsty relationship drama concerns Ryan (Lee) who's working in an L.A. coffee shop as he tries to become a screenwriter. He's living with Joel (Dayne) but that situation becomes tenuous when Ryan meets young college student Leo (Roessler) and begins to wonder what would happen if he left Joel to pursue this new relationship. Three talky scenarios are offered. **86m/C DVD.** *CA* R. T. Lee, Greyson Dayne, Jonathon Roessler; ***D:*** Quentin Lee; ***W:*** Quentin Lee; ***C:*** Quentin Lee; ***M:*** Steven Panoto.

Drift Fence 🦴🦴½ *Texas Desperadoes* **1936** Good early oater about a Texas ranger who goes in search of the man responsible for the murder of his buddy. Routine story saved by high quality production. Based on the story "Nevada" by Zane

Grey. **57m/B VHS.** Buster Crabbe, Katherine DeMille, Tom (George Duryea) Keene, Benny Baker; ***D:*** Otho Lovering; ***W:*** Stuart Anthony, Robert Yost.

The Drifter 🦴🦴 **1932** A lumberjack makes sacrifices for the love between his brother and the lumbermill owner's daughter. **56m/B VHS.** William Farnum, Noah Beery Sr., Phyllis Barrington.

The Drifter 🦴🦴½ **1988 (R)** It's psychos, psychos everywhere as a beautiful young woman learns to regret a one-night stand. A good, low-budget version of "Fatal Attraction." Director Brand plays the cop. **90m/C VHS, DVD.** Kim Delaney, Timothy Bottoms, Miles O'Keeffe, Al Shannon, Thomas Wagner, Larry Brand; ***D:*** Larry Brand; ***W:*** Larry Brand; ***C:*** David Sperling; ***M:*** Rick Conrad.

The Driftin' Kid 🦴 **1941** Poorly produced western has Keene posing as a rancher in order to nab a bunch of cattle rusters. So bad that even the sound of the punches are seconds off from the blows. **57m/B VHS.** Tom (George Duryea) Keene, Betty Miles, Frank Yaconelli, Slim Andrews, Stanley Price, Glenn Strange; ***D:*** Robert Emmett Tansey; ***W:*** Robert Emmett Tansey, Frances Kavanaugh.

Driftin' River 🦴🦴½ **1946** A shipment of horses bound for the Army is hijacked and the soldiers sent to investigate the theft are murdered. Investigators Deans and Ates are sent to take care of the culprits. Routine oater. **57m/B VHS.** Eddie Dean, Roscoe Ates, Shirley Patterson, William "Bill" Fawcett, Dennis Moore, Bob Callahan, Lottie Harrison, Forrest Taylor; ***D:*** Robert Emmett Tansey; ***W:*** Frances Kavanaugh.

Drifting 🦴🦴½ *Nagooa* **1982** A controversial Israeli film about a homosexual filmmaker surviving in modern-day Jerusalem. First such movie to be made in Israel. In Hebrew with English titles. **103m/C VHS.** *IS* Jonathan Sagalle, Ami Traub, Ben Levine, Dita Arel; ***D:*** Amos Guttman.

Drifting Souls 🦴🦴 **1932** In order to save her father's life, a beautiful young woman marries for money instead of love. **65m/C VHS.** Lois Wilson, Theodore von Eltz, Shirley Grey, Raymond Hatton, Gene Gowing, Bryant Washburn; ***D:*** Louis King.

Drifting Weeds 🦴🦴🦴½ *Floating Weeds; The Duckweed Story; Ukigusa* **1959** A remake by Ozu of his 1934 silent film about a troupe of traveling actors whose leader visits his illegitimate son and his lover after years of separation. Classic Ozu in his first color film. In Japanese with English subtitles. **128m/B VHS.** *JP* Ganjiro Nakamura, Machiko Kyo, Haruko Sugimura, Ayako Wakao; ***D:*** Yasujiro Ozu.

Driller Killer woof! **1979 (R)** Frustrated artist goes insane and begins to kill off Manhattan residents with a carpenter's drill. Likewise, the plot is full of holes. Director Ferrara starred in his own film under the name Jimmy Laine. **94m/C VHS, DVD.** Carolyn Marz, Bob DeFrank, Abel Ferrara, Peter Yellen, Baybi Day, Harry Schultz; ***D:*** Abel Ferrara; ***W:*** Nicholas St. John; ***C:*** Ken Kelsch; ***M:*** Joe Delia.

Drive 🦴🦴 **1996 (R)** A technologically enhanced man (Dacascos), running from biotech corporate hitmen, offers a down-on-his-luck stranger (Hardison) $5 million to drive him from San Franscisco to L.A. And he won't take no for an answer. **99m/C VHS, DVD.** Mark Dacascos, Kadeem Hardison, Brittany Murphy, John Pyper-Ferguson, Tracey Walter, James Shigeta, Masaya Kato; ***D:*** Steve Wang.

Drive-In woof! **1976 (PG)** A low-budget bomb showing a night in the life of teenage yahoos at a Texas drive-in. **96m/C VHS.** Lisa Lemole, Glenn Morshower, Gary Cavagnaro; ***D:*** Rod Amateau.

Drive-In Massacre woof! **1974 (R)** Two police detectives investigate a bizarre series of slasher murders at the local drive-in. Honk the horn at this one. **78m/C VHS.** Jake Barnes, Adam Lawrence, Austin Johnson, Douglas Gudbye, Valdesta; ***D:*** Stu Segall; ***W:*** George "Buck" Flower, John Goff.

Drive Me Crazy 🦴🦴 **1999 (PG-13)** Nicole (Hart) and Chase (Grenier) have grown up next door to each other and attend the same high school, but that's all they think they have in common. Pep rallying Nicole yearns to date BMOC Brad (Carpenter), but he's only interested in a rival cheerleader. Slacker-type Chase just wants to hang out at the coffeehouse with his animal activist girlfriend Dulcie (Larter), but he gets dumped hard. They conspire to win their dream dates to the prom by pretending to be a couple in order to provoke jealousy. As the two grow closer, they inevitably fall in love. Unfortunately, they don't do it in a very entertaining or amusing manner. Slow paced, unfunny and trite is no way to go through life, son. Based on the novel "How I Created My Perfect Prom Date" by Todd Strasser. **91m/C VHS, DVD, Wide.** Melissa Joan Hart, Adrian Grenier, Stephen Collins, Faye Grant, Susan May Pratt, Kris Park, Mark Webber, Ali Larter, Mark Metcalf, William Converse-Roberts, Gabriel Carpenter; ***D:*** John Schultz; ***W:*** Rob Thomas; ***C:*** Kees Van Oostrum; ***M:*** Greg Kendall.

Driven 🦴🦴 **2001 (PG-13)** Hotshot rookie racer Jimmy Bly (Pardue) is slipping in the rankings thanks to pressure from his promoter brother (Leonard) and his ongoing affair with Sophia (Warren), the girlfriend of top rival Beau (Schweiger). Owner Henry (Reynolds) brings in former hotshot Joe Tanto (Stallone) to straighten the kid out, but Joe has his own demons, including a horrific, nearlydeadly crash, an ex married to his arch-rival (De la Fuente), and a hovering female reporter (Edwards). There's a lot going on, what with all the CGI-created car crashes, the bed-hopping, and the tempers flaring, but it's all over the road, so as not to tax anyone's attention span. It doesn't get anywhere, but at least it gets there fast. **117m/C VHS, DVD, Wide.** *US* Sylvester Stallone, Burt Reynolds, Kip Pardue, Til Schweiger, Gina Gershon, Robert Sean Leonard, Stacy Edwards, Estella Warren, Christian de la Fuente, Brent Briscoe; ***D:*** Renny Harlin; ***W:*** Sylvester Stallone; ***C:*** Mauro Fiore; ***M:*** BT (Brian Transeau).

Driven to Kill 🦴🦴 **1990** No-name cast assemble in low-rent suspenser portraying the ugly side of love: bent on revenge, a man is out to obliterate the thugs who made his life a horrible experience highlighted by misery and boredom. **?m/C VHS.** Jake Jacobs, Chip Campbell, Michele McNeil.

The Driver 🦴½ **1978 (PG)** A police detective will stop at nothing to catch "The Driver," a man who has the reputation of driving the fastest getaway car around. Chase scenes win out over plot. **131m/C VHS.** Ryan O'Neal, Bruce Dern, Isabelle Adjani, Ronee Blakley, Matt Clark; ***D:*** Walter Hill; ***W:*** Walter Hill.

Driver's Seat woof! *Psychotic; Identikit* **1973 (R)** Extremely bizarre film with a cult following that was adapted from the novel by Muriel Spark. Liz stars as a deranged woman trying to keep a rendezvous with her strange lover in Rome. In the meantime she wears tacky clothes and delivers stupid lines. **101m/C VHS.** *IT* Elizabeth Taylor, Ian Bannen, Mona Washbourne, Andy Warhol, Guido Mannari, Maxence Mailfort; ***D:*** Giuseppe Patroni-Griffi; ***W:*** Giuseppe Patroni-Griffi, Raffaele La Capria; ***M:*** Franco Mannino.

Driving Force 🦴 **1988 (R)** In an effort to capitalize on the popularity of the "Road Warrior" movies, features a lone trucker battling a gang of roadhogs in another post-holocaust desert. Ultimately, runs off the road. **90m/C VHS.** Sam Jones, Catherine Bach, Don Swayze; ***D:*** A.J. Prowse; ***W:*** Patrick Edgeworth.

Driving Me Crazy 🦴½ **1991 (PG-13)** When an East German car inventor comes to America, it's laughs in the fast lane in this all-star comedy. **88m/C VHS.** Billy Dee Williams, Thomas Gottschalk, Dom DeLuise, Milton Berle, Steve Kanaly, Michelle Johnson, Richard Moll, Morton Downey Jr., George Kennedy; ***D:*** Jon Turteltaub.

Driving Miss Daisy 🦴🦴🦴½ **1989 (PG)** Tender and sincere portrayal of a 25-year friendship between an aging Jewish woman and the black chauffeur forced upon her by her son. Humorous and thought-provoking, skillfully acted and directed, it subtly explores the effects of prejudice in the South. The development of Aykroyd as a top-notch character actor is further evidenced here. Part of the fun is watching the changes in fashion and auto design. Adapted from the play by Alfred Uhry. **99m/C VHS, DVD, 8mm, Wide.** Jessica Tandy, Morgan Freeman, Dan Aykroyd, Esther Rolle, Patti LuPone; ***D:*** Bruce Beresford; ***W:*** Alfred Uhry; ***C:*** Peter James; ***M:*** Hans Zimmer. Oscars '89: Actress (Tandy), Adapt. Screenplay, Makeup, Picture; British Acad. '90: Actress (Tandy); Golden Globes '90: Actor—Mus./Comedy (Freeman), Actress—Mus./Comedy (Tandy), Film—Mus./Comedy; Natl. Bd. of Review '89: Actor (Freeman); Writers Guild '89: Adapt. Screenplay.

Drop Dead Fred woof! **1991 (PG-13)** As a little girl, Lizzie Cronin had a manic, imaginary friend named Fred, who protected her from her domineering mother. When her husband dumps her 20 years later, Fred returns to "help" as only he can. Although the cast is fine, incompetent writing and direction make this a truly dismal affair. Plus, gutter humor and mean-spirited pranks throw the whole "heart-warming" premise out the window. Filmed in Minneapolis. **103m/C VHS.** Phoebe Cates, Rik Mayall, Tim Matheson, Marsha Mason, Carrie Fisher, Daniel Gerroll, Ron Eldard; ***D:*** Ate De Jong; ***W:*** Carlos Davis, Anthony Fingleton; ***M:*** Randy Edelman.

Drop Dead Gorgeous 🦴🦴½ *Dairy Queens* **1999 (PG-13)** Oh, the ambitions of stage moms and their daughters in this mockumentary of small-town Minnesota beauty pageants. Satire takes the lowest road whenever possible, because that's where the laughs happen to be. Naive Amber (Dunst) has a trailer-trash babe, Annette (Barkin), for a mom, while rival rich bitch, Becky (Richards), is stuck with the horror that is Gladys (Alley). And someone is taking the contest way too seriously, since other contestants are dropping like flies. Piles it on a little thick sometimes, but overall it works. Watch for Richards' cringe-inducing talent show dance number. **97m/C VHS, DVD.** Denise Richards, Kirsten Dunst, Kirstie Alley, Ellen Barkin, Allison Janney, Sam McMurray, Mindy Sterling, Amy Adams, Tara Redepenning, Sara Stewart, Shannon Nelson, Matt Malloy, Michael McShane, Brooke Bushman, Will Sasso, Brittany Murphy, Mo Gaffney, Nora Dunn, Amanda Detmer; ***Cameos:*** Adam West; ***D:*** Michael Patrick Jann; ***W:*** Lona Williams; ***C:*** Michael Spiller; ***M:*** Mark Mothersbaugh.

Drop-Out Mother 🦴🦴 **1988** A woman gives up her executive position to become a housewife and full-time mom; expected domestic turmoil follows. Standard TV fare and sort of a sequel to "Drop-Out Father," shown in 1982. **100m/C VHS.** Valerie Harper, Wayne Rogers, Carol Kane, Kim Hunter, Danny Gerard; ***D:*** Charles S. Dubin. **TV**

DROP Squad 🦴🦴 **1994 (R)** Not quite on target social satire revolving around buppie Burford Jackson Jr. (La Salle), a token minority ad exec who's job is to push questionable products, using gross stereotypes, to the black community. His family's appalled and Buford becomes a prime target of D.R.O.P. (Deprogramming and Restoration of Pride), a vigilante organization that kidnaps erring black bretheren and leads them back to their cultural heritage. Frequently intense performances but the script raises some serious issues it doesn't deliver on. Based on the short story "The Deprogrammer" by David Taylor. **88m/C VHS, DVD, Wide.** Eriq La Salle, Vondie Curtis-Hall, Ving Rhames, Kasi Lemmons, Vanessa Williams, Nicole Powell, Afemo Omilami, Spike Lee; ***D:*** David Johnson; ***W:*** David Johnson, Butch Robinson, David Taylor; ***C:*** Ken Kelsch; ***M:*** Michael Bearden.

Drop Zone 🦴🦴½ **1994 (R)** Routine action-thriller finds U.S. marshal Pete Nessip (Snipes) and his brother Terry (Warner) assigned to protect drug cartel snitch Earl Leedy (Jeter). The plane they're on is skyjacked by criminal Moncrief (Busey) who parachutes off with Leedy, Terry's killed, and while Pete's on suspension he decides to go undercover into the world of sky-driving with the aid of ex-con cutie Jessie (Butler). Plot holes are big enough to pilot a plane through but the stunts are good and Snipes is never less than professional. **101m/C VHS, DVD.** Wesley Snipes, Gary Busey, Yancy Butler, Michael Jeter, Corin "Corky" Nemec, Kyle Secor, Luca Bercovici, Malcolm Jamal Warner, Rex Linn, Grace Zabriskie, Sam Hennings, Claire Stansfield, Mickey Jones, Andy Romano; ***D:*** John Badham; ***W:*** John Bishop, Peter Barsocchini; ***C:*** Roy Wagner; ***M:*** Hans Zimmer.

The Dropkick 🦴🦴🦴 **1927** Erstwhile D.W. Griffith leading man Barthelmess stars in this pigskin whodunnit: a coach's suicide looks like murder, and the prime suspect is the team's most valuable player. Cast includes ten bona fide university football players and Hedda "nobody's interested in sweetness and light" Hopper, while The Duke makes cameo. Webb later went on to direct a musical with Eddie Cantor and Rudy Vallee ("Glorifying the American Girl"). Silent. Based on the story "Glitter" by Katherine Brush. **62m/B VHS.** Richard Barthelmess, Barbara Kent, Dorothy Revier, Eugene Strong, Alberta Vaughn, Brooks Benedict, Hedda Hopper; ***Cameos:*** John Wayne; ***D:*** Millard Webb; ***W:*** Winifred Dunn.

Drowning by Numbers 🦴🦴🦴½ **1987 (R)** Three generations of women, each named Cissie Colpitts, solve their marital problems by drowning their husbands and making deals with a bizarre coroner. Further strange visions from director Greenaway, complemented by stunning cinematography courtesy of Sacha Vierny. A treat for those who appreciate Greenaway's uniquely curious cinematic statements. **121m/C VHS.** *GB* Bernard Hill, Joan Plowright, Juliet Stevenson, Joely Richardson; ***D:*** Peter Greenaway; ***W:*** Peter Greenaway; ***C:*** Sacha Vierny; ***M:*** Michael Nyman.

Drowning Mona 🦴🦴 **2000 (PG-13)** Strident comedy about the low-IQ denizens of small town Verplanck, New York, where everybody still drives a Yugo (the town was a test market). Nasty Mona Dearly (Midler) drives her car into the Hudson River and drowns. It turns out to be murder and Chief Wyatt Rash (DeVito) must investigate. He's not lacking in suspects since Mona was the most hated woman in the community. Everyone in the cast looks like they're enjoying themselves which may be more than the viewer will say. **95m/C VHS, DVD, Wide.** Danny DeVito, Bette Midler, Jamie Lee Curtis, Casey Affleck, Neve Campbell, William Fichtner, Peter Dobson, Marcus Thomas, Kathleen Wilhoite, Tracey Walter, Paul Ben-Victor, Paul Schulze, Mark Pellegrino; ***D:*** Nick Gomez; ***W:*** Peter Steinfeld; ***C:*** Bruce Douglas Johnson; ***M:*** Michael Tavera.

The Drowning Pool 🦴🦴 **1975 (PG)** Newman returns as detective Lew Harper (of "Harper" by Ross MacDonald) to solve a blackmail case. Uneventful script and stodgy direction, but excellent character work from all the cast members keep this watchable. Title is taken from a trap set for Newman, from which he must escape using most of his female companion's clothing. Adapted from a character created by Ross MacDonald. **109m/C VHS.** Paul Newman, Joanne Woodward, Anthony (Tony) Franciosa, Murray Hamilton, Melanie Griffith, Richard Jaeckel; ***D:*** Stuart Rosenberg; ***W:*** Tracy Keenan Wynn, Walter Hill; ***C:*** Gordon Willis; ***M:*** Charles Fox.

Drug Wars 2: The Cocaine Cartel 🦴🦴 **1992** Muddled drama featuring crazy unpredictable DEA agents executing the downfall of Colombia's Medellin drug kingpins. Average sequel to the award-winning miniseries "Drug Wars." **200m/C VHS.** Alex McArthur, Dennis Farina, Julie Carmen, John Glover, Karen Young, Michele Placido, Gustav Vintas, Geno Silva; ***D:*** Paul Krasny.

Drugstore Cowboy 🦴🦴🦴½ **1989 (R)** A gritty, uncompromising depiction of a pack of early 1970s drugstore-robbing junkies as they travel around looking to score. Brushes with the law and tragedy encourage them to examine other life-styles, but the trap seems impossible to leave. A perfectly crafted piece that reflects the "me generation" era, though it tends to glamorize addiction. Dillon's best work to date. Based on a novel by prison inmate James Fogle. **100m/C VHS, DVD.** Matt Dillon, Kelly Lynch, James Remar, James LeGros, Heather Graham, William S. Burroughs, Beah Richards, Grace Zabriskie, Max Perlich; ***D:*** Gus Van Sant; ***W:*** Gus Van Sant, Daniel Yost; ***C:*** Robert Yeoman; ***M:*** Elliot Goldenthal. Ind. Spirit '90: Actor (Dillon), Cinematog., Screenplay, Support. Actor (Perlich); L.A. Film Critics '89: Screenplay;

N.Y. Film Critics '89: Screenplay; Natl. Soc. Film Critics '89: Director (Van Sant), Film, Screenplay.

Druids 🦴🦴½ *Vercingetorix* **2001 (R)** Gallic chieftain Vercingetorix (Lambert) must rally his people when they are threatened by Roman army commander Julius Caesar (Brandauer) in 60 B.C. The action is well-done even if the story drags occassionally. **115m/C VHS, DVD, Wide.** Christopher Lambert, Klaus Maria Brandauer, Max von Sydow, Ines Sastre, Stefan Ivanov, Barnard Pierre Donnadieu; *D:* Jacques Dorfman; *W:* Jacques Dorfman, Rospo Pallenberg, Norman Spinrad; *M:* Pierre Charvet. **VIDEO**

Drum woof! **1976 (R)** This steamy sequel to "Mandingo" deals with the sordid interracial sexual shenanigans at a Southern plantation. Bad taste at its best. **101m/C VHS.** Ken Norton, Warren Oates, Pam Grier, Yaphet Kotto, Fiona Lewis, Isela Vega, Cheryl "Rainbeaux" Smith; *D:* Steve Carver; *C:* Lucien Ballard.

Drum Beat 🦴🦴 **1954** An unarmed Indian fighter sets out to negotiate a peace treaty with a renegade Indian leader. Bronson is especially believable as chief. Based on historical incident. **111m/C VHS.** Alan Ladd, Charles Bronson, Marisa Pavan, Robert Keith, Rodolfo Acosta, Warner Anderson, Elisha Cook Jr., Anthony Caruso; *D:* Delmer Daves.

Drum Taps 🦴🦴 **1933** Maynard saves the day for a young girl who is being pushed off her land by a group of speculators. **55m/B VHS.** Ken Maynard, Dorothy Dix, Frank "Junior" Coghlan, Kermit Maynard; *D:* J(ohn) P(aterson) McGowan.

Drums 🦴🦴½ *The Drum* **1938** A native prince helps to save the British army in India from being annihilated by a tyrant. Rich melodrama with interesting characterizations and locale. **96m/B VHS.** *GB* Sabu, Raymond Massey, Valerie Hobson, Roger Livesey, David Tree; *D:* Zoltan Korda.

Drums Along the Mohawk 🦴🦴🦴½ **1939** Grand, action-filled saga about pre-Revolutionary America, detailing the trials of a colonial newlywed couple as their village in Mohawk Valley is besieged by Indians. Based on the Walter Edmonds novel, and vintage Ford. **104m/C VHS.** Henry Fonda, Claudette Colbert, Edna May Oliver, Eddie Collins, John Carradine, Dorris Bowdon, Arthur Shields, Ward Bond, Jessie Ralph, Robert Lowery; *D:* John Ford; *C:* Ray Rennahan.

Drums in the Deep South 🦴🦴 **1951** A rivalry turns ugly as two former West Point roommates wind up on opposite sides when the Civil War breaks out. Historical drama hampered by familiar premise. **87m/C VHS.** James Craig, Guy Madison, Craig Stevens, Barbara Payton, Barton MacLane; *D:* William Cameron Menzies; *W:* Philip Yordan.

Drums of Fu Manchu 🦴🦴🦴 **1940** Fu Manchu searches for the scepter of Genghis Khan, an artifact that would give him domination over the East. Brandon smoothly evil as the Devil Doctor. Originally a serial in 15 chapters. **150m/B VHS.** Henry (Kleinbach) Brandon, Robert Kellard, George Cleveland, Dwight Frye, Gloria Franklin, Tom Chatterton; *D:* William Witney, John English.

Drums of Jeopardy 🦴 *Mark of Terror* **1931** A father wanders through czarist Russia and the U.S. to seek revenge on his daughter's killer. Cheap copy of "Dr. Fu Manchu." **65m/B VHS.** Warner Oland, June Collyer, Lloyd Hughes, George Fawcett, Mischa Auer; *D:* George B. Seitz.

Drums O'Voodoo woof! *She Devil* **1934** A voodoo princess fights to eliminate the town bad guy in this all-black feature that is greatly hampered by shoddy production values. **70m/B VHS.** Laura Bowman, J. Augustus Smith, Edna Barr; *D:* Arthur Hoerl.

Drunken Angel 🦴🦴🦴 *Yoidore tenshi* **1948** Alcoholic doctor gets mixed up with local gangster. Kurosawa's first major film aided by strong performances. With English subtitles. **108m/B VHS.** *JP* Toshiro Mifune, Takashi Shimura, Choko Iida; *D:* Akira Kurosawa; *W:* Keinosuke Uegusa; *C:* Takeo Ito; *M:* Fumio Hayasaka.

Drunks 🦴🦴 **1996 (R)** Ensemble story set in a church basement in Manhattan where a diverse group of people go to their Alcoholics Anonymous meetings. Recovering alcoholic Jim (Lewis) has gone on a bender after his wife's death; Rachel's (Wiest) an overworked doctor with drug and alcohol dependencies; alcoholic Becky's (Dunaway) a divorcee with problem kids; Brenda's (Hamilton) an ex-heroin addict who's HIV positive; Joseph's (Rollins) still haunted by his son's death, which he caused while driving drunk. There's more and everyone gets their chance at the spotlight. Adapted from Lennon's play "Blackout." **88m/C VHS, DVD.** Richard Lewis, Faye Dunaway, Dianne Wiest, Lisa Gay Hamilton, Howard E. Rollins Jr., Parker Posey, Spalding Gray, Amanda Plummer, Calista Flockhart, George Martin, Anna Thomson; *D:* Peter Cohn; *W:* Gary Lennon; *C:* Peter Hawkins; *M:* Joe Delia.

Dry Cleaning 🦴🦴 *Nettoyage a Sec* **1997** Marrieds Nicole (Miou-Miou) and Jean-Marie (Berling) Kunstler are sharing a midlife crisis. The hard-working owners of a dry cleaning establishment are bored by their routine and decide to visit a racy nightclub where the featured performers are a brother/sister drag act. And before the Kunstlers know quite how it happened, they are both involved with handsome Loic (Merhar), whose sister has suddenly broken up their performing partnership. So Loic is now both working for and living with the Kunstlers and the erotic waters are getting very murky indeed. French with subtitles. **97m/C VHS.** *FR* Miou-Miou, Charles Berling, Stanislas Merhar, Mathilde Seigner; *D:* Anne Fontaine; *W:* Anne Fontaine, Gilles Taurand; *C:* Caroline Champetier.

A Dry White Season 🦴🦴🦴 **1989 (R)** A white Afrikaner living resignedly with apartheid confronts the system when his black gardener, an old friend, is persecuted and murdered. A well-meaning expose that, like many others, focuses on white people. **105m/C VHS.** Donald Sutherland, Marlon Brando, Susan Sarandon, Zakes Mokae, Janet Suzman, Juergen Prochnow, Winston Ntshona, Susannah Harker, Thoko Ntshinga, Rowan Elmes; *D:* Euzhan Palcy; *W:* Colin Welland, Euzhan Palcy; *M:* Dave Grusin.

Drying Up the Streets 🦴 **1976** Tepid message tale of a police drug squad out to terminate the pattern that has young women turning to a life of prostitution and drugs. **90m/C VHS.** *CA* Len Cariou, Don Francks, Sarah Torgov, Calvin Butler; *D:* Robin Spry.

D3: The Mighty Ducks 🦴🦴 **1996 (PG)** Estevez proves that he'll quack for a dollar in the latest redux of the Disney franchise. This time the members of the rag-tag team are drafted by an exclusive prep school where, once again, they don't fit in. Go figure! Although billed as the star, Estevez only appears briefly at the beginning and end of the movie, leaving team captain Charlie (Jackson) as the focus of the story. Facing off against the new coach and the snooty elitist varsity team, the players learn lessons about maturity, responsibility and whacking people with sticks. In all probability, Disney will not be happy with just the hat trick, so don't be surprised if you see "D4: Mighty Old to Still Be Playing Kids" in a theatre near you soon. Cameo from professional Mighty Duck and fellow Disney employee Paul Kariya. **104m/C VHS.** Emilio Estevez, Jeffrey Nordling, Joshua Jackson, David Selby, Heidi Kling, Joss Ackland, Elden (Ratliff) Henson, Shaun Weiss, Matt Doherty, Michael Cudlitz, Vincent A. Larusso, Colombe Jacobsen, Aaron Lohr, Christopher Orr; *D:* Robert Lieberman; *W:* Steven Brill, Jim Burnstein; *C:* David Hennings; *M:* J.A.C. Redford.

D2: The Mighty Ducks 🦴🦴 *The Mighty Ducks 2* **1994 (PG)** When an injury forces Gordon (Estevez) out of the minor leagues, he is tapped by promotor Tibbles (Tucker) to coach Team U.S.A. in the Junior Goodwill Games. Upon arriving in LA, the coach's head is turned by the money to be made in endorsements, and he soon gets a lesson in character-building (hey, it's Disney). The duck redux premise is lame, but kids will want ice time to see more of the hockey action that made the first a hit. **107m/C VHS.** Emilio Estevez, Michael Tucker, Jan Rubes, Kathryn Erbe, Shaun Weiss, Kenan Thompson, Ty O'Neal; ***Cameos:*** Kristi Yamaguchi, Kareem Abdul-Jabbar, Wayne Gretzky; *D:* Sam Weisman; *W:* Steven Brill; *M:* J.A.C. Redford.

Dual Alibi 🦴🦴 **1947** Identical twin trapeze artists murder a colleague for a winning lottery ticket. Lom plays the brothers in a dual role. **87m/B VHS.** *GB* Herbert Lom, Terence de Marney, Phyllis Dixey, Ronald Frankau, Abraham Sofaer, Harold Berens, Sebastian Cabot; *D:* Alfred Travers.

Dubarry 🦴🦴½ **1930** Early sound version of the romantic experiences of Madame Dubarry, the alluring French heroine of David Belasco's "DuBarry." Talmadge's last film. **81m/B VHS.** Norma Talmadge, Conrad Nagel, William Farnum, Hobart Bosworth, Alison Skipworth; *D:* Sam Taylor.

DuBarry Was a Lady 🦴🦴½ **1943** Skelton is a washroom attendant who daydreams that he is King Louis XV of France. Dorsey's band gets to dress in period wigs and costumes. ♫DuBarry Was a Lady; Do I Love You, Do I?; Friendship; Well, Did You Evah; Taliostro's Dance; Katie Went to Haiti; Madame, I Love Your Crepes Suzettes; Thinking of You; A Cigarette, Sweet Music and You. **112m/C VHS.** Lucille Ball, Gene Kelly, Red Skelton, Virginia O'Brien, Zero Mostel, Dick Haymes, Rags Ragland, Donald Meek, George Givot, Louise Beavers; *D:* Roy Del Ruth; *W:* Irving Brecher; *C:* Karl Freund.

Dubeat-E-O 🦴½ **1984** A filmmaker races against time to finish making a documentary about the Los Angeles underground hardcore punk scene, and becomes immersed in the subculture. Somewhat of a haphazard exercise in filmmaking that is best appreciated by rock fans. **84m/C VHS.** Ray Sharkey, Joan Jett, Derf Scratch, Len Lesser, Nora Gaye; *D:* Alan Sacks.

The Duchess and the Dirtwater Fox 🦴½ **1976 (PG)** Period western strung together with many failed attempts at humor, all about a music-hall hooker who meets a bumbling card shark on the make. **105m/C VHS.** George Segal, Goldie Hawn, Conrad Janis, Thayer David; *D:* Melvin Frank; *W:* Barry Sandler; *C:* Joseph Biroc; *M:* Charles Fox.

The Duchess of Duke Street 🦴🦴🦴 **1978** Cockney Rosa Lewis (Jones), a clockmaker's daughter born in 1869, goes into service with the ambition to become the best cook in London. She learns from a society household's French chef, where she was a kitchen maid, and eventually won success by an unexpected opportunity to cook for Edward, the Prince of Wales. A marriage-of-convenience and a mysterious legacy allows Rosa to buy the rundown Bentinck Hotel (actually the Cavendish) and cater fashionable dinners. By unceasing hard work, Rosa turns her establishment into an exclusive and discreet haunt for aristocrats, the wealthy, and various celebrities. British series on seven cassettes. **880m/C VHS.** *GB* Gemma Jones, Christopher Cazenove, John Welsh, George Pravda, June Brown, Victoria Plucknett, Richard Vernon, Doreen Mantle, Elizabeth Bennett, Donald Burton, John Cater, Holly DeJong, John Rapley; *D:* Cyril Coke, Gerry Mill, Simon Langton, Bill Bain, Raymond Menmuir; *W:* Julian Bond, Julia Jones, Rosemary Anne Sisson, Maggie Wadey, Jeremy Paul, Jack Rosenthal, Bill Craig, John Hawkesworth. **TV**

The Duchess of Idaho 🦴🦴½ **1950** Williams tries to help her roommate patch up a romance gone bad, but ends up falling in love herself. MGM guest stars liven up an otherwise routine production. ♫Baby Come Out of the Clouds; You Can't Do Wrong Doin' Right; Let's Choo Choo to Idaho; Of All Things; Or Was It Spring; Warm Hands, Cold Heart; Single-foot Serenade; You Won't Forget Me. **98m/C VHS.** Esther Williams, Van Johnson, John Lund, Paula Raymond, Amanda Blake, Eleanor Powell, Lena Horne; *D:* Robert Z. Leonard.

Duck Soup 🦴🦴🦴🦴 **1933** The Marx Brothers satiric masterpiece (which failed at the box office). Groucho becomes the dictator of Freedonia, and hires Chico and Harpo as spies. Jam-packed with the classic anarchic and irreverent Marx shtick; watch for the mirror scene. Zeppo plays a love-sick tenor, in this, his last film with the brothers. **70m/B VHS, DVD.** Groucho Marx, Chico Marx, Harpo Marx, Zeppo Marx, Louis Calhern, Margaret Dumont, Edgar Kennedy, Raquel Torres, Leonid Kinskey, Charles Middleton; *D:* Leo McCarey; *W:* Harry Ruby, Nat Perrin, Bert Kalmar, Arthur Sheekman; *C:* Henry Sharp; *M:* Harry Ruby, Bert Kalmar. AFI '98: Top 100, Natl. Film Reg. '90.

DuckTales the Movie: Treasure of the Lost Lamp 🦴🦴½ **1990 (G)** Uncle Scrooge and company embark on a lost-ark quest, ala Harrison Ford, for misplaced treasure (a lamp that can make the sky rain ice cream). Based on the daily Disney cartoon of the same name, it's more like an extended-version Saturday morning sugar smacks'n'milk 'toon. See it with someone young. **74m/C VHS.** *D:* Bob Hathcock; *W:* Alan Burnett; *M:* David Newman; *V:* Alan Young, Christopher Lloyd, Rip Taylor, June Foray, Chuck McCann, Richard Libertini, Russi Taylor, Joan Gerber, Terence McGovern.

Dude Bandit 🦴🦴 **1932** An unscrupulous money-lender tries to gain control of a ranch but Gibson comes to the rescue. Gibson actually plays three roles: the rancher's best friend, an aw-shucks cowpoke disguise in order to find out what's going on, and the title character used to bedevil the crooks. **68m/B VHS.** Hoot Gibson, Gloria Shea.

Dude Ranger 🦴🦴½ **1934** Well-acted Zane Grey story about an easterner who gets caught up in a range war and cattle rustling when he takes possession of some property out west. **58m/B VHS.** Smiley Burnette, George O'Brien, Irene Hervey; *D:* Edward F. (Eddie) Cline.

Dude, Where's My Car? 🦴🦴 **2000 (PG-13)** Slow-witted roommates Jesse and Chester wake one morning to a bizarre, seemingly unexplainable situation. To make matters worse, they appear to have trashed their girlfriends' home the night before and, of course, their car is missing. Dude. Too hung over to remember how this all came to be, the two boys set out to piece things together and, in the process, involve themselves with angry transsexuals, ostriches, and extraterrestrials. Follows the grand tradition of stoned and/or goofball duos like Cheech and Chong, Bill and Ted, and Wayne and Garth, but just can't reach their level. **83m/C VHS, DVD, Wide.** Ashton Kutcher, Seann William Scott, Jennifer Garner, Marla Sokoloff, Kristy Swanson, David Herman, Charlie O'Connell, Hal Sparks; *D:* Danny Leiner; *W:* Philip Stark; *C:* Robert Stevens; *M:* David Kitay.

Dudes 🦴 **1987 (R)** Three city kids head for the desert and run afoul of some rednecks. Tired grade-6 revenge story. **90m/C VHS.** Jon Cryer, Catherine Mary Stewart, Daniel Roebuck, Flea, Lee Ving, Calvin Bartlett, Pete Willcox, Glenn Withrow; *D:* Penelope Spheeris; *M:* Charles Bernstein.

Dudley Do-Right 🦴🦴½ **1999 (PG)** Lightening didn't strike twice for Fraser, who successfully starred as Jay Ward's 60s cartoon character "George of the Jungle" and then decided to tackle Ward's brainless-but-noble Canadian Mountie, Dudley. The big goof is still protecting Semi-Happy Valley from the dastardly Snidely Whiplash (Molina), who manages to take over the town and rename it Whiplash City. Snidely is also twirling his mustache in the direction of Dudley's sweetie, fair maiden Nell Fenwick (Parker), which the right-minded Mountie won't allow. Unfortunately, the film only manages a few chuckles. **75m/C VHS, DVD.** Brendan Fraser, Sarah Jessica Parker, Alfred Molina, Robert Prosky, Eric Idle, Alex Rocco, Jack Kehler, Louis Mustillo, Regis Philbin, Kathie Lee Gifford; *D:* Hugh Wilson; *W:* Hugh Wilson; *C:* Donald E. Thorin; *M:* Steve Dorff; *Nar:* Corey Burton.

Duel 🦴🦴🦴 **1971 (PG)** Spielberg's first notable film, a made-for-TV exercise in paranoia. A docile traveling salesman is repeatedly attacked and threatened by a huge, malevolent tractor-trailer on an open desert highway. Released theatrically in Europe. **90m/C VHS.** Dennis Weaver, Lucille Benson, Eddie Firestone, Cary Loftin, Jacqueline Scott, Lou Frizzell, Gene Dynarski; ***D:*** Steven Spielberg; ***W:*** Richard Matheson; ***C:*** Jack Marta; ***M:*** Billy Goldenberg. **TV**

Duel at Diablo 🦴🦴🦴 **1966** An exceptionally violent film that deals with racism in the Old West. Good casting; western fans will enjoy the action. **103m/C VHS.** James Garner, Sidney Poitier, Bibi Andersson, Dennis Weaver, Bill Travers; ***D:*** Ralph Nelson.

Duel at Silver Creek 🦴🦴½ **1952** A group of claim jumpers murder anyone who gets in their way, including the family of the Silver Kid (Murphy), who's deputized by Sheriff Lightning (McNally) to help him get the varmints. **76m/B VHS.** Audie Murphy, Faith Domergue, Stephen McNally, Susan Cabot, Gerald Mohr, Eugene Iglesias, Kyle James, Lee Marvin; ***D:*** Donald Siegel; ***W:*** Gerald Drayson Adams; ***C:*** Irving Glassberg; ***M:*** Hans J. Salter.

Duel in the Sun 🦴🦴🦴 **1946** A lavish, lusty David O. Selznick production of a minor western novel about a vivacious half-breed Indian girl, living on a powerful dynastic ranch, who incites two brothers to conflict. Selznick's last effort at outdoing his epic success with "Gone With the Wind." **130m/C VHS, DVD.** Gregory Peck, Jennifer Jones, Joseph Cotten, Lionel Barrymore, Lillian Gish, Butterfly McQueen, Harry Carey Sr., Walter Huston, Charles Bickford, Herbert Marshall; ***D:*** King Vidor; ***W:*** Oliver H.P. Garrett, David O. Selznick; ***C:*** Ray Rennahan; ***M:*** Dimitri Tiomkin.

Duel of Champions 🦴 *Orazi e Curiazi* **1961** It's ancient Rome, and the prodigal gladiator has come home. Now the family must have a duel to decide who will rule. **90m/C VHS.** *IT SP* Alan Ladd, Francesca Bett; ***D:*** Ferdinando Baldi.

Duel of Fists 🦴 **1989** When the owner of a boxing institute dies, he instructs his son in his will to go searching for his long-lost brother in Thailand. All he can go on is an old photograph and the knowledge that his brother is a Thai boxer. **111m/C VHS.** David Chiang, Chen Hsing, Ti Lung, Tang Ti.

Duel of Hearts 🦴🦴 **1992 (PG-13)** Beautiful Caroline falls in love with wealthy Lord Vane Brecon, who unfortunately is accused of murder. When Caroline tries to help him clear his name she discovers he's hiding a number of secrets. Based on the romance novel "Duel of Love" by Barbara Cartland. Nothing too inspiring here, although regency romance fans will appreciate the attention to detail. **95m/C VHS.** *GB* Alison Doody, Michael York, Geraldine Chaplin, Benedict Taylor, Billie Whitelaw, Virginia McKenna, Richard Johnson, Jeremy Kemp, Beryl Reid, Suzanna Hamilton, Jolyon Baker, Julie Kate; ***D:*** John Hough. **CABLE**

The Duellists 🦴🦴🦴 **1977 (PG)** A beautifully photographed picture about the long-running feud between two French officers during the Napoleonic wars. Based on "The Duel" by Joseph Conrad. **101m/C VHS, Wide.** *GB* Keith Carradine, Harvey Keitel, Albert Finney, Edward Fox, Tom Conti, Christina Raines, Diana Quick; ***D:*** Ridley Scott.

Duet for One 🦴🦴 **1986 (R)** A famous concert violinist learns she is suffering from multiple sclerosis and is slowly losing her ability to play. Convinced that her life is meaningless without music, she self-destructively drifts into bitter isolation. From the play by Tom Kempinski. **108m/C VHS.** Julie Andrews, Max von Sydow, Alan Bates, Liam Neeson; ***D:*** Andrei Konchalovsky.

Duets 🦴🦴 **2000 (R)** Bruce Paltrow misuses the talents of his fine ensemble cast (including daughter Gwyneth) in this off-key comedy-melodrama about karaoke culture. The three subplots each center on a pair of misfits en route to a karaoke contest in Omaha. Ricky (Lewis) is a karaoke hustler who meets his daughter Liv (Paltrow) for the first time after the death of her mother in Las Vegas. Suzi (Bello) is a steely waitress who bullies and beguiles mild cab driver Billy (Speedman) into taking her halfway across the country with the promise of sex. Todd's (Giamatti) a freaked-out businessman fleeing his family and Reggie's (Braugher) a deep-thinking escaped convict with a killer voice. Flashes of feeling and humor offset some of the hokiness of the characters, but not enough to save the movie. **112m/C VHS, DVD, Wide.** Gwyneth Paltrow, Maria Bello, Scott Speedman, Andre Braugher, Paul Giamatti, Huey Lewis, Marian Seldes, Kiersten Warren, Angie Phillips, Angie Dickinson; ***D:*** Bruce Paltrow; ***W:*** John Byrum; ***C:*** Paul Sarossy; ***M:*** David Newman.

The Duke 🦴🦴½ **1999 (G)** Talk about the dog who has everything! Hubert is the faithful bloodhound companion to the Duke of Dingwall (Neville). When the Duke dies, Hubert inherits everything—even the title! Trusted butler Clive (Doohan) and his niece Charlotte (Draper) are there to make certain Hubert is safe from the plots of the late Duke's sniveling nephew, Cecil (Muirhead), who wants the estate for himself and even tries to arrange a doggie wedding to get the riches. **88m/C VHS.** *CA* James Doohan, John Neville, Courtnee Draper, Oliver Muirhead, Sophie Heyman, Judy Geeson; ***D:*** Philip Spink; ***W:*** Craig Detweiler, Anne Vince, Robert Vince; ***C:*** Mike Southon; ***M:*** Brahm Wenger. **VIDEO**

The Duke Is Tops 🦴🦴½ **1938** In Horne's earliest existing film appearance, she's off to attempt the "big-time," while her boyfriend joins a traveling medicine show. ♫I Know You Remember. **80m/C VHS.** Ralph Cooper, Lena Horne, Marie Bryant.

Duke of the Derby 🦴🦴 *Le Gentleman d'Epsom* **1962** A scheming racehorse handicapper bets over his head and ruins his higher-than-means lifestyle. In French with English subtitles. **83m/C VHS.** *FR* Jean Gabin; ***D:*** Gilles Grangier.

The Duke of West Point 🦴🦴 **1938** Conceited but ultimately good-hearted Brit Earley (Hayward) immigrates to the States and enrolls at West Point. He immediately alienates everyone with his superior attitude but eventually shows his good side. Fontaine provides a fine performance; plus, she's about the only one who's young enough to make a convincing college student. Hokey and predictable, but pleasant enough if you're wondering why they don't make 'em like that anymore. **109m/B VHS.** Louis Hayward, Joan Fontaine, Richard Carlson, William "Billy" Bakewell, Donald (Don "Red") Barry, Charles D. Brown, Tom Brown, Alan Curtis, Emma Dunn, Edward Earle, Marjorie Gateson, Jonathan Hale, Kenneth Harlan, Mary MacLaren; ***D:*** Alfred E. Green; ***W:*** George Bruce; ***C:*** Robert Planck.

Dumb & Dumber 🦴🦴½ **1994 (PG-13)** Moronic limo driver Lloyd Christmas (Carrey) and equally dense dog groomer Harry Dunne (Daniels) travel (in the hilarious "sheep dog" van) from Rhode Island to Colorado—at one point going east!—to return a briefcase full of cash to a beautiful socialite (Holly). Engaging in all sorts of gross-out bathroom, bodily function, and slapstick humor, this one will definitely not appeal to the stuffy critic or arthouse snob. It will provide plenty of laughs, however embarrassingly rendered, for everyone else. Daniels proves a convincing dimwit sidekick, while Carrey mugs shamelessly. Occasional "Seinfeld" writer Farrelly makes his directorial debut. **110m/C VHS, DVD.** Jim Carrey, Jeff Daniels, Lauren Holly, Teri Garr, Karen Duffy, Mike Starr, Charles Rocket, Victoria Rowell, Felton Perry, Harland Williams, Rob Moran, Cam Neely, Lin Shaye, Fred Stoller; ***D:*** Peter Farrelly; ***W:*** Bennett Yellin, Bobby Farrelly, Peter Farrelly; ***C:*** Mark Irwin; ***M:*** Todd Rundgren. MTV Movie Awards '95: Comedic Perf. (Carrey), Kiss (Jim Carrey/Lauren Holly); Blockbuster '96: Comedy Actor, V. (Carrey).

Dumb Waiter **1987** A mini-play by Harold Pinter about two hitmen awaiting instructions for a job in an empty boardinghouse, and getting comically mixed messages. **60m/C VHS.** John Travolta, Tom Conti; ***D:*** Robert Altman; ***W:*** Harold Pinter. **TV**

Dumbo 🦴🦴🦴🦴 **1941** Animated Disney classic about a baby elephant growing up in the circus who is ridiculed for his large ears, until he discovers he can fly. The little elephant who could fly then becomes a circus star. Expressively and imaginatively animated, highlighted by the hallucinatory dancing pink elephants sequence. Endearing songs by Frank Churchill, Oliver Wallace, and Ned Washington, including "Baby Mine," "Pink Elephants on Parade," and "I See an Elephant Fly." **63m/C VHS, DVD.** ***D:*** Ben Sharpsteen; ***W:*** Joe Grant, Dick Huemer; ***M:*** Frank Churchill, Oliver Wallace; ***V:*** Sterling Holloway, Edward Brophy, Verna Felton, Herman Bing, Cliff Edwards. Oscars '41: Scoring/Musical.

The Dummy Talks 🦴🦴 **1943** When a ventriloquist is murdered, a midget goes undercover as a dummy to find the killer. Watch closely and you might see his lips move. **85m/B VHS.** *GB* Jack Warner, Claude Hulbert, Beryl Orde, Derna Derna-Hazell, Ivy Benson, Manning Whiley; ***D:*** Oswald Mitchell.

Dune 🦴🦴 **1984 (PG-13)** Lynch sci-fi opus based on the Frank Herbert novel boasting great set design, muddled scripting, and a good cast. The story: controlling the spice drug of Arrakis permits control of the universe in the year 10991. Paul, the heir of the Atreides family, leads the Freemen in a revolt against the evil Harkhonens who have violently seized control of Arrakis, also known as Dune, the desert planet. That's as clear as it ever gets. **137m/C VHS, DVD.** Kyle MacLachlan, Francesca Annis, Jose Ferrer, Sting, Max von Sydow, Juergen Prochnow, Linda Hunt, Freddie Jones, Dean Stockwell, Virginia Madsen, Brad Dourif, Kenneth McMillan, Silvana Mangano, Jack Nance, Sian Phillips, Paul Smith, Richard Jordan, Everett McGill, Sean Young, Patrick Stewart; ***D:*** David Lynch; ***W:*** David Lynch; ***C:*** Freddie Francis; ***M:*** Brian Eno.

Dune 🦴🦴½ *Frank Herbert's Dune* **2000** Frank Herbert's 1965 sci-fi classic was previously made into a disappointing 1984 film by David Lynch. This miniseries more successfully combines visuals with character, although the complicated plot is still somewhat overwhelming. Duke Leto (Hurt) of the House of Atreides has been appointed by the Emperor to harvest and export Spice—the most prized commodity on the desert planet of Arrakis (or Dune). But a rival faction, led by Baron Harkonnen (McNeice), causes trouble for Atreides and his heir, Paul (Newman), who must look to Dune's native inhabitants for support. **270m/C VHS, DVD, Wide.** Alec Newman, William Hurt, Saskia Reeves, Ian McNeice, P. H. Moriarty, Julie Cox, Matt Keeslar, Giancarlo Giannini, Barbara Kodetova, Robert Russell, Miljen Kreka Kljakovic; ***D:*** John Harrison; ***W:*** John Harrison; ***C:*** Vittorio Storaro, Harry B. Miller III; ***M:*** Graeme Revell. **CABLE**

Dune Warriors 🦴½ **1991 (R)** Earth is a parched planet in the year 2040. Renegade bands cruise the desert, making short shrift of civilized people who band together in remote villages. When peaceful farmer Carradine's family falls prey to the pillagers, surely he and the most evil warlord of all must clash. Good action and stunts, if the dummy plot doesn't get you first. **77m/C VHS.** David Carradine, Richard (Rick) Hill, Luke Askew, Jillian McWhirter, Blake Boyd; ***D:*** Cirio H. Santiago.

The Dunera Boys 🦴🦴🦴 **1985 (R)** Hoskins shines in this story about Viennese Jews who, at the onset of WWII, escape to England where they are suspected as German spies. Subsequently, the British shipped them all to an Australian prison camp, where they recreated in peace their Viennese lifestyle. **150m/C VHS.** *AU* Bob Hoskins, Joe Spano, Warren Mitchell, Joseph Furst, Moshe Kedem, Dita Cobb, John Meillon, Mary-Anne Fahey, Simon Chilvers, Steven Vidler; ***D:*** Sam Lewin.

Dungeon of Harrow 🦴 **1964** Unbelievably cheap tale of shipwrecked comrades who encounter a maniacal family on an otherwise deserted island. Not your stranded-on-a-desert-island fantasy come true. Filmed in San Antonio; a harrowing bore. **74m/B VHS.** Russ Harvey, Helen Hogan, Bill McNulty, Pat Boyette; ***D:*** Pat Boyette.

Dungeonmaster 🦴½ *Ragewar* **1983 (PG-13)** A warlord forces a computer wiz to participate in a bizarre "Dungeons and Dragons" styled game in order to save a girl held captive. Consists of seven segments, each by a different director. Save yourself the trouble. **80m/C VHS.** Jeffrey Byron, Richard Moll, Leslie Wing, Danny Dick; ***D:*** John Carl Buechler, Charles Band, David Allen, Stephen Ford, Peter Manoogian, Ted Nicolaou, Rosemarie Turko; ***W:*** Allen Actor; ***M:*** Richard Band.

Dungeons and Dragons 🦴½ **2000 (PG-13)** Based (probably very loosely) on the role-playing game of the same name, "D & D" tells the story of the land of Izmer, whose reformer ruler, Empress Savina (Birch), wants to empower the lowly commoners and put them on equal footing with the ruling Mages. An elitist Mage, Profion (Irons, in an obvious pay-the-bills role) wants to overthrow her. Luckily, she's aided by young hero Ridley (Whalin) and his sidekick Snails (Wayans). It's hard to decide what's more ridiculous: plot, dialogue, settings, effects, costumes, or the idea that anyone would pay to see this mess. The mere title is enough to turn off anyone who never played the game as a kid, and the target audience will probably nit-pick it to death with "that's not like in the game"-type complaints. **107m/C VHS, DVD, Wide.** Justin Whalin, Marlon Wayans, Jeremy Irons, Thora Birch, Zoe McLellan, Kristen Wilson, Lee Arenberg, Bruce Payne, Richard O'Brien, Tom Baker, Robert Miano; ***D:*** Courtney Solomon; ***W:*** Topper Lilien, Carroll Cartwright; ***C:*** Doug Milsome; ***M:*** Justin Caine Burnett.

Dunston Checks In 🦴🦴½ **1995 (PG)** This just in: Hollywood thinks monkeys are funny. But, as far as "stupid people learn important life lessons from a monkey who wears clothes" movies go, this one's not bad. Robert Grant (Alexander) is the manager of a five-star hotel. His Leona Helmsley-esque boss (Dunaway) is convinced that aristocratic guest Lord Rutledge (Everett) is a travel guide critic who is there to bestow an elusive sixth star on the hotel. Actually he's a jewel thief, and Dunston the orangutan is his accomplice. When Dunston flees from his abusive owner, he's adopted by Grant's two children. Together, Dunston and the kids are left to straighten out the whole mess. **88m/C VHS.** Jason Alexander, Faye Dunaway, Eric Lloyd, Rupert Everett, Graham Sack, Paul (Peewee Herman) Reubens, Glenn Shadix, Nathan Davis, Jennifer Bassey; ***D:*** Ken Kwapis; ***W:*** Bruce Graham, John Hopkins; ***C:*** Peter Collister; ***M:*** Miles Goodman.

The Dunwich Horror 🦴🦴 **1970** Young warlock acquires a banned book of evil spells, starts trouble on the astral plane. Stockwell hammy. Loosely based on H. P. Lovecraft story. **90m/C VHS, DVD, Wide.** Sandra Dee, Dean Stockwell, Lloyd Bochner, Ed Begley Sr., Sam Jaffe, Joanna Moore, Talia Shire, Barboura Morris, Beach Dickerson, Michael Fox, Donna Baccala; ***D:*** Daniel Haller; ***W:*** Curtis Hanson, Henry Rosenbaum, Ronald Silkosky; ***C:*** Richard C. Glouner; ***M:*** Les Baxter.

Duplicates 🦴🦴 **1992 (PG-13)** Harrison and Greist are a married couple whose young son has disappeared. When the boy is found he has no memory of his former life or parents. The couple discover he's the victim of secret experiments which transfer human memories into computer banks. Will they become the next targets? **92m/C VHS.** Gregory Harrison, Kim Greist, Cicely Tyson, Lane Smith, William Lucking, Kevin McCarthy; ***D:*** Sandor Stern.

Dupont Lajoie 🦴🦴 *Rape of Innocence* **1974** At a tourist campground Lajoie (Carmet) accidentally kills his son's girlfriend when she resists his sexual advances. To save his life he accuses Arabs of committing the crime and begins a racist campaign of vengeance. French with subtitles. **103m/C VHS.** *FR* Jean Carmet; ***D:*** Yves Boisset.

Durango 🦴🦴½ **1999** Okay, the title sounds western and there is a cattle drive but this whimsical romance is set in the Irish countryside in 1939. Mark Doran (Keeslar) and his neighbors get together to drive their cattle to the railway (40 miles distant) when the local buyer tries to cheat them. He's also in love with a lassie (St. Alban) but is worried about her fearsome father (Bergin). Maybe, if Mark's plan succeeds, he'll have the confidence to get the girl as well. Based on the novel by John B. Keane. **98m/C VHS.** Matt Keeslar, Patrick Bergin, Brenda Fricker, Nancy St. Alban, George Hearn, Paul Ronan, Dermot Martin, Mark Lambert; ***D:*** Brent Shields; ***W:*** Walter Bernstein; ***C:*** Shelly Johnson; ***M:*** Mark McKenzie. **TV**

Durango Valley Raiders 🦴½ **1938** Sheriff is the leader of the outlaws, and a young cowboy finds out. **55m/B VHS.** Bob Steele; ***D:*** Sam Newfield.

Dust 🦴🦴🦴 **1985** A white woman in South Africa murders her father when he shows affection for a young black servant. Controversial and intense. **87m/C VHS.** *FR BE* Jane Birkin, Trevor Howard, John Matshikiza, Nadine Uwampa, Lourdes Christina Sayo, Rene Diaz; ***D:*** Marion Hansel; ***W:*** Marion Hansel; ***M:*** Martin St. Pierre.

Dust Devil 🦴🦴 **1993 (R)** Three travelers find themselves in Namibia's vast desert: a policeman, a woman on the run, and her abusive husband. They all have the misfortune of meeting up with a supernatural being known as the "Dust Devil," who kills humans in order to steal their souls and increase his other worldly powers. **87m/C VHS.** *GB* Robert John Burke, Chelsea Field, Zakes Mokae, Rufus Swart, John Matshikiza, William Hootkins, Marianne Saegebrecht; ***D:*** Richard Stanley; ***W:*** Richard Stanley; ***C:*** Steven Chivers; ***M:*** Simon Boswell.

Dust to Dust **1985** A short mystery about an aging gentleman who answers a request for correspondence and discovers ulterior, and evil, motives. **60m/C VHS.** *GB* Patricia Hodge, Michael Jayston, Judy Campbell. **TV**

Dusty 🦴🦴 **1985** Touching story of a wild dingo dog raised by an Australian rancher and trained to herd sheep. Filmed in the Australian bush and based on the children's book by Frank Dalby Davison. **89m/C VHS.** *AU* Bill Kerr, Noel Trevarthen, Carol Burns, Nicholas Holland, John Stanton; ***D:*** John Richardson.

Dutch 🦴½ **1991 (PG-13)** Working class boob attempts to pick up his girlfriend's son from boarding school. Their trip together gives them an unexpected chance to connect, if they don't kill each other first. Silly premise from the Hughes factory has little innovation and uses type-casting instead of acting. **107m/C VHS.** Ed O'Neill, Ethan (Randall) Embry, JoBeth Williams, Elizabeth (E.G. Dailey) Daily; ***D:*** Peter Faiman; ***W:*** John Hughes.

Dutch Girls woof! **1987** Muddled mayhem as a horny high school field hockey team travels through Holland, cavorts about, and discovers the meaning of life. **83m/C VHS.** *GB* Bill Paterson, Colin Firth, Timothy Spall; ***D:*** Giles Foster.

Dutch Treat 🦴 **1986 (R)** Two nerds con a sultry, all-girl rock band into thinking they're powerful record company execs. Nobody's buying. **95m/C VHS.** Lorin Dreyfuss, David Landsberg; ***D:*** Boaz Davidson.

The Dybbuk 🦴🦴🦴½ *Der Dibuk* **1937** A man's bride is possessed by a restless spirit. Set in the Polish-Jewish community before WWI and based on the play by Sholom Anski. Considered a classic for its portrayal of Jewish religious and cultural mores. In Yiddish with English subtitles. **123m/B VHS.** *PL* Abraham Morewski, Isaac Samberg, Moshe Lipman, Lili Liliana, Dina Halpern, Leon Liebgold; ***D:*** Michal Waszynski; ***W:*** S.A. Kacyzna, Marek Arenstein; ***C:*** Albert Wywerka; ***M:*** Krzysztof Komeda.

Dying Game 🦴🦴 **1994** Sorority girls are being stalked and murdered and the detective investigating the crimes falls for the sorority's president. Now, he has to find the killer before his girlfriend becomes the next victim. **85m/C VHS.** Michael Hughes, Mathea Webb, D.J. Boozer; ***D:*** Kris Hughes.

Dying Room Only 🦴🦴½ **1973** Travelling through the desert, a woman's husband suddenly disappears after they stop at a secluded roadside diner. A real spooker. **74m/C VHS.** Cloris Leachman, Ross Martin, Ned Beatty, Louise Latham, Dana Elcar, Dabney Coleman; ***D:*** Philip Leacock; ***W:*** Richard Matheson; ***M:*** Charles Fox. **TV**

Dying to Get Rich 🦴🦴 *Susan's Plan* **1998 (R)** Slow pacing stunts the humor but doesn't manage to destroy it. Divorced Susan (Kinski) wants her lover, Sam (Zane), to knock off her ex-husband (Paul) so she can collect his life insurance policy. He hires the job out to a couple of losers (Schneider, Biehn), who fail. So the lovers hire a crazy biker (Aykroyd) to finish the job. **90m/C VHS, DVD.** Nastassia Kinski, Billy Zane, Dan Aykroyd, Rob Schneider, Lara Flynn Boyle, Adrian Paul, Michael Biehn, Carl Ballantine, Thomas Haden Church, Bill Duke, Sheree North; ***D:*** John Landis; ***W:*** John Landis; ***C:*** Ken Kelsch; ***M:*** Peter Bernstein.

Dying to Remember 🦴½ **1993 (PG-13)** A fashion designer (Gilbert) regresses to a past life during hypnotherapy and discovers she was murdered in 1963. She flies to San Francisco to discover more about her past but finds that someome wants to keep things secret—and is willing to kill again. Tedious and predictable. **87m/C VHS.** Melissa Gilbert, Ted Shackleford, Scott Plank, Christopher Stone, Jay Robinson; ***D:*** Arthur Seidelman; ***W:*** George Schenck, Frank Cardea, Brian Ross.

The Dying Truth 🦴🦴 **1991** A wrongfully accused prisoner lies dying in his cell. Trouble is, he can't die in peace until he solves the murder they say he committed. Interesting mix of the supernatural and mystery, although perhaps not one of Carradine's more memorable roles. **80m/C VHS.** David Carradine, Stephanie Beacham, Stephen Greif, Stephan Chase, Larry Carby, Lesley Dunlop; ***D:*** John Hough.

Dying Young 🦴½ **1991 (R)** Muted romance has a wealthy leukemia victim hire a spirited, unschooled beauty as his nurse. They fall in love, but the film is either too timid or too unimaginative to mine emotions denoted by the title. Nobody dies, in fact, a grim ending (faithful to the Marti Leimbach novel on which this was based) got scrapped after testing poorly with audiences. The actors try their best, photography is lovely, and Kenny G's mellow music fills the soundtrack, but this is basically overmelodramatic drivel. Scott is the late Dewhurst's son. **111m/C VHS.** Julia Roberts, Campbell Scott, Vincent D'Onofrio, Colleen Dewhurst, Ellen Burstyn, David Selby; ***D:*** Joel Schumacher; ***W:*** Richard Friedenberg; ***C:*** Juan Ruiz-Anchia.

Dynamite 🦴 **1949** Romance explodes as two young demolitions experts vie for the same girl. Stand back. **68m/B VHS.** William Gargan, Virginia Welles, Richard Crane, Irving Bacon; ***D:*** William H. Pine.

Dynamite and Gold 🦴🦴 *Where the Hell's the Gold?* **1988 (PG)** Nelson and crew embark on a search for lost gold, battling hostile Indians, the Mexican army and assorted bandits along the way. A mediocre TV movie. **91m/C VHS.** Willie Nelson, Delta Burke, Jack Elam, Alfonso Arau, Gregory Sierra, Michael Wren, Gerald McRaney; ***D:*** Burt Kennedy; ***W:*** Burt Kennedy. **TV**

The Dynamite Brothers 🦴 **1974 (R)** Two tough guys, one a Hong Kong immigrant with martial arts skills, the other a brother from the streets of the ghetto, team up to rid Los Angeles of a Chinese crimelord. **90m/C VHS.** James Hong, Aldo Ray, Alan Tang, Timothy Brown, Carolyn Ann Speed, Don Oliver; ***D:*** Al Adamson; ***M:*** Charles Earland.

Dynamite Canyon 🦴🦴 **1941** Average oater has villain Price committing murder in order to keep secret the location of a lode of copper. Standard western fare. **58m/B VHS.** Tom (George Duryea) Keene, Evelyn Finley, Sugar Dawn, Stanley Price, Kenne Duncan; ***D:*** Robert Emmett Tansey; ***W:*** Robert Emmett Tansey, Frances Kavanaugh.

Dynamite Chicken 🦴🦴 **1970 (R)** Melange of skits, songs, and hippie satire is dated. Includes performances by Joan Baez, Lenny Bruce, B.B. King, and others. **75m/C VHS.** Joan Baez, Richard Pryor, Lenny Bruce, Jimi Hendrix; ***D:*** Ernest Pintoff.

Dynamite Dan 🦴½ **1924** A man knocks out the heavyweight boxing champion after he flirts with his girlfriend and decides to give up his day job to become a championship boxer. He is a success, and in the end he has to face the champion again. Will he win? **62m/B VHS.** Kenneth McDonald, Frank Rice, Boris Karloff, Eddie Harris, Diana Alden, Harry Woods, Jack (H.) Richardson; ***D:*** Bruce Mitchell.

Dynamite Pass 🦴🦴 **1950** Offbeat oater about disgruntled ranchers attempting to stop the construction of a new road. **61m/B VHS.** Tim Holt, Richard Martin, Regis Toomey, Lynne Roberts, Denver Pyle; ***D:*** Lew (Louis Friedlander) Landers.

Dynamite Ranch 🦴 **1932** Ranchers fight tooth and nail to keep their rights and property in this Maynard oater. **60m/B VHS.** Ken Maynard.

Dynasty 🦴🦴 **1977** A leader of the Ming Dynasty is killed by evil Imperial Court eunuch and his son the monk sets out to avenge him. In 3-D. Run-of-the-mill kung-fu stunts. **94m/C VHS.** Bobby Ming, Lin Tashing, Pai Ying, Tang Wei, Jin Gang; ***D:*** Zhang Meijun.

Dynasty 🦴🦴 **1982** Pulitzer Prize-winning author James Michener creates the usual sweeping saga of a family torn by jealousy, deception, and rivalry in love and business as husband, wife, and brother-in-law seek their fortune in the Ohio frontier of the 1820s. **90m/C VHS.** Sarah Miles, Harris Yulin, Stacy Keach.

Dynasty of Fear 🦴½ *Fear in the Night; Honeymoon of Fear* **1972 (PG)** Matters get rather sticky at a British boys' school when the headmaster's wife seduces her husband's assistant. Together they conspire to murder her husband and share his fortune. **93m/C VHS.** *GB* Peter Cushing, Joan Collins, Ralph Bates, Judy Geeson, James Cossins, John Bown, Brian Grellis, Gillian Lind; ***D:*** Jimmy Sangster; ***W:*** Jimmy Sangster, Michael Syson; ***C:*** Arthur Grant.

E. Nick: A Legend in His Own Mind **1984** Satire of videos and magazines designed for adults. **75m/C VHS.** Don Calfa, Cleavon Little, Andra Akers, Pat McCormick; ***D:*** Robert Hegyes.

Each Dawn I Die 🦴🦴½ **1939** Cagney stars as a reporter who is a fervent critic of the political system. Framed for murder and imprisoned, he is subsequently befriended by fellow inmate, Raft, a gangster. Once hardened by prison life, Cagney shuns his friend and becomes wary of the system. Despite its farfetched second half and mediocre script, the film makes interesting viewing thanks to a stellar performance from Cagney. **92m/B VHS.** James Cagney, George Raft, George Bancroft, Jane Bryan, Maxie "Slapsie" Rosenbloom, Alan Baxter, Thurston Hall, Stanley Ridges, Victor Jory; ***D:*** William Keighley; ***W:*** Norman Reilly Raine.

The Eagle 🦴🦴🦴 **1925** In this tale of a young Cossack "Robin Hood," Valentino assumes the persona of the Eagle to avenge his father's murder. The romantic rogue encounters trouble when he falls for the beautiful Banky much to the chagrin of the scorned Czarina Dresser. Fine performances from Valentino and Dresser. Silent, based on a Alexander Pushkin story. Released on video with a new score by Davis. **77m/B VHS.** Rudolph Valentino, Vilma Banky, Louise Dresser, George Nicholls Jr., James A. Marcus; ***D:*** Clarence Brown; ***C:*** George Barnes; ***M:*** Carl Davis.

The Eagle and the Hawk 🦴🦴🦴 **1933** Americans Jerry Young (March), Henry Crocker (Grant), and Mike Richards (Oakie) volunteer for flying duty with the British Army in 1918. Jerry is a heroic pilot but becomes depressed by the horrors of war, while gung ho Henry, who's serving as his observer/gunner, also becomes his rival. On leave, Jerry briefly finds solace with a society babe (Lombard) only to discover on his return that Henry's cockiness has gotten their buddy Mike killed. He denounces the war but Henry manages to ensure Jerry's status as a hero despite his actions. **73m/B VHS.** Fredric March, Cary Grant, Jack Oakie, Carole Lombard, Guy Standing, Forrester Harvey, Kenneth Howell, Leyland Hodgson; ***D:*** Stuart Walker; ***W:*** Seton I. Miller, Bogart Rogers; ***C:*** Harry Fischbeck.

The Eagle Has Landed 🦴🦴🦴 **1977 (PG)** Duvall, portraying a Nazi colonel in this WWII spy film, commissions Sutherland's Irish, English-hating character to aid him in his mission to kill Prime Minister Winston Churchill. Adapted from the best-selling novel by Jack Higgins. A restored version is available at 134 minutes. **123m/C VHS, DVD, Wide.** Michael Caine, Donald Sutherland, Robert Duvall, Larry Hagman, Jenny Agutter, Donald Pleasence, Treat Williams, Anthony Quayle; ***D:*** John Sturges; ***W:*** Tom Mankiewicz; ***C:*** Anthony B. Richmond; ***M:*** Lalo Schifrin.

The Eagle Has Two Heads 🦴🦴🦴 *L'Aigle a Deux Tetes; The Eagle with Two Heads* **1948** Set during the 19th century, poet/anarchist Marais sets out to assassinate the queen, but when he sees the beautiful monarch, it's love at first sight. Adapted from Cocteau's hugely successful play. In French with English subtitles. **93m/B VHS.** *FR* Edwige Feuillere, Jean Marais; ***D:*** Jean Cocteau; ***W:*** Jean Cocteau.

Eagles Attack at Dawn 🦴½ **1974 (PG)** After escaping from an Arab prison, an Israeli soldier vows to return with a small commando force to kill the sadistic warden. **96m/C VHS.** *IS* Rick Jason, Peter Brown, Joseph Shiloah.

Eagle's Shadow 🦴 **1984** After a poor orphan boy rescues an aged beggar, the grateful old man tutors the lad in Snake-Fist techniques. **101m/C VHS.** Jackie Chan, Juan Jan Lee, Simon Yuen, Roy Horan; ***D:*** Yuen Woo Ping.

Eagle's Wing 🦴½ **1979** John Briley, screenwriter of the award-winning epic "Gandhi," attempts to weave the threads of allegory smoothly in this white man vs. red man Western from England. The mediocre story finds Native American Waterston dueling white trapper Sheen in a quest to capture an elusive, exotic white stallion. **111m/C VHS.** *GB* Martin Sheen, Sam Waterston, Harvey Keitel, Stephane Audran, Caroline Langrishe; ***D:*** Anthony Harvey; ***W:*** John Briley; ***C:*** Billy Williams.

Early Days 🦴🦴 **1981** A cantankerous, salty, once-powerful politician awaits death. **67m/C VHS.** Ralph Richardson.

Early Frost 🦴½ **1984** Near suspenseful whodunit centering around a simple divorce investigation that leads to the discovery of a corpse. **95m/C VHS.** Diana McLean, Jon Blake, Janet Kingsbury, David Franklin; ***D:*** Terry O'Connor.

An Early Frost 🦴🦴🦴½ **1985** Highly praised, surprisingly intelligent drama following the anguish of a successful lawyer who tells his closed-minded family that he is gay and dying of AIDS. Sensitive performance by Quinn in one of the first TV films to focus on the devastating effects of HIV. Rowlands adeptly displays her acting talents as the despairing mother. **97m/C VHS.** Aidan Quinn, Gena Rowlands, Ben Gazzara, John Glover, D.W. Moffett, Sylvia Sidney; ***D:*** John Erman. **TV**

Early Summer 🦴🦴🦴 *Bakushu* **1951** A classic from renowned Japanese director Ozu, this film chronicles family tensions in post-WWII Japan caused by newly independent women rebelling against the social conventions they are expected to fulfill. Perhaps the best example of this director's work. Winner of Japan's Film of the Year Award. In Japanese with English subtitles. **150m/B VHS.** *JP* Ichiro Sugai, Chishu Ryu, Setsuko Hara, Chikage Awashima, Chieko Higashiyama, Haruko Sugimura, Kuniko Miyake, Kan Nihon-yanagi, Shuji Sano, Toyoko Takahashi, Seiji Miyaguchi; ***D:*** Yasujiro Ozu.

The Earrings of Madame De... 🦴🦴🦴🦴 *Diamond Earrings; Madame De* **1954** A simple story about a society woman who sells a pair of diamond earrings that her husband gave her, then lies about it. Transformed by Ophuls into his most opulent, overwrought masterpiece, the film displays a triumph of form over content. In French with English subtitles. **105m/C VHS.** *FR* Charles Boyer, Danielle Darrieux, Vittorio De Sica, Lea di Lea, Jean Debucourt; ***D:*** Max Ophuls; ***W:*** Max Ophuls, Marcel Archand, Annette Wademant; ***C:*** Christian Matras; ***M:*** Oscar Straus, Georges Van Parys.

Earth 🦴🦴🦴🦴 *Zemlya; Soul* **1930** Classic Russian silent film with English subtitles. Problems begin in a Ukrainian village when a collective farm landowner resists handing over his land. Outstanding camera work. Kino release runs 70 minutes. **101m/B VHS, DVD.** *RU* Semyon Svashenko, Mikola Nademsy, Stephan Shkurat, Yelena Maximova, Yulia Solntseva; ***D:*** Alexander Dovzhenko; ***W:*** Alexander Dovzhenko; ***C:*** Daniil Demutsky.

Earth 🦴🦴 **1998** The second of Mehta's projected trilogy (after 1997's "Fire"), "Earth" follows the events surrounding the partitioning of India in 1947, forcing neighbors to take sides in a ferocious religious conflict. The story is seen through the eyes of eight-year-old Lenny (Sthna), the daughter of a wealthy Parsi family in Lahore who are trying to remain neutral. But Lenny is cared for by her lovely Hindu nanny, Shanta (Das), whose Muslim suitors are deeply affected by the violence. Based on the novel "Cracking India" by Bapsi Sidhwa. Hindi, Urdu, Parsi, and Punjabi with subtitles. **101m/C VHS.** *CA* Aamir Khan, Nandita Das, Rahul Khanna, Maia Sethna; ***D:*** Deepa Mehta; ***W:*** Deepa Mehta; ***C:*** Giles Nuttgens; ***M:*** A.R. Rahman.

Earth Entranced 🦴🦴 *Terra em Transe* **1966** A complex political lamentation from Rocha, the premiere director of Brazil's own new wave cinema. Here a writer switches his allegiance from one politician to another, only to find that he (and the masses) lose either way. In Portuguese with English subtitles. **105m/C VHS.** *BR* Jose Lewgoy, Paulo Gracindo, Jardel Filho, Glauce Rocha; ***D:*** Glauce Rocha; ***W:*** Glauce Rocha.

Earth Girls Are Easy 🦴🦴½ **1989 (PG)** Valley girl Valerie is having a bad week: first she catches her fiancee with another woman, then she breaks a nail, then furry aliens land in her swimming pool. What more could go wrong? When the aliens are temporarily stranded, she decides to make amends by giving them a head-to-toe makeover. Devoid of their excessive hairiness, the handsome trio of fun-loving extraterrestrials set out to experience the Southern California lifestyle. Sometimes hilarious sci-fi/musical, featuring bouncy shtick and a gleeful dismantling of modern culture. **100m/C VHS, DVD, Wide.** *GB* Geena Davis, Jeff Goldblum, Charles Rocket, Julie Brown, Jim Carrey, Damon Wayans, Michael McKean, Angelyne, Larry Linville, Rick Overton, Diane Stilwell, Terrance McNally; ***D:*** Julien Temple; ***W:*** Charlie Coffey, Julie Brown, Terrance McNally; ***C:*** Oliver Stapleton; ***M:*** Nile Rodgers.

Earth vs. the Flying Saucers 🦴🦴½ *Invasion of the Flying Saucers* **1956** Extraterrestrials land on Earth and issue an ultimatum to humans concerning their constant use of bombs and missiles. Peace is threatened when the military disregards the extraterrestrials' simple warning. Superb special effects by Ray Harryhausen. **83m/B VHS.** Hugh Marlowe, Joan Taylor, Donald Curtis, Morris Ankrum; ***D:*** Fred F. Sears; ***W:*** George Worthing Yates, Bernard Gordon.

Earth vs. the Spider 🦴 *The Spider* **1958** Man-eating giant mutant (teenage ninja?) tarantula makes life miserable for a small town in general and high school partyers in particular. Silly old drive-in fare is agony for many, camp treasure for a precious few. **72m/B VHS.** Edward Kemmer, June Kenney, Gene Persson, Gene Roth, Hal Torey, Mickey Finn; ***D:*** Bert I. Gordon; ***W:*** Laszlo Gorog, George Worthing Yates; ***C:*** Jack Marta.

Earth vs. the Spider 🦴🦴 **2001 (R)** Shares the title of the 1958 drive-in feature but not much else. Nerdy comic book fanatic Quentin (Gummersall) works as a security guard at a biotech research lab. After his partner is killed during a break-in, Quentin injects himself with a drug made from a mutated lab spider. Soon Quentin begins to mutate and no one is safe! **90m/C VHS, DVD, Wide.** Devon Gummersall, Dan Aykroyd, Amelia Heinle, Christopher Cousins, John Cho, Theresa Russell, Mario Roccuzzo; ***D:*** Scott Ziehl; ***W:*** Cary Solomon, Chuck Konzelman, Max Enscoe, Annie de Young; ***C:*** Thomas Callaway; ***M:*** Charles Bernstein. CABLE

Earthling 🦴🦴½ **1980 (PG)** A terminally ill Holden helps a young Schroder survive in the Australian wilderness after the boy's parents are killed in a tragic accident. Lessons of life and the power of the human heart are passed on in this panoramic, yet mildly sentimental film. **102m/C VHS.** *AU* William Holden, Rick Schroder, Jack Thompson, Olivia Hamnett, Alwyn Kurts; ***D:*** Peter Collinson; ***W:*** Lanny Cotler.

Earthly Possessions 🦴🦴½ **1999 (R)** Sarandon can't really pass for a drab housewife but she does her best in this adaptation of Anne Tyler's novel. Charlotte Emory (Sarandon) is the very sheltered wife of a smalltown minister (Sanders), who longs for a break from her tedious routine. She gets her chance when she's unexpectedly taken hostage by would-be bankrobber, Jake Simms Jr. (Dorff), who suffers from impulse control problems and continual bad luck. Both their fortunes change when Jake forces Charlotte on the road with him (he wants to see his pregnant girlfriend) and an increasingly close bond forms between the two strangers as they try to stay out of police custody. **120m/C VHS, DVD.** Susan Sarandon, Stephen Dorff, Jay O. Sanders, Elissabeth (Elisabeth, Elizabeth, Liz) Moss, Margo Martindale; ***D:*** James Lapine; ***W:*** Steven Rogers; ***C:*** David Franco; ***M:*** Stephen Endelman. CABLE

Earthquake 🦴🦴 **1974 (PG)** Less-than-mediocre drama centers on a major earthquake in Los Angeles and its effect on the lives of an engineer, his spoiled wife, his mistress, his father-in-law, and a suspended policeman. Filmed in much-hyped Sensurround—a technique intended to shake up the theatre a bit, but which will have no effect on your TV set. Good special effects, but not enough to compensate for lackluster script. **123m/C VHS, DVD.** Charlton Heston, Ava Gardner, George Kennedy, Lorne Greene, Genevieve Bujold, Richard Roundtree, Marjoe Gortner, Barry Sullivan, Victoria Principal, Lloyd Nolan, Walter Matthau, Scott Hylands; ***D:*** Mark Robson; ***W:*** Mario Puzo; ***C:*** Philip Lathrop; ***M:*** John Williams. Oscars '74: Sound, Visual FX.

Earthworm Tractors 🦴🦴½ **1936** Ambitious tractor salesman Alexander Botts will do anything to make a sale. Brown excels as the fast-talking lead. Comedy is strengthened by its supporting cast. Based on characters first appearing in the "Saturday Evening Post." **63m/B VHS.** Joe E. Brown, June Travis, Guy Kibbee, Dick Foran, Carol Hughes, Gene Lockhart, Olin Howlin; ***D:*** Ray Enright.

East and West 🦴🦴🦴 *Ost und West* **1924** Morris Brown, a worldly New York Jew, returns home to Galicia with his daughter Mollie for a traditional family wedding. She teaches the young villagers to dance and box but meets her romantic match in a young yeshiva scholar who forsakes tradition to win her heart. Picon shines as the exuberant flapper. With English and Yiddish intertitles. **85m/B VHS.** *AT* Molly Picon, Jacob Kalish, Sidney Goldin; ***D:*** Ivan Abramson, Sidney Goldin.

East Is East 🦴🦴🦴 **1999 (R)** Culture clash comedy is set in 1971 in the northern working-class community of Salford, England. Pakistani immigrant George Khan (Puri) is the would-be stern patriarch to a brood of six sons and one daughter. While he wants to raise his kids traditionally, they're rebelling. Especially in the marriage department: despite his own long marriage to the English Ella (Bassett), George tries to arrange marriages to fellow Pakistanis for his two eldest sons, with disastrous results. Story is swift-paced, definitely not p.c., and is told in amusingly broad strokes. Based on Khan-Din's play. **96m/C VHS, DVD, Wide.** *GB* Om Puri, Linda Bassett, Archie Panjabi, Chris Bisson, Jimi Mistry, Ian Aspinall, Jordan Routledge, Raji James; ***D:*** Damien O'Donnell; ***W:*** Ayub Khan-Din; ***C:*** Brian Tufano; ***M:*** Deborah Mollison. British Acad. '99: Film.

East L.A. Warriors 🦴½ **1989** A mobster, Hilton-Jacobs, manipulates Los Angeles gangs in this non-stop action adventure. **90m/C VHS.** Tony Bravo, Lawrence-Hilton Jacobs, Kamar Reyes, William Smith; ***D:*** Addison Randall.

East of Borneo 🦴½ **1931** Tropical adventure involving a "lost" physician whose worried wife sets out to find him in the jungle. She locates her love only to discover he has a prestigious new job tending to royalty and didn't want to be found. **76m/B VHS.** Charles Bickford, Rose Hobart, Georges Renavent; ***D:*** George Melford.

East of Eden 🦴🦴🦴🦴 **1954** Steinbeck's contemporary retelling of the biblical Cain and Abel story receives superior treatment from Kazan and his excellent cast. Dean, in his first starring role, gives a reading of a young man's search for love and acceptance that defines adolescent pain. Though filmed in the 1950s, this story still rivets today's viewers with its emotional message. **115m/C VHS, Wide.** James Dean, Julie Harris, Richard (Dick) Davalos, Raymond Massey, Jo Van Fleet, Burl Ives, Albert Dekker; ***D:*** Elia Kazan; ***W:*** Paul Osborn; ***M:*** Leonard Rosenman. Oscars '55: Support. Actress (Van Fleet); Golden Globes '56: Film—Drama.

East of Eden 🦴🦴½ **1980** Remade into a TV mini series, this Steinbeck classic tells the tale of two brothers who vie for their father's affection and the woman who comes between them. Seymour is notable as the self-serving mother who abandons her babies to lead a disreputable life. Rife with biblical symbolism and allusions. **375m/C VHS.** Jane Seymour, Bruce Boxleitner, Warren Oates, Lloyd Bridges, Anne Baxter, Timothy Bottoms, Soon-Teck Oh, Karen Allen, Hart Bochner, Sam Bottoms, Howard Duff, Richard Masur, Wendell Burton, Nicholas Pryor, Grace Zabriskie, M. Emmet Walsh, Matthew "Stymie" Beard; ***D:*** Harvey Hart. TV

East of Elephant Rock 🦴½ **1976** In 1948, a young first secretary of the British Embassy returns from leave in England to a tense atmosphere in a colony in southeast Asia. Beautiful scenery can't make up for weak plot. **93m/C VHS.** *GB* John Hurt, Jeremy Kemp, Judi Bowker, Christopher Cazenove; ***D:*** Don Boyd; ***W:*** Don Boyd.

East of Kilimanjaro 🦴🦴 *The Big Search* **1957** A freelance photographer and a doctor search frantically to find the carrier of a fatal disease near the slopes of the majestic Mt. Kilimanjaro. Routine killer virus flick filmed in Africa. **75m/C VHS.** Marshall Thompson, Gaby Andre, Fausto Tozzi; ***D:*** Arnold Belgard.

East Palace, West Palace 🦴🦴 *Behind the Forbidden City; Donggong, Xigong* **1996** Bold and controversial examination of a shadow world in Chinese society. A-Lan (Han) is a young homosexual, cruising the park outside the Forbidden Palace in Beijing. He's detained in a roundup by a cop, Xiao Shi (Jun), who takes him to the park's police station for interrogation. A-Lan is unashamed of his lifestyle and the cop presses him to tell his life story. It soon becomes clear that the Xiao Shi, though outwardedly homophobic, is actually sexually intrigued by A-Lan's presence as the duo mentally and verbally dance around the charged situation. Chinese with subtitles. **95m/C VHS.** *CH* Si Han, Hu Jun; ***D:*** Zhang Yuan; ***W:*** Zhang Yuan, Wang Xiaobo; ***C:*** Zheng Jian; ***M:*** Xiang Min.

East Side Kids 🦴🦴 **1940** Early East Side kids. A hoodlum wants to prevent his brother from beginning a similar life of crime. **60m/B VHS.** Leon Ames, Harris Berger, Dennis Moore, Joyce Bryant; ***D:*** Robert F. "Bob" Hill.

East Side, West Side 🦴🦴 **1949** Stanwyck and Mason try hard to make this simple-minded soaper work, with mixed results. A wealthy couple experiences marital woes, aggravated by a ambitious young woman and a soft-hearted man suffering from unrequited love. Based on the popular novel by Marcia Davenport. **110m/B VHS.** Barbara Stanwyck, James Mason, Ava Gardner, Van Heflin, Gale Sondergaard, William Frawley, Nancy Davis; ***D:*** Mervyn LeRoy; ***C:*** Charles Rosher; ***M:*** Miklos Rozsa.

East-West 🦴🦴 *Est-Ouest* **1999 (PG-13)** In 1946, Stalin offered amnesty to any Russians who left the country after the 1917 revolution. But he executed or imprisoned many of the homesick expatriates and others found their gray motherland hard to bear (and impossible to leave). Russian doctor Alexei Golovin (Menshikov) bows to circumstances while his marriage to French wife Marie (Bonnaire) becomes increasingly strained. Marie befriends a champion swimmer, Sasha (Bodrov), with the hopes that they can both escape but things don't go as planned. Old-fashioned storytelling hampers the drama and the story (which leaps ahead months and years) becomes confused. French and Russian with subtitles. **125m/C VHS, DVD, Wide.** *FR* Sandrine Bonnaire, Oleg Menshikov, Sergei Bodrov Jr., Catherine Deneuve, Tatiana Dogileva; ***D:*** Regis Wargnier; ***W:*** Regis Wargnier, Sergei Bodrov, Rustam Ibragimbekov, Louis Gardel; ***C:*** Laurent Dailland; ***M:*** Patrick Doyle.

Easter Parade 🦴🦴🦴½ **1948** Big musical star Don Hewes (Astaire) splits with his partner Nadine (Miller) claiming that he could mold any girl to replace her in the act. He tries and finally succeeds with clumsy chorus girl Hannah Brown (Garland) after much difficulty. Astaire and Garland in peak form, aided by a classic Irving Berlin score. ♫Happy Easter; Drum Crazy; It Only Happens When I Dance With You; Everybody's Doin' It; I Want to Go Back to Michigan; Beautiful Faces Need Beautiful Clothes; A Fella With an Umbrella; I Love a Piano; Snookey Ookums. **103m/C VHS.** Fred Astaire, Judy Garland, Peter Lawford, Ann Miller, Jules Munshin, Joi Lansing; ***D:*** Charles Walters; ***W:*** Sidney Sheldon, Frances Goodrich, Albert Hackett; ***C:*** Harry Stradling Sr.; ***M:*** Irving Berlin. Oscars '48: Scoring/Musical.

Eastern Condors 🦴🦴 **1987** At the end of the Vietnam War, a band of Chinese convicts are recruited by the U.S. Army (and promised their freedom) if they can destroy an ammunition dump before the Viet Cong can make use of it. Considered a Hong Kong version of "The Dirty Dozen," with the requisite level of high energy and blood. Dubbed or Chinese with English subtitles. **94m/C VHS, DVD.** *HK* Sammo Hung, Joyce Godenzi, Yuen Biao, Haing S. Ngor; ***D:*** Sammo Hung.

Eastside 🦴🦴 **1999** After being released from prison, Antonio Lopez pays a visit to his successful lawyer brother and learns that he's a mouthpiece for the mob. So Antonio gets an in with East L.A. kingpin De La Rosa as a strongarm guy. Only when he's asked to intimidate the owner of an inner-city youth center, Antonio's latent conscience begins to bother him. Of course, if he betrays De La Rosa, he's dead. **94m/C VHS, DVD.** Mario Lopez, Efrain Figueroa, Mark Espinoza, Elizabeth Bogush, Gulsham Grover, Richard Lynch, Carlos Gallardo; ***D:*** Lorena David; ***W:*** Eric P. Sherman; ***C:*** Lisa Wiegard; ***M:*** Armando Avila. VIDEO

Easy Come, Easy Go 🦴🦴 **1967 (PG)** Elvis, as a Navy frogman, gets excited when he accidentally discovers what he believes is a vast sunken treasure. Music is his only solace when he finds his treasure to be worthless copper coins. ♫Easy Come, Easy Go; The Love Machine; Yoga Is As Yoga Goes; Sing, You Children; You Gotta Stop; I'll Take Love. **96m/C VHS.** Elvis Presley, Dodie Marshall, Pat Priest, Elsa Lanchester, Frank McHugh, Pat Harrington, Sonny Tufts; ***D:*** John Rich.

Easy Kill 🦴½ **1989** A man takes the law into his own hands to exact revenge on drug lords. **100m/C VHS.** Jane Badler, Cameron Mitchell, Frank Stallone; ***D:*** Josh Spencer.

The Easy Life 🦴🦴🦴 **1963** Haunting film about a hedonistic man from a small Italian village who takes a mild-mannered student pleasure-seeking. The ride turns sour and the playboy is ultimately destroyed by his own brutality. **105m/B VHS.** *IT* Vittorio Gassman, Catherine Spaak, Jean-Louis Trintignant, Luciana Angiolillo; ***D:*** Dino Risi.

Easy Living 🦴🦴🦴 **1937** Exasperated Wall Street millionaire J.B. Ball (Arnold) throws his spoiled wife's (Nash) fur coat out their apartment window and it just happens to land on poor-but-hardworking secretary Mary Smith (Arthur). Ball insists Mary keep the coat and even buys her a matching hat. Soon, rumors are flying that Mary is the millionaire's tootsie. She meets cute with John (Milland), who turns out to be Ball's son and, after the usual misunderstandings, the twosome realize that they're meant for each other. **91m/B VHS.** Jean Arthur, Edward Arnold, Ray Milland, Franklin Pangborn, Mary Nash, William Demerest; ***D:*** Mitchell Leisen; ***W:*** Preston Sturges; ***C:*** Ted Tetzlaff; ***M:*** Boris Morros.

Easy Living 🦴🦴½ **1949** Compromised melodrama about an over-the-hill football player who must cope with his failing marriage and looming retirement. Based on an Irwin Shaw story. **77m/B VHS.** Victor Mature, Lucille Ball, Jack Paar, Lizabeth

Scott, Sonny Tufts, Lloyd Nolan, Paul Stewart; *D:* Jacques Tourneur.

Easy Money ✂✂ 1983 (R) A basic slob has the chance to inherit $10 million if he can give up his loves: smoking, drinking, and gambling among others. Dangerfield is surprisingly restrained in this harmless, though not altogether unpleasing comedy. **95m/C VHS, DVD.** Rodney Dangerfield, Joe Pesci, Geraldine Fitzgerald, Jennifer Jason Leigh, Tom Ewell, Candice Azzara, Taylor Negron; *D:* James Signorelli; *W:* Rodney Dangerfield, Dennis Blair.

Easy Rider ✂✂✂½ 1969 (R) Slim-budget, generation-defining movie. Two young men in late 1960s undertake a motorcycle trek throughout the Southwest in search of the real essence of America. Along the way they encounter hippies, rednecks, prostitutes, drugs, Nicholson, and tragedy. One of the highest-grossing pictures of the decade, undoubtedly an influence on two generations of "youth-oriented dramas," which all tried unsuccessfully to duplicate the original accomplishment. Psychedelic scenes and a great role for Nicholson are added bonuses. Look for the graveyard dancing scene in New Orleans. Features one of the best '60s rock scores around, including "Mean Streets" and "The Wanderers." **94m/C VHS, DVD, 8mm, Wide.** Peter Fonda, Dennis Hopper, Jack Nicholson, Karen Black, Toni Basil, Robert Walker Jr., Luana Anders, Luke Askew, Warren Finnerty, Mac Mashorian, Antonio Mendoza, Sabrina Scharf, Phil Spector; *D:* Dennis Hopper; *W:* Terry Southern, Peter Fonda, Dennis Hopper; *C:* Laszlo Kovacs. AFI '98: Top 100, Natl. Film Reg. '98;, N.Y. Film Critics '69: Support. Actor (Nicholson); Natl. Soc. Film Critics '69: Support. Actor (Nicholson).

Easy Street ✂✂✂ 1916 Chaplin portrays a derelict who, using some hilarious methods, reforms the residents of Easy Street. Chaplin's row with the town bully is particularly amusing. Silent with musical soundtrack added. **20m/B VHS.** Charlie Chaplin; *D:* Charlie Chaplin.

Easy to Love ✂✂½ 1953 Williams is in love with her boss, but he pays her no attention until a handsome singer vies for her affections. Set at Florida's Cypress Gardens, this aquatic musical features spectacular water ballet productions choreographed by Busby Berkeley, and the title song penned by Cole Porter. ♫Easy to Love; Coquette; Beautiful Spring; That's What Rainy Day is For; Look Out! I'm Romantic; Didja Ever. **96m/C VHS.** Esther Williams, Van Johnson, Tony Martin, John Bromfield, King Donovan, Carroll Baker; *D:* Charles Walters; *W:* William Roberts.

Easy Virtue ✂✂½ 1927 Hitchcock directs this adaptation of a Noel Coward play as a social melodrama. Larita is an unhappily married socialite with a lover. When her husband discovers her infideltiy they divorce and she is marked as a woman of loose morals. Her reputation is not enhanced by her marriage to a younger man whose family diapproves. **79m/B VHS.** *GB* Isabel Jeans, Ian Hunter, Franklin Dyall, Eric Bransby Williams, Robin Irvine, Violet Farebrother; *D:* Alfred Hitchcock.

Easy Wheels ✂✂½ 1989 Like most decent biker movies, "Wheels" is propelled by bad taste and a healthy dose of existentialist nihilism. But there's an unusual plot twist in this parody. A biker named She-Wolf and her gang kidnap female babies and let wolves rear the children. Their elaborate plan is to create a race of super women who will subdue the troublesome male population. But can this "noble" plan succeed? **94m/C VHS.** Paul LeMat, Eileen Davidson, Marjorie Bransfield, Jon Menick, Mark Holton, Karen Russell, Jami Richards, Roberta Vasquez, Barry Livingston, George Plimpton; *D:* David O'Malley; *W:* Ivan Raimi, Celia Abrams, David O'Malley; *M:* John Ross.

Eat a Bowl of Tea ✂✂✂ 1989 (PG-13) Endearing light drama-comedy concerning a multi-generational Chinese family. They must learn to deal with the problems of life in America and in particular, marriage, when Chinese women are finally allowed to immigrate with their husbands to the United States following WWII. Adaptation of Louis Chu's story, directed by the man who brought us "Dim Sum." A PBS "American Playhouse" presentation. **102m/C VHS.** Cora Miao, Russell Wong, Lau Siu Ming, Eric Tsiang Chi Wai, Victor Wong, Jessica Harper, Lee Sau Kee; *D:* Wayne Wang; *W:* Judith Rascoe; *C:* Amir M. Mokri; *M:* Mark Adler.

Eat and Run ✂ 1986 (R) A bloody comedy about a 400-pound alien with a taste for Italian (people, that is). **85m/C VHS.** Ron Silver, R.L. Ryan, Sharon Schlarth; *D:* Christopher Hunt.

Eat Drink Man Woman ✂✂✂½ 1994 (R) In Taipei, widowed master chef serves weekly feast of elaborate food and familial guilt to his three grown daughters, all of whom still live at home. They spend their time sorting out professional and romantic difficulties, searching for independence, and fulfilling traditional family obligations. Each character has a lot going on, but no one's story gets lost in the mix. Lee uses irony to great effect, introducing us to the culinary artist who has lost his sense of taste and has a daughter who works at a Wendy's. Food preparation scenes (more than 100 recipes are served up) illustrate a careful attention to detail (and are guaranteed to make you hungry). Lee's follow-up to "The Wedding Banquet" is a finely observed, comic tale of generational drift, the richness of tradition, and the power of love to redeem or improve. In Chinese with subtitles or dubbed. **123m/C VHS, DVD, Wide.** *TW* Sihung Lung, Kuei-Mei Yang, Yu-Wen Wang, Chien-Lien Wu, Sylvia Chang, Winston Chao, Ah-Leh Gua, Lester Chen; *D:* Ang Lee; *W:* Ang Lee, James Schamus, Hui-Ling Wang; *C:* Jong Lin; *M:* Mader. Natl. Bd. of Review '94: Foreign Film.

Eat My Dust ✂✂ 1976 (PG) Teenage son of a California sheriff steals the best stock cars from a race track to take the town's heartthrob for a joy ride. Subsequently he leads the town on a wild car chase. Brainless but fast-paced. **89m/C VHS, DVD.** Ron Howard, Christopher Norris, Warren Kemmerling, Dave Madden, Robert Broyles, Jessica Potter, Don Brodie, Evelyn Russell, Clint Howard, Paul Bartel, Rance Howard, Corbin Bernsen; *D:* Charles B. Griffith; *W:* Charles B. Griffith; *C:* Eric Saarinen; *M:* David Grisman.

Eat the Peach ✂✂½ 1986 An idiosyncratic Irish comedy about two young unemployed rebels who attempt to break free from their tiny coast town by becoming motorcycle champs after seeing the Elvis Presley film "Roustabout." Together they create the "wall of death,"—a large wooden barrel in which they can perform various biker feats. **90m/C VHS.** *IR* Stephen Brennan, Eamon Morrissey, Catherine Byrne, Niall Toibin, Tony Doyle, Joe Lynch; *D:* Peter Ormrod; *W:* Peter Ormrod, John Kelleher; *M:* Donal Lunny.

Eat the Rich ✂ 1987 (R) A British farce about a group of terrorists who take over the popular London restaurant, Bastard's. Led by a former, disgruntled transvestite employee, they turn diners into menu offerings. Music by Motorhead. **89m/C VHS.** *GB* Nosher Powell, Lanah Pellay, Fiona Richmond, Ronald Allen, Sandra Dorne, Paul McCartney, Linda McCartney, Bill Wyman, Koo Stark, Miranda Richardson, Angie Bowie, Sandie Shaw; *D:* Peter Richardson; *W:* Peter Richardson; *C:* Witold Stok.

Eat Your Heart Out ✂✂½ 1996 (R) Routine romantic comedy about talented but struggling young chef Daniel (Oliver) who gets his shot at success with his own TV cooking show. He doesn't realize his best gal pal (Seagall) loves him, while Daniel becomes intrigued by his sexy agent (San Giacomo). **96m/C VHS, DVD.** Christian Oliver, Laura San Giacomo, Pamela Segall, Linda Hunt; *D:* Felix Adlon; *W:* Felix Adlon; *C:* Judy Irola; *M:* Alex Wurman.

Eaten Alive ✂✂ *Death Trap; Starlight Slaughter; Legend of the Bayou; Horror Hotel Massacre* 1976 (R) A Southerner takes an unsuspecting group of tourists into a crocodile death trap. Director Tobe Hooper's follow-up to "The Texas Chainsaw Massacre." Englund is more recognizable with razor fingernails as Freddy Krueger of the "Nightmare on Elm Street" films. **96m/C VHS, DVD, Wide.** Neville Brand, Mel Ferrer, Carolyn Jones, Marilyn Burns, Stuart Whitman, Robert Englund, William Finley, Roberta Collins, Kyle Richards, Janus Blythe; *D:* Tobe Hooper; *W:* Marti Rustam, Alvin L. Fast, Kim Henkel; *C:* Robert Caramico; *M:* Wayne Bell.

Eating ✂✂½ 1990 (R) Set in Southern California, women gather to celebrate birthdays for three of their friends who are turning 30, 40 and 50. As the party commences, women from two generations discuss their attitudes towards food and men...and discover hilarious parallels. **110m/C VHS.** Nelly Alard, Frances Bergen, Mary Crosby, Lisa Richards, Gwen Welles, Daphna Kastner, Elizabeth Kemp, Marlena Giovi, Marina Gregory, Toni Basil; *D:* Henry Jaglom; *W:* Henry Jaglom; *C:* Hanania Baer.

Eating Raoul ✂✂✂½ 1982 (R) The Blands are a happily married couple who share many interests: good food and wine, entrepreneurial dreams, and an aversion to sex. The problem is, they're flat broke. So, when the tasty swinger from upstairs makes a pass at Mary and Paul accidentally kills him, they discover he's got loads of money; Raoul takes a cut in the deal by disposing of—or rather recycling—the body. This may just be the way to finance that restaurant they've been wanting to open. Wonderful, offbeat, hilariously dark comedy. **83m/C VHS.** Mary Woronov, Paul Bartel, Robert Beltran, Buck Henry, Ed Begley Jr., Edie McClurg, John Paragon, Richard Blackburn, Hamilton Camp, Billy Curtis, Susan Saiger, Richard Paul, Don Steele, Mark Woods; *D:* Paul Bartel; *W:* Paul Bartel, Richard Blackburn; *C:* Gary Thieltges; *M:* Arlon Ober.

Eban and Charley ✂½ 2001 Draggy romance about a couple of misfits—one of whom is underage. 29-year-old Eban (Fellows) returns to his parents' home in a coastal Oregon community after leaving his job as a soccer coach. He's hanging around town when he meets the 15-year-old Charley (Andrade), who's been sent to live with his resentful divorced father after Charley's mother dies. Eventually, the relationship becomes physical (there are no depictions of sex) and they're headed for trouble. **88m/C VHS, DVD.** Brent Fellows, Giovanni Andrade, Nolan V. Chard, Ron Upton, Pam Munter; *D:* James Bolton; *W:* James Bolton; *C:* Judy Irola; *M:* Stephen Merritt.

The Ebb-Tide ✂✂½ 1997 Capt. Chisholm (Coltrane) is bothered by a scandalous past, so he doesn't ask a lot of questions about transporting a secret cargo to Australia. A storm strands Chisholm and two sailors on an uncharted island that's inhabited by the malevolent Ellstrom (Terry) and has Chisholm in a battle of good versus evil. Based on a novel by Robert Louis Stevenson. **104m/C VHS.** Robbie Coltrane, Nigel Terry, Steven Mackintosh, Chris Barnes, John Waters; *D:* Nicholas Renton; *W:* Simon Donald. **CABLE**

Ebbtide ✂✂½ 1994 (R) Lawyer Jeff Warren (Hamlin) takes on the case of a mother who says her son's died from chemicals dumped by the Poseidon Pacific Co. Jeff got the case when the previous lawyer died mysteriously but this doesn't stop him checking out the chemical company or its beautiful president. **90m/C VHS.** Harry Hamlin, Judy McIntosh, Susan Lyons, John Gregg, Frankie J. Holden; *D:* Craig Lahiff; *W:* Robert Ellis, Peter Goldsworthy.

Ebenezer ✂✂½ 1997 (PG) Ebenezer (Palance) is a crumedgeonly crook in the wild west who doesn't believe in Christmas and even cheats at poker. He's told by the ghostly Jacob Marlowe (Halliday) to change his ways or else—and Ebenezer is visited by several spirits that show him the error of his ways. A western version of Charles Dickens' "A Christmas Carol" that's quite colorful. **94m/C VHS.** Jack Palance, Rick Schroder, Amy Locane, Albert Schultz, Richard Halliday, Richard Comar, Michelle Thrush, Susan Coyne, Joshua Silberg, Morris Chapdelaine; *D:* Ken Jubenvil; *W:* Donald Martin; *C:* Henry Lebo; *M:* Bruce Leitl. **CABLE**

Ebony Dreams 1980 WWII documentary focuses on the experience of female factory workers during and after the war. Five contemporary women relate their personal endeavors and struggles to retain their jobs once the war ended. Excellent use of newsreel footage and interesting interviews with the women. **85m/C VHS.** Philomena Nowlin; *D:* Bill Brame.

Ebony Tower ✂✂½ 1986 Based on the John Fowles novel about a crusty old artist who lives in a French chateau with two young female companions. They are visited by a handsome young man, thereby initiating sexual tension and recognizably Fowlesian plot puzzles. Features some partial nudity. **80m/C** *GB* Laurence Olivier, Roger Rees, Greta Scacchi, Toyah Wilcox; *D:* Robert Knights; *M:* Richard Rodney Bennett. **TV**

Echo Murders ✂½ 1945 A Sexton Blake mystery wherein he investigates a mine owner's mysterious death, opening up a veritable can of murdering, power-hungry worms. **75m/B VHS.** David Farrar, Dennis Price.

Echo of Murder ✂✂ *Who Killed Atlanta's Children?* 2000 Docudrama focuses on the 29 child murders in Atlanta, which took place in the late '70s and early '80s, from the point of view of investigative journalists Hines and Belushi. Their theory is that convicted killer Wayne Williams is the scapegoat for a police conspiracy and the killings were purpetrated by the Ku Klux Klan. But they seem to spend most of their time yelling at each other so the story's emotional impact is lost. **105m/C VHS, DVD.** James Belushi, Gregory Hines; *D:* Charles Robert Carner; *W:* Charles Robert Carner; *C:* Michael Goi; *M:* James Verboort. **CABLE**

The Echo of Thunder ✂✂½ 1998 It's a hard life in the Australian outback for Gladwyn (Davis) and Larry (Sheridan) Ritchie who, with their three children, raise specialty palm trees on their small farm. It's a struggle that's made more uncomfortable for Gladwyn when 15-year-old Lara (Hewett) arrives. Lara is Larry's daughter by his late first wife and Gladwyn doesn't think the city-bred girl will fit in, and she's also worried that Lara's presence will stir up old memories for her husband. Indeed, Lara's only friend seems to be the stray Dingo dog she adopts and names Thunderwith. Based on the novel "Thunderwith" by Libby Hathorn. **98m/C VHS.** Judy Davis, Jamey Sheridan, Bill Hunter, Lauren Hewett, Ernie Dingo, Michael Caton; *D:* Simon Wincer; *W:* H. Haden Yelin; *M:* Laurence Rosenthal. **TV**

Echo Park ✂✂½ 1986 (R) An unsung sleeper comedy about three roommates living in Los Angeles' Echo Park: a body builder, a single-mother waitress, and an itinerant songwriter. Charts their struggles as they aim for careers in showbiz. Offbeat ensemble effort. **93m/C VHS, DVD, Wide.** *AU* Tom Hulce, Susan Dey, Michael Bowen, Richard "Cheech" Marin, Christopher Walker, Shirley Jo Finney, Cassandra Peterson, Yana Nirvana, Timothy Carey; *D:* Robert Dornhelm; *W:* Michael Ventura; *C:* Karl Kofler; *M:* David Rickets.

Echoes ✂✂ 1983 (R) A young painter's life slowly comes apart as he is tormented by nightmares that his stillborn twin brother is attempting to murder him. **90m/C VHS.** Gale Sondergaard, Mercedes McCambridge, Richard Alfieri, Ruth Roman, John Spencer, Nathalie Nell; *D:* Arthur Seidelman; *W:* Richard Alfieri, Richard J. Anthony; *C:* Hanania Baer.

Echoes ✂✂½ 1988 Shopkeeper's daughter Clare O'Brien (Garahy) and doctor's son David Power (Hines) both want to escape from their 1950s Irish seaside town. They meet again at university in Dublin where their friendship turns to romance but their return home comes complete with family troubles and differing dreams. Based on the novel by Maeve Binchy. **208m/C VHS.** *GB* Siobhan Garahy, Robert Hines, Geraldine James, Stephen Holland, Alison Doody, Dermot Crowley; *W:* Donald Churchill, Barbara Rennie. **TV**

Echoes in the Darkness ✂✂½ 1987 Miniseries based on the true-life Joseph Wambaugh bestseller about the "Main Line" murder investigation in Pennsylvania in 1979. Police are baffled when a teacher is murdered and her children vanish. Suspicion falls on a charismatic coworker and the school's principal. **234m/C VHS.** Peter Coyote, Robert Loggia, Stockard

Channing, Peter Boyle, Cindy Pickett, Gary Cole, Zeljko Ivanek, Alex Hyde-White, Treat Williams; *D:* Glenn Jordan. **TV**

Echoes of Paradise 🦴½ *Shadows of the Peacock* **1986 (R)** After a series of earth-shattering events, a depressed woman journeys to an island where she falls for a Balinese dancer. Soon she must choose between returning home or beginning life anew in paradise. **90m/C VHS.** *AU* Wendy Hughes, John Lone, Rod Mullinar, Peta Toppano, Steve Jacobs, Gillian Jones; *D:* Phillip Noyce; *C:* Peter James.

The Eclipse 🦴🦴🦴½ *L'eclisse* **1966** The last of Antonioni's trilogy (after "L'Avventura" and "La Notte"), wherein another fashionable and alienated Italian woman passes from one lover to another searching unsuccessfully for truth and love. Highly acclaimed. In Italian with subtitles. **123m/B VHS.** *IT* Monica Vitti, Alain Delon, Francesco Rabal, Louis Seigner; *D:* Michelangelo Antonioni; *W:* Tonino Guerra, Elio Bartolini, Ottiero Ottieri, Michelangelo Antonioni; *C:* Gianni Di Venanzo; *M:* Giovanni Fusco.

Eclipse 🦴½ **1994** Sexual roundelay set in Toronto shortly before a total solar eclipse, which is apparently affecting all the generally listless characters in such a way that they meet and mate in joyless abandon. First feature for Podeswa. **96m/C VHS.** *CA GE* Von Flores, John Gilbert, Pascale Montpetit, Manuel Aranguiz, Maria Del Mar, Matthew Ferguson, Earl Pastko, Greg Ellwand, Daniel MacIvor, Kirsten Johnson; *D:* Jeremy Podeswa; *W:* Jeremy Podeswa; *C:* Miroslaw Baszak; *M:* Ernie Tollar.

Ecstasy 🦴🦴½ *Extase; Ekstase; Symphony of Love* **1933** A romantic, erotic story about a young woman married to an older man, who takes a lover. Features Lamarr, then Hedy Kiesler, before her discovery in Hollywood. Film subsequently gained notoriety for Lamarr's nude scenes. In Czech with English subtitles. **90m/B VHS, DVD, 8mm.** *CZ* Hedy Lamarr, Jaromir Rogoz, Aribert Mog; *D:* Gustav Machaty; *W:* Gustav Machaty.

Ecstasy woof! **1984 (R)** Soft core fluff about a film director's wife's erotic adventures. **82m/C VHS.** Tiffany Bolling, Franc Luz, Jack Carter, Britt Ekland, Julie Newmar.

Ed woof! **1996 (PG)** A must see for all fans of flatulent animatronic chimpanzees who play third base. Everyone else should stay away. LeBlanc (who should've been tipped off when they couldn't even get a real chimp to appear) plays Coop, a phenom pitcher stuck on a losing team in the minor leagues. After Ed the chimpanzee is bequeathed to the team by the late Mickey Mantle, (forgive them Mick, they know not what they do) he starts playing the hot corner like Brooks Robinson. Surprise! Ed becomes a national sensation, the team goes on a winning streak and sets up the showdown game climax. Most of the humor is derived from Ed tearing things up and passing gas, while LeBlanc yells in pop-eyed exasperation. Cameo from Tommy Lasorda playing a fat major league manager. **94m/C VHS.** Matt LeBlanc, Jayne Brook, Bill Cobbs, Jack Warden, Doren Fein, Patrick Kerr, Charlie Schlatter, Carl Anthony Payne II, Curt Kaplan, Zack (Zach) Ward, Mike McGlone, James Caviezel, Valente Rodriguez; *D:* Bill Couturie; *W:* David Mickey Evans; *C:* Alan Caso; *M:* Stephen Endelman.

Ed and His Dead Mother 🦴🦴 **1993 (PG-13)** Ed's just an average guy who happens to really love his mother. So much so that when she dies Ed tries to bring her back from the dead—and succeeds. Only death has made a few changes in Mom's personality. Now she's a bug-eating, chainsaw-wielding fiend. Just what's a good son supposed to do? **93m/C VHS.** Ned Beatty, Steve Buscemi, John Glover, Miriam Margolyes, Sam Jenkins; *D:* Jonathan Wacks; *W:* Chuck Hughes.

Ed Gein 🦴 **2001** Considering the subject matter, this is a mild account of murdering, grave-robbing, dismembering psycho/cannibal Ed Gein (Railsback) and the Wisconsin farm community who just can't believe what their neighbor has been up to. **88m/C VHS, DVD.** Steve Railsback, Carrie Snodgress, Pat Skipper, Sally Champlin; *D:* Chuck Parello; *W:* Stephen Johnston; *C:* Vanja Cernjul; *M:* Robert F. McNaughton.

Ed Wood 🦴🦴🦴½ **1994 (R)** Leave it to Burton to bring to the screen the story of a director many consider to be the worst of all time (he's at least in the top three) and who now occupies a lofty position as a cult icon. In this hilarious and touching tribute to a Hollywood maverick with grade-Z vision, detailed homage is paid to Wood's single-mindedness and optimism in the face of repeated failure and lack of financing, even down to the black and white photography. Depp is convincing (and engaging) as Ed Wood, Jr., the cross-dressing, angora-sweater-wearing, low-budget auteur of such notoriously "bad" cult films as "Glen or Glenda" and "Plan 9 From Outer Space." Depp is supported by terrific portrayals of the motley Wood crew, led by Landau's morphine-addicted, down-on-his-luck Bela Lugosi. Burton focuses on Wood's relationship with Lugosi, whose career is over by the time Wood befriends him. Based on Rudolph Grey's book, "Nightmare of Ecstasy: The Life and Art of Edward D. Wood Jr." **127m/B VHS.** Max Casella, Johnny Depp, Sarah Jessica Parker, Martin Landau, Bill Murray, Jim Myers, Patricia Arquette, Jeffrey Jones, Lisa Marie, Vincent D'Onofrio, Ned Bellamy, Conrad Brooks, Rance Howard, Juliet Landau, G.D. Spradlin, Mike Starr, George "The Animal" Steele, Gregory Walcott; *D:* Tim Burton; *W:* Scott M. Alexander, Larry Karaszewski; *C:* Stefan Czapsky; *M:* Howard Shore. Oscars '94: Makeup, Support. Actor (Landau); Golden Globes '95: Support. Actor (Landau); L.A. Film Critics '94: Cinematog., Support. Actor (Landau), Score; N.Y. Film Critics '94: Cinematog., Support. Actor (Landau); Natl. Soc. Film Critics '94: Cinematog., Support. Actor (Landau); Screen Actors Guild '94: Support. Actor (Landau).

Eddie 🦴🦴 **1996 (PG-13)** Basketball nut Edwina (Goldberg) wins a chance to be honorary coach of her beloved Knicks in a free throw contest. When some of her courtside advice works, and the other fans seem to respond to her, the publicity-seeking maverick owner (Langella) gives her the job full-time. Predictable comedy with the usual "new team member leads underdogs to contention" characters won't suprise, or particularly thrill, anyone. Goldberg's lively performance somewhat redeems standard script but reduces everyone around her, including an All-Star roster of NBA players, to window dressing. Basically the hoops version of "Little Big League." **100m/C VHS, DVD.** Whoopi Goldberg, Frank Langella, Dennis Farina, Richard Jenkins, Lisa Ann Walter, John Benjamin Hickey, John Salley; *D:* Steve Rash; *W:* Jon Connolly, David Loucka, Eric Champnella, Keith Mitchell, Steve Zacharias, Jeff Buhai; *C:* Victor Kemper; *M:* Stanley Clarke.

Eddie and the Cruisers 🦴🦴 **1983 (PG)** In the early 1960s, rockers Eddie and the Cruisers score with one hit album. Amid their success, lead singer Pare dies mysteriously in a car accident. Years later, a reporter decides to write a feature on the defunct group, prompting a former band member to begin a search for missing tapes of the Cruisers' unreleased second album. Questions posed at the end of the movie are answered in the sequel. Enjoyable soundtrack by John Cafferty and the Beaver Brown Band. **90m/C VHS, DVD, 8mm, Wide.** Tom Berenger, Michael Pare, Ellen Barkin, Joe Pantoliano, Matthew Laurance, Helen Schneider, David Wilson, Michael "Tunes" Antunes, Joe Cates, John Stockwell, Barry Sand, Vebe Borge, Howard Johnson, Robin Karfo, Rufus Harley, Bruce Brown, Louis D'Esposito, Michael Toland, Bob Garrett, Joanne Collins; *D:* Martin Davidson; *W:* Martin Davidson, Arlene Davidson; *C:* Fred Murphy; *M:* John Cafferty.

Eddie and the Cruisers 2: Eddie Lives! 🦴½ **1989 (PG-13)** A sequel to the minor cult favorite, in which a rock star believed to be dead emerges under a new name in Montreal to lead a new band. The Beaver Brown Band again provides the music. **106m/C VHS.** *CA* Michael Pare, Marina Orsini, Matthew Laurance, Bernie Coulson, Anthony Sherwood; ***Cameos:*** Larry King, Bo Diddley, Martha Quinn, Merrill Shindler; *D:* Jean-Claude Lord; *W:* Charles Zev Cohen; *C:* Rene Verzier; *M:* Leon Aronson.

Eddie Macon's Run 🦴🦴 **1983 (PG)** Based on a true story; Eddie Macon has been unjustly jailed in Texas and plans an escape to run to Mexico. He is followed by a tough cop who is determined to catch the fugitive. Film debut of Goodman. **95m/C VHS.** Kirk Douglas, John Schneider, Lee Purcell, John Goodman, Leah Ayres; *D:* Jeff Kanew; *M:* Wendy Blackstone.

The Eddy Duchin Story 🦴🦴 **1956** Glossy tearjerker that profiles the tragic life of Eddy Duchin, the famous pianist/bandleader of the 30s and 40s. Features almost 30 songs, including classics by Cole Porter, George and Ira Gershwin, Hammerstein, Chopin, and several others. **123m/C VHS, Wide.** Tyrone Power, Kim Novak, Victoria Shaw, James Whitmore, Rex Thompson; *D:* George Sidney; *W:* Samuel A. Taylor; *C:* Harry Stradling Sr.; *M:* George Duning.

Eden 🦴🦴 **1992** Eden is a luxury resort designed to cater to personal fantasies and filled with numerous intrigues. Part-owner Eve Sinclair faces a number of professional and personal complications, including the tragic death of her husband, a brother-in-law who's interested in more than business, and an old friend with uncertain motives. Lots of sex in beautiful settings. **?m/C VHS.** Barbara Alyn Woods, Jack Armstrong, Steve Chase, Darcy Demoss, Jeff Griggs; *D:* Victor Lobl; *W:* Stephen Black, Henry Stern. **CABLE**

Eden 🦴🦴 **1998 (R)** Frustrated, Multiple Sclerosis-afflicted housewife Helen (Going) deals with the physical and emotional limitations of her life with dreams of astral projection. Husband Bill (Walsh) is a prep school teacher who doesn't want her to work even though she reaches one of his problem students (Flanery) more effectively than he can. First-time director Goldberg won a Sundance competition for his screenplay, but can't quite deliver on its promise. A tight budget and too many unanswered questions keep this one on the intriguing but ultimately disappointing level. **106m/C VHS, DVD.** Joanna Going, Dylan Walsh, Sean Patrick Flanery; *D:* Howard Goldberg; *W:* Howard Goldberg; *C:* Hubert Taczanowski; *M:* Brad Fiedel.

Eden 2 🦴🦴 **1993 (R)** The continuing saga of the luxury resort Eden. Owner Eve is still having erotic dreams of late husband Grant while fending off the very real advances of his brother Josh and becoming attracted to Paul, her late husband's best friend. The guests are equally caught up in erotic dilemmas involving sexual blackmail. **102m/C VHS.** Barbara Alyn Woods, Jack Armstrong, Steve Chase, Darcy Demoss, Jeff Griggs; *D:* Kristine Peterson; *W:* Stephen Black, Henry Stern. **CABLE**

Eden 3 🦴🦴 **1993 (R)** Yet another chapter in this sexy cable saga. Eve Sinclair risks losing her share of the tropical resort unless she remarries, which she doesn't want to do, although fitness trainer Randi would be delighted to pick up the option. Meanwhile, an heiress discovers her new bridegroom has murderous intentions. **?m/C VHS.** Barbara Alyn Woods, Jack Armstrong, Steve Chase, Darcy Demoss, Jeff Griggs, Dean Scofield; *D:* Victor Lobl. **CABLE**

Eden 4 🦴🦴 **1993 (R)** Further adventures in the cable series. Eve, Eden's co-owner, must cope with both Josh's jealous rage and Randi's continuing scheming as she tries to keep her guests happy at the posh resort. One of the guests, a beautiful author, gets too caught up in her sexual fantasies and may find herself in danger. **?m/C VHS.** Barbara Alyn Woods, Jack Armstrong, Steve Chase, Darcy Demoss, Jeff Griggs, Dean Scofield; *D:* Kristine Peterson. **CABLE**

Eden Valley 🦴🦴🦴 **1994** A low-key intensity marks this northeast England drama that's produced, written, and directed by an eight-member film cooperative, the Amber Production Team. Troubled Newcastle teenager Billy (Bell) is put on probation for drug and theft charges and in a last-ditch chance at turning his life around goes to live with his estranged father, Hoggy (Hogg). They haven't seen each other in 10 years and Hoggy lives on a farm in County Durham where he raises and trains horses for harness racing. Naturally, their relationship is strained and there aren't any easy solutions (kinda like in real life). **95m/C VHS.** *GB* Darren Bell, Brian Hogg, Mike Elliott, Jimmy Killeen.

The Edge 🦴🦴½ *Bookworm* **1997 (R)** Wealthy Charles Morse (Hopkins) isn't too pleased that fashion photog Bob Greene (Baldwin) takes such an interest in his lovely fashion model wife (Macpherson) and feels the two are out to kill him. Despite his conspiracy theory, Morse and Greene end up depending on each other for survival when their plane crashes in the Alaskan wilderness. To compound their problems, they must do battle with a stalking killer bear. Mamet screenplay dices things up a bit with cutting dialogue which leads to the mind games Mamet is so famous for. Hopkins and Baldwin give understated, intact performances, with an intensity shared only by Bart the Bear, in this small comtemporary parable on the meaning of life. The splendid Alaskan scenery is actually breathtaking aerial and ground footage in Canada. **120m/C VHS, DVD.** Anthony Hopkins, Alec Baldwin, Elle Macpherson, Harold Perrineau Jr., L.Q. (Justus E. McQueen) Jones; *D:* Lee Tamahori; *W:* David Mamet; *C:* Donald McAlpine; *M:* Jerry Goldsmith.

Edge of Darkness 🦴🦴🦴½ **1943** Compelling war-drama about the underground movement in Norway during Nazi takeover of WWII. Flynn plays a Norwegian fisherman who leads the local underground movement and Sheridan is his loyal fiancee. Although several problems occurred throughout filming, this picture earned high marks for its superb performances and excellent camera work. Based on the novel by William Woods. **120m/B VHS.** Errol Flynn, Ann Sheridan, Walter Huston, Nancy Coleman, Helmut Dantine, Judith Anderson, Ruth Gordon, John Beal; *D:* Lewis Milestone; *W:* Robert Rossen.

Edge of Darkness 🦴🦴 **1986** Miniseries mystery involves a police detective who investigates his daughter's murder and uncovers a web of espionage and intrigue. **307m/C VHS.** *GB* Bob Peck, Joe Don Baker, Jack Woodson, John Woodvine, Joanne Whalley; *D:* Martin Campbell; *M:* Eric Clapton, Michael Kamen. **TV**

Edge of Honor 🦴½ **1991 (R)** Young Eagle Scouts camping in the Pacific Northwest discover a woodland weapons cache and wage guerilla war against killer lumberjacks out to silence them. A boneheaded, politically correct action bloodbath; you don't have to like the logging industry to disapprove of the broad slurs against its men shown here. **92m/C VHS.** Corey Feldman, Meredith Salenger, Scott Reeves, Ken Jenkins, Christopher Neame, Don Swayze; *D:* Michael Spence; *W:* David O'Malley.

Edge of Sanity 🦴½ **1989 (R)** An overdone Jekyll-Hyde reprise, with cocaine serving as the villainous substance. Dr. Jekyll (Perkins) is working in his lab, testing cocaine for use as an anaesthetic, when a lab monkey knocks a liquid into the coke and the fumes cause the doc to turn into Jack Hyde, a prototype for Jack the Ripper. Perkins knows the schizoid territory and the production values are good but this is not for the easily queazy. Available in a 90 minute, unrated version. **85m/C VHS.** *GB* Anthony Perkins, Glynis Barber, David Lodge, Sarah Maur-Thorp, Ben Cole, Lisa Davis, Jill Melford; *D:* Gerard Kikoine; *W:* J.P. Felix, Ron Raley; *C:* Tony Spratling; *M:* Frederic Talgorn.

Edge of Seventeen 🦴🦴½ **1999** Perceptive gay coming of age tale set in 1984 Ohio. Naive 16-year-old Eric (Stafford) is eager to explore his burgeoning sexuality with the help of college man, Rod (Gabrych). Unfortunately for Eric, Rod's the love 'em and leave 'em type. Disillusioned, Eric tries to remake himself in Brit-pop, New Wave fashion (think Boy George and Duran Duran), while turning to best friend Maggie (Holmes), without realizing the depths of her feelings for him. Eric's coming out tellingly provides confusion not just for himself but for everyone around him. **100m/C VHS, DVD.** Chris Stafford, Tina Holmes, Andersen Gabrych, Stephanie McVay, Lea DeLaria, John Eby; *D:* David Moreton;

W: Todd Stephens; *C:* Gina DeGirolamo; *M:* Tom Bailey.

Edge of the Axe 1989 A small town is held in the grip of terror by a demented slasher. **91m/C VHS.** Barton Faulks, Christina Marie Lane, Page Moseley, Fred Hollyday; *D:* Joseph (Jose Ramon Larraz) Braunstein.

Edge of the World 𝒮𝒮𝒮 1937 Moody, stark British drama of a mini-society in its death throes, expertly photographed on a six-square-mile island in the Shetlands. A dwindling fishing community of fewer than 100 souls agonize over whether to migrate to the mainland; meanwhile the romance of a local girl with an off-islander takes a tragic course. Choral effects were provided by the Glasgow Orpheus Choir. **80m/B VHS.** *GB* Finlay Currie, Niall MacGinnis, Grant Sutherland, John Laurie, Michael Powell; *D:* Michael Powell; *W:* Michael Powell.

Edie & Pen 𝒮𝒮½ 1995 (PG-13) Tilly seems to be making a career of playing the ditz who's smarter than she seems as she shows here as Edie, who meets Pen (Channing) in Reno where both are looking for quickie divorces. They hit a bar to celebrate and hook up with soft-hearted Harry (Glenn), who's been dumped by his wife. Some drunken life discussions follow and then Edie finds out that her fiance is Pen's cold-hearted, newly ex hubby (Wilson). Slight script, charming performances. **97m/C VHS.** Jennifer Tilly, Stockard Channing, Scott Glenn, Stuart Wilson; ***Cameos:*** Beverly D'Angelo, Louise Fletcher, Joanna Gleason, Michael McKean, Martin Mull, Michael O'Keefe, Chris Sarandon, Randy Travis, Jean Smart, Victoria Tennant; *D:* Matthew Irmas; *W:* Victoria Tennant; *C:* Alicia Weber; *M:* Shawn Colvin.

Edie in Ciao! Manhattan 𝒮𝒮 *Ciao! Manhattan* 1972 (R) Real-life story of Edie Sedgwick, Warhol superstar and international fashion model, whose life in the fast lane led to ruin. **84m/C VHS.** Edie Sedgwick, Baby Jane Holzer, Roger Vadim, Paul America, Viva.

Edison the Man 𝒮𝒮½ 1940 Story of Tommy Edison's early years of experimentation in the basement. The young genious eventually invents light bulbs, motion pictures, and a sound recording device. Well played by Tracy. **108m/C VHS.** Spencer Tracy, Rita Johnson, Lynne Overman, Charles Coburn, Gene Lockhart, Henry Travers, Felix Bressart; *D:* Clarence Brown.

Edith & Marcel 𝒮½ 1983 A fictionalization of the love affair between chanteuse Edith Piaf and boxer Marcel Cerdan (played by his son, Marcel Cerdan Jr.). French with English subtitles. **104m/C VHS.** *FR* Evelyne Bouix, Marcel Cerdan Jr., Charles Aznavour, Jacques Villeret; *D:* Claude Lelouch.

Ed's Next Move 𝒮𝒮½ 1996 (R) Genial indie NYC comedy with a Woody Allen feel is littered with whimsical one-liners. Title character Ed (Ross) moves from small-town Wisconsin to New York after a break-up with his girlfriend. Being that he's a rice geneticist, it's not a big leap to conclude that Ed's a bit uptight, so it's imperative that Ed's big city roommate, the suave Ray (Carroll), hip him up to better meet the ladies. Soon, Ed falls for boho Lee (Thorne) leader of a band called "Ed's Redeeming Qualities." Fun fantasy sequence involving Ed, his old girlfriend and two translators is a highlight. Low-budgeter, with a first time writer/director (Walsh), and it shows, but in a good-natured way. Though more could be asked visually, picture does boast good performers and well-drawn characters. **88m/C VHS.** Matt Ross, Callie (Calliope) Thorne, Kevin Carroll, Ramsey Faragallah, Nina Shevaleva, James (Jimmy) Cummings; *D:* John Walsh; *W:* John Walsh; *C:* Peter Nelson.

EDtv 𝒮𝒮½ 1999 (PG-13) Ed (McConaughey) is a scruffy redneck video clerk who agrees to have his life broadcast 24/7 for a reality show produced by DeGeneres. Of course the show becomes a hit, and an entire nation watches breathlessly as Ed steals his brother's girlfriend Shari (Elfman), restocks shelves and goes to the bathroom with the door open. His family life immediately turns melodramatic, with Ed learning "shocking secrets" about his mom (Kirkland), dad (Landau) and brother (Harrelson). Compared to the "The Truman Show" thanks to their back-to-back release in theaters, but director (and TV child star survivor) Ron Howard's version lacks the biting satire. **122m/C VHS, DVD.** Ellen DeGeneres, Sally Kirkland, Martin Landau, Elizabeth Hurley, Rob Reiner, Dennis Hopper, Adam Goldberg, Viveka Davis, Clint Howard, Larry "Flash" Jenkins, Donny Most, Rick Overton, RuPaul Charles, Gedde Watanabe, Harry Shearer, Jennifer Elise Cox, Matthew McConaughey, Jenna Elfman, Woody Harrelson; *D:* Ron Howard; *W:* Lowell Ganz, Babaloo Mandel; *C:* John Schwartzman; *M:* Randy Edelman.

Educating Rita 𝒮𝒮𝒮½ 1983 (PG) Walters and Caine team beautifully in this adaptation of the successful Willy Russell play which finds Rita, an uneducated hairdresser, determined to improve her knowledge of literature. In so doing, she enlists the aid of tutor Frank: a disillusioned alcoholic, adeptly played by Caine. Together, the two find inspiration in one another's differences and experiences. Ultimately, the teacher receives a lesson in how to again appreciate his work and the classics as he observes his pupil's unique approach to her studies. Some deem this a "Pygmalion" for the '80s. **110m/C VHS, 8mm.** *GB* Michael Caine, Julie Walters, Michael Williams, Maureen Lipman; *D:* Lewis Gilbert; *W:* Willy Russell. British Acad. '83: Actor (Caine), Actress (Walters), Film; Golden Globes '84: Actor—Mus./Comedy (Caine), Actress—Mus./Comedy (Walters).

The Education of Little Tree 𝒮𝒮𝒮 1997 (PG) Child's eye view of a large scale epic on par with modern classics like "The Secret Garden." In 1935, poor, orphaned, and part Native American Little Tree (Ashton) is sent to live with his grandfather (Cromwell) and Native American grandmother (Cardinal) in the Smokey Mountains of Tennessee. There he learns "The Way" of his Cherokee ancestors and how to make moonshine from his Scottish/Irish grandfather. A nosy, Bible-thumping Aunt tips off authorities and soon Little Tree is shipped off to an evil state institution to cure him of his inappropriate Indian ways. There, the old-fashioned discipline runs fierce and abusive. Adapted from a children's book by Forrest Carter. Cardinal and Cromwell carve out memorable performances alongside first-rate newcomer Joseph Ashton. **112m/C VHS, DVD, Wide.** James Cromwell, Tantoo Cardinal, Joseph Ashton, Graham Greene; *D:* Richard Friedenberg; *W:* Richard Friedenberg; *C:* Anastas Michos; *M:* Mark Isham.

The Education of Sonny Carson 𝒮𝒮½ 1974 (R) Chilling look at the tribulations of a black youth living in a Brooklyn ghetto amid drugs, prostitution, crime, and other forms of vice. Based on Sonny Carson's autobiography. Still pertinent some 20 years after its theatrical release. **104m/C VHS.** Rony Clanton, Don Gordon, Paul Benjamin; *D:* Michael Campus.

Edward Munch 𝒮𝒮 1974 Biographical portrait of the Norwegian Expressionist painter and his tormented life in the stuffy society of 19th-century Oslo. Concentrates mainly on his early years, including the deaths of his mother and younger sister, his brother's suicide, Munch's affair with a married woman, and his struggle to maintain his sanity. Based on Munch's memoirs. In German and Norwegian with English subtitles. **167m/C VHS.** *NO* Geir Westby, Gro Fraas, Eli Ryg; *D:* Peter Watkins; *W:* Peter Watkins; *C:* Odd Geir Saether.

Edward and Mrs. Simpson 𝒮𝒮 1980 Dramatic reconstruction of the years leading to the abdication of King Edward VIII, who forfeited the British throne in 1936 so that he could marry American divorcee Wallis Simpson. Originally aired on PBS. **270m/C VHS.** Edward Fox, Cynthia Harris; *D:* Waris Hussein. **TV**

Edward Scissorhands 𝒮𝒮𝒮 1990 (PG-13) Depp's a young man created by loony scientist Price, who dies before he can attach hands to his boy-creature. Then the boy is rescued from his lonely existence outside of suburbia by an ingratiating Avon lady. With scissors in place of hands, he has more trouble fitting into suburbia than would most new kids on the block, and he struggles with being different and lonely in a cardboard-cutout world. Visually captivating fairy tale full of splash and color, however predictable the Hollywood-prefab denouement. **100m/C VHS, DVD, Wide.** Johnny Depp, Winona Ryder, Dianne Wiest, Vincent Price, Anthony Michael Hall, Alan Arkin, Kathy Baker, Conchata Ferrell, Caroline Aaron, Dick Anthony Williams, Robert Oliveri, John Davidson; *D:* Tim Burton; *W:* Tim Burton, Caroline Thompson; *C:* Stefan Czapsky; *M:* Danny Elfman.

Edward II 𝒮𝒮½ 1992 (R) Jarman's controversial adaptation of Christopher Marlowe's play "The Troublesome Reign of Edward II" portrays the weak-willed monarch as neglecting his kingdom for love. Unfortunately, it's not for his queen but for his commoner male lover. His neglect of both queen and country lead to a swift and brutal downfall. Jarman's use of contemporary anachronisms, stream of conscienceness approach, and heavy symbolism may leave more than one viewer wondering what's going on. **91m/C VHS.** *GB* Steven Waddington, Kevin Collins, Andrew Tiernan, John Lynch, Dudley Sutton, Tilda Swinton, Jerome Flynn, Jody Graber, Nigel Terry, Annie Lennox; *D:* Derek Jarman; *W:* Derek Jarman; *M:* Simon Fisher Turner. Venice Film Fest. '92: Actress (Swinton).

Edward the King 𝒮𝒮½ 1975 British miniseries follows the long life of Prince Edward, who waited some 60 years for his overbearing mother, Queen Victoria, to die so he could ascend the throne. Bertie scandalized with his affairs and carousing but, nevertheless, proved his worth as king-in-waiting. On six cassettes. **708m/C VHS.** *GB* Timothy West, Annette Crosbie, John Gielgud, Francesca Annis, Robert Hardy; *D:* John Gorrie; *C:* Tony Imi. **TV**

Edwin 𝒮𝒮½ 1984 Sir Fennimore Truscott (Guinness) is a retired High Court Judge who suspects that his neighbor once had an affair with Truscott's wife. These long-fermenting fears assert themself as Truscott presents his case (to the audience) and even suspects the paternity of his son, Edwin. When Edwin comes for a visit, Truscott's obsessions are forced into the open. **78m/C VHS.** *GB* Alec Guinness, Paul Rogers, Renee Asherson; *D:* Rodney Bennett; *W:* John Mortimer. **TV**

Eegah! woof! 1962 Another Arch Hall-directed (under the Nicholas Merriwether pseud.) epic in which an anachronistic Neanderthal falls in love in '60s California. Reputed to be one of the worst films of all time. **93m/C VHS, DVD.** Marilyn Manning, Richard Kiel, Arch Hall Jr., William Waters, Carolyn Brandt, William Lloyd, Ray Dennis Steckler; *D:* Arch (Archie) Hall Sr.; *W:* Bob Wehling; *C:* Vilis Lapenieks; *M:* Arch Hall Jr.

The Eel 𝒮𝒮𝒮 *Unagi* 1996 Yamashita (Yakusho) has just been paroled after spending eight years in prison for killing his adulterous wife in a jealous rage. While there, he found and cared for an eel, which became his only confidante, and which accompanies him to his new life as a barber in a small town outside Tokyo. The newcomer is soon befriended by the locals but Yamashita's life changes most when he saves the suicidal Keiko (Shimizu) from drowning. She comes to work in his shop and would obviously like a more intimate relationship but some secrets in her past and some strange incidents in the town may jepordize Yamashita's hopes for a normal life. Based on the novel "Glimmering in the Dark" by Akira Yoshimura. Japanese with subtitles. **117m/C VHS, DVD, Wide.** *JP* Koji Yakusho, Misa Shimizu, Mitsuko Baisho, Shou Aikawa, Fujio Tsuneta, Akira (Tsukamoto) Emoto, Etsuko Ichihara, Tomoroh Taguchi, Ken Kobayashi, Sabu Kawara; *D:* Shohei Imamura; *W:* Shohei Imamura, Motofumi Tomikawa, Daisuke Tengan; *C:* Shigeru Komatsubara; *M:* Shinichiro Ikebe. Cannes '97: Film.

The Effect of Gamma Rays on Man-in-the-Moon Marigolds 𝒮𝒮𝒮 1973 (PG) A wonderful drama based on the Pulitzer Prize winning play by Paul Zindel. The story centers around eccentric young Matilda and her depressed family. Matilda is preparing her experiment for the school science fair, determined to beat her competition. Her exhibit shows how radiation sometimes kills the helpless marigolds, but sometimes causes them to grow into even more beautiful mutations. This mirrors Matilda, who flowers even amidst the drunkenness of her mother and the dullness of her sister. **100m/C VHS.** Joanne Woodward, Nell Potts, Roberta Wallach, Judith Lowry, Richard Venture; *D:* Paul Newman. Cannes '73: Actress (Woodward).

Effi Briest 𝒮𝒮𝒮½ *Fontane Effi Briest* 1974 A 19th-century tragedy well-played by Schygulla and empowered with Fassbinder's directorial skills. Effi (Schygulla) is a 17 year-old beauty, unhappily married to a much older man. She drifts into a brief affair, which is not discovered for several years. When her husband does discover her past infidelity, the Prussian legal code permits him a chilling revenge. Based on a popular 19th-century novel by Theodor Fontane. In German with English subtitles. **135m/B VHS.** *GE* Hanna Schygulla, Wolfgang Schenck, Lilo Pempeit, Ulli Lommel; *D:* Rainer Werner Fassbinder; *W:* Rainer Werner Fassbinder; *C:* Jurgen Jurges, Dietrich Lohmann.

The Efficiency Expert 𝒮𝒮½ *Spotswood* 1992 (PG) Lighthearted Australian comedy about a dingy moccasin factory where a rigid efficiency consultant is invited to save the eccentric family-run company from bankruptcy. Predictable ending contains a nevertheless timely message about the importance of the bottom line. **97m/C VHS.** *AU* Anthony Hopkins, Ben Mendelsohn, Alwyn Kurts, Bruno Lawrence, Angela Punch McGregor, Russell Crowe, Rebecca Rigg, Toni Collette; *D:* Mark Joffe; *W:* Andrew Knight, Max Dann; *M:* Ricky Fataar.

Egg 𝒮𝒮½ 1988 Striking film from Holland chronicles the life of a quiet, middle-aged baker who answers a personal ad from a schoolteacher. After much correspondence, the teacher visits the baker in his village, and the townspeople take great interest in what happens next. In Dutch with English subtitles. **58m/C VHS.** *NL* Johan Leysen, Marijke Vengelers; *D:* Danniel Danniel; *W:* Danniel Danniel.

Egg and I 𝒮𝒮𝒮 1947 Based on the true-life adventures of best-selling humorist Betty MacDonald. A young urban bride agrees to help her new husband realize his life-long dream of owning a chicken farm. A dilapidated house, temperamental stove, and suicidal chickens test the bride's perseverance, as do the zany antics of her country-bumpkin neighbors, Ma and Pa Kettle, who make their screen debut. Plenty of old-fashioned laughs. **104m/B VHS.** Claudette Colbert, Fred MacMurray, Marjorie Main, Percy Kilbride, Louise Allbritton, Richard Long, Billy House, Donald MacBride; *D:* Chester Erskine; *C:* Milton Krasner.

The Egyptian 𝒮𝒮½ 1954 Based on the sword-and-sandal novel by Mika Waltari, this is a ponderous big-budget epic about a young Egyptian in Akhnaton's epoch who becomes physician to the Pharaoh. **140m/C VHS.** Edmund Purdom, Victor Mature, Peter Ustinov, Bella Darvi, Gene Tierney, Henry Daniell, Jean Simmons, Michael Wilding, Judith Evelyn, John Carradine, Carl Benton Reid; *D:* Michael Curtiz; *W:* Philip Dunne, Casey Robinson; *C:* Leon Shamroy.

An Egyptian Story 𝒮𝒮 *Hadduta Misriya* 1982 An Egyptian film director (Dine) goes to London for open-heart surgery and as he hovers between life and death, he remembers his past. Scenes from Chahine's other films highlight the director's reminiscences. Part 2 of the Alexandria trilogy, preceded by "Alexandria...Why?" and followed by "Alexandria Again and Forever." Arabic with subtitles. **127m/C VHS, DVD, Wide.** *EG* Mohiel Dine, Nour (el-Sherif) el-Cherif, Oussama Nadir, Magda El Khatib; *D:* Youssef Chahine; *W:* Youssef Chahine; *C:* Mohsen Nasr; *M:* Gamal Salama.

The Eiger Sanction 𝒮𝒮 1975 (R) An art teacher returns to the CII (a fictionalized version of the CIA) as an exterminator hired to assassinate the killers of an American agent. In the process, he finds himself climbing the Eiger. Beautiful Swiss

Alps scenery fails to totally compensate for several dreary lapses. Based on the novel by Trevanian. **125m/C VHS, DVD, Wide.** Clint Eastwood, George Kennedy, Vonetta McGee, Jack Cassidy, Thayer David; ***D:*** Clint Eastwood; ***W:*** Hal Dresner, Warren B. Murphy, Rod Whitaker; ***C:*** Frank Stanley; ***M:*** John Williams.

8-A 🦴🦴 *Ochoa* **1992** Reconstructs the 1989 trial and execution of Cuban general Arnaldo Ochoa Sanchez, a hero of the revolution who, along with other government officials, advocated the resignation of Fidel Castro as the solution to the country's economic and political crises. At the trial Ochoa and four other officials were convicted of illegal drug trafficking and shot by a firing squad. Spanish with subtitles. **84m/C VHS.** *CU* ***D:*** Orlando Jiminez-Leal.

8 1/2 🦴🦴🦴🦴 *Otto E Mezzo; Federico Fellini's 8 1/2* **1963** The acclaimed Fellini self-portrait of a revered Italian film director struggling with a fated film project wanders through his intermixed life, childhood memories, and hallucinatory fantasies. Subtitled in English. **135m/B VHS, DVD, Wide.** *IT* Marcello Mastroianni, Claudia Cardinale, Anouk Aimee, Sandra Milo, Barbara Steele, Rossella Falk, Eddra Gale, Mark Herron, Madeleine LeBeau, Caterina Boratto; ***D:*** Federico Fellini; ***W:*** Tullio Pinelli, Ennio Flaiano, Brunello Rondi, Federico Fellini; ***C:*** Gianni Di Venanzo; ***M:*** Nino Rota. Oscars '63: Costume Des. (B&W), Foreign Film; N.Y. Film Critics '63: Foreign Film.

8 1/2 Women 🦴½ **1999 (R)** A typically baffling presentation from Greenaway concerns wealthy Swiss businessman Philip Emmeenthal (Standing), who is grief-stricken over the recent death of his wife. His son, Storey (Delamere), comes to Geneva to console his father. After seeing Fellini's "8 1/2" they suddenly decide to assemble their own harem of decidedly offbeat females and pursue sexual fantasies. Remarkably unappealing and dull. **122m/C VHS, DVD.** *GB* John Standing, Vivian Wu, Annie Shizuka Inoh, Matthew Delamere, Toni Collette, Amanda Plummer, Manna Fujiwara, Barbara Sarafian, Polly Walker, Karina Mano, Natacha Amal; ***D:*** Peter Greenaway; ***W:*** Peter Greenaway; ***C:*** Sacha Vierny.

Eight Days a Week 🦴½ **1997 (R)** Shy, nerdy high-schooler Peter (Schaefer) is obsessed with Erica (Russell), the popular babe who lives across the street. Peter decides a sit-in on her front lawn and constant protestations about his devotion is the way to get her attention. Title comes from the Beatles tune and is the cleverest thing in the movie. **92m/C VHS.** Joshua Schaefer, Keri Russell, R.D. Robb, Mark L. Taylor, Catherine Hicks; ***D:*** Michael Paul Davis; ***W:*** Michael Paul Davis; ***C:*** James Lawrence Spencer; ***M:*** Kevin Bassinson.

8 Heads in a Duffel Bag 🦴🦴 **1996 (R)** Mob bag man Tommy (Pesci, in a real stretch) loses his heads, the evidence of a successful hit, to med student Charlie Pritchett (Comeau), who's headed for a Mexican vacation with his fiance's (Swanson) uptight family. Desperate, Tommy "persuades" Charlie's roommates (Spade and Louiso) to help him find some replacement noggins. Excellent premise is almost done in by a timid script that relies a little too much on slapstick. Schulman's uneven directorial debut does little to mask the problem. Newcomer Comeau tries for a "Bachelor Party" era Tom Hanks thing, but doesn't quite get there. Pesci and Spade save flick from disaster, and get most of the good lines, pitted in a generational "battle of the smart-asses," but neither one strays from their previous screen personas. Louiso hilariously makes the most of his role as the naive roommate. **95m/C VHS.** Joe Pesci, David Spade, Andy Comeau, Kristy Swanson, George Hamilton, Dyan Cannon, Todd Louiso, Frank Roman, Anthony Mangano, Joe Basile, Ernestine Mercer, Howard George; ***D:*** Tom Schulman; ***W:*** Tom Schulman; ***C:*** Adam Holender; ***M:*** Andrew Gross.

800 Leagues Down the Amazon 🦴½ **1993 (PG-13)** A 19th-century journey down the Amazon on a raft with a planter, his daughter, and various complications. Based on a novel by Jules Verne. **100m/C VHS, DVD.** Daphne Zuniga, Barry Bostwick, Adam Baldwin, Tom Verica, E.E. Bell; ***D:*** Luis Llosa; ***W:*** Laura Schiff, Jackson Barr; ***C:*** Pili Flores-Guerra; ***M:*** Jorge Tafur.

Eight Legged Freaks **2002 (PG-13)** Chemical spill causes spiders to mutate into the size of SUVs in a rural mining town. Mining engineer Arquette and sheriff Wuhrer round up the townsfolk to battle the beasties. Not yet reviewed. **?m/C VHS, DVD.** David Arquette, Kari Wuhrer, Scott Terra, Scarlett Johansson, Doug E. Doug, Riley Smith, Leon Rippy; ***D:*** Ellory Elkayem; ***W:*** Jesse Alexander, Ellory Elkayem.

Eight Men Out 🦴🦴🦴½ **1988 (PG)** Taken from Eliot Asinof's book, a moving, full-blooded account of the infamous 1919 "Black Sox" scandal, in which members of the Chicago White Sox teamed to throw the World Series for $80,000. A dirge of lost innocence, this is among Sayles' best films. Provides an interesting look at the "conspiracy" that ended "Shoeless" Joe Jackson's major-league career. The actual baseball scenes are first-rate, and Straithairn, Sweeney, and Cusack give exceptional performances. Sayles makes an appearance as Ring Lardner. Enjoyable viewing for even the non-sports fan. **121m/C VHS, DVD, Wide.** John Cusack, D.B. Sweeney, Perry Lang, Jace Alexander, Bill Irwin, Clifton James, Michael Rooker, Michael Lerner, Christopher Lloyd, Studs Terkel, David Strathairn, Charlie Sheen, Kevin Tighe, John Mahoney, John Sayles, Gordon Clapp, Richard Edson, James Read, Don Harvey, John Anderson, Maggie Renzi, Michael Mantell, Nancy Travis, Michael Laskin; ***D:*** John Sayles; ***W:*** John Sayles; ***C:*** Robert Richardson; ***M:*** Mason Daring.

8mm 🦴🦴½ **1998 (R)** Surveillance expert Tom Welles (Cage) leads a normal family life until he's hired by widow Mrs. Christian (Carter). She wants him to find out the identity of a young girl apparently slashed to death in a porno film found in her late husband's safe. He descends into the underbelly of the pornography industry, guided by sleazeballs with names like Max California (Phoenix) and Dino Velvet (Stormare), and is both disgusted and fascinated by what he sees and learns. After he ferrets out the villain, he is forced into a showdown in order to save his family. Scripted by "Seven" writer Andrew Kevin Walker, but lacks some of the psychological punch of his previous effort. **123m/C VHS, DVD.** Nicolas Cage, Joaquin Rafael (Leaf) Phoenix, James Gandolfini, Peter Stormare, Anthony Heald, Catherine Keener, Chris Bauer, Myra Carter, Amy Morton; ***D:*** Joel Schumacher; ***W:*** Andrew Kevin Walker; ***C:*** Robert Elswit; ***M:*** Mychael Danna.

8 Million Ways to Die 🦴🦴 **1985 (R)** An ex-cop hires himself out to rescue a pimp-bound hooker, and gets knee-deep in a mess of million-dollar drug deals, murder, and prostitution. Slow-moving but satisfying. Based on the book by Lawrence Block. **115m/C VHS.** Jeff Bridges, Rosanna Arquette, Andy Garcia, Alexandra Paul; ***D:*** Hal Ashby; ***W:*** Oliver Stone; ***C:*** Stephen Burum; ***M:*** James Newton Howard.

Eight on the Lam 🦴 **1967 (PG)** Unfunny comedy features widower Henry Dimsdale (Hope) taking off with his kids and family maid Golda (Diller) when he's accused of embezzling bank funds. Jasper Lynch (Winters) is on their trail until Henry can prove who the real culprit is. **103m/C VHS.** Bob Hope, Phyllis Diller, Jonathan Winters, Jill St. John, Shirley Eaton; ***D:*** George Marshall; ***W:*** Albert Lewin, Arthur Marx, Bob Fisher, Burt Styler; ***C:*** Alan Stenvold; ***M:*** George Romanis.

8 Seconds 🦴🦴½ *The Lane Frost Story* **1994 (PG-13)** Love, not sports, dominates the true-life story of rodeo star Lane Frost (Perry), a world champion bull rider killed in the ring at the age of 25 in 1990. A decent guy, he finds quick success on the rodeo circuit, marries (to Geary), and finds his career getting in the way of their happiness. Bull-riding sequences are genuinely stomach churning, the performances low-key. Title refers to the amount of time a rider must stay aboard his animal. **104m/C VHS, DVD.** Luke Perry, Cynthia Geary, Stephen Baldwin, James Rebhorn, Carrie Snodgress, Red Mitchell, Ronnie Claire Edwards; ***D:*** John G. Avildsen; ***W:*** Monte Merrick; ***C:*** Victor Hammer; ***M:*** Bill Conti.

Eight Witnesses 🦴🦴 **1954** Suspense thriller about a man being murdered in front of eight blind witnesses. **?m/C VHS.** Peggy Ann Garner.

18 Again! 🦴🦴½ **1988 (PG)** After a bump on the head, an 81-year-old man and his 18-year-old grandson mentally switch places, giving each a new look at his life. Lightweight romp with Burns in especially good form, but not good enough to justify redoing this tired theme. **100m/C VHS, DVD, Wide.** George Burns, Charlie Schlatter, Anita Morris, Jennifer Runyon, Tony Roberts, Red Buttons, Miriam Flynn, George DiCenzo, Pauly Shore, Anthony Starke; ***D:*** Paul Flaherty; ***W:*** Jonathan Prince, Josh Goldstein; ***C:*** Stephen M. Katz; ***M:*** Billy Goldenberg.

1860 🦴🦴 **1933** During the Battle of Calatafimi in May of 1860, Sicilian peasants revolted against the King of Naples' army. The story focuses on four people caught up in the fighting: the spouse of a revolutionary, a foppish intellectual, a rebel priest, and the young shepherd who is sent with a message to Genoa asking for assistance. Blasetti made great use of location filming and natural light. In Italian with English subtitles. **72m/C VHS.** *IT* ***D:*** Alessandro Blasetti.

The Eighteenth Angel 🦴🦴 **1997 (R)** The unexpected death of his wife (Crewson) finds Hugh Stanton (McDonald) clinging to his 15-year-old daughter Lucy (Cook), who has fallen into a deep depression. Then a mysterious modeling agent "discovers" Lucy, claiming she has the face of an angel, and offers Lucy a trip to Italy. Unexplainable things happen during their stay and when Hugh investigates it seems that good and evil are in a battle for Lucy's soul. **90m/C VHS.** Christopher McDonald, Rachael Leigh Cook, Maximilian Schell, Stanley Tucci, Wendy Crewson, Ted Rusoff; ***D:*** William Bindley; ***W:*** David Seltzer; ***C:*** Thomas Ackerman.

The Eighth Day 🦴🦴½ *Le Huitieme Jour* **1995** Sugary story about workaholic businessman Harry (Auteuil), whose wife Julie (Miou-Miou) has just left him, taking their daughters. Driving home, Harry finds Georges (Duquenne) by the side of the road. Georges, who has Downs syndrome, has left the institution he's been living in and, though Harry tries to take him to the nearest police station, Georges refuses to leave him. Naturally, the emotionally deprived Harry begins to loosen up and, when Georges is finally returned to his group home, all his friends decide to help with Harry's attempts to win back his family. Thick with whimsy but the lead performances are excellent. French with subtitles. **108m/C VHS.** *FR BE* Daniel Auteuil, Pascal Duquenne, Miou-Miou, Henri Garcin, Fabienne Loriaux, Isabelle Sadoyan, Helene Roussel, Michele Maes; ***D:*** Jaco Van Dormael; ***W:*** Jaco Van Dormael; ***C:*** Walther Vanden Ende; ***M:*** Pierre Van Dormael. Cannes '96: Actor (Auteuil), Actor (Duquenne).

The Eighties 🦴🦴½ **1983** A comic, pseudo-documentary romp through the making of a musical. Not just another dime-a-dozen song-and-dance flick, but plays with the genre with humor and intelligence, treating us to an insider's view of a performance arranged at a shopping plaza, from the rigorous auditions to the tedium of the production of songs and routines. Treated in a light-hearted, sensitive, just on the verge of laughable manner, it concludes with 30 minutes of song and dance. In French with English subtitles. **86m/C VHS.** *FR* Aurore Clement, Lio, Magali Noel, Pascale Salkin; ***D:*** Chantal Akerman; ***W:*** Chantal Akerman, Jean Gruault.

84 Charing Cross Road 🦴🦴🦴 **1986 (PG)** A lonely woman in New York and a book-seller in London begin corresponding for business reasons. Over a 20-year period, their relationship grows into a friendship, and then a romance, though they communicate only by mail. Based on a true story and adapted from the book by Helene Hanff. **100m/C VHS, DVD.** Anne Bancroft, Anthony Hopkins, Judi Dench, Jean De Baer, Maurice Denham, Eleanor David, Mercedes Ruehl, Daniel Gerroll, Hugh Whitemore; ***D:*** David Hugh Jones; ***W:*** Hugh Whitemore; ***C:*** Brian West; ***M:*** George Fenton. British Acad. '87: Actress (Bancroft).

84 Charlie MoPic 🦴🦴🦴 **1989 (R)** A widely acclaimed drama about the horrors of Vietnam seen through the eyes of a cameraman assigned to a special front-line unit. Filled with a cast of unknowns, this is an unsettling film that sheds new light on the subject of the Vietnam war. Powerful and energetic; music by Donovan. **89m/C VHS.** Richard Brooks, Christopher Burgard, Nicholas Cascone, Jonathan Emerson, Glenn Morshower, Jason Tomlins, Byron Thames; ***D:*** Patrick Sheane Duncan; ***W:*** Patrick Sheane Duncan; ***C:*** Alan Caso; ***M:*** Donovan.

Eijanaika 🦴🦴🦴½ *Why Not?* **1981** A gripping story of a poor Japanese man who returns to his country after a visit to America in the 1860s. Memorable performances make this an above-average film. In Japanese with English subtitles. **151m/C VHS.** *JP* Ken Ogata, Shigeru Izumiya; ***D:*** Shohei Imamura.

El 🦴🦴 *This Strange Passion* **1952** Bizarre black-comedy finds virginal middle-aged Francisco (De Cordova) marrying a beautiful young woman (Garces) and becoming jealously paranoid when he believes she's been unfaithful. He's eventually driven to insanity and attempted murder. Spanish with subtitles. **88m/B VHS.** *MX* Arturo de Cordova, Delia Garces, Luis Beristain, Aurora Walker; ***D:*** Luis Bunuel; ***W:*** Luis Bunuel, Luis Alcoriza; ***C:*** Gabriel Figueroa; ***M:*** Luis Hernandez Breton.

El Amor Brujo 🦴🦴🦴 *Love, the Magician* **1986** An adaptation of the work of Miguel de Falla, in which flamenco dancers enact the story of a tragic romance. **100m/C VHS.** Antonio Gades, Cristina Hoyos, Laura Del Sol; ***D:*** Carlos Saura.

El Barbaro 🦴 **1984** In the beginning of civilization, when evil powers rule, a barbarian has two ambitions in life: to seek revenge for his friend's death and to rescue the world from a sorcerer's power. **88m/C VHS.** *SP* Andrea Occhipinti, Maria Scola, Violeta Cela, Sabrina Siani.

El Bruto 🦴🦴½ *The Brute* **1952** A mid-Mexican-period Bunuel drama, about a brainless thug who is used as a bullying pawn in a struggle between a brutal landlord and discontented tenants. In Spanish with English titles. **83m/B VHS.** *MX* Pedro Armendariz Sr., Katy Jurado, Andres Soler, Rosita (Rosa) Arenas; ***D:*** Luis Bunuel.

El Cid 🦴🦴🦴 **1961** Charts the life of Rodrigo Diaz de Bivar, known as El Cid, who was the legendary 11th-century Christian hero who freed Spain from Moorish invaders. Noted for its insanely lavish budget, this epic tale is true to its setting and features elaborate battle scenes. **184m/C VHS.** Charlton Heston, Sophia Loren, Raf Vallone, Hurd Hatfield, Genevieve Page; ***D:*** Anthony Mann; ***W:*** Philip Yordan; ***C:*** Robert Krasker; ***M:*** Miklos Rozsa.

El Cochecito 🦴🦴🦴 *The Wheelchair* **1960** Great Spanish actor Isbert stars as the head of a large family whose closest friends are all joined together in a kind of fraternity defined by the fact that they each use a wheelchair. He feels excluded because he does not have or need one, so he goes to great lengths to gain acceptance in this "brotherhood." In Spanish with English subtitles. **90m/B VHS.** *SP* Jose Isbert; ***D:*** Marco Ferreri.

El Condor 🦴½ **1970 (R)** Two drifters search for gold buried in a Mexican fort. **102m/C VHS.** *SP* Jim Brown, Lee Van Cleef, Patrick O'Neal, Marianna Hill, Iron Eyes Cody, Elisha Cook Jr.; ***D:*** John Guillermin; ***W:*** Larry Cohen, Steven W. Carabatsos; ***M:*** Maurice Jarre.

El Diablo 🦴🦴½ **1990 (PG-13)** A young man finds the West more wild than he expected. He finds "help" in the shape of Gossett as he tries to free a young girl who's being held by the notorious El Diablo. Better than average. **107m/C VHS, DVD, Wide.** Louis Gossett Jr., Anthony Edwards, John Glover, Robert Beltran, M.C. Gainey, Miguel (Michael) Sandoval, Sarah Trigger, Joe Pantoliano; ***D:*** Peter Markle; ***W:*** John Carpenter, Bill Phillips; ***C:*** Ron Garcia; ***M:*** William Olvis. **CABLE**

El Diablo Rides 🦴½ **1939** A fierce feud between cattlemen and sheepmen develops, with touches of comedy in between. **57m/B VHS.** Bob Steele, Carleton Young, Kit Guard.

El Diputado 🦴🦴🦴 *The Deputy* **1978** A famous politician jeopardizes his career when he has an affair with a young man. In Spanish with English subtitles. **111m/C VHS.** *SP* Jose Sacristan, Maria Luisa San Jose, Jose Alonso; ***D:*** Eloy De La Iglesia.

El Dorado 🦴🦴🦴 **1967** A gunfighter rides into the frontier town of El Dorado to aid a reckless cattle baron in his war with farmers over land rights. Once in town, the hired gun meets up with an old friend—the sheriff—who also happens to be the town drunkard. Switching allegiances, the gunslinger helps the lawman sober up and defend the farmers. This Hawks western displays a number of similarities to the director's earlier "Rio Bravo" (1959), staring Wayne, Dean Martin, and Ricky Nelson—who charms viewers as the young sidekick "Colorado" much like Caan does as "Mississippi" in El Dorado. **126m/C VHS, DVD.** John Wayne, Robert Mitchum, James Caan, Charlene Holt, Ed Asner, Arthur Hunnicutt, Christopher George, R.G. Armstrong, Jim Davis, Paul Fix, Johnny Crawford, Michele Carey; ***D:*** Howard Hawks.

El Mariachi 🦴🦴🦴 **1993 (R)** Extremely low-budget but clever mixture of humor and violence in a tale of mistaken identity set in a small Mexican border town. Unemployed singer/musician Gallardo wanders into a small town and is mistaken for a hitman who carries his weapons in a guitar case. Eventually, the real hitman also shows up. 24-year-old director Rodriguez makes his feature film debut with this $7000 feature, originally intended only for the Spanish-language market. Film festival awards and critical attention brought the work to wider release. Spanish with subtitles or dubbed. **81m/C VHS, DVD.** *MX* Carlos Gallardo, Consuelo Gomez, Peter Marquardt, Jaime de Hoyos, Reinol Martinez, Ramiro Gomez; ***D:*** Robert Rodriguez; ***W:*** Robert Rodriguez, Carlos Gallardo; ***C:*** Robert Rodriguez; ***M:*** Eric Guthrie. Ind. Spirit '94: First Feature; Sundance '93: Aud. Award.

El Muerto 🦴½ **1975** In 19th-century Buenos Aires, a young man flees his home after killing an enemy. Arriving in Montevideo, he becomes a member of a smuggling ring. In Spanish with English subtitles. **103m/C VHS.** *SP* Thelma Biral, Juan Jose Camero, Francisco Rabal; ***D:*** Hector Olivera.

El Norte 🦴🦴🦴🦴 **1983 (R)** Gripping account of a Guatemalan brother and sister, persecuted in their homeland, who make an arduous journey north ("El Norte") to America. Their difficult saga continues as they struggle against overwhelming odds in an attempt to realize their dreams. Passionate, sobering, and powerful. In English and Spanish with English subtitles. Produced in association with the "American Playhouse" series for PBS. Produced by Anna Thomas who also co-wrote the story with Nava. **139m/C VHS.** *SP* David Villalpando, Zaide Silvia Gutierrez, Ernesto Cruz, Eracio Zepeda, Stella Quan, Alicia del Lugo, Lupe Ontiveros; ***D:*** Gregory Nava; ***W:*** Anna Thomas, Gregory Nava. Natl. Film Reg. '95.

El Paso Stampede 🦴½ **1953** Cowboy investigates raids on cattle herds used to feed Americans fighting in the Spanish-American War. **50m/B VHS.** Allan "Rocky" Lane, Eddy (Eddie, Ed) Waller, Phyllis Coates; ***D:*** Harry Keller.

El Super 🦴🦴🦴 **1979** A Cuban refugee, still homesick after many years, struggles to make a life for himself in Manhattan as an apartment superintendent. In Spanish with English subtitles; an American production shot on location in New York City. **90m/C VHS.** *SP* Raymundo Hidalgo-Gato, Orlando Jiminez-Leal, Zully Montero, Raynaldo Medina, Juan Granda, Hilda Lee, Elizabeth Pena; ***D:*** Leon Ichaso; ***W:*** Leon Ichaso, Manuel Arce.

Ele, My Friend 🦴🦴½ **1993** The British Raj still rules India in the 1920s, when 10-year-old Charles comes across a herd of wild elephants living in the jungle. Charles befriends a baby elephant he names Ele but what can he do when hunters also discover the animals? Filmed on location in south India. **104m/C VHS.** Jacob Paul Guzman, Gazan Khan, R.S. Shivaji, Amjad Khan, Prabhu; ***D:*** Dharan Mandrayar; ***W:*** Dharan Mandrayar; ***M:*** Barry Phillips.

Eleanor & Franklin 🦴🦴🦴½ **1976** An exceptional dramatization of the personal lives of President Franklin D. Roosevelt and his wife Eleanor. Based on Joseph Lash's book, this Emmy award-winning film features stunning performances by Alexander and Herrmann in the title roles. **208m/C VHS.** Jane Alexander, Edward Herrmann, Ed Flanders, Rosemary Murphy, MacKenzie Phillips, Pamela Franklin, Anna Lee, Linda Purl, Linda Kelsey, Lindsay Crouse; ***D:*** Daniel Petrie; ***M:*** John Barry. **TV**

Eleanor: First Lady of the World 🦴🦴½ **1982 (G)** Stapleton plays the former first lady after her husband's death as she goes on to work at the United Nations and emerges as even more of an influential public figure. **96m/C VHS.** Jean Stapleton, E.G. Marshall, Coral Browne, Joyce Van Patten, Gail Strickland, Kenneth Kimmins; ***D:*** John Erman; ***M:*** John Addison. **TV**

Election 🦴🦴🦴 **1999 (R)** Payne uses a high school student council election to skewer the American political system in general and the election process in particular. Smart comedy has wildly ambitious Tracy (Witherspoon) running for council president unopposed until dedicated but flawed civics teacher Mr. McAllister (Broderick) decides she must be stopped. He recruits likeable but dim jock Paul (Klein) to run against her. Then Paul's lesbian (and anarchic) sister Tammy (Campbell) joins the race. As in Payne's previous effort, "Citizen Ruth," no side of the political spectrum is spared. Everyone's foibles and hypocrisy are shown, to great effect. Witherspoon gives an energized performance, while Broderick is excellent as the respected, conflicted mentor with a touch of Bueller in him. **105m/C VHS, DVD.** Matthew Broderick, Reese Witherspoon, Chris Klein, Jessica Campbell, Mark Harelik, Molly Hagan, Colleen Camp, Frankie Ingrassia, Matt Malloy, Holmes Osborne, Phil Reeves, Delaney Driscoll, Jeanine Jackson; ***D:*** Alexander Payne; ***W:*** Alexander Payne, Jim Taylor; ***C:*** James Glennon; ***M:*** Rolfe Kent. Ind. Spirit '00: Director (Payne), Film, Screenplay; N.Y. Film Critics '99: Screenplay; Natl. Soc. Film Critics '99: Actress (Witherspoon); Writers Guild '99: Adapt. Screenplay.

Elective Affinities 🦴🦴½ **1996** Adaptation of Goethe's 1809 novel, which the Taviani brothers transport to their native Tuscany. Aristocratic Charlotte (Huppert) and Edouard (Anglade) reunite after 20 years and decide to marry, retiring to a country villa. Their idyll is interrupted by the arrival of Edouard's best friend, Othon (Bentivoglio), and Charlotte's goddaughter Ottilie (Gillain). Soon, the married duo find themselves in love with their respective houseguests. But though the characters pursue their relationships, tragedy haunts them. French with subtitles. **98m/C VHS.** *FR IT* Isabelle Huppert, Jean-Hugues Anglade, Fabrizio Bentivoglio, Marie Gillain; ***D:*** Paolo Taviani, Vittorio Taviani; ***W:*** Paolo Taviani, Vittorio Taviani; ***C:*** Giuseppe Lanci; ***M:*** Carlo Crivelli.

Electra 🦴🦴 **1995** Sex-bomb Lorna (Tweed) does her oedipal best with stepson Billy (Tab), who was implanted with the secret of physical regeneration by his late scientist dad. Cybervillian Roach (Erik) wants the info, which can only be obtained through intimate contact, and Lorna's the right woman for the job. Funny how Billy's just so uncooperative. Very over-the-top. **85m/C VHS.** Shannon Tweed, Joe Tab, Sten Eirik; ***D:*** Julian Grant; ***W:*** Damian Lee; ***C:*** Gerald R. Goozie.

Electra Glide in Blue 🦴🦴🦴 **1973 (R)** An Arizona motorcycle cop uses his head in a world that's coming apart at the seams. Good action scenes; lots of violence. **113m/C VHS.** Robert (Bobby) Blake, Billy Green Bush, Mitchell Ryan, Jeannine Riley, Elisha Cook Jr., Royal Dano; ***D:*** James W. Guercio; ***W:*** Robert Boris; ***C:*** Conrad L. Hall.

Electric Dreams 🦴🦴½ **1984 (PG)** A young man buys a computer that yearns to do more than sit on a desk. First it takes over his apartment, then it sets its sights on the man's cello-playing neighbor—the same woman his owner is courting. To win her affections, the over-eager computer tries to dazzle her with a variety of musical compositions from his unique keyboard. Cort supplies the voice of Edgar the computer in this film that integrates a rock-music video format. **95m/C VHS.** Lenny Von Dohlen, Virginia Madsen, Maxwell Caulfield, Bud Cort, Koo Stark; ***D:*** Steven Barron.

The Electric Horseman 🦴🦴½ **1979 (PG)** Journalist Fonda sets out to discover the reason behind the kidnapping of a prized horse by an ex-rodeo star. The alcoholic cowboy has taken the horse to return it to its native environment, away from the clutches of corporate greed. As Fonda investigates the story she falls in love with rebel Redford. Excellent Las Vegas and remote western settings. **120m/C VHS, DVD, Wide.** Robert Redford, Jane Fonda, John Saxon, Willie Nelson, Valerie Perrine, Wilford Brimley, Nicolas Coster, James B. Sikking; ***D:*** Sydney Pollack; ***W:*** Robert Garland; ***C:*** Owen Roizman; ***M:*** Dave Grusin.

The Electronic Monster 🦴🦴 *Escapement; The Electric Monster* **1957** Insurance claims investigator Cameron looks into the death of a Hollywood starlet and discovers an exclusive therapy center dedicated to hypnotism. At the facility, people vacation for weeks in morgue-like body drawers, while evil Dr. Illing uses an electronic device to control the sleeper's dreams and actions. Eerie. Intriguingly, it is one of the first films to explore the possibilities of brainwashing and mind control. **72m/B VHS.** *GB* Rod Cameron, Mary Murphy, Meredith Edwards, Peter Illing; ***D:*** Montgomery Tully.

The Elegant Criminal 🦴🦴½ **1992** Based on the true story of France's most infamous killer, Pierre Lacenaire. The film begins with Lacenaire in prison, writing his memoirs, receiving his admirers, and awaiting his execution (in 1836). A series of flashbacks detail his life and the supposed social clime which hindered his better instincts and turned him to the criminal life. However, Auteuil has such a wonderful time playing the charming bad guy that any blame to society fails to convince. In French with English subtitles. **120m/C VHS.** *FR* Daniel Auteuil, Jean Poiret, Jacques Weber, Marie-Armelle DeGuy, Maiwenn Le Besco, Patrick Pineau; ***D:*** Francis Girod; ***W:*** George Conchon, Francis Girod.

The Element of Crime 🦴🦴½ *Forbrydelsens Element* **1984** In a monochromatic, post-holocaust future, a detective tracks down a serial killer of young girls. Made in Denmark, this minor festival favorite features an impressive directional debut and awaits cult status. Filmed in Sepiatone. **104m/C VHS, DVD, Wide.** *DK* Michael Elphick, Esmond Knight, Jerold Wells, Meme Lei, Astrid Henning-Jensen, Preben Leerdorff-Rye, Gotha Andersen; ***D:*** Lars von Trier; ***W:*** Lars von Trier, Niels Vorsel; ***C:*** Tom Elling; ***M:*** Bo Holten.

Element of Doubt 🦴🦴½ **1996** Beth Murray's (McKee) family have always been suspicious of her ambitious husband, Richard (Havers). Although Beth desperately wants children, Richard has persuaded her to wait until after he's closed some mysterious business deal. Suddenly, Richard promises Beth a home in the country and the family she desires. Then, Beth discovers her husband has been in close contact with his ex-wife. So, is Beth merely suffering from hysterics or is Richard actually contemplating murder? **90m/C VHS, DVD.** *GB* Nigel Havers, Gina McKee, Polly Adams, Judy Parfitt, Sarah Berger, Michael Jayston, Dennis (Denis) Lill, Robert Reynolds; ***D:*** Christopher Morahan; ***C:*** Brian Tufano; ***M:*** Stephen Warbeck. **TV**

The Elementary School 🦴🦴 *Obecna Skola* **1991** Screenwriter Sverak's memories of his childhood are the basis for this child's eye view of the mysteries surrounding the adult world. In 1945, 10-year-old Eda (Jakoubek) is living in a village outside Prague. His school class is so wild that the teacher quits and is replaced by the strict Igor Hnizdo (Triska), who turns out to have a weakness for young women. Czech with subtitles. **100m/C VHS.** *CZ* Jan Triska, Vaclav Jakoubek, Zdenek Sverak, Radoslav Budas, Libuse Safrankova, Rudolf Hrusinsky, Petr Cepek; ***D:*** Jan Sverak; ***W:*** Zdenek Sverak; ***C:*** F.A. Brabec.

Elena and Her Men 🦴🦴🦴 *Paris Does Strange Things; Elena et les Hommes* **1956** The romantic entanglements and intrigues of a poor Polish princess are explored in this enjoyable French film. Beautiful cinematography by Claude Renoir. In French with subtitles. **98m/C VHS.** *FR* Ingrid Bergman, Jean Marais, Mel Ferrer, Jean Richard, Magali Noel, Pierre Bertin, Juliette Greco; ***D:*** Jean Renoir; ***C:*** Claude Renoir.

Eleni 🦴🦴 **1985 (PG)** The true story of "New York Times" reporter Nicholas Gage and his journey to Athens to discover the truth about his mother's execution by Communists during the Greek rebellion after WWII. Adapted by Steve Tesich from Gage's bestselling book. **117m/C VHS, 8mm.** John Malkovich, Kate Nelligan, Linda Hunt, Oliver Cotton, Ronald Pickup, Dimitra Arliss, Rosalie Crutchley; ***D:*** Peter Yates; ***W:*** Steve Tesich; ***C:*** Billy Williams; ***M:*** Bruce Smeaton.

Elephant Boy 🦴🦴🦴 **1937** An Indian boy helps government conservationists locate a herd of elephants in the jungle. Sabu's first film. Available in digitally remastered stereo. **80m/B VHS.** *GB* Sabu, Walter Hudd, W.E. Holloway; ***D:*** Robert Flaherty, Zoltan Korda. Venice Film Fest. '37: Director (Flaherty).

An Elephant Called Slowly 🦴🦴½ **1969 (G)** In a sequel of sorts to the 1966 hit "Born Free," McKenna and Travers star as an English couple who trek to Africa to meet game warden George Adamson (here playing himself). Once in Africa, they are introduced to a menagerie of animals, such as lions and hippos. Along the way, the meet Pole Pole (Swahili for "Slowly"), a baby elephant who adopts McKenna and Travers and attempts to travel with them. The first 20 minutes are rather slow, but the last 70 are very watchable with gorgeous cinematography and astounding nature shots. **91m/C VHS, DVD.** *GB* Virginia McKenna, Bill Travers, George Adamson, Joab Collins, Vinay Inambar, Ali Twaha; ***D:*** James Hill; ***W:*** Bill Travers, James Hill; ***C:*** Simon Trevor; ***M:*** Howard Blake, Bert Kaempfert.

The Elephant Man 🦴🦴🦴🦴 **1980 (PG)** A biography of John Merrick, a severely deformed man who, with the help of a sympathetic doctor, moved from freak shows into posh London society. Lynch's first mainstream film, shot in black and white, it presents a startlingly vivid picture of the hypocrisies evident in the social mores of the Victorian era. Moving performance from Hurt in title role. **125m/B VHS, DVD, Wide.** Michael Elphick, Anthony Hopkins, John Hurt, Anne Bancroft, John Gielgud, Wendy Hiller, Freddie Jones, Kenny Baker; ***D:*** David Lynch; ***W:*** Eric Bergren, Christopher DeVore, David Lynch; ***C:*** Freddie Francis; ***M:*** John Morris, Samuel Barber. British Acad. '80: Actor (Hurt), Film; Cesar '82: Foreign Film.

Elephant Walk 🦴🦴½ **1954** Sri Lanka's balmy jungles provide the backdrop for a torrid love triangle in this post-prime Dieterle effort. Taylor, ignored by her wealthy drunkard hubby, finds solace in the arms of her spouse's sexy right-hand man. As if keeping the affair secret weren't a big enough task, she also braves a cholera epidemic and a pack of vengeful elephants who take an unscheduled tour of her humble home. Lethargic lead performances make this more of a sleep walk, but Sofaer and Biberman's supporting roles are worth the price of rental. Taylor replaced Vivian Leigh early in the filming after she fell ill, but footage of Leigh in faraway shots is included. **103m/C VHS.** Elizabeth Taylor, Dana Andrews, Peter Finch, Abraham Sofaer, Abner Biberman; ***D:*** William Dieterle; ***C:*** Loyal Griggs.

11 Harrowhouse 🦴🦴🦴 *Anything for Love; Fast Fortune* **1974 (PG)** The Consolidated Selling System at 11 Harrowhouse, London, controls much of the world's diamond trade. Four adventurous thieves plot a daring heist relying on a very clever cockroach. A rather successful stab at spoofing detailed "heist" films. **95m/C VHS.** *GB* Charles Grodin, Candice Bergen, James Mason, Trevor Howard, John Gielgud; *D:* Aram Avakian; *W:* Jeffrey Bloom.

Eli Eli ☆☆½ **1940** An American Yiddish film about a family forced to live apart because of their farm's failure. Lighthearted and fun. In Yiddish with English titles. **85m/B VHS.** Esther Field, Lazar Fried, Muni Serebroff; *D:* Joseph Seiden; *M:* Sholom Secunda.

The Eliminators ☆ **1986 (PG)** A cyborgian creature endeavors to avenge himself on his evil scientist creator with help from a kung fu expert and a Mexican. The group uses time travel and other devices to achieve their mission. **95m/C VHS.** Roy Dotrice, Patrick Reynolds, Denise Crosby, Andrew Prine, Conan Lee; *D:* Peter Manoogian; *W:* Danny Bilson, Paul DeMeo; *M:* Richard Band.

Elisa ☆☆ **1994** Teenaged sexpot Marie (Paradis) has grown up in a reform school, thanks to her mother Elisa's suicide. Along with friends Solange (Courau) and Ahmed (Sall), Marie spends her time on the Paris streets shoplifting and flirting. Obsessed with finding her long-gone father, Marie discovers that Lebovitch (Depardieu), the writer of the popular song "Elisa," is daddy dearest. He's now a drunk, living on a fishing island, and Marie sets out to right the wrongs she believes drove her mother to suicide. Based on the song by Serge Gainsbourg. French with subtitles. **111m/C VHS.** *FR* Vanessa Paradis, Gerard Depardieu, Clotilde Courau, Sekkou Sall, Florence Thomassin; *D:* Jean Becker; *W:* Jean Becker, Fabrice Carazo; *C:* Etienne Becker; *M:* Zbigniew Preisner. Cesar '95: Support. Actress (Courau), Score.

Elisa, Vida Mia ☆☆ *Elisa, My Love; Elisa, My Life* **1977** A long-estranged father and daughter are reunited when he falls ill. She stays to help him write his biography and gradually begins to see things through his perspective. The shifting narrative can confuse but worth seeing are Rey and Chaplin's subtle performances. Spanish with subtitles. **125m/C VHS.** *SP* Fernando Rey, Geraldine Chaplin, Norman Brisky, Isabel Mestres, Joaquin Hinojosa; *D:* Carlos Saura; *W:* Carlos Saura; *M:* Erik Satie. Cannes '77: Actor (Rey).

Elizabeth ☆☆☆ **1998 (R)** And you thought modern day politics were dirty! Indian director Kapur takes a look at the turbulent life of Queen Elizabeth I of England (a brilliant Blanchett) from her uncertain days as a beseiged Protestant Princess to her ascension to the throne and the machinations surrounding her early reign. Elizabeth indeed proves to be her father's daughter as she must keep her head (literally) while dealing with religion, war, assassination, and the vexing question of a political marriage. Rush is notable as spidery spymaster Walsingham and Eccleston's hissably evil as the arrogant Catholic Duke of Norfolk. Wonderful shadowy cinematography by Adefarasin adds to the atmosphere but it does help to know some history in order to keep the plots and plotters straight. **124m/C VHS, DVD.** *GB* Cate Blanchett, Geoffrey Rush, Joseph Fiennes, Christopher Eccleston, Richard Attenborough, Fanny Ardant, Vincent Cassel, Daniel Craig, Kathy Burke, James Frain, Edward Hardwicke, Eric Cantona, John Gielgud, Emily Mortimer; *D:* Shekhar Kapur; *W:* Michael Hirst; *C:* Remi Adefarasin; *M:* David Hirschfelder. Oscars '98: Makeup; British Acad. '98: Actress (Blanchett), Cinematog., Film, Score; Golden Globes '99: Actress—Drama (Blanchett); Natl. Bd. of Review '98: Director (Kapur); Broadcast Film Critics '98: Actress (Blanchett).

Elizabeth of Ladymead ☆☆☆ **1948** Four generations of a British family live through their experiences in the Crimean War, Boer War, WWI, and WWII. Neagle, playing the wives in all four generations, aptly explores the woman's side of war. Enjoyable performances from husband and wife team Neagle and Wilcox. **97m/C VHS.** Anna Neagle, Hugh Williams, Bernard Lee, Michael Lawrence, Nicholas Phipps, Isabel Jeans; *D:* Herbert Wilcox.

Elizabeth R ☆☆☆ **1972** Jackson is outstanding in the title role of this TV drama focusing on the life of Elizabeth I, from 17 to 70. Constantly besieged by court intrigue and political machinations, the Virgin Queen managed to restore England to glory and power amidst private and public turmoil. Six 90-minute cassettes. **540m/C VHS.** *GB* Glenda Jackson, Rosalie Crutchley, Robin Ellis, Robert Hardy, Peter Jeffrey, Stephen Murray, Vivian Pickles, Sarah Frampton, Ronald Hines; *D:* Claude Whatham, Herbert Wise, Roderick Graham, Richard Martin, Donald Whatham; *W:* Hugh Whitemore, John Hale, Julian Mitchell, John Prebble, Ian Rodger, Rosemary Anne Sisson.

Elizabeth, the Queen ☆☆ *The Private Lives of Elizabeth and Essex* **1968** Historical drama recreates the struggle for power by Robert Devereaux, Earl of Essex, whom the aging Queen Elizabeth I both loved and feared, and whose downfall she finally invoked. Part of "George Schaefer's Showcase Theatre." **76m/C VHS.** Judith Anderson, Charlton Heston; *D:* George Schaefer. **TV**

Eliza's Horoscope ☆☆½ **1970** A frail Canadian woman uses astrology in her search for love in Montreal, and experiences bizarre and surreal events. An acclaimed Canadian film. **120m/C VHS.** *CA* Tommy Lee Jones, Elizabeth Moorman; *D:* Gordon Sheppard.

Ella Cinders ☆☆☆ **1926** The American mania for breaking into the movies is satirized in this look at a girl who wins a trip to Hollywood in a small-town beauty contest. Silent with original organ score. **60m/B VHS.** Colleen Moore, Harry Langdon, Lloyd Hughes, Jed Prouty, Vera Lewis; *D:* Alfred E. Green.

Ellen Foster ☆☆½ **1997 (PG-13)** Coming-of-age TV drama concerns 10-year-old Ellen (Malone), who lives with her abusive, drunken dad (Levine) and her gentle mom (O'Connor). After mom dies, Ellen is shuffled between uncaring relatives, including a nasty grandma, Leonora (Harris), while trying to draw strength from the few friends and teachers who do care about her. Based on the book by Kaye Gibbons. **97m/C VHS.** Jena Malone, Julie Harris, Ted Levine, Glynnis O'Connor, Debra Monk, Barbara Garrick, Kate Burton, Zeljko Ivanek, Lynne Moody, Bill Nunn, Amanda Peet, Allison Jones, Timothy Olyphant; *D:* John Erman; *W:* Maria Nation, William Hanley; *C:* Brian West; *M:* John Morris. **TV**

Ellie ☆½ **1984 (R)** A murderous widow's stepdaughter tries to save her father from being added to the woman's extensive list of dearly departed husbands. **90m/C VHS.** Shelley Winters, Sheila Kennedy, Pat Paulsen, George Gobel, Edward Albert; *D:* Peter Wittman.

Elmer ☆½ **1976 (G)** Follows the adventures of a temporarily blinded youth and a lovable hound dog who meet in the wilderness and together set off in search of civilization. **82m/C VHS.** Elmer Swanson, Phillip Swanson; *D:* Christopher Cain.

Elmer Gantry ☆☆☆½ **1960** The classic multi-Oscar-winning adaptation of the Sinclair Lewis novel written to expose and denounce the flamboyant, small-town evangelists spreading through America at the time. In the film, Lancaster is the amoral Southern preacher who exacts wealth and power from his congregation, and takes a nun as a mistress. Jones stars as his ex-girlfriend who resorts to a life of prostitution. **146m/C VHS.** Burt Lancaster, Shirley Jones, Jean Simmons, Dean Jagger, Arthur Kennedy, Patti Page, Edward Andrews, John McIntire, Hugh Marlowe, Rex Ingram; *D:* Richard Brooks; *W:* Richard Brooks; *C:* John Alton; *M:* Andre Previn. Oscars '60: Actor (Lancaster), Adapt. Screenplay, Support. Actress (Jones); Golden Globes '61: Actor—Drama (Lancaster); Natl. Bd. of Review '60: Support. Actress (Jones); N.Y. Film Critics '60: Actor (Lancaster).

Elmore Leonard's Gold Coast ☆☆½ *Gold Coast* **1997 (R)** Miami mobster Frank DiCilia (Bradford) is dead and his widow Karen (Helgenberger) is not happy. Yes, she's inherited $15 mil but Frank's will also stipulates that she has to remain faithful to him forever. Too bad Karen and smalltime con man Maguire (Caruso) are instantly attracted to one another. And too bad Frank's also left behind loathsome hit man Roland (Kober) to enforce the edict (although if Karen wants him, Roland's willing to be flexible). Based on the novel by Elmore Leonard. **109m/C VHS.** David Caruso, Marg Helgenberger, Jeff Kober, Barry Primus, Richard Bradford, Wanda De Jesus; *D:* Peter Weller; *W:* Harley Peyton; *C:* Jacek Laskus; *M:* Peter Harris. **CABLE**

Elsa, Elsa **1985** Satire of moviemaking life finds a scriptwriter-director distracted by the loss of his girlfriend and unable to concentrate on writing a memoir of his career as a child actor. He creates a subplot dealing with his romantic problems, and puts the film in jeopardy. Fine acting and witty dialogue. In French with English subtitles. **85m/C VHS.** *FR* *D:* Didier Haudepin.

The Elusive Corporal ☆☆☆½ *Le Caporal Epingle* **1962** Set in a P.O.W. camp on the day France surrendered to Germany, this is the story of the French and Germans, complete with memories of a France that is no more. **108m/B VHS.** Jean-Pierre Cassel, Claude Brasseur, O.E. Hasse, Claude Rich; *D:* Jean Renoir.

The Elusive Pimpernel ☆☆½ *The Fighting Pimpernel* **1950** Niven sparkles in this otherwise undistinguished adaptation of Baroness Orczy's "The Scarlet Pimpernel." **109m/C VHS.** *GB* David Niven, Margaret Leighton, Jack Hawkins, Cyril Cusack, Robert Coote, Edmund Audran, Danielle Godet, Patrick Macnee; *D:* Michael Powell; *W:* Michael Powell, Emeric Pressburger.

Elves ☆ **1989 (PG-13)** A group of possessed, neo-Nazi elves performs serious human harm at Christmas time in this tongue-in-check thriller. **95m/C VHS.** Dan Haggerty, Deanna Lund, Julie Austin, Borah Silver; *D:* Jeffrey Mandel.

Elvira Madigan ☆☆☆ **1967 (PG)** Chronicles the true 19th-century Swedish romance between teenaged Elvira (Degermark), a beautiful circus tight-rope walker, and young Army officer Sixten Sparre (Berggren) who leaves his wife and children to be with her. Exceptional direction and photography and a notable use of classical music by Mozart and Vivaldi. Swedish with subtitles. **90m/C VHS, DVD.** *SW* Pia Degermark, Thommy Berggren, Lennart Malmer, Nina Widerberg, Cleo Jensen; *D:* Bo Widerberg; *W:* Johan Lindstroem Saxon, Bo Widerberg; *C:* Jorgen Persson; *M:* Ulf Bjorlin. Cannes '67: Actress (Degermark).

Elvira, Mistress of the Dark ☆☆ **1988 (PG-13)** A manic comedy based on Peterson's infamous B-movie horror-hostess character. The mega-busted terror-queen inherits a house in a conservative Massachusetts town and causes double-entendre chaos when she attempts to sell it. **96m/C VHS.** Cassandra Peterson, Jeff Conaway, Susan Kellerman, Edie McClurg, Daniel Greene, W. Morgan Shepherd, Kurt Fuller, Pat Crawford Brown, William Duell, William Cort, John Paragon; *D:* James Signorelli; *W:* Sam Egan, Cassandra Peterson, John Paragon; *C:* Hanania Baer; *M:* James Campbell.

Elvis and Me ☆½ **1988** TV mini series based on Priscilla Beaulieu Presley's autobiography about her life with the Pelvis. Features many of Presley's biggest hits, sung by country star Ronnie McDowell. Film may aggravate Elvis fans, however, as the King is often depicted negatively from his ex-wife's point of view. **187m/C VHS.** Dale Midkiff, Susan Walters, Billy Green Bush, Linda Miller, Jon Cypher; *D:* Larry Peerce.

Elvis in Hollywood ☆☆☆ **1993** A tribute highlighting Presley's first four films, "Love Me Tender," "Loving You," "Jailhouse Rock," and "King Creole," completed prior to his reporting for active duty in the army. Features his 1956 screen test at Paramount Studios; photos from the movie sets; interviews with co-stars, directors, writers, business associates, songwriters, and friends; and home movies as well as out-take footage from "Jailhouse Rock." **65m/C VHS.** *D:* Frank Martin.

Elvis Meets Nixon ☆½ **1998 (PG-13)** Based on the bizarre (but true) visit of Elvis Presley (Peters) to the Nixon (Gunton) White House. **103m/C VHS.** Richard Beymer, Edwin Newman, Graham Nash, Wayne Newton, Bob Gunton, Rick Peters, Jackie Burroughs, Curtis Armstrong; *D:* Allan Arkush; *W:* Alan Rosen; *C:* Michael Storey; *M:* Larry Brown. **CABLE**

Elvis: The Movie ☆☆½ **1979** Biography of the legendary singer, from his high school days to his Las Vegas comeback. Russell gives a convincing performance and lip syncs effectively to the voice of the King (provided by country singer Ronnie McDowell). Also available in 150-minute version. **117m/C VHS.** Kurt Russell, Season Hubley, Shelley Winters, Ed Begley Jr., Dennis Christopher, Pat Hingle, Bing Russell, Joe Mantegna; *D:* John Carpenter. **TV**

Emanon ☆½ **1986 (PG-13)** A coming-of-age tale about a young kid and the Christ-like vagabond, named Emanon (or "no name" if spelled in reverse), he befriends. **101m/C VHS.** Stuart Paul, Cheryl Lynn, Jeremy Miller; *D:* Stuart Paul.

Embassy ☆☆ *Target: Embassy* **1972** In this mediocre espionage thriller, von Sydow is a Soviet defector under asylum at the U.S. embassy in Beirut. Colonel Connors, a Russian spy, penetrates embassy security and wounds von Sydow. He is caught, escapes, is captured, escapes, and is caught again. Great cast, but script is often too wordy and contrived. **90m/C VHS.** *GB* Richard Roundtree, Chuck Connors, Max von Sydow, Ray Milland, Broderick Crawford, Marie-Jose Nat; *D:* Gordon Hessler.

Embassy ☆☆ **1985** An American family in Rome unknowingly possesses a secret computer chip, and thus is pursued by ruthless agents. **104m/C VHS.** Nick Mancuso, Blanche Baker, Eli Wallach, Sam Wanamaker, Richard Gilliland, Mimi Rogers, George Grizzard, Richard Masur, Kim Darby; *D:* Robert Lewis. **TV**

Embrace of the Vampire ☆☆ **1995 (R)** Innocent young Charlotte (Milano) must make a choice between her college boyfriend Chris (Pruett) and a new night-time lover (Kemp) with some decidedly different habits. Seems Charlotte looks exactly like a love lost hundreds of years ago and he's not going to take no for an answer. Also available in an unrated version. **92m/C VHS, DVD.** Alyssa Milano, Martin Kemp, Harrison Pruett, Charlotte Lewis, Jordan Ladd, Rachel True, Jennifer Tilly; *D:* Anne Goursaud; *W:* Halle Eaton, Nicole Coady, Rick Bitzelberger; *C:* Suki Medencevic; *M:* Joseph Williams. **VIDEO**

Embryo ☆☆ *Created to Kill* **1976 (PG)** An average sci-fi drama about a scientist who uses raw genetic material to artificially produce a beautiful woman, with ghastly results. **108m/C VHS, DVD.** Rock Hudson, Barbara Carrera, Diane Ladd, Roddy McDowall, Ann Schedeen, John Elerick, Dr. Joyce Brothers; *D:* Ralph Nelson; *W:* Anita Doohan, Jack W. Thomas; *C:* Fred W. Koenekamp; *M:* Gil Melle.

The Emerald Forest ☆☆☆ **1985 (R)** Bill (Boothe) moves his family to Brazil where he has a job as an engineer working on a dam project. His young son Tommy wanders into the rainforest and is taken in by a primitive tribe of Amazons. Bill searches 10 years for him, finally discovering a happily adjusted teenager named Tomme (Boorman, the director's son), who may not want to return to so-called civilization. An engrossing look at tribal life in the vanishing jungle. Beautifully photographed and based upon a true story. **113m/C VHS, DVD, Wide.** Powers Boothe, Meg Foster, Charley Boorman, Dira Pass, Rui Polonah; *D:* John Boorman; *W:* Rospo Pallenberg; *C:* Philippe Rousselot.

Emerald Jungle ☆½ *Eaten Alive by Cannibals; Eaten Alive; Mangiati Vivi dai Cannibali* **1980** While searching for her missing sister in the jungle, Agren encounters cannibal tribes and a colony of brainwashed cult followers. This Italian feature was cut for its U.S. release. **92m/C VHS.** *IT* Robert Kerman, Janet Agren, Mel Ferrer, Luciano Martino, Mino Loy, Ivan Rassimov, Paola Senatore, Me Me Lay, Meg Fleming, Franco Fantasia; *D:* Umberto Lenzi; *W:* Umberto Lenzi; *C:* Frederico Zanni.

Emerald of Artama ☆ **1967** Anyone viewing the most precious and sought after stone in the history of man does not live to tell about it. **93m/C VHS.** Rory Calhoun.

The Emigrants ☆☆☆ *Utvandrarna* **1972 (PG)** Farmer von Sydow decides to gather his wife (Ullmann) and family together and leave 19th-century Sweden for the promise of a new life in America. Film is divided into their leaving, the voyage over, and the journey to a settlement in

Minnesota. Pacing is somewhat slow; notable cinematography (by director Troell). Adapted from the novels by Vilhelm Moberg. Dubbed into English. Followed by "The New Land." Also edited with the sequel for TV as "The Emigrant Saga." **151m/C VHS.** *SW* Max von Sydow, Liv Ullmann, Allan Edwall, Eddie Axberg, Svenolof Bern, Aina Alfredsson, Monica Zetterlund, Pierre Lindstedt; ***D:*** Jan Troell; ***W:*** Jan Troell, Bengt Forslund; ***C:*** Jan Troell; ***M:*** Erik Nordgren. N.Y. Film Critics '72: Actress (Ullmann).

Emil and the Detectives 🦴🦴½ *Emil Und Die Detektive* **1964** A German ten-year-old is robbed of his grandmother's money by gangsters, and subsequently enlists the help of pre-adolescent detectives to retrieve it. Good Disney dramatization of the Erich Kastner children's novel. Remake of the 1931 German film starring Rolf Wenkhaus. **99m/C VHS.** Bryan Russell, Walter Slezak, Roger Mobley; ***D:*** Peter Tewkesbury; ***W:*** A.J. Carothers.

Emily woof! **1977** Returning from her exclusive Swiss finishing school, licentious young Emily discovers mama is a prostitute and deals with the scalding news by delving into a series of erotic encounters at the hands of her willing "instructors." Stark's first venture into the realm of soft porn. **87m/C VHS.** Koo Stark; ***D:*** Henry Herbert; ***C:*** Jack Hildyard.

Emily Bronte's Wuthering Heights 🦴🦴½ *Wuthering Heights* **1992 (PG)** Miscast version of the tragic tale of doomed lovers Cathy (Binoche) and Heathcliff (Fiennes). While Fiennes may seem too refined for the role, he manages to be both brooding and brutal. However, the beautiful Binoche can't successfully supress her French accent enough to pass for a heedless Yorkshire lass. Good supporting cast, with O'Connor posing as writer/narrator Bronte. **107m/C VHS.** *GB* Ralph Fiennes, Juliette Binoche, Janet McTeer, Sophie Ward, Simon Shepherd, Jeremy Northam, Jason Riddington, Jonathan Firth, Paul Geoffrey, Sinead O'Connor; ***D:*** Peter Kosminsky; ***W:*** Anne Devlin; ***C:*** Mike Southon; ***M:*** Ryuichi Sakamoto.

Eminent Domain 🦴🦴½ **1991 (PG-13)** A communist party member wakes up to find himself stripped of power in a Kafkaesque purge, not knowing what he is accused of—or why. A potent premise, indifferently handled despite filming on location in Poland. Based on actual events that befell the family of scriptwriter Androej Krakowski. **102m/C VHS.** Donald Sutherland, Anne Archer, Paul Freeman, Bernard Hepton, Francoise Michaud, Jodhi May; ***D:*** John Irvin; ***W:*** Andrzej Krakowski, Richard Greggson; ***M:*** Zbigniew Preisner.

Emissary 🦴🦴 **1989 (R)** An American politician and his wife are blackmailed in Africa by the Russians into revealing state secrets that could spark WWIII. **98m/C VHS.** *SA* Robert Vaughn, Ted Leplat, Terry Norton, Andre Jacobs; ***D:*** Jan Scholtz.

Emma 🦴🦴½ **1972** BBC TV version of the Jane Austen saga with young Emma trying her matchmaking skills on all her friends and neighbors—with disastrous results. Mr. Knightly tries to provide both a voice of reason and romance, if only Emma could realize it. **257m/C VHS.** *GB* Doran Goodwin, Vivienne Moore, John Carson, Donald Eccles, Debbie Bowen; ***D:*** John Glenister.

Emma 🦴🦴🦴 **1996 (PG)** Jane Austen's 1816 novel about wealthy, 21-year-old Emma Woodhouse (Paltrow) who makes it her goal to "fix" the lives of all her friends, while ignoring her own problems (the modern adaptation was "Clueless"). Emma focuses much of her attention on Harriet Smith (Collete), a simple young woman who Emma believes is in need of the perfect mate. Meanwhile, Emma neglects to notice the attractive, and exasperated, Mr. Knightley (Northam). McGrath's screenplay makes Emma and Knightley more likable than in the book, but otherwise stays true. After the success of "Sense and Sensibility," Austen's name is making it in the movies in the footsteps of the likes of John Grisham. **120m/C VHS, DVD, Wide.** Gwyneth Paltrow, Jeremy Northam, Greta Scacchi, Toni Collette, Alan Cumming, Juliet Stevenson, Polly Walker, Ewan McGregor, James Cosmo, Sophie Thompson, Phyllida Law; ***D:*** Douglas McGrath; ***W:*** Douglas McGrath; ***C:*** Ian Wilson; ***M:*** Rachel Portman. Oscars '96: Orig. Score.

Emma 🦴🦴🦴 *Jane Austen's Emma* **1997** British TV adaptation of the Jane Austen novel featuring young, matchmaking Emma (Beckinsale) wrecking havoc amongst her friends and neighbors with her would-be romantic alliances. Screenplay is truer to the book, with slightly less likable personalities than the 1996 big-screen version. Excellent cast, and beautiful locations and costumes make this one worth seeing. A&E Network offered "Emma" after the overwhelming success of their miniseries "Pride and Prejudice," also adapted from Austen. **107m/C VHS, DVD.** *GB* Kate Beckinsale, Mark Strong, Samantha Bond, Prunella Scales, Bernard Hepton, Raymond Coulthard, Dominic Rowan, James Hazeldine, Samantha Morton, Lucy Robinson, Olivia Williams; ***D:*** Diarmuid Lawrence; ***W:*** Andrew Davis.

Emmanuelle 🦴🦴½ **1974** Filmed in Bangkok, a young, beautiful woman is introduced by her husband to an uninhibited world of sensuality. Above-average soft-core skin film, made with sophistication and style. Kristel maintains a vulnerability and awareness, never becoming a mannequin. **92m/C VHS, DVD.** *FR* Sylvia Kristel, Alain Cuny, Marika Green, Daniel Sarky; ***D:*** Just Jaeckin; ***W:*** Jean-Louis Richard; ***C:*** Richard Suzuki; ***M:*** Pierre Bachelet.

Emmanuelle 4 🦴 **1984 (R)** Emmanuelle flees a bad relationship and undergoes plastic surgery to mask her identity. Ultimately, she becomes a beautiful young model in the form of a different actress, of course. **95m/C VHS.** *FR* Sylvia Kristel, Mia Nygren, Patrick Bauchau; ***D:*** Francis Giacobetti.

Emmanuelle 5 🦴½ **1987 (R)** This time around sexy Emmanuelle flees aboard a convenient yacht when she's chased by adoring fans at the Cannes Film Festival. But she winds up being forced to join an Arab sheik's harem of slaves. A good example of a series that should have quit while it was ahead. **78m/C VHS, DVD.** *FR* Monique Gabrielle, Charles Foster; ***D:*** Steve Barnett, Walerian Borowczyk; ***M:*** Pierre Bachelet.

Emmanuelle 6 🦴 **1992 (R)** The saga of the sexy beauty continues. This time Emmanuelle and a group of models head for the paradise of an Amazon jungle where they promptly become the prized captives of a drug lord. **80m/C VHS, DVD.**

Emmanuelle & Joanna 🦴 **1986** A mistreated newlywed bride goes to her sister's whorehouse and stumbles across lots of soft-core antics. **90m/C VHS.** *FR* Sherry Buchanan, Danielle Dublino.

Emmanuelle in the Country 🦴 **1978** Emmanuelle becomes a nurse in an attempt to bring comfort and other pleasures to those in need. **90m/C VHS.** *FR* Laura Gemser.

Emmanuelle on Taboo Island 🦴½ **1976 (R)** Marooned young man discovers a beautiful woman on his island. This delights him. **95m/C VHS.** *FR* Laura Gemser, Paul(o) Giusti, Arthur Kennedy.

Emmanuelle, the Joys of a Woman 🦴 *Emmanuelle l'Antivierge; Emmanuelle's 7th Heaven; Emmanuelle 2* **1976** The amorous exploits of a sensuous, liberated couple take them and their erotic companions to exotic Hong Kong, Bangkok, and Bali. **92m/C VHS, DVD, 8mm.** *FR* Sylvia Kristel, Umberto Orsini, Catherine Rivet, Frederic Lagache, Laura Gemser, Henri Czarniak, Tom Clark, Caroline Laurence; ***D:*** Francis Giacobetti; ***W:*** Francis Giacobetti, Jean-Marc Vasseur; ***C:*** Robert Fraisse; ***M:*** Pierre Bachelet, Francis Lai.

Emmanuelle, the Queen 🦴 **1975** Seeking revenge, Emmanuelle plots the murder of her sadistic husband. The lecherous assassin she hires tries to blackmail her, and she challenges him at his own game of deadly seduction. **90m/C VHS.** Laura Gemser.

Emmanuelle's Daughter 🦴 **1979** A Greek-made thriller in which a vapidly sensuous heroine cavorts amid episodes of murder, blackmail, and rape. **91m/C** *GR* Laura Gemser, Gabriele Tinti, Livia Russa, Vagelis Varton, Nadia Neri.

Emma's Shadow 🦴🦴🦴 *Skyggen af Emma* **1988** In the 1930s, a young girl fakes her own kidnapping to get away from her inattentive family and comes to befriend an ex-convict sewer worker. In Danish with English subtitles. Winner of the Prix de la Jeunesse at Cannes, it was voted 1988's Best Danish Film. **93m/C VHS.** *DK* Borje Ahlstedt, Line Kruse; ***D:*** Soeren Kragh-Jacobsen; ***W:*** Soeren Kragh-Jacobsen; ***C:*** Dan Laustsen.

The Emperor and the Assassin 🦴🦴 **1999 (R)** Sumptuous historical drama (and a complicated storyline) concerns a united China's first emperor. Set in 320 B.C., China is a collection of seven rival kingdoms with Ying Zheng, the King of Qin (Xuejian) obsessed with uniting the country and then dividing it into provinces for proper ruling (with himself as supreme head). Naturally, this means war. Also involved is his lover, Lady Zhao (Li), who plans a fake assassination attempt to aid Zheng. But the assassin she chooses, Jing Ke (Fengyi), is trying to reform and things don't go exactly according to plan. Remember—power corrupts. Mandarin with subtitles. **161m/C VHS, DVD, Wide.** *CH* Li Xuejian, Gong Li, Zhang Fengyi, Wang Zhiwen, Sun Zhou, Chen Kaige; ***D:*** Chen Kaige; ***W:*** Chen Kaige, Wang Peigong; ***C:*** Zhao Fei; ***M:*** Zhao Jiping.

Emperor Jones 🦴🦴½ **1933** Loosely based on Eugene O'Neill's play, film portrays the rise and fall of a railroad porter whose exploits take him from a life sentence on a chain gang to emperor of Haiti. Robeson recreates his stage role in his first screen appearance. **72m/B VHS.** Paul Robeson, Dudley Digges, Frank Wilson, Fredi Washington, Ruby Elzy; ***D:*** Dudley Murphy. Natl. Film Reg. '99.

Emperor of the Bronx 🦴 **1989** A look at crime, sleaze, violence, and the actions of bad guys in the inner-city. **90m/C VHS.** William Smith.

Emperor of the North Pole 🦴🦴🦴 *Emperor of the North* **1973 (PG)** Violent and well-done tale of hobos riding the rails during the Depression has Marvin as A#1, a legendary hobo who can get on any train, and his protege Cigaret (Carradine), trying to catch a ride on the train of sadistic conductor Shack (Borgnine), who's been known to kill to keep the hobos away. Tense and gritty, with the usual tight direction of Aldridge, beautiful cinematography, and a gripping screenplay. Borgnine is exceptional among a very strong cast. **118m/C VHS.** Lee Marvin, Ernest Borgnine, Keith Carradine, Charles Tyner, Malcolm Atterbury, Simon Oakland, Harry Caesar, Hal Baylor, Matt Clark, Elisha Cook Jr., Liam Dunn, Robert Foulk, Ray Guth, Sid Haig, Vic Tayback; ***D:*** Robert Aldrich; ***W:*** Christopher Knopf; ***C:*** Joseph Biroc.

Emperor Waltz 🦴🦴½ **1948** Typical Hollywood musical finds phonograph salesman Crosby travelling to Vienna, hoping to sell his goods to the Austrian royal family of Emperor Franz Joseph. He meets up with the Emperor's snobby niece (Fontaine) and attempts to charm her into an audience with her royal uncle. Naturally the two fall in love and everything ends in a happy fade-out. ♫The Emperor's Waltz; Friendly Mountains; Get Yourself a Phonograph; The Kiss in Your Eyes; I Kiss Your Hand, Madame; The Whistler and His Dog. **106m/C VHS.** Bing Crosby, Joan Fontaine, Roland Culver, Richard Haydn, Lucile Watson, Sig Rumann, Harold Vermilyea; ***D:*** Billy Wilder; ***W:*** Billy Wilder, Charles Brackett; ***C:*** George Barnes; ***M:*** Victor Young.

The Emperor's New Clothes **1984** The story of an emperor and the unusual outfit he gets from his tailor. A "Faerie Tale Theatre" presentation. **60m/C VHS.** Art Carney, Alan Arkin, Dick Shawn; ***D:*** Peter Medak; ***Nar:*** Timothy Dalton. CABLE

The Emperor's New Groove 🦴🦴🦴 **2000 (G)** Animated fantasy about self-centered young emperor Kusco (Spade) who gets turned into a llama by sorceress Yzma (Kitt) and must team up with peasant Pacha (Goodman) to get his throne back. Refreshingly devoid of "important lessons" and sappy pop tunes, the only mission here is to provide laughs, and that it does. Like the great Warner Bros. cartoons of old, sarcastic and sophisticated humor abounds (Spade really helps out here), and the sidekicks get plenty of face (and hero) time, not to mention some of the best lines, including Warburton as Yzma's distracted and clumsy right-hand villain, Kronk. **79m/C VHS, DVD, Wide.** ***D:*** Mark Dindal; ***W:*** Dave Reynolds; ***M:*** John Debney; ***V:*** David Spade, John Goodman, Eartha Kitt, Patrick Warburton, Wendie Malick, Patti Deutsch, John Fiedler, Kellyann Kelso, Eli Russell Linnetz. Broadcast Film Critics '00: Song ("My Funny Friend and Me").

The Emperor's Shadow 🦴🦴 *Qin Song* **1996** Saga of two boyhood friends in China around 220 BC. Gao Jianli (You) is a famous musician and the childhood friend of powerful Emperor Ying Sheng (Wen). Jianli basically wants to be left alone to work on his music but the Emperor demands he stick around and compose a stirring imperial anthem. Add into the mix Yueyang (Qing), the Emperor's daughter who has the hots for the musician (and vice versa) although she's betrothed to another, and tragedy is bound to be the result. Mandarin with subtitles. **123m/C VHS, DVD.** *CH* Ge You, Jiang Wen, Xu Qing; ***D:*** Zhou Xiaowen; ***W:*** Wei Lu; ***C:*** Lu Gengxin; ***M:*** Jiping Zhao.

The Empire of Passion 🦴🦴🦴 **1976** A peasant woman and her low-life lover kill the woman's husband, but find the future they planned with each other is not to be. The husband's ghost returns to haunt them, and destroy the passionate bond which led to the murder. Oshima's follow-up to "In the Realm of the Senses." In Japanese with English subtitles. **110m/C VHS.** *JP* Nagisa Oshima, Kazuko Yoshiyuki, Tatsuya Fuji, Takahiro Tamura, Takuzo Kawatani; ***D:*** Nagisa Oshima. Cannes '78: Director (Oshima).

Empire of the Ants 🦴½ **1977 (PG)** A group of enormous, nuclear, unfriendly ants stalk a real estate dealer and prospective buyers of undeveloped oceanfront property. Story originated by master science-fiction storyteller H. G. Wells. **90m/C VHS, DVD.** Joan Collins, Robert Lansing, John David Carson, Albert Salmi, Jacqueline Scott, Robert Pine; ***D:*** Bert I. Gordon; ***W:*** Bert I. Gordon; ***C:*** Reginald Morris.

Empire of the Sun 🦴🦴🦴 **1987 (PG)** Spielberg's mature, extraordinarily vivid return to real storytelling, from the best-selling J.G. Ballard novel. Yearns to be a great film, but occasional flat spots keep it slightly out of contention. Young, wealthy British Jim (Bale) lives in Shanghai, but is thrust into a life of poverty and discomfort when China is invaded by Japan at the onset of WWII and he's separated from his family and interred in a prison camp. A mysterious, breathtaking work, in which Spielberg's heightened juvenile romanticism has a real, heartbreaking context. Two other 1987 releases explore the WWII memories of young boys: "Au Revoir Les Enfants" and "Hope and Glory." **153m/C VHS, DVD, 8mm, Wide.** Christian Bale, John Malkovich, Miranda Richardson, Nigel Havers, Joe Pantoliano, Leslie Phillips, Rupert Frazer, Ben Stiller, Robert Stephens, Burt Kwouk, Masato Ibu, Emily Richard, David Neidorf, Ralph Seymour, Emma Piper, Peter Gale, Zhai Nai She, Guts Ishimatsu, J.G. Ballard; ***D:*** Steven Spielberg; ***W:*** Tom Stoppard, Menno Meyjes; ***C:*** Allen Daviau; ***M:*** John Williams. Natl. Bd. of Review '87: Director (Spielberg).

Empire Records 🦴🦴 **1995 (PG-13)** Well, the soundtrack's good and that's about all this frantic movie has going for it (besides a photogenic cast). Joe's (LaPaglia), the manager of an independent record store about to be taken over by a faceless conglomerate unless he and his young-and-crisis-prone staff can come up with the cash to buy the place within 24 hours. **91m/C VHS, DVD, Wide.** Anthony LaPaglia, Rory Cochrane, Liv Tyler, Renee Zellweger, Johnny Whitworth, Robin Tunney, Ethan (Randall) Embry, Maxwell Caulfield, Debi Mazar; ***D:*** Allan Moyle; ***W:*** Carol Heikkinen; ***C:*** Walt Lloyd; ***M:*** Mitchell Leib.

Empire State 1987 (R) When his friend disappears from a posh London nightclub, a young man searches for him and finds more action and intrigue than he can handle. Even so, this movie's still pretty bland. **102m/C VHS.** *GB* Cathryn Harrison, Martin Landau, Ray McAnally; *D:* Ron Peck.

The Empire Strikes Back *Star Wars: Episode 5—The Empire Strikes Back* 1980 (PG) Second film in the epic "Star Wars" trilogy finds young Luke Skywalker and the Rebel Alliance plotting new strategies as they prepare to battle the evil Darth Vader and the forces of the Dark Side. Luke learns the ways of a Jedi knight from master Yoda, while Han and Leia find time for romance and a few adventures of their own. Introduces the charismatic Lando Calrissian and a mind-numbing secret from Vadar. Offers the same superb special effects and hearty plot as set by 1977's excellent "Star Wars." Followed by "Return of the Jedi" in 1983. **124m/C VHS, Wide.** Mark Hamill, Carrie Fisher, Harrison Ford, Billy Dee Williams, Alec Guinness, David Prowse, Kenny Baker, Frank Oz, Anthony Daniels, Peter Mayhew, Clive Revill, Julian Glover, John Ratzenberger, Jeremy Bulloch; *D:* Irvin Kershner; *W:* Leigh Brackett, Lawrence Kasdan; *C:* Peter Suschitzsky; *M:* John Williams; *V:* James Earl Jones. Oscars '80: Sound, Visual FX.

Employees' Entrance 1933 William stars as a ruthless department store manager in this story about commerce and compromise during the Depression. Young gives an excellent performance as the wife of one of his employees. Outrageous, and racy, this pre-Code film was expertly directed by veteran craftsman Del Ruth. Based on a play by David Boehm. **74m/B VHS.** Warren William, Loretta Young, Wallace Ford, Alice White, Allen Jenkins; *D:* Roy Del Ruth; *W:* Robert Presnell.

The Empty Beach ½ 1985 A tough private detective investigates the disappearance of a wealthy business tycoon. **87m/C VHS.** *AU* Bryan Brown, Anna Maria Monticelli; *D:* Chris Thomson.

An Empty Bed 1990 Award-winning independent production depicting Bill Frayne, an older homosexual, and the challenges of his everyday life. Told mostly in flashbacks as Bill encounters people and places during the course of one day, this is a delicate drama with important statements about homosexuality, aging and honesty. **60m/C VHS.** John Wylie, Mark Clifford Smith, Conan McCarty, Dorothy Stinnette, Kevin Kelly, Thomas Hill, Harriet Bass; *D:* Mark Gasper; *W:* Mark Gasper.

Empty Canvas ½ *La Noia: L'Ennui Et Sa Diversion, L'Erotisme* 1964 A spiritually bankrupt artist becomes obsessively jealous of his mistress who refuses to marry him in the hope that someone better will come along. Based on the Alberto Moravia novel. **118m/B VHS.** *FR IT* Horst Buchholz, Catherine Spaak, Bette Davis; *D:* Damiano Damiani; *M:* Luis Bacalov.

The Empty Mirror 1999 (PG-13) Boring fictionalized account of Hitler's (Rodway) final hours, hidden away in his bunker, as he realizes his Third Reich dreams have come to nothing. He does a lot of ranting but what is more interesting are the clips from Leni Riefenstahl's "Triumph of the Will" that are screened behind him. **108m/C VHS.** Norman Rodway, Joel Grey, Camilla Soeberg, Glenn Shadix, Peter Michael Goetz, Doug McKeon; *D:* Barry J. Hershey; *W:* Barry J. Hershey, R. Buckingham; *C:* Frederick Elmes; *M:* John (Gianni) Frizzell.

Enchanted April ½ 1992 (PG) Lotte (Lawrence) and Rose (Richardson), tired of their overbearing husbands, rent a villa in Portofino, Italy, for a month with two other very different women—Lady Caroline (Walker), a beautiful but bored socialite, and crusty old Mrs. Fisher (Plowright), who has an impeccable literary pedigree. The effects of the charming villa, with plenty of wisteria and sunshine, do wonders for the women. A charming and romantic period piece. Based on the 1922 novel by Elizabeth von Arnim. **93m/C VHS.** *GB* Miranda Richardson, Joan Plowright, Josie Lawrence, Polly Walker, Alfred Molina, Jim Broadbent, Michael Kitchen, Adriana Fachetti; *D:* Mike Newell; *W:* Peter Barnes; *C:* Richard Maidment; *M:* Richard Rodney Bennett. Golden Globes '93: Actress—Mus./Comedy (Richardson), Support. Actress (Plowright).

The Enchanted Cottage ½ 1945 Represents Hollywood's "love conquers all" fantasy hokum, as a disfigured war vet and a homely girl retreat from the horrors of the world into a secluded cottage, where they both regain youth and beauty. A four-tissue heart-tugger. Adopted from the Arthur Pinero play. **91m/B VHS.** Dorothy McGuire, Robert Young, Herbert Marshall, Mildred Natwick, Spring Byington, Hillary Brooke, Richard Gaines, Robert Clarke; *D:* John Cromwell.

The Enchanted Forest ½ 1945 An elderly man teaches a boy about life and the beauty of nature when the boy gets lost in a forest. **78m/C VHS, DVD.** *AR* Harry Davenport, Edmund Lowe, Brenda Joyce; *D:* Lew (Louis Friedlander) Landers.

Enchanted Island ½ 1958 Sailor stops on an island to find provisions and ends up falling in love with a cannibal princess. Thinly based upon Herman Melville's "Typee." **94m/C VHS.** Jane Powell, Dana Andrews, Arthur Shields; *D:* Allan Dwan.

The Enchantress ½ *I Skiachtra* 1985 A daring boy experiences his first true loves and passions when he journeys through a mystical land in order to find a beautiful fairy. In Greek with subtitles. **93m/C VHS.** *GR* Alkis Kourkoulos, Sofia Aliberti, Lily Kokodi, Antogone Amanitou, Vicky Koulianou, Nicols Papaconstantinou, Stratos Pachis; *D:* Manoussos Manoussakis.

Encino Man *California Man* 1992 (PG) Two, like, totally uncool Valley dudes dig up a 10,000-year-old caveman in the backyard. After giving him a makeover and teaching him the necessities like the four basic food groups (Milk Duds in the dairy group, Sweet Tarts in the fruit group), they use the gnarly caveman as their ticket to popularity and dates to the prom. Juvenile humor appealing to teens; strictly brain candy. **88m/C VHS, DVD.** Sean Astin, Brendan Fraser, Pauly Shore, Megan Ward, Robin Tunney, Ric(k) Ducommun, Mariette Hartley, Richard Masur, Michael DeLuise; *D:* Les Mayfield; *W:* Shawn Schepps; *C:* Robert Brinkmann. Golden Raspberries '92: Worst New Star (Shore).

Encore 1952 The third W. Somerset Maugham omnibus (following "Quartet" and "Trio") which includes: "Winter Cruise," "The Ant and the Grasshopper," and "Gigolo and Gigolette." **85m/B VHS.** *GB* Nigel Patrick, Kay Walsh, Roland Culver, John Laurie, Glynis Johns, Ronald Squire, Noel Purcell, Peter Graves; *D:* Pat Jackson, Anthony Pelissier, Harold French; *W:* Eric Ambler.

Encounter at Raven's Gate ½ 1988 (R) Punk rockers and extraterrestrials meet amid hard rock and gallons of gore. **85m/C VHS.** Eddie Cleary, Steven Vidler; *D:* Rolf de Heer.

Encounter with the Unknown ½ 1975 Relates three fully documented supernatural events including a death prophesy and a ghost. **90m/C VHS.** Rosie Holotik, Gene Ross; *D:* Harry Z. Thomason; *Nar:* Rod Serling.

The End 1978 (R) Reynolds plays a young man who discovers he is terminally ill. He decides not to prolong his suffering and attempts various tried-and-true methods for committing suicide, receiving riotous but incompetent help from the crazed DeLuise. **100m/C VHS, DVD, Wide.** Burt Reynolds, Sally Field, Dom DeLuise, Carl Reiner, Joanne Woodward, Robby Benson, Kristy McNichol, Norman Fell, Pat O'Brien, Myrna Loy, David Steinberg; *D:* Burt Reynolds; *W:* Jerry Belson; *C:* Bobby Byrne; *M:* Paul Williams.

End of August 1982 (PG) A spinster of New Orleans Creole aristocracy, circa 1900, breaks out of her sheltered life and experiences new sexual and romantic awareness. Adapted from "The Awakening" by Kate Chopin. **104m/C VHS.** Sally Sharp, David Marshall Grant, Paul Roebling; *D:* Bob Graham; *W:* Anna Thomas, Gregory Nava; *C:* Robert Elswit.

End of Days 1999 (R) Alcoholic ex-cop Jericho Cane (Schwarzenegger) becomes a reluctant savior, who must battle a literal Satan (Byrne) who has the opportunity to rule both Heaven and Hell if he can make young Christine (Tunney) his bride before the millennial midnight. There's lots of action, Arnold looks great (post heart surgery), and Byrne is a very sexy devil but there's also an excessive amount of gore and silly mumbo-jumbo to suffer through. **123m/C VHS, DVD.** Arnold Schwarzenegger, Gabriel Byrne, Robin Tunney, Kevin Pollak, CCH Pounder, Rod Steiger, Derrick O'Connor, Miriam Margolyes, Udo Kier; *D:* Peter Hyams; *W:* Andrew Marlowe; *C:* Peter Hyams; *M:* John Debney.

End of Desire 1962 Schell discovers that her husband, Marquand, has married her for her money and is having an affair with the maid in this melodrama based on De Maupassant's story, "Une Vie." A period piece that is a little on the slow side. In French with English subtitles. **86m/C VHS.** *FR* Maria Schell, Christian Marquand, Pascale Petit, Ivan Desny; *D:* Alexandre Astruc.

The End of Innocence 1990 (R) In her attempts to please everyone in her life, a woman experiences a nervous breakdown. Released two years after Schaeffer's murder. **102m/C VHS.** Dyan Cannon, John Heard, George Coe, Lola Mason, Rebecca Schaeffer, Stephen Meadows, Billie Bird, Michael Madsen, Madge Sinclair, Renee Taylor, Viveka Davis; *D:* Dyan Cannon; *W:* Dyan Cannon; *M:* Michael Convertino.

The End of St. Petersburg ½ 1927 A Russian peasant becomes a scab during a workers' strike in 1914. He is then forced to enlist in the army prior to the 1917 October Revolution. Fascinating, although propagandistic film commissioned by the then-new Soviet government. Silent. **75m/B VHS.** Ivan Chuvelov; *D:* Vsevolod Pudovkin.

End of Summer ½ 1997 (R) Bisset's performance is the highlight of this romantic drama. She's spinster Christine Van Buren who is spending the summer at a Saratoga Springs resort, circa 1890. She's stunned to encounter Theo (Weller), the man she loved and lost 20 years before. Christine and Theo are both willing to take a second chance but soon others are complicating the situation. **95m/C VHS.** Jacqueline Bisset, Peter Weller, Julian Sands, Amy Locane, Elizabeth Shepherd, Michael Hogan; *D:* Linda Yellen; *W:* Linda Yellen, Jonathan Platnick; *C:* David Bridges; *M:* Patrick Seymour. **CABLE**

End of the Affair 1955 In WWII London, Sarah (Kerr), the wife of a British civil servant (Cushing), falls in love with her neighbor Maurice (Johnson). The two make plans for their future together, but suddenly and mysteriously, Sarah brings the affair to an end. **105m/B DVD, Wide.** *GB* Deborah Kerr, Van Johnson, John Mills, Peter Cushing; *D:* Edward Dmytryk; *W:* Lenore Coffee; *C:* Wilkie Cooper; *M:* Benjamin Frankel.

The End of the Affair 1999 (R) During the Blitz of WWII, married Londoner Sarah Miles (Moore) suddenly breaks off her affair with writer Maurice Bendrix (Fiennes). An unexpected meeting with her husband, Henry (Rea), leads Bendrix to believe Sarah is having a new affair and he hires a detective (Hart) to follow her. Instead, Bendrix discovers her reasons for breaking off with him and her spiritual reawakening. Compellingly adult drama about love, faith, and moral dilemmas that is based on the 1955 novel by Graham Greene. **101m/C VHS, DVD, Wide.** *GB* Ralph Fiennes, Julianne Moore, Stephen Rea, Ian Hart, Sam Bould, Jason Isaacs; *D:* Neil Jordan; *W:* Neil Jordan; *C:* Roger Pratt; *M:* Michael Nyman. British Acad. '99: Adapt. Screenplay.

End of the Line ½ 1988 (PG) Two old-time railroad workers steal a locomotive for a cross-country jaunt to protest the closing of the local railroad company. Produced by Steenburgen. **103m/C VHS.** Wilford Brimley, Levon Helm, Mary Steenburgen, Kevin Bacon, Holly Hunter, Barbara Barrie, Bob Balaban, Howard Morris, Bruce McGill, Clint Howard, Trey Wilson, Rita Jenrette; *D:* Jay Russell; *W:* John Wohlbruck; *M:* Andy Summers.

End of the Road ½ 1970 (X) Keach is a troubled college professor whose bizarre treatment by his psychologist (Jones) produces tragic results. He eventually enters into an affair with the wife of a co-worker. Fascinating, if uneven script adapted from John Barth's story. Rated X upon release for adult story and nudity. **110m/C VHS.** Stacy Keach, James Earl Jones, James Coco, Harris Yulin, Dorothy Tristan; *D:* Aram Avakian; *W:* Terry Southern; *C:* Gordon Willis.

End of the World woof! 1976 (PG) A coffee machine explodes, sending a man through a window and into a neon sign, where he is electrocuted. A priest witnesses this and retreats to a convent where he meets his alien double and heads for more trouble with outer space invaders. Interesting premise. **88m/C VHS.** Christopher Lee, Sue Lyon, Lew Ayres, MacDonald Carey, Dean Jagger, Kirk Scott; *D:* John Hayes; *M:* Andrew Belling.

The End of Violence 1997 (R) Slick, manipulative action-movie producer Mike Max (Pullman) evolves from his Hollywood roots to tranquility as a gardener after his own life is touched by the violence so pervasive in his pictures. There's a sinister government agent (Benzali) and a reclusive surveillance expert (Byrne) and Max gets kidnapped, only the kidnappers mysteriously wind up dead, and then he disappears. And, no, the plot doesn't really make much sense and all the characters are paranoid anyway. But it does give you something to try to figure out. Director Wenders drastically re-edited his movie after its lukewarm work-in-progress appearance at the 1997 Cannes Film Festival. **122m/C VHS, DVD.** *FR* Bill Pullman, Gabriel Byrne, Andie MacDowell, Daniel Benzali, Traci Lind, Rosalind Chao, Loren Dean, Nicole Parker, Enrique Castillo, K. Todd Freeman, John Diehl, Pruitt Taylor Vince, Peter Horton, Udo Kier, Marshall Bell, Frederic Forrest, Henry Silva, Samuel Fuller; *D:* Wim Wenders; *W:* Nicholas Klein; *C:* Pascal Rabaud; *M:* Ry Cooder.

Endangered ½ 1994 Environmentalists battle bad guys for survival in the wilderness. **91m/C VHS.** Rick Aiello, Martin Kove, Sandra Hess, Tim Quill, Richard Hench, Dale Dye, Craig Alan, Kent MacLachlan, Renee Estevez; *D:* Nick Kellis; *W:* Nick Kellis.

Endangered Species ½ 1982 (R) Offbeat thriller with sci-fi leanings about a retired New York cop on vacation in America's West who is drawn into a female sheriff's investigation of a mysterious series of cattle killings. Could it be UFOs? Based on a true story. **97m/C VHS.** Robert Urich, JoBeth Williams, Paul Dooley, Hoyt Axton, Peter Coyote, Harry Carey Jr., Dan Hedaya, John Considine; *D:* Alan Rudolph; *W:* Alan Rudolph, John Binder.

Endgame 1985 Grotesquely deformed survivors of WWIII fight their way out of radioactive New York City to seek a better life. **98m/C VHS.** Al Oliver, Moira Chen, Jack Davis, Bobby Rhodes, Jill Elliot; *D:* Steve Benson.

Endless Descent woof! *La Grieta* 1990 (R) At least it seems endless. A group of scientist-types set out in search of a sunken sub, but somehow take a wrong turn into the rift, the deepest chasm at the bottom of the sea. There, they discover unimaginable horrors—that is, if you've never seen "Alien," or just about any other icky-monster flick. A Spanish film, shot in English, by director Simon, whose other works of art include "Pieces" and "Slugs." **79m/C VHS.** *SP* Jack Scalia, R. Lee Ermey, Ray Wise, Deborah Adair, Ely Pouget; *D:* J(uan) Piquer Simon; *W:* David Coleman.

The Endless Game 1989 (PG-13) Cold War suspenser has British secret-agent-man Finney attempting to solve the murder of his erstwhile fellow agent-lover, much to the dismay of the government. Written by director Forbes, this cable would-be thriller is a decidedly mediocre waste of a talented cast. Also of note, it was actor-director Sir Anthony Quayle's final appearance. **123m/C VHS.** *GB* Albert Finney, George Segal, Derek De Lint, Monica Guerritore, Ian Holm, John Standing, Anthony

Quayle, Kristin Scott Thomas; ***M:*** Ennio Morricone. **CABLE**

Endless Love 🦴🦴 **1981 (R)** Although only 17, David and Jade are in love. Her parents think they are too serious and demand that the two spend time apart. David attempts to win her parents' affection and approval, goes mad in the process, and commits a foolish act (he burns the house down) that threatens their love forever. Based on the novel by Scott Spencer. Of interest only to those with time on their hands or smitten by a love so bad that this movie will seem grand in comparison. Features Cruise's first film appearance. **115m/C VHS.** Brooke Shields, Martin Hewitt, Don Murray, Shirley Knight, Beatrice Straight, Richard Kiley, Tom Cruise, James Spader, Robert Moore, Jami Gertz; ***D:*** Franco Zeffirelli; ***W:*** Judith Rascoe; ***C:*** David Watkin.

Endless Night 🦴🦴 *Agatha Christie's Endless Night* **1971** An adaptation of an Agatha Christie tale. Focuses on a young chauffeur who wants to build a dream house, and his chance meeting with an American heiress. **95m/C VHS, DVD, Wide.** *GB* Hayley Mills, Hywel Bennett, Britt Ekland, George Sanders, Per Oscarsson, Peter Bowles; ***D:*** Sidney Gilliat; ***W:*** Sidney Gilliat; ***C:*** Harry Waxman; ***M:*** Bernard Herrmann.

The Endless Summer 🦴🦴🦴 **1966** Classic surfing documentary about the freedom and sense of adventure that surfing symbolizes. Director Brown follows two young surfers around the world in search of the perfect wave. (They finally find it at a then-unknown break off Cape Saint Francis in South America.) Besides the excellent surfing photography, Big Kahuna Brown provides the amusing tongue-in-cheek narrative. Considered by many to be the best surf movie ever. **90m/C VHS, DVD.** Mike Hynson, Robert August; ***D:*** Bruce Brown; ***W:*** Bruce Brown; ***Nar:*** Bruce Brown.

The Endless Summer 2 🦴🦴🦴 *Bruce Brown's The Endless Summer 2* **1994 (PG)** You don't have to personally hang ten to get stoked about this long-awaited sequel that once again follows two surfer dudes in their quest for the perfect wave. This time out pro surfers O'Connell and Weaver circle the globe seeking adventure and the world's best waves. Traces the evolution of surfing from the lazy, golden days of the '60s to the worldwide phenomenon it is today, complete with its own pro tour circuit. Breathtaking scenery and spectacular surfing sequences highlight this look at a unique subculture. Thirty years later and it's still a great ride, though the travelogue wears thin and the sub-culture's now fairly well exploited. **107m/C VHS.** Robert "Wingnut" Weaver, Pat O'Connell, Robert August; ***D:*** Bruce Brown; ***W:*** Bruce Brown, Dana Brown; ***Nar:*** Bruce Brown.

Endplay 🦴🦴½ **1975** An Australian-made crime/horror drama in which two brothers cover for each other in a series of murders involving blonde hitchhikers. Based on a novel by Russell Braddon. **110m/C VHS.** *AU* George Mallaby, John Waters, Ken Goodiet, Delvene Delaney, Charles Tingwell, Robert Hewett, Kevin Miles; ***D:*** Tim Burstall.

Enemies, a Love Story 🦴🦴🦴½ **1989 (R)** A wonderfully resonant, subtle tragedy based on the novel by Isaac Bashevis Singer. A post-Holocaust Jew, living in Coney Island, can't choose between three women—his current wife (who hid him during the war), his tempestuous lover, and his reappearing pre-war wife he presumed dead. A hilarious, confident tale told with grace and patience. **119m/C VHS.** Ron Silver, Lena Olin, Anjelica Huston, Margaret Sophie Stein, Paul Mazursky, Alan King, Judith Malina, Rita Karin, Phil Leeds, Elya Baskin, Marie-Adele Lemieux; ***D:*** Paul Mazursky; ***W:*** Paul Mazursky; ***C:*** Fred Murphy; ***M:*** Maurice Jarre. N.Y. Film Critics '89: Director (Mazursky), Support. Actress (Olin); Natl. Soc. Film Critics '89: Support. Actress (Huston).

The Enemy 🦴🦴½ **2001 (R)** Mike Ashton (Perry) lives in Canada with his retired chemist father (Buchholz) who has been keeping secrets from his son. But they don't stay hidden when the bad guys come looking for dad and his work on bio-weapons making. A kidnapping attempt and a murder bring in the authorities, including Penny (d'Abo) who has a past with Mike and isn't adverse to fanning some flames. Story gets too convoluted for its own good but the pace is fast. **98m/C VHS, DVD, Wide.** Luke Perry, Olivia D'Abo, Roger Moore, Horst Buchholz, Tom Conti, Hendrick Haese; ***D:*** Tom Kinninmont, Charlie Watson; ***W:*** John Penney; ***C:*** Mike Garfath; ***M:*** Gast Waltzing.

Enemy at the Gates 🦴🦴 **2000 (R)** World War II saga set during the siege of Stalingrad in 1942 as Russian sniper Zaitsev (Law) tracks his equal in German sniper Konig (Harris). Law is also involved in a romantic triangle with a female Russian soldier (Weisz) and smarmy commissar Danilov (Fiennes). Only the sniper story is based on actual events and real people, from William Craig's historical account. Otherwise, the story as put on screen leaves out a lot, namely any real exploration of either the German or the Russian social and political stances of the time. We're left with good-looking men shooting it out in front of dramatic scenery, and a World War II lacking historical commentary. **131m/C VHS, DVD, Wide.** *GE GB IR US* Jude Law, Ed Harris, Joseph Fiennes, Rachel Weisz, Bob Hoskins, Gabriel Marshall-Thomson, Eva Mattes, Ron Perlman, Matthias Habich; ***D:*** Jean-Jacques Annaud; ***W:*** Jean-Jacques Annaud, Alain Godard; ***C:*** Robert Fraisse; ***M:*** James Horner.

Enemy Below 🦴🦴🦴 **1957** Suspenseful WWII sea epic, in which an American destroyer and a German U-Boat chase one another and square off in the South Atlantic. **98m/C VHS.** Robert Mitchum, Curt Jurgens, David Hedison, Theodore Bikel, Doug McClure, Russell Collins; ***D:*** Dick Powell.

Enemy Gold 🦴½ **1993 (R)** A crime czar and a beautiful killer without a conscience go after federal agents who have stumbled across a cache of Confederate gold. Basically, a babes-with-guns blowout. **92m/C VHS.** Bruce Penhall, Rodrigo Obregon, Mark Barriere, Suzi Simpson, Tai Collins, Julie Strain; ***D:*** Drew Sidaris; ***W:*** Wess Rahn, Christian Sidaris.

Enemy Mine 🦴🦴 **1985 (PG-13)** A space fantasy in which two pilots from warring planets, one an Earthling, the other an asexual reptilian Drac, crash land on a barren planet and are forced to work together to survive. **108m/C VHS, DVD, Wide.** Dennis Quaid, Louis Gossett Jr., Brion James, Richard Marcus, Lance Kerwin, Carolyn McCormick; ***D:*** Wolfgang Petersen; ***W:*** Edward Khmara; ***C:*** Tony Imi; ***M:*** Maurice Jarre.

Enemy of the Law 🦴🦴½ **1945** Texas rangers battle evil in an old frontier town. **59m/B VHS.** Tex Ritter, Dave O'Brien; ***D:*** Harry Fraser.

Enemy of the State 🦴🦴½ **1998 (R)** Paranoia-thriller shows what the nerds would do if they really wanted revenge. After a friend slips him a videocassette without his knowledge, lawyer Robert Dean (Smith) is targeted by a surveillance-and-gizmo-happy government agency headed by the sinister Reynolds (Voight). They hound Dean relentlessly, cutting him off from everything he holds dear by ruining his career and marriage, forcing him underground. Just when he has no place left to turn, he is aided by Brill (Hackman), a remorseful ex-agent who helped create the cyber-surveillance monster. From this point, our two heroes bicker, buddy-film fashion, and things blow up until the inevitable shootout crescendo. Smith's good guy vibe sustains interest in tale of technology run amok. **132m/C VHS, DVD.** Bodhi (Pine) Elfman, Will Smith, Gene Hackman, Jon Voight, Jason Lee, Regina King, Gabriel Byrne, Barry Pepper, Scott Caan, Loren Dean, Jake Busey, Lisa Bonet, Stuart Wilson, Tom Sizemore, James LeGros, Ian Hurt, Daniel Butler, Jamie Kennedy, Rebeca Silva, Jason Robards Jr., Bobby Boriello, Anna Gunn, Seth Green, Philip Baker Hall, Lillo Brancato, John Capodice, Jack Black; ***D:*** Tony Scott; ***W:*** David Marconi; ***C:*** Dan Mindel; ***M:*** Trevor Rabin, Harry Gregson-Williams.

Enemy of Women 🦴½ *The Private Life of Paul Joseph Goebbels* **1944** Chronicles the life and loves of Nazi propagandist Dr. Joseph Goebbels. **90m/B VHS.** Claudia Drake, Paul Andor, Donald Woods, H.B. Warner, Sigrid Gurie, Ralph Morgan, Gloria Stuart, Charles Halton; ***D:*** Alfred Zeisler; ***W:*** Alfred Zeisler.

Enemy Territory 🦴🦴 **1987 (R)** A handful of citizens trapped in a New York City housing project after dark are stalked by a violent, murderous street gang. **89m/C VHS.** Ray Parker Jr., Jan-Michael Vincent, Gary Frank, Frances Foster; ***D:*** Peter Manoogian.

Enemy Unseen 🦴 **1991 (R)** A bickering squad of merceneries slog through the African jungle to find a girl abducted by crocodile-worshipping natives. Dull Jungle-Jim-style adventure, notable for the hilariously phony crocs that occasionally clamp onto the characters. **90m/C VHS.** Vernon Wells, Stack Pierce, Ken Gampu, Michael McCabe, Angela O'Neill; ***D:*** Elmo De Witt.

The Enemy Within 🦴🦴½ **1994** Cable TV remake of the 1964 political thriller "Seven Days in May." Set in the late 1990s, President William Foster's (Waterston) approval rating is at an all-time low and his heavy defense cuts have certain government officials plotting a coup. Hero of the tale is Joint Chief of Staffs officer, Col. Mac Casey (Whitaker), whose military career is warring with his sense of ethics. The updating is fairly clunky; for true suspense stick with the original. **86m/C VHS.** Forest Whitaker, Sam Waterston, Josef Sommer, Jason Robards Jr., Dana Delany, George Dzundza; ***D:*** Jonathan Darby; ***W:*** Darryl Ponicsan, Ronald Bass; ***C:*** Kees Van Oostrum. **CABLE**

The Enforcer 🦴🦴½ *Murder, Inc* **1951** A district attorney goes after an organized gang of killers in this film noir treatment of the real-life "Murder, Inc." case. **87m/B VHS.** Humphrey Bogart, Zero Mostel, Ted de Corsia, Everett Sloane, Roy Roberts, Michael (Lawrence) Tolan, King Donovan, Bob Steele, Adelaide Klein, Don Beddoe, Tito Vuolo, John Kellogg; ***D:*** Bretaigne Windust, Raoul Walsh; ***W:*** Martin Rackin; ***C:*** Robert Burks.

The Enforcer 🦴🦴½ **1976 (R)** Dirty Harry takes on a female partner and a vicious terrorist group that is threatening the city of San Francisco. See how many "punks" feel lucky enough to test the hand of the tough cop. **96m/C VHS, DVD, Wide.** Clint Eastwood, Tyne Daly, Harry Guardino, Bradford Dillman, John Mitchum, Albert "Poppy" Popwell; ***D:*** James Fargo; ***W:*** Stirling Silliphant, Stuart Hagmann; ***C:*** Charles W. Short; ***M:*** Jerry Fielding.

Enforcer from Death Row 🦴 **1978** An ex-con is recruited by a secret international peacekeeping organization to track down and eliminate a band of murderous spies. **87m/C VHS.** Cameron Mitchell, Leo Fong, Darnell Garcia, Booker T. Anderson, John Hammond, Mariwin Roberts.

The English Patient 🦴🦴🦴🦴 **1996 (R)** Filled with flashbacks and moral ambiguities, this adult romance is a complicated WWII saga that finds fragile French-Canadian nurse Hana (Binoche) caring for Almasy (Fiennes), an enigmatic, dying burn patient, in an abandoned monastery in Tuscany. Hana's joined by thief-turned-spy Caravaggio (Dafoe), who has a private score to settle with Almasy, and two British bomb disposal experts, Kip (Andrews), a Sikh who falls in love with Hana, and Sgt. Hardy (Whately). Almasy spends his days recalling his illicit love affair with Katharine Clifton (Scott Thomas), the wife of fellow cartographer, Geoffrey (Firth), as they map the North African desert. Exquisitely photographed in a golden glow by Seale with wonderful performances by the entire cast. Based on the novel by Michael Ondaatje. **162m/C VHS, DVD.** Ralph Fiennes, Kristin Scott Thomas, Juliette Binoche, Willem Dafoe, Naveen Andrews, Colin Firth, Julian Wadham, Juergen Prochnow, Kevin Whately, Clive Merrison, Nino Castelnuovo; ***D:*** Anthony Minghella; ***W:*** Anthony Minghella; ***C:*** John Seale; ***M:*** Gabriel Yared. Oscars '96: Art Dir./Set Dec., Cinematog., Costume Des., Director (Minghella), Film Editing, Picture, Sound, Support. Actress (Binoche), Orig. Dramatic Score; British Acad. '96: Adapt. Screenplay, Cinematog., Film, Support. Actress (Binoche), Score; Directors Guild '96: Director (Minghella); Golden Globes '97: Film—Drama, Score; L.A. Film Critics '96: Cinematog.; Natl. Bd. of Review '96: Support. Actress (Binoche), Support. Actress (Scott Thomas); Broadcast Film Critics '96: Director (Minghella), Screenplay.

An Englishman Abroad 🦴🦴🦴 **1983** During the Cold War, a British actress visits Moscow and chances to meet a notorious English defector. Behind their gossip and small talk is a tragicomic portrait of the exiled traitor/spy. He was the infamous Guy Burgess; the actress was Coral Browne, here playing herself in a pointed recreation. Made for British TV; nuances may be lost on yank viewers. Winner of several British awards. **63m/C VHS.** *GB* Alan Bates, Coral Browne, Charles Gray; ***D:*** John Schlesinger; ***W:*** Alan Bennett; ***M:*** George Fenton. **TV**

The Englishman Who Went up a Hill But Came down a Mountain 🦴🦴🦴 **1995 (PG)** Charming if slight tale of town pride based on writer/director Monger's family stories. In 1917 two English cartographers—pompous George (McNeice) and naive Reginald (Grant)—travel into Wales to measure the height of Ffynnon Garw (a running gag has the surveyors struggling with the Welsh language). To the proud locals it is the first mountain in Wales, and without that designation they might as well redraw the maps and be part of England—God forbid. But in order to be designated a mountain Ffynnon Garw must be 1000 feet high, and she measures only 984. Grant stammers boyishly as the Englishman who is not only captivated by the village, but by spirited local lass Betty (Fitzgerald, with whom he starred in "Sirens"). Meaney slyly shines as innkeeper Morgan the Goat, leading the townful of color characters. Wales is shown to great advantage by cinematographer Layton. **96m/C VHS, DVD.** *GB* Hugh Grant, Tara Fitzgerald, Colm Meaney, Ian McNeice, Ian Hart, Kenneth Griffith; ***D:*** Christopher Monger; ***W:*** Christopher Monger; ***C:*** Vernon Layton; ***M:*** Stephen Endelman.

Enid Is Sleeping 🦴🦴 *Over Her Dead Body* **1990 (R)** Well-done comedy noir in the now-popular there's-a-corpse-in-the-closet subgenre. A woman in a mythical New Mexican town tries to hide the body of her sister Enid, who she's accidentally killed. Enid, it turns out, wasn't thrilled to discover her sister sleeping with her police-officer husband. Phillips and Perkins restored the film to its original state after it was ruthlessly gutted by the studio. **105m/C VHS.** Elizabeth Perkins, Judge Reinhold, Rhea Perlman; ***D:*** Maurice Phillips; ***W:*** Maurice Phillips; ***C:*** Alfonso Beato.

Enigma 🦴🦴 **1982 (PG)** Trapped behind the Iron Curtain, a double agent tries to find the key to five pending murders by locating a Russian coded microprocessor holding information that would unravel the assassination scheme. **101m/C VHS.** *FR GB* Martin Sheen, Brigitte Fossey, Sam Neill, Derek Jacobi, Frank Finlay, Michael (Michel) Lonsdale, Warren Clarke; ***D:*** Jeannot Szwarc; ***W:*** John Briley.

Enigma 🦴🦴½ **2001 (R)** Tom Jericho (Scott) is a British codebreaker working at Bletchley Park during WWII. He has a breakdown after a romantic breakup with colleague Claire (Burrows), who's mysteriously dispeared. Could she have been working for the Germans? Tom is determined to find out, aided by Claire's roommate Hester (Winslet). Meanwhile, intelligence operative Wigram (Northam) is keeping an eye on them both, thinking they know more than they appear to. Excessive subplots make for some confusion but the story's still compelling. Based on a novel by Robert Harris. **117m/C VHS, DVD.** *GB* Dougray Scott, Kate Winslet, Saffron Burrows, Jeremy Northam, Nikolaj Waldau, Tom Hollander, Corin Redgrave, Robert Pugh, Matthew MacFadyen; ***D:*** Michael Apted; ***W:*** Tom Stoppard; ***C:*** Seamus McGarvey; ***M:*** John Barry.

Enigma Secret 🦴🦴 **1979** Three Polish mathematicians use their noggins to break the Nazi secret code machine during WWII. Based on a true story; in Polish with English subtitles. **158m/C VHS.** *PL* Tadeusz Borowski, Piotr Fronczewski, Piotr Garlicki.

Enjo 🦴🦴 *Conflagration; The Flame of Torment* **1958** True story of a tormented young monk, studying at the Golden Pavilion in Kyoto, who becomes disillusioned by the pervasive corruption of the temple. In desperation, he sets fire to the national shrine in an attempt to preserve the monument from further contamination. Very disturbing yet beautiful to watch. Adapted from Mishima's novel "Temple of the Golden Pavilion." Japanese with subtitles. **98m/B VHS.** *JP* Raizo Ichikawa, Ganjiro Nakamura, Tatsuya Nakadai; *D:* Kon Ichikawa; *W:* Natto Wada, Keiji Hasebe, Toshiro Mayazumi; *C:* Kazuo Miyagawa.

Enola Gay: The Men, the Mission, the Atomic Bomb ✓✓ **1980** Based on the best-selling book by Gordon Thomas and Max Gordon Witts, this drama tells the story of the airmen aboard the B-29 that dropped the first atomic bomb. Details the events during WWII leading up to the decision to bomb Hiroshima and the concerns of the crew assigned the task. **150m/C VHS.** Patrick Duffy, Billy Crystal, Kim Darby, Gary Frank, Gregory Harrison, Ed Nelson, Robert Walden, Stephen Macht, Robert Pine, James Shigeta, Henry Wilcoxon; *D:* David Lowell Rich; *M:* Maurice Jarre. **TV**

Enormous Changes ✓✓✓ *Enormous Changes at the Last Minute* **1983** Three stories about New York City women and their personal relationships. Based on the stories of Grace Paley. **115m/C VHS.** Ellen Barkin, David Strathairn, Ron McLarty, Maria Tucci, Lynn Milgrim, Kevin Bacon; *D:* Mirra Bank; *W:* John Sayles.

Enough ✓✓ **2002 (PG-13)** Revenge fantasy that's been compared to both "Sleeping with the Enemy" (Julia Roberts) and "Double Jeopardy" (Ashley Judd). Working-class waitress Slim (Lopez) marries wealthy contractor Mitch (Campbell) and for a while everything appears perfect. But Mitch turns out to be an abusive, cheating, control freak who forces Slim to take their daughter and run. When Mitch finds and threatens her, Slim decides to literally toughen up and give Mitch a taste of his own medicine. Okay, it's nice to see Lopez kick butt but this movie has a very nasty taste and some lame advice for battered women (who probably won't discover that their biological fathers are filthy rich and can help them out financially). **115m/C** *US* Jennifer Lopez, Billy Campbell, Juliette Lewis, Dan Futterman, Noah Wyle, Tessa Allen, Fred Ward, Bill Cobbs, Christopher Maher; *D:* Michael Apted; *W:* Nicholas Kazan; *C:* Rogier Stoffers; *M:* David Arnold.

Enrapture ✓½ **1990 (R)** A chauffeur is the prime suspect when a promiscuous passenger is murdered in his limousine. The driver did it? **87m/C VHS.** Ona Simms, Harvey Siegel, Richard Parnes; *D:* Chuck Vincent.

Ensign Pulver ✓✓ **1964** A continuation of the further adventures of the crew of the U.S.S. Reluctant from "Mister Roberts," which was adapted from the Broadway play. **104m/C VHS.** Walter Matthau, Robert Walker Jr., Larry Hagman, Jack Nicholson, Millie Perkins, James Coco, James Farentino, Burl Ives, Gerald S. O'Loughlin, Al Freeman Jr.; *D:* Joshua Logan.

Entangled ✓✓ **1993 (R)** David Mirkin (Nelson) is a struggling writer living in Paris with his beautiful girlfriend Annabelle (Treil). As she becomes ever more successful as a fashion model, David becomes ever more jealous and mistrustful. So he hires a detective (Brosnan) to spy on her. And then there's the small matter of a murder. Adapted from the novel "Les Veufs" by Boileau Narcejac. **98m/C VHS.** Judd Nelson, Pierce Brosnan, Laurence Treil, Roy Dupuis; *D:* Max Fischer.

Enter Laughing ✓✓ **1967** Based on Reiner's semi-autobiographical novel and play, depicts the botched efforts of a Bronx-born schlump to become an actor. Worthwhile, but doesn't live up to the original. **112m/C VHS.** Reni Santoni, Jose Ferrer, Elaine May, Shelley Winters, Jack Gilford, Don Rickles, Michael J. Pollard, Janet Margolin, Rob Reiner; *D:* Carl Reiner; *W:* Carl Reiner; *C:* Joseph Biroc; *M:* Quincy Jones.

Enter the Dragon ✓✓✓ *The Deadly Three* **1973 (R)** The American film that broke Bruce Lee worldwide combines Oriental conventions with 007 thrills. Spectacular fighting sequences including Karate, Judo, Tae Kwon Do, and Tai Chi Chuan are featured as Lee is recruited by the British to search for opium smugglers in Hong Kong. **98m/C VHS, DVD, Wide.** Bruce Lee, John Saxon, Jim Kelly, Ahna Capri, Shih Kien, Bob Wall, Angela (Mao Ying) Mao, Betty Chung, Jackie Chan, Tony Liu, Chuck Norris; *D:* Robert Clouse; *W:* Michael Allin; *C:* Gil Hubbs; *M:* Lalo Schifrin.

Enter the Ninja ✓✓ **1981 (R)** First and most serious of the Cannon canon of relatively well-done ninja epics (faint praise) that created original boxoffice stir for genre (mostly among adolescents needing outlet). Ninja Nero visits old friend in Philippines who's being pressured by ruthless evil guy George to give up the farm. Nero dispatches numerous thugs before indulging in ninja slugfest with Kosugi. **99m/C VHS.** Franco Nero, Susan George, Sho Kosugi, Christopher George, Alex Courtney; *D:* Menahem Golan; *W:* Judd Bernard.

The Entertainer ✓✓✓½ **1960** Splendid drama of egotistical, third-rate vaudevillian Archie Rice (Olivier), who tries vainly to gain the fame his dying father Billy (Livesey) once possessed. His blatant disregard for his alcoholic wife Phoebe (De Banzie), his superficial sons (Bates and Finney), and his loyal daughter (Plowright) brings his world crashing down around him, as Archie discovers how self-destructive his life has been. Adapted from the play by John Osborne. Remade for TV in 1975 with Jack Lemmon. **104m/B VHS, DVD, Wide.** *GB* Laurence Olivier, Brenda de Banzie, Roger Livesey, Joan Plowright, Daniel Massey, Alan Bates, Shirley Anne Field, Albert Finney, Thora Hird; *D:* Tony Richardson; *W:* Nigel Kneale, John Osborne; *C:* Oswald Morris; *M:* John Addison.

Entertaining Angels: The Dorothy Day Story ✓✓½ **1996 (PG-13)** Dorothy Day (Kelly) was a social activist who founded the left-wing publication The Catholic Worker and was dedicated to sheltering and feeding the poor, founding soup kitchens across America. A radical journalist and New York bohemian, Day converts to Catholicism in the '20s and is soon working with the city's poor and homeless. Episodic story works mainly on indignation and its heroine's compassion. **110m/C VHS.** Moira Kelly, Martin Sheen, Melinda Dillon, Lenny Von Dohlen, Heather Graham, Geoffrey Blake, Boyd Kestner, Allyce Beasley, Brian Keith; *D:* Michael Ray Rhodes; *W:* John Wells; *C:* Mike Fash; *M:* Bill Conti, Ashley Irwin.

Entertaining Mr. Sloane ✓✓½ **1970** Playwright Joe Orton's masterpiece of black comedy concerning a handsome criminal who becomes the guest and love interest of a widow and her brother. **90m/C VHS.** *GB* Beryl Reid, Harry Andrews, Peter McEnery, Alan Webb; *D:* Douglas Hickox; *W:* Clive Exton, Joe Orton; *C:* Wolfgang Suschitzky.

The Entity ✓✓ **1983 (R)** Supposedly based on a true story about an unseen entity that repeatedly rapes a woman. Hershey's the victim whom nobody believes. She eventually ends up at a university for talks with parapsychologist Silver. Pseudo-science to the rescue as the oversexed creature is frozen dead in its tracks. Exploitative violence, gore, and nudity aplenty, balanced to a degree by Hershey's strong performance. **115m/C VHS.** Barbara Hershey, Ron Silver, Alex Rocco; *D:* Sidney J. Furie; *W:* Frank De Felitta; *C:* Stephen Burum; *M:* Charles Bernstein.

Entr'acte **1924** Clair's famous dada-surrealist classic short, reflecting his sense of humor, as various eccentric characters become involved in a crazy chase. Silent. **21m/B VHS.** *FR* *D:* Rene Clair.

Entrapment ✓✓½ **1999 (PG-13)** Too tricky for its own good crime caper features insurance investigator Virginia Baker (Zeta-Jones) convincing her boss, Hector Cruz (Patton), that master thief Mac MacDougall (Connery) is behind the theft of a Rembrandt. Only when Gin catches up to Mac, she convinces him that she's also a thief and she has a very elaborate, very rich heist in mind, that needs his expertise. However, nobody involved in anything that goes on in this movie is exactly what they seem. Nice scenery (and not just that offered by the beautiful Zeta-Jones). **112m/C VHS, DVD.** Sean Connery, Catherine Zeta-Jones, Ving Rhames, Will Patton, Maury Chaykin; *D:* Jon Amiel; *W:* Ronald Bass, William Broyles Jr.; *C:* Phil Meheux; *M:* Christopher Young.

Entre-Nous ✓✓✓½ *Between Us; Coup de Foudre; At First Sight* **1983 (PG)** Two attractive, young French mothers find in each other the fulfillment their husbands cannot provide. One of the women was confined in a concentration camp during WWII; the other is a disaffected artist. In French with English subtitles. **112m/C VHS, DVD.** *FR* Jean-Pierre Bacri, Patrick Bauchau, Jacqueline Doyen, Isabelle Huppert, Miou-Miou, Guy Marchand; *D:* Diane Kurys; *W:* Alain Henry, Diane Kurys; *C:* Bernard Lutic; *M:* Luis Bacalov.

Entropy ✓✓ **1999** Dorff gives a gifted lead performance in this excessively stylistic romantic drama. It spans a year in the life of arrogant moviemaker Jake Walsh (Dorff), who describes how he meets French model Stella (Godreche) and experiences love at first sight. Although they live together, their careers frequently keep them apart and Jake's emotional immaturity eventually separates them. The cliched film-within-a-film narrative only manages to slow the main story down. **104m/C VHS.** Stephen Dorff, Judith Godreche, Kelly Macdonald, Lauren Holly, Jon Tenney, Frank Vincent, Paul Guilfoyle, Hector Elizondo; *D:* Phil Joanou; *W:* Phil Joanou; *C:* Carolyn Chen; *M:* George Fenton.

Epoch ✓✓½ **2000 (PG-13)** Alien monolith suddenly appears and hovers over Bhutan, seemingly causing worldwide power disruptions and earthquakes. National security adviser Lysander (O'Neal) assigns special ops Kasia Czaban (Niznik) and weapons specialist Mason Rand (Keith) to figure out just what the object is—and wants—and, if necessary, to destroy it. **97m/C VHS, DVD.** David Keith, Stephanie Niznik, Ryan O'Neal, James Hong, Brian Thompson, Craig Wasson, Donna Magnani, Shannon Lee; *D:* Matt Cold; *C:* Ken Stipe. **CABLE**

Equalizer 2000 ✓ **1986 (R)** A warrior in a post-holocaust future plots to overthrow a dictatorship by using a high-powered gun. **85m/C VHS.** Richard Norton, Corinne Wahl, William (Bill) Steis; *D:* Cirio H. Santiago.

Equinox ✓✓✓ *The Beast* **1971 (PG)** Young archaeologists uncover horror in a state forest. The ranger, questing for a book of spells that the scientists have found, threatens them with wonderful special effects, including winged beasts, huge apes, and Satan. Though originally an amateur film, it is deemed a minor classic in its genre. **80m/C VHS.** Edward Connell, Barbara Hewitt, Frank Bonner, Robin Christopher, Jack Woods, Fritz Leiber, Patrick Burke, Jim Phillips; *D:* Dennis Muren, Jack Woods; *W:* Jack Woods; *C:* Mike Hoover; *M:* John Caper Jr.

Equinox ✓✓ **1993 (R)** Modine gets to try his hand (and does well) at a dual role, with his portrayal of identical twins, separated at birth and raised in completely different environs. Garage worker Henry lives in a tenement while slick brother Freddie is a gangster's chauffeur married to the materialistic Sharon (Singer). Fate brings the brothers together when a janitor discovers a letter that reveals their parentage and the fact that a fortune has been left to them. Set in the near future, in the surreal and decaying city of Empire, this is typical Rudolph with its moody stylized appearance and convoluted plot. **110m/C VHS, Wide.** Matthew Modine, Lara Flynn Boyle, Lori Singer, Marisa Tomei, Fred Ward, M. Emmet Walsh, Tyra Ferrell, Tate Donovan, Kevin J. O'Connor, Gailard Sartain; *D:* Alan Rudolph; *W:* Alan Rudolph; *C:* Elliot Davis.

Equinox Flower ✓✓ **1958** Ozu's first color film tells the sensitive story of two teenage girls who make a pact to protect each other from the traditional prearranged marriages their parents have set up. Lovely film that focuses on the generation gap between young and old in the Japanese family. In Japanese with English subtitles. **118m/C VHS.** *JP* Shin Saburi, Kinuyo Tanaka, Ineko Arima, Miyuki Kuwano, Chishu Ryu; *D:* Yasujiro Ozu.

Equus ✓✓½ **1977 (R)** A psychiatrist undertakes the most challenging case of his career when he tries to figure out why a stable-boy blinded horses. Based upon the successful play by Peter Shaffer, but not well transferred to film. **138m/C VHS.** Richard Burton, Peter Firth, Jenny Agutter, Joan Plowright, Colin Blakely, Harry Andrews; *D:* Sidney Lumet; *W:* Peter Shaffer; *C:* Oswald Morris; *M:* Richard Rodney Bennett. British Acad. '77: Support. Actress (Agutter); Golden Globes '78: Actor—Drama (Burton), Support. Actor (Firth).

Era Notte a Roma ✓✓✓ **1960** An American, Russian, and British soldier each escape from a concentration camp in the waning days of WWII and find refuge in the home of a young woman. **145m/C VHS.** *IT* *D:* Roberto Rossellini; *W:* Roberto Rossellini.

Eraser ✓✓½ **1996 (R)** Arnold returns to familiar big-budget action territory and looks right at home. He plays elite U.S. Marshal John Kruger, who protects federal witnesses by "erasing" their previous identities. When a beautiful witness uncovers a high-level conspiracy, the two go on the run to stay alive long enough to expose the truth. Fans of the big bang Schwarzenegger of yore will not be disappointed. Rumors of production delays and budget overruns, not to mention difficulties between director Russell and producer Kopelson, brought up the spectre of "Waterworld," but the final result is more reminiscent of the success of "True Lies." **115m/C VHS, DVD.** Joe (Johnny) Viterelli, Michael (Mike) Papajohn, Arnold Schwarzenegger, Vanessa L(ynne) Williams, James Caan, James Coburn, Robert Pastorelli, Andy Romano, James Cromwell, Danny Nucci, Nicholas Chinlund, Mark Rolston, Gerry Becker; *D:* Chuck Russell; *W:* Walon Green, Tony Puryear; *C:* Adam Greenberg; *M:* Alan Silvestri.

Eraserhead ✓✓✓ **1978** The infamous cult classic about a numb-brained everyman wandering through what amounts to a sick, ironic parody of the modern urban landscape, innocently impregnating his girlfriend and fathering a pestilent embryonic mutant. Surreal and bizarre, the film has an inner, completely unpredictable logic all its own. Lynch's first feature-length film stars Nance, who later achieved fame in Lynch's "Twin Peaks" as Pete the Logger. **90m/B VHS.** Jack Nance, Charlotte Stewart, Allen Joseph, Jeanne Bates, Judith Anna Roberts, Laurel Near, V. Phipps-Willson, Jack Fisk, Jean Lange, Darwin Joston, Hal Landon Jr., Jennifer Lynch, Gill Dennis; *D:* David Lynch; *W:* David Lynch; *C:* Frederick Elmes, Herbert Cardwell; *M:* David Lynch, Fats Waller, Peter Ivers.

Erendira ✓✓½ **1983** Based on Gabriel Garcia-Marquez's story about a teenage girl prostituting herself to support her witch-like grandmother after accidentally torching the elder's house. The film follows the two as they travel across the desert trying out new and inventive ways to survive. Unusual ending tops off a creative, if not eclectic, movie. In Spanish with English subtitles. **103m/C VHS.** *FR MX GE* Sergio Calderon, Blanca Guerra, Ernesto Cruz, Pierre Vaneck, Irene Papas, Claudia Ohana, Michael (Michel) Lonsdale, Rufus, Jorge Fegan; *D:* Ruy Guerra; *W:* Gabriel Garcia Marquez; *C:* Denys Clerval; *M:* Maurice Lecouer.

Eric ✓✓✓ **1975** Tear-jerker about a young athlete who fights for his life after he's diagnosed with leukemia. Based on the true-life account written by Eric's mother, Doris Lund. **100m/C VHS.** Patricia Neal, John Savage, Claude Akins, Sian Barbara Allen, Mark Hamill, Nehemiah Persoff, Tom Clancy; *D:* James Goldstone; *M:* Dave Grusin. **TV**

Erik ✓✓ **1990** An ex-government agent working in Central America finds his loyalties divided when he is approached by a female activist and his old CIA friends. They want him to help expose his current boss as a drug smuggler. **90m/C VHS.** Stephen McHattie, Deborah Van Valkenburgh.

Erik, the Viking ✓ **1972** The Norse Warrior discovers not only the New World but traitorous subordinates among his crew, calling for drastic measures. **95m/C VHS.** Giuliano Gemma, Gordon Mitchell.

Erik the Viking 🦴½ 1989 (PG-13) A mediocre Monty Pythonesque farce about a Viking who grows dissatisfied with his barbaric way of life and decides to set out to find the mythical Asgaard, where Norse gods dwell. Great cast of character actors is wasted. **104m/C VHS.** *GB* Tim Robbins, Terry Jones, Mickey Rooney, John Cleese, Imogen Stubbs, Anthony Sher, Gordon John Sinclair, Freddie Jones, Eartha Kitt, Gary Cady, Neil Innes, Jim Broadbent, Andrew MacLachlan, Charles McKeown; ***D:*** Terry Jones; ***W:*** Terry Jones; ***C:*** Ian Wilson; ***M:*** Neil Innes.

Erin Brockovich 🦴🦴🦴 2000 (R) Erin Brockovich (Roberts) is a divorced mom desperate for a job. She bullies her way into a file clerk position at the small law office of Ed Masry (Finney) where her salty language, take-no-prisoners attitude, and scanty attire unnerve her co-workers. But that's just the appeal that Erin needs when she uncovers and investigates some shady corporate dealings that eventually lead to a multimillion dollar settlement against a public utility over contaminated water. Standout role for Roberts who's ably backed-up by the rumpled Finney. Based on a true story and yes, the real Erin is a looker who dresses every bit as provocatively as her screen counterpart. **131m/C VHS, DVD, Wide.** Julia Roberts, Albert Finney, Aaron Eckhart, Marg Helgenberger, Cherry Jones, Veanne Cox, Conchata Ferrell, Tracey Walter, Peter Coyote; ***D:*** Steven Soderbergh; ***W:*** Susannah Grant; ***C:*** Edward Lachman; ***M:*** Thomas Newman. Oscars '00: Actress (Roberts); British Acad. '00: Actress (Roberts); Golden Globes '01: Actress—Drama (Roberts); L.A. Film Critics '00: Actress (Roberts), Director (Soderbergh); Natl. Bd. of Review '00: Actress (Roberts), Director (Soderbergh); N.Y. Film Critics '00: Director (Soderbergh); Natl. Soc. Film Critics '00: Director (Soderbergh); Screen Actors Guild '00: Actress (Roberts), Support. Actor (Finney); Broadcast Film Critics '00: Actress (Roberts), Director (Soderbergh).

Ermo 🦴🦴 1994 Hard-working noodle-maker Ermo (Alia) supports her slothful husband, Chief (Zhijun), and their son in their northern China village. Her smitten truck-driver neighbor Blindman (Peiqi) has an equally unpleasant wife, Fat Woman (Haiyan), with whom Ermo has an ongoing rivalry. They own a color TV (the only one in the village) and Ermo becomes determined to get a bigger and better set by selling her noodles in a nearby town and compulsively saving her money. Of course, her entrepreneurship has some unexpected consequences. Mandarin Chinese with subtitles. **93m/C VHS.** *CH* Alia, Liu Peiqi, Ge Zhijun, Zhang Haiyan; ***D:*** Zhou Xiaowen; ***W:*** Lang Yun; ***C:*** Lu Gengxin; ***M:*** Zhou Xiaowen.

Ernest Goes to Africa 🦴½ 1997 (PG) Ernest P. Worrel (Varney) finds himself in a heap 'o trouble when he's accused of buying some stolen diamonds and he and would-be girlfriend Renee are kidnapped and taken to Africa where a prince wants his property returned. Lots of sight gags and low humor. **90m/C VHS.** Jim Varney, Linda Kash, Jamie Bartlett; ***D:*** John R. Cherry III; ***W:*** John R. Cherry III; ***C:*** James Robb.

Ernest Goes to Camp 🦴½ 1987 (PG) Screwball, slapstick summer camp farce starring the character Ernest P. Worrell as an inept camp counselor. When progress threatens the camp, Ernest leads the boys on a turtle-bombing, slop-shooting attack on the construction company. Followed by "Ernest Saves Christmas" and "Ernest Goes to Jail." **92m/C VHS.** Richard Speight Jr., Jim Varney, Victoria Racimo, John Vernon, Iron Eyes Cody, Lyle Alzado, Gailard Sartain, Daniel Butler, Hakeem Abdul-Samad; ***D:*** John R. Cherry III; ***W:*** John R. Cherry III.

Ernest Goes to Jail 🦴🦴 1990 (PG) The infamous loon Ernest P. Worrell winds up in the jury box and the courtroom will never be the same again. Jury duty suddenly becomes hard-time in the slammer for poor Ernest when he is mistaken for a big-wig organized crime boss. Sequel to "Ernest Goes to Camp" and "Ernest Saves Christmas." **81m/C VHS.** Jim Varney, Gailard Sartain, Randall "Tex" Cobb, Bill Byrge, Barry Scott, Charles Napier; ***D:*** John R. Cherry III; ***W:*** Charlie Cohen; ***M:*** Bruce Arntson.

Ernest Goes to School 🦴🦴½ 1994 (PG) Ernest must finish high school if he wants to keep his job as school janitor. He's "aided" by two crazy science teachers who give him an experimental IQ booster. **89m/C VHS.** Jim Varney, Linda Kash, Bill Byrge; ***D:*** Coke Sams.

The Ernest Green Story 🦴🦴½ 1993 Drama based on the integration of Central High in Little Rock, Arkansas, by nine black students in 1957. Green was the only senior in the group and the movie follows a year of verbal and physical abuse, vandalism, and unfair academic treatment, as he struggles to withstand every difficulty in order to graduate. **92m/C VHS.** Sonny Shroyer, Morris Chestnut, CCH Pounder, Gary Grubbs, Tina Lifford, Avery Brooks, Ruby Dee, Ossie Davis; ***D:*** Eric Laneuville. **CABLE**

Ernest in the Army 🦴½ 1997 (PG) Ernest is talked into joining the Army reserves and promptly causes all sorts of trouble when he's assigned to drive various military vehicles. **85m/C VHS.** Jim Varney, Hayley Tyson, David Muller, Ivan Lucas; ***D:*** John R. Cherry III; ***W:*** Jeffrey Pillars; ***C:*** James Robb; ***M:*** Mark Adler.

Ernest Rides Again 🦴🦴½ 1993 (PG) Ernest P. "Knowwhutimean?" Worrell (Varney) is back, aiding a college professor friend who has a cockamamie theory that the British crown jewels were hidden in a Revolutionary War cannon. Naturally he's right and Ernest must battle British spies and a greedy antiquities collector to get the gems back. Goofy slapstick sticks to the formula of the other films. **93m/C VHS.** Jim Varney, Ron James, Duke Ernsberger, Jeffrey Pillars, Linda Kash, Tom Butler; ***D:*** John R. Cherry III; ***W:*** John R. Cherry III, William M. Akers; ***M:*** Bruce Arntson, Kirby Shelstad.

Ernest Saves Christmas 🦴½ 1988 (PG) Ernest P. Worrell is back. When Santa decides that it's time to retire, Ernest must help him recruit a has-been children's show host who is a bit reluctant. For Ernest fans only, and only the most dedicated of those. Second in the series featuring the nimble-faced Varney, the first of which was "Ernest Goes to Camp," followed by "Ernest Goes to Jail." **91m/C VHS.** Jim Varney, Douglas Seale, Oliver Clark, Noelle Parker, Billie Bird; ***D:*** John R. Cherry III.

Ernest Scared Stupid 🦴½ 1991 (PG) Pea-brained Ernest P. Worrell returns yet again in this silly comedy. When he accidentally releases a demon from a sacred tomb a 200-year-old curse threatens to destroy his hometown, unless Ernest can come to the rescue. Would you want your town depending on Ernest's heroics? Who would have thought that the annoying Ernest P. Worrell could appear in one movie, let alone four? **93m/C VHS.** Jim Varney, Eartha Kitt, Austin Nagler, Jonas Moscartolo, Shay Astar; ***D:*** John R. Cherry III; ***W:*** John R. Cherry III; ***C:*** Hanania Baer; ***M:*** Bruce Arntson.

Ernesto 🦴🦴½ 1979 A lushly erotic Italian film depicting the troubled relationship between a young, devil-may-care gay youth and his older, coolly seducing lover. In Italian with subtitles. **98m/C VHS.** *IT* Martin Halm, Michele Placido; ***D:*** Salvatore Samperi.

Ernie Kovacs: Between the Laughter 🦴🦴 1984 The television comic's life and career, ending with his tragic death in a car accident in 1962. Shows the brand of humor that made Kovacs famous as well as the devastation that he suffered after the tragic kidnapping of his children by his first wife during divorce proceedings. Kovac's second wife, Edie Adams, makes a brief appearance. **95m/C VHS.** Jeff Goldblum, Cloris Leachman, Melody Anderson, Madolyn Smith, John Glover; ***Cameos:*** Edie Adams; ***D:*** Lamont Johnson; ***M:*** Ralph Burns. **TV**

Erotic Escape 🦴 1986 Soft-core fun about party girls taking over a small French town. Originally in French, but dubbed in English. Check your brain at the door. **86m/C VHS.** *FR* Marie-Claire Davy, Pauline Larrieu.

Erotic House of Wax 🦴½ 1997 Young woman inherits her uncle's bizarre wax museum upon his death and discovers that the museum's inhabitants have this habit of coming to life and acting out their sexual fantasies. **90m/C VHS.** Jacqueline Lovell, Josie Hunter; ***D:*** Sybil Richards.

Erotic Images woof! 1985 (R) A beautiful psychology teacher publishes her doctoral thesis on sex and becomes a best-selling author, which threatens her marriage. **93m/C VHS.** Britt Ekland, Edd Byrnes, John McCann; ***D:*** Declan Langan.

Erotic Touch of Hot Skin 🦴 1965 Sex, murder, false identities, car crashes, and striptease in the Riviera. **78m/B VHS.** Fabienne Dali, Sophie Hardy, Jean Valmont, Francois Dryek; ***D:*** Max Pecas.

Erotique 🦴🦴 1994 Sex quartet from female filmmakers. "Let's Talk About Sex" finds struggling Latina actress Rosie (Lopez-Dawson) supporting herself by working at a phone sex agency where a caller (Cranston) wants to know about her sexual fantasies. "Taboo Parlor" finds lesbian lovers Claire (Barnes) and Julia (Soeberg) picking up boy toy Victor (Carr) and planning some s/m games. "Wonton Soup" has Australian-born Chinese Adrian (Lounibos) reuniting with his lover Ann (Man) in Hong Kong and deciding to hold her interest by practicing some ancient Chinese sexual techniques. And in "Final Call," a school teacher (Ohana) tries a sexual adventure with a stranger. **120m/C VHS, DVD.** Kamala Lopez, Bryan Cranston, Priscilla Barnes, Camilla Soeberg, Michael Carr, Tim Lounibos, Hayley Man, Claudia Ohana; ***D:*** Lizzie Borden, Monika Treut, Clara Law, Ana Maria Magalhaes; ***W:*** Lizzie Borden, Monika Treut, Susie Bright, Eddie L.C. Fong; ***C:*** Larry Banks, Elfi Mikesch, Arthur Wong.

The Errand Boy 🦴🦴½ 1961 Jerry Lewis' patented babbling schnook hits Hollywood in search of a job. When he lands a position as an errand boy, Hollywood may never be the same again in this prototypical comedy; a must for Lewis fans only. **92m/B VHS, Wide.** Jerry Lewis, Brian Donlevy, Dick Wesson, Howard McNear, Felicia Atkins, Fritz Feld, Sig Rumann, Renee Taylor, Doodles Weaver, Mike Mazurki, Lorne Greene, Michael Landon, Dan Blocker, Pernell Roberts, Snub Pollard, Kathleen Freeman; ***D:*** Jerry Lewis; ***W:*** Jerry Lewis.

The Errors of Youth 🦴🦴 *Wild Oats* 1978 Dimitri (Zhdanko), a construction worker in Siberia, is disillusioned over a failed love affair and moves to Leningrad where he falls in with black marketeers and a marriage of convenience. Because of political problems, director Frumin left the film unfinished when he emigrated to the U.S. and it wasn't until 1989 that he returned to Leningrad to complete the project. Russian with subtitles. **87m/C VHS.** *RU* Stanislav Zhdanko, Marina Neyelova, Natalia Varley, Mikhail Vaskov; ***D:*** Boris Frumin.

Erskinville Kings 🦴🦴½ 1999 The plot borders on the cliched but White's debut feature has strong performances to carry it along. It's summer in a grimy Sydney suburb filled with run-down stores, bars, and neglected houses. Barky (screenwriter Chooney acting under the pseudonyn Martin Denniss) is returning home after two years for his drunken, abusive father's funeral. He's hoping to have some kind of reconciliation with his brother Wace (Jackman) but Wace's bitterness may prevent that. **85m/C VHS.** *AU* Anik (Martin Denniss) Chooney, Hugh Jackman, Leah Vandenberg, Aaron Blabey, Andrew Wholley, Joel Edgerton; ***D:*** Alan White; ***W:*** Anik (Martin Denniss) Chooney; ***C:*** John Swaffield; ***M:*** Don Miller-Robinson.

Escanaba in da Moonlight 🦴🦴 2001 (PG-13) If you're not a "Yooper" or familiar with those denizens of Michigan's Upper Penisula, Daniels's film (based on his play) will probably be lost on you. This is the kind of local humor that rarely travels well. The story is basically a tall tale—middleaged Reuben Soady (Daniels) has reached his advanced years without ever having bagged a deer on his annual hunting trip with his dad (Presnell) and brother (Albright). He is a community laughingstock but that is about to change. **90m/C VHS.** *US* Jeff Daniels, Harve Presnell, Joey Albright, Wayne David Parker, Randall Goodwin, Kimberly Norris Guerrero; ***D:*** Jeff Daniels; ***W:*** Jeff Daniels; ***C:*** Richard Brawer.

Escapade 🦴🦴🦴 1955 Sons thinking their parents are en route to divorce court create a scheme to achieve peace worldwide. The pacifist father's reaction juxtaposes idealistic youth with the cynicism of adulthood. Adapted from a play by Roger MacDougall. **87m/B VHS.** *GB* John Mills, Yvonne Mitchell, Alastair Sim, Jeremy Spenser, Andrew Ray, Marie Lohr, Peter Asher; ***D:*** Philip Leacock; ***W:*** Donald Ogden Stewart.

Escapade in Florence 🦴🦴 1962 As two students in Florence paint their way to immortality, an elaborate art-forging ring preys upon their talents. **81m/C VHS.** Tommy Kirk, Ivan Desny; ***D:*** Steve Previn.

Escapade in Japan 🦴🦴 1957 A Japanese youth helps an American boy frantically search the city of Tokyo for his parents. Shot in Japan. **93m/C VHS.** Cameron Mitchell, Teresa Wright, Jon(athan) Provost, Roger Nakagawa, Philip Ober, Clint Eastwood; ***D:*** Arthur Lubin; ***M:*** Max Steiner.

Escape 🦴½ 1990 (R) A woman attempts to track down her brother's killer and finds an entire town mysteriously controlled by a sadistic and powerful man. Features General Hospital's bad-boy Shriner. **100m/C VHS.** Elizabeth Jeager, Kim Richards, Kin Shriner; ***D:*** Richard Styles.

Escape 🦴🦴 1990 (PG) A fun-loving, care-free Irish officer is sent to oversee the toughest POW prison in Scotland. There, he becomes consumed with keeping the facility secure despite the intricate escape plans laid out by a group of rioters. **90m/C VHS.** Brian Keith, Helmut Griem; ***D:*** Lamont Johnson.

The Escape 🦴½ 1995 Prisoner Clayton (Dempsey) manages to escape incarceration and is then on the lam from sadistic prison guard, Hickman (Feore). Moody flashbacks show that his crime, while in the present Clayton finds some sexual solace with the accommodating Sarah (Bako) as he tries to outwit his pursuers. **91m/C VHS.** Patrick Dempsey, Brigitte Bako, Colm Feore, Vincent Gale, Nathaniel DeVeaux, W. Morgan Shepherd; ***D:*** Stuart Gillard; ***W:*** Scott Busby; ***C:*** Tobias Schliessler; ***M:*** Loek Dikker. **VIDEO**

The Escape Artist 🦴🦴🦴 1982 (PG) Award-winning cinematographer Deschanel's first directorial effort is this quirky film about a teenage escape artist who sets out to uncover the identity of his father's killers. **96m/C VHS.** Griffin O'Neal, Raul Julia, Teri Garr, Joan Hackett, Desi Arnaz Sr., Gabriel Dell, Huntz Hall, Jackie Coogan, Elizabeth (E.G. Dailey) Daily; ***D:*** Caleb Deschanel; ***W:*** Melissa Mathison; ***C:*** Stephen Burum; ***M:*** Georges Delerue.

Escape Clause 🦴🦴 1996 (R) Insurance exec Richard Ramsay (McCarthy) gets a call from a hitman informing him that his wife Sarah (McNeil) has hired him to kill Richard. The hitman says if Richard will pay him, the contract's off. Instead Richard tries to figure out what's going on, with some help from police detective Ferrand (Sorvino), who discovers Richard has been treated for paranoid delusions. Fast-paced mystery with a few too many twists. **131m/C VHS.** Andrew McCarthy, Paul Sorvino, Kate McNeil, Peter Donaldson, Kenneth Welsh, Connie Britton, Stan(ford) Egi, John Evans; ***D:*** Brian Trenchard-Smith; ***W:*** Danilo Bach; ***M:*** Ken Thorne, Rick Marvin. **VIDEO**

Escape from Alcatraz 🦴🦴🦴 1979 (PG) A fascinating account of the one and only successful escape from the maximum security prison at Alcatraz in 1962. The three men were never heard from again. **112m/C VHS, DVD.** Clint Eastwood, Patrick McGoohan, Roberts Blossom, Fred Ward, Danny Glover; ***D:*** Donald Siegel; ***W:*** Richard Tuggle; ***C:*** Bruce Surtees; ***M:*** Jerry Fielding.

Escape from Atlantis 🦴🦴½ 1997 (PG-13) Workaholic attorney and single dad, Matt Spencer (Speakman), charters a sailboat and plans a cruise to the Bahamas so he and his three teenagers can have some quality time. The sailboat heads into the Bermuda Triangle and capsizes in a hurricane; when the Spencers come to, they're in the land of Atlantis, where fantasy is reality. **93m/C VHS.** Jeff Speakman, Brian Bloom, Tim Thomerson, Mercedes McNab, Michael Lee Goggin, Justin Burnette, Breck Wilson; ***D:*** Strathford Hamilton; ***W:*** Arne Olsen.

Escape from Cell Block 3 **1978** Five escaped female convicts take it on the lam for Mexico and freedom. **82m/C VHS.** Carolyn Judd, Teri Guzman, Bonita Kalem.

Escape from Death Row **1976 (R)** Convicted criminal mastermind, sentenced to die, devises a brilliant and daring plan of escape on the eve of his execution. **85m/C VHS.** Lee Van Cleef, James Lane, Barbara Moore, Alice Belios.

Escape from DS-3 **198?** Bostwick and "Police Academy" alumnus Smith team up in a familiar story: framed for a serious crime, a man attempts to escape from a maximum security satellite prison. About as good as you'd expect. **88m/C VHS.** Jackson Bostwick, Bubba Smith.

Escape from El Diablo **1983 (PG)** Two juvenile delinquents harass guards at a Mexican prison. Being from California, they use frisbees and skateboards to help their escape. **92m/C VHS.** *SP GB* Jimmy (James Vincent) McNichol, Timothy Van Patten, John Ethan Wayne; ***D:*** Gordon Hessler.

Escape from Fort Bravo **1953** A Civil War era western set in an Arizona stockade. Holden is the hard-bitten Union cavalry officer who ruthlessly guards his Confederate prisoners, who are led by Forsythe. Parker is a southern spy whose job is to break the rebels out of jail by seducing Holden from his duty, which she does. When Holden discovers what's happened, he recaptures his prisoners only to be beset by hostile Mescalero Indians while trying to get everyone back to the fort. It's an old story but well-executed with lots of action. **98m/C VHS.** William Holden, Eleanor Parker, John Forsythe, William Demarest, William Campbell, Polly Bergen, Richard Anderson, Carl Benton Reid, John Lupton, Howard McNear, Alex Montoya, Forrest Lewis, Fred Graham, William "Billy" Newell; ***D:*** John Sturges; ***W:*** Frank Fenton; ***C:*** Robert L. Surtees.

Escape from Galaxy Three **1976 (G)** A pair of space travelers fight off a bevy of evil aliens. **90m/C VHS.** James Milton, Cheryl Buchanan.

Escape from Hell woof! *Hellfire on Ice, Part 2: Escape from Hell; Femmine Infernali* **1989** Two scantily clad women escape from a jungle prison and are pursued by their sadistic warden. **?m/C VHS, DVD.** *IT SP* Anthony Steffen, Ajita Wilson; ***D:*** Edward (Edoardo Mulargia) Muller.

Escape from L.A. *John Carpenter's Escape from L.A* **1996 (R)** Well, Snake Plissken is back (Russell once again) and so's Carpenter, who did the original "Escape from New York" saga, and technology's advanced a lot in 15 years, so sit back and enjoy the action. In 2013, L.A.'s been turned into a gang-infested island, thanks to a 9.6 earthquake, where Snake is forced to find a doomsday weapon in just 10 hours. Seems he's been injected with a virus that will kill him unless he can complete his job and escape to get the antidote. Naturally, there's lots of bad guys who'll try to stop him. Russell not only reprises his old role but found Snake's original leathers, which still fit, and wore the outfit in some scenes of the sequel. **101m/C VHS, DVD.** Kurt Russell, Georges Corraface, Stacy Keach, Peter Fonda, Steve Buscemi, Pam Grier, Valeria Golino, Cliff Robertson, Michelle Forbes, Bruce Campbell, A.J. (Allison Joy) Langer; ***D:*** John Carpenter; ***W:*** Kurt Russell, John Carpenter, Debra Hill; ***C:*** Gary B. Kibbe; ***M:*** John Carpenter, Shirley Walker.

Escape from Mars **1999 (PG)** Astronauts make the first manned trip to Mars in the 21st century and must battle any number of internal and external problems to survive. **90m/C VHS.** *CA* Christine Elise, Peter Outerbridge, Allison Hossack, Michael Shanks; ***D:*** Neill Fearnley; ***W:*** Jim Henshaw; ***C:*** Peter Woeste; ***M:*** Peter Allen. **TV**

Escape from New York **1981 (R)** The ultimate urban nightmare: a ruined, future Manhattan is an anarchic prison for America's worst felons. When convicts hold the President hostage, a disgraced war hero unwillingly attempts an impossible rescue mission. Cynical but largely unexceptional sci-fi action, putting a good cast through tight-lipped peril. **99m/C VHS, DVD, Wide.** Kurt Russell, Lee Van Cleef, Ernest Borgnine, Donald Pleasence, Isaac Hayes, Adrienne Barbeau, Harry Dean Stanton, Season Hubley, Tom Atkins, Charles Cyphers, George "Buck" Flower; ***D:*** John Carpenter; ***W:*** John Carpenter, Nick Castle; ***C:*** Dean Cundey; ***M:*** John Carpenter; ***V:*** Jamie Lee Curtis.

Escape from Planet Earth *The Doomsday Machine* **1967** A spaceship is damaged deep in space and only a few of the crew can make it back to Earth. But who will decide who lives or dies? (Unfortunately, the Earth has been totally destroyed so who cares anyway.) Lousy special effects. **91m/B VHS.** Grant Williams, Bobby Van, Ruta Lee, Henry Wilcoxon, Mala Powers, Casey Kasem, Mike Farrell, Harry Hope; ***D:*** Lee Sholem.

Escape from Safehaven woof! **1988 (R)** Brutal slimeballs rule a mad, sadistic world in the post-apocalyptic future, and a family tries to escape them. In very poor taste. **87m/C VHS.** Rick Gianasi, Mollie O'Mara, John Wittenbauer, Roy MacArthur, William Beckwith; ***D:*** Brian Thomas Jones, James McCalmont.

Escape from Sobibor **1987 (PG-13)** Nail-biting, true account of the largest successful escape from a Nazi prison camp, adapted from Richard Rashke's book. Made for TV. **120m/C VHS, DVD.** Alan Arkin, Joanna Pacula, Rutger Hauer, Hartmut Becker, Jack Shepherd; ***D:*** Jack Gold; ***M:*** Georges Delerue. **TV**

Escape from the Bronx **1985 (R)** Invading death squads seek to level the Bronx. Local street gangs cry foul and ally to defeat the uncultured barbarians. Sequel to "1990: The Bronx Warriors." **82m/C VHS.** Mark Gregory, Henry Silva, Valeria (Valerie Dobson) D'Obici, Giancarlo (Timothy Brent) Prete, Andrea Coppola; ***D:*** Enzo G. Castellari.

Escape from the KGB woof! **1987** A CIA agent escapes from a Soviet prison, taking plans for a new space installation with him. **99m/C VHS.** Thomas Hunter, Ivan Desny, Marie Versini, Walter Barns; ***D:*** Harald Phillipe.

Escape from the Planet of the Apes **1971 (G)** Reprising their roles as intelligent, English-speaking apes, McDowall and Hunter flee their world before it's destroyed, and travel back in time to present-day America. In L.A. they become the subjects of a relentless search by the fearful population, much like humans Charlton Heston and James Franciscus were targeted for experimentation and destruction in simian society in the earlier "Planet of the Apes" and "Beneath the Planet of the Apes." Sequelled by "Conquest of..." and a TV series. **98m/C VHS, DVD, Wide.** Roddy McDowall, Kim Hunter, Sal Mineo, Ricardo Montalban, William Windom, Bradford Dillman, Natalie Trundy, Eric (Hans Gudegast) Braeden, Jason Evers, Harry Lauter, John Randolph, M. Emmet Walsh; ***D:*** Don Taylor; ***W:*** Paul Dehn; ***C:*** Joseph Biroc; ***M:*** Jerry Goldsmith.

Escape from Wildcat Canyon **1999** Grandfather Weaver and his young grandson must fight for survival after their small plane crashes in the mountains. **96m/C VHS.** Dennis Weaver, Michael Caloz, Peter Keleghan, Frank Schorpion, Vlasta Vrana; ***D:*** Marc Voizard. **CABLE**

Escape: Human Cargo *Human Cargo* **1998** Suspenseful and fact-based drama set in 1977. Texan John McDonald (Williams) thinks he's scored big when he gets a contract to build housing in Dhahran, Saudi Arabia. Despite government warnings, McDonald decides to travel there himself to oversee the deal. But his partners prove deceitful and when McDonald tries to enforce the contract, he's the one that winds up in prison. He's eventually released, but with his passport confiscated, the only way for McDonald to get out of the Middle East is to try smuggling himself home as cargo. Based on the book "Flight from Dhahran" by John McDonald and Clyde Burleson. **110m/C VHS, DVD.** Treat Williams, Stephen Lang, Sasson Gabai; ***D:*** Simon Wincer; ***W:*** William Mickelberry, Dan Vining; ***C:*** David Burr; ***M:*** Eric Colvin. **CABLE**

Escape Me Never **1947** Flynn plays a struggling composer in this sappy period piece about poverty-stricken artists in Italy at the turn of the century. Flynn falls for his brother's wealthy fiancee (Parker), although he is married to the faithful Lupino. Atypical role for Flynn and definitely not one of his best. Based on the novel "The Fool of the Family," by Margaret Kennedy and the play "Escape Me Never" by Kennedy. **101m/B VHS.** Errol Flynn, Ida Lupino, Eleanor Parker, Gig Young, Reginald Denny, Isobel Elsom; ***D:*** Peter Godfrey; ***W:*** Thomas Williamson.

Escape to Athena **1979 (PG)** A motley group is stuck in a German P.O.W. camp on a Greek island during WWII. **102m/C VHS.** *GB* Roger Moore, Telly Savalas, David Niven, Claudia Cardinale, Richard Roundtree, Stefanie Powers, Sonny Bono, Elliott Gould, William Holden; ***D:*** George P. Cosmatos; ***W:*** Edward Anhalt; ***M:*** Lalo Schifrin.

Escape to Burma **1955** A man on the run for a murder he did not commit finds refuge and romance in an isolated jungle home. **86m/C VHS.** Barbara Stanwyck, Robert Ryan, Reginald Denny; ***D:*** Allan Dwan.

Escape to Love **1982** Beautiful student helps a famous dissident escape from Poland, only to lose him to another heroic venture. **105m/C** Clara Perryman, Louis Jourdan; ***D:*** Herbert Stein.

Escape to Paradise **1939** The last of Breen's films for RKO has him as a South American motorcycle-taxi driver acting as a guide for tourist Taylor. When Breen sets Taylor up with Shelton, trouble ensues. ♫Tra-La-La; Rhythm of the Rio; Ay, Ay, Ay. **60m/B VHS.** Bobby Breen, Kent Taylor, Marla Shelton, Joyce Compton, Rosina Galli, Frank Yaconelli; ***D:*** Erle C. Kenton.

Escape to the Sun *Habricha el Hashemesh* **1972 (PG)** Pair of Russian university students plan to flee their homeland so they can be allowed to live and love free from oppression. **94m/C VHS.** *IS* Laurence Harvey, Josephine Chaplin, John Ireland, Jack Hawkins, Lila Kedrova, Clive Revill; ***D:*** Menahem Golan.

Escape to Witch Mountain **1975 (G)** Two young orphans with supernatural powers find themselves on the run from a greedy millionaire who wants to exploit their amazing gift. Adapted from a novel by Alexander Key. **97m/C VHS.** Kim Richards, Ike Eisenmann, Eddie Albert, Ray Milland, Donald Pleasence; ***D:*** John Hough.

Escape 2000 woof! *Turkey Shoot* **1981 (R)** In a future society where individuality is considered a crime, those who refuse to conform are punished by being hunted down in a jungle. Gross, twisted takeoff of Richard Connell's "The Most Dangerous Game." **80m/C VHS.** *AU* Steve Railsback, Olivia Hussey, Michael Craig; ***D:*** Brian Trenchard-Smith; ***W:*** George Schenck; ***M:*** Brian May.

Escape under Pressure **2000 (R)** Cheapie version of "Die Hard" holds interest thanks to lots of action. Engineer John Spencer (Lowe) and wife Chloe (Miller) are aboard a Greek ferry that get hijacked by lowlifes who are after a priceless ancient statue of Artemis. They manage to protect the statue but have to save themselves as well from the killers. **90m/C VHS, DVD.** Rob Lowe, Larisa Miller, Craig Wasson, Harry Van Gorkum, Stanley Kamel; ***D:*** Jean Pellerin; ***W:*** James Christopher; ***C:*** Richard Clabaugh. **CABLE**

Escape Velocity **1999 (R)** Scientists Cal (Bergin), Billie (Crewson) and their daughter Ronnie (Beaudoin) are on a deep space project when they discover a seemingly abandoned space ship. They find one crewman, Nash (Outerbridge), in suspended animation and make the mistake of bringing him out of his deep sleep. Of course, he turns out to be a psychotic. **100m/C VHS, DVD.** Patrick Bergin, Wendy Crewson, Peter Outerbridge, Michelle Beaudoin; ***D:*** Lloyd A. Simandl; ***M:*** Peter Allen. **VIDEO**

Escapes **1986** In the tradition of "The Twilight Zone," Vincent Price introduces five short thrillers featuring time travel, aliens, and telepathy. Produced with computer assistance for sharper, more contrasted images. **72m/C VHS.** Vincent Price, Jerry Grisham, Lee Canfield, John Mitchum, Gil Reade; ***D:*** David Steensland.

Escapist woof! **1983** A professional escape artist becomes involved in a perverted corporate plot and must escape to save his life and livelihood. **87m/C VHS.** Bill Shirk, Peter Lupus; ***D:*** Eddie Beverly Jr.

The Escort **1997 (R)** Debra Grey (Hall) runs a highly successful (and respectable) escort service and has just hired the charming Suzanne Lane (O'Brien). But behind Suzanne's charm lies the dreaded face of a psycho and she takes a very personal interest in Debra and her family. The unrated version is 90 minutes. **85m/C VHS.** Shauna O'Brien, Landon Hall; ***D:*** Gary Graver; ***W:*** Sean O'Bannon; ***C:*** Gary Graver. **VIDEO**

Esmeralda Comes by Night *De Noche Vienes, Esmeralda* **1998 (R)** Fluff Mexican comedy about a very nuturing nurse named Esmeralda (Rojo) who just loves men so much that she's married to five of them—at the same time. When she decides to take a sixth spouse, that's one man too many for one of her jealous hubbies and he formally accuses her of polyandry. She gets arrested and must explain herself to a grim inspector (Obregon), who will naturally fall under her considerable spell. Based on a story by Elena Poniatowska. Spanish with subtitles. **107m/C VHS.** *MX* Maria Rojo, Claudio Obregon, Roberto Cobo, Ernesto Laguardia, Humberto Pineda, Pedro Armendariz Jr., Alberto Estrella; ***D:*** Jaime Humberto Hermosillo; ***W:*** Jaime Humberto Hermosillo; ***C:*** Xavier Perez Grobet; ***M:*** Omar Guzman.

E.S.P. **1983** A young man is given the amazing power of extra-sensory perception. **96m/C VHS.** Jim Stafford, George Deaton.

Essex Boys **1999 (R)** British gangster movie inspired by the true-crime 1995 murders of three criminals. Ambitious young Billy (Creed-Miles) is hired to chauffeur violent Jason Locke (Bean), who's just out of prison. Jason partnered with John Dyke (Wilkinson) in the drug trade but times have changed and double-crosses are the new name of the game. Billy gets sucked in and betrayed, but beware, because the female (Kingston) does turn out to be deadlier than the male. **102m/C VHS, DVD, Wide.** *GB* Charlie Creed-Miles, Sean Bean, Tom Wilkinson, Alex Kingston, Larry Lamb, Terence Rigby, Billy Murray, Amelia Lowdell; ***D:*** Terry Winsor; ***W:*** Terry Winsor, Jeff Pope; ***C:*** John Daly; ***M:*** Colin Towns.

Estate of Insanity **1970** An English lord and his second wife become involved in a web of death when a maniac stalks their ancient estate. **90m/C VHS.** John Turner, Heather Sears, Ann Lynn; ***D:*** Robert Hartford-Davis.

Esther **1998** Biblical story of a young Jewish girl named Esther who is sought as the bride of Ahasuerus, the King of Persia. She persuades him to stop the slaughter of her people. **91m/C VHS, DVD.** Louise Lombard, Thomas Kretschmann, F. Murray Abraham, Juergen Prochnow, Ornella Muti; ***D:*** Raffaele Mertes. **CABLE**

Esther and the King **1960** Biblical costumer with Egan as Persian king and Collins as the Judean maiden he wants in place of the murdered queen. Long, rambling, and torturous. **109m/C VHS.** *IT* Joan Collins, Richard Egan, Denis O'Dea, Sergio Fantoni; ***D:*** Raoul Walsh; ***W:*** Raoul Walsh, Michael Elkins; ***M:*** Angelo Francesco Lavagnino.

E.T.: The Extra-Terrestrial **1982 (PG)** Spielberg's famous fantasy, one of the most popular films in history, portrays a limpid-eyed alien stranded on earth and his special bonding relationship with a young boy. A modern fairy tale providing warmth, humor and sheer wonder. Held the first place spot as the highest grossing movie of all time for years until a new Spielberg hit replaced it—"Jurassic Park." Debra Winger contributed to the voice of E.T. **115m/C VHS, Wide.** Erika Eleniak, Henry Thomas, Dee Wallace Stone, Drew Barrymore, Robert MacNaughton, Peter Coyote, C. Thomas Howell, Sean Frye, K.C. Martel; ***D:*** Steven Spielberg; ***W:*** Melissa Mathison; ***C:*** Allen Daviau; ***M:*** John Williams; ***V:*** Debra Winger. Oscars '82: Visual FX, Orig. Score; AFI '98: Top 100; Golden Globes '83: Film—Drama, Score; L.A. Film Critics '82: Director (Spielberg), Film, Natl. Film Reg. '94;; Natl. Soc. Film Critics '82: Director (Spielberg); Writers Guild '82: Orig. Screenplay.

The Eternal 🦴🦴 *The Eternal Kiss of the Mummy* **1999 (R)** Nora (Elliott) plays a young wife and mother who's tormented by blinding headaches and dizziness. Along with her husband and young son, she decides to return to her childhood home in Ireland to visit her ailing grandmother. But her symptoms worsen the closer she gets to her ancestral home, and Elliott discovers that her creepy uncle (Walken) has retrieved the body of a witch who died hundreds of years before. Only she's not quite dead. **95m/C VHS, DVD.** Alison Elliott, Jared Harris, Christopher Walken, Lois Smith, Karl Geary; ***D:*** Michael Almereyda; ***W:*** Michael Almereyda; ***C:*** Jim Denault; ***M:*** Simon Fisher Turner.

Eternal Evil 🦴 **1987 (R)** A bored TV director is taught how to have out-of-body experiences by his devil-worshipping girlfriend. He eventually realizes that when he leaves his body, it runs around killing people. **85m/C VHS, DVD.** Karen Black, Winston Rekert, Lois Maxwell; ***D:*** George Mihalka; ***W:*** Robert Geoffrion; ***C:*** Paul Van der Linden.

Eternal Return 🦴🦴½ *L'Eternel Retour; Love Eternal* **1943** A lush modern retelling of the Tristan/Isolde legend. Patrice (Marais) brings the beautiful Nathalie (Sologne) to his family's castle, as his uncle's (Murat) intended bride. But thanks to a love potion, it's Nathalie and Patrice who fall in love—with tragic results. In French with English subtitles. **111m/B VHS.** *FR* Jane (Jeanne) Marken, Alex(andre) Rignault, Roland Toutain, Yvonne de Bray, Jean Marais, Madeleine Sologne, Jean Murat; ***D:*** Jean Delannoy; ***W:*** Jean Cocteau; ***C:*** Roger Hubert; ***M:*** Georges Auric.

The Eternal Waltz 🦴🦴 *Ewiger Walzer* **1954** Overly sentimental chronicle of the life of composer Johann Strauss. Only director Verhoeven's touch holds the viewer's interest, though the production values are excellent. **97m/C VHS.** Bernhard Wicki, Hilde Krahl, Annemarie Duerringer, Friedl Loor, Eduard Strauss Jr., Gert Frobe, Arnulf Schroeder; ***D:*** Paul Verhoeven.

Eternally Yours 🦴🦴½ **1939** A witty magician's career threatens to break up his marriage. **95m/B VHS.** David Niven, Loretta Young, Hugh Herbert, Broderick Crawford, Sir C. Aubrey Smith, Billie Burke, Eve Arden, ZaSu Pitts; ***D:*** Tay Garnett.

Eternity 🦴 **1990 (R)** While trying to uncover corrupt corporate America, a TV reporter falls in love with a model who works for a media king and puts his credibility on the line. He believes he and the woman shared romance in a past life. **122m/C VHS.** Jon Voight, Armand Assante, Wilford Brimley, Eileen Davidson, Kaye Ballard, Lainie Kazan, Joey Villa, Steven Keats, Eugene Roche, Frankie Valli, John P. Ryan; ***D:*** Steven Paul.

Eternity and a Day 🦴🦴 *Mia Eoniotita Ke Mia Mera* **1997** Seriously ill writer Alexander (Ganz) is putting his affairs in order and revisiting his past, particularly moments with his beloved late wife, Anna (Renauld). But the present isn't finished with Alexander yet. He rescues a young boy (Skevis), an illegal immigrant from Albania, who says he was taken from his grandmother. Alexander decides to take the boy home and the two set out on the journey that will surely be Alexander's last. Greek with subtitles. **134m/C VHS.** *GR FR* Bruno Ganz, Isabelle Renauld, Achileas Skevis; ***D:*** Theo Angelopoulos; ***W:*** Theo Angelopoulos; ***C:*** Yorgos Arvanitis, Andreas Sinani; ***M:*** Eleni Karaindrou. Cannes '98: Film.

Ethan 🦴½ **1971** A missionary in the Philippines falls in love with a woman and exiles himself for his fall from grace. **91m/C VHS.** Robert Sampson, Rosa Rosal, Eddie Infante; ***D:*** Michael DuPont.

Ethan Frome 🦴🦴½ **1992 (PG)** Neeson stars as the lonely, poverty-stricken 19th-century New England farmer who has long and faithfully cared for his bitter, invalid wife. When his wife's distant young cousin comes to take over as housekeeper they both succumb to their forbidden passion with tragic results. The performers carry the burden of the film's sluggish pacing, where the bleak setting of Massachusetts in winter tends to overwhelm the events. Based on the novel by Edith Wharton. **107m/C VHS.** Liam Neeson, Patricia Arquette, Joan Allen, Tate Donovan, Katharine Houghton, Stephen Mendillo; ***D:*** John Madden; ***W:*** Richard Nelson; ***C:*** Bobby Bukowski.

Eubie! **1982** The popular Broadway musical revue based on the life and songs of Eubie Blake is presented in a video transfer. Some of Eubie's best known songs, performed here by members of the original cast, include "I'm Just Wild About Harry," "Memories of You," "In Honeysuckle Time" and "The Charleston Rag." **100m/C VHS.** Gregory Hines, Maurice Hines, Leslie Dockery, Alaina Reed, Lynnie Godfrey, Mel Johnson Jr., Jeffrey V. Thompson; ***D:*** Julianne Boyd.

Eureka! 🦴🦴½ **1981 (R)** A bizarre, wildly symbolic slab of Roegian artifice that deals with the dream-spliced life of a rich, bored gold tycoon who becomes tortured over his daughter's marriage and his own useless wealth. Eventually he is bothered by the Mafia and led to the courtroom by business competitors. From the book by Paul Mayersberg. **130m/C VHS.** *GB* Gene Hackman, Theresa Russell, Joe Pesci, Rutger Hauer, Mickey Rourke, Ed Lauter, Jane Lapotaire; ***D:*** Nicolas Roeg.

Eureka Stockade 🦴🦴 *Massacre Hill* **1949** Four early Australian gold prospectors join forces to fight their governor and the police for the rights to dig on the continent. **103m/B VHS.** *AU* Chips Rafferty, Peter Finch, Jane Barrett, Peter Illing; ***D:*** Harry Watt.

Europa, Europa 🦴🦴🦴½ *Hitlerjunge Salomon* **1991 (R)** The incredible, harrowing and borderline-absurdist true story of Solomon Perel, a young Jew who escaped the Holocaust by passing for German at an elite, Nazi-run academy. Such a sharp evocation of the era that the modern German establishment wouldn't submit it for the Academy Awards. In German and Russian with English subtitles. **115m/C VHS.** *GE* Marco Hofschneider, Klaus Abramowsky, Michele Gleizer, Rene Hofschneider, Nathalie Schmidt, Delphine Forest, Julie Delpy; ***D:*** Agnieszka Holland; ***W:*** Agnieszka Holland; ***C:*** Jacek Petrycki, Jacek Zaleski; ***M:*** Zbigniew Preisner. Golden Globes '92: Foreign Film; Natl. Bd. of Review '91: Foreign Film; N.Y. Film Critics '91: Foreign Film.

Europa '51 🦴🦴½ *The Greatest Love* **1952** The despairing portrait of post-war malaise, as an American woman, whose son committed suicide, lives in Rome searching for some semblance of meaning, and ends up in an asylum. One of Bergman & Rossellini's least-loved films. In Italian with subtitles. **110m/B VHS.** Ingrid Bergman, Alexander Knox, Ettore Giannini, Giulietta Masina; ***D:*** Roberto Rossellini.

The Europeans 🦴🦴🦴 **1979** Fine adaptation of Henry James's satiric novel. British brother and sister visit their staid American cousins in 19th-century New England in an effort to improve their prospects through fortuitous marriages. **90m/C VHS.** Lee Remick, Lisa Eichhorn, Robin Ellis, Wesley Addy, Tim Woodward; ***D:*** James Ivory; ***W:*** Ruth Prawer Jhabvala.

Eva 🦴🦴½ *Eva the Devil's Woman* **1962** Writer Tyvian (Baker) becomes obsessed with prostitute Eva (Moreau), spends all his money on her, leaves his fiancee Francesca (Lisi) for her, but all she does is taunt and abandon him. He marries Francesca but leaves his bride (who kills herself) for Eva, who discards him again, leaving Tyvian broke and betrayed. Based on the novel "Eve" by James Hadley Chase. **103m/B VHS, DVD, Wide.** *FR IT* Jeanne Moreau, Stanley Baker, Virna Lisi, James Villiers, Giorgio Albertazzi, Riccardo Garrone; ***D:*** Joseph Losey; ***W:*** Hugo Butler, Evan Jones; ***C:*** Gianni Di Venanzo; ***M:*** Michel Legrand.

Evangeline 🦴🦴½ **1929** Based on the Henry Wadsworth Longfellow poem about the struggles of Evangeline and the tragedy of lost love. Evangeline lives in an Acadian (with ties to France) village in Nova Scotia and is engaged to Gabriel. But when France and England declare war, the village sides with France and the men are forcibly deported to Louisiana. But Evangeline is determined to be reunited with her love. **90m/B VHS, DVD.** Dolores Del Rio, Roland (Walter Goss) Drew, Alec B. Francis, George F. Marion Sr., Donald Reed; ***D:*** Edwin Carewe; ***W:*** Finis Fox; ***C:*** Robert B. Kurrle; ***M:*** Hugo Riesenfeld, Philip Carli.

Eve of Destruction woof! **1990 (R)** Hell knows no fury like a cutting-edge android-girl on the warpath. Modeled after her creator, Dr. Eve Simmons, Eve VII has android-babe good looks and a raging nuclear capability. Wouldn't you know, something goes haywire during her trial run, and debutante Eve turns into a PMS nightmare machine, blasting all the good Doctor's previous beaux. That's where military agent Hines comes in, though you wonder why. Dutch actress Soutendijk plays dual Eves in her first American film. **101m/C VHS.** Gregory Hines, Renee Soutendijk, Kurt Fuller, Ross Malinger, Eugene Glazer, John M. Jackson, Loren Haynes, Michael Greene; ***D:*** Duncan Gibbins; ***W:*** Duncan Gibbins, Yale Udoff; ***C:*** Alan Hume.

Evel Knievel 🦴🦴 **1972 (PG)** The life of motorcycle stuntman Evel Knievel is depicted in this movie, as portrayed by George Hamilton. Stunts will be appreciated by Evel Knievel fans. **90m/C VHS, DVD.** George Hamilton, Bert Freed, Rod Cameron, Sue Lyon; ***D:*** Marvin J. Chomsky; ***W:*** John Milius; ***C:*** David M. Walsh; ***M:*** Patrick Williams.

Evelyn Prentice 🦴🦴½ **1934** Powell and Loy again team up as a married couple (after their "The Thin Man" success) but this time things aren't so rosy. He is an attorney with a wandering eye who has an affair with Russell (in her film debut). Loy finds out and turns for sympathy to Stephens but then she decides to stay with her husband after all. Only she's written some steamy letters to Stephens and he tries blackmailing her—and winds up dead. Dramatic courtroom scene straightens things out. Adapted from the novel by W.E. Woodward. Film was remade as "Stronger Than Desire" in 1939. **78m/B VHS.** Myrna Loy, William Powell, Harvey Stephens, Isabel Jewell, Una Merkel, Rosalind Russell, Henry Wadsworth, Edward Brophy, Cora Sue Collins, Jessie Ralph, Sam Flint, Pat O'Malley; ***D:*** William K. Howard; ***W:*** Lenore Coffee.

Even Angels Fall 🦴🦴 **1990** One of heartthrob singer Humperdinck's scattered dramatic projects, a mystery thriller about a romance novelist moving into a New York brownstone whose previous inhabitant committed suicide—or was it murder? **?m/C VHS.** Morgan Fairchild, Engelbert Humperdinck; ***D:*** Thomas Calabrese.

Even Cowgirls Get the Blues 🦴½ **1994 (R)** '70s counterculture loses its ill-defined charm in a meandering adaptation of cult author Tom Robbins' 1976 novel. An interesting failure, but likely to alienate both Van Sant and Robbins fans. Sissy Hackshaw (Thurman) possesses enormous thumbs which she hopes will make her the greatest hitchhiker in the world. But first they take her to a NYC modeling career for The Countess (Hurt in a high camp performance), who sends her to the Rubber Rose ranch, recently liberated by female cowhands, who are happy to welcome her. Theatrical release was delayed numerous times as Van Sant recut but it doesn't matter—the only successful feature is the soundtrack. **106m/C VHS.** Uma Thurman, John Hurt, Rain Phoenix, Lorraine Bracco, Noriyuki "Pat" Morita, Angie Dickinson, Keanu Reeves; ***Cameos:*** Sean Young, Crispin Glover, Roseanne, Ed Begley Jr.; ***D:*** Gus Van Sant; ***W:*** Gus Van Sant; ***C:*** Eric Alan Edwards, John Campbell; ***M:*** k.d. lang, Ben Mink.

The Evening Star 🦴🦴½ **1996 (PG-13)** Sequel to 1983's "Terms of Endearment" starts in 1988 and finds the overbearing Aurora (MacLaine) now wreacking havoc on the lives of her three grown grandchildren (and vice versa). And Aurora's lovelife is as active as ever—old beau Hector Scott (Moffat) is hanging around, young psychiatrist Jerry Bruckner (Paxton) becomes her lover, and former astronaut flame Garrett Breedlove (Nicholson) also makes a brief appearance to cock an eyebrow at the shenanigans. Last screen role for Johnson as neighbor Arthur Cotten. Based on the novel by Larry McMurtry. Bring a hankie for the tears. **128m/C VHS, DVD, Wide.** Shirley MacLaine, Juliette Lewis, George Newbern, MacKenzie Astin, Bill Paxton, Miranda Richardson, Marion Ross, Ben Johnson, Donald Moffat, Scott Wolf, China Kantner, Jack Nicholson; ***D:*** Robert Harling; ***W:*** Robert Harling; ***C:*** Don Burgess; ***M:*** William Ross.

Event Horizon 🦴🦴½ **1997 (R)** Cross between "Alien" and "The Shining" has Fishburne heading an ensemble cast out to rescue a prototype spaceship that's been missing for seven years. Their own ship is sabotaged by their own demons and certain extraterrestial ones, too, that cause much mayhem on their once peaceful mission. **97m/C VHS, DVD.** Laurence "Larry" Fishburne, Sam Neill, Kathleen Quinlan, Joely Richardson, Richard T. Jones, Jack Noseworthy, Sean Pertwee, Jason Isaacs; ***D:*** Paul Anderson; ***W:*** Philip Eisner; ***C:*** Adrian Biddle; ***M:*** Michael Kamen.

Ever After: A Cinderella Story 🦴🦴🦴 **1998 (PG-13)** The adorable Barrymore takes on Cinderella, renamed Danielle and very capable, in this not-quite-a-fairytale version set in 16th-century France. Huston's the peeved stepmom, Rodmilla, who reduces Danielle to the role of servant in her own home after her beloved father (Krabbe) dies. Danielle still falls for handsome Prince Henry (Scott), only she's not above trying to change the arrogant snob's opinions and tweak him about his privileged upbringing. Artist/genius Leonardo da Vinci (Godfrey) serves as the prince's confidante and there's still a lovely masked ball and a shoe to be lost (and found). **122m/C VHS, DVD, Wide.** Drew Barrymore, Anjelica Huston, Dougray Scott, Patrick Godfrey, Megan Dodds, Melanie Lynskey, Timothy West, Judy Parfitt, Jeroen Krabbe; ***Cameos:*** Jeanne Moreau; ***D:*** Andy Tennant; ***W:*** Andy Tennant, Susannah Grant, Rick Parks; ***C:*** Andrew Dunn; ***M:*** George Fenton.

Evergreen 🦴🦴½ **1934** The daughter of a retired British music hall star is mistaken for her mother and it is thought that she has discovered the secret of eternal youth. ♫Daddy Wouldn't Buy Me a Bow-Wow; When You've Got a Little Springtime in Your Heart; If I Give in to You; Tinkle, Tinkle, Tinkle; Dear, Dear; Dancing on the Ceiling; Just by Your Example; Over My Shoulder. **91m/B VHS.** *GB* Jessie Matthews, Sonnie Hale, Betty Balfour, Barry Mackay, Ivor McLaren, Hartley Power, Patrick Ludlow, Marjorie Gaffney; ***D:*** Victor Saville; ***W:*** Emlyn Williams; ***C:*** Glen MacWilliams; ***M:*** Richard Rodgers, Harry Woods, Lorenz Hart, Harry Woods.

An Everlasting Piece 🦴🦴½ **2000 (R)** Director Levinson moves from working-class Baltimore to working-class Belfast in the 1980s in this goofball comedy. Best pals and fellow barbers Colm (McEvoy) and George (O'Byrne) don't let their different religions come between them. In fact, they decide it will be an advantage when they take on a new toupee business (called The Piece People)—Colm can sell to the Catholics and George will handle the Protestants. But it turns out they have a rival firm, Toupee or Not Toupee, and then Colm winds up with a substantial order from the IRA. He's willing to separate politics for business but is anyone else? **103m/C VHS, DVD, Wide.** *US* Barry McEvoy, Brian F. O'Byrne, Anna Friel, Billy Connolly, Pauline McLynn, Laurence Kinlan, Ruth McCabe; ***D:*** Barry Levinson; ***W:*** Barry McEvoy; ***C:*** Seamus Deasy; ***M:*** Hans Zimmer.

The Everlasting Secret Family 𝒜𝒜 1988 Politics and family life make strange bedfellows. A top political figure joins a secret homosexual organization in his search for power. **93m/C VHS.** *AU* Arthur Dignam, Mark Lee, Dennis Miller, Heather Mitchell; ***D:*** Michael Thornhill.

Eversmile New Jersey 𝒜½ 1989 (PG) A dentist travels through Patagonia, offering dental care and advice to anyone in need, and a young woman, taken with the dental knight, dumps her boyfriend and stows away with him. When he discovers his admirer, he is less than ecstatic, but a chance tooth extraction on the road reveals the young woman's natural dental talents, and the two bond. From the director of "The Official Story." **88m/C VHS.** *AR* Daniel Day-Lewis, Mirjana Jokovic; ***D:*** Carlos Sorin; ***W:*** Jorge Goldenberg, Roberto Scheuer, Carlos Sorin.

Every Breath 𝒜𝒜 1993 (R) A kinky couple's games can be deadly and now they have someone new to play with. Jimmy couldn't resist the wife's seductive allure and if he wants to survive, he'll have to beat them at their own game. **88m/C VHS.** Judd Nelson, Joanna Pacula, Patrick Bauchau; ***D:*** Steve Bing; ***W:*** Judd Nelson, Andrew Fleming, Steve Bing; ***M:*** Nils Lofgren.

Every Day's a Holiday 𝒜𝒜½ 1938 In the 1890s, West stars as confidence woman Peaches O'Day, who sells the Brooklyn Bridge and is run out of New York City. But she comes back, in disguise as a French singer, to expose some crooked cops. The Hays office again came down heavily on Mae's suggestive behavior, which left her with little to rely on. West's last film for Paramount. **79m/B VHS.** Mae West, Edmund Lowe, Charles Butterworth, Charles Winninger, Walter Catlett, Lloyd Nolan, Herman Bing; ***D:*** Edward Sutherland; ***W:*** Mae West.

Every Girl Should Be Married 𝒜𝒜½ 1948 A shopgirl sets her sights on an eligible bachelor doctor. **84m/B VHS.** Cary Grant, Betsy Drake, Diana Lynn, Franchot Tone; ***D:*** Don Hartman.

Every Girl Should Have One 𝒜½ 1978 A rambunctious comedy about a chase following a million-dollar diamond theft. **90m/C VHS.** Zsa Zsa Gabor, Robert Alda, Alice Faye, Sandra Vacey, John Lazar.

Every Man for Himself & God Against All 𝒜𝒜𝒜𝒜 *The Mystery of Kaspar Hauser; Jeder fur Sich und Gott gegen Alle; The Enigma of Kaspar Hauser* 1975 Kaspar Hauser is a young man who mysteriously appears in the town square of Nuremberg, early in the 19th century. He cannot speak or stand upright and is found to have been kept in a dungeon for the first 18 years of his life. He becomes an attraction in society with his alternate vision of the world and attempts to reconcile with reality. A lovely, though demanding film which is based on a true story. In German with English subtitles. **110m/C VHS.** *GE* Bruno S, Brigitte Mira, Walter Ladengast, Hans Musaus, Willy Semmelrogge, Michael Kroecher, Henry van Lyck; ***D:*** Werner Herzog; ***W:*** Werner Herzog; ***C:*** Jorge Schmidt-Reitwein; ***M:*** Orlando Di Lasso.

Every Man's Law 𝒜½ 1935 A cowboy who poses as a hired gunman is almost lynched by ranchers who think he is a murderer. **60m/B VHS.** Johnny Mack Brown.

Every Mother's Worst Fear 𝒜𝒜 1998 (PG-13) When her boyfriend dumps her, 16-year-old Martha Hoagland (Jordan Ladd) checks out the Internet chat rooms. She begins an online romance with Drew (Gale) but doesn't realize that hacker Mitch Carson (McGinley) is manipulating the entire situation. Soon Martha decides to slip away and meet Drew, and winds up Mitch's prisoner and the latest potential victim of his porn business. But it's mom Connie (Cheryl Ladd) to the rescue! **92m/C VHS.** Cheryl Ladd, Jordan Ladd, Ted McGinley, Vincent Gale, Robert Wisden, Tom Butler; ***D:*** Bill W.L. Norton; ***W:*** John Robert Bensink. CABLE

Every Other Weekend 𝒜𝒜𝒜 *Un Week-end sur Deux* 1991 Camille Valmont (Baye) is an actress who has sacrified everything for her now-fading career. She's divorced loving husband Adrian (Manojlovic) and given him custody of their two young children—often ignoring her every other weekend visitation rights. In financial straits, Camille takes a job out of town and decides to take the kids with her, without telling Adrian. Self-centered and easily distracted, Camille tries to get close but manages to destroy what little rapport she has with her children. Camille isn't likable but Baye is such a gifted actress that you'll still feel pity. Director Garcia's debut; French with subtitles. **100m/C VHS.** *FR* Nathalie Baye, Miki (Predrag) Manojlovic, Joachim Serreau, Felicie Pasotti; ***D:*** Nicole Garcia; ***W:*** Nicole Garcia, Jacques Fieschi; ***C:*** William Lubtchansky; ***M:*** Oswald D'Andrea.

Every Time We Say Goodbye 𝒜𝒜½ 1986 (PG-13) In 1942, Jerusalem, an American flyboy falls in love with a young Sephardic Jewish girl, whose family resists the match. **97m/C VHS.** Tom Hanks, Christina Marsillach, Benedict Taylor, Anat Atzmon, Gila Almagor; ***D:*** Moshe Mizrahi; ***W:*** Moshe Mizrahi, Leah Appet; ***M:*** Philippe Sarde.

Every Which Way But Loose 𝒜𝒜 1978 (R) Fairly pointless Eastwood foray featuring Clint as a beer-guzzling, country-music loving truck driver earning a living as a barroom brawler. He and his orangutan travel to Colorado in pursuit of the woman he loves. Behind him are a motorcycle gang and an L.A. cop. All have been victims of his fists. Sequel is "Any Which Way You Can." **119m/C VHS, DVD, Wide.** Clint Eastwood, Sondra Locke, Geoffrey Lewis, Beverly D'Angelo, Ruth Gordon; ***D:*** James Fargo; ***W:*** Jeremy Joe Kronsberg; ***C:*** Rexford Metz; ***M:*** Steve Dorff.

Everybody Sing 𝒜𝒜 1938 A down-on-their-luck theatrical family, including Garland (who is kicked out of boarding school for singing Mendelssohn with a swing beat) decides to put on a show in hopes of making a comeback. Dumb plot and boring songs make this one for die-hard Garland fans only. ♫Swing, Mr. Mendelssohn, Swing; The One I Love; Down on Melody Farms; The Show Must Go On; I Wanna Swing; Never Was There Such a Perfect Day; Quainty Dainty Me; Why? Because; Snooks. **80m/B VHS.** Allan Jones, Fanny Brice, Judy Garland, Reginald Owen, Billie Burke, Reginald Gardiner, Lynne Carver, Monty Woolley; ***D:*** Edwin L. Marin; ***M:*** George Bassman.

Everybody Wins 𝒜 1990 (R) A mystery-romance about a befuddled private eye trying to solve a murder and getting caught up with the bizarre prostitute who hired him. Arthur Miller based this screenplay on his stage drama "Some Kind of Love Story." Confused and, given its pedigree, disappointing mystery. **110m/C VHS.** Nick Nolte, Debra Winger, Will Patton, Jack Warden, Kathleen Wilhoite, Frank Converse, Frank Military, Judith Ivey; ***D:*** Karel Reisz; ***W:*** Arthur Miller; ***C:*** Ian Baker.

Everybody's All American 𝒜𝒜 1988 (R) Shallow, sentimental melodrama about a college football star and his cheerleader wife whose lives, subsequent to their youthful glories, is a string of disappointments and tragedies. Decently acted and based on Frank Deford's novel. **127m/C VHS, 8mm.** Jessica Lange, Dennis Quaid, Timothy Hutton, John Goodman, Carl Lumbly, Ray Baker, Savannah Smith; ***D:*** Taylor Hackford; ***M:*** James Newton Howard.

Everybody's Dancin' 𝒜½ 1950 A ballroom proprietor's business is marred by random killings in her establishment as the bands play on. ♫Foolish Tears; Oblivious; Deep Freeze Dinah; I Shook; Rhumba Boogie. **66m/B VHS.** Spade Cooley, Dick Lane, Hal Derwin, Roddy McDowall; ***D:*** Will Jason.

Everybody's Famous! 𝒜𝒜½ *Iedereen Beroemd!* 2000 (R) Factory worker Jean (De Pauw) is convinced that his teenaged daughter Marva (Van der Gucht) has the talent to become a famous singer, though she suffers from stage fright and seems hopeless. Devoted dad goes to the extreme of kidnapping Debbie (Reuten), a Belgian pop star burned out by her successful career. Jean's demand is that Debbie's lowlife manager (Loew) make Marva a star. Meanwhile, Debbie falls for her young co-kidnapper Willy (De Smedt). It's all played for laughs as it skewers the idea of media madness and fame at any price but there's a warped sweetness at the core as well. Dutch, Flemish, and French with subtitles. **99m/C VHS, DVD, Wide.** *BE* Josse De Pauw, Eva Van der Gucht, Werner De Smedt, Thekla Reuten, Victor Low, Gert Portael; ***D:*** Dominique Deruddere; ***W:*** Dominique Deruddere; ***C:*** Willy Stassen; ***M:*** Raymond van het Groenewoud.

Everybody's Fine 𝒜𝒜½ *Stanno Tutti Bene* 1990 (PG-13) Mastroianni stars in this bittersweet story of a father on a mission to reunite his five grown children. His journey takes him all over Italy as he tries to bring them together in this touching film about enduring family love. In Italian with English subtitles. **115m/C VHS.** *IT* Marcello Mastroianni, Salvatore Cascio, Valeria Cavalli, Norma Martelli, Marino Cenna, Roberto Nobile, Michele Morgan, Fabio Iellini; ***D:*** Giuseppe Tornatore; ***W:*** Giuseppe Tornatore, Tonino Guerra; ***M:*** Ennio Morricone.

Everyone Says I Love You 𝒜𝒜𝒜 1996 (R) Woody sings! Granted, he doesn't sing very well, but who else could twist a story of love among the neurotic rich with lavish production numbers from the golden age of movie musicals? The excellent cast (who weren't told that they were in a musical until after they signed) prove that as singers, they're pretty good actors. The plot centers around the wandering love lives of Steffi (Hawn), her husband Bob (Alda), her ex-husband Joe (Allen) and their assorted children; especially the preppy Skylar (Barrymore) and her fiance Holden (Norton). Some of the musical productions are shaky (Allen's duet with Julia Roberts is straight out of Tin Ear Alley), but the feeling behind them is genuine; Besides, where else are you going to hear Groucho's "Hooray for Captain Spaulding" sung in French or a chorus of pregnant women sing "Makin' Whoopee"? **105m/C VHS, DVD.** Woody Allen, Alan Alda, Drew Barrymore, Goldie Hawn, Gaby Hoffman, Edward Norton, Natalie Portman, Julia Roberts, Tim Roth, Natasha Lyonne, Lukas Haas, David Ogden Stiers; ***D:*** Woody Allen; ***W:*** Woody Allen; ***C:*** Carlo Di Palma; ***M:*** Dick Hyman. L.A. Film Critics '96: Support. Actor (Norton); Natl. Bd. of Review '96: Support. Actor (Norton).

Everything Happens at Night 𝒜𝒜𝒜 1939 Rival reporters Milland and Cummings are torn between the woman they love and the story of a lifetime. One of Henie's best romantic skating vehicles due to the strong performances by the leading men. Henie does take to the ice for a couple of numbers, but this film was largely designed to expand her image as a serious actress. Although it failed to do that, it's good entertainment nonetheless. **76m/B VHS.** Sonja Henie, Ray Milland, Robert Cummings, Maurice (Moscovitch) Moscovich, Leonid Kinskey, Alan Dinehart, Fritz Feld; ***D:*** Irving Cummings; ***W:*** Art Arthur, Robert Harari.

Everything Put Together 𝒜𝒜½ 2000 Suburban housewife Angie (Mitchell) is pregnant as are her best friends Judith (Burns) and Barbie (Mullally). But Angie seems overly anxious and her worst fears are realized when her seemingly healthy son dies in the hospital from SIDS. Although husband Russ (Louis) tries to be as understanding and caring as possible, Anglie sinks into severe depression, especially when her friends, in their discomfort, begin to withdraw from her. **85m/C VHS, DVD.** Radha Mitchell, Megan Mullally, Justin Louis, Catherine Lloyd Burns, Alan Ruck, Matt Malloy, Michele Hicks; ***D:*** Marc Forster; ***W:*** Catherine Lloyd Burns, Adam Forgash; ***C:*** Roberto Schaefer; ***M:*** Thomas Koppel.

Everything Relative 𝒜𝒜½ 1996 Seven college buddies reunite and spend a weekend in the country together in this lesbian twist on "The Big Chill." A bris held by partners Katie and Sarah for their new baby brings the mostly single forty-something women together, and bring out the unfulfilled desires and regrets of the six lesbians and one straight woman. Standouts include Weber as the stunt woman mourning the loss of a lover to a car accident 15 years prior, as well as the relationship between Josie (McLaughlin) and Maria (Negron), the woman who left her to get married and have children, and is now divorced and losing her children in the custody battle. Low budget ($100,000) indie debut of writer/director Pollack is right on the mark emotionally and manages to keep the characters and their stories engaging, but loses something with neatly pat solutions to the intricate problems facing these women. **110m/C VHS.** Stacey Nelkin, Ellen McLaughlin, Olivia Negron, Monica Bell, Andrea Weber, Gabriella Messina, Carol Schneider; ***D:*** Sharon Pollack; ***W:*** Sharon Pollack; ***C:*** Rachel Othmer; ***M:*** Frank London.

Everything That Rises 𝒜𝒜½ 1998 Quaid directs (his debut) and stars in this movie about tough rancher Jim Clay who struggles to hold onto the land that's been in his family for generations. An uncommunicative man, Jim is forced to reexamine his life when his young son Nathan (Merriman) is rendered a paraplegic after an auto accident caused by his dad. Winningham is devoted, stoic wife Kyle and Presnell is aging cowpoke/family friend Garth. **90m/C VHS.** Dennis Quaid, Mare Winningham, Harve Presnell, Ryan Merriman, Meat Loaf Aday, Bruce McGill; ***D:*** Dennis Quaid; ***W:*** Mark Spragg; ***C:*** Jack Conroy; ***M:*** David Robbins. CABLE

Everything You Always Wanted to Know about Sex (But Were Afraid to Ask) 𝒜𝒜𝒜 1972 (R) Satiric comical sketches about sex includes a timid sperm cell, an oversexed court jester, a sheep folly, and a giant disembodied breast. Quite entertaining in its own jolly way. Based on the book by Dr. David Reuben. **88m/C VHS, DVD, Wide.** Woody Allen, John Carradine, Lou Jacobi, Louise Lasser, Anthony Quayle, Geoffrey Holder, Lynn Redgrave, Tony Randall, Burt Reynolds, Gene Wilder, Robert Walden, Jay Robinson; ***D:*** Woody Allen; ***W:*** Woody Allen; ***C:*** David M. Walsh; ***M:*** Mundell Lowe.

Eve's Bayou 𝒜𝒜𝒜½ 1997 (R) Eve (newcomer Smollett) comes from the upper-middle class Batiste family that seems all too perfect on the outside, but secrets and lies slowly surface when she mistakenly catches her doctor father Louis (Jackson) doing more than a routine check-up with a female patient. With her innocence shattered by the discovery, Eve's torment soon affects her emotionally strained mother Roz (Whitfield) and adolescent tease older sister Cisely (Good). Set in Louisiana 1962, and told in flashback, film presents a mesmerizing and complex story with haunting visuals. Ghostly appearance from Carroll adds a touch of voodoo and heightens the melodramatic intensity. Jackson is solid as the charming, yet flawed womanizer and Whitfield his equal as the suspecting wife. Impressive, multi-layered directorial debut from Lemmons didn't draw much attention during theatrical run, but has gained a following since. **109m/C VHS, DVD.** Samuel L. Jackson, Lynn Whitfield, Debbi (Deborah) Morgan, Diahann Carroll, Jurnee Smollett, Meagan Good, Vondie Curtis-Hall, Lisa Nicole Carson, Jake Smollett, Ethel Ayler; ***D:*** Kasi Lemmons; ***W:*** Kasi Lemmons; ***C:*** Amy Vincent; ***M:*** Terence Blanchard; ***Nar:*** Tamara Tunie. Ind. Spirit '98: First Feature, Support. Actress (Morgan).

The Evictors woof! 1979 (PG) Young couple moves into an abandoned, haunted farmhouse in a small Louisiana town. Unfortunately, they don't know anything about its horrible bloody history. And the real estate agent acts kinda funny. AIP Amityville scare-a-thon. **92m/C VHS.** Vic Morrow, Michael Parks, Jessica Harper, Sue Ane Langdon, Dennis Fimple; ***D:*** Charles B. Pierce; ***W:*** Charles B. Pierce.

Evidence of Blood 𝒜𝒜½ 1997 (PG-13) Crime writer investigates a 40-year-old murder in a small town that would rather keep its secrets to itself. Based on the book by Thomas H. Cook. **109m/C VHS.**

David Strathairn, Mary McDonnell; *D:* Andrew Mondshein; *W:* Dalene Young; *C:* Philip Linzey; *M:* Mason Daring.

The Evil 🦴🦴 **1978 (R)** A psychologist must destroy an evil force that is killing off the members of his research team residing at an old mansion. **80m/C VHS.** Richard Crenna, Joanna Pettet, Andrew Prine, Victor Buono, Cassie Yates, George O'Hanlon Jr., Lynne Moody, Mary Louise Weller, Milton Selzer; *D:* Gus Trikonis; *W:* Donald G. Thompson; *C:* Mario DiLeo.

Evil Altar 🦴 **1989 (R)** A man controls a small town, but only so long as he offers sacrifices to the devil! **90m/C VHS.** William Smith, Robert Z'Dar, Pepper Martin, Theresa Cooney, Ryan Rao; *D:* James R. Winburn.

The Evil Below 🦴 **1987** A couple hits the high seas in search of the lost treasure ship "El Diablo," resting on the ocean floor. In the process they trigger an evil curse and then must attempt to thwart it. **90m/C VHS.** *SA* June Chadwick, Wayne Crawford; *D:* Jean-Claude Dubois.

Evil Clutch 🦴½ **1989 (R)** A young couple vacationing in the Alps encounter several creepy locals when they find themselves in the midst of a haunted forest. The cinematography is extremely amateurish in this Italian gorefest and the English dubbing is atrocious. However, the special makeup effects are outstanding and the musical score adds a touch of class to this otherwise inept horror film. **88m/C VHS.** *IT* Coralina Cataldi Tassoni, Diego Riba, Elena Cantarone, Luciano Crovato, Stefano Molinari; *D:* Andreas Marfori; *W:* Andreas Marfori; *C:* Marco Isoli.

Evil Dead 🦴🦴½ **1983 (NC-17)** Five college students, vacationing in the Tennessee mountains, take refuge in an abandoned cabin. They find a tape and a Book of the Dead, which unwittingly lets them resurrect demons, which transform the students into evil monsters until only Ash (Campbell) remains to fight the evil. Exuberantly gory low-budgeter followed by two sequels. **85m/C VHS, DVD.** Bruce Campbell, Ellen Sandweiss, Betsy Baker, Hal Delrich, Sarah York, Theodore (Ted) Raimi, Sam Raimi, Scott Spiegel; *D:* Sam Raimi; *W:* Sam Raimi; *C:* Tim Philo; *M:* Joseph LoDuca.

Evil Dead 2: Dead by Dawn 🦴🦴½ **1987 (R)** A gory, tongue-in-cheek sequel/remake of the original festival of gag and gore, in which an ancient book of magic invokes a crowd of flesh-snacking, joke-tossing ghouls. Followed by yet a third bloodfest. **84m/C VHS, DVD, Wide.** Bruce Campbell, Sarah Berry, Dan Hicks, Kassie Wesley, Theodore (Ted) Raimi, Denise Bixler, Richard Domeier, Scott Spiegel, Josh Becker, Lou Hancock; *Cameos:* Sam Raimi; *D:* Sam Raimi; *W:* Sam Raimi, Scott Spiegel; *C:* Peter Deming; *M:* Joseph LoDuca.

Evil Dead Trap 🦴🦴🦴½ **1988** Nami (Miyuki Ono), a Japanese late-night TV show host, is sent a tape that appears to show a brutal murder. Her cheap boss refuses to do anything, but she and her female crew decide to follow up on the tape and find the location where it was made. What follows in an abandoned factory owes much to Argento with even more visceral sex and violence. Director Ikeda's camera is almost never still. The script combines supernatural elements with a realistic setting and believable characters. **90m/C VHS, DVD.** *JP* Miyuki Ono, Fumi Katsuragi, Hitomi Kobayashi, Eriko Nakagawa; *D:* Toshiharu Ikeda; *W:* Takashi Ishii.

Evil Ed 🦴½ **1996 (R)** Formerly mild-mannered film editor Ed (Ruebeck) becomes obsessed with the horror series he's working on, goes off the deep end, and begins a series of killings that mimic the ones from the films. Lots of splatter. **90m/C VHS, DVD.** *SW* Johan Ruebeck, Olof Rhodin, Pete Lofbergh; *D:* Anders Jacobsson; *W:* Anders Jacobsson; *C:* Anders Jacobsson; *M:* Goran Lundstrom.

Evil Has a Face 🦴🦴½ **1996 (R)** Chicago police sketch artist Gwen McGarrell (Young) travels to rural Minnesota to help investigator Tom Sawyer (Moses) locate a child molester. But the face she draws turns out to be that of her abusive stepfather (Ross), who's been presumed dead. **92m/C VHS.** Sean Young, William R. Moses, Joe Guzaldo, Chelcie Ross, Brighton Hertford, Dick Cusack; *D:* Robert M. Fresco; *W:* Robert M. Fresco; *C:* Stephen Lighthill; *M:* Joseph Vitarelli. **CABLE**

Evil Judgment 🦴½ **1985** A young girl investigates a series of murders and finds the culprit is a psychopathic judge. **93m/C VHS.** Pamela Collyer, Jack Langedijk, Nanette Workman; *D:* Claude Castravelli.

Evil Laugh woof! **1986 (R)** Medical students and their girlfriends party at an abandoned orphanage, until a serial killer decides to join them. **90m/C VHS.** Tony Griffin, Kim McKamy, Jody Gibson, Dominick Brascia; *D:* Dominick Brascia.

Evil Lives 🦴🦴½ *Soulmates* **1992** Now here's a horror premise you don't run into every day. Horror novelist Richard Wayborn (Rodgers) leaves a trail of dead women during his lecture tours. Seems he's really 700-years-old and his long-dead wife can temporarily resurrect herself using the nubile forms of other women. Now, Wayborn has chosen a new babe but so far she's managing to elude his deadly charms. **90m/C VHS, DVD.** Tristan Rogers, Arabella Holzbog, Tyrone Power Jr., Sonia Curtis, Griffin O'Neal, Melissa Moore, Wendy Barry, Paul Bartel, Dawn Wells; *D:* Thunder Levin.

The Evil Mind 🦴🦴½ *The Clairvoyant* **1934** A fraudulent mind reader predicts many disasters that start coming true. **80m/B VHS.** *GB* Claude Rains, Fay Wray, Jane Baxter, Felix Aylmer; *D:* Maurice Elvey; *W:* Charles Bennett.

Evil Obsession 🦴 **1996** Disturbed Homer (Feldman) obsessed with supermodel Margo (Stevens) and later becomes a suspect in the murders of 12 other models. **93m/C VHS.** Corey Feldman, Kimberly Stevens, Mark Derwin, Brion James, Stacie Randall; *D:* Richard W. Munchkin. **VIDEO**

The Evil of Frankenstein 🦴🦴 **1964** The third of the Hammer Frankenstein films, with the mad doctor once again finding his creature preserved in ice and thawing him out. Preceded by "The Revenge of Frankenstein" and followed by "Frankenstein Created Woman." **84m/C VHS.** *GB* Peter Cushing, Duncan Lamont, Peter Woodthorpe, Sandor Eles, Kiwi Kingston, Katy Wild; *D:* Freddie Francis; *W:* John (Anthony Hinds) Elder; *C:* John Wilcox; *M:* Don Banks.

Evil Roy Slade 🦴🦴🦴 **1971** Goofy family comedy (a failed TV pilot) that's a parody of every western cliche imaginable. Roy (Astin) is the meanest gunslinger in the west (he was raised by vultures) who's trying to turn over a new leaf after he falls for a pretty schoolteacher. He's aided by a shrink, who wants Roy to give up his weapons fetish, but singing glamour boy lawman Bing Bell (Shawn) has a score to settle with Roy. **97m/C VHS.** John Astin, Dick Shawn, Mickey Rooney, Pam Austin, Henry Gibson, Edie Adams, Milton Berle, Dom DeLuise, Noriyuki "Pat" Morita, Penny Marshall, John Ritter; *Cameos:* Jerry Paris; *D:* Jerry Paris; *W:* Garry Marshall, Jerry Belson; *C:* Sam Leavitt; *Nar:* Pat Buttram. **TV**

Evil Spawn 🦴 *Deadly Sting; Alive by Night; Alien Within* **1987** A fading movie queen takes an experimental drug to restore her youthful beauty, but it only turns her into a giant silverfish. Releases under several alternate titles, and with varying running times. **70m/C VHS.** Bobbie Bresee, John Carradine, Drew Godderis, John Terrance, Dawn Wildsmith, Jerry Fox, Pamela Gilbert, Forrest J Ackerman; *D:* Kenneth J. Hall; *W:* Kenneth J. Hall; *C:* Christopher Condon.

Evil Spirits 🦴½ **1991 (R)** Boarding-house tenants are murdered while the crazy landlady cashes their social security checks. This seedy horror cheapie doesn't take itself seriously, and like-minded genre buffs may enjoy the cult-film cast. **95m/C VHS.** Karen Black, Arte Johnson, Virginia Mayo, Michael Berryman, Martine Beswick, Bert Remsen, Yvette Vickers, Robert Quarry, Mikel Angel, Debra Lamb; *D:* Gary Graver; *W:* Mikel Angel.

The Evil That Men Do 🦴🦴 **1984 (R)** A hitman comes out of retirement to break up a Central American government's political torture ring and, in the process, brings a friend's killer to justice. Based on the novel by R. Lance Hill. **90m/C VHS, DVD, Wide.** Charles Bronson, Theresa Saldana, Joseph Maher, Jose Ferrer, Rene Enriquez, John Glover, Raymond St. Jacques, Antoinette Bower, Enrique Lucero, Jorge Luke; *D:* J. Lee Thompson; *W:* John Crowther; *C:* Xavier Cruz; *M:* Ken Thorne.

Evil Toons 🦴½ **1990 (R)** A quartet of lovely coeds on a cleaning job venture into a deserted mansion. There they accidentally release a vulgar, lustful, animated demon who proceeds to cause their clothes to fall off. Can the girls escape the haunted mansion with their sanity, virtue and wardrobes intact? **86m/C VHS.** David Carradine, Dick Miller, Monique Gabrielle, Suzanne Ager, Stacy Nix, Madison Stone, Don Dowe, Arte Johnson, Michelle (McClellan) Bauer; *D:* Fred Olen Ray.

Evil Town 🦴 **1987 (R)** In this poorly made film, a wandering guy discovers a town overrun with zombies created by a mad doctor. **88m/C VHS.** Dean Jagger, James Keach, Robert Walker Jr., Doria Cook, Michele Marsh; *D:* Edward Collins.

Evil under the Sun 🦴🦴 **1982 (PG)** An opulent beach resort is the setting as Hercule Poirot attempts to unravel a murder mystery. Based on the Agatha Christie novel. **112m/C VHS, DVD, Wide.** *GB* Peter Ustinov, Jane Birkin, Maggie Smith, Colin Blakely, Roddy McDowall, Diana Rigg, Sylvia Miles, James Mason, Nicholas Clay; *D:* Guy Hamilton; *W:* Anthony Shaffer; *C:* Christopher Challis; *M:* Cole Porter.

The Evil Within woof! *Baby Blood* **1994 (R)** Parasitic beast, with an unquenchable thirst for blood, slithers from the center of the earth into the convenient womb of a young woman. She takes to murdering everyone within reach while preparing to give birth. As disgusting as it sounds. **88m/C VHS.** Emmanuelle Escourrou, Jean-Francois Guillotte; *D:* Alain Robak; *W:* Alain Robak, Serge Cukier.

Evil's Commandment 🦴🦴½ **1956** Original vampire film which started the classic Italian horror cycle. A gorgeous Countess needs blood to stay young, otherwise she reverts to a 200-year-old vampire. **?m/B VHS.** *IT* Gianna Maria Canale; *D:* Riccardo (Robert Hampton) Freda.

Evils of the Night 🦴 **1985** Teenage campers are abducted by sex-crazed alien vampires. Bloody naked mayhem follows. **85m/C VHS.** John Carradine, Julie Newmar, Tina Louise, Neville Brand, Aldo Ray, Karrie Emerson, Bridget Hollman; *D:* Marti Rustam; *W:* Marti Rustam, Phillip D. Connors.

Evilspeak woof! **1982 (R)** Bumbling misfit enrolled at a military school is mistreated by the other cadets. With the help of his computer, he retaliates with satanic power. Bits, bytes, and gore. **89m/C VHS.** Clint Howard, Don Stark, Lou Gravance, Lauren Lester, R.G. Armstrong, Joe Cortese, Claude Earl Jones, Haywood Nelson; *D:* Eric Weston.

Evita 🦴🦴½ **1996 (PG)** Webber/Rice rock opera about the life and death of Eva Peron finally comes to the big screen with all its extravaganza intact. Madonna's in the title role (in fine voice, lavishly costumed but unflatteringly lit) about an ambitious poor girl willing to do anything to make her mark—in this version by sleeping her way up the ladder of power to Argentine strongman Juan Peron (Pryce as wax dummy). Evita becomes a would-be champion of the people, even as the government ruthlessly suppresses their freedoms. The surprisingly strong-voiced Banderas (perhaps his emphatic enunciation is to make his English as clear as possible) is everyman narrator Che (changed from the stage version's revolutionary Che Guevera). The highlight is still Madonna's balcony scene, singing "Don't Cry for Me, Argentina," but some of the other songs are drowned by loud orchestration. Director Parker has a cameo as a frustrated film director trying to work with Evita. ♫A Cinema in Buenos Aires; Requiem for Evita; Oh, What a Circus; On This Night of a Thousand Stars; Eva and Magadi; Eva Beware of the City; Buenos Aires; Another Suitcase in Another Hall; Goodnight and Thank You. **133m/C VHS, DVD, Wide.** Madonna, Antonio Banderas, Jonathan Pryce, Jimmy Nail, Victoria Sus, Julian Littman, Olga Meediz, Laura Pallas, Julia Worsley; *Cameos:* Alan Parker; *D:* Alan Parker; *W:* Oliver Stone, Alan Parker; *C:* Darius Khondji; *M:* Andrew Lloyd Webber, Tim Rice. Oscars '96: Song ("You Must Love Me"); Golden Globes '97: Actress—Mus./Comedy (Madonna), Film—Mus./Comedy, Song ("You Must Love Me").

Evolution 🦴½ **2001 (PG-13)** A meteor containing microscopic organisms crashes in the New Mexico desert and they begin evolving at an enormous rate. A misfit team consisting of community college prof Duchovny, government scientist Moore, wannabe fireman Scott, and kooky geologist Jones try to prevent the spores (which evolve into a number of crazy critters) from taking over the planet. It's supposed to be sci-fi comedy, but the effectively scary monsters eliminate whatever comedic elements the writers and Reitman forgot to kill. **101m/C VHS, DVD, Wide.** *US* David Duchovny, Julianne Moore, Orlando Jones, Seann William Scott, Ted Levine, Ethan Suplee, Michael Ray Bower, Katharine Towne, Dan Aykroyd, Richard Moll, Gregory Itzin, Ty Burrell; *D:* Ivan Reitman; *W:* David Diamond, David Weissman, Don Jakoby; *C:* Michael Chapman; *M:* John Powell.

Evolver 🦴½ **1994 (R)** Teenager Kyle Baxter (Randall) wins a robot patterned after a video arcade game but the robot has a secret military weapon's program built into its brain, causing it to evolve into a killing machine. **90m/C VHS, DVD.** Ethan (Randall) Embry, John de Lancie, Cassidy Rae, Cindy Pickett, Paul Dooley; *D:* Mark Rosman; *W:* Mark Rosman; *C:* Jacques Haitkin; *V:* William H. Macy.

The Ewok Adventure 🦴🦴½ **1984 (G)** Those adorable, friendly and funny characters from "Return of the Jedi" make the jump from film to TV in a new adventure from George Lucas. In this installment, the Ewoks save a miraculous child from harm with the help of a young human. This fun-filled adventure has Lucas's thumbprint all over it and great special effects. Followed by "Ewoks: The Battle for Endor." **96m/C VHS.** Warwick Davis, Eric Walker, Aubree Miller, Fionnula Flanagan; *D:* John Korty; *M:* Elmer Bernstein, Peter Bernstein; *Nar:* Burl Ives. **TV**

The Ewoks: Battle for Endor 🦴🦴½ **1985** TV movie based on the furry creatures from "Return of the Jedi," detailing their battle against an evil queen to retain their forest home. Preceded by "The Ewok Adventure." **98m/C VHS.** Wilford Brimley, Warwick Davis, Aubree Miller, Sian Phillips, Paul Gleason, Eric Walker, Carel Struycken, Niki Bothelo; *D:* Jim Wheat, Ken Wheat; *M:* Peter Bernstein. **TV**

The Ex 🦴🦴½ **1996 (R)** Architect David Kenyon (Mancuso) has a new life, with a sweet second wife (Amis) and a five-year-old son. Then the ex, Deirdre (Butler), comes sauntering back and it seems she and David had a very kinky relationship. Now Deirdre decides it's time to get revenge. Familiar plotline is given a high gloss and some chills. **87m/C VHS.** Yancy Butler, Nick Mancuso, Suzy Amis; *D:* Mark L. Lester; *W:* John Lutz, Larry Cohen; *C:* Richard Letterman; *M:* Paul Zaza.

Ex-Cop 🦴🦴 **1993** Pete Danberg is a cop with a drinking problem. He's fired from the force but not before he puts away the "Las Vegas Slasher." Unfortunately for Pete the Slasher makes parole and is out for revenge—using Pete's kidnapped daughter as bait. **97m/C VHS.** Rick Savage, Sandy Hackett, Joan Chamberlain, Douglas Terry, Angi Davidson, Richard Cornell, Jim Williams; *D:* Patrick Kerby; *W:* Daniel S. Sample.

Ex-Lady 🦴🦴 **1933** Davis stars as a liberated woman who loves advertising writer Raymond, but doesn't want to marry him. However, she believes living together is the most suitable arrangement. The two open up an ad agency and complications ensue. Remake of "Illicit," which was filmed only two years earlier with Barbara Stanwyck in the lead role. **65m/B VHS.** Bette Davis, Gene Raymond, Frank McHugh, Claire Dodd, Monroe Owsley, Ferdinand Gottschalk; *D:* Robert Florey.

Ex-Mrs. Bradford 🦴🦴🦴 **1936** Amateur sleuth Dr. Bradford teams up with his ex-wife to solve a series of murders at the race track. Sophisticated comedy-mystery; witty dialogue. **80m/B VHS.** William Powell, Jean Arthur, James Gleason, Eric Blore, Robert Armstrong; ***D:*** Stephen Roberts.

Excalibur 🦴🦴🦴½ **1981 (R)** A sweeping, visionary retelling of the life of King Arthur, from his conception, to the sword in the stone, to the search for the Holy Grail and the final battle with Mordred. An imperfect, sensationalized version, but still the best yet filmed. **140m/C VHS, DVD, Wide.** Robert Addie, Keith Buckley, Niall O'Brien, Nigel Terry, Nicol Williamson, Nicholas Clay, Helen Mirren, Cherie Lunghi, Paul Geoffrey, Gabriel Byrne, Liam Neeson, Patrick Stewart, Charley Boorman, Corin Redgrave; ***D:*** John Boorman; ***W:*** Rospo Pallenberg, John Boorman; ***C:*** Alex Thomson; ***M:*** Trevor Jones.

Excellent Cadavers 🦴🦴½ **1999 (R)** Giovanni Falcone (Palminteri) was an incorruptible Italian prosecutor who took on the Mafia in Sicily in the 1980s. By the end of the decade, and with the help of informer Tommaso Buscetta (Abraham), Falcone had 300 convictions and sealed his own grim fate. Title refers to the corpses of public officials who challenged the mobsters. Based on the book by Alexander Stille. **86m/C VHS, DVD.** Chazz Palminteri, F. Murray Abraham, Anna Galiena; ***D:*** Ricky Tognazzi; ***W:*** Peter Pruce; ***M:*** Joseph Vitarelli. CABLE

Excess Baggage 🦴½ **1996 (PG-13)** Attention-seeking rich girl Emily (Silverstone) fakes her own kidnapping to get back at dear old dad, involving car thief Vincent Roche (del Toro) in the crime. Things get out of control when her creepy "Uncle" Ray (Walken), who's an ex-CIA assassin, is hired by Emily's father to get her back. Silverstone's character is alternately whiny and pouting, you'll wonder why dad would want her back and why Vincent hangs on at all. First picture in Silverstone's pricey production deal with Columbia went through the rumor mill (for supposed clashes between Silverstone and director Brambilla) and was originally scheduled for release in the fall of '96. **101m/C VHS, DVD.** Alicia Silverstone, Benicio Del Toro, Christopher Walken, Harry Connick Jr., Jack Thompson, Nicholas Turturro, Michael Bowen, Leland Orser, Robert Wisden, Sally Kirkland; ***D:*** Marco Brambilla; ***W:*** Mikhaila Max Adams, Dick Clement, Ian LaFrenais; ***C:*** Jean-Yves Escoffier; ***M:*** John Lurie.

Excessive Force 🦴½ **1993 (R)** Routine actioner lives up to its title by offering lots of violence, but little else. Gang leader Young seeks revenge on the cops who he believes ruined a $3 million drug deal. Loner cop Griffith is the only one to survive the grudge killings and goes after Young himself. Talented cast underachieves. Limited theatrical release sent this one almost straight to video. **87m/C VHS.** Thomas Ian Griffith, Lance Henriksen, James Earl Jones, Charlotte Lewis, Tony Todd, Burt Young, W. Earl Brown; ***D:*** Jon Hess; ***W:*** Thomas Ian Griffith; ***C:*** Donald M. Morgan; ***M:*** Charles Bernstein.

Excessive Force 2: Force on Force 🦴½ **1995 (R)** Special agent Harly Cordell (Randall) volunteers to hunt down an assassination squad that is turning L.A. into murder central. Seems her former lover Francis Lydell (Gauthier) is head killer and Harly's got a score to settle. Lots of action and nifty weapons. **88m/C VHS.** Stacie Randall, Dan Gauthier, Jay Patterson, John Mese; ***D:*** Jonathan Winfrey; ***W:*** Mark Sevi; ***C:*** Russ Brandt; ***M:*** Kevin Kiner.

The Execution 🦴½ **1985** Five female friends who discover that the Nazi doctor who brutalized them in a concentration camp during WWII is now living a normal life in California. Together they plot his undoing. **92m/C VHS.** Loretta Swit, Valerie Harper, Sandy Dennis, Jessica Walter, Rip Torn, Barbara Barrie, Robert Hooks, Michael Lerner; ***D:*** Paul Wendkos; ***M:*** Georges Delerue.

Execution of Justice 🦴🦴 **1999 (R)** Emily Mann's play focused on the 1978 voluntary manslaughter verdict in the trial of city supervisor Dan White for the deaths of San Francisco Mayor George Moscone (Young) and openly gay elected official Harvey Milk (Coyote). You may remember the infamous "Twinkie Defense." This sporadically compelling cable docudrama delves into the mind of White (Daly) himself. **103m/C VHS.** Timothy Daly, Peter Coyote, Stephen Young, Amy Van Nostrand, Tyne Daly, Khalil Kain, Frank Pellegrino, Shannon Hile; ***D:*** Leon Ichaso; ***W:*** Michael Butler; ***C:*** Claudio Chea. CABLE

The Execution of Private Slovik 🦴🦴🦴½ **1974** This quiet powerhouse of a TV movie recounts in straightforward terms the case of Eddie Slovik, a WWII misfit who became the only American soldier executed for desertion since the Civil War. The Levinson/Link screenplay (based on the book by William Bradford Huie) ends up deifying Slovik, which some might find hard to take. But there's no arguing the impact of the drama, or of Sheen's unaffected lead performance. **122m/C VHS.** Martin Sheen, Mariclare Costello, Ned Beatty, Gary Busey, Matt Clark, Ben Hammer, Warren Kemmerling; ***D:*** Lamont Johnson; ***W:*** Richard Levinson, William Link; ***C:*** Bill Butler. TV

Execution of Raymond Graham 🦴🦴½ **1985** The lawyers and family of Raymond Graham struggle to keep him from being executed for murder. Based on a true story. **104m/C VHS.** Morgan Freeman, Jeff Fahey, Kate Reid, Laurie Metcalf, Josef Sommer; ***D:*** Daniel Petrie. TV

The Executioner 🦴🦴 **1970 (PG)** A thriller wherein a British spy must prove that his former colleague is a double agent. Elements of backstabbing, betrayal, and espionage abound. **107m/C VHS.** *GB* Judy Geeson, Oscar Homolka, Charles Gray, Nigel Patrick, George Peppard, Joan Collins, Keith Michell; ***D:*** Sam Wanamaker.

The Executioner 🦴 *Like Father, Like Son; Massacre Mafia Style* **1978 (R)** A very cheap, very "Godfather"-like story of a mafia family gone awry. **84m/C VHS.** Duke Mitchell, Vic Caesar, Dominic Micelli, John Strong, Jim Williams, Lorenzo Dodo; ***D:*** Duke Mitchell; ***W:*** Duke Mitchell.

Executioner of Venice 🦴 **1963** Marauding pirates with time on hands swarm in from the Adriatic Sea and attempt to rob the Venetians blind. The Doge and his godson come to the rescue. **90m/C VHS.** Guy Madison, Lex Barker, Alessandra Panaro; ***D:*** Louis Capauno.

The Executioner, Part 2: Frozen Scream 🦴 **1984 (R)** Brutal feud rocks the Mafia, and a crime kingpin's passionate son seeks revenge on his father's slayers. Not a sequel to any other films bearing similar titles. Strange thing is, no "Executioner, Part I" was ever made. Pretty laughable. **150m/C VHS.** Chris Mitchum, Aldo Ray, Antoine John Mottet, Renee Harmon; ***D:*** James Bryant.

The Executioners 🦴½ **1993** When a nuclear explosion contaminates most of the city's drinking water, the remainder falls under the harsh control of the Black Knight. Now, it's up to the Heroic Trio to defeat their nemesis. Chinese with subtitles. **100m/C VHS, DVD.** *HK* Anita (Yim-Fong) Mui, Michelle Yeoh, Maggie Cheung; ***D:*** Ching Siu Tung; ***W:*** Susan Chan; ***C:*** Poon Hang-Seng; ***M:*** Cacine Wong.

The Executioner's Song 🦴🦴½ **1982** European version of the TV movie based on Norman Mailer's Pulitzer Prize-winner, recounting the life and death of convicted murderer Gary Gilmore. Features adult-minded footage not seen in the U.S. version. **157m/C VHS.** Tommy Lee Jones, Rosanna Arquette, Eli Wallach, Christine Lahti, Jenny Wright, Jordan Clark, Steven Keats; ***D:*** Lawrence Schiller.

Executive Action 🦴🦴½ **1973 (PG)** Political thriller providing a different look at the events leading to the assassination of JFK. In this speculation, a millionaire pays a professional spy to organize a secret conspiracy to kill President Kennedy. Ryan's final film. Adapted by Dalton Trumbo from Mark Lane's "Rush to Judgement." **91m/C VHS.** Burt Lancaster, Robert Ryan, Will Geer, Gilbert Green, John Anderson; ***D:*** David Miller; ***C:*** Robert Steadman; ***M:*** Randy Edelman.

Executive Decision 🦴🦴 **1996 (R)** Those wacky terrorists are at it again. You would think that after getting their butts kicked in almost every action picture since 1980 that they would learn. But here they are, hijacking a 747, cutting off communications, and affixing a nerve gas bomb to the plane. This time a group of high tech commandos, led by Russell and (briefly) Seagal, must sneak onto the plane and generally mess up the bad guys' plans. Brave stewardess Berry helps tango with the central casting mad dog terrorists. The title refers to the President's decision on whether or not to blow the plane up in order to avert disaster. Or maybe "Die Hard: Ad Nauseum" wasn't available. **132m/C VHS, DVD.** Mary Ellen Trainor, Kurt Russell, Halle Berry, Oliver Platt, John Leguizamo, Steven Seagal, Joe Morton, David Suchet, B.D. Wong, Len Cariou, Whip Hubley, J.T. Walsh; ***D:*** Stuart Baird; ***W:*** Jim Thomas, John Thomas; ***C:*** Alex Thomson; ***M:*** Jerry Goldsmith.

Executive Suite 🦴🦴🦴 **1954** One of the first dog-eat-dog dramas about high finance and big business. The plot centers on the question of a replacement for the freshly buried owner of a gigantic furniture company. **104m/B VHS.** William Holden, June Allyson, Barbara Stanwyck, Fredric March, Walter Pidgeon, Louis Calhern, Shelley Winters, Paul Douglas, Nina Foch, Dean Jagger; ***D:*** Robert Wise; ***W:*** Ernest Lehman; ***C:*** George J. Folsey.

Executive Target 🦴🦴 **1997 (R)** Stunt-car driver Nick James (Madsen) is grabbed by a gang of mercenaries who want him as their getaway man when they attempt to kidnap the president (Scheider) and overthrow the U.S. government. He agrees because the gang have also taken his wife as a hostage. Lots of action sequences show where the money went. **96m/C VHS.** Michael Madsen, Keith David, Angie Everhart, Roy Scheider, Dayton Callie, Kathy Christopherson; ***D:*** Joseph Merhi; ***W:*** Dayton Callie; ***C:*** Ken Blakey. VIDEO

Exiled in America 🦴🦴 **1990** A Central American freedom fighter (Albert) flees his country for the United States, settling in a small town with his wife. She gets a waitressing job at a local diner, telling the owner her husband died in an accident, and the owner's son winds up falling in love with her. Things get complicated when the death squad, led by a corrupt CIA agent, follows Albert to his hiding place, and the local sheriff threatens to blow his cover. **84m/C VHS.** Maxwell Caulfield, Edward Albert, Viveca Lindfors, Kamala Lopez, Stella Stevens, Wings Hauser; ***D:*** Paul Leder; ***W:*** Paul Leder.

Exiled to Shanghai 🦴🦴½ **1937** A couple of newsreel men invent a television device that revolutionizes the business. **65m/B VHS.** Wallace Ford, June Travis, Dean Jagger, William "Billy" Bakewell, Arthur Lake, Jonathan Hale, William Harrigan, Sarah Padden; ***D:*** Nick Grinde.

eXistenZ 🦴🦴½ **1999 (R)** Typically scary and weird Cronenberg production finds security guard Law saving the life of computer-game designer Leigh. They both get sucked into one of her alternate-reality creations and are pursued by assassins. In this future world, game players are literally hooked up to their computer with an umbilical-like cord plugged directly into their spines—no doubt the fantasy of teenage boys everywhere. Surreal visuals and excellent performances won't help the viewer keep track of what's going on, but for Cronenberg linear plotting is rarely the point. **97m/C VHS, DVD.** *CA* Jennifer Jason Leigh, Jude Law, Ian Holm, Willem Dafoe, Sarah Polley, Christopher Eccleston, Don McKellar, Callum Keith Rennie; ***D:*** David Cronenberg; ***W:*** David Cronenberg; ***C:*** Peter Suschitzsky; ***M:*** Howard Shore. Genie '99: Film Editing.

Exit 🦴½ **1995 (R)** Gang of criminals, lead by pscho Charles (Bradley), take a strip club's dancers as hostages when their robbery attempt goes bad. Exotic dancer Diane (Whirry) manages to escape and hook up with ex-ATF agent Alex (Bucci) to stop the creeps. Lame action, silly dialogue, very attractive Whirry. **90m/C VHS.** Shannon Whirry, David Bradley, Larry Manetti, Joe Bucci; ***D:*** Ric Roman Waugh; ***W:*** Joe Augustyn, Brent Friedman, David Robinson; ***C:*** David B. Nowell; ***M:*** Kevin Kiner.

Exit in Red 🦴½ **1997 (R)** Beverly Hills psychiatrist Ed Altman (Rourke) is hiding out after the suicide of one of his patients lead to professional misconduct charges. But he just can't leave the women alone and gets involved with unhappily married Ally (Schofield). When her husband turns up dead, Ed's charged with murder. It's a frame but just how's he going to prove it. **96m/C VHS.** Mickey Rourke, Annabel Schofield, Anthony Michael Hall, Carre Otis; ***D:*** Yurek Bogayevicz; ***W:*** David Womack; ***C:*** Ericson Core; ***M:*** Michael Lorenc.

Exit to Eden 🦴½ **1994 (R)** Anne Rampling's (AKA Anne Rice) novel focused on fulfilling S&M sexual fantasies, but director Marshall goes for laughs with a buddy cops-out-of-water sitcom subplot, as undercover cops Aykroyd and O'Donnell track a suspected jewel thief to the fantasy resort of Eden, run by dominatrix Delany. (What was the pitch for this one? Think "Another Stakeout" meets "Tie Me Up, Tie Me Down." It'll be great. Really.) Neither plot works, resulting in a kinky movie with no kink, and a comedy with few laughs. O'Donnell holds up her end, providing what few yuks there are. Everyone else, especially Aykroyd and Delany, seem to be sleepwalking. Lucky for them. **113m/C VHS.** Dan Aykroyd, Rosie O'Donnell, Dana Delany, Paul Mercurio, Hector Elizondo, Stuart Wilson, Iman, Sandi Korn; ***D:*** Garry Marshall; ***W:*** Deborah Amelon, Bob Brunner; ***M:*** Patrick Doyle. Golden Raspberries '94: Worst Support. Actress (O'Donnell).

Exit Wounds 🦴🦴 **2001 (R)** Unpredictable, unorthodox Detroit police detective Orin Boyd (Seagal, of course) gets sent to the baddest part of town after successfully, but unconventionally, breaking up a plot to kill the Vice President. There, along with his rambunctious new partner (Washington), he uncovers corrupt cops and a drug-running scheme involving the notorious crime lord Walker (DMX). Lots of martial arts sequences and loads of gunfire from, presumably, really bad shots. Romance also blossoms between Mr. Loose Canon and a precinct commander played by Hennessy. Typical Seagal flick, sure to be enjoyed by fans. Others should be wary. **98m/C VHS, DVD, Wide.** *US* Steven Seagal, DMX, Isaiah Washington IV, Anthony Anderson, Michael Jai White, Bill Duke, Jill(ian) Hennessey, Tom Arnold, Bruce McGill, David Vadim, Eva Mendez; ***D:*** Andrzej Bartkowiak; ***W:*** Ed Horowitz, Richard D'Ovidio; ***C:*** Glen MacPherson; ***M:*** Jeff Rona, Damon Blackman.

Exodus 🦴🦴🦴 **1960** Chronicles the post-WWII partition of Palestine into a homeland for Jews; the anguish of refugees from Nazi concentration camps held on ships in the Mediterranean; the struggle of the tiny nation with forces dividing it from within and destroying it from the outside; and the heroic men and women who saw a job to be done and did it. Based on the novel by Leon Uris; filmed in Cyprus and Israel. Preminger battled the Israeli government, the studio, and the novel's author to complete this epic. Cost more than $4 million, a phenomenal amount at the time. **208m/C VHS.** Paul Newman, Eva Marie Saint, Lee J. Cobb, Sal Mineo, Ralph Richardson, Hugh Griffith, Gregory Ratoff, Felix Aylmer, Peter Lawford, Jill Haworth, John Derek, David Opatoshu, Marius Goring, Alexandra Stewart, Michael Wager, Martin Benson, Paul Stevens, George Maharis; ***D:*** Otto Preminger; ***W:*** Dalton Trumbo; ***M:*** Ernest Gold. Oscars '60: Orig. Dramatic Score; Golden Globes '61: Support. Actor (Mineo).

Exorcism 🦴½ *Exorcismo* **1974** A satanic cult in a small English village commits a series of gruesome crimes that have the authorities baffled. **90m/C VHS.** *SP* Paul (Jacinto Molina) Naschy, Maria Perschy, Jacinto (Jack) Molina, Maria Kosti, Grace Mills, Jorge Torras, Marta Avile; ***D:*** Juan Bosch; ***W:*** Juan Bosch, Jacinto (Jack) Molina; ***C:*** Francisco Sanchez.

Exorcism's Daughter 🦴 *House of Insane Women* **1974 (R)** While running an insane asylum, a man discovers that a woman has lost her mind because as a child, she witnessed her mother's death during an exorcism. Pretty grim but interesting for genre fans. A natural double feature with "House of Psychotic Women." **93m/C VHS.** *SP* Amelia Gade, Francesco Rabal, Espartaco (Spartaco) Santoni; ***D:*** Rafael Morena Alba.

The Exorcist 🦴🦴🦴½ **1973 (R)** Truly terrifying story of a young girl who is possessed by a malevolent spirit. Brilliantly directed by Friedkin, with underlying themes of the workings and nature of fate. Impeccable casting and unforgettable, thought-provoking performances. A rare film that remains startling and engrossing with every viewing, it spawned countless imitations and changed the way horror films were made. Based on the bestseller by Blatty, who also wrote the screenplay. Not for the squeamish. When first released, the film created mass hysteria in theatres, with people fainting and paramedics on the scene. **120m/C VHS, DVD, Wide.** Ellen Burstyn, Linda Blair, Jason Miller, Max von Sydow, Jack MacGowran, Lee J. Cobb, Kitty Winn, Barton Heyman, Peter Masterson; ***D:*** William Friedkin; ***W:*** William Peter Blatty; ***C:*** Owen Roizman, Billy Williams; ***M:*** Jack Nitzsche; ***V:*** Mercedes McCambridge. Oscars '73: Adapt. Screenplay, Sound; Golden Globes '74: Director (Friedkin), Film—Drama, Screenplay, Support. Actress (Blair).

The Exorcist 2: The Heretic 🦴🦴 **1977 (R)** Unnecessary sequel to the 1973 hit "The Exorcist" which featured extensive recutting by Boorman. After four years, Blair is still under psychiatric care, suffering from the effects of being possessed by the devil. Meanwhile, a priest investigates the first exorcist's work as he tries to help the head-spinning lass. Decent special effects. **118m/C VHS.** Richard Burton, Linda Blair, Louise Fletcher, Kitty Winn, James Earl Jones, Ned Beatty, Max von Sydow, Paul Henreid; ***D:*** John Boorman; ***W:*** William Goodhart; ***C:*** William A. Fraker; ***M:*** Ennio Morricone.

Exorcist 3: Legion 🦴🦴 **1990 (R)** Apparently subscribing to the two wrongs make a right school of sequels, this time novelist Blatty is the director. The result is slightly better than the first sequel, but still a far cry from the original. Fifteen years later, Detective Kinderman (Scott) is faced with a series of really gross murders bearing the mark of a serial killer who was flambeed in the electric chair on the same night as the exorcism of the pea-soup expectorating devil of the original. With the aid of priests Flanders and Dourif, the detective stalks the transmigratory terror—without the help of Linda Blair, who was at the time spoofing "The Exorcist" in "Repossessed." **105m/C VHS, DVD, Wide.** George C. Scott, Ed Flanders, Jason Miller, Nicol Williamson, Scott Wilson, Brad Dourif, Nancy Fish, George DiCenzo, Viveca Lindfors, Patrick Ewing, Fabio; ***D:*** William Peter Blatty; ***W:*** William Peter Blatty; ***C:*** Gerry Fisher; ***M:*** Barry de Vorzon.

Exotica 🦴🦴🦴 **1994 (R)** Daunting look at eroticism, secrecy, and despair. Christina (Kirshner) is at the center of some complicated relationships. She dresses as a schoolgirl while working at the Exotica strip club in Toronto, where her former lover Eric (Koteas) is the creepily suggestive DJ. Christina's also the obsession of seemingly mild-mannered tax man Francis (Greenwood), who has turned her table dancing into a strange private ritual. Lest this seem to make sense be assured that director Egoyan has much, much more going on—not all of it clear and most of it disturbing. **104m/C VHS, DVD.** *CA* Mia Kirshner, Elias Koteas, Bruce Greenwood, Don McKellar, Victor Garber, Arsinee Khanjian, Sarah Polley, Calvin Green, David Hemblen; ***D:*** Atom Egoyan; ***W:*** Atom Egoyan; ***C:*** Paul Sarossy; ***M:*** Mychael Danna. Genie '94: Art Dir./Set Dec., Cinematog., Costume Des., Director (Egoyan), Film, Orig. Screenplay, Support. Actor (McKellar), Score; Toronto-City '94: Canadian Feature Film.

Expect No Mercy 🦴 **1995 (R)** Government agent must rescue a fellow agent being held in a virtual reality center that trains assassins to commit murder. **91m/C VHS.** Billy Blanks, Jalal Merhi.

Expectations 🦴🦴 *Swedish Heroes; Svenska Hjaltar* **1997** Several interconnected tales follow a divorcing couple, a man trying to reconcile with his father, two young lovers, and an older man and woman poised on the edge of an affair. Swedish with subtitles. **95m/C VHS.** *SW* Niclas Olund, Kent-Arne Dahlgren, Stefan Sundstrom, Emma Warg, Anki Liden, Cajsa-Lisa Ejemyr, Janne Carlsson, Hans Klinga; ***D:*** Daniel Bergman; ***W:*** Reider Jonsson; ***C:*** Esa Vuorinen; ***M:*** Nicklas Frisk.

The Expendables 🦴½ **1989 (R)** A rugged captain turns a platoon of criminals and misfits into a tough fighting unit for a particularly dangerous mission from which they might not return. See the "Dirty Dozen" instead. **89m/C VHS.** Anthony Finetti, Peter Nelson, Loren Haynes, Kevin Duffis; ***D:*** Cirio H. Santiago; ***W:*** Phillip Alderton.

Experience Preferred... But Not Essential 🦴🦴½ **1983 (PG)** An English schoolgirl gets her first job at a resort where she learns about life. **77m/C VHS.** *GB* Elizabeth Edmonds, Sue Wallace, Geraldine Griffith, Karen Meagher, Ron Bain, Alun Lewis, Robert Blythe; ***D:*** Peter Duffell; ***W:*** June Roberts; ***C:*** Phil Meheux. **TV**

Experiment in Terror 🦴🦴🦴 **1962** A psychopath kidnaps a girl in order to blackmail her sister, a bank teller, into embezzling $100,000. **123m/B VHS.** Lee Remick, Glenn Ford, Stefanie Powers, Ross Martin; ***D:*** Blake Edwards; ***M:*** Henry Mancini.

Experiment Perilous 🦴🦴🦴 **1945** A psychologist and a recently widowed woman band together to find her husband's murderer. An atmospheric vintage mystery. **91m/B VHS.** Hedy Lamarr, Paul Lukas, George Brent, Albert Dekker; ***D:*** Jacques Tourneur.

The Expert 🦴🦴 **1995 (R)** Special operations expert John Lomax (Speakman) helps catch the creep who murdered his sister. But the killer gets a slap-on-the-wrist sentence, ticking Lomax off mightily. Now, the duo prepare for a deadly last confrontation. **92m/C VHS.** Jeff Speakman, James Brolin, Michael Shaner, Alex Datcher, Wolfgang Bodison, Elizabeth (Ward) Gracen, Red West, Jim Varney; ***D:*** Rick Avery; ***W:*** Max Allan Collins; ***C:*** Levie Isaacks; ***M:*** Ashley Irwin.

Expert Weapon 🦴½ **1993** It's a low-budget, male version of "La Femme Nikita" with an imprisoned cop killer recruited as an assassin by a secret government org (are there any other kind in these flicks). He even falls in love and then wants out. Fat chance. **90m/C VHS, DVD.** Ian Jacklin, Sam Jones, Mel Novak, Judy Landers, Joe Estevez; ***D:*** Steve Austin.

The Experts 🦴🦴 **1989 (PG-13)** When the KGB needs real Americans for their spies to study, they kidnap two out-of-work New Yorkers who mistakenly believe that they have been hired to open a nightclub in Nebraska. Shot on location in Canada. Sometimes funny and directed by former Second City TV MacKenzie Brother, Dave Thomas. **94m/C VHS, 8mm.** John Travolta, Arye Gross, Charles Martin Smith, Kelly Preston, James Keach, Deborah Foreman, Brian Doyle-Murray; ***D:*** Dave Thomas; ***W:*** Nick Thiel, Eric Alter; ***M:*** Marvin Hamlisch.

Explorers 🦴🦴½ **1985 (PG)** Intelligent family fare involving three young boys who use a contraption from their makeshift laboratory to travel to outer space. From the director of "Gremlins," displaying Dante's characteristic surreal wit and sense of irony. **107m/C VHS.** Ethan Hawke, River Phoenix, Jason Presson, Amanda Peterson, Mary Kay Place, Dick Miller, Robert Picardo, Dana Ivey, Meshach Taylor, Brooke Bundy; ***D:*** Joe Dante; ***W:*** Eric Luke; ***M:*** Jerry Goldsmith.

Explosion 🦴½ **1969 (R)** Distraught and disturbed young man evades the draft after losing a brother in Vietnam. Arriving in Canada, he meets another draft-dodger with whom he embarks on a murderous rampage. **96m/C VHS.** Don Stroud, Gordon Thomson, Michele Chicione, Richard Conte; ***D:*** Jules Bricken.

Expose woof! **1997** Congressman's daughter Tiffany gets mistaken for a call girl and propositioned by one of dad's colleagues. When the geezer pays her off to keep quiet, Tiff decides extortion is a viable career option. **78m/C VHS.** Tracy Tutor, Kevin E. West, Daneen Boone, Libby George; ***D:*** B.A. Rudnick.

Exposed 🦴🦴 **1983 (R)** High fashion model Kinski falls in with a terrorist gang through a connection with violinist Nureyev. Weak plotting undermines the end of this political thriller. However, Kinski is brilliant, stripping the barrier between performance and audience. **100m/C VHS.** Nastassia Kinski, Rudolf Nureyev, Harvey Keitel, Ian McShane, Bibi Andersson; ***D:*** James Toback; ***W:*** James Toback; ***C:*** Henri Decae; ***M:*** Georges Delerue.

Exposure 🦴 **1991 (R)** A rugged American photographer (Coyote) on assignment in Rio turns vigilante to locate the vicious killer of a young prostitute. Coyote and his girlfriend (Pays) get caught up in the deadly underworld of international arms trading and drug running as they search for the murderer. **99m/C VHS.** Peter Coyote, Amanda Pays, Tcheky Karyo; ***M:*** Todd Boekelheide.

Express to Terror 🦴½ **1979** Passengers aboard an atomic-powered train en route to Los Angeles attempt to kill a sleazy theatrical agent. Pilot for the "Supertrain" series. **120m/C VHS.** Steve Lawrence, George Hamilton, Vic Morrow, Broderick Crawford, Robert Alda, Don Stroud, Fred Williamson, Stella Stevens, Don Meredith; ***D:*** Dan Curtis. **TV**

Expresso Bongo 🦴🦴½ **1959** Soho singer/bongo player (Richards) is "discovered" by seedy talent agent Johnny Jackson (Harvey) who manages the young man into a teen idol with a 50-50 contract. But women come between the duo and Johnny finds himself without a star. **111m/B VHS, DVD, Wide.** *GB* Laurence Harvey, Sylvia Syms, Yolande Donlan, Cliff Richard; ***D:*** Val Guest; ***W:*** Wolf Mankowitz; ***C:*** John Wilcox.

Exquisite Corpses 🦴½ **1988** An Oklahoma hayseed charges to New York with a new, slick image. He meets the wife of a wealthy man, and together they organize a murderous operation. **95m/C VHS.** Zoe Tamerlaine Lund, Gary Knox, Daniel Chapman, Ruth (Coreen) Collins; ***D:*** Temistocles Lopez.

The Exterminating Angel 🦴🦴🦴½ *El Angel exterminador* **1962** A fierce, funny surreal nightmare, wherein dinner guests find they cannot, for any definable reason, leave the dining room; full of dream imagery and characteristically scatological satire. One of Bunuel's best, in Spanish with English subtitles. **95m/B VHS.** *MX SP* Claudio Brook, Cesar del Campo, Lucy Gallardo, Enrique Garcia Alvarez, Tito Junco, Ofelia Montesco, Bertha Moss, Pancho Cordova, Silvia Pinal, Enrique Rambal, Jacqueline Andere, Jose Baviera, Augusto Benedico, Luis Beristain; ***D:*** Luis Bunuel; ***W:*** Luis Alcoriza, Luis Bunuel; ***C:*** Gabriel Figueroa; ***M:*** Raul Lavista, Domenico Scarletti.

Exterminator 🦴 **1980 (R)** Vietnam veteran hunts down the gang that assaulted his friend and becomes the target of the police, the CIA and the underworld in this bloody banal tale of murder and intrigue. Followed by creatively titled "Exterminator II." **101m/C VHS, DVD.** Christopher George, Samantha Eggar, Robert Ginty, Steve James, Tony DiBenedetto, Dick Boccelli, Patrick Farrelly, Michele Harrell, Stan Getz, Roger Grimsby; ***D:*** James Glickenhaus; ***W:*** James Glickenhaus; ***C:*** Robert M. "Bob" Baldwin Jr.; ***M:*** Joe Renzetti.

Exterminator 2 🦴 **1984 (R)** The Exterminator battles the denizens of New York's underworld after his girlfriend is crippled, then murdered by the ruthless Mr. X. Violence galore. **88m/C VHS.** Robert Ginty, Mario Van Peebles, Deborah Geffner, Frankie Faison; ***D:*** Mark Buntzman; ***W:*** Mark Buntzman.

Exterminators in the Year 3000 woof! **1983 (R)** The Exterminator and his mercenary girlfriend battle with nuclear mutants over the last remaining tanks of purified water on Earth. Low-budget Road Warrior rip-off. **91m/C VHS.** *IT SP* Robert Jannucci, Alicia Moro, Alan Collins, Fred Harris; ***D:*** Jules Harrison.

The External 🦴🦴 *Michael Almereyda's The Mummy; Trance* **1999 (R)** Alcoholic Nora (Elliott) keeps experiencing strange trances that have nothing to do with her drinking. So, Nora, her husband (Harris) and their young son travel to Ireland to visit Nora's freaky uncle (Walken) in hopes of some kind of explanation. Yep, it all has something to do with a 2,000-year-old druid he's keeping in the basement of the family castle. No, it doesn't make much sense. **?m/C VHS, DVD.** Alison Elliott, Jared Harris, Christopher Walken, Karl Geary; ***D:*** Michael Almereyda.

Extra Girl 🦴🦴 **1923** A silent melodrama/farce about a farm girl, brilliantly played by Normand, who travels to Hollywood to be a star. Once in the glamour capital, she gets used and abused for her trouble. **87m/B VHS, 8mm.** Mabel Normand, Ralph Graves, Vernon Dent; ***D:*** F. Richard Jones; ***W:*** Mack Sennett.

Extramarital 🦴🦴 **1998 (R)** Magazine editor Fahey assigns reporter Lords to investigate a woman whose affair with a mystery man turns deadly. **90m/C VHS, DVD.** Jeff Fahey, Traci Lords, Brian Bloom, Maria Diaz; ***D:*** Yael Russcol. **VIDEO**

Extramuros 🦴🦴 **1985** A nun (Maura), living in a convent during the Spanish Inquisition, tries to repress her lesbian desires while the convent vies for fame and money through faked visions. Spanish with subtitles. **120m/C VHS.** *SP* Carmen Maura; ***D:*** Miguel Picazo.

The Extraordinary Adventures of Mr. West in the Land of the Bolsheviks 🦴🦴 **1924** The first achievement from the Kuleshov workshop, a wacky satire on American insularity depicting a naive and prejudiced American visiting Russia and being taken advantage of. Silent. **55m/B VHS.** Vsevolod Pudovkin, Boris Barnet; ***D:*** Lev Kuleshov.

The Extreme Adventures of Super Dave 🦴½ **1998 (PG)** Cable TV character Super Dave Osborne (Einstein) comes to the big screen as Super Dave comes out of retirement for one last megastunt. He and protege Van Wormer plot a death-defying leap to raise money for neighbor Carides who has an ill son (Lindner). **91m/C VHS, DVD, Wide.** Bob Einstein, Gia Carides, Carl Michael Lindner, Steve Van Wormer, Dan Hedaya; ***D:*** Peter Macdonald; ***W:*** Lorne Cameron, Don Lake; ***C:*** Bernd Heinl; ***M:*** Andrew Gross.

Extreme Honor 🦴 **2001 (R)** This is an action movie with little action until the finale and a too-familiar storyline. Brascoe (Anderson) is forced out of the Navy SEALS when he's framed by his partner (Gruner). Now he needs a lot of cash in order to pay for his son's cancer treatments. So Brascoe teams up with some crooks (Madsen, Bush) to rip off a billionaire (Ironside). **95m/C VHS, DVD.** Dan Anderson, Michael Ironside, Michael Madsen, Olivier Gruner, Grand Bush, Martin Kove, Antonio Fargas, Edward Albert, Charles Napier, Odile Corso; ***D:*** Steven Rush; ***W:*** Steven Rush; ***C:*** Ken Blakey; ***M:*** David Powell, Geoff Levin. **VIDEO**

Extreme Justice 🦴🦴½ **1993 (R)** A violent expose of the Special Investigations Section of the Los Angeles Police Department, an elite, undercover squad which specialized in catching violent repeat offenders. But their tactics left something to be desired. They were accused of stalking their prey until they committed a crime and then dealing with the criminal by shooting them in the act. Lots of gunplay. Originally a theatrical film that was pulled for release in the wake of the Rodney King verdict. **96m/C VHS, DVD.** Stephen (Steve) Root, Lou Diamond Phillips, Scott Glenn, Yaphet Kotto, Ed Lauter, Chelsea Field; ***D:*** Mark L. Lester; ***W:*** Robert Boris; ***C:*** Mark Irwin; ***M:*** David Michael Frank.

Extreme Limits 🦴🦴 **2001 (R)** CIA agent Williams heads to Alaska to find a plane that has crashed in the mountains. As well as helping the survivors, he must find a mystery bomb that's also being sought by terrorists. Typical action fare. Wynorski directed under the pseudonym Jay Andrews. **105m/C VHS, DVD, Wide.** Treat Williams, Hannes Jaenicke, John Beck, Susan Blakely, Gary Hudson, Julie St. Clair; ***D:*** Jim Wynorski; ***C:*** Andrea V. Rossotto. **VIDEO**

Extreme Measures 🦴🦴½ **1996 (R)** Dr. Grant, Action Guy! Cast against type, Grant takes on action-suspense in this urbane medical thriller, and it works. Plot is pretty standard for the genre—doctor Luthan (Grant) suspects foul play when homeless people are turning up with mysterious symptoms before expiring in his ward. Seeking to expose what he believes is a medical conspiracy, his "darn meddling" gets him in all kinds of trouble. Enter Dr. Lawrence Myrick (Hackman), a genius neurologist who reeks of suspicion. Luthan must get by him to uncover the dangerous human experimentation that's been going on. Producer and real-life love Hurley may have had something to do with the fact that Grant pulls off a mostly convincing turn, where his normally comic persona is used to humanize an otherwise cardboard hero. Adapted from a book by Michael Palmer. **118m/C VHS, DVD.** J.K. Simmons, Hugh Grant, Gene Hackman, Sarah Jessica Parker, David Cronenberg, Bill Nunn, Debra Monk, John Toles-Bey, Paul Guilfoyle, Andre De Shields, Shaun Austin-Olsen, Peter Appel; ***D:*** Michael Apted; ***W:*** Tony Gilroy; ***C:*** John Bailey; ***M:*** Danny Elfman.

Extreme Prejudice 🦴🦴 **1987 (R)** A redneck Texas Ranger fights a powerful drug kingpin along the U.S.-Mexican border. Once best friends, they now fight for justice and the heart of the woman they both love. **104m/C VHS.** Nick Nolte, Powers Boothe, Maria Conchita Alonso, Michael Ironside, Rip Torn, Clancy Brown, Matt Mulhern, William Forsythe, Tommy (Tiny) Lister, Larry B. Scott; ***D:*** Walter Hill; ***W:*** Deric Washburn; ***M:*** Jerry Goldsmith.

Extreme Vengeance 🦴🦴 **1993** Police officer David puts mafia crime boss Mario Blanco away for ten years, then exposes police corruption and goes into hiding. When Blanco gets out, he seeks revenge on David's family, forcing David out of hiding to protect what is his. Available in Spanish subtitles. **97m/C VHS.**

Extremedays 🦴½ **2001 (PG)** Four buddies take an aimless road California trip after graduating from college, indulging in their love of extreme sports such as surfing, skateboarding, dirt bike racing, and snowboarding. But when one of the guys learns of his grandfather's death, they decide to make the trip into a pilgrimage to pay their respects. For the most part it's silly fluff. **93m/C VHS, DVD.** Dante Basco, Ryan Browning, A.J. Buckley, Derek Hamilton, Cassidy Rae; ***D:*** Eric Hannah. **VIDEO**

Extremely Dangerous 🦴🦴½ **1999** Convoluted thriller that originated as a four-part British miniseries. Neil Byrne (Bean) was a British intelligence agent working deep undercover after infiltrating a group of gangsters. But his life is blown apart when Neil is convicted of the brutal murders of his wife and daughter. Naturally, he's innocent and when he makes his escape from prison transport, he heads back to find the true killers and get his revenge while being pursued by mobsters, police, and the agency he worked for. Some of the violence is very nasty. **200m/C VHS, DVD.** *GB* Sean Bean, Juliet Aubrey, Ralph Brown, Anthony Booth, Ron Donachie, Sean Gallagher; ***D:*** Sallie Aprahamian; ***C:*** Peter Middleton; ***M:*** Rupert Gregson-Williams. **TV**

Extremities 🦴🦴 **1986 (R)** An adaptation of the topical William Mastrosimone play about an intended rape victim who turns on her attacker, captures him, and plots to kill him. Violent and exploitive. **83m/C VHS, DVD, 8mm, Wide.** Farrah Fawcett, Diana Scarwid, James Russo, Alfre Woodard; ***D:*** Robert M. Young; ***W:*** William Mastrosimone; ***C:*** Curtis Clark; ***M:*** J.A.C. Redford.

Eye 🦴🦴 *Dead Innocent* **1996 (R)** When attorney Suzanne St. Laurent's (Bujold) daughter is kidnapped, only mom can outwit the video-obsessed culprit before her child is killed. **90m/C VHS, DVD.** *CA* Genevieve Bujold, Graham Greene, Jonathan Scarfe, Emily Hampshire, Nancy Beatty, Susan Glover; ***D:*** Sara Botsford; ***W:*** Mort Pattigo, Dolores Payne; ***C:*** Rodney Gibbons; ***M:*** David Findlay.

The Eye Creatures 🦴 **1965** Alien creatures in the form of eyeballs are fought off by a teenager and his girlfriend. A low-budget, gory, science fiction feature. **80m/B VHS.** John Ashley, Cynthia Hull, Warren Hammack, Chet Davis, Bill Peck; ***D:*** Larry Buchanan.

An Eye for an Eye 🦴🦴 **1981 (R)** A story of pursuit and revenge with Norris as an undercover cop pitted against San Francisco's underworld and high society. **106m/C VHS, DVD.** Chuck Norris, Christopher Lee, Richard Roundtree, Matt Clark, Mako, Maggie Cooper; ***D:*** Steve Carver; ***W:*** James Bruner; ***C:*** Roger Shearman; ***M:*** William Goldstein.

An Eye for an Eye 🦴 **1995 (R)** A made-for-TV script that ended up on the feature film pile (and we do mean pile). Manipulative story has Karen McCann (Field) listening on the phone as her daughter is raped and killed by a scuzzball drifter (Sutherland). He's caught, but released on a technicality, driving Mom to join a vigilante group and plot revenge. Not a great career move for the director or surprisingly distinguished cast, who are given nothing but cardboard characters and push-button emotional cliches to work with. Shamelessly plays on middle class fears of crime and doubts about the judicial system. Based on the novel by Erika Holzer. **102m/C VHS, DVD, Wide.** Sally Field, Ed Harris, Kiefer Sutherland, Beverly D'Angelo, Joe Mantegna, Keith David; ***D:*** John Schlesinger; ***W:*** Amanda Silver, Rick Jaffa; ***C:*** Amir M. Mokri; ***M:*** James Newton Howard.

Eye of God 🦴🦴🦴 **1997 (R)** Darkly dramatic story of lonely small-town waitress Ainsley (Plimpton), who marries newly released, born-again ex-con Jack (Anderson) with whom she has been corresponding. Movie kicks off when veteran sherrif (Holbrook) questions a shaken up youth, Tommy (Stahl), who is mysteriously covered in blood but rendered mute by the experience. It soon becomes apparent in the deluge of frequent flashbacks and fast forwards that no good will come of this unlikely union, although the mere fate of the hapless Ainsley is not the point. First-time director Nelson's spare narrative seeks to explore deeper issues like faith and violence in the Bible Belt locale. Performances are universally powerful, especially Plimpton's lovable dim-bulb and Anderson's maniacal Jack, giving credence to the clever but sometimes overly flashy cinematic style. **88m/C VHS.** Martha Plimpton, Kevin Anderson, Hal Holbrook, Nick Stahl, Richard Jenkins, Margo Martindale, Maggie Moore, Mary Kay Place; ***D:*** Tim Blake Nelson; ***W:*** Tim Blake Nelson; ***C:*** Russell Fine; ***M:*** David Van Tiegham.

Eye of the Beholder 🦴 **1999 (R)** Disengaged surveillence expert, known only as "The Eye" (McGregor), works for British intelligence out of their embassy in Washington. His latest assignment is to keep track of blackmailing Joanna (Judd), who turns out to be a psychotic serial killer of many identities. This must provide some strange turn-on, since instead of calling the cops, he proceeds to track her cross-country, protecting her from capture. Judd's an attractive femme fatale but the picture makes little sense and soon falls into the jaw-dropping, I-don't-believe-what-I'm-seeing category. Based on the novel by Marc Behm. **101m/C VHS, DVD, Wide.** Ewan McGregor, Ashley Judd, Patrick Bergin, k.d. lang, Jason Priestley, Genevieve Bujold; ***D:*** Stephan Elliott; ***W:*** Stephan Elliott; ***C:*** Guy Dufaux; ***M:*** Marius De Vries.

Eye of the Demon 🦴 **1987** A couple moves to a small town in Massachusetts and discovers that the area had once been a haven for witchcraft. To their horror, they soon find that old habits die hard, and the spellcasting continues in a nearby graveyard. **92m/C VHS.** Tim Matheson, Pamela Sue Martin, Woody Harrelson, Barbara Billingsley, Susan Ruttan; ***D:*** Carl Schenkel. **CABLE**

Eye of the Eagle 🦴½ **1987 (R)** A special task force is given a dangerous assignment during the Vietnam war. **84m/C VHS.** Brett (Baxter) Clark, Ed Crick, Robert Patrick, William (Bill) Steis, Cec Verrell; ***D:*** Cirio H. Santiago.

Eye of the Eagle 2 🦴 **1989 (R)** When his platoon is betrayed and killed in Vietnam, a surviving soldier joins with a beautiful girl and seeks revenge. **79m/C VHS.** Todd Field, Andy Wood, Ken Jacobson, Ronald Lawrence; ***D:*** Carl Franklin.

Eye of the Eagle 3 🦴½ **1991 (R)** Filipino-made Vietnam-War shoot-em-up, rack-em-up, shoot-em-up again, with U.S. forces pinned down against seemingly overwhelming odds. Violent. **90m/C VHS.** Steve Kanaly, Ken Wright, Peter Nelson, Carl Franklin; ***D:*** Cirio H. Santiago; ***W:*** Carl Franklin.

Eye of the Killer 🦴🦴½ **1999 (R)** Mickey Hayden is a drunken detective who is forced to re-open the serial killer case that led to his present wretched state. But this time Mickey finds himself having psychic visions when he touches the victims' belongings that put him into the mind of the killer. Now he's tracking a serial killer that may tie into a ten-year-old case. **100m/C VHS, DVD, Wide.** Kiefer Sutherland, Henry Czerny, Polly Walker, Gary Hudson; ***D:*** Paul Marcus; ***W:*** Jeff Miller; ***C:*** Brian Pearson; ***M:*** Michael Hoenig.

Eye of the Needle 🦴🦴½ **1981 (R)** Based on Ken Follett's novel about a German spy posing as a shipwrecked sailor on a deserted English island during WWII. Lonely, sad, yet capable of terrible violence, he is stranded on an isolated island while en route to report to his Nazi commander. He becomes involved with an English woman living on the island, and begins to contemplate his role in the war. **112m/C VHS, DVD.** Donald Sutherland, Kate Nelligan, Ian Bannen, Christopher Cazenove, Philip Brown, Stephen MacKenna, Faith Brook, Colin Rix, Alex McCrindle, John Bennett, Sam Kydd, Rik Mayall, Bill Fraser; ***D:*** Richard Marquand; ***W:*** Stanley Mann; ***C:*** Alan Hume; ***M:*** Miklos Rozsa.

Eye of the Storm 🦴🦴½ **1991 (R)** At the highway gas station/motel/diner where they live, two young brothers witness their parent's murder. Their younger brother is blinded in the same incident. Ten years later both brothers are still there and the tragedy may have turned one of them psychotic. When the abusive Gladstone and his young and sexy wife are stranded at the gas station it brings out the worst in everyone, with a violent climax during an equally violent thunderstorm. **98m/C VHS.** Craig Sheffer, Bradley Gregg, Lara Flynn Boyle, Dennis Hopper, Leon Rippy; ***D:*** Yuri Zeltser.

Eye of the Storm 🦴½ *The Farmhouse* **1998 (R)** What's the elegant Danner during in this horror mishmash? (Maybe it worked better as a stage play.) College student Jenny (Kendall) is in rural Kansas during research on a typical American family. That turns out not to be the Millers—the farming family Jenny is forced to shelter with because of a tornado. Seems mom Irma (Danner) went whacko and killed daughter Sally and the event was covered up by her husband and adult son. Now, Irma's delusions mistake Jenny for Sally and the local sheriff is also snooping into Sally's disappearance. Adapted by co-scripter Watson from his play "The Farmhouse." **100m/C VHS, DVD.** Katherine Kendall, Blythe Danner, Leo Burmester, Guy Ale, Kurt Deutsch, Keith Reddin; ***D:*** Marcus Spiegel; ***W:*** Marcus Spiegel, Randy Watson; ***C:*** Horacio Marquinez; ***M:*** Anton Sanko.

Eye of the Stranger 🦴½ **1993 (R)** Suspenser about a nameless stranger who sets out to solve the mystery of a small western town and its corrupt mayor. **96m/C VHS.** David Heavener, Sally Kirkland, Martin Landau, Don Swayze, Stella Stevens, John Pleshette, Joe Estevez, Thomas F. Duffy; ***D:*** David Heavener; ***W:*** David Heavener; ***M:*** Robert Garrett.

Eye of the Tiger 🦴🦴 **1986 (R)** A righteous ex-con battles a crazed, crack-dealing motorcycle gang that terrorized and murdered his wife, and is moving on to infest his town. **90m/C VHS.** Gary Busey, Yaphet Kotto, Seymour Cassel, Bert Remsen, William Smith; ***D:*** Richard Sarafian; ***C:*** Peter Collister.

Eye of the Wolf 🦴🦴½ **1995 (PG-13)** Zoologist (Fahey) brings a wild wolf into civilization and then must fight to save the animal from execution. Kazan (a wolf-dog mix) is the true star—and rightly so. **96m/C VHS.** Jeff Fahey, Sophie Duez.

Eye on the Sparrow 🦴🦴½ **1991 (PG)** A couple (Winningham and Carradine) desperately want to raise a child of their own, but the system classifies them as unfit parents since they are both blind. Together they successfully fight the system in this inspiring movie that was based on a true story. **94m/C VHS.** Mare Winningham, Keith Carradine, Conchata Ferrell, Sandy McPeak, Karen Lee, Bianca Rose; ***D:*** John Korty. **TV**

Eye Witness 🦴🦴½ *Your Witness* **1949** An American attorney goes abroad to free a friend from the British legal system. A book of poems becomes the necessary device in deducing the whereabouts of the witness testifying to his friend's alibi. **104m/B VHS.** *GB* Robert Montgomery, Felix Aylmer, Leslie Banks, Michael Ripper, Patricia Wayne; ***D:*** Robert Montgomery; ***M:*** Malcolm Arnold.

Eye Witness 🦴🦴 *Sudden Terror* **1970 (PG)** The murder of an African dignitary is witnessed by a young boy who has trouble convincing his parents and the police about the incident. Suspenseful but less than original. Shot on location in Malta. **95m/C VHS, DVD, Wide.** *GB* Mark Lester, Lionel Jeffries, Susan George, Tony Bonner; ***D:*** John Hough; ***W:*** Bryan Forbes; ***C:*** David Holmes.

Eyeball woof! *Gatto Rossi In Un Labirinto Do Vetro* **1978 (R)** An intrepid policeman is stumped by a madman who is removing eyeballs from his victims. At least they won't have to watch this movie. **87m/C VHS.** *IT* John Richardson, Martine Brochard; ***D:*** Umberto Lenzi.

Eyes Behind the Stars 🦴 **1972** A news photographer accidentally gets a few pictures of invading aliens, but nobody takes him seriously, particularly the government. **95m/C VHS.** *IT* Martin Balsam, Robert Hoffman, Nathalie Delon, Sherry Buchanan; ***D:*** Roy Garrett.

Eyes of a Stranger woof! **1981 (R)** Terrifying maniac stalks his female prey by watching their every move. Tewes is cast as a journalist, the stronger of the two sisters in this exploitative slasher. **85m/C VHS.** Lauren Tewes, John Disanti, Jennifer Jason Leigh; ***D:*** Ken Wiederhorn; ***W:*** Eric L. Bloom; ***M:*** Richard Einhorn.

Eyes of a Witness 🦴🦴½ **1994** American businessman Roy Baxter (Travanti) travels to Kenya to rescue his daughter (Grey) from danger in the African bush. But Roy is falsely charged with murdering a government official and must take on the police to prove his innocence. **90m/C VHS.** Daniel J. Travanti, Jennifer Grey, Carl Lumbly.

Eyes of an Angel 🦴🦴½ **1991 (PG-13)** A widower (Travolta), who's heavily involved in gambling, is forced to go on the run with his young daughter (Raab) when a deal goes sour. She must abandon the family dog, who manages to follow them from Chicago to California anyway. Talk about loyalty! **91m/C VHS.** John Travolta, Elie Raab, Jeffrey DeMunn; ***D:*** Robert Harmon.

Eyes of Fire 🦴🦴 **1984 (R)** In early rural America, a group of pioneers set up camp in the wilderness and are besieged during the night by Indian witchcraft. **86m/C VHS.** Dennis Lipscomb, Rebecca Stanley, Fran Ryan, Rob Paulsen, Guy Boyd, Karlene Crockett; ***D:*** Avery Crounse; ***W:*** Avery Crounse; ***M:*** Brad Fiedel.

Eyes of Julia Deep 🦴🦴 **1918** Rare silent film featuring the ill-fated Minter as Julia, a woman who prevents Terry (Forrest) from killing himself. Piano scored. **54m/B VHS.** Mary Miles Minter, Alan Forrest, Alice Wilson, George Periolat; ***D:*** Lloyd Ingraham.

Eyes of Laura Mars 🦴🦴½ **1978 (R)** A photographer exhibits strange powers—she can foresee a murder before it happens through her snapshots. In time she realizes that the person responsible for a series of killings is tracking her. Title song performed by Barbra Streisand. **104m/C VHS, DVD, Wide.** Faye Dunaway, Tommy Lee Jones, Brad Dourif, Rene Auberjonois, Raul Julia, Darlanne Fluegel, Michael Tucker; ***D:*** Irvin Kershner; ***W:*** John Carpenter, David Zelag Goodman; ***C:*** Victor Kemper.

Eyes of Texas 🦴½ **1948** Bryant, a lawyer who uses a pack of killer dogs to get the land she wants, is pursued by a U.S Marshal played decently by Rogers. **54m/B VHS.** Roy Rogers, Lynne Roberts, Andy Devine, Nana Bryant, Roy Barcroft; ***D:*** William Witney.

The Eyes of the Amaryllis 🦴½ **1982 (R)** A young girl becomes involved in a mysterious game when she arrives in Nantucket to care for her insane, invalid grandmother. Based on the story by Natalie Babbitt and filmed on location on Nantucket Island. **94m/C VHS.** Martha Byrne, Ruth Ford, Guy Boyd, Jonathan Bolt, Katharine Houghton; *D:* Frederick King Keller.

Eyes of the Beholder ✌✌ **1992 (R)** Janice is a psychopathic serial killer who suffered brain damage from a botched surgical attempt to reverse his insanity. Now he's escaped from the state mental institution, heading straight for the secluded home of the doctor who made him crazier than ever. During a raging storm, Janice stalks the doctor, his wife, and their two hapless dinner guests in a sadistic game of cat-and-mouse. **89m/C VHS.** Lenny Von Dohlen, Joanna Pacula, Matt McCoy, George Lazenby, Kylie Travis, Charles Napier; *D:* Lawrence L. Simeone; *W:* Lawrence L. Simeone; *M:* Greg Turner.

Eyes of the Panther **1990** One of Shelley Duvall's "Nightmare Classics" series, this adaptation of an Ambrose Bierce story concerns a pioneer girl haunted for years by the animal urges of a wild cat. **60m/C VHS.** Daphne Zuniga, C. Thomas Howell, John Stockwell; *D:* Noel Black.

The Eyes of Youth ✌✌ **1919** A young woman searches her soul for answers: to marry or not to marry is the question. A little foresight, in the form of a glimpse into the hypothetical future, helps her make the right choice. Very early Valentino fare in which the sheik plays a cad. **78m/B VHS.** Clara Kimball Young, Edmund Lowe, Rudolph Valentino.

Eyes Right! ✌✌ **1926** Based on a story by Ernest Grayman, this portrayal of life in a military prep school has its main character experience struggle, recognition, love, jealousy, and triumph. Silent. **46m/B VHS.** Francis X. Bushman.

The Eyes, the Mouth ✌✌ **1983 (R)** A young man has an affair with his dead twin brother's fiancee. Happiness eludes them as they are haunted by the deceased's memory and the family's grief. In Italian with English subtitles. **100m/C VHS.** *FR IT* Lou Castel, Angela Molina; *D:* Marco Bellocchio; *W:* Marco Bellocchio.

Eyes Wide Shut ✌✌ **1999 (R)** Kubrick's psychosexual drama (two years in the making), and last film, turned out to be visual interesting (if just because you know everything was done on soundstages) but less than compelling. Society doc William Harford (Cruise) and wife Alice (Kidman) seem to have it all, until a stoned Alice confesses to having lustful thoughts for others besides her hubby. Bill can't admit to the same (he's kind of a chilly guy), but this revelation sends him reeling out into the Manhattan night looking for adventure. He ends his evening observing, but not joining in, an aristocratic, anonymous orgy before heading home, presumably a wiser man. Kidman's role basically fades out after her bravura confessional and Cruise seems more like an interested bystander than a man whose known world has crumbled. Based on Arthur Schnitzler's 1926 novel "Traumnovelle." **159m/C VHS, DVD.** Treva Etienne, Tom Cruise, Nicole Kidman, Sydney Pollack, Marie Richardson, Vinessa Shaw, Todd Field, Rade Serbedzija, Leelee Sobieski, Alan Cumming, Thomas Gibson, Sky Dumont, Fay Masterson; *D:* Stanley Kubrick; *W:* Stanley Kubrick; *C:* Larry Smith; *M:* Jocelyn Pook.

Eyewitness ✌✌½ *The Janitor* **1981 (R)** When a murder occurs in the office building of a star-struck janitor, he fabricates a tale in order to initiate a relationship with the TV reporter covering the story. Unfortunately the killers think he's telling the truth, which plunges the janitor and reporter into a dangerous and complicated position, pursued by both police and foreign agents. Somewhat contrived, but Hurt and Weaver are always interesting. Woods turns in a wonderful performance as Hurt's somewhat-psychotic best friend. **102m/C VHS.** William Hurt, Sigourney Weaver, Christopher Plummer, James Woods, Kenneth McMillan, Pamela Reed, Irene Worth, Steven Hill, Morgan Freeman; *D:* Peter Yates; *W:* Steve Tesich.

Eyewitness to Murder ✌½ **1993** Stevens plays a cop who is assigned to protect beautiful artist Wolter. They both have their tragic flaws: he is a grieving widower, she has been blinded by an unknown attacker. Their flaws may draw them together. Somewhat more engaging than a TV police action drama. **75m/C VHS.** Andrew Stevens, Adrian Zmed, Sherilyn Wolter, Carl Strano, Robin Drue; *D:* Jag Mundhra.

F. Scott Fitzgerald in Hollywood ✌✌ **1976** Dramatization begins in the late 1930s when Fitzgerald was lured to Hollywood to work in the burgeoning film industry. It covers the period when, with his wife in a mental institution, he lived with Sheila Graham and struggled against alcoholism. Interesting story made dull and depressing by Miller's uninspired performance, but it's almost saved by Weld's portrayal of Zelda. **98m/C VHS.** Jason Miller, Tuesday Weld, Julia Foster, Dolores Sutton, Michael Lerner, James Woods; *D:* Anthony Page. **TV**

F/X ✌✌✌ **1986 (R)** Rollie Tyler (Brown) is a New York-based special effects expert who is contracted by government agent Lipton (DeYoung) to fake an assassination in order to protect mob informer DeFranco (Orbach). After completing the assignment, Rollie learns that he's become involved in a real crime and is forced to reach into his bag of F/X tricks to survive, aided by tough cop Leo McCarthy (Dennehy), who's trying to figure out just what's going on. Twists and turns abound in this fast-paced story that was the sleeper hit of the year. Followed by a sequel. **109m/C VHS, DVD, Wide.** Bryan Brown, Cliff DeYoung, Diane Venora, Brian Dennehy, Jerry Orbach, Mason Adams, Joe Grifasi, Martha Gehman, Angela Bassett; *D:* Robert Mandel; *W:* Robert T. Megginson, Gregory Fleeman; *C:* Miroslav Ondricek; *M:* Bill Conti.

F/X 2: The Deadly Art of Illusion ✌✌ **1991 (PG-13)** Weak follow-up finds the special-effects specialist set to pull off just one more illusion for the police. Once again, corrupt cops use him as a chump for their scheme, an overcomplicated business involving a stolen Vatican treasure. **107m/C VHS, DVD, Wide.** Bryan Brown, Brian Dennehy, Rachel Ticotin, Philip Bosco, Joanna Gleason; *D:* Richard Franklin; *W:* Bill Condon; *C:* Victor Kemper; *M:* Michael Boddicker, Lalo Schifrin.

Fabiola ✌✌✌ **1948** The first of the big Italian spectacle movies, this one opened the door for a flood of low-budget imitators. Fabiola, the daughter of a Roman senator, becomes a Christian when her father's Christian servants are accused of murdering him. In the meantime, the Emperor Constantine speeds toward Rome to convert it to Christian status. You can bet plenty of Christians will lose their heads, be thrown to the lions and generally burn at the stake before he does. **96m/C VHS.** *IT* Michel Simon, Henri Vidal, Michele Morgan, Gino Cervi; *D:* Alessandro Blasetti.

The Fable of the Beautiful Pigeon Fancier ✌✌½ *Fabula de la Bella Palomera* **1988** A powerful man who has always gotten what he wanted spies a beautiful young married woman and sets out to make her his own. Based on the Gabriel Gracia Marquez novel "Love in the Time of Cholera." In Spanish with English subtitles. **73m/C VHS.** *SP* Ney Latorraca, Claudia Ohana, Tonia Carrero, Dina Stat, Chico Diaz; *D:* Ruy Guerra; *W:* Ruy Guerra, Gabriel Garcia Marquez; *C:* Edgar Moura.

Fabulous Adventures of Baron Munchausen ✌✌ *Baron Munchausen; The Fabulous Baron Munchausen; The Original Fabulous Adventures of Baron Munchausen; Baron Prasil* **1961** The legendary Baron Munchausen, known for his tall tales, relates the story of his trek to the strange and beautiful land of Trukesban in a mixture of live action and animation. Wonderful special effects but a boring storyline. In German with English subtitles. **84m/C VHS.** *GE* Milos Kopecky, Hana Brejchova, Rudolph Jelinek, Jan Werich; *D:* Karel Zeman; *W:* Karel Zeman; *C:* Jiri Tarantik; *M:* Zdenek Liska.

The Fabulous Baker Boys ✌✌✌ **1989 (R)** Two brothers have been performing a tired act as nightclub pianists for 15 years. When they hire a sultry vocalist to revitalize the routine, she inadvertently triggers long-suppressed hostility between the "boys." The story may be a bit uneven, but fine performances by the three leading actors, the steamy atmosphere, and Pfeiffer's classic rendition of "Makin' Whoopee," are worth the price of the rental. **116m/C VHS, DVD, 8mm, Wide.** Michelle Pfeiffer, Jeff Bridges, Beau Bridges, Elie Raab, Jennifer Tilly; *D:* Steven Kloves; *W:* Steven Kloves; *C:* Michael Ballhaus; *M:* Dave Grusin. Golden Globes '90: Actress—Drama (Pfeiffer); L.A. Film Critics '89: Actress (Pfeiffer), Cinematog.; Natl. Bd. of Review '89: Actress (Pfeiffer); N.Y. Film Critics '89: Actress (Pfeiffer); Natl. Soc. Film Critics '89: Actress (Pfeiffer), Cinematog., Support. Actor (Bridges).

The Fabulous Dorseys ✌✌ **1947** The musical lives of big band leaders Tommy and Jimmy Dorsey are portrayed in this less than fabulous biography that's strong on song but weak on plot. Guest stars include Art Tatum, Charlie Barnet, Ziggy Elman, Bob Eberly and Helen O'Connell. Highlights are the tunes. ♫At Sundown; I'll Never Say Never Again; To Me; Green Eyes; Dorsey Concerto; Art's Blues; Everybody's Doin' It; The Object of My Affection; Runnin' Wild. **91m/B VHS.** Tommy Dorsey, Jimmy Dorsey, Janet Blair, Paul Whiteman, Sara Allgood, Arthur Shields; *D:* Alfred E. Green.

Fabulous Joe ✌✌ **1947** A talking dog named Joe gets involved in the life of a hen-pecked husband. **54m/C VHS.** Walter Abel, Donald Meek, Margot Grahame, Marie Wilson; *D:* Harve Foster.

Facade ✌✌ **1998 (R)** American real-estate whiz, Colin Wentworth, and Frenchman Frederic Colbert team up for a shady business deal to build a luxury hotel in Malibu. They use murder, so no one will stand in their way. Frederic even encourages Colin to kill his murdered partner's wife, Caroline. But strange things keep happening and what Colin believes to be true, turns out to be very far from reality. **93m/C VHS.** Eric Roberts, Angus Macfadyen, Camilla Overbye Roos, Joe (Johnny) Viterelli; *D:* Carl Colpaert; *W:* Carl Colpaert, Lance Smith. **VIDEO**

Face ✌✌ **1997 (R)** A violent Brit-take on "Reservoir Dogs" has a group of East End armed robbers realizing someone in their gang has betrayed them after a heist goes wrong. Chief among the crooks are Ray (Carlyle) and his partner Dave (Winstone), plus three rookies and the unexpected involvement of a crooked cop. Lots of energy but not much that's new. **107m/C VHS.** *GB* Robert Carlyle, Steven Waddington, Ray Winstone, Philip Davis, Damon Albarn, Peter Vaughan, Lena Headey, Andrew Tiernan; *D:* Antonia Bird; *W:* Ronan Bennett; *C:* Fred Tammes; *M:* Andy Roberts.

The Face at the Window ✌✌ **1939** Melodramatic crime story of a pair of ne'er-do-well brothers who terrorize Paris to conceal their bank robberies. **65m/B VHS.** Tod Slaughter, Marjorie Taylor, John Warwick, Robert Adair, Harry Terry; *D:* George King.

Face Down ✌✌ **1997 (R)** You've got your standard wisecracking New York ex-cop-turned-PI Bob Signorelli (Mantegna), who has a one-nighter with your blonde bombshell type client Merre (Maroney), who has ties to a mystery man (Ant). There's a murder, there's Bob's ex-partner Lt. Cooper (Riegert), who's no friend, investigating the murder, and there's Bob trying to find the killer first. And you've certainly seen it all before. **107m/C VHS.** J.K. Simmons, Joe Mantegna, Peter Riegert, Kelli Maroney, Adam Ant; *D:* Thom Eberhardt; *W:* Thom Eberhardt; *C:* John Holosko; *M:* Gunther Schuller. **CABLE**

A Face in the Crowd ✌✌✌½ **1957** Journalist (Neal) discovers a down-home philosopher (Griffith) and puts him on her TV show. His aw-shucks personality soon wins him a large following and increasing influence—even political clout. Off the air he reveals his true nature to be insulting, vengeful, and power-hungry—all of which Neal decides to expose. Marks Griffith's spectacular film debut as a thoroughly despicable character and debut of Remick as the pretty cheerleader in whom he takes an interest. Schulburg wrote the screenplay from his short story "The Arkansas Traveler." He and director Kazan collaborated equally well in "On the Waterfront." **126m/B VHS.** Andy Griffith, Patricia Neal, Lee Remick, Walter Matthau, Anthony (Tony) Franciosa; *D:* Elia Kazan; *W:* Budd Schulberg; *C:* Harry Stradling Sr.

A Face in the Fog ✌✌ **1936** Two newspaper reporters set out to solve a number of murders that have plagued the cast of a play. Also interested is the playwright. Good low-budget thriller. **66m/B VHS.** June Collyer, Lloyd Hughes, Lawrence Gray, Al "Fuzzy" St. John, Jack Mulhall, Jack Cowell, John Elliott, Sam Flint, Forrest Taylor, Edward Cassidy; *D:* Robert F. "Bob" Hill.

A Face in the Rain ✌✌ **1963** American spy Rand (Calhoun) is hiding out in German-occupied Italy during WWII. It turns out Anna (Berti), the wife of his contact, is having an affair with the German officer (MacGinnis) who's hunting Rand. Mediocre. **82m/B VHS.** Rory Calhoun, Marina Berti, Niall MacGinnis, Massimo Giuliani; *D:* Irvin Kershner; *W:* Hugo Butler, Jean Rouveral; *C:* Haskell Wexler; *M:* Richard Markowitz.

Face of Another ✌✌ *Tanin no kao; I Have a Stranger's Face; Stranger's Face* **1966** A severely burned man gets a second chance when a plastic surgeon makes a mask to hide the disfigurement. Unfortunately this face leads him to alienation, rape, infidelity, and murder. In Japanese with English subtitles. **124m/B VHS.** *JP* Minoru Chiaki, Robert Dunham, Kyoko Kishida, Beverly Maeda, Eiji Okada, Koreya Senda, Tatsuya Nakadai, Machiko Kyo; *D:* Hiroshi Teshigahara; *W:* Kobe Abe; *C:* Hiroshi Segawa; *M:* Toru Takemitsu.

Face of the Screaming Werewolf ✌½ *La Casa Del Terror; House of Terror* **1959** Originally a Mexican horror/comedy that was bought for U.S. distribution by Jerry Warren, who earned his spot in the horror hall of fame with "The Incredible Petrified World" and "Teenage Zombies." A scientist brings a mummy back to life, but when he removes the bandages (gasp), the subject turns out to be of the canine persuasion. Suffers from comic evisceration; not much to scream about. **60m/B VHS.** *MX* Lon Chaney Jr., Landa Varle, Raymond Gaylord; *D:* Gilberto Martinez Solares, Jerry Warren.

Face/Off ✌✌✌½ **1997 (R)** Woo returns to his blood-soaked, violence-as-poetry-in-motion roots with the story of a fed who assumes the identity of the presumed-dead terrorist who killed his son. When the master criminal wakes up, he "steals" the cop's identity. Travolta's back for another wild ride, eating up the scenery when he takes on the bad-guy role. Cage, fresh from action hits in "The Rock" and "Con Air" gets to study the nature of good and evil (another Woo specialty) while he learns the nuances of the "leap across the room with two pistols blazing" move. Woo's Hong Kong efforts have always explored the blurry line between the good guys and the bad guys, and with Cage and Travolta, he has the perfect actors to display his findings. Woo cultists will welcome the return to the old style, while those only familiar with his stateside work will understand what all the fuss was about. **140m/C VHS, DVD.** John Travolta, Nicolas Cage, Joan Allen, Alessandro Nivola, Gina Gershon, Nick Cassavetes, Dominique Swain, Harve Presnell, Margaret Cho, CCH Pounder, Colm Feore, John Carroll Lynch, Matt Ross; *D:* John Woo; *W:* Mike Werb, Michael Colleary; *C:* Oliver Wood; *M:* John Powell. MTV Movie Awards '98: On-Screen Duo (John Travolta/Nicolas Cage), Action Seq.

Face the Evil ✌½ **1997 (R)** TV star Sharon (Tweed) gets taken hostage in an art gallery where she's filming by a gang of thieves. But that's not the real problem—seems their leader, Dangler (Henriksen), wants to retrieve a shipment of nerve gas that's been hidden in some art work. **92m/C VHS, DVD.** Shannon Tweed, Lance Henriksen, Bruce Payne, Jayne Heitmeyer; *D:*

Paul Lynch; *W:* Richard Beattie; *C:* Barry Gravelle; *M:* Paul Zaza. **VIDEO**

Face the Music ½ **1992 (PG-13)** Ringwald and Dempsey were once stormily married and pursuing successful, collaborative careers as singer/songwriters for the movies. But they've abandoned the work, along with the marriage, until a movie producer makes them a very lucrative offer for a new song. Only Dempsey's new girlfriend has some voracious objections. **93m/C VHS.** Patrick Dempsey, Molly Ringwald, Lysette Anthony.

Face to Face ½ **1952** Dramatic adaptation of two short stories, "The Secret Sharer," by Joseph Conrad, and Stephen Crane's "The Bride Comes to Yellow Sky." The Conrad story features Mason as a sea captain who discovers a fugitive stowaway aboard his ships. The Crane story features Preston as a sheriff threatened by an old-time gunfighter. **92m/B VHS.** Bretaigne Windust, James Mason, Michael Pate, Robert Preston, Marjorie Steele, Gene Lockhart, Minor Watson; *D:* John Brahm.

Face to Face *Ansikte mot Ansikte* **1976** Bergman's harrowing tale of a mental breakdown. Ullmann has a bravura role as a psychiatrist deciding to vacation at her grandparent's house in the country. Once there she begins to experience depression and hallucinations tied to her past with both her mother and grandmother. Her deeply repressed feelings eventually lead to a suicide attempt, which brings some much needed help. Originally a four-hour series made for Swedish TV; subtitled. **136m/C VHS.** *SW* Liv Ullmann, Erland Josephson, Gunnar Bjornstrand, Aino Taube-Henrikson, Sven Lindberg, Kary Sylway, Sif Ruud; *D:* Ingmar Bergman; *W:* Ingmar Bergman; *C:* Sven Nykvist. Golden Globes '77: Foreign Film; L.A. Film Critics '76: Actress (Ullmann), Foreign Film; Natl. Bd. of Review '76: Actress (Ullmann); N.Y. Film Critics '76: Actress (Ullmann). **TV**

A Face to Kill For **1999 (PG-13)** Bernard has a horse farm, which her compulsive gambler husband Savant needs to sell to get some cash. So, he frames her for a crime and she's sent to prison. A fight with another inmate leads to facial disfigurement and when she does get out, Bernard decides plastic surgery will give her a whole new look. And with a new face, she plans to take some very sweet revenge. **91m/C VHS.** Crystal Bernard, Doug Savant, Barry Corbin, Billy Dean. **CABLE**

Faces ½ **1968 (R)** Cassavettes' first independent film to find mainstream success portrays the breakup of the 14-year marriage of middle-aged Richard (Marley) and Maria (Carlin) Forst. Both seek at least momentary comfort with others—Richard with prostitute Jeannie (Rowlands) and Maria with aging hippie Chet (Cassel). The director's usual improvisational and documentary style can either be viewed as compelling or tedious but the performances are first-rate. **129m/B VHS, DVD.** John Marley, Lynn Carlin, Gena Rowlands, Seymour Cassel, Val Avery, Dorothy Gulliver, Joanne Moore Jordan, Fred Draper, Darlene Conley; *D:* John Cassavetes; *W:* John Cassavetes; *C:* Al Ruban; *M:* Jack Ackerman. Natl. Soc. Film Critics '68: Screenplay, Support. Actor (Cassel).

Faces of Women **1985** Two stories about women in contemporary Africa. In the first, an unhappy young woman is married to a very jealous man. When her brother-in-law visits, she decides to give her husband something to worry about. The second story finds a businesswoman running into problems when she tries to open a restaurant—problems that her daughter helps to solve. French and indigenous languages with English subtitles. **103m/C VHS.** Eugenie Cisse Roland, Sidiki Bakaba, Albertine N'Guessan; *D:* Desire Ecare.

Facing the Enemy **2000 (R)** Harlan Moss (Caulfield) believes in revenge and he blames Detective Griff McCleary (Ashby) for the death of his wife (Preston). So his idea is to seduce McCleary's estranged wife (Paul)—and then kill her. The surprise ending isn't very and it's a familiar ride but if you're in the mood for a cop thriller, this one will pass the time. **98m/C VHS, DVD.** Linden Ashby, Maxwell Caulfield, Alexandra Paul, Cynthia Preston, Max Gail, Bruce Weitz, Melanie Wilson; *D:* Rob Malenfant; *W:* Martin Kitrosser; *C:* Steve Adcock; *M:* Richard Bowers. **VIDEO**

The Facts of Life ½ **1960 (PG-13)** Risque bedroom comedy finds Larry Gilbert (Hope) and Kitty Weaver (Ball) running off from boredom in suburbia and their respective spouses (Hussey and DeFore) to have a little interlude together. **103m/B VHS.** Bob Hope, Lucille Ball, Ruth Hussey, Don DeFore, Louis Nye, Philip Ober; *D:* Melvin Frank; *W:* Melvin Frank, Norman Panama; *C:* Charles B(ryant) Lang Jr.; *M:* Leigh Harline. Oscars '60: Costume Des. (B&W).

The Faculty ½ **1998 (R)** Nerd (Wood), beauty queen (Brewster), jock (Hatosy), new girl (Harris), rebel (Hartnett), and lovelorn girl (DuVall) come up against the greatest challenge of their lives. No, not the SATs. Parasitic aliens have nested in their high school and replaced the rumpled, frumpy staff with pleasure-seeking sexpots out for excitment. It's "The Breakfast Club" against "Them" in a battle royale! More style, less substance dictates the union between indie director Rodriguez and screenwriter Williamson. As expected, the dialogue is hip, the fashions are crisp, and kids are spunky, but pic never explains the aliens' visit. The multi-generational cast is enjoyable enough and the scares (however recycled they may be) are effective if you like icky scenes of alien projectiles sprouting from a human orifice or two. **102m/C VHS, DVD.** Jon Abrahams, Elijah Wood, Robert Patrick, Bebe Neuwirth, Salma Hayek, Jon Stewart, Piper Laurie, Famke Janssen, Christopher McDonald, Jordana Brewster, Clea DuVall, Laura Harris, Josh Hartnett, Usher Raymond; *D:* Robert Rodriguez; *W:* Kevin Williamson; *C:* Enrique Chediak; *M:* Marco Beltrami.

Fade to Black woof! **1980 (R)** Young man obsessed with movies loses his grip on reality and adopts the personalities of cinematic characters (Hopalong Cassidy and Dracula among them) to seek revenge on people who have wronged him. Thoroughly unpleasant, highlighted by clips from old flicks. **100m/C VHS, DVD.** Dennis Christopher, Tim Thomerson, Linda Kerridge, Mickey Rourke, Melinda Fee, Gwynne Gilford, Norman Burton, Morgan Paull, James Luisi, John Steadman, Marcie Barkin, Eve Brent Ashe; *D:* Vernon Zimmerman; *W:* Vernon Zimmerman; *C:* Alex Phillips Jr.; *M:* Craig Safan.

Fade to Black **1993 (R)** Busfield stars as a college professor with voyeuristic tendencies and a handy camcorder. After viewing his latest tape, he realizes he's filmed his neighbor's murder and that he can recognize the killer. Before he can warn the killer's girlfriend, she disappears and our nosy prof is framed for the death. **84m/C VHS.** Timothy Busfield, Heather Locklear, Michael Beck, Louis Giambalvo, Cloris Leachman, David Byron; *D:* John McPherson; *W:* Douglas Barr.

Fahrenheit 451 **1966** Chilling adaptation of the Ray Bradbury novel about a totalitarian futuristic society that has banned all reading material and the firemen whose job it is to keep the fires at 451 degrees: the temperature at which paper burns. Werner is Montag, a fireman who begins to question the rightness of his actions when he meets the book-loving teacher Clarisse (Christie)—who also plays the dual role of Werner's TV-absorbed wife, Linda. Truffaut's first color and English-language film. **112m/C VHS, DVD.** *FR GB* Oskar Werner, Julie Christie, Cyril Cusack, Anton Diffring, Alex Scott, Anna Palk, Ann Bell, Mark Lester; *D:* Francois Truffaut; *W:* Francois Truffaut, Helen Scott, Jean-Louis Richard, David Rudkin; *C:* Nicolas Roeg; *M:* Bernard Herrmann.

Fail-Safe ½ **1964** A nail-biting nuclear age nightmare, in which American planes have been erroneously sent to bomb the USSR, with no way to recall them. An all-star cast impels this bitterly serious thriller, the straight-faced flipside of "Dr. Strangelove." **111m/B VHS, DVD, Wide.** Henry Fonda, Dan O'Herlihy, Walter Matthau, Larry Hagman, Fritz Weaver, Dom DeLuise; *D:* Sidney Lumet; *W:* Walter Bernstein; *C:* Gerald Hirschfeld.

Fair Game woof! **1982 (R)** Three young women decide to ditch their private school for a weekend of fun but find out the resort town they've chosen is run by sociopaths who get their kicks by stalking our chicks. **90m/C VHS.** *AU* Kim Trengove, Kerry Mack, Marie O'Loughlina, Karen West; *D:* Christopher Fitchett.

Fair Game woof! **1985** In the Australian outback, three loathesome excuses for human beings come across a beautiful woman alone on a remote farm. Naturally, they try to do despicable things but she fights back. **83m/C VHS, DVD.** *AU* Cassandra Delaney, Peter Ford, David Sandford, Gary Who; *D:* Mario Andreacchio; *W:* Rob George; *C:* Andrew Lesnie; *M:* Ashley Irwin.

Fair Game woof! *Mamba Snakes* **1989 (R)** A psychotic but imaginative exboyfriend locks his former girlfriend in her apartment with a lethal giant Mamba snake. Understandably uninterested in its serpentine attention, the young woman must trespass against the Hollywood code and keep her wits in the face of danger. Guaranteed not to charm you. **81m/C VHS, DVD.** *IT* Gregg Henry, Trudie Styler, Bill Moseley; *D:* Mario Orfini; *W:* Mario Orfini, Linda Ravera; *C:* Dante Spinotti; *M:* Giorgio Moroder.

Fair Game ½ **1995 (R)** Miami police detective Max (Baldwin) defies orders so he can protect family attorney Kate (Crawford, in her big-screen debut) from high-tech assassins. Nice work if you can get it. Generic action plot provides Crawford and first-time director Sipes with relatively safe proving ground. Cindy wears the "Die Hard" dirty white tank top look fetchingly enough (and showers when the action slackens), while Baldwin is no slouch in the babe department (male division) either. Based on Paula Gosling's 1978 novel "Fair Game," which was previously filmed as 1986's "Cobra." **91m/C VHS, DVD.** William Baldwin, Cindy Crawford, Steven Berkoff, Miguel (Michael) Sandoval, Christopher McDonald, Johann Carlo, Salma Hayek, John Bedford Lloyd, Jenette Goldstein; *D:* Andrew Sipes; *W:* Charlie Fletcher; *C:* Richard Bowen; *M:* Mark Mancina.

Fairy Tales *Fairytales* **1976 (R)** A ribald musical fantasy follows the equally risque "Cinderella." In order to save the kingdom, the prince must produce an heir. The problem is that only the girl in the painting of "Princess Beauty" can "interest" the prince and she must be found. Good-natured smut. **83m/C VHS.** Don Sparks, Prof. Irwin Corey, Brenda Fogarty, Sy Richardson, Nai Bonet, Martha Reeves; *D:* Harry (Hurwitz) Tampa.

FairyTale: A True Story ½ *Illumination* **1997 (PG)** Discovery of hope and fantasy in bleak reality when two girls in 1917 war-torn England claim to have photographed fairies in their garden. Skeptical debunker Harry Houdini (Keitel) and spiritual believer Sir Arthur Conan Doyle (O'Toole) show up to investigate the photos of cousins Elsie (Hoath) and Frances (Earl). The issues of science and spiritualism are profusely debated between the two men, getting a little in the way of the girls and their story. Tries to appeal to both adults and children, which may leave both feeling a bit unsatisfied. Perky pixies flitting about throughout picture, courtesy of special f/x wizard Tim Webber, are bound to delight even hardened audience skeptics. Don't blink for Mel Gibson's cameo as Frances' father. This same true story, known as the Cottingley Fairies, is also part of the plotline in the surreal British film "Photographing Fairies." **99m/C VHS.** Harvey Keitel, Peter O'Toole, Florence Hoath, Elizabeth Earl, Paul McGann, Phoebe Nicholls, Bill Nighy, Bob Peck, Tim (McInnerny) McInnery; ***Cameos:*** Mel Gibson; *D:* Charles Sturridge; *W:* Ernie Contreras; *C:* Michael Coulter; *M:* Zbigniew Preisner.

Faith **1992 (R)** When young dancer Faith's parents are killed in an accident she winds up in a frightening foster home. Running away, she meets a gentlemanly mobster who helps her attain her dance dreams. Laughably implausible. **104m/C VHS.** Sylvia Seidel, Ami Dolenz, Richard Maldone.

Faithful ½ **1995 (R)** Black comedy about depressed, rich housewife Margaret (Cher) who is rudely interrupted by Tony the hitman (Palminteri) while trying to commit suicide on her 20th wedding anniversary. Unfaithful hubby Jack (O'Neal), who has put the contract out on Margaret, is conveniently away on business. As Margaret sits tied to a chair and Tony waits for a call to confirm the hit, the two connect and decide to turn the tables. Director Mazursky succeeds in bringing Palminteri's three-character play to the screen, even if it does suffer at times from too much stage talk and not enough action. First film for Cher since 1990's "Mermaids" and the first for O'Neal since 1989's "Chances Are." Big rift between Mazursky and the film's producers over final cut led him to threaten to pull his name from the credits. Mazursky cameos as the hitman's therapist. **91m/C VHS.** Cher, Ryan O'Neal, Chazz Palminteri; ***Cameos:*** Paul Mazursky; *D:* Paul Mazursky; *W:* Chazz Palminteri; *C:* Fred Murphy.

Fake Out *Nevada Heat* **1982** Nightclub singer is caught between the mob and the police who want her to testify against her gangland lover. Typical vanity outing for Zadora. **89m/C VHS.** Pia Zadora, Telly Savalas, Desi Arnaz Jr.; *D:* Matt Cimber.

Falcon **1974** Brave knight battles for the honor of a beautiful maiden; with or without the Falcon's help. **105m/C VHS.** Franco Nero.

The Falcon and the Snowman **1985 (R)** True story of Daulton Lee and Christopher Boyce, two childhood friends who, almost accidentally, sell American intelligence secrets to the KGB in 1977. Hutton and Penn are excellent, creating a relationship we care about and strong characterizations. **110m/C VHS, DVD.** Sean Penn, Timothy Hutton, Lori Singer, Pat Hingle, Dorian Harewood, Richard Dysart, David Suchet, Jennifer Runyon, Priscilla Pointer, Nicholas Pryor, Joyce Van Patten, Mady Kaplan, Michael Ironside; *D:* John Schlesinger; *W:* Steven Zaillian; *C:* Allen Daviau; *M:* Lyle Mays, Pat Metheny.

The Falcon in Hollywood ½ **1944** The falcon gets caught up with the murder of an actor who was part of a Tinseltown love triangle. The film takes place on RKO's back lot for a behind-the-scenes view of Hollywood. Part of the popular "Falcon" series from the 1940s. **67m/B VHS.** Tom Conway, Barbara Hale, Veda Ann Borg, Sheldon Leonard, Frank Jenks, Rita (Paula) Corday, John Abbott; *D:* Gordon Douglas.

The Falcon in Mexico ½ **1944** When paintings from a supposedly dead artist turn up for sale in New York City, the Falcon and the artist's daughter wind up journeying to Mexico to solve the mystery. Part of "The Falcon" series. **70m/B VHS.** Tom Conway, Mona Maris, Nestor Paiva; *D:* William Berke.

The Falcon's Brother **1942** Enemy agents intent on killing a South American diplomat are foiled by the Falcon's brothers at a steep personal cost. The plot enabled Sanders' real-life brother Conway to take over the title role in "The Falcon" mystery series, a role which he played nine more times. **64m/B VHS.** Tom Conway, George Sanders, Keye Luke, Jane Randolph; *D:* Stanley Logan.

Fall **1997** Brainy supermodel falls for literary cabbie in this portrait of life in the Big Apple. Within minutes of a chance encounter in a cab, married fare Sarah Easton (DeCadenet) is whiling the hours that her gorgeous, rich, doting husband is away, listening to romantic hack Michael's poetry and writhing seductively while feasting on carry-out like it's "9 1/2 Weeks." Schaeffer places himself opposite yet another gorgeous model and egotistically pens his character as a supersensitive writer (who does this guy think he is, Woody Allen?) faced with overwhelming acclaim after his first novel, who decides to chuck it all and drive a cab. Although nicely acted and not bad to look at, the main characters and both their dilemmas are just a little hard to relate to. **92m/C VHS.** Eric Schaeffer, Amanda DeCadenet,

Francie Swift, Lisa Vidal, Rudolf Martin; *D:* Eric Schaeffer; *W:* Eric Schaeffer; *C:* Joe DeSalvo; *M:* Amanda Kravat.

The Fall 🦴🦴 **1998 (R)** Or should that be "The Patsy"? American novelist Sheffer, who's living in Budapest, gets chosen as the savior of femme de Fougerolles, who is being stalked by Prochnow. Or so she says—and she wants Sheffer to kill her tormenter. **90m/C VHS, DVD.** Craig Sheffer, Juergen Prochnow, Helene de Fougerolles; *D:* Andrew Piddington. **VIDEO**

Fall from Grace 🦴🦴½ **1994** American and British intelligence officers take deadly risks in 1943 Europe in an effort to convince Hitler to end the war. **180m/C VHS.** *GB* James Fox, Michael York, Patsy Kensit, Gary Cole; *D:* Waris Hussein.

Fall from Innocence 🦴½ **1988** A girl is driven to a life of prostitution and drugs by the sexual abuse inflicted upon her by her father. **81m/C VHS.** Isabelle Mejias, Thom Haverstock, Amanda Smith, Rob McEwan; *D:* Carey Connor.

The Fall of the House of Usher 🦴 **1949** Lord Roderick Usher is haunted by his sister's ghost in this poor adaptation of the Poe classic. **70m/B VHS.** *GB* Kay Tendeter, Gwen Watford, Irving Steen, Lucy Pavey; *D:* Ivan Barnett.

The Fall of the House of Usher 🦴🦴🦴 *House of Usher* **1960** The moody Roger Corman/Vincent Price interpretation, the first of their eight Poe adaptations, depicting the collapse of the famous estate due to madness and revenge. Terrific sets and solid direction as well as Price's inimitable presence. **85m/C VHS, DVD, Wide.** Vincent Price, Myrna Fahey, Mark Damon, Harry Ellerbe, Bill Borzage, Nadajan; *D:* Roger Corman; *W:* Richard Matheson; *C:* Floyd Crosby; *M:* Les Baxter.

The Fall of the House of Usher 🦴½ **1980 (PG)** Another version of Edgar Allan Poe's classic tale of a family doomed to destruction. Stray to the Roger Corman/Vincent Price version to see how it should have been done. **101m/C VHS.** Martin Landau, Robert Hays, Charlene Tilton, Ray Walston; *D:* James L. Conway.

The Fall of the Roman Empire 🦴🦴🦴 **1964** An all-star, big budget extravaganza set in ancient Rome praised for its action sequences. The licentious son of Marcus Aurelius arranges for his father's murder and takes over as emperor while Barbarians gather at the gate. Great sets, fine acting, and thundering battle scenes. **187m/C VHS, Wide.** Sophia Loren, Alec Guinness, James Mason, Stephen Boyd, Christopher Plummer, John Ireland, Anthony Quayle, Eric Porter, Mel Ferrer, Omar Sharif; *D:* Anthony Mann; *W:* Philip Yordan; *C:* Robert Krasker. Golden Globes '65: Score.

Fall Time 🦴🦴 *Falltime* **1994 (R)** Crime drama set in small-town Minnesota, circa 1957. Three high schoolers set in motion a prank that turns bad when they pull up in front of the local bank. David (Arquette), Joe (Blechman), and Tim (London) intend to stage a mock robbery—but a real robbery is going down and the teens wind up the terrified hostages of creepy criminals Florence (Rourke) and Leon (Baldwin). Promising premise derailed by narrative inadequacies. **88m/C VHS, DVD.** Mickey Rourke, Stephen Baldwin, Jason London, David Arquette, Jonah Blechman, Sheryl Lee; *D:* Paul Warner; *W:* Steve Alden, Paul Skemp; *C:* Mark J. Gordon; *M:* Hummie Mann.

Fallen 🦴🦴 **1997 (R)** Take a police-story suspense thriller, add the occult and a big dose of the supernatural, stir in a heaping helping of philosophy, a dash of a wrong-man subplot, shake vigorously, and out pours the bitter "Fallen." After the execution of serial killer Edgar Reese (Koteas), crack cop Hobbes (Washington) is soon chasing down copycat killings springing up everywhere. The real culprit is not Reese, but a fallen angel who inhabits body after body, creating new killers with each new host. Washington manages to hold his own as the pic gets messy and overly complicated. Goodman's character provides needed earthbound common sense when the banter gets a bit too lofty, debating things like the meaning of life, existence of God, and other issues that don't belong here. Hoblit's second feature tries to take on way too much in it's already lengthy span. With a mish-mash of conflicting film styles and dicey dialogue, film manages to land on the careers of an otherwise talented cast and crew. **124m/C VHS, DVD, Wide.** Denzel Washington, Donald Sutherland, John Goodman, Elias Koteas, Embeth Davidtz, James Gandolfini, Robert Joy, Gabriel Casseus; *D:* Gregory Hoblit; *W:* Nicholas Kazan; *C:* Newton Thomas (Tom) Sigel; *M:* Tan Dun.

Fallen Angel 🦴🦴½ **1981** Relationship between a child pornographer and a particular young girl he finds easily exploitable because of her unbalanced home situation. Fine cast, solid direction. **100m/C** Dana Hill, Richard Masur, Melinda Dillon, Ronny Cox; *D:* Robert Lewis; *M:* Richard Bellis. **TV**

Fallen Angels 🦴🦴 *Duoluo Tianshi* **1995** The visuals dazzle but the disjointed narrative proves a challenge in what Kar-Wai originally intended to be a third story for his film "Chungking Express." Contract killer Wong Chi-Ming (Lai) has been getting his assignments from a nameless female agent (Reis) who's fallen for him. Wong wants to retire, which upsets her. Then there's mute ex-con He Zhiwo (Kaneshiro) who gets involved with a strange young woman named Cherry (Young) who still loves her ex-boyfriend, and everybody crosses paths but there's really no connection and nothing makes much sense anyway. **97m/C VHS, DVD.** *HK* Leon Lai, Michelle Reis, Takeshi Kaneshiro, Charlie Young, Karen Mok; *D:* Wong Kar-Wai; *W:* Wong Kar-Wai; *C:* Christopher Doyle; *M:* Frankie Chan.

Fallen Angels 1 🦴🦴🦴 **1993** Trilogy of hard-boiled, film noirish tales set in Los Angeles. "The Frightening Frammis" concerns a grifter (Gallagher) who meets his match in a mystery woman (Rossellini) in this adaptation of a Jim Thompson story. Cruise's directorial debut. "Murder, Obliquely" finds a plain Jane (Dern) falling for a heel (Rickman) who may have murdered his previous girl in a Cornell Woolrich tale. "Since I Don't Have You" has Buzz Meeks (Busey) hired to find a dame sought by both Howard Hughes (Matheson) and gangster Mickey Cohen (Woods). From a story by James Elroy. **90m/C VHS.** Peter Gallagher, Isabella Rossellini, Nancy Travis, John C. Reilly, Bill Erwin, Laura Dern, Alan Rickman, Diane Lane, Robin Bartlett, Gary Busey, Tim Matheson, James Woods, Aimee Graham, Dick Miller, Ken Lerner; *D:* Tom Cruise, Alfonso Cuaron, Jonathan Kaplan; *W:* Jon Robin Baitz, Howard A. Rodman, Amanda Silver, Steven Katz; *M:* Elmer Bernstein. **CABLE**

Fallen Angels 2 🦴🦴🦴 **1993** Three more film noir stories set in L.A. "Dead End for Delia" finds a police detective (Oldman) arriving at a murder scene to find his estranged wife (Anwar) the victim. Based on a short story by William Campbell Gault. "I'll Be Waiting" has Kirby as a hapless hotel detective who falls for a beautiful guest (Helgenberger) and winds up a mob pawn. Adaptation of a Raymond Chandler tale. "The Quiet Room" has Bedelia and Mantegna as a pair of corrupt cops who find their shakedown schemes going very wrong. From a story by Jonathan Craig. **90m/C VHS.** Gary Oldman, Gabrielle Anwar, Meg Tilly, Patrick Massett, Vondie Curtis-Hall, Paul Guilfoyle, Dan Hedaya, John Putch, Wayne Knight, Bruno Kirby, Marg Helgenberger, Jon Polito, Peter Scolari, Dick Miller, Joe Mantegna, Bonnie Bedelia, Vinessa Shaw, J.E. Freeman, Peter Gallagher, Patrick Breen, Genia Michaela, Wayne Grace; *Cameos:* Tom Hanks; *D:* Phil Joanou, Tom Hanks, Steven Soderbergh; *W:* Scott Frank, C. Gaby Mitchell, Howard A. Rodman. **CABLE**

Fallen Champ: The Untold Story of Mike Tyson 🦴🦴🦴 **1993** Director Kopple's provocative documentary on the boxing champ, from his roots in a Brooklyn ghetto to his conviction for rape in 1991. Tyson is shown as pathetic, vulnerable, and violent—psychologically unprepared for both acclaim and responsibility, as well as easily manipulated by promoters and opportunists. A mixture of ring footage and interviews with sportswriters, promoters, trainers, and others as well as media coverage of Tyson. **93m/C VHS.** *D:* Barbara Kopple. **TV**

The Fallen Idol 🦴🦴🦴 *The Lost Illusion* **1949** A young boy wrongly believes that a servant he admires is guilty of murdering his wife. Unwittingly, the child influences the police investigation of the crime so that the servant becomes the prime suspect. Richardson as the accused and Henrey as the boy are notable. Screenplay adapted by Greene from his short story, "The Basement Room." **92m/B VHS.** *GB* Ralph Richardson, Bobby Henrey, Michele Morgan, Sonia Dresdel, Jack Hawkins, Bernard Lee, Denis O'Dea, Dora Bryan, Walter Fitzgerald, Karel Stepanek, Geoffrey Keen, James Hayter, Dandy Nichols, George Woodbridge, John Ruddock, Joan Young, Gerard Heinz; *D:* Carol Reed; *W:* Graham Greene, Lesley Storm, William Templeton; *C:* Georges Perinal. British Acad. '48: Film; Natl. Bd. of Review '49: Actor (Richardson); N.Y. Film Critics '49: Director (Reed).

The Fallen Sparrow 🦴🦴🦴 **1943** Garfield is superb as a half-mad veteran of the Spanish Civil War. Captured and brutalized, he never revealed the whereabouts of a valuable possession. His return to the U.S. continues his torture as Nazi agent Slezak uses the woman Garfield loves to set a trap and finish the job. Solid performances and good plot are highlights. **94m/B VHS.** John Garfield, Maureen O'Hara, Walter Slezak, Patricia Morison, Martha O'Driscoll, Bruce Edwards, John Miljan, John Banner, Hugh Beaumont; *D:* Richard Wallace.

Falling Down 🦴🦴 **1993 (R)** Douglas is "D-FENS" (taken from his license plate), a normally law-abiding white-collar geek who snaps while stuck in a traffic jam on a hot day in LA. Like Charles Bronson in "Death Wish," he decides to take matters into his own hands. Unlike Bronson, he is not avenging an attack by a specific criminal, but raging against whomever gets in his way. Duvall is a detective on his last day before retirement, Hershey has the thankless role of Douglas' ex. Essentially a revenge fantasy that was vilified by some for catering to the baser emotions. **112m/C VHS, DVD, Wide.** Michael Douglas, Robert Duvall, Barbara Hershey, Rachel Ticotin, Tuesday Weld, Frederic Forrest, Lois Smith, D.W. Moffett, Dedee Pfeiffer, Vondie Curtis-Hall, Michael Paul Chan, Raymond J. Barry, Jack Kehoe, John Diehl; *D:* Joel Schumacher; *W:* Ebbe Roe Smith; *C:* Andrzej Bartkowiak; *M:* James Newton Howard.

Falling Fire 🦴🦴½ *The Cusp* **1997 (R)** Good visual effects highlight this cable sci-fier that combines terrorists and asteroids. Daryl Boden (Pare) has the task of getting his spacecraft to steer an asteroid into earth orbit for the purpose of mining its resources. But an eco-terrorist group, led by Lopez (Vidosa), want to force the asteroid to crash into the planet, thus "cleansing" it of man. Oh, there's a terrorist aboard Boden's craft to help things along, while his ex-wife Marilyn (von Palleske) fights the eco-villians back on earth. **84m/C VHS.** *CA* Michael Pare, Heidi von Palleske, Christian Vidosa, Zehra Leverman; *D:* Daniel D'or; *W:* Daniel D'or; *C:* Jonathan Freeman; *M:* Donald Quan. **CABLE**

Falling for a Dancer 🦴🦴½ **1998** When young Elizabeth Sullivan (Dermot-Walsh) gets pregnant after a brief affair, there's not much she can do since she lives in Ireland during the 1930s. She's forced by her family into marriage with a drunken widower and resigns herself to loneliness until love is found again. Purcell adapted from her own novel. **200m/C VHS, DVD.** *GB* Elisabeth Dermot-Walsh, Dermot Crowley, Liam Cunningham, Rory Murray, Brian McGrath, Maureen O'Brien, Colin Farrell; *D:* Richard Standeven; *W:* Deirdre Purcell; *C:* Kevin Rowley; *M:* Stephen McKeon. **TV**

Falling from Grace 🦴🦴½ **1992 (PG-13)** Bud Parks (Mellencamp) is a successful country singer who, accompanied by his wife and daughter, returns to his small Indiana hometown to celebrate his grandfather's 80th birthday. He's tired of both his career and his marriage and finds himself taking up once again with an old girlfriend (Lenz), who is not only married to Bud's brother but is also having an affair with his father. Bud believes he's better off staying in his old hometown but the problems caused by his return may change his mind. Surprisingly sedate, although literate, family drama with good ensemble performances. Actor-director debut for Mellencamp. **100m/C VHS.** John Cougar Mellencamp, Mariel Hemingway, Kay Lenz, Claude Akins, Dub Taylor, Brent Huff, Deirdre O'Connell, Larry Crane; *D:* John Cougar Mellencamp; *W:* Larry McMurtry.

Falling in Love 🦴🦴½ **1984 (PG-13)** Two married New Yorkers unexpectedly fall in love after a coincidental meeting at the Rizzoli Book Store. Weak but gracefully performed reworking of "Brief Encounter," where no one seems to ever complete a sentence. An unfortunate re-teaming for Streep and De Niro after their wonderful work in "The Deer Hunter." **106m/C VHS, DVD, Wide.** Robert De Niro, Meryl Streep, Harvey Keitel, Dianne Wiest, George Martin, Jane Kaczmarek, David Clennon; *D:* Ulu Grosbard; *W:* Michael Cristofer; *C:* Peter Suschitzsky; *M:* Dave Grusin.

Falling in Love Again 🦴½ *In Love* **1980 (PG)** Romantic comedy about middle-aged dreamer Gould and realistic wife York. They travel from Los Angeles to their hometown of New York for his high school reunion, where Gould is suddenly attacked by nostalgia vibes for his youth, seen in countless flashbacks, and prominently featuring Pfeiffer, notable in her film debut. Like watching a home movie about people you don't care about. **103m/C VHS, DVD.** Elliott Gould, Susannah York, Michelle Pfeiffer; *D:* Steven Paul; *W:* Ted Allan; *C:* Michael Mileham; *M:* Michel Legrand.

Fallout 🦴🦴½ **2001** It is horribly ironic that filmmaker Palumbo chose to film the introduction to his independent feature on top of one of the World Trade Center towers. His film concerns the interplay among four high-rise office workers who flee a disaster of uncertain origin and find themselves trapped in a basement fallout shelter. His story really has nothing to do with the 9/11/01 atrocities. It's a well-made character study that attempts to work with some serious ideas within the limitations of a modest budget. It's mostly successful, too, and certainly doesn't need any extra baggage. Parallels to reality are difficult to ignore, however. **88m/C DVD.** Claire Beckman, Mark Deakins, Keith Randolph Smith, David Wasson; *D:* Robert Palumbo; *W:* Robert Palumbo, Mark Gallini; *C:* Wolfgang Held; *M:* Frank Ferrucci.

False Arrest 🦴🦴½ **1992** A woman is falsely accused of killing her husband's business partner and winds up in prison where she continues to fight to prove her innocence. Mills does well in this less-than-glamorous role. Based on a true story. **102m/C VHS.** Donna Mills, Steven Bauer, James Handy, Lane Smith, Lewis Van Bergen, Dennis Christopher, Robert Wagner; *D:* Bill W.L. Norton. **TV**

False Colors 🦴 **1943** Hopalong Cassidy unmasks a crook posing as a ranch heir. This was the 49th Hopalong Cassidy feature. **54m/B VHS.** William Boyd, Robert Mitchum, Andy Clyde, Jimmy Rogers; *D:* George Archainbaud.

False Faces 🦴🦴½ **1918** Secret agent known as The Lone Wolf is working in France for the Allies when he learns a German master spy is headed for the U.S. to cause trouble. So he heads for New York to stop him. Lots of thrills. **65m/B VHS.** Henry B. Walthall, Lon Chaney Sr., Mary Anderson, Milton Ross; *D:* Irvin Willat.

False Faces 🦴½ **1932** A ruthless, money-hungry quack is hounded by the law and the victims of his unscrupulous plastic surgery. **80m/B VHS.** Lowell Sherman, Peggy Shannon, Lila Lee, Joyce Compton, Berton Churchill, David Landau, Eddie Anderson, Ken Maynard, Veda Ann Borg; *D:* Lowell Sherman.

False Identity 🦴½ **1990 (PG-13)** A radio psychologist buys a Purple Heart medal at a garage sale and then tries to find out about the original recipient. But her questions are making a number of folks uneasy, including a potentially dangerous stranger. **97m/C VHS.** Genevieve Bujold, Stacy Keach, Veronica Cartwright, Tobin Bell, Mimi Maynard; *D:* James Keach; *W:* Sandra K. Bailey.

False Witness 🦴🦴½ 1989 A New Orleans district attorney and her lover, a private investigator, find themselves working the same rape-murder case. When their methods disagree both find themselves in danger. Adapted from a novel by Dorothy Uhnak. **96m/C VHS.** Phylicia Rashad, Philip Michael Thomas, Terri Austin, George Grizzard; ***D:*** Arthur Seidelman; ***M:*** Charles Fox. **TV**

Fame 🦴🦴🦴 1980 **(R)** Follows eight talented teenagers from their freshmen year through graduation from New York's High School of Performing Arts. Insightful and absorbing, director Parker allows the kids to mature on screen, revealing the pressures of constantly trying to prove themselves. A faultless parallel is drawn between these "special" kids and the pressures felt by high schoolers everywhere. Great dance and music sequences. Basis for a TV series. ♫Fame; Red Light; I Sing the Body Electric; Dogs in the Yard; Hot Lunch Jam; Out Here On My Own; Is It OK If I Call You Mine?. **133m/C VHS.** Irene Cara, Barry Miller, Paul McCrane, Anne Meara, Joanna Merlin, Richard Belzer, Maureen Teefy, Albert Hague; ***D:*** Alan Parker; ***M:*** Michael Gore. Oscars '80: Song ("Fame"), Orig. Score; Golden Globes '81: Song ("Fame").

Fame Is the Spur 🦴🦴½ 1947 A lengthy but interesting look at the way power corrupts, plus an insight into the Conservative versus Labor dynamics of British government. Redgrave is a poor, idealistic worker who decides to help his fellow workers by running for Parliament. There, he falls prey to the trappings of office with surprising consequences. Look hard for Tomlinson, who went on to star in "Mary Poppins" and "Bedknobs and Broomsticks" for Disney. **116m/B VHS.** *GB* Michael Redgrave, Rosamund John, Bernard Miles, Hugh Burden, Guy Verney, Carla Lehmann, Sir Seymour Hicks, David Tomlinson; ***D:*** Roy Boulting.

The Family 🦴½ 1973 As a New Orleans hit-man who resists joining the mob, Bronson initiates an all-out war on the syndicate and its boss, played by Savalas. A poorly dubbed Italian action film. **94m/C VHS.** *IT* Charles Bronson, Jill Ireland, Telly Savalas; ***D:*** Sergio Sollima.

The Family 🦴🦴🦴 *La Famiglia* 1987 An 80-year-old patriarch prepares for his birthday celebration reminiscing about his family's past triumphs, tragedies and enduring love. The charming flashbacks, convincingly played, all take place in the family's grand old Roman apartment. In Italian with English subtitles or dubbed. **128m/C VHS.** *IT* Vittorio Gassman, Fanny Ardant, Philippe Noiret, Stefania Sandrelli, Andrea Occhipinti, Jo Champa; ***D:*** Ettore Scola; ***W:*** Ettore Scola, Ruggero Maccari, Furio Scarpelli; ***M:*** Armando Trovajoli.

Family Business 🦴🦴½ 1989 **(R)** A bright Ivy Leaguer, impressed by the exploits and vitality of his criminal grandfather, recruits him and his ex-con dad to pull off a high-tech robbery, which goes awry. Caper film, with its interest in family relationships and being true to one's nature. Casting Connery, Hoffman, and Broderick as the three leaves a big believability problem in the family department. **114m/C VHS, 8mm.** Sean Connery, Dustin Hoffman, Matthew Broderick, Rosana De Soto, Janet Carroll, Victoria Jackson, Bill McCutcheon, Deborah Rush, Marilyn Cooper, Salem Ludwig, Rex Everhart, James Tolkan; ***D:*** Sidney Lumet; ***W:*** Vincent Patrick; ***C:*** Andrzej Bartkowiak; ***M:*** Cy Coleman.

Family Enforcer 🦴 *Death Collector* 1976 **(R)** A small-time hoodlum is bent on becoming the best enforcer in an underworld society. **82m/C VHS, DVD.** Joe Cortese, Lou Criscuola, Joe Pesci, Anne Johns, Keith Davis; ***D:*** Ralph De Vito; ***W:*** Ralph De Vito; ***C:*** Bob Bailin.

The Family Game 🦴🦴🦴 *Kazoku gaimu; Kazoku Game* 1983 An obsessive satire about a poor, belligerent college student hired by a wealthy contemporary Japanese family to tutor their spoiled teenage son. Provides an all-out cultural assault on the Japanese bourgeoisie. From an original story by Yohei Honma. In Japanese with English subtitles. **107m/C VHS.** *JP* Junichi Tsujita, Yusaku Matsuda, Juzo Itami, Saori Yuki, Ichirota Miyagawa; ***D:*** Yoshimitsu Morita; ***W:*** Yoshimitsu Morita; ***C:*** Yonezo Maeda.

Family Jewels 🦴🦴 1965 A spoiled child-heiress has to choose among her six uncles to decide which should be her new father. If you like Jerry Lewis, you can't miss this! In addition to playing all six uncles, Lewis plays the chauffeur, as well as serving as producer, director, and coauthor of the script. **100m/C VHS.** Jerry Lewis, Donna Butterworth, Sebastian Cabot, Robert Strauss; ***D:*** Jerry Lewis; ***W:*** Jerry Lewis.

Family Life 🦴🦴 *Zycie Rodzinne* 1971 Melancholy mood piece finds an engineer reluctantly returning to his family's delapidated country mansion after six years in Warsaw. He must confront his own life as well as his alcoholic father and slightly mad sister. Polish with subtitles. **93m/C VHS.** *PL* Daniel Olbrychski, Jan Nowicki, Jan Kreczmar, Maja Komorowska, Halina Mikolajska; ***D:*** Krzysztof Zanussi; ***W:*** Krzysztof Zanussi; ***M:*** Wojciech Kilar.

Family Life 🦴🦴½ *Wednesday's Child* 1971 A portrait of 19-year-old Janice Baldwin, who's forced to get an abortion by her parents and battles them constantly to establish her own identity. She is eventually sent to a mental institution for depression, where she is subjected to increasingly vigorous psychological interventions, including electro-shock. Documentary-style effort originally made for British TV. **108m/C VHS.** *GB* Sandy Ratcliff, Bill Dean, Grace Cave; ***D:*** Ken Loach. **TV**

The Family Man 🦴🦴 1979 A brief encounter-between a married Manhattanite (Asner) and a much younger single woman (Baxter Birney) is sensitively handled in this film which explores their passionate affair. **98m/C VHS.** Ed Asner, Meredith Baxter, Paul Clemens, Mary Joan Negro, Anne Jackson, Martin Short, Michael Ironside; ***D:*** Glenn Jordan; ***M:*** Billy Goldenberg. **TV**

Family Man 🦴🦴 2000 **(PG-13)** With the help of a guardian angel/taxi driver (Cheadle), money-loving investment banker Jack Campbell (Cage) gets to see how life could have been if he'd married college sweetie Leoni, had kids, and was living in New Jersey and working as a tire salesman. Lost in this new world of responsibility and funnel cakes, Jack can't help but pine for his old life. But, in the end, will he choose ambition and "freedom" over love? Darker and not as tidy as "It's a Wonderful Life," its obvious inspiration, "Family Man" seeks to teach Jack a lesson we see coming miles off. **125m/C VHS, DVD, Wide.** Nicolas Cage, Tea Leoni, Don Cheadle, Amber Valletta; ***D:*** Brett Ratner; ***W:*** David Diamond, David Weissman; ***C:*** Dante Spinotti; ***M:*** Danny Elfman.

A Family Matter 🦴🦴 *Vendetta: Secrets of a Mafia Bride* 1991 **(R)** A Mafia chieftain adopts a child whose father was killed by hit men. She grows into a beautiful woman bent on revenge. Melodramatic Italian-American co-production, made for TV. **100m/C VHS.** Eric Roberts, Carol Alt, Eli Wallach, Burt Young. **TV**

Family of Cops 🦴🦴½ 1995 **(PG-13)** Trouble comes calling on Inspector Paul Fein's (Bronson) close-knit Milwaukee family when his party girl daughter Jackie (Featherstone) comes home to visit. She's soon accused of murdering a wealthy businessman she picked up in a drunken stupor and her cop family gets deeply involved in the investigation. Made for TV. **90m/C VHS, DVD.** Charles Bronson, Daniel Baldwin, Angela Featherstone, Sebastian Spence, Lesley-Anne Down, Barbara Williams, Simon MacCorkindale; ***D:*** Ted Kotcheff; ***W:*** Joel Basberg. **TV**

Family of Cops 2: Breach of Faith 🦴🦴½ *Breach of Faith: A Family of Cops 2* 1997 **(PG-13)** The investigation of a priest's murder makes Inspector Paul Fein (Bronson) and his cop family the target of Russian mobsters. TV movie once again filmed in Toronto, which substitutes for Milwaukee. **90m/C VHS, DVD.** Charles Bronson, Joe Penny, Diane Ladd, Sebastian Spence, Angela Featherstone, Barbara Williams, Andrew Jackson, Matt Birman, Kim Weeks, David Hemblen, Mimi Kuzyk, Real Andrews; ***D:*** David Greene; ***W:*** Joel Basberg; ***C:*** Ronald Orieux; ***M:*** Peter Manning Robinson. **TV**

Family of Cops 3 🦴🦴½ 1998 **(PG-13)** Police inspector Paul Fein (Bronson) decides to run for chief while detective son Ben (Penny) investigates the murder of a banker. There's also a corruption problem and time for a little romance. **90m/C VHS, DVD.** Charles Bronson, Joe Penny, Kim Weeks, Sebastian Spence, Barbara Williams, Torri Higginson, Nikki DeBoer; ***D:*** Sheldon Larry; ***W:*** Noah Jubelirer; ***C:*** Bert Dunk. **TV**

Family Pictures 🦴🦴🦴 1993 A photographer remembers growing up in the '50s with her autistic brother, the mother who lavished her attention on him almost to the exclusion of her five other children, and the father who blamed his wife for their son's deficiencies. Interesting portrait of an American family, which eventually cracks under pressure and splits up. Adapted from the novel by Sue Miller (no relation to screenwriter Jennifer). **240m/C VHS.** Anjelica Huston, Sam Neill, Kyra Sedgwick, Dermot Mulroney, Gemma Barry, Tara Charendoff, Torri Higginson, Jamie Harold; ***D:*** Philip Saville; ***W:*** Jennifer Miller.

Family Plot 🦴🦴½ 1976 **(PG)** Alfred Hitchcock's last film focuses on the search for a missing heir which is undertaken by a phony psychic and her private-eye boyfriend, with all becoming involved in a diamond theft. Campy, lightweight mystery that stales with time and doesn't fit well into Hitchcock's genre. **120m/C VHS, DVD, Wide.** Karen Black, Bruce Dern, Barbara Harris, William Devane, Ed Lauter, Katherine Helmond, Cathleen Nesbitt, Warren Kemmerling, Edith Atwater, William Prince, Nicholas Colasanto, Alfred Hitchcock; ***D:*** Alfred Hitchcock; ***W:*** Ernest Lehman; ***C:*** Leonard J. South; ***M:*** John Williams.

Family Prayers 🦴🦴½ 1991 **(PG)** Coming-of-age drama, set in 1969 Los Angeles, about 13-year-old Andrew and his family troubles. His father Martin (Mantegna) is a compulsive gambler which causes wife Rita (Archer) untold anxiety and constant friction between the two. Tension is heightened by Nan (LuPone), Rita's opinionated older sister who has bailed the family out of their money problems more than once. Meanwhile, Andrew tries to look out for his younger sister and prepare for his bar-mitzvah. A little too much of a nostalgic golden glow surrounds what is essentially a family tragedy. **109m/C VHS.** Tzvi Ratner-Stauber, Joe Mantegna, Anne Archer, Patti LuPone, Paul Reiser, Allen (Goorwitz) Garfield, Conchata Ferrell, David Margulies; ***D:*** Scott Rosenfelt; ***W:*** Steven Ginsburg.

Family Reunion 🦴½ 1979 The Andrews family is on vacation and visiting the ghost town of Sutterville. Grandpa Henry didn't want to stop and for good reason—it seems the town was once in the grip of a satanic cult. Forty years before, when Tom Andrews was a child, he was the designated satanic sacrifice and was rescued by Henry, who adopted him. Now Tom's real father has willed the family back to Sutterville to complete the ritual. **88m/C VHS, DVD.** Mel Novak, John Andes, A.J. Woods, Kaylin Cool, Pam Phillips, Mark McTague; ***D:*** Michael Hawes; ***W:*** Michael Hawes; ***C:*** Jack Anderson.

Family Reunion 🦴½ 1988 A young man brings a pretty hitchhiker to his family reunion where they mistake her for his fiancee (who recently dumped him). **97m/C VHS.** David Eisner, Rebecca Jenkins, Henry Beckman, Linda Sorensen; ***D:*** Dick Sarin.

Family Secrets 🦴🦴½ 1984 Drama about a daughter, mother, and grandmother overprotecting and manipulating each other during a weekend together. **96m/C** Maureen Stapleton, Stefanie Powers, Melissa Gilbert, James Spader; ***D:*** Jack Hofsiss. **TV**

Family Sins 🦴🦴 1987 A domineering father dotes on his sports-oriented son while willfully neglecting the other. Eventually this leads to calamity. **93m/C VHS.** James Farentino, Jill Eikenberry, Andrew Bendarski, Mimi Kuzyk, Brent Spiner, Michael Durrell, Tom Bower; ***D:*** Jerrold Freedman. **TV**

A Family Thing 🦴🦴🦴 1996 **(PG-13)** Racial issues are addressed in this character-driven story of two brothers. Southerner Earl Pilcher (Duvall) learns his biological mother was black and that she died during his birth. In a letter written by the recently deceased woman who raised him, Earl discovers he also has a half brother, Ray (Jones), who is black and living in Chicago. He drives to Chicago, and seeks out Ray, who to Earl's surprise knows about him already, and is not exactly thrilled about the family ties, either. As the two brothers, expertly played by Duvall and Jones, slowly find common ground, Hall steals the show as the irascible Aunt T. **109m/C VHS, DVD, Wide.** Robert Duvall, James Earl Jones, Irma P. Hall, Michael Beach, Grace Zabriskie, Regina Taylor, Mary Jackson, Paula Marshall, Jim Harrell; ***D:*** Richard Pearce; ***W:*** Billy Bob Thornton, Tom Epperson; ***C:*** Fred Murphy.

Family Tree 🦴½ 2000 **(G)** Slow-paced and preachy. A small town, suffering from high unemployment, is happy when a plastics company agrees to build a new factory. Only problem is that it means cutting down the town landmark—an ancient oak tree with generations of initials carved into its bark. However, young Mitch (Lawrence) decides to start a save-the-tree movement. **90m/C VHS.** Robert Forster, Cliff Robertson, Naomi Judd, Andy Laurence, Mathew Lawrence; ***D:*** Duane Clark; ***W:*** Paul Canterna; ***C:*** John Peters; ***M:*** Michael Curb, Randy Miller.

Family Upside Down 🦴🦴🦴 1978 An aging couple fight their separation after the husband has a heart attack and is put into a nursing home. The fine cast received several Emmy nominations, with Astaire the winner. **100m/C VHS.** Helen Hayes, Fred Astaire, Efrem Zimbalist Jr., Patty Duke; ***D:*** David Lowell Rich; ***M:*** Henry Mancini. **TV**

Family Viewing 🦴🦴🦴 1987 Surrealistic depiction of a family—obsessed with television and video—whose existence is a textbook model of home sweet dysfunctional home. An early, experimental film from Canada's Egoyan, it won considerable praise for its social commentary. **92m/C VHS, DVD.** *CA* David Hemblen, Adian Tierney, Gabrielle Rose, Arsinee Khanjian; ***D:*** Atom Egoyan; ***W:*** Atom Egoyan; ***C:*** Robert MacDonald, Peter Mettler; ***M:*** Mychael Danna. Toronto-City '87: Canadian Feature Film.

Famous Five Get into Trouble 🦴🦴 1987 Four precocious youngsters and a dog get involved with a criminal plot and cutely wile their way out of it. Scandinavian; dubbed in English. **90m/C VHS.** Astrid Villaume, Ove Sprogoe, Lily Broberg; ***D:*** Trine Hedman.

The Fan 🦴🦴 1981 **(R)** A Broadway star is threatened and her immediate circle cut down when a lovestruck fan feels he has been rejected by his idol. The stellar cast makes this bloody and familiar tale seem better than it is. **95m/C VHS.** Lauren Bacall, Maureen Stapleton, James Garner, Hector Elizondo, Michael Biehn, Griffin Dunne; ***D:*** Edward Bianchi; ***W:*** Priscilla Chapman; ***C:*** Dick Bush; ***M:*** Pino Donaggio.

The Fan 🦴🦴½ 1996 **(R)** Obsessed baseball fan Gil Renard (De Niro, who owns the copyright on playing deranged) stalks favorite player Bobby Rayburn (Snipes) who just signed a big contract with the hometown team. When Rayburn goes into a slump, Renard figures he can help his idol—by any means necessary. As an added bonus, Gil's a knife salesman. De Niro does the psycho thing with his usual aplomb, while Snipes successfully returns to the diamond. Scott keeps the familiar storyline from becoming tedious. Based on the book by Peter Abrahams. **117m/C VHS, DVD, 8mm.** Robert De Niro, Wesley Snipes, Ellen Barkin, John Leguizamo, Benicio Del Toro, Patti D'Arbanville; ***D:*** Tony Scott; ***W:*** Phoef Sutton; ***C:*** Darius Wolski; ***M:*** Hans Zimmer.

Fanatic woof! *The Last Horror Film* 1982 **(R)** Beautiful queen of horror films is followed to the Cannes Film Festival by her number one fan who, unbeknownst to her, is slowly murdering members of her entourage in a deluded and vain attempt to capture her attentions. Title refers to lack of plans for a sequel. **87m/C VHS, DVD.** Caroline Munro, Joe Spinell, Judd Hamilton, Devin Goldenberg, David Winters; *D:* David Winters; *W:* Tom Klassen, Judd Hamilton, David Winters; *C:* Thomas Denove; *M:* Jesse Frederick.

Fanci's Persuasion 𝄞½ **1995** San Francisco-set gay farce features lesbian Fanci (Patton) 24 hours away from marrying lover Loretta (Boa) and in panic mode. Her parents refuse to come to the ceremony and there are numerous and inexplicable complications to deal with. Deliberately over-the-top performances and contrived dialogue and situations can't really take the strain despite the pic's good looks. **78m/C VHS.** Jessica Patton, Boa, Justin Bond, Robert Coffman, Charles Herman-Wurmfeld; *D:* Charles Herman-Wurmfeld; *W:* Charles Herman-Wurmfeld; *C:* David Rush Morrison.

Fancy Pants 𝄞𝄞½ **1950** Remake of "Ruggles of Red Gap" features Hope, a British actor posing as a butler. Also featuring Ball, an amusing contrast. Fine performances all around. ♫Fancy Pants; Home Cookin'. **92m/C VHS.** Bob Hope, Lucille Ball, Bruce Cabot, Jack Kirkwood, Lea Penman, Eric Blore, John Alexander, Norma Varden; *D:* George Marshall; *C:* Charles B(ryant) Lang Jr.

Fandango 𝄞𝄞½ **1985 (PG)** Five college friends take a wild weekend drive across the Texas Badlands for one last fling before graduation and the prospect of military service. Expanded by Reynolds with assistance from Steven Spielberg, from his student film. Provides a look at college and life during the Vietnam crisis. **91m/C VHS.** Judd Nelson, Kevin Costner, Sam Robards, Chuck Bush, Brian Cesak, Elizabeth (E.G. Dailey) Daily, Suzy Amis, Glenne Headly, Pepe Serna, Marvin J. McIntyre; *D:* Kevin Reynolds; *W:* Kevin Reynolds; *M:* Alan Silvestri.

Fanfan la Tulipe 𝄞𝄞𝄞 *Fanfan the Tulip; Fearless Little Soldier* **1951** Fanfan (Philipe) escapes an unwanted marriage by joining the army of Louis XV (Herrand), after being promised an illustrious career and a royal marriage. And after many heroics, it all comes true. Amusing satire of swashbucklers and historical romance movies. French with subtitles. **98m/B VHS.** *FR* Gerard Philipe, Gina Lollobrigida, Marcel Herrand, Sylvia Pelayo, Genevieve Page, Noel Roquevert; *D:* Christian-Jaque; *W:* Rene Wheeler, Jean Fallet, Christian-Jaque; *C:* Christian Matras; *M:* Georges Van Parys, Maurice Thiriet. Cannes '52: Director (Christian-Jaque).

Fangs 𝄞½ **1975 (R)** Unfriendly reptile-stomping villagers take the life of Mr. Snakey's favorite serpent. He sends his slithering pets on a vengeful and poisonous spree. **90m/C VHS.** Les Tremayne, Janet Wood, Bebe Kelly, Marvin Kaplan, Alice Nunn; *D:* Vittorio Schiraldi.

Fangs of Fate 𝄞½ **1925** A gang of bad guys battles the town's new marshal. **67m/B VHS, 8mm.** Bill(y) (William Patten) Patton, Dorothy Donald.

Fangs of the Living Dead 𝄞½ *Malenka, the Vampire; La Nipote del Vampiro; The Niece of the Vampire; The Vampire's Niece* **1968** When a young woman inherits a castle, her uncle, who happens to be a vampire, tries to persuade her to remain among the undead. **80m/C VHS.** *SP IT* Anita Ekberg, Rossana Yanni, Diana Lorys, Fernando Bilbao, Paul Muller, Julian Ugarte, Andriana Ambesi; *D:* Armando de Ossorio; *W:* Armando de Ossorio.

Fangs of the Wild 𝄞𝄞 *Follow the Hunter* **1954** When a young boy witnesses a murder at his father's hunting lodge, no one but the killer believes him. When the killer decides to get rid of the boy, Buck the Wonder Dog gets involved. **72m/B VHS.** Charles Chaplin Jr., Onslow Stevens, Margia Dean, Freddy Ridgeway, Phil Tead, Robert Stevenson; *D:* William Claxton.

Fanny 𝄞𝄞𝄞𝄞 **1932** Second part of Marcel Pagnol's trilogy depicting the lives of the people of Provence, France. The poignant tale of Fanny, a young woman who marries an older man when Marius, her young lover, leaves her pregnant when he goes to sea. Remade several times but the original holds its own very well. "Marius" was first in the trilogy; "Cesar" was third. **128m/B VHS.** *FR* Raimu, Charpin, Orane Demazis, Pierre Fresnay, Alida Rauffe; *D:* Marc Allegret; *W:* Marcel Pagnol; *M:* Vincent Scotto.

Fanny 𝄞𝄞𝄞 **1961** Young girl falls in love with an adventurous sailor, and finds herself pregnant after he returns to the sea. With the help of the sailor's parents, she finds, marries, and eventually grows to love a much older man, who in turn cares for her and adores her son as if he were his own. When the sailor returns, all involved must confront their pasts and define their futures. Beautifully made, with fine performances and a plot which defies age or nationality. Part of the "A Night at the Movies" series, this tape simulates a 1961 movie evening, with a Tweety Pie cartoon, a newsreel and coming attractions for "Splendor in the Grass" and "The Roman Spring of Mrs. Stone." **148m/C VHS.** *FR* Leslie Caron, Maurice Chevalier, Charles Boyer, Horst Buchholz, Lionel Jeffries; *D:* Joshua Logan; *W:* Julius J. Epstein; *C:* Jack Cardiff.

Fanny and Alexander 𝄞𝄞𝄞𝄞 *Fanny Och Alexander* **1983 (R)** The culmination of Bergman's career, this autobiographical film is set in a rural Swedish town in 1907. It tells the story of one year in the lives of the Ekdahl family, as seen by the young children, Fanny and Alexander. Magic and religion, love and death, reconciliation and estrangement are skillfully captured in this carefully detailed, lovingly photographed film. In Swedish with English subtitles or dubbed. **197m/C VHS.** *SW* Pernilla Allwin, Bertil Guve, Gunn Walgren, Allan Edwall, Ewa Froling, Erland Josephson, Harriet Andersson, Jarl Kulle, Jan Malmsjo; *D:* Ingmar Bergman; *W:* Ingmar Bergman; *C:* Sven Nykvist; *M:* Daniel Bell. Oscars '83: Art Dir./Set Dec., Cinematog., Costume Des., Foreign Film; Cesar '84: Foreign Film; Golden Globes '84: Foreign Film; L.A. Film Critics '83: Cinematog., Foreign Film; N.Y. Film Critics '83: Director (Bergman), Foreign Film.

Fanny Hill 𝄞𝄞 **1983 (R)** A softcore adaptation of the racy Victorian classic. **80m/C VHS.** *GB* Lisa Raines, Shelley Winters, Wilfrid Hyde-White, Oliver Reed.

Fanny Hill: Memoirs of a Woman of Pleasure woof! **1964** Sexual exploits of an innocent in bawdy 18th-century London, as directed by notorious "Super Vixen" Meyer (though by Meyer standards, proceedings are fairly innocuous, if inept). Based on the novel. **105m/B VHS.** *GE US* Miriam Hopkins, Walter Giller, Alexander D'Arcy, Leticia Roman, Billy Frick, Heidi Hansen, Chris Howland, Ulli Lommel; *D:* Russ Meyer; *W:* Robert J. Hill; *C:* Heinz Hoelscher; *M:* Erwin Halletz.

Fantasia 𝄞𝄞𝄞𝄞 **1940** Disney's most personal animation feature first bombed at the boxoffice and irked purists who couldn't take the plotless, experimental mix of classical music and cartoons. It became a cult movie, embraced by more liberal generations of moviegoers. Reissue of the original version, painstakingly restored, ceased because of a planned remake. ♫Toccata & Fugue in D; The Nutcracker Suite; The Sorcerer's Apprentice; The Rite of Spring; Pastoral Symphony; Dance of the Hours; Night on Bald Mountain; Ave Maria; The Cossack Dance. **116m/C VHS, DVD.** *D:* Ben Sharpsteen, James Nelson Algar, Samuel Armstrong, Ford Beebe, Jim Handley, T. Hee, Wilfred Jackson, Hamilton Luske, Bill Roberts, Paul Satterfield; *W:* Lee Blair, Phil Dike, Otto Englander, Carl Fallberg, Campbell Grant, Albert Heath, Graham Heid, Arthur Heinemann, Bianca Majolie, William Martin, John McLeish, Sylvia Moberly-Holland, Perce Pearce, Bill Peet, Edward Penner, Joseph Sabo, Webb Smith, Leo Thiele, Norman Wright; *M:* Leopold Stokowski; *V:* Walt Disney; *Nar:* Deems Taylor. AFI '98: Top 100, Natl. Film Reg. '90.

Fantasia/2000 𝄞𝄞½ **2000 (G)** Lightweight continuation of Disney's 1940 film hangs on to Mickey Mouse's popular "The Sorcerer's Apprentice" and adds seven new animated sequences of varying charm with celebrity introductions. Probably the most fun sequence is that of the yo-yo-ing flamingo set to Saint-Saens' "Carnvial of the Animals." Music is conducted by James Levine and performed by the Chicago Symphony Orchestra. Originally released in the IMAX format. ♫Symphony No. 5 (Ludwig Van Beethoven); Pines of Rome (Ottorino Respighi); Rhapsody in Blue (George Gershwin); Piano Concerto No. 2, Allegro, Opus 102 (Dmitri Shostakovich); Carnvial of the Animals (Camille Saint-Saens); The Sorcerer's Apprentice (Paul Dukas); Pomp and Circumstance (Edward Elgar); Firebird Suite (Igor Stravinsky). **75m/C VHS, DVD, Wide.** *D:* Hendel Butoy, Eric Goldberg, James Nelson Algar, Gaetan Brizzi, Paul Brizzi, Pixote Hunt, Francis Glebas.

Fantasies woof! *And Once Upon a Love* **1973 (R)** Teenage lovers Derek and Hooten return to their Greek island home and decide to improve their village by turning it into a tourist haven. First collaboration of the Dereks is a loser, lacking plot, direction, and decent acting. Bo shows no talent but the obvious one and is actually credited as Kathleen Collins. **81m/C VHS.** Bo Derek, Peter Hooten, Anna Alexiades; *D:* John Derek.

The Fantasist 𝄞 **1989 (R)** Sex crime thriller features a deranged killer who makes obscene, yet seductive phone calls to young ladies before murdering them. **98m/C VHS.** Timothy Bottoms, Christopher Cazenove; *D:* Robin Hardy.

Fantastic Balloon Voyage 𝄞 **198? (G)** Three men embark on a journey across the equator in a balloon, experiencing myriad adventures along the way. Much hot air. **100m/C VHS.** Hugo Stiglitz, Jeff Cooper.

The Fantastic Night 𝄞𝄞𝄞 *La Nuit Fantastique* **1942** Considering that this film was made in France during the Nazi occupation, it is a remarkably clear work. It's a fantasy about Denis (Gravey), who is visited by a beautiful woman (Presle) as he sleeps and then follows her through a series of adventures. According to the box copy, the star was working with the Resistance while he was making the film. French with subtitles. **90m/B VHS, DVD.** *FR* Fernand Gravet, Micheline Presle, Marcel Levesque, Christiane Nere; *D:* Marcel L'Herbier; *W:* Louis Chavance, Marcel L'Herbier; *C:* Pierre Montazel; *M:* Maurice Thiriet.

Fantastic Planet 𝄞𝄞𝄞 *La Planete Sauvage; Planet of Incredible Creatures; The Savage Planet* **1973 (PG)** A critically acclaimed French, animated, sci-fi epic based on the drawings of Roland Topor. A race of small humanoids are enslaved and exploited by a race of giants on a savage planet, until one of the small creatures manages to unite his people and fight for equality. **72m/C VHS, DVD.** *FR* *D:* Roland Topor, Rene Laloux; *W:* Roland Topor, Steve Hayes, Rene Laloux; *C:* Boris Baromykin, Lubomir Rejthar; *M:* Alain Goraguer; *V:* Barry Bostwick.

Fantastic Seven 𝄞½ **1982** The Fantastic Seven is a daredevil team sent to rescue a Hollywood sex symbol who has been kidnapped and held for ransom while shooting on location off the coast of Miami. **96m/C VHS.** Elke Sommer, Christopher Connelly.

Fantastic Voyage 𝄞𝄞𝄞 *Microscopia; Strange Journey* **1966** An important scientist, rescued from behind the Iron Curtain, is so severely wounded by enemy agents that traditional surgery is impossible. After being shrunk to microscopic size, a medical team journeys inside his body where they find themselves threatened by the patient's natural defenses. Great action, award-winning special effects. **100m/C VHS, DVD, Wide.** Stephen Boyd, Edmond O'Brien, Raquel Welch, Arthur Kennedy, Donald Pleasence, Arthur O'Connell, William Redfield, James Brolin, Barry Coe, Brendan Fitzgerald, Shelby Grant, Ken Scott; *D:* Richard Fleischer; *W:* Harry Kleiner; *C:* Ernest Laszlo; *M:* Leonard Rosenman. Oscars '66: Art Dir./Set Dec., Color, Visual FX.

The Fantastic World of D.C. Collins 𝄞𝄞 **1984** Gary Coleman plays a daydreaming teenager who thinks he is being pursued by mysterious strangers seeking a videotape that was unknowingly slipped to him. **100m/C VHS.** Gary Coleman, Bernie Casey, Shelley Smith, Fred (John F.) Dryer, Marilyn McCoo, Philip Abbott, George Gobel, Michael Ansara; *D:* Leslie Martinson. **TV**

The Fantasticks 𝄞𝄞½ **1995 (PG)** The stage's longest-running musical gets the big-screen treatment with a story about two fathers (Grey and Hughes) who decide to matchmake for their children Matt (McIntyre) and Luisa (Kelly). They hire the members of a traveling carnival (called the Fantasticks) to kidnap Luisa, so that Matt can play the hero and rescue her. The plan seems to work but the course of true love never runs that smoothly. Adapted by Jones and Schmidt from their play. **86m/C VHS, DVD.** Jonathan Morris, Joel Grey, Barnard Hughes, Jean (Louisa) Kelly, Joe McIntyre; *D:* Michael Ritchie; *W:* Tom Jones, Harvey Schmidt; *C:* Fred Murphy; *M:* Harvey Schmidt.

Fantasy Island 𝄞 **1976** Three people fly ("De plane, boss!") to an island paradise and get to live out their fantasies for a price. Pilot for the TV series. **100m/C VHS.** Ricardo Montalban, Bill Bixby, Sandra Dee, Peter Lawford, Carol Lynley, Hugh O'Brian, Eleanor Parker, Dick Sargent, Victoria Principal; *D:* Richard Lang. **TV**

Fantasy Man 𝄞½ **1984** A restless middle-aged man tries to relieve his mid-life crisis with the help of three women. **100m/C VHS.** *AU* Harold Hopkins, Jeanie Drynan, Kerry Mack, Kate Fitzpatrick; *D:* John Meagher; *W:* John Meagher.

Fantasy Mission Force 𝄞 **1984** In this indescribably silly action comedy, Japanese troops capture an international group of generals (some in Civil War-era uniforms). An invasion of Canada is underway. Jackie is part of a group trying to rescue them. UN troops wear kilts; others wear armor. **90m/C VHS, DVD.** *HK* Jackie Chan, Brigitte (Lin Chinag-hsia) Lin, Adam Cheng, Jimmy Wang Yu; *D:* Yen Ping Chu.

Far and Away 𝄞𝄞½ **1992 (PG-13)** Meandering old-fashioned epic about immigrants, romance, and settling the American West. In the 1890s, Joseph Donelly (Cruise) is forced to flee his Irish homeland after threatening the life of his landlord, and emigrates to America in the company of the landlord's daughter, feisty Shannon Christie (Kidman). Particularly brutal scenes of Cruise earning his living as a bare-knuckled boxer contrast with the expansiveness of the land rush ending. Slow, spotty, and a little too slick for its own good, though real-life couple Cruise and Kidman are an attractive pair. Filmed in 70-mm Panavision on location in Ireland and Montana. Also available in a letterboxed version. **140m/C VHS, DVD, Wide.** Tom Cruise, Nicole Kidman, Thomas Gibson, Robert Prosky, Barbara Babcock, Colm Meaney, Eileen Pollock, Michelle Johnson, Cyril Cusack, Clint Howard, Rance Howard; *D:* Ron Howard; *W:* Bob Dolman; *C:* Mikael Salomon; *M:* John Williams.

Far Away and Long Ago 𝄞𝄞½ **1974** Based on the autobiographical novel by Guillermo Hudson which details the memories which haunted his childhood—the Argentinian pampas, its gauchos, witchcraft, and women. In Spanish with English subtitles. **91m/C VHS.** *AR* Juan Jose Camero, Leonor Manso; *D:* Manuel Antin.

Far Country 𝄞𝄞𝄞 **1955** Cattlemen must battle the elements and frontier lawlessness in this classic. Stewart leads his herd to the Yukon in hopes of large profits, but ends up having to kidnap it back from the crooked sheriff and avenging the deaths of his friends. Entertaining and the Yukon setting takes it out of the usual Western arena. **97m/C VHS.** James Stewart, Ruth Roman, Walter Brennan, Harry (Henry) Morgan, Corinne Calvet, Jay C. Flippen, John McIntire; *D:* Anthony Mann; *C:* William H. Daniels; *M:* Henry Mancini.

Far Cry from Home 𝄞 **197?** A battered wife attempts to escape from her domineering husband before it's too late. **87m/C VHS.** Mary Ann McDonald, Richard Monette.

Far East 𝄞½ **1985** Two ex-lovers meet in Southeast Asia and join forces to find the woman's missing husband, a reporter. **105m/C VHS.** Bryan Brown, Helen Morse; *D:* John Duigan.

Far from Home 🦴🦴 **1989 (R)** Drew Barrymore is the seductive teen being scoped by a psychotic killer while on vacation with her father. Lots of over-the-top performances by the familiar cast. **86m/C VHS.** Matt Frewer, Drew Barrymore, Richard Masur, Karen Austin, Susan Tyrrell, Anthony Rapp, Jennifer Tilly, Andras Jones, Dick Miller; ***D:*** Meiert Avis; ***C:*** Paul Elliott; ***M:*** Jonathan Elias.

Far from Home: The Adventures of Yellow Dog 🦴🦴 **1994 (PG)** Stalwart lad Angus (Bradford) and his faithful pooch Yellow (Dakotah) battle the elements, wild animals and fatigue as they try to get back home after being shipwrecked on a remote island in British Columbia. Good thing Dad (Davidson) gave them all those cool survival tips before they left, or else they never would've known that you can eat bugs. (Okay, the dog probably knew that already.) Mom (Rogers) does her bit by making sure the search mission stays focused. You usually can't go wrong with a kid and his dog lost in the wilderness, but this one is really short—on time and drama. Nice scenery, though. **81m/C VHS.** Jesse Bradford, Bruce Davison, Mimi Rogers, Tom Bower; ***D:*** Phillip Borsos; ***W:*** Phillip Borsos.

Far from the Madding Crowd 🦴🦴🦴 **1967 (PG)** A lavish, long adaptation of Thomas Hardy's 19th-century classic about the beautiful Bathsheba (Christie) and the three very different men who love her. Her first love is handsome and wayward soldier Sgt. Troy (Stamp), her second the local noble lord William Boldwood (Finch), and her third the ever-loving and long-patient farmer Gabriel Oaks (Bates). Christie is well cast as the much-desired beauty. Gorgeous cinematography by Nicolas Roeg. Remade for British TV in 1997. **165m/C VHS, Wide.** *GB* Julie Christie, Terence Stamp, Peter Finch, Alan Bates, Prunella Ransome; ***D:*** John Schlesinger; ***W:*** Frederic Raphael; ***C:*** Nicolas Roeg; ***M:*** Richard Rodney Bennett. Natl. Bd. of Review '67: Actor (Finch).

Far from the Madding Crowd 🦴🦴🦴 **1997** TV version of the Thomas Hardy novel (filmed for the big screen in 1967) that follows the adventures of young Bathsheba (Baeza), who's the object of desire for three very different men in 19th-century rural England. Independent-minded Bathsheba Everdene inherits a farm and insists on managing it herself. She's aided by steadfast head man Gabriel Oak (Parker), who loves her but doesn't feel he can offer her anything; wealthy older neighbor William Boldwood (Terry), whose love for Bathesheba becomes an obsession; and rakish Sgt. Frank Troy (Firth), who captivates Bathsheba but proves to be a scoundrel. **200m/C VHS.** *GB* Paloma Baeza, Nigel Terry, Nathaniel Parker, Jonathan Firth; ***D:*** Nicholas Renton; ***W:*** Philomena McDonagh. **TV**

Far Frontier 🦴🦴 **1948** Roy Rogers saves the day by thwarting a band of outlaws who are being smuggled across the border in soybean oil cans. Includes musical numbers and horse tricks. **60m/B VHS.** Roy Rogers, Andy Devine, Clayton Moore.

Far Harbor 🦴🦴 **1996** An attractive cast of yuppie failures gather in a Long Island mansion to whine and snipe at each other over dinner. Among them is Frick (Atterton), a persona non grata English filmmaker, who becomes obsessed with a moored yacht that belongs to a Hollywood studio bigwig, and fragile hostess, Ellie (Connelly), who's written a screenplay based on her own traumas. **99m/C VHS.** Edward Atterton, Jennifer Connelly, Dan Futterman, Marcia Gay Harden, George Newbern, Jim True, Andrew Lauren, Tracee Ellis Ross; ***D:*** John Huddles; ***W:*** John Huddles; ***C:*** Tami Reiker.

Far North 🦴🦴½ **1988 (PG-13)** Quirky comedy about a woman who returns to her rural family homestead after her father is seriously injured by a horse, and tries to deal with her eccentric family's travails. Fine cast never reaches its potential. Shepard's directing debut. **96m/C VHS, 8mm.** Jessica Lange, Charles Durning, Tess Harper, Donald Moffat, Ann Wedgeworth, Patricia Arquette, Nina Draxton; ***D:*** Sam Shepard; ***W:*** Sam Shepard; ***C:*** Robbie Greenberg.

A Far Off Place 🦴🦴 **1993 (PG-13)** Adolescent boy, adolescent girl, adolescent bushperson, and mature dog set out across the African desert to escape elephant poachers who want to kill them. The boy and girl find romance in the sand, bushperson finds water by listening, and dog gets very nice walk. Strong performances by the youthful leads lend charm to this Disney/Amblin flick, particularly Bok as the bushperson. Unusually violent film for studios involved (animals and people bite sand), though care is taken to edit actual blood shed on screen. Filmed in Zimbabwe and Namibia and based on the books "A Story Like the Wind" and "A Far Off Place" by Laurens van der Post. **107m/C VHS, Wide.** Reese Witherspoon, Ethan (Randall) Embry, Sarel Bok, Jack Thompson, Maximilian Schell, Robert John Burke, Patricia Kalember, Daniel Gerroll, Miles Anderson; ***D:*** Mikael Salomon; ***W:*** Robert Caswell, Jonathan Hensleigh, Sally Robinson; ***C:*** Juan Ruiz-Anchia; ***M:*** James Horner.

Far Out Man woof! *Soul Man 2* **1989 (R)** An unalterable middle-aged hippie is sent by his worried family and his psychiatrist on a cross-country journey to rediscover himself. The script makes no sense and has very few laughs. **81m/C VHS.** Thomas Chong, Rae Dawn Chong, C. Thomas Howell, Shelby Chong, Martin Mull, Paris Chong, Paul Bartel, Judd Nelson, Michael Winslow, Richard "Cheech" Marin; ***D:*** Thomas Chong; ***W:*** Thomas Chong.

The Far Pavilions 🦴🦴½ *Blade of Steel* **1984** A British officer falls in love with an Indian princess during the second Afghan War. Cross is appropriately noble and stiff-upper-lipped but Irving is miscast as his ethnic love. This lavish production was based on the romantic bestseller by M.M. Kaye. **108m/C VHS, DVD.** *GB* Ben Cross, Amy Irving, Omar Sharif, Benedict Taylor, Rossano Brazzi, Christopher Lee, John Gielgud, Rupert Everett; ***D:*** Peter Duffell; ***C:*** Jack Cardiff; ***M:*** Carl Davis. **CABLE**

Faraway, So Close! 🦴🦴 *In Weiter Ferne, So Nah!* **1993 (PG-13)** Wenders' erratic follow-up to his magnificent "Wings of Desire." Cassiel (Sander), the angel left behind when Damiel (Ganz) chose to become human, once again surveys Berlin, noticing the changes (not necessarily for the better). Angelic companion Raphaela (Kinski) watches events passively, including an old man's (Ruhamnn) reflections on life and the philosophical musings of Emit Flesti (Dafoe, Time Itself, get it?), even as Cassiel impulsively chooses humanity over his heavenly world. Falk makes a return appearance to little effect. Overlong and under-developed. **146m/C VHS, DVD.** *GE* Otto Sander, Peter Falk, Horst Buchholz, Nastassia Kinski, Heinz Ruhmann, Bruno Ganz, Solveig Dommartin, Ruediger Vogler, Willem Dafoe, Lou Reed; ***D:*** Wim Wenders; ***W:*** Ulrich Zieger, Richard Reitinger, Wim Wenders; ***C:*** Jurgen Jurges; ***M:*** David Darling, Laurent Petitgrand. Cannes '93: Grand Jury Prize.

Farewell My Concubine 🦴🦴 *Bawang Bie Ji* **1993 (R)** Exotic film covers 50 years of sexual, social, and political Chinese history wrapped around the story of two male Peking Opera stars. Deposited as boys at the Opera's training school Douzi and Shitou become fast friends in their hermetically sealed world, but their friendship is tested during the chaos of Communism and the cultural revolution. Sumptuous and well-acted, but the sheer length and emotional detachment prove to be drawbacks. Adapted from a novel by Lee, who based the work on a 2,000-year-old Chinese opera about an imperial concubine. Filmed on location in Beijing. In Mandarin Chinese with subtitles. **157m/C VHS, DVD.** *HK* Leslie Cheung, Zhang Fengyi, Gong Li, Lu Qi, Ying Da, Ge You, Fei Yang, Ma Mingwei; ***D:*** Chen Kaige; ***W:*** Lilian Lee, Lu Wei; ***C:*** Gu Changwei; ***M:*** Zhao Jiping. British Acad. '93: Foreign Film; Cannes '93: Film; Golden Globes '94: Foreign Film; L.A. Film Critics '93: Foreign Film; Natl. Bd. of Review '93: Foreign Film; N.Y. Film Critics '93: Foreign Film, Support. Actress (Li).

Farewell, My Lovely 🦴🦴🦴 **1975 (R)** A remake of the 1944 Raymond Chandler mystery, "Murder, My Sweet," featuring private eye Phillip Marlowe hunting for an ex-convict's lost sweetheart in 1941 Los Angeles. Perhaps the most accurate of Chandler adaptations, but far from the best, this film offers a nicely detailed production. Mitchum is a bit too world-weary as the seen-it-all detective. **95m/C VHS, DVD.** *GB* Robert Mitchum, Charlotte Rampling, Sylvia Miles, John Ireland, Anthony Zerbe, Jack O'Halloran, Harry Dean Stanton, Sylvester Stallone, Cheryl "Rainbeaux" Smith; ***D:*** Dick Richards; ***W:*** David Zelag Goodman; ***C:*** John A. Alonzo; ***M:*** David Shire.

A Farewell to Arms 🦴🦴🦴 **1932** The original film version of Ernest Hemingway's novel about the tragic love affair between an American ambulance driver and an English nurse during the Italian campaign of WWI. The novelist disavowed the ambiguous ending, but the public loved the film. Fine performances and cinematography. **85m/B VHS, DVD.** Helen Hayes, Gary Cooper, Adolphe Menjou, Mary (Phillips) Philips, Jack LaRue, Blanche Frederici; ***D:*** Frank Borzage; ***W:*** Oliver H.P. Garrett, Benjamin Glazer; ***C:*** Charles B(ryant) Lang Jr. Oscars '33: Cinematog., Sound.

Farewell to the King 🦴🦴½ **1989 (PG-13)** During WWII, a ship-wrecked American deserter becomes the chief of a tribe of Borneo headhunters until his jungle kingdom is caught between the forces of the U.S. and Japanese. With the help of a British officer he helps them defend themselves when the Japanese invade. An old-fashioned war epic with a beautiful location and solid if uninspired-performances by the leads. Based on Pierre Schoendoerffer's novel "L'Adieu Au Roi." **114m/C VHS.** Nick Nolte, Nigel Havers, Marius Weyers, Frank McRae, Marilyn Tokuda, Elan Oberon, William Wise, James Fox, Aki Aleong; ***D:*** John Milius; ***W:*** John Milius; ***C:*** Dean Semler; ***M:*** Basil Poledouris.

Fargo 🦴🦴🦴 **1996 (R)** Another malicious, extra-dark comedy from the Coen brothers. Car salesman Jerry Lundegaard (Macy) hires a couple of losers to kidnap his wife so he can swindle the ransom money out of his father-in-law. Naturally, the scheme begins to unravel and the very pregnant police chief Marge Gunderson (McDormand) treks through the frozen tundra of Minnesota to put the pieces of the puzzle together. McDormand's performance as the chatty competent chief is first rate. Needling the flat-accented Midwesterners of their youth, the Coens have also returned to their filmmaking roots after the disappointing big-budget "Hudsucker Proxy." Because Minneapolis was having its warmest, driest winter in 100 years, the Coens were forced to shoot most of the exteriors in wintery North Dakota. **97m/C VHS, DVD, Wide.** William H. Macy, Frances McDormand, Steve Buscemi, Peter Stormare, Harve Presnell, Steve Reevis, John Carroll Lynch, Kristin Rudrud, Steve Park, Jose Feliciano; ***D:*** Joel Coen; ***W:*** Ethan Coen, Joel Coen; ***C:*** Roger Deakins; ***M:*** Carter Burwell. Oscars '96: Actress (McDormand), Orig. Screenplay; AFI '98: Top 100; Australian Film Inst. '96: Foreign Film; British Acad. '96: Director (Coen); Cannes '96: Director (Coen); Ind. Spirit '97: Actor (Macy), Actress (McDormand), Cinematog., Director (Coen), Film, Screenplay; Natl. Bd. of Review '96: Actress (McDormand), Director (Coen); N.Y. Film Critics '96: Film; Screen Actors Guild '96: Actress (McDormand); Writers Guild '96: Orig. Screenplay; Broadcast Film Critics '96: Actress (McDormand), Film.

Fargo Express 🦴½ **1932** When the kid brother of Maynard's true love is falsely accused of robbing a stagecoach, Maynard works to clear his name. Routine stuff. **60m/B VHS.** Ken Maynard, Helen Mack, Paul Fix; ***D:*** Alan James.

Farinelli 🦴🦴 *Farinelli the Castrato; Farinelli Il Castrato* **1994 (R)** A movie to make men cringe. Floridly depicts the complex professional and personal ties of 18th-century opera composer Riccardo Broschi (Lo Verso) and his younger brother Carlo (Dionisi), a celebrated castrato singer under the stage name "Farinelli." In part, because of an early church prohibition against women singing in public, boys were castrated before puberty to preserve their pure soprano voices while vocal power and agility grew as they became men. Castrati were the rock stars of their day and Farinelli lived a flamboyant life before retiring to the Spanish court of Philip V. The castrato voice heard in the movie is an electronic mixture of counter-tenor Derek Lee Ragin and soprano Ewa Mallas Godlewska. French and Italian with subtitles. **110m/C VHS, DVD, Wide.** *FR IT BE* Stefano Dionisi, Enrico Lo Verso, Jeroen Krabbe, Elsa Zylberstein, Caroline Cellier, Omero Antonutti, Jacques Boudet; ***D:*** Gerard Corbiau; ***W:*** Gerard Corbiau, Andree Corbiau, Marcel Beaulieu; ***C:*** Walther Vanden Ende; ***M:*** Christopher Rousset. Cesar '95: Art Dir./Set Dec., Sound; Golden Globes '95: Foreign Film.

Farmer & Chase 🦴🦴 **1996 (R)** It's always nice to see an old pro like Gazzara but it's a shame it couldn't have been in something less predictable. Farmer's (Gazzara) a hold-up man who's been working with partner Ollie (Jones) for 20 years. But when Ollie's killed, Farmer, who wants to pull one last job before retiring, makes the mistake of teaming up with his pacifist son Chase (Field). And then Chase involves his new gal pal Hillary (Boyle) in on the scheme. Dumb move, dumb movie. **97m/C VHS.** Ben Gazzara, Todd Field, Lara Flynn Boyle, Steven Anthony Jones, Ron Kaell, David Booth; ***D:*** Michael Seitzman; ***W:*** Michael Seitzman; ***C:*** Michael Maley; ***M:*** Tony Saunders.

The Farmer Takes a Wife 🦴🦴½ **1935** Henry Fonda's first film, recreating his stage role, as a mid-19th century farmer at odds with the Erie canal builders and struggling to court the woman he loves. Remade as a musical in 1953. **91m/B VHS.** Janet Gaynor, Henry Fonda, Charles Bickford, Slim Summerville, Jane Withers; ***D:*** Victor Fleming.

The Farmer Takes a Wife 🦴🦴 **1953** Poor musical remake of the 1935 drama, about the trials of a struggling 1850s farmer and the Erie canal boat cook he loves. Contains no memorable music and Robertson can't compete with Henry Fonda's original role as the farmer. ♫We're in Business; On the Erie Canal; We're Doing it for the Natives in Jamaica; When I Close My Door; Today I Love Everybody; Somethin' Real Special; With The Sun Warm Upon Me; Can You Spell Schenectady?. **81m/C VHS.** Betty Grable, Dale Robertson, Thelma Ritter, John Carroll, Eddie Foy Jr.; ***D:*** Henry Levin.

The Farmer's Daughter 🦴🦴🦴 **1947** Young portrays Katrin Holmstrom, a Swedish farm girl who becomes a maid to Congressman Cotten and winds up running for office herself (not neglecting to find romance as well). The outspoken and multi-talented character charmed audiences and was the basis of a TV series in the 1960s. **97m/B VHS.** Loretta Young, Joseph Cotten, Ethel Barrymore, Charles Bickford, Harry Davenport, Lex Barker, James Arness, Rose Hobart; ***D:*** H.C. Potter; ***C:*** Milton Krasner. Oscars '47: Actress (Young).

The Farmer's Other Daughter 🦴🦴 *Farm Girl* **1965** A rural comedy about Farmer Brown whose lovely daughter is eyed by all the farmhands. He also has to contend with dastardly Mr. Barksnapper who wants to take his farm away from him until one of his daughter's beaus comes to the rescue. **84m/C VHS.** Ernest Ashworth, Judy Pennebaker, Bill Michael; ***D:*** John Patrick Hayes.

The Farmer's Wife 🦴🦴½ **1928** Silent British comedy about a recently widowed farmer searching for a new wife. Meanwhile, his lovely housekeeper would be the perfect candidate. Based on Eden Philpott's play. **97m/B VHS, DVD.** *GB* Jameson Thomas, Lillian Hall-Davis, Gordon Harker; ***D:*** Alfred Hitchcock; ***W:*** Alfred Hitchcock; ***C:*** Jack Cox.

Fashions of 1934 🦴🦴 *Fashions* **1934** A typical, lightweight '30s musical with impressive choreography by Busby Berkeley. Powell plays a disreputable clothing designer who goes to Paris to steal the latest fashion designs and winds up costuming a musical and falls in love. ♫Spin a Little Web of Dreams; Broken

Melody. **78m/B VHS.** Bette Davis, William Powell, Frank McHugh, Hugh Herbert, Reginald Owen, Busby Berkeley; ***D:*** William Dieterle.

Fass Black **1977 (R)** Yet another man against the mob flick straight out of Bartlett's familiar plotlines. Amidst gratuitous music and violence, a disco owner locks horns with the syndicate after they try to take over his place. There's a good reason disco is dead. **105m/C VHS.** John Poole, Jeannie Bell, Cal Wilson, Harold Nicholas, Nicholas Lewis; ***D:*** D'Urville Martin.

The Fast and the Furious **1954** On the lam after being falsely charged with murder, Ireland picks up a fast car and a loose woman (or is it a loose car and a fast woman?) and makes a run for the border by entering the Pebble Beach race. **73m/B VHS, DVD.** John Ireland, Dorothy Malone, Bruce Carlisle, Iris Adrian, Jean Howell; ***D:*** Edwards Sampson, John Ireland; ***W:*** Jerome Odlum, Jean Howell; ***C:*** Floyd Crosby; ***M:*** Alexander Gerens.

The Fast and the Furious ½ **2001 (PG-13)** Rookie L.A. cop Brian (Walker) goes undercover to infiltrate a street gang that adapts sports cars for illicit street racing and other, even less legal, uses. But first he has to earn the respect and trust of their leader, Dominic (Diesel), and the love of Dom's sister Mia (Brewster). Dominic is the head of a tight-knit "family" of quirky thieves hopped up on car exhaust and adrenaline, very much in the B-movie tradition of "Gone in 60 Seconds" (the original), "Eat My Dust," and "Grand Theft Auto." And hey, let's face it, kids. That's all this is, a summer B-movie where reality, plot, and dialogue have no place. Diesel does impress (again) in the patriarch-philosopher-thief role. **101m/C VHS, DVD, Wide.** *US* Vin Diesel, Paul Walker, Jordana Brewster, Michelle Rodriguez, Rick Yune, Ted Levine, Ja Rule, Thom Barry, Chad Lindberg, Johnny Strong, Matt Schulze, Vyto Ruginis; ***D:*** Rob Cohen; ***W:*** Gary Scott Thompson, Erik Bergquist, David Ayer; ***C:*** Ericson Core; ***M:*** BT (Brian Transeau).

Fast Break ½ **1979 (PG)** New York deli clerk who is a compulsive basketball fan talks his way into a college coaching job. He takes a team of street players with him, with predictable results on and off the court. Kaplan's screen debut. **107m/C VHS.** Gabe Kaplan, Harold Sylvester, Randee Heller; ***D:*** Jack Smight; ***M:*** David Shire.

Fast Bullets ½ **1944** Texas Rangers fight a gang of smugglers and rescue a kidnap victim in this typical western. **52m/B VHS.** Tom Tyler, Rex Lease.

Fast, Cheap & Out of Control ½ **1997 (PG)** Director Morris' use of odd camera angles, unusual editing, and dark humor increases with each outing but always seems to enhance interest in the subject matter rather than detract from it. While his previous films have focused on just one subject, this one features four: a wild-animal trainer, a topiary gardener, a scientist who creates robotic insects, and a man who studies mole rats. Through inter-cutting and the overlapping of the subjects (at times audio from one is played over the visuals of another), Morris gives the impression that they are all linked together. Old movie footage is used to add an unreal quality, and the score by Caleb Sampson of the Alloy Orchestra hypnotically completes the surrealism. This is the story of four obsessed men, but none as obsessed as director Morris himself, with his need to show that truth is stranger than fiction. **82m/C VHS.** ***D:*** Errol Morris; ***C:*** Robert Richardson; ***M:*** Caleb Sampson. Natl. Bd. of Review '97: Feature Doc.; N.Y. Film Critics '97: Feature Doc.; Natl. Soc. Film Critics '97: Feature Doc.

Fast Company **1978** The life story of champion race car driver Lonnie Johnson including women, money, and the drag racing sponsors. **90m/C VHS.** William Smith, John Saxon, Claudia Jennings, Nicholas (Nick) Campbell, Don Francks; ***D:*** David Cronenberg; ***W:*** David Cronenberg.

Fast Food **1989** A super-cheap, strangulated attempt at low comedy, wherein an entrepreneurial hamburger peddler invents a secret aphrodisiac sauce. Look for former porn-star Traci Lords. **90m/C VHS.** Clark Brandon, Tracy Griffith, Randal Patrick, Traci Lords, Kevin McCarthy, Michael J. Pollard, Jim Varney; ***D:*** Michael A. Simpson; ***W:*** Clark Brandon.

Fast Forward ½ **1984 (PG)** A group of eight teenagers from Ohio learn how to deal with success and failure when they enter a national dance contest in New York City. A break-dancing variation on the old show business chestnut. ♫Fast Forward; How Do You Do; As Long As We Believe; Pretty Girl; Mystery; Curves; Showdown; Do You Want It Right Now?; Hardrock. **110m/C VHS.** John Scott Clough, Don Franklin, Tracy Silver, Cindy McGee; ***D:*** Sidney Poitier; ***W:*** Richard Wesley; ***M:*** Tom Bahler.

Fast Getaway **1991 (PG)** Chases scenes proliferate when a teen criminal mastermind plots bank heists for his outlaw father. Relatively painless adolescent action-comedy, cleverly acted, quickly forgotten. **91m/C VHS, 8mm.** Corey Haim, Cynthia Rothrock, Leo Rossi, Ken Lerner, Marcia Strassman; ***D:*** Spiro Razatos.

Fast Getaway 2 ½ **1994 (PG-13)** Ex-bank robber Nelson (Haim) has given up a life of crime to open a business with gal pal Patrice (Buxton) while waiting for his partner/dad Sam (Rossi) to get out of jail. Then Nelson gets set up by Lily (Rothrock) and finds himself trying to convince an FBI agent of his innocence. Innocuous. **90m/C VHS.** Corey Haim, Sarah Buxton, Leo Rossi, Cynthia Rothrock, Peter Paul Liapis; ***D:*** Oley Sassone; ***W:*** Mark Sevi; ***M:*** David Robbins.

Fast Gun ½ **1993 (R)** Weapons-loving ex-CIA spook decides to take over a town—with your basic one lone hero to stop him. **90m/C VHS.** Richard (Rick) Hill, Kaz Garas, Robert Dryer, Brenda Bakke, Cirio H. Santiago.

Fast Kill **1973** A terrorist plot begins to fall apart when the conspirators fight among themselves. **94m/C VHS.** Tom Adams, Susie Hampton, Michael Culver, Peter Halliday; ***D:*** Lindsay Shonteff.

Fast Money ½ **1983** Three pals can't resist the temptation of big bucks from flying drugs in from Mexico, but they find danger along the way. **92m/C VHS.** Sammy Allred, Sonny Carl Davis; ***D:*** Doug Holloway.

Fast Money **1996 (R)** Car thief Francesca Marsh (Butler) and journalist Jack Martin (McCoy) go on the lam from the mob (and everyone else) with a briefcase containing $2.7 million. **93m/C VHS.** Yancy Butler, Matt McCoy, John Ashton, Trevor Goddard, Andy Romano, Carole Cook, Patrika Darbo; ***D:*** Alexander Wright; ***W:*** Alexander Wright; ***C:*** Thomas Jewett; ***M:*** Tony Riparetti.

Fast Sofa **2001 (R)** Lowlife, smalltime L.A. drug dealer Rick (Busey) has a one-nighter with porn actress Ginger (Tilly) and decides to follow her to Palm Springs. Too bad her jealous (and violent) movie-producer husband (Roberts) is also about to show up. Based on the book by Bruce Craven. **95m/C VHS, DVD, Wide.** Jake Busey, Jennifer Tilly, Eric Roberts, Adam Goldberg, Crispin Glover, Natasha Lyonne, Bijou Phillips; ***D:*** Salome Breziner; ***W:*** Salome Breziner, Peter Chase, Bruce Craven; ***C:*** Dean Lent; ***M:*** William V. Malpede.

Fast Talking **1986** The story of a quick-talking, incorrigible, 15-year-old Australian boy's humorous though tragic criminal schemes. The young protagonist slides his way through a life marked by a degenerate home life, a brother who forces him to sell drugs, and a future that holds no promise. **93m/C VHS.** *AU* Steve Bisley, Tracey Mann, Peter Hehir, Dennis Moore, Rod Zuanic, Toni Allaylis, Chris Truswell; ***D:*** Ken Cameron; ***W:*** Ken Cameron.

Fast Times at Ridgemont High **1982 (R)** Teens at a Southern California high school revel in sex, drugs, and rock 'n' roll. A full complement of student types meet at the Mall—that great suburban microcosm percolating with angst-ridden teen trials—to contemplate losing their virginity, plot skipping homeroom, and move inexorably closer to the end of their adolescence. The talented young cast became household names: Sean Penn is most excellent as the California surfer dude who antagonizes teacher, Walston, aka "Aloha Mr. Hand." Based on the best-selling book by Cameron Crowe, it's one of the best of this genre. **91m/C VHS, DVD, Wide.** Sean Penn, Jennifer Jason Leigh, Judge Reinhold, Robert Romanus, Brian Backer, Phoebe Cates, Ray Walston, Scott Thomson, Vincent Schiavelli, Amanda Wyss, Forest Whitaker, Kelli Maroney, Eric Stoltz, Pamela Springsteen, James Russo, Martin Brest, Anthony Edwards, Nicolas Cage; ***D:*** Amy Heckerling; ***W:*** Cameron Crowe; ***C:*** Matthew F. Leonetti.

Fast Walking **1982 (R)** A prison guard is offered $50,000 to help a militant black leader escape from jail, the same man his cousin has contracted to kill. **116m/C VHS.** James Woods, Kay Lenz, M. Emmet Walsh, Robert Hooks, Tim McIntire, Timothy Carey, Susan Tyrrell; ***D:*** James B. Harris.

Faster, Pussycat! Kill! Kill! *The Leather Girls; Pussycat* **1965** It doesn't get any better than this! Three sexy go-go dancers get their after-work kicks by hot-rodding in the California desert. They soon find themselves enveloped in murder, kidnapping, lust and robbery after a particular race gets out of hand. Easily the most watchable, fun and funny production to spring from the mind of Russ Meyer. Those who haven't seen this cannot truly be called "cool." **83m/B VHS.** Tura Satana, Haji, Lori Williams, Susan Bernard, Stuart Lancaster, Paul Trinka, Dennis Busch, Ray Barlow, Mickey Foxx; ***D:*** Russ Meyer; ***W:*** Jack Moran, Russ Meyer; ***C:*** Walter Schenk; ***M:*** Paul Sawtell, Bert Shefter, The Bostweeds.

Fastest Guitar Alive ½ **1968** Debut of the legendary Orbison is strictly for inveterate fans only. Rebel operative/crooner during the Civil War, whose rhythm is good but timing is bad, steals a Union gold supply, but the war ends before he makes it back to the land of Dixie. Seems that makes him a common thief. **88m/C VHS.** Roy Orbison, Sammy Jackson, Margaret Pierce, Joan Freeman; ***D:*** Michael Moore; ***M:*** Fred Karger.

Fastest Gun Alive **1956** Suspenseful western with ex-gunfighter Ford challenged to a showdown by Crawford. **89m/C VHS.** Glenn Ford, Jeanne Crain, Broderick Crawford, Russ Tamblyn, Allyn Joslyn, Leif Erickson, John Dehner, Noah Beery Jr., J.M. Kerrigan, Rhys Williams; ***D:*** Russell Rouse; ***W:*** Russell Rouse, Frank D. Gilroy; ***C:*** George J. Folsey; ***M:*** Andre Previn.

Fat City ½ **1972 (PG)** One of Huston's later triumphs, a seedy, street-level drama based on the Leonard Gardner novel about an aging alcoholic boxer trying to make a comeback and his young worshipful protege. Highly acclaimed. Tyrrell earned an Oscar nomination as the boxer's world-weary lover. **93m/C VHS.** Stacy Keach, Jeff Bridges, Susan Tyrrell, Candy Clark, Nicholas Colasanto; ***D:*** John Huston; ***C:*** Conrad L. Hall; ***M:*** Marvin Hamlisch.

Fat Guy Goes Nutzoid woof! *Zeisters* **1986** A crude farce about an obese mental patient who escapes from the mental hospital and joins two teenagers on a wild trip to New York City. **85m/C VHS.** Tibor Feldman, Peter Linari, John MacKay, Joan Allen; ***D:*** John Golden; ***M:*** Leo Kottke.

Fat Man and Little Boy ½ **1989 (PG-13)** A lavish, semi-fictional account of the creation of the first atomic bomb, and the tensions between J. Robert Oppenheimer and his military employer, Gen. Leslie Groves. Overlong but interesting. Cusack, whose character never existed, is especially worthwhile as an idealistic scientist. **127m/C VHS, 8mm.** Paul Newman, Dwight Schultz, Bonnie Bedelia, John Cusack, Laura Dern, John C. McGinley, Natasha Richardson, Ron Frazier; ***D:*** Roland Joffe; ***W:*** Bruce Robinson, Tony Garnett, Roland Joffe; ***M:*** Ennio Morricone.

Fatal Attraction *Head On* **1980 (R)** Couple meet after an auto accident. They begin an affair which turns dark and bizarre. Fine cast doesn't get far with this peculiar premise, although every one tries hard. **90m/C VHS.** *CA* Sally Kellerman, Stephen Lack, John Huston, Lawrence Dane; ***D:*** Michael Grant.

Fatal Attraction **1987 (R)** When a very married New York lawyer is seduced by a beautiful blonde associate, the one-night stand leads to terror as she continues to pursue the relationship. She begins to threaten his family and home with possessive, violent acts. An expertly made, manipulative thriller; one of the most hotly discussed films of the 1980s. A successful change of role for Close as the sexy, scorned, and deadly other woman. Also available in a special "director's series" edition, featuring Lyne's original, controversial ending. **120m/C VHS, DVD, 8mm, Wide.** Michael Douglas, Glenn Close, Anne Archer, Stuart Pankin, Ellen Hamilton-Latzen, Ellen Foley, Fred Gwynne, Meg Mundy, J.J. Johnston; ***D:*** Adrian Lyne; ***W:*** James Dearden; ***C:*** Howard Atherton; ***M:*** Maurice Jarre.

Fatal Beauty ½ **1987 (R)** A female undercover cop in Los Angeles tracks down a drug dealer selling cocaine (from which the title is taken). Elliott is the mob bodyguard who helps her out. Violent and sensational, the film tries to capitalize on the success of "Beverly Hills Cop" and fails miserably. Goldberg is wasted in this effort and the picture tiptoes around the interracial romance aspects that are implied. **104m/C VHS, DVD, Wide.** Whoopi Goldberg, Sam Elliott, Ruben Blades, Harris Yulin, Richard "Cheech" Marin, Brad Dourif; ***D:*** Tom Holland; ***W:*** Hilary Henkin, Dean Riesner; ***C:*** David M. Walsh; ***M:*** Harold Faltermeyer.

Fatal Bond ½ **1991 (R)** Blair plays a small-town hairdresser caught in an obsessive love affair with a drifter. When she suspects her boyfriend is committing a string of rape-murders, will she turn him in or protect him? Or is she next? **89m/C VHS.** Linda Blair, Jerome Elhers, Stephen Leeder, Donal Gibson, Caz Lederman, Tao Gerbert, Penny Pederson, Joe Bugner; ***D:*** Vincent Monton; ***W:*** Phillip Avalon.

Fatal Charm **1992 (R)** There's a serial killer at work in a small town. So far six women have been raped and murdered. But cute-teen Valerie can't believe it when the townspeople accuse that sweet guy Adam, especially since he's the one boy Valerie is so very attracted to. **90m/C VHS.** Christopher Atkins, Amanda Peterson, Mary Frann, James Remar, Andrew (Andy) Robinson, Peggy Lipton; ***D:*** Alan Smithee; ***W:*** Nicholas Niciphor.

Fatal Chase *Nowhere to Hide* **1977** Van Cleef is a U.S. Marshal assigned to protect ex-hitman Musante from his vengeful former employers. And you thought you didn't get along with your boss. Typical made-for-TV fodder written by Anhalt, who usually manages to be a trifle more entertaining. **78m/C VHS.** Lee Van Cleef, Tony Musante, Charles Robinson, Lelia Goldoni, Noel Fournier, Russell Johnson, Edward Anhalt; ***D:*** Jack Starrett; ***W:*** Edward Anhalt.

Fatal Chase ½ **1992** Police investigation Marcus Lee and undercover cop Robin investigate drug dealer Dion. Robin and fellow officer Cynthia apprehend Dion in Hong Kong and bring him back to face charges in the Philippines. But Dion escapes and the duo are forced to deal with local officer Philip in order to get Dion back. Dubbed into English. **96m/C VHS.** *HK* Robin Shou, Yukari Oshima, Waise Lee; ***D:*** Ki Yee Chik.

Fatal Combat ½ **1996 (R)** Reclusive billionaire Houston Armstrong (Fitzpatrick) privately broadcasts a program called "No Exit" that features combat-to-the-death. (Live on TV!) But Armstrong tends to run out of combatants so when he hears about John Stoneman (Wincott), a master martial artist, he has his minions kidnap him along with Stoneman's pupil, Jason (Demambro). Now, it's fight or die. **93m/C VHS.** Jeff Wincott, Richard Fitzpatrick, Joe Demambro, Sven-Ole Thorsen; ***D:*** Damian Lee; ***W:*** Damian Lee, John Howard Lawson; ***C:*** Gerald R. Goozie. **VIDEO**

Fatal Confinement ½ **1964** Wrenching drama finds Crawford, having lived 15 years in seclusion with her young daughter, forced to sell her land to a giant corporation bent on expansion. Interesting also for the similarities to Crawford's real-life "Mommie Dearest" lifestyle. **70m/C**

VHS. *GB* Joan Crawford; Paul Burke, Charles Bickford; ***D:*** Robert Guest.

Fatal Error 🦴½ *Outsider in Amsterdam; The Outsider; Grijpstra and de Gier* **1983** Dutch police thriller about the investigation of a cop killing. Based on the mystery series by Janwillem van de Wetering. Dubbed. **85m/C VHS.** *NL* Rutger Hauer, Rijk de Gooyer, Willeke Van Ammelrooy, Donald M. Jones; ***D:*** Wim Verstappen; ***M:*** Ennio Morricone.

Fatal Error 🦴🦴½ **1999** Digicron, the world's largest media company, is about to connect all the televisions and computers worldwide. But Dr. Nick Baldwin (Sabato Jr.) and Army medical researcher Samantha Carter (Turner) discover that people are dying from an untraceable virus. So is the virus linked to Digicron. Well, what do you think? Adapted from the novel "Reaper" by Ben Mezrich. **91m/C VHS, DVD.** Antonio Sabato Jr., Janine Turner, Robert Wagner, Malcolm Stewart; ***D:*** Armand Mastroianni; ***W:*** Rockne S. O'Bannon; ***C:*** David Geddes; ***M:*** Ron Ramin. **CABLE**

Fatal Exposure 🦴🦴 **1990** The insatiably sanguinary Jack the Ripper lives on in the form of his great grandson, who avails himself of modern technology to capture those magic moments on videotape. Just goes to show home movies don't have to be bland. **?m/C VHS.** Blake Bahner, Ena Henderson, Julie Austin, Dan Schmale, Renee Cline, Gary Wise, Joy Ovington.

Fatal Exposure 🦴🦴 **1991 (PG-13)** A divorcee on vacation with her young sons accidentally picks up the wrong snapshots at the developers'. It turns out she has her hands on some incriminating photos, and the subject will resort to anything, even murder, to keep her quiet. **89m/C VHS.** Mare Winningham, Nick Mancuso, Christopher McDonald, Geoffrey Blake, Christopher Pettiet; ***D:*** Alan Metzger. **TV**

Fatal Fix 🦴½ **198?** A French film expose of urban heroin addiction. Music by the Pretenders. **90m/C VHS.** *FR* Helmut Berger, Corinne Clery; ***D:*** Massimo Pirri.

Fatal Games 🦴½ **1984** Young female athletes are mysteriously disappearing at the Falcon Academy of Athletics and a crazed killer is responsible. **88m/C VHS.** Sally Kirkland, Lynn Banashek, Sean Masterson.

The Fatal Hour 🦴½ **1940** Karloff is enlisted to aid police in solving the murder of a detective. As Karloff is rounding up suspects, three more murders take place. Feeble. **68m/B VHS, DVD, 8mm.** Boris Karloff, Marjorie Reynolds, Grant Withers, Charles Trowbridge, John Hamilton, Frank Puglia, Jason Robards Sr.; ***D:*** William Nigh; ***W:*** Scott Darling, George Waggner; ***C:*** Harry Neumann.

The Fatal Image 🦴🦴½ **1990** A mother and daughter on vacation in Paris inadvertantly videotape an international mob hit, making them the target of ruthless assassins. Filmed on location in Paris. **96m/C VHS, DVD.** Michele Lee, Justine Bateman, Francois Dunoyer, Jean-Pierre Cassel, Sonia Petrovna; ***D:*** Thomas J. Wright; ***C:*** Jean-Yves Le Mener. **TV**

Fatal Images 🦴 **1989** A camera mysteriously causes all the models who pose for it to die, prompting the photographer to investigate. **90m/C VHS.** Lane Coyle; ***D:*** Dennis Devine; ***W:*** Dennis Devine, Mike Bowler, Steve Jarvis.

Fatal Instinct 🦴½ **1992 (R)** A tough-guy cop trying to solve a murder instead finds himself a victim of sexual obsession in this erotic thriller. Also available in an unrated version. Not to be confused with (but doesn't everything sound familiar) "Basic Instinct." **93m/C VHS.** Michael Madsen, Laura Johnson, Tony Hamilton; ***D:*** John Dirlam.

Fatal Instinct 🦴🦴 **1993 (PG-13)** Spoof on erotic thrillers such as "Fatal Attraction" and "Basic Instinct." Suave Assante plays a guy with dual careers—he's both cop and attorney, defending the criminals he's arrested. Young plays a lovelorn psycho who's lost her panties. Plot is worth mentioning only in passing, since the point is to mercilessly skewer the entire film noir tradition. The gags occasionally hit deep-chuckle level, though for every good joke there's at least three that misfire. Clemmons of "E Street Band" fame wanders around with sax for background music purposes, typical of the acute self-consciousness of the film. **90m/C VHS.** Armand Assante, Sean Young, Sherilyn Fenn, Kate Nelligan, Christopher McDonald, James Remar, Tony Randall; ***Cameos:*** Clarence Clemons, Doc Severinsen; ***D:*** Carl Reiner; ***W:*** David O'Malley; ***M:*** Richard Gibbs.

A Fatal Inversion 🦴🦴½ **1992** When 19-year-old Hodge inherits a remote English estate from his great-uncle, he invites best friend Northam to spend a carefree summer, after both have told their parents they're vacationing in Greece. The boys are soon joined by Todd, Ford, and Warnecke in an informal commune but several disasters cause them to break off all contact for 12 years—until the remains of two bodies are discovered on the grounds and a police investigation is started. Made for British TV; based on the psychological thriller by Ruth Rendell (writing as Barbara Vine). **150m/C VHS.** *GB* Douglas Hodge, Jeremy Northam, Saira Todd, Julia Ford, Gordon Warnecke, Nicholas Woodeson, Peter Attard, Rachel Joyce, Nicholas Le Prevost, Ben Chaplin; ***D:*** Tim Fywell; ***W:*** Sandy Welch; ***C:*** Barry McCann; ***M:*** David Ferguson. **TV**

Fatal Justice 🦴 **199?** Mars is a topnotch assassin who's been in the business too long and knows too much so the agency he works for decides to kill him off. They send young and beautiful professional Diana to do the job but will she be able to when she discovers Mars is actually her father? **90m/C VHS.** Joe Estevez.

Fatal Mission 🦴 **1989 (R)** A Vietnam soldier captures a female Chinese guerilla and uses her as his hostage and guide through the jungle. **84m/C VHS.** Peter Fonda, Mako, Tia Carrere, Ted Markland, Jim Mitchum; ***D:*** George Rowe; ***C:*** Phil Parmet.

Fatal Passion 🦴🦴 **1994** Two sisters escape from the city after an accidental murder but run straight into the middle of a sacrifical backwoods cult. **90m/C VHS.** Lisa Hayland, Joe Pilato.

Fatal Past 🦴🦴 **1994 (R)** Bodyguard gets up close and personal with his client—who happens to be a mobster's mistress. As if this weren't trouble enough their pasts provide doom and gloom as well. **85m/C VHS.** Costas Mandylor, Kasia (Katarzyna) Figura; ***D:*** Clive Fleury; ***W:*** Richard Ryan.

Fatal Pulse woof! **1988** Sorority girls are being killed off in grisly ways. Basic slasher/gore. **90m/C VHS.** Michelle McCormick, Ken Roberts, Joe Phelan, Alex Courtney.

Fatal Skies 🦴 **1990** An evil schemer plots to dump toxic waste in a small town's water supply until a group of teens comes to the rescue. **88m/C VHS.** Timothy Leary.

Fatal Vision 🦴🦴½ **1984** Vresion of Joe McGinniss's controversial book about the murder trial of Dr. Jeffrey MacDonald, the former Green Berets physician accused of murdering his whole family and blaming the killings on crazed hippies. McGinniss first believed MacDonald may have been innocent but his subsequent investigation, and his book, proved otherwise. The starring debut for Cole. MacDonald still protests his innocence. **192m/C VHS.** Gary Cole, Karl Malden, Eva Marie Saint, Andy Griffith, Barry Newman; ***D:*** David Greene. **TV**

Fatally Yours 🦴🦴 **1995** Real-estate agent Danny (Rossovich) decides to restore a long-vacant house where a mob massacre occurred in 1928. While in the house, he's "contacted" by the ghostly Sara (MacDonnell), whose husband and gangster father were among the dead. Sara tells him about a hidden treasure of jewels, which leads some present-day gangsters to take an interest in Danny's new property. **90m/C VHS.** Rick Rossovich, George Lazenby, Roddy McDowall, Sage Stallone, Sarah MacDonnell; ***D:*** Tim Everitt; ***C:*** Tim Everitt.

Fate 🦴🦴½ **1990 (PG-13)** Sweet comedy. A young man plans his love-affair carefully, but his biggest problem is meeting the girl of his dreams. Cheerful acting from Lynn and Paul. Stylish and charming. **115m/C VHS.** Cheryl Lynn, Stuart Paul, Kaye Ballard, Susannah York; ***D:*** Stuart Paul.

Father 🦴🦴🦴 *Apa* **1967** After WWII, a Hungarian youth makes up stories about his dead father's heroism that enhance his own position. Eventually he becomes obsessed with the facts surrounding his father's death at the hands of the enemy and, learning the truth, lays the past to rest. In Hungarian with English subtitles. **85m/B VHS.** *HU* Andras Balint, Miklos Gabor; ***D:*** Istvan Szabo; ***W:*** Istvan Szabo.

Father 🦴🦴 **1990 (PG-13)** A woman receives an anonymous telephone call telling her to watch a TV news program and learn the truth about her beloved father. What she sees is her father's face superimposed over that of a young Nazi soldier and an aging, unstable woman accusing her father of war crimes. The daughter fiercely believes her father to be a victim of mistaken identity but questions keep nagging at her. Very similiar in plot to "Music Box" and just as pedestrian in spite of some good performances. **106m/C VHS.** *AU* Max von Sydow, Carol Drinkwater, Julia Blake, Steve Jacobs; ***D:*** John Power. Australian Film Inst. '90: Actor (von Sydow), Actress (Blake).

Father and Scout 🦴🦴½ **1994 (PG)** Would-be Eagle Scout Michael (Bonsall) has a problem when he takes his city-bred, whiny, basically incompetent, dad Spenser (Saget) on a camping trip. Made for TV. **92m/C VHS.** Bob Saget, Brian Bonsall, Heidi Swedberg, Stuart Pankin, David Graf, Troy Evans; ***D:*** Richard Michaels; ***M:*** David Kitay. **TV**

The Father Clements Story 🦴🦴½ **1987** The true story of a black priest in Chicago who battled the Roman Catholic hierarchy in order to adopt a troubled teenager. **100m/C VHS.** Louis Gossett Jr., Malcolm Jamal Warner, Carroll O'Connor, Leon Robinson, Rosetta LeNoire, Ron McClarty; ***D:*** Edwin Sherin. **TV**

Father Figure 🦴½ **1980** When a divorced man attends his ex-wife's funeral, he discovers that he must take care of his estranged sons. Well-done drama based on young adult writer Richard Peck's novel. **94m/C VHS.** Hal Linden, Timothy Hutton, Cassie Yates, Martha Scott, Jeremy Licht; ***D:*** Jerry London; ***M:*** Billy Goldenberg. **TV**

Father Goose 🦴🦴½ **1964** During WWII, a liquor-loving plane-spotter stationed on a remote Pacific isle finds himself stuck with a group of French refugee schoolgirls and their teacher. Some predictable gags, romance, and heroism fill out the running time pleasantly. Scriptwriters Stone and Tarloff, who were competitors, not collaborators on the project, shared an Oscar. **116m/C VHS, DVD.** Cary Grant, Leslie Caron, Trevor Howard; ***D:*** Ralph Nelson; ***W:*** Peter Stone, Frank Tarloff; ***C:*** Charles B(ryant) Lang Jr.; ***M:*** Cy Coleman. Oscars '64: Story & Screenplay.

Father Hood 🦴 **1993 (PG-13)** Family drama has Swayze playing a small-time criminal whose daughter tracks him down after leaving the foster-care shelter where she and her brother are being abused. The family takes to the road, running from both the police and a journalist (Berry) who wants to expose the corrupt foster-care system. The children are obnoxious, Swayze is miscast, and the entire film is a misfire. **94m/C VHS.** Patrick Swayze, Halle Berry, Sabrina Lloyd, Brian Bonsall, Diane Ladd, Michael Ironside, Bob Gunton; ***D:*** Darrell Roodt; ***W:*** Scott Spencer.

Father of the Bride 🦴🦴🦴½ **1950** A classic, quietly hilarious comedy about the tribulations of a father preparing for his only daughter's wedding. Tracy is suitably overwhelmed as loving father Stanley Banks and Taylor radiant as the bride, Kay. A warm vision of American family life, accompanied by the 1940 MGM short "Wedding Bills." Followed by "Father's Little Dividend" (1951) and later a TV series. Remade in 1991. **106m/C VHS.** Spencer Tracy, Elizabeth Taylor, Joan Bennett, Billie Burke, Leo G. Carroll, Russ Tamblyn, Don Taylor, Moroni Olsen; ***D:*** Vincente Minnelli; ***W:*** Frances Goodrich, Albert Hackett; ***C:*** John Alton.

Father of the Bride 🦴🦴½ **1991 (PG)** Remake of the 1950 comedy classic portrays one of the most overextravagant weddings in recent film history, but falls short of the original. Predictable plot and characters don't hide any surprises, but nothing detracts from the purpose of the film: to be a nice, charming movie. Martin is fine as the reluctant dad but Keaton is little more than window dressing as the bride's mom; Short is annoying as a pretentious wedding coordinator. Williams pulls off a nice film debut—and was almost immediately cast in a TV ad as a young-bride-to-be calling her dad long distance to tell him she's engaged. Adapted from a novel by Edward Streeter. **105m/C VHS, DVD, Wide.** Steve Martin, Diane Keaton, Kimberly Williams, Kieran Culkin, George Newbern, Martin Short, B.D. Wong, Peter Michael Goetz, Kate McGregor Stewart, Martha Gehman; ***Cameos:*** Eugene Levy; ***D:*** Charles Shyer; ***W:*** Charles Shyer, Nancy Meyers; ***C:*** John Lindley; ***M:*** Alan Silvestri.

Father of the Bride Part II 🦴🦴½ **1995 (PG)** Sweetly sentimental update of the 1951 film "Father's Little Dividend" finds George Banks (Martin) once again thrown for a loop—first by his beloved daughter Annie's (Williams) pregnancy and then by wife Nina's (the radiant Keaton) announcement that they are about to become parents themselves. George doesn't deal very well with either situation but, aided by fey party planner Franck (Short), he manages to get through the predictable chaos. Martin's physical expressiveness and sly charm are a big plus. **106m/C VHS, DVD, Wide.** Steve Martin, Diane Keaton, Kimberly Williams, Martin Short, George Newbern, Kieran Culkin, Peter Michael Goetz, Kate McGregor Stewart, Eugene Levy, B.D. Wong, Jane Adams; ***D:*** Charles Shyer; ***W:*** Nancy Myers, Charles Shyer; ***C:*** William A. Fraker; ***M:*** Alan Silvestri.

Father Was a Fullback 🦴🦴½ **1949** College football coach (MacMurray) has a losing team, problems with the administration and alumni, and two daughters with growing pains at home. Wife O'Hara supplies the sympathetic shoulder. **99m/B VHS.** Fred MacMurray, Maureen O'Hara, Betty Lynn, Rudy Vallee, Thelma Ritter, Natalie Wood, Jim Backus; ***D:*** John M. Stahl.

Fatherland 🦴🦴½ **1994** It's 1964 and 20 years earlier Hitler has won WWII in this what-if TV movie. The Nazi leader is about to sign a historic alliance with the U.S. President in Berlin when a series of murders of high-ranking Third Reich officers begins. SS detective Xavier March (Hauer) investigates, along with visiting American journalist Charlie Maguire (Richardson), leading the two to the Gestapo coverup of the Holocaust. If the secret gets out it could ruin the summit, so guess who's in big danger? Intriguing premise but the thriller fails to sustain tension. Based on the novel by Robert Harris. Filmed in Prague, Czech Republic. **106m/C VHS.** Rutger Hauer, Miranda Richardson, Peter Vaughan, Jean Marsh, Michael Kitchen, John Woodvine, John Shrapnel, Clare Higgins; ***D:*** Christopher Menaul; ***W:*** Stanley Weiser, Ron Hutchinson; ***C:*** Peter Sova; ***M:*** Gary Chang.

Fathers and Sons 🦴½ **1992 (R)** Max is a brooding, former bad-boy movie director living on the Jersey Shore. His wife's death causes him to rethink his life and deal with his drinking problem. He also tries to get to know his equally brooding teenage son, Ed. Turns out addiction may run in the family as Ed experiments with drugs. Ill-fitting subplot deals a serial killer stalking the community. Goldblum brings an uneasy gentleness to the father's role in an otherwise slow, talky, and obviously symbolic flick. **100m/C VHS.** Jeff Goldblum, Rory Cochrane, Mitchell Marchand, Famke Janssen, Natasha Gregson Wagner, Ellen Greene, Samuel L. Jackson, Joie Lee, Rosanna Arquette, Michael Disend; ***D:*** Paul Mones; ***W:*** Paul Mones; ***C:*** Ron Fortunato; ***M:*** Mason Daring.

Father's Day 🦴🦴½ **1996 (PG-13)** The comedy team of Williams and Crystal makes its feature film debut in this affable take on fatherhood. Freelance writer Putley (Williams) unites with attorney Lawrence (Crystal) to help their mutual ex-girlfriend Kinski search for her runaway son (she's led each man to believe he's the boy's father). Their quest leads to some inevitable sticky situations, but the erratic, adolescent Williams is wonderfully balanced by the calm, upstanding Crystal. Who needs a son when you have to deal with Williams? Together, they're fun to watch and almost make you forget the contrived plot. Almost. Remake of the 1984 French film "Les Comperes." **98m/C VHS, DVD.** Louis Lombardi, Robin Williams, Billy Crystal, Nastassia Kinski, Julia Louis-Dreyfus, Charlie Hofheimer, Bruce Greenwood, Jared Harris, Patti D'Arbanville, Charles Rocket, Dennis Burkley; *D:* Ivan Reitman; *W:* Lowell Ganz, Babaloo Mandel; *C:* Stephen Burum; *M:* James Newton Howard.

Father's Little Dividend 𝒮𝒮𝒮 **1951** Tracy expects a little peace and quiet now that he's successfully married off Taylor in this charming sequel to "Father of the Bride." However, he's quickly disillusioned by the news he'll soon be a grandfather—a prospect that causes nothing but dismay. Reunited the stars, director, writers, and producer from the successfull first film. **82m/B VHS, DVD.** Spencer Tracy, Joan Bennett, Elizabeth Taylor, Don Taylor, Billie Burke, Russ Tamblyn, Moroni Olsen; *D:* Vincente Minnelli; *W:* Frances Goodrich, Albert Hackett; *C:* John Alton; *M:* Albert Sendry.

A Father's Revenge 𝒮𝒮½ **1988 (R)** Dennehy is the only reason to bother with this average hostage drama. He's the father of a stewardess who's one of a group being held by terrorists. They're scheduled to die in 72 hours unless Dennehy can find a way to rescue them. **93m/C VHS.** Brian Dennehy, Joanna Cassidy, Ron Silver; *D:* John Herzfeld; *M:* Klaus Doldinger. **TV**

Fathom 𝒮𝒮½ **1967** Welch and her bikini fill out the title role as Fathom Harvill, a parachutist who is hired to find a nuclear triggering device that has been lost in the Mediterranean. She eventually hooks up with spy guy Peter Merriweather (Franciosa) and gets involved in a case involving priceless jewelry stolen from China. Spy spoof is oh so sixties. Based on the novel by Larry Forrester. **104m/C VHS, DVD.** *GB* Raquel Welch, Anthony (Tony) Franciosa, Ronald Fraser, Clive Revill, Richard Briers, Tom Adams; *D:* Leslie Martinson; *W:* Lorenzo Semple Jr.; *C:* Douglas Slocombe; *M:* John Dankworth.

Fatso 𝒮½ **1980 (PG)** After the shocking death of his obese cousin, an obsessive overeater struggles to overcome his neurosis with the aid of his sister and a self-help group called "Chubby Checkers." Bancroft's first work as both writer and director. **93m/C VHS.** Dom DeLuise, Anne Bancroft, Ron Carey, Candice Azzara; *D:* Anne Bancroft; *W:* Anne Bancroft.

Fatty Finn 𝒮½ **1984** A children's gagfest about young kids and bullies during the Depression, based on Syd Nicholls' comic strip. **91m/C VHS.** *AU* Ben Oxenbould, Bart Newton; *D:* Maurice Murphy.

Faust 𝒮𝒮𝒮½ *Faust-Eine deutsche Volkssage* **1926** The classic German silent based upon the legend of Faust, who sells his soul to the devil in exchange for youth. Based on Goethe's poem, and directed by Murnau as a classic example of Germanic expressionism. Remade as "All That Money Can Buy" in 1941. **117m/B VHS, DVD.** *GE* Emil Jannings, Warner Fuetterer, Gosta Ekman, Camilla Horn; *D:* F.W. Murnau; *W:* Hans Kyser; *C:* Carl Hoffmann; *M:* Timothy Brock, Werner R. Heymann.

Faust: Love of the Damned 𝒮𝒮 **2000 (R)** Very gory, visually impressive horror flick finds artist John Jaspers (Frost) selling his soul to Lucifer minion "M" (Divoff) in exchange for revenge on his wife's killers. Eventually, he gets sent to hell but returns as avenger Faust (in a red rubber suit). There's also a good guy detective (Combs) and a troubled shrink named Jade (Brook) involved in the action. Based on the comic book by Tim Vigil and David Quinn. An unrated version is also available. **96m/C VHS, DVD.** Mark Frost, Andrew Divoff, Jeffrey Combs, Isabel Brook; *D:* Brian Yuzna; *W:* David Quinn; *C:* Jacques Haitkin; *M:* Xavier Capellas.

The Favor 𝒮𝒮½ **1992 (R)** Lighthearted romance rife with comic confusion, vivid fantasies, secrets, and the all-important favor. Kathy (Kozak) seeks to relieve the boredom of her marriage through best friend Emily's (McGovern) tryst with Kathy's old beau, Tom. Or so she thinks, until Em spills all the juicy details. In a change of pace, the males take a back seat to the women. Good comic performances from Kozak and McGovern and witty dialogue help overcome the plot's sheer silliness. Damian Elwes (actor Cary's brother) provided Pitt's paintings. Theatrical release was delayed three years due to financial crisis at Orion Pictures. **97m/C VHS, DVD, Wide.** Harley Jane Kozak, Elizabeth McGovern, Bill Pullman, Brad Pitt, Ken Wahl, Larry Miller, Holland Taylor; *D:* Donald Petrie; *W:* Josann McGibbon, Sara Parriott; *C:* Tim Suhrstedt; *M:* Thomas Newman.

The Favor, the Watch, & the Very Big Fish 𝒮𝒮 **1992 (R)** Set in a fairytale version of Paris. Hoskins is a photographer of religious subjects searching for a man to pose as Jesus. He discovers his subject in the hirsute Goldblum, a mad bar pianist who actually thinks he's the savior. Richardson plays the object of Hoskin's shy affections, an actress who does dubbing work by providing the moaning and groaning for porno flicks. Messy attempt at screwball-comedy with some brief humorous moments. **89m/C VHS.** *GB FR* Bob Hoskins, Jeff Goldblum, Natasha Richardson, Michel Blanc, Jacques Villeret, Angela Pleasence, Jean-Pierre Cassel, Bruce Altman; *D:* Ben Lewin; *W:* Ben Lewin; *C:* Bernard Zitzermann; *M:* Vladimir Cosma.

The Favorite Son 𝒮𝒮𝒮 *Le Fils Prefere* **1994** Troubled family history is examined between three adult French brothers and their Italian immigrant father. A dutiful son, hotel manager Jean-Paul (Lanvin) regularly visits elderly father Raphael (Herlitzka). But Jean-Paul has problems. Desperate for cash to pay his loan shark, he approaches estranged younger brother Philippe (Barr), a wealthy lawyer, who is loath to help, while older schoolteacher brother Francis (Giraudeau) has little spare cash. Jean-Paul decides to take out a life insurance policy on dad—who promptly disappears—leaving the brothers to reluctantly come to terms in order to find him. French with subtitles. **100m/C VHS.** *FR* Gerard Lanvin, Jean-Marc Barr, Bernard Giraudeau, Roberto Herlitzka, Margherita Buy; *D:* Nicole Garcia; *W:* Nicole Garcia; *C:* Eric Gautier; *M:* Philippe Sarde. Cesar '95: Actor (Lanvin).

FBI Girl 𝒮𝒮 **1952** An FBI clerk is used as bait to trap a murderer and break up a gang. Burr, pre-Perry Mason, plays a bad guy. **74m/B VHS.** Cesar Romero, George Brent, Audrey Totter, Raymond Burr, Tom Drake; *D:* William Berke.

The FBI Story 𝒮𝒮𝒮 **1959** Mr. Stewart goes to Washington in this anatomy of the Federal Bureau of Investigation. If you're a fan of the gangster genre (LeRoy earlier directed "Little Caesar"), and not especially persnickety about fidelity to the facts, this actioner offers a pseudo-factual (read fictional) glimpse—based on actual cases from the 1920s through the 1950s—into the life of a fictitious agent-family man. **149m/C VHS.** James Stewart, Vera Miles, Nick Adams, Murray Hamilton, Larry Pennell; *D:* Mervyn LeRoy; *C:* Joseph Biroc; *M:* Max Steiner.

Fear 𝒮𝒮 **1946** An impoverished medical student murders the professor he believes is tormenting him and his life suddenly gets better. He falls in love and gets a scholarship but the police are closing in on his crime. Except...did any of it really happen? Or is he suffering from hallucinations. Low-budget psycho-drama with some good paranoid moments. **68m/B VHS.** Peter Cookson, Warren William, Anne Gwynne, James B. Cardwell, Nestor Paiva; *D:* Alfred Zeisler.

Fear 𝒮 *Honor Betrayed* **1988 (R)** A vacationing family is plagued by a murderous Vietnam vet and other psychotic cons. **96m/C VHS.** Edward (Eddie) Bunker, Frank Stallone, Cliff DeYoung, Kay Lenz, Robert Factor; *D:* Robert A. Ferretti.

Fear 𝒮𝒮½ **1990 (R)** A young psychic (Sheedy) delves into the minds of serial killers and writes novels about her experiences. But what happens when the next killer is also a psychic and decides to play mind-games with her? Above-average suspense sustains this cable thriller. **98m/C VHS.** Ally Sheedy, Lauren Hutton, Michael O'Keefe, Stan Shaw, Dina Merrill, John Agar, Marta DuBois; *D:* Rockne S. O'Bannon; *M:* Henry Mancini. **CABLE**

The Fear 𝒮½ **1994 (R)** Student psychologist (Bowz) takes a group to a remote cabin to explore their fears as part of his research project. Then, they begin to die horribly and gradually figure out that the cabin's wooden mascot, Morty (Weiss), is coming to life and doing them in. **98m/C VHS, DVD.** Eddie Bowz, Darin Heames, Anna Karin, Leland Hayward, Monique Mannen, Heather Medway, Antonio Todd, Erick Weiss, Vince Edwards, Ann Turkel, Wes Craven; *D:* Vincent Robert; *W:* Ron Ford; *C:* Bernd Heinl; *M:* Robert O. Ragland.

Fear 𝒮½ *No Fear* **1996 (R)** Wahlberg (the former Marky Mark) is a parents' worse nightmare: the violent, obsessed boyfriend of a 16-year-old girl (Witherspoon) as "Fatal Attraction" goes to the prom. Some cleverness, but ultimately follows a familiar, cliched path littered with one-dimensional characters and predictable plot twists. Gory, unconvincing climax kills any credibility that was left. The one standout is Petersen as the girl's protective father. **96m/C VHS, DVD, Wide.** Reese Witherspoon, Mark Wahlberg, William L. Petersen, Amy Brenneman, Alyssa Milano, Tracy Fraim, Christopher Gray, Todd Caldecott; *D:* James Foley; *W:* Christopher Crowe; *C:* Thomas Kloss; *M:* Carter Burwell. MTV Movie Awards '97: Song ("Machinehead").

Fear and Loathing in Las Vegas 𝒮𝒮 **1998 (R)** Hunter S. Thompson's 1971 cult memoir arrives on the big screen about 20 years too late to have any meaning or much entertainment value. Director Gilliam, never one to shy away from weirdness, overdoes everything in trying to capture the wretched excess of the book. Thompson's screen alter-ego Duke (Depp) packs his Caddy with illicit drugs and his equally wasted lawyer (Del Toro), and heads for his next writing assignment—to cover a drug enforcement conference in Vegas. Depp does a great job of impersonating the completely wasted and unlikable Thompson, while Del Toro passes out and pukes a lot in the sidekick role. It's most definitely a one-of-a-kind trip, but not one that most people will be willing to take. **119m/C VHS, DVD, Wide.** Johnny Depp, Benicio Del Toro, Christina Ricci, Gary Busey, Craig Bierko, Ellen Barkin, Cameron Diaz, Flea, Mark Harmon, Katherine Helmond, Michael Jeter, Penn Jillette, Lyle Lovett, Tobey Maguire, Harry Dean Stanton, Tim Thomerson; *D:* Terry Gilliam; *W:* Terry Gilliam, Alex Cox, Tony Grisoni, Tod Davies; *C:* Nicola Pecorini.

Fear, Anxiety and Depression 𝒮½ **1989 (R)** A neurotic aspiring playwright in New York has various problems with his love life. Sub-Woody Allen comedy attempt, with a few bright spots. The dregs of New York, with all the violence and degradation, are brought to the screen here. **84m/C VHS.** Todd Solondz, Stanley Tucci; *D:* Todd Solondz; *W:* Todd Solondz.

The Fear Chamber woof! *Torture Zone; Chamber of Fear; La Camara del Terror; Torture Chamber* **1968** Hardly a Karloff vehicle. Boris shot the footage for this and three other Mexican "horror" films in LA, an unfortunate swan song to his career, though he was fortunate to be quickly written out of this story. The near plot concerns a mutant rock that thrives on human fear. Doctor Karloff and his assistants make sure the rock is rolling in sacrificial victims (women, of course). A prodigious devaluation of the "B"-grade horror flick, it's so bad it's just bad. **88m/C VHS, DVD, Wide.** *MX* Boris Karloff, Yerye Beirut, Julissa, Carlos East, Sandra Chavez, Eva Muller, Pamela Rosas, Santanon, Isela Vega; *D:* Juan Ibanez, Jack Hill; *W:* Jack Hill, Luis Enrique Vergara; *C:* Austin McKinney, Raul Dominguez.

Fear City 𝒮½ **1985 (R)** Two partners who own a talent agency are after the psychopath who is killing off their prized strippers with the aid of a local cop. Sleazy look at Manhattan low life. **93m/C VHS, DVD, Wide.** Billy Dee Williams, Tom Berenger, Jack Scalia, Melanie Griffith, Rae Dawn Chong, Joe Santos, Maria Conchita Alonso, Rossano Brazzi; *D:* Abel Ferrara; *W:* Nicholas St. John; *C:* James (Momel) Lemmo; *M:* Dick Halligan.

The Fear: Halloween Night 𝒮𝒮 *Fear 2; Fear: Resurrection* **1999 (R)** Mike Hawthorne, the son of a psycho killer, has been plagued by blackouts. According to a friend, a Halloween eve ritual where a group of friends all face their worst fears could help Mike get rid of the fear of his father that continues to haunt him. Only when Mike awakens from another blackout, it's to discover a murdered friend. Palmer played another serial killer's mom (Jason) in "Friday the 13th." **87m/C VHS, DVD.** Gordon Currie, Stacy Grant, Brendan Beiser, Betsy Palmer, Emmanuelle Vaugier, Rachel Hayward, Larry Pennell, Phillip Rhys, Myc Agnew, Kelly Benson; *D:* Chris Angel; *W:* Kevin Richards. **VIDEO**

Fear in the City 𝒮 **1981** The Sicilian Mafia and a black crime gang battle for control of the streets. **90m/C VHS.** *IT* Michael Constantine, Fred Williamson, Gianni Manera; *D:* Gianni Manera.

Fear in the Night 𝒮𝒮𝒮 **1947** Suspenseful tale of a murder committed by a man under hypnosis. Fearing his nightmares are real Kelley talks his detective friend into investigating his "crime," which leads them to a mansion, a mirrored room, and a plot that takes some clever and unexpected twists. Remade in 1956 as "Nightmare." **72m/B VHS.** Paul Kelly, DeForest Kelley, Ann Doran, Kay Scott, Robert Emmett Keane; *D:* Maxwell Shane.

The Fear Inside 𝒮𝒮½ **1992 (R)** Lahti plays a woman suffering from agoraphobia who, because of her fear, has not left her home in more than a year. To help out, Lahti invites a seemingly charming college student to live with her. When the young woman's equally charming "brother" comes to visit, Lahti discovers the two aren't so charming after all. A standard woman-in-terror film with a better-than-average cast. **100m/C VHS.** Christine Lahti, Jennifer Rubin, Dylan McDermott, David Ackroyd, Thomas Ian Nicholas, Paul (Link) Linke, Leon Ichaso; *D:* Leon Ichaso; *W:* David Birke; *C:* Bojan Bazelli. **CABLE**

Fear No Evil 𝒮𝒮 **1980 (R)** A teenager who is the human embodiment of the demon Lucifer commits acts of demonic murder and destruction. His powers are challenged by an 18-year-old girl, who is the embodiment of the archangel Gabriel. First feature from La Loggia is better than it sounds. **90m/C VHS.** Stefan Arngrim, Kathleen Rowe McAllen, Elizabeth Hoffman; *D:* Frank Laloggia; *W:* Frank Laloggia.

Fear of a Black Hat 𝒮𝒮 **1994 (R)** Think "Spinal Tap" as gangsta rap and you've the plot of this good-natured imitator. The dim-witted Ice Cold (Cundieff), Tone-Def (Lawrence), and Tasty-Taste (Scott), the trio known as NWH (Niggaz With Hats), are touring in support of their album and trying to convince filmmaker Nina Blackburn (Lemmons) of their street cred. Like Tap's metalheads, the more they explain themselves, the less sense they make. **87m/C VHS.** Larry B. Scott, Mark Christopher Lawrence, Kasi Lemmons, Rusty Cundieff; *D:* Rusty Cundieff; *W:* Rusty Cundieff; *C:* John L. Demps Jr.

Fear Runs Silent 𝒮𝒮 **1999 (R)** High school class heads to the woods for an overnight campout. They get stranded. Can you guess what happens? Yes, someone or something tries to kill them! Busy production tries to make up for lack of storyline freshness. **90m/C VHS, DVD.** Stacy Keach, Billy Dee Williams, Dan Lauria, Bobby Jacoby, Suzanne Davis, Ethan Erickson, Elizabeth Low; *D:* Serge Rodnunsky; *W:* Serge Rodnunsky; *C:* Pierre Chemaly. **VIDEO**

Fear Strikes Out 𝒮𝒮𝒮 **1957** Perkins plays Jimmy Piersall, star outfielder for the Boston Red Sox, and Malden, his demanding father, in the true story of the baseball star's battle for sanity. One of Perkins' best screen performances. **100m/B VHS.** Anthony Perkins, Karl Malden, Norma Moore, Adam Williams, Perry Wilson; ***D:*** Robert Mulligan; ***W:*** Raphael David Blau; ***M:*** Elmer Bernstein.

Fearless 🦴 **1978** An Italian detective has found a Viennese banker's daughter, but continues to pursue the unanswered questions of the case, embroiling himself in a web of intrigue and plotting. **89m/C VHS.** Joan Collins, Maurizio Merli, Franz Antel.

Fearless 🦴🦴🦴 **1993 (R)** Two plane crash survivors reach out to each other as they try and cope with everday life. Bridges is riveting as the transformed Max, and Perez compelling as the sorrowful Carla. Hulce provides dead-on amusement as a casualty lawyer who knows he's slime but can't help himself. Opening sequences of smoke in the corn fields are haunting as are flashbacks of the crash itself. Weir provides an engrossing look at facing death, both psychological and spiritual, but the ending is something of a letdown in its sappiness. Based on the novel by Yglesias. **122m/C VHS, DVD, Wide.** Jeff Bridges, Isabella Rossellini, Rosie Perez, Tom Hulce, John Turturro, Benicio Del Toro, Deirdre O'Connell, John de Lancie; ***D:*** Peter Weir; ***W:*** Rafael Yglesias; ***C:*** Allen Daviau; ***M:*** Maurice Jarre. L.A. Film Critics '93: Support. Actress (Perez).

Fearless Tiger 🦴½ **1994 (R)** Martial arts action flick includes the usual combination of fierce swordplay, hand-to-hand showdowns, and the intrigue of exotic locations. **?m/C VHS.** Bolo Yeung, Monika Schnarre, Jamie Farr, Jalal Merhi; ***D:*** Ron Hulme; ***W:*** Ron Hulme; ***M:*** Varouje.

The Fearless Vampire Killers 🦴🦴🦴 *Pardon Me, Your Teeth Are in My Neck; Dance of the Vampires* **1967** Underrated, off-off-beat, and deliberately campy spoof of vampire films in which Tate is kidnapped by some fangy villains. Vampire trackers MacGowran and Polanski pursue the villains to the haunted castle and attempt the rescue. Only vampire movie with a Jewish bloodsucker ("Boy, have you got the wrong vampire," he proclaims to a maiden thrusting a crucifix at him). Inside the castle, Polanski is chased by the count's gay vampire son. Highlight is the vampire ball with a wonderful mirror scene. Many other amusing moments. **98m/C VHS, Wide.** *GB* Jack MacGowran, Roman Polanski, Alfie Bass, Jessie Robbins, Sharon Tate, Ferdinand "Ferdy" Mayne, Iain Quarrier, Terry Downes, Fiona Lewis, Ronald Lacey; ***D:*** Roman Polanski; ***W:*** Gerard Brach, Roman Polanski; ***C:*** Douglas Slocombe; ***M:*** Krzysztof Komeda.

Fearmaker 🦴½ *House of Fear; Violent Rage* **1989 (PG)** After the mysterious death of her father, the heiress to his fortune is tangled in a web of treachery created by other potential inheritors. **90m/C VHS.** *MX* Katy Jurado, Paul Picerni, Sonia Amelio, Carlos East; ***D:*** Anthony Carras.

Feast for the Devil 🦴½ **197?** A woman searches for her missing sister in a mysterious coastal village, only to fall under the occult spell of a mad doctor. **90m/C VHS.** Krista Nell, Teresa Gimpera.

Feast of July 🦴🦴 **1995 (R)** Victorian-era drama, adapted from an H. E. Bates novel, has young Bella (Davidtz) pregnant and abandoned by super-cad Arch (Wise) whom she sets out to find. After a miscarriage, she is taken in by the Wainwright family where she becomes the object of the affections of the three grown sons. Predictably, she falls for and weds the troubled loafer, Con (Chaplin). Naturally (this being Victorian England) tragedy results. Well-crafted, a given considering the producers, but ultimately a familiar telling of an average story. Feature film debut for director Menaul, after an award-winning career in British TV. **116m/C VHS.** Embeth Davidtz, Ben Chaplin, Tom Bell, Gemma Jones, James Purefoy, Kenneth Anderson, Greg Wise; ***D:*** Christopher Menaul; ***W:*** Christopher Neame; ***C:*** Peter Sova; ***M:*** Zbigniew Preisner.

Federal Agent 🦴🦴 **1936** Lots of cliches fill this crime film about a federal agent chasing foreign spys who are looking for a new explosive. **53m/B VHS.** William Boyd, Charles A. Browne, Irene Ware, George Cooper, Lentia Lace, Dan Alvarado; ***D:*** Sam Newfield.

Federal Agents vs. Underworld, Inc. *Golden Hands of Kurigal* **1949** Super G-Man Dave Worth goes up against Nila, a greedy villainess bent on finding the golden hands of Kurigal so she may rule the world. A 12-episode serial edited onto two cassettes. **167m/B VHS.** Kirk Alyn, Rosemary La Planche, Roy Barcroft, Carol Forman, James Dale, Bruce Edwards; ***D:*** Fred Brannon.

Federal Hill 🦴🦴 **1994 (R)** Familiar plot and characters are still well-handled by cast and first time writer/director Corrente. Federal Hill is a working-class, Little Italy section of Providence, Rhode Island. Five buddies, mostly losers, hang out together at a weekly card game. Nicky's (De Sando) a small-time dealer who meets his uptown Brown University sweetie, Wendy (Langdon), when he sells her cocaine. His friends try to warn him, especially short-fused burglar Ralphie (Turturro). And, of course, things go very wrong for practically everyone. The video is available colorized or in the director's version in B&W. **100m/B VHS.** Anthony De Sando, Nicholas Turturro, Libby Langdon, Michael Raynor, Jason Andrews, Frank Vincent, Robert Turano, Michael Corrente; ***D:*** Michael Corrente; ***W:*** Michael Corrente; ***C:*** Richard Crudo; ***M:*** Bob Held, David Bravo.

Federal Operator 99 🦴🦴½ **1945** A fortune in stolen jewels, a chemical plant, and a priceless violin all figure in this 12 chapter serial. And it's up to Jerry Blake, Federal Operator 99, to save the day. Part of "The Cliffhanger Serials" series. **169m/B VHS.** Marten Lamont, Helen Talbot, George Lewis.

Federal Protection 🦴½ **2002 (R)** Chicago mobster Frank Carbone (Assante) decides to go into the witness protection program after barely surviving a hit. But his suburban neighborhood heats up when next-door neighbor Leigh (Featherstone) finds out her husband is cheating on her with her own sister (Meyer) and she turns to Frank for comfort. Meanwhile, Frank is finding life a little too quiet and decides to stir things up by contacting his former partners. Slickly-made genre piece if you don't mind watching a familiar story. **94m/C VHS, DVD.** Armand Assante, Angela Featherstone, Dina Meyer, David Lipper, Maxim Roy, Tony Calabretta; ***D:*** Anthony Hickox; ***W:*** Craig Smith.

Feds 🦴½ **1988 (PG-13)** Two women enter the FBI Academy and take on the system's inherent sexism with feebly comic results. **82m/C VHS.** Rebecca DeMornay, Mary Gross, Ken Marshall, Fred Dalton Thompson, Larry Cedar, James Luisi, Raymond Singer; ***D:*** Dan Goldberg; ***W:*** Dan Goldberg, Len Blum; ***M:*** Randy Edelman.

Feel My Pulse 🦴🦴 **1928** Silent comedy about a rich fanatic who leaves everything in his will to his young niece on the stipulation that she lead a germ-free life; when she reaches 21, she moves into the sanitarium she's inherited, not knowing it has become a base for prohibition-era rum runners. **86m/B VHS.** Bebe Daniels, Richard Arlen, William Powell; ***D:*** Gregory La Cava.

Feel the Motion 🦴 **1986** A female auto-mechanic wants to make it big in the music biz. She sees her chance when she slips her demo tape onto a hit TV-music show. **98m/C VHS.** Sissy Kelling, Frank Meyer-Brockman, Ingold Locke, Falco, Meat Loaf Aday.

Feelin' Screwy 🦴 **1990** A couple of misfit dweebs attempt to rid their town of the local drug dealer in order to impress a couple of babes in this limp coming-of-ager. **90m/C VHS.** Quincy Reynolds, Larry Gamal, Darin McBride, Hassan Jamal, Marsha Carter, Brooks Morales, Anna Fuentes; ***D:*** Riffat A. Khan; ***W:*** Riffat A. Khan.

Feelin' Up woof! **1976 (R)** A young man sells all his possessions to come to New York in search of erotic adventures. **84m/C VHS.** Malcolm Groome, Kathleen Seward, Rhonda Hansome, Tony Collado, Charles Douglass; ***D:*** David Secter.

Feeling Minnesota 🦴 **1996 (R)** A truly stupid movie about truly stupid, mostly nasty people. Petty criminal Jjaks (Reeves) shows up at sleazy older brother Sam's (D'Onofrio) wedding and promptly falls for beautiful-but-unhappy bride Freddie (Diaz), who's being forced into the marriage by local crime boss Red (Lindo). Manipulative Freddie easily convinces Jjaks to run away to Vegas with her but Sam isn't willing to let his bride go so easily. The only character who comes off with any dignity is the diner waitress played by Love. A very lame first effort from Baigelman. Title's from a Soundgarden song about "looking California and feeling Minnesota." **96m/C VHS, DVD.** Keanu Reeves, Cameron Diaz, Vincent D'Onofrio, Delroy Lindo, Dan Aykroyd, Courtney Love, Tuesday Weld, Levon Helm; ***D:*** Steven Baigelman; ***W:*** Steven Baigelman; ***C:*** Walt Lloyd.

Feet First 🦴🦴½ **1930** A shoe salesman puts on "upper crust" airs as he begins a shipboard romance with a girl who thinks he's wealthy. Lloyd's second sound film shows him grappling with technique and has scenes that recall highlights of his silent hits. **85m/B VHS.** Harold Lloyd, Barbara Kent, Robert McWade; ***D:*** Clyde Bruckman.

Felicia's Journey 🦴🦴🦴 **1999 (PG-13)** Joseph Ambrose Hilditch (Hoskins) is a mild-mannered, fastidious, middle-aged Brit whose mother problems have turned him into a serial killer. He's a catering manager who watches tapes of his flamboyant late mother Gala's (Khanjian) cooking show, where young Hilditch was an embarassed foil. Into his structured world stumbles pregnant Irish teen, Felicia (Cassidy), who's trying to find the father of her baby. Hilditch begins to take a warped interest in Felicia, who may be naive but who isn't dumb. Cold and elegant adaptation of William Trevor's novel. **111m/C VHS, DVD, Wide.** *CA GB* Bob Hoskins, Elaine Cassidy, Arsinee Khanjian, Peter McDonald, Gerard McSorley, Brid Brennan, Claire Benedict; ***D:*** Atom Egoyan; ***W:*** Atom Egoyan; ***C:*** Paul Sarossy; ***M:*** Mychael Danna. Genie '99: Actor (Hoskins), Adapt. Screenplay, Cinematog., Score.

Felix the Cat: The Movie 🦴½ **1991** Classic cartoon creation Felix returns in a trite feature. The feline and his bag of tricks enter a dimension filled with He-Man/Mutant Ninja Turtles leftovers; new-age princess, comic reptiles, robots and a Darth Vader clone who's defeated with ridiculous ease. Strictly for undemanding kids. **83m/C VHS.** ***D:*** Tibor Hernadi; ***V:*** Chris Phillips, Alice Playten, Maureen O'Connell.

Fellini Satyricon 🦴🦴🦴 *Satyricon* **1969 (R)** Fellini's famous, garish, indulgent pastiche vision of ancient Rome, based on the novel "Satyricon" by Petronius, follows the adventures of two young men through the decadences of Nero's reign. Actually an exposition on the excesses of the 1960s, with the actors having little to do other than look good and react to any number of sexual situations. Crammed with excesses of every variety. In Italian with English subtitles. **129m/C VHS, DVD, Wide.** *IT FR* Martin Potter, Capucine, Hiram Keller, Salvo Randone, Max Born, Alain Cuny; ***D:*** Federico Fellini; ***W:*** Federico Fellini, Barnardino Zapponi; ***C:*** Giuseppe Rotunno; ***M:*** Nino Rota.

Fellini's Roma 🦴🦴½ *Roma* **1972 (R)** Fellini reviews his youth in this stream-of-consciousness homage to Rome and Italy. Best left for fervent Fellini fans. **128m/C VHS, Wide.** *FR IT* Peter Gonzales, Britta Barnes, Pia de Doses, Fiona Florence, Marne Maitland, Renato Giovannoli; ***Cameos:*** Gore Vidal, Anna Magnani, Marcello Mastroianni; ***D:*** Federico Fellini; ***W:*** Federico Fellini; ***C:*** Giuseppe Rotunno; ***M:*** Nino Rota; ***V:*** Federico Fellini.

Fellow Traveler 🦴🦴🦴 **1989** Two old friends, an actor and a screenwriter, both successful, get blacklisted for reputed Communist leanings in 1950s Hollywood. Good performances and a literate script. **97m/C VHS.** Ron Silver, Hart Bochner, Daniel J. Travanti, Imogen Stubbs, Katherine Borowitz, Jonathan Hyde; ***D:*** Philip Saville; ***M:*** Colin Towns. CABLE

Felony 🦴½ **1995 (R)** Police seek revenge when 12 cops are murdered. Turns out the culprit is a rogue CIA agent, whose spree was captured on video by a tabloid-show cameraman. **90m/C VHS.** Lance Henriksen, Leo Rossi, Joe Don Baker, Charles Napier, Ashley Laurence, Cory Everson; ***D:*** David A. Prior; ***W:*** David A. Prior; ***M:*** Jan A.P. Kaczmarek.

Female 🦴🦴½ **1933** Feminist look at life in the '30s stars Chatterton as the wealthy president of an auto factory who wines and dines the office men and then gives them the strictly business line the next day. However, she finally meets her match when Brent walks through the door. (The two stars were a real-life married couple at the time.) Funny, role-reversal story directed by Curtiz of "Casablanca" fame. Based on a story by Donald Henderson Clark. **60m/B VHS.** Ruth Chatterton, George Brent, Philip Reed, Ruth Donnelly, Johnny Mack Brown, Lois Wilson, Gavin Gordon, Ferdinand Gottschalk; ***D:*** Michael Curtiz, William Dieterle; ***W:*** Gene Markey, Kathryn Scola.

The Female Bunch woof! **1969 (R)** The man-free world of an all-woman settlement is shattered by the arrival of a handsome stranger. Some of this garbage was filmed on location at the notorious Charles Manson ranch, and that's the least of its flaws. **86m/C VHS.** Jennifer Bishop, Russ Tamblyn, Lon Chaney Jr., Nesa Renet, Geoffrey Land, Regina Carrol; ***D:*** Al Adamson, John Cardos.

The Female Jungle 🦴 *The Hangover* **1956** Below-average whocares whodunit directed by Roger Corman stock-company actor Ve Sota. Police sergeant Tierney is caught between a rock and a hard place. The prime suspect in a murder case, Tierney discovers a series of clues that implicate his friend Carradine. Interesting only for the screen debut of the nympho-typecast Miss Jayne—of whom Bette Davis said "Dramatic art in her opinion is knowing how to fill a sweater." **56m/B VHS.** Lawrence Tierney, John Carradine, Jayne Mansfield, Burt Kaiser, Kathleen Crowley, James Kodl, Duane Grey, Jack Hill, Bruno VeSota; ***D:*** Bruno VeSota; ***W:*** Burt Kaiser, Bruno VeSota; ***C:*** Elwood "Woody" Bredell; ***M:*** Nicholas Carras.

Female Perversions 🦴🦴 **1996 (R)** Psycho-sexual story of Los Angeles attorney Eve Stephens (Swinton), who, because of bizarre dreams and fantasies, leads a dual life. Successful Eve is being considered for appointment as a judge, but her enormous insecurity and neuroses only increase, landing her in kinky relationships with both sexes. During an unlikely reunion with her sister, Madelyn (Madigan), a kleptomaniac with a Ph.D., Eve is forced to spend time with Madelyn's motley roommates—her landlady and the landlady's odd daughter and sister. This semi-reunion brings about some self-realization on the part of both sisters about their dysfunctional behavior. Filled with detailed symbolism, powerful imagery, and dream sequences. Rife with Freudian psychology, movie is based on Louise J. Kaplan's feminist study on female behavior and sexuality, "Female Perversions: The Temptations of Emma Bovary." Extremely glossy visuals and rich production design brings life to this rather heavy story. **110m/C VHS.** Tilda Swinton, Amy Madigan, Karen Sillas, Laila Robins, Clancy Brown, Frances Fisher, Paulina Porizkova, Lisa Jane Persky, Dale Shuger; ***D:*** Susan Streitfeld; ***W:*** Susan Streitfeld, Julie Hebert; ***C:*** Teresa Medina; ***M:*** Debbie Wiseman.

Female Trouble 🦴🦴½ **1974 (R)** Divine leads a troublesome existence in this $25,000 picture. She turns to a life of crime and decadence, seeking to live out her philosophy: "Crime is beauty." Look closely at the Divine rape scene where she plays both rapist and victim. Climax of her deviant ways comes with her unusual night club act, for which the law shows no mercy. Trashy, campy; for die-hard Waters fans. **95m/C VHS, DVD, Wide.** Divine, David Lochary, Mary Vivian Pearce, Mink Stole, Edith Massey, Cookie Mueller, Susan Walsh, Michael Potter, Ed Peranio, Paul Swift, George Figgs, Susan Lowe, Channing Wilroy, Pat Moran, Elizabeth Coffey, George Stover; ***D:*** John Waters; ***W:*** John Waters; ***C:*** John Waters.

Female Vampire *Erotikill; The Loves of Irina; Les Avaleuses; The Bare Breasted Contessa* **1973** Franco's dreamy, sanguine, produced-on-a-dime tale of a vampiress. She cruises the Riviera, seducing and nibbling on a variety of men and women. Not for most tastes. **95m/C VHS, DVD, Wide.** *FR SP GE* Lina Romay, Monica Swin, Jack Taylor, Alice Arno; ***D:*** Jess (Jesus) Franco; ***C:*** Jess (Jesus) Franco; ***M:*** Daniel White.

Femalien **1996 (R)** Advanced alien beings, composed of pure light energy, travel to earth to assume corporal form so they can once again experience sensual pleasure. **90m/C VHS, DVD.** Vanessa Taylor, Jacqueline Lovell, Matt Schue; ***D:*** Cybil Richards, David DeCoteau; ***W:*** Cybil Richards, David DeCoteau. **VIDEO**

Femme Fatale ½ *Fatal Woman* **1990 (R)** When a man's new bride disappears he teams up with an artist pal to track her down. Their search reveals her secret double life and takes them to L.A.'s avant-garde art scene—and deeper into deception and mystery. Billy Zane (Elijah) and Lisa Zane are brother and sister. **96m/C VHS.** Colin Firth, Lisa Zane, Billy Zane, Scott Wilson, Lisa Blount; ***D:*** Andre Guttfreund; ***W:*** John Brancato.

Femme Fontaine: Killer Babe for the C.I.A. woof! **1995 (R)** Beautiful assassin Drew "Killer Babe" Fontaine (Hope) gets help from CIA-agent-turned-monk Master Sun (Hong) in order to avenge her father's death. Fishnet-clad women with big guns are always a Troma treat. **93m/C VHS.** Margot Hope, James Hong, Arthur Roberts, Catherine Dao, David Shark, Kevin Fry, Harry Mok; ***D:*** Margot Hope; ***W:*** Margot Hope; ***C:*** Gary Graver; ***M:*** Gardner Cole.

Femmes de Paris **1953** A funny and risque French musical comedy about the comings and goings of the cast of a naughty nightclub shows. In French with English subtitles. **79m/C VHS.** *FR* Robert Dhery, Collette Brosset, Louis de Funes.

The Fence ½ **1994** Interesting presentation of standard bad boy grows up, attempts to go straight. Terry Griff (Wirth) has been bounced from juvenile detention to prison since he was 15. On the streets for the first time in 14 years, Terry wants to lead a clean life with potential girlfriend Jackie (Gimp). But when Terry gets on the wrong side of his dishonest parole officer, the harsh world of the streets pulls him back. Bleak urban drama with sincere performances. **90m/C VHS, DVD.** Billy Wirth, Erica Gimpel, Marc Alaimo, Paul Benjamin, Lorenzo Clemons; ***D:*** Peter Pistor; ***W:*** Peter Fedorenko; ***C:*** John Newby; ***M:*** Jeff Beal.

The Fencing Master ½ **1992** The fencing master is the aristocratic Don Jaime de Astarloa (Antonutti) who secretly takes on female pupil, Adela de Otero (Serna), with whom he begins to fall in love. But when another pupil is murdered by de Astarloa's signature thrust to the throat, Don Jaime finds himself caught up in a bewildering world of political intrigue. Adapted from the novel by Antonio Perez Reverte. Spanish with subtitles. **88m/C VHS.** *SP* Assumpta Serna, Omero Antonutti, Joaquim de Almeida; ***D:*** Pedro Olea; ***W:*** Pedro Olea; ***C:*** Alfredo Mayo.

Fer-De-Lance ½ *Operation Serpent* **1974** A stricken submarine is trapped at the bottom of the sea, with a nest of deadly snakes crawling through the ship. **120m/C VHS.** David Janssen, Hope Lange, Ivan Dixon, Jason Evers; ***D:*** Russ Mayberry. **TV**

Fergie & Andrew: Behind Palace Doors **1993** More soap-opera from the British royals in this tale of feisty redhead, Sarah Ferguson, and the neglectful Prince Andrew. He's away a lot, she's bored by all the palace propriety and causes too many scandals, and their marriage falls apart. **92m/C VHS.** Pippa Hinchley, Sam Miller, Peter Cellier, Harold Innocent, Edita Brychta; ***D:*** Michael Switzer. **TV**

Fernandel the Dressmaker ½ **1957** Fernandel dreams of designing exquisite dresses, but when the opportunity arises, he finds his cheating partners get in the way. In French with English subtitles. **95m/B VHS, 8mm.** *FR* Fernandel, Suzy Delair, Francoise Fabian, Georges Chamarat; ***D:*** Jean Boyer.

Ferngully: The Last Rain Forest ½ **1992 (G)** Animated eco-musical follows the adventures of independent-minded flying sprite Crysta, who lives in a rain forest beset by pollution. She discovers the outside world and becomes smitten with the human Zak, who is helping to cut down the forest. Crysta decides to reduce him to her size and show him the error of his ways. She's aided by fellow sprite, Pips, and a crazy bat (Batty Koda with a voice provided by the lively Williams). So-so script with politically pristine environmental message may grow tiresome for both adults and children, though decent animation and brilliant coloring enlivens the tale. **80m/C VHS, DVD, Wide.** ***D:*** Bill Kroyer; ***W:*** Jim Cox; ***M:*** Alan Silvestri; ***V:*** Samantha Mathis, Christian Slater, Robin Williams, Tim Curry, Jonathan Ward, Grace Zabriskie, Richard "Cheech" Marin, Thomas Chong, Tone Loc, Jim Cox.

Ferocious Female Freedom Fighters **1988** A typical foreign-made action flick with female wrestlers is spoofed by the L.A. Connection comedy troupe which did the totally ridiculous dubbed dialog. **90m/C VHS.** Eva Arnaz, Barry Prima, Leyli Sagita, Wieke Widowati, Ruth Pelupessi, Aminah Cendrakasih; ***D:*** Yopi Burnama; ***W:*** Deddy Armand, Charles Kaufman, Joey Gaynor; ***C:*** Asmawi; ***M:*** Gatot Sudarto.

Ferris Bueller's Day Off **1986 (PG-13)** It's almost graduation and if Ferris can get away with just one more sick day—it had better be a good one. He sweet talks his best friend into borrowing his dad's antique Ferrari and sneaks his girlfriend out of school to spend a day in Chicago. Their escapades lead to fun, adventure, and almost getting caught. Broderick is charismatic as the notorious Bueller with Grey amusing as his tattletale sister doing everything she can to see him get caught. Early Sheen appearance as a juvenile delinquent who pesters Grey. Led to TV series. One of Hughes' more solid efforts. **103m/C VHS, DVD, 8mm.** Matthew Broderick, Mia Sara, Alan Ruck, Jeffrey Jones, Jennifer Grey, Cindy Pickett, Edie McClurg, Charlie Sheen, Del Close, Virginia Capers, Max Perlich, Louie Anderson, Richard Edson, Lyman Ward, Kristy Swanson, Larry "Flash" Jenkins, Ben Stein; ***D:*** John Hughes; ***W:*** John Hughes; ***C:*** Tak Fujimoto; ***M:*** Ira Newborn.

Ferry to Hong Kong ½ **1959** World-weary, heavy drinking traveler comes aboard the "Fat Annie," a ship skippered by the pompous Captain Hart. The two men clash, until an act of heroism brings them together. Embarrassingly hammy performance by Welles as the ferry skipper. **103m/C VHS.** Curt Jurgens, Orson Welles, Sylvia Syms; ***D:*** Lewis Gilbert.

The Feud **1990 (R)** Wacky comedy about the ultimate "family feud." The Bullards of Millville and the Bealers of Hornbeck engage in a battle of the witless, and no one in either town is safe. A silly, irreverent comedy of the slapstick variety. Based on a novel by Thomas Berger. **87m/C VHS.** Rene Auberjonois, Ron McLarty, Joe Grifasi, David Strathairn, Gale Mayron; ***D:*** Bill D'Elia; ***W:*** Bill D'Elia.

Feud Maker ½ **1938** Steele rides to the rescue in this range war between the bad guys and the cowmen. Hackett plays a schemer who falsely befriends both sides, plotting to buy up cheap land when the participants have killed each other off. Based on a story by Harry F. Olmsted. **55m/B VHS.** Bob Steele, Marion Weldon, Karl Hackett, Frank Ball, Budd Buster, Lew Meehan, Roger Williams; ***D:*** Sam Newfield; ***W:*** George Plympton.

Feud of the Trail **1937** A cowboy saves a range family's gold and falls in love with their daughter in the process. Tyler plays both the hero and the villain here. **56m/B VHS.** Tom Tyler, Harlin Wood, Guinn "Big Boy" Williams; ***D:*** Robert F. "Bob" Hill.

Feud of the West ½ **1935** Old West disagreements settled with guns in this outing for cowboy star Gibson, here portraying a rodeo performer. **60m/B VHS.** Hoot Gibson, Buzz Barton, Robert F. (Bob) Kortman, Edward Cassidy, Joan Barclay, Nelson McDowell, Reed Howes, Lew Meehan; ***D:*** Harry Fraser.

Fever **1981** Controversial Polish film based on Andrzej Strug's novel "The Story of One Bomb." Focusing on a period in Polish history marked by anarchy, violence, resistance, and revolution, it was banned before it won eventual acclaim at the Gdansk Film Festival. In Polish with English subtitles. **115m/C VHS.** *PL* ***D:*** Agnieszka Holland.

Fever **1988 (R)** A once-honest cop trades his good life in for a shot at dealing drugs. Meanwhile, his wife's lover wants to murder him. **83m/C VHS.** Bill Hunter, Gary Sweet, Mary Regan, Jim Holt; ***D:*** Craig Lahiff.

Fever **1991 (R)** An ex-con and a high-powered lawyer join forces to rescue the woman both of them love from a vicious killer. Available in Spanish. **99m/C VHS.** Armand Assante, Sam Neill, Marcia Gay Harden, Joe Spano; ***D:*** Larry Elikann; ***W:*** Larry Brothers. **CABLE**

Fever **1999 (R)** Twenty-something Nick Parker (Thomas) is a struggling artist living in a Brooklyn tenement and fighting a losing battle to keep both his physical health and his sanity. Neither are helped when his landlord's murder leads to a police investigation; a suspicious new tenant moves into the apartment above Nick's; and Nick realizes that he's been sleepwalking. Since the film is told from his fractured point-of-view, the viewer can never be sure just what's real. **90m/C VHS, DVD, Wide.** Henry Thomas, David O'Hara, Bill Duke, Teri Hatcher, Sandor Tecsi, Irma St. Paul, Marisol Padilla Sanchez; ***D:*** Alex Winter; ***W:*** Alex Winter; ***C:*** Joe DeSalvo; ***M:*** Joe Delia.

Fever Mounts at El Pao ½ *Los Ambiciosos* **1959** A minor effort from director Bunuel about the regime of a dictator in an imaginary South American country. In Spanish with English subtitles. **97m/B VHS.** *MX* Gerard Philipe, Jean Servais; ***D:*** Luis Bunuel.

Fever Pitch woof! **1985 (R)** Sordid story of a sports writer (O'Neal) who becomes addicted to gambling. Very poor script. **95m/C VHS.** Ryan O'Neal, Catherine Hicks, Giancarlo Giannini, Bridgette Andersen, Chad Everett, John Saxon, William Smith, Patrick Cassidy, Chad McQueen; ***D:*** Richard Brooks; ***W:*** Richard Brooks; ***M:*** Thomas Dolby.

Fever Pitch ½ **1996 (R)** Mildly amusing sports/romance based on Nick Hornby's 1992 sports memoir and set in late '80s London. English teacher/school coach Paul Ashworth (Firth) is an obsessed fan of the Arsenal football (soccer) club. Although completely oppposite in temperament, Paul begins a romance with fellow teacher, Sarah (Gemmell), who's only mildly interested in sports. When Sarah gets pregnant, they drift apart as Sarah begins more and more to resent Paul's perpetual adolescent behavior. Finally, it all comes down to Arsenal's championship match and how they both react. **103m/C VHS, DVD, Wide.** *GB* Colin Firth, Ruth Gemmell, Neil Pearson, Mark Strong, Holly Aird, Ken Stott, Stephen Rea, Lorraine Ashbourne; ***D:*** David Evans; ***W:*** Nick Hornby; ***C:*** Chris Seager; ***M:*** Neil MacColl, Boo Hewerdine.

A Few Good Men ½ **1992 (R)** Strong performances by Cruise and Nicholson carry this story of a peacetime military coverup. Cruise is a smart aleck Navy lawyer sleepwalking through his comfortable career in DC. He's ready to write off two soldiers pinned for the murder of their cohort until he interviews their commanding officer, Nicholson. Cruise smells a rat, but Nicholson practically dares him to prove it. Moore is another military lawyer assigned to the case, though her function seems to be holding Kaffee's hand (there's no actual romance between the two). Incredible fireworks between Cruise and Nicholson in the courtroom. Based on the play by Sorkin, who also wrote the screenplay. **138m/C VHS, DVD, Wide.** Tom Cruise, Jack Nicholson, Demi Moore, Kevin Bacon, Kevin Pollak, Kiefer Sutherland, James Marshall, J.T. Walsh, Christopher Guest, J.A. Preston, Matt Craven, Wolfgang Bodison, Xander Berkeley, Cuba Gooding Jr., Noah Wyle; ***D:*** Rob Reiner; ***W:*** Aaron Sorkin; ***C:*** Robert Richardson; ***M:*** Marc Shaiman. MTV Movie Awards '93: Film; Natl. Bd. of Review '92: Support. Actor (Nicholson).

ffolkes *Assault Force; North Sea Hijack* **1980 (PG)** Rufus Excalibur Ffolkes is an eccentric underwater expert who is called upon to stop a madman (Perkins, indulging himself) from blowing up an oil rig in the North Sea. Entertaining farce with Moore playing the opposite of his usual suave James Bond character. **99m/C VHS.** Roger Moore, James Mason, Anthony Perkins, David Hedison, Michael Parks; ***D:*** Andrew V. McLaglen.

The Fiance **1996 (R)** Faith (Anthony) suspects husband Richard (Cassidy) of being unfaithful and confides her suspicions to the friendly Walter (Moses). Only the unbalanced guy then becomes unhealthily involved in Faith's life. **94m/C VHS.** William R. Moses, Lysette Anthony, Patrick Cassidy, Alina Thompson, Wanda Acuna, Gordon Thomson; ***D:*** Martin Kitrosser; ***W:*** Greg Walker, Frank Rehwaldt; ***C:*** M. David Mullen; ***M:*** Richard Bowers. **VIDEO**

Fiances *The Engagement; I Fidanzati* **1963** Young man from Milan takes a welding job in Sicily that will separate him from his fiancee for 18 months. He thinks the separation will be good for them but loneliness and the strange environment makes him long for her. Non-professional leads provide strength. Italian with subtitles. **84m/B VHS.** *IT* Carlo Carbrini, Anna Canzi; ***D:*** Ermanno Olmi; ***W:*** Ermanno Olmi; ***C:*** Lamberto Caimi; ***M:*** Gianni Ferrio.

Fiction Makers **1967** Roger Moore stars as Simon Templar, also known as "The Saint," a sophisticated detective who is hired to help Amos Klein. Klein turns out to be an alias for a beautiful novelist who is being threatened by the underworld crime ring. Based on the Leslie Chateris' character. **102m/C VHS.** Roger Moore, Sylvia Syms.

Fictitious Marriage **1988** Eldad Ilan, a high school teacher experiencing a mid-life crisis, travels to Israel to get away from his family in order to consider his life's direction. In Hebrew with English subtitles. **90m/C VHS.** Shlomo Bar-Aba, Irit Sheleg, Ofra Veingarten; ***D:*** Haim Bouzaglo.

Fiddler on the Roof ½ **1971 (G)** Based on the long-running Broadway musical. The poignant story of Tevye, a poor Jewish milkman at the turn of the century in a small Ukrainian village, and his five dowry-less daughters, his lame horse, his wife, and his companionable relationship with God. Topol, an Israeli who played the role in London, is charming, if not quite as wonderful as Zero Mostel, the Broadway star. Finely detailed set decoration and choreography, strong performances from the entire cast create a sense of intimacy in spite of near epic proportions of the production. Play was based on the Yiddish stories of Tevye the Dairyman, written by Sholem Aleichem. ♫Tradition; Matchmaker, Matchmaker; If I Were a Rich Man; Sabbath Prayer; To Life; Miracle of Miracles; Tevye's Dream; Sunrise, Sunset; Wedding Celebration. **184m/C VHS, DVD, Wide.** Chaim Topol, Norma Crane, Leonard Frey, Molly Picon, Paul Mann, Rosalind Harris, Michele Marsh, Neva Small, Paul Michael Glaser, Ray Lovelock; ***D:*** Norman Jewison; ***W:*** Joseph Stein; ***C:*** Oswald Morris; ***M:*** John Williams. Oscars '71: Cinematog., Sound, Orig. Song Score and/or Adapt.; Golden Globes '72: Actor—Mus./Comedy (Topol), Film—Mus./Comedy.

The Fiddlin' Buckaroo ½ **1933** Maynard plays a government agent who disguises himself as a musical ventriloquist to capture Kohler and his band of outlaws. Everybody sings a lot. **63m/B VHS.** Ken Maynard, Gloria Shea, Fred Kohler Sr., Frank Rice, Jack Mower, Charles "Slim" Whitaker, Robert F. (Bob) Kortman, Hank Bell, Jack Rockwell; ***D:*** Ken Maynard; ***W:*** Nate Gatzert.

Fidel **2002** Excellent bio of Fidel Castro's rise to power in Cuba loses a little steam in its later moments but keeps interest with a strong performance by Martin in the title role. The politics are also kept simple; Castro is an idealistic lawyer who fights for the underdog as a rebel leader after his country's military takeover by Batista (Plana). But once he himself takes power, Castro blurs the lines into a dictatorship of his own. Based on the books "Guerilla Prince" by Georgie Anne Geyer and "Fidel Castro" by Robert E. Quirk. **140m/C VHS, DVD.** Victor Huggo Martin, Gael Garcia Bernal, Patricia Velasquez, Maurice Compte, Tony Plana, Guillermo Diaz, Margarita d'Francisco, Enrique Arce; ***D:*** David Attwood; ***W:*** Stephen Tolkin; ***C:*** Checco Varese; ***M:*** John Altman. CABLE

The Field 🦴🦴🦴½ **1990 (PG-13)** After an absence from the big screen, intense and nearly over the top Harris won acclaim as an iron-willed peasant fighting to retain a patch of Irish land he's tended all his life, now offered for sale to a wealthy American. His uncompromising stand divides the community in this glowing adaptation of John B. Keane's classic play, an allegory of Ireland's internal conflicts. **113m/C VHS, DVD, Wide.** *GB* Richard Harris, Tom Berenger, John Hurt, Sean Bean, Brenda Fricker, Frances Tomelty, John Cowley, Sean McGinley, Jenny Conroy; ***D:*** Jim Sheridan; ***W:*** Jim Sheridan; ***C:*** Jack Conroy; ***M:*** Elmer Bernstein.

Field of Dreams 🦴🦴🦴½ **1989 (PG)** Uplifting mythic fantasy based on W.P. Kinsella's novel "Shoeless Joe." Iowa corn farmer Ray Kinsella (Costner) heeds a mysterious voice that instructs "If you build it, he will come" and cuts a baseball diamond in his corn field. Soon the ball field is inhabited by the spirit of Joe Jackson (Liotta) and others who were disgraced in the notorious 1919 "Black Sox" baseball scandal. Jones is Terence Mann, a character based on reclusive author J.D. Salinger, is reluctantly pulled into the mystery. It's all about chasing a dream, maintaining innocence, finding redemption, reconciling the child with the adult, and celebrating the mythic lure of baseball. Costner and Madigan (as wife Anni) are strong, believable characters. **106m/C VHS, DVD, Wide.** Kevin Costner, Amy Madigan, James Earl Jones, Burt Lancaster, Ray Liotta, Timothy Busfield, Frank Whaley, Gaby Hoffman, Dwier Brown; ***D:*** Phil Alden Robinson; ***W:*** Phil Alden Robinson; ***C:*** John Lindley; ***M:*** James Horner.

Field of Fire 🦴🦴 **1992 (R)** One of America's top military experts has been taken hostage and it's up to a top general to rescue him. But the rescue doesn't come off as planned and all must fight their way through the Cambodian jungle to safety. **96m/C VHS.** David Carradine; ***D:*** Cirio H. Santiago; ***W:*** Thomas McKelvey Cleaver.

Field of Honor 🦴🦴½ **1986 (R)** A look at the harrowing experience of jungle combat through the eyes of a Dutch infantryman in Korea. **93m/C VHS.** Everett McGill, Ron Bradsteder, Hey Young Lee; ***D:*** Hans Scheepmaker.

Field of Honor 🦴🦴½ *Champ d'Honneur* **1987 (PG)** A quiet French anti-war drama set during the Franco-Prussian war in 1869 in which a peasant boy volunteers to fight in place of a rich man's son. He is befriended behind enemy lines by a young boy and both try to avoid capture. In French with English subtitles. **87m/C VHS.** *FR* Cris Campion, Eric Wapler, Pascale Rocard, Frederic Mayer; ***D:*** Jean-Pierre Denis. Cesar '88: Score.

The Fiend 🦴 **1971 (R)** A religious cultist, already unbalanced, grabs a knife and starts hacking away Jack-the-Ripper style. **87m/C VHS.** *GB* Ann Todd, Patrick Magee, Tony Beckley, Madeline Hinde, Suzanna Leigh, Percy Herbert; ***D:*** Robert Hartford-Davis.

Fiend woof! **1983** Glowing supernatural thing flits around graveyard before animating dead guy who needs to kill in order to go on living. Murderous dead guy becomes a small-town music teacher feeding parasitically on his students to satisfy his supernatural hunger. His neighbor suspects some discord. Low-budget time waster. **93m/C VHS.** Don Leifert, Richard Nelson, Elaine White, George Stover; ***D:*** Donald M. Dohler.

Fiend without a Face 🦴🦴 **1958** An isolated air base in Canada is the site for a scientist using atomic power in an experiment to make a person's thoughts materialize. Only his thoughts are evil and reveal themselves as flying brains with spinal cords that suck human brains right out of the skull. Tons of fun for '50s SF fans and anyone who appreciates the sheer silliness of it all. **77m/B VHS, DVD, Wide.** Marshall Thompson, Kim Parker, Terence (Terry) Kilburn, Michael Balfour, Gil Winfield, Shane Cordell, Kynaston Reeves; ***D:*** Arthur Crabtree; ***W:*** Herbert J. Leder; ***C:*** Lionel Banes; ***M:*** Buxton Orr.

The Fiendish Plot of Dr. Fu Manchu woof! **1980 (PG)** A sad farewell from Sellers, who in his last film portrays Dr. Fu in his desperate quest for the necessary ingredients for his secret life-preserving formula. Sellers portrays both Dr. Fu and the Scotland Yard detective on his trail, but it's not enough to save this picture, flawed by poor script and lack of direction. **100m/C VHS.** *GB* Peter Sellers, David Tomlinson, Sid Caesar, Helen Mirren, Simon Williams, Steve Franken, Stratford Johns, John Le Mesurier, John Sharp, Clement Harari; ***D:*** Piers Haggard; ***W:*** Rudy Dochtermann, Jim Moloney; ***C:*** Jean Tournier; ***M:*** Marc Wilkinson.

Fierce Creatures 🦴🦴 **1996 (PG-13)** This not-really-a-sequel features the same cast as "A Fish Called Wanda" and was jokingly known as "Death Fish II" until a more appropriate title was thought of. A failing London zoo gets a new lease on life, and officious new manager Rollo Lee (Cleese) by stocking only man-eating predators. This plan has kindly, insect house manager Bugsy (Palin) tongue-tied at the thought of destroying the zoo's cuddly current occupants. Kline is again in fine form with his dastardly dual role of zoo's Aussie owner Rod McCain and his idiot son, Vince. Curtis displays her obvious talents as Willa Weston, Vince's more sympathetic partner. Despite inspired moments, flick's not as tightly told or as wickedly funny as "Fish," (an admittedly tough act to follow). A family-friendlier attitude has effectively declawed this "Creature." Many scenes were reshot after unfavorable advance screenings, necessitating a new director and the recall of the actors from far and wide. **93m/C VHS, DVD.** John Cleese, Jamie Lee Curtis, Kevin Kline, Michael Palin, Ronnie Corbett, Robert Lindsay, Carey Lowell, Bille Brown, Derek Griffiths, Cynthia Cleese; ***D:*** Robert M. Young, Fred Schepisi; ***W:*** John Cleese, Iain Johnstone; ***C:*** Adrian Biddle, Ian Baker; ***M:*** Jerry Goldsmith.

Fiesta 🦴🦴½ **1995** Young, idealistic Spanish aristocrat Rafael (Colin) has been studying in France during the years since the Spanish Republic was declared. Now, it's 1936 and he has been summoned home to fight against the Communists under the command of Col. Masagual (Trintignant). Masagual assigns Rafael to the firing squad to toughen him up but Rafael eventually rediscovers his convictions and double-crosses his mentor. Based on an autobiographical novel by Jose Luis de Vilallonga. French with subtitles. **108m/C VHS.** *FR* Jean-Louis Trintignant, Gregoire Colin, Dayle Haddon, Marc Lavoine, Jean-Philippe Ecoffey, Laurent Terzieff; ***D:*** Pierre Boutron; ***W:*** Pierre Boutron; ***C:*** Javier Aguirresarobe; ***M:*** Wim Mertens.

15 Minutes 🦴🦴½ **2001 (R)** New York cop and publicity hound De Niro teams up with arson investigator Burns to hunt down a couple of violent criminals who are videotaping their crimes for celebrity purposes. Is writer/director Herzfeld exploring our culture's fascination with violence, nihilism, and fame, or just using images of those ideas to sell tickets? Most likely it's the latter, but either way, Warhol would probably approve. Grammer tries his hand at playing the sleazy, Jerry Springerish shock-TV host, and mostly pulls it off. **120m/C VHS, DVD, Wide.** *US* Robert De Niro, Edward Burns, Kelsey Grammer, Avery Brooks, Melina Kanakaredes, Vera Farmiga, Karel Roden, Oleg Taktarov, John DiResta, James Handy, Darius McCrary, Charlize Theron, Kim Cattrall, David Alan Grier; ***D:*** John Herzfeld; ***W:*** John Herzfeld; ***C:*** Jean-Yves Escoffier; ***M:*** Anthony Marinelli, J. Peter Robinson.

Fifth Avenue Girl 🦴½ **1939** An unhappy millionaire brings home a poor young woman to pose as his mistress to make his family realize how they've neglected him. As this below-par social comedy drones toward its romantic conclusion, the rich folks see the error of their ways and love conquers all. **83m/B VHS.** Ginger Rogers, Walter Connolly, Tim Holt, James Ellison, Franklin Pangborn; ***D:*** Gregory La Cava.

Fifth Day of Peace 🦴🦴 **1972 (PG)** In the aftermath of the WWI armistice, two German soldiers are tried and executed for desertion by their commander, even though the Allies forbade German military trials. An interesting plot that is marred by too obvious plot twists. Based on a true story. **95m/C VHS, DVD.** *IT* Richard Johnson, Franco Nero, Larry Aubrey, Helmut Schneider; ***D:*** Guiliano Montaldo.

The Fifth Element 🦴🦴½ **1997 (PG-13)** Besson's view of the future is colorful, loud and fashionable. Dressed in costumes by Jean Paul Gaultier, Willis (in a blonde dye job) is New York City cab driver turned unwilling hero Korban Dallas, who must save earth from destruction at the hands of evil arms dealer Zorg (Oldman). Bruce is up to the old heroics that made him a household name, and takes time to romance orange-haired nymph Jovovich, who holds the key to all the madness going on. Oldman is over-the-top as the icy villain with a distinct southern accent, which makes him more of a bad gag than a bad guy. Jumbled story fortunately takes a backseat to weird aliens and stunning visuals which makes this an eye-catching (albeit confusing) sci-fi trip. **125m/C VHS, DVD, Wide.** Bruce Willis, Gary Oldman, Ian Holm, Milla Jovovich, Luke Perry, Lee Evans, Chris Tucker, Brion James, Tommy (Tiny) Lister, John Neville, John Bluthal, Maiwenn Le Besco, Mathieu Kassovitz; ***D:*** Luc Besson; ***W:*** Luc Besson; ***C:*** Thierry Arbogast; ***M:*** Eric Serra. British Acad. '97: Visual FX; Cesar '98: Art Dir./Set Dec., Cinematog., Director (Besson).

The Fifth Floor woof! **1980 (R)** College disco dancer overdoses on drugs and winds up in an insane asylum, complete with menacing attendant Hopkins and apathetic doctor Ferrer. Pathetic, exploitative trash. **90m/C VHS.** Bo Hopkins, Dianne Hull, Patti D'Arbanville, Mel Ferrer; ***D:*** Howard (Hikmet) Avedis; ***W:*** Howard (Hikmet) Avedis.

The Fifth Monkey 🦴½ **1990 (PG-13)** A man embarks on a journey to sell four monkeys in order to fill a dowry for his bride, but along the way he encounters all sorts of obstacles and adventures. Filmed on location in Brazil **93m/C VHS.** Ben Kingsley; ***D:*** Eric Rochant; ***W:*** Eric Rochant.

The Fifth Musketeer 🦴🦴 *Behind the Iron Mask* **1979 (PG)** A campy adaptation of Dumas's "The Man in the Iron Mask," wherein a monarch's evil twin impersonates him while imprisoning the true king. A good cast and rich production shot in Austria make for a fairly entertaining swashbuckler. **90m/C** *GB* Beau Bridges, Sylvia Kristel, Ursula Andress, Cornel Wilde, Ian McShane, Alan Hale Jr., Helmut Dantine, Olivia de Havilland, Jose Ferrer, Rex Harrison; ***D:*** Ken Annakin; ***W:*** David Ambrose; ***C:*** Jack Cardiff.

The Fifth Seal 🦴🦴 **1976** A group of friends are arrested when one makes a casual remark that offends a commandant. This leads to a series of tasks that test their commitment to their moral ideals. Set at the close of WWII in Hungary. In Hungarian with English subtitles. **116m/C VHS.** *HU* ***D:*** Zoltan Fabri.

$50,000 Reward 🦴½ **1925** Maynard's first western finds him being victimized by an unscrupulous banker who wants Maynard's land deeds for property on which a new dam is being built. **49m/B VHS.** Ken Maynard, Esther Ralston.

52 Pick-Up 🦴🦴½ **1986 (R)** After a fling, a wealthy industrialist is blackmailed by a trio of repulsive criminals and determines to save himself. First he becomes deeply caught in their web of murder. Based on an Elmore Leonard novel with lots of gruesome violence and good performances. **111m/C VHS.** Roy Scheider, Ann-Margret, Vanity, John Glover, Doug McClure, Clarence Williams III, Kelly Preston, Robert Trebor, Lonny (Loni) Chapman; ***D:*** John Frankenheimer; ***W:*** John Steppling, Elmore Leonard; ***M:*** Gary Chang.

54 🦴½ **1998 (R)** The days of '70s disco, drugs, and hedonism rear their heads in this look back at New York's infamous Studio 54. Myers takes the drama route as druggie club co-owner Steve Rubell, while Phillippe starts off as innocent New Jersey boy Shane O'Shea, who gets a job as a bartender and is soon taking the low road to debauchery. Others hitting the dance floor include pouty soap star Julie (Campbell), coat-check girl/would-be disco diva Anita (Hayek), and her busboy hubby Greg (Meyer). But Shane is a dunce and his story a bore, while the effective Myers takes a decided backseat storywise. Film went through a lot of last-minute re-editing but it didn't seem to help. **92m/C VHS, DVD.** Mike Myers, Ryan Phillippe, Breckin Meyer, Salma Hayek, Neve Campbell, Sela Ward, Sherry Stringfield, Ellen A. Dow, Heather Matarazzo, Skipp (Robert L.) Sudduth; ***Cameos:*** Lauren Hutton, Michael York; ***D:*** Mark Christopher; ***W:*** Mark Christopher; ***C:*** Alexander Grusynski.

55 Days at Peking 🦴🦴🦴 **1963** A costume epic depicting the Chinese Boxer Rebellion and the fate of military Britishers caught in the midst of the chaos. Standard fare superbly handled by director Ray and an all-star cast. **150m/C VHS, Wide.** Charlton Heston, Ava Gardner, David Niven, John Ireland, Flora Robson, Paul Lukas, Jacques Sernas; ***D:*** Nicholas Ray; ***W:*** Philip Yordan; ***C:*** Jack Hildyard.

The Fig Tree **1987** After her mother passes away, Miranda becomes tormented by the fear of death. Now her aunt must help her cope with this difficult part of life. Adapted from the short story by Katherine Anne Porter. Aired on PBS as part of the "Wonderworks" family movie series. **58m/C VHS.** Olivia Cole, William Converse-Roberts, Doris Roberts, Teresa Wright, Karron Graves; ***D:*** Calvin Skaggs.

Fight Club 🦴🦴🦴½ **1999 (R)** Young, male, repressed rage comes in the form of Norton's disillusioned yuppie, emotionally numbed by chronic insomnia, who meets the answer to all his pent-up frustrations in malcontent Pitt. Tyler's his name and anarchy's his game as the duo eventually establish fight clubs where the participants beat each other up and stage massive acts of terrorism to undermine the allure of consumerism. Bonham Carter plays a kinky, death-obsessed woman both men fancy. Fincher heads for the dark side again and puts a middle finger on the pulse of several hot topics without missing a beat or skirting the issues. Film's dark humor and stylistic vision of young male malaise is made even more biting by newcomer Uhl's faithful adaptation of Chuck Palahniuk's debut novel. Performances by all three leads are equal to the powerful subject matter. **139m/C VHS, DVD, Wide.** Brad Pitt, Edward Norton, Helena Bonham Carter, Meat Loaf Aday, Jared Leto, Eion Bailey; ***D:*** David Fincher; ***W:*** Jim Uhls; ***C:*** Jeff Cronenweth; ***M:*** Howard Shore.

Fight for Gold 🦴 **1986** In the frozen wastes of the North, a man becomes embroiled in a violent quest for gold. **107m/C VHS.** *GE* Doug McClure, Harald Leipnitz, Heinz Reinl, Roberto Bianco, Angelica Ott, Kristina Nel; ***D:*** Harald Reinl.

A Fight for Jenny 🦴🦴 **1990 (PG)** Miami Viceroy Thomas and Warren play an interracial couple who fight for custody of the wife's child from a previous marriage. Standard made-for-TV meaningful drama (bite-sized issues served with a modicum of melodrama). **95m/C VHS.** Philip Michael Thomas, Lesley Ann Warren, Jean Smart, Lynne Moody, William Atherton; ***D:*** Gilbert Moses.

Fight for the Title 🦴🦴 **1957** Benny Leonard's reign as the lightweight boxing champ has just begun when WWII is declared. Against his manager's wishes, Benny decides to enlist. **30m/C VHS, DVD.** Michael Landon, George Brenlin; ***D:*** Eric Kenton.

Fight for Us 🦴½ *L'Insoumis* **1989 (R)** A social activist, recently released from prison, takes on the death squads terrorizing the countryside in post-Marcos Philippines. In Spanish with English subtitles. **92m/C VHS.** Phillip Salvador, Dina Bonnevie, Gina Alajar, Benbol Roco.

Fight for Your Life 🦴 **1979** Three escaped convicts—a white bigot, an Asian, and a Chicano—take a black minister's family hostage. After suffering all manner of vicious torture, the family exacts an equally brutal revenge. Shades of "The Desperate Hours" and "Extremities," but with much more graphic violence and a racial twist. **89m/C VHS.** *CA* William Sanderson, Robert Judd, Lela Small.

The Fighter 🦴🦴🦴 *The First Time* **1952** A Mexican patriot, involved in a struggle to overthrow a dictator, falls for a co-revolutionist. Flashbacks show the destruction of his family and village, and his pugilistic expertise, which he uses to fight for a huge purse to help the cause. Adapted from Jack London's "The Mexican." **78m/B VHS, DVD.** Richard Conte, Vanessa Brown, Lee J. Cobb, Frank Silvera, Roberta Haynes, Hugh Sanders, Claire Carleton, Martin Garralaga; ***D:*** Herbert Kline; ***W:*** Herbert Kline, Aben Kandel; ***C:*** Floyd Crosby, James Wong Howe; ***M:*** Vincente Gomez.

The Fighter 🦴½ **1995 (R)** French soldier Charlemont (Gruner) gets involved with desperate farmers opposing a greedy landlord (Ermey) and is forced to compete against former rival Ziegfield (Singer). Strange western/kickboxing hybrid that does have lots of action. **91m/C VHS.** Olivier Gruner, Marc Singer, R. Lee Ermey, Ian Ziering, James Brolin, Ashley Laurence; ***D:*** Isaac Florentine.

Fighter Attack 🦴🦴 **1953** Story of a WWII pilot, based in Corsica, who is shot down during a mission to destroy a Nazi supply station. He meets with a woman of the Italian underground, and succeeds in destroying his target with her help. **80m/C VHS.** Sterling Hayden, J. Carrol Naish, Joy Page; ***D:*** Lesley Selander.

Fightin' Ranch 🦴🦴 **1930** A famous lawman saves his reputation, previously tainted. A Maynard classic. **60m/B VHS.** Ken Maynard.

The Fighting American 🦴🦴 **1924** A frat boy proposes to a girl on a brotherly dare, and, unflattered by the fraternal proposal, the girl flees to the Far East to return to the bosom of her family. But it turns out the boy really does love the girl, by golly, and he's got just enough of that fighting American spirit to prove it. Predates Oland's Charlie Chan career by seven years. **65m/B VHS.** Pat O'Malley, Mary Astor, Raymond Hatton, Warner Oland; ***D:*** Tom Forman.

Fighting Back 🦴🦴 *Death Vengeance* **1982 (R)** Reactionary tale of an angry resident in a crime-ridden Philadelphia neighborhood who organizes a patrol of armed civilian vigilantes. The police attempt to head off a racial confrontation in this effective drama graced with some fine performances. **96m/C VHS.** Tom Skerritt, Patti LuPone, Michael Sarrazin, Yaphet Kotto; ***D:*** Lewis Teague; ***W:*** David Zelag Goodman; ***C:*** Franco Di Giacomo.

Fighting Black Kings 🦴 **1976 (PG)** Martial arts and karate masters appear in this tale of action. **90m/C VHS.** William Oliver, Charles Martin, Willie Williams, Mas Oyama.

Fighting Caballero 🦴 **1935** Lease and his pals effectively handle a gang of mine-harassing outlaws. **60m/B VHS.** Rex Lease; ***D:*** Elmer Clifton.

Fighting Caravans 🦴🦴 *Blazing Arrows* **1931** In this early big-budget western, based on a story by Zane Grey, a wagon train sets out west from Missouri. Cooper emerges as the hero after warding off an Indian attack that takes the lives of the original leaders. **80m/B VHS.** Gary Cooper, Ernest Torrence, Tully Marshall, Fred Kohler Sr., Lili Damita; ***D:*** Otto Brower, David Burton.

Fighting Champ 🦴 **1933** Cow-punching gives way to boxing as Steele steps into the ring and takes on all comers. Poor combination of riding and boxing makes for a disappointing Western. **57m/B VHS.** Bob Steele, Arletta Duncan, George "Gabby" Hayes, Charles "Blackie" King, Lafe (Lafayette) McKee, Kit Guard, George Chesebro; ***D:*** John P. McCarthy; ***W:*** Wellyn Totman.

Fighting Cowboy 🦴 **1933** Bill settles a tungsten mine dispute with a greedy miner and some outlaws. **50m/B VHS.** Buffalo Bill Jr.; ***D:*** Victor Adamson.

Fighting Devil Dogs **1938** Two Marine lieutenants are assigned the task of obtaining a deadly secret weapon controlled by crooks. A serial in 12 chapters. **195m/B VHS.** Lee Powell, Bruce (Herman Brix) Bennett; ***D:*** John English, William Witney.

Fighting Elegy 🦴🦴 *Kenka Ereji* **1966** A high school boy longs for an unattainable girl and channels all those teenaged hormones into brawling with street gangs. Then he has an encounter with an ultra-right wing militarist that changes his life and sets him on the path to fascism. Japanese with subtitles. **86m/B VHS, Wide.** *JP* Hideki Takahashi, Yusuke Kawazu, Jinko Asano, Mitsuo Kataoka; ***D:*** Seijun Suzuki.

Fighting Father Dunne 🦴🦴 **1948** Mega-hokey Hollywood steamroller about a tough priest caring for St. Louis newsboys in the early 1900s. Based on a true story. **92m/B VHS.** Pat O'Brien, Darryl Hickman, Charles Kemper, Una O'Connor, Arthur Shields, Harry Shannon, Joseph (Joe) Sawyer, Anna Q. Nilsson, Donn Gift, Myrna Dell; ***D:*** Ted Tetzlaff.

Fighting Fists of Shanghai Joe 🦴 **1965** Fearsome fighting man from the Far East engages a vile American land baron in a battle of honor. **94m/C VHS.** Klaus Kinski, Gordon Mitchell, Carla Romanelli, Robert Hundar, Chen Lee; ***D:*** Mario Caiano.

Fighting Fool 🦴 **1932** Average oater has McCoy as a sheriff constantly in pursuit of an outlaw named "The Shadow." Of course, romance blossoms between McCoy and Day, too. The real identity of "The Shadow" turns out to be quite a surprise for McCoy. **57m/B VHS.** Tim McCoy, Marceline Day, Robert Ellis, Arthur (L.) Rankin, Dorothy Granger; ***D:*** Lambert Hillyer.

Fighting Jack 🦴🦴 **1926** After he saves a girl from a watery death, a man is accused of horse stealing and trespassing. **52m/B VHS.** Bill (William N.) Bailey, Hazel Deane, Frona Hale, John Byron, Sailor Sharkey, Herma Cordova; ***D:*** Louis Chaudet.

The Fighting Kentuckian 🦴🦴½ **1949** Homeward bound from the Battle of New Orleans in 1814, a Kentucky rifleman lingers in a French settlement in Alabama. His romance with the daughter of a French general is blocked by the father until the American saves the community from an assault by land grabbers. Hardy as a frontiersman is well worth the view. An action-packed, well-photographed hit. **100m/B VHS.** John Wayne, Oliver Hardy, Vera (Hruba) Ralston, Marie Windsor, Philip Dorn, John Howard, Hugo Haas, Grant Withers; ***D:*** George Waggner.

The Fighting Legion 🦴🦴 **1930** Maynard shows his foresight here, making this one of the first westerns to fully exploit sound by adding music and singing. Standard plot has Maynard going after the villain who murdered his brother. **69m/B VHS.** Ken Maynard, Dorothy Dwan, Ernie Adams, Stanley Blystone, Frank Rice; ***D:*** Harry Joe Brown.

Fighting Mad 🦴½ **1939** A singing Mountie tangles with border-crossing robbers and saves the reputation of a woman they exploit. One of the "Renfrew of the Mounties" series. **57m/B VHS.** James Newill, Milburn Stone, Sally Blane; ***D:*** Sam Newfield.

Fighting Mad 🦴🦴½ **1976 (R)** A peaceful land owner is driven to violence when he discovers that the business men who want his property are planning to murder two of his family members in order to get it. The local sheriff's apathy forces the man to take the law into his own hands. Unlike other Fonda films of the time which consist of chaotic violence and car crashes, this story is a well performed character study. **90m/C VHS.** Peter Fonda, Lynn Lowry, John Doucette, Phil Carey, Scott Glenn, Kathleen Miller; ***D:*** Jonathan Demme; ***W:*** Jonathan Demme.

Fighting Mad 🦴½ *Fierce* **1977 (R)** Soldiers leave their buddy for dead in wartime Vietnam. He is alive, but captured by Japanese soldiers who believe they are still fighting in WWII. **96m/C VHS.** James Iglehart, Jayne Kennedy, Leon Isaac Kennedy; ***D:*** Cirio H. Santiago.

Fighting Marines 🦴½ **1936** U.S. Marines are trying to establish an air base on Halfway Island in the Pacific, but are thwarted by the "Tiger Shark," a modern-day pirate. First appeared as a serial. **69m/B VHS.** Jason Robards Sr., Grant Withers, Ann Rutherford, Pat O'Malley; ***D:*** Joseph Kane, B. Reeves Eason.

The Fighting Marshal 🦴🦴 **1932** After serving time for a crime he didn't commit, McCoy assumes the identity of a dead sheriff and tries to find the felons who done him wrong. **58m/B VHS.** Tim McCoy, Dorothy Gulliver, Mary Carr, Matthew Betz, Pat O'Malley; ***D:*** David Ross Lederman.

Fighting Parson 🦴 **1935** In order to infiltrate a lawless town Gibson, a gun-sliging cowboy, dresses as a revivalist preacher. **65m/B VHS.** Hoot Gibson, Marceline Day, Robert Frazer, Stanley Blystone, Skeeter Bill Robbins, Charles "Blackie" King; ***D:*** Harry Fraser.

Fighting Pilot **1935** Talmadge is a real fighter in this classic talkie. His assignment is to rescue the plans for a secret aircraft from ill fate. **62m/B VHS.** Richard Talmadge, Victor Mace, Gertrude Messinger, Eddie Davis, Robert Frazer; ***D:*** Noel Mason Smith.

The Fighting Prince of Donegal 🦴🦴½ **1966** An Irish prince battles the invading British in 16th Century Ireland. Escaping their clutches, he leads his clan in rescuing his mother and his beloved in this Disney swashbuckler. Based on the novel "Red Hugh, Prince of Donegal" by Robert T. Reilly. **110m/C VHS.** Peter McEnery, Susan Hampshire, Tom Adams, Gordon Jackson, Andrew Keir; ***D:*** Michael O'Herlihy; ***M:*** George Bruns.

The Fighting Rats of Tobruk 🦴🦴 *The Rats of Tobruk* **1944** Australian film about the Egyptian campaign against Rommel in World War II attempts to take a slightly documentary approach to the subject. It's notable mostly for providing an early role for Peter Finch. **71m/B VHS, DVD.** *AU* Grant Taylor, Peter Finch, Chips Rafferty, Pauline Garrick; ***D:*** Charles Chauvel; ***C:*** George Heath.

The Fighting Redhead 🦴🦴 **1950** Final entry in the "Red Ryder" series has Hart as a cattle rustling murderer and Bannon as the hero, Red Ryder. Based on the comic strip, "Red Ryder." **55m/C VHS.** Jim Bannon, Don Reynolds, Emmett Lynn, Marin Sais, Peggy Stewart, John Hart, Lane Bradford; ***D:*** Lewis D. Collins; ***W:*** Paul Franklin, Jerry Thomas.

Fighting Renegade 🦴½ **1939** The search for an Indian burial ground in Mexico prompts two murders and McCoy, disguised as a notorious bandit part of the time, is wrongly accused. Justice triumphs in the end. **60m/B VHS.** Tim McCoy; ***D:*** Sam Newfield.

The Fighting Rookie 🦴½ **1934** LaRue, better known for playing hoods, is a rookie cop set up and disgraced by the mob. But he fights back to regain his honor and bring the gang to justice. **65m/B VHS, 8mm.** Jack LaRue; ***D:*** Spencer Gordon Bennet.

Fighting Seabees 🦴🦴½ **1944** As a hot-tempered construction foreman who battles Navy regulations as well as the Japanese, Wayne emerges as a larger-than-life hero in this action-packed saga of the Pacific theater of WWII. Extremely popular patriotic drama depicts the founding of the Seabees, the naval construction corps, amidst the action and the would-be romance with a woman reporter. Also available colorized. **100m/B VHS, DVD.** John Wayne, Susan Hayward, Dennis O'Keefe, William Frawley, Grant Withers, Tom London, Wally Wales, Paul Fix, William Forrest, J.M. Kerrigan, Leonid Kinskey, Duncan Renaldo, Addison Richards, Ben Welden, Crane Whitley, Charles Trowbridge; ***D:*** Edward Ludwig; ***W:*** Borden Chase, Aeneas MacKenzie; ***C:*** William Bradford; ***M:*** Walter Scharf, Roy Webb.

Fighting Shadows 🦴½ **1935** McCoy plays a tough lawman who rids his town of an unscrupulous bandit gang guilty of harassing the locals. Highlighted by some excellent trick riding—for which Western star McCoy was known. **58m/B VHS.** Tim McCoy, Robert "Tex" Allen, Geneva Mitchell, Ward Bond, Si Jenks; ***D:*** David Selman; ***W:*** Ford Beebe.

The Fighting Sheriff 🦴 **1931** Routine oater mixes action and romance when a sheriff is thrown together with a society debutante. **65m/B VHS.** Buck Jones, Loretta Sayers, Robert Ellis, Harlan E. Knight, Paul Fix, Lilian Worth; ***D:*** Louis King; ***W:*** Stuart Anthony.

The Fighting 69th 🦴🦴🦴 **1940** Cornball but entertaining WWI drama with lots of action. Cagney is a Brooklyn street tough who joins the all-Irish 69th New York regiment but could care less about its famed military history. He promptly defies his superiors and barely scrapes through his training. Sent to France, the swaggering Cagney turns coward when confronted by the horrors of war but eventually redeems himself. O'Brien is the famed regimental chaplain Father Duffy, while Brent is commander "Wild Bill" Donovan, who would later found the OSS in WWII. Lots of heart-tugging emotion backed with a fine supporting cast. **90m/B VHS.** James Cagney, Pat O'Brien, George Brent, Jeffrey Lynn, Alan Hale, Frank McHugh, Dennis Morgan, William Lundigan, Dick Foran, Guinn "Big Boy" Williams, Henry O'Neill, John Litel, George Reeves, Frank "Junior" Coghlan, Sammy Cohen, Joseph Crehan, Eddie Dew, William Hopper, Frank Mayo, Herbert Anderson, Byron Nelson, Harvey Stephens, Charles Trowbridge, Roland Varno; ***D:*** William Keighley; ***W:*** Fred Niblo, Norman Reilly Raine, Dean Franklin; ***C:*** Gaetano Antonio "Tony" Gaudio; ***M:*** Adolph Deutsch.

The Fighting Stallion 🦴🦴🦴 **1926** Canutt stars as a drifter hired by a rancher who's determined to capture a beautiful wild stallion (played by Boy the Wonder Horse). Silent with original organ score. **76m/B VHS, 8mm.** Yakima Canutt, Neva Gerber, Bud Osborne.

The Fighting Sullivans 🦴🦴🦴½ *The Sullivans* **1942** The true story of five brothers killed on the Battleship Juneau at Guadalcanal during WWII. The tale tells of the fury felt by the siblings after Pearl Harbor, their enlistment to fight for their country, and their tragic fate in the heat of battle. Truly a stirring tribute to all lives lost in combat. **110m/B VHS, DVD.** Anne Baxter, Thomas Mitchell, Selena Royle, Eddie Ryan, Trudy Marshall, James B. Cardwell, Roy Roberts, Ward Bond, Mary McCarty, Bobby Driscoll, Addison Richards, Selmer Jackson, Mae Marsh, Harry Strang, Barbara Brown, George Offerman Jr., John Campbell, John Alvin, Patrick Curtis, Nancy June Robinson, Marvin Davis; ***D:*** Lloyd Bacon; ***W:*** Edward Doherty, Mary C. McCall, Jules Schermer; ***C:*** Lucien N. Andriot; ***M:*** Cyril Mockridge, Alfred Newman.

Fighting Texans 🦴 **1933** An entire town invests in an oil well, on the advice of young salesman Bell, that the bankers are sure is a dud. Imagine their surprise when it turns out to be a gusler. **60m/B VHS.** Rex Bell, Luana Walters, Betty Mack, Gordon DeMain; ***D:*** Armand Schaefer.

Fighting Thru 🦴 *California in 1878* **1930** Maynard fights off the bad guys and wins the girl after some nifty riding in his first all-talkie western. **60m/B VHS.** Ken Maynard, Jeanette Loff; ***D:*** William Nigh.

The Fighting Trooper 🦴½ **1934** Based on the James Oliver Curwood story, "Footprints," this frontier tale presents a Mountie who goes undercover as a trapper in the Northwest. He is out to catch a murderer. **57m/B VHS.** Kermit Maynard.

Fighting Valley 🦴🦴 **1943** Texas Rangers O'Brien, Newill, and Wilkerson ride off to break up an outlaw gang that is trying to monopolize the ore smelting business. O'Brien later went on to directing for TV and also wrote for Red Skelton. **60m/B VHS.** Dave O'Brien, James Newill, Guy Wilkerson, Patti McCarty, John Merton, Curly Dresden; ***D:*** Oliver Drake; ***W:*** Oliver Drake.

Fighting Vigilantes 🦴🦴 **1947** A villainous food distributor is terrorizing his rivals until LaRue whips him. Holt and her father put together a committee called "The Vigilantes" to help out. Holt is the daughter of movie good guy Jack Holt. **61m/B VHS.** Lash LaRue, Al "Fuzzy" St. John, Jennifer Holt, George Chesebro, Lee Morgan, Russell Arms, Steve Clark; ***D:*** Ray Taylor.

The Fighting Westerner 🦴½ *Rocky Mountain Mystery* **1935** Scott stars as a mining engineer who becomes entangled in mysterious murders. Mrs. Leslie Carter stars in a rare screen role. **54m/B VHS, 8mm.** Randolph Scott, Charles "Chic" Sale, Ann Sheridan, Charles T. Barton.

Fighting with Kit Carson **1933** Famous guide and Indian fighter lead bands of settlers westward. Action-packed. Twelve chapters. **230m/B VHS.** Johnny Mack Brown, Noah Beery Sr., Noah Beery Jr., Betsy King Ross; ***D:*** Armand Schaefer, Colbert Clark.

The Filth and the Fury 🦴🦴½ **1999 (R)** British punk anarchists The Sex Pistols get their documentary due. Combines new and old footage and interviews of the (surviving) band members (Sid Vicious died of a heroin overdose). Director Temple previously covered the group in 1980's "The Great Rock 'n' Roll Swindle," which was told from the viewpoint of their former manager, Malcolm McLaren. **105m/C VHS, DVD, Wide.** *GB* John (Johnny Rotten) Lydon, Paul Cook, Steve Jones, Malcolm McLaren, Sid Vicious, Glen Matlock, Nancy Spungen; ***D:*** Julien Temple; ***M:*** John (Johnny Rotten) Lydon.

Final 🦴🦴½ **2001 (R)** Bill (Leary) wakes up confused in a Connecticut psychiatric hospital after an apparent suicide attempt. He's assigned to Ann (Davis), a young staff therapist who tries to help Bill sort out his memories from his delusions, which include the fear that he's to be executed by lethal injection and must escape. The story takes on some strange twists, including patients' rights and conspiracy theories. **111m/C VHS, DVD, Wide.** Denis Leary, Hope Davis, J.C. MacKenzie, Jim Gaffigan; ***D:*** Campbell Scott; ***W:*** Bruce McIntosh; ***C:*** Dan Gillham; ***M:*** Guy Davis.

The Final Alliance 🦴 **1989 (R)** A tough loner takes on a vicious motorcycle gang that's terrorizing a small town, and realizes that they're also responsible for his family's death. **90m/C VHS.** David Hasselhoff, John Saxon, Bo Hopkins, Jeanie Moore; ***D:*** Mario Di Leo.

Final Analysis 🦴🦴½ **1992 (R)** Glossy thriller starring Gere as a San Francisco psychiatrist who falls for the glamorous sister of one of his patients. Basinger plays the femme fatale and Thurman is Gere's sexually neurotic patient. Although heavily influenced by "Vertigo," this film never comes close to attaining the depth of Hitchcock's cinematic masterpiece. Roberts gives the most gripping performance in this slick suspense movie as Basinger's sleazy gangster husband. **125m/C VHS, DVD.** Richard Gere, Kim Basinger, Uma Thurman, Eric Roberts, Paul Guilfoyle, Keith David, Robert Harper, Jolyon Baker, Harris Yulin, Agustin Rodriguez; ***D:*** Phil Joanou; ***W:*** Wesley Strick, Robert Berger; ***C:*** Jordan Cronenweth; ***M:*** George Fenton.

Final Appeal 🦴🦴½ **1993 (PG-13)** Christine Biondi (Williams) is an abused wife, living in terror of her drug-addicted doctor husband, Ed. When Christine walks in on Ed and his mistress, she's forced to kill him in self-defense. But Ed's mistress swears it was murder and Christine's on trial. Now her only chance is her hard-drinking lawyer brother Perry (Dennehy)—who doesn't believe her story. Fact-based made for TV fare. **94m/C VHS.** JoBeth Williams, Brian Dennehy, Lindsay Crouse, Tom Mason, Eddie Jones, Ashley Crow, Betsy Brantley, Michael Beach; ***M:*** Charles Bernstein. **TV**

Final Approach 🦴🦴 **1991 (R)** Test pilot Jason Halsey (Sikking) crashes in the desert and awakens in the office of psychiatrist Dio Gottlieb (Elizondo). Halsey can't remember anything about his past, or his own name for that matter, but through word association games and psychological tests, he begins to remember as Gottlieb tries to pry information from his brain. Showy computer effects are excellent, but they only serve to fill holes in a story that has an unsatisfying ending. Notable as first film made with digital sound. Also available in a letterboxed version. **100m/C VHS, Wide.** James B. Sikking, Hector Elizondo, Madolyn Smith, Kevin McCarthy, Cameo Kneuer, Wayne Duvall; ***D:*** Eric Steven Stahl.

Final Assignment 🦴 *The Moscow Chronicle* **1980** A Canadian TV reporter agrees to smuggle a dissident Soviet scientist's ill granddaughter out of Russia for treatment along with a videotape documenting tragic experiments on children with steroids. She manages to evade the KGB while carrying on with a Russian press officer, and enlists the support of a Jewish fur trader. Location shooting in Canada instead of Russia is just one pitfall of this production. **101m/C VHS.** *CA* Genevieve Bujold, Michael York, Burgess Meredith, Colleen Dewhurst; ***D:*** Paul Almond.

Final Comedown 🦴 **1972 (R)** A black revolutionary attempts to get white radicals behind his war against racism. He fails and starts a racial bloodbath. **84m/C VHS.** Billy Dee Williams, D'Urville Martin, Celia Kaye, Raymond St. Jacques, Pamela Jones, R.G. Armstrong; ***D:*** Oscar Williams.

The Final Countdown 🦴🦴🦴 **1980 (PG)** A U.S. nuclear-powered aircraft carrier, caught in a time warp, is transported back to 1941, just hours before the bombing of Pearl Harbor. The commanders face the ultimate decision—leave history intact or stop the incident and thus avoid WWII. Excellent photography and a surprise ending. **92m/C VHS.** Kirk Douglas, Martin Sheen, Katharine Ross, James Farentino, Charles Durning; ***D:*** Don Taylor; ***W:*** Thomas Hunter, David Ambrose.

Final Cut 🦴½ **1988** While filming in a secluded swampland, a crew stumbles on a local sheriff's crooked scheme and one by one, the crew members disappear. **92m/C VHS.** Carla De Lane, T.J. Kennedy, Joe Rainer, Brett Rice, Jordan Williams; ***D:*** Larry G. Brown.

The Final Cut 🦴🦴🦴 **1995** Follows "House of Cards" and "To Play the King" in portraying the political adventures of Francis Urquardt (Richardson), Prime Minister. At 65, Urquardt has two goals: he wants to beat Margaret Thatcher's 11-year reign and he wants to establish a secret retirement fund (the plot involves Cyprus and could—finally—leads to Urquardt's downfall). Author Michael Dobbs objected to the adaptation and insisted his name be removed from the script. On two cassettes. **200m/C VHS.** *GB* Ian Richardson, Diane Fletcher, Paul Freeman, Isla Blair, Nick Brimble, Erika Hoffman, Nickolas Grace, Julian Fellowes; ***D:*** Mike Vardy; ***W:*** Andrew Davies; ***C:*** Ian Punter; ***M:*** Jim Parker.

The Final Cut 🦴🦴 **1996 (R)** John Pierce (Elliott) is a retired bomb squad specialist who's unwillingly called back to active duty to stop a bomber who's targeting Seattle. Along with ambitious officer Kathleen Hardy (Ramsay), Pierce tries to discover the bomber's next move—only to have suspicion fall upon himself. **99m/C VHS.** Sam Elliott, Charles Martin Smith, Anne Elizabeth Ramsay, Matt Craven, Ray Baker, John Hannah, Amanda Plummer; ***D:*** Roger Christian; ***W:*** Raul Inglis; ***C:*** Mike Southon; ***M:*** Ross Vannelli.

The Final Days 🦴🦴½ **1989 (PG)** TV drama follows the presidency of Richard Nixon (Smith) from Watergate through his resignation. Based on the Pulitzer Prize-winning book by Bob Woodward and Carl Bernstein. **150m/C VHS.** Lane Smith, Richard Kiley, David Ogden Stiers, Ed Flanders, Theodore Bikel; ***D:*** Richard Pearce.

Final Destination 🦴🦴 **2000 (R)** Teenager Alex (Sawa) predicts that a plane filled with classmates will explode. It does but he and some others manage to make it off the plane beforehand. Things get interesting (and a little philosophical) when the survivors start dying. Seems Death feels cheated and is getting even. Typical body count slasher genre gets a twist from the machinations of fate...or whatever. Filmmakers paid tribute to some of their favorite horror stars and directors with the characters' surnames. **97m/C VHS, DVD, Wide.** Devon Sawa, Ali Larter, Kristen (Kristin) Cloke, Daniel Roebuck, Roger Guenveur Smith, Chad E. Donella, Seann William Scott, Tony Todd, Kerr Smith, Amanda Detmer; ***D:*** James Wong; ***W:*** Glen Morgan, James Wong, Jeffrey Reddick; ***C:*** Robert McLachlan; ***M:*** Shirley Walker.

Final Embrace 🦴½ **1992 (R)** When Laurel's famous sister is murdered she decides to do a little investigating on her own. She's aided by a young cop who just happened to be obsessed with the murdered woman. **88m/C VHS.** Robert Rusler, Nancy Valen, Dick Van Patten, Linda Dona; ***D:*** Oley Sassone; ***W:*** R.J. Robertson, Jim Wynorski; ***M:*** Daniel Licht.

Final Equinox 🦴½ **1995** Mysterious alien artifact, which has the power to spontaneously create new life, is stolen and both the government and the mob try to be the first to find—and control—it. Cop Kove opposes them both. **90m/C VHS.** Martin Kove, Joe Lara, David Warner, Gary Kasper; ***D:*** Serge Rodnunsky; ***W:*** Serge Rodnunsky.

Final Exam woof! **1981 (R)** Psychotic killer stalks college students during exam week. This one's too boring to be scary. You root for the psycho to off everyone just to have the movie over. **90m/C VHS.** Cecile Bagdadi, Joel Rice; ***D:*** Jimmy Huston.

Final Exam 🦴½ **1998** Ghetto drama about racism. High school basketball star Javon Robinson (McCray) is counting on getting a scholarship to college to get away from the drugs and violence that surrounds him. But when he fails English, he takes his teacher hostage at gunpoint and blames his failure on racism. **93m/C VHS.** Alvin O. McCray, John Mollica, Mario Velasquez, Gregor Manns, Augustina Montesino; ***D:*** John Mollica; ***W:*** John Mollica; ***C:*** Mike Dolgetta. **VIDEO**

The Final Executioner 🦴 *The Last Warrior* **1983** A valiant man finds a way to stop the slaughter of innocent people in a post-nuclear world. **95m/C VHS.** William Mang, Marina Costa, Harrison Muller, Woody Strode; ***D:*** Romolo Guerrieri.

Final Fantasy: The Spirits Within 🦴🦴½ **2001 (PG-13)** Photorealistic computer-generated animation may be the highlight of this fantasy adventure, which is based on the videogame series. In the year 2065, life on Earth is threatened by aliens who steal energy from all living things on the planet. A team of scientists, led by Aki Ross (Ming-Na) and Dr. Sid (Sutherland) are at odds with the military, in the form of General Hein (Woods) over how to deal with the creatures. Plot, dialogue, and characterization, the movie's obvious weaknesses, definitely take a back seat to the visuals. The human characters, while not completely lifelike, are the closest anyone's come so far. Where the techology shines is in the landscapes and non-human creatures, which are all striking. **104m/C VHS, DVD, Wide.** *US* ***D:*** Hironobu Sakaguchi; ***W:*** Al Reinert, Jeff Vintar; ***M:*** Elliot Goldenthal; ***V:*** Ming Na, Alec Baldwin, Steve Buscemi, Peri Gilpin, Ving Rhames, Donald Sutherland, James Woods, Keith David, Jean Simmons, Matt McKenzie.

The Final Goal 🦴½ **1994 (R)** Evil businessman (and ex-soccer star) Paulo Ramirez (Estrada) meddles with his country's current soccer star, who's playing in the Global Cup of Soccer. He wants the player to throw the game and thinks death threats will accomplish his goal. **85m/C VHS.** Erik Estrada, Steven Nijjar, Dean Butler; ***D:*** Jon Cassar.

The Final Hit 🦴🦴 **2002 (R)** Washed-up Hollywood producer Sonny Wexler (Reynolds) prefers to reminisce about his past success than raise the money to option a hot script and get back in the game. Maybe he should stick with his memories, since Sonny hooks up with a shady businessman who expects a guaranteed return on his investment—or else. **90m/C VHS, DVD.** Burt Reynolds, Lauren Holly, Benjamin Bratt, Sean Astin; ***D:*** Burt Reynolds.

Final Impact 🦴½ **1991 (R)** Nick Taylor seeks vengeance on reigning kickboxing champ Jake Gerard through his prodigy, Danny Davis. Will sweet revenge for the wicked beating, suffered at the hands of Gerard years earlier, be his? **99m/C VHS.** Lorenzo Lamas, Kathleen Kinmont, Mimi Lesseos, Kathrin Lautner, Jeff Langton, Mike Worth; ***D:*** Joseph Merhi, Stephen Smoke; ***M:*** John Gonzalez.

Final Judgment 🦴🦴 **1992 (R)** Daniel Tyrone (Dourif) is a former gang member, now a troubled priest, who's the prime suspect in the Los Angeles murder of a beautiful stripper. Determined to find the killer Father Tyrone heads into L.A.'s underground sex industry to search for clues, which brings him face to face with evil and his own desires. **90m/C VHS.** Brad Dourif, Isaac Hayes, Maria Ford, Karen Black, Orson Bean, David Ledingham; ***D:*** Louis Morneau; ***W:*** Kirk Honeycutt, Louis Morneau.

Final Justice 🦴 **1984 (R)** A small-town Texan sheriff wages a war against crime and corruption that carries him to Italy and the haunts of Mafia hitmen. **90m/C VHS, DVD.** Joe Don Baker, Rossano Brazzi, Patrizia Pellegrino, Venantino Venantini; ***D:*** Greydon Clark; ***W:*** Greydon Clark; ***C:*** Nicholas Josef von Sternberg; ***M:*** David Bell.

Final Justice 🦴 **1994 (R)** Icky revenge drama has bad guys Red (Huff) and Bobby (Marotta) hiding out in a woodsy cabin that's owned by lawyer Alan Massard (Brolin) and his wife Amy (Fitzgerald). Unfortunately for them, the Massards have chosen to invite some friends and hang out at the cabin for the weekend, where the bad guys do nasty things before Alan manages to kill Bobby and trap Red. Then there's a stupid debate on just what to do with Red and more violence. **92m/C VHS.** James Brolin, Annie Fitzgerald, Brent Huff, Rick Marotta, Beau Billingslea; ***D:*** Brent Huff; ***W:*** Brent Huff.

Final Justice 🦴🦴½ **1998** Teacher Gwen (O'Toole) is outraged when a sleazy attorney (McKean) gets her murdered gay brother's killer acquitted. So she kidnaps him for some rough justice of her own but then winds up on trial herself. **120m/C VHS, DVD.** Annette O'Toole, Michael McKean, CCH Pounder, Brian Wimmer; ***D:*** Tommy Lee Wallace; ***W:*** Babs Greyhosky; ***M:*** Brian Tyler. **CABLE**

Final Mission 🦴 **1984** Vengeful one-man army follows the professional hit man who slaughtered his family from L.A. to Laos. His pursuit leads to a jungle showdown. Gee, sounds like "Rambo, First Blood," though obviously less grand and glorious. **97m/C VHS.** Richard Young, John Dresden, Kaz Garas, Christine Tudor; ***D:*** Cirio H. Santiago.

Final Mission 🦴🦴 **1993 (R)** Virtual reality becomes a weapon in a military conspiracy when pilots start dying. Air Force jets are supposed to be unstoppable thanks to the new technology and a general is only too willing to blame the deaths on pilot error but one fly boy is out to find the truth. **91m/C VHS.** Billy Wirth, Corbin Bernsen, Elizabeth (Ward) Gracen, Steve Railsback.

Final Notice 🦴 **1989** A detective tracking a serial killer has as his only evidence a trail of shredded photos of nude women. Not released theatrically. **91m/C VHS.** Gil Gerard, Steve Landesberg, Jackie Burroughs, Melody Anderson, Louise Fletcher, David Ogden Stiers, Kevin Hicks; ***D:*** Steven Hilliard Stern; ***W:*** John Gay; ***M:*** Tom Scott.

The Final Option 🦴 *Who Dares Wins* **1982 (R)** An agent of England's Special Air Services team goes undercover as one of a band of anti-nuclear terrorists that take over the U.S. Embassy in London. Violent, but unconvincing. **125m/C VHS.** *GB* Lewis Collins, Judy Davis, Richard Widmark, Robert Webber, Edward Woodward, Ingrid Pitt, Kenneth Griffith, Tony Doyle, John Duttine; ***D:*** Ian Sharp; ***W:*** Reginald Rose; ***C:*** Phil Meheux.

Final Payback woof! **1999** A cast of faded TV stars long since past their prime time (Richard Grieco of "21 Jump Street," Corbin Bernsen of "L.A. Law," Martin Kove of "Cagney and Lacey," Priscilla Barnes of "Three's Company") collect their paychecks for this ineptly directed thriller that leaves no direct-to-video cliche unturned. Grieco stars as an ex-cop who finds himself "pushed over the fence" after he is framed for the murder of the police chief's wife. Gee, you think the police chief himself (B-movie vet John Saxon) may be involved in the conspiracy? No nudity and only one car explosion. Why bother? **102m/C VHS, DVD.** Richard Grieco, Corbin

Bernsen, Martin Kove, Priscilla Barnes, John Saxon; *D:* Art Camacho.

The Final Programme 🦴🦴½ *The Last Days of Man on Earth* **1973** In this futuristic story, a man must rescue his sister—and the world—from their brother, who holds a microfilmed plan for global domination. Meanwhile, he must shield himself from the advances of a bisexual computer programmer who wants to make him father to a new, all-purpose human being. Based on the Michael Moorcock "Jerry Cornelius" stories, the film has gained a cult following. **85m/C VHS, DVD, Wide.** *GB* Hugh Griffith, Harry Andrews, Jon Finch, Jenny Runacre, Sterling Hayden, Patrick Magee, Sarah Douglas; *D:* Robert Fuest; *W:* Robert Fuest; *C:* Norman Warwick; *M:* Gerry Mulligan, Paul Beaver, Bernard Krause.

Final Round 🦴½ **1993 (R)** A kickboxer and his girlfriend are kidnapped by a millionaire who stages hunt the humans games for the pleasure of his gambling syndicate. Stiff but with a few good action sequences. **90m/C VHS.** Lorenzo Lamas, Anthony de Longis, Kathleen Kinmont, Clark Johnson, Isabelle Jamieson; *D:* George Erschbamer; *W:* Arne Olsen; *M:* Graeme Coleman.

Final Sanction 🦴🦴½ **1989** After a nuclear holocaust exhausts their military resources, the U.S. and the Soviets each send one-man armies to battle each other for final control of the world. **90m/C VHS.** Robert Z'Dar, Ted Prior; *D:* David A. Prior; *W:* David A. Prior.

Final Shot: The Hank Gathers Story 🦴🦴½ **1992** Inspirational story of Gathers, who rose from the ghetto to become one of America's top college basketball stars at Loyola Marymount, until tragedy strikes during a game. **92m/C VHS.** Victor Love, Duane Davis, Nell Carter, George Kennedy.

The Final Terror 🦴🦴 *Campsite Massacre; Bump in the Night; The Forest Primeval* **1983 (R)** Group of young campers is stalked by a mad killer in a desolate, backwoods area. Better-than-average stalked-teens entry is notable for the presence of some soon-to-be stars. **90m/C VHS.** John Friedrich, Rachel Ward, Adrian Zmed, Daryl Hannah, Joe Pantoliano, Ernest Harden, Mark Metcalf, Lewis Smith, Cindy Harrel, Akosua Busia; *D:* Andrew Davis.

Final Verdict 🦴🦴½ **1991** A trial lawyer defends a man he knows is guilty, throwing his life and his family into turmoil. **93m/C VHS.** Treat Williams, Glenn Ford, Amy Wright, Olivia Burnette; *D:* Jack Fisk; *C:* Paul Elliott. **CABLE**

Final Voyage 🦴🦴 **1999 (R)** Hijackers, led by Ice-T, take over the cruise ship Britannica and their robbery of the ship's vault leads to a threat to sink the boat as well. Bodyguard Walsh manages to escape and wages a one-man war against the bad guys throughout the ship. It's better than "Speed 2." Wynorski directed under the pseudonym Jay Andrews. **95m/C VHS, DVD.** Ice-T, Dylan Walsh, Erika Eleniak, Claudia Christian, Ric(k) Ducommun; *D:* Jim Wynorski; *W:* Jim Wynorski, J. Everitt Morley; *C:* Ken Blakey; *M:* David Wurst, Eric Wurst. **VIDEO**

Final Warning 🦴🦴½ *Chernobyl: The Final Warning* **1990** A dramatization of actual events surrounding the 1986 melt-down of the nuclear power plant at Chernobyl. **94m/C VHS.** Jon Voight, Jason Robards Jr., Sammi Davis; *D:* Anthony Page. **TV**

Find the Lady 🦴½ *Call the Cops; Kopek and Broom* **1975 (R)** Candy assumes a supporting role as a bumbling cop who is part of an incompetent police team trying to rescue a kidnapped socialite. **100m/C VHS.** *CA* John Candy, Peter Cook, Mickey Rooney, Lawrence Dane, Alexandra Bastedo; *D:* John Trent.

Finders Keepers 🦴🦴 **1984 (R)** A wild assortment of characters on board a train en route from California to Nebraska search for $5 million hidden in the baggage car. **96m/C VHS.** Michael O'Keefe, Beverly D'Angelo, Ed Lauter, Louis Gossett Jr., Pamela Stephenson, Jim Carrey, David Wayne, Brian Dennehy, John Schuck; *D:* Richard Lester; *W:* Ronny Graham.

Finding Buck McHenry 🦴🦴½ **2000** When 11-year-old Jason (Schiffman) gets cut from Little League, he decides to form his own team. He persuades school custodian Buck McHenry (Davis) to coach but the man's knowledge about the game leads Jason to suspect that Buck is a Negro League legend who's long dropped out of sight and he decides to uncover the truth. **88m/C VHS, DVD.** Ossie Davis, Ruby Dee, Ernie Banks, Michael Schiffman, Duane McLaughlin, Karl Pruner, Megan Bower, Catherine Blythe; *D:* Charles Burnett; *W:* Alfred Slote; *C:* John L. Demps Jr.; *M:* Stephen James Taylor. **CABLE**

Finding Forrester 🦴🦴 **2000 (PG-13)** Underprivileged kid Brown from the Bronx, who has smarts and basketball skills, wins a scholarship to an Upper East Side prep school where he's befriended by wealthy classmate Paquin and eccentric writer Connery. Predictable, cloying script almost undermines excellent performances by Connery and newcomer Brown. The only good thing about the screenplay is their dialogue together. **133m/C VHS, DVD, Wide.** Anna Paquin, Sean Connery, Robert Brown, F. Murray Abraham, Busta Rhymes, April Grace, Michael Nouri, Zane R. (Lil' Zane) Copeland Jr.; *D:* Gus Van Sant; *W:* Mike Rich; *C:* Harris Savides; *M:* Hal Willner.

Finding Graceland 🦴🦴½ **1998 (PG-13)** Down-on-his-luck Byron (Schaech) is driving his 1959 Cadillac convertible through New Mexico when he stops for a hitchhiker and Elvis impersonator (Keitel), who's on his way to Memphis. Except this Elvis believes he's the real thing and he's heading for his Graceland home. Odd things seem to happen to Byron as long as Elvis is around. Not the least being his finding Marilyn Monroe impersonator, Ashley (Fonda). **97m/C VHS, DVD.** Johnathon Schaech, Harvey Keitel, Bridget Fonda, Gretchen Mol; *D:* David Winkler; *W:* Jason Horwitch; *C:* Elliot Davis; *M:* Stephen Endelman.

Finding North 🦴🦴 **1997** Predictable dramedy about the friendship between a straight woman and gay man. Talkative, bored bank clerk Rhonda (Makkena) meets suicidal yuppie, Travis (Hickey), who's just lost his lover to AIDS, and decides to help him regain his emotional balance. Even if this means following him from New York to the small Texas town where Travis' late lover grew up. **95m/C VHS, DVD, Wide.** Wendy Makkena, John Benjamin Hickey, Angela Pietropinto, Freddie Roman, Molly McClure; *D:* Tanya Wexler; *W:* Kim Powers; *C:* Michael Barrett; *V:* Jonathan Walker.

Fine Gold 🦴🦴 **1988** A false charge of embezzlement leaves a man without home and family, so he decides to turn the tables on those who betrayed him. **91m/C VHS.** Andrew Stevens, Ray Walston, Ted Wass, Stewart Granger, Lloyd Bochner, Jane Badler; *D:* J. Anthony (Jose Antonio de la Loma) Loma.

A Fine Madness 🦴🦴🦴 **1966** A near-classic comedy about a lusty, rebellious poet thrashing against the pressures of the modern world, and fending off a bevy of lobotomy-happy psychiatrists. Shot on location in New York City, based on Elliot Baker's novel. **104m/C VHS.** Sean Connery, Joanne Woodward, Jean Seberg, Patrick O'Neal, Colleen Dewhurst, Clive Revill, John Fiedler; *D:* Irvin Kershner; *M:* John Addison.

A Fine Mess 🦴½ **1986 (PG)** Two buffoons cash in when one overhears a plan to dope a racehorse, but they are soon fleeing the plotters' slapstick pursuit. The plot is further complicated by the romantic interest of a gangster's wife. The TV popularity of the two stars did not translate to the big screen; perhaps it's Edwards's fault. **100m/C VHS.** Ted Danson, Howie Mandel, Richard Mulligan, Stuart Margolin, Maria Conchita Alonso, Paul Sorvino; *D:* Blake Edwards; *W:* Blake Edwards; *C:* Harry Stradling Jr.; *M:* Henry Mancini.

A Fine Romance 🦴🦴 **1992 (PG-13)** An improbable romance set in Paris features Andrews and Mastroianni as abandoned spouses falling in love. Andrews is the prim English Pamela who has been abandoned by her docter husband. Mastroianni is the irrepresible Cesareo, whose wife has just happened to run off with the aforementioned doctor. They meet to plan how to get their spouses back and wind up with opposites attracting. Not much story and the charm is spread thin. Based on the play "Tchin, Tchin" by Francois Billetdoux. **83m/C VHS.** Julie Andrews, Marcello Mastroianni, Ian Fitzgibbon, Jean-Pierre Castaldi, Jean-Jacques Dulon, Maria Machado, Jean-Michel Cannone, Catherine Jarrett, Gene Saks; *W:* Ronald Harwood; *M:* Pino Donaggio.

The Finest Hour 🦴½ **1991 (R)** Two Navy buddies have a falling out when they both fall for the same woman. But they must put aside their differences when their next mission sends them to Iraq to deal with the deadly threat of biological warfare. **105m/C VHS.** Rob Lowe, Gale Hansen, Tracy Griffith, Eb Lottimer; *D:* Shimon Dotan; *W:* Shimon Dotan.

The Finger Man 🦴🦴½ **1955** An ex-con cooperates with the feds rather than return to jail. The deal is that he gets the dirt on an underworld crime boss. Solid performances. **82m/B VHS.** Frank Lovejoy, Forrest Tucker, Peggy Castle, Timothy Carey, Glenn Gordon; *D:* Harold Schuster.

Finger on the Trigger 🦴🦴 *El Dedo En El Gatillo* **1965** Veterans from both sides of the Civil War are after a hidden supply of gold, but find that they must band together to fend off an Indian attack. Routine. **89m/C VHS.** Rory Calhoun, James Philbrook, Todd Martin, Silvia Solar, Brad Talbot; *D:* Sidney Pink.

Fingerprints Don't Lie 🦴 **1951** A fingerprint expert pins the murder of the town mayor on an innocent guy, then suspects a frame-up. **56m/B VHS.** Richard Travis, Sheila Ryan, Tom Neal; *D:* Sam Newfield.

Fingers 🦴🦴🦴 **1978 (R)** Keitel is Johnny Fingers, a mobster's son, reluctantly working as a mob debt-collector, all the while dreaming of his ambitions to be a concert pianist. The divisions between his dreams and reality cause him to crack. Toback's first film generates psychological tension and excellent performances. **89m/C VHS.** Harvey Keitel, Tisa Farrow, Jim Brown, Danny Aiello, Tanya Roberts, Marian Seldes, Michael V. Gazzo, James Toback; *D:* James Toback; *W:* James Toback; *C:* Michael Chapman; *M:* George Barrie.

Finian's Rainbow 🦴🦴🦴 **1968 (G)** A leprechaun comes to America to steal back a pot of gold taken by an Irishman and his daughter in this fanciful musical comedy based on a 1947 Broadway hit. Both the sprite and the girl find romance; the share-cropping locals are saved by the cash; a bigot learns the error of his ways; and Finian (Astaire) dances off to new adventures. The fine production and talented cast are not used to their best advantage by the director who proved much better suited for "The Godfather." Entertaining, nonetheless. ♫How Are Things in Glocca Morra?; Look To the Rainbow; That Old Devil Moon; If This Isn't Love; Something Sort of Grandish; The Be-Gat; This Time of Year; The Great Come and Get It Day; When I'm Not Near the Girl I Love. **141m/C VHS, Wide.** Fred Astaire, Petula Clark, Tommy Steele, Keenan Wynn, Al Freeman Jr., Don Francks, Susan Hancock, Dolph Sweet; *D:* Francis Ford Coppola.

Finish Line 🦴🦴½ **1989** A high school track star turns to steroids to enhance his performance after being pushed by an overzealous father. The father-and-son Brolins play the pair. **100m/C VHS.** James Brolin, Josh Brolin, Mariska Hargitay, Kristoff St. John, John Finnegan, Billy Vera, Stephen Lang; *D:* John Nicolella. **CABLE**

Finishing School 🦴½ **1933** Girls' school roommates Rogers and Dee experience heartaches and loves lost while enduring disinterested parents and snobbish peers. Boxoffice bomb when released, despite a strong cast. **73m/B VHS.** Ginger Rogers, Frances Dee, George Nicholls Jr., Beulah Bondi, Bruce Cabot, Billie Burke, John Halliday, Sara Haden, Jack Norton, Joan Barclay, Jane Darwell; *D:* George Nicholls Jr.; *M:* Max Steiner.

The Finishing Touch 🦴🦴 **1992 (R)** Someone is stalking L.A.'s most gorgeous women and Detective Sam Stone (Nader) is assigned to the case. Stone discovers his prime suspect is a video artist with a taste for pornography. When Stone's investigation is cut short, his ex-wife, Detective Hannah Stone (Hack) is brought in to take over the case. Unfortunately, she finds herself falling for the suspect in this erotic thriller. **82m/C VHS.** Michael Nader, Shelley Hack, Arnold Vosloo, Art Evans, Clark Johnson, Theodore (Ted) Raimi; *D:* Fred Gallo.

Finnegan Begin Again 🦴🦴 **1984** A middle-aged schoolteacher and a grouchy, 65-year-old newspaper editor find romance despite their other obligations. Winning performances add charm to this cable TV movie. **112m/C VHS.** Mary Tyler Moore, Robert Preston, Sam Waterston, Sylvia Sidney, David Huddleston; *D:* Joan Micklin Silver. **CABLE**

Finnegan's Wake *Passages from "Finnegans Wake"; Passages from James Joyce's "Finnegans Wake"* **1963** Portions of the filmed adaptation of James Joyce's novel are shown in this program along with an interview with producer/director Mary Ellen Bute. **92m/B VHS.**

Fiona 🦴½ **1998** Fiona was abandoned as a baby, raised in an abusive foster home, and is now a crack-smoking hooker on the streets of New York. After casually killing three cops, she hides out in a crackhouse where she hooks up with Anita—who naturally turns out to be Fiona's long-lost mama. Film is a blend of fiction and documentary footage of real prostitutes and drug houses. **85m/C VHS, DVD.** Anna Thomson, Mike Hodge, Anna Grace, Felicia Maguire; *D:* Amos Kollek; *W:* Amos Kollek; *C:* Ed Talavera; *M:* Alison Gordy.

Fiorile 🦴🦴🦴 *Wild Flower* **1993 (PG-13)** Covers several generations of a Tuscan clan living under a family curse which dates back to Napoleon's invasion of Italy. At that time Jean, a handsome French lieutenant, falls in love with Tuscan peasant girl Elisabetta, nicknamed Fiorile. When Jean is executed for a theft committed by her brother, the pregnant Fiorile vows revenge. Throughout sucessive generations, haunted by the past, the family's personal bad luck persists. Several of the actors play their character's ancestors, lending continuity. Attractive cast does well with the Taviani brothers' visual style and romantic narrative. In Italian with English subtitles. **118m/C VHS.** *IT* Michael Vartan, Galatea Ranzi, Claudio Bigagli, Lino Capolicchio, Constanze Engelbrecht, Athina Cenci, Giovanni Guidelli, Chiara Caselli; *D:* Paolo Taviani, Vittorio Taviani; *W:* Paolo Taviani, Vittorio Taviani, Sandro Petraglia; *C:* Giuseppe Lanci; *M:* Nicola Piovani.

Fire 🦴½ **1977** A fire started by an escaped convict rages through Oregon timberland in this suspenseful Irwin Allen disaster drama. **98m/C VHS.** Ernest Borgnine, Vera Miles, Patty Duke, Alex Cord, Donna Mills; *D:* Earl Bellamy. **TV**

Fire 🦴🦴½ **1996** Follows the relationship of two sisters-in-law in New Delhi—both stuck in frustrating, loveless marriages—while examining the harsh patriarchal culture of India. Radha (Azmi) is married to Ashok (Kharbanda), a video store clerk who has taken a vow of celibacy under the teachings of a scruffy swami. Sita (Das) is married to Ashok's brother Jatin (Jaaferi), who is openly having an affair with a Chinese Canadian woman. As her frustration grows, the younger Sita acts on her attraction to her sister-in-law and the two begin a lesbian affair, which is taboo in the strict Hindu culture. Dialogue is in "Hinglish," or English with occasional Hindi phrases thrown in. The attitudes portrayed must exist, because the film was banned in India. **104m/C VHS, DVD, Wide.** *CA* Shabana Azmi, Nandita Das, Kulbashan Kharbanda, Jaaved Jaaferi, Ranjit (Chaudry) Chowdhry, Kushal Rekhi; *D:* Deepa Mehta; *W:* Deepa Mehta; *C:* Giles Nuttgens; *M:* A.R. Rahman.

Fire Alarm 🦴 **1932** A change of scene for Western star Brown as he portrays a fireman who, in-between his work, romances a career girl. **67m/B VHS, DVD.** Johnny Mack Brown, Noel Francis; *D:* Karl Brown; *W:* Karl Brown, I.E. Chadwick.

Fire and Ice 🦴🦴½ **1983 (PG)** An animated adventure film that culminates in a tense battle between good and evil, surrounded by the mystical elements of the ancient past. Designed by Frank Frazetta. **81m/C VHS.** Randy Norton, Cynthia Leake; ***D:*** Ralph Bakshi; ***W:*** Ralph Bakshi, Willy Bogner, Gerry Conway; ***V:*** Susan Tyrrell, William Ostrander.

Fire and Ice 🦴 **1987 (PG)** A tale of love on the slopes. Two skiers realize that their feelings for each other are perhaps even stronger than their feelings about skiing. You won't care though, except for some fine ski footage. **83m/C VHS.** Suzy Chaffee, John Eaves; ***D:*** Willy Bogner; ***W:*** George Schlatter; ***M:*** Harold Faltermeyer; ***Nar:*** John Denver.

Fire and Rain 🦴🦴 **1989** Based on the real-life crash of a Delta Airlines plane in Dallas and the rescue efforts made following the disaster. Familiar cast-members turn in decent performance. **89m/C VHS.** Angie Dickinson, Charles Haid, Tom Bosley, David Hasselhoff, Robert Guillaume, Susan Ruttan, John Beck, Patti LaBelle, Dean Jones, Lawrence Pressman, Penny Fuller; ***D:*** Jerry Jameson; ***W:*** Gary Sherman. **TV**

Fire and Sword 🦴 **1982** A Cornish knight must choose between loyalty for king and country and the love of an Irish woman in this medieval drama. A not very inspired retelling of the Tristan and Isolde legend. **84m/C VHS.** *GB* Peter Firth, Leigh Lawson, Antonia Preser, Christopher Waitz; ***D:*** Veith von Furstenberg.

Fire Birds 🦴 *Wings of the Apache* **1990 (PG-13)** Army attack helicopters and the people who fly them are used in the war on drugs in South America. Failed to match the exciting flight sequences, the romantic interest, or the boxoffice of "Top Gun." **85m/C VHS.** Nicolas Cage, Tommy Lee Jones, Sean Young, Bryan Kestner, Dale Dye, Mary Ellen Trainor, J.A. Preston, Peter Onorati; ***D:*** David Green; ***W:*** Dale Dye, Nick Thiel, Paul F. Edwards; ***M:*** David Newman.

Fire Down Below 🦴½ **1957** Hayworth is the been-around-the-block beauty who persuades Mitchum and Lemmon, two small-time smugglers, to take her to a safe haven, no questions asked. Both men fall for her obvious charms, causing them to have a falling out until a life or death situation puts their friendship to the test. An unoriginal melodrama indifferently acted by everyone but Lemmon. Good location work in Trinidad and Tobago. **116m/C VHS.** *GB* Robert Mitchum, Jack Lemmon, Rita Hayworth, Herbert Lom, Anthony Newley; ***D:*** Robert Parrish.

Fire Down Below 🦴 **1997 (R)** Seagal comes armed with his trademark ponytail, martial arts expertise, big leather jackets, and environment-friendly message to the Appalachians in this hoedown showdown. As undercover (yeah, he blends right in) EPA agent Jack Taggart, Seagal must stop evil industrialist Hanner (Kristofferson) from dumping toxic waste. Of course, the company town sends the usual band of thugs (thoughtfully attacking one at a time) to make him go away. He finds allies in the local outcasts (Helgenberger and Stanton) en route to the final confrontation. Not Seagal's worst, but that's not saying much. Even the usually-impressive fight scenes become tedious after a while. At least he didn't try to direct this one. Originally conceived as a Bruce Willis project at Columbia. **105m/C VHS, DVD, Wide.** Steven Seagal, Marg Helgenberger, Kris Kristofferson, Harry Dean Stanton, Stephen Lang, Levon Helm, Brad Hunt, Richard Masur, Ed Bruce, Randy Travis, Mark Collie, Alex Harvey; ***D:*** Feliz Alcala; ***W:*** Jeb Stuart; ***C:*** Tom Houghton; ***M:*** Nick Glennie-Smith.

Fire, Ice and Dynamite 🦴½ **1991 (PG)** Moore is onscreen only briefly as an eccentric tycoon who fakes suicide to watch several teams of challengers scramble in a madcap winter-sports contest for his millions. A German-made avalanche of crazy stunts, bad jokes, and product plugs for countless European companies, commencing with a literal parade of guests, from astronaut Buzz Aldrin to soul man Isaac Hayes. Numbing; must be seen to be believed. **105m/C VHS.** Roger Moore, Shari Belafonte, Simon Shepherd, Uwe Ochsenknecht, Marjoe Gortner; ***D:*** Willy Bogner.

Fire in the Night 🦴½ **1985** In a small Southern town, a beautiful and sure-footed woman battles the limitless resources of the town's predominant dynastic family. **89m/C VHS.** Graciela Casillas, John Martin.

Fire in the Sky 🦴🦴 **1993 (PG-13)** Mysterious disappearance of Sweeney sparks a criminal investigation, until he returns, claiming he was abducted by aliens. Though everybody doubts his story, viewers won't, since the alleged aliens have already made an appearance, shifting the focus to Sweeney as he tries to convince skeptics that his trauma is genuine. Perhaps this mirrors what director Lieberman went through while trying to convince backers the film should be made. He could have benefitted by understanding the difference between what he was telling viewers and what he was showing them. Captivating special effects are one of the few bright spots. Based on a story that might be true. **98m/C VHS, Wide.** D.B. Sweeney, Robert Patrick, Craig Sheffer, Peter Berg, James Garner, Henry Thomas; ***D:*** Robert Lieberman; ***W:*** Tracy Torme; ***M:*** Mark Isham.

The Fire in the Stone 🦴🦴 **1985** A young boy discovers an opal mine and dreams of using the treasure to reunite his family. However, when the jewels are stolen from him, he enlists his friends to help get them back. Based on the novel by Colin Thiele. **97m/C VHS.** *AU* Paul Smith, Linda Hartley, Theo Pertsindis.

Fire Maidens from Outer Space 🦴 **1956** Fire maidens prove to be true to the space opera code that dictates that all alien women be in desperate need of male company. Astronauts on an expedition to Jupiter's 13th moon discover the lost civilization of Atlantis, which, as luck would have it, is inhabited by women only. Possibly an idea before its time, it might've been better had it been made in the '60s, when space-exploitation came into its own. **80m/B VHS.** *GB* Anthony Dexter, Susan Shaw, Paul Carpenter, Harry Fowler, Jacqueline Curtiss, Sydney Tafler, Maya Koumani, Jan Holden, Kim Parker, Rodney Diak, Owen Berry; ***D:*** Cy Roth; ***W:*** Cy Roth; ***C:*** Ian Struthers.

Fire Monsters Against the Son of Hercules 🦴🦴 **1962** The son of the muscular one does battle with a hydra-headed monster in this average sword and sandal adventure. **?m/C VHS.** Reg Lewis.

The Fire Next Time 🦴🦴½ **1993** In the year 2017, the United States is being ravaged by an ecological holocaust caused by a deadly combination of pollution and global warming. Nelson, Bedelia, and their children are forced from their Louisiana home by a natural disaster and decide to head for better times in Canada. Their travels aren't easy. **195m/C VHS.** Craig T. Nelson, Bonnie Bedelia, Juergen Prochnow, Richard Farnsworth, Justin Whalin, Charles Haid, Sal Lopez, Shawn Toovey, Ashley Jones; ***Cameos:*** Odetta; ***D:*** Tom McLoughlin; ***W:*** James Henerson. **TV**

Fire on the Amazon 🦴½ **1993 (R)** Really dumb "save-the-environment" movie with Bullock the rainforest activist and Sheffer the photojournalist. The duo hook up to investigate the assassination of an environmentalist. The big woo-hoo is Bullock's brief nude sex scene with Sheffer. **81m/C VHS, DVD.** Sandra Bullock, Craig Sheffer, Judith Chapman, Juan Fernandez; ***D:*** Luis Llosa; ***W:*** Catherine Cyran, Jane Gray; ***C:*** Pili Flores-Guerra; ***M:*** Roy J. Ravio.

Fire Over England 🦴🦴🦴 **1937** Young naval officer volunteers to spy at the Spanish court to learn the plans for the invasion of his native England and to identify the traitors among the English nobility. He arouses the romantic interest of his queen, Elizabeth I, one of her ladies, and a Spanish noblewoman who helps with his missions, and later leads the fleet to victory over the huge Spanish Armada. The first on-screen pairing of Olivier and Leigh is just one of the many virtues of this entertaining drama. **81m/B VHS, DVD.** *GB* Flora Robson, Raymond Massey, Laurence Olivier, Vivien Leigh, Leslie Banks, James Mason; ***D:*** William K. Howard; ***W:*** Clemence Dane, Sergei Nolbandov; ***C:*** James Wong Howe; ***M:*** Richard Addinsell.

Fire with Fire 🦴🦴 **1986 (PG-13)** A boy at a juvenile detention center and a Catholic school girl fall in love. However, they find themselves on the run from the law when he escapes to be with her. Sheffer and Madsen are appealing in this otherwise unspectacular film. **103m/C VHS.** Craig Sheffer, Virginia Madsen, Jon Polito, Kate Reid, Jean Smart, D.B. Sweeney; ***D:*** Duncan Gibbins; ***W:*** Bill Phillips, Paul Boorstin, Sharon Boorstin; ***M:*** Howard Shore.

The Fire Within 🦴🦴🦴 *Le Feu Follet; Fuoco Fatuo* **1964** Ronet plays an alcoholic writer recently released from a sanitorium after a breakdown. Believing his life will only continue its downward spiral, he pays a final visit to friends and calmly plots his suicide. Malle clearly and pitilessly describes a man beyond despair. Based on a novel by Pierre Drieu La Rochelle, which itself fictionalized the suicide of writer Jacques Rigaut. In French with English subtitles. **104m/B VHS.** *FR* Bernard Noel, Jeanne Moreau, Alexandra Stewart, Henri Serre, Maurice Ronet, Lena Skerla, Yvonne Clech, Hubert Deschamps, Jean-Paul Moulinot; ***D:*** Louis Malle; ***W:*** Louis Malle; ***C:*** Ghislan Cloquet; ***M:*** Erik Satie.

Fireback 🦴½ **1978** A Vietnam vet's wife is kidnapped by the mob, causing him to take up arms and spill blood yet again. **90m/C VHS.** Bruce Baron, Richard Harrison.

Fireball Forward 🦴🦴½ **1972 (PG)** A battalion fighting in France during WWII is having a bad time until Gazzara takes over and turns them into a crack fighting team. Uses some battle footage from the movie "Patton." **100m/C VHS.** Ben Gazzara, Eddie Albert, Ricardo Montalban, Dana Elcar, L.Q. (Justus E. McQueen) Jones, Anne Francis; ***D:*** Marvin J. Chomsky. **TV**

Fireballs 🦴½ **1990** Sexploitaton pic set at a firehouse, where a batch of female recruits turn up the heat for three stud hose-bearers. The title should give you some idea of the intellectual level. **89m/C VHS.** Mike Shapiro, Goren Kalezik; ***D:*** Mike Shapiro.

Firebird 2015 A.D. 🦴 **1981 (PG)** Dreary action adventure set in a 21st century society where automobile use is banned because of an extreme oil shortage. Private cars are hunted down for destruction by the Department of Vehicular Control. One over-zealous enforcer decides to make it a package deal and throws in the owners as well. Everyone connected with effort should have been cited for running stop sign. **97m/C VHS.** Darren McGavin, George Touliatos, Doug McClure; ***D:*** David Robertson.

Firecracker 🦴 **1971** Female martial arts expert retaliates against the crooks who murdered her sister. **83m/C VHS.** Jillian Kesner, Darby Hinton; ***D:*** Cirio H. Santiago.

Firecreek 🦴🦴½ **1968** Fonda and his thugs terrorize a small town protected by part-time sheriff Stewart. Beautiful photography and competent cast, but meandering and long. **104m/C VHS.** Henry Fonda, James Stewart, Inger Stevens, Gary Lockwood, Dean Jagger, Ed Begley Sr., Jay C. Flippen, Jack Elam, Barbara Luna; ***D:*** Vincent McEveety; ***C:*** William Clothier.

Firefall 🦴🦴 *Freefall* **1994** Wildlife photog Katy Mazur (Gidley) has a brief affair with sportsman Grant Orion (Roberts) while on assignment in Africa. When they meet again, Orion tells Katy he's actually an Interpol agent who's assigned to protect her—although she has no idea why. Katy's fiance (Fahey) thinks this is strange. **95m/C VHS.** Pamela Gidley, Eric Roberts, Jeff Fahey; ***D:*** John Irvin.

Firefight 🦴 **1987** After a nuclear holocaust, convicted criminals endeavor to rule the wasteland. **100m/C VHS.** James Pfeiffer, Janice Carraher, Jack Tucker; ***D:*** Scott Pfeiffer.

The Firefly 🦴🦴½ **1937** Although slow-paced and long, this adaptation of the 1912 Rudolf Friml operetta was one of MacDonald's most popular films. Co-star Jones gets to sing the best song in the film, "Donkey Serenade," while MacDonald sings most of the others. ♫Love Is Like a Firefly; English March; A Woman's Kiss; He Who Loves and Runs Away; When a Maid Comes Knocking at Your Heart; When the Wine Is Full of Fire; The Donkey Serenade; Giannina Mia; Sympathy. **140m/B VHS.** Jeanette MacDonald, Allan Jones, Warren William, Billy Gilbert, Henry Daniell, Douglass Dumbrille, George Zucco; ***D:*** Robert Z. Leonard.

Firefox 🦴🦴½ **1982 (PG)** A retired pilot sneaks into the Soviet Union for the Pentagon to steal a top-secret, ultra-sophisticated warplane and fly it out of the country. Best for the low-altitude flight and aerial battle sequences, but too slow on character and much too slow getting started. **136m/C VHS.** Clint Eastwood, Freddie Jones, David Huffman, Warren Clarke, Ronald Lacey, Kenneth Colley, Nigel Hawthorne, Kai Wulff; ***D:*** Clint Eastwood; ***C:*** Bruce Surtees; ***M:*** Maurice Jarre.

Firehawk 🦴🦴 **1992 (R)** Several American soldiers survive the crash of their helicopter into the jungles of Vietnam. They think their only enemy is the Vietcong but when they discover the copter has been sabotaged the hunt is on for the traitor among them. **92m/C VHS.** Martin Kove, Matt Salinger, Vic Trevino; ***D:*** Cirio H. Santiago; ***W:*** Jeff Yonis.

Firehead 🦴🦴½ **1990 (R)** A pyrokinetic Soviet defector begins using his powers to destroy American munitions in the name of peace. When a clandestine pro-war organization hears of this, they attempt to capture the man and use him for their own evil purposes. **88m/C VHS.** Christopher Plummer, Chris Lemmon, Martin Landau, Gretchen Becker, Brett Porter; ***D:*** Peter Yuval.

Firehouse 🦴🦴 **1972** Tempers ignite in a lily-white firehouse when a black rookie replaces an expired veteran. March—of "Paper Lion" renown—directed this made-for-TV emergency clone, which ran ever-so-briefly as an adventure series on TV in 1974 (with a largely different cast). **73m/C VHS, DVD.** Richard Roundtree, Vince Edwards, Andrew Duggan, Richard Jaeckel, Sheila Frazier, Val Avery, Paul LeMat, Michael Lerner; ***D:*** Alex March; ***M:*** Tom Scott. **TV**

Firehouse 🦴 **1987 (R)** In the style of "Police Academy," three beautiful and sex-starved fire-fighting recruits klutz up an urban firehouse. A softcore frolic. **91m/C VHS, DVD.** Barrett Hopkins, Shannon Murphy, Violet Brown, John Anderson, Julia Roberts; ***D:*** J. Christian Ingvordsen; ***W:*** J. Christian Ingvordsen, Steven Kaman, Rick Marx; ***C:*** Steven Kaman; ***M:*** Michael Montes.

Firelight 🦴🦴½ **1997 (R)** Governess Elisabeth (Marceau) needs to pay off her father's debts and makes a deal with married British aristocrat Charles Godwin (Dillane) to give him a child since his own wife is comatose from a riding accident. She gives her baby daughter up but, seven years later, is still so haunted by her memories that she decides to seek them out. So Elisabeth gets hired as her own spoiled daughter's governess. Charles is at least momentarily outraged but soon they can't keep their sexual desires quiescent any longer. Set in 1838. **104m/C VHS.** Sophie Marceau, Stephen (Dillon) Dillane, Joss Ackland, Kevin Anderson, Lia Williams, Dominique Belcourt; ***D:*** William Nicholson; ***W:*** William Nicholson; ***C:*** Nic Morris; ***M:*** Christopher Gunning.

The Fireman 🦴🦴½ **1916** Chaplin portrays a fireman who becomes a hero. Silent with musical soundtrack added. **20m/B VHS.** Eric Campbell, Edna Purviance, Charlie Chaplin; ***D:*** Charlie Chaplin.

The Firemen's Ball 🦴🦴🦴 *Hori, ma panenko* **1968** A critically acclaimed comedy about a small-town ball held for a retiring fire chief. Plans go amusingly awry as beauty contestants refuse to show themselves, raffle prizes and other items—including the gift for the guest of honor—are stolen, and the firemen are unable to prevent an old man's house from burning down. Forman's second film is sometimes interpreted as political allegory; Czech with subtitles. **73m/C VHS, DVD.** *CZ* Vaclav Stockel, Josef Svet; ***D:*** Milos Forman; ***W:*** Ivan Passer, Jaroslav Papousek, Vaclav Sasek, Milos Forman; ***C:*** Miroslav Ondricek; ***M:*** Karel Mares.

Firepower 🦴½ 1979 (R) Loren blames her chemist husband's death on a rich industrialist and hires hitman Coburn to take care of the matter. Less than compelling. **104m/C VHS.** Dominic Chianese, Sophia Loren, James Coburn, O.J. Simpson, Christopher F. Bean; ***D:*** Michael Winner; ***W:*** Michael Winner; ***M:*** Gato Barbieri.

Firepower 🦴½ 1993 (R) Two cops chase "The Swordsman" into a federally sanctioned area of legalized gambling, prostitution and crime (Las Vegas?), risking life and limb in the treacherous "Caged Ring of Death." **?m/C VHS.** Chad McQueen, Gary Daniels, Jim Hellwig, Joseph Ruskin, George Murdock.

Fires on the Plain 🦴🦴🦴 *Nobi* 1959 A grueling Japanese antiwar film about an unhinged private in the Philippines during WWII who roams the war-torn countryside encountering all manner of horror and devastation. In Japanese with English subtitles. **105m/B VHS.** *JP* Eiji Funakoshi, Osamu Takizawa, Mickey Custis, Asao Sano, Kyu Sazanka, Yoshihiro Hamaguchi, Hikaru Hoshi, Yasushi Sugita, Masaya Tsukida, Mantaro Ushio; ***D:*** Kon Ichikawa; ***W:*** Natto Wada; ***C:*** Setsuo Kobayashi; ***M:*** Yashushi Akutagawa.

Fires Within 🦴🦴 1991 (R) A curiously flat romance with political overtones. After eight years as a political prisoner in Cuba, Nestor (Smits) is released and goes to Miami to be reunited with his wife and daughter. Once there he finds his wife has fallen in love with another man. Now Nestor must choose between his politics and the chance to win back his family. Secondary plotlines fizzle out and a talented cast is largely wasted. Scacchi is beautiful but hardly believable as the Cuban wife. **90m/C VHS, DVD, Wide.** Jimmy Smits, Greta Scacchi, Vincent D'Onofrio; ***D:*** Gillian Armstrong; ***W:*** Cynthia Cidre; ***C:*** David Gribble; ***M:*** Maurice Jarre.

Firestarter 🦴🦴 1984 (R) A C.I.A.-like organization is after a little girl who has the ability to set anything on fire in this filmed adaptation of Stephen King's bestseller. Good special effects help a silly plot. **115m/C VHS, DVD.** David Keith, Drew Barrymore, Freddie Jones, Martin Sheen, George C. Scott, Heather Locklear, Louise Fletcher, Moses Gunn, Art Carney, Antonio Fargas, Drew Snyder; ***D:*** Mark L. Lester; ***W:*** Stanley Mann; ***C:*** Giuseppe Ruzzolini; ***M:*** Tangerine Dream.

Firestarter 2: Rekindled 🦴🦴 2002 Original sequel to the 1984 film, based on the Stephen King novel. A now-adult Charlie (Moreau) is researching the project that sparked her fire-starting powers, without realizing that her former mentor (McDowell) wants to eliminate all survivors of the Lot 6 project. Meanwhile, insurance agent Vincent Sforza (Nucci) is looking for Charlie and a mysterious scientist (Hopper) is also involved. **168m/C VHS, DVD, Wide.** Marguerite Moreau, Malcolm McDowell, Danny Nucci, Dennis Hopper, Skye McCole Bartusiak, John Dennis Johnston, Darnell Williams, Deborah Van Valkenburgh; ***D:*** Robert Iscove; ***W:*** Philip Eisner; ***C:*** David Boyd. **CABLE**

Firestorm 🦴½ 1997 (R) Ex-NFL tough guy Long plays Jesse Graves, a parachuting firefighter with a really square head in his first starring role. Jesse, along with "smoke jumping" mentor Wynt (Glenn), must drop into a raging Wyoming forest fire in order to save a group of trapped firemen. Except they aren't really firemen, they're convicts in disguise who have escaped through a hole in the plot. Ringleader Shaye (Forsythe) had his lawyer set the fire so that he could use the volunteer murderer/fire fighter release program to escape and find the $37 million he has hidden. Happens all the time. The smoky chain gang also stumble across beautiful bird-watcher Jennifer (Amis) and take her hostage. Jesse must foil the bad guys, save the girl and douse the fire; all the while lugging around his humongous chin and speaking in monotone. Fire effects were enhanced by computer generated graphics. **89m/C VHS, DVD.** Howie Long, Scott Glenn, William Forsythe, Suzy Amis, Christianne Hirt, Garwin Sanford, Sebastian Spence, Michael Greyeyes, Benjamin Ratner, Barry Pepper, Vladimir Kulich, Tom McBeath; ***D:*** Dean Semler; ***W:*** Chris Soth; ***C:*** Stephen Windon; ***M:*** J. Peter Robinson.

Firestorm: 72 Hours in Oakland 🦴🦴½ 1993 Residents of an Oakland community face the threat of a big brush fire. **94m/C VHS.** LeVar Burton, Jill Clayburgh, Michael Gross; ***D:*** Michael Tuchner.

Firetrap 🦴🦴½ 2001 (R) Combo heist/disaster flick is routine material. Thief Jack (Cain) is hired to steal a computer chip from a L.A. high-rise corporate headquarters but is double-crossed by a crooked company insider (Tyson) who sets fire to the building, trapping Jack and the other occupants. **99m/C VHS, DVD.** Dean Cain, Richard Tyson, Lori Petty, Mel Harris, James Storm, Vanessa Angel, John O'Hurley, Elena Sahagun, Steven Williams; ***D:*** Harris Done; ***W:*** Richard Preston Jr., Diane Fine; ***C:*** Mark W. Gray; ***M:*** Sean Murray. **VIDEO**

Firewalker 🦴 1986 (PG) An "Indiana Jones" clone about three mercenaries endeavoring to capture a fortune in hidden gold. Paper-mache sets and a villain with an eye patch that consistently changes eyes are just some of the gaffes that make this one of the worst edited movies in history. **106m/C VHS.** Chuck Norris, Louis Gossett Jr., Melody Anderson; ***D:*** J. Lee Thompson; ***W:*** Norman Aladjem; ***M:*** Gary Chang.

Fireworks 🦴🦴 *Hana-Bi* 1997 Idiosyncratic mixture of drama, comedy, violence, and sentiment. Nishi (Kitano) is a tough detective whose wife, Miyuki (Kishimoto), is dying from leukemia. He's visiting her in the hospital when his partner Horibe (Osugi) is gunned down and paralyzed. Deciding to get justice on his own terms, Nishi quits the force and decides to settle his debts with the yakuza by robbing a bank (which also funds a last trip with his wife). Kitano (who uses his acting alias of Beat Takeshi) is the strong, silent, violent type and a very visual director. Those are Kitano's own paintings in the scenes where Horibe takes up art as his new hobby. Japanese with subtitles. **103m/C VHS, DVD, Wide.** *JP* Takeshi "Beat" Kitano, Kayoko Kishimoto, Ren Osugi, Susumu Terajima, Tetsu Watanabe; ***D:*** Takeshi "Beat" Kitano; ***W:*** Takeshi "Beat" Kitano; ***C:*** Hideo Yamamoto; ***M:*** Joe Hisaishi.

The Firing Line 🦴🦴 1991 The Central American government hires a mercenary rebel-buster to squash insurgents. Everything's great until he finds out he agrees with the rebel cause, and he trains them to fight the government. Below average renegade-with-a-hidden-heart warpic. **93m/C VHS, DVD.** Reb Brown, Shannon Tweed, Michael Monty, Kathlena Marie, Melvin Davidson, Carl Terry, Andy Jacobson; ***D:*** John Gale; ***W:*** John Gale, Sonny Sanders; ***C:*** Carl Sommers; ***M:*** Martia Manuel.

The Firm 🦴🦴🦴 1993 (R) Top-flight cast promises a good time—the script based on the top-selling 1991 novel by John Grisham nearly guarantees it. Ambitious, idealistic Ivy League law school grad Cruise accepts a great offer from a small but wealthy Memphis law firm. As with anything that seems too good to be true, he discovers too late that nothing in life is free. Good performances by nearly everyone involved makes up for predictability. Sorvino has an uncredited cameo as a mob boss. Book fans beware: the script is fairly faithful until the end. The movie rights were snapped up before the book was published. Placed third in the 1993 race for top boxoffice gross. **154m/C VHS, DVD, CD-I, Wide.** Joe (Johnny) Viterelli, Tom Cruise, Jeanne Tripplehorn, Gene Hackman, Hal Holbrook, Terry Kinney, Wilford Brimley, Ed Harris, Holly Hunter, David Strathairn, Gary Busey, Steven Hill, Tobin Bell, Barbara Garrick, Jerry Hardin, Karina Lombard, John Beal; ***Cameos:*** Paul Sorvino; ***D:*** Sydney Pollack; ***W:*** Robert Towne, David Rayfiel; ***C:*** John Seale; ***M:*** Dave Grusin.

First a Girl 🦴🦴½ 1935 Delivery girl Elizabeth (Matthews) is dropping off costumes at the local theater, which is where she meets a female impersonator with throat trouble. He gets Elizabeth to take his place on stage and she becomes famous overnight. So she keeps up the charade until a princess (Lee) and her boyfriend (Jones) become suspicious and decide to uncover the truth. If the plot sounds familiar, it's because the film was remade as "Victor/Victoria" (1982). **93m/B VHS.** *GB* Jessie Matthews, Sonnie Hale, Anna Lee, Griffith Jones, Alfred Drayton, Martita Hunt; ***D:*** Victor Saville; ***W:*** Marjorie Gaffney; ***C:*** Glen MacWilliams.

First Affair 1983 A young girl undergoes the pressures of freshman life at college, including her first love affair, which is with the husband of a female professor. **95m/C VHS.** Loretta Swit, Melissa Sue Anderson, Joel Higgins; ***D:*** Gus Trikonis. **TV**

First & Ten 🦴🦴 1985 A failing football team emphasizes sexual, rather than athletic conquests, under the guidance of their female owner. Followed by "First & Ten: The Team Scores Again." **88m/C VHS.** Delta Burke, Geoffrey Scott, Reid Shelton, Ruta Lee, Fran Tarkenton; ***D:*** Donald Kushner. **CABLE**

First & Ten: The Team Scores Again 🦴 1985 A sequel to the cable comedy "First and Ten" about a football team's relationship with their female owner. **101m/C VHS.** Delta Burke, Geoffrey Scott, Ruta Lee, Reid Shelton, Clayton Landey, Fran Tarkenton. **CABLE**

First Blood 🦴🦴 1982 (R) Stallone is a former Green Beret survivor of Vietnam whose nightmares of wartime horrors are triggered by a wrongful arrest in a small town. He escapes into the mountains of the Northwest and leads his pursuers to all manner of bloody ends. Finally, the Army is summoned to crush him. Extremely violent and frequently confused, fueled on the revenge fantasy and not much concerned with the rules of plot realism. Screen debut of Caruso. Based on David Morrell's novel. A boxoffice hit that launched the "Rambo" series. Followed by "Rambo: First Blood, Part 2." **96m/C VHS, DVD, Wide.** Sylvester Stallone, Richard Crenna, Brian Dennehy, Jack Starrett, David Caruso; ***D:*** Ted Kotcheff; ***W:*** Sylvester Stallone; ***C:*** Andrew Laszlo; ***M:*** Jerry Goldsmith.

First Born 🦴🦴½ 1984 (PG-13) In search of romance, divorced mother Garr finds an intriguing man, Weller. Trouble erupts when her son learns Weller is a cocaine dealer. Talented cast makes most of story. **100m/C VHS.** Teri Garr, Peter Weller, Christopher Collet, Corey Haim, Sarah Jessica Parker, Robert Downey Jr.; ***D:*** Michael Apted; ***C:*** Ralf Bode.

First Daughter 🦴🦴½ 1999 Alex McGregor (Hemingway) is a Secret Service agent who saves President Johnathan Hayes's (Harrison) life and is rewarded for her efforts by being assigned to protect his bratty teen daughter, Jess (Keena), on a Colorado rafting trip. (Actually filmed in Australia.) The teen gets kidnapped by a paramilitary group and agent Alex, aided by river guide Grant Carlson (Savant), is determined to get her back. **94m/C VHS.** Mariel Hemingway, Doug Savant, Monica Keena, Gregory Harrison; ***D:*** Armand Mastroianni; ***W:*** Carey Hayes, Chad Hayes; ***C:*** Mark Wareham; ***M:*** Louis Febre. **CABLE**

The First Deadly Sin 🦴½ 1980 (R) Police lieutenant Sinatra tracks down a homicidal killer in spite of wife Dunaway's illness and his impending retirement. Read Lawrence Sanders' bestselling novel; it's a lot more exciting than this. **112m/C VHS, DVD.** Frank Sinatra, Faye Dunaway, David Dukes, Brenda Vaccaro, James Whitmore; ***D:*** Brian G. Hutton; ***W:*** Mann Rubin; ***C:*** Jack Priestley; ***M:*** Gordon Jenkins.

First Degree 🦴½ 1995 (R) N.Y.C. homicide detective Rick Mallory (Lowe) goes up against the mob while investigating the murder of a rich man and falling for the widow. **98m/C VHS.** *CA* Rob Lowe, Leslie Hope, Tom McCamus, Nadia Capone, Brett Halsey; ***D:*** Jeff Woolnough; ***W:*** Ron Base; ***C:*** Glen MacPherson. **CABLE**

First Degree 🦴🦴 *Charades; Felons* 1998 (R) Quinn (Wilder) and wife Lara (Kates) invite some friends and co-workers to their house for a barbecue. But there's more than hamburgers about to be grilled. Seems widow Jude (Black) is convinced that her husband Paul's killer is attending the festivities. And she soon has everyone turning on each other. **80m/C VHS, DVD.** Erika Eleniak, C. Thomas Howell, Jack Scalia, James Wilder, James Russo, Karen Black, Kimberley Kates, James Andronica; ***D:*** Stephen Eckelberry; ***W:*** S.P. Somtow; ***C:*** Susan Emerson. **VIDEO**

First Do No Harm 🦴🦴½ 1997 (PG-13) Well-intentioned but routine TV movie depicts the crisis of the farming Reimuller family when the youngest child, four-year-old Robbie (Adkins), is diagnosed with epilepsy. Their health insurance won't cover Robbie's drug treatment and the bank is about to foreclose on the farm so dad Dave (Ward) takes up truck driving while mom Lori (Streep) tries to hold things together. Dismayed at Robbie's doctors, Lori also pursues an unorthodox treatment for Robbie that involves diet therapy rather than drugs. Director Abraham's own son has his epilepsy controlled by this alternative method. **94m/C VHS.** Meryl Streep, Fred Ward, Seth Adkins, Allison Janney, Michael Yarmush; ***D:*** Jim Abrahams; ***W:*** Ann Beckett; ***C:*** Pierre Letarte. **TV**

First Encounter 🦴½ 1997 Warning—when exploring space and encountering a mysteriously abandoned, apparently deserted ship—Leave It Alone! This crew decides to go sightseeing and it doesn't work out well. **88m/C VHS.** Roddy Piper, Trevor Goddard. **VIDEO**

First Family 🦴½ 1980 (R) Flat satire of life in the White House. The humor is weak and silly at best, despite the excellent comedy cast. Henry's first directorial effort. **100m/C VHS.** Bob Newhart, Madeline Kahn, Gilda Radner, Richard Benjamin; ***D:*** Buck Henry; ***W:*** Buck Henry; ***M:*** Ralph Burns.

First Kid 🦴🦴 1996 (PG) Formulaic "Home Alone Guarding Tess" does have its moments, but if you're over 14, probably not enough of them. Latest in a bevy of films to be inaugurated into the white hot "White House" genre-of-the-moment. Innocuous family comedy casts Sinbad as Sam Simms, an offbeat Secret Service agent who is given the menial job of guarding Prez's bratty son Luke (Pierce). Simms sees that Luke is merely a misunderstood misfit like himself, and helps the lad have more fun than a Presidential son is allowed. Flick's clean, inoffensive humor makes it hard to dislike. Watch for cameo from Sonny Bono. **101m/C VHS.** Sinbad, Brock Pierce, James Naughton, Blake Boyd, Timothy Busfield, Art LaFleur, Robert Guillaume, Lisa Eichhorn, Zachery Ty Bryan, Bill Cobbs; ***D:*** David Mickey Evans; ***W:*** Tim Kelleher; ***C:*** Anthony B. Richmond; ***M:*** Richard Gibbs.

First Knight 🦴½ 1995 (PG-13) King Arthur/Camelot legend comes to life again, but isn't worth the time it takes to watch. Wandering swordsman Lancelot (Gere) saves beautiful Guinevere (Ormond), soon to be Arthur's (Connery) queen, from evil renegade knight Malagant. They yearn, they gaze, they kiss—you gag. Written like a Harlequin romance, the dialogue (especially when uttered by Gere) is unintentionally funny, and the plot will cause much eye-rolling. Connery's regal (he knows his costume epics) and Ormond's lovely, but Gere is badly miscast. He offers a contemporary take on the flawed hero complete with American accent, an amazing feat in the 13th century. Big-scale battles, betrayals, passion, even Disneyland-like Camelot sets—the pieces for a tremendous epic are all here, it just doesn't work. **134m/C VHS, DVD, 8mm, Wide.** Sean Connery, Richard Gere, Julia Ormond, Ben Cross, John Gielgud, Liam Cunningham, Christopher Villiers, Valentine Pelka; ***D:*** Jerry Zucker; ***W:*** William Nicholson; ***C:*** Adam Greenberg; ***M:*** Jerry Goldsmith.

First Legion 🦴🦴½ 1951 Boyer and Addy are seminarians struggling with their faith when they are confronted with a supposed miracle. Low-key examination of religion and conflict within a religious community. **77m/B VHS.** Charles Boyer, Barbara Rush, William Demarest, Leo G. Carroll; ***D:*** Douglas Sirk.

First Love 🦴🦴½ 1939 Best known for Durbin's first screen kiss, this lightweight romance finds orphaned Connie Harding moving to New York to live with her wealthy Uncle James Clinton (Pallette) and his family. Connie meets handsome rich boy Ted Drake (Stack's screen debut) but her snobby debutante cousin Barbara

(Parrish) already has Ted in her sights. Barbara tries to prevent Connie from going to the Drakes fancy dance but, in Cinderella fashion, the Clinton family servants help her become the belle of the ball. Durbin also does some singing. ♫One Fine Day; Amapola; Sympathy; A Change of Heart; Deserted; Spring In My Heart; Home Sweet Home. **85m/B VHS.** Deanna Durbin, Robert Stack, Eugene Pallette, Helen Parrish, Leatrice Joy, June Storey, Frank Jenks, Kathleen Howard, Charles Coleman, Mary Treen; ***D:*** Henry Koster; ***W:*** Bruce Manning, Lionel Houser; ***C:*** Joseph Valentine; ***M:*** Frank Skinner.

First Love 🦴🦴½ **1970 (R)** A 16-year-old lad falls in love with a slightly older woman only to have his feelings rejected and to discover that she's his father's mistress. Actor Schell's directorial debut. **90m/C VHS.** *GE SI* John Moulder-Brown, Dominique Sanda, Maximilian Schell, Valentina Cortese; ***D:*** Maximilian Schell; ***C:*** Sven Nykvist.

First Love 🦴🦴½ **1977 (R)** A story of an idealistic college student who takes love (and especially making love) more seriously than the rest of his peers, including his girlfriend. Based on Harold Brodkey's story "Sentimental Education." Darling's directorial debut. **92m/C VHS.** William Katt, Susan Dey, John Heard, Beverly D'Angelo, Robert Loggia; ***D:*** Joan Darling; ***M:*** John Barry.

First Love and Other Pains / One of Them 🦴🦴½ **1999** Two gay shorts explore first love. In "First Love" (50 minutes), Hong Kong college student Mark begins an English lit course with a stern British professor, Hugh Graham. Depressed by creative burnout, Hugh is flattered by Mark's attentions and they have a one-nighter—at least in Hugh's mind because Mark is looking for a longer-lasting romance. Cantonese and English with subtitles. In "One of Them" (47 minutes), two gay teens in the 60s strike up a friendship that makes their small, boring town almost bearable. **97m/C VHS, DVD, Wide.** Edward Strode, Alex Wong, Ciaran Pennington, Cameron J. Watt; ***D:*** Simon Chung, Stewart Main; ***W:*** Simon Chung, Peter Wells; ***C:*** Ping Hung Wong, Stewart Main.

First Love, Last Rites 🦴🦴½ **1998 (R)** Peretz moved his atmospheric debut feature (adapted from a short story by Ian McEwan) from the English coast to the bayous of Louisiana. There local gal Sissel (Gregson Wagner) is shacking up with fish-out-of-water Brooklyn boy Joey (Ribisi). They have a lot of sex. Sissel finally introduces Joey to her crazy father Henry (Burke) and the two men get involved in an eel-catching business. Then Sissel and Joey start spatting and soon they're not having sex anymore and their romance drifts away. The film does look really good. **93m/C VHS.** Natasha Gregson Wagner, Giovanni Ribisi, Robert John Burke, Eli Marienthal; ***D:*** Jesse Peretz; ***W:*** Jesse Peretz, David Ryan; ***C:*** Tom Richmond; ***M:*** Craig (Shudder to Think) Wedren.

First Man into Space 🦴🦴 *Satellite of Blood* **1959** An astronaut returns to Earth covered with strange space dust and with an organism feeding inside him (shades of "Alien"). The alien needs human blood to survive and starts killing in order to get it. **78m/B VHS, DVD.** Marshall Thompson, Marla Landi, Bill Edwards; ***D:*** Robert Day; ***W:*** John C. Cooper, Lance Z. Hargreaves; ***C:*** Geoffrey Faithfull; ***M:*** Buxton Orr.

First Men in the Moon 🦴🦴 **1964** A fun, special effects-laden adaptation of the H. G. Wells novel about an Edwardian civilian spacecraft visiting the moon and the creature found there. Visual effects by Ray Harryhausen. Finch makes a brief appearance. **103m/C VHS, DVD, Wide.** *GB* Martha Hyer, Edward Judd, Lionel Jeffries, Erik Chitty, Peter Finch; ***D:*** Nathan (Hertz) Juran; ***W:*** Nigel Kneale, Jan Read; ***C:*** Wilkie Cooper; ***M:*** Laurie Johnson.

First Monday in October 🦴🦴½ **1981 (R)** A comedy concerning the first woman appointed to the Supreme Court, a conservative, and her colleague, a crusty but benign liberal judge. Though based on a Broadway hit, it ended up seeming to foreshadow the real-life appointment of Sandra Day O'Connor, which occurred at about the time the film was released. The title refers to the date the court begins its sessions. **99m/C VHS.** Walter Matthau, Jill Clayburgh, Barnard Hughes, James Stephens, Jan Sterling; ***D:*** Ronald Neame; ***C:*** Fred W. Koenekamp.

First Name: Carmen 🦴🦴🦴 *Prenom: Carmen* **1983** Carmen, although posing as an aspiring filmmaker, really is a bank robber and terrorist. She is also such a femme fatale that during a bank robbery one of the guards decides to run away with her. Godard cast himself as Carmen's uncle. Amusing late Godard. French with subtitles. **95m/C VHS, DVD.** *FR* Maruschka Detmers, Jacques Bonaffe, Jean-Luc Godard, Myriem Roussel, Christophe Odent; ***D:*** Jean-Luc Godard; ***W:*** Anne-Marie Mieville; ***C:*** Raoul Coutard.

The First 9 1/2 Weeks woof! **1998 (R)** Prequel to "9 1/2 Weeks" finds investor Matt Wade trying to close the biggest deal of his career with eccentric New Orleans businessman Francois Dubois. But Dubois' wife starts raising Wade's temperature even more than steamy New Orleans. **99m/C VHS, DVD.** Paul Mercurio, Clara Bellar, Malcolm McDowell, Frederic Forrest, Dennis Burkley, James Black, Anna Jacyszyn, William Keane, Richard Durden; ***D:*** Alexander Wright; ***W:*** Alexander Wright; ***C:*** John Tarver; ***M:*** Norman Orenstein.

The First Nudie Musical 🦴🦴 **1975 (R)** A producer tries to save his studio by staging a 1930s style musical, but with a naked cast and risque lyrics. Has attained semi-cult/trash status. ♫The First Nudie Musical; The Lights and the Smiles; Orgasm; Lesbian Butch Dyke; Dancing Dildos; Perversion; Honey, What Ya Doin' Tonight; Let 'Em Eat Cake; I Don't Have to Hide Anymore. **93m/C VHS.** Cindy Williams, Stephen Nathan, Diana Canova, Bruce Kimmel, Alan Abelew, Alexandra Morgan, Frank Doubleday, Kathleen Hietala, Leslie Ackerman, Ron Howard; ***D:*** Mark Haggard, Bruce Kimmel; ***W:*** Bruce Kimmel; ***C:*** Douglas Knapp; ***M:*** Bruce Kimmel.

The First Olympics: Athens 1896 🦴🦴½ **1984** Recounts the organization and drama surrounding the first modern-day Olympic games when the inexperienced American team shocked the games with their success. **260m/C VHS.** Louis Jourdan, Angela Lansbury, David Ogden Stiers, Virginia McKenna, Jason Connery, Alex Hyde-White, Honor Blackman, Bill Travers; ***D:*** Alvin Rakoff; ***M:*** Bruce Broughton. **TV**

The First Power 🦴½ **1989** A detective and psychic join forces to track down a serial killer who, after being executed, uses his satanic powers to kill again. **90m/C VHS, DVD, 8mm, Wide.** Lou Diamond Phillips, Tracy Griffith, Jeff Kober, Mykelti Williamson, Elizabeth Arlen; ***D:*** Robert Resnikoff; ***W:*** Robert Resnikoff; ***C:*** Theo van de Sande; ***M:*** Stewart Copeland.

First Spaceship on Venus 🦴🦴🦴 *Der Schweigende Stern; Milczaca Gwiazda* **1960** Eight scientists from various countries set out for Venus and find the remains of a civilization far in advance of Earth's that perished because of nuclear weapons. A sometimes compelling anti-nuclear sci-fi effort made with German and Polish backing. Originally released at 130 minutes. **78m/C VHS, DVD, Wide.** *GE PL* Yoko Tani, Oldrich Lukes, Ignacy Machowski, Julius Ongewe, Michal Postnikow, Kurt Rackelmann, Gunther Simon, Tang-Hua-Ta, Lucyna Winnicka; ***D:*** Kurt Maetzig; ***C:*** Joachim Hasler.

First Strike 🦴 **1985** The United States and the USSR engage in nuclear submarine warfare when the Soviets hijack a U.S. sub and aims its weapons at Arab oil fields. **90m/C VHS.** Stuart Whitman, Persis Khambatta.

The First Time 🦴½ *You Don't Need Pajamas at Rosie's; The Beginners Three; The Beginners; They Don't Wear Pajamas at Rosie's; Doin' It* **1969 (R)** It's pre-Porky's zaniness as a vacationing youth understandably wants to spend his "first time" with Bisset. Other than her presence, this film has little to offer. **90m/C VHS.** Jacqueline Bisset, Wes Stern, Rick Kelman, Wink Roberts; ***D:*** James Neilson.

First Time 🦴🦴½ *Doin' It* **1982 (R)** A comedy about a college student who can't quite succeed with women, despite coaching from his roommate and counseling from a psychology professor whose assistance is part of a research project. **96m/C VHS.** Tim Choate, Krista Errickson, Marshall Efron, Wallace Shawn, Wendie Jo Sperber, Cathryn Damon; ***D:*** Charles Loventhal.

First Time Felon 🦴🦴½ **1997 (R)** Based on the true story of a young Chicago drug dealer Greg Yance (Epps), who's convicted as a first-time offender and sent to a prison boot camp to straighten up. But the real challenge is when he's released and returns to his old neighborhood, with its old temptations, and tries to find an honest job. **106m/C VHS, DVD, Wide.** Omar Epps, William Forsythe, Rachel Ticotin, Delroy Lindo; ***D:*** Charles S. Dutton; ***W:*** Daniel Therriault. **CABLE**

The First to Go 🦴🦴 **1997 (PG-13)** Impulsive Adam is the first of his crowd to get engaged. His friends don't approve of his decision and decide to take him on vacation to get him to change his mind. Only his fiancee decides to come along too and she has plans of her own. **91m/C VHS, DVD.** Zach Galligan, Laurel Holloman, Mark Harmon, Corin "Corky" Nemec, Steve Parlavecchio, Jennifer Jostyn, Lisanne Falk; ***D:*** John Jacobs.

First Turn On 🦴 **1983 (R)** Not to be confused with "The Thomas Edison Story," this sex-comedy follows the adventures of several young campers who decide to die happy when an avalanche leaves them trapped in a cave. A longer unrated version is available. **88m/C VHS, DVD.** Georgia Harrell, Michael Sanville, Googy Gress, Jenny Johnson, Heide Basset, Vincent D'Onofrio, Sheila Kennedy; ***D:*** Michael Herz, Lloyd Kaufman; ***W:*** Michael Herz, Lloyd Kaufman, Stuart Strutin, Georgia Harrell; ***C:*** Lloyd Kaufman.

The First Wives Club 🦴🦴½ **1996 (PG)** As the first Mrs. Trump, who makes a most appropriate cameo, so wisely puts it, "Don't get mad, get everything." But to the three rich, middle-aged friends who are dumped by their husbands so the guys can marry younger "trophy" wives, there's just nothing like revenge. Comedy begins in 1969 with the young and idealistic Annie (Keaton), Brenda (Midler), Elise (Hawn) and Cynthia graduating college, then moves to the present with the wronged Cynthia (Channing) ledge-diving from her swanky Manhattan apartment because her husband left her. The remaining mistreated trio goes into action, using their exes' own money, businesses, power, and various mistresses against them. This film's appeal and success had Hollywood tongues wagging, predicting the dawn of new roles for older actresses. Based on the book by Olivia Goldsmith. **104m/C VHS, DVD, Wide.** Goldie Hawn, Diane Keaton, Bette Midler, Sarah Jessica Parker, Heather Locklear, Marcia Gay Harden, Elizabeth Berkley, Victor Garber, Dan Hedaya, Stephen Collins, Maggie Smith, Stockard Channing, Bronson Pinchot, Jennifer (Jennie) Dundas Lowe, Eileen Heckart, Philip Bosco, Rob Reiner, James Naughton; ***D:*** Hugh Wilson; ***W:*** Robert Harling; ***C:*** Donald E. Thorin; ***M:*** Marc Shaiman.

First Yank into Tokyo 🦴🦴 *Mask of Fury* **1945** An American army pilot who grew up in Japan undergoes plastic surgery in order to infiltrate Japanese lines and get information from an American scientist. Some last minute editing to capitalize on current events made this the first American film to deal with the atomic bomb. **83m/B VHS.** Tom Neal, Richard Loo, Barbara Hale, Marc Cramer; ***D:*** Gordon Douglas.

A Fish Called Wanda 🦴🦴🦴 **1988 (R)** Absurd, high-speed farce about four criminals trying to retrieve $20 million they've stolen from a safety deposit box—and each other. Meanwhile, barrister Archie Leech (Cleese) falls in love with the female thief, Wanda (Curtis). Some sick, but tastelessly funny, humor involves Palin's problem with stuttering and some very dead doggies. Written by Monty Python alum Cleese and director Crichton, who understand that silence is sometimes funnier than speech, and that timing is everything. Wickedly funny. **98m/C VHS, DVD, Wide.** John Cleese, Kevin Kline, Jamie Lee Curtis, Michael Palin, Tom Georgeson, Maria Aitken, Patricia Hayes, Geoffrey Palmer, Andrew MacLachlan; ***D:*** Charles Crichton; ***W:*** Charles Crichton, John Cleese; ***C:*** Alan Hume; ***M:*** John Du Prez. Oscars '88: Support. Actor (Kline); British Acad. '88: Actor (Cleese), Support. Actor (Palin).

Fish Hawk 🦴½ **1979 (G)** When an alcoholic Indian, Fish Hawk, meets a young boy in the forest, they strike up a friendship and he attempts to clean up his act. Attempts to be heartwarming. **95m/C VHS.** *CA* Will Sampson, Charlie Fields; ***D:*** Donald Shebib.

The Fish that Saved Pittsburgh 🦴🦴 **1979 (PG)** A floundering basketball team hires an astrologer to try and change their luck. She makes sure all the team members' signs are compatible with their star's Pisces sign (the fish). Produced a disco soundtrack with several Motown groups who also performed in the movie. **104m/C VHS.** Jonathan Winters, Stockard Channing, Flip Wilson, Julius Erving, Margaret Avery, Meadowlark Lemon, Nicholas Pryor, James Bond III, Kareem Abdul-Jabbar, Jack Kehoe, Debbie Allen; ***D:*** Gilbert Moses; ***M:*** Thom Bell.

The Fisher King 🦴🦴🦴 **1991 (R)** In derelict-infested Manhattan a down-and-out radio deejay meets a crazed vagabond (Williams) obsessed with medieval history and in search of the Holy Grail. At first the whimsical mix of Arthurian myth and modern urban hell seems amazingly wrongheaded. In retrospect it still does. But while this picture runs it weaves a spell that pulls you in, especially in its quiet moments. Your reaction to the silly ending depends entirely on how well you're bamboozled by a script that equates madness with enlightment and the homeless with holy fools. Filmed on the streets of New York, with many street people playing themselves. **138m/C VHS, DVD, Wide.** Robin Williams, Jeff Bridges, Amanda Plummer, Mercedes Ruehl, Michael Jeter, Harry Shearer, John de Lancie, Kathy Najimy, David Hyde Pierce; ***D:*** Terry Gilliam; ***W:*** Richard LaGravenese; ***C:*** Roger Pratt; ***M:*** George Fenton. Oscars '91: Support. Actress (Ruehl); Golden Globes '92: Actor—Mus./Comedy (Williams), Support. Actress (Ruehl); L.A. Film Critics '91: Actress (Ruehl).

Fisherman's Wharf 🦴½ **1939** Breen stars as an orphan adopted by a San Francisco fisherman who runs away when his aunt and bratty cousin come to live with them. **72m/B VHS.** Bobby Breen, Leo Carrillo, Henry Armetta, Lee Patrick, Rosina Galli, Leon Belasco; ***D:*** Bernard Vorhaus.

The Fishing Trip 🦴🦴 **1998** Jessie (Hood) and her younger sister Kristi (Erwin) are determined to track down the stepfather who molested them as children. They discover he's on a fishing trip at a remote British Columbia cabin and head after him, joined by Murdoch (Henry), their dope-smoking friend. The troubled trio are seeking resolution for their various problems and find it in an unexpected manner. **?m/C VHS.** *CA* Jhene Erwin, Melissa Hood, Anna Henry, Jim Kenney, Diana Tayback, T.J. Grist; ***D:*** Amnon Buchbinder; ***C:*** Derek Rogers. Genie '98: Song ("River Blue").

F.I.S.T. 🦴🦴½ **1978 (R)** A young truck driver turns union organizer for idealistic reasons, but finds himself teaming with gangsters to boost his cause. His rise to the top of the union comes at the cost of his integrity, as Stallone does a character resembling Jimmy Hoffa. **145m/C VHS.** Sylvester Stallone, Rod Steiger, Peter Boyle, David Huffman, Melinda Dillon, Tony LoBianco, Kevin Conway, Peter Donat, Cassie Yates, Brian Dennehy; ***D:*** Norman Jewison; ***W:*** Sylvester Stallone; ***M:*** Bill Conti.

Fist 🦴 **1979 (R)** Street fighter battles his way through the urban jungle seeking personal freedom and revenge. **84m/C VHS.** Richard Lawson, Annazette Chase, Dabney Coleman.

Fist Fighter 🦴½ **1988 (R)** The ups and downs of a professional bare-knuckle fighter as he avenges a friend's murder. **99m/C VHS.** Jorge (George) Rivero, Edward Albert, Brenda Bakke, Mike Connors, Simon Andrew, Matthias Hues; ***D:*** Frank Zuniga; ***W:*** Max Bloom.

Fist of Fear, Touch of Death 🦴 *Fist of Fear; The Dragon and the Cobra* **1980 (R)** Madison Square Garden is the scene for a high stakes martial arts face-off. Standard kung-fu film highlighted by short clips of the late Bruce Lee. **81m/C VHS, DVD, Wide.** Fred Williamson, Ron Van Cliff, Adolph Caesar, Aaron Banks, Bill Louie; ***D:*** Matthew Mallinson; ***W:*** Ron Harvey; ***C:*** John Hazard; ***M:*** Keith Mansfield.

Fist of Glory 🦴½ **1995 (R)** In the waning days of the Vietnam War, a commando searches for the comrade who saved his life. He discovers his pal is a drug-addicted POW who's forced to fight in order to survive. **93m/C VHS.** Dale "Apollo" Cook, Maurice Smith, Robert Marius, Eric Hahn; ***D:*** Joe Mari Avellana.

Fist of Honor 🦴 **1992 (R)** A young boxer seeks to avenge his fiance's death, a beautiful girl squares off against a bad-cop, and two mobster leaders try to take control of one the same city. When a member of one family breaks a truce and begins killing rival family members, the violence escalates and old scores will be settled. **90m/C VHS.** Sam Jones, Joey House, Harry Guardino, Nicholas Worth, Frank Sivero, Abe Vigoda, Bubba Smith; ***D:*** Richard Pepin; ***W:*** Charles Kanganis.

Fist of Legend 🦴🦴 **1994 (R)** Chen Zuen (Li) is a martial arts practitioner studying abroad during WWII, who returns to his homeland to avenge his teacher's death at the hands of the invading Japanese. Homage to Bruce Lee's 1972 "Fists of Fury" AKA "Chinese Connection." Cantonese with subtitles or dubbed. **92m/C VHS, DVD, Wide.** *HK* Jet Li, Yasuka Kurata; ***D:*** Woo-ping Yuen, Gordon Chan; ***M:*** Joseph Koo.

Fist of Steel 🦴½ **1993** In this futuristic martial arts film, modern day gladiators fight to the death in tournaments run by a vicious syndicate. When top gladiator Amp makes an escape bid he's hunted by henchman Mainframe, who plans to meet Amp in a fixed fight in order to become the new champion. **97m/C VHS.** Dale "Apollo" Cook, Greg Douglass, Cynthia Khan, Don Nakaya Neilsen, Jim Gaines, Ned Hourani, Nick Nicholson, Kris Aguilar; ***D:*** Irvin Johnson; ***W:*** Anthony Jesu.

Fist of the North Star 🦴🦴 **1995 (R)** Legendary warrior Kenshiro (Daniels) returns from the grave to avenge the death of his father (McDowell) and restore his North Star clan. He must battle evil Lord Shin (Mandylor) and his henchmen in a post-apocalyptic future. Based on the Japanese comic book series, which is also available in anime form. **90m/C VHS, DVD.** Gary Daniels, Costas Mandylor, Christopher Penn, Julie Brown, Malcolm McDowell, Melvin Van Peebles, Isako Washio; ***D:*** Tony Randel; ***W:*** Tony Randel; ***C:*** Jacques Haitkin; ***M:*** Christopher Stone.

Fistful of Death 🦴 **1967** Kinski portrays a vengefully violent and desperate cowpoke in the days of the old West. **84m/C VHS.** Klaus Kinski.

A Fistful of Dollars 🦴🦴🦴 **1964 (R)** The epitome of the "spaghetti western" pits Eastwood as "the man with no name" against two families who are feuding over land. A remake of Kurosawa's "Yojimbo," and followed by Leone's "For a Few Dollars More," and "The Good, The Bad, and The Ugly." **101m/C VHS, DVD, Wide.** *IT* Clint Eastwood, Gian Marie Volonte, Marianne Koch; ***D:*** Sergio Leone; ***W:*** Sergio Leone, Victor Andres Catena, Duccio Tessari, G. Schock; ***C:*** Massimo Dallamano, Federico G. Larraya; ***M:*** Ennio Morricone.

A Fistful of Dynamite 🦴🦴🦴 *Duck, You Sucker; Giu la Testa* **1972 (PG)** A spaghetti western, with Leone's trademark humor and a striking score by Morricone. An Irish demolitions expert and a Mexican peasant team up to rob a bank during a revolution in Mexico. **138m/C VHS, Wide.** *IT* James Coburn, Rod Steiger, Romolo Valli; ***D:*** Sergio Leone; ***M:*** Ennio Morricone.

Fists of Blood 🦴½ **1987** A martial arts expert seeks revenge on the drug baron who murdered his friend and kidnapped his girl. **90m/C VHS.** *AU* Eddie Stazak; ***D:*** Brian Trenchard-Smith.

Fists of Fury 🦴🦴🦴 *The Big Boss; Tang Shan da Xiong* **1973 (R)** Bruce Lee stars in this violent but charming Kung Fu action adventure in which he must break a solemn vow to avoid fighting in order to avenge the murder of his teacher by drug smugglers. **102m/C VHS, DVD, Wide.** Bruce Lee, Maria Yi; ***D:*** Lo Wei; ***W:*** Lo Wei, Bruce Lee; ***C:*** Chen Ching Chu; ***M:*** Fu-ling Wang.

Fists of Fury 2 🦴½ **1980 (R)** Chen Shan must survive the Organizations' onslaughts to kill him. He escapes their perilous plots only to return to battle against them after they kill his mother for her inability to disclose Chen's hiding place. Finally Chen defeats the Evil Organization himself. **90m/C VHS.** Bruce Li, Ho Chung Do, Shum Shim Po.

Fists of Iron 🦴½ **1994 (R)** Tough guy, skilled in martial arts, seeks revenge on the fighter and promoter who caused the death of his best friend. **94m/C VHS.** Mike Worth, Matthias Hues, Sam Jones, Marshall Teague, Jenilee Harrison.

Fit for a King 🦴🦴 **1937** A reporter becomes a princess' knight in shining armor when he foils an assassination plot in this screwball romance. **73m/B VHS.** Joe E. Brown, Leo Carrillo, Helen Mack, Paul Kelly, Harry Davenport; ***D:*** Edward Sedgwick; ***C:*** Paul Vogel.

Fit to Kill 🦴½ **1993 (R)** Once again special agents Donna Hamilton and Nicole Justine (former Playboy centerfolds Speir and Vasquez) reteam for an adventure that matches them with an old enemy, double agents, diamonds, and revenge. Filmed on location in Hawaii. **94m/C VHS.** Dona Speir, Roberta Vasquez, R.J. Moore, Bruce Penhall, Julie Strain, Rodrigo Obregon, Cynthia Brimhall, Tony Peck; ***D:*** Andy Sidaris; ***W:*** Andy Sidaris.

Fitzcarraldo 🦴🦴🦴🦴 **1982 (PG)** Although he failed to build a railroad across South America, Fitzcarraldo is determined to build an opera house in the middle of the Amazon jungles and have Enrico Caruso sing there. Based on a true story of a charismatic Irishman's impossible quest at the turn of the century. Of note: No special effects were used in this movie—everything you see actually occurred during filming, including hauling a large boat over a mountain. **157m/C VHS, DVD, Wide.** *GE* Klaus Kinski, Claudia Cardinale, Jose Lewgoy, Miguel Angel Fuentes, Paul Hittscher; ***D:*** Werner Herzog; ***W:*** Werner Herzog; ***C:*** Thomas Mauch; ***M:*** Popul Vuh. Cannes '82: Director (Herzog).

Five Came Back 🦴🦴 **1939** When a plane with 12 passengers crashes in the South American jungle, only five can ride in the patched-up wreck. Since the remainder will be left to face head hunters, intense arguments ensue. Same director remade this as "Back from Eternity" in 1956. **93m/B VHS.** Lucille Ball, Chester Morris, John Carradine, Wendy Barrie, Kent Taylor, Joseph Calleia, Sir C. Aubrey Smith, Patric Knowles; ***D:*** John Farrow.

Five Card Stud 🦴½ **1968 (PG)** Five members of a lynching party are being killed one by one, and a professional gambler, who tried to prevent the lynching, attempts to ensnare the killer with the aid of a preacher with a gun. The poor script was based on a novel by Ray Gaulden. **103m/C VHS, DVD.** Robert Mitchum, Dean Martin, Inger Stevens, Roddy McDowall, Yaphet Kotto, John Anderson, Katherine Justice; ***D:*** Henry Hathaway; ***W:*** Marguerite Roberts; ***C:*** Daniel F. Fapp; ***M:*** Maurice Jarre.

Five Cartridges 🦴🦴 *Funf Patronenhulsen* **1960** Five soldiers during the Spanish Civil War hide their dying commander's final message in five empty bullet casings to keep the message from falling into enemy hands. Now, they have to survive the fighting in order to deliver the message. German with subtitles. **85m/B VHS.** *GE* Erwin Geschonneck, Manfred Krug, Armin Mueller-Stahl, Ulrich Thein, Edwin Marran, Ernst-Georg Schwill; ***D:*** Frank Beyer; ***W:*** Walter Gorrish; ***C:*** Gunter Marczinkowski.

Five Corners 🦴🦴🦴 **1988 (R)** A quixotic, dramatic comedy about the inhabitants of the 5 Corners section of the Bronx in 1964, centering around a girl being wooed by a psychotic rapist, her crippled boyfriend, and the hero-turned-racial-pacifist who cannot rescue her out of principle. **92m/C VHS, DVD.** Jodie Foster, John Turturro, Todd Graff, Tim Robbins, Elizabeth Berridge, Rose Gregorio, Gregory Rozakis, Rodney Harvey, John Seitz; ***D:*** Tony Bill; ***W:*** John Patrick Shanley; ***C:*** Fred Murphy; ***M:*** James Newton Howard. Ind. Spirit '89: Actress (Foster).

5 Dark Souls 🦴½ **1996** Three high schoolers, anxious to be part of the "in" crowd, are sent by five members of the most popular clique on a sinister woodland adventure as stars in a snuff film. **90m/C VHS.** Tina Ona Paukstelis, Mick Wynhoff, Matthew Winkler, Christopher D. Harder, Karen Dilloo, Sy Stevens, William Krekling; ***D:*** Jason Paul Collum.

Five Days One Summer 🦴🦴 **1982 (PG)** Set in 1932, the story of a haunting and obsessive love affair between a married Scottish doctor and a young woman who happens to be his niece. While on vacation in the Swiss Alps, the doctor must vie for her love with their handsome young mountain climbing guide. Based on a story by Kay Boyle. **108m/C VHS.** Sean Connery, Betsy Brantley, Lambert Wilson; ***D:*** Fred Zinnemann; ***W:*** Michael Austin; ***M:*** Elmer Bernstein.

Five Dolls for an August Moon 🦴🦴 **1970** A group of investment speculators try to talk scientist Gerry Farrell (Berger) into selling them the rights to a new formula, while at a wild weekend retreat on an isolated island. As the competitors try to cheat one another with secret bids, Farrell seems disinterested, and tempers rise with the stakes. The wives and girlfriends along for the fun and games feel the tension as their men stray, or try to get them to use sex to close a deal. But once the murders begin, the possibility of anyone trusting anyone is left far behind. Allegedly a professional assignment given Bava with just two days' notice, the film is a fair murder mystery in which even this director's visual tricks can't sustain interest. The cast of connivers is interchangeable and hard to keep straight, and in some cases more easily identifiable by their now-hideous 1970 fashions than their faces. **78m/C DVD, Wide.** *IT* William Berger, Ira von Furstenberg, Edwige Fenech, Howard (Red) Ross, Helena Ronee, Teodoro Corra, Ely Galleani, Edith Meloni, Mauro Bosco, Maurice Poli; ***D:*** Mario Bava; ***W:*** Mario di Nardo; ***C:*** Antonio Rinaldi; ***M:*** Pierro Umiliani.

Five Easy Pieces 🦴🦴🦴🦴 **1970 (R)** Nicholson's superb acting brings to life this character study of a talented musician who has given up a promising career and now works on the oil rigs. After 20 years he returns home to attempt one last communication with his dying father and perhaps, reconcile himself with his fear of failure and desire for greatness. Black, Anspach, and Bush create especially memorable characters. Nicholson ordering toast via a chicken salad sandwich is a classic. **98m/C VHS, DVD, 8mm, Wide.** Jack Nicholson, Karen Black, Susan Anspach, Lois Smith, Billy Green Bush, Fannie Flagg, Ralph Waite, Sally Struthers, Helena Kallianiotes, Richard Stahl, Lorna Thayer; ***D:*** Bob Rafelson; ***W:*** Adrien (Carole Eastman) Joyce, Bob Rafelson; ***C:*** Laszlo Kovacs. Golden Globes '71: Support. Actress (Black); Natl. Bd. of Review '70: Support. Actress (Black), Natl. Film Reg. '00;; N.Y. Film Critics '70: Director (Rafelson), Film, Support. Actress (Black); Natl. Soc. Film Critics '70: Support. Actress (Smith).

Five Fingers 🦴🦴🦴½ *Operation Cicero* **1952** Under the alias "Cicero," Albanian valet Mason joins the espionage ring, selling highly confidential British war papers to the Germans during WWII. True story with odd real-life ending—unconvinced of document authenticity, the Nazis never acted on the information, even when they had the time and date of the European invasion! Fast-paced and absorbing. Adapted from the book "Operation Cicero" by L.C. Moyzisch. **108m/B VHS.** James Mason, Danielle Darrieux, Michael Rennie, Walter Hampden, Oscar Karlweis, Herbert Berghof, John Wengraf, Michael Pate, Ivan Triesault, Hannelore Axman, David Wolfe, Nestor Paiva, Richard Loo, Keith McConnell; ***D:*** Joseph L. Mankiewicz; ***W:*** Michael Wilson; ***M:*** Bernard Herrmann; ***Nar:*** John Sutton. Golden Globes '53: Screenplay.

Five for Hell 🦴 **1967** The army picks five of its meanest men for a suicide mission during WWII. They must go behind German lines and find the plans for the enemy offensive. Parolini used the pseudonym Frank Kramer. **88m/C VHS.** *IT* Klaus Kinski, Gianni "John" Garko, Nick Jordan, Margaret Lee; ***D:*** Gianfranco Parolini.

Five Giants from Texas 🦴 *I Cinque Della Vendetta* **1966** El cheapo spaghetti western features Madison, TV's former Wild Bill Hickock, as a rancher fighting off displaced Mexican peasants and outlaws. **103m/C VHS.** *IT* Guy Madison, Monica Randall; ***D:*** Aldo Florio.

Five Golden Dragons 🦴 **1967** A typical action film about an American running afoul of ruthless gold trafficking in Hong Kong. Even this stellar cast can't help the script. **92m/C VHS.** *GB* Robert Cummings, Christopher Lee, Brian Donlevy, Klaus Kinski, George Raft, Dan Duryea, Margaret Lee; ***D:*** Jeremy Summers.

Five Graves to Cairo 🦴🦴🦴 **1943** Tense WWII thriller finds British soldier John Bramble (Tone) stranded in a small desert town after the defeat of the British garrison by General Rommel's (Von Stroheim) Afrika Korps. Arab hotel owner Farid (Tamiroff) agrees to let Bramble assume the identity of a dead hotel waiter, much to the dismay of French maid Moush (Baxter), whose only interest is in getting her brother out of a German POW camp. The real waiter turns out to have been a secret Nazi spy, fortunately known to Rommel only by name, so Bramble attempts to learn where the German supply depots have been hidden (the "five graves" of the title)—that is, unless Moush decides to betray him to win her brother's release. Based on the play "Hotel Imperial" by Lajos Biro. **97m/B VHS.** Franchot Tone, Anne Baxter, Erich von Stroheim, Akim Tamiroff, Peter Van Eyck, Fortunio Bonanova, Miles Mander, Konstantin Shayne, Leslie Denison, Ian Keith, Frederick Giermann, Fred Nurney; ***D:*** Billy Wilder; ***W:*** Billy Wilder, Charles Brackett; ***C:*** John Seitz; ***M:*** Miklos Rozsa.

The Five Heartbeats 🦴🦴🦴 **1991 (R)** Well told story of five black singers in the 1960s, their successes and failures as a group and as individuals. Although every horror story of the music business is included, the story remains fresh and the acting excellent. Music is fine, but secondary to the people. Well written characters with few cliches. Skillfully directed by Townsend (of "Hollywood Shuffle") who did research by talking to the Dells. Less than memorable showing at the boxoffice but fun and entertaining. **122m/C VHS, DVD, Wide.** Robert Townsend, Tressa Thomas, Michael Wright, Harry J. Lennix, Diahann Carroll, Leon, Hawthorne James, Chuck Patterson, Roy Fegan, Tico Wells, John Canada Terrell, Harold Nicholas, Paul Benjamin, Norma Donaldson, Eugene Glazer; ***D:*** Robert Townsend; ***W:*** Robert Townsend, Keenen Ivory Wayans; ***C:*** Bill Dill; ***M:*** Stanley Clarke.

Five Minutes to Love 🦴 *The Rotten Apple; It Only Take Five Minutes* **1963** McClanahan (one of TV's "Golden Girls") plays a young, sleazy hussy named "Poochie, the girl from the shack." This exploitation schlocker appears to be McClanahan's first film. **85m/B VHS.** Rue McClanahan, Paul Leder, King Moody; ***D:*** John Hayes.

The Five of Me 🦴🦴½ **1981** A man with five personalities finds that livin' ain't easy and seeks professional help. Based on the autobiography of Henry Hawksworth. **100m/C VHS.** David Birney, Dee Wallace Stone, Mitchell Ryan, John McLiam, James Whitmore Jr., Ben Piazza; ***D:*** Paul Wendkos. **TV**

The Five Pennies 🦴🦴½ **1959** Sentimental biography starring Kaye as famed jazzman Red Nichols features performances by legendary musicians Bob Crosby, Bobby Troup, Ray Anthony and Louis Armstrong. This movie marked Weld's film debut. ♫Good Night Sleep Tight; The Five Pennies; Battle Hymn of the Republic; When the Saints Go Marching In; The Music Goes 'Round and Around; Jingle Bells; Carnival of Venice; Paradise. **117m/C VHS.** Danny Kaye, Louis

Armstrong, Barbara Bel Geddes, Tuesday Weld, Harry Guardino; **D:** Melville Shavelson; **W:** Melville Shavelson, Jack Rose; **C:** Daniel F. Fapp.

The Five Senses **1999** Follows the trials of five urbanites, each of whom is linked to a missing child, as well as being linked to one of the five senses. Massage therapist Ruth (Rose) is losing her sense of touch; cake baker Rona (Parker) has an impaired sense of taste; housecleaner Robert (MacIvor) believes his acute sense of smell will lead to love; optholmologist Richard (Volter) is losing his hearing; and teenager Rachel (Litz) is drawn into spying games (sight) with a voyeur. Suprisingly accessible given the complex construct, each story is not only well-acted but frequently warm and witty. **105m/C VHS, DVD, Wide.** *CA* Mary-Louise Parker, Phillipe Volter, Gabrielle Rose, Daniel MacIvor, Molly Parker, Pascale Bussieres, Marco Leonardi, Brendan Fletcher, Nadia Litz; **D:** Jeremy Podeswa; **W:** Jeremy Podeswa; **C:** Gregory Middleton; **M:** Alex Pauk, Alexina Louie. Genie '99: Director (Podeswa); Toronto-City '99: Canadian Feature Film.

The 5000 Fingers of Dr. T **1953 (G)** In Dr. Seuss' only non-animated movie, a boy tries to evade piano lessons and runs right into the castle of the evil Dr. Terwilliger, where hundreds of boys are held captive for piano lessons. Worse yet, they're forced to wear silly beanies with "happy fingers" waving on top. Luckily, the trusted family plumber is on hand to save the day through means of an atomic bomb. Wonderful satire, horrible music, mesmerizing Seussian sets. The skating brothers (who are joined at their beards) are a treat. **88m/C VHS, DVD.** Peter Lind Hayes, Mary Healy, Tommy Rettig, Hans Conried, Noel Cravat; **D:** Roy Rowland; **W:** Theodore "Dr. Seuss" Geisel, Allan Scott; **C:** Franz Planer; **M:** Frederick "Friedrich" Hollander, Hans J. Salter.

The $5.20 an Hour Dream **1980** Lavin is a divorced mother and factory worker burdened with debt and determined to get and keep a job on the higher-paying, traditionally all-male assembly line. Lesser feminist drama on the heels of "Norma Rae." **96m/C VHS.** Linda Lavin, Richard Jaeckel, Nicholas Pryor, Pamela McMyler, Mayf Nutter, Taurean Blacque, Robert Davi, Dennis Fimple, Dana Hill, Ernie Hudson; **D:** Russ Mayberry. **TV**

Five Weeks in a Balloon **1962 (PG)** This adaptation of the Jules Verne novel follows the often-comic exploits of a 19th-century British expedition that encounters many adventures on a balloon trek across Africa. Pleasant fluff with a good cast. **101m/C VHS, Wide.** Fabian, Peter Lorre, Red Buttons, Cedric Hardwicke, Barbara Eden; **D:** Irwin Allen; **W:** Charles Bennett, Irwin Allen; **C:** Winton C. Hoch.

The Fix *The Agitators* **1984** A group of cocaine smugglers get their just desserts as the federal government catches them in a sting operation. **95m/C VHS.** Vince Edwards, Richard Jaeckel, Julie Hill, Charles Dierkop, Byron Cherry, Robert Tessier; **D:** Will Zens.

The Fixer **1968 (PG-13)** Based on the true story of a Jewish handyman (Bates) in 1911 Tsarist Russia who's accused of murdering a gentile boy. Wrongly imprisoned he's tortured to confess to the crime, which he refuses to do. Bogarde is the lawyer who tries to help him. Strong direction and acting in an unrelenting drama. Adapted from Bernard Malamud's Pulitzer Prize-winning novel. **132m/C VHS.** Alan Bates, Dirk Bogarde, Georgia Brown, Hugh Griffith, Elizabeth Hartman, Ian Holm, David Opatoshu, David Warner, Carol White, Murray Melvin, Peter Jeffrey, William Hutt; **D:** John Frankenheimer; **W:** Dalton Trumbo; **M:** Maurice Jarre.

The Fixer ½ **1997** Jack Killoran (Voight) is a corrupt Chicago lawyer who can get anything done for a price. But after he's temporarily paralyzed in an accident, Jack has a crisis of conscience and decides he'd like to go legit. However, his bosses decide he knows too much to let him go. **105m/C VHS.** Jon Voight, Brenda Bakke, J.J. Johnston, Miguel (Michael) Sandoval, Karl Pruner, Brent Jennings, Jack Wallace; **D:** Charles Robert Carner; **W:** Charles Robert Carner; **C:** Michael Goi; **M:** Lennie Niehaus. **CABLE**

Flambards ½ **1978** In the early 1900s, teenaged orphan Christine is sent to live with her tyrannical Uncle Russell and his two sons on their crumbling English estate, Flambards. Bitter rivalries and jealousies abound between arrogant, tradition-bound Mark and younger brother William, who's obsessed with the new-fangled airplane. Quarrels intensify as both young men fall in love with Christine and WWI begins, leading to sacrifice and tragedy. Based on the trilogy by K.M. Peyton. **676m/C VHS, DVD.** *GB* Christine McKenna, Stephen Grives, Alan Parnaby, Edward Judd, Sebastian Abineri, Peter Settelen, Carol Leader, Frank Mills; **D:** Lawrence Gordon Clark, Peter Duffell. **TV**

The Flame & the Arrow **1950** Dardo the Arrow, a Robin Hood-like outlaw in medieval Italy, leads his band of mountain fighters against a mercenary warlord who has seduced his wife and kidnapped his son. Spectacular acrobatics, with Lancaster performing his own stunts, add interest to the usual swashbuckling. **88m/C VHS.** Burt Lancaster, Virginia Mayo, Aline MacMahon, Nick Cravat, Robert Douglas, Frank Allenby; **D:** Jacques Tourneur; **M:** Max Steiner.

The Flame Is Love ½ **1979** Adaptation of one of Barbara Cartland's romantic novels. A turn-of-the-century American heiress falls tragically in love with a Parisian journalist despite her engagement to an Englishman. **98m/C VHS.** Linda Purl, Timothy Dalton, Shane Briant; **D:** Michael O'Herlihy. **TV**

Flame of Araby ½ **1951** When Princess Tanya's (O'Hara) father is murdered, she's threatened with an unwanted marriage and loss of the throne. But if she can win a horse race, Tanya has a chance for freedom. Now, if she can only convince handsome Bedouin chief Tamerlane (Chandler), who has the fastest black stallion in the desert, to come to her aid. **78m/C VHS.** Maureen O'Hara, Jeff Chandler, Lon Chaney Jr., Buddy Baer, Maxwell Reed, Susan Cabot, Royal Dano, Richard Egan; **D:** Charles Lamont; **W:** Gerald Drayson Adams; **C:** Russell Metty.

The Flame of New Orleans **1941** Dietrich is naturally the flame in question as Claire, Countess of New Orleans. She becomes engaged to Girard (Young) but then is attracted to sailor Robert (Cabot) and strings both men along while she tries to decide what to do. Claire's temporary solution is a harebrained plan involving her posing as a lookalike cousin, just come to town. French director Clair's first U.S. film was critically panned upon its release. **79m/B VHS.** Marlene Dietrich, Bruce Cabot, Roland Young, Mischa Auer, Andy Devine, Frank Jenks, Franklin Pangborn, Laura Hope Crews; **D:** Rene Clair; **W:** Norman Krasna; **C:** Rudolph Mate; **M:** Frank Skinner.

Flame of the Barbary Coast ½ **1945** A rancher from Montana vies with a gambling czar for a beautiful dance hall queen and control of the Barbary Coast district of San Francisco. The great earthquake of 1906 provides the plot with a climax. Also available colorized. **91m/B VHS.** John Wayne, Ann Dvorak, Joseph Schildkraut, William Frawley; **D:** Joseph Kane.

Flame of the Islands **1955** De Carlo plays a smoldering, passionate chanteuse who struggles with love and gangsters for possession of a Bahamian casino in this tropical heat wave. **92m/C VHS.** Yvonne De Carlo, Howard Duff, Zachary Scott, James Arness, Kurt Kasznar, Barbara O'Neil; **D:** Edward Ludwig.

Flame Over India *Northwest Frontier* **1960** When Moslems lay siege to a British fortress in India, Governess Wyatt (Bacall) and Captain Scott (More) save the Maharaja's son and escape by commandeering a train. Along the way they find treason, adventure and love. **130m/C VHS.** *GB* Kenneth More, Lauren Bacall, Herbert Lom, Wilfrid Hyde-White, I.S. Johar, Ursula Jeans, Ian Hunter, Eugene Deckers, Jack (Gwyllam) Gwillim, Govind Raja Ross, Frank Olegario; **D:** J. Lee Thompson; **C:** Geoffrey Unsworth.

Flame to the Phoenix ½ **1985** A WWII drama about the Polish cavalry forces' decimation to German Panzer tanks. **80m/C VHS.** *GB* Paul Geoffrey, Ann(e) Firbank, Frederick Treves; **D:** William Brayne.

The Flame Trees of Thika **1981** In 1913, a British family travels to East Africa to start a coffee plantation. Seen through the eyes of the young daughter, her childhood consists of the local Masai and Kikuyu tribes, the eccentric and sometimes unhappy English neighbors, and the wild animals that roam the plains. Based on the memoirs of writer Elspeth Huxley. Four cassettes; shown on PBS "Masterpiece Theatre." **366m/C VHS.** *GB* Hayley Mills, Holly Aird, David Robb, Ben Cross.

Flaming Bullets **1945** Last of the Texas Rangers series has solid action scenes, but little else. Ritter leads the Texas Rangers in breaking up a gang with a devious scheme: breaking men out of jail, then killing them for the cash reward. **55m/B VHS.** Tex Ritter, Dave O'Brien, Guy Wilkerson, Charles "Blackie" King, Patricia Knox, I. Stanford Jolley; **D:** Harry Fraser; **W:** Harry Fraser; **C:** Robert C. Cline.

Flaming Frontiers **1938** A frontier scout matches wits against gold mine thieves. In 15 episodes. **300m/B VHS.** Johnny Mack Brown, Eleanor Hanson, Ralph Bowman; **D:** Ray Taylor.

Flaming Lead ½ **1939** A hard-drinkin' ranch owner hires a nightclub cowboy to help him get an Army horse contract. **57m/B VHS.** Ken Maynard, Eleanor Stewart, Walter Long, Tom London; **D:** Sam Newfield.

Flaming Signal ½ **1933** Featuring Flash the Wonder Labrador, this action-packed film deals with a pilot who crash-lands near a Pacific island, just as the natives, provoked by an exploitative German trader, are rising up against the whites. Both Flash and his master manage to rescue the missionary's pretty daughter. **64m/B VHS.** Noah Beery Sr., Marceline Day, Carmelita Geraghty, Mischa Auer, Henry B. Walthall.

Flaming Star **1960** In 1870s Texas, a family with a white father and an Indian mother is caught in the midst of an Indian uprising. The mixed-blood youth, excellently played by Presley, must choose a side with tragic results for all. A stirring, well-written drama of frontier prejudice and one of Presley's best films. **101m/C VHS.** Elvis Presley, Dolores Del Rio, Barbara Eden, Steve Forrest, John McIntire, Richard Jaeckel, L.Q. (Justus E. McQueen) Jones, Douglas Dick, Rodolfo Acosta, Ford Rainey, Karl Swenson; **D:** Donald Siegel; **W:** Nunnally Johnson, Clair Huffaker; **C:** Charles Clarke; **M:** Cyril Mockridge.

The Flaming Teen-Age **1956** Schlocky pseudo-documentary demonstrating the evils of drugs and alcohol. Exploitative, and the teenagers look really old. Cheaply made, and it shows. **67m/B VHS.** Noel Reyburn, Ethel Barrett, Jerry Frank, Shirley Holmes; **D:** Irvin S. Yeaworth Jr., Charles Edwards.

The Flaming Urge **1953** A small town is plagued by mysterious fires. Could a pyromaniac be on the loose? **67m/B VHS.** Harold Lloyd Jr., Cathy Downs.

The Flamingo Kid **1984 (PG-13)** Brooklyn teen Jeffrey Willis (Dillon) gets a summer job at a fancy beach club on Long Island. His plumber father, Arthur (Elizondo), remembers how to dream but is also aware of how rough the world is on dreamers. Suddenly making lots of money at a mostly easy job, the kid's attracted to the high style of local sports car dealer Phil Brody (Crenna), and finds his father's solid life a bore. By the end of the summer, he's learned the true value of both men, and the kind of man he wants to be. Excellent performances all around, nice ensemble acting among the young men who play Dillon's buddies. Great sound track. Film debut of Jones, who seems a little old for her part as a California college sophomore. **100m/C VHS, DVD.** Matt Dillon, Hector Elizondo, Molly McCarthy, Martha Gehman, Richard Crenna, Jessica Walter, Carole (Raphaelle) Davis, Janet Jones, Fisher Stevens, Bronson Pinchot; **D:** Garry Marshall; **W:** Garry Marshall, Neil Marshall; **C:** James A. Contner; **M:** Curt Sobel.

The Flamingo Rising ½ **2001** Impetuous Herbert T. Lee (Benben) decides to build the world's largest drive-in movie theater in his '60s Florida community. Unfortunately, the spot he picks is right across the street from the funeral parlor run by Turner Knight (Hurt), who doesn't see it as an appropriate venue. Caught in the middle are Lee's two adopted children and his wife, Edna (McGovern), who tries to make both men see reason. Based on the novel by Larry Baker. **98m/C VHS.** Brian Benben, William Hurt, Elizabeth McGovern, Angela Bettis, Erin Broderick, Joe Torry, Chris Larkin, Olivia Oguma; **D:** Martha Coolidge; **W:** Richard Russo; **C:** Johnny E. Jensen; **M:** David Newman. **TV**

Flamingo Road **1949** A scandalously entertaining melodrama in which Crawford portrays a carnival dancer who intrigues Scott and Brian in a small Southern town where the carnival stops. Crawford shines in a role that demands her to be both tough and sensitive in a corrupt world full of political backstabbing and sleazy characters. Remade as a TV movie and television soap-opera series in 1980. **94m/B VHS.** Joan Crawford, Zachary Scott, David Brian, Sydney Greenstreet, Gertrude Michael, Gladys George, Virginia Huston, Fred Clark, Alice White; **D:** Michael Curtiz; **W:** Edmund H. North, Robert Wilder; **M:** Max Steiner.

The Flash **1990** When police scientist Barry Allen is accidentally doused by chemicals and then struck by lightening the combination makes him into a new superhero. His super quickness help his quest in fighting crime in Central City where he's aided by fellow scientist Tina McGee (the only other person to know his secret). In this adventure, the Flash seeks out the violent and mesmerizing leader of a biker gang who caused the death of Barry's brother. Based on the DC comic book character, this is the pilot episode for the short-lived TV series. The look is dark and stylized and not played for camp. **94m/C VHS.** John Wesley Shipp, Amanda Pays, Michael Nader; **M:** Danny Elfman. **TV**

Flash **1998** Fourteen-year-old Connor's (Black) best friend is a horse named Flash. When his family hits hard times, Connor's dad (Kerwin) joins the merchant marines, his grandmother (Burstyn) goes to work in a factory, and Connor is forced to sell Flash. The teen takes a job in the new owner's stables and when he sees how badly the animal is treated, Connor steals Flash and sets off to meet his father's ship in New York. **90m/C VHS, DVD.** Lucas Black, Ellen Burstyn, Brian Kerwin, Shawn Toovey, Tom Nowicki, Dan Biggers; **D:** Simon Wincer. **TV**

Flash & Firecat **1975 (PG)** A beautiful blonde and a crazy thief steal and race their way across the country in a dune buggy with the police hot on their trail. **90m/C VHS.** Roger Davis, Tricia Sembera, Dub Taylor, Richard Kiel; **D:** Ferd Sebastian.

Flash Gordon **1980 (PG)** Camp version of the adventures of Flash Gordon in outer space. This time, Flash and Dale Arden are forced by Dr. Zarkov to accompany him on a mission to far-off Mongo, where Ming the Merciless is threatening the destruction of Earth. Music by Queen. **111m/C VHS, DVD, Wide.** Sam Jones, Melody Anderson, Chaim Topol, Max von Sydow, Ornella Muti, Timothy Dalton, Brian Blessed; **D:** Mike Hodges; **W:** Lorenzo Semple Jr.; **C:** Gilbert Taylor; **M:** Howard Blake.

Flash Gordon Conquers the Universe *Purple Death from Outer Space* **1940** Ravaging plague strikes the earth and Flash Gordon undertakes to stop it. A serial in 12 chapters. **240m/B VHS, DVD.** Buster Crabbe, Carol Hughes, Charles Middleton, Frank Shannon.

Flash Gordon: Mars Attacks the World *The Deadly Rays from Mars; Flash Gordon's Trip to Mars* **1939** The earth is plagued by the evil Ming, but Flash Gordon steps in. From the serial. **97m/B VHS, DVD.** Buster Crabbe, Jean Rogers, Charles Middleton; **D:** Robert F. "Bob" Hill, Ford Beebe.

Flash Gordon: Rocketship 🦴🦴½ *Spaceship to the Unknown; Perils from Planet Mongo; Space Soldiers; Atomic Rocketship* **1940** Re-edited from the original Flash Gordon serial in which Flash and company must prevent the planet Mongo from colliding with Earth. Good character acting and good clean fun. **82m/B VHS.** Buster Crabbe, Jean Rogers, Frank Shannon, Charles Middleton, Priscilla Lawson, Jack Lipson; ***D:*** Frederick Stephani.

A Flash of Green 🦴🦴 **1985** A crooked politician is helping a construction firm exploit valuable waterfront property. He enlists the influence of a hesitant local journalist, who then falls for the woman leading the homeowner's conservation drive against the development plan. Made for American Playhouse and produced by costar Jordon. Based on the work of John D. MacDonald. **122m/C VHS.** Ed Harris, Blair Brown, Richard Jordan, George Coe; ***D:*** Victor Nunez; ***W:*** Victor Nunez; ***M:*** Charles Engstrom.

Flashback 🦴🦴🦴 **1989 (R)** FBI agent Sutherland's assignment sounds easy: escort aging 1960s radical Hopper to prison. But Hopper is cunning and decides not to go without a fight. He uses his brain to outwit the young Sutherland and to turn him against himself. Good moments between the two leads and with Kane, as a woman who never left the '60s behind. **108m/C VHS.** Dennis Hopper, Kiefer Sutherland, Carol Kane, Cliff DeYoung, Paul Dooley, Michael McKean, Richard Masur; ***D:*** Franco Amurri; ***M:*** Barry Goldberg.

Flashdance 🦴🦴 **1983 (R)** 18-year-old Alex (Beals) wants to dance. She works all day as a welder, has a hot affair going with her boss Nick (Nouri), dances at a local bar at night, and hopes someday to get enough courage to audition for a spot at the School of Ballet. Glossy music video redeemed somewhat by exciting choreography with Marine Jahan doing the dancing for Beals. Oscar-winning title song sung by Irene Cara. Inspired the torn-sweatshirt trend in fashion of the period. ♫Flashdance...What a Feeling; I Love Rock 'n Roll; Manhunt; Gloria; Lady, Lady, Lady; Seduce Me Tonight. **95m/C VHS, 8mm.** Jennifer Beals, Michael Nouri, Belinda Bauer, Lilia Skala, Cynthia Rhodes, Sunny Johnson, Lee Ving, Kyle T. Heffner, Ron Karabatsos, Robert Wuhl, Elizabeth Sagal; ***D:*** Adrian Lyne; ***W:*** Joe Eszterhas; ***C:*** Don Peterman; ***M:*** Giorgio Moroder. Oscars '83: Song ("Flashdance...What a Feeling"); Golden Globes '84: Song ("Flashdance...What a Feeling"), Score.

Flashfire 🦴🦴½ **1994 (R)** The torching of an apartment building and the murder of a cop seem unrelated until troubled detective Jack Flinder (Zane) becomes involved. Soon, he and murder witness Lisa (Minter) are on the run from the arsonists and crooked police. **88m/C VHS, DVD.** Billy Zane, Kristin Minter, Louis Gossett Jr.; ***D:*** Elliot Silverstein; ***W:*** John Warren, Dan York; ***C:*** Albert J. Dunk; ***M:*** Sylvester Levay.

Flashpoint 🦴🦴 **1984 (R)** A pair of Texas border patrolmen discover an abandoned jeep that contains a fortune in cash, apparently from the 1960s. As they try to figure out how it got there, they become prey to those who want to keep the secret. With this cast, flick ought to be better. **95m/C VHS.** Terry Alexander, Treat Williams, Kris Kristofferson, Tess Harper, Rip Torn, Miguel Ferrer, Roberts Blossom; ***D:*** William Tannen; ***W:*** Michael Butler.

Flashpoint Africa 🦴½ **1984** When a news team follows a terrorist group's activities it winds up in a power struggle with terrifying consequences. **99m/C VHS.** Trevor Howard, Gayle Hunnicutt, James Faulkner.

Flat Top 🦴🦴½ **1952** The training of Navy fighter pilots aboard "flat top" aircraft carriers during WWII provides the drama here. A strict commander is appreciated only after the war when the pilots realize his role in their survival. The film makes good use of actual combat footage; fast-paced and effective. **85m/C VHS.** Sterling Hayden, Richard Carlson, Keith Larsen, John Bromfield; ***D:*** Lesley Selander.

Flatbed Annie and Sweetiepie: Lady Truckers 🦴🦴½ *Flatbed Annie* **1979** A couple of good ol' gals hit the road and encounter a variety of bad guys out to steal their truck. **100m/C VHS.** Annie Potts, Kim Darby, Harry Dean Stanton, Arthur Godfrey, Rory Calhoun, Bill Carter; ***D:*** Robert Greenwald. **TV**

Flatfoot 🦴🦴 *The Knock-Out Cop* **1978 (PG)** Tough police officer will let nothing stop him from finding and arresting drug smugglers. Good for laughs as well as lots of action. **113m/C VHS.** *IT GE* Bodo, Werner Pochath, Bud Spencer, Enzo Cannavale, Dagmar Lassander, Joe Stewardson; ***D:*** Steno.

Flatliners 🦴🦴 **1990 (R)** A group of medical students begin after-hours experimentation with death and out-of-body experiences. Some standard horror film images but Roberts and Sutherland create an energy that makes it worth watching. **111m/C VHS, DVD, 8mm, Wide.** Kiefer Sutherland, Julia Roberts, William Baldwin, Oliver Platt, Kevin Bacon, Kimberly Scott, Joshua Rudoy, Aeryk Egan; ***D:*** Joel Schumacher; ***W:*** Peter Filardi; ***C:*** Jan De Bont; ***M:*** James Newton Howard.

Flawless 🦴🦴 **1999 (R)** Former New York City cop and resident tough guy Walt Koontz (De Niro) lives across the hall from nosily outrageous drag queen Rusty (Hoffman). The odd couple have a mutual animosity that's put to the test when Walt suffers a stroke and it's recommended that he take singing lessons to help him recover his ability to speak. So he makes an offer to Rusty who needs the cash. Soon they're not only tolerating each other but bonding as well. There are distracting subplots about hidden drug money and a drag queen beauty contest that take the focus off of what could have worked as a two-character study about an unlikely friendship. **111m/C VHS, DVD, Wide.** Robert De Niro, Philip Seymour Hoffman, Barry Miller, Chris Bauer, Skipp (Robert L.) Sudduth, Wanda De Jesus, Daphne Rubin-Vega, Rory Cochrane; ***D:*** Joel Schumacher; ***W:*** Joel Schumacher; ***C:*** Declan Quinn; ***M:*** Bruce Roberts.

Fled 🦴🦴 **1996 (R)** Charles Piper (Fishburne) and Luke Dodge (Baldwin) are combative prison escapees who need to find a stash of cash and a computer disk that could save them from both the Cuban mob and the cops. Bombshell Cora (Hayek) decides to help the duo and tries to get steamy with Piper. Lots of chases, lots of violence, not much sense. The climatic battle (the film was shot around Atlanta) takes place in a sightseeing gondola at Georgia's Stone Mountain. **98m/C VHS, DVD.** Laurence "Larry" Fishburne, Stephen Baldwin, Salma Hayek, Will Patton, Robert John Burke; ***D:*** Kevin Hooks; ***W:*** Preston A. Whitmore II; ***C:*** Matthew F. Leonetti; ***M:*** Graeme Revell.

Flesh 🦴🦴🦴 *Andy Warhol's Flesh* **1968** An Andy Warhol-produced seedy urban farce about a bisexual street hustler who meets a variety of drug-addicted, deformed, and sexually deviant people. Dallesandro fans will enjoy his extensive exposure (literally). **90m/C VHS, DVD.** Joe Dallesandro, Geraldine Smith, Patti D'Arbanville, Candy Darling, Jackie Curtis, Geri Miller, Barry Brown; ***D:*** Paul Morrissey; ***W:*** Paul Morrissey; ***C:*** Paul Morrissey.

Flesh and Blood 🦴🦴 **1922** An unjustly convicted lawyer is released from prison to find out his wife has died. He vows revenge on those who falsely imprisoned him and assumes the disguise of a crippled beggar to begin his plot. Silent with musical score. **75m/B VHS, 8mm.** Lon Chaney Sr.; ***D:*** Irving Cummings.

Flesh and Blood 🦴🦴½ *The Rose and the Sword* **1985 (R)** A rowdy group of 16th Century hellions makes off with a princess who is already spoken for and pillage and plunder their way to revenge. Hauer leads the motley group through sword fights, raids, and the like. Dutch director Verhoeven's first English language film. Not for children; with rape scenes, nudity, and graphic sex. **126m/C VHS.** Rutger Hauer, Jennifer Jason Leigh, Tom Burlinson, Susan Tyrrell, Jack Thompson, Ronald Lacey, Brion James, Bruno Kirby; ***D:*** Paul Verhoeven; ***W:*** Paul Verhoeven, Gerard Soeteman; ***C:*** Jan De Bont; ***M:*** Basil Poledouris.

Flesh and Blood Show 🦴 *Asylum of the Insane* **1973 (R)** Rehearsal turns into an execution ritual for a group of actors at a mysterious seaside theatre. Truth in titling: features blood, gore, and some sex. Shot in part in 3-D. **93m/C VHS.** *GB* Robin Askwith, Candace Glendenning, Tristan Rogers, Ray Brooks, Jenny Hanley, Luan Peters, Patrick Barr, Judy Matheson, Penny Meredith; ***D:*** Pete Walker; ***W:*** Alfred Shaughnessy; ***C:*** Peter Jessop.

Flesh and Bone 🦴🦴🦴 **1993 (R)** Quaid is exact as a vending machine distributor with a desolate rural Texas circuit, haunted by the memory of a decades-old murder committed by his father (Caan) during a botched farm-house robbery. Alcoholic Ryan (Quaid's real-life wife) emerges from a bad marriage and helps Quaid rebuild his life, never suspecting that they may have met before. Challenging but successful role for Ryan, better known for her girlish, romantic-comedy appeal. Paltrow's unforgettable as a heartless casket robber and Caan's partner/girlfriend. Director Kloves extracts moments of earthy beauty from the bleak, humble West Texas setting. **127m/C VHS, DVD, Wide.** Dennis Quaid, Meg Ryan, James Caan, Gwyneth Paltrow, Scott Wilson, Christopher Rydell; ***D:*** Steven Kloves; ***W:*** Steven Kloves; ***M:*** Thomas Newman.

The Flesh and the Devil 🦴🦴🦴½ **1927** Classic Garbo at her seductive best as a woman who causes a feud between two friends. Gilbert is an Austrian officer, falls for the married Garbo and winds up killing her husband in a duel. Banished to the African Corps he asks his best friend (Hanson) to look after his lady love. But Hanson takes his job too seriously, falling for the lady himself. Great silent movie with surprise ending to match. The first Gilbert and Garbo pairing. **112m/B VHS.** John Gilbert, Greta Garbo, Lars Hanson, Barbara Kent, George Fawcett, Eugenie Besserer; ***D:*** Clarence Brown; ***C:*** William H. Daniels.

The Flesh and the Fiends 🦴🦴½ *Mania; Fiendish Ghouls; Psycho Killers* **1960** Fine adaptation of the Burke and Hare grave robbing legend. Cushing is the doctor who needs corpses and Pleasence and Rose provide them by any means. Highly atmospheric representation of dismal, 19th century Edinburgh. Very graphic for its time. **87m/B VHS, DVD.** *GB* Peter Cushing, June Laverick, Donald Pleasence, George Rose, Dermot Walsh, Renee Houston, Billie Whitelaw, John Cairney, Michael Balfour; ***D:*** John Gilling; ***W:*** John Gilling, Leon Griffiths; ***C:*** Monty Berman; ***M:*** Stanley Black.

Flesh and the Spur 🦴½ **1957** A cowboy tracks the killer of his brother. Future Mannix Mike Connors (nicknamed 'Touch' at the time) joins the search. Unedifying western with oddball touches, notably a theme song by Chipmunks creator Ross Bagdasarian. **78m/C VHS.** John Agar, Marla English, Mike Connors, Raymond Hatton, Maria Monay, Joyce Meadows, Kenne Duncan; ***D:*** Edward L. Cahn.

The Flesh Eaters 🦴½ **1964** A claustrophobic low-budget thriller about a film queen and her secretary who crash-land on an island inhabited by your basic mad scientist. His latest experiment is with tiny flesh-eating sea creatures. Shock ending. **87m/C VHS.** Martin Kosleck, Rita Morley, Byron Sanders, Barbara Wilkin, Ray Tudor; ***D:*** Jack Curtis; ***W:*** Arnold Drake; ***C:*** Carson Davidson.

Flesh Eating Mothers 🦴 **1989** Housewives are transformed into cannibals after a mystery virus hits their town. Their kids must stop the moms from eating any more people. **90m/C VHS.** Robert Lee Oliver, Donatella Hecht, Valorie Hubbard, Neal Rosen, Terry Hayes; ***D:*** James Aviles Martin.

Flesh Feast woof! **1969 (R)** Classically horrendous anti-Nazi bosh, in which a mad female plastic surgeon (Lake) rejuvenates Hitler and then tortures him to death with maggots to avenge her mother's suffering. Lake's last film, and the sorriest sign-off any actress ever had. **72m/C VHS.** Veronica Lake, Phil Philbin, Heather Hughes, Martha Mischon, Yanka (Doris Keating) Mann, Dianne Wilhite, Chris Martell; ***D:*** Brad F. Ginter.

Flesh Gordon 🦴 **1972** Soft-core spoof of the "Flash Gordon" series. Flesh takes it upon himself to save Earth from the evil Wang's sex ray; Wang, of course, being the leader of the planet Porno. Lackluster special effects and below par story dull an already ridiculous movie. Look for cameo by real-life porn starlet Candy Samples. The restored (90-minute) version also includes the theatrical trailer; a 72-minute R-rated version is also available. **90m/C VHS, DVD, Wide.** Jason Williams, Suzanne Fields, Joseph Hudgins, John Hoyt, Howard Zieff, Michael Benveniste; ***Cameos:*** Candy Samples; ***D:*** Howard Ziehm, Michael Benveniste; ***W:*** Michael Benveniste; ***C:*** Howard Ziehm; ***M:*** Ralph Ferraro; ***V:*** Craig T. Nelson.

Flesh Gordon 2: Flesh Gordon Meets the Cosmic Cheerleaders 🦴 **1990** Emperor Wang (Hunt) threatens the Universe with his powerful Impotence ray. Flesh (Murdocco), along with Dale (Kelly) and Dr. Flexi Jerkoff (Travis), do battle with a belt of farting assteroids and other weirdos. Director Ziehm delivers this one on a shoestring of under $1 million, even improving technically on the original. The sex scenes are, however, more watered down in an apparent attempt to gain a wider audience. Scatological jokes are the basis for much of the humor. **98m/C VHS, DVD.** *CA* Vince Murdocco, Tony Travis, William Dennis Hunt, Robyn Kelly, Morgan Fox, Melissa Mounds; ***D:*** Howard Ziehm; ***W:*** Howard Ziehm; ***C:*** Danny Nowak.

Fleshburn 🦴🦴 **1984 (R)** An Indian Vietnam War veteran escapes from a mental institution to get revenge on the four psychiatrists who committed him. **91m/C VHS, DVD.** Steve Kanaly, Karen Carlson, Sonny Landham, Macon McCalman; ***D:*** George Gage; ***W:*** George Gage, Beth Gage, Brian Garfield; ***M:*** Arthur Kempel.

Fleshpot on 42nd Street 🦴 **1971** Stark, realistic look at the streetwalking profession. Dusty leaves her blue collar boyfriend to move in with a transvestite and then she meets a dashing young Staten Island native (like the director). Their romance blooms until he is run over by a car, sending Dusty into a tailspin which lands her back on 42nd Street. Along the way, various rustic hookers and venerable old floozies liven up director Mulligan's version of New York. Less emphasis on the sleaze than the grittiness. **78m/C VHS.** Diana Lewis, Lynn Flanagan, Bob Walters; ***D:*** Andy Milligan.

Fleshtone 🦴🦴 **1994 (R)** Artist Matthew Greco's (Kemp) work is not for the faint-hearted since he paints grisly suicides and murders. No wonder he's lonely—so lonely that he answers a phone-sex ad and is hooked up with Edna (Cutter), who becomes an obsession. Matthew even depicts her murder in one of his paintings and then she's found dead—only it turns out not to be Edna, who doesn't exist. Just what has Matthew gotten himself into? Provocative but ending is a letdown. An unrated version is also available. **89m/C VHS.** Martin Kemp, Lise Cutter, Tim Thomerson; ***D:*** Harry Hurwitz; ***W:*** Harry Hurwitz.

Fletch 🦴🦴 **1985 (PG)** Somewhat charming comedy. When newspaper journalist Fletch goes undercover to get the scoop on the local drug scene, a wealthy young businessman enlists his help in dying. Something's rotten in Denmark when the man's doctor knows nothing of the illness and Fletch comes closer to the drug scene than he realizes. Throughout the entire film, Chevy Chase assumes a multitude of flippant comic characters to discover the truth. Based on Gregory McDonald's novel. **98m/C VHS, DVD.** Chevy Chase, Tim Matheson, Joe Don Baker, Dana Wheeler-Nicholson, M. Emmet Walsh, Kenneth Mars, Geena Davis, Richard Libertini, George Wendt, Kareem Abdul-Jabbar, Alison La Placa, George Wyner, Tony Longo, James Avery, William Sanderson, Beau Starr, Ralph Seymour, Larry "Flash" Jenkins; ***D:*** Michael Ritchie; ***W:*** Andrew Bergman; ***C:*** Fred Schuler; ***M:*** Harold Faltermeyer.

Fletch Lives 🦴🦴 **1989 (PG)** In this sequel to "Fletch," Chase is back again as the super-reporter. When Fletch learns of his inheritance of a Southern estate he is eager to claim it. During his down-home trip he becomes involved in a murder and must use his disguise skills to solve it before he becomes the next victim. Based on the novels of Gregory MacDonald. **95m/C VHS.** Chevy Chase, Hal Holbrook, Julianne Phillips, Richard Libertini, R. Lee Ermey, Cleavon Little, Randall "Tex" Cobb, Richard Belzer, Geoffrey Lewis, Patricia Kalember, Phil Hartman, George Wyner; ***D:*** Michael Ritchie; ***W:*** Leon Capetanos; ***M:*** Harold Faltermeyer.

Flicks *Hollyweird; Loose Joints* **1985 (R)** A compilation of skits parodying the tradition of Saturday afternoon matinees, including coming attractions and a cartoon. Never released theatrically. **79m/C VHS.** Martin Mull, Joan Hackett, Pamela Sue Martin, Betty Kennedy, Richard Belzer; ***D:*** Peter Winograd.

The Flight 🦴🦴 **1989** A non-narrative view of glider planes as they soar over the countryside and rivers of the Laurentians and Canadian Rockies. Useful in language arts classes. **96m/C VHS.** Eli Danker, Sandy McPeak, Lindsay Wagner; ***D:*** Paul Wendkos.

Flight from Glory 🦴🦴½ **1937** A group of pilots fly supplies over the Andes from their isolated base camp to even more isolated mines. Morris is their leader who watches as, one by one, the men are killed on their dangerous flights. To make a bad situtation worse, Heflin arrives as a new recruit—along with his pretty wife. **66m/B VHS.** Chester Morris, Onslow Stevens, Whitney Bourne, Van Heflin; ***D:*** Lew (Louis Friedlander) Landers.

Flight from Singapore 🦴½ **1962** Transporting desperately needed blood to Malaysia, a flight crew is forced to crash land in the jungle. Nicely done if trite. **74m/B VHS.** *GB* Patrick Allen, Patrick Holt, William Abney, Harry Fowler; ***D:*** Dudley Birch; ***W:*** Dudley Birch.

Flight from Vienna 🦴🦴 **1958** A high-ranking Hungarian security officer, disenchanted with communism, stages a daring escape from his country. In Vienna, he asks the British for political asylum, but is sent back to Hungary to help a scientist escape in order to prove his loyalty. Cold war drama hangs together on strength of Bikel's performance. **54m/B VHS.** Theodore Bikel, John Bentley, Donald Gray.

Flight of Black Angel 🦴🦴½ **1991 (R)** Wacked-out F-16 pilot fancies himself an angel of death, and, after annihilating a number of trainees, sets out to make Las Vegas a nuked-out ghost town. Squadron commander Strauss, however, is not pleased with his pilot's initiative. Made-for-cable script runs out of gas and heads into a nosedive. **102m/C VHS.** Peter Strauss, William O'Leary, James O'Sullivan, Michael Keys Hall; ***D:*** Jonathan Mostow; ***W:*** Henry Dominick. CABLE

Flight of Dragons 🦴🦴½ **1982** Animated tale takes place between the Age of Magic and the Age of Science, in a century when dragons ruled the skies. **98m/C VHS.** ***D:*** Arthur Rankin Jr., Jules Bass; ***V:*** John Ritter, Victor Buono, James Earl Jones, Donald E. Messick, Larry Storch.

A Flight of Rainbirds 🦴🦴 **1981** In a dual role, Krabbe plays a biologist who dreams he must lose his virginity within a week or die and his alter ego who joins him in the search for the perfect woman. In Dutch with English subtitles. **94m/C VHS.** *NL* Jeroen Krabbe; ***D:*** Ate De Jong.

Flight of the Eagle 🦴🦴½ **1982** Based on the actual ill-fated expedition of Salomon Andree who, with two friends, attempted to fly from Sweden to the North Pole in a hydrogen balloon in 1897. The last half of the film drags somewhat as the three struggle to survive in the frozen north after their balloon crashes. Beautifully photographed adventure. In Swedish with English subtitles. **115m/C VHS.** *SW* Max von Sydow, Goran Stangertz, Clement Harari, Sverre Anker; ***D:*** Jan Troell.

Flight of the Grey Wolf 🦴½ **1976** A tame, innocent wolf is mistaken for a killer and must run for his life with the help of his boy-owner. **82m/C VHS.** Bill Williams, Barbara Hale, Jeff East.

Flight of the Innocent 🦴🦴½ **1993 (R)** The innocent 10-year-old Vito comes from a family who make their living as kidnappers. He is the only witness (and the only survivor) when his family is massacred by a rival gang. Vito flees the carnage and sets off to find his cousin who lives in Rome. But his journey truly ends when he is taken in by a wealthy industrialist family whose own son has been kidnapped. Directorial debut of Carlei who tends to rely on striking visuals rather than his characters. In Italian with English subtitles. **105m/C VHS.** *IT* Manuel Colao, Francesca Neri, Jacques Perrin, Frederico Pacifici, Sal Borgese; ***D:*** Carlo Carlei; ***W:*** Carlo Carlei, Gualtiero Rosella.

Flight of the Intruder 🦴½ **1990 (PG-13)** Vietnam naval pilots aboard an aircraft carrier don't like the way the war is being handled, so they go rogue and decide to go on a mission to bomb an enemy air base in Hanoi. Loads of male bonding. **115m/C VHS, Wide.** Danny Glover, Willem Dafoe, Brad Johnson, Rosanna Arquette, Tom Sizemore, Ving Rhames, David Schwimmer; ***D:*** John Milius; ***W:*** Robert Dillon; ***C:*** Fred W. Koenekamp; ***M:*** Basil Poledouris.

Flight of the Navigator 🦴🦴½ **1986 (PG)** A boy boards an alien spacecraft and embarks on a series of time-travel adventures with a crew of wisecracking extraterrestrial creatures. When he returns home eight years later, a NASA investigation ensues. Paul Reubens, better known as Pee-wee Herman, provides the voice of the robot. **90m/C VHS.** Joey Cramer, Veronica Cartwright, Cliff DeYoung, Sarah Jessica Parker, Matt Adler, Howard Hesseman; ***D:*** Randal Kleiser; ***W:*** Michael Burton, Matt MacManus; ***M:*** Alan Silvestri; ***V:*** Paul (Pee-wee Herman) Reubens.

The Flight of the Phoenix 🦴🦴🦴 **1965** A group of men stranded in the Arabian desert after a plane crash attempt to rebuild their plane in order to escape before succumbing to the elements. Big budget, all-star survival drama based on the novel by Elleston Trevor. **147m/C VHS.** James Stewart, Richard Attenborough, Peter Finch, Hardy Kruger, Dan Duryea, George Kennedy, Ernest Borgnine, Ian Bannen; ***D:*** Robert Aldrich; ***C:*** Joseph Biroc.

Flight to Fury 🦴½ **1966** A cheap independent adventure film, featuring the novice Hellman-Nicholson team, about a few assorted mercenaries searching for a horde of diamonds when their plane crashes in the wilderness of the Philippines. Based on a story by director/producer Hellman. **73m/B VHS.** Jack Nicholson, Dewey Martin, Fay Spain, Vic Diaz, Jacqueline Hellman; ***D:*** Monte Hellman; ***W:*** Jack Nicholson.

Flight to Mars 🦴🦴 **1952** An expedition crash lands on the red planet and discovers an advanced underground society that wants to invade earth using the U.S. spacecraft. Includes previews of coming attractions from classic science fiction films. First movie of this genre to be shot in color. **72m/C VHS, DVD.** Cameron Mitchell, Marguerite Chapman, Arthur Franz, Virginia Huston; ***D:*** Lesley Selander; ***W:*** Arthur Strawn; ***C:*** Harry Neumann; ***M:*** Marlin Skiles.

Flight to Nowhere woof! **1946** An FBI agent tracks down a stolen map of atomic bomb source material with the help of a charter pilot and a dizzy blonde. Muddled plot and no discernable acting. **74m/B VHS.** Alan Curtis, Evelyn Ankers, Jack Holt; ***D:*** William Rowland.

Flim-Flam Man 🦴🦴 *One Born Every Minute* **1967** A con man teams up with an army deserter to teach him the fine art of flim-flamming as they travel through small southern towns. Love may lead the young man back to the straight and narrow, but not his reprobate mentor. Scott is wonderful; and the slapstick episodes move at a good pace. **104m/C VHS.** George C. Scott, Michael Sarrazin, Slim Pickens, Sue Lyon, Jack Albertson, Harry (Henry) Morgan; ***D:*** Irvin Kershner; ***C:*** Charles B(ryant) Lang Jr.; ***M:*** Jerry Goldsmith.

Flinch 🦴🦴 **1994 (R)** Two models, who work as live mannequins, witness a murder and wonder if they'll be the next victims. **90m/C VHS.** Judd Nelson, Nick Mancuso, Gina Gershon; ***D:*** George Erschbamer.

The Flintstones 🦴🦴½ **1994 (PG)** Preceded by massive hype, popular '60s cartoon comes to life thanks to a huge budget and creative sets and props. Seems that Fred's (Goodman) being set up by evil corporate types Cliff Vandercave (MacLachlan) and Miss Rosetta Stone (Berry) to take the fall for their embezzling scheme. Soon he gives up dining at RocDonald's for Cavern on the Green and cans best buddy Barney (Moranis). Forget the lame plot (32 writers took a shot at it) and sit back and enjoy the spectacle. Goodman's an amazingly true-to-type Fred, O'Donnell has Betty's giggle down pat, and Perkins looks a lot like Wilma. Wilma's original voice, VanderPyl, has a cameo as Mrs. Feldspar; listen for Korman's voice as the Dictabird. Add half a bone if you're under 12. **92m/C VHS, DVD, Wide.** John Goodman, Rick Moranis, Elizabeth Perkins, Rosie O'Donnell, Elizabeth Taylor, Kyle MacLachlan, Halle Berry, Jonathan Winters, Richard Moll, Irwin Keyes, Dann Florek; ***Cameos:*** Laraine Newman, Jean Vander Pyl, Jay Leno; ***D:*** Brian Levant; ***W:*** Tom S. Parker, Jim Jennewein, Steven E. de Souza; ***C:*** Dean Cundey; ***M:*** David Newman; ***V:*** Harvey Korman. Golden Raspberries '94: Worst Support. Actress (O'Donnell), Worst Screenplay.

The Flintstones in Viva Rock Vegas 🦴🦴 **2000 (PG)** In a prequel to the 1994 film, a young Fred (Addy) and his best pal Barney (Baldwin) take their girlfriends Wilma (Johnson) and Betty (Krakowski) on a would-be romantic weekend to Rock Vegas. There's a whole lot going on, as runaway society girl Wilma is being wooed by playboy Chip Rockefeller (Gibson), Chip's trying to bankrupt and frame Fred, and the Great Gazoo (Cumming) is on hand to observe earthly mating habits. Everything is appropriately cartoonish, including the story and the acting. Unfortunately, the only ones who'll be entertained are the ones who are too young to remember the original series (or the original movie for that matter). **90m/C VHS, DVD, Wide.** Mark Addy, Kristen Johnston, Stephen Baldwin, Jane Krakowski, Thomas Gibson, Joan Collins, Alan Cumming, Harvey Korman, Alex Meneses; ***D:*** Brian Levant; ***W:*** Harry Elfont, Deborah Kaplan, Jim Cash, Jack Epps Jr.; ***C:*** Jamie Anderson; ***M:*** David Newman.

Flipper 🦴🦴🦴 **1963** A fisherman's son befriends an injured dolphin, is persuaded to return him to the wild, and earns the animal's gratitude. Prime kids' fare, as its sequels and TV series attest. **87m/C VHS.** Chuck Connors, Luke Halpin, Kathleen Maguire, Connie Scott; ***D:*** James B. Clark.

Flipper 🦴🦴🦴 **1996 (PG)** They still call him Flipper! Flipper, who in some scenes is played by a robot dolphin, reappears in a feature film for the first time since 1966. Sullen 14-year-old city boy Sandy Ricks (Wood) must spend the summer with crusty bachelor uncle Porter (Hogan), who would rather fish than look after his troublesome nephew. The duo witness the heartless killing of Flipper's family and are adopted by him. In addition to causing their seafood bill to skyrocket, the dolphin helps them uncover an illegal toxic waste dumper, who happens to be the same guy who made Flipper's mama sleep with the fishes. Updated along with the story is the soundtrack, which features a version of the famous theme song by Matthew Sweet. **97m/C VHS.** Elijah Wood, Paul Hogan, Chelsea Field, Isaac Hayes, Jonathan Banks, Luke Halpin; ***D:*** Alan Shapiro; ***W:*** Alan Shapiro; ***C:*** Bill Butler; ***M:*** Joel McNeely.

Flipper's New Adventure 🦴🦴🦴 *Flipper and the Pirates* **1964** Believing they are to be separated, Flipper and Sandy travel to a remote island. Little do they know, a British family is being held for ransom on the island they have chosen. It's up to the duo to save the day. An enjoyable, nicely done family adventure. **103m/C VHS.** Luke Halpin, Pamela Franklin, Tom Helmore, Francesca Annis, Brian Kelly, Joe Higgins, Ricou Browning; ***D:*** Leon Benson.

Flipper's Odyssey 🦴🦴 **1966** Flipper has disappeared and his adopted family goes looking for him, but when one of the boys gets trapped in a cave, Flipper is his only hope. **77m/C VHS.** Luke Halpin, Brian Kelly, Tommy Norden; ***D:*** Paul Landres.

Flipping 🦴🦴 **1996 (R)** Quartet of none-too-bright wiseguy wanna-bes serve as debt collectors for gangster Leo Richards (David). Turns out gay undercover cop Billy (Proval) has infiltrated the gang—only to fall for ambitious hoodlum Michael (Amos)—and violent double-crosses abound. Debut for writer/director Mitchell. **102m/C VHS.** David Amos, David Proval, Gene Mitchell, Keith David, Shant Benjamin, Barry Primus, Mike Starr, Tony Burton, Paul Klar; ***D:*** Gene Mitchell; ***W:*** Gene Mitchell; ***C:*** Phil Parmet.

Flirt 🦴🦴½ **1995 (R)** Three variations on the same theme: love, jealousy, and the problems of committing are what comprise this interesting portrait of modern romance in three countries. One character in each of the three stories is faced with an ultimatum to commit and is given a 90-minute deadline. Each are already involved in various other romantic entanglements. The best scenes show the confused flirts receiving very amusing advice from strangers. First episode is the best, as the pace subsequently slows. **84m/C VHS.** *GE JP* William Sage, Parker Posey, Martin Donovan, Dwight Ewell, Dominik Bender, Geno Lechner, Miho Nikaido, Toshizo Fujisawa; ***D:*** Hal Hartley; ***W:*** Hal Hartley; ***C:*** Michael Spiller; ***M:*** Ned Rifle.

Flirtation Walk 🦴🦴½ **1934** West point musical that has cadet Powell falling in love with the general's daughter (Keeler), who is already engaged to lieutenant Eldredge. Some fairly good numbers, including "Mr. and Mrs. Is The Name," and "Flirtation Walk." In an attempt to change her image, Keeler hardly dances at all, which is too bad for the viewer. Based on a story by Lou Edelman and Delmer Daves. **98m/B VHS.** Dick Powell, Ruby Keeler, Pat O'Brien, Ross Alexander; ***D:*** Frank Borzage; ***W:*** Delmer Daves.

Flirting 🦴🦴🦴 **1989 (R)** Set in an Australian boarding school in 1965, a charming story following the misadventures of the adolescent Danny Embling, who has the misfortune to be both bright and sensitive, putting him seriously at odds with his masculine peers. He finds love with an outcast at the neighboring girls boarding school, the daughter of a diplomat from Uganda. Kidman has a supporting role as a snobbish older boarding school girl, not quite as bad as she seems. Tender and amusing. The second of director Duigan's coming-of-age trilogy, preceded by "The Year My Voice Broke" (the third film isn't yet completed). **100m/C VHS.** *AU* Noah Taylor, Thandie Newton, Nicole Kidman, Bartholomew Rose, Felix Nobis, Josh Picker, Kiri Paramore, Marc Gray, Joshua Marshall, David Wieland, Craig Black, Leslie Hill; ***D:*** John Duigan; ***W:*** John Duigan. Australian Film Inst. '90: Film.

Flirting with Disaster 🦴🦴🦴 **1995 (R)** Mel Coplin (Stiller) is your average neurotic New York entomologist searching for his birth parents so he can finally name his four-month-old child and make love to his wife. Tagging along on his bumpy ride are his wife Nancy (Arquette), a beautiful quirky adoption agency shrink (Leoni), and a pair of bisexual FBI agents. The excellent cast also features Moore as Mel's bra-baring adoptive mother, Segal as his weirdly paranoid adoptive father, and Alda and Tomlin as hilarious send-ups of ex-hippie mentality. As events spin madly out of control, every type of relationship is satirized, and every character is left in their underwear. This is director Russell's first big-budget movie, and is as close to a vintage screwball comedy as you'll see in the '90s. **92m/C VHS, DVD, Wide.** Ben Stiller, Patricia Arquette, Tea Leoni, Alan Alda, Mary Tyler Moore, George Segal, Lily Tomlin, Josh Brolin, Richard Jenkins, Celia Weston, Glenn Fitzgerald, Beth Ostrosky, Cynthia Lamontagne, David Patrick Kelly, John Ford Noonan, Charles Oberly; ***D:*** David O. Russell;

W: David O. Russell; *C:* Eric Alan Edwards; *M:* Stephen Endelman.

Flirting with Fate ✂✂✂ **1916** Early Fairbanks-cum-acrobat vehicle. Having hired a hitman to rub himself out, a young man decides he doesn't want to die, after all. Seems there's a girl involved... **51m/B VHS.** Douglas Fairbanks Sr., Jewel Carmen, Howard Gaye, William E. Lawrence, George Beranger, Dorothy Hadel, Lillian Langdon; *D:* Christy Cabanne.

Floating ✂✂ **1997** Van (Reedus) is a moody 20-year-old ex-high school swimming champ who's basically treading water. He looks after his drunken paraplegic father (Lyman) in their run-down cottage and drifts into home burglaries with two equally loser friends. It's Van's idea to stash their ill-gotten gains in the basement of his former family home—of course the empty dwelling immediately gets a new owner—and Van winds up befriending the family's son, Doug (Lowe), who's not only a swimming champ but has Dad problems as well. This male bonding leads to some (predictable) attitude changes but the sincerity of the cast goes a long way in overcoming the cliches. **91m/C VHS, DVD.** Norman Reedus, Chad Lowe, Will Lyman, Jonathan Quint, Josh Marchette, Sybil Temchen; *D:* William Roth; *W:* William Roth; *C:* Wolfgang Held; *M:* David Mansfield.

Floating Life ✂✂ **1995** The Chans have decided to emigrate from Hong Kong before the mainland China takeover and join daughter Bing (Yip) and her family in Sydney. High-strung Bing's determined to assimilate as much as possible into Australian society and bullies her newly arrived family, who are naturally disoriented. The arrival of laggard son Gar Ming (Wong) and easy-going daughter Yen (Shun-Wah), who's been living in Germany, only provide further complications for a family completely adrift in their new world. Cantonese, German, and English dialogue. **95m/C VHS.** *AU* Annie Yip, Annete Shun-Wah, Anthony Wong, Edwin Pang, Cecilia Fong Sing Lee, Toby Wong, Toby Chan, Bruce Poon; *D:* Clara Law; *W:* Clara Law, Eddie L.C. Fong; *C:* Dion Beebe; *M:* Davood A. Tabrizi.

Flood! ✂✂ **1976** Irwin Allen's first made-for-TV disaster film. A dam bursts and devastates a small town, so a helicopter pilot must save the day. Good cast is swept along in a current of disaster-genre cliches. **98m/C VHS.** Robert Culp, Martin Milner, Barbara Hershey, Richard Basehart, Carol Lynley, Roddy McDowall, Cameron Mitchell, Teresa Wright, Francine York; *D:* Earl Bellamy. **TV**

Flood: A River's Rampage ✂✂½ **1997 (PG-13)** Community struggles to rebuild after a devastating flood. **92m/C VHS, DVD.** Richard Thomas, Kate Vernon, Jan Rubes; *D:* Bruce Pittman. **TV**

Flooding ✂✂½ **1997** Clever homage to Alfred Hitchcock on a budget. Joyce Calloway (Gibson) has become agoraphobic after the unsolved murder of her husband and has spent the past six months in her house. She is working with a new doctor (who comes to the house, of course) to get over her fear of the outside world, and she better hurry, because her parents are selling the house in an effort to get her to go outside. After a fling, a man comes to her back door, falls inside, and dies after uttering a name she doesn't recognize. The tension mounts as it becomes clear that her subconscious mind is holding out on her and that someone wants her dead or at least out of the way. The why of the story is the weak link in the film; it is the journey to the answer that is absorbing. This is not a perfect film, but it is worth watching for fans of suspense. **86m/C DVD, Wide.** Brenna Gibson, Lauren Bailey, Kary Cawley; *D:* Todd Portugal; *W:* Todd Portugal.

The Floorwalker ✂✂✂ **1917** Chaplin becomes involved with a dishonest floorwalker in a department store. Silent. **20m/B VHS.** Charlie Chaplin; *D:* Charlie Chaplin.

Flor Silvestre ✂ *Wild Flower* **1958** The son of a rich rancher romances a young woman against the background of the Mexican Revolution. **90m/B VHS.** *MX* Dolores Del Rio, Pedro Armendariz Sr.; *D:* Emilio Fernandez.

The Florentine ✂✂ **1998 (R)** A decaying steel town is home to a bar called The Florentine, its owner Whitey (Madsen), and the usual drinking denizens. But with profits sinking, Whitey may lose his livelihood. And then there's his sister Molly's (Madsen) problems. Her wedding to Frankie (Perry) is in jeopardy because of a con man (Belushi) and her ex-fiance, Teddy (Sizemore), who's back in town. **104m/C VHS, DVD.** Michael Madsen, Virginia Madsen, Luke Perry, Tom Sizemore, James Belushi, Mary Stuart Masterson, Christopher Penn; *D:* Nick Stagliano. **VIDEO**

The Florida Connection ✂ **1974** An action thriller set in the Florida Swamps with a collection of villains and a vague plot about smuggling. **90m/C VHS.** Dan Pastorini, June Wilkinson.

Florida Straits ✂✂ **1987 (PG-13)** A recently released Cuban prisoner hires a few losers and their boat to return to the island, supposedly to find the girl he loves. The real quest is for gold buried during the Bay-of-Pigs invasion in this none-too-original cable movie that at least offers a good cast. **98m/C VHS.** Raul Julia, Fred Ward, Daniel H. Jenkins, Antonio Fargas; *D:* Mike Hodges; *W:* Stephen Metcalfe; *M:* Michel Colombier. **CABLE**

Floundering ✂½ **1994 (R)** Misguided satire uses the 1992 L.A. riots as a backdrop to tell the saga of unemployed James Boyz (LeGros), whose life is a walking disaster. He owes the IRS, his unemployment compensation has run out, his brother (Hawke) has fled from a drug rehab clinic, and he finds his girlfriend (Zane) in bed with another man. John drags himself among the city's downtrodden as he fantasizes about life. Drag pretty much sums up the film despite good performances by LeGros and Hawke. **97m/C VHS, DVD.** James LeGros, Ethan Hawke, Steve Buscemi, John Cusack, Lisa Zane, Sy Richardson, Jeremy Piven, Billy Bob Thornton; *D:* Peter McCarthy; *W:* Peter McCarthy; *C:* Denis Maloney; *M:* Pray for Rain.

Flower Drum Song ✂✂ **1961** The Rodgers and Hammerstein musical played better on Broadway than in this overblown adaptation of life in San Francisco's Chinatown. Umeki plays the young girl who arrives from Hong Kong for an arranged marriage. Her intended (Soo) is a fast-living nightclub owner already enjoying the love of singer Kwan. Meanwhile Umeki falls for the handsome Shigeta. Naturally, everything comes together in a happy ending. ♫I Enjoy Being A Girl; Don't Marry Me; Grant Avenue; You Are Beautiful; A Hundred Million Miracles; Fan Tan Fanny; Chop Suey; The Other Generation; I Am Going to Like It Here. **133m/C VHS.** Nancy Kwan, Jack Soo, James Shigeta, Miyoshi Umeki, Juanita Hall; *D:* Henry Koster; *C:* Russell Metty; *M:* Richard Rodgers, Oscar Hammerstein.

The Flower of My Secret ✂✂✂ *La Flor de My Secreto* **1995 (R)** Emotional yet restrained story about middle-aged Leo (Paredes), whose longtime marriage is fast ending (and it's not her idea). Leo writes hugely popular romance novels under a pseudonym but her current work is so bleak it's unpublishable. So, Leo gets a job at a newspaper where editor Angel (Echanove) immediately falls for her, and indeed, lives up to his name as her guardian. Willfully myopic about her own life, Leo undergoes further trials until she slowly realizes the mess she's in and becomes willing to change. Surprisingly subdued given Almodovar's usual flamboyance but it's a welcome change of pace. Spanish with subtitles. **107m/C VHS.** *SP FR* Marisa Paredes, Juan Echanove, Imanol Arias, Carmen Elias, Rossy de Palma, Chus (Maria Jesus) Lampreave, Joaquin Cortes, Manuela Vargas; *D:* Pedro Almodovar; *W:* Pedro Almodovar; *C:* Alfonso Beato; *M:* Alberto Iglesias.

Flowers in the Attic ✂½ **1987 (PG-13)** Based on the V.C. Andrews bestseller, a would-be thriller about four young siblings locked for years in their family's old mansion by their grandmother with their mother's selfish acquiescence. A chicken-hearted, clumsy flop that skimps on the novel's trashier themes. **93m/C VHS, DVD, Wide.** Victoria Tennant, Kristy Swanson, Louise Fletcher, Jeb Stuart Adams; *D:* Jeffrey Bloom; *W:* Jeffrey Bloom; *C:* Gil Hubbs; *M:* Christopher Young.

Flowers of Reverie ✂✂ **1984** A former soldier is imprisoned for his work in the resistance during the Hungarian Revolution (1848-9), leading to tragedy. In Hungarian with English subtitles. **106m/C VHS.** *HU* *D:* Laszlo Lugossy.

The Flowers of St. Francis ✂✂✂ *Francesco, giullare di Dio; Francis, God's Jester* **1950** Rossellini's presentation of St. Francis and his friars' attainment of spiritual harmony. In Italian with English subtitles. This is the British release version, 10-15 minutes longer than the U.S. version. **75m/B VHS.** *IT* Aldo Fabrizi, Brother Nazario Gerardi, Arabella Lemaitre; *D:* Roberto Rossellini; *W:* Father Antonio Lisandrini, Father Felix Morion, Federico Fellini, Roberto Rossellini; *C:* Otello Martelli; *M:* Enrico Buondonno, Renzo Rossellini.

Flowers of Shanghai ✂✂ *Haishang Hua* **1998** Slow costume drama/soap opera set in the brothels of late 19th-century Shanghai. In this self-contained world, the elegant "flower girls" depend on their ability to hold onto wealthy clients and Crimson (Hada) seems to be losing her charms. Her longtime patron, Wang (Leung Chui Wai), is also seeing Jasmin (Wei). Meanwhile, among the other ladies, Emerald (Reis) is working to buy her freedom and Jade (Hsuan) is refusing other clients because she believes Zhu (Chang) will marry her. Based on the novel "Biographies of Flowers of Shanghai" by Han Ziyun. Mandarin with subtitles. **125m/C VHS, DVD, Wide.** *JP TW* Tony Leung Chiu-Wai, Michiko Hada, Hsiao-hui Wei, Jack Kao, Michelle Reis, Annie Shizuka Inoh, Fang Hsuan, Simon Chang; *D:* Chien Hsiao Hou; *W:* Tien-wen Chu; *C:* Mark Lee Ping-Bin; *M:* Yoshihiro Yanno.

Flubber ✂✂ **1997 (PG)** Bland remake of Disney's "The Absent-Minded Professor" with Williams as the befuddled, yet brilliant Prof. Brainard. Putting his wedding on the back Bunsen burner, much to the dismay of his fiancee Sara Jean (Harden), Brainard invents a bouncy, flying green slime named "flubber." As the substance becomes the cure-all for romantic turmoil and fledging school basketball teams, it also attracts the attention of a corrupt businessman and his moronic henchmen. Due to the dull subplots, kids and adults will be disappointed that the main attraction (the cute green goo) doesn't have much screen time. Williams, oddly enough, seems comfortable playing second banana to a substance that could describe his comedic skills. **93m/C VHS, DVD.** Robin Williams, Marcia Gay Harden, Christopher McDonald, Raymond J. Barry, Clancy Brown, Ted Levine, Wil Wheaton, Edie McClurg; *D:* Les Mayfield; *W:* John Hughes; *C:* Dean Cundey; *M:* Danny Elfman.

The Fluffer ✂✂ **2001** Naive aspiring filmmaker Sean (Cunio) has his romantic illusions destroyed and is rather rudely forced to grow up. Gay Sean gets a job with a Hollywood porn production company and falls for one of the company's stars—the immature and self-destructive gay-for-pay Mikey (Gurney) whose nom-de-porn is Johnny Rebel. Mikey's on a downward slide despite Sean's admiration and the love of his stripper girlfriend Julie (Day) and if the two aren't careful, Mikey will take them with him. Title refers to one of the personal services Sean is expected to offer Mikey. **94m/C VHS.** Michael Cunio, Scott Gurney, Rozanne Day, Richard Riehle, Taylor Negron, Tim Bagley, Adina Porter, Deborah Harry; *D:* Richard Glatzer, Wash West; *W:* Wash West; *C:* Mark Putnam.

Fluke ✂✂ **1995 (PG)** "Ghost" meets "Oh, Heavenly Dog" as Tom (Modine) dies in a suspicious car accident and is reincarnated as a dog who remembers his past life. He returns to his former family (Travis and Pomeranc) to protect them from his former business partner (Stoltz), battling such puppy perils as cosmetic testing labs and dogcatchers along the way. While there's plenty of squishy sentimentality to go around, some of the scenes involving animal abuse may be a little much for the target audience of preteen kids. Jackson and Stoltz trade "Pulp Fiction" for pup fiction, but this dog won't hunt. Based on the novel by James Herbert. **96m/C VHS, DVD.** Matthew Modine, Nancy Travis, Eric Stoltz, Max Pomeranc, Ron Perlman, Jon Polito, Bill Cobbs, Frederico Pacifici, Collin Wilcox-Paxton; *D:* Carlo Carlei; *W:* James Carrington, Carlo Carlei; *C:* Raffaele Mertes; *M:* Carlo Siliotto; *V:* Samuel L. Jackson.

Flush ✂✂ **1981** Unorthodox comedy involving funny noises. **90m/C VHS.** William Calloway, William Bronder, Jeannie Linero; *D:* Andrew J. Kuehn.

The Fly ✂✂✂ **1958** The historic, chillingly original '50s sci-fi tale about a hapless scientist experimenting with teleportation who accidentally gets anatomically confused with a housefly. Campy required viewing; two sequels followed, and a 1986 remake which itself has spawned one sequel. **94m/C VHS, DVD, Wide.** David Hedison, Patricia Owens, Vincent Price, Herbert Marshall, Kathleen Freeman, Betty Lou Gerson, Charles Herbert; *D:* Kurt Neumann; *W:* James Clavell; *C:* Karl Struss; *M:* Paul Sawtell.

The Fly ✂✂✂ **1986 (R)** A sensitive, humanistic remake of the 1958 horror film about a scientist whose flesh is genetically intermixed with a housefly via his experimental transportation device. A thoughtful, shocking horror film, with fine performances from Goldblum and Davis and a brutally emotional conclusion. Followed by "The Fly II" in 1989. **96m/C VHS, DVD, Wide.** Jeff Goldblum, Geena Davis, John Getz, Joy Boushel, Cosette Lee; *D:* David Cronenberg; *W:* David Cronenberg, Charles Edward Pogue; *C:* Mark Irwin; *M:* Howard Shore. Oscars '86: Makeup.

The Fly 2 ✂½ **1989 (R)** Inferior sequel to Cronenberg's opus, in which the offspring of Seth Brundle achieves full genius maturity in three years, falls in love, and discovers the evil truth behind his father's teleportation device and the corporate auspices that backed it. **105m/C VHS, DVD, Wide.** Eric Stoltz, Daphne Zuniga, Lee Richardson, John Getz, Harley Cross; *D:* Chris Walas; *W:* Ken Wheat, Frank Darabont, Mick Garris, Jim Wheat; *C:* Robin Vidgeon; *M:* Christopher Young.

Fly Away Home ✂✂✂ *Father Goose; Flying Wild* **1996 (PG)** Does for geese what "Babe" did for pigs. Young Amy (Paquin) withdraws when she loses her mother in a car crash and is forced to live with her estranged father, Thomas (Daniels), a scruffy sculptor/inventor, in rural Ontario. Still dealing with her own mother's death, Amy suddenly becomes a mother herself to a tiny gaggle of goslings when she happens upon a nest of uprooted eggs. Extraordinary technical achievements make up for some unnecessary melodrama in the second half as the geese head South, led by Amy, in a glider built by her father. Touching but unsentimental, mostly well scripted and acted, and extraordinarily shot. Based on the true story of inventor Bill Lishman, who led domesticated geese on a winter migration from Toronto, Canada to North Carolina, leading the formation in his motor-powered glider. **107m/C VHS, DVD, Wide.** Jeff Daniels, Anna Paquin, Dana Delany, Terry Kinney, Jeremy Ratchford; *D:* Carroll Ballard; *W:* Robert Rodat, Vince McKewin; *C:* Caleb Deschanel; *M:* Mark Isham.

Fly Boy ✂✂½ **1999 (PG)** Gramps (Karen) is a still-adventurous WWII vet whose remote-controlled model airplanes are the terror of the neighborhood and the delight of his 10-year-old grandson, Ray (Hughes). In fact, Ray would like to help Gramps fulfill his big dream—to fly a real plane one last time. **86m/C VHS.** Miko Hughes, James Karen, Kathleen Lloyd, Gregory Itzin; *D:* Richard Stanley. **VIDEO**

Fly by Night ✂✂ **1993 (PG-13)** Mismatched New York rappers Rich and I join forces to make it big as hard-core gangstas. When they're propelled to the top of the charts, forces both personal and professional work to tear them apart. **93m/C VHS.** Jeffrey D. Sams, Ron Brice, Darryl (Chill)

Mitchell, Todd Graff, Leo Burmester, Soulfood Jed, Lawrence Gilliard, Omar Carter, Maura Tierney, Yul Vazquez, M.C. Lyte, Christopher-Michael Gerrard, Ebony Jo-Ann; *D:* Steve Gomer; *W:* Todd Graff; *C:* Larry Banks; *M:* Kris Parker, Sidney Mills, Dwayne Sumal. Sundance '93: Filmmakers Trophy.

Fly with the Hawk 19?? A troubled teenager gets lost in the wilderness for a year, and learns some important things from nature to take back to civilization. **90m/C VHS.** Peter Ferri, Peter Snook, Shelley Lynne Speigel; *D:* Robert Tanos.

Flying Blind ½ 1941 Foreign agents are thwarted in their attempt to steal a vital air defense secret. Unconvincing espionage plot cobbled into a story about a Los Angeles-Las Vegas puddle jumper. **69m/B VHS.** Richard Arlen, Jean Parker, Marie Wilson.

The Flying Deuces *Flying Aces* 1939 Ollie's broken heart lands Laurel and Hardy in the Foreign Legion. The comic pair escape a firing squad only to suffer a plane crash that results in Hardy's reincarnation as a horse. A musical interlude with a Laurel soft shoe while Hardy sings "Shine On, Harvest Moon" is one of the film's highlights. **65m/B VHS, DVD.** Stan Laurel, Oliver Hardy, Jean Parker, Reginald Gardiner, James Finlayson; *D:* Edward Sutherland; *W:* Ralph Spence, Charles R. Rogers, Harry Langdon, Alfred Schiller; *C:* Elmer Dyer, Art Lloyd; *M:* Leo Shuken, John Leopold.

Flying Down to Rio ½ 1933 The first Astaire-Rogers musical, although they are relegated to supporting status behind Del Rio and Raymond. Still, it was enough to make them stars and a team that epitomizes the height of American musical films. The slim story revolves around singer Del Rio's two suitors and receives a splendid, art deco production. Showgirls dancing on plane wings in flight provide another memorable moment. ♫Music Makes Me; The Carioca; Orchids in the Moonlight; Flying Down to Rio. **89m/B VHS.** Fred Astaire, Ginger Rogers, Dolores Del Rio, Eric Blore, Gene Raymond, Franklin Pangborn; *D:* Thornton Freeland; *M:* Vincent Youmans, Max Steiner.

The Flying Fool 1929 Ace pilot Bill returns from the war to find his younger brother has fallen for a singer. When Bill meets the lady, he also notices her charms and the two brothers have a duel in the skies to see who'll get the girl. **75m/B VHS.** William Boyd, Marie Prevost, Russell Gleason; *D:* Tay Garnett; *W:* James Gleason.

Flying from the Hawk ½ 1986 A 12-year-old boy sees something he shouldn't and soon finds that his friends and relatives are mysteriously vanishing. **110m/C VHS.** John Ireland, Diane McBain.

Flying Leathernecks 1951 Tough squadron leader Wayne fights with his fellow officer Ryan in Guadalcanal when their leadership styles clash. But when the real fighting begins all is forgotten as Wayne leads his men into victorious battle, winning the admiration and devotion of his fliers. Memorable WWII film deals with war in human terms. **102m/C VHS.** John Wayne, Robert Ryan, Janis Carter, Don Taylor, James Bell, James Dobson, Jay C. Flippen, Gordon Gebert, William Harrigan, Brett King, Adam Williams, Carleton Young, Dick Wessel, Gail Davis, Harlan Warde, Michael (Steve Flagg) St. Angel, Maurice Jara, John Mallory, Britt Nelson, Lynn Stalmaster; *D:* Nicholas Ray; *W:* Kenneth Gamet, James Edward Grant; *C:* William E. Snyder; *M:* Roy Webb.

The Flying Saucer ½ 1950 U.S. and Russian scientists clash over their search for a huge flying saucer that is hidden under a glacier. The first movie to deal with flying saucers. The cassette includes animated opening and closing sequences plus previews of coming attractions. **71m/B VHS, DVD.** Mikel Conrad, Pat Garrison, Hanz von Teuffen; *D:* Mikel Conrad; *W:* Howard Irving Young, Mikel Conrad; *C:* Philip Tannura; *M:* Darrell Calker.

The Flying Scotsman ½ 1929 A fired railroad worker tries to wreck an express train on the engineer's last journey. The daughter of the intended victim saves the day. Silent, with sound added. **60m/B VHS.** Ray Milland, Pauline Johnson, Moore Marriott; *D:* Castleton Knight.

Flying Tigers ½ 1942 Salutes the All-American Volunteer Group which flew for China under General Claire Chennault against the Japanese before the U.S. entered WWII. A squadron leader and a brash new recruit both vie for the affections of a pretty nurse in-between their flying missions. Romance and a few comic touches take a back seat to graphic scenes of aerial battles and dramatization of heroic sacrifice in this rousing war film. **101m/B VHS, DVD.** John Wayne, Paul Kelly, John Carroll, Anna Lee, Mae Clarke, Gordon Jones; *D:* David Miller.

Flying Wild ½ 1941 A gang of saboteurs is out to steal top-secret airplane blueprints. Who else but the Bowery Boys could conceivably stop them? **62m/B VHS.** Leo Gorcey, Bobby Jordan, Donald Haines, Joan Barclay, David Gorcey, Bobby Stone, Sammy (Earnest) Morrison; *D:* William West.

Flynn ½ *My Forgotten Man* 1996 Details the adventurous early years of Tasmania-born Errol Flynn (Pearce) before he became the swashbuckling hero of Hollywood films. His sexual exploits get him kicked out of school and he makes his way as gigolo, thief, liar, and alleged spy. **96m/C VHS, DVD.** *AU* Guy Pearce, Claudia Karvan, Steven Berkoff; *D:* Frank Howson; *W:* Frank Howson; *C:* John Wheeler; *M:* Anthony Marinelli.

Flypaper 1997 (R) Parking-lot bigshot Marvin (Loggia) and his business associate Jack (Brolly) help out junkie Natalie (Frost), who is being pressured by low-rent hood Bobby Ray (Sheffer). There's actually three separate but connected stories revolving around a big score and the various lowlifes who want to get their hands on it one California afternoon. **111m/C VHS, DVD.** Robert Loggia, Sadie Frost, Craig Sheffer, Shane Brolly, Lucy Alexis Liu, James Wilder, Illeana Douglas, Talisa Soto, John C. McGinley; *D:* Klaus Hoch; *W:* Klaus Hoch; *C:* Jurgen Baum; *M:* Peter Manning Robinson.

FM *Citizen's Band* 1978 (PG-13) The disc jockeys at an L.A. radio station rebel in the name of rock'n'roll. Despite the promising cast and setting (Mull makes his movie debut as a memorable space case), this is just disjointed and surprisingly unhip; one producer took his name off it due to creative difficulties. The decent soundtrack includes concert footage of Jimmy Buffet and Linda Ronstadt. ♫FM; Do It Again; FM Reprise; Livingston Saturday Night; The Key To My Kingdom; Green Grass and High Tides; Life In The Fast Lane; Bad Man; Poor, Poor, Pitiful Me. **104m/C VHS, DVD, Wide.** Eileen Brennan, Alex Karras, Cleavon Little, Martin Mull, Cassie Yates, Linda Ronstadt, Jimmy Buffett; *D:* John A. Alonzo; *W:* Ezra Sacks; *C:* David Myers.

Focus ½ 2001 (PG-13) Based on a 1945 novel by playwright Arthur Miller, this exploration of anti-Semitism and bigotry features Macy as Larry Newman, a nebbish personnel worker who lives with his invalid mother. After twenty years on the job, he is demoted after he gets glasses because they make him look "too Jewish" to his bosses. After quitting his job in protest, he is interviewed for a new job by Gertrude (Dern), a woman that he had turned away from his firm because she may or may not have been a Jew. A whirlwind romance ensues, and the two are soon married as their neighborhood is becoming a battleground of ethnic tension. Strong-arm tactics are used on local newsstand owner Finkelstein (Paymer), and he warns the Newmans about collective hate. Macy gives a great performance, but the material is a bit blunt and preachy. **106m/C VHS, DVD, Wide.** William H. Macy, Laura Dern, David Paymer, Meat Loaf Aday, Michael Copeman, Kenneth Welsh, Kay Hewtrey, Joseph Ziegler, Arlene Meadows; *D:* Neil Slavin; *W:* Kendrew Lascelles; *C:* Juan Ruiz-Anchia; *M:* Mark Adler.

The Fog 1978 (R) John Carpenter's blustery follow-up to his success with "Halloween." An evil fog containing murderous, vengeful ghosts envelops a sleepy seaside town and subjects the residents to terror and mayhem. **91m/C VHS, 8mm.** Hal Holbrook, Adrienne Barbeau, Jamie Lee Curtis, Janet Leigh, John Houseman, Tom Atkins; *D:* John Carpenter; *W:* John Carpenter, Debra Hill; *C:* Dean Cundey; *M:* John Carpenter.

Fog Island ½ 1945 Murder and terror lurk after a greedy inventor, who was framed for fraud by his business partner, is released from prison. He plots revenge by inviting his foes to his island home. **72m/B VHS, DVD.** George Zucco, Lionel Atwill, Terry Morse, Jerome Cowan, Veda Ann Borg; *D:* Terry Morse; *W:* Pierre Gendron; *C:* Ira Morgan.

Folks! 1992 (PG-13) Selleck is a Chicago stockbroker whose wife and kids have left him, the FBI is after him, and, worst of all, his parents have moved in with him. His parents don't want to be a burden, so Selleck decides that the best way to solve his financial woes is to help his parents commit suicide so he can collect on their insurance policies. Tasteless comedy that makes fun of aging and Alzheimer's Disease. Selleck is too sweet and cuddly for his role, but Ameche is good as the senile father, and Ebersole is great as Selleck's unpleasant sister. **109m/C VHS.** Tom Selleck, Don Ameche, Anne Jackson, Christine Ebersole, Wendy Crewson, Robert Pastorelli, Michael Murphy, Kevin Timothy Chevalia, Margaret Murphy; *D:* Ted Kotcheff; *M:* Michel Colombier.

Follies Girl 1943 There's folly in expecting that this wartime tuner would hold up today. An army private romances a dress designer and a musical show somehow results. ♫Keep the Flag A-Flying; No Man In The House; Someone to Love; I Told A Lie; Shall We Gather at the Rhythm?; Fascination; I Knew Your Father's Son; Thoity Poiple Boids. **74m/B VHS.** Wendy Barrie, Doris Nolan, Gordon Oliver, Anne Barrett, Arthur Pierson; *D:* William Rowland.

Follies in Concert 1985 A filmed record of the famed Stephen Sondheim musical play, performed at Lincoln Center in New York with an all-star cast. Songs include "I'm Still Here," "Losing My Mind," "Broadway Baby" and "The Ladies Who Lunch." **90m/C VHS.** Carol Burnett, Lee Remick, Betty Comden, Andre Gregory, Adolph Green, Mandy Patinkin, Phyllis Newman, Elaine Stritch, Jim Walton, Licia Albanese.

Follow Me 1969 (G) Round-the-world odyssey of three moon doggies searching for adventure—and the perfect wave. Spectacular surfing scenes are complemented by songs performed by Dino, Desi, and Billy. **90m/C VHS.** Claude Codgen, Mary Lou McGinnis, Bob Purvey; *D:* Gene McCabe.

Follow Me, Boys! 1966 A Disney film about a simple man who decides to put down roots and enjoy the quiet life, after one year too many on the road with a ramshackle jazz band. That life is soon interrupted when he volunteers to lead a high-spirited boy scout troop. **120m/C VHS.** Fred MacMurray, Vera Miles, Lillian Gish, Charlie Ruggles, Elliott Reid, Kurt Russell, Luana Patten, Ken Murray; *D:* Norman Tokar; *W:* Louis Pelletier; *M:* George Bruns.

Follow Me Quietly 1949 Serial strangler who only kills in the rain is stalked by Lundigan. Very good little thriller which packs a punch in less than an hour. **59m/B VHS.** William Lundigan, Dorothy Patrick, Jeff Corey, Nestor Paiva, Charles D. Brown, Paul Guilfoyle; *D:* Richard Fleischer.

Follow That Camel ½ *Carry On Follow That Camel* 1967 Foreign Legion sergeant who invents acts of heroism finally gets a chance to really help out a friend in need. Part of the "Carry On" series. **95m/C VHS.** *GB* Phil Silvers, Kenneth Williams, Anita Harris, Jim Dale; *D:* Gerald Thomas.

Follow That Car 1980 (PG) Three southern kids become FBI agents and begin a thigh-slappin', rip-snortin' down-home escapade. **96m/C VHS.** Dirk Benedict, Tanya Tucker, Teri Nunn; *D:* Daniel Haller.

Follow That Dream 1961 (G) Elvis plays a musical hillbilly whose family is trying to homestead on government land along the sunny Florida coast. Based on Richard C. Powell's novel "Pioneer Go Home." The songs—the only reason to see this movie—include "Angel," "What a Wonderful Life," and the title track. **111m/C VHS, Wide.** Elvis Presley, Arthur O'Connell, Anne Helm, Simon Oakland, Jack Kruschen, Joanna Moore, Howard McNear; *D:* Gordon Douglas.

Follow That Rainbow 1966 Believing that her long-lost father is a popular touring singer, a young lass pursues him from Switzerland to South Africa. **90m/C VHS.** Joe Stewardson, Memory Jane, Joan Bickhill.

Follow the Boys 1944 Vaudeville performer Tony West (Raft) heads out to California to try his luck and gets a double break when he's noticed by leading lady Gloria Vance (Zorina). Not only does he become a star but he marries Gloria as well. When WWII breaks out Tony's turned down for military service, so he organizes camp shows for the soldiers. They're a big success but misunderstandings have put his marriage in jeopardy. Plot's merely an excuse to have haute Hollywood (including Marlene Dietrich, Orson Welles, Jeanette MacDonald, and W.C. Fields) sing, dance, and tell jokes. ♫Beyond the Blue Horizon; I'll See You In My Dreams; The Bigger the Army and the Navy; Some of These Days; I'll Get By; I'll Walk Alone; Mad About Him Blues; The House I Live In. **111m/B VHS.** George Raft, Vera Zorina, Grace McDonald, Charles Butterworth, Martha O'Driscoll, Charley Grapewin, Elizabeth Patterson; *D:* Edward Sutherland; *W:* Lou Breslow, Gertrude Purcell.

Follow the Fleet 1936 A song-and-dance man joins the Navy and meets two sisters in need of help in this Rogers/Astaire bon-bon featuring a classic Berlin score. Look for Betty Grable, Lucille Ball, and Tony Martin in minor roles. Hilliard went on to be best known as the wife of Ozzie Nelson in TV's "The Adventures of Ozzie and Harriet." ♫Let's Face the Music and Dance; We Saw the Sea; I'm Putting All My Eggs In One Basket; Get Thee Behind Me, Satan; But Where Are You?; I'd Rather Lead a Band; Let Yourself Go. **110m/B VHS.** Fred Astaire, Ginger Rogers, Randolph Scott, Harriet Hilliard Nelson, Betty Grable, Lucille Ball; *D:* Mark Sandrich; *M:* Irving Berlin, Max Steiner.

Follow the Leader *East of the Bowery* 1944 On leave from the Army, Hall and Gorcey discover that one of the gang has been jailed on a trumped-up charge and set about finding the real culprit. ♫Now and Then; All I Want to Do Play the Drums. **65m/B VHS.** Leo Gorcey, Huntz Hall, Gabriel Dell, Jack LaRue, Joan Marsh, William Benedict, Mary Gordon, Sammy (Earnest) Morrison; *D:* William Beaudine; *M:* Gene Austin.

Follow the River ½ 1995 (PG) It's 1775 and Mary Ingles (Lee) is living with her husband and family on a frontier farm in the Blue Ridge Mountains. The community is raided by the Shawnee, lead by Wildcat (Schweig), who take Mary and several other settlers miles away to their home camp. Once there, Mary befriends another captive, the older Gretl (Burstyn), proves her courage to the smitten Wildcat, and plots to escape and find her way home. Based on the 1981 novel by James Alexander Thom; filmed in North Carolina. **93m/C VHS.** Sheryl Lee, Eric Schweig, Ellen Burstyn, Tim Guinee, Renee O'Connor; *D:* Martin Davidson.

Follow the Stars Home ½ 2001 Dianne (Williams) falls for charming fisherman Mark McCune (Close), they get married, and she's soon pregnant. But when Dianne learns that their baby daughter will be born will severe disabilities, Mark can't cope and leaves her. Flash forward six years, with Dianne making a life for herself and Julia—aided by her mother (Brown) and Mark's steadfast pediatrician brother, David (Scott), who obviously loves her. Then an accident brings Mark back into their lives, but will Dianne make a different choice this time? Based on the novel by Luanne Rice. A Hallmark Hall of Fame production that's a predictable tearjerker. **97m/C VHS, DVD.** Kimberly Williams, Campbell Scott, Eric Close, Blair Brown, Alexa Vega, Roxanne Hart; *D:* Dick Lowry; *W:* Sally Robinson. **TV**

Following 🦴🦴 **1999 (R)** Nolan's feature debut is an odd little neo-noir about a young man named Bill (Theobald) who likes to follow strangers. He picks the wrong guy in burglar Cobb (Haw) who has his own voyeuristic tastes. Cobb turns the tables on Bill and decides to become his mentor in crime. And sticking with the noir tradition, there's a mysterious blonde femme (Russell) whose relationship to the men is gradually revealed. As in his 2001 film "Memento," Nolan plays twister with the chronology, which means more than one viewing may be necessary to figure things out. **71m/B VHS, DVD.** Jeremy Theobald, Alex Haw, Lucy Russell, John Nolan; ***D:*** Christopher Nolan; ***W:*** Christopher Nolan; ***C:*** Christopher Nolan; ***M:*** David Julyan.

Food of the Gods woof! **1976 (PG)** On a secluded island giant rats, chickens, and other creatures crave human flesh, blood, bones, etc. This cheap, updated version of the H. G. Wells novel suffers from lousy performances and a lack of imagination. **88m/C VHS.** Marjoe Gortner, Pamela Franklin, Ralph Meeker, Ida Lupino, Jon Cypher; ***D:*** Bert I. Gordon.

Food of the Gods: Part 2 woof! *Gnaw: Food of the Gods 2* **1988 (R)** The killer beasts and animals of the first film (and of H.G. Wells' classic novel) strike again; gigantic rats maim young girls. Easily as bad as the original. **93m/C VHS.** Paul Coufos, Lisa Schrage; ***D:*** Damian Lee; ***W:*** E. Kim Brewster.

A Fool and His Money 🦴🦴½ **1988 (R)** Adman Morris Codman (Penner) decides to market a shady new religion based on greed but, naturally, finds the true road. Bullock is skeptical girlfriend Debby. **84m/C VHS.** Jonathan Penner, Sandra Bullock, Gerald Orange, George Plimpton; ***D:*** Daniel Adams; ***W:*** Daniel Adams.

Fool for Love 🦴🦴 **1986 (R)** Explores the mysterious relationship between a modern-day drifter and his long-time lover, who may or may not be his half-sister, as they confront each other in a seedy New Mexico motel. Adapted by Shepard from his play. **108m/C VHS.** Sam Shepard, Kim Basinger, Randy Quaid, Harry Dean Stanton; ***D:*** Robert Altman; ***W:*** Sam Shepard; ***M:*** George Burt.

The Fool Killer 🦴🦴½ *Violent Journey* **1965** In the post-Civil War south, a 12 year-old boy learns that a terrifying legend about an axe-murderer may be all too real. Offbeat film with striking visuals and photography. Debut film for Albert and another choice psycho role for Perkins. **100m/B VHS.** Anthony Perkins, Edward Albert, Dana Elcar, Henry Hull, Salome Jens, Arnold Moss; ***D:*** Servando Gonzalez.

A Fool There Was 🦴🦴½ **1914** The rocket that blasted Theda Bara to stardom and launched the vamp film genre. One of the few extant Bara films, it tells the now familiar story of a good man whom crumbles from the heights of moral rectitude thanks to the inescapable influence of an unredeemable vamp. Bette Davis described Bara as "divinely, hysterically, insanely malevolent." Much heavy emoting; subtitled (notoriously) "Kiss Me, My Fool!" Based on Rudyard Kipling's "The Vampire." **70m/B VHS, DVD.** Mabel Frenyear, Victor Benoit, Theda Bara, Edward Jose, Runa Hodges, Clifford Bruce; ***D:*** Frank Powell; ***W:*** Roy L. McCardell; ***C:*** George Schneiderman.

Foolin' Around 🦴🦴½ **1980 (PG)** An innocent Oklahoma farm boy arrives at college and falls in love with a beautiful heiress. He will stop at nothing to win her over, including crashing her lavish wedding ceremony. **101m/C VHS.** Gary Busey, Annette O'Toole, Eddie Albert, Tony Randall, Cloris Leachman; ***D:*** Richard T. Heffron; ***W:*** Michael Kane; ***M:*** Charles Bernstein.

Foolish woof! **1999 (R)** Foolish? You bet it is. Eddie Griffin stars as the title character, a struggling comic who rips off old Eddie Murphy routines to a hip-hop beat. He butts heads with his brother Fifty Dollah, played by rapper/sports agent/bad actor Master P, who also wrote and executive produced this clunker. The boom mike falls into the picture so often that you expect Master P to grab it and bust a rhyme at any given moment. Strictly for sucka MCs. **96m/C VHS, DVD.** Eddie Griffin, Percy (Master P) Miller, Frank Sivero, Amy Petersen, Jonathan Banks, Andrew (Dice Clay) Silverstein, Marla Gibbs, Daphnee Lynn Duplaix, Sven-Ole Thorsen, Bill Nunn, Bill Duke; ***D:*** Dave Meyers; ***W:*** Percy (Master P) Miller; ***C:*** Steve Gainer; ***M:*** Wendy Melvoin, Lisa Coleman.

Foolish Wives 🦴🦴🦴½ **1922** A remake of Von Stroheim's classic depicting the confused milieu of post-war Europe as reflected through the actions of a bogus count and his seductive, corrupt ways. Comes as close as possible to the original film. **107m/B VHS, DVD.** Erich von Stroheim, Mae Busch, Maud(e) (Ford) George, Cesare Gravina, Harrison Ford; ***D:*** Erich von Stroheim; ***W:*** Erich von Stroheim; ***C:*** William H. Daniels; ***M:*** Sigmund Romberg.

Fools 🦴 **1970 (PG)** Two lonely people—he an aging horror film actor and she a young woman estranged from her husband—start a warm romance when they meet in San Francisco. The husband reacts violently. Good cast seems lost. **93m/C VHS.** Jason Robards Jr., Katharine Ross, Scott Hylands; ***D:*** Tom Gries.

Fools of Fortune 🦴🦴½ **1990 (PG-13)** Adaptation of William Trevor's novel depicting Willie Clinton's childhood and adult experiences of family dramatics played against the backdrop of post-WWI Ireland. During the Irish war for independence, a family is attacked by British soldiers, creating emotional havoc for the survivors. Though well-acted and poignant, it's a rather disjointed and straying shamrock opera. **104m/C VHS.** *GB* Mary Elizabeth Mastrantonio, Iain Glen, Julie Christie, Michael Kitchen, Sean McClory, Frankie McCafferty; ***D:*** Pat O'Connor; ***W:*** Michael Hirst; ***M:*** Hans Zimmer.

Fools Rush In 🦴🦴 **1997 (PG-13)** Uptight eastern yuppie Alex Whitman (Perry) meets cute in Vegas with beautiful Latina casino worker Isabel Fuentes (Hayek) and the duo spend the night together. Three months later, Isabel shows up at Alex's New York door to announce her pregnancy and say she's keeping the baby. Movie cliches collide with movie stereotypes when they decide to marry but find the relationship suffers over their vast ethnic and cultural differences. At least the leads are attractive. Perry's real-life dad plays his character's father. **110m/C VHS, DVD.** Matthew Perry, Salma Hayek, Jon Tenney, Carlos Gomez, Tomas Milian, John Bennett Perry, Jill Clayburgh, Stanley DeSantis, Anne Betancourt; ***D:*** Andy Tennant; ***W:*** Katherine Reback; ***C:*** Robbie Greenberg; ***M:*** Alan Silvestri.

Footlight Frenzy 🦴🦴 **1984** The Law Moan Spectacular comedy troupe are at it again as they perform a benefit play where everything goes wrong. **110m/C VHS.** *GB* Alan Shearman, Diz White, Ron House, Frances Tomelty, Michael Aldridge, Ron Pember.

Footlight Glamour 🦴🦴 **1943** Dagwood is actually hired to run a new tool manufacturing plant but Blondie causes trouble when she casts the boss' daughter in a local play against the man's wishes. **68m/B VHS.** Penny Singleton, Arthur Lake, Larry Simms, Jonathan Hale, Thurston Hall, Ann Savage, Marjorie Ann Mutchie, Irving Bacon, Danny Mummert; ***D:*** Frank Strayer; ***W:*** Karen De Wolf, Connie Lee; ***C:*** Philip Tannura.

Footlight Parade 🦴🦴🦴 **1933** Broadway producer Cagney is out of work. Sound films have scared off his backers until his idea for staging live musical numbers before the cinema features lures them back. Lots of authentic backstage action precedes three spectacular Busby Berkeley-choreographed numbers that climax the film, including the giant water ballet featuring more than 100 performers. ♫Ah, the Moon is Here; Sittin' on a Backyard Fence; Honeymoon Hotel; By A Waterfall; Shanghai Lil. **104m/B** James Cagney, Joan Blondell, Dick Powell, Ruby Keeler, Guy Kibbee, Ruth Donnelly; ***D:*** Lloyd Bacon; ***C:*** George Barnes. Natl. Film Reg. '92.

Footlight Serenade 🦴🦴½ **1942** A boxer falls for a beautiful dancer with whom he's costarring in a Broadway play. Unfortunately, she's secretly married to another of the actors and her husband is becoming jealous of the boxer's intentions. Light, fun musical. One of a series of Grable movies made to boost morale during WWII. ♫Are You Kidding?; I'm Still Crazy About You; I Hear the Birdies Sing; Living High; I'll Be Marching to a Love Song; Land On Your Feet; I'm Stepping Out With a Memory Tonight. **80m/B VHS.** Betty Grable, Victor Mature, John Payne, Jane Wyman, Phil Silvers, James Gleason, Mantan Moreland; ***D:*** Gregory Ratoff; ***C:*** Lee Garmes.

Footloose 🦴🦴½ **1984 (PG)** When a city boy moves to a small Midwestern town, he discovers some disappointing news: rock music and dancing have been forbidden by the local government. Determined to bring some '80s-style life into the town, he sets about changing the rules and eventually enlists the help of the daughter of the man responsible for the law. Rousing music, talented young cast, and plenty of trouble make this an entertaining musical-drama. ♫Footloose; Let's Hear it for the Boy; The Girl Gets Around; Dancing in the Sheets; Somebody's Eyes; Almost Paradise; I'm Free; Never; Holding Out for a Hero. **107m/C VHS, 8mm.** Kevin Bacon, Lori Singer, Christopher Penn, John Lithgow, Dianne Wiest, John Laughlin, Sarah Jessica Parker; ***D:*** Herbert Ross; ***M:*** Miles Goodman.

Footsteps 🦴🦴 *Expose* **1998 (R)** Reporter Jason Davis (Chapa) gets a tip that makes him an eyewitness to a judge's murder. Separated from wife Nancy (Alonso), Jason gets involved with photographer Amber (Lombard), who is also connected to D.A. Steve Carlen (Schanley). When Jason turns up evidence that links Amber and Carlen to the murdered judge and he begins to receive threatening messages, Jason can trust only himself to catch the killer. **93m/C VHS, DVD.** Damian Chapa, Karina Lombard, Tom Schanley, Maria Conchita Alonso, Steven Schub, Sandra Bernhard, Tippi Hedren; ***D:*** Daphna Edwards; ***W:*** Daphna Edwards; ***C:*** David J. Miller; ***M:*** Alex Wurman. **VIDEO**

Footsteps in the Dark 🦴🦴½ **1941** Fairly amusing comedy-mystery with investment counselor Flynn doubling as detective. Based on the play "Blondie White" by Ladislaus Fodor, Bernard Merivale, and Jeffrey Dell. **96m/B VHS.** Errol Flynn, Brenda Marshall, Ralph Bellamy, Alan Hale, Lee Patrick, Allen Jenkins, Lucile Watson, William Frawley, Roscoe Karns, Grant Mitchell, Maris Wrixon, Noel Madison, Jack LaRue, Turhan Bey; ***D:*** Lloyd Bacon, Hugh MacMullen; ***W:*** Lester Cole, John Wexley.

For a Few Dollars More 🦴🦴½ **1965 (PG)** The Man With No Name returns as a bounty hunter who teams up with a gunslinger/rival to track down the sadistic leader of a gang of bandits. Violent. Sequel to "A Fistful of Dollars" (1964) and followed by "The Good, The Bad, and The Ugly." **127m/C VHS, DVD, Wide.** *IT* Clint Eastwood, Lee Van Cleef, Klaus Kinski, Gian Marie Volonte; ***D:*** Sergio Leone; ***W:*** Sergio Leone, Luciano Vincenzoni; ***C:*** Massimo Dallamano; ***M:*** Ennio Morricone.

For a Lost Soldier 🦴🦴 *Voor een Verloren Soldaat* **1993** Middle-aged Dutch choreographer Jeroen (Krabbe), working on a piece about the Allied liberation, recalls his relationship with a Canadian soldier more than 40 years before. During WWII, the 13-year-old Jeroen (Smit) is sent from Amsterdam to live in the country with a foster family. With the first twinges of puberty and sexuality he longs for a special friend, whom he finds in Walt (Kelley), a young gay Canadian soldier who is part of the Allied liberation forces. Very provocative subject, delicately handled, without any implication of child abuse. In English and Dutch with subtitles. **92m/C VHS.** *NL* Marten Smit, Andrew Kelley, Jeroen Krabbe, Feark Smink, Elsje de Wijn, Derk-Jan Kroon; ***D:*** Roeland Kerbosch; ***W:*** Roeland Kerbosch; ***C:*** Nils Post; ***M:*** Joop Stokkermans.

For Better and for Worse 🦴🦴½ **1992 (PG)** A nice young couple is planning to have your average nice wedding when one of their friends gets hold of an invitation and decides to jokingly invite the Pope to attend. But the joke is on them when the Pope accepts. Talk about upstaging the bride! **94m/C VHS.** Patrick Dempsey, Kelly Lynch.

For Better or Worse 🦴🦴 **1995 (PG-13)** Pathetic loser Michael Makeshift (Alexander, also making his directorial debut) falls in love with his new sister-in-law Valerie (Davidovich) even as he gets entangled in his brother Reggie's (Woods) business scams. **95m/C VHS.** Jason Alexander, Lolita (David) Davidovich, James Woods, Joe Mantegna, Jay Mohr, Beatrice Arthur, Robert Costanzo, John Amos, Eda Reiss Merin; ***Cameos:*** Rob Reiner, Rip Torn; ***D:*** Jason Alexander; ***W:*** Jeff Nathanson; ***C:*** Wayne Keenan; ***M:*** Miles Goodman. **CABLE**

For Ever Mozart 🦴🦴 **1996** Godard's film puzzle makes references to literature, music, and cinema itself without making any particular sense. Veteran film director Vicky Vitalis (Messica) agrees to help his daughter Camille (Assas) stage a comedic play by Alfred de Musset in Sarajevo, in order to cheer up its war-tired residents. This doesn't go well, but the director has already abandoned the project to return to his latest film idea, which also turns out to be a disaster. French with subtitles. **85m/C VHS.** *FR SI* Vicky Messica, Madeleine Assas, Frederic Pierrot, Ghalia Lacroix; ***D:*** Jean-Luc Godard; ***W:*** Jean-Luc Godard; ***C:*** Christophe Pollock.

For Heaven's Sake 🦴🦴🦴 **1926** Lloyd's first film for Paramount has him making an accidental donation to a skid row mission, then marrying the preacher's daughter and converting all the neighborhood tough guys. **60m/B VHS.** Harold Lloyd, Jobyna Ralston, Noah Young, James Mason, Paul Weigel; ***D:*** Sam Taylor.

For Heaven's Sake 🦴½ **1979** A bumbling basketball team is lent some heavenly assistance in the form of a meddling angel. But can he hit the jumper? **90m/C VHS.** Ray Bolger, Kent McCord. **TV**

For Hire 🦴🦴½ **1998** Suffering from cancer and with a pregnant wife, Chicago cabbie Mitch Lawrence (Lowe) is desperate for money. So, he agrees to kill an associate of famous writer Louis Webber (Mantegna) for $50,000. When the job is done, Mitch learns just why he was chosen to do the deed. **96m/C VHS, DVD.** Rob Lowe, Joe Mantegna, Dominic Philie, Bronwen Black; ***D:*** Jean Pellerin; ***M:*** Alan Reeves.

For Keeps 🦴½ **1988 (PG-13)** Two high school sweethearts on the verge of graduating get married after the girl becomes pregnant, and suffer all the trials of teenage parenthood. Tends toward the unrealistic and trite. **98m/C VHS.** Molly Ringwald, Randall Batinkoff, Kenneth Mars; ***D:*** John G. Avildsen; ***W:*** Tim Kazurinsky, Denise DeClue; ***M:*** Bill Conti.

For Ladies Only 🦴🦴 **1981** A struggling actor takes a job as a male stripper to pay the rent. Among the leering ladies is Davis, daughter of former President Reagan. **100m/C VHS.** Gregory Harrison, Patricia Davis, Dinah Manoff, Louise Lasser, Lee Grant, Marc Singer, Viveca Lindfors, Steven Keats; ***D:*** Mel Damski. **TV**

For Love Alone 🦴🦴 **1986** A young Australian college co-ed in the 1930s falls in love with a handsome, controversial teacher and follows him to London, only to discover he's not her Mr. Right after all. **102m/C VHS.** *AU* Helen Buday, Sam Neill, Hugo Weaving; ***D:*** Stephen Wallace.

For Love of Ivy 🦴🦴 **1968 (PG)** Poitier is a trucking executive who has a gambling operation on the side. Ivy is the Black maid of a rich white family who is about to leave her job to look for romance. The two are brought together but the road to true love doesn't run smooth. Based on a story by Poitier. **102m/C VHS, DVD.** Sidney Poitier, Abbey Lincoln, Beau Bridges, Carroll O'Connor, Nan Martin; ***D:*** Daniel Mann; ***M:*** Quincy Jones.

For Love of the Game 🦴🦴½ **1999 (PG-13)** The baseball glove has long been gold for Costner. In his third baseball outing, he moderately scores as veteran Detroit Tigers pitcher Billy Chapel, facing a crossroad in his professional and personal life. In 1-2-3 manner, he learns that the team he's played on for 20 years has been sold, the new owners want to trade him, and his longtime girlfriend, Jane (Preston), is dumping him prior to an important game with the Yankees. Magically, he's this close to pitching a perfect game, as the last five years of his life flash before him. Sudsy, predictable romance overshadows the game action, but harder-edged Raimi, with his own love for the game, injects some striking visual flair. Costner pitched a fit against the studio for editing out his infamous penis shot to ensure a kid-friendly rating. Based on the novel by Michael Shaara. **137m/C VHS, DVD, Wide.** Michael (Mike) Papajohn, Kevin Costner, Kelly Preston, John C. Reilly, Jena Malone, Brian Cox, J.K. Simmons, Bill Rogers, Vin Scully, Carmine D. Giovinazzo, Hugh Ross, Steve Lyons; ***D:*** Sam Raimi; ***W:*** Dana Stevens; ***C:*** John Bailey; ***M:*** Basil Poledouris.

For Love or Country: The Arturo Sandoval Story 🦴🦴½ **2000 (PG-13)** Biopic of Cuban trumpeter Arturo Sandoval (Garcia) who stays in Cuba for the sake of wife Marianela (Maestro) and their children, all the while chafing under his artistic restrictions. Finally, his wife agrees to defect and during a tour in Athens, Sandoval asks for political asylum. Both Garcia and Maestro have a believable chemistry but also look for Dutton's portrayal of Dizzy Gillespie, who hired Sandoval for his U.N. Orchestra, allowing the musician to travel abroad. **120m/C VHS, DVD, Wide.** Andy Garcia, Mia Maestro, Charles S. Dutton, David Paymer, Gloria Estefan, Tomas Milian, Freddy Rodriguez, Jose Zuniga, Steven Bauer, Fionnula Flanagan, Michael O'Hagan; ***D:*** Joseph Sargent; ***W:*** Timothy J. Sexton; ***C:*** Donald M. Morgan; ***M:*** Arturo Sandoval. **CABLE**

For Love or Money 🦴🦴 **1963** A super-rich hotel owner wants her lawyer to find her three beautiful daughters. However, she doesn't trust him enough not to meddle in the search. Lavish production and a good cast can't overcome the mediocrity of the script and direction. **108m/C VHS.** Kirk Douglas, Mitzi Gaynor, Thelma Ritter, William Bendix, Julie Newmar, Gig Young, Leslie Parrish, William Windom, Dick Sargent; ***D:*** Michael Gordon.

For Love or Money 🦴½ **1984** Game-show contestants find money and romance. **91m/C VHS.** Jamie Farr, Suzanne Pleshette, Gil Gerard, Ray Walston, Lawrence Pressman, Mary Kay Place; ***D:*** Terry Hughes; ***M:*** Billy Goldenberg. **TV**

For Love or Money 🦴🦴 **1988 (PG)** A real estate man with Career on the mind has to choose between the woman in his life and the condo development that stands firmly between them and happily-ever-afterdom. **?m/C VHS.** Timothy Daly, Haviland (Haylie) Morris, Kevin McCarthy.

For Love or Money 🦴🦴½ **1993 (PG)** Struggling hotel concierge with a heart of gold finds himself doing little "favors" for a slimy entrepreneur who holds the key to his dreams—the cash to open an elegant hotel of his own. Romantic comedy is reminiscent of the classic screwball comedies of the '30s and '40s, but lacks the trademark tight writing and impeccable timing. Fox is appealing and likable as the wheeling and dealing concierge, a role undermined by a mediocre script offering too few laughs. **89m/C VHS.** Michael J. Fox, Gabrielle Anwar, Isaac Mizrahi, Anthony (Corlan) Higgins, Michael Tucker, Bobby Short, Dan Hedaya, Bob Balaban, Udo Kier, Patrick Breen, Paula Laurence; ***D:*** Barry Sonnenfeld; ***W:*** Mark Rosenthal, Larry Konner; ***M:*** Bruce Broughton.

For Me and My Gal 🦴🦴½ **1942** In his film debut, Kelly plays an opportunistic song-and-dance man who lures a young vaudevillian (Garland) away from her current partners. WWI interrupts both their career and romance, but you can count on them being reunited. Loaded with vintage tunes. ♫For Me and My Gal; They Go Wild, Simply Wild Over Me; The Doll Shop; Oh, Johnny, Oh; Oh, You Beautiful Doll; When You Wore A Tulip; Don't Leave Me Daddy; Do I Love You; By The Beautiful Sea. **104m/B VHS.** Gene Kelly, Judy Garland, George Murphy, Martha Eggerth, Ben Blue, Richard Quine, Keenan Wynn, Stephen McNally; ***D:*** Busby Berkeley; ***M:*** George Bassman.

For Pete's Sake 🦴🦴 *July Pork Bellies* **1974 (PG)** Topsy-turvy comedy about a woman whose efforts to get together enough money to put her husband through school involve her with loan sharks, a madame, and even cattle rustling in NYC. Not one of Streisand's best. **90m/C VHS, DVD, Wide.** Barbra Streisand, Michael Sarrazin, Estelle Parsons, William Redfield, Molly Picon; ***D:*** Peter Yates; ***W:*** Stanley Shapiro, Maurice Richlin; ***C:*** Laszlo Kovacs; ***M:*** Artie Butler.

For Richer, for Poorer 🦴½ *Father, Son and the Mistress* **1992 (PG)** A very rich, successful businessman notices his son is happy just to sit back and let dad earn all the dough while he waits for his share. In order to teach his son a lesson, Dad decides to give all his money away. But the plan backfires when both realize that earning a second fortune may not be as easy as they assumed. Below average cable fare. **90m/C VHS.** Jack Lemmon, Talia Shire, Joanna Gleason, Jonathan Silverman, Madeline Kahn, George Wyner; ***D:*** Jay Sandrich; ***W:*** Stan Daniels. **CABLE**

For Richer or Poorer 🦴 **1997 (PG-13)** Definitely poorer. Don't pity the Amish because they can't defend themselves against movies like this—envy them because they don't have to see it. Shallow New York real-estate hustler Brad (Allen) is supposed to be divorcing socialite wife Caroline (Alley). Their inept accountant (Knight), however, has cooked the books, causing them to head for the Pennsylvania hills. They hide out with a community of Amish people, rediscovering their love along with a bunch of manure jokes. Proves once again the inherent unfunniness of butter churns and barn raisings. **122m/C VHS, DVD.** Tim Allen, Kirstie Alley, Wayne Knight, Larry Miller, Jay O. Sanders, Michael Lerner, Miguel Nunez, Megan Cavanagh, John Pyper-Ferguson, June Claman, Katie Moore; ***D:*** Bryan Spicer; ***W:*** Jana Howington, Steve Lukanic; ***C:*** Buzz Feitshans IV; ***M:*** Randy Edelman.

For Roseanna 🦴🦴½ *Roseanna's Grave* **1996 (PG-13)** Romantic comedy (despite the subject matter) about Marcello (Reno), the owner of a trattoria in an Italian village and his ailing wife Cecilia (Ruehl), whose dream is to be buried next to their daughter in one of the three remaining plots in their ancient local cemetery. Marcello goes to great lengths to ensure the health of the town's more at-risk citizens to save his wife's spot. Pleasant enough comedy boasts a fine job by an excellent cast, and the Italian scenery is beautiful. Overlooked at the time of its theatrical release, but worth a look for the sentimentally-inclined. **99m/C VHS.** Jean Reno, Mercedes Ruehl, Polly Walker, Mark Frankel, Trevor Peacock, Fay Ripley, Giuseppe Cederna, Luigi Diberti, Renato Scarpa, George Rossi, Roberto Della Casa, Romano Ghini; ***D:*** Paul Weiland; ***W:*** Saul Turteltaub; ***C:*** Henry Braham; ***M:*** Trevor Jones.

For Sale 🦴🦴 *A Vendre* **1998** After France (Kiberlain) leaves her groom-to-be at the altar, he hires private detective Luigi (Castellito) to track her down and bring her back. Luigi discovers France has left a string of lovers in her wake and that she has been charging them for her favors. The more he learns, the more obsessed he becomes with a woman he has yet to meet in the flesh. French with subtitles. **116m/C VHS, DVD, Wide.** *FR* Sandrine Kiberlain, Sergio Castellitto, Jean-Francois Stevenin, Chiara Mastroianni, Aurore Clement, Samuel Le Bihan; ***D:*** Laetitia Masson; ***W:*** Laetitia Masson; ***C:*** Antoine Hebale; ***M:*** Siegfried.

For the Boys 🦴🦴 **1991 (R)** Midler stars as Dixie Leonard, a gutsy singer-comedian who hooks up with Eddie Sparks (Caan) to become one of America's favorite USO singing, dancing, and comedy teams. The movie spans 50 years and three wars—including Korea and Vietnam—and raises such issues as the blacklist and the role of politics in showbiz. Glitzy Hollywood entertainment falters despite Midler's strong performance. ♫Billy-A-Dick; Come Rain or Come Shine; In My Life; Stuff Like That There. **120m/C VHS, DVD, Wide.** Bette Midler, James Caan, George Segal, Patrick O'Neal, Christopher Rydell, Arye Gross, Norman Fell, Rosemary Murphy, Dori Brenner, Bud Yorkin, Jack Sheldon, Melissa Manchester, Brandon Call, Arliss Howard; ***D:*** Mark Rydell; ***W:*** Marshall Brickman, Neal Jimenez, Lindy Laub; ***C:*** Stephen Goldblatt; ***M:*** Dave Grusin. Golden Globes '92: Actress—Mus./Comedy (Midler).

For the First Time 🦴🦴½ **1959** In his last film, Lanza plays an opera singer who tours European cities to raise money for his deaf girlfriend's medical treatment. ♫Oh Mon Amour; Bavarian Drinking Song; Ave Maria; Vesti La Giubba; La Donna e Mobile; Niun Mi Tema; Grand March; O Solo Mio; Ich Liebe Dich. **97m/C VHS.** Mario Lanza, Zsa Zsa Gabor, Johanna von Koczian, Kurt Kasznar, Hans Sohnker, Peter Capell, Renzo Cesana, Sandro Giglio; ***D:*** Rudolph Mate; ***W:*** Andrew Solt.

For the Love of Angela 🦴½ **1986** Pretty and young shop clerk involves herself with both the shopkeeper and his son. **90m/C** Louis Jourdan.

For the Love of Benji 🦴🦴 **1977 (G)** In this second "Benji" film, the adorable little dog accompanies his human family on a Greek vacation. He is kidnapped to be used as a messenger for a secret code, but escapes, to have a series of comic adventures in this entertaining family fare. **85m/C VHS, DVD.** Benji, Patsy Garrett, Cynthia Smith, Allen Finzat, Ed Nelson; ***D:*** Joe Camp; ***W:*** Joe Camp; ***C:*** Don Reddy; ***M:*** Euel Box.

For the Love of It 🦴½ **1980** TV stars galore try to hold together this farce about car chases in California, stolen secret documents, and (of course) true love. Outstandingly mediocre. **100m/C VHS.** Deborah Raffin, Jeff Conaway, Tom Bosley, Norman Fell, Don Rickles, Henry Gibson, Noriyuki "Pat" Morita, William (Bill) Christopher, Lawrence-Hilton Jacobs, Adrian Zmed, Barbi Benton, Adam West; ***D:*** Hal Kanter. **TV**

For the Love of Mary 🦴🦴½ **1948** Durbin retired after this fluff romantic comedy (with some musical numbers) in which she played White House switchboard operator Mary Peppertree. Mary has three potential suitors and juggling her romances causes job-related problems. Includes a second ending and song, which runs an additional eight minutes. ♫Moonlight Bay; Let Me Call You Sweetheart; I'll Take You Home Again, Kathleen; On the Wings of a Song; Largo al Factotum. **91m/B VHS.** Deanna Durbin, Edmond O'Brien, Don Taylor, Jeffrey Lynn, Harry Davenport, Ray Collins, Hugo Haas; ***D:*** Fred de Cordova; ***W:*** Oscar Brodney; ***C:*** William H. Daniels.

For the Moment 🦴🦴½ **1994 (PG-13)** Aussie aviator Lachlan (Crowe) has joined the British Commonwealth Training Plan in 1942, a crash course for fighter pilots that drew men from several countries to bases across Canada. Stationed with best buddy Johnny (Outerbridge) in Manitoba, Lachlan falls for the married Lill (Hirt), sister of Johnny's honey Kate (McMillan), whose husband is away fighting. The emotional stakes are high for all concerned since they know the fliers will soon be sent off to combat. Old-fashioned (and sometimes slow-moving) romance with excellent performances and some gorgeous scenery. **120m/C VHS.** *CA* Russell Crowe, Christianne Hirt, Peter Outerbridge, Sara McMillan, Wanda Cannon, Scott Kraft; ***D:*** Aaron Kim Johnston; ***W:*** Aaron Kim Johnston; ***C:*** Ian Elkin; ***M:*** Victor Davies.

For Us, the Living 🦴🦴🦴 **1988** The life and assassination of civil rights activist Medgar Evers are dramatically presented in this production of "American Playhouse" for PBS. Provides insight into Evers' character, not just a recording of the events surrounding his life. Adapted from the biography written by Evers' widow. **84m/C VHS.** Howard E. Rollins Jr., Rocky Aoki, Paul Winfield, Irene Cara, Margaret Avery, Roscoe Lee Browne, Laurence "Larry" Fishburne, Janet MacLachlan, Dick Anthony Williams; ***D:*** Michael A. Schultz.

For Which He Stands 🦴🦴 **1998** Johnny Rochetti (Forsythe) is a popular Vegas club owner with a loving wife (Alonso) and child. Then his life comes undone one night when he protects a young woman and kills her attacker in the process. Although vindicated by the cops, Johnny finds his troubles are just beginning when he learns the dead man was the brother of a Columbian druglord (Davi). Johnny's wife and child are taken hostage in order to force a deadly showdown between the two men. **94m/C VHS.** William Forsythe, Robert Davi, Maria Conchita Alonso, Ernie Hudson, John Ashton, Robert Costanzo, Ed Lauter, Jose Zuniga, Robert Miranda, Anthony John (Tony) Denison, Ed McMahon; ***D:*** Nelson McCormick; ***W:*** Gianni Russo, Nelson McCormick; ***C:*** Larry Blanford. **VIDEO**

For Whom the Bell Tolls 🦴🦴🦴½ **1943** Hemingway novel, gorgeously translated to the big screen, features a star-crossed romantic tale of derring-do. American schoolteacher Robert Jordan (Cooper) decides to join the Spanish Civil War and fight the fascists. He's ordered to rendezvous with peasant guerillas, to aid in blowing up a bridge, and in the rebel camp Jordan meets the beautiful Maria (Bergman). Lots of heroics (and some romance under the stars). Both leads were personally selected by the author. Originally released at 170 minutes. **130m/C VHS, DVD.** Gary Cooper, Ingrid Bergman, Akim Tamiroff, Katina Paxinou, Arturo de Cordova, Vladimir Sokoloff, Mikhail Rasumny, Fortunio Bonanova, Victor Varconi, Joseph Calleia, Alexander Granach, Yakima Canutt, George Coulouris, Yvonne De Carlo, Martin Garralaga, Soledad Jiminez, Duncan Renaldo, Tito Renaldo, Pedro de Cordoba, Frank Puglia, John (Jack) Mylong, Eric Feldary, Lilo Yarson, Leo Bugakov, Antonio Molina; ***D:*** Sam Wood; ***W:*** Dudley Nichols; ***C:*** Ray Rennahan; ***M:*** Victor Young. Oscars '43: Support. Actress (Paxinou).

For Your Eyes Only 🦴🦴🦴 **1981 (PG)** In this James Bond adventure, 007 must keep the Soviets from getting hold of a valuable instrument aboard a sunken British spy ship. Sheds the gadgetry of its more recent predecessors in the series in favor of some spectacular stunt work and the usual beautiful girl and exotic locale. Glen's first outing as director, though he handled second units on previous Bond films. Sheena Easton sang the hit title tune. **136m/C VHS, DVD, Wide.** *GB* Roger Moore, Carole Bouquet, Chaim Topol, Lynn-Holly Johnson, Julian Glover, Cassandra Harris, Jill Bennett, Michael Gothard, John Wyman, Jack Hedley, Lois Maxwell, Desmond Llewelyn, Geoffrey Keen, Walter Gotell, Charles Dance; ***D:*** John Glen; ***W:*** Michael G. Wilson; ***C:*** Alan Hume; ***M:*** Bill Conti.

For Your Love Only 🦴🦴 **1979** A beautiful young student falls in love with her teacher and is blackmailed, leading her to murder her tormentor. Soap opera made for German TV. Dubbed in English. **90m/C VHS.** *GE* Nastassia Kinski, Christian Quadflieg, Judy Winter, Klaus Schwarzkopf; ***D:*** Wolfgang Petersen. **TV**

Forbidden 🦴🦴½ **1985** In Nazi Germany, a German countess has an affair with a Jewish intellectual, and she winds up hiding him from the S.S. Based on the novel "The Last Jews of Berlin" by Leonard Gross. Slow made-for-cable movie. **116m/C VHS.** Jacqueline Bisset, Juergen Prochnow, Irene Worth, Peter Vaughan, Amanda Cannings, Avis Bunnage; ***D:*** Anthony Page; ***W:*** Leonard Gross. **CABLE**

Forbidden Choices 🦴🦴 *The Beans of Egypt, Maine* **1994 (R)** Problems and attractions of the white trash Bean family as observed by enthralled neighbor girl Earlene (Plimpton). Hot-tempered Reuben Bean (Hauer) has just landed a long prison term, leaving his brood of nine in the care of lover Roberta (Lynch), who's also involved with Bean nephew Beal (McGaw). Downtrodden Earlene is only too eager to give in to handsome Beal's charms, leading to more heartbreak. Based on Carolyn Chute's novel "The Beans of Egypt, Maine." Directorial debut of Warren. **109m/C VHS.** Martha Plimpton, Kelly Lynch, Rutger Hauer, Patrick McGaw, Richard Sanders; ***D:*** Jennifer Warren; ***W:*** Bill Phillips; ***C:*** Stevan Larner; ***M:*** Peter Manning Rob.

The Forbidden Christ 🦴🦴 *Il Cristo Proibito* **1950** Bruno (Vallone) returns from the war to his Tuscan village after years as a POW, only to learn his younger brother, a Resistance fighter, was killed by the Nazis after being betrayed by someone in the town. Bruno wants revenge but when no one will help him find the truth, his rage leads him to kill the wrong man. The only film made by writer Malaparte, which was inspired by actual events, was a boxoffice disaster and caused him to abandon future film plans. Italian with subtitles. **98m/B VHS.** *IT* Raf Vallone, Gino Cervi, Alain Cuny, Elena Varzi; ***D:*** Curzio Malaparte; ***W:*** Curzio Malaparte; ***C:*** Gabor Pogany; ***M:*** Curzio Malaparte.

The Forbidden City 🦴🦴 **1918** San San is a young Chinese maiden who has the misfortune to fall in love with a Western diplomat. After he is sent away on business San San keeps secret the fact she has born her lover a child but her actions are unforgiven by her father, a deposed mandarin. **72m/B VHS.** Norma Talmadge, Thomas Meighan; ***D:*** Sidney Franklin.

The Forbidden Dance woof! **1990 (PG-13)** The first of several quickies released in 1990 applying hackneyed plots to the short-lived Lambada dance craze. The nonsensible plot has a Brazilian princess coming to the U.S. in order to stop further destruction of the rain forest. Instead, she winds up falling for a guy, teaching him to Lambada, and going on TV for a dance contest. Features an appearance by Kid Creole and the Coconuts. **90m/C VHS.** Laura Herring, Jeff James, Sid Haig, Richard Lynch; ***D:*** Greydon Clark.

Forbidden Fruit 🦴🦴🦴 *Le Fruit Defendu* **1952** Widowed country doctor (Fernandel), who lives with his domineering mother (Sylvie), marries an equally demanding woman (Nollier) and then finds himself involved with a compliant young prostitute (Arnoul). Comic Fernandel does very well with his change of pace role as a man whose illusions of middle-class respectibility are destroyed. Based on "Letter a Mon Juge" by Georges Simenon. French with subtitles. **103m/B VHS.** *FR* Fernandel, Francoise Arnoul, Claude Nollier, Sylvie, Jacques Castelot; ***D:*** Henri Verneuil; ***W:*** Jacques Companeez, Jean Manse, Henri Verneuil; ***C:*** Henri Alekan; ***M:*** Paul Durand.

Forbidden Games 🦴🦴🦴🦴 *Les Jeux Interdits* **1952** Famous anti-war drama about two French children play-acting the dramas of war amid the carnage of WWII. Young refugee Fossey sees her parents and dog killed. She meets a slightly older boy whose family takes the girl in. The children decide to bury the animals they have seen killed in the same way that people are buried—even stealing crosses from the cemetery to use over the animal graves. Eventually they are discovered and Fossey is again separated from her newfound home. Acclaimed; available in both dubbed and English-subtitled versions. **90m/B VHS.** *FR* Brigitte Fossey, Georges Poujouly, Amedee, Louis Herbert, Suzanne Courtal, Jacques Marin, Laurence Badie, Andre Wasley, Louis Sainteve; ***D:*** Rene Clement; ***W:*** Rene Clement, Jean Aurenche, Pierre Bost, Francois Boyer; ***C:*** Robert Juillard; ***M:*** Narciso Yepes. Oscars '52: Foreign Film; British Acad. '53: Film; N.Y. Film Critics '52: Foreign Film; Venice Film Fest. '52: Film.

Forbidden Love 🦴 **1982** A man in his early 20s falls in love with a woman twice his age, much to the chagrin of her daughters. **96m/C VHS.** Andrew Stevens, Yvette Mimieux, Dana Elcar, Lisa Lucas, Jerry Hauser, Randi Brooks, Lynn Carlin, Hildy Brooks, John Considine; ***D:*** Steven Hilliard Stern; ***M:*** Hagood Hardy. **TV**

Forbidden Passion: The Oscar Wilde Movie 🦴🦴½ **1987** A British-made look at Wilde's later years, emphasizing his homosexuality and the Victorian repression that accompanied it. **120m/C VHS.** *GB* Michael Gambon, Robin Lermitte.

Forbidden Planet 🦴🦴🦴½ **1956** In A.D. 2200, a space cruiser visits the planet Altair-4 to uncover the fate of a previous mission of space colonists. They are greeted by Robby the Robot and discover the only survivors of the Earth colony which has been preyed upon by a terrible space monster. A classic science-fiction version of the Shakespearean classic "The Tempest." **98m/C VHS, DVD, Wide.** Walter Pidgeon, Anne Francis, Leslie Nielsen, Warren Stevens, Jack Kelly, Richard Anderson, Earl Holliman, George D. Wallace, Robert Dix, Frankie Darro; ***D:*** Fred M. Wilcox; ***W:*** Cyril Hume; ***C:*** George J. Folsey; ***M:*** Bebe Barron, Louis Barron; ***V:*** Marvin Miller; ***Nar:*** Les Tremayne.

The Forbidden Quest 🦴🦴 **1993** In 1941, a journalist (Ward) tracks down the only survivor of the Hollandia's 1905 expedition to Antarctica, ship's carpenter Sullivan (O'Conor), to find out about the tragic journey. Director Delpeut mixes archival footage of actual turn-of-the-century voyages to reveal the Hollandia's murderous secrets. **75m/C VHS.** *NL* Joseph O'Conor, Roy Ward; ***D:*** Peter Delpeut; ***W:*** Peter Delpeut.

Forbidden Sins 🦴🦴 **1999 (R)** Defense attorney Maureen Doherty (Tweed) is hired to defend an arrogant multi-millionaire accused of murdering a stripper during kinky sex games. Maureen's search for the truth soon takes her into forbidden territory, in opposition to her exhusband, the detective assigned to the case. **87m/C VHS, DVD.** Shannon Tweed, Corbin Timbrook; ***D:*** Robert Angelo; ***W:*** Daryl Haney, Hel Styverson; ***C:*** Michael Goi; ***M:*** Herman Beeftink. **VIDEO**

Forbidden Sun 🦴 **1989 (R)** An Olympic gymnastics coach and her dozen beautiful students go to Crete to train. When one of them is brutally raped, vengeance is meted out by the girls. **88m/C VHS.** Lauren Hutton, Cliff DeYoung, Renee Estevez; ***D:*** Zelda Barron.

Forbidden Trails 🦴½ **1941** Rough Riders adventure has Silver the horse saving his owner from the vengeance of two outlaws. Two more heroes go under cover to bring the bad guys to justice. **60m/B VHS.** Buck Jones, Tim McCoy, Raymond Hatton; ***D:*** Robert North Bradbury.

Forbidden World woof! *Mutant* **1982 (R)** Lives of a genetic research team become threatened by the very life form they helped to create: a man-eating organism capable of changing its genetic structure as it grows and matures. Corman-produced quickie follow-up to "Galaxy of Terror" is a graphically violent ripoff of "Alien." **82m/C VHS.** Jesse Vint, Dawn Dunlap, June Chadwick, Linden Chiles, Scott Paulin, Michael Bowen; ***D:*** Allan Holzman; ***W:*** Jim Wynorski, R.J. Robertson, Tim Curnen; ***C:*** Tim Suhrstedt; ***M:*** Susan Justin.

Forbidden Zone 🦴½ **1980 (R)** A sixth dimension kingdom is ruled by the midget, King Fausto, and inhabited by dancing frogs, bikini-clad tootsies, robot boxers, and degraded beings of all kinds. Original music by Oingo Boingo, and directed by founding member Elfman. **75m/B VHS.** Herve Villechaize, Susan Tyrrell, Viva, Marie-Pascale Elfman, Joe Spinell, Richard Elfman, Danny Elfman; ***D:*** Richard Elfman; ***W:*** Matthew Bright, Richard Elfman; ***C:*** Gregory Sandor; ***M:*** Danny Elfman.

Forbidden Zone: Alien Abduction 🦴 **1996 (R)** Three babes sharing a sauna also share sexual confidences and discover they've each had an encounter with the same unusual man. Then one of the girls figures out they've had an alien encounter of the very close kind. **90m/C VHS.** Darcy Demoss, Pia Reyes, Dumitri Bogmaz, Carmen Lacatus, Alina Chivulescu, Florin Chiriac, Meredyth Holmes; ***D:*** Lucian S. Diamonde; ***W:*** Vernon Lumley; ***C:*** Adolfo Bartoli; ***M:*** Reg Powell.

The Force 🦴🦴 **1994 (R)** Rookie LAPD cop Cal Warner (Gedrick) crosses paths with maverick homicide detective Des Flynn (Hudson), who's on the trail of a brutal killer. But when Flynn dies mysteriously, it's Cal who's haunted by bizarre dreams—and finding the truth could be equally deadly. **94m/C VHS.** Jason Gedrick, Gary Hudson, Cyndi Pass, Kim Delaney.

Force Five 🦴🦴 **1975** A group of excons form an anti-crime undercover force turning their skills toward justice. Nothing new in this TV pilot. **78m/C VHS.** Gerald Gordon, Nicholas Pryor, James Hampton, David Spielberg, Leif Erickson, Bradford Dillman; ***D:*** Walter Grauman. **TV**

Force: Five 🦴 **1981 (R)** Mercenary gathers a group of like-minded action groupies together to rescue the daughter of a powerful man from a religious cult. All action and no brains. **95m/C VHS.** Joe Lewis, Pam Huntington, Master Bong Soo Han; ***D:*** Robert Clouse; ***W:*** Robert Clouse; ***M:*** William Goldstein.

Force of Evil 🦴🦴🦴 **1949** A cynical attorney who works for a mob boss and for Wall Street tries to save his brother from the gangster's takeover of the numbers operation. The honorable, though criminal, brother refuses the help of the amoral lawyer, and he is finally forced to confront his conscience. Garfield's sizzling performance and the atmospheric photography have made this a film noir classic. **82m/B VHS.** John Garfield, Thomas Gomez, Marie Windsor, Sheldon Leonard, Roy Roberts; ***D:*** Abraham Polonsky; ***W:*** Abraham Polonsky; ***C:*** George Barnes. Natl. Film Reg. '94.

Force of Evil 🦴 **1977** A paroled murderer returns to his hometown to brutalize the family that refused to fabricate an alibi for him. **100m/C VHS.** Lloyd Bridges, Eve Plumb, William Watson, Pat(ricia) Crowley; ***D:*** Richard Lang. **TV**

Force of Impulse 🦴🦴 **1960** J.D. schlocker featuring an impressive cast involved with everything from hot rods to robbery to parental problems. **?m/C VHS.** J. Carrol Naish, Robert Alda, Tony Anthony, Christina Crawford, Jody McCrea, Lionel Hampton.

Force of One 🦴🦴 **1979 (PG)** A team of undercover narcotics agents is being eliminated mysteriously, and karate expert Norris saves the day in this sequel to "Good Guys Wear Black." **91m/C VHS.** Chuck Norris, Bill Wallace, Jennifer O'Neill, Clu Gulager; ***D:*** Paul Aaron.

Force of the Ninja **1997** When Kazuko Tokugawa (Ball), the daughter of a member of Japan's imperial family, is kidnapped and two of her friends are killed, Kenji (Ivan) is forced to take action. A U.S. agent studying the art of the ninja, he learns that the kidnapping is part of an international arms deal lead by a mercenary named Ryan (Williams). Now Kenji must return home and save the situation using his new warrior skills. **?m/C VHS.** Douglas Ivan, Robert B. Williams, Patricia Ball, Brook Lynne, Lee Thomas.

Force on Thunder Mountain 🦴 **1977** A father and son go camping and encounter ancient Indian lore and flying saucers. **93m/C VHS.** Christopher Cain, Todd Dutson.

Force 10 from Navarone 🦴🦴 **1978 (PG)** So-so sequel to Alistair MacLean's "The Guns of Navarone," follows a group of saboteurs whose aim is to blow up a bridge vital to the Nazi's in Yugoslavia. Keep an eye out for Ford, Nero, and Bach. Lots of double-crosses and action sequences, but doesn't quite hang together. **118m/C VHS, DVD, Wide.** Robert Shaw, Harrison Ford, Barbara Bach, Edward Fox, Carl Weathers, Richard Kiel, Franco Nero; ***D:*** Guy Hamilton; ***W:*** Robin Chapman; ***C:*** Christopher Challis; ***M:*** Ronald Goodwin.

Forced Entry 🦴 *The Last Victim* **1975 (R)** Psychopathic killer-rapist hesitates over one of his victims, and she murders him instead. **92m/C VHS.** Tanya Roberts, Ron Max, Nancy Allen; ***D:*** Jim Sotos.

Forced March 🦴🦴½ **1990** On location in Hungary, an actor portrays a poet who fought in WWII and became a victim of the Holocaust. However, the deeper he gets into his role, the thinner the line between illusion and reality becomes. Flat drama. **104m/C VHS.** Chris Sarandon, Renee Soutendijk, Josef Sommer, John Seitz; ***D:*** Rick King.

Forced to Kill 🦴½ **1993 (R)** A repo man is on his way to deliver a Jaguar when he's captured by a bizarre family and forced to fight in an illegal bare-fist tournament run by the local lunatic sheriff. Professional stuntman Eubanks has his work cut out for him in this actioner. **91m/C VHS.** Corey Michael Eubanks, Michael Ironside, Rance Howard, Don Swayze, Clint Howard, Brian Avery, Kari Whitman, Mickey Jones, Carl Ciarfalio, Cynthia J. Blessington, Alan Gelfant; ***D:*** Russell Solberg; ***W:*** Corey Michael Eubanks; ***M:*** Martin D. Bolin.

Forced Vengeance 🦴🦴 **1982 (R)** Vietnam vet pits himself against the underworld in Hong Kong. With Norris in the lead, you can take it for granted there will be plenty of martial arts action. **103m/C VHS.** Chuck Norris, Mary Louise Weller; ***D:*** James Fargo; ***M:*** William Goldstein.

Forces of Nature 🦴🦴 **1999 (PG-13)** Lightweight romantic screwball comedy has straight-laced nice guy Ben (Affleck) trying to get to Savannah in time for his wedding with Tierney. When his plane skids off the runway, he's paired up with free spirit Sarah (Bullock) on an obstacle-filled trip down south. Some fine moments and unusually well done characterization are undone by inconsistency and a lack of chemistry. Enjoyment of the conclusion depends on your opinion of romantic comedy conventions. **104m/C VHS, DVD.** Sandra Bullock, Ben Affleck, Maura Tierney, Steve Zahn, Blythe Danner, Ronny Cox, Michael Fairman, Janet Carroll, Richard Schiff, Meredith Scott Lynn, George D. Wallace, John Doe, Steve Hytner, David Strickland; ***D:*** Bronwen Hughes; ***W:*** Marc Lawrence; ***C:*** Elliot Davis; ***M:*** John Powell.

Ford: The Man & the Machine 🦴½ **1987** Episodic biography of ruthless auto magnate Henry Ford I from the building of his empire to his personal tragedies. The cast lacks spark and Robertson (Ford) is positively gloomy. The only one appearing to have any fun is Thomas (Ford's mistress). Based on the biography by Robert Lacey. **200m/C VHS.** Cliff Robertson, Hope Lange, Heather Thomas, Michael Ironside, Chris Wiggins, R.H. Thomson; ***D:*** Allan Eastman; ***C:*** Thomas Burstyn.

A Foreign Affair 🦴🦴🦴 **1948** Amusing comedy finds straitlaced congresswoman Phoebe Frost (Arthur) heading a committee that travels to Berlin to check on the morale (and morals) of American troops stationed there. Phoebe is suspicious of sultry singer Erika Von Schluetow (Dietrich), whose under the protection of a mysterious American officer. After Phoebe falls for Captain John Pringle (Lund), guess who turns out to be the heel in question? Of course, he's got a perfectly reasonable explanation. **115m/B VHS.** Marlene Dietrich, Jean Arthur, John Lund, Millard Mitchell, Stanley Prager, Peter Von Zerneck; ***D:*** Billy Wilder; ***W:*** Billy Wilder, Charles Brackett, Richard L. Breen; ***C:*** Charles B(ryant) Lang Jr.; ***M:*** Frederick "Friedrich" Hollander.

Foreign Affairs 🦴🦴🦴 **1993** Vinnie Miller (Woodward) is a prim New England college teacher off to London on a research sabbatical. On the flight Vinnie's seatmate is boisterous good-ole-boy Chuck Mumpson (Dennehy), with whom she appears to have nothing in common. Naturally the two middle-aged romantics find a funny, though bittersweet, love together. A rather distracting subplot find's Vinnie's young colleague Fred (Stolz) involved in an affair with an older, eccentric British actress (Beacham). Based on the novel by Alison Lurie. **100m/C VHS.** Joanne Woodward, Brian Dennehy, Eric Stoltz, Stephanie Beacham, Ian Richardson, Robert Hands; ***D:*** Jim O'Brien; ***W:*** Chris Bryant; ***C:*** Michael Coulter. **CABLE**

Foreign Body 🦴🦴½ **1986 (PG-13)** An Indian (played by "Passage to India" star, Banerjee) visiting London pretends to be a doctor and finds women flocking to him. Excellent overlooked British comedy. Based on the novel by Roderick Mann. **108m/C VHS.** *GB* Victor Banerjee, Warren Mitchell, Trevor Howard, Geraldine McEwan, Amanda Donohoe, Denis Quilley, Eve Ferret, Anna Massey; ***D:*** Ronald Neame; ***W:*** Celine La Freniere; ***M:*** Ken Howard.

Foreign Correspondent 🦴🦴🦴🦴 **1940** A classic Hitchcock tale of espionage and derring-do. A reporter is sent to Europe during WWII to cover a pacifist conference in London, where he becomes romantically involved with the daughter of the group's founder and befriends an elderly diplomat. When the diplomat is kidnapped, the reporter uncovers a Nazi spy-ring headed by his future father-in-law. **120m/B VHS.** Joel McCrea, Laraine Day, Herbert Marshall, George Sanders, Robert Benchley, Albert Bassermann, Edmund Gwenn, Eduardo Ciannelli, Harry Davenport, Martin Kosleck, Charles Halton; *D:* Alfred Hitchcock; *W:* Robert Benchley, Charles Bennett, Joan Harrison, James Hilton; *M:* Alfred Newman.

A Foreign Field ½ **1993** Comedy/drama focuses on several WW2 veterans returning to the Normandy beaches in honor of the 50th anniversary of the invasion. Blustery British Cyril (McKern) and equally demanding Yank Waldo (Randolph) also must deal with their 50-year rivalry over their wartime love, the cheerfully vulgar Angelique (Moreau). Veteran performers get the chance to show their stuff but film descends into pathos. **90m/C VHS.** *GB* Leo McKern, John Randolph, Jeanne Moreau, Lauren Bacall, Alec Guinness, Edward Herrmann, Geraldine Chaplin; *D:* Charles Sturridge; *W:* Roy Clarke; *M:* Geoffrey Burgon.

Foreign Land *Terra Estrangeira* **1995** Twenty-one-year-old Paco is an impoverished student living in Sao Paulo who naively agrees to take a suitcase to Lisbon for shady businessman Igor (Melo) and give it to his compatriot, Miguel (Borges). But Paco discovers Miguel has been murdered—leading him to the dead man's girlfriend, unhappy Brazilian exile, Alex (Torres). The two bond while seeking to avoid the newly arrived Igor and Miguel's other treacherous associates. Portuguese with subtitles. **100m/B VHS, DVD.** *BR PT* Alexandre Borges, Tcheky Karyo, Fernanda Torres, Laura Cardoso, Joao Lagarto, Luis Mello, Fernando Pinto; *D:* Walter Salles; *W:* Walter Salles, Marcos Bernstein, Daniela Thomas; *C:* Walter Carvalho; *M:* Jose Miguel Wisnik.

Foreign Student ½ **1994 (R)** In 1956 Philippe (Hofschneider) is a French exchange student at a tradition-bound Virginia college. At a professor's home he meets part-time housekeeper April (Givens), who wants to practice her schoolbook French (among other things). They begin a romance but, since April is black, there's trouble. Hofschneider is charming though Givens appears too glamorous and self-aware. Dutton and Battle are notable in their small roles as blues musicians Howlin' Wolf and Sonny Boy Williamson. Directorial debut for Sereny. Based on the novel "The Foreign Student" by Philippe Labro. **96m/C VHS.** Marco Hofschneider, Robin Givens, Jack Coleman, Edward Herrmann, Rick Johnson, Charlotte Ross, Charles S. Dutton, Hinton Battle; *D:* Eva Sereny; *W:* Menno Meyjes; *C:* Franco Di Giacomo; *M:* Jean-Claude Petit.

The Foreigner **1978** Secret agent who comes to New York City to meet his contact becomes entrapped in a series of mysterious events revolving around the underground club scene. **90m/B VHS.** Eric Mitchell, Patti Astor, Deborah Harry; *D:* Amos Poe; *W:* Amos Poe.

The Foreman Went to France ½ *Somewhere in France* **1942** Industrial engineer travels to France during WWII to help prevent secret machinery from falling into the hands of the Nazis and their allies. **88m/B VHS.** *GB* Clifford Evans, Constance Cummings, Robert Morley; *D:* Charles Frend.

Foreplay woof! *The President's Women* **1975** Inane trilogy of comedy segments involving characters with White House connections. Stories are introduced by former President Mostel discussing his downfall in a TV interview. Lame rather than risque, wasting talents of all involved. Each segment was scripted and directed by a different team. **100m/C VHS.** Pat Paulsen, Jerry Orbach, Estelle Parsons, Zero Mostel; *D:* Bruce Malmuth, John G. Avildsen; *C:* Ralf Bode.

Forest of Little Bear **1979** A man returns to his impoverished family in 1928 and decides to seek the reward put on the head of a one-eared man-eating bear. He kills the bear but faces a dilemma when he sees the bear left a helpless cub behind. In Japanese with English subtitles. **124m/C VHS.** *JP D:* Toshio Goto.

Forest Warrior **1995 (PG)** Children fight to save the local forests of Tanglewood Mountain from greedy developer Kiser with the help of ghostly mountain man John McKenna (Norris), who was murdered in the same woods a century before. Mild adventure with good ecology theme. **98m/C VHS.** Chuck Norris, Terry Kiser, Max Gail, Roscoe Lee Browne, William Sanderson; *D:* Aaron Norris; *W:* Ron Swanson; *C:* Joao Fernandes.

Forever ½ **1978** A teenage girl experiences true love for the first time and struggles with its meaning. Adaptation of Judy Blume's novel. **100m/C VHS.** Stephanie Zimbalist, Dean Butler, John Friedrich, Beth Raines, Diana Scarwid; *D:* John Korty. **TV**

Forever: A Ghost of a Love Story ½ **1992 (R)** Coogan is a hot-shot music video director who moves into a haunted house and soon meets the resident ghost, who just happens to be a beautiful woman. He falls for the ghostly presence but his all-too-real female agent is also making her moves. **93m/C VHS.** Keith Coogan, Sean Young, Diane Ladd, Sally Kirkland, Terence Knox, Nicholas Guest, Renee Taylor, Steve Railsback; *D:* Thomas Palmer Jr.; *W:* Thomas Palmer Jr.

Forever Amber ½ **1947** Seventeenth century rags to riches story features Darnell as the poverty stricken girl who uses sex to gain wealth and status. She makes it to the bed of King Charles II, only to lose the one man she ever really loved (Wilde). The censorship of the 1940s hindered the film's erotic potential. Adapted from the best-selling novel by Kathleen Winsor. **140m/C VHS.** Linda Darnell, Cornel Wilde, Richard Greene, George Sanders, Richard Haydn, Jessica Tandy, Anne Revere, John Russell, Leo G. Carroll, Robert Coote, Margaret Wycherly, Alma Kruger, Edmund Breon, Alan Napier, Bill Ward, Richard Bailey, Skelton Knaggs, Norma Varden, Edith Evanson, Ellen Corby; *D:* Otto Preminger; *W:* Philip Dunne, Ring Lardner Jr.; *C:* Leon Shamroy; *M:* David Raksin.

Forever and a Day **1943** Tremendous salute to British history centers around a London manor originally built by an English admiral during the Napoleonic era and the exploits of succeeding generations. The house even manages to survive the blitz of WWII showing English courage during wartime. Once-in-a-lifetime casting and directing. **104m/B VHS, DVD.** Brian Aherne, Robert Cummings, Ida Lupino, Charles Laughton, Herbert Marshall, Ray Milland, Anna Neagle, Merle Oberon, Claude Rains, Victor McLaglen, Buster Keaton, Jessie Matthews, Roland Young, Sir C. Aubrey Smith, Edward Everett Horton, Elsa Lanchester, Edmund Gwenn; *D:* Rene Clair, Edmund Goulding, Cedric Hardwicke, Frank Lloyd, Victor Saville, Robert Stevenson, Herbert Wilcox, Kent Smith; *W:* Christopher Isherwood, Gene Lockhart, Donald Ogden Stewart, Charles Bennett, Michael Hogan, Peter Godfrey; *C:* Robert De Grasse, Lee Garmes, Russell Metty, Nicholas Musuraca; *M:* Anthony Collins.

Forever Darling **1956** Mixed effort from the reliable comedy duo sees Desi playing a dedicated chemist who neglects his wife while pursuing the next great pesticide. Lucy calls on her guardian angel (Mason) to help her rekindle her marriage. He advises her to go with Desi when he tests his new bug killer, and a series of hilarious, woodsy calamities occur. Lucy and Desi are always fun to watch, but '60s TV sitcom fans will enjoy the fact that Mrs. Howell (Schaefer) and Jane Hathaway (Kulp) appear in the same picture. **91m/C VHS.** Lucille Ball, Desi Arnaz Sr., James Mason, Louis Calhern, John Emery, John Hoyt, Natalie Schafer, Nancy Kulp; *D:* Alexander Hall.

Forever Emmanuelle **1982 (R)** Sensual young woman finds love and the ultimate erotic experience in the wilds of the South Pacific in this sequel to the porn-with-production-values "Emmanuelle." **89m/C VHS.** Annie Belle, Emmanuelle Arsan, Al Cliver.

Forever Evil **1987** The vacationing denizens of a secluded cabin are almost killed off by the cult followers of a mythic god. **107m/C VHS.** Red Mitchell, Tracey Huffman, Charles Trotter, Howard Jacobsen, Kent Johnson.

Forever Female **1953** Bright comedy about show business, egos, and love. Holden is a young playwright whose first play is accepted by stage producer Douglas on the condition that the lead role, featuring a 19-year-old heroine, be rewritten for his ex-wife Rogers. She's an aging leading lady smitten by Holden's charms—as is the ingenue Crowley, who would be perfect for the role as written. Complications and manipulations abound as the play makes its way to production. Adaptation of the Sir James Barrie play "Rosalind." **93m/B VHS.** Ginger Rogers, William Holden, Paul Douglas, Pat(ricia) Crowley, James Gleason, Jesse White, George Reeves, Marjorie Rambeau, King Donovan, Vic Perrin, Marion Ross; *D:* Irving Rapper; *W:* Julius J. Epstein, Philip G. Epstein.

Forever Love ½ **1998** Lizzie Brooks (McEntire) is a wife and mother who has just awakened from a 20-year coma. Her daughter Emma (Stephens) is a grownup, her husband Peter (Matheson) is a stranger, and she discovers her best friend Gail (Armstrong) has taken her place in both her home and Peter's heart. Now Lizzie seeks to find her own place in a totally new world. Based on a true story. **120m/C VHS.** Reba McEntire, Tim Matheson, Bess Armstrong, Heather Stephens, Richard Biggs, Scott Foley; *D:* Michael Switzer; *W:* Joyce Heft Brotman. **TV**

Forever, Lulu *Crazy Streets* **1987 (R)** A down-on-her-luck novelist winds up involved with the mob and a gangster's girlfriend. Completely laughless comedy with amateurish direction. **86m/C VHS.** Hanna Schygulla, Deborah Harry, Alec Baldwin, Annie Golden, Paul Gleason, Dr. Ruth Westheimer; *D:* Amos Kollek.

Forever Mary *Mery per Sempre* **1989** A teacher tries to better the lives of the boys sentenced to a reformatory in Palermo, Sicily, when a teenage transvestite prostitute (the title character) is admitted to the school. In Italian with English subtitles. **100m/C VHS.** *IT* Michele Placido, Alesandro DiSanzo, Francesco Benigno; *D:* Marco Risi; *W:* Sandro Petraglia.

Forever Mine **1999 (R)** In 1973, cabana boy Alan (Fiennes) meets Ella (Mol), the seductive young wife of politico Mark (Liotta) at the Miami Beach resort where he works. It's lust at first sight but ends badly when Mark discovers the affair. But in 1987, Alan re-enters both their lives with a new identity, a new occupation, and a desire for revenge. Noir wannabe whose story doesn't always hold together (but is at least titillating for the sex scenes). **117m/C VHS, DVD, Wide.** Joseph Fiennes, Ray Liotta, Gretchen Mol, Vincent Laresca; *D:* Paul Schrader; *W:* Paul Schrader; *C:* John Bailey; *M:* Angelo Badalamenti.

Forever Together ½ *Can't Be Heaven* **2000 (PG)** The perils of young, first love are sweetly explored as fatherless seventh-grader Danny (Burke) thinks he's falling in love with best friend, Julie (Tractenberg). His widowed mom (Ticotin) is having her own romantic troubles, so Danny turns for advice to a friendly jazz musician (Macchio). **88m/C VHS, DVD.** Michelle Trachtenberg, Rachel Ticotin, Ralph Macchio, Bryan Burke, Matt McCoy, Diane Ladd, Garry Marshall; *D:* Richard S. Friedman. **VIDEO**

Forever Young **1985** A young boy immerses himself in Catholicism. Admiring a priest, he is unaware that the priest's friend is involved with his mother. Tangled, but delicate handling of the coming-of-age story. **85m/C VHS.** *GB* James Aubrey, Nicholas Gecks, Alec McCowen; *D:* David Drury; *W:* Ray Connolly. **TV**

Forever Young ½ **1992 (PG)** When test pilot Gibson's girlfriend is hit by a car and goes into a coma, he volunteers to be cryogenically frozen for one year. Oops!—he's left frozen for 50 years, until he is accidentally thawed out by a couple of kids. Predictable, designed to be a tear jerker, though it serves mostly as a star vehicle for Gibson who bumbles with '90s technology, finds his true love, and escapes from government heavies, adorable as ever. Through all the schmaltz, the relationship Gibson develops with the young Wood turns out to be the most authentic and endearing love in the film. **102m/C VHS, DVD, 8mm, Wide.** Mel Gibson, Jamie Lee Curtis, Elijah Wood, Isabel Glasser, George Wendt, Joe Morton, Nicolas Surovy, David Marshall Grant, Art LaFleur, John David (J.D.) Cullum; *D:* Steve Miner; *W:* Jeffrey Abrams; *C:* Russell Boyd; *M:* Jerry Goldsmith.

Forger of London **1961** Edgar Wallace tale in which Scotland Yard investigates a counterfeit ring connected to a prime suspect, an amnesiac playboy. **91m/C VHS.** *GE* Eddi Arent, Karin Dor, Viktor de Kowa, Hellmut Lange, Robert Graf; *D:* Harald Reinl.

Forget Mozart *Zabudnite na Mozarta* **1985** On the day of Mozart's death, the head of the secret police gathers a group together for questioning. They include the composer's wife, his lyricist, the head of a Masonic lodge, and Salieri, Mozart's rival. Each has a different story to tell to the investigator about the composer's life and death. The film makes use of a number of sets and costumes from "Amadeus" and was also filmed on location in Prague. In German with English subtitles. **93m/C VHS.** *GE* Armin Mueller-Stahl, Catarina Raacke; *D:* Salvo Luther.

Forget Paris ½ **1995 (PG-13)** Pro basketball referee Mickey (Crystal) and airline executive Ellen (Winger) meet in Paris, fall in love and get married. But once the honeymoon is over, the marital bliss unravels due to conflicting work schedules and the lack of romantic scenery. This look at yuppie love and courtship finds Crystal in pre-"City Slickers 2" form, launching three-point one-liners and "When Harry Met Sally" sentiment. Bland direction and an obligation to be cute intensify the "been-there-seen-that" feeling. Winger's presence may hint of miscasting, but she has one of the films funniest scenes involving a stray pet and a pigeon. **101m/C VHS, DVD.** Billy Crystal, Debra Winger, Joe Mantegna, Cynthia Stevenson, Richard Masur, Julie Kavner, William Hickey, Cathy Moriarty, John Spencer; *D:* Billy Crystal; *W:* Billy Crystal, Lowell Ganz, Babaloo Mandel; *C:* Don Burgess; *M:* Marc Shaiman.

Forgive and Forget **1999** Macho London construction worker David (Shepherd) can't admit to himself or anyone else that he's gay, including his best mate since childhood, Theo (Simon). But when Theo decides to move in with his girlfriend Hannah (Fraser), David schemes to break them up. He also decides to publicly declare his love by appearing with Theo on a TV talk show, with unforgetable consequences. **96m/C VHS, DVD, Wide.** *GB* Steve John Shepherd, John Simm, Laura Fraser, Maurice Roeves, Ger Ryan, Meera Syal; *D:* Aisling Walsh; *W:* Mark Burt; *C:* Kevin Rowley; *M:* Hal Lindes.

The Forgotten **1989** After 17 years as POWs, six Green Berets are freed, only to face a treacherous government conspiracy aimed at eliminating them. **96m/C VHS.** Keith Carradine, Steve Railsback, Stacy Keach, Pepe Serna, Don Opper, Richard Lawson; *D:* James Keach; *W:* Keith Carradine, Steve Railsback, James Keach. **TV**

Forgotten City *The Vivero Letter* **1998 (R)** James Wheeler is out to uncover a city from the Mayan civilization but he faces a rival expedition, an unhappy native tribe, and mysterious disappearances and deaths that point to someone—or something—wanting the city and its treasures to remain undisturbed. Based on the novel "The Vivero Letter" by Desmond Bagley. Filmed on location in Costa Rica. **96m/C VHS, DVD.** Robert Patrick, Fred Ward, Chiara Caselli; *D:* H. Gordon Boos; *W:* Denne Bart Petitclerc, Arthur Sellers; *C:* Fabrizio Lucci. **VIDEO**

The Forgotten One ½ **1989 (R)** An uninspired author and a female reporter become mixed up in a century-old murder and the restless ghost it spawned. **89m/C VHS.** Kristy McNichol, Terry O'Quinn, Blair Parker, Elisabeth Brooks; *D:* Phillip Badger; *W:* Phillip Badger; *C:* James Mathers.

Forgotten Prisoners *Forgotten Prisoners: The Amnesty Files* **1990 (R)** Celluloid proof that conviction and true grit do not always entertainment make. Greenwald—whose credits range from "Xanadu" to "The Burning Bed"—directed this righteous but stationary drama about an

Amnesty International official (Silver) who's assigned to look into the incarceration and egregious mistreatment of Turkish citizens. **92m/C VHS.** Ron Silver, Roger Daltrey, Hector Elizondo; *D:* Robert Greenwald; *M:* Brad Fiedel. **CABLE**

Forgotten Silver 1996 Jackson's mockumentary finds the director and co-director Botes "discovering" the lost films of Colin McKenzie, a pioneering New Zeland filmmaker of the early 1900s. These include McKenzie's epic film "Salome" which the duo decide to restore. The entire escapade is a fiction, including the silent film footage that's shown. The tape also includes the short film "Signing Off" about the final show for a radio DJ and the special request he has trouble fulfilling. **70m/C VHS, DVD, Wide.** *NZ* Costa Botes, Sam Neill, Leonard Maltin, Harvey Weinstein, John O'Shea, Hannah McKenzie, Lindsay Shelton, Johnny Morris, Marguerite Hurst; *D:* Peter Jackson, Costa Botes, Robert Sarkies; *W:* Peter Jackson, Costa Botes; *C:* Alun Bollinger; *Nar:* Jeffrey Thomas.

A Forgotten Tune for the Flute ♂♂♂ 1988 A delightful, Glasnost-era romantic comedy. A bureaucrat caught up in a dull, stuffy existence has a heart attack and winds up falling in love with his nurse. He then must decide between his comfortable, cared-for life or the love which beckons him. In Russian with English subtitles. **131m/C VHS.** *RU* Leonid Filatov, Tatiana Dogileva, Irina Kupchenko; *D:* Edgar Ryazanov.

Forgotten Warrior ♂½ 1986 (R) Vengeance is the name of the game as a Vietnam vet tracks down the fellow officer who tried to kill him and shot his commander. **76m/C VHS.** Quincy Frazer, Sam T. Lapuzz, Ron Marchini, Joe Meyer; *D:* Nick Cacas, Charlie Ordonez.

Forlorn River ♂½ 1937 Nevada and Weary, two law-abiding men, seek to return their hometown to peace by eliminating a gang of outlaws. Based on a novel by Zane Grey. **62m/B VHS.** Buster Crabbe, June Martel, John D. Patterson, Harvey Stephens, Chester Conklin, Lew Kelly, Syd Saylor; *D:* Charles T. Barton.

The Formula ♂½ 1980 (R) Convoluted story about a secret formula for synthetic fuel that meanders it's way from the end of WWII to the present. A U.S. soldier waylays, and then joins forces with, a German general entrusted with the formula. Years later, after the American is murdered, his friend, a hard-nosed L.A. cop, starts investigating, meeting up with spies and a reclusive oil billionaire. Scott and Brando have one good confrontation scene but the rest of the movie is just hot air. From the novel by Steve Shagan. **117m/C VHS.** Marlon Brando, George C. Scott, Marthe Keller, G.D. Spradlin, Beatrice Straight, John Gielgud, Richard Lynch; *D:* John G. Avildsen; *M:* Bill Conti.

Formula for a Murder ♂ 1985 A very rich but paralyzed woman marries a scheming con artist who plots to kill her and inherit everything. **89m/C VHS.** Christina Nagy, David Warbeck, Rossano Brazzi.

Forrest Gump ♂♂♂½ 1994 (PG-13) Grandly ambitious and slightly flawed, amounting to a wonderful bit of movie magic. As the intelligence-impaired Gump with a heart of gold and more than enough character and dignity, Hanks supplies another career highlight. Field contributes a nice turn as his dedicated mama (they were last together in "Punchline"), while Sinise is particularly effective as a handicapped Vietnam veteran with a bad attitude. Incredible special effects put Gump in the middle of historic events over a four decade period, but the real story is the life-affirming, non-judgmental power of Gump to transform the lives of those around him. From the novel by Winston Groom. **142m/C VHS, DVD, Wide.** Sonny Shroyer, Mary Ellen Trainor, Tom Hanks, Robin Wright Penn, Sally Field, Gary Sinise, Mykelti Williamson; *D:* Robert Zemeckis; *W:* Eric Roth; *C:* Don Burgess; *M:* Alan Silvestri. Oscars '94: Actor (Hanks), Adapt. Screenplay, Director (Zemeckis), Film Editing, Picture, Visual FX; AFI '98: Top 100; Directors Guild '94: Director (Zemeckis); Golden Globes '95: Actor—Drama (Hanks), Director (Zemeckis), Film—Drama; Natl. Bd. of Review '94: Actor (Hanks), Film, Support. Actor (Sinise); Screen Actors Guild '94: Actor (Hanks); Writers Guild '94: Adapt. Screenplay; Blockbuster '95: Movie, T., Drama Actor, T. (Hanks); Blockbuster '96: Drama Actor, V. (Hanks).

The Forsaken ♂ 2001 (R) Vampire films need a little smarts to go with their gore but this film has only the latter. It was apparently gutted by the studio prior to release so maybe there was a story at some point. Sean (Smith) is driving from L.A. to Miami when he picks up hitchhiker Nick (Fehr) and the dirsoriented Megan (Miko). Both turn out to be infected by a blood disease thanks to a vampire's bite. They have to kill the sire if they don't want to become bloodsuckers themselves and then Megan bites Sean, so now it's personal. The vamp in question is suave Kit (Schaech), who has the usual band of trashy minions. The whole movie is trashy but not in a fun way. **90m/C VHS, DVD, Wide.** *US* Kerr Smith, Izabella Miko, Johnathon Schaech, Brendan Fehr, Simon Rex, Carrie Snodgress, Phina Oruche; *D:* J.S. Cardone; *W:* J.S. Cardone; *C:* Steven Bernstein; *M:* Johnny Lee Schell, Tim Jones.

Forsaking All Others ♂♂½ 1935 Screwball comedy featuring several MGM superstars. Friends since childhood, Gable has been in love with Crawford for 20 years, but she never realizes it and plans to marry Montgomery. Crawford is very funny in this delightful story of a wacky romantic triangle. **84m/B VHS.** Joan Crawford, Clark Gable, Robert Montgomery, Charles Butterworth, Billie Burke, Rosalind Russell, Frances Drake; *D:* Woodbridge S. Van Dyke; *W:* Joseph L. Mankiewicz; *C:* George J. Folsey.

Fort Apache ♂♂♂½ 1948 The first of director Ford's celebrated cavalry trilogy, in which fanatical Lt. Col. Owen Thursday (a decidely unsympathetic Fonda) leads his reluctant men to an eventual slaughter when he battle Apache cheif Cochise (Inclan), recalling George Custer at Little Big Horn. Wayne is his seasoned second-in-command Kirby Yorke, who's unable to prevent what occurs. In residence: Ford hallmarks of spectacular landscapes and stirring action, as well as many vignettes of life at a remote outpost. Don't forget to catch "She Wore a Yellow Ribbon" and "Rio Grande," the next films in the series. **125m/B VHS.** Henry Fonda, John Wayne, Shirley Temple, John Agar, Pedro Armendariz Sr., Victor McLaglen, Ward Bond, Anna Lee, Guy Kibbee, Miguel Incian, Mae Marsh; *D:* John Ford; *W:* Frank Nugent; *C:* Archie Stout; *M:* Richard Hageman.

Fort Apache, the Bronx ♂♂♂ 1981 (R) A police drama set in the beleaguered South Bronx of NYC, based on the real-life experiences of two former New York cops who served there. Newman is a decent cop who goes against every kind of criminal and crazy and against his superiors in trying to bring law and justice to a downtrodden community. **123m/C VHS, DVD, Wide.** Paul Newman, Ed Asner, Ken Wahl, Danny Aiello, Rachel Ticotin, Pam Grier, Kathleen Beller; *D:* Daniel Petrie; *W:* Heywood Gould; *C:* John Alcott; *M:* Jonathan Tunick.

Fort Saganne ♂♂ 1984 Charles Saganne (Depardieu), a soldier from a peasant background, is posted to the French Sahara, where he becomes a natural leader. He gains fame and fortune, marries, and then WWI begins. Good, if cliched, adventure saga. Based on the novel by Louis Gardel. French with subtitles. **180m/C VHS.** *FR* Gerard Depardieu, Catherine Deneuve, Philippe Noiret, Sophie Marceau, Michael Duchaussoy; *D:* Alain Corneau; *W:* Alain Corneau, Louis Gardel; *M:* Philippe Sarde.

Fortress ♂ 1985 (R) A teacher and her class are kidnapped from their one-room schoolhouse in the Australian outback. They must use their ingenuity and wits to save their lives in this violent suspense drama. **90m/C VHS.** *AU* Rachel Ward, Sean Garlick, Rebecca Rigg; *D:* Arch Nicholson; *M:* Danny Beckerman. **CABLE**

Fortress ♂♂ 1993 (R) How come the future is never a place you'd want to be? Thanks to overpopulation a woman is only allowed one pregnancy. When John and Karen Brennick are caught trying to have a second child they are shipped to the Fortress, an underground prison in the middle of the desert. Discipline is enforced with numerous sadistic toys, including the intestinator, so-called because it's implanted in the stomach of each prisoner and infractions result in excruciating laser-activated pain. Lambert does well with his action hero but it's character actor Smith as the warden, a techno-human with some sick fantasies, who has the real fun in this horrific depiction of the future. **91m/C VHS, DVD.** Christopher Lambert, Kurtwood Smith, Loryn Locklin, Lincoln Kilpatrick; *D:* Stuart Gordon; *W:* Steve Feinberg, Troy Neighbors, Terry Curtis Fox; *C:* David Eggby.

Fortress 2: Re-Entry ♂♂ 1999 (R) John Brennick (Lambert) and his wife and son have escaped from a maximum security prison known as The Fortress. But Brennick is re-captured and his new prison is in orbit, 26,000 miles from Earth. Brennick wants to escape but there's mucho surveillance to overcome (including a camera placed inside his body) and the problem of returning to Earth. **92m/C VHS, DVD.** Christopher Lambert, Pam Grier, Patrick Malahide, Nick Brimble; *D:* Geoff Murphy; *W:* Steve Feinberg, Troy Neighbors. **VIDEO**

Fortress of Amerikka ♂½ 1989 In the not-too-distant future, mercenaries get their hands on a secret weapon that could allow them to take over the USA. **?m/C VHS.** Gene Le Brock, Kellee Bradley.

Fortune and Men's Eyes ♂♂ 1971 (R) Exploitative and depressing film about life in a Canadian prison. A naive young man is sent to prison for marijuana possession and has to make a difficult choice—be regularly sodomized by a man who will protect him or be raped by everyone else. Based on the play by John Herbert. **102m/C VHS.** Wendell Burton, Michael Greer, Zooey Hall, Danny Freedman; *D:* Harvey Hart; *W:* John Herbert.

The Fortune Cookie ♂♂♂ *Meet Whiplash Willie* 1966 After receiving a minor injury during a football game, a TV cameraman is convinced by his seedy lawyer brother-in-law to exaggerate his injury and start an expensive lawsuit. A classic, biting comedy by Wilder. First of several Lemmon-Matthau comedies. **125m/B VHS, Wide.** Jack Lemmon, Walter Matthau, Ron Rich, Cliff Osmond, Judi West, Lurene Tuttle; *D:* Billy Wilder; *W:* Billy Wilder, I.A.L. Diamond; *C:* Joseph LaShelle; *M:* Andre Previn. Oscars '66: Support. Actor (Matthau).

Fortune Dane ♂½ 1986 (PG) Police detective Fortune Dane goes undercover to clear his name after he is framed for murder. **83m/C VHS.** Carl Weathers, Adolph Caesar; *D:* Nicholas Sgarro; *W:* Charles Correll.

Fortune's Fool ♂♂ 1921 A beef king and profiteer marries a younger woman and soon discovers the problems that ambition can cause. Silent. **60m/B VHS.** *GE* Emil Jannings, Daguey Servaes, Reinhold Schunzel; *D:* Reinhold Schunzel.

Fortunes of War ♂♂♂ 1987 British professor Guy Pringle arrives with his bride, Harriet, to take up a teaching post in the Balkans in 1939. The idealistic Guy soon becomes enmeshed in anti-fascist politics and involved with the local members of the British embassy. When threatened by war they travel to Athens and then Cairo, where Guy's increasing involvement in the political situation, and his neglect of Harriet, causes a crisis in their marriage. Slow-moving drama with some self-centered characters is redeemed by the acting skills of those involved. Based on the autobiographial novels of Olivia Manning. Originally shown on "Masterpiece Theater" on PBS. **160m/C VHS.** *GB* Kenneth Branagh, Emma Thompson, Rupert Graves, Ronald Pickup, Robert Stephens, Charles Kay, James Villiers, Harry Burton, Ciaran Madden, Diana Hardcastle, Greg Hicks, Alan Bennett, Jeremy Brundell, Jeremy Sinden; *D:* James Cellan Jones; *W:* Alan Plater.

Fortunes of War ♂♂ 1994 (R) Peter Kernan (Salinger) is a burned-out relief worker in Thailand. Desperate for money, he agrees to smuggle a rare medicine across the Cambodian border to a rural war lord. Travelling with refugee Khoy Thoun (Ngor) and French Red Cross worker, Johanna (Jenkins), Peter begins to realize his need to do the right thing, even if the cost is high. Filmed on location in Manila. **107m/C VHS.** Matt Salinger, Michael Ironside, Haing S. Ngor, Sam Jenkins, Martin Sheen, Michael Nouri; *D:* Thierry Notz; *W:* Mark Lee.

Forty Carats ♂♂½ 1973 (PG) Ullmann plays the just-turned 40 divorcee who has a brief fling with the half-her-age Albert while on vacation in Greece. She figures she'll never see him again but, back in New York, he turns up on the arm of her beautiful daughter (Raffin). Except he's still interested in mom. The rest of the movie is spent trying to convince Ullmann that love can conquer all. Ullmann's very attractive but not well-suited for the part; Raffins's screen debut. Based on the Broadway hit. **110m/C VHS.** Liv Ullmann, Edward Albert, Gene Kelly, Binnie Barnes, Deborah Raffin, Nancy Walker; *D:* Milton Katselas; *W:* Jay Presson Allen, Mary St. Feint; *C:* Charles B(ryant) Lang Jr.

40 Days and 40 Nights ♂♂½ 2002 (R) Abstinence comedy has womanizer Matt (Hartnett) suffering from a brutal romantic break-up, so for Lent he vows to go cold turkey in the sack. His always-supportive friends and co-workers rush to place odds on when Matt's self-control will eventually crumble, even posting his progress on the Internet. With babes aplenty seemingly everywhere, Matt's vow is really tested when, of course, he meets the girl of his dreams (Sossamon). Director Lehmann deftly directs the crew of likeable characters, keeping things light and moving along. Memorable funny scenes includes a dinner with Matt's dad describing sex with a hip replacement, and any with Bagel Guy (Maronna). **94m/C VHS, DVD.** *US* Josh Hartnett, Shannyn Sossamon, Maggie Gyllenhaal, Vinessa Shaw, Paulo Costanzo, Glenn Fitzgerald, Emmanuelle Vaugier, Michael Maronna, Mary Gross, Stanley Anderson, Adam Trese, Barry Newman, Griffin Dunne, Monet Mazur, Dylan Neal, Chris Gauthier; *D:* Michael Lehmann; *W:* Rob Perez; *C:* Elliot Davis; *M:* Rolfe Kent.

Forty Days of Musa Dagh ♂♂ 1985 Based on the true story of Armenia's fight for freedom against Turkey in the 1914 uprising and the dreadful cost. From the novel by Franz Werfel. **120m/C VHS.** Michael Constantine, David Opatoshu.

The Forty-Niners ♂ 1932 A forgettable oater about the hysteria surrounding the finding of gold in California. **59m/B VHS.** Tom Tyler, Betty Mack, Alan Bridge, Fern Emmett, Gordon Wood, Frank Ball; *D:* John P. McCarthy.

The Forty-Ninth Parallel ♂♂♂ *The Invaders* 1941 Six Nazi servicemen, seeking to reach neutral American land, are trapped and their U-boat sunk by Royal Canadian Air Force bombers, forcing them into Canada on foot, where they run into an array of stalwart patriots. Dated wartime propaganda made prior to the U.S. entering the war; riddled with entertaining star turns. **90m/B VHS.** *GB* Laurence Olivier, Leslie Howard, Eric Portman, Raymond Massey, Glynis Johns, Finlay Currie, Anton Walbrook; *D:* Michael Powell; *W:* Emeric Pressburger, Rodney Ackland. Oscars '42: Story.

40 Pounds of Trouble ♂♂½ 1962 Lake Tahoe casino/hotel manager Steve McCluskey (Curtis) likes to avoid complications in his life. But first he's charmed by his boss' niece Chris (Pleshette), the hotel's new headliner, and then he becomes a surrogate father to five-year-old Penny (Wilcox), abandoned by her debt-ridden dad. So what does Steve decide to do? Why take them to Disneyland, of course! Director Jewison's feature film debut. **106m/C VHS.** Tony Curtis, Suzanne Pleshette, Claire Wilcox, Phil Silvers, Larry Storch, Howard Morris, Stubby Kaye, Edward Andrews, Mary Murphy, Kevin McCarthy, Sharon Farrell; *D:* Norman Jewison; *W:* Marion Hargrove; *M:* Mort Lindsey.

Forty Thousand Horsemen 🦴🦴½ **1941** The story of the ANZACS of Australia, created to fight Germany in the Middle East during WWII. This Australian war drama is full of cavalry charges, brave young lads, and "Waltzing Matilda." **86m/B VHS.** *AU* Chips Rafferty, Grant Taylor, Betty Bryant, Pat Twohill.

42nd Street 🦴🦴🦴🦴 **1933** A Broadway musical producer faces numerous problems in his efforts to reach a successful opening night. Choreography by Busby Berkeley. A colorized version of the film is also available. ♫You're Getting to Be a Habit with Me; Shuffle off to Buffalo; Young and Healthy; 42nd Street; It Must Be June. **89m/B VHS, DVD.** Warner Baxter, Ruby Keeler, Bebe Daniels, George Brent, Dick Powell, Guy Kibbee, Ginger Rogers, Una Merkel, Busby Berkeley, Ned Sparks, George E. Stone; ***D:*** Lloyd Bacon; ***W:*** Rian James, James Seymour; ***C:*** Sol Polito; ***M:*** Harry Warren, Al Dubin. Natl. Film Reg. '98.

47 Ronin, Part 1 🦴🦴🦴 *The Loyal 47 Ronin; 47 Samurai* **1942** Turn of the 18th-century epic chronicling the samurai legend. The warriors of Lord Asano set out to avenge their leader, tricked into committing a forced seppuku, or hara-kiri. The photography is generously laden with views of 18th century gardens as well as panoramic vistas. This is the largest and most popular film of the Kabuki version of the story by Seika Mayama. In Japanese with English subtitles. **111m/C VHS, DVD.** *JP* Yoshisaburo Arashi, Utaemon Ichikawa, Chojuro Kawarazaki, Kunitaro Kawarazaki, Mantoyo Mimasu, Mieko Takamine; ***D:*** Kenji Mizoguchi; ***W:*** Yoshikata Yoda, Kenchiro Hara; ***C:*** Kohei Sugiyama; ***M:*** Shiro Fukai.

47 Ronin, Part 2 🦴🦴🦴 **1942** Second half of the film in which the famous Japanese folklore tale of Lord Asano and his warriors is told. The film follows Asano's samurai as they commit themselves to avenging their leader in 1703. In Japanese with English subtitles. **108m/C VHS, DVD.** *JP* Yoshisaburo Arashi, Utaemon Ichikawa, Chojuro Kawarazaki, Kunitaro Kawarazaki, Mantoyo Mimasu; ***D:*** Kenji Mizoguchi; ***W:*** Kenchiro Hara, Yoshikata Yoda; ***C:*** Kohei Sugiyama; ***M:*** Shiro Fukai.

48 Hrs. 🦴🦴🦴 **1982 (R)** An experienced San Francisco cop (Nolte) springs a convict (Murphy) from jail for 48 hours to find a vicious murdering escaped con. Murphy's film debut is great and Nolte is perfect as his gruff foil. **97m/C VHS, DVD.** Ned Dowd, Nick Nolte, Eddie Murphy, James Remar, Annette O'Toole, David Patrick Kelly, Sonny Landham, Brion James, Denise Crosby; ***D:*** Walter Hill; ***W:*** Walter Hill, Larry Gross, Steven E. de Souza, Roger Spottiswoode; ***M:*** James Horner.

48 Hours to Live 🦴 *Man in the Middle* **1960** A reporter travels to a nuclear scientist's secluded island only to find the scientist held hostage by nuclear weapon-seeking terrorists. **86m/B VHS.** Anthony Steel, Ingemar Johannson, Marlies Behrens.

Foul Play 🦴🦴 **1976** Bearing no similarity to the Goldie Hawn vehicle of the same name, this Polish crimer is based on a true story, and stars two of Poland's Olympic boxers. A young man, accused of theft, is coerced by the Warsaw police to go undercover in return for having the charges against him dropped. With English subtitles. **98m/C VHS.** *PL* Marek Powowski, Jan Szczepanski, Jerzy Kulej.

Foul Play 🦴🦴🦴 **1978 (PG)** Hawn is a librarian who picks up a hitchhiker which leads to nothing but trouble. She becomes involved with San Francisco detective Chase in an effort to expose a plot to kill the Pope during his visit to the city. Also involved is Moore as an English orchestra conductor with some kinky sexual leanings. Chase is charming (no mugging here) and Hawn both bubbly and brave. A big winner at the boxoffice; features Barry Manilow's hit tune "Ready to Take a Chance Again." **116m/C VHS, 8mm.** Goldie Hawn, Chevy Chase, Dudley Moore, Burgess Meredith, Billy Barty, Rachel Roberts, Eugene Roche, Brian Dennehy, Chuck McCann, Bruce Solomon; ***D:*** Colin Higgins; ***M:*** Charles Fox.

Found Alive 🦴 **1934** After a painful divorce, a woman kidnaps her son and steals away into the Mexican jungle, with only the help of her faithful butler. **65m/B VHS.** Barbara Bedford, Maurice Murphy, Robert Frazer, Edwin Cross; ***D:*** Charles (Hutchison) Hutchinson.

The Fountainhead 🦴🦴🦴 **1949** Cooper is an idealistic, uncompromising architect who refuses to change his designs. When he finds out his plans for a public housing project have been radically altered he blows up the building and winds up in court defending his actions. Neal is the sub-plot love interest. Based on the novel by Ayn Rand. **113m/C VHS.** Gary Cooper, Patricia Neal, Raymond Massey, Ray Collins, Henry Hull; ***D:*** King Vidor; ***C:*** Robert Burks; ***M:*** Max Steiner.

Four Adventures of Reinette and Mirabelle 🦴🦴🦴 **1989** Small but touching Rohmer tale of the friendship between two women—one a naive country girl (Miquel, as Reinette), the other a sophisticated Parisian (Forde, as Mirabelle)—who share an apartment and a number of experiences, but who have a very different manner of inhabiting those experiences. A thoroughly French human comedy, one of Rohmer's better studies. In French with English subtitles. **95m/C VHS.** *FR* Joelle Miquel, Jessica Forde, Philippe Laudenbach, Marie Riviere, Beatrice Romand, Yasmine Haury; ***D:*** Eric Rohmer; ***W:*** Eric Rohmer.

Four Bags Full 🦴🦴½ **1956** A bitter comedy about two smugglers during WWII who try to get a slaughtered pig to the black market under the Nazis' noses. In French with English subtitles. **82m/C VHS.** *FR* Jean Gabin, Louis de Funes, Bourvil, Jeanette Batti; ***D:*** Claude Autant-Lara.

Four Daughters 🦴🦴🦴 **1938** Classic, three-hankie outing in which four talented daughters of music professor Rains fall in love and marry. Garfield shines, in a role tailor-made for him, as the world-weary suitor driven to extremes in the name of love. Great performances from all. Based on the novel "Sister Act" by Fannie Hurst. **90m/B VHS.** Claude Rains, John Garfield, May Robson, Priscilla Lane, Lola Lane, Rosemary Lane, Gale Page, Dick Foran, Jeffrey Lynn; ***D:*** Michael Curtiz; ***M:*** Max Steiner. **TV**

Four Days 🦴🦴½ **1999 (R)** Fourteen-year-old Simon (Zegers) is devoted to his smalltime crook dad Milt (Forsythe) who's just doublecrossed his partner, Fury (Meany), in a bank robbery after arranging for Simon to get the money and meet him in a pre-selected location. But unbeknowst to Simon, Milt has been killed and Fury is on his trail—at least Simon has gotten a lift from over-sexed Crystal (Davidovitch), so things may not be so bad. Based on the novel by John Buell. **88m/C VHS.** *CA* Kevin Zegers, Lolita (David) Davidovich, Colm Meaney, William Forsythe, Anne-Marie Cadieux, Patrick Goyette; ***D:*** Curtis Wehrfritz; ***W:*** Pickney Benedict; ***C:*** Miroslaw Baszak; ***M:*** Tom Third.

Four Days in July 🦴🦴 **1985** Two couples from Belfast, one Catholic and one Protestant, find they have something in common when they meet in the maternity ward as both couples become first-time parents. Script and dialog were mainly improvised, which provides both dull stretches and the film's charm. **99m/C VHS.** *GB* Des McAleer, Brid Brennan, Charles Lawson, Paula Hamilton, Shane Connaughton, Eileen Pollock, Stephen Rea; ***D:*** Mike Leigh. **TV**

Four Days in September 🦴🦴 **1997 (R)** Based on the true story of Charles Burke Elbrick (Arkin), the American ambassador to Brazil who, in 1969, was kidnapped by four idealistic students, part of a Marxist revolutionary group protesting their government's military dictatorship. Their leader, Fernando Gabeira (Cardoso), wants the release of political prisoners and gives the government four days to meet his terms. Adapted from the book "What's Up, Comrade?" by Gabeira. **105m/C VHS.** *BR* Alan Arkin, Pedro Cardoso, Marco Ricca, Fernanda Torres; ***D:*** Bruno Barreto; ***W:*** Leopoldo Serran; ***C:*** Felix Monti; ***M:*** Stewart Copeland.

Four Deuces 🦴½ **1975** Gang war is underway between the Chico Hamilton mob and Vic Morano and the Four Deuces during the Depression. Comedy and action combine with elements of strong language, strong sex, and strong violence. **87m/C VHS.** Jack Palance, Carol Lynley, Warren Berlinger, Adam Roarke; ***D:*** William H. Bushnell Jr.

Four Dogs Playing Poker 🦴½ **2000 (R)** Four friends plan an art heist and then lose the prize, which gets them into trouble with the gangster who's expecting the goods. So they come up with another scheme that involves collecting on one of the group's life insurance policies (to pay off the gangster)—which means one of them will have to die. Sketchy thriller. **98m/C VHS, DVD, Wide.** Olivia Williams, Balthazar Getty, Stacy Edwards, Daniel London, Tim Curry, Forest Whitaker, George Lazenby, John Taylor; ***D:*** Paul Rachman; ***W:*** Thomas Durham, William Quist; ***C:*** Claudio Rocha; ***M:*** Brian Tyler, Scott Hackwith.

Four Eyes and Six Guns 🦴🦴½ **1993** In 1882 a New York optometrist, who's a fan of the popular dime-store western novels, moves to Tombstone, Arizona, in search of adventure. He's just in time, too, because Sheriff Wyatt Earp is trying to rid the town of those pesky Doom Brothers but is having a problem with his eyesight (causing his gunshots to go astray). Now if the greenhorn can just get Earp to wear his new glasses. Silly but harmless fluff. **92m/C VHS.** Judge Reinhold, Patricia Clarkson, Dan Hedaya, M. Emmet Walsh, Austin Pendleton, Fred Ward; ***D:*** Piers Haggard; ***W:*** Leon Prochnik. **CABLE**

Four Faces West 🦴🦴½ *They Passed This Way* **1948** McCrea is an honest rancher who nevertheless robs the local bank in order to save his father's ranch from foreclosure. His humanity in helping a diphtheria-ridden family leads to his capture, but the sheriff promises a light sentence, since he is not a typical bad guy. Fine performances strengthen this low-key western. **90m/B VHS.** Joel McCrea, Frances Dee, Charles Bickford; ***D:*** Alfred E. Green.

The Four Feathers 🦴🦴🦴🦴 **1939** A grand adventure from a story by A.E.W. Mason. After resigning from the British Army a young man is branded a coward and given four white feathers as symbols by three of his friends and his lady love. Determined to prove them wrong he joins the Sudan campaign of 1898 and rescues each of the men from certain death. They then take back their feathers as does his girl upon learning of his true courage. Excellent performances by Smith and Richardson. **99m/C VHS.** *GB* Alexander Knox, John Clements, Ralph Richardson, Sir C. Aubrey Smith, June Duprez, Donald Gray, Jack Allen, Allan Jeayes, Frederick Culley, Hal Walters, Henry Oscar, John Laurie, Clive Baxter, Robert Rendel, Derek Elphinstone, Norman Pierce, Amid Taftazani, Archibald Batty, Hay Petrie; ***D:*** Zoltan Korda; ***W:*** R.C. Sherriff, Lajos Biro, Arthur Wimperis; ***C:*** Osmond H. Borradaile, Georges Perinal, Jack Cardiff; ***M:*** Miklos Rozsa.

The Four Feathers 🦴🦴 **1978** Determined to return the symbols of cowardice, four feathers, to his friends and fiancee, a man courageously saves his friends' lives during the British Sudan campaign and regains the love of his lady, in this fifth remake of the story. **95m/C VHS.** Beau Bridges, Jane Seymour, Simon Ward, Harry Andrews, Richard Johnson, Robert Powell; ***D:*** Don Sharp. **TV**

Four for Texas 🦴 **1963** Perhaps Aldrich's later success with "The Dirty Dozen" can be attributed, in part, to this exercise in how not to make a comic western; poorly made, over long, and far too dependant on the feminine charisma of Ekberg and Andress. Slow-moving Sinatra-Martin vehicle tells the tale of con men in the Old West who battle bandits and bad bankers for a stash of loot. **124m/C VHS, DVD, Wide.** Frank Sinatra, Dean Martin, Anita Ekberg, Ursula Andress, Charles Bronson, Victor Buono, Jack Elam, Arthur Godfrey, Moe Howard, Larry Fine, Joe DeRita; ***D:*** Robert Aldrich; ***W:*** Robert Aldrich, Teddi Sherman; ***C:*** Ernest Laszlo; ***M:*** Nelson Riddle.

Four Friends 🦴🦴🦴 *Georgia's Friends* **1981 (R)** The magical good and bad dream of the 1960s is remembered in this story of four friends. A young woman and the three men in love with her first come together in high school and then separate, learning from college, war and drug abuse, and each other in this ambitious movie from Steve Tesich, the writer of "Breaking Away." Good performances by all. **114m/C VHS.** James Leo Herlihy, Craig Wasson, Jodi Thelen, Michael Huddleston, Jim Metzler, Reed Birney; ***D:*** Arthur Penn; ***W:*** Steve Tesich; ***C:*** Ghislan Cloquet.

The Four Horsemen of the Apocalypse 🦴🦴🦴½ **1921** Silent classic and star maker for Valentino concerning an Argentine family torn apart by the outbreak of WWI. Valentino is a painter who moves from his native Argentina to France and is persuaded to enlist by a recruiter who invokes the image of the Biblical riders. His excellence as a soldier, however, proves to be his undoing. The 1962 remake can't hold a candle to original, adapted from a novel by Vicente Blasco-Ibanez. **110m/B VHS.** Rudolph Valentino, Alice Terry, Pomeroy Cannon, Josef Swickard, Alan Hale, Mabel van Buren, Nigel de Brulier, Bowditch Turner, Wallace Beery, Bridgetta Clark, Virginia Warwick, Stuart Holmes, John St. Polis, Mark Fenton, Derek Ghent; ***D:*** Rex Ingram; ***W:*** June Mathis; ***C:*** John Seitz; ***M:*** Louis F. Gottschalk. Natl. Film Reg. '95.

The Four Horsemen of the Apocalypse 🦴🦴½ **1962** The members of a German family find themselves fighting on opposite sides during WWII. This remake of the vintage Valentino silent failed at the boxoffice, with complaints about its length, disjointed script, and uninspired performances. The title refers to the horrors of conquest, pestilence, war, and death. Adapted from the book by Vincente Blasco-Ibanez. **153m/C VHS.** Glenn Ford, Charles Boyer, Lee J. Cobb, Paul Henreid, Yvette Mimieux; ***D:*** Vincente Minnelli; ***W:*** John Gay; ***C:*** Milton Krasner; ***M:*** Andre Previn.

The 400 Blows 🦴🦴🦴🦴 *Les Quartre Cents Coups* **1959** The classic, groundbreaking semi-autobiography that initiated Truffaut's career and catapulted him to international acclaim, about the trials and rebellions of 12-year-old French schoolboy, Antoine Doinel (Leaud). One of the greatest and most influential of films, and the first of Truffaut's career-long Doinel series. French with subtitles. **97m/B VHS, DVD, Wide.** *FR* Francois Truffaut, Jean-Pierre Leaud, Claire Maurier, Albert Remy, Guy Decomble, Georges Flament, Patrick Auffay, Jeanne Moreau, Jean-Claude Brialy, Jacques Demy, Robert Beauvais; ***D:*** Francois Truffaut; ***W:*** Francois Truffaut, Marcel Moussey; ***C:*** Henri Decae; ***M:*** Jean Constantin. Cannes '59: Director (Truffaut); N.Y. Film Critics '59: Foreign Film.

Four in a Jeep 🦴🦴½ **1951** In Vienna in 1945, soldiers from different countries are serving as an international military police force. They clash as a result of political demands and their love for the same woman. Shot on location in Austria. **83m/B VHS.** Ralph Meeker, Viveca Lindfors, Joseph Yadin, Michael Medwin; ***D:*** Leopold Lindtberg.

Four Jacks and a Jill 🦴🦴 **1941** Four musicians are left in the lurch when their band singer leaves them for her gangster boyfriend and they must frantically search for a replacement. Not completely uninteresting, but rather bland and old now. Earlier versions of the story were released as "Street Girl" and "That Girl from Paris." ♫I'm in Good Shape For the Shape I'm In; You Go Your Way and I'll Go Crazy; I Haven't A Thing to Wear; Wherever You Are; Boogie Woogie Conga. **68m/B VHS.** Anne Shirley, Ray Bolger, Desi Arnaz Sr., Jack Durant, June Havoc, Eddie Foy Jr., Fritz Feld; ***D:*** Jack Hively.

The Four Minute Mile 🦴🦴 **1992** Four athletes become determined to break the record of running the mile in under four minutes. **186m/C VHS.** *GB* Richard Huw, Nique Needles, John Philbin, Lewis Fitz-Gerald, Michael York.

The Four Musketeers *The Revenge of Milady* **1975 (PG)** A fun-loving continuation of "The Three Musketeers," reportedly filmed simultaneously. Lavish swashbuckler jaunts between France, England, and Italy, in following the adventures of D'Artagnan and his cohorts. Pictures give an amusing depiction of Lester-interpreted 17th-century Europe, with fine performances especially by Dunaway as an evil countess seeking revenge on our heroes and Welch as the scatterbrained object of York's affections. Followed, in 1989, by "The Return of the Musketeers." **108m/C VHS, DVD, Wide.** Michael York, Oliver Reed, Richard Chamberlain, Frank Finlay, Raquel Welch, Christopher Lee, Faye Dunaway, Jean-Pierre Cassel, Geraldine Chaplin, Simon Ward, Charlton Heston, Roy Kinnear, Nicole Calfan; ***D:*** Richard Lester; ***W:*** George MacDonald Fraser; ***C:*** David Watkin; ***M:*** Lalo Schifrin.

Four Robbers **197?** The ruthless Ma initiates his series of crimes throughout the Far East, somehow staying ahead of the cops. When the final showdown occurs, it's an all out kung fu massacre. **90m/C VHS.** Lau Chun, Shek Hon, Kong Seng, Lee Wing Shan.

Four Rode Out **1969** A Mexican outlaw is pursued by his girlfriend, one-time partner, and the law. Brutal, inferior western. **99m/C VHS.** Pernell Roberts, Sue Lyon, Leslie Nielsen, Julian Mateos; ***D:*** John Peyser.

Four Rooms **1995 (R)** Four stories by four hot indie filmers set in the same L.A. hotel on New Year's Eve are tied together by bellboy Roth, stumbling around in a Jerry/Carrey-like stupor. Leading off is Anders's roomful of witches trying to resurrect spirit of '50s stripper DeCadenet. After this disappointing start is Rockwell's bland look at infidelity, with wife Beals tied and gagged by her husband (Proval) over an alleged fling with Roth. Bandaras heads the best seg as a mobster who leaves his demonic children in Roth's hands. Tarantino is the anchor man with his take on Hitchcock, dealing with a macabre bet involving the removal of body parts. Altogether disjointed and uninspired. **98m/C VHS, DVD, Wide.** Tim Roth, Antonio Banderas, Jennifer Beals, Paul Calderon, Sammi Davis, Valeria Golino, Madonna, Ione Skye, Marisa Tomei, Tamlyn Tomita, Bruce Willis, David Proval, Lili Taylor, Alicia Witt, Amanda DeCadenet, Danny Verduzco, Lana McKissack, Quentin Tarantino; ***Cameos:*** Salma Hayek; ***D:*** Quentin Tarantino, Alexandre Rockwell, Robert Rodriguez, Allison Anders; ***W:*** Quentin Tarantino, Alexandre Rockwell, Robert Rodriguez, Allison Anders; ***C:*** Phil Parmet, Guillermo Navarro, Andrzej Sekula, Rodrigo Garcia; ***M:*** Combustible Edison, Esquivel. Golden Raspberries '95: Worst Support. Actress (Madonna).

The Four Seasons ½ **1981 (PG)** Three upper-middle-class New York couples share their vacations together, as well as their friendship, their frustrations and their jealousies. Alda's first outing as a film director is pleasant and easy on the eyes. **108m/C VHS.** Alan Alda, Carol Burnett, Sandy Dennis, Len Cariou, Jack Weston, Rita Moreno, Bess Armstrong; ***D:*** Alan Alda; ***W:*** Alan Alda.

Four Sided Triangle **1953** Two mad scientists find their friendship threatened when they discover that they are both in love with the same woman. So they do what anyone would do in this situation—they invent a machine and duplicate her. **81m/B VHS, DVD.** *GB* James Hayter, Barbara Payton, Stephen Murray, John Van Eyssen, Percy Marmont; ***D:*** Terence Fisher; ***W:*** Terence Fisher, Paul Tabori; ***C:*** Reg Wyer; ***M:*** Malcolm Arnold.

Four Times That Night *Quante Volte...Quella Notte* **1969 (R)** Though he's known for his work in horror, Mario Bava also made one sex comedy and it's not a bad little movie, though its appeal is mostly nostalgia. Technically, it's a "Rashomon" story with the events of one night told from different points of view. What happens when Gianni (Halsey) takes the lovely Tina (Giordano) to his bachelor pad? Is it date rape or does she seduce him? The film is still grand stuff for '60s fans. The shagadelic apartment must be seen to be believed. **83m/C DVD, Wide.** *IT* Brett Halsey, Daniela Giordano, Pascale Petit, Brigitte Skay; ***D:*** Mario Bava; ***M:*** Lallo Gori.

Four Ways Out ½ **1957** Four average guys are fed up by their lot in life and stage a boxoffice robbery of their local soccer stadium. They don't get to enjoy their ill-gotten gains. In Italian with subtitles or dubbed. **77m/B VHS.** *IT* Gina Lollobrigida, Renato Baldini, Paul Muller; ***D:*** Pietro Germi.

Four Weddings and a Funeral **1994 (R)** Refreshing, intelligent adult comedy brimming with stiff upper-lip wit and sophistication. Thirtyish Brit bachelor Charles (Grant) spends his time attending the weddings of his friends, but manages to avoid taking the plunge himself. Then he falls for American Carrie (MacDowell), who's about to wed another. Great beginning offers loads of laughs as the first two weddings unfold, then becomes decidedly bittersweet. While Grant makes this a star turn as the romantic bumbler, MacDowell charms without seeming particularly needed. Supporting characters are superb, especially Coleman as the "flirty" Scarlett and Atkinson as a new minister. Surprising boxoffice hit found a broad audience. **118m/C VHS, DVD, Wide.** *GB* Hugh Grant, Andie MacDowell, Simon Callow, Kristin Scott Thomas, James Fleet, John Hannah, Charlotte Coleman, David Bower, Corin Redgrave, Rowan Atkinson, Rosalie Crutchley, Kenneth Griffith, Jeremy Kemp, Sophie Thompson; ***D:*** Mike Newell; ***W:*** Richard Curtis; ***C:*** Michael Coulter; ***M:*** Richard Rodney Bennett. Australian Film Inst. '94: Foreign Film; British Acad. '94: Actor (Grant), Director (Newell), Film, Support. Actress (Scott Thomas); Golden Globes '95: Actor—Mus./Comedy (Grant); Writers Guild '94: Orig. Screenplay.

The 4D Man ½ **1959** A physicist makes two fateful discoveries while working on a special project that gets out of control, leaving him able to pass through matter and see around corners. He also finds that his touch brings instant death. Cheap but effective sci-fier. Young Duke has a small part. **85m/C VHS, DVD.** Robert Lansing, Lee Meriwether, James Congdon, Guy Raymond, Robert Strauss, Patty Duke; ***D:*** Irvin S. Yeaworth Jr.; ***W:*** Theodore Simonson, Cy Chermack; ***C:*** Theodore J. Pahle; ***M:*** Ralph Carmichael.

1492: Conquest of Paradise ½ **1992 (PG-13)** Large-scale Hollywood production striving for political correctness is a drawn-out account of Columbus's (Depardieu) discovery and subsequent exploitation of the "New World." Skillful directing by Ridley Scott and impressive scenery add interest, yet don't make up for a script which chronicles events but tends towards trite dialogue and characterization. Available in both pan-and-scan and letterbox formats. **142m/C VHS, Wide.** Gerard Depardieu, Sigourney Weaver, Armand Assante, Frank Langella, Loren Dean, Angela Molina, Fernando Rey, Michael Wincott, Steven Waddington, Tcheky Karyo, Kario Salem; ***D:*** Ridley Scott; ***W:*** Roselyne Bosch; ***M:*** Vangelis.

The 4th Floor **1999 (R)** Lewis, who's engaged to older and successful TV weatherman Hurt, inherits a rent-controlled apartment and is then terrorized by her neighbor, who may be working for someone else. Twist ending leaves viewer with more questions than answers. **90m/C VHS, DVD, Wide.** Juliette Lewis, William Hurt, Austin Pendleton, Shelley Duvall, Artie Lange, Tobin Bell; ***D:*** Josh Klausner; ***W:*** Josh Klausner; ***C:*** Michael Slovis; ***M:*** Brian Tyler.

The 4th Man ½ *Die Vierde Man* **1979** Steeped in saturated colors and jet black comedy, with an atmospheric score, Verhoeven's nouveau noir mystery enjoyed considerable art-house success but was not released in the US until 1984. The story is decidedly non-linear, the look stylish and symbolic. Krabbe is an alcoholic bisexual Catholic writer who inadvertently becomes the hypotenuse of a love triangle involving Herman, a young man he encounters at a railway station, and his lover Christine, who owns the Sphinx beauty parlor and whose three husbands died, shall we say, mysteriously. In Dutch with English subtitles. **102m/C VHS, DVD, Wide.** *NL* Jeroen Krabbe, Renee Soutendijk, Thom Hoffman, Jon (John) DeVries, Geert De Jong; ***D:*** Paul Verhoeven; ***W:*** Gerard Soeteman; ***C:*** Jan De Bont; ***M:*** Loek Dikker. L.A. Film Critics '84: Foreign Film.

The Fourth Protocol **1987 (R)** Well-made thriller based on the Frederick Forsyth bestseller about a British secret agent trying to stop a young KGB agent from destroying NATO and putting the world in nuclear jeopardy. Brosnan, as the totally dedicated Russkie, gives his best performance to date while Caine, as usual, is totally believable as he goes about the business of tracking down the bad guys. **119m/C VHS.** *GB* Michael Caine, Pierce Brosnan, Ned Beatty, Joanna Cassidy, Julian Glover, Ray McAnally, Michael Gough, Ian Richardson, Betsy Brantley, Matt Frewer, Peter Cartwright, David Conville; ***D:*** John MacKenzie; ***W:*** Frederick Forsyth, Richard Burridge, George Axelrod; ***C:*** Phil Meheux; ***M:*** Lalo Schifrin, Francis Shaw.

The Fourth Sex ½ *Le Quatrieme Sexe* **1961** Wealthy American, Sand, spends her time in Paris painting her girlfriends in the nude and throwing very wild parties. When she meets newcomer Caroline, she immediately sets out to add her to her harem. **82m/B VHS.** *FR* Nicole Burgot, Brigette Juslin, Richard Winckler; ***D:*** Michel Wichard.

Fourth Story **1990 (PG-13)** A misfit detective is hired by a beautiful woman to find her missing husband. The investigation reveals some unseemly facts about the gentleman. Characterizations and plot twists keep this mystery interesting. **91m/C VHS.** Mark Harmon, Mimi Rogers, Cliff DeYoung, Paul Gleason, M. Emmet Walsh; ***D:*** Ivan Passer; ***W:*** Andrew Guerdat. **CABLE**

The Fourth War **1990 (R)** Scheider and Prochnow are American and Russian colonels, respectively, assigned to guard the West German-Czechoslovakian border against each other. With the end of the cold war looming, these two frustrated warriors begin to taunt each other with sallies into the other's territory, threatening to touch off a major superpower conflict. **109m/C VHS.** Roy Scheider, Juergen Prochnow, Tim Reid, Lara Harris, Harry Dean Stanton, Dale Dye; ***D:*** John Frankenheimer; ***M:*** Bill Conti.

Fourth Wise Man **1985** A Biblical Easter story about a rich physician searching for Christ in Persia. **72m/C VHS.** Martin Sheen, Lance Kerwin, Alan Arkin, Harold Gould, Eileen Brennan, Ralph Bellamy, Adam Arkin, Richard Libertini.

Fourth Wish **1975** When a single father learns that his son is dying, he vows to make his son's last months as fulfilling as possible. Bring lots of hankies. **107m/C VHS.** John Meillon, Robert Bettles, Robyn Nevin; ***D:*** Don Chaffey; ***C:*** Geoff Burton. Australian Film Inst. '75: Actor (Meillon).

Fowl Play woof! **1983** An unlikely threesome encounter various hardships and mishaps on their way to the first cockfighting Olympics. Let's hope it's the last cock-fighting Olympics. **90m/C VHS.** Nancy Kwan.

Fox and His Friends ½ *Faustrecht der Freiheit; Fist Right of Freedom* **1975** Fassbinder's breakthrough tragi-drama, about a lowly gay carnival barker who wins the lottery, thus attracting a devious, exploiting lover, who takes him for everything he has. In German with English subtitles. **123m/C VHS.** *GE* Rainer Werner Fassbinder, Peter Chatel, Karl-Heinz Boehm, Adrian Hoven, Harry Baer, Ulla Jacobsson, Kurt Raab; ***D:*** Rainer Werner Fassbinder; ***C:*** Michael Ballhaus.

The Fox and the Hound **1981 (G)** Sweet story of the friendship shared by a fox and hound. Young and naive, the animals become friends and swear their allegiance to one another when they are separated for a season. Upon return, the hound has become his master's best hunting dog and warns his friend the fox to stay clear of their hunting grounds, for the master is determined to catch the docile fox. Saddened, the fox retreats but soon finds himself boldly standing his ground against a bear that attacks the hound, and the hound inevitably protects the fox from the mean-spirited hunter. Very good animation, but not in the same class as other Disney favorites like "Beauty and the Beast." **83m/C VHS, DVD.** ***D:*** Art Stevens, Ted Berman, Richard Rich; ***W:*** Art Stevens, Peter Young, Steve Hulett, Earl Kress, Vance Gerry, Laury Clemmons, Dave Michener, Burny Mattinson; ***M:*** Buddy (Norman Dale) Baker; ***V:*** Mickey Rooney, Kurt Russell, Pearl Bailey, Jack Albertson, Sandy Duncan, Jeanette Nolan, Pat Buttram, John Fiedler, John McIntire, Richard Bakalyan, Paul Winchell, Keith Mitchell, Corey Feldman.

Foxes **1980 (R)** Four young California girls grow up with little supervision from parents still trying to grow up themselves. They rely on each other in a world where they have to make adult choices, yet are not considered grown-up. They look for no more than a good time and no tragic mistakes. **106m/C VHS.** Jodie Foster, Cherie Currie, Marilyn Kagan, Scott Baio, Sally Kellerman, Randy Quaid, Laura Dern; ***D:*** Adrian Lyne; ***W:*** Gerald Ayres.

Foxfire **1987 (PG)** In the role that won her Tony and Emmy awards, Tandy stars as Annie Nations, a woman who has lived her entire life in the Blue Ridge Mountains. Widowed, all she has left are the memories of her beloved husband, with whom she regularly communes. Her son tries to convince her to move, and it becomes a clash of the wills as Annie tries to decide to stay in her past or change her future. **118m/C VHS.** Jessica Tandy, Hume Cronyn, John Denver, Gary Grubbs, Harriet Hall; ***D:*** Jud Taylor; ***C:*** Thomas Burstyn. **TV**

Foxfire **1996 (R)** Not much more than "The Craft" without the hocus-pocus. Lusty Legs Sadovsky (Jolie) is a liberated drifter who empowers a quartet of abused teens to take action against their molester, who happens to be their biology teacher. Based on the book by Joyce Carol Oates originally written in the 1950s, modern adaptation suffers from time warp, most notably when the girls expose their teacher's behavior to their principal and he promptly suspends them without further ado. After some bonding and tattooing in an abandoned house, flick descends into the more masculine and mundane territory of car chases, kidnapping and gunplay. Filmmakers rather timidly back off of leather-clad Legs' obvious lesbianism and her relationship with the adoring Maddy (Burress). Decent acting by most would've benefitted from a more cohesive screenplay. **102m/C VHS, DVD, Wide.** Angelina Jolie, John Diehl, Jenny Lewis, Cathy Moriarty, Richard Beymer, Hedy Burress, Jenny Shimizu, Sarah Rosenberg, Peter Facinelli; ***D:*** Annette Haywood-Carter; ***W:*** Elizabeth White; ***C:*** Newton Thomas (Tom) Sigel; ***M:*** Michel Colombier.

Foxfire Light **1982 (PG)** A young woman vacationing in the Ozarks is drawn into a romance with a cowboy. But her mother's social ambitions and her own indecesion may tear them apart. **102m/C VHS.** Tippi Hedren, Lara Parker, Leslie Nielsen, Barry Van Dyke; ***D:*** Allen Baron; ***C:*** Thomas Ackerman.

Foxstyle ½ **1973** A wealthy nightclub owner struggles with his country roots and his city sophistication. **84m/C VHS.** Juanita Moore, Richard Lawson, John Taylor, Jovita Bush; ***D:*** Clyde Houston.

Foxtrap **1985** An L.A. courier is hired to find a runaway girl and, upon finding her in Europe, discovers he's been led into a trap. A low budget Italian co-production. **89m/C VHS.** *IT* Fred Williamson, Christopher Connelly, Arlene Golonka; ***D:*** Fred Williamson.

Foxtrot *The Other Side of Paradise* **1976 (R)** A wealthy count isolates himself, his wife, and their two servants, on an island but cannot escape his past or the horrors of WWII. Even the good cast can't save the pretentious script and inadequate production. **91m/C VHS.** *SI MX* Peter O'Toole, Charlotte Rampling, Max von Sydow, Jorge Luke; ***D:*** Arturo Ripstein.

Foxy Brown **1974 (R)** A bitter woman poses as a prostitute to avenge the mob-backed deaths of her drug dealer brother and undercover cop boyfriend. Extremely violent black exploitation flick. **92m/C VHS, DVD, Wide.** Pam Grier, Terry Carter,

Antonio Fargas, Kathryn Loder, Peter Brown, Sid Haig, Juanita Brown; *D:* Jack Hill; *W:* Jack Hill; *C:* Brick Marquard; *M:* Willie Hutch.

F.P. 1 🦴🦴 **1933** An artifical island (Floating Platform 1) in the Atlantic is threatened by treason. This slow-moving 1930s technothriller is the English-language version of the German "F.P. 1 Antwortet Nicht" ("F.P. 1 Doesn't Answer"). Both were directed at the same time by Hartl, using different casts. **74m/B VHS.** *GE* Leslie Fenton, Conrad Veidt, Jill Esmond; *D:* Karl Hartl.

F.P. 1 Doesn't Answer 🦴🦴 *F.P. 1 Antwortet Nicht* **1933** A mid-Atlantic refueling station (Floating Platform 1) is threatened by treason and a pilot sets out to put things right. Features pre-Hollywood vintage Lorre; Albers was Germany's number one boxoffice draw at the time. In German. **74m/B VHS.** *GE* Hans Albers, Sybille Schmitz, Paul Hartmann, Peter Lorre, Hermann Speelmanns; *D:* Karl Hartl.

Frailty 🦴🦴🦴 **2002 (R)** Impressive directorial debut by Paxton has him as Dad, a seemingly normal West Texas widower. One day, however, he tells his boys that their family has been chosen by God to destroy demons who are disguised as normal people. This sounds okay by impressionable nine year old Adam (Sumpter), but older Fenton (O'Leary) seems skeptical. Told mostly in flashback, from the point of view of now-grown, haunted Fenton (McConaughey), the story keeps the gore mostly offscreen, while focusing on the such lofty ideas as the wages of religious fanaticism, the trust between parents and their kids, and toll of insanity. Screenwriting debut for Hanley. Paxton acquits himself well on both sides of the camera, but it's O'Leary who shines. McConaughey turns in his best performance to date. **100m/C VHS, DVD.** *US* Bill Paxton, Matthew McConaughey, Powers Boothe, Luke Askew, Matt O'Leary, Jeremy Sumpter, Derk Cheetwood, Missy (Melissa) Crider, Alan Davidson, Cynthia Ettinger, Vincent Chase, Levi Kreis; *D:* Bill Paxton; *W:* Brent Hanley; *C:* Bill Butler; *M:* Brian Tyler.

Frame by Frame 🦴🦴½ **1995 (R)** Cop partners Ekberg (Helgenberger) and Stash (Biehn), who share a passion on and off the job, become implicated in the mob-style murder of Stash's wife. **97m/C VHS.** Michael Biehn, Marg Helgenberger, Ron White, Dan Lett, Von Flores; *D:* Douglas Barr; *W:* Douglas Barr; *C:* Rodney Charters; *M:* Mark Snow. **CABLE**

Frame Up 🦴🦴 **1991 (R)** A small town sheriff is trying to investigate a murder tied to a fraternity's initiation. However, he runs into opposition from the most powerful man in town. **90m/C VHS.** Wings Hauser, Bobby DiCicco, Frances Fisher, Dick Sargent, Robert Picardo; *D:* Paul Leder.

Framed 🦴🦴 **1975 (R)** A nightclub owner is framed for murder, which understandably irks him. He's determined to get paroled and then seek revenge on the crooked cops responsible for his incarceration. This action melodrama features the writer, director and star of "Walking Tall." **106m/C VHS.** Joe Don Baker, Gabriel Dell, Brock Peters, Conny Van Dyke, John Marley; *D:* Phil Karlson; *W:* Mort Briskin.

Framed 🦴🦴 **1990** An art forger gets tripped up by a beautiful con artist. However, when they meet again he is willingly drawn into her latest swindle. **87m/C VHS.** Jeff Goldblum, Kristin Scott Thomas, Todd Graff; *D:* Dean Parisot.

Framed 🦴🦴🦴 **1993** British miniseries about a mediocre cop and a master criminal. Sgt. Larry Jackson (Morrissey) is on vacation in Spain when he spots the supposedly dead master thief/murderer Eddie Myers (Dalton). Once back in London, Larry's assigned the dubious task of guarding Eddie and finding out the names of his associates. Only the sophisticated Eddie starts to dangle temptation in front of the younger man until Larry begins to waver in his duty. Intricate plotting, with Dalton particular fine as the suave, immoral crook. LaPlante also wrote the very successful "Prime Suspect" police dramas for TV. **115m/C VHS, DVD.** *GB* Timothy Dalton, David Morrissey, Timothy West, Annabelle Apsion, Penelope Cruz, Rowena King, Francis Johnson, Glyn Grimstead, Wayne Foskett, Trevor Cooper; *D:* Geoffrey Sax; *W:* Lynda La Plante; *M:* Nick Bicat. **TV**

Fran 🦴🦴 **1985** A young woman is torn between her desperate need for a male companion and the care of her children. Well made, albeit depressing, Australian production. **92m/C VHS.** *AU* Noni Hazlehurst, Annie Byron, Alan Fletcher; *D:* Glenda Hambly. Australian Film Inst. '85: Actress (Hazlehurst).

Frances 🦴🦴🦴 **1982** The tragic story of Frances Farmer, the beautiful and talented screen actress of the '30s and early '40s, who was driven to a mental breakdown by bad luck, drug and alcohol abuse, a neurotic, domineering mother, despicable mental health care, and her own stubbornness. After being in and out of mental hospitals, she is finally reduced to a shadow by a lobotomy. Not nearly as bleak as it sounds, this film works because Lange understands this character from the inside out, and never lets her become melodramatic or weak. **134m/C VHS, DVD, Wide.** Jessica Lange, Kim Stanley, Sam Shepard, Jeffrey DeMunn, Gerald S. O'Loughlin, Chris Pennock, John Randolph, Lane Smith; *D:* Graeme Clifford; *W:* Christopher DeVore, Nicholas Kazan, Eric Bergren; *C:* Laszlo Kovacs; *M:* John Barry.

Francesco 🦴🦴 **1993 (PG-13)** Set in 13th-century Italy and depicting the life of St. Francis of Assisi. Follows the pleasure-loving son of a wealthy merchant through his religious awakening, and the founding of the Franciscan order of monks. Rourke, in a definite change-of-pace role, is actually believable, while Bonham Carter offers fine support as a devoted disciple. **119m/C VHS, DVD.** Mickey Rourke, Helena Bonham Carter, Paolo Bonacelli, Andrea Ferreol, Hanns Zischler, Peter Berling; *D:* Liliana Cavani; *W:* Liliana Cavani; *C:* Giuseppe Lanci, Ennio Guarnieri; *M:* Vangelis.

The Franchise Affair 🦴🦴 **1952** A teenage girl in need of an alibi accuses two reclusive women of kidnapping and abusing her. It's up to a lawyer to sort out the truth. Based on the novel by Josephine Tey. **149m/C VHS.** *GB* Michael Denison, Dulcie Gray, Anthony Nicholls, Marjorie Fielding, Athene Seyler, Ann Stephens, Patrick Troughton; *D:* Lawrence Huntington.

The Franchise Affair 🦴🦴½ **19??** A scandal is about to overtake the sleepy village of Milford in 1947. An elderly lady and her daughter, the owners of a forbidding country house, are accused of kidnapping and beating a teenaged girl until she agreed to work as their servant. A British TV production based on the novel by Josephine Tey and previously filmed for the big screen in 1952. **155m/C VHS.** *GB* Patrick Malahide, Rosalie Crutchley, Joanna McCallum.

Francis Covers the Big Town 🦴🦴½ **1953** The fourth in the series finds Peter Stirling (O'Connor) trying to become an ace reporter with a New York newspaper. Thanks to Francis he gets some big scoops but then runs afoul of the mob and is accused of murder. And it's up to his smarter pal to come to the rescue. **86m/B VHS.** Donald O'Connor, Yvette Dugay, Gene Lockhart, Nancy Guild, Larry Gates, Gale Gordon; *D:* Arthur Lubin; *W:* Oscar Brodney; *C:* Carl Guthrie; *M:* Joseph Gershenson; *V:* Chill Wills.

Francis Gary Powers: The True Story of the U-2 Spy 🦴🦴½ **1976** Dramatization of the true experiences of Gary Powers, a CIA spy pilot whose plane was shot down over the Soviet Union in 1960. His capture, trial, and conviction are all portrayed in detail, taken from Power's own reminiscences. **120m/C VHS.** Lee Majors, Noah Beery Jr., Nehemiah Persoff, Lew Ayres, Brooke Bundy; *D:* Delbert Mann. **TV**

Francis Goes to the Races 🦴🦴½ **1951** The second in the talking-mule series finds O'Connor and Francis taking up residence on Kellaway's failing horse ranch. When mobsters seize control of the property to pay off a debt, Francis decides to check with the horses at the Santa Anita race track and find a sure winner to bet on. **88m/B VHS.** Donald O'Connor, Piper Laurie, Cecil Kellaway, Jesse White, Barry Kelley, Hayden Rorke, Vaughn Taylor, Larry Keating; *D:* Arthur Lubin; *W:* Oscar Brodney; *M:* Frank Skinner; *V:* Chill Wills.

Francis Goes to West Point 🦴🦴½ **1952** Peter (O'Connor) and Francis get into West Point where the unfortunate freshman winds up last in his class. But thanks to Francis, Peter makes it past school hazing, grades, and other campus hijicks. Look for Leonard Nimoy in the bit role of a football player. Third in the series. **81m/B VHS.** Donald O'Connor, Lori Nelson, William Reynolds, Gregg (Hunter) Palmer, Alice Kelley, Les Tremayne, David Janssen, Paul Burke; *D:* Arthur Lubin; *W:* Oscar Brodney; *C:* Carl Guthrie; *M:* Joseph Gershenson; *V:* Chill Wills.

Francis in the Haunted House 🦴½ **1956** The sixth and last entry in the series finds star Donald O'Connor, director Arthur Lubin, and even Chill Wills (the voice of Francis) all abandoning the sinking series. So, its left to Rooney (as hapless David Prescott) to get himself into trouble (trapped in a haunted house with thieves) and for Francis to get him out. Ho-hum. **80m/B VHS.** Mickey Rooney, Virginia Welles, James Flavin, Paul Cavanagh, David Janssen, Richard Deacon; *D:* Charles Lamont; *W:* Herbert Margolis, William Raynor; *C:* George Robinson; *M:* Joseph Gershenson; *V:* Paul Frees.

Francis in the Navy 🦴🦴 **1955** The precocious talking mule, Francis, is drafted, and his buddy, played by O'Connor, comes to the rescue. The loquacious beast proves he has the superior grey matter however, and ends up doing all the thinking. Look for Clint Eastwood in his second minor role. **80m/B VHS.** Donald O'Connor, Martha Hyer, Jim Backus, Paul Burke, David Janssen, Clint Eastwood, Martin Milner; *D:* Arthur Lubin.

Francis Joins the WACs 🦴🦴½ **1954** The fifth entry in the series finds O'Connor working as a bank clerk when he is mistakenly drafted back into the military—and sent to a WAC base. Francis tries to keep him out of trouble with the ladies. Wills, the voice of Francis, also turns up as a general. **94m/B VHS.** Donald O'Connor, Julie Adams, Chill Wills, Mamie Van Doren, Lynn Bari, ZaSu Pitts, Joan Shawlee, Mara Corday, Allison Hayes; *D:* Arthur Lubin; *V:* Chill Wills.

Francis the Talking Mule 🦴🦴🦴 *Francis* **1949** The first of the silly but funny series about, what else, a talking mule. Peter Stirling (O'Connor) is the dim-bulb G.I. who hooks up with Francis while fighting in Burma. Francis helps Peter become a war hero but of course everyone thinks he's crazy when Peter insists the mule can talk. The joke is that Francis is smarter than any of the humans. O'Connor starred in six of the films, with Mickey Rooney taking over the final adventure. Director Lubin went on to create the TV series "Mr. Ed," about a talking horse. Watch for Tony Curtis in a small role. **91m/B VHS.** Donald O'Connor, Patricia Medina, ZaSu Pitts, Ray Collins, John McIntire, Eduard Franz, Howland Chamberlain, Frank Faylen, Tony Curtis; *D:* Arthur Lubin; *M:* Frank Skinner; *V:* Chill Wills.

Frank and Jesse 🦴🦴½ **1994 (R)** Another revisionist western finds outlaw Jesse James (Lowe) brooding about his violent existence while brother Frank (Paxton) keeps the gang together and they all try to avoid capture by a vengeful Alan Pinkerton (Atherton) and his detective agency. **106m/C VHS, DVD, Wide.** Rob Lowe, Bill Paxton, Randy Travis, William Atherton, Alexis Arquette; *D:* Robert Boris; *W:* Robert Boris; *C:* Walt Lloyd; *M:* Mark McKenzie.

Frankenhooker 🦴½ **1990 (R)** Jeffrey Franken is a nice guy; he didn't mean to mow his fiancee down on the front lawn. But sometimes bad things just happen to good people. Luckily Jeff thought to save her head and decides to pair it up with the body of some sexy streetwalkers. Voila! You have Frankenhooker: the girlfriend with more than a heart. The posters say it best, "A Terrifying Tale of Sluts and Bolts." **90m/C VHS, DVD.** James Lorinz, Patty Mullen, Charlotte J. Helmkamp, Louise Lasser, Shirley Stoler, Joseph Gonzalez, Beverly Bonner, John Zacherle; *D:* Frank Henenlotter; *W:* Frank Henenlotter, Robert Martin; *C:* Robert M. "Bob" Baldwin Jr.; *M:* Joe Renzetti.

Frankenstein 🦴🦴🦴🦴 **1931** The definitive expressionistic Gothic horror classic that set the mold. Adapted from the Mary Shelley novel about Dr. Henry Frankenstein (Clive), the scientist who creates a terrifying, yet strangely sympathetic monster aided by his hunchbacked assistant, Fritz (Frye). Great performance by Karloff as the creation, which made him a monster star (in part, thanks to Jack Pierce's makeup). Several powerful scenes, excised from the original version, have been restored, including that of young Maria (Marilyn Harris), who is spotted by the monster innocently picking flowers by a pond. The first in the Universal series. **71m/B VHS, DVD.** Boris Karloff, Colin Clive, Mae Clarke, John Boles, Dwight Frye, Edward Van Sloan, Frederick Kerr, Lionel Belmore, Arletta Duncan; *D:* James Whale; *W:* Garrett Fort, John Lloyd Balderston, Robert Florey, Francis Edwards Faragoh; *C:* Arthur Edeson; *M:* David Broeckman. AFI '98: Top 100, Natl. Film Reg. '91.

Frankenstein 🦴🦴½ **1973** A brilliant scientist plays God, unleashing a living monster from the remains of the dead. A TV movie version of the legendary horror story. Good atmosphere provided by producer Dan "Dark Shadows" Curtis. **130m/C VHS, DVD.** Robert Foxworth, Bo Svenson, Willie Aames, Susan Strasberg; *D:* Glenn Jordan.

Frankenstein 🦴🦴½ **1982** A remake of the horror classic, closely following the original story, wherein the creature speaks (and waxes philosophical), the doctor sees him as his dark subconscious, and the two die in an arctic confrontation. **81m/C VHS.** Robert Powell, Carrie Fisher, David Warner, John Gielgud; *D:* James Ormerod.

Frankenstein 🦴🦴½ **1993** Yet another remake of Mary Shelley's 1818 novel. Bergin stars as Dr. Victor Frankenstein, fanatically believing in the power of science to solve all mankind's ills. This leads him to prove his theories on the "secret of life" with his creation of the monster (Quaid), which Frankenstein finds he cannot ultimately control. Slow-moving story but while the monster isn't really terrifying, he's vengeful and intelligent enough to be a good enemy. **117m/C VHS.** Patrick Bergin, Randy Quaid, John Mills, Lambert Wilson, Fiona Gilles, Jacinta Mulcahy, Timothy Stark; *D:* David Wickes; *W:* David Wickes. **CABLE**

Frankenstein and Me 🦴🦴½ **1996 (PG)** Monster-mad 12-year-old Earl Williams (Boulanger) lives in a small Mojave desert town and dreams about bringing Frankenstein's creature back to life. On Halloween, Earl and his friends visit a traveling carnival that claims to have the "authentic" monster, which happens to fall off the truck when the show leaves. Earl finds the dummy and makes numerous attempts to bring the creature back to life. Lots of fantasy sequences and the picture's fun without being too scary. **91m/C VHS.** *CA* Jamieson Boulanger, Ricky Mabse, Louise Fletcher, Burt Reynolds, Myriam Cyr; *D:* Robert Tinnell; *W:* David Sherman, Richard Goudreau; *C:* Roxanne Di Santo; *M:* Normand Corbeil.

Frankenstein and the Monster from Hell 🦴🦴 **1974 (R)** A young doctor is discovered conducting experiments with human bodies and thrown into a mental asylum run by none other than Dr. Frankenstein himself. They continue their gruesome work together, creating a monster who develops a taste for human flesh. This really lame film was the last of the Hammer Frankenstein series. **93m/C VHS.** *GB* Peter Cushing, Shane Briant, Madeleine Smith, David Prowse, John Stratton, Bernard Lee, Patrick Troughton, Sydney Bromley; *D:* Terence Fisher; *W:* John (Anthony Hinds) Elder; *C:* Brian Probyn; *M:* James Bernard.

Frankenstein Created Woman 🦴🦴🦴 *Frankenstein Made Woman* **1966** In Hammer's fourth take on the Frankenstein story, traditional lab scenes are replaced with less expensive "soul" translocations, though the filmmakers retain an ongoing fascination with decapitations. Oddly, the story has a warmth that's often lacking in the genre, and it's aimed at a younger audience, reflecting the changes that were going on when it was made. **86m/C DVD, Wide.** Peter Cushing, Susan Denberg, Thorley Walters, Robert Morris, Duncan Lamont, Peter Blythe, Alan McNaughton, Peter Madden, Barry Warren, Derek Fowlds; ***D:*** Terence Fisher; ***W:*** John (Anthony Hinds) Elder; ***C:*** Arthur Grant.

Frankenstein '80 woof! *Mosaic* **1979** Guy named Frankenstein pieces together a monster who goes on a killing spree. Bottom of the barrel Italian production with funky music and lots of gore. **88m/C VHS.** *IT GE* John Richardson, Gordon Mitchell, Leila Parker, Dada Galloti, Marisa Travers, Xiro Papas, Renato Romano; ***D:*** Mario Mancini; ***W:*** Mario Mancini, Ferdinando De Leone; ***C:*** Emilio Varriano.

Frankenstein General Hospital woof! **1988** A completely laughless horror spoof wherein the 12th grandson of the infamous scientist duplicates his experiments in the basement of a modern hospital. A must see for Frankenstein fans; considered by some the worst Frankenstein movie ever made. **90m/C VHS.** Mark Blankfield, Kathy Shower, Leslie Jordan, Irwin Keyes, Jonathan Farwell, Hamilton Mitchell, Lou (Cutel) Cutell, Bobby "Boris" Pickett; ***D:*** Deborah Roberts; ***W:*** Robert Deel, Michael F. Kelly; ***C:*** Tom Fraser.

Frankenstein Island woof! **1981 (PG)** Four balloonists get pulled down in a storm and end up on a mysterious island. They are greeted by one Sheila Frankenstein and encounter monsters, amazons, and other obstacles. Completely inept; Carradine "appears" in a visionary sequence wearing his pajamas. **97m/C VHS.** Cameron Mitchell, Andrew Duggan, John Carradine; ***D:*** Jerry Warren.

Frankenstein Meets the Space Monster woof! *Mars Invades Puerto Rico; Frankenstein Meets the Spacemen; Duel of the Space Monsters* **1965** A classic grade-Z epic about a space robot gone berserk among Puerto Rican disco dancers. **80m/B VHS.** James Karen, Nancy Marshall, Marilyn Hanold, David Kerman, Robert Reilly, Lou (Cutel) Cutell; ***D:*** Robert Gaffney; ***W:*** George Garret; ***C:*** Saul Midwall.

Frankenstein Meets the Wolfman 🦴🦴🦴 **1942** The two famous Universal monsters meet and battle it out in this typical grade-B entry, the fifth from the series. The Werewolf wants Dr. Frankenstein to cure him, but only his monster (played by Lugosi) remains. **73m/C VHS, DVD.** Lon Chaney Jr., Bela Lugosi, Patric Knowles, Lionel Atwill, Maria Ouspenskaya, Ilona Massey, Dwight Frye; ***D:*** Roy William Neill; ***W:*** Curt Siodmak; ***C:*** George Robinson.

Frankenstein Must Be Destroyed 🦴🦴½ **1969** Evil Dr. Frankenstein (Cushing) gets interested in brain transplants but discovers the expert, Dr. Pravda, he hoped to work with has gone mad and is in an asylum. He forces a young medical couple to help him free Pravda but the man is accidentally killed. Nevertheless, Frankenstein transplants Pravda's brain into the body of an asylum inmate that Frankenstein has murdered. These things never work out as intended. Followed by "The Horror of Frankenstein." **97m/C VHS.** *GB* Peter Cushing, Veronica Carlson, Freddie Jones, Maxine Audley, Simon Ward, Thorley Walters, George Pravda, Colette O'Neil; ***D:*** Terence Fisher; ***W:*** Bert Batt; ***C:*** Arthur Grant.

Frankenstein Reborn 🦴½ **1998 (PG)** Thirteen-year-old Anna Frankenstein is impressed with her eccentric scientist uncle, Victor, but things get a little spooky when she meets his latest creation. Yes, Uncle Vic is still working on creating a man from stitched together parts of dead bodies and this time his creature has a human soul. DeCoteau used the pseudonym Julian Breen. **70m/C VHS, DVD.** Jaason Simmons, Ben Gould, Haven Burton, Ethan Wilde; ***D:*** David DeCoteau. **VIDEO**

Frankenstein Sings...The Movie 🦴½ **1995 (PG)** Musical horror spoof finds young couple seeking shelter in a creepy mansion that happens to belong to Dr. Frankenstein. Also visiting (it just happens to be Halloween) are Mr. and Mrs. Dracula, the Wolfman and his mother, and the mummified remains of Elvis and his agent. Some amusing one-liners and mediocre music; adapted from a stage musical. **83m/C VHS.** Candace Cameron, Ian Bohen, Jimmie Walker, Anthony Crivello; ***D:*** Joel Cohen, Alec Sokolow.

Frankenstein Unbound 🦴🦴🦴 *Roger Corman's Frankenstein Unbound* **1990 (R)** Corman returns after nearly 20 years with a better than ever B movie. Hurt plays Dr. Joseph Buchanan, a nuclear physicist time traveler who accidentally goes back to 1816 and runs into Lord Byron (Patric), Percy (Hutchence) and Mary (Fonda) Shelley and their neighbor Baron Frankenstein (Julia) and his monster (Brimble). But Frankenstein is not done experimenting just yet. Great acting, fun special effects, intelligent and subtle message, with a little sex to keep things going. **86m/C VHS.** John Hurt, Raul Julia, Bridget Fonda, Jason Patric, Michael Hutchence, Catherine Rabett, Nick Brimble, Catherine Corman, Mickey Knox; ***D:*** Roger Corman; ***W:*** F.X. Feeney, Roger Corman; ***C:*** Michael Scott, Armando Nannuzzi; ***M:*** Carl Davis; ***V:*** Terri Treas.

Frankenstein's Daughter 🦴 *She Monster of the Night* **1958** Demented descendant of Dr. Frankenstein sets a den of gruesome monsters loose, including the corpse of a teenaged girl he revitalizes, as he continues the mad experiments of his forefathers. **85m/B VHS, DVD.** John Ashley, Sandra Knight, Donald Murphy, Felix Locher, Sally Todd, Harry Wilson; ***D:*** Richard Cunha; ***C:*** Meredith Nicholson; ***M:*** Nicholas Carras.

Frankenstein's Great Aunt Tillie woof! **1983** An excrutiatingly bad send up of the Frankenstein saga with the good doctor about to be evicted from his estate because of back taxes. Gabor appears for a few seconds in a flashback. **99m/C VHS.** Donald Pleasence, Yvonne Furneaux, Aldo Ray, June Wilkinson, Zsa Zsa Gabor; ***D:*** Myron G. Gold; ***W:*** Myron G. Gold.

Frankenweenie 🦴🦴½ **1984 (PG)** "Frankenweenie" is the tale of a lovable spunky dog named Sparky and his owner, Victor Frankenstein. When Sparky is hit by a car, Victor brings him back to life through the use of electric shock. This affectionate parody of "Frankenstein" launched renowned director Burton's career. **27m/B VHS.** Shelley Duvall, Daniel Stern, Barret Oliver, Paul Bartel, Joseph Maher, Jason Hervey; ***D:*** Tim Burton; ***W:*** Tim Burton; ***C:*** Thomas Ackerman; ***M:*** Michael Convertino, David Newman.

Frankie and Johnny 🦴 **1936** Based on the song of the same name, famed torch singer Morgan portrays a singer in a bordello who shoots her unfaithful lover. Release was delayed two years by the Hays Office's intervention in how a house of prostitution could be portrayed on screen. Too bad they reached an agreement. Not even Morgan's rendition of the title song redeems this. **68m/B VHS.** Helen Morgan, Chester Morris; ***D:*** Chester Erskine.

Frankie and Johnny 🦴🦴½ **1965** Elvis is a riverboat gambler/singer with lousy luck until Kovack changes the odds. This upsets his girlfriend Douglas who shoots him (but not fatally). Elvis wears period costumes, but this is otherwise similar to his contemporary films. ♫When the Saints Go Marching In; Look Out Broadway; Shout It Out; Frankie and Johnny; Chesay; Come Along; Petunia; The Gardner's Daughter; Beginner's Luck. **88m/C VHS, DVD, Wide.** Elvis Presley, Donna Douglas, Harry (Henry) Morgan, Audrey Christie, Anthony Eisley, Sue Ane Langdon, Robert Strauss, Nancy Kovack; ***D:*** Fred de Cordova; ***W:*** Alex Gottlieb; ***C:*** Jacques "Jack" Marquette; ***M:*** Fred Karger.

Frankie and Johnny 🦴🦴🦴 **1991 (R)** Ex-con gets a job as a short-order cook and falls for a world-weary waitress. She doesn't believe in romance, but finally gives into his pleas for a chance and finds out he may not be such a bad guy after all. Nothing can make Pfeiffer dowdy enough for this role, but she and Pacino are charming together. In a change of pace role, Nelligan has fun as a fellow waitress who loves men. Based on the play "Frankie and Johnny in the Clair de Lune" by McNally who also wrote the screenplay. **117m/C VHS, DVD, Wide.** Al Pacino, Michelle Pfeiffer, Hector Elizondo, Nathan Lane, Kate Nelligan, Jane Morris, Greg Lewis, Al Fann, K. Callan, Phil Leeds, Tracy Reiner, Dey Young; ***D:*** Garry Marshall; ***W:*** Terrance McNally; ***C:*** Dante Spinotti; ***M:*** Marvin Hamlisch. British Acad. '91: Support. Actress (Nelligan); Natl. Bd. of Review '91: Support. Actress (Nelligan).

Frankie Starlight 🦴🦴½ **1995 (R)** Bernadette (Parillaud) leaves France after WWII, smuggled aboard an American troop ship. By the time the ship reaches Ireland, she's pregnant and gives birth to her dwarf son, Frankie, in Dublin. She's taken in by the family of customs officer Jack Kelly (Byrne), who instills in the boy a lifelong love of the stars. The adult Frankie (Walker) becomes a celebrity when he writes a novel combining his obsession with the cosmos and his mother's erotic history. Raymo adapts from his 1993 novel "The Dork of Cork." Great performances by both Pentony and Walker as the child and adult Frankies. **100m/C VHS.** *IR* Corban Walker, Alan Pentony, Gabriel Byrne, Anne Parillaud, Matt Dillon, Georgina Cates, Darbnia Molloy, Niall Toibin, Rudi Davies; ***D:*** Michael Lindsay-Hogg; ***W:*** Chet Raymo, Ronan O'Leary; ***C:*** Paul Laufer; ***M:*** Elmer Bernstein.

Frantic 🦴🦴🦴 *Elevator to the Gallows; Ascenseur pour L'Echafaud* **1958** From Louis Malle comes one of the first French New Wave film noir dramas. A man kills his boss with the connivance of the employer's wife, his lover, and makes it look like suicide. Meanwhile, teenagers have used his car and gun in the murder of a tourist couple and he is indicted for that crime. Their perfectly planned murder begins to unravel into a panic-stricken nightmare. A suspenseful and captivating drama. Director Malle's first feature film. Musical score by jazz legend Miles Davis. **92m/B VHS, 8mm.** *FR* Maurice Ronet, Jeanne Moreau, Georges Poujouly; ***D:*** Louis Malle; ***C:*** Henri Decae; ***M:*** Miles Davis.

Frantic 🦴🦴🦴 **1988 (R)** While in Paris, an American surgeon's wife is kidnapped when she inadvertantly picks up the wrong suitcase. Her kidnappers want their hidden tresure returned, which forces the husband into the criminal underground and into unexpected heroism when he seeks to rescue her. Contrived ending weakens on the whole, but Polanski is still master of the dark film thriller. **120m/C VHS, DVD.** Harrison Ford, Betty Buckley, John Mahoney, Emmanuelle Seigner, Jimmie Ray Weeks, Yorgo Voyagis, David Huddleston, Gerard Klein; ***D:*** Roman Polanski; ***W:*** Roman Polanski, Gerard Brach; ***C:*** Witold Sobocinski; ***M:*** Ennio Morricone.

Franz 🦴 **1972** A French mercenary and an insecure woman struggle with a doomed love affair. In French with English subtitles. **90m/C VHS.** *FR* Jacques Brel; ***D:*** Jacques Brel.

Frasier the Sensuous Lion 🦴🦴 *Frasier the Lovable Lion* **1973 (PG)** A zoology professor is able to converse with Frasier, a lion known for his sexual stamina and whose potency is coveted by a billionaire (shadow of monkey glands rejuvenation therapy). A fairly typical, if slightly risque, talking critter film. **97m/C VHS.** Michael Callan, Katherine Justice, Frank De Kova, Malachi Throne, Victor Jory, Peter Lorre Jr., Marc Lawrence; ***D:*** Pat Shields.

Fraternity Vacation 🦴 **1985 (R)** Two college fraternity men show a nerd the greatest time of his life while he's on vacation in Palm Springs. **95m/C VHS, DVD, Wide.** Stephen Geoffreys, Sheree J. Wilson, Cameron Dye, Leigh McCloskey, Tim Robbins, Matt McCoy, Amanda Bearse, John Vernon, Nita Talbot, Barbara Crampton, Kathleen Kinmont, Max Wright, Julie Payne, Franklin Ajaye, Charles Rocket, Britt Ekland; ***D:*** James Frawley; ***W:*** Lindsay Harrison; ***C:*** Paul Ryan; ***M:*** Brad Fiedel.

Frauds 🦴½ **1993 (R)** Collins is an immoral insurance investigator who takes his victims for everything he can. Then he meets a couple who are out to beat him at his own game. **94m/C VHS.** Phil Collins, Hugo Weaving, Josephine Byrnes.

Freaked 🦴🦴 *Hideous Mutant Freekz* **1993 (PG-13)** Bizarre little black comedy throws everything at the screen, hoping some of the gross-out humor will prove amusing (and some does). Greedy TV star Ricky Coogin (Winter) agrees to be the spokesman for E.E.S. Corporation, which markets a toxic green slime fertilizer to the third world. He's sent to South America to promote the product and is captured by the mad scientist proprietor (Quaid) of a mysterious sideshow, who douses him with the fertilizer. Before you know it he's an oozing half-man, half-beast, perfect to join other freaks as the latest attraction. Lots of yucky makeup. Reeves has an uncredited cameo as the Dog Boy. **80m/C VHS.** Alex Winter, Randy Quaid, Megan Ward, Michael Stoyanov, Brooke Shields, William Sadler, Derek McGrath, Alex Zuckerman, Karyn Malchus, Mr. T, Morgan Fairchild; ***Cameos:*** Keanu Reeves, Tom Stern, Tim Burns; ***D:*** Alex Winter, Tom Stern; ***W:*** Alex Winter, Tom Stern, Tim Burns; ***C:*** Jamie Thompson, Jene Omens; ***M:*** Kevin Kiner; ***V:*** Bob(cat) Goldthwait.

The Freakmaker 🦴🦴 *Mutations; The Mutation* **1973 (R)** Mad professor attempts to breed plants with humans in his lab and has the usual bizarre results. Experiments that fail go to Dunn, a dwarf who runs a freak show. Shamelessly includes real freaks as if plot was not strange enough. **90m/C VHS.** *GB* Donald Pleasence, Tom Baker, Brad Harris, Julie Ege, Michael Dunn, Jill Haworth, Olga Anthony, Lisa Collings, Scott Antony; ***D:*** Jack Cardiff; ***W:*** Edward Andrew (Santos Alcocer) Mann, Robert D. Weinbach; ***C:*** Paul Beeson; ***M:*** Basil Kirchin.

Freaks 🦴🦴🦴½ *Nature's Mistakes; Forbidden Love; The Monster Show* **1932** The infamous, controversial, cult-horror classic about a band of circus freaks that exact revenge upon a beautiful aerialist and her strongman lover after enduring humiliation and exploitation. Based on Ted Robbins story "Spurs." It was meant to out-horror "Frankenstein" but was so successful that it was repeatedly banned. Browning's film may be a shocker but it is never intended to be exploitative since the "Freaks" are the only compassionate, loyal, and loving people around. **66m/B VHS.** Wallace Ford, Olga Baclanova, Leila Hyams, Roscoe Ates, Harry Earles, Henry Victor, Daisy Earles, Madame Rose (Dion) Dione, Daisy Hilton, Violet Hilton; ***D:*** Tod Browning; ***W:*** Al Boasberg, Willis Goldbeck, Leon Gordon, Edgar Allen Woolf; ***C:*** Merritt B. Gerstad. Natl. Film Reg. '94.

Freakshow 🦴🦴 **1995 (R)** Two teens wander into the sideshow at a local carnival and meet the Freakmaster (Hansen), whose grisly exhibits have equally grisly stories to tell. Campy horror with routine special effects. **102m/C VHS.** Gunnar Hansen, Veronica Carlson, Brian D. Kelly, Shannon Michelle Parsons; ***D:*** William Cooke, Paul Talbot.

Freaky Friday 🦴🦴½ **1976 (G)** A housewife and her teenage daughter inadvertently switch bodies and each then tries to carry on the other's normal routine. Mary Rodgers' popular book is brought to the screen with great charm in this above average Disney film. **95m/C VHS.** Barbara Harris, Jodie Foster, Patsy Kelly, John Astin, Dick Van Patten, Ruth Buzzi, Kaye Ballard, Charlene Tilton, James Van Patten; ***D:*** Gary Nelson; ***W:*** Mary Rogers.

Freddie the Frog 🦴🦴½ *Freddie as F.R.O.7* **1992 (G)** Prince Frederick's life is shattered when his father is killed by his evil Aunt Messina, who wants to rule the kingdom. She even changes Frederick into a frog—but he manages to escape her with the help of friendly sea monster Nessie. But Freddie discovers that he has also been given super-frog powers, just in time to save Britain's landmarks, which are disappearing thanks to Aunt Messina's spells. **72m/C VHS.** *GB* ***D:*** Jon Acevski; ***W:*** Jon Acevski, David Ashton; ***V:*** Ben Kingsley, Nigel Hawthorne, Jenny Agutter, John Sessions, Brian Blessed, Billie Whitelaw, Jonathan Pryce, Phyllis Logan, Michael Hordern; ***Nar:*** James Earl Jones.

Freddy Got Fingered woof! **2001 (R)** Green, making his feature directorial debut, is our hero, Gord, a dedicated slacker who refuses to get a job and move out of his father's (Torn) house. Green the director loves Green the "actor," almost as much as he loves human and animal bodily fluids—all of them. What he does to horses and elephants will poison forever your fond memories of trips to the zoo. He also enjoys oral sex, performed by a wheelchair-bound girlfriend, of course. Then, just to appeal to the family-values crowd, he falsely accuses his overbearing father of sexually abusing his younger brother. Taken in small doses, Green's act can induce "I can't believe I'm laughing at this"-type chuckles, but an hour and a half could cause permanent brain damage. Look what its apparently done to him! To say "Freddy" wallows in the gutter is to besmirch the gutter's good name. **88m/C VHS, DVD, Wide.** *US* Tom Green, Rip Torn, Harland Williams, Eddie Kaye Thomas, Julie Hagerty, Anthony Michael Hall, Marisa Coughlan; ***D:*** Tom Green; ***W:*** Tom Green, Derek Harvie; ***C:*** Mark Irwin; ***M:*** Mike Simpson. Golden Raspberries '01: Worst Picture, Worst Actor (Green), Worst Director (Green), Worst Screenplay.

Freddy's Dead: The Final Nightmare 🦴🦴 *A Nightmare on Elm Street 6: Freddy's Dead* **1991 (R)** Freddy's daughter journeys to Springwood, Ohio, to put a stop to her father's evil ways. Will she be able to destroy this maniac, or is a new reign of terror just beginning? The sixth film in the "Nightmare" series; followed by "Wes Craven's New Nightmare." **96m/C VHS, DVD.** Robert Englund, Lisa Zane, Shon Greenblatt, Lezlie (Dean) Deane, Ricky Dean Logan, Breckin Majer, Yaphet Kotto, Elinor Donahue, Roseanne, Johnny Depp, Alice Cooper, Tom Arnold; ***D:*** Rachel Talalay; ***W:*** Michael De Luca; ***C:*** Declan Quinn.

Free Amerika Broadcasting **1989** A drama about an alternate reality in which Richard Nixon was assassinated, leaving Spiro Agnew president. As a result, the country turns to violent revolution. **80m/C VHS.** Brian Kincaid; ***D:*** Dean Wilson.

Free and Easy 🦴🦴½ *Easy Go* **1930** Keaton plays the incompetent manager of a beauty contest winner (Page) from Gopher City, Kansas. Page and her overbearing mother, accompanied by Keaton, go to Hollywood to make the girl a star. They gate-crash the MGM studio where all cause havoc and it turns out Keaton is the one who lands in front of the cameras (Page has to settle for romancing Montgomery). Provides a behind-the-scenes look at the MGM studio, with a number of MGM stars making cameo appearances. **92m/B VHS.** Buster Keaton, Anita Page, Robert Montgomery, Trixie Friganza, Fred Niblo; ***Cameos:*** Cecil B. DeMille, Jackie Coogan, Lionel Barrymore, William Haines; ***D:*** Edward Sedgwick.

Free Enterprise 🦴🦴½ **1998 (R)** Funny and inventive semi-autobiographical tale of a couple of aspiring filmmakers facing thirty without a clue about becoming adults. Schlock screenwriter Robert (Weigel) and best bud, film editor Mark (McCormack), filter their existence through sci fi and '70s TV shows. The two are completely geeked by a chance meeting with their "Star Trek" idol William Shatner (who slyly pokes fun at his own persona), who offers them enouragement. The duo actually make some attempts at that grown-up thing by the clever finale. **114m/C VHS, DVD.** Eric McCormack, Rafer Weigel, William Shatner, Audie England, Patrick Van Horn, Jonathan Slavin, Phil LaMarr, Deborah Van Valkenburgh; ***D:*** Robert Meyer Burnett; ***W:*** Robert Meyer Burnett, Mark Altman; ***C:*** Charles L. Barbee; ***M:*** Scott Spock.

Free Grass 🦴 *Scream Free!* **1969** A gang of thoughtless hippie drug smugglers and abusers escape from the police, drink acid-spiked wine, shoot each other, and have love-ins. **82m/C VHS.** Russ Tamblyn, Richard Beymer, Casey Kasem, Lana Wood, Warren Finnerty.

Free Money 🦴🦴 **1999 (R)** Kinda dumb buddy comedy finds Bud (Sheen) and Larry (Church) stuck in North Dakota and forced to marry the twin daughters of local prison warden The Swede (Brando, overacting as usual). The two losers decide the best way to get away from their father-in-law's watchful eye is to rob a train loaded with cash. **94m/C VHS, DVD.** Charlie Sheen, Marlon Brando, Donald Sutherland, Thomas Haden Church, Mira Sorvino, David Arquette; ***D:*** Yves Simoneau; ***W:*** Tony Peck, Joseph Brutsman; ***C:*** David Franco.

Free of Eden 🦴🦴½ **1998** Successful New York businessman Poitier reluctantly agrees to mentor a troubled inner-city teeanged girl (played by Poitier's daughter). **97m/C VHS, DVD.** Sidney Poitier, Sydney Tamiia Poitier, Phylicia Rashad, Robert Hooks; ***D:*** Leon Ichaso; ***W:*** Delle Chatman, Yule Caise; ***C:*** Claudio Chea; ***M:*** Terence Blanchard. **CABLE**

Free Ride 🦴 **1986 (R)** A kooky kid steals a sportscar to impress a girl, and gets involved with local hoods. They chase each other around. **92m/C VHS.** Gary Hershberger, Reed Rudy, Dawn Schneider, Peter DeLuise, Brian MacGregor; ***W:*** Robert Bell, Ron Zwang.

A Free Soul 🦴🦴½ **1931** Tippling litigator Barrymore helps low-life mobster Gable beat a murder rap, only to discover the hood has stolen his daughter's heart. Bargaining with his ditzy daughter, he vows to eschew the bottle if she'll stay away from good-for-nothing Gable. Directed by Brown, best known for his work with Garbo, and based on the memoirs of Adela Rogers St. John. The final courtroom scene—a cloak-and-gavel classic—cinched Barrymore's Oscar. Remade with Liz Taylor as "The Girl Who Had Everything" (although, ironically, the earlier version is the racier of the two). **94m/B VHS.** Norma Shearer, Leslie Howard, Lionel Barrymore, Clark Gable, James Gleason, Lucy Beaumont; ***D:*** Clarence Brown; ***C:*** William H. Daniels. Oscars '31: Actor (Barrymore).

Free to Love 🦴🦴 **1925** Screen idol Bow plays a young woman, fresh out of prison, who is taken in by a kindly, affluent patron. But, as the silent drama axiom would have it, there's no escaping the past, and she's forced to defend her former life when her guardian is murdered. **61m/B VHS.** Clara Bow, Donald Keith, Raymond (Ray) McKee; ***D:*** Frank O'Connor.

Free, White, and 21 🦴🦴 **1962** A black motel owner is accused of raping a white civil rights worker. Produced in a "pseudo-documentary" form which sometimes drags. **104m/B VHS.** Frederick O'Neal, Annalena Lund, George Edgely, John Hicks, Hugh Crenshaw, George Russell; ***D:*** Larry Buchanan.

Free Willy 🦴🦴½ **1993 (PG)** Sentimental story about a 12-year-old runaway (Richter) who befriends a whale. Should appeal to children for its heartwarming story and delightful sea acrobatics. An electronically operated stand-in whale was used for far-off shots; a domesticated performing whale named Keiko for the close-ups. Director Wincer was known to grumble about the temperamental Keiko during shooting. Suggested viewing for students of animal behavior. Proof that family films can make money, "Free Willy" placed tenth for total boxoffice receipts in 1993. **112m/C VHS, DVD, 8mm, Wide.** Jason James Richter, Lori Petty, Jayne Atkinson, August Schellenberg, Michael Madsen; ***D:*** Simon Wincer; ***W:*** Keith A. Walker, Corey Blechman; ***C:*** Robbie Greenberg; ***M:*** Basil Poledouris. MTV Movie Awards '94: Song ("Will You Be There").

Free Willy 2: The Adventure Home 🦴🦴½ **1995 (PG)** While camping in the Pacific Northwest, Jesse is reunited with his orca-pal Willy, who has found a new home along with his whale siblings. But an offshore oil spill separates Willy from his family and threatens their lives, so his human friends must once again come to the rescue. All the principal characters are back, except for Willy (real name Keiko), who is recuperating from a skin virus in Mexico. Animatronics and Gump-like digital effects were used to replicate the real Willy. **98m/C VHS.** Jason James Richter, Michael Madsen, Jayne Atkinson, August Schellenberg, Jon Tenney, Elizabeth Pena; ***D:*** Dwight Little; ***W:*** Corey Blechman, John Mattson; ***C:*** Laszlo Kovacs; ***M:*** Basil Poledouris.

Free Willy 3: The Rescue 🦴🦴½ **1997 (PG)** Isn't this poor whale ever going to be left in peace? This time around an illegal whaling operation threatens Willie and his orca pod. But 17-year-old Jesse (Richter), who has a summer job as a whale tracker on a research vessel, is determined to rescue his friend, aided by 10-year-old Max (Berry), who's horrified to discover his commercial fisherman father (Kilpatrick) is one of the whalers. **86m/C VHS.** Jason James Richter, Vincent Berry, August Schellenberg, Annie Corley, Patrick Kilpatrick; ***D:*** Sam Pillsbury; ***W:*** John Mattson; ***C:*** Tobias Schliessler; ***M:*** Cliff Eidelman.

Freebie & the Bean 🦴½ **1974 (R)** Two San Francisco cops nearly ruin the city in their pursuit of a numbers-running mobster. Top-flight car chases and low-level, bigoted humor combine. Watch for Valerie Harper's appearance as Arkin's wife. Followed by a flash-in-the-pan TV series. **113m/C VHS, Wide.** Alan Arkin, James Caan, Loretta Swit, Valerie Harper, Jack Kruschen, Mike Kellin; ***D:*** Richard Rush.

Freedom 🦴½ **1981** A young man finds the price of freedom to be very high when he tries to escape from Australian society in a silver Porsche. **102m/C VHS.** Jon Blake, Candy (Candida) Raymond, Jad Capelja, Reg Lye, John Clayton.

Freedom Is Paradise 🦴🦴🦴 **1989** With his mother dead and his father missing, 13-year-old Sasha is growing up in a bleak reform school. Every time he runs away he is caught and severely beaten upon his return. When Sasha learns of his father's whereabouts he sets out on a 1,000 mile journey to the gulag-style prison where is father is being held. Bodrov's directorial debut. In Russian with English subtitles. **75m/C VHS.** *RU* ***D:*** Sergei Bodrov. Montreal World Film Fest. '89: Film.

Freedom Road 🦴🦴 **1979** Drama about a Reconstruction Era ex-slave, portrayed by heavyweight champion Ali, who is elected to the U.S. Senate and subsequently killed while trying to obtain total freedom for his race. Based on a novel by Howard Fast. **186m/C VHS.** Ron O'Neal, Edward Herrmann, John McLiam, Ernest Dixon, Alfre Woodard, Kris Kristofferson, Muhammad Ali; ***D:*** Jan Kadar. **TV**

Freedom Song 🦴🦴🦴 **2000** In Mississippi in 1961, Will Walker (Glover) is a black man both angry and afraid. Civil rights, freedom rights and increasing racial violence make for tense times for the Walker family as teenaged Owen (Shannon) is drawn to organizer Daniel Wall (Curtis-Hall). Complex, conflicted people and situations make for a fine drama. **150m/C VHS.** Danny Glover, Vondie Curtis-Hall, Vicellous Reon Shannon, Loretta Devine, Glynn Turman, Stan Shaw, Michael Jai White, Rae'ven (Alyia Larrymore) Kelly, John Beasley, Jason Weaver, Marcello Thedford, David Strathairn; ***D:*** Phil Alden Robinson; ***W:*** Phil Alden Robinson, Stanley Weiser; ***M:*** James Horner. **CABLE**

Freedom Strike 🦴½ **1998 (R)** Navy pilots Stone and MacDonald are sent on a covert mission to sabotage an Iraqui nuclear reactor before terrorists can use it. **93m/C VHS, DVD.** Michael Dudikoff, Tone Loc, Felicity Waterman; ***D:*** Jerry P. Jacobs. **VIDEO**

Freejack 🦴🦴½ **1992 (R)** Futuristic thriller set in the year 2009, where pollution, the hole in the ozone layer, and the financial gap between the social classes have grown to such horrific proportions that the rich must pillage the past to find young bodies to replace their own. Estevez is a young race car driver whose sudden death makes him an ideal candidate for this bizarre type of surgery. Once transported to the future, he becomes a "Freejack" who must run for his life. Good cast including Jagger and Hopkins brings this one up slightly. Adapted from the novel "Immortality Inc." by Robert Sheckley. **110m/C VHS, DVD, Wide.** Emilio Estevez, Mick Jagger, Rene Russo, Anthony Hopkins, Jonathan Banks, David Johansen, Amanda Plummer, Grand Bush, Frankie Faison, Esai Morales, John Shea; ***D:*** Geoff Murphy; ***W:*** Dan Gilroy, Ronald Shusett, Steven Pressfield; ***C:*** Amir M. Mokri; ***M:*** Michael Boddicker, Trevor Jones.

Freeway 🦴🦴½ **1988 (R)** A nurse attempts to find the obsessive killer who shot her husband. The murderer phones a radio psychiatrist from his car, using Biblical quotes, while cruising for new victims. Okay thriller, based on the L.A. freeway shootings. **91m/C VHS.** Darlanne Fluegel, James Russo, Billy Drago, Richard Belzer, Michael Callan, Steve Franken, Kenneth Tobey, Clint Howard; ***D:*** Francis Delia; ***W:*** Larry Ketron, Darrell Fetty, Francis Delia; ***M:*** Joe Delia.

Freeway 🦴½ **1995 (R)** Grubby modern retelling of "Little Red Riding Hood" finds surly 16-year-old Vanessa (Witherspoon) escaping from her parole officer to avoid foster care when the cops arrest her mom and stepdad. She takes the family car and heads off to grandma's but car trouble on the freeway leads to a ride from the big bad wolf—Bob Wolverton (Sutherland)—a serial killer preying on young women. Lots of lurid unpleasantness. **102m/C VHS, DVD.** Reese Witherspoon, Kiefer Sutherland, Brooke Shields, Wolfgang Bodison, Dan Hedaya, Amanda Plummer, Bokeem Woodbine, Brittany Murphy; ***D:*** Matthew Bright; ***W:*** Matthew Bright; ***C:*** John Thomas; ***M:*** Danny Elfman.

Freeway 2: Confessions of a Trickbaby 🦴 **1999 (R)** The 1995 film was a violent modern update of "Little Red Riding Hood" and the sequel is a twisted fairytale "Hansel and Gretel." Crystal (Lyonne) escapes from juvenile prison with cell buddy Cyclona (Celedonio) and heads to Tijuana where she hopes psychic Sister Gomez (Gallo) can cure her of her compulsion to murder. The body count rises a lot on their journey. As grubby and unappealing as its predecessor. **90m/C VHS, DVD.** Natasha Lyonne, Maria Celedonio, Vincent Gallo, David Alan Grier, Michael T. Weiss, John Landis, Max Perlich; ***D:*** Matthew Bright; ***W:*** Matthew Bright; ***C:*** Joel Ransom; ***M:*** Kennard Ramsey. **VIDEO**

The Freeway Maniac 🦴 **1988 (R)** A low budget thriller about an escaped convict who ends up on a movie set where he continues his former career: murder. Music by former "Doors" guitarist Robby Krieger. **94m/C VHS.** Loren Winters, James Courtney, Shepard Sanders, Donald Hotton; ***D:*** Paul Winters; ***M:*** Robby Krieger.

Freeze-Die-Come to Life 🦴🦴🦴½ *Zamri Oumi Voskresni* **1990** First feature film from Kanevski, who spent eight years in a labor camp before glasnost. The story of two children who overcome the crushing poverty and bleakness of life in a remote mining community with friendship and humor. Beautifully filmed images, fine acting, touching but never overly sentimental story. The title comes from a children's game of tag. In Russian with English subtitles. **105m/B VHS.** *RU* Pavel Nazarov, Dinara Drukarova; ***D:*** Vitaly Kanevski; ***W:*** Vitaly Kanevski; ***C:*** Vladimir Brylyakov; ***M:*** Sergei Banevich.

Freeze Frame 🦴🦴½ **1992** Doherty is a high school TV reporter who's determined to capture a biotech conspiracy on video in this funny, fast-paced action flick. Nothing objectionable here. **78m/C VHS.** Shannen Doherty, Charles Haid, Robyn Douglass, Seth Michaels; ***D:*** William Bindley; ***W:*** William Bindley.

French Can-Can 🦴🦴🦴 *Only the French Can!* **1955** Dramatically sparse but visually stunning depiction of the can-can's revival in Parisian nightclubs. Gabin plays the theatre impressario who discovers laundress Arnoul and decides to turn her into the dancing star of his new revue at the Moulin Rouge. In French with English subtitles. **93m/C VHS.** *FR* Jean Gabin, Francoise Arnoul, Maria Felix, Jean-Roger Caussimon, Edith Piaf, Patachou; ***D:*** Jean Renoir.

The French Connection 🦴🦴🦴½ **1971 (R)** Popeye Doyle (Hackman) and his partner Buddy Russo (Scheider) are a couple of hard-nosed NYC narcotics detectives who stumble onto what turns out to be one of the biggest narcotics rings of all time, involving French mastermind Alain Charnier (Rey). Cat-and-mouse thriller will keep you on the edge of your seat; contains one of the most exciting chase scenes ever filmed. Hackman's portrayal of Doyle is exact and the teamwork with Scheider special. Based on a true story from the book by Robin Moore. Followed in 1975 by "French Connection 2." **102m/C VHS, DVD, Wide.** Gene Hackman, Roy Scheider, Fernando Rey, Tony LoBianco, Eddie Egan, Sonny Grosso, Marcel Bozzuffi; ***D:*** William Friedkin; ***W:*** Ernest Tidyman; ***C:*** Owen Roizman; ***M:*** Don Ellis.

Oscars '71: Actor (Hackman), Adapt. Screenplay, Director (Friedkin), Film Editing, Picture; AFI '98: Top 100; British Acad. '72: Actor (Hackman); Directors Guild '71: Director (Friedkin); Golden Globes '72: Actor—Drama (Hackman), Director (Friedkin), Film—Drama; Natl. Bd. of Review '71: Actor (Hackman); N.Y. Film Critics '71: Actor (Hackman); Writers Guild '71: Adapt. Screenplay.

French Connection 2 🦴🦴🦴 **1975 (R)** New York policeman "Popeye" Doyle goes to Marseilles to crack a heroin ring headed by his arch nemesis, Frog One, whom he failed to stop in the United States. Dour, super-gritty sequel to the 1971 blockbuster, and featuring one of Hackman's most uncompromising performances. **118m/C VHS, DVD, Wide.** Gene Hackman, Fernando Rey, Bernard Fresson; ***D:*** John Frankenheimer; ***W:*** Robert Dillon; ***C:*** Claude Renoir; ***M:*** Don Ellis.

The French Detective 🦴🦴🦴 **1975** Two detectives, one an old-time tough guy and the other a young cynic, are after a ruthless politician and his pet hood. Grim but entertaining. **90m/C VHS.** *FR* Lino Ventura, Patrick Dewaere, Victor Lanoux; ***D:*** Pierre Granier-Deferre.

French Exit 🦴🦴 **1997 (R)** Another "meet cute" Hollywood romantic comedy. Neophyte screenwriters David Lake (Silverman) and Zina Hart (Amick) have a fender bender in an L.A. intersection. Flirtatious sparks fly amid their bickering but later they discover they're vying for the same big break script job. So will professional rivalry destroy the romantic fire? What do you think. **88m/C VHS.** Kurt Fuller, Beth Broderick, Jonathan Silverman, Madchen Amick, Molly Hagen; ***D:*** Daphna Kastner; ***W:*** Daphna Kastner, Michael Alan Lerner; ***C:*** Geza Sinkovics; ***M:*** Alex Wurman.

French Fried Vacation **1979** Zany antics erupt when a group of unattached and consenting adults vacation in Africa. French with English subtitles. **90m/C VHS.** Josiane Balasko, Michel Blanc, Mariann (Marie-Anne) Chazel; ***D:*** Patrice Leconte.

French Intrigue 🦴🦴 **197? (R)** International agents track drug lords from the U.S. to France in a so-so spy thriller. **90m/C VHS.** Jane Birkin, Curt Jurgens.

French Kiss 🦴🦴½ **1995 (PG-13)** Ultra cute Kate (Ryan) has a fear of flying but she's more afraid of losing her fiance (Hutton) to a newly met French babe. She jets off to Paris and on the way meets a dashing, but disheveled, French rogue (Kline). What happens next is predictable, but amusing just the same. Plot drags a bit in the middle, but the scenery and banter between Ryan and Kline are a pleasant enough diversion. Kline is at his charming best, while Ryan is typically perky. Watch for Spielvogel's stereotypically rude French hotel concierge. He's a hoot. **111m/C VHS, DVD, Wide.** Meg Ryan, Kevin Kline, Timothy Hutton, Jean Reno, Francois Cluzet, Renee Humphrey, Michael Riley, Susan Anbeh, Laurent Spielvogel; ***D:*** Lawrence Kasdan; ***W:*** Adam Brooks; ***C:*** Owen Roizman; ***M:*** James Newton Howard.

The French Lesson 🦴🦴½ *The Frog Prince* **1986 (PG)** A romantic British farce from a screenplay by cartoonist Simmonds, dealing with an English girl who goes to school in Paris and finds love. **90m/C VHS.** *GB* Alexandre Sterling, Jane Snowdon; ***D:*** Brian Gilbert; ***W:*** Posy S. Simmonds.

The French Lieutenant's Woman 🦴🦴🦴½ **1981 (R)** Romantic love and tragedy in the form of two parallel stories, that of an 19th-century woman who keeps her mysterious past from the scientist who loves her, and the lead actor and actress in the film of the same story managing an illicit affair on the set. Extraordinary performances and beautifully shot. Based on the John Fowles novel. **124m/C VHS, DVD, Wide.** Meryl Streep, Jeremy Irons, Leo McKern, Lynsey Baxter; ***D:*** Karel Reisz; ***W:*** Harold Pinter; ***C:*** Freddie Francis; ***M:*** Carl Davis. British Acad. '81: Actress (Streep); Golden Globes '82: Actress—Drama (Streep); L.A. Film Critics '81: Actress (Streep).

The French Line 🦴🦴 **1954** A millionairess beauty travels incognito while trying to sort out which men are after her money, and which ones aren't. The 3-D presentation of Russell's physique in skimpy costumes earned this the condemnation of the Catholic Legion of Decency, which pumped the boxoffice even higher. Lacks the charm of "Gentlemen Prefer Blonds," which it imitates. ♫Comment Allez-Vous; Well, I'll Be Switched; Any Gal From Texas; What Is This That I Feel?; With A Kiss; By Madame Fuelle; Wait Till You See Paris; Poor Andre; The French Line. **102m/C VHS.** Jane Russell, Gilbert Roland, Craig Stevens, Kim Novak, Arthur Hunnicutt, Scott Elliott, Joi Lansing; ***D:*** Lloyd Bacon.

French Postcards 🦴🦴 **1979 (PG)** Three American students study all aspects of French culture when they spend their junior year of college at the Institute of French Studies in Paris. By the same writers who penned "American Graffiti" a few years earlier. **95m/C VHS.** Miles Chapin, Blanche Baker, Valerie Quennessen, Debra Winger, Mandy Patinkin, Marie-France Pisier; ***D:*** Willard Huyck; ***W:*** Gloria Katz, Willard Huyck.

French Quarter 🦴🦴½ **1978 (R)** A dual story about a young girl in the modern-day French Quarter of New Orleans who is also the reincarnation of a turn-of-the-century prostitute. Everyone gets to play two roles but this film is more curiosity than anything else. **101m/C VHS.** Bruce Davison, Virginia Mayo, Lindsay Bloom, Alisha Fontaine, Lance LeGault, Anne Michelle; ***D:*** Dennis Kane.

French Quarter Undercover 🦴 **1985 (R)** Two undercover cops in New Orleans thwart a terrorist plot aimed at the World's Fair. **84m/C VHS.** Michael Parks, Bill Holiday; ***D:*** Joe Catalanotto.

French Silk 🦴🦴½ **1994 (PG-13)** Homicide detective (Horsley) falls for a lingerie designer (Lucci) who's a murder suspect. Filmed on location in New Orleans. Made for TV production with additional footage. "R" rating is for nudity (not Lucci's). Based on the novel by Sandra Brown. **90m/C VHS.** Susan Lucci, Lee Horsley, Shari Belafonte, R. Lee Ermey, Sarah Marshall, Bobby Hosea, Jim Metzler, Joe Warfield, Paul Rosenberg; ***D:*** Noel Nosseck. **TV**

The French Touch 🦴🦴½ **1954** Fernandel stars in this French farce about a shepherd who decides to open his own clip joint as a hairdresser and finds himself a hit among the Parisiennes. Fair to middling comedy. **84m/B VHS.** *FR* Fernandel, Renee Devillers, Georges Chamarat; ***D:*** Jean Boyer.

French Twist 🦴🦴½ *Bushwhacked; Gazon Maudit* **1995 (R)** Romantic comedy about housewife Loli (Abril), tiredly coping with her realtor/husband Laurent (Chabat) and their two sons. Then Loli meets appealing stranger Marijo (Balasko), a very matter-of-fact lesbian, and when she discovers her hubby is a chronic philanderer, Loli gets revenge by inviting Marijo to move in with them. Laurent realizes he loves his wife but she's having too much fun and there's finally an interesting showdown between Laurent and Marijo over Loli. The French title, which translates literally to "Cursed Lawn," is an old slang term for lesbian. French with subtitles. **100m/C VHS.** *FR* Victoria Abril, Alain Chabat, Josiane Balasko, Ticky Holgado; ***D:*** Josiane Balasko; ***W:*** Josiane Balasko, Telsche Boorman; ***C:*** Gerard de Battista; ***M:*** Manuel Malou. Cesar '96: Writing.

The French Way 🦴🦴½ **1940** One of the legendary Baker's few films, in which she portrays a Parisian nightclub owner playing matchmaker for a young couple. In French with English subtitles. **72m/B VHS.** *FR* Josephine Baker, Micheline Presle, Georges Marchal; ***D:*** Jacques de Baroncelli.

The French Woman 🦴 **1979 (R)** Soft-core story of blackmail, murder, and sex involving French cabinet ministers mixing passion and politics. From the director of "Emmanuelle." **97m/C VHS.** Francoise Fabian, Klaus Kinski; ***D:*** Just Jaeckin; ***M:*** Serge Gainsbourg.

Frenchman's Creek 🦴🦴½ **1944** Adventure set in the 17th century features English noblewoman Lady Dona (Fontaine) fleeing her spineless husband Harry St. Columb (Forbes) and his lecherous friend, Lord Rockingham (Rathbone). She finds a Frenchman's ship anchored in a creek off her country estate and becomes dazzled by its dashing pirate captain (de Cordova). Unfortunately, the pirate is also a spy (since the Frenchies and the Brits are fighting as usual) and Rockingham discovers their secrets. When the Frenchman is captured, Lady Dona risks all to rescue him. Based on the novel by Daphne du Maurier and remade for British TV in 1998. **112m/C VHS.** Joan Fontaine, Arturo de Cordova, Basil Rathbone, Ralph Forbes, Nigel Bruce, Cecil Kellaway, Moyna MacGill; ***D:*** Mitchell Leisen; ***W:*** Talbot Jennings; ***C:*** George Barnes; ***M:*** Victor Young. **TV**

Frenchman's Creek 🦴🦴½ **1998** Lady Dona St. Columb (Fitzgerald) is bored both with London society and her husband, Sir Harry (Fleet), so she and her children head for her family's estate on the Cornish coast. There, Dona discovers dashing French privateer, Jean Aubrey (Delon), is using a nearby cove to anchor his ship while he spies on the English. Dona and the pirate get very, very close and she decides to help him outwit the authorities. But soon Dona must choose between passion and duty. **120m/C VHS.** *GB* Tara Fitzgerald, Anthony Delon, Tim Dutton, James Fleet, Danny Webb, Jeremy Child; ***D:*** Ferdinand Fairfax; ***W:*** Patrick Harbinson; ***C:*** Chris Seager. **TV**

Frenchman's Farm 🦴½ **1987 (R)** A young woman witnesses a killing at a deserted farmhouse. When she tells the police, they tell her that the murder happened 40 years before. Average thriller that probably won't keep you on the edge of your seat. **90m/C VHS.** *AU* Tracey Tanish, David Reyne, John Meillon, Norman Kaye, Tui Bow; ***D:*** Ron Way.

Frenzy 🦴🦴½ *Latin Quarter* **1946** A sculptor, pushed over the brink of sanity when he discovers that his wife is having an affair, turns to his art for solace...and seals his wife's corpse in a statue. Creepy. **75m/B VHS.** *GB* Derrick DeMarney, Frederick Valk, Joan Greenwood, Joan Seton, Valentine Dyall, Martin Miller; ***D:*** Vernon Sewell; ***W:*** Vernon Sewell.

Frenzy 🦴🦴🦴 **1972 (R)** The only film in which Hitchcock was allowed to totally vent the violence and perverse sexuality of his distinctive vision, in a story about a strangler stalking London women in the late '60s. Finch plays the convicted killer-only he's innocent and must escape prison to find the real killer. McGowen is wonderful as the put-upon police inspector. A bit dated, but still ferociously hostile and cunningly executed. **116m/C VHS, DVD, Wide.** *GB* Jon Finch, Barry Foster, Barbara Leigh-Hunt, Anna Massey, Alec McCowen, Vivien Merchant, Billie Whitelaw, Jean Marsh, Bernard Cribbins, Michael Bates, Rita Webb, Jimmy Gardner, Clive Swift, Madge Ryan, George Tovey, Noel Johnson; ***D:*** Alfred Hitchcock; ***W:*** Anthony Shaffer; ***C:*** Gilbert Taylor; ***M:*** Ronald Goodwin.

Frequency 🦴🦴½ **2000 (PG-13)** In 1999, New York cop John (Caviezel) finds he can communicate with his dead father (Quaid) in 1969 through dad's old ham radio. Since his father was a fireman who died in a warehouse fire almost exactly 30 years ago, John decides to tell him how not to get killed. This leads to changes in the present (messing with the past always does), including the murder of John's mother by a serial killer. Father and son must solve and prevent the killings in the past and the present using their respective skills and, amazingly, John's knowledge of the 1969 World Series. It's all very convoluted and ridiculous (especially the ending), but the underlying sentiment, and the fine work of Caviezel and Quaid make it easy to suspend disbelief and go along for the ride. **117m/C VHS, DVD, Wide.** Dennis Quaid, James Caviezel, Elizabeth Mitchell, Andre Braugher, Shawn Doyle, Noah Emmerich, Jordan Bridges, Melissa Errico, Daniel Henson; ***W:*** Toby Emmerich; ***C:*** Alar Kivilo; ***M:*** Michael Kamen.

Fresh 🦴🦴½ **1994 (R)** Intelligent 12-year-old boy runs heroin in the morning and sells crack after school in a tough Brooklyn neighborhood. Enterprising young man draws life lessons from chess-hustler father Jackson and heroin-dealing mentor Esposito, so he looks for a way out of the dead-end business. First time director Yakin plays it straight, foregoing the usual Hollywood-style rap and automatic weapons approach to convey the message that circumstances can kill innocence just as effectively as a bullet. Startling but subdued atmosphere allows the plot and characters to become more complicated than first suspected. Excellent performance by newcomer Nelson as the kid. **114m/C VHS, DVD.** *FR* Samuel L. Jackson, Giancarlo Esposito, Sean Nelson, N'Bushe Wright, Ron Brice, Jean LaMarre, Luis Lantigua, Yul Vazquez, Cheryl Freeman; ***D:*** Boaz Yakin; ***W:*** Boaz Yakin; ***C:*** Adam Holender. Ind. Spirit '95: Debut Perf. (Nelson); Sundance '94: Special Jury Prize, Filmmakers Trophy.

Fresh Horses 🦴🦴 **1988 (PG-13)** A wrong-side-of-the-tracks Depression-era romance. McCarthy is the engaged college boy who falls for backwoods girl Ringwald, who turns out to have a destructive secret. **92m/C VHS.** Molly Ringwald, Andrew McCarthy, Patti D'Arbanville, Ben Stiller, Viggo Mortensen; ***D:*** David Anspaugh; ***M:*** David Foster.

Fresh Kill 🦴 **1987** A young guy from Chicago goes to Hollywood, and gets mixed up in drugs and murder. **90m/C VHS.** Flint Keller, Patricia Parks; ***D:*** Joseph Merhi. **VIDEO**

The Freshman 🦴🦴🦴🦴 **1925** Country boy Lloyd goes to college and, after many comic tribulations, saves the day with the winning touchdown at the big game and wins the girl of his dreams. This was one of the comedian's most popular films. **75m/B VHS.** Harold Lloyd, Jobyna Ralston, Brooks Benedict, James Anderson, Hazel Keener; ***D:*** Fred Newmeyer, Sam Taylor; ***W:*** Sam Taylor. Natl. Film Reg. '90.

The Freshman 🦴🦴½ **1990 (PG)** Brando, in an incredible parody of his Don Corleone character, makes this work. Broderick is a college student in need of fast cash, and innocent enough to believe that any work is honest. A good supporting cast and a twisty plot keep things interesting. Sometimes heavy handed with its sight gags, but Broderick and Brando push the movie to hilarious conclusion. Don't miss Bert Parks's musical extravaganza. **102m/C VHS, DVD, Wide.** Marlon Brando, Matthew Broderick, Penelope Ann Miller, Maximilian Schell, Bruno Kirby, Frank Whaley, Jon Polito, Paul Benedict, Richard Gant, B.D. Wong, Bert Parks; ***D:*** Andrew Bergman; ***W:*** Andrew Bergman; ***C:*** William A. Fraker; ***M:*** David Newman.

Freud Leaving Home 🦴🦴 **1991** Freud (Roor) is the nickname of 25-year-old Angelique, who lives with her Jewish family in Stockholm. Problems erupt when her sister and brother return home for their mother's 60th birthday and all learn of her fatal illness. The siblings are forced to confront themselves and their relationships with each other and their mother. Swedish with subtitles. **100m/C VHS.** *SW* Gunilla Roor, Ghita Norby, Philip Zanden, Jessica Zanden; ***D:*** Suzanne (Susanne) Bier.

Frida 🦴🦴½ **1984** The life of controversial Mexican painter Frido Kahlo is told via deathbed flashbacks using the artist's paintings to set the scenes. In Spanish with English subtitles. **108m/C VHS.** *SP* Ofelia Medina, Juan Jose Gurrola, Max Kerlow; ***D:*** Paul Leduc.

Friday 🦴🦴½ **1995 (R)** It's "Boyz N' the Hood" meets "Good Times." Ice Cube wrote and stars as Craig in this humorous look into life in the 'hood. Craig's just lost his job and spends his time sitting on the porch with his pot smoking sidekick Smokey (Tucker), with the two getting mixed up in a variety of crazy antics involving their kooky neighbors. The laughs come at the expense of overworn cliches and sterotypical characters, but there's originality in the movie's energy and boldness (i.e. the local dope dealer is also the neighborhood ice cream man). To some, this "Friday" could be something to look forward to. **91m/C VHS, DVD.** Ice Cube, Chris Tucker, Bernie Mac, John Witherspoon, Regina King, Nia Long, Tommy (Tiny) Lister, Anna Maria Horsford, LaWanda Page; ***D:*** F. Gary Gray; ***W:*** DJ Pooh, Ice Cube; ***C:*** Gerry Lively; ***M:*** Frank Fitzpatrick.

Friday Foster ☝½ 1975 (R) A beautiful, young photographer investigates an assassination attempt and uncovers a conspiracy against black politicians. Based on the Chicago Tribune comic strip. **90m/C VHS, DVD, Wide.** Pam Grier, Yaphet Kotto, Thalmus Rasulala, Carl Weathers, Godfrey Cambridge; *D:* Arthur Marks; *W:* Orville H. Hampton; *C:* Harry J. May; *M:* Luchi De Jesus.

Friday the 13th ☝☝ 1980 (R) Notable as among the first in a very long series of slasher flicks, with effects by Tom Savini. A New Jersey camp reopens after it's been closed for 20 years after a history of "accidental" deaths. And the horror begins again. Six would-be counselors arrive to get the place ready. Each is progressively murdered: knifed, speared, and axed. Followed by numerous, equally gory sequels. **95m/C VHS, DVD, Wide.** Betsy Palmer, Adrienne King, Harry Crosby, Laurie Bartram, Mark Nelson, Kevin Bacon, Jeannine Taylor, Robbi Morgan, Peter Brouwer, Walt Gorney; *D:* Sean S. Cunningham; *W:* Victor Miller; *C:* Barry Abrams; *M:* Harry Manfredini.

Friday the 13th, Part 2 woof! 1981 (R) New group of teen camp counselors are gruesomely executed by the still undead Jason. Equally as graphic as the first installment; followed by several more gorefests. **87m/C VHS, DVD, Wide.** Amy Steel, John Furey, Adrienne King, Betsy Palmer, Kirsten Baker, Stu Charno, Warrington Gillette, Walt Gorney, Marta Kober, Bill Randolph, Jack Marks; *D:* Steve Miner; *W:* Ron Kurz; *C:* Peter Stein; *M:* Harry Manfredini.

Friday the 13th, Part 3 woof! 1982 (R) Yet another group of naive counselors at Camp Crystal Lake fall victim to the maniacal Jason. The 3-D effects actually helped lessen the gory effects, but this is still awful. Followed by more disgusting sequels. **96m/C VHS, DVD, Wide.** Dana Kimmell, Paul Kratka, Richard Brooker, Catherine Parks, Jeffrey Rogers, Tracie Savage, Larry Zerner; *D:* Steve Miner; *W:* Martin Kitrosser, Carol Watson; *C:* Gerald Feil.

Friday the 13th, Part 4: The Final Chapter woof! 1984 (R) Jason escapes from the morgue to once again slaughter and annihilate teenagers at a lakeside cottage. Preceded by three earlier "Friday the 13th" films, equally as graphic. The title's also a lie since there's several more sequels to look forward to. **90m/C VHS, DVD, Wide.** Erich Anderson, Judie Aronson, Kimberly Beck, Peter Barton, Tom Everett, Corey Feldman, Crispin Glover, Richard Brooker; *D:* Joseph Zito; *W:* Barney Cohen; *C:* Joao Fernandes.

Friday the 13th, Part 5: A New Beginning woof! 1985 (R) Jason rises from the dead to slice up the residents of a secluded halfway house. The sequels, and the sameness, never stop. See Part 6... **92m/C VHS, DVD, Wide.** John Shepherd, Melanie Kinnaman, Shavar Ross, Richard Young, Juliette Cummins, Corey Feldman, Carol Lacatell, Vernon Washington; *D:* Danny Steinmann; *W:* Danny Steinmann, David M. Cohen, Martin Kitrosser; *C:* Stephen Posey.

Friday the 13th, Part 6: Jason Lives woof! 1986 (R) One of the few youths not butchered by Jason digs him up and discovers he's not (and never will be) dead. Carnage ensues...and the sequels continue. **87m/C VHS, DVD, Wide.** Thom Mathews, Jennifer Cooke, David Kagen, Kerry Noonan, Renee Jones, Tom Fridley, C.J. Graham, Darcy Demoss; *D:* Tom McLoughlin; *W:* Tom McLoughlin; *C:* Jon Kranhouse; *M:* Harry Manfredini.

Friday the 13th, Part 7: The New Blood woof! 1988 (R) A young camper with telekinetic powers accidentally unchains Jason from his underwater lair with the now-familiar results. There's still another bloody sequel to go. **90m/C VHS.** Lar Park Lincoln, Kevin Blair Spirtas, Susan Blu, Terry Kiser, Kane Hodder, Elizabeth Kaitan, John Otrin, Heidi Kozak; *D:* John Carl Buechler; *W:* Daryl Haney; *C:* Paul Elliott.

Friday the 13th, Part 8: Jason Takes Manhattan ☝ 1989 (R) Yet another sequel, with the hockey-masked walking slaughterhouse transported to New York. Most of the previous action in the movie takes place on a cruise ship. This one is less gruesome than others in the series. Followed by "Jason Goes to Hell: The Final Friday." **96m/C VHS.** Kelly Hu, Jensen Daggett, Scott Reeves, Peter Mark Richman, Barbara Bingham, Kane Hodder, Martin Cummins, Sharlene Martin, Vincent Craig Dupree; *D:* Rob Hedden; *W:* Rob Hedden; *C:* Bryan England.

Fridays of Eternity ☝☝ 1981 A romantic comedy about loyalty, fidelity, love, and lovers all with a tinge of the supernatural. In Spanish with English subtitles. **89m/C VHS.** *AR* Thelma Biral, Hector Alterio; *D:* Hector Olivera.

Fried Green Tomatoes ☝☝☝ 1991 (PG-13) Two stories about four women, love, friendship, Southern charm, and eccentricity are untidily held together by wonderful performances. Unhappy, middle-aged Evelyn (Bates), meets the talkative 83-year-old Ninny Threadgoode (Tandy). Ninny reminisces about her Depression-era life in the town of Whistle Stop, Alabama and the two women, Idgie (Masterson) and Ruth (Parker), who ran the local cafe. Back-and-forth narrative as it tracks multiple storylines is occasionally confusing, though strong character development holds interest. Surprising box office hit adapted by Fannie Flagg from her novel "Fried Green Tomatoes at the Whistle Stop Cafe." **130m/C VHS, DVD, Wide.** Kathy Bates, Jessica Tandy, Mary Stuart Masterson, Mary-Louise Parker, Cicely Tyson, Chris O'Donnell, Stan Shaw, Gailard Sartain, Timothy Scott, Gary Basaraba, Lois Smith, Grace Zabriskie; *D:* Jon Avnet; *W:* Fannie Flagg, Carol Sobieski; *C:* Geoffrey Simpson; *M:* Thomas Newman.

Frieda ☝☝½ 1947 An RAF officer brings his German wife home after the war and she is naturally distrusted by his family and neighbors. An interesting look at post-war bigotry. **97m/B VHS.** *GB* David Farrar, Glynis Johns, Mai Zetterling, Flora Robson, Albert Lieven; *D:* Basil Dearden.

Friend of the Family ☝½ *Elke* 1995 While backpacking across the U.S., Elke (O'Brien) is invited to stay in Malibu with the Stillman family—husband Jeff, wife Linda, and their 20-something children, Josh and Montana. Naturally, the sexy Elke becomes very involved with the family. **98m/C VHS, DVD.** Shauna O'Brien, C.T. Miller, Griffin (Griffen) Drew, Lisa Boyle; *D:* Edward Holzman; *W:* Edward Holzman, April Moskowitz; *C:* Kim Haun; *M:* Richard Bronskill.

Friend of the Family 2 ☝ 1996 (R) Disturbed young woman decides to get revenge on the man who used and abandoned her by becoming his family's nanny. Also available in an unrated version. Ray used the pseudonym Nicholas Medina. **90m/C VHS, DVD.** Shauna O'Brien, Paul Michael Robinson, Jenna Bodnar, Jeff Rector; *D:* Fred Olen Ray; *W:* Henry Krinkle; *C:* Gary Graver.

Friendly Fire ☝☝☝ 1979 Based on a true story of an American family in 1970 whose soldier son is killed by "friendly fire" in Vietnam, and their efforts to uncover the circumstances of the tragedy. Touching and powerful, with an excellent dramatic performance by Burnett. **146m/C VHS.** Carol Burnett, Ned Beatty, Sam Waterston, Timothy Hutton; *D:* David Greene. **TV**

Friendly Persuasion ☝☝☝ *Except for Me and Thee* 1956 Earnest, solidly acted tale about a peaceful Quaker family struggling to remain true to its ideals in spite of the Civil War which touches their farm life in southern Indiana. Cooper and McGuire are excellent as the parents with Perkins fine as the son worried he's using his religion to hide his cowardice. Based on a novel by Jessamyn West. **140m/C VHS, DVD, Wide.** Gary Cooper, Dorothy McGuire, Anthony Perkins, Marjorie Main, Charles Halton; *D:* William Wyler; *W:* Michael Wilson; *C:* Ellsworth Fredericks; *M:* Dimitri Tiomkin. Cannes '57: Film.

Friends ☝ 1971 (R) Ho-hum drama about an orphaned French girl and an unloved English boy who meet, become friends, and decide to run away together, setting up house in a deserted beach cottage. They even have a baby before they're discovered. Provides no insight into the teenagers dilemmas. Followed by "Paul and Michelle." **101m/C VHS.** *GB* Sean Bury, Anicee Alvina, Pascale Roberts, Sady Rebbot, Ronald Lewis; *D:* Lewis Gilbert; *M:* Elton John.

Friends ☝☝ 1995 Story of three South African women sharing an apartment in Johannesburg. Fox is a white political activist, Burgers, an Afrikaner archaeologist, and Kente, a black teacher. When Fox plants a bomb that takes two innocent lives, their loyalties are tested. Debut for director Proctor. **109m/C VHS.** Kerry Fox, Michele Burgers, Dambisa Kente; *D:* Elaine Proctor; *W:* Elaine Proctor.

Friends & Lovers ☝½ 1999 Nonsensical and mediocre would-be romantic comedy about wealthy widower, Richard (Rasche), who invites his estranged son, Ian (Newbern), and his son's L.A. friends to spend Christmas with him at his Park City chalet. Everyone has some kind of sexual agenda except for Richard, who just wants to come to terms with Ian. **104m/C VHS, DVD.** David Rasche, George Newbern, Stephen Baldwin, Danny Nucci, Robert Downey Jr., Leon, Alison Eastwood, Suzanne Cryer, Neill Barry, Claudia Schiffer; *D:* George Haas; *W:* George Haas; *C:* Carlos Montaner; *M:* Emilio Kauderer.

Friends Forever ☝☝☝ 1986 Conformity, sexuality, and friendship are explored in this coming-of-age drama. Kristian is a shy, conformist 16-year-old, starting off at a new school. He finds himself drawn to two different young men who equally dominate his class. Henrik's androgynous sexual charm is equaled by his independence while the moody Patrick is the leader of a band of troublemakers. Kristian gains in self-confidence by their friendship but is tested when he learns Patrick is gay. **95m/C VHS.** *DK* *D:* Stefan Christian Henszelman.

Friends, Lovers & Lunatics ☝½ *Crazy Horse; She Drives Me Crazy* 1989 A weekend turns into a romantic nightmare/laugh-fest when a man visits his ex-girlfriend and her new "friend," and winds up in a new romance himself. **87m/C VHS.** *CA* Daniel Stern, Deborah Foreman, Sheila McCarthy, Page Fletcher, Elias Koteas; *D:* Stephen Withrow.

A Friendship in Vienna ☝☝½ 1988 The friendship of two young teenage girls, one Jewish, and the other the daughter of a Nazi collaborator, is tested as WWII looms over Europe and the Nazis begin their persecution of Austrian Jews. Adapted from the book "Devil in Vienna" by Doris Orgel. **100m/C VHS.** Jenny Lewis, Ed Asner, Jane Alexander, Stephen Macht, Rosemary Forsyth, Ferdinand "Ferdy" Mayne, Kamie Harper; *D:* Arthur Seidelman; *W:* Richard Alfieri; *Nar:* Jean Simmons. **CABLE**

Fright ☝ *Spell of the Hypnotist* 1956 A woman—convinced that she died in 1889 as part of a suicide pact with Prince Rudolph of Austria—seeks help from a psychiatrist who promptly falls in love with her (didn't Freud say it was supposed to be the other way around?). **?m/B VHS.** Nancy Malone, Eric Fleming, Frank Marth, Humphrey Davis, Ned Glass, Norman Burton; *D:* W. Lee Wilder.

Fright ☝☝ *Night Legs* 1971 A baby-sitter is menaced by a mental hospital escapee. He turns out to be the father of the boy she is watching. Tense but violent thriller. **87m/C VHS, DVD, Wide.** *GB* Susan George, Honor Blackman, Ian Bannen, John Gregson, George Cole, Dennis Waterman, Tara Collinson, Maurice Kaufmann, Michael Brennan, Roger Lloyd Pack; *D:* Peter Collinson; *W:* Tudor Gates; *C:* Ian Wilson; *M:* Harry Robinson.

Fright House ☝ 1989 (R) Two stories of terror. "Fright House" features witches preparing an old mansion for a visit from the Devil. "Abandon" explains the prolonged youth of a teacher to her young student. **110m/C VHS.** Al Lewis, Duane Jones; *D:* Len Anthony.

Fright Night ☝☝½ 1985 (R) It's Dracula-versus-the-teens time when Charley suspects that his new neighbor descends from Count Vlad's line. He calls in the host of "Fright Night," the local, late-night, horror-flick series, to help de-ghoul the neighborhood. But they have a problem when the vampire discovers their plans (and nobody belives them anyway). Sarandon is properly seductive as the bloodsucker. Followed by sequel. **106m/C VHS, DVD, Wide.** William Ragsdale, Chris Sarandon, Amanda Bearse, Roddy McDowall, Stephen Geoffreys, Jonathan Stark, Dorothy Fielding, Art Evans; *D:* Tom Holland; *W:* Tom Holland; *C:* Jan Kiesser; *M:* Brad Fiedel.

Fright Night 2 ☝☝ 1988 (R) The sequel to the 1985 release "Fright Night," in which the harassed guy from the original film learns slowly that the vampire's sister and her entourage have come to roost around his college. Not quite as good as the original but the special effects are worth a look. **108m/C VHS.** Roddy McDowall, William Ragsdale, Traci Lind, Julie Carmen, Jonathan (Jon Francis) Gries, Russ Clark, Brian Thompson; *D:* Tommy Lee Wallace; *W:* Tommy Lee Wallace, Tim Metcalfe, Miguel Tejada-Flores; *C:* Mark Irwin; *M:* Brad Fiedel.

The Frightened City ☝☝½ 1961 Waldo Zhernikov (Lom) decides to unite all six of London's crime syndicates into one conglomerate that would control the city. But when he gets power-mad, rival gangster Harry Foulcher (Marks) breaks away and forms his own organization. Naturally, there's a war between the factions. Paddy Damion (Connery in an early role), one of Waldo's gunsels, is sent to get rid of Foulcher. **91m/B VHS.** *GB* Herbert Lom, John Gregson, Sean Connery, Alfred Marks, Yvonne Romain, Kenneth Griffith, Olive McFarland, Frederick Piper, John Stone, David Davies, Tom Bowman, Robert Cawdron, Norrie Paramor; *D:* John Lemont; *W:* Leigh Vance; *C:* Desmond Dickinson; *M:* Norrie Paramor.

The Frightened Woman ☝☝ 1971 Wealthy Sayer (Leroy) likes to get his sexual kicks by playing master and slave in his villa outside Rome. When his usual hired call girl isn't available, he decides to lure a lovely journalist (Lassander) into his domination games. Dubbed into English. **90m/C VHS, DVD, Wide.** *IT* Phillippe LeRoy, Dagmar Lassander; *D:* Piero Schivazappa; *W:* Piero Schivazappa; *M:* Stelvio Cipriano.

The Frighteners ☝☝½ 1996 (R) Con man Frank Bannister (Fox) has a unique scam—he works with a group of ghosts who haunt a home until Frank comes along to drive them out, for the right price. But the small town of Fairwater is plagued by a serial killer's evil spirit and Frank and his spiritual cronies face the challenge of getting rid of the ghost before the police decide to get rid of Frank. Interesting horror-comedy takes a lot of twists and turns to get where its going, but the payoff in gore and humor is worth it for fans of the genre. New Zealand helmer Jackson makes his American directorial debut. **106m/C VHS, DVD, Wide.** Michael J. Fox, Trini Alvarado, Peter Dobson, Dee Wallace Stone, John Astin, Jeffrey Combs, Troy Evans, Chi McBride, Jake Busey, R. Lee Ermey, Jim Fyfe; *D:* Peter Jackson; *W:* Peter Jackson, Frances Walsh; *C:* Alun Bollinger, John Blick; *M:* Danny Elfman.

Frightmare ☝☝½ *Frightmare 2* 1974 (R) A seemingly quiet British couple do indulge in one strange habit—they're cannibals. Released on video as "Frightmare 2" to avoid confusion with the 1981 film. **86m/C VHS, DVD.** *GB* Deborah Fairfax, Kim Butcher, Rupert Davies, Sheila Keith; *D:* Pete Walker; *W:* David McGillivray; *C:* Peter Jessop; *M:* Stanley Myers.

Frightmare ☝ 1981 (R) Great horror star dies, but he refuses to give up his need for adoration and revenge. **84m/C VHS.** Ferdinand "Ferdy" Mayne, Luca Bercovici, Nita Talbot, Peter Kastner; *D:* Norman Thaddeus Vane.

The Fringe Dwellers ☝☝½ 1986 (PG) An Aborigine family leave their shantytown and move to the white, middle-class suburbs of Australia, encountering prejudice and other difficulties. Well acted and interesting but the ending's a letdown. **98m/C VHS.** *AU* Kristina Nehm, Justine Saunders, Bob Maza, Kylie Belling, Denis Walker, Ernie Dingo; *D:* Bruce Beresford; *W:* Bruce Beresford, Rhoisin Beresford; *M:* George Dreyfus.

The Frisco Kid ☝☝ *No Knife* 1979 (R) An innocent orthodox rabbi (Wilder) from Poland is sent to the wilds of San Francisco during the 1850s gold rush to lead a new congregation. He lands in Philadelphia, joins a wagon train and is promptly robbed and abandoned. He eventually meets up with a not-too-bright robber (Ford) who finds himself unexpectedly befriending the man and undergoing numerous tribulations in order to get them both safely to their destination. This isn't a laugh riot and some scenes fall distinctly flat but Wilder is sweetness personified and lends the movie its charm. **119m/C VHS.** Gene Wilder, Harrison Ford, Ramon Bieri, Val Bisoglio, George DiCenzo, Penny Peyser, William Smith; ***D:*** Robert Aldrich; ***W:*** Michael Elias; ***C:*** Robert B. Hauser.

Frisk 🦴🦴 **1995** Disturbing depictions of sex/murder fantasies come courtesy of letters written by Dennis (Gunther), a part of the L.A. S&M scene, to his former boyfriend, Julian (Laplante). Just exactly how far Dennis has gone with some of his like-minded sexual partners is the question. Has he become the killer he claims to be? Adapted from Dennis Cooper's 1991 novel. **87m/C VHS.** Michael Gunther, Jaie Laplante, Craig Chester, Parker Posey, James Lyons, Alexis Arquette, Raoul O'Connell, Michael Stock; ***D:*** Todd Verow; ***W:*** Todd Verow, Jim Dwyer, George LaVoo; ***C:*** Greg Watkins.

Fritz the Cat 🦴🦴🦴 **1972** Ralph Bakshi's animated tale for adults about a cat's adventures as he gets into group sex, college radicalism, and other hazards of life in the '60s. Loosely based on the underground comics character by Robert Crumb. Originally X-rated. **77m/C VHS, DVD, Wide.** ***D:*** Ralph Bakshi; ***W:*** Ralph Bakshi; ***C:*** Ted C. Bemiller, Gene Borghi; ***M:*** Ed Bogas, Ray Shanklin; ***V:*** Skip Hinnant, Rosetta Le Noire, John McCurry.

Frog and Wombat 🦴🦴½ **1998** Alli, whose codename is "Frog," tries to convince her best friend Jane, code named "Wombat," that their new school principal (Cox) is up to no good, especially when she discovers the man's niece is missing. So the intrepid duo prepare to investigate. **90m/C VHS.** Katie Stuart, Ronny Cox, Lindsay Wagner, Ross Malinger, Emily Lipoma.

Frogs 🦴🦴½ **1972 (PG)** An environmental photographer working on a small island in Florida interrupts the birthday celebration of a patriarch. He and the folks at the party soon realize that various amphibians animals in the surrounding area are going berserk and attacking humans. One of the first environmentally motivated animal-vengeance films, and one of the best to come out of the '70s. **91m/C VHS.** Ray Milland, Sam Elliott, Joan Van Ark, Adam Roarke, Judy Pace, Lynn Borden, Mae Mercer, David Gilliam, George Skaff, Holly Irving; ***D:*** George McCowan; ***W:*** Robert Blees, Robert Hutchison; ***C:*** Mario Tosi; ***M:*** Les Baxter.

Frogs for Snakes 🦴🦴 **1998 (R)** Self-conscious black comedy about New York loan shark Al Santana (Coltrane) who also spends his time as a wanna-be East Village theatrical impressario. And how everybody who works for Al as a collector is even more desperate to be an actor, including his struggling ex-wife Eva (Hershey). And how all the characters suddenly break into monologues from their favorite movies. And how none of this makes much sense and the actors have really done better work elsewhere. **98m/C VHS.** Barbara Hershey, Robbie Coltrane, Harry Hamlin, Ian Hart, John Leguizamo, Lisa Marie, Debi Mazar, David Deblinger, Ron Perlman, Clarence Williams III, Justin Theroux, Nicholas Chinlund, Mike Starr, Taylor Mead; ***D:*** Amos Poe; ***W:*** Amos Poe; ***C:*** Enrique Chediak.

Frolics on Ice 🦴🦴 **1940** Pleasant musical-comedy about a family man saving to buy the barber shop at which he works. Irene Dare is featured in several ice skating production numbers. **65m/B VHS.** Roscoe Karns, Lynne Roberts, Irene Dare, Edgar Kennedy.

From a Far Country: Pope John Paul II 🦴🦴 **1981** TV biography of Polish Pope John Paul II begins in 1926 as Karol Wojtila celebrates Christmas with his father and continues through the important highlights of his life. **120m/C VHS.** *PL GB* Sam Neill, Christopher Cazenove, Warren Clarke, Kathleen Byron, Maurice Denham, Lisa Harrow; ***D:*** Krzysztof Zanussi; ***W:*** Krzysztof Zanussi; ***C:*** Slawomir Idziak; ***M:*** Wojciech Kilar; ***Nar:*** Michael Jayston. **TV**

From Beyond 🦴🦴🦴 **1986 (R)** A gruesome, tongue-in-cheek adaptation of the ghoulish H.P. Lovecraft story. Scientists discover another dimension through experiments with the pineal gland. From the makers of "Re-Animator," and just as funny. **90m/C VHS.** Jeffrey Combs, Barbara Crampton, Ted (Theodore) Sorel, Ken Foree, Carolyn Purdy-Gordon, Bunny Summers, Bruce McGuire; ***D:*** Stuart Gordon; ***W:*** Dennis Paoli, Brian Yuzna; ***C:*** Mac Ahlberg; ***M:*** Richard Band.

From Beyond the Grave 🦴🦴 *Creatures* **1973 (PG)** This horror compendium revolves around a mysterious antique shop whose customers experience various supernatural phenomena, especially when they try to cheat the shop's equally mysterious owner. **98m/C VHS.** *GB* Peter Cushing, David Warner, Ian Bannen, Donald Pleasence, Margaret Leighton, Lesley-Anne Down, Diana Dors, Ian Ogilvy; ***D:*** Kevin Connor.

From Dusk Till Dawn 🦴🦴½ **1995 (R)** Escaped cons Seth and Richie Gecko (Clooney and Tarantino) pick up an ex-preacher (Keitel) and his two kids (Lewis and Liu) as hostages en route to their Mexican rendezvous spot, a raunchy biker joint run (unbenownst to them) by vampires. Feels like two movies in one, as Rodriguez's and Tarantino's styles don't necessarily mesh as much as they coexist. The first half features Tarantino's gift for snappy dialogue and somewhat sympathetic scumbags while the barroom finale shows off Rodriguez's mastery of the go-for-broke action set piece. Clooney proves the jump from TV to movies can be made successfully. Penned by Tarantino in 1990 during his video store days, he used the fee to get "Reservoir Dogs" off the ground. **108m/C VHS, DVD, Wide.** George Clooney, Quentin Tarantino, Harvey Keitel, Juliette Lewis, Ernest Liu, Fred Williamson, Richard "Cheech" Marin, Salma Hayek, Michael Parks, Tom Savini, Kelly Preston, John Saxon, Danny Trejo; ***D:*** Robert Rodriguez; ***W:*** Quentin Tarantino; ***C:*** Guillermo Navarro; ***M:*** Graeme Revell. MTV Movie Awards '96: Breakthrough Perf. (Clooney).

From Dusk Till Dawn 2: Texas Blood Money 🦴🦴 *Texas Blood Money* **1998 (R)** Buck (Patrick) and his partner-in-crime Luther (Whitaker) decide to get a few bad men together and knock over a bank in Mexico. However, the group unwittingly come into contact with the vampire denizens of the Titty Twister bar and soon join the ranks of the undead. Except for Buck, who's somehow managed to avoid having the bite put on him—for now. Direct-to-video sequel is set two weeks after the first film's carnage. **88m/C VHS, DVD.** Robert Patrick, Bo Hopkins, Muse Watson, Duane Whitaker, Raymond Cruz, Tiffani-Amber Thiessen, Brett Harrelson, Danny Trejo, Bruce Campbell; ***D:*** Scott Spiegel; ***W:*** Duane Whitaker, Scott Spiegel; ***C:*** Philip Lee; ***M:*** Joseph Williams. **VIDEO**

From Dusk Till Dawn 3: The Hangman's Daughter 🦴🦴 **1999 (R)** This is actually a prequel to the "From Dusk Till Dawn" mayhem. In 1914, a group of refugees wind up in an isolated Mexican saloon, "La Tetilla del Diablo," that's the home of Santanico Pandemonium, the Queen of the Vampires (Braga). Oh, and the hangman's daughter is lovely Esmeralda (Celi), who doesn't know that Santanico is her mom. **94m/C VHS, DVD.** Michael Parks, Sonia Braga, Marco Leonardi, Rebecca Gayheart, Temuera Morrison, Lenny Y. Loftin, Danny Trejo, Ara Celi; ***D:*** P.J. Pesce. **VIDEO**

From Hell 🦴🦴🦴 **2001 (R)** The Hughes brothers take on the legend of Jack the Ripper in this grisly period thriller. Inspector Abberline (Depp) is the fictional opium-addled detective charged with finding the notorious killer of London's ladies of the night in 1888. With the help of his police sidekick Godley (Coltrane) and the cockney hooker-with-a-heart-of-gold Mary (Graham), Abberline pries into the medical community, the royal family and other less respectable areas in his search for the Ripper. Beautiful visuals and taut suspense raise this effort a notch above other adaptions of the material. Based on a graphic novel (a.k.a. fancy-schmancy comic book) by Alan Moore and Eddie Campbell. **121m/C VHS, DVD, Wide.** *US* Johnny Depp, Heather Graham, Ian Holm, Robbie Coltrane, Ian Richardson, Jason Flemyng, Katrin Cartlidge, Terence Harvey, Susan Lynch, Leslie Sharp, Annabelle Apsion; ***D:*** Albert Hughes, Allen Hughes; ***W:*** Terry Hayes, Rafael Yglesias; ***C:*** Peter Deming; ***M:*** Trevor Jones.

From Hell to Borneo 🦴½ **1964 (PG)** A mercenary must defend his secluded island from pirates and gangsters. **90m/C VHS.** George Montgomery, Torin Thatcher, Julie Gregg, Lisa Moreno; ***D:*** George Montgomery.

From Hell to Victory 🦴🦴 **1979 (PG)** Group of friends of different nationalities vow to meet each year in Paris on the same date but WWII interrupts their lives and friendships. Director Lenzi used the alias Hank Milestone. Good battle scenes but nothing special. **100m/C VHS.** *SP FR* George Peppard, George Hamilton, Horst Buchholz, Jean-Pierre Cassel, Capucine, Sam Wanamaker, Anny (Annie Legras) Duperey, Ray Lovelock; ***D:*** Umberto Lenzi.

From Here to Eternity 🦴🦴🦴🦴 **1953** Complex, hard-hitting look at the on and off-duty life of soldiers at the Army base in Honolulu in the days before the Pearl Harbor attack. There's sensitive Pvt. Pruitt (Clift), his always in trouble best friend Maggio (Sinatra), and their good-guy top sergeant (Lancaster) who just happens to be having a torrid affair with the commander's wife (Kerr). Pruitt, meanwhile, is introduced to a club "hostess" (Reed) who is a lot more vulnerable than she's willing to admit. A movie filled with great performances. Still has the best waves-on-the-beach love scene in filmdom. Based on the novel by James Jones, which was toned down by the censors. **118m/B VHS, 8mm.** Burt Lancaster, Montgomery Clift, Frank Sinatra, Deborah Kerr, Donna Reed, Ernest Borgnine, Philip Ober, Jack Warden, Mickey Shaughnessy, George Reeves, Claude Akins, Harry Bellaver, John Dennis, Tim Ryan, John Bryant, John Cason, Doug(las) Henderson, Robert Karnes, Robert J. Wilke, Carleton Young, Merle Travis, Arthur Keegan, Barbara Morrison, Tyler McVey; ***D:*** Fred Zinnemann; ***W:*** Daniel Taradash; ***C:*** Burnett Guffey; ***M:*** George Duning. Oscars '53: B&W Cinematog., Director (Zinnemann), Film Editing, Picture, Screenplay, Sound, Support. Actor (Sinatra), Support. Actress (Reed); AFI '98: Top 100; Directors Guild '53: Director (Zinnemann); Golden Globes '54: Support. Actor (Sinatra); N.Y. Film Critics '53: Actor (Lancaster), Director (Zinnemann), Film.

From Here to Eternity 🦴🦴½ **1979 (PG-13)** From here to eternity...and back on the silver screen. Remake of the 1953 classic is based on James Jones's novel about life on a Hawaiian military base just before WWII. Decent actioner, but no Oscar-winner this time around. **110m/C VHS.** Natalie Wood, Kim Basinger, William Devane, Steve Railsback, Peter Boyle, Will Sampson, Andy Griffith, Roy Thinnes, Barbara Hershey; ***D:*** Buzz Kulik. **TV**

From Here to Maternity 🦴🦴½ **1985** A soap opera-based spoof about modern maternity. Three women want to be pregnant but their significant others aren't interested in paternity. **40m/C VHS.** Carrie Fisher, Arleen (Arlene) Sorkin, Lauren Hutton, Griffin Dunne, Paul Reiser. **TV**

From Hollywood to Deadwood 🦴🦴 **1989 (R)** A beautiful starlet is kidnapped and the private eye searching for her discovers blackmail and danger. **90m/C VHS.** Scott Paulin, Jim Haynie, Barbara Schock; ***D:*** Rex Pickett; ***W:*** Rex Pickett; ***C:*** Peter Deming.

From Noon Till Three 🦴🦴½ **1976 (PG)** A change of pace role for Bronson as a two-bit gunfighter in a spoof of western legends. Bronson has a brief romance with Ireland who, believing him dead, fictionalizes their relationship in a series of books and builds the mediocre Dorsey into a western hero. When he turns up alive no one, including Ireland, believes that he is the real Dorsey and he's gradually driven crazy. Good script, weak direction but Bronson is likeable. **99m/C VHS.** Charles Bronson, Jill Ireland, Douglas Fowley, Stan Haze, Damon Douglas; ***D:*** Frank D. Gilroy; ***W:*** Frank D. Gilroy; ***C:*** Lucien Ballard; ***M:*** Elmer Bernstein.

From Russia with Love 🦴🦴🦴½ **1963 (PG)** Bond is back and on the loose in exotic Istanbul looking for a super-secret coding machine. He's involved with a beautiful Russian spy and has the SPECTRE organization after him, including villainess Rosa Klebb (she of the killer shoe). Lots of exciting escapes but not an overreliance on the gadgetry of the later films. The second Bond feature, thought by many to be the best. **125m/C VHS, DVD, Wide.** *GB* Sean Connery, Daniela Bianchi, Pedro Armendariz Sr., Lotte Lenya, Robert Shaw, Eunice Gayson, Walter Gotell, Lois Maxwell, Bernard Lee, Desmond Llewelyn, Nadja Regin, Alizia Gur, Martine Beswick, Leila; ***D:*** Terence Young; ***W:*** Johanna Harwood, Richard Maibaum; ***C:*** Ted Moore; ***M:*** John Barry.

From the Dead of Night 🦴🦴🦴 **1989** A spooky chiller about a near-death experience. Fashion designer Wagner narrowly escapes death but gets close enough to the other side that six of the dead feel cheated that she didn't join them. They decide to rectify the mistake and Wagner is pursued by the shadowy figures. Based on the novel "Walkers" by Gary Bradner. **192m/C VHS.** Lindsay Wagner, Bruce Boxleitner, Diahann Carroll, Robert Prosky, Robin Thomas, Merritt Butrick, Joanne Linville; ***D:*** Paul Wendkos. **TV**

From the Earth to the Moon 🦴🦴 **1958** A mad scientist invents a new energy source and builds a rocket which takes him, his daughter, and two other men for some adventures on the moon. Based on the novel by Jules Verne. **100m/C VHS.** George Sanders, Joseph Cotten, Debra Paget, Don Dubbins; ***D:*** Byron Haskin; ***W:*** Robert Blees.

From the Earth to the Moon 🦴🦴🦴 **1998** Executive producer Tom Hanks shows off his fascination with the space program in this 12-part series covering the Apollo space program through the 1960s and '70s. Covers behind-the-scenes at NASA, the heroics of the astronauts and their missions, and the families that are left behind to wait and worry. On six cassettes. **720m/C VHS, DVD.** David Andrews, Bryan Cranston, Timothy Daly, Al Franken, Tony Goldwyn, Chris Isaak, Cary Elwes, Brett Cullen, Robert John Burke, Peter Scolari, Nick Searcy, Lane Smith, Dan Lauria, Mark Rolston, Mason Adams, Ronny Cox, Dakin Matthews, Kevin Pollak, Ben Marley, Joe Spano, Daniel Hugh-Kelly, Stephen (Steve) Root, Dann Florek, John Slattery, Ted Levine, Ann Cusack, Jo Anderson, James Rebhorn, Mark Harmon, Rita Wilson, Tom Amandes, John Aylward, Dylan Baker, Adam Baldwin, Reed Birney, Betsy Brantley, Bart Braverman, David Brisbin, Jimmy Buffett, Dan Butler, David Clennon, Gary Cole, Matt Craven, Wendy Crewson, Blythe Danner, Dave Foley, Jack Gilpin, John Michael Higgins, Peter Horton, Clint Howard, Zeljko Ivanek, Tcheky Karyo, John Carroll Lynch, Ann Magnuson, Joshua Malina, Andrew Masset, DeLane Matthews, Paul McCrane, Doug McKeon, Jay Mohr, Kieran Mulroney, Holmes Osborne, Conor O'Farrell, Elizabeth Perkins, Ethan Phillips, Andrew Rubin, Alan Ruck, Diana Scarwid, Grant Shaud, Cynthia Stevenson, Tom Verica, Gareth Williams, JoBeth Williams, Max Wright, Steve Zahn; ***D:*** Tom Hanks, David Frankel, Lili Fini Zanuck, Graham Yost, Frank Marshall, Jon Turteltaub, Gary Fleder, David Carson, Sally Field, Jonathan Mostow; ***W:*** Tom Hanks, Graham Yost, Stephen Katz, Remi Aubuchon, Al Reinert, Andy Wolk, Jeffrey Alladin Fiskin, Karen Janszen, Jonathan Marc Feldman; ***C:*** Gale Tattersall; ***M:*** Michael Kamen, Mark Mancina. **CABLE**

From the Edge of the City 🦴🦴 **1998** Sasha (Papadopoulos) is a teenaged emigre from Russia, who's working the Athens streets as a hustler. His older (and ruthless) mentor Giorgos (Papoulidis) is a pimp and offers Sasha the chance to move up by temporarily turning over the management of one of his girls—fellow emigre, Natasha (Tzimou). But Sasha, who isn't nearly as hardened as some of his friends, struggles not to become emotionally involved with the girl, to disastrous effect. Greek with subtitles. **94m/C VHS, DVD.** *GR* Stathis Papadopoulos, Dimitris Papoulidis, Theadora Tzimou, Costas Cotsianidis; ***D:*** Constantine Giannaris; ***W:*** Constantine Giannaris; ***C:*** George Argiroilipoulos; ***M:*** Akis Daoutis.

From the Hip 🦴🦴 **1986 (PG)** A young lawyer (Nelson) gets the chance of a lifetime when his office assigns a murder case to him. The only problem is that he suspects his client is very guilty indeed and must discover the truth without breaking his code of ethics. Nelson's courtroom theatrics are a bit out of hand, as he flares his nostrils at every opportunity. The movie is encumbered by a weak script and plot as well as a mid-story switch from comedy to drama. **111m/C VHS, DVD, Wide.** Judd Nelson, Elizabeth Perkins, John Hurt, Ray Walston; *D:* Bob (Benjamin) Clark; *W:* Bob (Benjamin) Clark, David Kelly; *C:* Dante Spinotti; *M:* Paul Zaza.

From the Journals of Jean Seberg 🦴🦴 **1995** An imaginary look at the life of the ill-fated actress, who began her career as a 17-year-old, miscast in Otto Preminger's "Saint Joan," achieved fame in Godard's "Breathless," and became a suicide at age 40 in 1979. Seberg (Hurt) dispassionately narrates her life story as she views film clips, from small-town Iowa teenager to would-be star, through abusive relationships, drugs and drinking, political activisim, and FBI harassment. **97m/C VHS, DVD.** Mary Beth Hurt; *D:* Mark Rappaport; *W:* Mark Rappaport; *C:* Mark Daniels.

From the Life of the Marionettes 🦴🦴🦴 **1980 (R)** A repressed man in a crumbling marriage rapes and kills a young prostitute. Another look at the powers behind individual motivations from Bergman, who uses black and white and color to relate details of the incident. **104m/C VHS.** *SW* Robert Atzorn, Christine Buchegger, Martin Benrath, Rita Russek, Lola Muethel, Walter Schmidinger, Heinz Bennent; *D:* Ingmar Bergman; *W:* Ingmar Bergman; *C:* Sven Nykvist.

From the Manger to the Cross 🦴🦴 **1915** This version of the Passion play was the first film to be done on location in Palestine. Re-enacts the Nativity, the flight into Egypt, and the crucifixion. Color-tinted. **71m/B VHS.** R. Henderson-Bland, Alice Hollister, Gene Gauthier; *D:* Sidney Olcott; *W:* Gene Gauthier, Sidney Olcott. Natl. Film Reg. '98.

From the Mixed-Up Files of Mrs. Basil E. Frankweiler 🦴🦴½ **1995 (PG)** Runaway siblings (Barnwell and Lee) secretly hide out in a New York art museum. They get caught up in trying to determine the authenticity of a sculpture (could it be the work of Michelangelo?) and turn to the statue's last owner, elusive art patron Mrs. Basil E. Frankweiler (Bacall). Based on the Newbery Award-winning novel by E.L. Konigsburg. Made for TV. **92m/C VHS, DVD.** Lauren Bacall, Jean Marie Barnwell, Jesse Lee; *D:* Marcus Cole. **TV**

From the Terrace 🦴🦴½ **1960** Newman is a wealthy Pennsylvania boy who goes to New York and marries into even more money and social position when he weds Woodward. He gets a job with her family's investment company and neglects his wife for business. She turns to another man and when he goes home for a visit he also finds a new romance which leads to some emotional soul searching. The explicitness of O'Hara's very long novel was diluted by the censors and Newman's performance is a stilted disappointment. Loy, as Newman's alcoholic mother, earned the best reviews. **144m/C VHS.** Paul Newman, Joanne Woodward, Myrna Loy, Ina Balin, Felix Aylmer, Leon Ames, George Grizzard, Patrick O'Neal, Barbara Eden, Mae Marsh; *D:* Mark Robson; *W:* Ernest Lehman; *M:* Elmer Bernstein.

The Front 🦴🦴🦴 **1976 (PG)** Woody is the bookmaker who becomes a "front" for blacklisted writers during the communist witch hunts of the 1950s in this satire comedy. The scriptwriter and several of the performers suffered blacklisting themselves during the Cold War. Based more or less on a true story. **95m/C VHS.** Woody Allen, Zero Mostel, Herschel Bernardi, Michael Murphy, Danny Aiello, Andrea Marcovicci; *D:* Martin Ritt; *W:* Walter Bernstein; *C:* Michael Chapman; *M:* Dave Grusin.

The Front Page 🦴🦴🦴½ **1931** The original screen version of the Hecht-MacArthur play about the shenanigans of a battling newspaper reporter and his editor in Chicago. O'Brien's film debut here is one of several hilarious performances in this breathless pursuit of an exclusive with an escaped death row inmate. **101m/B VHS, DVD.** Adolphe Menjou, Pat O'Brien, Edward Everett Horton, Mae Clarke, Walter Catlett; *D:* Lewis Milestone; *C:* Hal Mohr.

The Front Page 🦴🦴½ **1974 (PG)** A remake of the Hecht-MacArthur play about the managing editor of a 1920s Chicago newspaper who finds out his ace reporter wants to quit the business and get married. But first an escaped convicted killer offers the reporter an exclusive interview. **105m/C VHS, DVD.** Jack Lemmon, Walter Matthau, Carol Burnett, Austin Pendleton, Vincent Gardenia, Charles Durning, Susan Sarandon; *D:* Billy Wilder; *W:* I.A.L. Diamond, Billy Wilder; *C:* Jordan Cronenweth; *M:* Billy May.

Frontier Days 🦴½ **1934** Cody goes undercover to capture the leader of a gang of stagecoach robbers. He also manages to capture a killer along the way. **60m/B VHS.** Bill Cody, Ada Ince, Wheeler Oakman; *D:* Sam Newfield.

Frontier Fugitives 🦴½ **1945** When a trapper is murdered—allegedly by Indians—the Texas Rangers ride in to investigate. **58m/B VHS.** Tex Ritter, Dave O'Brien, Guy Wilkerson, Lorraine Miller, I. Stanford Jolley, Jack Ingram; *D:* Harry Fraser.

Frontier Horizon 🦴🦴 **1939** Wayne and the Three Mesquiteers help out ranchers whose land is being bought up by crooked speculators. **55m/B VHS.** John Wayne, Jennifer Jones, Ray Corrigan, Raymond Hatton; *D:* George Sherman.

Frontier Justice 🦴🦴 **1935** Gibson is the foolish son of a cattle owner who has been forced into an insane asylum because of a battle over water rights. Naturally, he must take on responsibility and rescue his father. **56m/B VHS.** Hoot Gibson, Richard Cramer; *D:* Robert McGowan.

Frontier Law 🦴½ **1943** Hayden and the boys ride into town to clean out the bad guys and clear a friend wrongly accused of murder. **55m/B VHS.** Russell Hayden, Jennifer Holt, Dennis Moore, Fuzzy Knight, Jack Ingram, Hal Taliaferro; *D:* Elmer Clifton; *W:* Elmer Clifton.

Frontier Outlaws 🦴🦴 **1944** A gang of villains is selling stolen cattle, and Crabbe poses as an interested buyer to catch them in the act. Laughs are provided by Lynn as a judge, and "Fuzzy" St. John as Crabbe's sidekick. **58m/B VHS.** Buster Crabbe, Al "Fuzzy" St. John, Frances Gladwin, Marin Sais, Charles "Blackie" King, Jack Ingram, Kermit Maynard, Edward Cassidy, Emmett Lynn, Budd Buster; *D:* Sam Newfield.

Frontier Pony Express 🦴🦴 **1939** Roy and Trigger do their best to help the Pony Express riders who are being attacked by marauding gangs in California during the time of the Civil War. Plenty of action here. **54m/B VHS.** Roy Rogers; *D:* Joseph Kane.

Frontier Scout 🦴🦴 **1938** Action-packed western has Wild Bill Hickock, portrayed by former opera singer Houston, forcing Lee's surrender in the Civil War before pursuing cattle rustlers out West. **60m/B VHS.** George Houston, Mantan Moreland; *D:* Sam Newfield.

Frontier Uprising 🦴½ **1961** Stunning cinematography makes up for weak narrative in this otherwise routine oater. Davis stars as a frontier scout battling hordes of Mexicans and Indians while trying to gain control of California for the U.S. Based on the short story "Kit Carson" by George Bruce. **68m/B VHS.** Jim Davis, Nancy Hadley, Ken Mayer, Nestor Paiva, Don O'Kelly; *D:* Edward L. Cahn; *W:* Owen Harris.

Frontier Vengeance 🦴½ **1940** Barry is falsely accused of murder and works to clear his name while at the same time romancing a stagecoach driver who's trying to win a race with a rival stagecoach line. **54m/B VHS.** Donald (Don "Red") Barry, Nate Watt.

The Frontiersmen 🦴🦴 **1938** Things plod along at the little red schoolhouse until Hoppy and the guys have to take off after some rustlers. Features the members of the St. Brendan Boys Choir as the schoolboys. Unusual for its lack of gunplay until near the end. **71m/B VHS.** William Boyd, George "Gabby" Hayes, Russell Hayden, Evelyn Venable, Clara Kimball Young, Charles Hughes, Dick(ie) Jones, Roy Barcroft, Emily Fitzroy; *D:* Lesley Selander.

Frostbiter: Wrath of the Wendigo 🦴 **1994 (R)** Disappointing Troma entry takes itself a bit too seriously. It wants to be an "Evil Dead on Ice" (we even see a movie poster for same in the flick); the plot involves hunters trapped in the frozen woods of Northern Michigan by the evil spirit "Wendigo." It's short on original horror and the laff-factor is not up to usual Troma standards (although the killer chili was a nice touch). The only saving grace is the quirky soundtrack, including said chili's theme song by Randall and Allan Lynch, "March of the Undead" by the 3-D Invisibles, and "I'm a Hellbilly" by Elvis Hitler. Based on the comic book character of the same name. **90m/C VHS, DVD.** Ron Asheton, Lori Baker, Patrick Butler, Devlin Burton; *D:* Tom Chaney; *W:* Tom Chaney; *C:* Tom Chaney.

Frozen 🦴🦴 **1998** Flashback look at the suicide of struggling Beijing performance artist Qi Lei (Hongshen), who dies by freezing himself to death in an "ice burial" as part of his art. Focuses on the aftermath of Tienanmen Square and its disaffected younger generation. Mandarin with subtitles. Working without authorization, the director hid behind a pseudonym that translates as "No Name." The film was smuggled out of China and completed in Amsterdam. **90m/C VHS.** *CH* Jia Hongshen, Ma Xiaoqing, Bai Yu, Li Geng, Wei Ye; *D:* Xiaoshuai Wang; *W:* Xiaoshuai Wang, Pang Ming; *C:* Yang Shu; *M:* Roeland Dol.

Frozen Alive 🦴 **1964** A scientist experiments with suspended animation but, wouldn't you know, someone murders his wife while he's on ice. Apparently being frozen stiff does not an alibi make, and he becomes the prime suspect. Much unanimated suspense. **80m/B VHS.** *GB GE* Mark Stevens, Marianne Koch, Delphi Lawrence, Joachim Hansen, Walter Rilla, Wolfgang Lukschy; *D:* Bernard Knowles.

Frozen Assets 🦴 **1992 (PG-13)** Pathetic attempt at comedy from Long and Bernsen. He's an ambitious executive who finds the "bank" of his corporation's latest acquisition deals in sperm and not cash. Still, he expects this acquisition to be a success and comes up with a number of tacky ways, much to the horror of the facility's administrator, to make that profit margin grow. **93m/C VHS.** Corbin Bernsen, Shelley Long, Larry Miller, Dody Goodman, Gerrit Graham, Paul Sand, Teri Copley, Matt Clark, John Bloom; *D:* George Miller; *W:* Don Klein, Tom Kartozian.

Frozen in Fear 🦴🦴 *The Flying Dutchman* **2000** Variation on the 1933 film "The Mystery of the Wax Museum" and the Vincent Price 1953 remake "House of Wax." Admiring art dealer Oxenberg tracks reclusive painter Roberts down to his remote cabin in Montana. Turns out the artist uses real female bodies for his work—killing young women, arranging them in provocative poses, and then encasing them in ice. Will Oxenberg become part of his next tableau? **91m/C VHS, DVD.** Eric Roberts, Catherine Oxenberg, Rod Steiger, Scott Plank, Barry Sigismondi, Joan Benedict, Douglas Sebern; *D:* Robin P. Murray. **VIDEO**

The Fugitive 🦴🦴🦴🦴 **1948** Fonda is a priest devoted to God and the peasants under his care when he finds himself on the run after religion is outlawed in this nameless South-of-the-border dictatorship. Despite the danger of capture, he continues to minister to his flock. His eventual martyrdom unites the villagers in prayer. Considered Fonda's best performance; Ford's favorite film. Shot on location in Mexico. Excellent supporting performances. Based on the Graham Greene novel "The Power and the Glory" although considerably cleaned up for the big screen—Greene's priest had lost virtually all of his faith and moral code. Here the priest is a genuine Ford hero. A gem. **99m/B VHS.** Henry Fonda, Dolores Del Rio, Pedro Armendariz Sr., J. Carrol Naish, Leo Carrillo, Ward Bond, Robert Armstrong, John Qualen; *D:* John Ford; *W:* Dudley Nichols.

The Fugitive 🦴🦴🦴½ **1993 (PG-13)** Exciting big-screen version of the '60s TV series with the same basic storyline: Dr. Richard Kimble's (Ford) wife (Ward) is murdered and he's convicted, so he escapes and goes on the lam to find the real killer, the mysterious one-armed man. Dogged marshal Sam Gerard (Jones) is determined to retrieve his man. Lots of mystery and action, particularly a spectacular train/bus crash sequence, keeps the tension high. Due to illness, Richard Jordan was replaced by Krabbe after production had begun. Alec Baldwin was originally slated to star as Kimble, but backed out and Ford was cast. Sound familiar? Ford also replaced Baldwin as Jack Ryan in "Patriot Games." **127m/C VHS, DVD.** Harrison Ford, Tommy Lee Jones, Jeroen Krabbe, Julianne Moore, Sela Ward, Joe Pantoliano, Andreas Katsulas, Daniel Roebuck; *D:* Andrew Davis; *W:* David N. Twohy, Jeb Stuart; *C:* Michael Chapman; *M:* James Newton Howard. Oscars '93: Support. Actor (Jones); Golden Globes '94: Support. Actor (Jones); L.A. Film Critics '93: Support. Actor (Jones); MTV Movie Awards '94: On-Screen Duo (Harrison Ford/Tommy Lee Jones), Action Seq.; Blockbuster '95: Action Actor, V. (Ford).

Fugitive Among Us 🦴🦴 **1992** Dedicated cop is determined to return an escaped rapist to a life behind bars and he's aided by a victim who would really rather forget the whole thing. Made for TV. **97m/C VHS.** Peter Strauss, Eric Roberts, Elizabeth Pena, Lauren Holly. **TV**

Fugitive Champion 🦴🦴 **1999** Gangsters bust motor-cross champion Jake McKnight (Mayer) out of a chain-gang so that he can search for his kidnapped daughter, a participant in an internet sex site. The silly plot is a framework upon which to hang some inventive lively chase scenes. Standard action for a video premiere with a generic title. **94m/C DVD.** Chip Mayer, Charlene Blaine, Thomas Burr, Carlos Cervantes; *D:* Max Kleven; *W:* Steven Baio, Jack Burkhead Jr.; *C:* Jason C. Poteet; *M:* Ennio di Berardo. **VIDEO**

The Fugitive Kind 🦴🦴½ **1960** A young drifter walks into a sleepy Mississippi town and attracts the attention of three of its women with tragic results. Based upon the Tennessee Williams' play "Orpheus Descending." good performances but the writing never hangs well-enough together for coherence. **122m/B VHS.** Marlon Brando, Anna Magnani, Joanne Woodward, Victor Jory, R.G. Armstrong, Maureen Stapleton; *D:* Sidney Lumet; *C:* Boris Kaufman.

Fugitive Mind 🦴½ **1999 (PG-13)** Robert Dean (Dudikoff) is suffering from severe memory loss. As he begins to piece together his past, Dean discovers his mind has been programmed to carry out bizarre crimes. So now what does he do? **94m/C VHS, DVD.** Michael Dudikoff, Heather Langenkamp. **VIDEO**

Fugitive Rage 🦴🦴 **1996 (R)** Tara McCormick (Schumacher) winds up behind bars when she shoots the mobster who was acquitted for murdering her sister. She teams up with her cellmate Josie (O'Brien) to fight back against the mob who's put a bounty on her head and a covert government agency also out to use her. Prerequisite prison shower sequences, tough babes, and lots of action. **90m/C VHS.** Wendy Schumacher, Shauna O'Brien, Jay Richardson; *D:* Fred Olen Ray.

Fugitive Road 🦴🦴 **1934** The great von Stroheim stars as a crusty but soft-hearted border guard who arbitrarily detains people at the crossing. **69m/B VHS.** Erich von Stroheim, Wera Engels, Leslie Fenton, Harry Holman; *D:* Frank Strayer.

The Fugitive: Taking of Luke McVane 🦴🦴 **1915** An early silent western in which Hart upholds the cowboy code of honor. **28m/B VHS.** William S. Hart, Enid Markey.

Fugitive Valley 1941 Muddled plot has villains-turned-heroes on the trail of some outlaws and stolen money. Terhune shows off some of his vaudeville skills, and King sings some songs. **61m/B VHS.** Ray Corrigan, John "Dusty" King, Max Terhune, Julie Duncan, Glenn Strange, Robert F. (Bob) Kortman, Tom London, Reed Howes; ***D:*** S. Roy Luby.

Fugitive X 1996 Advertising exec gets to be the prey for a group of thrill-seeking hunters. He's got a handgun, a small head start, and the slime taking bets on how long he'll last. You've seen this before. **97m/C VHS.** David Heavener, Richard Norton, Lynn-Holly Johnson, William Windom, Chris Mitchum, Robert Z'Dar; ***D:*** David Heavener; ***W:*** David Heavener.

Fulfillment *The Fulfillment of Mary Gray* 1989 (PG-13) Ladd stars as Mary Gray, a turn-of-the-century woman comfortably married to good but unexciting farmer, Jonathan (Levine). He's unable to give his wife the child they both desperately want and when his younger brother, Aaron (Smith), visits, the hope is Aaron can be persuaded to help out. The naturally volatile situation is heightened by the fact Mary is very drawn to the handsome Aaron anyway, and the feeling is mutual. Based on the novel "The Fulfillment" by LaVyrle Spencer. **96m/C VHS.** Cheryl Ladd, Ted Levine, Lewis Smith; ***D:*** Piers Haggard. **TV**

Full Body Massage 1995 (R) Wealthy art gallery owner Nina (Rogers) spends much of her time alone at her California dream home—except for a weekly appointment with young masseur Douglas (Burgard). But one week, the older Fitch (Brown) comes instead and begins discussing life and personal spirituality while he massages away the self-indulgent cares of the world-weary Nina. Good work by the leads in a chatty cable movie. **93m/C VHS.** Mimi Rogers, Bryan Brown, Christopher Burgard, Elizabeth Barondes; ***D:*** Nicolas Roeg; ***W:*** Dan Gurskis; ***C:*** Anthony B. Richmond; ***M:*** Harry Gregson-Williams. **CABLE**

Full Circle *The Haunting of Julia* 1977 (R) Peter Straub wrote this eerie tale about a grief-stricken young woman whose child has recently died. To overcome her loss, she moves into a new house—which is haunted by the ghost of a long-dead child. **96m/C VHS.** *CA GB* Mia Farrow, Keir Dullea, Tom Conti, Jill Bennett, Robin Gammell; ***D:*** Richard Loncraine; ***M:*** Colin Towns.

Full Contact *Xia dao Gao Fei* 1992 Nightclub bouncer Jeff helps his friend Sam escape from a loan shark. But Sam has doublecrossed him and now thinks that Jeff is dead in an arranged explosion. But Jeff's survived and plans to seek a suitable revenge. Cantonese with subtitles. **99m/C VHS, DVD, Wide.** *HK* Chow Yun-Fat, Anthony Wong, Simon Yam, Bonnie Fu, Franklin Chin, Ann Bridgewater, Chan Chi Leung; ***D:*** Ringo Lam; ***W:*** Yin Nam; ***M:*** Teddy Robin Kwan.

Full Contact 1993 (R) Farmhand Luke Powers heads for the decadence of Los Angeles to find his older brother. When three thugs make the mistake of trying to rob him, Luke shows off his martial arts skills. When Luke finds out his brother has been murdered by gamblers involved in an illegal back alley kickboxing circuit, he vows to get revenge. **97m/C VHS.** Jerry Trimble, Howard Jackson, Alvin Prouder, Gerry Blanck, Denise Buick; ***D:*** Rick Jacobson; ***W:*** Beverly Gray.

Full Disclosure 2000 (R) Veteran journalist McWhirter (Ward) gets an incredible opportunity when a group of radicals he sent to prison ask him to protect a Palestinian operative (Ticotin) involved in the murder of a pro-Israeli media mogul. But neither an FBI agent (Plummer) nor an assassin (Miller) want McWhirter in the way and he'll have to decide just how badly he wants this story. **137m/C VHS, DVD.** Fred Ward, Christopher Plummer, Penelope Ann Miller, Rachel Ticotin, Virginia Madsen, Kim Coates, Nicholas (Nick) Campbell, Dan Lauria, Roberta Maxwell; ***D:*** John Bradshaw; ***W:*** Tony Johnston; ***C:*** Barry Stone; ***M:*** Claude Desjardins, Eric N. Robertson. **VIDEO**

Full Eclipse 1993 (R) Max Dire (Van Peebles) is seduced by the fetching Casey (Kensit) into joining a fierce elite group of underground cops whose mission is to wipe out crime. However, Max soon learns that the secret of their power is a serum which turns them into werewolves. Max is now faced with a decision: join forces with them, or expose them. Either way, blood will flow. Interesting special effects. Unrated version also available. **97m/C VHS, DVD.** Mario Van Peebles, Patsy Kensit, Bruce Payne, Anthony John (Tony) Denison; ***D:*** Anthony Hickox; ***W:*** Richard Christian Matheson; ***C:*** Sandi Sissel.

Full Exposure: The Sex Tape Scandals 1989 (R) Sleazy drama about a murdered call girl who was blackmailing her clients with sex videos. A cop and his inexperienced female partner are assigned to catch the killer. **95m/C VHS.** Jennifer O'Neill, Lisa Hartman Black, Vanessa L(ynne) Williams, Anthony John (Tony) Denison, Peter Jurasik; ***D:*** Noel Nosseck; ***W:*** Stephen Zito; ***M:*** Dana Kaproff. **TV**

Full Fathom Five 1990 (PG) Central American militants, angered by America's invasion of Panama, hijack a submarine and threaten a nuclear assault on Houston. Boring and dumb. **81m/C VHS.** Michael Moriarty, Maria Rangel, Michael Cavanaugh, John Lafayette, Todd Field, Daniel Faraldo; ***D:*** Carl Franklin; ***W:*** Bart Davis.

Full Frontal 2002 (R) Love is all its confusions, and Soderbergh's unofficial sequel to "sex, lies and videotape," tracks the lives of various Los Angelenos over a 24-hour period. Not yet reviewed. **?m/C VHS, DVD.** David Duchovny, Nicky Katt, Catherine Keener, Mary McCormack, David Hyde Pierce, Julia Roberts, Blair Underwood, Brad Pitt; ***D:*** Steven Soderbergh; ***W:*** Coleman Hough.

Full Hearts & Empty Pockets 1963 Follows the happy-go-lucky adventures of a young, handsome, impoverished gentleman on the loose in Rome. Dubbed in English. **88m/B VHS.** *IT GE* Linda Christian, Gino Cervi, Senta Berger; ***D:*** Camillo Mastrocinque.

Full Metal Jacket 1987 (R) A three-act Vietnam War epic, about a single Everyman impetuously passing through basic training then working in the field as a Marine Corps photojournalist and fighting at the onset of the Tet offensive. First half of the film is the most realistic bootcamp sequence ever done. Unfocused but powerful. Based on the novel by Hasford, who also co-scripted. **116m/C VHS, DVD, 8mm.** Matthew Modine, R. Lee Ermey, Vincent D'Onofrio, Adam Baldwin, Dorian Harewood, Arliss Howard, Kevyn Major Howard, Ed O'Ross, John Terry, Jon Stafford, Marcus D'Amico, Kieron Jecchinis, Bruce Boa, Kirk Taylor, Tim Colceri, Ian Tyler, Gary Landon Mills, Sal Lopez, Ngoc Le, Peter Edmund, Tan Hung Francione, Leanne Hong, Costas Dino Chimona; ***D:*** Stanley Kubrick; ***W:*** Stanley Kubrick, Michael Herr, Gustav Hasford; ***C:*** Doug Milsome; ***M:*** Abigail Mead.

Full Metal Ninja 1989 When his family is kidnapped, a trained martial artist trails their abductors and swears revenge. **90m/C VHS.** Patrick Allen, Pierre Kirby, Sean Odell, Jean Paul, Renato Sala; ***D:*** Charles Lee.

The Full Monty 1996 (R) A group of laid off Yorkshire mill workers come up with a unique way to earn some money in this amusing Britcom. When exuberant Gaz (Carlyle) notices the local women lining up to see the Chippendale dancers, he persuades his mates to launch a striptease act themselves. But these guys are hardly cover boy material—they're variously overweight, middle-aged, depressed, and shy. Nevertheless, they turn out to be an unexpected success despite numerous mishaps and misunderstandings. Title refers to the fact that they strip down to their birthday suits. The film audience merely gets the moon view. **90m/C VHS, DVD.** *GB* Robert Carlyle, Tom Wilkinson, Mark Addy, Steve Huison, William Snape, Paul Barber, Hugo Speer, Lesley Sharp, Emily Woof, Deirdre Costello; ***D:*** Peter Cattaneo; ***W:*** Simon Beaufoy; ***C:*** John de Borman; ***M:*** Anne Dudley. Oscars '97: Orig. Mus./Comedy Score; British Acad. '97: Actor (Carlyle), Film, Support. Actor (Wilkinson); Screen Actors Guild '97: Cast.

Full Moon in Blue Water 1988 (R) His wife's been dead a year, he owes back taxes on his bar, his father has Alzheimer's, and his only form of entertainment is watching old home movies of his wife. Floyd has problems. Enter Louise, a lonely spinster who feels that it is her personal duty to change his life. If she doesn't do it, the bizarre things that happen after her arrival will. **96m/C VHS, DVD, Wide.** Gene Hackman, Teri Garr, Burgess Meredith, Elias Koteas, Kevin Cooney, David Doty; ***D:*** Peter Masterson; ***W:*** Bill Bozzone; ***C:*** Fred Murphy; ***M:*** Phil Marshall.

Full Moon in Paris *Les Nuits de la Pleine* 1984 (R) A young woman in Paris moves out on her architect lover in order to experience freedom. Through a couple of random relationships, she soon finds that what she hoped for is not what she really wanted. The fourth of Rohmer's Comedies and Proverbs series. French with subtitles. **101m/C VHS, DVD.** *FR* Pascale Ogier, Tcheky Karyo, Fabrice Luchini; ***D:*** Eric Rohmer; ***W:*** Eric Rohmer; ***C:*** Renato Berta. Venice Film Fest. '84: Actress (Ogier).

Full of Life 1956 Holliday stars in this domestic comedy about a non-religious young woman who had married, in a civil ceremony, into a strict, Italian-Catholic family. Although Emily is now eight months pregnant the family still wants her and husband Nick (Conte) to have a church wedding. Holliday is a winning personality and the humor is lightly handled. Fante adapts from his own novel. **91m/B VHS.** Judy Holliday, Richard Conte, Salvatore Baccaloni, Esther Minciotti; ***D:*** Richard Quine; ***W:*** John Fante.

Full Speed *A Toute Vitesse* 1996 Quentin (Cervo) has published a semi-autobiographical novel about disenfranchised youth that's based on his friends from a Lyon housing project, including drug-dealing DJ, Jimmy (Rideau). Although he has a girlfriend, Julie (Bouchez), Quentin flirts with Algerian-born Samir (Bardadi) in order to learn about Samir's murdered boyfriend, so he can use the story in his writing. Julie, meanwhile, becomes involved with the charismatic Jimmy when Quentin decides to go to Paris. There are several melodramatic twists in Morel's feature debut about live-for-today youth and racial tensions. French with subtitles. **84m/C VHS.** *FR* Pascal Cervo, Stephane Rideau, Elodie Bouchez, Meziane Bardadi; ***D:*** Gael Morel; ***W:*** Gael Morel, Catherine Corsini; ***C:*** Jeanne Lapoirie.

Full Tilt Boogie 1997 (R) Director Sarah Kelly's documentary films the making of hipster crime-vampire flick "From Dusk Till Dawn" by Quentin Tarantino and Robert Rodriguez. Watching this clash of show biz egos is actually more fun than watching the movie they made. Probes the inner workings of big shots Tarantino, Clooney, Keitel, and the interns that hate to go to Taco Bell for them. Keitel, in his best "I can't believe you talked me into making this movie" tone, has a brief monologue about...well, he probably had a point when he started talking. Also shows the problems that went on during the production, including the destruction of a set by fire and the process of saving it. **110m/C VHS.** ***D:*** Sarah Kelly; ***C:*** Chris Gallo; ***M:*** Cary Berger, Dominic Kelly.

The Fuller Brush Girl 1950 Lots of slapstick with Ball as a door-to-door saleswoman unexpectedly involved in a murder. She and dim-bulb boyfriend Albert are chased by cops, murderers, and smugglers in this frantic farce. Sequel to Red Skelton's (who has a cameo) 1948 film "The Fuller Brush Man." **84m/B VHS.** Lucille Ball, Eddie Albert, Carl Benton Reid, Gale Robbins, Jeff Donnell, John Litel, Fred Graham, Lee Patrick; ***Cameos:*** Red Skelton; ***D:*** Lloyd Bacon; ***W:*** Frank Tashlin.

The Fuller Brush Man *That Man Mr. Jones* 1948 A newly hired Fuller Brush man becomes involved in murder and romance as he tries to win the heart of his girlfriend. A slapstick delight for Skelton fans. **93m/B VHS.** Red Skelton, Janet Blair, Don McGuire, Adele Jergens; ***D:*** Frank Tashlin.

Fun 1994 Another in the thrill kill genre. 14-year-old Bonnie (Witt) and 15-year-old Hillary (Humphrey) are best friends (and possibly lovers) who have stabbed to death an old woman—seemingly for kicks and to cement their loyalty to each other. (Can you say Leopold and Loeb?) Convicted and in a reformatory, they're documenting their actions, separately (in black & white sequences), to counselor Jane (Hope) and tabloid journalist John (Moses). Bleak dysfunction adapted by Bosley from his play. **95m/C VHS.** Alicia Witt, Renee Humphrey, Leslie Hope, William R. Moses, Ania Suli; ***D:*** Rafal Zielinski; ***W:*** James Bosley; ***C:*** Jens Sturup; ***M:*** Marc Tschantz.

Fun & Fancy Free 1947 (G) Part-animated, part-live-action Disney feature is split into two segments: "Bongo" with Dinah Shore narrating the story of a happy-go-lucky circus bear looking for love; and "Mickey and the Beanstalk"—a "new" version of an old fairy tale. Disney's last performance as the voice of Mickey and the only film to star Mickey, Donald Duck, Jiminy Cricket and Goofy. **73m/C VHS, DVD.** ***D:*** Jack Kinney, Hamilton Luske, William M. Morgan; ***C:*** Charles P. Boyle; ***M:*** Paul J. Smith, Oliver Wallace, Eliot Daniel; ***V:*** Walt Disney, Cliff Edwards, Billy Gilbert, Clarence Nash, Anita Gordon; ***Nar:*** Edgar Bergen, Dinah Shore.

Fun Down There woof! 1988 This smalltown boy-comes-to-the-big city is so bad, it's—bad. A naive—and unsympathetic—gay man from upstate New York moves to Greenwich Village and has fun down there (and they don't mean Australia). **110m/C VHS.** Michael Waite, Nickolas Nagurney, Gretschen Somerville, Martin Goldin, Kevin Och; ***D:*** Roger Stigliano; ***W:*** Michael Waite, Roger Stigliano.

Fun in Acapulco 1963 (PG) Former trapeze artist Elvis romances two beauties and acts as a part-time lifeguard and night club entertainer. He must conquer his fear of heights for a climactic dive from the Acapulco cliffs. Features ten musical numbers. ♫Fun in Acapulco; Vino, Dinero y Amor; Mexico; The Bullfighter Was A Lady; El Toro; Marguerita; (There's) No Room To Rhumba (In A Sports Car); I Think I'm Going To Like It Here; You Can't Say No In Acapulco. **97m/C VHS.** Elvis Presley, Ursula Andress, Elsa Cardenas, Paul Lukas, Alejandro Rey, Larry Domasin, Howard McNear; ***D:*** Richard Thorpe; ***C:*** Daniel F. Fapp.

Fun with Dick and Jane 1977 (PG) An upper-middle class couple turn to armed robbery to support themselves when the husband is fired from his job. Though it has good performances, the film never develops its intended bite. **104m/C VHS.** George Segal, Jane Fonda, Ed McMahon; ***D:*** Ted Kotcheff; ***W:*** Jerry Belson, David Giler, Mordecai Richler; ***C:*** Fred W. Koenekamp; ***M:*** Ernest Gold.

The Funeral *Funeral Rites; Ososhiki* 1984 A sharp satire of the clash of modern Japanese culture with the old. The hypocrisies, rivalries and corruption in an average family are displayed at the funeral of its patriarch who also happened to own a house of ill repute. Itami's breakthrough film; Japanese with subtitles. **112m/C VHS, DVD.** *JP* Tsutomu Yamazaki, Nobuko Miyamoto, Kin Sugai, Ichiro Zaitsu, Nekohachi Edoya, Shoji Otake; ***D:*** Juzo Itami; ***W:*** Juzo Itami; ***C:*** Yonezo Maeda; ***M:*** Joji Yuasa.

The Funeral 1996 (R) Ferrara fuels fantastic performances from his famous thesps in this fatalistic tale of a family of gangsters in 1930s New York. Flashbacks from the opening funeral scene show a complex and troubled family of Italian brothers (Walken, Penn, and Gallo), from their formative years through their quest for justice after youngest brother Johnny is murdered. Not just another mob movie; characters are multi-dimensional with interesting quirks and Penn, especially, sprints into his role. More subtle than "Bad Lieutenant" and less pretentious than "The Addiction," this Ferrara flick is the one to see. **96m/C VHS, DVD.** Christopher Walken, Benicio Del Toro, Vincent Gallo, Christopher Penn, Isabella Rossellini, Annabella Sciorra, John Ventimiglia, Paul Hipp, Gretchen Mol; *D:* Abel Ferrara; *W:* Nicholas St. John; *C:* Ken Kelsch; *M:* Joe Delia.

Funeral for an Assassin ½ **1977 (PG)** A professional assassin seeks revenge for his imprisonment by the government of South Africa, a former client. Planning to kill all of the country's leading politicians, he masquerades as a black man, a cover which is designed to fool the apartheid establishment. **92m/C VHS.** Vic Morrow, Peter Van Dissel; *D:* Ivan Hall.

Funeral Home ½ *2 Cries in the Night* **1982** Terrified teen spends her summer vacation at her grandmother's tourist home, a former funeral parlor. Rip-off of "Psycho." **90m/C VHS.** *CA* Lesleh Donaldson, Kay Hawtry; *D:* William Fruet.

Funeral in Berlin **1966 (R)** Second of the Caine/Harry Palmer espionage films (following up "Ipcress File"), in which the deadpan antihero British secret serviceman arranges the questionable defection of a Russian colonel (Homolka). Good look at the spy biz and postwar Berlin. Based on the novel by Len Deighton. "Billion Dollar Brain" continues the series. **102m/C VHS, DVD, Wide.** Michael Caine, Eva Renzi, Oscar Homolka, Paul (Christian) Hubschmid, Guy Doleman, Hugh Burden; *D:* Guy Hamilton; *W:* Evan Jones; *C:* Otto Heller; *M:* Konrad Elfers.

The Funhouse ½ **1981 (R)** Four teenagers spend the night at a carnival funhouse, witness a murder, and become next on the list of victims. From the director of cult favorite "The Texas Chainsaw Massacre," but nothing that hasn't been seen before. **96m/C VHS, DVD, Wide.** Elizabeth Berridge, Shawn Carson, Cooper Huckabee, Largo Woodruff, Sylvia Miles, Miles Chapin, Kevin Conway, William Finley, Wayne Doba; *D:* Tobe Hooper; *W:* Larry Block; *C:* Andrew Laszlo; *M:* John Beal.

Funland **1989 (PG-13)** In the world's weirdest amusement park a clown goes nuts over the new corporate owners' plans for the place and decides to seek revenge. **86m/C VHS.** David Lander, William Windom, Bruce Mahler, Michael McManus; *D:* Michael A. Simpson.

Funny About Love ½ **1990 (PG-13)** Fairly absurd tale with dashes of inappropriate black humor about a fellow with a ticking biological clock. Nimoy sheds his Spock ears to direct a star-studded cast in this lame tale of middle-aged cartoonist Wilder who strays from wife Lahti after having problems on the conception end into the welcoming arms of fertile college co-ed Masterson in his quest to contribute to the population count. **107m/C VHS, 8mm.** Gene Wilder, Christine Lahti, Mary Stuart Masterson, Robert Prosky, Stephen Tobolowsky, Anne Jackson, Susan Ruttan, David Margulies; *D:* Leonard Nimoy; *W:* Norman Steinberg, David Frankel.

Funny Bones **1994 (R)** Struggling comedian Tommy Fawkes (Platt) bombs in Vegas big-time while his Mr. Showbiz father George (Lewis) easily overshadows him at every turn. So Tommy decides to head back to his childhood home in Blackpool, England and figure out his life. What he discovers are the Parkers, a family of British vaudevillians, and the fact that his father stole their routines and, briefly, Mrs. Parker (Caron), resulting in half-brother Jack (Evans) who has all the natural talent Tommy can only dream about. Serious, funny, and hostile with notable performances from Platt and Evans. **128m/C VHS.** Oliver Platt, Lee Evans, Leslie Caron, Jerry Lewis, Oliver Reed, Ian McNeice, Ruta Lee, Richard Griffith, George Carl, Freddie Davies; *D:* Peter Chelsom; *W:* Peter Chelsom, Peter Flannery; *C:* Eduardo Serra; *M:* John Altman.

Funny, Dirty Little War ½ *No Hambra mas Penas ni Olvido; Funny Little Dirty War* **1983** An Argentinian farce about the petty rivalries in a small village erupting into a violent, mini-civil war. Based on the novel by Osvaldo Soriano. In Spanish with English subtitles. **80m/C VHS, DVD.** *AR* Federico Luppi, Julio de Grazia, Miguel Angel Sola; *D:* Hector Olivera; *W:* Hector Olivera, Roberto Cassa; *C:* Leonardo Solis; *M:* Oscar Cardozo Ocampo.

Funny Face **1957** Musical satire on beatniks and the fashion scene also features the May-December romance between Astaire and the ever-lovely Hepburn. He is a high-fashion photographer (based on Richard Avedon); she is a Greenwich Village bookseller fond of shapeless, drab clothing. He decides to take her to Paris and show her what modeling's all about. The elegant musical score features classic Gershwin. ♫Let's Kiss and Make Up; He Loves and She Loves; Funny Face; How Long Has This Been Going On?; Clap Yo' Hands; S'Wonderful; Bonjour Paris; On How To Be Lovely; Marche Funebre. **103m/C VHS, 8mm, Wide.** Fred Astaire, Audrey Hepburn, Kay Thompson, Suzy Parker; *D:* Stanley Donen; *W:* Mary St. Feint; *M:* George Gershwin, Ira Gershwin.

The Funny Farm ½ **1982** Comedy about a group of ambitious young comics striving to make it in the crazy world of comedy at Los Angeles' famous comedy club, The Funny Farm. **90m/C VHS.** *CA* Miles Chapin, Eileen Brennan, Peter Aykroyd; *D:* Ron Clark; *W:* Ron Clark.

Funny Farm **1988 (PG)** Chevy Chase as a New York sportswriter finds that life in the country is not quite what he envisioned. The comedy is uneven throughout, with the best scenes coming at the end. **101m/C VHS, DVD.** Chevy Chase, Madolyn Smith, Joseph Maher, Jack Gilpin, Brad Sullivan, MacIntyre Dixon; *D:* George Roy Hill; *W:* Jeffrey Boam; *C:* Miroslav Ondricek; *M:* Elmer Bernstein.

Funny Games **1997** Georg (Muhe), his wife, Anna (Lothar), and young son, Georgie (Clapczynski) are vacationing at their lakeside cottage when their peace is invaded by psycho Paul (Frisch) and his sniveling partner Frank (Giering). The family is tied up and forced to play humiliating games with a couple of amoral killers. Most of the physical violence occurs off-screen but the psychological torture is relentless. German with subtitles. **103m/C VHS, DVD.** *AT* Susanne Lothar, Ulrich Muhe, Frank Giering, Arno Frisch, Stefan Clapczynski; *D:* Michael Haneke; *W:* Michael Haneke; *C:* Jurgen Jurges.

Funny Girl **1968 (G)** Follows the early career of comedian Fanny Brice, her rise to stardom with the Ziegfeld Follies, and her stormy romance with gambler Nick Arnstein in a fun and funny look at back stage music hall life in the early 1900s. Streisand's film debut followed her auspicious performance of the role on Broadway. Score was augmented by several tunes sung by Brice during her performances. Excellent performances from everyone, captured beautifully by Wyler in his musical film debut. Followed by "Funny Lady." ♫My Man; Second Hand Rose; I'd Rather Be Blue Over You; People; Don't Rain On My Parade; I'm The Greatest Star; Sadie, Sadie; His Love Makes Me Beautiful; You Are Woman, I Am Man. **151m/C VHS, DVD, Wide.** Barbra Streisand, Omar Sharif, Walter Pidgeon, Kay Medford, Anne Francis; *D:* William Wyler; *W:* Isobel Lennart; *C:* Harry Stradling Sr.; *M:* Jule Styne, Walter Scharf. Oscars '68: Actress (Streisand); Golden Globes '69: Actress—Mus./Comedy (Streisand).

Funny Lady ½ **1975 (PG)** A continuation of "Funny Girl," recounting Fanny Brice's tumultuous marriage to showman Billy Rose in the 1930s and her lingering affection for first husband Nick Arnstein. One of the rare sequels which are just as good, or at least almost, as the original. ♫How Lucky Can You Get?; Great Day; More Than You Know; Blind Date; So Long, Honey Lamb; Isn't This Better; Let's Hear It For Me; I Like Him/I Like Her; It's Only a Paper Moon. **137m/C VHS, DVD, Wide.** Barbra Streisand, Omar Sharif, James Caan, Roddy McDowall, Ben Vereen, Carole Wells, Larry Gates, Heidi O'Rourke; *D:* Herbert Ross; *W:* Jay Presson Allen, Arnold Schulman; *C:* James Wong Howe.

Funny Money **1982** Pointed, satirical look at the British habit of financing life with the almighty credit card. Sometimes uneven comedy. **92m/C VHS.** *GB* Gregg Henry, Elizabeth (E.G. Dailey) Daily, Gareth Hunt, Derren Nesbitt, Annie Ross; *D:* James Kenelm Clarke.

A Funny Thing Happened on the Way to the Forum **1966** A bawdy Broadway farce set in ancient Rome where a conniving, slave plots his way to freedom by aiding in the romantic escapades of his master's inept son. Terrific performances by Mostel and Gilford. Keaton's second-to-last film role. The Oscar-winning score includes such highlights as "Comedy Tonight," "Lovely," and "Everybody Ought to Have a Maid." **100m/C VHS, DVD, Wide.** Zero Mostel, Phil Silvers, Jack Gilford, Buster Keaton, Michael Hordern, Michael Crawford, Annette Andre; *D:* Richard Lester; *W:* Melvin Frank, Michael Pertwee; *C:* Nicolas Roeg; *M:* Ken Thorne. Oscars '66: Adapt. Score.

Funnyman **1994 (R)** Cartoon splatter courtesy of a demon dressed in classic British jester regalia. Rock 'n' roll mogul Young obtains Lee's creepy ancestral home in a card game but when he visits with his family, everyone but Young is killed by the Funnyman, who uses his victims own weaknesses to dispatch them. A second set of likely candidates arrive when Young's brother Devitt shows up with a motley collection of hangers-on, including psychic Black, who's the only one to realize something's seriously off. **89m/C VHS.** *GB* Tim James, Benny Young, Matthew Devitt, Pauline Black, Ingrid Lacey; ***Cameos:*** Christopher Lee; *D:* Simon Sprackling; *W:* Simon Sprackling.

The Further Adventures of Tennessee Buck **1988 (R)** Mercenary adventurer travels through tropical jungles acting as a guide to a dizzy couple. Along the way, they encounter cannibals, headhunters, and other bizarre jungle things in this lame take on "Indiana Jones." Shot on location in Sri Lanka. **90m/C VHS.** David Keith, Kathy Shower, Brant Van Hoffman; *D:* David Keith; *M:* John Debney.

Further Adventures of the Wilderness Family, Part 2 ½ *Wilderness Family, Part 2* **1977 (G)** Depicts the Robinson family who left civilization for the freedom of the Colorado wild. Predictable retread, but more good family adventure drama from the makers of "Adventures of the Wilderness Family." **104m/C VHS.** Heather Rattray, Ham Larsen, George "Buck" Flower, Robert F. Logan, Susan Damante Shaw; *D:* Frank Zuniga.

Fury ½ **1936** Tracy gives an excellent performance as an innocent young man framed for kidnapping and then nearly murdered by a lynch mob. His plans for revenge are thwarted by his girlfriend, who fears that he will turn into the murderer he has been accused of being. Powerful anti-violence message is well-made, with strong ensemble acting. Lang's favorite of his American-made films. **96m/B VHS.** Spencer Tracy, Sylvia Sidney, Walter Abel, Bruce Cabot, Edward Ellis, Walter Brennan, Frank Albertson; *D:* Fritz Lang; *C:* Joseph Ruttenberg. Natl. Film Reg. '95.

The Fury **1978 (R)** The head of a government institute for psychic research finds that his own son is snatched by supposed terrorists who wish to use his lethal powers. The father tries to use another a young woman with psychic power to locate him, with bloody results. A real chiller. **117m/C VHS, DVD, Wide.** Kirk Douglas, John Cassavetes, Carrie Snodgress, Andrew Stevens, Amy Irving, Charles Durning, Carol Rossen, Rutanya Alda, William Finley, Jane Lambert, Joyce Easton, Daryl Hannah, Dennis Franz, James Belushi; *D:* Brian DePalma; *W:* John Farris; *C:* Richard H. Kline; *M:* John Williams.

Fury **198?** A man and woman meet in the Amazonian jungle and the sparks begin to fly. **75m/C VHS.** Stuart Whitman, Laura Gemser.

The Fury of Hercules ½ *La Furia Di Ercole; Fury of Samson* **1961** It's up to the mighty son of Zeus to free an enslaved group of people from an oppressive, evil ruler. Surely all who stand in his way will be destroyed. Another Italian muscleman film. **95m/C VHS.** *IT* Brad Harris, Brigitte Corey, Mara Berni, Carlo Tamberlani, Serge Gainsbourg, Elke Arendt, Alan Steel; *D:* Gianfranco Parolini.

The Fury of the Wolfman *La Furia del Hombre Lobo* **1970** A murdering werewolf is captured by a female scientist who tries to cure his lycanthropy with drugs and brain implants. Pretty slow going, but hang in there for the wolfman versus werewoman climax. **80m/C VHS.** *SP* Paul (Jacinto Molina) Naschy, Jacinto (Jack) Molina, Perla Cristal, Michael Rivers, Mark Stevens, Veronica Lujan; *D:* Jose Maria Zabalza; *W:* Jacinto (Jack) Molina.

Fury on Wheels **1971 (PG)** Tale of men who race cars and wreak havoc and vice versa. **89m/C VHS.** Judd Hirsch, Tom Ligon, Paul Sorvino, Logan Ramsey, Collin Wilcox-Paxton.

Fury to Freedom: The Life Story of Raul Ries **1985** A young man raised in the volatile world of abusive and alcoholic parents grows into an abusive and violent adult. One night, however, he meets something he can't beat up, and it changes his life. **78m/C VHS.** Gil Gerard, John Quade, Tom Silardi.

The Fury Within **1998 (PG-13)** Mike (Mandylor) and Jo (Sheedy) Hanlon are an estranged couple who, along with their two young children, are terrorized by the supernatural. Turns out the poltergeist is a manifestation of Jo's anger about her upcoming divorce. Gives new meaning to the saying about scorned women. **91m/C VHS.** Ally Sheedy, Costas Mandylor, Vincent Berry; *D:* Noel Nosseck. **CABLE**

Future Cop *Trancers* **1976** A hard-nosed, old-fashioned cop is forced to team with the ultimate partner—a robot. Silly made-for-TV movie, but likable leads. **78m/C VHS.** Ernest Borgnine, Michael J. Shannon, John Amos, John Larch, Herbert Nelson, Ronnie Clair Edwards; *D:* Jud Taylor; *W:* Danny Bilson, Paul DeMeo.

Future Fear ½ **1997 (R)** Genetic scientist Dr. John Denniel (Wincott) has to find a solution for a flesh-eating virus that threatens mankind. Along with wife Anna (Ford), John tries cominbing human DNA with that of other species. But it turns out the virus was engineered by maniacal General Wallace (Keach) as a form of human cleansing—and he's not happy when he hears about a potential cure. **82m/C VHS.** Shawn Thompson, Jeff Wincott, Maria Ford, Stacy Keach; *D:* Lewis Baumander; *W:* Lewis Baumander; *C:* Graeme Mears; *M:* Donald Quan. **VIDEO**

Future Force **1989 (R)** In the crime-filled future cops can't maintain order. They rely on a group of civilian mercenaries to clean up the streets. **90m/C VHS.** David Carradine, Robert Tessier, Anna Rapagna, William Zipp.

Future Hunters **1988** In the holocaust-blitzed future, a young couple searches for a religious artifact that may decide the future of the planet. **96m/C VHS.** Robert Patrick, Linda Carol, Ed Crick, Bob Schott; *D:* Cirio H. Santiago.

Future Kill **1985 (R)** Anti-nuclear activists battle fraternity brothers in this grim futuristic world. Shaky political alliances form between revenge-seeking factions on both sides. **83m/C VHS.** Edwin Neal, Marilyn Burns, Doug Davis; *D:* Ronald W. Moore; *W:* Ronald W. Moore.

Future Shock **1993 (PG-13)** Dr. Russell Langdon is a psychiatrist who has been experimenting with virtual reality technology. Unbeknownst to three of his patients he decides to use them as guinea pigs in his work. But confronting their deepest fears only leads to new terrors. Also available in an unrated version. **93m/C VHS.** Bill Paxton, Vivian Schilling, Brion James, Martin Kove; *D:* Eric Parkinson, Matt Reeves, Oley Sassone; *W:* Vivian Schilling.

Future Zone **1990 (R)** In an attempt to save his father from being murdered, a young man travels backwards in time. **88m/C VHS.** David Carradine, Charles Napier, Ted Prior; *D:* David A. Prior.

Futurekick ½ **1991 (R)** In the not so distant future, a kickboxer with an attitude and cyborg capabilities must use every ounce of strength in a battle against evil. **80m/C VHS.** Don "The Dragon" Wilson, Meg Foster, Christopher Penn, Eb Lottimer, Linda Dona, Maria Ford; *D:* Damian Klaus; *W:* Damian

Klaus, Catherine Cyran; **C:** Ken Arlidge; **M:** Stan Ridgway.

Futuresport 🦴🦴½ **1998 (R)** In 2025, Tre Ramsey (Cain) is the arrogant star of a popular violent sport that's a combo of skateboarding and basketball. Only the key game turns out to have more on the line than endorsements when terrorists take over the arena. Tre's mentor, and Futuresport creator Orbike Fixx (Snipes), suggests it's just a gigantic turf war and that matters can be settled by an arena match to the death. Caught in the middle is newscaster Alejandra (Williams), the woman Tre once loved and left behind. **89m/C VHS, DVD.** Dean Cain, Vanessa L(ynne) Williams, Wesley Snipes, Bill Smitrovich, Francoise Yip; **D:** Ernest R. Dickerson; **W:** Robert Hewitt Wolfe. **TV**

Futureworld 🦴🦴 **1976 (PG)** In the sequel to "Westworld," two reporters junket to the new "Futureworld" theme park, where they first support a scheme to clone and control world leaders. Includes footage shot at NASA locations. **107m/C VHS.** Peter Fonda, Blythe Danner, Arthur Hill, Yul Brynner, Stuart Margolin; **D:** Richard T. Heffron; **W:** George Schenck.

Futz 🦴½ **1969** Story from off-Broadway is of a man who loves his pig and the world that can't understand the attraction. Better in original stage production. **90m/C VHS.** John Pakos, Victor Lipari, Sally Kirkland; **D:** Tom O'Horgan.

Fuzz 🦴🦴½ **1972 (PG)** Reynolds in the Boston cop on the track of a bomber killing policemen, punks setting winos on fire, and some amorous fellow officers. Combines fast action and some sharp-edged humor. **92m/C VHS.** Burt Reynolds, Tom Skerritt, Yul Brynner, Raquel Welch, Jack Weston; Charles Martin Smith, Albert "Poppy" Popwell; **D:** Richard A. Colla; **M:** Dave Grusin.

Fyre 🦴½ **1978 (R)** Young beautiful girl moves from the Midwest to Los Angeles and becomes a prostitute. **90m/C VHS.** Allen (Goorwitz) Garfield, Lynn Theel, Tom Baker, Cal Haynes, Donna Wilkes, Bruce Kirby; **D:** Richard Grand.

"G" Men 🦴🦴🦴½ **1935** Powerful story based loosely on actual events that occurred during FBI operations in the early 1930s, with Cagney on the right side of the law, though still given to unreasonable fits of anger. Raised and educated by a well-known crime kingpin, a young man becomes an attorney. When his friend the FBI agent is killed in the line of duty, he joins the FBI to seek vengeance on the mob. But his mob history haunts him, forcing him to constantly prove to his superiors that he is not under its influence. Tense and thrilling classic. **86m/B VHS.** James Cagney, Barton MacLane, Ann Dvorak, Margaret Lindsay, Robert Armstrong, Lloyd Nolan, William Harrigan, Regis Toomey; **D:** William Keighley.

G-Men Never Forget *Code 645* **1948** Moore, former stunt-man and future Lone Ranger, stars in this 12-part serial about FBI agents battling the bad guys. Lots of action. On two cassettes. **167m/B VHS.** Clayton Moore, Roy Barcroft, Ramsay Ames, Drew Allen, Tommy Steele, Eddie Acuff; **D:** Fred Brannon, Yakima Canutt.

G-Men vs. the Black Dragon **1943** Reedited serial of "Black Dragon of Manzanar" stars Cameron as Fed who battles Asian Axis agents during WWII. Action-packed. **244m/B VHS.** Rod Cameron, Roland Got, Constance Worth, Nino Pipitone, Noel Cravat; **D:** William Witney.

G2: Mortal Conquest 🦴🦴 **1999 (R)** In the year 2003, Steven Colin (Bernhardt) unknowingly possesses the secret of an ancient martial arts power he learned in a former incarnation. Now the foes from the ancient battle have returned and Colin must remember his past if he's to save his present. **93m/C VHS, DVD.** Daniel Bernhardt, James Hong. **VIDEO**

G. Whilliker! 🦴🦴 **1993** Brothers have decided a guy named Gus Whilliker is the perfect match for their older sister/guardian. Too bad she's already dating someone. **93m/C VHS.** Dan Brook, Robin Brooks, Matthew Tompkins, Jay Michael Ferguson, William Ryan Tilk, Chris Lloyd, Jody Miller; **D:** David McClendon; **W:** Brenda Brown-Canary, Michael Helderman; **M:** Drew F. Barlow.

Gabbeh 🦴🦴🦴½ **1996** Gabbeh is not only the name of the film's heroine (Djobat), it is also the name of the finely embroidered woolen rugs that the nomadic Ghashgai tribe is known for. Gabbeh has a simple desire—she wishes to marry a mysterious horseman but her father keeps placing obstacles in her path. She tells her story to an old married couple, who are washing their own gabbeh in a stream. The film is visually lush but a challenge for Western sensibilities with its slow pace and allegorical content. Farsi with subtitles. **75m/C VHS, Wide.** *IA* Shaghayeh Djodat, Hossein Moharami, Rogheih Moharami, Abbas Sayah; **D:** Mohsen Makhmalbaf; **W:** Mohsen Makhmalbaf; **C:** Mahmoud Kalari; **M:** Hossein Alizadeh.

Gabriel Over the White House 🦴🦴🦴 **1933** Part political satire, part fantasy, and completely fascinating. Huston is venal politician Judson Hammond, completely in thrall to his crooked cohorts, who manages to get elected President. While recuperating from an auto accident Hammond thinks he's sees a vision of the Archangel Gabriel, who essentially tells him to change his crooked ways. From bought man Hammond changes to righteous do-gooder, much to the dismay of his criminal companions, who'll stop at nothing to get rid of the man they think has simply gone insane. Huston gives a powerful performance in this decidedly oddball film. **86m/B VHS.** Walter Huston, Karen Morley, Arthur Byron, Franchot Tone, Dickie Moore, C. Henry Gordon, David Landau, Samuel S. Hinds, Jean Parker; **D:** Gregory La Cava; **W:** Carey Wilson.

Gabriela 🦴🦴 **1984 (R)** A sultry romance develops between a Brazilian tavern keeper and the new cook he's just hired. Derived from Jorge Amado's novel. In Portuguese with English subtitles. **102m/C VHS.** *BR* Sonia Braga, Marcello Mastroianni, Nelson Xavier, Antonio Cantafora; **D:** Bruno Barreto; **W:** Bruno Barreto; **C:** Carlo Di Palma; **M:** Antonio Carlos.

Gabriela 🦴🦴½ **2001 (R)** Student Gabriela (Lopez) takes a job at a mental health clinic where she meets social worker Mike (Gomez). She's pretty, he's handsome, there's a strong mutual attraction but Gabriela is engaged to Pat (Galligan) even though she doesn't really love him and only agreed to please her strict mother (Fernandez). So will this twosome manage to overcome their romantic obstacles and be together? Expect the expected. **93m/C VHS, DVD.** Seidy Lopez, Jaime Gomez, Zach Galligan, Troy Winbush, Evelina Fernandez, Lupe Ontiveros, Stacy Haiduk; **D:** Vincent Jay Miller; **W:** Vincent Jay Miller; **C:** Adrian Rudomin; **M:** Craig Stuart Garfinkle.

Gaby: A True Story 🦴🦴🦴 **1987 (R)** The story of a woman with congenital cerebral palsy who triumphs over her condition with the help of family and loved ones, and ends up a college graduate and acclaimed author. Based on a true story. **115m/C VHS.** Rachel Levin, Liv Ullmann, Norma Aleandro, Robert Loggia, Lawrence Monoson, Robert Beltran, Tony Goldwyn; **D:** Luis Mandoki; **W:** Martin Salinas, Michael James Love; **C:** Lajos Koltai; **M:** Maurice Jarre.

Gal Young 'Un 🦴🦴🦴 **1979** Set during the Prohibition era, a rich, middle-aged woman living on her property in the Florida backwoods finds herself courted by a much younger man. She discovers she is being used to help him set up a moonshining business. Unsentimental story of a strong woman. Based on a Marjorie Kinnan Rawlings story. **105m/C VHS.** Dana Preu, David Peck, J. Smith, Timothy McCormack, Gene Densmore, Jenny Stringfellow; **D:** Victor Nunez; **W:** Victor Nunez; **C:** Victor Nunez. Sundance '81: Grand Jury Prize.

Galactic Gigolo woof! **1987 (R)** An alien broccoli (yes, the vegetable) descends to earth on vacation, and discovers he's irresistible to Connecticut women. Must be something in the water. Amateurish effort intended as science-fiction satire, but there's more sleaze than humor. **80m/C** Carmine Capobianco, Debi Thibeault, Ruth (Coreen) Collins, Angela Nicholas, Frank Stewart; **D:** Gorman Bechard.

Galaxies Are Colliding 🦴🦴½ *Planet of Love* **1992 (R)** Adam (Brown) is so afraid of tying the knot that he abandons his bride at the altar and takes off on a journey of enlightenment, accompanied by best friend Peter (Grammer). They naturally meet any number of eccentrics along the way. **97m/C VHS.** Dwier Brown, Kelsey Grammer, Susan Walters, Karen Medak; **D:** John Ryman; **W:** John Ryman; **C:** Philip Lee; **M:** Stephen Barber.

Galaxina 🦴½ **1980 (R)** In the 31st century, a beautiful robot woman capable of human feelings is created. Stumbling parody of superspace fantasies features murdered Playmate Stratten in one of few film appearances. **95m/C VHS, DVD.** Dorothy Stratten, Avery Schreiber, Stephen Macht, James D. Hinton, Ronald J. Knight, Lionel Smith, Tad Horino, Herb Kaplowitz, Nancy McCauley; **D:** William Sachs; **W:** William Sachs; **C:** Dean Cundey.

Galaxis 🦴½ **1995 (R)** The physically impressive Nielsen stars as space- and time-traveling freedom fighter Landera, who beams down to Earth to battle your basic evil, intergalatic villain Kyla (Moll) who has the power source that could save her civilization. **91m/C VHS.** Brigitte Nielsen, Richard Moll, Craig Fairbrass; **D:** William Mesa.

Galaxy Invader 🦴 **1985 (PG)** Chaos erupts when an alien explorer crash lands his spacecraft in a backwoods area of the United States. **90m/C VHS.** Richard Ruxton, Faye Tilles, Don Leifert.

Galaxy of Terror 🦴½ *Mindwarp: An Infinity of Terror; Planet of Horrors* **1981 (R)** Astronauts sent to rescue a stranded spaceship get killed by vicious aliens. Big first: Moran (Joanie on "Happy Days") explodes. Inferior Corman-produced "Alien" imitation still manages to shock and displays generous gore. Followed by "Forbidden World." **85m/C VHS.** Erin Moran, Edward Albert, Ray Walston, Grace Zabriskie, Zalman King, Taaffe O'Connell, Robert Englund, Bernard Behrens, Jack Blessing, Sid Haig; **D:** Bruce (B.D.) Clark; **W:** Bruce (B.D.) Clark, Mark Siegler; **C:** Jacques Haitkin; **M:** Barry Schrader.

Galaxy Quest 🦴🦴½ **1999 (PG)** An ingratiating goof on "Star Trek" and other cheesy TV shows that draw rabid fans and typecast actors. At a sci-fi convention, the actors from the campy '70s TV space series "Galaxy Quest" are mistaken for real space traveling heroes by naive aliens who need them to aid in an intergalactic war and whisk the troupe off to a galaxy far, far away (or thereabouts). Naturally, the "crew" is ill-prepared for their latest mission. Playful acting includes Allen's vain leader Peter Nesmith, blond bosomy babe Gwen DeMarco (Weaver), and cynical Brit, Alexander Dane (Rickman). **104m/C VHS, DVD, Wide.** Tim Allen, Sigourney Weaver, Alan Rickman, Tony Shalhoub, Sam Rockwell, Darryl (Chill) Mitchell, Robin Sachs, Enrico Colantoni, Missi Pyle; **D:** Dean Parisot; **W:** David Howard, Robert Gordon; **C:** Jerzy Zielinski; **M:** David Newman.

Gale Force 🦴🦴½ **2001 (R)** The reality TV show "Treasure Hunt" involves eight contestants, one of whom is L.A. detective Sam Garrett (Williams), competing to find 10 million buried on the remote island on which they are marooned. But Sam is suspicious of executive producer Stuart McMahon (DeYoung), who'll do anything for ratings, and show host Jack MacRae (Nozick), who has a plot to get the money for himself. Oh, and then Mother Nature decides to make things even more interesting. Lots of action, including a good storm sequence. Wynorski directs under his Jay Andrews pseudonym. **96m/C VHS, DVD.** Treat Williams, Michael Dudikoff, Tim Thomerson, Curtis Armstrong, Cliff DeYoung, Bruce Nozick; **D:** Jim Wynorski. **VIDEO**

Galgameth 🦴🦴½ *The Adventures of Galgameth* **1996 (PG)** Old-fashioned tale of a boy-hero and a friendly monster. 14-year-old Prince Davin (Oatway) accidentally injures his father during a joust and blames himself when the king suddenly dies. But his majesty's actually been poisoned by knight El El (Macht), who declares himself regent and terrorizes the kingdom. Davin's only hope to restore peace is a magical statue called Galgameth that the prince is able to bring to life. Romanian location provides proper storybook castles and medieval villages. **99m/C VHS.** Devin Oatway, Stephen Macht, Sean McNamara, Johna Stewart, Tom Dugan; **D:** Sean McNamara; **W:** James Angeli; **C:** Christian Sebaldt; **M:** Rick Marvin.

Gallagher's Travels 🦴 **1987** A screwball male/female reporting team chase an animal smuggling ring through the wilds of Australia. **94m/C VHS.** *AU* Ivar Kants, Joanne Samuel, Stuart Campbell, Jennifer Hagan; **D:** Michael Caulfield.

The Gallant Fool 🦴½ **1933** A man is wrongly accused of murder and tries to clear his name while eluding the law. **57m/B VHS.** Bob Steele, Arletta Duncan, George "Gabby" Hayes, John Elliott; **D:** Robert North Bradbury; **W:** Robert North Bradbury.

The Gallant Hours 🦴🦴🦴 **1960** Biography of Admiral "Bull" Halsey (Cagney) covers five weeks, October 18 through December 1, 1942, in the WWII battle of Guadalcanal in the South Pacific. Director Montgomery forgoes battle scenes to focus on the human elements in a war and what makes a great leader. Fine performance by Cagney. **115m/B VHS.** James Cagney, Dennis Weaver, Ward (Edward) Costello, Richard Jaeckel, Les Tremayne, Robert Burton, Raymond Bailey, Karl Swenson, Harry Landers, James T. Goto, Walter Sande, Vaughn Taylor, Leon Lontoc, Carleton Young, James Yagi, Carl Benton Reid, Selmer Jackson, Nelson Leigh, John McKee, Tyler McVey, William Schallert, John Zaremba, Richard Carlyle, Herbert Lylton, Sydney Smith, Art Gilmore; **D:** Robert Montgomery; **W:** Frank D. Gilroy, Beirne Lay Jr.; **C:** Joe MacDonald; **M:** Roger Wagner.

Gallipoli 🦴🦴🦴🦴 **1981 (PG)** History blends with the destiny of two friends as they become part of the legendary WWI confrontation between Australia and the German-allied Turks. A superbly filmed, gripping commentary on the wastes of war. Haunting score; excellent performances by Lee and a then-unknown Gibson. Remake of a lesser 1931 effort "Battle of Gallipoli." **111m/C VHS, DVD.** *AU* Mel Gibson, Mark Lee, Bill Kerr, David Argue, Tim McKenzie, Robert Grubb, Graham Dow, Stan Green, Heath Harris, Harold Hopkins, Charles Yunupingu, Ronny Graham, Gerda Nicolson; **D:** Peter Weir; **W:** Peter Weir, David Williamson; **C:** Russell Boyd; **M:** Brian May. Australian Film Inst. '81: Actor (Gibson), Film.

Galloping Dynamite 🦴½ **1937** Early western based on a James Oliver Curwood story. A ranger avenges the death of his brother killed for gold. **58m/B VHS.** Kermit Maynard; **D:** Harry Fraser.

The Galloping Ghost 🦴🦴½ **1931** A 12-chapter serial starring football great "Red" Grange about big games, gambling, and underworld gangs. Grange is ousted from football when he's accused of throwing a game and he sets out to prove his innocence. **226m/B VHS.** Harold "Red" Grange, Dorothy Gulliver, Walter Miller, Tom Dugan; **D:** B. Reeves Eason.

Galloping Romeo 🦴½ **1933** Steele stars as a heartthrob on horseback in this romantic Western. Steele had a hard time pulling off the light comedy he was asked to do, so clips from his previous films were used to pad the movie. **59m/B VHS.** Bob Steele, Doris Hill, George "Gabby" Hayes, Frank Ball, Ernie Adams; **D:** Robert North Bradbury; **W:** Harry Fraser.

Gallowglass 🦴🦴🦴 **1995** A "gallowglass" is an ancient Gaelic term for a servant willing to sacrifice his life for his master. In this moody TV mystery that is dim Joe (Sheen), whose life was saved by manipulative, handsome Sandor (Rhys), who now demands his absolute loyalty. Sandor needs his help in kidnapping Nina (Whitely), an unhappy ex-model who was the victim of a kidnapping years before in Italy and now lives with her husband in wealthy seclusion in the country. There, Nina is under the protection of bodyguard/chauffeur Paul (McArdle), and their mutual attraction leads to unexpected complications. Based on the thriller by Ruth Rendell (writing as Barbara Vine). **150m/C VHS.** *GB* Paul Rhys, Michael Sheen, Arkie Whiteley,

John McArdle, Claire Hackett, Gary Waldhorn; *D:* Tim Fywell. **TV**

Galyon 🦴 **1977 (PG)** Soldier of fortune is recruited by an oil tycoon to find his daughter and son-in-law who have been kidnapped by terrorists in South America. **92m/C VHS.** Stan Brock, Lloyd Nolan, Ina Balin.

Gambit 🦴🦴½ **1966** Caine's first Hollywood film casts him as a burglar who develops a "Topkapi"-style scheme to steal a valuable statue with MacLaine as the lure and Lom as the equally devious owner. Once Caine's careful plan is put into operation, however, everything begins to unravel. **109m/C VHS.** Shirley MacLaine, Michael Caine, Herbert Lom, Roger C. Carmel; *D:* Ronald Neame; *W:* Alvin Sargent, Jack Davies; *M:* Maurice Jarre.

The Gamble 🦴🦴 **1988 (R)** A young man (Modine) seeks to rescue his father from gambling debts by wagering himself against a lustful countess (Dunaway). When he loses the bet, however, he flees and joins up with a runaway (Beals) with the countess and her henchmen in close pursuit. **108m/C VHS.** Matthew Modine, Jennifer Beals, Faye Dunaway; *D:* Carlo Vanzina.

Gamble on Love 🦴 **1986** Woman returns to her father's Las Vegas casino and falls for the man who manages the gaming room. **90m/C** Beverly Garland; *D:* Jim Balden.

The Gambler 🦴🦴🦴 **1974 (R)** College professor Axel Freed has a gambling problem so vast that it nearly gets him killed by his bookies. He goes to Las Vegas to recoup his losses and wins big, only to blow the money on stupid sports bets that get him deeper into trouble. Excellent character study of a compulsive loser on a downward spiral. **111m/C VHS, DVD, Wide.** James Caan, Lauren Hutton, Paul Sorvino, Burt Young, James Woods, Jacqueline Brookes, M. Emmet Walsh; *D:* Karel Reisz; *W:* James Toback; *C:* Victor Kemper; *M:* Jerry Fielding.

The Gambler 🦴🦴 **1997** In St. Petersburg in 1866, Russian writer Dostoyevsky (Gambon) is a middle-aged compulsive gambler who is currently indebted to his publisher Stellovsky (Jansen) and must now write a new novel in 27 days to pay him off. He hires poverty-stricken Anna (May) to be his secretary and the dictated novel turns out to be the story of a gambling couple who are trying to get out of hock at a German resort. The real and fictional intertwine as Anna becomes more and more protective of Dostoyevsky and is determined to help him succeed. **97m/C VHS, DVD.** *GB NL HU* Michael Gambon, Jodhi May, Polly Walker, Dominic West, Luise Rainer, John Wood, Johan Leysen, Thom Jansen, Angeline Ball; *D:* Karoly Makk; *W:* Charles Cohen, Nick Dear, Katharine Odgen; *C:* Jules Van Den Steenhoven; *M:* Brian Lock.

The Gambler & the Lady 🦴½ **1952** A successful London-based gambler and casino owner endeavors to climb the social ladder by having an affair with a member of the British aristocracy. He not only has to contend with his jilted nightclub singer girlfriend but also with the gangsters who would like to take over his clubs. Dull direction and a mediocre script. **72m/B VHS.** *GB* Dane Clark, Naomi Chance, Kathleen Byron; *D:* Patrick Jenkins.

The Gambler Returns: The Luck of the Draw 🦴🦴½ **1993** You'll see lots of familiar western TV stars as Rogers returns yet again as debonair gambler Brady Hawkes. This time he's on a cross country trip to San Francisco and the biggest card game around—only some varmints are out to stop him playing that first hand. **180m/C VHS.** Kenny Rogers, Reba McEntire, Rick Rossovich, Chuck Connors, Patrick Macnee, Linda Evans, James Drury, Mickey Rooney, Jere Burns, Clint Walker, Claude Akins, Gene Barry, Doug McClure, Hugh O'Brian, Brian Keith, Park Overall, Jack Kelly, David Carradine, Johnny Crawford, Marianne Rogers; *D:* Dick Lowry. **TV**

Gambler's Choice 🦴🦴 **1944** A police lieutenant and his boyhood friend find themselves on opposite sides of the law in this crime drama. Even though both men are romantically involved with the same woman, their friendship remains intact. **66m/B VHS.** Chester Morris, Nancy Kelly, Russell Hayden, Sheldon Leonard, Lee Patrick, Lloyd Corrigan, Tom Dugan, Lyle Talbot, Charles Arnt; *D:* Frank McDonald.

The Gambling Samurai 🦴🦴 *Kunisada Chuji* **1960** A samurai returns to his village to find it besieged by a ruthless government. Instead of attacking, he bides his time and works to undermine the government—finally achieving his revenge. In Japanese with English subtitles. **101m/C VHS.** *JP* Toshiro Mifune, Michiyo Aratama; *D:* Senkichi Taniguchi.

The Gambling Terror 🦴🦴 **1937** A cowboy goes after a mobster selling protection to hapless ranchers. **53m/B VHS.** Johnny Mack Brown, Charles "Blackie" King; *D:* Sam Newfield.

The Game 🦴 **1989** Three friends arrange a puzzle-murder-mystery for a selected group of guilty people, with $1 million as the prize—and death for the losers. **91m/C VHS.** Tom Blair, Debbie Martin; *D:* Curtis Brown; *W:* Curtis Brown.

The Game 🦴🦴🦴 **1997 (R)** Investment banker Nicholas Van Orton (Douglas) is an uptight corporate control freak. He receives a dangerous birthday present from his blacksheep younger brother Conrad (Penn). It's a subscription to Consumer Recreation Services, a real life-and-death version of a role-playing game that is designed to tap the hidden emotional and physical resources of the client. His life is overrun with an escalating series of traps and terrors, with the game reaching into every facet of his life. Excellent portrayal by Douglas as a man stuck in a Hitchcockian nightmare. **128m/C VHS, DVD, Wide.** Michael Douglas, Sean Penn, Deborah Kara Unger, Armin Mueller-Stahl, James Rebhorn, Peter Donat, Carroll Baker, Anna (Katerina) Katarina; *D:* David Fincher; *W:* John Brancato, Michael Ferris; *C:* Harris Savides; *M:* Howard Shore.

Game for Vultures 🦴½ **1986 (R)** Racial unrest in Rhodesia is the backdrop for this tale of a black revolutionary who fights racist sanctions. The noble topic suffers from stereotypes and oversimplification. **113m/C VHS.** *GB* Richard Harris, Richard Roundtree, Joan Collins, Ray Milland; *D:* James Fargo.

The Game Is Over 🦴🦴½ **1966 (R)** A wealthy neglected wife falls in love with her grown stepson, causing her to divorce her husband and shatter her life. A good performance by Fonda, then Vadim's wife. Modern version of Zola's "La Curee." **96m/C VHS.** *FR* Jane Fonda, Peter McEnery, Michel Piccoli; *D:* Roger Vadim; *M:* Jean Bouchety.

Game of Death 🦴🦴 *Goodbye Bruce Lee: His Last Game of Death; Bruce Lee's Game of Death* **1979 (R)** Bruce Lee's final kung fu thriller about a young martial arts movie star who gets involved with the syndicate. Lee died halfway through the filming of this movie and it was finished with outtakes and a double. **100m/C VHS, Wide.** Bruce Lee, Dean Jagger, Kareem Abdul-Jabbar, Colleen Camp, Chuck Norris; *D:* Robert Clouse; *M:* John Barry.

The Game of Love 🦴🦴 **1990 (PG)** Olin presides over Henry's bar, the lost and found of lonely hearts and lust, where people go to quench that deep thirst for love. **94m/C VHS.** Ed Marinaro, Belinda Bauer, Ken Olin, Robert Rusler, Tracy Nelson, Max Gail, Janet Margolin, Brynn Thayer; *D:* Bobby Roth.

Game of Seduction 🦴 **1986** A murdering, womanizing playboy pursues a married woman and gets caught up in a treacherous cat-and-mouse game. Dubbed. **81m/C VHS.** Sylvia Kristel, Jon Finch, Nathalie Delon; *D:* Roger Vadim.

Game of Survival 🦴 **1989** A young rebel warrior from another planet is sent to earth to battle six of the galaxy's most brutal warriors. **85m/C VHS.** Nikki Hill, Cindy Coatman, Roosevelt Miller Jr.; *D:* Armand Gazarian.

Gamera, the Invincible 🦴½ *Gamera; Gammera; Daikaiju Gamera* **1966** This Japanese monster flick features the ultimate nuclear super-turtle who flies around destroying cities and causing panic. First in the series of notoriously bad films, this one is cool in black and white and has some impressive special effects. Dubbed in English. **86m/B VHS.** *JP* Eiji Funakoshi, Harumi Kiritachi, Junichiro Yamashiko, Yoshiro Uchida, Brian Donlevy, Albert Dekker, Diane Findlay, John Baragrey, Dick O'Neill; *D:* Noriaki Yuasa; *W:* Fumi Takahashi; *C:* Nobuo Munekawa.

Gamera vs. Barugon 🦴½ *Gamera Tai Barugon; Gambara vs. Barugon; The War of the Monsters* **1966** The monstrous turtle returns to Earth from his outer space prison, now equipped with his famous leg-jets. He soon wishes he had stayed airborne, however, when he is forced to do battle with 130-foot lizard Barugon and his rainbow-melting ray. Tokyo and Osaka get melted in the process. **101m/C VHS.** *JP* Kojiro Hongo, Kyoko Enami; *D:* Shigeo Tanaka.

Gamera vs. Gaos 🦴½ *The Return of the Giant Monsters; Gamera vs. Gyaos; Boyichi and the Supermonster; Gamera Tai Gaos* **1967** Now fully the good guy, Gamera slugs it out with a bat-like critter named Gaos. Suspense rules the day when Gaos tries to put out the super turtle's jets with his built-in fire extinguisher but luckily for Earth, Gamera has a few tricks of his own up his shell. **87m/C VHS.** *JP* Kojiro Hongo, Kichijiro Ueda, Naoyuki Abe; *D:* Noriaki Yuasa.

Gamera vs. Guiron 🦴 *Attack of the Monsters; Gamera Tai Guiron* **1969** Gamera risks it all to take on an evil, spear-headed monster on a distant planet. Highlight is the sexy, leotard clad aliens who want to eat the little Earth kids' brains. **88m/C VHS.** *JP* Nobuhiro Kashima, Christopher Murphy, Miyuki Akiyama, Yuko Hamada, Eiji Funakoshi; *D:* Noriaki Yuasa.

Gamera vs. Zigra 🦴 *Gamera Tai Shinkai Kaiju Jigara; Gamera vs. the Deep Sea Monster Zigra* **1971** Gamera the flying turtle chose an ecological theme for this, his final movie. It seems that the alien Zigrans have come to Earth to wrest the planet from the hands of the pollutive humans who have nearly destroyed it. The aliens kill the staunch turtle, but the love and prayers of children revive him that he may defend Earth once more. **91m/C VHS.** *JP* Reiko Kasahara, Mikiko Tsubouchi, Koji Fujiyama, Arlene Zoellner, Gloria Zoellner; *D:* Noriaki Yuasa.

Games 🦴🦴½ **1967** Bored married Manhattanites Paul (Caan) and Jennifer (Ross), who are looking for some kinky entertainment, get involved with amateur medium Lisa (Signoret). Suddenly what's "real," isn't and there's more than one double-cross to cope with. Lots of atmosphere but not enough suspense. **100m/C VHS.** Simone Signoret, James Caan, Katharine Ross, Don Stroud, Kent Smith, Estelle Winwood, Marjorie Bennett, Ian Wolfe; *Cameos:* Florence Marly, Luana Anders; *D:* Curtis Harrington; *W:* Gene R. Kearney; *C:* William A. Fraker; *M:* Samuel Matlovsky.

Games Girls Play 🦴½ *The Bunny Caper; Sex Play* **1975** The daughter of an American diplomat organizes a contest at a British boarding school to see which of her classmates can seduce important dignitaries. **90m/C VHS.** Christina Hart, Jane Anthony, Jill Damas, Drina Pavlovic; *D:* Jack Arnold.

The Gamma People woof! **1956** A journalist discovers a Balkan doctor shooting children with gamma rays, creating an army of brainless zombies. Cult-renowned grade-Z tripe. **83m/B VHS.** *GB* Walter Rilla, Paul Douglas, Eva Bartok; *D:* John Gilling; *C:* Ted Moore.

Gandhi 🦴🦴🦴½ **1982 (PG)** The biography of Mahatma Gandhi from the prejudice he encounters as a young attorney in South Africa, to his role as spiritual leader to the people of India and his use of passive resistance against the country's British rulers, and his eventual assassination. Kingsley is a marvel in his Academy Award-winning role and the picture is a generally riveting epic worthy of its eight Oscars. **188m/C VHS, DVD, Wide.** *GB* Ben Kingsley, Candice Bergen, Edward Fox, John Gielgud, John Mills, Saeed Jaffrey, Trevor Howard, Ian Charleson, Roshan Seth, Athol Fugard, Martin Sheen, Daniel Day-Lewis, Rohini Hattangady; *D:* Richard Attenborough; *W:* John Briley; *C:* Billy Williams; *M:* George Fenton. Oscars '82: Actor (Kingsley), Art Dir./Set Dec., Cinematog., Costume Des., Director (Attenborough), Film Editing, Orig. Screenplay, Picture, Sound; British Acad. '82: Actor (Kingsley), Director (Attenborough), Film, Support. Actress (Hattangady); Directors Guild '82: Director (Attenborough); Golden Globes '83: Actor—Drama (Kingsley), Director (Attenborough), Foreign Film, Screenplay; L.A. Film Critics '82: Actor (Kingsley); Natl. Bd. of Review '82: Actor (Kingsley); N.Y. Film Critics '82: Actor (Kingsley), Film.

Gang Boys 🦴½ **1997** When a young man is brutally beaten by an L.A. street gang, mom Blair does not take things lying down. She contacts her estranged, ex-cop husband Hauser and he organizes a group of local victims to fight back. This time it's the gang members who should watch out. **87m/C VHS.** Wings Hauser, Linda Blair, Cole Hauser, Daryl Roach, Carmen Zapata, Ernest Harden Jr., Talbert Morton, Dave Buzzotta; *D:* Wings Hauser; *W:* Maria Dylan, Wings Hauser; *C:* Francis Grumman; *M:* Geoff Levin, Chris Many. **VIDEO**

Gang Bullets 🦴 **1938** Mobster tries to continue his dirty systems in a new town, but finds the legal force incorruptible. **62m/B VHS.** Anne Nagel, Robert Kent, Charles Trowbridge, Morgan Wallace, J. Farrell MacDonald, Arthur Loft, John Merton; *D:* Lambert Hillyer.

Gang Busters 🦴½ **1955** Prisoners plan a breakout. Slow and uninteresting adaptation of the successful radio series. Filmed in Oregon. **78m/B VHS.** Myron Healey, Sam Edwards, Frank Gerstle; *D:* Bill Karn.

Gang in Blue 🦴🦴½ **1996 (R)** Black officer Michael Rhoades (Van Peebles) is secretly investigating a white supremacist group of cops, called the Phantoms, within the LAPD. Marine Corp vet and police rookie Keith DeBruler (Brolin) becomes Rhoades's new partner and his racial comments make him a likely initiate for the Phantoms. So can he be trusted to be Rhoades's inside man and help Michael expose the corruption within the ranks? **99m/C VHS.** Mario Van Peebles, Josh Brolin, Melvin Van Peebles, J.T. Walsh, Cynda Williams, Stephen Lang, Sean McCann; *D:* Mario Van Peebles, Melvin Van Peebles; *W:* David Fuller, Rick Natkin; *C:* Rhett Morita; *M:* Larry Brown. **CABLE**

Gang Justice 🦴 **1994** Low-budget melodrama finds sensitive Asian student Paul (Kim) battling racists at school and his crippled alcoholic father at home. Some martial arts fight scenes but this is amateur time. **92m/C VHS.** Joon Kim, Jonathan Gorman, Erik Estrada, Angel Dashek; *D:* Richard W. Park.

Gang Related 🦴½ **1996 (R)** Rodriguez (Shakur) and Divinci (Belushi) are a couple of scuzzball homicide cops who set up drug deals with impounded dope, then kill the customers. They keep the dope and the money, and call the murders "gang-related." Their plan unravels when they whack an undercover DEA agent posing as a dealer. They try to play a game of "pin the crime on the wino" with a derelict (Quaid) who the duo thinks is easy prey. As their scheming spins out of control, Rodriguez tries to hold things together, while Divinci rips them apart. Shakur rises above the average material as the most likable of the entirely distasteful cast of characters. **109m/C VHS, DVD, Wide.** James Belushi, Tupac Shakur, Dennis Quaid, Lela Rochon, James Earl Jones, David Paymer, Wendy Crewson, Gary Cole, Terrence "T.C." Carson, Brad Greenquist, James Handy, Victor Love, Robert LaSardo, Gregory Scott Cummins; *D:* Jim Kouf; *W:* Jim Kouf; *C:* Brian Reynolds; *M:* Mickey Hart.

Gang War 🦴 **1940** Low-budget gangster film with an all-black cast about two gangs fighting for control of the city's jukebox business. **60m/B VHS.** Ralph Cooper, Gladys Snyder, Reggie Fenderson, Lawrence Criner, Monte Hawley, Jesse C. Brooks, Maceo B. Sheffield; *D:* Leo Popkin.

Gang Wars 🦴 *Devil's Express* **1975 (R)** There's a riot going on as Puerto Rican, Black, and Chinese gangs fight it out for control of the city. **82m/C VHS.** Warhawk Tanzania, Larry Fleishman, Sam DeFazio, Wilfred Roldan, Elsie Roman, Sarah Nyrick; *D:* Barry Rosen.

Gangbusters 1938 Men battle crime in the city in this serial in 13 episodes based on the popular radio series of the same name. **253m/B VHS.** Kent Taylor, Irene Hervey, Robert Armstrong.

The Gang's All Here ½ 1940 Darro joins a trucking firm whose rigs are being run off the road and hijacked by a competitor. Features "Charlie Chan" regulars Luke and Moreland. **63m/B VHS.** Frankie Darro, Marcia Mae Jones, Jackie Moran, Mantan Moreland, Keye Luke; ***D:*** Jean Yarbrough.

Gangs, Inc. *Crimes, Inc.; Paper Bullets* **1941** A woman is sent to prison for a hit-and-run accident, actually the fault of a wealthy playboy. When she learns his identity she vows revenge and turns to crime to achieve her evil ends. Okay thriller suffers from plot problems. Ladd has a minor role filmed before he became a star. **72m/B VHS.** Joan Woodbury, Lash LaRue, Linda Ware, John Archer, Vince Barnett, Alan Ladd; ***D:*** Phil Rosen.

The Gangster ½ 1947 Sullivan plays a small-time slum-bred hood who climbs to the top of the underworld, only to lose his gang because he allows his fears to get the better of him. (There's nothing to fear except when someone knows you're afeared.) Noir crimer with an interesting psychological perspective, though a bit sluggish at times. **84m/B VHS.** Barry Sullivan, Joan Lorring, Akim Tamiroff, Harry (Henry) Morgan, John Ireland, Fifi d'Orsay, Shelley Winters; ***D:*** Gordon Wiles.

Gangster Wars 1981 A specially edited-for-video version of the TV miniseries "The Gangster Chronicles." Based on fact, it deals with the growth of organized crime in America from the early days of this century, through the eyes of three ghetto kids who grow up to become powerful mobsters. **121m/C VHS.** Michael Nouri, Joe Penny, Brian Benben, Kathleen Lloyd, Madeleine Stowe, Robert Davi; ***D:*** Richard Sarafian. **TV**

Gangster World 1998 (R) In the 21st century, Gangster World is an adult theme part that caters to fulfilling a human's most decadent fantasies—aided by cyborgs in a 1930s setting. But with a name like that, it's easy to believe that a battle for control turns the park into the most dangerous place in the universe. Lots of action and decent enough special effects. **91m/C VHS, DVD.** Xavier DeClie, David Leisure, Gabriel Dell Jr., Stacey Williams, Bridget Flannery; ***D:*** David Bishop. **VIDEO**

Gangsters 1979 City is ruled by the mob and nothing can stop their bloody grip except "The Special Squad." **90m/C VHS.** *IT* Michael V. Gazzo, Tony Page, Vicki Sue Robinson, Nai Bonet; ***D:*** Mac Ahlberg.

Gangster's Den 1945 A gang of renegades scare a woman out of buying a gold-laden piece of land and Billy the Kid comes to her rescue. **56m/B VHS.** Buster Crabbe, Kermit Maynard, Al "Fuzzy" St. John, Charles "Blackie" King; ***D:*** Sam Newfield.

Gangster's Law woof! 1986 A look at a seedy gangster's downfall. Filmed on location in Italy. Dubbed. **89m/C VHS.** Klaus Kinski, Maurice Poli, Susy Andersen, Max Delys; ***D:*** Siro Marcellini.

Gangsters of the Frontier **1944** The people of Red Rock are forced to work in the town mines by two prison escapees until Ritter and his friends ride to the rescue. Part of the "Texas Ranger" series. **56m/B VHS.** Tex Ritter, Dave O'Brien; ***D:*** Elmer Clifton; ***W:*** Elmer Clifton.

Gangway ½ 1937 Pat Wayne (Matthews), a London newspaper reporter, is mistaken for a jewel thief and kidnapped by gangsters aboard a New York-bound ocean liner. In the meantime, the real thief is aboard posing as a Hollywood actress (Blakeney), and it's up to Scotland Yard inspector Bob Deering (Mackay) to solve the crime. Matthews was considered by many to be the English equivalent of America's Eleanor Powell. Based on an original story by Dwight Taylor. **90m/B VHS.** *GB* Jessie Matthews, Barry Mackay, Olive Blakeney, Liane Ordeyne, Patrick Ludlow, Nat Pendleton, Noel Madison, Alastair Sim, Doris Rogers, Laurence Anderson, Bennie Dorn; ***D:*** Sonnie Hale; ***W:*** Sonnie Hale, Lesser Samuels.

Ganja and Hess ½ *Blood Couple; Black Vampire; Double Possession; Black Out: The Moment of Terror; Black Evil* **1973 (R)** Jones plays a professor of African studies who is turned into a vampire by another vampire. He then marries the villain's ex-wife, played by Clark, a veteran of Russ Meyer films. Not much of a story but the acting is actually quite good and there are some creepy moments thanks mainly to an interesting score. **110m/C VHS, DVD, Wide.** Duane Jones, Marlene Clark, Bill Gunn, Sam Waymon, Leonard Jackson, Candece Tarpley, Mabel King; ***D:*** Bill Gunn; ***W:*** Bill Gunn; ***C:*** James E. Hinton; ***M:*** Sam Waymon.

Ganjasaurus Rex 1987 (R) Monster spoof about a giant green dinosaur emerging from the pot-laden hills of California. Maybe it's all in your head, man. **100m/C VHS.** Paul Bassis, Dave Fresh, Rosie Jones; ***D:*** Ursi Reynolds.

Gappa the Trifibian Monster ½ *Daikyoju Gappa; Monster from a Prehistoric Planet* **1967 (PG)** Researchers visiting a tropical island find a giant egg and take it back to Tokyo with them, dismaying the egg's giant monster parents. Dubbed. **90m/C VHS, DVD, Wide.** *JP* Tamio Kawaji, Yoko Yamamoto, Tatsuya Fuji, Koji Wada, Yuji Okada; ***D:*** Haruyasu Noguchi; ***W:*** Ryuzo Nakanishi; ***C:*** Muneo Ueda.

The Garbage Pail Kids Movie woof! 1987 (PG) The disgusting youngsters, stars of bubblegum cards, make their first and last film appearance in this live action dud. The garbage is where it should be thrown. **100m/C VHS.** Anthony Newley, MacKenzie Astin, Katie Barberi; ***D:*** Rod Amateau; ***W:*** Rod Amateau.

The Garbage-Picking, Field Goal-Kicking Philadelphia Phenomenon ½ 1998 Sports recruiters discover the natural kicking talents of sanitation engineer Barney Gorman (Danza) and turn his life upside down by giving him the chance to be the new place-kicker for the Philadelphia Eagles. TV movie. **85m/C VHS.** Tony Danza, Jessica Tuck, Art LaFleur, Al Ruscio, Ray Wise, Chris Berman; ***D:*** Tom Kelleher. **TV**

Garbo Talks 1984 (PG-13) A dying eccentric's last request is to meet the reclusive screen legend Greta Garbo. Bancroft amusingly plays the dying woman whose son goes to extreme lengths in order to fulfill his mother's last wish. **104m/C VHS.** Anne Bancroft, Ron Silver, Carrie Fisher, Catherine Hicks, Steven Hill, Howard da Silva, Dorothy Loudon, Harvey Fierstein, Hermione Gingold; ***D:*** Sidney Lumet; ***C:*** Andrzej Bartkowiak; ***M:*** Cy Coleman.

The Garden 1990 Eternally provocative director Jarman does another take on sex and religion. He examines the role of the Church in the persecution of homosexuality by recreating the story of the Passion and replacing the figure of Christ in some sequences with two male lovers, who are arrested, humiliated, and tortured. **90m/C VHS.** *GB* Tilda Swinton, Johnny Mills, Philip MacDonald, Roger Cook, Kevin Collins, Pete Lee-Wilson, Spencer Lee, Jody Graber; ***D:*** Derek Jarman; ***W:*** Derek Jarman; ***M:*** Simon Fisher Turner.

The Garden of Allah **1936** Dietrich finds hyper-romantic encounters in the Algerian desert with Boyer, but his terrible secret may doom them both. This early Technicolor production, though flawed, is an absolute must for Dietrich fans. Yuma, Arizona substituted for the exotic locale. **85m/C VHS, DVD.** Alan Marshal, Marlene Dietrich, Charles Boyer, Basil Rathbone, Sir C. Aubrey Smith, Tilly Losch, Joseph Schildkraut, Henry (Kleinbach) Brandon, John Carradine; ***D:*** Richard Boleslawski; ***W:*** W.P. Lipscomb, Lynn Riggs; ***C:*** William Howard Greene; ***M:*** Max Steiner.

The Garden of Delights **1970** A wicked black comedy about a millionaire, paralyzed and suffering from amnesia after a car accident. His horrendously greedy family tries to get him to remember and reveal his Swiss bank account number. Acclaimed; in Spanish with English subtitles. **95m/C VHS.** *SP* Jose Luis Lopez Vasquez, Lina Canelajas, Luchy Soto, Francisco Pierra, Charo Soriano; ***D:*** Carlos Saura.

The Garden of Eden **1928** Milestone—whose "Two Arabian Nights" had won an Academy Award the previous year, and who went on to direct "All Quiet on the Western Front" and "Of Mice and Men"—directed this sophisticated ersatz Lubitsch sex comedy. Griffith, the so-called "Orchid Lady," is a young girl who dreams of diva-dom but falls deep into the underbelly of the seedy side of Budapest. With the aid of a fallen baroness, however, she finds her way to Monte Carlo and has her turn in the limelight. A handsome production designed by William Cameron Menzies, art director for "Gone With the Wind." **115m/B VHS, 8mm.** Corine Griffith, Louise Dresser, Charles Ray, Lowell Sherman; ***D:*** Lewis Milestone.

The Garden of Redemption ½ 1997 (PG-13) Italian priest Don Paolo (LaPaglia) has his faith tested when his Tuscan village is occupied in 1944 by German troops and he has to decide whether to overcome his fears and join with the partisan resistance movement. That village beauty Adriana (Davidtz) is eager to help him with the decision only complicates matters more. **99m/C VHS.** Anthony LaPaglia, Embeth Davidtz, Dan Hedaya, Peter Firth, David Neal, Jorge Sanz, James Acheson; ***D:*** Thomas Michael Donnelly; ***W:*** Thomas Michael Donnelly; ***C:*** Jacek Laskus; ***M:*** John Altman. **CABLE**

The Garden of the Finzi-Continis *Il Giardino Del Finzi-Contini* **1971 (R)** Acclaimed film by De Sica about an aristocratic Jewish family living in Italy under increasing Fascist oppression on the eve of WWII. The garden wall symbolizes the distance between the Finzi-Continis and the Nazi reality about to engulf them. Flawless acting and well-defined direction. Based on the novel by Giorgio Bassani, who collaborated on the script but later repudiated the film. Music by De Sica's son, Manuel. In Italian with English subtitles or dubbed. **94m/C VHS, DVD, Wide.** *IT* Dominique Sanda, Helmut Berger, Lino Capolicchio, Fabio Testi, Romolo Valli; ***D:*** Vittorio De Sica; ***W:*** Cesare Zavattini; ***C:*** Ennio Guarnieri; ***M:*** Bill Conti, Manuel De Sica. Oscars '71: Foreign Film; Berlin Intl. Film Fest. '71: Golden Berlin Bear.

Gardens of Stone 1987 (R) A zealous young cadet during the Vietnam War is assigned to the Old Guard patrol at Arlington Cemetery, and clashes with the patrol's older officers and various pacifist civilians. Falls short of the mark, although Jones turns in an excellent performance. **112m/C VHS.** James Caan, James Earl Jones, D.B. Sweeney, Anjelica Huston, Dean Stockwell, Lonette McKee, Mary Stuart Masterson, Bill Graham, Sam Bottoms, Casey Siemaszko, Laurence "Larry" Fishburne, Dick Anthony Williams, Elias Koteas, Peter Masterson, Carlin Glynn, Eric Holland; ***D:*** Francis Ford Coppola; ***W:*** Ronald Bass; ***C:*** Jordan Cronenweth; ***M:*** Carmine Coppola.

Gargantua ½ 1998 Marine biologist Jack Ellway (Baldwin) and his son are studying the effects of seismic activity on marine life on a Polynesian island, that's also been the scene of a number of mysterious drownings. Then Jack discovers a nearby underwater trench houses a family of giant reptiles. When a two-foot long baby lizard comes ashore, it's clear mom and dad must be close behind. Kinda the small screen version of "Godzilla," and you know how successful that was. **91m/C VHS.** Adam Baldwin, Julie Carmen, Bobby Hosea, Emile Hirsch; ***D:*** Bradford May; ***W:*** Ronald Parker; ***C:*** John Stokes. **TV**

Gargoyles, The Movie: The Heroes Awaken ½ 1994 (G) Mythical crimefighting creatures, trapped in stone by day thanks to a sorcerer's spell but released to live at night, are displaced in time from their medieval Scottish home, winding up in modern-day New York City. But they discover they still have old enemies to fight. First aired as a five-episode part of the animated TV series. **80m/C VHS, DVD.** ***V:*** Ed Asner, Keith David, Jonathon Frakes, Marina Sirtis, Bill Fagerbakke, Salli Richardson, Frank Welker, Thom Adcox, Jeff Bennett.

Garringo 1969 Lawmen attempt to bring to justice a man who is intent on killing the soldiers responsible for his father's death. **95m/C VHS.** *IT SP* Anthony Steffen, Peter Lee Lawrence, Jose Bodalo; ***D:*** Rafael Romero Marchent.

Gas woof! 1981 (R) This dog has tycoon Hayden buying up all the gas stations in town to create a crisis that will make him richer. Everyone in the cast wastes their time, especially Sutherland as a hip DJ reporting on the gas shortage. **94m/C VHS.** *CA* Donald Sutherland, Susan Anspach, Sterling Hayden, Peter Aykroyd, Howie Mandel, Helen Shaver; ***D:*** Les Rose; ***W:*** Dick Wolf.

Gas Food Lodging 1992 (R) Saga casts Adams as Nora, a weary waitress in Laramie, New Mexico, trying her best to raise two teenaged daughters on her own. The daughters, Skye and Balk, are disillusioned about love and family. Balk's special friend is Darius, an eccentric window dresser, played by Leitch, Skye's brother. Nothing works out quite as intended but multi-dimensional characters, poignant situtations, and enormous emotional appeal highlight the directorial debut of Anders. Based on the Richard Peck novel "Don't Look and It Won't Hurt." **100m/C VHS, Wide.** Brooke Adams, Ione Skye, Fairuza Balk, James Brolin, Rob Knepper, Donovan Leitch, David Lansbury, Jacob Vargas, Chris Mulkey, Tiffany Anders; ***D:*** Allison Anders; ***W:*** Allison Anders; ***C:*** Dean Lent; ***M:*** J. Mascis, Barry Adamson. Ind. Spirit '93: Actress (Balk).

Gas Pump Girls ½ 1979 (R) Comedy about five lovely ladies who manage a gas station and use their feminine wiles to win the battle against a shady oil sheik. **102m/C VHS.** Kirsten Baker, Dennis Bowen, Huntz Hall, Steve Bond, Leslie King, Linda Lawrence; ***D:*** Joel Bender.

Gas-s-s-s! ½ *Gas-s-s-s... or, It May Become Necessary to Destroy the World in Order to Save It* **1970 (PG)** A gas main leak in an Alaskan defense plant kills everyone beyond 30-something and the post-apocalyptic pre-boomer survivors are left to muddle their way through the brume. Trouble is, AIP edited the heck out of the movie, much to Corman's chagrin, and the result is a truncated comedy; Corman was so displeased, in fact, he left to create New World studios. **79m/C VHS.** Robert Corff, Elaine Giftos, Pat Patterson, George Armitage, Alex Wilson, Ben Vereen, Cindy Williams, Bud Cort, Talia Shire; ***D:*** Roger Corman; ***W:*** George Armitage; ***C:*** Ron Dexter; ***M:*** Barry Melton.

Gaslight ½ *Angel Street* **1940** A forgotten British classic that fell victim to the American production of the same title and theme that was filmed only five years later. Set in late Victorian London, Wynyard is the rich innocent married to the calculating Walbrook, who slowly tries driving his bride insane in order to discover some hidden family jewels. She comes under the protection of a Scotland Yard detective (Pettingell) who suspects Walbrook has already murdered once. An outstandingly eerie psychological thriller. Based on the play "Angel Street" by Patrick Hamilton. **88m/C VHS.** *GB* Anton Walbrook, Diana Wynyard, Frank Pettingell, Cathleen Cordell, Robert Newton, Jimmy Hanley, Minnie Rayner, Mary Hinton, Marie Wright, Jack Barty, Moyna MacGill, Darmora Ballet; ***D:*** Thorold Dickinson; ***W:*** A.H. Rawlinson, Bridget Boland; ***C:*** Bernard Knowles; ***M:*** Richard Addinsell.

Gaslight ½ *The Murder in Thorton Square* **1944** Lavish remake of the 1939 film, based on the Patrick Hamilton play "Angel Street." A man tries to drive his beautiful wife insane while searching for priceless jewels. Her only clue to his evil acts is the frequent dimming of their gaslights. A suspenseful Victorian era mystery. Lansbury's film debut, as the tarty maid. **114m/B VHS.** Charles Boyer, Ingrid Bergman, Joseph Cotten, Angela Lansbury, Terry Moore, May Whitty, Barbara Everest, Emil Rameau, Edmund Breon, Halliwell Hobbes, Tom Stevenson; ***D:*** George Cukor; ***C:*** Joseph Ruttenberg. Oscars '44: Actress (Bergman); Golden Globes '45: Actress—Drama (Bergman).

The Gate 1987 (PG-13) Kids generally like to explore and Dorff and Tripp are no exception. When a large hole is exposed in their backyard, it would be a childhood sin not to see what's in it, right? What they don't know is that this hole is actually a gateway to and from Hell. The terror they unleash includes more than just run-of-the-mill demons. Good special effects. Followed by "Gate 2." **85m/C VHS.** Christa Denton, Stephen Dorff, Louis Tripp, Kelly Rowan, Jennifer Irwin; ***D:*** Tibor Takacs; ***W:*** Michael Nankin; ***C:*** Thomas Vamos.

Gate 2 ½ **1992 (R)** Tripp returns in his role as Terry, a young student of demonology in this lame sequel to "The Gate." Terry and a few of his teen buddies call up a group of demons that have been confined behind a gate for billions of years. The demons are used to grant modest wishes, but the wishes end up having very evil effects. Incredibly weak plot saved only by the special monster effects, which include live action and puppetry. **90m/C VHS.** Louis Tripp, Simon Reynolds, Pamela Segall, James Villemaire, Neil Munro, James Kidnie, Andrea Ladanyi; ***D:*** Tibor Takacs; ***W:*** Michael Nankin; ***C:*** Bryan England; ***M:*** George Blondheim.

Gate of Flesh *Nikutai No Mon* **1964** In postwar Japan, four prostitutes survive the American Occupation by sticking to their own code of conduct, including a restriction on anyone giving away their services for free. However, conduct becomes a flexible point when the women harbor a wounded black marketeer whom each comes to desire. Based on a novel by Taijiro Tamura. Japanese with subtitles. **90m/C VHS, Wide.** *JP* Joe Shishido, Yumiko Nogawa, Kayo Matsuo, Satoko Kasai, Misako Tominaga, Tomiko Ishi; ***D:*** Seijun Suzuki.

Gate of Hell ½ *Jigokumen* **1954** Set in 12th-century Japan. A warlord desires a beautiful married woman and seeks to kill her husband to have her. However, he accidentally kills her instead. Filled with shame and remorse, the warlord abandons his life to seek solace as a monk. Heavily awarded and critically acclaimed; the first Japanese film to use color photography. In Japanese with English subtitles. **89m/C VHS, 8mm.** *JP* Kazuo Hasegawa, Machiko Kyo, Isao Yamagata, Koreya Senda; ***D:*** Teinosuke Kinugasa; ***W:*** Teinosuke Kinugasa; ***C:*** Kohei Sugiyama; ***M:*** Yashushi Akutagawa. Oscars '54: Costume Des. (C), Foreign Film; Cannes '54: Film.

Gates of Hell woof! *Paura Nella Citta Dei Morti Viventi; City of the Living Dead; The Fear; Twilight of the Dead; Fear in the City of the Living Dead* **1980** The Seven Gates of Hell have been opened and in three days the dead will rise and walk the earth. A reporter (George) and a psychic (MacColl) fight to close the portals before Salem, Massachusetts is overrun by the risen dead. A gorefest that tried to disguise itself under many other titles. **93m/C VHS, DVD.** *IT* Christopher George, Janet Agren, Katherine (Katriona) MacColl, Robert Sampson, Carlo de Mejo, Antonella Interlenghi, Lucio Fulci, Michele (Michael) Soavi; ***D:*** Lucio Fulci; ***W:*** Dardano Sacchetti, Lucio Fulci; ***C:*** Sergio Salvati; ***M:*** Fabio Frizzi.

Gates of Hell 2: Dead Awakening **1996** Occultists performing an initiation rite reopen the portal to hell and a creature from its depths reawakens to cause the usual unholy terror. **87m/C VHS.** Tom Campitelli, Tamara Hext, Randy Strickland; ***D:*** G.D. Marcum.

The Gathering ½ **1977** A dying man seeks out the wife and family he has alienated for a final Christmas gathering. James Poe authored this well-acted holiday tearjerker that won the 1977-78 Emmy for outstanding TV drama special. **94m/C VHS.** Ed Asner, Maureen Stapleton, Lawrence Pressman, Stephanie Zimbalist, Bruce Davison, Gregory Harrison, Veronica Hamel, Gail Strickland; ***D:*** Randal Kleiser; ***M:*** John Barry. **TV**

A Gathering of Eagles ½ **1963** Hudson portrays a hard-nosed Air Force colonel during peacetime whose British wife must adjust to being a military spouse. **115m/C VHS.** Rock Hudson, Rod Taylor, Mary Peach, Barry Sullivan, Kevin McCarthy, Henry Silva, Leif Erickson; ***D:*** Delbert Mann; ***M:*** Jerry Goldsmith.

The Gathering: Part 2 **1979** Sequel in which a widow has a Christmas reunion with her family, but conflict arises when she introduces a new man in her life. Not as effective as the original, also made for TV. **98m/C VHS.** Maureen Stapleton, Efrem Zimbalist Jr., Jameson Parker, Bruce Davison, Lawrence Pressman, Gail Strickland, Veronica Hamel; ***D:*** Charles S. Dubin. **TV**

The Gathering Storm **1974** Based on the first book of memoirs from Sir Winston Churchill, this drama examines the pre-WWII years. **72m/C** Richard Burton, Virginia McKenna, Ian Bannen; ***D:*** Herbert Wise.

The Gatling Gun ½ *King Gun* **1972 (PG)** Poor tale of the Cavalry, Apache Indians, and renegades all after the title weapon. **93m/C VHS.** Guy Stockwell, Woody Strode, Patrick Wayne, Robert Fuller, Barbara Luna, John Carradine, Pat Buttram, Phil Harris; ***D:*** Robert Gordon.

Gator **1976 (PG)** Sequel to "White Lightning" (1973) follows the adventures of Gator (Reynolds), who is recruited to gather evidence to convict a corrupt political boss who also happens to be his friend. Reynolds in his good ole' boy role with lots of chase scenes. Talk show host Michael Douglas made his film debut in the role of the governor. First film Reynolds directed. **116m/C VHS.** Sonny Shroyer, Mike Douglas, Burt Reynolds, Jerry Reed, Lauren Hutton, Jack Weston, Alice Ghostley, Dub Taylor; ***D:*** Burt Reynolds; ***W:*** William W. Norton Sr.; ***M:*** Charles Bernstein.

Gator Bait ½ **1973 (R)** The Louisiana swamp is home to the beautiful Desiree, and woe be unto any man who threatens her family. Aims to please fans of the raunchy and violent. Followed by an equally vile sequel. **91m/C VHS.** Claudia Jennings, Clyde Ventura, Bill (Billy) Thurman, Janit Baldwin; ***D:*** Ferd Sebastian, Beverly Sebastian; ***W:*** Ferd Sebastian, Beverly Sebastian.

Gator Bait 2: Cajun Justice **1988 (R)** A city girl comes to the Louisiana swamp and turns violent in an effort to exact revenge on the men who have been tormenting her. **94m/C VHS.** Jan MacKenzie, Tray Loren, Paul Muzzcat, Brad Kepnick, Jerry Armstrong, Ben Sebastian; ***D:*** Ferd Sebastian, Beverly Sebastian; ***W:*** Ferd Sebastian, Beverly Sebastian.

Gator King ½ **1970 (R)** Villainous Santos (Fargas) imports Chinese crocodiles to serve them up as dinner at his restaurant and for other nefarious purposes. Spunky journalist Maureen (Foley) and her ex-beau Ranger Ronny (Richardson) decide to investigate. It's a standard-issue micro-budget action flick with nothing really to recommend it, even to fans of the genre. **86m/C DVD.** Antonio Fargas, Jay Richardson, Shannon K. Foley, Michael Berryman, Joe Estevez; ***D:*** Grant Austin Waldman; ***W:*** John L. Denk; ***C:*** Richard Lacy; ***M:*** Joe Pegram.

Gattaca **1997 (PG-13)** It's a future world where genetic tinkering allows parents to tweak their children's DNA before birth and a caste system of "perfect" humans exists. Vincent (Hawke) dreams of employment with the aerospace corporation Gattaca, so he assumes the identity of the genetically superior Jerome (Law). Soon Vincent is falling for icy co-worker Thurman and getting involved in a murder investigation, which could uncover his true identity. Thinking man's sci-fi (read: no spaceships or explosions) along the lines of George Lucas' "THX-1138." **112m/C VHS, DVD, Wide.** Ethan Hawke, Uma Thurman, Jude Law, Gore Vidal, Alan Arkin, Loren Dean, Jayne Brook, Elias Koteas, Tony Shalhoub, Ernest Borgnine; ***D:*** Andrew Niccol; ***W:*** Andrew Niccol; ***C:*** Slawomir Idziak; ***M:*** Michael Nyman.

The Gaucho **1927** Fairbanks stars as the title character, an immoral swashbuckler who lusts after a virginal religious (Greear) before undergoing a change of heart (but not before dancing a red-hot tango with the less-than-virginal Velez). **?m/B VHS.** Douglas Fairbanks Sr., Lupe Velez, Geraine Greear, Gustav von Seyffertitz; ***D:*** F. Richard Jones; ***W:*** Lotta Woods; ***C:*** Gaetano Antonio "Tony" Gaudio.

Gaucho Serenade ½ **1940** Former rodeo stars Gene (Autry) and Frog (Burnette) set out to help the son of their ex-partner, who's the kidnapping target of gangsters. Lots of singing, not much action. ♫Gaucho Serenade; A Song at Sunset; The Singing Hills; Give Out with a Song; Wooing of Kitty MacFuty. **66m/B VHS.** Gene Autry, Smiley Burnette, Duncan Renaldo, June Storey, Mary Lee; ***D:*** Frank McDonald; ***W:*** Bradford Ropes; ***C:*** Reggie Lanning.

The Gauntlet **1977 (R)** Clint is a broken-down cop ordered to Las Vegas to bring back a key witness for an important trial—but the witness turns out to be a beautiful prostitute being hunted by killers. Violence-packed action with some decent set-pieces. **111m/C VHS, DVD.** Clint Eastwood, Sondra Locke, Pat Hingle, Bill McKinney; ***D:*** Clint Eastwood; ***W:*** Michael Butler; ***C:*** Rexford Metz; ***M:*** Jerry Fielding.

The Gay Deceivers **1969 (R)** Unmistakably grounded in the '60s, the performances of this comedy are still fresh, but the script is a little stale. Danny (Coughlin) and Elliot (Casey) are two straight guys who avoid the draft by posing as a loving couple. When an army Colonel appears to be investigating the duo, they move into a gay apartment complex to carry on their scam. Naturally, hilarity ensues. The jokes are stereotype-based and show no true skill from the writer or director. Unfortunately, the film is credited with ruining the careers of its leads. **97m/C DVD.** Kevin Coughlin, Lawrence Casey, Brooke Bundy; ***D:*** Bruce Kessler; ***W:*** Gil Lasky, Jerome Wish; ***C:*** Richard C. Glouner; ***M:*** Stu Phillips.

The Gay Desperado ½ **1936** Mexican bandit Pablo (Carrillo), who styles himself after American screen gangsters, kidnaps singing caballero Chivo (Martini) and heiress Jane (Lupino). The reason everybody is so gay is that they're always singing in this goofy musical comedy. **85m/B VHS, DVD.** Leo Carrillo, Ida Lupino, Harold Huber, Nino Martini, Stanley Fields, Mischa Auer; ***D:*** Rouben Mamoulian; ***W:*** Wallace Smith; ***C:*** Lucien N. Andriot; ***M:*** Alfred Newman.

The Gay Divorcee *The Gay Divorce* **1934** Astaire pursues Rogers to an English seaside resort, where she mistakes him for the hired correspondent in her divorce case. Based on the musical play "The Gay Divorce" by Dwight Taylor and Cole Porter. The title was slightly changed for the movie because of protests from the Hays Office. ♫Don't Let It Bother You; A Needle in a Haystack; Let's K-nock K-nees; Night and Day; The Continental. **107m/B VHS.** Fred Astaire, Ginger Rogers, Edward Everett Horton, Eric Blore, Alice Brady, Erik Rhodes, Betty Grable; ***D:*** Mark Sandrich; ***M:*** Max Steiner. Oscars '34: Song ("The Continental").

The Gay Lady ½ *Trottie True* **1949** Light romantic comedy set in the 1890s about an actress who climbs to stardom in London theatre and winds up marrying into the aristocracy. Look for Christopher Lee and Roger Moore in early bit parts. **95m/C VHS.** *GB* Jean Kent, James Donald, Hugh Sinclair, Lana Morris, Bill Owen, Michael Medwin, Andrew Crawford; ***D:*** Brian Desmond Hurst.

Gay Purr-ee **1962** Delightful tale of feline romance in the City of Lights. For all ages. **85m/C VHS.** ***D:*** Abe Levitow; ***W:*** Chuck Jones; ***M:*** Harold Arlen; ***V:*** Judy Garland, Robert Goulet, Red Buttons, Hermione Gingold, Mel Blanc.

The Gay Ranchero **1942** Rogers, without Dale Evans, in an average tale of old west meets new crooks. Rogers is the sheriff who foils gangsters trying to take over an airport. The action doesn't stop him from singing a duet with leading lady Frazee on "Wait'll I Get My Sunshine in the Moonlight." **55m/B VHS.** Roy Rogers, Andy Devine, Tito Guizar, Jane Frazee, Estelita Rodriguez; ***D:*** William Witney.

The Gazebo **1959** Wacky comedy about a TV writer who is being blackmailed by someone who has nude photos of his Broadway star wife. He decides murder is the only solution to this problem. Reynolds sings "Something Called Love." Based on a play by Alec Coppel from a story by Myra and Alec Coppel. **102m/B VHS.** Glenn Ford, Debbie Reynolds, Carl Reiner, John McGiver, Doro Merande, Bert Freed, Martin Landau; ***D:*** George Marshall; ***W:*** George Wells.

Geek Maggot Bingo *The Freak from Suckweasel Mountain* **1983** It's too bad director Zed waited until mid-"Bingo" to post a sign warning "Leave Now, It Isn't Going Get Any Better!" Conceived by the New York underground's don of the "Cinema of Transgression" to be an off-the-rack cult classic, this horror spoof is too long on in-jokes and short on substance to earn its number in the cult hall of fame. It does, however, boast Death as Scumbalina the vampire queen and Hell as a punk cowboy crooner (before alternative country hit the airwaves). TV horror-meister Zacherle narrates. **70m/C VHS.** Robert Andrews, Richard Hell, Donna Death, Brenda Bergman, Tyler Smith, Bruno Zeus, John Zacherle; ***D:*** Nick Zedd; ***W:*** Nick Zedd; ***C:*** Nick Zedd.

Geheimakte WB1 *Secret Paper WB1* **1942** Historical drama centering on the invention of the U-boat by Sergeant Wilhelm Bauer during Denmark's WWII blockade of the ports of Schleswig-Holstein. In German with no subtitles. **91m/B VHS.** *GE* Alexander Golling; ***D:*** Herbert Selpin.

A Geisha *Gion Bayashi; Gion Festival Music* **1953** Miyoharu (Kogure) is a passive elderly geisha who agrees to train the naive young Eiko (Wakao) in her new role. But Eiko discovers her romantic notions of the geisha life are far from it's modern reality. Poignant look at the changing status of the geisha in Japan after WWII and the country's social upheavals. In Japanese with English subtitles. **86m/B VHS.** *JP* Michiyo Kogure, Ayako Wakao, Seizaburo Kawazu, Chieko Naniwa, Eitaro Shindo; ***D:*** Kenji Mizoguchi; ***W:*** Yoshikata Yoda; ***M:*** Ichiro Saito.

The Geisha Boy **1958** Jerry is a floundering magician who joins the USO and tours the Far East. His slapstick confrontations with the troupe leader and an officer who dreams of attending his own funeral provide hearty laughs, plus Lewis finds romance with a Japanese widow after her son claims him as a father. Pleshette's film debut, with an appearance by the Los Angeles Dodgers. **98m/C VHS.** Jerry Lewis, Marie McDonald, Sessue Hayakawa, Barton MacLane, Suzanne Pleshette, Nobu McCarthy; ***D:*** Frank Tashlin.

Geisha Girl ½ **1952** Forgotten sci-fi film about a mad scientist and his Japanese cohorts who develop small explosive pills that are more powerful than nuclear bombs. Their plans of world conquest are thwarted when the pills inadvertently fall into the hands of two American G.I.s. **67m/B VHS.** Martha Hyer, William Andrews, Archer MacDonald, Kekao Yokoo, Teddy Nakamura; ***D:*** George Breakston, C. Ray Stahl; ***W:*** C. Ray Stahl.

Gemini Affair **198?** Two women go to Hollywood to become rich and famous but end up being very disappointed. **88m/C VHS.** Marta Kristen, Kathy Kersh, Anne Seymour.

Gen-X Cops *Tejing Xinrenlei* **1999 (R)** Hong Kong police break a ring of smugglers, who are selling a massive shipment of explosives. But the cops then lose the goods to major criminal, Akatura (Nakamura). So a rebellious trio of young cops go undercover and discover the bad guy has very sinister plans. Cantonese with subtitles. **113m/C VHS, DVD, Wide.** *HK* Nicholas Tse, Stephen Fung, Sam Lee, Grace Kip, Toru Nakamura, Jackie Chan; ***D:*** Benny Chan; ***W:*** Benny Chan; ***C:*** Arthur Wong.

The Gene Krupa Story ½ **1959** The story of the famous jazz drummer and his career plunge after a drug conviction. Krupa recorded the soundtrack, mimed by Mineo, who was too young for a convincing portrayal. Gavin McLeod (of "Love Boat" fame) has a small part as Mineo's dad. **101m/B VHS.** Sal Mineo, James Darren, Susan Kohner, Susan Oliver, Anita O'Day, Red Nichols; ***D:*** Don Weis.

Genealogies of a Crime *Genealogies d'un Crime* **1997** Complex puzzle with the ever-beautiful Deneuve in dual roles. In one role, she's Solange, a criminal lawyer who agrees to defend a young man, Rene (Poupaud), who's accused of murdering his psychologist aunt Jeanne (Deneuve again, in flashback). Jeanne, who raised Rene, long suspected him of homicidal tendencies, became his shrink, and even expected to be killed by him. Solange believes Jeanne's ministrations programmed Rene to kill. As Solange investigates Rene's background, she becomes too involved with the unstable young man—leading her down the path to madness as well. French with subtitles. **114m/C VHS.** *FR* Catherine Deneuve, Melvil Poupaud, Michel Piccoli, Andrzej Seweryn, Bernadette LaFont, Hubert Saint Macary; ***D:*** Raul Ruiz; ***W:*** Raul Ruiz, Pascal Bonitzer; ***C:*** Stefan Ivanov; ***M:*** Jorge Arriagada.

The General 🦴🦴🦴🦴 **1926** Keaton's masterpiece and arguably the most formally perfect and funniest of silent comedies. Concerns a plucky Confederate soldier who single-handedly retrieves a pivotal train from Northern territory. Full of eloquent man-vs-machinery images and outrageous sight gags. Remade as "The Great Locomotive Chase" in 1956 with Fess Parker. **78m/B VHS, DVD.** Buster Keaton, Marion Mack, Glen Cavender, Jim Farley, Joe Keaton, Frederick Vroom, Charles Smith, Frank Barnes, Mike Donlin; ***D:*** Clyde Bruckman, Buster Keaton; ***W:*** Clyde Bruckman, Al Boasberg, Charles Henry Smith, Buster Keaton; ***C:*** Bert Haines, Devereaux Jennings. Natl. Film Reg. '89.

The General 🦴🦴🦴 **1998 (R)** Biopic of maverick Dublin crime lord Martin Cahill (Gleeson), nicknamed "The General" for his planning abilities. Film is one long flashback as it begins in 1994 with Cahill's assassination. Cahill supports his family through various burglaries, making a mockery of the local cops, including Ned Kenny (Voight). But Cahill's rise from petty criminal to local mobster is noted by the IRA and when he refuses to cut them in on his profits, things turn very dicey for the cocky, ruthless Cahill. **123m/B VHS, DVD.** *IR GB* Brendan Gleeson, Adrian Dunbar, Sean McGinley, Jon Voight, Maria Doyle Kennedy, Angeline Ball, Ciaran Fitzgerald, Eamon Owens; ***D:*** John Boorman; ***W:*** John Boorman; ***C:*** Seamus Deasy; ***M:*** Richie Buckley. Cannes '98: Director (Boorman).

The General Died at Dawn 🦴🦴🦴 **1936** A clever, atmospheric suspense film about an American mercenary in Shanghai falling in love with a beautiful spy as he battles a fierce Chinese warlord who wants to take over the country. Playwright-to-be Odets' first screenplay; he, O'Hara and '30s gossip hound Skolsky have cameos as reporters. **93m/B VHS.** Gary Cooper, Madeleine Carroll, Akim Tamiroff, Dudley Digges, Porter Hall, William Frawley, Philip Ahn; ***Cameos:*** John O'Hara, Clifford Odets, Sidney Skolsky; ***D:*** Lewis Milestone; ***W:*** Clifford Odets; ***C:*** Victor Milner.

The General Line 🦴🦴🦴🦴 *The Old and the New* **1929** Eisenstein's classic pro-Soviet semi-documentary about a poor farm woman who persuades her village to form a cooperative. Transgresses its party-line instructional purpose by vivid filmmaking. The director's last silent film. **90m/B VHS.** *RU* Marfa Lapkina; ***D:*** Sergei Eisenstein.

General Spanky 🦴🦴 **1936** The only feature "Our Gang" comedy goofed by transplanting them to a Civil War milieu popular at the time. Confederate kids Spanky and Alfalfa play soldier, ultimately outsmarting Union troops. The rascals are still funny sometimes, but Buckwheat's role as an eager slave is disturbing today. **73m/B VHS.** George "Spanky" McFarland, Phillips Holmes, Ralph Morgan, Irving Pichel, Rosina Lawrence, Billie "Buckwheat" Thomas, Carl "Alfalfa" Switzer, Louise Beavers; ***D:*** Fred Newmeyer.

Generale Della Rovere 🦴🦴🦴½ *Il Generale Della-Rovere* **1960** A WWII black marketeer is forced by the Nazis to go undercover in a local prison. To find out who the resistance leaders are, he poses as a general. But when prisoners begin to look to him for guidance, he finds the line between his assumed role and real identity diminished, leading to a tragic conclusion. Acclaimed film featuring a bravura lead performance by veteran director De Sica. In Italian with English subtitles. **139m/B VHS.** *IT* Vittorio De Sica, Otto Messmer, Sandra Milo; ***D:*** Roberto Rossellini; ***W:*** Roberto Rossellini, Sergio Amidei, Diego Fabbri, Indro Montanelli; ***C:*** Carlo Carlini; ***M:*** Renzo Rossellini.

The General's Daughter 🦴🦴 **1999 (R)** Disturbing and convoluted military thriller based on the 1992 bestseller by Nelson DeMille. Paul Brenner (Tavolta) is an Army criminal investigator whose latest case is the rape and murder of Capt. Elisabeth Campbell (Stefanson), whose father (Cromwell) is a legendary general. Elisabeth specialized in psychological warfare but she had more than a few mental problems of her own. Naturally, for the good of the service, everyone but Brenner would like a quick and tidy solution to the sleazy goings-on. Goes a little too over the top (including some performances) and you may come out wondering just who done what. **116m/C VHS, DVD.** John Travolta, Madeleine Stowe, James Cromwell, Timothy Hutton, James Woods, Leslie Stefanson, Clarence Williams III, Daniel von Bargen, Boyd Kestner, Mark Boone Jr., John Beasley, Peter Weireter, John Benjamin Hickey, Rick Dial, Brad Beyer; ***D:*** Simon West; ***W:*** William Goldman, Christopher Bertolini; ***C:*** Peter Menzies Jr.; ***M:*** Carter Burwell.

A Generation 🦴🦴🦴 *Pokolenie* **1954** During WWII, a young man escapes from the Warsaw Ghetto and finds his way to the Polish Resistance. He falls in love with the leader of the local group and finds the courage to fight for his freedom. Strong directorial debut from Wajda. Part 1 of his "War Trilogy," followed by "Kanal" and "Ashes and Diamonds." Scripted by Czeszko from his novel "Pokolenie." Polish with subtitles. **90m/B VHS.** *PL* Tadeusz Lomnicki, Urszula Modrzynska, Zbigniew Cybulski, Roman Polanski; ***D:*** Andrzej Wajda; ***W:*** Bohdan Czeszko; ***C:*** Jerzy Lipman; ***M:*** Andrzej Markowski.

Generation 🦴🦴 *A Time For Caring* **1969** A very pregnant bride informs everyone she'll give birth at home without doctors, and creates a panic. Based on the Broadway play by William Goodhart. **109m/C VHS.** David Janssen, Kim Darby, Carl Reiner, Peter Duel, Andrew Prine, James Coco, Sam Waterston; ***D:*** George Schaefer; ***W:*** William Goodhart; ***C:*** Lionel Lindon; ***M:*** Dave Grusin.

Genevieve 🦴🦴🦴 **1953** A 1904 Darracq roadster is the title star of this picture which spoofs "classic car" owners and their annual rally from London to Brighton. Two married couples challenge each other to a friendly race which becomes increasingly intense as they near the finish line. **86m/C VHS.** *GB* John Gregson, Dinah Sheridan, Kenneth More, Kay Kendall, Geoffrey Keen, Reginald Beckwith, Arthur Wontner, Joyce Grenfell, Leslie Mitchell, Michael Medwin, Michael Balfour, Edie Martin, Harold Siddons; ***D:*** Henry Cornelius; ***W:*** William Rose; ***C:*** Christopher Challis; ***M:*** Larry Adler. British Acad. '53: Film; Golden Globes '55: Foreign Film.

Genghis Cohn 🦴🦴½ **1993** Black comedy follows the misadventures of a former Nazi concentration camp commander (Lindsay) who has settled in a small Bavarian town and taken on the position of police chief. But his quiet life is rocked by a series of murders, an affair with a kinky Baroness (Rigg), and by the ghost of Jewish comedian Genghis Cohn (Sher), a victim of the camps whose haunting presence exacts a particularly appropriate revenge. Adapted from Romain Gary's novel "The Dance of Genghis Cohn." Made for British TV. **100m/C VHS.** *GB* Robert Lindsay, Diana Rigg, Anthony Sher; ***D:*** Elijah Moshinsky; ***W:*** Stanley Price. **TV**

Genie of Darkness 🦴 **1960** The ashes of Nostradamus himself are retrieved in a bid to destroy his vampiric descendent. Edited from a Mexican serial; if you were able to sit through this one, look for "Curse of Nostradamus" and "The Monster Demolisher." **?m/B VHS.** *MX* German Robles; ***D:*** Frederick Curiel.

Gentle Giant 🦴🦴 **1967** An orphaned bear is taken in by a boy and his family and grows to be a 750 pound giant who must be returned to the wild. "Gentle Ben" TV series was derived from this feature. **93m/C VHS.** Dennis Weaver, Vera Miles, Ralph Meeker, Clint Howard, Huntz Hall; ***D:*** James Neilson.

Gentle Savage 🦴🦴½ *Camper John* **1973 (R)** When an Indian is wrongly accused of raping and beating a white woman, the white community seeks revenge. The vengeful mob, led by the victim's step-father, is unaware that it's really their ringleader who is responsible for the crime. When the accused's brother is slain, the Indian community retaliates. Violent but well-crafted. **85m/C VHS.** William Smith, Gene Evans, Barbara Luna, Joe Flynn; ***D:*** Sean McGregor.

A Gentle Woman 🦴🦴 *A Gentle Creature; Une Femme Douce* **1969** Adaptation of Dostoevsky's short story about a young married woman who kills herself. Sanda marries pawnbroker Frangin, is miserable in her marriage, toys with killing her husband, and commits suicide instead, leaving the bewildered Frangin to try to figure out why. Several theories are offered but nothing is ever made clear. Debut of Sanda; Bressons' first film in color. French with subtitles. **89m/C VHS.** *FR* Dominique Sanda, Guy Frangin, Jane Lobre; ***D:*** Robert Bresson; ***W:*** Robert Bresson; ***C:*** Ghislan Cloquet; ***M:*** Jean Wiener.

A Gentleman After Dark 🦴🦴 **1942** Poor script but a good lead performance by Donlevy. Harry Melton escapes from prison in order to protect his daughter (who was raised by others) from his blackmailing wife, Flo (Hopkins). This monster mom is threatening to spoil the girl's upcoming marriage by revealing her sordid antecedents. A remake of 1936's "Forgotten Faces." **78m/B VHS.** Brian Donlevy, Miriam Hopkins, Preston Foster, Harold Huber, Philip Reed, Gloria Holden, Douglass Dumbrille, Sharon Douglas; ***D:*** Edwin L. Martin; ***W:*** George Bruce, Patterson McNutt; ***C:*** Milton Krasner; ***M:*** Dimitri Tiomkin.

Gentleman Bandit 🦴🦴 **1981** So-so drama about Father Bernard Pagano, a Boston priest mistakenly arrested as a stickup artist. Based on a true story. **96m/C VHS.** Ralph Waite, Julie Bovasso, Jerry Zaks, Joe Grifasi, Estelle Parsons, Tom Aldredge; ***D:*** Jonathan Kaplan. **TV**

The Gentleman from California 🦴 *The Californian* **1937** The dashing son of a Mexican landowner returns home and finds his people's land stolen from them by greedy tax collectors. **56m/B VHS, 8mm.** Ricardo Cortez, Marjorie Weaver, Katherine DeMille; ***D:*** Gus Meins.

Gentleman from Dixie 🦴🦴 **1941** After LaRue is released from prison, he looks to change his life by joining his brother on a farm and seeking revenge on the man who put him in the pokey. **61m/B VHS.** Jack LaRue, Marian Marsh, Clarence Muse, Mary Ruth, Robert Kellard, John Holland, Herbert Rawlinson; ***D:*** Al(bert) Herman.

Gentleman from Texas 🦴 **1946** Ropin', ridin', and romance figure in this less than dramatic oater. **55m/B VHS.** Johnny Mack Brown, Raymond Hatton, Claudia Drake, Reno Blair, Christine McIntyre; ***D:*** Lambert Hillyer.

Gentleman Jim 🦴🦴🦴½ **1942** A colorful version of the life of old-time heavyweight boxing great Jim Corbett, transformed from a typical Warner Bros. bio-pic by director Walsh into a fun-loving, anything-for-laughs donnybrook. Climaxes with Corbett's fight for the championship against the great John L. Sullivan. One of Flynn's most riotous performances. **104m/B VHS.** Errol Flynn, Alan Hale, Alexis Smith, Jack Carson, Ward Bond, Arthur Shields, William Frawley; ***D:*** Raoul Walsh.

The Gentleman Killer 🦴 **1978** A man-with-no-name clears a ravaged border town of murdering bandits. **95m/C VHS.** Anthony Steffen, Silvia Solar.

Gentleman's Agreement 🦴🦴🦴 **1947** Magazine writer Phil Green (Peck) looks for a new angle when he agrees to write a series of articles on anti-Semitism for publisher John Minify (Dekker). Phil pretends to be Jewish, and his new identity pervades his life in unexpected ways, almost destroys his relationships. Garfield has a small but powerful role as Phil's Jewish friend Dave, who has long had to deal with both overt and covert prejudice. This movie was Hollywood's first major attack on anti-Semitism. Controversial in its day, yet still timely. **118m/B VHS, DVD.** Gregory Peck, Dorothy McGuire, John Garfield, Celeste Holm, Anne Revere, June Havoc, Albert Dekker, Jane Wyatt, Dean Stockwell, Nicholas Joy; ***D:*** Elia Kazan; ***W:*** Moss Hart; ***C:*** Arthur C. Miller; ***M:*** Alfred Newman. Oscars '47: Director (Kazan), Picture, Support. Actress (Holm); Golden Globes '48: Director (Kazan), Film—Drama, Support. Actress (Holm); N.Y. Film Critics '47: Director (Kazan), Film.

Gentlemen Prefer Blondes 🦴🦴🦴 **1953** Amusing satire involving two show-business girls from Little Rock trying to make it big in Paris. Seeking rich husbands or diamonds, their capers land them in police court. Monroe plays Lorelei Lee, Russell is her sidekick. Despite an occasionally slow plot, the music, comedy, and performances are great fun. Film version of a Broadway adaption of a story by Anita Loos. Followed by (but without Monroe) "Gentlemen Marry Brunettes." ♫A (Two) Little Girl(s) From Little Rock; Bye, Bye Baby; Ain't There Anyone Here For Love?; When Love Goes Wrong; Diamonds Are A Girl's Best Friend. **91m/C VHS, DVD.** Marilyn Monroe, Jane Russell, Charles Coburn, Elliott Reid, Tommy Noonan, George Winslow; ***D:*** Howard Hawks; ***W:*** Charles Lederer; ***C:*** Harry Wild; ***M:*** Leo Robin, Jule Styne, Lionel Newman.

Genuine Risk 🦴½ **1989 (R)** Gorgeous young woman turns off her crime boss boyfriend bigtime when she seduces his bodyguard. Genuine tripe. **89m/C VHS.** Terence Stamp, Michelle Johnson, Peter Berg, Michael (M.K.) Harris; ***D:*** Kurt Voss; ***W:*** Kurt Voss.

George! 🦴½ **1970 (G)** A carefree bachelor takes his girlfriend and his 250-pound St. Bernard on a trip to the Swiss Alps where he proves that a dog is not always man's best friend. **87m/C VHS.** Marshall Thompson, Jack Mullaney, Inge Schoner; ***D:*** Wallace C. Bennett; ***W:*** Wallace C. Bennett.

George Balanchine's The Nutcracker 🦴🦴½ *The Nutcracker* **1993 (G)** Pas de deux redeux. Tchaikovsky's classic ballet about the magic of Christmas and a little girl (Cohen) who dreams on Christmas Eve that she is in an enchanted kingdom. Culkin lamely grins through his wooden performance as the Nutcracker Prince, but the talent of the Sugarplum Fairy (Kistler) and the other dancers is such that conventional camera techniques sometimes fail to keep up with their exacting moves. Adapted from the 1816 book by E.T.A. Hoffmann. **93m/C VHS, DVD, 8mm.** Macaulay Culkin, Jessica Lynn Cohen, Bart Robinson Cook, Darci Kistler, Damian Woetzel, Kyra Nichols, Wendy Whelan, Gen Horiuchi, Margaret Tracey; ***D:*** Emile Ardolino; ***W:*** Susan Cooper; ***C:*** Ralf Bode; ***Nar:*** Kevin Kline.

George of the Jungle 🦴🦴🦴 **1997 (PG)** The '60s cartoon hero goes big screen and live-action with Fraser starring as the clumsy (but very hunky) jungle hero. While on safari, socialite Ursula (Mann) falls in love with George and takes him back to San Francisco, leaving behind obnoxious fiancee Lyle (Church). But when poachers capture George's "brother" Ape (voiced by Cleese), he returns to save the day (aided by various jungle companions). Fraser is an appealing lead, and the script is sweetly funny while retaining creator Ward's smart, subversive edge. The stunts are more impressive than you'd usually expect from a cartoon adaptation. **91m/C VHS, DVD.** Brendan Fraser, Leslie Mann, Thomas Haden Church, Holland Taylor, Richard Roundtree, Greg Cruttwell, Abraham Benrubi, John Bennett Perry, Kelly Miller; ***D:*** Sam Weisman; ***W:*** Dana Olsen, Audrey Wells; ***C:*** Thomas Ackerman; ***M:*** Marc Shaiman; ***V:*** John Cleese; ***Nar:*** Keith Scott.

George Wallace 🦴🦴½ **1997** Follows 20 years (1955-1975) in the life of politician George Wallace (Sinise) from his career as a state circuit judge, his four terms as Alabama's hard-line segregationist governor, to the first years after he was paralyzed by a would-be assassin while campaigning for the presidency. Some elements are disturbingly dramatized, including Archie (Williams), the fictional black manservant who serves as Wallace's conscience. Based on the book "Wallace" by co-scripter Frady. **178m/C**

VHS. Gary Sinise, Mare Winningham, Clarence Williams III, Joe Don Baker, Angelina Jolie, Mark Valley, Cliff DeYoung, Skipp (Robert L.) Sudduth, Mark Rolston, William Sanderson, Terry Kinney; ***D:*** John Frankenheimer; ***W:*** Marshall Frady, Paul Monash; ***C:*** Alan Caso; ***M:*** Gary Chang. **CABLE**

George Washington 🦴🦴½ **1984** Bostwick stars as the father of our country in this made TV adaptation of James Thomas Flexner's biography. The destitute young Washington develops a close friendship with the wealthy Will Fairfax (Dukes), who provides him with the support to pursue his dreams, even though Washington has secretly fallen in love with Sally (Smith), Will's flirtatious wife. George himself has married the widowed Martha (Duke) and begins his military career, leading the American colonies against the Brits in the Revolutionary War. **398m/C VHS.** Barry Bostwick, David Dukes, Jaclyn Smith, Patty Duke, Hal Holbrook, Lloyd Bridges, Jose Ferrer, Trevor Howard, Richard Kiley, James Mason, Clive Revill, Robert Stack; ***W:*** Richard Fielder. **TV**

George Washington Slept Here 🦴🦴🦴 **1942** Hilarious side-splitter about a couple who moves from their Manhattan apartment to an old, broken-down country home in Connecticut. It's one catastrophe after another as the couple tries to renovate their home and deal with a greedy neighbor. Based on the play by George S. Kaufman and Moss Hart. **93m/B VHS.** Jack Benny, Ann Sheridan, Charles Coburn, Percy Kilbride, Hattie McDaniel, William Tracy; ***D:*** William Keighley.

George Washington: The Forging of a Nation 🦴🦴½ **1986** Sequel to the "George Washington" miniseries finds Bostwick and Duke reprising their roles as George and Martha. Unfortunately, the later part of Washington's life isn't nearly as exciting. **208m/C VHS.** Barry Bostwick, Patty Duke, Penny Fuller, Jeffrey Jones, Richard Bekins; ***D:*** William A. Graham; ***M:*** Bruce Broughton. **TV**

George White's Scandals 🦴🦴 **1945** A lightweight musical comedy look at the show biz world and why the show must go on. Based on White's Broadway extravaganzas. Jazz numbers by Gene Krupa and his band. Preceded by "George White's Scandals" of 1934 and 1935. ♫Bolero in the Jungle; E.H.S.; Leave Us Leap; I Want to be a Drummer in the Band; How Did You Get Out of My Dreams?; I Wake Up in the Morning; Who Killed Vaudeville?; Scandals; Liza. **95m/B VHS.** Joan Davis, Jack Haley, Jane Greer, Phillip Terry, Margaret Hamilton, Martha Holliday; ***D:*** Felix Feist.

George's Island 🦴🦴🦴 **1991 (PG)** When young George is placed with the worst foster parents in the world, his eccentric grandfather helps him escape. They wind up on Oak's Island, where, legend has it, Captain Kidd's ghost and buried treasure reside. They soon find out the legends are true! **89m/C VHS.** Ian Bannen, Sheila McCarthy, Maury Chaykin, Nathaniel Moreau, Vicki Ridler, Brian Downey, Gary Reineke; ***D:*** Paul Donovan; ***W:*** J. William Ritchie; ***M:*** Marty Simon.

Georgia 🦴🦴 **1987** Tough lawyer Nina Bailey (Davis) explores her past when she begins a search for information on her biological mother, Georgia White, a photographer who drowned herself years before. Only Nina has no idea about the Pandora's box of secrets she's about to unleash. Frequent flashbacks to Georgia's mysterious life and death (Davis well plays both roles). **90m/C VHS.** *AU* Judy Davis, Julia Blake, John Bach; ***D:*** Ben Lewin.

Georgia 🦴🦴🦴 **1995 (R)** Character study about sibling rivalry, self-destruction, and the Seattle music scene. Struggling rock singer Sadie (Leigh), who relies on booze, drugs, and men to help her make it through the night, returns to Seattle to crash with big-sister Georgia (Winningham). Settled, with loving husband and kids, the much more talented Georgia is also a popular folk icon and has the type of personal/career success angry and ambitious Sadie can only dream about. Fine performances—particularly from the chameonlike Leigh; both leads do their own singing. Screenwriter Turner is Leigh's mother. **117m/C VHS, DVD.** Mina (Badiyi) Badie, Jennifer Jason Leigh, Mare Winningham, Ted Levine, Max Perlich, John Doe, John C. Reilly, Jimmy Witherspoon; ***D:*** Ulu Grosbard; ***W:*** Barbara Turner; ***C:*** Jan Kiesser. Ind. Spirit '96: Support. Actress (Winningham); Montreal World Film Fest. '95: Actress (Leigh), Film; N.Y. Film Critics '95: Actress (Leigh).

Georgia, Georgia 🦴½ **1972 (R)** Sands is a black entertainer on tour in Sweden who falls for a white photographer. Her traveling companion, who hates whites, takes drastic action to separate the lovers. Poor acting, script, and direction. Based on a book by Maya Angelou. **91m/C VHS.** Diana Sands, Dirk Benedict, Minnie Gentry; ***D:*** Stig Bjorkman; ***W:*** Maya Angelou.

Georgy Girl 🦴🦴🦴 **1966** Redgrave finely plays the overweight ugly-duckling Georgy who shares a flat with the beautiful and promiscuous Meredith (Rampling). Georgy is, however, desired by the wealthy and aging Mason and soon by Meredith's lover (Bates) who recognizes her good heart. When Meredith becomes pregnant, Georgy persuades her to let her raise the baby, leaving Georgy with the dilemma of marrying the irresponsible Bates (the baby's father) or the settled Mason. The film and title song (sung by the Seekers) were both huge hits. Based on the novel by Margaret Foster who also co-wrote the screenplay. **100m/B VHS.** *GB* Lynn Redgrave, James Mason, Charlotte Rampling, Alan Bates, Bill Owen, Claire Kelly, Rachel Kempson, Denise Coffey, Dorothy Alison, Peggy Thorpe-Bates, Dandy Nichols; ***D:*** Silvio Narizzano; ***W:*** Margaret Forster, Peter Nichols; ***C:*** Ken Higgins. Golden Globes '67: Actress—Mus./Comedy (Redgrave); N.Y. Film Critics '66: Actress (Redgrave).

Gepetto 🦴🦴 **2000** Kinda goopy Pinocchio update that focuses on toymaker dad, Geppetto (Carey). His longing for a kid of his own is granted by the Blue Fairy (Louis-Dreyfus), who makes puppet Pinocchio (Adkins) come alive. But Geppetto's parenting skills leave something to be desired and soon his new son disappears with travelling showman, Stromboli (Spiner), and gets into all kinds of trouble. Some catchy tunes. **90m/C VHS.** Drew Carey, Seth Adkins, Julia Louis-Dreyfus, Brent Spiner, Rene Auberjonois, Usher Raymond, Ana Gasteyer, Wayne Brady; ***D:*** Tom (Thomas R.) Moore; ***W:*** David Stern; ***C:*** Stephen M. Katz; ***M:*** Stephen Schwartz. **TV**

Germany in Autumn 🦴🦴 *Deutschland im Herbst* **1978** Twelve West German filmmakers offer political statements and artistic commentary on the political situation in their country after the kidnapping and murder of industrialist Hans Martin Schleyer. In German with English subtitles. **124m/C VHS.** *GE* ***D:*** Volker Schlondorff, Rainer Werner Fassbinder, Alf Brustellin, Alexander Kluge, Maximiliane Mainka, Edgar Reitz, Katja Rupe, Hans Peter Cloos, Bernhard Sinkel, Beate Mainka-Jellinghaus, Peter Schubert, Heinrich Boll; ***W:*** Heinrich Boll.

Germany, Pale Mother 🦴🦴 *Deutschland, Bleiche Mutter* **1980** In 1939, young, pregnant German hausfrau Lene (Mattes) sends her husband, Hans (Jacobi), to the front lines. Lene and her daughter struggle for survival through the war years until she has a bittersweet reunion with the embittered Hans. Director Sanders-Brahms based her story on her own mother's wartime experiences but the film suffers from the relentless parade of atrocities. German with subtitles. **123m/C VHS.** *GE* Eva Mattes, Ernst Jacobi; ***D:*** Helmer Sanders-Brahms; ***W:*** Helmer Sanders-Brahms; ***C:*** Jurgen Jurges; ***M:*** Jurgen Knieper.

Germicide 🦴 **1974** Scientist tries to warn the world of the threat posed by a horrifying bacterial weapon. Terrorists and his mistress hatch plots against him. **90m/C** Rod Taylor, Bibi Andersson.

Germinal 🦴🦴🦴 **1993 (R)** Recounts the struggle of working-class coal miners in France, led by Depardieu and wife Miou-Miou, to stave off poverty. While greedy investors debate how far they should lower miners' wages, the Maheu family, spurred on by newly arrived Marxist and off-camera French pop star Renaud, lead a strike. Minor themes revolving around management's adulterous adventures provide some momentary relief to relieve short attention spans. Seems so self-consciously an epic drama, however, that the overall effect is ponderous. Adaptation of the 19th century novel by Zola. In French with English subtitles. **158m/C VHS.** *FR* Gerard Depardieu, Miou-Miou, Bernard Fresson, Jean Carmet, Laurent Terzieff, Anny (Annie Legras) Duperey, Renaud, Jacques Dacqmine, Judith Henry; ***D:*** Claude Berri; ***W:*** Claude Berri, Arlette Langmann; ***C:*** Yves Angelo; ***M:*** Jean-Louis Roques. Cesar '94: Cinematog., Costume Des.

Geronimo 🦴🦴½ **1962** In typical Hollywood casting Connors stars as the Indian leader on the warpath against the cavalry over broken treaties. Lots of action and the Indians are actually the good guys. **101m/C VHS, Wide.** Chuck Connors, Ross Martin, Pat Conway, Kamala Devi, Adam West, Lawrence (Larry) Dobkin, Denver Pyle, Enid Jaynes, Armando Silvestre, John Anderson; ***D:*** Arnold Laven.

Geronimo 🦴🦴🦴 **1993** Not to be confused with the big screen version, this made-for-cable drama uses three actors to portray the legendary Apache warrior (1829-1909) at various stages of his life. The intrepid teenager who leads attacks on Mexican troops, the adult fighting the duplicitous bluecoats, and the aged man witnessing the destruction of his way of life. The true story is told from the point of view of Native American culture and historical records. Somewhat overly earnest. **120m/C VHS.** Joseph Runningfox, Jimmy Herman, Ryan Black, Nick Ramus, Michelle St. John, Michael Greyeyes, Tailinh Forest Flower, Kimberly Norris, August Schellenberg, Geno Silva, Harrison Lowe; ***D:*** Roger Young; ***W:*** J.T. Allen; ***M:*** Patrick Williams. **CABLE**

Geronimo: An American Legend 🦴🦴½ **1993 (PG-13)** Well-intentioned bio-actioner about the legendary Apache leader who fought the U.S. Army over forcing Native Americans onto reservations. The division of young Army officer Gatewood (Patric) is to round up the renegades led by Geronimo (Studi), whom Gatewood naturally comes to admire. Hackman and Duvall (as a General and a scout respectively) steal any scene they're in although the leads manage to hold their own. An unknown Damon plays the narrator, Lt. Britton Davis. Too noble for its own good and somewhat plodding. Great location filming around Moab, Utah. **115m/C VHS, DVD, 8mm.** Wes Studi, Jason Patric, Robert Duvall, Gene Hackman, Matt Damon, Rodney A. Grant, Kevin Tighe, Carlos Palomino, Stephen McHattie; ***D:*** Walter Hill; ***W:*** John Milius, Larry Gross; ***C:*** Lloyd Ahern; ***M:*** Ry Cooder.

Geronimo's Revenge 🦴½ **1960** When Geronimo starts a battle with the settlers, a rancher he has befriended finds himself caught in the middle. The fourth soggy Disney TV oater from the "Tales of Texas John Slaughter" series. **77m/C VHS.** Tom Tryon, Darryl Hickman; ***D:*** Harry Keller.

Gertrud 🦴🦴🦴½ **1964** The simple story of an independent Danish woman rejecting her husband and lovers in favor of isolation. Cold, dry, minimalistic techniques make up Dreyer's final film. In Danish with subtitles. **116m/B VHS, DVD, Wide.** *DK* Nina Pens Rode, Bendt Rothe, Ebbe Rode, Baard Owe; ***D:*** Carl Theodor Dreyer; ***W:*** Carl Theodor Dreyer; ***C:*** Arne Abrahamsen, Henning Bendtsen; ***M:*** Jorgen Jersild.

Gervaise 🦴🦴🦴 **1956** The best of several films of Emile Zola's "L'Assommoir." A 19th-century middle-class family is destroyed by the father's plunge into alcoholism despite a mother's attempts to save them. Well acted but overwhelmingly depressing. In French with English subtitles. **89m/B VHS.** *FR* Maria Schell, Francois Perier, Suzy Delair, Armand Mestral; ***D:*** Rene Clement; ***M:*** Georges Auric. British Acad. '56: Actor (Perier), Film; N.Y. Film Critics '57: Foreign Film; Venice Film Fest. '56: Actress (Schell).

Get Carter 🦴🦴🦴 **1971 (R)** Tough and stylish crime drama that has gained in stature since its release. Small-timer London hood Jack Carter (Caine) arrives in Newcastle determined to find out who killed his brother. After meeting local crime boss Cyril Kinnear (Osborne), Carter is told to go back home and leave things alone. But he doesn't and things (and the film) don't turn out exactly as expected. Caine shows just how ruthless he can make a character. Film debut for director Hodges. Based on the novel "Jack's Return Home" by Ted Lewis. Remade in 1972 as "Hit Man" and in 2000. **112m/C VHS, DVD, Wide.** *GB* Michael Caine, Ian Hendry, John Osborne, Geraldine Moffatt, Glynn Edwards, Dorothy White, Petra Markham, Bryan Mosley, Britt Ekland, Tony Beckley, George Sewell, Alun Armstrong, Bernard Hepton, Terence Rigby; ***D:*** Mike Hodges; ***W:*** Mike Hodges; ***C:*** Wolfgang Suschitzky; ***M:*** Roy Budd.

Get Carter 🦴🦴 **2000 (R)** Stallone is Las Vegas tough guy Jack Carter, who goes home to Seattle for his brother's funeral and decides that his death wasn't natural. Hoping to redeem himself in the eyes of sister-in-law Gloria (Richardson) and niece Doreen (Cook), Carter searches the seedy underbelly for the killers. Or he may be searching for some decent lighting, since most of the scenes are dark even for a seedy underbelly. His injury-inducing tour of the underworld leads him to a sleazy pornographer (Roarke) and whiny billionaire (Cumming), setting the stage for a climactic showdown involving Doreen. Remake fails because Stallone's catalog of cinematic carnage waters down the feeling of nihilistic violence of the original 1971 Brit thriller. Michael Caine (who had the original title role) makes an appearance as a wily bar owner. **104m/C VHS, DVD, Wide.** Sylvester Stallone, Michael Caine, Rachael Leigh Cook, Alan Cumming, Miranda Richardson, Mickey Rourke, John C. McGinley, Rhona Mitra, Johnny Strong, John Cassini, Garwin Sanford, Gretchen Mol; ***D:*** Stephen Kay; ***W:*** David McKenna; ***C:*** Mauro Fiore; ***M:*** Tyler Bates.

Get Christie Love! 🦴🦴 **1974** Vintage blaxploitation from the genre's halcyon days, when going undercover meant a carte blanche for skimpy outfits. Based on Dorothy Uhnak's detective novel, the eponymous policewoman goes undercover to bring a thriving drug empire to it knees. The outcome: a TV series. Graves previously appeared on TV as one of the "Laugh-In" party girls. **95m/C VHS.** Teresa Graves, Harry Guardino, Louise Sorel, Paul Stevens, Andy Romano, Debbie Dozier; ***D:*** William A. Graham. **TV**

Get Crazy 🦴🦴½ *Flip Out* **1983** The owner of the Saturn Theatre is attempting to stage the biggest rock-and-roll concert of all time on New Year's Eve 1983, and everything is going wrong in this hilarious, off-beat film. **90m/C VHS.** Malcolm McDowell, Allen (Goorwitz) Garfield, Daniel Stern, Gail Edwards, Ed Begley Jr., Lou Reed, Bill Henderson, Fabian, Bobby Sherman, Miles Chapin, Howard Kaylan, Franklin Ajaye, Mary Woronov, Paul Bartel, Jackie Joseph, Dick Miller, Lee Ving, Clint Howard; ***D:*** Allan Arkush; ***W:*** Henry Rosenbaum, Danny Opatoshu, David Taylor; ***C:*** Thomas Del Ruth; ***M:*** Michael Boddicker.

Get On the Bus 🦴🦴🦴 **1996 (R)** Lee looks at the personal side of the Million Man March through a fictional group of men who board a bus in south central L.A. and head for Washington, D.C. Practically ignoring the event itself, Lee and writer Bythewood focus on the the men who participated, their reasons, and their interaction with each other. Standouts in the melting pot of characters include Dutton as the attentive bus driver, a brash young actor (Braugher), a likable old man (Davis), an absentee father (Byrd) and his potentially delinquent son (Bonds), and a cop (Smith). Despite low budget (2.4 mil) and tight shooting schedule (21 days), Lee manages to drive the story home with fine dialogue and characterization that (for the most part) avoids stereotypes. **122m/C VHS, DVD, Wide.** Andre Braugher, Ossie Davis, Charles S. Dutton, De'Aundre Bonds, Gabriel Casseus, Albert Hall, Hill Harper, Harry J. Lennix, Bernie Mac, Wendell Pierce, Roger Guenveur Smith, Isaiah Washington IV, Steve White, Thomas Jefferson Byrd, Richard Belzer, Randy Quaid; ***D:*** Spike Lee; ***W:*** Reggie Rock Bythewood; ***C:*** Elliot Davis; ***M:*** Terence Blanchard.

Get Out Your Handkerchiefs 🦴🦴🦴½ *Preparez Vous Mouchoirs* **1978 (R)** Unconventional comedy about a husband desperately attempting to make his sexually frustrated wife happy. Determined to go to any lengths, he asks a Mozart-loving teacher to become her lover. She is now, however, bored by both men. Only when she meets a 13-year-old genius at the summer camp where the three adults are counselors does she come out of her funk and find her sexual happiness. Laure is a beautiful character, but Depardieu and Dewaere are wonderful as the bewildered would-be lovers. Academy Award winner for Best Foreign Film. In French with English subtitles. **109m/C VHS, DVD, Wide.** *FR* Gerard Depardieu, Patrick Dewaere, Carole Laure; ***D:*** Bertrand Blier; ***W:*** Bertrand Blier; ***C:*** Jean Penzer; ***M:*** Georges Delerue. Oscars '78: Foreign Film; Cesar '79: Score; Natl. Soc. Film Critics '78: Film.

Get Over It! 🦴½ **2001 (PG-13)** Professes to be thematically related to "A Midsummer Night's Dream," but don't let this get your hopes up. Thankfully, there's little chance of that happening, as the practice of basing teen comedies on Shakespeare plays reached the saturation point not too long ago and audiences realized that a film claiming to have been inspired by the Bard rarely met such high expectations. So it goes with this below-average kiddie comedy, which follows the sad breakup of Berke Landers (Foster), the nice but slightly dull boy, and Alison (Sagemiller), his popular former girlfriend, who soon takes up with Striker (West), the hot new boy in school. Berke's obsession with his old flame seems unrelenting until Kelly (Dunst) enters the scene. **90m/C VHS, DVD, Wide.** *US* Kirsten Dunst, Ben Foster, Colin Hanks, Melissa Sagemiller, Sisqo, Shane West, Martin Short, Swoosie Kurtz, Ed Begley Jr., Zoe Saldana, Mila Kunis, Carmen Electra; ***Cameos:*** Coolio, Colleen (Ann) (Vitamin C) Fitzpatrick; ***D:*** Tommy O'Haver; ***W:*** R. Lee Fleming Jr.; ***C:*** Maryse Alberti; ***M:*** Steve Bartek.

Get Real 🦴🦴½ **1999 (R)** Gay coming of age tale about Brit suburban teen, Steven (Silverstone), deciding to come out of the closet. Steven's only confidante is fellow outsider Linda (Brittain). Then he has an unexpected encounter with popular jock John (Gorton), who's confused about his sexuality and terrified that anyone will suspect he's gay, even to the point of helping his jock buddies gay-bash Steven. Eventually, Steven decides secrecy is not worth the pain. Good performances in a somewhat self-conscious drama. Adapted from Wilde's play "What's Wrong with Angry?" **111m/C VHS, DVD.** *GB* Ben Silverstone, Brad Gorton, Charlotte Brittain, Stacy A. Hart, Kate McEnery, Jacquetta May, David Lumsden, Louise J. Taylor, Tim Harris; ***D:*** Simon Shore; ***W:*** Patrick Wilde; ***C:*** Alan Almond; ***M:*** John Lunn.

Get Rita 🦴🦴 *Gun Moll; Poopsie; Oopsie Poopsie; La Puppa del Gangster* **1975** Italian prostitute sets up her gangster boyfriend for a murder she committed and she winds up as mob boss. **90m/C VHS.** Sophia Loren, Marcello Mastroianni; ***D:*** Tom Rowe.

Get Shorty 🦴🦴🦴 **1995 (R)** Low-level Miami loan shark and film buff Chili Palmer (Travolta) heads to Hollywood via Las Vegas, looking for a deadbeat dry-cleaner (Paymer) and a grade-Z movie producer (Hackman) who owes Vegas $150,000. Aided by B-movie scream-queen (Russo), Palmer is pitted against a variety of shady Hollywood-types, including egomaniacal star (DeVito) while trying to get into showbiz himself. Snappy scripting and performances finally do screen justice to an Elmore Leonard novel. DeVito, with the smaller title role, was originally cast as Chili Palmer, a role Travolta twice turned down until the ubiquitous Quentin Tarantino advised him to take it. **105m/C VHS, DVD.** John Travolta, Gene Hackman, Danny DeVito, Rene Russo, Dennis Farina, Delroy Lindo, David Paymer, James Gandolfini; ***Cameos:*** Bette Midler, Harvey Keitel, Penny Marshall; ***D:*** Barry Sonnenfeld; ***W:*** Scott Frank; ***C:*** Don Peterman; ***M:*** John Lurie. Golden Globes '96: Actor—Mus./Comedy (Travolta).

Get Smart, Again! 🦴🦴½ **1989** Would you believe Maxwell Smart is back again as CONTROL's most incompetent agent? How about Agent 99 as his sidekick? Hymie the robot and those no-goodniks at KAOS? Well, it's all true. This second reunion movie (following "The Nude Bomb") from the '60s TV show highlights all the wacky gadgetry, including the shoe phone, but fails to find the show's original outlandishness. **93m/C VHS.** Don Adams, Barbara Feldon, Dick Gautier, Bernie Kopell, Kenneth Mars, Harold Gould, Roger Price, Fritz Feld, Robert Karvelas, King Moody; ***D:*** Gary Nelson. **TV**

Get That Girl 🦴 **1932** Minor western action pic marred by former silent-screen player Talmadge's heavy German accent which soon lead to him giving up acting for a directing career. **54m/B VHS.** Richard Talmadge, Shirley Grey, Carl Stockdale; ***D:*** George Crone.

Get That Man 🦴🦴 **1935** When a cabby is mistaken for the murdered heir to a vast fortune, his life suddenly becomes complex. **57m/B VHS.** Wallace Ford, Leon Ames, Lillian Miles, E. Alyn Warren; ***D:*** Spencer Gordon Bennet.

Get Well Soon 🦴½ **2001 (R)** Disjointed romantic comedy finds midnight TV talk show host Bobby Bishop (Gallo) suffering a nervous breakdown that results in a number of scandals. Bobby takes off to see ex-girlfriend Lily (Cox) in New York but she's not happy to see him when he arrives and neither is her new boyfriend (Donovan). **95m/C VHS, DVD.** Vincent Gallo, Courteney Cox Arquette, Jeffrey Tambor, Tate Donovan, Elina Lowensohn, Anne Meara; ***D:*** Justin McCarthy; ***W:*** Justin McCarthy; ***M:*** Vincent Gallo, Ric Markmann.

The Getaway 🦴🦴 **1972 (PG)** McQueen plays a thief released on a parole arranged by his wife (McGraw) only to find out a corrupt politician wants him to rob a bank. After the successful holdup, McQueen finds out his cohorts are in the politician's pocket and trying to doublecross him. McQueen and McGraw are forced into a feverish chase across Texas to the Mexican border, pursued by the politician's henchmen and the state police. Completely amoral depiction of crime and violence with McQueen taciturn as always and McGraw again showing a complete lack of acting skills. Based on a novel by Jim Thompson. McQueen and McGraw had a romance during filming and later married. Remade in 1993. **123m/C VHS, DVD.** Steve McQueen, Ali MacGraw, Ben Johnson, Sally Struthers, Al Lettieri, Slim Pickens, Jack Dodson, Dub Taylor, Bo Hopkins; ***D:*** Sam Peckinpah; ***W:*** Walter Hill; ***C:*** Lucien Ballard; ***M:*** Quincy Jones.

The Getaway 🦴½ **1993 (R)** It was a bad movie in 1972 and the remake hasn't improved the situation. Doc and Carol are husband and wife crooks (played by marrieds Basinger and Baldwin). Doc gets double-crossed and winds up in a Mexican jail; Carol gets a well-connected crook (Woods) to spring her hubby—by sleeping with him and promising Doc will pull off another heist. The robbery's botched, there are double-crosses galore, and the couple go on the run. The stars are pretty but everything's predictable. An unrated version is also available. **110m/C VHS, DVD, Wide.** Alec Baldwin, Kim Basinger, James Woods, Michael Madsen, Jennifer Tilly, David Morse; ***D:*** Roger Donaldson; ***W:*** Walter Hill, Amy Holden Jones; ***C:*** Peter Menzies Jr.; ***M:*** Mark Isham.

Getting Away With Murder woof! **1996 (R)** An utterly distasteful bomb that proves the Holocaust just isn't as funny as it used to be. College professor Aykroyd takes matters into his own hands when he learns that his kindly neighbor (Lemmon) is a Nazi war criminal. After finding out he may have been a wee bit hasty, he marries the coot's daughter as penance. Writer-director Miller tries to squeeze gags out of such topics as Nazi death camps and Holocaust denial. Definitely career lows for everyone involved. (What were they thinking?) One of the last films released (with no advance warning and no advance screenings) by Savoy pictures. **92m/C VHS.** Dan Aykroyd, Lily Tomlin, Jack Lemmon, Bonnie Hunt, Brian Kerwin; ***D:*** Harvey Miller; ***W:*** Harvey Miller; ***C:*** Frank Tidy; ***M:*** John Debney.

Getting Even 🦴½ *Hostage: Dallas* **1986 (R)** A maniac threatens to poison the entire population of Texas with a deadly gas unless he gets $50 million. An adventurous businessman sets out to stop him. **90m/C VHS.** Edward Albert, Joe Don Baker, Audrey Landers; ***D:*** Dwight Little; ***C:*** Peter Collister.

Getting Even 🦴🦴 **1992 (R)** Dundee and Evans served together in Vietnam. Fifteen years later they're reunited by the FBI to track a former Marine, who once betrayed Evans to the enemy. Seems he's now a drug traffiker and arms dealer who also gets his sadistic pleasures by killing women. The two ex-Marines find they have one last battle to fight. **93m/C VHS.** Richard Roundtree, Michael J. Aronin; ***D:*** Leandro Lucchetti.

Getting Even with Dad 🦴½ **1994 (PG)** Crook Danson can't find the money he stole in his last heist. Why? because his precocious son has hidden it with the intention of blackmailing dear old dad into going straight and acting like a real father. Title is unintentionally funny in light of Mac's domineering dad Kit, who makes everybody in Hollywood want to go hide when he appears. Fairly bland family film squanders charm of Danson and Culkin, running formulaic plot into ground. Headly is likewise wasted as district attorney who prosecutes and then falls for Pops. And hey, Macaulay's precocious days are down to a precious few. **108m/C VHS, DVD.** Macaulay Culkin, Ted Danson, Glenne Headly, Hector Elizondo, Saul Rubinek, Gailard Sartain, Kathleen Wilhoite, Sam McMurray; ***D:*** Howard Deutch; ***W:*** Tom S. Parker, Jim Jennewein; ***C:*** Tim Suhrstedt; ***M:*** Miles Goodman.

Getting Gotti 🦴🦴½ **1994 (R)** Story of the seven-year investigation and six-month trial by U.S. Attorney's Office prosecutor Diane Giacalone (Bracco) against reputed mobster "Teflon Don" John Gotti. (She lost.) **93m/C VHS.** Lorraine Bracco, Anthony John (Tony) Denison, Kathleen Lasky, August Schellenberg, Kenneth Welsh, Ellen Burstyn, Lawrence Bayne; ***D:*** Roger Young; ***W:*** James Henerson; ***M:*** Patrick Williams. **TV**

Getting In 🦴½ *Student Body* **1994 (R)** Pressured by the family tradition of attending Johns Hopkins Medical School, Gabriel Higgs (Mailer) decides to bribe the rivals ahead of him on the waiting list. But one of them (McCarthy) decides the easiest thing to do is murder the other candidates and frame Gabe. **94m/C VHS.** Steven Mailer, Kristy Swanson, Andrew McCarthy, Dave Chappelle; ***D:*** Doug Liman; ***W:*** P.J. Posner, Joel Posner, Jonathan Lewin.

Getting It On 🦴 **1983 (R)** High school student uses his new-found video equipment for voyeuristic activity. **100m/C VHS.** Martin Yost, Heather Kennedy, Jeff Edmond, Kathy Rockmeier, Mark Alan Ferri; ***D:*** William Olsen.

Getting It Right 🦴🦴½ **1989 (R)** A sweet-natured British comedy about an inexperienced, shy adult male who is quite suddenly pursued by a middle-aged socialite, a pregnant, unstable rich girl, and a modest single mother. Novel and screenplay by Elizabeth Jane Howard. **101m/C VHS.** *GB* Jesse Birdsall, Helena Bonham Carter, Lynn Redgrave, Peter Cook, John Gielgud, Jane Horrocks, Richard Huw, Shirley Anne Field, Pat Haywood, Judy Parfitt, Bryan Pringle; ***D:*** Randal Kleiser; ***W:*** Elizabeth Jane Howard; ***M:*** Colin Towns, Steve Tyrell.

The Getting of Wisdom 🦴🦴½ **1977** A 13-year-old girl from the Australian outback tries to establish her identity, and her individuality, within the restricting confines of a Victorian girl's boarding school. Based on the novel by Henry Handel Richardson. **100m/C VHS.** *AU* Susannah Fowle, Hilary Ryan, Alix Longman, Sheila Helpmann, Patricia Kennedy, Barry Humphries, John Waters; ***D:*** Bruce Beresford.

Getting Out 🦴🦴½ **1994** Arlie (DeMornay) is an ex-con on her way home to Georgia after an eight year prison stint and what she hopes will be a reunion with the son she bore in jail. She thinks he's in a foster home but instead her mother (Burstyn) had the child adopted and if she interferes, Arlie's parole will be revoked. Arlie's trying desperately to rehabilitate herself but the system and old contacts are close to dragging her back down. TV movie adapted from Marsha Norman's 1977 play. **92m/C VHS.** Rebecca DeMornay, Ellen Burstyn, Rob Knepper, Richard Jenkins, Carol Mitchell-Leon, Tandy Cronyn, Norman Skaggs; ***D:*** John Korty; ***W:*** Eugene Corr, Ruth Shapiro; ***M:*** Mason Daring.

Getting Over 🦴 **1981** A black promoter is hired as a figurehead by a bigoted record company president and proceeds to try to run the company his own way. He develops an all-girl group called "The Love Machine" and gets involved in a singer's kidnapping and a record company run by gangsters. Filled with cliches and stereotypes. **108m/C VHS.** John Daniels, Gwen Brisco, Mary Hopkins, John Goff, Andrew "Buzz" Cooper; ***D:*** Bernie Rollins; ***W:*** Bernie Rollins.

Getting Physical 🦴½ **1984** After being mugged, a secretary decides to get in shape and enters the world of female body building. Crammed with workout scenes and disco music. **95m/C VHS.** Alexandra Paul, Sandahl Bergman, David Naughton; ***D:*** Steven Hilliard Stern; ***M:*** William Goldstein. **TV**

Getting Straight 🦴🦴 **1970 (R)** A returning Vietnam soldier (Gould) goes back to his alma mater to secure a teaching degree and gets involved in the lives of his fellow students and the turbulence of the end of the '60s, including campus riots. A now-dated "youth" picture somewhat watchable for Gould's performance. **124m/C VHS.** Elliott Gould, Candice Bergen, Jeff Corey, Cecil Kellaway, Jeannie Berlin, Harrison Ford, John Rubinstein, Robert F. Lyons, Max Julien; ***D:*** Richard Rush.

Getting Up and Going Home 🦴🦴½ **1992** Jack (Skerritt) is a married man with a midlife crisis. So what does he do? Get involved with not one, but two, other women. Is he asking for trouble or what? Adapted from the book by Robert Anderson. **93m/C VHS.** Tom Skerritt, Blythe Danner, Roma Downey, Julianne Phillips, Bruce Kirby, Gary Frank, Dorian Harewood, Paul Sand; ***D:*** Steven Schachter; ***W:*** Peter Nelson.

Getting Wasted 🦴½ **1980 (PG)** Set in 1969 at a military academy for troublesome young men, chaos ensues when the cadets meet hippies. **98m/C VHS.** Brian Kerwin, Stephen Furst, Cooper Huckabee.

Gettysburg 🦴🦴🦴½ **1993 (PG)** Civil War buff Ted Turner (who has a cameo as a Confederate soldier) originally intended Michael Shaara's Pulitzer Prize-winning novel "The Killer Angels" to be adapted as a three-part miniseries for his "TNT" network, but the lure of the big screen prevailed, marking the first time the battle has been committed to film and the first time a film crew has been allowed to film battle scenes on the Gettysburg National Military Park battlefield. The greatest battle of the war and the bloodiest in U.S. history is realistically staged by more than 5,000 Civil War re-enactors. The all-male cast concentrates on presenting the human cost of the war, with Daniels particularly noteworthy as the scholarly Colonel Chamberlain, determined to hold Little Round Top for the Union. Last film role for Jordan, to whom the movie is co-dedicated. The full scale recreation of Pickett's Charge is believed to be the largest period scale motion-picture sequence filmed in North America since D.W. Griffith's "Birth of a Nation." **254m/C VHS, DVD, Wide.** Jeff Daniels, Martin Sheen, Tom Berenger, Sam Elliott, Richard Jordan, Stephen Lang, Kevin Conway, C. Thomas Howell, Maxwell Caulfield, Andrew Prine, James Lancaster, Royce D. Applegate, Brian Mallon, Cooper Huckabee, Bo Brinkman, Kieran Mulroney, Patrick Gorman, William Morgan Sheppard, James Patrick Stuart, Tim Ruddy, Joseph Fuqua, Ivan Kane, Warren Burton, MacIntyre Dixon, George Lazenby, Alex Harvey, John Diehl, John Rothman, Richard Anderson, Billy Campbell, David Carpenter, Donal Logue, Dwier Brown, Mark Moses, Ken Burns, Ted Turner; ***D:*** Ronald F. Maxwell; ***W:*** Ronald F. Maxwell; ***C:*** Kees Van Oostrum; ***M:*** Randy Edelman.

The Ghastly Ones woof! **1968** Three couples must stay in a haunted mansion to inherit an estate, but they're soon being violently killed off. No budget and no talent. Remade as "Legacy of Blood." **81m/C VHS.** Don Williams, Maggie Rogers, Hal Belsoe, Veronica Redburn, Hal Sherwood; ***D:*** Andy Milligan; ***W:*** Andy Milligan, Hal Sherwood; ***C:*** Andy Milligan.

Ghetto Blaster 🦴 **1989 (R)** A Vietnam vet takes on out-of-control street gangs to make his neighborhood safe. **86m/C VHS.** R.G. Armstrong, Richard Hatch, Richard Jaeckel, Harry Caesar, Rose Marie; ***D:*** Alan L. Stewart.

Ghetto Revenge **19??** An embittered Vietnam vet gets caught between white supremacists and black radical activists in this coming home story. He returns and tries to build a life but succumbs to the desire for vengeance and things are never the same. **?m/C VHS.** Mike Sims.

Ghidrah the Three Headed Monster 🦴🦴½ *Ghidorah Sandai Kaiju Chikyu Saidai No Kessan; Ghidora, the Three-Headed Monster; Ghidrah; The Greatest Battle on Earth; The Biggest Fight on Earth; Monster of Monsters* **1965** When a three-headed monster from outer-space threatens the world, humans, having nowhere else to turn, appeal to the friendly Mothra, Rodan, and Godzilla. Rock'em, sock 'em giant thrashing about as Tokyo once again gets trampled. Dependable afternoon monster fare complete with usual dubious dubbing. **85m/C VHS.** *JP* Akiko Wakabayashi, Yosuke Natsuki, Yuriko Hoshi, Hiroshi Koizumi, Takashi Shimura, Emi Ito, Yumi Ito, Kenji Sahara, Hisaya Ito; ***D:*** Inoshiro Honda; ***W:*** Shinichi Sekizawa; ***C:*** Hajime Koizumi; ***M:*** Akira Ifukube.

The Ghost 🦴½ *Lo Spettro; Lo Spettro de Dr. Hitchcock; The Spectre* **1963** A woman is driven mad by her supposedly dead husband and their evil housekeeper. Sequel to "The Horrible Dr. Hichcock." **96m/C VHS.** *IT* Barbara Steele, Peter Baldwin, Leonard Eliott, Harriet White, Harriet Medin, Umberto Raho; ***D:*** Riccardo (Robert Hampton) Freda; ***W:*** Riccardo (Robert Hampton) Freda, Oreste Biancoli; ***C:*** Raffaele Masciocchi; ***M:*** Franco Mannino, Roman Vlad.

Ghost 🦴🦴🦴 **1990 (PG-13)** Zucker, known for overboard comedies like "Airplane!" and "Ruthless People," changed tack and directed this undemanding romantic thriller, which was the surprising top grosser of 1990. Murdered investment consultant Sam Wheast (Swayze) attempts (from somewhere near the hereafter) to protect his lover, Molly (Moore), from imminent danger when he learns he was the victim of a hit gone afoul. Goldberg is medium Oda Mae Brown, who suddenly discovers that the powers she's been faking are real. A winning blend of action, special effects (from Industrial Light and Magic) and romance. **127m/C VHS, DVD, 8mm, Wide.** Stephen (Steve) Root, Patrick Swayze, Demi Moore, Whoopi Goldberg, Tony Goldwyn, Rick Aviles, Vincent Schiavelli, Gail Boggs, Armelia McQueen, Phil Leeds; ***D:*** Jerry Zucker; ***W:*** Bruce Joel Rubin; ***C:*** Adam Greenberg; ***M:*** Maurice Jarre. Oscars '90: Orig. Screenplay, Support. Actress (Goldberg); British Acad. '90: Support. Actress (Goldberg); Golden Globes '91: Support. Actress (Goldberg).

The Ghost and Mrs. Muir 🦴🦴🦴 **1947** A charming, beautifully orchestrated fantasy about a feisty widow who, with her young daughter, buys a seaside house and refuses to be intimidated by the crabby ghost of its former sea captain owner. When the widow falls into debt, the captain dictates his sea adventures, which she adapts into a successful novel. The ghost also falls in love with the beautiful lady. Tierney is exquisite and Harrison is sharp-tongued and manly. Based on R. A. Dick's novel. **104m/B VHS.** Gene Tierney, Rex Harrison, George Sanders, Edna Best, Anna Lee, Vanessa Brown, Robert Coote, Natalie Wood, Isobel Elsom; ***D:*** Joseph L. Mankiewicz; ***W:*** Philip Dunne; ***C:*** Charles B(ryant) Lang Jr.; ***M:*** Bernard Herrmann.

The Ghost and Mr. Chicken 🦴🦴½ **1966** Fraidy cat Luther Heggs (Knotts) works for a small town newspaper and longs to be a hot-shot reporter. One night he thinks he sees a woman's corpse at the vacant Simmons mansion but of course there's no body when the cops come. The house is considered haunted and there is a 20-year-old murder scandal, so Luther is very reluctantly persuaded to spend the night and solve the sinister goings-on. **90m/C VHS.** Don Knotts, Joan Staley, Dick Sargent, Liam Redmond, Skip Homeier, Reta Shaw, Lurene Tuttle, Philip Ober; ***D:*** Alan Rafkin; ***W:*** James Fritzell; ***C:*** William Margulies; ***M:*** Vic Mizzy.

The Ghost and the Darkness 🦴🦴½ **1996 (R)** Based on the true story of two man-eating lions who killed 130 people and nearly derailed the building of the East African railroad in 1896. Engineer John Patterson (Kilmer) is sent to build a bridge over the Tsavo river, but as African liaison Samuel (Kani) informs him, Tsavo prophetically means place of slaughter. The workers become convinced the lions, nicknamed "The Ghost" and "The Darkness" are actually demons and, try as he might, Patterson has little luck killing the beasts. Then, legendary big game hunter Remington (Douglas) is called in—but the lions still seem to have the advantage. Lots of crunching bones, slurping blood, and quick cut editing is used to depict the lions' attacks. **110m/C VHS, DVD, Wide.** Val Kilmer, Michael Douglas, John Kani, Bernard Hill, Om Puri, Brian McCardie, Tom Wilkinson, Emily Mortimer, Henry Cele; ***D:*** Stephen Hopkins; ***W:*** William Goldman; ***C:*** Vilmos Zsigmond; ***M:*** Jerry Goldsmith. Oscars '96: Sound FX Editing.

The Ghost and the Guest 🦴🦴½ **1943** Newlyweds spend their honeymoon in a house in the country only to find that gangsters are using the place as a hideout. Chases involving secret passages ensue. **59m/B VHS.** James Dunn, Florence Rice, Mabel Todd; ***D:*** William Nigh; ***W:*** Morey Amsterdam.

The Ghost Breakers 🦴🦴🦴 **1940** As a follow-up to the Hope/Goddard 1939 comedy thriller "The Cat and the Canary," this spooky comedy was even better. Lots of laughs and real chills as Hope and Goddard investigate a haunted mansion that she's inherited in Cuba. Effective horror scenes are expertly handled by director Marshall. Remade in 1953 as "Scared Stiff" with Dean Martin and Jerry Lewis. Based on the play by Paul Dickey and Charles Goddard. **83m/B VHS, DVD.** Bob Hope, Paulette Goddard, Richard Carlson, Paul Lukas, Willie Best, Pedro de Cordoba, Noble Johnson, Anthony Quinn; ***D:*** George Marshall; ***W:*** Walter DeLeon; ***C:*** Charles B(ryant) Lang Jr.

The Ghost Brigade 🦴🦴½ *The Killing Box* **1993 (R)** Civil War ghost story finds a Union general (Sheen) trying to discover who's slaughtering both Confederate and Union soldiers on the battlefield. So he sends Captain Harling (Pasdar) to investigate, with the help of rebel prisoner Strayn (Bernsen) and a slave (Williams). What they find is an evil brigade of soldiers—who already happen to be dead—and are eager for new recruits. **80m/C VHS.** Adrian Pasdar, Corbin Bernsen, Martin Sheen, Cynda Williams, Ray Wise, Roger Wilson; ***D:*** George Hickenlooper; ***W:*** Matt Greenberg; ***C:*** Kent Wakeford.

The Ghost Camera 🦴🦴½ **1933** Slight story of a man falsely accused of murder. A photograph taken at the murder scene can prove his innocence if only the missing camera can be discovered. **68m/B VHS.** *GB* Henry Kendall, Ida Lupino, John Mills; ***D:*** Bernard Vorhaus.

Ghost Chase 🦴½ **1988 (PG-13)** A young filmmaker desperate for funds inherits his dead relative's clock, from which issues the ghost of the deceased's butler. The ghostly retainer aids in a search for the departed's secret fortune. Neither scary nor funny. **89m/C VHS, DVD.** Jason Lively, Jill Whitlow, Tim McDaniel, Paul Gleason, Chuck "Porky" Mitchell; ***D:*** Roland Emmerich; ***W:*** Roland Emmerich, Oliver Eberle; ***C:*** Karl Walter Lindenlaub.

Ghost Chasers 🦴🦴½ **1951** The Bowery Boys become mixed up in supernatural hijinks when a seance leads to the appearance of a ghost that only Sach can see. **70m/B VHS.** Leo Gorcey, Huntz Hall, William Benedict, David Gorcey, Buddy Gorman, Bernard Gorcey, Jan Kayne, Philip Van Zandt, Lloyd Corrigan; ***D:*** William Beaudine.

Ghost City 🦴 **1932** Our hero must deal with a masked gang that is "haunting" a town. **60m/B VHS.** Bill Cody, Helen Foster, Ann Rutherford, John Shelton, Reginald Owen; ***D:*** Harry Fraser.

Ghost Crazy 🦴🦴 **1944** Three wild comedians and a gorilla create mayhem in a haunted house. **?m/C VHS.** Shemp Howard, Billy Gilbert, Maxie "Slapsie" Rosenbloom.

Ghost Dad 🦴 **1990 (PG)** A widowed workaholic dad is prematurely killed and returns from the dead to help his children prepare for the future. Cosby walks through doors, walls, and other solid objects for the sake of comedy—only none of it is funny. **84m/C VHS, DVD.** Bill Cosby, Denise Nicholas, Ian Bannen, Christine Ebersole, Dana Ashbrook, Arnold Stang; ***D:*** Sidney Poitier; ***W:*** S.S. Wilson, Brent Maddock; ***M:*** Henry Mancini.

Ghost Dance 🦴 **1983** Sacred Indian burial ground is violated, with grim results. **93m/C VHS.** Sherman Hemsley, Henry Ball, Julie Amato; ***D:*** Peter Bufa.

Ghost Dog: The Way of the Samurai 🦴🦴½ **1999 (R)** Jarmusch takes a Far Eastern approach to the Mob-hit man genre with "Dog," whose title character, a contract killer played excellently by Whitaker, pledges himself to small-time hood Louie in the tradition of the Samurai after Louie saves his life. When one of his hits goes wrong, Ghost Dog is targeted for elimination, which leads to many dead bodies. Like most Jarmusch offerings, this one's quirky, disjointed, and not for everyone, but Whitaker's performance, and the offbeat humor make up for a lot. **116m/C VHS, DVD, Wide.** Forest Whitaker, Cliff Gorman, Henry Silva, John Tormey, Isaach de Bankole, Tricia Vessey, Victor Argo, Gene Ruffini, Richard Portnow, Camille Winbush; ***D:*** Jim Jarmusch; ***W:*** Jim Jarmusch; ***C:*** Robby Muller.

Ghost Fever woof! **1987 (PG)** Two bumbling cops try to evict the inhabitants of a haunted house and get nowhere. A bad rip-off of "Ghostbusters." Alan Smithee is a pseudonym used when a director does not want his or her name on a film—no wonder. **86m/C VHS.** Sherman Hemsley, Luis Avalos; ***D:*** Alan Smithee; ***W:*** Oscar Brodney.

The Ghost Goes West 🦴🦴🦴 **1936** A brash American family buys a Scottish castle and transports the pieces to the United States along with the Scottish family ghost (Donat). Also along is the ghost's modern-day descendant (also played by Donat) who is the new castle caretaker and in love with the new owner's daughter. It turns out to be up to the ghost to get the two lovers together and find his own eternal rest. A rather lovable fantasy. Rene Clair's first English film. Available in digitally remastered stereo with original movie trailer. **90m/B VHS.** *GB* Robert Donat, Jean Parker, Eugene Pallette, Elsa Lanchester, Ralph Bunker, Patricia Hilliard, Everley Gregg, Morton Selten, Chili Bouchier, Mark Daly, Herbert Lomas, Elliot Mason, Jack Lambert, Hay Petrie; ***D:*** Rene Clair; ***W:*** Robert Sherwood, Geoffrey Kerr; ***C:*** Harold Rosson.

Ghost in the Machine 🦴½ **1993 (R)** Serial killer dies while undergoing an X-ray scan and somehow, because of a lightning storm and a power outage, his soul manages to infiltrate the hospital's computer and go on to terrorize more victims via their home computers and appliances. (You expect this to make sense?) Outlandish, predictable flick hovers between high-tech horror and satiric comedy and wastes some pretty decent talent. Horror buffs may get a kick out of it but be forewarned: You may never view your microwave, dishwasher, or electrical outlets in quite the same way again. **104m/C VHS.** Karen Allen, Chris Mulkey, Ted Marcoux, Jessica Walter, Ric(k) Ducommun, Wil Horneff, Nancy Fish, Brandon Adams; ***D:*** Rachel Talalay; ***W:*** William Davies, William Osborne; ***M:*** Graeme Revell.

Ghost in the Noonday Sun woof! **1974** Crew of a treasure-seeking pirate ship sets sail for high sea silliness in this slapstick adventure film. Not a theatrical release for one obvious reason—it's terrible. **90m/C VHS.** *GB* Peter Sellers, Spike Milligan, Anthony (Tony) Franciosa, Clive Revill, Rosemary Leach, Peter Boyle; ***D:*** Peter Medak.

Ghost in the Shell 🦴🦴🦴 *Kouka-ku Kidoutai* **1995** Major Motoko Kusanagi of the Security Police Section 9 is on the trail of a super hacker known as the Puppet Master. His techniques are so advanced that almost nothing is known about him. The time is 2029 and many people are cybernetically enhanced which allows the Puppet Master to make almost anyone his pawn. The more the Major works on the case, the more conflicted she becomes, for all that remains of her original body is a small slice of brain. In a world where the only humanity some people have are their ghosts (or souls), where they may or may not be within the shells (or bodies) they were born with, what happens when a ghost exists where it should not? Along with the philosophical questions about the nature of humanity that are heavily interlaced within the plot, this anime features a slick science fiction story and top-quality animation. Based on the story by Masamune Shirow. A special edition is available which includes the 30-minutes documentary "The Making of Ghost in the Shell." **82m/C VHS, DVD.** *JP* ***D:*** Mamoru Oshii; ***W:*** Kazunori Ito.

Ghost Keeper 🦴 **1980** Three girls are trapped in a mansion with an old hag and various supernatural apparitions. **87m/C VHS.** Riva Spier, Murray Ord, Georgie Collins; ***D:*** Vernon Sewell.

The Ghost of Fletcher Ridge **198?** Two friends on a hunting trip run into some backwoodsmen and uncover their moonshining operation. When one of the men is killed, the other flees to the forest in a desperate bid for survival. **90m/C VHS.** Campbell Scott, Bernie White, Virginia Lantry, Len Lesser; ***D:*** Michael Bordon.

The Ghost of Frankenstein 🦴🦴½ **1942** Fourth Frankenstein film in the Universal Studios series with Chaney filling in for Karloff as the monster. Not as good as its predecessors, but the cast is enjoyable, especially Lugosi as the monster's deformed sidekick, Ygor. Based on a story by Eric Taylor. **68m/B VHS, DVD.** Cedric Hardwicke, Lon Chaney Jr., Lionel Atwill, Ralph Bellamy, Bela Lugosi, Evelyn Ankers, Dwight Frye; ***D:*** Erle C. Kenton; ***W:*** W. Scott Darling; ***C:*** Milton Krasner; ***M:*** Charles Previn.

The Ghost of Rashmon Hall 🦴 *Night Comes Too Soon* **1947** Doctor tries to rid his home of the ghosts of a sailor, his wife and her lover. **52m/B VHS.** Valentine Dyall, Anne Howard, Alex Flavorsham, Howard Douglas, Beatrice Marsden, Arthur Brander.

The Ghost of Spoon River 🦴🦴 *The Mystery of Spoon River* **2000 (R)** Chicago lawyer Emma Masters (Sinclair) heads home to defend her brother-in-law Jesse (McNamara) who's been accused of killing the local game warden. A killing that seems racially motivated and seems to tie into the town's dark past and a 1941 lynching. And despite the title, this standard thriller has really nothing to do with Edgar Lee Masters' "Spoon River Anthology." **90m/C VHS, DVD.** Lauren Sinclair, Brian McNamara, Richard Portnow, Michael Monks; ***D:*** Scott A. Meehan. **VIDEO**

The Ghost of Yatsuya 🦴½ **1958** Based on the Japanese legend of a man who must betray his wife to get the power he seeks. When he does, however, what follows is a horrifying revenge. In Japanese with English subtitles. **100m/C VHS.** *JP* Shigeru Amachi.

Ghost on the Loose **1943** The Bowery Boys take on Nazi spies. **65m/C VHS.** Leo Gorcey, Huntz Hall, Bela Lugosi; ***D:*** William Beaudine.

Ghost Patrol 🦴½ **1936** A cowboy duo kidnaps the inventor of a ray gun in order to hijack mail planes, but they're stopped by G-Man McCoy and friends. An odd hybrid of science fiction and western, to say the least. **57m/B VHS.** Tim McCoy, Walter Miller, Wheeler Oakman; ***D:*** Sam Newfield.

Ghost Rider ☠ **1935** A lawman is aided in his outlaw-nabbing efforts by the ghost of a gunfighter. **56m/B VHS.** Rex Lease, Bobby Nelson, Franklyn Farnum, Lloyd Ingraham, Eddie (Ed, Eddy, Edwin) Parker, Lafe (Lafayette) McKee; ***D:*** Jack Levine.

Ghost Rider ☠☠ **1943** Former footballer Brown rides the range once again, this time with an element of the supernatural nipping at his heels. **58m/B VHS.** Johnny Mack Brown, Raymond Hatton, Tim Seidel, Beverly Boyd, Milburn (Milt) Morante; ***D:*** Wallace Fox.

Ghost Ship ☠½ **1953** Young couple is tortured by ghostly apparitions when they move into an old yacht with a dubious past. Grade-B haunting featuring the murdered wife of the ship's former owner as the poltergeist. **69m/B VHS.** *GB* Dermot Walsh, Hazel Court, Hugh Burden, John Robinson; ***D:*** Vernon Sewell.

Ghost Story ☠☠ **1981 (R)** Four elderly men, members of an informal social club called the Chowder Society, share a terrible secret buried deep in their pasts—a secret that comes back to haunt them to death. Has moments where it's chilling, but unfortunately they're few. Based on the best-selling novel by Peter Straub. **110m/C VHS, DVD.** Fred Astaire, Melvyn Douglas, Douglas Fairbanks Jr., John Houseman, Craig Wasson, Alice Krige, Patricia Neal; ***D:*** John Irvin; ***W:*** Lawrence D. Cohen; ***C:*** Jack Cardiff; ***M:*** Philippe Sarde.

Ghost Town ☠ **1937** Good guy Carey saves a mine from claim jumpers, but not before he is mistakenly incarcerated as his friend's murderer, and then proved innocent. **65m/B VHS.** Harry Carey Sr.; ***D:*** Harry Fraser.

Ghost Town ☠☠½ **1988 (R)** Fine sleeper about a modern sheriff who follows a gal through a supernatural sandstorm and discovers a literal ghost town of bad guys. **85m/C VHS.** Franc Luz, Catherine Hickland, Jimmie F. Skaggs, Penelope Windust, Bruce Glover, Blake Conway, Laura Schaefer; ***D:*** Richard Governor; ***W:*** Duke Sandefur; ***M:*** Harvey R. Cohen.

Ghost Town Gold ☠ **1936** The Three Mesquiteers series continues as the trio outwits bank robbers who have hidden their loot in a ghost town. **53m/B VHS.** Robert "Bob" Livingston, Ray Corrigan, Max Terhune; ***D:*** Joseph Kane.

Ghost Town Law ☠½ **1942** The Rough Riders step in to save the day when a group of outlaws defend their hideout by murdering anyone who approaches. **62m/B VHS.** Buck Jones, Tim McCoy, Raymond Hatton; ***D:*** Howard Bretherton.

Ghost Town Renegades ☠ **1947** A pair of government agents prevent a crook from gaining control of a mining town. **57m/B VHS.** Lash LaRue, Al "Fuzzy" St. John, Jennifer Holt; ***D:*** Ray Taylor.

Ghost Town Riders ☠½ **1938** An outlaw gang is holed up in an abandoned town, threatening to steal Shannon's gold mine, until Baker comes to the rescue. **55m/B VHS.** Bob Baker, Fay McKenzie, George Cleveland, Glenn Strange, Forrest Taylor, Hank Worden, Murdock McQuarrie; ***D:*** George Waggner.

The Ghost Train ☠☠ **1941** Passengers stranded at a train station are told tales of a haunted train. Forced to stay at the station overnight, they encounter a number of comically spooky situations. **85m/B VHS.** *GB* Arthur Askey, Richard Murdock, Kathleen Harrison; ***D:*** Walter Forde.

Ghost Valley ☠☠½ **1932** When Keene and Kennedy inherit land rich in unmined ore, the administrator (Harris) attempts to scare them off. To foil his plan, Keene conceals his identity and takes a job as the administrator's assistant. Based on a story by Adele Buffington. **54m/B VHS.** Tom (George Duryea) Keene, Merna Kennedy, Mitchell Harris, Billy Franey, Harry Bowen, Kate Campbell, Ted Adams, Buck Moulton, Harry Semels, Al Taylor, Charles "Slim" Whitaker; ***D:*** Fred Allen.

The Ghost Walks ☠☠ **1934** A playwright has his new masterpiece acted out in front of an unsuspecting producer, who thinks that a real murder has taken place. But when the cast really does start disappearing, who's to blame? **69m/B VHS.** John Miljan, June Collyer, Richard Carle, Spencer Charters, Johnny Arthur, Henry Kolker; ***D:*** Frank Strayer.

Ghost World ☠☠☠½ **2001 (R)** Zwigoff makes his feature debut with this dark comedy that contains echoes of his documentary "Crumb." Enid (Birch) and Rebecca (Johansson) are not your typical acid-tongued teenage outsiders. Instead of struggling to fit in, they wear their contempt for the empty mall culture that surrounds them like a badge of honor. On a whim, the girls answer a personal ad from Seymour, a middle-aged schmoe who collects old records. Seymour, whose personal quirks are similar to those of former Zwigoff documentary subject R. Crumb, is also baffled by modern culture and Enid is eventually drawn to him. She decides to help him in his attempt to find a woman, developing a special yet strange bond with him. Swinging from bleak to hilarious, the plot refuses to follow your standard romantic formula. That would be, like, so mainstream. Based on the underground comics of Daniel Clowes. **111m/C VHS, DVD, Wide.** *US* Thora Birch, Scarlett Johansson, Steve Buscemi, Brad Renfro, Illeana Douglas, Bob Balaban, Teri Garr, Stacy Travis, Dave Sheridan, Brian George; ***D:*** Terry Zwigoff; ***W:*** Daniel Clowes, Terry Zwigoff; ***C:*** Alfonso Beato; ***M:*** David Kitay. Ind. Spirit '02: Support. Actor (Buscemi); N.Y. Film Critics '01: Support. Actor (Buscemi); Natl. Soc. Film Critics '01: Support. Actor (Buscemi).

Ghost Writer ☠ **1989 (PG)** A writer discovers the ghost of a movie star haunting her beach house, and together they solve the dead vamp's murder. **94m/C VHS.** Audrey Landers, Judy Landers, Jeff Conaway, David Doyle, Anthony (Tony) Franciosa, Joey Travolta, John Matuszak, David Paul, Peter Paul; ***D:*** Kenneth J. Hall.

Ghostbusters ☠☠☠ **1984 (PG)** After losing their scholastic funding, a group of "para-normal" investigators decide to go into business for themselves, aiding New York citizens in the removal of ghosts, goblins and other annoying spirits. Comedy-thriller about Manhattan being overrun by ghosts contains great special effects, zany characters, and some of the best laughs of the decade. Oscar nominated title song written and sung by Ray Parker Jr. Followed by a sequel. **103m/C VHS, DVD, Wide.** Bill Murray, Dan Aykroyd, Harold Ramis, Rick Moranis, Sigourney Weaver, Annie Potts, Ernie Hudson, William Atherton, David Margulies, Steven Tash, Reginald Vel Johnson, Timothy Carhart; ***D:*** Ivan Reitman; ***W:*** Dan Aykroyd, Harold Ramis; ***C:*** Laszlo Kovacs; ***M:*** Elmer Bernstein.

Ghostbusters 2 ☠☠½ **1989 (PG)** After being sued by the city for the damages they did in the original "Ghostbusters," the boys in khaki are doing kiddie shows at birthday parties. When a river of slime that is actually the physical version of evil is discovered running beneath the city, the Ghostbusters are back in action. They must do battle with a wicked spirit in a painting or the entire world will fall pray to its ravaging whims. Murray is the highlight of this serviceable sequel, although MacNicol gives him a good run as the painting's henchman. **102m/C VHS, DVD, 8mm, Wide.** Mary Ellen Trainor, Bill Murray, Dan Aykroyd, Sigourney Weaver, Harold Ramis, Rick Moranis, Ernie Hudson, Peter MacNicol, David Margulies, Wilhelm von Homburg, Harris Yulin, Annie Potts, Ben Stein, Richard "Cheech" Marin, Brian Doyle-Murray, Janet Margolin; ***D:*** Ivan Reitman; ***W:*** Dan Aykroyd, Harold Ramis; ***C:*** Michael Chapman; ***M:*** Randy Edelman.

Ghosthouse ☠ **1988** It looks like an average suburban house, but it's haunted by the ghost of a little girl—and when she comes, evil is sure to follow. **91m/C VHS.** Lara Wendel, Gregg Scott; ***D:*** Humphrey Humbert.

Ghostriders ☠ **1987** One hundred years after their hanging, a band of ghostly outlaws take revenge on the townfolk's descendents. **85m/C VHS.** Bill Shaw, Jim Peters, Ricky Long, Cari Powell, Mike Ammons, Arland Bishop; ***D:*** Alan L. Stewart.

Ghosts Can Do It ☠½ **1990** The Hound doesn't like jumping to conclusions, but is it possible this obscurity was titled to be reminiscent of the more publicized Bo Derek vehicle "Ghosts Can't Do It" comedy about a man who returns to his sexy wife despite her efforts at killing him. **88m/C VHS.** Garry McDonald, Pamela Stephenson.

Ghosts Can't Do It ☠ **1990 (R)** Another wet-shirted, Bo-dacious softcore epic, involving a young woman who would like to have the spirit of her virile, but unfortunately dead, husband return to inhabit a living body. **91m/C VHS.** Bo Derek, Anthony Quinn, Don Murray, Leo Damian; ***D:*** John Derek. Golden Raspberries '90: Worst Picture, Worst Actress (Derek), Worst Director (Derek).

Ghosts of Berkeley Square ☠☠½ **1947** The ghosts of two retired soldiers of the early 18th century are doomed to haunt their former home, and only a visit from a reigning monarch can free them. **85m/B VHS.** Wilfrid Hyde-White, Robert Morley, Felix Aylmer; ***D:*** Vernon Sewell.

The Ghosts of Hanley House ☠½ **1968** No-budget spooker with no-brain plot. Several unlucky guests spend an evening in a creepy mansion...sound familiar? Shot in Texas. **80m/C VHS.** Barbara Chase, Wilkie De Martel, Elsie Baker, Cliff Scott.

Ghosts of Mississippi ☠☠ *Ghosts from the Past* **1996 (PG-13)** Director Reiner attempts to tell the story of civil rights leader Medgar Evers, murdered in 1963, and the three trials of Byron De la Beckwith (Woods), who was finally convicted (after two hung juries) in 1994. Unfortunately, he filters the story through the eyes of white assistant D.A. Bobby De Laughter (Baldwin) while ignoring Evers' accomplishments almost completely. Woods chews up the scenery as the wily old racist, bringing perhaps a little too much glee into a portrait of true evil. Goldberg sleepwalks through her role as Evers' widow, Myrlie; Evers' sons, Darrell and Van, play themselves; daughter Reena plays a juror while her character is played by Yolanda King, the daughter of slain civil rights leader Martin Luther King, Jr. Filmed on location in Jackson, Mississippi. **123m/C VHS, DVD, Wide.** Alec Baldwin, Whoopi Goldberg, James Woods, Craig T. Nelson, Wayne Rogers, William H. Macy, Michael O'Keefe, Yolanda King, Susanna Thompson, Lucas Black, James Pickens Jr., Virginia Madsen, Bill Cobbs; ***D:*** Rob Reiner; ***W:*** Lewis Colick; ***C:*** John Seale; ***M:*** Marc Shaiman.

Ghosts That Still Walk ☠ **1977** Spooky phenomena occur. The demons possessing a young lad's soul may be responsible. **92m/C VHS.** Ann Nelson, Matt Boston, Jerry Jenson, Caroline Howe, Rita Crafts; ***D:*** James T. Flocker.

Ghostwarrior ☠ *Swordkill* **1986 (R)** A 16th-century samurai warrior's ice-packed body is revived and runs amuck in the streets of modern-day Los Angeles. **86m/C VHS.** Hiroshi Fujioka, Janet (Johnson) Julian, Andy Wood, John Calvin; ***D:*** Larry Carroll; ***W:*** Tim Curnen; ***C:*** Mac Ahlberg.

Ghostwriter ☠☠ **1984** Based on Philip Roth's best-selling novel, the story is of a writer coming to terms with his past. Roth co-wrote the screenplay. First seen on PBS. **90m/C VHS.** Sam Wanamaker, Claire Bloom, Rose Arrick, MacIntyre Dixon, Cecile Mann, Joseph Wiseman, Mark Linn-Baker, Paulette Smit; ***D:*** Tristam Powell; ***W:*** Phillip J. Roth.

The Ghoul ☠☠½ **1934** An eccentric English Egyptologist desires a sacred jewel to be buried with him and vows to come back from the grave if the gem is stolen. When that happens, he makes good on his ghostly promise. A minor horror piece with Karloff only appearing at the beginning and end of the film. This leaves the middle very dull. **73m/B VHS.** *GB* Boris Karloff, Cedric Hardwicke, Ernest Thesiger, Dorothy Hyson, Ralph Richardson, Anthony Bushell, Kathleen Harrison, Harold Huth, D. A. Clarke-Smith, Jack Raine; ***D:*** T. Hayes Hunter; ***W:*** Roland Pertwee, John Hastings Turner, Rupert Downing; ***C:*** Gunther Krampf.

The Ghoul ☠☠ **1975 (R)** A defrocked clergyman has a cannibal son to contend with—especially after the drivers in a local auto race begin to disappear. Hurt is the lunatic family gardener. **88m/C VHS.** *GB* Peter Cushing, John Hurt, Alexandra Bastedo, Don Henderson, Stewart Bevan; ***D:*** Freddie Francis.

Ghoul School ☠ **1990 (R)** A spoof of horror films and college flicks, with lots of scantily clad women and bloody creatures in dark hallways. **90m/C VHS.** Joe Franklin, Nancy Siriani, William Friedman.

Ghoulies ☠ **1984 (PG-13)** A young man gets more than he bargained for when he conjures up a batch of evil creatures when dabbling in the occult. Ridiculous but successful. Followed by three sequels. **81m/C VHS.** Lisa Pelikan, Jack Nance, Scott Thomson, Tamara DeTreaux, Mariska Hargitay, Bobbie Bresee; ***D:*** Luca Bercovici; ***W:*** Luca Bercovici; ***C:*** Mac Ahlberg; ***M:*** Richard Band.

Ghoulies 2 ☠ **1987 (R)** Inept sequel to "Ghoulies" (1985), wherein the little demons haunt a failing carnival horror house, whose revenues begin to soar. Followed by a second sequel. **89m/C VHS, DVD.** Damon Martin, Royal Dano, Phil Fondacaro, J. Downing, Kerry Remsen; ***D:*** Albert Band.

Ghoulies 3: Ghoulies Go to College woof! **1991 (R)** Third in the series has the best special effects and the worst storyline. Not satisfied with ripping off "Gremlins," this one imposes Three Stooges personae upon a trio of demons at large on a beer- and babe-soaked campus. **94m/C VHS.** Kevin McCarthy, Griffin O'Neal, Evan Mackenzie; ***D:*** John Carl Buechler.

Ghoulies 4 ☠½ **1993 (R)** Dopey series continues with the satanic creatures roaming the streets of Los Angeles, searching for a way to return to their netherworld home. They get their chance when they meet a Satan-worshipping dominatrix out on a killing spree. **84m/C VHS.** Bobby DiCicco, Barbara Alyn Woods, Peter Paul Liapis; ***D:*** Jim Wynorski; ***W:*** Mark Sevi.

G.I. Blues ☠☠ **1960 (PG)** Three G.I.'s form a musical combo while stationed in Germany. Prowse is the nightclub singer Presley falls for. Presley's first film after his military service. ♫Shopping Around; Tonight Is So Right For Love; What's She Really Like?; Frankfurt Special; Didya Ever; Big Boots; Pocketful of Rainbows; Doin' the Best I Can; Blue Suede Shoes. **104m/C VHS, DVD.** Elvis Presley, Juliet Prowse, Robert Ivers, Leticia Roman, Ludwig Stossel, James Douglas, Jeremy Slate; ***D:*** Norman Taurog; ***C:*** Loyal Griggs.

G.I. Executioner ☠ *Wit's End; Dragon Lady* **1971 (R)** An adventure set in Singapore featuring a Vietnam veteran turned executioner. **86m/C VHS.** Tom Kenna, Victoria Racimo, Angelique Pettyjohn, Janet Wood, Walter Hill; ***D:*** Joel M. Reed.

G.I. Jane ☠ **1951** A TV producer faints when he gets his draft notice and dreams his company is stranded at a desert post with a company of WACs. **62m/B VHS.** Jean Porter, Tom Neal, Iris Adrian, Jimmy Lloyd, Mara Lynn, Michael Whalen; ***D:*** Reginald LeBorg; ***W:*** Henry Blankfort.

G.I. Jane ☠☠½ *In Pursuit of Honor; Navy Cross* **1997 (R)** Moore is buffed, bold and bald in this modern day fable of the first female to become a Navy SEAL. As Jordan O'Neil, Moore endures grueling training exercises and sexist remarks from male collegues that are tortuous for her, but enjoyable for those who sat through Moore's three previous films. Impressive supporting cast, including Mortensen as the vicious and misogynist master chief and Bancroft as a fiesty senator with a secret political agenda, pick things up when the story flags in the middle. The beginning holds the most interest, but the movie's length encourages improbable plot points. Scott shows he still knows how to make a movie look great, even if the writing doesn't quite measure up. **124m/C VHS, DVD.** Demi Moore, Viggo Mortensen, Anne Bancroft, Jason Beghe, Scott Wilson, Morris Chestnut, Lucinda Jenney, James Caviezel; ***D:*** Ridley Scott; ***W:*** David N. Twohy, Danielle Alexandra; ***C:*** Hugh Johnson; ***M:*** Trevor Jones. Golden Raspberries '97: Worst Actress (Moore).

Gia 🦴🦴 **1998 (R)** Based on the life of self-destructive supermodel/drug addict Gia Carangi (Jolie), who died from AIDS at the age of 26. Gia grew up in an abusive Philadelphia family and hid her insecurities under a tough and wanton persona. Taken under the wing of New York modeling exec Wilhelmina Cooper (Dunaway), Gia's exoticness gets her noticed but the hedonistic lifestyle of the late '70s quickly leads to her downfall. Jolie goes all out for the title role. **120m/C VHS, DVD.** Angelina Jolie, Mercedes Ruehl, Kylie Travis, Faye Dunaway, Elizabeth Mitchell, Louis Giambalvo, John Considine, Scott Cohen; ***D:*** Michael Cristofer; ***W:*** Michael Cristofer, Jay McInerney; ***C:*** Rodrigo Garcia; ***M:*** Terence Blanchard. **CABLE**

Giant 🦴🦴🦴½ **1956** Based on the Edna Ferber novel, this epic saga covers two generations of a wealthy Texas cattle baron (Hudson) who marries a strong-willed Virginia woman (Taylor) and takes her to live on his vast ranch. It explores the problems they have adjusting to life together, as well as the politics and prejudice of the time. Dean plays the resentful ranch hand (who secretly loves Taylor) who winds up striking oil and beginning a fortune to rival that of his former boss. Dean's last movie—he died in a car crash shortly before filming was completed. **201m/C VHS.** Elizabeth Taylor, Rock Hudson, James Dean, Carroll Baker, Chill Wills, Dennis Hopper, Rod Taylor, Earl Holliman, Jane Withers, Sal Mineo, Mercedes McCambridge; ***D:*** George Stevens; ***C:*** William Mellor. Oscars '56: Director (Stevens); AFI '98: Top 100; Directors Guild '56: Director (Stevens).

The Giant Claw 🦴½ **1957** Giant, winged (and stringed) bird attacks from outer space and scientists Morrow, Corday and Ankrum attempt to pluck it. Good bad movie; Corday was Playboy's Miss October, 1958. **76m/B VHS.** Jeff Morrow, Mara Corday, Morris Ankrum, Louis D. Merrill, Edgar Barrier, Robert Shayne, Morgan Jones, Clark Howat; ***D:*** Fred F. Sears.

Giant from the Unknown woof! **1958** Giant conquistador is revived after being struck by lightning and goes on a murderous rampage. Unbelievably bad. **80m/B VHS, DVD.** Edward Kemmer, Buddy Baer, Bob Steele, Sally Fraser, Morris Ankrum; ***D:*** Richard Cunha; ***W:*** Ralph Brooke, Frank Hart Taussig; ***C:*** Richard Cunha; ***M:*** Albert Glasser.

The Giant Gila Monster 🦴½ **1959** A giant lizard has the nerve to disrupt a local record hop, foolishly bringing upon it the wrath of the local teens. Rear-projection monster isn't particularly effective, but the film provides many unintentional laughs. **74m/B VHS, DVD, Wide.** Don Sullivan, Lisa Simone, Shug Fisher, Jerry Cortwright, Beverly Thurman, Don Flournoy, Pat Simmons; ***D:*** Ray Kellogg; ***W:*** Jay Simms; ***C:*** Wilfrid M. Cline; ***M:*** Jack Marshall.

The Giant of Marathon 🦴🦴 **1960** Reeves shrugs off the role of Hercules to play Philippides, a marathoner (who uses a horse) trying to save Greece from invading Persian hordes. Lots of muscle on display, but not much talent. **90m/C VHS.** *IT* Steve Reeves, Mylene Demongeot, Daniela Rocca, Ivo Garrani, Alberto Lupo, Sergio Fantoni; ***D:*** Jacques Tourneur; ***C:*** Mario Bava.

The Giant of Metropolis 🦴🦴 *Il Gigante Di Metropolis* **1961** Muscle-bound hero goes shirtless to take on the evil, sadistic ruler of Atlantis (still above water) in 10,000 B.C. Ordinary Italian adventure, but includes interesting sets and bizarre torture scenes. **92m/C VHS.** *IT* Gordon Mitchell, Roldano Lupi, Bella Cortez, Liana Orfei; ***D:*** Umberto Scarpelli.

The Giant Spider Invasion 🦴 **1975 (PG)** A meteorite carrying spider eggs crashes to Earth and soon the alien arachnids are growing to humongous proportions. Notoriously bad special effects, but the veteran "B" cast has a good time. **76m/C VHS.** Steve Brodie, Barbara Hale, Leslie Parrish, Robert Easton, Alan Hale Jr., Dianne Lee Hart, Bill Williams, Christiane Schmidtmer, Kevin Brodie; ***D:*** Bill Rebane; ***W:*** Bill Rebane, Richard L. Huff, Robert Easton; ***C:*** Jack Willoughby.

Giant Steps 🦴🦴 **19??** Williams plays Slate Hopson, a moody jazz legend idolized by a talented young trumpet player. When the two meet Hopson clues the boy into some of life's lessons and rediscovers his own joy at making music. **94m/C VHS.** Billy Dee Williams, Michael Mahonen; ***M:*** Eric Leeds.

Giants of Rome woof! **1963** Rome is in peril at the hands of a mysterious secret weapon that turns out to be a giant catapult. Ludicrous all around. **87m/C VHS.** *IT* Richard Harrison, Ettore Manni.

The Giants of Thessaly 🦴🦴 **1960** Jason and Orpheus search for the Golden Fleece, encountering and defeating monsters, wizards, and a scheming witch. **86m/C VHS.** *IT* Roland Carey, Ziva Rodann, Massimo Girotti, Alberto (Albert Farley) Farnese; ***D:*** Riccardo (Robert Hampton) Freda.

Gideon's Trumpet 🦴🦴½ **1980** True story of Clarence Earl Gideon, a Florida convict whose case was decided by the Supreme Court and set the precedent that everyone is entitled to defense by a lawyer, whether or not they can pay for it. Based on the book by Anthony Lewis. **104m/C VHS.** Henry Fonda, Jose Ferrer, John Houseman, Dean Jagger, Sam Jaffe, Fay Wray; ***D:*** Robert E. Collins. **TV**

Gidget 🦴🦴 **1959** A plucky, boy-crazy teenage girl (whose nickname means girl midget) discovers romance and wisdom on the beaches of Malibu when she becomes involved with a group of college-aged surfers. First in a series of Gidget/surfer films. Based on a novel by Frederick Kohner about his daughter. **95m/C VHS.** Sandra Dee, James Darren, Cliff Robertson, Mary Laroche, Arthur O'Connell, Joby Baker; ***D:*** Paul Wendkos; ***W:*** Gabrielle Upton; ***C:*** Burnett Guffey.

Gidget Goes Hawaiian 🦴🦴 **1961** Gidget is off to Hawaii with her parents and is enjoying the beach (and the boys) when she is surprised by a visit from boyfriend "Moondoggie." Sequel to "Gidget" and followed by "Gidget Goes to Rome." **102m/C VHS.** Deborah Walley, James Darren, Carl Reiner, Peggy Cass, Michael Callan, Eddie Foy Jr.; ***D:*** Paul Wendkos.

Gidget Goes to Rome 🦴½ **1963** Darren returns in his third outing as boyfriend "Moondoggie" to yet another actress playing "Gidget" as the two vacation in Rome and find themselves tempted by other romances. Second sequel to "Gidget." **104m/C VHS.** Cindy Carol, James Darren, Jeff Donnell, Cesare Danova, Peter Brooks, Jessie Royce Landis; ***D:*** Paul Wendkos; ***M:*** John Williams.

The Gift 🦴🦴½ **1982 (R)** Story of a 55-year-old man who chooses early retirement in the hopes of changing his dull and boring life. Unbeknownst to him, his co-workers arrange the ultimate retirement gift—a woman. Silly French sexual farce. Dubbed. **105m/C VHS.** *FR* Pierre Mondy, Claudia Cardinale, Clio Goldsmith, Jacques Francois, Cecile Magnet, Remy Laurent; ***D:*** Michael (Michel) Lang.

The Gift 🦴🦴 **2000 (R)** Widowed mom Blanchett uses her psychic gifts to help find the murderer of rich girl Holmes in their Georgia town. Among those involved are battered wife Swank, abuser Reeves, Holmes's fiance Kinnear and mentally slow tow-truck driver Ribisi. By-the-numbers thriller loses steam after a promising start, but is saved by the performances of a fine cast. The characters are stock Southern Gothic types, but they're given dimension by the portrayals. Raimi shows (early on) that he still knows how to startle an audience and create a creepy atmosphere. **112m/C VHS, DVD, Wide.** Cate Blanchett, Katie Holmes, Hilary Swank, Keanu Reeves, Greg Kinnear, Giovanni Ribisi, Michael Jeter, Gary Cole, Kim Dickens, Rosemary Harris, J.K. Simmons, Chelcie Ross, John Beasley; ***D:*** Sam Raimi; ***W:*** Billy Bob Thornton, Tom Epperson; ***C:*** Jamie Anderson; ***M:*** Christopher Young.

The Gift Horse 🦴🦴 *Glory at Sea* **1952** A WWII British naval officer dispatches his duties with an iron hand in an attempt to overturn the legacy of a court-martial eight years earlier. Angry rumblings from his crew threaten to upset the ship's stability. Against this foreboding backdrop, the Nazis give battle. Not historically accurate, but exciting. Based on a story by Ivan Goff and Ben Roberts. **99m/B VHS.** *GB* Trevor Howard, Richard Attenborough, Sonny Tufts, Bernard Lee; ***D:*** Compton Bennett.

The Gift of Love 🦴½ **1990** Saccharine TV adaption of O. Henry's Christmas romance "The Gift of the Magi." **96m/C VHS.** James Woods, Marie Osmond, Timothy Bottoms, June Lockhart, David Wayne; ***D:*** Don Chaffey. **TV**

The Gig 🦴🦴½ **1985** In this small, independently made film, a band of middle-aged amateur jazz musicians give up their stable occupations for a once-in-a-lifetime shot at a two-week gig in the Catskills. Film succeeds on the strength of it's well fleshed-out characters. **95m/C VHS.** Wayne Rogers, Cleavon Little, Warren Vache, Joe Silver, Daniel Nalbach, Andrew Duncan, Jay Thomas, Jerry Matz; ***D:*** Frank D. Gilroy; ***W:*** Frank D. Gilroy.

Gigi 🦴🦴🦴🦴 **1958** Based on Colette's story of a young Parisian girl (Caron) trained to become a courtesan to the wealthy Gaston (Jourdan). But he finds out he prefers her to be his wife rather than his mistress. Chevalier is Gaston's roguish uncle, who casts an always admiring eye on the ladies. Gingold is Gigi's grandmother and former Chevalier flame, and Gabor amuses as Gaston's current, and vapid, mistress. One of the first MGM movies to be shot on location, this extravaganza features some of the best tributes to the French lifestyle ever filmed. Score includes memorable classics. ♫Gigi; Ah Yes, I Remember It Well; Thank Heaven For Little Girls; The Night They Invented Champagne; She's Not Thinking of Me; It's a Bore; Gossip; I'm Glad I'm Not Young Anymore; The Parisians. **119m/C VHS, DVD, 8mm, Wide.** Leslie Caron, Louis Jourdan, Maurice Chevalier, Hermione Gingold, Eva Gabor, Isabel Jeans, Jacques Bergerac; ***D:*** Vincente Minnelli; ***W:*** Alan Jay Lerner; ***C:*** Joseph Ruttenberg; ***M:*** Frederick Loewe. Oscars '58: Adapt. Screenplay, Art Dir./Set Dec., Color Cinematog., Costume Des., Director (Minnelli), Film Editing, Picture, Song ("Gigi"), Scoring/Musical; Directors Guild '58: Director (Minnelli); Golden Globes '59: Director (Minnelli), Film—Mus./Comedy, Support. Actress (Gingold), Natl. Film Reg. '91.

Gilda 🦴🦴🦴½ **1946** An evil South American gambling casino owner hires young American Ford as his trusted aide, unaware that Ford and his sultry wife Hayworth have engaged in a steamy affair. Hayworth does a striptease to "Put the Blame on Mame" in this prominently sexual film. This is the film that made Hayworth into a Hollywood sex goddess. **110m/B VHS, DVD.** Rita Hayworth, Glenn Ford, George Macready, Joseph Calleia, Steven Geray; ***D:*** Charles Vidor; ***W:*** Jo Eisinger, Marion Parsonnet; ***C:*** Rudolph Mate.

The Gilded Cage 🦴🦴 **1954** Two brothers are falsely accused of art theft and must find the real crooks in order to clear their names. **77m/B VHS.** *GB* Alex Nicol, Veronica Hurst, Clifford Evans, Ursula Howells, Elwyn Brook-Jones, John Stuart; ***D:*** John Gilling.

Gimme an F woof! *T & A Academy 2* **1985 (R)** The handsome cheerleading instructor at Camp Beaver View ruffles a few pom-poms when he discovers that the camp's owner is about to enter into a shady deal with some foreigners. The film certainly deserves an "F" for foolishness if nothing else. **100m/C VHS.** Stephen Shellen, Mark Keyloun, John Karlen, Jennifer Cooke; ***D:*** Paul Justman.

Gimme Shelter **1970** The '60s ended as violence occurred at a December 1969 free Rolling Stones concert attended by 300,000 people in Altamont, California. This "Woodstock West" became a bitter remembrance in rock history, as Hell's Angels (hired for security) do some ultimate damage to the spectators. A provocative look at an out-of-control situation. **91m/C VHS, DVD.** Mick Jagger, Keith Richards, Charlie Watts, Bill Wyman, Mick Taylor, Marty Balin, Grace Slick, Paul Kantner, Jerry Garcia, David Crosby, Stephen Stills, Graham Nash, Tina Turner, Ike Turner, Melvin Belli, Bill Graham; ***D:*** David Maysles, Albert Maysles, Charlotte Zwerlin; ***C:*** Haskell Wexler; ***M:*** Rolling Stones.

Gin Game 🦴🦴🦴 **1984** Taped London performance of the Broadway play about an aging couple who find romance in an old age home. Two-character performance won awards; touching and insightful. **82m/C VHS.** Jessica Tandy, Hume Cronyn; ***D:*** Mike Nichols.

Ginger 🦴 **1972** Fabulous super-sleuth Ginger faces the sordid world of prostitution, blackmail and drugs. Prequel to "The Abductors" and followed eventually by "Girls Are for Loving." **90m/C VHS.** Cheri Caffaro, William Grannel, Calvin Culver, Cindy Barnett, Lise Mauer, Michele Norris, Linda Susoeff; ***D:*** Don Schain; ***W:*** Don Schain; ***C:*** R. Kent Evans; ***M:*** Robert G. Orpin.

Ginger Ale Afternoon 🦴 **1989** A smutty comedy revolving around a triangle formed by a married couple and their sexy next-door neighbor. The film tries for fizz but only comes up flat. **88m/C VHS.** Dana Anderson, John M. Jackson, Yeardley Smith; ***D:*** Rafal Zielinski; ***W:*** Gina Wendkos; ***M:*** Willie Dixon.

Ginger & Fred 🦴🦴🦴 **1986 (PG-13)** An acclaimed story of Fellini-esque poignancy about an aging dance team. Years before they had gained success by reverently impersonating the famous dancing duo of Astaire and Rogers. Now, after 30 years, they reunite under the gaudy lights of a high-tech TV special. Wonderful performances by the aging Mastroianni and the still sweet Masina. Italian with English subtitles. **126m/C VHS.** *IT* Marcello Mastroianni, Giulietta Masina, Franco Fabrizi, Frederick Von Ledenberg, Martin Blau, Toto Mignone; ***D:*** Federico Fellini; ***W:*** Federico Fellini, Tonino Guerra, Tullio Pinelli; ***C:*** Tonino Delli Colli; ***M:*** Nicola Piovani.

Ginger in the Morning 🦴🦴 **1973** A salesman is enamored of a young hitchhiker whom he picks up on the road. This is the same year Spacek played the innocent-gone-twisted in "Badlands." **90m/C VHS.** Sissy Spacek, Slim Pickens, Monte Markham, Susan Oliver, Mark Miller; ***D:*** Gordon Wiles.

Ginger Snaps 🦴🦴 **2001 (R)** Modern teen horror goes for quite a ride. Teenaged sisters Ginger (Isabelle) and Brigitte (Perkins) are proud misfits in their quiet Canadian community. Then they're attacked by a werewolf in the woods and Ginger starts behaving very strangely (even for her). Brigitte turns to local pot dealer Sam (Lemche) for help while Ginger just gets more and more aggressive. **107m/C VHS, DVD.** *CA* John Bourgeois, Peter Keleghan, Emily Perkins, Katharine Isabelle, Kris Lemche, Mimi Rogers, Jesse Moss, Danielle Hampton; ***D:*** John Fawcett; ***W:*** Karen Walton; ***C:*** Thom Best; ***M:*** Michael Shields.

The Gingerbread Man 🦴🦴½ **1997 (R)** Lawyer Rick Macgruder (Branagh) falls for a scheming femme (Davidtz) who hires him to have her deranged, stalker father (Duvall) committed. Set in the new hot spot of filmdom, steamy Savannah, it becomes clear that nothing is clear and plot takes on noirish twists and turns of intrigue and suspense before the cigarette smoke clears. Shakespeare savant Branagh proves he can also master a Southern accent. Hannah, as Rick's mousy partner, surprises with an unusually good performance. Grisham's first original screenplay. Studio Polygram disliked Altman's original cut, replaced his editor, and recut the movie to its own specifications, angering Altman who threatened to remove his name from the film. Though not an Altman masterpiece, sly thriller doesn't fail to entice. **114m/C VHS, DVD.** Sonny Shroyer, Kenneth Branagh, Embeth Davidtz, Robert Duvall, Tom Berenger, Daryl Hannah, Robert Downey Jr., Famke Janssen, Mae Whitman, Jesse James Jr.; ***D:*** Robert Altman; ***W:*** John Grisham, Al Hayes; ***C:*** Gu Changwei; ***M:*** Mark Isham.

The Girl 🦴🦴🦴 **1968** The first of Meszaros' trilogy, dealing with a young girl who leaves an orphanage to be reunited with her mother, a traditional country peasant. In Hungarian with English subtitles. Meszaros' first film. Followed by "Riddance" (1973) and "Adoption" (1975). **86m/B VHS.** *HU* ***D:*** Marta Meszaros.

The Girl 🦴½ **1986 (R)** Nero is a wealthy attorney who agrees to pay Powney 300 crowns to have his way with her. Although somewhat ambivalent because of her scandalous age, he takes her anyway. Soon he informs his wife he needs to go on a long business trip, which fits in with her own adulterous plans. A snooping reporter (Brennan) out for some dirt upsets the apple cart, eventually leading to murder. **104m/C VHS.** Franco Nero, Christopher Lee, Bernice Stegers, Clare Powney, Frank Brennan; ***D:*** Arne Mattson.

Girl 🦴🦴½ **1998 (R)** Suburban 18-year-old Andrea Marr (Swain) is bored by her usual life and her virginity. She decides to try on the local club scene and spots musician Todd Sparrow (Flanery), becoming his groupie, and also taking up with cool chick singer Cybil (Reid) and her friends who are in a band. This try at self-discovery ultimately proves less-than-satisfying for Andrea. Lots of cliched issues are dealt with in the most cursory fashion. Based on the novel by Blake Nelson. **99m/C VHS, DVD, Wide.** Dominique Swain, Sean Patrick Flanery, Tara Reid, Summer Phoenix, Selma Blair, Channon Roe, Portia de Rossi, Christopher K. Masterson, Rosemary Forsyth, James Karen; ***D:*** Jonathan Kahn; ***W:*** David E. Tolchinsky; ***C:*** Tami Reiker; ***M:*** Michael Tavera.

A Girl, 3 Guys and a Gun 🦴🦴 **2001 (R)** Best buds Neil (Leffler), Frank (Florence), and Joey (Luper) want to blow out of their smalltown by getting involved in a botched robbery that leads to an unexpected kidnapping. An indie that starts off as larky and then turns serious (and somewhat confusing). **88m/C VHS, DVD.** Christian Leffler, Josh Holland, Tracy Zahoryin, Michael Trucco, Tava Smiley, Kenny Luper, Brent Florence; ***D:*** Brent Florence; ***W:*** Brent Florence; ***C:*** Matt Davis.

A Girl, a Guy and a Gob 🦴🦴 *The Navy Steps Out* **1941** A shy rich boy falls in love with a girl who has her sights on another. Silly but enjoyable cast. **91m/B VHS.** Lucille Ball, Edmond O'Brien, George Murphy, Franklin Pangborn, Henry Travers, Lloyd Corrigan; ***D:*** Richard Wallace.

The Girl Can't Help It 🦴🦴½ **1956** Satiric rock and roll musical comedy about a retired mobster who hires a hungry talent agent to promote his girlfriend, a wanna-be no-talent singer. Mansfield's first starring role. Classic performances by some of the early greats including Eddie Cochran, Gene Vincent, the Platters, Little Richard, and Fats Domino. **99m/B VHS.** Jayne Mansfield, Tom Ewell, Edmond O'Brien, Julie London, Ray Anthony, Henry Jones, John Emery, Juanita Moore, Barry J. Gordon, Fats Domino, Abbey Lincoln, Eddie Fontaine, Little Richard, Eddie Cochran, Gene Vincent; ***D:*** Frank Tashlin; ***W:*** Frank Tashlin, Herbert Baker; ***C:*** Leon Shamroy; ***M:*** Lionel Newman.

Girl Crazy 🦴🦴🦴 *When the Girls Meet the Boys* **1943** A wealthy young playboy is sent to an all-boy school in Arizona to get his mind off girls. Once there, he still manages to fall for a local girl who can't stand the sight of him. The eighth film pairing for Rooney and Garland. ♫Sam and Delilah; Embraceable You; I Got Rhythm; Fascinating Rhythm; Treat Me Rough; Bronco Busters; Bidin' My Time; But Not For Me; Do. **99m/B VHS.** Mickey Rooney, Judy Garland, Nancy Walker, June Allyson; ***D:*** Norman Taurog; ***C:*** William H. Daniels; ***M:*** George Gershwin, Ira Gershwin.

Girl from Calgary 🦴 **1932** A female rodeo champ ropes her boyfriends much like she ropes her cows, but not without a knock-down, drag-out fight between the two which forces our cowgirl to make the choice she seems to know is fated. Stock rodeo footage is intercut with the heroine riding an obviously mechanical bucking bronc. **66m/B VHS.** Fifi d'Orsay, Paul Kelly; ***D:*** Philip H. (Phil, P.H.) Whitman.

Girl from Chicago 🦴🦴 **1932** In this crime melodrama a secret service agent falls in love while on assignment in Mississippi. When he's back in New York he finds a good friend of his girl's in serious trouble with the numbers racket. **69m/C VHS.** Starr Calloway, Grace Smith, Eugene Brooks, Frank Wilson; ***D:*** Oscar Micheaux.

Girl from Hunan 🦴🦴🦴 **1986** Turn-of-the-century China, a 12-year-old girl is married to a two-year-old boy in a typical arranged marriage. She grows into womanhood treating her toddler husband with sibling affection, but conducts a secret love affair with a farmer. Intolerant village laws against adultry place her life in jeopardy. In Mandarin with English subtitles. **99m/C VHS.** Na Renhua, Deng Xiaotuang, Yu Zhang; ***D:*** Xie Fei.

The Girl from Missouri 🦴🦴🦴 *One Hundred Percent Pure* **1934** Cute comedy in which Harlow tries to snag a millionaire without sacrificing her virtues. Lots of laughs and hilarious action, especially the scene where Harlow arrives at the yacht in Florida. Kelly is great as Harlow's wise-cracking girlfriend. Witty dialogue by Emerson and Loos, who also wrote "Gentleman Prefer Blondes." **75m/B VHS.** Jean Harlow, Lionel Barrymore, Franchot Tone, Lewis Stone, Patsy Kelly, Alan Mowbray, Clara Blandick, Russell Hopton; ***D:*** Jack Conway; ***W:*** Anita Loos, John Emerson.

The Girl from Petrovka 🦴½ **1974 (PG)** A high-spirited Russian ballerina falls in love with an American newspaper correspondent. Their romance is complicated by the suspicious KGB. Bittersweet with a bleak ending. **103m/C VHS.** Goldie Hawn, Hal Holbrook, Anthony Hopkins; ***D:*** Robert Ellis Miller; ***W:*** Chris Bryant, Allan Scott; ***M:*** Henry Mancini.

The Girl from Tobacco Row 🦴 **1966** A Southern slut involved with a cache of stolen cash fools with both a convict and the sheriff. **90m/C VHS.** Tex Ritter, Rachel Romen, Earl Richards, Tim Ormond, Rita Faye, Ralph Emery; ***D:*** Ron Ormond.

The Girl Getters 🦴🦴 *The System* **1966** Tinker (Reed) and his rowdy London pals take a vacation at a seaside resort, where they proceed to pick fights, chase girls, and cause general (minor) mayhem. Tinker's busy chasing Nicola (Merrow) but surprises himself when he actually starts to fall for her. **79m/B VHS, Wide.** *GB* Oliver Reed, Jane Merrow, David Hemmings, John Alderton, Harry Andrews; ***D:*** Michael Winner; ***W:*** Peter Draper; ***C:*** Nicolas Roeg.

Girl Happy 🦴🦴 **1965** The King's fans will find him in Fort Lauderdale, Florida this time as the leader of a rock 'n' roll group. His mission: to chaperone the daughter of a Chicago mobster who naturally falls for him. Why not? ♫Girl Happy; Cross My Heart and Hope to Die; Do Not Disturb; Spring Fever; Wolf Call; Do the Clam; Fort Lauderdale Chamber of Commerce; Puppet On a String; I've Got to Find About My Baby. **96m/C VHS.** Elvis Presley, Harold J. Stone, Shelley Fabares, Gary Crosby, Nita Talbot, Mary Ann Mobley, Jackie Coogan; ***D:*** Boris Sagal; ***W:*** Harvey Bulloch.

Girl Hunters 🦴🦴½ **1963** That intrepid private eye, Mike Hammer (played by his creator, Spillane), is caught up with communist spies, wicked women, and a missing secretary. Hammer is his usual judge-and-jury character but the action is fast-paced. **103m/B VHS, DVD.** Mickey Spillane, Lloyd Nolan, Shirley Eaton, Hy Gardner, Scott Peters; ***D:*** Roy Rowland; ***W:*** Roy Rowland, Robert Fellows; ***C:*** Ken Talbot; ***M:*** Philip Green.

A Girl in a Million 🦴🦴 **1946** Williams dumps his verbose wife and seeks peace and quiet in a men-only War Department office. All is well until the arrival of a colonel and his daughter, mute from trauma. Finding her silence appealing, he marries her, but another trauma restores her speech. Sexist comedy may have played better in its day. **90m/B VHS.** *GB* Hugh Williams, Joan Greenwood, Naunton Wayne, Wylie Watson, Garry Marsh; ***D:*** Francis Searle.

The Girl in a Swing 🦴½ **1989 (R)** An Englishman impulsively marries a beautiful German girl and both are subsequently haunted by phantoms from her past—are they caused by her psychic powers? Cliche-ridden silliness. Based on the Richard Adams novel. **119m/C VHS.** Meg Tilly, Rupert Frazer, Elspet Gray, Lynsey Baxter, Nicholas Le Prevost, Jean Both; ***D:*** Gordon Hessler.

Girl in Black 🦴🦴 *To Koritsi Me Ta Mavra* **1956** The shy daughter of a once wealthy household gets the chance to escape her genteel poverty when she falls in love with the young man boarding with her family. He is attracted to her but a shocking tragedy changes everything. In Greek with English subtitles. **100m/B VHS, DVD.** *GR* Ellie Lambetti, Eleni Zafirou, Georges Foundas, Dimitri Horne, Stefanos Stratigos; ***D:*** Michael Cacoyannis; ***W:*** Michael Cacoyannis; ***C:*** Walter Lassally; ***M:*** Manos Hadjidakis.

Girl in Black Stockings 🦴🦴 **1957** Beautiful women are mysteriously murdered at a remote, Utah hotel. Interesting, little known thriller similar to Hitchcock's "Psycho," but pre-dating it by three years. **75m/B VHS.** Lex Barker, Anne Bancroft, Mamie Van Doren, Ron Randell, Marie Windsor, John Dehner, John Holland, Diana Van Der Vlis; ***D:*** Howard W. Koch; ***M:*** Les Baxter.

The Girl in Blue 🦴🦴 **1974 (R)** A lawyer, ill at ease with his current romance, suddenly decides to search for a beautiful woman he saw once, and instantly fell in love with, years before. **103m/C VHS.** *CA* Maud Adams, David Selby, Gay Rowan, William Osler, Diane Dewey, Michael Kirby; ***D:*** George Kaczender.

A Girl in Every Port 🦴🦴½ **1952** Navy buddies acquire an ailing racehorse and try to conceal it aboard ship along with a healthy horse they plan to switch it with in an upcoming race. Groucho flies without his brothers in this zany film. **86m/B VHS.** Groucho Marx, William Bendix, Marie Wilson, Don DeFore, Gene Lockhart; ***D:*** Chester Erskine.

Girl in Gold Boots 🦴 **1969** Aspiring starlet meets up with a draft evader and a biker on her way to Hollywood where she gets a job as a go-go dancer in a sleazy club. But things don't go smoothly when a murder and a drug theft are revealed. ♫Do You Want to Laugh or Cry?; For You; Hello, Michelle; One Good Time, One Good Place; Lonesome Man; You Gotta Come Down; Everything I Touch Turns to Gold; Cowboy Santa; Wheels of Love. **91m/C VHS, DVD, Wide.** Jody Daniels, Leslie McRae, Tom Pace, Mark Herron; ***D:*** Ted V. Mikels; ***W:*** Art Names, Leighton J. Peatman, John T. Wilson; ***C:*** Robert Maxwell; ***M:*** Nicholas Carras.

Girl in His Pocket 🦴🦴 *Amour de Poche; Nude in His Pocket* **1957** Mad scientist creates a potion that turns things into three-inch statues. He uses it mostly to have trystes with his lab assistant so his fiancee won't find out. Based on "The Diminishing Draft" by Waldemar Kaempfert. **82m/C VHS.** *FR* Jean Marais, Genevieve Page, Agnes Laurent; ***D:*** Pierre Kast; ***C:*** Ghislan Cloquet.

The Girl in Lover's Lane 🦴🦴 **1960** A drifter falls in love with a small town girl but becomes a murder suspect when she turns up dead. Interesting mainly for Elam's uncharacteristic portrayal of a village idiot. **78m/B VHS.** Brett Halsey, Joyce Meadows, Lowell Brown, Jack Elam; ***D:*** Charles R. Rondeau.

The Girl in Room 2A woof! **1976 (R)** A young woman is trapped in a mansion with the elderly owner and her demented son. Routine horrorfest. **90m/C VHS.** Raf Vallone, Daniela Giordano; ***D:*** William Rose.

Girl in the Cadillac 🦴🦴½ **1994 (R)** Modern-day B-movie wanna-be loosely adapted from the James M. Cain novella "The Enchanted Isle." 17-year-old freespirited Amanda (Eleniak) wants to get out of stifling small town Texas. She buys a bus ticket to find her long-gone daddy and winds up with not-too-smart cowpoke Rick (McNamara) instead. A bank robbery gone bad finds the twosome on the loose with $75 thou, a cherry red El Dorado convertible, and Rick's partners after them. Appealing lead performers can't overcome the cliches. **89m/C VHS.** Erika Eleniak, William McNamara, Michael Lerner, Bud Cort, Valerie Perrine, Ed Lauter, William Shockley; ***D:*** Lucas Platt; ***W:*** John Warren; ***C:*** Nancy Schreiber; ***M:*** Anton Sanko.

The Girl in the Picture 🦴🦴½ **1986 (PG-13)** Sinclair stars in this light comedy as an unlucky photo clerk who discovers only too late that his ex-girlfriend may be the woman of his dreams. Typical understated but entertaining effort. **89m/C VHS.** *GB* John Gordon-Sinclair, Irina Brook, David McKay, Catherine Guthrie, Paul Young, Gregory Fisher; ***D:*** Cary Parker.

Girl, Interrupted 🦴🦴½ **1999 (R)** Ryder stars as neurotic 18-year-old Susanna who, after making a half-hearted suicide attempt, is diagnosed with borderline personality disorder. So, in 1967, she's sent to Claymoore, a psychiatric hospital outside Boston, where she'll spend the next two years. There, Susanna meets some young woman who are truly disturbed, including compelling sociopath, Lisa (Jolie). Yes, the story's predictable but it's also touching—just don't expect the fireworks of "One Flew Over a Cuckoo's Nest." Based on the 1993 memoir by Susanna Kaysen. **127m/C VHS, DVD, Wide.** Winona Ryder, Angelina Jolie, Vanessa Redgrave, Whoopi Goldberg, Clea DuVall, Brittany Murphy, Elissabeth (Elisabeth, Elizabeth, Liz) Moss, Jared Leto, Jeffrey Tambor, Mary Kay Place; ***D:*** James Mangold; ***W:*** James Mangold, Anna Hamilton Phelan, Lisa Loomer; ***C:*** Jack N. Green; ***M:*** Mychael Danna. Oscars '99: Support. Actress (Jolie); Golden Globes '00: Support. Actress (Jolie); Screen Actors Guild '99: Support. Actress (Jolie); Broadcast Film Critics '99: Support. Actress (Jolie).

The Girl Most Likely 🦴🦴½ **1957** Light musical comedy about a romance-minded girl who dreams of marrying a wealthy, handsome man. She runs into a problem when she finds three prospects. Remake of 1941's "Tom, Dick and Harry" with Ginger Rogers. Choreography by great Gower Champion. ♫The Girl Most Likely; All the Colors of the Rainbow; I Don't Know What I Want; Balboa; We Gotta Keep Up With the Joneses; Crazy Horse. **98m/C VHS.** Jane Powell, Cliff Robertson, Tommy Noonan, Kaye Ballard, Una Merkel; ***D:*** Mitchell Leisen; ***W:*** Paul Jarrico.

The Girl Next Door 🦴🦴 **1998 (R)** Married doctor Czerny agrees to keep an eye on his neighbor's 18-year-old hot-babe daughter (Shannon) while her parents are out of town. Only he takes the good neighbor relationship too far. When the teen winds up dead, the local Sheriff (Busey) is out to discover just what happened. **100m/C VHS, DVD.** *CA* Henry Czerny, Gary Busey, Polly Shannon, Robin Gammell, Alberta Watson, Simon MacCorkindale; ***D:*** Eric Till.

Girl of the Golden West 🦴🦴 **1938** A musical version of the David Belasco chestnut about a Canadian frontier girl loving a rogue. One of Eddy and MacDonald's lesser efforts but features Ebsen's song and dance talents. ♫Camptown Races; Shadows on the Moon; Soldiers of Fortune; Soldiers of Fortune Reprise; Shadows on the Moon Reprise; The Wind in the Trees; Liebestraum; Ave Maria; Senorita. **120m/B VHS.** Jeanette MacDonald, Nelson Eddy, Walter Pidgeon, Leo Carrillo, Buddy Ebsen, Leonard Penn, Priscilla Lawson, Bob Murphy, Olin Howlin, Cliff Edwards, Billy Bevan; ***D:*** Robert Z. Leonard.

A Girl of the Limberlost **1990** A young Indiana farmgirl fights to bring her estranged parents back together, in spite of a meddling aunt and the unexplained phenomena that haunt her. Fine acting and beautiful scenery. Originally broadcast as part of PBS's "Wonderworks" family movie series, it's best appreciated by young teens. Adapted from Gene Stratton Porter's much-filmed novel. **120m/C VHS.** Annette O'Toole, Joanna Cassidy, Heather Fairfield. **TV**

Girl on a Chain Gang woof! **1965** A girl on the run gets caught by police and does her time on a chain gang—an otherwise all-male chain gang. Predictable. **96m/B VHS.** William Watson, Julie Ange, R.K. Charles; ***D:*** Jerry Gross; ***W:*** Jerry Gross.

The Girl on a Motorcycle 🦴🦴 *Naked under Leather; La Motocyclette* **1968 (R)** Singer Faithfull is a bored housewife who dons black leather and hops on her motorcycle to meet up with her lover (Delon), all the while remembering their other erotic encounters. **92m/C VHS, DVD.** *GB* Alain Delon, Marianne Faithfull, Roger Mutton; ***D:*** Jack Cardiff; ***W:*** Gillian Freeman, Ronald Duncan; ***C:*** Jack Cardiff; ***M:*** Les Reed.

A Girl on Her Own 🦴🦴 **1976** A young actress embarking on her first big role in Paris must also deal with family and political considerations in this drama set during the political upheaval of 1935. **112m/C VHS.** *FR* Sophie Chemineau, Bruno La Brasca; ***D:*** Philippe Nahon.

The Girl on the Bridge 🦴🦴🦴 *Le Fille sure le Pont* **1998 (R)** An unconventional romance that finds middle-aged professional knife-thrower Gabor (Auteuil) calmly engaging in conversation with suicidal Adele (Paradis), the titular character. After a young lifetime of perpetual bad luck, what could be better for Adele than to risk everything every night by becoming Gabor's new partner. The duo seem to have a telepathic communication that makes them a great success but luck has a way of changing. Great chemistry between the world-weary Auteuil and the gamine Paradis that is all the more apparent because their characters maintain a hands-off relationship. French with subtitles. **92m/B VHS, Wide.** *FR* Daniel Auteuil, Vanessa Paradis, Demetre Georgalas, Isabelle Petit-Jacques; ***D:*** Patrice Leconte; ***W:*** Serge Frydman; ***C:*** Jean-Marie Dreujou. Cesar '00: Actor (Auteuil).

Girl Rush 🦴 **1944** Two bad vaudeville comics are stuck in California during the gold rush and are promised sacks of gold if they can persuade some women to come to a rowdy mining town. ♫Annabella's Bustle; Rainbow Valley; If Mother Could Only See Us Now; Walking Arm in Arm With Jim. **65m/B VHS.** Wally Brown, Alan Carney, Frances Langford, Vera Vague, Robert Mitchum, Paul Hurst, Patti Brill, Sarah Padden, Cy Kendall; ***D:*** Gordon Douglas.

The Girl Said No 🦴½ *With Words and Music* **1937** A sleazy bookie poses as a theatrical producer in order to get even with a dance hall floozy who once stiffed him. **72m/B VHS.** Robert Armstrong, Irene Hervey, William Haines; ***D:*** Andrew L. Stone; ***W:*** Andrew L. Stone.

Girl Shy 🦴🦴🦴 **1924** Harold is a shy tailor's apprentice who is trying to get a collection of his romantic fantasies published. Finale features Lloyd chasing wildly after girl of his dreams. **65m/B VHS.** Harold Lloyd, Jobyna Ralston, Richard Daniels; ***D:*** Fred Newmeyer; ***W:*** Sam Taylor.

Girl 6 🦴🦴½ **1996 (R)** Aspiring actress (Randle) takes job as a phone sex operator in order to make ends meet. After finally finding stardom in the world of titillating telecommunications, she starts to take her work home. Bound to be compared, unfairly and probably unfavorably, to Lee's debut "She's Gotta Have It." Terrific performance by Randle is hampered by the lack of a strong story and too many unresolved subplots. Features the obligatory Lee cameo, while Tarantino shows up as a young hotshot director. Prince provides old and new tunes (as well as his previous moniker, apparently) to the proceedings. **107m/C VHS.** Theresa Randle, Isaiah Washington IV, Ron Silver, John Turturro, Naomi Campbell, Halle Berry, Madonna, Quentin Tarantino, Debi Mazar, Peter Berg, Richard Belzer, Spike Lee, Jenifer Lewis, Michael Imperioli, Kristen Wilson, Dina Pearlman, Maggie Rush, Desi Moreno, Susan Batson; ***D:*** Spike Lee; ***W:*** Suzan-Lori Parks; ***C:*** Malik Hassan Sayeed; ***M:*** Prince.

The Girl, the Body and the Pill 🦴 **1967** Sexploitation pic from director Lewis has a high school instructor getting fired for her sex education lectures—so she continues them in the privacy of her own home. Meanwhile, her students take up playing musical beds and learn about "the pill." **80m/C VHS.** Pamela Rhea, Bill Rogers, Nancy Lee Noble, George Brown, Roy Collodi, Todd Harris, James Nelson, Ray Sager, Valedia Hill; ***D:*** Herschell Gordon Lewis; ***W:*** Allison Louise Downe; ***C:*** Roy Collodi; ***M:*** Larry Wellington.

A Girl Thing 🦴🦴 **2001** In four individual stories, shrink Dr. Noonan (Channing) listens to her female patients' dreams and woes. Macpherson is a successful lawyer who finds herself attracted to Capshaw in a complicated affair. Headly and her sisters DeMornay and Janney bicker over their mother's final request—they must spend a week together in her house in order to collect their inheritance. Whitfield suspects her husband Bakula is having an affair and hires Hamilton to check things out. Manheim stars as a deeply disturbed patient who forces the doctor to re-evaluate her own life and profession. **237m/C VHS, DVD, Wide.** Stockard Channing, Elle Macpherson, Kate Capshaw, Glenne Headly, Rebecca DeMornay, Allison Janney, Lynn Whitfield, Linda Hamilton, Camryn Manheim, Scott Bakula, Bruce Greenwood, Brent Spiner, Mia Farrow; ***D:*** Lee Rose. **CABLE**

A Girl to Kill For 🦴½ **1990 (R)** A temptress lures a randy college guy into a plot of murder and betrayal. **85m/C VHS.** Sasha Jenson, Karen Austin, Alex Cord, Rod McCary, Karen Medak; ***D:*** Richard Oliver.

Girl Under the Sheet 🦴 **196?** A con-man/archaeologist moves into an ancient castle and begins romancing a beautiful resident ghost. **89m/C VHS.** Chelo Alonso, Walter Chiari.

The Girl Who Had Everything 🦴🦴½ **1953** Good melodrama with top cast, intelligent script and smooth direction. Taylor plays the spoiled daughter of a criminal lawyer (Powell) who falls for her father's client (Lamas), a suave, underground syndicate boss. Remake of the 1931 film "A Free Soul," which starred Norma Shearer, Clark Gable, and Lionel Barrymore. Based on the novel of the same name by Adela Rogers St. John. **69m/B VHS.** Elizabeth Taylor, Fernando Lamas, William Powell, Gig Young, James Whitmore, Robert Burton; ***D:*** Richard Thorpe; ***M:*** Andre Previn.

The Girl Who Knew Too Much 🦴🦴½ *La Ragazza Che Sapeva Troppo; The Evil Eye* **1963** Ten years ago in Italy a string of "alphabet murders" began on "A" and ended on "C." Now a pretty young American named Nora Davis (Roman) is visiting a family friend in Italy. When the friend dies and Nora goes for help—in the middle of the night, in the rain, wearing only a raincoat, alone, through an empty plaza—she witnesses a murder that happened ten years ago or does she? She shouldn't worry, though, because handsome young Dr. Marcello Bassi (Saxon speaking fluent Italian) wants to help her. Typically fun and frightening Bava fare with the script, cinematography and direction working much more smoothly than usual. **86m/B DVD, Wide.** *IT* Leticia Roman, John Saxon, Valentina Cortese, Robert Buchanan; ***D:*** Mario Bava; ***W:*** Mario Bava, Ennio de Concini, Mino Guerrini; ***C:*** Mario Bava.

The Girl Who Spelled Freedom 🦴🦴🦴 **1986** A young Cambodian girl, speaking little English, strives to adjust to life in Chattanooga, Tennessee. She faces her challenges by becoming a champion at the national spelling bee. Based on a true story. **90m/C VHS.** Wayne Rogers, Mary Kay Place, Jade Chinn, Kieu Chinh, Kathleen Sisk; ***D:*** Simon Wincer. **TV**

The Girl with a Suitcase 🦴🦴 *La Ragazza con la Valgia* **1960** Young nightclub singer Aida (Cardinale) falls for rich cad Marcello (Pani) and leaves her job to follow him to his family home in Parma. He was just stringing her along and instructs his 16-year-old brother Lorenzo (Perrin) to get rid of Aida. But instead Lorenzo decides to become her protector and the unlikely duo fall in love. Italian with subtitles; the original release was 135 minutes. **111m/B VHS.** *IT* Claudia Cardinale, Jacques Perrin, Corrado Pani, Luciana Angelillo, Romolo Valli, Gian Marie Volonte; ***D:*** Valerio Zurlini; ***W:*** Valerio Zurlini; ***C:*** Tito Santoni; ***M:*** Mario Nascimbene.

Girl with Green Eyes 🦴🦴½ **1964** Kate Brady (Tushingham) is a young Catholic farm girl who comes to Dublin for work and falls in love with much older divorced writer Eugene Gaillard (Finch). She moves in with him despite her moral misgivings but both discover their differences are too great to sustain their relationship. O'Brien adapted the screenplay from her novel "The Lonely Girl." **91m/B VHS, DVD, Wide.** *GB* Peter Finch, Rita Tushingham, Lynn Redgrave, Marie Kean, Julian Glover, T.P. McKenna, Yolande Finch, Arthur O'Sullivan; ***D:*** Desmond Davis; ***W:*** Edna O'Brien; ***C:*** Manny Wynn; ***M:*** John Addison.

The Girl with the Hat Box 🦴🦴 **1927** Early Russian production about a poor working girl who's paid with a lottery ticket rather than rubles (an ironic pre-communist theme?). When she strikes it rich in the lottery, her boss gives chase and silent antics ensue. Silent with orchestral score. **67m/B VHS.** *RU* Anna Sten, Vladimar Fogel, Serafina Birman, Ivan Koval-Samborsky; ***D:*** Boris Barnet.

The Girl with the Hungry Eyes 🦴🦴 **1994 (R)** In 1937, top fashion model and hotel owner Louise (Fulton) kills herself over a cheating fiancee. Except Louise doesn't die, instead she becomes a vampire and, in the present-day, decides to return to her now-derelict haunts. Louise is determined to restore her hotel to its former glory and get her revenge on men in general. Filmed in Miami's South Beach. Adapted from a short story by Fritz Leiber. **84m/C VHS.** Christina (Kristina) Fulton, Isaac Turner, Leon Herbert, Bret Carr, Susan Rhodes; ***D:*** Jon Jacobs; ***W:*** Jon Jacobs; ***M:*** Paul Inder.

Girlfight 🦴🦴🦴 **1999 (R)** Scrappy feminist coming-of-age drama is the feature debut from director Karyn Kusama. Diana (Rodriguez) is a high-school senior with a bad temper and a penchant for trouble. Her single dad, Sandro (Calderon), encourages her brother Tiny (Santiago) to work with a boxing trainer but refuses to allow his daughter to participate. Diana decides to train anyway, and her determination finds her becoming the gym's first female champ. She falls in love with fellow promising amateur Adrian (Douglas), setting the stage for an unlikely mixed gender bout between the two. The movie strains reality when it has Diana fight Adrian, but the feeling throughout is heartfelt without being overly sentimental. And at least she doesn't howl "Yo Adrian" afterwards. **90m/C VHS, DVD, Wide.** Jamie Tirelli, Michelle Rodriguez, Santiago Douglas, Ray Santiago, Elisa Bacanegra, Paul Calderon, John Sayles; ***D:*** Karyn Kusama; ***W:*** Karyn Kusama; ***C:*** Patrick Cady; ***M:*** Theodore Shapiro. Ind. Spirit '01: Debut Perf. (Rodriguez); Sundance '00: Director (Kusama), Grand Jury Prize.

Girlfriend from Hell 🦴 **1989 (R)** The Devil inhabits the body of a teenage wallflower and turns her into an uncontrollable vamp. **95m/C VHS.** Liane (Alexandra) Curtis, Dana Ashbrook, Lezlie (Dean) Deane, James Daughton, Anthony Barrile, James Karen; ***D:*** Daniel M. Peterson; ***W:*** Daniel M. Peterson.

Girlfriends 🦴🦴🦴 **1978 (PG)** Bittersweet story of a young Jewish photographer learning to make it on her own. Directorial debut of Weill reflects her background in documentaries as the true-to-life episodes unfold. **87m/C VHS.** Melanie Mayron, Anita Skinner, Eli Wallach, Christopher Guest, Amy Wright, Viveca Lindfors, Bob Balaban, Kathryn Walker, Kristopher Tabori, Mike Kellin, Kenneth McMillan; ***D:*** Claudia Weill; ***W:*** Vicki Polon; ***C:*** Fred Murphy. Sundance '78: Grand Jury Prize.

Girls Are for Loving 🦴 **1973** Undercover agent Ginger faces real adventure when she battles it out with her counterpart, a seductive enemy agent. Her third adventure following "Ginger" (1970) and "The Abductors" (1971). **90m/C VHS.** Cheri Caffaro, Timothy Brown, William Grannel, Scott Ellsworth, Robert C. Jefferson, Jocelyn Peters, Yuki Shimoda, Fred Vincent; ***D:*** Don Schain; ***W:*** Don Schain; ***M:*** Robert G. Orpin.

A Girl's Folly 🦴🦴½ **1917** A country girl falls in love with the leading man of a film shooting on location. She wants to become a rich actress, but fails miserably. The actor offers her all the luxuries she wants if she'll become his mistress. When she finally agrees, her mother shows up. What will our country maid do now? **66m/B VHS, 8mm.** Robert Warwick, Doris Kenyon, June Elvidge, Johnny Hines; ***D:*** Maurice Tourneur.

Girls! Girls! Girls! 🦴🦴 **1962 (PG)** Poor tuna boat fisherman Elvis moonlights as a nightclub singer to get his father's boat out of hock. He falls for a rich girl pretending to be poor; and after some romantic trials, there's the usual happy ending. ♫The Nearness of You; Never Let Me Go; Girls, Girls, Girls; Return to Sender; We're Coming in Loaded; A Boy Like Me, A Girl Like You; Song of the Shrimp; Earth Boy; The Walls Have Ears. **106m/C VHS.** Elvis Presley, Stella Stevens, Laurel Goodwin, Jeremy Slate, Benson Fong, Robert Strauss, Ginny Tiu, Guy Lee, Beulah Quo, Frank Puglia, Nestor Paiva, Alexander Tiu, Elizabeth Tiu, Lili Valenty; ***D:*** Norman Taurog; ***W:*** Edward Anhalt; ***C:*** Loyal Griggs; ***M:*** Joseph J. Lilley.

Girls in Chains 🦴½ **1943** Girls in a reformatory, a teacher, a corrupt school official, and the detective trying to nail him. There's also a murder with the killer revealed at the beginning of the film. **72m/B VHS.** Arline Judge, Roger Clark, Robin Raymond, Barbara Pepper, Dorothy Burgess, Clancy Cooper, Sid Melton, Betty Blythe, Peggy Stewart, Francis Ford; ***D:*** Edgar G. Ulmer; ***W:*** Albert Beich; ***C:*** Ira Morgan; ***M:*** Leo Erdody.

Girls in Prison 🦴½ **1956** Anne Carson is sent to prison for a bank robbery she didn't commit, and although the prison chaplain believes her story, the other prisoners think she knows where the money is hidden. They plan a prison break, forcing Carson to go with them and get the money, but they soon run across the real robber, also searching for the loot. A below-average "B" prison movie, lacking the camp aspects of so many of these films. **87m/B VHS.** Richard Denning, Joan Taylor, Adele Jergens, Helen Gilbert, Lance Fuller, Jane Darwell, Raymond Hatton; ***D:*** Edward L. Cahn.

Girls in Prison 🦴🦴 **1994 (R)** Not exactly a remake of the same-titled 1956 film (although it's still set in the '50s) but it's a familiar "babes behind bars" saga. Aspiring country singer Aggie (Crider) is wrongfully convicted of murdering a record company exec and winds up in the big house. Then she learns an inmate has been contracted to kill her. Can she find the hit girl before it's too late (and find out who's framing her)? **82m/C VHS.** Missy (Melissa) Crider, Ione Skye, Anne Heche, William Boyett, Tom Towles, Miguel (Michael) Sandoval, Jon Polito, Richmond Arquette; ***D:*** John McNaughton; ***W:*** Christa Lang, Samuel Fuller; ***C:*** Jean De Segonzac; ***M:*** Hummie Mann. **CABLE**

Girls Just Want to Have Fun 🦴½ **1985 (PG)** An army brat and her friends pull out all the stops and defy their parents for a chance to dance on a national TV program. **90m/C VHS, DVD, Wide.** Sarah Jessica Parker, Helen Hunt, Ed Lauter, Holly Gagnier, Morgan Woodward, Lee Montgomery, Shannen Doherty, Biff Yeager; ***D:*** Alan Metter; ***W:*** Janice Hirsch, Amy Spies; ***C:*** Thomas Ackerman; ***M:*** Thomas Newman.

Girls Next Door 🦴 **1979 (R)** A bevy of boisterous beauties cavort and cause havoc in buffoon-cluttered suburbia. **85m/C VHS.** Kirsten Baker, Perry Lang, Leslie Cederquist, Richard Singer; ***D:*** James Hong.

Girls' Night 🦴🦴½ **1997** The acting's fine but the story's weak in this old-fashioned weepie. Brit wives Dawn (Blethyn) and Jackie (Walters) are best friends and in-laws, who even work at the same factory. Both women are also suffering from the marriage blues and find solace at the local bingo parlor. When Dawn wins very big, she splits the money with Jackie and then discovers that she has cancer. The duo decide this is the time for their dream Las Vegas vacation, where they even meet a Prince Charming—in the form of cowpoke Cody (Kristofferson). **106m/C VHS.** *GB* Brenda Blethyn, Julie Walters, Kris Kristofferson, George Costigan, James Gaddas, Philip Jackson; ***D:*** Nick Hurran; ***W:*** Kay Mellor; ***C:*** David Odd; ***M:*** Ed Shearmur.

Girls Night Out 🦴 *The Scaremaker* **1983 (R)** Ex-cop must stop a killer who is murdering participants in a sorority house scavenger hunt and leaving cryptic clues on the local radio station. **96m/C VHS.** Hal Holbrook, Rutanya Alda, Julia Montgomery, James Carroll; ***D:*** Robert Deubel.

The Girls of Huntington House 🦴🦴 **1973** A teacher in a school for unwed mothers finds herself becoming increasingly absorbed in her students' lives. **73m/C VHS.** Shirley Jones, Mercedes McCambridge, Sissy Spacek, William Windom, Pamela Sue Martin, Darrell Larson; ***D:*** Alf Kjellin. **TV**

Girls of the White Orchid 🦴 *Death Ride to Osaka* **1985** A naive American girl thinks she's getting a job singing in a Japanese nightclub, but it turns out to be a front for a prostitution ring run by the Japanese Yakuza. Based on real stories, though the producers concentrate on the seamy side. **96m/C VHS, DVD.** Thomas Jefferson Byrd, Carolyn Seymour, Mako, Ann Jillian, Jennifer Jason Leigh; ***D:*** Jonathan Kaplan; ***C:*** John Lindley; ***M:*** Brad Fiedel. **TV**

Girls on the Road 🦴½ **1973 (PG)** Two girls are just out for fun cruising the California coast, but that handsome hitchhiker turns out to be a deadly mistake. **91m/C VHS.** *CA* Kathleen (Kathy) Cody, Michael Ontkean, Dianne Hull, Ralph Waite, Rigg Kennedy; ***D:*** Thomas J. Schmidt.

Girls Riot 🦴 **1988** Young, female juvenile delinquents have had enough! They decide to give their warden-like headmistress a taste of her own violence. **100m/C VHS.** Jocelyne Boisseau, Cornelia Calwer, Angelica Domrose, Ute Freight; ***D:*** Manfred Purzer.

Girls School Screamers 🦴 **1986 (R)** Six young women and a nun are assigned to spend the weekend checking the contents for sale in a scary mansion bequeathed to their school. Unfortunately, the psychotic killer inhabiting the place doesn't think that's a good idea. **85m/C VHS, DVD.** Mollie O'Mara, Sharon Christopher, Vera Gallagher; ***D:*** John P. Finegan; ***W:*** John P. Finegan; ***C:*** Albert R. Jordan; ***M:*** John Hodian.

Girls' Town 🦴 *The Innocent and the Damned* **1959** Typical bad girls and drag racing '50s flick has Van Doren sent to a correctional institute, run by nuns. This tough girl sees the error of her wicked ways and turns into a goody-two-shoes. **90m/B VHS.** Mamie Van Doren, Mel Torme, Paul Anka, Ray Anthony, Maggie Hayes, Cathy Crosby, Elinor Donahue, Gigi Perreau, Jim Mitchum, Gloria Talbott, Harold Lloyd Jr., Charles Chaplin Jr., Peggy Moffitt; ***D:*** Charles Haas; ***W:*** Robert Smith, Robert D. (Robert Hardy) Andrews; ***C:*** John L. "Jack" Russell; ***M:*** Van Alexander, Paul Anka.

Girls Town 🦴🦴 **1995 (R)** Tough look at the lives of three working-class high school seniors who are shattered by the suicide of Nikki (Ellis), the fourth member of their group, who killed herself from guilt over an undisclosed rape. Single mom Patti (Taylor), ambitious Emma (Grace), and strong-willed Angela (Harris) argue, commiserate, battle their foes (Patti's abusive boyfriend, Nikki's rapist), and lean on each other as they struggle to figure out themselves and their ambiguous futures. Lots of time's spent in the girls' bathroom at school (how realistic can you get?) **90m/C VHS.** Lili Taylor, Anna Grace, Bruklin Harris, Aunjanue Ellis, Guillermo Diaz, John Ventimiglia; ***D:*** Jim McKay; ***W:*** Denise Casano, Jim McKay, Lili Taylor, Anna Grace, Bruklin Harris, Aunjanue Ellis; ***C:*** Russell Fine. Sundance '96: Filmmakers Trophy.

Girly 🦴 *Mumsy, Nanny, Sonny, and Girly* **1970 (R)** An English gothic about an excessively weird family that lives in a crumbling mansion and indulges in murder, mental aberration, and sexual compulsion. **101m/C VHS.** *GB* Michael Bryant, Ursula Howells, Pat Heywood, Howard Trevor, Vanessa Howard, Michael Ripper; ***D:*** Freddie Francis.

Git! 🦴½ **1965** A young runaway and his faithful dog are taken in by a wealthy dog-breeder and trained by him into a crack hunting team. **90m/C VHS.** Jack Chaplain, Richard Webb, Heather North; ***D:*** Ellis Kadison.

Git Along Little Dogies 🦴½ **1937** It's cattle ranchers versus oil men with Autry caught in the middle of the petro/cow war. But Gene still finds a little time to romance the town banker's pretty daughter. **60m/B VHS.** Gene Autry, Judith Allen, Smiley Burnette, William Farnum; ***D:*** Joseph Kane.

Give a Girl a Break 🦴🦴½ **1953** Three talented but unknown babes vie for the lead in a stage production headed for Broadway after the incumbent prima donna quits. After befriending one of the various men associated with the production, each starlet thinks she's a shoe-in for the part. Entertaining but undistinguished musical with appealing dance routines of Fosse and the Champions. Ira Gershwin, collaborating for the first and only time with Burton Lane, wrote the lyrics to two of the songs. ♫Give the Girl a Break; In Our United State; It Happens Every Time; Nothing is Impossible; Applause, Applause; Challenge Dance. **84m/C VHS.** Marge Champion, Gower Champion, Debbie Reynolds, Helen Wood, Bob Fosse, Kurt Kasznar, Richard Anderson, William Ching, Larry Keating, Donna (Dona Martel) Martell; ***D:*** Stanley Donen; ***M:*** Andre Previn.

Give 'Em Hell, Harry! **1975** James Whitmore's one-man show as Harry S. Truman filmed in performance on stage; Whitmore was nominated for a Tony. **103m/C VHS.** James Whitmore; ***D:*** Steve Binder.

Give Me a Sailor 🦴🦴½ **1938** Hope and Whiting play brothers, and fellow Naval officers, who meet sisters Grable and Raye on shore leave. Naturally, there's comic romantic complications until a double wedding ends the farce. Not much of a musical score from Ralph Rainger and Leo Robin but the movie's fun. Based on a play by Anne Nichols. ♫What Goes Here in My Heart?; A Little Kiss at Twilight; Give Me a Sailor; The US and You; It Don't Make Sense. **71m/B VHS.** Bob Hope, Martha Raye, Betty Grable, Jack Whiting, Clarence (C. William) Kolb, Nana Bryant, Emerson Treacy; ***D:*** Elliott Nugent; ***W:*** Frank Butler, Doris Anderson.

Give My Regards to Broad Street 🦴🦴 **1984 (PG)** McCartney film made for McCartney fans. Film features many fine versions of the ex-Beatle's songs that accompany his otherwise lackluster portrayal of a rock star in search of his stolen master recordings. ♫Eleanor Rigby; Ballroom Dancing; Good Day, Sunshine; Silly Love Songs; No Values; No More Lonely Nights; Yesterday; Not Such a Bad Boy; The Long and Winding Road. **109m/C VHS.** *GB* Paul McCartney, Bryan Brown, Ringo Starr, Barbara Bach, Tracey Ullman, Ralph Richardson, Linda McCartney; ***D:*** Peter Webb.

The Gladiator 🦴🦴🦴½ **1938** Brown stars as a mild-mannered collegiate who accidently ingests a serum which turns him into a real he-man. Things take a turn for the funniest when the effects wear off, just as he is to wrestle Man Mountain Dean. Chock-full of Brown's trademark physical humor. **70m/B VHS.** Joe E. Brown, Man Mountain Dean, June Travis, Dickie Moore, Lucien Littlefield, Robert Kent, Ethel Wales; ***D:*** Edward Sedgwick.

The Gladiator 🦴½ **1986** An angry Los Angeles citizen turns vigilante against drunk drivers after his brother is one of their victims. **94m/C VHS.** Ken Wahl, Nancy Allen, Robert Culp, Stan Shaw, Rosemary Forsyth; ***D:*** Abel Ferrara. **TV**

Gladiator 🦴½ **1992 (R)** When suburban Golden Gloves boxing champion Tommy Riley (Marshall) is forced to move to the inner city because of his father's gambling debts, he becomes involved with an evil boxing promotor who thrives on pitting different ethnic races against each other in illegal boxing matches. Eventually Riley is forced to fight his black friend Lincoln (Gooding), even though Lincoln has been warned that another blow to the head could mean his life. Although this film tries to serve some moral purpose, it falls flat on the mat. **98m/C VHS, DVD, Wide.** Cuba Gooding Jr., James Marshall, Robert Loggia, Ossie Davis, Brian Dennehy, Cara Buono, John Heard, Jon Seda, Lance Slaughter; ***D:*** Rowdy Herrington; ***W:*** Lyle Kessler, Robert Mark Kamen; ***C:*** Tak Fujimoto; ***M:*** Brad Fiedel.

Gladiator 🦴🦴🦴 **2000 (R)** Emperor Marcus Aurelius (Harris) decides to name victorious general Maximus (Crowe) his heir over the ruler's own son, the decadent Commodus (Phoenix). But Commodus manages to take over the Empire anyway. Maximus is betrayed, his family killed, and he is sold as a slave, eventually learning the ways of a gladiator. Then he returns to Rome to fight before the new Emperor and get his revenge. Last role for Reed (playing owner/trainer Proximo), who died during production. Unlike the cheesy Italian muscle epics of the early sixties this is swords, sandals, and killer beasts for a new generation, with a compelling hero in Crowe. **154m/C VHS, DVD, Wide.** Russell Crowe, Joaquin Rafael (Leaf) Phoenix, Connie Nielsen, Djimon Hounsou, Ralph (Ralf) Moeller, Derek Jacobi, Oliver Reed, Richard Harris, David Schofield, John Shrapnel, Tomas Arana, Spencer (Treat) Clark, Tommy Flanagan, David Hemmings, Sven-Ole Thorsen; ***D:*** Ridley Scott; ***W:*** David Franzoni, John Logan, William Nicholson; ***C:*** John Mathieson; ***M:*** Hans Zimmer. Oscars '00: Actor (Crowe), Costume Des., Film, Sound, Visual FX; British Acad. '00: Cinematog., Film; Golden Globes '01: Film—Drama, Score; Natl. Bd. of Review '00: Support. Actor (Phoenix); Broadcast Film Critics '00: Actor (Crowe), Cinematog., Film, Support. Actor (Phoenix).

Gladiator Cop: The Swordsman 2 🦴½ **1995 (R)** A legendary sword, believed to have magic powers, is stolen and an ex-detective winds up fighting modern-day gladiators and a man who believes himself to be a reincarnation of Alexander the Great. **92m/C VHS.** Lorenzo Lamas.

Gladiator of Rome 🦴 *Il Gladiatore Di Roma* **1963** A gladiator flexes his pecs to save a young girl from death at the hands of evil rulers. **105m/C VHS.** *IT* Gordon Scott, Wandisa Guida, Roberto Risso, Ombretta Colli, Alberto (Albert Farley) Farnese; ***D:*** Mario Costa.

The Gladiators 🦴 *The Peace Game; Gladiatorerna* **1970** Televised gladiatorial bouts are designed to subdue man's violent tendencies in a futuristic society until a computer makes a fatal error. **90m/C VHS.** Arthur Pentelow, Frederick Danner; ***D:*** Peter Watkins.

Gladiators 7 🦴½ **1962** Sparta must be freed from the tyrannical rule of the Romans. In lieu of samurai or cowboys, who better than the Gladiators 7 to do the deed? Plenty of sword-to-sword action and scantily clad Italian babes. **92m/C VHS.** *SP IT* Richard Harrison, Loredana Nusciak, Livio Lorenzon, Gerard Tichy, Edoardo Toniolo, Joseph Marco, Barta Barry; ***D:*** Pedro Lazaga.

Glam 🦴🦴 **1997 (R)** Eccentric writer Sonny Daye (McNamara) arrives in L.A. and is promptly exploited. His cousin Franky (Frank) takes Sonny's journal to a pair of schlocky producers who are impressed by the writing. So vain and ruthless Sid Dalgren (Danza) decides to control Sonny even while his tootsie, Vanessa (Wagner), begins to fall for the oddball's sweetness. Very talky. Director Evan's mom, Ali McGraw, has a cameo. **93m/C VHS, DVD.** William McNamara, Frank Whaley, Natasha Gregson Wagner, Tony Danza, Valerie Kaprisky, Caroline Lagerfelt, Lou (Cutel) Cutell, Robert DoQui, Jon Cryer, Donal Logue; ***Cameos:*** Ali MacGraw; ***D:*** Josh Evans; ***W:*** Josh Evans; ***M:*** Josh Evans.

Glass 🦴½ **1990** A normally complacent man is driven to the brink of savagery when a killer begins stalking his employees. **92m/C VHS.** Alan Lovell, Lisa Peers, Adam Stone, Natalie McCurry.

The Glass Bottom Boat 🦴🦴½ **1966** A bubbly but transparent Doris Day comedy, in which she falls in love with her boss at an aerospace lab. Their scheme to spend time together get her mistaken for a spy. Made about the time they stopped making them like this anymore, it's innocuous slapstick romance with a remarkable 1960s cast, including a Robert Vaughn cameo as the Man From U.N.C.L.E. Doris sings "Que Sera, Sera" and a few other numbers. **110m/C VHS, Wide.** Doris Day, Rod Taylor, Arthur Godfrey, Paul Lynde, Eric Fleming, Alice Pearce, Ellen Corby, John McGiver, Dom DeLuise, Dick Martin, Edward Andrews; ***Cameos:*** Robert Vaughn; ***D:*** Frank Tashlin; ***W:*** Everett Freeman; ***C:*** Leon Shamroy.

The Glass Cage 🦴🦴 **1996 (R)** Ex-CIA agent Paul Yeager (Tyson) takes a bartending job in New Orleans' French Quarter in order to get back his exotic dancer girlfriend Jacqueline (Lewis) but the bar's jealous owner and dirty cop Montrachet (Roberts) have other plans in mind for the duo. **96m/C VHS.** Richard Tyson, Charlotte Lewis, Eric Roberts, Stephen Nichols, Joseph Campanella, Richard Moll, Maria Ford, Lisa Marie Scott; ***D:*** Michael Schroeder; ***W:*** David Keith Miller; ***C:*** John Aronson.

The Glass House 🦴🦴🦴 *Truman Capote's The Glass House* **1972** Alda stars as a middle-aged college professor, convicted on a manslaughter charge, who is sent to a maximum security prison and must learn to deal with life inside. Filmed at Utah State Prison, real-life prisoners as supporting cast add to the drama. Still has the power to chill, with Morrow particularly effective as one of the inmate leaders. Adapted from a Truman Capote story. **92m/C VHS.** Alan Alda, Vic Morrow, Clu Gulager, Billy Dee Williams, Dean Jagger, Kristopher Tabori; ***D:*** Tom Gries; ***M:*** Billy Goldenberg. **TV**

The Glass House 🦴½ **2001 (PG-13)** With a brittle plot you can see right through, this flick is aptly named. After their parents are killed in a car accident, 16-year-old Ruby (Sobieski) and her little brother Rhett (Morgan) are sent to live with their former neighbors Erin and Terry Glass (Lane and Skarsgaard). The Glasses live in a swanky glass mansion with all the charm of a Windex bottle. Although they lavish the kids with clothes and gadgets, Ruby begins to suspect what we already know: evil stepparents! Ruby then tries to tell all the adults in her life that the Glasses have ugly streaks, but no one believes her or even suggests a rinsing agent. Obvious plot devices and cliched techniques (including the ever-popular "tinkling danger piano music") shatter what could have been a great thriller given the cast and concept. **111m/C VHS, DVD, Wide.** *US* Leelee Sobieski, Stellan Skarsgard, Diane Lane, Trevor Morgan, Bruce Dern, Kathy Baker, Christopher Noth, Rita Wilson, Michael O'Keefe, Vyto Ruginis; ***D:*** Daniel Sackheim; ***W:*** Wesley Strick; ***C:*** Alar Kivilo; ***M:*** Christopher Young.

The Glass Jungle **1988** Will a cab driver save Los Angeles? When armed terrorists and the FBI battle it out in the sunny California city an innocent cabby seems to hold the solution to survival. **94m/C VHS.** Lee Canalito, Joe Filbeck, Diana Frank, Mark High, Frank Scala; ***D:*** Joseph Merhi.

The Glass Key 🦴🦴🦴 **1942** Previously filmed in 1935, this version of Dashiell Hammet's novel is a vintage mystery concerning nominally corrupt politician Madvig (Donlevy) being framed for murder, and his assistant Ed Beaumont (Ladd) sleuthing out the real culprit. One of Ladd's first starring vehicles; Lake is the mystery woman who loves him, and Bendix a particularly vicious thug. **85m/B VHS.** Alan Ladd, Veronica Lake, Brian Donlevy, William Bendix, Bonita Granville, Richard Denning, Joseph Calleia, Moroni Olsen, Dane Clark; ***D:*** Stuart Heisler; ***W:*** Jonathan Latimer; ***C:*** Theodor Sparkuhl; ***M:*** Victor Young.

The Glass Menagerie 🦴🦴🦴 **1987 (PG)** An aging Southern belle deals with her crippled daughter Laura, whose one great love is her collection of glass animals. The third film adaptation of the Tennessee Williams classic, which preserves the performances of the Broadway revival cast, is a solid-but-not-stellar adaptation of the play. All-star acting ensemble. **134m/C VHS.** Joanne Woodward, Karen Allen, John Malkovich, James Naughton; ***D:*** Paul Newman; ***W:*** Tennessee Williams; ***C:*** Michael Ballhaus; ***M:*** Henry Mancini, Max Steiner.

The Glass Shield 🦴🦴½ **1995 (PG-13)** Timely look at racism and corruption in the Los Angeles sheriff's department as seen through the eyes of African American rookie J.J. Johnson (Boatman). His dream of being a police officer turns to disillusionment when he slowly realizes his own department is framing a black man (Ice Cube) for a murder he did not commit. First half grabs your attention, but the momentum is lost in murky plot twists and a rushed ending. Made on a shoestring, but has an interesting cast, including the reliably slimy Ironside as (what else) one of the bad cops and an almost unrecognizable Petty, who becomes Johnson's only ally on the force. **109m/C VHS, DVD, Wide.** Michael Boatman, Lori Petty, Michael Ironside, M. Emmet Walsh, Ice Cube, Richard Anderson, Elliott Gould; ***D:*** Charles Burnett; ***W:*** Charles Burnett; ***C:*** Elliot Davis; ***M:*** Stephen James Taylor.

The Glass Slipper 🦴🦴 **1955** In this version of the "Cinderella" saga, Caron plays an unglamourous girl gradually transformed into the expected beauty. Winwood is the fairy godmother who inspires the girl to find happiness, rather then simply providing it for her magically. The film is highlighted by the stunning dance numbers, choreographed by Roland Petit and featuring the Paris ballet. **93m/C VHS.** Leslie Caron, Michael Wilding, Keenan Wynn, Estelle Winwood, Elsa Lanchester, Barry Jones, Amanda Blake, Lurene Tuttle; ***D:*** Charles Walters; ***Nar:*** Walter Pidgeon.

Glass Tomb 🦴🦴 *The Glass Cage* **1955** At a circus, a man performs the world's longest fast inside a glass cage, and becomes the raison d'etre for murder. **59m/B VHS.** John Ireland, Honor Blackman, Eric Pohlmann, Tonia Bern, Sidney James; ***D:*** Montgomery Tully.

Gleaming the Cube 🦴½ **1989 (PG-13)** A skateboarding teen investigates his brother's murder. Film impresses with its stunt footage only. For those with adolescent interests. **102m/C VHS, DVD.** Christian Slater, Steven Bauer, Min Luong, Art Chudabala, Le Tuan; ***D:*** Graeme Clifford; ***W:*** Michael Tolkin; ***M:*** Jay Ferguson.

Glen and Randa 🦴🦴½ **1971 (R)** Two young people experience the world after it has been destroyed by nuclear war. Early McBride, before the hired-gun success of "The Big Easy." **94m/C VHS.** Steven Curry, Shelley Plimpton; ***D:*** Jim McBride; ***W:*** Rudy Wurlitzer, Jim McBride.

Glen or Glenda? woof! *He or She; I Changed My Sex; I Led Two Lives; The Transvestite; Glen or Glenda: The Confessions of Ed Wood* **1953** An appalling, quasi-docudrama about transvestism, interspersed with meaningless stock footage, inept dream sequences and Lugosi sitting in a chair spouting incoherent prattle at the camera. Directorial debut of Wood, who, using a pseudonym, played the lead; one of the phenomenally bad films of this century. An integral part of the famous anti-auteur's canon. **67m/B VHS, DVD.** Edward D. Wood Jr., Bela Lugosi, Lyle Talbot, Timothy Farrell, Dolores Fuller, Charles Crafts, Tommy Haynes, Captain DeZita, Evelyn Wood, Shirley Speril, Conrad Brooks, Henry Bederski, William C. Thompson, Mr. Walter, Harry Thomas, George Weiss; ***D:*** Edward D. Wood Jr.; ***W:*** Edward D. Wood Jr.; ***C:*** William C. Thompson.

Glengarry Glen Ross 🦴🦴🦴 **1992 (R)** A seven-character study chronicling 48-hours in the lives of some sleazy real estate men in danger of getting the ax from their hard-driving bosses. A standout cast includes Pacino as the glad-handing sales leader, Lemmon as the hustler fallen on dim prospects, and Baldwin, briefly venomous, as the company hatchet-man. Brutal and hard-edged with very strong language. Mamet scripted from his Tony-award winning Broadway play. **100m/C VHS, Wide.** Al Pacino, Jack Lemmon, Ed Harris, Alec Baldwin, Alan Arkin, Kevin Spacey, Jonathan Pryce, Bruce Altman, Jude Ciccolella; ***D:*** James Foley; ***W:*** David Mamet; ***C:*** Juan Ruiz-Anchia; ***M:*** James Newton Howard. Natl. Bd. of Review '92: Actor (Lemmon); Venice Film Fest. '93: Actor (Lemmon).

The Glenn Miller Story 🦴🦴🦴 **1954 (G)** The music of the Big Band Era lives again in this warm biography of the legendary Glenn Miller, following his life from the late '20s to his untimely death in a WWII plane crash. Stewart's likably convincing and even fakes the trombone playing well. ♫Moonlight Serenade; In the Mood; Tuxedo Junction; Little Brown Jug; Adios; String of Pearls; Pennsylvania 6-5000; Stairway to the Stars; American Patrol. **113m/C VHS.** James Stewart, June Allyson, Harry (Henry) Morgan, Gene Krupa, Louis Armstrong, Ben Pollack; ***D:*** Anthony Mann; ***W:*** Oscar Brodney, Valentine Davies; ***C:*** William H. Daniels; ***M:*** Henry Mancini. Oscars '54: Sound.

The Glimmer Man 🦴½ **1996 (R)** When a vicious LA serial killer starts dispatching whole families, NY detective Jack Cole (Seagal) is teamed with local homicide detective Jim Campbell (Wayans). Since, however, this is a Seagal movie, things have to be a little different. Cole, for example, is an ex-CIA operative who has been convinced by a Buddhist monk to stop killing people and start wearing goofy Nehru jackets and prayer beads. Campbell is a couch potato who cries over old movies (or perhaps he was watching the dailies from this one). After Cole's ex-wife is killed, he's implicated; and then somehow the Russian Mafia and the CIA are brought into the mix. Cole uses his unique brand of non-violence to slash, chop and impale his way to justice. Predictable when it's not being unbelievable, this could have been called "Hard to Watch." **92m/C VHS, DVD.** Steven Seagal, Keenen Ivory Wayans, Michelle Johnson, Brian Cox, Bob Gunton, Stephen Tobolowsky, Johnny Strong, Ryan Cutrona; ***D:*** John Gray; ***W:*** Kevin Brodbin; ***C:*** Rick Bota; ***M:*** Trevor Rabin.

A Glimpse of Hell 🦴🦴½ **2001 (PG-13)** Excellent depiction of the 1989 explosion aboard the USS Iowa, and the subsequent investigations by the Navy, Congress. Lt. Dan Meyer (Leonard) is put in charge of a gun turret but soon finds equipment problems, unauthorized munitions experiments, and lax training of the gunnery crew. When one of the turrets is rocked by an explosion and 47 men are killed, the Navy, and the ship's commander, Capt. Moosally (Caan), ignore the mounting physical evidence of accidental explosion to focus on a sabotage scenario involving one of the crew, Clay Hartwig (Eaves), supposedly distraught over the end of a homosexual affair with a fellow crewmember. As the investigations progress, Moosally comes to defend his men, and both he and Meyer must struggle with the question of truth vs. career. **85m/C VHS, DVD, Wide.** Robert Sean Leonard, James Caan, Daniel Roebuck, Jamie Harrold, Cherie Devanney, Dashiell Eaves; ***D:*** Mikael Salomon; ***W:*** Charles C. Thompson II, David Freed. **TV**

Glitch! 🦴½ **1988 (R)** A throng of beautiful Hollywood hopefuls draw two youngsters unconnected with the film into posing as the film's director and producer in the hopes of conducting personal interviews on the casting couch. **88m/C VHS, DVD.** Julia Nickson-Soul, Will Egan, Steve Donmyer, Dan Speaker, Dallas Cole, Ji-Tu Cumbuka, Dick Gautier, Ted Lange, Teri Weigel, Fernando Carzon, John Kreng, Lindsay Carr; ***D:*** Nico Mastorakis; ***W:*** Nico Mastorakis; ***C:*** Peter C. Jensen; ***M:*** Tom Marolda. **VIDEO**

Glitter woof! **2001 (PG-13)** Following in the footsteps of "Cool as Ice" and "Spice World," this may be the third in the pop star "why was this allowed to happen?" trilogy. Mariah Carey, showing her acting range of two emotions ("Yay!" and "Huh?"), stars as Billie Frank, a backup singer who climbs to stardom with the help from her svengali boyfriend Dice (Beesley). Together they struggle through the hard times and the wooden dialogue. Will success and the crappy plot stolen from "A Star is Born" tear them apart? You'll be wishing that wild dogs will tear them apart before the end of this mess. So bad it's nearly unintentionally funny. The key word is nearly. **104m/C VHS, DVD, Wide.** *US* Mariah Carey, Max Beesley, Tia Texada, Da Brat, Valarie Pettiford, Ann Magnuson, Terrence DaShon Howard, Dorian Harewood, Grant Nickalls, Eric Benet, Padma Lakshmi, Isabel Gomes; ***D:*** Vondie Curtis-Hall; ***W:*** Kate Lanier; ***C:*** Geoffrey Simpson; ***M:*** Terence Blanchard. Golden Raspberries '01: Worst Actress (Carey).

The Glitter Dome 🦴½ **1984** Two policemen discover the sleazier side of Hollywood when they investigate the murder of a pornographer. Based upon the novel by Joseph Wambaugh. **90m/C VHS.** Stuart Margolin, John Marley, James Garner, John Lithgow, Margot Kidder, Colleen Dewhurst; ***D:*** Stuart Margolin. **TV**

Glitz 🦴🦴½ **1988** A Miami cop and an Atlantic City lounge singer team up to investigate a call-girl's death and wind up too close to a drug ring. Based on the novel by Elmore Leonard. **96m/C VHS.** Jimmy Smits, John Diehl, Markie Post, Ken Foree, Madison Mason, Robin Strasser; ***D:*** Sandor Stern. **TV**

A Global Affair 🦴½ **1963** Hope is a department head in the United Nations who finds an abandoned baby in the building. The inept bachelor is wooed by a number of international beauties seeking to adopt the child for their various countries but he becomes increasingly attached to the little tyke. **84m/B VHS.** Bob Hope, Lilo (Liselotte) Pulver, Michele Mercier, Yvonne De Carlo, Miiko Taka, Robert Sterling, Nehemiah Persoff, John McGiver, Mickey Shaughnessy; ***D:*** Jack Arnold; ***W:*** Charles Lederer, Arthur Marx, Bob Fisher; ***C:*** Joseph Ruttenberg.

Gloria 🦴🦴½ **1980 (PG)** She used to be a Mafia moll, now she's outrunning the Mob after taking in the son of a slain neighbor. He's got a book that they want, and they're willing to kill to get it. Trademark Cassavetes effort in which he has actors plumb their souls to discomfiting levels. **123m/C VHS.** Gena Rowlands, John Adams, Buck Henry, Julie Carmen; ***D:*** John Cassavetes; ***M:*** Bill Conti. Venice Film Fest. '80: Film; Golden Raspberries '80: Worst Support. Actor (Adams).

Gloria 🦴🦴 **1998 (R)** Remake of the 1980 Cassavetes film, with Stone as title character, a gang moll who reluctantly becomes the guardian of a boy whose parents were killed by her low-life boyfriend Kevin (Northam). Entertainment value is derived from listening to Stone mangle her Noo Yawk accent. Stick with the original. **108m/C VHS, DVD.** Sharon Stone, Jeremy Northam, Cathy Moriarty, George C. Scott, Mike Starr, Don Billett, Tony DiBenedetto, Bonnie Bedelia, Jean-Luke Figueroa, Barry McEvoy, Jerry Dean, Teddy Atlas; ***D:*** Sidney Lumet; ***W:*** Steve Antin; ***C:*** David Watkin; ***M:*** Howard Shore.

Glorifying the American Girl 🦴🦴 **1930** Eaton's a chorus girl performing in the Ziegfeld Follies, which lends itself to numerous production numbers. The only film Ziegfeld ever produced. ♫What I Wouldn't Do For That Man; Blue Skies; I'm Just a Vagabond Lover; Baby Face; At Sundown; Beautiful Changes; Sam the Old Accordian Man; There Must Be Someone Waiting For Me. **96m/B VHS.** Mary Eaton, Dan Healey, Eddie Cantor, Rudy Vallee; ***D:*** Millard Webb.

Glory 🦴🦴 **1956** O'Brien is a racehorse owner who tussles with her grandmother over how to keep the family farm open on a shoestring budget. Brennan enters the picture as the financial guru who lands them back on track, with enough left over to enter their prize filly in the Kentucky Derby. Lupton plays O'Brien's love interest. No surprises here. **100m/C VHS.** Margaret O'Brien, Walter Brennan, Charlotte Greenwood; ***D:*** David Butler.

Glory 🦴🦴🦴½ **1989 (R)** A rich, historical spectacle chronicling the 54th Massachusetts, the first black volunteer infantry unit in the Civil War. The film manages to artfully focus on both the 54th and their white commander, Robert Gould Shaw. Based on Shaw's letters, the film uses thousands of accurately costumed "living historians" (re-enactors) as extras in this panoramic production. A haunting, bittersweet musical score pervades what finally becomes an anti-war statement. Stunning performances throughout, with exceptional work from Freeman and Washington. **122m/C VHS, DVD, 8mm, Wide.** Matthew Broderick, Morgan Freeman, Denzel Washington, Cary Elwes, Jihmi Kennedy, Andre Braugher, John Finn, Donovan Leitch, John David (J.D.) Cullum, Bob Gunton, Jane Alexander, Raymond St. Jacques, Cliff DeYoung, Alan North, Jay O. Sanders, Richard Riehle, Ethan Phillips, RonReaco Lee, Peter Michael Goetz; ***D:*** Edward Zwick; ***W:*** Kevin Jarre, Marshall Herskovitz; ***C:*** Freddie Francis; ***M:*** James Horner. Oscars '89: Cinematog., Sound, Support. Actor (Washington); Golden Globes '90: Support. Actor (Washington).

Glory & Honor 🦴🦴½ **1998** Covers explorer Robert Peary's (Czerny) treks to the North Pole (he was finally successful in 1909). Peary was accompanied by his black valet Matthew Henson (Lindo), who proved to be resourceful and a source of calm to the driven explorer, and was eventually credited as a co-discoverer. Filmed on location near the Arctic Circle. **94m/C VHS.** Henry Czerny, Delroy Lindo; ***D:*** Kevin Hooks; ***W:*** Susan Rhinehart. **CABLE**

The Glory Boys 🦴½ **1984** A secret agent is hired to protect an Israeli scientist who is marked for assassination by the PLO and IRA. **78m/C VHS.** Rod Steiger, Anthony Perkins, Gary Brown, Aaron Harris; ***D:*** Michael Ferguson.

Glory Daze 🦴🦴 **1996 (R)** Gen-X comedy about graduation week for five Santa Cruz college friends/housemates. There's Jack (Affleck), Mickey (DeRamus), Rob (Rockwell), Josh (Hong), and Dennis (Stewart) who basically party and kvetch about their uncertain futures, with various girlfriends, professors, and parents around to nag the boys. Not much you haven't seen before, although a number of the cast have gone on to bigger and better things. **100m/C VHS.** Ben Affleck, Sam Rockwell, French Stewart, Vinnie DeRamus, Vien Hong, Alyssa Milano, Megan Ward, John Rhys-Davies, Elizabeth Ruscio, Spalding Gray, Mary Woronov; ***Cameos:*** Matthew McConaughey, Brendan Fraser, Matt Damon, Meredith Salenger; ***D:*** Rich Wilkes; ***W:*** Rich Wilkes; ***C:*** Christopher Taylor.

Glory Enough for All: The Discovery of Insulin 🦴🦴½ **1992** The drama behind the discovery of insulin in the 1920s focuses on the research of four men, sometimes not-so-friendly rivals, searching for a treatment for diabetes mellitus. Dr. Frederick Banting and science student Charles Best are granted permission by James Macleod, a Professor of Physiology at the University of Toronto, to conduct experiments on the pancreas. Macleod then assigns biochemist James Collip to assist them on developing a viable serum, an extract named insulin. Banting and Macleod were awarded the Nobel prize in 1923 for their discovery (though Banting felt Macleod was undeserving). Adapted from "The Discovery of Insulin" by Michael Bliss. **196m/C VHS.** *CA* R.H. Thomson, Robert Wisden, John Woodvine, Michael Zelniker, Martha Henry, Heather Hess; ***D:*** Eric Till; ***W:*** Grahame Woods. **TV**

Glory! Glory! 🦴🦴🦴 **1990 (R)** Slashing satire about TV evangelism. Thomas as the meek son of founder of Church of the Champions of Christ brings in lewd female rock singer to save the money-machine ministry from financial ruin. Rock music, sex, and MTV-like camera work make it worth seeing. Whitmore is a treat. **152m/C VHS.** Ellen Greene, Richard Thomas, Barry Morse, James Whitmore, Winston Rekert; ***D:*** Lindsay Anderson; ***W:*** Stan Daniels.

The Glory Stompers woof! **1967** Hopper prepares for his Easy Rider role as the leader of a motorcycle gang who battles with a rival leader over a woman. Very bad, atrocious dialogue, and a "love-in" scene that will be best appreciated by insomniacs. **85m/C VHS.** Dennis Hopper, Jody McCrea, Chris Noel, Jock Mahoney, Lindsay Crosby, Robert Tessier, Casey Kasem; ***D:*** Anthony M. Lanza.

The Glory Trail 🦴½ *Glorious Sacrifice* **1936** A group of railroad workers and soldiers are constantly harassed by Indian attacks. **63m/B VHS.** Tom (George Duryea) Keene, Joan Barclay, James Bush, Frank Melton, Walter Long; ***D:*** Lynn Shores.

Glory Years 🦴 **1987** Three old friends find themselves in charge of the scholarship fund at their 20th high school reunion. Unfortunately, they decide to increase the fund by gambling in Las Vegas and lose it all on a fixed fight! **150m/C VHS.** George Dzundza, Archie Hahn, Tim Thomerson, Tawny Kitaen, Donna Pescow, Donna Denton; ***D:*** Arthur Seidelman.

The Glove 🦴½ *The Glove: Lethal Terminator; Blood Mad* **1978 (R)** Ex-cop turned bounty hunter has his toughest assignment ever. It's his job to bring in a six-and-a-half foot, 250-pound ex-con who's been wreaking havoc with an unusual glove—it's made of leather and steel. **93m/C VHS.** John Saxon, Roosevelt "Rosie" Grier, Joanna Cassidy, Joan Blondell, Jack Carter, Aldo Ray; ***D:*** Ross Hagen.

The Gnome-Mobile 🦴🦴 **1967** A lumber baron and his two grandchildren attempt to reunite a pair of forest gnomes with a lost gnome colony. Brennan has a dual role as both a human and a gnome grandfather. Wynn's last film. Based on a children's novel by Upton Sinclair. **84m/C VHS.** Walter Brennan, Richard Deacon, Ed Wynn, Karen Dotrice, Matthew Garber; ***D:*** Robert Stevenson; *C:* Edward Colman; *M:* Buddy (Norman Dale) Baker.

Go 1999 (R) Episodic tale of Christmas Eve in L.A. and Vegas follows grocery clerk Ronna (Polley) as she takes over a shift for Vegas-bound co-worker Simon (Askew) and also agrees to sub as a go-between for a drug deal between two actors (Mohr and Wolf) and Simon's dealer Todd (Olyphant). Three-part narrative also shows Simon's wild ride in Vegas with his buddies and the actors' involvement with a weird cop (Fichtner). Everybody seems to be doing everything at a break-neck pace, and the fact that all the activity is dangerous or illegal makes it that much more fun. Liman does a fine job of sorting out characters and plotlines, and the performances tag this as a star maker for a few of the cast members, most notably Polley and Diggs. **103m/C VHS, DVD.** Sarah Polley, Katie Holmes, Scott Wolf, Jay Mohr, Desmond Askew, Taye Diggs, William Fichtner, Breckin Meyer, Jane Krakowski, Timothy Olyphant, J.E. Freeman, James Duval, Nathan Bexton, Jay Paulson, Jimmy Shubert; *D:* Doug Liman; *W:* John August; *C:* Doug Liman.

The Go-Between ½ 1971 (PG) Wonderful tale of hidden love. Young boy Guard acts as a messenger between the aristocratic Christie and her former lover Bates. But tragedy befalls them all when the lovers are discovered. The story is told as the elderly messenger (now played by Redgrave) recalls his younger days as the go-between and builds to a climax when he is once again asked to be a messenger for the lady he loved long ago. Based on a story by L.P. Hartley. **116m/C VHS.** *GB* Julie Christie, Alan Bates, Dominic Guard, Margaret Leighton, Michael Redgrave, Michael Gough, Edward Fox; *D:* Joseph Losey; *W:* Harold Pinter; *C:* Gerry Fisher; *M:* Michel Legrand. British Acad. '71: Screenplay, Support. Actor (Fox), Support. Actress (Leighton); Cannes '71: Film.

Go Down Death ½ 1941 In this early all-black film, a minister is caught in a moral dilemma literally between Heaven and Hell. Scenes of the afterlife are taken from early silent films. **63m/B VHS.** Myra D. Hemmings, Samuel H. James, Eddy L. Houston, Spencer Williams Jr., Amos Droughan; *D:* Spencer Williams Jr.

Go Fish 1994 (R) Low-budget girl-meets-girl romantic comedy finds Kia (McMillan) playing matchmaker for her roommate, energetic Max (Turner), by setting her up with shy Ely (Brodie). The opposites do, eventually, attract, with their friends eager for every detail. Good-natured and candid, with a welcome lack of melodrama. **87m/B VHS, DVD.** Guinevere Turner, V.S. Brodie, T. Wendy McMillan, Anastasia Sharp, Migdalia Melendez; *D:* Rose Troche; *W:* Guinevere Turner, Rose Troche; *C:* Ann T. Rossetti; *M:* Brendan Dolan, Jennifer Sharpe.

Go for Broke! ½ 1951 Inexperienced officer Johnson heads a special WWII attack force which is made up of Japanese Americans. Sent to fight in Europe, they prove their bravery and loyalty to all. Good, offbeat story. **92m/B VHS, DVD.** Van Johnson, Gianna Maria Canale, Warner Anderson, Lane Nakano, George Miki; *D:* Robert Pirosh; *W:* Robert Pirosh; *C:* Paul Vogel; *M:* Alberto Colombo.

Go for It 1983 (PG) Oddball supercops go after a mad scientist—who has created a deadly "K"-bomb—and they encounter killer whales, karate busboys and malevolent Shirley Temple clones along the way. **109m/C VHS.** *IT* Bud Spencer, Terence Hill, David Huddleston; *D:* E.B. (Enzo Barboni) Clucher.

Go for the Gold 1984 A young marathon runner risks his girlfriend's love when he decides to pursue fame and fortune. **98m/C VHS.** James Ryan, Cameron Mitchell, Sandra Horne.

Go-Get-'Em-Haines 1935 Newsman Boyd follows a fleeing bankrupt utilities tycoon onto an ocean liner for an interview only to end up trying to solve the tycoon's murder. **61m/C VHS.** William Boyd, Sheila Terry, Eleanor Hunt, Leroy Mason, Lloyd Ingraham, Jimmy Aubrey, Clarence Geldert, Louis Natheaux, Lee Shumway; *D:* Sam Newfield.

The Go-Getter 1954 Wild slapstick fun in the world of business. **78m/C VHS.** Hank McCune, Beverly Garland, Thurston Hall, Ray Collins, Andrew Tombes; *D:* Leslie Goodwins, Leigh Jason; *W:* Earl Baldwin, Charles Maxwell; *C:* Charles Straumer.

Go, Johnny Go! 1959 Rock promoter Alan Freed molds a young orphan into rock sensation "Johnny Melody." Musical performances include Ritchie Valens (his only film appearance), Eddie Cochran, Jackie Wilson. **75m/B VHS.** Alan Freed, Sandy Stewart, Chuck Berry, Jimmy Clanton, Eddie Cochran, Jackie Wilson, Ritchie Valens; *D:* Paul Landres.

Go Kill and Come Back 1968 (PG) A bounty hunter tracks down a notoriously dangerous train robber. **95m/C VHS.** Gilbert Roland, George Helton, Edd Byrnes; *D:* Enzo G. Castellari.

The Go-Masters *Mikan No Taikyoku* 1982 Historic co-production between Japan and China, centering on the ancient strategy board game "Go." A young competitor becomes obsessed with winning at any price. Episodic tale of the relationships between a Japanese and Chinese family spans 30 years and was critically acclaimed in both China and Japan. In Japanese and Chinese with English subtitles. **134m/C VHS.** *JP CH* Huang Zong-Ying, Du Peng, Yu Shao-Kang, Lui Xin, Yoshiko Mita, Keiko Matsuzaka, Mayumi Ogawa, Rentaro Mikuni, Sun Dao-Lin, Shen Guan-Chu, Misako Honno; *D:* Junya Sato, Duan Jishun. Montreal World Film Fest. '83: Film.

Go Now ½ 1996 Regular guy Nick (Carlyle), a soccer-playing construction worker meets and falls in love with hotel management trainee Karen (Aubrey). All is going well until Nick starts experiencing physical problems—dropping things, double vision, numbness. As his condition worsens, it's confirmed that he's been stricken with Multiple Sclerosis. Nick goes through the usual stages of dealing with the disease, but Winterbottom's film doesn't go through the usual disease-of-the-week motions. Straightforward look at the effects of a debilitating disease doesn't create martyrs or heroes, opting instead for realistic characters and honest emotions and situations. First-rate performance by Carlyle. **87m/C VHS.** *GB* Robert Carlyle, Juliet Aubrey, James Nesbitt, Sophie Okonedo, Berwick Kaler; *D:* Michael Winterbottom; *W:* Jimmy McGovern, Paul Powell; *C:* Daf Hobson; *M:* Alastair Gavin.

Go Tell It on the Mountain ½ 1984 Young black boy tries to gain the approval of his stern stepfather in this fine adaptation of James Baldwin's semiautobiographical novel. Set in the 1930s; originally a PBS "American Playhouse" presentation. **100m/C VHS.** Paul Winfield, Olivia Cole, Ruby Dee, Alfre Woodard, James Bond III, Rosalind Cash, Linda Hopkins; *D:* Stan Lathan.

Go Tell the Spartans 1978 (R) In Vietnam, 1964, a hard-boiled major is ordered to establish a garrison at Muc Wa with a platoon of burned out Americans and Vietnamese mercenaries. Blundering but politically interesting war epic pre-dating the flood of 1980s American-Vietnam apologetics. Based on Daniel Ford's novel. **114m/C VHS.** Burt Lancaster, Craig Wasson, David Clennon, Marc Singer, Jonathan Goldsmith, Joe Unger, Dennis Howard, Evan C. Kim, John Megna, Hilly Hicks, Dolph Sweet, Clyde Kusatsu, James Hong; *D:* Ted Post; *W:* Wendell Mayes; *C:* Harry Stradling Jr.; *M:* Dick Halligan.

Go West ½ *Marx Brothers Go West* 1940 The brothers Marx help in the making and un-making of the Old West. Weak, late Marx Bros., but always good for a few yucks. **80m/B VHS, DVD.** Groucho Marx, Chico Marx, Harpo Marx, John Carroll, Diana Lewis, Walter Woolf King, George Lessey, Robert Barrat, June MacCloy; *D:* Edward Buzzell; *W:* Irving Brecher; *C:* Leonard Smith; *M:* George Bassman, Roger Edens.

Go West, Young Man ½ 1936 West is a movie star whose latest film is premiering in a small town, where she's naturally a sensation. Scott is the muscular farm boy who catches her eye and she decides to hang around in order to catch the rest of him as well. The censors again cut West's most overt sexual and satiric barbs. **80m/B VHS.** Mae West, Randolph Scott, Warren William, Alice Brady, Elizabeth Patterson, Lyle Talbot, Isabel Jewell; *D:* Henry Hathaway; *W:* Mae West; *C:* Karl Struss.

The Goalie's Anxiety at the Penalty Kick ½ *Die Angst Tormannes beim Elfmeter* 1971 A chilling landmark film that established Wenders as one of the chief film voices to emerge from post-war Germany. The story deals with a soccer player who wanders around Vienna after being suspended, commits a random murder, and slowly passes over the brink of sanity and morality. A suspenseful, existential adaptation of the Peter Handke novel. In German with English subtitles. **101m/C VHS.** *GE* Arthur Brauss, Erika Pluhar, Kai Fischer; *D:* Wim Wenders; *W:* Peter Handke, Wim Wenders; *C:* Robby Muller; *M:* Jurgen Knieper.

Goblin woof! 1993 Newlywed couple regret the purchase of their new home when the devilish creature once brought to life by the previous homeowner, a witchcraft performing farmer, is raised from the depths of hell to rip to pieces anyone in its view. Any movie whose promo says "You won't believe your eyes...until he rips them from their sockets" is sure to be a crowd pleaser. Enjoy. **75m/C VHS.** Bobby Westrick, Jenny Admire.

God Bless the Child 1988 A young single mother loses her home and she and her seven-year-old daughter are forced to live on the streets. Harrowing TV drama providing no easy answers to the plight of the homeless. **93m/C VHS.** Mare Winningham, Dorian Harewood, Grace Johnston, Charlaine Woodard, Obba Babatunde, L. Scott Caldwell; *D:* Larry Elikann; *W:* Dennis Nemec; *M:* David Shire. **TV**

God, Man and Devil ½ 1949 A wager between God and Satan begins this allegory of money versus the spirit. A poor Torah scribe, Hershele Dubrovner, has a life that glorifies God until Satan, disguised as a business partner, turns him greedy and dishonest. Dubrovner's success destroys both his religion and his community leaving only betrayal and abandonment. In Yiddish with English subtitles. **100m/B VHS.** Mikhal Mikhalesko, Gustav Berger; *D:* Joseph Seiden.

God Said "Ha!" 1999 (PG-13) Julia Sweeney recounts a very trying year in her life in this adaptation of her one-woman Broadway show. She tells of her brother's fight with lymphoma, which caused him (as well as her parents) to move in with her, as well as her own battle with cervical cancer. Sweeney's wry observations and loving rememberances prevent melodrama from seeping in. As with most monologues-turned-movies, this one works much better in the small-screen setting. **87m/C VHS.** Julia Sweeney; *D:* Julia Sweeney; *W:* Julia Sweeney; *C:* John Hora; *M:* Anthony Marinelli.

God Told Me To ½ *Demon* 1976 (R) A religious New York cop is embroiled in occult mysteries while investigating a series of grisly murders. He investigates a religious cult that turns out to be composed of half-human, half-alien beings. A cult-fave Larry Cohen epic. **89m/C VHS, Wide.** Tony LoBianco, Deborah Raffin, Sylvia Sidney, Sandy Dennis, Richard Lynch, Sam Levene, Andy Kaufman, Robert Drivas, Mike Kellin; *D:* Larry Cohen; *W:* Larry Cohen; *C:* Paul Glickman; *M:* Frank Cordell.

The Goddess 1958 Sordid story of a girl who rises to fame as a celluloid star by making her body available to anyone who can help her career. When the spotlight dims, she keeps going with drugs and alcohol to a bitter end. **105m/B VHS.** Kim Stanley, Lloyd Bridges, Patty Duke; *D:* John Cromwell; *W:* Paddy Chayefsky.

The Godfather 1972 (R) Coppola's award-winning adaptation of Mario Puzo's novel about a fictional Mafia family in the late 1940s. Revenge, envy, and parent-child conflict mix with the rituals of Italian mob life in America. Minutely detailed, with excellent performances by Pacino, Brando, and Caan as the violence-prone Sonny. Film debut of Coppola's daughter Sophia, the infant in the baptism scene, who returns in "Godfather III." The horrific horse scene is an instant chiller. Indisputably an instant piece of American culture. Followed by two sequels. **171m/C VHS, 8mm, Wide.** Marlon Brando, Al Pacino, Robert Duvall, James Caan, Diane Keaton, John Cazale, Talia Shire, Richard Conte, Richard S. Castellano, Abe Vigoda, Alex Rocco, Sterling Hayden, John Marley, Al Lettieri, Sofia Coppola, Al Martino, Morgana King; *D:* Francis Ford Coppola; *W:* Mario Puzo, Francis Ford Coppola; *C:* Gordon Willis; *M:* Nino Rota. Oscars '72: Actor (Brando), Adapt. Screenplay, Picture; AFI '98: Top 100; Directors Guild '72: Director (Coppola); Golden Globes '73: Actor—Drama (Brando), Director (Coppola), Film—Drama, Screenplay, Score; Natl. Bd. of Review '72: Support. Actor (Pacino), Natl. Film Reg. '90;; N.Y. Film Critics '72: Support. Actor (Duvall); Natl. Soc. Film Critics '72: Actor (Pacino); Writers Guild '72: Adapt. Screenplay.

The Godfather 1902-1959: The Complete Epic 1981 Coppola's epic work concerning the lives of a New York crime family. Comprises the first two "Godfather" films, reedited into a chronological framework of the Corleone family history, with much previously discarded footage restored. **386m/C VHS.** Marlon Brando, Al Pacino, Robert Duvall, James Caan, Richard S. Castellano, Diane Keaton, Robert De Niro, John Cazale, Lee Strasberg, Talia Shire, Michael V. Gazzo, Troy Donahue, Joe Spinell, Abe Vigoda, Alex Rocco, Sterling Hayden, John Marley, Richard Conte, G.D. Spradlin, Bruno Kirby, Harry Dean Stanton, Roger Corman, Al Lettieri; *D:* Francis Ford Coppola; *W:* Mario Puzo, Francis Ford Coppola; *M:* Nino Rota.

The Godfather, Part 2 1974 (R) A continuation and retracing of the first film, interpolating the maintenance of the Corleone family by the aging Michael, and its founding by the young Vito (De Niro, in a terrific performance) 60 years before in NYC's Little Italy. Often considered the second half of one film, the two films stand as one of American film's greatest efforts, and as a 1970s high-water mark. Combined into one work for TV presentation. Followed by a sequel. **200m/C VHS, 8mm, Wide.** Dominic Chianese, Frank Sivero, Gianni Russo, Peter Donat, Al Pacino, Robert De Niro, Diane Keaton, Robert Duvall, James Caan, Danny Aiello, John Cazale, Lee Strasberg, Talia Shire, Michael V. Gazzo, Troy Donahue, Joe Spinell, Abe Vigoda, Marianna Hill, Fay Spain, G.D. Spradlin, Bruno Kirby, Harry Dean Stanton, Roger Corman, Kathleen Beller, John Aprea, Morgana King; *D:* Francis Ford Coppola; *W:* Mario Puzo, Francis Ford Coppola; *C:* Gordon Willis; *M:* Nino Rota, Carmine Coppola. Oscars '74: Adapt. Screenplay, Art Dir./Set Dec., Director (Coppola), Picture, Support. Actor (De Niro), Orig. Dramatic Score; AFI '98: Top 100; Directors Guild '74: Director (Coppola), Natl. Film Reg. '93;; Natl. Soc. Film Critics '74: Director (Coppola); Writers Guild '74: Adapt. Screenplay.

The Godfather, Part 3 1990 (R) Don Corleone (Pacino), now aging and guilt-ridden, determines to buy his salvation by investing in the Catholic Church, which he finds to be a more corrupt brotherhood than his own. Meanwhile, back on the homefront, his young daughter discovers her sexuality as she falls in love with her first cousin. Weakest entry of the trilogy is still a stunning and inevitable conclusion to the story; Pacino adds exquisite finishing touches to his time-worn character. Beautifully photographed in Italy by Gordon Willis. Video release contains the final director's cut featuring nine minutes of footage not included in the theatrical release. **170m/C VHS, 8mm, Wide.** Al Pacino, Diane Keaton, Andy Garcia, Joe Mantegna, George Hamilton, Talia Shire, Sofia Coppola, Eli Wallach, Don Novello, Bridget Fonda, John Savage, Al Martino, Raf Vallone, Franc D'Ambrosio, Donal Donnelly, Richard Bright, Helmut Berger; *D:* Francis Ford Coppola; *W:* Mario Puzo, Francis Ford Coppola; *C:* Gordon Willis; *M:* Nino Rota, Carmine Coppola. Golden Raspberries '90: Worst Support. Actress (Coppola), Worst New Star (Coppola).

Godmoney ½ 1997 (R) Nathan (Rodney) is a New York street kid who tries to clean up his life of drugs and crime by moving to the Los Angeles suburbs where he is recruited by Matthew (Field), a dealer who tries to get him back into his old ways. Director Doane's debut made an impression on the festival circuit, and it deserves its reputation. Despite a background in music videos, he is able to tell a coherent story about interesting characters without letting style overpower substance. **99m/C VHS, DVD, Wide.** Rick Rodney, Bobby Field, Christi Allen; ***D:*** Darren Doane; ***W:*** Darren Doane, Sean Atkins, Sean Nelson; ***M:*** Nicholas Rivera.

Gods and Monsters 🦴🦴🦴½ **1998** Although British director James Whale (McKellen) had a varied (if short) Hollywood career in the '30s and '40s, his name rested on his Universal horror films: "The Invisible Man," "Frankenstein," and "The Bride of Frankenstein." Now long-retired and suffering from ill-health, the openly gay Whale lives quietly in L.A. with his protective housekeeper, Hanna (Redgrave). Whale does enjoy the company of his new gardener—hunky, hetero ex-Marine Clayton Boone (Fraser)—but a stroke has left the director with a confusing sense of reality—returning him to his soldiering days in WWI and "Frankenstein" re-creations. Brilliant performance from McKellen, with solid support from Fraser and Redgrave. Based on the novel "Father of Frankenstein" by Christopher Bram. **105m/C VHS, DVD, Wide.** Ian McKellen, Brendan Fraser, Lynn Redgrave, Lolita (David) Davidovich, David Dukes, Kevin J. O'Connor, Brandon Kleyla, Jack Plotnick, Rosalind Ayres, Arthur Dignam, Jack Betts, Martin Ferrero; ***D:*** Bill Condon; ***W:*** Bill Condon; ***C:*** Stephen M. Katz; ***M:*** Carter Burwell. Oscars '98: Adapt. Screenplay; Golden Globes '99: Support. Actress (Redgrave); Ind. Spirit '99: Actor (McKellen), Film, Support. Actress (Redgrave); L.A. Film Critics '98: Actor (McKellen); Natl. Bd. of Review '98: Actor (McKellen), Film; Broadcast Film Critics '98: Actor (McKellen).

God's Bloody Acre woof! **1975 (R)** Three backwoods mountain-dwelling brothers kill construction workers in order to defend their land, and then begin preying on vacationers. **90m/C VHS.** Scott Lawrence, Jennifer Gregory, Sam Moree, Shiang Hwa Chyang; ***D:*** Harry Kerwin.

God's Comedy 🦴🦴 *A Comedia de Deus* **1995** Joao de Deus (Monteiro) is a lecherous ice-cream maker who indulges himself with the ice cream counter girls and some nighttime fantasies. But when he asks the daughter of the local butcher to indulge him as well, her father decides that Joao needs to be taught a lesson. Portuguese with subtitles. **163m/C VHS, DVD, Wide.** *PT* Joao Cesar Monteiro, Claudia Teixeira, Manuela de Freitas, Raquel Ascensao, Saraiva Serrano; ***D:*** Joao Cesar Monteiro; ***W:*** Joao Cesar Monteiro; ***C:*** Mario Barroso.

God's Country 🦴🦴 **1946** A loner kills a man in self-defense and escapes the pursuing law by disappearing into California Redwood country with his dog. **62m/C VHS.** Robert Lowery, Helen Gilbert, William Farnum, Buster Keaton; ***D:*** Robert Emmett Tansey.

God's Country and the Man 🦴🦴 **1937** Typical western adventurer about a cowboy out to nab a gunman who's been threatening the life of a dance hall girl. Plenty of two-fisted action when law-abiding Keene shows up. **56m/B VHS.** Tom (George Duryea) Keene, Betty Compson, Charlotte Henry, Charles "Blackie" King, Billy Bletcher, Eddie (Ed, Eddy, Edwin) Parker; ***D:*** Robert North Bradbury; ***W:*** Robert Emmett.

God's Gun 🦴 *A Bullet from God* **1975 (R)** Preacher who was once a gunfighter seeks revenge on the men who tried to kill him. Parolini used the pseudonym Frank Kramer. **93m/C VHS.** Richard Boone, Lee Van Cleef, Jack Palance, Sybil Danning; ***D:*** Gianfranco Parolini.

God's Little Acre 🦴🦴🦴 **1958** Delves into the unexpectedly passionate lives of Georgia farmers. One man, convinced there's buried teasure on his land, nearly brings himself and his family to ruin trying to find it. Based on the novel by Erskine Caldwell. **110m/B VHS, DVD, Wide.** Robert Ryan, Tina Louise, Michael Landon, Buddy Hackett, Vic Morrow, Jack Lord, Aldo Ray, Fay Spain; ***D:*** Anthony Mann; ***W:*** Philip Yordan; ***C:*** Hans J. Haller; ***M:*** Elmer Bernstein.

The Gods Must Be Crazy 🦴🦴🦴½ **1984 (PG)** An innocent and charming film. A peaceful Bushman travels into the civilized world to return a Coke bottle "to the gods." Along the way he meets a transplanted schoolteacher, an oafishly clumsy microbiologist and a gang of fanatical terrorists. A very popular film, disarmingly crammed with slapstick and broad humor of every sort. Followed by a weak sequel. **109m/C VHS.** *SA* N!xau, Marius Weyers, Sandra Prinsloo, Louw Verwey, Jamie Uys, Michael Thys, Nic de Jager; ***D:*** Jamie Uys; ***W:*** Jamie Uys; ***C:*** Robert M. Lewis, Buster Reynolds; ***M:*** John Boshoff, Johnny Bishop.

The Gods Must Be Crazy 2 🦴🦴½ **1989 (PG)** A slapdash sequel to the original 1981 African chortler, featuring more ridiculous shenanigans in the bush. This time the bushman's children find themselves in civilization and N!xau must use his unique ingenuity to secure their safe return. **90m/C VHS.** N!xau, Lena Farugia, Hans Strydom, Eiros Nadies, Eric Bowen; ***D:*** Jamie Uys; ***M:*** Charles Fox.

Gods of the Plague 🦴🦴🦴 *Gotter der Pest* **1969** Fassbinder goes noir—or grey with lots of sharp lighting—in this gangster-auteur tale of robbery gone awry. The requisite trappings of the crime genre (guys and dolls and cops and robbers) provide a vague backdrop (and a vague plot) for a moody story full of teutonic angst and alienation, and that certain Fassbinder feeling (which, need we say, isn't to everyone's taste). An early effort by the director, who remade the story later the same year as "The American Soldier" (Fassbinder acts in both). In German with (difficult-to-read) English subtitles. **92m/C VHS.** *GE* Hanna Schygulla, Harry Bear; ***D:*** Rainer Werner Fassbinder.

The Godsend 🦴 **1979 (R)** "Omen" rip-off about a little girl who is thrust upon a couple. After adopting her, they lose their natural family to her evil ways. **93m/C VHS.** *CA* Cyd Hayman, Malcolm Stoddard, Angela Pleasence, Patrick Barr; ***D:*** Gabrielle Beaumont.

Godson 🦴🦴🦴 **1972** Emotionless assassin lives a barren life under the surveillance of Paris police who suspect him in a recent killing. He suddenly discovers that his boss has a contract out on his life. Delon's performance raises this to an above-average crime drama. **103m/C VHS.** *FR* Alain Delon, Nathalie Delon, Francois Perier; ***D:*** Jean-Pierre Melville.

The Godson 🦴 **1998 (PG-13)** When Guiseppe "the Guppy" Calzone becomes the head of his crime family, he realizes his son and heir will need some tutoring to become the next big boss. So he sends the kid to Mafia U. to pick up some tricks of the trade. But the head of a rival family sees this as the perfect opportunity to get rid of the Calzone clan. Really, really dumb, despite the comic cast. **100m/C VHS, DVD.** Rodney Dangerfield, Dom DeLuise, Kevin McDonald, Fabiana Udenio, Lou Ferrigno, Barbara Crampton; ***D:*** Bob Hoge; ***W:*** Bob Hoge; ***C:*** Tom Lappin; ***M:*** Boris Elkis. VIDEO

Godspell 🦴🦴½ **1973 (G)** Musical retelling of the story of Jesus, set in New York City. Adapted from an enjoyable Broadway play but the film version comes off as silly. Good dancing and interesting score. ♫Day by Day; By My Side; Alas For You; On the Willows; O, Bless the Lord My Soul; Prepare Ye the Way of the Lord; Turn Back O Man; Beautiful City; Save the People. **103m/C VHS, DVD.** Victor Garber, David Haskell, Jerry Sroka, Lynne Thigpen, Gilmer McCormick; ***D:*** David Greene; ***M:*** Stephen Schwartz.

Godzilla 🦴🦴½ **1998 (PG-13)** Over-the-top remake of the 1954 cult classic has nuclear testing in France creating a giant mutant lizard to destroy all boats, piers, people, and buildings that happen to get in its way. Gone are the days of a man in a rubber suit menacing Tokyo, replaced by state-of-the-art special effects. Third rate storyline has wimpy biologist Niko Tatopoulos (Broderick) hired to track down and connect with the beast, only to realize that Godzilla has chosen the Big Apple as the birthing place for its huge brood. When various supporting characters (including Reno as a French secret agent out to destroy Godzilla) cross paths with the creature, what results looks amazingly similar to one hugely successful dinosaur movie and its sequel. Ending leaves door wide open for an inevitable sequel of its own. **138m/C VHS, DVD, Wide.** Matthew Broderick, Jean Reno, Maria Pitillo, Hank Azaria, Kevin Dunn, Michael Lerner, Harry Shearer, Arabella Field, Vicki Lewis, Doug Savant, Malcolm Danare; ***D:*** Roland Emmerich; ***W:*** Roland Emmerich, Dean Devlin; ***C:*** Ueli Steiger; ***M:*** David Arnold. Golden Raspberries '98: Worst Remake/Sequel, Worst Support. Actress (Pitillo).

Godzilla, King of the Monsters 🦴🦴½ *Gojira* **1956** An underwater prehistoric reptile emerges from the depths to terrorize Tokyo after he has been awakened by atomic testing. Burr's scenes are intercut in the American version, where he serves as a narrator telling the monster's tale in flashbacks. Ridiculously primitive special effects even in its own day. One of the first post-WWII Japanese films to break through commercially in the U.S. **80m/B VHS, DVD.** *JP* Raymond Burr, Takashi Shimura, Akira Takarada, Akihiko Hirata, Momoko Kochi, Sachio Sakai, Fuyuki Murakami, Ren Yamamoto; ***D:*** Inoshiro Honda, Terry Morse; ***W:*** Inoshiro Honda, Takeo Murata; ***C:*** Masao Tamai, Guy Roe; ***M:*** Akira Ifukube.

Godzilla 1985 🦴½ **1985 (PG)** Godzilla is awakened from underwater slumber by trolling nuclear submarines belonging to the superpowers near Japan. The giant monster's newly acquired appetite for nuclear energy inadvertently precipitates an international incident. Burr is called in (as the only living American witness to Godzilla's destructive 1955 outburst) to help mediate the conflict. Film released to coincide with the 30th anniversary of the original. **91m/C VHS.** *JP* Keiju Kobayashi, Ken Tanaka, Raymond Burr, Yasuka Sawaguchi, Shin Takumaa; ***D:*** Kohji Hashimoto, Robert J. Kizer; ***W:*** Shuichi Nagahara, Lisa Tomei; ***C:*** Kazutami Hara; ***M:*** Reijiro Koroku.

Godzilla on Monster Island 🦴🦴 *Godzilla vs. Gigan* **1972** Even Godzilla himself cannot hope to take on both Ghidra and Gigan alone and hope to succeed. Therefore he summons his pal Angillus for help. Together, they offer Earth its only hope of survival. Though the terror may repel you, the movie is a must for Godzilla fans; it's his first speaking part. **89m/C VHS.** *JP* Hiroshi Ichikawa, Tomoko Umeda, Yuriko Hishimi, Minoru Takashima, Zan Fujita; ***D:*** Jun Fukuda.

Godzilla Raids Again 🦴🦴 *Gigantis, the Fire Monster; Godzilla's Counter Attack* **1959** Warner Bros. had a problem securing rights to Godzilla's name. Yearning for a change of pace, the King of Monsters opts to destroy Osaka instead of Tokyo, but the spiny Angorous is out to dethrone our hero. Citizens flee in terror when the battle royale begins. The first Godzilla sequel. **78m/B VHS.** *JP* Hugo Grimaldi, Makayama, Minoru Chiaki.

Godzilla 2000 🦴🦴🦴 **1999 (PG)** Any other bigger-than-life movie-house hero staring in a series of films that span almost 50 years would have to answer some serious questions about plot repetition—but not Godzilla. The familiarity is what you pay to see. If Godzilla didn't clumsily destroy Tokyo office buildings and knock commuter trains off their elevated tracks, you'd be asking for a refund, pronto. So, with the latest Japanese flick to make it to our shores—featuring the REAL Godzilla, not that sophisticated American excuse for a Godzilla from a couple of years back—all is well. Funny dubbing, rubber suits, miniature sets—perfect comfort food on a rainy afternoon. As far as the plot goes...in short, spacecraft attacks Tokyo—the radioactive dinosaur comes to the rescue. **97m/C VHS, DVD, Wide.** *JP* Takehiro Murata, Shiro Sano, Hiroshi Abe, Naomi Nishida, Mayu Suzuki; ***D:*** Takao Okawara; ***W:*** Hiroshi Kashiwabara, Waturu Mimura; ***C:*** Katsuhiro Kato; ***M:*** Takayuki Hattori.

Godzilla vs. Biollante 🦴🦴 *Gojira tai Biorante* **1989 (PG)** Five years after Japan was destroyed, scientists are studying Godzilla's cells. Desparate spies, who apparently can't find their own Godzilla cells on all the ruined buildings, relaease Godzilla from his volcanic prison. When one scientist's attempt to create a super-plant goes awry and creates the behemoth Biollante, the monsters go at it in a giant territorial rumble. Japan (or a really small model thereof) is once again underfoot. Sequel to "Godzilla 1985." **104m/C VHS.** *JP* Koji Takahashi, Yoshiko Tanaka, Megumi Odaka, Kunihiko Mitamura, Masahiro Takashima, Kenpachiro Satsuma; ***D:*** Kazuki Ohmori; ***W:*** Kazuki Ohmori; ***C:*** Yudai Kato.

Godzilla vs. King Ghidora 🦴½ **1991** Tokyo begins to panic when aliens from the 23rd century make an appearance. But these aliens supposedly come in peace—warning that Godzilla will soon reawaken and destroy Japan unless he can be destroyed first. But it turns out these beings aren't so benign and soon Godzilla is confronted by his arch-enemy—flying, three-headed King Ghidora. **89m/C VHS.** *JP* Richard Berger, Kinako Harada, Kent Gilbert, Shoji Kobayashi; ***D:*** Kazuki Omori; ***W:*** Kazuki Omori; ***C:*** Yoshinori Sekiguchi; ***M:*** Akira Ifukube.

Godzilla vs. Mechagodzilla II 🦴½ **1993** Mechagodzilla II, a mammoth robot fueled by a nuclear reactor and sheathed in a synthetic diamond shield, is supposed to protect Japan from Godzilla. The mechanical monster has its work cut out for it now that Godzilla and Rodan have both arrived to claim the recently hatched baby Godzilla from a team of scientists. **108m/C VHS.** *JP* Masahiro Takashima, Leo Mangetti; ***D:*** Takao Okawara.

Godzilla vs. Megalon 🦴½ *Gojira tai Megaro* **1976 (G)** Godzilla's creators show their gratitude to misguided but faithful American audiences by transforming the giant monster into a good guy. This time, the world is threatened by Megalon, the giant cockroach, and Gigan, a flying metal creature, simultaneously. Fortuneately, the slippery hero's robot pal Jet Jaguar is on hand to slug it out side by side with Tokyo's ultimate defender. **80m/C VHS.** *JP* Katsuhiko Sasakai, Hiroyuki Kawase, Yutaka Hayashi, Robert Dunham, Kotaro Tomita; ***D:*** Jun Fukuda; ***W:*** Jun Fukuda, Shinichi Sekizawa; ***C:*** Yuzuru Aizawa; ***M:*** Richiro Manabe.

Godzilla vs. Monster Zero 🦴🦴 *Monster Zero; Battle of the Astros; Invasion of the Astro-Monsters; Invasion of the Astros; Invasion of Planet X; Kaiju Daisenso; The Great Monster War; War of the Monsters* **1968 (G)** Novel Godzilla adventure with the big guy and Rodan in outer space. Suspicious denizens of Planet X require the help of Godzilla and Rodan to rid themselves of the menacing Ghidra, whom they refer to as Monster Zero. Will they, in return, help Earth as promised, or is this just one big, fat double cross? **93m/C VHS, DVD.** *JP* Akira Takarada, Nick Adams, Kumi Mizuno, Jun Tazaki, Akira Kubo, Keiko Sawai, Yoshio Tsuchiya, Noriko Sengoku, Fuyuki Murakami; ***D:*** Inoshiro Honda; ***W:*** Shinichi Sekizawa; ***C:*** Hajime Koizumi; ***M:*** Akira Ifukube.

Godzilla vs. Mothra 🦴🦴 *Godzilla vs. the Thing; Godzilla vs. the Giant Moth; Godzilla Fights the Giant Moth; Mothra vs. Godzilla; Mosura tai Gojira* **1964** Mighty Mothra is called in to save the populace from Godzilla, who is on a rampage; and he's aided by two junior Mothras who hatch in the nick of time. The hesitant moth avoids the fire-breathing behemoth until succumbing to the pleadings of the Peanut Sisters to save humanity. Hilarious special effects inspire more laughter from derision than anything else. **88m/C VHS, DVD.** *JP* Akira Takarada, Yuriko Hoshi, Hiroshi Koizumi, Emi Ito, Yumi Ito, Yoshifumi Tajima, Kenji Sahara, Yu Fujiki; ***D:*** Inoshiro Honda; ***W:*** Shinichi Sekizawa; ***C:*** Hajime Koizumi; ***M:*** Akira Ifukube.

Godzilla vs. the Cosmic Monster 🦴🦴 *Godzilla Versus the Bionic Monster; Godzilla vs. Mechagodzilla; Gojira Tai Meka-Gojira* **1974 (G)** Godzilla's worst nightmares become a reality as he is forced to take on the one foe he cannot defeat—a metal clone of himself! To make matters worse, Earth is in dire peril at the hands of cosmic apes. We all need friends, and Godzilla is never more happy to see his buddy King Seeser, who gladly lends a claw. **80m/C VHS.** *JP* Masaki Daimon, Kazuya Aoyama, Reiko Tajima, Barbara Lynn, Akihiko Hirata; ***D:*** Jun Fukuda.

Godzilla vs. the Sea Monster woof! *Nankai No Kai Ketto; Ebirah, Terror of the Deep; Big Duel in the North* **1966** Godzilla makes friends with former rival Mothra (a giant moth) and together they bash on Ebirah, an enormous lobster backed by an evil cadre of (human) totalitarians. The unrepentant crusteacean turns the tables on our heroes, however, by growing a new tentacle everytime one is ripped off. Meanwhile, a frenzied batch of helpless humans are trapped on an island about to explode, if they aren't drowned first in a shower of reptilian backwash. **80m/C VHS.** *JP* ***D:*** Jun Fukuda.

Godzilla vs. the Smog Monster 🦴 *Gojira Tai Hedora; Godzilla vs. Hedora* **1972 (G)** Godzilla battles a creature borne of pollution, a 400-pound sludge blob named Hedora. Early 1970s period piece conveys interesting attitude towards pollution; it's treated as a sinister force that people are powerless to stop. Japanese teenagers marshal their dancing talents to combat the threat amid the hypnotic swirl of disco lighting. Great opening song: "Save the Earth." Dubbed in English. **87m/C VHS.** *JP* Akira Yamauchi, Hiroyuki Kawase, Toshio Shibaki; ***D:*** Yoshimitu Banno.

Godzilla's Revenge 🦴 *Oru Kaiju Daishingeki* **1969** A young boy who is having problems dreams of going to Monster Island to learn from Minya, Godzilla's son. Using the lessons in real life, the boy captures some bandits and outwits a bully. Uses footage from "Godzilla vs. the Sea Monster" and "Son of Godzilla" for battle scenes. One of the silliest Godzilla movies around. **70m/C VHS, DVD.** *JP* Kenji Sahara, Tomonori Yazaki, Machiko Naka, Sachio Sakai, Chotaro Togin, Yoshifumi Tajima, Eisei Amamoto, Ikio Sawamura; ***D:*** Inoshiro Honda; ***W:*** Shinichi Sekizawa; ***C:*** Sokei Tomioka; ***M:*** Kunio Miyauchi.

Goin' Coconuts 🦴 **1978 (PG)** Donny and Marie are miscast as Donny and Marie in this smarmy story of crooks and jewels. Seems someone covets the chanteuse's necklace, and only gratuitous crooning can spare the twosome from certain swindling. Big bore on the big island. **93m/C VHS.** Donny Osmond, Marie Osmond, Herb Edelman, Kenneth Mars, Ted Cassidy, Marc Lawrence, Harold Sakata; ***D:*** Howard Morris.

Goin' South 🦴🦴🦴 **1978 (PG)** An outlaw is saved from being hanged by a young woman who agrees to marry him in exchange for his help working a secret gold mine. They try to get the loot before his old gang gets wind of it. A tongue-in-cheek western that served as Nicholson's second directorial effort. Movie debuts of Steenburgen and Belushi. **109m/C VHS, DVD, Wide.** Jack Nicholson, Mary Steenburgen, John Belushi, Christopher Lloyd, Veronica Cartwright, Richard Bradford, Danny DeVito, Luana Anders, Ed Begley Jr., Anne Ramsey; ***D:*** Jack Nicholson; ***W:*** Charles Shyer; ***C:*** Nestor Almendros; ***M:*** Perry Botkin.

Goin' to Town 🦴🦴½ **1935** Complicated yarn with West as a woman who inherits an oil field and becomes the wealthiest woman in the state. She falls for British engineer Cavanagh and decides to become a "lady" in order to get his attention. There's a subplot about Buenos Aires and a crooked horse race, an in-name-only marriage to a high society type, and a murder before Mae finally gets her man. **71m/B VHS.** Mae West, Paul Cavanagh, Gilbert Emery, Ivan Lebedeff, Marjorie Gateson, Tito Coral, Monroe Owsley; ***D:*** Alexander Hall; ***W:*** Mae West; ***C:*** Karl Struss.

Going All the Way 🦴🦴½ **1997 (R)** Korean War vets Sonny Burns (Davies) and Gunner Casselman (Affleck) find themselves becoming best buds after returning to their Indianapolis hometown in 1954. Gunner's the self-confident stud, who vaguely wants to be an artist, while aspiring photographer Sonny's an anxious geek. The boys have mom troubles (Sonny's is a bible-thumper while Gunner's is a seductive flirt) and chase girls with varying success but the true bonding is strictly male. Davies is appropriately twitchy while Affleck gets to effectively use his natural charisma. Wakefield adapted from his 1970 novel. **110m/C VHS, DVD.** Jeremy Davies, Ben Affleck, Jill Clayburgh, Lesley Ann Warren, Rose McGowan, Rachel Weisz, Amy Locane; ***D:*** Mark Pellington; ***W:*** Dan Wakefield; ***C:*** Bobby Bukowski.

Going Ape! 🦴🦴 **1981 (PG)** Danza inherits a bunch of orangutans. If the apes are treated well, a legacy of $5 million will follow. This is all you need to know. **87m/C VHS.** Tony Danza, Jessica Walter, Danny DeVito, Art Metrano, Rick Hurst; ***D:*** Jeremy Joe Kronsberg; ***M:*** Elmer Bernstein.

Going Back 🦴½ **1983** Four friends reunite after college to relive a memorable summer they spent together after graduating from high school. **85m/C VHS.** Bruce Campbell, Christopher Howe, Perry Mallette, Susan W. Yamasaki; ***D:*** Ron Teachworth.

Going Bananas 🦴🦴 **1988 (PG)** Wacky adventure about a chimp who is being chased by a sinister circus owner. The monkey runs through Africa dragging along a boy, his caretaker, and a guide. The cast says it all. **95m/C VHS.** Dom DeLuise, Jimmie Walker, David Mendenhall, Herbert Lom; ***D:*** Boaz Davidson.

Going Berserk 🦴🦴½ **1983 (R)** The members of SCTV's television comedy troupe are featured in this comedy which lampoons everything from religious cults to kung fu movies. Has moments of inspired lunacy, interspersed with more pedestrian fare. Includes wicked send-up of "Father Knows Best," with former cast member Donahue. **85m/C VHS.** *CA* John Candy, Joe Flaherty, Eugene Levy, Paul Dooley, Pat Hingle, Richard Libertini, Ernie Hudson, Alley Mills, Dixie Carter, Murphy Dunne, Elinor Donahue; ***D:*** David Steinberg.

Going for the Gold: The Bill Johnson Story 🦴🦴 **1985** Biographical tale of the American downhill skier who went from hard-luck punk to Olympic champion in the 1984 games at Sarajevo, Yugoslavia. **100m/C VHS.** Anthony Edwards, Dennis Weaver, Sarah Jessica Parker, Deborah Van Valkenburgh, Wayne Northrop; ***D:*** Don Taylor.

Going Hollywood 🦴🦴🦴 **1933** Amusing musical/romantic fluff about a French teacher (Davies) who falls in love with a radio crooner (Crosby in his first MGM film). He's got the movie bug and heads for Hollywood, where he becomes an overnight sensation with a sultry costar (D'Orsay). Davies follows and proceeds to get Crosby out of D'Orsay's clutches and winds up replacing her rival in the film, promptly becoming a star herself. The underrated Davies was a fine light comedienne and supplied glamour to the production as well. Kelly, in her film debut, supplied the slapstick. The last Hearst-Cosmopolitan production made with MGM. ♫Temptation; We'll Make Hay While the Sun Shines; Going Hollywood; Our Big Love Scene; After Sundown; Cinderella's Fella; Beautiful Girl; Just an Echo in the Valley. **78m/B VHS.** Marion Davies, Bing Crosby, Fifi d'Orsay, Stuart Erwin, Patsy Kelly, Ned Sparks; ***D:*** Raoul Walsh; ***W:*** Donald Ogden Stewart; ***C:*** George J. Folsey.

Going Home 🦴🦴½ **1986** During WWI, Canadian soldiers held in British camps awaiting transport back home stage a riot over the endless delays and intolerable conditions. A fact-based story of the events leading up to this tragedy. **100m/C VHS.** Nicholas (Nick) Campbell, Paul Maxwell, Eugene Lipinski.

Going in Style 🦴🦴🦴½ **1979 (PG)** Three elderly gentlemen, tired of doing nothing, decide to liven up their lives by pulling a daylight bank stick-up. They don't care about the consequences because anything is better than sitting on a park bench all day long. The real fun begins when they get away with the robbery. Great cast makes this a winner. **91m/C VHS.** George Burns, Art Carney, Lee Strasberg; ***D:*** Martin Brest; ***W:*** Martin Brest.

Going My Way 🦴🦴🦴½ **1944** A musical-comedy about a progressive young priest assigned to a downtrodden parish who works to get the parish out of debt, but clashes with his elderly curate, who's set in his ways. Followed by "The Bells of St. Mary's." Fitzgerald's Oscar-winning Supporting Actor performance was also nominated in the Best Actor category. ♫The Day After Forever; Swinging on a Star; Too-ra-loo-ra-loo-ra; Going My Way; Silent Night; Habanera; Ave Maria. **126m/B VHS, DVD.** Bing Crosby, Barry Fitzgerald, Rise Stevens, Frank McHugh, Gene Lockhart, Porter Hall; ***D:*** Leo McCarey; ***W:*** Frank Butler, Frank Cavett, Leo McCarey; ***C:*** Lionel Lindon. Oscars '44: Actor (Crosby), Director (McCarey), Picture, Screenplay, Song ("Swinging on a Star"), Story, Support. Actor (Fitzgerald); Golden Globes '45: Director (McCarey), Film—Drama, Support. Actor (Fitzgerald); N.Y. Film Critics '44: Actor (Fitzgerald), Director (McCarey), Film.

Going Overboard 🦴 *Babes Ahoy* **1989 (R)** Cruise ship waiter dreams of becoming a comedian and gets his big break when the ship's comic disappears. **99m/C VHS, DVD.** Adam Sandler, Burt Young, Billy Zane, Peter Berg; ***D:*** Valerie Breiman.

Going Places 🦴🦴🦴 *Les Valseuses; Making It* **1974 (R)** A cynical, brutal satire about two young thugs traversing the French countryside raping, looting and cavorting as they please. Moreau has a brief role as an ex-con trying to go straight. An amoral, controversial comedy that established both its director and two stars. In French with English subtitles or dubbed. **122m/C VHS, DVD, Wide.** *FR* Gerard Depardieu, Patrick Dewaere, Miou-Miou, Isabelle Huppert, Jeanne Moreau, Brigitte Fossey; ***D:*** Bertrand Blier; ***W:*** Bertrand Blier; ***C:*** Bruno Nuytten; ***M:*** Stephane Grappelli.

Going to Town 🦴 **1944** Radio team Lum and Abner in one of their last films, as two conmen who scheme to make money from a phony oil well. **77m/B VHS.** Barbara Hale, Grady Sutton, Florence Lake.

Going Under **1991 (PG)** Subsurface military satire about the U.S.S. Sub Standard, the worst nuclear vessel in the Navy. It's so poorly constructed that the brass would rather sink than inspect it—if only they could. Interesting cast sinks with script headed for dry dock. **81m/C VHS.** Bill Pullman, Wendy Schaal, Ned Beatty, Robert Vaughn, Bud Cort, Michael Winslow.

Going Undercover 🦴 **1988 (PG-13)** A bumbling private investigator is hired to protect a rich, beautiful, and spoiled young woman on her European vacation. Poor excuse for a comedy. **90m/C VHS, DVD.** Lea Thompson, Jean Simmons, Chris Lemmon; ***D:*** James Kenelm Clarke.

The Gold & Glory 🦴 **1988 (PG-13)** Two brothers, one a musician, the other an athlete, vie for the affections of the same girl by competing in a footrace for a golden purse. **102m/C VHS.** Colin Friels, Josephine Smulders, Grant Kenny.

Gold Diggers of 1933 🦴🦴🦴½ **1933** In this famous period musical, showgirls help a songwriter save his Busby Berkeley-choreographed show. Followed by two sequels. ♫We're in the Money; Shadow Waltz; I've Got to Sing a Torch Song; Pettin' in the Park; Remember My Forgotten Man. **96m/B VHS.** Joan Blondell, Ruby Keeler, Aline MacMahon, Dick Powell, Guy Kibbee, Warren William, Ned Sparks, Ginger Rogers; ***D:*** Mervyn LeRoy.

Gold Diggers of 1935 🦴🦴🦴 **1935** The second Gold Diggers film, having something to do with a New England resort, romance, and a charity show put on at the hotel. Plenty of Berkeleian large-scale drama, especially the bizarre, mock-tragic "Lullaby on Broadway" number, which details the last days of a Broadway baby. ♫I'm Going Shopping With You; The Words Are in My Heart; Lullaby of Broadway. **95m/B VHS.** Dick Powell, Adolphe Menjou, Gloria Stuart, Alice Brady, Frank McHugh, Glenda Farrell, Grant Mitchell, Hugh Herbert, Wini Shaw; ***D:*** Busby Berkeley; ***C:*** George Barnes. Oscars '35: Song ("Lullaby of Broadway").

Gold Diggers: The Secret of Bear Mountain 🦴🦴½ **1995 (PG)** Thirteen-year-old Beth (Ricci) moves to the small town of Wheaton, Washington, and forms an unlikely friendship with rebellious tomboy Jody (Chlumsky). Together, the girls set out on a treasure hunt that takes them into a dangerous trek through sea-coast mountain terrain. The grownups are dumb (and the story's fairly boring) but the two heroines have real appeal. **94m/C VHS.** Christina Ricci, Anna Chlumsky, Polly Draper, Brian Kerwin, Diana Scarwid, David Keith; ***D:*** Kevin James Dobson; ***W:*** Barry Glasser; ***C:*** Ross Berryman; ***M:*** Joel McNeely.

The Gold of Naples 🦴🦴🦴 *L'Oro Di Napoli* **1954** A four-part omnibus film about life in Naples, filled with romance and family tragedies, by turns poignant, funny and pensive. Originally six tales; two were trimmed for U.S. release. In Italian with subtitles. **107m/B VHS.** *IT* Vittorio De Sica, Eduardo de Filippo, Paolo Stoppa, Sophia Loren, Silvana Mangano; ***D:*** Vittorio De Sica.

Gold of the Amazon Women 🦴 *Amazon Women* **1979** When two explorers set out to find gold, they stumble onto a society of man-hungry women who follow them into the urban jungle of Manhattan. There is also a European "R" rated version. **94m/C VHS, DVD.** Bo Svenson, Anita Ekberg, Bond Gideon, Donald Pleasence; ***D:*** Mark L. Lester; ***W:*** Stanley Ralph Ross; ***C:*** David Quaid; ***M:*** Gil Melle. **TV**

Gold Raiders 🦴 **1951** Larry, Moe, and Shemp team up with an insurance agent to take on the bad guys in the wild west. The Stooges are long past their prime. **56m/B VHS.** George O'Brien, Moe Howard, Moe Howard, Shemp Howard, Larry Fine, Sheila Ryan, Clem Bevans, Lyle Talbot; ***D:*** Edward L. Bernds.

Gold Raiders 🦴½ **1984** Team of secret agents are sent to the Jungles of Laos to find a plane carrying $200 million worth of gold, and nothing will get in their way. **106m/C VHS.** Robert Ginty, Sarah Langenfeld, William Steven.

The Gold Rush 🦴🦴🦴🦴 **1925** Chaplin's most critically acclaimed film. The best definition of his simple approach to film form; adept maneuvering of visual pathos. The "Little Tramp" searches for gold and romance in the Klondike in the mid-1800s. Includes the dance of the rolls, pantomime sequence of eating the shoe, and Chaplin's lovely music. **85m/B VHS, DVD, 8mm.** Charlie Chaplin, Mack Swain, Tom Murray, Georgia Hale; ***D:*** Charlie Chaplin; ***W:*** Charlie Chaplin; ***C:*** Roland H. Totheroh, Jack Wilson; ***M:*** Charlie Chaplin. AFI '98: Top 100, Natl. Film Reg. '92.

The Golden Bowl 🦴🦴🦴 **1972** Wealthy widower Adam Verver (Morris) and his naive daughter, Maggie (Townsend), are utterly devoted to each other. A situtation that doesn't change with Maggie's marriage to an impoverished Italian prince (Massey). Then Maggie decides her lonely father should also remarry and who could be better than Maggie's old chum, the beautiful Charlotte (Hunnicutt). But what the Ververs don't realize is how well the Prince and Charlotte already know each other. However, a gilded crystal cup—The Golden Bowl—will bring unwelcome knowledge. Based on the novel by Henry James. **270m/C VHS.** *GB* Barry Morse, Jill Townsend, Daniel Massey, Gayle Hunnicutt, Cyril Cusack, Kathleen Byron; ***D:*** James Cellan Jones; ***W:*** Jack Pulman. **TV**

The Golden Bowl 🦴🦴½ **2000 (R)** Beautiful but bloodless Merchant/Ivory adaptation of Henry James' complex 1904 novel set in turn-of-the-century London. Wealthy American aesthete Adam Verver (Nolte) dotes on his only daughter, Maggie (Beckinsale), and even buys her a husband—an impoverished Italian aristocrat, Prince Amerigo (a miscast Northam), whom she loves. But, unknown to both Ververs, the prince and Maggie's best friend, the equally poor Charlotte (Thurman), had a long ago affair that gets rekindled, even though Charlotte has become the wife of Adam. A studied menage a quartre where just what anyone knows (or suspects) is never made clear. **130m/C VHS, DVD, Wide.** *GB US FR* Nick Nolte, Uma Thurman, Kate Beckinsale, Jeremy Northam, Anjelica Huston, James Fox, Madeleine Potter, Peter Eyre; ***D:*** James Ivory; ***W:*** Ruth Prawer Jhabvala; ***C:*** Tony Pierce-Roberts; ***M:*** Richard Robbins.

Golden Boy 🦴🦴🦴 **1939** Holden plays a young and gifted violinist who earns money for his musical education by working as a part-time prizefighter. Fight promoter Menjou has Stanwyck cozy up to the impressionable young man to convince him to make the fight game his prime concern. She's successful but it leads to tragedy. Holden's screen debut, with Cobb as his immigrant father and Stanwyck successfully slinky as the corrupting love interest. Classic pugilistic drama with well-staged fight scenes. Based on Clifford Odets' play with toned down finale. **99m/B VHS.** William Holden, Adolphe Menjou, Barbara Stanwyck, Lee J. Cobb, Joseph Calleia, Sam Levene, Don Beddoe, Charles Halton; ***D:*** Rouben Mamoulian; ***W:*** Daniel Taradash, Victor Heerman, Sarah Y. Mason.

The Golden Child 🦴🦴 **1986 (PG-13)** When a Tibetan child with magic powers is kidnapped and transported to Los Angeles, Chandler, a professional "finder of lost children" must come to the rescue. The search takes him through Chinatown in a hunt that cliches every Oriental swashbuckler ever made. Good fun. **94m/C VHS, DVD, 8mm.** Eddie Murphy, Charlotte Lewis, Charles Dance, Victor Wong, Randall "Tex" Cobb, James Hong; ***D:*** Michael Ritchie; ***W:*** Dennis Feldman; ***C:*** Donald E. Thorin; ***M:*** Michel Colombier.

The Golden Coach 🦴🦴🦴 *Le Carrosse D'Or* **1952** Based on a play by Prosper Merimee, the tale of an 18th-century actress in Spanish South America who takes on all comers, including the local viceroy who creates a scandal by presenting her with his official coach. Rare cinematography by Claude Renoir. **101m/C VHS.** *FR* Anna Magnani, Odoardo Spadaro, Nada Fiorelli, Dante Rino, Duncan Lamont; ***D:*** Jean Renoir; ***W:*** Ginette Doynel, Jack Kirkland, Giulio Macchi, Jean Renoir; ***C:*** Claude Renoir, Ronald Hill; ***M:*** Antonio Vivaldi.

Golden Demon 🦴🦴½ *Konjiki Yasha* **1953** An acclaimed Japanese epic, from the novel by Koyo Ozaki, about the destructive powers of wealth on the lives of two star-crossed lovers in medieval Japan. In Japanese with English subtitles. **95m/C VHS.** *JP* Jun Negami, Fujiko Yamamoto; ***D:*** Koji Shima.

Golden Earrings 🦴🦴½ **1947** Enjoyable, yet incredulous story about British agent Milland joining up with gypsy Dietrich for espionage work. Absurd film was so bad it became a camp classic overnight. Although Dietrich and Milland couldn't stand each other and battled constantly during production, the movie did quite well at the boxoffice. Based on a novel by Yolanda Foldes. **95m/B VHS.** Ray Milland, Marlene Dietrich, Bruce Lester, Dennis Hoey, Quentin Reynolds, Reinhold Schunzel, Ivan Triesault; ***D:*** Mitchell Leisen; ***W:*** Abraham Polonsky, Frank Butler, Helen Deutsch; ***C:*** Daniel F. Fapp.

Golden Gate 🦴🦴 **1993 (R)** Young Fed Dillon is thrown into the hysteria of the communist witch hunt in 1952 San Francisco. He snares Song, a Chinese labor activist, on some very dubious charges. Ten years later he finds himself getting involved with Song's daughter Marilyn (Chen), who knows nothing about her lover's involvement with her family. Then she finds out. Everchanging moods, sometimes film noir, sometimes a love story, sometimes a nostalgic look back, are confusing. Promising storyline meanders and fades as Director Madden tries to do too much in a short time. Beware of broad stereotypes in every character. **95m/C VHS.** Matt Dillon, Joan Chen, Bruno Kirby, Teri Polo, Tzi Ma, Stan(ford) Egi, Peter Murnik, Jack Shearer, George Giudall; ***D:*** John Madden; ***W:*** David Henry Hwang; ***C:*** Bobby Bukowski; ***M:*** Elliot Goldenthal.

Golden Lady 🦴½ **1979** Beautiful woman leads her female gang in a deadly game of international intrigue. **90m/C VHS.** Christina World, Suzanne Danielle, June Chadwick; ***D:*** Joseph (Jose Ramon) Larraz.

Golden Rendezvous 🦴🦴 *Nuclear Terror* **1977** A tale of treachery aboard a "gambler's paradise" luxury liner which is hijacked and held for ransom. Based on Alistair MacLean's novel. **103m/C VHS.** Richard Harris, David Janssen, John Carradine, Burgess Meredith, Ann Turkel, John Vernon; ***D:*** Ashley Lazarus.

The Golden Salamander 🦴🦴 **1951** Howard shines in otherwise lackluster adventure about archaeologist searching for ancient ruins in Tunisia who must deal with gun runners and their evil leader, while torridly romancing a beautiful Tunisian girl. Filmed on location in Tunis. Based on the novel by Victor Canning. **96m/B VHS.** *GB* Trevor Howard, Anouk Aimee, Herbert Lom, Miles Malleson, Walter Rilla, Jacques Sernas, Wilfrid Hyde-White, Peter Copley, Eugene Deckers, Henry Edwards, Marcel Poncin, Percy Walsh, Sybilla Binder, Kathleen Boutall, Valentine Dyall; ***D:*** Ronald Neame; ***C:*** Oswald Morris.

The Golden Seal 🦴🦴½ **1983 (PG)** Tale of a small boy's innocence put in direct conflict, because of his love of a rare wild golden seal and her pup, with the failed dreams, pride and ordinary greed of adults. **94m/C VHS, 8mm.** Steve Railsback, Michael Beck, Penelope Milford, Torquil Campbell; ***D:*** Frank Zuniga; ***M:*** John Barry.

The Golden Spiders: A Nero Wolfe Mystery 🦴🦴½ **2000** It's actually not much of a mystery but writer Rex Stout's eccentric Wolfe (Chaykin) and his idiosyncratic cast of helpers as well as the setting (Manhattan in the late forties) make for some amusing moments. Gourmand and orchid grower Wolfe never leaves his brownstone, preferring righthand man Archie Goodwin (Hutton) take care of the leg work. The golden spiders of the title are a pair of flashy earrings worn by a damsel in distress that leads to several hit-and-run deaths, blackmail, and fraud. **100m/C VHS.** Maury Chaykin, Timothy Hutton, Bill Smitrovich, Saul Rubinek, Mimi Kuzyk, Beau Starr, Robert Clark, Larissa Lapchinski, Gary Reineke, Nicky Guadagni, Robert Bockstael, Trent McMullen; ***D:*** Bill Duke; ***W:*** Paul Monash; ***C:*** Mike Fash; ***M:*** Michael Small. **CABLE**

The Golden Stallion 🦴½ **1949** Trigger falls in love with a stunning mare. He sees her villainous owners abusing her and kills them. Roy takes the blame for his equine pal, but true love triumphs to save the day. **67m/B VHS.** Roy Rogers, Dale Evans, Estelita Rodriguez, Pat Brady, Douglas Evans, Frank Fenton; ***D:*** William Witney.

Golden Voyage of Sinbad 🦴🦴½ **1973 (G)** In the mysterious ancient land of Lemuria, Sinbad and his crew encounter magical and mystical creatures. A statue of Nirvana comes to life and engages in a sword fight with Sinbad. He later meets up with a one-eyed centaur and a griffin. Ray Harryhausen can once again claim credit for the unusual and wonderful mythical creatures springing to life. **105m/C VHS, DVD, Wide.** John Phillip Law, Caroline Munro, Tom Baker, Douglas Wilmer, Martin Shaw, John David Garfield, Gregoire Aslan; ***D:*** Gordon Hessler; ***W:*** Brian Clemens; ***C:*** Ted Moore; ***M:*** Miklos Rozsa.

Goldeneye 🦴🦴🦴 **1995 (PG-13)** Bond is back, in the long-awaited (eight years) debut of Brosnan as legendary Brit agent 007. Since we're through the Cold War, Bond has to make do with the villainy of the Russian Mafia, who are planning to sabotage global financial markets utilizing the "Goldeneye" satellite weapon. There's a spectacularly impossible stunt to start things out in familiar territory and lots more noisy (if prolonged) action pieces. Brosnan (who looks great in a tux) is slyly self-aware that his character is more myth than man and Janssen does a suitably over-the-top job as bad Bond girl Xenia Onatopp. Tina Turner sings the dreary title track. **130m/C VHS, DVD.** Pierce Brosnan, Famke Janssen, Sean Bean, Izabela Scorupco, Joe Don Baker, Robbie Coltrane, Judi Dench, Tcheky Karyo, Gottfried John, Alan Cumming, Desmond Llewelyn, Michael Kitchen, Serena Gordon, Samantha Bond, Minnie Driver; ***D:*** Martin Campbell; ***W:*** Jeffrey Caine, Michael France; ***C:*** Phil Meheux; ***M:*** Eric Serra. Blockbuster '96: Action Actor, T. (Brosnan).

Goldeneye: The Secret Life of Ian Fleming 🦴🦴½ *Spymaster* **1989** James Bond's creator lead quite an interesting life himself. The debonair author joins His Majesty's Secret Service and gets involved in numerous romantic exploits. Not to be confused with the British TV movie "Spymaker," which also covered Fleming's early career. **103m/C VHS.** *GB* Charles Dance, Phyllis Logan, Julian Fellowes, Patrick Ryecart, Ed Devereaux; ***D:*** Don Boyd; ***W:*** Reg Gadney; ***C:*** Mike Southon; ***M:*** Michael Berkeley. **TV**

Goldengirl 🦴🦴 **1979 (PG)** A neo-Nazi doctor tries to make a superwoman of his daughter who has been specially fed, exercised, and emotionally conditioned since childhood to run in the Olympics. Anton's starring debut. **107m/C VHS.** Susan Anton, James Coburn, Curt Jurgens, Robert Culp, Leslie Caron, Harry Guardino, Jessica Walter; ***D:*** Joseph Sargent; ***M:*** Bill Conti.

Goldenrod 🦴½ **1977** A successful rodeo champion is forced to reevaluate his life when he sustains a crippling accident in the ring. **100m/C VHS.** *CA* Tony LoBianco, Gloria Carlin, Donald Pleasence, Donnelly Rhodes; ***D:*** Harvey Hart. **TV**

Goldfinger 🦴🦴🦴 **1964 (PG)** Ian Fleming's James Bond, Agent 007, attempts to prevent international gold smuggler Goldfinger and his pilot Pussy Galore from robbing Fort Knox. Features villainous assistant Oddjob and his deadly bowler hat. The third in the series is perhaps the most popular. Shirley Bassey sings the theme song. **117m/C VHS, DVD, Wide.** *GB* Sean Connery, Honor Blackman, Gert Frobe, Shirley Eaton, Tania Mallet, Harold Sakata, Cec Linder, Bernard Lee, Lois Maxwell, Desmond Llewelyn, Nadja Regin; ***D:*** Guy Hamilton; ***W:*** Paul Dehn, Richard Maibaum; ***C:*** Ted Moore; ***M:*** John Barry. Oscars '64: Sound FX Editing.

Goldilocks & the Three Bears **1983** Entry from "Faerie Tale Theatre" tells the story of Goldilocks, who wanders through the woods and finds the home of three bears—only in this version Goldilocks is a nasty child, and it's the bears who'll get your sympathy. **60m/C VHS.** Tatum O'Neal, Alex Karras, Brandis Kemp, Donovan Scott, Hoyt Axton, John Lithgow, Carole King; ***D:*** Gilbert Cates.

Goldrush: A Real Life Alaskan Adventure 🦴🦴½ **1998** Well-bred Frances (Milano) decides to leave New York society life behind and join an expedition to Alaska (as a would-be gold miner) during the 1899 gold rush. **89m/C VHS.** Alyssa Milano, Bruce Campbell, Stan Cahill, Tom Scholte, William Morgan Sheppard; ***D:*** John Power; ***W:*** Jacqueline Feather, David Seidler. **TV**

The Goldwyn Follies 🦴🦴 **1938** Lavish disjointed musical comedy about Hollywood. A movie producer chooses a naive girl to give him advice on his movies. George Gershwin died during the filming. ♫Romeo and Juliet; Water Nymph; Here, Pussy, Pussy; Serenade To a Fish; Love Walked In; Love is Here to Stay; Spring Again; I Was Doing Alright; La Serenata. **115m/C VHS, DVD.** Adolphe Menjou, Vera Zorina, Al Ritz, Harry Ritz, Jimmy Ritz, Helen Jepson, Phil Baker, Bobby Clark, Ella Logan, Andrea Leeds, Edgar Bergen; ***D:*** George Marshall; ***C:*** Gregg Toland; ***M:*** George Gershwin, Ira Gershwin.

The Golem 🦴🦴🦴½ *Der Golem, wie er in die Welt kam* **1920** A huge clay figure is given life by a rabbi in hopes of saving the Jews in the ghetto of medieval Prague. Rarely seen Wegener expressionist mythopus that heavily influenced the "Frankenstein" films of the sound era. **80m/B VHS, DVD.** *GE* Paul Wegener, Albert Steinruck, Ernst Deutsch, Lyda Salmonava, Otto Gebuehr, Max Kronert, Loni Nest, Greta Schroder, Hans Sturm; ***D:*** Carl Boese, Paul Wegener; ***W:*** Henrik Galeen, Paul Wegener; ***C:*** Karl Freund; ***M:*** Hans Landberger.

Goliath Against the Giants 🦴½ *Goliath Contro I Giganti; Goliat Contra Los Gigantes; Goliath and the Giants* **1963** Goliath takes on Bokan, who has stolen his throne. Goliath must fight Amazons, storms, and sea monsters to save the lovely Elea. Goliath conquers all. **95m/C VHS.** *IT SP* Brad Harris, Gloria Milland, Fernando Rey, Barbara Carroll; ***D:*** Guido Malatesta.

Goliath and the Barbarians 🦴🦴 *Il Terror Dei Baraberi* **1960** Goliath and his men go after the barbarians who are terrorizing and ravaging the Northern Italian countryside during the fall of the Roman Empire. A basic Reeves muscleman epic. **86m/C VHS.** *IT* Steve Reeves, Bruce Cabot; ***D:*** Carlo Campogalliani; ***M:*** Les Baxter.

Goliath and the Dragon woof! *La Vendetta di Ercole* **1961** Even Goliath must have doubts as he is challenged by the evil and powerful King Eurystheus. A must for fans of ridiculous movies with ridiculous monsters. **90m/C VHS, DVD, Wide.** *IT FR* Bruce Cabot, Mark Forest, Broderick Crawford, Gaby Andre, Leonora Ruffo; ***D:*** Vittorio Cottafavi; ***W:*** Marco Piccolo, Archibald Zounds Jr.; ***C:*** Mario Montuori; ***M:*** Les Baxter.

Goliath and the Sins of Babylon 🦴🦴 *Maciste, L'Eroe Piu Grande Del Mondo* **1964** Well-sculpted Forest plays yet another mesomorph to the rescue in this poorly dubbed spaghetti legend. Goliath must spare 24 virgins whom the evil Crisa would submit as human sacrifice. Forest—who played the mythic Maciste in a number of films—was randomly assigned the identity of Goliath, Hercules, or Samson for U.S. viewing; go figure. **80m/C VHS.** *IT* Mark Forest, Eleanora Bianchi, Jose Greco, Giuliano Gemma, Paul Muller; ***D:*** Michele Lupo.

Goliath Awaits 🦴🦴 **1981** Harmon plays an oceanographer who discovers a ship that was sunk by German U-boats during WWI. Nothing much new there, except that the survivors still reside on board the vessel, some 40 years after the oceanliner was torpedoed. And get this: they're living a quasi-Utopian existence. Kind of hard to swallow. Made for TV, it originally aired in two parts. **110m/C VHS.** Mark Harmon, Robert Forster, Christopher Lee, Eddie Albert, John Carradine, Alex Cord, Emma Samms, Jean Marsh; ***D:*** Kevin Connor; ***M:*** George Duning. **TV**

Gone Are the Days 🦴🦴½ *The Man From C.O.T.T.O.N., Purlie Victorious* **1963** Shaky adaptation of the play, "Purlie Victorious." A black preacher wants to cause the ruin of a white plantation owner. Alda's screen debut. **97m/B VHS.** Ossie Davis, Ruby Dee, Sorrell Booke, Godfrey Cambridge, Alan Alda, Beah Richards; ***D:*** Nicholas Webster; ***W:*** Ossie Davis; ***C:*** Boris Kaufman.

Gone Are the Days 🦴🦴 **1984** Government agent (Korman) is assigned to protect a family who witnessed an underworld shooting, but the family would like to get away from both the mob and the police. Disney comedy is well-acted but done in by cliches. **90m/C VHS.** Harvey Korman, Susan Anspach, Robert Hogan; ***D:*** Gabrielle Beaumont. **CABLE**

Gone Fishin' woof! **1997 (PG)** Long delayed comedy (thanks to some on-set disasters and well founded doubts about quality) finds best friends and bassmasters of disaster Gus (Glover) and Joe (Pesci) thinking they're going on a peaceful fishing trip. Instead they meet two women (Arquette and Whitfield) who are on the trail of a dangerous British con artist (Brimble). Pesci and Glover have reeled in one stinky old shoe of a movie here. Granted, it's not entirely their fault, but they should've known better. There are no surprises (or laughs) as every joke and set piece is tipped way ahead of time, just so you won't miss it. Less fun than a fish hook in the eye. **94m/C VHS.** Danny Glover, Joe Pesci, Rosanna Arquette, Lynn Whitfield, Willie Nelson, Nick Brimble, Gary Grubbs, Carol Kane, Edythe Davis; ***D:*** Christopher Cain; ***W:*** Jeffrey Abrams, Jill Mazurzsky Cody; ***C:*** Dean Semler; ***M:*** Randy Edelman.

Gone in 60 Seconds 🦴½ **1974** Car thief working for an insurance adjustment firm gets double-crossed by his boss and chased by the police. Forty minutes are consumed by a chase scene which destroyed more than 90 vehicles. **105m/C VHS, DVD, Wide.** H.B. Halicki, Marion Busia, George Cole, James McIntyre, Jerry Daugirda; ***D:*** H.B. Halicki; ***W:*** H.B. Halicki; ***C:*** Jack Vacek; ***M:*** Philip Kachaturian.

Gone in 60 Seconds 🦴🦴 **2000 (PG-13)** Cage is an ex-car thief who must steal 50 cars in one night in order to save his ne'er-do-well brother (Ribisi) while gung-ho cop Castleback (Lindo) stays on his tail. "Rounding-up-the-old-crew" montage ensues, followed by much highway mayhem and the odd humorous one-liner. As with most Bruckheimer-produced epics, flash and stunts run roughshod over plot and character, but the target audience won't care because the cars just look so damn cool. Jolie is woefully underutilized in the girlfriend/partner-in-crime role. Remake of the 1974 film notable for its 40-minute chase scene. **117m/C VHS, DVD, Wide.** Nicolas Cage, Angelina Jolie, Giovanni Ribisi, Robert Duvall, Scott Caan, Vinnie Jones, Will Patton, Delroy Lindo, Chi McBride, Christopher Eccleston, Timothy Olyphant, William Lee Scott, Frances Fisher, Grace Zabriskie, James Duval, TJ Cross, Arye Gross, Bodhi (Pine) Elfman, Percy (Master P) Miller; ***D:*** Dominic Sena; ***W:*** Scott Rosenberg; ***C:*** Paul Cameron; ***M:*** Trevor Rabin.

Gone to Ground **1976** Mad killer terrorizes a group of vacationers who are trapped in an isolated beach house. **74m/C VHS.** Charles Tingwell, Elaine Lee, Eric Oldfield, Marion Johns, Robyn Gibbes, Judy Lynne, Dennis Grosvenor, Alan Penney, Marcus Hale.

Gone with the West ½ **1972** Little Moon and Jud McGraw seek revenge upon the man who stole their cattle. **92m/C VHS.** James Caan, Stefanie Powers, Sammy Davis Jr., Aldo Ray, Michael Conrad, Michael Walker Jr.; ***D:*** Bernard Giraudeau.

Gone with the Wind **1939** Epic Civil War drama focuses on the life of petulant southern belle Scarlett O'Hara. Starting with her idyllic lifestyle on a sprawling plantation, the film traces her survival through the tragic history of the South during the Civil War and Reconstruction, and her tangled love affairs with Ashley Wilkes and Rhett Butler. Classic Hollywood doesn't get any better than this; one great scene after another, equally effective in intimate drama and sweeping spectacle. The train depot scene, one of the more technically adroit shots in movie history, involved hundreds of extras and dummies, and much of the MGM lot was razed to simulate the burning of Atlanta. Based on Margaret Mitchell's novel, screenwriter Howard was assisted by producer Selznick and novelist F. Scott Fitzgerald. For its 50th anniversary, a 231-minute restored version was released that included the trailer for "The Making of a Legend: GWTW." **231m/C VHS, DVD.** Clark Gable, Vivien Leigh, Olivia de Havilland, Leslie Howard, Thomas Mitchell, Hattie McDaniel, Butterfly McQueen, Evelyn Keyes, Harry Davenport, Jane Darwell, Ona Munson, Barbara O'Neil, William "Billy" Bakewell, Rand Brooks, Ward Bond, Laura Hope Crews, Yakima Canutt, George Reeves, Marjorie Reynolds, Ann Rutherford, Victor Jory, Carroll Nye, Paul Hurst, Isabel Jewell, Cliff Edwards, Eddie Anderson, Oscar Polk, Eric Linden, Violet Kemble-Cooper, Fred Crane, Howard Hickman, Leona Roberts, Cammie King, Mary Anderson, Frank Faylen; ***D:*** Victor Fleming; ***W:*** Sidney Howard; ***C:*** Ray Rennahan; ***M:*** Max Steiner. Oscars '39: Actress (Leigh), Color Cinematog., Director (Fleming), Film Editing, Picture, Screenplay, Support. Actress (McDaniel); AFI '98: Top 100, Natl. Film Reg. '89;; N.Y. Film Critics '39: Actress (Leigh).

Gonza the Spearman ½ **1986** A gifted samurai lancer is accused of having an affair with the wife of the lord of his province. The lancer must leave to save the woman's honor, because to stay would mean death to them both. In Japanese with English subtitles. **126m/C VHS, Wide.** *JP* Hiromi Goh, Shima Iwashita; ***D:*** Masahiro Shinoda.

Good Advice ½ **2001 (R)** Stockboker Ryan Turner (Sheen) loses all his money on a bad stock tip and decides to ghostwrite his ex-girlfriend's (Richards) lame newspaper advice column. Suddenly the column is hot and the newspaper's publisher (Harmon) is showing interest in more than newsprint. **93m/C VHS, DVD, Wide.** Charlie Sheen, Denise Richards, Angie Harmon, Jon Lovitz, Rosanna Arquette, Estelle Harris, Barry Newman; ***D:*** Steve Rash; ***W:*** Robert Horn, Daniel Margosis; ***C:*** Daryn Okada; ***M:*** Teddy Castellucci.

A Good Baby ½ **1999** In a sparsely populated North Carolina community, loner Raymond Toker (Thomas) dicovers an abandoned newborn in the woods. He rescues the infant and attempts to find the baby's parents but no one will claim her. Toker gets more and more attached to the baby when slick traveling salesman Truman Lester (Strthairn) suddenly appears in town and the child's origins are finally revealed. Hasty ending mars an otherwise notably affecting debut for director Dieckmann. **98m/C VHS, DVD.** Henry Thomas, David Strathairn, Cara Seymour, Danny Nelson; ***D:*** Katherine Dieckmann; ***W:*** Katherine Dieckmann, Leon Rooke; ***C:*** Jim Denault; ***M:*** David Mansfield.

Good Burger ½ **1997 (PG)** Teen actors Kel and Kenan from Nickelodeon fame make their feature film debut in this innocent, silly romp as employees trying to prevent the takeover of their fast food restaurant by the mega burger conglomerate across the street. Similar to comedy teams of the past, Kel is the dimwitted Ed and Kenan is the schemer Dexter, always looking for a quick way out of hard labor. The pre-adolescent humor of the film is as goofy as it is charming and the energetic duo of K&K serves up an entertaining meal for the kiddies. Shaquille O'Neal makes a cameo as does funk meister George Clinton. And yes, that is Abe Vigoda by that fry machine! **95m/C VHS, Wide.** Kenan Thompson, Kel Mitchell, Sinbad, Abe Vigoda, Dan Schneider, Shar Jackson, Jan Schweiterman, Ron Lester; ***Cameos:*** Shaquille O'Neal, George Clinton; ***D:*** Brian Robbins; ***W:*** Kevin Kopelow, Heather Seifert, Dan Schneider; ***C:*** Mac Ahlberg; ***M:*** Stewart Copeland.

Good Day for a Hanging ½ **1958** Marshal Ben Cutler (MacMurray) finds unexpectedly opposition from the townspeople when he captures killer Eddie Campbell (Vaughn). The charismatic outlaw gains their sympathy and Cutler is going to have trouble when Campbell is sentenced to hang. **85m/C VHS.** Fred MacMurray, Robert Vaughn, Joan Blackman, Maggie Hayes, James Drury, Wendell Holmes, Emile Meyer, Bing Russell; ***D:*** Nathan (Hertz) Juran; ***W:*** Daniel Ullman, Maurice Zimm; ***C:*** Henry Freulich.

A Good Day to Die ½ *Children of the Dust* **1995 (R)** Western made-for-TV saga, set during the 1880s land rush of the Oklahoma Territory, and adapted from the novel by Clancy Carlile. Half-black, half-Cherokee gunslinger Gypsy Smith (Poitier) reluctantly agrees to lead a wagontrain of freed slaves west to found their own community. Naturally, there's trouble with the Klan and Gypsy isn't the only one involved—young Cherokee brave White Wolf (Wirth), who has been raised among whites, has a forbidden romance with his foster sister, Rachel (Going), leading to lots of heartbreak. Fawcett has a brief role as the young Rachel's high-strung mother. Filmed in Alberta, Canada. **120m/C VHS, DVD.** Sidney Poitier, Michael Moriarty, Joanna Going, Billy Wirth, Regina Taylor, Hart Bochner, Shirley Knight, Robert Guillaume, Farrah Fawcett; ***D:*** David Greene; ***W:*** Joyce Eliason; ***C:*** Ronald Orieux; ***M:*** Mark Snow.

The Good Earth ½ **1937** Pearl S. Buck's classic recreation of the story of a simple Chinese farm couple beset by greed and poverty. Outstanding special effects. MGM's last film produced by master Irving Thalberg and dedicated to his memory. Rainer won the second of her back-to-back Best Actress Oscars for her portrayal of the self-sacrificing O-Lan. **138m/B VHS.** Paul Muni, Luise Rainer, Charley Grapewin, Keye Luke, Walter Connolly; ***D:*** Sidney Franklin; ***C:*** Karl Freund. Oscars '37: Actress (Rainer), Cinematog.

Good Evening, Mr. Wallenberg ½ **1993** Raoul Wallenberg was an upper-class Swede who imported luxury goods from Hungary. He was also responsible for saving thousands of Hungarian Jews from extermination by the Nazis. Using phony documents he first had small groups of Jews smuggled to safety but when he learns that the 65,0000 Jews of the Budapest ghetto are to be killed he uses a bluff to prevent the deaths. Later taken prisoner by the Soviet Army, Wallenberg's fate has never been determined. Characters are dwarfed by the immensity of the events and Wallenberg remains an enigma. In Swedish, German, and Hungarian with English subtitles. **115m/C VHS.** *SW* Stellan Skarsgard, Erland Josephson, Katharina Thalbach; ***D:*** Kjell Grede; ***W:*** Kjell Grede.

The Good Father **1987 (R)** An acclaimed British TV movie about a bitter divorced man trying to come to terms with his son, his ex-wife, and his own fury by supporting the courtroom divorce battle of a friend. **90m/C VHS.** *GB* Anthony Hopkins, Jim Broadbent, Harriet Walter, Frances Viner, Joanne Whalley, Simon Callow, Michael Byrne; ***D:*** Mike Newell; ***W:*** Christopher Hampton; ***C:*** Michael Coulter; ***M:*** Richard Hartley.

The Good Fight ½ **1992** Grace Cragin (Lahti) is a lawyer at a small firm who's asked by her son's best friend to represent him in a tough case against a powerful corporation. The young man is dying of mouth cancer and he wants to sue the tobacco company that makes the chewing tobacco he blames for his illness. Grace is wary of the high-powered litigation necessary but with the increasingly personal aid of her prominent lawyer ex-husband (O'Quinn), she is ready to battle the odds. Another fine performance by Lahti in this cable drama. **91m/C VHS.** Christine Lahti, Terry O'Quinn, Kenneth Welsh, Lawrence Dane, Adam Trese, Tony Rosato, Andrea Roth, Jonathan Crombie; ***D:*** John David Coles; ***W:*** Beth Gutcheon; ***M:*** W.G. Snuffy Walden. CABLE

The Good Girl **2002 (R)** Dowdy smalltown cashier Aniston is bored with her marriage to pothead house painter hubby Reilly and has an affair with teen Gyllenhaal. Not yet reviewed. **?m/C VHS, DVD.** Jennifer Aniston, Jake Gyllenhaal, John C. Reilly, Tim Blake Nelson, Zooey Deschanel; ***D:*** Miguel Arteta; ***W:*** Mike White.

Good Girls Don't ½ **1995** Jeannie (Estevez) and Bettina (Parton) are framed for murder and take it on the lam in a red convertible with a half million in cash. It's a comedy. **85m/C VHS.** Renee Estevez, Julia Parton, Mary Woronov, Christopher Knight; ***D:*** Rick Sloane; ***W:*** Rick Sloane.

The Good Guys and the Bad Guys ½ **1969 (PG)** When Kennedy is abandoned by his gang of outlaws for being too old to keep up, he finds himself being hunted by lifelong marshall nemesis Mitchum. **91m/C VHS.** Robert Mitchum, George Kennedy, David Carradine, Tina Louise, Douglas Fowley, Lois Nettleton, Martin Balsam, John Carradine; ***D:*** Burt Kennedy; ***W:*** Ronald M. Cohen; ***C:*** Harry Stradling Jr.

Good Guys Wear Black **1978 (PG)** A mild-mannered professor keeps his former life as leader of a Vietnam commando unit under wraps until he discovers that he's number one on the CIA hit list. Sequel is "A Force of One." **96m/C VHS, DVD, Wide.** Chuck Norris, Anne Archer, James Franciscus; ***D:*** Ted Post; ***W:*** Mark Medoff; ***M:*** Craig Safan.

Good Luck ½ **1996 (R)** Inspirational buddy movie that manages to avoid the worst of sentimental excess. Tony Olezniak (D'Onofrio) is a football player left blind because of a game injury. He's on a downward spiral and winds up in jail, which is where paraplegic Bernard Lemley (Hines), once Tony's tutor, finds him. Bernard wants to enter a rigorous whitewater raft race held on Oregon's Rogue River and he needs Tony's strength to help him do it. The emotional payoff comes as the two bicker and bond instead of from the challenge of the raft race, which in itself is a change of pace. Lots of charm. **95m/C VHS, DVD.** Vincent D'Onofrio, Gregory Hines, Max Gail, James Earl Jones, Sarah Trigger, Joe Theisman; ***D:*** Richard LaBrie; ***W:*** Bob Comfort; ***C:*** Maximo Munzi; ***M:*** Tim Truman.

A Good Man in Africa **1994 (R)** Bumbling low-level British diplomat gets caught up in the high-level political turmoil of a newly independent African state. Confusing plot has borderline incompetent blackmailed by corrupt politician into bribing respected doctor for local land rights. Wow, corrupt officials, ineffectual bureaucrats—go figure! Does to the British diplomatic corps what "A Fish Called Wanda" did to England's legal community, without the humor. Performances by Connery, Gossett and Lithgow almost make up for shortcomings in key areas such as writing and direction. Adapted from the novel by William Boyd. **95m/C VHS.** Colin Friels, Sean Connery, Louis Gossett Jr., John Lithgow, Joanne Whalley, Diana Rigg; ***D:*** Bruce Beresford; ***W:*** William Boyd; ***C:*** Andrzej Bartkowiak.

Good Morning *Ohayo* **1959** One of Ozu's first color efforts, "Good Morning" is a light social comedy revolving around two young Japanese boys who try to talk their parents into buying them one of those new-fangled television sets. Not likely, since the Dad feels that the boob tube will dull the senses of the Japanese youth...talk about your ESP. The kids feel that there's too much small talk going on. Ozu keeps the camera at kids' eye-level, emphasizing the sympathetic perspective of the children and giving a unique look to the film. Bold colors populate the screen and Ozu keeps the story whimsical while commenting on Japanese society (very much like Juzo Itami would years later). The characters are well-fleshed out and likable. **94m/C DVD.** *JP* Masahiko Shimazu, Koji Shigaragi, Chishu Ryu, Kuniko Miyake; ***D:*** Yasujiro Ozu; ***W:*** Yasujiro Ozu, Kogo Noda; ***C:*** Yushun Atsuta; ***M:*** Toshiro Mayuzumi.

Good Morning, Babylon *Good Morning Babilonia* **1987 (PG-13)** The Taviani brothers' first American film. Two young Italian brothers skilled in cathedral restoration come to America and find success building the sets to D.W. Griffith's "Intolerance." Eventually, their fortune is shattered by the onslaught of WWI. **113m/C VHS.** Vincent Spano, Joaquim de Almeida, Greta Scacchi, Charles Dance, Desiree Becker, Omero Antonutti, David Brandon; ***D:*** Paolo Taviani, Vittorio Taviani; ***W:*** Paolo Taviani, Vittorio Taviani, Tonino Guerra; ***M:*** Nicola Piovani.

Good Morning, Vietnam **1987 (R)** Based on the story of Saigon DJ Adrian Cronauer, although Williams' portrayal is reportedly a bit more extroverted than the personality of Cronauer. Williams spins great comic moments that may have been scripted but likely were not as a man with no history and for whom everything is manic radio material. The character ad-libs, swoops, and swerves, finally accepting adult responsibility. Engaging all the way with an outstanding period soundtrack. **121m/C VHS, DVD, 8mm.** Robin Williams, Forest Whitaker, Bruno Kirby, Richard Edson, Robert Wuhl, J.T. Walsh, Noble Willingham, Floyd Vivino, Tung Thanh Tran, Chintara Sukapatana, Richard Portnow, Juney Smith, Cu Ba Nguyen, Dan Stanton, Don Stanton; ***D:*** Barry Levinson; ***W:*** Mitch Markowitz; ***C:*** Peter Sova; ***M:*** Alex North. Golden Globes '88: Actor—Mus./Comedy (Williams).

The Good Mother ½ **1988 (R)** A divorced mother works at creating a fulfilling life for herself and her daughter, with an honest education for her daughter about every subject, including sex. But her ex-husband, unsure of how far this education is being taken, fights her for custody of their eight-year-old daughter after allegations of sexual misconduct against the mother's new lover. Based on Sue Miller's bestselling novel. Well acted, weakly edited and scripted. **104m/C VHS.** Diane Keaton, Liam Neeson, Jason Robards Jr., Ralph Bellamy, James Naughton, Teresa Wright, Asia Vieira, Joe Morton, Katey Sagal, Tracy Griffith, Charles Kimbrough, Matt Damon; ***D:*** Leonard Nimoy; ***W:*** Michael Bortman; ***C:*** David Watkin; ***M:*** Elmer Bernstein.

Good Neighbor Sam **1964** A married advertising executive (Lemmon) agrees to pose as a friend's husband in order for her to collect a multi-million-dollar inheritance. Complications ensue when his biggest client mistakes the friend for his actual wife and decides they're the perfect couple to promote his wholesome product—milk. **130m/C VHS.** Jack Lemmon, Romy Schneider, Dorothy Provine, Mike Connors, Edward G. Robinson, Joyce Jameson; ***D:*** David Swift.

Good News ½ **1947** A vintage Comden-Green musical about the love problems of a college football star, who will flunk out if he doesn't pass his French exams. Revamping of the 1927 Broadway smash features the unlikely sight of Lawford in a song-and-dance role. ♪Varsity Drag; He's a Lady's Man; Good News; Tait Song; Students Are We; Just Imagine; If You're Not Kissing Me; Football; I Feel Pessimistic. **92m/C VHS, DVD.** June Allyson, Peter Lawford, Joan McCracken, Mel Torme; ***D:*** Charles Walters; ***W:*** Betty Comden; ***C:*** Charles E. Schoenbaum; ***M:*** Hugh Martin, Ralph Blane, Roger Edens.

The Good Old Boys 🦴🦴½ **1995** Debuting as both director and co-writer, Jones also stars as aging cowpoke Hewey Calloway. The n'er-do-well Hewey makes a surprise visit to the hardscrabble 1906 Texas farm of brother Walter (Kinney), whose wife Eve (McDormand) is none too happy to see the wanderer. But Walter needs help, the local banker (Brimley) is about to foreclose, and Hewey is also taken with spirited schoolmarm Spring Renfro (Spacek, who also starred with Jones in "Coal-Miner's Daughter"). And even Hewey realizes that the 20th century is going to change his way of life forever. Easy-going drama with a fine cast. **118m/C VHS.** Tommy Lee Jones, Sissy Spacek, Terry Kinney, Frances McDormand, Wilford Brimley, Sam Shepard, Walter Olkewicz, Matt Damon, Bruce McGill, Park Overall, Richard Jones; ***D:*** Tommy Lee Jones; ***W:*** J.T. Allen, Tommy Lee Jones; ***C:*** Alan Caso; ***M:*** John McEuen.

Good Sam 🦴🦴 **1948** An incurable "Good Samaritan" finds himself in one jam after another as he tries too hard to help people. Lots of missed opportunities for laughs with McCrarey's mediocre direction. **116m/B VHS.** Gary Cooper, Ann Sheridan, Ray Collins, Edmund Lowe, Joan Lorring, Ruth Roman; ***D:*** Leo McCarey.

The Good Son 🦴🦴 **1993 (R)** In a grand departure from cute, Culkin tackles evil as a 13-year-old obsessed with death and other unseemly hobbies. During a stay with his uncle, Mark (Wood) watches as his cousin (Culkin) gets creepier and creepier, and tries to alert the family. But will they listen? Nooo—they choose to ignore the little warning signs like the doll hanging by a noose in Culkin's room. And then there's the untimely death of a sibling. Hmmm. Culkin isn't as bad as expected, but doesn't quite get all the way down to bone-chilling terror either. Original star Jesse Bradford was dropped when Papa Culkin threatened to pull Mac off "Home Alone 2" if he wasn't cast in the lead. **87m/C VHS.** Macaulay Culkin, Elijah Wood, Wendy Crewson, David Morse, Daniel Hugh-Kelly, Quinn Culkin; ***D:*** Joseph Ruben; ***W:*** Ian McEwan; ***C:*** John Lindley; ***M:*** Elmer Bernstein.

The Good, the Bad, and Huckleberry Hound **1988** Journeying out West to begin a ranch, Huckleberry Hound winds up becoming a sheriff in the small town of Two-Bit. Huckleberry stands up against a group of bully brothers who have been terrorizing the town. **94m/C VHS.** ***D:*** Ray Patterson; ***V:*** Daws Butler.

The Good, the Bad and the Ugly 🦴🦴🦴½ **1967** Leone's grandiloquent, shambling tribute to the American Western. Set during the Civil War, it follows the seemingly endless adventures of three dirtbags in search of a cache of Confederate gold buried in a nameless grave. Violent, exaggerated, beautifully crafted, it is the final and finest installment of the "Dollars" trilogy: a spaghetti Western chef d'oeuvre. **161m/C VHS, DVD, Wide.** *IT* Clint Eastwood, Eli Wallach, Lee Van Cleef, Chelo Alonso, Luigi Pistilli, Rada Rassimov, Livio Lorenzon, Mario Brega; ***D:*** Sergio Leone; ***W:*** Sergio Leone, Sergio Donati, Furio Scarpelli, Luciano Vincenzoni, Agenore Incrocci; ***C:*** Tonino Delli Colli; ***M:*** Ennio Morricone.

Good Times 🦴🦴½ **1967** Pop silliness as Sonny and Cher (playing themselves) are offered a movie deal by an eccentric tycoon (Sanders). Sonny thinks the script is terrible and dreams up various parts that he and Cher could play. Friedkin's directorial debut. **91m/C VHS, DVD.** Cher, Sonny Bono, George Sanders, Norman Alden, Edy Williams, China Lee, Larry Duran; ***D:*** William Friedkin; ***W:*** Tony Barrett; ***C:*** Robert Wyckoff; ***M:*** Sonny Bono.

The Good Wife 🦴🦴½ *The Umbrella Woman* **1986 (R)** A bored and sexually frustrated wife scandalizes her small Australian town by taking up with the new hotel barman. There's no denying Ward's sexuality, but overall the movie is too predictable. **97m/C VHS, DVD, Wide.** *AU* Rachel Ward, Bryan Brown, Sam Neill, Steven Vidler, Bruce Barry, Jennifer Claire; ***D:*** Ken Cameron; ***W:*** Peter Kenna; ***C:*** James Bartle; ***M:*** Cameron Allan.

Good Will Hunting 🦴🦴½ **1997 (R)** Good, if predictable, first effort from screenwriting actors Damon and Affleck. Troubled, young Will Hunting (Damon) is a janitor at MIT who also happens to be an unsung mathematical genius. This gift is discovered by big-shot Professor Lambeau (Skarsgard), who must vouch for Will with the parole board by giving him weekly math sessions and taking him to a therapist to work on his anger. Naturally, only the equally troubled shrink Sean Maguire (Williams) is willing to help Hunting get beyond his blue-collar roots. But Will resists the help—not sure that he wants to leave his neighborhood and best friends behind. The Damon/Williams scenes are affecting but the southie Boston accents offer an unexpected challenge. **126m/C VHS, DVD.** Matt Damon, Robin Williams, Ben Affleck, Stellan Skarsgard, Minnie Driver, Casey Affleck, Cole Hauser; ***D:*** Gus Van Sant; ***W:*** Matt Damon, Ben Affleck; ***C:*** Jean-Yves Escoffier; ***M:*** Danny Elfman. Oscars '97: Orig. Screenplay, Support. Actor (Williams); Golden Globes '98: Screenplay; Screen Actors Guild '97: Support. Actor (Williams); Broadcast Film Critics '97: Breakthrough Perf. (Damon), Orig. Screenplay.

Goodbye Again 🦴🦴½ *Aimez-Vous Brahms* **1961** A romantic drama based on the novel by Francoise Sagan. Bergman is a middle-aged interior decorator whose lover, Montand, has a roaming eye. She finds herself drawn to the son (Perkins) of a client and begins an affair—flattered by the young man's attentions. Montand is outraged and vows to change his ways and marry Bergman if she will give up the young man. A bit soapy, but a must for Bergman fans. **120m/B VHS.** Jessie Royce Landis, Ingrid Bergman, Anthony Perkins, Yves Montand, Diahann Carroll; ***D:*** Anatole Litvak; ***W:*** Samuel A. Taylor. Cannes '61: Actor (Perkins).

The Goodbye Bird 🦴🦴½ **1993 (G)** Frank is accused by his school principal of stealing her prized talking parrot. With the aid of a kindly veterinarian Frank tries to discover who the thief really is. **91m/C VHS.** Cindy Pickett, Concetta Tomei, Wayne Rogers, Christopher Pettiet; ***D:*** William Clark.

Goodbye Charlie 🦴🦴 **1964** Very much a product of its time with its swingin' sixties, playboy aura. Hollywood writer Charlie Sorel is murdered by film producer Leopold Sartori (Matthau) when he catches Charlie with his wife. But the playboy is reincarnated as a woman (Reynolds)—much to the confusion of the male Charlie's best friend, George (Curtis). And the female Charlie decides to see how the other half lives, loves, and gets revenge. Based on the play by George Axelrod. **117m/C VHS.** Debbie Reynolds, Tony Curtis, Pat Boone, Walter Matthau, Joanna Barnes, Ellen Burstyn, Laura Devon, Martin Gabel, Roger C. Carmel; ***D:*** Vincente Minnelli; ***W:*** Harry Kurnitz; ***C:*** Milton Krasner; ***M:*** Andre Previn.

Goodbye Columbus 🦴🦴🦴 **1969 (PG)** Philip Roth's novel about a young Jewish librarian who has an affair with the spoiled daughter of a nouveau riche family is brought to late-'60s life, and vindicated by superb performances all around. Benjamin and McGraw's first starring roles. **105m/C VHS.** Richard Benjamin, Ali MacGraw, Jack Klugman, Nan Martin, Jaclyn Smith; ***D:*** Larry Peerce; ***M:*** Charles Fox. Writers Guild '68: Adapt. Screenplay.

Goodbye Cruel World 🦴½ **1982 (R)** Black comedy about a suicidal TV anchorman who decides to spend his last day filming the relatives who drove him to the brink. **90m/C VHS.** Dick Shawn, Cynthia Sikes, Chuck "Porky" Mitchell; ***D:*** David Irving.

Goodbye Emmanuelle 🦴½ **1979 (R)** Follows the further adventures of Emmanuelle in her quest for sexual freedom and the excitement of forbidden pleasures. The second sequel to "Emmanuelle." **92m/C VHS.** Sylvia Kristel.

The Goodbye Girl 🦴🦴🦴 **1977 (PG)** Neil Simon's story of a former actress, her precocious nine-year-old daughter and the aspiring actor who moves in with them. The daughter serves as catalyst for the other two to fall in love. While Mason's character is fairly unsympathetic, Dreyfuss is great and Simon's dialogue witty. **110m/C VHS, DVD.** Richard Dreyfuss, Marsha Mason, Quinn Cummings, Barbara Rhoades, Marilyn Sokol; ***D:*** Herbert Ross; ***W:*** Neil Simon; ***M:*** Dave Grusin. Oscars '77: Actor (Dreyfuss); British Acad. '78: Actor (Dreyfuss); Golden Globes '78: Actor—Mus./Comedy (Dreyfuss), Actress—Mus./Comedy (Mason), Film—Mus./Comedy, Screenplay; L.A. Film Critics '77: Actor (Dreyfuss).

Goodbye Love 🦴½ **1934** Dull comedy about a group of ex-husbands who refuse to pay alimony and end up in jail. **65m/B VHS, DVD.** Charlie Ruggles, Verree Teasdale, Sidney Blackmer, Mayo Methot, Phyllis Barry, Ray Walker, John Kelly, Hale Grace, Luis Alberni; ***D:*** Herbert Ross.

Goodbye, Lover 🦴🦴 **1999 (R)** Sandra (Arquette) and Ben (Johnson) are hot 'n' heavy lovers. Jake (Mulrony) is husband to one and brother to the other. Peggy (Parker) has eyes for Ben and works with Jake. Since this is a contemporary noir comedy, there's plot twists, betrayal, blackmail, murder, a fortune in insurance money, and two cops (DeGeneres and McKinnon) trying to piece it all together. Overshoots comedy and ultimately lands in silly territory, but looks good doing it. Johnson comes out the best, kicking pic up a notch whenever he's on screen. DeGeneres (as the jaded cop) and McKinnon (the wide-eyed newbie) plod through the odd-couple schtick. **104m/C VHS, DVD.** Don Johnson, Patricia Arquette, Dermot Mulroney, Ellen DeGeneres, Mary-Louise Parker, Ray McKinnon, Alex Rocco, Andre Gregory, John Neville, Nina Siemaszko, David Brisbin, Lisa Eichhorn, George Furth, Barry Newman, Max Perlich, Frances Bay; ***D:*** Roland Joffe; ***W:*** Joel Cohen, Alec Sokolow, Ron Peer; ***C:*** Dante Spinotti; ***M:*** John Ottman.

Goodbye, Miss 4th of July 🦴🦴½ **1988** Inspired by the true story of the teenage daughter of Greek immigrants living in pre-WWI West Virginia, the prejudice they encounter, the relationship that begins between the family and an aging African-American ex-boxer, and the girl's efforts in the influenza epidemic. Based on the 1985 book by her brother. **89m/C VHS.** Richard Speight Jr., Roxana Zal, Louis Gossett Jr., Chris Sarandon, Chantal Contouri, Chynna Phillips, Mitchell Anderson, Conchata Ferrell, Ed Lauter; ***D:*** George Miller.

Goodbye, Mr. Chips 🦴🦴🦴½ **1939** An MGM classic, the sentimental rendering of the James Hilton novel about shy Latin professor Charles Chipping (Donat), who teaches in an English public school, marrying the vivacious Katherine (Garson) only to tragically lose her. He spends the rest of his life devoting himself to his students and becoming a school legend. Multi award-winning soaper featuring Garson's first screen appearance, which was Oscar nominated. Remade in 1969 as a fairly awful musical starring Peter O'Toole. **115m/B VHS, Wide.** Robert Donat, Greer Garson, Paul Henreid, John Mills, Terence (Terry) Kilburn; ***D:*** Sam Wood; ***W:*** R.C. Sherriff, Sidney Franklin, Claudine West, Eric Maschwitz; ***C:*** Frederick A. (Freddie) Young. Oscars '39: Actor (Donat).

Goodbye, Mr. Chips 🦴🦴 **1969** Ross debuted as director with this big-budget (but inferior musical re-make) of the classic James Hilton novel about a gentle teacher at an English all-boys private school and the woman who helps him demonstrate his compassion and overcome his shyness. O'Toole, although excellent, is categorically a non-singer, while Clark, a popular singer at the time ("Downtown"), musters very little talent in front of the camera. The plot is altered unnecessarily and updated to the WWII era for little reason; the music is thoroughly forgettable. ♪Fill The World With Love; Where Did My Childhood Go; London is London; And the Sky Smiled; When I Am Older; Walk Through the World; What Shall I Do with Today?; What a Lot of Flowers; Schooldays. **151m/C VHS, Wide.** Peter O'Toole, Petula Clark, Michael Redgrave, George Baker, Sian Phillips, Michael Bryant, Jack Hedley, Elspeth March, Herbert Ross; ***D:*** Herbert Ross; ***C:*** Oswald Morris; ***M:*** Leslie Bricusse, John Williams. Golden Globes '70: Actor—Mus./Comedy (O'Toole); Natl. Bd. of Review '69: Actor (O'Toole); Natl. Soc. Film Critics '69: Support. Actress (Phillips).

Goodbye, My Lady 🦴🦴 **1956** Based on the novel by James Street, this is a tear-jerking film about a young Mississippi farmboy who finds and cares for a special dog that he comes to love but eventually must give up. **95m/B VHS.** Brandon de Wilde, Walter Brennan, Sidney Poitier, Phil Harris, Louise Beavers; ***D:*** William A. Wellman.

Goodbye, New York 🦴🦴 **1985 (R)** A New York yuppie on a vacation finds herself penniless and stranded in Israel. She makes the best of the situation by joining a kibbutz and falling for a part-time soldier. Well, of course. **90m/C VHS.** *IS* Julie Hagerty, Amos Kollek, Shmuel Shilo; ***D:*** Amos Kollek; ***M:*** Michael Abene.

Goodbye, Norma Jean 🦴 **1975 (R)** Detailed and sleazy recreation of Marilyn Monroe's early years in Hollywood. Followed by "Goodnight, Sweet Marilyn." **95m/C VHS.** Misty Rowe, Terrence Locke, Patch MacKenzie; ***D:*** Larry Buchanan; ***M:*** Joe Beck.

The Goodbye People 🦴🦴½ **1983** Balsam is an elderly man who decides to reopen his Coney Island hot dog stand that folded 22 years earlier. Hirsch and Reed help him realize his impossible dream in this sweetly sentimental film. **104m/C VHS.** Judd Hirsch, Martin Balsam, Pamela Reed, Ron Silver; ***D:*** Herb Gardner; ***W:*** Herb Gardner.

Goodbye Pork Pie 🦴½ **1981 (R)** With the police on their trail, two young men speed on a 1000-mile journey in a small, brand-new, yellow stolen car. Remember: journey of thousand miles always begin in stolen car. **105m/C VHS.** *NZ* Tony Barry, Kelly Johnson; ***D:*** Geoff Murphy; ***C:*** Alun Bollinger.

Goodbye South, Goodbye 🦴🦴 *Nanguo Zaijian, Nanguo* **1996** Restless camera follows equally restless losers through Taiwan's sprawling suburbs. Kao (Kao) and his sidekick Flathead (Giong) are minor gangsters running gambling dens and various scams. A kickback scheme involving corrupt bureaucrats and cops goes awry, Flathead gets beaten, and retaliation is in order. Thin characters tend not to hold a viewer's interest. Taiwanese with subtitles. **116m/C VHS, DVD, Wide.** *JP TW* Jack Kao, Lim Giong, Kuei-ying Hsu, Annie Shizuka Inoh; ***D:*** Chien Hsiao Hou; ***W:*** Tien-wen Chu; ***C:*** Mark Lee Ping-Bin, Hwai-en Chen; ***M:*** Lim Giong.

Goodfellas 🦴🦴🦴🦴 **1990 (R)** Quintessential picture about "wiseguys," at turns both violent and funny. A young man grows up in the mob, works hard to advance himself through the ranks, and enjoys the life of the rich and violent, oblivious to the horror of which he is a part. Cocaine addiction and many wiseguy missteps ultimately unravel his climb to the top. Excellent performances (particularly Liotta and Pesci, with De Niro pitching in around the corners), with visionary cinematography and careful pacing. Watch for Scorsese's mom as Pesci's mom. Based on the life of Henry Hill, ex-mobster now in the Witness Protection Program. Adapted from the book by Nicholas Pileggi. **146m/C VHS, DVD, Wide.** Robert De Niro, Ray Liotta, Joe Pesci, Paul Sorvino, Lorraine Bracco, Frank Sivero, Mike Starr, Frank Vincent, Samuel L. Jackson, Tony Darrow, Chuck Low, Frank DiLeo, Christopher Serrone, Illeana Douglas, Debi Mazar, Michael Imperioli, Peter Onorati, Beau Starr, Angela Pietropinto, Joseph D'Onofrio, Jerry Vale, Henny Youngman, Catherine Scorsese; ***D:*** Martin Scorsese; ***W:*** Nicholas Pileggi, Martin Scorsese; ***C:*** Michael Ballhaus. Oscars '90: Support. Actor (Pesci); AFI '98: Top 100; British Acad. '90: Adapt. Screenplay, Director (Scorsese), Film; L.A. Film Critics '90: Cinematog., Director (Scorsese), Film, Support. Actor (Pesci), Support. Actress (Bracco); Natl. Bd. of Review '90: Support. Actor (Pesci), Natl. Film Reg. '00;; N.Y. Film Critics '90: Actor (De Niro), Director (Scorsese), Film; Natl. Soc. Film Critics '90: Director (Scorsese), Film.

Goodnight, Michelangelo 🦴🦴½ **1989 (R)** Funny, engaging and somewhat confusing story of the life of an Italian immigrant family as seen through the eyes of its youngest member, eight-year-old Michelangelo. Winner of the 1990 Best Comedy Award at the Greater Fort Lauderdale Film Festival. **91m/C VHS.** *IT* Lina Sastri, Kim Cattrall, Giancarlo Giannini, Daniel Desanto; *D:* Carlo Liconti; *W:* Carlo Liconti.

Goodnight, Mr. Tom 🦴🦴½ **1999** Tom Oakley (Thaw) is an elderly widower, living reclusively in rural England at the onset of WWII. When abused, nine-year-old Londoner Willie Beech (Robinson) is evacuated to the countryside with a number of other children, he winds up in Tom's care. Naturally, the curmudgeonly old man and the wary young boy develop a strong friendship, which is threatened when Willie's mother unexpectedly turns up. Based on the novel by Michelle Magorian. **90m/C VHS.** *GB* John Thaw, Nick Robinson; *D:* Jack Gold; *W:* Brian Finch.

Goodnight, Sweet Marilyn 🦴 **1989 (R)** Supposed "never-before-told" story of Marilyn Monroe's tragic death. According to this, her death was the result of pre-arranged "mercy-killing." Follow-up to director Buchanan's "Goodbye, Norma Jean" (1977) with Lane as the 1960s Marilyn intercut with scenes of Rowe from the first film as young Marilyn. You'd be better off leaving "Sweet Marilyn" to rest in peace. **100m/C VHS.** Paula Lane, Jeremy Slate, Misty Rowe; *D:* Larry Buchanan.

Goof Balls woof! **1987 (R)** The tourist denizens of a island golf resort putt and cavort about, and golf isn't all that's on their minds. **87m/C VHS.** Ben Gordon, Laura Robinson.

A Goofy Movie 🦴🦴½ **1994 (G)** The dog finally gets his day. After 63 years of supporting roles, Disney's Goofy stars in his own movie along with his teenage son Max. When it comes to Goofy's attention that his rock music obsessed son is goofing off in school, Goofy decides to spend some quality time with Max via a road trip through the country. Their journey is plagued with mishaps, but through the obstacles, father and son bridge their generational gap and bond in the true Disney sense. A modest animated treat with six new songs that may induce some finger snapping and toe tapping. **78m/C VHS, DVD.** *D:* Kevin Lima; *W:* Jymn Magon, Brian Pimental, Chris Matheson; *V:* Bill Farmer, Jason Marsden, Jim (Jonah) Cummings, Kellie Martin, Rob Paulsen, Wallace Shawn, Florence Stanley, Jo Anne Worley.

Goon Movie 🦴🦴 *Stand Easy* **1953** The cast of "The Goon Show," Britain's popular radio comedy series, perform some of their best routines in this, their only film appearance. **75m/B VHS.** Peter Sellers, Spike Milligan, Harry Secombe.

The Goonies 🦴🦴½ **1985 (PG)** Two brothers who are about to lose their house conveniently find a treasure map. They pick up a couple of friends and head for the "X." If they can recover the treasure without getting caught by the bad guys, then all will be saved. Steven Spielberg produced this high-energy action fantasy for kids of all ages. **114m/C VHS, DVD, Wide.** Sean Astin, Josh Brolin, Jeff B. Cohen, Corey Feldman, Martha Plimpton, John Matuszak, Robert Davi, Anne Ramsey, Mary Ellen Trainor, Jonathan Ke Quan, Kerri Green, Joe Pantoliano; *D:* Richard Donner; *W:* Chris Columbus, Steven Spielberg; *C:* Nick McLean; *M:* Dave Grusin.

Gor 🦴½ **1988 (PG)** Sword and sorcery: a magic ring sends a meek college professor to "Gor," a faraway world in which survival goes to the fittest and the most brutal. Followed by "Outlaw of Gor." **95m/C VHS.** Urbano Barberini, Rebecca Ferratti, Jack Palance, Paul Smith, Oliver Reed; *D:* Fritz Kiersch; *W:* R.J. Marx.

Gorath 🦴🦴 *Yosei Gorasu* **1964** The world's top scientists are racing to stop a giant meteor from destroying the Earth. **77m/C VHS.** *JP D:* Inoshiro Honda.

Gordon's War 🦴🦴 **1973 (R)** When a Vietnam vet returns to his Harlem home, he finds his wife overdosing on the drugs that have infiltrated his neighborhood. He leads a vigilante group in an attempt to clean up the area, which makes for a lot of action; however, there's also an excessive amount of violence. **89m/C VHS.** Paul Winfield, Carl Lee, David Downing, Tony King, Grace Jones; *D:* Ossie Davis; *M:* Angelo Badalamenti.

Gordy 🦴½ **1995 (G)** Perky talking porker Gordy manages to escape his fate as future bacon and find a couple of equally perky kids—motherless country-song-singing Jinnie Sue (Young) and lonely rich boy Hanky (Roescher), whom the pig manages to save from drowning. Plot scarcely matters and all the 25 piggies who performed as Gordy generally manage to outshine the humans, though country singer Stone (in his film debut) displays an easy charm. **90m/C VHS.** Doug Stone, Michael Roescher, Kristy Young, James Donadio, Deborah Hobart, Tom Lester, Ted Manson; *D:* Mark Lewis; *W:* Leslie Stevens; *C:* Richard Michalak; *M:* Tom Bahler; *V:* Justin Garms.

The Gore-Gore Girls 🦴 *Blood Orgy* **1972** Splatter horror director Lewis' final film follows a detective's search for a madman who's been mutilating and killing beautiful young bar dancers. **84m/C VHS, DVD.** Frank Kress, Amy Farrel, Hedda Lubin, Henny Youngman, Russ Badger, Nora Alexis, Phil Laurensen, Frank Rice, Jackie Kroeger, Corlee Bew, Emily Mason, Lena Bousman, Ray Sager; *D:* Herschell Gordon Lewis; *W:* Alan J. Dachman; *C:* Alex Ameri.

Gore-Met Zombie Chef from Hell woof! **1987** A demon/vampire opens up a seafood restaurant and slaughters his customers. Deliberately campy and extremely graphic. **90m/C VHS.** Theo Depuay, Kelley Kunicki, C.W. Casey, Alan Marx, Michael O'Neill; *D:* Don Swan; *W:* Don Swan, Jeff Baughn, William Highsmith; *C:* Don Swan; *M:* Don Swan, Steve Cunningham, Dan Smith.

Gore Vidal's Billy the Kid 🦴🦴½ **1989** An unusual treatment of the William Bonney legend in which the Kid is merely a misunderstood teenager caught up in the midst of the brutal range wars. **100m/C VHS.** Val Kilmer, Duncan Regehr, Wilford Brimley, Julie Carmen, Michael Parks, Rene Auberjonois, Albert Salmi; *D:* William A. Graham. **CABLE**

Gore Vidal's Lincoln 🦴🦴½ *Lincoln* **1988** Waterston is a low-key but sympathetic Lincoln, with Moore as his high-strung wife Mary, in this made for TV adaptation of the Vidal best-seller. Follows the couple from their first day in Washington, through the Civil War, family tragedies, up to the day of the President's burial. **190m/C VHS.** Sam Waterston, Mary Tyler Moore, John Houseman, Richard Mulligan, John McMartin, Ruby Dee, Cleavon Little, Jeffrey DeMunn, James Gammon, Deborah Adair, Robin Gammell; *D:* Lamont Johnson; *W:* Ernest Kinoy; *M:* Ernest Gold. **TV**

Gorgeous 🦴🦴½ *Glass Bottle; Bor Lei Jun* **1999 (PG-13)** Ah Bu (Shu), a young woman from a small Taiwan fishing village, finds a glass bottle with a romantic message inside. An adventurous spirit, she travels to Hong Kong to find the author of the note. Albert (Leung Chui Wai), the missive's writer, turns out to be a gay make-up artist but Ah Bu also meets millionaire businessman, C.N. Chan (Chan), who manages to fall for Ah Bu while battling corporate rival, Yi Lung (Jen). There may be romance amongst the action but Jackie is more than up to the challenge. Cantonese with subtitles. **99m/C VHS, DVD, Wide.** *HK* Jackie Chan, Tony Leung Chiu-Wai, Qi Shu, Hsein-Chi Jen; *D:* Vincent Kok; *W:* Vincent Kok; *C:* Man Po Cheung; *M:* Dang-Yi Wong.

The Gorgeous Hussy 🦴 **1936** Crawford stars in this fictionalized biography of Peggy Eaton, Andrew Jackson's notorious belle, who disgraces herself and those around her. A star-studded cast complete with beautiful costumes isn't enough to save this overly long and dull picture. **102m/B VHS.** Joan Crawford, Robert Taylor, Lionel Barrymore, Melvyn Douglas, James Stewart, Franchot Tone, Louis Calhern; *D:* Clarence Brown; *C:* George J. Folsey.

Gorgo 🦴🦴½ **1961** An undersea explosion off the coast of Ireland brings to the surface a prehistoric sea monster, which is captured and brought to a London circus. Its irate mother appears looking for her baby, creating havoc in her wake. **76m/C VHS, DVD, Wide.** *GB* Bill Travers, William Sylvester, Vincent Winter, Bruce Seton, Christopher Rhodes; *D:* Eugene Lourie; *W:* Robert L. Richards, Daniel James; *C:* Frederick A. (Freddie) Young; *M:* Angelo Francesco Lavagnino.

The Gorgon 🦴🦴 **1964** In pre-WWI Germany, the lovely assistant to a mad brain surgeon moonlights as a snake-haired gorgon, turning men to stone. A professor arrives in the village to investigate, only to become another victim. **83m/C VHS.** *GB* Peter Cushing, Christopher Lee, Richard Pasco, Barbara Shelley, Michael Goodliffe, Patrick Troughton, Jack Watson, Jeremy Longhurst, Toni Gilpin, Prudence Hyman; *D:* Terence Fisher; *W:* John Gilling; *C:* Michael Reed; *M:* James Bernard.

The Gorilla 🦴🦴 **1939** Bumbling Ritzes are hired to protect a country gentleman receiving threats from a killer. Lugosi portrays the menacing butler. Derived from the play by Ralph Spence. **67m/B VHS.** Al Ritz, Harry Ritz, Jimmy Ritz, Anita Louise, Patsy Kelly, Lionel Atwill, Bela Lugosi; *D:* Allan Dwan.

Gorilla 🦴🦴 **1956** A rampaging gorilla is sought by the local game warden and a journalist researching the natives. Filmed on location in the Belgian Congo. **79m/B VHS.** *SW* Gio Petre, Georges Galley; *D:* Sven Nykvist, Lar Henrik Ottoson.

Gorillas in the Mist 🦴🦴🦴 **1988 (PG-13)** The life of Dian Fossey, animal rights activist and world-renowned expert on the African gorilla, from her pioneering contact with mountain gorillas to her murder at the hands of poachers. Weaver is totally appropriate as the increasingly obsessed Fossey, but the character moves away from us, just as we need to see and understand more about her. Excellent special effects. **117m/C VHS, DVD, Wide.** Sigourney Weaver, Bryan Brown, Julie Harris, Iain Cuthbertson, John Omirah Miluwi, Constantin Alexandrov, Waigwa Wachira; *D:* Michael Apted; *W:* Anna Hamilton Phelan; *C:* John Seale; *M:* Maurice Jarre. Golden Globes '88: Actress—Drama (Weaver); Golden Globes '89: Score.

Gorky Park 🦴🦴🦴 **1983 (R)** Adaptation of Martin Cruz Smith's bestseller. Three strange, faceless corpses are found in Moscow's Gorky Park. There are no clues for the Russian police captain investigating the incident. He makes the solution to this crime his personal crusade, and finds himself caught in a web of political intrigue. Excellent police procedure yarn. **127m/C VHS, DVD, Wide.** William Hurt, Lee Marvin, Brian Dennehy, Joanna Pacula; *D:* Michael Apted; *W:* Dennis Potter; *C:* Ralf Bode; *M:* James Horner.

Gorp woof! **1980 (R)** Sex, fun, and lewd, sophomoric humor reign at a summer camp. For the bored and witless or those who aspire. **90m/C VHS.** Dennis Quaid, Rosanna Arquette, Michael Lembeck, Philip Casnoff, Frank Drescher; *D:* Joseph Ruben.

Gosford Park 🦴🦴🦴 **2001 (R)** Altman's ensemble take on a British country house murder mystery set in 1932 that showcases both the upstairs and downstairs inhabitants. Actually, the murder is given short shrift in this look at the manners and mores of the snobs and their servants. Sir William McCordle (Gambon), a self-made man, is giving a weekend shooting party whose guests seem mainly to be the grasping relatives of his cold, aristocratic wife, Lady Sylvia (Scott Thomas). He's the murder victim but nobody really seems to care much (he's not a very nice guy). There's even a couple of American interlopers—movie producer Morris Weissman (Balaban) and his "valet" Henry (Phillippe). Keeping who's who straight is confusing and the pacing is sedate but the cinematography is gorgeous and the cast are all-pro. **137m/C VHS, DVD.** *GB* Michael Gambon, Kristin Scott Thomas, Maggie Smith, Helen Mirren, Eileen Atkins, Alan Bates, Bob Balaban, Ryan Phillippe, Kelly Macdonald, Clive Owen, Jeremy Northam, Emily Watson, Richard E. Grant, Charles Dance, Geraldine Somerville, Tom Hollander, James Wilby, Sophie Thompson, Stephen Fry, Ron Webster, Camilla Rutherford, Claudie Blakley, Natasha Wightman, Jeremy Swift, Teresa Churcher; *D:* Robert Altman; *W:* Julian Fellowes; *C:* Andrew Dunn; *M:* Patrick Doyle. Oscars '01: Orig. Screenplay; British Acad. '01: Costume Des., Film; Golden Globes '02: Director (Altman); N.Y. Film Critics '01: Director (Altman), Screenplay, Support. Actress (Mirren); Natl. Soc. Film Critics '01: Director (Altman), Screenplay, Support. Actress (Mirren); Screen Actors Guild '01: Support. Actress (Mirren); Screen Actors Guild '03: Cast; Writers Guild '01: Orig. Screenplay; Broadcast Film Critics '01: Cast.

Gospa 🦴🦴½ **1994 (PG)** Based on the true story of Father Jozo Zovko (Sheen), who was put on trial for treason by the communist government in Yugoslavia in 1981 when he protected six Croatian children who repeatedly claimed that they saw visions of the Virgin Mary. Somewhat ponderous but well-meaning story that also suffers from a plethora of accents. "Gospa" means "Our Lady" in Croatian. **121m/C VHS.** Paul Guilfoyle, Martin Sheen, Michael York, Morgan Fairchild, Frank Finlay; *D:* Jakov Sedlar; *W:* Ivan Aralica, Paul Gronseth; *C:* Vjekoslav Vrdoljak; *M:* Nona Hendryx.

The Gospel According to St. Matthew 🦴🦴🦴🦴 *Il Vangelo Secondo Matteo; L'Evangile Selon Saint-Matthieu* **1964** Perhaps Pasolini's greatest film, retelling the story of Christ in gritty, neo-realistic tones and portraying the man less as a divine presence than as a political revolutionary. The yardstick by which all Jesus-films are to be measured. In Italian with English subtitles or dubbed. **142m/B VHS, DVD, 8mm, Wide.** *IT* Enrique Irazoqui, Susanna Pasolini, Margherita Caruso, Marcello Morante, Mario Socrate; *D:* Pier Paolo Pasolini; *W:* Pier Paolo Pasolini; *C:* Tonino Delli Colli; *M:* Luis Bacalov.

The Gospel According to Vic 🦴🦴 *Heavenly Pursuits* **1987 (PG-13)** A Scottish comedy about a skeptical teacher at a remedial school, who, having survived miraculously from a fall, is taken for proof of the sainthood of the school's patron namesake. **92m/C VHS.** *GB* Tom Conti, Helen Mirren; *D:* Charles Gormley; *C:* Michael Coulter.

Gossip 🦴🦴 **1999 (R)** Intriguing premise goes over-the-top. Bored rich boy Derrick (Marsden) share his pad with fellow college students Cathy (Headey) and Travis (Reedus). They all take a class where the prof (Bogosian) rants about the blurring of gossip and news. Then Derrick sees campus ice queen Naomi (Hudson) passed out a party with her jock boyfriend Beau (Jackson). So Derrick persuades his pals that they should all spread a rumor that Naomi did the wild thing with Beau and see how the slander takes on a life of its own. Only what no one anticipates is that Naomi comes to believe she's been raped and Beau gets arrested. **91m/C VHS, DVD.** James Marsden, Lena Headey, Norman Reedus, Kate Hudson, Joshua Jackson, Marisa Coughlan, Edward James Olmos, Sharon Lawrence, Eric Bogosian; *D:* Davis Guggenheim; *W:* Gregory Poirier, Theresa Rebeck; *C:* Andrzej Bartkowiak; *M:* Graeme Revell.

Gotcha! 🦴🦴½ **1985 (PG-13)** The mock assassination game "Gotcha!" abounds on the college campus and sophomore Edwards is one of the best. What he doesn't know is that his "assassination" skills are about to take on new meaning when he meets up with a female Czech graduate student who is really an international spy. **97m/C VHS.** Anthony Edwards, Linda Fiorentino, Alex Rocco, Nick Corri, Marla Adams, Klaus Loewitsch, Christopher Rydell; *D:* Jeff Kanew; *W:* Dan Gordon; *M:* Bill Conti.

Gotham 🦴🦴🦴 **1988** A wealthy financier hires private-eye Jones to track down beautiful wife Madsen. It seems that she keeps dunning her husband for money. Sounds easy enough to Jones until he learns that she has been dead for some time. Mystery ventures into the afterlife and back as it twists its way to its surprise ending. Intriguing throwback to '40s detective flicks. **100m/C VHS.** Tommy Lee Jones, Virginia Madsen, Colin Bruce, Kevin Jarre, Denise Stephenson, Frederic Forrest; ***D:*** Lloyd Fonvielle; ***C:*** Michael Chapman; ***M:*** George S. Clinton. **TV**

Gothic 🦴🦴🦴 **1987 (R)** Mary Shelley (Richardson), Lord Byron (Byrne), Percy Bysshe Shelley (Sands), Claire Clairmont (Cyr), and Dr. John Polidori (Spall) spend the night of June 16, 1816 in a Swiss villa telling each other ghost stories and experimenting with laudanum and sexual partner combinations. The dreams and realizations of the night will color their lives ever after. Interesting premise, well-carried out, although burdened by director Russell's typical excesses. **87m/C VHS, DVD.** Julian Sands, Gabriel Byrne, Timothy Spall, Natasha Richardson, Myriam Cyr; ***D:*** Ken Russell; ***W:*** Stephen Volk; ***C:*** Mike Southon; ***M:*** Thomas Dolby.

Gotti 🦴🦴½ **1996 (R)** Follows the career of the New York mobster known as the "Teflon Don." Gotti's (Assante) mentor is Neil Dellacroce (Quinn), underboss to the aging head of the Gambino crime family. When Gambino (Lawrence) dies, Gotti is incensed that Paul Castellano (Sarafian) is named as family successor and eventually has him killed. He then grabs power (and lots of tabloid headlines), manages to beat his first federal racketeering rap, but is brought down with the aid of his own underboss, Sammy the Bull (Forsythe), whom the feds get into court. **118m/C VHS, DVD.** Dominic Chianese, Armand Assante, William Forsythe, Anthony Quinn, Richard Sarafian, Vincent Pastore, Robert Miranda, Frank Vincent, Marc Lawrence, Al Waxman, Alberta Watson, Silvio Oliviero, Nigel Bennett; ***D:*** Robert Harmon; ***W:*** Steve Shagan; ***C:*** Alar Kivilo; ***M:*** Mark Isham. **CABLE**

The Governess 🦴🦴½ **1998 (R)** Rosina da Silva (Driver) is a young Jewish woman living in 1840s London. After her doting father dies, she changes her name to Mary Blackchurch in order to pass herself off as a Gentile and secure a position as a governess. Rosina then gets a job with the Cavendish family in remote Scotland, with her charges being randy teenager Henry (Rhys Meyers) and spoiled brat Clementina (Hoath). Her free-spirit entrances stodgy father Charles (Wilkinson), whom she aids in his obsession with the new art of photography. Where there's a dark room and chemistry, more than photos are bound to develop; and soon Mr. Cavendish comes up with a fixation of his own. Starts as a depiction of a woman adapting to different surroundings, but ends up like a history of the first girlie photos. In the end, her Jewishness isn't that big of a deal, leaving that portion of the story a dead end. **114m/C VHS, DVD.** Minnie Driver, Tom Wilkinson, Harriet Walter, Florence Hoath, Jonathan Rhys Meyers, Arlene Cockburn, Emma Bird, Adam Levy, Bruce Meyers; ***D:*** Sandra Goldbacher; ***W:*** Sandra Goldbacher; ***C:*** Ashley Rowe; ***M:*** Ed Shearmur.

Government Agents vs. Phantom Legion **1951** Agent Hal Duncan must stop an evil group who is stealing uranium shipments from under the government's nose. Edited from 12 episodes of the original serial on two cassettes. **167m/B VHS.** Walter Reed, Mary Ellen Kay, Dick Curtis, John Pickard.

Goya in Bordeaux 🦴🦴 **1999 (R)** On the eve of his death at age 82 in 1828, Spanish artist Fracisco De Goya Lucientes (Rabal), living in political exile in France, remembers the wild creative days of his youth, particularly his passionate affair with the Duchess of Alba (Verdu), his struggles as a court painter to King Charles of Spain, and the deafness that afflicted him from the age of 46. This is a lavish production, filled with sumptuous sets and costumes. It's also a fairly standard bio-pic that settles back on cliches in the second half. **105m/C VHS, DVD, Wide.** *SP IT* Francesco Rabal, Jose Coronado, Maribel Verdu, Daphne Fernandez, Eulalia Ramon; ***D:*** Carlos Saura; ***W:*** Carlos Saura; ***C:*** Vittorio Storaro; ***M:*** Roque Banos.

Grace & Glorie 🦴🦴½ **1998** Somewhat sappy and predictable story adapted from the play by Tom Ziegler. Aging Grace (Rowlands) is fiercely independent and resents having to have help in her country home as she recovers from a broken hip. But help she gets—in the form of ex-New Yorker turned hospice volunteer Glorie (Lane). Naturally, the younger woman has some hurts of her own to deal with and Grace decides to help her. **98m/C VHS.** Gena Rowlands, Diane Lane, Neal McDonough, Chris Beetem; ***D:*** Arthur Allan Seidelman; ***W:*** Grace McKeaney; ***C:*** Mike Fash; ***M:*** J.A.C. Redford. **TV**

The Grace Kelly Story 🦴🦴½ **1983** Ladd stars as the beautiful Philadelphia society girl who became an Oscar-winning actress and a seemingly fairy tale princess when she leaves Hollywood behind to marry Prince Rainier of Monaco. Standard TV bio but Ladd does look the part. **104m/C VHS.** Cheryl Ladd, Diane Ladd, Lloyd Bridges, Ian McShane, Alejandro Rey, William Schallert, Marta DuBois, Salome Jens, Edith Fellows; ***D:*** Anthony Page; ***W:*** Cynthia Mandelberg.

Grace of My Heart 🦴🦴½ **1996 (R)** Edna Buxton (Douglas), from a rich Philadelphia family, wins a song contest and winds up in New York at Manhattan's Brill Building, pop music's '60s song factory, where she's transformed into Denise Waverly and told to write the music—not sing it. She pens a lot of hits, winds up in hippie Malibu, and finally gets the courage to record her own concept album (think Carole King's "Tapestry"). Along the way there's a succession of wrong men and heartbreak before her independent triumph. Douglas does a fine job (her singing's dubbed by Kristen Vigard) but last minute melodrama turns this into typical showbiz kitsch. **116m/C VHS, DVD, Wide.** Illeana Douglas, John Turturro, Matt Dillon, Eric Stoltz, Bruce Davison, Patsy Kensit, Bridget Fonda, Jennifer Leigh Warren, Chris Isaak; ***D:*** Allison Anders; ***W:*** Allison Anders; ***C:*** Jean-Yves Escoffier; ***M:*** Larry Klein; ***V:*** Peter Fonda.

Grace Quigley 🦴½ *The Ultimate Solution of Grace Quigley* **1984 (PG)** An elderly woman, tired of life, hires a hitman to kill her. Instead they go into business together, bumping off other elderly folk who decide they'd rather be dead. Notoriously inept black comedy noted for being the career embarrassment for both of its stars. **87m/C VHS.** Katharine Hepburn, Nick Nolte, Walter Abel, Chip Zien, Elizabeth Wilson, Kit Le Fever, William Duell, Jill Eikenberry; ***D:*** Anthony Harvey; ***M:*** John Addison.

Grad Night 🦴 **1981 (R)** The anticipation for graduation in a small town high school brings surprises no one could have predicted, unless they've seen all the other typical adolescent films. **85m/C VHS.** Joey Johnson, Suzanna Fagan, Barry Stolze, Sam Whipple, Caroline Bates; ***D:*** John Tenorio; ***C:*** Arledge Armenaki.

The Graduate 🦴🦴🦴🦴 **1967 (PG)** Famous, influential slice of comic Americana stars Hoffman as Benjamin Braddock, a shy, aimless college graduate who, without any idea of responsibility or ambition, wanders from a sexual liaison with a married woman (the infamous Mrs. Robinson) to pursuit of her engaged daughter. His pursuit of Elaine right to her wedding has become a film classic. Extremely popular and almost solely responsible for establishing both Hoffman and director Nichols. The career advice given to Benjamin, "plastics," became a catchword for the era. Watch for Dreyfuss in the Berkeley rooming house, Farrell in the hotel lobby, and screenwriter Henry as the desk clerk. Based on the novel by Charles Webb. **106m/C VHS, DVD, 8mm, Wide.** Dustin Hoffman, Anne Bancroft, Katharine Ross, Murray Hamilton, Brian Avery, Marion Lorne, Alice Ghostley, William Daniels, Elizabeth Wilson, Norman Fell, Buck Henry, Richard Dreyfuss, Mike Farrell; ***D:*** Mike Nichols; ***W:*** Buck Henry, Calder Willingham; ***C:*** Robert L. Surtees; ***M:*** Paul Simon, Art Garfunkel, Dave Grusin. Oscars '67: Director (Nichols); AFI '98: Top 100; British Acad. '68: Director (Nichols), Film, Screenplay; Directors Guild '67: Director (Nichols); Golden Globes '68: Actress—Mus./Comedy (Bancroft), Director (Nichols), Film—Mus./Comedy, Natl. Film Reg. '96;; N.Y. Film Critics '67: Director (Nichols).

Graduation Day 🦴 **1981 (R)** Another teen slasher about the systematic murder of members of a high school track team. Notable mainly for brief appearance by Vanna White. **85m/C VHS.** Christopher George, Patch MacKenzie, E. Danny Murphy, Vanna White; ***D:*** Herb Freed.

Graffiti Bridge 🦴½ **1990 (PG-13)** Prince preaches love instead of sex and the result is boring. The Lavender One is a Minneapolis nightclub owner who battles with Day over the love of a beautiful woman. Chauvinistic attitudes toward women abound, but the females in the film don't seem to mind. Which must mean they were "acting." Visually interesting, although not as experimental as "Purple Rain." Music made Top Ten. **90m/C VHS.** Prince, Morris Day, Jerome Benton, Jill Jones, Mavis Staples, George Clinton, Ingrid Chavez; ***D:*** Prince; ***W:*** Prince; ***C:*** Bill Butler.

Grain of Sand 🦴🦴🦴 **1984** Based on a true story, an understated French drama about a troubled woman searching her past, and her home town in Corsica, for the man of her dreams. Directorial debut of Meffre. In French with English subtitles. **90m/C VHS.** *FR* Delphine Seyrig, Genevieve Fontanel, Coralie Seyrig, Michel Aumont; ***D:*** Pomme Meffre.

Grambling's White Tiger 🦴🦴½ **1981** The true story of Jim Gregory, the first white man to play on Grambling College's all-black football team. Jenner's a little too old, but Belafonte, in his TV acting debut, is fine as legendary coach Eddie Robinson. Based on book by Bruce Behrenberg. **98m/C VHS, DVD.** Bruce Jenner, Harry Belafonte, LeVar Burton, Ray Vitte, Byron Stewart; ***D:*** Georg Stanford Brown; ***M:*** John D'Andrea. **TV**

Grand Canyon 🦴🦴🦴 **1991 (R)** Diverse group of characters is thrown together through chance encounters while coping with urban chaos in L.A. The main focus is the growing friendship between an immigration lawyer (Kline) and a tow-truck driver (Glover) who meet when Kline's car breaks down in a crime-ridden neighborhood. First-rate performances by the cast make up for numerous moral messages thrown at viewers with the subtlety of a brick. Sometimes funny, sometimes preachy became more relevant in light of the violence that exploded in L.A. during the summer of '92. **134m/C VHS, DVD, Wide.** Danny Glover, Kevin Kline, Steve Martin, Mary McDonnell, Mary-Louise Parker, Alfre Woodard, Jeremy Sisto, Tina Lifford, Patrick Malone, Mary Ellen Trainor; ***D:*** Lawrence Kasdan; ***W:*** Lawrence Kasdan, Meg Kasdan; ***C:*** Owen Roizman; ***M:*** James Newton Howard.

Grand Canyon Trail 🦴½ **1948** Our hero is the owner of a played-out silver mine who is the target of an unscrupulous engineer who thinks there's silver to be found if you know where to look. The first appearance of the Riders of the Purple Sage, who replaced the Sons of the Pioneers. **68m/B VHS.** Roy Rogers, Andy Devine, Charles Coleman, Jane Frazee, Robert "Bob" Livingston; ***D:*** William Witney.

The Grand Duchess and the Waiter 🦴🦴🦴 **1926** Menjou is a French millionaire who disguises himself as a waiter in order to enter the service of a grand duchess with whom he has fallen in love. **70m/B VHS.** Adolphe Menjou, Florence Vidor, Lawrence Grant; ***D:*** Malcolm St. Clair.

The Grand Duel 🦴🦴 **1973** More spaghetti thrills as Lee plays a mysterious gunman who also acts as protector of a young ruffian falsely accused of murder. **?m/C VHS.** *IT* Lee Van Cleef, Peter O'Brien, Jess Hahn, Horst Frank.

Grand Hotel 🦴🦴🦴½ **1932** A star-filled cast is brought together by unusual circumstances at Berlin's Grand Hotel and their lives become hopelessly intertwined over a 24 hour period. Adapted (and given the red-carpet treatment) from a Vicki Baum novel; notable mostly for Garbo's world-weary ballerina. Time has taken its toll on the concept and treatment, but still an interesting star vehicle. **112m/B VHS.** Greta Garbo, John Barrymore, Joan Crawford, Lewis Stone, Wallace Beery, Jean Hersholt, Lionel Barrymore; ***D:*** Edmund Goulding; ***C:*** William H. Daniels. Oscars '32: Picture.

Grand Illusion 🦴🦴🦴🦴 *La Grande Illusion* **1937** Unshakably classic anti-war film by Renoir, in which French prisoners of war attempt to escape from their German captors during WWI. An indictment of the way Old World, aristocratic nobility was brought to modern bloodshed in the Great War. Renoir's optimism remains relentless, but was easier to believe in before WWII. In French, with English subtitles. **111m/B VHS, DVD.** *FR* Jean Gabin, Erich von Stroheim, Pierre Fresnay, Marcel Dalio, Julien Carette, Gaston Modot, Jean Daste, Dita Parlo, Georges Peclet, Werner Florian, Sylvain Itkine, Jacques Becker; ***D:*** Jean Renoir; ***W:*** Jean Renoir, Charles Spaak; ***C:*** Christian Matras; ***M:*** Joseph Kosma. N.Y. Film Critics '38: Foreign Film.

Grand Isle 🦴🦴½ **1992** At the turn of the century Grand Isle is the place Louisiana gentry leisurely spend their summers. This is where Edna Pontellier (McGillis), the wife of a rich stockbroker, meets sensitive Creole artist Robert LeBrun (Pasdar). Robert gives Edna all the attention sorely lacking in her marriage and they fall in love. However, Edna's attempts to liberate herself from the strictures of society lead her to tragedy. Based on "The Awakening" by Kate Chopin. **94m/C VHS.** Kelly McGillis, Adrian Pasdar, Julian Sands, Jon (John) DeVries, Glenne Headly, Anthony De Sando, Ellen Burstyn; ***D:*** Mary Lambert; ***W:*** Hesper Anderson; ***C:*** Toyomichi Kurita. **CABLE**

Grand Larceny 🦴🦴 **1992** The daughter of a millionaire/thief has to prove that she can take over the family "business." Lots of action and stunts. **95m/C VHS.** Marilu Henner, Omar Sharif, Ian McShane, Louis Jourdan; ***D:*** Jeannot Szwarc.

Grand Prix 🦴🦴 **1966** A big-budget look at the world of Grand Prix auto racing, as four top competitors circle the world's most famous racing circuits. Strictly for those who like cars racing round and round; nothing much happens off the track. **161m/C VHS, Wide.** James Garner, Eva Marie Saint, Yves Montand, Toshiro Mifune, Brian Bedford; ***D:*** John Frankenheimer; ***C:*** Lionel Lindon; ***M:*** Maurice Jarre. Oscars '66: Film Editing, Sound, Sound FX Editing.

Grand Theft Auto 🦴🦴 **1977 (PG)** In Howard's initial directorial effort, a young couple elopes to Las Vegas in a Rolls Royce owned by the bride's father. The father, totally against the marriage and angered by the stolen Rolls, offers a reward for their safe return and a cross-country race ensues. **84m/C VHS, DVD.** Ron Howard, Nancy Morgan, Marion Ross, Barry Cahill, Clint Howard, Elizabeth Rogers, Paul Bartel, Rance Howard; ***D:*** Ron Howard; ***W:*** Ron Howard, Rance Howard; ***C:*** Gary Graver; ***M:*** Peter Ivers.

Grand Tour: Disaster in Time 🦴🦴 **1992 (PG-13)** Greenglen is a quiet, small Midwestern town, until it is visited by a sinister group of time-traveling aliens. Daniels plays a widowed innkeeper who must save the town from destruction and save his daughter from being kidnapped by the fiends. **98m/C VHS.** Jeff Daniels, Ariana Richards, Emilia Crow, Jim Haynie, Nicholas Guest, Marilyn Lightstone, George Murdock; ***D:*** David N. Twohy; ***W:*** David N. Twohy. **CABLE**

The Grandfather 🦴🦴 *El Abuelo* **1998 (PG)** Frail and nearly blind, old Count Albrit (Fernan-Gomez) returns to Spain from Peru, having lost the family's money. While he was away, the Count's only son died and from his belongings, the old man learned that his daughter-in-law was unfaithful and one of his lovely granddaughters is not his flesh-and-blood. He becomes determined to discover who is true heir, while his equally determined daughter-in-law wants to protect her children and what remains of their inheritance. Based on the novel by Benito Perez-Galdos. Spanish with subtitles. **145m/C VHS, DVD, Wide.** *SP* Fernando Fernan-Gomez, Cayetana Guillen Cuervo, Rafael Alonso, Augustin Gonzalez; ***D:*** Jose Luis Garci; ***W:*** Jose Luis Garci, Horacio Valcarcel; ***C:*** R(aul) P. Cubero; ***M:*** Manuel Balboa.

Grandma's House 🦴 *Grandmother's House* **1988 (R)** A brother and sister discover that the house in which they live with their grandmother is chock-full of secrets and strange happenings, including madness, incest, and murder. **90m/C VHS, DVD.** Eric Foster, Kim Valentine, Brinke Stevens, Ida Lee, Len Lesser; *D:* Peter Rader; *W:* Peter C. Jensen; *C:* Peter C. Jensen.

Grandview U.S.A. 🦴🦴½ **1984 (R)** A low-key look at low-rent middle America, centering on a foxy local speedway owner and the derby-obsessed boys she attracts. Pre-"Dirty Dancing" choreography from Patrick Swayze and wife Lisa Niemi. **97m/C VHS.** Jamie Lee Curtis, Patrick Swayze, C. Thomas Howell, M. Emmet Walsh, Troy Donahue, William Windom, Jennifer Jason Leigh, Ramon Bieri, John Cusack, Joan Cusack, Jason Court; *D:* Randal Kleiser; *M:* Thomas Newman.

The Granny 🦴½ **1994 (R)** Evil Granny Gargoli (Stevens) is so mean that just before she dies she swallows an ancient potion, enabling her to haunt her survivors. When Kelly (Whirry), the only one to really care for Granny, is cheated out of her inheritance, the rest of the family is in for some nasty shocks from the zombiefied oldster. Can't decide whether to be camp or horrific. **85m/C VHS.** Shannon Whirry, Stella Stevens; *D:* Luca Bercovici; *W:* Luca Bercovici.

The Grapes of Wrath 🦴🦴🦴½ **1940** John Steinbeck's classic American novel about the Great Depression. We follow the impoverished Joad family as they migrate from the dust bowl of Oklahoma to find work in the orchards of California and as they struggle to maintain at least a little of their dignity and pride. A sentimental but dignified, uncharacteristic Hollywood epic. **129m/B VHS.** Henry Fonda, Jane Darwell, John Carradine, Charley Grapewin, Zeffie Tilbury, Dorris Bowdon, Russell Simpson, John Qualen, Eddie Quillan, O.Z. Whitehead, Grant Mitchell; *D:* John Ford; *W:* Nunnally Johnson; *C:* Gregg Toland. Oscars '40: Director (Ford), Support. Actress (Darwell); AFI '98: Top 100, Natl. Film Reg. '89;; N.Y. Film Critics '40: Director (Ford), Film.

The Grass Harp 🦴🦴½ **1995 (PG)** Rather dull retelling (with an excellent cast) of the Truman Capote novella covering the eccentricities of small town Southern life in the '30s and '40s. Teenaged Collin Fenwick (Furlong) is sent to live with his maiden aunts, artistic, impractical Dolly (Laurie) and shrewd, hard businesswoman Verena (Spacek). Charlie Cool's (Matthau) the retired judge who's sweet on Dolly, Morris Ritz (Lemmon) is a shady Chicago entrepreneur with plans for Verena's money, and there are various opinionated townspeople with stories to tell as well. Screen nostalgia directed by Matthau's son Charles. **107m/C VHS.** Sissy Spacek, Piper Laurie, Edward Furlong, Walter Matthau, Nell Carter, Jack Lemmon, Mary Steenburgen, Roddy McDowall, Joe Don Baker, Charles Durning, Sean Patrick Flanery, Mia Kirshner; *D:* Charles Matthau; *W:* Stirling Silliphant; *C:* John A. Alonzo; *M:* Patrick Williams.

The Grass Is Always Greener Over the Septic Tank 🦴🦴 **1978** Based on Erma Bombeck's best-seller. A city family's flight to the supposed peace of the suburbs turns out to be a comic compilation of complications. **98m/C VHS.** Carol Burnett, Charles Grodin, Linda Gray, Alex Rocco, Robert Sampson, Vicki Belmonte, Craig Richard Nelson, Anrae Walterhouse, Eric Stoltz; *D:* Robert Day. **TV**

The Grass Is Greener 🦴🦴½ **1961** An American millionaire invades part of an impoverished Earl's mansion and falls in love with the lady of the house. The Earl, who wants to keep his wife, enlists the aid of an old girlfriend in a feeble attempt to make her jealous. The two couples pair off properly in the end. **105m/C VHS, DVD, Wide.** Cary Grant, Deborah Kerr, Jean Simmons, Robert Mitchum; *D:* Stanley Donen; *W:* Hugh Williams; *C:* Christopher Challis; *M:* Noel Coward.

The Grave 🦴🦴½ **1995 (R)** Rednecks King (Scheffer) and Tyn (Charles) escape from a North Carolina prison farm after learning about a possible fortune buried in a grave. Unfortunately, they can't keep their mouths shut and soon every other lowlife around them is hunting as well. **90m/C VHS.** Craig Sheffer, Josh Charles, Gabrielle Anwar, Donal Logue, John Diehl, Anthony Michael Hall, Eric Roberts; *D:* Jonas Pate; *W:* Jonas Pate, Josh Pate; *C:* Frank Prinzi.

Grave Indiscretions 🦴🦴 *The Grotesque; Gentlemen Don't Eat Poets* **1996 (R)** Eccentric aristocrat, and amateur paleontologist, Sir Hugo Coal (Bates) is much more interested in the dinosaur skeleton he's attempting to assemble than in his crumbling estate or unsatisfied wife Harriet (Russell). Although he does take a dislike to the married servants his wife hires—sly butler Fledge (Sting) and his dipso cook/wife Doris (Styler). And then there's daughter Cleo (Headey) who's about to marry useles poet Sidney (Mackintosh) until he suddenly disappears. Which raises all sorts of questions, including just what the pigs have been eating recently. Based on McGrath's 1989 novel, "The Grotesque." **97m/C VHS.** *GB* Sting, Alan Bates, Theresa Russell, Trudie Styler, Lena Headey, Steven Mackintosh, Anna Massey, Jim Carter, James Fleet, Maria Aitken; *D:* John-Paul Davidson; *W:* Patrick McGrath; *C:* Andrew Dunn; *M:* Anne Dudley.

Grave of the Fireflies 🦴🦴🦴 *Hotaru no Haka* **1988** In post-war Japan, in the city of Kobe's train station, a young boy lies dying. A janitor finds a metal canister lying next to the boy and when he opens it ashes fall out. As fireflies gather around, ghostly figures of the boy and his little sister appear, as the story flashes back to the orphaned, homeless Seita and his sister. The two youngsters struggle in the Japanese countryside but find they cannot escape the hardships of war and have no chance for survival. Stunning animated testimony to the human spirit. Based on the novel by Akiyuki Nosaka. In Japanese with English subtitles. **88m/C VHS, DVD, Wide.** *JP D:* Isao Takahata; *W:* Isao Takahata.

Grave of the Vampire 🦴 *Seed of Terror* **1972 (R)** A vampire rapes and impregnates a modern-day girl. Twenty years later, their son, who grows up to be a bitter bloodsucker, sets out to find his father and kill him. **95m/C VHS.** William Smith, Michael Pataki, Lyn Peters, Diane Holden, Jay Adler, Kitty Vallacher, Jay Scott, Lieux Dressler; *D:* John Hayes.

Grave Secrets 🦴½ **1989 (R)** A professor of psychic phenomena teams up with a medium to find out who—or what—is controlling the life of a young woman. **90m/C VHS.** Paul LeMat, Renee Soutendijk, David Warner, Olivia Barash, Lee Ving; *D:* Donald P. Borchers.

Grave Secrets: The Legacy of Hilltop Drive 🦴🦴 **1992** The Williams family finds out their dream house is built on the site of an old graveyard. The spirits are not only restless, they're deadly. Based on a true story. **94m/C VHS.** Jonelle Allen, Patty Duke, David Selby, David Soul, Blake Clark; *D:* John D. Patterson.

Gravesend 🦴🦴½ **1997 (R)** Big cajones, puny budget: mini-Scorsese Stabile delivers the goods. Tracks a night in the life of four delinquent Brooklyn buddies who find themselves with a dead body on their hands. To avoid police involvement, the boys recruit local drug dealer JoJo (Aquilino) to aid in the body's disposal. JoJo demands $500 and a finger from the victim in return. Rest of pic deals with the fellows' quest for the cash and incorporates a deluge of dark humor which, outside of the pat, in your face dialogue and action, is the picture's real draw. Nineteen at the time of shooting, film school dropout's $5,000 auspicious first picture grabbed the attention of such heavyweights as Spielberg (Stabile now has a two picture deal with his Dreamworks SKG) and Oliver Stone. **85m/C VHS, DVD.** Tony Tucci, Michael Parducci, Tom Malloy, Thomas Brandise, Macky Aquilino; *D:* Salvatore Stabile; *W:* Salvatore Stabile; *C:* Joseph Dell'Olio; *M:* Bill Laswell.

The Graveyard 🦴🦴 *Persecution; Terror of Sheba; Sheba* **1974** A mommy spends many years torturing her little boy, David. In one blood-filled day, the fellow seeks his revenge. **90m/C VHS.** Lana Turner, Trevor Howard, Ralph Bates, Olga Georges-Picot, Suzan Farmer; *D:* Don Chaffey.

Graveyard of Horror 🦴 **1971** His wife and baby dead, a man seeking revenge discovers a horrible secret: his brother, a doctor, is stealing the heads from corpses. Dubbed. **105m/C VHS.** *SP* Bill Curran, Francisco (Frank) Brana, Beatriz Lacy; *D:* Miguel Madrid.

Graveyard Shift 🦴½ **1987 (R)** A New York cabby on the night shift is actually a powerful vampire who uses his fares to build an army of vampires. Not to be confused with the 1990 Stephen King scripted film. Followed by "Understudy: Graveyard Shift II." **89m/C VHS.** *IT* Silvio Oliviero, Helen Papas, Cliff Stoker; *D:* Gerard Ciccoritti.

Graveyard Shift 🦴 *Stephen King's Graveyard Shift* **1990 (R)** Just because Stephen King wrote the original story doesn't mean its celluloid incarnation is guaranteed to stand your hair on end; unless that's your response to abject boredom. When a man takes over the night shift at a recently reopened textile mill, he starts to find remnants...and they aren't fabric. Seems there's a graveyard in the neighborhood. **89m/C VHS, DVD, Wide.** David Andrews, Kelly Wolf, Stephen Macht, Brad Dourif; *D:* Ralph S. Singleton; *W:* Stephen King, John Esposito; *C:* Peter Stein; *M:* Brian Banks.

Gray Lady Down 🦴🦴 **1977 (PG)** A nuclear submarine sinks off the coast of Cape Cod and with their oxygen running out, a risky escape in an experimental diving craft seems to be their only hope. Dull, all-semi-star suspenser. **111m/C VHS.** Charlton Heston, David Carradine, Stacy Keach, Ned Beatty, Ronny Cox, Christopher Reeve, Michael O'Keefe, Rosemary Forsyth; *D:* David Greene.

Grayeagle 🦴🦴 **1977 (PG)** When a frontier trapper's daughter is kidnapped by Cheyenne Indians, he launches a search for her recovery. More style than pace in this Western, but worth a look for fans of Johnson. **104m/C VHS.** Ben Johnson, Iron Eyes Cody, Lana Wood, Alex Cord, Jack Elam, Paul Fix, Cindy Butler, Charles B. Pierce; *D:* Charles B. Pierce; *W:* Charles B. Pierce.

Gray's Anatomy **1996** Yet another monologue from Gray, this time about his medical crisis involving a rare eye disease. **80m/C VHS, DVD.** Spalding Gray; *D:* Steven Soderbergh.

Grease 🦴🦴🦴 **1978 (PG)** Film version of the hit Broadway musical about summer love. Set in the 1950s, this spirited musical follows a group of high-schoolers throughout their senior year. The story offers a responsible moral: act like a tart and you'll get your guy; but, hey, it's all in fun anyway. Followed by a weak sequel. ♫Grease; Summer Nights; Hopelessly Devoted to You; You're the One That I Want; Sandy; Beauty School Dropout; Look at Me, I'm Sandra Dee; Greased Lightnin'; It's Raining on Prom Night. **110m/C VHS, DVD.** John Travolta, Olivia Newton-John, Jeff Conaway, Stockard Channing, Didi Conn, Eve Arden, Frankie Avalon, Sid Caesar, Dinah Manoff, Joan Blondell, Alice Ghostley, Dody Goodman, Kelly Ward, Michael Tucci, Barry Pearl, Edd Byrnes, Susan Buckner, Lorenzo Lamas, Fannie Flagg, Eddie Deezen, Michael Biehn; *D:* Randal Kleiser; *W:* Allan Carr; *C:* Bill Butler; *M:* John Farrar, Barry Gibb.

Grease 2 🦴🦴 **1982 (PG)** Continuing saga of the T-Birds, the Pink Ladies, and young love at Rydell High. Newton-John and Travolta have graduated, leaving Pfeiffer to lead on love-struck book-neb Caulfield. Some okay tunes, though lame story lacks good-humor flair of the original. **115m/C VHS.** Maxwell Caulfield, Michelle Pfeiffer, Adrian Zmed, Lorna Luft, Didi Conn, Eve Arden, Sid Caesar, Tab Hunter, Christopher McDonald; *D:* Patricia Birch; *M:* Artie Butler.

Greased Lightning 🦴🦴½ **1977 (PG)** The story of the first black auto racing champion, Wendell Scott, who had to overcome racial prejudice to achieve his success. Slightly better-than-average Pryor comedy vehicle. **95m/C VHS.** Richard Pryor, Pam Grier, Beau Bridges, Cleavon Little, Vincent Gardenia; *D:* Michael A. Schultz; *W:* Leon Capetanos, Melvin Van Peebles.

Greaser's Palace 🦴🦴½ *Zoot Suit Jesus* **1972** Seaweedhead Greaser, owner of the town's saloon, faces his arch-nemesis in this wide-ranging satiric Christ allegory from the director of "Putney Swope." **91m/C VHS, DVD, Wide.** Albert Henderson, Allan Arbus, Michael Sullivan, Luana Anders, James Antonio, Ronald Nealy, Larry Moyer, John Paul Hudson, Herve Villechaize; *D:* Robert Downey; *W:* Robert Downey; *C:* Peter Powell; *M:* Jack Nitzsche.

The Great Adventure 🦴🦴🦴½ *Det Stora Aventyret* **1953** Two farm boys capture and attempt to train a wild otter. Unfortunately, the otter longs to once again join his kind despite the boys' efforts. Arne Sucksdorff won an Oscar for his arresting view of animal life. **73m/B VHS.** *SW* Anders Norberg, Kjell Sucksdorff, Arne Sucksdorff; *D:* Arne Sucksdorff; *W:* Arne Sucksdorff.

Great Adventure 🦴🦴 **1975 (PG)** In the severe environment of the gold rush days on the rugged Yukon territory, a touching tale unfolds of a young orphan boy and his eternal bond of friendship with a great northern dog. Based on a Jack London story. Baldanello used the pseudonym Paul Elliotts and Fred Romer is actually Fernando Romero. **90m/C VHS.** *IT SP* Jack Palance, Joan Collins, Fred Romer, Elisabetta Virgili, Remo de Angelis, Manuel de Blas; *D:* Gianfranco Baldanello.

The Great Alligator 🦴 *Il Fiume del Grande Caimano; Alligators* **1981** As if you couldn't guess, this one's about a huge alligator who does what other huge alligators do...terrorizes the people at a resort. **89m/C VHS.** Barbara Bach, Mel Ferrer, Richard Johnson, Claudio Cassinelli, Romano Puppo; *D:* Sergio Martino; *W:* Sergio Martino, Ernesto Gastaldi, Luigi Montefiore, Maria Chiaretta; *C:* Giancarlo Ferrando.

The Great American Broadcast 🦴🦴🦴 **1941** Two WWI vets want more than anything to strike it rich. After many failed endeavors, the two try that new-fangled thing called radio. The station takes off, as does the plot. The girlfriend of one vet falls for his partner and numerous other misunderstandings and complications ensue. Charming and crazy musical with an energetic cast. ♫I've Got a Bone To Pick With You; It's All In a Lifetime; I Take to You; Long Ago Last Night; Where You Are; The Great American Broadcast; Albany Bound; Give My Regards to Broadway; If I Didn't Care. **92m/B VHS.** Alice Faye, John Payne, Jack Oakie, Cesar Romero, James Newill, Mary Beth Hughes; *D:* Archie Mayo; *C:* Leon Shamroy.

The Great American Sex Scandal 🦴🦴½ *Jury Duty* **1994 (PG-13)** Sanford Lagelfust (Pinchot) is an meek accountant on trial for embezzlement, but when the prosecution's main witness turns out to be his sexy girlfriend Hope (Scoggins) the case turns into a courtroom sex scandal. Silly Canadian TV production. **94m/C VHS.** *CA* Bronson Pinchot, Tracy Scoggins, Heather Locklear, Stephen Baldwin, Lynn Redgrave, Alan Thicke, Madchen Amick, Barbara Bosson, Ilene Graff, Mark Blankfield, Danny Pintauro, Reginald Vel Johnson, Jacklyn Zeman; *D:* Michael A. Schultz.

Great American Traffic Jam 🦴½ *Gridlock* **1980 (PG)** Farce about the humorous variety of characters interacting on the interstate during a massive California traffic jam. **97m/C VHS.** Ed McMahon, Vic Tayback, Howard Hesseman, Abe Vigoda, Noah Beery Jr., Desi Arnaz Jr., John Beck, Shelley Fabares, James Gregory; *D:* James Frawley. **TV**

The Great Armored Car Swindle 🦴🦴 **1964** An anonymous English businessman becomes involved in international intrigue when he becomes a pawn in a plan to transfer money to a Middle Eastern government under communist rule. But thanks to his wife things don't go off as planned. **58m/B VHS.** Peter Reynolds, Dermot Walsh, Joanna Dunham, Lisa Gastoni, Brian Cobby; *D:* Lance Comfort.

Great Balls of Fire 🦴🦴½ **1989 (PG-13)** A florid, comic-book film of the glory days of Jerry Lee Lewis, from his first band to stardom. Most of the drama is derived from his marriage to his 13-year-old cousin. Somewhat overacted but full of energy. The soundtrack features many of the "Killer's" greatest hits re-recorded by Jerry Lee Lewis for the film. **108m/C VHS, DVD, Wide.** Dennis Quaid, Winona Ryder, Alec Baldwin, Trey Wilson, John Doe, Lisa Blount, Steve Allen, Stephen Tobolowsky, Lisa Jane Persky, Michael St. Gerard, Peter Cook; ***D:*** Jim McBride; ***W:*** Jack Baran, Jim McBride; ***C:*** Alfonso Beato; ***M:*** Jack Baran, Jim McBride.

Great Bank Hoax 🦴🦴½ *The Great Georgia Bank Hoax; Shenanigans* **1978 (PG)** Three bank managers decide to rob their own bank to cover up the fact that all the assets have been embezzled. **89m/C VHS.** Richard Basehart, Ned Beatty, Burgess Meredith, Michael Murphy, Paul Sand, Arthur Godfrey; ***D:*** Joseph Jacoby; ***C:*** Walter Lassally.

Great Bikini Off-Road Adventure 🦴½ **1994 (R)** Duke Abbey is about to lose his jeep tour company because business is so slow that he can't pay the rent. Then Duke's niece Lori decides to get her bikini-clad friends to hire on as drivers, showing lots of sights on their desert tours. **90m/C VHS.** Avalon Anders, Lauren Hays, Floyd Irons, Laura Hudspeth, Dan Frank; ***D:*** Gary Orona.

The Great Caruso 🦴🦴½ **1951** The story of opera legend Enrico Caruso's rise to fame, from his childhood in Naples, Italy, to his collapse on the stage of the Metropolitan Opera House. Lanza is superb as the singer, and there are 27 musical numbers to satisfy the opera lover. ♫The Loveliest Night of the Year; Over the Waves; Vesti la Giubba; M'Appari; Celeste Aida; Numi, Pieta; La Fatal Pietra; Sextet from Lucia di Lammermoor; La Donne a Mobile. **113m/C VHS.** Mario Lanza, Ann Blyth, Dorothy Kirsten; ***D:*** Richard Thorpe; ***C:*** Joseph Ruttenberg. Oscars '51: Sound.

The Great Commandment 🦴 **1941** Young man throws himself into a revolution against the overbearing Roman Empire in A.D. 30. His brother joins him but is killed. The man, who has become influenced by the teachings of Christ, decides to give up his revolution and go off with his brother's widow. (He always loved her anyway.) **78m/B VHS.** John Beal, Maurice (Moscovitch) Moscovich, Albert Dekker, Marjorie Cooley, Warren McCollum; ***D:*** Irving Pichel.

Great Dan Patch 🦴½ **1949** The story of the great Dan Patch, the horse that went on to become the highest-earning harness racer in history. **92m/B VHS.** Dennis O'Keefe, Gail Russell, Ruth Warrick; ***D:*** Joseph M. Newman.

Great Day 🦴½ **1946** A soap opera set around the wartime visit of first lady Eleanor Roosevelt to a small British town. It focuses mainly on the wife and daughter of a bitter, alcoholic WWI vet. **62m/B VHS.** Eric Portman, Flora Robson, Sheila Sim, Isabel Jeans, Walter Fitzgerald, Philip Friend, Marjorie Rhodes, Maire O'Neill, Beatrice Varley; ***D:*** Lance Comfort.

Great Day in the Morning 🦴🦴½ **1956** A rebel sympathizer and a Northern spy are both after Colorado gold to help finance the Civil War. But our Southern gentlemen soon find themselves equally interested in the local ladies. **92m/C VHS.** Robert Stack, Ruth Roman, Raymond Burr, Virginia Mayo, Alex Nicol, Regis Toomey; ***D:*** Jacques Tourneur.

The Great Dictator 🦴🦴🦴🦴 **1940** Chaplin's first all-dialogue film, a searing satire on Nazism in which he has dual roles as a Jewish barber with amnesia who is mistaken for a Hitlerian dictator, Adenoid Hynkel. A classic scene involves Hynkel playing with a gigantic balloon of the world. Hitler banned the film's release to the German public due to its highly offensive portrait of him. The film also marked Chaplin's last wearing of the Little Tramp's (and Hitler's equally little) mustache. **126m/B VHS, DVD.** Charlie Chaplin, Paulette Goddard, Jack Oakie, Billy Gilbert, Reginald Gardiner, Henry Daniell, Maurice (Moscovitch) Moscovich, Emma Dunn, Bernard Gorcey, Paul Weigel, Chester Conklin, Grace Hayle, Carter DeHaven; ***D:*** Charlie Chaplin; ***W:*** Charlie Chaplin; ***C:*** Roland H. Totheroh, Karl Struss; ***M:*** Meredith Willson. Natl. Film Reg. '97;; N.Y. Film Critics '40: Actor (Chaplin).

The Great Elephant Escape 🦴🦴½ **1995** Vacationing American teen Gordon-Levitt teams up with Kenyan M'Cormac, who works at an animal orphanage, to save a baby elephant from an unscrupulous businessman and his poacher friends. Made for TV. **90m/C VHS.** Joseph Gordon-Levitt, Frederick M'Cormac, Stephanie Zimbalist, Leo Burmester, Julian Sands; ***D:*** George Miller; ***W:*** John Sweet, Christopher Canaan. **TV**

The Great Escape 🦴🦴🦴½ **1963** During WWII, troublesome allied POWs are thrown by the Nazis into an escape-proof camp, where they join forces in a single mass break for freedom. One of the great war movies, with a superb ensemble cast and lots of excitement. The story was true, based on the novel by Paul Brickhill. McQueen performed most of the stunts himself, against the wishes of director Sturges. Followed by a made for TV movie 25 years later. **170m/C VHS, DVD, Wide.** Tom Adams, Steve McQueen, James Garner, Richard Attenborough, Charles Bronson, James Coburn, Donald Pleasence, David McCallum, James Donald, Gordon Jackson, Hannes Messemer, John Leyton, Nigel Stock, Jud Taylor, Hans Reiser, Robert Freitag, Karl Otto Alberty, Angus Lennie, Robert Graf, Harry Riebauer; ***D:*** John Sturges; ***W:*** James Clavell, W.R. Burnett; ***C:*** Daniel F. Fapp; ***M:*** Elmer Bernstein.

The Great Escape 2: The Untold Story 🦴🦴 **1988** Bland actioner can't decide whether it's a remake of the original or a sequel; it pretends to be a sequel yet spends a lot of time retelling—poorly—the first great escape. Once it gets around to the sequel part, it dispenses with protocol: Pleasence, an escapee in the original, is a Nazi bad guy in this go-round. Poor casting, especially Reeves, unconvincing as a German-speaking British officer who rallies the surviving escapees in revenge against their WWII captors. TV movie was originally shown in two parts, but mercifully shortened for video. **93m/C VHS.** Christopher Reeve, Judd Hirsch, Ian McShane, Donald Pleasence, Anthony John (Tony) Denison, Michael Nader, Charles Haid; ***D:*** Jud Taylor, Paul Wendkos. **TV**

Great Expectations 🦴🦴½ **1934** Weak Hollywood adaptation of the Dickens novel, easily dwarfed by the brilliant 1946 version. Holmes is Pip, the orphan who rises in the world thanks to a mysterious benefactor (Hull), with Wyatt as Pip's disdainful love, Estrella. **102m/B VHS.** Phillips Holmes, Henry Hull, Jane Wyatt, Florence Reed, Francis L. Sullivan, Alan Hale; ***D:*** Stuart Walker; ***W:*** Gladys Unger; ***C:*** George Robinson.

Great Expectations 🦴🦴🦴🦴 **1946** Lean's magisterial adaptation of the Dickens tome, in which a young English orphan is graced by a mysterious benefactor and becomes a well-heeled gentleman. Hailed and revered over the years; possibly the best Dickens on film. Well-acted by all, but especially notable is Hunt's slightly mad and pathetic Miss Havisham. Remake of the 1934 film. **118m/B VHS, DVD.** *GB* John Mills, Valerie Hobson, Anthony Wager, Alec Guinness, Finlay Currie, Jean Simmons, Bernard Miles, Francis L. Sullivan, Martita Hunt, Freda Jackson, Torin Thatcher, Hay Petrie, Eileen Erskine, George "Gabby" Hayes, Everley Gregg, O.B. Clarence; ***D:*** David Lean; ***W:*** David Lean, Ronald Neame; ***C:*** Guy Green; ***M:*** Walter Goeher. Oscars '47: Art Dir./Set Dec., B&W, B&W Cinematog.

Great Expectations 🦴🦴 **1981** Miniseries adaptation of the Dickens epic about Pip and his mysterious benefactor in Victorian London. **300m/C VHS.** *GB* Gerry Sundquist, Stratford Johns, Joan Hickson. **TV**

Great Expectations 🦴🦴🦴 **1989** Dickens classic retold on three cassettes. A mysterious benefactor turns a poor orphan boy into a gentleman of means. **325m/C VHS.** *GB* Jean Simmons, Anthony Hopkins, John Rhys-Davies; ***D:*** Kevin Connor. **TV**

Great Expectations 🦴🦴 **1997 (R)** Expecting "Great Expectations?" The title and basic storyline are about all the filmmakers took for their contemporary updating of Dickens' story. The artistic, orphaned Finn (Hawke) is living a meager existence with his trashy sister and his "uncle" Joe in a Florida fishing town. His destiny is intertwined with an escaped convict (De Niro) he aids, the rich and loony Ms. Dinsmoor (Bancroft) and Dinsmoor's beautiful niece Estella (Paltrow). After being spurned by Estella as a teen, Finn quits painting and drawing entirely. Years later a mysterious art dealer offers him a one-man show in New York if he will move there and start creating again. Estella inevitably reappears in his life, providing more than a little inspiration. More style than substance. Although the visuals are stunning, the director should have learned that beauty on the surface isn't all it's cracked up to be from, say...hmm... "Great Expectations" by Charles Dickens maybe? **112m/C VHS, DVD, Wide.** Ethan Hawke, Robert De Niro, Gwyneth Paltrow, Hank Azaria, Anne Bancroft, Chris Cooper, Josh Mostel, Kim Dickens, Nell Campbell, Stephen Spinella; ***D:*** Alfonso Cuaron; ***W:*** Mitch Glazer; ***C:*** Emmanuel Lubezki; ***M:*** Patrick Doyle.

Great Expectations 🦴🦴½ **1999** British TV version of the Dickens story about the expectations of Pip (Gruffudd). As a boy, he helps escaped convict Magwitch (Hill), a kindness that will change the course of Pip's life, though he doesn't realize it. Also a continuing part of his life is haughty beauty, Estella (Waddell), who has been raised by the eccentric Miss Havisham (Rampling) to wreak havoc on the male gender. A respectable retelling and rather dull. **180m/C VHS, DVD.** Ioan Gruffudd, Justine Waddell, Charlotte Rampling, Bernard Hill, Clive Russell, Laila Morse, Nicholas Woodeson, Leslie Sharp, Emma Cunniffe, Daniel Evans; ***D:*** Julian Jarrold; ***W:*** Tony Marchant. **TV**

Great Expectations: The Untold Story 🦴🦴½ **1987** Magwitch is an escaped convict, hiding out in the Victorian English countryside, who is aided by the young orphan, Pip. Captured and sent to the penal colonies in Australia, Magwitch serves his time and then discovers a fortune in gold, which he decides to use to make Pip into a gentleman. But Magwitch's enemies would like to get Pip's inheritance for themselves. Based on the Dickens classic, this three-tape miniseries is also available in a 102-minute feature length version. **287m/C VHS.** John Stanton, Sigrid Thornton, Robert Coleby, Todd Boyce, Anne Louise Lambert, Ron Haddrick, Noel Ferrier; ***D:*** Tim Burstall. **TV**

Great Flamarion 🦴🦴½ **1945** A woman-hating trick-shot artist is nevertheless duped into murdering the husband of his femme fatale assistant after he comes to believe she loves him. He's wrong. **78m/B VHS.** Dan Duryea, Erich von Stroheim, Mary Beth Hughes; ***D:*** Anthony Mann.

The Great Gabbo 🦴🦴 **1929** A ventriloquist can express himself only through his dummy, losing his own identity and going mad at the end. Von Stroheim's first talkie. May quite possibly be the first mentally-twisted-ventriloquist story ever put on film. Von Stroheim hated the movie, believing it to be analogous to his own life. When he tried to buy the rights to the film, presumably to destroy the prints, he found that the property had been already purchased by real-life ventriloquist, Edgar Bergen. Based on a story by Ben Hecht. ♫The New Step; I'm Laughing Ickey; I'm in Love With You; The Ga-Ga Bird; The Web of Love; Every Now and Then. **82m/B VHS.** Erich von Stroheim, Betty Compson, Don Douglas, Marjorie "Babe" Kane; ***D:*** James Cruze.

The Great Gatsby 🦴🦴½ **1949** Follows the silent 1926 version of F. Scott Fitzgerald's Jazz Era novel. Mysterious Jay Gatsby (Ladd) is a wealthy gangster and bootlegger who tries to buy his way into fast-living New York society. He befriends well-bred but penniless Nick Carraway (Carey), who serves as Gatsby's one true friend and eyewitness to the unfolding events. Gatsby rekindles his love for decorative Daisy (Field), who married into money and society and merely toys with leaving it all behind for Gatsby. Finally, the shallowness and selfishness all about prove to be Gatsby's undoing. **92m/B VHS.** Alan Ladd, Betty Field, MacDonald Carey, Ruth Hussey, Barry Sullivan, Howard da Silva, Shelley Winters, Henry Hull, Ed Begley Sr., Elisha Cook Jr.; ***D:*** Elliott Nugent; ***W:*** Cyril Hume, Richard Maibaum; ***C:*** John Seitz; ***M:*** Robert Emmett Dolan.

The Great Gatsby 🦴🦴½ **1974 (PG)** Adaptation of F. Scott Fitzgerald's novel of the idle rich in the 1920s. A mysterious millionaire crashes Long Island society, and finds his heart captured by an impetuous and emotionally impoverished girl. Skillful acting and directing captures the look and feel of this era, but the movie doesn't have the power of the book. **144m/C VHS.** Robert Redford, Mia Farrow, Bruce Dern, Karen Black, Patsy Kensit, Sam Waterston, Howard da Silva, Edward Herrmann; ***D:*** Jack Clayton; ***W:*** Francis Ford Coppola; ***M:*** Nelson Riddle. Oscars '74: Costume Des., Orig. Song Score and/or Adapt.; Golden Globes '75: Support. Actress (Black).

The Great Gatsby 🦴🦴½ **2001** Wealthy Jay Gatsby (Stephens) was a poor boy with a questionable past who fell in love with rich girl Daisy (Sorvino), who married another (Donovan). Now Jay, who wants to make it in Jazz Age Newport society, renews his involvement with superficial Daisy, which leads to tragedy. All the drama is observed by Daisy's cousin Nick (Rudd). Adapted from the 1925 F. Scott Fitzgerald novel. **100m/C VHS, DVD.** Toby Stephens, Mira Sorvino, Martin Donovan, Paul Rudd, Francie Swift, Matt Malloy; ***D:*** Robert Markowitz; ***W:*** John McLaughlin; ***C:*** Guy Dufaux; ***M:*** Carl Davis. **CABLE**

The Great Gildersleeve 🦴🦴 **1943** Throckmorton P. Gildersleeve adds another problem to his list; the sister of a local judge wants to marry him. His niece and nephew won't allow it and his attempts to juggle everyone's desires make for fine fun. Peary was also the voice for the popular radio series of the same name. **62m/B VHS.** Harold (Hal) Peary, Jane Darwell, Nancy Gates, Charles Arnt, Thurston Hall; ***D:*** Gordon Douglas.

Great Gold Swindle 🦴🦴 **1984** A dramatization of the 1982 swindling of the Perth Mint in Australia of over $650,000 worth of gold. **101m/C VHS.** John Hargreaves, Robert C. Hughes, Tony Rickards, Barbara Llewellyn.

The Great Gundown 🦴½ **1975** A violent tale set in the Old West. The peace of frontier New Mexico erupts when a half-breed Indian leads a brutal assault on an outlaw stronghold. **98m/C VHS.** Robert Padilla, Richard Rust, Milila St. Duval; ***D:*** Paul Hunt.

Great Guns 🦴🦴 **1941** Stan and Ollie enlist in the army to protect a spoiled millionaire's son but wind up being targets at target practice instead. Not one of their better efforts. **74m/B VHS.** Stan Laurel, Oliver Hardy, Sheila Ryan, Dick Nelson; ***D:*** Montague (Monty) Banks.

Great Guy 🦴½ *Pluck of the Irish* **1936** One of Cagney's lesser roles as an ex-boxer turned food inspector who wipes out graft in his town. **50m/B VHS.** James Cagney, Mae Clarke, Edward Brophy; ***D:*** John Blystone.

The Great Impostor 🦴🦴½ **1961** The true story of Ferdinand Waldo Demara Jr. who, during the 1950s, hoodwinked people by impersonating a surgeon, a college professor, a monk, a prison warden, and a schoolteacher, with the FBI always one step behind him. **112m/C VHS.** Tony Curtis, Edmond O'Brien, Arthur O'Connell, Gary Merrill, Raymond Massey, Karl Malden, Mike Kellin, Frank Gorshin; ***D:*** Robert Mulligan; ***C:*** Robert Burks; ***M:*** Henry Mancini.

Great Jesse James Raid 🦴½ **1949** Jesse James comes out of retirement to carry out a mine theft. Routine. **73m/C VHS.** Willard Parker, Barbara Payton, Tom Neal, Wallace Ford; ***D:*** Reginald LeBorg.

Great K & A Train Robbery 🦴🦴½ **1926** A railroad detective is hired to find and stop the bandits who have been preying on the K & A Railroad. Silent. **55m/B VHS.** Tom Mix, Dorothy Dwan, William Walling, Harry Grippe, Carl Miller; ***D:*** Lewis Seiler.

The Great Land of Small 🦴🦴 **1986 (G)** Two children enter a fantasy world and try to save it from Evil. For kids. **94m/C VHS.** Karen Elkin, Michael Blouin, Michael Anderson Jr., Ken Roberts; ***D:*** Vojtech Jasny.

The Great Lie 🦴🦴🦴 1941 A great soaper with Davis and Astor as rivals for the affections of Brent, an irresponsible flyer. Astor is the concert pianist who marries Brent and then finds out she's pregnant after he's presumed dead in a crash. The wealthy Davis offers to raise the baby so Astor can continue her career. But when Brent does return, who will it be to? Sparkling, catty fun. Astor's very short, mannish haircut became a popular trend. **107m/B VHS.** Bette Davis, Mary Astor, George Brent, Lucile Watson, Hattie McDaniel, Grant Mitchell, Jerome Cowan; ***D:*** Edmund Goulding; ***C:*** Gaetano Antonio "Tony" Gaudio; ***M:*** Max Steiner. Oscars '41: Support. Actress (Astor).

The Great Locomotive Chase 🦴🦴½ *Andrews' Raiders* 1956 During the Civil War, Parker and his fellow Union soldiers head into Confederate territory to disrupt railroad supply lines. They take over a locomotive, but are pursued by Confederate Hunter, the conductor of another train; and soon a pursuit is underway. Based on the true story of Andrews' Raiders. **85m/C VHS, DVD.** Fess Parker, Jeffrey Hunter, Kenneth Tobey; ***D:*** Francis D. Lyon; ***W:*** Lawrence Edward Watkin; ***C:*** Charles P. Boyle; ***M:*** Paul J. Smith.

The Great Los Angeles Earthquake 🦴½ *The Big One: The Great Los Angeles Earthquake* 1991 Made-for-TV disaster movie is the same old story; multiple soap-opera plotlines are spun around terrifying special effects, as L.A. is devastated by three major earth tremors and attendant disasters. Condensed from a two-part miniseries. **106m/C VHS.** Ed Begley Jr., Joanna (Joanna DeVarona) Kerns; ***D:*** Larry Elikann.

Great Love Experiment 🦴 1984 Everyone in a high school learns a valuable lesson about beauty and friendship when four popular students try to change the personality of an awkward classmate. **52m/C VHS.** Tracy Pollan, Esai Morales, Kelly Wolf, Scott Benderer.

The Great Lover 🦴🦴½ 1949 Aboard an ocean liner, a bumbler chaperoning school kids gets involved with a gambler, a duchess and a murder. Vintage Bob Hope. **80m/B VHS, DVD.** Bob Hope, Rhonda Fleming, Roland Young, Roland Culver, George Reeves, Jim Backus, Jack Benny; ***D:*** Alexander Hall; ***W:*** Edmund Beloin, Melville Shavelson, Jack Rose; ***C:*** Charles B(ryant) Lang Jr.

The Great Madcap 🦴🦴 1949 A wealthy man believes in lavishly indulging himself which drives his excessively conservative family crazy. Bunuel satirizes behavioral extremes, Christianity, advertising, sex, and a number of other popular absurdities. In Spanish with English subtitles. **90m/B VHS.** *MX* Fernando Soler, Rosario Granados, Ruben Rogo; ***D:*** Luis Bunuel.

The Great Man Votes 🦴🦴🦴 1938 Alcoholic college professor Barrymore falls into a deep depression after his wife's death. His children then plan to create a situation wherein his vote will decide the fate of the new town mayor, thus instilling in him a newly found sense of importance for himself and his children. Satiric and funny. **72m/B VHS.** John Barrymore, Peter Holden, Virginia Weidler, Katherine Alexander, Donald MacBride, Elisabeth Risdon, Granville Bates, Luis Alberni, J.M. Kerrigan, William Demarest, Roy Gordon; ***D:*** Garson Kanin; ***C:*** Russell Metty.

The Great Man's Lady 🦴🦴½ 1942 Stanwyck stars in a "stand by your man" story in which she supported and was responsible for the good deeds of a now past town hero. Told in flashback sequence, Stanwyck's character, 109-year-old Hanna Sampler, reveals to a young biographer the trials and tribulations of her life with Ethan Hoyt, founder of Hoyt City, who is being honored with the dedication of a statue in the opening of the film. The picture reveals their secrets and the truth about the woman behind the man. Based on the story "The Human Side" by Vina Delmar. **91m/B VHS.** Barbara Stanwyck, Joel McCrea, Brian Donlevy; ***D:*** William A. Wellman; ***W:*** Seena Owen, W.L. Rivers, Adela Rogers St. John; ***C:*** William Mellor; ***M:*** Victor Young.

The Great McGinty 🦴🦴🦴½ *Down Went McGinty* 1940 Sturges' directorial debut, about the rise and fall of a small-time, bribe-happy politician is an acerbic, ultra-cynical indictment of modern politics that stands, like much of his other work, as bracingly courageous as anything that's ever snuck past the Hollywood censors. Political party boss Tamiroff chews the scenery with gusto while Donlevy, in his first starring role, is more than his equal as the not-so-dumb political hack. **82m/B VHS.** Brian Donlevy, Muriel Angelus, Akim Tamiroff, Louis Jean Heydt, Arthur Hoyt, William Demarest; ***D:*** Preston Sturges; ***W:*** Preston Sturges; ***C:*** William Mellor. Oscars '40: Orig. Screenplay.

Great McGonagall 🦴½ 1975 Tale of an unemployed Scot trying to become Britain's poet laureate. Sellers adds a semi-bright spot with his portrayal of Queen Victoria! **95m/C VHS.** *GB* Peter Sellers, Spike Milligan, Julia Foster; ***D:*** Joseph McGrath.

The Great Mike 🦴🦴½ 1944 Unlikely but moving story of a young boy who convinces track management that his work horse has a chance against the touted thoroughbred. Sentimental, with little innovation, but generally well-acted. **72m/B VHS.** Stuart Erwin, Robert "Buzzy" Henry, Pierre Watkin, Gwen Kenyon, Carl "Alfalfa" Switzer, Edythe Elliott, Marion Martin; ***D:*** Wallace Fox.

Great Missouri Raid 🦴🦴 1951 Follows the famous adventures of the James/Younger gang and their eventual demise. **81m/C VHS.** Wendell Corey, MacDonald Carey, Ellen Drew, Ward Bond; ***D:*** Gordon Douglas; ***C:*** Ray Rennahan.

The Great Moment 🦴🦴 1944 Story of the Boston dentist who discovered ether's use as an anesthetic in 1845. Confusing at times, changing from comedy to drama and containing flashbacks that add little to the story. Surprisingly bland result from ordinarily solid cast and director. **87m/B VHS.** Joel McCrea, Betty Field, Harry Carey Sr., William Demarest, Franklin Pangborn, Porter Hall; ***D:*** Preston Sturges; ***C:*** Victor Milner.

The Great Mouse Detective 🦴🦴🦴 *The Adventures of the Great Mouse Detective* 1986 (G) Animated version of the book "Basil of Baker Street" by Eve Titus. Fun adventure concerning the Sherlock-of-the-mouse-world, Basil, who must prevent his arch nemesis, Professor Ratigan, from overthrowing Queen Mousstoria. Not as good as some of the other Disney animated features, but kids will enjoy it nonetheless. **74m/C VHS.** ***D:*** John Musker, Ron Clements, Dave Michener, Burny Mattinson; ***W:*** Ron Clements, Dave Michener; ***M:*** Henry Mancini; ***V:*** Vincent Price, Barrie Ingham, Val Bettin, Susanne Pollatschek, Candy Candido, Eve Brenner, Alan Young, Melissa Manchester.

The Great Muppet Caper 🦴🦴🦴 1981 (G) A group of hapless reporters (Kermit, Fozzie Bear, and Gonzo) travel to London to follow up on a major jewel robbery. **95m/C VHS, DVD, Wide.** Charles Grodin, Diana Rigg, John Cleese, Robert Morley, Peter Ustinov, Peter Falk, Jack Warden; ***D:*** Jim Henson; ***W:*** Jack Rose; ***C:*** Oswald Morris; ***V:*** Frank Oz.

The Great Northfield Minnesota Raid 🦴🦴½ 1972 (PG) The Younger/James gang decides to rob the biggest bank west of the Mississippi, but everything goes wrong. Uneven, offbeat western, but Duvall's portrayal of the psychotic Jesse James and Robertson's cunning Cole Younger are notable. **91m/C VHS.** Cliff Robertson, Robert Duvall, Elisha Cook Jr., Luke Askew, R.G. Armstrong, Donald Moffat, Matt Clark; ***D:*** Philip Kaufman; ***W:*** Philip Kaufman; ***C:*** Bruce Surtees; ***M:*** Dave Grusin.

The Great Outdoors 🦴🦴 1988 (PG) Good cast is mostly wasted in another John Hughes's tale of vacation gone bad. A family's peaceful summer by the lake is disturbed by their uninvited, trouble-making relatives. Aykroyd and Candy are two funny guys done in by a lame script that awkwardly examines friendship and coming of age and throws in a giant bear when things get unbearably slow. May be fun for small fry. **91m/C VHS, DVD.** Dan Aykroyd, John Candy, Stephanie Faracy, Annette Bening, Chris Young, Lucy Deakins, John Bloom; ***D:*** Howard Deutch; ***W:*** John Hughes; ***C:*** Ric Waite; ***M:*** Thomas Newman.

The Great Race 🦴🦴½ 1965 A dastardly villain, a noble hero, and a spirited suffragette are among the competitors in an uproarious New York-to-Paris auto race circa 1908, complete with pie fights, saloon brawls, and a confrontation with a feisty polar bear. Overly long and only sporadically funny. **160m/C VHS.** Jack Lemmon, Tony Curtis, Natalie Wood, Peter Falk, Keenan Wynn, George Macready; ***D:*** Blake Edwards; ***M:*** Henry Mancini. Oscars '65: Sound FX Editing.

Great Ride 🦴 1978 State police are after two dirt bikers who are riding through areas where bike riding is illegal. **90m/C VHS.** Perry Lang, Michael MacRae, Michael Sullivan; ***D:*** Don Hulette.

The Great Riviera Bank Robbery 🦴🦴½ 1979 A genius executes a bank robbery on the French Riviera netting $15 million. Based on a true story, the film chronicles the unfolding of the heist. **98m/C VHS.** Ian McShane, Warren Clarke, Stephen Greif, Christopher Malcolm; ***D:*** Francis Megahy.

The Great Rupert 🦴🦴🦴 1950 Durante and family are befriended by a helpful squirrel (a puppet) in obtaining a huge fortune. Good fun; Durante shines. **86m/B VHS, DVD.** Jimmy Durante, Terry Moore, Tom Drake, Frank Orth, Sara Haden, Queenie Smith; ***D:*** Irving Pichel; ***W:*** Laszlo Vadnay; ***C:*** Lionel Lindon.

The Great St. Louis Bank Robbery 🦴🦴½ 1959 Three career criminals (Denton, Clarke, Dukas) and young turk McQueen are brought together for a bank heist. They don't trust each other, which proves fatal when the heist goes bad. Based on a true story and filmed in semi-documentary style. Nineteen-year-old McQueen's follow-up to "The Blob." **86m/B VHS, DVD, Wide.** Graham Denton, David Clarke, James Dukas, Steve McQueen, Molly McCarthy; ***D:*** Charles Guggenheim; ***W:*** Richard T. Heffron; ***C:*** Victor Duncan; ***M:*** Bernardo Segall.

The Great St. Trinian's Train Robbery 🦴🦴 1966 Train robbers hide their considerable loot in an empty country mansion only to discover, upon returning years later, it has been converted into a girls' boarding school. When they try to recover the money, the thieves run up against a band of pestiferous adolescent girls, with hilarious results. Based on the cartoon by Ronald Searle. Sequel to "The Pure Hell of St. Trinian's." **90m/C VHS.** *GB* Dora Bryan, Frankie Howerd, Reg Varney, Desmond Walter Ellis; ***D:*** Sidney Gilliat, Frank Launder; ***M:*** Malcolm Arnold.

The Great Santini 🦴🦴🦴 *Ace* 1980 (PG) Lt. Col. Bull Meechum, the "Great Santini," a Marine pilot stationed stateside, fights a war involving his frustrated career goals, repressed emotions, and family. His family becomes his company of marines, as he abuses them in the name of discipline, because he doesn't allow himself any other way to show his affection. With a standout performance by Duvall, the film successfully blends warm humor and tenderness with the harsh cruelties inherent with dysfunctional families and racism. Based on Pat Conroy's autobiographical novel, the movie was virtually undistributed when first released, but re-released due to critical acclaim. **118m/C VHS, DVD, 8mm.** Robert Duvall, Blythe Danner, Michael O'Keefe, Julie Ann Haddock, Lisa Jane Persky, David Keith; ***D:*** Lewis John Carlino; ***W:*** Lewis John Carlino; ***C:*** Ralph Woolsey; ***M:*** Elmer Bernstein. Montreal World Film Fest. '80: Actor (Duvall).

Great Scout & Cathouse Thursday 🦴½ *Wildcat* 1976 (PG) Marvin and Reed vow to take revenge on their third partner, Culp, who made off with all their profits from a gold mine. The title refers to Marvin's May-December romance with prostitute Lenz. Already forgotten, unfunny, all-star comedy with cutesy title. **96m/C VHS.** Lee Marvin, Oliver Reed, Robert Culp, Elizabeth Ashley, Kay Lenz; ***D:*** Don Taylor.

The Great Skycopter Rescue 🦴 1982 Ruthless businessmen hire a motorcycle gang to terrorize and scare away the inhabitants of an oil-rich town. A local teenage flying enthusiast organizes his friends into an attack force to fight back. **96m/C VHS.** William Marshall, Aldo Ray, Russell Johnson, Terry Michos, Terry Taylor; ***D:*** Lawrence Foldes.

Great Smokey Roadblock 🦴🦴 *Last of the Cowboys* 1976 (PG) While in the hospital, a 60-year-old truck driver's rig is repossessed by the finance company. Deciding that it's time to make one last perfect cross country run, he escapes from the hospital, steals his truck, picks up six prostitutes, heads off into the night with the police on his tail, and becomes a folk hero. **84m/C VHS.** Henry Fonda, Eileen Brennan, Susan Sarandon, John Byner; ***D:*** John Leone.

The Great Texas Dynamite Chase 🦴½ *Dynamite Women* 1976 (R) Two sexy young women drive across Texas with a carload of dynamite. They leave a trail of empty banks with the cops constantly on their trail. **90m/C VHS, DVD.** Claudia Jennings, Jocelyn Jones, Johnny Crawford, Chris Pennock, Tara Strohmeier, Miles Watkins, Bart Braverman; ***D:*** Michael Pressman; ***C:*** Jamie Anderson; ***M:*** Craig Safan.

The Great Train Robbery 🦴🦴🦴 *The First Great Train Robbery* 1979 (PG) A dapper thief arranges to heist the Folkstone bullion express in 1855, the first moving train robbery. Well-designed, fast-moving costume piece based on Crichton's best-selling novel. **111m/C VHS, DVD.** *GB* Sean Connery, Donald Sutherland, Lesley-Anne Down, Alan Webb; ***D:*** Michael Crichton; ***W:*** Michael Crichton; ***C:*** Geoffrey Unsworth; ***M:*** Jerry Goldsmith.

Great Treasure Hunt 🦴 197? Four Western rogues help a blind man steal a wealthy crook's gold. **90m/C VHS.** Mark Damon, Stan Cooper, Luis Marin; ***D:*** Tonino Ricci.

The Great Waldo Pepper 🦴🦴🦴 1975 (PG) Low key and (for Hill) less commercial film about a WWI pilot-turned-barnstormer who gets hired as a stuntman for the movies. Features spectacular vintage aircraft flying sequences. **107m/C VHS, DVD.** Robert Redford, Susan Sarandon, Margot Kidder, Bo Svenson, Scott Newman, Geoffrey Lewis, Edward Herrmann; ***D:*** George Roy Hill; ***W:*** William Goldman; ***C:*** Robert L. Surtees; ***M:*** Henry Mancini.

A Great Wall 🦴🦴🦴 *The Great Wall is a Great Wall* 1986 (PG) A Chinese-American family travels to mainland China to discover the country of their ancestry and to visit relatives. They experience radical culture shock. Wang's first independent feature. In English and Chinese with subtitles. **103m/C VHS.** Peter Wang, Sharon Iwai, Kelvin Han Yee, Lin Qinqin, Hy Xiaoguang; ***D:*** Peter Wang; ***W:*** Peter Wang, Shirley Sun; ***M:*** David Liang, Ge Ganru.

The Great Wallendas 🦴🦴 1978 The true story of the tragedies and triumphs of the Wallendas, a seven-person acrobatic family, who were noted for creating a pyramid on the high wire without nets below them. **96m/C VHS.** Lloyd Bridges, Britt Ekland, Cathy Rigby; ***D:*** Larry Elikann. **TV**

The Great Waltz 🦴🦴🦴 1938 The first of two musical biographies on the life of Johann Strauss sees the musician quit his banking job to pursue his dream of becoming a successful composer. A fine, overlooked production rich with wonderful music and romantic comedy. ♫Tales of Vienna Woods; There'll Come A Time; One Day When We Were Young; Voices of Spring; Du und Du; The Bat; I'm In Love With Vienna; Revolutionary March. **102m/B VHS.** Luise Rainer, Fernand Gravet, Milza Korjus, Hugh Herbert, Lionel Atwill, Curt Bois, Leonid Kinskey, Al Shean, Minna Gombell, George Houston, Bert Roach, Herman Bing, Alma Kruger, Sig Rumann; ***D:*** Julien Duvivier; ***C:*** Joseph Ruttenberg. Oscars '38: Cinematog.

The Great War 🦴🦴 *La Grande Guerre* 1959 Two Italian soldiers find themselves in the midst of WWI, much against their will. They try a number of schemes to get out of fighting and working, but their circumstance dictates otherwise. Slightly muddled, but generally good acting. **118m/B VHS.** *FR IT* Vittorio Gassman, Alberto Sordi, Silvana Mangano, Folco Lulli; ***D:*** Mario Monicelli; ***M:*** Nino Rota.

The Great White Hope ½ **1970 (PG-13)** A semi-fictionalized biography of boxer Jack Johnson, played by Jones, who became the first black heavyweight world champion in 1910. Alexander makes her film debut as the boxer's white lover, as both battle the racism of the times. Two Oscar-nominated performances in what is essentially an "opened-out" version of the Broadway play. **103m/C VHS.** James Earl Jones, Jane Alexander, Lou Gilbert, Joel Fluellen, Chester Morris, Robert Webber, Hal Holbrook, R.G. Armstrong, Moses Gunn, Scatman Crothers; *D:* Martin Ritt; *C:* Burnett Guffey.

The Great White Hype ½ **1996 (R)** Screenwriter Shelton, who penned "Bull Durham" and "White Men Can't Jump," returns to the sports arena with this satire of the sleazy world of boxing. Jackson's the Don King-esque promoter and manager of heavyweight champ Wayans. Noticing that pay-per-view revenues are slipping, he searches for a white boxer to generate interest and dollars and finds boxer-turned-musician Berg, who beat the champ in their Golden Glove days, and the publicity machine is cranked up for a veritable Lollapalooka. Jackson's performance as the flamboyant Rev. Fred Sultan fuels the entire movie. Concentrating on the shady wheeling and dealing, the boxing action is kept to a minimum. **95m/C VHS.** Samuel L. Jackson, Damon Wayans, Peter Berg, Jeff Goldblum, Jon Lovitz, Corbin Bernsen, Richard "Cheech" Marin, John Rhys-Davies, Salli Richardson, Rocky Carroll, Jamie Foxx, Michael Jace; *D:* Reginald (Reggie) Hudlin; *W:* Ron Shelton, Tony Hendra; *C:* Ron Garcia; *M:* Marcus Miller.

The Great Ziegfeld ½ **1936** Big bio-pic of the famous showman; acclaimed in its time as the best musical biography ever done, still considered the textbook for how to make a musical. Look for cameo roles by many famous stars, as well as a walk-on role by future First Lady Pat Nixon. The movie would have stood up as a first-rate biography of Ziegfeld, even without the drop-dead wonderful songs. ♫Won't You Come Play With Me?; It's Delightful to be Married; If You Knew Susie; Shine On Harvest Moon; A Pretty Girl is Like a Melody; You Gotta Pull Strings; She's a Follies Girl; You; You Never Looked So Beautiful. **179m/B VHS.** William Powell, Luise Rainer, Myrna Loy, Frank Morgan, Reginald Owen, Nat Pendleton, Ray Bolger, Virginia Bruce, Harriet Hocter, Ernest Cossart, Robert Greig, Gilda Gray, Leon Errol, Dennis Morgan, Mickey Daniels, William Demarest; ***Cameos:*** Fanny Brice; *D:* Robert Z. Leonard; *W:* William Anthony McGuire. Oscars '36: Actress (Rainer), Picture; N.Y. Film Critics '36: Actress (Rainer), Actress (Rainer).

The Greatest ½ **1977 (PG)** Autobiography of Cassius Clay, the fighter who could float like a butterfly and sting like a bee. Ali plays himself, and George Benson's hit "The Greatest Love of All" is introduced. **100m/C VHS, DVD, Wide.** Muhammad Ali, Robert Duvall, Ernest Borgnine, James Earl Jones, John Marley, Roger E. Mosley, Dina Merrill, Paul Winfield; *D:* Tom Gries; *W:* Ring Lardner Jr.; *C:* Harry Stradling Jr.; *M:* Michael Masser.

The Greatest Question ½ **1919** Gish is a girl menaced by a married couple whom she saw commit a murder years before. A rush job by Griffith to fulfill his studio obligations but Gish's performance is fine. **80m/B VHS.** Lillian Gish, Robert "Bobbie" Harron, Ralph Graves, Eugenie Besserer, George Fawcett, George Nicholls Jr., Josephine Crowell, Carl Stockdale; *D:* D.W. Griffith.

The Greatest Show on Earth **1952** DeMille is in all his epic glory here in a tale of a traveling circus wrought with glamour, romance, mysterious clowns, a tough ringmaster, and a train wreck. **149m/C VHS.** Betty Hutton, Cornel Wilde, James Stewart, Charlton Heston, Dorothy Lamour, Lawrence Tierney, Gloria Grahame; *D:* Cecil B. DeMille. Oscars '52: Picture, Story; Golden Globes '53: Director (DeMille), Film—Drama.

The Greatest Story Ever Told **1965** Christ's journey from Galilee to Golgotha is portrayed here in true international-all-star-epic treatment by director Stevens. A lackluster version of Christ's life, remarkable only for Heston's out-of-control John the Baptist. **196m/C VHS, DVD, Wide.** Max von Sydow, Charlton Heston, Sidney Poitier, Claude Rains, Jose Ferrer, Telly Savalas, Angela Lansbury, Dorothy McGuire, John Wayne, Donald Pleasence, Carroll Baker, Van Heflin, Robert Loggia, Shelley Winters, Ed Wynn, Roddy McDowall, Pat Boone; *D:* George Stevens; *W:* George Stevens, James Lee Barrett; *C:* William Mellor, Loyal Griggs; *M:* Alfred Newman.

Greed **1924** A wife's obsession with money drives her husband to murder. Although the original version's length (eight hours) was trimmed to 140 minutes, it remains one of the greatest and most highly acclaimed silent films ever made. Effective use of Death Valley locations. Adapted from the Frank Norris novel, "McTeague." **140m/B VHS.** Dale Fuller, Gibson Gowland, ZaSu Pitts, Jean Hersholt, Chester Conklin; *D:* Erich von Stroheim. Natl. Film Reg. '91.

The Greed of William Hart *Horror Maniacs* **1948** Reworking of the Burke and Hare legend has grave robbers providing Edinburgh medical students with the requisite cadavers. **78m/B VHS.** *GB* Tod Slaughter, Henry Oscar, Jenny Lynn, Winifred Melville; *D:* Oswald Mitchell.

Greedy ½ **1994 (PG-13)** Money-grubbing family suck up to elderly millionaire uncle (Douglas) when they fear he'll leave his money to the sexy, young former pizza delivery girl (d'Abo) he's hired as his nurse. Fox is the long-lost nephew who comes to the rescue. Wicked comedy from veterans Ganz and Mandel should zing, but instead falls flat thanks to a descent into the maudlin. Fox bares his backside and Douglas has fun as the mean old miser, but check out Hartman, a riot as a snarky relative. **109m/C VHS, DVD, Wide.** Mary Ellen Trainor, Kirk Douglas, Michael J. Fox, Olivia D'Abo, Phil Hartman, Nancy Travis, Ed Begley Jr., Bob Balaban, Colleen Camp, Jere Burns, Khandi Alexander, Jonathan Lynn; *D:* Jonathan Lynn; *W:* Lowell Ganz, Babaloo Mandel; *C:* Gabriel Beristain; *M:* Randy Edelman.

Greedy Terror **1978** A cross-country motorcycle trip becomes a real nightmare when two young men realize they're being stalked by a maniac with a thirst for blood. **90m/C VHS.** Michael MacRae, Perry Lang.

Greek Street *Latin Love* **1930** The owner of small cafe in London discovers a poor girl singing in the street for food. He takes her in and spotlights her songs in his cafe. **51m/B VHS.** *GB* Sari Maritza, Arthur Ahmbling, Martin Lewis; *D:* Sinclair Hill.

The Greek Tycoon ½ **1978 (R)** Old familiar story about widow of an American president who marries a billionaire shipping magnate and finds that money cannot buy happiness. A transparent depiction of the Onassis/Kennedy marriage, done to a turn. **106m/C VHS.** Anthony Quinn, Jacqueline Bisset, James Franciscus, Raf Vallone, Edward Albert; *D:* J. Lee Thompson.

Green Archer **1940** Fifteen episodes of the famed serial, featuring a spooked castle complete with secret passages and tunnels, trapdoors, and the mysterious masked figure, the Green Archer. **283m/B VHS.** Victor Jory, Iris Meredith, James Craven, Robert (Fisk) Fiske; *D:* James W. Horne.

The Green Berets woof! **1968 (G)** Cliched wartime heroics co-directed by Wayne and based on Robin Moore's novel. The Duke stars as a Special Forces colonel, leading his troops against the Viet Cong. Painfully insipid pro-war propaganda, notable as the only American film to come out in support of U.S. involvement in Vietnam. Truly embarrassing but did spawn the hit single "Ballad of the Green Beret" by Barry Sadler. **135m/C VHS, DVD, Wide.** John Wayne, David Janssen, Jim Hutton, Aldo Ray, George Takei, Raymond St. Jacques, Bruce Cabot, Jack Soo, Patrick Wayne, Luke Askew, Irene Tsu, Edward Faulkner, Jason Evers, Mike Henry, Chuck Roberson, Eddy Donno; *D:* John Wayne; *W:* James Lee Barrett; *C:* Winton C. Hoch; *M:* Miklos Rozsa.

Green Card ½ **1990 (PG-13)** Some marry for love, some for money, others for an apartment in the Big Apple. Refined, single MacDowell covets a rent-controlled apartment in Manhattan, but the lease stipulates that the apartment be let to a married couple. Enter brusque and burly Depardieu, who covets the elusive green card. The counterpoint between MacDowell, as a stuffy horticulturist, and Depardieu, as a French composer works well, and the two adroitly play a couple whose relationship covers the romantic continuum. Director Weir wrote the screenplay with Depardieu in mind. Depardieu's English-language debut. **108m/C VHS.** Gerard Depardieu, Andie MacDowell, Bebe Neuwirth, Gregg Edelman, Robert Prosky, Jessie Keosian, Ann Wedgeworth, Ethan Phillips, Mary Louise Wilson, Lois Smith, Simon Jones; *D:* Peter Weir; *W:* Peter Weir; *M:* Hans Zimmer. Golden Globes '91: Actor—Mus./Comedy (Depardieu), Film—Mus./Comedy.

Green Dolphin Street ½ **1947** Flimsy romantic epic set in 19th century New Zealand. A young girl marries the beau she and her sister are battling over in this Oscar-winning special effects show which features one big earthquake. Based on the Elizabeth Goudge novel, this was one of MGM's biggest hits in 1947. **161m/B VHS.** Lana Turner, Van Heflin, Donna Reed, Edmund Gwenn; *D:* Victor Saville; *C:* George J. Folsey.

Green Dragon Inn **1982** When trying to escort an accused murderer to trial, a Ming court emissary finds himself battling against Kung Fu masters. **94m/C VHS.** Yue Hwa, Lo Lei, Shangkuan Ling-Feng.

Green Eyes ½ **1934** A costume party in a country mansion sets the scene for a routine murder mystery when the guests find their host stabbed to death in a closet. Based on the novel "The Murder of Stephen Kester" by H. Ashbrook. **68m/B VHS.** Shirley Grey, Charles Starrett, Claude Gillingwater, John Wray, Dorothy Revier; *D:* Richard Thorpe; *W:* Melville Shyer.

Green Eyes ½ **1976** Winfield, an ex-GI, returns to postwar Vietnam to search for his illegitimate son who he believes will have green eyes. A highly acclaimed drama featuring moving performances from Winfield and Jonathan Lippe. **100m/C VHS.** Paul Winfield, Rita Tushingham, Jonathon Lippe, Victoria Racimo, Royce Wallace, Claudia Bryar; *D:* John Erman. **TV**

Green Fields ½ *Grine Felder; Gruner Felder* **1937** A quiet romance based on Peretz Hirschbein's legendary tale of a young scholar of the Talmud who leaves the shelter of the synagogue in order to learn about people in the real world. The search takes him to the countryside where he finds himself in the middle of a battle between two families who both want him as a tutor and a suitor for their daughters. In Yiddish with English subtitles. **95m/B VHS.** Michael Goldstein, Herschel Bernardi, Helen Beverly; *D:* Jacob Ben-Ami.

Green Fire ½ **1955** The screen sizzles when emerald miner Granger meets plantation-owner Kelly in the exotic jungles of South America. Usual plot complications muddle the story, but who cares when the stars are this attractive? **100m/C VHS.** Stewart Granger, Grace Kelly, Paul Douglas, John Ericson, Murvyn Vye, Jose Torvay, Robert Tafur, Nacho Galindo; *D:* Andrew Marton; *W:* Ivan Goff, Ben Roberts; *M:* Miklos Rozsa.

Green for Danger **1947** A detective stages a chilling mock operation to find a mad killer stalking the corridors of a British hospital during WWII. Sim's first great claim to fame (pre-"A Christmas Carol"). **91m/B VHS.** *GB* Trevor Howard, Alastair Sim, Leo Genn; *D:* Sidney Gilliat.

The Green Glove ½ **1952** A jewel thief steals a beautiful relic from a tiny church. WWII makes it impossible for him to fence it and the church finds a relentless ally to track the thief. Excellent action sequences lift this standard plot slightly above the ordinary. **88m/B VHS.** Glenn Ford, Geraldine Brooks, Cedric Hardwicke, George Macready, Gaby Andre, Roger Treville, Juliette Greco, Jean Bretonniere; *D:* Rudolph Mate; *W:* Charles Bennett.

Green Grow the Rushes *Brandy Ashore* **1951** The English government tries to put a stop to brandy smuggling on the coast, but the townspeople drink up the evidence. A young Burton highlights this watered-down comedy. Based on a novel by co-scripter Harold Clewes. **77m/B VHS.** *GB* Roger Livesey, Honor Blackman, Richard Burton, Frederick Leister; *D:* Derek Twist.

Green Horizon ½ *Afurika Monogatari; A Tale of Africa* **1983** A bucolic old codger faces a dilemma when he must choose between his granddaughter's future and his disaster-prone natural environment. **80m/C VHS.** James Stewart, Philip Sayer, Elenora Vallone.

The Green Hornet **1939** The feature version of the original serial, in which the Green Hornet and Kato have a series of crime-fighting adventures. **100m/B VHS.** Gordon Jones, Keye Luke, Anne Nagel, Wade Boteler, Walter McGrail, Douglas Evans, Cy Kendall.

The Green House *The Greenhouse; Le Jardin des Plantes* **1996** Fernand Bonard (Rich) is the aged caretaker of the Paris zoo's botanical gardens during the waning days of WWII. His son Armand (Labarthe) is a collaborator who arrives at his father's home with eight-year-old daughter, Philippine (Stevenin), to celebrate her birthday. When Armand is suddenly killed by the Gestapo, Fernand begins an elaborate deception for his granddaughter, portraying her father as a hero of the French Resistance but his illusions take an unexpected turn. French with subtitles. **93m/C VHS.** *FR* Claude Rich, Salomee Stevenin, Samuel Labarthe, Catherine Jacob, Rose Thiery; *D:* Philippe de Broca; *W:* Philippe de Broca, Alexandre Jardin; *C:* Janos Kende; *M:* Charles Court.

Green Ice ½ **1981** An American electronics expert gets involved with a brutal South American government dealing with emeralds and plans a heist with his girlfriend and other cohorts. A little bit of romance, a little bit of action, a lot of nothing much. **109m/C VHS.** *GB* Ryan O'Neal, Anne Archer, Omar Sharif, John Larroquette; *D:* Ernest Day; *W:* Edward Anhalt, Robert De Laurentis.

Green Inferno **198?** A wealthy eccentric who lives deep in the South American jungle incites the natives to rebel. Mercenary agents are then hired to kill him. **90m/C VHS.** Richard Yesteran, Didi Sherman, Caesar Burner.

The Green Man **1991** Maurice Allington (Finney), the alcoholic and randy owner of the Green Man Inn in rural England, jokes about the spirits that supposedly haunt the inn. It's not too funny, however, when he discovers the spirits are real and he has to figure out who the spirit of a 17th-century murderer is inhabiting before he kills again. A classy ghost story based on the novel by Kingsley Amis. **150m/C VHS.** *GB* Albert Finney, Sarah Berger, Linda Marlowe, Michael Hordern, Nickolas Grace, Michael Culver; *D:* Elijah Moshinsky; *W:* Malcolm Bradbury.

Green Mansions **1959** Screen adaptation of W. H. Hudson's novel suffers due to miscasting of Hepburn as Rima the Bird Girl, who is not permitted to leave her sanctuary. Perkins is good as the male lead who fled to the jungle in search of wealth and instead finds a powerful love. Hepburn was married to director Ferrer at the time. **104m/C VHS.** Audrey Hepburn, Anthony Perkins, Lee J. Cobb, Sessue Hayakawa, Henry Silva, Nehemiah Persoff, Michael Pate; *D:* Mel Ferrer; *W:* Dorothy Kingsley; *C:* Joseph Ruttenberg.

The Green Mile ½ **1999 (R)** Lightning didn't exactly strike twice when Darabont directed this follow-up to "The Shawshank Redemption," another period prison drama by Stephen King. Paul Edgecomb (Hanks) is the decent head guard at Louisiana's Cold Mountain Penitentiary in 1935. He works E block, which is death row (title refers to the color of the floor). Among his prisoners is hulking black man John Coffey (Duncan), whose intimidating size belies a sweet nature. And something else—it seems Coffey has the power to heal. Overlong and watching the executions takes a strong stomach; characters are more symbols than human beings. **187m/C VHS, DVD.** Tom Hanks, Michael Clarke Duncan, David Morse, Bonnie Hunt, Michael Jeter,

Sam Rockwell, James Cromwell, Patricia Clarkson, Graham Greene, Barry Pepper, Doug Hutchison, Jeffrey DeMunn, Harry Dean Stanton, Dabbs Greer, Eve Brent, William Sadler, Gary Sinise; *D:* Frank Darabont; *W:* Frank Darabont; *C:* David Tattersall; *M:* Thomas Newman. Broadcast Film Critics '99: Adapt. Screenplay, Support. Actor (Duncan).

Green Pastures 𝒿𝒿𝒿 **1936** An adaptation of Marc Connelly's 1930 Pulitzer Prize-winning play, which attempts to retell Biblical stories in black English vernacular of the '30s. Southern theatre owners boycotted the controversial film which had an all-Black cast. **93m/C VHS.** Rex Ingram, Oscar Polk, Eddie Anderson, George Reed, Abraham Graves, Myrtle Anderson, Frank Wilson; *D:* William Keighley, Marc Connelly; *C:* Hal Mohr.

The Green Promise 𝒿𝒿 *Raging Waters* **1949** A well-meaning but domineering farmer and his four motherless children face disaster as a result of the father's obstinacy. But when he is laid up, the eldest daughter takes over, tries modern methods and equipment, and makes the farm a success. **90m/B VHS.** Walter Brennan, Marguerite Chapman, Robert Paige, Natalie Wood; *D:* William D. Russell.

The Green Room 𝒿𝒿 *La Chambre Verte* **1978 (PG)** Truffaut's haunting tale of a man who, valuing death over life, erects a shrine to all the dead he has known. Offered a chance at love, he cannot overcome his obsessions to take the risk. Based on the Henry James story "Altar of the Dead." In French with subtitles. **95m/C VHS.** *FR* Antoine Vitez, Jane Lobre, Marcel Berbert, Francois Truffaut, Nathalie Baye, Jean Daste; *D:* Francois Truffaut; *W:* Jean Gruault; *C:* Nestor Almendros; *M:* Maurice Jaubert.

The Green Slime woof! *Gamma Sango Uchu Daisakusen; Battle Beyond the Stars; Death and the Green Slime* **1968 (G)** Danger and romance highlight the journey of a space ship assigned to intercept an oncoming asteroid. Little do the astronauts realize, but they have brought aboard the ship the malevolent alien creatures known as green slime (and we ain't talking jello here). Cheap, U.S./Japanese co-production will leave you feeling lousy in the morning. The title song is legendary among genre aficionados. **90m/C VHS.** *JP* Robert Horton, Richard Jaeckel, Luciana Paluzzi, Bud Widom, Ted Gunther, Robert Dunham; *D:* Kinji Fukasaku; *W:* Ivan Reiner, Charles Sinclair, Bill Finger; *C:* Yoshikazu Yamasawa; *M:* Charles Fox, Toshiaki Tsushima.

Green Snake 𝒿𝒿 **1993** Combo of mysticism and action based on a Chinese fable. Green Snake (Cheung) and Son Ching (Wong) are actual reptiles who have been practicing taking human form. When self-righteous Buddhist monk Fa-Hai discovers them, he thinks it's a sin to tamper with the natural order. The snakes don't appreciate his lack of compassion and plot destruction. Cantonese with subtitles. **102m/C VHS.** *HK* Maggie Cheung, Joey Wong; *D:* Tsui Hark.

The Green Wall 𝒿𝒿𝒿 **1970** A city-dwelling young man attempts to homestead with his family in the Amazon. A lovely and tragic film with stunning photography of the Peruvian forests. First Peruvian feature to be shown in the U.S. In Spanish with English subtitles. **110m/C VHS.** *SP* Julio Aleman, Sandra Riva; *D:* Armando Robles Godoy; *W:* Armando Robles Godoy.

Greenfingers 𝒿𝒿½ **2000 (R)** One of those strange-but-true stories that barely stays ahead of being twee, thanks to its cast. Surly prisoner Colin Briggs (Owen) has just been transferred to Edgefield, an "open" prison that aims at building job skills. When Colin accidentally turns out to be a prime gardener (with greenfingers in British parlance), warden Hodge (Clarke) assigns him to garden detail along with his twinkly, dying, elderly cellmate Fergus (Kelly). Then the prison garden comes to the attention of TV star gardener Georgina Woodhouse (Mirren) and she sponsors their efforts in a very prestigious flower show. Remember the Brits take their gardening very seriously indeed. **90m/C VHS, DVD, Wide.** *GB US* Clive Owen, Helen Mirren, David Kelly, Warren Clarke, Danny Dyer, Paterson Joseph, Natasha Little, Adam Fogerty; *D:* Joel Hershman; *W:* Joel Hershman; *C:* John Daly; *M:* Guy Dagul.

Greetings 𝒿𝒿𝒿 **1968 (R)** De Niro stars in this wild and crazy comedy about a man who tries to help his friend flunk his draft physical. One of DePalma's first films, and a pleasantly anarchic view of the late '60s, wrought with a light, intelligent tone. Followed by the sequel "Hi, Mom." **88m/C VHS.** Robert De Niro, Jonathan Warden, Gerrit Graham, Allen (Goorwitz) Garfield, Megan McCormick, Bettina Kugel, Jack Cowley, Richard Hamilton; *D:* Brian DePalma; *W:* Brian DePalma, Charles Hirsch; *C:* Robert Fiore.

Gregory's Girl 𝒿𝒿𝒿½ **1980** Sweet, disarming comedy established Forsyth. An awkward young Scottish schoolboy falls in love with the female goalie of his soccer team. He turns to his 10-year-old sister for advice, but she's more interested in ice cream than love. His best friend is no help, either, since he has yet to fall in love. Perfect mirror of teenagers and their instantaneous, raw, and all-consuming loves. Very sweet scene with Gregory and his girl lying on their backs in an open space illustrates the simultaneous simplicity and complexity of young love. **91m/C VHS, DVD, Wide.** *GB* Gordon John Sinclair, Dee Hepburn, Jake D'Arcy, Chic Murray, Alex Norton, John Bett, Clare Grogan; *D:* Bill Forsyth; *W:* Bill Forsyth; *C:* Michael Coulter. British Acad. '81: Screenplay.

Gremlins 𝒿𝒿𝒿 **1984 (PG)** Comedy horror with deft satiric edge. Produced by Spielberg. Fumbling gadget salesman Rand Peltzer is looking for something really special to get his son Billy. He finds it in a small store in Chinatown. The wise shopkeeper is reluctant to sell him the adorable "mogwai" but relents after fully warning him "Don't expose him to bright light, don't ever get him wet, and don't ever, ever feed him after midnight." Naturally, this all happens and the result is a gang of nasty gremlins who decide to tear up the town on Christmas Eve. Followed by "Gremlins 2: The New Batch" which is less black comedy, more parody, and perhaps more inventive. **106m/C VHS, DVD, 8mm, Wide.** Zach Galligan, Phoebe Cates, Hoyt Axton, Polly Holliday, Frances Lee McCain, Keye Luke, Dick Miller, Corey Feldman, Judge Reinhold, Glynn Turman, Scott Brady, Jackie Joseph; *D:* Joe Dante; *W:* Chris Columbus; *C:* John Hora; *M:* Jerry Goldsmith; *V:* Howie Mandel.

Gremlins 2: The New Batch 𝒿𝒿𝒿½ **1990 (PG-13)** The sequel to "Gremlins" is superior to the original, which was quite good. Set in a futuristic skyscraper in the Big Apple, director Dante presents a less violent but far more campy vision, paying myriad surreal tributes to scores of movies, including "The Wizard of Oz" and musical extravaganzas of the past. Also incorporates a Donald Trump parody, takes on TV news, and body slams modern urban living. Great fun. **107m/C VHS, 8mm, Wide.** Zach Galligan, Phoebe Cates, John Glover, Christopher Lee, Robert Prosky, Robert Picardo, Haviland (Haylie) Morris, Dick Miller, Jackie Joseph, Keye Luke, Belinda Balaski, Paul Bartel, Kenneth Tobey, John Astin, Henry Gibson, Leonard Maltin, Hulk Hogan; ***Cameos:*** Jerry Goldsmith; *D:* Joe Dante; *W:* Charles Haas; *C:* John Hora; *M:* Jerry Goldsmith; *V:* Howie Mandel, Tony Randall.

Grendel, Grendel, Grendel 𝒿𝒿 **1982** An utterly urbane dragon wants to be friends, but for some reason people are just terrified of Grendel. It's true, he bites a head off once in a while, but nobody's perfect! An ingenious, animated retelling of Beowulf. **90m/C VHS.** *AU* *D:* Alexander Stitt; *M:* Bruce Smeaton; *V:* Peter Ustinov, Arthur Dignam, Julie McKenna, Keith Michell.

Greta 𝒿𝒿𝒿 **1986** During WWII, a young Polish boy escapes from a detention camp. Now on the run, several bizarre twists of fate place him in the care of Greta, a young girl whose father is an officer in the S.S. In Polish with English subtitles. **60m/C VHS.** *PL* Janusz Grabowski, Agnieszka Kruszewska, Eva Borowik, Tomasz Grochoczki, Andrzej Precig; *D:* Krzysztof Gruber.

The Grey Fox 𝒿𝒿𝒿½ **1983 (PG)** Based on the true story of Canada's most colorful and celebrated outlaw. Gentlemanly old stagecoach robber Bill Miner (Farnsworth) tries to pick up his life after 30 years in prison. Unable to resist another heist, he tries train robbery, and winds up hiding out in British Columbia where he meets photographer Kate Flynn (Burroughs), come to document the changing West. Farnsworth is perfect as the man who suddenly finds himself in the 20th century trying to work at the only craft he knows. Borso's first feature film after his work as a documentary filmmaker. **92m/C VHS.** *CA* Richard Farnsworth, Jackie Burroughs, Wayne Robson, Timothy Webber, Ken Pogue; *D:* Phillip Borsos; *W:* John Hunter; *C:* Frank Tidy; *M:* Michael Conway Baker. Genie '83: Director (Borsos), Film, Support. Actress (Burroughs).

Grey Owl 𝒿𝒿½ **1999 (PG-13)** Interesting old-fashioned biopic suffers from miscasting (and it's not Brosnan, although he takes a little getting used to). Based on the true story of Archie Grey Owl (Brosnan), an Ojibway trapper in 1930's Canada who changes his occupation and becomes an ardent early environmentalist and celebrity lecturer and writer. Only after his death does the truth come out—Archie was in fact Englishman Archibald Belaney. Film bogs down in its romantic aspects with Galipeau, as Grey Owl's young Mohawk girlfriend, sadly out of her depths. **117m/C VHS, DVD, Wide.** *GB CA* Pierce Brosnan, Annie Galipeau, Vlasta Vrana, Nathaniel Arcand, David Fox, Charles Powell, Renee Asherson, Stephenie Cole, Graham Greene; *D:* Richard Attenborough; *W:* William Nicholson; *C:* Roger Pratt; *M:* George Fenton. Genie '99: Costume Des.

Greyfriars Bobby 𝒿𝒿½ **1961** A true story of a Skye terrier named Bobby who, after his master dies, refuses to leave the grave. Even after being coaxed by the local children into town, he still returns to the cemetery each evening. Word of his loyalty spreads, and Bobby becomes the pet of 19th century Edinburgh. Nicely told, with fine location photography and good acting. Great for children and animal lovers. **91m/C VHS.** Donald Crisp, Laurence Naismith, Kay Walsh; *D:* Don Chaffey.

Greystoke: The Legend of Tarzan, Lord of the Apes 𝒿𝒿 **1984 (PG)** The seventh Earl of Greystoke becomes a shipwrecked orphan and is raised by apes. Ruling the ape-clan in the vine-swinging persona of Tarzan, he is discovered by an anthropologist and returned to his ancestral home in Scotland, where he is immediately recognized by his grandfather. The contrast between the behavior of man and ape is interesting, and Tarzan's introduction to society is fun, but there's no melodrama or cliff-hanging action, as we've come to expect of the Tarzan genre. Due to her heavy southern accent, Andie MacDowell (as Jane) had her voice dubbed by Glenn Close. **130m/C VHS, Wide.** Christopher Lambert, Ralph Richardson, Ian Holm, James Fox, Andie MacDowell, Ian Charleson, Cheryl Campbell, Nigel Davenport; *D:* Hugh Hudson; *W:* Michael Austin. N.Y. Film Critics '84: Support. Actor (Richardson).

Gridlock'd 𝒿𝒿𝒿 **1996 (R)** Junkies and sometime-musicians Spoon (Shakur) and Stretch (Roth) decide to kick the habit after their singer Cookie (Newton) overdoses and slips into a coma. The hapless pair are thrown into the switches of social services programs and government offices where they shuffle endlessly but nothing happens. Think "Waiting for Godot" meets "Waiting for the Man." Meanwhile, their dealer is murdered and they're the prime suspects, pursued by the cops and the actual killers, who believe that they've stolen said dealer's stash. Shakur shows flashes of the brilliance that might have been as the more sensitive and sane of the pair, while Roth complements him perfectly as his bug-crazy short-sighted partner. Fellow actor Curtis-Hall's directorial debut. **91m/C VHS, DVD, Wide.** Tim Roth, Tupac Shakur, Thandie Newton, Charles Fleischer, Howard Hesseman, James Pickens Jr., John Sayles, Tom Towles, Eric Payne; ***Cameos:*** Vondie Curtis-Hall; *D:* Vondie Curtis-Hall; *W:* Vondie Curtis-Hall; *C:* Bill Pope; *M:* Stewart Copeland.

Grief 𝒿𝒿 **1994** Mark (Chester) is a writer on the syndicated daytime TV show "The Love Judge." Still numb from his lover's death from AIDS the previous year, Mark begins to take an interest in fellow writer Bill (Arquette), while writer Paula (Gutteridge) desires to become the show's new producer and secretary Leslie (Douglas) wants to take her place as the new writer. Present producer Jo (Beat) tries to keep her office family in line while sorting out her personal life. Writer-director Glatzer knows his territory since he spent five years writing for "Divorce Court." **86m/C VHS.** Craig Chester, Alexis Arquette, Lucy Gutteridge, Illeana Douglas, Jackie Beat, Carlton Wilborn, Paul Bartel, Mary Woronov; *D:* Richard Glatzer; *W:* Richard Glatzer; *C:* David Dechant.

Grievous Bodily Harm 𝒿𝒿 **1989 (R)** Morris Martin's wife Claudine is missing. When he finds a videotape of Claudine in very compromising positions, he becomes murderously determined to find out where she has gone. **136m/C VHS.** John Waters, Colin Friels, Bruno Lawrence; *D:* Mark Joffe.

Griffin and Phoenix: A Love Story 𝒿𝒿½ **1976** A sentimental film about the mortality of two vital people. Falk deserts his family when he learns he has terminal cancer. Clayburgh, also terminally ill, meets him for a short but meaningful affair. Good performances help overcome the tear-jerker aspects of the story. **110m/C VHS.** Peter Falk, Jill Clayburgh, Dorothy Tristan, John Lehne; *D:* Daryl Duke. **TV**

The Grifters 𝒿𝒿𝒿½ **1990 (R)** Evocative rendering of a terrifying sub-culture. Huston, Cusak, and Bening are con artists, struggling to stay on top in a world where violence, money, and lust are the prizes. Bening and Huston fight for Cusak's soul, while he's determined to decide for himself. Seamless performances and dazzling atmosphere, along with superb pacing, make for a provocative film. Based on a novel by Jim Thompson. **114m/C VHS, DVD.** Anjelica Huston, John Cusack, Annette Bening, Pat Hingle, J.T. Walsh, Charles Napier, Henry Jones, Gailard Sartain, Jeremy Piven; *D:* Stephen Frears; *W:* Donald E. Westlake; *C:* Oliver Stapleton; *M:* Elmer Bernstein. Ind. Spirit '91: Actress (Huston), Film; L.A. Film Critics '90: Actress (Huston); Natl. Soc. Film Critics '90: Actress (Huston), Support. Actress (Bening).

Grim 𝒿 **1995 (R)** Lives up to its title as an extremely icky and evil subterranean creature is awakened from a long sleep by miners. Apparently not long enough, since he proceeds to rip apart anyone he comes in contact with. **86m/C VHS, DVD.** Emmanuel Xuereb, Tres Handley, Peter Tregloan; *D:* Paul Matthews; *W:* Paul Matthews; *C:* Alan M. Trow; *M:* Dennis Michael Tenney.

Grim Prairie Tales 𝒿𝒿 **1989 (R)** A city slicker and a crazed mountain man meet by a campfire in the high plains one night and pass the time sharing four tales of Western horror. Dourif and Jones are fun, the stories scary, making for an interesting twist on both the horror and the Western genres. **90m/C VHS.** Brad Dourif, James Earl Jones, Marc McClure, William Atherton, Scott Paulin, Lisa Eichhorn; *D:* Wayne Coe; *W:* Wayne Coe; *C:* Janusz Kaminski.

The Grim Reaper 𝒿𝒿𝒿 *La Commare Secca* **1962** 22-year-old Bertolucci directed his first feature with this grim and brutal treatment of the investigation of the murder of a prostitute, told via flashbacks and from the disparate perspectives of three people who knew the woman. A commercial bust, the critics were no kinder than the public at the time; not until two years later, with "Before the Revolution," did Bertolucci earn his directorial spurs. The script was written by Pasolini, with whom the erstwhile poet had collaborated on "Accattone" the previous year (as assistant). In Italian with English subtitles. **100m/B VHS.** *IT* Francesco Rulu, Giancarlo de Rosa; *D:* Bernardo Bertolucci; *W:* Pier Paolo Pasolini.

Grim Reaper 𝒿½ **1981 (R)** Mia Farrow's sister is one of a group of American students vacationing on a Greek island. Farrow learns of the twisted cannibalistic murderer who methodically tries to avenge the tragic deaths of his family. **81m/C VHS.** *IT* Tisa Farrow, George Eastman; ***D:*** Joe D'Amato.

Grind 🦴🦴 **1996** Dysfunctional blue-collar family saga set in New Jersey. Eddie Dolan (Crudup), just out of the joint, moves in with brother Terry (Schulze) and sister-in-law Janey (Shelly). He gets a dull factory job and fixes up old cars to go drag-racing on the weekend—as well as helping out Terry, who has a sideline working with a car theft ring. Since gorgeous Eddie works nights, he and sulky stay-at-home-with-the-baby Janey get to be real close daytime buddies. Naturally their affair causes trouble for all. A paint-by-numbers plot with some decent acting. **96m/C VHS, DVD.** Billy Crudup, Adrienne Shelly, Paul Schulze, Frank Vincent, Saul Stein, Amanda Peet, Steven Beach, Tim Devlin; ***D:*** Chris Kentis; ***W:*** Chris Kentis, Laura Lau; ***C:*** Stephen Kazmierski; ***M:*** Brian Kelly.

Grisbi 🦴🦴 *Hands Off the Loot; Honour Among Thieves; Touchez Pas Au Grisbi* **1953** King of the French underworld, Gabin finds there's no honor among thieves when a gold heist goes wrong and the loot comes up missing. Moreau is the quintessential moll. French with subtitles. **94m/B VHS.** *FR* Jean Gabin, Jeanne Moreau, Lino Ventura, Daniel Cauchy, Gaby Basset; ***D:*** Jacques Becker; ***W:*** Jacques Becker, Maurice Griffe; ***M:*** Jean Wiener. Venice Film Fest. '54: Actor (Gabin).

The Grissom Gang 🦴🦴🦴 **1971 (R)** Remake of the 1948 British film "No Orchids for Miss Blandish." Darby is a wealthy heiress kidnapped by a family of grotesques, led by a sadistic mother. The ransom gets lost in a series of bizarre events, and the heiress appears to be falling for one of her moronic captors. Director Robert Aldrich skillfully blends extreme violence with dark humor. Superb camera work, editing, and 1920s period sets. **127m/C VHS, DVD, Wide.** Kim Darby, Scott Wilson, Tony Musante, Ralph Waite, Connie Stevens, Robert Lansing, Wesley Addy; ***D:*** Robert Aldrich; ***W:*** Leon Griffiths; ***C:*** Joseph Biroc; ***M:*** Gerald Fried.

Grizzly 🦴 *Killer Grizzly* **1976 (PG)** Giant, killer grizzly terrorizes a state park in this blatant "Jaws" rip-off. From the same folks who produced "Abby," a blatant "Exorcist" rip-off. Filmed in Georgia. **92m/C VHS, DVD.** Christopher George, Richard Jaeckel, Andrew Prine, Victoria (Vicki) Johnson, Charles Kissinger; ***D:*** William Girdler; ***W:*** Harvey Flaxman, David Sheldon; ***M:*** Robert O. Ragland.

Grizzly Adams: The Legend Continues 🦴½ **1990** A small town is saved from three desperados by Grizzly and his huge grizzly bear pet, Martha. **90m/C VHS.** Gene Edwards, Link Wyler, Red West, Tony Caruso, Acquanetta, L.Q. (Justus E. McQueen) Jones; ***D:*** Ken Kennedy.

Grizzly Falls 🦴🦴½ **1999 (PG)** Old-fashioned family fare, set in 1913, finds 13-year-old Harry (Clark) setting out on a wilderness adventure in the Canadian Rockies with his dad, Tyrone (Brown). Tyrone is out to capture a grizzly and bring it back (alive) for study. But when Tyrone finds a female grizzly and captures the bear's two cubs, Mom Grizzly gets back at him by making off with Harry. The boy and the bear bond but this interspecies relationship can't last and eventually boy and cubs end up with the right species of parent. **94m/C VHS, DVD.** *CA GB* Daniel Clark, Bryan Brown, Tom Jackson, Oliver Tobias, Richard Harris; ***D:*** Stewart Raffill; ***W:*** Richard Beattie; ***C:*** Thom Best; ***M:*** Paul Zaza, David Reilly.

Grizzly Mountain 🦴🦴½ **1997 (G)** Dylan (Dylan Haggerty) and his sister Nicole (Lund) are camping in Oregon with their parents when they decide to explore a cave. After some mysterious rumbling and shaking, the siblings emerge in the 1870s. They meet mountain man Jeremiah (Haggerty), who promises to help them return home, but he's got problems of his own—bad guy Burt (Stephens) wants to dynamite the mountain so the railroad can come through. Pic wanders back and forth between the two time periods and the kids learn a lesson in ecology (and are reunited with their parents). Easy-going; some beautiful scenery. **96m/C VHS.** Dan Haggerty, Dylan Haggerty, Nicole Lund, Perry Stephens, Kim Morgan Greene, Martin Kove, Robert Budaska, E.E. Bell, Marguerite Hickey, Don Borza; ***D:*** Jeremy Haft; ***W:*** Peter White, Jeremy Haft; ***C:*** Andy Parke; ***M:*** John McCallum.

Groove 🦴🦴🦴½ **2000 (R)** Editor Greg Harrison's directorial debut is an economically paced examination of the "rave" scene. It features a terrific ensemble cast, but at heart, the film is an old-fashioned boy-meets-girl romance. The setting is an abandoned building on a San Francisco pier. That's where the squarish David (Linklater) is attending his first rave. Leyla (Glaudini) has perhaps been to too many. Over the course of the night they and the other rave kids go through a series of changes fueled by drugs, emotion, and sexual indecision. In another time, the same story with more limited sexual roles and consciousness-altering substances could have been told about a homecoming dance or spring break. The changes and discoveries the characters make have not changed. Even though the film was made on a restricted budget—actually shot in Super 16mm.—it looks very good. **86m/C VHS, DVD, Wide.** Steve Van Wormer, Lola Glaudini, Hamish Linklater, Denny Kirkwood, Rachel True, MacKenzie Firgens, Nick Offerman, Ari Gold; ***D:*** Greg Harrison; ***W:*** Greg Harrison; ***C:*** Matthew Irving.

The Groove Tube 🦴🦴½ **1972 (R)** A TV series called "The Groove Tube" is the context for these skits that spoof everything on TV from commercials to newscasts. Chevy Chase's movie debut. **75m/C VHS, DVD.** Lane Sarasohn, Chevy Chase, Richard Belzer, Marcy Mendham, Bill Kemmill, Ken Shapiro, Alex Stephens, Berkeley Harris, Buzzy Linhart, Richmond Baier; ***D:*** Ken Shapiro; ***W:*** Lane Sarasohn, Ken Shapiro; ***C:*** Bob Bailin.

Gross Anatomy 🦴🦴½ **1989 (PG-13)** Lightweight comedy/drama centers on the trials and tribulations of medical students. Modine is the very bright, but somewhat lazy, future doctor determined not to buy into the bitter competition among his fellow students. His lack of desire inflames Lahti, a professor dying of a fatal disease who nevertheless believes in modern medicine. She pushes and inspires him to focus on his potential, and his desire to help people. Worth watching, in spite of cheap laughs. Interesting cast of up-and-comers. **107m/C VHS.** Matthew Modine, Daphne Zuniga, Christine Lahti, John Scott Clough, Alice Carter, Robert Desiderio, Zakes Mokae, Todd Field; ***D:*** Thom Eberhardt; ***W:*** Ron Nyswaner; ***M:*** David Newman.

Gross Misconduct 🦴🦴 **1993 (R)** Charismatic university professor Justin Thorne (Smits) makes the nearly fatal mistake of getting involved with his student, Jennifer (Watts). Seems she's one of those obsessive types and when Thorne wants to break off the affair for the sake of his marriage, Jennifer goes over the edge. Thorne's charged with rape and unless Jennifer changes her story his life is over. Based on a true story that happened in the '50s but this version is set in the '90s. **97m/C VHS.** *AU* Jimmy Smits, Naomi Watts, Sarah Chadwick, Adrian Wright, Alan Fletcher; ***D:*** George Miller; ***W:*** Lance Peters, Gerard Maguire; ***C:*** David Connell.

Grosse Fatigue 🦴🦴🦴 *Dead Tired* **1994 (R)** Diminutive comic everyman Blanc successfully takes up the challenge of a dual role of mistaken identity (as well as directing and writing chores). He first plays himself, bewildered by accusations of lechery and other escapades, who learns he has a psychopath double who's stolen his celebrity. So it's up to Michel and pal Carole (the gorgeous Bouquet) to track down the mischief-maker before Blanc's reputation is in complete tatters. French with subtitles. **85m/C VHS.** *FR* Michel Blanc, Carole Bouquet, Philippe Noiret, Josiane Balasko; ***Cameos:*** Charlotte Gainsbourg, Mathilda May, Thierry Lhermitte, Roman Polanski; ***D:*** Michel Blanc; ***W:*** Michel Blanc; ***C:*** Eduardo Serra; ***M:*** Rene Marc Bini.

Grosse Pointe Blank 🦴🦴🦴 **1997 (R)** Stressed-out Martin Q. Blank (Cusack) debates with his nervous shrink (Arkin) about whether to attend his 10-year high school reunion. He doesn't want to deal with the Debi (Driver), the girl he ditched on prom night, the incessant small talk, or the prospect of telling his classmates that he's a professional hit man. Then there's the matter of rival pro Grocer (Aykroyd), who wants to start an assassins union. Dark comedy with excellent writing, a charmingly off-center lead by Cusack, who attended his own reunion as research, and a surprising amount of action. Pasadena fills in for most of Grosse Pointe, but the Detroit shots are real. **107m/C VHS, DVD.** John Cusack, Minnie Driver, Dan Aykroyd, Alan Arkin, Joan Cusack, Jeremy Piven, Mitchell Ryan, Hank Azaria, Michael Cudlitz, Benny "The Jet" Urquidez, Barbara Harris, Ann Cusack, K. Todd Freeman; ***D:*** George Armitage; ***W:*** Tom Jankiewicz, D.V. DeVincentis, Steve Pink, John Cusack; ***C:*** Jamie Anderson; ***M:*** Joe Strummer.

Grotesque woof! **1987 (R)** After slaughtering a young woman's family as they vacationed in a remote mountain cabin, a gang of bloodthirsty punks are attacked by the family secret, the deformed son. The title says it all. **79m/C VHS.** Linda Blair, Tab Hunter, Guy Stockwell, Donna Wilkes, Nels Van Patten, Brad Wilson, Sharon Hughes, Robert Z'Dar, Billy Frank, Michelle Bensoussan, Mikel Angel; ***D:*** Joe Tornatore; ***W:*** Mikel Angel.

Ground Control 🦴🦴 **1998 (PG-13)** Jack Harris (Sutherland) is a former air traffic controller, who retired after a fatal plane crash. Years later, a old friend asks Jack to help out during a busy night at the Phoenix airport and Jack finds himself being forced to aid a plane with no radar, contact or control. **98m/C VHS, DVD.** Kiefer Sutherland, Robert Sean Leonard, Kelly McGillis, Henry Winkler, Michael Gross, Margaret Cho, Charles Fleischer, Farrah Forke, Bruce McGill, Kristy Swanson; ***D:*** Richard Howard.

Ground Zero 🦴🦴🦴 **1988 (R)** Political thriller, set in the Australian outback in the '50s, in which a man searches for the reasons for his father's murder in the films of the British nuclear tests. **109m/C VHS.** *AU* Colin Friels, Jack Thompson, Donald Pleasence, Natalie Bate, Simon Chilvers, Neil Fitzpatrick, Bob Maza, Peter Cummins; ***D:*** Bruce Myles, Michael Pattinson.

Ground Zero 🦴½ **1988 (R)** Ground Zero is the term used to describe the site of a nuclear explosion. San Francisco is threatened with just such a new name in this story of nuclear blackmail. Someone plants an atomic bomb on the Golden Gate Bridge. It must be defused and the culprit caught. **90m/C VHS.** Ron Casteel, Melvin Belli, Yvonne D'Angiers; ***D:*** James T. Flocker.

Groundhog Day 🦴🦴🦴 **1993 (PG)** Phil (Murray), an obnoxious weatherman, is in Punxatawney, PA to cover the annual emergence of the famous rodent from its hole. After he's caught in a blizzard that he didn't predict, he finds himself trapped in a time warp, doomed to relive the same day over and over again until he gets it right. Lighthearted romantic comedy takes a funny premise and manages to carry it through to the end. Murray has fun with the role, although he did get bitten by the groundhog during the scene when they're driving. Elliott, who has been missed since his days as the man under the seats on "Late Night with David Letterman" is perfectly cast as a smart-mouthed cameraman. **103m/C VHS, DVD, Wide.** Bill Murray, Andie MacDowell, Chris Elliott, Stephen Tobolowsky, Brian Doyle-Murray, Marita Geraghty, Angela Paton; ***D:*** Harold Ramis; ***W:*** Harold Ramis, Daniel F. Rubin; ***C:*** John Bailey; ***M:*** George Fenton. British Acad. '93: Orig. Screenplay.

The Groundstar Conspiracy 🦴🦴🦴 **1972 (PG)** Spy thriller brings to life L.P. Davies' novel, "The Alien." After an explosion kills all but one space project scientist, Peppard is sent to investigate suspicions of a cover-up. Meanwhile, the surviving scientist (Sarrazin) suffers from disfigurement and amnesia. He pursues his identity while Peppard accuses him of being a spy. Splendid direction by Lamont Johnson. Sarrazin's best role. **96m/C VHS, DVD, Wide.** *CA* George Peppard, Michael Sarrazin, Christine Belford, Cliff (Potter) Potts, James Olson, Tim O'Connor, James McEachin, Alan Oppenheimer; ***D:*** Lamont Johnson; ***W:*** Matthew Howard; ***C:*** Michael Reed; ***M:*** Paul Hoffert.

The Group 🦴🦴½ **1966** Based upon the novel by Mary McCarthy, the well-acted story deals with a group of graduates from a Vassar-like college as they try to adapt to life during the Great Depression. Has some provocative subject matter, including lesbianism, adultery, and mental breakdowns. Soapy, but a good cast with film debuts of Bergen, Hackett, Pettet, Widdoes, and Holbrook. **150m/C VHS.** Candice Bergen, Joanna Pettet, Shirley Knight, Joan Hackett, Elizabeth Hartman, Jessica Walter, Larry Hagman, James Broderick, Kathleen Widdoes, Hal Holbrook, Mary-Robin Redd, Richard Mulligan, Carrie Nye; ***D:*** Sidney Lumet; ***C:*** Boris Kaufman.

Group Marriage 🦴🦴½ **1972 (R)** Six young professionals fall into a marriage of communal convenience and rapidly discover the many advantages and drawbacks of their thoroughly modern arrangement. **90m/C VHS.** Victoria Vetri, Aimee (Amy) Eccles, Zack Taylor, Jeff Pomerantz, Claudia Jennings, Jayne Kennedy, Milt Kamen; ***D:*** Stephanie Rothman.

Growing Pains 🦴½ **1982** A young couple discover that their newly adopted son possesses extraordinary powers. **60m/C VHS.** Gary Bond, Barbara Keilermann, Norman Beaton.

Grown Ups 🦴🦴 **1980** A newly married couple move into their first home only to discover that the wife's ditzy sister expects to live with them and that their next door neighbor was their former high school teacher. **95m/C VHS.** *GB* Philip Davis, Leslie Manville, Sam Kelly, Lindsay Duncan, Brenda Blethyn, Janine Duvitsky; ***D:*** Mike Leigh; ***W:*** Mike Leigh. **TV**

Grown Ups 🦴🦴 **1986** A journalist watches his family slowly disintegrating around him in this adaptation of Jules Feiffer's play. **106m/C VHS.** Jean Stapleton, Martin Balsam, Charles Grodin, Marilu Henner, Kerry Segal; ***D:*** John Madden.

Gruesome Twosome 🦴 **1967** Another guts/cannibalism/mutilation funfest by Lewis, about someone who's marketing the hair of some very recently deceased college coeds. **75m/C VHS, DVD.** Elizabeth Davis, Gretchen Wells, Chris Martell, Rodney Bedell, Ronnie Cass, Karl Stoeber, Dianne Wilhite, Andrea Barr, Dianne Raymond, Sherry Robinson, Barrie Walton, Michael Lewis, Ray Sager; ***D:*** Herschell Gordon Lewis; ***W:*** Allison Louise Downe; ***C:*** Roy Collodi; ***M:*** Larry Wellington.

Grumpier Old Men 🦴🦴 **1995 (PG-13)** Max (Matthau) and John (Lemmon) are back at each other's throats, but with John happily married to Ariel (Ann-Margaret), he's not much of an adversary. Enter Maria (Loren), who wants to turn the boys' favorite bait shop into an Italian restaurant. In a twist that should surprise no one, Max soon falls for the beautiful Maria, and she with him. Jokes are similar but more adolescent than in the first, and subplots involving John and Max's kids' wedding and Grandpa's (Meredith) romantic interests are forced. Suffers the standard sequel fate of not measuring up to the original. **101m/C VHS, DVD.** Jack Lemmon, Walter Matthau, Ann-Margret, Sophia Loren, Kevin Pollak, Burgess Meredith, Daryl Hannah, Ann Guilbert; ***D:*** Howard Deutch; ***W:*** Mark Steven Johnson; ***C:*** Tak Fujimoto; ***M:*** Alan Silvestri.

Grumpy Old Men 🦴🦴🦴 **1993 (PG-13)** Lemmon and Matthau team for their seventh movie, in parts that seem written just for them. Boyhood friends and retired neighbors, they have been feuding for so long that neither of them can remember why. Doesn't matter much, when it provides a reason for them to spout off at each other every morning and play nasty practical jokes every night. This, and ice-fishing, is life as they know it, until feisty younger woman Ann-Margret moves into the neighborhood and lights some long-dormant fires. 83-year-old Meredith is a special treat playing Lemmon's 90-something father. Filmed in Wabasha, Minnesota, and grumpy, in the most pleasant way. **104m/C VHS, DVD, 8mm, Wide.** Jack Lemmon, Walter Matthau, Ann-Margret, Burgess Meredith, Daryl Hannah, Kevin Pollak, Ossie Davis, Buck Henry, Christopher McDonald; ***D:***

Donald Petrie; **W:** Mark Steven Johnson; **C:** Johnny E. Jensen; **M:** Alan Silvestri.

Grunt! The Wrestling Movie woof! **1985 (R)** A spoof of documentaries about the behind-the-scenes world of wrestling. For fans only. **91m/C VHS.** Wally Greene, Steven Cepello, Dick Murdoch, John Tolos; **D:** Allan Holzman.

Gryphon **1988** Ricky's new teacher can do all sorts of magical things. Hidden among her tricks are lessons about creativity, beauty, and imagination. Adapted from the short story by Charles Baxter. Aired on PBS as part of the "Wonderworks" family movie series. **58m/C VHS.** Amanda Plummer, Sully Diaz, Alexis Cruz; **D:** Mark Cullingham.

Guadalcanal Diary && ½ **1943** A vintage wartime flag-waver, with a typical crew of Marines battling the "Yellow Menace" over an important base on the famous Pacific atoll. Based on Richard Tregaskis' first-hand account. **93m/B VHS, DVD.** Preston Foster, Lloyd Nolan, William Bendix, Richard Conte, Anthony Quinn, Richard Jaeckel, Roy Roberts, Minor Watson, Miles Mander, Ralph Byrd, Lionel Stander, Reed Hadley, John Archer, Eddie Acuff, Selmer Jackson, Paul Fung; **D:** Lewis Seiler; **W:** Lamar Trotti, Jerome Cady; **C:** Charles Clarke; **M:** David Buttolph.

Guantanamera &&& **1995** A famous singer returns to her hometown of Guantanamo for the first time in 50 years, is reunited with her first sweetheart, and promptly dies. Her niece Georgina (Ibarra) comes to take her remains back to Havana, along with her husband Adolfo (Cruz), an oafish Communist Party worker who has devised a bizarre relay system to transport corpses in order to save gasoline. Also in the caravan is Mariano (Perugorria), a former student of Georgina's who had a crush on her. Mariano attempts to seduce Georgina, while Adolfo attempts to get a clue. Celebrates the lives of everyday Cubans and skewers bumbling government bureaucrats. The final collaboration between directors Gutierrez Alea, who died in 1996, and Tabio. Spanish with subtitles. **104m/C VHS, DVD.** *CU* Carlos Cruz, Mirta Ibarra, Jorge Perugorria, Raul Eguren, Pedro Fernandez; **D:** Tomas Gutierrez Alea, Juan Carlos Tabio; **W:** Tomas Gutierrez Alea, Juan Carlos Tabio, Eliseo Alberto Diego; **C:** Hans Burman; **M:** Jose Nieto.

The Guardian &½ **1984 (R)** Residents of a chic New York apartment building hire a security expert/ex-military man to aid them in combatting their crime problem. But one of the liberal tenants thinks their guard's methods may come at too high a cost. **102m/C VHS.** Martin Sheen, Louis Gossett Jr., Arthur Hill; **D:** David Greene; **M:** Jonathan Goldsmith. CABLE

The Guardian & **1990 (R)** A young couple unwittingly hires a human sacrificing druid witch as a babysitter for their child. Based on the book "The Nanny" by Dan Greenburg. **92m/C VHS, DVD.** Jenny Seagrove, Dwier Brown, Carey Lowell, Brad Hall, Miguel Ferrer, Natalija Nogulich, Pamela Brull, Gary Swanson; **D:** William Friedkin; **W:** William Friedkin, Stephen Volk, Dan Greenberg; **C:** John A. Alonzo; **M:** Jack Hues.

The Guardian &½ **2000 (R)** Uninspired actioner finds Marine John Kross (Van Peebles) witnessing some freaky stuff during Desert Storm. He winds up in the hospital with a strange map carved on his chest. Flash-forward 12 years and Kross is an L.A. cop chasing down some new street drug that's made from a mystery powder from Iraq. And then there's something about a demon, a young prophet who needs protection, and his guardian who is Kross of course. Who cares. **89m/C VHS, DVD, Wide.** Mario Van Peebles, James Remar, Ice-T, Daniel Hugh Kelly, Stacy Oversier; **D:** John Terlesky; **W:** John Terlesky, Jeff Yagher, Gary J. Tunnicliffe; **C:** Maximo Munzi. VIDEO

Guardian &½ **2001 (R)** So soldier Van Peebles witnesses the escape of a demon while stationed in the middle east (although he doesn't know what he's really seen) and 12 years later must battle said demon to save the world. There are other plot threads but they don't make much sense either. **89m/C VHS.** James Remar, Ice-T, Mario Van Peebles; **D:** John Terlesky, Gary J. Tunnicliffe; **W:** Jeff Yagher. VIDEO

Guardian Angel && ½ *Beyond Justice* **1994 (R)** Detective Christy McKay (Rothrock) quits the force after her partner/lover is killed by icy seductress Nina (Denier), who manages to escape from jail. When McKay is hired to protect playboy Lawton Hobbs (McVicar), she finds that the threat comes from a psycho exgirlfriend. Guess who. **97m/C VHS, DVD.** Cynthia Rothrock, Lydie Denier, Daniel McVicar, Kenneth McLeod, Marshall Teague, John O'Leary, Dale Jacoby; **D:** Richard W. Munchkin.

Guardian of the Abyss & **1982** A young couple who buy an antique mirror get more than they bargained for when they discover that it is the threshold to Hell and the devil wants to come through. **60m/C VHS.** Ray Lonnen, Rosalyn Landor, Paul Darrow, Barbara Ewing; **D:** Don Sharp.

Guarding Tess && **1994 (PG-13)** Long-suffering Secret Service agent Cage is nearing the end of his three-year assignment to crotchety widowed First Lady MacLaine when the Prez extends his tour of duty. Feels like a TV movie, not surprising since writers Torokvei and Wilson have several sitcoms to their credit, including "WKRP in Cinncinnati." Nice chemistry between Cage and MacLaine results in a few funny moments, but there are too many formulaic plot twists. End result: a pleasant, if somewhat slow buddy comedy. **98m/C VHS, DVD, 8mm, Wide.** Shirley MacLaine, Nicolas Cage, Austin Pendleton, Edward Albert, Richard Griffiths, Dale Dye; **D:** Hugh Wilson; **W:** Hugh Wilson, Peter Torokvei; **C:** Brian Reynolds; **M:** Michael Convertino.

The Guardsman &&& **1931** Broadway's illustrious couple Lunt and Fontanne shine in this adaptation of the clever marital comedy by French playwright Molnar in which they also starred. This sophisticated comedy was their only starring film, although they were offered large sums of money to appear in other movies—they just couldn't tear themselves away from the stage. Remade as "The Chocolate Soldier" and "Lily in Love." **89m/B VHS.** Alfred Lunt, Lynn Fontanne, Roland Young, ZaSu Pitts, Maude Eburne, Herman Bing, Ann Dvorak; **D:** Sidney Franklin.

Guerilla Brigade && ½ *Riders* **1939** A rarely seen Ukrainian epic about Russian/Ukrainian solidarity during the Civil War. In Russian with English subtitles. **90m/B VHS.** *RU* **D:** Igor Savchenko.

Guess What We Learned in School Today? woof! **1970 (R)** Parents in a conservative suburban community protest sex education in the schools. Intended as a satire, but it only reinforces stereotypes. **85m/C VHS.** Richard Carballo, Devin Goldenberg; **D:** John G. Avildsen.

Guess Who's Coming to Dinner &&& **1967** Controversial in its time. A young white woman brings her black fiance home to meet her parents. The situation truly tests their open-mindedness and understanding. Hepburn and Tracy (in his last film appearance) are wonderful and serve as the anchors in what would otherwise have been a rather sugary film. Houghton, who portrays the independent daughter, is the real-life niece of Hepburn. **108m/C VHS, DVD.** Katharine Hepburn, Spencer Tracy, Sidney Poitier, Katharine Houghton, Cecil Kellaway, Beah Richards; **D:** Stanley Kramer; **W:** William Rose; **C:** Sam Leavitt; **M:** Frank DeVol. Oscars '67: Actress (Hepburn), Story & Screenplay; AFI '98: Top 100; British Acad. '68: Actor (Tracy), Actress (Hepburn).

Guest in the House && ½ **1944** A seemingly friendly young female patient is invited to stay in the family home of her doctor. She skillfully attempts to dissect the family's harmony in the process. **121m/B VHS.** Anne Baxter, Ralph Bellamy, Ruth Warrick, Marie McDonald, Margaret Hamilton, Aline MacMahon, Scott McKay, Jerome Cowan, Percy Kilbride, Connie Laird; **D:** John Brahm; **W:** Ketti Frings; **C:** Lee Garmes; **M:** Werner Janssen.

Guest Wife && ½ **1945** Determined to impress his sentimental boss, a quick-thinking bachelor talks his best friend's wife into posing as his own wife, but the hoax gets a bit out of hand and nearly ruins the real couple's marriage. **90m/B VHS.** Claudette Colbert, Don Ameche, Dick Foran, Charles Dingle, Wilma Francis; **D:** Sam Wood; **C:** Joseph Valentine.

A Guide for the Married Man &&& **1967** One suburban husband instructs another in adultery, with a cast of dozens enacting various slapstick cameos. Based on Frank Tarloff's novel of the same name. Followed by "A Guide for the Married Woman." **91m/C VHS.** Walter Matthau, Robert Morse, Inger Stevens, Sue Ane Langdon, Claire Kelly, Elaine Devry; **Cameos:** Lucille Ball, Sid Caesar, Jack Benny, Wally Cox, Jayne Mansfield, Louis Nye, Carl Reiner, Phil Silvers, Terry-Thomas, Sam Jaffe, Jeffrey Hunter, Polly Bergen; **D:** Gene Kelly; **W:** Frank Tarloff; **M:** John Williams.

A Guide for the Married Woman &½ **1978** A bored housewife tries to take the romantic advice of a girlfriend to add a little spice to her life. A poor TV follow-up to "A Guide for the Married Man." **96m/C VHS.** Cybill Shepherd, Barbara Feldon, Eve Arden, Chuck Woolery, Peter Marshall, Charles Frank; **D:** Hy Averback. TV

The Guilty && **1999 (R)** Lawyer Callum Crane (Pullman) has a drunken sexual tryst with his new secretary, Sophie (Anwar), and suddenly his life is spiraling out-of-control. Sophie tries to blackmail him when Crane is appointed a federal judge and he decides to hire Nathan (Sawa), a young man who's just been released from prison, to bump her off. But Nathan's not exactly who he seems and, of course, nothing goes exactly as planned. It's a complex thriller with a good ensemble cast. **112m/C VHS, DVD.** Bill Pullman, Gabrielle Anwar, Devon Sawa, Angela Featherstone, Joanne Whalley, Jaimz Woolvett, Ken Tremblett, Camilla Overbye Roos; **D:** Anthony Waller; **W:** William Davies; **C:** Tobias Schliessler; **M:** Debbie Wiseman.

Guilty as Charged &½ **1992 (R)** A butcher rigs his own private electric chair and captures and executes paroled killers in his personal quest for justice. But when a politician frames an innocent man for murder how far will this vigilante go? **95m/C VHS.** Rod Steiger, Lauren Hutton, Heather Graham, Isaac Hayes; **D:** Sam Irvin; **M:** Steve Bartek.

Guilty as Sin && **1993 (R)** Johnson is a ruthless Casanova accused of murdering his very wealthy wife and decides lawyer DeMornay is just the woman to defend him. Question is, who'll defend DeMornay from him? Johnson has fun as the menacing smoothie but DeMornay's supposedly hotshot criminal attorney is just plain dumb. It sounds like "Jagged Edge" but there's no sexual involvement between client and lawyer and no thrill in this thriller. **120m/C VHS, Wide.** Don Johnson, Rebecca DeMornay, Jack Warden, Stephen Lang, Dana Ivey, Ron White, Sean McCann, Luis Guzman; **D:** Sidney Lumet; **W:** Larry Cohen; **C:** Andrzej Bartkowiak.

Guilty by Suspicion && ½ **1991 (PG-13)** Examination of the 1950s McCarthy investigations by the House Un-American Activities Committee comes off like a bland history lesson. De Niro plays a director who attended a Communist party meeting in the '30s but who otherwise doesn't have any red connections. He takes the moral high ground and refuses to incriminate his buddy (Wendt) to get off the hook and finds himself blacklisted. Characterized by average performances (excepting Wettig who goes overboard) and a lightweight script. "The Front" (1976) does a better job on this topic. Directorial debut for producer Winkler. **105m/C VHS, DVD, 8mm, Wide.** Stephen (Steve) Root, Robert De Niro, Annette Bening, George Wendt, Patricia Wettig, Sam Wanamaker, Chris Cooper, Ben Piazza, Martin Scorsese, Barry Primus, Gailard Sartain, Stuart Margolin, Barry Tubb, Roxann Biggs-Dawson, Robin Gammell, Brad Sullivan, Luke Edwards, Adam Baldwin; **D:** Irwin Winkler; **W:** Irwin Winkler; **C:** Michael Ballhaus; **M:** James Newton Howard.

Guilty of Innocence && **1987 (PG)** A young African-American man finds he's guilty until proven innocent when he runs into the law in Texas. A bold lawyer joins his fight for justice. Based on a true story. **95m/C VHS.** Dorian Harewood, Dabney Coleman, Hoyt Axton, Paul Winfield, Dennis Lipscomb, Debbi (Deborah) Morgan, Marshall Colt, Victor Love; **D:** Richard T. Heffron. TV

Guilty of Treason && ½ **1950** A documentary on the life and times of Joszef Cardinal Mindszenty of Hungary, who was imprisoned by the communists as an enemy of the state for speaking out against the totalitarian regime. At the trial, it was revealed that the Cardinal's confession was obtained only by the use of drugs, hypnosis, and torture. A realistic look at the dark side of Communism. **86m/B VHS.** Charles Bickford, Paul Kelly, Bonita Granville, Richard Derr, Berry Kroeger, Elisabeth Risdon, Roland Winters, John Banner; **D:** Felix Feist.

The Guinea Pig && ½ *The Outsider* **1948** Jack Read (Attenborough), the son of a tobacconist, is sent to a posh public school as an experiment but finds problems between his simple upbringing and the reactions of teachers and other students. **97m/B VHS.** *GB* Richard Attenborough, Joan Hickson, Bernard Miles, Sheila Sim, Robert Flemyng, Timothy Bateson; **D:** Roy Boulting; **W:** Bernard Miles, Roy Boulting.

Guinevere &&& **1999 (R)** Harper (Polley) is an uncertain, inexperienced 20-year-old in San Francisco who ditches family responsibilites at her sister's wedding reception in order to talk to 40-something photographer Connie Fitzpatrick (Rea). Worldly wise and a natural charmer, Connie soon has Harper as his latest "Guinevere," the innocent young women he beds and nurtures until they outgrow the need for his guidance. Harper certainly doesn't seem to have much personality on her own but Connie also needs something of a lifeline as his drinking increases while his job prospects decline. Polished production with compelling performances by both Polley and Rea. **104m/C VHS, DVD, Wide.** Stephen Rea, Sarah Polley, Jean Smart, Gina Gershon, Paul Dooley, Francis Guinan, Jasmine Guy, Sandra Oh, Emily (Proctor) Procter, Gedde Watanabe; **D:** Audrey Wells; **W:** Audrey Wells; **C:** Charles Minsky; **M:** Christophe Beck. Sundance '99: Screenplay.

Guitarman & **1995** Modern version of "The Pied Piper of Hamlin" finds a mysterious musician saving a farming community's crops from a plague of locusts. But when the mayor reneges on paying the piper (so to speak), he takes the town's children instead. **92m/C VHS.** Nicholas (Nick) Campbell, Donnelly Rhodes, Andrea Martin, Shawn Ashmore, Jack Semple; **D:** Will Dixon.

Gulag && ½ **1985** An American sportscaster is wrongly sentenced to ten years of hard labor in a Soviet prison, and plans his escape from the cruel guards. Good suspense. **130m/C VHS.** *GB* David Keith, Malcolm McDowell, David Suchet, Warren Clarke, John McEnery; **D:** Roger Young; **M:** Elmer Bernstein. TV

Gulliver's Travels && ½ **1939** The Fleischer Studio's animated version of Jonathan Swift's classic about the adventures of Gulliver, an English sailor who is washed ashore in the land of Lilliput, where everyone is about two inches tall. **74m/C VHS, DVD.** **D:** Dave Fleischer; **W:** Dan Gordon, Tedd Pierce, Edmond Seward, Izzy Sparber; **C:** Charles Schettler; **V:** Lanny Ross, Jessica Dragonette.

Gulliver's Travels && **1977 (G)** In this partially animated adventure the entire land of Lilliput has been constructed in miniature. Cartoon and real life mix in a 3-dimensional story of Dr. Lemuel Gulliver and his discovery of the small people in the East Indies. From the classic by Jonathan Swift. **80m/C VHS.** *GB* Richard Harris, Catherine Schell; **D:** Peter Hunt.

Gulliver's Travels && ½ **1995 (PG)** Faithful TV version of Jonathan Swift's 1726 satiric novel. Lemuel Gulliver (Danson) is confined to Bedlam, an English insane asylum, after having been lost at sea for eight years. While in the asylum he relates his very odd adventures—in the tiny land of Lilliput, among the giants of Brobdingnag, with the silly and impractical intellectuals of Laputa, and finally amidst the brutish human Yahoos, who are ruled by rational talking horses, the

Houyhnhnms. Meanwhile, Gulliver's wife Mary (Steenburgen) and son Tom (Sturridge) struggle to prove his sanity and win his release. On two cassettes. **187m/C VHS, DVD.** Ted Danson, Mary Steenburgen, Edward Fox, Thomas Sturridge, Edward Woodward, Nicholas Lyndhurst, Peter O'Toole, Phoebe Nicholls, Ned Beatty, Kate Maberly, Alfre Woodard, Geraldine Chaplin, John Gielgud, Kristin Scott Thomas, Omar Sharif, John Standing, Warwick Davis, Robert Hardy, Shashi Kapoor, Karyn Parsons, Edward Petherbridge; ***D:*** Charles Sturridge; ***W:*** Simon Moore; ***C:*** Howard Atherton; ***M:*** Trevor Jones. **TV**

Gumball Rally 🦴🦴 **1976 (PG)** An unusual assortment of people converge upon New York for a cross country car race to Long Beach, California where breaking the rules is part of the game. **107m/C VHS.** Michael Sarrazin, Gary Busey, Raul Julia, Nicholas Pryor, Tim McIntire, Susan Flannery; ***D:*** Charles "Chuck" Bail; ***W:*** Leon Capetanos.

Gumby: The Movie 🦴🦴½ **1995 (G)** Gumby and his musical group, the Clayboys, seek to save their neighbors' farms from foreclosure by putting on a benefit concert. And yes, pal Pokey is along to help out. But 90 minutes of our gentle clay hero stretches the patience of even the most enthusiastic fan. **90m/C VHS.** ***D:*** Art Clokey; ***W:*** Art Clokey.

Gummo woof! **1997 (R)** "Kids" scripter and first time helmer Korine shamelessly parades out the freaks and calls it entertainment. More like a series of grisly images than a cohesive narrative when nihilism pervades a group of disaffected Xenia, Ohio teens who explore every brand of atrocity for kicks. Disturbing, not only in the graphic violence of the bored juvies but also in the frightening lack of a point to this uneven and self-indulgent shock-fest. Touted as modern movie's golden-boy, 23 year-old Korine doesn't let any dark humor slip in to detract from the purely revolting scenarios. The images that do summon up some truth about growing up in a dead-end town are far overshadowed by the collection of images as a whole. Renowned French cinematographer Escoffier lends style to this lost cause. **88m/C VHS, DVD, Wide.** Chloe Sevigny, Jacob Reynolds, Jacob Sewell, Nick Sutton, Carisa Bara, Darby Dougherty, Max Perlich, Linda Manz; ***D:*** Harmony Korine; ***W:*** Harmony Korine; ***C:*** Jean-Yves Escoffier.

Gumshoe 🦴🦴½ **1972 (G)** An homage to American hard-boiled detectives. Finney plays a small-time worker in a Liverpool nightclub who decides to become a detective like his movie heroes. He bumbles through a number of interconnecting cases, but finds his way in the end. Good satire of film noir detectives. **85m/C VHS.** *GB* Albert Finney, Billie Whitelaw, Frank Finlay, Janice Rule, Carolyn Seymour; ***D:*** Stephen Frears; ***W:*** Neville Smith; ***C:*** Chris Menges; ***M:*** Andrew Lloyd Webber.

The Gumshoe Kid 🦴 *The Detective Kid* **1989 (R)** A college-bound kid enters the family detective business to prevent his mother from being evicted. He gets in over his head though, trying to track the fiancee of a wealthy mobster. **98m/C VHS.** Jay Underwood, Tracy Scoggins, Vince Edwards, Arlene Golonka, Pamela Springsteen; ***D:*** Joseph Manduke.

A Gun, a Car, a Blonde 🦴🦴 **1997** Paraplegic Richard Spraggins (Metzler) escapes from his pain-filled life by imagining himself to be living in a '50s film noir world, where he takes on the persona of tough private eye Rick Stone. Naturally, as in all good noir worlds, he must save a femme fatale blonde (Thompson) from a killer. **101m/C VHS, DVD.** Jim Metzler, Billy Bob Thornton, Andrea Thompson, John Ritter, Kay Lenz, Victor Love, Paula Marshall; ***D:*** Stefani Ames; ***W:*** Stefani Ames, Tom Epperson; ***C:*** Carlos Gaviria; ***M:*** Harry Manfredini.

Gun Cargo 🦴 **1949** Muddled story about a conniving shipowner who fires his crew for demanding shore leave. He replaces them with assorted low-lifes, resulting in the usual hijinks. A terrible performance by an otherwise great cast. **49m/C VHS, 8mm.** Rex Lease, Smith Ballew, William Farnum, Gibson Gowland.

Gun Code 🦴½ **1940** The white-hatted cowboy-hero puts a stop to small-town racketeering. **52m/B VHS.** Tim McCoy, Ina Guest; ***D:*** Sam Newfield.

Gun Crazy 🦴🦴🦴 *Deadly Is the Female* **1949** Annie Laurie Starr—Annie Oakley in a Wild West show—meets gun-lovin' Bart Tare, who says a gun makes him feel good inside, "like I'm somebody." Sparks fly, and the two get married and live happily ever after—until the money runs out and fatal femme Laurie's craving for excitement and violence starts to flare up. The two become lovebirds-on-the-lam. Now a cult fave, it's based on a MacKinlay Kantor story. Ex-stuntman Russell Harlan's photography is daring; the realism of the impressive robbery scenes is owed in part to the technical consultation of former train robber Al Jennings. And watch for a young Tamblyn as the 14-year-old Bart. **87m/B VHS.** Peggy Cummins, John Dall, Berry Kroeger, Morris Carnovsky, Anabel Shaw, Nedrick Young, Trevor Bardette, Russ Tamblyn, Harry Lewis, Mickey Little, Paul Frison, Dave Bair, Stanley Prager, Virginia Farmer, Anne O'Neal, Frances Irwin, Don Beddoe, Robert Osterloh, Shimen Ruskin, Harry Hayden; ***D:*** Joseph H. Lewis; ***W:*** Dalton Trumbo; ***C:*** Russell Harlan; ***M:*** Victor Young. Natl. Film Reg. '98.

Gun Crazy 🦴🦴½ *A Talent for Loving* **1969** A gambler becomes enmeshed in an arranged marriage with a cursed Mexican family. Lightweight comedy, good cast. **110m/C VHS.** Richard Widmark, Chaim Topol, Cesar Romero, Genevieve Page, Judd Hamilton, Caroline Munro; ***D:*** Richard Quine.

Gun Fight at Red Sands 🦴🦴 *Gringo; Duello Nel Texas* **1963** Landmark western in the history of Italian cinema. Long before Leone's Eastwood trilogy, this film introduced the theme of an avenging stranger to the genre. Harrison stars as the dark, brooding hero who is out for revenge after learning that his family has been attacked by a gang of bandits. **?m/C VHS.** *IT* Richard Harrison, Giacomo "Jack" Rossi-Stuart, Sara Lezana; ***M:*** Ennio Morricone.

Gun Fury 🦴🦴½ **1953** A panoramic western about a Civil War veteran pursuing the bandits who kidnapped his beautiful bride-to-be. First screened as a 3-D movie. **83m/C VHS.** Rock Hudson, Donna Reed, Phil Carey, Lee Marvin; ***D:*** Raoul Walsh.

Gun Girls 🦴 **1956** Campy exploitation flick about a gun-toting gang of girls who rob anything or anyone. The guy who fences their goods ends up getting one of them pregnant. **?m/C VHS.** Timothy Farrell, Jean Ferguson, Jacquelyn Park, Jean Ann Lewis; ***D:*** Robert Deltano.

Gun Glory 🦴🦴½ **1957** Granger plays Tom Early, a gunslinger who returns home after three years to find the town would rather not have him. He regains the town's respect when he stops a murderer from invading the town with his cattle herd. Based on the novel "Man of the West" by Philip Yordan. **88m/C VHS.** Stewart Granger, Rhonda Fleming, Chill Wills, Steve Rowland, James Gregory, Jacques Aubuchon, Arch Johnson, William "Bill" Fawcett, Lane Bradford, Michael Dugan, Bud Osborne, May McAvoy, Charles Herbert, Carl Pitti; ***D:*** Roy Rowland; ***W:*** William Ludwig; ***M:*** Jeff Alexander.

Gun Grit 🦴½ **1936** An FBI agent is sent west to break up a protection racket. **51m/B VHS.** Jack Perrin, Ethel Beck, David Sharpe, Roger Williams, Budd Buster; ***D:*** William Berke.

The Gun in Betty Lou's Handbag 🦴🦴 **1992 (PG-13)** Shy, small town librarian with a dull marriage is looking for excitement when she stumbles across a gun used in a murder. She decides excitement will follow her (false) confession to the crime leaving her husband thunderstruck, the police confused, and the gossip line humming. She also intrigues the real bad guy, who comes looking for her. Lame silliness is redeemed somewhat by Miller, but there's some surprisingly nasty violence given the comedy label. **99m/C VHS.** Penelope Ann Miller, Eric Thal, Alfre Woodard, Cathy Moriarty, William Forsythe, Julianne Moore, Xander Berkeley, Michael O'Neill, Christopher John Fields; ***D:*** Allan Moyle; ***W:*** Grace Cary Bickley; ***M:*** Richard Gibbs.

A Gun in the House 🦴 **1981** While being attacked in her own home, a woman shoots one of her assailants. The police find no conclusive evidence of attack and arrest the woman for murder. Exploitive drama on gun control. **100m/C VHS.** Sally Struthers, David Ackroyd, Joel Bailey, Jeffrey Tambor; ***D:*** Ivan Nagy. **TV**

Gun Law 🦴½ **1933** The hero tackles the Sonora Kid, an outlaw terrorizing Arizona folk. One of the few sound westerns with Hoxie, a silent-era star who hung up his spurs when his voice proved non-photogenic. **59m/B VHS.** Jack Hoxie, Paul Fix, Mary Carr, Edmund Cobb, Robert Burns; ***D:*** Lewis D. Collins.

Gun Lords of Stirrup Basin 🦴🦴 **1937** A cattleman and the daughter of a homesteader are in love in the Old West, but a seedy lawyer wants to douse their flame. Bullets and fists fly as a result. **55m/B VHS.** Bob Steele, Louise Stanley, Karl Hackett, Ernie Adams, Frank LaRue, Frank Ball, Steve Clark; ***D:*** Sam Newfield.

Gun Packer 🦴🦴 **1938** When an outlaw gang robs stagecoaches of their gold and uses the booty to salt barren mine shafts so the unsuspecting can be swindled out of their money on worthless gold mine certificates, hard-riding Randall is called in to save the day. **51m/B VHS.** Addison "Jack" Randall, Louise Stanley, Charles "Blackie" King, Glenn Strange; ***D:*** Wallace Fox; ***W:*** Robert Emmett.

Gun Play 🦴🦴 *Lucky Boots* **1936** Brother and sister venture west to run their father's ranch. Mexican bandits believe the ranch's property houses a revolutionary fortune, and set about recovering it. The brother defends his father's ranch along with a sidekick, who sweeps the sister off her feet. **59m/B VHS.** Guinn "Big Boy" Williams, Frank Yaconelli, Marion Shilling, Wally Wales, Charles French; ***D:*** Al(bert) Herman.

The Gun Ranger 🦴½ **1934** Our hero plays a Texas Ranger who becomes fed up with soft judges and shady prosecutors and decides to take the law into his own hands. **56m/B VHS.** Bob Steele, Eleanor Stewart, John Merton, Ernie Adams, Budd Buster; ***D:*** Robert North Bradbury.

Gun Riders 🦴½ *Five Bloody Graves; Five Bloody Days to Tombstone; Lonely Man* **1969** Gunman must seek out and stop a murderer of innocent people. **98m/C VHS.** Scott Brady, Jim Davis, John Carradine; ***D:*** Al Adamson.

Gun Shy 🦴🦴 **2000 (R)** Psychiatry and organized crime collide again, but this time it's the cops in therapy. Well, one of 'em at least. Charlie (Neeson) is a burned-out DEA agent forced back undercover as a go-between for an Italian gangster (Platt) who knows he's a cliche and a Colombian drug cartel leader (Zuniga) who believes investing in bean futures is some sort of ethnic no-no. Charlie's work problems lead him to a men's therapy group and a nurse (Bullock) dubbed the "Enema Queen." Yep, it's mostly that kind of humor. The crime figures are thin, and Blakeney needs to work on his comic and scene timing, but Neeson fares pretty well. The group sessions are highlights, but the payoff isn't as big as one would hope. **102m/C VHS, DVD, Wide.** Liam Neeson, Oliver Platt, Sandra Bullock, Jose Zuniga, Richard Schiff, Andrew Lauer, Mitch Pileggi, Paul Ben-Victor, Mary McCormack, Frank Vincent, Michael Mantell, Louis Giambalvo, Gregg Daniel, Michael Delorenzo; ***D:*** Eric Blakeney; ***W:*** Eric Blakeney; ***C:*** Tom Richmond; ***M:*** Rolfe Kent.

Gunblast 🦴 **197?** A convict is released from San Quentin and wastes no time in getting involved with mob-powered drug smuggling. **70m/C VHS.** Lloyd Allan, Christine Cardan, James Cunningham.

Guncrazy 🦴🦴 **1992 (R)** Girl from the wrong side of the tracks, abused her entire life, finds her freedom in a gun. She winds up killing the man who raped her, takes up with an equally lost ex-con, and the two armed misfits go on the run from the law. Barrymore's convincing and the movie is another well-made variation on the lovers-on-the-run theme. Film was inspired by, but is not a remake of, the 1949 movie "Gun Crazy." **97m/C VHS, DVD.** Drew Barrymore, James LeGros, Billy Drago, Rodney Harvey, Ione Skye, Joe Dallesandro, Michael Ironside; ***D:*** Tamra Davis; ***W:*** Matthew Bright; ***C:*** Lisa Rinzler.

A Gunfight 🦴🦴 **1971 (PG)** When Cash is stranded in a small Western town, he meets up with fellow old-time gunfighter Douglas. The two strike up a friendship, but discover the town folk expect a gun battle. Needing money, the two arrange a gunfight for paid admission — winner take all. Cash makes his screen debut. **90m/C** Kirk Douglas, Johnny Cash, Jane Alexander, Karen Black, Dana Elcar, Keith Carradine, Raf Vallone; ***D:*** Lamont Johnson; ***W:*** Harold Jack Bloom.

Gunfight at the O.K. Corral 🦴🦴🦴 **1957** The story of Wyatt Earp and Doc Holliday joining forces in Dodge City to rid the town of the criminal Clanton gang. Filmed in typical Hollywood style, but redeemed by its great stars. **122m/C VHS.** Burt Lancaster, Kirk Douglas, Rhonda Fleming, Jo Van Fleet, John Ireland, Kenneth Tobey, Lee Van Cleef, Frank Faylen, DeForest Kelley, Earl Holliman; ***D:*** John Sturges; ***W:*** Leon Uris; ***C:*** Charles B(ryant) Lang Jr.

The Gunfighter 🦴🦴🦴½ **1950** A mature, serious, Hollywood-western character study about an aging gunfighter searching for peace and quiet but unable to avoid his reputation and the duel-challenges it invites. One of King's best films. **85m/B VHS.** Gregory Peck, Helen Westcott, Millard Mitchell, Jean Parker, Karl Malden, Skip Homeier, Mae Marsh; ***D:*** Henry King; ***C:*** Arthur C. Miller.

Gunfighter 🦴🦴 **1998 (PG-13)** Gunfighter Sheen is out to avenge the murder of some townsfolk. Then an outlaw kidnaps his girlfriend and things get even more personal. **94m/C VHS, DVD, Wide.** Robert Carradine, Martin Sheen, Clu Gulager; ***D:*** Christopher Coppola.

The Gunfighters 🦴½ **1987** Lackluster pilot of a proposed Canadian series pits three individualistic relatives against a powerful empire-builder. **100m/C VHS, DVD.** *CA* Art Hindle, Reiner Schoene, Anthony Addabbo, George Kennedy, Michael Kane, Lori Hallier; ***D:*** Clay Borris. **TV**

Gunfighter's Moon 🦴🦴½ **1996 (PG-13)** Legendary gunslinger Frank Morgan (Henriksen) is called on by former lover, Linda (Lenz), to help her sheriff husband prevent a jailbreak. Frank's tired of his constant challengers but can't seem to make another life for himself. **95m/C VHS.** Lance Henriksen, Kay Lenz, David McIlwraith, Ivan Sergei, Nikki Deloach; ***D:*** Larry Ferguson; ***W:*** Larry Ferguson; ***C:*** James L. Carter; ***M:*** Lee Holdridge.

Gunfire 🦴½ **1950** A Frank James look-alike cavorts, robs and loots the countryside until the real James decides to set things straight. **59m/B VHS.** Donald (Don "Red") Barry, Robert Lowery, Pamela Blake, Wally Vernon; ***D:*** William Berke.

Gunfire 🦴🦴 *China 9, Liberty 37* **1978** A gunfighter is rescued from the hangman's noose by railroad tycoons who want him to kill a farmer. He doesn't kill the man, but runs off with his wife instead, and the incensed railway honchos send assassins after the double-crossing gunman. Peckinpah's part is pretty puny in this leisurely horse opera. **94m/C VHS.** *IT* Fabio Testi, Warren Oates, Jenny Agutter, Sam Peckinpah; ***D:*** Monte Hellman; ***M:*** Pino Donaggio.

Gung Ho! 🦴🦴 **1943** Carlson's Raiders are a specially trained group of Marine jungle fighters determined to retake the Pacific island of Makin during WWII. **88m/B VHS, DVD.** Robert Mitchum, Randolph Scott, Noah Beery Jr., Alan Curtis, Grace McDonald; ***D:*** Ray Enright; ***C:*** Milton Krasner.

Gung Ho 🦴🦴½ **1985 (PG-13)** A Japanese firm takes over a small-town U.S. auto factory and causes major cultural collisions. Keaton plays the go-between for employees and management while trying to keep both groups from killing each other. From the director of "Splash" and "Night Shift." Made into a short-lived TV series. **111m/C VHS, 8mm.** Michael Keaton, Gedde Watanabe, George Wendt, Mimi Rogers, John Turturro, Clint Howard, Michelle Johnson, So Yamamura, Sab Shimono; ***D:*** Ron Howard; ***W:*** Babaloo Mandel, Lowell Ganz; ***M:*** Thomas Newman.

Gunga Din 🦴🦴🦴🦴 **1939** The prototypical "buddy" film. Three veteran British sergeants in India try to suppress a native uprising, but it's their water boy, the intrepid Gunga Din, who saves the day. Friendship, loyalty, and some of the best action scenes ever filmed. Based loosely on Rudyard Kipling's famous poem, the story is credited to Ben Hecht, Charles MacArthur, and William Faulkner (who is uncredited). Also available colorized. **117m/B VHS.** Cary Grant, Victor McLaglen, Douglas Fairbanks Jr., Sam Jaffe, Eduardo Ciannelli, Montagu Love, Joan Fontaine, Abner Biberman, Robert Coote, Lumsden Hare, Cecil Kellaway, Roland Varno, George Regas, Reginald (Reggie, Reggy) Sheffield, Clive Morgan; ***D:*** George Stevens; ***W:*** Fred Guiol, Joel Sayre, Ben Hecht, William Faulkner; ***C:*** Joseph August; ***M:*** Alfred Newman. Natl. Film Reg. '99.

Gunman from Bodie 🦴½ *Gun Man from Bodie* **1941** Second of the Rough Rider series. Jones, McCoy, and Hatton rescue a baby orphaned by rustlers and then go after the bad guys. **62m/B VHS.** Tim McCoy, Buck Jones, Raymond Hatton; ***D:*** Spencer Gordon Bennet.

Gunman's Walk 🦴🦴½ **1958** Rancher Lee Hackett (Heflin) gained his power through his gunslinging skill but wants his two sons to be respectable citizens. However, hot-tempered eldest son Ed (Hunter) wants to best the old man's reputation while younger son Davy (Darren) has his own problems when he falls for Sioux half-breed Clee (Grant), whose brother was murdered by Ed. As Ed gets more ruthless, his father must decide how far he's willing to go to protect him. **95m/C VHS.** Van Heflin, Tab Hunter, James Darren, Kathryn Grant, Mickey Shaughnessy, Robert F. Simon, Edward Platt, Bert Convy; ***D:*** Phil Karlson; ***W:*** Frank Nugent; ***C:*** Charles Lawton Jr.

Gunmen 🦴🦴 **1993 (R)** A reluctant buddy team face down some bad guys. DEA agent Cole (Van Peebles) teams up with smuggler Dani (Lambert) to find stolen drug money also wanted by wheelchair-bound villain Loomis (Stewart) and his violence-loving henchman (Leary). Adds comedy to the mix as well as shameless action rip-offs from spaghetti westerns. **90m/C VHS.** Christopher Lambert, Mario Van Peebles, Denis Leary, Patrick Stewart, Kadeem Hardison, Sally Kirkland; ***Cameos:*** Big Daddy Kane, Ed Lover, Eric B. Rakim, Dr. Dre; ***D:*** Deran Sarafian; ***W:*** Stephen Sommers; ***M:*** John Debney.

Gunners & Guns 🦴 **1934** Vintage western starring King. **51m/B VHS.** Black King, Edmund Cobb, Edna Asetin, Eddie Davis; ***D:*** Robert Hoyt.

Gunplay 🦴½ **1951** Two cowboys befriend a boy whose father has been killed and search for the murderer. **61m/B VHS.** Tim Holt, Joan Dixon, Richard Martin.

Gunpowder 🦴 **1984** Two Interpol agents endeavor to stop a crime lord from causing the collapse of the world economy. **85m/C VHS.** David Gilliam, Martin Potter, Gordon Jackson, Anthony Schaeffer.

The Gunrunner 🦴½ **1984 (R)** Costner plays a Canadian mobster, involved in liquor smuggling, who aids a Chinese rebellion in this 1920s drama. Interesting concept. Received more attention after Costner gained notoriety in later films. **92m/C VHS.** *CA* Kevin Costner, Sara Botsford, Paul Soles; ***D:*** Nardo Castillo.

Guns 🦴🦴 **1990 (R)** An international gunrunner puts the moves on buxom women between hair-raising adventures. **95m/C VHS.** Erik Estrada, Dona Speir; ***D:*** Andy Sidaris; ***W:*** Andy Sidaris.

The Guns and the Fury 🦴½ **1983** Two American oil riggers in the Middle East, circa 1908, are forced to fight off an attack by a vicious Arab sheik and his tribe. **90m/C VHS.** Peter Graves, Cameron Mitchell, Michael Ansara, Albert Salmi; ***D:*** Tony Zarindast.

Guns at Batasi 🦴🦴½ **1964** Attenborough plays a tough British Sergeant Major stationed in Africa during the anti-colonial 1960s. Ultimately the regiment is threatened by rebel Africans. Fine performances make this rather predictable film watchable. **103m/B VHS.** *GB* Richard Attenborough, Jack Hawkins, Mia Farrow, Flora Robson, John Leyton; ***D:*** John Guillermin; ***M:*** John Addison.

Guns Don't Argue 🦴🦴 **1957** Entertaining schlocker about the rise and fall of famous criminal Dillinger. Non-stop action also features Bonnie and Clyde, Pretty Boy Floyd and Baby Face Nelson. **?m/C VHS.** Myron Healey, Jim Davis, Richard Crane.

Guns for Dollars 🦴🦴 *They Call Me Hallelujah* **1973** Mex-Western has four men, including a secret agent and a cossack, tangled up in the Mexican Revolution as they search for a fortune in smuggled jewels. **94m/C VHS.** *MX* George Hilton, Charles Southwood, Agata Flory, Roberto Camardiel, Paolo Gozlino, Rick Boyd; ***D:*** Anthony (Giuliano Carnimeo) Ascot.

Guns in the Dark 🦴 **1937** A cowboy vows never to use a gun again when he believes that he accidentally shot his best friend. **60m/C VHS.** Johnny Mack Brown, Claire Rochelle; ***D:*** Sam Newfield.

Guns of Diablo 🦴🦴 **1964** Wagon train master Bronson has to fight a gang that controls the supply depot, all the while showing his young helper (beardless boy Russell) the fascinating tricks of the trade. **91m/C VHS.** Charles Bronson, Kurt Russell, Susan Oliver; ***D:*** Boris Sagal.

Guns of Fury 🦴½ **1945** Cisco and Pancho solve the troubles of a small boy in this standard oater. **60m/B VHS.** Duncan Renaldo.

Guns of Justice 🦴 *Colorado Ranger* **1950** Undercover Colorado rangers stop a swindler from forcing homesteaders off their land. **60m/B VHS.** James Ellison, Russell Hayden, Tom Tyler, Raymond Hatton; ***D:*** Thomas Carr.

The Guns of Navarone 🦴🦴🦴½ **1961** During WWII, British Intelligence in the Middle East sends six men to the Aegean island of Navarone to destroy guns manned by the Germans. Consistently interesting war epic based on the Alistair MacLean novel, with a vivid cast. **159m/C VHS, DVD, Wide.** Gregory Peck, David Niven, Anthony Quinn, Richard Harris, Stanley Baker, Anthony Quayle, James Darren, Irene Papas, Gia Scala, James Robertson Justice, Bryan Forbes, Allan Cuthbertson, Michael Trubshawe, Percy Herbert, Walter Gotell, Tutte Lemkow; ***D:*** J. Lee Thompson; ***W:*** Carl Foreman; ***C:*** Oswald Morris; ***M:*** Dimitri Tiomkin. Golden Globes '62: Film—Drama, Score.

Guns of the Law 🦴½ **1944** The Texas Rangers try to stop a shifty lawyer who attempts to swindle a family out of a potential fortune in property. **56m/B VHS.** Dave O'Brien, James Newill, Guy Wilkerson, Jack Ingram, Robert F. (Bob) Kortman, Bob Barron; ***D:*** Elmer Clifton; ***W:*** Elmer Clifton.

Guns of the Magnificent Seven 🦴🦴½ **1969 (G)** The third remake of "The Seven Samurai." Action-packed western in which the seven free political prisoners and train them to kill. The war party then heads out to rescue a Mexican revolutionary being held in an impregnable fortress. **106m/C VHS.** George Kennedy, Monte Markham, James Whitmore, Reni Santoni, Bernie Casey, Joe Don Baker, Scott Thomas, Michael Ansara, Fernando Rey; ***D:*** Paul Wendkos; ***M:*** Elmer Bernstein.

Gunshy 🦴🦴🦴 **1998 (R)** Familiar crime genre has some fine performances and an intelligent script. Journalist Jake Bridges (Petersen) heads to Atlantic City after catching his wife cheating on him. His drunken ranting gets him trouble, but Jake is rescued by likeable smalltime mob guy Frankie (Wincott) and his hot girlfriend, Melissa (Lane). Jake hangs around watching Frankie work and making passes at Melissa but it just might be that Jake has his own hidden agenda, as well. **101m/C VHS, DVD.** William L. Petersen, Michael Wincott, Diane Lane, Kevin Gage, Michael Byrne, Meat Loaf Aday, Eric Schaeffer, Musetta Vander, John Fleck, Badja (Medu) Djola, R. Lee Ermey, Natalie Canerday; ***D:*** Jeff Celentano; ***W:*** Larry Gross; ***C:*** John Aronson; ***M:*** Hal Lindes.

The Gunslinger 🦴½ **1956** A woman marshall struggles to keep law and order in a town overrun by outlaws. Unique western with a surprise ending. **83m/C VHS.** John Ireland, Beverly Garland, Allison Hayes, Jonathan Haze, Dick Miller, Bruno VeSota, William Schallert; ***D:*** Roger Corman; ***W:*** Charles B. Griffith, Mark Hanna; ***C:*** Frederick E. West; ***M:*** Ronald Stein.

Gunslinger 🦴½ **197?** Armed to the teeth with weaponry, Sartana shows a mining town's heavies how to sling a gun or two. **90m/C VHS.** Gianni "John" Garko, Antonio Vilar; ***D:*** Anthony (Giuliano Carnimeo) Ascot.

Gunsmoke 🦴🦴½ **1953** Reb Kittredge (Murphy) is a gun-for-hire who's offered a job by greedy rancher Matt Telford (Randolph). Instead, Kittredge decides to go with Telford's enemy, Dan Saxon (Kelly), so Telford hires another gunslinger (Drake) to get rid of them both. Cabot provides the usual romantic lure as Saxon's daughter. Based on the novel "Roughshod" by Norman A. Fox. **78m/C VHS.** Audie Murphy, Susan Cabot, Paul Kelly, Donald Randolph, Charles Drake, Mary Castle, Jack Kelly, Jesse White, William Reynolds; ***D:*** Nathan (Hertz) Juran; ***W:*** D.D. Beauchamp; ***C:*** Charles P. Boyle.

Gunsmoke: Return to Dodge 🦴🦴½ **1987** The first of the TV movies that reunited most of the cast of the classic TV western. Matt Dillon returns to Dodge and Miss Kitty after 12 years only to be trailed by a ruthless adversary. **100m/C VHS.** James Arness, Amanda Blake, Buck Taylor, Fran Ryan, Earl Holliman, Steve Forrest; ***D:*** Vincent McEveety. **TV**

Gunsmoke Trail 🦴½ **1938** Cowpoke Randall saves an heiress from losing her estate to a phony uncle in low-budget Western. Also features the prolific "Fuzzy" St. John in his cowboy's sidekick stage (interestingly, St. John, a nephew of Fatty Arbuckle, later co-starred in the "Lone Rider" series with Randall's brother, Robert Livingston). **59m/C VHS.** Addison "Jack" Randall, Al "Fuzzy" St. John.

Gus 🦴🦴½ **1976 (G)** A Disney film about the California Atoms, a football team that has the worst record in the league until they begin winning games with the help of their field goal kicking mule of a mascot, Gus. The competition then plots a donkey-napping. Enjoyable comedy for the whole family. **96m/C VHS.** Ed Asner, Tim Conway, Dick Van Patten, Ronnie Schell, Bob Crane, Tom Bosley; ***D:*** Vincent McEveety; ***W:*** Arthur Alsberg; ***M:*** Robert F. Brunner.

GUY: Awakening of the Devil 🦴🦴 **1993** Guy and Raina, two despicable intergalactic soldiers of fortune, embark on a continuous sky-raid adventure. Available in general release and uncut versions. Japanese with English subtitles. **?m/C VHS.** *JP*

The Guy from Harlem 🦴🦴 **1977** He's mad, he's from Harlem, and he's not going to take it any more. **86m/C VHS.** Loye Hawkins, Cathy Davis, Patricia Fulton, Wanda Starr; ***D:*** Rene Martinez Jr.

A Guy Named Joe 🦴🦴½ **1944** A sentimental, patriotic Hollywood fantasy about the angel of a dead WWII pilot guiding another young pilot through battle and also helping him to romance his girl, who's still too devoted to his memory. Remade in 1989 as "Always." **121m/B VHS.** Spencer Tracy, Irene Dunne, Van Johnson, Ward Bond, James Gleason, Lionel Barrymore, Esther Williams; ***D:*** Victor Fleming; ***W:*** Dalton Trumbo; ***C:*** Karl Freund.

A Guy Thing **2002** Marketing exec Lee wakes up with Stiles after his wild bachelor party and she's not his fiancee. Not yet reviewed. **?m/C VHS, DVD.** Jason Lee, Julia Stiles, Selma Blair, Shawn Hatosy, James Brolin, Diana Scarwid; ***D:*** Chris Koch; ***W:*** Matt Tarses, Bill Wrubel.

The Guyana Tragedy: The Story of Jim Jones 🦴🦴 **1980** Dramatization traces the story of the Reverend Jim Jones and the People's Temple from its beginnings in 1953 to the November 1978 mass suicide of more than 900 people. Boothe is appropriately hypnotic as the Reverend. **240m/C VHS.** Powers Boothe, Ned Beatty, Randy Quaid, Brad Dourif, Brenda Vaccaro, LeVar Burton, Colleen Dewhurst, James Earl Jones; ***D:*** William A. Graham; ***C:*** Gil Hubbs; ***M:*** Elmer Bernstein. **TV**

Guys and Dolls 🦴🦴🦴 **1955** New York gambler Sky Masterson takes a bet that he can romance a Salvation Army lady. Based on the stories of Damon Runyon with Blaine, Kaye, Pully, and Silver recreating their roles from the Broadway hit. Brando's not-always-convincing musical debut. ♫More I Cannot Wish You; My Time of Day; Guys and Dolls; Fugue for Tinhorns; Follow the Fold; Sue Me; Take Back Your Mink; If I Were a Bell; Luck Be a Lady. **150m/C VHS, DVD, Wide.** Marlon Brando, Jean Simmons, Frank Sinatra, Vivian Blaine, Stubby Kaye, Sheldon Leonard, Veda Ann Borg, Regis Toomey; ***D:*** Joseph L. Mankiewicz; ***W:*** Joseph L. Mankiewicz; ***C:*** Harry Stradling Sr.; ***M:*** Frank Loesser. Golden Globes '56: Actress—Mus./Comedy (Simmons), Film—Mus./Comedy.

The Guyver 🦴½ **1991** A young college student is transformed into a superhuman fighting machine thanks to his discovery of an alien device, "The Guyver." A CIA agent (Hamill) must keep the secret device from falling into the hands of human mutants, the Zoanoids. Based on a Japanese comic book. **92m/C VHS.** Mark Hamill, Vivian Wu, David Gale, Jeffrey Combs, Michael Berryman; ***D:*** Steve Wang.

Guyver 2: Dark Hero 🦴½ **1994 (R)** The Guyver discovers an alien ship filled with weapons capable of destroying the planet. Naturally, he must battle the evil mutant Zoanoids in order to save the world. Adapted from a Japanese comic book. **127m/C VHS.** David Hayter, Kathy Christopherson, Christopher Michael; ***D:*** Steve Wang; ***W:*** Nathan Long.

Gymkata 🦴 **1985 (R)** A gymnast (Olympian Thomas) must use his martial arts skills to conquer and secure a military state in a hostile European country. **89m/C VHS.** Kurt Thomas, Tetchie Agbayani, Richard Norton, Conan Lee; ***D:*** Robert Clouse; ***W:*** Charles Robert Carner.

Gypsy 🦴🦴🦴 **1962** The life story of America's most famous striptease queen, Gypsy Rose Lee (Wood). Russell gives a memorable performance as the infamous Mama Rose, Gypsy's stage mother. Based on both Gypsy Rose Lee's memoirs and the hit 1959 Broadway play by Arthur Laurents. ♫Small World; All I Need is the Girl; You'll Never Get Away From Me; Let Me Entertain You; Some People; Everything's Coming Up Roses; You Gotta Have a Gimmick; Baby Jane and the Newsboys; Mr. Goldstone, I Love You. **144m/C VHS, DVD, Wide.** Rosalind Russell, Natalie Wood, Karl Malden, Ann Jillian, Parley Baer, Paul Wallace, Betty Bruce; ***D:*** Mervyn LeRoy; ***W:*** Arthur Laurents, Leonard Spigelgass; ***C:*** Harry Stradling Sr.; ***M:*** Jule Styne, Stephen Sondheim. Golden Globes '63: Actress—Mus./Comedy (Russell).

Gypsy 🦴🦴 **1975** A modern day gypsy-blooded Robin Hood cavorts between heists and romantic trysts. Dubbed. **90m/C VHS.** Alain Delon, Annie Girardot, Paul Meurisse; ***D:*** Jose Giovanni.

Gypsy 🦴🦴½ **1993** If you like Bette brassy and larger than life, as only she can be, than this is the production for you. This TV re-creation of the 1959 Broadway musical stars Midler as notorious stage mother Mama Rose, who tries to realize all her frustrated ambitions by pushing her two young daughters, June and Louise, into vaudeville show biz. Her wish eventually comes true, in an unexpected fashion, when an adult Louise (Gibb) transforms herself into stripper Gypsy Rose Lee. ♫Everything's Coming Up Roses; You've Gotta Have a Gimmick; All I Need Is the Girl; Rose's Turn; Some People; Mr. Goldstone, I Love You; You'll Never Get Away From Me; Together, Wherever We Go. **150m/C VHS, DVD.** Bette Midler, Peter Riegert, Cynthia Gibb, Ed Asner, Christine Ebersole, Michael Jeter, Andrea Martin, Jennifer Beck, Linda Hart, Rachel Sweet; ***D:*** Emile Ardolino; ***W:*** Arthur Laurents; ***C:*** Ralf Bode; ***M:*** Jule Styne, Stephen Sondheim. **TV**

Gypsy Angels 🦴 **1994 (R)** A daredevil stunt pilot has a terrifying accident and develops amnesia. With the help of a stripper (who is in love with him), he tries to rebuild his life, this time with her in it. White's no actress and unless you like stunt flying (and there's a lot of it), fly by this one. (You'll note the director won't admit to this, since Smithee is a pseudonym.) **92m/C VHS.** Vanna White, Richard Roundtree, Gene Bicknell; ***D:*** Alan Smithee.

Gypsy Blood 🦴🦴 **1918** One of the first screen versions of "Carmen," closer to Prosper Merrimee's story than to the opera, depicting the fated love between a dancing girl and a matador. Lubitsch's first notable film. Silent. **104m/B VHS.** Pola Negri; ***D:*** Ernst Lubitsch.

Gypsy Colt 🦴🦴½ **1954 (G)** Gypsy is the horse beloved by the young Corcoran. But a drought forces her family to sell the animal to a racing stable 500 miles from their home. Gypsy is having none of this, escapes the stables, and returns home to be with Corcoran. Both horse and child actress are naturally appealing. **72m/C VHS.** Donna Corcoran, Ward Bond, Frances Dee, Lee Van Cleef, Larry Keating; ***D:*** Andrew Marton.

The Gypsy Warriors 🦴½ **1978** Two Army captains during WWII infiltrate Nazi-occupied France in order to prevent the distribution of a deadly toxin and are aided by a band of Gypsies. **77m/C VHS.** Tom Selleck, James Whitmore Jr., Joseph Ruskin, Lina Raymond; ***D:*** Lou Antonio. **TV**

H 🦴🦴 **1990** Two junkies try to kick their heroin addiction and face the difficult withdrawal period. Includes glimpses into their past that shed light on the reasons they turned to drugs. Contains explicit footage. **93m/C VHS.** *CA* Martin Neufeld, Pascale Montpetit; ***D:*** Darrell Wasyk. Genie '91: Actress (Montpetit); Toronto-City '90: Canadian Feature Film.

H-Bomb WOOF! **1971** Mitchum stars as a CIA agent who is sent to Bangkok to retrieve two stolen nuclear warheads from a terrorist. It just so happens that his ex-girlfriend's father is the terrorist he must contend with in this stupid movie. **98m/C VHS.** Olivia Hussey, Chris Mitchum, Krung Savilai; ***D:*** P. (Philip) Chalong.

H-Man WOOF! *Bijo to Ekitainigen* **1959** A Japanese sci-fi woofer about a radioactive mass of slime festering under Tokyo. Extremely lame special effects get quite a few unintentional laughs. Dubbed. **79m/C VHS.** *JP* Koreya Senda, Kenji Sahara, Yumi Shirakawa, Akihiko Hirata; ***D:*** Inoshiro Honda.

Habit 🦴🦴 **1997** A very low-budget New York vampire tale that tweaks tradition. Wastrel Sam (Fessenden) is at loose ends when he meets intriguing Anna (Snaider). This first encounter is a bust (Sam's very drunk) but a later meeting leads to an intense sexual encounter—and Sam waking up alone in Battery Park with a prominently cut lip and some hazy memories. All their encounters are similarly intense (and in public places) but Anna refuses to reveal anything about herself. Sam is soon a confused physical wreck but when Anna's around, he just doesn't care. **112m/C VHS, DVD.** Larry Fessenden, Meredith Snaider, Aaron Beall, Heather Woodbury, Patricia Coleman; ***D:*** Larry Fessenden; ***W:*** Larry Fessenden; ***C:*** Frank DeMarco; ***M:*** Geoffrey Kidde.

Habitat 🦴🦴½ **1997 (R)** Nature goes wild when high school student Andreas (Getty) moves with his scientist parents, Hank (Karyo) and Clarissa (Krige), to the small Southwestern burg of Pleasanton. Hank's experiment with accelerated evolution takes some unexpected blips, with Hank turning into particles of matter, their house transformed into a vegetation-covered fortress, and Clarissa becoming a very earthy earth mother. Some eerie special effects. **103m/C VHS, DVD.** Alice Krige, Balthazar Getty, Tcheky Karyo, Kenneth Welsh, Lara Harris; ***D:*** Renee Daalder; ***W:*** Renee Daalder; ***C:*** Jean Lepine; ***M:*** Ralph Grierson. **CABLE**

The Habitation of Dragons 🦴½ **1991** Family fueds and melodrama in 1930s West Texas. Wandering lawyer George Tolliver (Davis) argues with successful businessman brother Leonard (Forrest) while matriarch Leonora (Stapleton) presides and family skeletons rattle. Confusing hodgepodge. **94m/C VHS.** Jean Stapleton, Frederic Forrest, Brad Davis, Pat Hingle, Hallie Foote, Maureen O'Sullivan; ***D:*** Michael Lindsay-Hogg; ***W:*** Horton Foote; ***M:*** David Shire. **TV**

Hack O'Lantern 🦴 **1987** Granddad worships Satan, and gets his grandson involved; the result is much bloodshed, violence, and evil. **90m/C VHS.** ***D:*** Jag Mundhra.

Hackers 🦴🦴 **1995 (PG-13)** Group of teenaged computer cyber-geeks surf the 'net and become the prime suspects in an industrial conspiracy when hacker Dade (Miller) breaks into the computer at Ellingson Oil Company. It's really an inside job but just try getting anyone (read "adult") to believe him. So the techno whiz kids band together, with cops and security all wanting to shut them down. Jolie (hacker Acid Burn) is the daughter of actor Jon Voight. **105m/C VHS, DVD, Wide.** Felicity Huffman, Jonny Lee Miller, Angelina Jolie, Fisher Stevens, Lorraine Bracco, Jesse Bradford, Wendell Pierce, Alberta Watson, Laurence Mason, Renoly Santiago, Matthew Lillard, Penn Jillette; ***D:*** Iain Softley; ***W:*** Rafael Moreu; ***C:*** Andrzej Sekula; ***M:*** Simon Boswell.

Hadley's Rebellion 🦴½ **1984 (PG)** A Georgia farm boy adjusts to relocation at an elitist California boarding school by flaunting his wrestling abilities. **96m/C VHS.** Griffin O'Neal, Charles Durning, William Devane, Adam Baldwin, Dennis Hage, Lisa Lucas; ***D:*** Fred Walton; ***W:*** Fred Walton.

Haiku Tunnel 🦴🦴 **2000 (R)** Josh (Kornbluth) takes a temp job with high-powered attorney Bob Shelby (Keith) and then accepts an offer for a permanent position. This soon begins to freak commitment-phobic Josh out, resulting in his inability to complete the simple task of mailing out 17 important letters. As his anxiety grows, Josh has even more trouble dealing with his chipper co-workers and his impatient boss. **88m/C VHS, DVD, Wide.** Josh Kornbluth, Warren Keith, Helen Shumaker, June Lomena, Amy Resnick; ***D:*** Josh Kornbluth, Jacob Kornbluth; ***W:*** Josh Kornbluth, Jacob Kornbluth, John Bellucci; ***C:*** Don Matthew Smith.

Hail 🦴🦴 *Hail to the Chief; Washington, B.C* **1973 (PG)** A biting satire of what-might-have-been if certain key cabinet members had their way. **85m/C VHS.** Richard B. Shull, Dick O'Neill, Phil Foster, Joseph Sirola, Dan Resin, Willard Waterman, Gary Sandy; ***D:*** Fred Levinson.

Hail Caesar 🦴🦴½ **1994 (PG)** His job at an eraser factory is the only thing standing between Julius Caesar MacGruder (Hall) and fame and fortune as a rock 'n' roll singer. **93m/C VHS.** Anthony Michael Hall, Robert Downey Jr., Frank Gorshin, Samuel L. Jackson, Judd Nelson, Nicholas Pryor, Leslie Danon, Bobbie Phillips; ***D:*** Anthony Michael Hall; ***W:*** Robert Mittenthal; ***M:*** Roger Tallman.

Hail, Hero! 🦴½ **1969 (PG)** A dated Vietnam War era drama about a confused hippie rebelling against his parents and the draft. First film for both Douglas and Strauss. Adapted from the novel by John Weston. Includes music by Gordon Lightfoot. **97m/C VHS.** Michael Douglas, Arthur Kennedy, Teresa Wright, John Larch, Charles Drake, Deborah Winters, Peter Strauss; ***D:*** David Miller; ***C:*** Robert B. Hauser.

Hail Mary 🦴🦴½ *Je Vous Salue Marie* **1985 (R)** A modern-day virgin named Mary inexplicably becomes pregnant in this controversial film that discards notions of divinity in favor of the celebration of a lively, intellectual humanism. Godard rejects orthodox narrative structure and bourgeois prejudices. Very controversial, but not up to his breathless beginning work. In French with English subtitles. **107m/C VHS.** *FR SI GB* Myriem Roussel, Thierry Rode, Philippe Lacoste, Manon Anderson, Juliette Binoche, Johan Leysen; ***D:*** Jean-Luc Godard; ***W:*** Jean-Luc Godard.

Hail the Conquering Hero 🦴🦴🦴½ **1944** A slight young man is rejected by the Army. Upon returning home, he is surprised to find out they think he's a hero. Biting satire with Demarest's performance stealing the show. **101m/B VHS.** Eddie Bracken, Ella Raines, William Demarest, Franklin Pangborn, Raymond Walburn; ***D:*** Preston Sturges.

Hair 🦴🦴🦴½ **1979 (PG)** Film version of the explosive 1960s Broadway musical about the carefree life of the flower children and the shadow of the Vietnam War that hangs over them. Great music, as well as wonderful choreography by Twyla Tharp help portray the surprisingly sensitive evocation of the period so long after the fact. Forman has an uncanny knack for understanding the textures of American life. Watch for a thinner Nell Carter. **122m/C VHS, DVD, Wide.** Treat Williams, John Savage, Beverly D'Angelo, Annie Golden, Nicholas Ray, Nell Carter; ***D:*** Milos Forman; ***W:*** Michael Weller; ***C:*** Miroslav Ondricek; ***M:*** Galt MacDermot.

The Hairdresser's Husband 🦴🦴 *Le Mari de la coiffeuse* **1992 (R)** Antoine (Rochefort) has had an odd obsession since boyhood—hairdressers—and in middle age he finds love with Mathilde (Galiena), a hairdresser he meets and proposes to as she cuts his hair. She accepts, and the two live their quiet lives in her barber shop as she cuts hair and he watches, occasionally breaking out in Arabian dances. A dark and odd yet refreshing film with fine performances by Rochefort and Galiena in this story about fetishism, obsession, and hair. In French with English subtitles. **84m/C VHS.** *FR* Jean Rochefort, Anna Galiena, Roland Bertin, Maurice Chevit, Philippe Clevenot, Jacques Mathou, Claude Aufaure; ***D:*** Patrice Leconte; ***W:*** Claude Klotz, Patrice Leconte; ***C:*** Eduardo Serra; ***M:*** Michael Nyman.

Hairspray 🦴🦴🦴 **1988 (PG)** Waters' first truly mainstream film, if that's even possible, and his funniest. Details the struggle among teenagers in 1962 Baltimore for the top spot in a local TV dance show. Deals with racism and stereotypes, as well as typical "teen" problems (hair-do's and don'ts). Filled with refreshingly tasteful, subtle social satire (although not without typical Waters touches that will please die-hard fans). Lake is lovable and appealing as Divine's daughter; Divine, in his last film, is likeable as an iron-toting mom. Look for Waters in a cameo and Divine as a man. Great '60s music, which Waters refers to as "the only known remedy to today's Hit Parade of Hell." **94m/C VHS, DVD, Wide.** Ricki Lake, Divine, Jerry Stiller, Colleen (Ann) (Vitamin C) Fitzpatrick, Sonny Bono, Deborah Harry, Ruth Brown, Leslie Ann Powers, Michael St. Gerard, Shawn Thompson, Clayton Prince, Pia Zadora, Ric Ocasek, Mink Stole, Mary Vivian Pearce, Alan J. Wendl, Susan Lowe, George Stover, Toussaint McCall; ***Cameos:*** John Waters; ***D:*** John Waters; ***W:*** John Waters; ***C:*** David Insley; ***M:*** Kenny Vance.

The Hairy Ape 🦴🦴 **1944** Screen adaptation of the Eugene O'Neill play. A beast-like coal stoker becomes obsessed with a cool and distant passenger aboard an ocean liner. **90m/B VHS.** William Bendix, Susan Hayward, John Loder, Dorothy Comingore, Roman Bohnen, Alan Napier; ***D:*** Alfred Santell.

Half a Lifetime **1986** The stakes are too high for four friends playing a game of poker. **85m/C VHS.** Keith Carradine, Gary Busey, Nick Mancuso, Saul Rubinek.

Half a Loaf of Kung Fu 🦴 *Dian Zhi Gong Fu Gan Chian Chan* **1985** The worthy bodyguards of Sern Chuan are called upon to deliver a valuable jade statue. Thwarted again and again by ruthless robbers, they falter. Only Chan carries on, meeting the enemy alone. Fast action, good story. **98m/C VHS, DVD.** *HK* Jackie Chan, James Tien.

Half a Sixpence 🦴🦴 **1967** Former musician Sidney, who earlier directed "Showboat" and "Kiss Me Kate," shows a bit less verve in this production. Based on H.G. Wells' 1905 novel, "Kipps," it sports much of the original cast from its Broadway incarnation. Edwardian orphan Steele, a cloth-dealer-in-training, comes into a large sum of money and proceeds to lose it with great dispatch. Somewhere along the way he loses his girlfriend, too, but she takes him back because musicals end happily. ♫Half a Sixpence; Flash, Bang, Wallop!; All In The Cause Of Economy; I'm Not Talking To You; Money To Burn; The Race Is On; I Don't Believe A Word Of It; A Proper Gentleman; She's Too Far Above Me. **148m/B VHS.** Tommy Steele, Julia Foster, Penelope Horner, Cyril Ritchard, Grover Dale; ***D:*** George Sidney; ***W:*** Beverley Cross; ***C:*** Geoffrey Unsworth.

Half a Soldier 🦴🦴 **1940** A spoiled girl gets a big surprise when she steals a car and discovers the body of a gangster in the trunk. **59m/B VHS.** Heather Angel, John "Dusty" King.

Half-Baked 🦴 **1997 (R)** Four seedy roommates whose problems stem from their love of marijuana float through life with loser jobs that give them just enough money to buy their next bag. When Kenny (H.Williams) is arrested for killing a diabetic police horse during a munchies run, the three remaining friends must put their resinated brains together and come up with a way to bail him out. Thurgood (Chapelle), a custodian for a pharmaceutical company, decides to steal some high-grade grass from the lab; and along with Brian (Breuer, doing a very convincing stoned) and Scarface (Diaz), he begins dealing. This puts them afoul of the law as well as local drug lord Samson Simpson (C. Williams). Just say no. Trust me, dude, this stuff is bogus and it won't get you off. **83m/C VHS, DVD, Wide.** Tracy Morgan, Harland Williams, Dave Chappelle, Jim Breuer, Guillermo Diaz, Rachel True, Clarence Williams III, Thomas Chong, Jon Stewart, Stephen Baldwin, Willie Nelson, Janeane Garofalo, Steven Wright, Laura Silverman, Snoop Dogg; ***D:*** Tamra Davis; ***W:*** Neal Brennan, Dave Chappelle; ***C:*** Steven Bernstein; ***M:*** Alf Clausen.

The Half-Breed 🦴🦴 **1951** Routine oater with settlers and Apaches fighting, and the obligatory half-breed stuck in the middle. **81m/B VHS.** Robert Young, Jack Buetel, Janis Carter, Barton MacLane, Reed Hadley, Porter Hall, Connie Gilchrist; ***D:*** Stuart Gilmore.

Half Human 🦴½ **1958** Dull Japanese monster movie about an ape-human who terrorizes Northern Japan. When released in the U.S., Carradine and Morris were added. Without subtitles, just Carradine's narration. Director Honda made better movies before and after, with Godzilla and Rodan. **78m/B VHS.** *JP* John Carradine, Akira Takarada, Morris Ankrum; ***D:*** Inoshiro Honda.

Half Moon Street 🦴🦴 *Escort Girl* **1986 (R)** A brilliant woman scientist supplements her paltry fellowship salary by becoming a hired escort and prostitute, which leads her into various incidents of international intrigue. Adapted from a story by Paul Theroux, "Dr. Slaughter." **90m/C VHS, 8mm.** Sigourney Weaver, Michael Caine, Keith Buckley, Ian MacInnes; ***D:*** Bob Swaim.

Half of Heaven 🦴🦴🦴 *La Mitad del Cielo* **1986** A critically popular film about a young Spanish woman who begins to share certain telepathic powers with her wizened grandmother. In Spanish with English subtitles. **95m/C VHS.** *SP* Angela Molina, Margarita Lozano; ***D:*** Manuel Gutierrez Aragon.

Half-Shot at Sunrise 🦴🦴 **1930** Madcap vaudeville comedians play AWOL soldiers loose in 1918 Paris. Continuous one-liners, sight gags, and slapstick nonsense. First film appearance of comedy team Wheeler and Woolsey. **78m/B VHS.** Bert Wheeler, Robert Woolsey, Dorothy Lee, Robert Rutherford, Edna May Oliver; ***D:*** Paul Sloane; ***M:*** Max Steiner.

Half Slave, Half Free 🦴🦴½ *Solomon Northrup's Odyssey* **1985** The true story of a free black man in the 1840s who is kidnapped and forced into slavery for 12 years. Part of the "American Playhouse" series on PBS. Followed by "Charlotte Forten's Mission: Experiment in Freedom." **113m/C VHS.** Avery Brooks, Mason Adams, Petronia Paley, John Saxon, Joe Seneca, Michael (Lawrence) Tolan, Lee Bryant, Rhetta Greene, Janet League; ***D:*** Gordon Parks. **TV**

The Halfback of Notre Dame 🦴🦴½ **1996 (G)** Star football player (and coach's son) Craig Modeau (Hogan) is a lumbering misfit, ripe for high school teasing, anywhere but on the gridiron. But French exchange student Esmeralda (Vaugier) thinks he's sweet—much to the dismay of current boyfriend, obnoxious quarterback Archie (Cutler). Then Craig decides to quit the team right before the big game when dad says no fraternizing and it's up to his French flame to get the jock to change his mind. Made for TV reworking of Victor Hugo's "The Hunchback of Notre Dame." **97m/C VHS.** Gabriel Hogan, Emmanuelle Vaugier, Scott Hylands, Sandra Nelson, Allen (Culter) Cutler; ***D:*** Rene Bonniere; ***W:*** Richard Clark, Mark Trafficante; ***C:*** Maris Jansons; ***M:*** George Blondheim. **TV**

Halfmoon 🦴🦴 *Paul Bowles: Halbmond* **1995** Trilogy of stories by Paul Bowles. "Merkala Beach" looks at the friendship of two young Moroccan men who are both seduced by the same mysterious woman. "Call at Corazon" finds the honeymoon journey of a mismatched British couple turning into a nightmare as they sail up the Amazon on a crowded cargo boat. "Allal" is a Moroccan boy who's an outcast in his village because of his illegitimacy. He befriends an old snake dealer and steals one of his cobras in order to charm the reptile. Then Allal winds up in a magical transformation with the creature. English and Arabic with subtitles. **90m/C VHS.** *GE GE* Samir Guesmi, Khalid Ksouri, Sondos Belhassan, Veronica Quilligan, Sam Cox, Said Zakir, Mohammed Belfquih; ***D:*** Irene von Alberti, Frieder Schlaich; ***W:*** Irene von Alberti, Frieder Schlaich; ***C:*** Volker Tittel; ***M:*** Roman Bunka; ***Nar:*** Paul Bowles.

Hallelujah! 🦴🦴🦴½ **1929** Haynes plays an innocent young man who turns to religion and becomes a charasmatic preacher after a family tragedy. He retains all his human weaknesses, however, including falling for the lovely but deceitful McKinney. Great music included traditional spirituals and songs by Berlin, such as "At the End of the Road" and "Swanee Shuffle." Shot on location in Tennessee. The first all-black feature film and the first talkie for director Vidor was given the go-ahead by MGM production chief Irving Thalberg, though he knew the film would be both controversial and get minimal release in the deep South. **90m/B VHS.** Daniel L. Haynes, Nina Mae McKinney, William Fontaine, Harry Gray, Fannie Belle DeKnight, Everett McGarrity; ***D:*** King Vidor; ***M:*** Irving Berlin.

Hallelujah, I'm a Bum 🦴🦴½ *Hallelujah, I'm a Tramp; The Heart of New York; Happy Go Lucky; Lazy Bones* **1933** A happy-go-lucky hobo reforms and begins a new life for the sake of a woman. Bizarre Depression-era musical with a Rodgers and Hart score and continuously rhyming dialogue. The British version, due to the slang meaning of "bum," was retitled, substituting "tramp." ♫You Are Too Beautiful; I'll Do It Again; I've Got To Get Back To New York; What Do You Want With Money?; Hallelujah, I'm A Bum; My Pal Bumper; Dear June; Bumper Found a Grand. **83m/B VHS, DVD.** Al Jolson, Madge Evans, Frank Morgan, Chester Conklin, Edgar Connor; ***D:*** Lewis Milestone; ***W:*** Ben Hecht, S.N. Behrman; ***M:*** Richard Rodgers, Lorenz Hart.

The Hallelujah Trail 🦴🦴 **1965** Denver mining town in the late 1800s is about to batten down the hatches for a long winter, and there's not a drop of whiskey to be had. The U.S. Cavalry sends a shipment to the miners, but temperance leader Cora Templeton Massingale (Remick) and her bevy of ladies against liquor stand between the shipment and the would-be whistle whetters. Limp Western satire directed by Preston Sturges' brother, who fared much better when he kept a straight face (he also directed "The Great Escape"). Based on Bill Gulick's novel, "The Hallelujah Train." **166m/C VHS, DVD, Wide.** Burt Lancaster, Lee Remick, Jim Hutton, Pamela Tiffin, Donald Pleasence, Brian Keith, Martin Landau; ***D:*** John Sturges; ***W:*** John Gay; ***C:*** Robert L. Surtees; ***M:*** Elmer Bernstein; ***Nar:*** John Dehner.

Halloween 🦴🦴🦴½ **1978 (R)** John Carpenter's horror classic has been acclaimed "the most successful independent motion picture of all time." A deranged youth returns to his hometown with murderous intent after 15 years in an asylum. Very, very scary—you feel this movie more than see it. **90m/C VHS, DVD.** Jamie Lee Curtis, Donald Pleasence, Nancy Loomis, P.J. Soles, Charles Cyphers, Kyle Richards, Brian Andrews, John Michael Graham, Nancy Stephens, Arthur Malet, Mickey Yablans, Brent Le Page, Adam Hollander, Robert Phalen, Sandy Johnson, David Kyle, Nick Castle; ***D:*** John Carpenter; ***W:*** John Carpenter, Debra Hill; ***C:*** Dean Cundey; ***M:*** John Carpenter.

Halloween 2: The Nightmare Isn't Over! 🦴½ **1981 (R)** Trying to pick up where "Halloween" left off, the sequel begins with the escape of vicious killer Michael, who continues to murder and terrorize the community of Haddonfield, Illinois. Lacking the innovative intentions of its predecessor, it relies on old-fashioned buckets of blood. No chills, just trauma. Co-scripted by Carpenter, director of the original. **92m/C VHS, DVD, Wide.** Jamie Lee Curtis, Donald Pleasence, Jeffrey Kramer, Charles Cyphers, Lance Guest; ***D:*** Rick Rosenthal; ***W:*** John Carpenter, Debra Hill; ***C:*** Dean Cundey; ***M:*** John Carpenter.

Halloween 3: Season of the Witch 🦴🦴 **1982 (R)** Modern druid plans to kill 50 million children with his specially made Halloween masks. Produced by John Carpenter, this second sequel to the 1978 horror classic is not based on the events or characters of its predecessors or successors. Followed by Halloweens 4, 5, and 6. **98m/C VHS, DVD.** Tom Atkins, Stacey Nelkin, Dan O'Herlihy, Ralph Strait, Michael Currie; ***D:*** Tommy Lee Wallace; ***W:*** Tommy Lee Wallace; ***C:*** Dean Cundey; ***M:*** John Carpenter.

Halloween 4: The Return of Michael Myers 🦴 **1988 (R)** The third sequel, wherein the lunatic that won't die returns home to kill his niece. **89m/C VHS, DVD, Wide.** Donald Pleasence, Ellie Cornell, Danielle Harris, Michael Pataki, George P. Wilbur, Beau Starr, Kathleen Kinmont, Sasha Jenson, Gene Ross; ***D:*** Dwight Little; ***W:*** Alan B. McElroy; ***C:*** Peter Collister; ***M:*** Alan Howarth, John Carpenter.

Halloween 5: The Revenge of Michael Myers 🦴½ **1989 (R)** Fifth in the series, this Halloween is an improvement over 2, 3, and 4, thanks to a few well directed scare scenes. Unfortunately, the plot remains the same: a psycho behemoth chases down and kills more teens. An open ending promises yet another installment. **96m/C VHS, DVD, Wide.** Donald Pleasence, Ellie Cornell, Danielle Harris, Don Shanks, Betty Carvalho, Beau Starr, Wendy Kaplan, Jeffrey Landman; ***D:*** Dominique Othenin-Girard; ***W:*** Dominique Othenin-Girard, Shem Bitterman, Michael Jacobs; ***C:*** Rob Draper; ***M:*** John Carpenter, Alan Howarth.

Halloween 6: The Curse of Michael Myers 🦴 *Halloween: The Origin of Michael Myers* **1995 (R)** First the return. Then his revenge. And now, his curse, aimed square at the viewer. Lame series entry connects Michael Meyers to an ancient Celtic ritual that drives him to murder whole families in his old stompin' grounds of Haddonfield. Before he finishes his reign of terror, Meyers has to contend with Dr. Loomis (Pleasence), the man who knows his true evil. Though still a profit-making monster (the entire franchise had a combined budget of $20 million and grossed over $200 million), Michael should probably join Freddy and Jason at the old slashers' retirement home. Film marks the final screen appearance of Pleasence, who died shortly after its completion. **88m/C VHS, DVD.** Donald Pleasence, Mitchell Ryan, Marianne Hagan, Leo Geter, George P. Wilbur, Kim Darby, Bradford English, Devin Gardner; ***D:*** Joe Chappelle; ***W:*** Daniel Farrands; ***C:*** Billy Dickson; ***M:*** Alan Howarth.

Halloween: H20 🦴🦴🦴 *Halloween: H20 (Twenty Years Later); Halloween 7* **1998 (R)** Jamie Lee Curtis treads familiar water in this return to the wellspring of the slasher genre. She reprises her role as Laurie Strode, sister of relentless psycho-killer Michael Myers. After faking her own death and changing her name, she becomes the headmistress of a private school in California. Now an overprotective single mom, she battles with the spirit of her brother, as well as the spirit of vodka. Her rebellious son John (Harnett) blows off a field trip for a romantic weekend with girlfriend Molly (Williams). They are accompanied by fellow lust-ridden Michael fodder Charlie (Hann-Byrd) and Sarah (O'Keefe) on the dimly lit campus. Either Laurie extracts her final revenge or you can anticipate "Halloween 8: The Social Security Checks of Michael Myers." Also features Curtis' mother Janet Leigh in a family reunion of screaming divas. **86m/C VHS, DVD.** Jamie Lee Curtis, Adam Arkin, Josh Hartnett, Michelle Williams, Adam Hann-Byrd, Jodi Lyn O'Keefe, Janet Leigh, L.L. Cool J., Joseph Gordon-Levitt, Nancy Stephens, Branden Williams, Chris Durand; ***D:*** Steve Miner; ***W:*** Matt Greenberg, Robert Zappia; ***C:*** Daryn Okada; ***M:*** John Ottman, John Carpenter.

Halloween Night 🦴🦴 **1990 (R)** Ancient evil rises up to destroy the perfect small town. **90m/C VHS.** Hy Pyke, Katrina Garner; ***D:*** Emilio P. Miraglio.

Halloween: Resurrection **2002 (R)** So why is this film (the 8th in the series) being released in the summer instead of, oh, say, at Halloween? Anyway, Internet entrepreneur Rhymes arranges for a group of stupid kids to stay in Michael Myers' house as a publicity stunt for a live webcast. Naturally, Mike doesn't like the interlopers and proceeds to do what he does best. Curtis and Rosenthal, who directed "Halloween 2," also return. Not yet reviewed. **?m/C VHS, DVD.** Busta Rhymes, Sean Patrick Thomas, Jamie Lee Curtis, Bianca Kajlich, Tyra Banks, Thomas Ian Nicholas; ***D:*** Rick Rosenthal; ***W:*** Larry Brand, Sean Hood.

Halloween with the Addams Family woof! **1979** A really pathetic production spawned during the "reunion" craze of the late '70s, sparked only by the lively performance of Coogan's Uncle Fester and the always lovable Lurch. **87m/C VHS.** John Astin, Carolyn Jones, Jackie Coogan, Ted Cassidy. **TV**

The Halls of Montezuma 🦴🦴½ **1950** Large, bombastic WWII combat epic. Depicts the Marines fighting the Japanese in the Pacific. **113m/C VHS, DVD.** Richard Widmark, Jack Palance, Reginald Gardiner, Robert Wagner, Karl Malden, Richard Boone, Richard Hylton, Skip Homeier, Jack Webb, Neville Brand, Martin Milner, Bert Freed; ***D:*** Lewis Milestone; ***W:*** Michael Blankfort; ***C:*** Winton C. Hoch, Harry Jackson; ***M:*** Sol Kaplan.

Hallucination woof! *Hallucination Generation* **1967** Early flower-power exploiter about expatriate acid heads who murder an antique dealer under the influence of LSD and then attempt to hide at a monastery. Depicts LSD as the catalyst in bringing out the group's criminal behavior. In sepia while everyone's cool, breaking into color during the head trips. **90m/C VHS.** George Montgomery, Danny Stone; ***D:*** Edward Andrew (Santos Alcocer) Mann; ***W:*** Edward Andrew (Santos Alcocer) Mann.

Hallucinations of a Deranged Mind 🦴 *Delirios de Um Anormal* **1970** A compilation of all the magic moments ever censored by the Brazilian military dictatorship. Includes scenes banned from over 10 different Mojica Marins films, including his "Coffin Joe" character. In Portugese with English subtitles. **?m/C VHS.** *BR* Jose Mojica Marins; ***D:*** Jose Mojica Marins.

Hambone & Hillie 🦴🦴 **1984 (PG)** An elderly woman makes a 3000-mile trek across the United States to search for the dog she lost in an airport. **97m/C VHS.** Lillian Gish, Timothy Bottoms, Candy Clark, O.J. Simpson, Robert Walker Jr., Jack Carter, Alan Hale Jr., Anne Lockhart; ***D:*** Roy Watts; ***W:*** Sandra K. Bailey.

Hamburger Hill 🦴🦴½ **1987 (R)** Popular war epic depicting the famous battle between Americans and Viet Cong over a useless hill in Vietnam. Made in the heyday of 1980s Vietnam backlash, and possibly the most realistic and bloodiest of the lot. **104m/C VHS, DVD.** Michael Dolan, Daniel O'Shea, Dylan McDermott, Tommy Swerdlow, Courtney B. Vance, Anthony Barille, Michael Boatman, Don Cheadle, Tim Quill, Don James, Michael A. (M.A.) Nickles, Harry O'Reilly, Steven Weber, Tegan West, Kieu Chinh, Doug Goodman, J.C. Palmore; ***D:*** John Irvin; ***W:*** James (Jim) Carabatsos; ***C:*** Peter Macdonald; ***M:*** Philip Glass.

Hamburger...The Motion Picture 🦴 **1986 (R)** The life and times of students at Busterburger U., the only college devoted to hamburger franchise management. **90m/C VHS.** Leigh McCloskey, Dick Butkus, Randi Brooks, Sandy Hackett; ***D:*** Mike Marvin; ***M:*** Elmer Bernstein.

Hamlet 🦴🦴🦴🦴 **1948** Splendid adaptation of Shakespeare's dramatic play. Hamlet vows vengeance on the murderer of his father in this tight version of the four hour stage play. Some scenes were cut out, including all of Rosencrantz and Guildenstern. Beautifully photographed in Denmark. An Olivier triumph. Remade several times. **153m/B VHS, DVD.** *GB* Laurence Olivier, Basil Sydney, Felix Aylmer, Jean Simmons, Stanley Holloway, Peter Cushing, Christopher Lee, Eileen Herlie, John Laurie, Esmond Knight, Anthony Quayle; ***D:*** Laurence Olivier; ***W:*** Alan Dent; ***C:*** Desmond Dickinson; ***M:*** William Walton; ***V:*** John Gielgud. Oscars '48: Actor (Olivier), Art Dir./Set Dec., B&W, Costume Des. (B&W), Picture; British Acad. '48: Film; Golden Globes '49: Actor—Drama (Olivier); N.Y. Film Critics '48: Actor (Olivier).

Hamlet 🦴🦴½ **1969 (G)** Williamson brings to the screen his stage performance as the classic Shakespeare character. Something is lost in the process, although there are some redeeming moments including those with Faithfull as Ophelia. **114m/C VHS.** *GB* Nicol Williamson, Anthony Hopkins, Marianne Faithfull, Gordon Jackson, Judy Parfitt, Mark Dingham, Anjelica Huston; ***D:*** Tony Richardson.

Hamlet 🦴🦴🦴½ **1990 (PG)** Zeffirelli—in his fourth attempt at Shakespeare—creates a surprisingly energetic and accessible interpretation of the Bard's moody play. Gibson brings charm, humor and a carefully calculated sense of violence, not to mention a good deal of solid flesh, to the eponymous role, and handles the language skillfully (although if you seek a poetic Dane, stick with Olivier). Exceptional work from Scofield and Bates; Close seems a tad hysterical (not to mention too young to play Gibson's mother), but brings insight and nuance to her role. Purists beware: this isn't a completely faithful adaptation. Beautifully costumed; shot on location in Northern Scotland. **135m/C VHS, 8mm, Wide.** Mel Gibson, Glenn Close, Alan Bates, Paul Scofield, Ian Holm, Helena Bonham Carter, Nathaniel Parker, Pete Postlethwaite; ***D:*** Franco Zeffirelli; ***W:*** Franco Zeffirelli, Christopher DeVore; ***C:*** David Watkin.

Hamlet 🦴🦴🦴🦴 **1996 (PG-13)** Branagh tackles Shakespeare once again with the uncut, four-hour long story of the melancholy Dane (played by you-know-who). Branagh's decision to use the complete text, and move the action ahead 600 years to the 19th century adds an interesting external political dimension to the palace intrigue and gives this sixth screen adaptation the stature of Olivier's 1948 masterpiece. Jacobi and Christie stand out among a very large and brilliant cast. Lemmon and Crystal, however, should stick to American comedy. A two and a half hour version was also prepared for those with shorter attention spans, but the uncut version is well worth the time invested. **242m/C VHS.** *GB* Kenneth Branagh, Kate Winslet, Julie Christie, Derek Jacobi, Richard Briers, Brian Blessed, Michael Maloney, Timothy Spall, Reece Dinsdale, Jack Lemmon, Nicholas Farrell, Charlton Heston, Rosemary Harris, Gerard Depardieu, Robin Williams, Billy Crystal, Simon Russell Beale, Michael Bryant, John Gielgud, Richard Attenborough, Rufus Sewell, Judi Dench, Ian McElhinney, John Mills; ***D:*** Kenneth Branagh; ***W:*** Kenneth Branagh; ***C:*** Alex Thomson; ***M:*** Patrick Doyle.

Hamlet 🦴🦴🦴 **2000 (R)** It's mopey Hawke's turn as the title character but in this update he's hardly a Danish prince. Instead he's an experimental filmmaker in New York whose murderous uncle Claudius (MacLachlan) runs the family conglomerate, Denmark, Inc. Thanks to Almereyda's respect for Shakespeare's language, as well as his excellent adaptation to present-day corporate America, this interpretation loses none of the play's power, and adds some insights that prove its timelessness. **111m/C VHS, DVD, Wide.** Ethan Hawke, Kyle MacLachlan, Sam Shepard, Diane Venora, Bill Murray, Julia Stiles, Liev Schreiber, Karl Geary, Paula Malcomson, Steve Zahn, Dechen Thurman, Jeffrey Wright, Paul Bartel, Rome Neal, Casey Affleck; ***D:*** Michael Almereyda; ***W:*** Michael Almereyda; ***C:*** John de Borman; ***M:*** Carter Burwell.

Hamlet 🦴🦴½ **2001** Every actor wants to play Shakespeare's melancholy Dane and in this cable adaptation, it's Scott (co-directing as well) who takes on the title role. This version is set at the turn of the 20th century. Good cast and some clever supernatural visuals for enchancement. **179m/C VHS, DVD.** Campbell Scott, Jamey Sheridan, Blair Brown, Roscoe Lee Browne, Lisa Gay

Hamilton, John Benjamin Hickey, Roger Guenveur Smith, Sam Robards, Michael Imperioli, Byron Jennings; *D:* Campbell Scott, Eric Simonson; *C:* Dan Gillham. CABLE

Hammers over the Anvil 𝒮𝒮½ 1991 Young Alan Marshall (Outhred) has a case of hero worship for local horse trainer East Driscoll (Crowe). But East has also caught the eye of the upper-class (and married) English beauty, Grace McAlister (Rampling), with whom he is having an affair, and which Alan witnesses. But East wants Grace more than just part-time and is determined to force her to run away with him—with disastrous consequences. **98m/C VHS, DVD.** *AU* Charlotte Rampling, Russell Crowe, Alexander Outhred, John Rafter Lee, Kirsty McGregor, Jake Frost; *D:* Ann Turner; *W:* Ann Turner, Peter Hepworth; *C:* James Bartle.

Hammersmith Is Out 𝒮½ 1972 (R) A violent lunatic cons an orderly into letting him escape. Chases, romance and craziness follow. **108m/C VHS.** Richard Burton, Elizabeth Taylor, Peter Ustinov, Beau Bridges, John Schuck; *D:* Peter Ustinov.

Hammett 𝒮𝒮 1982 (PG) After many directors and script rewrites, Wenders was assigned to this arch neo-noir what-if scenario. Depicts Dashiell Hammett solving a complex crime himself, an experience he uses in his novels. Interesting, but ultimately botched studio exercise, like many from executive producer Francis Coppola, who is said to have reshot much of the film. **98m/C VHS.** Frederic Forrest, Peter Boyle, Sylvia Sidney, Elisha Cook Jr., Marilu Henner; *D:* Wim Wenders; *C:* Joseph Biroc; *M:* John Barry.

Hamsin 𝒮𝒮𝒮 1983 A Jewish landowner and an Arab worker encounter difficulties in their relationship when the government announces plans to confiscate Arab land. In Hebrew with English subtitles. **90m/C VHS.** Shlomo Tarshish, Yasin Shawap, Hemda Levy, Ruth Geler; *D:* Daniel Wachsmann.

Hamsun 𝒮𝒮 1996 Highly-regarded Norwegian Nobel Prize-winning writer Knut Hamsun (von Sydow) stunned his countrymen when he sided with the Nazis in WWII and urged them to stop resisting the invaders of their homeland. An ardent nationalist, the elderly Hamsun apparently heard only what he wanted to about Hitler's policies and regarded Britain as the greater threat to Europe. After the war Hamsun and his equally outspoken pro-German wife, Marie (Norby), are deemed traitors and are put on trial. Based on a book by Thorkild Hansen. Swedish, Danish, and Norwegian with subtitles. **154m/C VHS.** *NO DK SW* Max von Sydow, Ghita Norby, Sverre Anker Ousdal, Ernst Jacobi, Anette Hoff, Erik Hivju; *D:* Jan Troell; *W:* Per Olof Enquist; *C:* Jan Troell; *M:* Arvo Part.

The Hand 𝒮½ 1960 During WWII, three British POWs are tortured by the Japanese. Refusing to give information, two of them have their right hands cut off. The third opts to talk, thereby keeping his hand. After the war, a series of murders occur in London where the victims have their hands amputated. Could there be a connection? **61m/B VHS.** *GB* Derek Bond, Ronald Lee Hunt, Reed de Rouen, Ray Cooney, Brian Coleman; *D:* Henry Cass.

The Hand 𝒮𝒮𝒮 1981 (R) A gifted cartoonist's hand is severed in a car accident. Soon, the hand is on the loose with a mind of its own, seeking out victims with an obsessive vengeance. Stone's sophomore directorial outing is a unique, surreal psycho-horror pastiche consistently underrated by most critics. **105m/C VHS.** *GB* Michael Caine, Andrea Marcovicci, Annie McEnroe, Bruce McGill, Viveca Lindfors; ***Cameos:*** Oliver Stone; *D:* Oliver Stone; *W:* Oliver Stone; *C:* King Baggot; *M:* James Horner.

Hand Gun 𝒮𝒮½ 1993 (R) Jack McCallister (Cassel) is wounded in a shoot-out with police but still manages to get away with half-a-million from a robbery. When word gets out, everybody begins looking for Jack, including his two sons—gun happy George (Williams) and small time con artist Michael (Schulze). **90m/C VHS, DVD.** Seymour Cassel, Treat Williams, Paul Schulzie, Michael Rapaport; *D:* Whitney Ransick; *W:* Whitney Ransick; *C:* Michael Spiller; *M:* Douglas J. Cuomo.

The Hand that Rocks the Cradle 𝒮𝒮½ 1992 (R) DeMornay is Peyton Flanders, the nanny from hell, in an otherwise predictable thriller. Sciorra's role is a thankless one as pregnant and unbelievably naive Claire Bartel, who unwittingly starts a horrific chain of events when she levels charges of molestation against her obstetrician. Transparent plot preys on the worst fears of viewers, and doesn't offer anything innovative or new. See this one for DeMornay's Jekyll and Hyde performance. **110m/C VHS, DVD.** Annabella Sciorra, Rebecca DeMornay, Matt McCoy, Ernie Hudson, Julianne Moore, Madeline Zima, John de Lancie, Mitchell Laurance; *D:* Curtis Hanson; *W:* Amanda Silver; *C:* Robert Elswit; *M:* Graeme Revell. MTV Movie Awards '92: Villain (DeMornay).

A Handful of Dust 𝒮𝒮 1988 (PG) A dry, stately adaptation of the bitter Evelyn Waugh novel about a stuffy young aristocrat's wife's careless infidelity and how it sends her innocent husband to a tragic downfall. A well-meaning version that captures Waugh's cynical satire almost in spite of itself. Set in post-WWI England. **114m/C VHS.** *GB* James Wilby, Kristin Scott Thomas, Rupert Graves, Alec Guinness, Anjelica Huston, Judi Dench, Cathryn Harrison, Pip Torrens, John Junkin; *D:* Charles Sturridge; *W:* Charles Sturridge, Tim Sullivan, Derek Granger; *C:* Peter Hannan; *M:* George Fenton. British Acad. '88: Support. Actress (Dench).

The Handmaid's Tale 𝒮𝒮½ 1990 (R) A cool, shallow but nonetheless chilling nightmare based on Margaret Atwood's bestselling novel, about a woman caught in the machinations of a near-future society so sterile it enslaves the few fertile women and forces them into being child-bearing "handmaids." **109m/C VHS, DVD, Wide.** Natasha Richardson, Robert Duvall, Faye Dunaway, Aidan Quinn, Elizabeth McGovern, Victoria Tennant, Blanche Baker, Traci Lind; *D:* Volker Schlondorff; *W:* Harold Pinter; *C:* Igor Luther; *M:* Ryuichi Sakamoto.

Hands Across the Border 𝒮½ 1943 A musical western in which Roy helps a woman find the men who killed her father. **72m/B VHS, DVD.** Roy Rogers, Ruth Terry, Guinn "Big Boy" Williams, Onslow Stevens, Mary Treen, Joseph Crehan; *D:* Joseph Kane.

Hands Across the Table 𝒮𝒮𝒮 1935 Regi Allen (Lombard) is a fortune-hunting manicurist in a swanky hotel barber shop. Has-been millionaire playboy Theodore Drew III (MacMurray) falls for her but he's about to marry money (Allwyn) and Regi's got a wheelchair-bound rich man (Bellamy) just waiting for her to say "I do." Snappy dialogue and light-hearted performances. Based on the story "Bracelets" by Vina Delmar. **80m/B VHS.** Carole Lombard, Fred MacMurray, Ralph Bellamy, Astrid Allwyn, Ruth Donnelly, Marie Prevost, William Demarest, Edward (Ed) Gargan; *D:* Mitchell Leisen; *W:* Norman Krasna, Vincent Lawrence, Herbert Fields; *C:* Ted Tetzlaff.

Hands of a Murderer 𝒮𝒮½ *Sherlock Holmes and the Prince of Crime* 1990 Sherlock Holmes (Woodward) and the faithful Dr. Watson (Hillerman) are in pursuit of the great detective's most evil nemesis—the nefarious Moriarty (Andrews). This time, the fiend has escaped the gallows and stolen government secrets from the safe of Holmes' brother Mycroft. TV movie. **100m/C VHS.** Edward Woodward, John Hillerman, Anthony Andrews, Kim Thomson, Peter Jeffrey, Warren Clarke; *D:* Stuart Orme; *W:* Charles Edward Pogue.

Hands of a Stranger 𝒮𝒮 1962 Another undistinguished entry in the long line of remakes of "The Hands of Orlac." A pianist who loses his hands in an accident is given the hands of a murderer, and his new hands want to do more than tickle the ivories. Kellerman has a very small role as does former "Sheena" McCalla. **95m/B VHS.** Paul Lukather, Joan Harvey, James Stapleton, Sally Kellerman, Irish McCalla; *D:* Newton Arnold.

Hands of a Stranger 𝒮𝒮½ 1987 Policeman's wife is raped during an adulterous tryst. As the painful truth dawns on the cop, he himself dallies with a compassionate lady D.A. while hunting the attacker. About as sordid as a network TV-movie gets without toppling into sleaze; strong acting and a sober script pull it through. But the plot, from Robert Daly's novel, doesn't justify miniseries treatment; the two-cassette package is excessively long. **179m/C VHS.** Armand Assante, Beverly D'Angelo, Blair Brown, Michael Lerner, Philip Casnoff, Arliss Howard; *D:* Larry Elikann; *W:* Arthur Kopit. TV

The Hands of Orlac 𝒮𝒮 *Orlacs Hände* 1925 Classic silent film about a pianist whose hands are mutilated in an accident. His hands are replaced by those of a murderer, and his urge to kill becomes overwhelming. Contains restored footage. **92m/B VHS.** *AT* Conrad Veidt, Fritz Kortner, Carmen Cartellieri, Paul Askonas, Alexandra Sorina, Fritz Strassny; *D:* Robert Wiene; *W:* Ludwig Nerz; *C:* Gunther Krampf, Hans Androschin.

The Hands of Orlac 𝒮𝒮 *Hands of the Strangler; Hands of a Strangler* 1960 Third remake of Maurice Renard's classic tale. When a concert pianist's hands are mutilated in an accident, he receives a graft of a murderer's hands. Obsession sweeps the musician, as he believes his new hands are incapable of music, only violence. Bland adaptation of the original story. **95m/B VHS.** *GB FR* Mel Ferrer, Christopher Lee, Felix Aylmer, Basil Sydney, Donald Wolfit, Donald Pleasence, Danny Carrel, Lucile Saint-Simon, Peter Reynolds, Campbell Singer, David Peel; *D:* Edmond T. Greville; *W:* Edmond T. Greville, John Baines, Donald Taylor; *C:* Desmond Dickinson; *M:* Claude Bolling.

Hands of Steel woof! 1986 (R) A ruthless cyborg carries out a mission to find and kill an important scientist. Terrible acting, and lousy writing: an all-around woofer! **94m/C VHS.** Daniel Greene, John Saxon, Janet Agren, Claudio Cassinelli, George Eastman; *D:* Sergio Martino.

Hands of the Ripper 𝒮𝒮½ 1971 (R) Jack the Ripper's daughter returns to London where she works as a medium by day and stalks the streets at night. Classy Hammer horror variation on the perennial theme. **85m/C VHS.** *GB* Eric Porter, Angharad Rees, Jane Merrow, Keith Bell, Derek Godfrey, Dora Bryan, Marjorie Rhodes, Norman Bird; *D:* Peter Sasdy; *W:* L.W. Davidson; *C:* Ken Talbot; *M:* Christopher Gunning.

Hands Up 𝒮𝒮½ 1926 Jaunty Confederate spy (played by much-overlooked American comedian Griffith) attempts, amidst much comic nonsense, to thwart Yankee gold mining during the Civil War. Silent. **50m/B VHS.** Raymond Griffith, Mack Swain, Marion (Marian) Nixon, Montagu Love; *D:* Clarence Badger.

Hands Up 𝒮𝒮𝒮 *Rece do Gory* 1981 Famed Polish film finished in 1967 but not released until 1981 for political reasons (prologue shot in '81 included). Doctors at a medical school reunion reflect upon the effect of Stalinist rule on their education and lives. In Polish with English subtitles. **78m/C VHS.** *PL* *D:* Jerzy Skolimowski.

Hang 'Em High 𝒮𝒮½ 1967 (PG-13) A cowboy is saved from a lynching and vows to hunt down the gang that nearly killed him in this American-made spaghetti western. Eastwood's first major vehicle made outside of Europe. **114m/C VHS, DVD, Wide.** *IT* Clint Eastwood, Inger Stevens, Ed Begley Sr., Pat Hingle, James MacArthur; *D:* Ted Post; *W:* Leonard Freeman, Mel Goldberg; *C:* Richard H. Kline, Leonard J. South; *M:* Dominic Frontiere.

Hangar 18 𝒮½ *Invasion Force* 1980 (PG) Silly sci-fi drama about two astronauts who collide with a UFO during a shuttle flight. Later they learn that the government is hiding it in a hangar and they try to prove its existence. Shown on TV as "Invasion Force" with an entirely new ending. **97m/C VHS.** Darren McGavin, Robert Vaughn, Gary Collins, James Hampton, Philip Abbott, Pamela Bellwood, Tom Hallick, Cliff Osmond, Joseph Campanella; *D:* James L. Conway; *W:* David O'Malley.

The Hanged Man 𝒮𝒮 1974 Tale of a gunslinger in the Old West who mystically escapes death by hanging. Reborn, he re-evaluates the meaning of justice. **78m/C VHS.** Steve Forrest, Cameron Mitchell, Sharon Acker, Dean Jagger, Will Geer, Barbara Luna, Rafael Campos; *D:* Michael Caffey. TV

Hangfire 𝒮𝒮 1991 (R) When a New Mexican prison is evacuated thanks to a nasty chemical explosion, several prisoners decide it's time for a furlough, and they elect the local sheriff's wife as a traveling companion. Another mediocre actioner from director Maris, it gets an extra bone for stunts kids shouldn't try at home. **91m/C VHS.** Brad Davis, Yaphet Kotto, Lee DeBroux, Jan-Michael Vincent, George Kennedy, Kim Delaney; *D:* Peter Maris; *W:* Brian D. Jeffries.

Hangin' with the Homeboys 𝒮𝒮𝒮 1991 (R) One night in the lives of four young men. Although the Bronx doesn't offer much for any of them, they have little interest in escaping its confines, and they are more than willing to complain. Characters are insightfully written and well portrayed, with strongest work from Serrano as a Puerto Rican who is trying to pass himself off as Italian. Lack of plot may frustrate some viewers. **89m/C VHS.** Mario Joyner, Doug E. Doug, John Leguizamo, Nestor Serrano, Kimberly Russell, Mary B. Ward, Christine Claravall, Rosemark Jackson, Reggie Montgomery; *D:* Joseph B. Vasquez; *W:* Joseph B. Vasquez; *C:* Anghel Decca. Sundance '91: Screenplay.

The Hanging Garden 𝒮𝒮 1997 (R) Bizarre family drama mixes the matter-of-fact and the surreal. Gay 25-year-old Sweet William (Leavins) returns to his rural Nova Scotia home and family after a 10-year absence for the marriage of his sister, Rosemary (Fox). The reunion brings up lots of painful memories and flashes back to the 15-year-old Sweet William (Veinotte), when he was emotionally and physically abused by his psycho father Whiskey Mac (MacNeill). After more crises, the teen hangs himself from a backyard tree. Oh yes, everyone in the present can still see the teen's ghost hanging there, including the adult William. You figure it out. **91m/C VHS.** *CA* Chris Leavins, Peter MacNeill, Kerry Fox, Seana McKenna, Troy Veinotte, Sarah Polley, Christine Dunsworth, Joel S. Keller, Joan Orenstein; *D:* Thom Fitzgerald; *W:* Thom Fitzgerald; *C:* Daniel Jobin. Genie '97: Screenplay, Support. Actor (MacNeill), Support. Actress (McKenna); Toronto-City '97: Canadian Feature Film.

Hanging on a Star 𝒮 1978 (PG) A small rock band encounters many comic adventures as it climbs its way up the charts. Raffin stars as the band's persistent and competent road agent. **92m/C VHS.** Deborah Raffin, Lane Caudell, Wolfman Jack, Jason Parker, Danil Torppe; *D:* Mike MacFarland.

The Hanging Tree 𝒮𝒮𝒮 1959 Cooper plays a frontier doctor who rescues a thief (Piazza) from a lynch mob and nurses a temporarily blind girl (Schell). Malden is the bad guy who tries to attack Schell and Cooper shoots him. The townspeople take Cooper out to "The Hanging Tree" but this time it's Schell and Piazza who come to his rescue. Slow-paced western with good performances. Scott's screen debut. **108m/B VHS.** Gary Cooper, Maria Schell, Ben Piazza, Karl Malden, George C. Scott, Karl Swenson, Virginia Gregg, King Donovan; *D:* Delmer Daves; *W:* Wendell Mayes, Halsted Welles; *M:* Max Steiner.

Hanging Up 𝒮½ 1999 (PG-13) Strident, schmaltzy comedy about family. Married working mom and middle sister Eve (Ryan) seems to be the one that has to deal with family dilemmas, in this case her cantankerous dying father Lou (Matthau). Older sis Georgia (Keaton) is a workaholic Manhattan magazine exec while ditzy younger sis Maddy (Kudrow) is an actress working on a soap. They check in by phone but duck out on their share of the responsibilities although sibling rivalry rears its head. Based on the novel by Delia Ephron. **93m/C VHS, DVD, Wide.** Meg Ryan, Diane Keaton, Lisa Kudrow, Walter Matthau, Adam Arkin, Cloris Leachman, Jesse James, Duke Moosekian, Ann Bortolotti; *D:* Diane Keaton; *W:*

Delia Ephron, Nora Ephron; ***C:*** Howard Atherton; ***M:*** David Hirschfelder.

The Hanging Woman 🦴🦴½ *Return of the Zombies; Beyond the Living Dead; La Orgia de los Muertos; Dracula, the Terror of the Living Dead; Orgy of the Dead; House of Terror* **1972 (R)** A man is summoned to the reading of a relative's will, and discovers the corpse of a young woman hanging in a cemetery. As he investigates the mystery, he uncovers a local doctor's plans to zombify the entire world. Not bad at all and quite creepy once the zombies are out in force. Euro-horror star Naschy plays the necrophiliac grave digger, Igor. **91m/C VHS.** *SP IT* Stan Cooper, Vickie Nesbitt, Marcella Wright, Catherine Gilbert, Gerard Tichy, Paul (Jacinto Molina) Naschy, Dianik Zurakowska, Maria Pia Conte, Carlos Quiney, Jacinto (Jack) Molina; ***D:*** Jose Luis Merino; ***W:*** Jose Luis Merino.

Hangman 🦴🦴 **2000 (R)** A serial killer plays a lethal game of hangman, sending a videotape of each murder to detective Nick Roos (Phillips). Roos joins psychiatrist Grace Mitchell (Amick) to catch the killer but she may be the killer's next intended victim. **96m/C VHS, DVD, Wide.** Lou Diamond Phillips, Madchen Amick, Dan Lauria, Mark Wilson, Vincent Coraza; ***D:*** Ken Girotti; ***W:*** Vladimir Nemirovsky; ***C:*** Gerald Packer; ***M:*** Steven Stern. **VIDEO**

Hangman's Knot 🦴🦴½ **1952** Members of the Confederate Cavalry rob a Union train, not knowing that the war is over. Now facing criminal charges, they are forced to take refuge in a stagecoach stop. Well-done horse opera with a wry sense of humor. **80m/C VHS.** Randolph Scott, Donna Reed, Claude Jarman Jr., Frank Faylen, Glenn Langan, Richard Denning, Lee Marvin, Jeanette Nolan; ***D:*** Roy Huggins.

Hangmen woof! **1987 (R)** Ex-CIA agents battle it out on the East side of New York. If you're into very violent, very badly acted films, then this one's for you. **88m/C VHS, DVD.** Jake La Motta, Rick Washburne, Doug Thomas, Sandra Bullock; ***D:*** J. Christian Ingvordsen; ***W:*** J. Christian Ingvordsen, Steven Kaman; ***C:*** Steven Kaman; ***M:*** Michael Montes.

Hangmen Also Die 🦴🦴½ **1942** Lang's anti-Nazi propaganda film was inspirated by the actual May, 1942 assassination of Reinhard Heydrich. Franz Svoboda (Donlevy) is the member of the Czech resistance who assassinates Heydrich. The Nazis seek revenge and begin rounding up and executing Czech citizens, aided by the traitorous Emil (Lockhart). Franz wants to give himself up to prevent further slaughter but is persuaded to turn the tables on Emil and make him appear to be the assassin. Bertolt Brecht had a hand in the original screenplay but did not receive screen credit and later said most of his work was cut out. **134m/B VHS, DVD.** Brian Donlevy, Gene Lockhart, Walter Brennan, Anna Lee, Dennis O'Keefe, Alexander Granach, Jonathan Hale, Margaret Wycherly, Hans von Twardowski; ***D:*** Fritz Lang; ***W:*** John Wexley; ***C:*** James Wong Howe; ***M:*** Hanns Eisler.

Hank Aaron: Chasing the Dream 🦴🦴🦴 **1995** Docudrama combines archival footage, interviews, and reenactments to tell the story of the life and career of Henry Aaron. Follows Aaron's development as a Hall of Fame outfielder for the Milwaukee and Atlanta Braves and as a leader in the civil rights movement. Emphasis on personal and societal issues, as well as on-the-field accomplishments, raises this one above most sports biography documentaries. **120m/C VHS.** ***Nar:*** Dorian Harewood.

Hanky Panky 🦴½ **1982 (PG)** Insipid comic thriller in which Wilder and Radner become involved in a search for top-secret plans. **107m/C VHS.** Gene Wilder, Gilda Radner, Richard Widmark, Kathleen Quinlan; ***D:*** Sidney Poitier.

Hanna K. 🦴🦴 **1983 (R)** Story of divided passions set in the tumultuous state of Israel. American lawyer Clayburgh tries to settle her personal and political affairs with various Middle-Eastern men. Mediocre Disappointing. Release generated controversy over pro-Palestine stance. **111m/C VHS.** *FR* Jill Clayburgh, Gabriel Byrne, Jean Yanne, Muhamad Bakri, David Clennon, Oded Kotler; ***D:*** Constantin Costa-Gavras.

Hannah and Her Sisters 🦴🦴🦴½ **1986 (PG)** Allen's grand epic about a New York showbiz family, its three adult sisters and their various complex romantic entanglements. Excellent performances by the entire cast, especially Caine and Hershey. Classic Allen themes of life, love, death, and desire are explored in an assured and sensitive manner. Witty, ironic, and heartwarming. **103m/C VHS, DVD, Wide.** Mia Farrow, Barbara Hershey, Dianne Wiest, Michael Caine, Woody Allen, Maureen O'Sullivan, Lloyd Nolan, Sam Waterston, Carrie Fisher, Max von Sydow, Julie Kavner, Daniel Stern, Tony Roberts, John Turturro; ***D:*** Woody Allen; ***W:*** Woody Allen; ***C:*** Carlo Di Palma. Oscars '86: Orig. Screenplay, Support. Actor (Caine), Support. Actress (Wiest); British Acad. '86: Director (Allen), Orig. Screenplay; Golden Globes '87: Film—Mus./Comedy; L.A. Film Critics '86: Film, Screenplay, Support. Actress (Wiest); Natl. Bd. of Review '86: Director (Allen), Support. Actress (Wiest); N.Y. Film Critics '86: Director (Allen), Film, Support. Actress (Wiest); Natl. Soc. Film Critics '86: Support. Actress (Wiest); Writers Guild '86: Orig. Screenplay.

Hanna's War 🦴🦴½ **1988 (PG-13)** A moving film about Hanna Senesh, a young Hungarian Jew living in Palestine, who volunteered for a suicide mission behind Nazi lines during WWII. After her capture by the Germans, she was killed, and is now considered by many to have been a martyr. Detmers is very believable as Hanna and Burstyn puts in a good performance as her mother. **148m/C VHS.** Ellen Burstyn, Maruschka Detmers, Anthony Andrews, Donald Pleasence, David Warner, Denholm Elliott, Vincenzo Ricotta, Ingrid Pitt; ***D:*** Menahem Golan; ***W:*** Menahem Golan; ***M:*** Dov Seltzer.

Hannibal 🦴🦴 **2001 (R)** The long-awaited sequel to the much loved "Silence of the Lambs," and the lesser-known but equally praised "Manhunter," is more gruesome than scary, but it still managed to bring loads of people to the theatre, most likely to enjoy a heapin' helping of Hopkins's Hannibal. This time the infamous Dr. Lecter and FBI agent Clarice Starling (now played by Moore) are brought together by one of Hannibal's vengeful victims, the severely disfigured Verger (played by Oldman, under layers of prosthetics), and his trained wild pigs. Based on the novel by Thomas Harris. **131m/C VHS, DVD, Wide.** *US* Anthony Hopkins, Julianne Moore, Gary Oldman, Ray Liotta, Frankie Faison, Giancarlo Giannini, Francesca Neri, Zeljko Ivanek, Hazelle Goodman, David Andrews, Francis Guinan, Enrico Lo Verso; ***D:*** Ridley Scott; ***W:*** David Mamet, Steven Zaillian; ***C:*** John Mathieson; ***M:*** Hans Zimmer.

Hannie Caulder 🦴🦴 **1972 (R)** A woman hires a bounty hunter to avenge her husband's murder and her own rape at the hands of three bandits. Excellent casting but uneven direction. Boyd is uncredited as the preacher. **87m/C VHS.** Raquel Welch, Robert Culp, Ernest Borgnine, Strother Martin, Jack Elam, Christopher Lee, Diana Dors, Stephen Boyd; ***D:*** Burt Kennedy; ***W:*** Burt Kennedy.

Hanoi Hilton 🦴½ **1987 (R)** A brutal drama about the sufferings of American POWs in Vietnamese prison camps. Nonstop torture, filth, and degradation. **126m/C VHS.** Michael Moriarty, Paul LeMat, Jeffrey Jones, Lawrence Pressman, Stephen Davies, David Soul, Rick Fitts, Aki Aleong, Gloria Carlin; ***D:*** Lionel Chetwynd; ***W:*** Lionel Chetwynd.

Hanover Street 🦴🦴 **1979 (PG)** An American bomber pilot and a married British nurse fall in love in war-torn Europe. Eventually the pilot must work with the husband of the woman he loves on a secret mission. A sappy, romantic tearjerker. **109m/C VHS, DVD, Wide.** Harrison Ford, Lesley-Anne Down, Christopher Plummer, Alec McCowen; ***D:*** Peter Hyams; ***W:*** Peter Hyams; ***C:*** David Watkin; ***M:*** John Barry.

Hans Brinker 🦴🦴½ **1969** Young Hans Brinker and his sister participate in an ice skating race, hoping to win a pair of silver skates. A musical version of the classic tale. **103m/C VHS.** Robin Askwith, Eleanor Parker, Richard Basehart, Cyril Ritchard, John Gregson; ***D:*** Robert Scheerer.

Hans Christian Andersen 🦴🦴 **1952** Sentimental musical story of Hans Christian Andersen, a young cobbler who has a great gift for storytelling. Digitally remastered editions available with stereo sound and original trailer. ♫The King's New Clothes; I'm Hans Christian Andersen; Wonderful Copenhagen; Thumbelina; The Ugly Duckling; Anywhere I Wander; The Inch Worm; No Two People. **112m/C VHS, DVD.** Danny Kaye, Farley Granger, Zizi Jeanmarie, Joey Walsh; ***D:*** Charles Vidor; ***W:*** Moss Hart; ***C:*** Harry Stradling Sr.; ***M:*** Frank Loesser.

Hansel and Gretel **1982** From Shelly Duvall's "Faerie Tale Theatre" comes the story of two young children who get more than they bargained for when they eat a gingerbread house. **51m/C VHS.** Rick Schroder, Joan Collins, Paul Dooley, Bridgette Andersen; ***D:*** James Frawley. **CABLE**

Hanussen 🦴🦴🦴½ **1988 (R)** The third of Szabo and Brandauer's price-of-power trilogy (after "Mephisto" and "Colonel Redl"), in which a talented German magician and clairvoyant (based on a true life figure) collaborates with the Nazis during their rise to power in the 1930s, although he can foresee the outcome of their reign. In German with English subtitles. **110m/C VHS.** *GE HU* Klaus Maria Brandauer, Erland Josephson, Walter Schmidinger; ***D:*** Istvan Szabo; ***W:*** Peter Dobai, Istvan Szabo; ***C:*** Lajos Koltai; ***M:*** Gyorgy Vukan.

Happenstance 🦴🦴½ *The Beating of the Butterfly's Wings; Le Battement d'Ailes du Papillon* **2000 (R)** Is it fate? destiny? chance? that brings people together? Clerk Irene (Tautou) chats with a woman on the subway who tells her that she will meet her true love that day. He turns out to be Faudel (Younes) but of course the made-for-each-other duo's actually getting together is a maze of complications. Amusing romantic comedy; French with subtitles. **97m/C VHS, DVD, Wide.** *FR* Audrey Tautou, Faudel, Eric Savin, Eric Feldman, Nathalie Besancon, Lysaine Meis, Lily Boulogne, Francoise Bertin, Frederique Bouraly, Irene Ismailoff; ***D:*** Laurent Firode; ***W:*** Laurent Firode; ***C:*** Jean-Rene Duveau; ***M:*** Peter Chase.

The Happiest Days of Your Life 🦴🦴🦴 **1950** During the London Blitz, a girls' academy is evacuated to the country and mistakeningly billeted with a boys' school. The headmaster and headmistress clash and the bewildered students all try to get along. Good cast, lots of laughs. Adapted from a play by John Dighton. **81m/B VHS.** *GB* Alastair Sim, Margaret Rutherford, Joyce Grenfell, Edward Rigby, Guy Middleton, John Bentley, Bernadette O'Farrell, Richard Wattis, Muriel Aked, Patricia Owens, John Turnbull, Arthur Howard; ***D:*** Frank Launder; ***W:*** Frank Launder, John Dighton; ***M:*** Mischa Spoliansky.

The Happiest Millionaire 🦴🦴 **1967** A Disney film about a newly immigrated lad who finds a job as butler in the home of an eccentric millionaire. Based on the book "My Philadelphia Father," by Kyle Chrichton. ♫What's Wrong With That?; Watch Your Footwork; Valentine Candy; Strengthen the Dwelling; I'll Always Be Irish; Bye-Yum Pum Pum; I Believe in This Country; Detroit; There Are Those. **118m/C VHS, DVD.** Fred MacMurray, Tommy Steele, Greer Garson, Geraldine Page, Lesley Ann Warren, John Davidson; ***D:*** Norman Tokar; ***W:*** A.J. Carothers; ***C:*** Edward Colman; ***M:*** Richard M. Sherman, Robert B. Sherman.

Happily Ever After 🦴🦴 **1982** Las Vegas star-maker recruits and manipulates two green performers. Show business life in Vegas is given a truthful treatment in this drama. **95m/C VHS.** Suzanne Somers, John Rubinstein, Eric (Hans Gudegast) Braeden; ***D:*** Robert Scheerer. **TV**

Happily Ever After 🦴🦴 *Alem Da Paixao* **1986** A Brazilian housewife meets a bisexual transvestite and has a passionate affair, bringing her into the depths of the criminal underworld. In Portuguese with English subtitles. Contains nudity. **106m/C VHS.** *BR* Regina Duarte, Paul Castelli; ***D:*** Bruno Barreto; ***C:*** Alfonso Beato.

Happily Ever After 🦴½ **1993 (G)** Sequel to "Snow White" begins where the original ends, but isn't connected to the Walt Disney classic. Snow White and her Prince prepare for their wedding when the Wicked Queen is found dead by her brother, who vows revenge. So it's up to Snow and the Dwarfelles (Disney said no to using the Dwarfs), female cousins of the original Dwarfs, to rescue him. Interesting choices from the casting department: Diller is Mother Nature and Asner provides the voice of a rapping owl. Poorly animated drivel designed to ride in on Disney's coattails. While the kids might enjoy it, save your money for the original, finally slated for a video release. **74m/C VHS.** ***D:*** John Howley; ***W:*** Martha Moran, Robby London; ***V:*** Dom DeLuise, Phyllis Diller, Zsa Zsa Gabor, Ed Asner, Sally Kellerman, Irene Cara, Carol Channing, Tracey Ullman.

Happiness 🦴🦴 **1934** Another zany comedy from the land of the hammer and sickle. Banned in Russia for 40 years, it was deemed to be risque and a bit too biting with the social satire. Silent with orchestral score. **69m/B VHS, DVD.** *RU* ***D:*** Alexander Medvedkin.

Happiness 🦴🦴🦴 **1998** Very disturbing film made for the "love it or hate it" category. There are three middleclass New Jersey sisters—perky housewife Trish (Stevenson), underachieving Joy (Adams) and glamourous writer Helen (Boyle). Trish is married to shrink Bill (Baker) and they have an 11-year-old son, Billy (Read), who's getting curious about sex. His dad is the wrong person to ask since he's a pedophile who abuses his son's friends. Then there's Allen (Hoffman), one of Bill's patients. He makes obscene phone calls to Helen, who turns out to be turned on by the dirty talk. Suburban hell, indeed. Some riveting performances, especially Baker and Hoffman. **139m/C VHS, DVD, Wide.** Dylan Baker, Cynthia Stevenson, Lara Flynn Boyle, Jane Adams, Philip Seymour Hoffman, Ben Gazzara, Louise Lasser, Rufus Read, Jared Harris, Jon Lovitz, Camryn Manheim, Elizabeth Ashley, Marla Maples; ***D:*** Todd Solondz; ***W:*** Todd Solondz; ***C:*** Maryse Alberti; ***M:*** Robbie Kondor.

Happy Accidents 🦴🦴½ **2000 (R)** Quirky sci-fi/romance offers a breath of fresh air by going against the grain of both genres. Ruby (Tomei) is a neurotic loser in romance who always tries to "fix" the men she dates. She meets Sam (D'Onofrio), who appears to be the well-adjusted guy she doesn't have to change. They fall for each other, and then Sam drops the other shoe. He claims to be a time-traveler from the year 2470, and he's come back to save her life by breaking the "causal chain of events" that will result in a fatal accident. Ruby then has to decide whether to believe him or write him off as another lunatic. D'Onofrio amusingly goes from seemingly normal to spouting surreal "history" without blinking. Light on the special effects (especially for sci-fi), but they're effective when they are used. Pic went through a time warp of its own, as it was shot in 1999, debuted at Sundance in 2000 and released in theaters in 2001. **110m/C VHS, DVD.** *US* Marisa Tomei, Vincent D'Onofrio, Tovah Feldshuh, Nadia Dajani, Holland Taylor, Richard Portnow, Sean Gullette, Cara Buono, Liana Pai, Tamara Jenkins, Jose Zuniga; ***Cameos:*** Anthony Michael Hall; ***D:*** Brad Anderson; ***W:*** Brad Anderson; ***C:*** Terry Stacy; ***M:*** Evan Lurie.

Happy Birthday, Gemini 🦴½ **1980 (R)** A coming-of-age comedy about a young man on his 21st birthday worrying about his sexual identity. Based on the play "Gemini" by Albert Innaurato. The closeness of the characters on stage did not translate to the screen. **107m/C VHS.** Robert Viharo, Madeline Kahn, Rita Moreno, Alan Rosenberg, Sarah Holcomb, David Marshall Grant, David McIlwraith; ***D:*** Richard Benner; ***W:*** Richard Benner.

Happy Birthday to Me 🦴½ **1981 (R)** Several elite seniors at an exclusive private school are mysteriously killed by a deranged killer who has a fetish for cutlery. **108m/C VHS.** *CA* Melissa Sue Anderson, Glenn Ford, Tracy Bregman, Jack Blum, Matt Craven, Lawrence Dane, Lenore Zann, Sharon Acker,

Frances Hyland, Earl Pennington, David Eisner, Richard Rebrere, Lesleh Donaldson; ***D:*** J. Lee Thompson; ***W:*** Timothy Bond, Peter Jobin, John C.W. Saxton, John Beaird; ***C:*** Miklos Lente; ***M:*** Bo Harwood, Lance Rubin.

Happy Campers 🦴🦴 **2001 (R)** Director of Camp Bleeding Dove (Stormare) is sidelined by an injury, so his teen counselors take charge and seek to spice up their boring daily routines. Routine summer camp flick with a better-than-average cast. **94m/C VHS, DVD, Wide.** Brad Renfro, Dominique Swain, Emily Bergl, James King, Jordan Bridges, Peter Stormare, Justin Long, Keram Malicki-Sanchez; ***D:*** Daniel Waters; ***W:*** Daniel Waters; ***C:*** Elliot Davis; ***M:*** Rolfe Kent. **VIDEO**

The Happy Ending 🦴🦴½ **1969 (PG)** Woman struggles with a modern definition of herself and her marriage, causing pain and confusion for her family. Simmons is solid as the wife and mother seeking herself. Michel LeGrand's theme song "What Are You Doing With the Rest of Your Life?" was a big hit. **112m/C VHS.** Jean Simmons, John Forsythe, Lloyd Bridges, Shirley Jones, Teresa Wright, Dick Shawn, Nanette Fabray, Bobby Darin, Tina Louise; ***D:*** Richard Brooks; ***W:*** Richard Brooks; ***C:*** Conrad L. Hall.

The Happy Face Murders 🦴🦴½ **1999 (R)** A puzzling murder and witnesses who keep changing their stories are the problem in this mystery, inspired by true events, that doesn't quite live up to its potential. Dowdy grandmother Lorraine Petrovich (Ann-Margaret) accuses abusive younger boyfriend Rusty (Campbell) of murder. Cynical detective Jen Powell (Helgenberger) and her naive assistant, Dylan (Thomas), must try and find the truth as everyone else keeps lying. The murder is brutal and each retelling only dramatizes the gore. **99m/C VHS.** Ann-Margret, Marg Helgenberger, Henry Thomas, Nicholas (Nick) Campbell, Rick Peters, David McIlwraith, Bruce Gray, Emily Hampshire; ***D:*** Brian Trenchard-Smith; ***W:*** John Pielmeier; ***C:*** Albert J. Dunk; ***M:*** Elmer Bernstein. **CABLE**

Happy Gilmore 🦴🦴 **1996 (PG-13)** Skating-impaired hockey player Gilmore (Sandler) translates his slap shot into a 400-yard tee shot and joins the pro golf tour. His unique style brings a new, less refined breed of fan to the game and upsets the reigning tour hotshot (McDonald). Sandler improves on "Billy Madison," which isn't saying much. There's still plenty of ammo for his many detractors, but the laughs are more frequent and consistent. Replacing bathroom humor with abusive behavior, the mis-named Happy swears at or beats up about 90% of the supporting cast, including Bob Barker in a charity pro-am. **92m/C VHS, DVD.** Adam Sandler, Christopher McDonald, Carl Weathers, Julie Bowen, Frances Bay, Ben Stiller, Richard Kiel, Joe Flaherty, Kevin Nealon, Allen Covert, Robert Smigel, Bob Barker, Dennis Dugan; ***D:*** Dennis Dugan; ***W:*** Adam Sandler, Tim Herlihy; ***C:*** Arthur Albert; ***M:*** Mark Mothersbaugh. MTV Movie Awards '96: Fight (Adam Sandler/Bob Barker).

Happy Go Lovely 🦴🦴 **1951** An unscrupulous theatrical producer casts a chorus girl in a leading role in order to get closer to her boyfriend's fortune. Tired plot, but good performances in this lightweight musical. ♫One-Two-Three; Would You, Could You; London Town. **95m/C VHS.** Vera-Ellen, David Niven, Cesar Romero, Bobby Howes; ***D:*** H. Bruce Humberstone.

The Happy Hooker 🦴🦴½ **1975 (R)** Xaviera Hollander's cheeky (and bestselling) memoir of her transition from office girl to "working girl" has been brought to the screen with a sprightly (though sanitary) air of naughtiness, with Redgrave enjoyable in title role. Followed by "The Happy Hooker Goes to Washington" and "The Happy Hooker Goes Hollywood." **96m/C VHS.** Lynn Redgrave, Jean-Pierre Aumont, Nicholas Pryor; ***D:*** Nicholas Sgarro.

The Happy Hooker Goes Hollywood 🦴 **1980 (R)** Third film inspired by the title of Xaviera Hollander's memoirs, in which the fun-loving Xaviera comes to Hollywood with the intention of making a movie based on her book, but soon meets up with a series of scheming, would-be producers. **86m/C VHS.** Martine Beswick, Chris Lemmon, Adam West, Phil Silvers; ***D:*** Alan Roberts.

The Happy Hooker Goes to Washington 🦴½ **1977 (R)** Further adventures of the world's most famous madam. Heatherton (not Redgrave) is Xaviera Hollander this time, testifying before the U.S. Senate in defense of sex. Fairly stupid attempt to milk boxoffice of original. Second in the holy trilogy of Happy Hooker pictures, which also include "The Happy Hooker" and "The Happy Hooker Goes Hollywood." **89m/C VHS.** Joey Heatherton, George Hamilton, Ray Walston, Jack Carter; ***D:*** William A. Levey.

Happy Hour 🦴½ **1987 (R)** A young brewing scientist discovers a secret formula for beer, and everyone tries to take it from him. Little turns in a good performance as a superspy. **88m/C VHS.** Richard Gilliland, Jamie Farr, Tawny Kitaen, Ty Henderson, Rich Little; ***D:*** John DeBello; ***W:*** John DeBello.

Happy Landing 🦴🦴½ **1938** Predictable, yet entertaining Henie vehicle about a plane that makes a forced landing in Norway near Henie's home. Romance follows with bandleader Romero and manager Ameche. ♫Hot and Happy; Yonny and his Oompah; You Are The Music to the Words in my Heart; A Gypsy Told Me; You Appeal to Me. **102m/B VHS.** Sonja Henie, Don Ameche, Jean Hersholt, Ethel Merman, Cesar Romero, Billy Gilbert, Wally Vernon, El Brendel; ***D:*** Roy Del Ruth; ***W:*** Milton Sperling, Boris Ingster.

Happy New Year 🦴🦴🦴 *The Happy New Year Caper; La Bonne Annee* **1973** Charming romantic comedy in which two thieves plan a robbery but get sidetracked by the distracting woman who works next door to the jewelry store that's their target. Available in both subtitled and dubbed versions. Remade in 1987. **114m/C VHS.** *FR IT* Francoise Fabian, Lino Ventura, Andre Falcon, Charles Gerard; ***D:*** Claude Lelouch; ***W:*** Claude Lelouch, Pierre Uytterhoeven.

A Happy New Year! 🦴🦴 **1979** Two men and a woman, all engineers in a chemical plant, try to fight off a hangover as they deal with the comings and goings of friends throughout the day and night. In Hungarian with English subtitles. **84m/C VHS.** *HU* Istvan Bujtor, Erika Bodnar, Cecilia Esztergalyos, Andras Balint; ***D:*** Reszo Szoreny; ***W:*** Peter Modos, Reszo Szoreny.

Happy New Year 🦴🦴½ **1987 (PG)** Two sophisticated thieves plan and execute an elaborate jewel heist that goes completely awry. Remake of the 1974 French film of the same name. **86m/C VHS.** Peter Falk, Wendy Hughes, Tom Courtenay, Charles Durning, Joan Copeland; ***D:*** John G. Avildsen; ***W:*** Warren Lane; ***M:*** Bill Conti.

Happy Since I Met You 🦴🦴🦴 **1989** Comedy-drama about a scatter-brained drama teacher and a struggling young actor who become romantically involved. **55m/C VHS.** *GB* Julie Walters, Duncan Preston; ***Cameos:*** Tracey Ullman, Jim Bowen; ***D:*** Baz Taylor; ***W:*** Victoria Wood.

Happy, Texas 🦴🦴🦴 **1999 (PG-13)** Producer/director Mark Illsley's quirky little debut hearkens back to such classic Hollywood comedies as "Some Like It Hot." Escaped prisoners Harry Sawyer (Northam) and Wayne Wayne Wayne Jr. (Zahn) steal a camper and assume the identity of its owners in order to evade the law. The trouble is that the owners are a pair of gay men who organize kiddie beauty pageants. When they arrive in the town of Happy, Texas, the populace thinks that they're there to stage the Little Miss Fresh Squeezed contest and greet them with open arms. Wayne is forced to summon up fashion and choreography skills not commonplace in your average hardened criminal, while Harry hobnobs with the local gentry while plotting to knock over the town bank. Romantic complications involving a schoolmarm (Douglas), lady banker (Walker) and a sexually confused sheriff (Macy) arise, setting the stage for a happy (but unnecessarily tidy) ending. **104m/C VHS, DVD, Wide.** Steve Zahn, Jeremy Northam, Ally Walker, Illeana Douglas, William H. Macy, M.C. Gainey, Ron Perlman, Michael Hitchcock, Paul Dooley; ***D:*** Mark Illsley; ***W:*** Phil Reeves, Ed Stone, Mark Illsley; ***C:*** Bruce Douglas Johnson; ***M:*** Peter Harris. Ind. Spirit '00: Support. Actor (Zahn).

Happy Together 🦴 **1989 (PG-13)** An eager freshman accidentally gets a beautiful, impulsive girl as his roommate. Together they meet the challenges of secondary education. **102m/C VHS, DVD.** Helen Slater, Patrick Dempsey, Dan Schneider, Marius Weyers, Barbara Babcock, Brad Pitt; ***D:*** Mel Damski; ***M:*** Robert Folk.

Happy Together 🦴🦴 *Cheun Gwong Tsa Sit* **1996** Lovers Lai Yiu-Fai (Leung) and Ho Po-Wing (Cheung) travel to Argentina from Hong Kong looking for adventure but soon go their separate ways. Lai is working as a doorman at a tango bar when a badly beaten Ho unexpectedly re-enters his life. Lai looks after the self-destructive Ho but his restlessness causes him to desert Lai once again, even as Lai befriends young Taiwanese Chang (Chen). After Chang returns to Taipei, Lai begins to suffer from depression and serious homesickness, as well as still worrying about Ho. Edgy visuals and playful performances bely a serious nature. Chinese and Spanish with subtitles. **92m/C VHS, DVD.** *HK* Leslie Cheung, Tony Leung Chiu-Wai, Chang Chen; ***D:*** Wong Kar-Wai; ***W:*** Wong Kar-Wai; ***C:*** Christopher Doyle; ***M:*** Danny Chung. Cannes '97: Director (Kar-Wai).

Hard-Boiled 🦴🦴½ *Lashou Shentan* **1992** Police Inspector Yuen (Woo regular Yun-Fat) is investigating, with his usual excessive force, the Triads organized crime syndicate and a group of gun smugglers who killed his partner. He joins forces with Tony, an undercover cop who's working as a gangster hitman. There's lots of gunplay and betrayals among all the participants. Usual Woo way with violence and action sequences although the plot is more contrived. In Mandarin and Chinese with English subtitles. **126m/C VHS, DVD, Wide.** *HK* Chow Yun-Fat, Tony Leung Chiu-Wai, Philip Chan, Anthony Wong, Teresa Mo, Bowie Lam, Hoi-Shan Kwan, Philip Kwok, John Woo; ***D:*** John Woo; ***W:*** Barry Wong, John Woo; ***C:*** Wing-Heng Wang; ***M:*** Michael Gibbs.

Hard-Boiled Mahoney 🦴🦴½ **1947** Slip, Sach, and the rest of the Bowery Boys try to solve a mystery involving mysterious women and missing men. The last film in the series for Bobby Jordan, whose career was ended when he was injured in an accident involving a falling elevator. **64m/B VHS.** Leo Gorcey, Huntz Hall, Bobby Jordan, William Benedict, David Gorcey, Gabriel Dell, Teala Loring, Dan Seymour, Bernard Gorcey, Patti Brill, Betty Compson; ***D:*** William Beaudine.

Hard Bounty 🦴🦴½ **1994 (R)** After five years of chasing desperadoes, bounty hunter Martin B. Kanning hangs up his guns to open a saloon—complete with frontier prostitutes. When one of his ladies is murdered, the other gals decide to chase after the killer. Naturally, Kanning can't let them go alone. **90m/C VHS, DVD.** Matt McCoy, Kelly Le Brock, Rochelle Swanson, Felicity Waterman, Kimberly Kelley; ***D:*** Jim Wynorski; ***W:*** Karen Kelly; ***C:*** Zoran Hochstatter; ***M:*** Taj.

Hard Cash 🦴½ *Run for the Money* **2001 (R)** Thief Tom Taylor (Slater) wants to go legit after being released from prison but instead hooks up with a new crew for a job. When they discover the money is marked, Taylor finds himself embroiled with corrupt FBI agent Mark Cornell (Kilmer). Despite the billing, Kilmer has limited screen time and this caper film is a predictable yawner. **98m/C VHS, DVD, Wide.** Christian Slater, Bokeem Woodbine, Val Kilmer, Daryl Hannah, Verne Troyer, Balthazar Getty, Vincent Laresca, Peter Woodward, William Forsythe, Sara Downing; ***D:*** Pedrag (Peter) Antonijevic; ***W:*** Willie Dreyfus; ***C:*** Phil Parmet; ***M:*** Stephen Edwards.

Hard Choices 🦴🦴🦴 **1984** A 15-year-old Tennessee boy is unjustly charged as an accessory to murder, until a female social worker decides to help him. From then on, nothing is predictable. Excellent work by Klenck, McCleery, and Seitz. Don't miss Sayles as an unusual drug dealer. Intelligent, surprising, and powerful. Based on a true story, this is a low profile film that deserves to be discovered. **90m/C VHS.** Margaret Klenck, Gary McCleery, John Seitz, John Sayles, Liane (Alexandra) Curtis, J.T. Walsh, Spalding Gray; ***D:*** Rick King; ***W:*** Rick King.

Hard Core Logo 🦴🦴 **1996 (R)** Mockumentary about a group of Canadian veteran punk rock musicians who, at 30-something, have reunited for one last benefit concert. The semi-legendary Vancouver band are so pleased by how well the concert goes that they decide to head back on the road (in a decrepit van) for one last shot at glory, trailed by a documentary film crew (led by director McDonald). The documentary inserts reveal the band's ups and downs and the ego trips that ultimately drove them apart. Adapted from a novel by Michael Turner. McDonald describes "Hard Core Logo" as the last of his rock 'n' roll road trilogy, following "Roadkill" and "Highway 61." **96m/C VHS, DVD, Wide.** *CA* Hugh Dillon, Callum Keith Rennie, John Pyper-Ferguson, Bernie Coulson; ***D:*** Bruce McDonald; ***W:*** Noel S. Baker; ***C:*** Danny Nowak; ***M:*** Shaun Tozer. Genie '96: Song ("Swamp Baby, Who the Hell Do You Think You Are?").

Hard Country 🦴🦴½ **1981 (PG)** Caught between her best friend's success as a country singer and the old values of a woman's place, a small town girl questions her love and her life style. A warm and intelligent rural drama. Basinger's debut. **104m/C VHS.** Jan-Michael Vincent, Kim Basinger, Michael Parks, Gailard Sartain, Tanya Tucker, Ted Neeley, Daryl Hannah, Richard Moll; ***D:*** David Greene; ***W:*** Michael Kane; ***M:*** Michael Martin Murphy.

A Hard Day's Night 🦴🦴🦴½ **1964** The Beatles' first film is a joyous romp through an average "day in the life" of the Fab Four, shot in a pseudo-documentary style with great flair by Lester and noted as the first music video. ♫A Hard Day's Night; Tell Me Why; I Should Have Known Better; She Loves You; I'm Happy Just to Dance with You; If I Fell; And I Love Her; This Boy; Can't Buy Me Love. **90m/B VHS, DVD, CD-I.** *GB* John Lennon, Paul McCartney, George Harrison, Ringo Starr, Wilfrid Brambell, Norman Rossington, John Junkin, Victor Spinetti, Anna Quayle, Deryck Guyler, Richard Vernon, Lionel Blair, Eddie Malin, Robin Ray, Alison Seebohm, David Saxon, Patti Boyd; ***D:*** Richard Lester; ***W:*** Alun Owen; ***C:*** Gilbert Taylor; ***M:*** George Martin, John Lennon, Paul McCartney.

Hard Drive 🦴½ **1994** A high tech, interactive network offers shared fantasies to Will and Delilah. Then they become obsessed with making their dreams a reality. **92m/C VHS, DVD.** Matt McCoy, Christina (Kristina) Fulton, Edward Albert, Leo Damian, Stella Stevens; ***D:*** James Merendino; ***W:*** James Merendino; ***C:*** Sead Muhtarevic; ***M:*** Nels Cline.

Hard Drivin' 🦴 **1960** Rowdy action featuring Southern stock car drivers with well shot race scenes from the Southern 500. **92m/C VHS.** Rory Calhoun, John Gentry, Alan Hale Jr.; ***D:*** Paul Helmick.

Hard Eight 🦴🦴🦴 *Sydney* **1996 (R)** Performances are the highlight of this low-key story set in Reno, Nevada. Sydney (Hall) is a professional gambler who decides to take under his wing the destitute John (Reilly) and teach him the trade. John falls for waitress/hooker Clementine (Paltrow) but there has to be some snake in this gambler's would-be paradise and it shows up in the malevolent form of the scary Jimmy (Jackson), who the dim John befriends despite Sydney's warnings. Debut for writer/director Anderson. **101m/C VHS, DVD, Wide.** Philip Baker Hall, John C. Reilly, Gwyneth Paltrow, Samuel L. Jackson, F. William Parker, Philip Seymour Hoffman, Nathanael Cooper, Wynn White, Robert Ridgely, Michael J. Rowe, Kathleen Campbell, Melora Walters; ***D:*** Paul Thomas Anderson; ***W:*** Paul Thomas Anderson; ***C:*** Robert Elswit; ***M:*** Michael Penn, Jon Brion.

Hard Evidence 🦴🦴½ **1994 (R)** Trent Turner (Harrison) winds up with major regrets when he joins his mistress (Timmins) on a business trip. Seems her "business" involves drug smuggling and he's forced to shoot a DEA agent to protect them. Some protection—now Turner and his wife (Severance) are caught up in murder, drugs, and blackmail. **100m/C VHS.** Gregory Harrison, Joan Severance, Cali Timmins,

Andrew Airlie, Nathaniel DeVeaux; *D:* Michael Kennedy; *W:* William Martell; *C:* Bruce Worrall; *M:* Barron Abramovitch.

Hard Frame 🦴½ *Hunters Are For Killing* **1970** An ex-con returns home hoping all will turn to sweetness and light when he attempts to make nice-nice with his stepdad, who wouldn't stick by him during his trial. Reynolds' debut into TV moviedom; could be the hirsute actor was thinking of this one when he said his movies were the kind they show in prisons and airplanes because nobody can leave. **100m/C VHS.** Burt Reynolds, Melvyn Douglas, Suzanne Pleshette, Larry Storch, Martin Balsam, Peter Brown, Jill Banner, Donald (Don "Red") Barry, Angus Duncan, Ivor Francis; *D:* Bernard Girard.

Hard Hombre 🦴🦴 **1931** Gibson rides and shoots across the screen in one of his best western adventures. **60m/B VHS.** Hoot Gibson, Lena Basquette, Skeeter Bill Robbins, Jack Byron, Glenn Strange; *D:* Otto Brower.

Hard Hunted 🦴½ **1992 (R)** Three macho undercover agents try to avoid death at the hands of high-tech guerillas trying to steal nuclear weapons. No-brain actioner, heavy on the display of feminine charms. **97m/C VHS.** Dona Speir, Roberta Vasquez, Cynthia Brimhall, Bruce Penhall, R.J. Moore, Tony Peck, Rodrigo Obregon, Al Leong, Michael J. Shane; *D:* Andy Sidaris; *W:* Andy Sidaris.

Hard Justice 🦴🦴 **1995 (R)** Bureau of Alcohol, Tobacco & Firearms agent Nick Adams (Bradley) goes undercover in prison to find his partner's killer and discovers that Warden Pike (Napier) is running an illegal gun operation. Now, who's he gonna trust? Lots of action thrills in a routine story. **95m/C VHS.** David Bradley, Charles Napier, Yuji Okumoto, Vernon Wells; *D:* Greg Yaitanes; *W:* Nicholas Amendolare, Chris Bold; *C:* Moshe Levin; *M:* Don Peake.

Hard Knocks 🦴🦴½ **1980** An ex-con goes from one tragic situation to another, and is eventually stalked by shotgun-wielding rednecks in this grim, powerful drama. Excellent performance by Mann holds this picture together. **85m/C** *AU* Tracey Mann, John Arnold, Bill Hunter, Max Cullen, Tony Barry; *D:* Don McLennan. Australian Film Inst. '80: Actress (Mann).

Hard Knocks 🦴 **19??** A young man on the run is tormented by an aging actress and her husband. His attempt to leave a past of violence and pain creates even more havoc. **90m/C VHS.** Michael Christian, John Crawford, Donna Wilkes, Keenan Wynn.

Hard Knox 🦴 **1983** A hard-nosed Marine pilot is dumped from the service and takes up command at a military school filled with undisciplined punks. A made-for-television movie. **96m/C VHS.** Robert Conrad, Frank Howard, Alan Ruck, Red West, Bill Erwin, Dean Hill, Joan Sweeney; *D:* Peter Werner.

Hard Labour 🦴🦴 **1973** Middle-aged housekeeper is humiliated at home by her children and tyrannical daughter-in-law. **70m/C VHS.** *GB* Alison Steadman, Ben Kingsley, Clifford Kershaw; *D:* Mike Leigh. **TV**

Hard Lessons 🦴🦴½ *The George McKenna Story* **1986** Washington stars as the newly appointed principal of George Washington High in Los Angeles. The school is located in South Central, a gang and drug-infested war zone where the students are armed for their own protection. The situation appears hopeless but McKenna refuses to give up. Based on a true story. **95m/C VHS, DVD.** Denzel Washington, Lynn Whitfield, Akosua Busia, Richard Masur; *D:* Eric Laneuville; *W:* Charles Eric Johnson; *C:* Isidore Mankofsky; *M:* Herbie Hancock. **TV**

Hard Luck 🦴🦴 **2001** Trevor "Lucky" O'Donnell's life certainly doesn't live up to his nickname. He's doing time in a mental ward when his childhood sweetheart Sheryl visits to let him know that his buddy, her brother Eric, is dying of cancer. So Lucky escapes and heads to his hometown of Gold Beach, Oregon, determined that the threesome will take one last trip together to their favorite childhood haunt. Too bad they're being pursued by Sheryl's cop husband Matt and her and Eric's dad, who just happens to be the Chief of Police. **85m/C VHS, DVD.** Kirk Harris, Renee Humphrey, Matthew Faber, Ron Gilbert, Gareth Williams, Karen Black, Joannne Baron, Darrell Bryan, Tony Longo, Luca Bercovici, Jon Jacobs; *D:* Jack Rubio; *W:* Kirk Harris.

Hard Part Begins 🦴 **198?** A naive country singer gets sucked into the pratfalls of show business. **87m/C VHS.** Donnelly Rhodes, Nancy Belle Fuller, Paul Bradley.

Hard Promises 🦴🦴 **1992 (PG)** Absence doesn't necessarily make the heart fonder, as Joey finds out when he's accidentally invited to his wife's wedding. He's been away from home for so long he doesn't even realize he's been divorced and hightails it home to win his sweetheart back. Average performances and script round out this innocuous domestic comedy-drama. **95m/C VHS, 8mm.** Sissy Spacek, William L. Petersen, Brian Kerwin, Mare Winningham, Peter MacNicol, Ann Wedgeworth, Amy Wright, Lois Smith, Rip Torn; *D:* Martin Davidson; *M:* George S. Clinton. **CABLE**

Hard Rain 🦴🦴 *Flood* **1997 (R)** Armored car guards Tom (Slater) and his uncle Charlie (Asner) are transporting $3 million to high ground during a flood in a small Indiana town. When their truck gets stuck in the mud, a band of jet-skiin' motor boatin' thieves arrive and try to steal the money. Tom hides the dough and alerts the local sheriff (Quaid) who, being your normal American elected official, decides he wants to steal it, too. Tom forms an uneasy alliance with head bad guy Jim (Freeman) to thwart the lawman and his toadies. While all this is happening, Tom manages to find love interest Karen (Driver), who's there to protect her church restoration work and wear wet blouses. And now the weather report: floods are the least cinematic disasters. Everything just gets soggy and waterlogged (especially the action sequences). Director Salomon created the huge flooded town set inside a tank in Palmdale, California. **96m/C VHS, DVD.** Morgan Freeman, Christian Slater, Randy Quaid, Minnie Driver, Ed Asner, Richard Dysart, Betty White, Mark Rolston, Peter Murnik, Dann Florek, Wayne Duvall, Michael Goorjian; *D:* Mikael Salomon; *W:* Graham Yost; *C:* Peter Menzies Jr.; *M:* Christopher Young.

The Hard Ride 🦴🦴½ **1971 (PG)** Above average biker movie about a Vietnam vet who brings the body of a black buddy back home, then tries to persuade the dead man's white girlfriend and the leader of his motorcycle gang to attend the funeral. **93m/C VHS.** Robert Fuller, Sherry Bain, Tony Russell, Marshall Reed, Biff (Elliott) Elliot, William Bonner, R.L. Armstrong; *D:* Burt Topper; *W:* Burt Topper.

Hard Rock Zombies 🦴½ **1985 (R)** Four heavy metal band members die horribly on the road and are brought back from the dead as zombies. This horror/heavy metal spoof is somewhat amusing in a goofy way. **90m/C VHS.** E.J. Curcio, Sam Mann; *D:* Krishna Shah; *W:* David Ball.

Hard Target 🦴🦴½ **1993 (R)** Van Damme continues his action-hero ways as Chance Boudreaux, a Cajun (which explains the accent) merchant seaman, who comes to the rescue of Natasha (Butler), albeit with lots of violence. Brimley provides the humor as Chance's bayou uncle. It's another variation of "The Most Dangerous Game" story but it moves. American directorial debut of over-the-top Hong Kong action director Woo who had to tone down his usual stylistic effects and repeatedly cut some of the more violent scenes to earn an "R" rating. **97m/C VHS, DVD, Wide.** Jean-Claude Van Damme, Lance Henriksen, Yancy Butler, Arnold Vosloo, Wilford Brimley, Kasi Lemmons, Eliott Keener, Theodore (Ted) Raimi, Chuck Pfarrer; *D:* John Woo; *W:* Chuck Pfarrer; *C:* Russell Carpenter; *M:* Graeme Revell.

Hard Ticket to Hawaii 🦴 **1987 (R)** A shot-on-video spy thriller about an agent trying to rescue a comrade in Hawaii from a smuggling syndicate. Supporting cast includes many Playboy Playmates. **96m/C VHS, DVD.** Ron Moss, Dona Speir, Hope Marie Carlton, Cynthia Brimhall, Harold Diamond, Rodrigo Obregon, Rustam Branaman, Kwan Hi Lim; *D:* Andy Sidaris; *W:* Andy Sidaris; *C:* Howard Wexler; *M:* Gary Stockdale.

Hard Times 🦴🦴🦴 **1975 (PG)** A Depression-era drifter becomes a bare knuckle street fighter, and a gambler decides to promote him for big stakes. One of grade-B meister Hill's first genre films. A quiet, evocative drama. **92m/C VHS, DVD.** Charles Bronson, James Coburn, Jill Ireland, Strother Martin; *D:* Walter Hill; *W:* Walter Hill, Bryan Gindoff, Bruce Henstell; *C:* Philip Lathrop; *M:* Barry DeVorzon.

Hard to Die 🦴 *Tower of Terror* **1990** Director Wynorski's comic homage to Carol Frank's "Sorority House Massacre." Five beauties (former Playboy Playmates Harris, Taylor, Dare, Moore, and Carney) find employment moving boxes in a deserted lingerie factory. The film takes off from there as they uncover a mysterious spirit called the Sorority House Killer in an ancient "Soul Box." Desperate to extinguish the evil threat, they focus their efforts in an armed struggle involving high-powered weaponry against the building maintenance man, whom they fear is possessed by the spirit. Accompanied by a lovely, touching group shower scene. **77m/C VHS.** Robin Harris, Melissa Moore, Debra (Deborah Dutch) Dare, Lindsay Taylor, Bridget Carney, Forrest J Ackerman, Orville Ketchum; *D:* Jim Wynorski.

Hard to Hold 🦴½ **1984 (PG)** Rockin' Rick's lukewarm film debut where he falls in love with a children's counselor after an automobile accident. Springfield sings "Love Somebody" with music by Peter Gabriel. **93m/C VHS.** Rick Springfield, Janet Eilber, Patti Hansen, Albert Salmi, Monique Gabrielle; *D:* Larry Peerce.

Hard to Kill 🦴🦴 **1989 (R)** Policeman Seagal is shot and left for dead in his bedroom, but survives against the odds, though his wife does not. After seven years, he is well enough to consider evening the score with his assailants. He hides while training in martial arts for the final battle. Strong outing from Seagal, with good supporting cast. **96m/C VHS, DVD, 8mm.** Steven Seagal, Kelly Le Brock, William Sadler, Frederick Coffin, Bonnie Burroughs, Zachary Rosencrantz, Dean Norris; *D:* Bruce Malmuth; *W:* Steven McKay; *C:* Matthew F. Leonetti; *M:* Charles Fox.

Hard Traveling 🦴🦴 **1985 (PG)** An unemployed Depression-era farmworker is accused of murder. He must fight a hostile court system to maintain his dignity and salvage the love and respect of his wife. Based on a novel by Alvah Bessie. **99m/C VHS.** J.E. Freeman, Ellen Geer, Barry Corbin, James Gammon, Jim Haynie; *D:* Dan Bessie; *W:* Dan Bessie; *C:* David Myers.

The Hard Truth 🦴🦴½ **1994 (R)** By-the-book actioner finds cop Jonah (Rooker) suspended for having an itchy trigger finger. His gal Lisa (Anthony) knows her sleazy boss has lots of mob money handy and proposes they grab it. But then Lisa gets a look at Chandler (Roberts), the electronic whiz blackmailed to assist in the heist, and the triangle leads to trouble. **100m/C VHS.** Michael Rooker, Eric Roberts, Lysette Anthony, Ray Baker, Don Yesso; *D:* Kristine Peterson; *W:* Jonathan Tydor; *C:* Ross Berryman.

Hard Vice 🦴½ **1994 (R)** Vice cops Joe Owens (Jones) and Andrea Thompson (Tweed) have their work cut out for them on their Las Vegas beat. When the bodies start piling up, the prime suspects turn out to be a group of high-priced hookers. **86m/C VHS, DVD.** Shannon Tweed, Sam Jones, James Gammon, Rebecca Ferratti; *D:* Joey Travolta; *W:* Joey Travolta; *C:* F. Smith Martin; *M:* Jeff Lass.

Hard Way 🦴🦴 **1980** A world-weary assassin is pressured by his boss to perform one last assignment. A surprise awaits him if he accepts. **88m/C VHS.** Patrick McGoohan, Lee Van Cleef, Donal McCann, Edna O'Brien; *D:* Mihael Dryhurst.

The Hard Way 🦴🦴🦴 **1991 (R)** Hollywood superstar Fox is assigned to hardened NYC cop Woods to learn the ropes as he trains for a role. Nothing special in the way of script or direction, but Woods and Fox bring such intensity and good humor to their roles that the package works. Fox pokes fun at the LA lifestyle as the annoying, self-absorbed actor, and Marshall has an entertaining appearance as his agent. Woods is on familiar over-the-edge turf as the brittle but dedicated detective. Silly finale almost destroys the film, but other small vignettes are terrific. **91m/C VHS, DVD, Wide.** James Woods, Michael J. Fox, Annabella Sciorra, Stephen Lang, Penny Marshall, L.L. Cool J., John Capodice, Christina Ricci, Karen (Lynn) Gorney, Luis Guzman; *D:* John Badham; *W:* Daniel Pyne, Lem Dobbs; *C:* Robert Primes; *M:* Arthur B. Rubinstein.

Hardball 🦴🦴 **2001 (PG-13)** Loosely based on Daniel Coyle's book "Hardball: A Season in the Projects," the plot plays like a watered down "Bad News Bears" with a dark edge. Conor O'Neill (Reeves) is a gambler who owes money all over Chicago. He asks broker pal Jimmy (McGlone) for financial help, but it comes at a cost. Jimmy has him take over a baseball team from the Cabrini-Green projects as part of his company's community outreach program. Conor and the foul-mouthed little tykes inevitably get off on the wrong foot, setting up the eventual "rag-tag bunch of misfits turn into champions" scenario. Grimmer overtones show up, however, with the realities of the projects and a tragedy that deeply affects Conor and the team. The kids' teacher Elizabeth (Lane) is the guiding influence/unfulfilled love interest. The kids, especially Griffith and Warren, steal pic from the grown-ups with their performances. **106m/C VHS, DVD, Wide.** *US* Keanu Reeves, Diane Lane, John Hawkes, Bryan C. Hearne, Julian Griffith, A. Delon Ellis Jr., DeWayne Warren, Michael Jordan, D.B. Sweeney, Mike McGlone, Graham Beckel, Mark Margolis; *D:* Brian Robbins; *W:* John Gatins; *C:* Tom Richmond; *M:* Mark Isham.

Hardbodies 🦴 **1984 (R)** Three middle-aged men hit the beaches of Southern California in search of luscious young girls. They find them. Mid-life crisis done stupidly. Followed by a sequel. **88m/C VHS.** Grant Cramer, Teal Roberts, Gary Wood, Michael Rapport, Sorrels Pickard, Roberta Collins, Cindy Silver, Courtney Gains, Kristi Somers, Crystal Shaw, Kathleen Kinmont, Joyce Jameson; *D:* Mark Griffiths; *W:* Eric Alter.

Hardbodies 2 WOOF! **1986 (R)** A sequel to the original comedy hit, dealing with film crew in Greece that is distracted by hordes of nude natives. Sophomoric humor dependent on nudity and profanity for laughs. **89m/C VHS.** Brad Zutaut, Brenda Bakke, Fabiana Udenio, James Karen; *D:* Mark Griffiths; *W:* Eric Alter; *M:* Eddie Arkin.

Hardcase and Fist 🦴🦴 **1989 (R)** A framed cop leaves prison with his mind on revenge. The godfather who used him is just his first target. **92m/C VHS, DVD, Wide.** Maureen Lavette, Ted Prior, Tony Zarindast, Christine Lunde, Carter Wong; *D:* Tony Zarindast; *W:* Tony Zarindast, Bud Fleischer; *C:* Robert Hayes; *M:* Matthew Tucciarone, Tom Tucciarone. **VIDEO**

Hardcore 🦴🦴½ *The Hardcore Life* **1979 (R)** A Midwestern businessman who is raising a strict Christian family learns of his daughter's disappearance while she is on a church trip. After hiring a streetwise investigator, he learns that his daughter has become an actress in pornographic films out in California. Strong performance by Scott and glimpse into the hardcore pornography industry prove to be convincing points of this film, though it exploits what it condemns. **106m/C VHS.** George C. Scott, Season Hubley, Peter Boyle, Dick Sargent; *D:* Paul Schrader; *W:* Paul Schrader; *C:* Michael Chapman; *M:* Jack Nitzsche.

The Harder They Come 🦴🦴½ **1972 (R)** A poor Jamaican youth becomes a success with a hit reggae record after he has turned to a life of crime out of desperation. Songs, which are blended nicely into the framework of the film, include "You Can Get It If You Really Want it" and "Sitting In Limbo." **93m/C VHS, DVD, Wide.** *JM* Jimmy Cliff, Janet Barkley, Carl Bradshaw, Bobby Charlton, Ras Daniel Hartman, Basil Keane, Winston Stona; *D:* Perry Henzell; *W:* Perry Henzell, Trevor D. Rhone; *C:* Peter Jessop, David McDonald; *M:* Desmond Dekker, Jimmy Cliff.

The Harder They Fall 🦴🦴🦴 **1956** A cold-eyed appraisal of the scum-infested boxing world. An unemployed reporter (Bogart in his last role) promotes a fighter for the syndicate, while doing an expose on the fight racket. Bogart became increasingly debilitated during filming and died soon afterward. Based on Budd Schulberg's novel. **109m/B VHS.** Humphrey Bogart, Rod Steiger, Jan Sterling, Mike Lane, Max Baer Sr., Albert "Poppy" Popwell; ***D:*** Mark Robson; ***W:*** Philip Yordan; ***C:*** Burnett Guffey.

Hardhat & Legs 🦴🦴 **1980** Comic complications arise when a New York construction worker falls in love with the woman who's teaching the modern sexuality course in which he's enrolled. **96m/C VHS.** Sharon Gless, Kevin Dobson, Raymond Serra, Elva Josephson, Bobby Short, Jacqueline Brookes, W.T. Martin; ***D:*** Lee Philips; ***W:*** Ruth Gordon; ***M:*** Brad Fiedel. **TV**

Hardly Working 🦴 **1981 (PG)** A circus clown finds it difficult to adjust to real life as he fumbles about from one job to another. Lewis's last attempt at resuscitating his directorial career. His fans will love it, but others need not bother. **90m/C VHS.** Jerry Lewis, Susan Oliver, Roger C. Carmel, Gary Lewis, Deanna Lund; ***D:*** Jerry Lewis; ***W:*** Jerry Lewis.

Hardware 🦴½ **1990 (R)** Rag-tag rip-off in which McDermott is a post-apocalyptic garbage picker who gives girlfriend Travis some robot remains he collected (ours is not to ask why), oblivious to the fact that the tidy android was a government-spawned population controller programmed to destroy warm bodies. Seems old habits die hard, and that spells danger, danger, Will Robinson. Much violence excised to avoid x-rating. **94m/C VHS.** Dylan McDermott, Stacy Travis, John Lynch, Iggy Pop; ***D:*** Richard Stanley; ***M:*** Simon Boswell.

Harem 🦴 **1985** A beautiful stockbroker gets kidnapped by a wealthy OPEC oil minister and becomes part of his harem. Kingsley stars as the lonely sheik who longs for the love of a modern woman. **107m/C VHS.** *FR* Ben Kingsley, Nastassia Kinski; ***D:*** Arthur Joffe.

Harem 🦴🦴 **1986** In the early 1900s, a dastardly Turkish sultan kidnaps an American beauty to add to his harem—mightily displeasing his jealous first wife. Lots of overwrought romance and drama until she is finally rescued. **200m/C VHS.** Omar Sharif, Nancy Travis, Ava Gardner, Julian Sands, Art Malik, Sarah Miles, Yaphet Kotto, Cherie Lunghi; ***D:*** Billy Hale. **TV**

Harlan County, U.S.A. **1976 (PG)** The emotions of 180 coal mining families are seen up close in this classic documentary about their struggle to win a United Mine Workers contract in Kentucky. Award-winning documentary. **103m/C VHS.** ***D:*** Barbara Kopple; ***C:*** Phil Parmet. Oscars '76: Feature Doc., Natl. Film Reg. '90.

Harlan County War 🦴🦴½ **2000** Ruby Kincaid (Hunter) is the wife of striking Kentucky coal miner Silas (Levine). After a court order severely restricts the union members' protests, Ruby leads the wives into action, even allowing her arrest to be used as propaganda by union rep Warren Jakopovich (Skarsgard) to her husband's dismay. Good lead performances, although the dramatic power of the story is subdued. Inspired by Barbara Kopple's 1976 documentary, "Harlan County, U.S.A." **104m/C VHS, DVD.** Holly Hunter, Stellan Skarsgard, Ted Levine, Wayne Robson; ***D:*** Tony Bill; ***W:*** Peter Silverman; ***C:*** Flavio Labiano; ***M:*** Van Dyke Parks. **CABLE**

Harlem Nights 🦴🦴 **1989 (R)** Two Harlem nightclub owners in the 1930s battle comically against efforts by the Mob and crooked cops to take over their territory. High-grossing, although somewhat disappointing effort from Murphy, who directed, wrote, produced, and starred in this film. **118m/C VHS, DVD, Wide.** Eddie Murphy, Richard Pryor, Redd Foxx, Danny Aiello, Jasmine Guy, Michael Lerner, Arsenio Hall, Della Reese, Eugene Glazer; ***D:*** Eddie Murphy; ***W:*** Eddie Murphy; ***C:*** Woody Omens; ***M:*** Herbie Hancock. Golden Raspberries '89: Worst Screenplay.

Harlem on the Prairie 🦴 *Bad Man of Harlem* **1938** This first-ever western with an all-black cast has Jeffries helping a young lady find hidden gold and foiling a villain. Even though the technical standards and acting are below par, this is worth watching for the singing and a comedy routine done by a well-known contemporary black team. ♫Harlem On The Prairie; Romance In The Rain. **54m/B VHS.** Herbert Jeffries, Mantan Moreland, F.E. (Flourney) Miller, Connie Harris, Maceo B. Sheffield, William Spencer Jr.; ***D:*** Sam Newfield.

Harlem Rides the Range 🦴½ **1939** Jeffries must outsmart villainous Brooks, who means to swindle a radium mine away from its rightful owner. Early oater of interest only because of its atypical all-black cast and crew. **58m/B VHS.** Herbert Jeffries, Lucius Brooks, Artie Young, F.E. (Flourney) Miller, Spencer Williams Jr., Clarence Brooks, Tom Southern, Wade Dumas, Leonard Christmas; ***D:*** Richard C. Kahn; ***W:*** F.E. (Flourney) Miller, Spencer Williams Jr.

Harley 🦴🦴 **1990 (PG)** Diamond is Harley, an L.A. thug-on-a-hog, who's on his way to an extended stay at one of the state's luxury institutions when he's sent to a Texas rehabilitation community. There, he bonds with an ex-biker, and may just find his way back down the straight and narrow. And the local longhorn rednecks applaud his efforts...not. **80m/C VHS.** Lou Diamond Phillips, Eli Cummins, DeWitt Jan, Valentine Kim; ***D:*** Fred Holmes; ***W:*** Frank Kuntz, Sandy Kuntz.

Harley Davidson and the Marlboro Man 🦴 **1991 (R)** An awful rehash of "Butch Cassidy and the Sundance Kid" with blatant vulgarity and pointless sci-fi touches. The title duo are near-future outlaws who rob a bank to save their favorite bar, then find they've stolen mob money. Some action, but it's mostly talk: lewd, meant-to-be-whimsical soul-probing chats between H.D. and M.M. that would bore even the biker crowd—and did. **98m/C VHS, DVD, Wide.** Kelly Hu, Mickey Rourke, Don Johnson, Chelsea Field, Tom Sizemore, Vanessa L(ynne) Williams, Robert Ginty, Daniel Baldwin; ***D:*** Simon Wincer; ***W:*** Don Michael Paul; ***C:*** David Eggby; ***M:*** Basil Poledouris.

Harlow 🦴🦴½ **1965** The more lavish of the two Harlow biographies made in 1965, both with the same title. A sensationalized "scandal sheet" version of Jean Harlow's rise to fame that bears little resemblance to the facts of her life. **125m/C VHS.** Carroll Baker, Martin Balsam, Red Buttons, Mike Connors, Angela Lansbury, Peter Lawford, Raf Vallone, Leslie Nielsen; ***D:*** Gordon Douglas; ***W:*** John Michael Hayes; ***C:*** Joseph Ruttenberg.

Harmon of Michigan 🦴🦴½ **1941** College football hero Harmon starred in this loosely adapted story of his life in and out of the pros and his career at Michigan. **65m/B VHS.** Tom Harmon, Anita Louise, Forest Evashevski, Oscar O'Shea, Warren Ashe, Stanley Crown, Ken Christy, Tim Ryan, Lloyd Bridges, William Hall, Chester Conklin, Larry Parks; ***D:*** Charles T. Barton; ***W:*** Howard J. Green.

The Harmonists 🦴🦴 **1999 (R)** Actor/singer Harry Frommermann (Noethen) is frustrated by his lack of success and decides to put together his own a cappella group—a musical sextet known as "The Comedian Harmonists," who find great success in Germany. Unfortunately, as the '20s give way to the '30s and the rise of Nazism, the group begins to run into trouble since three of its members are Jewish. Eventually, the political pressures force the group to disband and send its Jewish members into exile. German with subtitles. **114m/C VHS.** *GE* Ulrich Noethen, Ben Becker, Heino Ferch, Heinrich Schafmeister, Max Tidof, Kai Wiesinger, Meret Becker, Katja Riemann, Dana Vavrova; ***D:*** Joseph Vilsmaier; ***W:*** Klaus Richter; ***C:*** Joseph Vilsmaier; ***M:*** Harold Kloser.

Harmony Lane 🦴🦴 **1935** Highly romanticised rendition of the life of American composer, Stephen Collins Foster (1826-1864). Montgomery, as Foster, manages to lend a hint of credibility to the syrupy, melodramatic script. Very little attention is given to historical fact and almost every scene is orchestrated to showcase the composer's songs. The music steals the show. ♫Beautiful Dreamer; Old Folks at Home; Swanee River; Oh! Susanna; De Camptown Races. **84m/B VHS.** Douglass Montgomery, Evelyn Venable, Adrienne Ames, Joseph Cawthorn, William Frawley, Florence Roberts, Smiley Burnette, Hattie McDaniel; ***D:*** Joseph Santley.

Harnessing Peacocks 🦴🦴½ **1992** Hebe (Scott Thomas) has a one-night stand with a mystery man during carnival time in Venice, gets pregnant, and winds up living a very independent life with her son in a British seaside community. She supports herself as both a chef and as an expensive mistress, with a very select group of admirers, but always dreams of reuniting with her son's father. Based on the novel by Mary Wesley. **108m/C VHS.** *GB* Serena Scott Thomas, Peter Davison, Renee Asherson. **TV**

Harold and Maude 🦴🦴🦴🦴 **1971 (PG)** Cult classic pairs Cort as a deadpan disillusioned 20-year-old obsessed with suicide (his staged attempts are a highlight) and a loveable Gordon as a fun-loving 80-year-old eccentric. They meet at a funeral (a mutual hobby), and develop a taboo romantic relationship, in which they explore the tired theme of the meaning of life with a fresh perspective. The script was originally the 20-minute long graduate thesis of UCLA student Higgins, who showed it to his landlady, wife of film producer Lewis. Features music by the pre-Islamic Cat Stevens. **92m/C VHS, DVD, 8mm, Wide.** Ruth Gordon, Bud Cort, Cyril Cusack, Vivian Pickles, Charles Tyner, Ellen Geer, Eric Christmas, G(eorge) Wood, Gordon Devol; ***D:*** Hal Ashby; ***W:*** Colin Higgins; ***C:*** John A. Alonzo; ***M:*** Cat Stevens. Natl. Film Reg. '97.

Harold Robbins' Body Parts 🦴🦴 *Body Parts* **2001** An unsurprising formula revenge flick. Ty Kinnick (Grieco) is double-crossed by his best friend (Stewart) and wife (Massey) during a drug deal. Five years later, he's back and finds that the intrigues are still being played out. **?m/C DVD.** Richard Grieco, Will Foster Stewart, Athena Massey; ***D:*** Craig Corman; ***W:*** Craig Corman.

Harper 🦴🦴🦴 *The Moving Target* **1966** A tight, fast-moving genre piece about cynical LA private eye Lew Harper (Newman) who is hired by Mrs. Sampson (Bacall) to investigate the disappearance of her wealthy husband. Along the way he gets involved with an aging actress (Winter), a junkie singer (Harris), a religious nut (Martin), and a smuggling operation. From the Ross McDonald novel "The Moving Target." Later sequelled in "The Drowning Pool." **121m/C VHS, Wide.** Paul Newman, Shelley Winters, Lauren Bacall, Julie Harris, Robert Wagner, Janet Leigh, Arthur Hill, Pamela Tiffin; ***D:*** Jack Smight; ***W:*** William Goldman; ***C:*** Conrad L. Hall; ***M:*** Johnny Mandel.

Harper Valley P.T.A. 🦴🦴 **1978 (PG)** Eden raises hell in Harper Valley after the PTA questions her parental capabilities. Brain candy was adapted from a hit song; TV series followed. **93m/C VHS.** Barbara Eden, Nanette Fabray, Louis Nye, Pat Paulsen, Ronny Cox, Ron Masak, Audrey Christie, John Fiedler, Bob Hastings; ***D:*** Richard Bennett; ***W:*** Barry Schneider.

Harrad Experiment 🦴½ **1973 (R)** Adaptation of Robert Rimmer's love-power bestseller in which an experiment-minded college establishes a campus policy of sexual freedom. Famous for the Hedren/Johnson relationship, shortly before Johnson married Hedren's real-life daughter Melanie Griffith. Followed by "The Harrad Summer." **98m/C VHS, DVD.** James Whitmore, Tippi Hedren, Don Johnson, Bruno Kirby, Laurie Walters, Victoria Thompson, Elliot Street, Sharon Taggart, Robert Middleton, Billy (Billie) Sands, Melanie Griffith; ***D:*** Ted Post; ***W:*** Ted Cassedy, Michael Werner; ***C:*** Richard H. Kline; ***M:*** Artie Butler.

Harrad Summer 🦴🦴 **1974 (R)** Sequel to "The Harrad Experiment." College coeds take their sex-education to the bedroom where they can apply their knowledge by more intensive means. **103m/C VHS.** Richard Doran, Victoria Thompson, Laurie Walters, Robert Reiser, Bill Dana, Marty Allen; ***D:*** Steven Hilliard Stern.

Harriet Craig 🦴🦴🦴 **1950** Tailor-made Crawford role finds her as seemingly perfect wife Harriet Craig. In reality, she's a domineering shrew, who's also a bully and a clean freak. Harriet squelches husband Walter's (Corey) promotion because it means he'll be travelling abroad, ruins his relationship with best friend Billy (Joslyn), and manages to sabotage her young cousin Clare's (Stevens) romance before anybody stands up to her. Third film adaptation of George Kelly's 1925 play "Craig's Wife." **94m/B VHS.** Joan Crawford, Wendell Corey, Allyn Joslyn, William Bishop, K.T. Stevens, Lucile Watson, Raymond Greenleaf, Ellen Corby; ***D:*** Vincent Sherman; ***W:*** James Gunn; ***C:*** Joseph Walker; ***M:*** George Duning.

Harriet the Spy 🦴🦴½ **1996 (PG)** Sixth-grade, 11-year-old tomboy Harriet M. Welsch (Trachtenberg) spies on everyone around her and, encouraged by her nanny Ole Golly (O'Donnell), writes down everything going on in her secret notebook, because she's determined to become a great writer. Unfortunately, Harriet's imagination sometimes gets the best of her and when her notebook is found, her friends and family are not too happy about its contents. Based on the award-winning novel by Louise Fitzhugh. Lovers of the book may not be enthusiastic about some of the changes but generally it's enjoyable fare. **102m/C VHS.** Michelle Trachtenberg, Rosie O'Donnell, Vanessa Lee Chester, Gregory Edward Smith, Robert Joy, Eartha Kitt, J. Smith-Cameron; ***D:*** Bronwen Hughes; ***W:*** Douglas Petrie, Theresa Rebeck; ***C:*** Francis Kenny; ***M:*** Jamshield Sharifi.

Harrison's Flowers 🦴🦴 **2002 (R)** Sometimes goopy, sometimes harrowing story of a naive woman searching for her missing husband. Newsweek photojournalist Harrison Lloyd (Strathairn) promises wife Sarah (MacDowell) that his '91 assignment to Yugoslavia (at the beginning of the Balkan conflict) will be his last. Maybe in more ways than one, since he's reported missing, which Sarah doesn't believe. So she's takes off for Croatia and promptly gets a hard lesson in the confusion of war. Fellow correspondents Kyle (Brody), Stevenson (Gleeson), and Yeager (Koteas) agree to help Sarah even though they think she's nuts. Watch the guys, particularly Brody, since all MacDowell has to do is alternate between noble, frightened, and stubborn. **122m/C VHS, DVD.** *FR* Andie MacDowell, David Strathairn, Elias Koteas, Adrien Brody, Brendan Gleeson, Alun Armstrong, Caroline Goodall, Diane Baker, Gerard Butler, Marie Trintignant; ***D:*** Elie Chouraqui; ***W:*** Elie Chouraqui, Didier Le Pecheur, Isabel Ellsen; ***C:*** Nicola Pecorini; ***M:*** Cliff Eidelman.

Harry & Son 🦴🦴 **1984 (PG)** A widowed construction worker faces the problems of raising his son. Newman is miscast as the old man and we've all seen Benson play the young role too many times. **117m/C VHS.** Paul Newman, Robby Benson, Ellen Barkin, Wilford Brimley, Judith Ivey, Ossie Davis, Morgan Freeman, Joanne Woodward; ***D:*** Paul Newman; ***M:*** Henry Mancini.

Harry and the Hendersons 🦴🦴½ **1987 (PG)** Ordinary American family vacationing in the Northwest has a collision with Bigfoot. Thinking that the big guy is dead, they throw him on top of the car and head home. Lo and behold, he revives and starts wrecking the furniture and in the process, endears himself to the at-first frightened family. Nice little tale efficiently told, with Lithgow fine as the frustrated dad trying to hold his Bigfoot-invaded home together. Basis for the TV series. **111m/C VHS.** John Lithgow, Melinda Dillon, Don Ameche, David Suchet, Margaret Langrick, Joshua Rudoy, Kevin Peter Hall, Lainie Kazan, M. Emmet Walsh, John Bloom; ***D:*** William Dear; ***W:*** William Dear, William E. Martin, Ezra D. Rappaport; ***C:*** Allen Daviau; ***M:*** Bruce Broughton. Oscars '87: Makeup.

Harry and Tonto 🦴🦴🦴 **1974** A gentle comedy about an energetic septuagenarian who takes a cross-country trip with his cat, Tonto. Never in a hurry, still capable of feeling surprise and joy, he makes new friends and visits old lovers. Carney deserved his Oscar. Mazursky has seldom been better. **115m/C VHS.** Art Carney, Ellen Burstyn, Larry Hagman, Geraldine Fitzgerald, Chief Dan George, Arthur Hunnicutt, Josh Mostel; ***D:*** Paul Mazursky; ***W:*** Paul Mazursky; ***M:*** Bill Conti. Oscars '74: Actor (Carney); Golden Globes '75: Actor—Mus./Comedy (Carney).

Harry & Walter Go to New York **1976 (PG)** At the turn of the century, two vaudeville performers are hired by a crooked British entrepreneur for a wild crime scheme. The cast and crew try their hardest, but it's not enough to save this boring comedy. The vaudeville team of Caan and Gould perhaps served as a model for Beatty and Hoffman in "Ishtar." **111m/C VHS.** James Caan, Elliott Gould, Michael Caine, Diane Keaton, Burt Young, Jack Gilford, Charles Durning, Lesley Ann Warren, Carol Kane; ***D:*** Mark Rydell; ***W:*** John Byrum; ***M:*** David Shire.

Harry Black and the Tiger *Harry Black* **1958** Jungle adventure involving a one-legged hunter and a man-eating tiger. The hunter initally teams up with the old war buddy who cost him his leg. The motivation grows with each failure to catch the beast and to make matters worse, the friend's wife and son are lost somewhere in the perilous jungle. Filmed in India. **107m/C VHS.** *GB* Stewart Granger, Barbara Rush, Anthony Steel; ***D:*** Hugo Fregonese.

Harry Potter and the Sorcerer's Stone *Harry Potter and the Philosopher's Stone* **2001 (PG)** Much-anticipated screen adaptation of J.K. Rowling's first book about a Dickensian orphan who discovers his wizardly legacy, didn't disappoint its legions of built-in fans. Director Columbus remains painstakingly faithful to the book, although film plays, understandably, like a highlights version and sometimes lacks any personality of its own. This may have been intentional (directors Steven Spielberg and Terry Gilliam were perhaps passed over because their personal stamp would override the material), and it doesn't detract from the outstanding production and captivating storytelling. Stellar all-Brit cast is fun to watch, and the special effects are what you'd expect given a $125-million budget and use of no less than nine effects houses. Enen those not familiar with the book will enjoy the film's many charms. Good mix of entertainment for kids and adults, although a bit long for the very young. **152m/C VHS, DVD, Wide.** *US* Daniel Radcliffe, Rupert Grint, Emma Watson, Robbie Coltrane, Richard Harris, Maggie Smith, Zoe Wanamaker, Alan Rickman, Ian Hart, John Hurt, Tom Felton, Harry Melling, Richard Griffiths, Fiona Shaw, John Cleese, Warwick Davis, Julie Walters, Sean Biggerstaff, David Bradley, Matthew Lewis; ***D:*** Chris Columbus; ***W:*** Steven Kloves; ***C:*** John Seale; ***M:*** John Williams.

Harry Tracy ½ *Harry Tracy—Desperado* **1983 (PG)** Whimsical tale of the legendary outlaw whose escapades made him both a wanted criminal and an exalted folk hero. **111m/C VHS.** *CA* Bruce Dern, Gordon Lightfoot, Helen Shaver, Michael C. Gwynne; ***D:*** William A. Graham; ***C:*** Allen Daviau.

Harry's War **1984 (PG)** A middle-class, middle-aged American declares military war on the IRS in this overdone comedy. **98m/C VHS.** Edward Herrmann, Geraldine Page, Karen Grassle, David Ogden Stiers; ***D:*** Keith Merrill.

Hart's War ½ **2002 (R)** Willis is leathery Col. McNamara, ranking U.S. POW officer in a German stalag who clashes with newly imprisoned Lt. Thomas Hart (Farrell), Yale law student and son of a U.S. Senator. Hart is recruited to lead a court martial proceeding against African-American prisoner Scott (Howard), accused of killing racist fellow prisoner Bedford (Hauser). McNamara seems to have ulterior motives for this court martial, however, and seems to be undermining Hart at every turn. Howard shines as the accused who doesn't even begin to expect a fair trial, and lures is brilliant as the urbane, Yankee culture loving German Col. Visser, who also happens to be a Yale alum. Beautiful cinematography helps offset occasional heavy-handed direction and, at times, overwrought plot. **128m/C VHS, DVD.** *US* Bruce Willis, Colin Farrell, Terrence DaShon Howard, Cole Hauser, Marcel Iures, Linus Roache, Rory Cochrane, Michael Weston, Vicellous Reon Shannon, Scott Michael Campbell, Adrian Grenier, Jonathan Brandis, Joe Spano, Sam Worthington; ***D:*** Gregory Hoblit; ***W:*** Billy Ray, Terry George; ***C:*** Alar Kivilo; ***M:*** Rachel Portman.

Harum Scarum *Harem Holiday* **1965** Elvis tune-fest time! When a movie star (Presley) travels through the Middle East, he becomes involved in an attempted assassination of the king and falls in love with his daughter. He also sings at the drop of a veil: "Shake That Tambourine," "Harem Holiday," and seven others. **95m/C VHS.** Elvis Presley, Mary Ann Mobley, Fran Jeffries, Michael Ansara, Billy Barty, Theo Marcuse, Jay Novello; ***D:*** Gene Nelson.

Harvest *Regain* **1937** A classically Pagnolian rural pageant-of-life melodrama, wherein a pair of loners link up together in an abandoned French town and completely revitalize it and the land around it. From the novel by Jean Giono. In French with English subtitles. **128m/B VHS.** *FR* Fernandel, Gabriel Gabrio, Orane Demazis, Edouard Delmont, Henri Poupon; ***D:*** Marcel Pagnol; ***W:*** Marcel Pagnol; ***C:*** Willy; ***M:*** Arthur Honegger. N.Y. Film Critics '39: Foreign Film.

The Harvest ½ **1992 (R)** Sultry temptress Leilani sends Miguel's internal thermometer into convulsions with her preference for ice during lovemaking. However, their tryst turns sour (for him) when she takes Miguel to the beach where mystery thugs beat him unconscious and swipe his kidney. Bizarre story sure to ignite a small cult following. **97m/C VHS.** Miguel Ferrer, Leilani Sarelle Ferrer, Harvey Fierstein, Anthony John (Tony) Denison, Tim Thomerson, Matt Clark, Henry Silva; ***D:*** David Marconi; ***W:*** David Marconi; ***M:*** Dave Allen, Rick Boston.

Harvest **1999** Andy (Horneff) is shocked to discover that his seemingly straight-arrow parents (DeMunn and Emery) have held on to the family farm by growing and selling pot. And they're not the only ones, although the local sheriff (Slattery) has been neighborly looking the other way. But trouble arrives with a feisty DEA agent (McCormack). Not very memorable. **96m/C VHS.** Wil Horneff, Jeffrey DeMunn, John Slattery, Lisa Emery, Mary McCormack, James Van Der Beek, Evan Handler, Frederick Weller; ***D:*** Stuart Burkin; ***W:*** Stuart Burkin, James Biederman, David A. Korn; ***C:*** Oliver Bokelberg.

Harvest Melody **1943** Singing star Gilda Parker travels to farm country for a mere publicity stunt but decides to stay. Corny in more ways than one. ♫You Could Have Knocked Me Over With A Feather; Put It In Reverse; Let's Drive Out To The Drive-In; Tenderly. **70m/B VHS.** Rosemary Lane, Johnny Downs, Sheldon Leonard, Charlotte Wynters, Luis Alberni, Claire Rochelle, Syd Saylor; ***D:*** Sam Newfield.

Harvest of Fire ½ **1995 (PG)** A close-knit Amish farming community in Iowa has been the target of a series of barn burnings, which come under the investigation of FBI agent Sally Russell (Davidovich). But the community doesn't want an outsider around and Sally needs some help, which she finds with Amish widow Annie Beiler (Duke). And gradually the disparate duo find some common ground. A Hallmark Hall of Frame presentation. **90m/C VHS.** Patty Duke, Lolita (David) Davidovich, J.A. Preston, Jean (Louisa) Kelly, Tom Aldredge, James Read, Craig Wasson; ***D:*** Arthur Allan Seidelman; ***W:*** Richard Alfieri; ***C:*** Neil Roach; ***M:*** Lee Holdridge. **TV**

Harvey ½ **1950** Straightforward version of the Mary Chase play about a friendly drunk with an imaginary six-foot rabbit friend named Harvey, and a sister who tries to have him committed. A fondly remembered, charming comedy. Hull is a standout, well deserving her Oscar. **104m/B VHS, DVD.** James Stewart, Josephine Hull, Victoria Horne, Peggy Dow, Cecil Kellaway, Charles Drake, Jesse White, Wallace Ford, Nana Bryant; ***D:*** Henry Koster; ***W:*** Oscar Brodney; ***C:*** William H. Daniels; ***M:*** Frank Skinner. Oscars '50: Support. Actress (Hull); Golden Globes '51: Support. Actress (Hull).

The Harvey Girls **1946** Lightweight musical about a restaurant chain that sends its waitresses to work in the Old West. ♫In the Valley Where the Evening Sun Goes Down; Wait and See; On the Atchison, Topeka and Santa Fe; It's a Great Big World; The Wild Wild West. **102m/C VHS, DVD.** Judy Garland, Ray Bolger, John Hodiak, Preston Foster, Angela Lansbury, Virginia O'Brien, Marjorie Main, Chill Wills, Kenny L. Baker, Selena Royle, Cyd Charisse; ***D:*** George Sidney; ***C:*** George J. Folsey; ***M:*** Harry Warren, Johnny Mercer. Oscars '46: Song ("On the Atchison, Topeka and Santa Fe").

The Hasty Heart **1986** A rowdy, terminally ill Scotsman brings problems and friendships to a makeshift wartime hospital built in the jungles of Burma. Remake of 1949 flick with Richard Todd and Ronald Reagan in leading roles. **100m/C VHS.** Gregory Harrison, Cheryl Ladd, Perry King; ***D:*** Martin Speer.

Hat Box Mystery **1947** A detective's secretary is tricked into shooting a woman and private eye Neal is determined to save her from prison. Although not outstanding, it's worth seeing as perhaps the shortest detective film (a mere 44 min.) to ever make it as a feature. **44m/B VHS.** Tom Neal, Pamela Blake, Allen Jenkins; ***D:*** Lambert Hillyer.

Hatari! **1962** An adventure-loving team of professional big game hunters ventures to East Africa to round up animals for zoos around the world. Led by Wayne, they get into a couple of scuffs along the way, including one with lady photographer Martinelli who is doing a story on the expedition. Extraordinary footage of Africa and the animals brought to life by a fantastic musical score. **158m/C VHS, DVD, Wide.** John Wayne, Elsa Martinelli, Red Buttons, Hardy Kruger, Gerard Blain, Bruce Cabot; ***D:*** Howard Hawks; ***W:*** Leigh Brackett; ***C:*** Russell Harlan; ***M:*** Henry Mancini.

Hatchet for the Honeymoon *Blood Brides; Una Hacha para la Luna de Miel; Il Rosso Segmo della Follia; An Axe for the Honeymoon; The Red Sign of Madness* **1970** A rather disturbed young man goes around hacking young brides to death as he tries to find out who murdered his wife. Typical sick Bava horror flick; confusing plot, but strong on vivid imagery. **90m/C VHS, DVD, Wide.** *SP IT* Stephen Forsyth, Dagmar Lassander, Laura Betti, Gerard Tichy, Femi Benussi, Luciano Pigozzi, Jesus Puente; ***D:*** Mario Bava; ***W:*** Mario Bava, Santiago Moncada, Mario Musy; ***C:*** Mario Bava; ***M:*** Santa Maria Romitelli.

Hate *La Haine; Hatred* **1995** Twenty-hours in the lives of young, disenfranchised Said (Taghmaoui), Vinz (Cassel), and Hubert (Kounde), who are living in a housing project outside Paris. A riot breaks out, thanks to police brutality of an Arab resident, and Vinz finds a gun the cops lost. A Paris sojourn leads to a police interrogation of Hubert and Said, a fight with some skinheads, a return to their home turf, and an unexpected conclusion. Intelligent look at the idiocy engendered by societal oppression and a buildup of hatred. French with subtitles. **95m/B VHS.** *FR* Vincent Cassel, Hubert Kounde, Said Taghmaoui, Francois Levantal; ***D:*** Mathieu Kassovitz; ***W:*** Mathieu Kassovitz; ***C:*** Pierre Aim, Georges Diane. Cannes '95: Director (Kassovitz); Cesar '96: Film, Film Editing.

The Hatfields & the McCoys **1975** A re-telling of the most famous feud in American history—the legendary mountain war between the Hatfields and the McCoys. **90m/C VHS.** Jack Palance, Steve Forrest, Richard Hatch, Karen Lamm; ***D:*** Clyde Ware. **TV**

Hats Off **1937** Clarke and Payne star as opposing press agents in this tedious musical. The only bright spot is the finale, which features white-robed girls on a cloud-covered carousel. ♫Where Have You Been All My Life?; Little Old Rhythm; Twinkle, Twinkle, Little Star; Let's Have Another; Zilch's Hats; Hats Off. **65m/B VHS.** Mae Clarke, John Payne, Helen Lynd, Luis Alberni, Richard "Skeets" Gallagher, Franklin Pangbom; ***D:*** Boris L. Petroff.

The Haunted **1979** The ancient curse of an Indian woman haunts a present day family by possessing the body of a beautiful girl. Through the girl, a horrible vengeance is carried out. **81m/C VHS.** Aldo Ray, Virginia Mayo, Anne Michelle, Jim Negele; ***D:*** Michael de Gaetano.

Haunted ½ **1995 (R)** At their Sussex home, David Ash watches helplessly as his younger sister Juliet drowns. Flashforward to 1925 and the grownup David (Quinn) returns to teach a university course debunking the supernatural. Still, he's drawn to a supposedly haunted mansion, inhabited by artist Robert Mariell (Andrews), his sister Christina (Beckinsale), brother Simon (Lowe), and their elderly nanny (Massey). David starts experiencing visions of his dead sister, while mysterious fires and other unexplained manifestations occur—all of which seem tied to the unholy Mariell trio. Based on a novel by James Herbert. **108m/C VHS, DVD.** *GB* Aidan Quinn, Kate Beckinsale, Anthony Andrews, Alex Lowe, Anna Massey, Geraldine Somerville, Victoria Shalet; ***Cameos:*** John Gielgud; ***D:*** Lewis Gilbert; ***W:*** Lewis Gilbert, Bob Kellett, Tim Prager; ***C:*** Tony Pierce-Roberts; ***M:*** Debbie Wiseman.

Haunted ½ **1998** The first production of the play "Turpitude" resulted in a number of mysterious accidents and the opening night death of the star, Kay Taggert. Fifteen years later, producer Sol Brosky wants to take another shot mounting a new production at the original theater. Problems arise almost immediately and people claim the ghost of Kay Taggart is haunting the play. Parapsychologist Charles Mooreland is called in to discover whether it's a spirit or a corporeal form wreaking havoc. **91m/C VHS.** Peter Tomarken, Suzan Spann, Yvette McClendon; ***D:*** Dennis Devine; ***W:*** Steve Jarvis.

The Haunted Castle *Schloss Vogelod* **1921** One of Murnau's first films, and a vintage, if crusty, example of German expressionism. A nobleman entertains guests at his country mansion when strange things start to occur. Silent, with English titles. **56m/B VHS.** Arnold Korff, Lulu Keyser-Korff; ***D:*** F.W. Murnau.

Haunted Gold **1932** A young Wayne, in his first Western for Warners, battles gold-hungry desperadoes and a mysterious cloaked phantom. Remake of "The Phantom City." **57m/B VHS.** John Wayne, Sheila Terry, Harry Woods; ***D:*** Mack V. Wright; ***W:*** Adele Buffington.

Haunted Harbor ½ *Pirate's Harbor* **1944** A high-seas financier has been murdered by a crooked crony and Captain Jim Marsden's alibi is all wet. He's got to find the gold, the girl, and avoid the goons. Part of "The Cliffhanger Serials" series. **243m/B VHS.** Kane Richmond, Kay Aldridge, Roy Barcroft.

Haunted Honeymoon **1986 (PG)** Arthritic comedy about a haunted house and a couple trapped there. Sad times for the Mel Brooks alumni participating in this lame horror spoof. **82m/C VHS, DVD, Wide.** Gene Wilder, Gilda Radner, Dom DeLuise, Jonathan Pryce, Paul Smith, Peter Vaughan, Bryan Pringle, Roger Ashton-Griffiths, Jim Carter, Eve Ferret; ***D:*** Gene Wilder; ***W:*** Terence Marsh, Gene Wilder; ***C:*** Fred Schuler.

The Haunted Palace ½ **1963** Price plays both a 17th-century warlock burned at the stake and a descendant who returns to the family dungeon and gets possessed by the mutant-breeding forebearer. The movie has its own identity crisis, with title and ambience from Poe but story from H.P. Lovecraft's "The Case of Charles Dexter Ward." Respectable but rootless chills. **87m/C VHS.** Vincent Price, Debra Paget, Lon Chaney Jr., Frank Maxwell, Leo Gordon, Elisha Cook Jr., John Dierkes, Barboura Morris, Bruno VeSota; ***D:*** Roger Corman; ***W:*** Charles Beaumont, Floyd Crosby; ***M:*** Ronald Stein.

Haunted Ranch ½ **1943** Reno Red has been murdered and a shipment of gold bullion is missing. A gang on the lookout for the gold tries to convince people that Red's ranch is haunted by his ghost. **56m/B VHS.** John "Dusty" King, David

Sharpe, Max Terhune, Rex Lease, Julie Duncan; ***D:*** Robert Emmett Tansey.

The Haunted Sea 🦴🦴 **1997 (R)** The crew of the Patna discovered an abandoned ship that's filled with Aztec treasure. But when the Patna's crew members begin disappearing, those remaining must discover what's guarding the treasure. **74m/C VHS.** James Brolin, Joanna Pacula, Krista Allen, Don Stroud; ***D:*** Dan Golden; ***C:*** John Aronson; ***M:*** David Wurst, Eric Wurst.

The Haunted Strangler 🦴🦴½ *The Grip of the Strangler* **1958** Boris Karloff is a writer investigating a 20-year-old murder who begins copying some of the killer's acts. **78m/B VHS, DVD.** *GB* Boris Karloff, Anthony Dawson, Elizabeth Allan, Timothy Turner, Diane Aubrey, Dorothy Gordon, Jean Kent, Vera Day; ***D:*** Robert Day; ***W:*** John C. Cooper, Jan Read; ***C:*** Lionel Banes; ***M:*** Buxton Orr.

Haunted Summer 🦴🦴 **1988 (R)** Soft-focus, sex-and-drugs period piece of the bacchanalian summer of 1816 spent by free spirits Lord Byron, Percy Shelley, Mary Shelley, and John Polidori and others that led Mary Shelley to write "Frankenstein." Based on the novel of the same name by Anne Edwards. **106m/C VHS.** Alice Krige, Eric Stoltz, Philip Anglim, Laura Dern, Alex Winter; ***D:*** Ivan Passer; ***W:*** Lewis John Carlino.

Haunted Symphony 🦴🦴 *Blood Song; Last Resurrection; Hellfire* **1994 (R)** In the 18th century, a deranged composer (Wert) is discovered creating a symphony for the devil and killed by a mob. Years later, his niece Gabrielle (Burns) discovers the unfinished symphony hidden in an old piano and hires choir master Marius (Cross) to complete the score. But when he tries, demonic things begin to occur. **85m/C VHS.** Jennifer Burns, Ben Cross, Doug Wert, Beverly Garland; ***D:*** David Tausik; ***W:*** Beverly Gray, David Hartwell.

Haunted: The Ferryman 🦴🦴 **1974** Adapted by Julian Bond from a Kingsley Amis story, the film deals with a novelist who is mysteriously confronted with various events and macabre set-pieces from his own novel, including a dead ferryman rising from the grave. **50m/C VHS.** *GB* Jeremy Brett, Nastasha Parry, Lesley Dunlop; ***D:*** John Irvin.

HauntedWeen 🦴½ **1991** All trick, no treat, as a guy nailed by a frat house prank 20 years ago comes-back-for-revenge. **?m/C VHS.** Brien Blakely, Blake Pickett, Brad Hanks, Bart White, Leslee Lacey, Ethan Adler; ***D:*** Doug Robertson.

The Haunting 🦴🦴🦴½ **1963** A subtle, bloodless horror film about a weekend spent in a monstrously haunted mansion by a parapsychologist (Johnson), the mansion's skeptic heir (Tamblyn), and two mediums (Harris and Bloom). A chilling adaptation of Shirley Jackson's "The Haunting of Hill House," in which the psychology of the heroine is forever in question. There's a silly 1999 remake that's all special effects and no scares. **113m/B VHS.** *GB* Julie Harris, Claire Bloom, Russ Tamblyn, Richard Johnson, Fay Compton, Rosalie Crutchley, Lois Maxwell, Valentine Dyall, Diane Clare; ***D:*** Robert Wise; ***W:*** Nelson Gidding; ***C:*** David Boulton; ***M:*** Humphrey Searle.

The Haunting 🦴½ *The Haunting of Hill House* **1999 (PG-13)** Tiny Lili Taylor gets to play avenging angel with an assortment of ghosties and ghoulies in this silly would-be frightener based on the novel by Shirley Jackson and originally filmed in 1963. Dr. Marrow (Neeson) enlists three subjects to stay at Hill House for a study in insomnia that's (unknown to them) actually a study in fear response. There's brash Theo (Zeta-Jones), dopey Luke (Wilson), and fragile Nell (Taylor), who turns out to have unexpected ties to the haunted mansion. Big-budget doesn't make for big frights, just big, mocking laughter from the audience—certainly not what director De Bont must have intended. Dern appears briefly as the scruffy caretaker, with Seldes his Mrs. Danvers-like wife. **114m/C VHS, DVD.** Lili Taylor, Liam Neeson, Catherine Zeta-Jones, Owen C. Wilson, Bruce Dern, Marian Seldes, Virginia Madsen, Todd Field, Alix Koromzay; ***D:*** Jan De Bont; ***W:*** David Self; ***C:*** Caleb Deschanel; ***M:*** Jerry Goldsmith.

Haunting Fear 🦴 **1991** Poe's "The Premature Burial" inspired this pale cheapie about a wife with a fear of early interment. After lengthy nightmares and graphic sex, her greedy husband uses her phobia in a murder plot. **88m/C VHS.** Jan-Michael Vincent, Karen Black, Brinke Stevens, Michael Berryman; ***D:*** Fred Olen Ray; ***W:*** Sherman Scott.

Haunting of Harrington House 🦴 **1982** Tame teenage haunted house film. **50m/C VHS.** Dominique Dunne, Roscoe Lee Browne, Edie Adams, Phil Leeds; ***D:*** Murray Golden. **TV**

The Haunting of Hell House 🦴 *Henry James' The Ghostly Rental; The Ghostly Rental* **1999 (R)** Remember when Hammer Studios made all those horror movies based on Edgar Allan Poe stories and they were a lot of campy fun (if not truly creepy)? Well, that's what this Victorian Gothic wants to (or should) be and isn't. Tormented James (Bowen) took his girlfriend to an abortionist and she died. James seeks advice from the mysterious Professor Ambrose (York), whose family past is also filled with tragedy. **90m/C VHS.** Andrew Bowen, Michael York, Claudia Christian, Aideen O'Donnell; ***D:*** Mitch Marcus; ***W:*** Mitch Marcus, L.L. Shapira; ***C:*** Russ Brandt; ***M:*** Ivan Koutikov.

The Haunting of Morella 🦴 **1991 (R)** Poe-inspired cheapjack exploitation about a an executed witch living again in the nubile body of her teen daughter. Ritual murders result, in between lesbian baths and nude swims. Producer Roger Corman did the same story with more class and less skin in his earlier anthology "Tales of Terror." **82m/C VHS.** David McCallum, Nicole Eggert, Maria Ford, Lana Clarkson; ***D:*** Jim Wynorski; ***W:*** Jim Wynorski, R.J. Robertson.

Haunting of Sarah Hardy 🦴🦴 **1989** Ward, as a recently wed heiress, returns to the scene of her unhappy childhood home. In a standard plot, Ward is torn between an apparent haunting and the question of her own sanity. TV film is redeemed by the creditable acting. **92m/C VHS.** Sela Ward, Michael Woods, Roscoe Born, Polly Bergen, Morgan Fairchild; ***D:*** Jerry London; ***C:*** Bojan Bazelli. **TV**

The Haunting of Seacliff Inn 🦴🦴½ **1994 (PG-13)** Susan and Mark Enright struggle to start a bed-and-breakfast in their newly acquired Mendocino Victorian manse. But psychic Susie senses something—seems the former owner died violently, and, a hundred years ago, an owner was accused of murdering his wife in the house. Not-too-frightening ghost story but good cast work. **94m/C VHS.** Ally Sheedy, William R. Moses, Louise Fletcher, Lucinda Weist, Maxine Stuart, Tom McCleister, James Horan; ***D:*** Walter Klenhard; ***W:*** Walter Klenhard, Tom Walla. **CABLE**

The Haunting Passion 🦴🦴½ **1983** Newlywed Seymour moves into a haunted house only to be seduced by the ghost of the former occupant's dead lover. Effective and erotic presentation. **100m/C VHS.** Jane Seymour, Gerald McRaney, Millie Perkins, Ruth Nelson, Paul Rossilli, Ivan Bonar; ***D:*** John Korty. **TV**

Haunts 🦴½ *The Veil* **1977 (PG)** Tormented woman has difficulty distinguishing between fantasy and reality after a series of brutal slayings lead police to the stunning conclusion that dead people have been committing the crimes. **97m/C VHS.** Cameron Mitchell, Aldo Ray, May Britt, William Gray Espy, Susan Nohr; ***D:*** Herb Freed; ***M:*** Pino Donaggio.

Haunts of the Very Rich 🦴🦴½ **1972** A loose remake of "Outward Bound" in which a group of spoiled people on a vacation find themselves spiritually dead. Made for TV. **72m/C VHS.** Lloyd Bridges, Anne Francis, Donna Mills, Tony Bill, Robert Reed, Moses Gunn, Cloris Leachman, Ed Asner; ***D:*** Paul Wendkos. **TV**

Hav Plenty 🦴🦴🦴 **1997 (R)** Moving in the circles of young black professionals, Lee Plenty (Cherot) is an unemployed would-be writer who doesn't seem to care too much about getting a job. The materialistic and ambitious Havilland (Maxwell),a friend of his from college, invites him to a New Year's Eve party when she finds that her fiance Michael (Harper) is playing around on her. The sedate holiday weekend turns into a frenzy of surprises, as Lee is chased by Hav's hairdo-happy friend Caroline (Jones) and newlywed sister Leigh (Lee). Screwball romantic comedy comes off as a hybrid of Spike Lee and Woody Allen, with writer/director/editor Cherot's own personal touches thrown in. Performances are excellent, especially Cherot himself, who only starred when the actor hired to play his part bowed out as filming started. **87m/C VHS, DVD, Wide.** Christopher Scott Cherot, Chenoa Maxwell, Hill Harper, Tammi Katherine Jones, Robbine Lee, Betty Vaughn, Reginald James, Kenneth "Babyface" Edmonds; ***D:*** Christopher Scott Cherot; ***W:*** Christopher Scott Cherot; ***C:*** Kerwin Devonish; ***M:*** Wendy Melvoin, Lisa Coleman.

Havana 🦴🦴½ **1990 (R)** During the waning days of the Batista regime, a gambler travels to Havana in search of big winnings. Instead, he meets the beautiful wife of a communist revolutionary. Unable to resist their mutual physical attraction, the lovers become drawn into a destiny which is far greater than themselves. Reminiscent of "Casablanca." **145m/C VHS, DVD.** Robert Redford, Lena Olin, Alan Arkin, Raul Julia, Tomas Milian, Tony Plana, Betsy Brantley, Lise Cutter, Richard Farnsworth, Mark Rydell, Daniel Davis; ***D:*** Sydney Pollack; ***W:*** Judith Rascoe, David Rayfiel; ***C:*** Owen Roizman; ***M:*** Dave Grusin.

Have Rocket Will Travel 🦴🦴½ **1959** Three janitors (guess who) help a scientist who is about to lose her job if she can't send a rocket to Venus. They accidently initiate the launch while still on board and introduce their brand of slapstick to a whole new planet. First of the late '50s-early '60s feature films to capitalize on the renewed popularity of the Three Stooges. **76m/B VHS.** Moe Howard, Larry Fine, Joe DeRita, Anna-Lisa, Jerome Cowan, Bob Colbert; ***D:*** David Lowell Rich; ***W:*** Raphael Hayes.

Having It All 🦴🦴 **1982** A wry comedy about a love triangle. Dyan Cannon stars as a successful business woman with a husband on each coast, who finds dividing her time is more than she bargained for. **100m/C VHS.** Dyan Cannon, Barry Newman, Hart Bochner, Melanie Chartoff, Sylvia Sidney; ***D:*** Edward Zwick; ***M:*** Miles Goodman. **TV**

Having Our Say: The Delany Sisters' First 100 Years 🦴🦴½ **1999** Based on the book and the Broadway play that looks at life through the aging eyes of the black Delany sisters: 103-year-old Sadie (Carroll) and 101-year-old Bessie (Dee). They share their experiences with New York Times reporter Amy Hill Hearth (Madigan), who has come to interview them in 1991. Their father was born a slave but all 12 of the Delany children graduated from college, with Bessie becoming a teacher and Sadie a dentist in Harlem. (The real Bessie died in 1995 and Sadie in 1999.) **90m/C VHS.** Diahann Carroll, Ruby Dee, Mykelti Williamson, Lonette McKee, Lisa Anderson, Audra McDonald, Richard Roundtree, Della Reese; ***D:*** Lynne Littman; ***W:*** Emily Mann; ***C:*** Frank Byers. **TV**

Having Wonderful Crime 🦴🦴½ **1945** Madcap comedy-thriller about a newly married couple who combine sleuthing with a honeymoon. With their criminal lawyer friend along, the trio winds up searching for a magician who has vanished. Fast-paced action and quick dialogue. **70m/B VHS.** Pat O'Brien, George Murphy, Carole Landis, Lenore Aubert, George Zucco; ***D:*** Edward Sutherland.

Having Wonderful Time 🦴½ **1938** A young girl tries to find culture and romance on her summer vacation at a resort in the Catskills. Film debut of comic Red Skelton, who wasn't always as old as the hills. Based on a Broadway hit by Arthur Kober. **71m/B VHS.** Ginger Rogers, Lucille Ball, Eve Arden, Red Skelton, Douglas Fairbanks Jr.; ***D:*** Alfred Santell.

Hawaii 🦴🦴🦴 **1966** James Michener's novel about a New England farm boy who decides in 1820 that the Lord has commanded him to the island of Hawaii for the purpose of "Christianizing" the natives. Filmed on location. Also available in a 181 minute version with restored footage. Available in director's cut version with an additional 20 minutes. **161m/C VHS, Wide.** Max von Sydow, Julie Andrews, Richard Harris, Carroll O'Connor, Bette Midler, Gene Hackman, Jocelyn Lagarde; ***D:*** George Roy Hill; ***W:*** Daniel Taradash, Dalton Trumbo; ***M:*** Elmer Bernstein. Golden Globes '67: Support. Actress (Lagarde), Score.

Hawaii Calls 🦴🦴 **1938** Two young stowaways on a cruise ship are allowed to stay on after one of them (Breen) struts his stuff as a singer. The two then turn sleuth to catch a gang of spies. More ham than a can of Spam, but still enjoyable. ♫That's The Hawaiian In Me; Hawaii Calls; Down Where The Trade Winds Blow; Macushia; Aloha Oe. **72m/B VHS.** Bobby Breen, Ned Sparks, Irvin S. Cobb, Warren Hull, Gloria Holden, Pua Lani, Raymond Paige, Philip Ahn, Ward Bond; ***D:*** Edward F. (Eddie) Cline.

Hawaiian Buckaroo 🦴 **1938** A couple of cowboys fight to save their pineapple plantation from a sneaky foreman. **62m/B VHS.** Smith Ballew, Evalyn Knapp, Benny Burt, Harry Woods, Pat O'Brien; ***D:*** Ray Taylor.

The Hawk 🦴🦴½ **1993 (R)** Okay thriller about suburban housewife Annie (Mirren) who suspects that her husband Stephen (Costigan) is a serial killer known as the Hawk. Since Annie has a history of depression and her husband is a known louse, her suspicions are dismissed as delusional. Some surprise twists help the weak story along. Contains some graphic views of corpses. Based on the novel by Ransley. **84m/C VHS.** *GB* Helen Mirren, George Costigan, Owen Teale, Rosemary Leach; ***D:*** David Hayman; ***W:*** Peter Ransley; ***M:*** Nick Bicat.

Hawk and Castile **19??** Bandits murder, pillage, and terrorize the nobility in Medieval Europe until the Hawk comes onto the scene. **95m/C VHS.** Tom Griffith, Jerry Cobb, Nuria Forway, Mari Real.

The Hawk of Powder River 🦴 **1948** Cheapie western has Dean getting involved with a beautiful outlaw gang leader with a murderous streak. A large part of this film was lifted from earlier Dean oaters, as are all the tunes. **54m/B VHS.** Eddie Dean, Roscoe Ates, Jennifer Holt, June Carlson, Terry Frost, Lane Bradford; ***D:*** Ray Taylor.

Hawk of the Wilderness *Lost Island of Kioga* **1938** A man, shipwrecked as an infant and reared on a remote island by native Indians, battles modern day pirates after an explorer finds a cache of treasure. Serial in 12 episodes. **213m/B VHS.** Bruce (Herman Brix) Bennett, Mala, William Boyle; ***D:*** William Witney.

Hawk the Slayer 🦴½ **1981** A comic book fantasy. A good warrior struggles against his villainous brother to possess a magical sword that bestows upon its holder great powers of destruction. Violent battle scenes; Palance makes a great villain. **93m/C VHS.** Jack Palance, John Terry, Harry Andrews, Roy Kinnear, Ferdinand "Ferdy" Mayne; ***D:*** Terry Marcel.

Hawken's Breed 🦴🦴 **1987 (R)** Drifter meets American Indian beauty and hears her tale of woe; the two fall for each other and set out together to avenge the murder of the woman's husband and son. Nothing much to crow about. **93m/C VHS.** Peter Fonda, Serene Hedin, Jack Elam; ***D:*** Charles B. Pierce.

Hawkeye 🦴½ **1988** After his best friend is murdered by gangsters in a seedy drug deal, Hawkeye, a rough and tumble Texas cop, and his slick new partner hit the streets of Las Vegas with a vengeance. **90m/C VHS.** Troy Donahue, Chuck Jeffreys, George Chung, Stan Wertlieb; ***D:*** Leo Fong.

Hawks 🦴½ **1989 (R)** Somewhere on the road to black-comedy this film gets waylaid by triviality. Two terminally ill men break out of the hospital, determined to make their way to Amsterdam for some last-minute fun. Mediocre at best. **105m/C VHS, 8mm.** *GB* Anthony Edwards, Timothy Dalton, Janet McTeer, Jill Bennett, Sheila Hancock, Connie Booth, Camille Coduri; ***D:*** Robert Ellis Miller; ***W:*** Roy Clarke; ***C:*** Doug Milsome.

The Hawks & the Sparrows 🦴🦴 *Uccellacci e Uccellini* **1967** Shortly after "Mr. Ed" came Pasolini's garrulous crow, which follows a father and son's travels through Italy spouting pithy bits of politics. A comic Pasolinian allegory-fest full of then-topical political allusions, the story comes off a bit wooden. Worth watching to see Toto, the Italian comic, in his element. **91m/B VHS, Wide.** *IT* Toto, Ninetto Davoli, Femi Benussi; ***D:*** Pier Paolo Pasolini; ***W:*** Pier Paolo Pasolini; ***M:*** Ennio Morricone.

Hawk's Vengeance 🦴🦴 **1996 (R)** While investigating his police detective stepbrother's murder British Royal Marine Lt. Eric "Hawk" Kelly (Daniels) discovers a bizarre connection between a skinhead gang called the Death Skulls, a martial arts master crime boss (Magda), and the black market organ trade. **96m/C VHS.** Gary Daniels, Cass Magda.

Hawmps! woof! **1976 (G)** Idiotic comedy about a Civil War lieutenant who trains his men to use camels. When the soldiers and animals begin to grow fond of each other, Congress orders the camels to be set free. Hard to believe this was based on a real life incident. **98m/C VHS.** James Hampton, Christopher Connelly, Slim Pickens, Denver Pyle; ***D:*** Joe Camp; ***W:*** William Bickley; ***M:*** Euel Box.

Hawthorne of the USA 🦴🦴½ **1919** Reid stars as Anthony Hamilton Hawthorne, American extraordinaire. After gambling a fortune away in Monte Carlo, Hawthorne heads to mainland Europe for rest and revelry. Instead, he finds the love of a princess and a Communist coup in the making. Silent with orchestral score. **55m/B VHS.** Wallace Reid, Harrison Ford, Lila Lee, Tully Marshall; ***D:*** James Cruze.

Haxan: Witchcraft through the Ages 🦴🦴🦴 *Haxan; Witchcraft through the Ages* **1922** The demonic Swedish masterpiece in which witches and victims suffer against various historical backgrounds. Nightmarish and profane, especially the appearance of the Devil as played under much make-up by Christiansen himself. Silent. **74m/B VHS, DVD.** *SW* Maren Pedersen, Clara Pontoppidan, Oscar Stribolt, Benjamin Christiansen, Tora Teje, Elith Pio, Karen Winther, Emmy Schonfeld, John Andersen, Astrid Holm, Gerda Madsen; ***D:*** Benjamin Christiansen; ***W:*** Benjamin Christiansen; ***C:*** Johan Ankerstjerne; ***Nar:*** William S. Burroughs.

Hazel's People 🦴½ **1975 (G)** Bitter and hostile college student attends his friend's funeral in Mennonite country. He discovers not only a way of life he never knew existed, but a personal faith in a living Christ. From the Merle Good novel, "Happy as the Grass Was Green." **105m/C VHS.** Geraldine Page, Pat Hingle, Graham Beckel, Charles Davis.

He Got Game 🦴🦴½ **1998 (R)** Lee hops all over the place with this basketball drama that reveals more of his love for the game than cohesive filmmaking. Actually two movies in one: High school basketball great Jesus Shuttlesworth (newcomer and Milwaukee Bucks player Allen) must decide between college or a lucrative NBA contract. Then up pops his incarcerated pops, Jake, (a haggard Washington) to pressure him to chose his warden's alma mater, which turns the film into a shallow look at a strained father-son relationship. Washington is dynamic as the embittered father and Allen is evenly effective. Yet, the reunion is never fully developed and sometimes abandoned, while Lee scores visually by beautifully photographing the glorious hoop moves. Extraneous, stereotypical characters and rauchy sex sequences drag the film further from its dramatic resonance. **134m/C VHS, DVD, Wide.** Denzel Washington, Ray Allen, Milla Jovovich, Rosario Dawson, Hill Harper, Zelda Harris, Jim Brown, Ned Beatty, Lonette McKee, John Turturro, Michele Shay, Bill Nunn, Thomas Jefferson Byrd; ***D:*** Spike Lee; ***W:*** Spike Lee; ***C:*** Malik Hassan Sayeed.

He Is My Brother 🦴½ **1975 (G)** Two boys survive a shipwreck, landing on an island that houses a leper colony. **90m/C VHS.** Keenan Wynn, Bobby Sherman, Robbie (Reist) Rist; ***D:*** Edward Dmytryk.

He Kills Night After Night After Night 🦴½ **1970** British police are baffled as they seek the man who has been killing women in the style of Jack the Ripper. And he keeps doing it. **88m/C VHS.** Jack May, Linda Marlowe, Justine Lord.

He Knows You're Alone 🦴 **1980 (R)** Lame horror flick that focuses on a psychotic killer terrorizing a bride-to-be and her bridal party in his search for a suitable bride of his own. **94m/C VHS.** Don Scardino, Caitlin (Kathleen Heaney) O'Heaney, Tom Rolfing, Paul Gleason, Elizabeth Kemp, Tom Hanks, Patsy Pease, Lewis Arlt, James Rebhorn, Joseph Leon, James Carroll; ***D:*** Armand Mastroianni; ***W:*** Scott Parker; ***C:*** Gerald Feil; ***M:*** Alexander Peskanov, Mark Peskanov.

He Lives: The Search for the Evil One 🦴 **1988** A man who was imprisoned by Nazis as a child attempts to keep Hitler, now living in Buenos Aires, from starting a 4th Reich. **90m/C VHS.** Lee Patterson.

He Said, She Said 🦴🦴½ **1991 (R)** Romance is the topic, but this isn't a typical dating film, instead a couple's relationship unfolds from differing points of view: first, the guy's (by Kwapis) and then the girl's (by Silver). Bacon and Perkins, Baltimore journalists and professional rivals, tell how their romance wound up on the rocks, and why (or so they say). The end result is overlong and lacks the zing of other war between the sexes movies, but real-life couple Silver and Kwapis do humorously highlight the fact that men and women often view the same incidents very differently. Bacon overacts, Perkins overreacts, and Stone shines as Bacon's ex-girl. **115m/C VHS, DVD, Wide.** Elizabeth Perkins, Kevin Bacon, Sharon Stone, Nathan Lane, Anthony LaPaglia, Stanley Anderson, Charlaine Woodard, Danton Stone, Phil Leeds, Rita Karin; ***D:*** Marisa Silver, Ken Kwapis; ***W:*** Brian Hohlfield; ***C:*** Stephen Burum; ***M:*** Miles Goodman.

He Walked by Night 🦴🦴🦴½ **1948** Los Angeles homicide investigators track down cop killer Ray Morgan (Basehart) in this excellent drama. The final confrontation takes place in the L.A. County Flood Control System, consisting of some 700 miles of underground tunnels. Based on a true story from the files of the Los Angeles police, this first rate production reportedly inspired Webb to create "Dragnet." **80m/B VHS, DVD.** Richard Basehart, Scott Brady, Roy Roberts, Jack Webb, Whit Bissell; ***D:*** Alfred Werker, Anthony Mann; ***W:*** John C. Higgins; ***C:*** John Alton; ***M:*** Leonid Raab.

He Who Gets Slapped 🦴🦴🦴 **1924** Chaney portrays a brilliant scientist whose personal and professional humiliations cause him to join a travelling French circus as a masochistic clown (hence the title). There he falls in love with a beautiful circus performer and plans a spectacular revenge. Brilliant use of lighting and Expressionist devices by director Sjostrom (who used the Americanized version of his name-Seastrom-in the credits). Adapted from the Russian play "He, The One Who Gets Slapped" by Leonid Andreyev. **85m/B VHS.** Lon Chaney Sr., Norma Shearer, John Gilbert, Tully Marshall, Ford Sterling, Marc McDermott; ***D:*** Victor Sjostrom; ***W:*** Carey Wilson, Victor Sjostrom.

He Who Walks Alone 🦴🦴½ **1978** Documents the life of Thomas E. Gilmore, who became the South's first elected black sheriff in the 1960s. **74m/C VHS.** Louis Gossett Jr., Clu Gulager, Mary Alice, James McEachin, Barton Heyman, Barry Brown, Lonny (Loni) Chapman; ***D:*** Jerrold Freedman. **TV**

The Head 🦴🦴 **1959** A scientist comes up with a serum that can keep the severed head of a dog alive. Before too long, he tries the stuff out on a woman, transferring the head from her own hunchbacked body to that of a beautiful stripper. Weird German epic sports poor special effects and unintentional laughs, but is interesting nonetheless. **92m/B VHS.** *GE* Horst Frank, Michel Simon, Paul Dahlke, Karin Kernke, Helmut Schmidt; ***D:*** Victor Trivas; ***W:*** Victor Trivas.

Head 🦴🦴🦴 **1968 (G)** Infamously plotless musical comedy starring the TV fab four of the '60s, the Monkees, in their only film appearance. A number of guest stars appear and a collection of old movie clips are also included. ♫Circle Sky; Can You Dig It; Long Title: Do I Have to Do This All Over Again; Daddy's Song; As We Go Along; The Porpoise Song. **86m/C VHS, DVD.** Peter Tork, Mickey Dolenz, Davy Jones, Michael Nesmith, Frank Zappa, Annette Funicello, Teri Garr, Timothy Carey, Logan Ramsey, Victor Mature, Jack Nicholson, Bob Rafelson, Dennis Hopper; ***D:*** Bob Rafelson; ***W:*** Jack Nicholson, Bob Rafelson; ***C:*** Michael Hugo; ***M:*** Ken Thorne.

Head Above Water 🦴🦴 **1996 (PG-13)** Remake of same-titled 1993 Norwegian black comedy is now set on an island off the Maine coast where marrieds Nathalie (Diaz) and George (Keitel) are vacationing at her family's cottage. George goes off on an overnight fishing trip, but Nathalie isn't alone for long—former boyfriend Kent (Zane) shows up, the duo get drunk catching up on old times, and Nathalie wakes up the next morning with Kent's corpse. The unstable Nathalie hides the body, which is quickly found by George, who discards the corpse in a more permanent manner involving cement. Then Natalie suddenly decides George must have murdered Kent and is now after her. Plot doesn't hang together well and Keitel is frequently too low-key but Diaz is watchable. **92m/C VHS.** Cameron Diaz, Harvey Keitel, Craig Sheffer, Billy Zane; ***D:*** Jim Wilson; ***W:*** Theresa Marie; ***C:*** Richard Bowen; ***M:*** Christopher Young.

Head of the Family 🦴🦴½ **1971 (PG)** After a woman sacrifices her political ideals and career goals for her role as a family matriarch, she eventually falls apart. **105m/C VHS.** *IT FR* Nino Manfredi, Leslie Caron, Ugo Tognazzi, Claudine Auger; ***D:*** Nanni Loy; ***W:*** Nanni Loy.

Head of the Family 🦴½ **1996 (R)** Lance (Bailey) moves to Nob Hollow and discovers the Stackpool family's dreadful secrets—they're telepathic quadruplets under the control of brother Myron (Perra), who just happens to be a giant head that gets around in a wheelchair. Lance decides to use the whacko family to get rid of babe girlfriend Loretta's (Lovell) inconvenient husband. **82m/C VHS, DVD.** Blake Bailey, Jacqueline Lovell, Bob Schott, J.W. Perra; ***D:*** Robert Talbot; ***W:*** Benjamin Carr; ***C:*** Adolfo Bartoli; ***M:*** Richard Band.

Head Office 🦴🦴 **1986 (PG-13)** A light comedy revolving around the competition between corporate management and the lower echelon for the available position of chairman. **90m/C VHS.** Danny DeVito, Eddie Albert, Judge Reinhold, Rick Moranis, Jane Seymour; ***D:*** Ken Finkleman; ***M:*** James Newton Howard.

Head On 🦴🦴🦴 **1998** Nineteen-year-old Ari (Dimitriades) is forced to confront his Greek heritage and its idea of manhood with the homosexuality he keeps secret from his traditional family. Much of his day is spent killing time with his friends until he can meet Sean (Garner), the young man Ari is attracted to, at a bar that night. Bored and restless, Ari is out to have a good time with as little pain to himself as possible. Adapted from the book "Loaded" by Christos Tsiolkas. **104m/C VHS, DVD.** *AU* Alex Dimitriades, Paul Capsis, Julian Garner, Damien Fotiou, Elena Mandalis, Andrea Mandalis, Tony Nikolakopoulos, Eugenia Fragos, Maria Mercedes; ***D:*** Ana Kokkinos; ***W:*** Ana Kokkinos, Mira Robertson, Andrew Bovell; ***C:*** Jaems Grant; ***M:*** Ollie Olsen.

Head Over Heels 🦴🦴🦴 **1967** A model married to an older man has an affair with a younger one and cannot decide between them. In French with subtitles. **89m/C VHS.** *FR* Brigitte Bardot, Laurent Terzieff, Michael Sarne; ***D:*** Serge Bourguignon.

Head Over Heels 🦴½ **2001 (PG-13)** New York art restorer Amanda (Potter) has sworn off men after a bad breakup, but finds herself back in the game when she meets her dashing and mysterious neighbor, Jim (Prinze). Having conveniently taken up residence in an apartment that offers a perfect view of the one occupied by Jim, her attraction grows as she and her supermodel roommates follow the young man's every move. Works well during its romantic comedy stretches, but loses points for its reliance on an ill-conceived plot point revolving around a possible murder, and for lowering itself to much crude, scatological humor. **86m/C VHS, DVD, Wide.** *US* Monica Potter, Freddie Prinze Jr., Shalom Harlow, Ivana Milicevic, China Chow, Jay Brazeau, Sarah O'Hare, Tomiko Fraser, Stanley DeSantis; ***D:*** Mark Waters; ***W:*** Ron Burch, David Kidd; ***C:*** Mark Plummer; ***M:*** Randy Edelman, Steve Porcaro.

Head Winds 🦴🦴 **1925** Silent romance in which Mr. Right spares helpless girl against her will from marrying Mr. Wrong. **52m/B VHS.** House Peters Sr., Patsy Ruth Miller.

Headhunter 🦴½ **1989** Voodoo-esque killers are leaving headless bodies all around Miami. Plenty of prosthetic make-up. **92m/C VHS.** Kay Lenz, Wayne Crawford, John Fatooh, Steve Kanaly, June Chadwick, Sam Williams; ***D:*** Francis Schaeffer.

Headin' for the Rio Grande 🦴 **1936** A cowboy and his sheriff brother drive off cattle-rustlers in this Western saga. Ritter's film debut. Songs include "Campfire Love Song," "Jailhouse Lament," and "Night Herding Song." **60m/B VHS.** Tex Ritter, Eleanor Stewart, Syd Saylor, Warner Richmond, Charles "Blackie" King; ***D:*** Robert North Bradbury.

Headin' Home 🦴🦴½ **1924** A very early version of the Babe Ruth story—starring none other than the Babe himself. A fair print, this film is orchestra scored. **56m/B VHS, DVD.** Babe Ruth.

Heading for Heaven 🦴🦴 **1947** A mistaken medical report leaves a frazzled realtor believing he has only three months to live, and when he disappears the family suspects the worst. A minor comedy based on a play by Charles Webb. **65m/B VHS.** Stuart Erwin, Glenda Farrell, Russ Vincent, Irene Ryan, Milburn Stone, George O'Hanlon; ***D:*** Lewis D. Collins.

Headless Body in Topless Bar 🦴🦴½ **1996** Based on a famous New York Post headline and the crime that inspired it, this black comedy contains more than its lurid title lets on. Except for street footage at the opening and closing, the entire movie is set in a seedy strip club. After shooting the bartender in a robbery attempt, a crazed ex-con holds the patrons and employees hostage. He forces them to play a mind game called "Nazi truth," revealing the distasteful truth about the captives. Director Bruce and screenwriter Koper first worked together filming re-creations for "America's Most Wanted." The cast worked for "hostage scale," meaning if those playing captives stole the gun from the robber (a plot point), they got his pay for the day. If not, then he got their wages. **105m/C VHS.** Raymond J. Barry, Jennifer MacDonald, David Selby, Taylor Nichols, Paul Williams, Biff Yeager, Rustam Branaman, April Grace; ***D:*** James Bruce; ***W:*** Peter Koper; ***C:*** Kevin Morrisey; ***M:*** Charles P. Barnett.

Headless Eyes 🦴½ **1983** Gory entry into the psycho-artist category. An artist is miffed when mistaken by a woman as a burglar he loses an eye. Not one to forgive and forget, he becomes quite the eyeball fetishist, culling donations from unsuspecting women. An eye for an eye ad finitum. **78m/C VHS.** Bo Brundin, Gordon Raman, Mary Jane Early; ***D:*** Kent Bateman; ***W:*** Kent Bateman.

Headline Woman 🦴🦴 **1935** An ongoing feud between a police commissioner and a newspaper's city editor causes a reporter to make a deal with a policeman in exchange for news. A good cast makes this otherwise tired story tolerable. **75m/B VHS.** Heather Angel, Roger Pryor, Jack LaRue, Ford Sterling, Conway Tearle; ***D:*** William Nigh.

Heads 🦴🦴½ **1993 (R)** Unassuming copyreader Guy Franklin (Cryer) gets promoted to reporter and his first assignment is a doozy. He's to cover a series of decapitation murders in a small town. Can he do the job without become the next victim—or being accused of the crimes? Filmed in Manitoba, Canada. **102m/C VHS.** *CA* Jon Cryer, Jennifer Tilly, Ed Asner, Roddy McDowall; ***D:*** Paul Shapiro; ***W:*** Adam Brooks; ***M:*** Jonathan Goldsmith. **CABLE**

Healer 🦴½ *Little Pal* **1936** A doctor forgets his pledge to help the lame and becomes a fashionable physician. A young crippled lad helps him eventually remember his original purpose was to serve others. **80m/B VHS.** Mickey Rooney, Ralph Bellamy, Karen Morley, Judith Allen, Robert McWade; ***D:*** Reginald Barker.

Hear My Song 🦴🦴🦴½ **1991 (R)** Mickey O'Neill (Dunbar) is an unscrupulous club promoter, who books singers with names like Franc Cinatra, while trying to revive his failing nightclub in this charming, hilarious comedy. He hires the mysterious Mr. X, who claims he is really the legendary exiled singer Josef Locke, only to find out he is an imposter. To redeem himself with his fiance and her mother, he goes to Ireland to find the real Locke (Beatty) and bring him to Liverpool to sing. Dunbar is appealing in his role, and Beatty is magnificent as the legendary Locke—so much so that he was nominated for a Golden Globe for Best Supporting Actor. **104m/C VHS.** *GB* Ned Beatty, Adrian Dunbar, Shirley Anne Field, Tara Fitzgerald, William Hootkins, David McCallum, Gladys Sheehan; ***D:*** Peter Chelsom; ***W:*** Peter Chelsom; ***C:*** Sue Gibson; ***M:*** John Altman.

Hear No Evil 🦴½ **1993 (R)** Below average thriller with a deaf victim (Matlin) involved in a game of cat-and-mouse with a corrupt cop (Sheen) who's looking for a valuable coin. Weak script plays up the woman in jeopardy theme but lacks the crucial element of suspense. A waste of an otherwise talented cast. **98m/C VHS.** Marlee Matlin, D.B. Sweeney, Martin Sheen, John C. McGinley, Christina Carlisi, Greg Elam, Charley Lang; ***D:*** Robert Greenwald; ***W:*** Randall Badat, Kathleen Rowell; ***M:*** Graeme Revell.

Hearing Voices 🦴½ **1990** Joyless Erica is a commercial model who suffers from a form of scoliosis. If she capitalized on her infirmity by advertising medical aids, she could make a lot of money but she firmly refuses her lover's pleas to do this. When her doctor suggests reconstructive surgery, she storms out of his office but not before attracting the attention of Lee, his gay lover. Erica and Lee begin a complex emotional relationship, upsetting to everyone around them. Uninvolving characters, inert direction, and amateurish acting work against Greytak's feature film debut. **87m/C VHS.** Erika Nagy, Stephen Gatta, Tim Ahearn, Michael Davenport; ***D:*** Sharon Greytak; ***W:*** Sharon Greytak.

The Hearse woof! **1980 (PG)** Incredibly boring horror film in which a young school teacher moves into a mansion left to her by her late aunt and finds her life threatened by a sinister black hearse. **100m/C VHS, DVD, Wide.** Trish Van Devere, Joseph Cotten, Donald Hotton, David Gautreaux; ***D:*** George Bowers; ***W:*** William Bleich; ***C:*** Mori Kawa.

The Hearst and Davies Affair 🦴🦴½ **1985** Married, middle-aged newspaper tycoon William Randolph Hearst falls for teenage Ziegfeld girl Marion Davies and tries to turn her into a Hollywood star. Davies was generally thought to be talented as a comedienne but Hearst insisted on choosing ill-suited dramatic roles for the blonde and her career was problematic. Their lavish lifestyle was enhanced when Hearst built San Simeon for Davies and their scandalous affair lasted 35 years. **97m/C VHS.** Robert Mitchum, Virginia Madsen, Fritz Weaver; ***D:*** David Lowell Rich. **TV**

Heart 🦴½ **1987 (R)** A down-and-out small-time boxer is given a chance to make a comeback, and makes the Rocky-like most of it. **93m/C VHS.** Brad Davis, Jesse Doran, Sam Gray, Steve Buscemi, Frances Fisher; ***D:*** James (Momel) Lemmo.

Heart 🦴½ **1999 (R)** Gruesome wanna-ble thriller (told in flashback) finds Gary Ellis (Eccleston) suffering a jealousy-induced heart attack after discovering wife Tess's (Hardie) philandering with Alex (Ifans). Gary gets a heart transplant—the donor being a young man killed in a motorcycle accident—and contacts the man's mother, Maria Ann (Reeves) after he gets out of the hospital. Too bad she's crazy. **85m/C VHS, DVD.** *GB* Christopher Eccleston, Saskia Reeves, Kate Hardie, Rhys Ifans, Bill Paterson, Anna Chancellor, Matthew Rhys; ***D:*** Charles McDougall; ***W:*** Jimmy McGovern; ***C:*** Julian Court; ***M:*** Stephen Warbeck.

Heart and Souls 🦴🦴½ **1993 (PG-13)** Reincarnation comedy casts Downey Jr. as a mortal whose body is inhabited by four lost souls who died on the night he was born. Now an adult, he must finish what they could not, no matter how outrageous it may be. Talented cast wears plot that's old hat. Downey Jr. must be looking to do a trilogy of tired reincarnated soul roles—this is his second, "Chances Are" was his first. **104m/C VHS, DVD, Wide.** Robert Downey Jr., Charles Grodin, Tom Sizemore, Alfre Woodard, Kyra Sedgwick, Elisabeth Shue, David Paymer; ***D:*** Ron Underwood; ***W:*** Erik Hansen, Brent Maddock, S.S. Wilson, Gregory Hansen; ***C:*** Michael Watkins; ***M:*** Marc Shaiman.

Heart Beat 🦴🦴½ **1980 (R)** The fictionalized story of Jack Kerouac (author of "On the Road"), his friend and inspiration Neal Cassady, and the woman they shared, Carolyn Cassady. Based on Carolyn Cassady's memoirs. Strong performances, with Nolte as Cassady and Spacek as his wife, overcome the sometimes shaky narrative. **105m/C VHS.** Nick Nolte, John Heard, Sissy Spacek, Ann Dusenberry, Ray Sharkey, Tony Bill, Steve Allen, John Larroquette; ***D:*** John Byrum; ***W:*** John Byrum; ***M:*** Jack Nitzsche.

Heart Condition 🦴🦴½ **1990 (R)** A deceased black lawyer's heart is donated to a bigoted Los Angeles cop who was stalking the lawyer when he was alive. Soon afterwards the lawyer's ghost returns to haunt the police officer, hoping the officer will help to avenge his murder. Both Hoskins and Washington display fine performances given the unlikely script. **95m/C VHS.** Bob Hoskins, Denzel Washington, Chloe Webb, Ray Baker, Ja'net DuBois, Alan Rachins, Roger E. Mosley, Jeffrey Meek; ***D:*** James D. Parriott; ***C:*** Arthur Albert.

The Heart Is a Lonely Hunter 🦴🦴🦴 **1968 (G)** Set in the South, Carson McCuller's tale of angst and ignorance, loneliness and beauty comes to the screen with the film debuts of Keach and Locke. Arkin gives an instinctive, gentle performance as the deaf mute; Locke's screen debut. **124m/C VHS.** Alan Arkin, Cicely Tyson, Sondra Locke, Stacy Keach, Chuck McCann, Laurinda Barrett; ***D:*** Robert Ellis Miller; ***C:*** James Wong Howe; ***M:*** Dave Grusin. N.Y. Film Critics '68: Actor (Arkin).

Heart Like a Wheel 🦴🦴½ **1983 (PG)** The story of Shirley Muldowney, who rose from the daughter of a country-western singer to the leading lady in drag racing. The film follows her battles of sexism and choosing whether to have a career or a family. Bedelia's perfomance is outstanding. Fine showings from Bridges and Axton in supporting roles. **113m/C VHS.** Bonnie Bedelia, Beau Bridges, Bill McKinney, Leo Rossi, Hoyt Axton, Dick Miller, Anthony Edwards; ***D:*** Jonathan Kaplan; ***W:*** Ken Friedman.

Heart of a Champion: The Ray Mancini Story 🦴🦴 **1985** Made-for-TV movie based on the life of Ray "Boom Boom" Mancini, former lightweight boxing champion. Inspired by the career his father never had due to WWII, Mancini fought his way to the top. Sylvester Stallone staged the fight sequences. **94m/C VHS.** Robert (Bobby) Blake, Doug McKeon, Mariclare Costello; ***D:*** Richard Michaels.

Heart of a Nation 🦴🦴🦴 *Untel Pere et Fils* **1943** Saga of the Montmarte family and their life during three wars, beginning with the Franco-Prussian War and ending with the Nazi occupation in France. Although ordered to be destroyed by the Nazis, this film was saved, along with many others, by the French "Cinema Resistance." In French with English subtitles. **111m/B VHS.** *FR* Louis Jouvet, Raimu, Suzy Prim, Michele Morgan, Renee Devillers; ***D:*** Julien Duvivier; ***Nar:*** Charles Boyer.

Heart of Darkness 🦴🦴 **1993** Joseph Conrad's 1902 menacing novella set in the Belgian Congo is told through flashbacks by Marlow (Roth), whose employers, a Belgian trading company, hire him to find Kurtz (Malkovich), head of a remote trading station, who is rumored to be hoarding a huge cache of ivory. Marlow's journey up the river is beset by obstacles and Kurtz is rumored to be either insane or a prophet in his jungle kingdom. Filmed in Belize. Francis Ford Coppola's updated adaptation became "Apocalyse Now." **120m/C VHS.** Tim Roth, John Malkovich, James Fox, Isaach de Bankole, Patrick Ryecart, Geoffrey Hutchings, Peter Vaughan, Phoebe Nicholls, Allan Corduner, Alan Scarfe, Iman, Timothy Bateson; ***D:*** Nicolas Roeg; ***W:*** Benedict Fitzgerald; ***M:*** Stanley Myers. **TV**

The Heart of Dixie 🦴🦴 **1989 (PG)** Three college co-eds at a southern university in the 1950s see their lives and values change with the influence of the civil rights movement. College newspaper reporter Sheedy takes up the cause of a black man victimized by racial violence. Lightweight social-conscience fare. **96m/C VHS, DVD, Wide.** Virginia Madsen, Ally Sheedy, Phoebe Cates, Treat Williams, Kyle Secor, Francesca Roberts, Barbara Babcock, Don Michael Paul, Kurtwood Smith, Richard Bradford; ***D:*** Martin Davidson; ***W:*** Tom McCown; ***C:*** Robert Elswit; ***M:*** Kenny Vance.

Heart of Dragon 🦴🦴 **1985** Police officer Chan takes care of his mentally challenged brother Hung, who gets mistaken for a robbery suspect. So Chan has to track down the real crooks. Features a 20-minute fight finale. Chinese with subtitles or dubbed. **85m/C VHS, DVD.** *HK* Jackie Chan, Sammo Hung, Emily Chu; ***D:*** Sammo Hung; ***W:*** Barry Wong; ***C:*** Arthur Wong; ***M:*** Man Yee Lam.

Heart of Glass 🦴🦴🦴 *Herz aus Glas* **1974** A pre-industrial Bavarian village becomes deeply troubled when their glassblower dies without imparting the secret of making his unique Ruby glass. The townspeople go to extremes, from madness to murder to magic, to discover the ingredients. From German director Herzog (who hypnotized his cast daily), this somewhat apocalyptic tale is based on legend. The colors are incredible in their intensity. In German with English subtitles. **93m/C VHS, DVD, Wide.** *GE* Josef Bierbichler, Stefan Guttler, Clemens Scheitz, Volker Prechtel, Sonia Skiba; ***D:*** Werner Herzog; ***W:*** Werner Herzog, Herbert Achternbusch; ***C:*** Jorge Schmidt-Reitwein; ***M:*** Popul Vuh.

Heart of Humanity **1918** An intense drama of love, patriotism, and sacrifice just before the war in a small Canadian village. A traveler who is really a Prussian army lieutenant finds his way to the house of a young man who is about to wed. He ends up falling in love with his fiancee and war is declared just before the wedding. A silent film with music score. **133m/B VHS, 8mm.** Dorothy Phillips, Erich von Stroheim; ***D:*** Allen Holubar.

Heart of Light 🦴🦴 *Lysets Hjerte* **1997** Marginalized Inuit family, living in Danish-occupied Greenland, suffer from being cut off from their native culture. Teenager Nisi has a breakdown, goes on a killing spree, and then turns the gun on himself. His drunken father, Rasmus, decides to leave the community on an old dogsled and encounters a hermit who leads him on a mystical journey into the past. Filmed on location in Greenland. Inuit and Danish with subtitles. **92m/C VHS, DVD.** *DK* Rasmus Lyberth, Anda Kristensen, Vivi Nielsen, Niels Platow; ***D:*** Jacob Gronlykke; ***W:*** Jacob Gronlykke; ***C:*** Dan Laustsen; ***M:*** Joachim Holbek.

Heart of Midnight 🦴🦴½ **1989 (R)** An emotionally unstable young woman inherits a seedy massage parlor. She works hard to turn it, and herself, into something better. Nice performance by Leigh. **93m/C VHS.** Jennifer Jason Leigh, Brenda Vaccaro, Frank Stallone, Peter Coyote, Gale Mayron, Sam Schacht, Denise Dumont; ***D:*** Matthew Chapman; ***W:*** Matthew Chapman; ***M:*** Yanni.

Heart of Texas Ryan 🦴½ **1916** Flamboyant cowboy star fights with kidnappers and wins in this silent film. **50m/B VHS.** Tom Mix.

Heart of the Golden West 🦴🦴 **1942** Roy protects ranchers of Cherokee City from unjust shipping charges. **65m/B VHS.** Roy Rogers, Smiley Burnette, George "Gabby" Hayes, Bob Nolan, Ruth Terry; ***D:*** Joseph Kane.

Heart of the Rio Grande 🦴½ **1942** Spoiled young rich girl tries to trick her father into coming to her "rescue" at a western dude ranch. **70m/B VHS.** Gene Autry, Smiley Burnette, Fay McKenzie, Edith Fellows, Joseph Stauch Jr.; ***D:*** William M. Morgan.

Heart of the Rockies 🦴½ **1937** The Three Mesquiteers stop a mountain family's rustling and illegal game trappers. **54m/B VHS.** Robert "Bob" Livingston, Ray Corrigan, Max Terhune, Lynne Roberts, Yakima Canutt, J(ohn) P(aterson) McGowan; ***D:*** Joseph Kane.

Heart of the Rockies 🦴½ **1951** Roy, along with his trusty horse and dog, takes care of a highway construction project. **67m/B VHS.** Roy Rogers, Penny Edwards, Gordon Jones, Ralph Morgan, Fred Graham, Mira McKinney; ***D:*** William Witney.

Heart of the Stag 🦴🦴½ **1984 (R)** On an isolated sheep ranch in the New Zealand outback, a father and daughter suffer the repercussions of an incestuous relationship when she becomes enamored with a hired hand. **94m/C VHS.** *NZ* Bruno Lawrence, Mary Regan, Terence Cooper; ***D:*** Michael Firth.

Heartaches 🦴🦴 **1947** A reporter tries to track down a murderer who has killed twice. **71m/B VHS.** Chill Wills, Sheila Ryan, Edward Norris, James Seay.

Heartaches 🦴🦴🦴 **1982** A young pregnant woman (Potts) meets up with a crazy girlfriend (Kidder) in this touching film about love and friendship. Although a study in contrasts, the two end up sharing an apartment together in Toronto. Fine performances from Potts and Kidder give life to this romantic comedy. **90m/C VHS.** *CA* Margot Kidder, Annie Potts, Robert Carradine, Winston Rekert; ***D:*** Donald Shebib. Genie '82: Actress (Kidder).

Heartbeat 🦴🦴½ **1946** If you thought pointless Hollywood remakes of French films were a new phenomenon (see "Pure Luck," for example), then note this lighthearted remake of a 1940 Gallic farce. Rogers becomes the best student in a Parisian school for pickpockets, but when she tries out her skills on a dashing diplomat they fall in love instead. **100m/B VHS.** Ginger Rogers, Jean-Pierre Aumont, Adolphe Menjou, Basil Rathbone, Melville Cooper, Mona Maris, Henry Stephenson, Eduardo Ciannelli; ***D:*** Sam Wood; ***C:*** Joseph Valentine.

Heartbeeps 🦴½ **1981 (PG)** Mildly amusing romantic comedy about a couple of robot household servants (Kaufman and Peters) who fall in love, escape from domestic service, and begin a family of their own (they assemble a child robot from spare parts). **88m/C VHS.** Andy Kaufman, Bernadette Peters, Randy Quaid, Kenneth McMillan, Melanie Mayron, Christopher Guest, Richard B. Shull, Dick Miller, Kathleen Freeman, Mary Woronov, Paul Bartel; ***D:*** Allan Arkush; ***W:*** John Hill; ***C:*** Charles Rosher Jr.; ***M:*** John Williams.

Heartbreak Hotel 🦴🦴½ **1988 (PG-13)** Johnny Wolfe kidnaps Elvis Presley from his show in Cleveland and drives him home to his mother, a die-hard Elvis fan. Completely unbelievable, utterly ridiculous, and still a lot of fun. **101m/C VHS.** David Keith, Tuesday Weld, Charlie Schlatter, Angela Goethals, Jacque Lynn Colton, Chris Mulkey, Karen Landry, Tudor Sherrard, Paul Harkins; ***D:*** Chris Columbus; ***W:*** Chris Columbus; ***M:*** Georges Delerue.

Heartbreak House 🦴🦴½ **1986** A production of George Bernard Shaw's classic play about a captain and his daughter who invite an odd assortment of people into their home for a few days. In the course of their visit, each person shares his ambitions, hopes, and fears. From the "American Playhouse" TV series. **118m/C VHS.** Rex Harrison, Rosemary Harris, Amy Irving; ***D:*** Anthony Page. **TV**

The Heartbreak Kid 1972 (PG) Director May's comic examination of love and hypocrisy. Grodin embroils himself in a triangle with his new bride and a woman he can't have, an absolutely gorgeous and totally unloving woman he shouldn't want. Walks the fence between tragedy and comedy, with an exceptional performance from Berlin. Based on Bruce Jay Friedman's story. **106m/C VHS, DVD.** Charles Grodin, Cybill Shepherd, Eddie Albert, Jeannie Berlin, Audra Lindley, Art Metrano; ***D:*** Elaine May; ***W:*** Neil Simon; ***C:*** Owen Roizman; ***M:*** Garry Sherman, Cy Coleman, Sheldon Harnick. N.Y. Film Critics '72: Support. Actress (Berlin); Natl. Soc. Film Critics '72: Support. Actor (Albert), Support. Actress (Berlin).

Heartbreak Ridge 1986 (R) An aging Marine recon sergeant is put in command of a young platoon to whip them into shape to prepare for combat in the invasion of Grenada. Eastwood whips this old story into shape too, with a fine performance of a man who's given everything to the Marines. The invasion of Grenada, though, is not epic material. (Also available in English with Spanish subtitles.) **130m/C VHS, 8mm.** Clint Eastwood, Marsha Mason, Everett McGill, Arlen Dean Snyder, Bo Svenson, Moses Gunn, Eileen Heckart, Boyd Gaines, Mario Van Peebles, Vincent Irizarry, Ramon Franco, Tom Villard, Pete Koch, Richard Venture, J.C. Quinn, Peter Jason, Thom Sharp; ***D:*** Clint Eastwood; ***W:*** James (Jim) Carabatsos; ***C:*** Jack N. Green; ***M:*** Lennie Niehaus.

Heartbreaker ½ 1983 (R) Eastern Los Angeles explodes with vicious turf wars when Beto and Hector battle for the affection of Kim, the neighborhood's newest heartbreaker. **90m/C VHS.** Fernando Allende, Dawn Dunlap, Michael D. Roberts, Robert Dryer, Apollonia; ***D:*** Frank Zuniga.

Heartbreakers 1984 (R) Two male best friends find themselves in the throes of drastic changes in their careers and romantic encounters. On target acting makes this old story new, with a fine performance by Wayne, in her last film before her death. **98m/C VHS.** Peter Coyote, Nick Mancuso, Carole Laure, Max Gail, James Laurenson, Carol Wayne, Jamie Rose, Kathryn Harrold; ***D:*** Bobby Roth; ***W:*** Bobby Roth; ***C:*** Michael Ballhaus; ***M:*** Tangerine Dream.

Heartbreakers ½ 2001 (PG-13) Max and Page, played by Weaver and Hewitt, are a mother-daughter con-artist team who delight in seducing men right out of their bank accounts and billfolds. Tobacco billionaire William B. Tensy is Max's latest target, but proves to be a tougher case than she realized. Meanwhile, daughter Page has her sights set on Jack, the handsome Palm Beach bar owner, but can't decide if it's just another con, or true love. Hackman excels as the obnoxious Tensy. Director Mirkin's first feature since "Romy and Michelle's High School Reunion." **123m/C VHS, DVD, Wide.** *US* Sigourney Weaver, Jennifer Love Hewitt, Gene Hackman, Ray Liotta, Jason Lee, Anne Bancroft, Jeffrey Jones, Nora Dunn, Julio Mechoso, Ricky Jay; ***D:*** David Mirkin; ***W:*** Paul Guay, Robert Dunn, Steve Mazur; ***C:*** Dean Semler; ***M:*** John Debney.

Heartburn 1986 (R) Based on Nora Ephron's own semi-autobiographical novel about her marital travails with writer Carl Bernstein, this is a tepid, bitter modern romance between writers already shell-shocked from previous marriages. **109m/C VHS, 8mm.** Meryl Streep, Jack Nicholson, Steven Hill, Richard Masur, Stockard Channing, Jeff Daniels, Milos Forman, Catherine O'Hara, Maureen Stapleton, Karen Akers, Joanna Gleason, Mercedes Ruehl, Caroline Aaron, Yakov Smirnoff, Anna Maria Horsford, Wilfrid Hyde-White; ***D:*** Mike Nichols; ***W:*** Nora Ephron; ***C:*** Nestor Almendros; ***M:*** Carly Simon.

Heartland ½ 1981 (PG) Set in 1910, this film chronicles the story of one woman's life on the Wyoming frontier, when she contracts to become a housekeeper for a rancher. Elinore (Ferrell) and her young daughter arrive at the home of Clyde Stewart (Torn) and face any number of hazards, which test her courage and spirit. Stunningly realistic and without cliche. Based on the diaries of Elinore Randall Stewart. **95m/C VHS, DVD.** Conchata Ferrell, Rip Torn, Barry Primus, Lilia Skala, Megan Folson; ***D:*** Richard Pearce; ***W:*** Beth Ferris; ***C:*** Fred Murphy. Sundance '81: Grand Jury Prize.

Hearts & Armour 1983 A holy war between Christians and Moors erupts when a Moorish princess is kidnapped. Based on Ludovico Ariosto's "Orlando Furioso." **101m/C VHS.** *IT* Tanya Roberts, Leigh McCloskey, Ron Moss, Rick Edwards, Giovanni Visentin; ***D:*** Giacomo Battiato.

Heart's Desire ½ 1937 Opera great Tauber stars in this musical of an unknown Viennese singer who falls in love with an English girl. **79m/B VHS.** *GB* Richard Tauber, Lenora Corbett, Kathleen Kelly, Paul Graetz; ***D:*** Paul Stein.

Heart's Haven ½ 1922 An insensitive wife (Adams), who doesn't appreciate how wonderful her husband is, winds up running away with another man. **61m/B VHS.** Claire Adams, Robert McKim, Carl Gantvoort, Jean Hersholt; ***D:*** Benjamin B. Hampton.

Hearts in Atlantis ½ 2001 (PG-13) Coming-of-age tale tinged with creeps benefits from the odd combination of a story by Stephen King and direction from Scott Hicks, who also directed "Shine" and "Snow Falling on Cedars." Bobby (Yelchin) is an 11-year-old boy living in lower middle class Connecticut circa 1960 with his widowed mother Liz (Davis). When enigmatic Ted (Hopkins) rents a room in their attic, he offers the boy a job reading him the daily newspaper. He also has Bobby keep an eye out for the "low men" (CIA agents? Mafia?) he believes are pursuing him. Ted offers the male role model and adult attention Bobby craves and the two quickly become close. Ted, it seems, has some kind of psychic ability, which he also sees in Bobby. Although lushly filmed, the plot seems a bit stagnant and listless for a story about young people. **101m/C VHS, DVD, Wide.** *US* Anthony Hopkins, Anton Yelchin, Hope Davis, Mika Boorem, David Morse, Alan Tudyk, Tom Bower, Celia Weston, Adam LeFevre, Timothy Reifsnyder, Deirdre O'Connell, Will Rothhaar; ***D:*** Scott Hicks; ***W:*** William Goldman; ***C:*** Piotr Sobocinski; ***M:*** Mychael Danna.

Hearts of Darkness: A Filmmaker's Apocalypse 1991 (R) This riveting, critically acclaimed documentary about the making of Francis Ford Coppola's masterpiece "Apocalypse Now" is based largely on original footage shot and directed by his wife Eleanor. Also included are recent interviews with cast and crew members including Coppola, Martin Sheen, Robert Duvall, Frederic Forrest and Dennis Hopper. **96m/C VHS.** Sam Bottoms, Eleanor Coppola, Francis Ford Coppola, Robert Duvall, Laurence "Larry" Fishburne, Frederic Forrest, Albert Hall, Dennis Hopper, George Lucas, John Milius, Martin Sheen; ***D:*** Fax Bahr, George Hickenlooper; ***W:*** Fax Bahr, George Hickenlooper; ***M:*** Todd Boekelheide. Natl. Bd. of Review '91: Feature Doc.

Hearts of Fire 1987 A trio of successful rock 'n' roll stars work out their confused romantic entanglements. Barely released at all, and not even in the U.S. Sad outing for the cast, especially legendary Dylan. **90m/C VHS.** Bob Dylan, Fiona, Rupert Everett, Julian Glover; ***D:*** Richard Marquand; ***W:*** Joe Eszterhas; ***M:*** John Barry.

Hearts of Humanity 1932 Mawkish melodrama concerning a Jewish antique dealer and his relationship with the son of an Irish cop. An early "Chico and the Man" variant. **56m/B VHS.** Jean Hersholt, Jackie Searl, J. Farrell MacDonald, Claudia Dell, Charles Delaney, Lucille LaVerne, George Humbert; ***D:*** Christy Cabanne.

Hearts of the West ½ *Hollywood Cowboy* 1975 (PG) A fantasy-filled farm boy travels to Hollywood in the 1930s and seeks a writing career. Instead, he finds himself an ill-suited western movie star in this small offbeat comedy-drama that's sure to charm. **103m/C VHS.** Jeff Bridges, Andy Griffith, Donald Pleasence, Alan Arkin, Blythe Danner; ***D:*** Howard Zieff; ***W:*** Rob Thompson. N.Y. Film Critics '75: Support. Actor (Arkin).

Hearts of the World 1918 A vintage Griffith epic about a young boy who goes off to WWI and the tribulations endured by both him and his family on the homefront. Overly sentimental but powerfully made melodrama, from Griffith's waning years. Silent with music score. **152m/B VHS, 8mm.** Lillian Gish, Robert "Bobbie" Harron, Dorothy Gish, Erich von Stroheim, Ben Alexander, Josephine Crowell, Noel Coward, Mary Gish; ***D:*** D.W. Griffith.

Heartstopper 1992 Benjamin Latham, an innocent physician in Pittsburgh, was accused of being a vampire in colonial times and hung. 200 years later, he emerges from the grave, unscathed. While trying to figure out what has happened, he falls in love with a photojournalist, who helps him find his own descendent, Matthew Latham. Unfortunately, his deep freeze has left him with the compulsion to kill, but only evil members of society. **96m/B VHS.** Moon Zappa, Tom Savini, Kevin Kindlin.

Heartstrings 1995 Melissa wants everything in her life to be perfect, including having the perfect man, which she thinks is New York gallery owner Peter. But will Melissa's heart compromise her ambitions? **94m/C VHS.** Michelle Little, Phyllis Diller.

Heartwood 1998 (PG-13) Frank (Mills) is an outcast living in the woods of a failing lumber town. He falls for Sylvia (Swank), the daughter of the engineer hired by mill owner Logan Reese (Robards) to save the mill and the town as well. But when Frank discovers gold, he's the one who comes up with a plan. **92m/C VHS, DVD.** Eddie Mills, Hilary Swank, Jason Robards Jr., Randall Batinkoff, Stanley DeSantis; ***D:*** Lanny Cotler.

Heat *Andy Warhol's Heat* 1972 Another Andy Warhol-produced journey into drug-addled urban seediness. Features a former child actor/junkie and a has-been movie star barely surviving in a run-down motel. This is one of Warhol's better film productions; even non-fans may enjoy it. **102m/C VHS, DVD.** Joe Dallesandro, Sylvia Miles, Pat Ast, Andrea Feldman, Ray Vestal; ***D:*** Paul Morrissey; ***W:*** Paul Morrissey; ***C:*** Paul Morrissey; ***M:*** John Cale.

Heat ½ 1987 (R) A Las Vegas bodyguard avenges the beating of an old flame by a mobster's son, and incites mob retaliation. Based on the William Goldman novel. **103m/C VHS.** Burt Reynolds, Karen Young, Peter MacNicol, Howard Hesseman; ***D:*** R.M. Richards; ***W:*** William Goldman; ***M:*** Michael Gibbs.

Heat ½ 1995 (R) Pacino and De Niro in the same scene. Together. Finally. Obsessive master thief McCauley (De Niro) leads a crack crew on various military-style heists across L.A. while equally obsessive detective Hanna (Pacino) tracks him. Each man recognizes and respects the other's ability and dedication, even as they express the willingness to kill each other, if necessary. Excellent script with all the fireworks you'd expect, as well as a surprising look into emotional and personal sacrifice. Beautiful cinematography shows industrial landscape to great effect. Writer-director Mann held onto the screenplay for 12 years. **171m/C VHS, DVD.** Robert De Niro, Al Pacino, Val Kilmer, Jon Voight, Diane Venora, Ashley Judd, Wes Studi, Tom Sizemore, Mykelti Williamson, Amy Brenneman, Ted Levine, Dennis Haysbert, William Fichtner, Natalie Portman, Hank Azaria, Henry Rollins, Kevin Gage; ***Cameos:*** Tone Loc, Bud Cort, Jeremy Piven; ***D:*** Michael Mann; ***W:*** Michael Mann; ***C:*** Dante Spinotti; ***M:*** Elliot Goldenthal.

Heat and Dust 1982 (R) A young bride joins her husband at his post in India and is inexorably drawn to the country and its prince of state. Years later her great niece journeys to modern day India in search of the truth about her scandalous and mysterious relative. More than the story of two romances, this is the tale of women rebelling against an unseen caste system which keeps them second-class citizens. Ruth Jhabvala wrote the novel and screenplay. **130m/C VHS.** *GB* Julie Christie, Greta Scacchi, Shashi Kapoor, Christopher Cazenove, Nickolas Grace, Julian Glover, Susan Fleetwood, Patrick Godfrey, Jennifer Kendal, Madhur Jaffrey, Barry Foster, Amanda Walker, Sudha Chopra, Sajid Khan, Zakir Hussain, Ratna Pathak, Charles McCaughan, Parveen Paul; ***D:*** James Ivory; ***W:*** Ruth Prawer Jhabvala, Saeed Jaffrey, Harish Khare; ***C:*** Walter Lassally; ***M:*** Richard Robbins. British Acad. '83: Adapt. Screenplay.

Heat and Sunlight ½ 1987 A photographer becomes obsessively jealous of his lover as their relationship comes to an end. Director Nilsson again used a unique improvisational, video-to-film technique, as he did with his previous film, "Signal 7." **98m/B VHS.** Rob Nilsson, Consuelo Faust, Bill Bailey, Don Bajema, Ernie Fosselius; ***D:*** Rob Nilsson; ***W:*** Rob Nilsson; ***C:*** Tomas Tucker; ***M:*** Mark Adler. Sundance '88: Grand Jury Prize.

Heat of Desire *Plein Sud* 1984 (R) A philosophy professor abandons everything (including his wife) for a woman he barely knows and is conned by her "relatives." With English subtitles. **90m/C VHS.** *FR* Clio Goldsmith, Patrick Dewaere, Jeanne Moreau, Guy Marchand; ***D:*** Luc Beraud.

The Heat of the Day ½ 1991 A British officer is accused of treason. As he attempts to find those who framed him, he meets a lovely woman all too willing to help. But whose side is she really on? Set in WWII. Tense and well-acted; made for TV. **120m/C VHS.** Michael York, Patricia Hodge, Peggy Ashcroft, Anna Carteret, Michael Gambon; ***W:*** Harold Pinter. **TV**

Heat of the Flame 1982 A vicious woodsman captures and rapes a beautiful girl. Psychological games, eroticism and exploitive nudity ensue. **88m/C VHS.** Tony Ferrandis, Ellie MacLure, Raymond Young, Anthony (Jose, J. Antonio, J.A.) Mayans.

Heat of the Sun 1999 Former Scotland Yard detective Albert Tyburn (Eve) has been sent to work in Nairobi, Kenya in the hedonistic expatriate community of the 1930s, known as "Happy Valley." But despite his disdain for the community's racial and social lines, Tyburn is soon involved in murder and mayhem. In "Private Lives," Tyburn investigates the death of Lady Ellesmere and discovers drug-running, adultery, and murder. "Hide in Plain Sight" finds Tyburn investigating the death of a native girl and the disappear of other girls from the local Christian mission. "The Sport of Kings" finds Tyburn involved in the murder of a young boy against the backdrop of Nairobi's premier social event, Race Week. **360m/C VHS.** *GB* Trevor Eve, Michael Byrne, Susannah Harker, Tim Woodward, Daniel Betts, James Callis, Freddie Annobil-Dodoo, Kate McKenzie, Hugh Bonneville, Cathryn Harrison, Julian Rhind-Tutt, Diana Quick, Deborah Findlay, Joss Ackland, Richard McCabe, Sonya Walger; ***D:*** Adrian Shergold, Diarmuid Lawrence, Paul Seed; ***W:*** Russell Lewis, Tim Prager. **TV**

Heat Street 1987 Two thugs exact revenge on street gangs for the murders of loved ones. Made for video. **90m/C VHS.** Quincy Adams, Deborah Gibson, Wendy MacDonald, Del Zamora; ***D:*** Joseph Merhi. **VIDEO**

Heat Wave ½ 1954 A writer gets involved with a "femme fatale" who kills her wealthy husband for the love of a young pianist. **60m/B VHS.** *GB* Alex Nicol, Hillary Brooke, Sidney James, Susan Stephen, Paul Carpenter; ***D:*** Ken Hughes; ***W:*** Ken Hughes.

Heat Wave 1990 (R) The Watts ghetto uprising of 1965 is a proving ground for a young black journalist. Excellent cast and fine script portrays the anger and frustration of blacks in Los Angeles and the U.S. in the 1960s and the fear of change felt by blacks and whites when civil rights reform began. Strong drama with minimal emotionalism. **92m/C VHS.** Blair Underwood, Cicely Tyson, James Earl Jones, Sally Kirkland, Margaret Avery, David Strathairn, Robert Hooks, Adam Arkin, Paris Vaughan, Charlie Korsmo. **CABLE**

Heated Vengeance 1987 (R) A Vietnam vet returns to the jungle to find the woman he left behind, and runs into some old enemies. **91m/C VHS.** Richard Hatch, Michael J. Pollard, Dennis Patrick, Mills Watson, Cameron Dye; ***D:*** Edward Murphy.

Heathers 1989 (R) Clique of stuck-up girls named Heather rule the high school social scene until the newest member (not a Heather) decides that enough is enough. She and her outlaw boyfriend embark (accidentally on her part, intentionally on his) on a murder spree disguised as a rash of teen suicides. Dense, take-no-prisoners black comedy with buckets of potent slang, satire and unforgiving hostility. Humor this dark is rare; sharply observed and acted, though the end is out of place. Slater does his best Nicholson impression. **102m/C VHS, DVD, Wide.** Winona Ryder, Christian Slater, Kim Walker, Shannen Doherty, Lisanne Falk, Penelope Milford, Glenn Shadix, Lance Fenton, Patrick Laborteaux, Jeremy Applegate, Renee Estevez; ***D:*** Michael Lehmann; ***W:*** Daniel Waters; ***C:*** Francis Kenny; ***M:*** David Newman. Ind. Spirit '90: First Feature.

The Heat's On *Tropicana* 1943 Gaxton is a broadway producer with a failing musical and an unhappy star in West. He cranks up the publicity machine and gets the show declared immoral by the Legion of Purity which results in its closing (not what he expected). Gaxton then runs a scam to become the producer of West's new show, which just happens to be financed by some Legion members. Very uneven plot and performances with thrown-in musical numbers. West wrote her own dialogue but unlike her early films she had little control over the production and it showed. West didn't make another movie for 27 years (the appalling "Myra Breckenridge"). ♫Just a Stranger in Town; Hello, Mi Amigo; The White Keys and the Black Keys; There Goes That Guitar; Antonio; The Caissons Go Rolling Along; There Goes My Heart. **79m/B VHS.** Mae West, William Gaxton, Victor Moore, Almira Sessions, Lester Allen, Mary Roche, Alan Dinehart, Lloyd Bridges; ***D:*** Gregory Ratoff; ***W:*** Fitzroy Davis, George S. George, Fred Schiller.

Heatseeker 1995 (R) Corporations use mechanical fighters to participate in brutal kickboxing contests in 2019 New America. Human Chance (Cooke) must battle cyborg opponent Xao if he wants to save his kidnapped trainer. Lots of action and even some intentional humor. **91m/C VHS.** Keith Cooke, Gary Daniels, Norbert Weisser, Thom Mathews; ***D:*** Albert Pyun.

Heatwave 1983 (R) Local residents oppose a multi-million dollar residential complex in Australia. Davis portrays a liberal activist, who wages war with the developers, and, in return, becomes involved with a possible murder case. **92m/C VHS.** *AU* Judy Davis, Richard Moir, Chris Haywood, Bill Hunter, John Gregg, Anna Jemison; ***D:*** Phillip Noyce.

Heaven 1987 (PG-13) An exploration of "heaven" including the idea, the place, and people's views about it. Questions such as "How do you get there?" and "What goes on up there?" are discussed. Offbeat interviews mixed with a collage of celestial images. **80m/C VHS.** ***D:*** Diane Keaton; ***M:*** Howard Shore.

Heaven 1999 (R) Robert Marling (Donovan) is an architect with a broken marriage and a compulsion to gamble (and lose) at a sleazy strip joint owned by the odious and brutual Stanner (Schiff). One of the performers is a psychic transvestite named Heaven (Edwards), who predicts that Robert will win big in the lottery. This info gets back to evil shrink Melrose (Malahide), who has both Robert and Heaven as patients, and who just happens to be having an affair with Robert's bitter wife, Jennifer (Going). And the coincidental silliness doesn't stop there. Based on a novel by Chad Taylor. **103m/C VHS, DVD.** *NZ* Martin Donovan, Joanna Going, Patrick Malahide, Danny Edwards, Richard Schiff; ***D:*** Scott Reynolds; ***W:*** Scott Reynolds; ***C:*** Simon Raby; ***M:*** Victoria Kelly.

Heaven & Earth 1990 (PG-13) A samurai epic covering the battle for the future of Japan between two feuding warlords. The overwhelming battle scenes were actually filmed on location in Canada. In Japanese with English subtitles. **104m/C VHS.** *JP* Masahiko Tsugawa, Takaai Enoki, Atsuko Asano, Tsunehiko Watase, Naomi Zaizen, Binpachi Ito; ***Nar:*** Stuart Whitman.

Heaven and Earth 1993 (R) Conclusion of Stone's Vietnam trilogy (after "Platoon" and "Born on the Fourth of July") focuses on Vietnamese woman (film debut of Le) and her life under the French and American occupations. Jones is the American soldier who marries her and eventually brings her to the U.S. Not one for subtleties, Stone chases melodramatic excess with finesse of lumberjack, sawing away at guilt and remorse from a "woman's point of view." Cranky Tommy Lee shows up too late to save flick and is saddled with a perplexing I.D. to boot. Flawed, ambitious, and interesting if a student of Stone. Based on the two autobiographies of Le Ly Haslip, "When Heaven and Earth Changed Places" and "Child of War, Woman of Peace." Filmed on location in Thailand. **142m/C VHS, DVD, Wide.** Hiep Thi Le, Tommy Lee Jones, Joan Chen, Haing S. Ngor, Debbie Reynolds, Conchata Ferrell, Dustin Nguyen, Liem Whatley, Dale Dye; ***D:*** Oliver Stone; ***W:*** Oliver Stone; ***C:*** Robert Richardson; ***M:*** Kitaro. Golden Globes '94: Score.

Heaven Before I Die 1996 (PG) Sheltered Jacob (Velasquez) travels from the Middle East to Toronto and is taken under the questionable wing of a small-time thief (Giannini) and a beautiful waitress (Pacula). But when Jacob finds a measure of success as a Charlie Chaplin impersonator, his innocence gets a dose of culture shock. **98m/C VHS.** *CA* Andy Velasquez, Giancarlo Giannini, Catherine Oxenberg; ***Cameos:*** Joanna Pacula, Omar Sharif, Burt Young, Joseph Bologna; ***D:*** Izidore K. Musallam.

Heaven Can Wait 1943 Social satire in which a rogue tries to convince the Devil to admit him into Hell by relating the story of his philandering life and discovers that he was a more valuable human being than he thought. A witty Lubitsch treat based on the play "Birthdays." **112m/C VHS.** Don Ameche, Gene Tierney, Laird Cregar, Charles Coburn, Marjorie Main, Eugene Pallette, Allyn Joslyn, Spring Byington, Signe Hasso, Louis Calhern, Dickie Moore, Florence Bates, Scotty Beckett, Charles Halton; ***D:*** Ernst Lubitsch.

Heaven Can Wait 1978 (PG) A remake of 1941's "Here Comes Mr. Jordan." L.A. Rams quarterback Joe Pendleton (Beatty) is summoned to heaven before his time. When archangel Mr. Jordan (Mason) realizes the mistake, Joe is returned to Earth but it's in the body of a wealthy industrialist who's about to be murdered by his unfaithful wife Julia (Cannon) and his nervous secretary, Tony (Grodin). But Joe is about to let a little thing like murder prevent him from playing in the Super Bowl—new body or not. Christie's the new love interest; Warden's the gruff coach. Not to be confused with the 1943 film of the same name. **101m/C VHS, DVD.** Warren Beatty, Julie Christie, Charles Grodin, Dyan Cannon, James Mason, Jack Warden, Buck Henry; ***D:*** Warren Beatty, Buck Henry; ***W:*** Elaine May, Warren Beatty; ***C:*** William A. Fraker; ***M:*** Dave Grusin. Oscars '78: Art Dir./Set Dec.; Golden Globes '79: Actor—Mus./Comedy (Beatty), Film—Mus./Comedy, Support. Actress (Cannon); Writers Guild '78: Adapt. Screenplay.

Heaven Help Us *Catholic Boys* 1985 (R) Three mischievous boys find themselves continually in trouble with the priests running their Brooklyn Catholic high school during the mid-1960s. Realistic and humorous look at adolescent life. **102m/C VHS.** Andrew McCarthy, Mary Stuart Masterson, Kevin Dillon, Malcolm Danare, Jennifer (Jennie) Dundas Lowe, Kate Reid, Wallace Shawn, Jay Patterson, John Heard, Donald Sutherland, Yeardley Smith, Sherry Steiner, Calvert Deforest, Philip Bosco, Patrick Dempsey, Christopher Durang; ***D:*** Michael Dinner; ***W:*** Charles Purpura; ***M:*** James Horner.

Heaven Is a Playground 1991 (R) On Chicago's South Side an inner city basketball coach and an idealistic young lawyer are determined to change the fate of a group of high school boys. The men use the incentive of athletic scholarships to keep their team in school and away from drugs and gangs. **104m/C VHS.** D.B. Sweeney, Michael Warren, Richard Jordan, Victor Love; ***D:*** Randall Fried; ***W:*** Randall Fried.

Heaven Knows, Mr. Allison 1957 Terrific two-character WWII drama finds tough (but tenderhearted) Marine sergeant Allison (Mitchum) stranded with Irish nun, Sister Angela (Kerr), on a Pacific island overrun by Japanese troops. The duo hide out during the day and forage for food by night, gradually revealing their pasts to each other. He falls hard while she resists his advances and they struggle to stay alive until U.S. forces invade the island. Lots of action and good performances. Based on the novel by Charles Shaw. **106m/C VHS.** Robert Mitchum, Deborah Kerr; ***D:*** John Huston; ***W:*** John Huston, John Lee Mahin; ***C:*** Oswald Morris; ***M:*** Georges Auric.

Heaven on Earth 1989 The story of two orphaned British children who, along with thousands of orphans shipped from England to Canada between 1867 and 1914, try to make new lives in the Canadian wilderness. **101m/C VHS.** *CA* R.H. Thomson, Sian Leisa Davies, Torquil Campbell, Fiona Reid; ***D:*** Allen Kroeker; ***W:*** Margaret Atwood.

Heaven or Vegas 1998 (R) Rachel (Bleeth) is a part-time Vegas prostitute who falls for gigolo Navy (Grieco), who offers her a new life with him in Montana. But first Rachel wants to visit the home she ran away from years before. Too bad Rachel's sister Lilli starts making eyes at her man and when Navy appears interested, Rachel runs away again. Can Navy find her and convince Rachel he loves only her? It's a modern-day fairytale so what do you think? **110m/C VHS.** Yasmine Bleeth, Richard Grieco; ***D:*** Gregory C. Haynes; ***W:*** Gregory C. Haynes. VIDEO

Heaven Tonight 1993 (R) Ex-rock star dad copes with midlife crisis by trying for his big comeback, this time with his son. **97m/C VHS.** *AU* John Waters, Rebecca Gilling, Guy Pearce, Kim Gyngell; ***D:*** Pino Amenta; ***C:*** David Connell.

Heavenly Bodies woof! 1984 (R) A young woman who dreams of owning a health club will stop at nothing to accomplish her goals. When a rival tries to put her out of business, a "dance-down" takes place in this lame low-budget aerobics musical. **99m/C VHS.** *CA* Cynthia Dale, Richard Rebrere, Laura Henry, Stuart Stone, Walter George Alton, Cec Linder; ***D:*** Lawrence Dane; ***W:*** Lawrence Dane, Ron Base; ***C:*** Thomas Burstyn.

Heavenly Creatures 1994 (R) Haunting and surreal drama chronicles the true-life case of two young schoolgirls, Pauline and Juliet, who were charged with clubbing to death Pauline's mother in Christchurch, New Zealand, in 1954. Opens two years before the murder, and follows the friendship as the two teens become obsessed with each other, retreating into a rich fantasy life. They create an elaborate, medieval kingdom where they escape to their dream lovers and romantic alter egos. Elaborate morphing and animation effects vividly express the shared inner fantasy world, while innovative camera work creates the sensations of hysteria and excitement that the girls experience as their infatuation becomes uncontrollable. Leads Lynsky and Winslet are convincing as the awkward, quiet Pauline and the pretty, intelligent, upper class Juliet. Bizarre crime story is stylish and eerily compelling, and made more so by real life events: after the film was released, mystery writer Anne Perry was revealed as Juliet Hulme. **110m/C VHS.** *NZ* Melanie Lynskey, Kate Winslet, Sarah Pierse, Diana Kent, Clive Merrison, Simon O'Connor; ***D:*** Peter Jackson; ***W:*** Peter Jackson, Frances Walsh; ***C:*** Alun Bollinger; ***M:*** Peter Dasent.

The Heavenly Kid 1985 (PG-13) Leather-jacketed "cool" guy who died in a '60s hot rod crash finally receives an offer to exit limbo and enter heaven. The deal requires that he educate his dull earthly son on more hip and worldly ways. A big problem is that the soundtrack and wardrobe are 1955, whereas the cocky cool greaser supposedly died 17 years ago in 1968. Mildly entertaining. **92m/C VHS.** Lewis Smith, Jane Kaczmarek, Jason Gedrick, Richard Mulligan; ***D:*** Cary Medoway; ***W:*** Cary Medoway, Martin Copeland.

Heaven's a Drag *To Die For* 1994 Low-budget British cross between a tearjerker and a supernatural comedy. HIV-positive London drag performer Mark (Williams) lives with Simon (Arklie), a TV repairman who keeps his sexuality a secret from his co-workers and his emotional distance from his stricken lover. When Mark dies, Simon is quick to get on with his life—too quick for Mark, who's ghostly presence puts a damper on Simon's dating possibilities and brings up some old resentments. **96m/C VHS.** *GB* Thomas Arklie, Ian Patrick Williams, Dilly Keane, Tony Slattery, Jean Boht, John Altman; ***D:*** Peter MacKenzie Litten; ***W:*** Johnny Byrne; ***C:*** John Ward; ***Nar:*** Ian McKellen.

Heavens Above 1963 A sharp, biting satire on cleric life in England. Sellers stars as the quiet, down-to-earth reverend who is appointed to a new post in space. **113m/B VHS.** *GB* Peter Sellers, Cecil Parker, Isabel Jeans, Eric Sykes, Ian Carmichael; ***D:*** John Boulting, Roy Boulting; ***M:*** Richard Rodney Bennett.

Heaven's Burning 1997 (R) Fast-paced road movie with some unexpected twists. Midori (Kudoh) is a young Japanese woman who is honeymooning in Sydney with new hubby Yukio (Isomura). But Midori fakes her own kidnapping to wait for her lover to arrive (who doesn't show). Yukio and the cops quickly discover her plotting but, in the meantime, Midori's been caught up in the midst of a bank robbery. When the robbery goes wrong, she becomes the quai-hostage of driver Colin (Crowe), who takes off across Australia, pursued by the cops, his ex-partners, and the humiliated husband who wants revenge. Midori and Colin bond and things get increasingly stranger. **96m/C VHS, DVD, Wide.** *AU* Youki Kudoh, Russell Crowe, Kenji Isomura, Ray Barrett, Robert Mammone, Petru Gheorghiu, Matthew Dyktynski, Anthony Phelan, Colin Hay, Susan Prior, Norman Kaye; ***D:*** Craig Lahiff; ***W:*** Louis Nowra; ***C:*** Brian J. Breheny; ***M:*** Michael Atkinson.

Heaven's Fire 1999 Dean (Roberts) finds himself trying to prevent former co-worker Quentin (Prochnow) from stealing U.S. currency engraving plates from the treasury building. Dean foils the getaway but the crooks (and a group of tourists) are trapped in the building by a couple of explosions. So Dean then tries to protect the innocent while keeping Quentin at bay. **91m/C VHS, DVD.** Eric Roberts, Juergen Prochnow, Cali Timmins; ***D:*** David Warry-Smith; ***W:*** Rob Kerchner, Charles Philip Moore; ***C:*** Gordon Verheul; ***M:*** Deddy Tzur. CABLE

Heaven's Gate 1981 (R) The uncut version of Cimino's notorious folly. A fascinating, plotless, and exaggerated account of the Johnson County cattle war of the 1880s. Ravishingly photographed, the film's production almost single-handedly put United Artists out of business. **220m/C VHS, DVD, Wide.** Kris Kristofferson, Christopher Walken, Isabelle Huppert, John Hurt, Richard Masur, Mickey Rourke, Brad Dourif, Joseph Cotten, Jeff Bridges, Sam Waterston, Terry O'Quinn, Geoffrey Lewis; ***D:*** Michael Cimino; ***W:*** Michael Cimino; ***C:*** Vilmos Zsigmond. Golden Raspberries '81: Worst Director (Cimino).

Heaven's Heroes 1987 Dennis Hill, a dedicated policeman, was killed in the line of duty on August 27, 1977. This film recalls his life and deep faith in Jesus. **72m/C VHS.** David Ralphe, Heidi Vaughn, James O'Hagen; ***D:*** Donald W. Thompson.

Heaven's Prisoners 1995 (R) Dave Robicheaux (Baldwin) is an ex-New Orleans homicide detective and recovering alcoholic, living a quiet life on a bayou with patient wife Annie (Lynch). They witness a plane crash and Dave rescues the only survivor, a young Salvadoran girl, whom they adopt. But the crash wasn't an accident and Dave's snooping around involves him with drug runners and local crime bosses, including old high school buddy, Bubba Rocque (Roberts), and his sirenish wife, Claudette (Hatcher). Convoluted plot with some moody touches but Baldwin scores as the flawed hero. Based on the mystery series by James Lee Burke. **135m/C VHS.** Paul Guilfoyle, Alec Baldwin, Kelly Lynch, Mary Stuart Masterson, Eric Roberts, Teri Hatcher, Vondie Curtis-Hall, Badja (Medu) Djola, Joe (Johnny) Viterelli, Hawthorne James; *D:* Phil Joanou; *W:* Scott Frank, Harley Peyton; *C:* Harris Savides; *M:* George Fenton.

Heavy ♂♂♂ **1994 (R)** Sensitive character study supported by an excellent ensemble, led by Vince as Victor, an obese, painfully withdrawn, 30-ish cook. He lives with his domineering mother (a subdued Winters) and helps her run their roadside diner, along with veteran waitress Delores (Harry). Then beautiful teenager Callie (Tyler) is hired and Victor develops a suitably massive crush. Tyler is all pout and promise as Callie, making it clear why a guy like Victor could fall hard for her. Harry brings a rich cynical and sexual edge to Delores. Director Mangold's feature debut is both eloquent and economical, though at times paced to a near stand-still. **104m/C VHS.** Pruitt Taylor Vince, Shelley Winters, Liv Tyler, Deborah Harry, Evan Dando, Joe Grifasi; *D:* James Mangold; *W:* James Mangold; *C:* Michael Barrow; *M:* Thurston Moore. Sundance '95: Special Jury Prize.

Heavy Metal ♂♂♂ **1981 (R)** Yes, the animated cult flick is now legally available on video, its copyright disputes finally resolved. A collection of science-fiction and fantasy stories, inspired by the same-titled magazine and offered in a variety of graphic styles, that all encompass the theme of good versus evil. And don't always bet on the good. Features a soundtrack compiled from the work of many top metal artists of the time as well as Bernstein's score with the London Philharmonic Orchestra. A three-minute transitional segment, called "Neverwhere Land," that was cut from the original version has been restored as an epilogue. **90m/C VHS, DVD, Wide.** *CA D:* Gerald Potterton; *W:* Dan Goldberg, Len Blum; *C:* Brian Tufano; *M:* Elmer Bernstein; *V:* John Candy, Joe Flaherty, Don Francks, Eugene Levy, Rodger Bumpass, Jackie Burroughs, Harold Ramis, Richard Romanus, Doug Kenney.

Heavy Metal 2000 ♂½ **2000 (R)** The original 1981 film was cutting edge but this video game-ish sequel is average at best. Warrior babe Julie is tracking a group of space pirates, led by villain Lord Tyler, who destroyed her home and forced her sister into slavery. Julie assumes a new name, F.A.K.K. (Federation Assigned Ketogenic Killzone), and the usual avenger mission. **88m/C VHS, DVD, Wide.** *D:* Michael Coldewey, Michel Lemire; *W:* Robert Payne Cabeen; *C:* Bruno Philip; *M:* Frederic Talgorn; *V:* Julie Strain, Michael Ironside, Billy Idol, Sonja Ball.

Heavy Petting ♂♂½ **1989** A hilarious compilation of "love scene" footage from feature films of the silent era to the '60s, newsreels, news reports, educational films, old TV shows, and home movies. **75m/C VHS.** David Byrne, Josh Mostel, Sandra Bernhard, Allen Ginsberg, Ann Magnuson, Spalding Gray, Laurie Anderson, John Oates, Abbie Hoffman, Jacki Ochs; *D:* Obie Benz; *C:* Sandi Sissel.

Heavy Traffic ♂♂♂ **1973** Ralph Bakshi's animated fantasy portrait of the hard-edged underside of city life. A young cartoonist draws the people, places, and paranoia of his environment. **77m/C VHS, DVD.** Joseph Kaufmann, Beverly Hope Atkinson, Michael Brandon, Frank DeKova, Terri Haven, Mary Dean Lauria, Lillian Adams, Jamie Farr, Robert Easton; *D:* Ralph Bakshi; *W:* Ralph Bakshi; *C:* Ted C. Bemiller, Gregg Heschong; *M:* Ed Bogas.

Heavyweights ♂ **1994 (PG)** A product of Disney's sometimes assembly line approach to family entertainment (think "Mighty Ducks"). Nothing new saga of overweight youngsters sent to a fat camp run by tyrannical fitness guru Tony Perkis (Stiller). His methods cause the kids to band together and overthrow him and his "evil" tactics. Oh, by the way, there's a baseball competition with the more athletic camp kids on the other side of the lake. Guess who wins. Stiller as the fame obsessed fitness fanatic, sporting a David Copperfield make-over, is the only highlight in this exercise of excess fluff. Directorial debut of Brill. **98m/C VHS.** Jeffrey Tambor, Ben Stiller, Jerry Stiller, Anne Meara, Shaun Weiss, Kenan Thompson; *D:* Steven Brill; *W:* Judd Apatow, Steven Brill; *C:* Victor Hammer; *M:* J.A.C. Redford.

Heck's Way Home ♂♂½ **1995** Heck is the Neufeld family dog and best friend of 11-year-old Luke (Krowchuk). The family is moving from Winnipeg to Australia and have a three-day layover in Vancouver. Heck is supposed to come along but instead, unbeknownst to the family, he gets captured by the local dogcatcher (Arkin) and the family are forced to leave without him. Naturally, Heck escapes and starts off on a 2000-mile journey to find his family before they fly away forever. **92m/C VHS, DVD.** Chad Krowchuk, Alan Arkin, Michael Riley, Shannon Lawson; *D:* Michael Scott; *C:* Maris Jansons. **CABLE**

Hedd Wyn ♂♂ **1992** True story of talented young poet Ellis Evans (Garmon), writing under the pseudonym Hedd Wyn, who dreams of winning a coveted literary prize. His hopes are put on hold when he's forced to fight in WWI, although he submits his antiwar poem "The Hero" to the competition. Welsh with subtitles. **123m/C VHS.** *GB* Huw Garmon, Catrin Fychan, Ceri Cunnington, Llio Silyn; *D:* Paul Turner; *W:* Alan Llwyd; *C:* Ray Orton; *M:* John E.R. Hardy.

Hedda ♂♂½ **1975** A dramatization of the Henrik Ibsen play, "Hedda Gabler," about a middle-class pregnant woman. The story finds her frustrated with her life and manipulating those around her with tragic results. **102m/C VHS.** *GB* Glenda Jackson, Peter Eyre, Timothy West, Jennie Linden, Patrick Stewart; *D:* Trevor Nunn.

Hedwig and the Angry Inch ♂♂♂ **2000 (R)** Creator-star Mitchell adapted and directed his Off Broadway stage rock musical along with composer-lyricist Trask (who's also in the film) and opened up his gender-bending '70s kitsch fantasy. Hedwig was once Hansel, an East Berlin boy, whose sex-change operation was botched and who was abandoned in a Kansas trailer park by her G.I. husband. Betrayed in love by teenaged boy toy Tommy (Pitt), who also steals Hedwig's songs, Hedwig and her band embark on a low-rent tour while Hedwig sings her life story to the disinterested and stalks a much-more successful Tommy. **95m/C VHS, DVD, Wide.** *US* John Cameron Mitchell, Michael Pitt, Andrea Martin, Miriam Shor, Alberta Watson, Maurice Dean Wint, Rob Campbell, Stephen Trask, Theodore Liscinski, Michael Aranov; *D:* John Cameron Mitchell; *W:* John Cameron Mitchell; *C:* Frank DeMarco; *M:* Stephen Trask.

Heidi ♂♂½ **1937** Johanna Spyri's classic tale puts Shirley Temple in the hands of a mean governess and the loving arms of her Swiss grandfather. Also available colorized. Remade in 1967. **88m/B VHS, DVD.** Shirley Temple, Jean Hersholt, Helen Westley, Arthur Treacher, Sidney Blackmer, Marcia Mae Jones, Mary Nash; *D:* Allan Dwan; *W:* Walter Ferris; *C:* Arthur C. Miller; *M:* Julien Josephson.

Heidi ♂♂½ **1952** The Swiss do their own version of the children's classic by Johanna Spyri. A precocious little girl enjoys life in the Swiss Alps with her grandfather, until her stern aunt takes her away to live in the village in the valley. **98m/B VHS.** *SI* Elsbeth Sigmund, Heinrich Gretler, Thomas Klameth, Elsie Attenoff; *D:* Luigi Comencini.

Heidi ♂♂♂ **1965** The classic story from Johanna Spyri's novel is filmed beautifully in the Swiss Alps in Eastmancolor. Heidi is kidnapped by her mean aunt and forced to work as a slave for a rich family. Her kindly old grandfather comes to her rescue. Family entertainment for all, dubbed in English. **95m/C VHS.** *AT GE* Eva Maria Singhammer, Gustav Knuth, Lotte Ledl; *D:* Werner Jacobs.

Heidi ♂♂ **1967** The second American adaptation of the classic Johanna Spyri novel tells the story of an orphaned girl who goes to the Swiss Alps to live with her grandfather. **100m/C VHS, DVD.** Maximilian Schell, Jennifer Edwards, Michael Redgrave, Jean Simmons; *D:* Delbert Mann; *W:* Earl Hamner; *M:* John Williams. **TV**

Heidi ♂♂♂ **1993 (G)** Yet another version of the children's classic, from German writer Johanna Spyri's 1881 novel. Thornton is charming as the orphan shuttled from relative to relative until she happily ends up with her crotchety grandfather (Robards) in his mountain cabin. Then her cousin comes along and whisks her off to the city to be a companion to the invalid Klara (Randall). Seymour is the snobbish, scowling governess. This "Heidi" is spunky enough to keep the sugar level tolerable. Filmed on location in Austria. **167m/C VHS.** Noley Thornton, Jason Robards Jr., Jane Seymour, Lexi (Faith) Randall, Sian Phillips, Patricia Neal, Benjamin Brazier, Michael Simkins, Andrew Bicknell, Jane Hazlegrove; *D:* Michael Rhodes; *W:* Jeanne Rosenberg; *M:* Lee Holdridge. **TV**

The Heidi Chronicles ♂♂½ **1995** Some 25 years of boomer angst and friendship are covered in this cable adaptation of Wasserstein's 1988 Pulitzer Prize-winning play. Heidi Holland (Curtis) goes from prep school to Vassar to an art history career while searching for self-fulfillment, feminist ideals, and some romance along the way. The romance is on-and-off, thanks to caddish journalist Scoop (Friedman), but Heidi can always depend on soul mate, gay pediatrician Peter (Hulce), and Susan (Cattrall), her follow-the-fads confidante. Heidi's sometimes too morose for her own good but you won't mind spending a couple of hours in her company. **94m/C VHS.** Jamie Lee Curtis, Tom Hulce, Kim Cattrall, Peter Friedman, Eve Gordon, Shari Belafonte, Sharon Lawrence, Julie White, Debra Eisenstadt, Roma Maffia; *D:* Paul Bogart; *W:* Wendy Wasserstein; *C:* Isidore Mankofsky; *M:* David Shire.

Height of the Sky ♂♂½ **1999** In rural Arkansas, 1935, the poor Jones family farms a small plot of land, which they rent from the rich Caldwells. When Gabriel Jones (Moninger) succumbs to tuberculosis, family patriarch Wendel Jones (Stewart) decides to hide Gabriel in an old cabin thereby leaving the strong-willed Leora (Weedon) in charge of the family. Jennifer must convince Mr. Caldwell (Palazzo) that all is well on their farm while she covers for her father's absence. Written and directed by Lyn Clinton, cousin of President Bill Clinton. **116m/C DVD, Wide.** Grant Moninger, Evan Palazzo, Jackie Stewart, Jennifer Weedon; *D:* Lyn Clinton; *W:* Lyn Clinton; *C:* John R. Zilles; *M:* Boris Zelkin.

Heimat **1** *Heimat-Eine deutsche Chronik* **1984** Sixteen-hour series follows the lives, loves, and tragedies of the German Simon family from the end of WWI to 1982. Based on Reitz's own family and his childhood. Shot over two years, the series has 28 lead performances and more than 140 speaking roles. German with subtitles; boxed 9-tape set. **924m/C VHS.** *GE* Marita Breuer; *D:* Edgar Reitz; *W:* Edgar Reitz, Peter F. Steinbach; *C:* Gernot Roll; *M:* Nikos Mamangakis.

Heimat 2 **198?** The continuation of the saga is composed of 25 half-hour segments and follows Hermann Simon's life in Munich from 1960 to 1970. A modernist musician and composer, Hermann falls in with a group of students, artists, and rebels. German with subtitles. **750m/C VHS.** *GE D:* Edgar Reitz.

The Heiress ♂♂♂♂½ **1949** Based on the Henry James novel "Washington Square." Catherine (de Havilland) is the plain, awkward daughter of wealthy widowed doctor Austin Sloper (Richardson), who is a belittling tyrant to his only child. Catherine has no suitors until handsome, fortune-seeking Morris Townsend (Clift) approaches her. Naturally, Dr. Sloper dismisses his interest and warns that his daughter will only end up with a broken heart. No happy endings here but the performances are superb. Remade as "Washington Square" in 1997. **115m/B VHS.** Olivia de Havilland, Montgomery Clift, Ralph Richardson, Miriam Hopkins, Vanessa Brown, Mona Freeman, Ray Collins, Selena Royle; *D:* William Wyler; *W:* Ruth Goetz, Augustus Goetz; *C:* Leo Tover; *M:* Aaron Copland. Oscars '49: Actress (de Havilland), Art Dir./Set Dec., B&W, Costume Des. (B&W), Orig. Dramatic Score; Golden Globes '50: Actress—Drama (de Havilland); Natl. Bd. of Review '49: Actor (Richardson), Natl. Film Reg. '96;; N.Y. Film Critics '49: Actress (de Havilland).

The Heist ♂♂ **1989** An ex-con, upon regaining his freedom, sets out to rip off the crook who framed him. Entertaining enough story with a first-rate cast. **97m/C VHS.** Pierce Brosnan, Tom Skerritt, Wendy Hughes; *D:* Stuart Orme. **CABLE**

The Heist ♂♂ *Hostile Force* **1996** Con artist plots the hijacking of a transport company's fleet and starts out by taking the firm's employees hostage. But one of the workers is an ex-cop who failed once to stop a robbery and is not about to fail again. **99m/C VHS, DVD.** *GE* Hannes Jaenicke, Cali Timmins, Andrew McCarthy, Cynthia Geary, Wolf Larson; *D:* Michael Kennedy; *W:* Michael January; *C:* Bruce Worrall. **TV**

Heist ♂♂♂ **2001 (R)** Hackman is Joe, a master thief who's planning to retire after his latest job, but fence Bergman (DeVito) has other ideas, holding Joe's payoff until he agrees to a big-time gold heist. And just to make things interesting, Bergman sends his nephew Silk (Rockwell) along. This complicates things even more, especially with Joe's wife, Fran (Pidgeon). In classic Mamet fashion, doublecrosses, plot twists, misdirection, great dialogue and perfect casting convene to create an excellent caper film. Lindo and Jay add plenty of spark as Joe's loyal crew members. **107m/C VHS, DVD, Wide.** *US* Gene Hackman, Danny DeVito, Delroy Lindo, Sam Rockwell, Rebecca Pidgeon, Ricky Jay, Patti LuPone, Jim Frangione; *D:* David Mamet; *W:* David Mamet; *C:* Robert Elswit; *M:* Theodore Shapiro.

Helas pour Moi ♂♂ *Oh Woe is Me* **1994** Perplexing, contemplative film on faith and love—and maybe a miracle. Told in flashback, publisher Alexander Klimt (Verley) travels to a Swiss lakeside town where it's rumored that the beautiful Rachel Donnadieu (Masliah) has been "visited" by God, who wishes to experience the pleasures of love, in the form of her own husband, simple fisherman Simon (Depardieu). Story is derived from the Greek myth concerning Zeus, who seduced Alcmene in the shape of her husband Amphitryon. French with subtitles. **84m/C VHS.** *FR SI* Gerard Depardieu, Laurence Masliah, Bernard Verley; *D:* Jean-Luc Godard; *W:* Jean-Luc Godard; *C:* Caroline Champetier.

Held for Murder ♂ *Her Mad Night* **1932** When a vacationing daughter is accused of murder, her mom lovingly takes the blame. Will the daughter come back to clear her mom, or will she let her fry in the electric chair? **67m/B VHS.** Irene Rich, Conway Tearle, Mary Carlisle, Kenneth Thomson, William B. Davidson; *D:* E. Mason Hopper.

Held Hostage ♂♂ **1991** The true story of Jerry Levin, a reporter kidnapped by terrorists while on assignment in Beirut, and his wife, Sis, who struggled with the State Department for his release. **95m/C VHS.** Marlo Thomas, David Dukes, G.W. Bailey, Edward Winter, Robert Harper, William Schallert; *D:* Roger Young. **TV**

Held Up ♂½ *Inconvenienced* **2000 (PG-13)** Engaged couple Foxx and Long are having a hard time staying together when after they have a fight and Foxx becomes a hostage during a botched convenience store robbery in a sleepy southwestern town. Broad comedy works in all the black-guy-meets-white-yokels gags, but they've all been done before by funnier writers. Foxx has some appeal, but not enough to overcome this mess. It could've been worse: Rob Schneider bailed after four days of filming. **88m/C VHS, DVD, Wide.** Jamie Foxx, Nia Long, Jake Busey, John Cullum, Barry Corbin, Eduardo Yanez, Mike Wiles, Sarah Paulson, Julie Hagerty; *D:* Steve Rash; *W:* Jeff Eastin; *C:* David Makin; *M:* Robert Folk.

Helen of Troy ♂½ **1956** Mythological fantasy finds Helen (Podesta), the beautiful daughter of Zeus, falling in love with Trojan prince Paris (Sernas)—an event that leads to the siege of Troy. Ignores script for lavish effects. Video includes behind-the-scenes footage. **135m/C**

VHS. Rossana Podesta, Jacques Sernas, Cedric Hardwicke, Stanley Baker, Niall MacGinnis, Nora Swinburne, Robert Douglas, Torin Thatcher, Harry Andrews, Janette Scott, Ronald Lewis, Brigitte Bardot; *D:* Robert Wise; *W:* John Twist, N. Richard Nash; *C:* Harry Stradling Sr.; *M:* Max Steiner.

Hell Comes to Frogtown 🦴 1988 (R) In a post-nuclear holocaust land run by giant frogs, a renegade who is one of the few non-sterile men left on earth must rescue some fertile women and impregnate them. Sci-fi spoof is extremely low-budget, but fun. Stars "Rowdy" Roddy Piper of wrestling fame. **88m/C VHS, DVD, Wide.** Roddy Piper, Sandahl Bergman, Rory Calhoun, Donald G. Jackson, Cec Verrell; *D:* Robert J. Kizer, Donald G. Jackson; *W:* Randall Frakes; *C:* Donald G. Jackson.

Hell Commandos 🦴½ 1969 Soldiers in WWII struggle to prevent the Nazis from releasing a deadly bacteria that will kill millions. Dubbed. **92m/C VHS.** *IT* Guy Madison, Stan Cooper; *D:* Jose Luis Merino.

Hell Fire Austin 🦴½ 1932 Maynard finds himself mixed up with outlaws in the Old West. **60m/B VHS.** Ken Maynard, Nat Pendleton, Jack Perrin; *D:* Forrest Sheldon.

Hell Harbor 🦴🦴 1930 Caribbean love, murder and greed combine to make this early talkie. Exterior shots were filmed on the west coast of Florida and the beauty of the Tampa area in the 1930s is definitely something to see. **65m/B VHS.** Lupe Velez, Gibson Gowland, Jean Hersholt, John Holland; *D:* Henry King.

Hell High 🦴 1986 (R) Four high schoolers plan a night of torture and humiliation for an annoying teacher, only to find she has some deadly secrets of her own. Dumber than it sounds. **84m/C VHS.** Christopher Stryker, Christopher Cousins, Millie Prezioso, Jason Brill; *D:* Douglas Grossman.

Hell Hounds of Alaska 🦴 1973 (G) The Yukon, Yugoslav-style. European co-production goes back to the Gold Rush days for an adventure about a frontiersman tracking down a stolen shipment of the precious ore while trying to save the life of an injured boy. **90m/C VHS.** Doug McClure, Harald Leipnitz, Angelica Ott; *D:* Harald Reinl.

Hell Hunters 🦴 1987 Nazi-hunters foil the plot of an old German doctor to poison the population of L.A. Meanwhile, a daughter avenges the death of her mother by blowing up the doctor's jungle compound. **98m/C VHS.** Stewart Granger, Maud Adams, George Lazenby, Candice Daly, Romulo Arantes, William Berger.

Hell in the Pacific 🦴🦴🦴 1969 (PG) A marvelously photographed (by Conrad Hall) psycho/macho allegory, about an American and a Japanese soldier stranded together on a tiny island and the mini-war they fight all by themselves. Overly obvious anti-war statement done with style. **101m/C VHS, DVD.** Lee Marvin, Toshiro Mifune; *D:* John Boorman; *W:* Eric Bercovici, Alexander Jacobs; *C:* Conrad L. Hall; *M:* Lalo Schifrin.

Hell Is for Heroes 🦴🦴🦴½ 1962 McQueen stars as the bitter leader of a small infantry squad outmanned by the Germans in this tight WWII drama. A strong cast and riveting climax make this a must for action fans. **90m/B VHS, DVD, Wide.** Steve McQueen, Bobby Darin, Fess Parker, Harry Guardino, James Coburn, Mike Kellin, Nick Adams, Bob Newhart, L.Q. (Justus E. McQueen) Jones, Don Haggerty, Joseph Hoover, Michele Montau, Bill Mullikin; *D:* Donald Siegel; *W:* Robert Pirosh, Richard Carr; *C:* Harold Lipstein; *M:* Leonard Rosenman.

Hell Night woof! 1981 (R) Several young people must spend the night in a mysterious mansion as part of their initiation into Alpha Sigma Rho fraternity in this extremely dull low-budget horror flick. **100m/C VHS, DVD.** Linda Blair, Vincent Van Patten, Kevin Brophy, Peter Barton, Jenny Neumann; *D:* Tom De Simone; *W:* Randy Feldman; *C:* Mac Ahlberg; *M:* Danny Wyman.

Hell of the Living Dead woof! *Apocalipsis Canibal; Night of the Zombies; Zombie Creeping Flesh* 1983 Staff of a scientific research center are killed and then resurrected as cannibals who prey on the living. The living will suffer again if trapped into watching. Mattel is pseudonym for director Vincent Dawn. Cheap, dubbed, and possessing minimal coherence. **103m/C VHS, DVD, Wide.** *IT SP* Margit Evelyn Newton, Frank Garfield, Selan Karay; *D:* Bruno Mattei; *W:* J.M. Cunilles, Claudio Fragasso; *C:* John Cabrera.

Hell on Frisco Bay 🦴🦴½ 1955 An ex-waterfront cop, falsely imprisoned for manslaughter, sets out to clear his name. His quest finds him taking on the Mob, in this '30s-style gangster film. Good performances all around, especially Robinson, who steals every scene he's in. **93m/C VHS.** Alan Ladd, Edward G. Robinson, Joanne Dru, Fay Wray, William Demarest, Jayne Mansfield; *D:* Frank Tuttle; *M:* Max Steiner.

Hell on the Battleground 🦴½ 1988 (R) Group of inexperienced recruits are led into combat by two battle-hardened veterans. Their only hope for survival is a counterattack by U.S. tanks. **91m/C VHS.** William Smith, Ted Prior, Fritz Matthews; *D:* David A. Prior; *W:* David A. Prior.

Hell on Wheels 🦴🦴 1967 Two successful brothers in the racing industry are torn apart by the same girl. Brotherly love diminishes into a hatred so deep that murder becomes the sole purpose of both. **96m/C VHS.** Marty Robbins, Jennifer Ashley, John Ashley, Gigi Perreau, Robert Dornan, Connie Smith, Frank Gerstle; *D:* Will Zens.

Hell Raiders 🦴½ 1968 A force invades a supposedly defenseless Pacific island, and finds itself fiercely attacked. **90m/C VHS.** John Agar, Richard Webb, Joan Huntington; *D:* Larry Buchanan.

Hell River 🦴🦴 1975 (PG) In 1941 Yugoslavia, Yugoslav partisans and Nazis battle it out at a place called Hell River. **100m/C VHS.** Rod Taylor, Adam West; *D:* Stole Jankovic.

Hell-Ship Morgan 🦴🦴½ 1936 Bancroft is a womanizing tuna boat captain who falls for and marries Sothern. When they set up married life on the boat, she starts eyeing first mate Jory. And Bancroft finds out. **65m/B VHS.** George Bancroft, Ann Sothern, Victor Jory, George Regas, Howard Hickman, Ralph Byrd; *D:* David Ross Lederman.

Hell Ship Mutiny 🦴½ 1957 Man comes to the aid of a lovely island princess, whose people have been forced to hand over their pearls to a pair of ruthless smugglers. Excellent cast in an unfortunately tepid production. **66m/B VHS.** Jon Hall, John Carradine, Peter Lorre, Roberta Haynes, Mike Mazurki, Stanley Adams; *D:* Lee Sholem, Elmo Williams.

Hell Squad 🦴½ 1958 Lost in North Africa during WWII, five American GIs wander through the desert. They find numerous pitfalls and unexpected help. Overall, dismal and disappointing. **64m/B VHS.** Wally Campo, Brandon Carroll; *D:* Burt Topper.

Hell Squad 🦴 1985 (R) Unable to release his son from the Middle Eastern terrorists who kidnapped him, a U.S. ambassador turns to the services of nine Las Vegas showgirls. These gals moonlight as vicious commandos in this low-budget action film with skin. **88m/C VHS.** Bainbridge Scott, Glen Hartford, Tina Lederman; *D:* Kenneth Hartford; *W:* Kenneth Hartford; *M:* Charles P. Barnett.

Hell to Eternity 🦴🦴½ 1960 The true story of how WWII hero Guy Gabaldon persuaded 2,000 Japanese soldiers to surrender. Features several spectacular scenes. **132m/B VHS.** Jeffrey Hunter, Sessue Hayakawa, David Janssen, Vic Damone, Patricia Owens; *D:* Phil Karlson.

Hell Up in Harlem woof! 1973 (R) A black crime lord recuperates from an assassination attempt and tries to regain his power. Poor sequel to the decent film "Black Caesar." **98m/C VHS, DVD, Wide.** Fred Williamson, Julius W. Harris, Margaret Avery, Gerald Gordon, Gloria Hendry; *D:* Larry Cohen; *W:* Larry Cohen; *C:* Fenton Hamilton; *M:* Fonce Mizell, Freddie Perren.

Hellbenders 🦴½ *Il Crudeli; Los Despiadados* 1967 (PG) A confederate veteran robs a Union train and must fight through acres of Civil War adversity. Dubbed. Poorly directed and acted. **92m/C VHS.** *IT SP* Joseph Cotten, Norma Bengell, Julian Mateos; *D:* Sergio Corbucci; *M:* Ennio Morricone.

Hellbent 1990 A crazed musician and a revenge-obsessed housewife embark on an unusual adventure that challenges their very sanity. **90m/C VHS.** Phil Ward, Lynn Levand, Cheryl Slean, David Marciano; *D:* Richard Casey; *W:* Richard Casey.

Hellblock 13 1997 Anthology of three low-budget short horror tales is told with grainy, raw-edged energy and a distinct regional flavor. Tara (Rochon) writes stories while she's on Death Row and shows them to her stolid guard (Hansen, "Leatherface" from "Texas Chainsaw Massacre"). Rochon brings a welcome note of humor to what might have been your basic madwoman stereotype. The individual films get better and funnier as they go along. **91m/C VHS, DVD.** Debbie Rochon, Gunnar Hansen, J.J. North, Jennifer Peluso, David G. Holland; *D:* Paul Talbot; *W:* Paul Talbot, Jeff Miller, Michael R. Smith.

Hellbound 🦴🦴½ 1994 (R) Prosatanos (Neame), a powerful 12th-century wizard, is imprisoned and the source of his power (a scepter) is supposedly destroyed. Fast-forward several hundred years when Prosatanos manages to free himself and seek out the pieces of his scepter. Which happens to lead him to Chicago and a couple of unsuspecting cops (Norris, Levels). **95m/C VHS.** Chuck Norris, Christopher Neame, Calvin Levels, Sheree J. Wilson; *D:* Aaron Norris.

Hellbound: Hellraiser 2 🦴🦴 *Hellraiser 2* 1988 (R) In this, the first sequel to Clive Barker's inter-dimensional nightmare, the traumatized daughter from the first film is pulled into the Cenobites' universe. Gore and weird imagery abound. An uncut, unrated version is also available. **96m/C VHS, DVD, Wide.** *GB* Ashley Laurence, Clare Higgins, Kenneth Cranham, Imogen Boorman, William Hope, Oliver Smith, Sean Chapman, Doug Bradley; *D:* Tony Randel; *W:* Peter Atkins; *C:* Robin Vidgeon; *M:* Christopher Young.

Hellcats woof! 1968 (R) A mob of sleazy, leather-clad female bikers terrorize small Midwestern towns in this violent girl-gang thriller. Even biker movie fans might find this one unworthy. **90m/C VHS.** Ross Hagen, Dee Duffy, Sharyn Kinzie, Sonny West, Bob Slatzer; *D:* Bob Slatzer.

Hellcats of the Navy 🦴½ 1957 Soggy true saga of the WWII mission to sever the vital link between mainland Asia and Japan. The only film that Ronald and Nancy Davis Reagan starred in together and the beginning of their grand romance. **82m/B VHS.** Ronald Reagan, Nancy Davis, Arthur Franz, Robert Arthur; *D:* Nathan (Hertz) Juran; *W:* Bernard Gordon, David Lang.

Helldorado 🦴🦴 *Heldorado* 1946 A lively western starring the singing cowboy, Roy Rogers. **54m/B VHS.** Roy Rogers, George "Gabby" Hayes, Dale Evans, Paul Harvey; *D:* William Witney.

Heller in Pink Tights 🦴🦴 1960 Offbeast western, based on a novel by Louis L'Amour, that follows the adventures of a seedy vaudeville troupe in the 1880s. Manager Tom Healy (Quinn) stays barely ahead of his creditors, with Angela (Loren) as his leading asset (and Loren's assets are the film's highlight). She dallys with gunslinger Clint Mabry (Forest), who pursues her out of town and there's an Indian attack and more gunslinging until the troupe manages to find a safe haven. The story was hardly sophisticated director Cukor's specialty, which may account for the unbelievable characters and confused plot. **100m/C VHS.** Sophia Loren, Anthony Quinn, Margaret O'Brien, Steve Forrest, Edmund Lowe, Ramon Novarro, Eileen Heckart; *D:* George Cukor; *W:* Walter Bernstein; *C:* Harold Lipstein; *M:* Daniele Amfitheatrof.

Hellfighters 🦴🦴 1968 (G) Texas oil well fire fighters experience trouble between themselves and the women they love. **121m/C VHS, DVD, Wide.** John Wayne, Katharine Ross, Jim Hutton, Vera Miles, Bruce Cabot, Jay C. Flippen; *D:* Andrew V. McLaglen; *W:* Clair Huffaker; *C:* William Clothier; *M:* Leonard Rosenman.

Hellfire 🦴🦴 1948 A gambler promises to build a church and follow the precepts of the Bible after a minister sacrifices his life for him. **90m/B VHS.** William Elliott, Marie Windsor, Forrest Tucker, Jim Davis; *D:* R.G. Springsteen.

The Hellfire Club 🦴🦴 1961 In 18th century Britain, a young man reaches adulthood and attempts to claim the estate of his father. No ordinary dad, his led the infamous Hellfire Club, an organization specializing in debauchery and depravity. His cousin challenges his claim and kidnaps his fiancee. Historical hokum, complete with swordplay. **88m/C VHS.** *GB* Keith Michell, Kai Fischer, Adrienne Corri, Peter Arne, David Lodge, Bill Owen, Peter Cushing, Francis Matthews, Desmond Walter Ellis; *D:* Robert S. Baker, Monty Berman; *W:* Jimmy Sangster.

Hellgate woof! 1989 (R) A woman hitchhiking turns out to be one of the living dead. Her benefactor lives to regret picking her up. **96m/C VHS.** Abigail Wolcott, Ron Palillo, Carel Trichardt, Petrea Curran, Evan J. Klisser, Joanne Ward; *D:* William A. Levey; *W:* Michael O'Rourke; *C:* Peter Palmer.

Hellhole 🦴 1985 (R) A young woman who witnesses her mother's murder is sent to a sanitarium where the doctors are perfecting chemical lobotomies. Extremely weak script and poor acting make this a suspenseless thriller. **93m/C VHS.** Judy Landers, Ray Sharkey, Mary Woronov, Marjoe Gortner, Edy Williams, Terry Moore, Dyanne Thorne, Lynn Borden; *D:* Pierre De Moro; *W:* Vincent Mongol; *C:* Stephen Posey; *M:* Jeff Sturges.

Hellmaster 🦴 1992 Your basic sicko mad scientist experiments on some unsuspecting college students by injecting them with an addictive drug. The drug also causes some horrifying mutations and makes its victims superhuman (but also super-ugly). Lots of gore. Creative special effects and make-up will appeal to fans of horror. **92m/C VHS.** John Saxon, David Emge, Amy Raasch; *D:* Douglas Schulze; *W:* Douglas Schulze.

Hello Again 🦴🦴 1987 (PG) The wife of a successful plastic surgeon chokes to death on a piece of chicken. A year later she returns to life, with comical consequences, but soon discovers that life won't be the same. **96m/C VHS.** Shelley Long, Corbin Bernsen, Judith Ivey, Gabriel Byrne, Sela Ward, Austin Pendleton, Carrie Nye, Robert Lewis, Madeleine Potter; *D:* Frank Perry; *M:* William Goldstein.

Hello, Dolly! 🦴🦴 1969 (G) Widow Dolly Levi, while matchmaking for her friends, finds a match for herself. Based on the hugely successful Broadway musical adapted from Thornton Wilder's play "Matchmaker." Lightweight story needs better actors with stronger characterizations. Original Broadway score helps. ♫Hello Dolly; Just Leave Everything to Me; Love is Only Love; Dancing; Walter's Gavotte; It Only Takes a Moment; Ribbons Down My Back; Elegance; It Takes a Woman. **146m/C VHS.** Barbra Streisand, Walter Matthau, Michael Crawford, Louis Armstrong, E.J. Peaker, Marianne McAndrew, Tommy Tune; *D:* Gene Kelly; *W:* Ernest Lehman; *C:* Harry Stradling Sr.; *M:* Jerry Herman. Oscars '69: Art Dir./Set Dec., Sound, Scoring/Musical.

Hello, Frisco, Hello 🦴🦴½ 1943 San Francisco's wild Barbary Coast is the setting for this romantic musical. Smoothie Payne opens up a saloon that features Faye, who's in love with him, as the star singing attraction. Unfortunately, Payne is involved with a society snob and Faye heads off to European success. When she returns, it's to a sadder and wiser man. ♫Hello, Frisco, Hello; You'll Never Know; San Francisco; Ragtime Cowboy Joe; Sweet Cider Time; Has Anybody Here Seen Kelly; King Chanticleer; When You Wore a Tulip; Strike Up the Band, Here Comes a Sailor. **98m/C VHS.** Alice Faye, John Payne, Jack Oakie, Lynn Bari, Laird Cregar, June Havoc, Ward Bond, Aubrey Mather, John Archer; *D:* H. Bruce Humberstone; *W:* Robert Ellis, Helen Logan. Oscars '43: Song ("You'll Never Know").

Hello Mary Lou: Prom Night 2 🦴½ *The Haunting of Hamilton High; Prom Night 2* 1987 (R) A sequel to the successful slasher flick, wherein a dead-for-30-years prom queen relegates the current queen to purgatory and comes back to life in order to avenge herself. Wild special effects. **97m/C VHS.** *CA* Michael Ironside, Wendy Lyon,

Justin Louis, Lisa Schrage, Richard Monette; *D:* Bruce Pittman; *W:* Ron Oliver; *C:* John Herzog.

Hello Trouble 1932 A Texas Ranger accidentally kills his friend, who was a former Ranger turned bandit, causing him to hang up his guns. **63m/C VHS.** Buck Jones, Lena Basquette, Wallace MacDonald, "Spec" (Walter) O'Donnell, Ward Bond, Frank Rice, Ruth Warren; *D:* Lambert Hillyer.

Hellraiser ☙☙½ 1987 (R) A graphic, horror fantasy about a woman who is manipulated by the monstrous spirit of her husband's dead brother. In order for the man who was also her lover to be brought back to life, she must lure and kill human prey for his sustenance. Grisly and inventive scenes keep the action fast-paced; not for the faint-hearted. **94m/C DVD, Wide.** *GB* Andrew (Andy) Robinson, Clare Higgins, Ashley Laurence, Sean Chapman, Oliver Smith, Robert Hines, Doug Bradley, Nicholas Vince, Dave Atkins; *D:* Clive Barker; *W:* Clive Barker; *C:* Robin Vidgeon; *M:* Christopher Young.

Hellraiser 3: Hell on Earth ☙☙ 1992 (R) Pinhead is back in this film based on characters created by horrormeister Clive Barker. A strange black box holds the key to sending Pinhead back to Hell and is sought by the heroine, a TV newswoman (Farrell). But Pinhead's human henchman, a nasty nightclub owner, isn't going to make things easy. Imaginative special effects and Bradley's commanding presence as Pinhead aid this shocker, which becomes unfortunately mired in excessive gore. An unrated version at 97 minutes is also available. **91m/C VHS.** Doug Bradley, Terry Farrell, Kevin Bernhardt, Paula Marshall, Ken Carpenter, Peter Boynton, Ashley Laurence; *D:* Anthony Hickox; *W:* Peter Atkins; *C:* Gerry Lively.

Hellraiser 4: Bloodline ☙ 1995 (R) You can't keep a bad Pinhead in Hell, as this unfortunate sequel demonstrates. Bradley reprises his role as the big bad S&M pincushion in the latest and supposedly last installment of Clive Barker's blood drenched series. Tracing the origin of the infernal Rubik's Cube that releases Pinhead, the plot jumps between 18th century France, present day New York, and a 22nd century space station. Along the way, the Pointy One gets to flay, skewer, and impale to his evil heart's content. Special f/x guru Kevin Yeagher was so embarrassed by this outing that he took his director's credit off of the picture. Bad acting, bad plot, bad complexion. **81m/C VHS.** Bruce Ramsey, Valentina Vargas, Doug Bradley, Kim Myers, Christina Harnos, Charlotte Chatton, Paul Perri, Mickey Cotrell; *D:* Alan Smithee, Kevin Yagher; *W:* Peter Atkins; *M:* Daniel Licht.

Hellraiser 5: Inferno ☙ 2000 (R) Los Angeles detective Joseph (Sheffer) wakes up one day literally in hell. In order to escape he must find the puzzle box, which is in Pinhead's possession. This one is not only boring, it's confusing, and Pinhead has little more than a cameo appearance. **99m/C VHS, DVD.** Craig Sheffer, Doug Bradley, Nicholas Turturro, James Remar, Lindsay Taylor; *D:* Scott Derrickson; *W:* Scott Derrickson, Paul Harris Boardman. VIDEO

Hellriders woof! 1984 (R) A motorcycle gang rides into a small town and subjects its residents to a reign of terror. **90m/C VHS.** Adam West, Tina Louise.

Hell's Angels ☙☙☙ 1930 Classic WWI aviation movie is sappy and a bit lumbering, but still an extravagant spectacle with awesome air scenes. Studio owner Hughes fired directors Howard Hawks and Luther Reed, spent an unprecedented $3.8 million, and was ultimately credited as director (although Whale also spent some time in the director's chair). Three years in the making, the venture cost three pilots their lives and lost a bundle. Harlow replaced Swedish Greta Nissen when sound was added and was catapulted into blond bombshelldom as a two-timing dame. And the tinted and two-color scenes—restored in 1989—came well before Ted Turner ever wielded a crayola. **135m/B VHS.** Jean Harlow, Ben Lyon, James Hall, John Darrow, Lucien Prival, Frank Clarke, Roy "Baldy" Wilson, Douglas Gilmore, Jane Winton, Evelyn Hall; *D:* Howard Hughes; *W:* Harry Behn, Howard Estabrook, Joseph Moncure March; *C:* Elmer Dyer, Harry Perry, E. Burton Steene, Dewey Wrigley, Gaetano Antonio "Tony" Gaudio; *M:* Hugo Riesenfeld.

Hell's Angels Forever 1983 (R) A revealing ride into the world of honor, violence, and undying passion for motorcycles on the road. Documentary was filmed with cooperation of the Angels. Features appearances by Willie Nelson, Jerry Garcia, Bo Diddley, Kevin Keating and Johnny Paycheck. **93m/C VHS.** Willie Nelson, Jerry Garcia, Johnny Paycheck, Bo Diddley; *D:* Richard Chase, Leon Gast, Kevin Keating.

Hell's Angels on Wheels ☙☙½ 1967 Low-budget, two-wheeled Nicholson vehicle that casts him as a gas station attendant who joins up with the Angels for a cross country trip. Laszlo Kovacs is responsible for the photography. One of the better 1960s biker films. **95m/C VHS.** Jack Nicholson, Adam Roarke, Sabrina Scharf, Jana Taylor, John Garwood, Sonny Barger, Bruno VeSota; *D:* Richard Rush; *W:* Robert W(right) Campbell; *C:* Laszlo Kovacs; *M:* Stu Phillips.

Hell's Angels '69 ☙☙ 1969 (PG) Figuring on robbing Caesar's Palace for the thrill, two wealthy brothers plot a deadly game by infiltrating the ranks of the Hell's Angels. Upon figuring out that they've been duped, the Angels seek revenge. Average biker epic filmed in Nevada features Hell's Angels Oakland chapter. **97m/C VHS.** Tom Stern, Jeremy Slate, Conny Van Dyke; *D:* Lee Madden; *W:* Tom Stern, Jeremy Slate.

Hell's Belles ☙½ *Girl in the Leather Suit* 1969 Biker has his ride stolen by a rival, who leaves a chick as payment. The two team up to get revenge, chasing the gang across the Arizona desert and picking them off one by one. **95m/C VHS.** Jeremy Slate, Adam Roarke, Jocelyn Lane, Angelique Pettyjohn, Michael Walker, William Lucking; *D:* Maury Dexter; *W:* James Gordon White, Robert McMullen; *M:* Les Baxter.

Hell's Belles woof! 1995 (R) The Devil's bored so he leaves hell for some mortal fun but in order to stay he and his henchmen must sacrifice five ladies. **90m/C VHS.** Terence Cooper, Nadine Kalmes, K.C. Kelly, Eric Liddy, Martin Howeller, Robert Mansbridge, Jeffrey Richardson; *D:* Ed Hansen; *W:* Ed Hansen, George "Buck" Flower, Simon Hartwell; *C:* Rick Lamb.

Hell's Brigade: The Final Assault woof! 1980 (PG) Low-budget, poorly acted film in which a small band of American commandos is ordered on the most dangerous and important mission of WWII. **99m/C VHS.** Jack Palance, John Douglas, Carlos Estrada; *D:* Henry Mankiewirk.

Hell's Gate ☙½ *Bad Karma* 2001 (R) Dangerous and crazy Agnes Thatcher (Kensit) believes her shrink, Dr. Trey Cambell (Muldoon), is the reincarnation of Jack the Ripper and that she was his mistress. She escapes from the looney bin and decides to eliminate Trey's family so that they can be reunited. Standard psycho-horror fare with some nudity for titillation (no pun intended). **92m/C VHS, DVD.** Patsy Kensit, Patrick Muldoon, Amy Locane, Damian Chapa; *D:* John Hough; *C:* Jacques Haitkin; *M:* Harry Manfredini. VIDEO

Hell's Headquarters ☙ 1932 A startling tale of murder and greed involving a hunt for a fortune in African ivory. **59m/B VHS.** Jack Mulhall, Barbara Weeks, Frank Mayo; *D:* Andrew L. Stone.

Hell's Hinges ☙☙ 1916 The next to last Hart western, typifying his good/bad cowboy character. This time he's a gunslinger who falls for the new preacher's sister, while the minister himself is led astray by a saloon gal. Perhaps Hart's best film. **65m/B VHS.** William S. Hart, Clara Williams, Jack Standing, Robert McKim; *D:* William S. Hart. Natl. Film Reg. '94.

Hell's House ☙☙ 1932 After his mother dies, young lad Durkin goes to the city to live with relatives, gets mixed up with moll Davis and her bootlegger boyfriend O'Brien, and is sent to a brutal reform school. Interesting primarily for early appearances by Davis and O'Brien (before he was typecast as the indefatigable good-guy). **80m/B VHS.** Junior Durkin, Pat O'Brien, Bette Davis, Frank "Junior" Coghlan, Charley Grapewin, Emma Dunn; *D:* Howard Higgin.

Hell's Kitchen NYC ☙☙½ 1997 (R) Ex-con Johnny Miles (Phifer) returns home to New York's notorious Hell's Kitchen after serving five years for a crime he did not commit, only to face grudges, guns, and the ramifications of his violent past. More or less a redemption drama, the film benefits from a good cast, especially Jolie as a revenge-driven street urchin and Arquette as her drugged-out mom. Despite the trappings of his "convict-into-street angel" role, Phifer exudes a quiet strength that never seems out of place, even when the action gets hysterical. Director Cinciripini scores points in creating scenes of drug addiction that invoke a kind of horrific absurdity, guiding seemingly over-the-top moments with a sure hand and a rock-solid purpose. It's in the more preachy aspects of his script where he loses control, the rising saccharine quotient potentially diluting the potency of his worthwhile message. **101m/C DVD.** Rosanna Arquette, William Forsythe, Michael Spiller, Angelina Jolie, Mekhi Phifer; *D:* Tony Cinciripini; *W:* Tony Cinciripini; *C:* Derek Wiesehahn; *M:* Tony Cinciripini, Nat Robinson.

The Hellstrom Chronicle ☙☙☙ 1971 (G) A powerful quasi-documentary about insects, their formidable capacity for survival, and the conjectured battle man will have with them in the future. **90m/C VHS.** Lawrence Pressman; *D:* Walon Green; *W:* David Seltzer. Oscars '71: Feature Doc.

Helltown ☙½ *Born to the West* 1938 A western programmer based on Zane Grey's novel in which Wayne tracks down a cattle rustler. **60m/B VHS, DVD.** John Wayne, Marsha Hunt, Johnny Mack Brown, Monte Blue, Syd Saylor, John D. Patterson; *D:* Charles T. Barton; *W:* Stuart Anthony, Robert Yost; *C:* Devereaux Jennings.

Help! ☙☙☙ *Eight Arms to Hold You* 1965 (G) Ringo's ruby ring is the object of a search by Arab cult members Clang (McKern) and Ahme (Bron) who chase the Fab Four all over the globe in order to acquire the bauble. A crazy scientist (Spinelli) and his assistant (Kinnear) also want the ring and join in the pursuit. ♫Help!; You're Gonna Lose That Girl; You've Got to Hide Your Love Away; The Night Before; Another Girl; Ticket to Ride; I Need You. **90m/C VHS, DVD.** *GB* John Lennon, Paul McCartney, Ringo Starr, George Harrison, Leo McKern, Eleanor Bron, Victor Spinetti, Roy Kinnear, John Bluthal, Patrick Cargill, Alfie Bass, Warren Mitchell, Peter Copley, Bruce Lacey; *D:* Richard Lester; *W:* Charles Wood, Marc Behm; *C:* David Watkin; *M:* George Martin, Ken Thorne, John Lennon, Paul McCartney, Ringo Starr, George Harrison.

Help Wanted Female ☙ 1968 Jo Jo, a prostitute with kung fu skills who likes to rob traveling salesmen, is in a quandary over her lesbian roommate's acid dropping friends, including Mr. Gregory, who has a penchant for murder. After recounting a previous trip in which he murdered an acquaintance, he succeeds in alienating his current companions, who must fight for their life to escape him. **71m/B VHS.** Sebastian Gregory, Inga Olsen; *D:* Harold Perkins.

Help Wanted: Male ☙½ 1982 When a magazine publisher discovers that her fiance cannot have children, she looks for someone else who can do the job right. **97m/C VHS.** Suzanne Pleshette, Gil Gerard, Bert Convy, Dana Elcar, Harold Gould, Caren Kaye; *D:* William Wiard. TV

Helter Skelter ☙☙½ 1976 The harrowing story of the murder of actress Sharon Tate and four others at the hands of Charles Manson and his psychotic "family." Based on the book by prosecutor Vincent Bugliosi, adapted by J.P. Miller. Features an outstanding performance by Railsback as Manson. **194m/C VHS.** Steve Railsback, Nancy Wolfe, George DiCenzo, Marilyn Burns, Christina Hart, Alan Oppenheimer, Cathy Paine; *D:* Tom Gries; *W:* J(ames) P(inckney) Miller; *M:* Billy Goldenberg. TV

Helter Skelter Murders woof! 1971 (R) An independently made version of the Charles Manson story, with sequences filmed at Spawn Ranch. Includes Manson's own recording of his songs "Mechanical Man" and "Garbage Dump" on the soundtrack. **83m/B VHS, DVD.** Brian Klinknett, Debbie Duff, Phyllis Estes; *D:* Frank Howard; *W:* J.J. Wilkie, Duke Howze; *C:* Frank Howard.

The Henderson Monster ☙☙½ 1980 Experiments of a genetic scientist are questioned by a community and its mayor. A potentially controversial drama turns into typical romantic fluff. **105m/C VHS.** Jason Miller, Christine Lahti, Stephen Collins, David Spielberg, Nehemiah Persoff, Larry Gates; *D:* Waris Hussein. TV

Hendrix ☙☙½ 2000 (R) Biopic of legendary rock guitarist Jimi Hendrix (Harris) from his first teenaged band to his drug overdose death in 1970. There are some fine re-creations of such notable Hendrix performances at the 1967 Monterey Pop Festival and Woodstock in 1969. **103m/C VHS, DVD.** Wood Harris, Vivica A. Fox, Billy Zane, Christian Potenza, Dorian Harewood, Kris Holdenried, Christopher Ralph, Michie Mee; *D:* Leon Ichaso; *W:* Art Washington, Hal Roberts, Butch Stein; *C:* Claudio Chea; *M:* Daniel Licht. CABLE

Hennessy ☙☙½ 1975 (PG) An IRA man plots revenge on the Royal family and Parliament after his family is violently killed. Tense political drama, but slightly far-fetched. **103m/C VHS.** *GB* Rod Steiger, Lee Remick, Richard Johnson, Trevor Howard, Peter Egan, Eric Porter; *D:* Don Sharp; *W:* John Gay.

Henry IV ☙☙½ 1985 The adaptation of the Luigi Pirandello farce about a modern-day recluse who shields himself from the horrors of the real world by pretending to be mad and acting out the fantasy of being the medieval German emperor Henry IV. In Italian with English subtitles. **94m/C VHS.** *IT* Marcello Mastroianni, Claudia Cardinale, Leopoldo Trieste, Paolo Bonacelli, Luciano Bartoli, Latou Chardons; *D:* Marco Bellocchio; *W:* Marco Bellocchio, Tonino Guerra, Astor Piazzolla.

Henry V ☙☙☙☙ 1944 Classic, epic adaptation of the Shakespeare play, and Olivier's first and most successful directorial effort, dealing with the medieval British monarch that defeated the French at Agincourt. Distinguished by Olivier's brilliant formal experiment of beginning the drama as a 16th Century performance of the play in the Globe Theatre, and having the stage eventually transform into realistic historical settings of storybook color. Filmed at the height of WWII suffering in Britain (and meant as a parallel to the British fighting the Nazis), the film was not released in the U.S. until 1946. **136m/C VHS, DVD.** *GB* Laurence Olivier, Robert Newton, Leslie Banks, Esmond Knight, Renee Asherson, Leo Genn, George Robey, Ernest Thesiger, Felix Aylmer, Ralph Truman, Harcourt Williams, Max Adrian, Valentine Dyall, Russell Thorndike, Roy Emerton, Robert Helpmann, Freda Jackson, Griffith Jones, John Laurie, Niall MacGinnis, Michael Shepley; *D:* Laurence Olivier; *W:* Alan Dent, Dallas Bower, Laurence Olivier; *C:* Robert Krasker; *M:* William Walton. Natl. Bd. of Review '46: Actor (Olivier); N.Y. Film Critics '46: Actor (Olivier).

Henry V ☙☙☙☙ 1989 Stirring, expansive retelling of Shakespeare's drama about the warrior-king of England. Branagh stars as Henry, leading his troops and uniting his kingdom against France. Very impressive production rivals Olivier's 1945 rendering but differs by stressing the high cost of war—showing the ego-mania, doubts, and subterfuge that underlie conflicts. Marvelous film-directorial debut for Branagh (who also adapted the screenplay). Wonderful supporting cast includes some of Britain's finest actors. **138m/C VHS, DVD, Wide.** *GB* Kenneth Branagh, Derek Jacobi, Brian Blessed, Alec McCowen, Ian Holm, Richard Briers, Robert Stephens, Robbie Coltrane, Christian Bale, Judi Dench, Paul Scofield, Michael Maloney, Emma Thompson, Patrick Doyle, Richard Clifford, Richard Easton, Paul Gregory, Harold Innocent, Charles Kay, Geraldine McEwan, Christopher Ravenscroft, John Sessions, Simon Shepherd, Jay Villiers, Danny Webb; *D:* Kenneth Branagh; *W:* Kenneth Branagh; *C:* Kenneth Macmillan; *M:* Patrick Doyle. Oscars '89: Costume Des.; British Acad. '89: Director (Branagh); Natl. Bd. of Review '89: Director (Branagh).

Henry & June 🦴🦴🦴½ **1990** **(NC-17)** Based on the diaries of writer Anais Nin which chronicled her triangular relationship with author Henry Miller and his wife June, a relationship that provided the erotic backdrop to Miller's "Tropic of Capricorn." Set in Paris in the early '30s, the setting moves between the impecunious expatriate's cheap room on the Left bank—filled with artists, circus performers, prostitutes, and gypsies—to the conservative, well-appointed home of Nin and her husband. Captures the heady atmosphere of Miller's gay Paris; no one plays an American better than Ward (who replaced Alec Baldwin). Notable for having prompted the creation of an NC-17 rating because of its adult theme. **136m/C VHS, DVD, Wide.** Fred Ward, Uma Thurman, Maria De Medeiros, Richard E. Grant, Kevin Spacey; ***D:*** Philip Kaufman; ***W:*** Philip Kaufman; ***C:*** Philippe Rousselot; ***M:*** Mark Adler.

Henry & Verlin 🦴🦴 **1994** Verlin (Macintosh) is a nine-year-old who doesn't talk. He lives in rural Ontario (during the Depression) with his overprotective mother Minnie (Beatty) and indifferent father Ferris (Joy), as well as Ferris' childlike brother Henry (Farmer) who befriends Verlin. The misfit duo develop a strong bond that includes disabled retired prostitute Mabel (Kidder)—much to the resentment of some of the less-enlightened townsfolk. There's some melodramatic events but the performances skirt maudlin excess. **87m/C VHS.** *CA* Gary Farmer, Keegan Macintosh, Nancy Beatty, Robert Joy, Margot Kidder, Eric Peterson; ***Cameos:*** David Cronenberg; ***D:*** Gary Ledbetter; ***W:*** Gary Ledbetter.

Henry Fool 🦴🦴🦴 **1998 (R)** Simon Grim (Urbaniak) is a socially inept garbage man treated with contempt by his depressed mother (Porter) and caustic sister (Posey). Henry Fool (Ryan), an alcoholic homeless man, claims to be a great writer and sees a bit of poet in Simon as well. After he moves Henry into the family's basement, Simon takes his first steps as a poet and Henry takes liberties with both of the women. Simon turns out to be a natural artist, and writes a poem that profoundly moves and/or shocks the public and creates a controversy on the Internet. As Simon is courted by publishers, he champions Henry's unread work as well. Their respective fortunes rise and fall as Henry's work is unveiled and the price of fame affects their lives. Director Hartley pulls very different elements such as the artistry of Samuel Beckett and the myth of Faust together to create a bizarre urban fable. **138m/C VHS.** Thomas Jay Ryan, James Urbaniak, Parker Posey, Maria Porter, Kevin Corrigan, James Saito; ***D:*** Hal Hartley; ***W:*** Hal Hartley; ***C:*** Michael Spiller; ***M:*** Hal Hartley.

Henry: Portrait of a Serial Killer 🦴🦴🦴🦴 **1990 (R)** Based on the horrific life and times of serial killer Henry Lee Lucas, this film has received wide praise for its straight-forward and uncompromising look into the minds of madmen. The film follows ex-cons Henry (Rooker) and his roommate Otis (Towles) as they set out on mindless murder sprees (one of which they videotape). Extremely disturbing and graphic film. Unwary viewers should be aware of the grisly scenes and use their own discretion when viewing this otherwise genuinely moving film. **90m/C VHS, DVD.** Michael Rooker, Tom Towles, Tracy Arnold, David Katz; ***D:*** John McNaughton; ***W:*** John McNaughton, Richard Fire; ***C:*** Charlie Lieberman; ***M:*** Robert F. McNaughton.

Henry: Portrait of a Serial Killer 2: Mask of Sanity 🦴 *Henry 2: Portrait of a Serial Killer* **1996 (R)** Michael Rooker gave a chilling performance as serial killer Henry in part 1 but Giuntoli is merely dull. A sullen drifter, Henry manages to get a job and fellow worker Kai (Komenich) invites him to crash at his place. Turns out Kai is a part-time arsonist for hire and Henry helps him out—also introducing Kai to the pleasures of casual murder. The gore is actually limited to a few bloody scenes (usually more is heard than shown) but the whole project is boring. **84m/C VHS, DVD.** Neil Giuntoli, Rich Komenich, Katherine Walsh, Carri Levinson, Penelope Milford; ***D:*** Chuck Parello; ***W:*** Chuck Parello; ***C:*** Michael Kohnhurst; ***M:*** Robert F. McNaughton.

Her Alibi 🦴🦴 **1988 (PG)** When successful murder-mystery novelist Phil Blackwood runs out of ideas for good books, he seeks inspiration in the criminal courtroom. There he discovers a beautiful Romanian immigrant named Nina who is accused of murder. He goes to see her in jail and offers to provide her with an alibi. Narrated by Blackwood in the tone of one of his thriller novels. Uneven comedy, with appealing cast and arbitrary plot. **95m/C VHS, DVD, 8mm.** Tom Selleck, Paulina Porizkova, William Daniels, James Farentino, Hurd Hatfield, Patrick Wayne, Tess Harper, Joan Copeland; ***D:*** Bruce Beresford; ***W:*** Charlie Peters; ***C:*** Freddie Francis; ***M:*** Georges Delerue.

Her and She and Him 🦴🦴 *Claude et Greta* **1969** Young Swedish beauty Greta arrives in Paris with only her guitar. Penniless, she takes up with another woman but soon feels she's only a sexual prisoner. So Greta seduces a young painter who is having an obsessive affair with a gay artist. Dubbed into English. **90m/C VHS.** *FR* Astrid Frank, Yves Vincent; ***D:*** Max Pecas; ***C:*** Robert Lefebvre.

Her First Romance 🦴🦴½ *The Right Man* **1940** Mixed-up romance with Fellows and Wells as sisters, Linden their cousin, and Ladd her fiance. The sisters fall for Evans and use Ladd in their schemes, causing him to believe Evans is actually after Linden. Eventually, everyone pairs up properly. **77m/B VHS.** Edith Fellows, Julie (Jacqueline Wells) Bishop, Alan Ladd, Judith Linden, Wilbur Evans, Roger Daniel; ***D:*** Edward Dmytryk; ***W:*** Adele Comandini.

Her Husband's Affairs 🦴 **1947** Tone is an advertising wonder and Ball is his loving wife who always gets credit for his work. Tone does the advertising for an inventor who is searching for the perfect embalming fluid in this rather lifeless comedy. **83m/B VHS.** Lucille Ball, Franchot Tone, Edward Everett Horton, Gene Lockhart, Larry Parks; ***D:*** Sylvan Simon; ***M:*** George Duning.

Her Life as a Man 🦴½ **1983** A female reporter is refused a job as a sportswriter because of her gender. She makes herself up as a man, gets the job, and creates havoc when she has to deal with lustful women on the job. **93m/C VHS.** Robyn Douglass, Joan Collins, Robert Culp, Marc Singer, Laraine Newman; ***D:*** Robert Ellis Miller. **TV**

Her Name Is Cat 🦴🦴½ **1999 (R)** Yet another Hong Kong hitwoman (Almen Wong) agrees to yet another "last job" before retiring...fans know the drill. Explosions and slo-mo shoot outs are plentiful, though the fight choreography isn't going to make anyone forget John Woo or Ringo Lam. **94m/C DVD, Wide.** *HK* Michael Wong, Almen Wong, Kent Masters King; ***D:*** Clarence (Fok) Ford; ***W:*** Wong Jing. **VIDEO**

Her Silent Sacrifice 🦴½ **1918** A silent melodrama about a French girl torn between material wealth and true love. **42m/B VHS.** Alice Brady, Henry Clive.

Herbie Goes Bananas 🦴½ **1980 (G)** While Herbie the VW is racing in Rio de Janeiro, he is bothered by the syndicate, a pickpocket, and a raging bull. The fourth and final entry in the Disney "Love Bug" movies, but Herbie later made his way to a TV series. **93m/C VHS.** Cloris Leachman, Charles Martin Smith, Harvey Korman, John Vernon, Alex Rocco, Richard Jaeckel, Fritz Feld; ***D:*** Vincent McEveety.

Herbie Goes to Monte Carlo 🦴🦴 **1977 (G)** While participating in a Paris-to-Monte-Carlo race, Herbie the VW takes a detour and falls in love with a Lancia. Third in the Disney "Love Bug" series. **104m/C VHS.** Dean Jones, Don Knotts, Julie Sommars, Roy Kinnear; ***D:*** Vincent McEveety; ***W:*** Arthur Alsberg.

Herbie Rides Again 🦴🦴½ **1974 (G)** In this "Love Bug" sequel, Herbie comes to the aid of an elderly woman who is trying to stop a ruthless tycoon from raising a skyscraper on her property. Humorous Disney fare. Two other sequels followed. **88m/C VHS.** Helen Hayes, Ken Berry, Stefanie Powers, John McIntire, Keenan Wynn; ***D:*** Robert Stevenson; ***M:*** George Bruns.

Hercules 🦴🦴½ *La Tatiche de Ercole* **1958** The one that started it all. Reeves is perfect as the mythical hero Hercules who encounters many dangerous situations while trying to win over his true love. Dubbed in English. **107m/C VHS, Wide.** *IT* Steve Reeves, Sylva Koscina, Fabrizio Mioni, Gianna Maria Canale, Arturo Dominici; ***D:*** Pietro Francisci; ***C:*** Mario Bava.

Hercules 🦴 **1983 (PG)** Lackluster remake of 1957 original finds legendary muscle guy Hercules in the person of Ferrigno's Hulkster fighting against the evil King Minos for his own survival and the love of Cassiopeia, a rival king's daughter. **100m/C VHS.** *IT* Lou Ferrigno, Sybil Danning, William Berger, Brad Harris, Ingrid Anderson; ***D:*** Lewis (Luigi Cozzi) Coates; ***W:*** Lewis (Luigi Cozzi) Coates; ***M:*** Pino Donaggio. Golden Raspberries '83: Worst Support. Actress (Danning), Worst New Star (Ferrigno).

Hercules 🦴🦴🦴½ **1997 (G)** After a couple of animated downers, Disney's latest adventure goes for a happy heroic tone by taking on Greek myths. Baby Herc is the son of Zeus, who rules on Mt. Olympus. Hades, Lord of the Underworld, plans a takeover and learns that only Hercules' strength will stand in his way. Hades manages to kidnap the tyke and turn him mortal but when the teenaged Herc learns his true origins, he also discovers that if he proves himself to be a hero he can regain his immortality and return to Mt. Olympus. He's aided by his flying horse Pegasus, satyr-like trainer Phil, and smart gal Meg, while Hades has his less-than-bright minions Pain and Panic. Lots of fun and lots of merchandising (even the movie makes fun of the inevitable tie-ins). ♫The Gospel Truth; Go the Distance; One Last Hope; I Won't Say; Zero to Hero. **92m/C VHS, DVD.** ***D:*** John Musker, Ron Clements; ***W:*** John Musker, Ron Clements, Bob Shaw, Donald McEnery, Irene Mecchi; ***M:*** Alan Menken, David Zippel; ***V:*** Tate Donovan, James Woods, Danny DeVito, Matt Frewer, Bob(cat) Goldthwait, Susan Egan, Rip Torn, Samantha Eggar, Paul Shaffer, Barbara Barrie, Hal Holbrook, Amanda Plummer, Carol(e) Shelley; ***Nar:*** Charlton Heston.

Hercules 2 🦴 *The Adventures of Hercules* **1985 (PG)** The muscle-bound demi-god returns to do battle with more evil foes amidst the same stunningly cheap special effects. **90m/C VHS, DVD.** *IT* Lou Ferrigno, Claudio Cassinelli, Milly Carlucci, Sonia Viviani, William Berger, Carlotta Green; ***D:*** Lewis (Luigi Cozzi) Coates; ***M:*** Pino Donaggio.

Hercules against the Moon Men 🦴 *Maciste la Regina di Samar* **1964** It's no holds barred for the mighty son of Zeus when evil moon men start killing off humans in a desperate bid to revive their dead queen. **88m/C VHS.** *IT FR* Alan Steel, Jany Clair, Anna Maria Polani, Nando Tamberlani, Delia D'Alberti, Jean-Pierre Honore; ***D:*** Giacomo Gentilomo; ***W:*** Arpad De Riso, Nino Scolaro; ***C:*** Oberdan Troiani; ***M:*** Carlo Franci.

Hercules and the Captive Women 🦴🦴 *Hercules and the Haunted Women; Hercules and the Conquest of Atlantis; Ercole Alla Conquista di Atlantide* **1963** Hercules' son is kidnapped by the Queen of Atlantis, and the bare-chested warrior goes on an all-out rampage to save the boy. Directed by sometimes-lauded Cottafavi. **93m/C VHS.** *IT* Reg Park, Fay Spain, Ettore Manni; ***D:*** Vittorio Cottafavi.

Hercules and the Princess of Troy 🦴🦴½ **1965** Hercules is up to his pecs in trouble as he battles a hungry sea monster in order to save a beautiful maiden. Originally a pilot for a prospective TV series, and shot in English, not Italian, with Hercules played by erstwhile Tarzan Scott. Highlights are special effects and color cinematography. **?m/C VHS.** *IT* Gordon Scott, Diana Hyland, Paul Stevens, Everett Sloane. **TV**

Hercules in New York 🦴½ *Hercules: The Movie; Hercules Goes Bananas* **1970 (G)** Motion picture debut of Schwarzenegger (his voice is dubbed) as a Herculean mass of muscle sent by dad Zeus to Manhattan, where he behaves likes a geek out of water and eventually becomes a professional wrestling superstar. 250 pounds of stupid, lighthearted fun. **93m/C VHS, DVD.** Arnold Schwarzenegger, Arnold Stang, Deborah Loomis, James Karen, Ernest Graves, Taina Elg; ***D:*** Arthur Seidelman; ***W:*** Aubrey Wisberg; ***C:*** Leo Lebowitz; ***M:*** John Balamos.

Hercules in the Haunted World 🦴🦴½ *Ercole al Centro Della Terra* **1964** Long before the days of 24-hour pharmacies, Hercules—played yet again by Reeves-clone Park—must journey to the depths of Hell in order to find a plant that will cure a poisoned princess. Better than most muscle operas, thanks to Bava. **91m/C VHS.** *IT* Reg Park, Leonora Ruffo, Christopher Lee, George Ardisson; ***D:*** Mario Bava.

Hercules, Prisoner of Evil 🦴 **1964** Spaghetti myth-opera in which Hercules battles a witch who is turning men into werewolves. Made for Italian TV by director Dawson (the nom-de-cinema of Antonio Margheriti). **?m/C VHS.** *IT* Reg Park; ***D:*** Anthony (Antonio Margheriti) Dawson. **TV**

Hercules the Legendary Journeys, Vol. 1: And the Amazon Women 🦴🦴½ **1994** Half-man, half-god Hercules (Sorbo) and his friend Ioleus (Hurst) are summoned to a village to kill the beasts stealing livestock. Turns out those responsible are the village's women, who are mad at their husbands and have formed a band of Amazons, lead by Hippolyta (Downey), who happens to be working for Hercules' immortal enemy, the goddess Hera. Now it's up to Herc to convince Hippolyta that men and women can work together and outsmart Hera at the same time. **91m/C VHS.** Kevin Sorbo, Michael Hurst, Roma Downey, Anthony Quinn, Lucy Lawless; ***D:*** Bill W.L. Norton; ***M:*** Joseph LoDuca. **TV**

Hercules the Legendary Journeys, Vol. 2: The Lost Kingdom 🦴🦴½ **1994** Hera has hidden the kingdom of Troy and only a magic compass can point Hercules (Sorbo) in the right direction. He rescues a sacrificial virgin (O'Connor) and the duo manage to find the compass and get into Troy where she learns her father was once its king. Turns out dad sent his daughter away so he wouldn't have to sacrifice her to Hera and lost his kingdom instead. Now she wants her kingdom back and Hera still wants her sacrifice—especially if it's Hercules. **91m/C VHS.** Kevin Sorbo, Michael Hurst, Anthony Quinn, Renee O'Connor, Robert Trebor; ***D:*** Harley Cokliss; ***M:*** Joseph LoDuca. **TV**

Hercules the Legendary Journeys, Vol. 3: The Circle of Fire 🦴🦴½ **1994** Hera's stolen fire from mankind, which is slowly freezing to death, keeping one eternal torch for herself. A villager named Deianeira (Kitaen) enlists Hercules (Sorbo) to search for Prometheus (Ferguson), the god of fire, but Hera's stolen his flame as well. When Herc finds the torch it's encircled in a ring of fire, which Hera knows can destroy Hercules' immortality. **92m/C VHS.** Kevin Sorbo, Michael Hurst, Anthony Quinn, Tawny Kitaen, Mark Ferguson; ***D:*** Doug Lefler; ***M:*** Joseph LoDuca. **TV**

Hercules the Legendary Journeys, Vol. 4: In the Underworld 🦴🦴½ **1994** Having married Deianeira (Kitaen), Herc's a pretty happy guy until a mysterious maiden, Iole, comes to him for help. Seems a deadly crack has opened up in the earth and is swallowing villagers. But Iole has actually been sent by Hera to destroy Hercules and when Deianeira discovers her treachery she goes to warn her husband. Only Hera manages to trick her into walking off a clift and falling to her death. Hercules must go into the underworld to save the world from Hera but when he learns Deianeira's fate, he accepts an impossible challenge from Hades (Ferguson) to bring his wife back to life. **91m/C VHS.** Kevin Sorbo, Michael Hurst, Anthony Quinn, Tawny Kitaen, Mark Ferguson; ***D:*** Bill W.L. Norton; ***M:*** Joseph LoDuca. **TV**

Hercules Unchained 🦴🦴 *Ercole e la Regina de Lidia* **1959** Sequel to "Hercules" finds superhero Reeves must use all his strength to save the city of Thebes and the woman he loves from the giant Antaeus. **101m/C VHS.** *IT* Steve Reeves, Sylva Koscina, Silvia Lopel, Primo Carnera; ***D:*** Pietro Francisci.

Hercules vs. the Sons of the Sun 🦴½ *Hercules Against the Sons of the Sun; Ercole Contro I Figli del Sole* **1964** Herc (Forest) battles the evil King of the Incas by building unstoppable fighting machines. Typical of the genre. **91m/C VHS.** *IT SP* Mark Forest, Giuliano Gemma, Riccardo Valle, Andrea Scotti, Anna Maria Pace, Angela Rhu, Giulio Donnini; ***D:*** Osvaldo Civirani; ***W:*** Osvaldo Civirani; ***C:*** Osvaldo Civirani, Julio Ortas; ***M:*** Coriolano Gori.

Here and Elsewhere *Ici et Ailleurs* **197?** Godard, Gorin, and Mieville contrast the story of a French family with a look at the Palestine revolution as seen through the media of television, books, and pictures. The film was originally titled "Until Victory" and commissioned by the Palestinians to examine life in the Palestinian camps. After the defeat of the Palestinian army in the Six Day War, Godard and his cohorts transformed the film with their French family ("Here") and their impressions of Palestine ("Elsewhere"). French with subtitles. **?m/C VHS.** *FR* Anne-Marie Mieville; ***D:*** Jean-Pierre Gorin, Jean-Luc Godard.

Here Come the Co-Eds 🦴🦴½ **1945** Bud & Lou are the caretakers of an all-girl college which is about to go bankrupt unless the boys can find a way to pay off the mortgage. And come to the rescue they do, including Bud getting into the wrestling ring with the "Masked Marvel" (Chaney Jr. as the villain). There's also a classic silent scene with Lou served a bowl of oyster stew containing a live oyster, which promptly grabs his tie, bites his fingers, and squirts in his face. **90m/B VHS.** Bud Abbott, Lou Costello, Lon Chaney Jr., Peggy Ryan, Martha O'Driscoll, June Vincent, Donald Cook, Charles Dingle; ***D:*** Jean Yarbrough; ***W:*** Arthur T. Horman, John Grant.

Here Come the Girls 🦴½ **1953** An unfunny musical-comedy about a chorus boy (Hope) fired for incompetence and then rehired to set a trap when the new singer (Martin) is stalked by a killer. Weak script, weak songs. ♫Girls Are Here To Stay; Never So Beautiful; You Got Class; Desire; When You Love Someone; Ali Baba Be My Baby; Heavenly Days; See the Circus; Peace. **100m/C VHS.** Bob Hope, Tony Martin, Arlene Dahl, Rosemary Clooney, Millard Mitchell, William Demarest, Fred Clark, Robert Strauss; ***D:*** Claude Binyon; ***W:*** Hal Kanter.

Here Come the Littles: The Movie 🦴½ **1985** A 12-year-old boy finds many new adventures when he meets The Littles—tiny folks who reside within the walls of people's houses. Adapted from the books and TV series. **76m/C VHS.** ***D:*** Bernard Deyries.

Here Come the Marines 🦴🦴 *Tell It To the Marines* **1952** The Bowery Boys accidentally join the marines and wind up breaking up a gambling ring. **66m/B VHS.** Leo Gorcey, Huntz Hall, Tim Ryan; ***D:*** William Beaudine.

Here Come the Nelsons 🦴🦴½ **1952** In between the radio show, "The Adventures of Ozzie and Harriet," and the TV series came this feature film. Ad man Ozzie is trying to develop a campaign for a women's wear company while the town's centennial celebration is causing problems on the homefront. Seems Harriet's houseguest for the festivities is Rock Hudson! **76m/B VHS.** Ozzie Nelson, Harriet Hilliard Nelson, David Nelson, Ricky Nelson, Rock Hudson, Barbara Lawrence, Sheldon Leonard, Jim Backus; ***D:*** Fred de Cordova; ***W:*** Don Nelson, Ozzie Nelson.

Here Come the Waves 🦴🦴🦴 **1945** Easy-going wartime musical finds Der Bingle as a singing idol drafted into the Navy, assigned to direct WAVE shows. The crooner meets identical twins (both played by Hutton) and falls hard. Only problem is he can't tell the gals apart—and one twin can't stand him. Amusing romantic complications mix well with some spoofing of a star's life. ♫Accent-tchu-ate the Positive; I Promise You; Let's Take the Long Way Home; That Old Black Magic; There's a Fellow Waiting in Poughkeepsie; Here Come the Waves; My Mama Thinks I'm a Star; Join the Navy. **99m/B VHS.** Bing Crosby, Betty Hutton, Sonny Tufts, Ann Doran, Noel Neill, Mae Clarke, Gwen Crawford, Catherine Craig; ***D:*** Mark Sandrich; ***W:*** Zion Myers.

Here Comes Cookie 🦴🦴½ **1935** Amusing farce finds Gracie (Allen) the daughter of wealthy Harrison Allen (Barbier), who's afraid of the fortune hunters eyeing other daughter Phyllis (Furness). So he temporarily turns over the family fortune to Gracie, who promptly turns their Park Avenue mansion into a home for down-on-their-luck vaudevillians. Lots of specialty acts and Burns is around as straight man. **65m/B VHS.** Gracie Allen, George Burns, George Barbier, Betty Furness; ***D:*** Norman Z. McLeod; ***W:*** Don Hartman, Sam Mintz; ***C:*** Gilbert Warrenton.

Here Comes Kelly 🦴½ **1943** Controlling his temper and hanging on to his job is more than our hero can handle. **63m/C VHS.** Eddie Quillan, Joan Woodbury, Maxie "Slapsie" Rosenbloom; ***D:*** William Beaudine.

Here Comes Mr. Jordan 🦴🦴🦴🦴 **1941** Montgomery is the young prizefighter killed in a plane crash because of a mix-up in heaven. He returns to life in the body of a soon-to-be murdered millionaire. Rains is the indulgent and advising guardian angel. A lovely fantasy/romance remade in 1978 as "Heaven Can Wait." **94m/B VHS.** Robert Montgomery, Claude Rains, James Gleason, Evelyn Keyes, Edward Everett Horton, Rita Johnson, John Emery; ***D:*** Alexander Hall; ***W:*** Sidney Buchman, Seton I. Miller; ***M:*** Frederick "Friedrich" Hollander. Oscars '41: Screenplay, Story.

Here Comes Santa Claus 🦴½ **1984** A young boy and girl travel to the North Pole to deliver a very special wish to Santa Claus. **78m/C VHS.** Karen Cheryl, Armand Meffre; ***D:*** Christian Gion.

Here Comes the Groom 🦴🦴 **1951** Late, stale Capra-corn, involving a rogue journalist who tries to keep his girlfriend from marrying a millionaire by becoming a charity worker. Includes a number of cameos. ♫In the Cool, Cool, Cool of the Evening; Bonne Nuit, Good Night; Misto Cristofo Columbo; Your Own Little House. **114m/B VHS.** Bing Crosby, Jane Wyman, Franchot Tone, Alexis Smith, James Barton, Connie Gilchrist, Robert Keith, Anna Maria Alberghetti, Charles Halton; ***Cameos:*** Dorothy Lamour, Phil Harris, Louis Armstrong; ***D:*** Frank Capra. Oscars '51: Song ("In the Cool, Cool, Cool of the Evening").

Here on Earth 🦴🦴 **2000 (PG-13)** Predictable teary teen romantic drama with a very pretty cast doing what they can with one-note roles. Smalltown beauty Samantha (Sobieski) waits tables at the family diner and hangs out with long-time boyfriend Jasper (Hartnett), who's rivals with snotty prep, Kelley (Klein). Their rivalry causes a disaster for Sam and her family that the boys must rectify, even as Kelley and Sam turn to each other. Oh yeah, and then Sam's recurring knee problems turn out to be cancer and everyone has to pull together. **96m/C VHS, DVD, Wide.** Chris Klein, Leelee Sobieski, Josh Hartnett, Michael Rooker, Annie Corley, Bruce Greenwood, Annette O'Toole, Stuart Wilson, Tac Fitzgerald; ***D:*** Mark Piznarski; ***W:*** Michael Seitzman; ***C:*** Michael D. O'Shea; ***M:*** Andrea Morricone.

Here We Go Again! 🦴🦴 **1942** Fibber McGee and Molly are planning a cross-country trip for their 20th anniversary celebration, but complications abound. Based on the popular NBC radio series. **76m/B VHS.** Marian Jordan, Jim Jordan, Harold (Hal) Peary, Gale Gordon, Edgar Bergen, Ray Noble; ***D:*** Allan Dwan.

Heritage of the Desert 🦴½ **1933** One of the earlier westerns made by the rugged Scott. **62m/B VHS.** Randolph Scott, Sally Blane, Guinn "Big Boy" Williams; ***D:*** Henry Hathaway.

The Hero 🦴½ *Bloomfield* **1971 (PG)** A popular soccer player agrees to throw a game for big cash, and then worries about losing the respect of a young boy who idolizes him. Nothing new in this overly sentimental sports drama. **97m/C VHS.** Richard Harris, Romy Schneider, Kim Burfield, Maurice Kaufmann; ***D:*** Richard Harris.

Hero 🦴🦴🦴 **1992 (PG-13)** Interesting twist on Cinderella fable and modern media satire has TV reporter Davis looking for the man who saved her life, expecting a genuine hero, and accepting without question the one who fits her vision. Critically considered disappointing, but wait—Garcia and Hoffman make a great team, and Davis is fetching as the vulnerable media person. Strong language and dark edges may keep away some of the kids, but otherwise this is a fine fable. **116m/C VHS, DVD, 8mm, Wide.** Geena Davis, Dustin Hoffman, Andy Garcia, Joan Cusack, Kevin J. O'Connor, Chevy Chase, Maury Chaykin, Stephen Tobolowsky, Christian Clemenson, Tom Arnold, Warren Berlinger, Susie Cusack, James Madio, Richard Riehle, Don Yesso, Darrell Larson; ***D:*** Stephen Frears; ***W:*** David Peoples; ***C:*** Oliver Stapleton; ***M:*** George Fenton.

A Hero Ain't Nothin' but a Sandwich 🦴🦴½ **1978 (PG)** A young urban black teenager gets involved in drugs and is eventually saved from ruin. Slow-moving, over-directed and talky. However, Scott turns in a fine performance. Based on Alice Childress' novel. **107m/C VHS.** Cicely Tyson, Paul Winfield, Larry B. Scott, Helen Martin, Glynn Turman, David Groh; ***D:*** Ralph Nelson.

Hero and the Terror 🦴½ **1988 (R)** Perennial karate guy Norris plays a sensitive policeman who conquers his fear of a not-so-sensitive maniac who's trying to kill him. Plenty of action and a cheesy subplot to boot. **96m/C VHS, DVD, Wide.** Chuck Norris, Brynn Thayer, Steve James, Jack O'Halloran, Ron O'Neal, Billy Drago; ***D:*** William Tannen; ***W:*** Michael Blodgett; ***C:*** Eric Van Haren Noman; ***M:*** David Michael Frank.

Hero at Large 🦴🦴½ **1980 (PG)** An unemployed actor foils a robbery while dressed in a promotional "Captain Avenger" suit, and instant celebrity follows. Lightweight, yet enjoyable. **98m/C VHS.** John Ritter, Anne Archer, Bert Convy, Kevin McCarthy, Kevin Bacon; ***D:*** Martin Davidson; ***W:*** A.J. Carothers.

Hero Bunker 🦴🦴 **1971** Hero bunk about a platoon of heroic Greek soldiers who attempt, at the expense of their personal longevity, to defend an important bunker from enemy invasion. **93m/C VHS.** John Miller, Maria Xenia; ***D:*** George Andrews.

Hero of Rome **1963** Rome has many who could be called "hero," but one stands biceps and pecs above the rest. **?m/C VHS.** *IT* Gordon Scott, Gabriella Pallotta.

Hero of the Year 🦴🦴 **1985** The characters from Falk's "Top Dog" return in this story of a Polish TV personality who loses his job and is forced to face unemployment and job-seeking. **115m/C VHS.** *PL* ***D:*** Feliks Falk.

Herod the Great 🦴 **1960** Biblical epic of the downfall of Herod, the ruler of ancient Judea. Scantily clad women abound. Dubbed. **93m/C VHS.** *IT* Edmund Purdom, Sandra Milo, Alberto Lupo; ***D:*** Arnaldo Genoino.

Heroes 🦴🦴 **1977 (PG)** An institutionalized Vietnam vet (Winkler) escapes, hoping to establish a worm farm which will support all his crazy buddies. On the way to the home of a friend he hopes will help him, he encounters Field. Funny situations don't always mix with serious underlying themes of mental illness and post-war adjustment. **97m/C VHS.** Henry Winkler, Sally Field, Harrison Ford; ***D:*** Jeremy Paul Kagan; ***W:*** James (Jim) Carabatsos; ***M:*** Jack Nitzsche.

Heroes Die Young 🦴½ **1960** A cheap independent feature depicting an American command mission with orders to sabotage German oil fields during WWII. **76m/B VHS.** Krika Peters, Scott Borland, Robert Getz, James Strother.

Heroes for Sale 🦴🦴🦴 **1933** Fascinating melodrama about a WWI veteran who returns home and manages to survive one disaster after another. Barthelmess is great in his performance as an American Everyman who must deal with everything from morphine addiction to finding work during the Depression. Fast-paced, patriotic film is helped by ambitious script and the expert direction of Wellman. **72m/B VHS.** Richard Barthelmess, Loretta Young, Aline MacMahon, Robert Barrat, Grant Mitchell, Douglass Dumbrille, Charley Grapewin, Ward Bond; ***D:*** William A. Wellman; ***W:*** Robert Lord, Wilson Mizner.

Heroes in Blue 🦴🦴 **1939** Two brothers join the police force, but one goes astray and hooks up with gangsters. Plenty of action distracts from the cliched story. **60m/B VHS.** Dick Purcell, Charles Quigley, Bernadene Hayes, Edward (Ed Kean, Keene) Keane; ***D:*** William Watson.

Heroes in Hell 🦴½ **1967** Two escaped WWII POWs join the Allied underground in an espionage conspiracy against the Third Reich. **90m/C VHS.** Klaus Kinski, Ettore Manni.

The Heroes of Desert Storm 🦴🦴 **1991** The human spirit of the people who fought in the high-tech Persian Gulf War is captured in this film that also features real war footage from ABC News. **93m/C VHS.** Daniel Baldwin, Angela Bassett, Marshall Bell, Michael Alan Brooks, William Bumiller, Michael Champion, Maria Diaz; ***D:*** Don Ohlmeyer; ***W:*** Lionel Chetwynd.

The Heroes of Telemark 🦴🦴½ **1965** In 1942, Norway is under Nazi occupation and Nazi scientists are dangerously close to producing an essential element for making an atomic bomb in a secret factory. Underground leader Knut Straud (Harris) enlists the help of Norwegian scientist Rolf Pedersen (Douglas) and a group of saboteurs to destroy the factory. But their raid only provides a short delay and our heroes must now prevent shipment of the component from ever reaching Germany. Filmed on location in Norway, with former members of the underground serving as technical advisors for director Mann. **130m/C VHS.** *GB* Richard Harris, Kirk Douglas, Michael Redgrave, Ulla Jacobsson, David Weston, Sebastian Breaks, Alan Howard, Roy Dotrice, Patrick Jordan, Anton Diffring, Eric Porter, Ralph Michael; ***D:*** Anthony Mann; ***W:*** Ben Barzman; ***C:*** Robert Krasker; ***M:*** Malcolm Arnold.

Heroes of the Alamo 🦴½ **1937** Remember the Alamo...but forget this movie. Dull, threadbare dramatization of the battle that was scorned even back in '37. **75m/B VHS.** Rex Lease, Lane Chandler, Roger Williams, Earle Hodgins, Julian Rivero; ***D:*** Harry Fraser.

Heroes of the Heart 🦴🦴½ **1994** Residents ofa West Viriginia trailer park are devastated when their homes are destroyed in a flood. But then Basquette claims she was visited by God, who's directed her to bring the poor community together so that each can be granted their most secret wish. Nicely eccentric characters, serious theme with some whimsical touches, and a country-music soundtrack. **102m/C VHS.** Lena Basquette, Larry Groce, Dusty Rhodes, Webb Wilder, John McIntire, Jennifer Gurney, Johnny Paycheck; ***D:*** Daniel Boyd; ***W:*** Daniel Boyd; ***C:*** Larry Kopelman; ***M:*** Michael Lipton.

Heroes of the Hills 🦴½ **1938** The Three Mesquiteers back up a plan that would allow trusted prisoners to work for neighboring ranchers. Part of "The Three Mesquiteers" series. **54m/B VHS.** Robert "Bob" Livingston, Ray Corrigan, Max Terhune.

Heroes Shed No Tears 🦴🦴 *Ying Xiong Wei Lei; The Sunset Warrior* **1986** Chinese mercenaries are hired by the Thai government to capture a drug lord from the Golden Triangle. Cantonese with subtitles. **93m/C VHS, DVD.** *HK* Eddy Ko, Ching-Ying Lam, Chen Yue Sang, Kuo Sheng; ***D:*** John Woo; ***W:*** John Woo.

Heroes Stand Alone 🦴 1989 (R) When a U.S. spy plane is downed in Central America, a special force is sent in to rescue the crew. Another "Rambo" rip-off. **84m/C VHS.** Bradford Dillman, Chad Everett, Wayne Grace, Rick Dean; ***D:*** Mark Griffiths; ***W:*** Thomas McKelvey Cleaver.

Heroes Three 🦴🦴 1984 When his crewmate is murdered while on leave in in the Far East, a Navy officer enlists the aid of a Chinese detective to track down the killer. **90m/C VHS.** Rowena Cortes, Mike Kelly, Laurens C. Postma, Lawrence Tan; ***D:*** S.H. Lau.

The Heroic Trio 🦴🦴½ *Dong Fang San Xia* 1993 Three superheroines battle the Lord of the Underground to prevent him from stealing any more human babies. Lots of martial arts and supernatural action. Chinese with subtitles or dubbed. **87m/C VHS, DVD.** *HK* Damian Lau, Michelle Yeoh, Maggie Cheung, Anita (Yim-Fong) Mui, Anthony Wong; ***D:*** Ching Siu Tung, Johnny To; ***W:*** Sandy Shaw; ***C:*** Poon Hang-Seng, Tom Lau; ***M:*** William Hu.

He's My Girl 🦴½ 1987 (PG-13) When a rock singer wins a trip for two to Hollywood, he convinces his agent to dress up as a woman so they can use the free tickets. **104m/C VHS.** David Hallyday, T.K. Carter, Misha McK, Jennifer Tilly; ***D:*** Gabrielle Beaumont; ***W:*** Terence H. Winkless, Taylor Ames, Charles F. Bohl; ***C:*** Peter Collister.

Hester Street 🦴🦴🦴½ 1975 Set at the turn of the century, the film tells the story of a young Jewish immigrant who ventures to New York City to be with her husband. As she re-acquaints herself with her husband, she finds that he has abandoned his Old World ideals. The film speaks not only to preserving the heritage of the Jews, but to cherishing all heritages and cultures. Highly regarded upon release, unfortunately forgotten today. **92m/B VHS.** Carol Kane, Doris Roberts, Steven Keats, Mel Howard, Dorrie Kavanaugh, Stephen Strimpell; ***D:*** Joan Micklin Silver; ***W:*** Joan Micklin Silver; ***C:*** Kenneth Van Sickle; ***M:*** William Bolcom.

Hexed 🦴½ 1993 (R) Walter Mitty lives in the person of bellboy Matthew Welsh, who enjoys masquerading as a debonair bon vivant. He finagles his way into the life of Hexina, a beautiful psychotic model who has checked into the hotel where Matthew works in order to murder her blackmailer. She tries to kill Matthew, apparently getting in a little practice, but he'll still follow her anywhere. Inane, charmless comedy that intends to satirize "Fatal Attraction" and similar films. **93m/C VHS.** Arye Gross, Claudia Christian, Adrienne Shelly, R. Lee Ermey, Norman Fell, Michael E. Knight; ***D:*** Alan Spencer; ***W:*** Alan Spencer.

Hey, Babu Riba 🦴🦴½ 1988 (R) A popular Yugoslavian fit of nostalgia about four men convening at the funeral of a young girl they all loved years before, and their happy, Americana-bathed memories therein. In Serbo-Croatian with English subtitles. **109m/C VHS.** *YU* Gala Videnovic, Nebojsa Bakocevic, Dragan Bjelogric, Marko Todorovic, Goran Radakovic, Relja Basic, Milos Zutic; ***D:*** Jovan Acin; ***W:*** Jovan Acin.

Hey Good Lookin' 1982 Ralph Bakshi's irreverent look at growing up in the 1950s bears the trademark qualities that distinguish his other adult animated features, "Fritz the Cat" and "Heavy Traffic." **87m/C VHS.** ***D:*** Ralph Bakshi; ***W:*** Ralph Bakshi.

Hey There, It's Yogi Bear 🦴🦴 1964 When Yogi Bear comes out of winter hibernation to search for food, he travels to the Chizzling Brothers Circus. The first feature-length cartoon to come from the H-B Studios. **98m/C VHS.** ***D:*** William Hanna; ***V:*** Daws Butler, James Darren, Mel Blanc, J. Pat O'Malley, Julie Bennett.

Hi-De-Ho 🦴🦴½ 1935 The great Cab Calloway and his red hot jazz are featured in this film, which has the band caught between rival gangsters. The plot is incidental to the music, anyway. ♫Hi-De-Ho; I Got A Gal Named Nettie; Little Old Lady From Baltimore; A Rainy Sunday. **60m/B VHS, DVD.** Cab Calloway, Ida James; ***D:*** Josh Binney.

Hi-Di-Hi 1988 Comedy about the shenanigans that inevitably follow when a stuffy Cambridge professor becomes the entertainment manager for a holiday camp. **91m/C VHS.** *GB* Simon Cadell, Ruth Madoc, Paul Shane, Jeffrey Holland, Leslie Dwyer. **TV**

Hi Diddle Diddle 🦴🦴½ *Diamonds and Crime; Try and Find It* 1943 Topsy-turvy comedy features young lovers who long for conventional happiness. Instead they are cursed with con-artist parents who delight in crossing that law-abiding line. **72m/B VHS.** Adolphe Menjou, Martha Scott, Dennis O'Keefe, Pola Negri; ***D:*** Andrew L. Stone.

Hi-Jacked 🦴 1950 When a parolee trucker's cargo is stolen, he inevitably becomes a suspect and must set out to find the true culprits. **66m/B VHS.** Jim Davis, Paul Cavanagh, Marsha Jones.

Hi-Life 🦴🦴½ 1998 (R) Talky, Christmastime, Manhattan-set ensemble comedy finds compulsive gambler and out of work actor Jimmy (Stoltz) owing bookie Fatty (Durning) $900. To get the money, he tells girlfriend Susan (Kelly) it's to finance an abortion for his slutty sis Maggie (Hannah). Then Maggie's ex-boyfriend Ray (Scott) gets involved and Fatty's associate Miner (Reigart) and numerous other players who all wind up at the Hi-Life Bar and discover Jimmy's scams. **82m/C VHS, DVD.** Eric Stoltz, Moira Kelly, Daryl Hannah, Campbell Scott, Peter Riegert, Katrin Cartlidge, Charles Durning, Saundra Santiago, Anne DeSalvo, Bruce MacVittie, Tegan West; ***D:*** Roger Hedden; ***W:*** Roger Hedden; ***C:*** John Thomas; ***M:*** David Lawrence.

The Hi-Lo Country 🦴🦴½ 1998 (R) For years, Sam Peckinpah wanted to make this movie. It took Martin Scorsese to resurrect the project and to secure Walon Green to adapt the 1961 Max Evans novel for the screen. Pete Calder (Crudup) returns to New Mexico from WWII. While waiting for buddy Big Boy Matson (Harrelson) to return from the Marines, Pete falls for Mona (Arquette), a saucy woman whose husband works for the area's biggest rancher, Jim Love (Elliott). When Big Boy does return, it becomes obvious that he and Mona are hot for each other, so Pete bows out. Big Boy is the last real cowboy (a favorite Peckinpah theme), who loves the land, fears no one, and knows his times are coming to an end. Director Frears may not completely understand the American mythic West, but thanks to Oliver Stapleton's cinematography, the film has a look close to what a Peckinpah or a Ford might have given it. **114m/C VHS, DVD.** Woody Harrelson, Patricia Arquette, Billy Crudup, Penelope Cruz, Sam Elliott, Cole Hauser, Darren E. Burrows, Jacob Vargas, James Gammon, Lane Smith, Katy Jurado, John Diehl, Enrique Castillo, Rosaleen Linehan; ***D:*** Stephen Frears; ***W:*** Walon Green; ***C:*** Oliver Stapleton; ***M:*** Carter Burwell.

Hi, Mom! 🦴🦴🦴 *Confessions of A Peeping John; Blue Manhattan* 1970 (R) DePalma's follow-up to "Greetings" finds amateur pornographer/movie maker De Niro being advised by a professional in the field (Garfield) of sleazy filmmaking. De Niro films the residents of his apartment building and eventually marries one of his starlets. One of De Palma's earlier and better efforts with De Niro playing a crazy as only he can. **87m/C VHS.** Robert De Niro, Charles Durnham, Allen (Goorwitz) Garfield, Lara Parker, Jennifer Salt, Gerrit Graham; ***D:*** Brian DePalma; ***W:*** Brian DePalma.

Hi-Riders 🦴 1977 (R) A revenge-based tale about large, mag-wheeled trucks and their drivers. **90m/C VHS.** Mel Ferrer, Stephen McNally, Neville Brand, Ralph Meeker; ***D:*** Greydon Clark.

The Hidden 🦴🦴🦴 1987 (R) A seasoned cop (Nouri) and a benign alien posing as an FBI agent (MacLachlan) team up to track down and destroy a hyper-violent alien who survives by invading the bodies of humans, causing them to go on murderous rampages. Much acclaimed, high velocity action film with state-of-the-art special effects (at least for the time). Followed by a minor 1994 sequel with a different cast. **98m/C VHS, DVD.** Kyle MacLachlan, Michael Nouri, Clu Gulager, Ed O'Ross, Claudia Christian, Clarence Felder, Richard Brooks, William Boyett, Chris Mulkey; ***D:*** Jack Sholder; ***W:*** Bob Hunt, Jim Kouf; ***C:*** Jacques Haitkin; ***M:*** Michael Convertino.

The Hidden 2 🦴🦴½ 1994 (R) The hyper-violent alien of the 1987 movie returns. With its love of fast cars, high-caliber weapons, and heavy metal music, this body-possessing creature appears to be unstoppable. **91m/C VHS.** Raphael Sbarge, Kate Hodge, Michael Nouri; ***D:*** Seth Pinsker; ***W:*** Seth Pinsker; ***M:*** David McHugh.

Hidden Agenda 🦴🦴½ 1990 (R) A human rights activist and an American lawyer uncover brutality and corruption among the British forces in Northern Ireland. Slow-paced but strong performances. The Northern Irish dialect is sometimes difficult to understand as are the machinations on the British police system. Generally worthwhile. **108m/C VHS, DVD, Wide.** Frances McDormand, Brian Cox, Brad Dourif, Mai Zetterling, John Benfield, Des McAleer, Jim Norton, Maurice Roeves; ***D:*** Ken Loach; ***W:*** Jim Allen; ***C:*** Clive Tickner; ***M:*** Stewart Copeland. Cannes '90: Special Jury Prize.

Hidden Agenda 🦴🦴 1999 (R) Arriving in Berlin, American tourist Dillon learns his brother has been murdered. He decides to do some investigating on his own and winds up caught between CIA spies and the German secret police. **97m/C VHS, DVD.** Kevin Dillon, Christopher Plummer, Andrea Roth, Michael Wincott, J.T. Walsh. **VIDEO**

Hidden Agenda 🦴🦴½ 2001 (R) Former NSA agent Jason Price (Lundgren) is still doing covert government work by making people vanish. His latest client is a mobster (Houde) but Price finds that a legendary hit man (Roy) has taken an unhealthy interest in his operation. **94m/C VHS, DVD.** Dolph Lundgren, Maxim Roy, Brigitte Paquette, Serge Houde, Patrick Kerton, Christian Paul; ***D:*** Marc S. Grenier; ***W:*** Les Weldon; ***C:*** Sylvain Brault. **VIDEO**

Hidden Assassin 🦴 *The Shooter* 1994 (R) French hit woman Simone (Detmers) supposedly shoots the Cuban ambassador to the U.N. and escapes back to her home base in Prague, followed by Czech-born U.S. Marshal Mickey Dane (Lundgren). Mickey starts to doubt that Simone is the killer (she claims she's long retired and is being set up) and the duo try to find the truth amid lots of double-crosses. Doesn't make much sense in any case. **89m/C VHS.** Dolph Lundgren, Maruschka Detmers, Assumpta Serna, Gavan O'Herlihy, John Ashton, Simon Andreu; ***D:*** Ted Kotcheff; ***W:*** Meg Thayer, Billy Ray, Yves Andre Martin; ***C:*** Fernando Arguelles; ***M:*** Stefano Mainetti.

Hidden City 🦴🦴 1987 A film archivist and a statistician become drawn into a conspiracy when a piece of revealing film is spliced onto the end of an innocuous government tape. **112m/C VHS.** Charles Dance, Cassie Stuart, Alex Norton, Tusse Silberg, Bill Paterson; ***D:*** Stephen Poliakoff.

Hidden Enemy 🦴½ 1940 During WWII, a scientist develops a new metal alloy that is stronger than steel yet lighter than aluminum. His nephew must protect his scientist/uncle from spies who would steal the formula to use against the Allies. **63m/B VHS.** Warren Hull, Kay Linaker, Wilhelm von Brinken, George Cleveland; ***D:*** Howard Bretherton.

Hidden Fears 🦴🦴½ 1993 Maureen Dietz (Foster) carries the gruesome memories of her husband's murder with her. Years later she goes to the police with new evidence to reopen her husband's case. Only the killers find out and return to finish off the eyewitnesses, and she's next! Based on the novel "Exercise in Terror" by Kaminsky, who also wrote the screenplay. **90m/C VHS.** Meg Foster, Frederic Forrest, Wally Taylor, Bever-Leigh Banfield, Marc Macaulay, Patrick Cherry, Scott Hayes; ***D:*** Jean Bodon; ***W:*** Stuart Kaminsky.

The Hidden Fortress 🦴🦴🦴½ *Kakushi Toride No San Akunin; Three Rascals in the Hidden Fortress; Three Bad Men in the Hidden Fortress* 1958 Kurosawa's tale of a warrior who protects a princess from warring feudal lords. An inspiration for George Lucas' "Star Wars" series and deserving of its excellent reputation. In Japanese with English subtitles. **139m/B VHS, DVD, Wide.** *JP* Toshiro Mifune, Misa Uehara, Kamatari (Keita) Fujiwara, Susumu Fujita, Eiko Miyoshi, Takashi Shimura, Kichijiro Ueda, Koji Mitsui, Minoru Chiaki, Toshiko Higuchi, Shiten Ohashi; ***D:*** Akira Kurosawa; ***W:*** Akira Kurosawa, Shinobu Hashimoto, Ryuzo Kikushima, Hideo Oguni; ***C:*** Kazuo Yamazaki; ***M:*** Masaru Sato. Berlin Intl. Film Fest. '59: Director (Kurosawa).

Hidden Gold 🦴½ 1933 Routine western for Mix, which has him going undercover to win the confidence of three outlaws and discover where they have hidden their loot. **57m/B VHS.** Tom Mix, Judith Barrie, Raymond Hatton; ***D:*** Arthur Rosson.

Hidden Guns 🦴🦴🦴 1956 Above-average tale of father-and-son lawmen out to reform a town and put the bad guys away. When dad is killed, son goes up against the villain alone. A Greek chorus adds an interesting twist to the action. Erich von Stroheim Jr. is listed as assistant director. **66m/B VHS.** Bruce (Herman Brix) Bennett, Richard Arlen, John Carradine, Faron Young, Angie Dickinson, Guinn "Big Boy" Williams; ***D:*** Albert C. Gannaway.

Hidden in America 🦴🦴½ 1996 (PG-13) Bill Januson (Bridges) has lost his auto-plant job because of downsizing and his wife to cancer. His savings exhausted and his prospects bleak, Januson struggles to put food on the table for his two kids, who increasingly begin to suffer the effects of poverty. Produced in conjunction with the End Hunger Network, whose co-founder, Jeff Bridges, has a cameo. **96m/C VHS.** Beau Bridges, Bruce Davison, Jena Malone, Shelton Dane, Alice Krige, Josef Sommer, Frances McDormand; ***Cameos:*** Jeff Bridges; ***D:*** Martin Bell; ***W:*** Peter Silverman, Michael deGuzman; ***C:*** James R. Bagdonas; ***M:*** Mason Daring. **CABLE**

Hidden Obsession 🦴½ 1992 (R) Newscaster Ellen is taking a much needed vacation at an isolated cabin when she learns that a serial killer has escaped from a nearby prison. Luckily, she has a hunky police officer neighbor for protection. But though the escaped killer is captured, the killings go on—with Ellen as the next target. **92m/C VHS.** Heather Thomas, Jan-Michael Vincent, Nicholas Celozzi; ***D:*** John Stewart; ***W:*** David Reskin.

The Hidden Room 🦴🦴🦴 *Obsession* 1949 A doctor finds out about his wife's affair and decides to get revenge on her lover. He kidnaps him, imprisons him in a cellar, and decides to kill him—slowly. Tense melodrama. **98m/B VHS.** *GB* Robert Newton, Sally Gray, Naunton Wayne, Phil Brown, Olga Lindo, Russell Waters, James Harcourt, Allan Jeayes, Stanley Baker; ***D:*** Edward Dmytryk; ***W:*** Alec Coppel; ***C:*** C.M. Pennington-Richards; ***M:*** Nino Rota.

Hidden Valley 🦴🦴 1932 Early Steele western in which everyone is fighting over a map that leads to hidden treasure in the valley. **60m/B VHS.** Bob Steele, Gertrude Messinger, Francis McDonald; ***D:*** Robert North Bradbury.

Hide and Go Shriek 🦴 1987 (R) Several high school seniors are murdered one by one during a graduation party. Also available in an unrated, gorier version. **90m/C VHS.** Annette Sinclair, Brittain Frye, Rebunkah Jones; ***D:*** Skip Schoolnik.

Hide and Seek 🦴 1977 When a high school hacker converts his computer into a nuclear weapon, he finds that it has developed a mind of its own. **60m/C VHS.** Bob Martin, Ingrid Veninger, David Patrick.

Hide and Seek 🦴 1980 A study of children living in the land that would soon become Israel. Although they play as normal children, life is particularly difficult. This adversity will lay the foundation for their Israeli citizenry. In Hebrew with English subtitles. **90m/C VHS.** Gila Almagor, Doron Tavori, Chaim Hadaya; ***D:*** Dan Wolman.

Hide and Seek 🦴🦴½ *Cord* 2000 (R) Pregnant Ann (Hannah) is kidnapped by a crazy childless couple (Tilly and Gallo) and it's no kids' game when husband Jack (Greenwood) tries to find her. **100m/C VHS, DVD, Wide.** Daryl Hannah, Jennifer Tilly, Vincent Gallo, Bruce Greenwood, Johanna Black;

D: Sidney J. Furie; *W:* Joel Hladecek, Yas Takata; *M:* Robert Carli. **VIDEO**

Hide in Plain Sight ♂♂♂ 1980 (PG) A distraught blue-collar worker searches for his children who disappeared when his ex-wife and her mobster husband are given new identities by federal agents. Caan's fine directorial debut is based on a true story. **96m/C VHS.** James Caan, Jill Eikenberry, Robert Viharo, Kenneth McMillan, Josef Sommer, Danny Aiello; *D:* James Caan.

Hide-Out ♂♂½ 1934 A man running from the law winds up at a small farm, falls in love, and becomes reformed by the good family that takes him in. Good supporting cast includes a very young Rooney. **83m/B VHS.** Robert Montgomery, Maureen O'Sullivan, Edward Arnold, Elizabeth Patterson, Mickey Rooney, Edward Brophy; *D:* Woodbridge S. Van Dyke.

Hideaway ♂♂ 1994 (R) Hodge podge movie finds Hatch Harrison (Goldblum) brought back from the other side after suffering injuries from a near-fatal car accident. He returns with the ability to psychically connect with Vassago (Sisto), a sadistic serial killer of young girls. Coincidentally, Harrison has a teenage daughter, Regina (Silverstone), and Vassago has her lined up as his next victim. The visual effects of spirits floating down a cosmic vortex are entertaining, but plot originality must have been hidden away to make room for the nifty special effects. Based on a novel by Dean R. Koontz. **103m/C VHS, DVD, Wide.** Jeff Goldblum, Christine Lahti, Alicia Silverstone, Jeremy Sisto, Rae Dawn Chong; *D:* Brett Leonard; *W:* Andrew Kevin Walker, Neal Jimenez; *C:* Gale Tattersall; *M:* Trevor Jones.

The Hideaways ♂♂½ *From the Mixed-Up Files of Mrs. Basil E. Frankweiler* 1973 (G) A 12-year-old girl and her younger brother run away and hide in the Metropolitan Museum of Art. The girl becomes enamored of a piece of sculpture and sets out to discover its creator. Based on the children's novel by E.L. Konigsburg. **105m/C VHS.** Richard Mulligan, George Rose, Ingrid Bergman, Sally Prager, Johnny Doran, Madeline Kahn; *D:* Fielder Cook.

Hideous ♂½ 1997 (R) Eccentric collector's greatest prize is a seemingly petrified toxic waste mutant that's not so petrified afterall. It manages to come to life and even spawn little mutants to go on a killing spree. **82m/C VHS, DVD.** Jacqueline Lovell, Michael Citrinti, Rhonda Griffin, Mel Johnson Jr., Traci May, Jerry O'Donnell; *D:* Charles Band; *W:* Benjamin Carr; *M:* Richard Band.

Hideous Kinky ♂♂½ 1999 (R) Julia (Winslet) is a free-spirited single mom who decides to leave London and take her two daughters, Bea and Lucy, to live in Morocco in 1972. She gets by on sales of homemade dolls and the occasional check from the girls' father. Julia believes that a conversion to the Sufi life will solve her problems, while Bea would rather they settle into a "normal" life. Julia meets, and has a passionate affair with, juggler and sometime con man Bilal, whom the girls adopt as a surrogate father figure. Winslet plays her character's mixture of naivete and motherly concern well, and looks good doing it, as does the whole movie. The Moroccan locales are brilliantly displayed. Character development and consistent narrative are sometimes lacking. **97m/C VHS, DVD.** *GB FR* Kate Winslet, Said Taghmaoui, Bella Riza, Carrie Mullan, Pierre Clementi, Abigail Cruttenden, Sira Stampe; *D:* Gilles Mackinnon; *W:* Billy Mackinnon; *C:* John de Borman; *M:* John Keane.

Hideous Sun Demon ♂½ *Blood on His Lips; Terror from the Sun; The Sun Demon* 1959 A physicist exposed to radiation must stay out of sunlight or he will turn into a scaly, lizard-like creature. Includes previews of coming attractions from classic sci-fi films. **75m/B VHS, DVD.** Robert Clarke, Patricia Manning, Nan Peterson, Patrick Whyte, Peter Similuk, Fred La Porta, Robert Garry, Del Courtney; *D:* Thomas Bontross, Robert Clarke; *W:* Doane R. Hoag, E. S. Seeley Jr.; *C:* Vilis Lapenieks, John Morrill, Stan Follis; *M:* John Seeley.

Hider in the House ♂♂½ 1990 (R) In a peaceful neighborhood a family is about to spend an evening of terror when they discover a psychopath is hiding in the attic of their home. **109m/C VHS.** Michael McKean, Gary Busey, Mimi Rogers, Kurt Christopher Kinder, Candy Hutson, Elizabeth Ruscio, Bruce Glover; *D:* Michael Patrick.

Hiding Out ♂♂ 1987 (PG-13) A young stockbroker testifies against the Mafia and must find a place to hide in order to avoid being killed. He winds up at his cousin's high school in Delaware, but can he really go through all these teenage troubles once again? **99m/C VHS, DVD, Wide.** Jon Cryer, Keith Coogan, Gretchen Cryer, Annabeth Gish, Tim Quill; *D:* Bob Giraldi; *W:* Jeff Rothberg, Joe Menosky; *C:* Daniel Pearl; *M:* Anne Dudley.

The Hiding Place ♂♂ 1975 True story of two Dutch Christian sisters sent to a concentration camp for hiding Jews during WWII. Film is uneven but good cast pulls it through. Based on the Corrie Ten Boom book and produced by Billy Graham's Evangelistic Association. **145m/C VHS.** Julie Harris, Eileen Heckart, Arthur O'Connell, Jeanette Clift; *D:* James F. Collier.

High & Low ♂♂♂½ *Tengoku To Jigoku* 1962 (R) Fine Japanese film noir about a wealthy businessman who is being blackmailed by kidnappers who claim to have his son. When he discovers that they have mistakenly taken his chauffeur's son he must decide whether to face financial ruin or risk the life of a young boy. Based on an Ed McBain novel. In Japanese with English subtitles. **143m/B VHS, DVD, Wide.** *JP* Toshiro Mifune, Tatsuya Mihashi, Tatsuya Nakadai; *D:* Akira Kurosawa; *W:* Evan Hunter, Ryuzo Kikushima, Hideo Oguni, Akira Kurosawa; *C:* Asakazu Nakai, Takao Saito; *M:* Masaru Sato.

High Anxiety ♂♂ 1977 (PG) Brooks tries hard to please in this lowbrow parody of Hitchcock films employing dozens of references to films like "Psycho," "Spellbound," "The Birds," and "Vertigo." Tells the tale of a height-fearing psychiatrist caught up in a murder mystery. The title song performed a la Sinatra by Brooks is one of the film's high moments. Brooks also has a lot of fun with Hitchcockian camera movements. Uneven (What? Brooks?) but amusing tribute. **92m/C VHS.** Mel Brooks, Madeline Kahn, Cloris Leachman, Harvey Korman, Ron Carey, Howard Morris, Dick Van Patten; *D:* Mel Brooks; *W:* Mel Brooks, Ron Clark, Barry Levinson, Rudy DeLuca.

High Art ♂♂ 1998 (R) A trio of women play romantic games in New York's art community. Ambitious magazine editor-in-training Syd (Mitchell) has a boyfriend, James (Mann), but feels something's missing. Noticing a leak in her apartment ceiling, Syd heads upstairs to confront her neighbor and meets Lucy Berliner (Sheedy), a once-celebrated, now-retired photographer with a heroin problem and an equally hooked girlfriend, Greta (Clarkson). Syd and Lucy begin a friendship that leads to an affair, while Syd also wants to revitalize Lucy's career. Ex-Brat Packer Sheedy's the real revelation with her standout performance. **102m/C VHS.** Radha Mitchell, Ally Sheedy, Patricia Clarkson, Tammy Grimes, Gabriel Mann, William Sage, David Thornton, Anh Duong; *D:* Lisa Cholodenko; *W:* Lisa Cholodenko; *C:* Tami Reiker; *M:* Craig (Shudder to Think) Wedren. Ind. Spirit '99: Actress (Sheedy); L.A. Film Critics '98: Actress (Sheedy); Natl. Soc. Film Critics '98: Actress (Sheedy); Sundance '98: Screenplay.

High Ballin' ♂♂ 1978 (PG) Truckers Fonda and Reed team up with lady trucker Shaver to take on the gang trying to crush the independent drivers. **100m/C VHS.** *CA* Peter Fonda, Jerry Reed, Helen Shaver; *D:* Peter Carter; *W:* Paul F. Edwards.

High Command ♂♂½ 1937 To save his daughter from an ugly scandal, the British general of an isolated Colonial African outpost traps a blackmailer's killer. **84m/B VHS.** *GB* Lionel Atwill, Lucie Mannheim, James Mason; *D:* Thorold Dickinson.

High Country ♂♂½ *The First Hello* 1981 (PG) Two misfits, one handicapped, the other an ex-con, on the run from society learn mutual trust as they travel through the Canadian Rockies. **101m/C VHS.** *CA* Timothy Bottoms, Linda Purl, George Sims, Jim Lawrence, Bill Berry; *D:* Harvey Hart.

High Crime ♂♂ 1973 A "French Connection"-style suspense story about the heroin trade. Features high-speed chases and a police commissioner obsessed with capturing the criminals. **91m/C VHS.** James Whitmore, Franco Nero, Fernando Rey; *D:* Enzo G. Castellari.

High Crimes ♂♂½ 2002 (PG-13) Military courtroom thriller is only average but does have Freeman, who's always worth watching. He's reteamed with "Kiss the Girls" co-star Judd, who plays spunky California attorney Claire Kubik. Claire gets a big surprise when her contractor hubby Tom (Caviezel) is suddenly arrested by the FBI and sent to a military prison. Turns out Tom, then known as Ron Chapman, was in an elite Marine special unit and is accused of a 1988 civilian massacre in El Salvador. She looks to recovering alcoholic and ex-JAG lawyer Charlie Grimes (Freeman) for assistance but sinister plots are afoot. Based on the 1998 novel by Joseph Finder. **115m/C VHS, DVD.** *US* Ashley Judd, James Caviezel, Morgan Freeman, Amanda Peet, Tom Bower, Adam Scott, Bruce Davison, Michael Gaston, Juan Carlos Hernandez, Jude Ciccolella, Michael Shannon; *D:* Carl Franklin; *W:* Yuri Zeltser, Cary Bickley; *C:* Theo van de Sande; *M:* Graeme Revell.

The High Crusade ♂½ 1992 (PG-13) A group of 13th-century English crusaders are heading for the Holy Land when they're interrupted on their journey by an alien spacecraft. They overpower the space guys and take over the vessel, hoping it will take them to Jerusalem, but since the spacecraft's on autopilot, the knights wind up heading for the aliens' home planet instead. **?m/C VHS, DVD.** *GB GE* John Rhys-Davies, Michael Des Barres, Rick Overton; *D:* Holger Neuhauser.

High Desert Kill ♂♂ 1990 (PG) A science-fiction tale that will keep you guessing. Aliens landing in the New Mexican desert want something totally unexpected, and a trio of friends will be the first to find out what it is. Writer Cook was also responsible for "The China Syndrome." **93m/C VHS.** Chuck Connors, Marc Singer, Anthony Geary, Micah Grant; *D:* Harry Falk; *W:* T.S. Cook. **CABLE**

High Fidelity ♂♂♂ 2000 (R) Frears, Cusack, and the writing team from "Grosse Pointe Blank" successfully bring Nick Hornby's 1995 novel to the screen, transplanting it from London to Chicago in the process. Cusack is Rob, a stuck-in-adolescence record store owner who just broke up with Laura (Hjejle), his long-time, live-in love. This gets him to thinking about his Top Five All-Time Breakups. Cue flashbacks. It also sends him on some hilarious conversations with his employees: know-it-all Barry (Black) who wields his musical tastes like a weapon, and Dick (Louiso), who's bashful to the point of invisibility. Cusack does his usual fine job, but Black and Louiso take over whenever they're on screen. **113m/C VHS, DVD.** John Cusack, Todd Louiso, Jack Black, Iben Hjejle, Tim Robbins, Joan Cusack, Lisa Bonet, Catherine Zeta-Jones, Lili Taylor, Natasha Gregson Wagner, Sara Gilbert, Chris Rehmann, Ben Carr, Joelle Carter, Bruce Springsteen; *D:* Stephen Frears; *W:* John Cusack, D.V. DeVincentis, Steve Pink, Scott Rosenberg; *C:* Seamus McGarvey; *M:* Howard Shore.

High Frequency ♂♂ 1988 Two young men monitoring a satellite relay station witness the murder of a woman. Believing they know who the killer's next victim will be, they set out to warn her. Lack of development mars what could have been a tidy little thriller. **105m/C VHS.** *IT* Oliver Benny, Vincent Spano, Isabelle Pasco, Anne Canovos; *D:* Faliero Rosati.

High Gear ♂ 1933 Heartstring-tugger about a race car driver, his girlfriend and the orphan son of a driver killed in a crash. Try to guess the outcome. **65m/B VHS.** James Murray, Joan Marsh, Jackie Searl, Theodore von Eltz, Lee Moran, Gordon DeMain; *D:* Leigh Jason.

High Heels ♂♂ *Docteur Popaul; Scoundrel in White* 1972 A black comedy about a doctor who believes beauty is only skin deep and marries a plain woman. However, when he meets her beautiful sister, he begins to wonder. In French with English subtitles. **100m/C VHS.** *FR* Laura Antonelli, Jean-Paul Belmondo, Mia Farrow, Daniel Ivernel; *D:* Claude Chabrol.

High Heels ♂♂♂ *Tacones Lejanos* 1991 (R) An outrageous combination murder-melodrama-comedy from Almodovar. Rebecca is a TV anchorwoman in Madrid whose flamboyant singer/actress mother has returned to the city for a concert. Rebecca happens to be married to one of her mother's not-so-ex-flames. When her husband winds up dead, Rebecca confesses to his murder during her newscast—but is she telling the truth or just covering up for mom? Mix in a drag queen/judge, a dancing chorus of women prison inmates, and a peculiar police detective, and see if the plot convolutions make sense. In Spanish with English subtitles. **113m/C VHS.** *SP* Victoria Abril, Marisa Paredes, Miguel Bose, Feodor Atkine, Bibi Andersen, Rocio Munoz; *D:* Pedro Almodovar; *W:* Pedro Almodovar; *C:* Alfredo Mayo; *M:* Ryuichi Sakamoto. Cesar '93: Foreign Film.

High Heels and Low Lifes ♂♂ 2001 (R) Brit nurse Shannon (Driver) and American actress Frances (McCormack) overhear a plot to rob a London safe deposit box center and immediately go to the cops. When the cops seem uninterested, the girls decide to blackmail the crooks into giving them a cut. Nice premise and an enjoyable performance by Driver are wasted by Smith's flat direction, which misses almost all comic payoff opportunities in the script. **85m/C VHS, DVD, Wide.** *US GB* Minnie Driver, Mary McCormack, Kevin McNally, Mark Williams, Danny Dyer, Michael Gambon, Kevin Eldon, Len Collin, Darren Boyd, Julian Wadham; *D:* Mel Smith; *W:* Kim Fuller; *C:* Steven Chivers; *M:* Charlie Mole.

High Hopes ♂♂♂ 1988 A moving yet nasty satiric comedy about a pair of ex-hippies maintaining their counterculture lifestyle in Margaret Thatcher's England, as they watch the signs of conservative "progress" overtake them and their geriatric, embittered Mum. Hilarious and mature. **110m/C VHS.** *GB* Philip Davis, Ruth Sheen, Edna Dore, Philip Jackson, Heather Tobias, Leslie Manville, David Bamber; *D:* Mike Leigh; *W:* Mike Leigh; *C:* Roger Pratt; *M:* Rachel Portman, Andrew Dixon.

High Ice ♂½ 1980 Forest ranger and a lieutenant colonel are involved in a clash of wills over a rescue mission high in the snow-capped Washington state peaks. **97m/C VHS.** David Janssen, Tony Musante; *D:* Eugene S. Jones.

High Lonesome ♂♂½ 1950 Barrymore is a drifter in Big Bend country, suspected in a series of mysterious murders. While he is being held captive, the real killers—thought dead—return to exact revenge on those they hold responsible for the range war in which they were wounded. This was LeMay's only stint as a director. **80m/C VHS.** John Blythe Barrymore Jr., Chill Wills, John Archer, Lois Butler, Kristine Miller, Basil Ruysdael, Jack Elam; *D:* Alan LeMay; *W:* Alan LeMay.

High Noon ♂♂♂♂ 1952 Landmark Western about Hadleyville town marshal Will Kane (Cooper) who faces four professional killers alone, after being abandoned to his fate by the gutless townspeople who profess to admire him. Cooper is the ultimate hero figure, his sheer presence overwhelming. Note the continuing use of the ballad written by Dimitri Tiomkin, "Do Not Forsake Me, Oh My Darlin'" (sung by Tex Ritter) to heighten the tension and action. ♫High Noon (Do Not Forsake Me, Oh My Darlin'). **85m/B VHS, DVD.** Gary Cooper, Grace Kelly, Lloyd Bridges, Lon Chaney Jr., Thomas Mitchell, Otto Kruger, Katy Jurado, Lee Van Cleef, Harry (Henry) Morgan, Robert J. Wilke, Sheb Wooley; *D:* Fred Zinnemann; *W:* Carl Foreman; *C:* Floyd Crosby; *M:* Dimitri Tiomkin. Oscars '52: Actor (Cooper), Film Editing, Song ("High Noon (Do Not Forsake Me, Oh My Darlin')"), Orig. Dramatic Score; AFI '98: Top 100; Golden Globes '53: Actor—Drama (Cooper), Support. Actress (Jurado), Score, Natl. Film Reg.

'89;; N.Y. Film Critics '52: Director (Zinnemann), Film.

High Noon ½ **2000 (PG-13)** Generally faithful but needless TV remake of the 1952 western classic. Stoic marshal Will Kane (Skerritt), having just married the Quaker Amy (Thompson), is about to give up his badge when he learns that outlaw Frank Miller (Madsen) will be coming in on the noon train with revenge on his mind. Everyone thinks Will should just skedaddle out of town and save them all some grief but, hey, he's a hero and has to do what's right! **93m/C VHS, DVD, Wide.** Tom Skerritt, Susanna Thompson, Reed Edward Diamond, Maria Conchita Alonso, Michael Madsen, Dennis Weaver, August Schellenberg; ***D:*** Rod Hardy; ***W:*** Carl Foreman, T.S. Cook; ***C:*** Robert McLachlan; ***M:*** Allyn Ferguson. **CABLE**

High Noon: Part 2 **1980** Majors attempts to fill Gary Cooper's shoes, as Marshal Kane returns a year after the events of the original "High Noon" to remove the corrupt marshal who replaced him. Subtitled "The Return of Will Kane." **96m/C VHS.** Lee Majors, David Carradine, Pernell Roberts, Katherine (Kathy) Cannon; ***D:*** Jerry Jameson. **TV**

High Plains Drifter ½ **1973 (R)** A surreal, violent western focusing on a drifter who defends a town from gunmen intent on meting out death. One of Eastwood's most stylistic directorial efforts, indebted to his "Man with No Name" days with Sergio Leone. Laser format is letterboxed and includes chapter stops and the original theatrical trailer. **105m/C VHS, DVD, Wide.** Clint Eastwood, Verna Bloom, Mitchell Ryan, Marianna Hill, Jack Ging, Stefan Gierasch; ***D:*** Clint Eastwood; ***W:*** Ernest Tidyman, Dean Riesner; ***C:*** Bruce Surtees; ***M:*** Dee Barton.

High Risk ½ **1981 (R)** Improbable action-adventure of four unemployed Americans who battle foreign armies, unscrupulous gunrunners, and jungle bandits in a harrowing attempt to steal $5 million from an expatriate American drug dealer living in the peaceful splendor of his Columbian villa. Interesting in its own run-on way. **94m/C VHS, DVD.** James Brolin, Anthony Quinn, Lindsay Wagner, James Coburn, Ernest Borgnine, Bruce Davison, Cleavon Little, Chick Vennera; ***D:*** Stewart Raffill; ***W:*** Stewart Raffill; ***C:*** Alex Phillips Jr.; ***M:*** Mark Snow.

High Road to China **1983 (PG)** A hard-drinking former WWI air ace is recruited by a young heiress who must find her father before his ex-partner takes over his business. Post-"Raiders of the Lost Ark" thrills and romance, but without that tale's panache. **105m/C VHS.** Bess Armstrong, Tom Selleck, Jack Weston, Robert Morley, Wilford Brimley, Brian Blessed; ***D:*** Brian G. Hutton; ***M:*** John Barry.

High Rolling in a Hot Corvette *High Rolling* **1977 (PG)** Two carnival workers leave their jobs and hit the road in search of adventure and excitement, eventually turning to crime. **82m/C VHS.** *AU* Joseph Bottoms, Greg Taylor, Judy Davis, Wendy Hughes; ***D:*** Igor Auzins.

High School Caesar **1956** A seedy teenage exploitation flick about a rich teenager, with no parental supervision, who starts his own gang to run his high school. **75m/B VHS.** John Ashley; ***D:*** O'Dale Ireland.

High School Confidential *Young Hellions* **1958** Teen punk Tamblyn transfers to Santo Bello high school from Chicago and causes havoc among the locals. He soon involves himself in the school drug scene and looks to be the top dog in dealing, but what no one knows is that he's really a narc! A must for midnight movie fans thanks to high camp values, "hep cat" dialogue and the gorgeous Van Doren as Tamblyn's sex-crazed "aunt." **85m/B VHS.** Russ Tamblyn, Jan Sterling, John Blythe Barrymore Jr., Mamie Van Doren, Diane Jergens, Jerry Lee Lewis, Ray Anthony, Jackie Coogan, Charles Chaplin Jr., Burt Douglas, Michael Landon, Jody Fair, Phillipa Fallon, Robin Raymond, James Todd, Lyle Talbot, William Wellman Jr.; ***D:*** Jack Arnold; ***W:*** Robert Blees, Lewis Meltzer; ***C:*** Harold Marzorati.

High School High ½ **1996 (PG-13)** Idealistic teacher Richard Clark (Lovitz) leaves the private school world for notorious inner city Marion Barry High. This school is so bad it has its own cemetery (it's a parody, folks), but Clark is determined to get through to the kids. "Clockers" star Phifer shows up as a helpful student. Penned by David Zucker of "Airplane!" fame, so don't expect a "Mr. Holland's Opus." **86m/C VHS, DVD, Wide.** Jon Lovitz, Tia Carrere, Mekhi Phifer, Louise Fletcher, Malinda Williams; ***D:*** Hart Bochner; ***W:*** Pat Proft, David Zucker, Robert Locash; ***C:*** Vernon Layton; ***M:*** Ira Newborn.

High School USA ½ **1984** A high-school class clown confronts the king of the prep-jock-bullies. Antics ensue in this flick that features many stars from '50s and '60s sitcoms. **96m/C VHS.** Michael J. Fox, Nancy McKeon, Bob Denver, Angela Cartwright, Elinor Donahue, Dwayne Hickman, Lauri Hendler, Dana Plato, Tony Dow, David Nelson; ***D:*** Rod Amateau; ***M:*** Miles Goodman. **TV**

High Season ½ **1988 (R)** A satire about a beautiful English photographer (Bisset) stranded on an idyllic Greek island with neither money nor inspiration, and the motley assembly of characters who surround her during the tourist season. **95m/C VHS, 8mm.** *GB* Jacqueline Bisset, James Fox, Irene Papas, Sebastian Shaw, Kenneth Branagh, Robert Stephens, Leslie Manville; ***D:*** Clare Peploe; ***W:*** Mark Peploe, Clare Peploe; ***C:*** Chris Menges; ***M:*** Jason Osborn.

High Sierra **1941** Bogart is Roy "Mad Dog" Earle, an aging gangster whose last job backfires, so he's hiding out from the police in the High Sierras. Bogart's first starring role. Based on the novel by W.R. Burnett. Remade in 1955 as "I Died A Thousand Times." Also available colorized. **96m/B VHS.** Humphrey Bogart, Ida Lupino, Arthur Kennedy, Joan Leslie, Cornel Wilde, Henry Travers, Henry Hull; ***D:*** Raoul Walsh; ***W:*** John Huston, W.R. Burnett; ***C:*** Gaetano Antonio "Tony" Gaudio.

High Society **1956** A wealthy man attempts to win back his ex-wife who's about to be remarried in this enjoyable remake of "The Philadelphia Story." ♫High Society Calypso; Little One; Who Wants to Be a Millionaire?; True Love; You're Sensational; I Love You, Samantha; Now You Has Jazz; Well, Did You Evah?; Mind if I Make Love to You?. **107m/C VHS, 8mm, Wide.** Frank Sinatra, Bing Crosby, Grace Kelly, Louis Armstrong, Celeste Holm, Sidney Blackmer, Louis Calhern; ***D:*** Charles Walters; ***C:*** Paul Vogel; ***M:*** Cole Porter.

High Spirits **1988 (PG-13)** An American inherits an Irish castle and a sexy 200-year-old ghost. A painful, clumsy comedy by the fine British director that was apparently butchered by the studio before its release. **99m/C VHS, DVD, Wide.** Daryl Hannah, Peter O'Toole, Steve Guttenberg, Beverly D'Angelo, Liam Neeson, Martin Ferrero, Peter Gallagher, Jennifer Tilly; ***D:*** Neil Jordan; ***W:*** Neil Jordan; ***C:*** Alex Thompson; ***M:*** George Fenton.

High Stakes *Melanie Rose* **1989 (R)** Kirkland stars as a prostitute who's battling the Mob and falling in love. Limited release in theatres but another fine performance from Kirkland. **102m/C VHS.** Sally Kirkland, Robert LuPone, Richard Lynch, Sarah Michelle Gellar, Kathy Bates, W.T. Martin, Eddie Earl Hatch, Betty Miller, Maia Danzinger, Jesse Corti, Samantha Louca, Larry Block, June Stein, Michael Steinhardt, Maggie Warner, William Kennedy; ***D:*** Amos Kollek; ***W:*** Amos Kollek; ***C:*** Marc Hirschfeld; ***M:*** Bob Dylan, Mira Spektor.

High Stakes ½ *The Disappearance of Nora* **1993** Nora Fremont (Hamel) wakes up in the Nevada desert bloodied and bruised from a beating and suffering from amnesia. She makes it to Vegas where she meets Denton (Farina), who does casino security, and he agrees to help her find out who she is. But when her husband (Collins) comes to claim her, Nora's nightmare is really just beginning. **98m/C VHS, DVD.** Veronica Hamel, Dennis Farina, Stephen Collins, Stan Ivar, Bryan Cranston; ***D:*** Joyce Chopra; ***W:*** Tom Cole, Alan Ormsby; ***C:*** James Glennon; ***M:*** Mark Snow. **TV**

High Strung ½ **1991 (PG)** Writer Thane Furrows (Oedekerk) thinks his life can't get any worse since he's plagued by a nagging mom, pressuring boss, and an insurance salesman. Then mysterious voices and images (played by Carrey) tell him he'll die that night. Naturally, Thane tries to think of a way out of his predicament. You'll hope he dies sooner since the movie is so lame. Beware, Carrey has very little screen time in spite of the advertising. **96m/C VHS.** Steve Oedekerk, Thomas F. Wilson, Fred Willard, Jim Carrey.

High Tide **1987 (PG-13)** A strong and strange drama once again coupling the star and director of "My Brilliant Career." A small-time rock 'n' roll singer who is stranded in a small, beach town fortuitously meets up with her previously abandoned teenage daughter. Acclaimed. **120m/C VHS, 8mm.** *AU* Judy Davis, Jan Adele, Claudia Karvan, Colin Friels, John Clayton, Mark Hembrow, Frankie J. Holden, Monica Trapaga; ***D:*** Gillian Armstrong; ***W:*** Laura Jones; ***C:*** Russell Boyd; ***M:*** Peter Best, Ricky Fataar, Mark Moffatt. Australian Film Inst. '87: Actress (Davis); Natl. Soc. Film Critics '88: Actress (Davis).

High Velocity ½ **1976 (PG)** Lame adventure about two mercenaries involved in the challenge of a lifetime—rescuing a kidnapped executive from Asian terrorists. Filmed in Manila. **105m/C VHS.** Ben Gazzara, Paul Winfield, Britt Ekland, Keenan Wynn; ***D:*** Remi Kramer; ***M:*** Jerry Goldsmith.

High Voltage **1929** A fast-moving comedy adventure set in the High Sierras. **62m/B VHS.** Carole Lombard, William Boyd, Gwen Moore, Billy Bevan; ***D:*** Howard Higgin.

High Voltage **1998 (R)** Tough guy Johnny Clay (Sabato Jr.) winds up in unexpected trouble when he and his cohorts rob a bank that's laundering money for the Asian mob. Mob boss Cheung decides they need to be taught a lesson. **92m/C VHS, DVD.** Antonio Sabato Jr., Lochlan Monroe, William Zabka, George Kee Cheung, Amy Smart, James Lew, Antonio (Tony) Sabato, Shannon Lee; ***D:*** Isaac Florentine; ***W:*** Mike Mains; ***C:*** Philip D. Schwartz; ***M:*** Steve Edwards. **VIDEO**

Higher and Higher **1944** Bankrupt aristocrat conspires with servants to regain his fortune, and tries to marry his daughter into money. Sinatra's first big-screen role. ♫You Belong in a Love Song; A Most Important Affair; The Music Stopped; Today I'm A Debutante; A Lovely Way To Spend An Evening; I Couldn't Sleep a Wink Last Night; You're On Your Own; I Saw You First; Disgustingly Rich. **90m/B VHS.** Frank Sinatra, Leon Errol, Michele Morgan, Jack Haley, Mary McGuire; ***D:*** Tim Whelan.

Higher Education **1988 (R)** Andy leaves his small town for a big city college and falls head over heels for a student and a teacher. He didn't know college could be so much fun. **83m/C VHS.** Kevin Hicks, Isabelle Mejias, Lori Hallier, Maury Chaykin, Richard Monette; ***D:*** John Sheppard.

Higher Learning **1994 (R)** Racism, idealism, and the struggle for identity converge in this stylistically shot but rarely enlightening commentary on campus life and strife, focusing on three very different freshmen at fictional Columbus University—a bright track star (Ebbs) who questions the exploitation of black student athletes; a sheltered, sexually confused beauty from the 'burbs (Swanson); and a goony, paranoid loner who falls in with a group of skinheads (Rapaport). Singleton's honorable intention—to make a movie that makes a difference—is marred by cardboard supporting characters, a penchant for in-your-face irony, and a predictable, simplistic conclusion. **127m/C VHS, DVD, Wide.** Omar Epps, Kristy Swanson, Michael Rapaport, Laurence "Larry" Fishburne, Jennifer Connelly, Ice Cube, Tyra Banks, Jason Wiles, Cole Hauser, Regina King; ***D:*** John Singleton; ***W:*** John Singleton; ***C:*** Peter Collister.

The Highest Honor ½ **1984 (R)** True story set during WWII of a friendship between an Australian army officer, captured while attempting to infiltrate Singapore, and a Japanese security officer. Too long, but gripping. **99m/C VHS.** *AU* John Howard, Atsuo Nakamura, Stuart Wilson, Michael Aitkens, Steve Bisley; ***D:*** Peter Maxwell.

Highlander **1986 (R)** A strange tale about an immortal 16th-century Scottish warrior who has had to battle his evil immortal enemy through the centuries. The feud comes to blows in modern-day Manhattan. Connery makes a memorable appearance as the good warrior's mentor. Spectacular battle and death scenes. A cult favorite which spawned a weak sequel and a TV series. Based on a story by Gregory Widen. **110m/C VHS, DVD.** Christopher Lambert, Sean Connery, Clancy Brown, Roxanne Hart, Beatie Edney, Alan North, Sheila Gish, Jon Polito; ***D:*** Russell Mulcahy; ***W:*** Gregory Widen, Peter Bellwood, Larry Ferguson; ***C:*** Gerry Fisher; ***M:*** Michael Kamen.

Highlander 2: The Quickening ½ *Highlander 2: Renegade Version* **1991 (R)** The saga of Connor MacLeod and Juan Villa-Lobos continues in this sequel set in the year 2024. An energy shield designed to block out the sun's harmful ultraviolet rays has left planet Earth in perpetual darkness, but there is evidence that the ozone layer has repaired itself. An environmental terrorist and her group begin a sabotage effort and are joined by MacLeod and Villa-Lobos in their quest to save Earth. Stunning visual effects don't make up for the lack of substance. The Renegade version is a director's cut, which has been reedited and contains some 19 additional minutes of footage. **90m/C VHS, DVD, 8mm, Wide.** Christopher Lambert, Sean Connery, Virginia Madsen, Michael Ironside, John C. McGinley; ***D:*** Russell Mulcahy; ***W:*** Peter Bellwood; ***C:*** Phil Meheux; ***M:*** Stewart Copeland.

Highlander: Endgame ½ **2000 (R)** Fourth series installment ignores the two middle films but harkens back to the 1985 original. Lambert returns as immortal Connor MacLeod, teaming up with his equally immortal clansman, Duncan (TV "Highlander" Paul), to battle baddie Jacob Kell (Payne). Kell has a long-standing grudge against Connor and doesn't follow the rules of the "game." Numerous flashbacks could be confusing for newcomers but fans will find enjoyment and there is much action and swordplay. Story is so fast-paced that some subplots and characters are left in the dust for the exploits of the three main immortals. The video release contains 12 more minutes of footage and a new ending. **101m/C VHS, DVD, Wide.** Christopher Lambert, Adrian Paul, Bruce Payne, Lisa Barbuscia, Peter Wingfield, Jim Byrnes, Donnie Yen, Beatie Edney, Sheila Gish; ***D:*** Douglas Aarniokoski; ***W:*** Joel Soisson; ***C:*** Doug Milsome; ***M:*** Stephen Graziano.

Highlander: The Final Dimension ½ *Highlander 3: The Magician; Highlander 3: The Sorcerer* **1994 (R)** Immortal Conner MacLeod (Lambert) battles master illusionist Kane (Van Peebles), who seeks to rule the world. Aiding MacLeod is Alex Smith (Unger), a research scientist who discovers Kane was once buried beneath a mystical mountain along with three other immortal warriors some 300 years before. MacLeod returns to his old Scottish stomping grounds to prepare for battle. Lots of action and special effects, really dumb storyline and overacting—even for a fantasy film. Original theatrical release was PG-13 and 94 minutes; the director's cut has been re-edited and footage added. **99m/C VHS, DVD, Wide.** Christopher Lambert, Mario Van Peebles, Deborah Kara Unger, Mako; ***D:*** Andrew Morahan; ***W:*** Paul Ohl; ***C:*** Steven Chivers; ***M:*** J. Peter Robinson.

Highlander: The Gathering ½ **1992 (PG-13)** Re-edited episodes from the syndicated TV series finds good immortals Connor MacLeod (Lambert) and distant relative Duncan (Paul) battling against an evil immortal (Moll as a particularly nasty villain) and a misguided human (Vanity). Lots of swordplay and a little bit of romance (courtesy of Vandernoot). **98m/C VHS.** Christopher Lambert, Adrian Paul, Richard Moll, Vanity, Alexandra Vandernoot, Stan Kirsch; ***D:*** Thomas J. Wright, Ray Austin; ***W:*** Lorain Despres, Dan Gordon. **TV**

Highpoint 1980 (PG) When an unemployed man becomes the chauffeur of a wealthy family, he finds himself in the middle of a mysterious murder and part of an international CIA plot. Hard to figure what's happening in this one. **91m/C VHS.** *CA* Richard Harris, Christopher Plummer, Beverly D'Angelo, Kate Reid, Saul Rubinek; ***D:*** Peter Carter.

Highway 2001 (R) Vegas pool cleaner Jack Hayes (Leto) decides to make make a quick getaway when he gets caught in bed with a mobster's wife. So he and best pal Pilot Kelson (Gyllenhaal) score some drugs and head out on the road, along with hitchhiking hooker Cassie (Blair). And they even have a destination—to attend a vigil for the recently deceased Kurt Cobain in Seattle. **97m/C VHS, DVD, Wide.** Jared Leto, Selma Blair, Jake Gyllenhaal, Kimberley Kates, Jeremy Piven, John C. McGinley; ***D:*** James Cox; ***W:*** Scott Rosenberg; ***C:*** Mauro Fiore. **VIDEO**

Highway Hitcher *The Pass* 1998 (R) Comic strip salesman Charles Duprey (Forsythe) is in the midst of a mid-life crisis, including having his wife Shirley (Allen) leave him. Charles' friend Willie (McKean) convinces him to hit the road to Reno for a little R&R. On a backroad Charles crosses paths with Hunter (LeGros), who's having car trouble, and reluctantly offers him a ride. He should have trusted his instincts, since this is only the beginning of trouble. **93m/C VHS, DVD.** William Forsythe, James LeGros, Elizabeth Pena, Jamie Kennedy, Nancy Allen, Michael McKean, Jaason Simmons, John Doe; ***D:*** Kurt Voss; ***W:*** Kurt Voss; ***C:*** Denis Maloney; ***M:*** Vinnie Golia. **VIDEO**

The Highway Man 1999 (R) Middleaged Frank Drake (McHattie) is running telephone scams and winds up getting framed by his nasty boss (Gossett) for fraud and then accused of murder. Into this mess strolls Ziggy (Harris), who thinks Frank is her daddy, along with her boyfriend/thief Walter (Priestly), who's just made a big score. It plays more like two separate stories that never really come together. **97m/C VHS, DVD, Wide.** Jason Priestley, Louis Gossett Jr., Stephen McHattie, Laura Harris, Callum Keith Rennie, Gordon Michael Woolvett, Bernie Coulson; ***D:*** Keoni Waxman; ***W:*** Richard Beattie.

Highway Patrolman *El Patrullero* 1991 Young Pedro Rojas (Sosa) has just graduated from the National Highway Patrol Academy and he and best friend Anibal (Bichir) have been assigned to the isolated roads of northern Durango. He quickly learns that most of the people he stops for minor violations are too poor to pay for licenses and fines. What Pedro does get is a wife, Griselda (Gutierrez), who's soon complaining about Pedro's meager wages. Pedro's resistance to bribery begins to weaken and he becomes more depressed as his ideals are destroyed and his rage increases. Spanish with subtitles. **104m/C VHS.** *MX* Roberto Sosa, Zaide Silvia Gutierrez, Bruno Bichir, Vanessa Bauche; ***D:*** Alex Cox; ***W:*** Lorenzo O'Brien; ***C:*** Miguel Garzon; ***M:*** Zander Schloss.

Highway 61 1991 (R) Shy barber Pokey Jones lives in the small Canadian town of Pickerel Falls and becomes a celebrity when he discovers the frozen corpse of an unknown young man in his backyard. Jackie Bangs, a rock roadie who's stolen her band's stash of drugs, finds herself stranded in the same small town. So begins a wild road trip. Lackluster direction undercuts much of the first-rate acting and amusing story quirks. **110m/C VHS.** Valerie Buhagiar, Don McKellar, Earl Pastko, Peter Breck, Art Bergmann; ***D:*** Bruce McDonald; ***W:*** Don McKellar.

Highway 13 ½ 1948 When a trucker witnesses an "accidental" death at the loading warehouse, he falls under suspicion. He then sets out to clear his name. **60m/B VHS.** Robert Lowery, Pamela Blake, Lyle Talbot, Michael Whalen, Maris Wrixon, Clem Bevans; ***D:*** William Berke.

Highway to Hell 1992 (R) Bergen plays the devil in a horror-comedy about going to hell—even if you're not dead yet. Lowe and Swanson are newlyweds on their way to Las Vegas when they're stopped by a "hellcop," who kidnaps the bride and takes her to the netherworld to be the devil's new plaything. Her human hubby doesn't take kindly to this and goes to hell to rescue his bride. Campy flick is played for laughs and has some good special effects. **93m/C VHS.** Patrick Bergin, Adam Storke, Chad Lowe, Kristy Swanson, Richard Farnsworth, C.J. Graham, Lita Ford, Kevin Peter Hall, Pamela Gidley, Brian Helgeland; ***Cameos:*** Gilbert Gottfried; ***D:*** Ate De Jong.

Hijacking Hollywood 1997 Modest Hollywood satire finds naive Kevin Conroy (Thomas) using family ties to land a menial job with distant relative Michael Lawrence (Metcalf), a tyrannical producer. Kevin's supervisor is the petty Russell (Thompson), who enjoys sending the kid on useless errands. Kevin's one important task is to pick up film rushes at the airport and he tells hustling roommate Tad (Mandt) that if someone took the dailies, a production could be held hostage. Naturally, Tad is all for the idea. **91m/C VHS, DVD.** Henry Thomas, Scott Thompson, Mark Metcalf, Paul Hewitt, Art LaFleur, Neil Mandt; ***D:*** Neil Mandt; ***W:*** Jim Rossow, Neil Mandt; ***C:*** Anton Floquet.

Hilary and Jackie 1998 (R) Based on the true story of cover girl cellist Jacqueline Du Pre (Watson) and her relationship with her sister Hilary (Griffiths). As Jackie takes the world of classical music by storm, Hilary gives up her musical ambitions and marries conductor Kiffer (Morrissey). The story switches perspectives between the two women after Jackie arrives at Hilary's doorstep and asks if she may sleep with her husband. Hilary reluctantly agrees, and there go all those stereotypes you had about girls who play classical music. The second half details Jackie's decline and eventual death from multiple sclerosis and the sisters' mutual bonds developed during her illness. Excellent performances and music, including some actual Du Pre performances, make this a pleaser for those who liked "Shine." **124m/C VHS, DVD.** *GB* Emily Watson, Rachel Griffiths, James Frain, David Morrissey, Charles Dance, Celia Imrie, Rupert Penry-Jones, Nyree Dawn Porter, Bill Paterson, Vernon Dobtcheff, Auriol Evans, Keeley Flanders; ***D:*** Anand Tucker; ***W:*** Frank Cottrell-Boyce; ***C:*** David Johnson; ***M:*** Barrington Pheloung.

Hill Number One 1951 A dramatization of the story of Easter, featuring Dean in one of his first major roles as John the Baptist. **57m/B VHS, DVD.** James Dean, Michael Ansara, Leif Erickson, Ruth Hussey, Roddy McDowall; ***D:*** Arthur Presson. **TV**

Hill 24 Doesn't Answer 1955 Four Zionist soldiers defend a strategic entrance to Jerusalem. While at their posts, they reflect on their lives and devotion to the cause. Made in Israel, in English. The first Israeli feature film. **101m/B VHS.** *IS* Edward Mulhare, Haya Harareet, Michael Wager; ***D:*** Thorold Dickinson.

Hillbillies in a Haunted House woof! *Hillbillys in a Haunted House* 1967 Two country and western singers en route to the Nashville jamboree encounter a group of foreign spies "haunting" a house. Features Rathbone's last film performance. Sequel to "Las Vegas Hillbillies" (1966). Giant step down for everyone involved. **88m/C VHS, DVD.** Ferlin Husky, Joi Lansing, Don Bowman, John Carradine, Lon Chaney Jr., Basil Rathbone, Merle Haggard, Sonny James, Linda Ho, Molly Bee, George Barrows; ***D:*** Jean Yarbrough; ***W:*** Duke Yelton; ***C:*** Vaughn Wilkins; ***M:*** Hal Borne.

Hillbilly Blitzkrieg *Enemy Round-Up* 1942 Two soldiers are sent to the boonies to guard a top-secret missile site from enemy agents. Come-to-life comic strip characters Snuffy Smith, Barney Google and Spark Plug join in the antics. **63m/B VHS.** Bud Duncan, Cliff Nazarro, Edgar Kennedy, Doris Linden, Lucien Littlefield, Alan Baldwin; ***D:*** Roy Mack.

The Hills Have Eyes woof! 1977 (R) Desperate family battles for survival and vengeance against a brutal band of inbred hillbilly cannibals. Craven gorefest followed by Hills II. **83m/C VHS.** Susan Lanier, Robert Houston, Martin Speer, Dee Wallace Stone, Russ Grieve, John Steadman, James Whitworth, Michael Berryman, Virginia Vincent, Janus Blythe; ***D:*** Wes Craven; ***W:*** Wes Craven; ***C:*** Eric Saarinen; ***M:*** Don Peake.

The Hills Have Eyes, Part 2 1984 Craven reprises Hills with Eyes number one to ill effect. Ignorant teens disregard warnings of a "Hills Have Eyes" refugee, and go stomping into the grim reaper's proving grounds. Predictably bad things happen. **86m/C VHS.** Michael Berryman, Kevin Blair Spirtas, John Bloom, Janus Blythe, John Laughlin, Tamara Stafford, Peter Frechette; ***D:*** Wes Craven; ***W:*** Wes Craven; ***C:*** David Lewis.

The Hills of Home *Master of Lassie* 1948 (G) Warm sentimental tale about a Scottish doctor and his beloved pet collie. One of the better films in the "Lassie" series. **97m/C VHS.** Edmund Gwenn, Donald Crisp, Tom Drake, Janet Leigh; ***D:*** Fred M. Wilcox; ***W:*** William Ludwig.

Hills of Oklahoma 1950 Allen stars as the leader of a cattlemen's association who decides not to deal with dishonest meatpacker Keane, so he drives his herd across the desert to a slaughterhouse run by an honest businesswoman. Based on an original story by Cooper. **67m/B VHS.** Rex Allen, Elisabeth Fraser, Elisabeth Risdon, Fuzzy Knight, Roscoe Ates, Robert Emmett Keane, Trevor Bardette; ***D:*** R.G. Springsteen; ***W:*** Olive Cooper, Victor Arthur.

Hills of Utah ½ 1951 Autry finds himself in the middle of a feud between the local mine operator and a group of cattlemen, while searching for his father's murderer. **70m/B VHS.** Gene Autry, Pat Buttram, Denver Pyle; ***D:*** John English.

The Hillside Strangler ½ *The Case of the Hillside Stranglers* 1989 Crime-of-the-week drama about the investigation to apprehend the serial killer responsible for 10 deaths in 1977-78. **91m/C VHS.** Richard Crenna, Dennis Farina, Billy Zane, Tony Plana, James Tolkan, Tasia Valenza; ***D:*** Steven Gethers. **TV**

Himalaya *Himalaya - L'Enfance d'un Chef; Himalaya - The Youth of a Chief; Caravan* 1999 The age-old struggle of generations deciding between tradition and progress plays itself out once more against the spectacular scenery of the Tibetan mountains. Although the story is nothing new, the film gives a detailed look into a traditional lifestyle that is fast dying out, using non-professional actors, location shooting, and not an ounce of special effects. A bit of the film's grandeur is lost on the small screen, but it is still breathtaking. **104m/C VHS, DVD, Wide.** *FR SI GB* Thinlen Lhondup, Karma Wangiel, Lhakpa Tsamchoe; ***D:*** Eric Valli; ***W:*** Eric Valli, Olivier Dazat; ***C:*** Eric Guichard, Jean-Paul Meurisse; ***M:*** Bruno Coulais.

Himatsuri *Fire Festival* 1985 An acclaimed film detailing the conflicts between man and nature, as a lumberjack in a Japanese forest believes he's the protector of the mountains through his divine relationship with the ancient gods. Outraged by the destruction, pollution, and commercial exploitation of the land he turns to violence. In Japanese with English subtitles. **120m/C VHS.** *JP* Kinya Kitaoji, Kwako Taichi, Ryota Nakamoto, Norihei Miki; ***D:*** Mitsuo Yanagimachi; ***W:*** Kenji Nakagami; ***C:*** Masaki Tamura; ***M:*** Toru Takemitsu.

The Hindenburg 1975 (PG) A dramatization of what might have happened on the fateful night the Hindenburg exploded. Scott plays an investigator who is aware that something is up, and has numerous suspects to interrogate. The laser edition features widescreen format, digital Stereo Surround, the original trailer, and chapter stops. **126m/C VHS, DVD, Wide.** George C. Scott, Anne Bancroft, William Atherton, Roy Thinnes, Gig Young, Burgess Meredith, Charles Durning, Richard Dysart; ***D:*** Robert Wise; ***W:*** Nelson Gidding, Richard Levinson, William Link; ***C:*** Robert L. Surtees; ***M:*** David Shire. Oscars '75: Sound FX Editing, Visual FX.

Hindsight 1997 Ah, Hollywood. Joanne (Shower), the bored wife of studio exec Vincent (Law), is having an affair with younger, not-too-bright, aspiring actor Jason (Steadman). Joanne's finally agreed to run off when Jason happens to meet party girl Cassandra (Pass). Thanks to her studio connections, Jason soon has an important agent (Forster) and a studio deal that leaves Joanne in the back lot. But Cassandra is a wild woman with an agenda that doesn't bode well for our selfish himbo. **93m/C VHS.** Ken Steadman, Cyndi Pass, Kathy Shower, John Phillip Law, Robert Forster; ***D:*** John Bowen; ***W:*** Steve Tymon; ***C:*** Keith Holland; ***M:*** Jimmy Hodges. **VIDEO**

Hip Hip Hurrah! 1987 At the end of the 19th-century, a group of famous painters travel each summer to the northernmost cape of Skagen in Denmark to capture the beauty around them. The most talented of their group is Soren Kroyer (Skarsgard) who has a beautiful wife, Marie (Vieth), and a mistress Lille (Brondum). But his bright surface has a tragic core—Soren's mother was mad, he was born to her in an insane asylum, and he feels his own sanity is slipping away as the very light dims around him. Danish with subtitles. **110m/C VHS.** *DK* Stellan Skarsgard, Lene Brondum, Pia Vieth, Helge Jordal; ***D:*** Kjell Grede; ***W:*** Kjell Grede.

Hips, Hips, Hooray ½ 1934 Two supposed "hot shot" salesmen are hired by a cosmetic company to sell flavored lipstick. This lavish musical comedy is one of Wheeler and Woolsey's best vehicles. ♫Tired of It All; Keep Romance Alive; Keep On Doin' What You're Doin'. **68m/B VHS.** Robert Woolsey, Bert Wheeler, Ruth Etting, Thelma Todd, Dorothy Lee; ***D:*** Mark Sandrich.

Hired Hand ½ 1971 Two drifters settle on a farm belonging to one of their wives, only to leave again seeking to avenge the murder of a friend. TV prints include Larry Hagman in a cameo role. **93m/C VHS.** Peter Fonda, Warren Oates, Verna Bloom, Severn Darden, Robert Pratt; ***Cameos:*** Larry Hagman; ***D:*** Peter Fonda.

Hired to Kill ½ *The Italian Connection* 1973 (R) A pair of Mafia hoods plot against each other over a $6 million drug shipment. **90m/C** Henry Silva, Woody Strode, Adolfo Celi, Mario Adorf.

Hired to Kill ½ 1991 (R) The granite-hewn Thompson plays a male-chauvinist commando grudgingly leading a squad of beautiful mercenary-ettes on an international rescue mission. Not as bad as it sounds (mainly because the ladies aren't complete bimbos), but between senseless plotting, gratuitous catfights, and a love scene indistinguishable from rape, the Hound found plenty to dislike. **91m/C VHS.** Brian Thompson, George Kennedy, Jose Ferrer, Oliver Reed, Penelope Reed, Michelle Moffett, Barbara Lee (Niven) Alexander, Jordanna Capra; ***D:*** Nico Mastorakis, Peter Rader; ***W:*** Nico Mastorakis.

Hiroshima 1995 (PG) Haunting depiction re-reates the circumstances surrounding the dropping of the first atomic bomb in 1945. Juxtaposes scenes between the U.S., Japan, and their leaders—President Truman (Welsh) and Emperor Hirohito (Umewaka)—with the development of the Manhattan Project, the bombing itself, and its consequences. Filmed primarily in B&W, with newsreel and contemporary witness interviews in color; Japanese sequences are subtitled in English. Filmed on location in Montreal and Tokyo. **180m/C VHS, DVD.** *JP CA* Kenneth Welsh, Naohiko Umewaka, Wesley Addy, Richard Masur, Hisashi Igawa, Ken Jenkins, Jeffrey DeMunn, Leon Pownall, Saul Rubinek, Timothy West, Koji Takahashi, Kazuo Kato; ***D:*** Roger Spottiswoode, Koreyoshi Kurahara; ***W:*** John Hopkins, Toshiro Ishido; ***C:*** Pierre Mignot, Shohei Ando. **CABLE**

Hiroshima Maiden 1988 An American family gains new perspective when they meet a young survivor of the atomic bomb. Based on true stories of Japanese women who stayed with Americans while undergoing surgery to minimize their scars. Originally aired on PBS as part of the "Wonderworks" family movie series.

58m/C VHS. Susan Blakely, Richard Masur, Tamlyn Tomita; *D:* Joan Darling.

Hiroshima, Mon Amour 𝒥𝒥𝒥𝒥 1959 Presented in a complex network of flashbacks this profoundly moving drama explores the shadow of history over the personal lives of a lonely French actress (Riva), who's working in Hiroshima, and the Japanese architect (Okada) with whom she's having an affair. She has suffered during the war in occupied France, while he has survived the city's bombing—and their pasts deeply affect their present. Resnais' first feature film and highly influential; adapted by Marguerite Duras from her book. Japanese with subtitles. **88m/B VHS.** *JP FR* Emmanuelle Riva, Eiji Okada, Bernard Fresson, Stella Dassas, Pierre Barbaud; *D:* Alain Resnais; *W:* Marguerite Duras; *C:* Sacha Vierny, Michio Takahashi; *M:* Georges Delerue, Giovanni Fusco. N.Y. Film Critics '60: Foreign Film.

Hiroshima: Out of the Ashes 𝒥𝒥𝒥 1990 (PG) The terrible aftermath of the bombing of Hiroshima, August, 1945, as seen through the eyes of American and Japanese soldiers, the Japanese people, and a priest. Carefully detailed and realistic, creates an amazing emotional response. Don't miss the scene in which Nelson and his buddy find themselves surrounded by Japanese—the enemy—only to realize that their "captors" have been blinded by the blast. Created as an homage for the 45th anniversary of the bombing. **98m/C VHS.** Max von Sydow, Judd Nelson, Mako, Tamlyn Tomita, Stan(ford) Egi, Sab Shimono, Noriyuki "Pat" Morita, Kim Miyori; *D:* Peter Werner.

His Bodyguard 𝒥𝒥½ 1998 (PG-13) A deaf young man (Natale) is witness to a break-in at the pharmaceutical lab that his family owns, where thieves steal a secret experimental drug. Jenny Farrell (Kapture), the head of lab security, is assigned to protect him from the perpetrators and the two end up running from the bad guys and getting quite friendly. **88m/C VHS.** Mitzi Kapture, Robert Guillaume, Anthony Natale, Vanessa Vaughan, Michael Copeman, Robin Gammell; *D:* Artie Mandelberg; *W:* Emma Samms. **CABLE**

His Brother's Ghost 𝒥𝒥 1945 When Fuzzy is rubbed out by bandits, Billy Carson (no longer called Billy the Kid thanks to mothers' protestations) convinces his twin brother to impersonate him in order to make the bandits believe they are the victims of hocus pocus from the otherworld. Crabbe—who dressed noir before it was chic—made this during his post sci-fi western period, when he slugged it through some 50 low-rent oaters (usually under the direction of Newfield at PRC studios). **54m/C VHS.** Buster Crabbe, Al "Fuzzy" St. John, Charles "Blackie" King, Bud Osborne, Karl Hackett, Arch (Archie) Hall Sr.; *D:* Sam Newfield.

His Butler's Sister 𝒥𝒥 1944 Bachelor composer Charles Gerard (Tone) lives a sybarite's life in his Manhattan penthouse, which is run by his butler Martin Murphy (O'Brien). When Murphy's stepsister Ann Carter (Durbin) arrives unexpectedly, she's delighted to hear who Murphy works for because she's a singer and wants an audition—an absolute taboo in Gerard's household. So she fools him into thinking she's the new maid until she can get her big break. Nothing new but Durbin does get to work her pretty pipes. ♫Nessun Dorma; In the Spirit of the Moment; When You're Away; Is It True What They Say About Dixie?. **87m/B VHS.** Deanna Durbin, Franchot Tone, Pat O'Brien, Evelyn Ankers, Akim Tamiroff, Alan Mowbray, Frank Jenks, Walter Catlett, Hans Conried, Florence Bates, Roscoe Karns, Franklin Pangborn; *D:* Frank Borzage; *W:* Samuel Hoffenstein, Bety Reinhardt; *C:* Elwood "Woody" Bredell; *M:* Hans J. Salter.

His Double Life 𝒥𝒥½ 1933 When a shy gentleman's valet dies, his master assumes the dead man's identity and has a grand time. From the play "Buried Alive" by Arnold Bennett. Remade in 1943 as "Holy Matrimony." **67m/B VHS.** Roland Young, Lillian Gish, Montagu Love; *D:* Arthur Hopkins.

His Fighting Blood 𝒥½ 1935 Northwest Mounties in action. Based on a James Oliver Curwood story. **63m/B VHS.** Kermit Maynard.

His First Command 𝒥½ 1929 An early talkie wherein a playboy falls in love with the daughter of a cavalry officer, and enlists in order to win her affections. **60m/B VHS, 8mm.** William Boyd, Dorothy Sebastian, Gavin Gordon; *D:* Gregory La Cava.

His First Flame 𝒥𝒥𝒥 1926 A classic Langdon silent romantic comedy. **62m/B VHS.** Harry Langdon, Vernon Dent, Natalie Kingston; *W:* Frank Capra.

His Girl Friday 𝒥𝒥𝒥𝒥 1940 Classic, unrelentingly hilarious war-between-the-sexes comedy. Cynical newspaper editor Walter Burns (Grant) wants to get a big scoop on political corruption, which involves convincing star reporter (and ex-wife) Hildy Johnson (Russell), to come back to work and put off her marriage to dull Bruce Baldwin (Bellamy). Hildy can't resist covering a good story, even when it mean helping a condemned man (Qualen) escape the law. One of Hawks's most furious and inventive screen combats in which women are given uniquely equal (for Hollywood) footing, with staccato dialogue and wonderful performances. Based on the Hecht-MacArthur play "The Front Page," which was filmed in 1931, remade in 1974, and again in 1988 (as "Switching Channels"). **92m/B VHS, DVD.** Cary Grant, Rosalind Russell, Ralph Bellamy, Gene Lockhart, John Qualen, Porter Hall, Roscoe Karns, Abner Biberman, Cliff Edwards, Billy Gilbert, Helen Mack, Ernest Truex, Clarence (C. William) Kolb, Frank Jenks; *D:* Howard Hawks; *W:* Charles Lederer; *C:* Joseph Walker; *M:* Morris Stoloff. Natl. Film Reg. '93.

His Kind of Woman 𝒥𝒥𝒥 1951 Sleazy, campy crime drama that turns out to be compelling fun. Unlucky gambler Dan Milner (Mitchum) accepts a big payday for an unknown job that takes him to a Mexican resort. He gets an eyeful of chanteuse Lenore (Russell) and the hot twosome hook-up, even though her married boyfriend, Mark (Price), is also hanging around. Then Dan learns his job is to be the fall guy for racketeer Nick Ferraro (Burr), who wants to get back into the States, and he doesn't go for the idea. **120m/B VHS.** Robert Mitchum, Jane Russell, Vincent Price, Tim Holt, Charles McGraw, Raymond Burr, Jim Backus, Marjorie Reynolds; *D:* John Farrow; *W:* Frank Fenton, Jack Leonard; *C:* Harry Wild; *M:* Leigh Harline.

His Majesty O'Keefe 𝒥𝒥½ 1953 Lancaster stars as a South Seas swashbuckler dealing in the lucrative coconut-oil trade of the mid-1800s. The natives see him as a god and allow him to marry a beautiful maiden. When his reign is threatened by unscrupulous traders, Lancaster springs into action to safeguard his kingdom. Based on a real-life American adventurer, this was the first movie ever filmed in the Fiji Islands. **92m/C VHS.** Burt Lancaster, Joan Rice, Benson Fong, Philip Ahn, Grant Taylor; *D:* Byron Haskin.

His Majesty, the American 𝒥𝒥½ 1919 William Brooks (Fairbanks) is a young man whose heritage is unknown to him. It turns out he's an heir to a small European kingdom. When Brooks arrives in Alaine he discovers the war minister is trying to overthrow the present king. With his usual dash, our hero saves the day and also wins the hand of a beautiful princess. First picture released by United Artists studios, formed by Fairbanks, Mary Pickford, Charles Chaplin, and D.W. Griffith. **100m/B VHS.** Douglas Fairbanks Sr., Marjorie Daw, Lillian Langdon, Frank Campeau; *D:* Joseph Henabery.

His Name Was King woof! 1985 A man goes after the gang who murdered his brother and raped his young wife in the old West. **90m/C VHS.** *IT* Richard Harrison, Klaus Kinski, Anne Puskin; *D:* Don Reynolds.

His Picture in the Papers 𝒥𝒥 1916 An early silent comedy wherein the robust, red-meat-eating son of a health food tycoon must get his father's permission to marry by getting his picture favorably in the paper for advertising's sake. **68m/B VHS, 8mm.** Douglas Fairbanks Sr., Clarence Handysides, Rene Boucicault, Jean Temple, Charles Butler, Homer Hunt, Loretta Blake, Helena Rupport; *D:* John Emerson; *W:* John Emerson, Anita Loos.

His Private Secretary 𝒥½ 1933 Wayne plays the jet-setting son of a wealthy businessman who wants his boy to settle down. And he does—after he meets the minister's beautiful daughter. **68m/B VHS.** John Wayne, Evalyn Knapp, Alec B. Francis, Reginald Barlow, Natalie Kingston, Arthur Hoyt, Al "Fuzzy" St. John; *D:* Philip H. (Phil, P.H.) Whitman.

His Wife's Lover 𝒥𝒥𝒥 *Zayn Vaybs Lubovnik* 1931 An actor disguised as an old man wins the heart of a lovely young woman. He decides to test her fidelity by reverting to his handsome young self and attempting to seduce her. An enchanting comedy in Yiddish with English subtitles. **77m/B VHS.** Ludwig Satz, Michael Rosenberg, Isadore Cashier, Lucy Levine; *D:* Sidney Goldin.

History Is Made at Night 𝒥𝒥𝒥 1937 A wife seeks a divorce from a jealous husband while on an Atlantic cruise; she ends up finding both true love and heartbreak in this story of a love triangle at sea. **98m/B VHS.** Charles Boyer, Jean Arthur, Leo Carrillo, Colin Clive; *D:* Frank Borzage; *C:* Gregg Toland.

History of the World: Part 1 𝒥𝒥 1981 (R) More misses than hits in this Brooks' parody of historic epics. A bluntly satiric vision of human evolution, from the Dawn of Man to the French Revolution told in an episodic fashion. Good for a few laughs. **90m/C VHS, DVD, Wide.** Mel Brooks, Dom DeLuise, Madeline Kahn, Harvey Korman, Cloris Leachman, Gregory Hines, Pamela Stephenson, Paul Mazursky, Beatrice Arthur, Fritz Feld, John Hurt, Jack Carter, John Hillerman, John Gavin, Barry Levinson, Ron Carey, Howard Morris, Sid Caesar, Jackie Mason, Charlie Callas, Henny Youngman, Hugh Hefner; *D:* Mel Brooks; *W:* Mel Brooks; *C:* John Morris, Woody Omens; *M:* Shecky Greene; *Nar:* Orson Welles.

Hit! 𝒥𝒥 1973 (R) When the 15-year-old daughter of a government agent dies of a drug overdose, he deals his revenge to top French heroin traffickers. **135m/C VHS.** Billy Dee Williams, Richard Pryor, Gwen Welles, Paul Hampton, Warren Kemmerling, Sid Melton; *D:* Sidney J. Furie; *W:* Alan R. Trustman, David M. Wolf; *M:* Lalo Schifrin.

The Hit 𝒥𝒥½ 1985 (R) A feisty young hooker gets mixed-up with two strong-armed hired killers as they escort an unusual stool-pigeon from his exile in Spain to their angry mob bosses. Minor cult-noir from the director of "My Beautiful Launderette" and "Dangerous Liaisons." **105m/C VHS.** *GB* Terence Stamp, John Hurt, Laura Del Sol, Tim Roth, Fernando Rey, Bill Hunter; *D:* Stephen Frears; *W:* Peter Prince; *C:* John A. Alonzo; *M:* Eric Clapton.

Hit & Run 𝒥 *Revenge Squad* 1982 David Marks, a Manhattan cab driver, is haunted by recurring flashbacks of a freak hit-and-run accident in which his wife was struck down on a city street. **96m/C VHS.** Paul Perri, Claudia Cron; *D:* Charles Braverman; *M:* Brad Fiedel.

Hit Lady 𝒥𝒥 1974 An elegant cultured woman becomes a hit lady for the syndicate in this predictable, yet slick gangster movie. **74m/C VHS, DVD.** Yvette Mimieux, Dack Rambo, Clu Gulager, Keenan Wynn; *D:* Tracy Keenan Wynn; *W:* Yvette Mimieux; *M:* George Aliceson Tipton. **TV**

The Hit List 𝒥𝒥 1988 (R) A regular guy fights back brutally when his wife and child are mistakenly kidnapped by the Mafia. Fast-paced action makes up for thin plot. **87m/C VHS.** Jan-Michael Vincent, Leo Rossi, Lance Henriksen, Charles Napier, Rip Torn; *D:* William Lustig; *W:* Peter Brosnan.

The Hit List 𝒥𝒥½ 1993 (R) Charles Pike (Fahey) is a professional hitman working for attorney Peter Mayhew (Coburn) to wipe out drug lords. Then Mayhew gives Pike a new assignment. He introduces him to sexy widow Jordan Henning (Butler), who wants Pike to kill the man who murdered her husband. Pike finds himself mixing business with pleasure in a deadly combination that sees him dodging crooked cops and trained assassins. **97m/C VHS.** Jeff Fahey, Yancy Butler, James Coburn; *D:* William Webb; *W:* Reed Steiner.

The Hit Man 𝒥𝒥 *Il Sicario* 1961 A crime drama that profiles the crisis of a man unfit to commit murder but who does for a price. **100m/B VHS.**

Hit Men 𝒥½ 1973 Double crosses and gun battles highlight this tale of inner-city crime. **90m/C VHS.** Henry Silva, Mario Adorf, Woody Strode, Adolfo Celi.

Hit the Deck 𝒥½ 1955 Second-rate studio musical about sailors on leave and looking for romance. Based on the 1927 Broadway musical. ♫Sometimes I'm Happy; Hallelujah; Why, Oh Why; Keeping Myself For You; More Than You Know; I Know That You Know; Lucky Bird. **112m/C VHS, Wide.** Jane Powell, Tony Martin, Debbie Reynolds, Walter Pidgeon, Vic Damone, Gene Raymond, Ann Miller, Russ Tamblyn, J. Carrol Naish, Kay Armen, Richard Anderson; *D:* Roy Rowland; *C:* George J. Folsey; *M:* Vincent Youmans.

Hit the Dutchman 𝒥𝒥 1992 (R) Routine gangster flick about Dutch Schultz trying to rise to the top of the New York crime community—with or without the help of underworld pals Legs Diamond and Lucky Luciano. An unrated version is also available. **116m/C VHS.** Bruce Nozick, Sally Kirkland, Will Kempe; *D:* Menahem Golan.

Hit the Ice 𝒥𝒥 1943 Newspaper photographers Bud and Lou are mistaken as gangsters in Chicago and the usual complications ensue. Includes an appearance by Johnny Long & His Orchestra. ♫I'm Like A Fish Out Of Water; Happiness Bound; I'd Like to Set You to Music; Slap Polka. **89m/C VHS.** Bud Abbott, Lou Costello, Patric Knowles, Elyse Knox, Ginny Simms; *D:* Charles Lamont.

Hit the Saddle 𝒥𝒥 1937 The Three Mesquiteers track down a gang involved in capturing wild horses in protected areas although one of three is more interested in the charms of a dance hall girl (played by starlet Rita Cansino who would soon become Rita Hayworth). **54m/B VHS.** Robert "Bob" Livingston, Ray Corrigan, Max Terhune, J(ohn) P(aterson) McGowan, Yakima Canutt, Rita Hayworth; *D:* Mack V. Wright.

Hit Woman: The Double Edge 𝒥𝒥½ 1993 (R) Lucci plays a dual role as an FBI agent and the look-alike killer-for-hire that she's tracking. Originally made for TV; the video version contains additional footage that earned the "R" rating. **92m/C VHS.** Susan Lucci, Robert Urich, Michael Woods, Robert Prosky. **TV**

The Hitch-Hiker 𝒥𝒥𝒥 1953 Two young men off on the vacation of their dreams pick up a psychopathic hitchhiker with a right eye that never closes, even when he sleeps. Taut suspense makes this flick worth seeing. **71m/B VHS, DVD.** Edmond O'Brien, Frank Lovejoy, William Talman, Jose Torvay; *D:* Ida Lupino. Natl. Film Reg. '98.

Hitched 𝒥𝒥 2001 Housewife Eve (Lee) doesn't suspect that her salesman hubby Ed (Hall) is cheating on her. But then he winds up in the hospital after a drunk-driving accident that also involved his lady friend of the moment. So Eve decides to get even by shackling him in their soundproof basement and filing a missing person's report. Detective Cary Grant (Carter) is immediately smitten and makes his move on Eve but gets confused when Ted reappears and Eve goes missing. **89m/C VHS, DVD.** Sheryl Lee, Anthony Michael Hall, Alex Carter; *D:* Wesley Strick; *W:* Wesley Strick; *C:* Jonathan Freeman; *M:* Randy Miller. **CABLE**

The Hitcher 𝒥𝒥½ 1986 (R) A young man picks up a hitchhiker on a deserted stretch of California highway only to be tormented by the man's repeated appearances: is he real or a figment of his imagination? Ferociously funny, sadomasochistic comedy with graphic violence. **98m/C VHS, DVD, Wide.** Rutger Hauer, C. Thomas Howell, Jennifer Jason Leigh, Jeffrey DeMunn, John M. Jackson, Billy Green Bush; *D:* Robert Harmon; *W:* Eric Red; *C:* John Seale; *M:* Mark Isham.

Hitchhikers woof! **1972 (R)** Trash film about a bunch of scantily clad female hitchhikers who rob the motorists who stop to pick them up. Keep right on going when you spot this roadkill. **90m/C VHS.** Misty Rowe, Norman Klar, Linda Avery; ***D:*** Ferd Sebastian.

The Hitchhiker's Guide to the Galaxy **1981** The six-episode BBC TV adaptation of Douglas Adams's hilarious science-fiction books. Features the intergalatic Ford Prefect, sent to Earth to update its planetary listing in the Hitchhiker's Guide; hapless hero Arthur Dent, a typical Englishman caught up in space mayhem; and an odd assortment of aliens, including Marvin the Paranoid Android. The show's sheer cheesiness is part of the charm. **194m/C VHS.** *GB* Simon Jones, David Dixon, Sandra Dickinson, Mark Wing-Davey; ***D:*** Alan Bell. **TV**

Hitler ½ *Women of Nazi Germany* **1962** The true story of the infamous Nazi dictator's rise to power and his historic downfall. **103m/B VHS.** Richard Basehart, Maria Emo, Cordula Trantow; ***D:*** Stuart Heisler.

Hitler: Dead or Alive **1943** Three ex-cons devise a scheme to gain a million-dollar reward for capturing Adolf Hitler in this low-budget production. **64m/B VHS.** Ward Bond, Dorothy Tree, Bruce Edwards, Warren Hymer, Paul Fix, Russell Hicks, Bobby Watson; ***D:*** Nick Grinde.

Hitler: The Last Ten Days **1973 (PG)** Based on an eyewitness account, the story of Hitler's last days in an underground bunker gives insight to his madness. **106m/C VHS.** Alec Guinness, Simon Ward, Adolfo Celi, Phyllida Law; ***D:*** Ennio de Concini.

Hitler's Children **1943** Two young people, a German boy and an American girl, are caught in the horror of Nazi Germany. He's attracted to Hitler's rant, she's repelled. Exploitative yet engrossing. **83m/B VHS.** Tim Holt, Bonita Granville, Otto Kruger, H.B. Warner, Irving Reis, Hans Conried, Lloyd Corrigan; ***D:*** Edward Dmytryk.

Hitler's Daughter **1990 (R)** Made for TV movie following the trials and tribulations of the illegitimate daughter of Adolf Hitler. She's all grown up now...and wants to rule the United States. She secures a position of power during an election and now Nazi-hunters must figure out her identity before she takes over the world! **88m/C VHS.** Kay Lenz, Veronica Cartwright, Melody Anderson, Patrick Cassidy, Carolyn Dunn, Lindsay Merrithew, George R. Robertson; ***D:*** James A. Contner. **TV**

The Hitman **1991 (R)** Norris plays a cop undercover as a syndicate hit man in Seattle, where he cleans up crime by triggering a three-way mob bloodbath between beastly Italian mafiosi, snooty French-Canadian hoods, and fanatical Iranian scum. But he teaches a black kid martial arts, so you know he's politically correct. Action addicts will give this a passing grade; all others need not apply. **95m/C VHS, 8mm.** Chuck Norris, Michael Parks, Al Waxman, Alberta Watson, Salim Grant, Ken Pogue, Marcel Sabourin, Bruno Gerussi, Frank Ferrucci; ***D:*** Aaron Norris; ***C:*** Joao Fernandes.

Hitman's Journal *18 Shades of Dust* **1999 (R)** Vincent Dianni (Aiello) is a mob enforcer for Don Cucci and his son Tommy (Forsythe). But when info leaked to the feds gets the Don life in prison, Vincent comes under suspicion as the squealer. All Vincent wants to do is quietly retire but first he has to square things with his bosses. **95m/C VHS, DVD.** Danny Aiello, William Forsythe, Polly Draper, Vincent Pastore, Aida Turturro; ***D:*** Danny Aiello III. **VIDEO**

Hitman's Run **1999 (R)** Former Mafia hitman Roberts has double-crossed his bosses and is now in the FBI's Witness Protection Program. However, his safety is hardly guaranteed. **93m/C VHS, DVD.** Eric Roberts, Damian Chapa, Esteban Louis Powell. **VIDEO**

The Hitter **1979 (R)** A former prizefighter, his girlfriend, and a washed-up promoter are all on the run in this adventure tale. **94m/C VHS.** Ron O'Neal, Adolph Caesar, Sheila Frazier; ***D:*** Christopher Leitch.

Hittin' the Trail **1937** The Good Cowboy is mistaken for a murdering varmint, and must prove his innocence. **57m/B VHS.** Tex Ritter, Charles "Blackie" King, Ray Whitley, The Range Ramblers; ***D:*** Robert North Bradbury.

Hitz ½ **1992 (R)** In a Los Angeles barrio, Musico, a Loco gang member, kills two rival gang members. Arrested and convicted when a young boy named Pepe is coerced into testifying against him, Musico is killed in the courtroom. But the violence doesn't stop. The judge, who wants to reform the juvenile court system, tries to protect Pepe, and both are targeted for death by the Loco gang. **90m/C VHS.** Elliott Gould, Emilia Crow, Karen Black, Cuba Gooding Jr.

The Hobbit **1978** An animated interpretation of J.R.R. Tolkien's novel of the same name. The story follows Bilbo Baggins and his journeys in Middle Earth and encounters with the creatures who inhabit it. He joins comrades to battle against evil beings and creatures. **76m/C VHS, DVD, 8mm.** ***D:*** Arthur Rankin Jr., Jules Bass; ***M:*** Maury Laws; ***V:*** Orson Bean, John Huston, Otto Preminger, Richard Boone. **TV**

Hobgoblins **1987** Little creatures escape from a studio vault and wreak havoc. **92m/C VHS.** Jeffrey Culver, Tom Bartlett; ***D:*** Rick Sloane.

Hobo's Christmas **1987** A man who left his family to become a hobo comes home for Christmas 25 years later. Hughes turns in a delightful performance as the hobo. **94m/C VHS.** Barnard Hughes, William Hickey, Gerald McRaney, Wendy Crewson; ***D:*** Will MacKenzie. **TV**

Hobson's Choice **1953** A prosperous businessman in the 1890s tries to keep his daughter from marrying, but the strong-willed daughter has other ideas. **107m/B VHS.** *GB* Charles Laughton, John Mills, Brenda de Banzie; ***D:*** David Lean; ***C:*** Jack Hildyard; ***M:*** Malcolm Arnold. British Acad. '54: Film.

Hobson's Choice **1983** Remake of the old family comedy about a crusty, penny-pinching businessman whose headstrong daughter proves to him she'll not become an old maid. Instead she marries one of his employees. Not bad, but not as good as the original. **95m/C VHS.** Jack Warden, Sharon Gless, Richard Thomas, Lillian Gish; ***D:*** Gilbert Cates. **TV**

Hockey Night ½ **1984** A movie for pre- and early teens in which a girl goalie makes the boys' hockey team. **77m/C VHS.** *CA* Megan Follows, Rick Moranis, Gail Youngs, Martin Harburg, Henry Ramer; ***D:*** Paul Shapiro.

Hocus Pocus ½ **1993 (PG)** The divine Miss M is back, but this time she's not so sweet. Midler, Najimy, and Parker are 17th century witches accidentally conjured up in the 20th century, appropriately enough on Halloween in Salem, Massachusetts. Seems they were hung 300 years back and they take their revenge in some surprisingly gruesome ways, given the Disney label. They rant, they rave, they sing (only once), they fly. See this one for the three stars who make up for the lack of substance with their comedic talents. **95m/C VHS.** Bette Midler, Kathy Najimy, Sarah Jessica Parker, Thora Birch, Doug Jones, Omri Katz, Vinessa Shaw, Stephanie Faracy, Charles Rocket; ***Cameos:*** Penny Marshall, Garry Marshall; ***D:*** Kenny Ortega; ***W:*** Neil Cuthbert, Mick Garris; ***M:*** John Debney.

Hoffa **1992 (R)** The story of union organizer James R. Hoffa, who oversaw the rise of the Teamsters, a labor union composed mostly of truck drivers, from its fledgling infancy during the Great Depression to a membership of 2 million by the 1970s. Powerful performances by Nicholson in the title role and DeVito, who plays a union aide, a fictitious composite of several men who actually served Hoffa. This almost affectionate biographical treatment stands out in contrast from a career bristling with tension and violence. Proceeds through a series of flashbacks from the day Hoffa disappeared, July 30, 1975. **140m/C VHS, Wide.** Paul Guilfoyle, Jack Nicholson, Danny DeVito, Armand Assante, J.T. Walsh, Frank Whaley, Kevin Anderson, John P. Ryan, Robert Prosky, Natalija Nogulich, Nicholas Pryor, John C. Reilly, Karen Young, Cliff Gorman; ***D:*** Danny DeVito; ***W:*** David Mamet; ***C:*** Stephen Burum; ***M:*** David Newman.

Hog Wild ½ **1980 (PG)** A clique of high school nerds exact revenge on bullies from the local mean motorcycle gang, and a girl is torn between the two factions. **97m/C VHS.** *CA* Patti D'Arbanville, Tony Rosato, Michael Biehn; ***D:*** Les Rose.

The Holcroft Covenant **1985 (R)** Based upon the complex Robert Ludlum novel. Details the efforts of a man trying to release a secret fund that his Nazi father humanistically set up to relieve the future sufferings of Holocaust survivors. Confusing, and slow, but interesting, nonetheless. **112m/C VHS, DVD.** *GB* Michael Caine, Victoria Tennant, Anthony Andrews, Lilli Palmer, Mario Adorf, Michael (Michel) Lonsdale; ***D:*** John Frankenheimer; ***W:*** Edward Anhalt, John Hopkins, George Axelrod.

Hold 'Em Jail ½ **1932** Some good laughs with Wheeler and Woolsey starting a competitive football team at Kennedy's Bidemore Prison. **65m/B VHS.** Bert Wheeler, Robert Woolsey, Edgar Kennedy, Betty Grable, Edna May Oliver; ***D:*** Norman Taurog.

Hold Me, Thrill Me, Kiss Me ½ **1993 (R)** "Offbeat" barely begins to describe this comedy about a hapless loser who finds true love. Eli (Parrish) has escaped marriage to a rich girl named Twinkle (Young), unfortunately it took a little shooting to do it and now Eli's hiding out in a tacky pink trailer park where Sabra (Naschak), an insatiable stripper with a fondness for sex toys, immediately goes after Eli's bod. But he falls for her naive (and virginal) sister, Dannie (Shelly). Hershman manages to keep all the free-wheeling goings on under control. Film debut of former model Parrish; directorial debut feature of Hershman. **92m/C VHS.** Max Parrish, Adrienne Shelly, Andrea Naschak, Sean Young, Diane Ladd, Bela Lehoczky, Ania Suli; ***Cameos:*** Timothy Leary; ***D:*** Joel Hershman; ***W:*** Joel Hershman; ***C:*** Kent Wakeford; ***M:*** Gerald Gouriet.

Hold That Ghost *Oh, Charlie* **1941** Abbott and Costello inherit an abandoned roadhouse where the illicit loot of its former owner, a "rubbed out" mobster, is supposedly hidden. **86m/B VHS.** Bud Abbott, Lou Costello, Joan Davis, Richard Carlson, Mischa Auer, The Andrews Sisters, Shemp Howard, Evelyn Ankers, Nestor Paiva; ***D:*** Arthur Lubin; ***W:*** Robert Lees, Frederic Rinaldo, John Grant; ***C:*** Elwood "Woody" Bredell; ***M:*** Hans J. Salter.

Hold the Dream ½ **1986** Barbara Taylor Bradford's sequel to "A Woman of Substance." Kerr plays the adult Emma Harte while Seagrove, who played young Emma in the original miniseries, now plays her granddaughter Paula, who has been chosen to take over the family's retailing empire. But will her ambitions clash with her romantic possibilities? **200m/C VHS.** Jenny Seagrove, Deborah Kerr, Claire Bloom, James Brolin, Stephen Collins, Nicholas Farrell, Nigel Havers, John Mills, Liam Neeson, Valentine Pelka; ***D:*** Don Sharp; ***C:*** John Coquillon; ***M:*** Barrie Guard. **TV**

Hold Your Man **1933** Great star vehicle that turns from comedy to drama with Harlow falling for hustler Gable. Harlow and Gable are at their best in this unlikely story of a crooked couple. Direction drags at times, but snappy dialogue and the stars' personalities more than make up for it. **86m/B VHS.** Jean Harlow, Clark Gable, Stuart Erwin, Dorothy Burgess, Garry Owen, Paul Hurst, Elizabeth Patterson, Laura La Plante; ***D:*** Sam Wood; ***W:*** Anita Loos, Howard Emmett Rogers.

A Hole in the Head ½ **1959** A comedy-drama about a shiftless but charming lout who tries to raise money to save his hotel from foreclosure and learn to be responsible for his young son. Notable for the introduction of the song "High Hopes." ♫High Hopes; All My Tomorrows. **120m/C VHS, DVD, Wide.** Frank Sinatra, Edward G. Robinson, Thelma Ritter, Carolyn Jones, Eleanor Parker, Eddie Hodges, Keenan Wynn, Joi Lansing; ***D:*** Frank Capra; ***W:*** Arnold Schulman; ***C:*** William H. Daniels. Oscars '59: Song ("High Hopes").

Hole in the Sky ½ *The Ranger, the Cook and a Hole in the Sky* **1995 (PG)** Teenaged Mac (O'Connell) is working for the Montana forestry service in the summer of 1919 under the tutelage of taciturn legend Bill Bell (a mustache-less Elliott). Mac learns some lessons about growing up, first love, card-playing—and never to rile the camp cook. Based on an autobiographical story by Norman MacLean. Made for TV; filmed on location in British Columbia. **94m/C VHS, DVD.** Sam Elliott, Jerry O'Connell, Ricky Jay, Molly Parker; ***D:*** John Kent Harrison; ***W:*** Robert W. Lenski. **TV**

The Holes ½ *Les Gaspards* **1972 (PG)** A Parisian book shop owner's daughter vanishes along with other local citizens and American tourists, and he decides to investigate when the police won't. In French with subtitles. **92m/C VHS.** *FR* Philippe Noiret, Charles Denner, Michel Serrault, Gerard Depardieu.

Holiday ½ *Free to Live; Unconventional Linda* **1938** The classically genteel screwball comedy about a rich girl who steals her sister's fiance. A yardstick in years to come for sophisticated, urbane Hollywood romanticism. Based on the play by Philip Barry who later wrote "The Philadelphia Story." **93m/B VHS.** Cary Grant, Katharine Hepburn, Doris Nolan, Edward Everett Horton, Ruth Donnelly, Lew Ayres, Binnie Barnes; ***D:*** George Cukor; ***W:*** Donald Ogden Stewart, Sidney Buchman.

Holiday Affair ½ **1949** Hollywood yuletide charmer about a pretty widow being courted by two very different men. **86m/B VHS.** Robert Mitchum, Janet Leigh, Griff Barnett, Wendell Corey, Esther Dale, Henry O'Neill, Harry (Henry) Morgan, Larry J. Blake; ***D:*** Don Hartman.

Holiday Affair ½ **1996** Remake of the 1949 film finds Manhattan department store clerk Steve Mason (Elliott) intrigued by widowed mom Jodie Ennis (Gibb). Although she inadvertently gets him fired, Steve still expresses interest in Jodie and her son. But Jodie's accepted the marriage proposal of regular guy boyfriend Paul (Irwin) because he offers her security. It's up to Jodie's son Timmy (Blanck) and some Christmastime truthfulness to get Jodie to see the light. **93m/C VHS.** David James Elliott, Cynthia Gibb, Curtis Blanck, Tom Irwin, Al Waxman, Patricia Hamilton, Victor Ertmanis, Pam Hyatt; ***D:*** Alan Myerson; ***M:*** Lee Holdridge. **CABLE**

Holiday Heart **2000 (R)** **1946** Macho big man Rhames may not be the first actor to spring to mind to play a drag queen but he does a fine job in this melodramatic adaptation of the play by West. Holiday Heart (Rhames) comes to the rescue of ex-addict Wanda (Woodard) who has a 12-year-old daughter, Niki (Reynolds), and lousy taste in men. Wanda just can't make that final break with her dealer boyfriend Silas (Williamson), even though it leads to her sliding back into crack addiction and means that Heart has to draw on his maternal skills to give Niki a stable home. **97m/C VHS, DVD.** Ving Rhames, Alfre Woodard, Mykelti Williamson, Jesika Reynolds; ***D:*** Robert Thompson; ***W:*** Cheryl L. West; ***C:*** Jan Kiesser; ***M:*** Stephen James Taylor. **CABLE**

Holiday Hotel **1977 (R)** A group of wild French vacationers let loose at their favorite little resort hotel along the Brittany coast. Available in French with English subtitles or dubbed into English. **109m/C VHS.** *FR* Sophie Barjae, Daniel Ceccaldi; ***D:*** Michael (Michel) Lang.

Holiday in Havana **1949** Desi Arnaz is back in Cuba winning hearts and dance contests. Watch only for Desi's presence. ♫Holiday in Havana; The Arnaz Jam; Straw Hat Song; Rhumba Rumbero; Copacobana; Made For Each Other; I'll Take Romance. **73m/B VHS.** Desi Arnaz Sr., Lolita Valdez, Mary Hatcher, Ann Doran; ***D:*** Jean Yarbrough.

Holiday in Mexico ½ **1946** Pidgeon plays the U.S. ambassador to Mexico whose teenage daughter (Powell) tries to run his life along with his household. He falls for a singer while she develops a crush on an older, respected pianist (Iturbi playing himself). Lots of lively production numbers featuring Xavier Cugat and his orchestra. ♫I Think Of You; Walter Winchell Rhumba; Yo Te Amo Mucho—And That's That; And Dreams Remain; Holiday in Mexico; Ave Maria; Les Filles de Cadiz; Italian Street Song; Polonaise in A Flat Major. **127m/C VHS.** Walter Pidgeon, Jane Powell, Ilona Massey, Jose Iturbi, Roddy McDowall, Xavier Cugat, Hugo Haas; ***D:*** George Sidney; ***W:*** Isobel Lennart; ***C:*** Harry Stradling Sr.; ***M:*** Georgie Stoll.

Holiday Inn ♪♪♪ **1942** Fred Astaire and Bing Crosby are rival song-and-dance men who decide to work together to turn a Connecticut farm into an inn, open only on holidays. Remade in 1954 as "White Christmas." ♫White Christmas; Be Careful, It's My Heart; Plenty to Be Thankful For; Abraham, Abraham; Let's Say It With Firecrackers; I Gotta Say I Love You Cause I Can't Tell A Lie; Let's Start the New Year Right; Happy Holidays; Song of Freedom. **101m/B VHS, DVD.** Bing Crosby, Fred Astaire, Marjorie Reynolds, Walter Abel, Virginia Dale; ***D:*** Mark Sandrich. Oscars '42: Song ("White Christmas").

Holiday Rhythm ♪½ **1950** A TV promoter is knocked out and dreams of a world-wide trip full of entertainment, comedy, and insanity. **61m/B VHS.** Mary Beth Hughes, Tex Ritter, David Street, Donald MacBride.

Hollow Gate **1988** Trick or Treat?? Four kids find out when they run into a guy with hungry dogs. **90m/C VHS.** Addison Randall.

The Hollow Man ♪♪ **2000 (R)** Scientist Caine (Bacon) heads a team that discovers the ability to make humans invisible. He decides to test it on himself and the process works, in fact it's irreversible, and his newfound power has unexpected side effects when he gives into his worst impulses and terrorizes his colleagues, including ex-girlfriend Linda (Shue) and her new beau (Brolin). Stunning visual effects can't hide script's lack of imagination and creepy sexual kink. Degenerates into body-count slasher flick as the intriguing moral questions are dropped in favor of cheap scares. **114m/C VHS, DVD, Wide.** Kevin Bacon, Elisabeth Shue, Josh Brolin, William Devane, Kim Dickens, Greg Grunberg, Mary Jo Randle, Joey Slotnick; ***D:*** Paul Verhoeven; ***W:*** Andrew Marlowe; ***C:*** Jost Vacano; ***M:*** Jerry Goldsmith.

Hollow Point ♪♪ **1995 (R)** After FBI agent Diane Norwood (Carrere) and DEA agent Max Perish (Griffith) get in each other's way, they reluctantly team up to bring down crime kingpin Oleg Krezinsky (Hemblen). Only Krezinsky and his partner Livingston (Lithgrow) learns she's a fed and hire assassin Lawton (Sutherland) to teach her a lesson. **103m/C VHS.** Thomas Ian Griffith, Tia Carrere, John Lithgow, Donald Sutherland, David Hemblen; ***D:*** Sidney J. Furie; ***C:*** David Franco; ***M:*** Brahm Wenger.

Hollow Reed ♪♪♪ *Believe Me* **1995** Heart-wrenching, though not maudlin, drama revolves around nine-year-old Oliver Wyatt (Bould). His parents, Martyn (Donovan) and Hannah (Richardson), have bitterly divorced after Martyn finally acknowledges his homosexuality and moves in with his lover, Tom (Hart). Hannah's new live-in boyfriend Frank (Flemyng) turns out to be abusive towards Oliver, who's reluctant to say anything to destroy his mother's new happiness. But when Martyn discovers what's happening, he instigates a custody battle for his son that has everyone at each other's throats, with the terrified Oliver caught in the crossfire. Compelling performances. **105m/C VHS.** *GB* Martin Donovan, Joely Richardson, Ian Hart, Jason Flemyng, Sam Bould, Edward Hardwicke, Annette Badland, Douglas Hodge; ***D:*** Angela Pope; ***W:*** Paula Milne; ***C:*** Remi Adefarasin; ***M:*** Anne Dudley.

Hollywood after Dark ♪ **1965** McClanahan plays a young starlet trying to make it big in Hollywood. Pure exploitation schlock. Not released theatrically until 1968. **74m/C VHS.** Anthony (Tony) Vorno, Rue McClanahan, Paul Bruce, Ernest Macias, John Barrick; ***D:*** John Patrick Hayes; ***W:*** John Patrick Hayes; ***C:*** Vilis Lapenieks; ***M:*** Bill Marx.

Hollywood Boulevard ♪♪½ **1976 (R)** Behind-the-scenes glimpse of shoestring-budget movie making offers comical sex, violence, sight gags, one-liners, comedy bits, and mock-documentary footage. Commander Cody and His Lost Planet Airmen are featured. **93m/C VHS, DVD.** Candice Rialson, Mary Woronov, Rita George, Jonathan Kaplan, Jeffrey Kramer, Dick Miller, Paul Bartel, Charles B. Griffith, Richard Doran; ***D:*** Joe Dante, Allan Arkush; ***W:*** Patrick Hobby; ***C:*** Jamie Anderson; ***M:*** Andrew Stein.

Hollywood Boulevard 2 ♪ **1989 (R)** A "B" movie studio finds its top actresses being killed off and terror reigns supreme as the mystery grows more intense. Could that psycho-bimbo from outer space have something to do with it? **82m/C VHS.** Ginger Lynn Allen, Kelly Monteith, Eddie Deezen, Ken Wright, Steve Vinovich; ***D:*** Steve Barnett.

Hollywood Canteen ♪♪♪♪ **1944** Star-studded extravaganza with just about every Warner Bros. lot actor in this tribute to love and nationalism. Lovesick G.I. Hutton falls for Leslie, wins a date with her in a phony raffle set up at the Hollywood Canteen, and the sparks fly right away. But he thinks she tricked him as he boards his train and she's not there to see him off. Lame story is redeemed by the talented cast and wonderful musical numbers which make this picture fly with charm and style. Before production began there were arguments over "unpatriotic" actors—labeled as such due to their lack of participation in this, and other similar movies produced at the time. ♫Don't Fence Me In; Sweet Dreams, Sweetheart; You Can Always Tell A Yank; We're Having a Baby; What Are You Doin' the Rest of Your Life; The General Jumped At Dawn; Gettin' Corns For My Country; Voodoo Moon; Tumblin' Tumbleweeds. **124m/B VHS.** Robert Hutton, Dane Clark, Janis Paige, Jonathan Hale, Barbara Brown, James Flavin, Eddie Marr, Ray Teal, Bette Davis, Joan Leslie, Jack Benny, Jimmy Dorsey, Joan Crawford, John Garfield, Barbara Stanwyck, Ida Lupino, Eddie Cantor, Jack Carson, Eleanor Parker, Alexis Smith, S.Z. Sakall, Peter Lorre, Sydney Greenstreet, Helmut Dantine; ***D:*** Delmer Daves; ***W:*** Delmer Daves.

Hollywood Chainsaw Hookers ♪♪ **1988 (R)** A campy, sexy, very bloody parody about attractive prostitutes who dismember their unsuspecting customers. **90m/C VHS, DVD, Wide.** Linnea Quigley, Gunnar Hansen, Jay Richardson, Michelle (McClellan) Bauer, Dawn Wildsmith, Dennis Mooney, Jerry Fox; ***D:*** Fred Olen Ray; ***W:*** Fred Olen Ray, T.L. Lankford; ***C:*** Scott Ressler; ***M:*** Michael Perilstein.

Hollywood Chaos ♪½ **1989** Director Ballantine's stars quit his production before it even starts, so he gets the next best thing—star look-alikes. However, his problems are just beginning. One of his new "stars" is kidnapped, and his reclusive stage manager is hunted as the object of desire for a female motorcycle gang. **90m/C VHS.** Carl Ballantine, Tricia Leigh Fisher, Kathleen Freeman; ***D:*** Sean McNamara.

Hollywood Confidential ♪♪ **1997 (R)** TV movie stars Olmos as former LAPD cop Stan Navarro, who now runs a struggling detective agency specializing in the seamier sides of Hollywood. His latest cases involve getting dirt on a studio acting coach, seeing if a bartender at the newest hotspot is skimming the receipts, and "persuading" the mistress of a well-known director to take a hike. **90m/C VHS, DVD.** Edward James Olmos, Anthony Yerkovich, Rick Aiello, Richard T. Jones, Charlize Theron, Angela Alvarado, Christina Harnos, Thomas Jane, Amanda Pays; ***D:*** Reynaldo Villalobos; ***W:*** Anthony Yerkovich; ***C:*** Reynaldo Villalobos; ***M:*** Marc Bonilla. **TV**

Hollywood Cop ♪½ **1987 (R)** A tough cop in Hollywood goes up against the mob for the sake of a kidnapped boy. **101m/C VHS.** Jim Mitchum, David Goss, Cameron Mitchell, Troy Donahue, Aldo Ray; ***D:*** Amir Shervan.

The Hollywood Detective ♪♪ **1989 (PG)** An average TV movie that spoofs "Kojak." A TV detective tries it out for real, and gets into troubles for which he can't pause "for a message from our sponsor." **88m/C VHS.** Telly Savalas, Helene Udy, George Coe, Joe Dallesandro, Tom Reese; ***D:*** Kevin Connor. **TV**

Hollywood Dreams ♪½ **1994 (R)** Starlet on the Hollywood casting couch saga of a midwestern girl that comes to California with dreams of making it big. **90m/C VHS, DVD.** Kelly Cook, Danny Smith, Debra Beatty; ***D:*** Ralph Portillo.

Hollywood Ending ♪♪ **2002 (PG-13)** Allen continues two recent disturbing trends: making mediocre comedies, and making creepy casting choices when picking his female leads. This time he's Val Waxman, a a down-on-his-luck, nuerotic director about ten years past his prime with a hot ex-wife, Ellie (Leoni) who's engaged to a smarmy studio head (Williams). He's also managed to snag a hot dim-bulb wannabe-actress girlfriend (Messing). When Ellie uses her connections to get Val a job directing an "Ode to New York" pic, his hypochodriac tendencies go into haywire and he goes blind. Woody's made some great comedies in the past, and if this was 10-15 years ago, this one might've been great, too. But his overwhelmingly annoying screen persona, and the missed execution of some pretty good setups, this one goes to the forgettable file. Leoni, Williams, and Rydell do well with what they're given. **114m/C VHS, DVD.** *US* Woody Allen, Tea Leoni, Treat Williams, Debra Messing, George Hamilton, Tiffani-Amber Thiessen, Mark Rydell, Isaac Mizrahi, Marian Seldes, Peter Gerety, Greg Mottola, Mark Webber, Lu Yu, Barney Cheng, Jodie Markell; ***D:*** Woody Allen; ***W:*** Woody Allen; ***C:*** Wedigo von Schultzendorff.

Hollywood Harry ♪ *Harry's Machine* **1986 (PG-13)** A private-eye mystery/parody, about an inept detective who searches for a missing porn actress. **99m/C VHS.** Robert Forster, Kathrine (Kate) Forster, Joe Spinell, Shannon Wilcox; ***D:*** Robert Forster; ***W:*** Curt Allen.

Hollywood Heartbreak ♪♪ **1989** It's heartbreak in tinseltown for a young writer who's trying to pitch his movie script but winds up defending himself from slimy agents and persistent starlets. Another entry for Bartlett's familiar plotlines. **90m/C VHS.** Mark Moses, Carol Mayo Jenkins, Ron Karabatsos, Richard Romanus, James LeGros; ***D:*** Lance Dickson.

Hollywood High ♪ **1977 (R)** Four attractive teen couples converge on the mansion of an eccentric silent-film star for an unusual vacation experience in this teenage skin flick. Followed by a sequel. **81m/C VHS.** Marcy Albrecht, Sherry Hardin, Rae Sperling, Susanne Kevin Mead; ***D:*** Patrick Wright.

Hollywood High, Part 2 ♪ **1981 (R)** Ignored by their boyfriends for the lure of sun and surf, three comely high school students try their best to regain their interest. **86m/C VHS.** April May, Donna Lynn, Camille Warner, Lee Thomburg; ***D:*** Caruth C. Byrd.

Hollywood Hot Tubs ♪ **1984 (R)** Teen sex romp has adolescent picking up some extra cash and a lot of fun repairing the hot tubs of the rich and famous. **103m/C VHS.** Donna McDaniel, Michael Andrew, Katt Shea, Paul Gunning, Edy Williams, Jewel Shepard; ***D:*** Chuck Vincent.

Hollywood Hot Tubs 2: Educating Crystal ♪ **1989 (R)** A softcore comedy about a well-tanned ingenue learning about business in Hollywood during numerous hot tub trysts. **103m/C VHS.** Jewel Shepard, Patrick Day, Remy O'Neill, David Tiefen, Bart Braverman; ***D:*** Ken Raich.

Hollywood in Trouble ♪ **1987** A bumbling middle-aged fool decides to break into the wacky movie-making business. **90m/C VHS.** Vic Vallard, Jean Levine, Jerry Tiffe, Pamela Dixon, Jerry Cleary.

The Hollywood Knights ♪♪ **1980 (R)** Cheap imitation of "American Graffiti" is not without its funny moments. Beverly Hills teens, lead by Newbomb Turk (Wuhl), are displeased that their hangout—Tubby's Drive-in—is being shut down by those no-fun adults. So they decide to retaliate. Set on Halloween Night, 1965. **91m/C VHS, DVD, Wide.** Robert Wuhl, Michelle Pfeiffer, Tony Danza, Fran Drescher, Leigh French, Gary (Rand) Graham, James Jeter, Stuart Pankin, Gailard Sartain, Mike Binder, T.K. Carter, Moosie Drier, Debra Feuer, Garry Goodrow, Joyce Hyser, Roberta Wallach, Doris Hargrave, Walter Janovitz, Art LaFleur, Glenn Withrow, Sandy Helberg; ***D:*** Floyd Mutrux; ***W:*** Floyd Mutrux; ***C:*** William A. Fraker.

Hollywood Man ♪♪ **1976 (R)** A Hollywood actor wants to make his own film but when his financial support comes from the mob there's trouble ahead. **90m/C VHS.** William Smith, Don Stroud, Jennifer Billingsley, Mary Woronov; ***D:*** Jack Starrett.

Hollywood Mystery ♪½ *Hollywood Hoodlum* **1934** A publicity agent stops at nothing to promote his would-be starlet girlfriend. **53m/B VHS.** June Clyde, Frank Albertson, Joe Crespo; ***D:*** B. Reeves Eason.

Hollywood or Bust ♪♪½ **1956** The zany duo take their act on the road as they head for Tinsel Town in order to meet Lewis' dream girl Ekberg. This was the last film for the Martin & Lewis team and it's not the swan song their fans would have hoped for. **95m/C VHS.** Dean Martin, Jerry Lewis, Anita Ekberg, Pat(ricia) Crowley, Maxie "Slapsie" Rosenbloom, Willard Waterman; ***D:*** Frank Tashlin.

Hollywood Party ♪♪½ **1934** Durante plays a film star who decides to throw a Hollywood bash. Any plot is incidental as it is mainly an excuse to have numerous stars of the day appear in brief comic bits or musical numbers. Mickey Mouse and the Big Bad Wolf of Disney fame also appear in color animated footage combined with live action. Numerous MGM directors worked on parts of the film but Dwan was given the task of trying to pull the various scenes together (he is uncredited onscreen). ♫Hollywood Party; Hello; Reincarnation; I've Had My Moments; Feeling High; Hot Chocolate Soldiers. **72m/B VHS.** Jimmy Durante, Stan Laurel, Oliver Hardy, Lupe Velez, Ted Healy, Moe Howard, Curly Howard, Larry Fine, Robert Young, Charles Butterworth, Polly Moran, George Givot, Tom Kennedy, Arthur Treacher; ***D:*** Allan Dwan, Richard Boleslawski; ***W:*** Howard Dietz, Arthur Kober; ***C:*** James Wong Howe; ***V:*** Walt Disney, Billy Bletcher.

Hollywood Safari ♪♪½ **1996 (PG)** Jane (Boone) and Troy (Leisure) Johnson train animals for the movies. But Kensho the mountain lion escapes into the woods after a transport accident and is eventually captured by the police who think it's the wild cat that recently attacked a local teen. The Johnsons try to prevent the sheriff's deputy (Savage) from having Kensho killed before they can prove their claims, but their best defense would be to find the renegade cougar. It's a pleasant enough time-waster, with Muddy, the Johnson's dog, providing some fine heroics. **89m/C VHS.** John Savage, Ted Jan Roberts, David Leisure, Debbie Boone, Ken Tigar, Don "The Dragon" Wilson; ***D:*** Henri Charr; ***W:*** Robert Newcastle; ***C:*** Guido Verweyen. **VIDEO**

Hollywood Shuffle ♪♪½ **1987 (R)** Townsend's autobiographical comedy about a struggling black actor in Hollywood trying to find work and getting nothing but stereotypical roles. Written, directed, financed by Townsend, who created this often clever and appealing film on a $100,000 budget. **81m/C VHS, DVD, Wide.** Robert Townsend, Anne-Marie Johnson, Starletta DuPois, Helen Martin, Keenen Ivory Wayans, Damon Wayans, Craigus R. Johnson, Eugene Glazer; ***D:*** Robert Townsend; ***W:*** Robert Townsend, Keenen Ivory Wayans; ***C:*** Peter Deming; ***M:*** Patrice Rushen, Udi Harpaz.

Hollywood Stadium Mystery ♪♪ **1938** A boxer turns up dead before a big match and a D.A. investigates. Performances hold this one up, especially by Hamilton who later played Commissioner Gordon on TV's "Batman." **66m/B VHS.** Neil Hamilton, Evelyn Venable, Jimmy Wallington, Barbara Pepper, Lucien Littlefield, Lynne Roberts, Charles Williams, James Spottswood, Reed Hadley, Smiley Burnette; ***D:*** David Howard.

The Hollywood Strangler Meets the Skid Row Slasher woof! *The Model Killer* **1979 (R)** Voiced-over narration, canned music, and an unfathomable plot are but a few of this would-be fright fest's finer points. Uninhibited by any narrative connection, two terrors strike fear in the heart of Tinseltown. While a psycho photographer cruises L.A. taking pictures of models he subsequently strangles, a woman working in a barebums magazine store takes a stab (with a knife) at lowering the city's derelict population. There's a word for this sort of dribble, and it isn't versimilitude. Steckler used an alias (not surprisingly) for this one—Wolfgang Schmidt. **72m/C VHS.** Pierre Agostino, Carolyn Brandt, Forrest Duke, Chuck Alford; ***D:*** Ray Dennis Steckler, Wolfgang Schmidt.

Hollywood Vice Sqaud 𝒹 **1986 (R)** Explores the lives of Hollywood police officers and the crimes they investigate. Contains three different storylines involving prostitution, child pornography, and organized crime. The film can't decide to be a comedy send-up of crime stories or a drama and is also crippled by a poor script. Written by the real-life chief of the Hollywood Vice Squad. **90m/C VHS, DVD.** Trish Van Devere, Ronny Cox, Frank Gorshin, Leon Isaac Kennedy, Carrie Fisher, Ben Frank, Robin Wright Penn; ***D:*** Penelope Spheeris; ***W:*** James J. Docherty; ***M:*** Michael Convertino.

Hollywood Zap woof! **1986 (R)** Two losers, one a Southern orphan, the other a video game nut, hit Hollywood and engage in antics that are meant to be funny, but are actually tasteless. **85m/C VHS.** Ben Frank, Ivan E. Roth, De Waldron, Annie Gaybis, Chuck "Porky" Mitchell; ***D:*** David M. Cohen; ***W:*** David M. Cohen.

Hollywood's New Blood 𝒹 **1988** Young actors making a movie are haunted by a film crew from hell. **90m/C VHS.** Bobby Johnson, Francine Lapensee; ***D:*** James Shyman.

Holocaust 𝒹𝒹𝒹½ **1978** The war years of 1935 to 1945 are relived in this account of the Nazi atrocities, focusing on the Jewish Weiss family, destroyed by the monstrous crimes, and the Dorf family, Germans who thrived under the Nazi regime. Highly acclaimed riveting miniseries with an exceptional cast. Won eight Emmys. **475m/C VHS.** Michael Moriarty, Fritz Weaver, Meryl Streep, James Woods, Joseph Bottoms, Tovah Feldshuh, David Warner, Ian Holm, Michael Beck, Marius Goring; ***D:*** Marvin J. Chomsky. **TV**

Holocaust Survivors...Remembrance of Love 𝒹𝒹 *Remembrance of Love* **1983** A concentration camp survivor and his daughter attend the 1981 World Gathering of Holocaust Survivors in Tel-Aviv and both find romance. **100m/C VHS.** Kirk Douglas, Pam Dawber, Chana Eden, Yoram Gal, Robert Clary; ***D:*** Jack Smight; ***M:*** William Goldstein. **TV**

Hologram Man 𝒹𝒹 **1995 (R)** Futuristic thriller finds psycho/terrorist Slash Gallagher (Lurie) captured by rookie cop Kurt Decoda (Lara). His prison term is to be served in Holographic Stasis, which means his mind is stored on a computer. Slash's gang manges to break his mind out of the computer but since his body is destroyed, Slash roams as a powerful electro-magnetic hologram. And it's up to cop Decoda to get Slash back. **96m/C VHS.** Joe Lara, Evan Lurie, William Sanderson, Tommy (Tiny) Lister, Michael Nouri, John Amos; ***D:*** Richard Pepin; ***W:*** Evan Lurie; ***M:*** John Gonzalez.

Holt of the Secret Service **1942** Secret service agent runs afoul of saboteurs and fifth-columnists in this 15-episode serial. **290m/B VHS.** Jack Holt, Evelyn Brent, C. Montague Shaw, Tristram Coffin, John Ward, George Chesebro; ***D:*** James W. Horne.

The Holy Innocents 𝒹𝒹𝒹 *Los Santos Inocentes* **1984 (PG)** A peasant family is torn asunder by their feudal obligations to their patrons. Set in the 1960s in Franco's Spain. In Spanish with English subtitles. **108m/C VHS.** *SP* Alfredo Landa, Francesco Rabal; ***D:*** Mario Camus. Cannes '84: Actor (Landa), Actor (Rabal).

Holy Man 𝒹𝒹 **1998 (PG)** This satire of home shopping networks is supposed to shell American consumerism, but ends up shooting itself in the foot instead. Murphy is G, a New Age-babble spouting wise man who is used by home shopping execs Goldblum and Preston to boost flagging sales. G lectures about the joy of spiritual over material happiness, but sales soar anyway. Misuses Murphy's wisecracking ability in what could have been a good premise, and reduces his character to a sight gag. **113m/C VHS, DVD.** Eddie Murphy, Jeff Goldblum, Kelly Preston, Robert Loggia, Jon Cryer, Eric McCormack, Marc Macaulay, Sam Kitchin, Robert Small, Morgan Fairchild; ***D:*** Stephen Herek; ***W:*** Tom Schulman; ***C:*** Adrian Biddle; ***M:*** Alan Silvestri.

Holy Matrimony 𝒹𝒹½ **1994 (PG-13)** Mild-mannered and pleasant comedy in spite of its potentially salacious plot. Thieves Peter (Donovan) and Havana (Arquette) take off to Canada to hide out in the Hutterite religious community where Peter grew up and where he's welcomed as the prodigal son. Peter hides their stolen loot but neglects to pass the word on before he's killed in an accident. Wanting to stay and search for the money, Havana uses the colony's reliance on biblical law to marry Peter's brother, Zeke (Gordon-Levitt). Only problem is Zeke is 12 and doesn't even like girls. Strictly brother-sister affection develops between the two. Amusing performances by both. **93m/C VHS.** Patricia Arquette, Joseph Gordon-Levitt, Armin Mueller-Stahl, Tate Donovan, John Schuck, Lois Smith, Courtney B. Vance, Jeffrey Nordling, Richard Riehle; ***D:*** Leonard Nimoy; ***W:*** David Weisberg, Douglas S. Cook; ***C:*** Bobby Bukowski; ***M:*** Bruce Broughton.

Holy Smoke 𝒹𝒹 **1999 (R)** Free-spirited Ruth (Winslet) travels to India and finds would-be spiritual enlightenment with an Indian guru. Her behavior terrifies her parents and her mother (Hamilton) manages to lure Ruth back home to Australia. They've hired American cult specialist, macho PJ Waters (Keitel), to rescue and deprogram her. Isolated in the Australian bush, the balance of power between Ruth and PJ begins to shift as sexual obsession takes hold. Complex characters but the strident storytelling gets annoying and some scenes seem staged for needless shock value. Based on the novel by the Campion sisters. **114m/C VHS, DVD, Wide.** *AU* Harvey Keitel, Kate Winslet, Julie Hamilton, Tim Robertson, Sophie Lee, Pam Grier, Paul Goddard, Daniel Wyllie; ***D:*** Jane Campion; ***W:*** Jane Campion, Anna Campion; ***C:*** Dion Beebe; ***M:*** Angelo Badalamenti.

Holy Terror 𝒹𝒹 **1965** The story of Florence Nightingale, who shocked Victorian society by organizing a nursing staff to aid British soldiers in the Crimean War, is told in this presentation from "George Schaefer's Showcase Theatre." **76m/C VHS.** Julie Harris, Denholm Elliott, Torin Thatcher, Kate Reid; ***D:*** George Schaefer. **TV**

Homage 𝒹𝒹 **1995 (R)** Archie's (Whaley) an emotionally disturbed mathematical nerd who needs a break from academia and persuades widowed ex-teacher Katherine Samuel (Danner) to hire him as caretaker for her New Mexico ranch. The duo achieve a strange serenity that shatters when Katherine's TV star daughter, self-absorbed Lucy (Lee), arrives seeking shelter because of her drug and drinking problems. A nasty triangle ensues as Lucy makes the mistake of sexually enticing, then rejecting, the needy Archie. In fact, the mistake's fatal. Based on Medoff's play "The Homage That Follows." **100m/C VHS.** Frank Whaley, Blythe Danner, Sheryl Lee, Bruce Davison, Danny Nucci; ***D:*** Ross Kagen Marks; ***W:*** Mark Medoff; ***C:*** Tom Richmond; ***M:*** W.G. Snuffy Walden.

Hombre 𝒹𝒹𝒹 **1967** A white man in the 1880s, raised by a band of Arizona Apaches, is forced into a showdown. In helping a stagecoach full of settlers across treacherous country, he not only faces traditional bad guys, but prejudice as well. Based on a story by Elmore Leonard. **111m/C VHS, Wide.** Paul Newman, Fredric March, Richard Boone, Diane Cilento, Cameron Mitchell, Barbara Rush, Martin Balsam; ***D:*** Martin Ritt; ***W:*** Harriet Frank Jr., Irving Ravetch; ***C:*** James Wong Howe.

Hombres Armados 𝒹𝒹𝒹 *Men with Guns* **1997 (R)** Fiercely independent filmmaker John Sayles' men with guns are not characters; they're an inevitable force like time or the weather that the characters have learned to accept. Set in a fictional Latin American country, story follows a well-to-do physician (Luppi) who trains doctors to work in the countryside among the local Mayan Indians. What he doesn't realize is that a civil war is engulfing his country, the Indians are practically enslaved, and his students have been murdered by the government that trained them. He picks up a ragged bunch of stragglers whose lives have been shattered by ever-present soldiers from either side of the war. Together they trudge through the jungle, searching for a place devoid of war or politics. Sayles based his idea on the 36-year-long civil war in Guatemala, which began in 1960. Spanish with subtitles. **128m/C VHS.** Federico Luppi, Damian Delgado, Dan Rivera Gonzalez, Tania Cruz, Damian Alcazar, Iguandili Lopez, Nandi Luna Ramirez, Rafael De Quevedo, Mandy Patinkin, Kathryn Grody, Roberto Sosa; ***D:*** John Sayles; ***W:*** John Sayles; ***C:*** Slawomir Idziak; ***M:*** Mason Daring.

Hombres Complicados 𝒹𝒹 **1997** Petty crook Roger (De Pauw) can't pay his debts to a group of gangsters. So he convinces gullible brother Bruno (Roofthooft) that they should use the small inheritance left to them by their mother to take a bonding road trip. Roger wants to buy some time until he can come up with a get-rich-quick scheme but, as usual in his sad-sack life, Roger's scheming leads to some bizarre happenings. Flemish and French with subtitles. **83m/C VHS.** *BE* Josse De Pauw, Dirk Roofthooft, Lies Pauwels; ***D:*** Dominique Deruddere; ***W:*** Dominique Deruddere, Marc Didden; ***C:*** Willy Stassen.

Home Alone 𝒹𝒹𝒹 **1990 (PG)** Eight-year-old Kevin is accidentally left behind when his entire (and large) family makes a frantic rush for the airport. That's the plausible part. Alone and besieged by burglars, Culkin turns into a pint-sized Rambo defending his suburban castle with the wile and resources of a boy genius with perfect timing and unlimited wherewithal. That's the implausible part. Pesci and Stern, the targets of Macauley's wrath, enact painful slapstick with considerable vigor, while Candy has a small but funny part as the leader of a polka band traveling cross-country with mom O'Hara. The highest-grossing picture of 1990, surpassing "Ghost" and "Jaws." **105m/C VHS, DVD, Wide.** Macaulay Culkin, Catherine O'Hara, Joe Pesci, Daniel Stern, John Heard, Roberts Blossom, John Candy, Billie Bird, Angela Goethals, Devin Ratray, Kieran Culkin; ***D:*** Chris Columbus; ***W:*** John Hughes; ***C:*** Julio Macat; ***M:*** John Williams.

Home Alone 2: Lost in New York 𝒹𝒹½ **1992 (PG)** In an almost exact duplication of the original blockbuster, the harebrained McCallister family leaves Kevin behind in the shuffle to start their Florida vacation. Boarding the wrong plane, Kevin lands in NYC, where wonder of wonders, he meets crooks Pesci and Stern, prison escapees who somehow survived the torture meted out in the first film. And they want revenge. Loaded with cartoon violence and shameless gag replicas from HA1, mega-hit still produces genuine laughs and manages to incorporate fresh material. Culkin is as adorable as ever, with supporting cast all delivering fine performances. Filmed in New York City. **120m/C VHS, DVD.** Macaulay Culkin, Joe Pesci, Daniel Stern, Catherine O'Hara, John Heard, Tim Curry, Brenda Fricker, Devin Ratray, Hillary Wolf, Eddie Bracken, Dana Ivey, Rob Schneider, Kieran Culkin, Gerry Bamman, Donald Trump; ***D:*** Chris Columbus; ***W:*** John Hughes; ***C:*** Julio Macat; ***M:*** John Williams.

Home Alone 3 𝒹 **1997 (PG)** Regardless of the new faces, the story and cartoon violence seems all too familar. Linz (taking over for the teenaged Culkin) is stricken with the chicken pox but able to booby trap his suburban house with to foil the plans of international criminals trying to recover a microchip stashed in a toy car. Film fails to carry the charm of its predecessors and sends the wrong messages: it's okay for parents to leave underaged kids home by themselves and electrocuting people is fun. Writer Hughes should be left home alone to rethink his skills as a screenwriter. **102m/C VHS, DVD.** Alex D. Linz, Kevin Kilner, Olek Krupa, Rya Kihlstedt, Lenny Von Dohlen, David Thornton, Haviland (Haylie) Morris, Marian Seldes, Scarlett Johansson, Christopher Curry, Baxter Harris, Seth Smith; ***D:*** Raja Gosnell; ***W:*** John Hughes; ***C:*** Julio Macat; ***M:*** Nick Glennie-Smith.

The Home and the World 𝒹𝒹𝒹½ *Ghare Baire* **1984** Another masterpiece from India's Ray, this film deals with a sheltered Indian woman who falls in love with her husband's friend and becomes politically committed in the turmoil of 1907-08. Based on Rabindranath Tagore's novel. In Bengali with English subtitles. **130m/C VHS.** *IN* Victor Banerjee, Soumitra Chatterjee; ***D:*** Satyajit Ray.

Home at Last **1988** An orphan in turn of the century New York finds himself shipped to Nebraska on an orphan train. There he works on the farm of his adopted family, whose own son has died. The boy finds that he must adjust to a new lifestyle as well as strive to be accepted as someone other than a replacement for the couple's son. From the "Wonderworks" series. **58m/C VHS.** Adrien Brody, Frank Converse, Caroline Lagerfelt, Sascha Radetsky.

Home Before Midnight 𝒹½ **1984** A young songwriter falls in love with a 14-year-old, is discovered, and is subsequently charged with statutory rape. **115m/C VHS.** James Aubrey, Alison Elliott; ***D:*** Pete Walker.

Home for Christmas 𝒹𝒹½ **1990** An elderly homeless man, with the love of a young girl, teaches a wealthy family the spirit of Christmas. **96m/C VHS.** Mickey Rooney, Joel Kaiser; ***D:*** Peter McCubbin.

Home for Christmas 𝒹𝒹½ *Little Miss Millions* **1993 (PG)** A 12-year-old has run away from her wicked stepmom who hires a bounty hunter to bring her back—for a half a million bucks. Only when he finds the girl stepmom doesn't want to pay up and she tells anyone who will listen that the bounty hunter actually kidnapped the girl. Bounty hunter turns to friends, including the 12-year-old who isn't a fool and knows stepmom is a lying witch, for help. **90m/C VHS, DVD.** Howard Hesseman, Anita Morris, Jennifer Love Hewitt; ***D:*** Jim Wynorski; ***W:*** Jim Wynorski, R.J. Robertson; ***C:*** Zoran Hochstatter; ***M:*** Joel Goldsmith.

Home for the Holidays 𝒹𝒹 *Deadly Desires* **1972** Four daughters are called home on Christmas by their father who is convinced that his second wife is trying to poison him. **74m/C VHS.** Eleanor Parker, Walter Brennan, Sally Field, Jessica Walter, Julie Harris; ***D:*** John Llewellyn Moxey. **TV**

Home for the Holidays 𝒹𝒹½ **1995 (PG-13)** Frantic dysfunctional family saga finds eldest daughter Claudia Larson (Hunter) on her way to Baltimore to spend Thanksgiving with her family. Frazzled Claudia must deal with badly bewigged mom Adele (Bancroft), genial dad Henry (Durning), and her siblings—frenzied gay brother Tommy (Downey Jr.) and self-righteous sister Joanne (Stevenson), as well as screwy Aunt Glady (Chaplin) and Tommy's handsome friend Leo Fish (McDermott). Yes, there are moments of deja vu about your very own family holidays but the film seems badly paced and ultimately irritating. Adapted from a short story by Chris Radant. **103m/C VHS, DVD, Wide.** Holly Hunter, Anne Bancroft, Charles Durning, Robert Downey Jr., Dylan McDermott, Cynthia Stevenson, Geraldine Chaplin, Steve Guttenberg, Claire Danes, David Strathairn, Austin Pendleton; ***D:*** Jodie Foster; ***W:*** W.D. Richter; ***C:*** Lajos Koltai; ***M:*** Mark Isham.

Home Free All 𝒹𝒹½ **1984** A Vietnam vet turned revolutionary, turned writer, tries to reacquaint himself with childhood friends only to find one has joined the mob and another is settled in suburbia and none of them are dealing well with adulthood. **92m/C VHS.** Allan Nicholls, Roland Caccavo, Maura Ellyn, Shelley Wyant, Lucille Rivim; ***D:*** Stuart Bird.

Home Fries 𝒹𝒹 **1998 (PG-13)** Things go from bad to worse for pregnant fast-food cashier, Sally (Drew Barrymore), as she learns that the father of her child is not only married, but dead! The catch is that the philanderer's stepsons are responsible and believe that Sally may have overheard their dastardly deed on her drive-through headset. Brother Dorian (Luke Wilson) takes a job at the Burger-Matic to find out just what Sally knows, but predictably falls in love with her instead. Tries to be a quirky dark comedy in a sweet love story, but the result is a bad mix of bleak humor and saccarine-sweet puppy love. Barrymore's cute and convincing performance manages to keep the whole thing from spoiling. Unfortunately, first-time director Parisot leaves the audience thinking, "this isn't what I ordered." **94m/C VHS, DVD, Wide.** Drew Barrymore, Luke Wilson, Catherine O'Hara, Jake Busey, Shelley Duvall, Kim Robillard, Darryl (Chill) Mitchell, Lanny Flaherty, Chris Ellis, Edward "Blue" Deckert; ***D:*** Dean Parisot; ***W:*** Vince Gilligan; ***C:*** Jerzy Zielinski; ***M:*** Rachel Portman.

Home from the Hill 🦴🦴🦴 **1960** A solemn, brooding drama about a southern landowner and his troubled sons, one of whom is illegitimate. This one triumphs because of casting. **150m/C VHS, Wide.** Robert Mitchum, George Peppard, George Hamilton, Eleanor Parker, Everett Sloane, Luana Parker, Constance Ford; ***D:*** Vincente Minnelli; ***W:*** Harriet Frank Jr., Irving Ravetch; ***C:*** Milton Krasner. Natl. Bd. of Review '60: Actor (Mitchum).

Home in Oklahoma 🦴🦴 **1947** A boy will be swindled out of his inheritance and a killer will escape justice until Roy comes to the rescue. Standard series fare. **72m/B VHS.** Roy Rogers, Dale Evans, George "Gabby" Hayes, Carol Hughes; ***D:*** William Witney.

Home Is Where the Hart Is 🦴🦴 **1988 (PG-13)** A rich 103-year-old is kidnapped by a nurse wanting to marry him and become heir to his estate. It's up to his sons, all in their 70s, to rescue him. **94m/C VHS.** Martin Mull, Leslie Nielsen, Valri Bromfield, Stephen E. Miller, Eric Christmas, Ted Stidder; ***D:*** Rex Bromfield; ***W:*** Rex Bromfield.

Home Movies 🦴½ **1979 (PG)** Brian DePalma and his film students at Sarah Lawrence College devised this loose, sloppy comedy which hearkens back to DePalma's early films. Tells the story of a nebbish who seeks therapy to gain control of his absurdly chaotic life. **89m/C VHS.** Kirk Douglas, Nancy Allen, Keith Gordon, Gerrit Graham, Vincent Gardenia, Mary Davenport; ***D:*** Brian DePalma; ***W:*** Brian DePalma; ***C:*** James L. Carter; ***M:*** Pino Donaggio.

Home of Angels 🦴🦴½ **1994** Billy sneaks his granddad out of his nursing home in Philadelphia and together the twosome begin a perilous journey back to Billy's home in Long Island, New York so they can have a family Christmas. They're aided by a homeless man when they run into trouble with a street gang. **90m/C VHS.** Lance Robinson, Abe Vigoda, Sherman Hemsley, Joe Frazier; ***D:*** Nick Stagliano.

A Home of Our Own **1975** An American priest sets up a home in Mexico for orphan boys and changes their lives for the better. A true story of Father William Wasson. **100m/C VHS.** Jason Miller.

A Home of Our Own 🦴🦴½ **1993 (PG-13)** Semi-autobiographical tearjerker based on screenwriter Duncan's childhood. Widowed and poor mother of six (Bates) is fired from her job at a Los Angeles potato chip factory, packs up the tribe and heads for a better life and a home to call their own. They end up in Idaho, in a ramshackle house owned by lonely Mr. Moon (Oh) and what follows is a winter of discontent. Bates provides an intense performance as a poor but proud woman with a tough exterior. Furlong provides the story's narration as the eldest son. A story of spiritual triumph, this one is sure to make your heart weep. **104m/C VHS, DVD, Wide.** Kathy Bates, Edward Furlong, Soon-Teck Oh, Amy Sakasitz, Tony Campisi; ***D:*** Tony Bill; ***W:*** Patrick Duncan; ***C:*** Jean Lepine; ***M:*** Michael Convertino.

Home of the Brave 🦴🦴🦴 **1949** A black soldier is sent on a top secret mission in the South Pacific, but finds that he must battle with his white comrades as he is subjected to subordinate treatment and constant racial slurs. Hollywood's first outstanding statement against racial prejudice. **86m/B VHS.** Lloyd Bridges, James Edwards, Frank Lovejoy, Jeff Corey, Douglas Dick, Steve Brodie, Cliff Clark; ***D:*** Mark Robson; ***W:*** Carl Foreman; ***C:*** Robert De Grasse; ***M:*** Dimitri Tiomkin.

Home Remedy 🦴🦴 **1988** An introverted New Jersey bachelor's isolated lifestyle is invaded by a flirtatious housewife and her jealous husband. **92m/C VHS.** Seth Barrish, Maxine Albert; ***D:*** Maggie Greenwald.

Home Sweet Home 🦴🦴½ **1914** Suggested by the life of John Howard Payne (actor, poet, dramatist, critic, and world-wanderer) who wrote the title song amid the bitterness of his sad life. Silent with musical score. **62m/B VHS.** Lillian Gish, Dorothy Gish, Henry B. Walthall, Mae Marsh, Blanche Sweet, Donald Crisp, Robert "Bobbie" Harron; ***D:*** D.W. Griffith.

Home Sweet Home 🦴½ *Slasher in the House* **1980** A murdering psychopath escapes from the local asylum, and rampages through a family's Thanksgiving dinner. **84m/C VHS.** Jake Steinfeld, Sallee Elyse, Peter de Paula; ***D:*** Nettie Pena.

Home Sweet Home 🦴🦴 **1982** Postman Stan fancies himself a ladies man, but his wife has left him. So Stan decides to assuage his loneliness by seducing his co-workers' wives. Black comedy look at British social classism. **90m/C VHS.** *GB* Eric Richard, Timothy Spall, Tim Barker, Su Elliot, Frances Barber, Kay Stonham; ***D:*** Mike Leigh; ***W:*** Mike Leigh. **TV**

Home Team 🦴🦴½ **1998 (PG)** Gambling addict and ex-con Henry Butler (Guttenberg) is required to perform community service as part of his parole. Since he's a former soccer coach, he finds a job at a boys' home where administor Karen (Lorain) figures a soccer team will teach the kids teamwork and sportsmanship. Familiar plot but that's not necessarily bad. **94m/C VHS, DVD.** Steve Guttenberg, Sophie Lorain, Ryan Slater, Johnny Morina; ***D:*** Allan Goldstein. **CABLE**

Home to Stay 🦴🦴 **1979** A farmer who has suffered a stroke is fighting off repeated lapses into senility. His son and daughter have conflicting interests as to whether he should be committed to a nursing home. **74m/C VHS.** Henry Fonda, Frances Hyland, Michael McGuire; ***D:*** Delbert Mann; ***M:*** Hagood Hardy. **TV**

Home Town Story 🦴🦴 **1951** A politician is convinced big business is behind his election loss. Fair drama. Watch for Monroe in a bit part. **61m/B VHS.** Jeffrey Lynn, Donald Crisp, Marjorie Reynolds, Alan Hale Jr., Marilyn Monroe, Barbara Brown, Melinda Plowman; ***D:*** Arthur Pierson.

Homebodies 🦴🦴 **1974 (PG)** Six senior citizens, disgusted when they learn that they will be callously tossed out of their home, become violent murderers in their shocking attempt to solve their problem. An odd little film made in Cincinnati. **96m/C VHS.** Ruth McDevitt, Linda Marsh, William Hansen, Peter Brocco, Frances Fuller; ***D:*** Larry Yust.

Homeboy 🦴🦴 **1988 (R)** A small-time club boxer who dreams of becoming middleweight champ is offered his big break, but the opportunity is jeopardized by his dishonest manager's dealings. Never released theatrically. **118m/C VHS.** Mickey Rourke, Christopher Walken, Debra Feuer, Kevin Conway, Antony Alda, Ruben Blades; ***D:*** Michael Seresin; ***M:*** Eric Clapton, Michael Kamen.

Homeboy 🦴½ **198?** A Black boxer owes his career to the mob. When he tries to break free his wife is murdered—and he seeks revenge. **93m/C VHS.** Dabney Coleman, Philip Michael Thomas.

Homeboys 🦴 **1992** Two East L.A. brothers find themselves on opposite sides of the law in this quickie designed to cash in on gang violence and ghetto dramas. **91m/C VHS.** Todd Bridges, David Garrison, Ron Odriozola, Ken Michaels; ***D:*** Lindsay Norgard.

Homecoming 🦴🦴🦴 **1928** Two German prisoners of war escape from a Siberian lead mine. One reaches home first and has an affair with his comrade's wife. Silent. **74m/B VHS.** *GE* Dita Parlo, Lars Hanson, Gustav Froehlich; ***D:*** Joe May.

Homecoming 🦴🦴 **1948** Average soap opera starring Gable and Turner set amidst the trenches of WW II. Gable plays a selfish doctor who leaves behind his wife and colleague to enlist in the Medical Corps as a major. Turner is the battlefield nurse who forever changes his life. Film is hindered by a story which is far below the talents of the excellent cast. Although voted by the New York Critics as one of the ten worst movies of 1948, the public loved it. Based on the story "The Homecoming of Ulysses" by Sidney Kingsley. **113m/B VHS.** Clark Gable, Lana Turner, Anne Baxter, John Hodiak, Ray Collins, Gladys Cooper, Cameron Mitchell, Art Baker, Lurene Tuttle; ***D:*** Mervyn LeRoy; ***W:*** Paul Osborn, Jan Lustig.

Homecoming 🦴🦴½ **1996 (PG)** Mentally ill mother abandons her four children at a Connecticut shopping mall in the care of 13-year-old eldest daughter Dicey (Peterson). The children slowly make their way to a relative's (Bedelia) home in Bridgeport, but when she proves equally uncaring Dicey decides to continue the family trek to their maternal grandmother Ab's (Bancroft) house in Chrisfield, Maryland. No surprise when crazy grandma doesn't want them either but this time Dicey is determined to make them all a home. Based on the Newbery Medal-winning children's novel by Cynthia Voight. **105m/C VHS, DVD.** Anne Bancroft, Kimberlee Peterson, Bonnie Bedelia, Trever O'Brien, Hanna Hall, William Greenblatt. **CABLE**

Homecoming: A Christmas Story 🦴🦴½ **1971** Heart-tugger that inspired the television series "The Waltons." A depression-era Virginia mountain family struggles to celebrate Christmas although the whereabouts and safety of their father are unknown. Adapted from the autobiographical novel by Earl Hamner Jr. **98m/C VHS.** Richard Thomas, Patricia Neal, Edgar Bergen, Cleavon Little, Ellen Corby; ***D:*** Fielder Cook. **TV**

Homegrown 🦴🦴½ **1997 (R)** Engaging comedy-noir has three dense Norther California pot growers (Thornton, Azaria, Phillippe) witness their Boss's (Lithgow) murder. Seeing this as a bad omen, they take off, with the crop, to the operation's packaging department (Lynch) and decide to carry on as if the boss is still alive. Amid many cameos (Danson, Curtis) they set up a big deal with a seemingly laid-back wholesaler (Bon Jovi). **101m/C VHS, DVD, Wide.** Billy Bob Thornton, Hank Azaria, Ryan Phillippe, Kelly Lynch, Jon Bon Jovi, John Lithgow, Jon Tenney, Matt Clark; ***Cameos:*** Ted Danson, Jamie Lee Curtis, Judge Reinhold; ***D:*** Stephen Gyllenhaal; ***W:*** Stephen Gyllenhaal, Nicholas Kazan; ***C:*** Greg Gardiner; ***M:*** Trevor Rabin.

Homer and Eddie 🦴 **1989 (R)** A witless road comedy with Goldberg as a dying sociopath and a mentally retarded Belushi. They take off cross-country to make a little trouble, learn a little about life, and create a less than entertaining movie. **100m/C VHS.** Whoopi Goldberg, James Belushi, Karen Black; ***D:*** Andrei Konchalovsky; ***W:*** Patrick Cirillo; ***C:*** Lajos Koltai; ***M:*** Eduard Artemyev.

Homesteaders of Paradise Valley 🦴½ **1947** The Hume brothers oppose Red Ryder and a group of settlers building a dam in Paradise Valley. **54m/B VHS.** Allan "Rocky" Lane, Robert (Bobby) Blake.

Hometown Boy Makes Good 🦴🦴½ **1993 (R)** Smalltown boy Boyd Geary moved to the big city to go to medical school. But what he never told his proud mom was that he dropped out and doesn't have the successful psychiatry practice she thinks he has, instead he's a barely surviving waiter. But when Boyd travels back home to confess to mom, the local mayor makes him an offer to set up his own practice and won't take no for an answer. **88m/C VHS.** Anthony Edwards, Grace Zabriskie, Cynthia Bain; ***D:*** David Burton Morris; ***W:*** Allen Rucker; ***M:*** Barry Goldberg.

Hometown U.S.A. woof! **1979 (R)** Set in L.A. in the late '50s, this teenage cruising movie is the brainchild of director Baer, better known as Jethro from that madcap TV series "The Beverly Hillbillies." **97m/C VHS, DVD.** Brian Kerwin, Gary Springer, David Wilson, Cindy Fisher, Sally Kirkland; ***D:*** Max Baer Jr.

Homeward Bound 🦴 **1980 (G)** A dying teenager tries to reunite his long-estranged father and grandfather. **96m/C VHS.** David Soul, Moosie Drier, Barnard Hughes; ***D:*** Richard Michaels. **TV**

Homeward Bound 2: Lost in San Francisco 🦴🦴½ **1996 (G)** House pets Chance, the feisty bulldog (Fox), Sassy the sophisticated feline (Field), and Shadow the sage golden retriever (Waite) find themselves on the loose again, this time in the tough streets of San Francisco. The animals escape from the airport as the family departs for a Canadian holiday, and on their way back home, encounter some tough mutts—a gang of streetwise dogs, (most notably comedian Sinbad as Riley) and, of course, some dog nappers. Chance even finds romance along the way with Delilah (Gugino). Not too scary for the little ones, flick carries the same charm of the first adventure. **88m/C VHS.** Robert Hays, Kim Greist, Veronica Lauren, Kevin Timothy Chevalia, Michael Rispoli, Max Perlich; ***D:*** David R. Ellis; ***W:*** Julie Hickson, Chris Hauty; ***C:*** Jack Conroy; ***V:*** Michael J. Fox, Sally Field, Ralph Waite, Al Michaels, Tommy Lasorda, Bob Uecker, Jon Polito, Adam Goldberg, Sinbad, Carla Gugino.

Homeward Bound: The Incredible Journey 🦴🦴🦴 **1993 (G)** Successful remake of the 1963 Disney release "The Incredible Journey." Two dogs and a cat once again try to find their way home after their family relocates, armed with greater depth of character than the original. Hard not to shed a tear for the brave animal trio who develop a trusting bond through assorted misadventures. Based on the novel by Sheila Burnford. Superior family fare. **85m/C VHS, DVD, Wide.** Robert Hays, Kim Greist, Jean Smart, Benj Thall, Veronica Lauren, Kevin Timothy Chevalia; ***D:*** Duwayne Dunham; ***W:*** Linda Woolverton, Caroline Thompson; ***C:*** Reed Smoot; ***M:*** Bruce Broughton; ***V:*** Don Ameche, Michael J. Fox, Sally Field.

Homework 🦴 **1982 (R)** Young man's after-school lessons with a teacher are definitely not part of the curriculum. Yawning sexploitation. **90m/C VHS.** Joan Collins, Michael Morgan, Betty Thomas, Shell Kepler, Wings Hauser, Lee Purcell; ***D:*** James Beshears.

Homewrecker 🦴🦴 **1992 (PG-13)** Benson stars as a scientist who invents a computer, with a female voice, as the ultimate domestic worker. Only the computer turns possessive and against Benson's estranged wife. **88m/C VHS.** Robby Benson, Sydney Walsh, Sarah Rose Karr; ***D:*** Fred Walton; ***W:*** Eric Harlacher; ***V:*** Kate Jackson.

Homicidal 🦴🦴🦴 **1961** Castle's "Psycho" imitation makes a belated debut on home video. He takes all the key elements of Hitchcock's original and reshuffles them: the big old house with the steep staircase, the creepy invalid older woman, a troubled young man, the blonde who's up to something, the cheap hotel, the vaguely threatening cops, the unexpectedly graphic knife violence, the young couple who investigates. And a central gimmick which is cheesily transparent; most viewers will tumble to it early on and that's part of the fun, too. With enthusiastic overacting from all the leads, the whole thing becomes a minor camp masterpiece. **87m/B DVD.** Glenn Corbett, Patricia Breslin, Alan Bunce, James Westerfield; ***D:*** William Castle; ***W:*** Robb White; ***C:*** Burnett Guffey; ***M:*** Hugo Friedhofer.

Homicidal Impulse 🦴½ **1992 (R)** When Assistant D.A. Tim Casey has an affair with his boss' ambitious niece he doesn't realize the danger he's in. His lover decides to kill her uncle so boyfriend Tim will get his job. Some women will do anything for love. Also available in an unrated version. **84m/C VHS.** Scott Valentine, Vanessa Angel.

Homicide 🦴🦴🦴½ **1991 (R)** Terrific police thriller with as much thought as action; a driven detective faces his submerged Jewish identity while probing an anti-Semitic murder and a secret society. Playwright/filmmaker Mamet creates nail-biting suspense and shattering epiphanies without resorting to Hollywood glitz. Rich (often profane) dialogue includes a classic soliloquy mystically comparing a lawman's badge with a Star of David. **100m/C VHS, 8mm.** Joe Mantegna, William H. Macy, Natalija Nogulich, Ving Rhames, Rebecca Pidgeon; ***D:*** David Mamet; ***W:*** David Mamet; ***C:*** Roger Deakins.

Homicide: The Movie 🦴🦴 **2000 (PG-13)** Rather a disappointment for fans of the intelligent NBC cop series but at least the TV movie tied up some loose ends. Giardello (Kotto) is gunned down at a rally where he's campaigning for mayor of Baltimore. While G hovers between life and death, the tragedy brings Pembleton (Braugher) back to town and gets Giardello's old squad—some of whom have retired or been re-assigned—back to work on his case. A somewhat surreal ending has cameos by cast members from previous seasons. **89m/C VHS, DVD.** Yaphet Kotto, Andre Braugher, Kyle Secor, Richard Belzer, Giancarlo Esposito, Peter Gerety, Clark Johnson, Zeljko Ivanek, Michael Michele, Reed Edward Diamond, Michelle Forbes, Isabella Hofmann, Melissa Leo, Callie (Calliope) Thorne, Jon Seda, Max Perlich, Jason Priestley, Daniel Baldwin, Ned Beatty, Jon Polito, Toni Lewis; ***D:*** Jean De Segonzac; ***W:*** Eric Overmyer, Tom Fontana, James Yoshimura; ***C:*** Jean De Segonzac; ***M:*** Douglas J. Cuomo. **TV**

Hondo 🦴🦴🦴 **1953** In 1874, whites have broken their treaty with the Apache nation who are now preparing for war. Calvary dispatch rider Hondo Lane (Wayne) encounters Angie (Page) and her young son at an isolated ranch and warns her of the danger but she refuses to leave. After various Indian attacks, Hondo persuades Angie (they've fallen in love) to leave for California with him. Based on the story "The Gift of Cochise" by Louis L'Amour. **84m/C VHS, DVD.** John Wayne, Geraldine Page, Ward Bond, Michael Pate, James Arness, Rodolfo Acosta, Leo Gordon, Lee Aaker, Paul Fix; ***D:*** John Farrow; ***W:*** James Edward Grant; ***C:*** Robert Burks, Archie Stout.

Honey 🦴½ **1981** Attractive writer pays an unusual visit to the home of a distinguished publisher. Brandishing a pistol, she demands that he read aloud from her manuscript. As he reads, a unique fantasy unfolds, a dreamlike erotic tale that may be the writer's own sexual awakening. Or maybe not. **89m/C VHS.** *IT SP* Clio Goldsmith, Fernando Rey, Catherine Spaak; ***D:*** Gianfranco Angelucci.

Honey & Ashes 🦴🦴 *Miel et Cendres* **1996** Three women in Islamic Tunisia try to overcome their patriarchal society and control their own lives with bitter consequences. Leila flees to the city when her father disapproves of the boy she loves; Naima may be a successful doctor but she still can't avoid a pre-arranged marriage; and Amina suffers constant abuse from her husband. French and Arabic with subtitles. **80m/C VHS, DVD.** *SI* Nozha Khouadra, Amel Hedhili, Samia Mzali, Lara Chaouachi, Naji Najeh, Slim Larnaout, Jamel Sassi; ***D:*** Nadia Fares; ***W:*** Nadia Fares, Yves Kropf; ***C:*** Ismael Ramirez; ***M:*** Slim Larnaout, Jean-Francois Bovard, Mami Azairez.

Honey, I Blew Up the Kid 🦴🦴½ **1992 (PG)** Screwball suburban inventor Moranis reverses his shrinking process and this time manages to enlarge his two-year-old into a 112-foot giant who gets bigger every time he comes in contact with electricity. Yikes! Loaded with great special effects, this is a charming and funny film that's fit for the whole family. Sequel to "Honey I Shrunk the Kids." **89m/C VHS, Wide.** Rick Moranis, Marcia Strassman, Robert Oliveri, Daniel Shalikar, Joshua Shalikar, Lloyd Bridges, John Shea, Keri Russell, Gregory Sierra, Julia Sweeney, Kenneth Tobey, Peter Elbling; ***D:*** Randal Kleiser; ***W:*** Thom Eberhardt, Garry Goodrow; ***M:*** Bruce Broughton.

Honey, I Shrunk the Kids 🦴🦴½ **1989 (G)** The popular Disney fantasy about a suburban inventor. His shrinking device accidentally reduces his kids to 1/4 inch tall, and he subsequently throws them out with the garbage. Now they must journey back to the house through the jungle that was once the back lawn. Accompanied by "Tummy Trouble," the first of a projected series of Roger Rabbit Maroon Cartoons. Followed by "Honey, I Blew Up the Kids." **101m/C VHS.** Rick Moranis, Matt Frewer, Marcia Strassman, Kristine Sutherland, Thomas Wilson Brown, Jared Rushton, Amy O'Neill, Robert Oliveri; ***D:*** Joe Johnston, Rob Minkoff; ***W:*** Ed Naha, Tom Schulman, Stuart Gordon; ***C:*** Hiro Narita; ***M:*** James Horner; ***V:*** Charles Fleischer, Kathleen Turner, Lou Hirsch, April Winchell.

The Honey Pot 🦴🦴½ *It Comes Up Murder; Anyone for Venice?; Mr. Fox of Venice* **1967** A millionaire feigns death to see the reaction of three of his former lovers. Amusing black comedy with fine performances from all. Based on Moliere's "Volpone." **131m/C VHS.** Rex Harrison, Susan Hayward, Cliff Robertson, Capucine, Edie Adams, Maggie Smith, Adolfo Celi; ***D:*** Joseph L. Mankiewicz; ***W:*** Joseph L. Mankiewicz; ***M:*** John Addison.

Honey, We Shrunk Ourselves 🦴🦴½ **1997 (PG)** Scientist Wayne Szalinsky (Moranis) manages to shrink himself, his wife, his brother, and his sister-in-law. The kids just think their parents are out of town for the weekend (so they go nuts). The third in the "Honey" series, this one was released directly to video. Though adults may find it dull, it was made with the kids in mind. **76m/C VHS.** Rick Moranis, Stuart Pankin, Robin Bartlett, Eve Gordon, Bug Hall; ***D:*** Dean Cundey; ***W:*** Karey Kirkpatrick, Nell Scovell, Joel Hodgson; ***C:*** Raymond N. Stella. **VIDEO**

Honeybaby 🦴🦴 **1974 (PG)** A smooth international soldier of fortune and a bright, sexy American interpreter are entangled in Middle-Eastern turbulence when they must rescue a politician kidnapped by terrorists. **94m/C VHS.** Calvin Lockhart, Diana Sands; ***D:*** Michael A. Schultz.

Honeyboy 🦴½ **1982** Estrada tries to win fame, fortune, and a ticket out of the barrio as an up-and-coming boxer. Outstanding fight scenes, but little else in this drama of the boxing scene. **100m/C VHS.** Erik Estrada, Morgan Fairchild, James McEachin, Robert Costanzo, Yvonne Wilder; ***D:*** John Berry. **TV**

Honeymoon 🦴🦴 **1987** A young French woman visiting New York learns she will be deported when her boyfriend is arrested for drug-smuggling. To stay, she is set up in a marriage of convenience and told her new husband will never see or bother her. But hubby has other plans! **96m/C VHS.** John Shea, Nathalie Baye, Richard Berry, Peter Donat; ***D:*** Patrick Jamain; ***W:*** Phillip Setbon.

Honeymoon Academy 🦴🦴 *For Better or For Worse* **1990 (PG-13)** Newly married man has lots to learn in this comic outing. His new wife never told him about her unusual line of business—as an undercover agent! **94m/C VHS.** Robert Hays, Kim Cattrall, Leigh Taylor-Young; ***D:*** Gene Quintano; ***W:*** Gene Quintano; ***M:*** Robert Folk.

Honeymoon Horror 🦴 **197?** Stranded on an island, three honeymooning couples soon realize their romantic retreat is a nightmare. A crazy man with an axe is tracking them down. Minimally effective. **90m/C VHS.** Cheryl Black, William F. Pecchi, Bob Wagner.

Honeymoon in Vegas 🦴🦴½ **1992 (PG-13)** Romantic comedy turns frantic after Cage loses his fiancee to Caan in a high stakes Vegas poker game. Cage displays lots of talent for manic comedy as the distraught young groom-to-be who encounters numerous obstacles on his way to the altar. Lightweight and funny, featuring a bevy of Elvis impersonators in every size, shape, and color and new versions of favorite Elvis tunes. Look for former Las Vegas U basketball coach Jerry Tarkanian as one of Caan's gambling buddies. **95m/C VHS, DVD.** James Caan, Nicolas Cage, Sarah Jessica Parker, Noriyuki "Pat" Morita, John Capodice, Robert Costanzo, Anne Bancroft, Peter Boyle, Seymour Cassel, Tony Shalhoub, Ben Stein, Angela Pietropinto; ***D:*** Andrew Bergman; ***W:*** Andrew Bergman; ***C:*** William A. Fraker; ***M:*** David Newman.

Honeymoon Killers 🦴🦴🦴 *The Lonely Hearts Killers* **1970 (R)** A grim, creepy filmization of a true multiple-murder case wherein an overweight woman and slimy gigolo living on Long Island seduce and murder one lonely woman after another. Independently made and frankly despairing. **103m/C VHS.** Tony LoBianco, Shirley Stoler, Mary Jane Higby, Dortha Duckworth, Doris Roberts, Marilyn Chris, Kip McArdle, Mary Breen, Barbara Cason, Ann Harris, Guy Sorel; ***D:*** Leonard Kastle; ***W:*** Leonard Kastle; ***C:*** Oliver Wood; ***M:*** Gustav Mahler.

The Honeymoon Machine 🦴🦴½ **1961** A lightweight comedy about two American sailors and a computer scam. McQueen and Mullaney hook up with computer expert Hutton to use their ship's computer to beat the gambling odds at an Italian casino. Their commander misinterprets the signals and thinks the ship is being attacked. Fast paced and the computer angle was new territory in '61. **87m/C VHS.** Steve McQueen, Jack Mullaney, Jim Hutton, Dean Jagger, Paula Prentiss, Brigid Bazlen, Jack Weston; ***D:*** Richard Thorpe.

Honeysuckle Rose 🦴🦴½ *On the Road Again* **1980 (PG)** A road-touring country-Western singer whose life is a series of one night stands, falls in love with an adoring young guitar player who has just joined his band. This nearly costs him his marriage when his wife, who while waiting patiently for him at home, decides she's had enough. Easygoing performance by Nelson, essentially playing himself. **120m/C VHS.** Willie Nelson, Dyan Cannon, Amy Irving, Slim Pickens, Joey Floyd, Charles Levin, Priscilla Pointer; ***D:*** Jerry Schatzberg; ***W:*** William D. Wittliff, John Binder, Carol Sobieski; ***M:*** Willie Nelson, Richard Baskin. Golden Raspberries '80: Worst Support. Actress (Irving).

Hong Kong Nights 🦴🦴½ **1935** Two agents attempt to break up a Chinese smuggling ring run by an unscrupulous madman. Good, action-packed low-budget film. **59m/B VHS.** Tom (George Duryea) Keene, Wera Engels, Warren Hymer, Tetsu Komai, Cornelius Keefe; ***D:*** E. Mason Hopper.

Hong Kong 1941 🦴🦴½ **1984** Yip Kim Fay (Yun-Fat) arrives in Hong Kong on the eve of war in 1941 and befriends peasant Wong Hak Keung (Man). Fay and Keung plan to leave Hong Kong with Keung's girlfriend, Ah Nam (Yip), but fall victim to the Japanese invasion. An early role for Yun-Fat, who's the romantic hero here rather than the action star he later became. Chinese with subtitles. **118m/C VHS, DVD, Wide.** *HK* Cecilia Yip, Alex Man, Chow Yun-Fat; ***D:*** Po-Chi Leung; ***W:*** Koon-Chung Chan.

Hong Kong '97 🦴🦴 **1994 (R)** On the eve of China's takeover of Hong Kong from Great Britain, special agent Reg Cameron (Patrick) murders a Chinese general. With a $10 million bounty on his head, Cameron tries to escape with his partners and girlfriend in tow. Lots of action, good use of Hong Kong setting. **91m/C VHS.** Robert Patrick, Ming Na, Brion James, Tim Thomerson; ***D:*** Albert Pyun.

Honky 🦴½ **1971 (R)** An innocent friendship between a black woman and a white man develops into a passionate romance that has the whole town talking. **92m/C VHS.** Brenda Sykes, John Neilson, Maria Donzinger; ***D:*** William A. Graham; ***M:*** Quincy Jones.

Honky Tonk 🦴🦴🦴 **1941** A western soap opera in which ne'er do well Clark marries Lana and tries to live a respectable life. In this, the first of several MGM teamings between Gable and Turner, the chemistry between the two is evident. So much so in fact that Gable's then wife Carole Lombard let studio head Louis B. Mayer know that she was not at all thrilled. The public was pleased however, and made the film a hit. **106m/B VHS.** Clark Gable, Lana Turner, Frank Morgan, Claire Trevor, Marjorie Main, Albert Dekker, Chill Wills, Henry O'Neill, John Maxwell, Morgan Wallace, Betty Blythe, Francis X. Bushman, Veda Ann Borg; ***D:*** Jack Conway.

Honky Tonk Freeway 🦴 **1981 (PG)** An odd assortment of people become involved in a small town Mayor's scheme to turn a dying hamlet into a tourist wonderland. You can find better things to do with your evening than watch this accident. **107m/C VHS, DVD.** Teri Garr, Howard Hesseman, Beau Bridges, Hume Cronyn, William Devane, Beverly D'Angelo, Geraldine Page; ***D:*** John Schlesinger; ***W:*** Edward Clinton; ***C:*** John Bailey; ***M:*** Elmer Bernstein, Steve Dorff.

Honkytonk Man 🦴🦴 **1982 (PG)** Unsuccessful change-of-pace Eastwood vehicle set during the Depression. Aging alcoholic country singer tries one last time to make it to Nashville, hoping to perform at the Grand Ole Opry. This time he takes his nephew (played by Eastwoood's real-life son) with him. **123m/C VHS.** Clint Eastwood, Kyle Eastwood, John McIntire, Alexa Kenin, Verna Bloom; ***D:*** Clint Eastwood; ***W:*** Clancy Carlile; ***C:*** Bruce Surtees; ***M:*** Steve Dorff.

Honkytonk Nights 🦴 **197? (R)** A honky-tonkin' romp through an evening in a country/western bar, featuring legendary topless dancer Carol Doda, Georgina ("Devil in Mrs. Jones") Spelvin, and the music of The Hot Licks (minus front man Dan Hicks). **90m/C VHS.** Carol Doda, Georgina Spelvin, Ramblin' Jack Elliot.

Honolulu 🦴🦴½ **1939** A screwball comedy with Powell providing the musical numbers. Young takes on the dual role of a Hollywood star who meets his exact double, a Hawaii plantation owner. They decide to switch identities to give their lives a little oomph. The star sails to Hawaii, falling for fellow passenger Powell, only to discover he's expected to get married upon his arrival in Honolulu. Anderson and Burns and Allen provide the comic relief. ♫The Leader Doesn't Like Music; This Night Was Made For Dreaming; Honolulu; Hymn To The Sun. **83m/B VHS.** Robert Young, Eleanor Powell, George Burns, Gracie Allen, Rita Johnson, Eddie Anderson, Clarence (C. William) Kolb; ***D:*** Edward Buzzell; ***W:*** Frank Partos, Herbert Fields; ***M:*** Franz Waxman.

Honor Among Thieves 🦴½ *Farewell, Friend* **1968 (R)** Two former mercenaries reteam for a robbery that doesn't come off as planned. Not as fast paced as others in Bronson canon. **115m/C VHS, DVD.** *FR IT* Charles Bronson, Alain Delon, Brigitte Fossey, Olga Georges-Picot, Bernard Fresson; ***D:*** Jean Herman; ***W:*** Sebastien Japrisot; ***C:*** Jean-Jacques Tarbes; ***M:*** Francois de Roubaix.

Honor and Glory 🦴🦴 **1992 (R)** Tracy Pride, an FBI agent and martial arts expert, teams up with an Interpol agent, who doubles as a TV anchorwoman, to stop an international banker from getting his greedy hands on the key to a nuclear arsenal. These fighting gals are up against a team of assassins but they can more than handle themselves. **90m/C VHS.** Cynthia Rothrock, Donna Jason, Chuck Jeffreys, Gerald Klein, Robin Shou, Richard Yuen; ***D:*** Godfrey Hall; ***W:*** Herb Borkland.

Honor of the Range 🦴🦴 **1934** The good sheriff's lady is whisked away by his evil twin brother and the sheriff must go undercover to get her back. Odd plot twists for a seemingly normal western. **60m/B VHS.** Ken Maynard, Cecilia Parker, Fred Kohler Sr.; ***D:*** Ken Maynard.

Honor Thy Father 🦴🦴 **1973** The everyday life of a real-life Mafia family as seen through the eyes of Bill Bonanno, the son of mob chieftain Joe Bonanno. Adapted from the book by Gay Talese. **97m/C DVD.** Raf Vallone, Richard S. Castellano, Brenda Vaccaro, Joseph Bologna; ***D:*** Paul Wendkos; ***M:*** George Duning. **TV**

Honor Thy Father and Mother: The True Story of the Menendez Brothers 🦴🦴½ **1994** First Amy Fisher won the true-sleaze-on-TV award and now its the turn of Lyle and Erik Menendez. Accused of the gruesome 1989 shotgun murders of their wealthy parents, the trial provided numerous sordid details, including alleged sexual abuse of the brothers by both parents. (Both Menendez trials ended in hung juries and will be retried). Composite characters and compressed time sequences play fast and loose with the facts of the case. Based on public records and on the book "Blood Brothers," by reporters John Johnson and Ronald L. Soble. **90m/C VHS.** Billy Warlock, David Beron, Jill Clayburgh, James Farentino, Susan Blakely, Erin Gray, Elaine Joyce, John Beck, John David Conti, Stanley Kamel; ***D:*** Paul Schneider; ***W:*** Michael J. Murray. **TV**

Hooch 🦴½ **1976 (PG)** Comedy about three members of the New York Mafia who get some unexpected southern hospitality when they try to muscle in on a southern family's moonshine operation. **96m/C VHS.** Gil Gerard, Erika Fox, Melody Rogers, Danny Aiello, Mike Allen, Raymond Serra; ***D:*** Edward Andrew (Santos Alcocer) Mann.

The Hooded Terror **1938** A merciless group of murderers take on a G-man. **70m/B VHS.** Tod Slaughter, Greta Gynt.

The Hoodlum 🦴🦴 **1951** A criminal does his best to rehabilitate and, with a little help from his brother, is able to hold a steady job. However the crime bug dies hard and when he spots an armored car, he just can't resist the temptation. Tierney's real brother, Edward, plays his screen brother. **61m/B VHS, DVD, Wide.** Lawrence Tierney, Allene Roberts, Marjorie (Reardon) Riordan, Lisa Golm, Edward Tierney; ***D:*** Max Nosseck.

Hoodlum 🦴🦴½ *Gangster; Hoods* **1996 (R)** Highly fictionalized tale of '30s gangster "Bumpy" Johnson (Fishburne, reprising his role from "The Cotton Club"), who refuses to allow Dutch Schultz (Roth) and Lucky Luciano (Garcia) to muscle into the Harlem numbers rackets. Duke makes the proceedings nice to look at, and does well by the eclectic cast, but the uneven screenplay occasionally lets everybody down, especially during the cheesy time-passage montage (complete with Tommy Gun fire and flipping calendar pages). Roth is ruthless as ever and Garcia is smooth as ever. But it's definitely Fishburne's show, as he explores Johnson's professional triumphs and the personal toll they take. Fishburne previously worked with director Duke on "Deep Cover." Singer Michael McCary from Boyz II Men makes his film debut as an explosives expert. **130m/C VHS, DVD, Wide.** Laurence "Larry" Fishburne, Tim Roth, Andy Garcia, Vanessa L(ynne) Williams, Cicely Tyson, Clarence Williams III, William Atherton, Chi McBride, Richard Bradford, Loretta Devine, Queen Latifah, Paul Benjamin, Mike Starr, Beau Starr, Joe Guzaldo, Ed O'Ross; ***D:*** Bill Duke; ***W:*** Chris Brancato; ***C:*** Frank Tidy; ***M:*** Elmer Bernstein.

Hoodlum Empire 🦴🦴 **1952** A senator enlists the aid of a former gangster, now a war hero, in his battle against the syndicate. Loosely based on the Kefauver investigations of 1950-51. **98m/B VHS.** Brian Donlevy, Claire Trevor, Forrest Tucker, Vera (Hruba) Ralston, Luther Adler, John Russell, Gene Lockhart, Grant Withers, Taylor Holmes, Roy Barcroft, Richard Jaeckel; ***D:*** Joseph Kane.

The Hoodlum Priest 🦴🦴🦴 **1961** Biography of the Rev. Charles Dismas Clark (Murray), a Jesuit priest who dedicated his life to working with juvenile delinquents and ex-cons in St. Louis. Dullea made his screen debut as Billy Lee Jackson, a thief who finds the straight and narrow is a hard road with more detours than he can handle. Fine performances with Murray co-scripting under the pseudonym Don Deer. **101m/B VHS.** Don Murray, Keir Dullea, Larry Gates, Logan Ramsey, Cindi Wood; ***D:*** Irvin Kershner; ***W:*** Don Murray, Joseph Landon; ***C:*** Haskell Wexler.

Hoodoo Ann 🦴🦴 **1916** The story of Hoodoo Ann, from her days in the orphanage to her happy marriage. Silent. **27m/B VHS.** Mae Marsh, Robert "Bobbie" Harron.

Hoods 🦴🦴½ **1998 (R)** Mob comedy features a bunch of pros that make it worth watching. Smalltime mobster Martinelli (Mantegna) suffers a midlife crisis on his 50th birthday when he learns that his floozy girlfriend (Tilly) is cheating on him and his aging father wants him to whack someone named Carmine—who turns out to be a nine-year-old boy. **92m/C VHS, DVD.** Joe Mantegna, Kevin Pollak, Joe Pantoliano, Jennifer Tilly; ***D:*** Mark Malone; ***W:*** Mark Malone; ***C:*** Tobias Schliessler; ***M:*** Anthony Marinelli.

Hook 🦴🦴 **1991 (PG)** Although he said he was never gonna to do it, Peter Pan has grown up. Uptight Peter Banning places work before family and has forgotten all about Neverland and the evil Captain Hook, until Hook kidnaps the Banning kids and takes them to Neverland. With the help of Tinkerbell, her magic pixie dust, and happy thoughts, Peter rescues his kids and rediscovers his youth while visiting with the Lost Boys. The sets and special effects are spectacular; the direction less so. Big-budget fantasy lacks the charm it needs to really fly. Still, kids seem to love it. You'll have to look hard to spot pirates Crosby and Close. Futurizes the J.M. Barrie classic. **142m/C VHS, DVD, 8mm, Wide.** Dustin Hoffman, Robin Williams, Julia Roberts, Bob Hoskins, Maggie Smith, Charlie Korsmo, Caroline Goodall, Amber Scott, Phil Collins, Arthur Malet, Dante Basco, Gwyneth Paltrow, Glenn Close, David Crosby; ***D:*** Steven Spielberg; ***W:*** Nick Castle; ***C:*** Dean Cundey; ***M:*** John Williams.

Hook, Line and Sinker 🦴🦴 **1930** A couple of insurance investigators try to help a young woman restore a hotel, and they find romance and run-ins with crooks. Directed by Cline, who later directed W.C. Fields in "The Bank Dick," "My Little Chickadee," and "Never Give a Sucker an Even Break." **75m/B VHS.** Bert Wheeler, Robert Woolsey, Dorothy Lee, Jobyna Howland, Ralf Harolde, Natalie Moorhead, George F. Marion Sr., Hugh Herbert; ***D:*** Edward F. (Eddie) Cline; ***W:*** Rod Amateau.

The Hooked Generation 🦴 **1969 (R)** A group of drug pushers kidnap defenseless victims, rape innocent girls, and even murder their own Cuban drug contacts (and all without the aid of a cohesive plot). Many gory events precede their untimely deaths; few will be entertained. **92m/C VHS.** Jeremy Slate, Steve Alaimo.

Hoop Dreams 🦴🦴🦴🦴 **1994 (PG-13)** Exceptional documentary follows two inner-city basketball phenoms' lives through high school as they chase their dreams of playing in the NBA. We meet Arthur Agee and William Gates as they prepare to enter St. Joseph, a predominantly white Catholic school that has offered them partial athletic scholarships. The coach tabs Gates as the "next Isiah Thomas," alluding to the school's most famous alum. There's plenty of game footage, but the more telling and fascinating parts of the film deal with the kids' families and home life. Both players encounter dramatic reversals of fortune on and off the court, demonstrating the incredibly long odds they face. **169m/C VHS.** Arthur Agee, William Gates; ***D:*** Steve James; ***C:*** Peter Gilbert. Directors Guild '95: Feature Doc. (James); L.A. Film Critics '94: Feature Doc.; MTV Movie Awards '95: New Filmmaker (James); Natl. Bd. of Review '94: Feature Doc.; N.Y. Film Critics '94: Feature Doc.; Natl. Soc. Film Critics '94: Feature Doc.; Sundance '94: Aud. Award.

Hooper 🦴🦴½ **1978 (PG)** Lightweight behind-the-scenes satire about the world of movie stuntmen. Reynolds is a top stuntman who becomes involved in a rivalry with an up-and-coming young man out to surpass him. Dated good-ole-boy shenanigans. **94m/C VHS, DVD.** Burt Reynolds, Jan-Michael Vincent, Robert Klein, Sally Field, Brian Keith, John Marley, Adam West; ***D:*** Hal Needham; ***W:*** Bill Kerby, Tom Rickman; ***C:*** Bobby Byrne; ***M:*** Bill Justis.

Hoopla 🦴🦴 **1933** Bow's last film has her portraying the seductive older woman in a number of scanty outfits. Carnival femme Lou (Bow) seduces teen Chris (Cromwell) and makes him a man. Climax (not that kind!) takes place at the Chicago World's Fair. Adapted from the Kenyon Nicholson play "The Barker." **85m/B VHS.** Clara Bow, Richard Cromwell, Preston Foster, Herbert Mundin, James Gleason, Minna Gombell, Florence Roberts, Roger Imhof; ***D:*** Frank Lloyd; ***W:*** Joseph Moncure March, Bradley King; ***C:*** Ernest Palmer; ***M:*** Louis De Francesco.

Hoosiers 🦴🦴🦴 **1986 (PG)** In Indiana, where basketball is the sport of the gods, a small town high school basketball team gets a new, but surprisingly experienced coach. He makes the team, and each person in it, better than they thought possible. Classic plot rings true because of Hackman's complex and sensitive performance coupled with Hopper's touching portrait of an alcoholic basketball fanatic. **115m/C VHS, DVD, Wide.** Gene Hackman, Barbara Hershey, Dennis Hopper, David Neidorf, Sheb Wooley, Fern Parsons, Brad Boyle, Steve Hollar, Brad Long; ***D:*** David Anspaugh; ***W:*** Angelo Pizzo; ***C:*** Fred Murphy; ***M:*** Jerry Goldsmith. L.A. Film Critics '86: Support. Actor (Hopper), Natl. Film Reg. '01.

Hootch Country Boys 🦴 *Redneck County; The Great Lester Boggs* **1975 (PG)** A film packed with moonshine, sheriffs, busty country girls, and chases. **90m/C VHS.** Alex Karras, Scott MacKenzsie, Dean Jagger, Willie Jones, Bob Ridgely, Susan Denbo, Bob Ginnaven, David Haney; ***D:*** Harry Z. Thomason.

Hopalong Cassidy 🦴🦴🦴 *Hopalong Cassidy Enters* **1935** In this first of a long series of "Hopalong Cassidy" films, Hoppy and his pals intervene in a brewing range war. A gang of rustlers is helped by a two-timing foreman who's playing both sides off each other. After a career in silent films, Boyd was pretty much washed up before taking on the role of Cassidy. He was originally asked to play the villain and declined, but agreed to be the good guy if the character was cleaned up. "Gabby" Hayes' stock character was killed off in this episode, but was brought back for later installments. **60m/B VHS, DVD.** William Boyd, James Ellison, Paula Stone, Robert Warwick, Charles Middleton, Frank McGlynn, Kenneth Thomson, George "Gabby" Hayes, James Mason, Franklyn Farnum, Doris Schroeder; ***D:*** Howard Bretherton; ***C:*** Archie Stout.

Hopalong Cassidy: Borrowed Trouble 🦴½ **1948** Hoppy must save a righteous teacher from the clutches of kidnappers who plan to place a saloon right next to the school. **61m/B VHS.** William Boyd, Andy Clyde, Rand Brooks, Elaine Riley, John Kellogg, Helen Chapman; ***D:*** George Archainbaud.

Hopalong Cassidy: Dangerous Venture 🦴🦴 **1948** "Dangerous Venture" was one of Hoppy's last ventures, produced the final year of the series' 13-year tenure. Hoppy and the gang hunt for Aztec ruins in the great Southwest, and have to deal with renegade Indians and a band of treacherous looters along the way. **55m/B VHS.** William Boyd, Andy Clyde, Rand Brooks.

Hopalong Cassidy: False Paradise 🦴🦴 **1948** Another late Hopalong has the noir-clad cowboy rushing to the aid of a girl and her dad when control of their ranch is threatened by swindlers with false mining claims. **59m/B VHS.** William Boyd, Andy Clyde, Rand Brooks; ***D:*** George Archainbaud.

Hopalong Cassidy: Hoppy's Holiday 🦴🦴 **1947** Boyd—the only celluloid incarnation of Clarence Mulford's pulp hero—plays the Hopster yet again. This time, the non-drinking, non-smoking (what does he do for kicks?) hero and a passel of Bar-20 cowboys visit Mesa City for some well-earned R and R, but find themselves caught in a web of corruption. **60m/B VHS.** William Boyd, Andy Clyde, Rand Brooks, Jeff Corey; ***D:*** George Archainbaud.

Hopalong Cassidy: Renegade Trail 🦴🦴 **1939** Hoppy comes to the aid of both a small town sheriff and a widow. **61m/B VHS.** William Boyd, George "Gabby" Hayes, Russell Hayden, Charlotte Wynters, Russell Hopton, Sonny Bupp, Jack Rockwell, Roy Barcroft, John Merton, Robert F. (Bob) Kortman; ***D:*** Lesley Selander.

Hopalong Cassidy Returns 🦴🦴½ **1936** In the seventh entry in the "Hopalong Cassidy" series, Hoppy (Boyd) faces a lady outlaw, Lilli Marsh (Brent), who, of course, falls hard for our stalwart hero. If this is not one of the best in the series, it maintains the high production standards, and it contains the debut of series regular Morris Ankrum as a villain. **74m/B DVD.** William Boyd, George "Gabby" Hayes, Evelyn Brent, Morris Ankrum, William Janney; ***D:*** Nate Watt; ***W:*** Doris Schroeder; ***C:*** Archie Stout.

Hopalong Cassidy: Riders of the Deadline 🦴🦴 **1943** Hoppy turns into a baddie in this episode in order to infiltrate a treacherous gang and apprehend their leader. **70m/B VHS.** William Boyd, Andy Clyde, Jimmy Rogers, Robert Mitchum; ***D:*** Lesley Selander.

Hopalong Cassidy: Silent Conflict 🦴🦴 **1948** Lucky is tricked and hypnotized by a traveling medicine man who commands him to rob and kill Hoppy. **61m/B VHS.** William Boyd, Andy Clyde, Rand Brooks; ***D:*** George Archainbaud.

Hopalong Cassidy: Sinister Journey 🦴🦴 **1948** Mysterious accidents are plaguing a railroad where an old friend of Hoppy's works, so Hoppy, California, and Lucky take railroad jobs to find out what gives. **58m/B VHS.** William Boyd, Andy Clyde, Rand Brooks; ***D:*** George Archainbaud.

Hopalong Cassidy: The Dead Don't Dream 🦴🦴 **1948** Hoppy's sidekick Lucky decides to get married, but happily-ever-afterdom is threatened when the father of Mrs. Lucky-to-be is murdered. When Hoppy sets out to find the killer, he finds himself suspected of the dastardly deed. **55m/B VHS.** William Boyd, Andy Clyde, Rand Brooks, John Parrish; ***D:*** George Archainbaud.

Hopalong Cassidy: The Devil's Playground 🦴🦴 **1946** Strange things are afoot in a peaceful valley adjacent to a desolate, forbidding wasteland. When Hoppy and a young woman set out across the wasteland to make a gold delivery, they encounter a band of desperados and begin to unravel the secrets of a dishonest political ring. **65m/B VHS.** William Boyd, Andy Clyde, Rand Brooks, Elaine Riley; ***D:*** George Archainbaud.

Hopalong Cassidy: The Marauders 🦴🦴 **1947** After seeking shelter in an abandoned church one rainy night, Hoppy and the boys must defend the kirk when it is threatened by a marauder and his gang. **64m/B VHS.** William Boyd, Andy Clyde, Rand Brooks; ***D:*** George Archainbaud.

Hopalong Cassidy: Unexpected Guest 🦴🦴½ **1947** When a small fortune is left to a California family, the head count starts to dwindle, and Hoppy aims to find out why. **59m/B VHS.** William Boyd, Andy Clyde, Rand Brooks, Una O'Connor; ***D:*** George Archainbaud.

Hope 🦴🦴½ **1997** Thirteen-year-old Lily Kate Burns (Malone) is living in the small southern town of Hope in 1962. Her mother's had a severe stroke and the only family she has to turn to are racist Uncle Ray (Walsh) and fragile Aunt Emma (Lahti). Amidst the town's segregation and fears about the Cuban Missile Crisis, Lily Kate is also more open to befriending new town residents than her elders, including visiting black preacher Jediah (Sams). Hawn's directorial debut. **100m/C VHS.** Mary Ellen Trainor, Christine Lahti, Jena Malone, J.T. Walsh, Jeffrey D. Sams, Catherine O'Hara; ***D:*** Goldie Hawn; ***W:*** Kerry Kennedy. **CABLE**

Hope and Glory 🦴🦴🦴½ **1987 (PG-13)** Boorman turns his memories of WWII London into a complex and sensitive film. Father volunteers, and mother must deal with the awakening sexuality of her teenage daughter, keep her son in line, balance the ration books, and try to make it to the bomb shelter in the middle of the night. Seen through the boy's eyes, war creates a playground of shrapnel to collect and wild imaginings come true. Nice companion film to "Empire of the Sun" and "Au Revoir Les Enfants," two more 1987 releases that explore WWII from the recollections of young boys. **97m/C VHS, DVD, 8mm, Wide.** *GB* Sebastian Rice-Edwards, Geraldine Muir, Sarah Miles, Sammi Davis, David Hayman, Derrick O'Connor, Susan Wooldridge, Jean-Marc Barr, Ian Bannen, Jill Baker, Charley Boorman, Annie Leon, Katrine Boorman, Gerald James, Amelda Brown, Colin Higgins; ***D:*** John Boorman; ***W:*** John Boorman; ***C:*** Philippe Rousselot; ***M:*** Peter Martin. British Acad. '87: Film, Support. Actress (Wooldridge); Golden Globes '88: Film—Mus./Comedy; L.A. Film Critics '87: Director (Boorman), Film, Screenplay; Natl. Soc. Film Critics '87: Cinematog., Director (Boorman), Film, Screenplay.

Hope Floats 🦴🦴½ **1998 (PG-13)** Former small town Texas beauty queen Birdee Pruitt (Bullock) finds out her husband Bill (Pare) is having an affair with her best friend (Arquette) live on TV, thanks to a tabloid talk show expose. Completely humiliated, she takes her daughter Bernice (Whitman) and heads home to her own rather spaced-out mom Ramona (Rowlands). She's trying to gain some perspective on her life—and maybe, slowly, find a new love with the help of handsome cowpoke Justin (Connick Jr.) Movie is sweet, sentimental, obvious, and has an appealing cast and a happy ending. Perfect girlfriend fare. **114m/C VHS, DVD.** Sandra Bullock, Harry Connick Jr., Gena Rowlands, Mae Whitman, Cameron Finley, Michael Pare, Rosanna Arquette, Kathy Najimy, Bill Cobbs; ***D:*** Forest Whitaker; ***W:*** Steven Rogers; ***C:*** Caleb Deschanel; ***M:*** Dave Grusin.

Hoppity Goes to Town *Mr. Bug Goes to Town* **1941** Full-length animated feature from the Max Fleischer studios tells the story of the inhabitants of Bugville, who live in a weed patch in New York City. **77m/C VHS.** ***D:*** Dave Fleischer; ***M:*** Frank Loesser, Hoagy Carmichael.

Hoppy Serves a Writ 🦴🦴 **1943** In this last of the series to be based on the writings of the original author, Texas sheriff Cassidy tries to bring a gang of outlaws to justice. Look for a young Robert Mitchum as one of the villains. **67m/B VHS.** William Boyd, Andy Clyde, Jay Kirby, Victor Jory, George Reeves, Hal Taliaferro, Robert Mitchum, Byron Foulger, Earle Hodgins, Roy Barcroft; ***D:*** George Archainbaud.

Hopscotch 🦴🦴🦴 **1980 (R)** A C.I.A. agent drops out when his overly zealous chief demotes him to a desk job. When he writes a book designed to expose the dirty deeds of the CIA, he leads his boss and KGB pal on a merry chase. Amiable comedy well-suited for Matthau's rumpled talents. **107m/C VHS.** Walter Matthau, Glenda Jackson, Ned Beatty, Sam Waterston, Herbert Lom; ***D:*** Ronald Neame.

Horatio Hornblower 🦴🦴🦴 **1999** Adventure on the high seas in these adaptations of C.S. Forester's popular novels, which are set in the late 18th-century. Hornblower (Gruffudd) is a young recruit who rises through the ranks of the King's Navy as the British battle the French. "The Duel" provides the introduction to Hornblower and his mentor, Captain Pellew (Lindsay). "The Fire Ships" has Hornblower preparing for his lieutenant's exam. "The Duchess and the Devil" finds Hornblower escorting the Duchess of Wharfedale (Lunghi) to England with important naval dispatches. "The Wrong War" finds the Brits preparing a coup against the French Republican government. **400m/C VHS, DVD.** *GB* Ioan Gruffudd, Robert Lindsay, Denis Lawson, Cherie Lunghi, Anthony Sher, Samuel West, Andrew Tiernan, Ronald Pickup; ***D:*** Andrew Grieve; ***W:*** Russell Lewis, Mike Cullen, Patrick Harbinson; ***C:*** Alec Curtis, Neve Cunningham. **TV**

Horatio Hornblower: The Adventure Continues 🦴🦴🦴 **2001** The adventures of young British naval officer Hornblower (Gruffud) continue with two linked stories: "Mutiny" and "The Retribution." Horatio recounts to his mentor, Captain Pellew (Lindsay), the reasons for his imprisonment on mutiny charges after confining his insane captain (Warner) to his quarters to prevent his sending the crew into a suicidal battle. But Hornblower must also lead a force to recapture an enemy fort. Based on C.S. Forrester's novel, "Lieutenant Hornblower." **200m/C VHS, DVD.** *GB* Ioan Gruffudd, Robert Lindsay, David Warner, Jamie Bamber, Paul McGann, Nicholas Jones, Philip Glenister, David Rintoul; ***D:*** Andrew Grieve; ***C:*** Chris O'Dell; ***M:*** John Keane. **TV**

Horizons West 🦴🦴½ **1952** Two brothers go their separate ways after the Civil War. One leads a peaceful life as a rancher but the other, corrupted by the war, engages in a violent campaign to build his own empire. Ryan's outstanding performance eclipses that of the young Hudson. **81m/C VHS.** Robert Ryan, Julie Adams, Rock Hudson, Raymond Burr, James Arness, John McIntire, Dennis Weaver, Frances Bavier; ***D:*** Budd Boetticher; ***M:*** Henry Mancini.

The Horizontal Lieutenant 🦴🦴½ **1962** Hutton and Prentiss team up again in this moderately funny romantic-comedy about an officer's escapades during WWII. Based on the novel "The Bottletop Affair" by Gordon Cotler. **90m/C VHS.** Jim Hutton, Paula Prentiss, Jack Carter, Jim Backus, Charles McGraw, Miyoshi Umeki; ***D:*** Richard Thorpe; ***W:*** George Wells.

The Horn Blows at Midnight 🦴🦴🦴 **1945** A band trumpeter falls asleep and dreams he's a bumbling archangel, on Earth to blow the note bringing the end of the world. But a pretty girl distracts him, and...A wild, high-gloss, well-cast fantasy farce, uniquely subversive in its lighthearted approach to biblical Doomsday. Benny made the film notorious by acting ashamed of it in his later broadcast routines. **78m/B VHS.** Jack Benny, Alexis Smith, Dolores Moran, Allyn Joslyn, Reginald Gardiner, Guy Kibbee, John Alexander, Margaret Dumont; ***D:*** Raoul Walsh.

Hornet's Nest 🦴🦴½ **1970** Captain Turner (Hudson) is the lone survivor of an Army commando unit which parachuted into the Italian countryside in an effort to blow up a dam being held by the Nazis. He's rescued by a group of boys, the survivors of a German massacre of their nearby town. Turner wants the boys to help him blow up the dam—and they want his help in getting revenge on the Nazis who have occupied their homes. **110m/C VHS.** Rock Hudson, Sylva Koscina, Sergio Fantoni, Jacques Sernas, Giacomo "Jack" Rossi-Stuart, Andrea Bosic, Gerard Herter, Tom Felleghi; ***D:*** Phil Karlson; ***W:*** S.S. Schweitzer.

The Horrible Dr. Bones 🦴🦴 **2000 (R)** Dr. Bones (Igus) is a record producer who gives the young Urban Protectors band their big break, but it turns out that he's exploiting them in a supernatural scheme involving human sacrifice and zombies. The plotting is amateurish. Some of the effects have shock value. The low-budget horror doesn't rise much above the studio's bare-bones production. **72m/C DVD, Wide.** Darrow Igus, Larry Bates, Sarah Scott, Rhonda Claebaut, Nathaniel Lamar; ***D:*** Art Carnage; ***W:*** Raymond Forchon; ***C:*** Adolfo Bartoli.

The Horrible Dr. Hichcock 🦴🦴½ *L'Orribile Segreto del Dr. Hichcock* **1962** A sicko doctor, who accidentally killed his first wife while engaged in sexual antics, remarries to bring the first missus back from the dead using his new wife's blood. Genuinely creepy. Sequelled by "The Ghost." **76m/C VHS.** *IT* Robert Flemyng, Barbara Steele, Montgomery Glenn, Harriet Medin, Ernesto Gastaldi, Maria Teresa Vianello; ***D:*** Riccardo (Robert Hampton) Freda; ***W:*** Perry (Ernesto Gastaldi) Julyan; ***C:*** Raffaele Masciocchi; ***M:*** Roman Vlad.

The Horror Chamber of Dr. Faustus 🦴🦴🦴½ *Eyes without a Face; Les Yeux sans Visage; Occhi senza Volto* **1959** A wickedly intelligent, inventive piece of Grand Guignol about a mad doctor who kills young girls so he may graft their skin onto the face of his accidentally mutilated daughter. In French with English subtitles. **84m/B VHS.** *FR* Alida Valli, Pierre Brasseur, Edith Scob, Francois Guerin, Juliette Mayniel, Alex(andre) Rignault, Claude Brasseur, Charles Blavette; ***D:*** Georges Franju; ***W:*** Jean Redon; ***C:*** Eugene (Eugen Shufftan) Shuftan; ***M:*** Maurice Jarre.

Horror Express 🦴🦴½ *Panic on the Trans-Siberian Express; Panico en el Transiberiano; Panic in the Trans-Siberian Train* **1972 (R)** A creature from prehistoric times, that was removed from its tomb, is transported on the Trans-Siberian railroad. Passengers suddenly discover strange things happening—such as having their souls sucked out of them. **88m/C VHS, DVD.** *SP GB* Christopher Lee, Peter Cushing, Telly Savalas, Alberto De Mendoza, Sylvia Tortosa, Julio Pena, Angel Del Pozo, Helga Line, Jorge (George) Rigaud, Jose Jaspe; ***D:*** Eugenio (Gene) Martin; ***W:*** Julian Zimet, Arnaud d'Usseau; ***C:*** Alejandro Ulloa.

Horror Hospital 🦴 *Computer Killers; Doctor Blood Bath* **1973 (R)** Patients are turned into zombies by a mad doctor in this hospital where no anesthesia is used. Those who try to escape are taken care of by the doctor's guards. **91m/C VHS, DVD, Wide.** *GB* Michael Gough, Robin Askwith, Vanessa Shaw, Ellen Pollock, Skip Martin, Dennis Price; ***D:*** Antony Balch; ***W:*** Antony Balch, Alan Watson; ***C:*** David McDonald.

Horror Hotel 🦴🦴½ *The City of the Dead* **1960** A young witchcraft student visits a small Massachusetts town which has historic ties to witch burnings and discovers a new, and deadly, coven is now active. Well done and atmospheric. **76m/B VHS, DVD, Wide.** *GB* Christopher Lee, Patricia Jessel, Betta St. John, Dennis Lotis, Venetia Stevenson, Valentine Dyall; ***D:*** John Llewellyn Moxey; ***W:*** George L. Baxt; ***C:*** Desmond Dickinson.

Horror House on Highway 5 woof! **1986** Someone in a Nixon mask kills people in this extremely cheap dud. **90m/C VHS.** ***D:*** Richard Casey; ***W:*** Richard Casey.

The Horror of Dracula 🦴🦴🦴½ *Dracula* **1958** The first Hammer Dracula film, in which the infamous vampire is given a new, elegant and ruthless persona, as he battles Prof. Van Helsing after coming to England. Possibly the finest, most inspired version of Bram Stoker's macabre chestnut, and one that single-handedly revived the horror genre. **82m/C VHS.** *GB* Peter Cushing, Christopher Lee, Michael Gough, Melissa Stribling, Carol Marsh, John Van Eyssen, Valerie Gaunt, Charles Lloyd Pack, Miles Malleson; ***D:*** Terence Fisher; ***W:*** Jimmy Sangster; ***C:*** Jack Asher; ***M:*** James Bernard.

The Horror of Frankenstein 🦴🦴 **1970** Spoof of the standard Frankenstein story features philandering ex-med student Baron Frankenstein, whose interest in a weird and esoteric branch of science provides a shocking and up-to-date rendition of the age-old plot. Preceded by "Frankenstein Must Be Destroyed" and followed by "Frankenstein and the Monster from Hell." **93m/C VHS, DVD.** *GB* Ralph Bates, Kate O'Mara, Dennis Price, David Prowse, Veronica Carlson, Joan Rice, Bernard Archard, Graham James; ***D:*** Jimmy Sangster; ***W:*** Jimmy Sangster, Jeremy Burnham; ***C:*** Moray Grant.

Horror of Party Beach woof! *Invasion of the Zombies* **1964** Considered to be one of the all-time worst films. Features a mob of radioactive seaweed creatures who eat a slew of nubile, surf-minded teenagers. ♫Zombie Stomp. **71m/C VHS.** John Scott, Alice Lyon, Allen Laurel, Marilyn Clarke, Augustin Mayer, Eulabelle Moore; ***D:*** Del Tenney; ***W:*** Richard Hilliard; ***C:*** Richard Hilliard; ***M:*** Bill Holmes.

Horror of the Blood Monsters woof! *Vampire Men of the Lost Planet; Horror Creatures of the Prehistoric Planet; Creatures of the Prehistoric Planet; Creatures of the Red Planet; Flesh Creatures of the Red Planet; The Flesh Creatures; Space Mission of the Lost Planet* **1970 (PG)** John Carradine made a career out of being in bad movies, and this one competes as one of the worst. This is an editor's nightmare, made up of black & white film spliced together and colorized. Vampires from outer space threaten to suck all the blood from the people of Earth. **85m/C VHS.** *PH* John Carradine, Robert Dix, Vicki Volante, Jennifer Bishop; ***D:*** Al Adamson, George Joseph.

Horror of the Zombies 🦴 *El Buque Maldito* **1974 (R)** Bikinied models are pursued by hooded zombies on board a pleasure yacht...the horror. Effete final installment in the "blind dead" trilogy; see also "Tombs of the Blind Dead" and "Return of the Evil Dead." **90m/C VHS.** *SP* Maria Perschy, Jack Taylor; ***D:*** Armando de Ossorio; ***W:*** Armando de Ossorio.

Horror Rises from the Tomb 🦴🦴 *El Espanto Surge de la Tumba* **1972** A 15th century knight and his assistant are beheaded for practicing witchcraft. Five hundred years later, they return to possess a group of vacationers and generally cause havoc. **89m/C VHS.** *SP* Paul (Jacinto Molina) Naschy, Vic Winner, Emma Cohen, Helga Line, Cristina Suriani, Jacinto (Jack) Molina; ***D:*** Carlos Aured; ***W:*** Jacinto (Jack) Molina.

The Horror Show 🦴 *House 3* **1989 (R)** Serial killer fries in electric chair, an event that really steams him. So he goes after the cop who brought him in. Standard dead guy who won't die and wants revenge flick. **95m/C VHS.** Terry Alexander, Brion James, Lance Henriksen, Rita Taggart, Dedee Pfeiffer, Aron Eisenberg, Matt Clark, Thom Bray; ***D:*** James Isaac; ***W:*** Alan Smithee, Leslie Bohem; ***C:*** Mac Ahlberg.

Horrors of Burke & Hare 🦴 **1971** A gory tale about the exploits of a bunch of 19th-century grave robbers. **94m/C VHS.** Derren Nesbitt, Harry Andrews, Yootha Joyce; ***D:*** Vernon Sewell.

Horrors of Spider Island 🦴 *It's Hot in Paradise; Ein Toter Hing im Netz; A Corpse Hangs in the Web* **1959** D'Arcy is a Hollywood talent scout who sniffs a goldmine in a team of young female dancers whom he schedules to perform for him in Singapore. Their transport plane crashes in the Pacific Ocean and he and the girls are forced to take refuge on an uncharted isle. Upon landing there they discover it is infested with giant crab-sized spiders. Lots of potential for both shock and arousal, which was probably why it was originally released in both "horror" and "girlie" versions. D'Arcy later admitted to taking over for director Bottger and adding all the horror sequences himself. Dubbed from the German. **77m/C VHS, DVD.** *GE* Alexander D'Arcy, Ursula Lederstger, Barbara Valentin, Harold Maresch, Helga Franck; ***D:*** Fritz Bottger; ***W:*** Fritz Bottger.

Horrors of the Red Planet 🦴 *The Wizard of Mars* **1964** Cheapo epic sees astronauts crash on Mars, meet its Wizard, and stumble into a few Oz-like creatures. Technically advised by Forrest J. Ackerman. **81m/C VHS.** John Carradine, Roger Gentry, Vic McGee; ***D:*** David L. Hewitt.

The Horse 🦴🦴🦴½ *Horse, My Horse* **1982** A moving, mature Turkish film about a father and son trying to overcome socio-economic obstacles and their own frailties in order to make enough money to send the boy to school. In Turkish with English subtitles. **116m/C VHS.** *TU* ***D:*** Ali Ozgenturk.

Horse Feathers 🦴🦴🦴½ **1932** Huxley College has to beef up its football team to win the championship game which has been rigged by local gamblers in the opposition's favor, and the corrupt new college president (Groucho) knows just how to do it. Features some of the brothers' classic routines, and the songs "Whatever It Is, I'm Against It" and "Everyone Says I Love You." **67m/B VHS, DVD.** Groucho Marx, Chico Marx, Harpo Marx, Zeppo Marx, Thelma Todd, David Landau, Nat Pendleton; ***D:*** Norman Z. McLeod; ***W:*** Bert Kalmar, S.J. Perelman, Harry Ruby; ***C:*** Ray June; ***M:*** Harry Ruby.

A Horse for Danny 🦴🦴½ **1995 (G)** Horse trainer Eddie (Urich), dogged by bad luck, and his 11-year-old niece Danny (Sobieski), come across a thoroughbred named Tom Thumb, who may be their chance at racing's winners circle. TV movie. **92m/C VHS.** Robert Urich, Leelee Sobieski, Ron Brice, Karen Carlson, Gary Basaraba; ***D:*** Dick Lowry; ***C:*** Steven Fierberg.

The Horse in the Gray Flannel Suit 🦴🦴½ **1968 (G)** Disney comedy portrays an advertising executive who links his daughter's devotion to horses with a client's new ad campaign. **114m/C VHS.** Dean Jones, Ellen Janov, Fred Clark, Diane Baker, Lloyd Bochner, Kurt Russell; ***D:*** Norman Tokar; ***W:*** Louis Pelletier; ***M:*** George Bruns.

The Horse of Pride 🦴🦴½ *Le Cheval D'Orgeuil* **1980** Chabrol takes a telling look at the everyday life of the peasants of Breton—both their pleasures and their sorrows. In French with English subtitles. French script booklet available. **118m/C VHS.** *FR* Jacques Dufilho, Francois Cluzet; ***D:*** Claude Chabrol.

The Horse Soldiers 🦴🦴½ **1959** An 1863 Union cavalry officer is sent 300 miles into Confederate territory to destroy a railroad junction and is accompanied by a fellow officer who is also a pacifist doctor. Based on a true Civil War incident. **114m/C VHS, DVD, Wide.** John Wayne, William Holden, Hoot Gibson, Constance Towers, Russell Simpson, Strother Martin, Anna Lee, Judson Pratt, Denver Pyle, Jack Pennick, Althea Gibson, William Forrest, Willis Bouchey, Bing Russell, Ken Curtis, O.Z. Whitehead, Walter Reed, Hank Worden, Carleton Young, Cliff Lyons; ***D:*** John Ford; ***W:*** John Lee Mahin, Martin Rackin; ***C:*** William Clothier; ***M:*** David Buttolph.

The Horse Thief 🦴🦴🦴 *Daoma Zei* **1987** Noted as the first movie from the People's Republic of China to be released on video, this epic tells the tale of Norbu, a man who, exiled from his people for horse thievery, is forced to wander the Tibetan countryside with his family in search of work. His son dies while he is in exile, and he, a devout Buddhist, is ultimately forced to accept tribal work in a ritual exorcism, after which he pleads to be accepted back into his clan. Beautiful and image-driven, offering a rare glimpse into the Tibet you won't see in travel brochures. Filmed on location with locals as actors. In Mandarin with English subtitles. **88m/C VHS.** *CH* Daiba, Jiji Dan, Drashi, Gaoba, Jamco Jayang, Rigzin Tseshang; ***D:*** Tian Zhuangzhuang; ***W:*** Rui Zhang; ***C:*** Fei Zhao, Hou Yong; ***M:*** Xiao-Song Qu.

The Horse Whisperer 🦴🦴½ **1997 (PG-13)** After her teenaged daughter Grace (Johansson) is injured in a riding accident, determined mom Annie (Thomas), believeing that the girl's recovery is tied to the horse's, takes child and horse to Montana to seek the help of horse healer Tom (Redford) in the big-screen adaptation of the Nicholas Evans novel. While there, chilly New York editor Annie warms up to Tom and the possibility of love. Like "The Bridges of Madison County," this adaptation removes the overwrought syrupy melodrama of its source novel to concentrate on mature themes like fidelity, trust, and fate. Fine performances by all (although Redford could be seen as a bit self-indulgent at times) and the beautiful Montana backdrop make up for the lack of sustained dramatic impact, which is probably due to the almost three-hour run time and some dramatic changes from the book. **168m/C VHS, DVD.** Robert Redford, Kristin Scott Thomas, Scarlett Johansson, Sam Neill, Chris Cooper, Dianne Wiest, Cherry Jones, Jeanette Nolan, Don Edwards, Ty Hillman, Kate (Catherine) Bosworth, Steve Frye; ***D:*** Robert Redford; ***W:*** Eric Roth, Richard LaGravenese; ***C:*** Robert Richardson; ***M:*** Thomas Newman.

The Horse Without a Head 🦴🦴½ **1963** Stolen loot has been hidden in a discarded toy horse which is now the property of a group of poor children. The thieves, however, have different plans. Good family fare from the Disney TV show. **89m/C VHS.** Jean-Pierre Aumont, Herbert Lom, Leo McKern, Pamela Franklin, Vincent Winter; ***D:*** Don Chaffey. **TV**

The Horseman on the Roof 🦴🦴½ *Le Hussard sur le Toit* **1995 (R)** Lavish costume drama set in Provence in the 1830s, during a cholera epidemic. Italian officer/revolutionary Angelo (Martinez) is on the run and eventually meets up with beautiful Pauline de Theus (Binoche), who hides him in a quarantined French village. Pauline's in search of her husband and Angelo reluctantly agrees to help her. Together they manage to escape a military cordon and travel to another plague town. There's lots of riding through the countryside and hiding out and not much actually happens. Nice scenery, attractive stars. Based on the 1951 novel by Jean Giono. French with subtitles; originally released at 135 minutes. **119m/C VHS.** *FR* Olivier Martinez, Juliette Binoche, Francois Cluzet, Isabelle Carre, Jean Yanne, Claudio Amendola, Pierre Arditti; ***Cameos:*** Gerard Depardieu; ***D:*** Jean-Paul Rappeneau; ***W:*** Jean-Paul Rappeneau, Jean-Claude Carriere, Nina Companeez; ***C:*** Thierry Arbogast; ***M:*** Jean-Claude Petit. Cesar '96: Cinematog., Sound.

Horsemasters 🦴🦴 **1961** A group of young riders enter a special training program in England to achieve the ultimate equestrian title of horsemaster, with Annette having to overcome her fear of jumping. Originally a two-part Disney TV show, and released as a feature film in Europe. **85m/C VHS.** Tommy Kirk, Annette Funicello, Janet Munro, Tony Britton, Donald Pleasence, Jean Marsh, John Fraser, Millicent Martin; ***D:*** William Fairchild. **TV**

The Horsemen 🦴½ **1970 (PG)** An Afghani youth enters the brutal buzkashi horse tournament to please his macho-minded father. Beautifully shot in Afghanistan and Spain by Claude Renoir. **109m/C VHS.** Omar Sharif, Leigh Taylor-Young, Jack Palance, David De, Peter Jeffrey; ***D:*** John Frankenheimer; ***W:*** Dalton Trumbo; ***M:*** Georges Delerue.

The Horseplayer 🦴½ **1991 (R)** A loner is drawn into a mysterious triangle of decadence and desire in this riveting psychothriller. **?m/C VHS.** Brad Dourif, Sammi Davis, Michael (M.K.) Harris, Vic Tayback; ***D:*** Kurt Voss.

The Horse's Mouth 🦴🦴🦴 *The Oracle* **1958** An obsessive painter discovers that he must rely upon his wits to survive in London. A hilarious adaptation of the Joyce Cary novel. **93m/C VHS, DVD, Wide.** *GB* Alec Guinness, Kay Walsh, Robert Coote, Renee Houston, Michael Gough; ***D:*** Ronald Neame; ***W:*** Alec Guinness; ***C:*** Arthur Ibbetson; ***M:*** Kenneth V. Jones. Natl. Bd. of Review '58: Support. Actress (Walsh).

Horsey 🦴🦴 **1999** Young Delilah makes no apologies for any of her passions—those of her art or the men or women she chooses to love. Then she starts a relationship with volatile Ryland Yale, a rock 'n' roller with a heroin addiction who still manages to fill all Delilah's emotional and physical needs. But is Delilah ready to deal with what Ryland will cost her? **93m/C VHS, DVD.** Holly Ferguson, Todd Kerns, Ryan Robbins, Victoria Deschanel; ***D:*** Kirsten Clarkson; ***W:*** Kirsten Clarkson; ***C:*** Glen Winter; ***M:*** Helen Keller.

Horton Foote's Alone 🦴🦴½ *Alone* **1997** John Webb (Cronyn) is an elderly Texas farmer, lost after the death of his wife of 52 years. His nephews (Forrest, Cooper) want him to sell his land to an interested oil company and his daughters (Miles, Hart) want to cry on his shoulder. Then Webb's former tenant farmer (Jones) comes back to visit and is the only one to ask the old man what he wants to do. **107m/C VHS, DVD.** Hume Cronyn, James Earl Jones, Chris Cooper, Frederic Forrest, Joanna Miles, Roxanne Hart, Shelley Duvall, Hallie Foote, Ed Begley Jr., David Selby, Piper Laurie; ***D:*** Michael Lindsay-Hogg; ***W:*** Horton Foote; ***C:*** Jeffrey Jur; ***M:*** David Shire. **CABLE**

The Hospital 🦴🦴🦴½ **1971 (PG)** Cult favorite providing savage, unrelentingly sarcastic look at the workings of a chaotic metropolitan hospital beset by murders, witchdoctors, madness, and plain ineptitude. Scott's suicidal chief surgeon Herbert Bock, who falls in love with free-spirited Barbara Drummond (Riggs), a patient's daughter. **101m/C VHS.** George C. Scott, Diana Rigg, Barnard Hughes, Stockard Channing, Nancy Marchand, Richard Dysart, Stephen Elliott, Rehn Scofield, Katherine Helmond, Roberts Blossom; ***D:*** Arthur Hiller; ***W:*** Paddy Chayefsky; ***C:*** Victor Kemper. Oscars '71: Story & Screenplay; Berlin Intl. Film Fest. '72: Silver Prize; British Acad. '72: Screenplay; Golden Globes '72: Screenplay, Natl. Film Reg. '95;, Writers Guild '71: Orig. Screenplay.

Hospital Massacre woof! *X-Ray; Ward 13; Be My Valentine, Or Else* **1981 (R)** Psychopathic killer is loose in a hospital. Seems he holds a grudge against the woman who laughed at his valentine when they were children 20 years earlier, and too bad for her that she just checked in as a patient. Former "Playboy" and Hefner playmate Benton frolics in dangerous health care situation presented by the Cannon organization. **89m/C VHS.** Barbi Benton, Jon Van Ness, Chip Lucio; ***D:*** Boaz Davidson; ***W:*** Marc Behm.

Hospital of Terror 🦴🦴 *Nurse Sherri; Terror Hospital; Beyond the Living* **1978 (R)** A transmigratory religious fanatic who died on the operating table manages to possess a nurse (Jacobson) before he kicks the bucket, and once in his candystripe incarnation, vents his spleen on the doctors who botched his operation. It's got a little more plasma than Adamson's "Astro-Zombies," considered by many to be a world-class boner. **88m/C VHS.** Jill Jacobson, Geoffrey Land, Marilyn Joi, Mary Kay Pass, Prentiss Moulden, Clayton Foster; ***D:*** Al Adamson.

The Hostage 🦴🦴½ **1967 (PG)** A young teenager is witness to a gruesome and clandestine burial. The two murderers responsible take it upon themselves to see that their secret is never told. **84m/C VHS.** Don O'Kelly, Harry Dean Stanton, John Carradine, Danny Martins; ***D:*** Russell S. Doughten Jr.

Hostage 🦴½ **1987 (R)** Arab terrorists hijack a plane and the passengers start to fight back. Filmed in South Africa. **94m/C VHS.** Karen Black, Kevin McCarthy, Wings Hauser; ***D:*** Hanro Mohr; ***M:*** Brad Fiedel.

Hostage 🦴🦴 **1992 (R)** British Secret Service agent John Rennie is fed up after a difficult mission in Argentina. He thinks he can walk away clean but his superiors beg to differ. He's marked for murder but Rennie has a dangerous plan that could guarantee his safety—only if he returns to Argentina to set things in motion. Based on the novel "No Place to Hide" by Ted Allbeury. **100m/C VHS.** Sam Neill, Talisa Soto, James Fox; ***D:*** Robert W. Young.

Hostage for a Day 🦴🦴½ **1994** Married to a shrew, toiling for an overbearing father-in-law, and suffering a midlife crisis, Wendt decides to fake his own kidnapping, take the ransom money, and head off for a better life. A series of comedic complications abound. Candy's directorial debut. Made for TV. **92m/C VHS.** George Wendt, John Vernon, Robin Duke, Peter Torokvei, Don Lake, Frank Moore, John Hemphill, Christopher Templeton; ***Cameos:*** John Candy; ***D:*** John Candy; ***W:*** Peter Torokvei, Robert Crane, Kari Hildebrand; ***M:*** Ian Thomas. **TV**

Hostage High 🦴🦴 *Detention: The Siege at Johnson High* **1997 (R)** Jason Copeland (Schroeder) returns to his former high school with a gun in order to take revenge on the teachers who failed him. The students, including Aaron (Prinze Jr.), he holds hostage inside the building have entirely different tactics for negotiation from the adults who are outside. Based on a true story. **93m/C VHS, DVD.** Rick Schroder, Henry Winkler, Freddie Prinze Jr., Ren Woods, Katie Wright, Alexis Cruz, Patrick Malone; ***D:*** Michael W. Watkins; ***W:*** Larry Golin; ***C:*** Bill Roe; ***M:*** Brian Adler. **TV**

Hostage Hotel 🦴🦴 **2000 (R)** Ex-cop Logan McQueen (Reynolds) tries to outmanouever a kidnapper who's holding a congressman's daughter and McQueen's old partner hostage in an abandoned old hotel. **95m/C VHS.** Burt Reynolds, Charles Durning, Keith Carradine, David Rasche; ***D:*** Hal Needham; ***W:*** Nicholas Factor. **CABLE**

The Hostage Tower 🦴🦴 **1980 (PG)** In France, a group of international crime figures capture the visiting U.S. president's mother, hold her hostage in the Eiffel Tower and demand $30 million in ransom. **97m/C VHS.** Peter Fonda, Maud Adams, Britt Ekland, Billy Dee Williams, Keir Dullea, Douglas Fairbanks Jr., Rachel Roberts, Celia Johnson; ***D:*** Claudio Guzman. **TV**

Hostages 🦴 **1979** A gang of criminals kidnap a family on vacation at a Caribbean island. **93m/C VHS.** Stuart Whitman, Marisa Mell.

Hostages 🦴🦴🦴 **1993 (R)** Harrowing docudrama about the Beirut hostage crisis combines acutal news footage with scenes of the prisoners and their families. Under desperate conditions hostages John McCarthy, Brian Keenan, Terry Anderson, Thomas Sutherland, Frank Reed, and Terry Waite try to hold on to their sanity and humanity as their families struggle for their release. Filmed on location in England, Israel, and Lebanon. **90m/C VHS.** Colin Firth, Ciaran Hinds, Jay O. Sanders, Josef Sommer, Harry Dean Stanton, Kathy Bates, Natasha Richardson, Conrad Asquith; ***D:*** David Wheatley; ***W:*** Bernard MacLaverty. **CABLE**

Hostile Guns 🦴🦴½ **1967** A law man discovers a woman he once loved is now an inmate he is transporting across the Texas badlands. Routine with the exception of cameos by veteran actors. Based on a story by Sloan Nibley and James Edward Grant. **91m/C VHS.** George Montgomery, Yvonne De Carlo, Tab Hunter, John Russell; ***Cameos:*** Brian Donlevy, Richard Arlen, Fuzzy Knight, Donald (Don "Red") Barry; ***D:*** R.G. Springsteen; ***W:*** Steve Fisher, Sloan Nibley.

Hostile Intent 🦴🦴 **1997 (R)** Computer whiz Mike Cleary (Lowe) has designed a new program to counter a computer chip that will allow the government access to everyone's computer. Naturally, this does not make the feds happy and when Mike and his team are off in the woods playing wargames for relaxation, someone is using real bullets to pick off the workers. **90m/C VHS.** Rob Lowe, John Savage, Sofia Shinas, James Kidnie; ***D:*** Jonathan Heap; ***W:*** Manny Coto; ***C:*** Gerald R. Goozie; ***M:*** Christophe Beck. **VIDEO**

Hostile Intentions 🦴🦴 **1994 (R)** Three girlfriends head for a weekend of fun in the sun in Tijuana and find themselves turned into fugitives through a series of misunderstandings. In order to get home, they must risk a night border crossing with a group of illegal immigrants. **90m/C VHS.** Tia Carrere, Lisa Dean Ryan, Tricia Leigh Fisher, Carlos Gomez, Rigg Kennedy; ***D:*** Catherine Cyran; ***W:*** Catherine Cyran; ***C:*** Azusa Ohno; ***M:*** Marcos Loya.

Hostile Takeover 🦴½ *Office Party* **1988 (R)** A mild-mannered accountant finally cracks and takes his co-workers hostage. He faces the police in a tense showdown. **93m/C VHS.** David Warner, Michael Ironside, Kate Vernon, Jayne (Jane) Eastwood; ***D:*** George Mihalka.

Hostile Waters 🦴🦴½ **1997 (PG)** Based on Soviet accounts of an October 1986 incident that nearly set off a nuclear holocaust. A Russian and a U.S. sub play a game of cat-and-mouse 500 miles east of Bermuda. There's a collision and a fire aboard the Soviet sub threatens their cargo of thermonuclear missiles. Soviet captain Igor Britanov (Hauer) tries to control the situation while the U.S. skipper (Sheen) tries to figure out just what's going on. **92m/C VHS.** Rutger Hauer, Martin Sheen, Colm Feore, Rob Campbell, Harris Yulin, Max von Sydow, Regina Taylor, John Rothman; ***D:*** David Drury; ***W:*** Troy Kennedy Martin; ***C:*** Alec Curtis; ***M:*** David Ferguson. **CABLE**

Hot Blood **1989** Two bank robbers take an innocent woman hostage and thrust her in the midst of a huge family battle. Another lukewarm entry from the director of "The Arrogant." **89m/C VHS.** Sylvia Kristel, Alicia Moro, Aldo Sambrel, Gaspar Cano; ***D:*** Philippe Blot.

Hot Blooded 🦴 *Hit & Run; Red Blooded American Girl 2* **1998 (R)** Trent Colbert (Winters) is a naive college freshman driving back to his family at Thanksgiving. Pulling into a truck stop he's makes the mistake of offering alluring hooker Miya (Wuhrer) a ride. But Miya's a twisted soul and all this means for the libidinous Trent is trouble. **95m/C VHS, DVD.** Kari Wuhrer, Kristoffer Ryan Winters, David Keith, Burt Young; ***D:*** David Blyth; ***W:*** Nicolas Stiliadis; ***C:*** Edgar Egger; ***M:*** Paul Zaza. **VIDEO**

Hot Box woof! **1972 (R)** A Filipino-shot, low budget woofer. Prison flick about women who break out and foment a revolution. **85m/C VHS.** Andrea Cagan, Margaret Markov, Rickey Richardson, Laurie Rose; ***D:*** Joe Viola; ***W:*** Joe Viola, Jonathan Demme.

Hot Bubblegum 🦴 **1981 (R)** Three teenagers discover sex, the beach, rock 'n' roll, sex, drag racing, and sex. **94m/C VHS.** Jonathan Segall, Zachi Noy, Yftach Katzur.

Hot Child in the City 🦴 **1987** A country girl goes to Los Angeles and searches through the city's fleshpots for her sister's killer. Music by Nick Glider, Lou Reed, Billy Idol, and Fun Boy Three. **85m/C VHS.** Leah Ayres Hendrix, Shari Shattuck, Geof Pryssir; ***D:*** John Florea; ***M:*** Michael W. Lewis.

Hot Chocolate 🦴🦴 **1992 (PG-13)** Derek is a sultry Texas tycoon who wants to buy out the French chocolate factory run by Hays. After getting a look at her, work isn't all that's on his mind. **93m/C VHS.** Bo Derek, Robert Hays.

Hot Dog ... The Movie! 🦴½ **1983 (R)** There's an intense rivalry going on between an Austrian ski champ and his California challenger during the World Cup Freestyle competition in Squaw Valley. Snow movie strictly for teens or their equivalent. **96m/C VHS.** David Naughton, Patrick Houser, Shannon Tweed, Tracy N. Smith; ***D:*** Peter Markle; ***M:*** Peter Bernstein.

Hot Lead 🦴🦴 **1951** Typical Holt oater which has the cowpoke and his sidekick Martin trying to avenge the death of a close friend who was killed by a gang of train robbers. **60m/B VHS.** Tim Holt, Joan Dixon, Ross Elliott, John Dehner; ***D:*** Stuart Gilmore.

Hot Lead & Cold Feet 🦴🦴 **1978 (G)** Twin brothers (one a gunfighter, the other meek and mild) compete in a train race where the winner will take ownership of a small western town. Dale not only plays both brothers, but also their tough father. Standard Disney fare. **89m/C VHS.** Jim Dale, Don Knotts, Karen Valentine; ***D:*** Robert Butler; ***W:*** Arthur Alsberg; ***M:*** Buddy (Norman Dale) Baker.

The Hot Line 🦴½ *The Day the Hot Line Got Hot; Le Rouble a Deux Faces; El Rublo de las dos Caras* **1969** The world's two superpowers become befuddled when the hot line connecting Washington and Moscow breaks down. Taylor's final film. **87m/C VHS.** Robert Taylor, Charles Boyer, George Chakiris, Dominique Fabre, Gerard Tichy; ***D:*** Etienne Perier.

Hot Millions 🦴🦴🦴 **1968** Hysterical comedy about high-class swindling operation with Ustinov as a refined embezzler. Excellent cast and sharp script. Although it didn't do well at the boxoffice, this amusing romp became one of the biggest sleepers of the year. **106m/C VHS.** *GB* Peter Ustinov, Maggie Smith, Karl Malden, Bob Newhart, Robert Morley, Cesar Romero, Melinda May, Ann Lancaster, Margaret Courtenay, Lynda Baron, Billy Milton, Peter Jones, Raymond Huntley, Kynaston Reeves; ***D:*** Eric Till; ***W:*** Ira Wallach, Peter Ustinov; ***C:*** Ken Higgins.

Hot Money 🦴 **1979** A small-town drama about an ex-con who poses as an assistant sheriff and plots a million-dollar robbery during the town's 4th of July parade. Made shortly before Welles' death, and kept on the shelf for more than five years. **78m/C VHS.** Orson Welles, Michael Murphy, Bobby "Boris" Pickett, Michelle Finney.

Hot Moves 🦴 **1984 (R)** Four high school boys make a pact to lose their virginity before the end of the summer. **89m/C VHS.** Michael Zorek, Adam Silbar, Jill Schoelen, Deborah Richter, Monique Gabrielle, Tami Holbrook, Virgil Frye; ***D:*** Jim Sotos.

Hot Potato 🦴 **1976 (PG)** Black Belt Jones rescues a senator's daughter from a megalomaniacal general by using skull-thwacking footwork. **87m/C VHS.** Jim Kelly, George Memmoli, Geoffrey Binney; ***D:*** Oscar Williams.

Hot Pursuit 🦴½ **1984 (PG)** A woman who has been framed for murder runs from the law and a relentless hitman. **94m/C VHS.** Mike (Michael) Preston, Dina Merrill, Kerrie Keane.

Hot Pursuit 🦴½ **1987 (PG-13)** A prep-school bookworm resorts to Rambo-like tactics in tracking down his girlfriend and her family after being left behind for a trip to the tropics. **93m/C VHS, DVD, Wide.** Monte Markham, Shelley Fabares, Ben Stiller, John Cusack, Robert Loggia, Jerry Stiller, Wendy Gazelle; ***D:*** Steven Lisberger; ***W:*** Steven W. Carabatsos; ***C:*** Frank Tidy; ***M:*** Joseph Conlan.

Hot Resort 🦴½ **1985 (R)** Young American lads mix work and play when they sign on as summer help at an island resort. Typical teen sex fantasy. **92m/C VHS.** Bronson Pinchot, Tom Parsekian, Michael Berz, Linda Kenton, Frank Gorshin; ***D:*** John Robins; ***W:*** John Robins, Boaz Davidson.

The Hot Rock 🦴🦴🦴 *How to Steal a Diamond in Four Easy Lessons* **1970 (PG)** A motley crew of bumbling thieves conspire to steal a huge, priceless diamond; a witty, gritty comedy that makes no moral excuses for its characters and plays like an early-'70s crime thriller gone awry. Adapted from the novel by Donald E. Westlake. The sequel, 1974's "Bank Shot," stars George C. Scott in the role created by Redford. **97m/C VHS, Wide.** Robert Redford, George Segal, Ron Leibman, Zero Mostel, Moses Gunn, William Redfield, Charlotte Rae, Topo Swope; ***M:*** Quincy Jones.

Hot Rod 🦴 *Rebel of the Road* **1979** A young California hotrodder battles the evil sponsor of a drag race championship. **97m/C VHS.** Gregg Henry, Robert Culp, Pernell Roberts, Robin Mattson, Grant Goodeve; ***D:*** George Armitage.

Hot Rod Girl 🦴 *Hot Car Girl* **1956** A concerned police officer (Conners) organizes supervised drag racing after illegal drag racing gets out of hand in his community. **75m/B VHS, DVD.** Lori Nelson, Chuck Connors, John W. Smith; ***D:*** Leslie Martinson; ***W:*** John McGreevey; ***C:*** Sam Leavitt.

Hot Shot 🦴½ **1986 (PG)** An inspirational tale involving a young soccer player who goes to great lengths to take training from a soccer star, played—of course—by Pele. **90m/C VHS, DVD.** Pele, Jim Youngs, Billy Warlock, Weyman Thompson, Mario Van Peebles, David Groh; ***D:*** Rick King.

Hot Shots! 🦴🦴🦴 **1991 (PG-13)** Another entry from "The Naked Gun" team of master movie parodists, this has lots of clever sight gags but the verbal humor often plummets to the ground. Spoofs "Top Gun" and similar gung-ho air corps adventures but doesn't forget other popular films including "Dances with Wolves" and "The Fabulous Baker Boys." Sheen is very funny as ace fighter pilot Sean "Topper" Harley who's to avenge the family honor. Great when you're in the mood for laughs that don't require thought. **83m/C VHS.** Charlie Sheen, Cary Elwes, Valeria Golino, Lloyd Bridges, Kevin Dunn, Jon Cryer, William O'Leary, Kristy Swanson, Efrem Zimbalist Jr., Bill Irwin, Heidi Swedberg, Judith Kahan, Pat Proft; ***Cameos:*** Charles Barkley, Bill Laimbeer; ***D:*** Jim Abrahams; ***W:*** Pat Proft, Jim Abrahams; ***C:*** Bill Butler; ***M:*** Sylvester Levay.

Hot Shots! Part Deux 🦴🦴½ **1993 (PG-13)** Second "Hot Shots" outing doesn't live up to the first, but it's not bad either. Admiral Tug Benson (Bridges) is elected President (yes, of the U.S.) and calls on Sheen's newly pumped-up Topper to take on Saddam Hussein Rambo-style. Love interest Ramada (Golino), returns but this time she's competing with Michelle (Bakke), a sexy CIA agent. Crenna spoofs his role in the "Rambo" films as Sheen's mentor; look for real-life dad Martin in a take-off of "Apocalypse Now." Shtick flies as fast and furious as the bodies, with Bridges getting a chance to reprise his glory days of "Sea Hunt." Don't miss the credits. **89m/C VHS.** Charlie Sheen, Lloyd Bridges, Valeria Golino, Brenda Bakke, Richard Crenna, Miguel Ferrer, Rowan Atkinson, Jerry Haleva, Mitchell Ryan, Gregory Sierra, Ryan Stiles, Michael Colyar; ***Cameos:*** Martin Sheen, Bob Vila; ***D:*** Jim Abrahams; ***W:*** Pat Proft, Jim Abrahams; ***M:*** Basil Poledouris.

Hot Spell 🦴½ **1958** In an attempt to repair her marriage and unify her family, a mother plans a reunion-birthday party for her husband. Despair reigns in this sultry, Southern melodrama. **86m/B VHS.** Shirley Booth, Anthony Quinn, Shirley MacLaine, Earl Holliman, Eileen Heckart; ***D:*** Daniel Mann; ***C:*** Loyal Griggs; ***M:*** Alex North.

The Hot Spot 🦴🦴½ **1990 (R)** An amoral drifter arrives in a small Texas town and engages in affairs with two women, including his boss's over-sexed wife and a young woman with her own secrets. Things begin to heat up when he decides to plot a bank robbery. Based on Charles Williams' 1952 novel "Hell Hath No Fury." **120m/C VHS, DVD.** Don Johnson, Virginia Madsen, Jennifer Connelly, Charles Martin Smith, William Sadler, Jerry Hardin, Barry Corbin, Leon Rippy, Jack Nance; ***D:*** Dennis Hopper; ***W:*** Charles Williams, Nona Tyson; ***C:*** Ueli Steiger; ***M:*** Jack Nitzsche.

Hot Stuff 🦴 **1980 (PG)** Officers on a burglary task force decide the best way to obtain convictions is to go into the fencing business themselves. **91m/C VHS.** Dom DeLuise, Jerry Reed, Suzanne Pleshette, Ossie Davis; ***D:*** Dom DeLuise; ***W:*** Donald E. Westlake, Michael Kane.

Hot Summer 🦴🦴 *Heisser Sommer* **1968** A group of high school girls and boys meet on their way to a Baltic Sea vacation and begin their own version of the war between the sexes, especially since there's one more girl than boy. Then Kai (Schoel) and Brit (Doerk) decide they're in love, causing trouble for everyone else. Goofy teen romp starring pop stars Schoebel and Doerk that was the East German version of the sixties American beach movie. German with subtitles. **91m/C VHS, DVD.** *GE* Frank Schobel, Chris Doerk, Madeleine Lierck, Hanns-Michael Schmidt, Regine Albrecht; ***D:*** Joachim Hasler.

Hot Summer in Barefoot County 🦴🦴 **1974 (R)** A state law enforcement officer on the search for illegal moonshiners finds more than he bargained for. **90m/C VHS.** Sherry Robinson, Tonia Bryan, Dick Smith; ***D:*** Will Zens.

Hot T-Shirts woof! **1979 (R)** A small town bar owner needs a boost for business, finding the answer in wet T-shirt contests. Softcore trash. **86m/C VHS.** Ray Holland, Stephanie Lawlor, Pauline Rose, Corinne Alphen; ***D:*** Chuck Vincent.

Hot Target 🦴 **1985 (R)** An ideal mother becomes obsessed with the stranger who seduced her, even after she finds out he's a thief planning to rob her home. **93m/C VHS.** *NZ* Simone Griffeth, Steve Marachuk; ***D:*** Denis Lewiston.

Hot Times 🦴 **1974 (R)** Low-budget comedy about a high school boy who, after striking out with the high school girls, decides to go to New York and have the time of his life. **80m/C VHS.** Gail Lorber, Amy Farber, Henry Cory; ***D:*** Jim McBride; ***W:*** Jim McBride.

Hot to Trot! 🦴 **1988 (PG)** A babbling idiot links up with a talking horse in an updated version of the "Francis, the Talking Mule" comedies, by way of Mr. Ed. The equine voice is provided by Candy. Some real funny guys are wasted here. **90m/C VHS.** Bob(cat) Goldthwait, Dabney Coleman, Virginia Madsen, Jim Metzler, Cindy Pickett, Tim Kazurinsky, Santos Morales, Barbara Whinnery, Garry Kluger; ***D:*** Michael Dinner; ***W:*** Charlie Peters; ***M:*** Danny Elfman; ***V:*** John Candy.

Hot Touch woof! **198?** An art forger with a large heist is besieged by a slashing maniac, and must discover the culprit. **92m/C VHS.** Wayne Rogers, Samantha Eggar, Marie-France Pisier, Melvyn Douglas.

Hot Under the Collar 🦴½ **1991 (R)** Jerry is a weasel who tries to seduce the luscious Monica by using hypnosis. But his plans backfire and instead Monica enters a convent and takes a vow of chastity. This isn't going to stop Jerry, he tries posing as a priest and even dressing as a nun in order to get her out. Things get even more complicated when a mobster, looking for a fortune in stolen diamonds, sneaks into the convent. **87m/C VHS.** Richard Gabai, Angela Visser, Daniel Friedman, Melinda (Mindy) Clarke, Tane McClure; ***D:*** Richard Gabai.

Hot Wire 🦴½ **197?** Tired comedy about the unscrupulous side of the car repossession racket. **92m/C VHS.** George Kennedy, Strother Martin.

Hotel 🦴½ **1967 (PG)** A pale rehash of the "Grand Hotel" formula about an array of rich characters interacting in a New Orleans hotel. From the Arthur Hailey potboiler; basis for the TV series. **125m/C VHS.** Rod Taylor, Catherine Spaak, Karl Malden, Melvyn Douglas, Merle Oberon, Michael Rennie, Richard Conte, Kevin McCarthy; ***D:*** Richard Quine; ***W:*** Wendell Mayes; ***C:*** Charles B(ryant) Lang Jr.

Hotel Colonial 🦴½ **1988 (R)** A young Italian idealist ventures to Columbia to retrieve the body of his brother, who reportedly killed himself. Once there, he finds the dead man is not his brother, and decides to investigate. **103m/C VHS, 8mm.** *IT* Robert Duvall, John Savage, Rachel Ward, Massimo Troisi; ***D:*** Cinzia Torrini; ***W:*** Ira Barmak, Enzo Monteleone; ***M:*** Pino Donaggio.

Hotel de Love 🦴🦴½ **1996 (R)** Seventeen-year-old fraternal twin brothers Rick (Young) and Stephen Dunne (Bossell) both fall for beautiful Melissa (Burrows) and she has a short-lived romance with the more-aggressive Rick. Ten years later, mopey stockbroker Stephen shows up at the tacky theme honeymoon hotel Rick now manages and who should show up (besides the twins bickering parents) but Melissa and her fiance Norman (O'Brien). So the twins renew their competition while Melissa decides if Norman is the right guy for her, Mrs. Dunne gets mash notes from a secret admirer, and fortuneteller Alison (Grandison), who happens to be Rick's ex-girlfriend, offers romantic advice to Stephen. **93m/C VHS.** *AU* Aden Young, Simon Bossell, Saffron Burrows, Julia Blake, Ray Barrett, Pippa Grandison, Alan Hopgood, Peter O'Brien; ***D:*** Craig Rosenberg; ***W:*** Craig Rosenberg; ***C:*** Stephen Windon; ***M:*** Brett Rosenberg.

Hotel du Lac 🦴🦴 **1986** Adaptation of the Anita Brookner novel about a woman writer languishing at a Swiss lakefront hotel. **75m/C VHS.** *GB* Anna Massey, Denholm Elliott, Googie Withers; ***D:*** Giles Foster; ***M:*** Carl Davis. **TV**

Hotel Imperial 🦴🦴 **1927** Set in 1917 Budapest, six Hungarian soldiers ride into a frontier town and find it occupied by Russians. Hall plays Lieutenant Almasy, who takes refuge in the Hotel Imperial. Orchestra scored. **84m/B VHS.** Pola Negri, James Hall, George Siegmann, Max Davidson; ***D:*** Mauritz Stiller.

The Hotel New Hampshire 🦴🦴 **1984 (R)** The witless, amoral adaptation of John Irving's novel about a very strange family's adventures in New Hampshire, Vienna and New York City, which include gang rape, incest, and Kinski in a bear suit. **110m/C VHS, DVD, Wide.** Jodie Foster, Rob Lowe, Beau Bridges, Nastassia Kinski, Wallace Shawn, Wilford Brimley, Amanda Plummer, Anita Morris, Matthew Modine, Lisa Banes, Seth Green, Jennifer (Jennie) Dundas Lowe; ***D:*** Tony Richardson; ***W:*** Tony Richardson; ***C:*** David Watkin; ***M:*** Jacques Offenbach.

Hotel Paradiso 🦴🦴½ **1966** Slightly amusing bedroom farce has timid Guinness trying to carry on affair with Italian sexpot Lollibrigida. Guinness fans won't be disappointed, although it's not a top-rate production. Based on the play "L'Hotel du Libre Echange" by Georges Feydeau and Maurice Desvalliers. **100m/C VHS.** *GB* Alec Guinness, Gina Lollobrigida, Akim Tamiroff, Marie Bell, Derek Fowlds; ***D:*** Peter Glenville; ***W:*** Peter Glenville, Jean-Claude Carriere.

Hotel Reserve 🦴🦴🦴 **1944** A Nazi spy is reportedly afoot in a French resort during WWII, and tension mounts as the guests attempt to flush him out. Critical response to this film is wildly split; some find it obvious, while others call it well-done and suspenseful. Based on the novel "Epitaph for a Spy" by Eric Ambler. **79m/B VHS.** *GB* James Mason, Lucie Mannheim, Raymond Lovell, Julien Mitchell, Martin Miller, Herbert Lom, Frederick Valk, Valentine Dyall, Patricia Medina; ***D:*** Victor Hanbury, Lance Comfort, Max Greene.

Hotel Room 🦴🦴½ *David Lynch's Hotel Room* **1993** A trilogy of stories set in the same drab New York hotel room in three different time periods. "Getting Rid of Robert," set in 1992, has three girlfriends swilling champagne and discussing Sasha's slick, movie exec boyfriend whom she wants to dump. "Tricks," set in 1969, features Darlene, a bored, druggy prostitute; her client, Moe; and the sudden appearance of Moe's talkative friend, Lou. "Blackout" is set in 1936 and features a young husband trying to cope with the madness of his beautiful wife. Unfortunately, all three stories are rambling and lacking in energy. **100m/C VHS.** Deborah Kara Unger, Mariska Hargitay, Chelsea Field, Griffin Dunne, Glenne Headly, Harry Dean Stanton, Freddie Jones, Crispin Glover, Alicia Witt, Clark Heathcliffe Brolly, Camilla Overbye Roos; ***D:*** James Signorelli, David Lynch; ***W:*** Barry Gifford, Jay McInerney; ***M:*** Angelo Badalamenti. **CABLE**

Hothead 🦴🦴 *Coup de Tete* **1978** A heedless, impulsive soccer player's behavior gets him cut from the team, fired from his mill job, and booted out of his favorite bar. In French with English subtitles or dubbed. **98m/C VHS.** *FR* Patrick Dewaere, Jean Bouise, Michel Aumont, France Dougnac; ***D:*** Jean-Jacques Annaud; ***W:*** Francis Veber. Cesar '80: Support. Actor (Bouise).

Hotline 🦴🦴 **1982** After taking a job answering phones at a crisis center, a woman becomes the next target of a psychotic killer. **96m/C VHS.** Lynda Carter, Steve Forrest, Granville Van Dusen, Monte Markham, James Booth; ***D:*** Jerry Jameson. **TV**

H.O.T.S. 🦴 *T & A Academy* **1979 (R)** A sex-filled sorority rivalry film, starring a slew of ex-Playboy Playmates in wet shirts. Screenplay co-written by exploitation star Caffaro. **95m/C VHS, DVD, Wide.** Susan Kiger, Lisa London, Kimberly Cameron, Danny Bonaduce, Steve Bond; ***D:*** Gerald Seth Sindell; ***W:*** Cheri Caffaro, Joan Buchanan; ***C:*** Harvey Genkins; ***M:*** David Davis.

Houdini ½ **1953** Historically inaccurate but entertaining biopic of the infamous magician and escapologist. Chronicles his rise to stardom, his efforts to contact his dearly departed mother through mediums (a prequel to "Ghost"?), and his heart-stopping logic-defying escapes. First screen teaming of Leigh and Curtis, who had already been married for two years. **107m/C VHS.** Tony Curtis, Janet Leigh, Torin Thatcher, Angela Clark, Stefan Schnabel, Ian Wolfe, Sig Rumann, Michael Pate, Connie Gilchrist, Mary Murphy, Tor Johnson; ***D:*** George Marshall; ***W:*** Philip Yordan.

Houdini ½ **1999** New York Jewish youth Erich Weiss transforms himself into vaudeville magician/illusionist Harry Houdini (Schaech) and marries Bess (Edwards), who becomes his assistant. Houdini soon becomes a famed escape artist, pushing himself into ever-more dangerous stunts. After his beloved mother's death, Houdini then goes on a crusade to expose fake spiritualists who had promised him contact with her. **94m/C VHS.** Johnathon Schaech, Stacy Edwards, Grace Zabriskie, Paul Sorvino, Rhea Perlman, George Segal, David Warner, Mark Ruffalo, Ron Perlman, Judy Geeson; ***D:*** Pen Densham; ***W:*** Pen Densham; ***C:*** Gordon C. Lonsdale; ***M:*** Don Harper. **CABLE**

The Hound of London ½ *Sherlock Holmes in The Hound of London* **1993** Inspector Lestrade brings Sherlock Holmes (Macnee) his latest case, a double murder that has taken place at the Strand Theatre. And among the suspects is the only woman Holmes has ever admired, the lovely Irene Adler. Eccentric characters, a sword duel, backstage mischief, and Holmes and Watson together once more. Based on the play by Craig Bowlsby. **72m/C VHS.** *CA* Patrick Macnee, John Scott-Paget, Colin Skinner, Jack McCreath, Carolyn Wilkinson, Sophia Thornley, Drew Kemp, Ned Lemley, Craig Bowlsby; ***D:*** Gil Letourneau, Peter Reynolds-Long; ***W:*** Craig Bowlsby.

The Hound of the Baskervilles **1939** The curse of a demonic hound threatens descendants of an English noble family until Holmes and Watson solve the mystery. **80m/B VHS.** *GB* Basil Rathbone, Nigel Bruce, Richard Greene, John Carradine, Wendy Barrie, Lionel Atwill, E.E. Clive; ***D:*** Sidney Lanfield.

The Hound of the Baskervilles ½ **1959** Cushing's not half bad as Sherlock Holmes as he investigates the mystery of a supernatural hound threatening the life of a Dartmoor baronet. Dark and moody. **86m/C VHS, DVD, Wide.** *GB* Peter Cushing, Christopher Lee, Andre Morell; ***D:*** Terence Fisher; ***W:*** Peter Bryan; ***C:*** Jack Asher; ***M:*** James Bernard.

The Hound of the Baskervilles woof! **1977** Awful spoof of the Sherlock Holmes classic with Cook as Holmes and Moore as Watson (and Holmes' mother). Even the cast can't save it. **84m/C VHS.** Dudley Moore, Peter Cook, Denholm Elliott, Joan Greenwood, Spike Milligan, Jessie Matthews, Roy Kinnear; ***D:*** Paul Morrissey; ***W:*** Dudley Moore, Peter Cook, Paul Morrissey; ***C:*** Dick Bush; ***M:*** Dudley Moore.

The Hound of the Baskervilles **1983** Another remake of the Sherlock Holmes story which finds the great detective investigating the murder of Sir Charles Baskerville and a mysterious haunted moor. **100m/C VHS, DVD.** *GB* Ian Richardson, Donald Churchill, Martin Shaw, Nicholas Clay, Denholm Elliott, Brian Blessed, Ronald Lacey; ***D:*** Douglas Hickox; ***W:*** Charles Edward Pogue; ***C:*** Ronnie Taylor; ***M:*** Michael Lewis.

The Hound of the Baskervilles ½ **2000** Frewer takes on the role of Sherlock Holmes, emphasizing the character's cynical humor as well as his sometimes insufferable intelligence. Welsh ably backs him up as Watson and this version closely follows the Conan Doyle story. Sir Henry Baskerville (London) has inherited an estate with a curse and a devilish hound that terrorizes the moors. Holmes investigates. **90m/C VHS.** *CA* Matt Frewer, Kenneth Welsh, Jason London, Emma Campbell, Robin Wilcock, Arthur Holden, Leni Parker, Gordon Masten; ***D:*** Rodney Gibbons; ***W:*** Joe Wiesenfeld; ***C:*** Eric Cayla; ***M:*** Marc Ouellette. **CABLE**

Hour of Decision ½ **1957** When a newspaper columnist turns up dead, a reporter investigates the murder. Things get hairy when he finds the prime suspect is his own wife. **81m/B VHS.** *GB* Jeff Morrow, Hazel Court, Lionel Jeffries, Anthony Dawson, Mary Laura Wood; ***D:*** C.M. Pennington-Richards.

Hour of the Assassin ½ **1986 (R)** A mercenary is hired to assassinate a South American ruler, and a CIA operative is sent to stop him. Shot in Peru. **96m/C VHS.** Erik Estrada, Robert Vaughn; ***D:*** Luis Llosa.

Hour of the Gun **1967** Western saga chronicles what happens after the gunfight at the OK Corral. Garner plays the grim Wyatt Earp on the trail of vengeance after his brothers are killed. Robards is excellent as the crusty Doc Holliday. **100m/C VHS.** James Garner, Jason Robards Jr., Robert Ryan, Albert Salmi, Charles Aidman, Steve Ihnat, Jon Voight; ***D:*** John Sturges; ***W:*** Edward Anhalt; ***M:*** Jerry Goldsmith.

The Hour of the Star ½ *A Hora Da Estrela* **1985** The poignant, highly acclaimed feature debut by Amaral, about an innocent young woman moving to the city of Sao Paulo from the impoverished countryside of Brazil, and finding happiness despite her socioeconomic failures. Based on Clarice Lispector's novel. In Portuguese with English subtitles. **96m/C VHS.** *BR* Marcelia Cartaxo; ***D:*** Suzana Amaral. Berlin Intl. Film Fest. '85: Actress (Cartaxo).

Hour of the Wolf ½ *Vargtimmen* **1968** An acclaimed, surreal view into the tormented inner life of a painter as he and his wife are isolated on a small northern island. In Swedish with English subtitles. **89m/B VHS.** *SW* Max von Sydow, Liv Ullmann, Ingrid Thulin, Erland Josephson, Gertrud Fridh, Gudrun Brost, Georg Rydeberg, Naima Wifstrand, Bertil Anderberg, Ulf Johansson; ***D:*** Ingmar Bergman; ***W:*** Ingmar Bergman; ***C:*** Sven Nykvist; ***M:*** Lars Johan Werle. Natl. Bd. of Review '68: Actress (Ullmann); Natl. Soc. Film Critics '68: Director (Bergman).

Hourglass **1995 (R)** Fashion industry honcho Michael Jardine (Howell) risks his reputation and his life when he becomes involved with deadly, revenge-minded seductress Dara (Shinas), who blames the Jardines for her father's suicide. Another in a long line of be careful who you sleep with movies. **91m/C VHS.** C. Thomas Howell, Sofia Shinas, Ed Begley Jr., Timothy Bottoms, Anthony Clark; ***D:*** C. Thomas Howell; ***W:*** C. Thomas Howell, Darren Dalton; ***C:*** John Lambert; ***M:*** Chris Saranec.

The Hours and Times **1992** A concise drama based on one point of fact used to quietly evoke differences in class, talent, sexual orientation, and unrequited love. The fact is that in the spring of 1963 Brian Epstein, the Beatles brilliant homosexual manager, shared a four-day Barcelona vacation with John Lennon. Director Munch speculates that the sophisticated Epstein was hopelessly in love with the younger, working-class Lennon who is friendly but unresponsive to the courtship. A tender and rueful depiction of friendship longing to be something more. **60m/B VHS.** David Angus, Ian Hart, Stephanie Pack, Robin McDonald, Sergio Moreno, Unity Grimwood; ***D:*** Christopher Munch; ***W:*** Christopher Munch. Sundance '92: Special Jury Prize.

House **1986 (R)** Horror novelist Roger Cobb (Katt) moves into his dead aunt's supposedly haunted house only to find that the monsters don't necessarily stay in the closets. His worst nightmares come to life as he writes about his Vietnam experiences and is forced to relive the tragic events, but these aren't the only visions that start springing to life. It sounds depressing, but is actually a funny, intelligent "horror" flick. Followed by several lesser sequels. **93m/C VHS, DVD, Wide.** William Katt, George Wendt, Richard Moll, Kay Lenz, Michael Ensign, Mary Stavin, Susan French; ***D:*** Steve Miner; ***W:*** Ethan Wiley; ***C:*** Mac Ahlberg; ***M:*** Harry Manfredini.

House 2: The Second Story **1987 (PG-13)** The flaccid sequel to the haunted-house horror flick concerns two innocent guys who move into the family mansion and discover Aztec ghosts. Has none of the humor which helped the first movie along. **88m/C VHS, DVD, Wide.** John Ratzenberger, Arye Gross, Royal Dano, Bill Maher, Jonathan Stark, Lar Park Lincoln, Amy Yasbeck, Devin Devasquez; ***D:*** Ethan Wiley; ***W:*** Ethan Wiley; ***C:*** Mac Ahlberg.

House 4: Home Deadly Home ½ **1991 (R)** Another bad real estate epic on a par with the other unusually inept "House" efforts. When her husband (Katt) is killed in an auto accident, a young woman and her daughter move into a mysterious old house. Terror begins to confront them at every turn, threatening to destroy them both. We can only hope. **93m/C VHS.** Terri Treas, Scott Burkholder, Melissa Clayton, William Katt, Ned Romero; ***D:*** Lewis Abernathy.

House Across the Bay ½ **1940** Raft, an imprisoned nightclub owner, finds that he is being duped by his attorney who's eager to get his hooks into the lingerie-clad prisoner's wife. But prison isn't going to stop the bitter husband from getting his revenge. **88m/B VHS.** George Raft, Walter Pidgeon, Joan Bennett, Lloyd Nolan, Gladys George; ***D:*** Archie Mayo.

House Arrest ½ **1996 (PG)** Another tired kids-think-they-know-best formula film. When Grover Beindorf (Howard) and his younger sister learn that their constantly fighting parents (Curtis and Pollak) are separating, they lock them in the basement so they'll be forced to sort things out. Word gets around and some school pals kidnap their problem parents and stash them in the basement with the Beindorfs. Most of the movie was actually shot in a basement; watch for Curtis hanging upside down in a laundry chute "True Lies" style. **107m/C VHS, DVD.** Jamie Lee Curtis, Kevin Pollak, Christopher McDonald, Jennifer Tilly, Caroline Aaron, Wallace Shawn, Sheila McCarthy, Ray Walston, Kyle Howard, Amy Sakasitz, Jennifer Love Hewitt; ***D:*** Harry Winer; ***W:*** Michael Hitchcock; ***C:*** Ueli Steiger; ***M:*** Bruce Broughton.

The House by the Cemetery *Quella Villa Accanto Al Cimitero* **1983 (R)** When a family moves into a house close to a cemetery, strange things start to happen to them. **84m/C VHS, DVD, Wide.** *IT* Katherine (Katriona) MacColl, Paolo Malco, Giovanni Frezza; ***D:*** Lucio Fulci; ***W:*** Lucio Fulci, Dardano Sacchetti; ***C:*** Sergio Salvati; ***M:*** Walter Rizzati.

House Calls **1978 (PG)** A widowed surgeon turns into a swinging bachelor until he meets a witty but staid English divorcee. Wonderful dialogue. Jackson is exceptional. Made into a short-lived TV series. **98m/C VHS.** Walter Matthau, Glenda Jackson, Art Carney, Richard Benjamin, Candice Azzara; ***D:*** Howard Zieff; ***W:*** Charles Shyer; ***M:*** Henry Mancini.

A House Divided ½ **2000 (R)** Amanda (Beals) is the beloved only child of wealthy Georgia plantation owner David Dickson (Waterson) and is named as his heir when her father dies. But when Dickson's estranged brother (White) contests the will, family secrets come to light, including the devastating fact that Amanda's real mother is Julia (Hamilton), who was one of Dickson's slaves. And although it may be 1874, race is still definitely an issue. Based on a true court case described in the book "Woman of Color, Daughter of Privilege" by Kent Anderson Leslie. **99m/C VHS.** Sam Waterston, Jennifer Beals, Lisa Gay Hamilton, Timothy Daly, Ron White, Shirley Douglas, Sean McCann, Gerard Parkes, Colin Fox; ***D:*** John Kent Harrison; ***W:*** Paris Qualles; ***C:*** Kees Van Oostrum; ***M:*** Lawrence Shragge. **CABLE**

The House in Marsh Road **1960** A faithless husband decides to rid himself of She Who Must Be Obeyed, but his wife's ghost-friend intervenes. **70m/B VHS.** *GB* Tony Wright, Patricia Dainton, Sandra Dorne, Derek Aylward, Sam Kydd; ***D:*** Montgomery Tully.

A House in the Hills **1993 (R)** A struggling actress is housesitting at a luxurious estate and innocently lets in the exterminator. Except he's an ex-con looking for revenge on the home's current occupant (whom the actress is pretending to be) and may just exterminate her instead. **91m/C VHS.** Helen Slater, Michael Madsen, Jeffrey Tambor, James Laurenson, Elyssa Davalos, Toni Barry; ***D:*** Ken Wiederhorn; ***W:*** Ken Wiederhorn; ***C:*** Josep Civit; ***M:*** Richard Einhorn.

House of Angels *Anglagard; Colin Nutley's House of Angels* **1992 (R)** Charming comedy, with some serious overtones, about what happens to the gossipy inhabitants of a small Swedish village when two free-spirited newcomers come to stay. Fanny and her friend Zac, who are cabaret performers, show up at the funeral of eccentric Erik, who turns out to be the grandfather Fanny never knew. With her outrageous clothes and attitude, Fanny has most of the neighbors scandalized but what the generous Fanny wants is some information about her past, including who her father might be. What the neighbors want is for Fanny and Zac to leave as quickly as possible. In Swedish with English subtitles. **119m/C VHS.** *SW* Helena Bergstrom, Rikard Wolff, Sven Wollter, Jakob Eklund, Viveka Seldahl, Ernst Gunter, Reine Brynolfsson, Per Oscarsson; ***D:*** Colin Nutley; ***W:*** Susanne Falck.

House of Cards **1990** Depicts the political machinations of Machiavellian Tory whip Francis Urquhart (Richardson), who schemes to bring down the present government so that he can become the next Prime Minister. And there's absolutely nothing "F.U." (as he's appropriately known) won't do to achieve power. Followed by "To Play the King" and "The Final Cut"; based on the novel Michael Dobbs. On two cassettes. **200m/C VHS.** *GB* Ian Richardson, Susannah Harker.

House of Cards ½ **1992 (PG-13)** Precocious six-year-old Sally (Menina) suddenly stops talking after her father is killed in an accident at an archeological site in Mexico. Mom Ruth (Turner) fights to bring her daughter out of her fantasy world and seeks medical advice from a psychiatrist (a sympathetic Jones) but ignores it when it clashes with her own theories. The ethereal Menina, in her acting debut, gives the best performance in this weakly plotted and confusing family saga. **109m/C VHS.** Kathleen Turner, Asha Menina, Tommy Lee Jones, Shiloh Strong, Esther Rolle, Park Overall, Michael Horse, Anne Pitoniak; ***D:*** Michael Lessac; ***W:*** Michael Lessac; ***C:*** Victor Hammer.

House of Dark Shadows **1970 (PG)** Gory, intense feature-film version of the gothic TV daytime soap "Dark Shadows." Released from his coffin by a handyman seeking treasure, 150-year-old vampire Barnabas Collins (Frid) avails himself of the hospitality of his descendents and moves into a house on their property. As a series of vampire attacks plague the area, Barnabas finds himself involved with a love-smitten doctor who wants to cure him (Hall) and a young girl who resembles his lost love, Josette (Scott). A violent and exciting film, long on shocks but short on continuity and character development. **97m/C VHS.** Jonathan Frid, Joan Bennett, Grayson Hall, Kathryn Leigh Scott, Roger Davis, Nancy Barrett, John Karlen, Thayer David, Louis Edmonds; ***D:*** Dan Curtis; ***W:*** Sam Hall, Gordon Russell; ***C:*** Arthur Ornitz.

House of Death **1982 (R)** The ex-Playmate of the Year runs in hysterical fear from a knife-wielding lunatic. **88m/C VHS.** Susan Kiger, William T. Hicks, Jody Kay, Martin Tucker, Jennifer Chase.

The House of Dies Drear **1988** A modern-day African American family moves into an old house that turns out to be haunted by the ghost of a long dead abolitionist. The family is transported back to the days of slavery as they interact with the ghost. Based on the story by Virginia Hamilton. Aired on PBS as part of the "Wonderworks" family movie series. **107m/C VHS.** Howard E. Rollins Jr., Moses Gunn, Shavar Ross, Gloria Foster, Clarence Williams III; *D:* Allan Goldstein.

House of Dracula 🦴🦴 **1945** Sequel to "House of Frankenstein" features several of the Universal monsters. Overly ambitious story gets a bit hokey, but it's entertaining, nonetheless. **67m/B VHS.** Lon Chaney Jr., Martha O'Driscoll, John Carradine, Lionel Atwill, Onslow Stevens, Glenn Strange, Jane Adams, Ludwig Stossel; *D:* Erle C. Kenton; *W:* Edward T. Lowe; *C:* George Robinson.

House of Dreams 🦴 **1964** Berry is a blocked writer coping with domestic difficulties whose dreams reveal a disturbing future. Contains a bit part for Goodnow, now a CNN talking head. **80m/B VHS.** Robert Berry, Pauline Elliott, Charlene Bradley, Lance Bird, David Goodnow; *D:* Robert Berry.

The House of Eliott **1992** BBC miniseries set in 1920s London finds the orphaned Beatrice and Evangeline Eliott struggling to begin their fashion business as couturiers to the rich and influential, which eventually leads to their founding of the House of Eliott. Lots of romance and intrigue along the way. Boxed set of six cassettes. **600m/C VHS.** *GB* Stella Gonet, Louise Lombard, Aden (John) Gillett, Richard Lintern.

House of Errors 🦴½ **1942** Two deliverymen pose as reporters to safeguard a prototype machine gun from the bad guys. Contrived plot consisting of outdated comic routines. This was Marsh's last film. **63m/B VHS.** Harry Langdon, Marian Marsh, Ray Walker, Betty Blythe, John Holland; *D:* Bernard B. Ray.

House of Fear 🦴🦴½ **1945** Holmes and Watson investigate the murders of several members of the Good Comrades Club, men who were neither good nor comradely. **69m/B VHS.** Basil Rathbone, Nigel Bruce, Dennis Hoey, Aubrey Mather, Paul Cavanagh, Gavin Muir; *D:* Roy William Neill.

House of Frankenstein 🦴🦴½ **1944** An evil scientist (Karloff) escapes from prison, and, along with his hunchback manservant, revives Dracula, Frankenstein's monster, and the Wolfman to carry out his dastardly deeds. An all-star cast helps this horror fest along. **71m/B VHS, DVD.** Boris Karloff, J. Carrol Naish, Lon Chaney Jr., John Carradine, Elena Verdugo, Anne Gwynne, Lionel Atwill, Peter Coe, George Zucco, Glenn Strange, Sig Rumann; *D:* Erle C. Kenton; *W:* Edward T. Lowe; *C:* George Robinson.

House of Games 🦴🦴🦴 **1987 (R)** The directorial debut of playwright Mamet is a tale about an uptight female psychiatrist who investigates the secret underworld of con-artistry and becomes increasingly involved in an elaborate con game. She's led along her crooked path by smooth-talking con-master Mantegna. A taut, well plotted psychological suspense film with many twists and turns. Stylishly shot, with dialogue which has that marked Mamet cadence. Most of the leads are from Mamet's theatre throng (including his wife, Crouse). **102m/C VHS, DVD, Wide.** Joe Mantegna, Lindsay Crouse, Lilia Skala, J.T. Walsh, Meshach Taylor, Ricky Jay, Mike Nussbaum, Willo Hausman; *D:* David Mamet; *W:* David Mamet; *C:* Juan Ruiz-Anchia; *M:* Alaric Jans.

House of Horrors 🦴🦴½ **1946** Deformed murderer "The Creeper" (Hatton) is used by a mad sculptor in a twisted revenge plot. Marcel De Lange (Kosleck) believes his work has been vilely abused by art critics so he uses his friend's homicidal urges to get rid of anyone who stands in his way. **76m/B VHS.** Martin Kosleck, Rondo Hatton, Robert Lowery, Virginia Grey, Bill Goodwin, Alan Napier, Joan Shawlee, Howard Freeman; *D:* Jean Yarbrough; *W:* George Bricker.

House of Mirth 🦴🦴🦴 **2000 (PG-13)** The treacherous world of high society is the backdrop for savvy social climber Lily Bart (Anderson), who seeks to match her wits with an eligible bachelor's money in early 20th-century N.Y.C. Stoltz plays friend Selden who is not quite up to snuff financially for Lily, and Aykroyd, a well-heeled and seemingly well-meaning married "friend" who offers her investment advice...but at a hefty price. To make matter worse, a high-profile social maven (Linney) uses Lily to distract her husband from her own infidelities which puts Lily's reputation in jeopardy. With powerful friends lining up against her and her gambling debts piling up, the innocent Lily soon finds her once promising social position compromised. Disturbing but involving story made all the more so by Anderson's performance. Based on the novel by Edith Wharton. **140m/C VHS, DVD, Wide.** *GB US* Gillian Anderson, Eric Stoltz, Dan Aykroyd, Eleanor Bron, Terry Kinney, Anthony LaPaglia, Laura Linney, Jodhi May, Elizabeth McGovern; *D:* Terence Davies; *W:* Terence Davies; *C:* Remi Adefarasin.

House of Mystery 🦴🦴 **1934** For a shot at some priceless jewels stolen by the host from a Hindu princess, several guests gather for a weekend in a spine-tingling mansion. A creepy curse keeps them looking over their shoulders. **62m/C VHS.** Ed Lowry, Verna Hillie, Brandon Hurst, George "Gabby" Hayes; *D:* William Nigh.

House of Mystery 🦴🦴½ *At the Villa Rose* **1941** Splendid British remake of 1934 film in which the detective does some true sleuthing to catch the culprits. An old widow is killed for her jewels, but the murderers can't locate the goods. After they try a series of fiendish plans to retrieve them, the detective must work to stop the crooks. **61m/B VHS.** *GB* Kenneth Kent, Judy Kelly, Peter Murray Hill, Walter Rilla, Ruth Maitland; *D:* Walter Summers.

The House of 1000 Dolls 🦴 *Haus Der Tausend Freuden* **1967** Doleful, not dollful, exploitation thriller as magician Price drugs young girls and sells them to slavery rings. An international production set in Tangiers; dialogue is dubbed. **79m/C VHS.** *GE SP GB* Vincent Price, Martha Hyer, George Nader, Ann Smyrner, Maria Rohm; *D:* Jeremy Summers.

House of Psychotic Women woof! *Los Ojos Azules de la Muneca Rota; Blue Eyes of the Broken Doll* **1973 (R)** Naschy, Spain's premier horror movie star, plays a studly drifter who winds up in the home of three sisters, one with an artifical arm, one confined to a wheelchair and the other a nymphomaniac. No problemo thinks the hirsute Spaniard, until a series of bizarre murders—in which the victims eyes are ripped out—spoils his fun. Naschy, who usually sprouts fur and fangs, actually doesn't turn into a werewolf. Catchy but inappropriate score. A must for Naschy/bad movie fans. **87m/C VHS.** *SP* Paul (Jacinto Molina) Naschy, Maria Perschy, Diana Lorys, Eva Leon, Ines Morales, Tony Pica, Jacinto (Jack) Molina; *D:* Carlos Aured; *W:* Jacinto (Jack) Molina; *C:* Francisco Sanchez.

The House of Secrets 🦴🦴 **1937** A Yank travels to Britain to collect an inheritance and stays in a dusty old mansion filled with an odd assortment of characters. **70m/B VHS.** Leslie Fenton, Muriel Evans, Noel Madison, Sidney Blackmer, Morgan Wallace, Holmes Herbert; *D:* Roland D. Reed.

The House of Seven Corpses 🦴🦴 **1973 (PG)** A crew attempts to film a horror movie in a Victorian manor where seven people died in a variety of gruesome manners. Things take a turn for the ghoulish when a crew member becomes possesed by the house's evil spirits. Good, low budget fun with a competent "B" cast. Filmed in what was the Utah governor's mansion. **90m/C VHS, DVD, Wide.** John Ireland, Faith Domergue, John Carradine, Carole Wells; *D:* Paul Harrison; *W:* Paul Harrison, Thomas J. Kelly.

House of Shadows 🦴½ **1983** A 20-year-old murder comes back to haunt the victim's friends in this tale of mystery and terror. **90m/C VHS.** John Gavin, Yvonne De Carlo, Leonor Manso; *D:* Richard Wulicher.

House of Strangers 🦴🦴🦴½ **1949** Conte, in a superb performance, swears vengeance on his brothers, whom he blames for his father's death. Robinson, in a smaller part than you'd expect from his billing, is nevertheless excellent as the ruthless banker father who sadly reaps a reward he didn't count on. Based on Philip Yordan's "I'll Never Go There Again." **101m/B VHS.** Edward G. Robinson, Susan Hayward, Richard Conte, Luther Adler, Efrem Zimbalist Jr., Debra Paget; *D:* Joseph L. Mankiewicz; *W:* Philip Yordan; *C:* Milton Krasner. Cannes '49: Actor (Robinson).

House of Terror 🦴 *The Five at the Funeral; Scream Bloody Murder* **1987** A woman and her boyfriend plot to kill her rich boss, while they too are being stalked by some undefined horror. **91m/C VHS.** Jennifer Bishop, Arell Blanton, Jacquelyn Hyde; *D:* Sergei Goncharoff.

The House of the Arrow 🦴🦴🦴 **1953** Investigating the murder of a French widow, who was killed by a poisoned arrow, a detective must sort through a grab bag of potential suspects. Superior adaptation of the A.E.W. Mason thriller. **73m/B VHS.** *GB* Oscar Homolka, Yvonne Furneaux, Robert Urquhart; *D:* Michael Anderson Sr.

House of the Black Death 🦴½ *Blood of the Man Devil; Night of the Beast* **1965** Horror titans Chaney and Carradine manage to co-star in this as warring warlocks, yet they share no scenes together! Chaney is the evil warlock (the horns are a giveaway) holding people hostage in the title edifice. **89m/B VHS.** Lon Chaney Jr., John Carradine, Katherine Victor, Tom Drake, Andrea King; *D:* Harold Daniels, Reginald LeBorg.

House of the Damned 🦴½ **1971** A young woman, a mental hospital, a murdered father, a priceless gold statue—mix together and you get a mystery horror movie. A woman tries to solve her father's murder. **89m/C VHS.** Donald Pleasence, Michael Dunn; *D:* Gonzalo Suarez.

House of the Dead 🦴 **1980** Man is trapped inside a haunted house. Scary. **100m/C VHS.** John Ericson, Charles Aidman, Bernard Fox, Ivor Francis.

House of the Living Dead 🦴 *Doctor Maniac* **1973 (PG)** Brattling Manor harbors a murderous and flesh-eating secret ready to lure the unsuspecting. Don't you be one. **87m/C VHS.** *SA* Mark Burns, Shirley Anne Field, David Oxley; *D:* Ray Austin.

House of the Long Shadows 🦴½ **1982 (PG)** Comedy mixes with gore, as four of the horror screen's best leading men team up for the first time, although they have only minor roles. Might have been a contender, but Arnaz is miscast as author who stays in spooky house on a bet with Todd. Some wit but not enough. Based on the play "Seven Keys to Baldpate" by George M. Cohan (and novel by Earl Derr Biggers). **96m/C VHS.** *GB* Vincent Price, Christopher Lee, Peter Cushing, John Carradine, Desi Arnaz Jr., Sheila Keith, Richard Todd; *D:* Pete Walker; *W:* Michael Armstrong; *C:* Norman G. Langley.

House of the Rising Sun 🦴½ **1987** A Los Angeles reporter goes under cover for a story on an exclusive brothel only to discover the owner is a psychopath who has very permanent ways of dealing with troublesome employees. **86m/C VHS.** John York, Bud Davis, Deborah Wakeham, Frank Annese; *D:* Greg Gold; *M:* Tina Turner, Bryan Ferry.

The House of the Seven Gables 🦴🦴½ **1940** Nathaniel Hawthorne's brooding novel about greed and a family curse. Jaffrey Pyncheon (Sanders) frames his brother Clifford (Price) for the murder of their father so that he can search in peace for the fortune Jaffrey believes is hidden somewhere in the family mansion, Seven Gables. But, eventually, Clifford gets out of prison and returns to claim his birthright. The studio built an exact duplicate of the original Salem house. **89m/B VHS.** George Sanders, Vincent Price, Margaret Lindsay, Dick Foran, Nan Grey, Cecil Kellaway, Alan Napier; *D:* Joe May; *W:* Harold Greene; *C:* Milton Krasner.

The House of the Spirits 🦴🦴 **1993 (R)** Star-studded adaptation of the novel by Isabel Allende is a multi-generational saga following the fortunes of the powerful Trueba family. The ambitious Esteban (Irons) marries the clairvoyant Clara (Streep), exploits the peasants on his property, and becomes a conservative senator. Their rebellious daughter Blanca (Ryder) falls for rabble-rousing peasant Pedro (Banderas), and the country undergoes a bloody revolution. Magical realism of the novel is lost in screen melodrama, with the international cast ill-served by tepid direction. The child Clara is played by Streep's daughter, Mary Willa (listed in the credits as Jane Gray). **109m/C VHS, DVD, Wide.** Meryl Streep, Jeremy Irons, Glenn Close, Winona Ryder, Antonio Banderas, Armin Mueller-Stahl, Vanessa Redgrave, Sarita Choudhury, Maria Conchita Alonso, Vincent Gallo, Miriam Colon, Jan Niklas, Teri Polo, Jane Gray; *D:* Bille August; *W:* Bille August; *C:* Jorgen Persson; *M:* Hans Zimmer.

House of the Yellow Carpet 🦴½ **1984** A couple try to sell an ancient Persian carpet heirloom, and in doing so transgress some unwritten mystical law. Havoc ensues. **90m/C VHS.** Roland Josephson, Beatrice Romand; *D:* Carlo Lizzani.

The House of Usher 🦴 *Edgar Allen Poe's House of Usher; The Fall of the House of Usher* **1988 (R)** Some serious overacting by Reed (as Roderick) and Pleasence (as his balmy brother) almost elevate this Poe retread to "so bad it's good" status, and there are a few admirably grisly moments. But, without other camp virtues, it's merely dreary. Adapted by Michael J. Murray and filmed in South Africa. **92m/C VHS.** *SA* Oliver Reed, Donald Pleasence, Romy Windsor, Rufus Swart, Norman Coombes, Anne Stradi; *D:* Alan Birkinshaw; *W:* Michael J. Murray; *C:* Yossi Wein; *M:* Gary Chang.

House of Wax 🦴🦴🦴 **1953 (PG)** A deranged sculptor (Price, who else?) builds a sinister wax museum which showcases creations that were once alive. A remake of the early horror flick "Mystery of the Wax Museum," and one of the '50s most popular 3-D films. This one still has the power to give the viewer the creeps, thanks to another chilling performance by Price. Look for a very young Charles Bronson, as well as Carolyn "Morticia Addams" Jones as a victim. **88m/C VHS.** Vincent Price, Frank Lovejoy, Carolyn Jones, Phyllis Kirk, Paul Cavanagh, Charles Bronson, Paul Picerni, Angela Clarke; *D:* Andre de Toth; *W:* Crane Wilbur; *C:* Bert Glennon; *M:* David Buttolph.

House of Whipcord woof! **1975** Beautiful young women are kidnapped and tortured in this British gore-o-rama. Awful and degrading. **102m/C VHS, DVD.** *GB* Barbara Markham, Patrick Barr, Ray Brooks, Penny Irving, Anne Michelle, Ivor Salter, Robert Tayman; *D:* Pete Walker; *W:* David McGillivray; *C:* Peter Jessop; *M:* Stanley Myers.

The House of Yes 🦴🦴 **1997 (R)** Thanksgiving certainly brings out the worst in families although the Pascal clan is dysfunction personified. Marty (Hamilton) brings home fiancee Lesley (Spelling) to meet his eccentric mom (Bujold) and siblings. Younger brother Anthony's (Prinze) a dropout with no direction and Marty's twin sister Jackie-O (Parker) is bonkers. She's recreated herself as Jackie Kennedy Onassis and has had a very intimate relationship with Marty that Lesley probably doesn't know about. **90m/C VHS, DVD.** Parker Posey, Josh Hamilton, Tori Spelling, Freddie Prinze Jr., Genevieve Bujold, Rachael Leigh Cook; *D:* Mark Waters; *W:* Mark Waters; *C:* Michael Spiller; *M:* Jeff Rona.

The House on Carroll Street 🦴½ **1988 (PG)** New York 1951, the middle of the McCarthy era. A young woman overhears a plot to smuggle Nazi war criminals into the U.S. She's already lost her job because of accusations of subversion, and it's not easy persuading FBI agent Daniels that she knows what she's talking about. Contrived plot and melodramatic finale help sink this period piece. **111m/C VHS.** Kelly McGillis, Jeff Daniels, Mandy Patinkin, Jessica Tandy; *D:* Peter Yates; *W:* Walter Bernstein; *C:* Michael Ballhaus; *M:* Georges Delerue.

The House on Chelouche Street 🦴🦴½ **1973** In Tel-Aviv, during the summer of 1946, 15-year-old Sami, an Egyptian immigrant, tries to help support his mother and family during the upheavals of Palestine under the British mandate. A well thought-out story detailing the struggles of a North African Jewish family before the creation of the country of Israel. In Hebrew with English subtitles. **111m/C**

VHS. *IS* Gila Almagor, Michal Bat-Adam, Shai K. Ophir; *D:* Moshe Mizrahi.

The House on Garibaldi Street 🦴🦴½ **1979** Spy drama about the capture of Nazi war criminal Adolph Eichmann in Argentina and his extradition to Israel for trial. Based on the book by Isser Harel. **96m/C VHS.** Chaim Topol, Nick Mancuso, Martin Balsam, Janet Suzman, Leo McKern, Charles Gray, Alfred Burke; *D:* Peter Collinson; *M:* Charles Bernstein. **TV**

House on Haunted Hill 🦴🦴½ **1958** A wealthy man throws a haunted house party and offers $10,000 to anyone who can survive the night there. Vintage cheap horror from the master of the macabre Castle. Remembered for Castle's in-theatre gimmick of dangling a skeleton over the audiences' heads in the film's initial release. **75m/B VHS, DVD.** Vincent Price, Carol Ohmart, Richard Long, Alan Marshal, Carolyn Craig, Elisha Cook Jr., Julie Mitchum, Howard Hoffman; *D:* William Castle; *W:* Robb White; *C:* Carl Guthrie; *M:* Von Dexter.

House on Haunted Hill 🦴🦴½ **1999 (R)** This remake of William Castle's 1958 B-movie doesn't reach too far above its predecessor. In an homage to original star Vincent Price, Geoffrey Rush plays mincing amusement park tycoon Stephen Price, who invites a few friends over for his wife Evelyn's (Janssen) birthday. However, he invites them to a haunted former insane asylum, and offers them a million bucks if they can stick it out for the entire night. Stephen and the scheming Evelyn have a few tricks rigged for the guests, who all end up having some connection to the horrors that went on in the house in the bad old days. Soon, however, actual supernatural creepiness starts thinning the ranks of the guests. Unashamedly bloody and cheesy. **96m/C VHS, DVD.** Geoffrey Rush, Famke Janssen, Taye Diggs, Peter Gallagher, Chris Kattan, Ali Larter, Bridgette Wilson, Max Perlich, Jeffrey Combs; *D:* William Malone; *W:* Dick Beebe; *C:* Rick Bota; *M:* Don Davis.

House on 92nd Street 🦴🦴🦴 **1945** Documentary-style thriller finds federal investigator George Briggs (Nolan) contacted by German-American student Bill Dietrich (Eythe), who's been sought out by Nazi spies. Briggs encourages Dietrich to play along and report their nefarious activities to the feds. What Dietrich discovers is that a scientist, working on the atomic bomb project, is actually a Nazi agent. Lots of atmosphere and action, with director Hathaway incorporating newsreel footage to highlight the true-to-life feel. Title refers the the house where the head of the Nazi spies resides. **89m/B VHS.** William Eythe, Lloyd Nolan, Signe Hasso, Gene Lockhart, Leo G. Carroll, William Post Jr., Harry Bellaver; *D:* Henry Hathaway; *W:* Barre Lyndon, John Monks Jr., Charles G. Booth; *C:* Norbert Brodine; *M:* David Buttolph. Oscars '45: Story.

The House on Skull Mountain 🦴½ **1974 (PG)** The four surviving relatives of a deceased voodoo priestess are in for a bumpy night as they gather at the House on Skull Mountain for the reading of her will. **85m/C VHS.** Victor French, Janee Michelle, Mike Evans, Jean Durand; *D:* Ron Honthaner.

The House on Sorority Row 🦴½ *House of Evil; Seven Sisters* **1983** Less-than-harrowing story of what happens when seven sorority sisters have a last fling and get back at their housemother at the same time. **90m/C VHS, DVD, Wide.** Eileen Davidson, Kate McNeil, Robin Meloy, Lois Kelso Hunt, Christopher Lawrence, Janis Zido; *D:* Mark Rosman; *W:* Mark Rosman; *C:* Tim Suhrstedt; *M:* Richard Band.

The House on Straw Hill 🦴½ *Expose; Trauma* **1976 (R)** A successful novelist is intrigued by an attractive woman who lives in an isolated farmhouse. Her presence inspires gory hallucinations, lust, and violence. **84m/C VHS.** *GB* Udo Kier, Linda Hayden, Fiona Richmond, Karl Howman, Patsy Smart; *D:* James Kenelm Clarke; *W:* James Kenelm Clarke; *C:* Denis Lewiston.

House on the Edge of the Park woof! *La Casa Nel Parco* **1984** A frustrated would-be womanizer takes revenge on a parade of women during an all-night party. **91m/C VHS.** *IT* David A(lexander) Hess, Annie Belle, Lorraine (De Sette) De Selle; *D:* Ruggero Deodato.

The House on Todville Road 🦴 **1995 (R)** Fact-based story about a dangerous cult and its followers. **94m/C VHS.** David Harrod, Terri Harrel, Lisa Marie Newmyer.

The House on Tombstone Hill 🦴½ **1992** An old, abandoned mansion seems like a good investment to a group of friends. Wrong! The original owner is still around and doesn't like strangers coming to visit. **95m/C VHS.** Doug Gibson, John Dayton (J.D.) Cerna, Sarah Newhouse; *D:* J. Riffel; *W:* J. Riffel.

House Party 🦴🦴🦴 **1990 (R)** Lighthearted, black hip-hop version of a '50s teen comedy with rap duo Kid 'n' Play. After his father grounds him for fighting, a high-schooler attempts all sorts of wacky schemes to get to his friend's party. Sleeper hit features real-life music rappers and some dynamite dance numbers. **100m/C VHS, DVD, Wide.** Christopher Reid, Christopher Martin, Martin Lawrence, Tisha Campbell, Paul Anthony, A.J. (Anthony) Johnson, Robin Harris; *D:* Reginald (Reggie) Hudlin; *W:* Reginald (Reggie) Hudlin; *C:* Peter Deming; *M:* Marcus Miller. Sundance '90: Cinematog.

House Party 2: The Pajama Jam 🦴🦴½ **1991 (R)** Rap stars Kid 'N' Play are back in this hip-hop sequel to the original hit. At Harris University Kid 'N' Play hustle up overdue tuition by holding a campus "jammie jam jam." A stellar cast shines in this rap-powered pajama bash. **94m/C VHS, DVD, Wide.** Christopher Reid, Christopher Martin, Tisha Campbell, Iman, Queen Latifah, Georg Stanford Brown, Martin Lawrence, Eugene Allen, George Anthony Bell, Kamron, Tony Burton, Helen Martin, William Schallert; *D:* Doug McHenry, George Jackson; *W:* Rusty Cundieff, Daryl G. Nickens; *M:* Vassal Benford.

House Party 3 🦴 **1994 (R)** Kid is engaged to be married and Play tries to set up a blowout bachelor party. The duo are also working on their record producer careers by trying to sign a feisty female rap group (real life TLC). Strikes out early for easy profanity while never coming within spitting distance of first two flicks. **93m/C VHS, DVD, Wide.** Christopher Reid, Christopher Martin, Angela Means, Tisha Campbell, Bernie Mac, Barbara (Lee) Edwards, Michael Colyar, David Edwards, Betty Lester, Chris Tucker; *D:* Eric Meza; *W:* Takashi Bufford; *M:* David Allen Jones.

The House that Bled to Death 🦴 **1981** Strange things happen to a family when they move into a rundown house where a murder occurred years before. **60m/C VHS.** Nicholas Ball, Rachel Davies, Brian Croucher, Pat Maynard, Emma Ridley.

The House that Dripped Blood 🦴🦴½ **1971 (PG)** A Scotland Yard inspector discovers the history of an English country house while investigating an actor's disappearance. Four horror tales comprise the body of this omnibus creeper, following the successful "Tales from the Crypt" mold. Duffell's debut as director. **101m/C VHS.** *GB* Christopher Lee, Peter Cushing, Jon Pertwee, Denholm Elliott, Ingrid Pitt, John Bennett, Tom Adams, Joss Ackland, Chloe Franks; *D:* Peter Duffell; *W:* Robert Bloch.

The House that Vanished 🦴 *Scream and Die; Psycho Sex Fiend* **1973 (R)** Semi-exploitative fare about a beautiful young model who witnesses a murder in a house but later can't find the place. Her boyfriend is skeptical. **84m/C VHS.** *GB* Andrea Allan, Karl Lanchbury, Judy Matheson, Maggie Walker, Alex Leppard; *D:* Joseph (Jose Ramon) Larraz.

House Where Evil Dwells 🦴½ **1982 (R)** An American family is subjected to a reign of terror when they move into an old Japanese house possessed by three deadly samurai ghosts. The setting doesn't upgrade the creepiness of the plot. Based on a novel by James Hardiman. **88m/C VHS.** Edward Albert, Susan George, Doug McClure, Amy Barett, Mako Hattori, Toshiya Maruyama, Henry Mitowa, Tsuyako Okajima, Tsuiyuki Sasaki; *D:* Kevin Connor; *W:* Robert Suboksky; *C:* Jacques Haitkin.

A House without a Christmas Tree 🦴🦴½ **1972** A frustrated middle-aged man denies his young daughter her one desire—a Christmas tree. Charming TV holiday fare. **90m/C VHS.** Jason Robards Jr., Lisa Lucas, Mildred Natwick; *D:* Paul Bogart. **TV**

Houseboat 🦴🦴½ **1958** Widower Grant with three precocious kids takes up residence on a houseboat with Italian maid Loren who is actually a socialite, incognito. Naturally, they fall in love. Light, fun Hollywood froth. **110m/C** Cary Grant, Sophia Loren, Martha Hyer, Eduardo Ciannelli, Murray Hamilton, Harry Guardino; *D:* Melville Shavelson; *W:* Melville Shavelson, Jack Rose; *M:* George Duning.

Houseguest 🦴🦴 **1994 (PG)** Dumb comedy about mistaken identity finds hard luck dreamer Kevin Franklin (Sinbad) on the run from loan sharks. Fortunately, while trying to make a getaway at the airport, he's mistaken for the childhood buddy (who's also an eminent dentist prompting some hygiene humor) of family guy/lawyer Gary Young (Hartman), who opens his suburban home to his long lost pal. Street smart Kevin naturally manages to solve every dysfunctional family problem that arises while avoiding some inept Mafia thugs. Everyone is oh-so-good-natured but there's nothing new to hold much interest. **109m/C VHS.** Sinbad, Phil Hartman, Jeffrey Jones, Kim Greist, Stan Shaw, Tony Longo, Mason Adams, Paul Ben-Victor, Chauncey Leopardi, Ron Glass, Talia Seider, Kim Murphy; *D:* Randall Miller; *W:* Michael J. Di Gaetano, Laurence Gay; *C:* Jerzy Zielinski; *M:* John Debney.

Household Saints 🦴🦴🦴 **1993 (R)** Chronicling one family from post-WWII Little Italy through the 1970s, this is a quirky little story about sausage, religion, women, and families (not necessarily in that order). Joseph (D'Onofrio) wins his bride (Ullman) in a pinochle game, much to his superstitious Catholic mother's (Malina) chagrin. The product of that union is a slightly obsessive girl (Taylor), who sees visions and wants to be a saint. Interesting study of Italian-American families, and the roles religion and food play in the culture of Little Italy. **124m/C VHS.** Tracey Ullman, Vincent D'Onofrio, Lili Taylor, Judith Malina, Michael Rispoli, Victor Argo, Michael Imperioli, Rachael Bella, Illeana Douglas, Joe Grifasi, Sebastien Roche; *D:* Nancy Savoca; *W:* Nancy Savoca, Richard Guay; *C:* Bobby Bukowski; *M:* Stephen Endelman. Ind. Spirit '94: Support. Actress (Taylor).

The Householder 🦴🦴 *Gharbar* **1963** An early Merchant-Ivory collaboration featuring a young Indian schoolteacher whose widowed mother arranges his marriage to a woman he doesn't know. The immature couple find their adjustment to marriage fraught with, sometimes amusing, complications. **101m/B VHS.** *IN* Shashi Kapoor, Leela Naidu, Durga Khote; *D:* James Ivory; *W:* Ruth Prawer Jhabvala.

The Housekeeper 🦴🦴 *A Judgement in Stone* **1986 (R)** Tushingham's portrayal of a deranged housekeeper brings this movie to life even as she kills off her employers. **97m/C VHS.** *CA* Rita Tushingham, Ross Petty, Jackie Burroughs, Tom Kneebone, Shelly Peterson, Jessica Steen, Jonathan Crombie; *D:* Ousama Rawi.

Housekeeping 🦴🦴🦴 **1987 (PG)** A quiet but bizarre comedy by Forsyth (his first American film). A pair of orphaned sisters are cared for by their newly arrived eccentric, free-spirited aunt in a small and small-minded community in Oregon in the 1950s. Conventional townspeople attempt to intervene, but the sisters' relationship with their offbeat aunt has become strong enough to withstand the coercion of the townspeople. May move too slowly for some viewers. Based on novel by Marilynne Robinson. **117m/C VHS.** Christine Lahti, Sarah Walker, Andrea Burchill; *D:* Bill Forsyth; *W:* Bill Forsyth; *C:* Michael Coulter; *M:* Michael Gibbs.

Housemaster 🦴🦴½ **1938** In a British boys' school the housemaster is kind and understanding of his sometimes-unruly charges. The stern new headmaster is not, and the students conspire against him. An okay but dated comedy, featuring characters with names like Bimbo and Button. Based on "Bachelor Born" by Ian Hay, a London stage hit at the time. **95m/B VHS.** Otto Kruger, Diana Churchill, Phillips Holmes, Rene Ray, Walter Hudd, George L. Baxt, Cecil Parker, Michael Shepley, Jimmy Hanley, Rosamund Barnes; *D:* Herbert Brenon.

Housesitter 🦴🦴½ **1992 (PG)** Newton Davis (Martin), an architect/dreamer, builds his high school sweetheart (Delany) a beautiful house and surprises her with a marriage proposal. Delany says no, he has a one-night stand with Gwen (Hawn), and Hawn moves into his empty house and assumes the position of Davis's wife, unbeknownst to him. Gwen spins whoppers of lies and soon has the entire town, including Davis's parents and ex-girlfriend, believing her wacky stories. This romantic screwball comedy is a delight, not only because of Martin and Hawn, but also because of the array of other characters who complicate the stories they spin. **102m/C VHS, DVD.** Steve Martin, Goldie Hawn, Dana Delany, Julie Harris, Donald Moffat, Peter MacNicol, Richard B. Shull, Laurel Cronin, Christopher Durang; *D:* Frank Oz; *W:* Mark Stein, Brian Grazer; *C:* John A. Alonzo; *M:* Miles Goodman.

Housewife 🦴🦴 *Bone; Beverly Hills Nightmare; Dial Rat for Terror* **1972 (R)** Bone (Kotto) is a vengeful black man, who holds an unhappily married Beverly Hills couple (Duggan and Van Patten) hostage in their home. **96m/C VHS.** Yaphet Kotto, Andrew Duggan, Joyce Van Patten, Jeannie Berlin; *D:* Larry Cohen; *W:* Larry Cohen; *C:* George Folsey Jr.; *M:* Gil Melle.

How Come Nobody's On Our Side? 🦴 **1973 (PG)** Two out-of-work stuntmen try astrology to find the best time to make some easy money smuggling marijuana out of Mexico. **84m/C VHS.** Adam Roarke, Larry Bishop, Alexandra Hay, Rob Reiner, Penny Marshall; *W:* Leigh Chapman.

How Funny Can Sex Be? 🦴🦴 **1976 (R)** Eight risque sketches about love and marriage Italian style. **97m/C VHS.** *IT* Giancarlo Giannini, Laura Antonelli, Dulio Del Prete; *D:* Dino Risi.

How Green Was My Valley 🦴🦴🦴🦴 **1941** Compelling story of the trials and tribulations of a Welsh mining family, from the youthful perspective of the youngest child (played by a 13-year-old McDowall). Spans 50 years, from the turn of the century, when coal mining was a difficult but fair-paying way of life, and ends, after unionization, strikes, deaths, and child abuse, with the demise of a town and its culture. Considered by many to be director Ford's finest work. When WWII prevented shooting on location, producer Zanuck built a facsimile Welsh valley in California (although Ford, born Sean Aloysius O'Fearna, was said to have been thinking of his story as taking place in Ireland rather than Wales). Based on the novel by Richard Llewellyn. **118m/C VHS, DVD.** Walter Pidgeon, Maureen O'Hara, Donald Crisp, Anna Lee, Roddy McDowall, John Loder, Sara Allgood, Barry Fitzgerald, Patric Knowles, Rhys Williams, Arthur Shields, Ann E. Todd, Mae Marsh; *D:* John Ford; *W:* Philip Dunne; *C:* Arthur C. Miller; *M:* Alfred Newman; *Nar:* Irving Pichel. Oscars '41: B&W Cinematog., Director (Ford), Picture, Support. Actor (Crisp), Natl. Film Reg. '90;; N.Y. Film Critics '41: Director (Ford).

How High 🦴🦴½ **2001 (R)** Genial stoner comedy finds tokers Silas (Method Man) and Jamal (Redman) smoking some extra-potent "smart" ganja that magically gets them into Harvard. There the laid back homeboys clash with uptight Dean Cain (Babatunde) but find time for some fine chicks. **93m/C VHS, DVD, Wide.** Method Man, Redman, Obba Babatunde, Chuck Davis, Anna Maria Horsford, Fred Willard, Lark Voorhies, Essence Atkins, Jeffrey Jones, Mike Epps, Hector Elizondo, Chris Elwood, Spalding Gray, Tracey Walter; *D:* Jesse Dylan; *W:* Dustin Lee Abraham; *C:* Francis Kenny; *M:* Rockwilder.

How I Got into College 🦴🦴 **1989 (PG-13)** A slack, uninspired satire about doofus high school senior Marion Browne (Parker) who is eager to attend the same college as brainy Jessica (Boyle). But both run into problems from the snooty college recruiter (Rocket). More interesting for what the cast went on to do in the nineties. **87m/C VHS.** Corey Parker, Lara Flynn Boyle, Christopher Rydell, Anthony Edwards, Phil Hartman, Brian Doyle-Murray, Nora Dunn, Finn Carter, Charles Rocket; *D:* Steve Holland; *W:* Terrel Seltzer; *C:* Robert Elswit; *M:* Joseph Vitarelli.

How I Learned to Love Women 196? A British comedy of errors involving a car-loving youth who learns about women and love. **95m/C VHS.** *GB* Anita Ekberg.

How I Spent My Summer Vacation 1997 Squabbling college sweethearts Perry (Lea) and Stephanie (Davis) have decided their battles have blighted their romance and they split up right before their senior year. Perry moves into an apartment with a couple of buddies and pines for his ex, who's independently getting on with her life, although the dating scene turns out to be trying for them both. Sweetly amusing debut for writer/director Fisher. **75m/C VHS.** RonReaco Lee, Deanna Davis, E. Roger Mitchell, Mike Ngaujah, Jade Janise Dixon; *D:* John Fisher; *W:* John Fisher; *C:* Charles Mills; *M:* Johnny Barrow.

How I Won the War 1967 (PG) An inept officer must lead his battalion out of England into the Egyptian desert to conquer a cricket field. Indulgent, scarcely amusing Richard Lester comedy; Lennon, in a bit part, provides the brightest moments. **111m/C VHS.** *GB* Roy Kinnear, John Lennon, Michael Crawford, Michael Hordern; *D:* Richard Lester; *W:* Charles Wood; *C:* David Watkin; *M:* Ken Thorne.

How Many Miles to Babylon? 1982 During WWI, two young men become friends despite their different backgrounds. But one is court-martialed for desertion, and the other is supposed to oversee his execution. **106m/C VHS.** *GB* Daniel Day-Lewis, Christopher Fairbank; *D:* Moira Armstrong. **TV**

How Stella Got Her Groove Back 1998 (R) Underneath the flawless physique and upscale way of life, fortyish single mom Stella (Bassett) is sad; too much work and no love life is to blame. Coaxed by her best friend Delilah (Goldberg), Stella takes a trip to Jamaica where she falls in love with 20-year-old islander Winston (Diggs in his film debut). A flipside to the May-December romance that is purely more gloss (picturesque shots of the Carribean landscape) than grit. Bassett glows in a tailor-made role and muscular hunk Diggs is a find, but perfection in casting can't rescue this hollow romance that woefully missteps after a promising beginning. Based on the novel by Terry McMillan. **124m/C VHS, DVD.** Angela Bassett, Whoopi Goldberg, Taye Diggs, Regina King, Suzzanne Douglass, Richard Lawson, Michael J. Pagan, Barry (Shabaka) Henley, Sicily; *D:* Kevin Rodney Sullivan; *W:* Ronald Bass, Terry McMillan; *C:* Jeffrey Jur; *M:* Michel Colombier.

How Sweet It Is! 1968 Typical American family takes a zany European vacation. Looks like a TV sitcom and is about as entertaining. National Lampoon's version is a lot more fun. **99m/C VHS.** James Garner, Debbie Reynolds, Maurice Ronet, Paul Lynde, Erin Moran, Marcel Dalio, Terry-Thomas; *D:* Jerry Paris; *W:* Jerry Belson; *C:* Lucien Ballard.

How Tasty Was My Little Frenchman *Como Era Gostoso O Meu Frances* 1971 French explorer is captured by a cannibal tribe in the jungles of Brazil. He's treated very well and attempts to learn tribal customs to avoid his fate—he's going to be the main course in a ceremonial dinner. French and Tupi with subtitles. **80m/C VHS.** *BR* Arduino Colasanti, Ana Maria Magalhaes, Ital Natur, Eduardo Embassahy; *D:* Nelson Pereira dos Santos.

How the West Was Fun ½ 1995 The Olsen gals are visiting great godmother Natty's dude ranch, which is in financial difficulty, and must outsmart her greedy son Bart (Mull), a land grabber who wants to turn the ranch into an environmentally unfriendly western theme park. Made for TV. **93m/C VHS.** Mary-Kate Olsen, Ashley (Fuller) Olsen, Martin Mull, Michele Greene, Patrick Cassidy, Leon Pownall, Peg Phillips; *D:* Stuart Margolin; *M:* Richard Bellis. **TV**

How the West Was Won 1963 (G) A panoramic view of the American West, focusing on the trials, tribulations and travels of three generations of one family, set against the background of wars and historical events. Particularly notable for its impressive cast list and expansive western settings. **165m/C VHS, DVD, Wide.** John Wayne, Carroll Baker, Lee J. Cobb, Spencer Tracy, Gregory Peck, Karl Malden, Robert Preston, Eli Wallach, Henry Fonda, George Peppard, Debbie Reynolds, Carolyn Jones, Richard Widmark, James Stewart, Walter Brennan, Andy Devine, Raymond Massey, Agnes Moorehead, Harry (Henry) Morgan, Thelma Ritter, Russ Tamblyn; *D:* John Ford, Henry Hathaway, George Marshall; *W:* James R. Webb; *C:* Milton Krasner, Charles B(ryant) Lang Jr. Oscars '63: Film Editing, Sound, Story & Screenplay, Natl. Film Reg. '97.

How to Be a Woman and Not Die in the Attempt *How to Be a Woman and Not Die Trying; Como ser Mujer y No Morir en El* 1991 Carmen has just turned 42, is married to her third husband, and is raising three children. She's also very serious about her journalistic career on the local paper. So, she's a modern woman with too much to do and too little time, trying to juggle her home and her work and still keep a sense of humor. Based on the novel by Carmen Rico-Godoy. Spanish with subtitles. **96m/C VHS, DVD.** *SP* Carmen Maura, Antonio Resines; *D:* Ana Belen; *W:* Carmen Rico Godoy; *C:* Juan Amoros.

How to Beat the High Cost of Living ½ 1980 (PG) Three suburban housewives decide to beat inflation by taking up robbery, and they start by planning a heist at the local shopping mall. Comedic talent can't salvage whipped script and direction. **105m/C VHS.** Jessica Lange, Susan St. James, Jane Curtin, Richard Benjamin, Eddie Albert, Dabney Coleman, Fred Willard, Cathryn Damon, Art Metrano; *D:* Robert Scheerer.

How to Break Up a Happy Divorce 1976 A divorced woman starts a vigorous campaign to win her exhusband back by dating another man to make him jealous. Lightweight comedy. **74m/C VHS.** Barbara Eden, Hal Linden, Peter Bonerz, Marcia Rodd, Harold Gould; *D:* Jerry Paris. **TV**

How to Commit Marriage ½ 1969 (PG) Hope and Wyman have been married for 20 years when they decide to divorce—just when their daughter (Cameron) decides to marry her college boyfriend (Matheson). His father (Gleason) tries to stop the wedding, fails, but sticks around to cause more trouble. Subplots involve the divorced duo's new loves and the fact that they're about to become grandparents but the comedy is completely uninspired. **96m/C VHS, DVD.** Bob Hope, Jane Wyman, Jackie Gleason, Joanna Cameron, Tim Matheson, Beatrice Arthur, Leslie Nielsen, Tina Louise, Paul Stewart, Prof. Irwin Corey; *D:* Norman Panama; *W:* Ben Starr, Michael Kanin; *C:* Charles B(ryant) Lang Jr.; *M:* Joseph J. Lilley.

How to Frame a Figg ½ 1971 (G) Bookkeeper Hollis A. Figg (Knotts) is working at Dalton's corrupt city hall where he's setup to be the patsy in the fradulent doings of the mayor and city council. But his best friends Prentiss (Welker) and Ema Letha (Joyce) set out to prove the bumbler's innocence. **103m/C VHS.** Don Knotts, Elaine Joyce, Frank Welker, Joe Flynn, Edward Andrews, Yvonne Craig, Parker Fennelly, Fay DeWitt; *D:* Alan Rafkin; *W:* George Tibbles; *C:* William Margulies; *M:* Vic Mizzy.

How to Get Ahead in Advertising 1989 (R) A cynical, energetic satire about a manic advertising idea man who becomes so disgusted with trying to sell a pimple cream that he quits the business. Ultimately he grows a pimple of his own that talks and begins to take over his life. Acerbic and hilarious. **95m/C VHS, DVD, Wide.** *GB* Richard E. Grant, Rachel Ward, Susan Wooldridge, Mick Ford, Richard Wilson, John Shrapnel, Jacqueline Tong; *D:* Bruce Robinson; *W:* Bruce Robinson; *C:* Peter Hannan; *M:* David Dundas, Rick Wentworth.

How to Kill 400 Duponts 1965 Bumbling Scotland Yard detective is off to France to stop a master criminal from trying to kill off the rich Dupont family. Why? So he'll be the only one left with any claim to the remaining family fortune. **98m/C VHS.** Terry-Thomas, Johnny Dorelli, Margaret Lee.

How to Kill Your Neighbor's Dog 2001 (R) Critically acclaimed playwright Peter McGowen (Branagh) has fallen on hard times after a string of flops and is feeling the pressure from his sunny-natured wife Melanie (Wright Penn) to have kids. He's trying to fix his latest work but his neighbor's incessantly barking dog keeps him awake nights. The grouch also finds he must befriend a neighbor's daughter, Amy (Hofrichter), because he needs a model for the child role in his play, although Amy's presence does some not entirely unexpected reexamination of Peter and Melanie's marriage. Branagh is amusingly sharp-tongued but the film has a squishy center. **108m/C VHS, DVD.** Kenneth Branagh, Robin Wright Penn, Jared Harris, Suzi Hofrichter, Johnathon Schaech, Peter Riegert, Lynn Redgrave; *D:* Michael Kalesniko; *W:* Michael Kalesniko; *C:* Hubert Taczanowski; *M:* David Robbins.

How to Make a Doll 1968 Lewis' sex farce about an extremely shy professor whose ineptness with women inspires him to invent android females to satisfy his sexual needs. **81m/C VHS.** Robert Wood, Bobbi West, Jim Vance, Pamela Rhea; *D:* Herschell Gordon Lewis; *W:* Herschell Gordon Lewis, Bert Ray.

How to Make a Monster 1958 In-joke from the creators of youth-oriented '50s AIP monster flicks; a mad makeup man's homebrew greasepaint brainwashes the actors. Disguised as famous monsters, they kill horror-hating movie execs. Mild fun if—and only if—you treasure the genre. Conway repeats his role as Teenage Frankenstein, but the studio couldn't get Michael Landon for the Teenage Werewolf. **73m/B VHS.** Robert Harris, Paul Brinegar, Gary Conway, Gary Clarke, Malcolm Atterbury, Dennis Cross, John Ashley, Morris Ankrum, Walter Reed, Heather Ames; *D:* Herbert L. Strock.

How to Make a Monster 2001 (R) Computer game company hires three ambitious programmers to finish a game and bring it to market in four weeks. A telemetry suit is used to render a 3-D version of the game's villain but a power-surge brings the program to life. Now the game's killer cyborg (AKA the telemetry suit) goes after the threesome, thinking they're players in the game. Basically takes only the title from the 1958 A.I.P. flick. **90m/C VHS, DVD.** Steven Culp, Clea DuVall, Jason Marsden, Tyler Mane, Julie Strain, Karim Prince; *D:* George Huang; *W:* George Huang; *C:* Steven Firestone; *M:* David Reynolds. **CABLE**

How to Make an American Quilt ½ 1995 (PG-13) Slow-moving take on female friendship and marriage revolves around perennial grad student Finn (the mopey Ryder), who is frantic to both finish her third attempted thesis and to answer a marriage proposal from practically perfect beau Sam (Mulroney). She takes a summer refuge with her grandmother (Burstyn), where a variety of family friends work on her wedding quilt as they tell stories of loves lost and won. Lots of (somewhat overextended) flashbacks and with so many characters, naturally some get the short end of the script. Based on the novel by Whitney Otto. **109m/C VHS, DVD.** Winona Ryder, Ellen Burstyn, Anne Bancroft, Lois Smith, Jean Simmons, Kate Nelligan, Maya Angelou, Alfre Woodard, Dermot Mulroney, Kate Capshaw, Rip Torn, Derrick O'Connor, Loren Dean, Samantha Mathis, Joanna Going, Tim Guinee, Johnathon Schaech, Claire Danes, Jared Leto, Esther Rolle, Melinda Dillon, Alicia (Lecy) Goranson, Maria Celedonio, Mykelti Williamson; *D:* Jocelyn Moorhouse; *W:* Jane Anderson; *C:* Janusz Kaminski; *M:* Thomas Newman.

How to Marry a Millionaire ½ 1953 Three models pool their money and rent a lavish apartment in a campaign to trap millionaire husbands. Clever performances by three lead women salvage a vehicle intended primarily to bolster Monroe's career. The opening street scene, with the accompanying theme music, was a state-of-the-art achievement of screen and sound in the one of the first movies to be filmed in CinemaScope ("The Robe" was the first). Remake of "The Greeks Had a Word for Them." **96m/C VHS, DVD, Wide.** Lauren Bacall, Marilyn Monroe, Betty Grable, William Powell, David Wayne, Cameron Mitchell; *D:* Jean Negulesco; *W:* Nunnally Johnson; *C:* Joe MacDonald; *M:* Alfred Newman.

How to Murder Your Wife 1964 While drunk, a cartoonist marries an unknown woman and then frantically tries to think of ways to get rid of her — even contemplating murder. Frantic comedy is tailored for Lemmon. **118m/C VHS.** Jack Lemmon, Terry-Thomas, Virna Lisi, Eddie Mayehoff, Sidney Blackmer, Claire Trevor, Mary Wickes, Jack Albertson; *D:* Richard Quine; *W:* George Axelrod; *C:* Harry Stradling Sr.

How to Pick Up Girls 1978 Comic tale based on Eric Weber's bestseller follows the exploits of a small-town boy who moves to New York City and finds the secret to picking up women. Made for television. **93m/C VHS.** Desi Arnaz Jr., Bess Armstrong, Fred McCarren, Polly Bergen, Richard Dawson, Alan King, Abe Vigoda, Deborah Raffin; *D:* Bill Persky. **TV**

How to Seduce a Woman woof! 1974 A playboy attempts to bed five supposedly unattainable women. **108m/C VHS.** Angus Duncan, Marty Ingels, Lillian Randolph.

How to Steal a Million *How to Steal a Million Dollars and Live Happily Ever After* 1966 Sophisticated comedy-crime caper involving a million-dollar heist of a sculpture in a Paris art museum. Hepburn and O'Toole are perfectly cast as partners in crime and Griffith gives a good performance as Hepburn's art-forging father. A charming, lightweight script and various Parisian locales combine for fun, above-average fluff. Based on the story "Venus Rising" by George Bradshaw. **127m/C VHS.** Audrey Hepburn, Peter O'Toole, Eli Wallach, Hugh Griffith, Charles Boyer, Fernand Gravet, Marcel Dalio, Jacques Marin; *D:* William Wyler; *W:* Harry Kurnitz; *C:* Charles B(ryant) Lang Jr.; *M:* John Williams.

How to Stuff a Wild Bikini 1965 Tired next to last feature in the overlong tradition of Frankie and Annette doing the beach thing, featuring a pregnant Funicello (though this is hidden and not part of the plot). Avalon actually has only a small role as the jealous boyfriend trying to see if Annette will remain faithful while he's away on military duty. Keaton is the witch doctor who helps Frankie keep Annette true. "Playboy" playmates wander about in small swimsuits, garage band extraordinare "The Kingsmen" play themselves, and Brian Wilson of the "Beach Boys" drops by. Followed by "Ghost in the Invisible Bikini," the only movie in the series that isn't on video. ♫After the Party; Better Be Ready; Follow Your Leader; Give Her Lovin'; How About Us?; How to Stuff a Wild Bikini; I'm the Boy Next Door; Madison Avenue; The Perfect Boy. **90m/C VHS, DVD.** Annette Funicello, Dwayne Hickman, Frankie Avalon, Beverly Adams, Buster Keaton, Harvey Lembeck, Mickey Rooney, Brian Donlevy, Jody McCrea, John Ashley, Marianne Gaba, Len Lesser, Irene Tsu, Bobbi Shaw, Luree Holmes; *D:* William Asher; *W:* William Asher, Leo Townsend; *C:* Floyd Crosby; *M:* Les Baxter.

How to Succeed in Business without Really Trying ½ 1967 Classic musical comedy about a window-washer who charms his way to the top of a major company. Robert Morse repeats his Tony winning Broadway role. Loosely based on a non-fiction book of the same title by Shepherd Mead, which Morse purchases on his first day of work. Excellent transfer of stage to film, with choreography by Moreda expanding Bob Fosse's original plan. Dynamite from start to finish. ♫I Believe In You; The Company Way; Coffee Break; The Brotherhood of

Man; A Secretary Is Not A Toy; Grand Old Ivy; Been A Long Day; Rosemary; Finch's Frolic. **121m/C VHS, DVD, Wide.** Robert Morse, Michele Lee, Rudy Vallee, Anthony Teague, George Fenneman, Maureen Arthur; ***D:*** David Swift; ***W:*** David Swift, Abe Burrows; ***C:*** Burnett Guffey; ***M:*** Frank Loesser.

How to Succeed with Girls **1964** Marginally funny comedy about pious wax salesman (Leder) with a secret fantasy life who unwittingly enlists the aid of his wife's lover (Schrier) to help him overcome his shyness. Several fantasy sequences (in color; the rest of the film is B&W) include an Arabian harem, an old West saloon, and a science laboratory. Brubaker's secretary (Mathes) was Playboy's Miss June 1962. Pete's girlfriend (McClanahan of TV's "Golden Girls") is credited as either Patty Leigh or Helen Goodman. **83m/C VHS.** Marissa Mathes, Rue McClanahan, Paul Leder, Leon Schrier; ***D:*** Edward A. Biery.

How U Like Me Now? **1992 (R)** Comedy set on Chicago's south side focuses on Thomas, an attractive but unmotivated guy with low earning potential, and his girl Valerie, a pretentious overachiever who wants much more than he's able to offer. Robert's second directorial effort offers a fresh look at African Americans on film with plenty of lively supporting characters and witty dialogue. Filmed on a $600,000 budget. **109m/C VHS.** Darnell Williams, Salli Richardson, Daniel Gardner, Raymond Whitefield, Debra Crable, Jonelle Kennedy, Byron Stewart, Charnele Brown, Daryll Roberts; ***D:*** Daryll Roberts; ***W:*** Daryll Roberts; ***M:*** Kahil El Zabar, Chuck Webb.

Howard the Duck **1986 (PG)** Big-budget Lucasfilm adaptation of the short-lived Marvel comic book about an alien, resembling a cigar-chomping duck, who gets sucked into a vortex, lands on Earth and saves it from the Dark Overlords. While he's at it, he befriends a nice young lady in a punk rock band and starts to fall in love. A notorious boxoffice bomb and one of the '80s' worst major films, although it seems to work well with children, given the simple storyline and good special effects. **111m/C VHS.** Elizabeth Sagal, Thomas Dolby, Paul Guilfoyle, Lea Thompson, Jeffrey Jones, Tim Robbins; ***D:*** Willard Huyck; ***W:*** Gloria Katz, Willard Huyck; ***C:*** Richard H. Kline; ***M:*** John Barry, Sylvester Levay; ***V:*** Chip Zien. Golden Raspberries '86: Worst Picture, Worst Screenplay.

Howard's End **1992 (PG)** E.M. Forster's 1910 novel about property, privilege, class differences, and Edwardian society is brought to enchanting life by the Merchant Ivory team. A tragic series of events occurs after two impulsive middleclass sisters, Margaret (Thompson) and Helen (Bonham Carter), become involved with the working class Basts (West, Duffett), and the wealthy Wilcox family (Hopkins, Redgrave). Tragedy aside, this is a visually beautiful effort with subtle performances where a glance or a gesture says as much as any dialog. The winner of numerous awards and wide critical acclaim. Thompson is especially notable as the compassionate Margaret, while Hopkins plays the repressed English gentleman brilliantly. **143m/C VHS, DVD, 8mm, Wide.** *GB* Anthony Hopkins, Emma Thompson, Helena Bonham Carter, Vanessa Redgrave, James Wilby, Samuel West, Jemma Redgrave, Nicola Duffett, Prunella Scales, Joseph Bennett; ***Cameos:*** Simon Callow; ***D:*** James Ivory; ***W:*** Ruth Prawer Jhabvala; ***C:*** Tony Pierce-Roberts; ***M:*** Richard Robbins. Oscars '92: Actress (Thompson), Adapt. Screenplay, Art Dir./Set Dec.; British Acad. '92: Actress (Thompson); Golden Globes '93: Actress—Drama (Thompson); L.A. Film Critics '92: Actress (Thompson); Natl. Bd. of Review '92: Actress (Thompson), Director (Ivory), Film; N.Y. Film Critics '92: Actress (Thompson); Natl. Soc. Film Critics '92: Actress (Thompson).

The Howards of Virginia ½ *Tree of Liberty* **1940** A lavish Hollywood historical epic, detailing the adventures of a backwoodsman and the rich Virginia girl he marries as their families become involved in the Revolutionary War. **117m/B VHS.** Cary Grant, Martha Scott, Cedric Hardwicke, Alan Marshal, Richard Carlson, Paul Kelly, Irving Bacon, Tom Drake, Anne Revere, Ralph Byrd, Alan Ladd; ***D:*** Frank Lloyd.

The Howling **1981 (R)** A pretty TV reporter takes a rest at a clinic and discovers slowly that its denizens are actually werewolves. Crammed with inside jokes, this horror comedy pioneered the use of the body-altering prosthetic makeup (by Rob Bottin) now essential for onscreen man-to-wolf transformations. At last count, followed by six sequels. **91m/C VHS, DVD, Wide.** Dee Wallace Stone, Patrick Macnee, Dennis Dugan, Christopher Stone, Belinda Balaski, Kevin McCarthy, John Carradine, Slim Pickens, Elisabeth Brooks, Robert Picardo, Dick Miller, Kenneth Tobey, Meshach Taylor; ***Cameos:*** John Sayles, Roger Corman, Forrest J Ackerman; ***D:*** Joe Dante; ***W:*** John Sayles, Terence H. Winkless; ***C:*** John Hora; ***M:*** Pino Donaggio.

Howling 2: Your Sister Is a Werewolf *Howling 2: Stirba—Werewolf Bitch* **1985 (R)** A policeman (the brother of one of the first film's victims) investigates a Transylvanian werewolf-ridden castle and gets mangled for his trouble. Followed by four more sequels. **91m/C VHS.** *FR IT* Sybil Danning, Christopher Lee, Annie McEnroe, Marsha A. Hunt, Reb Brown, Ferdinand "Ferdy" Mayne, Judd Omen, Jimmy Nail; ***D:*** Philippe Mora; ***W:*** Gary Brandner, Robert Sarno; ***C:*** Geoffrey Stephenson.

Howling 3: The Marsupials *The Marsupials: Howling 3* **1987 (PG-13)** Australians discover a pouch-laden form of lycanthrope. Third "Howling" (surprise), second from Mora and better than his first. **94m/C VHS, DVD, Wide.** *AU* Barry Otto, Imogen Annesley, Dasha Blahova, Max Fairchild, Ralph Cotterill, Leigh Biolos, Frank Thring Jr., Michael Pate; ***D:*** Philippe Mora; ***W:*** Philippe Mora; ***C:*** Louis Irving; ***M:*** Allan Zavod.

Howling 4: The Original Nightmare **1988 (R)** A woman novelist hears the call of the wild while taking a rest cure in the country. This werewolf tale has nothing to do with the other sequels. **94m/C VHS.** Romy Windsor, Michael T. Weiss, Antony Hamilton, Susanne Severeid, Lamya Derval, Dennis Folbigge; ***D:*** John Hough.

Howling 5: The Rebirth **1989 (R)** The fifth in the disconnected horror series, in which a varied group of people stranded in a European castle are individually hunted down by evil. **99m/C VHS.** Philip Davis, Victoria Catlin, Elizabeth She, Ben Cole, William Shockley; ***D:*** Neal Sundstrom; ***C:*** Arledge Armenaki.

Howling 6: The Freaks ½ **1990 (R)** Hideous werewolf suffers from multiple sequels, battles with vampire at freak show, and discovers that series won't die. Next up: "Howling 7: The Nightmare that Won't Go Away." **102m/C VHS.** Brendan Hughes, Michelle Matheson, Sean Gregory Sullivan, Antonio Fargas, Carol Lynley, Jered Barclay, Bruce Payne; ***D:*** Hope Perello.

The Howling: New Moon Rising ½ *Howling 7* **1995 (R)** Small desert town is plagued by a series of terrifying murders believed to be the work of a werewolf, whose victims then join his vicious pack. **92m/C VHS.** Clive Turner, John Ramsden, Ernest Kester, Elizabeth She, Jacqueline Armitage, Romy Windsor; ***D:*** Clive Turner; ***W:*** Clive Turner.

H.P. Lovecraft's Necronomicon: Book of the Dead *Necronomicon* **1993 (R)** Trilogy of stories: Payne encounters a demon who resurrects his late wife and son in "The Drowning"; "The Cold" finds a reporter investigating a series of murders and uncovers crazed doctor Warner, who's discovered the secret to immortality; and a female cop discovers a subterranean alien in "Whispers." Combs serves as narrator, Lovecraft. **96m/C VHS.** Bruce Payne, Belinda Bauer, Bess Meyer, David Warner, Signy Coleman, Richard Lynch, Dennis Christopher, Jeffrey Combs, Maria Ford, Don Calfa; ***D:*** Brian Yuzna, Shusuke (Shu) Kaneko, Christophe Gans; ***W:*** Brian Yuzna, Christophe Gans, Brent Friedman, Kazunori Ito; ***C:*** Russ Brandt; ***M:*** Joseph LoDuca, Daniel Licht.

Huck and the King of Hearts ½ **1993 (PG)** When a cardshark and his young friend Huck travel the country searching for Huck's long-lost grandfather, they find adventure everywhere from Hannibal, Missouri to L.A. to Vegas. Loose, contemporary adaptation of Mark Twain's "The Adventures of Huckleberry Finn." **103m/C VHS.** Chauncey Leopardi, Graham Greene, Dee Wallace Stone, Joe Piscopo, John Astin, Gretchen Becker; ***D:*** Michael Keusch; ***W:*** Christopher Sturgeon; ***M:*** Chris Saranec.

Huckleberry Finn **1974 (G)** The musical version of the Mark Twain story about the adventures a young boy and a runaway slave encounter along the Mississippi River. **114m/C VHS, Wide.** Jeff East, Paul Winfield, Harvey Korman, David Wayne, Arthur O'Connell, Gary Merrill, Natalie Trundy, Lucille Benson; ***D:*** J. Lee Thompson.

Huckleberry Finn ½ **1975 (G)** Whitewashed version of the Twain classic features post Opie Howard as the incredible Huck and Dano as the sharp witted short storyist. Stars four members of the Howard clan. Made for TV. **74m/C VHS.** Ron Howard, Donny Most, Royal Dano, Antonio Fargas, Jack Elam, Merle Haggard, Rance Howard, Jean Howard, Clint Howard, Shug Fisher, Sarah Selby, Bill Erwin; ***D:*** Robert Totten. **TV**

Huckleberry Finn ½ **1981** A version of the classic Mark Twain novel about the adventures a young boy and a runaway slave encounter as they travel down the Mississippi River. **72m/C VHS.**

The Hucksters **1947** Account of a man (Gable) looking for honesty and integrity in the radio advertising world and finding little to work with. All performances are excellent; but Greenstreet, as the tyrannical head of a soap company, is a stand out. Deborah Kerr's American debut. Based on the novel by Frederic Wakeman. **115m/B VHS.** Clark Gable, Deborah Kerr, Sydney Greenstreet, Adolphe Menjou, Ava Gardner, Keenan Wynn, Edward Arnold; ***D:*** Jack Conway; ***W:*** Edward Chodorov, Luther Davis, George Wells; ***C:*** Harold Rosson; ***M:*** Lennie Hayton.

Hud **1963** Newman is a hard-driving, hard-drinking, woman-chasing young man whose life is a revolt against the principles of stern father Douglas. Neal is outstanding as the family housekeeper. Excellent photography. Based on the Larry McMurtry novel "Horseman, Pass By." **112m/B VHS.** Paul Newman, Melvyn Douglas, Patricia Neal, Brandon de Wilde, John Ashley; ***D:*** Martin Ritt; ***W:*** Irving Ravetch, Harriet Frank Jr.; ***C:*** James Wong Howe; ***M:*** Elmer Bernstein. Oscars '63: Actress (Neal), B&W Cinematog., Support. Actor (Douglas); British Acad. '63: Actress (Neal); Natl. Bd. of Review '63: Actress (Neal), Support. Actor (Douglas); N.Y. Film Critics '63: Actress (Neal), Screenplay.

Hudson Hawk **1991 (R)** A big-budget star vehicle with little else going for it. Willis plays a master burglar released from prison, only to find himself trapped by the CIA into one last theft. Everyone in the cast tries to be extra funny, resulting in a disjointed situation where no one is. Weakly plotted, poorly paced. **95m/C VHS, DVD, 8mm.** Bruce Willis, Danny Aiello, Andie MacDowell, James Coburn, Sandra Bernhard, Richard E. Grant, Frank Stallone; ***D:*** Michael Lehmann; ***W:*** Steven E. de Souza, Daniel Waters; ***C:*** Dante Spinotti; ***M:*** Michael Kamen, Robert Kraft. Golden Raspberries '91: Worst Picture, Worst Director (Lehmann), Worst Screenplay.

The Hudsucker Proxy **1993 (PG)** In an effort to scare off would-be investors in a public stock offering dim bulb mailboy Robbins is installed as the Prez of Hudsucker Industries (in 1958) by Board Director Newman after corporate magnate Hudsucker (Durning) takes a swan dive from the 44th floor. First truly mainstream effort from the maverick Coen brothers is peppered with obscure references to numerous points on the historical map of cinematic style, and trots out an equally old but instantly recognizable story. Will delight Coen fans, but may be too dark for others. Destined to keep art history profs busy for decades. **115m/C VHS, DVD, Wide.** Tim Robbins, Paul Newman, Jennifer Jason Leigh, Charles Durning, John Mahoney, Jim True, Bill Cobbs, Bruce Campbell, Steve Buscemi; ***Cameos:*** Peter Gallagher; ***D:*** Joel Coen; ***W:*** Ethan Coen, Joel Coen, Sam Raimi; ***C:*** Roger Deakins; ***M:*** Carter Burwell.

Hue and Cry **1947** Nobody believes a young boy when he discovers crooks are sending coded messages in a weekly children's magazine. A detective writer finally believes his story and they set off to capture the crooks. **82m/B VHS.** *GB* Alastair Sim, Jack Warner, Frederick Piper, Jack Lambert, Joan Dowling; ***D:*** Charles Crichton.

Hugh Hefner: Once Upon a Time **1992 (R)** Fascinating look at the "Bunny" king and Playboy Enterprises. His celebrated life of isolation and excess at the Playboy mansions is portrayed as is the founding of "Playboy" magazine in 1953 and the Playboy clubs (with their notorious Bunnies). Includes interviews, home movies, and photographs. Admiring yet not without a few sharp edges. **91m/C VHS.** Hugh Hefner; ***D:*** Robert Heath; ***Nar:*** James Coburn.

Hughes & Harlow: Angels in Hell **1977 (R)** The story of the romance that occurred between Howard Hughes and Jean Harlow during the filming of "Hell's Angels" in 1930. **94m/C VHS.** Lindsay Bloom, Victor Holchak, David McLean, Royal Dano, Adam Roarke, Linda Cristal; ***D:*** Larry Buchanan.

Hugo Pool ½ **1997 (R)** Pool cleaner Hugo Dugay (Milano) has to clean the pools of 44 backyard eccentrics. Reluctantly, she must enlist the aid of her gambler mom (Moriarty) and drug addict father (McDowell). Bizarre characters abound, including Downey Jr. overacting as Hungarian film director Franz Mazur, whose accent changes with each line. Most interesting is Dempsey as ALS-afflicted Floyd Galen. The romance between Floyd and Hugo supplies the most sensitive and well-acted sequences. Disappointing, long-anticipated outing from director Downey Sr. (this is his first directorial effort in six years) who shared writing duties with wife Laura, who died of ALS in 1994. **92m/C VHS, DVD.** Alyssa Milano, Patrick Dempsey, Robert Downey Jr., Malcolm McDowell, Cathy Moriarty, Sean Penn, Richard Lewis, Chuck Barris; ***D:*** Robert Downey; ***W:*** Laura Downey; ***C:*** Joe Montgomery; ***M:*** Danilo Perez.

Hugo the Hippo **1976 (G)** Animated musical about a forlorn baby hippo who struggles to survive in the human jungle of old Zanzibar. **90m/C VHS.** ***W:*** Thomas Baum; ***V:*** Paul Lynde, Burl Ives, Robert Morley, Marie Osmond.

Hula ½ **1928** Unflappable flapper Bow and her gang frolic on a Pacific island. **64m/B VHS.** Clara Bow, Clive Brook, Patricia Dupont, Arnold Kent, Agaslino Borgato; ***D:*** Victor Fleming.

Hullabaloo over Georgie & Bonnie's Pictures ½ **1978** A young maharajah has inherited a priceless collection of Indian miniature paintings he doesn't appreciate and which his greedy sister is anxious for him to sell. They're beseiged by art dealers and collectors who learn about the treasure trove and will do anything to possess it. Among them are the British Ashcroft, who wants the art for the British Museum, and competing American collector Pine. **85m/C VHS.** *GB* Victor Banerjee, Aparna Sen, Larry Pine, Saeed Jaffrey, Peggy Ashcroft; ***D:*** James Ivory; ***W:*** Ruth Prawer Jhabvala; ***C:*** Walter Lassally. **TV**

Human Beasts **1980** Jewel robbers face a tribe of hungry cannibals. **90m/C VHS.** *SP JP* Paul (Jacinto Molina) Naschy, Eiko Nagashima, Jacinto (Jack) Molina; ***D:*** Jacinto (Jack) Molina; ***W:*** Jacinto (Jack) Molina.

Human Bomb ½ **1997 (PG-13)** After her husband dies, Marcia Weller (Kensit) moves to Germany to be near her mother. Marcia's only been at her new teaching job a few days when she and her class of third-graders are taken hostage by a masked gunman. Captain Gerhardt (Prochnow) is brought in to resolve the crisis, but the terrorist won't negogiate, so Gerhardt must come up with a rescue plan before the bomber decides to carry out his threats. **93m/C VHS.** Patsy Kensit, Juergen Prochnow, Dorian Healy, Richard Moore; *D:* Anthony Page.

The Human Comedy 🦴🦴🦴½ **1943** A small-town boy experiences love and loss and learns the meaning of true faith during WWII. Straight, unapologetically sentimental version of the William Saroyan novel. **117m/B VHS.** Mickey Rooney, Frank Morgan, James Craig, Fay Bainter, Ray Collins, Donna Reed, Van Johnson, Barry Nelson, Robert Mitchum, Jackie "Butch" Jenkins; *D:* Clarence Brown; *W:* William Saroyan; *C:* Harry Stradling Sr. Oscars '43: Story.

The Human Condition: A Soldier's Prayer 🦴🦴🦴 **1961** A Japanese pacifist escapes from his commanders and allows himself to be captured by Russian troops, hoping for better treatment as a P.O.W. The final part of the trilogy preceded by "The Human Condition: No Greater Love" and "The Human Condition: Road to Eternity." In Japanese with English subtitles. **190m/B VHS, DVD.** *JP* Tatsuya Nakadai, Michiyo Aratama, Yusuke Kawazu, Tamao Nakamura, Chishu Ryu, Taketoshi Naito, Reiko Hitomi, Kyoko Kishida, Keijiro Morozumi, Koji Kiyomura, Nobuo Kaneko, Fujio Suga; *D:* Masaki Kobayashi.

The Human Condition: No Greater Love 🦴🦴🦴 **1958** First of a three-part series of films. A pacifist is called into military service and subsequently sent to a run a military mining camp. A gripping look at one man's attempt to retain his humanity in the face of war. Followed by "The Human Condition: Road to Eternity" and "The Human Condition: A Soldier's Prayer." In Japanese with English subtitles. **200m/B VHS, DVD.** *JP* Tatsuya Nakadai, Michiyo Aratama, So Yamamura, Eitaro (Sakae, Saka Ozawa) Ozawa, Akira Ishihama, Chikage Awashima, Ineko Arima, Keiji Sada, Shinji Nambara, Seiji Miyaguchi, Toru Abe, Masao Mishima, Eijiro Tono, Yasushi Nagata, Yoshio Kosugi; *D:* Masaki Kobayashi; *W:* Masaki Kobayashi, Zenzo Matsuyama; *C:* Yoshio Miyajima; *M:* Chuji Kinoshita.

The Human Condition: Road to Eternity 🦴🦴🦴 *No Greater Love; Ningen No Joken* **1959** A Japanese pacifist is on punishment duty in Manchuria where he is beaten by sadistic officers who try to destroy his humanity. The second part of the trilogy, preceded by "The Human Condition: No Greater Love" and followed by "The Human Condition: A Soldier's Prayer." In Japanese with English subtitles. **180m/B VHS, DVD.** *JP* Tatsuya Nakadai, Michiyo Aratama, Kokinji Katsura, Jun Tatara, Michio Minami, Keiji Sada, Minoru Chiaki, Ryohei Uchida, Kan Yanagidani, Kenjiro Uemura, Yusuke Kawazu, Susumu Fujita; *D:* Masaki Kobayashi; *W:* Masaki Kobayashi, Zenzo Matsuyama; *C:* Yoshio Miyajima; *M:* Chuji Kinoshita.

Human Desire 🦴🦴½ **1954** Femme fatale Grahame and jealous husband Crawford turn out the lights on Crawford's boss (seems there's some confusion about how Miss Gloria managed to convince the guy to let her hubby have his job back). Ford's wise to them but plays see no evil because he's gone crackers for Grahame, who by now has decided she'd like a little help to rid herself of an unwanted husband. Bleak, melodramatic, full of big heat, its Lang through and through. Based on the Emile Zola novel "La Bete Humaine," which inspired Renoir's 1938 telling as well. **90m/B VHS.** Glenn Ford, Gloria Grahame, Broderick Crawford, Edgar Buchanan, Kathleen Case; *D:* Fritz Lang; *C:* Burnett Guffey.

Human Desires 🦴🦴 **1997 (R)** A lingerie beauty contest provides a bevy of beauties for P.I. Dean Thomas (Noble) to investigate when one of them turns up dead. The death is ruled a suicide but a fellow contestant thinks it was murder and Thomas is around to check things out—very closely. **95m/C VHS, DVD.** Shannon Tweed, Christian Noble, Dawn Ann Billings, Duke Stroud; *D:* Ellen Earnshaw; *W:* Todd Smith; *C:* Carl Oakwood; *M:* Ed Korvin.

The Human Duplicators 🦴½ **1964** Kiel is an alien who has come to Earth to make androids out of important folk, thus allowing the "galaxy beings" to take over. Cheap stuff, but earnest performances make this more fun than it should be. **82m/C VHS.** George Nader, Barbara Nichols, George Macready, Dolores Faith, Hugh Beaumont, Richard Kiel, Richard Arlen; *D:* Hugo Grimaldi.

Human Experiments 🦴 **1979 (R)** Psychiatrist in a women's prison conducts a group of experiments in which he destroys the "criminal instinct" in the inmates through brute fear. **82m/C VHS.** Linda Haynes, Jackie Coogan, Aldo Ray; *D:* Gregory Goodell.

The Human Factor 🦴½ **1975 (R)** Kennedy stars as a computer expert who tracks down his family's murderers using technology. Bloody and violent. **96m/C VHS.** *GB IT* George Kennedy, John Mills, Raf Vallone, Rita Tushingham, Barry Sullivan, Arthur Franz; *D:* Edward Dmytryk; *M:* Ennio Morricone.

The Human Factor 🦴🦴½ **1979 (R)** Unexciting spy caper has a British Secret Service agent (Williamson) betraying his country in order to aid a friend. As a result of his actions an innocent man is killed and Williamson is forced to defect to the Soviet Union. Based on a novel by Graham Greene. **115m/C VHS.** *GB* Nicol Williamson, Richard Attenborough, John Gielgud, Derek Jacobi, Robert Morley, Ann Todd, Richard Vernon, Iman; *D:* Otto Preminger; *W:* Tom Stoppard.

Human Gorilla 🦴 *Behind Locked Doors* **1948** A thriller involving a mad scientist, an insane asylum, a reporter, and various other mysterious trappings. **58m/B VHS.** Richard Carlson, Lucille Bremer, Tor Johnson.

Human Hearts 🦴🦴 **1922** A creaky old silent starring "Phantom of the Opera" leading lady Philbin. A family is torn apart by a con man and his femme fatale. **99m/B VHS, 8mm.** House Peters Sr., Russell Simpson, Mary Philbin.

The Human Monster 🦴🦴½ *Dark Eyes of London* **1939** Scotland Yard inspector investigates five drownings of the blind patients a phony Dr. Orloff (Lugosi) is exploiting for insurance money. Superior Lugosi effort that's modestly violent and tasteless. Based on the Edgar Wallace novel. **73m/B VHS, DVD.** *GB* Bela Lugosi, Hugh Williams, Greta Gynt; *D:* Walter Summers; *W:* Walter Summers.

Human Nature 🦴🦴½ **2002 (R)** Offbeat and charming screwball comedy stars Arquette as Lila, a sweet kid with a hairy problem—extreme hirsutism—which forces her to become a reclusive nature writer living in the woods. Her sex drive finally forces her back to civilization, where she finds a sympathetic electrologist (Perez) who sets her up with repressed scientist Nathan (Robbins). As a result of his uber-repressed upbringing, Nathan is on a quest to teach mice good table manners, but when the couple finds a woods-dwelling wildman (Ifans), he has something new to experiment on and tries to teach nature-boy to be civilized, despite his raging libido. Eccentric feature debut of Gallic director Gondry is a quirky study of three characters at odds with their own true nature and trying to fit into a judgmental society. In keeping with the offbeat humor of writer/co-producer Kaufman's "Being John Malkovich." **96m/C VHS, DVD.** *US FR* Tim Robbins, Rhys Ifans, Patricia Arquette, Miranda Otto, Robert Forster, Mary Kay Place, Miguel (Michael) Sandoval, Toby Huss, Peter Dinklage, Rosie Perez; *D:* Michel Gondry; *W:* Charlie Kaufman; *C:* Tim Maurice-Jones; *M:* Graeme Revell.

The Human Shield 🦴🦴 **1992 (R)** A man risks his life on a mission to save his brother during the Persian Gulf War. **88m/C VHS.** Michael Dudikoff, Tommy Hinkley, Steve Inwood; *D:* Ted Post.

Human Traffic 🦴½ **1999 (R)** It's kinda like "Groove" only these club kids are spending their oblivious weekend in Cardiff, Wales. They have various personal dilemmas that they try to overcome by taking E and dancing the hours away and they're all one step away from insufferable. Writer/director Kerrigan was just 25 when he recorded his debut film so he's got time to grow up. Or maybe the Hound is just getting old. **84m/C VHS, DVD, Wide.** *GB* John Simm, Lorraine Pilkington, Shaun Parkes, Nicola Reynolds, Danny Dyer, Dean Davies; *D:* Justin Kerrigan; *W:* Justin Kerrigan; *C:* David Bennett; *M:* Matthew Herbert, Rob Mellow.

Humanity 🦴🦴 *L'Humanite* **1999** Overly long and raw look at a few days in the life naive cop Pharon De Winter (Schotte), who suffers from an overabundance of empathy for the pain of others. His latest assignment is certain to plunge Pharon into despair as he investigates the rape and murder of an 11-year-old girl. Pharon is also hopelessly attracted to his young neighbor Domino (Caneele), whose sexual interludes with boyfriend Joseph (Tullier) leave nothing to the viewers' imagination. French with subtitles. **142m/C VHS, DVD, Wide.** *FR* Emmanuel Schotte, Severine Caneele, Philippe Tullier, Ghislain Ghesquiere, Ginette Allegre; *D:* Bruno Dumont; *W:* Bruno Dumont; *C:* Yves Cape; *M:* Richard Cuvillier. Cannes '99: Actor (Schotte), Actress (Caneele), Grand Jury Prize.

Humanoid Defender 🦴🦴 **1985** A a scientist and an android rebel against the government that wants to use the android as a warfare prototype. **94m/C VHS.** Terence Knox, Gary Kasper, Aimee (Amy) Eccles, William Lucking; *D:* William Lucking. **TV**

Humanoids from the Deep woof! *Monster* **1980 (R)** Mutated salmon-like monsters rise from the depths of the ocean and decide to chomp on some bikinied babes. Violent and bloody. **81m/C VHS, DVD.** Doug McClure, Ann Turkel, Vic Morrow, Cindy Weintraub, Anthony Penya, Denise Balik, Hoke Howell, Meegan King, Rob Bottin; *D:* Barbara Peeters; *W:* Frank Arnold, Frederick James, Martin B. Cohen; *C:* Daniel Lacambre; *M:* James Horner.

Humanoids from the Deep 🦴🦴 *Roger Corman Presents: Humanoids from the Deep* **1996 (R)** Remake of the 1980 Corman culter finds fishery manager Wade Parker (Carradine) and researcher Dr. Drake (Samms) dealing with a coastal town's battle against killers whose DNA has been genetically combined with that of fish. When the fish monsters escape the lab, their mutations are further altered by toxic waste and they go on a rampage. **90m/C VHS.** Robert Carradine, Emma Samms, Mark Rolston, Clint Howard, Kaz Garas, Warren Burton, Bert Remsen; *D:* Jeff Yonis; *W:* Jeff Yonis; *C:* Christopher Baffa; *M:* Christopher Lennertz. **CABLE**

Humongous woof! **1982 (R)** Braindead bevy of teens shipwreck on an island where they encounter a deranged mutant giant who must kill to survive. You'll be rooting for the monster. **93m/C VHS.** *CA* Janet (Johnson) Julian, David Wallace, Janit Baldwin, Joy Boushel, Page Fletcher; *D:* Paul Lynch; *W:* William Gray; *C:* Brian R.R. Hebb.

Humoresque 🦴🦴🦴½ **1946** Talented but struggling young musician Paul Boray (Garfield) finds a patron in the married, wealthy, and older Helen Wright (Crawford). His appreciation is not as romantic as she hoped. Stunning performance from Crawford, with excellent supporting cast (Levant supplies the witty comebacks), including a young Robert Blake as a young Paul. Fine music sequences (Isaac Stern dubbed the violin), and lush production values. **123m/B VHS.** Joan Crawford, John Garfield, Oscar Levant, J. Carrol Naish, Joan Chandler, Tom D'Andrea, Peggy Knudsen, Ruth Nelson, Craig Stevens, Paul Cavanagh, Richard Gaines, John Abbott, Robert (Bobby) Blake; *D:* Jean Negulesco; *W:* Clifford Odets, Zachary Gold; *C:* Ernest Haller; *M:* Franz Waxman.

The Hunchback 🦴🦴½ **1997** Cable version of Victor Hugo's ever-popular "The Hunchback of Notre Dame." In 15th-century Paris, hunchbanked Notre Dame bell-ringer Quasimodo (Patinkin) loves spirited and kind gypsy Esmeralda (Hayek), who's the lustful obsession of evil archdeacon Frollo (Harris). Properly melodramatic, with Harris stealing the film as the cold cleric. **98m/C VHS.** Mandy Patinkin, Richard Harris, Salma Hayek, Jim Dale, Edward Atterton; *D:* Peter Medak; *W:* John Fasano; *C:* Elemer Ragalyi; *M:* Ed Shearmur. **CABLE**

The Hunchback of Notre Dame 🦴🦴🦴 **1923** The first film version of Victor Hugo's novel about the tortured hunchback bellringer of Notre Dame Cathedral, famous for the contortions of Lon Chaney's self-transformations via improvised makeup. Also available at 68 minutes. **100m/B VHS, DVD.** Lon Chaney Sr., Patsy Ruth Miller, Norman Kerry, Ernest Torrence, Kate Lester, Brandon Hurst; *D:* Wallace Worsley II; *W:* Edward T. Lowe; *C:* Tony Kornman, Robert S. Newhard.

The Hunchback of Notre Dame 🦴🦴🦴🦴 **1939** Best Hollywood version of the Victor Hugo classic, infused with sweep, sadness, and an attempt at capturing a degree of spirited, Hugoesque detail. Laughton is Quasimodo, a deformed Parisian bellringer, who provides sanctuary to young gypsy Esmeralda (O'Hara) accused by church officials of being a witch. The final scene of the townspeople storming the cathedral remains a Hollywood classic. Great performances all around; the huge facade of the Notre Dame cathedral was constructed on a Hollywood set for this film. Remake of several earlier films, including 1923's Lon Chaney silent, and followed by several remakes for both the big screen (included an animated Disney version) and for TV. **117m/B VHS, DVD.** Charles Laughton, Maureen O'Hara, Edmond O'Brien, Cedric Hardwicke, Thomas Mitchell, George Zucco, Alan Marshal, Walter Hampden, Harry Davenport, Curt Bois, George Tobias, Rod La Rocque; *D:* William Dieterle; *W:* Sonya Levien, Bruno Frank; *C:* Joseph August; *M:* Alfred Newman.

The Hunchback of Notre Dame 🦴🦴½ *Notre Dame de Paris* **1957 (PG)** Slow retelling of the Victor Hugo novel, filmed entirely in France in CinemaScope. Quinn's the tragic Quasimodo with bombshell Lollobrigida appropriatley hot-blooded as gypsy Esmerelda. **104m/C VHS, DVD, Wide.** *FR* Anthony Quinn, Gina Lollobrigida, Alain Cuny, Jean Danet, Robert Hirsch, Jean Tissier; *D:* Jean Delannoy; *W:* Jacques Prevert, Jean Aurenche; *C:* Michel Kelber; *M:* Georges Auric.

The Hunchback of Notre Dame 🦴🦴🦴 *Hunchback* **1982 (PG)** It's not often that a classic novel is remade into a classic movie that's remade into a made-for-TV reprise, and survives its multiple renderings. But it's not often a cast so rich in stage trained actors is assembled on the small screen. Hopkins gives a textured, pre-Hannibal Lecter interpretation of Quasimodo, the Hunchback in Hugo's eponymous novel. Impressive model of the cathedral by production designer John Stoll. **102m/C VHS.** Anthony Hopkins, Derek Jacobi, Lesley-Anne Down, John Gielgud, Tim Pigott-Smith, Rosalie Crutchley, Robert Powell; *D:* Michael Tuchner.

The Hunchback of Notre Dame 🦴🦴🦴 **1996 (G)** Animated/musical version of Victor Hugo's story about deformed bellringer Quasimodo (Hulce) and his love for the beautiful gypsy Esmerelda (Moore). The original isn't exactly fun fare but you expect Disney to find a way to leave everybody humming (and happy). The sweeping music was provided by "Pocahontas" tunesmiths Menken and Schwartz. Comic relief is supplied by three gargoyles, companions to Quasimodo, who are voiced wonderfully by Alexander, Kimbrough and Wickes. Wickes, 85, died six weeks after voicing her role. Looks like another boatload of boxoffice, merchandising, and video sale cash is making its way into old Walt's vaults. **91m/C VHS, DVD, Wide.** *D:* Kirk Wise, Gary Trousdale; *W:* Irene Mecchi, Tab Murphy, Jonathan Roberts, Bob Tzudiker, Noni White; *M:* Stephen Schwartz, Alan Menken; *V:* Tom Hulce, Demi Moore, Kevin Kline, Tony Jay, Charles Kimbrough, Jason Alexander, Mary Wickes, David Ogden Stiers.

Hundra 🦴 **1985** A warrior queen vows revenge when her all-female tribe is slain by men. Nothing can stop her fierce vendetta—except love. **96m/C VHS.** *IT* Laurene Landon, John Gaffari, Ramiro Oliveros, Marissa Casel; *D:* Matt Cimber; *M:* Ennio Morricone.

A Hungarian Fairy Tale 🦴🦴🦴 *Hol Volt, Hol Nem Volt* **1987** Political satire meets fantasy in a magical tale of a fatherless young boy searching for a surrogate dad. Unusual characters as well as an homage to Mozart's "The Magic Flute." In Hungarian with English subtitles. **97m/B VHS.** *HU* Arpad Vermes, Maria Varga, Frantisek Husak, Eszter Csakanyi, Szilvia Toth, Judith Pogany, Geza Balkay; *D:* Gyula Gazdag.

Hungarian Rhapsody **1978** In 1911, a Hungarian nobleman joins the ranks of the rebelling peasants in order to oppose his brother, who represents aristocratic repression. One of Jancso's clearest political films, and one that continues the filmmaker's experiments with long, uncut sequences and dynamic mise-en-scene. In Hungarian with English subtitles. **101m/C VHS.** *HU* Gyorgy Cserhalmi, Lajos Balaszovits, Gabor Koncz, Bertalan Solti; *D:* Miklos Jancso.

Hunger *Sult* **1966** In the late 1800s, a starving Norwegian writer, unable to sell his work, rejects charity out of pride, and retains his faith in his talent. Based on a novel "Sult" by Knut Hamsun. In Danish with English subtitles. **115m/B VHS.** *DK* Per Oscarsson, Gunnel Lindblom; *D:* Henning Carlsen; *W:* Henning Carlsen. Cannes '66: Actor (Oscarsson); Natl. Soc. Film Critics '68: Actor (Oscarsson).

The Hunger **1983 (R)** A beautiful 2000-year-old vampire needs new blood when she realizes that her current lover, Bowie, is aging fast. Visually sumptuous but sleepwalking modern vampire tale, complete with soft-focus lesbian love scenes between Deneuve and Sarandon. **100m/C VHS, Wide.** Catherine Deneuve, David Bowie, Susan Sarandon, Cliff DeYoung, Ann Magnuson, Dan Hedaya, Willem Dafoe, Beth Ehlers, Suzanne Bertish, Rufus Collins, James Aubrey; *D:* Tony Scott; *W:* Michael Thomas, Ivan Davis; *C:* Stephen Goldblatt, Tom Mangravite; *M:* Denny Jaeger, Michel Rubini.

Hunk **1987 (PG)** A computer nerd sells his soul to the devil for a muscular, beach-blonde physique. Answers the question, "Was it worth it?" **102m/C VHS.** John Allen Nelson, Steve Levitt, Deborah Shelton, Rebecca Bush, James Coco, Avery Schreiber; *D:* Lawrence Bassoff; *W:* Lawrence Bassoff; *C:* Bryan England.

The Hunley ½ **1999** Based on the true story of the Confederate submarine that was used to defend Charleston harbor against Union forces in 1864. The experimental craft has already claimed the lives of two crews but General Beauregard (Sutherland) is desperate to break the blockade of the city and gives command to Lt. George E. Dixon (Assante), an engineer. As usual, Dixon's crew is a ragged bunch of misfits but Dixon perseveres. **120m/C VHS.** Armand Assante, Donald Sutherland, Alex Jennings, Sebastien Roche, Michael Dolan, Chris Bauer, Michael Stuhlbarg, Jack Baun, Kevin Robertson; *D:* John Gray; *W:* John Gray; *C:* John Thomas; *M:* Randy Edelman. CABLE

The Hunt *La Caza* **1965** A teenage boy accompanies three Spanish Civil War veterans on what is supposed to be a friendly rabbit hunt. Things turn violent, however, when old rivalries and tensions begin to surface. In Spanish with English subtitles. **87m/B VHS.** *SP* Alfredo Mayo, Ismael Merlo, Jose Maria Prada, Emilio Gutierrez-Caba, Fernando Sanchez Polack; *D:* Carlos Saura.

The Hunt for Red October **1990 (PG)** Based on Tom Clancy's blockbuster novel, a high-tech Cold War yarn about a Soviet nuclear sub (commanded by Connery) turning rogue and heading straight for U.S. waters, as both the U.S. and the U.S.S.R. try to stop it. Complicated, ill-plotted potboiler that succeeds breathlessly due to the cast and McTiernan's tommy-gun direction. Introduces the character of CIA analyst Jack Ryan (Baldwin) who returns in "Patriot Games," though in the guise of Harrison Ford. **137m/C VHS, DVD, 8mm, Wide.** Sean Connery, Alec Baldwin, Richard Jordan, Scott Glenn, Joss Ackland, Sam Neill, James Earl Jones, Peter Firth, Tim Curry, Courtney B. Vance, Jeffrey Jones, Fred Dalton Thompson; *D:* John McTiernan; *W:* Larry Ferguson, Donald Stewart; *C:* Jan De Bont; *M:* Basil Poledouris. Oscars '90: Sound FX Editing.

The Hunt for the Night Stalker *Manhunt: The Search for the Night Stalker* **1991 (PG-13)** Another one of those True-Detective quickies so beloved by network TV, following two hardworking L.A. cops who tracked down satanic serial killer Richard Ramirez in the mid-1980s. It originally aired (under the title "Manhunt: The Search for the Night Stalker") on the date of the killer's death-sentence verdict; the videotape lacks that particular timely sparkle. **95m/C VHS.** Richard Jordan, A. Martinez, Lisa Eilbacher, Julie Carmen, Alan Feinstein; *D:* Bruce Seth Green. TV

Hunt the Man Down ½ **1950** An innocent man is charged with murder, and a public defender must find the real killer before time runs out. **68m/B VHS.** Gig Young, Lynne Roberts, Gerald Mohr; *D:* George Archainbaud.

Hunted **1988 (PG)** WWII prisoner attempts to escape from demented officer who seems to enjoy bugging him. Hunted by the MPs, he relies on unorthodox guide to sustain feature length footage. **75m/C VHS.** Andrew Buckland, Richard Carlson, Ron Smerczak, Mercia Van Wyk; *D:* David Lister.

The Hunted ½ **1994 (R)** American businessman in Japan meets, beds, and witnesses the assassination of a mysterious woman and is forced on the run by the modern-day ninja clan that committed the crime. Only a notch above the low-budget, badly dubbed martial arts flicks of the '70s, this shameless bloodfest features unintentionally campy performances by Lambert and Lone and lots of silly dialogue. Beware, the cliches pile up as quickly as the bodies. **110m/C VHS, DVD, Wide.** Christopher Lambert, John Lone, Joan Chen, Yoshio Harada, Yoko Shimada, Mari Natsuki, Tak Kubota; *D:* J.F. Lawton; *W:* J.F. Lawton; *C:* Jack Conroy; *M:* Motofumi Yamaguchi.

The Hunted **1998 (R)** Insurance investigator Samantha Clark (Amick) needs to recover $12 million from a crash site in the Pacific Northwest. She meets reclusive Doc (Hamlin), who offers to help her out and then discovers she's become the prey in a deadly hunt. **96m/C VHS.** Harry Hamlin, Madchen Amick, Hannes Jaenicke; *D:* Stuart Cooper; *W:* Bennett Cohen, David Ives; *C:* Curtis Petersen. VIDEO

The Hunted Lady ½ **1977** In this TV pilot, Mills is an undercover policewoman who is framed by the mob. Tired and predictable. **100m/C VHS.** Donna Mills, Robert Reed, Lawrence Casey, Andrew Duggan, Will Sampson, Alan Feinstein; *D:* Richard Lang. TV

Hunter ½ **1973** Unsuccessful TV pilot in which a government agent uncovers an enemy brainwashing scam. **90m/C VHS.** John Vernon, Steve Ihnat, Fritz Weaver, Edward Binns, Sabrina Scharf, Barbara Rhoades; *D:* Leonard Horn. TV

Hunter **1977** An attorney is falsely accused of a crime and imprisoned. Released after eight years, he sets out to even the score with the mysterious millionaire who set him up. **120m/C VHS.** James Franciscus, Linda Evans, Broderick Crawford. TV

The Hunter ½ **1980 (PG)** Action drama based on the real life adventures of Ralph (Papa) Thorson, a modern day bounty hunter who makes his living by finding fugitives who have jumped bail. McQueen's last. **97m/C VHS, DVD, Wide.** Steve McQueen, Eli Wallach, Kathryn Harrold, LeVar Burton; *D:* Buzz Kulik; *W:* Peter Hyams; *C:* Fred W. Koenekamp; *M:* Charles Bernstein.

Hunter in the Dark **1980** Set in 18th-century Japan, where power, betrayal, and corruption are the dark side of the samurai world. Tanuma is a powerful shogunate minister who becomes involved with Gomyo, the leader of a secret underworld organization of thieves and murderers with a violent honor code. In Japanese with English subtitles. **138m/C VHS, Wide.** *JP* Tatsuya Nakadai, Tetsuro Tamba, Sonny Chiba; *D:* Hideo Gosha.

The Hunters ½ **1958** A motley crew of pilots learn about each other and themselves in this melodrama set during Korean war. Incredible aerial photography sets this apart from other films of the genre. **108m/C VHS.** Robert Mitchum, Robert Wagner, Richard Egan, May Britt, Lee Philips, John Gabriel, Stacy Harris, John Doucette, Jay Jostyn, Leon Lontoc, Ralph Manza, Alena Murray, Robert Reed, Victor Sen Yung, Candace Lee; *D:* Dick Powell; *W:* Wendell Mayes; *C:* Charles Clarke; *M:* Paul Sawtell.

Hunter's Blood ½ **1987 (R)** Five urbanites plunge into the Southern wilderness to hunt deer, and are stalked by maniacal hillbillies. **102m/C VHS.** Sam Bottoms, Kim Delaney, Clu Gulager, Mayf Nutter, Eugene Glazer; *D:* Robert C. Hughes; *W:* Emmett Alston.

Hunter's Moon ½ **1997 (R)** Reynolds plays a very bad guy (very well) as a Depression era, Kentucky backwoods moonshiner who has no intention of letting his lovely daughter, Flo (Du Mond), fall for a city boy (Carradine) who's trying to make a new life for himself. **104m/C VHS, DVD.** Burt Reynolds, Keith Carradine, Hayley Du Mond, Ann Wedgeworth, Pat Hingle, Brion James, Charles Napier; *D:* Richard Weinman; *W:* Richard Weinman, L. Ford Neale, John Huff, William Kemper; *C:* Suki Medencevic.

Hunters of the Golden Cobra **1982 (R)** Two American soldiers plot to recover the priceless golden cobra from the Japanese general who stole the prized relic during the last days of WWII. **95m/C VHS.** David Warbeck, Almanta Suska, Alan Collins, John Steiner; *D:* Anthony (Antonio Margheriti) Dawson.

The Hunting **1992 (R)** A married woman falls for a ruthless businessman and is drawn into a web of blackmail and murder in this low-budget erotic thriller. **97m/C VHS.** John Savage, Kerry Armstrong, Guy Pearce, Rebecca Rigg; *D:* Frank Howson; *W:* Frank Howson.

Hurlyburly **1998 (R)** Casting agents Eddie (Penn) and Mickey (Spacey) share a Hollywood apartment with out-of-work actor Phil (Palminteri). Eddie uses cocaine almost constantly, Phil has just been dumped by his wife, and Mickey (Spacey), although more low key, is himself ready to explode. They're all desperate to be huge "Hollywood" successes. Plot pretty much consists of the men venting their spleens and treating women like crap, particularly Bonnie (Ryan), a slutty exotic dancer traded between the boys. Snappy dialogue-happy script might have worked on the stage, but here, with the camera in close, the mean spirit becomes tiring very quickly. Paquin shows confidence in her first adult role, as a drifter girl-toy. **122m/C VHS, DVD, Wide.** Sean Penn, Kevin Spacey, Chazz Palminteri, Meg Ryan, Robin Wright Penn, Anna Paquin, Garry Shandling; *D:* Tony Drazan; *W:* David Rabe; *C:* Gu Changwei; *M:* David Baerwald.

The Hurricane **1937** A couple on the run from the law are aided by a hurricane and are able to build a new life for themselves on an idyllic island. Filmed two years before the Academy's "special effects" award came into being, but displaying some of the best effects of the decade. Boringly remade in 1979. **102m/B VHS, DVD.** Jon Hall, Dorothy Lamour, Mary Astor, Sir C. Aubrey Smith, Raymond Massey, Thomas Mitchell, John Carradine; *D:* John Ford; *W:* Oliver H.P. Garrett, Dudley Nichols; *C:* Bert Glennon, Paul Eagler, Archie Stout; *M:* Alfred Newman. Oscars '37: Sound.

Hurricane **1974** TV's answer to the disaster movie craze of the early 1970s. Realistic hurricane footage and an adequate cast cannot save this catastrophe. **78m/C VHS.** Larry Hagman, Martin Milner, Jessica Walter, Barry Sullivan, Will Geer, Frank Sutton; *D:* Jerry Jameson. TV

Hurricane woof! *Forbidden Paradise* **1979 (PG)** And the wind cried, "turkey." Robards is the governor of a tropical island beset with environmental and personal concerns. Virginal daughter Farrow falls for hunky native, standard colonial power/indigenous people complications ensue, vital explanatory footage is cut, and overacting reaches epidemic heights. Then too late the big wind blows in, leveling the place. Expensive (most of the $22 million must have gone to catering) and essentially misdirected remake of the 1937 semi-classic. **120m/C VHS.** Mia Farrow, Jason Robards Jr., Trevor Howard, Max von Sydow, Timothy Bottoms, James Keach; *D:* Jan Troell; *C:* Sven Nykvist; *M:* Nino Rota.

The Hurricane *Lazarus and the Hurricane* **1999 (R)** Moving, albeit truncated account of the true story of middleweight boxing champ Rubin "Hurricane" Carter (Washington—in peak physical and professional form), who was falsely accused and convicted of murder and who spent 20 years in prison. Anchored by a transcendent performance by Washington, pic came under fire for its liberal rearrangement of the facts behind the case. If you want a full lowdown on the case, read one of several books written about this unique court battle by Carter himself ("The Sixteenth Round") or "Lazurus and the Hurricane," which served as the basis for the film; but if you want to see acting that can lift one to a higher spirtual plane, give "The Hurricane" a look. Carter was immortalized in Bob Dylan's 1976 protest song, "Hurricane." **125m/B VHS, DVD, Wide.** Denzel Washington, Vicellous Reon Shannon, Deborah Kara Unger, Liev Schreiber, John Hannah, David Paymer, Dan Hedaya, Debbi (Deborah) Morgan, Clancy Brown, Harris Yulin, Vincent Pastore, Rod Steiger; *D:* Norman Jewison; *W:* Armyan Bernstein, Dan Gordon; *C:* Roger Deakins; *M:* Christopher Young. Golden Globes '00: Actor—Drama (Washington).

Hurricane Express **1932** Twelve episodes of the vintage serial, in which the Duke pits his courage against an unknown, powerful individual out to sabotage a railroad. **223m/B VHS.** John Wayne, Joseph Girard, Conway Tearle, Shirley Grey; *D:* J(ohn) P(aterson) McGowan, Armand Schaefer.

Hurricane Smith **1992 (R)** Weathers stars as a roughneck Texan who travels to Australia's Gold Coast in search of his missing sister. While in the land of Oz, he gets entangled in a Mafia-style drug and prostitution ring around the "Surfer's Paradise" section of the Gold Coast. Packed with mind-blowing stunts and a good performance from Weathers, this fast-paced action thriller won't disappoint fans of this genre. **86m/C VHS.** Carl Weathers, Juergen Prochnow, Tony Bonner, Cassandra Delaney; *D:* Colin Budds.

Hurricane Streets ½ *Hurricane* **1996** Freeman's directorial debut centers on a group of young teenagers getting into trouble in lower Manhattan. 15-year-old Marcus (Sexton) is on the edge—his dad is dead, his mother's in jail, he's being ineffectually looked after by his working grandma, and the authorities are already eyeing this petty thief. He hangs with three buddies, one of whom, Chip (Frank), wants to start them stealing cars. Meanwhile, Marcus falls for 14-year-old Melena (Vega), whose father is both possessive and abusive, and tries to plan an escape for them both. **89m/C VHS.** Terry Alexander, Brendan Sexton III, Isidra Vega, David Roland Frank, L.M. Kit Carson, Jose Zuniga, Lynn Cohen, Edie Falco, Shawn Elliot, Heather Matarazzo; *D:* Morgan J. Freeman; *W:* Morgan J. Freeman; *C:* Enrique Chediak. Sundance '97: Cinematog., Director (Freeman), Aud. Award.

Hurry, Charlie, Hurry **1941** Husband gets in trouble when he bows out of a trip with his social-climber wife when he tells her he must travel to Washington to see the Vice President. **65m/B VHS.** Leon Errol.

Hurry Up or I'll Be Thirty **1973** A Brooklyn bachelor celebrates his 30th birthday by becoming morose, depressed, and enraged. His friends try to help; they fail, but he finds love anyway. For those seeking a better life through celluloid. **87m/C VHS.** Danny DeVito, John Lefkowitz, Steve Inwood, Linda DeCoff, Ronald Anton, Maureen Byrnes, Francis Gallagher; *D:* Joseph Jacoby.

Husband Hunting **196?** Working girls hit the beach in search of husbands, and find that love isn't easy to find or hold on to. **90m/C VHS.** *IT* Walter Chiari.

Husbands ½ **1970 (PG-13)** When Stuart (Rowlands) dies suddenly of a heart attack, his three equally middleaged buddies—Harry (Gazzara), Archie (Falk), and Gus (Cassavettes)—are reluctantly confronted with their own mortality. These suburban married men decide to cut loose and go on a spree, with Harry even persuading his buddies they should carry their frantic merriment across the pond in a trip to London. Meanders on a bit too long, thanks to Cassavettes usual reliance on improv and reluctance to edit. **140m/C VHS.** Ben Gazzara, Peter Falk, John Cassavetes, Jenny Runacre, David Rowlands, Jenny Lee Wright, Noelle Kao; ***D:*** John Cassavetes; ***W:*** John Cassavetes; ***C:*** Victor Kemper.

Husbands and Lovers **1991 (R)** Controversial and confusing film focuses on a couple's untraditional marriage. Stephen (Sands) and Alina (Pacula) have agreed to be totally honest with each other and when Alina decides to take a lover, Stephen agrees on the condition that she report back to him every intimate detail of her affair. In the confusion and excitement of this kinky love triangle, everyone starts losing control as sexual boundaries are pushed to the limit. Also available in an unrated version. **91m/C VHS.** Julian Sands, Joanna Pacula, Tcheky Karyo; ***D:*** Mauro Bolognini; ***W:*** Sergio Bazzini; ***M:*** Ennio Morricone.

Husbands and Wives ½ **1992 (R)** Art imitates life as Allen/Farrow relationship dissolves onscreen (and off) and Woody becomes involved with young student. Mature, penetrating look at modern pair bonding and loneliness offers more painful honesty and sadness than outright laughs, though still retains essential Allen charm. Stylistically burdened by experiment with pseudo-documentary telling of tale and spasmodic hand-held cameras that annoy more than entertain. Excellent, intriguing cast, notably Davis as the overwhelming, overbearing wife/friend. Trailers became unintentionally funny in light of the highly publicized personal problems of Allen and Farrow. **107m/C VHS, DVD, Wide.** Woody Allen, Mia Farrow, Judy Davis, Sydney Pollack, Liam Neeson, Juliette Lewis, Lysette Anthony, Blythe Danner; ***D:*** Woody Allen; ***W:*** Woody Allen; ***C:*** Carlo Di Palma. British Acad. '92: Orig. Screenplay; L.A. Film Critics '92: Support. Actress (Davis); Natl. Bd. of Review '92: Support. Actress (Davis); Natl. Soc. Film Critics '92: Support. Actress (Davis).

Husbands, Wives, Money, and Murder **1986** A couple is pushed over the edge by a nosey census taker and then must dispose of the consequences. **92m/C VHS.** Garrett Morris, Greg Mullavey, Meredith MacRae, Timothy Bottoms; ***D:*** Bruce Cook Jr.

Hush ½ *Kilronan; Bloodline* **1998 (PG-13)** Stinky thriller stars Paltrow as a working-class gal who marries wealthy dreamboat Jackson (Schaech) and moves to his family's Kentucky estate, Kilronan. There, smother-in-law Lange camps it up (albeit unknowingly) as she turns psycho on the pregnant bride while coming on to her dim-witted son who doesn't have a clue. Apparently, neither did filmmaker Darby, whose film was held from release pending two years of pasting Band-Aids on this gaping wound of a movie. Foch's crusty grandmother is the sole highlight of this horror of a film. **96m/C VHS, DVD.** Gwyneth Paltrow, Jessica Lange, Johnathon Schaech, Nina Foch, Debi Mazar, Kaiulani Lee, David Thornton, Hal Holbrook; ***D:*** Jonathan Darby; ***W:*** Jonathan Darby, Jane Rusconi; ***C:*** Andrew Dunn; ***M:*** Christopher Young.

Hush, Hush, Sweet Charlotte **1965** A fading southern belle finds out the truth about her married lover's murder when the case is reopened 37 years later by her cousin in an elaborate plot to drive her crazy. Grisly, superbly entertaining Southern Gothic horror tale, with vivid performances from the aging leads. **134m/B VHS.** Bette Davis, Olivia de Havilland, Joseph Cotten, Agnes Moorehead, Mary Astor, Bruce Dern, Cecil Kellaway, Victor Buono; ***D:*** Robert Aldrich; ***W:*** Lukas Heller, Henry Farrell; ***C:*** Joseph Biroc. Golden Globes '65: Support. Actress (Moorehead).

Hush Little Baby, Don't You Cry **1986** Drama about a seemingly normal middle-aged family man who is in actuality a child abuser/murderer. **110m/C VHS.** Emery L. Kedocia, Gary Giem, Tony Grant, Burt Douglas; ***D:*** Don Hawks. **TV**

Hussy **1980 (R)** Hooker and her boyfriend find themselves trapped in a web of gangsters and drugs. **95m/C VHS.** *GB* Helen Mirren, John Shea, Jenny Runacre; ***D:*** Matthew Chapman; ***W:*** Matthew Chapman; ***M:*** George Fenton.

The Hustle **1975 (R)** Gritty urban adventure with Reynolds as an L.A. detective investigating a young call girl's death. He becomes romantically entangled with high-priced call girl Deneuve. **120m/C VHS.** Burt Reynolds, Catherine Deneuve; ***D:*** Robert Aldrich; ***C:*** Joseph Biroc.

The Hustler **1961** The original story of Fast Eddie Felsen and his adventures in the seedy world of professional pool. Newman plays the naive, talented and self-destructive Felsen perfectly, Laurie is oustanding as his lover, and Gleason epitomizes the pool great Minnesota Fats. Rivetingly atmospheric, and exquisitely photographed. Parent to the reprise "The Color of Money," made 25 years later. **134m/B VHS.** Paul Newman, Jackie Gleason, Piper Laurie, George C. Scott, Myron McCormick, Murray Hamilton, Michael Constantine, Jake La Motta, Vincent Gardenia; ***D:*** Robert Rossen; ***W:*** Robert Rossen; ***C:*** Eugene (Eugen Shufftan) Shuftan. Oscars '61: Art Dir./Set Dec., B&W, B&W Cinematog.; British Acad. '61: Actor (Newman), Film; Natl. Bd. of Review '61: Support. Actor (Gleason), Natl. Film Reg. '97;; N.Y. Film Critics '61: Director (Rossen).

Hustler Squad **1976 (R)** U.S. Army major and Philippine guerrilla leader stage a major operation to help rid the Philippines of Japanese Occupation forces: they have four combat-trained prostitutes infiltrate a brothel patronized by top Japanese officers. Verrrrry clever. **98m/C VHS.** John Ericson, Karen Ericson, Lynda Sinclaire, Nory Wright; ***D:*** Ted V. Mikels.

Hustler White **1996** Outrageous underground actor/filmmaker LaBruce stars as pretentious German writer Jurgen Anger, who comes to Hollywood to research the gay scene for a book. Cruising Santa Monica Boulevard he becomes obsessively intrigued by local hustler Montgomery Ward (Ward), who serves as a tour guide to the city's sexual kinks. Yes, it's racy, but it's also not as hardcore as the subject matter might imply. **80m/C VHS.** Tony Ward, Bruce La Bruce; ***D:*** Rick Castro, Bruce La Bruce; ***W:*** Rick Castro, Bruce La Bruce; ***C:*** James Carman.

Hustling **1975** A reporter writing a series of articles on prostitution in New York City takes an incisive look at their unusual and sometimes brutal world. Notable performance by Remick as the reporter and Clayburgh as a victimized hooker. Made for TV and based on a novel by Gail Sheehy. **96m/C VHS.** Jill Clayburgh, Lee Remick, Alex Rocco, Monte Markham; ***D:*** Joseph Sargent. **TV**

Hybrid ½ **1997 (R)** Another bleak apocalyptic future flick, which finds a handful of survivors stumbling across a remote desert lab where they decide to take shelter. Big mistake since the lab still houses a living alien hybrid that's bent on reproduction and destruction. **87m/C VHS.** Brinke Stevens, Tim Abell, John Barrymore III.

Hyena of London **1962** A doctor steals the hyena of London's corpse and injects the rabid protoplasm into his own brain with deadly results. **?m/C VHS.** Diana Martin, Bernard Price.

Hyper-Sapien: People from Another Star ½ **1986 (PG)** Two cuddly aliens run away from home, are befriended by a lonely farmboy, and are chased all over the wilds of Wyoming. **93m/C VHS.** Sydney Penny, Keenan Wynn, Gail Strickland, Ricky Paull Goldin, Peter Jason, Talia Shire; ***D:*** Peter Hunt; ***W:*** Richard Adcock, Christopher Blue.

Hyper Space ½ *Black Forest: Rage in Space* **1989** Six people awaken from cryogenic sleep to discover that their spaceship has become marooned lightyears from earth and only a single passenger shuttle is available to get someone home. Naturally, everyone wants that one chance. **90m/C VHS, DVD.** Richard Norton, Don Stroud, Lynn-Holly Johnson, James Van Patten, Ron O'Neal, Rebecca Cruz; ***D:*** David Huey; ***W:*** Richard Dominguez; ***C:*** Roger Olkowski.

The Hypothesis of the Stolen Painting *L'Hypothese du Tableau Vole* **1978** An art collector guides an interviewer around six paintings by Frederic Tonnerre, an academic 19th century painter, in an attempt to solve the mysterious disappearance of a seventh painting. The film presents the paintings as tableaux vivants in which the actors hold poses as they are examined. Based on the novel "Baphomet" by Pierre Klossowski. In French with English subtitles. **87m/B VHS.** ***D:*** Raul Ruiz; ***W:*** Raul Ruiz.

Hysteria ½ **1964 (PG)** When an American becomes involved in an accident and has amnesia, a mysterious benefactor pays all his bills and gives the man a house to live in. But a series of murders could mean he's the murderer—or the next victim. **85m/B VHS.** *GB* Robert Webber, Sue Lloyd, Maurice Denham; ***D:*** Freddie Francis; ***W:*** Jimmy Sangster; ***M:*** Don Banks.

Hysterical **1983 (PG)** Odd little attempt at a horror flick parody features the Hudson Brothers and involves a haunted lighthouse occupied by the vengeful spirit of a spurned woman. Late-night fun. **86m/C VHS, DVD.** Brett Hudson, Bill Hudson, Mark Hudson, Cindy Pickett, Richard Kiel, Julie Newmar, Bud Cort; ***D:*** Chris Bearde; ***W:*** Trace Johnston, Brett Hudson, Bill Hudson, Mark Hudson; ***C:*** Thomas Del Ruth; ***M:*** Robert Alcivar.

I, a Woman *Jag, en Kvinna* **1966** Siv (Persson) is a seductive young nurse who likes to have sex with every man she meets—and then leave them after they fall in love with her. Based on the novel by the pseudononomous Siv Holm. Dubbed. **90m/B VHS, DVD.** *SW* Essy Persson, Jorgen Reenberg, Preben Mahrt; ***D:*** Mac Ahlberg; ***W:*** Peer Guldbrandsen; ***C:*** Mac Ahlberg.

I Accuse My Parents ½ **1945** Juvenile delinquent tries to blame a murder and his involvement in a gang of thieves on his mom and dad's failure to raise him properly. **70m/B VHS.** Mary Beth Hughes, Robert Lowell, John Miljan, Edward Earle, Patricia Knox, George Meeker, George Lloyd; ***D:*** Sam Newfield; ***W:*** Marjorie Dudley; ***C:*** Robert C. Cline; ***M:*** Lee Zahler.

I Am a Camera **1955** A young English writer develops a relationship with a reckless young English girl in Berlin during the 1930s. Based on the Berlin stories by Christopher Isherwood, later musicalized as "Cabaret." **99m/B VHS.** *GB* Julie Harris, Shelley Winters, Laurence Harvey, Patrick McGoohan; ***D:*** Henry Cornelius; ***C:*** Guy Green; ***M:*** Malcolm Arnold.

I Am a Fugitive from a Chain Gang *I Am a Fugitive From the Chain Gang* **1932** WWI veteran Muni returns home with dreams of traveling across America. After a brief stint as a clerk, he strikes out on his own. Near penniless, Muni meets up with a tramp who takes him to get a hamburger. He becomes an unwilling accomplice when the bum suddenly robs the place. Convicted and sentenced to a Georgia chain gang, he's brutalized and degraded, though he eventually escapes and lives the life of a criminal on the run. Based on the autobiography by Robert E. Burns. Brutal docu-details combine with powerhouse performances to create a classic. Timeless and thought-provoking. **93m/B VHS.** Paul Muni, Glenda Farrell, Helen Vinson, Preston Foster, Edward Ellis, Allen Jenkins; ***D:*** Mervyn LeRoy; ***W:*** Howard J. Green. Natl. Film Reg. '91.

I Am Cuba *Soy Cuba; Ja Cuba* **1964** Agitprop Russian-Cuban co-production illustrates different aspects of the Cuban revolution from the toppling of Batista's decadent Havana to idealistic soldiers and student revolutionaries. Lots of oratory and deliberate artificiality combined with cinematographer Urusevky's stunning high-contrast photography. Spanish and Russian with subtitles. **141m/B VHS, DVD.** *CU RU* Luz Maria Collazo, Jose Gallardo, Sergio Corrieri, Jean Bouise, Raul Garcia, Celia Rodriguez; ***D:*** Mikhail Kalatozov; ***W:*** Yevgeny Yevtushenko, Enrique Pineda Barnet; ***C:*** Sergei Urusevsky; ***M:*** Carlos Farinas.

I Am Curious (Yellow) ½ *Jag ar nyfiken-gul; Jag ar nyfiken-en film i gult* **1967** A woman sociologist is conducting a sexual survey on Swedish society, which leads her to have numerous sexual encounters in all sorts of places. Very controversial upon its U.S. release because of the nudity and sexual content but tame by today's standards. Followed by "I Am Curious (Blue)" which was filmed at the same time. In Swedish with English subtitles. **95m/B VHS.** *SW* Lena Nyman, Peter Lindgren, Borje Ahlstedt, Marie Goranzon, Magnus Nilsson; ***D:*** Vilgot Sjoman; ***W:*** Vilgot Sjoman; ***M:*** Bengt Ernryd.

I Am Frigid...Why? *Je Suis Frigide...Pourquoi?; She Should Have Stayed in Bed; Comment le Desir Vient aux Filles* **1972** Eighteen-year-old Doris is the gardener's daughter. She is raped by Eric Chambon, the estate owner's son, and is then sent to boarding school to hush up the scandal. But Doris can't forget and befriends an older woman who runs an expensive call girl operation in Paris. Doris joins her other girls and one of her clients turns out to be Eric's father. French with subtitles. **90m/C VHS.** *FR* Joelle Coeur, Sandra Julien, Anne Kerylen, Stephane Machanovitch, Marie-Georges Pascal, Thierry Murzeau, Jean-Luc Terrade, Virginie Vignon; ***D:*** Max Pecas; ***W:*** Max Pecas; ***C:*** Robert Lefebvre; ***M:*** Derry Hall.

I Am Sam ½ **2001 (PG-13)** Single father Penn has the mental capacity of a seven-year-old which makes authorities question his ability to raise young daughter Fanning. Pfeifer's the hard-edged lawyer who comes to his aid and becomes a better person for it. Overly sentimental and sweet, with not much new to offer except the obvious talent of Fanning. **93m/C VHS, DVD, Wide.** Sean Penn, Michelle Pfeiffer, Dakota Fanning, Dianne Wiest, Loretta Devine, Richard Schiff, Laura Dern, Brad Allan Silverman, Stanley DeSantis, Doug Hutchison, Joseph Rosenberg, Mary Steenburgen; ***D:*** Jessie Nelson; ***W:*** Jessie Nelson, Kristine Johnson; ***C:*** Elliot Davis; ***M:*** John Powell.

I Am the Cheese **1983** An institutionalized boy undergoes psychiatric treatment; with the aid of his therapist (Wagner) he relives his traumatic childhood and finds out the truth about the death of his parents. A bit muddled, but with its moments. Adapted from a Robert Cormier teen novel. **95m/C VHS.** Robert MacNaughton, Hope Lange, Don Murray, Robert Wagner, Sudie Bond; ***D:*** Robert Jiras.

I Am the Law **1938** Robinson is given the task of stopping gangster activity in the city. Although regularly a law professor, he is made special prosecutor and starts canvassing for people to testify. His witnesses become murder victims as an enemy on the inside attempts to thwart the game plan. Robinson is dismissed from the case but continues to pursue justice in streetclothes. Fine performances but somewhat predictable. **83m/B VHS.** Edward G. Robinson, Otto Kruger, John Beal, Barbara O'Neil, Wendy Barrie, Arthur Loft, Marc Lawrence, Charles Halton; ***D:*** Alexander Hall; ***W:*** Jo Swerling.

I Beheld His Glory **1953** Story based on the experience of Cornelius, the Roman centurion who guarded Christ's tomb. **53m/C VHS.** George Macready, Robert Wilson, Virginia Wave.

I Bombed Pearl Harbor **1960** Mifune stars in this epic that shows events of WWII through Japanese eyes. Dramatic battle scenes boast the most ships destroyed per minute of film. Dubbed from Japanese. **98m/C VHS.** *JP* Toshiro Mifune; ***D:*** Shue Matsubayashi.

I Bury the Living **1958** A cemetery manager sticks pins in his map of a graveyard and people mysteriously start to die. Well-done suspense film. **76m/B VHS, DVD.** Richard Boone, Theodore Bikel, Peggy Maurer, Herbert Anderson, Howard Smith, Robert Osterloh, Russ Bender, Matt Moore, Ken Drake, Glenn Vernon, Lynn Bernay, Cyril Delevanti; ***D:*** Albert Band; ***W:*** Louis Garfinkle; ***C:*** Frederick Gately; ***M:*** Gerald Fried.

I Can't Escape **1934** A man attempts to piece his life back together after serving time for a crime he didn't commit. To prove himself to his girlfriend, he tries to break up an illegal stock scam. **60m/B VHS.** Onslow Stevens, Lila Lee, Russell Gleason, Otis Harlan, Hooper Atchley, Clara Kimball Young; ***D:*** Otto Brower.

I Can't Sleep 🦴🦴 *J'ai Pas Sommeil* **1993** Serial killers, French style. Gay, black Camille (Courcet), an immigrant from Martinique, and his white lover Raphael (Dupont) live in a Paris hotel and murder elderly women. Though they also rob them, the motive for their horrific crimes is vague (seemingly even to themselves). Not much actually happens—Camille visits his brother, who longs to return home, and their status as outsiders is juxtaposed against another immigrant, Daiga (Golubeva) from Lithuania, who takes little interest in the crimes but unwittingly crosses paths with Camille. Atmospheric if nothing else. Based on the 1987 "Granny Killer" slayings of 20 women. French with subtitles. **110m/C VHS.** *FR* Richard Courcet, Vincent Dupont, Katerina Golubeva, Alex Descas, Beatrice Dalle, Laurent Grevill; *D:* Claire Denis; *W:* Claire Denis, Jean-Pol Fargeau; *C:* Agnes Godard; *M:* Jean Murat.

I Come in Peace 🦴🦴 *Dark Angel* **1990 (R)** A tough, maverick Texas cop embarks on a one-way ride to Nosebleed City when he attempts to track down a malevolent alien drug czar who kills his victims by sucking their brains. Mindless thrills. **92m/C VHS.** Dolph Lundgren, Brian Benben, Betsy Brantley, Jesse Vint, Michael J. Pollard; *D:* Craig R. Baxley; *M:* Jan Hammer.

I Confess 🦴🦴½ **1953** Interesting but overly serious mid-career Hitchcock, adapted from Paul Anthelme's 1902 play, "Our Two Consciences." Father Michael Logan (Clift) is a young curate in Quebec, who hears the murder confession of Otto Keller (Hasse). Keller knows Father Logan can tell no one because of the sanctity of the confessional, even when Logan himself comes under suspicion for the crime. Unfortunately, the resolution to the conflict is not up to the master's usual standards. **95m/B VHS.** Montgomery Clift, Anne Baxter, Karl Malden, Brian Aherne, O.E. Hasse, Dolly Haas, Roger Dann; *D:* Alfred Hitchcock; *W:* William Archibald, George Tabori; *C:* Robert Burks; *M:* Dimitri Tiomkin.

I Conquer the Sea 🦴½ **1936** Two brothers, who works as whalers, cast their affection on the same woman. Drowns in its own melodrama. **68m/B VHS, 8mm.** Steffi Duna, Dennis Morgan, Douglas Walton, George Cleveland, Johnny Pirrone; *D:* Victor Halperin.

I Could Go on Singing 🦴🦴½ **1963** An aging American songstress, on a tour in Britain, becomes reacquainted with her illegitimate son and his British father, but eventually goes back to the footlights. Garland's last film. Songs include "By Myself" and "It Never Was You." A must for Garland fans. Letterboxed. **99m/C VHS, Wide.** Judy Garland, Dirk Bogarde, Jack Klugman, Aline MacMahon; *D:* Ronald Neame.

I Cover the Waterfront 🦴🦴½ **1933** A reporter is assigned to write about a boatman involved in a fishy scheme to smuggle Chinese immigrants into the country wrapped in shark skins. While trying to get the story, the journalist falls in love with the fisherman's daughter. Torrance passed away before its release. **70m/B VHS.** Claudette Colbert, Ben Lyon, Ernest Torrence, Hobart Cavanaugh; *D:* James Cruze.

I Died a Thousand Times 🦴🦴 **1955** Aging gangster Mad Dog Earle (pushup prince Palance) plans one last death-defying heist while hiding from police in the mountains. Meanwhile, the hard boiled gangster softens a bit thanks to surgery-needing girlfriend, but moll Winters doesn't seem to think that three's company. A low rent "High Sierra." From the novel by W.R. Burnett. **109m/C VHS, Wide.** Jack Palance, Shelley Winters, Lori Nelson, Lee Marvin, Earl Holliman, Lon Chaney Jr., Howard St. John; *D:* Stuart Heisler; *W:* W.R. Burnett.

I Dismember Mama woof! *Poor Albert and Little Annie* **1974 (R)** Classless story of an asylum inmate who escapes to kill his mother. Although he hates women, he likes little girls as evidenced by his nine-year-old love interest. Notably lacking in bloody scenes. **81m/C VHS.** Zooey Hall, Joanne Moore Jordan, Greg Mullavey, Marlene Tracy, Geri Reischl, Frank Whiteman; *D:* Paul Leder; *W:* William W. Norton Sr.; *C:* Andreas Mannkopff; *M:* Herschel Burke Gilbert.

I Do! I Do! **1984** This Los Angeles production of the Broadway musical covers 50 years of a marriage, beginning just before the turn of the century. **116m/C VHS.** Lee Remick, Hal Linden.

I Don't Buy Kisses Anymore 🦴🦴½ **1992 (PG)** Heartwarming story starring Alexander and Peeples as two mismatched lovers who end up realizing that they're made for each other. Alexander plays Bernie Fishbine, an overweight Jewish shoe store owner who falls for a psychology graduate student (Peeples). Little does he know, but Peeples is studying him for her term paper, appropriately titled "The Psychological Study of an Obese Male." Alexander gives a great performance, as do Kazan and Jacobi who play Bernie's parents. **112m/C VHS.** Jason Alexander, Nia Peeples, Lainie Kazan, Lou Jacobi, Eileen Brennan, Larry Storch, Arleen (Arlene) Sorkin; *D:* Robert Marcarelli; *W:* Jonnie Lindsell; *C:* Michael Ferris; *M:* Cobb Bussinger. **TV**

I Don't Give a Damn 🦴🦴 **1988 (R)** An embittered wounded soldier returns home to his loved ones, rejects them, and becomes more and more uninterested in life itself. Subtitled. **94m/C VHS.** *IS* Ika Sohar, Anat Waxman; *D:* Shmuel Imberman.

I Don't Want to Be Born 🦴 *The Devil Within Her* **1975 (R)** It's got all the right ingredients for overnight camp: a spurned dwarf, a large, howling babything, slice and dice murder and mayhem, and Collins. It could've been so bad. Instead, this "Rosemary's Baby" rehash is just stupid bad. **90m/C VHS.** *GB* Joan Collins, Eileen Atkins, Donald Pleasence, Ralph Bates, Caroline Munro; *D:* Peter Sasdy.

I Don't Want to Talk About It 🦴🦴½ *De Eso No Se Habla* **1994** Fable set in a small South American town in the '30s. The widowed Leonor (Brando) is the community leader, a woman determined to see that her daughter Charlotte (Podesta) be as happy and accomplished as possible. Leonor refuses to acknowledge Charlotte is a dwarf and size is never permitted to be mentioned in her presence. Her zealous protectiveness is challenged by worldly and charming newcomer Ludovico (Mastroianni) who becomes entranced by Charlotte. Mastroianni is masterly as always but the moody film proves slight. Based on story by Julio Llinas. Spanish with subtitles. **102m/C VHS.** *AR* Marcello Mastroianni, Luisina Brando, Alejandra Podesta; *D:* Maria-Luisa Bemberg; *W:* Maria-Luisa Bemberg, Jorge Goldenberg.

I Dood It 🦴🦴 *By Hook or By Crook* **1943** Young tailor's assistant Skelton falls hard for young actress Powell working near his shop. She agrees to date, and eventually marry him, but only to spite her boyfriend who has just run off with another woman. All's well however, when Skelton stumbles across a spy ring, is hailed a hero and helps Powell realize she really loves him. ♫Star Eyes; Taking a Chance on Love; Jericho; One O'Clock Jump; So Long Sarah Jane; Hola E Pae; Swing the Jinx Away. **102m/B VHS.** Red Skelton, Eleanor Powell, Richard Ainley, Patricia Dane, Sam Levene, Thurston Hall, Lena Horne, Butterfly McQueen; *D:* Vincente Minnelli.

I Dream of Jeannie 🦴 **1952** The third and worst bio of Stephen Foster has Foster as a bookkeeper-cum-songwriter alternating between writing tunes and chasing Lawrence. When she dumps him, he goes into a funk. Will he be able to complete the title song? The suspense will kill you. Lots of singing, but not much else. **90m/C VHS.** Ray Middleton, Bill (William) Shirley, Muriel Lawrence, Lynn Bari, Rex Allen; *D:* Allan Dwan.

I Dream Too Much 🦴🦴 **1935** A musical vehicle for opera star Pons, as a French singer who marries an American composer played by Fonda. Songwriter falls into wife's shadow after pushing her into a singing career; she then raises his spirits a couple of octaves by helping him sell a musical comedy. Went into production after a rival company, Columbia, launched opera singer Grace Moore's acting career. Ball later bought this studio, where she was given her second starring role. ♫The Jockey on the Carousel; I'm the Echo; I Got Love; I Dream Too Much; Bell Song; Caro Nome. **90m/B VHS.** Lily Pons, Henry Fonda, Eric Blore, Lucille Ball, Mischa Auer, Scotty Beckett; *D:* John Cromwell; *M:* Max Steiner.

I Dreamed of Africa 🦴🦴½ **2000 (PG-13)** Okay the scenery is beautiful (it was filmed in Kenya), including blonde Basinger, but the story is predictable and trite despite being based on the autobiography of Italian socialite Kuki Gallmann. Gallmann (Basinger) trades in her designer duds for safari khaki when she, her young son, Emanuele (Aiken), and her second husband, Paolo (Perez), decide they need a fresh start. The somewhat irresponsible Paolo likes to go big game hunting with his friends, leaving Kuki alone, and she eventually becomes a conservationist after some personal tragedies. Most of the roles, except Basinger's, are one-dimensional. **114m/C VHS, DVD, Wide.** Kim Basinger, Vincent Perez, Eva Marie Saint, Daniel Craig, Lance Reddick, Liam Aiken, Garrett Strommen; *D:* Hugh Hudson; *W:* Paula Milne, Susan Shilliday; *C:* Bernard Lutic; *M:* Maurice Jarre.

I Drink Your Blood 🦴½ **1971 (R)** Hippie satanists looking for kicks spike an old man's drink with LSD. To get revenge, the old codger's grandson sells the nasty flower children meat pies injected with the blood of a rabid dog. The hippies then turn into cannibalistic maniacs, infecting anyone they bite. From the man responsible for "I Spit on Your Grave"; originally played on a double bill with "I Eat Your Skin." **83m/C VHS.** Bhasker, Jadine Wong, Ronda Fultz, Elizabeth Marner-Brooks, George Patterson, Riley Mills, Iris Brooks, John Damon, Bruno Damon; *D:* David E. Durston; *W:* David E. Durston; *C:* Jacques Demarecaux; *M:* Clay Pitts.

I Eat Your Skin woof! *Voodoo Blood Bath; Zombie; Zombies* **1964** Cannibalistic zombies terrorize a novelist and his girlfriend on a Caribbean island. Blood and guts, usually shown on a gourmet double bill with "I Drink Your Blood." **82m/B VHS.** William Joyce, Heather Hewitt, Betty Hyatt Linton, Robert Stanton, Dan Stapleton; *D:* Del Tenney; *W:* Del Tenney; *C:* Francois Farkas; *M:* Lon Norman.

I Got the Hook-Up 🦴½ **1998 (R)** Inner-city hustlers Black (Master P) and Blue (Johnson) have their own "department store" in a vacant lot where they sell various goods of dubious quality and origin. When a truckload of cell phones is mistakenly delivered to them, it ushers them into a new business venture. All hell breaks loose when a thug (Lister) has a money pick-up go bad because of the defective phones. Sporadically amusing comedy plays gang violence and misogyny for laughs, while the leads do nothing to make their characters interesting or even likable. **93m/C VHS.** Percy (Master P) Miller, A.J. (Anthony) Johnson, Gretchen Palmer, Frantz Turner, Tommy (Tiny) Lister, Helen Martin, John Witherspoon, Harrison White, Ice Cube, Anthony Boswell, Lola Mae; *D:* Michael Martin; *W:* Percy (Master P) Miller; *C:* Antonio Calvache; *M:* Tommy Coster, Brad Fairman.

I Hate Blondes 🦴🦴½ *Odio le Bionde* **1983** A group of criminals use a ghostwriter's burglaring stories as instructional manuals. The writer becomes involved with the gang. Relies heavily on visual humor. Notably among the comedy scenes is the author's search for jewels at a get-together. **90m/C VHS.** *IT* *D:* Giorgio Capitani, Giorgio Capitani.

I Heard the Owl Call My Name 🦴🦴½ **1973** Poignant story of an Anglican priest who is relocated to an Indian fishing village on the ouskirts of Vancouver, British Columbia. Based on a Margaret Craven book. **74m/C** Tom Courtenay, Dean Jagger, Paul Stanley; *D:* Daryl Duke. **TV**

I Killed Rasputin 🦴½ **1967** The "Mad Monk" who rose to power before the Russian Revolution lost his life in a bizarre assassination by Felix Youssoupoff. Film deals with the friendship between the men that ended in betrayal. Well-intentioned, but overwrought. Dubbed. **95m/C VHS.** *FR IT* Geraldine Chaplin, Gert Frobe, Peter McEnery; *D:* Robert Hossein; *M:* Don Banks.

I Killed That Man 🦴🦴½ **1942** A prisoner scheduled to die in the electric chair is given an early ticket out when he is found poisoned. Evidence points to an unusual group of suspects. Effective low-budget thriller offers a few unexpected surprises. **72m/B VHS.** Ricardo Cortez, Joan Woodbury, Iris Adrian, George Pembroke, Herbert Rawlinson, Pat Gleason, Ralf Harolde, Jack Mulhall, Vince Barnett, Gavin Gordon, John Hamilton; *D:* Phil Rosen.

I Know What You Did Last Summer 🦴🦴🦴 **1997 (R)** Four teens get involved in a fatal hit-and-run accident and think they've managed to keep it a secret. Good girl Julie (Hewitt), beauty queen Helen (Gellar), arrogant jock Barry (Cox), and regular guy Ray (Prinze) make a pact to take the secret to their graves, which may be sooner than they thought. One year later, the quartet receive letters which give the movie its title and set them against each other. After a few youngsters are made into bait on rather large fishing hooks, they band together to stop the bloodthirsty killer. Hint: It's not Mrs. Paul. Another quality slasher throwback written by Kevin Williamson, the man who made you "Scream." **100m/C VHS, DVD, Wide.** Jennifer Love Hewitt, Sarah Michelle Gellar, Ryan Phillippe, Freddie Prinze Jr., Muse Watson, Anne Heche, Bridgette Wilson, Johnny Galecki, Dan Albright; *D:* Jim Gillespie; *W:* Kevin Williamson; *C:* Denis Crossan; *M:* John Debney.

I Know Where I'm Going 🦴🦴🦴 **1945** A young woman (Hiller), who believes that money brings happiness, is on the verge of marrying a rich old man, until she meets a handsome naval officer (Livesey) and finds a happy, simple life. Early on the female lead appears in a dream sequence filmed in the mode of surrealist painter Salvador Dali and avant garde director Luis Bunuel. Scottish setting and folk songs give a unique flavor. Brown provides a fine performance as a native Scot. **91m/B VHS, DVD.** *GB* Roger Livesey, Wendy Hiller, Finlay Currie, Pamela Brown, George Carney, Walter Hudd; *D:* Michael Powell, Emeric Pressburger; *W:* Michael Powell, Emeric Pressburger; *C:* Erwin Hillier; *M:* Allan Gray.

I Know Why the Caged Bird Sings 🦴🦴🦴 **1979** A black writer's memories of growing up in the rural South during the 1930s. Strong performances from Rolle and Good. Based on the book by Maya Angelou. **100m/C VHS.** Diahann Carroll, Ruby Dee, Esther Rolle, Roger E. Mosley, Paul Benjamin, Constance Good; *D:* Fielder Cook. **TV**

I Like Bats **1985** Can a psychiatrist help a vampire become a human? Polish dialogue with English subtitles. **90m/C VHS.** *D:* Grzegorz Warchol.

I Like It Like That 🦴🦴🦴 **1994 (R)** Chaotic family life and loves in the Bronx are the setting for this tale of a Cinderella in the record industry. Strong-willed black-Latina Lisette (Velez) has been married for 10 years to macho Latin, Chino (Seda), who has a wandering eye. When Chino is jailed for looting during a blackout, Lisette, needing to support their three kids, talks her way into a job with WASP record promoter Stephen Price (Dunne). When local gossips make it seem Lisette is having an affair, the newly sprung Chino retaliates by turning to lusty Magdalena (Vidal). Lisette, meanwhile, gathers support from her transvestite brother and proves to have inner resources previously unnoticed. Great Latino soundtrack illuminates the complications. Modest-budget sleeper quickly exited the theatre but proves to be a strong debut for director/writer Martin, reputed to be the first African-American woman to be given the reins by a major studio. **106m/C VHS.** Lauren Velez, Jon Seda, Lisa Vidal, Jesse Borrego, Griffin Dunne, Rita Moreno, Tomas Melly, Desiree Casado, Isaiah Garcia; *D:* Darnell Martin; *W:* Darnell Martin; *C:* Alexander Grusynski; *M:* Sergio George.

I Like to Play Games 𝒮½ **1995 (R)** Michael is looking for a woman who enjoys playing sexual games—and he seems to have the perfect partner in Suzanne. But just how far will their kinks take them? Also available unrated. **95m/C VHS, DVD.** Lisa Boyle, Ken Steadman; ***D:*** Moctezuma Lobato; ***W:*** David Keith Miller; ***C:*** Kim Haun; ***M:*** Herman Beeftink.

I Live in Fear 𝒮𝒮𝒮 *Record of a Living Being; Kimono No Kiroku* **1955** Nakajima, an elderly, wealthy owner of a foundry, becomes increasingly fearful of atomic war and the threats to his family's safety. He tries to persuade them to leave Japan and move with him to Brazil but they fear the family will be ruined financially. Nakajima then burns down his foundry to force his children to move but instead they go to court and have him declared mentally incompetent. He is placed in an institution where he finds peace in the delusion that he has escaped to another planet and that the Earth has indeed suffered a nuclear holocaust. Provocative look at the fear of atomic warfare and radiation. In Japanese with English subtitles. **105m/C VHS.** *JP* Toshiro Mifune, Takashi Shimura, Eiko Miyoshi, Haruko Togo; ***D:*** Akira Kurosawa; ***W:*** Akira Kurosawa, Shinobu Hashimoto, Hideo Oguni; ***C:*** Asakazu Nakai; ***M:*** Fumio Hayasaka.

I Live in Grosvenor Square 𝒮𝒮 *A Yank In London* **1946** An American soldier in Great Britain falls in love with a major's fiancee. Entertaining if a bit drawn out. **106m/B VHS.** *GB* Anna Neagle, Rex Harrison, Dean Jagger, Robert Morley, Jane Darwell; ***D:*** Herbert Wilcox.

I Live My Life 𝒮½ **1935** Stylish glossy flick with Crawford playing a bored New York debutante who travels to Greece and meets a dedicated archaelogist (Aherne). A love/hate relationship ensues in this typical Crawford vehicle where she is witty and parades around in sophisticated fashions, but there is little substance here. **92m/B VHS.** Joan Crawford, Brian Aherne, Frank Morgan, Aline MacMahon, Eric Blore, Fred Keating, Jessie Ralph, Arthur Treacher, Frank Conroy, Sterling Holloway, Vince Barnett, Hedda Hopper, Lionel Stander; ***D:*** Woodbridge S. Van Dyke; ***W:*** Joseph L. Mankiewicz, Gottfried Reinhardt, Ethel B. Borden; ***C:*** George J. Folsey.

I Live with Me Dad 𝒮½ **1986** A vagrant drunk and his son fight the authorities for the right to be together. **86m/C VHS.** *AU* Peter Hehir, Haydon Samuels; ***D:*** Paul Maloney.

I Love All of You 𝒮𝒮½ **1983** Deneuve relives experiences with three former lovers—a composer, a well-intentioned nobody, and a rock star—as she enters into a relationship with a widower. **103m/C VHS.** *FR* Catherine Deneuve, Jean-Louis Trintignant, Gerard Depardieu, Serge Gainsbourg; ***D:*** Claude Berri.

I Love Melvin 𝒮𝒮½ **1953** Reynolds wants to be a Tinseltown goddess, and O'Connor just wants Reynolds; so he passes himself off as chief lenseman for a famous magazine and promises her a shot at the cover of "Look." Seems he has a little trouble on the follow through. Choreographed by Robert Alton, it's got a best ever football ballet (with Reynolds as pigskin). ♫A Lady Loves; Saturday Afternoon Before The Game; I Wanna Wander; We Have Never Met As Of Yet; Life Has Its Funny Little Ups And Downs; Where Did You Learn To Dance?; And There You Are. **77m/C VHS.** Donald O'Connor, Debbie Reynolds, Una Merkel, Richard Anderson, Jim Backus, Allyn Joslyn, Les Tremayne, Noreen Corcoran, Robert Taylor, Howard Keel; ***D:*** Don Weis.

I Love My...Wife 𝒮𝒮 **1970 (R)** A medical student plays doctor with hospital nurses when he and his wife stop having sex during her pregnancy. The marriage becomes more strained when their son is born and his mother-in-law moves in. A comedy without the proper dosage of laughs. **98m/C VHS.** Elliott Gould, Brenda Vaccaro, Angel Tompkins; ***D:*** Mel Stuart.

I Love N.Y. 𝒮 **1987** A young metropolitan couple struggles to find true love amidst disapproving parents and doubting friends. Choppy direction and poor writing contribute to its failure. **100m/C VHS.** Scott Baio, Kelley Van Der Velden, Christopher Plummer, Jennifer O'Neill, Jerry Orbach, Virna Lisi; ***D:*** Alan Smithee; ***M:*** Bill Conti.

I Love Trouble 𝒮𝒮½ **1994 (PG)** Veteran reporter Peter Brackett (sexy veteran Nolte) and ambitious cub reporter Sabrina Petersen (young and sexy Roberts) are competitors working for rival Chicago newspapers. When they begin to secretly exchange information on a big story, they find their lives threatened and their rivalry turning to romance. Some action, simplistic retro script, one big star, one sorta big star, and you've got the perfect movie package for the Prozac decade. Written, produced and directed by husband/wife team Meyers and Shyer. **123m/C VHS, DVD.** Julia Roberts, Nick Nolte, Saul Rubinek, Robert Loggia, James Rebhorn; ***D:*** Charles Shyer; ***W:*** Nancy Myers, Charles Shyer; ***C:*** John Lindley; ***M:*** David Newman.

I Love You 𝒮½ **1981 (R)** Man down on his luck mistakenly assumes that a woman he meets is a hooker. She plays along, only to find that they are becoming emotionally involved. Pretentious cat-and-mouse game. **104m/C VHS.** *BR* Sonia Braga, Paulo Cesar Pereio, Vera Fischer, Tarcisio Meria; ***D:*** Arnaldo Jabor.

I Love You Again 𝒮𝒮𝒮½ **1940** A classic screwball comedy with Powell and Loy working together (wonderfully) in something other than their "Thin Man" series. Powell is a gloomy businessman who's about to be divorced by Loy. But after an accident it turns out Powell had been suffering from amnesia and has now regained his memory (which he keeps a secret). It seems Mr. Respectable used to be a con man and he decides to revert to his criminal ways. He also doesn't remember Loy but falls instantly in love with her and must decide what kind of life he wants. Witty dialog, amusing situations, fine direction. **97m/B VHS.** William Powell, Myrna Loy, Frank McHugh, Edmund Lowe; ***D:*** Woodbridge S. Van Dyke.

I Love You, Alice B. Toklas! 𝒮𝒮½ *Kiss My Butterfly* **1968** A straight uptight lawyer decides to join the peace and love generation in this somewhat maniacal satire of the hippie culture. Authored by Paul Mazursky and Larry Tucker. Incidentally, the title's Alice B. Toklas was actually the lifemate of "Lost Generation" author Gertrude Stein. **94m/C VHS.** Peter Sellers, Jo Van Fleet, Leigh Taylor-Young, Joyce Van Patten; ***D:*** Hy Averback; ***W:*** Paul Mazursky; ***M:*** Elmer Bernstein.

I Love You, Don't Touch Me! 𝒮𝒮½ **1997 (R)** Katie (Schafel) is a smart-mouthed, 25-year-old would-be singer in L.A., who also happens to be a virgin. She wants everything to be perfect her first time but all the guys she meets are just wrong. Her best friend Ben (Whitfield) would like to be the one, but Katie just can't see him in a romantic like. Then Katie finally gets involved with an older composer (Webber) who takes an interest in her career and all the romantic complications just get worse. **85m/C VHS.** Maria Schaffel, Mitchell Whitfield, Michael (M.K.) Harris, Nancy Sorel, Meredith Scott Lynn, Darryl Theirse; ***D:*** Julie Davis; ***W:*** Julie Davis; ***C:*** Mark Putnam.

I Love You ... Goodbye 𝒮𝒮 **1973** A frustrated housewife, fed up with the constant role of wife and mother, leaves her family in an effort to find a more challenging and fulfilling life. A good performance by Lange compensates for some of its muddledness. **74m/C VHS.** Hope Lange, Earl Holliman.

I Love You, I Love You Not 𝒮𝒮½ **1997 (PG-13)** The Holocaust becomes a metaphor for one teen's survival of her first painful romance. Daisy (Danes) is a Jewish student at a snobby and anti-Semetic Manhattan prep school, where she falls in love with the ultimate gentile, Ethan (Law) in a "Kids" meets "The Way We Were" spin. Moreau is Nana, Daisy's grandmother and a Holocaust survivor, whom Daisy visits every weekend. The two share their painful stories (Danes also plays Nana as a young girl). Danes does what she does best as a misunderstood teen coming of age. Moreau shines in her role as the beloved grandmother. What misfires is the trite handling of the serious subject matter as Daisy's romance scores far more screen time than Nana's suffering. Hopkins, an established casting director, makes his feature debut. **92m/C VHS, DVD.** *FR GE GB* Claire Danes, Jeanne Moreau, Jude Law, James Van Der Beek, Robert Sean Leonard, Kris Park, Lauren Fox, Emily Burkes-Nossiter, Carrie Slaza; ***D:*** Billy Hopkins; ***W:*** Wendy Kesselman; ***C:*** Maryse Alberti; ***M:*** Gil Goldstein.

I Love You Rosa 𝒮𝒮½ **1972** Rosa, a young Jewish widow, wrestles big time with old world values. Required by custom to marry her dearly departed's eldest brother, she's not enamored with her newly betrothed. Not that he's not a nice guy; he seems to plan to take his marital duties very seriously. It's just that he's a tad youthful (11 years old, to be exact). Much rabbi consulting and soul searching. **90m/C VHS.** Michal Bat-Adam, Gabi Oterman, Joseph Shiloah; ***D:*** Moshe Mizrahi; ***W:*** Moshe Mizrahi.

I Love You to Death 𝒮𝒮½ **1990 (R)** Dry comedy based on a true story, concerns a woman who tries to kill off her cheating husband. Lots of stars, but they never shine. Hurt and Reeves are somewhat amusing as drugged up hit men who struggle with the lyrics to the National Anthem. Watch for director Kasdan as Devo's lawyer. Cates, Kline's real-life wife, has an unbilled part as one of his one-night stands. **110m/C VHS, Wide.** Kevin Kline, Tracey Ullman, Joan Plowright, River Phoenix, William Hurt, Keanu Reeves, James Gammon, Victoria Jackson, Miriam Margolyes, Heather Graham; ***Cameos:*** Phoebe Cates; ***D:*** Lawrence Kasdan; ***W:*** John Kostmayer; ***C:*** Owen Roizman; ***M:*** James Horner.

I, Madman 𝒮𝒮 **1989 (R)** A novel-loving horror actress is stalked by the same mutilating madman that appears in the book she's presently reading. We call that bad luck. **90m/C VHS.** Jenny Wright, Clayton Rohner, William Cook; ***D:*** Tibor Takacs; ***W:*** David Chaskin; ***C:*** Bryan England.

I Married a Centerfold 𝒮𝒮 **1984** Fluff about a young man's amorous pursuit of a model. **100m/C VHS.** Teri Copley, Timothy Daly, Diane Ladd, Bert Remsen, Anson Williams; ***D:*** Peter Werner. **TV**

I Married a Dead Man 𝒮𝒮 *J'ai Epouse une Ombre; I Married a Shadow* **1982** When the train she's travelling on is involved in a terrible crash, abandoned, pregnant Helene (Baye) decides to assume the identity of a wealthy young woman who was killed in the wreck. But soon Helene is receiving anonymous threats from someone who knows who she really is. Based on a book by Cornell Woolrich and also filmed as "No Man of Her Own" (1950) and "Mrs. Winterbourne" (1996). French with subtitles. **110m/C VHS.** *FR* Nathalie Baye, Richard Bohringer, Victoria Abril, Francis Huster, Madeleine Robinson, Guy Trejan, Humbert Balsan, Veronique Genest; ***D:*** Robin Davis; ***W:*** Patrick Laurent; ***C:*** Bernard Zitzermann; ***M:*** Philippe Sarde.

I Married a Monster 𝒮𝒮½ **1998 (PG-13)** Update of the 1958 sci-fi film "I Married a Monster from Outer Space." The title tells the story—small town newlywed (Walters) finds out her hubby (Burgi) has been possessed by an alien intent on procreating its dying race. **90m/C VHS.** Susan Walters, Richard Burgi, Richard Herd, Barbara Niven; ***D:*** Nancy Malone; ***W:*** Duane Poole. **TV**

I Married a Monster from Outer Space 𝒮𝒮½ **1958** The vintage thriller about a race of monster-like aliens from another planet who try to conquer earth. Despite its head-shaking title, an effective '50s sci-fi creeper. **78m/B VHS.** Tom Tryon, Gloria Talbott, Maxie "Slapsie" Rosenbloom, Mary Treen, Ty Hardin, Ken Lynch, John Eldridge, Jean Carson, Alan Dexter; ***D:*** Gene Fowler Jr.; ***W:*** Louis Vittes; ***C:*** Haskell Boggs.

I Married a Vampire 𝒮𝒮 **1987** A country girl in the city is romanced and wed by a dashing vampire. Troma-produced hyper-camp. **85m/C VHS.** Rachel Gordon, Brendan Hickey, Ted Zalewski, Deborah Carroll, Temple Aaron; ***D:*** Jay Raskin; ***W:*** Jay Raskin; ***C:*** Oren Rudavsky.

I Married a Witch 𝒮𝒮𝒮 **1942** Jennifer (Lake) and her father Daniel (Kellaway) are burned at the stake during the Salem witch trials but not before cursing their persecutors, the Wooley family, vowing that no male of the line will ever find happiness. When Jennifer and Daniel are accidentally freed from their burial place centuries later, Jennifer locates Wallace Wooley (March) and tries to get him to fall in love with her so that she can remain on the mortal plane. Wonderfully played fantasy/comedy. **77m/B VHS.** Veronica Lake, Fredric March, Susan Hayward, Robert Benchley, Cecil Kellaway, Elizabeth Patterson, Robert Warwick, Eily Malyon, Mary Field, Nora Cecil, Emory Parnell, Helen St. Rayer, Aldrich Bowker, Emma Dunn, Harry Tyler, Ralph Peters, Ann Carter; ***D:*** Rene Clair; ***W:*** Robert Pirosh, Marc Connelly; ***C:*** Ted Tetzlaff; ***M:*** Roy Webb.

I Married a Woman 𝒮𝒮 **1956** Advertising executive marries beautiful blonde woman, but finds it very difficult to balance his career and marriage. Low on laughs. Shot in black and white, but includes a fantasy scene in color that features John Wayne. Pay attention to see young Angie Dickinson. **84m/B VHS.** George Gobel, Diana Dors, Adolphe Menjou, Nita Talbot; ***D:*** Hal Kanter.

I Married an Angel 𝒮½ **1942** The last MacDonald/Eddy film. A playboy is lured away from his usual interests by a beautiful angel. Adapted from Rodgers and Hart Broadway play. Strange and less than compelling. ♫I Married An Angel; I'll Tell the Man in the Street; Spring is Here; Tira Lira La; A Twinkle in Your Eye; Aloha Oe; Caprice Viennoise; Chanson Boheme; Anges Purs. **84m/C VHS.** Jeanette MacDonald, Nelson Eddy, Binnie Barnes, Edward Everett Horton, Reginald Owen, Mona Maris, Janis Carter, Inez Cooper, Douglass Dumbrille, Leonid Kinskey, Marion Rosamond, Anne Jeffreys, Marek Windheim, Veda Ann Borg; ***D:*** Woodbridge S. Van Dyke; ***W:*** Anita Loos; ***M:*** Richard Rodgers, Lorenz Hart.

I Met a Murderer 𝒮𝒮½ **1939** A man kills his nagging wife after a bitter argument and flees from her vengeful brother. Fine fugitive drama with a number of interesting twists. **79m/B VHS.** James Mason, Pamela Kellino, Sylvia Coleridge, William Devlin, Esma Cannon, James Harcourt; ***D:*** Roy Kellino; ***W:*** Roy Kellino; ***C:*** Roy Kellino.

I, Mobster 𝒮𝒮½ **1958** Cochran tells a Senate Sub-Committee of his rise in the ranks of the Underworld—from his humble beginning as a bet collector for a bookie to his position as kingpin of the crime syndicate. **80m/B VHS.** Steve Cochran, Lita Milan, Robert Strauss, Celia Lovsky; ***D:*** Roger Corman; ***C:*** Floyd Crosby.

I, Monster 𝒮𝒮𝒮 **1971** The character names may have changed but this is still Robert Louis Stevenson's "Dr. Jekyll and Mr. Hyde." Lee tackles the title characters with his usual sinister savoir faire as Dr. Marlowe, who is obsessed with the nature of the id, the ego, and the superego and whether they can be separated within an individual. He injects himself with his secret formula and is transformed into Mr. Blake, who prowls the seedy sections of Victorian London to satisfy his violent desires. Frequent co-star Cushing shows up as a suspicious colleague. **74m/C VHS.** *GB* Christopher Lee, Peter Cushing, Mike Raven, George Merritt, Richard Hurndall, Kenneth J. Warren, Michael Des Barres, Susan Jameson; ***D:*** Stephen Weeks; ***W:*** Milton Subotsky; ***C:*** Moray Grant; ***M:*** Carl Davis.

I Never Promised You a Rose Garden 𝒮𝒮𝒮 **1977 (R)** A disturbed 16-year-old girl spirals down into madness and despair while a hospital psychiatrist struggles to bring her back to life. Based on the Joanne Greenberg bestseller. Compelling and unyielding exploration of the clinical treatment of schizophrenia. **90m/C VHS, DVD.** Kathleen Quinlan, Bibi Andersson, Sylvia Sidney, Diane Varsi, Dennis Quaid, Jeff Conaway; ***D:*** Anthony Page; ***W:*** Gavin Lambert, Lewis John Carlino; ***C:*** Bruce Logan; ***M:*** Paul Chihara.

I Never Sang for My Father 🦴🦴🦴½ 1970 (PG) A devoted son must choose between caring for his cantankerous but well-meaning father, and moving out West to marry the divorced doctor whom he loves. While his mother wants him to stay near home, his sister, who fell out of her father's favor by marrying out of the family faith, argues that he should do what he wants. An introspective, stirring story based on the Robert Anderson play. **90m/C VHS.** Gene Hackman, Melvyn Douglas, Estelle Parsons, Dorothy Stickney; ***D:*** Gilbert Cates; ***W:*** Robert Anderson. Writers Guild '70: Adapt. Screenplay.

I Only Want You to Love Me 🦴🦴 *Ich Will Doch Nur, Dass Ihr Mich Liebt* 1976 Peter's (Zeplichal) been denigrated by his family his entire life, so he decides to move with his wife (Aberle) to Munich and show them he can make something of himself. But his desires become compulsions and he falters under the strain of work and marriage, leading to a terrifying crackup. A true story, based on the book "Life Sentence" by Klaus Antes and Christine Eberhardt. Originally produced for TV; German with subtitles. **104m/C VHS.** *GE* Vitus Zeplichal, Elke Aberle, Ernie Mangold, Joanna Hofe, Alexander Allerson; ***D:*** Rainer Werner Fassbinder; ***W:*** Rainer Werner Fassbinder; ***C:*** Michael Ballhaus; ***M:*** Peer Raben.

I Ought to Be in Pictures 🦴🦴 1982 (PG) After hitchhiking from New York to Hollywood to break into the movies, a teenage actress finds her father, a screenwriter turned alcoholic-gambler. Late, desperately unfunny Neil Simon outing, adapted from a Simon play. **107m/C VHS.** Walter Matthau, Ann-Margret, Dinah Manoff, Lance Guest, Michael Dudikoff; ***D:*** Herbert Ross; ***W:*** Neil Simon; ***M:*** Marvin Hamlisch.

I Posed for Playboy 🦴🦴 1991 (R) Three women—one a college co-ed, one a stockbroker, and one a 37-year-old mother—quench their private passions by posing for "Playboy" magazine. Made for TV with additional footage added to give it an "R" rating. **98m/C VHS.** Lynda Carter, Michele Greene, Amanda Peterson, Brittany York; ***D:*** Stephen Stafford. **TV**

I Remember Mama 🦴🦴🦴½ 1948 A true Hollywood heart tugger chronicling the life of a Norwegian immigrant family living in San Francisco during the early 1900s. Dunne triumphs as the mother, with a perfect Norwegian accent, and provides her family with wisdom and inspiration. A kindly father and four children round out the nuclear family. A host of oddball characters regularly pop in on the household—three high-strung aunts and an eccentric doctor who treats a live-in uncle. Adapted from John Van Druten's stage play, based on Kathryn Forbes memoirs, "Mama's Bank Account"; a TV series ran from 1946-57. **95m/B VHS.** Irene Dunne, Barbara Bel Geddes, Oscar Homolka, Ellen Corby, Cedric Hardwicke, Edgar Bergen, Rudy Vallee, Barbara O'Neil, Florence Bates; ***D:*** George Stevens; ***W:*** DeWitt Bodeen. Golden Globes '49: Support. Actress (Corby).

I See a Dark Stranger 🦴🦴🦴 *The Adventuress* 1946 Cynical yet whimsical postwar British spy thriller about an angry Irish lass who agrees to steal war plans for the Nazis in order to battle her native enemies, the British—then she falls in love with a British officer. A sharply performed, decidedly jaded view of nationalism and wartime "heroism." **112m/B VHS.** *GB* Deborah Kerr, Trevor Howard, Raymond Huntley; ***D:*** Frank Launder.

I Sent a Letter to My Love 🦴🦴🦴 1981 An aging spinster, faced with the lonely prospect of the death of her paralyzed brother, places a personal ad for a companion in a local newspaper, using a different name. Unknown to her, the brother is the one who answers it, and they begin a romantic correspondence. Well-acted, touching account of relationships that change lives, but it takes its time in telling the story. **102m/C VHS.** *FR* Simone Signoret, Jean Rochefort, Delphine Seyrig; ***D:*** Moshe Mizrahi; ***W:*** Moshe Mizrahi, Gerard Brach; ***C:*** Ghislan Cloquet.

I Shot a Man in Vegas 🦴½ 1996 (R) Low-budget variation of "Rashomon." Drinking buddies Johnny (Cubitt) and Grant (Stockwell) wind up in a back alley brawl and Johnny takes a bullet, supposedly shot dead by Grant. Only their friends, Gale (Garofalo), Martin (Drillinger), and Amy (Lippman), who witnessed the fight all saw it differently. So they decide to stash the corpse in their car trunk and head out across the desert to California. There's a last-minute revelation and a big finale but the strain shows. **84m/C VHS.** John Stockwell, Janeane Garofalo, Brian Drillinger, Noelle Lippman, David Cubitt; ***D:*** Keoni Waxman; ***W:*** Keoni Waxman; ***C:*** Steven Firestone.

I Shot Andy Warhol 🦴🦴🦴 1996 (R) Based on a true story, this black comedy focuses on the 15 minutes of fame achieved by Valerie Solanas, the woman who shot pop artist Andy Warhol for ignoring her in 1968. Taylor manages to recreate the more unpleasant aspects of Solanas without making her completely unsympathetic. Writer/director Harron, making her feature film debut, does a wonderful job of recreating the drugged-out world Warhol and his cohorts inhabited. Her script succeeds by attempting to understand Solanas's actions, while not excusing or sensationalizing them. Features music by former Velvet Underground member, John Cale. **100m/C VHS, DVD, Wide.** Lili Taylor, Jared Harris, Stephen Dorff, Martha Plimpton, Donovan Leitch, Tahnee Welch, Michael Imperioli, Lothaire Bluteau, Anna Thompson, Peter Friedman, Jill(ian) Hennessey, Craig Chester, James Lyons, Reginald Rodgers, Jamie Harrold, Edoardo Ballerini, Lynn Cohen, Myriam Cyr, Isabel Gillies, Eric Mabius; ***D:*** Mary Harron; ***W:*** Mary Harron, Daniel Minahan; ***C:*** Ellen Kuras; ***M:*** John Cale.

I Shot Billy the Kid 🦴½ 1950 Billy the Kid decides to turn over a new leaf and live a decent life. The cards are stacked against him though: He's killed a man for nearly every year of his life, and old habits are hard to break. **58m/B VHS.** Donald (Don "Red") Barry, Robert Lowery, Tom Neal, Jack Perrin; ***D:*** William Berke.

I Shot Jesse James 🦴🦴🦴 1949 In his first film, director Fuller breathes characteristically feverish, maddened fire into the story of Bob Ford (Ireland) after he killed the notorious outlaw. An essential moment in Fuller's unique, America-as-tabloid-nightmare canon, and one of the best anti-westerns ever made. **83m/B VHS.** John Ireland, Barbara Britton, Preston Foster, Reed Hadley; ***D:*** Samuel Fuller; ***W:*** Samuel Fuller.

I Spit on Your Corpse woof! *Girls for Rent* 1974 (R) A vicious female hired killer engages in a series of terrorist activities. Stars Spelvin in a non-pornographic role. **90m/C VHS.** Georgina Spelvin, Susan McIver, Kent Taylor, Rosalind Miles, Preston Pierce, Robert "Bob" Livingston; ***D:*** Al Adamson.

I Spit on Your Grave woof! *Day of the Woman* 1977 (R) Woman vacationing at a Connecticut lake house (on the Housatonic River) is brutally attacked and raped by four men. Left for dead, she recovers and seeks revenge. Not to be confused with the 1962 film of the same title, this one is worth zero as a film; lots of violent terror and gory death, totally irresponsibly portrayed. Also available in a 102-minute version. **98m/C VHS, DVD, Wide.** Camille Keaton, Eron Tabor, Richard Pace, Anthony Nichols, Gunter Kleeman, Alexis Magnotti; ***D:*** Mier Zarchi; ***W:*** Mier Zarchi; ***C:*** Yuri Haviv.

I Stand Alone 🦴🦴 *Seul contre tous* 1998 (R) Loud and RE-PUL-SIVE drama has unemployed butcher Chevalier (Nahon) descending into madness at warp speed when he can't find work. The brutal approach Noe takes distracts, rather than intrigues, as the "hero" is such a low-life loser. His hate-filled narration is accompanied by wild camera moves and loud gunshot booms ending each scene. A 30-second warning plastered before the film's grisly climax is not only unique but warranted when the least of Chevalier's crimes is maliciously kicking his pregnant girlfriend in the stomach. Considered a continuation to Noe's 1991 short feature entitled "Carne." French with English subtitles. **93m/C VHS.** Philippe Nahon, Blandine Lenoir, Frankye Pain, Martine Audrain; ***D:*** Gasper Noe; ***W:*** Gasper Noe; ***C:*** Dominique Colin.

I Stand Condemned 🦴🦴½ *Moscow Nights* 1936 A Russian officer is tricked into borrowing money from a spy and is condemned for treason. He's saved when a girl who loves him gives herself to a profiteer. Worth seeing only for young Olivier's performance. **90m/B VHS, 8mm.** *GB* Laurence Olivier, Penelope Dudley Ward, Robert Cochran; ***D:*** Anthony Asquith.

I Still Know What You Did Last Summer 🦴🦴 1998 (R) You know what the real problem with teenagers is? It's not the loud music or the messy room; it's that they can't finish off psychokillers who show up annually on a major holiday to wield the axe they've been grinding for the rest of the year. Perky survivor Julie James (Hewitt) and new best friend Karla (Brandy) win a vacation in the Bahamas, and take boyfriends Tyrell (Phifer) and Will (Settle) along for some fun in the monsoon. Along with the hurricane, the kids must cope with fish stick guy/killer Ben Willis, who's still pretty cranky. The scares come at such a regular interval, and sometimes with such a lame premise, that the viewer becomes numb to them. The young cast, especially the wet t-shirt adorned Hewitt, help to keep it afloat, however. **100m/C VHS, DVD, Wide.** Jennifer Love Hewitt, Freddie Prinze Jr., Brandy, Mekhi Phifer, Muse Watson, Matthew Sattle, Bill Cobbs, Jeffrey Combs, John Hawkes, Jennifer Esposito; ***D:*** Danny Cannon; ***W:*** Trey Callaway; ***C:*** Vernon Layton; ***M:*** John (Gianni) Frizzell.

I Take This Oath 🦴 1940 A cop is shocked to discover that his uncle is a wanted mobster, responsible for the death of a man. Hackneyed plot. **64m/B VHS.** Gordon Jones, Joyce Compton, Craig Reynolds, J. Farrell MacDonald, Robert E. Homans, Veda Ann Borg; ***D:*** Sam Newfield.

I, the Jury 🦴🦴 1982 (R) A remake of the 1953 Mike Hammer mystery in which the famed PI investigates the murder of his best friend. Assante mopes around as Hammer and looks out of place in this slowed-down version. **111m/C VHS.** Armand Assante, Barbara Carrera, Laurene Landon, Alan King, Geoffrey Lewis, Paul Sorvino, Jessica James, Leigh Anne Harris, Lynette Harris; ***D:*** Richard T. Heffron; ***W:*** Larry Cohen; ***M:*** Bill Conti.

I, the Worst of All 🦴🦴 *Yo, la Peor de Todas* 1990 Portrayal of 17th-century Mexican poet, Sister Juana Ines del la Cruz (Serna). She develops a passionate but chaste friendship with Maria Luisa (Sanda), the wife of the Spanish viceroy in Mexico, and writes love poems to her. However, the newly appointed archbishop (Murua) is a religious fanatic who condemns Juana's work, burns her books, and proceeds to persecute her. Adapted from the novel, "The Traps of Faith," by Octavio Paz. Spanish with subtitles. **105m/C VHS.** *SP* Assumpta Serna, Dominique Sanda, Lautaro Murua, Hector Alterio; ***D:*** Maria-Luisa Bemberg; ***W:*** Maria-Luisa Bemberg, Antonio Larreta; ***C:*** Felix Monti; ***M:*** Luis Maria Serra.

I Think I Do 🦴🦴 1997 Gay Bob (Arquette) has always had an unrequited crush on college roomie, Brendan (Maelen). Five years after graduation, the duo meet up at the wedding of mutual friends, Carol (Velez) and Matt (Harrold). Bob's brought along his boyfriend, Sterling (Watkins), and doesn't know that Brendan has come out and is anticipating their reunion. It seems no one's sure about any of their romantic entanglements and someone's bound to be disappointed. **92m/C VHS.** Alexis Arquette, Christian Maelen, Maddie Corman, Guillermo Diaz, Lauren Velez, Jamie Harrold, Marianne Hagan, Tuc Watkins, Marni Nixon, Dechen Thurman; ***D:*** Brian Sloan; ***W:*** Brian Sloan; ***C:*** Milton Kam; ***M:*** Gerry Gershman.

I Vampiri 🦴🦴 *The Devil's Commandment; Lust of the Vampires* 1956 A lurid melodrama about a Parisian newspaperman's journey into a network of crime and perversion. **78m/B VHS, DVD, Wide.** *FR* Gianna Maria Canale, Dario Michaelis, Carlo D'Angelo, Wandisa Guida, Paul Muller, Renato Tontini; ***D:*** Riccardo (Robert Hampton) Freda, Mario Bava; ***C:*** Mario Bava.

I Vitelloni 🦴🦴🦴½ *The Young and the Passionate; Vitelloni; Spivs* 1953 Fellini's semi-autobiographical drama, argued by some to be his finest work. Five young men grow up in a small Italian town. As they mature, four of them remain in Romini and limit their opportunities by roping themselves off from the rest of the world. The characters are multi-dimensional, including a loafer who is supported by his sister and a young stud who impregnates a local woman. The script has some brilliant insights into youth, adulthood and what's in between. **104m/B VHS.** *IT* Alberto Sordi, Franco Interlenghi, Franco Fabrizi, Leopoldo Trieste, Riccardo Fellini; ***D:*** Federico Fellini; ***W:*** Federico Fellini, Ennio Flaiano; ***C:*** Carlo Carlini, Otello Martelli; ***M:*** Nino Rota.

I Wake Up Screaming 🦴🦴🦴 *Hot Spot* 1941 An actress' promoter is accused of her murder. Entertaining mystery with a surprise ending. Remade as "Vicki." **82m/B VHS.** Betty Grable, Victor Mature, Carole Landis, Laird Cregar, William Gargan, Alan Mowbray, Allyn Joslyn; ***D:*** H. Bruce Humberstone.

I Walked with a Zombie 🦴🦴🦴½ 1943 The definitive and eeriest of the famous Val Lewton/Jacques Tourneur horror films. Dee, a young American nurse, comes to Haiti to care for the catatonic matriarch of a troubled family. Local legends bring themselves to bear when the nurse takes the ill woman to a local voodoo ceremony for "healing." Superb, startling images and atmosphere create a unique context for this serious "Jane Eyre"-like story; its reputation has grown through the years. **69m/B VHS.** Frances Dee, Tom Conway, James Ellison, Christine Gordon, Edith Barrett, Darby Jones, Sir Lancelot; ***D:*** Jacques Tourneur; ***W:*** Curt Siodmak, Ardel Wray; ***C:*** J. Roy Hunt; ***M:*** Roy Webb.

I Wanna Be a Beauty Queen 1985 Divine hosts the "Alternative Miss World" pageant featuring all sorts of bizarre contestants. **81m/C VHS.** Divine, Little Nell, Andrew Logan; ***D:*** Richard Gayer; ***M:*** Peter Logan.

I Wanna Hold Your Hand 🦴🦴½ 1978 (PG) Teenagers try to crash the Beatles' appearance on the Ed Sullivan show. **104m/C VHS.** Nancy Allen, Bobby DiCicco, Wendie Jo Sperber, Marc McClure, Susan Kendall Newman, Theresa Saldana, Eddie Deezen, William Jordan; ***D:*** Robert Zemeckis; ***W:*** Robert Zemeckis.

I Want to Live! 🦴🦴🦴 1958 Based on a scandalous true story, Hayward gives a riveting, Oscar-winning performance as a prostitute framed for the murder of an elderly woman and sentenced to death in the gas chamber. Producer Walter Wanger's seething indictment of capital punishment. **120m/B VHS, DVD, Wide.** Susan Hayward, Simon Oakland, Theodore Bikel, Virginia Vincent, Wesley Lau; ***D:*** Robert Wise; ***W:*** Nelson Gidding, Don Mankiewicz; ***C:*** Lionel Lindon; ***M:*** Johnny Mandel. Oscars '58: Actress (Hayward); Golden Globes '59: Actress—Drama (Hayward); N.Y. Film Critics '58: Actress (Hayward).

I Want What I Want 🦴🦴 1972 (R) A young Englishman wants a sex-change, lives as a woman, falls in love, complications ensue. Not as shocking to watch as it might seem, but more a melodramatic gender-bender. **91m/C VHS.** *GB* Anne Heywood, Harry Andrews, Jill Bennett; ***D:*** John Dexter.

I Want You 🦴🦴½ 1951 Small-town life in Greenhill is disturbed for various citizens by the gathering storm of the Korean War. WWII vet Martin Greer (Andrews) is uncertain about re-enlisting while his wife Nancy (McGuire) is totally against the idea. Young Jack (Granger) doesn't want to leave his girl and family while his dad (Keith) tries to instill some patriotic fervor in his son, while George's (Milner) father (Baldwin) doesn't want to let him go. Dated but not unaffecting. **102m/B VHS.** Dana Andrews, Dorothy McGuire, Farley Granger, Peggy Dow, Robert Keith, Mildred Dunnock, Martin Milner, Walter Baldwin, Jim Backus, Ray Collins; ***D:*** Mark Robson; ***W:*** Irwin Shaw; ***C:*** Harry Stradling Sr.; ***M:*** Leigh Harline.

I Want You 1998 (R) Smokey (Mitevska) and her mute brother Honda (Petrusic) are Central European refugees in the British seaside town of Haven. Honda is shyly entranced by Helen (Weisz), who is trying to deal with her old boyfriend, paroled con Martin (Nivola). Martin becomes increasingly violent towards Helen and Hondo comes to her rescue, but there's more to her relationship with Martin than Helen wants to admit. Winterbottom often flirts with the darker side of human nature and does so again in this rather thinly plotted Brit noir. **87m/C VHS.** *GB* Rachel Weisz, Luka Petrusic, Alessandro Nivola, Labina Mitevska, Ben Daniels, Carmen Ejogo, Graham Crowden, Geraldine O'Rawe, Des McAleer, Phyllida Law, Mary MacLeod; ***D:*** Michael Winterbottom; ***W:*** Eoin McNamee; ***C:*** Slawomir Idziak; ***M:*** Adrian Johnston.

I Was a Male War Bride 1949 Hilarious WWII comedy. French officer Grant falls in love with and marries WAC lieutenant Sheridan in occupied Europe. Planning to leave the continent and settle down in the U.S., the couple hits a roadblock of red tape and Grant must cross-dress in order to accompany his bride on the troop ship taking her home. Worth watching for Grant's performance alone. Based on the novel by Henri Rochard. **105m/B VHS.** Cary Grant, Ann Sheridan, Randy Stuart, Kenneth Tobey, William Neff, Marion Marshall; ***D:*** Howard Hawks; ***W:*** Charles Lederer, Leonard Spigelgass, William Neff; ***M:*** Cyril Mockridge.

I Was a Teenage TV Terrorist woof! *Amateur Hour* 1987 Two teenagers pull on-the-air pranks at the local cable television, blaming it all on an imaginary terrorist group. Poorly acted, cheaply made, and pointless. **85m/C VHS.** Adam Nathan, Julie Hanlon, John MacKay; ***D:*** Stanford Singer; ***W:*** Stanford Singer, Kevin McDonough; ***C:*** Lisa Rinzler; ***M:*** Cengiz Yaltkaya.

I Was a Teenage Werewolf ½ 1957 "Rebel Without a Cause" meets "The Curse of the Werewolf" in this drive-in rock 'n' roll horror. Troubled teen Tony (Landon in his first film appearance) suffers from teen angst and low production values, falling victim to shrink Dr. Brandon (Bissell). The doc's been exploring hypnosis and regression therapy that, when practiced on Tony, turn him positively prehistoric. Misconstrued and full of terrible longings, the hairy highschooler goes on a rampage despite the loyal love of girlfriend Arlene (Lime). Directorial debut of Fowler. **70m/B VHS.** Michael Landon, Yvonne Lime, Whit Bissell, Tony Marshall, Dawn Richard, Barney (Bernard) Phillips, Ken Miller, Cindy Robbins, Michael Rougas, Robert E. (Bob) Griffin, Joseph Mell, Malcolm Atterbury, Eddie Marr, Vladimir Sokoloff, Louise Lewis, S. John Launer, Guy Williams, Dorothy Crehan; ***D:*** Gene Fowler Jr.; ***W:*** Ralph Thornton; ***C:*** Joseph LaShelle; ***M:*** Paul Dunlap.

I Was a Teenage Zombie 1987 Spoof of high school horror films features a good zombie against a drug-pushing zombie. Forget the story and listen to the music by Los Lobos, the Fleshtones, the Waitresses, Dream Syndicate, and Violent Femmes. **92m/C VHS, DVD.** Michael Rubin, Steve McCoy, Cassie Madden, Allen Rickman; ***D:*** John E. Michalakis; ***W:*** George Seminara, Steve McCoy; ***C:*** Peter Lewnes; ***M:*** Jonathan Roberts, Craig Seeman.

I Was a Zombie for the FBI ½ 1982 Intelligence agency toughens its hiring criteria. Much McCarthyian mirth. **105m/B VHS.** James Raspberry, Larry Raspberry, John Gillick, Christina Wellford, Anthony Isbell, Laurence Hall, Rick Crowe; ***D:*** Maurice Penczner; ***W:*** Maurice Penczner, John Gillick; ***C:*** Rick Dupree.

I Was Born But... *Umarete Wa Mita Keredo* 1932 Two young brothers (Sugahara and Tokkankozo) are the leaders of the neighborhood gang of kids. Their office clerk father (Saito), who is trying to advance his position by playing up to the boss, insists the boys accompany him to his boss' house for a visit. The sons are embarassed by their father's ingratiating behavior, especially when they realize that the boss' son is a minor member of their gang. In retaliation, the brothers decide to go on a hunger strike. Charming social satire. Japanese with subtitles. **89m/B VHS.** *JP* Tatsuo Saito, Hideo Sugahara, Tokkankozo, Mitsuko Yoshikawa, Takeshi Sakamoto; ***D:*** Yasujiro Ozu; ***W:*** Akira Fushimi, Geibei Ibushiya; ***C:*** Hideo Shigehara.

I Was Nineteen *Ich War Neunzehn* 1968 Gregor Hecker left Germany with his parents as a eight-year-old. Now, at the end of WWII, he's returning at 19 in the uniform of a Russian Lieutenant and isn't sure of his identity anymore. Based on the diary kept by German filmmaker Wolf when he was in the Russian Army. German with subtitles. **115m/B VHS.** *GE* Jaecki Schwarz, Wassili Liwanow, Alexej Ejboshenko; ***D:*** Konrad Wolf.

I Went Down 1997 (R) The title of this dark comedy about Irish gangsters has many meanings, including a quote from Plato. Not too many caper movies can boast of a plug from the father of Western philosophy, but luckily director Breathnach and writer McPherson don't take anything too seriously. Their heroes are hapless Git (McDonald) and hair-trigger Bunny (Gleeson), a duo who show you what Laurel and Hardy might look like if they were cast as the hit men in "Pulp Fiction." Ordered by big boss Tom French (Doyle) to bring in Frank Grogan (Caffrey), a man who swindled him out of big bucks and also slept with his wife, they fumble through bad directions and a missed meeting with a sinister fellow called "The Friendly Face," but manage to nab Grogan anyway. The two then attempt to deliver the extremely gabby Grogan to French, leading to a showdown between all four men. More character and dialogue driven than action oriented, this went down as the highest grossing independent Irish film after its theatrical release. **105m/C VHS.** *IR GB* Brendan Gleeson, Peter McDonald, Tony Doyle, Peter Caffrey, Donal O'Kelly, Antoine Byrne; ***D:*** Paddy Breathnach; ***W:*** Conor McPherson; ***C:*** Cian de Buitlear; ***M:*** Dario Marianelli.

I Will Fight No More Forever 1975 A vivid recounting of the epic true story of the legendary Chief Joseph who led the Nez Perce tribe on a 1600-mile trek to Canada in 1877. Disturbing and powerful. **100m/C VHS.** James Whitmore, Ned Romero, Sam Elliott; ***D:*** Richard T. Heffron. **TV**

I Will, I Will for Now 1976 (R) Tacky sex clinic comedy with Keaton and Gould trying to save their marriage through kinky therapy. **109m/C VHS.** Diane Keaton, Elliott Gould, Paul Sorvino, Victoria Principal, Robert Alda, Warren Bellinger; ***D:*** Norman Panama; ***W:*** Norman Panama; ***C:*** John A. Alonzo.

I Wonder Who's Killing Her Now? 1976 Husband pays to have his wife murdered, then changes his mind. On-again, off-again comedy. **87m/C VHS.** Bob (Robert) Dishy, Joanna Barnes, Bill Dana, Vito Scotti; ***D:*** Steven Hilliard Stern.

Ice ½ 1993 (R) Charley and Ellen Reed are thieves whose latest heist is $60 million in diamonds from mob boss Vito Malta. There's trouble when they try to fence the goods and Ellen is left with the merchandise and on the run from Malta's henchmen. **91m/C VHS.** Traci Lords, Phillip Troy, Zach Galligan, Jorge (George) Rivero, Michael Bailey Smith, Jamie Alba, Jean Pflieger, Floyd Levine; ***D:*** Brook Yeaton; ***W:*** Sean Dash.

Ice Age 2002 (PG) Director Wedge (also the voice of Scrat the squirrel) has crafted a smart, sophisticated and touching animated comedy/adventure about a group of prehistoric beasts who find a human baby and then try to restore the tyke to his tribe. During the long march south during an ice age, the cuddly Manfred the Mammoth (Romano) and Sid the Sloth (the already animated Leguizamo) are joined by Diego the scheming Sabertooth Tiger (Leary) whose bond is solidified after the two save Diego's life. Amazing computer-animation technology and artistry are commendably top-notch. Characters are likeable but sometimes spew overly glib dialogue. Although not quite of the same caliber story-wise, this one fits right in with "Shrek," "Monsters, Inc." and "Toy Story." **81m/C VHS, DVD.** ***D:*** Chris Wedge; ***W:*** Michael Berg, Michael J. Wilson, Peter Ackerman; ***M:*** David Newman; ***V:*** John Leguizamo, Denis Leary, Ray Romano, Goran Visnjic, Jack Black, Cedric the Entertainer, Stephen (Steve) Root, Tara Strong, Diedrich Bader, Alan Tudyk, Lorri Bagley, Jane Krakowski, Chris Wedge.

Ice Castles 1979 (PG) A young figure skater's Olympic dreams are dimmed when she is blinded in an accident, but her boyfriend gives her the strength, encouragement, and love necessary to perform a small miracle. Way too schmaltzy. **110m/C VHS, DVD, Wide.** Robby Benson, Lynn-Holly Johnson, Tom Skerritt, Colleen Dewhurst, Jennifer Warren, David Huffman; ***D:*** Donald Wrye; ***W:*** Donald Wrye, Gary L. Bain; ***C:*** Bill Butler; ***M:*** Marvin Hamlisch.

Ice Cream Man 1995 (R) Quite disgusting horror tale of a dweeby, demented ice cream man who delivers gore and death along with his frozen treats. **96m/C VHS.** Clint Howard, Sandahl Bergman, Olivia Hussey, Lee Majors II, David Naughton, Jan-Michael Vincent, David Warner, Steve Garvey; ***D:*** Norman Apstein.

The Ice Flood 1926 Silent family type comedy of a son who proves to the old man that he wrote the book on life, wagering the successful supervision of dad's lumberjacks. **63m/B VHS.** Kenneth Harlan, Viola Dana; ***D:*** George B. Seitz.

Ice House 1989 A sophisticated young lady flees Texas for Hollywood, searching for a better life. When her exlover shows up and wants her to go back, the lackless turmoil begins. Pairs real-life couple Gilbert and Brinkman. **81m/C VHS.** Melissa Gilbert, Bo Brinkman, Andreas Manolikakis, Buddy Quaid; ***D:*** Bo Brinkman, Eagle Pennell; ***W:*** Bo Brinkman.

The Ice House 1997 Chilling TV adaptation of Minette Walters' first mystery. Ten years ago Phoebe Maybury's (Downie) abusive husband David disappeared. Locally condemned as a murderess, she and her friends Diana (Barber) and Anne (Aldridge) have been shunned by their small-minded community. Now a body has been discovered in an ice house located on Maybury property. Is it David? Inspector Walsh (Redgrave), who couldn't prove anything against Phoebe before, certainly thinks so, but his on-the-edge associate Sgt. McLoughlin (Craig) isn't so certain. **180m/C VHS.** *GB* Daniel Craig, Penny Downie, Corin Redgrave, Kitty Aldridge, Frances Barber; ***D:*** Tim Fywell; ***W:*** Lizzie Mickery.

Ice Palace 1960 Two rugged adventurers maintain a lifelong rivalry in the primitive Alaskan wilderness, their relationship dramatizing the development of the 49th state. Silly but entertaining. Based on Edna Ferber's novel. **143m/C VHS.** Richard Burton, Robert Ryan, Carolyn Jones, Shirley Knight, Martha Hyer, Jim Backus, George Takei; ***D:*** Vincent Sherman; ***C:*** Joseph Biroc; ***M:*** Max Steiner.

Ice Pawn 1992 Alex Dalton may finally get to realize his dream of becoming a gold medal ice skater if he can beat Misha, his Russian rival. He soon finds out that Misha isn't his only problem, as he unknowingly becomes a pawn in a game of corruption and greed that could totally ruin his career. **102m/C VHS.** Paul Cross, Dan Haggerty, Robert Budaska, Chris Thomas; ***D:*** Barry Samson; ***W:*** Paul Cross.

Ice Pirates ½ 1984 (PG) Space pirates in the far future steal blocks of ice to fill the needs of a thirsty galaxy. Cool plot has its moments. **91m/C VHS.** Robert Urich, Mary Crosby, Michael D. Roberts, John Matuszak, Anjelica Huston, Ron Perlman, John Carradine, Robert Symonds; ***D:*** Stewart Raffill; ***W:*** Stewart Raffill; ***M:*** Bruce Broughton.

The Ice Rink *La Patinoire* 1999 A director (Novembre) decides to make a movie about the romance between a French ice skater (Chaplin) and an American hockey player (Campbell) that is to be filmed on an ice skating rink. However, most of the cast and crew can't skate, the ice keeps melting, the supporting hockey players are Lithuanian and don't speak French, the two leads are having a torrid (and disruptive) affair, and that's just the beginning. A generally playful look at the tribulations of making a movie. French with subtitles. **80m/C VHS, DVD, Wide.** *FR* Tom Novembre, Marie-France Pisier, Bruce Campbell, Dolores Chaplin, Mireille Perrier, Jean-Pierre Cassel; ***D:*** Jean-Philippe Toussaint; ***W:*** Jean-Philippe Toussaint; ***C:*** Jean-Francois Robin.

The Ice Runner ½ 1993 (R) Low-key Cold War thriller, filmed in 1991, about a U.S. spy who escapes from the Soviet gulag. Jeffrey West (Albert) gets caught in a botched payoff to a Soviet minister and when the diplomats wash their hands of him a rigged trial has West sentenced to 12 years hard labor. A convenient train wreck lets him assume a different prisoner's name which gets him to a minimum security camp under the eyes of a suspicious commander. Now West needs to escape and cross 39 miles of icy tundra separating his Russian prison from American freedom. **116m/C VHS.** Edward Albert, Eugene Lazarev, Olga Kabo, Victor Wong, Alexander Kuznitsov, Basil Hoffman, Bill Bordy, Sergei Ruban; ***D:*** Barry Samson; ***W:*** Joyce Warren, Clifford Coleman, Joshua Stallings.

Ice Station Zebra ½ 1968 (G) A nuclear submarine races Soviet seamen to find a downed Russian satellite under a polar ice cap. Suspenseful Cold War adventure based on the novel by Alistair MacLean. **148m/C VHS, Wide.** Rock Hudson, Ernest Borgnine, Patrick McGoohan, Jim Brown, Lloyd Nolan, Tony Bill; ***D:*** John Sturges; ***C:*** Daniel F. Fapp; ***M:*** Michel Legrand.

The Ice Storm ½ 1997 (R) Excellent family drama/period piece (the 1970s!) directed by Ang Lee and based on the book by Rick Moody. Kline plays a husband and father too self-absorbed to notice his marriage (to Allen) unraveling into crisis, and his children (Maguire and Ricci) mimicking the sordid behavior that surrounds them. Skillfully fuses together a frank, unsympathetic look at family psychology, while also making a comment on the social situation of the early 1970s. Flirts with being overpoweringly negative and moody, but is elevated by Lee's insight and direction. Excellent job by the entire cast, especially Weaver, frighteningly dead-on as an emotionally reckless wife and mother, and Hann-Byrd and Wood as her eerie sons. **113m/C VHS, DVD, Wide.** Kevin Kline, Sigourney Weaver, Joan Allen, Christina Ricci, Tobey Maguire, Elijah Wood, Katie Holmes, Henry Czerny, Adam Hann-Byrd, David Krumholtz, Jamey Sheridan, Maia Danzinger, Kate Burton, John Benjamin Hickey, Allison Janney, Byron Jennings; ***D:*** Ang Lee; ***W:*** James Schamus; ***C:*** Frederick Elmes; ***M:*** Mychael Danna. British Acad. '97: Support. Actress (Weaver).

Icebox Murders woof! 198? A crazed, motiveless, faceless killer hangs his victims in a walk-in freezer. Store this one. **90m/C VHS.** Jack Taylor, Mirta Miller.

Iced 1988 Wild fun turns to horror on a ski trip as a group of college friends are hunted by a maniac on the loose. It's all downhill. **86m/C VHS.** Debra Deliso, Doug Stevenson, Ron Kologie, Elizabeth Gorcey, Alan Johnson; ***D:*** Jeff Kwitny.

Iceland 1942 Labored romance of an Iceland girl and a Marine with plenty of skating thrown in for good measure. Skating and singing interludes are the best part of an otherwise average film. ♫You Can't Say No to a Soldier; There Will Never Be Another You; Lover's Knot; Let's Bring New Glory to Old Glory; I Like a Military Tune. **79m/B VHS.** Sonja Henie, John Payne, Jack Oakie, Felix Bressart, Osa Massen, Fritz Feld; ***D:*** H. Bruce Humberstone; ***W:*** Robert Ellis, Helen Logan.

Iceman 1984 (PG) A frozen prehistoric man is brought back to life, after which severe culture shock takes hold. Underwritten but nicely acted, especially by Lone as the primal man. **101m/C VHS, Wide.** *CA* Timothy Hutton, Lindsay Crouse, John Lone, David Strathairn, Josef Sommer, Danny Glover; ***D:*** Fred Schepisi; ***W:*** Chip Proser; ***C:*** Ian Baker; ***M:*** Bruce Smeaton.

The Icicle Thief *Ladri di Saponette* 1989 "The Naked Gun" for the art-house crowd. As a stark, black-and-white neo-realist tragedy airs on TV, bright color commercials disrupt the narrative. Soon ads invade the the movie itself, and the film's director jumps into his picture to fix the damage. Study up on your postwar Italian cinema and this'll seem hilarious; otherwise the real fun doesn't kick in until the halfway point. In Italian with English subtitles. **93m/C VHS.** *IT* Maurizio Nichetti, Cateria Sylos Labini, Claudio G. Fava, Renato Scarpa, Heidi Komarek; ***D:*** Maurizio Nichetti; ***W:*** Maurizio Nichetti; ***C:*** Mario Battistoni; ***M:*** Manuel De Sica.

Icy Breasts **1975** A French psychiatrist tries to prevent his beautiful but psychotic patient from continuing her murdering spree. Dubbed. **105m/C VHS.** *FR* Alain Delon, Mireille Darc; ***D:*** Georges Lautner.

I'd Climb the Highest Mountain **1951** Sincere, sentimental piece of Americana about a country preacher (Lundigan) and his city wife (Hayward) as they adjust to life in a small town in Southern hill country. Filmed on location in Georgia. Film was a big hit, especially in the South. Based on the novel by Corra Harris. **88m/C VHS.** Susan Hayward, William Lundigan, Rory Calhoun, Gene Lockhart, Ruth Donnelly, Barbara Bates, Lynn Bari, Alexander Knox; ***D:*** Henry King; ***W:*** Lamar Trotti.

I'd Give My Life ½ **1936** A gangster's ex-wife is presently married to the governor. He tries to use their honest but framed son to blackmail her. **73m/B VHS.** Guy Standing, Frances Drake, Tom Brown, Janet Beecher; ***D:*** Edwin L. Marin.

Idaho ½ **1943** On a mission to close down houses of ill repute, Rodgers teams up with Autry's old sidekick Burnette. **70m/B VHS.** Roy Rogers, Harry Shannon, Virginia Grey, Smiley Burnette, Ona Munson; ***D:*** Joseph Kane.

Idaho Transfer woof! *Deranged* **1973 (PG)** Fonda's second directorial effort; Carradine's first screen appearance. An obnoxious group of teens travel through time to Idaho in the year 2044. Environmental wasteland story is dull and confused. **90m/C VHS.** Keith Carradine, Kelley Bohanan; ***D:*** Peter Fonda.

An Ideal Husband **1999 (PG-13)** Victorian comedy of manners adapted from the play by Oscar Wilde. The very proper Lady Gertrud Chiltern (Blanchett) discovers that her husband, Sir Robert (Northam), a member of Parliament, attained their fortune and power through questionable means. Robert is being blackmailed over a shady business deal by Gertrud's loathed ex-school mate, Laura Cheveley (Moore). Cynical social butterfly, Lord Arthur Goring (Everett), is drawn into the fray because of his friendship with Chiltern. It's rather exaggerated and very witty, as one would expect of Wilde. **96m/C VHS, DVD.** *GB* Cate Blanchett, Jeremy Northam, Minnie Driver, Rupert Everett, Julianne Moore, Jeroen Krabbe, Lindsay Duncan, Peter Vaughan, John Wood, Marsha Fitzalan, Benjamin Pullen; ***D:*** Oliver Parker; ***W:*** Oliver Parker; ***C:*** David Johnson; ***M:*** Charlie Mole. Natl. Bd. of Review '99: Support. Actress (Moore).

Identification of a Woman *Identificazione di una Donna* **1982** Niccolo (Milian) is a middle-aged film director who is searching for the perfect female image as the focus for his new movie. But his personal search alienates the flesh-and-blood women already in his life. Lots of visuals give the film a slow, dreamlike quality. Italian with subtitles. **131m/C VHS.** *IT* Tomas Milian, Christine Boisson, Daniela Silverio, Sandra Monteleoni; ***D:*** Michelangelo Antonioni; ***W:*** Michelangelo Antonioni, Gerard Brach; ***C:*** Carlo Di Palma; ***M:*** John Foxx.

Identity Crisis **1990 (R)** Campy fashion maven and flamboyant rapper switch identities causing much tedious overacting. Lifeless murder comedy from father and son Van Peebles. **98m/C VHS.** Mario Van Peebles, Ilan Mitchell-Smith, Nicholas Kepros, Shelly Burch, Richard Clarke; ***D:*** Melvin Van Peebles.

Identity Unknown ½ **1945** Shell-shocked veteran goes AWOL to discover who he is, meeting grieving relatives along the way. Interesting premise is sometimes moving. **70m/B VHS, 8mm.** Richard Arlen, Cheryl Walker, Roger Pryor, Bobby Driscoll; ***D:*** Walter Colmes.

The Idiot **1951** Dostoevski's Russian novel is transported by Kurosawa across two centuries to post-war Japan, where the madness and jealousy continue to rage. In Japanese with English subtitles. **166m/B VHS.** Toshiro Mifune, Masayuki Mori, Setsuko Hara, Yoshiko Kuga, Takashi Shimura; ***D:*** Akira Kurosawa.

Idiot Box **1997** Crazy youth comedy about lazy, brainless Kev (Mendelsohn) and Mick (Sims) who spend most of their unemployed time watching violent cop shows on TV and drinking beer. It's from the "idiot box" that the dim duo get the idea that they've learned enough to rob a bank, but it just so happens that a pair of crooks, who wear clown masks, are already on a bank crime spree. Naturally, both sets of robbers choose the same bank as their target and the cops just happen to be waiting. **83m/C VHS, DVD.** *AU* Ben Mendelsohn, Jeremy Sims, John Polson, Robyn Loau, Graeme Blundell, Deborah Kennedy, Stephen Rae, Andrew S. Gilbert, Amanda Muggleton, Paul Gleeson, Susie Porter; ***D:*** David Caesar; ***W:*** David Caesar; ***C:*** Joseph Pickering; ***M:*** Tim Rogers, Nick Launay.

The Idiots *Idioterne* **1999 (R)** Von Trier uses the stripped back camerawork of Dogma 95 to tell an annoying, pointless story involving a commune-like group of middle-class drop-outs around Copenhagen who spend their time deliberately acting like idiots in public places. They're trying to get in touch with their wounded inner child while you'll want to slap some sense into them. Film provoked controversy because of a group sex scene that (at least) borders on porn. Danish with subtitles. **115m/C VHS, DVD.** *DK* Bodil Jorgensen, Jens Albinus, Louise Hassing, Troels Lyby, Nikolaj Lie Kaas, Henrik Prip, Luis Mesonero, Louise Mieritz, Knud Romer Jorgensen, Trine Michelsen; ***D:*** Lars von Trier; ***W:*** Lars von Trier; ***C:*** Lars von Trier.

Idiot's Delight **1939** At an Alpine hotel, a song and dance man meets a gorgeous Russian countess who reminds him of a former lover. Incredibly, Gable sings and dances through "Puttin' on the Ritz," the film's big highlight. Based on the Pulitzer Prize-winning play by Robert Sherwood. **107m/B VHS.** Clark Gable, Norma Shearer, Burgess Meredith, Edward Arnold, Charles Coburn, Joseph Schildkraut; ***D:*** Clarence Brown; ***C:*** William H. Daniels.

Idle Hands ½ **1999 (R)** Pothead slacker Anton (Sawa) finds that his very idle hand is possessed by a demon, making him do things he doesn't want to do, like get up off the couch and kill his friends Mick (Green) and Pnub (Henson). When Anton cuts off the offending appendage, it's free to terroroze his girlfriend Molly (Alba). With the help of a Druid priestess (Fox) and his now undead friends, Anton must stop the hand from taking Molly's soul to Hell. Even if the release hadn't coincided with the Littleton tragedy, this tasteless horror-comedy wouldn't be funny. Relentless overacting tries to cover up for a lame script filled with pot jokes and gory high school slasher conventions. Green and Henson are the only bright spots. **90m/C VHS, DVD, Wide.** Devon Sawa, Seth Green, Elden (Ratliff) Henson, Jessica Alba, Christopher Hunt, Vivica A. Fox, Jack Noseworthy, Sean M. Whalen, Nicholas Sadler, Fred Willard, Katie Wright, Connie Ray; ***D:*** Rodman Flender; ***W:*** Terri Hughes, Ron Milbauer; ***C:*** Christopher Baffa; ***M:*** Graeme Revell.

The Idol Dancer ½ **1920** Romance and adventure in the South Seas with a drunken American beachcomber inspired by love to change his ways. There's also a native uprising for added excitement. Minor Griffith but nice Nassau scenery. **93m/B VHS.** Richard Barthelmess, Clarine Seymour, Creighton Hale, George MacQuarrie, Kate Bruce, Anders Randolf, Walter James, Thomas Carr; ***D:*** D.W. Griffith.

Idolmaker ½ **1980 (PG)** A conniving agent can make a rock star out of anyone. Well-acted fluff with Sharkey taking a strong lead. The first film by hack-meister Hackford and somewhat based on true-life teen fab Fabian. **119m/C VHS, DVD.** Ray Sharkey, Tovah Feldshuh, Peter Gallagher, Paul Land, Joe Pantoliano, Maureen McCormick, John Aprea, Richard Bright, Olympia Dukakis, Steven Apostlee Peck; ***D:*** Taylor Hackford; ***C:*** Adam Holender; ***M:*** Jeff Barry. Golden Globes '81: Actor—Mus./Comedy (Sharkey).

If... **1969 (R)** Three unruly seniors at a British boarding school refuse to conform. A popular, anarchic indictment of staid British society, using the same milieu as Vigo's "Zero de Conduite," with considerably more violence. The first of Anderson and McDowell's trilogy, culminating with "O Lucky Man!" and "Britannia Hospital." In color and black and white. **111m/C VHS.** *GB* Malcolm McDowell, David Wood, Christine Noonan, Richard Warwick, Robert Swann, Arthur Lowe, Mona Washbourne, Graham Crowden, Hugh Thomas, Guy Rose, Peter Jeffrey, Geoffrey Chater, Mary MacLeod, Anthony Nicholls, Ben Aris, Charles Lloyd Pack, Rupert Webster, Brian Pettifer, Sean Bury, Michael Cadman; ***D:*** Lindsay Anderson; ***W:*** David Sherwin; ***C:*** Miroslav Ondricek; ***M:*** Marc Wilkinson. Cannes '69: Film.

If Ever I See You Again **1978 (PG)** The creator of "You Light Up My Life" stars in the sentimental melodrama. Two adolescent lovers meet again years later and try to rekindle old passions. Done with as much skill as "Light" minus a hit song. **105m/C VHS.** Joseph Brooks, Shelley Hack, Jerry Keller, Jimmy Breslin; ***D:*** Joseph Brooks; ***W:*** Joseph Brooks; ***M:*** Joseph Brooks.

If I Die Before I Wake woof! **1998 (R)** Suburban family become the grisly victims of three intruders who enjoy terrorizing, torturing, and killing until teenaged LoriBeth (Jones), who has been hiding from the bad guys, gets revenge. Ick, ick, ick. **77m/C VHS, DVD.** Michael (Mick) McCleery, Muse Watson, Stephanie Jones, Anthony Nicosia; ***D:*** Brian Katkin; ***W:*** Brian Katkin; ***C:*** Zoran Hochstatter; ***M:*** Thomas Morse. **VIDEO**

If I Were King **1938** Colman, of the impeccable diction, stars as swashbuckling 15th-century French poet Francois Villon, who matches wits with King Louis XI (Rathbone), and falls in love with aristocratic Katherine de Vaucelles (Dee). He even manages to save Paris by leading a peasant army against the invading Burgundians. Probably the best scenes are the witty repartee between Colman and Rathbone, each trying to best the other. Also filmed as 1927's "The Beloved Rogue" (with John Barrymore) and the operetta "The Vagabond King." **102m/B VHS.** Ronald Colman, Basil Rathbone, Frances Dee, Henry Wilcoxon, C.V. France, Ellen Drew, Sidney Toler, Heather Thatcher, Stanley Ridges; ***D:*** Frank Lloyd; ***W:*** Preston Sturges; ***C:*** Theodor Sparkuhl; ***M:*** Richard Hageman.

If I Were Rich *Cash; For Love or Money* **1933** Gwenn is arranging a meeting at his home for a group of financiers he hopes will back a scheme to save his ailing business. Meanwhile he has to dodge bill collectors and others determined to ruin his plans. **63m/B VHS.** *GB* Edmund Gwenn, Wendy Barrie, Robert Donat, Clifford Heatherley; ***D:*** Zoltan Korda.

If It's a Man, Hang Up ½ **1975** A model is terrified by harrowing telephone calls from a stranger. **71m/C VHS.** Carol Lynley, Gerald Harper.

If It's Tuesday, This Must Be Belgium **1969 (G)** A fast-paced, frantic, and funny look at a group of Americans on a whirlwind European tour. The group does a nine-country, 18-day bus tour with clashing, comic personalities and lots of romantic possibilities. Remade in 1987 for TV. **99m/C VHS.** Suzanne Pleshette, Ian McShane, Mildred Natwick, Norman Fell, Michael Constantine, Peggy Cass, Murray Hamilton, Marty Ingels, Sandy Baron, Pamela Britton, Luke Halpin; ***D:*** Mel Stuart.

If Looks Could Kill **1986 (R)** Would-be film noir about a man spying on a female embezzler and falling in love. **90m/C VHS.** Alan Fisler, Tim Gail, Kim Lambert, Jeanne Marie; ***D:*** Chuck Vincent.

If Looks Could Kill ½ **1991 (PG-13)** TV stud Grieco makes film debut as a high school class cutup who travels to France with his class to parlez vous for extra credit. Mistaken for a CIA agent, he stumbles into a plot to take over all the money in the whole wide world, and much implausible action and eyelash batting follows. Extra kibbles for supporting characterizations. Oh, and don't be put off by the fact that the Parisian scenes were shot in Montreal. **89m/C VHS, 8mm.** Richard Grieco, Linda Hunt, Roger Rees, Robin Bartlett, Gabrielle Anwar, Roger Daltrey, Geraldine James, Carole (Raphaelle) Davis; ***D:*** William Dear; ***W:*** Fred Dekker; ***M:*** David Foster.

If Lucy Fell **1995 (R)** Schaeffer serves as writer/director/star of this predictable 90s-style romantic comedy. Ludicrous premise has psychotherapist Lucy (Parker) bent on realizing a 10-year-old pact with longtime friend Joe (Schaeffer) that stipulates they both jump off the Brooklyn Bridge if neither one has found true love by age 30. With the big birthday approaching, Lucy takes a desperate shot with eccentric painter Bwick (Stiller), while Joe finally goes for the object of his desire, asking beautiful neighbor Jane (MacPherson) to a showing of his paintings. Highlights come in the casting, with Parker a solid and energetic neurotic and MacPherson showing that there's something beyond her more obvious talents. **92m/C VHS, DVD, Wide.** Sarah Jessica Parker, Eric Schaeffer, Ben Stiller, Elle Macpherson, James Rebhorn, Dominic Chianese; ***D:*** Eric Schaeffer; ***W:*** Eric Schaeffer, Tony Spiridakis; ***C:*** Ron Fortunato; ***M:*** Amanda Kravat, Charles Pettis.

If These Walls Could Talk ½ **1996 (R)** Covers four decades, from the '50s to the present, telling the stories of three women and the different ways they deal with unexpected pregnancies. "1952" finds recently widowed nurse Claire (Moore) discovering she's pregnant—and it's not her late husband's. In some graphic scenes she tries to end the pregnancy herself with a knitting needle and later through a back-alley abortion. Happily married Barbara (Spacek) already has four children in "1974" and has just returned to college. Then she discovers she's pregnant again. Abortion's an option but does Barbara want one? Finally, college student Christine (Heche) gets pregnant by her married professor in "1996" and reluctantly opts for an abortion at a family planning clinic, which is besieged by pro-lifers and on the edge of some violent confrontations. **109m/C VHS, DVD.** Demi Moore, Catherine Keener, Jason London, Shirley Knight, Kevin Cooney, CCH Pounder, Robin Gammell, Sissy Spacek, Xander Berkeley, Joanna Gleason, Harris Yulin, Anne Heche, Jada Pinkett Smith, Cher, Diana Scarwid, Lindsay Crouse, Lorraine Toussaint, Rita Wilson, Eileen Brennan, Craig T. Nelson; ***D:*** Cher, Nancy Savoca; ***W:*** Nancy Savoca, Susan Manus, I. Marlene King; ***C:*** Ellen Kuras, Bobby Bukowski, John Stanier; ***M:*** Cliff Eidelman. **CABLE**

If These Walls Could Talk 2 ½ **2000 (R)** Anthology features the stories of three lesbian couples in America. "1961" shows the sedate lives of retired schoolteachers Edith (Redgrave) and Abby (Seldes), who have lived together for decades. But when Abby suddenly dies, Edith discovers she will be dispossesed by Abby's greedy nephew. "1972" finds Linda (Williams) living with a group of lesbian feminists who disapprove of butch-femme couples. But Linda is still drawn to the butch Amy (Sevigny), who refuses to apologize for how she chooses to live. "2000" has thirtysomething couple Fran (Stone) and Kal (DeGeneres) deciding to have a baby and having some comical problems with the sperm issue. **96m/C VHS, DVD.** Vanessa Redgrave, Marian Seldes, Paul Giamatti, Elizabeth Perkins, Michelle Williams, Chloe Sevigny, Nia Long, Natasha Lyonne, Heather McComb, Sharon Stone, Ellen DeGeneres, Regina King, Kathy Najimy, Mitchell Anderson, George Newbern, Amy Carlson; ***D:*** Jane Anderson, Martha Coolidge, Anne Heche, Alex Sichel; ***W:*** Jane Anderson, Sylvia Sichel, Anne Heche; ***C:*** Paul Elliott, Robbie Greenberg, Peter Deming; ***M:*** Basil Poledouris. **CABLE**

If Things Were Different ½ **1979** Feisty woman struggles to hold her family together after her husband is hospitalized with a nervous breakdown. **96m/C VHS.** Suzanne Pleshette, Tony Roberts, Arte Johnson, Chuck McCann, Don Murray; ***D:*** Robert Lewis.

If You Could See What I Hear 🦴½ 1982 (PG) Irritatingly upbeat true-life story of blind singer-musician, Tom Sullivan. Covers his life from college days to marriage. Sophomoric comedy centers around the hero's irresponsible, and often life-endangering, behavior. **103m/C VHS.** *CA* Marc Singer, R.H. Thomson, Sarah Torgov, Shari Belafonte; ***D:*** Eric Till. Genie '83: Support. Actor (Thomson).

If You Don't Stop It...You'll Go Blind 🦴½ 1977 (R) A series of gauche and tasteless vignettes from various little-known comedians. **80m/C VHS.** Pat McCormick, George Spencer, Patrick Wright; ***D:*** I. Robert Levy, Keefe Brasselle.

If You Knew Susie 🦴🦴 1948 Two retired vaudeville actors find a letter from George Washington which establishes them as descendants of a colonial patriot and the heirs to a $7 billion fortune. ♫If You Knew Susie; My Brooklyn Love Song; What Do I Want With Money?; We're Living the Life We Love; My, How the Time Goes By. **90m/B VHS.** Eddie Cantor, Joan Davis, Allyn Joslyn, Charles Dingle, Charles Halton; ***D:*** Gordon Douglas.

If You Only Knew 🦴🦴 2000 Struggling New York writer (are there any other kind?) Parker (Schaech) falls for painter Samantha (Eastwood) when he answers her ad for someone to share her loft. She has no problem rooming with a guy—as long as he's gay. So Parker moves in and finds the pretense an increasing struggle. Formulaic but Eastwood is a real charmer. **111m/C VHS, DVD.** Johnathon Schaech, Alison Eastwood, Gabrielle Anwar, James LeGros, Lainie Kazan; ***D:*** David Snedeker.

Igby Goes Down 2002 (R) Teenager Culkin has the weird family blues—a snotty older brother (Phillippe), a nutso godfather (Goldblum) and a crazy, dying mother (Sarandon). But his girlfriend Danes helps keep him together. Not yet reviewed. **?m/C VHS, DVD.** Kieran Culkin, Ryan Phillippe, Susan Sarandon, Claire Danes, Jeff Goldblum, Bill Pullman, Amanda Peet; ***D:*** Burr Steers; ***W:*** Burr Steers.

Igor & the Lunatics 🦴 1985 (R) Tasteless tale of a cannibal cult leader released from prison who picks up where he left off. **79m/C VHS, DVD.** Joseph Eero, Joe Niola, T.J. Michaels; ***D:*** Billy Parolini.

Iguana 🦴🦴 1989 The videocassette box art makes this look like a horror movie, but it's really a stiff, solemn period drama about a deformed sailor with lizardlike features. After a life of mistreatment he reigns mercilessly over a handful of island castaways. An international coproduction with mostly English dialogue, some Spanish and Portuguese with subtitles. **88m/C VHS, DVD, Wide.** *SI IT* Everett McGill, Michael Madsen, Joseph Culp, Fabio Teste; ***D:*** Monte Hellman; ***W:*** Monte Hellman, Jaime Comas Gil, Steven Gaydos; ***C:*** Josep Civit.

Ike 🦴🦴½ *Ike: The War Years* 1979 Duvall is top brass in this epic biography tracing Eisenhower's career during WWII. Originally a six-hour miniseries. **291m/C VHS.** Robert Duvall, Lee Remick, Darren McGavin, Dana Andrews, Laurence Luckinbill; ***D:*** Melville Shavelson. **TV**

Ikiru 🦴🦴🦴🦴 *To Live; Doomed; Living* 1952 When a clerk finds out he is dying of cancer, he decides to build a children's playground and give something of himself back to the world. Highly acclaimed, heartbreaking drama from the unusually restrained Kurosawa; possibly his most "eastern" film. In Japanese with English subtitles. **134m/B VHS.** *JP* Takashi Shimura, Nobuo Kaneko, Kyoko Seki, Miki Odagari, Yunosuke Ito; ***D:*** Akira Kurosawa; ***W:*** Akira Kurosawa, Shinobu Hashimoto, Hideo Oguni; ***C:*** Asakazu Nakai; ***M:*** Fumio Hayasaka.

Il Bell'Antonio 🦴🦴½ *Handsome Antonio* 1960 The boastful Antonio has a reputation as a womanizer but when he finally marries, to a lovely young woman, he faces the loss of his libido. Satire of machismo, marriage, and Catholicism. In Italian with English subtitles. **115m/C VHS.** *IT* Marcello Mastroianni, Claudia Cardinale, Pierre Brasseur, Tomas Milian, Rina Morelli; ***D:*** Mauro Bolognini; ***W:*** Pier Paolo Pasolini, Gino Vissentini; ***C:*** Armando Nannuzzi; ***M:*** Piero Piccioni.

Il Bidone 🦴🦴 *The Swindle* 1955 Three Italian conmen pull capers in Rome trying to make a better life for themselves. Dark overtones permeate one of Fellini's lesser efforts. Good cast can't bring up the level of this film. In Italian with English subtitles. **92m/C VHS, DVD.** *IT* Broderick Crawford, Giulietta Masina, Richard Basehart, Franco Fabrizi; ***D:*** Federico Fellini; ***W:*** Federico Fellini, Tullio Pinelli, Ennio Flaiano; ***C:*** Otello Martelli; ***M:*** Nino Rota.

Il Grido 🦴🦴 *The Cry; The Outcry* 1957 A jilted husband takes his young daughter from village to village in search of the woman who deserted them for another man. Set in the desolate Po Valley of director Antonioni's childhood. In Italian with English subtitles. **116m/B VHS, DVD.** *IT* Steve Cochran, Alida Valli, Dorian Gray, Betsy Blair, Gabriella Pallotta; ***D:*** Michelangelo Antonioni; ***W:*** Michelangelo Antonioni, Ennio de Concini; ***C:*** Gianni Di Venanzo; ***M:*** Giovanni Fusco.

Il Sorpasso 🦴🦴½ 1963 A braggart, who has failed at everything, spends all his time traveling around Italy in his sportscar. He takes a repressed law student under his wing and decides to teach him how to have fun. In Italian with English subtitles. **116m/B VHS.** *IT* Vittorio Gassman, Jean-Louis Trintignant; ***D:*** Dino Risi.

I'll Be Home for Christmas 🦴½ 1998 (PG) Snotty college kid Jake (Thomas) wants to teach his Dad a lesson by boycotting Christmas and stealing away to Mexico with his girlfriend (Biel). Jake thinks his Dad remarried too soon after his mother's death, but is bribed home with his Dad's prized Porshe (now there's a lesson for the kids) if he can arrive for Christmas Eve dinner. A series of absurd mishaps ensue (almost all of which occur because Jake is a lying, cheating jerk) as he makes his away cross-country while glued inside of a Santa suit. The characters are superficial and at times downright annoying. This run of the mill holiday stinker will likely only appeal to Thomas' legion of teenage groupies. **86m/C VHS, DVD, Wide.** Jonathan Taylor Thomas, Jessica Biel, Adam LaVorgna, Gary Cole, Eve Gordon, Sean O'Bryan, Andrew Lauer; ***D:*** Arlene Sanford; ***W:*** Harris Goldberg, Tom Nursall; ***C:*** Hiro Narita; ***M:*** John Debney.

I'll Be Yours 🦴🦴½ 1947 Small town Louise Ginglebusher (Durbin) moves to New York and becomes an usher at the Buckingham Theater (a fictional Radio City Music Hall). She gets involved with millionarie, J. Conrad Nelson (Menjou), and struggling lawyer, George Prescott (Drake). She falls for George and tries to help him get a job with Nelson by telling Nelson that they have just gotten married. Bendix plays the sympathetic coffee shop owner. Remake of 1935's "The Good Fairy," which was also a play by Ferenc Molnar. ♫It's Dreamtime; Cobbleskill School Song; Granada; Sari Waltz. **94m/B VHS.** Deanna Durbin, Tom Drake, Adolphe Menjou, William Bendix, Walter Catlett, Franklin Pangborn; ***D:*** William A. Seiter; ***W:*** Preston Sturges; ***C:*** Hal Mohr; ***M:*** Frank Skinner.

I'll Cry Tomorrow 🦴🦴🦴 1955 Hayward brilliantly portrays actress Lillian Roth as she descends into alcoholism and then tries to overcome her addiction. Based on Roth's memoirs. ♫Sing You Sinners; When The Red Red Robin Comes Bob Bob Bobbin' Along; Happiness Is Just a Thing Called Joe; Vagabond King Waltz. **119m/B VHS.** Susan Hayward, Richard Conte, Eddie Albert, Jo Van Fleet, Margo, Don Taylor, Ray Danton, Veda Ann Borg; ***D:*** Daniel Mann; ***M:*** Alex North. Oscars '55: Costume Des. (B&W); Cannes '56: Actress (Hayward).

I'll Do Anything 🦴🦴½ 1993 (PG-13) Hollywood satire finds unemployed actor Matt (Nolte) suddenly forced to care for his six-year-old daughter Jeannie (Wright), whom he hasn't seen in three years. Matt also finally gets a job—as a chauffeur to an obnoxious producer (well played by Brooks) whose company winds up making the manipulative demon Jeannie into a hot child star. Great work by Kavner as the owner of a test-screening service who romances Brooks. Originally intended as a musical, the test screenings were so disastrous that the numbers were axed. What's left is less jerky than expected; Brooks reportedly based his character in part on mega-mogul Joel Silver. **115m/C VHS, 8mm.** Nick Nolte, Albert Brooks, Julie Kavner, Whittni Wright, Joely Richardson, Tracey Ullman; ***D:*** James L. Brooks; ***W:*** James L. Brooks; ***C:*** Michael Ballhaus; ***M:*** Hans Zimmer.

I'll Get You 🦴🦴 *Escape Route* 1953 An FBI agent goes to England on the trail of a kidnapping ring. **79m/B VHS.** George Raft, Sally Gray, Clifford Evans; ***D:*** Seymour Friedman.

I'll Name the Murderer 🦴🦴 1936 Suspense film in which a gossip columnist starts his own investigation into the murder of a club singer. **?m/C VHS.** Ralph Forbes, Marion Shilling; ***D:*** Raymond K. Johnson.

I'll Never Forget What's 'Isname 🦴🦴🦴 1967 To some tastes, this overwrought and long-unseen comedy from the swinging '60s will be completely dated with characters whose mindsets are totally alien. Protagonist Andrew Quint (Reed) is a piggish young ad executive who tries to leave his even more piggish boss (Welles), and his two mistresses, though he's not sure he wants to divorce his wife. Why? He wants to go back to do something meaningful with his life, something like working for a literary magazine. It's actually a long midlife crisis (though the phrase did not exist when the film was made) that set standards for frankness in its sexual material. **99m/C DVD, Wide.** Oliver Reed, Orson Welles, Carol White, Marianne Faithfull, Michael Hordern, Frank Finlay; ***D:*** Michael Winner; ***W:*** Peter Draper; ***C:*** Otto Heller; ***M:*** Francis Lai.

I'll Remember April 🦴🦴½ 1999 In the days following the bombing of Pearl Harbor rumors abound that Japanese submarines are patrolling the Pacific and four 10-year-old California boys like to pretend they are Marines in search of the Japanese enemy. Imagine their surprise when they discover a Japanese soldier who washed up on the beach and is hiding out in their clubhouse. They keep him their prisoner while trying to decide what to do but when the soldier rescues one of the boys from drowning, the boys decide that they have to save him. **90m/C VHS, DVD.** Haley Joel Osment, Trevor Morgan, Richard Taylor Olson, Yuki Tokuhiro, Mark Harmon, Pam Dawber, Noriyuki "Pat" Morita, Yuji Okumoto, Troy Evans, Paul Dooley; ***D:*** Bob (Benjamin) Clark; ***W:*** Mark Sanderson; ***C:*** Stephen M. Katz; ***M:*** Paul Zaza.

I'll See You in My Dreams 🦴🦴½ 1951 Hokey but fun musical biography of songwriter Gus Kahn (Thomas) and his wife Grace LeBoy (Day). Kahn gets his start in Ziegfeld shows but loses both his career and wife after the 1929 crash. However, she soon returns and everything ends happily ever after. ♫Ain't We Got Fun; Ukelele Lady; The One I Love Belongs To Somebody Else; I'll See You In My Dreams; It Had To Be You; Swingin' Down the Lane; My Buddy; Makin' Whoopee!; Yes Sir, That's My Baby. **109m/B VHS.** Danny Thomas, Doris Day, Frank Lovejoy, Patrice Wymore, James Gleason, Mary Wickes, Jim Backus, Minna Gombell, William Forrest; ***D:*** Michael Curtiz; ***W:*** Melville Shavelson, Jack Rose.

I'll Take Sweden 🦴🦴½ 1965 Overprotective father Hope disapproves of teenaged daughter Weld's guitar-playing boyfriend (Avalon). So to keep her out of harm's way he finagles a company transfer to Sweden. Dad falls for an interior decorator (Merrill) while Weld gets involved with a Swedish playboy (Slate). Deciding Avalon is the lesser of two evils, Hope schemes to get the two back together. **96m/C VHS.** Bob Hope, Tuesday Weld, Frankie Avalon, Dina Merrill, Jeremy Slate, Walter Sande, John Qualen, Roy Roberts, Maudie Prickett; ***D:*** Fred de Cordova; ***W:*** Arthur Marx, Bob Fisher, Nat Perrin; ***C:*** Daniel F. Fapp.

Illegal 🦴🦴½ 1955 Crime melodrama stars Robinson as an attorney who risks all to acquit his assistant of murder. Early Mansfield appearance. Remake of "The Mouthpiece." **88m/B VHS.** Edward G. Robinson, Nina Foch, Hugh Marlowe, Jayne Mansfield, Albert Dekker, Ellen Corby, DeForest Kelley, Howard St. John; ***D:*** Lewis Allen.

Illegal Affairs 🦴 1996 The kind of film that almost makes you feel sorry for lawyers. The sleazy firm of Grimes and Peterson specializes in divorce cases—and seem personally responsible for any number of them on account of adultery. **87m/C VHS, DVD.** Jay Richardson, Monique Parent, Christian Noble; ***D:*** Michael Paul Girard; ***W:*** Michael Paul Girard; ***C:*** Denis Maloney; ***M:*** Miriam Cutler. **VIDEO**

Illegal Entry: Formula for Fear 🦴½ 1993 Tracie's scientist father has invented a formula that could change the world. When he's murdered the formula falls into her unsuspecting hands. Tracie might not know what she has but that doesn't stop some very ruthless efforts to get the information others want. **88m/C VHS.** Sabryn Gene't, Barbara Lee (Niven) Alexander, Gregory Vignolle, Arthur Roberts, Carol Hoyt; ***D:*** Henri Charr; ***W:*** John B. Pfeifer.

Illegal in Blue 🦴🦴 1995 (R) Chris (Gauthier) the cop falls for sultry blues singer Kari (Dash) and then realizes she could be a suspect in the murder he's investigating. Will libido win out over loyalty to the job? Also available unrated. **94m/C VHS.** Dan Gauthier, Stacey Dash, Louis Giambalvo, Michael Durrell, David Groh; ***D:*** Stu Segall; ***W:*** Noel Hynd; ***M:*** Steve Edwards.

Illegally Yours 🦴 1987 (PG) Miscast comedy about a college student serving on the jury in trial of old girlfriend. Bring down the gavel on this one. **94m/C VHS.** Rob Lowe, Colleen Camp, Kenneth Mars; ***D:*** Peter Bogdanovich.

Illicit 🦴🦴 1931 In love, Stanwyck fears that marrying Rennie will only ruin their wonderful relationship. Two years after their marriage her fears are realized when each searches for happiness with a past lover. A melodramatic performance that doesn't quite hit its mark. Remade two years later as "Ex-Lady" with Bette Davis in the lead. Based on the play by Edith Fitzgerald and Robert Riskin. **76m/B VHS.** Barbara Stanwyck, Ricardo Cortez, Natalie Moorhead, Charles Butterworth, Joan Blondell, Claude Gillingwater; ***D:*** Archie Mayo; ***W:*** Harvey Thew.

Illicit Behavior 🦴🦴½ 1991 (R) A dangerous manipulative woman (Severance) is out to claim a $2 million inheritance in this intricate and seductive police thriller. Included among her victims are her husband; a Hollywood vice cop suspended for use of excessive force; his partner; her husband's internal affairs adversary; and her own psychiatrist. Also available in an uncut, unrated version. **101m/C VHS.** Joan Severance, Robert Davi, James Russo, Jack Scalia, Kent McCord; ***D:*** Worth Keeter.

Illicit Dreams 🦴½ 1994 A lonely housewife fantasizes about a dream lover who then becomes real. Too bad her possessive and vicious tycoon hubby would rather kill than lose her. **93m/C VHS.** Shannon Tweed, Andrew Stevens.

Illtown 🦴🦴½ 1996 A happy trio of yuppy-ish Florida drug dealers, led by Rapaport's Dante, land in their own inferno when Dante's former business partner Gabriel (Trese), emerges from jail hell-bent on revenge. Danza plays the evil, effeminate underworld boss while Hayes takes the high road as the saintly detective. Abundance of metaphors aside and amid all the violence, the sluggish narrative style, with everything thrown in from dream sequences and flashbacks to dissolves and slow motion, is more effective at setting a mood than telling a story. Effective score and powerful performances, beautifully filmed by Denault, make a stylish pic that sacrifices substance. **103m/C VHS.** Michael Rapaport, Lili Taylor, Adam Trese, Kevin Corrigan, Paul Schulze, Angela Featherstone, Saul Stein, Tony Danza, Isaac Hayes; ***D:*** Nick Gomez; ***W:*** Nick Gomez; ***C:*** Jim Denault; ***M:*** Brian Keane.

Illuminata 🦴🦴 1998 (R) Comedy-drama about a struggling theater troupe in turn-of-the-century New York. Tuccio (Turturro) is the company's playwright—in love with manager/leading lady, Rachel (Turturro's wife Borowitz), and worried about the reception for his new work. Also involved are self-centered aging diva Celimene (Sarandon), theater owner Astergourd (D'Angelo), foppish critic Bevalaqua (Walken) and the unlikely object of his affections, the troupe's clown, Marco (Irwin), among many others. Adapted from the play by Brandon Cole. **111m/C VHS, DVD, Wide.** John Turturro, Katherine Borowitz, Christopher Walken, Susan Sarandon, Beverly D'Angelo, Bill Irwin, Rufus Sewell, Georgina Cates, Ben Gazzara, Donal McCann, Aida Turturro, Matthew Sussman, Leo Bassi; ***D:*** John Turturro; ***W:*** John Turturro, Brandon Cole; ***C:*** Harris Savides; ***M:*** William Bolcom, Arnold Black.

Illumination 🦴🦴 *Iluminacja* **1973** Cryptic drama about a young scientist who believes that rational analysis can solve every crisis. Until he must confront the accidental death of a close friend and his problematic affair with an older woman. Intercutting of documentary material can prove disconcerting. Polish with subtitles. **91m/C VHS.** *PL* Stanislaw Latallo, Monika Denisiewicz-Olbrzychska, Malgorzata Pritulak, Edward Zebrowski; ***D:*** Krzysztof Zanussi; ***W:*** Krzysztof Zanussi; ***C:*** Edward Klosinski; ***M:*** Wojciech Kilar.

The Illusion Travels by Streetcar 🦴🦴🦴 *La Illusion Viaja en Tranvia* **1953** Odd but enchanting story of two men who restore a streetcar, only to find that it will not be used by the city. In a gesture of defiance, they steal the streetcar and take it for one last ride, picking up an interesting assortment of characters along the way. In Spanish with English subtitles. Not released in the U.S. until 1977. **90m/B VHS.** *MX* Lilia Prado, Carlos Navarro, Domingo Soler, Fernando Soto Mantequilla, Agustin Isunza, Miguel Manzano; ***D:*** Luis Bunuel.

Illusions 🦴🦴 **1991 (R)** Jan (Locklear) is trying to recover from a nervous breakdown and improve her crumbling marriage when her husband's sexy sister arrives and things start to heat up. Jan thinks her husband and sister-in-law are just a little too close, but when she lets her landlord in on her suspicions, he reacts quite strangely. Will Jan have another nervous breakdown? Mysterious with lots of plot twists. Based on Colley's play "I'll Be Back Before Midnight." **95m/C VHS.** Robert Carradine, Heather Locklear, Emma Samms, Ned Beatty; ***D:*** Victor Kulle; ***W:*** Peter Colley.

The Illustrated Man 🦴🦴🦴 **1969 (PG)** A young drifter meets a tattooed man. Each tattoo causes a fantastic story to unfold. A strange, interesting, but finally limited attempt at literary sci-fi. Based on the story collection by Ray Bradbury. **103m/C VHS.** Rod Steiger, Claire Bloom, Robert Drivas, Don Dubbins; ***D:*** Jack Smight; ***M:*** Jerry Goldsmith.

Ilsa, Harem Keeper of the Oil Sheiks woof! **1976 (R)** The naughty Ilsa works for an Arab sheik in the slave trade. More graphic violence and nudity. Plot makes an appearance. **90m/C VHS, DVD, Wide.** Dyanne Thorne, Michael Thayer, Victor Alexander, Elke Von, Sharon Kelly, Haji, Tanya Boyd, Marilyn Joy, Bobby Woods; ***D:*** Don Edmonds; ***W:*** Langton Stafford; ***C:*** Dean Cundey, Glenn Roland.

Ilsa, She-Wolf of the SS woof! **1974 (R)** The torture-loving Ilsa runs a medical camp for the Nazis. Plot is incidental to nudity and violence. **45m/C VHS, DVD, Wide.** Dyanne Thorne, Greg Knoph, Sharon Kelly, Uschi Digart, Sandy Richman; ***D:*** Don Edmonds; ***W:*** Jonah Royston.

Ilsa, the Tigress of Siberia woof! *The Tigress* **1979** Everyone's favorite torturer has been working her wiles on political prisoners in Russia. After escaping to Canada, her past threatens to catch up with her. As usual, no plot, violence. **85m/C VHS.** Dyanne Thorne, Michel Morin, Jean-Guy Latour, Michael Mallot, Tony Angelo, Terry Coady, Joe Mattia, Sonny Forbes, Greg Giants, Howard Mauer; ***D:*** Jean LaFleur; ***W:*** Marven McGara; ***C:*** Richard Ciupka.

Ilsa, the Wicked Warden woof! *Ilsa, the Absolute Power; Greta the Mad Butcher* **1978 (R)** Ilsa is now a warden of a woman's prison in South America, behaving just as badly as she always has, until the prisoners stage an uprising. Lots of skin, no violence, no acting. Also: no plot. **90m/C VHS, DVD, Wide.** Dyanne Thorne, Lina Romay, Tania Busselier, Howard Maurer, Jess (Jesus) Franco; ***D:*** Jess (Jesus) Franco; ***W:*** Erwin C. Dietrich, Jess (Jesus) Franco; ***C:*** Ruedi Kuttel; ***M:*** Walter Baumgartner.

I'm All Right Jack 🦴🦴🦴 **1959** Sellers plays a pompous communist union leader in this hilarious satire of worker-management relations. Based on Alan Hackney's novel "Private Life." **101m/B VHS.** Peter Sellers, Ian Carmichael, Terry-Thomas, Victor Maddern; ***D:*** John Boulting. British Acad. '59: Actor (Sellers), Screenplay.

I'm Dancing as Fast as I Can 🦴🦴 **1982 (R)** A successful TV producer hopelessly dependent on tranquilizers tries to stop cold turkey. Good story could be better; based on Barbara Gordon's memoirs. **107m/C VHS.** Jill Clayburgh, Nicol Williamson, Dianne West, Joe Pesci, Geraldine Page, John Lithgow, Daniel Stern; ***D:*** Jack Hofsiss; ***W:*** David Rabe; ***C:*** Jan De Bont.

I'm Dangerous Tonight 🦴½ **1990 (R)** Wallflower Amick (Shelley the Waitress in "Twin Peaks") turns into party monster when she dons red dress made from evil ancient Aztec cloak. Many dead soldiers when this girl parties. Based on a Cornell Woolrich short story, it's another in a series of ever more disappointing entries from Hooper, whose cult fave "The Texas Chainsaw Massacre" had low as they come production values, but far better scares. **92m/C VHS.** Madchen Amick, Corey Parker, R. Lee Ermey, Mary Frann, Dee Wallace Stone, Anthony Perkins, Natalie Schafer, William Berger; ***D:*** Tobe Hooper; ***W:*** Alice Wilson. CABLE

I'm from Arkansas 🦴 **1944** The little town of Pitchfork, Arkansas, goes nuts when a pig gives birth to ten piglets. **68m/B VHS.** El Brendel, Slim Summerville, Iris Adrian, Harry Harvey, Bruce (Herman Brix) Bennett; ***D:*** Lew (Louis Friedlander) Landers.

I'm Gonna Git You Sucka 🦴🦴🦴 **1988 (R)** Parody of "blaxploitation" films popular during the '60s and '70s. Funny and laced with outright bellylaughs. A number of stars who made "blaxploitation" films, including Jim Brown, take part in the gags. **89m/C VHS, DVD, Wide.** Keenen Ivory Wayans, Bernie Casey, Steve James, Isaac Hayes, Jim Brown, Ja'net DuBois, Dawnn Lewis, Anne-Marie Johnson, John Vernon, Antonio Fargas, Eve Plumb, Clu Gulager, Kadeem Hardison, Damon Wayans, Gary Owens, Clarence Williams III, David Alan Grier, Kim Wayans, Robin Harris, Chris Rock, Jester Hairston, Eugene Glazer, Peggy Lipton, Robert Townsend; ***D:*** Keenen Ivory Wayans; ***W:*** Keenen Ivory Wayans; ***C:*** Tom Richmond; ***M:*** David Michael Frank.

I'm Losing You 🦴🦴 **1998 (R)** Confusing story with too many shocks and no point of view, which wastes a good cast. TV producer Perry Krohn (Langella) learns that he is dying of cancer. His wife, Diantha (Jens), takes the news badly, as do his wayward children Bertie (McCarthy) and Rachel (Arquette). But it seems everyone has a doom-laden revelation to deal with. Wagner adapts from his own novel. **102m/C VHS, DVD, Wide.** Frank Langella, Salome Jens, Rosanna Arquette, Andrew McCarthy, Amanda Donohoe, Elizabeth Perkins, Gina Gershon, Buck Henry, Ed Begley Jr.; ***D:*** Bruce Wagner; ***W:*** Bruce Wagner; ***C:*** Rob Sweeney; ***M:*** Daniel Catan.

I'm No Angel 🦴🦴🦴 **1933** "Beulah, peel me a grape." Well, you'd be hungry too if you spent your time eyeing playboy Grant as West does. She's a circus floozy who's prone to extorting money from her men (after hashing over their shortcomings with her seen-it-all-maid, the aforementioned Beulah). However, after wooing Grant, she sues for breach of promise. This leads to a comic courtroom scene with Grant bringing in all West's exlovers as witnesses. Grant's second film with West, following "She Done Him Wrong." **88m/B VHS, DVD.** Mae West, Cary Grant, Gregory Ratoff, Edward Arnold, Ralf Harolde, Kent Taylor, Gertrude Michael, Russell Hopton, Dorothy Peterson, William B. Davidson, Gertrude Howard, Hattie McDaniel; ***D:*** Wesley Ruggles; ***W:*** Lowell Brentano, Mae West; ***C:*** Leo Tover; ***M:*** Harvey Brooks.

I'm Not Rappaport 🦴🦴 **1996 (PG-13)** Matthau does some comic grump schtick as irascible, unrepentent 81-year-old New York Jewish radical Nat. He likes to vent his considerable opinions in Central Park and carries on a grumbling friendship with fellow octogenarian Midge (Davis), who stills works as a building superintendent, tending an equally ancient boiler. But Nat's fed-up daughter Clara (Irving) is threatening to put him in a home and Midge seems likely to lose his job when the boiler is scheduled for replacement. Gardner's 1986 stage play tends to show its weaknesses on the big screen. **135m/C VHS.** Walter Matthau, Ossie Davis, Amy Irving, Martha Plimpton, Craig T. Nelson, Boyd Gaines, Guillermo Diaz, Elina Lowensohn, Ron Rifkin; ***D:*** Herb Gardner; ***W:*** Herb Gardner; ***C:*** Adam Holender; ***M:*** Gerry Mulligan.

I'm the Girl He Wants to Kill 🦴½ **1974** A woman sees a murder committed, and the murderer sees her. Now he's after her. **71m/C VHS.** Julie Sommars, Anthony Steel.

I'm the One You're Looking For 🦴🦴½ **1988** A famous model obsessively combs Barcelona for the man who raped her. Suspenseful thriller based on a short story by Gabriel Garcia Marquez. In Spanish with English subtitles. **85m/C VHS.** *SP* Patricia Adriani, Chus (Maria Jesus) Lampreave, Ricard Borras, Toni Canto, Angel Alcazar, Marta Fedz, Frank Muro, Miriam DeMaeztu; ***D:*** Jaime Chavarri.

The Image 🦴🦴½ **1989** Anchorman Finney, the unscrupulous czar of infotainment, does a little soul delving when a man he wrongly implicated in a savings and loan debacle decides to check into the hereafter ahead of schedule. Seems the newsmonger's cut a few corners en route to the bigtime, and his public is mad as hell and...oops, wrong movie (need we say there are not a few echoes of "Network"?). Finney's great. **91m/C VHS.** Albert Finney, John Mahoney, Kathy Baker, Swoosie Kurtz, Marsha Mason, Spalding Gray; ***D:*** Peter Werner; ***M:*** James Newton Howard. CABLE

Image of Death 🦴 **1977** Woman plots to take the life of an old school chum, assume her identity, and then blow up the Capitol. **83m/C VHS.** Cathy Paine, Cheryl Waters, Tony Banner, Barry Pierce, Sheila Helpmann, Penne Hackforth-Jones; ***D:*** Kevin James Dobson.

Image of Passion 🦴 **1986** Weak account of male stripper/lovely advertising executive romance. **90m/C** James Horan, Susan Damante Shaw, Edward Bell; ***D:*** Susan Orlikoff-Simon.

Imagemaker 🦴½ **1986 (R)** Uneven story of a presidential media consultant who bucks the system and exposes corruption. **93m/C VHS.** Michael Nouri, Jerry Orbach, Jessica Harper, Farley Granger; ***D:*** Hal Wiener.

Imaginary Crimes 🦴🦴🦴 **1994 (PG)** Ray Weiler (Keitel) is a well-meaning salesman with dreams much bigger than his reach. After the death of his wife (Lynch), Ray tries to raise his two daughters, Sonya (Balk) and Greta (Moss). But gifted high school senior (in 1962) Sonya is resentful of being her sister's maternal anchor and having her father's schemes come to nothing even as she acknowledges how much Ray cares and how he wants to improve their lives. Remarkable performances by Keitel and Balk. From the novel by Sheila Ballantyne. **106m/C VHS, DVD, Wide.** Harvey Keitel, Fairuza Balk, Kelly Lynch, Vincent D'Onofrio, Elissabeth (Elisabeth, Elizabeth, Liz) Moss, Diane Baker, Christopher Penn, Seymour Cassel, Annette O'Toole; ***D:*** Tony Drazan; ***W:*** Kristine Johnson, Davia Nelson; ***C:*** John Campbell; ***M:*** Stephen Endelman.

Imitation of Life 🦴🦴½ **1934** Fannie Hurst novel tells the story of widowed Beatrice Pullman (Colbert) who uses maid Delilah's (Beaver) recipe for pancakes in order to have the women open a restaurant, which becomes a success. Both mothers suffer at the hands of their willfull teenaged daughters. Delilah's lightskinned daughter Peola (Washington) breaks away from her mother so she can continue to pass for white and Bea's daughter Jessie (Hudson) has a serious crush on her mother's beau, Stephen (William). Weepie was also successfully filmed in 1959. **106m/B VHS.** Claudette Colbert, Louise Beavers, Rochelle Hudson, Fredi Washington, Warren William, Ned Sparks, Alan Hale; ***D:*** John M. Stahl; ***W:*** Preston Sturges, William Hurlbut; ***C:*** Merritt B. Gerstad.

Imitation of Life 🦴🦴🦴 **1959** Remake of the successful 1939 Claudette Colbert outing of the same title, and based on Fanny Hurst's novel, with a few plot changes. Turner is a single mother, more determined to achieve acting fame and fortune than function as a parent. Her black maid, Moore, is devoted to her own daughter (Kohner), but loses her when the girl discovers she can pass for white. When Turner discovers that she and her daughter are in love with the same man, she realizes how little she knows her daughter, and how much the two of them have missed by not having a stronger relationship. Highly successful at the boxoffice. **124m/C VHS.** Lana Turner, John Gavin, Troy Donahue, Sandra Dee, Juanita Moore, Susan Kohner; ***D:*** Douglas Sirk; ***C:*** Russell Metty. Golden Globes '60: Support. Actress (Kohner).

Immediate Family 🦴🦴½ **1989 (PG-13)** Childless couple contact a pregnant, unmarried girl and her boyfriend in hopes of adoption. As the pregnancy advances, the mother has doubts about giving up her baby. A bit sugar-coated in an effort to woo family trade. **112m/C VHS.** Glenn Close, James Woods, Kevin Dillon, Mary Stuart Masterson, Linda Darlow, Jane Greer, Jessica James, Mimi Kennedy; ***D:*** Jonathan Kaplan; ***W:*** Barbara Benedek; ***M:*** Brad Fiedel. Natl. Bd. of Review '89: Support. Actress (Masterson).

The Immigrant 🦴🦴🦴½ **1917** Chaplin portrays a newly arrived immigrant who falls in love with the first girl he meets. Silent with musical soundtrack added. **20m/B VHS.** Charlie Chaplin, Edna Purviance, Eric Campbell, Kitty Bradbury; ***D:*** Charlie Chaplin; ***W:*** Charlie Chaplin. Natl. Film Reg. '98.

The Immoral One 🦴½ *Confessions of a Prostitute; L'Immorale* **1980** Lamo is suffering from amnesia. Fortunately, she's apparently taped her life story for a book deal and can learn all the sordid details. And sordid they are since she was a prostitute in Paris, involved with both men and women, and with a blackmailing madam. **90m/C VHS.** *FR* Sylvia Lamo, Yves Jouffroy, Isabelle Legentil; ***D:*** Claude Mulot; ***W:*** Claude Mulot.

Immortal Bachelor 🦴½ **1980 (PG)** Good cast can't overcome the silliness of this one. A juror daydreams about the dead husband of a cleaning woman on trial for killing her adulterous spouse. She decides the dead man seems a lot more exciting than her own dull and tiresome husband. **94m/C VHS.** *IT* Giancarlo Giannini, Monica Vitti, Claudia Cardinale, Vittorio Gassman; ***D:*** Marcello Fondato; ***C:*** Pasqualino De Santis.

Immortal Battalion 🦴🦴🦴 *The Way Ahead* **1944** Entertaining wartime psuedo-documentary follows newly recruited soldiers as they are molded from an ordinary group of carping civilians into a hardened battalion of fighting men by Niven. Some prints run to 116 minutes. **89m/B VHS, DVD.** *GB* David Niven, Stanley Holloway, Reginald Tate, Raymond Huntley, William Hartnell, James Donald, Peter Ustinov, John Laurie, Leslie Dwyer, Hugh Burden, Jimmy Hanley, Leo Genn, Renee Asherson, Mary Jerrold, Tessie O'Shea, Raymond Lovell, A.E. Matthews, Jack Watling; ***D:*** Carol Reed; ***W:*** Eric Ambler, Peter Ustinov; ***C:*** Guy Green; ***M:*** William Alwyn.

Immortal Beloved 🦴🦴 **1994 (R)** The death of Ludwig van Beethoven prompts his loyal secretary to seek the identity of a mystery love to whom the composer has bequeathed his estate. While Beethoven's genius is awesome and his music breathtaking, his lovelife is neither, and the ensuing confessions of the maestro's former loves only get in the way of flashbacks that hint at his torment and triumph. Oldman is darkly intense, and a scene in which the aged Beethoven remembers his terrifying childhood amid the strains of "Ode to Joy" is simply stunning, but an unfocused script undoes what might have been a fine tribute to the master. The London Symphony Orchestra and soloists Murray Perahia, Emanuel Ax, and Yo Yo Ma contributed to the splendid soundtrack. **121m/C VHS, DVD, Wide.** Gary Oldman, Jeroen Krabbe, Isabella Rossellini, Johanna Ter Steege, Marco Hofschneider, Miriam Margolyes, Barry Humphries, Valeria Golino, Christopher Fulford; ***D:*** Bernard Rose; ***W:*** Bernard Rose; ***C:*** Peter Suschitzsky.

Immortal Combat 🦴½ **1994 (R)** An army of men trained in ninja and guerilla warfare have seemingly immortal powers. Can our two violent heroes find an equally destructive way to stop the killing? **109m/C VHS, DVD.** Roddy Piper, Sonny Chiba, Tommy (Tiny) Lister, Meg Foster; ***D:*** Daniel Neira; ***W:*** Daniel Neira, Robert Crabtree; ***C:*** Henner Hofmann.

Immortal Sergeant 🦴🦴½ **1943** After the battle death of the squad leader, an inexperienced corporal takes command of North African troops during WWII. Fonda gives a strong performance. Based on a novel by John Brody. **91m/B VHS.** Henry Fonda, Thomas Mitchell, Maureen O'Hara, Allyn Joslyn, Reginald Gardiner, Melville Cooper, Morton Lowry, Peter Lawford, John Banner, Bud Geary, James Craven; ***D:*** John M. Stahl; ***W:*** Lamar Trotti; ***C:*** Clyde De Vinna, Arthur C. Miller; ***M:*** David Buttolph.

Immortal Sins 🦴 **1991 (R)** Michael and Susan inherited an old Spanish Castle, complete with its own curse, which comes in the form of a seductive women that has haunted families for centuries. **80m/C VHS.** Cliff DeYoung, Maryam D'Abo; ***W:*** Thomas McKelvey Cleaver.

Immortality 🦴🦴 *The Wisdom of Crocodiles* **1998 (R)** The vampire myth undergoes yet another postmodern twist. Steven Grlscz (Law) is a medical researcher, living in London, who stops Maria (Fox) from committing suicide and then sets out to seduce her. When he's convinced she's in love with him, he kills her and takes her blood. His next would-be victim is Anne (Lowensohn), but she's reluctant to commit to Steven and soon he becomes ill, which leads him to confess to Anne that his bloodsucking tendencies can only be satiated when he believes his victims love him. While Law is a charming seducer, he fails to chill as a vampire killer. **98m/C VHS, DVD, Wide.** *GB* Jude Law, Elina Lowensohn, Timothy Spall, Kerry Fox, Jack Davenport, Colin Salmon; ***D:*** Po Chich Leong; ***W:*** Paul Hoffman; ***C:*** Oliver Curtis; ***M:*** John Lunn, Orlando Gough.

The Immortalizer 🦴 **1989 (R)** A mad doctor transfers people's brains into young bodies for a price, although it's not as simple as it sounds. **85m/C VHS.** Ron Kay, Chris Crone, Melody Patterson, Clarke Lindsley, Bekki Armstrong; ***D:*** Joel Bender.

The Immortals 🦴🦴 **1995 (R)** Nightclub owner Jack (Roberts) recruits eight terminally ill criminals in an elaborate heist that calls for simultaneously hitting targets citywide. But when they compare notes, the team fear a doublecross. **92m/C VHS, DVD.** Louis Lombardi, Eric Roberts, Tia Carrere, William Forsythe, Joe Pantoliano, Clarence Williams III, Tony Curtis, Chris Rock, Kieran Mulroney, Kevin Bernhardt; ***D:*** Brian Grant; ***W:*** Kevin Bernhardt; ***C:*** Anthony B. Richmond.

Impact 🦴🦴🦴 **1949** A woman and her lover plan the murder of her rich industrialist husband, but the plan backfires. More twists and turns than a carnival ride. **111m/B VHS, DVD.** Brian Donlevy, Ella Raines, Charles Coburn, Helen Walker, Anna May Wong, Philip Ahn, Art Baker, Tony Barrett, Harry Cheshire, Lucius Cooke, Joel Friedkin, Sheilah Graham, Tom Greenway, Hans Herbert, Linda Johnson, Joe (Joseph) Kirk, Clarence (C. William) Kolb, Mary Landa, Mae Marsh; ***D:*** Arthur Lubin; ***W:*** Dorothy Reid, Jay Dratler; ***C:*** Ernest Laszlo; ***M:*** Michel Michelet.

The Imperial Japanese Empire 🦴🦴 **1985** Epic of the WWII Pacific seen through Japanese eyes. **130m/C VHS.** *JP* Tetsuro Tamba, Tomokazu Miura, Teruhiko Saigo, Teruhiko Aoi, Saburo Shinoda, Keiko Sekine, Masako Natsume, Akiko Kana.

Imperial Venus 🦴🦴 **1971 (PG)** Biography of Napoleon's sister, Paolina Boneparte—with particular focus on her many loves, lusts and tribulations. **121m/C VHS.** Gina Lollobrigida, Stephen Boyd, Raymond Pellegrin; ***D:*** Jean Delannoy.

Implicated 🦴🦴 **1998 (R)** Tom (McNamara) asks his new girlfriend Ann (Locane) to help him out by babysitting his boss' young daughter, Katie. But Ann soon realizes that Tom's kidnapped Katie and they're both pawns in an elaborate scheme that has gone out of control. Based on the book "Wishful Thinking" by Frank Wyka. **95m/C VHS.** Amy Locane, William McNamara, Frederic Forrest, Priscilla Barnes; ***D:*** Irving Belateche; ***W:*** Webb Millsaps, Irving Belateche. **VIDEO**

The Importance of Being Earnest 🦴🦴🦴 **1952** Fine production of classic Oscar Wilde comedy-of-manners. Cast couldn't be better or the story funnier. **95m/C VHS.** Michael Redgrave, Edith Evans, Margaret Rutherford, Michael Denison, Joan Greenwood; ***D:*** Anthony Asquith.

The Importance of Being Earnest 🦴🦴 **2002 (PG)** Jack Worthing (Firth) has invented a brother, Earnest, in order to leave the dull country and visit lovely Gwendolyn (O'Connor), the daughter of the formidable Lady Bracknell (Dench), in London. His best friend Algernon Montcrieff (Everett), who is Gwendolyn's cousin, also has a make-believe chum named Bunbury to get Algy out of boring situations. Then Algy decides to pose as Earnest in order to woo Jack's country ward, Cecily (Witherspoon). But when everyone ends up together, chaos threatens. Based on the play by Oscar Wilde and filled with bon mots, director Parker felt compelled to "open up" the production, which only works some of the time. But the performances are all delightful and Witherspoon manages her English accent quite nicely. **100m/C** *US GB* Colin Firth, Rupert Everett, Frances O'Connor, Reese Witherspoon, Judi Dench, Tom Wilkinson, Anna Massey, Edward Fox; ***D:*** Oliver Parker; ***W:*** Oliver Parker; ***C:*** Tony Pierce-Roberts; ***M:*** Charlie Mole.

The Imported Bridegroom 🦴🦴 **1989** A comedy set at the turn of the century about a man who returns to Poland in order to find his daughter a proper husband. **93m/C VHS.** Eugene Troobarck, Avi Hoffman, Greta Cowan, Annette Miller; ***D:*** Pamela Berger; ***W:*** Pamela Berger.

The Impossible Spy 🦴🦴🦴 **1987** True story of Elie Cohen, an unassuming Israeli who doubled as a top level spy in Syria during the 1960s. Cohen became so close to Syria's president that he was nominated to become the Deputy Minister of Defense before his double life was exposed. Well-acted spy thriller and is worth a look for espionage fans. **96m/C VHS, DVD.** *GB* John Shea, Eli Wallach, Michal Bat-Adam, Rami Danon, Sasson Gabray, Chaim Girafi; ***D:*** Jim Goddard; ***M:*** Richard Hartley. **CABLE**

The Impossible Years 🦴 **1968** Unattractive, leering sex farce about psychiatrist Nivens who has problems with his own young daughter. Dismal adaptation of the hit Broadway play by Bob Fisher and Arthur Marx. **97m/C VHS.** David Niven, Lola Albright, Chad Everett, Ozzie Nelson, Christina Ferrare, Jeff Cooper, John Harding; ***D:*** Michael Gordon; ***W:*** George Wells.

The Imposter 🦴½ **1984** Improbable tale of a con artist/ex-con who impersonates a high school principal in order to regain his estranged girlfriend, who works as a teacher. Complications ensue when he tackles the school's drug problems. **95m/C VHS.** Anthony Geary, Billy Dee Williams, Lorna Patterson; ***D:*** Michael Pressman. **TV**

Imposter 🦴 **2001 (PG-13)** When a movie is shelved for a year and a half, there's usually a reason. Earth in 2079 is dystopian and paranoid, and the neon-blue cave lighting makes it difficult to see. Which is not a huge loss. Talented cast is reduced to a collection of archetypes, including the usually solid Sinise as an elite military scientist accused of fighting (as a replicant) for the wrong team, namely, the sinister aliens who are laying waste to our earth. Citizens are monitored via spinal identification chips, yet a hooded sweatshirt and sunglasses are enough to shield public enemy #1 from detection. Tired sci-fi themes of soul and identity are not enough to keep things interesting. Adapted (and yawningly stretched) from a short story by perennial sci-fi source Philip K. Dick. **96m/C VHS, DVD.** Gary Sinise, Madeleine Stowe, Vincent D'Onofrio, Tony Shalhoub, Mekhi Phifer, Tim Guinee, Lindsay Crouse, Gary Dourdan, Erica Gimpel, Elizabeth Pena; ***D:*** Gary Fleder; ***W:*** Ehren Kruger, David N. Twohy, Caroline Case; ***C:*** Robert Elswit; ***M:*** Mark Isham.

Imposters 🦴🦴 **1984** A comedy centering on the romantic problems between a self-indulgent young man and the woman who cheats on him. **110m/C VHS.** Ellen McElduff, Charles Ludlam, Lisa Todd, Peter Evans.

The Imposters 🦴🦴 *Ship of Fools* **1998 (R)** Its the 1930s, and third-rate actors Arthur and Maurice (Tucci and Platt, respectively) are out of work. Inadvertently forced into hiding on a cruise ship, they encounter a virtual ship of fools while slinking around in an array of costumes. The wacky story unfolds as the stowaways run into various characters: the Nazi-like, crop-wielding head steward (Scott), a gay Scottish wrestler (Connolly), an anarchist bomber from an unnamed Eastern European nation (Shalhoub), his country's deposed queen (Rossellini), and a pair of murderous con artists posing as French tourists. Written and directed by Tucci, pic reunites much of the cast from Tucci and Scott's "Big Night." Unfortunately, they weren't as successful this time. Too much free-reign hamming by the big-name indie cast sinks this homage to Buster Keaton and the Marx Brothers. **101m/C VHS, DVD.** Stanley Tucci, Oliver Platt, Elizabeth Bracco, Steve Buscemi, Billy Connolly, Allan Corduner, Hope Davis, Dana Ivey, Allison Janney, Richard Jenkins, Matt McGrath, Alfred Molina, Isabella Rossellini, Campbell Scott, Tony Shalhoub, Lili Taylor, Lewis J. Stadlen, Woody Allen; ***D:*** Stanley Tucci; ***W:*** Stanley Tucci; ***C:*** Ken Kelsch; ***M:*** Gary DeMichele.

Impromptu 🦴🦴🦴 **1990 (PG-13)** A smart, sassy, romantic comedy set in 1830s Europe among the era's artistic greats—here depicted as scalawags, parasites and early beatniks. The film's ace is Davis in a lusty, dynamic role as mannish authoress George Sand, obsessively in love with the dismayed composer Chopin. Though he's too pallid a character for her attraction to be credible, a great cast and abundant wit make this a treat. Beautiful score featuring Chopin and Liszt. Film debut of stage director Lapine; screenplay written by his wife, Sarah Kernochan. **108m/C VHS, DVD, Wide.** Judy Davis, Hugh Grant, Mandy Patinkin, Bernadette Peters, Julian Sands, Ralph Brown, Georges Corraface, Anton Rodgers, Emma Thompson, Anna Massey, John Savident, Elizabeth Spriggs; ***D:*** James Lapine; ***W:*** Sarah Kernochan; ***C:*** Bruno de Keyzer. Ind. Spirit '92: Actress (Davis).

Improper Channels 🦴🦴 **1982 (PG)** Mediocre comedy about a couple trying to recover their daughter after being accused of child abuse. **91m/C VHS.** Monica Parker, Alan Arkin, Mariette Hartley; ***D:*** Eric Till; ***W:*** Adam Arkin.

Improper Conduct 🦴🦴 **1994 (R)** Ad agency employee is sexually harassed by her boss but loses her court case. Her sister decides to get revenge by getting hired and setting the slimeball up for a fall. **95m/C VHS.** Steven Bauer, Lee Ann Beaman, John Laughlin, Kathy Shower, Tahnee Welch, Nia Peeples, Stuart Whitman, Adrian Zmed, Patsy Pease; ***D:*** Jag Mundhra; ***W:*** Carl Austin.

Impulse 🦴½ **1955** When his wife leaves for a visit with her mother, a young man is thrust into cahoots with gangsters, and wrapped up in an affair with another woman. **81m/B VHS.** *GB* Arthur Kennedy, Constance Smith, Joy Shelton; ***D:*** Charles De Latour.

Impulse **woof!** *Want a Ride, Little Girl?; I Love to Kill* **1974 (PG)** Shatner, a crazed killer, is released from prison and starts to kill again in this low-budget, predictable, critically debased film about child-molesting. **85m/C VHS.** William Shatner, Ruth Roman, Harold Sakata, Kim Nicholas, Jennifer Bishop, James Dobson; ***D:*** William Grefe; ***W:*** Tony Crechales; ***C:*** Edwin Gibson; ***M:*** Lewis Perles.

Impulse 🦴🦴 **1984 (R)** Small town residents can't control their impulses, all because of government toxic waste in their milk. A woman worried about her mother's mental health returns to town with her doctor boyfriend to discover most of the inhabitants are quite mad. Starts strong but... **95m/C VHS, DVD.** Tim Matheson, Meg Tilly, Hume Cronyn, John Karlen, Bill Paxton, Amy Stryker, Claude Earl Jones, Sherri Stoner; ***D:*** Graham Baker; ***W:*** Bart Davis; ***C:*** Thomas Del Ruth; ***M:*** Paul Chihara.

Impulse 🦴🦴½ **1990 (R)** A beautiful undercover vice cop poses as a prostitute, and gives in to base desires. Russell gives a fine performance in this underrated sleeper. **109m/C VHS.** Theresa Russell, Nicholas Mele, Eli Danker, Charles McCaughan, Jeff Fahey, George Dzundza, Alan Rosenberg, Lynne Thigpen, Shawn Elliott; ***D:*** Sondra Locke; ***W:*** John DeMarco, Leigh Chapman; ***M:*** Michel Colombier.

Impure Thoughts 🦴🦴 **1986 (PG)** Four friends meet in the afterlife and discuss their Catholic school days. Odd premise never catches fire. **87m/C VHS.** Brad Dourif, Lane Davies, John Putch, Terry Beaver; ***D:*** Michael A. Simpson.

In a Class of His Own 🦴🦴½ **1999** School janitor Rich Donato (Phillips) is an ex-teen bad boy who has formed a close relationship with both the teachers and the students at the high school where he works. However, in order to keep his job, he learns he must pass his GED and this isn't an easy task. When his wife appeals for help, Rich finds himself becoming a school project. Based on a true story. **94m/C VHS, DVD.** Lou Diamond Phillips, Cara Buono, Joan Chen, Nathaniel DeVeaux; ***D:*** Robert Munic; ***W:*** Robert Munic; ***C:*** Ron Stannett; ***M:*** Sharon Farber. **CABLE**

In a Glass Cage 🦴🦴½ *Tras el Cristal* **1986** A young boy who was tortured and sexually molested by a Nazi official seeks revenge. Years after the war, he shows up at the Nazi's residence in Spain and is immediately befriended by his tormentor's family. Confined to an iron lung, the official is at the mercy of the young man who tortuously acts out the incidents detailed in the Nazi's journal. Suspenseful and extremely graphic, it's well crafted and meaningful but may be just too horrible to watch. Sexual and violent acts place it in the same league as Pasolini's infamous "Salo, or The 120 Days in Sodom." Definitely not for the faint of heart. In Spanish with English subtitles. **110m/C VHS.** *SP* Gunter Meisner, David Sust, Marisa Paredes, Gisela Echevarria; ***D:*** Agustin Villaronga; ***W:*** Agustin Villaronga.

In a Lonely Place 🦴🦴🦴½ **1950** Bogart is outstanding as a volatile Hollywood screenwriter who has an affair with starlet Grahame while under suspicion of murder. Offbeat, yet superb film noir entry became one of the most memorable of the genre. Expertly directed by Ray. Based on the novel by Dorothy B. Hughes and an adaptation by Edmund H. North. **93m/B VHS.** Humphrey Bogart, Gloria Grahame, Frank Lovejoy, Carl Benton Reid, Art Smith, Jeff Donnell; ***D:*** Nicholas Ray; ***W:*** Andrew Solt; ***C:*** Burnett Guffey.

In a Moment of Passion 🦴½ **1993 (R)** A two-bit actor wants to be a star—in the worst way possible. So he kills off the lead actor of a new film, takes his place, and proceeds to eliminate any obstacle that gets in his way. The problem comes in when an aspiring actress falls for the actor and then figures out what's going on. **100m/C VHS.** Maxwell Caulfield, Chase Masterson, Vivian Schilling, Julie Araskog, Joe Estevez, Robert Z'Dar, Zbigniew Kaminski; ***Cameos:*** Jeff Conaway; ***W:*** Charles Haigh.

In a Savage Land 🦴½ **1999** Interesting premise gets a laughable execution. Prim married anthropologists Philip (Donovan) and Evelyn (Stange) Spence travel to the South Seas in the late 1930s to study native society and find their marriage quickly unraveling. Philip refuses to acknowledge the sexuality and importance of the tribe's women, so Evelyn decides to take advantage (in more than one way) of pearl merchant Mick (Sewell) to continue her studies in another village. Pretty scenery courtesy of the Trobriand Islands is the only high point. **116m/C VHS.** *AU* Martin Donovan, Rufus Sewell, Maya Stange; ***D:*** Bill Bennett; ***W:*** Bill Bennett, Jennifer Bennett;

C: Danny Ruhlman; **M:** David Bridie. Australian Film Inst. '99: Sound, Score.

In a Shallow Grave 🦴🦴 **1988 (R)** Shallow treatment of James Purdy's novel about a WWII veteran, badly disfigured in combat at Guadalcanal, who returns to Virginia in an attempt to return to the life he once had with the woman he still loves. Handsome Biehn plays the disfigured vet, Mueller's his ex-fiancee, and Dempsey's the drifter who adds a bisexual hypotenuse to the love triangle. Pokey American Playhouse coproduction. **92m/C VHS.** Michael Biehn, Maureen Mueller, Patrick Dempsey, Michael Beach, Thomas Boyd Mason; **D:** Kenneth Bowser; **W:** Kenneth Bowser.

In a Stranger's Hand 🦴🦴½ **1992** Urich stars a respected businessman who happens to find a doll which belongs to a kidnapped young girl. The police have their suspicions but Urich teams up with the child's mother to find the girl and winds up uncovering a child-selling ring. **93m/C VHS.** Robert Urich, Megan Gallagher, Brett Cullen, Vondie Curtis-Hall, Dakin Matthews, Alan Rosenberg, Maria O'Brien; **D:** David Greene. **TV**

In a Year of 13 Moons 🦴🦴 *In a Year with 13 Moons; In Einem Jahr Mit 13 Monden* **1978** Notorious Fassbinder tale of Erwin who becomes Elvira and is subjected to a series of humiliating relationships with men. Finally, with the aid of his/her ex-wife and a prostitute, Elvira looks into the past in an effort to resolve the present. Alternatingly depressing and pretentious. German with subtitles. **119m/C VHS.** *GE* Volker Spengler, Ingrid Caven, Gottfried John, Elisabeth Trissenaar, Eva Mattes, Gunther Kaufman; **D:** Rainer Werner Fassbinder; **W:** Rainer Werner Fassbinder; **C:** Rainer Werner Fassbinder; **M:** Peer Raben.

In an Old Manor House 🦴🦴½ **1984** Residents of an old house are tormented by the vindictive ghost of a murdered adultress whose husband didn't approve of the, uh, affection she showed his son from a previous marriage. Based on the play by Stanislaw Witkiewicz. In Polish with English subtitles. **90m/C VHS.** *PL* **D:** Jerzy Kotkowski.

In and Out 🦴🦴🦴 **1997 (PG-13)** See what an Oscar can do? When Tom Hanks thanked, and inadvertently outed, his high school drama teacher during his Academy Awards speech (for "Philadelphia"), it lead to this feature. Popular high school English teacher Howard Brackett (Kline) has his sexuality come into question on the eve of his wedding thanks to a former-student-turned-movie-star (Dillon). As a media circus converges on the small town, Howard is forced to examine his sexuality by openly gay reporter Selleck (out to prove Howard's gay), his mother Reynolds (who wants the wedding to go on regardless of his orientation) and his tightly wound fiancee Cusack (who wants to put a serious hurtin' on Barbra Striesand). All-around excellent performances, especially by Kline and Cusack. **92m/C VHS, DVD.** Kevin Kline, Joan Cusack, Matt Dillon, Debbie Reynolds, Wilford Brimley, Bob Newhart, Tom Selleck, Deborah Rush, Lewis J. Stadlen, J. Smith-Cameron, Zak Orth, Gregory Jbara, Shalom Harlow, Kate McGregor-Stewart, Shawn Hatosy, Lauren Ambrose, Alexandra Holden; **D:** Frank Oz; **W:** Paul Rudnick; **C:** Rob Hahn; **M:** Marc Shaiman. N.Y. Film Critics '97: Support. Actress (Cusack); Broadcast Film Critics '97: Support. Actress (Cusack).

In Between 🦴🦴½ **1992 (PG-13)** When Margo, Jack, and Amy wake up they expect it to be another average day. Instead, these three strangers find themselves together in a peculiar house. An angel informs them that the house is a way station between life and the hereafter. The three must look at their pasts, imagine their futures, and decide whether to return to their old lives or accept death and go on to an afterlife. **92m/C VHS.** Wings Hauser, Robin Mattson, Alexandra Paul, Robert Forster.

In Celebration 🦴🦴🦴 **1975 (PG)** Three successful brothers return to the old homestead for their parents' 40th wedding celebration. Intense drama but somewhat claustrophobic. Based on a play by David Storey. **131m/C VHS.** *GB CA* Alan Bates, James Bolam, Brian Cox, Constance Chapman, Gabrielle Daye, Bill Owen; **D:** Lindsay Anderson; **W:** David Storey; **C:** Dick Bush.

In Cold Blood 🦴🦴🦴½ **1967** Truman Capote's supposedly factual novel provided the basis for this hard-hitting docu-drama about two ex-cons who ruthlessly murder a Kansas family in 1959 in order to steal their non-existent stash of money. Blake is riveting as one of the killers. **133m/B VHS.** Robert (Bobby) Blake, Scott Wilson, John Forsythe; **D:** Richard Brooks; **W:** Richard Brooks; **C:** Conrad L. Hall; **M:** Quincy Jones. Natl. Bd. of Review '67: Director (Brooks).

In Cold Blood 🦴🦴 **1996** Tv miniseries version of the Truman Capote true crime classic, which follows the 1959 murders of the four members of the Clutter family in Holcomb, Kansas by ex-cons Dick Hickock (Edwards) and Perry Smith (Roberts). The TV version covers more of the background of both the killers and the Holcombs, the relentless hunt by Al Dewey (Neill) of the Kansas Bureau of Investigation, and the duo's time on death row. **180m/C VHS.** Anthony Edwards, Eric Roberts, Sam Neill, Kevin Tighe, Gillian Barber, Robbie Bowen, Margot Finley, Bethel Leslie, Gwen Verdon, Stella Stevens, L.Q. (Justus E. McQueen) Jones, Louise Latham, Campbell Lane, Leo Rossi; **D:** Jonathan Kaplan; **W:** Benedict Fitzgerald. **TV**

In Country 🦴🦴½ **1989 (R)** Based on Bobbie Ann Mason's celebrated novel, the story of a young Kentuckian high schooler (perfectly played by Lloyd) and her search for her father, killed in Vietnam. Willis plays her uncle, a veteran still struggling to accept his own survival, and crippled with memories. Moving scene at the Vietnam Veterans Memorial. **116m/C VHS, DVD, 8mm.** Bruce Willis, Emily Lloyd, Joan Allen, Kevin Anderson, Richard Hamilton, Judith Ivey, Peggy Rea, John Terry, Patricia Richardson, Jim Beaver; **D:** Norman Jewison; **W:** Frank Pierson, Cynthia Cidre; **C:** Russell Boyd; **M:** James Horner.

The In Crowd 🦴🦴 **1988 (PG)** A bright high school student gets involved with a local TV dance show circa 1965, and must choose between uncertain fame and an Ivy League college. A fair nostalgic look at the period. Leitch is the son of psychedelic folk singer Donovan. **96m/C VHS.** Donovan Leitch, Jennifer Runyon, Scott Plank, Joe Pantoliano; **D:** Mark Rosenthal; **W:** Mark Rosenthal.

The In Crowd 🦴🦴 **2000 (PG-13)** Having been cured of her "erotomania," pretty, young Adrien (Heuring) is released from a psychiatric hospital, and, on the advice of her doctor, gains employment for the summer at a seaside country club. There Adrien is confronted by the in crowd, which is led by the ultra bitchy (what other name would suffice?) Brittany (Ward), who, with clearly ulterior motives, befriends the lovely Adrien. As Adrien is introduced to the ways of the privileged, things become stranger and stranger as our heroine discovers some unpleasant things about her new acquaintance. **98m/C VHS, DVD, Wide.** Susan Ward, Lori Heuring, Matthew Settle, Nathan Bexton, Tess Harper, Laurie Fortier, Kim Murphy; **D:** Mary Lambert; **W:** Mark Gibson, Philip Halprin; **C:** Tom Priestley; **M:** Jeff Rona.

In Custody 🦴🦴 *Hifazaat* **1994 (PG)** Producer Merchant makes his feature directorial debut with this dreamy tale of small-town teacher Deven (Puri) who's urged by a publishing friend to interview Nur (Kapoor), the greatest living poet in the disappearing Urdu language. The worshipful Deven is dismayed to find his idol a wreck, surrounded by sycophants and a shrewish second wife who's plagiarizing her husband's work, and soon finds himself hopelessly entangled in the writer's life. Unabashedly literary (the poetry recited is by Faiz Ahmed Faiz) with a star cast. Based on the 1987 novel by Anita Desai. Urdu with subtitles. **123m/C VHS.** *IN* Shashi Kapoor, Om Puri, Shabana Azmi, Sushma Seth, Neena Gupta, Ajay Sahni, Tinnu Anand; **D:** Ismail Merchant; **W:** Anita Desai, Shahrukh Husain; **C:** Larry Pizer; **M:** Zakir Hussain, Ustad Sultan Khan.

In Dangerous Company 🦴 **1988 (R)** Beautiful babe balances beaux and battles abound. A brow lowering experience. **92m/C VHS.** Tracy Scoggins, Cliff DeYoung, Chris Mulkey, Henry Darrow, Steven Keats, Richard Portnow; **D:** Ruben Preuss; **W:** Mitch Brown; **C:** James L. Carter.

In Dark Places 🦴🦴 **1997 (R)** Seductive artist Chapelle (Severance) visits long-estranged brother Chazz (Kestner) with more than familial feelings on her mind. As things between them heat up, Chazz loses his girl, best friend, and job before discovering his sister's true agenda. This one actually has a story to go along with the eroticism. **96m/C VHS.** Joan Severance, Bryan Kestner, John Vargas, Suzanne Turner; **D:** James Burke.

In Deadly Heat 🦴 **1987** Crime, revenge, murder, and urban warfare are done once again. **98m/C VHS.** William Dame, Catherine Dee, M.R. Murphy; **D:** Don Nardo.

In Desert and Wilderness 🦴🦴½ **1973** Two kidnapped children escape and are thrust into the wilds of Africa, where they must survive with wits and courage. Based on a novel by Nobel prize-winning author Henyk Sienkiewicz. In Polish with English subtitles. **144m/C VHS.** *PL* **D:** Wladyslaw Slesicki.

In Dreams 🦴🦴½ *Blue Vision* **1998 (R)** Bening is a small town wife and mother with a psychic connection to twisted child killer Downey, causing her to dream of his gruesome crimes before he commits them. After she dreams that her daughter is killed, her life begins to unravel, causing those around her to suspect her of insanity. Draws its chills from a more cerebral standpoint, so fans of big action may want to pass. The unnerving dream sequences are suitable murky and ominous thanks to cinematographer Darius Khondji, who also filmed "Seven." **99m/C VHS, DVD, Wide.** Annette Bening, Robert Downey Jr., Aidan Quinn, Stephen Rea, Paul Guilfoyle, Dennis Boutsikaris, Pamela Payton-Wright, Margo Martindale, Prudence Wright Holmes, Katie Sagona, Krystal Benn; **D:** Neil Jordan; **W:** Neil Jordan, Bruce Robinson; **C:** Darius Khondji; **M:** Elliot Goldenthal.

In for Treatment 🦴🦴🦴 **1982** A terminally ill cancer patient, lost in the bureaucracy of the hospital, fights to rediscover the joy of life. Strong and disturbing story. In Dutch with English subtitles. **92m/C VHS.** *NL* Helmut Woudenberg, Frank Groothof, Hans Man Int Veld; **D:** Eric Van Zuylen, Marja Kok.

In God We Trust woof! **1980 (PG)** Bleech. Monumentally unfunny comedy about innocent monk, Brother Ambrose (Feldman), who travels to Hollywood to raise money to save his monastery. He winds up getting involved with crooked TV evangelist Armageddon T. Thunderbird (Kaufman). Pryor plays G.O.D. **97m/C VHS.** Marty Feldman, Andy Kaufman, Richard Pryor, Peter Boyle, Louise Lasser, Wilfrid Hyde-White, Severn Darden; **D:** Marty Feldman; **W:** Marty Feldman, Chris Allen; **C:** Charles Correll; **M:** John Morris.

In God's Hands 🦴🦴 **1998 (PG-13)** Dude! Check it out! Three surfers (Dorian, George, and Liu) travel the world looking for (what else?) the perfect wave. Disjointed, plot-deprived, but beautifully shot flick has the trio busting out of prison (why they're there is never explained) to begin their quest. Moving from Madagascar to Bali to Hawaii, one finds love with a girl from Ipanema (!), another contracts malaria, and the other succumbs to the surf. What happens to whom doesn't really matter, because as actors, they're really great surfers. Besides, the "story" is just connective tissue for the killer surfing scenes. Gnarly. **98m/C VHS, DVD, Wide.** Patrick Shane Dorian, Matt George, Matty Liu, Brion James, Shaun Thompson, Maylin Pultar, Bret Michaels, Brian L. Keaulana, Darrick Doerner; **D:** Zalman King; **W:** Zalman King, Matt George; **C:** John Aronson.

In Gold We Trust 🦴½ **1991** Vincent leads an elite battalion of fighters against a group of rogue American MIAs (!) laying waste to the Vietnemese countryside. **89m/C VHS.** Jan-Michael Vincent, Sam Jones; **D:** P. (Philip) Chalong; **M:** Hummie Mann.

In Harm's Way 🦴🦴 **1965** Overdone story about two naval officers and their response to the Japanese attack at Pearl Harbor. Even the superb cast members (and there are plenty of them) can't overcome the incredible length and overly intricate plot. **165m/B VHS, DVD, Wide.** John Wayne, Kirk Douglas, Tom Tryon, Patricia Neal, Paula Prentiss, Brandon de Wilde, Burgess Meredith, Stanley Holloway, Henry Fonda, Dana Andrews, Franchot Tone, Jill Haworth, George Kennedy, Carroll O'Connor, Patrick O'Neal, Slim Pickens, Bruce Cabot, Larry Hagman, Hugh O'Brian, Jim Mitchum, Barbara Bouchet, Stewart Moss, Tod Andrews; **D:** Otto Preminger; **W:** Wendell Mayes; **C:** Loyal Griggs; **M:** Jerry Goldsmith. British Acad. '65: Actress (Neal).

In His Father's Shoes 🦴🦴½ **1997 (PG)** After his father (Gossett) dies, 15-year-old Clay (Ri'chard) takes a literal journey of self-discovery. Slipping on a pair of his dad's old wingtips, the teen is transported back to the '60s to revisit his father's past, and then further back to his grandfather's (Gossett again) day. Clay learns his granddad was a hard-working man who gave up his own dreams to support his family, which later caused a generational rift. Touching drama. **105m/C VHS.** Louis Gossett Jr., Robert Ri'chard, Rachael Crawford; **D:** Vic Sarin; **W:** Gary Gelt; **C:** Michael Storey; **M:** John Welsman. **CABLE**

In His Life: The John Lennon Story 🦴🦴½ **2000** Focuses on seven years in the life of John Lennon—from the purchase of his first guitar to the Beatles arrival in America. Flashbacks show a teenage John (McQuillian) in 1957 Liverpool teaming up with art school pal Stu Sutcliffe (Williams) and meeting Paul (McGowan) and George (Rice-Oxley). There's the trip to Hamburg, the group's meeting with eventual manager Brian Epstein (Glover), Ringo (Ealey) becoming the band's drummer, and the first recordings. Skims the surface but, of course, the music is excellent. **87m/C VHS, DVD.** Phillip McQuillan, Daniel McGowan, Mark Rice-Oxley, Lee Williams, Jamie Glover, Scot Williams, Blair Brown, Kristian Ealey, Christine Kavanagh, Gillian Kearney, Palina Jonsdottir; **D:** David Carson; **W:** Michael O'Hara; **C:** Lawrence Jones; **M:** Dennis McCarthy. **TV**

In Hot Pursuit 🦴½ **1982** Convicted for drug smuggling, two young men stage a daring but not too exciting escape from a southern prison. **90m/C VHS.** Bob Watson, Don Watson, Debbie Washington.

The In-Laws 🦴🦴🦴 **1979 (PG)** A wild comedy with Falk, who claims to be a CIA agent, and Arkin, a dentist whose daughter is marrying Falk's son. The fathers foil a South American dictator's counterfeiting scheme in a delightfully convoluted plot. **103m/C VHS.** Peter Falk, Alan Arkin, Richard Libertini, Nancy Dussault, Penny Peyser, Arlene Golonka, Michael Lembeck, Ed Begley Jr., Rosana De Soto, Art Evans; **D:** Arthur Hiller; **W:** Andrew Bergman; **M:** John Morris.

In Like Flint 🦴🦴½ **1967** Sequel to "Our Man Flint" sees our dapper spy confronting an organization of women endeavoring to take over the world. Spy spoofery at its low-level best. **107m/C VHS, DVD, Wide.** James Coburn, Lee J. Cobb, Anna Lee, Andrew Duggan, Jean Hale; **D:** Gordon Douglas; **C:** William H. Daniels; **M:** Jerry Goldsmith.

In Love and War 🦴🦴½ **1991 (R)** Woods plays Navy pilot Jim Stockdale, whose plane was grounded over hostile territory and who endured nearly eight years of torture as a POW. Meanwhile, wife Sybil is an organizer of POW wives back in the States. Low octane rendering of the US Navy Commander's true story. Aaron earlier directed "The Miracle Worker," and you may recognize Ngor from "The Killing Fields." **96m/C VHS.** James Woods, Jane Alexander, Haing S. Ngor, Concetta Tomei, Richard McKenzie, James Pax; **D:** Paul Aaron; **W:** Carol Schreder.

In Love and War 🦴½ **1996 (PG-13)** Tells the story of 19-year-old Ernest Hemingway's (O'Donnell) romance with 27-year-old Red Cross nurse Agnes (Bullock) while both were stationed in Italy during WWI. This romance later served as the basis for Hemingway's novel "A Farewell to Arms." Here's a thought. Read the book instead. The boyish O'Donnell is so miscast as testosterone-junkie Hemingway, the only analogy would be having Sylvester Stallone play Truman Capote.

The lack of passion and chemistry between the two stars is unsettling, and the action is just plain clunky. Bullock looks great in a nurse's uniform, though. Adapted from "Hemingway in Love and War: The Lost Diary of Agnes Von Kurowsky" by Henry Villard and James Nagel. **115m/C VHS, DVD.** Chris O'Donnell, Sandra Bullock, MacKenzie Astin, Ingrid Lacey, Emilio Bonucci, Margot Steinberg, Colin Stinton, Ian Kelly, Richard Blackburn; ***D:*** Richard Attenborough; ***W:*** Allan Scott, Anna Hamilton Phelan, Clancy Sigal, Dimitri Villard; ***C:*** Roger Pratt; ***M:*** George Fenton.

In Love and War 🦴🦴½ **2001** British commando Eric Newby (Blue) is captured by the Italian army in 1942 and held as a POW until the Italian Armistice in 1943. He is released just before the advancing German forces and is rescued by a group of anti-fascist farmers, including lovely Wanda (Bobulova). They fall in love but Eric is betrayed and Wanda risks her life to warn him so he can escape. But can he bear to leave her behind? Based on Newby's autobiography "Love and War in the Apennines." **98m/C VHS, DVD.** Callum Blue, Barbara Bobulova, Peter Bowles, Nick Reding, John Warnaby, Toby Jones, Robert Weatherby, Nicholas Gallagher; ***D:*** John Kent Harrison; ***W:*** John Mortimer; ***C:*** Giovanni Fiore Coltellacci; ***M:*** Nicola Piovani. **TV**

In Love with an Older Woman 🦴🦴 **1982** Ritter takes fewer pratfalls than usual in this film; after all, it's a romantic comedy. Adapted from "Six Months with an Older Woman," the novel by David Kaufelt. **100m/C VHS.** John Ritter, Karen Carlson, Jamie Rose, Robert Mandan, Jeff Altman, George Murdock; ***D:*** Jack Bender. **TV**

In Memoriam 🦴🦴½ **1976** Tragic and gripping drama about one man's ability, albeit too late, to cope with his unforgettable past. Based on a story by Adolfo Bioy Casares. In Spanish with English subtitles. **96m/C VHS.** *SP* Geraldine Chaplin, Jose Luis Gomez; ***D:*** Enrique Braso.

In 'n Out 🦴½ **1986** An American loser ventures to Mexico to recover a long-lost inheritance, meeting with mildly comic obstacles along the way. **85m/C VHS.** Sam Bottoms, Pat Hingle.

In Name Only 🦴🦴½ **1939** Somber drama about a heartless woman who marries for wealth and prestige and holds her husband to a loveless marriage. Based on "Memory of Love" by Bessie Brewer. **102m/B VHS.** Carole Lombard, Cary Grant, Kay Francis, Charles Coburn; ***D:*** John Cromwell.

In Old Caliente 🦴½ **1939** Rogers battles the bad guys in the frontier town of Caliente. **60m/B VHS.** Roy Rogers, Lynne Roberts, George "Gabby" Hayes.

In Old California 🦴🦴½ **1942** Plucky story of a young Boston pharmacist who searches for success in the California gold rush and runs into the local crime boss. Also available colorized. **88m/B VHS, DVD.** John Wayne, Patsy Kelly, Binnie Barnes, Albert Dekker, Charles Halton; ***D:*** William McGann.

In Old Cheyenne 🦴½ **1941** Bank holdups, cattle rustling, fist fights, and even car crashes mix with some good ol' guitar plunking in this western. **60m/B VHS.** Roy Rogers, George "Gabby" Hayes.

In Old Chicago 🦴🦴🦴 **1937** The O'Leary family travels to Chicago to seek their fortune, with mom working as a washerwoman to support her sons. Brothers Power and Ameche become power-broking rivals and when mom comes to break up a brawl between the two, she neglects to properly restrain the family cow. This leads to the great Chicago fire of 1871, supposedly started when the cow kicks over a latern and sets the barn ablaze. The city burns down in a spectacular 20-minute sequence. Based on the story "We the O'Learys" by Niven Busch. **115m/B VHS.** Tyrone Power, Alice Faye, Don Ameche, Alice Brady, Andy Devine, Brian Donlevy, Phyllis Brooks, Tom Brown, Sidney Blackmer, Gene Reynolds, Berton Churchill, Bobs Watson; ***D:*** Henry King; ***W:*** Lamar Trotti, Sonya Levien. Oscars '37: Support. Actress (Brady).

In Old Colorado 🦴🦴½ **1941** Ankrum and his cronies try to stir up trouble over water rights, but Boyd and his pals ride to the rescue. **67m/B VHS.** William Boyd, Russell Hayden, Andy Clyde, Margaret Hayes, Morris Ankrum, Sarah Padden, Cliff Nazarro, Stanley Andrews, James Seay, Morgan Wallace; ***D:*** Howard Bretherton.

In Old Montana 🦴 **1939** A Cavalry lieutenant tries to settle a cattleman vs. sheep-herding war. **60m/B VHS.** Fred Scott, Jeanne Carmen, Harry Harvey, John Merton; ***D:*** Raymond K. Johnson.

In Old New Mexico 🦴 **1945** The Cisco Kid and Pancho reveal the murderer of an old woman—a mysterious doctor who was after an inheritance. **60m/B VHS.** Duncan Renaldo, Martin Garralaga, Gwen Kenyon, Pedro de Cordoba.

In Old Santa Fe 🦴🦴½ **1934** Cowboy star Maynard's best western, and the first film ever with Autry and Burnette. Maynard is framed for murder and his pals save him. **60m/B VHS.** Ken Maynard, Gene Autry, Smiley Burnette, Evalyn Knapp, George "Gabby" Hayes, Kenneth Thomson, Wheeler Oakman, George Chesebro; ***D:*** David Howard, Joseph Kane.

In Person 🦴🦴½ **1935** Spry comedy about a movie star who disguises herself to take a vacation incognito and falls in love with a country doctor who is unaware of her identity. ♫Don't Mention Love To Me; Out of Sight, Out of Mind; Got a New Lease on Life. **87m/B VHS.** Ginger Rogers, George Brent, Alan Mowbray, Grant Mitchell; ***D:*** William A. Seiter; ***M:*** Oscar Levant.

In Praise of Older Women 🦴🦴 **1978** Berenger is just right as a young Hungarian who is corrupted by WWII and a large number of older women. Based on a novel by Stephen Vizinczey. **110m/C VHS.** *CA* Karen Black, Tom Berenger, Susan Strasberg, Helen Shaver, Alexandra Stewart; ***D:*** George Kaczender.

In Pursuit 🦴🦴 **2000 (R)** Attorney Rick Alvarez (Baldwin) is accused of murdering his lover Katherine's (Schiffer) rich husband (Stockwell) and goes on the lam to Mexico. Routine thriller. **91m/C VHS, DVD, Wide.** Daniel Baldwin, Claudia Schiffer, Coolio, Sarah Lassez, Dean Stockwell; ***D:*** Peter Pistor; ***W:*** Peter Pistor, John Penney; ***C:*** Richard Crudo. **VIDEO**

In Pursuit of Honor 🦴🦴½ **1995 (PG-13)** Based on the true story of five American cavalry soldiers who find themselves being phased out in the 1935 Army. Ordered by General Douglas MacArthur to destroy their horses, they instead try to outrun an elite tank division to get some 400 horses to safety in Canada. Rugged performances and the violence towards the horses is aptly disturbing. Filmed on location in Australia and New Zealand. **110m/C VHS, DVD, Wide.** Don Johnson, Craig Sheffer, Gabrielle Anwar, Bob Gunton, Rod Steiger, James B. Sikking, John Dennis Johnston, Robert Coleby; ***D:*** Ken Olin; ***W:*** Dennis Lynton Clark; ***C:*** Stephen Windon; ***M:*** John Debney. **CABLE**

In Search of a Golden Sky 🦴🦴 **1984 (PG)** Following their mother's death, a motley group of children move in with their secluded cabin-dwelling uncle, much to the righteous chagrin of the welfare department. **94m/C VHS.** Charles Napier, George "Buck" Flower, Cliff Osmond; ***D:*** Jefferson (Jeff) Richard.

In Search of Anna woof! **1979** When a convict is released from jail, he hits the road with a flighty model in search of the girlfriend who corresponded with him in prison. There auto be a law. **90m/C VHS.** *AU* Judy Morris, Richard Moir, Chris Hayward, Bill Hunter; ***D:*** Esben Storm.

In Search of the Castaways 🦴🦴🦴 **1962** Stirring adventure tale of a teenage girl and her younger brother searching for their father, a ship's captain lost at sea years earlier. Powerful special effects and strong cast make this a winning Disney effort. Based on a story by Jules Verne. **98m/C VHS.** *GB* Hayley Mills, Maurice Chevalier, George Sanders, Wilfrid Hyde-White, Michael Anderson Jr.; ***D:*** Robert Stevenson.

In Self Defense 🦴½ **1993 (PG)** Purl is supposed to be protected from the killer she testified against but it doesn't quite work out that way. **94m/C VHS.** Linda Purl, Yaphet Kotto, Billy Drago; ***D:*** Bruce Seth Green; ***M:*** Patrick Gleeson.

In Society 🦴🦴½ **1944** The duo play dim-witted plumbers who are mistakenly invited to a high society party, where they promptly create catastrophe. **84m/B VHS.** Bud Abbott, Lou Costello, Marion Hutton, Kirby Grant, Ann Gillis, Arthur Treacher, Thomas Gomez, Steven Geray, Margaret Irving, Thurston Hall; ***Cameos:*** Sid Fields; ***D:*** Jean Yarbrough; ***W:*** Sid Fields, Hal Fimberg, Edmund Hartmann, John Grant.

In the Aftermath: Angels Never Sleep 🦴½ **1987** Mix of animation and live-action in this post-nuclear wasteland tale never quite works. **85m/C VHS.** Tony Markes, Rainbow Dolan; ***D:*** Carl Colpaert.

In the Army Now 🦴 **1994 (PG)** Pauly dude gets his head shaved, man. Service comedy about a slacker who joins the Army hoping to cash in on military benefits but who winds up in combat instead. Shore drops the Valley Guy shtick and ventures into the land of action when he gets sent on a mission to the Sahara. Strictly for Shore's fans. **92m/C VHS.** Pauly Shore, Esai Morales, Lori Petty, David Alan Grier, Ernie Hudson, Andy Dick; ***D:*** Dan Petrie Jr.; ***W:*** Dan Petrie Jr., Ken Kaufman, Fax Bahr, Stu Krieger, Adam Small; ***M:*** Robert Folk.

In the Bedroom 🦴🦴🦴½ **2001 (R)** Spacek and Wilkinson are a middle age couple who lose their son to violence. The numbing grief, paralyzing emotional swirl, and long-simmering but long-denied marital resentments that follow combine to drastically alter their marriage and lives. Field's impressive, if gut-wrenching directorial debut shows trust for the script and in the actors by not overplaying the obvious emotional moments, or the dramatic twists. This trust is rewarded with exceptional performances by Spacek, Wilkinson, and Tomei (in her best performance to date), and by a film that doesn't miss a chance to be subtle when it's called for, or explosive when it's needed. **131m/C VHS, DVD.** Sissy Spacek, Tom Wilkinson, Nick Stahl, Marisa Tomei, William Mapother, William Wise, Celia Weston, Karen Allen; ***D:*** Todd Field; ***W:*** Todd Field, Rob Festinger; ***C:*** Antonio Calvache; ***M:*** Thomas Newman. Golden Globes '02: Actress—Drama (Spacek); Ind. Spirit '02: Actor (Wilkinson), Actress (Spacek), First Feature; L.A. Film Critics '01: Actress (Spacek), Film; Natl. Bd. of Review '01: Director (Field), Screenplay; N.Y. Film Critics '01: Actor (Wilkinson), Actress (Spacek), First Feature; Broadcast Film Critics '01: Actress (Spacek).

In the Cold of the Night 🦴 **1989 (R)** Another drowsy entry into the "to sleep perchance to have a nightmare genre." A photographer with a vivid imagination dreams he murders a woman he doesn't know, and when said dream girl rides into his life on the back of a Harley, Mr. Foto's faced with an etiquette quandary: haven't they met before? Cast includes Hedren (Hitchcock's Marnie and Melanie Griffith's mother). **112m/C VHS.** Jeff Lester, Adrienne Sachs, Shannon Tweed, David Soul, John Beck, Tippi Hedren, Marc Singer; ***D:*** Nico Mastorakis; ***W:*** Nico Mastorakis; ***C:*** Andreas Bellis.

In the Company of Men 🦴🦴 **1996 (R)** A couple of dissatisfied Yuppies, Chad (Eckhart) and Howard (Malloy), are sent on a six-week job out of town by their home office. Grumbling about the lack of control in their lives (and blaming it on women), Chad formulates a nasty plan (to which Howard eventually agrees)—they'll deliberately get involved with the same girl, secretary Christine (Edwards), string her along, and then abandon her when their job is done. But Chad actually has his own agenda and bigger corporate ideas in mind. Think misogynistic satire. **93m/C VHS, DVD.** Matt Malloy, Aaron Eckhart, Stacy Edwards, Mark Rector, Jason Dixie, Emily Cline, Michael Martin, Chris Hayes; ***D:*** Neil LaBute; ***W:*** Neil LaBute; ***C:*** Anthony P. Hettinger; ***M:*** Ken Williams. Ind. Spirit '98: Debut Perf. (Eckhart); Ind. Spirit '99: First Screenplay; Sundance '97: Filmmakers Trophy.

In the Company of Spies 🦴🦴½ **1999 (PG-13)** CIA operative Brown is captured and tortured by the North Koreans while his bosses back in Washington try to protect national security. Retired operative Berenger is called back to active service to retrieve the agent and the information in his possession. **102m/C VHS.** Tom Berenger, Clancy Brown, Elizabeth Arlen, Ron Silver, Alice Krige, Arye Gross, Al Waxman, Len Cariou, David McIlwraith; ***D:*** Tim Matheson; ***W:*** Roger Towne; ***C:*** Roy Wagner; ***M:*** Don Davis. **CABLE**

In the Country Where Nothing Happens 🦴🦴 *En el Pais de No Pasa Nada* **1999** Corrupt businessman Enrique is kidnapped but, thanks to a videotape, wife Elena discovers he has a young lover, Rita. Instead of getting angry, Elena befriends Rita and they both decide Enrique isn't worth the bother of rescuing, so he's left to deal with his inept kidnappers on his own. Spanish with subtitles. **92m/C VHS, DVD, Wide.** *MX* Fernando Lujan, Julieta Egurrola, Maria (Isasi-Isasmendi) Isasi, Alvaro Guerrero, Zaide Silvia Gutierrez; ***D:*** Maricarmen de Lara; ***W:*** Maricarmen de Lara, Laura Sosa; ***C:*** Arturo de la Rosa.

In the Custody of Strangers 🦴🦴🦴 **1982** A teenager's parents refuse to help when he is arrested for being drunk and he ends up spending the night in jail. Realistic handling of a serious subject. Real-life father and son Sheen and Estevez play father and son. **100m/C VHS.** Martin Sheen, Jane Alexander, Emilio Estevez, Kenneth McMillan, Ed Lauter, Matt Clark, John Hancock; ***D:*** Robert Greenwald. **TV**

In the Days of the Thundering Herd & the Law & the Outlaw **1914** In the first feature, a pony express rider sacrifices his job to accompany his sweetheart on a westward trek to meet her father. In the second show, a fugitive falls in love with a rancher's daughter and risks recognition. **76m/B VHS.** Tom Mix, Myrtle Stedman; ***D:*** Colin Campbell.

In the Dead of Space 🦴½ **1999 (R)** Confusing sci fier has the space station Tesla becoming the target of saboteurs, who are determined to crash the ship into Los Angeles. **85m/C VHS, DVD.** Michael Pare, Lisa Bingley, Tony Curtis Blondell; ***D:*** Eli Necakov. **VIDEO**

In the Deep Woods 🦴🦴 **1991** Children's author Joanna Warren (Arquette) gets too close to mayhem when a childhood friend is murdered by the Deep Woods Killer. A mysterious private detective (Perkins) is on the killer's trail but when Joanna comes into the picture will she be a suspect or a victim? Based on the book by Nicholas Conde. **96m/C VHS.** Rosanna Arquette, Anthony Perkins, Will Patton, D.W. Moffett, Christopher Rydell, Harold Sylvester, Kimberly Beck; ***D:*** Charles Correll; ***W:*** Robert Nathan, Robert Rosenbaum; ***C:*** James Glennon.

In the Doghouse 🦴🦴 **1998 (PG)** A valuable movie pooch is dognapped just before the start of his next film and his owners are out to discover whodunnit. **90m/C VHS.** Matt Frewer, Rhea Perlman, Trevor Morgan. **VIDEO**

In the Flesh 🦴🦴 **1997** Closeted Atlanta police detective Philip (Corbin) is working an undercover drug operation that puts him in a gay bar. Which is where he meets Oliver (Ritter), a student by day/hustler by night. When Oliver witnesses a murder, it's Philip who provides him with an alibi, a place to stay, and a new relationship, even though it nearly destroys his own career. But then it seems Philip and Oliver have other connections besides sex. **105m/C VHS, DVD.** Dane Ritter, Ed Corbin, Roxzane T. Mims, Adrian Roberts; ***D:*** Ben Taylor; ***W:*** Ben Taylor; ***C:*** Brian Gurley; ***M:*** Eddie Horst.

In the Gloaming 🦴🦴🦴 **1997 (PG)** Twentysomething Danny (Leonard) bitterly returns home to his suburban, wealthy, emotionally cold family because he is dying of AIDS. He and mother Janet (Close) renew their strained family ties but his businessman dad (Strathairn) doesn't know how to cope except with distance, and his sullen sister Anne (Fonda) is resentful. Wrenching story with fine work by all, including Goldberg in the small role of live-in nurse, Myrna. Based on a short story by Alice Elliot Dark. Reeve's directorial debut. **60m/C VHS.** Robert Sean Leonard, Glenn Close, David Strathairn, Bridget Fonda, Whoopi Goldberg; ***D:*** Christopher Reeve; ***W:*** Will Scheffer; ***C:*** Frederick Elmes; ***M:*** Dave Grusin. **CABLE**

In the Good Old Summertime 🦴🦴🦴 **1949** This pleasant musical version of "The Shop Around the Corner" tells the story of two bickering co-workers who are also anonymous lovelorn pen pals. Minnelli made her second screen appearance at 18 months in the final scene. ♫I Don't Care; Meet Me Tonight In Dreamland; Play That Barbershop Chord; In the Good Old Summertime; Put Your Arms Around Me Honey; Wait Till the Sun Shines Nellie; Chicago; Merry Christmas. **104m/C VHS.** Judy Garland, Van Johnson, S.Z. Sakall, Buster Keaton, Spring Byington, Liza Minnelli, Clinton Sundberg; ***D:*** Robert Z. Leonard; ***C:*** Harry Stradling Sr.

In the Heat of Passion 🦴½ **1991 (R)** A low-budget ripoff of "Body Heat" and "Fatal Attraction" starring Kirkland as a married woman who involves a much younger man in a very steamy affair that leads to murder. This movie wants to be a thriller, but is little more than a softcore sex flick. Also available in an unrated version that contains explicit footage. **84m/C VHS.** Sally Kirkland, Nick Corri, Jack Carter, Michael Greene; ***D:*** Rodman Flender; ***W:*** Rodman Flender.

In the Heat of Passion 2: Unfaithful 🦴½ **1994 (R)** Philip Donovan (Bostwick) is having an affair with his stepdaughter Casey (Hill) and the duo murder hapless wife/mother (Down) to get her money. But it seems someone else knows about their crime. **88m/C VHS.** Barry Bostwick, Teresa Hill, Lesley-Anne Down, Michael Gross; ***D:*** Catherine Cyran.

In the Heat of the Night 🦴🦴🦴½ **1967** A wealthy industrialist in a small Mississippi town is murdered. A black homicide expert is asked to help solve the murder, despite resentment on the part of the town's chief of police. Powerful script with underlying theme of racial prejudice is served well by taut direction and powerhouse performances. Poitier's memorable character Virgil Tibbs appeared in two more pictures, "They Call Me Mister Tibbs" and "The Organization." **109m/C VHS, DVD, Wide.** Sidney Poitier, Rod Steiger, Warren Oates, Lee Grant; ***D:*** Norman Jewison; ***W:*** Stirling Silliphant; ***C:*** Haskell Wexler; ***M:*** Quincy Jones. Oscars '67: Actor (Steiger), Adapt. Screenplay, Film Editing, Picture, Sound; British Acad. '67: Actor (Steiger); Golden Globes '68: Actor—Drama (Steiger), Film—Drama, Screenplay; N.Y. Film Critics '67: Actor (Steiger), Director (Nichols), Film; Natl. Soc. Film Critics '67: Actor (Steiger), Cinematog.

In the King of Prussia 🦴½ **1983** Recreation of the trial of the "Plowshares Eight" radicals who were jailed for sabotaging two nuclear missiles at an electric plant in Pennsylvania. **92m/C VHS.** Martin Sheen, Rev. Daniel Berrigan.

In the Kingdom of the Blind the Man with One Eye Is King 🦴🦴 **1994 (R)** The title doesn't seem to mean anything and you may feel the same way about this standard crime drama, despite a strong cast. Mobster Tony (Petersen) gets police assistance from detective Al (Vallelonga) in discovering who murdered a mob boss' brother. **99m/C VHS.** Nick Vallelonga, William L. Petersen, Michael Biehn, Paul Winfield, James Quarter; ***D:*** Nick Vallelonga; ***W:*** Nick Vallelonga.

In the Land of the Owl Turds **1987** The story of a decidely eccentric young man who drives a dada art gallery on wheels while searching for love. Blank's senior thesis film. **30m/C VHS.** ***D:*** Harrod Blank.

In the Line of Duty: A Cop for the Killing 🦴🦴 *A Cop for the Killing* **1990 (R)** Undercover L.A. narcotics squad is about to bust the city's biggest drug lord when their sting operation goes bad and one of the team is brutally murdered. So, squad leader Ray Wiltern (Farentino) decides to get even. One in a series of TV movies under the "In the Line of Duty" banner. **95m/C VHS.** James Farentino, Steven Weber, Charles Haid, Tony Crane, Harold Sylvester, Dan Lauria, Tony Plana; ***D:*** Dick Lowry; ***W:*** Philip Rosenberg; ***C:*** Frank Beascoechea; ***M:*** Mark Snow. **TV**

In the Line of Duty: Ambush in Waco 🦴🦴½ *Ambush in Waco* **1993 (R)** Insta-TV movie made by NBC even before the fire which engulfed the Texas compound and ended the standoff between self-proclaimed "prophet" David Koresh and the federal government. Daly does well as the manipulative, charasmatic Branch Davidian cult leader whose stockpiling of illegal weapons lead to an investigation by the Bureau of Alcoholol, Tobacco and Firearms and a botched raid which caused the ultimately fatal siege. Filmed on location outside Tulsa, Oklahoma. **93m/C VHS.** Timothy Daly, Dan Lauria, William O'Leary; ***D:*** Dick Lowry; ***W:*** Phil Penningroth. **TV**

In the Line of Duty: The FBI Murders 🦴🦴🦴 *The FBI Murders* **1988** A fact-based chiller about the bloody 1986 shootout between Miami FBI agents and a pair of violent killers (Soul and Gross playing against type). **95m/C VHS.** David Soul, Michael Gross, Ronny Cox, Bruce Greenwood, Doug Sheehan, Teri Copley; ***D:*** Dick Lowry; ***W:*** Tracy Keenan Wynn. **TV**

In the Line of Fire 🦴🦴🦴½ **1993 (R)** Aging Secret Service agent Frank Horrigan (Eastwood) meets his match in a spooky caller, ex-CIA assassin Mitch Leary (Malkovich), who threatens his honor and the president in an exciting, fast-paced cat and mouse game. Terrific performance by Eastwood includes lots of dry humor and an unscripted emotional moment, but is nearly overshadowed by Malkovich's menacing bad guy. Russo is agent Lily Raines, who begins a charmingly tentative romance with Horrigan. Eerie special effects add to the mood. The Secret Service cooperated and most scenes are believable, with a few Hollywood exceptions; the end result clearly pays homage to the agents who protect our presidents. **128m/C VHS, DVD, 8mm, Wide.** Clint Eastwood, John Malkovich, Rene Russo, Dylan McDermott, Gary Cole, Fred Dalton Thompson, John Mahoney, Gregory Alan Williams; ***D:*** Wolfgang Petersen; ***W:*** Jeff Maguire; ***C:*** John Bailey; ***M:*** Ennio Morricone.

In the Money 🦴 **1934** Veteran vaudevillian "Skeets" Gallagher introduces a muddled mass of acts, including a poor imitator of boxing great Gene Tunney, a mad scientist who talks to rabbits and writes rubber checks, and a limp-wristed lisper. **66m/B VHS.** Lois Wilson, Warren Hymer, Arthur Hoyt, Frank "Junior" Coghlan, Louise Beavers; ***D:*** Frank Strayer.

In the Mood 🦴🦴½ **1987 (PG-13)** Based on fact, this is the story of teenager Sonny Wisecarver, nicknamed "The Woo Woo Kid," who in 1944, seduced two older women and eventually landed in jail after marrying one of them. Look for Wisecarver in a cameo role as a mailman in the film. **98m/C VHS.** Patrick Dempsey, Beverly D'Angelo, Talia Balsam, Michael Constantine, Betty Jinnette, Kathleen Freeman, Peter Hobbs, Edith Fellows; ***Cameos:*** Ellsworth Wisecarver; ***D:*** Phil Alden Robinson; ***W:*** Phil Alden Robinson; ***M:*** Ralph Burns.

In the Mood for Love 🦴🦴½ **2000 (PG)** Romantic melodrama set in the Shanghai community of Hong Kong in 1962. Newspaper editor Chow (Leung Chiu-Wai) and his wife have just moved into a new apartment across the hall from Li-zhen (Cheung) and her husband. Both their respective spouses are away from home a great deal, traveling on business, so the lonely duo begin a tentative friendship. Then Chow begins to suspect his wife is having an affair and it quickly becomes apparent that it's with Li-zhen's husband. Gorgeous to look at, melancholy in tone, if somewhat oblique. Chinese with subtitles. **98m/C VHS, DVD, Wide.** *HK* Tony Leung Chiu-Wai, Maggie Cheung, Rebecca Pan, Lai Chen, Siu Ping-Lam; ***D:*** Wong Kar-Wai; ***W:*** Wong Kar-Wai; ***C:*** Christopher Doyle, Mark Lee Ping-Bin; ***M:*** Michael Galasso, Umebayashi Shigeru. Cannes '00: Actor (Leung Chiu-Wai); N.Y. Film Critics '01: Cinematog., Foreign Film.

In the Mouth of Madness 🦴🦴 **1995 (R)** Standard horror flick pays homage to or pokes fun at Stephen King (you decide) with story of successful horror novelist whose fans become a bit too engrossed in his stories—seems his readers tend to slip into dementia and carry out the grisly acts depicted within the pages. Neill plays an insurance investigator who must track down the missing author while combating the psychotic, axe-wielding residents of the seemingly quiet east coast hamlet where the author resides. Worth a look for the above-average special effects and makeup provided by Industrial Light and Magic (ILM). **95m/C VHS, DVD.** Sam Neill, Juergen Prochnow, Julie Carmen, Charlton Heston, David Warner, John Glover, Bernie Casey, Peter Jason, Frances Bay; ***D:*** John Carpenter; ***W:*** Michael De Luca; ***C:*** Gary B. Kibbe; ***M:*** John Carpenter, Jim Lang.

In the Name of the Father 🦴🦴🦴½ **1993 (R)** Compelling true story of Gerry Conlon and the Guildford Four, illegally imprisoned in 1974 by British officials after a tragic IRA bombing near London. The British judicial system receives a black eye, but so does the horror and cruelty of IRA terrorism. Politics and family life in a prison cell share the focus, as Sheridan captures superior performances from Day-Lewis and Postlethwaite (beware the thick Belfast brogue). Thompson was accused of pro-IRA sympathies in the British press for her role as the lawyer who believed in Conlon's innocence. Adapted from "Proved Innocent," Conlon's prison memoirs; reunites Sheridan and Day-Lewis after "My Left Foot." Includes original songs by U2's Bono, with a haunting theme sung by Sinead O'Connor. **127m/C VHS, DVD, Wide.** *GB IR* Daniel Day-Lewis, Pete Postlethwaite, Emma Thompson, John Lynch, Corin Redgrave, Beatie Edney, John Benfield, Paterson Joseph, Marie Jones, Gerard McSorley, Frank Harper, Mark Sheppard, Don Baker, Britta Smith, Aidan Grennell, Daniel Massey, Bosco Hogan; ***D:*** Jim Sheridan; ***W:*** Jim Sheridan, Terry George; ***C:*** Peter Biziou; ***M:*** Trevor Jones, Bono, Sinead O'Connor. Berlin Intl. Film Fest. '94: Golden Berlin Bear.

In the Name of the Pope-King 🦴🦴🦴 **1985** An acclaimed historical epic about the politics and warfare raging around the 1867 Italian wars that made the Pope the sole ruler in Rome. In Italian with English subtitles. **115m/C VHS.** Nino Manfredi, Danilo Mattei, Carmen Scarpitta, Giovannella Grifea, Carlo Bagno; ***D:*** Luigi Magni.

In the Navy 🦴🦴½ *Abbott and Costello in the Navy* **1941** Abbott and Costello join the Navy in one of four military-service comedies they cranked out in 1941 alone. The token narrative involves about a singing star (Powell) in uniform to escape his female fans, but that's just an excuse for classic A & C routines. With the Andrews Sisters. ♫Starlight, Starbright; You're Off To See The World; Hula Ba Lua; Gimme Some Skin; A Sailor's Life For Me; We're In The Navy; Anchors Aweigh (instrumental); You're A Lucky Fellow, Mr. Smith (instrumental). **85m/B VHS, DVD, Wide.** Lou Costello, Bud Abbott, Dick Powell, The Andrews Sisters; ***D:*** Arthur Lubin; ***W:*** Arthur T. Horman, John Grant; ***C:*** Joseph Valentine.

In the Presence of Mine Enemies 🦴🦴½ **1997 (PG-13)** Remake of Rod Serling's 1960 script for "Playhouse 90." Rabbi Adam Heller (Mueller-Stahl) and his daughter Rachel (Lowensohn) are living in the Warsaw ghetto in 1942, trying to deal with Nazi oppression. But the Rabbi's faith is put the test when his son Paul (McKellar), who's escaped from the Treblinka labor camp, returns for vengeance and Rachel becomes the sexual victim of a vicious German officer (Dance). **100m/C VHS.** Armin Mueller-Stahl, Elina Lowensohn, Don McKellar, Charles Dance, Chad Lowe; ***D:*** Joan Micklin Silver; ***W:*** Rod Serling. **CABLE**

In the Realm of Passion 🦴🦴 *Empire of Passion; Ai No Borei* **1980 (R)** A wife and her lover murder her husband and dump the body in an abandoned well. Guilt over their actions drive the lovers to return to the scene where they are greeted by the vengeful ghost of the betrayed husband—or is it only their consciences torturing them? In Japanese with English subtitles. **108m/C VHS, DVD.** Kazuko Yoshiyuki, Takahiro Tamura, Tatsuya Fuji; ***D:*** Nagisa Oshima; ***W:*** Nagisa Oshima; ***C:*** Yoshio Miyajima; ***M:*** Toru Takemitsu.

In the Realm of the Senses 🦴🦴🦴 *Ai No Corrida* **1976 (NC-17)** Taboo-breaking story of a woman and man who turn their backs on the militaristic rule of Japan in the mid-1930s by plunging into an erotic and sensual world all their own. Striking, graphic work that was seized by U.S. customs when it first entered the country. Violent with explicit sex, and considered by some critics as pretentious, while others call it Oshima's masterpiece. In Japanese with English subtitles. **105m/C VHS, DVD.** *JP FR* Tatsuya Fuji, Eiko Matsuda, Aio Nakajima, Meika Seri; ***D:*** Nagisa Oshima; ***W:*** Nagisa Oshima; ***C:*** Hideo Ito; ***M:*** Minoru Miki.

In the Region of Ice 🦴🦴🦴 **1976** Award-winning short reveals the complexities of the relationship between a nun and a disturbed student. **38m/B VHS.** Fionnula Flanagan, Peter Lempert; ***D:*** Peter Werner.

In the Secret State 🦴🦴 **19??** Inspector Strange finds himself faced with the apparent suicide of a colleague on the day of his own retirement from the force. His private investigation into the case finds him mired in murder and espionage. **107m/C VHS.** Frank Finlay, Matthew Marsh, Thorley Walters.

In the Shadow of Kilimanjaro woof! **1986 (R)** A pack of hungry baboons attacks innocent people in the wilderness of Kenya. Based on a true story but the characters are contrived and just plain stupid at times. Quite gory as well. Filmed on location in Kenya. **105m/C VHS.** *GB* John Rhys-Davies, Timothy Bottoms, Michele Carey, Irene Miracle, Calvin Jung, Donald Blakely; ***D:*** Raju Patel.

In the Shadows 🦴🦴½ *Under Heaven* **1998 (R)** Modern update of Henry James' 1902 novel "The Wings of the Dove." Lonely, wealthy divorcee Eleanor (Richardson) is dying from cancer and needs a caregiver. Cynthia (Parker) moves in along with her weak-willed boyfriend Buck (Young), who passes himself off as Cynthia's brother and takes a job as a gardener. Avaricious Cynthia decides Buck should make Eleanor fall in love and marry him, so they can inherit her fortune. Of course this menage is made for misery. **115m/C VHS, DVD.** Joely Richardson, Molly Parker, Aden Young; ***D:*** Meg Richman; ***W:*** Meg Richman; ***C:*** Claudio Rocha; ***M:*** Marc Olsen.

In the Shadows 🦴🦴 **2001 (R)** New York hitman Eric O'Byrne (Modine) is sent to Miami to kill veteran Hollywood stunt coordinator Lance Huston (Caan) in retaliation for an accident that killed stuntman Jimmy (Brancato), a mobster's nephew. But before he died, Jimmy managed to steal money and drugs from an undercover FBI agent (Gooding Jr.) who's posing as a dealer. So both the mob and the feds want to reclaim their property. And then Eric goes and falls for the doctor daughter (Adams) of his target just to complicate things further. **104m/C VHS, DVD.** James Caan, Joey Lauren Adams, Matthew Modine, Cuba Gooding Jr., Lillo Brancato, Jeffrey Chase; ***D:*** Ric Roman Waugh; ***W:*** Ric Roman Waugh; ***C:*** Chuck Cohen; ***M:*** Adam Gorgoni.

In the Soup 🦴🦴½ **1992 (R)** Adolpho is a naive New York filmmaker barely scraping by. He decides to sell his script in a classified ad which is answered by the fast-talking Joe, a would-be film producer who's true profession is as a con artist. The two then try numerous (and humorous) ways to raise the money to begin filming. Also available colorized. **93m/B VHS.** Steve Buscemi, Seymour Cassel, Jennifer Beals, Will Patton, Pat Moya, Stanley Tucci, Sully

Boyar, Rockets Redglare, Elizabeth Bracco, Ruth Maleczech, Debi Mazar, Steven Randazzo, Francesco Messina; *Cameos:* Jim Jarmusch, Carol Kane; *D:* Alexandre Rockwell; *W:* Tim Kissell, Alexandre Rockwell; *C:* Phil Parmet; *M:* Mader. Sundance '92: Grand Jury Prize.

In the Spirit 🦴🦴½ **1990 (R)** New Age couple move from Beverly Hills to New York, where they meet an air-headed mystic and are forced to hide from a murderer. Falk gives solid performance in sometimes rocky production. Berlin is the real-life daughter of May. **94m/C VHS.** Elaine May, Marlo Thomas, Jeannie Berlin, Peter Falk, Melanie Griffith, Olympia Dukakis, Chad Burton, Thurn Hoffman, Michael Emil, Christopher Durang, Laurie Jones; *D:* Sandra Seacat; *W:* Jeannie Berlin, Laurie Jones; *C:* Dick Quinlan; *M:* Patrick Williams.

In the Steps of a Dead Man 🦴½ **1974** A family grieving for a fallen soldier is earmarked for evil by a young man who bears an uncanny resemblance to the dead man. A friend of the family has her suspicions and must find out the truth before something terrible happens. **71m/C VHS.** Skye Aubrey, John Nolan.

In the Time of the Butterflies 🦴🦴½ **2001 (PG-13)** Based on the novel by Julia Alvarez, which was inspired by the true story of the three Mirabal sisters (collectively known as Las Mariposas) who fought against the Trujillo dictatorship in the Dominican Republic. After their father is murdered, Minerva (Hayek) persuades her sisters Mate (Maestro) and Patria (Cavazos) to join with the rebels in overthrowing the government to ultimately tragic consequences for the women. **92m/C VHS, DVD.** Salma Hayek, Lumi Cavazos, Mia Maestro, Edward James Olmos, Marc Anthony, Pilar Padilla, Demian Bichir, Fernando Becerril; *D:* Mariano Barroso; *W:* Judy Klass, David Klass; *C:* Xavier Perez Grobet; *M:* Van Dyke Parks. **CABLE**

In the White City 🦴🦴🦴 *Dans la Ville Blanche* **1983** A sailor jumps ship in Lisbon and uses a movie camera to record himself and his search through the twisted streets and alleys of the city for something or someone to connect to. In French, Portuguese, and German with English subtitles. **108m/C VHS.** *PT SI* Bruno Ganz, Teresa Madruga, Julia Vonderlinn, Jose Carvalho; *D:* Alain Tanner; *W:* Alain Tanner; *C:* Acacio De Almeida; *M:* Jean-Luc Barbier.

In the Winter Dark 🦴🦴 **1998** The isolation of a remote valley community (filmed in Australia's Blue Mountains) is enhanced by the discovery of a woman's body and the slaughter of livestock. Maurice (Barrett) and Ida (Blethyn) have scratched out a farm living but personally never recovered from the death of their baby son long before. Outcast Laurie (Roxburgh) spends his time drifting through the countryside while pregnant Ronnie (Otto) has been abandoned by her lover. The four are brought together by death and what (or who) might be causing it. Based on the novel by Tim Winton. **92m/C VHS.** *AU* Ray Barrett, Brenda Blethyn, Richard Roxburgh, Miranda Otto; *D:* James Bogle; *W:* James Bogle, Peter Rasmussen; *C:* Martin McGrath; *M:* Peter Cobbin.

In This House of Brede 🦴🦴🦴 **1975** A sophisticated London widow turns her back on her worldly life to become a cloistered Benedictine nun. Rigg is outstanding as the woman struggling to deal with the discipline of faith. Based on the novel by Rumer Godden. **105m/C VHS, DVD.** Diana Rigg, Pamela Brown, Gwen Watford, Denis Quilley, Judi Bowker; *D:* George Schaefer; *M:* Peter Matz. **TV**

In This Our Life 🦴🦴½ **1942** Histrionic melodrama handled effectively by Huston about a nutsy woman who steals her sister's husband, rejects him, manipulates her whole family and eventually leads herself to ruin. Vintage star vehicle for Davis, who chews scenery and fellow actors alike. Adapted by Howard Koch from the Ellen Glasgon novel. **101m/B VHS.** Bette Davis, Olivia de Havilland, Charles Coburn, Frank Craven, George Brent, Dennis Morgan, Billie Burke, Hattie McDaniel, Lee Patrick, Walter Huston, Ernest Anderson; *D:* John Huston; *M:* Max Steiner.

In Too Deep 🦴½ **1990 (R)** A rock star and a beautiful woman are physically drawn to one another in spite of the fact that any contact between them could have disasterous results. **106m/C VHS.** Hugo Race, Santha Press, Rebekah Elmaloglou, John Flaus, Dominic Sweeney; *D:* Colin South.

In Too Deep 🦴🦴 **1999 (R)** Omar Epps and LL Cool J rise above the tired formula in this by-the-book undercover cop/paranoid drug dealer crime drama. Young Cincinnati cop Jef Cole (Epps) is working undercover in a drug ring run by a none-too-humble crime lord who calls himself God (LL Cool J). As he tries to gain the confidence of God, Cole becomes so deeply mired in the gangster life that his commander Boyd (Tucci) begins to question his loyalty. Epps does an excellent job conveying the tension in his character's position, although the script is totally devoid of any kind of plot twist to help him out. Also shining in minor parts are Pam Grier as a veteran detective and Nia Long as the standard issue love interest. **104m/C VHS, DVD.** Omar Epps, Stanley Tucci, L.L. Cool J., Pam Grier, Veronica Webb, Nia Long, David Patrick Kelly, Hill Harper; *D:* Michael Rymer; *W:* Paul Aaron, Michael Henry Brown; *C:* Ellery Ryan; *M:* Christopher Young.

In Trouble woof! **1967** Hard-to-follow and frequently aimless story of a pregnant girl who invents a fake rape story that her dull-witted brothers take seriously, embarking on a cross-country search for the culprit. **82m/C VHS.** *CA* Julie LaChapelle, Katherine Mousseau, Daniel Pilon; *D:* Gilles Carle.

In Which We Serve 🦴🦴🦴½ **1943** Much stiff upper-lipping in this classic that captures the spirit of the British Navy during WWII. The sinking of the destroyer HMS Torrin during the Battle of Crete is told via flashbacks, with an emphasis on realism that was unusual in wartime flag-wavers. Features the film debuts of Johnson and Attenborough, and the first Lean directorial effort. Coward received a special Oscar for his "outstanding production achievement," having scripted, scored, codirected, and costarred. **114m/B VHS.** *GB* Noel Coward, John Mills, Bernard Miles, Celia Johnson, Kay Walsh, James Donald, Richard Attenborough, Michael Wilding, George Carney, Gerald Case; *D:* David Lean, Noel Coward; *W:* Noel Coward; *C:* Ronald Neame; *M:* Noel Coward. N.Y. Film Critics '42: Film.

In Your Face 🦴½ *Abar, the First Black Superman* **1977 (R)** Little known blaxploitation film about a black family harrassed in a white suburb. A black motorcycle gang comes to their rescue. **90m/C VHS.** J. Walter Smith, Tobar Mayo, Roxie Young, Tina James; *D:* Frank Packard.

The Incident 🦴🦴½ **1967** A gritty, controversial (at-the-time) drama about two abusive thugs who take over a New York subway car late at night, humiliating and terrorizing each passenger in turn. Film debut for Sheen and Musante as the thugs. **99m/B VHS.** Martin Sheen, Tony Musante, Beau Bridges, Ruby Dee, Jack Gilford, Thelma Ritter, Brock Peters, Ed McMahon, Gary Merrill, Donna Mills, Jan Sterling, Mike Kellin, Bob Bannard, Diana Van Der Vlis, Victor Arnold, Robert Fields; *D:* Larry Peerce; *W:* Charles Fox, Nicholas E. Baehr; *C:* Gerald Hirschfeld; *M:* Charles Fox.

The Incident 🦴🦴🦴 **1989** Political thriller set during WWII in Lincoln Bluff, Colorado. Matthau is excellent in his TV debut as a small-town lawyer who must defend a German prisoner of war accused of murder at nearby Camp Bremen. An all-star cast lends powerful performances to this riveting made for TV drama. **95m/C VHS.** Walter Matthau, Susan Blakely, Harry (Henry) Morgan, Robert Carradine, Barnard Hughes, Peter Firth, William Schallert; *D:* Joseph Sargent. **TV**

Incident at Channel Q 🦴½ **1986** A heavy-metal rock musical about a suburban neighborhood declaring war on a chain-and-leather deejay. **85m/C VHS.** Al Corley.

Incident at Deception Ridge 🦴🦴½ **1994 (R)** After five years in prison, Jack Bolder (O'Keefe) is finally a free man, and headed for Seattle by bus. Unfortunately, also aboard is weasely bank manager Jack Davis (Begley Jr.) who's bolted with the ransom money for his kidnapped wife, Helen (Purl). Now Helen is left at the mercy of her kidnappers, who've discovered where their money is and decide to go after it—no matter who gets in their way. Filmed in Vancouver, British Columbia. **94m/C VHS.** Michael O'Keefe, Ed Begley Jr., Linda Purl, Miguel Ferrer, Colleen Flynn, Michelle Johnson, Ian Tracey; *D:* John McPherson; *W:* Ken Hixon, Randy Kornfield; *C:* David Geddes. **CABLE**

Incident at Oglala: The Leonard Peltier Story 🦴🦴🦴 **1992 (PG)** Offers a detailed account of the violent events leading to the murder of two FBI agents in Oglala, South Dakota in 1975. American Indian activist Leonard Peltier was convicted of the murders and is presently serving two consecutive life sentences, but he's cited as a political prisoner by Amnesty International. The documentary examines the highly controversial trial and the tensions between the government and the Oglala Nation stemming back to the Indian occupation of Wounded Knee in 1973. Director Apted is sympathetic to Peltier and offers reasons why he should be allowed a retrial; he examined similar incidents in his film "Thunderheart." **90m/C VHS, DVD.** *D:* Michael Apted; *M:* John Trudell, Jackson Browne; *Nar:* Robert Redford.

Incognito 🦴½ **1997 (R)** Art forger Harry Donovan (Patric) is approached by a couple of British art dealers and a Japanese broker to forge a Rembrandt for a Japanese client. He checks out the painter's style by traveling to Amsterdam and Paris, where he falls for art expert Marieke (Jacob). Harry forges the painting and then gets doublecrossed and caught up in murder. Convoluted plot; lots of cliches. Original director Peter Weller was replaced by Badham after two weeks of filming. **107m/C VHS, DVD.** Jason Patric, Irene Jacob, Rod Steiger, Thomas Lockyer, Simon Chandler, Michael Cochrane, Ian Richardson, Pip Torrens, Togo Igawa; *D:* John Badham; *W:* Jordan Katz; *C:* Denis Crossan; *M:* John Ottman.

An Inconvenient Woman 🦴🦴 **1991** When an older married man has an affair with a young seductress, there's suicide, murder, a nasty gossip columnist, a reporter, a knowing society wife, and a lot of cover-ups among the rich and famous. Miniseries from the novel by Dominick Dunne and based on the Alfred Bloomingdale scandal. **126m/C VHS.** Rebecca DeMornay, Jason Robards Jr., Jill Eikenberry, Peter Gallagher, Roddy McDowall, Chad Lowe. **TV**

The Incredible Hulk 🦴🦴½ **1977** Bixby is a scientist who achieves superhuman strength after he is exposed to a massive dose of gamma rays. But his personal life suffers, as does his wardrobe. Ferrigno is the Hulkster. Pilot for a TV series; based on the Marvel Comics character. **94m/C VHS.** Bill Bixby, Susan Sullivan, Lou Ferrigno, Jack Colvin; *D:* Kenneth Johnson. **TV**

The Incredible Hulk Returns 🦴½ **1988** The beefy green mutant is back and this time he wages war against a Viking named Thor. Very little substance in this made for TV flick, so be prepared to park your brain at the door. Followed by "The Trial of the Incredible Hulk." **100m/C VHS.** Bill Bixby, Lou Ferrigno, Jack Colvin, Lee Purcell, Charles Napier, Steve Levitt; *D:* Nicholas J. Corea. **TV**

The Incredible Journey 🦴🦴½ **1963** A labrador retriever, bull terrier and Siamese cat mistake their caretaker's intentions when he leaves for a hunting trip, believing he will never return. The three set out on a 250 mile adventure-filled trek across Canada's rugged terrain. Entertaining family adventure from Disney taken from Sheila Burnford's book. **80m/C VHS.** *D:* Fletcher Markle.

The Incredible Journey of Dr. Meg Laurel 🦴🦴🦴 **1979** A young doctor returns to her roots to bring modern medicine to the Appalachian mountain people during the 1930s. Features Wagner in a strong performance. **143m/C VHS.** Lindsay Wagner, Jane Wyman, Dorothy McGuire, James Woods, Gary Lockwood; *D:* Guy Green. **TV**

Incredible Melting Man woof! **1977 (R)** Two transformations change an astronaut's life after his return to earth. First, his skin starts to melt, then he displays cannibalistic tendencies. Hard to swallow. Special effects by Rick Baker. Look for director Jonathan Demme in a bit part. Gross-out remake of 1958's "First Man Into Space." **85m/C VHS.** Alex Rebar, Burr de Benning, Cheryl "Rainbeaux" Smith; *Cameos:* Jonathan Demme; *D:* William Sachs.

The Incredible Mr. Limpet 🦴🦴 **1964** Limp comedy about a nebbish bookkeeper who's transformed into a fish, fulfilling his aquatic dreams. Eventually he falls in love with another fish, and helps the U.S. Navy find Nazi subs during WWII. Partially animated, beloved by some, particularly those under the age of seven. Based on Theodore Pratt's novel. **99m/C VHS.** Don Knotts, Jack Weston, Carole Cook, Andrew Duggan, Larry Keating, Elizabeth McRae; *D:* Arthur Lubin; *W:* Jameson Brewer.

The Incredible Petrified World woof! **1958** Divers are trapped in an underwater cave when volcanic eruptions begin. Suffocating nonsense. **78m/B VHS.** John Carradine, Allen Windsor, Phyllis Coates, Lloyd Nelson, George Skaff; *D:* Jerry Warren.

The Incredible Rocky Mountain Race 🦴🦴 **1977** The townspeople of St. Joseph, fed up with Mark Twain's destructive feud with a neighbor, devise a shrewd scheme to rid the town of the troublemakers by sending them on a road race through the West. Comedy starring the F-Troop. **97m/C VHS.** Christopher Connelly, Forrest Tucker, Larry Storch, Mike Mazurki; *D:* James L. Conway. **TV**

The Incredible Sarah 🦴🦴 **1976 (PG)** A limp adapted stage biography from "Reader's Digest" of the great actress Sarah Bernhardt. Jackson chews scenery to no avail. **105m/C VHS.** Glenda Jackson, Daniel Massey, Yvonne Mitchell, Douglas Wilmer; *D:* Richard Fleischer; *M:* Elmer Bernstein.

The Incredible Shrinking Man 🦴🦴🦴½ **1957** Adapted by Richard Matheson from his own novel, the sci-fi classic is a philosophical thriller about a man who is doused with radioactive mist and begins to slowly shrink. His new size means that everyday objects take on sinister meaning and he must fight for his life in an increasingly hostile, absurd environment. A surreal, suspenseful allegory with impressive special effects. Endowed with the tension usually reserved for Hitchcock films. **81m/B VHS.** Grant Williams, Randy Stuart, April Kent, Paul Langton, Raymond Bailey, William Schallert, Frank Scanell, Billy Curtis; *D:* Jack Arnold; *W:* Richard Matheson; *C:* Ellis W. Carter.

The Incredible Shrinking Woman 🦴🦴½ **1981 (PG)** "...Shrinking Man" spoof and inoffensive social satire finds household cleaners producing some strange side effects on model homemaker Tomlin, slowly shrinking her to doll-house size. She then encounters everyday happenings as big tasks and not so menial. Her advertising exec husband has a hand in the down-sizing. Sight gags abound but the cuteness wears thin by the end. **89m/C VHS.** Lily Tomlin, Charles Grodin, Ned Beatty, Henry Gibson; *D:* Joel Schumacher; *W:* Jane Wagner.

The Incredible Two-Headed Transplant woof! **1971 (PG)** Mad scientist Dern has a criminal head transplanted on to the shoulder of big John Bloom and the critter runs amuck. Low-budget special effects guaranteed to give you a headache or two. Watch for Pat "Marilyn Munster" Priest in a bikini. **88m/C VHS.** Bruce Dern, Pat Priest, Casey Kasem, Albert Cole, John Bloom, Berry Kroeger; *D:* Anthony M. Lanza; *W:* John Lawrence, James Gordon White;

C: Glen Gano, Paul Hipp, Jack Steely; *M:* John Barber.

Incredibly Strange Creatures Who Stopped Living and Became Mixed-Up Zombies woof! *The Teenage Psycho Meets Bloody Mary; The Incredibly Strange Creatures* **1963** The infamous, super-cheap horror spoof that established Sheckler (for whom Cash Flagg is a pseudonym), about a carny side show riddled with ghouls and bad rock bands. Assistant cinematographers include the young Laszlo Kovacs and Vilmos Zsigmond. A must-see for connoisseurs of cult and camp. **90m/C VHS.** Cash (Ray Dennis Steckler) Flagg, Ray Dennis Steckler, Carolyn Brandt, Brett O'Hara, Atlas King, Sharon Walsh, Toni Camel, Erina Enyo; *D:* Ray Dennis Steckler; *W:* Gene Pollock, Robert Silliphant; *C:* Laszlo Kovacs, Vilmos Zsigmond, Joseph Mascelli; *M:* Henry Price.

The Incredibly True Adventure of Two Girls in Love ½ **1995 (R)** Gentle low-budget romantic comedy about first love between two high school girls. Tomboyish working-class Randy (Holloman) lives with her lesbian aunt and works part-time at the local gas station where she spots the rich and beautiful Evie (Parker), one of the popular girls in school. Some sparks fly but Evie's confused, though she's willing to be wooed and, later, defend her new relationship. The issue of race (Randy's white, Evie's black) is only briefly alluded to—more is made of the differences between the girls' social classes and their vulnerability. Directorial debut for Maggenti. **95m/C VHS.** Laurel Holloman, Nicole Parker, Kate Stafford, Stephanie Berry; *D:* Maria Maggenti; *W:* Maria Maggenti.

Incubus **1965** One of the very few films made in the artificial language of Esperanto (so it's subtitled in English). Beautiful Kia (Ames) and Amael (Hardt) are sisters who retain their youth and beauty by sucking the life out of the corrupted souls who visit a supposedly magic well. Then Kia discovers the uncorrupted soldier Mark (Shatner) and falls big time. But her succubis sis doesn't like what's going on and casts a spell that calls an incubus to wreak havoc. Creepily atmospheric with striking cinematography by Hall. **76m/B VHS, DVD.** William Shatner, Allyson Ames, Eloise Hardt, Ann Atmar, Robert Fortier, Milos Milos; *D:* Leslie Stevens; *W:* Leslie Stevens; *C:* Conrad L. Hall; *M:* Dominic Frontiere.

Incubus woof! **1982 (R)** A doctor and his teenaged daughter settle in a quiet New England community, only to encounter the incubus, a terrifying, supernatural demon who enjoys sex murders. Offensive trash. **90m/C VHS.** *CA* John Cassavetes, Kerrie Keane, Helen Hughes, Erin Flannery, John Ireland, Duncan McIntosh; *D:* John Hough; *W:* George Franklin; *C:* Conrad L. Hall, Albert J. Dunk; *M:* Stanley Myers.

Indecency **1992 (PG-13)** Ellie (Beals) is still recovering from a mental breakdown when she goes to work for Marie (Clarkson) at her ad agency. There Ellie must deal with manipulative associate Nia (Davis) and Marie's charming, estranged husband Mick (Remar), who draws the fragile Ellie into an affair. Then Marie commits suicide—or maybe it was murder. **88m/C VHS.** Jennifer Beals, James Remar, Sammi Davis, Barbara Williams, Christopher John Fields, Ray McKinnon; *D:* Marisa Silver; *W:* Amy Holden Jones, Holly Goldberg Sloan, Alan Ormsby.

Indecent Behavior **1993 (R)** Tweed is a sex therapist who's accused of murder when one of her clients overdose's on the latest designer drug. Hudson, who plays the genre's hard-boiled cop figure, gets very personally involved investigating the allegations, which really upsets Tweed's hubby, Vincent. Also available in an unrated version. **93m/C VHS.** Shannon Tweed, Gary Hudson, Jan-Michael Vincent, Michelle Moffett, Lawrence-Hilton Jacobs, Penny Peyser; *D:* Lawrence Lanoff.

Indecent Behavior 2 ½ **1994 (R)** Sex therapist Rebecca is targeted for blackmail as she finds out all sorts of unhealthy things about her patients. Meanwhile, she's practicing her technique with a fellow therapist. Also available unrated. **96m/C VHS.** Shannon Tweed, James Brolin, Chad McQueen, Elizabeth Sandifer, Craig Stepp, Rochelle Swanson; *D:* Carlo Gustaff.

Indecent Behavior 3 **1995 (R)** Sex therapist becomes the obsessed object of desire for a decidedly deadly client. Also available unrated. **90m/C VHS.** Shannon Tweed, Sam Hennings, Colleen T. Coffey, Doug Jeffery, Beau Billingslea, Laura Rogers; *D:* Kelley Cauthen; *W:* Hel Styverson.

An Indecent Obsession ½ **1985** Colleen McCullough's bestseller about WWII Australian soldiers recuperating in a field hospital mental ward. Hughes plays the nurse everyone's in love with. **100m/C VHS.** *AU* Wendy Hughes, Gary Sweet, Richard Moir, Jonathan Hyde, Bill Hunter, Bruno Lawrence; *D:* Lex Marinos; *W:* Denise Morgan.

Indecent Proposal ½ **1993 (R)** High-gloss movie that had couples everywhere discussing the big question: Would you let your wife sleep with a billionaire in exchange for a million bucks? Probably, if all were as goodlooking as the weathered, yet ever gorgeous Redford. Moore and Harrelson are the financially down on their luck, but happy, couple who venture to Vegas on a last-ditch gambling effort. Surreally slick direction from Lyne, but an ultimately empty film that explores the values of marriage in a terribly angst-ridden fashion. Based on the novel by Jack Engelhard. Proof that average movies can make a killing at the boxoffice, landing in sixth place for 1993. **119m/C VHS, DVD, CD-I, Wide.** Robert Redford, Demi Moore, Woody Harrelson, Seymour Cassel, Oliver Platt, Billy Bob Thornton, Rip Taylor, Billy Connolly, Joel Brooks, Sheena Easton, Herbie Hancock; *D:* Adrian Lyne; *W:* Amy Holden Jones; *C:* Howard Atherton; *M:* John Barry. MTV Movie Awards '94: Kiss (Demi Moore/Woody Harrelson); Golden Raspberries '93: Worst Picture, Worst Support. Actor (Harrelson), Worst Screenplay.

Independence Day *Follow Your Dreams* **1983 (R)** Uneven romantic drama about a small-town photographer, yearning for the big city, who falls in love with a racing car enthusiast, whose sister is a battered wife. Strong cast, particularly Wiest as the abused wife, is left occasionally stranded by a script reaching too hard for social significance. **110m/C VHS.** Kathleen Quinlan, David Keith, Frances Sternhagen, Dianne Wiest, Cliff DeYoung, Richard Farnsworth, Josef Sommer, Cheryl "Rainbeaux" Smith; *D:* Robert Mandel; *M:* Charles Bernstein.

Independence Day **1996 (PG-13)** The biggest of the new wave of disaster flicks paying tribute to the Irwin Allen celebrity-fests of the '70s finds an alien armada descending on Earth to create some fireworks on the July 4th weekend. The fate of the world rests in the hands of an unlikely band of Earthlings led by President Whitmore (Pullman), a computer expert (Goldblum), and a Marine fighter pilot (Smith). Special effects, despite forgoing some of the more expensive newer technology, don't disappoint. Strong (if not A-list) cast and plenty of action. Devlin and Emmerich wrote the script while promoting "Stargate," after a reporter asked Emmerich if he believed in aliens. **135m/C VHS, DVD.** Richard Speight Jr., Adam Baldwin, Bill Smitrovich, Mae Whitman, Kiersten Warren, Giuseppe Andrews, Devon Gummersall, Leland Orser, Raphael Sbarge, Bobby Hosea, Dan Lauria, Robert Pine, John Capodice, Lyman Ward, Bill Pullman, Will Smith, Jeff Goldblum, Judd Hirsch, Margaret Colin, Randy Quaid, Mary McDonnell, Robert Loggia, Brent Spiner, James Rebhorn, Vivica A. Fox, James Duval, Harry Connick Jr., Harvey Fierstein; *D:* Roland Emmerich; *W:* Dean Devlin, Roland Emmerich; *C:* Karl Walter Lindenlaub; *M:* David Arnold. Oscars '96: Visual FX; MTV Movie Awards '97: Kiss (Vivica A. Fox/Will Smith).

The Indestructible Man **1956** Chaney, electrocuted for murder and bank robbery, is brought back to life by a scientist. Naturally, he seeks revenge on those who sentenced him to death. Chaney does the best he can with the material. **70m/B VHS, DVD, Wide.** Ross Elliott, Ken Terrell, Robert Shayne, Lon Chaney Jr., Marian Carr, Max (Casey Adams) Showalter; *D:* Jack Pollexfen; *W:* Sue Bradford, Vy Russell; *C:* John L. "Jack" Russell; *M:* Albert Glasser.

The Indian Fighter **1955** Exciting actioner has Douglas as a scout hired to lead a wagon train to Oregon in 1870. The train must past through dangerous Sioux territory and Douglas tries to make peace with the Sioux leader but a secret Indian gold mine and romance cause friction and keep things lively. **88m/C VHS.** Kirk Douglas, Elsa Martinelli, Walter Abel, Walter Matthau, Diana Douglas, Lon Chaney Jr., Eduard Franz, Alan Hale Jr., Elisha Cook Jr., Harry Landers; *D:* Andre de Toth; *W:* Ben Hecht, Robert L. Richards.

The Indian in the Cupboard ½ **1995 (PG)** On his ninth birthday, Omri receives a three-inch plastic indian named Little Bear and an old wooden medicine cabinet. (Guess they were out of Power Rangers.) When placed in the cabinet, Little Bear magically comes to life, taking Omri on adventures and teaching him important lessons. Blue screen techniques allow them to appear together on-screen although they were actually shot together only once. Based on the best-selling children's book by Lynne Reid Banks. **97m/C VHS, DVD, Wide.** Michael (Mike) Papajohn, Hal Scardino, Litefoot, Lindsay Crouse, Richard Jenkins, Rishi Bhat, David Keith; *D:* Frank Oz; *W:* Melissa Mathison; *C:* Russell Carpenter; *M:* Miles Goodman.

Indian Paint **1964** A pleasant children's film about an Indian boy's love for his horse and his rite of passage. Silverheels was Tonto on TV's "The Lone Ranger," while Crawford was the "Rifleman's" son. **90m/C VHS.** Jay Silverheels, Johnny Crawford, Pat Hogan, Robert Crawford Jr., George Lewis; *D:* Norman Foster.

The Indian Runner ½ **1991 (R)** Penn's debut as a writer-director tells the story of two brothers in Nebraska during the late '60s, who are forced to change their lives with the loss of their family farm. Joe is a good cop and family man who can't deal with the rage of his brother Frank, who has just returned from Vietnam and is turning to a life of crime. Penn does a decent job of representing the struggle between the responsible versus the rebellious side of human nature. Quiet and very stark. Based on the song "Highway Patrolman" by Bruce Springsteen. **127m/C VHS, Wide.** David Morse, Viggo Mortensen, Sandy Dennis, Charles Bronson, Valeria Golino, Patricia Arquette, Dennis Hopper, Benicio Del Toro; *D:* Sean Penn; *W:* Sean Penn.

The Indian Scarf **1963** Heirs to a dead man's fortune are being strangled one by one at the benefactor's country estate. An Edgar Wallace suspense tale. **85m/C VHS.** *GE* Heinz Drache, Gisela Uhlen, Klaus Kinski; *D:* Alfred Vohrer.

Indian Summer **1993 (PG-13)** Yet another addition to the growing 30-something nostalgia genre. Delete the big house, add a crusty camp director (Arkin), change the characters' names (but not necessarily their lives) and you feel like you're experiencing deja vu. This time seven friends and the requisite outsider reconvene at Camp Tamakwa, the real-life summer camp to writer/director Binder. The former campers talk. They yearn. They save Camp Tamakwa and experience personal growth. A must see for those who appreciate listening to situational jokes that are followed by "I guess you had to be there." **108m/C VHS.** Alan Arkin, Matt Craven, Diane Lane, Bill Paxton, Elizabeth Perkins, Kevin Pollak, Sam Raimi, Vincent Spano, Julie Warner, Kimberly Williams, Richard Chevolleau; *D:* Mike Binder; *W:* Mike Binder; *M:* Miles Goodman.

The Indian Tomb ½ *The Mission of the Yogi; The Tiger of Eschanapur* **1921** Silent film fare in two parts. Ayan (Veidt) is the Maharajah of Eschanapur. But all his wealth and power has not prevented Ayan's wife, Princess Savitri, from falling in love with British officer MacAllan. Ayan plots to built a massive tomb to imprison the woman who betrayed him but yogi Ramigani prophesizes that such revenge will destroy the prince's life. Huge budget (for the time) and lavish spectacle, which was all created at director May's German studio. Adapted from the novel by Thea von Haubou. **212m/B VHS, DVD.** *GE* Conrad Veidt, Paul Richter, Olaf Fonss, Mia May, Bernhard Goetzke, Lya de Putti, Erna Morena; *D:* Joe May; *W:* Fritz Lang; *C:* Werner Brandes.

The Indian Tomb *Das Indische Grabmal* **1959** Sequel to "The Tiger of Eschnapur" finds Harald Berger (Hubschmid) and Seetha (Paget) managing to elude Chandra's soldiers until Seetha's faith in her gods results in her capture and his apparent death. Berger's partner Dr. Rhode (Holm) and Berger's sister Irene (Bethmann) discover they're in the hands of a madman when Chandra lies about Berger's whereabouts. Along the way is another knockout exotic dance (with Ms. Paget in an even more revealing costume), encounters with a horde of lepers locked away in the catacombs, and a full-scale palace revolt. **102m/C DVD.** *GE* Debra Paget, Paul (Christian) Hubschmid, Walter Reyer, Sabine Bethmann; *D:* Fritz Lang; *W:* Werner Jorg Luddecke; *C:* Richard Angst; *M:* Michel Michelet.

Indian Uprising **1951** An army captain tries to keep local settlers from causing trouble with Geronimo and his people when gold is discovered on their territory. **75m/C VHS.** George Montgomery, Audrey Long, Carl Benton Reid, John Baer, Joseph (Joe) Sawyer; *D:* Ray Nazarro.

Indiana Jones and the Last Crusade **1989 (PG)** In this, the third and last (?) Indiana Jones adventure, the fearless archaeologist is once again up against the Nazis in a race to find the Holy Grail. Connery is perfectly cast as Indy's father; opening sequence features Phoenix as a teenage Indy and explains his fear of snakes and the origins of the infamous fedora. Returns to the look and feel of the original with more adventures, exotic places, dastardly villains, and daring escapes than ever before; a must for Indy fans. **126m/C VHS, 8mm, Wide.** Harrison Ford, Sean Connery, Denholm Elliott, Alison Doody, Julian Glover, John Rhys-Davies, River Phoenix, Michael Byrne, Alex Hyde-White; *D:* Steven Spielberg; *W:* Jeffrey Boam; *M:* John Williams.

Indiana Jones and the Temple of Doom **1984 (PG)** Daredevil archaeologist Indiana Jones is back. This time he's on the trail of the legendary Ankara Stone and a ruthless cult that has enslaved hundreds of children. More gore and violence than the original; Capshaw's whining character is an irritant, lacking the fresh quality that Karen Allen added to the original. Enough action for ten movies, special effects galore, and the usual booming Williams score make it a cinematic roller coaster ride, but with less regard for plot and pacing than the original. Though second in the series, it's actually a prequel to "Raiders of the Lost Ark." Followed by "Indiana Jones and the Last Crusade." **118m/C VHS, 8mm.** Harrison Ford, Kate Capshaw, Ke Huy Quan, Amrish Puri; *D:* Steven Spielberg; *W:* Willard Huyck, Gloria Katz; *M:* John Williams. Oscars '84: Visual FX.

Indictment: The McMartin Trial **1995 (R)** Woods stars as attorney Danny Davis, who has the unenviable task of providing a defense in the notorious McMartin child molestation trial. In 1983, Manhattan Beach, California was rocked by reports that some 60 preschoolers had been abused at a day-care center. Seven defendants were accused thanks to lurid videotaped interviews with the children. The trial lasted six years (the longest and most expensive on record) and all charges were eventually dismissed. It's clear from this telepic that public hysteria and media hype lead to a grave miscarriage of justice that put the legal system on trial as well. **132m/C VHS.** James Woods, Henry Thomas, Mercedes Ruehl, Shirley Knight, Sada Thompson, Mark Blum, Alison Elliott, Chelsea Field, Richard Bradford, Lolita (David) Davidovich; *D:* Mick Jackson; *W:* Abby Mann, Myra Mann; *C:* Rodrigo Garcia; *M:* Peter Melnick.

Indio **1990 (R)** A Marine-trained half-breed takes it on himself to save the Amazon rain forest. Not a peaceful demonstrator, his tactics are violent ones. **94m/C VHS.**

Marvin Hagler, Francesco Quinn, Brian Dennehy; ***D:*** Anthony (Antonio Margheriti) Dawson.

Indio 2: The Revolt 🦴 **1992 (R)** Greedy developers are cutting a highway into the Amazon jungle, destroying everything in their path. All is not lost though, because U.S. Marine Sgt. Iron is on top of things, continuing his struggle to unite the Amazon tribes and save the rainforest, no matter what it takes. **104m/C VHS.** Marvin Hagler, Charles Napier; ***M:*** Pino Donaggio.

Indiscreet 🦴½ **1931** Empty-headed romantic comedy about a fashion designer whose past catches up with her when her ex-lover starts romancing her sister. No relation to the classic 1958 film with Cary Grant and Ingrid Bergman. ♫Come To Me; If You Haven't Got Love. **81m/B VHS.** Gloria Swanson, Ben Lyon, Barbara Kent; ***D:*** Leo McCarey.

Indiscreet 🦴🦴🦴 **1958** A charming American diplomat in London falls in love with a stunning actress, but protects himself by saying he is married. Needless to say, she finds out. Stylish romp with Grant and Bergman at their sophisticated best. Adapted by Norman Krasna from his stage play "Kind Sir." **100m/C VHS, DVD, Wide.** Cary Grant, Ingrid Bergman, Phyllis Calvert; ***D:*** Stanley Donen; ***W:*** Norman Krasna; ***C:*** Frederick A. (Freddie) Young; ***M:*** Richard Rodney Bennett.

Indiscreet 🦴½ **1988 (PG)** Indistinctive made for TV rehash of the charming 1958 Grant/Bergman romantic comedy in which a suave American falls for an English actress. Both versions derive from the play "Kind Sir" by Norman Krasna, but this one suffers by comparison. **94m/C VHS.** Robert Wagner, Lesley-Anne Down, Maggie Henderson, Robert McBain, Jeni Barnett; ***D:*** Richard Michaels. **TV**

Indiscreet 🦴🦴½ **1998 (R)** Private eye Michael Nash (Perry) is hired by a suspicious millionaire to follow his wife, Eve (Reuben). When Nash winds up saving the desperately unhappy Eve from suicide, the two begin an affair. Then her husband is murdered and the cops find Nash a very handy suspect. **101m/C VHS.** Luke Perry, Gloria Reuben, Peter Coyote, Adam Baldwin; ***D:*** Marc Bienstock; ***W:*** Vladimir Nemirovsky.

Indiscretion of an American Wife 🦴🦴 *Indiscretion; Terminus Station; Terminal Station Indiscretion* **1954** Set almost entirely in Rome's famous Terminal Station, where an ill-fated couple say goodbye endlessly while the woman tries to decide whether to join her husband in the States. Trimmed down from 87 minutes upon U.S. release. **63m/C VHS.** *IT* Jennifer Jones, Montgomery Clift, Richard Beymer; ***D:*** Vittorio De Sica; ***W:*** Truman Capote; ***C:*** Oswald Morris.

Indochine 🦴🦴🦴 **1992 (PG-13)** Soapy melodrama follows the fortunes of Eliane (Deneuve), a Frenchwoman born and reared in Indochina, from 1930 to the communist revolution 25 years later. She contends with the changes to her country as well as her adopted daughter as she grows up and becomes independent. Deneuve's controlled performance (and unchanging beauty) is eminently watchable. Filmed on location in Vietnam with breathtaking cinematography by Francois Catonne. In French with English subtitles. **155m/C VHS, DVD, Wide.** *FR* Catherine Deneuve, Linh Dan Pham, Vincent Perez, Jean Yanne, Dominique Blanc, Henri Marteau, Carlo Brandt, Gerard Lartigau; ***D:*** Regis Wargnier; ***W:*** Erik Orsenna, Louis Gardel, Catherine Cohen, Regis Wargnier; ***C:*** Francois Catonne; ***M:*** Patrick Doyle. Oscars '92: Foreign Film; Cesar '93: Actress (Deneuve), Art Dir./Set Dec., Cinematog., Sound, Support. Actress (Blanc); Golden Globes '93: Foreign Film; Natl. Bd. of Review '92: Foreign Film.

Infamous Crimes 🦴🦴 *Philo Vance Returns* **1947** Philo investigates the murders of a playboy and his girlfriends. One of the last of the series whose character was based on the S.S. Van Dine stories. **64m/B VHS, 8mm.** William Wright, Terry Austin, Leon Belasco, Clara Blandick, Iris Adrian, Frank Wilcox; ***D:*** William Beaudine.

The Infernal Trio 🦴🦴½ *Le Trio Infernal* **1974** An attorney comes up with a plan involving two sisters (who are his lovers) which will make them both wealthy; but it will also make them both murderers. Sophisticated black comedy based on a true story. In French with English subtitles or dubbed. **100m/C VHS.** *FR IT* Romy Schneider, Michel Piccoli, Mascha Gonska; ***D:*** Francis Girod.

Inferno 🦴🦴 **1980 (R)** Uneven occult horror tale about a young man who arrives in New York to investigate the mysterious circumstances surrounding his sister's death. Dubbed. **106m/C VHS, DVD.** *IT* Leigh McCloskey, Elenora Giorgi, Irene Miracle, Sacha (Sascha) Pitoeff; ***D:*** Dario Argento; ***W:*** Dario Argento; ***C:*** Romano Albani; ***M:*** Keith Emerson.

Inferno 🦴🦴½ **1999 (R)** Jack Conley awakens in the middle of the desert with no idea who he is or what's happened to him. Taken in by a reclusive artist, Jack suffers violent flashbacks as he tries to piece together his identity, only remembering that he had a lot of money in his possession and it's gone. Then two of Jack's former associates track him down and he learns the dangerous truth about himself. **94m/C VHS, DVD, Wide.** Ray Liotta, Gloria Reuben, Armin Mueller-Stahl; ***D:*** Harley Cokliss; ***C:*** Stephen McNutt; ***M:*** Fred Mollin. **VIDEO**

Inferno 🦴½ **2001** Darcy Hamilton (Gunn) is an expert firejumper who leads her team in controlling a forest fire that Darcy suspects was arson. A second blaze erupts and heads for the nearest town and the local fire chief accuses Darcy's daughter and her boyfriend of being fire bugs. Now Darcy not only has to fight the fire but prove her daughter's innocence. **91m/C VHS, DVD.** Janet Gunn, Jeff Fahey, Dean Stockwell; ***D:*** Dusty Nelson; ***M:*** Jeff Marsh.

Inferno in Paradise 🦴 **1988** Mucho macho firefighter and bimbous gal pal photographer get hot while trailing a murderous pyromaniac. More like purgatory in the living room (that is, unless you thought Forsyth's earlier "Chesty Anderson, US Navy" was divine comedy). **115m/C VHS.** Richard Young, Betty Ann Carr, Jim Davis, Andy Jarrell, Dennis Chun; ***D:*** Ed Forsyth.

The Infiltrator 🦴🦴½ **1995 (R)** Based on the true story of Yaron Svoray (Platt), an Israeli journalist and the son of Holocaust survivors, whose latest assignment is to go to Berlin and investigate the rising Neo-Nazi movement. Eventually, Svoray manages to meet leaders of the Nationalist Front and then finds himself enmeshed in a worldwide political network. Based on the book "In Hitler's Shadow" by Yaron Svoray and Nick Taylor. **102m/C VHS.** Oliver Platt, Arliss Howard, Peter Riegert, Alan King, Tony Haygarth, Michael Byrne, Julian Glover, Alex Kingston; ***D:*** John MacKenzie; ***W:*** Guy Andrews; ***M:*** Hal Lindes. **CABLE**

Infinity 🦴🦴½ **1996 (PG)** Based on memoirs covering the early years of Nobel Prize-winning physicist Richard Feynman (Broderick) and his romance with aspiring artist Arline Greenbaum (Arquette). They marry despite the fact that Arline is diagnosed with tuberculosis, at this time in the '30s a contagious and incurable disease. Richard's recruited to work on the Manhattan Project at Los Alamos, New Mexico, and the narrative travels between his scientific endeavors and Arline's worsening illness in an Albuquerque hospital. Problem is it's neither a character study or a love story but a weak combo. Directing debut of Broderick; screenplay is written by his mother. **119m/C VHS, DVD.** Matthew Broderick, Patricia Arquette, James LeGros, Peter Riegert, Dori Brenner, Peter Michael Goetz, Zeljko Ivanek; ***D:*** Matthew Broderick; ***W:*** Patricia Broderick; ***C:*** Toyomichi Kurita; ***M:*** Bruce Broughton.

The Informant 🦴🦴🦴 **1997 (R)** In 1983, ex-IRA soldier Gingy McAnally (Brophy) has been tracked down by his cohorts and blackmailed (with threats to his family) into assassinating a Belfast judge. Recognized by British army officer Ferris (Elwes), Gingy is quickly arrested and interrogated by ruthless inspector Rennie (Dalton), who puts the pressure on Gingy to give up his comrades in exchange for immunity. Moved to a safe house, hapless Gingy has to live with being an informant and stay alive long enough to testify. Based on the novel "Field of Blood" by Gerald Seymour. **106m/C VHS.** *IR* Anthony Brophy, Timothy Dalton, Cary Elwes, Sean McGinley, Maria Lennon, John Kavanagh, Frankie McCafferty, Stuart Graham; ***D:*** Jim McBride; ***W:*** Nicholas Meyer; ***C:*** Alfonso Beato.

The Informer 🦴½ **1929** Hanson wants to flee Ireland's poverty for America, using the reward money he gets for turning in an IRA comrade. But things don't turn out as planned and instead he's haunted by the guilt of his betrayal. Based on the novel by Liam O'Flaherty and filmed to much greater effect by John Ford in 1935. **83m/B VHS.** *GB* Lars Hanson, Lya de Putti, Warwick Ward, Dennis Wynham; ***D:*** Arthur Robison; ***W:*** Benn W. Levy, Rolfe E. Vanlo.

The Informer 🦴🦴🦴🦴 **1935** Based on Liam O'Flaherty's novel about the Irish Sinn Fein Rebellion of 1922, it tells the story of a hard-drinking Dublin man (McLaglen) who informs on a friend (a member of the Irish Republican Army) in order to collect a 20-pound reward. When his "friend" is killed during capture, he goes on a drinking spree instead of using the money, as planned, for passage to America. Director Ford allowed McLaglen to improvise his lines during the trial scene in order to enhance the realism, leading to excruciating suspense. Wonderful score. **91m/B VHS.** Victor McLaglen, Heather Angel, Wallace Ford, Margot Grahame, Joseph (Joe) Sawyer, Preston Foster, Una O'Connor, J.M. Kerrigan, Donald Meek; ***D:*** John Ford; ***W:*** Dudley Nichols; ***M:*** Max Steiner. Oscars '35: Actor (McLaglen), Director (Ford), Screenplay, Score; N.Y. Film Critics '35: Director (Ford), Film.

Infra-Man woof! *The Super Inframan; The Infra Superman* **1976 (PG)** If you're looking for a truly bad, hokey flick, this could be it. Infra-man is a superhero who must rescue the galaxy from the clutches of the evil Princess Dragon Mom and her army of prehistoric monsters. Outlandish dialogue (delivered straight) combines with horrible special effects and costumes to create what may well be one of the best camp classics to date. Poorly dubbed in English. **92m/C VHS.** *HK* Li Hsiu-hsien, Wang Hsieh, Yuan Man-tzu, Terry Liu, Tsen Shu-yi, Huang Chienlung, Lu Sheng; ***D:*** Hua-Shan; ***W:*** Peter Fernandez.

Inherit the Wind 🦴🦴🦴½ **1960** Powerful courtroom drama, based on the Broadway play, is actually a fictionalized version of the infamous Scopes "Monkey Trial" of 1925. Tracy is the defense attorney for the schoolteacher on trial for teaching Darwin's Theory of Evolution to a group of students in a small town ruled by religion. March is the prosecutor seeking to put the teacher behind bars and restore religion to the schools. **128m/B VHS, DVD, Wide.** Spencer Tracy, Fredric March, Florence Eldridge, Gene Kelly, Dick York, Donna Anderson, Harry (Henry) Morgan, Elliott Reid, Philip Coolidge, Claude Akins, Noah Beery Jr., Norman Fell; ***D:*** Stanley Kramer; ***W:*** Nedrick Young, Harold Jacob Smith; ***C:*** Ernest Laszlo; ***M:*** Ernest Gold. Berlin Intl. Film Fest. '60: Actor (March).

Inherit the Wind 🦴🦴½ **1999 (PG)** Adaptation of the 1955 play by Jerome Lawrence and Robert E. Lee that was previously filmed in 1960 and that is based on the 1925 Scopes Monkey Trial. Tennessee science teacher Bertram Cates (Scott) is being prosecuted for teaching evolution. Agnostic attorney Henry Drummond (Lemmon) comes to town to defend Cates against respected, conservative prosecutor Matthew Harrison Brady (Scott) who wants to keep religious teachings in the school. **113m/C VHS.** Jack Lemmon, George C. Scott, Tom Everett Scott, Piper Laurie, Beau Bridges, John Cullum, Kathryn Morris, Lane Smith, Brad Greenquist, David Wells; ***D:*** Daniel Petrie; ***W:*** Nedrick Young, Harold Jacob Smith; ***C:*** James Bartle; ***M:*** Laurence Rosenthal. **CABLE**

Inheritance 🦴🦴🦴 *Uncle Silas* **1947** Victorian-era melodrama of a young heiress endangered by her guradian, who plots to murder his charge for her inheritance. Chilling and moody story based on a novel by Sheridan Le Fanu. **103m/B VHS.** *GB* Jean Simmons, Katina Paxinou, Derrick DeMarney, Derek Bond; ***D:*** Charles Frank.

The Inheritance 🦴🦴½ *L'Eredita Ferramonti* **1976 (R)** Wealthy partiarch becomes sexually involved with scheming daughter-in-law. Tawdry tale is nonetheless engaging. **121m/C VHS, DVD.** *IT* Anthony Quinn, Fabio Testi, Dominique Sanda; ***D:*** Mauro Bolognini; ***W:*** Sergio Bazzini; ***C:*** Ennio Guarnieri; ***M:*** Ennio Morricone. Cannes '76: Actress (Sanda).

The Inheritor 🦴🦴 **1990 (R)** Set in a small New England town, this mystery centers on the death of a young woman and her sister's attempts to uncover the murderer. The local celebrity, a writer, seems to be at the heart of the mystery and the sister finds herself growing interested. Keeps you guessing. **83m/C VHS.** Dan Haggerty; ***D:*** Brian Savegar.

The Inheritors 🦴½ **1985** Not-too-subtle tale of a young German boy who becomes involved with a Nazi youth group as his home life deteriorates. Heavy-going anti-fascism creates more message than entertainment. In German with English subtitles or dubbed. **89m/C VHS.** *GE* Nikolas Vogel, Roger Schauer, Klaus Novak, Johanna Tomek; ***D:*** Walter Bannert; ***W:*** Walter Bannert.

The Inheritors 🦴🦴 *Die Siebtelbauern* **1998 (R)** Seven peasants in 1930s rural Austria unexpectedly inherit the farm they've been working from its misanthropic owner, who was murdered by an elderly peasant woman. The foreman (Pruckner) tries to bully the others to sell the farm to the neighboring gentry, Danniger (Wildgruber). When they refuse, the twosome try to sabotage the property, which leads to the foreman's death and places the peasants in the murderous path of the intolerant locals. German with subtitles. **94m/C VHS, DVD.** *GE* Tito Pruckner, Ulrich Wildgruber, Simon Schwarz, Sophie Rois, Lars Rudolph, Julia Gschnitzer; ***D:*** Stefan Ruzowitzky; ***W:*** Stefan Ruzowitzky; ***C:*** Peter von Haller; ***M:*** Erik Satie.

Inhibition 🦴 **1986** A beautiful heiress has lots of sex with different people in exotic locales. Softcore soap. **90m/C VHS.** Claudine Beccaire, Ilona Staller.

Inhumanity 🦴 **2000** Serial killer thriller is indescribably inept. Though the lead performances are mostly all right, supporting work is amateur. The film is padded with shots of traffic and buildings in Dallas. Lighting, writing, and directing are substandard. **90m/C DVD, Wide.** Todd Bridges, Faizon Love, Carl Jackson, Georgia Foy, Billy Davis; ***D:*** Carl Jackson; ***W:*** Carl Jackson; ***C:*** Kurt Ugland; ***M:*** Damon Criswell.

The Initiation 🦴 **1984 (R)** Trying to rid herself of a troublesome nightmare, a coed finds herself face-to-face with a psycho. Gory campus slaughterfest. **97m/C VHS.** Vera Miles, Clu Gulager, James Read, Daphne Zuniga; ***D:*** Larry Stewart.

Initiation of Sarah 🦴 **1978** College freshman joins a sorority, undergoes abusive initiation, and gains a supernatural revenge. "Carrie" rip-off. **100m/C VHS.** Kay Lenz, Shelley Winters, Kathryn Crosby, Morgan Brittany, Tony Bill, Tisa Farrow, Robert Hays, Morgan Fairchild; ***D:*** Robert Day. **TV**

The Inkwell 🦴🦴½ **1994 (R)** Quiet teenager Drew Tate finds first love when his family spends their vacation with relatives on Martha's Vineyard. Drew is drawn into the party atmosphere of the Inkwell, the area where affluent black professionals have summered for decades. Meanwhile, political differences between Drew's former Black Panther father and his conservative uncle threaten family harmony. Everything about the film has a sugary aura, with conflicts handled tastefully. Rich directs broadly, leading to some overacting. Film is set in 1976. **112m/C VHS.** Larenz Tate, Joe Morton, Phyllis Stickney, Jada Pinkett Smith; ***D:*** Matty Rich; ***W:*** Paris Qualles, Tom Ricostronza; ***C:*** John L. Demps Jr.; ***M:*** Terence Blanchard.

Inn of Temptation 🦴 **1986** A bunch of bowling buddies take off for Bangkok on an impulsive weekend, and meet lots of Oriental women. **72m/C VHS.** Michael Jacot, Claude Martin.

Inn of the Damned 🦴½ 1974 Detective looks into an inn where no one ever gets charged for an extra day; they simply die. Anderson is watchable. **92m/C VHS.** *AU* Alex Cord, Judith Anderson, Tony Bonner, Michael Craig, John Meillon; ***D:*** Terry Burke.

The Inn of the Sixth Happiness 🦴🦴🦴 1958 Inspiring story of Gladys Aylward, an English missionary in 1930s' China, who leads a group of children through war-torn countryside. Donat's last film. **158m/C VHS.** Ingrid Bergman, Robert Donat, Curt Jurgens; ***D:*** Mark Robson; ***C:*** Frederick A. (Freddie) Young; ***M:*** Malcolm Arnold. Natl. Bd. of Review '58: Actress (Bergman).

Inn on the River 🦴🦴½ 1962 Scotland Yard investigates a series of murders taking place on the waterfront by the "Shark's" gang. Remake of "The Return of the Frog." **95m/C VHS.** *GE* Klaus Kinski, Joachim Fuchsberger, Brigitte Grothum, Richard Much; ***D:*** Alfred Vohrer.

The Inner Circle 🦴½ 1946 A private detective, framed for murder by his secretary, has a limited amount of time to find the real murderer. Confusing. **57m/B VHS.** Adele Mara, Warren Douglas, William Frawley, Ricardo Cortez, Virginia Christine; ***D:*** Philip Ford.

The Inner Circle 🦴🦴🦴 1991 (PG-13) Ivan Sanshin is a meek, married man working as a movie projectionist for the KGB in 1935 Russia. Sanshin is taken by the KGB to the Kremlin to show movies, primarily Hollywood features, to leader Joseph Stalin, a job he cannot discuss with anyone, even his wife. Under the spell of Stalin's personality, Sanshin sees only what he's told and overlooks the oppression and persecution of the times. Based on the life of the projectionist who served from 1935 until Stalin's death in 1953. Filmed on location at the Kremlin. **122m/C VHS, 8mm.** Tom Hulce, Lolita (David) Davidovich, Bob Hoskins, Alexandre Zbruev, Maria Baranova, Feodor Chaliapin Jr., Bess Meyer; ***D:*** Andrei Konchalovsky; ***W:*** Andrei Konchalovsky, Anatoli Usov; ***M:*** Eduard Artemyev.

Inner Sanctum 🦴🦴 1948 Adequate tale of a young girl accosted by a gypsy who claims that tragedy awaits her. Based on a radio show of the same name. **62m/B VHS.** Chuck Russell, Mary Beth Hughes, Lee Patrick, Nana Bryant; ***D:*** Lew (Louis Friedlander) Landers.

Inner Sanctum woof! 1991 (R) Cheating husband hires sensuous nurse to tend invalid wife. You can guess the rest; in fact, you have to because the plot ultimately makes no sense. Available in R-rated and sex-drenched unrated editions. **87m/C VHS.** Tanya Roberts, Margaux Hemingway, Joseph Bottoms, Valerie Wildman, William Butler, Brett (Baxter) Clark; ***D:*** Fred Olen Ray.

Inner Sanctum 2 🦴½ 1994 (R) Jennifer Reed (Swope) had a breakdown and killed her husband in the first film. Now under a doctor's (Warner) care, Jennifer is under siege from her brother-in-law's (Nouri) evil plot to send her over the edge again and claim her fortune. As if that's not enough, Jennifer's also being stalked by a murderer. Also available in an unrated version. **90m/C VHS.** Michael Nouri, Tracy Brooks Swope, Sandahl Bergman, David Warner, Jennifer Ciesar, Margaux Hemingway; ***D:*** Fred Olen Ray; ***W:*** Sherman Scott; ***M:*** Chuck Cirino.

Innerspace 🦴🦴½ 1987 (PG) A space pilot, miniaturized for a journey through a lab rat a la "Fantastic Voyage," is accidentally injected into a nebbish supermarket clerk, and together they nab some bad guys and get the girl. Award-winning special effects support some funny moments between micro Quaid and nerdy Short, with Ryan producing the confused romantic interest. **120m/C VHS, 8mm.** Dennis Quaid, Martin Short, Meg Ryan, Kevin McCarthy, Fiona Lewis, Henry Gibson, Robert Picardo, John Hora, Wendy Schaal, Orson Bean, Chuck Jones, William Schallert, Dick Miller, Vernon Wells, Harold Sylvester, Kevin Hooks, Kathleen Freeman, Kenneth Tobey; ***D:*** Joe Dante; ***W:*** Jeffrey Boam, Chip Proser; ***M:*** Jerry Goldsmith. Oscars '87: Visual FX.

Innocence Unprotected 🦴🦴½ 1968 A film collage that contains footage from the 1942 film "Innocence Unprotected," the story of an acrobat trying to save an orphan from her wicked stepmother, newsreels from Nazi-occupied Yugoslavia, and interviews from 1968 with people who were in the film. Confiscated by the Nazis during final production, "Innocence Unprotected" was discovered by director Makavejev, who worked it into the collage. Filmed in color and black and white; in Serbian with English subtitles. **78m/C VHS.** *YU* Dragoljub Aleksic, Ana Milosavljevic, Vera Jovanovic; ***D:*** Dusan Makavejev; ***W:*** Dusan Makavejev.

The Innocent 🦴🦴🦴½ *L'Innocente; The Intruder* 1976 (R) The setting: turn of the century Rome, ablaze with atheism and free love. The story: Giannini's a Sicilian aristocrat who ignores wife Antonelli and dallies with scheming mistress O'Neill. Discovering his wife's infidelity, he's profoundly disillusioned, and his manly notion of self disintegrates. Visconti's last film, it was an art house fave and is considered by many to be his best. Lavishly photographed, well set and costumed, and true to the Gabrielle D'Annunzio's novel. In Italian with English subtitles. **125m/C VHS.** *IT* Laura Antonelli, Jennifer O'Neill, Giancarlo Giannini, Didier Haudepin, Marc Porel; ***D:*** Luchino Visconti; ***W:*** Luchino Visconti, Suso Cecchi D'Amico; ***C:*** Pasqualino De Santis.

The Innocent 🦴🦴½ 1993 (R) Cold War thriller has naive British engineer Leonard Markham (Scott) sent to Berlin in 1955 by Brits who are warily cooperating with the U.S. forces. He's turned over to CIA operator Bob Glass (Hopkins) and asked to intercept communications between East Germany and the Soviet Union. Glass continually warns Markham not to trust anyone, including Maria (Rossellini), the married German woman with whom he begins an affair. Failure to build necessary suspense and performances leads to disappointing one-note display. Based on the novel by McEwan. **97m/C VHS.** *GE GB* Anthony Hopkins, Campbell Scott, Isabella Rossellini, Hart Bochner, James Grant, Jeremy Sinden, Ronald Nitschke; ***D:*** John Schlesinger; ***W:*** Ian McEwan; ***M:*** Gerald Gouriet.

Innocent Blood 🦴🦴 1992 (R) A mediocre modern-day vampire/gangster combo with the beautiful (though red-eyed) Parillaud as the woman with a taste for someone "Italian." Unfortunately, she doesn't finish off her latest meal—mobster Loggia—who finds being undead very useful to his vicious work. LaPaglia plays the bewildered, love-struck cop involved with the vamp. Parillaud appears nude in several scenes and the gore and violence are stomach-turning. **112m/C VHS, DVD, Wide.** Anne Parillaud, Anthony LaPaglia, Robert Loggia, David Proval, Don Rickles, Rocco Sisto, Kim Coates, Chazz Palminteri, Angela Bassett, Tom Savini, Frank Oz, Forrest J Ackerman, Sam Raimi, Dario Argento, Linnea Quigley; ***D:*** John Landis; ***W:*** Michael Wolk; ***C:*** Mac Ahlberg; ***M:*** Ira Newborn.

Innocent Lies 🦴🦴½ 1995 (R) In 1938, British policeman Alan Cross (Dunbar) heads for an island off the French coast to look into the suicide of a colleague who was investigating the expatriate Graves family. There are family tensions, skeletons in the closet, and some Nazi-sympathizers all mixed together in an old-fashioned but satisfying stew. **88m/C VHS.** *FR GB* Adrian Dunbar, Stephen Dorff, Gabrielle Anwar, Joanna Lumley; ***D:*** Patrick Dewolf; ***W:*** Kerry Crabbe, Patrick Dewolf; ***C:*** Patrick Blossier; ***M:*** Alexandre Desplat.

An Innocent Man 🦴🦴½ 1989 (R) Uneven story of Selleck, an ordinary family man and airline mechanic, framed as a drug dealer and sent to prison. **113m/C VHS.** Tom Selleck, F. Murray Abraham, Laila Robins, David Rasche, Richard Young, Badja (Medu) Djola; ***D:*** Peter Yates; ***W:*** Larry Brothers; ***M:*** Howard Shore.

Innocent Prey 🦴🦴 1988 (R) When a woman finally summons the courage to bid hasta la vista to her abusive husband, it turns out he's not so quick to say ciao. Definitely not a highlight in Balsam's career. **88m/C VHS.** *AU* P.J. Soles, Martin Balsam, Kit Taylor, Grigor Taylor, John Warnock, Susan Stenmark, Richard Morgan; ***D:*** Colin Eggleston.

The Innocent Sleep 🦴🦴½ 1995 (R) Adequate thriller that stays true to genre cliches. Homeless drunk Alan Terry (Graves) witnesses an execution (by hanging) from London's Tower Bridge, near where he's bedded down. He's spotted but manages to escape. When he tries to report the crime, Terry realizes that one of the killers is police investigator Matheson (Gambon). Terry then goes to tabloid journalist Billie Hayman (Sciorra) for help but her probing into the death leads to even more danger. **96m/C VHS.** *GB* Rupert Graves, Annabella Sciorra, Michael Gambon, Franco Nero, Graham Crowden, John Hannah; ***D:*** Scott Michell; ***W:*** Ray Villis; ***C:*** Alan Dunlop; ***M:*** Mark Ayres.

Innocent Sorcerers 🦴🦴 *Niewinni Czarodzieje* 1960 Ironic comedy about aimless '60s Polish youth that finds a young doctor having trouble committing himself to his superficial girlfriend and coping with the problems of his cynical friends. Polish with subtitles. **86m/B VHS.** *PL* Tadeusz Lomnicki, Zbigniew Cybulski, Roman Polanski, Krystyna Stypulkowska, Jerzy Skolimowski; ***D:*** Andrzej Wajda; ***W:*** Jerzy Skolimowski, Andrzej Wajda; ***M:*** Krzysztof Komeda.

Innocent Victim 🦴 *The Tree of Hands* 1990 (R) Convoluted tale of revenge and madness. Bacall plays a mad grandmother who kidnaps a boy to take the place of her dead grandson. The kidnapped boy's stepfather then is accused of murdering him, and starts murdering others to get the boy back. **100m/C VHS.** Lauren Bacall, Helen Shaver, Paul McGann, Peter Firth; ***D:*** Giles Foster.

The Innocents 🦴🦴🦴½ 1961 Incredibly creepy version of Henry James' "The Turn of the Screw." Minister's daughter, Miss Giddens (Kerr), is hired by Redgrave (known only as "The Uncle") as governess to young Flora (Franklin) and her brother Miles (Stephens) at his country estate. Miss Giddens begins to see the specters of a man and a woman and is told her descriptions match that of former estate manager Peter Quint and the last governess, his mistress, whose influence on the children was thought to be malevolent. Indeed, Miss Giddens believes the children are possessed by evil—but is it true or a product of her own hysteria? **85m/B VHS.** *GB* Deborah Kerr, Michael Redgrave, Pamela Franklin, Martin Stephens, Peter Wyngarde, Megs Jenkins, Clytie Jessop, Isla Cameron, Eric Woodburn; ***D:*** Jack Clayton; ***W:*** Truman Capote, William Archibald, John Mortimer; ***C:*** Freddie Francis; ***M:*** Georges Auric.

Innocents 🦴½ *Dark Summer* 2000 Boring thriller about French cellist Gerard (Anglade) who gets involved with beautiful Megan (Nielsen) and her disturbed younger sister, Dominique (Kirshner). After the sisters' father (Langella) dies, the trio head to Seattle to tell mom (Archer) she's now a widow. The road trip takes a turn for the worst when a judge (Culp) gets killed and Gerard gets blamed. Never does make much sense. **90m/C VHS, DVD.** *CA* Jean-Hugues Anglade, Connie Nielsen, Mia Kirshner, Robert Culp, Anne Archer, Keith David, Joseph Culp; ***Cameos:*** Frank Langella; ***D:*** Gregory Marquette; ***W:*** Gregory Marquette; ***C:*** Bruce Worrall; ***M:*** Michel Colombier.

The Innocents Abroad 🦴🦴½ 1984 Entertaining adaptation of Mark Twain's novel about a group of naive Americans cruising the Mediterranean. Ensemble cast offers some surprising performances. Originally produced for PBS. **116m/C VHS.** Craig Wasson, Brooke Adams, David Ogden Stiers.

Innocents in Paris 🦴🦴½ 1953 A group of seven Britons visit Paris for the first time. A bit long but enough ooo-la-la to satisfy. **89m/B VHS.** *GB* Alastair Sim, Laurence Harvey, Jimmy Edwards, Claire Bloom, Margaret Rutherford; ***D:*** Gordon Parry.

Innocents with Dirty Hands 🦴🦴 *Innocents aux Mains Sales* 1975 Pulp twists abound in this thriller based on the novel "The Damned Innocents" by Richard Neely and set in sunny St. Tropez. Wealthy Louis Wormser (Steiger) has an unhappy marriage to trophy wife, Julie (Schneider), who turns out to be having an affair with neighbor, Jeff (Giusti). The lovers decide to kill Louis, dump the body, and keep things quiet until Julie can inherit. Unfortunately, a couple of police detectives don't believe Julie's story and little clues keep popping up. Oh yeah, nobody stays dead in this film. French with subtitles. **?m/C VHS.** *FR* Rod Steiger, Romy Schneider, Paul(o) Giusti, Jean Rochefort, Pierre Santini, Francois Perrot, Hans-Christian Blech, Francois Maistre; ***D:*** Claude Chabrol; ***W:*** Claude Chabrol; ***C:*** Jean Rabier; ***M:*** Pierre Jansen.

The Inquiry 🦴🦴½ 1987 A new twist on the resurrection of Christ. Carradine senses a cover-up when he's sent from Rome to investigate the problem of Christ's missing corpse. He retraces Christ's final days to solve the case in this interesting, offbeat film. Dubbed. **107m/C VHS.** *IT* Keith Carradine, Harvey Keitel, Phyllis Logan, Angelo Infanti, Lina Sastri; ***D:*** Damiano Damiani.

Inquisition 🦴½ 1976 Naschy is a 16th century witch hunting judge who finds himself accused of witchcraft. **85m/C VHS.** *SP* Paul (Jacinto Molina) Naschy, Jacinto (Jack) Molina, Daniela Giordano, Juan Gallardo, Monica Randall; ***D:*** Jacinto (Jack) Molina; ***W:*** Jacinto (Jack) Molina.

Insanity 🦴 1982 A film director becomes violently obsessed with a beautiful actress. **101m/C VHS.** Terence Stamp, Fernando Rey, Corinne Clery.

The Insect Woman 🦴🦴🦴 *The Insect; Nippon Konchuki* 1963 Chronicles 45 years in the life of a woman who must work with the diligence of an ant in order to survive. Thoughtfully reflects the exploitation of women and the cruelty of human nature in Japanese society. Beautiful performance from Hidari, who ages from girlhood to middle age. In Japanese with English subtitles. **123m/B VHS.** *JP* Sachiko Hidari, Yitsuko Yoshimura, Hiroyuki Nagaes, Sumie Sasaki; ***D:*** Shohei Imamura.

Inseminoid woof! *Horror Planet* 1980 (R) Alien creature needs a chance to breed before moving on to spread its horror. When a group of explorers disturbs it, the years of waiting are over, and the unlucky mother-to-be will never be the same. Graphic and sensationalistic, capitalizing on the popularity of "Aliens." **93m/C VHS, DVD, Wide.** *GB* Robin Clarke, Jennifer Ashley, Stephanie Beacham, Judy Geeson, Stephen Grives, Victoria Tennant; ***D:*** Norman J. Warren; ***W:*** Gloria Maley, Nick Maley; ***C:*** John Metcalfe; ***M:*** John Scott.

Inserts 🦴 1976 (R) A formerly successful director has been reduced to making porno films in this pretentious, long-winded effort set in a crumbling Hollywood mansion in the 1930s. Affected, windbaggish performances kill it. **99m/C VHS.** *GB* Richard Dreyfuss, Jessica Harper, Veronica Cartwright, Bob Hoskins; ***D:*** John Byrum; ***W:*** John Byrum.

Inside 🦴🦴🦴 1996 (R) Harrowing anti-apartheid drama finds university professor and white Afrikaaner Peter Martin Strydom (Stoltz) being held in a Johannesburg government prison. He's being interrogated by Col. Kruger (Hawthorne), head of the prison security force, supposedly for conspiracy against the South African regime. Tortured, Strydom's will begins to break as the drama flashes forward ten years, with Colonel Kruger now subjected to interrogation by a nameless black questioner (Gossett Jr.) investigating human rights crimes, including Strydom's fate. **94m/C VHS, DVD.** Eric Stoltz, Nigel Hawthorne, Louis Gossett Jr.; ***D:*** Arthur Penn; ***W:*** Bima Stagg; ***C:*** Jan Weincke; ***M:*** Robert Levin. CABLE

Inside Daisy Clover 🦴🦴½ 1965 Wood is the self-sufficient, junior delinquent waif who becomes a teenage musical star and pays the price for fame in this Hollywood saga set in the 1930s. Discovered by tyrannical studio head Plummer, Daisy is given her big break and taken under his wing for grooming as Swan Studio's newest sensation. She falls for fellow performer, matinee idol Redford, who has some secrets of his own, and eventually has a breakdown from the career pressure. Glossy melodrama is filled with over-the-top performances but its sheer silliness makes it amusing. **128m/C VHS, Wide.** Natalie Wood, Christopher Plummer, Robert Redford, Ruth Gordon, Roddy McDowall, Katharine Bard; *D:* Robert Mulligan; *W:* Gavin Lambert; *C:* Charles B(ryant) Lang Jr.; *M:* Andre Previn. Golden Globes '66: Support. Actress (Gordon).

Inside Edge ✓✓ **1992 (R)** Urban crime thriller is a complex yet surprisingly uninteresting story of a police officer who falls for the girlfriend of the drug lord he is chasing. Filled with the standard genre violence. **84m/C VHS.** Michael Madsen, Richard Lynch, Rosie Vela, Tony Peck, George Jenesky, Branscombe Richmond; *D:* Warren Clark; *W:* William Tannen.

Inside Information ✓ **1934** With Tarzan's help, a cop searches out the leader of a ring of jewel thieves. **51m/B VHS.** Rex Lease, Marion Shilling, Philo (Philip, P.H., P.M.) McCullough.

The Inside Man ✓✓½ **1984** Double agents struggle to find a submarine-detecting laser device. Based on true incidents in which a soviet sub ran aground in Sweden. Made in Sweden; dubbed. **90m/C VHS, DVD.** *SW* Dennis Hopper, Hardy Kruger, Gosta Ekman Jr., David Wilson; *D:* Tom Clegg; *W:* Alan Plater; *C:* Jorgen Persson; *M:* Stefan Nilsson.

Inside Monkey Zetterland ✓✓ **1993 (R)** Monkey Zetterland (Antin) is a screenwriter and former actor with an eccentric family. His actress mother is neurotically insecure and a nag; his father is an aging hippie who only shows up at Thanksgiving; his lesbian sister Grace is trying to get over a failed relationship; and his brother Brent is totally self-absorbed. Add to this menage his equally lunatic friends: Imogene, the compulsive talker and exhibitionist; his vicious girlfriend Daphne; and frightening married couple Sophie and Sasha. Meanwhile, Monkey tries to survive amidst the chaos. Interesting cast but lots of camera tricks do not a successful film make and the effort to be hip is all too apparent. **92m/C VHS.** Steve Antin, Patricia Arquette, Sandra Bernhard, Sofia Coppola, Tate Donovan, Katherine Helmond, Bo Hopkins, Debi Mazar, Martha Plimpton, Rupert Everett, Ricki Lake, Lance Loud, Frances Bay, Luca Bercovici; *D:* Jefery Levy; *W:* John Boskovich, Steve Antin; *C:* Christopher Taylor; *M:* Rick Cox, Jeff Elmassian.

Inside Moves ✓✓½ **1980 (PG)** A look at handicapped citizens trying to make it in everyday life, focusing on the relationship between an insecure, failed suicide and a volatile man who is only a knee operation away from a dreamed-about basketball career. **113m/C VHS.** John Savage, Diana Scarwid, David Morse, Amy Wright; *D:* Richard Donner; *W:* Valerie Curtin, Barry Levinson; *M:* John Barry.

Inside Out ✓✓½ *The Golden Heist; Hitler's Gold* **1975 (PG)** An ex-GI, a jewel thief and a German POW camp commandant band together to find a stolen shipment of Nazi gold behind the Iron Curtain. To find the gold, they help a Nazi prisoner who knows the secret to break out of prison. Good action caper. **97m/C VHS.** *GB* Telly Savalas, Robert Culp, James Mason, Aldo Ray, Doris Kunstmann; *D:* Peter Duffell.

Inside Out ✓✓½ **1991 (R)** Hiding in his apartment from a world which terrifies him, Jimmy doesn't feel he's missing much—since he has the necessary women and bookies come to him. He soon finds he's not quite as safe as he thought, and the only way out is "out there." Fine performance from Gould, suspenseful pacing. **87m/C VHS.** Elliott Gould, Jennifer Tilly, Howard Hesseman, Beah Richards, Timothy Scott, Sandy McPeak, Dana Elcar, Meshach Taylor, Nicole Norman; *D:* Robert Taicher; *W:* Robert Taicher.

Inside the Law ✓✓ **1942** A gang of crooks takes over a bank and must stay "inside the law" and resist their natural inclinations. Lots of comic situations. **65m/B VHS.** Wallace Ford, Frank Sully, Harry Holman, Luana Walters, Lafe (Lafayette) McKee, Danny Duncan, Earle Hodgins; *D:* Hamilton MacFadden.

Inside the Lines ✓✓ **1930** A WWI tale of espionage and counter-espionage. **73m/B VHS.** Betty Compson, Montagu Love, Mischa Auer, Ralph Forbes.

Inside the Third Reich ✓✓½ **1982** Miniseries detailing the rise to power within the Third Reich of Albert Speer, top advisor to Hitler. Based on Speer's rather self-serving memoirs. **250m/C VHS.** Derek Jacobi, Rutger Hauer, John Gielgud, Blythe Danner, Maria Schell, Ian Holm, Trevor Howard, Randy Quaid, Viveca Lindfors, Robert Vaughn, Stephen Collins, Elke Sommer, Renee Soutendijk; *D:* Marvin J. Chomsky. **TV**

The Insider ✓✓✓½ **1999 (R)** Riveting and controversial film that caused a real-life snit at "60 Minutes" over the facts and portrayals in the story. After Jeffrey Wigand (Crowe) is fired from his top-level tobacco company job, he turns whistle-blower, claiming his former employers lied about the dangers of cigarettes. Veteran "60 Minutes" producer Lowell Bergman (Pacino) and newsman Mike Wallace (Plummer) pursue the story—only to be shot down by their own network. The fallout causes ethical consequences for all involved. Performances are outstanding—from the chameleon Crowe to the relatively subdued Pacino and the slyly pompous Plummer. Based on a "Vanity Fair" magazine article. **157m/C VHS, DVD.** Russell Crowe, Al Pacino, Christopher Plummer, Gina Gershon, Philip Baker Hall, Diane Venora, Lindsay Crouse, Debi Mazar, Stephen Tobolowsky, Colm Feore, Bruce McGill, Michael Gambon, Rip Torn, Lynne Thigpen, Hallie Kate Eisenberg, Michael Paul Chan, Wings Hauser, Pete Hamill, Nestor Serrano, Michael Moore; *D:* Michael Mann; *W:* Michael Mann, Eric Roth; *C:* Dante Spinotti; *M:* Graeme Revell. L.A. Film Critics '99: Actor (Crowe), Cinematog., Film, Support. Actor (Plummer); Natl. Bd. of Review '99: Actor (Crowe); Natl. Soc. Film Critics '99: Actor (Crowe), Support. Actor (Plummer); Broadcast Film Critics '99: Actor (Crowe).

Insignificance ✓✓✓ **1985** A film about an imaginary night spent in a New York hotel by characters who resemble Marilyn Monroe, Albert Einstein, Joe McCarthy, and Joe DiMaggio. Entertaining and often amusing as it follows the characters as they discuss theory and relativity, the Russians, and baseball among other things. **110m/C VHS.** *GB* Gary Busey, Tony Curtis, Theresa Russell, Michael Emil, Will Sampson; *D:* Nicolas Roeg; *W:* Terry Johnson; *C:* Peter Hannan; *M:* Hans Zimmer.

Insomnia ✓✓✓ **1997** After a young girl is murdered in northern Norway, Oslo detective Jonas Engstrom (Skarsgard) and his partner Erik Vik (Ousdal) are called in to solve the crime, aided by local cop Hilde Hagen (Armand). Engstrom accidentally shoots and kills his partner during a stakeout in the fog and attempts to cover up one killing while uncovering another. He begins to unravel when his conscience and the unrelenting sun cause not only insomnia, but a moral breakdown. His nerves jangle as he comes under suspicion from Hilde. He is also forced into a face-to-face climax with the killer, who witnessed the shooting. Excellent feature debut for Norwegian director Erik Skjoldbjaerg. **97m/C VHS, DVD.** *NO* Stellan Skarsgard, Sverre Anker Ousdal, Maria Bonnevie, Bjorn Floberg, Gisken Armand, Marianne O. Ulrichsen, Maria Mathiesen; *D:* Erik Skjoldbjaerg; *W:* Nikolaj Frobenius; *C:* Erling Thurmann-Andersen; *M:* Geir Jenssen.

Insomnia ✓✓✓½ **2002 (R)** American remake of a 1997 Norwegian films finds veteran police detective Will Dormer (Pacino), under Internal Affairs investigation back home, sent to a small Alaskan town to investigate the murder of a 17-year-old girl. Primary suspect Williams plays a game of psychological chicken after witnessing a moment of Dormer's increasing weakness. Pacino, in service to an excellent script, gives an outstanding performance as the guilt-ridden, exhausted supercop, and Swank impresses (again) as the idol-worshipping but self-assured local deputy. "Memento" helmer Nolan proves there doesn't have to be a letdown after a breakout, groundbreaking hit. **116m/C VHS, DVD.** *US* Al Pacino, Robin Williams, Hilary Swank, Maura Tierney, Martin Donovan, Nicky Katt, Paul Dooley, Jonathan Jackson, Katharine Isabelle, Larry Holden; *D:* Christopher Nolan; *W:* Hillary Seitz; *C:* Wally Pfister; *M:* David Julyan.

Inspector Gadget ✓✓ **1999 (PG)** Go-go gadget script rewrite! The popular cartoon character goes live-action with Broderick in the title role. Blown to pieces by the evil Dr. Claw (Everett), a naive security guard is put back together by scientist Brenda Bradford (Fisher) with a vast array of grafted-on gizmos. Gadget becomes the world's top detective and discovers that Claw also murdered Brenda's father. In his battle against Claw, he is forced to fight his evil robot twin in order to clear his own name. The computer generated effects are eye-catching but far too brief, and Broderick is forced to react lamely to them most of the time. **77m/C VHS, DVD.** Matthew Broderick, Rupert Everett, Joely Fisher, Michelle Trachtenberg, Dabney Coleman, Andy Dick, Michael G. (Mike) Hagerty, Rene Auberjonois, Frances Bay; *D:* David Kellogg; *W:* Kerry Ehrin, Zak Penn; *C:* Adam Greenberg; *M:* John Debney; *V:* Don Adams, D.L. Hughley.

The Inspector General ✓✓✓ *Happy Times* **1949** Classic Kaye craziness of mistaken identities with the master comic portraying a carnival medicine man who is mistaken by the villagers for their feared Inspector General. If you like Kaye's manic performance, you'll enjoy this one. ♫The Gypsy Drinking Song; Onward Onward; The Medicine Show; The Inspector General; Lonely Heart; Soliloquy For Three Heads; Happy Times; Brodny. **103m/C VHS.** Danny Kaye, Walter Slezak, Barbara Bates, Elsa Lanchester, Gene Lockhart, Walter Catlett, Alan Hale; *D:* Henry Koster; *W:* Harry Kurnitz, Philip Rapp; *C:* Elwood "Woody" Bredell; *M:* Johnny Green. Golden Globes '50: Score.

The Inspector General ✓✓½ **1954** The filmed performance of Gogol's great play by the Moscow Art Theatre, wherein a provincial town panics when they mistake a wandering moron for the Inspector come to check up on them. In Russian with English subtitles. **128m/B VHS.** *RU* *D:* Vladimir Petrov.

Inspector Hornleigh ✓✓½ **1939** A pair of bumbling detectives arrive on the scene when a Chancellor's fortune is stolen. Fine comedy, although the Scottish and British accents can be rather thick now and again. **76m/B VHS.** *GB* Gordon Harker, Alastair Sim, Miki Hood, Wally Patch, Steven Geray, Edward Underdown, Hugh Williams, Gibb McLaughlin; *D:* Eugene Forde.

The Inspectors ✓½ **1998** Remarkably dull thriller about postal inspectors Silverman and Gossett Jr., who are tracking a mail bomber. **91m/C VHS, DVD.** Louis Gossett Jr., Jonathan Silverman; *D:* Brad Turner; *W:* Bruce Zimmerman; *C:* Albert J. Dunk; *M:* Terry Frewer. **CABLE**

Instant Justice ✓½ *Marine Issue* **1986 (R)** A professional Marine jeopardizes his military career by avenging his sister's murder, vigilante style. Exclusive action. **101m/C VHS.** *GB* Michael Pare, Tawny Kitaen, Charles Napier; *D:* Craig T. Rumar.

Instant Karma ✓½ **1990** Would be comedy depicts young man's far fetched attempts to score babewise. Ask no more what happened to erstwhile teen heart throb Cassidy: he suffers from a major bout of bad karma. **94m/C VHS.** Craig Sheffer, Chelsea Noble, David Cassidy, Alan Blumenfeld, Glen Hirsch, Marty Ingels, Orson Bean; *D:* Roderick Taylor.

Instinct ✓✓ **1999 (R)** Primatologist Ethan Powell (Hopkins) has been in the African jungle studying gorillas a little too long, and has turned apeman, killing poachers threatening his primate friends. Since he's been returned to the U.S. and incarcerated in a Miami prison ward for for the insane, he's taken a vow of silence. Theo Caulder (Gooding) is an ambitious shrink who's sent to see if Powell is still (or ever was) a clinical whacko. Hopkins mainly gets to chew the scenery and leave Gooding wide-eyed in his wake. "Suggested" by the novel "Ishmael" by Daniel Quinn. **123m/C VHS, DVD.** Anthony Hopkins, Cuba Gooding Jr., Donald Sutherland, George Dzundza, Maura Tierney, John Ashton, Paul Bates, John Aylward; *D:* Jon Turteltaub; *W:* Gerald Di Pego; *C:* Philippe Rousselot; *M:* Danny Elfman.

Institue Benjamenta or This Dream People Call Human Life ✓✓ **1995** The Brothers Quay's first live-action feature is a surreal nightmareish fairytale based on the 1905 novel "Jakob von Gunten" by Robert Waiser. Jakob (Rylance) arrives at the secluded Institute Benjamenta, which is run by Lisa (Krige) and her brother Johannes (John), to train as a servant. He becomes a favorite of the enigmatic duo and tries to decide what is real and what isn't. Eccentric and wonderfully photographed by Knowland. **105m/B VHS, DVD, Wide.** *GB* Mark Rylance, Alice Krige, Gottfried John; *D:* Stephen Quay, Timothy Quay; *W:* Stephen Quay, Timothy Quay, Allan Passes; *C:* Nicholas D. Knowland; *M:* Lech Jankowski.

The Instructor ✓ **1983** The head of a karate school proves the value of his skill when threatened by the owner of a rival school. **91m/C VHS.** Don Bendell, Bob Chaney, Bob Saal, Lynday Scharnott; *D:* Don Bendell.

Interceptor ✓✓ **1992 (R)** Hijackers attempt to steal a Stealth Bomber in this action-adventure saga which features virtual reality computer-generated imagery in its combat sequences. **92m/C VHS, DVD.** Juergen Prochnow, Andrew Divoff, Elizabeth Morehead; *D:* Michael Cohn; *W:* John Brancato; *M:* Rick Marvin.

Interceptor Force ✓✓ **1999 (R)** The Interceptors are a top-secret group of soldiers trained for encounters with aliens. Their latest assignment involves a UFO in a remote community and a species that's capable of morphing into any form. And if they can't clean up the mess in 24 hours, the military will nuke the region. **91m/C VHS, DVD, Wide.** Olivier Gruner, Brad Dourif, Glenn Plummer, Ernie Hudson, Ken Olandt, Angel Boris, Holly Fields; *D:* Phillip J. Roth; *W:* Phillip J. Roth, Martin Lazarus. **VIDEO**

Interface ✓½ **1984** A computer game gets out of hand at a university, turning the tunnels beneath the campus into a battleground of good and evil. **88m/C VHS.** John Davies, Laura Lane, Matthew Sacks.

Interiors ✓✓✓½ **1978 (R)** Ultra serious, Bergmanesque drama about three neurotic adult sisters, coping with the dissolution of their family. When Father decides to leave mentally unbalanced mother for a divorcee, the daughters are shocked and bewildered. Depressing and humorless, but fine performances all the way around, supported by the elegant camera work of Gordon Willis. **95m/C VHS, DVD, Wide.** Diane Keaton, Mary Beth Hurt, E.G. Marshall, Geraldine Page, Richard Jordan, Sam Waterston, Kristin Griffith, Maureen Stapleton; *D:* Woody Allen; *W:* Woody Allen; *C:* Gordon Willis. British Acad. '78: Support. Actress (Page); L.A. Film Critics '78: Support. Actress (Stapleton).

Interlocked ✓½ *A Bold Affair* **1998 (R)** Another psycho-babe thriller. Pregnant Emily Anderson (Ferguson) and happy hubby Michael (Trachta) befriend Eva (Harrison), which turns into trouble. Harrison and Trachta previously worked together on TV soap "The Bold & the Beautiful." **94m/C VHS, DVD.** Jeff Trachta, Schae Harrison, Sandra Ferguson, George Alvarez, Bruce Kirby; *D:* Rick Jacobson; *W:* Al Sophianopoulos; *C:* Jesse Weathington. **VIDEO**

Intermezzo ✓✓✓ *Interlude* **1936** Married violinist Ekman meets pianist Bergman and they fall in love. He deserts his family to tour with Bergman, but the feelings for his wife and children become too much. When Bergman sees their love won't last, she leaves him. Shakily, he returns home and as his daughter runs to greet him, she is hit by a truck and he realizes that his family is his true love. One of the great grab-your-hanky melodramas. In Swedish with English subtitles. 1939 English re-make features Bergman's American film debut. **88m/B VHS, DVD.** *SW* Gosta Ekman, Inga Tidblad, Ingrid Bergman, Erik "Bullen" Berglund, Anders Henrikson, Hasse (Hans) Ekman, Britt Hagman, Hugo Bjorne; *D:* Gustaf Molander; *W:* Gustaf Molander, Gosta Stevens; *C:* Ake Dahlqvist; *M:* Heinz Provost.

Intermezzo 𝒮𝒮𝒮 *Intermezzo: A Love Story* **1939** Fine, though weepy, love story of a renowned, married violinist who has an affair with his stunningly beautiful protege (Bergman), but while on concert tour realizes that his wife and children hold his heart, and he returns to them. A re-make of the 1936 Swedish film, it's best known as Bergman's American debut. Howard's violin playing was dubbed by Jascha Heifetz. **70m/B VHS.** *IT* Ingrid Bergman, Leslie Howard, Edna Best, Ann E. Todd; ***D:*** Gregory Ratoff; ***C:*** Gregg Toland; ***M:*** Max Steiner.

Intern 𝒮½ **2000** Satire on the fashion industry is filled with insider chit-chat and cameos from fashionistas and designers, takes a lot of well-placed digs, and is finally as superficial and throw away as the world it depicts. Naive Jocelyn (Swain) is an intern at fashion magazine Skirt who is desperate to fit in. But everyone is more paranoid and mean-spirited than usual because there's an insider giving the rag's best ideas to archival Vogue. **93m/C VHS, DVD.** Dominique Swain, Benjamin Pullen, Peggy Lipton, Joan Rivers, David Deblinger, Dwight Ewell, Billy Porter, Anna Thompson, Paulina Porizkova, Kathy Griffin; ***D:*** Michael Lange; ***W:*** Caroline Doyle, Jill Kopelman; ***C:*** Rodney Charters; ***M:*** Jimmy Harry.

Internal Affairs 𝒮𝒮½ **1990 (R)** Wild, sexually charged action piece about an Internal Affairs officer for the L.A.P.D. (Garcia) who becomes obsessed with exposing a sleazy, corrupt street cop (Gere). Drama becomes illogical, but boasts excellent, strung out performances, especially Gere as the creepy degenerate you'd love to bust. **114m/C VHS, DVD, 8mm, Wide.** Elijah Wood, Arlen Dean Snyder, Faye Grant, John Capodice, Xander Berkeley, John Kapelos, Richard Gere, Andy Garcia, Laurie Metcalf, Ron Vawter, Marco Rodriguez, Nancy Travis, William Baldwin, Richard Bradford, Annabella Sciorra, Michael Beach, Mike Figgis; ***D:*** Mike Figgis; ***W:*** Henry Bean; ***C:*** John A. Alonzo; ***M:*** Brian Banks, Mike Figgis.

International Crime 𝒮𝒮 **1937** Radio hero The Shadow solves a tough crime in this adventure film. **62m/B VHS.** Rod La Rocque, Astrid Allwyn, Wilhelm von Brinken; ***D:*** Charles Lamont.

International House 𝒮𝒮½ **1933** A wacky Dada-esque Hollywood farce about an incredible array of travelers quarantined in a Shanghai hotel where a mad doctor has perfected television. Essentially a burlesque compilation of skits, gags, and routines. Guest stars Rudy Vallee, Baby Rose Marie, and Cab Calloway appear on the quaint "TV" device, in musical sequences. ♫Tea Cup; Thank Heaven For You; My Bluebirds are Singing the Blues; Reefer Man. **72m/B VHS.** W.C. Fields, Peggy Hopkins Joyce, Rudy Vallee, George Burns, Cab Calloway, Sari Maritza, Gracie Allen, Bela Lugosi, Sterling Holloway, Baby Rose Marie; ***D:*** Edward Sutherland.

International Lady 𝒮𝒮½ **1941** Sexy musician Carla (Massey) travels the world performing and spying for the Germans in the early days of WWII. Brent and Rathbone are the American and British agents sent to capture the spy. Things get complicated when Brent falls for her. Romantic spy thriller has its lighter moments. **102m/B VHS.** Ilona Massey, George Brent, Basil Rathbone, George Zucco, Gene Lockhart, Clayton Moore, Charles D. Brown, Marjorie Gateson, Gordon DeMain, Leyland Hodgson, Martin Kosleck, Jack Mulhall, Frederick Worlock, William Forrest, Marten Lamont, Selmer Jackson; ***D:*** Tim Whelan; ***W:*** Howard Estabrook; ***C:*** Hal Mohr; ***M:*** Lucien Moraweck.

Internationai Velvet 𝒮½ **1978 (PG)** Why did they bother? This dismal and long overdue sequel to "National Velvet," finds the adult Velvet, with live-in companion (Plummer), grooming her orphaned niece (O'Neal) to become an Olympic champanion horsewoman. O'Neal's way out of her league although Plummer and Hopkins give good performances and the sentiment is kept at a trot. **126m/C VHS.** *GB* Tatum O'Neal, Anthony Hopkins, Christopher Plummer; ***D:*** Bryan Forbes.

Internecine Project 𝒮𝒮½ **1973 (PG)** Stylistic espionage tale with Coburn's English professor acting as the mastermind behind an unusual series of murders where industrial spies kill each other, so Coburn can garner a top government job in D.C. Unexpected ending is worth the viewing. Based on Mort Elkind's novel. **89m/C VHS.** *GB* James Coburn, Lee Grant, Harry Andrews, Keenan Wynn; ***D:*** Ken Hughes; ***W:*** Barry Levinson; ***C:*** Geoffrey Unsworth.

Internes Can't Take Money 𝒮𝒮½ **1937** With the help of McCrea and gangster Nolan, widow Stanwyck is desperately trying to find the daughter her bank robber husband hid before he died. Young doctor McCrea must save the life of another gangster who knows the whereabouts of the toddler. The first film featuring writer Max Brand's Dr. Kildare characters, which later became part of a series starring Lew Ayres and Laraine Day. **79m/B VHS.** Barbara Stanwyck, Joel McCrea, Lloyd Nolan, Stanley Ridges, Lee Bowman, Irving Bacon; ***D:*** Alfred Santell; ***W:*** Rian James, Theodore Reeves; ***C:*** Theodor Sparkuhl; ***M:*** Gregory Stone.

The Interns 𝒮𝒮½ **1962** Finessed hospital soaper about interns on the staff of a large city hospital, whose personal lives are fraught with trauma, drugs, birth, death, and abortion. Good performances and direction keep this medical melodrama moving in a gurney-like manner. Followed by the "The New Interns" and the basis for a TV series. Adapted from a novel by Richard Frede. **120m/C VHS.** Cliff Robertson, James MacArthur, Michael Callan, Nick Adams, Stefanie Powers, Suzy Parker, Buddy Ebsen, Telly Savalas, Haya Harareet; ***D:*** David Swift.

Interpol Connection 𝒮½ **1992** International drug dealer Law Tak is being pursued by Hong Kong narcotics officer Ko Pang, international police officer Cynthia, and bumbling Philippine cop King-Kong. The cop trio reluctantly decide to work together to bring down the bad guy. Dubbed into English. **91m/C VHS.** *HK* Robin Shou, Yukari Oshima.

The Interrogation 𝒮𝒮𝒮 *Przesluchanie* **1982** Grueling depiction of Stalin-era Poland proves that nobody makes anti-communist movies better than those who knew tyranny firsthand. A 1950s cabaret starlet is arrested on false charges and endures years of torment in custody. Banned under Polish martial law in 1982, it circulated illegally in the country until 1989. Janda won an award at Cannes for her transformation from showgirl floozy to defiant heroine. In Polish with English subtitles. **118m/C VHS.** *PL* Krystyna Janda, Janusz Gajos, Adam Ferency, Agnieszka Holland, Anna Romantowska; ***D:*** Richard Bugajski; ***W:*** Richard Bugajski, Janusz Dymek; ***C:*** Jacek Petrycki.

Interrupted Journey 𝒮𝒮½ **1949** A married man runs away to start a new life with another woman. When she is killed in a train accident, he becomes the prime suspect in her murder. Lots of action and speed, but a disappointing ending. **80m/B VHS.** *GB* Richard Todd, Valerie Hobson; ***D:*** Daniel Birt.

Interrupted Melody 𝒮𝒮𝒮 **1955** True story of opera diva Marjorie Lawrence's courageous battle with polio and her fight to appear once more at the Metropolitan Opera. Parker was nominated for an Oscar in her excellent portrayal of the Australian singer who continues her career despite her handicap. Vocals dubbed by opera star Eileen Farrell. Based on the book by Marjorie Lawrence. **106m/C VHS.** Glenn Ford, Eleanor Parker, Roger Moore, Cecil Kellaway, Evelyn Ellis, Walter Baldwin; ***D:*** Curtis Bernhardt; ***W:*** William Ludwig, Sonya Levien; ***C:*** Paul Vogel. Oscars '55: Story & Screenplay.

Intersection 𝒮½ **1993 (R)** Successful architect Vincent (Gere) is torn between his aloof wife/partner, Sally (Stone), and a sexy journalist mistress, Olivia (Davidovitch). Whom to choose? Since he's a completely self-involved boor, you won't care either way. Another retooling of a French film ("Les Choses de la Vie") as a Hollywood star vehicle that doesn't work. Lousy dialogue doesn't help. Does boast some nice location shots of Vancouver, B.C. **98m/C VHS, DVD, Wide.** Richard Gere, Sharon Stone, Lolita (David) Davidovich, Martin Landau, David Selby, Jenny Morrison; ***D:*** Mark Rydell; ***W:*** Marshall Brickman, David Rayfiel; ***C:*** Vilmos Zsigmond; ***M:*** James Newton Howard. Golden Raspberries '94: Worst Actress (Stone).

Interval 𝒮𝒮 **1973 (PG)** A middle-aged, globe-trotting woman becomes involved with a young American painter while running from her past. Oberon, 62 at the time, produced and played in this, her last film. Filmed in Mexico. **84m/C VHS.** Merle Oberon, Robert Wolders; ***D:*** Daniel Mann.

The Interview 𝒮𝒮𝒮 **1998** Eddie Fleming (Weaving) is a seemingly ordinary bloke who is rudely awakened when armed police burst into his apartment and haul him off for questioning. His interrogators are tenacious Detective Steele (Martin) and his younger partner, Prior (Jeffery). It slowly becomes clear that the cops are interested in a serial killer and that Fleming isn't the only one under investigation. It seems the two detectives are being watched by an internal affairs unit who are suspicious of Steele himself. And maybe Fleming isn't quite as innocent as he protests. **101m/C VHS, DVD, Wide.** *AU* Hugo Weaving, Tony Martin, Aaron Jeffery, Paul Sonkkila, Michael Caton, Peter McCauley; ***D:*** Craig Monahan; ***W:*** Craig Monahan, Gordon Davie; ***C:*** Simon Duggan; ***M:*** David Hirschfelder. Australian Film Inst. '98: Actor (Weaving), Film, Orig. Screenplay.

Interview with the Vampire 𝒮𝒮 **1994 (R)** Portrayal of the elegantly decadent world of vampires and their prey, which features the perverse Lestat (Cruise) who decides to make 18th-century New Orleans aristocrat Louis (Pitt) his latest recruit. Only problem is Louis is horrified by his blood-sucking nature and whines about it for 200 years (it does get tedious). Lestat even makes a child-vampire, Claudia (Dunst), for their own very dysfunctional family but this doesn't turn out well. Director Jordan brings some much needed humor to the dark mix along with some overdone gore. The first book in Anne Rice's "The Vampire Chronicles" was a 17-year film project beset by controversy, including the casting of Cruise (who looks nothing like Rice's description of the character, although Pitt does), leading to an outcry among the cult book's fans though Rice finally came around. Slater replaced the late River Phoenix as the interviewer. **123m/C VHS, DVD.** Tom Cruise, Brad Pitt, Kirsten Dunst, Christian Slater, Antonio Banderas, Stephen Rea, Domiziana Giordano; ***D:*** Neil Jordan; ***W:*** Anne Rice; ***C:*** Philippe Rousselot; ***M:*** Elliot Goldenthal. MTV Movie Awards '95: Male Perf. (Pitt), Breakthrough Perf. (Dunst), Most Desirable Male (Pitt).

Intervista 𝒮𝒮𝒮 *Federico Fellini's Intervista* **1987** A pseudo-documentary look at director Fellini's love of the movies, "Intervista" is a mixture of recollection, parody, memoir, satire, self-examination and fantasy. Fellini himself is the master of ceremonies in this joyous celebration of the studio community that features actors, actresses, bit players, make-up artists, scene painters, publicity agents, technicians, and gate-crashers. The high point of the film arrives with the stars of "La Dolce Vita" re-screening the Fellini masterpiece at Ekberg's country villa. It's a special moment of fantasy vs. reality in this glorious tribute to cinema history. In Italian with English subtitles. **108m/C VHS.** *IT* Marcello Mastroianni, Anita Ekberg, Sergio Rubini, Lara Wendel, Antonio Cantafora, Antonella Ponziani, Maurizio Mein, Paola Liguori, Nadia Ottaviani, Federico Fellini; ***D:*** Federico Fellini; ***W:*** Federico Fellini, Gianfranco Angelucci; ***C:*** Tonino Delli Colli; ***M:*** Nicola Piovani.

Interzone 𝒮½ **1988** Humans battle mutants in a post-holocaust world. **97m/C VHS.** Bruce Abbott; ***D:*** Deran Sarafian.

Intimate Betrayal 𝒮½ **1996 (R)** Mack (Brown) is surprised when ex-friend Charlie (Edson) crashes his bachelor party. Charlie still wants the bride-to-be, Katie (Hecht), and has hired a hooker, Shelley (Conaway), to seduce Mack and then tell Katie all the dirty details. The wedding's off, Charlie makes his play, Shelley confesses the scam, blah, blah, blah. Neither of these guys is worth the time. **90m/C VHS.** Dwier Brown, Richard Edson, Cristi Conaway, Jessica Hecht; ***D:*** Andrew Behar; ***W:*** Sara Sackner; ***C:*** Hamid Shams; ***M:*** Peter Fish.

Intimate Contact 𝒮𝒮𝒮 **1987 (PG)** Top executive discovers he has AIDS after a business trip fling. Powerful drama as he and his wife try to cope. Excellent, understated performances from Massey and Bloom. **140m/C VHS.** *GB* Claire Bloom, Daniel Massey, Abigail Cruttenden, Mark Kingston, Sylvia Syms, Sally Jane Jackson; ***D:*** Waris Hussein; ***W:*** Alma Cullen. **CABLE**

Intimate Deception 𝒮𝒮 **1996** Artist Charles Michaels is in a crumbling marriage and having dreams about a murder that took place in his past. Into his confused life comes new neighbor John and beautiful model Tina and neither meeting is a coincidence. **96m/C VHS.** George Saunders, Lisa Boyle, Dan Frank, Nicole Gian; ***D:*** George Saunders; ***W:*** George Saunders.

Intimate Lighting 𝒮𝒮½ *Intimni Osvetleni* **1965** Professional cello player takes his fiancee to a provincial town to meet his friend, the local orchestra director. Slice of life comedy enjoys the simple pleasures of sharing food, music, and reminiscences, all tinged with melancholy. Czech with subtitles. **73m/B VHS.** *CZ* Zdenek Bezusek, Vera Kresadlova, Jan Vostrcil, Karel Blazek, Jaroslava Stedra, Vlastimila Vlkova; ***D:*** Ivan Passer; ***W:*** Ivan Passer, Jaroslav Papousek, Vaclav Sasek; ***C:*** Miroslav Ondricek, Jan Strecha; ***M:*** Oldrich Korte.

Intimate Power 𝒮𝒮½ **1989 (R)** True story of French schoolgirl sold into slavery to an Ottoman sultan who becomes the harem queen. She bears an heir and begins to teach her son about his people's rights, in the hope that he will bring about reform in Turkey where he grows up to be a sultan. Good cast supports the exotic storytelling in this cable drama. **104m/C VHS.** F. Murray Abraham, Maud Adams, Amber O'Shea; ***D:*** Jack Smight. **CABLE**

Intimate Relations 𝒮𝒮½ **1995 (R)** Fifties family dsyfunction—British style. Harold Guppy (Graves) is an orphaned merchant marine who winds up in an English coastal town where he takes rooms with the seemingly respectable Beasleys. Stanley Beasley (Walker) is a quiet nonentity whose life is run by homemaker extraordinaire Marjorie (Walters), with 14-year-old daughter Joyce (Sadler) rounding out the family. The needy Harold fits in fine, especially to the sexually hungry Marjorie who's soon offering her boarder unexpected services. But young Joyce won't be left out and then there's a blackmailing tug of war between the threesome. Based on the true story of a crime of passion that shocked Great Britain. **105m/C VHS.** *GB* Julie Walters, Rupert Graves, Laura Sadler, Matthew (Matt) Walker, Holly Aird, Les Dennis, Liz McKechnie; ***D:*** Philip Goodhew; ***W:*** Philip Goodhew; ***C:*** Andres Garreton; ***M:*** Lawrence Shragge. Montreal World Film Fest. '95: Actor (Graves).

Intimate Story 𝒮𝒮½ **1981** Intimate story of a husband and wife trying unsuccessfully to have a baby, amid the lack of privacy in a Kibbutz. Each blames the other for the problem and tries to escape the problems by focusing on personal fantasies. In Hebrew with English subtitles. **95m/C VHS.** *IS* Chava Alberstein, Alex Peleg; ***D:*** Israeli Nadav Levitan.

Intimate Stranger 𝒮½ **1991 (R)** Sexy, would-be rock star by day, Harry sets out in search of a steadier source of income. Rather than wait on tables all day, she chooses instead to become a phone-sex girl. This turns out to be an unwise career move, as she promptly finds herself the target of a phone-psycho who just can't take "no" for an answer. Will Debbie be able to shake this loser, or will he put a permanent end to her life-long dreams? **96m/C VHS.** Deborah Harry, James Russo, Tim Thomerson, Paige French, Grace Zabriskie; ***D:*** Allan Holzman. **TV**

Intimate Strangers 𝒳𝒳½ 1977 Taut expose on battering and its effects on the family. Weaver and Struthers outshine the material, but the finest performance is a cameo by Douglas as Weaver's irascible aged father. **96m/C VHS.** Dennis Weaver, Sally Struthers, Quinn Cummings, Tyne Daly, Larry Hagman, Rhea Perlman; ***Cameos:*** Melvyn Douglas; ***D:*** John Llewellyn Moxey. **TV**

Into the Badlands 𝒳𝒳 1992 (R) Mild thriller presents three suspense tales in "Twilight Zone" fashion, linked by the appearance of a mysterious Man in Black. No, it's not Johnny Cash, but Dern as a sinister bounty hunter in the old west, who inspires strange events on the trail. **89m/C VHS, DVD.** Bruce Dern, Mariel Hemingway, Helen Hunt, Dylan McDermott, Lisa Pelikan, Andrew (Andy) Robinson; ***D:*** Sam Pillsbury; ***W:*** Dick Beebe, Marjorie David, Gordon Dawson. **CABLE**

Into the Blue 𝒳𝒳½ 1997 Harry Barnett (Thaw) is a bankrupt businessman now working as a caretaker at a friend's estate on the Greek isle of Rhodes. He has a one-nighter with young Englishwoman Heather Mallender (Cruttenden) and when she mysteriously disappears, Harry becomes a suspect. Then he learns she was investigating the drowning death of her sister, which involves people Harry knows, and he returns to London to try and sort out the mess he's in. **120m/C VHS.** *GB* John Thaw, Abigail Cruttenden, Miles Anderson, Michael Culkin, Celia Imrie; ***D:*** Jack Gold. **TV**

Into the Darkness 𝒳½ 1986 In the world of fashion models, a maniacal, demented killer stalks his prey. **90m/C VHS.** Donald Pleasence, Ronald Lacey.

Into the Fire 𝒳 1988 (R) Thriller about a young drifter who, against the backdrop of a Canadian winter, happens upon a roadside lodge and diner, where he gets involved in sex and murder. Title gives a good idea of what to do with this one. **88m/C VHS.** *CA* Susan Anspach, Art Hindle, Olivia D'Abo, Lee Montgomery; ***D:*** Graeme Campbell.

Into the Homeland 𝒳𝒳 1987 Seasoned ex-cop (Boothe) infiltrates a white supremacist group which had kidnapped his teenage daughter. Failed "message" about neo-nazi ethics, but good confrontation between Boothe and his son (Howell) make this so-so viewing. **95m/C VHS.** Powers Boothe, C. Thomas Howell, Paul LeMat; ***D:*** Leslie Linka Glatter. **CABLE**

Into the Night 𝒳𝒳 1985 (R) Campy, off-beat thriller about a middle-aged, jilted deadbeat (Goldblum), who meets a beautiful woman (Pfeiffer) when she suddenly drops onto the hood of his car, with a relentless gang of Iranians pursuing. During their search through L.A. and other parts of California for the one person who can help her out of this mess, a whole crew of Hollywood directors make cameo appearances, making this a delight for film buffs, but occasionally tedious for general audiences. B.B. King sings the title song. **115m/C VHS.** Jeff Goldblum, Michelle Pfeiffer, David Bowie, Carl Perkins, Richard Farnsworth, Dan Aykroyd, Paul Mazursky, Roger Vadim, Irene Papas, Bruce McGill, Vera Miles, Clu Gulager, Don Steel, Kathryn Harrold; ***Cameos:*** Jim Henson, Paul Bartel, David Cronenberg, Jack Arnold, Jonathan Demme, Lawrence Kasdan, Amy Heckerling, Donald Siegel, Richard Franklin, Colin Higgins, Andrew Marton; ***D:*** John Landis; ***W:*** Ron Koslow; ***M:*** Ira Newborn.

Into the Sun 𝒳½ 1992 (R) Hall plays a Hollywood star who encounters real-life danger while hanging out with an Air Force pilot (Pare) to prepare for an upcoming role. Spectacular aerial scenes steal the show, which isn't hard to do in this lackluster movie. **101m/C VHS.** Anthony Michael Hall, Michael Pare, Terry Kiser, Deborah Maria Moore; ***D:*** Fritz Kiersch; ***W:*** John Brancato.

Into the West 𝒳𝒳𝒳 1992 (PG) Enchanting horse tale set amid the mystic isle of Eire. Brooding, drunken Riley (Byrne), once the leader of a band of travelers (the Irish version of gypsies), leaves the road after his wife's death and settles in a Dublin slum with his two boys. The boys are enraptured when their grandfather turns up with a beautiful white horse, but their happiness is shattered when the police take it away. Boys and horse eventually escape in a wild ride across Ireland and into the west. Spiritual and mythic, with an awe-inspiring performance by the horse. Fitzgerald and Conroy make a run at best performances by kids, while Byrne is convincingly sodden and sulky. Meany and Barkin shine in small parts as sibling travellers. **97m/C VHS.** *IR* Gabriel Byrne, Ellen Barkin, Ciaran Fitzgerald, Ruaidhri Conroy, David Kelly, Colm Meaney; ***D:*** Mike Newell; ***W:*** Jim Sheridan; ***M:*** Patrick Doyle.

Into Thin Air 𝒳𝒳𝒳 1985 A mother searches tirelessly for her college bound son who disappeared on a cross-country drive. Well-done TV drama with a good performance from Burstyn. **100m/C VHS.** Ellen Burstyn, Robert Prosky, Sam Robards, Tate Donovan, Caroline McWilliams, Nicholas Pryor, John Dennis Johnston; ***D:*** Roger Young; ***W:*** George Rubio, Larry Cohen; ***M:*** Brad Fiedel. **TV**

Into Thin Air: Death on Everest 𝒳𝒳 1997 Based on the book by Jon Krakauer (played in the telepic by McDonald) about the tragic May, 1996 climbing expedition to Mount Everest that resulted in the deaths of eight climbers. **90m/C VHS, DVD.** Peter Horton, Christopher McDonald, Nathaniel Parker, Richard Jenkins; ***D:*** Robert Markowitz; ***W:*** Robert J. Avrech. **TV**

Intolerance 𝒳𝒳𝒳𝒳 1916 Griffith's largest film in every aspect. An interwoven, four-story epic about human intolerance, with segments set in Babylon, ancient Judea, and Paris. One of the cinema's grandest follies, and greatest achievements. Silent with music score; B&W with some restored color footage. **175m/B VHS, DVD.** Lillian Gish, Mae Marsh, Constance Talmadge, Bessie Love, Elmer Clifton, Erich von Stroheim, Eugene Pallette, Seena Owen, Alfred Paget; ***D:*** D.W. Griffith; ***W:*** D.W. Griffith, Tod Browning; ***C:*** Billy (G.W.) Bitzer, Karl Brown. Natl. Film Reg. '89.

Intrigue 𝒳𝒳½ 1990 (PG) Former CIA agent (Loggia) defects to the KGB, but wants to return to the U.S. when he realizes he has a progressive illness. Underground agent and old buddy (Glenn) is recruited with orders to smuggle his former colleague out. Tension continues throughout as murder comes along with the orders. Loads of suspense and twist ending in this nail-biter. **96m/C VHS.** Scott Glenn, Robert Loggia, William Atherton, Martin Shaw, Cherie Lunghi, Eleanor Bron; ***D:*** David Drury. **TV**

Intrigue and Love 𝒳𝒳 *Kabale und Liebe* 1959 Luise, who's the daughter of the town musician, is in love with Ferdinand, the son of President von Walter. Von Walter wants his son to marry the Duke's mistress, in order to increase his own influence. Finding their romance impossible, the lovers come up with a drastic solution. Based on the drama by Friedrich Schiller. German with subtitles. **109m/B VHS.** *GE* ***D:*** Martin Hellberg.

Introducing Dorothy Dandridge 𝒳𝒳𝒳 1999 (R) Beautiful, sexy singer/actress Dorothy Dandridge (Berry) was the first African-American woman to be nominated for a best actress Oscar for her title role in 1955's "Carmen Jones." Ten years later, at the age of 42, she was dead from an overdose of antidepressants after suffering a lifetime of tragedies—an abusive childhood, two failed marriages, a brain-damaged child, tumultuous affairs, limited career choices, and bad financial decisions. Based on the book by Dandridge's loyal manager, Earl Mills. **115m/C VHS, DVD.** Halle Berry, Brent Spiner, Obba Babatunde, Loretta Devine, Cynda Williams, Latanya Richardson, Tamara Taylor, Klaus Maria Brandauer, D.B. Sweeney, William Atherton; ***D:*** Martha Coolidge; ***W:*** Scott Abbott, Shonda Rhimes; ***C:*** Robbie Greenberg; ***M:*** Elmer Bernstein. **CABLE**

Intruder 𝒳𝒳 1977 A man and his stepson are terrorized by a stranger in a panel truck as they travel from Rome to Paris. **98m/C VHS.** Jean-Louis Trintignant, Mireille Darc, Adolfo Celi.

Intruder 𝒳𝒳 1988 (R) A psychotic killer stalks an all-night convenience store shopping for fresh meat (customers beware). Slasher movie fans should get a kick out of the plot twist at the end. **90m/C VHS.** Elizabeth Cox, Renee Estevez, Alvy Moore; ***D:*** Scott Spiegel; ***W:*** Lawrence Bender.

Intruder in the Dust 𝒳𝒳𝒳½ 1949 A small southern community develops a lynch mob mentality when a black man is accused of killing a white man. Powerful, but largely ignored portrait of race relations in the South. Solid performances from the whole cast; filmed in Mississippi. Adapted from a novel by William Faulkner. **87m/B VHS.** David Brian, Claude Jarman Jr., Juano Hernandez, Porter Hall, Elizabeth Patterson; ***D:*** Clarence Brown; ***C:*** Robert L. Surtees.

Intruder Within 𝒳 1981 Half-baked thriller about crew on an isolated oil rig in Antarctica who, while drilling, unearth a nasty creature that goes around terrorizing the frost-bitten men and occasional stray woman. **91m/C VHS.** Chad Everett, Joseph Bottoms, Jennifer Warren; ***D:*** Peter Carter. **TV**

Intruders 𝒳𝒳 1992 Follows the story of three people who have unexplained lapses of time in their lives which they eventually believe are connected to visits by aliens. The three are brought together by a skeptical psychiatrist. The aliens are your typical bugged-eyed, white-faced spooks but part of the film is genuinely unsettling. **162m/C VHS.** Richard Crenna, Mare Winningham, Susan Blakely, Ben Vereen, Steven Berkoff, Daphne Ashbrook; ***D:*** Dan Curtis.

Intruso 𝒳𝒳½ *Intruder* 1993 Gloomy story set in a coastal city in northern Spain. Luisa (Abril) spots her destitute exhusband Angel (Arias) and persuades him to stay with her and her new family, husband Ramiro (Valero)—once Angel's good friend—and their two young children. Angel turns out to be terminally ill and decides to wreak vengeance on Ramiro by reclaiming Luisa for himself. In Spanish with English subtitles. **85m/C VHS.** *SP* Victoria Abril, Imanol Arias, Antonio Valero; ***D:*** Vicente Aranda; ***W:*** Vicente Aranda, Alvaro del Amo.

Invader 𝒳𝒳 1991 (R) When a news reporter is sent to cover a mysterious massacre, he begins to realize that the culprits are vicious aliens thirsty for blood...and now they're after him! **95m/C VHS.** Hans Bachman, A. Thomas Smith, Rich Foucheux, John Cooke, Robert Diedermann, Allison Sheehy, Ralph Bluemke; ***D:*** Phillip Cook.

The Invader 𝒳𝒳½ 1996 Schoolteacher Annie (Young) discovers she's pregnant by a mystery man (Cross), who turns out to be an alien from a dying race—and Annie's child may be their salvation. Only her ex-cop boyfriend (Baldwin) is on their trail as is an intergalactic bounty hunter (Mancuso). This one is on the romance rather than the action side. **97m/C VHS.** Sean Young, Ben Cross, Nick Mancuso, Daniel Baldwin; ***D:*** Mark Rosman; ***W:*** Mark Rosman; ***C:*** Gregory Middleton; ***M:*** Todd Hayen. **VIDEO**

The Invaders 𝒳𝒳½ 1995 TV mini is an updated continuation of the 1967 sci-fi series that finds the pollution-loving aliens gradually conquering Earth by allowing humans to destroy their own ecosystem (which we're so good at anyway). Bewildered hero Nolan Wood (Bakula) is trying to get everyone to believe in the alien invasion but since he's just gotten out of prison, it's an uphill climb. Still, the aliens (lead by effectively evil Thomas) would like to permanently shut Nolan up. Thinnes, who starred in the original series, briefly reprises his role as David Vincent. **180m/C VHS.** Scott Bakula, Richard Thomas, DeLane Matthews, Terence Knox, Elizabeth Pena, Raoul Trujillo, Richard Belzer, Jon Polito, Roy Thinnes, Jon Cypher, Todd Susman, Jack Kehler, Elinor Donahue; ***D:*** Paul Shapiro; ***W:*** James Dott; ***C:*** Alar Kivilo; ***M:*** Joseph Vitarelli.

Invaders from Mars 𝒳𝒳½ 1953 Young boy cries "martian" in this sci-fi cheapy classic. He can't convince the townspeople of this invasion because they've already been possessed by the alien beings. His parents are zapped by the little green things first, making this perhaps an allegory for the missing Eisenhower/Stepford years. Includes previews of coming attractions from classic science-fiction films. Remade in 1986 by Tobe Hooper. **78m/C VHS, DVD.** Helena Carter, Arthur Franz, Jimmy Hunt, Leif Erickson, Hillary Brooke, Morris Ankrum, Lock Martin; ***D:*** William Cameron Menzies; ***W:*** Richard Blake, John Tucker Battle; ***C:*** John Seitz; ***M:*** Raoul Kraushaar.

Invaders from Mars 𝒳½ 1986 (PG) A high-tech remake of Menzies' 1953 semi-classic about a Martian invasion perceived only by one young boy and a sympathetic (though hysterical) school nurse, played by mother and son Black and Carson. Instant camp. **102m/C VHS, DVD, Wide.** Hunter Carson, Karen Black, Louise Fletcher, Laraine Newman, Timothy Bottoms, Bud Cort, Dale Dye; ***D:*** Tobe Hooper; ***W:*** Dan O'Bannon, Don Jakoby; ***C:*** Daniel Pearl; ***M:*** Sylvester Levay, David Storrs, Christopher Young.

Invasion 𝒳𝒳½ 1965 A hospital opens its doors to an accident victim, and his attractive female visitors don't seem sympathetic to the idea of a long hospital stay. Turns out he's an escaped alien prisoner, and the alien babes, intent on intergalactic extradition, place a force field around the hospital and demand his return. Early effort of director Bridges, who later did "The Shooting Party." Interesting, creepy, atmospheric, with very cool camera moves. **82m/B VHS.** *GB* Edward Judd, Yoko Tani, Valerie Gearon, Lyndon Brook, Tsai Chin, Barrie Ingham; ***D:*** Alan Bridges.

Invasion! 𝒳𝒳½ *Top of the Food Chain* 1999 (PG-13) Deliberately tacky and frequently amusing spoof of alien invasion flicks. Atomic scientist Dr. Karel Lamonte (Scott) comes to the town of Exceptional Vista just after the local TV tower is hit by a big meteor. It's hard to tell if aliens have invaded since the townspeople are so weird to begin with, but they have. And they turn out to be the cannibalistic kind who take to munching on the locals. Oh, and it turns out that TV is the key to the aliens' destruction. **99m/C VHS, DVD.** *CA* Campbell Scott, Fiona Loewi, Tom Everett Scott, Hardee T. Lineham, Bernard Behrens, Nigel Bennett, Peter Donaldson, Robert Bockstael, Lorry Ayers, Ron Gabriel, James Allodi, Maggie Butterfield, Kathryn Kirkpatrick; ***D:*** John Paizs; ***W:*** Phil Bedard, Larry Lalonde; ***C:*** Bill Wong; ***M:*** David Krystal.

Invasion: Earth 𝒳𝒳½ 1998 Britain's Royal Air Force and U.S. Air Force officers discover that two alien races have invaded earth and only one of them is amenable to letting the current inhabitants remain. British sci-fi miniseries on 3 cassettes. **270m/C VHS.** *GB* Fred Ward, Maggie O'Neill, Phyllis Logan, Vincent Regan; ***D:*** Richard Laxton, Patrick Lau. **TV**

Invasion Earth: The Aliens Are Here! 𝒳 1987 A cheap spoof of monster movies, as an insectoid projectionist takes over the minds of a movie audience. Clips of Godzilla, Mothra and other beasts are interpolated. **84m/C VHS.** Janice Fabian, Christian Lee; ***D:*** George Maitland.

Invasion Force 𝒳 1990 A terrorist army parachutes into a remote region where a film crew is preparing to set up for an action movie. The moviemakers must scare away the terrorists with their smokepots and blanks. Sounds promising, but proves to be as empty as the movie props used to scare the terrorists. **93m/C VHS.** Richard Lynch, David Shark, Renee Cline, Douglas Hartier, Graham Times, Angie Synodis; ***D:*** David A. Prior.

The Invasion of Carol Enders 𝒳½ 1974 A woman, almost killed by a prowler, awakens with an expanded consciousness, and tries to convince her near husband that her death wasn't an accident. **72m/C VHS.** Meredith Baxter, Christopher Connelly, Charles Aidman.

Invasion of Privacy 𝒳𝒳 1992 (R) Alex is a psycho prison inmate obsessed with high profile journalist, Hilary. When Hilary interviews Alex for a magazine cover story, his obsession only grows stronger. Then Alex gets paroled and goes to work for Hilary. When he discovers Hilary isn't interested in him, Alex turns his fantasies to her daughter, who has no notion what she's getting into. An unrated version is also available. **95m/C VHS.** Robby Benson, Jennifer O'Neill, Lydie Denier, Ian Ogilvy, John Agar; ***D:*** Kevin Meyer; ***W:*** Kevin Meyer. **CABLE**

Invasion of Privacy **1996 (R)** Some hot-button topics take the thriller route. When Theresa (Avital) becomes pregnant, she discovers her boyfriend Josh (Schaech) is seriously unbalanced. She decides on an abortion but retreats for some quiet time to an isolated lakeside cabin. Mistake—the expectant dad shows up and holds her prisoner until Theresa is too far along to terminate the pregnancy. When Josh finally releases her, Theresa heads for the cops and charges him with kidnapping. He gets a hot female lawyer (Rampling), who turns the media attention into making him a cause celebre for parental rights. Once the baby is born, Josh is also detemined to gain custody—by whatever means necessary. **94m/C VHS.** Johnathon Schaech, Mili Avital, David Keith, Charlotte Rampling, Naomi Campbell, R.G. Armstrong; ***D:*** Anthony Hickox; ***W:*** Larry Cohen; ***C:*** Peter Wunstorf; ***M:*** Angelo Badalamenti.

Invasion of the Animal People **woof!** *Terror in the Midnight Sun; Space Invasion of Lapland; Horror in the Midnight Sun; Space Invasion from Lapland* **1962** Hairy monster from outer space attacks Lapland. Narrated by Carradine, the only American in the cast. Pretty silly. **73m/B VHS, DVD.** *SW* Robert Burton, Barbara Wilson, John Carradine; ***D:*** Jerry Warren, Virgil W. Vogel; ***W:*** Arthur C. Pierce; ***C:*** Hilding Bladh; ***M:*** Harry Arnold, Allan Johansson.

Invasion of the Bee Girls *Graveyard Tramps* **1973** California girls are mysteriously transformed into deadly nymphomaniacs in this delightful campy science fiction romp. Written by Meyer who later directed "Star Trek II: The Wrath of Khan." **85m/C VHS.** William Smith, Anitra Ford, Cliff Osmond, Victoria Vetri, Wright King, Ben Hammer, Cliff Emmich, Anna Aries; ***D:*** Denis Sanders; ***W:*** Nicholas Meyer; ***C:*** Gary Graver; ***M:*** Charles Bernstein.

Invasion of the Blood Farmers **woof!** **1972 (PG)** In a small New York town, members of an ancient Druidic cult murder young women, taking their blood in the hope of finding the precise, rare blood type to keep their queen alive. A real woofer. **86m/C VHS, DVD, Wide.** Norman Kelley, Tanna Hunter, Bruce Detrick, Jack Neubeck, Cythia Fleming, Paul Craig Jennings; ***D:*** Ed Adlum; ***W:*** Ed Adlum, Ed Kelleher.

Invasion of the Body Snatchers **1956** The one and only post-McCarthy paranoid sci-fi epic, where a small California town is infiltrated by pods from outer space that replicate and replace humans. A chilling, genuinely frightening exercise in nightmare dislocation. Based upon a novel by Jack Finney. Remade in 1978. **80m/B VHS, DVD, Wide.** Kevin McCarthy, Dana Wynter, Carolyn Jones, King Donovan, Larry Gates, Jean Willes, Whit Bissell, Richard Deacon, Pat O'Malley, Sam Peckinpah, Donald Siegel; ***D:*** Donald Siegel; ***W:*** Daniel Mainwaring, Sam Peckinpah; ***C:*** Ellsworth Fredericks; ***M:*** Carmen Dragon. Natl. Film Reg. '94.

Invasion of the Body Snatchers **1978 (PG)** One of the few instances where a remake is an improvement on the original, which was itself a classic. This time, the "pod people" are infesting San Francisco, with only a small group of people aware of the invasion. A ceaselessly inventive, creepy version of the alien-takeover paradigm, with an intense and winning performance by Sutherland. Features cameos by Don Siegel and Kevin McCarthy from the original, as well as an uncredited appearance by Robert Duvall. **115m/C VHS, DVD, Wide.** Donald Sutherland, Brooke Adams, Veronica Cartwright, Leonard Nimoy, Jeff Goldblum, Kevin McCarthy, Donald Siegel, Art Hindle, Robert Duvall; ***D:*** Philip Kaufman; ***W:*** W.D. Richter; ***C:*** Michael Chapman.

Invasion of the Body Stealers **woof!** *Thin Air; The Body Stealers* **1969 (PG)** Aliens are thought to be the captors when sky-divers begin vanishing in mid-air. Uneven sci-fi with nothing going for it. **115m/C VHS.** *GB* George Sanders, Maurice Evans, Patrick Allen; ***D:*** Gerry Levy.

Invasion of the Girl Snatchers **woof!** **1973** Aliens from another planet, in cahoots with a cult kingpin, subdue young earth girls and force them to undergo bizarre acts that may just rob them of their dignity. Save a bit of your own dignity by staying away. Cheap look, cheap feel, cheap thrills. **90m/C VHS.** Elizabeth Rush, Ele Grigsby, David Roster; ***D:*** Lee Jones.

Invasion of the Saucer Men *Hell Creatures; Spacemen Saturday Night* **1957** Suburban teenagers (Terrell, Castillo) are detained by a little green man at lovers lane. When they return with police to the scene, only the corpse of the town drunk (Gorshin) remains. Fortunately, the dead man's roommate (Osborn) believes them but the trio must convince authorities before the alien creatures multiply and take over the world. **69m/B VHS.** Steven Terrell, Gloria Castillo, Frank Gorshin, Lyn Osborn, Ed Nelson, Angelo Rossitto, Raymond Hatton, Russ Bender; ***D:*** Edward L. Cahn; ***W:*** Al Martin; ***C:*** Frederick E. West; ***M:*** Ronald Stein.

Invasion of the Space Preachers *Strangest Dreams: Invasion of the Space Preachers* **1990** Hideous creatures from outer space arrive on Earth with plans for conquest. Led by the seemingly human Reverend Lash, they prey on the innocent and trusting, fleecing God-fearing folk out of their hard earned cash! **100m/C VHS.** Jim Wolfe, Guy Nelson, Eliska Hahn, Gary Brown, Jesse Johnson, John Riggs, Jimmie Walker; ***D:*** Daniel Boyd; ***W:*** Daniel Boyd; ***C:*** Bill Hogan; ***M:*** Michael Lipton.

Invasion of the Vampires *La Invasion de Los Vampiros* **1961** Burrito bat fest has Count Frankenhausen doing his vampire thing in a small, 16th century village. Atmospheric sets are highlight. Not a good substitute for No Doze. **78m/B VHS.** *MX* Carlos Agosti, Rafael Etienne, Bertha Moss, Tito Junco, Erna Martha Bauman, Fernando Soto Mantequilla, Enrique Garcia Alvarez, David Reynoso; ***D:*** Miguel Morayta; ***W:*** Miguel Morayta.

Invasion of the Zombies **1961** Bare-fisted wrestler Santo faces of brace of zombies in order to prove that men with short necks can hug other men and still be mucho macho. **85m/B VHS.** *MX* Santo; ***D:*** Benito Alazraki.

Invasion U.S.A. **1952** Cheap Red Scare movie using tons of stock footage showing actual bombings and air battles. O'Herlihy is a stranger who visits a New York bar and convinces the patrons that the H-bomb has been unleashed on America, while Mohr romances Castle. Full of propaganda and overacting. Based on a story by Robert Smith and Franz Spencer. **73m/B VHS, DVD.** Gerald Mohr, Peggy Castle, Dan O'Herlihy, Robert Bice, Tom Kennedy, Phyllis Coates, Erik Blythe, Wade Crosby, William Schallert, Noel Neill; ***D:*** Alfred E. Green; ***W:*** Robert Smith; ***C:*** John L. "Jack" Russell; ***M:*** Albert Glasser.

Invasion U.S.A. **1985 (R)** A mercenary defends nothing less than the entire country against Russian terrorists landing in Florida and looking for condos. A record-setting amount of people killed. Count them—it's not like you'll miss anything important. Norris is a bit less animated than a wooden Indian, and the acting is more painful to endure than the violence. Glasnost saved the movie industry from additional paranoia movies of this kind. **108m/C VHS, DVD.** Chuck Norris, Richard Lynch, Melissa Prophet, Alex Colon, Billy Drago; ***D:*** Joseph Zito; ***W:*** James Bruner; ***C:*** Joao Fernandes; ***M:*** Jay Chattaway.

Inventing the Abbotts **1997 (R)** Appealing cast populates this sleepy, bittersweet coming-of-age story set in small town Illinois in 1957. Alice (Going), Eleanor (Connelly) and Pamela (Tyler) are the lovely daughters of wealthy Lloyd Abbott (Patton) who's determined that they'll marry well despite the temptations offered by the two working-class Holt boys. Surly stud Jacey (Crudup) holds a grudge against Lloyd for possibly cheating his deceased father in a business deal and causing whispers about his schoolteacher mother Helen's (Baker) reputation, while sweet-natured younger brother Doug (Phoenix) has his romantic ideals fixed on Pamela, who loves him in return. Not memorable, but not a complete waste of time, either. Based on the story by Sue Miller. **110m/C VHS, DVD, Wide.** Billy Crudup, Joaquin Rafael (Leaf) Phoenix, Liv Tyler, Will Patton, Kathy Baker, Jennifer Connelly, Joanna Going, Barbara Williams; ***D:*** Pat O'Connor; ***W:*** Ken Hixon; ***C:*** Kenneth Macmillan; ***M:*** Michael Kamen.

Investigation **1979** A Frenchman plans to murder his wife so he can marry his pregnant mistress, guaranteeing an heir. Subtle study of small town people so concerned with their own welfare that the dirty deeds of the lead character might be overlooked. Fine performances and story development make this worth investigating. In French with English subtitles. **116m/C VHS.** *FR* Victor Lanoux, Valerie Mairesse; ***D:*** Etienne Perier.

Invincible **1980 (R)** Martial arts student must find and correct another student who has turned evil. For Bruce Lee fans, as if they haven't already memorized all the memorable lines-"hiyaah," "ugh," "oof," etc. **93m/C VHS.** Chen Sing, Ho Chung Dao.

Invincible Barbarian **woof!** **1983** A young man leads a tribe of amazing Amazon warriors in a sneak attack against the tribe that annihilated his native village. One of those movies that presumes "primitivism" can be recreated through bad acting. **92m/C VHS.** Diana Roy, David Jenkins.

The Invincible Gladiator *Il Gladiatore Invincible* **1963** A gladiator who saves the evil man ruling a land for a boyking is given command of an army. He eventually leads the army in revolt when the evil man tries to take over the throne. Plodding with stock characters. **96m/C VHS.** *IT SP* Richard Harrison, Isabel Corey, Livio Lorenzon; ***D:*** Frank Gregory.

Invincible Gladiators **woof!** **1964** The sons of Hercules labor to aid a prince whose bride had been kidnapped by an evil queen. Laborious to watch. **87m/C VHS.** Richard Lloyd, Claudia Lange, Tony Freeman; ***D:*** Robert (Roberto) Mauri.

Invincible Mr. Disraeli **1963** Presentation from "George Schaefer's Showcase Theatre" deals with the life and career of Benjamin Disraeli, novelist, philosopher, first Earl of Beaconsfield, statesman, and Prime Minister. Basically a tribute. **76m/C VHS.** Trevor Howard, Greer Garson, Hurd Hatfield, Kate Reid; ***D:*** George Schaefer. **TV**

The Invincible Six *The Heroes* **1968** An unlikely band of thieves running from the law winds up protecting a small village from marauding bandits. Plenty of action, as you would expect when thieves take on bandits, but with no scene-stealers or sympathetic characters the story lacks interest. Unremarkable choreography by ballet great Rudolf Nureyev. Filmed in Iran. **96m/C VHS.** Stuart Whitman, Elke Sommer, Curt Jurgens, Jim Mitchum, Ian Ogilvy; ***D:*** Jean Negulesco.

Invisible Adversaries **1977** A photographer uncovers an extra-terrestrial plot to cause excessive aggression in humans. She and her lover attempt to hold on to their crumbling humanity. Movies like this make you mad enough to tear something up. Enjoyed a meek cult following. In German with English subtitles. **112m/C VHS.** *AT* Susanne Widl, Peter Weibel; ***D:*** Valie Export.

Invisible Agent **1942** Hall plays an agent using the secret formula to outwit the Nazis in this third sequel to "The Invisible Man." Especially enjoyable for the kids. Based on characters suggested in H.G. Wells' "The Invisible Man." **83m/B VHS.** Ilona Massey, Jon Hall, Peter Lorre, Cedric Hardwicke, J. Edward Bromberg, Albert Bassermann, John Litel, Holmes Herbert; ***D:*** Edwin L. Marin; ***W:*** Curt Siodmak.

The Invisible Avenger *Bourbon St. Shadows* **1958** Based on the vintage radio character "The Shadow." A detective who can make himself invisible investigates the murder of a New Orleans jazz musician. The mysterious element successful on radio is lost on film, and only the Shadow knows why. **60m/B VHS.** Richard Derr, Marc Daniels, Helen Westcott, Jeanne Neher; ***D:*** John Sledge, Ben Parker.

The Invisible Boy **1957 (G)** Science fiction story about a young boy and his robot (Robby the Robot from "Forbidden Planet"). Kids will enjoy this adventure as told through the viewpoint of the child. Based on a story by Edmund Cooper. **89m/B VHS.** Richard Eyer, Diane Brewster, Philip Abbott, Harold J. Stone, Robert Harris; ***D:*** Herman Hoffman; ***W:*** Cyril Hume; ***C:*** Harold E. Wellman; ***M:*** Les Baxter.

Invisible Circus **2000 (R)** Coming-of-age drama set in 1976 of a young woman, Phoebe (Brewster), who treks through Europe in an attempt to solve the mystery of her older sister Faith (Diaz), a radical hippie who died there seven years ago. Her Nancy Drew-like sleuthing leads her to the big, bad Wolf (Eccleston) in Paris, Faith's old boho boyfriend, now a bourgeois married. Somewhat unlikely tales emerge about Faith's dealings with German terrorists gone bad and bring Phoebe closer to the truth and danger. Story told much like many a late 1960s memory, in confusing flashback fashion, and lacks adequate pacing. Brewster has inspired moments, along with Danner as the girls' mother, while Diaz seems an unlikely terrorist. Based on the novel by Jennifer Egan. **98m/C VHS, DVD.** *US* Cameron Diaz, Jordana Brewster, Christopher Eccleston, Blythe Danner, Patrick Bergin, Moritz Bleibtreu, Isabelle Pasco; ***D:*** Adam Brooks; ***W:*** Adam Brooks; ***C:*** Henry Braham; ***M:*** Nick Laird-Clowes.

Invisible Dad **1997 (PG)** Doug Baily's dad invents a machine that makes him invisible and uses it to foil the evil designs of a co-worker. Unfortunately, the machine isn't perfect, and Mr. Baily tends to reappear at inopportune moments. When Doug discovers his dad is in danger, he figures it's time to help out. **90m/C VHS.** Daran Noris, William Meyers, Mary Elizabeth McGlynn, Charles Dierkop, Karen Black; ***D:*** Fred Olen Ray; ***W:*** Steve Latshaw; ***C:*** Gary Graver; ***M:*** Jeff Walton. **VIDEO**

The Invisible Dr. Mabuse *The Invisible Horror; Die Unsichtbaren Krallen des Dr. Mabuse* **1962** Possibly the best of the Dr. Mabuse series sees the mad scientist using an invisibility agent in an attempt to take over the world. Preiss also played the title villian in Fritz Lang's "The Thousand Eyes of Dr. Mabuse." **89m/B VHS.** *GE* Lex Barker, Karin Dor, Siegfried Lowitz, Wolfgang Preiss, Rudolf Fernau; ***D:*** Harald Reinl.

The Invisible Ghost **1941** A man carries out a series of grisly stranglings while under hypnosis by his insane wife. Typically bad low-budget exploiter about a fun-lovin' crazy couple bringing down property values in the neighborhood. **70m/B VHS, DVD.** Bela Lugosi, Polly Ann Young, John McGuire, Clarence Muse, Betty Compson; ***D:*** Joseph H. Lewis; ***W:*** Helen Martin, Al Martin; ***C:*** Marcel Le Picard.

Invisible Invaders **1959** Short, cheap, and silly aliens-try-to-take-over-the-earth flick. This time they're moonmen who use the bodies of dead earthlings (ugh) to attack the living until Agar can save the day. Carradine has a brief role as a formerly dead scientist. **67m/B VHS.** John Agar, Robert Hutton, Hal Torey, Jean Byron, Philip Tonge, John Carradine; ***D:*** Edward L. Cahn; ***W:*** Samuel Newman; ***C:*** Maury Gertsman.

The Invisible Kid **1988** A shy teen manages to make himself invisible, a feat which ironically permits him to get people to notice him. Now he can visit places he's only dreamed of, including the girls' locker room. For those who have dreamed about girls' locker rooms. **95m/C VHS.** Karen Black, Jay Underwood, Chynna Phillips, Wallace (Wally) Langham, Brother Theodore; ***D:*** Avery Crounse; ***W:*** Avery Crounse.

The Invisible Killer **1940** Someone is killing folks by sending poison through telephone lines. A detective and a reporter team up to find the scoundrel by setting up an answering machine that automatically plays back messages to the caller. Bad connection of events leads to a static resolution. **61m/B VHS.** Grace Bradley, Roland (Walter Goss) Drew, William "Billy" Newell; ***D:*** Sam Newfield.

The Invisible Man 🦴🦴🦴🦴 **1933** The vintage horror-fest based on H. G. Wells' novella about scientist Jack Griffin (Rains) whose formula for invisibility slowly drives him insane. His mind definitely wandering, Jack plans to use his recipe to rule the world. Rains' first role; though his body doesn't appear until the final scene, his voice characterization is magnificent. The visual detail is excellent, setting standards that are imitated because they are difficult to surpass; with special effects by John P. Fulton and John Mescall. **71m/B VHS, DVD.** Claude Rains, Gloria Stuart, Dudley Digges, William Harrigan, Una O'Connor, E.E. Clive, Dwight Frye, Henry Travers, Holmes Herbert, John Carradine, Walter Brennan; ***D:*** James Whale; ***W:*** R.C. Sherriff; ***C:*** Arthur Edeson; ***M:*** W. Franke Harling.

The Invisible Man Returns 🦴🦴🦴 **1940** Price stars as the original invisible man's brother. Using the same invisibility formula, Price tries to clear himself after being charged with murder. He reappears at the worst times, and you gotta love that floating gun. Fun sequel to 1933's classic "The Invisible Man." **81m/B VHS.** Cedric Hardwicke, Vincent Price, John Sutton, Nan Grey; ***D:*** Joe May; ***W:*** Lester Cole, Curt Siodmak; ***C:*** Milton Krasner.

The Invisible Maniac woof! **1990 (R)** A crazy voyeur perfects a serum for invisibility and promptly gets a job as a physics teacher in a high school. There he leers at girls taking showers and slaughters students when he is caught. For voyeurs. Get outta here, you maniac. Rifkin used the pseudonym Rif Coogan. **87m/C VHS.** Noel Peters, Shannon Wilsey, Melissa Moore, Robert Ross, Rod Sweitzer, Eric Champnella, Kalei Shellabarger, Gail Lyon, Debra Lamb; ***D:*** Adam Rifkin; ***W:*** Adam Rifkin; ***C:*** James Bay; ***M:*** Marc David Decker.

The Invisible Man's Revenge 🦴🦴½ **1944** Left for dead on a safari five years before, Robert Griffin (Hall) seeks revenge against wealthy English couple Lady Irene (Sondergaard) and Sir Jasper (Matthews) Herrick by taking over their estate and marrying their daughter, Julie (Akers). He's aided by scientist Peter Drury (Carradine) who renders Griffin invisible. Only problem is he doesn't stay that way. Fifth in Universal's "Invisible Man" film series. **78m/B VHS.** Jon Hall, John Carradine, Gale Sondergaard, Lester Matthews, Evelyn Ankers, Alan Curtis, Leon Errol, Doris Lloyd; ***D:*** Ford Beebe; ***W:*** Bertram Millhauser; ***C:*** Milton Krasner; ***M:*** Hans J. Salter.

Invisible Mom 🦴🦴½ **1996 (PG)** Dad (Livingston) invents an invisibility potion that his 10-year-old son decides will make him popular at school. Too bad Mom (Wallace Stone) accidentally swallows the concoction instead. **82m/C VHS, DVD.** Dee Wallace Stone, Barry Livingston, Trenton Knight, Russ Tamblyn, Stella Stevens; ***D:*** Fred Olen Ray; ***W:*** William Martell; ***C:*** Gary Graver; ***M:*** Jeff Walton.

The Invisible Monster *Slaves of the Invisible Monster* **1950** Special investigators Lane Carlson and Carol Richards battle a mad scientist ready to take over the world with his invisible army. Twelve episodes of the original serial edited onto two cassettes. **167m/B VHS.** Richard Webb, Aline Towne, Lane Bradford, Stanley Price, John Crawford, George Meeker; ***D:*** Fred Brannon.

The Invisible Ray 🦴🦴½ **1936** For a change, this horror film features Lugosi as the hero, fighting Karloff, a scientist who locates a meteor that contains a powerful substance. Karloff is poisoned and becomes a murdering megalomaniac. Watching Karloff and Lugosi interact, and the great special effects—including a hot scene where a scientist bursts into flames—helps you ignore a generally hokey script. **82m/B VHS.** Boris Karloff, Bela Lugosi, Frances Drake, Frank Lawton, Beulah Bondi, Walter Kingsford; ***D:*** Lambert Hillyer; ***W:*** John Colton; ***C:*** George Robinson.

The Invisible Strangler 🦴½ *The Astral Factor* **1976 (PG)** A death-row murderer can make himself invisible and rubs out witnesses who helped put him away; woman risks her life to expose him when the police fail to see the problem. Very violent collection of brutal scenes. Not released theatrically until 1984. **85m/C VHS, DVD.** Robert Foxworth, Stefanie Powers, Elke Sommer, Sue Lyon, Leslie Parrish, Marianna Hill; ***D:*** John Florea; ***W:*** Arthur C. Pierce; ***C:*** Alan Stensvold; ***M:*** Richard Hieronymous, Alan Oldfield.

The Invisible Terror 🦴🦴 **1963** A maniac steals a mad scientist's invisibility formula and uses it on a number of innocent victims. **?m/C VHS.** Herbert Stass, Ellen Scheirs.

Invisible: The Chronicles of Benjamin Knight 🦴🦴½ **1993 (R)** Scientist Benjamin Knight is rendered invisible during a terrible laboratory accident. His only hope of regaining his visible form is a desperate search by Knight and his fellow scientists for just the right chemical antidote. **80m/C VHS.** Brian Cousins, Jennifer Nash, Michael DellaFemina, Curt Lowens, David Kaufman, Alan Oppenheimer, Aharon Ipale; ***D:*** Joakim (Jack) Ersgard; ***W:*** Earl Kenton.

The Invisible Woman 🦴🦴🦴 **1940** Above average comedy about zany professor Gibbs (Barrymore) discovering the secret of invisibility and making luscious model Kitty (Bruce) transparent during his experiments. She tries some romance with Richard (Howard), the guy who financed the invention, and then gets involved with crooks who want to steal the machine for their own illicit gain. A very likeable movie with a good cast. Based on a story by Curt Siodmak and Joe May, the same team that wrote "The Invisible Man Returns." **73m/B VHS.** John Barrymore, Virginia Bruce, John Howard, Charlie Ruggles, Oscar Homolka, Margaret Hamilton, Donald MacBride, Edward Brophy, Shemp Howard, Charles Lane, Thurston Hall; ***D:*** Edward Sutherland; ***W:*** Robert Lees, Frederic Rinaldo, Gertrude Purcell; ***C:*** Elwood "Woody" Bredell.

Invitation au Voyage 🦴🦴½ **1982 (R)** Follows the journey of a twin who refuses to accept the death of his sister, a rock singer. The obsession is played fairly well, but it's a no-twin situation, even though the guy can't admit it. Perversity is played to the point of overkill. From the novel "Moi, Ma Soeur Images," by Jean Bany. In French with English subtitles. **90m/C VHS.** *FR* Laurent Malet, Nina Scott, Aurore Clement, Mario Adorf; ***D:*** Peter Del Monte.

Invitation to a Gunfighter 🦴🦴 **1964** Small town politics change when a paid assassin ambles into town and creates a lot of talk among the neighbors. Like a long joke in which the teller keeps forgetting the important details, the plot grows confusing though it's not complicated. Brynner is interesting as an educated, half-black/half-creole, hired gun. **92m/C VHS.** Yul Brynner, George Segal, Strother Martin, William Hickey, Janice Rule, Mike Kellin, Pat Hingle, John Alonzo; ***D:*** Richard Wilson.

Invitation to Hell 🦴½ **1984** "Faust" meets "All My Children" in celluloid suburbia. Never Emmied Lucci is the devil's dirty worker, persuading upwardly mobile suburbanites to join a really exclusive country club in exchange for a little downward mobility. Urich, a space scientist, and family are new in town, and soul searching Lucci's got her devil vixen sights set on space jock and brood. Bound to disappoint both fans of Craven's early independent work ("Last House on the Left") and his later high gloss ("Nightmare on Elm Street") formulas. Made for the small screen. **100m/C VHS.** Susan Lucci, Robert Urich, Joanna Cassidy, Kevin McCarthy, Patty McCormack, Joe Regalbuto, Soleil Moon Frye, Barret Oliver; ***D:*** Wes Craven. **TV**

Invitation to Hell woof! **1984** Tormented maiden has a devil of a time discovering a secret power that can enable her to gracefully decline a satanic summoning. The cliched evil is tormenting. **100m/C VHS.** Becky Simpson, Joseph Sheahan, Colin Efford, Stephen Longhurst.

Invitation to the Dance 🦴🦴½ **1956** Three classic dance sequences, "Circus," "Ring Around the Rosy," and "Sinbad the Sailor." For dance lovers, featuring excellent performances by Kelly. **93m/C VHS.** Gene Kelly, Igor Youskevitch, Tamara Toumanova; ***D:*** Gene Kelly. Berlin Intl. Film Fest. '56: Golden Berlin Bear.

Invitation to the Wedding 🦴🦴 **1973 (PG)** When the best friend of a bridegroom falls in love with the bride, he stops at nothing to halt the wedding. Not exactly the Gielgud movie of the year, but there are some excellent scenes between him and Richardson. **89m/C VHS.** John Gielgud, Ralph Richardson, Paul Nicholas, Elizabeth Shepherd; ***D:*** Joseph Brooks; ***M:*** Joseph Brooks.

The Ipcress File 🦴🦴🦴 **1965** The first of the Harry Palmer spy mysteries that made Caine a star. Based upon the best-seller by Len Deighton, it features the flabby, nearsighted spy investigating the kidnapping of notable British scientists. Solid scenes, including a scary brainwashing session, and tongue-firmly-in-British-cheek humor. Lots of camera play to emphasize Caine's myopia. Two sequels: "Funeral in Berlin" and "Billion Dollar Brain." **108m/C VHS, DVD.** *GB* Michael Caine, Nigel Green, Guy Doleman, Sue Lloyd, Gordon Jackson; ***D:*** Sidney J. Furie; ***W:*** Bill Canaway, James Doran; ***C:*** Otto Heller; ***M:*** John Barry. British Acad. '65: Film.

Iphigenia 🦴🦴🦴 **1977** Based on the classic Greek tragedy by Euripides, this story concerns the Greek leader Agamemnon, who plans to sacrifice his lovely daughter, Iphigenia, to please the gods. Mere mortals protest and start a save-the-babe movement, but Euripides' moral—you can't please 'em all—is devastatingly realized. Fine adaptation that becomes visually extravagant at times, with an equally fine musical score. In Greek with English subtitles. **130m/C VHS.** *GR* Irene Papas, Costa Kazakos, Tatiana Papamoskou, Costas Carras, Christos Tsangas, Panos Michalopoulas; ***D:*** Michael Cacoyannis; ***W:*** Michael Cacoyannis; ***C:*** Yorgos Arvanitis; ***M:*** Mikis Theodorakis.

I.Q. 🦴🦴½ **1994 (PG)** Albert Einstein (the irascible Matthau) thinks his co-ed niece (Ryan) is in need of a little romance, so he engineers a plan to get her into the arms of Robbins, a local auto mechanic. Robbins and Ryan are comfortable in their comic roles, although they're both above the material. Matthau shines as the famous physicist. Plot gets a little farfetched with its central contrivance of making Robbins look like a brilliant scientist, which leaves second half of story flat. However, chemistry between leads is undeniable and you can't help but cheer on the inevitable. Visually pleasing with Ryan costumed in cool, elegant '50s fashions. Filmed in Princeton, New Jersey. **95m/C VHS.** Tim Robbins, Meg Ryan, Walter Matthau, Lou Jacobi, Gene Saks, Joseph Maher, Stephen Fry, Tony Shalhoub, Frank Whaley; ***D:*** Fred Schepisi; ***W:*** Michael Leeson, Andy Breckman; ***C:*** Ian Baker; ***M:*** Jerry Goldsmith.

Iran: Days of Crisis 🦴🦴½ **1991** An insightful cable miniseries recounts America's humiliation at the hands of Iranian radicals in 1979, told from the vantage of a U.S. embassy official married to a Tehran woman. Former Carter administration aides Hamilton Jordan and Gerald Rafshoon devised the docudrama, which spares neither them nor their president in showing how bungled and shortsighted policies led to 52 Americans held hostage for over a year. **185m/C VHS.** Arliss Howard, Alice Krige, George Grizzard, Jeff Fahey, Tony Goldwyn, Ronald Guttman, Valerie Kaprisky, Daniel Gelin; ***D:*** Kevin Connor. **CABLE**

Irezumi 🦴🦴🦴 *Spirit of Tattoo* **1983** A Japanese woman has her body elaborately tattooed to please her lover. Things start off well enough. He's an inept lover, so she has directions tattooed, but then he discovers a "Dear John" letter on her foot just as she gives him the boot. Actually proves an interesting study in obsession and eroticism, with the tattoos drawing the lovers deeper and deeper until they get under each other's skin. In Japanese with English subtitles. **88m/C VHS.** *JP*

Iris 🦴🦴 **1989** Drama follows the passionate and tragic life of New Zealand writer Iris Wilkinson, an international novelist, poet, and journalist. Wilkinson achieved a great deal of acclaim as a writer, but suffered many personal tragedies, and eventually took her own life at age 33. Well intentioned but clunky treatment of powerful subject matter. **90m/C VHS.** *NZ* Helen Morse.

Iris 🦴🦴🦴 **2001 (R)** Enduring love story between novelist/philosopher Iris Murdoch and her husband John Bayley from their days at Oxford in the 1950s to Murdoch's long decline from Alzheimer's and death in 1999. Winslet and Bonneville play the young duo while Dench and Broadbent play the mature marrieds. The ladies have the showier roles, especially Winslet, since the young Iris was a sexual free-spirit and disdained conventional morality while John comes across as shy and rather awed by Murdoch's talents. Based on Bayley's memoirs "Iris: A Memoir" and "Elegy for Iris." **90m/C VHS, DVD.** *GB US* Judi Dench, Jim Broadbent, Kate Winslet, Hugh Bonneville, Penelope Wilton, Juliet Aubrey, Timothy West, Samuel West, Eleanor Bron; ***D:*** Richard Eyre; ***W:*** Richard Eyre, Charles Wood; ***C:*** Roger Pratt; ***M:*** James Horner. Oscars '01: Support. Actor (Broadbent); British Acad. '01: Actress (Dench); Golden Globes '02: Support. Actor (Broadbent); L.A. Film Critics '01: Support. Actor (Broadbent), Support. Actress (Winslet); Natl. Bd. of Review '01: Support. Actor (Broadbent).

Iris Blond 🦴🦴½ **1998 (R)** Bittersweet romantic comedy about a sadsack piano player named Romeo (Verdone), who's pushing 50 and is unlucky in love. Having been cuckholded by his girlfriend, Romeo asks a fortuneteller (Fumo) for some help. She tells him his future resides with a singer who has the name of a flower. Naturally, Romeo picks the wrong chick (Ferrerol), only to soon meet red-hot maneater, Iris (Gerini). Eventually things work out as they should. French and Italian with subtitles. **100m/C VHS.** *IT* Carlo Verdone, Andrea Ferreol, Claudia Gerini, Nuccia Fumo; ***D:*** Carlo Verdone; ***W:*** Carlo Verdone, Francesca Marciano, Pasquale Plastino; ***C:*** Giuseppe Di Biase.

Irish Cinderella 🦴🦴 **1922** A silent version of the Cinderella legend set in Ireland, with thematic stress on Irish politics and patriotism. **72m/B VHS, 8mm.** Pattie MacNamara.

Irish Luck 🦴🦴 **1939** A bellhop turns detective to figure out the mysterious happenings in his hotel. Becomes terminally cute by playing on a luck o' the Irish theme. **58m/B VHS.** Frankie Darro, Dick Purcell, Sheila (Rebecca Wassem) Darcy, Grant Withers; ***D:*** Howard Bretherton.

The Irishman 🦴🦴½ **1978** Set in 1920s Australia, the tale of a proud North Queensland family and their struggles to stay together. The Irish immigrant father is a teamster whose horse-drawn wagons are threatened by progress. His fight to preserve old ways is impressive, but gives way to sentimentality. **108m/C VHS, DVD.** *AU* Lou Brown, Michael Craig, Simon Burke, Robyn Nevin, Bryan Brown; ***D:*** Donald Crombie; ***W:*** Donald Crombie; ***C:*** Peter James; ***M:*** Charles Marawood.

Irma La Douce 🦴🦴½ **1963** A gendarme pulls a one-man raid on a backstreet Parisian joint and falls in love with one of the hookers he arrests. Lemmon is great as a well-meaning, incompetent boob, and MacLaine gives her all as the hapless hooker. A plodding pace, however, robs it of the original's zip, though it was a boxoffice smash. Broadway musical is lost without the music. **144m/C VHS, DVD, Wide.** Jack Lemmon, Shirley MacLaine, Herschel Bernardi; ***D:*** Billy Wilder; ***W:*** Billy Wilder, I.A.L. Diamond; ***M:*** Andre Previn. Oscars '63: Adapt. Score; Golden Globes '64: Actress—Mus./Comedy (MacLaine).

Irma Vep 🦴🦴 **1996** Satiric tweaking of French filmmaking begins with hasbeen director Rene Vidal (Leaud) hiring Hong Kong star Maggie Cheung to take the lead role of Irma Vep in a remake of the 1915 silent French classic "Les Vampires." But from the moment the actress arrives in Paris, it's one disaster after another. Cheung has trouble with the language barrier, Vidal is having a breakdown, lesbian costumer Zoe (Richard) is instantly smitten by Cheung and has her interest humiliatingly conveyed to everyone on the production. Then there's Jose Murano (Castel), a snobbish auteur who replaces Vidal and believes the Chinese actress can't play a French thief, not knowing that Cheung has become obsessed with her role and is practicing stealing from other hotel guests. English and French with subtitles. **96m/C VHS, DVD, Wide.** *FR* Maggie Cheung, Jean-Pierre Leaud, Nathalie Richard, Bulle Ogier, Lou Castel, Antoine Basler, Nathalie Boutefeu, Arsinee Khanjian, Alex Descas; ***D:*** Olivier Assayas; ***W:*** Olivier Assayas; ***C:*** Eric Gautier.

Iron & Silk 🦴🦴½ **1991 (PG)** A young American searches for himself while he teaches English and learns martial arts in mainland China. Based on the true story of Salzman's travels. His studies of martial arts and Chinese culture provide a model for his students in their studies of American language and culture. Beautiful photography. Fine performances. **94m/C VHS.** Mark Saltzman, Pan Qingfu, Jeanette Lin Tsui, Vivian Wu; ***D:*** Shirley Sun; ***W:*** Mark Saltzman, Shirley Sun; ***M:*** Michael Gibbs.

Iron Angel 🦴½ **1964** During the Korean War a squadron sets out to silence North Korean guns. They do. Judging by their eternal bickering they must have put the enemy to sleep. **84m/B VHS.** Jim Davis, Margo Woode, Donald (Don "Red") Barry, L.Q. (Justus E. McQueen) Jones; ***D:*** Ken Kennedy; ***W:*** Ken Kennedy.

Iron Cowboy 🦴🦴 **1968** Actor finds romance with film editor while audience stifles yawns. Filmed on the set of "Blue," this pre-"Deliverance" Reynolds comedy never made it to the theaters. (Smithee is actually director Jud Taylor.) **86m/C VHS.** Burt Reynolds, Barbara Loden, Terence Stamp, Noam Pitlik, Ricardo Montalban, Patricia Casey, Jane Hampton, Joseph V. Perry; ***D:*** Alan Smithee.

The Iron Crown 🦴🦴 **1941** A 13th-century legend inspired this sometime violent spectacle involving the title totem, a symbol of justice ignored by a powerful king at his peril. There's wonderful pagentry and a notable Tarzan imitator, but the pace is terribly slow. Italian dialogue with English subtitles. **100m/C VHS.** ***D:*** Alessandro Blasetti.

The Iron Duke 🦴🦴½ **1934** Fair to middlin' historical account of the life of the Duke of Wellington, victor over Napoleon at Waterloo. **88m/B VHS.** *GB* George Arliss, Gladys Cooper, A.E. Matthews, Emlyn Williams, Felix Aylmer; ***D:*** Victor Saville.

Iron Eagle 🦴🦴½ **1986 (PG-13)** A teenager teams with a renegade fighter pilot to rescue the youth's father from captivity in the Middle East. Predictable but often exciting. Followed by two sequels. **117m/C VHS, DVD.** Louis Gossett Jr., Jason Gedrick, Tim Thomerson, David Suchet, Larry B. Scott, Caroline Lagerfelt, Jerry Levine, Michael Bowen, Robbie (Reist) Rist, Bobby Jacoby, Melora Hardin; ***D:*** Sidney J. Furie; ***W:*** Kevin Elders, Sidney J. Furie; ***M:*** Basil Poledouris.

Iron Eagle 2 🦴🦴 **1988 (PG)** Lower-budget extended adventures of a maverick fighter pilot after he is reinstated in the Air Force. This time he links with an equally rebellious commie fighter and blasts away at nuke-happy Ivan. Yahoo fun for all overt Yankees! Followed by "Aces: Iron Eagle 3." Available in Spanish. **102m/C VHS.** *CA IS* Louis Gossett Jr., Mark Humphrey, Stuart Margolin, Alan Scarfe, Maury Chaykin, Sharon H. Brandon; ***D:*** Sidney J. Furie; ***W:*** Sidney J. Furie, Kevin Elders; ***C:*** Alan Dostie; ***M:*** Amin Bhatia.

Iron Eagle 4 🦴½ **1995 (PG-13)** Series has gotten old and tired though Gossett Jr. shows professionalism in his father figure role of retired Air Force General "Chappy" Sinclair. He's running the Iron Eagle Flight School—a training center/holding cell for troubled teens—along with pilot Doug Masters (Cadieux). Masters and his would-be pilots discover suspicious activities at a local air base, leading to biological weapons and an Air Force conspiracy. **95m/C VHS, DVD.** *CA* Louis Gossett Jr., Jason Cadieux, Al Waxman, Joanne Vannicola, Rachel Blanchard, Sean McCann, Ross Hill, Karen Gayle; ***D:*** Sidney J. Furie; ***W:*** Michael Stokes; ***C:*** Curtis Petersen; ***M:*** Paul Zaza.

Iron Giant 🦴🦴🦴½ **1999 (PG)** After a giant robot falls from the sky and frightens a small town, only a young boy is willing to befriend the iron man. With his new friend, he teaches the townspeople a lesson about being afraid of what is different. Jennifer Aniston provides the voice for the boy's mother, and Harry Connick Jr. that of the town beatnik. Great animation and story propel this tale above the level of most kiddie fare. Based on the 1968 children's book by Ted Hughes, which was also used for a 1989 concept album by Pete Townshend. **86m/C VHS, DVD.** ***D:*** Brad Bird; ***W:*** Tim McCanlies; ***M:*** Michael Kamen; ***V:*** Vin Diesel, Eli Marienthal, Jennifer Aniston, Harry Connick Jr., John Mahoney, M. Emmet Walsh, Cloris Leachman, James Gammon, Christopher McDonald.

Iron Horsemen 🦴 *J.C* **1971 (R)** A motorcycle gang leader has a prophetic vision while tripping on LSD, and returns to his former town to challenge its religious establishment. **97m/C VHS.** William F. McGaha, Hannibal Penny, Joanna Moore, Burr de Benning, Slim Pickens, Pat Delaney; ***D:*** William F. McGaha.

The Iron Major 🦴🦴½ **1943** Frank Cavanaugh, a famous football coach, becomes a hero in WWI. Standard flag-waving biography to increase morale back home, but fairly well-made. **85m/B VHS.** Pat O'Brien, Ruth Warrick, Robert Ryan, Leon Ames, Russell Wade, Bruce Edwards; ***D:*** Ray Enright.

The Iron Mask 🦴🦴½ **1929** Early swashbuckling extravaganza with a master swordsman defending the French king from a scheme involving substitution by a lookalike. Still fairly exciting, thanks largely to director Dwan's flair. Based on Alexandre Dumas's "Three Musketeers" and "The Man in the Iron Mask" with talking sequences. **103m/B VHS, DVD.** Douglas Fairbanks Sr., Nigel de Brulier, Marguerite de la Motte, Ullrich Haupt, William "Billy" Bakewell; ***D:*** Allan Dwan; ***W:*** Douglas Fairbanks Sr.; ***C:*** Henry Sharp.

Iron Maze 🦴½ **1991 (R)** A fascinating notion forms the center of this dramatic scrapheap; the classic Japanese "Rashomon" plot shifted to a rusting Pennsylvania steel town. When a Tokyo businessman is found bludgeoned, witnesses and suspects (including his American-born wife) tell contradictory stories. It's too convoluted and contrived to work, with a hollow happy ending tacked on. Oliver Stone helped produce. **102m/C VHS, DVD.** Jeff Fahey, Bridget Fonda, Hiroaki Murakami, J.T. Walsh, Gabriel Damon, John Randolph, Peter Allas; ***D:*** Hiroaki Yoshida; ***W:*** Tim Metcalfe; ***C:*** Morio Saegusa; ***M:*** Stanley Myers.

Iron Monkey 🦴🦴½ *Siunin Wong Feihung Tsi Titmalau; Shao Nian Huang Fei Hong Zhi Tie Ma Liu; Iron Monkey: The Young Wong Feihung* **1993 (PG-13)** Historical fantasy martial arts is built around the Iron Monkey (Rongguang Yu), a Robin-Hood figure who defeats whole armies of opponents and can leap tall buildings in a single bound. The humor and outstanding choreography of the fight scenes put this one a cut above the usual martial arts action flick. **87m/C VHS, DVD.** *HK* Rongguang Yu, Donnie Yen, Yam Sai-kun, Tsing-ying Wong; ***D:*** Wooping Yuen; ***W:*** Tseng Pik-Yin, Tsui Hark, Tai-Muk Lau, Cheung Tan, Pik-yin Tang; ***C:*** Arthur Wong; ***M:*** James L. Venable.

Iron Mountain Trail 🦴½ **1953** Postal inspector Allen is sent to California to see what's holding up mail delivery. He discovers a couple of nefarious types and he and his horse Koko put them in their place. **54m/B VHS.** Rex Allen, Slim Pickens, Roy Barcroft, Grant Withers, Nan Leslie, Forrest Taylor; ***D:*** William Witney; ***W:*** Gerald Geraghty; ***C:*** Bud Thackery; ***M:*** Stanley Wilson.

Iron Thunder 🦴½ **1989** Liberty is in peril and only much kicking and pec flexing will make the world a kinder gentler place. A thundering bore. **85m/C VHS.** Iron "Amp" Elmore, George M. Young, Julius Dorsey.

The Iron Triangle 🦴🦴 **1989 (R)** A U.S. officer taken prisoner by the Viet Cong forms a bond with one of his captors. Film lends the viewer an opportunity to see things from the other sides perspective. **94m/C VHS.** Beau Bridges, Haing S. Ngor, Liem Whatley; ***D:*** Eric Weston; ***W:*** John Bushelman.

Iron Warrior 🦴 **1987 (R)** A barbarian hacks his way through a fantastical world to get to a beautiful princess. **82m/C VHS.** Miles O'Keeffe, Savina Gersak, Tim Lane; ***D:*** Al (Alfonso Brescia) Bradley; ***W:*** Al (Alfonso Brescia) Bradley.

Iron Will 🦴🦴½ **1993 (PG)** Okay Disney family movie based on a true story. Will Stoneman is a 17-year-old farm kid from South Dakota. It's 1917 and because of his father's death there's no money to send Will to college. So he decides to enter the 500 mile winner-take-all dog sled race, with its $10,000 prize. Lots of obstacles, several villains, but Will perseveres. **109m/C VHS.** MacKenzie Astin, Kevin Spacey, David Ogden Stiers, August Schellenberg, George Gerdes, John Terry; ***D:*** Charles Haid; ***W:*** John Michael Hayes, Jeffrey Arch, Djordje Milicevic; ***M:*** Joel McNeely.

Ironclads 🦴🦴½ **1990** Memorable dramatization of the five-hour naval battle between the Confederate's Merrimac and the Union's Monitor during the Civil War. The special effects are the only thing worth watching in this overlong tale that includes standard subplots of loyalty, lost loves, and death from war. **94m/C VHS.** Virginia Madsen, Alex Hyde-White, Reed Edward Diamond, E.G. Marshall, Fritz Weaver, Philip Casnoff; ***D:*** Delbert Mann.

Ironheart 🦴½ **1992** Slimy Milverstead and his henchman meet lovely young women at dance clubs, drug them, and sell them into slavery. But the trouble really starts when they kill a cop and his former partner, John Keem (Lee), lashes out with his blazing martial arts skill to still the perpetrators. **?m/C VHS.** Britton Lee, Bolo Yeung, Richard Norton, Karman Kruschke; ***D:*** Robert Clouse; ***W:*** Lawrence Riggins.

Ironmaster 🦴 **1983** When a primitive tribesman is exiled from his tribe, he discovers a mysteriously power-filled iron staff on a mountainside. **98m/C VHS.** George Eastman, Pamela Field.

Ironweed 🦴🦴🦴 **1987 (R)** Grim and gritty drama about bums living the hard life in Depression-era Albany. Nicholson excels as a former ballplayer turned drunk bothered by visions of the past, and Streep is his equal in the lesser role of a tubercular boozer. Waits also shines. Another grim view from "Pixote" director Babenco. Kennedy scripted based on his Pulitzer Prize-winning tragedy. **135m/C VHS.** Jack Nicholson, Meryl Streep, Tom Waits, Carroll Baker, Michael O'Keefe, Fred Gwynne, Diane Venora, Margaret Whitton, Jake Dengel, Nathan Lane, James Gammon, Joe Grifasi, Bethel Leslie, Ted Levine, Frank Whaley; ***D:*** Hector Babenco; ***W:*** William Kennedy; ***M:*** John Morris. L.A. Film Critics '87: Actor (Nicholson); N.Y. Film Critics '87: Actor (Nicholson).

Irreconcilable Differences 🦴🦴½ **1984 (PG)** When her Beverly Hills parents spend more time working and fretting than giving hugs and love, a ten-year-old girl sues them for divorce on the grounds of "irreconcilable differences." The media has a field day when they hear that she would rather go live with the maid. Well cast, with well-developed characterizations. The script, by the creators of "Private Benjamin," is humanely comic rather than uproariously funny. **112m/C VHS.** Ryan O'Neal, Shelley Long, Drew Barrymore, Sam Wanamaker, Allen (Goorwitz) Garfield, Sharon Stone, Luana Anders; ***D:*** Charles Shyer; ***W:*** Charles Shyer, Nancy Meyers.

Irresistible Impulse 🦴🦴½ **1995** Sleazy real estate agent Jeffrey allows himself to become entangled in a wild scheme with bad girl Beaman. **107m/C VHS.** Doug Jeffery, Lee Anne Beavan; ***D:*** Jag Mundhra.

Is Money Everything? 🦴🦴 **1923** Man goes to the big city, becomes a success, and then has an affair with a married woman. **58m/B VHS.** Norman Kerry, Miriam Cooper, Martha Mansfield, William Bailey, Andrew Hicks, John Sylvester, Lawrence Brooke; ***D:*** Glen Lyons; ***W:*** Glen Lyons; ***C:*** Alvin Knechtel.

Is Paris Burning? 🦴🦴🦴 *Paris Brule-t-il?* **1966** A spectacularly star-studded but far too sprawling account of the liberation of Paris from Nazi occupation. The script, in which seven writers had a hand, is based on Larry Collins and Dominique Lapierre's best-seller. **173m/C VHS.** *FR* Jean-Paul Belmondo, Charles Boyer, Leslie Caron, Jean-Pierre Cassel, George Chakiris, Claude Dauphin, Alain Delon, Kirk Douglas, Glenn Ford, Gert Frobe, Daniel Gelin, E.G. Marshall, Yves Montand, Anthony Perkins, Claude Rich, Simone Signoret, Robert Stack, Jean-Louis Trintignant, Pierre Vaneck, Orson Welles, Bruno Cremer, Suzy Delair, Michael (Michel) Lonsdale; ***D:*** Rene Clement; ***W:*** Gore Vidal, Francis Ford Coppola; ***C:*** Marcel Grignon; ***M:*** Maurice Jarre.

Is There Life Out There? 🦴🦴½ **1994** Wife, mother, and waitress Lily Marshall (McEntire) decides it's time to do something for herself—so she goes to work on her college degree. But there's unexpected family resentments, a breast cancer scare, and the interest of a young teaching assistant to turn her head away from her studies. Filmed in Nashville, Tennessee. Based on a song by McEntire; made for TV. **92m/C VHS.** Reba McEntire, Keith Carradine, Mitchell Anderson, Donald Moffat, Genia Michaela; ***D:*** David Hugh Jones; ***W:*** Dalene Young. **TV**

Is There Sex After Death? 🦴🦴🦴 **1971 (R)** Often funny satire on the sexual revolution is constructed as a behind-the-scenes view of the porn film world. Odd cast includes Henry and Warhol superstar Woodlawn. Originally rated "X." **97m/C VHS.** Buck Henry, Alan Abel, Marshall Efron, Holly Woodlawn, Earl Doud; ***D:*** Alan Abel, Jeanne Abel.

Isaac Asimov's Nightfall 🦴🦴 *Nightfall* **2000 (R)** The planet Aeon has six suns and has never experienced night. But with an eclipse approaching, religious cultists are predicting catastrophe. Scientist Carradine tries to allay the population's fear. Low-budget and bland adaptation of Asimov's 1941 short story. **85m/C VHS, DVD.** David Carradine, Jennifer Burns, Joseph Hodge; ***D:*** Gwyneth Gibby; ***W:*** Gwyneth Gibby, John W. Corrington, Michael B. Druxman; ***C:*** Abhik Mukhopadhyay; ***M:*** Nicolas Tenbroek, Brad Segal. **VIDEO**

Isadora 🦴🦴🦴 *The Loves of Isadora* **1968** A loose, imaginative biography of Isadora Duncan, the cause celebre dancer in the 1920s who became famous for her scandalous performances, outrageous behavior, public love affairs, and bizarre, early death. Redgrave is exceptional in the lead, and Fox provides fine support. Restored from its original 131-minute print length by the director. **138m/C VHS.** *GB* Vanessa Redgrave, Jason Robards Jr., James Fox, Ivan Tchenko, John Fraser, Bessie Love, Cynthia Harris, Libby Glenn, Tony Vogel, Wallace Eaton, John Quentin, Nicholas Pennell, Ronnie Gilbert, Alan Gifford, Christian Duvaleix; ***D:*** Karel Reisz; ***W:*** Melvyn Bragg, Clive Exton; ***C:*** Larry Pizer; ***M:*** Maurice Jarre. Cannes '69: Actress (Redgrave); Natl. Soc. Film Critics '69: Actress (Redgrave).

Ishtar 🦴🦴 **1987 (PG-13)** Two astoundingly untalented performers have a gig in a fictional Middle Eastern country and become involved in foreign intrigue. A big-budget boxoffice bomb produced by Beatty offering few laughs, though it's not as bad as its reputation. Considering the talent involved, though, it's a disappointment, with Beatty and Hoffman laboring to create Hope and Crosby chemistry. Anyone for a slow night? **107m/C VHS.** Dustin Hoffman, Warren Beatty, Isabelle Adjani, Charles Grodin, Jack Weston, Tess Harper, Carol Kane, Matt Frewer; ***D:*** Elaine May; ***W:*** Elaine May; ***C:*** Vittorio Storaro; ***M:*** Dave Grusin, Bahjawa. Golden Raspberries '87: Worst Director (May).

The Island 🦴🦴🦴½ *Hadaka No Shima; Naked Island* **1961** Poetic examination of a peasant family's daily struggle for existence on a small island. No dialogue in this slow but absorbing work by one of Japan's master directors. **96m/B VHS, 8mm.** *JP* Nobuko Otowa, Taiji Tonoyama, Shinji Tanaka, Masanori Horimoto; ***D:*** Kaneto Shindo.

The Island woof! **1980 (R)** New York reporter embarks on a Bermuda triangle investigation, only to meet with the murderous but sterile descendants of 17th century pirates on a deserted island. Caine is designated as stud service for the last remaining fertile woman. Almost surreal in its badness. Adapted by Benchley from his novel. **113m/C VHS.** Michael Caine, David Warner, Angela Punch McGregor, Frank Middlemass, Don Henderson; ***D:*** Michael Ritchie; ***W:*** Peter Benchley; ***C:*** Henri Decae; ***M:*** Ennio Morricone.

The Island at the Top of the World ♪♪½ **1974 (G)** A rich Englishman, in search of his missing son, travels to the Arctic Circle in 1908. The rescue party includes an American archeologist, a French astronaut, and an Eskimo guide. Astonishingly, they discover an unknown, "lost" Viking kingdom. This Jules Verne-style adventure doesn't quite measure up, but kids will like it. **93m/C VHS, DVD, Wide.** David Hartman, Donald Sinden, Jacques Marin, Mako, David Gwillim; ***D:*** Robert Stevenson; ***W:*** John Whedon; ***C:*** Frank Phillips; ***M:*** Maurice Jarre.

Island Claw woof! *Night of the Claw* **1980** A group of marine biologists experimenting on a tropical island discover the "Island Claw," who evolved as the result of toxic waste seeping into the ocean. A festering, oozing woofer. **91m/C VHS.** Barry Nelson, Robert Lansing; ***D:*** Hernan Cardenas.

Island in the Sun ♪♪ **1957** Racial tension pulls apart the lives of the residents of a Caribbean island. Good cast, but a very poor adaptation of Alec Waugh's novel. Marvelous location shots. **119m/C VHS.** James Mason, Joan Fontaine, Dorothy Dandridge, John Williams, Harry Belafonte; ***D:*** Robert Rossen; ***C:*** Frederick A. (Freddie) Young; ***M:*** Malcolm Arnold.

Island Monster ♪½ *Monster of the Island* **1953** Deals with ruthless, kidnapping drug-smugglers led by "monster" Karloff, and the efforts to bring them to justice. **87m/B VHS.** *IT* Boris Karloff, Renata Vicario, Franca Marzi; ***D:*** Robert Montero.

Island of Blood ♪½ **1986** Buckets of blood abound on a remote island when a film crew's beset by berserk butcher. **84m/C VHS.** Jim Williams, Dean Richards.

Island of Desire ♪ *Saturday Island* **1952** An Army nurse, a doctor, and a young Navy Adonis are trapped on a deserted island. Not surprisingly, a love triangle develops. **93m/C VHS.** *GB* Tab Hunter, Linda Darnell, Donald Gray; ***D:*** Stuart Heisler.

The Island of Dr. Moreau ♪♪½ **1977 (PG)** This remake of the "Island of the Lost Souls" (1933) is a bit disappointing but worth watching for Lancaster's solid performance as the scientist who has isolated himself on a Pacific island in order to continue his chromosome research—he can transform animals into near-humans and humans into animals. Neat-looking critters. Adaptation of the H.G. Wells novel of the same title. **99m/C VHS, DVD, Wide.** Burt Lancaster, Michael York, Nigel Davenport, Barbara Carrera, Richard Basehart, Nick Cravat; ***D:*** Don Taylor; ***W:*** John Herman Shaner, Al Ramrus; ***C:*** Gerry Fisher.

The Island of Dr. Moreau ♪½ **1996 (PG-13)** What were they thinking? Not even the frightening "manimals" could prevent the unintentional laughs from this abomination of the horrifying 1896 H.G. Wells novel. Brando's enormous presence as the mad scientist Moreau walks a tight rope between puzzling and campy, especially as he explains his ghastly DNA experiments on a remote Pacific to a miscast Thewlis. A wasted Kilmer is the doctors's right-hand hybrid who often seems to be acting in a different movie. Filming hit some big rocks when "creative differences" caused original director Richard Stanley to be replaced and Rob Morrow (originally the lawyer) to ask for his release. Previously filmed under the same title in 1977 and (terrifically) as "Island of Lost Souls" in 1933. **91m/C VHS, DVD.** Marlon Brando, Val Kilmer, David Thewlis, Fairuza Balk, Marco Hofschneider, Temuera Morrison, Ron Perlman; ***D:*** John Frankenheimer; ***W:*** Richard Stanley, Ron Hutchinson; ***C:*** William A. Fraker; ***M:*** Gary Chang.

Island of Lost Girls woof! **1973 (R)** Young women are taken to an unknown location in the Far East to be sold as part of a white slave ring. **85m/C VHS.** Brad Harris, Tony Kendall, Monica Pardo.

Island of Lost Souls ♪♪♪½ **1932** Horrifying adaptation of H.G. Wells's "The Island of Dr. Moreau" was initially banned in parts of the U.S. because of its disturbing contents. Dr. Moreau (Laughton) is a mad scientist who lives on a remote island and is obsessed with making men out of jungle animals. When shipwreck survivor Edward Parker (Arlen) gets stranded on the island, little does he know that Moreau wants to mate him with Lota (Burke), the Panther Woman, to produce the first human-animal child. As unsettling today as it was in the '30s. Lugosi has the notable role of the hybrid "Sayer of the Law" while Burke beat out more than 60,000 young women in a nationwide search to play the Panther Woman, winning the role because of her "feline" look. Remade as "The Island of Dr. Moreau" in both 1977 and 1996. **71m/B VHS.** Charles Laughton, Bela Lugosi, Richard Arlen, Leila Hyams, Kathleen Burke, Stanley Fields, Robert F. (Bob) Kortman, Arthur Hohl; ***Cameos:*** Alan Ladd, Randolph Scott, Buster Crabbe; ***D:*** Erle C. Kenton; ***W:*** Philip Wylie, Waldemar Young; ***C:*** Karl Struss.

Island of Terror ♪♪♪ *Night of the Silicates; The Creepers* **1966** First-rate science fiction chiller about an island overrun by shell-like creatures that suck the bones out of their living prey. Good performances and interesting twists make for prickles up the spine. **90m/C VHS.** *GB* Peter Cushing, Edward Judd, Carole Gray, Sam Kydd, Niall MacGinnis; ***D:*** Terence Fisher.

Island of the Blue Dolphins ♪♪½ **1964** Based on a popular children's book by Scott O'Dell, this is a true story of a young Native American girl who, with her brother, are stranded on a deserted island when their people accidentally leave them. When the boy is killed, the girl learns to survive by her skills and by befriending the leader of a pack of wild dogs. Good family fare. **99m/C VHS.** Celia Kaye, Larry Domasin, Ann Daniel, George Kennedy; ***D:*** James B. Clark.

Island of the Burning Doomed ♪♪½ *Island of the Burning Damned; Night of the Big Heat* **1967** A brutal heat wave accompanies invading aliens in this British-made outing. Lee and Cushing carry the picture. **94m/C VHS.** *GB* Christopher Lee, Peter Cushing, Patrick Allen, Sarah Lawson, Jane Merrow; ***D:*** Terence Fisher.

Island of the Dead ♪♪ **2000 (R)** Now here's a storyline sure to be entertaining. One business tycoon, one policewoman, one prison warden, and three convicts are all trapped on a island burial ground. Just when the dead (in the form of maggots and killer flies) decide to rise up and strike a little terror. **91m/C VHS.** Malcolm McDowell, Talisa Soto, Bruce Ramsay, Mos Def, Devin Crannell; ***D:*** Tim Southam; ***W:*** Peter Koper, Tim Southam. **VIDEO**

Island of the Lost ♪½ **1968** An anthropologist's family must fight for survival when they become shipwrecked on a mysterious island. **92m/C VHS.** *GB* Richard Greene, Luke Halpin, Mart Hulswit, Jose De Vega, Robin Mattson, Irene Tsu, Sheilah Wells; ***D:*** John Florea, Ricou Browning; ***W:*** Richard Carlson, Ivan Tors; ***C:*** Howard Winner; ***M:*** George Bruns.

Island Trader ♪ **1971** Young lad battles pirates and a crooked tug captain who seek hidden gold that he knows about. **95m/C VHS.** John Ewart, Ruth Cracknell, Eric Oldfield; ***D:*** Harold Rubie.

The Islander ♪ **1988** Sixteen-year-old Inga comes of age among the commercial fishermen of Lake Michigan. **99m/C VHS.** Kit Wholihan, Jeff Weborg, Celia Klehr, Jacob Mills, Julie Johnson, Mary Ann McHugh, Michael Rock, Sheri Parish; ***D:*** Phyllis Berg-Pigorsch.

Islands ♪♪ **1987** Drama about a middle-aged ex-hippie and a young rebellious punk who clash during a summer together on a secluded island. **55m/C VHS.** Louise Fletcher. **TV**

Islands in the Stream ♪♪½ **1977 (PG)** Based on Ernest Hemingway's novel, this film is actually two movies in one. An American painter/sculptor, Thomas Hudson, lives a reclusive life on the island of Bimini shortly before the outbreak of WWII. The first part is a sensitive story of a broken family and the coming of the artist's three sons to live with their father after a four-year separation. The second part is a second rate action-adventure. **105m/C VHS, Wide.** George C. Scott, David Hemmings, Claire Bloom, Susan Tyrrell, Gilbert Roland; ***D:*** Franklin J. Schaffner; ***C:*** Fred W. Koenekamp; ***M:*** Jerry Goldsmith.

Isle of Forgotten Sins ♪♪ *Monsoon* **1943** Deep sea divers and an evil ship's captain vie for treasure. Good cast and direction but unremarkable material. **82m/B VHS, DVD, 8mm.** John Carradine, Gale Sondergaard, Sidney Toler, Frank Fenton, Veda Ann Borg; ***D:*** Edgar G. Ulmer.

Isle of Secret Passion ♪ **1985** A romance novel comes to video life as two lovers thrash out their problems on a Greek island. **90m/C VHS.** Patch MacKenzie, Michael MacRae, Zohra Lampert.

Isle of the Dead ♪♪½ **1945** A Greek general is quarantined with seemingly all manner of social vermin on a plague-infested island in the early 1900s. The fear is that vampires walk among them. Characteristically spooky Val Lewton production with some original twists. **72m/B VHS.** Boris Karloff, Ellen Drew, Marc Cramer, Katherine Emery, Helen Thimig, Alan Napier, Jason Robards Sr., Skelton Knaggs; ***D:*** Mark Robson; ***W:*** Josef Mischel, Ardel Wray; ***C:*** Jack MacKenzie; ***M:*** Leigh Harline.

Isn't Life Wonderful ♪♪♪♪ **1924** Inga's (Dempster) a Polish war orphan who struggles to provide for her family in post-WWI Germany. It means giving up her dream to marry former soldier, Paul (Hamilton), but he has a secret plan to reunite them. Filmed on location. **118m/B VHS.** Carol Dempster, Neil Hamilton, Lupino Lane, Hans von Schlettow; ***D:*** D.W. Griffith; ***W:*** D.W. Griffith.

Isn't She Great ♪♪ **2000 (R)** Irreverant biopic about the queen of sixties trash novels, Jacqueline Susann (Midler), and her hungry quest for flashy fame. Lane plays her ever-loyal husband and manager, Irving Mansfield. Susann's life was no bed of roses as she fought a long battle with breast cancer and had an austistic child, although she never let her personal tragedies become public fodder. Midler gives an overripe performance while Channing (as best friend Florence) proves to be the true scene-stealer. Unfortunately, the film is even more shallow than a Susann novel and lot less fun. Based on a memoir by Susann's editor, Michael Korda. **96m/C VHS, DVD, Wide.** Bette Midler, Nathan Lane, Stockard Channing, David Hyde Pierce, John Cleese, John Larroquette, Amanda Peet; ***D:*** Andrew Bergman; ***W:*** Paul Rudnick; ***C:*** Karl Walter Lindenlaub; ***M:*** Burt Bacharach.

Istanbul ♪♪½ **1957** Adventurer Jim Brennan (Flynn) finds a fortune in smuggled diamonds, which he hides in a hotel room. Unfortunately, he's deported before he can retrieve the gems and it takes him five years to make it back to Istanbul. Then he's hounded by the original smugglers who want their gems back and discovers his lost love Stephanie (Borchers). Cole croons a couple of songs in his role as a lounge singer. Remake of 1947's "Singapore." ♫When I Fall In Love; I Was a Little Too Lonely. **85m/C VHS.** Errol Flynn, Cornell Borchers, John Bentley, Torin Thatcher, Leif Erickson, Peggy Knudsen, Martin Benson, Nat King Cole, Werner Klemperer; ***D:*** Joseph Pevney; ***W:*** Seton I. Miller, Barbara Gray; ***C:*** William H. Daniels.

Istanbul ♪ **1985 (R)** An American charms a Belgian student into taking part in a kidnap scheme. **90m/C VHS.** *FR* Brad Dourif, Dominique Deruddere, Ingrid De Vos, Francois Beukelaers; ***D:*** Marc Didden.

Istanbul ♪ *Istanbul, Keep Your Eyes Open* **1990 (PG-13)** Believing he has stumbled upon the best story of his career, a journalist soon discovers that he has been pulled into a world of guns and violence. **88m/C VHS.** *TU SW* Robert Morley, Timothy Bottoms, Twiggy; ***D:*** Mats Arehn.

It ♪♪½ **1927** The film that established Bow as a prominent screen siren. Betty Lou (Bow) is a saucy lingerie sales clerk who sets her sights on department store owner Cyrus (Moreno), despite the fact that he has a fiancee. Adapted by Elinor Glyn from her own story; Glyn also makes an appearance. **71m/B VHS, DVD.** Clara Bow, Antonio Moreno, Jacqueline Gadsdon, William Austin, Gary Cooper, Julia Swayne Gordon; ***D:*** Clarence Badger, Josef von Sternberg; ***W:*** Hope Loring, Louis D. Lighton; ***C:*** Kinley Martin. Natl. Film Reg. '01.

It Ain't Hay ♪♪½ **1943** Grover (Abbott) and buddy Wilbur (Costello) accidentally kill their friend King O'Hara's (Kellaway) horse, so they steal a horse from the racetrack. Only the horse turns out to be a champion racer. Remake of the 1935 film "Princess O'Hara" and based on a Damon Runyon story. **79m/B VHS.** Bud Abbott, Lou Costello, Cecil Kellaway, Grace McDonald, Eugene Pallette, Shemp Howard, Eddie Quillan; ***D:*** Erle C. Kenton; ***W:*** Allen Boretz, John Grant; ***C:*** Charles Van Enger.

It Came from Beneath the Sea ♪♪♪ **1955** A giant octopus arises from the depths of the sea to scour San Francisco for human food. Ray Harryhausen effects are special. **80m/B VHS.** Kenneth Tobey, Faith Domergue, Ian Keith, Donald Curtis; ***D:*** Robert Gordon.

It Came from Outer Space ♪♪♪ **1953** Aliens take on the form of local humans to repair their spacecraft in a small Arizona town. Good performances and outstanding direction add up to a fine science fiction film. Based on the story "The Meteor" by Ray Bradbury, who also wrote the script. Originally filmed in 3-D. **81m/B VHS, DVD.** Richard Carlson, Barbara Rush, Charles Drake, Russell Johnson, Kathleen Hughes; ***D:*** Jack Arnold; ***W:*** Harry Essex, Ray Bradbury; ***C:*** Clifford Stine; ***M:*** Henry Mancini, Herman Stein, Irving Gertz.

It Came from Outer Space 2 ♪½ **1995 (PG-13)** Poorly updated cable version of the sci-fi film finds photographer Jack Putnam (Kerwin) heading home to his isolated desert community. A freakish blue lightning storm causes big changes amongst the desert dwellers who are sucked into a glowing ground mass and re-emerge possessed by shape-shifting aliens, who need the human bodies to rebuild their crashed space ship. Based on a story by Ray Bradbury and the 1953 screenplay by Harry Essex. **85m/C VHS.** Brian Kerwin, Elizabeth Pena, Bill McKinney, Jonathan Carrasco, Adrian Sparks, Howard Morris, Mickey Jones, Lauren Tewes; ***D:*** Roger Duchowny; ***W:*** Jim Wheat, Ken Wheat; ***M:*** Shirley Walker. **CABLE**

It Came from the Sky ♪♪ **1998 (R)** Eccentric strangers Jarvis Moody (Lloyd) and his girlfriend Pepper (Bleeth) invade the lives of bitter Donald (Ritter), his long-suffering wife Alice (Williams), and their brain-damaged teenage son (Zegers). Has fate sent the strange duo to intervene for good or is disaster about to strike? **92m/C VHS, DVD.** John Ritter, Christopher Lloyd, Yasmine Bleeth, JoBeth Williams, Kevin Zegers; ***D:*** Jack Bender.

It Came Upon a Midnight Clear ♪½ **1984** A heavenly miracle enables a retired (and dead) New York policeman to keep a Christmas promise to his grandson. **96m/C VHS.** Mickey Rooney, Scott Grimes, George Gaynes, Annie Potts, Lloyd Nolan, Barrie Youngfellow; ***D:*** Peter H. Hunt; ***C:*** Dean Cundey. **TV**

It Conquered the World ♪♪½ **1956** Vegetable critters from Venus follow a probe satellite back to Earth and drop in on scientist Van Cleef, who'd been their intergalactic pen pal (seems he thought a Venusian invasion would improve the neighborhood). Their travelling companions, little bat creatures, turn earth dwellers into murderous zombies, and it starts to look like the Venusians are trying to make earth their planetary exurbia. Early vintage zero-budget Corman, for schlock connoisseurs. Remade for TV as "Zontar, the Thing from Venus." **68m/B VHS.** Peter

Graves, Beverly Garland, Lee Van Cleef, Sally Fraser, Charles B. Griffith, Russ Bender, Jonathan Haze, Dick Miller, Karen Kadler, Paul Blaisdell; ***D:*** Roger Corman; ***W:*** Lou Rusoff, Charles B. Griffith; ***C:*** Frederick E. West; ***M:*** Ronald Stein.

It Could Happen to You 🦴½ **1937** Stepbrothers raised by a gentle immigrant take different paths in life. When one ends up killing someone during a botched robbery, the other—a lawyer—defends him. Standard '30s morality play. **64m/B VHS.** Alan Baxter, Andrea Leeds, Owen Davis Jr., Astrid Allwyn, Walter Kingsford, Al Shean; ***D:*** Phil Rosen.

It Could Happen to You 🦴🦴 **1939** A drunken advertising executive is charged with murder after a dead nightclub singer is found in his car. His wife sets out to clear him. **64m/C VHS.** Stuart Erwin, Gloria Stuart, Raymond Walburn, Douglas Fowley, June Gale, Paul Hurst, Richard Lane; ***D:*** Alfred Werker.

It Could Happen to You 🦴🦴½ *Cop Tips Waitress $2 Million* **1994 (PG)** NYC cop Charlie Lang (Cage) doesn't have any change to leave coffee shop waitress Yvonne (Fonda) a tip, so he promises to split his lottery ticket with her. When he nets $4 million, he makes good on the promise, much to the chargrin of his upwardly mobile wife (Perez). Capra-corn for the X-crowd is pleasant dinnertime diversion as Cage and Perez shine as henpecked nice guy and the wife committed to making him miserable. Don't look for the diner on your next trip to NYC; it was specially built in TriBeCa and dismantled after the shoot. **101m/C VHS, DVD, 8mm, Wide.** Bridget Fonda, Nicolas Cage, Rosie Perez, Red Buttons, Isaac Hayes, Seymour Cassel, Stanley Tucci, J.E. Freeman, Richard Jenkins, Ann Dowd, Wendell Pierce, Angela Pietropinto; ***D:*** Andrew Bergman; ***W:*** Andrew Bergman, Jane Anderson; ***C:*** Caleb Deschanel; ***M:*** Carter Burwell.

It Couldn't Happen Here 🦴 **1988 (PG-13)** Fans of the techno-pop duo The Pet Shop Boys can test their loyalty by enduring this feature music-video that actually played a few theatres. The dour pair journey across a surreal England, encountering a sinister blind priest, a philisophical ventriloquist's dummy, and more. Songs, sometimes presented only as muted incidental music, include the title track, "West End Girls," "It's a Sin," and "Always on My Mind." **87m/C VHS.** *GB* Neil Tennant, Chris Lowe, Joss Ackland, Neil Dickson, Carmen (De Sautoy) Du Sautoy, Gareth Hunt; ***D:*** Jack Bond.

It Happened at Nightmare Inn 🦴🦴 *A Candle for the Devil; Nightmare Hotel* **1970** Average thriller in which Geeson travels to Spanish inn and confronts two mad sisters who run the hotel. **95m/C VHS.** *SP* Judy Geeson, Aurora Bautista, Esperanza Roy, Victor Alcocer, Lone Fleming; ***D:*** Eugenio (Gene) Martin.

It Happened at the World's Fair 🦴🦴½ **1963** Fun and light romance comedy has Elvis and a companion (O'Brien) being escorted through the Seattle World's Fair by a fetching Chinese girl. ♫I'm Falling In Love Tonight; They Remind Me Too Much Of You; Take Me To The Fair; Relax; How Would You Like To Be; Beyond the Bend; One Broken Heart For Sale; Cotton Candy Land; A World Of Our Own. **105m/C VHS.** Elvis Presley, Joan O'Brien, Gary Lockwood, Kurt Russell, Edith Atwater, Yvonne Craig; ***D:*** Norman Taurog.

It Happened in Brooklyn 🦴🦴 **1947** Former sailor with blue eyes bunks with janitor with big nose in Brooklyn. Sailor and cronies encounter many musical opportunities. Lots of songs and falling in love, little entertainment. **104m/B VHS.** Frank Sinatra, Kathryn Grayson, Jimmy Durante, Peter Lawford, Gloria Grahame; ***D:*** Richard Whorf.

It Happened in New Orleans 🦴½ *Rainbow on the River* **1936** A young boy is cared for by a former slave in post-Civil War New Orleans until his Yankee grandmother claims him and takes him to New York. The boy is resented by his family but manages to overcome their hostilities. **86m/B VHS.** Bobby Breen, May Robson, Alan Mowbray, Benita Hume.

It Happened in the Park 🦴🦴½ **1956** A rare film exercise for De Sica, wherein the patrons of the Villa Borghese parks are surveyed for a 24-hour period. In French with English dialogue. **72m/B VHS.** *FR* ***D:*** Vittorio De Sica.

It Happened One Night 🦴🦴🦴🦴 **1934** Classic Capra comedy about an antagonistic couple determined to teach each other about life. Colbert is an unhappy heiress who runs away from her affluent home in search of contentment. On a bus she meets newspaper reporter Gable, who teaches her how "real" people live. She returns the favor in this first of the 1930s screwball comedies. The plot is a framework for an amusing examination of war between the sexes. Colbert and Gable are superb as affectionate foes. Remade as the musicals "Eve Knew Her Apples" and "You Can't Run Away From It." **105m/B VHS, DVD.** Clark Gable, Claudette Colbert, Roscoe Karns, Walter Connolly, Alan Hale, Ward Bond; ***D:*** Frank Capra; ***W:*** Robert Riskin; ***C:*** Joseph Walker. Oscars '34: Actor (Gable), Actress (Colbert), Adapt. Screenplay, Director (Capra), Picture; AFI '98: Top 100, Natl. Film Reg. '93.

It Happened Tomorrow 🦴🦴½ **1944** Now-familiar plotline will remind TV viewers of "Early Edition." Whimsical fantasy finds obituary writer Larry Stevens (Powell) receiving the next day's newspaper from his paper's librarian (Philliber). Stevens uses his knowledge of coming events to get some major scoops, win at the track, and impress beautiful spiritualist Sylvia (Darnell). Then, he reads his own obituary and tries to avoid his fate. **84m/B VHS.** Dick Powell, Linda Darnell, Jack Oakie, John Philliber, Edgar Kennedy, Edward Brophy, Sig Rumann, George Cleveland, Paul Guilfoyle, Eddie Acuff; ***D:*** Rene Clair; ***W:*** Rene Clair, Dudley Nichols; ***C:*** Archie Stout.

It Happens Every Spring 🦴🦴🦴½ **1949** Chemistry professor Vernon Simpson (Milland) is working on a bug repellant for trees and accidentally invents a potion that repels any kind of wood that it comes in contact with. Since he needs some big bucks to pop the question to his sweetie Deborah (Peters), Vernon, who also loves baseball, gets a tryout as a pitcher with a major league team and uses the solution on the baseballs he pitches. Naturally, it's strikeout time and the prof becomes a pitching phenom. Now, if he can only keep his little secret. Wacky baseball footage is a highlight. **87m/B VHS.** Ray Milland, Jean Peters, Paul Douglas, Ed Begley Sr., Ted de Corsia, Ray Collins, Jessie Royce Landis, Alan Hale Jr., Gene Evans; ***D:*** Lloyd Bacon; ***W:*** Valentine Davies; ***M:*** Leigh Harline.

It Means That to Me 🦴🦴 **1963** Espionage thriller in which Constantine plays a reporter who's hired by the government to transport top secret micro-film. **?m/C VHS.** *FR* Eddie Constantine, Jean-Louis Richard.

It Rained All Night the Day I Left 🦴🦴 **1978 (R)** Two drifters find their fortunes change when they are hired by a wealthy widow. Interesting romance adventure. **100m/C VHS.** Louis Gossett Jr., Sally Kellerman, Tony Curtis; ***D:*** Nicolas Gessner.

It Should Happen to You 🦴🦴🦴 **1954** An aspiring model attempts to boost her career by promoting herself on a New York City billboard. The results, however, are continually surprising. Fine comedy teamwork from master thespians Holliday and Lemmon in this, the latter's first film. **87m/B VHS.** Judy Holliday, Jack Lemmon, Peter Lawford; ***D:*** George Cukor; ***W:*** Ruth Gordon, Garson Kanin; ***C:*** Charles B(ryant) Lang Jr.

It Started in Naples 🦴🦴🦴 **1960** Good performances by both Gable and Loren in this comedy-drama about an American lawyer in Italy who, upon preparing his late brother's estate, finds that his brother's nephew is living with a stripper. A custody battle ensues, but love wins out in the end. Loren is incredible in nightclub scenes. **100m/C VHS.** Clark Gable, Sophia Loren, Marietto, Vittorio De Sica, Paolo Carlini, Claudio Ermelli, Giovanni Filidoro; ***D:*** Melville Shavelson; ***W:*** Melville Shavelson, Jack Rose.

It Started with a Kiss 🦴🦴½ **1959** Reynolds plays a showgirl who impulsively marries an Air Force sargeant (Ford). When he's transfered to Spain they try to make a go of their hasty marriage among numerous comic complications. Flimsy farce with likeable leads. **104m/C VHS.** Debbie Reynolds, Glenn Ford, Eva Gabor, Gustavo Rojo, Fred Clark, Edgar Buchanan, Robert Warwick, Harry (Henry) Morgan, Frances Bavier; ***D:*** George Marshall.

It Started with Eve 🦴🦴🦴 **1941** Funny comedy about grumpy old millionaire Jonathan Reynolds (Laughton) whose dying wish is to meet the young lady his son Johnny (Cummings) is to wed. Unfortunately, the bride-to-be is unavailable, so Johnny finds a replacement in hatcheck girl Anne (Durbin). Of course, Anne steals the old man's heart and he miraculously makes a full-blown recovery, which means big trouble for Johnny. Remade in 1964 as "I'd Rather Be Rich." Based on the story "Almost An Angel" by Hans Kraly. ♫Clavelitos; Going Home. **92m/B VHS.** Deanna Durbin, Charles Laughton, Robert Cummings, Guy Kibbee, Margaret Tallichet, Catherine Doucet, Walter Catlett, Charles Coleman, Clara Blandick; ***D:*** Henry Koster; ***W:*** Norman Krasna, Leo Townsend; ***C:*** Rudolph Mate; ***M:*** Hans J. Salter.

It Takes a Thief 🦴🦴 *The Challenge* **1959** Tough cookie Jayne's a buxom gangstress who does the hokey pokey with her criminal minions. A former lover who's been released from the big house seems to think she's been minding the mint for him. Au contraire. **93m/B VHS.** *GB* Jayne Mansfield, Anthony Quayle, Carl Mohner, Peter Reynolds, John Bennett, Barbara Mullen, Robert Brown, Dermot Walsh, Patrick Holt; ***D:*** John Gilling; ***W:*** John Gilling; ***C:*** Gordon Dines; ***M:*** Bill McGuffie.

It Takes Two 🦴🦴 **1988 (PG-13)** A young man spends his last ten days of bachelorhood cruising down Texas highways with a beautiful car saleswoman. Meanwhile, back at the altar, his bride waits patiently. Upbeat with some genuinely funny moments. From the director of "Pass the Ammo." **79m/C VHS.** George Newbern, Leslie Hope, Kimberly Foster, Barry Corbin, Anthony Geary; ***D:*** David Beaird; ***W:*** Thomas Szollosi, Richard Christian Matheson; ***C:*** Peter Deming; ***M:*** Carter Burwell.

It Takes Two 🦴 **1995 (PG)** Vapid sugary comedy finds the nine-year-old Olsen twins playing a duo from opposite sides of the tracks who change identities in an effort to get their respective adults (Guttenberg and Alley) together. See "The Parent Trap" instead. **100m/C VHS.** Ashley (Fuller) Olsen, Mary-Kate Olsen, Kirstie Alley, Steve Guttenberg, Philip Bosco, Jane Sibbett, Lawrence Dane, Gerard Parkes; ***D:*** Andy Tennant; ***W:*** Deborah Dean Davis; ***C:*** Kenneth Zunder; ***M:*** Sherman Foote, Ray Foote.

It! The Terror from Beyond Space 🦴🦴½ *It! The Vampire from Beyond Space* **1958** The sole survivor of a Martian expedition is believed to have murdered his colleagues. He's arrested and brought back to Earth via space ship. En route, a vicious alien, the actual culprit, is discovered on board and begins killing the crew members. A fun science fiction thriller which, 20 years later, would provide Ridley Scott with the plot for "Alien." **68m/B VHS, DVD.** Marshall Thompson, Shawn Smith, Kim Spalding, Ann Doran, Dabbs Greer, Paul Langton, Ray Corrigan; ***D:*** Edward L. Cahn; ***W:*** Jerome Bixby; ***C:*** Kenneth Peach Sr.; ***M:*** Paul Sawtell, Bert Shefter.

The Italian **1915** The story of an Italian immigrant family living in the slums of New York during the turn of the century. **78m/B VHS.** George Beban, Clara Williams, Leo Wills, J. Frank Burke, Fanny Midgley. Natl. Film Reg. '91.

Italian for Beginners 🦴🦴½ *Italiensk for Begyndere* **2001 (R)** Director Scherfig is the first woman to use the strict Dogma 95 filmmaking rules (hand-held cameras, natural light, live music, no studios scenes, no costumes, and no special effects) of her Danish colleagues. She's also the first to try to do a romantic comedy in the Dogma style, and she pulls it off nicely. Her tale brings together six quirky lonelyhearts: Andreas (Berthlesen), newly-widowed minister; Hall-Finn (Kaalund), a soccer-obsessed restaurant manager; his best friend Jorgen (Gantzler), who's convinced he's impotent; Olympia (Stovelbaek), who likes Andreas and cares for her abusive, ill father; Karen (Jorgensen) who cuts Hal-Finn's hair and cares for her alcoholic shrew of a mother; and Giulia (Jensen), an Italian waitress with a crush on Jorgen, in a Conversational Italian class. The seemingly lightweight plot is anchored by insight into everyday misery and hurt amid the giddy matchmaking and likeable characters. **112m/C VHS.** *DK* Anders W. Berthelsen, Peter Gantzler, Anette Stovelbaek, Ann Eleonora Jorgensen, Lars Kaalund, Sara Indrio Jensen; ***D:*** Lone Scherfig; ***W:*** Lone Scherfig; ***C:*** Jorgen Johansson.

The Italian Job 🦴🦴½ **1969 (G)** Caine and Coward pair up to steal $4 million in gold by causing a major traffic jam in Turin, Italy. During the jam, the pair steals the gold from an armored car. Silliness and chases through the Swiss mountains ensue, culminating in a hilarious ending. **99m/C VHS.** *GB* Michael Caine, Noel Coward, Benny Hill, Raf Vallone, Tony Beckley, Rossano Brazzi, Margaret Blye; ***D:*** Peter Collinson; ***M:*** Quincy Jones.

Italian Movie 🦴🦴 **1993** First-generation Italian immigrant Leonardo decides to become a male escort to pay off his gambling debts and support his large family but things get quite complicated. **95m/C VHS, DVD.** Michael DellaFemina, Rita Moreno, James Gandolfini, Caprice Benedetti; ***D:*** Roberto Monticello.

The Italian Stallion 🦴 **1973** Stallone plays a man with only one thing on his mind...sex! **90m/C VHS.** Sylvester Stallone, Henrietta Holm.

Italian Straw Hat 🦴🦴🦴 *Un Chapeau de Paille d'Italie* **1927** Classic silent about the chain of errors that ensues when a man's horse eats a woman's hat. His vast, unending struggle to replace the hat is the source of continual comedy. From Eugene Labiche's play. **114m/B VHS.** *FR* Albert Prejean, Olga Tschekowa; ***D:*** Rene Clair.

It's a Bundyful Life **1992** The outrageous family from TV's "Married with Children" does Christmas in their own inimitable fashion. This parody of "It's a Wonderful Life" features Kinison earning his wings as father Al's guardian angel. See what the family would have been like if Al had never been born...and what Al decides to do about it. Those seeking traditional family fare should look elsewhere. **47m/C VHS.** Ed O'Neill, Katey Sagal, Christina Applegate, David Faustino, Sam Kinison, Amanda Bearse, Ted McGinley; ***D:*** Gerry Cohen. **TV**

It's a Date 🦴🦴 **1940** A mother and daughter, both actresses, continually get their professional and romantic lives intertwined. It begins when Durbin (the daughter) is offered Kay's (the mother) Broadway role. It continues in Hawaii where the man that Kay is in love with tries to court Durbin. As it's a comedy, of course, all is put right in the end. ♫Musetta's Waltz; Ave Maria; Loch Lomond; Love Is All; It Happened in Kaloha; Rhythm of the Islands; Hawaiian War Chant. **103m/B VHS.** Deanna Durbin, Kay Francis, Walter Pidgeon, Samuel S. Hinds, S.Z. Sakall, Henry Stephenson, Charles Lane, Leon Belasco; ***D:*** William A. Seiter; ***W:*** Norman Krasna; ***C:*** Joseph Valentine.

It's a Dog's Life 🦴🦴½ *The Bar Sinister* **1955** The hero and narrator of this story is a wily bull terrier called Wildfire. Wildfire is a tough dog on the mean streets of the Bowery in turn-of-the-century New York. His master has him in dog fights in the local saloon but eventually abandons him. Wildfire is then taken in by the kindly employee of the rich and doghating Jagger but naturally manages to win the codger over. Based on the short story "The Bar Sinister" by Richard Harding Davis. **87m/C VHS.** Jeff Richards, Edmund Gwenn, Dean Jagger; ***D:*** Herman Hoffman; ***W:*** John Michael Hayes; ***M:*** Elmer Bernstein.

It's a Gift 🦴🦴🦴½ **1934** A grocery clerk moves his family west to manage orange groves in this classic Fields comedy. Several inspired sequences. The supporting cast shines too. A real find for the discriminating comedy buff. Remake of the silent "It's the Old Army Game." **71m/B VHS.** W.C. Fields, Baby LeRoy, Kathleen Howard, Jean Rouveral, Julian Madison, Tammany Young, Tommy Bupp; ***D:*** Norman Z. McLeod; ***W:*** Jack Cunningham; ***C:*** Henry Sharp.

It's a Great Feeling 🦴🦴½ **1949** Another Carson and Day team-up where Carson plays a camera-hogging show-off whom no one wants to direct. He's such an industry piranha that he ends up directing himself! He cons Day, a waitress and would-be actress, by promising her a part in his new film. Some executives hear her sing before she heads back home to Wisconsin, fed up with Hollywood. They make Carson track her down to star in the new picture, but when he arrives she is at the altar with her high school sweetheart. **85m/C VHS.** Dennis Morgan, Doris Day, Jack Carson, Bill Goodwin, Errol Flynn, Gary Cooper, Joan Crawford, Ronald Reagan, Sydney Greenstreet, Danny Kaye, Eleanor Parker, Edward G. Robinson, Jane Wyman; ***D:*** David Butler.

It's a Great Life 🦴🦴½ **1943** Blondie wants Dagwood to buy a house but instead he buys a horse. He's scheming to impress a client of Mr. Dither's by participating in a fox hunt. Blondie comes to the rescue. 13th entry in series. **75m/B VHS.** Penny Singleton, Arthur Lake, Larry Simms, Hugh Herbert, Jonathan Hale, Danny Mummert, Alan Dinehart, Irving Bacon, Douglas Leavitt, Marjorie Ann Mutchie; ***D:*** Frank Strayer; ***W:*** Karen De Wolf, Connie Lee.

It's a Joke, Son! 🦴🦴 **1947** Follows the fictional politician, Senator Claghorn from the Fred Allen radio show, during his first run for the U.S. Senate. **67m/B VHS.** Kenny Delmar, Una Merkel; ***D:*** Ben Stoloff.

It's a Mad, Mad, Mad, Mad World 🦴🦴 **1963** Overblown epic comedy with a cast of notables desperately seeking the whereabouts of stolen money. Ultimately exhausting film undone by its length and overbearing performances. **155m/C VHS, DVD, Wide.** Spencer Tracy, Sid Caesar, Milton Berle, Ethel Merman, Jonathan Winters, Jimmy Durante, Buddy Hackett, Mickey Rooney, Phil Silvers, Dick Shawn, Edie Adams, Dorothy Provine, Buster Keaton, Terry-Thomas, Moe Howard, Larry Fine, Joe DeRita, Jim Backus, William Demarest, Peter Falk, Leo Gorcey, Edward Everett Horton, Joe E. Brown, Carl Reiner, ZaSu Pitts, Eddie Anderson, Jack Benny, Jerry Lewis, Norman Fell, Stan Freberg, Don Knotts; ***D:*** Stanley Kramer; ***W:*** William Rose, Tania Rose; ***C:*** Ernest Laszlo; ***M:*** Ernest Gold. Oscars '63: Sound FX Editing.

It's a Wonderful Life 🦴🦴🦴🦴 **1946** American classic about a man saved from suicide by a considerate angel, who then shows the hero how important he's been to the lives of loved ones. Corny but inspirational and heartwarming, with an endearing performance by Travers as angel Clarence. Stewart and Reed are typically wholesome. Perfect film for people who want to feel good, joyfully teetering on the border between Hollywood schmaltz and genuine heartbreak. Available colorized. Also available in a 160-minute Collector's Edition with original preview trailer, "The Making of 'It's a Wonderful Life,'" and a new digital transfer from the original negative. **125m/B VHS, DVD.** Carl "Alfalfa" Switzer, James Stewart, Donna Reed, Henry Travers, Thomas Mitchell, Lionel Barrymore, Samuel S. Hinds, Frank Faylen, Gloria Grahame, H.B. Warner, Ellen Corby, Sheldon Leonard, Beulah Bondi, Ward Bond, Frank Albertson, Todd Karns, Mary Treen, Charles Halton; ***D:*** Frank Capra; ***W:*** Frances Goodrich, Albert Hackett, Jo Swerling; ***C:*** Joseph Biroc, Joseph Walker; ***M:*** Dimitri Tiomkin. AFI '98: Top 100; Golden Globes '47: Director (Capra), Natl. Film Reg. '90.

It's Alive! 🦴 **1968** Slow-moving dud about a farmer feeding passersby to the area's cave-dwelling lizard man. The ping pong ball-eyed monster puts in a belated appearance that's not worth the wait. **80m/C VHS.** Tommy Kirk, Shirley Bonne, Bill (Billy) Thurman, Annabelle MacAdams, Corveth Osterhouse; ***D:*** Larry Buchanan; ***W:*** Larry Buchanan; ***C:*** Robert Alcott.

It's Alive 🦴🦴🦴 **1974 (PG)** Cult film about a mutated baby, born to a normal Los Angeles couple, who escapes and goes on a bloodthirsty, murderous rampage. It's a sight to behold. Fantastic score by Bernard Herrmann makes this chilling film a memorable one. **91m/C VHS.** John P. Ryan, Sharon Farrell, Andrew Duggan, Guy Stockwell, James Dixon, Michael Ansara, William Wellman Jr., Shamus Locke; ***D:*** Larry Cohen; ***W:*** Larry Cohen; ***C:*** Fenton Hamilton; ***M:*** Bernard Herrmann.

It's Alive 2: It Lives Again woof! *It Lives Again* **1978 (R)** In this sequel to "It's Alive," the original hell-spun baby meets up with two more of the same and all three terrorize the city, murdering everyone they can find. Truly horrendous. **91m/C VHS.** Frederic Forrest, Kathleen Lloyd, John P. Ryan, Andrew Duggan, John Marley, Eddie Constantine, James Dixon, Bobby Ramsen; ***D:*** Larry Cohen; ***W:*** Larry Cohen; ***C:*** Fenton Hamilton; ***M:*** Bernard Herrmann.

It's Alive 3: Island of the Alive 🦴 *Island of the Alive* **1987 (R)** The second sequel to the tongue-in-cheek horror film, in which the infant mutant of the previous films has been left with other mutations to spawn on a desert island. **94m/C VHS.** Michael Moriarty, Karen Black, Laurene Landon, Gerrit Graham, James Dixon, Neal Israel, MacDonald Carey; ***D:*** Larry Cohen; ***W:*** Larry Cohen; ***C:*** Daniel Pearl; ***M:*** Laurie Johnson.

It's All True 🦴🦴 **1993 (G)** A look at auteur Welles' ill-fated WWII filmmaking project. Welles served as a special cultural ambassador to South America and, in 1942, began a documentary covering the area's complex political and social issues. Includes footage from "Four Men on a Raft," Welles' recreation about the peasant fishermen of Brazil; surviving excerpts from "The Story of Samba," a Technicolor musical about Carnaval in Rio de Janeiro; and footage from "My Friend Bonito," set against a backdrop of bullfighting in Mexico. **85m/C VHS.** ***D:*** Richard Wilson, Bill Krohn, Myron Meise, Orson Welles; ***W:*** Richard Wilson, Bill Krohn, Myron Meise; ***C:*** Gary Graver, George Fanto; ***M:*** Jorge Arriagada; ***Nar:*** Miguel Ferrer.

It's Always Fair Weather 🦴🦴 **1955** Three WWII buddies meet again at a 10-year reunion and find that they don't like each other very much. A surprisingly cynical film. Director Donen produced "Seven Brides for Seven Brothers" the previous year. ♫Stillman's Gym; March, March; Why Are We Here? (Blue Danube); Music Is Better Than Words; Once Upon A Time; The Time For Parting; I Like Myself; Baby You Knock Me Out; Thanks A Lot But No Thanks. **102m/C VHS, Wide.** Gene Kelly, Cyd Charisse, Dan Dailey, Michael Kidd; ***D:*** Stanley Donen; ***W:*** Betty Comden, Adolph Green; ***M:*** Betty Comden, Adolph Green, Andre Previn.

It's Called Murder, Baby 🦴 **1982 (R)** The famed porn star gives the viewer a lesson in English vocabulary in this tale of a blackmailed movie queen. **94m/C VHS.** John Leslie, Cameron Mitchell, Lisa Trego; ***D:*** Sam Weston.

It's Good to Be Alive 🦴🦴½ **1974** The true story of how Brooklyn Dodgers' catcher Roy Campanella learned to face life after an automobile accident left him a quadriplegic. Good performances. **100m/C VHS, DVD.** Ramon Bieri, Joe De Santis, Paul Winfield, Ruby Dee, Louis Gossett Jr.; ***D:*** Michael Landon; ***M:*** Michel Legrand. **TV**

It's in the Bag 🦴🦴½ *The Fifth Chair* **1945** A shiftless flea circus owner sells chairs he has inherited, not knowing that a fortune is hidden in one of them. **87m/B VHS.** Fred Allen, Don Ameche, Jack Benny, William Bendix, Binnie Barnes, Robert Benchley; ***D:*** Richard Wallace.

It's In the Water 🦴🦴 **1996** Small, conservative Azalea Springs, Texas is rocked by the opening of an AIDS hospice. The homophobia outrages society wife Alex, who begins working at the hospice alongside best friend (soon to be more) Grace. Then a rumor starts that the local drinking water turns you gay and things really get wild. Fast-moving and funny. **100m/C VHS, DVD.** Keri Jo Chapman, Teresa Garrett, Barbara Lasater, Larry Randolph; ***D:*** Kelli Herd.

It's Love Again 🦴🦴½ **1936** A streetwise chorus girl poses as a fictional socialite in a light music-hall comedy. ♫It's Love Again; Heaven In Your Arms. **83m/B VHS.** *GB* Jessie Matthews, Robert Young, Sonnie Hale; ***D:*** Victor Saville.

It's My Party 🦴🦴½ **1995 (R)** When L.A. architect Nick Stark (Roberts) learns that he's developed untreatable brain lesions from AIDS that will essentially leave him helpless, he decides to throw himself a monumental farewell bash before taking a drug overdose. Friends and family all turn up as does, awkwardly enough, Brandon Theis (Harrison), Nick's former live-in who couldn't handle his HIV-positive diagnosis but would like a last reapproachment. Fine, sympathetic performances, espcially by the two leads, and yes, it's a weepie. Based on a true story. **120m/C VHS.** Eric Roberts, Gregory Harrison, Marlee Matlin, Lee Grant, George Segal, Bronson Pinchot, Bruce Davison, Devon Gummersall, Roddy McDowall, Margaret Cho, Paul Regina, Olivia Newton-John, Christopher Atkins, Dennis Christopher, Ron Glass, Eugene Glazer; ***D:*** Randal Kleiser; ***W:*** Randal Kleiser; ***C:*** Bernd Heinl; ***M:*** Basil Poledouris.

It's My Turn 🦴🦴 **1980 (R)** A mathematics professor (Clayburgh) struggles in her relationship with live-in lover (Grodin) who sells real-estate in Chicago. She meets retired baseball player (Douglas) and falls in love. "Ho-hum" just about describes the rest. **91m/C VHS.** Jill Clayburgh, Michael Douglas, Charles Grodin, Beverly Garland, Steven Hill, Dianne Wiest, Daniel Stern; ***D:*** Claudia Weill; ***W:*** Eleanor Bergstein; ***C:*** Bill Butler.

It's My Turn, Laura Cadieux 🦴🦴 *C't'a Ton Tour, Laura Cadieux* **1998** One a week several women meet at the same doctor's office as they've done for the past 15 years. The social aspects far outweigh the medical benefits for the women as they gossip and talk about their restricted lives. But one week a series of misunderstandings unfold when Madame Therrien believes her friend Laura Cadieux's son has gone missing. Based on the novel by Michel Tremblay. French with subtitles. **92m/C VHS.** *CA* Ginette Reno, Donald Pilon, Pierrette Robitaille, Denise Dubois, Samuel Landry, Adele Reinhardt; ***D:*** Denise Filiatrault; ***W:*** Denise Filiatrault; ***C:*** Daniel Jobin; ***M:*** Francois Dompierre.

It's Not the Size That Counts woof! *Percy's Progress* **1974** After the Earth's drinking water is contaminated, Lawson is the only man on Earth not to be struck by impotency. Limp sequel to "Percy," the British comedy about the first man to receive a penis transplant. Promising comedy doesn't deliver. **90m/C VHS.** Leigh Lawson, Elke Sommer, Denholm Elliott, Vincent Price, Judy Geeson, Milo O'Shea, Julie Ege, George Coulouris, Bernard Lee; ***D:*** Ralph Thomas; ***W:*** Harry H. Corbett, Sid Colin, Ian La Frenais; ***C:*** Tony Imi; ***M:*** Tony Macaulay.

It's Pat: The Movie woof! **1994 (PG-13)** This movie is so bad, let's pray it sounds the death knell to big-screen versions of "Saturday Night Live" sketch characters—who possessed little humor to begin with. For what it's worth, the androgynous Pat (Sweeney) falls for the equally gender-suspect Chris (Foley, from Canada's version of SNL, "Kids in the Hall") and all sorts of embarrassing situations arise. Pat's quest to find Pat's self is sketch material stretched see-through thin. **78m/C VHS.** Julia Sweeney, Dave Foley, Charles Rocket, Kathy Griffin, Julie Haydon, Tim Meadows, Arleen (Arlene) Sorkin; ***Cameos:*** Sally Jesse Raphael, Kathy Najimy; ***D:*** Adam Bernstein; ***W:*** Julia Sweeney, Jim Emerson, Stephen Hibbert.

It's the Old Army Game **1926** Classic Fields gags in three of his best Ziegfeld Follies sketches: "The Drug Store," "A Peaceful Morning," and "The Family Flivver." The beautiful Brooks serves as his comic foil. **75m/B VHS.** W.C. Fields, Louise Brooks, Blanche Ring, William Gaxton; ***D:*** Edward Sutherland.

It's the Rage 🦴🦴½ *All the Rage* **1999 (R)** Glib ensemble comedy about the collision of guns and anger, with an interesting cast. Warren (Daniels) shoots an intruder who turns out to be his business partner, who may have been fooling around with Warren's prim wife, Helen (Allen). His lawyer, Tim (Braugher), has just been given a gun by his boyfriend (Schwimmer), and he has another client (Paquin) whose brother (Ribisi) is trigger-happy. Meanwhile, Helen takes a job with paranoid billionaire, Mr. Morgan (Sinise), while Warren's being investigated by a couple of detectives (Forster, Woodbine) for whom guns are job accessories. Reddin scripted from his play. **97m/C VHS, DVD.** Jeff Daniels, Joan Allen, Andre Braugher, David Schwimmer, Anna Paquin, Giovanni Ribisi, Gary Sinise, Josh Brolin, Robert Forster, Bokeem Woodbine; ***D:*** James D. Stern; ***W:*** Keith Reddin; ***C:*** Alex Nepomniaschy; ***M:*** Mark Mothersbaugh.

Ivan and Abraham 🦴🦴 **1994** Abraham (Alexandrovitch) is a nine-year-old Jewish boy, living on a shetl in 1930s eastern Poland, with his best friend being the family's 14-year-old Christian apprentice Ivan (Iakovlev). The boys sense the increasing family tensions and escape into the nearby forest, only to find politics and prejudice sweeping over them all. In Yiddish, Russian, Polish, and Romany, with English subtitles. **105m/B VHS.** Roma Aleksandrovitch, Sacha Iakovlev, Vladimir Machkov, Maria Lipkina, Rolan Bykov, Daniel Olbrychski; ***D:*** Yolande Zauberman; ***W:*** Yolande Zauberman; ***C:*** Jean-Marc Fabre.

Ivan the Terrible, Part 1 🦴🦴🦴🦴 *Ivan Groznyi* **1944** Contemplative epic of Russia's first czar is a classic, innovative film from cinema genius Eisenstein. Visually stunning, with a fine performance by Cherkassov. Ivan's struggles to preserve his country is the main concern of the first half of Eisenstein's masterwork (which he originally planned as a trilogy). In Russian with English subtitles. **100m/B VHS, DVD, 8mm, Wide.** *RU* Nikolai Cherkasov, Ludmila Tselikovskaya, Serafina Birman, Piotr Kadochnikev; ***D:*** Sergei Eisenstein; ***W:*** Sergei Eisenstein; ***C:*** Eduard Tisse; ***M:*** Sergei Prokofiev.

Ivan the Terrible, Part 2 🦴🦴🦴½ *Ivan the Terrible, Part 2: The Boyars' Plot; Ivan Groznyi 2* **1946** Landed gentry conspire to dethrone the czar in this continuation of the innovative epic. More stunning imagery from master Eisenstein, who makes no false moves in this one. Slow going, but immensely rewarding. Russian dialogue with English subtitles; contains color sequences. **87m/B VHS, DVD, 8mm, Wide.** *RU* Nikolai Cherkasov, Ludmila Tselikovskaya, Serafina Birman, Piotr Kadochnikev; ***D:*** Sergei Eisenstein; ***W:*** Sergei Eisenstein; ***C:*** Eduard Tisse, Andrei Moskvin; ***M:*** Sergei Prokofiev.

Ivanhoe 🦴🦴🦴 **1952** Knights fight each other and woo maidens in this chivalrous romance derived from the Sir Walter Scott classic. Taylor is suitably noble, while Sanders is familiarly serpentine. Remade in 1982. **107m/C VHS.** Robert Taylor, Elizabeth Taylor, Joan Fontaine, George Sanders, Finlay Currie, Felix Aylmer; ***D:*** Richard Thorpe; ***W:*** Marguerite Roberts, Noel Langley; ***C:*** Frederick A. (Freddie) Young; ***M:*** Miklos Rozsa.

Ivanhoe 🦴🦴½ **1982** A version of Sir Walter Scott's classic novel of chivalry and knighthood in 12th-century England. Remake of the 1953 film classic. **142m/C VHS.** Anthony Andrews, James Mason, Lysette Anthony, Sam Neill, Olivia Hussey, Michael Hordern, Julian Glover, George Innes, Ronald Pickup, John Rhys-Davies, Chloe Franks; ***D:*** Douglas Camfield. **TV**

Ivanhoe 🦴🦴🦴 **1997** TV miniseries version of Sir Walter Scott's epic tale of knights, chivalry, romance, and daring. Saxon knight Wilfred of Ivanhoe (Waddington), having fought for Richard the Lionheart (Edwards) during the Crusades, returns to England to battle the scheming Prince John (Brown) and sinister Grand Master of the Templars, Lucas De Beaumanoir (Lee) in order to regain his honor. His childhood sweetheart, Saxon heiress Rowena (Smurfit), is betrothed to another but Ivanhoe's also drawn to Jewish healer Rebecca (Lynch) as is scheming Knight Templar, Sir Brian Bois-Guilbert (Hinds). Lots of action. On six cassettes. **292m/C VHS, DVD.** *GB* Steven Waddington, Susan Lynch, Ciaran Hinds, Victoria Smurfit, Ralph Brown, Rory Edwards, Ronald Pickup, David Horovitch, Trevor Cooper, Valentine Pelka, Nick Brimble, Jimmy

Chisholm, Christopher Lee, Aden (John) Gillett, James Cosmo, Sian Phillips, Ciaran Madden; *D:* Stuart Orme; *W:* Deborah Cook; *C:* Clive Tickner; *M:* Colin Towns. **TV**

I've Always Loved You 🦴🦴½ *Concerto* **1946** The drama of love and jealousy explored in an extravagant production filled with classical music. **117m/C VHS.** Philip Dorn, Catherine McLeod; *D:* Frank Borzage; *C:* Gaetano Antonio "Tony" Gaudio.

I've Been Waiting for You 🦴🦴½ **1998 (PG-13)** California teen Sarah Zoltanne (Chalke), who has an interest in the occult, moves with her family to a New England town. Her fellow teens begin to believe that she's a witch out for revenge on the descendents of the townspeople who burned another witch, who had the same name. Then on Halloween, Sarah begins to see events beyond her knowledge or control. Based on the novel "Gallows Hill" by Lois Duncan. **90m/C VHS, DVD.** Sarah Chalke, Soleil Moon Frye, Markie Post, Christian Campbell, Tom Dugan; *D:* Christopher Leitch; *W:* Duane Poole. **TV**

I've Heard the Mermaids Singing 🦴🦴🦴 **1987** Independent Canadian semi-satiric romantic comedy details the misadventures of a klutzy woman who suddenly obtains a desirable job in an art gallery run by a lesbian on whom she develops a crush. Good-natured tone helped considerably by McCarthy's winning performance. **81m/C VHS.** *CA* Sheila McCarthy, Paule Baillargeon, Ann-Marie MacDonald, John Evans; *D:* Patricia Rozema; *M:* Mark Korven. Genie '88: Actress (McCarthy), Support. Actress (Baillargeon).

The Ivory Handled Gun **1935** The Wolverine Kid wants Buck Ward (Jones) dead because the Kid's father, John Plunkett, was rejected by Buck's mother in favor of Buck's dad, Bill, who killed the interloper in a fight. Bill also happens to be in position of one of Plunkett's ivory-handed guns and the Kid wants that back as well. In chapter 2 of "Gordon of Ghost City," Gordon and Mary Gray are observed by a mysterious, threatening figure and Mary gets caught in a stampede. **81m/B VHS.** Buck Jones, Charlotte Wynters, Walter Miller, Frank Rice, Carl Stockdale, Joseph Girard, Madge Bellamy; *D:* Ray Taylor.

Ivory Hunters 🦴🦴½ *The Last Elephant* **1990** Conservationists team up to thwart a massacre of elephants by poachers. Predictable made-for-cable entertainment co-produced by the National Audubon Society. **94m/C VHS.** John Lithgow, Isabella Rossellini, James Earl Jones, Tony Todd, Olek Krupa; *D:* Joseph Sargent; *W:* Richard Guttman, Bill Bozzone; *M:* Charles Bernstein. **CABLE**

Ivory Tower 🦴🦴 **1997** Anthony Daytona (Van Horn) is a hotshot marketing exec in charge of launching a new computer product. But then his new boss arrives and suddenly not only the project but Anthony's career and the company itself is in jeopardy. **107m/C VHS, DVD.** Patrick Van Horn, James Wilder, Kari Wuhrer, Michael Ironside, Donna Pescow, Keith Coogan, Ian Buchanan; *D:* Darin Ferriola; *W:* Darin Ferriola; *C:* Maida Sussman.

Izzy & Moe 🦴🦴½ **1985** Carney and The Great One are reunited for the last time on screen as former vaudevillians who become federal agents and create havoc amid speak-easies and bathtub gin during Prohibition. Based on true stories. **92m/C VHS.** Jackie Gleason, Art Carney, Cynthia Harris, Zohra Lampert, Drew Snyder, Dick Latessa; *D:* Jackie Cooper. **TV**

J. Edgar Hoover 🦴🦴 **1987** Cable adaptation from "My 30 years in Hoover's FBI" by William G. Sullivan and William S. Brown. Biographical drama deals with Hoover's 55-year career with the government. Included are his FBI days. **110m/C VHS.** Treat Williams, Rip Torn, David Ogden Stiers, Andrew Duggan, Art Hindle, Louise Fletcher; *D:* Robert E. Collins. **CABLE**

J-Men Forever! 🦴🦴🦴 **1979 (PG)** A spoof on early sci-fi/spy serials in which an alien takeover is attempted via rock-n-roll (your parents warned you). Employs an amusing technique of dubbing footage from dozens of Republic dramas intercut with new film featuring the "Firesign Theater" crew. **73m/B VHS.** Peter Bergman, Phil(ip) Proctor; *D:* Richard Patterson.

Jabberwocky 🦴🦴½ **1977 (PG)** Pythonesque chaos prevails in the medieval cartoon kingdom of King Bruno the Questionable, who rules with cruelty, stupidity, lust and dust. Jabberwocky is the big dragon mowing everything down in its path until hero Palin decides to take it on. Uneven, but real funny at times. **104m/C VHS, DVD, Wide.** *GB* Michael Palin, Eric Idle, Max Wall, Deborah Fallender, Terry Jones, John Le Mesurier, Annette Badland, Warren Mitchell, Harry H. Corbett, David Prowse, Neil Innes; *D:* Terry Gilliam; *W:* Charles Alverson, Terry Gilliam; *C:* Terry Bedford; *M:* De Wolfe.

J'Accuse 🦴🦴🦴 *I Accuse; That They May Live* **1937** A Frenchman creates a device he believes will stop the war but it is confiscated by the government and used as part of the national defense. Subsequently, he goes mad. Gance (known for his 1927 "Napoleon"), remade his 1919 silent film, retelling the powerful anti-war message with great sensitivity. Banned in Nazi Germany. **125m/B VHS.** *FR* Victor Francen, Jean Max, Deltaire, Renee Devillers; *D:* Abel Gance.

Jack 🦴🦴½ **1996 (PG-13)** Ten-year-old Jack Powell (Williams) suffers from a rare genetic disorder that causes him to age at four times the normal rate so he looks like a 40-year-old. His family, fearing ridicule, has kept him isolated but since Jack's so lonely, they finally agree to let him attend school. This new fourth grader isn't the only one with a lot to learn. **111m/C VHS.** Robin Williams, Bill Cosby, Diane Lane, Brian Kerwin, Fran Drescher, Michael McKean, Jennifer Lopez, Don Novello; *D:* Francis Ford Coppola; *W:* James DeMonaco, Gary Nadeau; *C:* John Toll; *M:* Michael Kamen.

Jack and His Friends 🦴🦴 **1992 (R)** Comic satire of the tribulations of Jack the shoe salesman (Garfield), who is shown the front door by his unfaithful wife. Beset by grief, he drives the streets aimlessly until he is kidnapped by a young couple (Rockwell and Reyes) on the run from the law, who force Jack to take them to his summer house where they all try to decide what to do with their lives. **93m/C VHS.** Allen (Goorwitz) Garfield, Sam Rockwell, Judy Reyes; *D:* Bruce Ornstein.

Jack and Sarah 🦴🦴½ **1995 (R)** Widowed London lawyer (Grant) hires American waitress (Mathis), to help raise his infant daughter Sarah. Complications arise because Amy has no child rearing skills and Jack's parents and in-laws disapprove of the whole situation. Performances are nice (especially the scene-stealing infants), and there's some fine moments combining tragedy with romance, but the plot is a little thin and the whole film is slow moving (it takes more than half the movie to get the three protagonists in place). An edited version is rated PG. **110m/C VHS, DVD.** *GB* Richard E. Grant, Samantha Mathis, Ian McKellen, Judi Dench, Cherie Lunghi, Eileen Atkins, Imogen Stubbs; *D:* Tim Sullivan; *W:* Tim Sullivan; *C:* Jean-Yves Escoffier; *M:* Simon Boswell.

Jack & the Beanstalk 🦴🦴 **1952** While baby-sitting, Lou falls asleep and dreams he's Jack in this spoof of the classic fairy tale. **78m/C VHS, DVD.** Bud Abbott, Lou Costello, Buddy Baer, Dorothy Ford, Barbara Brown, William Farnum; *D:* Jean Yarbrough; *W:* Nathaniel Curtis; *C:* George Robinson; *M:* Heinz Roemheld.

Jack & the Beanstalk **1983** From the "Faerie Tale Theatre" comes this classic tale of Jack, who sells his family's cow for five magic beans, climbs the huge beanstalk that sprouts from them, and encounters an unfriendly giant. **60m/C VHS.** Dennis Christopher, Katherine Helmond, Elliott Gould, Jean Stapleton, Mark Blankfield; *D:* Lamont Johnson.

Jack and the Beanstalk: The Real Story 🦴½ *Jim Henson's Jack and the Beanstalk* **2001** Attenuated and dull take on the familiar fairytale finds Modine's Jack a modern-day descendant of the Jack who stole the golden goose. That's how his family built an empire but it's payback time and Jack needs to climb that beanstalk and make reparations for his ancestor's crimes. **184m/C VHS, DVD, Wide.** Matthew Modine, Vanessa Redgrave, Mia Sara, Jon Voight, Daryl Hannah, Richard Attenborough; *D:* Brian Henson; *W:* Jim V. Hart, Brian Henson. **TV**

Jack Be Nimble 🦴🦴 **1994 (R)** Siblings Jack (Arquette) and Dora (Kennedy) were separated as children and adopted by different families. Jack's family turns out to be sadistic and he suffers much abuse, until he enacts a violent revenge; Dora begins to hear voices and soon realizes it's Jack crying out to her. The duo finally reunite but between Jack's rage and Dora's telepathic abilities, life takes on further bizarre twists. Much psychological terror rather than gore. **93m/C VHS, DVD.** *NZ* Alexis Arquette, Sarah Kennedy, Bruno Lawrence; *D:* Garth Maxwell; *W:* Garth Maxwell; *C:* Donald Duncan; *M:* Chris Neal.

The Jack Bull 🦴🦴½ **1999 (R)** Cusack's father adapted a 19th-century German novel, "Michael Kohlhaas" by Heinrich Von Kleist, into a 19th-century American western, set in Wyoming. Myrl Redding (Cusack) is a peaceful horse trader who demands justice when wealthy landowner Henry Ballard (Jones) beats two of Redding's horses and their Indian caretaker. Since Ballard has the local law in his pocket, Redding gets no satisfaction. Becoming obsessed, he decides to form a vigilante posse to get Ballard to pay for his actions. **120m/C VHS, DVD.** John Cusack, L.Q. (Justus E. McQueen) Jones, John Goodman, Rodney A. Grant, Miranda Otto, John C. McGinley, John Savage, Jay O. Sanders, Scott Wilson, Drake Bell, Glenn Morshower, Ken Pogue; *D:* John Badham; *W:* Dick Cusack; *C:* Gale Tattersall; *M:* Lennie Niehaus. **CABLE**

Jack Frost 🦴🦴½ **1943** Moving biographical drama that follows a man from the sweat factories of London to his eventual rise to success. **89m/B VHS, 8mm.** Michael O'Shea, Susan Hayward.

Jack Frost 🦴 **1997 (R)** Convicted serial killer Jack Frost (McDonald) mutates after accidental exposure to an experimental liquid DNA, becomes a killer snowman, and terrorizes a town preparing for the annual Snowman Festival. Snickering seasonal gore with a killer who uses icicles and a carrot nose to dispatch some of his latest victims. **89m/C VHS, DVD.** Scott McDonald, Christopher Allport, F. William Parker; *D:* Michael Cooney; *W:* Michael Cooney; *C:* Dean Lent. **VIDEO**

Jack Frost 🦴 **1998 (PG)** As emotionally realistic and cool as soap flake snow, alleged family feature has Keaton playing Jack Frost, a struggling musician who spends too much time away from wife Gabby (Preston) and son Charlie (Cross). He decides to blow off a Christmas Day gig to spend more time with the family, only to be killed on his way to their mountain cabin. One year later, forlorn Charlie makes a snowman, dresses it in his dead dad's duds, and blows a note on Jack's harmonica. Bingo! Now his dead father is back to life as a creepy-looking talking snowman! Keaton tries his best with the lame material; but with the use of four confused screenwriters, he didn't have a snowball's chance. Additional warning: Keaton sings. Not to be confused with the straight-to-video release of the same name about a murderous deranged talking snowman. **95m/C VHS, DVD.** Michael Keaton, Kelly Preston, Joseph Cross, Mark Addy, Eli Marienthal, Dweezil Zappa, Henry Rollins, Andy Lawrence, Ahmet Zappa, Jeff Cesario; *D:* Troy Miller; *W:* Mark Steven Johnson, Steven L. Bloom, Jonathan Roberts, Jeff Cesario; *C:* Laszlo Kovacs; *M:* Trevor Rabin.

Jack Frost 2: Revenge of the Mutant Killer Snowman woof! **2000 (R)** Snowy horror is returned to his evil ways by a lab accident that also makes him impervious to heat, bullets, and antifreeze. So Jack decides to get revenge on Sheriff Sam (who defeated him previously), who just happens to be on vacation in a tropical paradise. But Chilly Boy doesn't have to worry about that. **91m/C VHS, DVD, Wide.** Christopher Allport, David Allan Brooks, Chip Heller, Eileen Seeley, Adrienne Barbeau; *D:* Michael Cooney; *W:* Michael Cooney. **VIDEO**

Jack Higgins' Midnight Man 🦴½ *Midnight Man* **1996 (R)** Ex-terrorist Sean Dillon (Lowe) is reluctantly recruited by British intelligence to thwart a plot to kill Princes Harry and William in a scheme to overthrow the monarchy. Only Dillon soon realizes his target is a dangerous ex-colleague and a band of fanatics. Based on the Higgins novel "Eye of the Storm." **104m/C VHS.** Rob Lowe, Kenneth Cranham, Deborah Maria Moore, Michael Sarrazin, Hannes Jaenicke, Daphne Cheung, Jim Duggan; *D:* Lawrence Gordon Clark; *W:* Jurgen Wolff; *C:* Ken Westbury; *M:* Leon Aronson. **CABLE**

Jack Higgins' On Dangerous Ground 🦴 *On Dangerous Ground* **1995 (R)** A major miscast ruins thriller writer Higgins's chances in this cable movie. Ex-IRA assassin and all-around terrorist Sean Dillon (Lowe) nows works for a British intelligence agency, headed by Brigadier Ferguson (Cranham). A secret agreement documenting a WWII deal between Lord Mountbatten and Mao Tse-tung has come to murky light and could exacerbate the tensions between China and Britain over Hong Kong. Dillon not only is expected to retrieve the document but also prevent an assassination attempt while the U.S. prez visits England. Lowe's way too lightweight for the Dillon role and manages to throw what should have been a good action yarn completely off-balance. **105m/C VHS.** *CA GB LU* Rob Lowe, Kenneth Cranham, Juergen Prochnow, Deborah Maria Moore, Ingeborga Dapkounaite, Daphne Cheung, Richard Rees, Claude Blanchard; *D:* Laurence Gordon-Clark; *W:* Christopher Wickens; *C:* Ken Westbury; *M:* Leon Aronson. **CABLE**

Jack Higgins' The Windsor Protocol 🦴½ *The Windsor Protocol* **1997 (R)** The sequel to "Jack Higgins' Thunder Point" finds ex-terrorist Sean Dillon (MacLachlan), now working for British Intelligence, still trying to recover The Windsor Protocol, a Nazi-era document that has recently come to light and involves present-day Nazi sympathizers, money, power, and both the U.S. and British governments. **96m/C VHS.** Kyle MacLachlan, Alan Thicke, Macha Grenon, John Colicos, Chris Wiggins; *D:* George Mihalka; *W:* David Preston, Stephen Zoller; *C:* Peter Benison; *M:* Stanislas Syrewicz. **CABLE**

Jack Higgins' Thunder Point 🦴½ *Thunder Point* **1997 (R)** MacLachlan takes over from Rob Lowe as ex-IRA terrorist Sean Dillon and the casting still stinks. (Doesn't anybody read Higgins' books!) A treasure diver finds The Windsor Protocol, a Hitler directive that also contains info on hidden funds that neo-Nazis hope to use to resurrect the Reich. Dillon's hired to find the document but it eventually does winds up in the hands of Nazi sympathizers, leading to the sequel "Jack Higgins' The Windsor Protocol." **95m/C VHS.** Kyle MacLachlan, Michael Sarrazin, Kenneth Welsh, Pascale Bussieres, Chris Wiggins, John Colicos, Cedric Smith; *D:* George Mihalka; *W:* Morrie Ruvinsky; *C:* Peter Benison; *M:* Stanislas Syrewicz. **CABLE**

The Jack Knife Man 🦴🦴🦴 **1920** Sentimental silent treatment of the relationship between a boy and a man. A new mother close to death hands over her bundle of joy to a kindly old river man, and the two bond in a familial way despite incessant adversity. Made the year following Vidor's debut as a feature film director. **70m/B VHS.** Fred Turner, Harry Todd, Bobby Kelso, Willis Marks, Lillian (Lillianne, Lyllian) Leighton, James Corrigan; *D:* King Vidor; *W:* William Parker.

Jack London 🦴½ *The Adventures of Jack London; The Life of Jack London* **1944** Dramatizes London's most creative years during his careers as oyster pirate, prospector, war correspondent and author. Based on "The Book of Jack London" by Charmian London. **94m/B VHS.** Michael O'Shea, Susan Hayward, Harry Davenport, Virginia Mayo, Frank Craven; *D:* Alfred Santell.

Jack London's The Call of the Wild 🦴🦴½ *The Call of the Wild: Dog of the Yukon* **1997 (PG)** Adaptation of Jack London's 1903 adventure story is told from the view of Buck, an intelligent St. Bernard-Labrador mix who's kidnapped from his California home. He's sold in the Yukon and eventually winds up with prospector John Thornton (Hauer) but Buck is increasingly drawn to running free. **90m/C VHS.** Rutger Hauer, Luc Morrissette, Bronwyn Booth; ***D:*** Peter Svatek; ***W:*** Graham Ludlow; ***C:*** Sylvain Brault; ***M:*** Alan Reeves; ***Nar:*** Richard Dreyfuss. **CABLE**

Jack-O 🦴½ **1995 (R)** Halloween nightmares in the small town of Oakmoor Crossing. When warlock Walter Machen (Carradine) was hung 100 years before, he invoked a demon creature to take his revenge. Now partyers, fooling around in the local cemetery, have stumbled onto horrific Jack-O's remains and manage to once again unleash the evil within. Cheesy grade-Z horror features old footage of deceased actors Carradine and Mitchell incorporated into what little plot there is. **90m/C VHS, DVD.** Linnea Quigley, Ryan Latshaw, Cameron Mitchell, John Carradine, Dawn Wildsmith, Brinke Stevens; ***D:*** Steve Latshaw; ***W:*** Patrick Moran; ***C:*** Maxwell J. Beck; ***M:*** Jeff Walton.

Jack the Bear 🦴½ **1993 (PG-13)** Exercise in misery centers on a father and his two sons, trying to pick up the pieces after the death of wife and mother Marcovicci. Dad DeVito is the host of a late-night horror show who's cuddly as a bear—when he's not drinking. While the talent and circumstances might have been enough to create a sensitive study, the emotion is completely overwrought by contrived plot twists, including a kidnapping by the local Nazi. TV's "thirtysomething" director Herskovitz creates an effect not unlike a cement block being dropped on a card house. Point made, but so much for subtlety. Based on a novel by Dan McCall. **98m/C VHS, Wide.** Danny DeVito, Robert J. Steinmiller Jr., Miko Hughes, Gary Sinise, Art LaFleur, Andrea Marcovicci, Julia Louis-Dreyfus, Reese Witherspoon; ***D:*** Marshall Herskovitz; ***W:*** Steven Zaillian; ***C:*** Fred Murphy; ***M:*** James Horner.

Jack the Giant Killer 🦴🦴🦴 **1962 (G)** A young farmer joins a medieval princess on a journey to a distant convent. Along the way, they combat an evil wizard, dragons, sea monsters, and other mystical creatures, and are assisted by leprechauns, a dog, and a chimp. Generally considered a blatant rip-off of "The Seventh Voyage of Sinbad," the film nonetheless delivers plenty of fun and excitement. Jim Danforth of "Gumby" fame provided the stop-motion animation. **95m/C VHS, DVD.** Kerwin Mathews, Judi Meredith, Torin Thatcher, Walter Burke, Roger Mobley, Barry Kelley, Don Beddoe, Anna Lee, Robert Gist; ***D:*** Nathan (Hertz) Juran; ***W:*** Nathan (Hertz) Juran, Orville H. Hampton; ***C:*** David S. Horsley; ***M:*** Paul Sawtell, Bert Shefter.

Jack the Ripper 🦴🦴 **1960** An American detective joins Scotland Yard in tracking down the legendary and elusive Jack the Ripper. More gory than most. The last scene is in color. **88m/B VHS.** *GB* Lee Patterson, Betty McDowall, Barbara Burke, John Le Mesurier, George Rose; ***D:*** Monty Berman, Robert S. Baker; ***M:*** Stanley Black.

Jack the Ripper 🦴🦴 *Der Dirnenmoerder von London* **1976 (R)** The inimitable Kinski assumes the role of the most heinous criminal of modern history—Jack the Ripper. **82m/C VHS.** *SI GE* Klaus Kinski, Josephine Chaplin, Herbert (Fuchs) Fux, Ursula von Wiese, Lina Romay, Andreas Mannkopff; ***D:*** Jess (Jesus) Franco; ***W:*** Jess (Jesus) Franco; ***C:*** Peter Baumgartner.

Jack the Ripper 🦴🦴🦴 **1988** Another retelling of the life of the legendary serial killer. Caine is the Scotland Yard inspector who tracks down the murderer. Ending is based on recent evidence found by director/co-writer Wickes. Extremely well done TV film. **200m/C VHS.** Michael Caine, Armand Assante, Ray McNally, Susan George, Jane Seymour, Lewis Collins, Ken Bones; ***D:*** David Wickes; ***W:*** David Wickes. **TV**

The Jackal 🦴🦴½ **1997 (R)** The plot has more holes than Swiss cheese but thanks to a pro cast this film manages to be at least a workmanlike thriller. Willis stars as a killer-for-hire known only as "The Jackal." His latest employer, a Russian gangster, wants revenge for FBI interference in his business, and the Jackal's target is apparently the FBI's Director. Few know what the Jackal looks like and the most available is Declan Mulqueen (Gere), an IRA gunman imprisoned in the U.S. He's given a deal by good FBI guy Preston (Poitier) and the hunt is on. Unfortunately, the Jackal's elaborate preparations don't raise the tension, though they do provide some gross-out moments. The end game (in the D.C. subway) between the Jackal and Mulqueen provides a satisfying conclusion and Willis does excell as the ice-cold killer. Started off as a heavily reworked version of the 1973 assassination thriller "The Day of the Jackal" but most of the associations have been cut. **124m/C VHS, DVD.** Bruce Willis, Richard Gere, Sidney Poitier, Diane Venora, Mathilda May, Stephen Spinella, John Cunningham, J.K. Simmons, Tess Harper, Richard Lineback, Jack Black, David Hayman, Steve Bassett; ***D:*** Michael Caton-Jones; ***W:*** Chuck Pfarrer; ***C:*** Karl Walter Lindenlaub; ***M:*** Carter Burwell.

The Jackals 🦴🦴 **1967** Six bandits threaten miner Price and his granddaughter in order to get his gold. Set in South Africa. **105m/C VHS, DVD.** Vincent Price, Diana Ivarson, Robert Gunner, Bob Courtney, Patrick Mynhardt; ***D:*** Robert D. Webb.

Jackie Brown 🦴🦴🦴 **1997 (R)** Tarantino finally climbs back into the director's chair with his leisurely but satisfying adaptation of Elmore Leonard's "Rum Punch." No, it's not "Pulp Fiction," but it could do for Pam Grier what "Pulp" did for John Travolta. Grier stars as out-of-luck-and-options stewardess Jackie Brown, who runs money to Mexico for ruthless arms dealer Ordell (Jackson). Busted on one of her errands, she comes up with an intricate plan to get out from under, hopefully with the money and without getting caught or killed. Slower and less bloody than Quentin fans are used to, but as usual, he gets killer performances from everybody. Cool dialogue and chronological shifts are again key ingredients, along with a hightened sense of character development. Fonda and De Niro make the most of small (but crucial) roles, but it's Forster (another '70s whatever-happened-to refugee) who provides the standout performance. The look and feel of the movie reflects the dingy world it inhabits, as well as Tarantino's love of '70s blaxploitation flicks. **155m/C VHS.** Pam Grier, Robert Forster, Samuel L. Jackson, Robert De Niro, Bridget Fonda, Michael Keaton, Michael Bowen, Chris Tucker, Lisa Gay Hamilton, Tommy (Tiny) Lister, Hattie Winston, Aimee Graham, Sid Haig; ***D:*** Quentin Tarantino; ***W:*** Quentin Tarantino; ***C:*** Guillermo Navarro; ***M:*** Mary Ramos, Michelle Kuznetsky.

Jackie Chan's First Strike 🦴🦴🦴 *First Strike; Police Story 4* **1996 (PG-13)** Plot, schmot. The human hurricane that is Jackie Chan is once again amazing in this kung-fu comedy homage to '60s James Bond movies. Half Bruce Lee and half Charlie Chaplin, Chan reprises the role of the Hong Kong supercop named Jackie, who is this time loaned out by his superior officer "Uncle Bill" (Tung) to the CIA. He is sent to the Ukraine to spy on a beautiful young woman involved in smuggling nuclear weapons along with rogue CIA agent Tsui (Lou). He follows the villains to Australia, where he secures justice, peace, and sharp blows to the head. Enough about the plot. Listen to this! He holds bad guys at bay by whirling an aluminum stepladder like it was a drum major's baton! He kicks somebody off of a second story ledge while on stilts! He sings and dances while wearing koala bear underwear! Dubbed in English. **87m/C VHS, DVD.** *HK* Jackie Chan, Bill Tung, Jackson Lou, Annie (Chen Chun) Wu, Jouri (Yuri) Petrov, Grishajeva Nonna; ***D:*** Stanley Tong; ***W:*** Stanley Tong, Greg Mellott, Nick Tramontane, Elliot Tong; ***C:*** Jingle Ma; ***M:*** J. Peter Robinson.

Jackie Chan's Who Am I 🦴🦴½ *Who Am I; Ngo Hai Sui* **1998 (PG-13)** Jackie (Chan) is recruited by the CIA to join a team of commandos leading a raid on a secret weapons research lab in South Africa. The team hijack a piece of highly explosive experimental material and are betrayed by their leader. Only Jackie survives but he's got amnesia. When he finally returns home, he's still wondering who he is—an important question since he's being pursued by the bad guys who want him to stay dead. **108m/C VHS, DVD, Wide.** *HK* Jackie Chan, Ed Nelson, Ron Smerczak, Michelle Ferre, Mirai Yamamoto; ***D:*** Jackie Chan, Benny Chan; ***W:*** Jackie Chan, Lee Reynolds, Susan Chan; ***C:*** Poon Hang-Seng; ***M:*** Nathan Wang.

Jackie, Ethel, Joan: The Kennedy Women 🦴🦴½ *Jackie, Ethel, Joan: Women of Camelot* **2001** TV miniseries focuses on the Kennedy wives: Jackie (Hennessy), Ethel (Holly), and Joan (Stefanson) rather than on their husbands and the toll that politics and the spotlight took on them as individuals. Sudser follows the period from 1960 to 1980; based on the bestseller by J. Randy Taraborrelli. **172m/C VHS.** Jill(ian) Hennessey, Lauren Holly, Leslie Stefanson, Daniel Hugh-Kelly, Rob Knepper, Matt Letscher, Harve Presnell, Charmion King, Thom Christopher; ***D:*** Larry Shaw; ***W:*** David Stevens; ***C:*** Frank Byers; ***M:*** Martin Davich. **TV**

The Jackie Robinson Story 🦴🦴🦴 **1950** Chronicles Robinson's rise from UCLA to his breakthrough as the first black man to play baseball in the major league. Robinson plays himself; the film deals honestly with the racial issues of the time. **76m/B VHS, DVD.** Jackie Robinson, Ruby Dee, Minor Watson, Louise Beavers, Richard Lane, Harry Shannon, Joel Fluellen, Ben Lessy; ***D:*** Alfred E. Green; ***W:*** Arthur Mann, Lawrence Taylor; ***C:*** Ernest Laszlo; ***M:*** David Chudnow.

Jackie's Back 🦴🦴½ **1999 (R)** Mockumentary follows the stumbling comeback of forgotten pop diva, Jackie Washington (Lewis). Spoiled and temperamental, Jackie is followed by a supercilious British doumentary filmmaker, Edward Whatsett St. John (Curry), as she prepares for a big concert as everything is in chaos around her. Flashbacks reflect on Jackie's early career. **91m/C VHS, DVD.** Jenifer Lewis, Tim Curry, Tangie Ambrose, Whoopi Goldberg, David Hyde Pierce, Tom Arnold, Julie Hagerty, JoBeth Williams, Dolly Parton, Grace Slick, Liza Minnelli; ***D:*** Robert Townsend; ***W:*** Mark Brown, Dee La Duke; ***C:*** Charles Mills; ***M:*** Marc Shaiman. **CABLE**

Jacknife 🦴🦴🦴 **1989 (R)** The well-crafted story of a Vietnam veteran who visits his old war buddy and tries to piece together what's happened to their lives since their homecoming. During his visit he encounters anger and hostility from the other veteran, and tenderness from his friend's sister. A masterfully acted, small-scale drama, adapted by Stephen Metcalfe from his play. **102m/C VHS.** Robert De Niro, Kathy Baker, Ed Harris, Loudon Wainwright III, Charles S. Dutton; ***D:*** David Hugh Jones; ***W:*** Stephen Metcalfe; ***M:*** Bruce Broughton.

Jacko & Lise 🦴🦴 **1982 (R)** A French lad falls in love with a young girl, and abandons his previously decadent lifestyle to win her. Available with English subtitles or dubbed. **92m/C VHS.** *FR* Laurent Malet, Annie Girardot; ***D:*** Walter Bal.

The Jackpot 🦴🦴 **1950** An average Joe wins a bushel of money from a radio quiz show but can't pay the taxes. Maybe that was funny before the age of read-my-lips economics, but the all-star cast doesn't deliver on its promise. Lang, noted for mostly mediocre pictures, went on to direct "The King and I." **87m/C VHS.** James Stewart, Natalie Wood, Barbara Hale, James Gleason, Fred Clark, Patricia Medina; ***D:*** Walter Lang; ***C:*** Joseph LaShelle.

Jackpot 🦴🦴 **2001 (R)** Brothers Mark and Michael Polish follow up their critically lauded debut "Twin Falls Idaho" with this road tale of karaoke and crackpots. Sunny Holiday (Gries) is an aspiring country singer riding the back roads of the remote West with his manager Les (Morris), trying to break into Nashville via the untraveled karaoke route. Neither one seems to realize the futility of his dreams, but Bobbi (Hannah), the wife he's abandoned with their young child, does. The "Jackpot" of the title is his dream of making it big, the way he hopes to support his family (he sends them a lottery ticket each week in lieu of child support) and the name of the Nevada town where he hopes to be discovered. Tries way too hard to be arty in a folksy "look at these eccentric characters" way, but it's not without its own weird charm. **100m/C VHS, DVD, Wide.** *US* Jonathan (Jon Francis) Gries, Garrett Morris, Daryl Hannah, Peggy Lipton, Adam Baldwin, Mac Davis, Crystal Bernard, Anthony Edwards; ***D:*** Michael Polish; ***W:*** Michael Polish, Mark Polish; ***C:*** M. David Mullen; ***M:*** Stuart Matthewman; ***V:*** Patrick Bauchau.

Jack's Back 🦴🦴🦴 **1987 (R)** When a lunatic is killing Los Angeles prostitutes Jack-the-Ripper style, twin brothers get mistakenly involved (Spader in both roles). One of the brothers is accused of the murders and it is up to the other either to clear his name or to provide the final evidence of guilt. A well-thought out story with enough twists and turns for any suspense buff. **97m/C VHS.** James Spader, Cynthia Gibb, Rod Loomis, Rex Ryon, Robert Picardo, Jim Haynie, Chris Mulkey, Danitza Kingsley, Wendell Wright; ***D:*** Rowdy Herrington; ***W:*** Rowdy Herrington; ***C:*** Shelly Johnson.

Jackson County Jail 🦴🦴½ **1976 (R)** While driving cross-country, a young woman is robbed, imprisoned, and raped by a deputy, whom she kills. Faced with a murder charge, she flees, with the law in hot pursuit. Also known by its later remade-for-TV name, "Outside Chance," this is a minor cult film. **84m/C VHS, DVD.** Yvette Mimieux, Tommy Lee Jones, Robert Carradine, Severn Darden, Howard Hesseman, Mary Woronov, Ed Marshall, Cliff Emmich, Betty Thomas; ***D:*** Michael Miller; ***W:*** Donald Stewart; ***C:*** Bruce Logan; ***M:*** Loren Newkirk.

The Jacksons: An American Dream 🦴🦴½ **1992** Miniseries covering the career of the Jackson 5, the working-class family from Gary, Indiana, who became a celebrated show business success. The series begins with the courtship of Joseph and Katherine Jackson and ends with the group's farewell tour in 1984, covering both family and career turmoils. Simplistic, glossy biography. **225m/C VHS.** Lawrence-Hilton Jacobs, Angela Bassett, Wylie Draper, Angel Vargas, Jacen Wilkerson, Terrence DaShon Howard, Jason Weaver, Jermaine Jackson II, Billy Dee Williams, Vanessa L(ynne) Williams, Holly Robinson, Margaret Avery; ***D:*** Karen Arthur. **TV**

Jacob 🦴🦴½ **1994** Jacob (Modine), second son of Isaac (Ackland), tricks his father into giving him the blessing meant for eldest son Esau (Bean). Jacob is forced to run away to his Uncle Laban (Giannini), where he promptly falls in love with his cousin Rachel (Boyle). But Laban tricks Jacob into marrying eldest daughter Leah (Aubrey), before allowing his marriage to Rachel. Finally, Jacob settles on his own land with his wives and children (who will become the tribes of Israel). Dignified retelling of the biblical story; filmed on location in Morocco. **120m/C VHS.** Matthew Modine, Lara Flynn Boyle, Sean Bean, Juliet Aubrey, Giancarlo Giannini, Joss Ackland, Irene Papas, Christoph Waltz; ***D:*** Peter Hall; ***W:*** Lionel Chetwynd; ***M:*** Marco Frisina. **CABLE**

Jacob Have I Loved **1988** A teenage girl struggles to overcome her jealousy of her twin sister and find her own place in life as she comes of age on a Chesapeake island. Based on the book by Katherine Paterson. Part of the "Wonderworks" family movie series from PBS. **57m/C VHS.** Bridget Fonda, Jenny Robertson, John Kellogg; ***D:*** Victoria Hochberg.

Jacob the Liar 🦴🦴 *Jakob der Lugner* **1974 (PG-13)** When Jacob Heim is stopped for being out of the Jewish ghetto after curfew, he is sent to see the police commander. On the police radio, he hears that the Red Army is advancing and he returns to the ghetto to pass along the news, pretending that he heard it on his own hidden radio. Soon, Jacob is inventing news reports to give his fellow Jews hope. German with subtitles. A sentimental American remake came out in 1999. **101m/C VHS, DVD.** *GE* Armin Mueller-Stahl, Vlastimil Brodsky, Erwin Geschonneck, Henry Hubchen, Blanche Kommerell, Manuela Simon; ***D:***

Frank Beyer; ***W:*** Jurek Becker; ***C:*** Gunter Marczinkowski.

Jacob Two Two Meets the Hooded Fang 🦴🦴½ **1999** Edgy kids fantasy based on the book by Mordecai Richler. Jacob (Morrow) is nicknamed Jacob Two Two because he repeats everything since no one every listens to him the first time he says something. Because of this Jacob gets into unexpected trouble when shopping at the corner store, runs into the store basement, and knocks himself out in the darkness. Jacob dreams he's now on trial and is sentenced to Slimers' Island, which is run by a bizarre creature called the Hooded Fang (Busey) and his equally strange henchmen. **96m/C VHS, DVD.** *CA* Max Morrow, Gary Busey, Miranda Richardson, Ice-T, Mark McKinney, Maury Chaykin; ***D:*** George Bloomfield; ***W:*** Tim Burns; ***C:*** Gerald Packer; ***M:*** Jono Grant.

Jacob's Ladder 🦴🦴½ **1990 (R)** A man struggles with events he experienced while serving in Vietnam. Gradually, he becomes unable to separate reality from the strange, psychotic world into which he increasingly lapses. His friends and family try to help him before he's lost forever. Great story potential is flawed by too many flashbacks, leaving the viewer more confused than the characters. **116m/C VHS, DVD, Wide.** Tim Robbins, Elizabeth Pena, Danny Aiello, Matt Craven, Pruitt Taylor Vince, Jason Alexander, Patricia Kalember, Eriq La Salle, Ving Rhames, Macaulay Culkin; ***D:*** Adrian Lyne; ***W:*** Bruce Joel Rubin; ***C:*** Jeffrey L. Kimball; ***M:*** Maurice Jarre.

Jacqueline Bouvier Kennedy 🦴½ **1981** Biography of the former First Lady, from her childhood to "Camelot," the glorious years with JFK in the White House. Smith bears a physical resemblance to Jackie, but this drama is far too glossy. **150m/C VHS.** Jaclyn Smith, James Franciscus, Rod Taylor, Donald Moffat, Dolph Sweet, Stephen Elliott; ***D:*** Steven Gethers; ***M:*** Billy Goldenberg. **TV**

Jacquot 🦴🦴 *Jacquot de Nantes* **1991 (PG)** Director Varda offers a loving tribute to her husband, filmmaker Jacques Demy. Based on the memoirs of her husband's childhood as a boy obsessed with movies, Varda re-stages scenes and also uses clips from various Demy films to illustrate her points. In French with English subtitles. **118m/C VHS.** *FR* Philippe Maron, Edouard Joubeaud, Laurent Monnier, Brigitte de Villepoix, Daniel Dublet; ***D:*** Agnes Varda; ***W:*** Agnes Varda; ***C:*** Patrick Blossier; ***M:*** Joanne Bruzdowicz.

Jade 🦴½ **1995 (R)** Sleazy whodunnit scraped from the bottom of the Eszterhas barrel (and it's a deep one) has hot-shot San Francisco Assistant D.A. David Corelli (Caruso) tracking a trail of pubic hairs across San Francisco. Seems he's caught up in the murder of a millionaire that points to his ex-lover, psychologist Katrina Gavin (Fiorentino), as the killer. Oh yeah, she's also a kinky call girl of choice to California's rich and famous, and happens to be married to Corelli's best friend (Palminteri). Psycho-thriller with little of either injects lots of lurid details (and a car chase scene that Friedkin has done much better elsewhere) in an attempt to curtail boredom; it doesn't work. Combine it with "Showgirls" for the No Self-Respect Film Festival, then go to confession. **94m/C VHS, DVD.** David Caruso, Linda Fiorentino, Chazz Palminteri, Michael Biehn, Richard Crenna, Kenneth King, Angie Everhart; ***D:*** William Friedkin; ***W:*** Joe Eszterhas; ***C:*** Andrzej Bartkowiak; ***M:*** James Horner.

The Jade Mask 🦴½ **1945** Chan discovers a murderer and his wife use puppets and masks to make it appear their victims are still alive. Another in the detective series with nothing noteworthy about it. Luke, the brother of actor Keye Luke, takes on the role of Chan's Number Four son. **66m/B VHS.** Sidney Toler, Mantan Moreland, Edwin Luke, Janet Warren, Hardie Albright, Edith Evanson; ***D:*** Phil Rosen.

Jaded 🦴🦴½ **1996 (R)** Seemingly innocent Meg (Gugino) is befriended by a couple of uninhibited babes (Kihlstedt, Thompson) at the local bar and goes with them to a party where she's sexually assaulted. The two women are accused of rape and the case goes to trial but Meg's past secrets come to light and things don't seem so cut-and-dried anymore. The box art is the real tease since the film isn't the erotic thriller it might appear to be. **95m/C VHS, DVD.** Carla Gugino, Anna Thomson, Rya Kihlstedt, Christopher McDonald, Lorraine Toussaint; ***D:*** Caryn Krooth. **VIDEO**

JAG 🦴🦴½ **1995** TV pilot episode features Navy pilot-turned-lawyer Lt. Harmon Rabb, Jr. (Elliott) assigned to investigate the case of a young female pilot who disappears from an aircraft carrier. Seems some of her fellow sailors resented having women on board so was it an accident or murder? JAG stands for the office of the Judge Advocate General, whose Navy lawyers serve as investigators, prosecutors, and defense attorneys. **94m/C VHS.** David James Elliott, Andrea Parker, Terry O'Quinn, John Roselius, Katie Rich, Scott Jaeck, Patrick Laborteaux, Cliff DeYoung, Kevin Dunn; ***D:*** Donald P. Bellisario; ***W:*** Donald P. Bellisario; ***C:*** Thomas Del Ruth; ***M:*** Bruce Broughton. **TV**

The Jagged Edge 🦴🦴½ **1985 (R)** The beautiful wife of successful newspaper editor, Jack Forester, is killed and the police want to point the guilty finger at Jack. Attorney Teddy Barnes is brought in to defend him and accidentally falls in love. Taut murder mystery will keep you guessing "whodunit" until the very end. **108m/C VHS, DVD, 8mm, Wide.** Jeff Bridges, Glenn Close, Robert Loggia, Peter Coyote, John Dehner, Leigh Taylor-Young, Lance Henriksen, James Karen, Karen Austin, Michael Dorn, Guy Boyd, Marshall Colt, Louis Giambalvo; ***D:*** Richard Marquand; ***W:*** Joe Eszterhas; ***C:*** Matthew F. Leonetti; ***M:*** John Barry.

Jaguar **1956** Three men leave their homes in Niger in order to find jobs in the cities. When they return to their village, they bring back with them their experiences. **93m/C VHS.** ***D:*** Jean Rouch; ***M:*** Van Alexander.

Jaguar Lives 🦴 **1979 (PG)** A high-kicking secret agent tracks down bad boy drug kings around the world. **91m/C VHS.** Joe Lewis, Barbara Bach, Christopher Lee, Woody Strode, Donald Pleasence, Joseph Wiseman, John Huston, Capucine; ***D:*** Ernest Pintoff.

Jail Bait 🦴½ *Hidden Face* **1954** Early Wood film about a group of small-time crooks who are always in trouble with the law; they blackmail a plastic surgeon into using his talents to help them ditch the cops. Not as "bad" as Wood's "Plan 9 From Outer Space," but still bad enough for camp fans to love (check the cheesy score leftover from an equally cheesy Mexican mad-scientist flick). **80m/B VHS, DVD.** Timothy Farrell, Clancy Malone, Lyle Talbot, Steve Reeves, Herbert Rawlinson, Dolores Fuller, Theodora Thurman, Conrad Brooks, Mona McKinnon; ***D:*** Edward D. Wood Jr.; ***W:*** Edward D. Wood Jr., Alex Gordon; ***C:*** William C. Thompson.

Jailbait 🦴🦴 *Streetwise* **1993 (R)** A cop gets involved with an alleged murder witness, a teenaged runaway named Kyle. What they discover is an international crime syndicate that kidnaps runaways to exploit as sex slaves. Now they know too much. An unrated version is also available. **100m/C VHS.** C. Thomas Howell, Renee Humphrey; ***D:*** Rafal Zielinski; ***W:*** Robert Vincent O'Neil.

Jailbait! 🦴🦴 **2000 (R)** Popular high school jock Adam (Mundy), who's 18, cheats on his girlfriend and gets wrong side of the tracks 16-year-old Gynger (Purrott) preggers leading to a charge of statutory rape. Satire on teen sex, political platforms, and society. First original movie made for MTV. **94m/C VHS, DVD.** Kevin Mundy, Mo Gaffney, Alycia Purrott, Melody Johnson, Matt Frewer, Mary Gross, Reagan Pasternak; ***D:*** Allan Moyle. **CABLE**

Jailbait: Betrayed By Innocence 🦴½ **1986 (R)** A man is on trial for statutory rape. **90m/C VHS.** Barry Bostwick, Lee Purcell, Paul Sorvino, Cristen Kauffman, Isaac Hayes; ***D:*** Elliot Silverstein. **TV**

Jailbird Rock 🦴½ **1988** We'd like to tell you that this isn't really a sweet-young-thing-in-prison musical, but it is. When Antin shoots her stepfather (he told her to turn that damn noise down?) she tries to bring down the Big House with song and dance. No kidding. **90m/C VHS.** Robin Antin, Valchie Gene Richards, Robin Cleaver, Rhonda Aldrich, Jacquelyn Houston, Debra Laws, Erica Jordan, Perry Lang, Ronald Lacey; ***D:*** Phillip Schuman; ***W:*** Edward Kovach, Carole Stanley; ***C:*** Leonardo Solis; ***M:*** Rick Nowecs.

Jailbird's Vacation 🦴🦴½ *Les Grandes Gueules* **1965** From the director of the classic "An Occurrence at Owl Creek Bridge," comes this comedy-drama about a sawmill owner dealing with two ex-convicts hired as lumberjacks. They want to get revenge on the bum who put them away. French with subtitles. **125m/C VHS.** *FR* Lino Ventura, Bourvil, Marie DuBois; ***D:*** Robert Enrico.

Jailbreakers 🦴🦴 **1994 (R)** Another remake from Showtime's "Rebel Highway" series that takes little but the title from the 1960 A.I.P. flick. Cheerleader Angel (Doherty) falls for bad boy Tony (Sabato Jr.) and gets busted by the cops while they're out on a little crime spree. He goes to prison, she and her family must leave town. But boy can't get girl out of his head and he busts out of the big house to reunite with his true love. Then the crazy kids hit the road for the Mexican border. **76m/C VHS, DVD.** Shannen Doherty, Antonio Sabato Jr., Adrienne Barbeau, Adrien Brody, Vince Edwards, George Gerdes; ***D:*** William Friedkin; ***W:*** Debra Hill, Gigi Vorgan; ***C:*** Cary Fisher; ***M:*** Hummie Mann. **CABLE**

Jailbreakin' 🦴 **1972** A faded country singer and a rebellious youth team up to break out of jail. **90m/C VHS.** Erik Estrada.

Jailhouse Rock 🦴🦴🦴 **1957 (G)** While in jail for manslaughter, teenager Vince Everett (Presley) learns to play the guitar. After his release, he slowly develops into a top recording star. Probably the only film that captured the magnetic power of the young Elvis Presley; an absolute must for fans. Also available in a colorized version. ♫Jailhouse Rock; Treat Me Nice; Baby, I Don't Care; Young and Beautiful; Don't Leave Me Now; I Wanna Be Free; One More Day. **96m/B VHS, DVD, Wide.** Elvis Presley, Judy Tyler, Vaughn Taylor, Dean Jones, Mickey Shaughnessy, William Forrest, Glenn Strange, Jennifer Holden, Anne Neyland; ***D:*** Richard Thorpe; ***W:*** Guy Trosper; ***C:*** Robert J. Bronner; ***M:*** Jeff Alexander.

Jakarta 🦴½ **1988 (R)** Before gaining fame on the popular t.v. series "Law and Order," actor Chris Noth was action hero material. Sadly without much success in this dud. A love-hardened CIA operative (Noth) is whisked away to Jakarta for reasons unknown, only to find his thought-to-be-dead lover still alive and caught in a deadly game of espionage. **94m/C VHS.** Christopher Noth, Sue Francis Pai, Ronald Hunter; ***D:*** Charles Kaufman.

Jake Speed 🦴½ **1986 (PG)** Comic-book mercenary Jake and his loyal associate Remo rescue a beautiful girl from white slave traders. Supposedly a parody of the action adventure genre. **93m/C VHS, DVD, Wide.** Wayne Crawford, John Hurt, Karen Kopins, Dennis Christopher; ***D:*** Andrew Lane; ***W:*** Wayne Crawford; ***C:*** Bryan Loftus; ***M:*** Mark Snow.

Jakob the Liar 🦴🦴🦴 **1999 (PG-13)** Robin Williams reins in his usual manic personality in this touching tale set during the Holocaust. Jakob (Williams) is a Jew confined to the Polish ghetto by the Nazis. After he hears a radio broadcast describing German defeats while in a Nazi commandant's office, he relates the news to his friend Mischa (Schreiber). This leads to rumors that he owns a contraband radio, which is an offense punishable by death. He sees the excitement and hope that his news has brought and begins to make up new stories to encourage his oppressed community. Finally, the men become courageous enough to start a resistance movement, with Jakob as the leader. The realities of the Holocaust are shown with no attempt to sugarcoat them, and the performances are excellent all around. **114m/C VHS, DVD.** Robin Williams, Armin Mueller-Stahl, Alan Arkin, Bob Balaban, Michael Jeter, Liev Schreiber, Hannah Taylor Gordon, Nina Siemaszko, Mathieu Kassovitz, Mark Margolis; ***D:*** Peter Kassovitz; ***W:*** Peter Kassovitz, Didier Decoin; ***C:*** Elemer Ragalyi; ***M:*** Ed Shearmur.

Jalsaghar 🦴🦴 *The Music Room* **1958** Bisambhar Roy is the last in his aristocratic line and has inherited nothing but debts. But his position in society demands a certain style and he pawns family heirlooms in order to host expensive private concerts, even after tragedy strikes his family. Bengali with subtitles. **100m/B VHS.** *IN* Chhabi Biswas, Padma Devi, Tulsi Lahnin, Pinaki Sen Gupta, Kali Sarkar; ***D:*** Satyajit Ray; ***W:*** Satyajit Ray; ***C:*** Subrata Mitra; ***M:*** Satyajit Ray.

Jamaica Inn 🦴🦴 **1939** In old Cornwall, an orphan girl becomes involved with smugglers. Remade in 1982; based on the story by Daphne Du Maurier. **98m/B VHS, DVD.** *GB* Charles Laughton, Maureen O'Hara, Leslie Banks, Robert Newton; ***D:*** Alfred Hitchcock; ***W:*** Sidney Gilliat, Joan Harrison; ***C:*** Harry Stradling Sr.; ***M:*** Eric Fenby.

Jamaica Inn 🦴½ **1982** Miniseries based on the old Daphne Du Maurier adventure about highwaymen and moor-lurking thieves in Cornwall. Remake of the 1939 Hitchcock film. **192m/C VHS, DVD.** Patrick McGoohan, Jane Seymour; ***D:*** Lawrence Gordon Clark. **TV**

James and the Giant Peach 🦴🦴🦴 **1996 (PG)** Terrific combo of live action and stop-motion animation highlights this adaptation of Roald Dahl's 1961 children's book. Orphaned James is sent to live with his wicked aunts. When magic "crocodile tongues," given to James by a hobo, spill at the base of a peach tree, one fruit grows to such a tremendous size that James crawls inside, meets six insect friends, and goes on numerous adventures, all the while trying to face his fears. Dahl's books are creepy and since the people who brought you "Nightmare Before Christmas" are also doing "James," expect the visuals to be astonishing but too scary for the little ones. **80m/C VHS, DVD, Wide.** ***D:*** Henry Selick; ***C:*** Pete Kozachik, Hiro Narita; ***M:*** Randy Newman; ***V:*** Paul Terry, Pete Postlethwaite, Joanna Lumley, Miriam Margolyes, Richard Dreyfuss, Susan Sarandon, David Thewlis, Simon Callow, Jane Leeves.

James Dean 🦴🦴 *The Legend* **1976** Dean's friend Bast wrote this behind-the-scenes look at the short life of the enigmatic movie star. **99m/C VHS.** Stephen McHattie, Michael Brandon, Candy Clark, Amy Irving, Brooke Adams, Dane Clark, Jayne Meadows, Meg Foster; ***D:*** William Bast, Robert Butler; ***W:*** William Bast; ***M:*** Billy Goldenberg. **TV**

James Dean 🦴🦴½ **2001** The original rebel without a cause gets a superficial biopic treatment that doesn't have much time to explore the appeal of the young legend who died at the age of 24. Dean's (Franco) troubles stem from his unhappy relationship with his distant father (Moriarty) and even his impressive acting talents can't save him from self-destruction. Film focuses on the making of "East of Eden" and Dean's romance with fragile actress Pier Angeli (Cervi). Franco does well in the title role. **95m/C VHS, DVD.** James Franco, Michael Moriarty, Valentina Cervi, Enrico Colantoni, Edward Herrmann, Barry Primus, Mark Rydell, Joanne Linville, John Pleshette; ***D:*** Mark Rydell; ***W:*** Israel Horovitz; ***C:*** Robbie Greenberg. **CABLE**

James Dean: Live Fast, Die Young 🦴🦴 *James Dean: Race with Destiny* **1997 (PG-13)** Lightweight biopic of legendary acting rebel with a cause Dean (Van Dien). Film finds Dean troubled when girlfriend Pier Angeli (Carrie Mitchum, Robert's granddaughter) marries another, and in trouble with studio boss Jack Warner (Connors) and director George Stevens (Mitchum). **105m/C VHS, DVD.** Casper Van Dien, Robert Mitchum, Mike Connors, Carrie Mitchum, Diane Ladd, Connie Stevens, Monique Parent, Casey Kasem, Joseph Campanella; ***D:*** Marti Rustam; ***W:*** Dan Sefton; ***C:*** Gary Graver, Irv Goodnoff. **TV**

James Joyce: A Portrait of the Artist as a Young Man **1977** A moving, lyrical adaptation of the author's autobiography, told through the character of Stephen Dedalus. Joyce's characterizations, words, and scenes are beautifully translated to the medium of film. Excellent casting. **93m/C VHS.** John Gielgud, T.P. McKenna, Bosco Hogan; ***D:*** Joseph Strick.

James Joyce's Women 🦴🦴🦴 **1985 (R)** Adapted from her one-woman stage show as well as produced by Flanagan, this acclaimed film features enacted portraits of three real-life Joyce associates, including his wife (Nora Barnacle) and three of his famous characters. **91m/C VHS.** Fionnula Flanagan, Timothy E. O'Grady, Chris O'Neill; ***D:*** Michael Pearce; ***W:*** Fionnula Flanagan.

Jamon, Jamon 🦴🦴 *Ham Ham* **1993** Comedic melodrama satirizing various aspects of the Spanish character, including machismo, sex, and food. A small Spanish town is dominated by two businesses—an underwear factory and a brothel—both run by strong-minded women. The brothel's Carmen and the factory's Conchita clash when Carmen's daughter, Silvia, becomes pregnant by Conchita's son, Manuel. Conchita's appalled and hires stud Raul to seduce Silvia—only to fall for him herself. Oh yes, Raul attributes his sexual prowess to a steady diet of ham and garlic. In Spanish with English subtitles. **95m/C VHS.** *SP* Penelope Cruz, Anna Galiena, Javier Bardem, Stefania Sandrelli, Juan Diego, Jordi Molla; ***D:*** Bigas Luna; ***W:*** Bigas Luna, Cuca Canals; ***C:*** Jose Luis Alcaine; ***M:*** Nicola Piovani.

Jane & the Lost City 🦴🦴½ **1987 (PG)** A British farce based on the age-old, barely dressed comic-strip character, Jane, as she stumbles on ancient cities, treasures, villains, and blond/blue-eyed heroes. Low-budget camp fun. **94m/C VHS, DVD, Wide.** *GB* Kristen Hughes, Maud Adams, Sam Jones; ***D:*** Terry Marcel; ***W:*** Mervyn Haisman; ***C:*** Paul Beeson; ***M:*** Harry Robertson.

Jane Austen in Manhattan 🦴½ **1980** Two acting-teachers vie to stage a long-lost play written by a youthful Jane Austen. Dreary, despite the cast. Hodiak is the real-life daughter of Baxter. **108m/C VHS.** Anne Baxter, Robert Powell, Michael Wager, Sean Young, Kurt Johnson, Katrina Hodiak; ***D:*** James Ivory; ***W:*** Ruth Prawer Jhabvala.

Jane Doe 🦴🦴½ **1983** Valentine plays a young amnesia victim who is linked to a series of brutal slayings. Quite suspenseful for a TV movie. **100m/C VHS.** Karen Valentine, William Devane, Eva Marie Saint, Stephen E. Miller, Jackson Davies; ***D:*** Ivan Nagy. **TV**

Jane Doe 🦴🦴 *Pictures of Baby Jane Doe* **1996 (R)** Jane Doe (Flockhart) is a drug addict who's getting seriously involved with shy writer Horace (Peditto). Only her addictions begin to cause some serious trouble for this odd couple. Adapted from a play. **92m/C VHS, DVD.** Calista Flockhart, Elina Lowensohn, Joe Ragno, Christopher Peditto; ***D:*** Paul Peditto; ***W:*** Paul Peditto.

Jane Eyre 🦴🦴 **1934** Stiff, early version of Charlotte Bronte's classic gothic romance. English orphan grows up to become the governess of a mysterious manor. Notable as the first talkie version. Remade several times. **67m/B VHS.** Virginia Bruce, Colin Clive, Beryl Mercer, Jameson Thomas, Aileen Pringle, David Torrence; ***D:*** Christy Cabanne.

Jane Eyre 🦴🦴🦴 **1944** Excellent adaptation of the Charlotte Bronte novel about the plain governess with the noble heart and her love for the mysterious and tragic Mr. Rochester. Fontaine has the proper backbone and yearning in the title role but to accommodate Welles' emerging popularity the role of Rochester was enlarged. Excellent bleak romantic-Gothic look. Taylor, in her third film role, is seen briefly in the early orphanage scenes. **97m/B VHS.** Joan Fontaine, Orson Welles, Margaret O'Brien, Peggy Ann Garner, John Sutton, Sara Allgood, Henry Daniell, Agnes Moorehead, Aubrey Mather, Edith Barrett, Barbara Everest, Hillary Brooke, Elizabeth Taylor; ***D:*** Robert Stevenson; ***W:*** John Houseman, Aldous Huxley, Robert Stevenson; ***C:*** George Barnes; ***M:*** Bernard Herrmann.

Jane Eyre 🦴🦴🦴 **1983** Miniseries based on the famed Charlotte Bronte novel about the maturation of a homeless English waif, her love for the tormented Rochester, and her quest for permanent peace. **239m/C VHS.** *GB* Timothy Dalton, Zelah Clarke; ***D:*** Julian Aymes. **TV**

Jane Eyre 🦴🦴🦴 **1996 (PG)** Zeffirelli creates an eloquent yet spare interpretation of Charlotte Bronte's 1847 masterpiece, about a meek governess and her mysterious employer, in its fourth film incarnation. Everything about it, from the lighting to the score, is muted and somber. Still a beautiful film, it seems to lack a certain passion that earlier versions (especially the 1944 classic) brought to the screen. Strong performances all around, including Oscar-winner Paquin and French star Gainsbourg as the younger and older Jane, and Hurt as the tormented Rochester. **116m/C VHS.** William Hurt, Anna Paquin, Charlotte Gainsbourg, Joan Plowright, Elle Macpherson, Geraldine Chaplin, Fiona Shaw, John Wood, Amanda Root, Maria Schneider, Josephine Serre, Billie Whitelaw; ***D:*** Franco Zeffirelli; ***W:*** Franco Zeffirelli, Hugh Whitemore; ***C:*** David Watkin; ***M:*** Alessio Vlad, Claudio Capponi.

Jane Eyre 🦴🦴½ **1997** Charlotte Bronte's dark romance between meek-yet-strong-willed governess Jane (Morton) and her tormented-yet-dashing employer, Mr. Rochester (Hinds). This version dispenses quickly with many of the subplots to concentrate on the main duo. **108m/C VHS, DVD.** *GB* Samantha Morton, Ciaran Hinds, Gemma Jones, Abigail Cruttenden, Richard Hawley; ***D:*** Robert M. Young; ***W:*** Kay Mellor; ***M:*** Richard Harvey. **CABLE**

The January Man 🦴🦴 **1989 (R)** An unorthodox cop, previously exiled by a corrupt local government to the fire department, is brought back to the force in New York City to track down a serial killer. Written by the "Moonstruck" guy, Shanley, who apparently peaked with the earlier movie. **97m/C VHS, DVD, Wide.** Kevin Kline, Susan Sarandon, Mary Elizabeth Mastrantonio, Harvey Keitel, Rod Steiger, Alan Rickman, Danny Aiello; ***D:*** Pat O'Connor; ***W:*** Pat O'Connor, John Patrick Shanley; ***C:*** Jerzy Zielinski; ***M:*** Marvin Hamlisch.

The Jar **1984** A recluse discovers a disgusting creature in a jar. He keeps it, only to discover that it is out to kill him. **90m/C VHS.** Gary Wallace, Karen Sjoberg; ***D:*** Bruce Toscano; ***W:*** George Bradley.

Jason and the Argonauts 🦴🦴🦴 **1963 (G)** Jason, son of the King of Thessaly, sails on the Argo to the land of Colchis, where the Golden Fleece is guarded by a seven-headed hydra. Superb special effects and multitudes of mythological creatures; fun for the whole family. **104m/C VHS, DVD, Wide.** *GB* Todd Armstrong, Nancy Kovack, Gary Raymond, Laurence Naismith, Nigel Green, Michael Gwynn, Honor Blackman, Niall MacGinnis, Douglas Wilmer, Jack (Gwyllam) Gwillim; ***D:*** Don Chaffey; ***W:*** Jan Read, Beverley Cross; ***C:*** Wilkie Cooper; ***M:*** Bernard Herrmann.

Jason and the Argonauts 🦴🦴½ **2000** Elaborate retelling of the Greek myth of Jason and his quest for the golden fleece. Young Prince Jason (London) has had his heritage usurped by his evil Uncle Pelias (Hopper in braids), who has killed Jason's father and taken his throne. In order to reclaim it, Jason must retrieve the magical golden fleece from distant Colchis and bring it to Pelias. So Jason assembles the usual motley crew of would-be heroes and sets sail on the Argos for uncharted waters and numerous adventures. TV saga with lots of action and some good special effects. **179m/C VHS, DVD.** Jason London, Dennis Hopper, Angus Macfadyen, Olivia Williams, Brian Thompson, Adrian Lester, Derek Jacobi, Jolene Blalock, Frank Langella, Natasha Henstridge, Ciaran Hinds, Kieran O'Brien, Charles Cartmell; ***D:*** Nick Willing; ***W:*** Matthew Faulk, Mark Skeet; ***C:*** Sergei Kozlov; ***M:*** Simon Boswell. **TV**

Jason Goes to Hell: The Final Friday woof! **1993 (R)** The supposed last, at least so far, in the "Friday the 13th" gore series. Only through the bodies—dead or alive—of his Vorhees kin can supernatural killer Jason be reborn, and only at their hands can he truly die. One can only hope that this is finally true. An unrated, even gorier, version is also available. **89m/C VHS.** Kane Hodder, John D. LeMay, Kari Keegan, Steven Williams, Steven Culp, Erin Gray, Richard Gant, Leslie Jordan, Billy Green Bush, Rusty Schwimmer, Allison Smith, Julie Michaels; ***D:*** Adam Marcus; ***W:*** Dean Lorey, Jay Huguely-Cass; ***M:*** Harry Manfredini.

Jason X 🦴 **2001 (R)** This time it's Jason in space. The tenth installment of the "Friday the 13th" franchise is set in 2455, when Earth has been abandoned because of toxic damage. An archeological expedition discovers the cryogenically frozen Jason and a young woman and brings them back to their spaceship. Of course, if they'd just leave him on Earth with no one to kill, he'd die a horrible existential death that'd be really cool to see. Unfortunately, there's a passel of horny med students that needs killin' so here we go again. The space setting does give the series a bunch of new franchises to rip off, but that doesn't really help. **93m/C VHS, DVD.** *US* Lexa Doig, Lisa Ryder, Kane Hodder, Jonathan Potts, Chuck Campbell, Peter Mensah, Melyssa Ade, Melody Johnson, Dov Tiefenbach, David Cronenberg, Derwin Jordan; ***D:*** James Isaac; ***W:*** Todd Farmer; ***C:*** Derick Underschultz; ***M:*** Harry Manfredini.

Jason's Lyric 🦴🦴 **1994 (R)** A romantic triangle, sibling rivalry, family bonds, and neighborhood violence all set on the wrong side of the Houston tracks. Jason (Payne) is the responsible young man who works hard and helps out his mom; younger brother Joshua (Woodbine) has just gotten out of jail and is headed straight for more trouble. Between the two is Lyric (Pinkett), a soul-food waitress whose bad news half-brother Alonzo (Treach) is naturally one of Joshua's homies. Good-looking but ultimately empty storytelling. **119m/C VHS, DVD.** Allen Payne, Bokeem Woodbine, Jada Pinkett Smith, Suzzanne Douglass, Forest Whitaker, Treach (Anthony Criss); ***D:*** Doug McHenry; ***W:*** Bobby Smith Jr.; ***M:*** Matt Noble.

Java Head 🦴🦴🦴 **1935** Young Chinese wife commits suicide so her husband can marry an English girl. Set in mid-1800s England. Based on the novel by Joseph Hergesheimer. **70m/B VHS, 8mm.** *GB* Anna May Wong, Elizabeth Allan, John Loder, Edmund Gwenn, Ralph Richardson, George Curzon; ***D:*** J. Walter Ruben.

Jawbreaker 🦴🦴 **1998 (R)** Writer-director Darren Stein steals the plot from "Heathers" and adds a dash of S&M for this black comedy about high school clique queens. Courtney (McGowan) is the leader of a group of glam princesses who accidentally kill one of their own during a mock kidnapping. Fellow beautiful people Julie (Gayheart) and Marcie (Benz) help her cover up, but class nerd Fern (Greer) is a witness. Further complicating things are nosy detective Vera Cruz (Grier) and the upcoming prom, which provides a "Carrie" style finale. Although the movie treads familiar ground, McGowan's performance keeps it interesting. Cameo by rocker Marilyn Manson, billed as Brian Warner. **87m/C VHS, DVD, Wide.** Rose McGowan, Rebecca Gayheart, Julie Benz, Charlotte Roldan, Judy Greer, Chad Christ, Carol Kane, Pam Grier, William Katt, P.J. Soles, Jeff Conaway, Ethan Erickson; ***D:*** Darren Stein; ***W:*** Darren Stein; ***C:*** Amy Vincent.

Jaws 🦴🦴🦴½ **1975 (PG)** Early directorial effort by Spielberg from the Peter Benchley potboiler. A tight, very scary, and sometimes hilarious film about the struggle to kill a giant great white shark that is terrorizing an eastern beach community's waters. The characterizations by Dreyfuss, Scheider, and Shaw are much more endurable than the shock effects. Memorable score. Sequelled by "Jaws 2" in 1978, "Jaws 3" in 1983, and "Jaws: The Revenge" in 1987. Look for Benchley as a TV reporter. **124m/C VHS, DVD, Wide.** Roy Scheider, Robert Shaw, Richard Dreyfuss, Lorraine Gary, Murray Hamilton, Carl Gottlieb, Peter Benchley; ***D:*** Steven Spielberg; ***W:*** Carl Gottlieb, Peter Benchley; ***C:*** Bill Butler; ***M:*** John Williams. Oscars '75: Film Editing, Sound, Orig. Score; AFI '98: Top 100; Golden Globes '76: Score, Natl. Film Reg. '01.

Jaws 2 🦴🦴½ **1978 (PG)** Unsatisfactory sequel to "Jaws." It's been four years since the man-eating shark feasted on the resort town of Amity; suddenly a second shark stalks the waters and the terror returns. Scheider—who must by now wonder at his tendancy to attract large aquatic carnivores with lunch on their minds—battles without his compatriots from the original. And we haven't seen the last of the mechanical dorsal fin yet; two more sequels follow. **116m/C VHS, DVD, Wide.** Roy Scheider, Lorraine Gary, Murray Hamilton, Joseph Mascolo, Jeffrey Kramer, Collin Wilcox-Paxton, Keith Gordon; ***D:*** Jeannot Szwarc; ***W:*** Carl Gottlieb, Howard Sackler; ***C:*** Michael C. Butler; ***M:*** John Williams.

Jaws 3 🦴🦴 *Jaws 3-D* **1983 (PG)** Same monster, new setting: in a Sea World-type amusement park, a great white shark escapes from its tank and proceeds to cause terror and chaos. Little connection to the previous "Jaws" sagas. Followed by one more sequel, "Jaws: The Revenge." **98m/C VHS.** Dennis Quaid, Bess Armstrong, Louis Gossett Jr., Simon MacCorkindale, Lea Thompson, John Putch; ***D:*** Joe Alves; ***W:*** Richard Matheson, Carl Gottlieb; ***C:*** James A. Contner; ***M:*** John Williams.

Jaws of Death 🦴🦴 *Mako: The Jaws of Death* **1976** "Jaws"-like saga of shark terror. Jaeckel illogically strikes out to protect his "friends," the sharks. **91m/C VHS.** Richard Jaeckel, Harold Sakata, Jennifer Bishop, John Chandler, Buffy Dee; ***D:*** William Grefe.

Jaws of Justice 🦴½ **1933** A Canadian Mountie and his trusty German shepherd track down outlaws in the Canadian Northwest. **55m/B VHS, 8mm.** Richard Terry, Lafe (Lafayette) McKee.

Jaws of Satan woof! *King Cobra* **1981 (R)** Weaver is terrorized by a slimy snake who is, in actuality, the Devil. Not released for two years after it was filmed, and generally considered a bomb of the first caliber. Unfortunate work for usually worthwhile Weaver. **92m/C VHS.** Fritz Weaver, Gretchen Corbett, Jon Korkes, Norman Lloyd, Christina Applegate; ***D:*** Bob Claver; ***C:*** Dean Cundey.

Jaws: The Revenge 🦴 **1987 (PG-13)** The third sequel, in which Mrs. Brody is pursued the world over by a seemingly personally motivated Great White Shark. Includes footage not seen in the theatrical release. Each sequel in this series is progressively inferior to the original. **87m/C VHS, DVD, Wide.** Lorraine Gary, Lance Guest, Karen Young, Mario Van Peebles, Michael Caine, Judith Barsi, Lynn Whitfield; ***D:*** Joseph Sargent; ***W:*** Michael deGuzman; ***C:*** John McPherson; ***M:*** Michael Small.

Jay and Silent Bob Strike Back 🦴🦴½ **2001 (R)** The fifth (and last) in Smith's series of movies with ties to Red Bank, New Jersey, is a road movie as the boys go after Miramax studio (which is producing the film) when it makes a movie based on the comic book characters that are based on them without their permission. It makes more sense (and is probably more enjoyable) if you've seen Smith's entire ouvre. Besides Jay (Mewes) and Silent Bob (Smith himself), many of the characters and jokes are from Smith's previous movies. Subplots and detours abound for our heroes, allowing Smith to effectively parody and lampoon recent summer blockbusters, his own stars, and Hollywood in general. **95m/C VHS, DVD, Wide.** *US* Kevin Smith, Jason Mewes, Jason Lee, Ben Affleck, Shannon Elizabeth, Eliza Dushku, Ali Larter, Jennifer Schwalbach, Chris Rock, Will Ferrell, Brian O'Halloran, Seann William Scott, George Carlin, Carrie Fisher, Judd Nelson, Jon Stewart, Mark Hamill, Diedrich Bader; ***Cameos:*** Wes Craven, Gus Van Sant, Matt Damon, Shannen Doherty, Jason Biggs, James Van Der Beek, Joey Lauren Adams, Alanis Morissette, Renee Humphrey; ***D:*** Kevin Smith; ***W:*** Kevin Smith; ***C:*** Jamie Anderson; ***M:*** James L. Venable.

The Jayhawkers 🦴🦴 **1959** Chandler and Parker battle for power and women in pre-Civil War Kansas. **100m/C VHS.** Jeff Chandler, Fess Parker, Nicole Maurey, Henry Silva, Herbert Rudley, Frank De Kova, Don Megowan, Leo Gordon; ***D:*** Melvin Frank.

The Jayne Mansfield Story *Jayne Mansfield: A Symbol of the '50s* **1980** Recounts the blond bombshell's career from her first career exposure, through her marriage to a bodybuilder, to the famous car crash that beheaded her. **97m/C VHS.** Loni Anderson, Arnold Schwarzenegger, Raymond Buktenica, Kathleen Lloyd, G.D. Spradlin, Dave Shelley; ***D:*** Dick Lowry. **TV**

The Jazz Singer ½ **1927** A Jewish cantor's son breaks with his family to become a singer of popular music. Of historical importance as the first successful part-talkie; a very early Loy performance. With the classic line "You ain't heard nothing yet!" Remade several times. ♫Toot, Toot, Tootsie Goodbye; Blue Skies; My Gal Sal; Waiting for the Robert E. Lee; Dirty Hands, Dirty Face; Mother, I Still Have You; Kol Nidre; Yahrzeit; My Mammy. **89m/B VHS.** Al Jolson, May McAvoy, Warner Oland, William Demarest, Eugenie Besserer, Myrna Loy; ***D:*** Alan Crosland; ***C:*** Hal Mohr. AFI '98: Top 100, Natl. Film Reg. '96.

The Jazz Singer woof! **1980 (PG)** Flat and uninteresting (if not unintentionally funny) remake of the 1927 classic about a Jewish boy who rebels against his father and family tradition to become a popular entertainer. Stick with the original, this is little more than a vehicle for Diamond to sing. ♫America; You Baby Baby; Jerusalem; Love on the Rocks; Summer Love; On the Robert E. Lee; Louise; Songs of Life; Hello Again. **115m/C VHS, DVD, 8mm.** Neil Diamond, Laurence Olivier, Lucie Arnaz, Catlin Adams, Franklin Ajaye, Ernie Hudson; ***D:*** Richard Fleischer; ***W:*** Herbert Baker, Stephen H. Foreman; ***C:*** Isidore Mankofsky; ***M:*** Leonard Rosenman, Neil Diamond. Golden Raspberries '80: Worst Actor (Diamond), Worst Support. Actor (Olivier).

Jazzman **1984** A comedy set in the late 1920s with a young musician forming a jazz band with two street musicians and a saxophonist who played in the czar's marching band. Their music is condemned as a product of bourgeois society but that doesn't stop them. In Russian with English subtitles. **80m/C VHS.** *RU* Igor Sklyar, Alexander Chorny; ***D:*** Karen Chakhnazarov.

J.D.'s Revenge ½ **1976 (R)** Attorney in training Glynn Turman is possessed by the spirit of a gangster who was murdered on Bourbon Street in the early 1940s and grisly blaxploitation results. Ever so slightly better than others of the genre. Shot in New Orleans, with a soundtrack by a then-unknown Prince. **95m/C VHS, DVD, Wide.** Louis Gossett Jr., Glynn Turman, Joan Pringle, David McKnight, James L. Watkins; ***D:*** Arthur Marks; ***W:*** Jaison Starkes; ***C:*** Harry J. May; ***M:*** Prince.

Je Tu Il Elle ½ *I You She He* **1974** A hyperactive young woman desperately seeking the answers to life gradually gains experience and maturity as she travels around France. The directorial debut of Ackerman. In French with English subtitles. **90m/B VHS.** *FR* Niels Arestrup, Claire Wauthion, Chantal Akerman; ***D:*** Chantal Akerman.

Jealousy **1984** Three dramatic episodes dealing with jealousy. Made for TV. **95m/C VHS.** Angie Dickinson, Paul Michael Glaser, David Carradine, Bo Svenson; ***D:*** Jeffrey Bloom. **TV**

Jealousy *Celos* **1999** Antonio (Giminez Cacho) and Carmen (Sanchez-Gijon) seem to be happily engaged and making wedding plans when Antonio finds an old photo of Carmen with another man. Although he has no reason to be suspicious, he begins to investigate Carmen's past and becomes consumed by a jealous obsession that threatens to tear the couple apart. Spanish with subtitles. **105m/C VHS, DVD, Wide.** *SP* Daniel Gimenez Cacho, Aitana Sanchez-Gijon, Maria Botto, Luis Tosar; ***D:*** Vicente Aranda; ***W:*** Vicente Aranda, Alvaro del Amo; ***C:*** Jose Luis Alcaine; ***M:*** José Nieto.

Jean de Florette ½ **1987 (PG)** The first of two films (with "Manon of the Spring") based on Marcel Pagnol's novel. A single spring in drought-ridden Provence, France is blocked by two scheming countrymen (Montand and Auteuil). They await the imminent failure of the farm nearby, inherited by a city-born hunchback, whose chances for survival fade without water for his crops. A devastating story with a heartrending performance by Depardieu as the hunchback. Lauded and awarded; in French with English subtitles. **122m/C VHS, DVD, Wide.** *FR* Gerard Depardieu, Yves Montand, Daniel Auteuil, Elisabeth Depardieu, Ernestine Mazurowna, Margarita Lozano, Armand Meffre; ***D:*** Claude Berri; ***W:*** Claude Berri, Gerard Brach; ***C:*** Bruno Nuytten; ***M:*** Jean-Claude Petit. British Acad. '87: Adapt. Screenplay, Film, Support. Actor (Auteuil); Cesar '87: Actor (Auteuil), Support. Actress (Beart).

Jeanne and the Perfect Guy *Jeanne et le Garcon Formidable* **1998** Jeanne (Ledoyen) is a hopeless romantic looking for her perfect love and having a lot of sex as she "auditions" her would-be Romeos. Then she meets Olivier (Demy) in the subway and decides he's the one. Only Olivier tells Jeanne that he has AIDS. Oh yeah, and it's a musical, with everyone breaking into song and dancing through the Parisian streets. It's gawky romanticism is strangely appealing and Ledoyen has a lot of charisma. French with subtitles. **98m/C VHS, DVD.** *FR* Virginie Ledoyen, Mathieu Demy, Frederic Gorny, Jacques Bonnaffe, Valerie Bonneton; ***D:*** Olivier Ducastel, Jacques Martineau; ***W:*** Olivier Ducastel, Jacques Martineau; ***C:*** Mathieu Poirot-Delpech; ***M:*** Philippe Miller.

Jeanne la Pucelle *Joan the Maid: The Battles; Joan the Maid: The Prisons; Jeanne la Pucelle: Les Batailles; Jeanne la Purcelle: Les Prisons* **1994** Rivette's ambitious two-part production on the life of Joan of Arc. The first section, "The Battles," follows Joan (Bonnaire) as she becomes convinced that God has spoken to her, and that only she can lead the Dauphin's soldiers and end the English siege of Orleans. "The Prisons" finds the Dauphin crowned King Charles VII and no longer needing Joan's aid—in fact she becomes a hindrance to his plans and is sold to the English for trial and execution. French with subtitles. **241m/C VHS.** *FR* Sandrine Bonnaire, Andre Marcon, Jean-Louis Richard, Jean-Pierre Lorit; ***D:*** Jacques Rivette; ***W:*** Christine Laurent, Pascal Bonitzer; ***C:*** William Lubtchansky; ***M:*** Jordi Savall.

Jeepers Creepers ½ **1939** Rogers is strictly sidekick material in this story. Hall discovers coal on the Weaver's property and proceeds to, underhandedly, acquire the land for himself. **69m/B VHS.** Thurston Hall, Leon Weaver, Frank Weaver, June "Elviry" Weaver, Loretta Weaver, Roy Rogers, Lucien Littlefield; ***D:*** Frank McDonald; ***W:*** Dorrell McGowan, Stuart E. McGowan; ***C:*** Ernest Miller.

Jeepers Creepers **2001 (R)** Uneven horror entry that slips from mocking trite slasher flicks to becoming a trite slasher flick itself. Trish (Phillips) and her brother Darry (Long) are driving home from college during spring break when they're almost run down by a dilapidated cargo hauler. Further on down the abandoned desolate road, they see the driver of the van dumping what looks to be squirming human bodies into a drain pipe near a creepy church. They turn around to see if anyone needs help. Well, no one needs help, but a horror movie needs victims and they've just volunteered. The storyline then degrades into demonic, prophecy-laden voodoo nonsense while trying to keep its tongue firmly in cheek. Creature effects and make-up take over in no time. **89m/C VHS, DVD, Wide.** *US* Gina Phillips, Justin Long, Jonathan Breck, Patricia Belcher, Brandon Smith, Eileen Brennan; ***D:*** Victor Salva; ***W:*** Victor Salva; ***C:*** Don E. Fauntleroy; ***M:*** Bennett Salvay.

Jefferson in Paris ½ **1994 (PG-13)** Costume drama explores the impact Thomas Jefferson's (Nolte) five years in pre-revolutionary Paris (as American ambassador to Versailles) had on his private life. Jefferson confronts the personal and political issues of slavery in America, as well as his feelings for Sally Hemings (Newton), a Monticello slave brought to Paris by Jefferson's daughter. The Jefferson-Hemings legend may or may not be true (more likely not, according to many historians), but it seems to be the central theme here. Merchant Ivory's trademark tasteful production values and earnest characters can't camouflage the fact that they're playing fast and loose with the historical facts. **139m/C VHS.** Nick Nolte, Greta Scacchi, Gwyneth Paltrow, Thandie Newton, Jean-Pierre Aumont, Seth Gilliam, Todd Boyce, James Earl Jones; ***D:*** James Ivory; ***W:*** Ruth Prawer Jhabvala; ***M:*** Richard Robbins.

Jeffrey ½ **1995 (R)** AIDS-fearing Jeffrey (Weber) decides to give celibacy a try until a trip to the gym brings Mr. Right into the picture. Steve (Weiss) is a hunk, but he happens to be HIV-positive, which prompts Jeffrey to do some serious soul-searching. Hence the message: AIDS sucks, but don't let it destroy life's joys. Musical fantasy numbers, phallic fireworks, and a game show are a bit crass and the high theatrics can get annoying, but wicked barbs and one-liners score lots of laughs. Scene-stealer Stewart is caustically funny as Jeffrey's flamboyantly effeminate best friend Sterling, who works as an interior decorator and dates a "Cats" chorus boy. Adapted from the Paul Rudnick play. **92m/C VHS.** Steven Weber, Patrick Stewart, Michael T. Weiss, Bryan Batt, Sigourney Weaver, Olympia Dukakis, Kathy Najimy, Nathan Lane; ***Cameos:*** Victor Garber, Christine Baranski; ***D:*** Christopher Ashley; ***W:*** Paul Rudnick; ***C:*** Jeffery Tufano; ***M:*** Stephen Endelman.

Jekyll and Hyde ½ **1990** Unmemorable remake of the Robert Louis Stevenson tale of a doctor whose scientific experiments lead to a horrifyingly violent split personality. Caine does have a good time with his dual role. Made for TV. **100m/C VHS.** Michael Caine, Cheryl Ladd, Joss Ackland, Ronald Pickup, Kim Thomson, Lionel Jeffries, Kevin McNally, Lee Montague, Diane Keen, David Schofield; ***D:*** David Wickes; ***W:*** David Wickes; ***C:*** Norman G. Langley. **TV**

Jekyll & Hyde...Together Again **1982 (R)** New Wave comic version of the classic story. This time, a serious young surgeon turns into a drug-crazed punk rocker after sniffing a mysterious powder. Mad scientist Blankfield fires and misfires, occasionally eliciting a snort. **87m/C VHS.** Mark Blankfield, Bess Armstrong, Krista Errickson, Tim Thomerson; ***D:*** Jerry Belson; ***W:*** Monica Johnson, Michael Leeson, Harvey Miller, Jerry Belson.

Jennifer ½ *Jennifer (The Snake Goddess)* **1978 (PG)** Elaboration of that old "Carrie" theme: a teenage girl outcast who likes snakes wreaks havoc on her catty classmates in this supernatural thriller. **90m/C VHS.** Lisa Pelikan, Bert Convy, Nina Foch, John Gavin, Wesley Eure, Jeff Corey; ***D:*** Brice Mack; ***W:*** Kay Cousins Johnson, Steve Krantz.

Jennifer 8 **1992 (R)** Mix of familiar genres results in a film about a burned-out cop moving to the suburbs where he finds the eighth victim of a serial killer and falls in love with the chief witness. Garcia is John Berlin, the cop who discovers the hand of the blind female victim, which leads him to her school and Helena Robertson (Thurman), another blind woman who may have the information he needs. Dark and mysterious atmosphere is dramatic, but plot lacks logic and sense of thrill. **127m/C VHS, DVD, Wide.** Andy Garcia, Uma Thurman, Lance Henriksen, Kathy Baker, Graham Beckel, Kevin Conway, John Malkovich; ***D:*** Bruce Robinson; ***W:*** Bruce Robinson.

Jenny **1970 (PG)** A loveless marriage of convenience between a draft-dodger and a film buff gets turned around as they fall in love despite themselves. **90m/C VHS.** Marlo Thomas, Alan Alda, Marian Hailey, Elizabeth Wilson, Vincent Gardenia, Charlotte Rae; ***D:*** George Bloomfield.

Jenny Lamour *Quai des Orfevres* **1947** A dark mystery thriller about a singer accused of murdering a man he thought was stealing his woman. Acclaimed genre piece, dubbed into English. **95m/B VHS.** *FR* Louis Jouvet, Suzy Delair, Bernard Blier, Simone Renant; ***D:*** Henri-Georges Clouzot.

Jenny's War ½ **1985 (PG)** An unbelievable WWII adventure story of an American teacher (Cannon) who outwits the Gestapo and infiltrates a Nazi POW camp in search of her missing soldier son. Actually based on a true story. From the book by Jack Stoneley. **192m/C VHS.** Dyan Cannon, Elke Sommer, Robert Hardy, Nigel Hawthorne, Christopher Cazenove, Patrick Ryecart, Hartmut Becker; ***D:*** Steven Gethers; ***W:*** Steven Gethers. **TV**

Jeremiah ½ **1998** The prophet Jeremiah abandons his family and the woman he loves in order to proclaim God's message that the people of Judah must change their ways or be overcome by the Babylonians. He's deemed a traitor but the prophecy is fulfilled when Jerusalem is destroyed. **96m/C VHS, DVD.** Patrick Dempsey, Oliver Reed, Klaus Maria Brandauer; ***D:*** Harry Winer. **CABLE**

Jeremiah Johnson **1972 (PG)** The story of a man (Redford) who turns his back on civilization, circa 1830, and learns a new code of survival (thanks to a trapper, played by Geer) in a brutal land of isolated mountains and hostile Indians. In the process, Jeremiah becomes part of the wilderness, eventually taking an Indian wife and adopting a son. When hostile Crow warriors kill them, he begins a one-man revenge mission, gaining legendary status as a warrior. Based on the novel "Mountain Man" by Vardis Fisher and the story "Crow Killer" by Raymond W. Thorp and Robert Bunker. A notable and picturesque movie, filmed in Utah. **107m/C VHS, DVD.** Robert Redford, Will Geer, Stefan Gierasch, Allyn Ann McLerie, Joaquin Martinez, Charles Tyner, Paul Benedict, Josh Albie, Delle Bolton; ***D:*** Sydney Pollack; ***W:*** Edward Anhalt, John Milius; ***C:*** Duke Callaghan; ***M:*** John Rubinstein.

Jericho *Dark Sands* **1938** Jericho Jackson (Robeson) is a corporal in the black unit of the U.S.'s Expeditionary Forces in WWI France. After a fight with his sergeant leads to the man's accidental death, Jackson is court-martialed and sentenced to die. He manages to escape to North Africa and begin a new life but military authorities eventually discover his whereabouts. Despite the military drama, Robeson's vocal talents are still showcased. ♫My Way; Golden River; Silent Night; Deep Desert; Shortnin' Bread. **77m/B VHS.** *GB* Paul Robeson, Henry Wilcoxon, Wallace Ford; ***D:*** Thornton Freeland.

Jericho Fever ½ **1993 (PG-13)** A group of terrorists assassinate Palestinian and Israeli negotiators engaged in peace talks in Mexico. Infected with a deadly disease they escape to the U.S., tracked by Israeli Mossad agents, a border patrolman, and two investigators from the Centers for Disease Control who want to stop the spread of the plague. **88m/C VHS.** Stephanie Zimbalist, Perry King, Branscombe Richmond, Alan Scarfe, Elyssa Davalos, Ari Barak; ***D:*** Sandor Stern; ***W:*** I.C. Rapoport; ***M:*** Cameron Allan.

The Jericho Mile **1979** Drama about a track-obsessed convicted murderer who is given a chance at the Olympics. Powerful lead performance by Strauss. **97m/C VHS.** Peter Strauss, Roger E. Mosley, Brian Dennehy; ***D:*** Michael Mann. **TV**

The Jerk ½ **1979 (R)** A jerk tells his rags-to-riches-to-rags story in comedic flashbacks, from "I was born a poor Black child," through his entrepreneurial success in his invention of the "Optigrab," to his inevitable decline. Only film in history with a dog named "Shithead." Martin's first starring role, back in his wild and crazy days; his ridiculous misadventures pay tribute to Jerry Lewis movies of the late '60s. Followed by a TV version released in 1984 as "The Jerk Too," with Mark Blankfield as the Jerk. **94m/C VHS, DVD.** Carl Gottlieb, Steve Martin, Bernadette Peters, Catlin Adams, Bill Macy, Jackie Mason, Mabel King, Richard Ward, M. Emmet Walsh, Dick O'Neill, Maurice Evans, Pepe Serna, Trinidad Silva; ***Cameos:*** Carl Reiner, Rob Reiner; ***D:*** Carl Reiner; ***W:*** Carl Gottlieb, Michael Elias, Steve Martin; ***C:*** Victor Kemper; ***M:*** Jack Elliott.

The Jerky Boys woof! **1995 (R)** Quick! Let's make a Jerky Boys movie and exploit their popularity before everyone realizes what a lame, one-joke act it is! Too late, guys. In what passes for a plot, Johnny and Kamal prank call an irritable mob boss (Arkin), pretending to be Chicago hitmen in need of a hideout. The wiseguys soon figure out the truth, but the requisite dumb cop (Sullivan) pads the film by not catching on. All these "twists" serve only one purpose—to get our heroes to the next phone. Don't accept the charges for this one. **82m/C VHS.** Johnny Brennan, Kamal Ahmed, Alan Arkin, William Hickey, Alan North, James Lorinz, Brad Sullivan, Vincent Pastore, Ozzy Osbourne, Paul Bartel, Suzanne Shepherd; ***Cameos:*** Tom Jones; ***D:*** James Melkonian; ***W:*** Johnny Brennan, Kamal Ahmed, Rich Wilkes, James Melkonian.

Jerome 🦴🦴🦴 **1998** Well-acted indie with a compelling story that deserves a wider audience. After 15 soul-sucking years as a factory welder in California, Wade Hampton (Pillsbury) decides to just walk away from his life. He picks Jerome, Arizona as his destination because he's heard it has an artists' colony and Wade has secretly been making miniature metal sculptures. So Wade heads out on the highway and encounters restless hitchhiker, Jane (Malick), who has no destination in mind at all. The film is interspersed with interviews with people from Wade's past, so the viewer also anticipates trouble coming for the travelers as well. **91m/C VHS, DVD, Wide.** Wendie Malick, Drew Pillsbury, Scott McKenna, Beth Kennedy, James Keeley; ***D:*** Thomas Johnston, David Elton, Eric Tignini; ***W:*** Thomas Johnston, David Elton, Eric Tignini; ***C:*** Gina DeGirolamo.

Jerry and Tom 🦴🦴 **1998 (R)** Tom (Mantegna) is a veteran hitman breaking in an impatient protege, Jerry (Rockwell), on various assignments for a couple of old-time mobsters. The most important thing to remember is that it's just a job—nothing personal—but that kind of emotional vacuum isn't easy to maintain. Familiar story but it has the advantage of a talented cast and good direction. **97m/C VHS, DVD, Wide.** Joe Mantegna, Sam Rockwell, Maury Chaykin, Charles Durning, Peter Riegert, William H. Macy, Ted Danson; ***D:*** Saul Rubinek; ***W:*** Rick Cleveland; ***C:*** Paul Sarossy; ***M:*** David Buchbinder.

Jerry Maguire 🦴🦴🦴½ **1996 (R)** Romantic sports comedy focuses on the off-field action and makes an agent the good guy. Risky business in an era of strikes, lockouts, and astronomical salaries, but writer/director Crowe manages to pull it off. Cruise is well-used as the title character in the story of a shark-like sports agent who sees the error of his ways and transforms into...a more moral sports agent. Somewhat regretting his momentary twinge of honor (which gets him fired from his ultra-huge agency), he allies himself with his obnoxious and least important client Rod Tidwell (Gooding Jr.), as well as Dorothy, an adoring young accountant (Zellweger) with a lovable young son (Lipnicki, making a strong bid for Culkin-like stardom). Famously well-researched, film sports great dialogue, talented leads, great supporting cast and a mega-star currently riding a wave of $100-million-plus films (talk about "Show me the money!"). Pop culture bonus points for coining 1996's most memorable catch phrase, which Crowe took from real life ex-Phoenix Cardinal Tim McDonald, and is now being used to sell everything from magazines to t-shirts. **135m/C VHS, DVD, Wide.** Tom Cruise, Cuba Gooding Jr., Renee Zellweger, Kelly Preston, Bonnie Hunt, Jerry O'Connell, Jay Mohr, Regina King, Glenn Frey, Jonathan Lipnicki, Todd Louiso, Mark Pellington; ***Cameos:*** Eric Stoltz; ***D:*** Cameron Crowe; ***W:*** Cameron Crowe; ***C:*** Janusz Kaminski; ***M:*** Nancy Wilson. Oscars '96: Support. Actor (Gooding); Golden Globes '97: Actor—Mus./Comedy (Cruise); MTV Movie Awards '97: Male Perf. (Cruise); Natl. Bd. of Review '96: Actor (Cruise); Screen Actors Guild '96: Support. Actor (Gooding); Broadcast Film Critics '96: Breakthrough Perf. (Zellweger), Support. Actor (Gooding).

Jersey Girl 🦴🦴½ **1992 (PG-13)** Toby Mastellone (Gertz) is a bright single gal from the Jersey shore who wants something better in her life. Her hardworking dad (Bologna) has fixed her up with an apprentice plumber but she wants a Manhattan guy. And then Toby meets cute with Sal (McDemott), who seems just the ticket, but can you really take the Jersey out of the girl? **95m/C VHS.** Jami Gertz, Dylan McDermott, Joseph Bologna, Aida Turturro, Star Jasper, Sheryl Lee, Joseph Mazzello, Molly Price; ***D:*** David Burton Morris; ***W:*** Gina Wendkos; ***M:*** Stephen Bedell.

Jerusalem 🦴🦴 **1996 (PG-13)** Charismatic fundamentalist preacher Hellgum (Taube) travels to a small turn-of-the-century Swedish village preaching the end of the world and encouraging the people in his belief that all Christians should move to the Holy Land in order to build the new Jerusalem. He manages to convince the wealthy Karin (August) and to tempt young Gertrud (Bonnevie), whose fiance Ingmar (Friberg) is away trying to earn money so they can get married. Based on the novel by Selma Lagerlof who was inspired by Swedes who made a move to Palestine in 1900. Swedish with subtitles. **166m/C VHS.** *SW* Maria Bonnevie, Ulf Friberg, Lena Endre, Pernilla August, Olympia Dukakis, Max von Sydow, Sven-Bertil Taube; ***D:*** Bille August; ***W:*** Bille August; ***C:*** Jorgen Persson; ***M:*** Stefan Nilsson.

Jesse 🦴🦴 **1988 (PG)** A heroic nurse ministers to remote Death Valley residents, and state bureaucats hound her for practicing medicine without a license. Although based on a true case and well-acted, this made-for-TV drama just lacks import and impact. **94m/C VHS.** Lee Remick, Scott Wilson, Leon Rippy, Priscilla Lopez, Albert Salmi; ***D:*** Glenn Jordan; ***M:*** David Shire.

Jesse James 🦴🦴🦴 **1939** One of director King's best efforts is this Hollywood biography of the notorious outlaw. 24-year-old Power showed he was more than just his good looks in the title role but Fonda truly became a star in the role of brother Frank James. Screenwriter Johnson also focused more on the legend than the reality of the outlaw's career in post-Civil War Missouri. **105m/C VHS.** Henry Fonda, Tyrone Power, Randolph Scott, Henry Hull, Jane Darwell, Brian Donlevy, Charles Halton, John Carradine, Donald Meek, Slim Summerville; ***D:*** Henry King; ***W:*** Nunnally Johnson; ***C:*** George Barnes, William Howard Greene; ***M:*** Louis Silvers.

Jesse James at Bay 🦴🦴 **1941** Rogers is the do-good Jesse who's warring against some crooked railroad execs. Interesting perspective. **54m/B VHS.** Roy Rogers, George "Gabby" Hayes, Sally Payne; ***D:*** Joseph Kane.

Jesse James Meets Frankenstein's Daughter 🦴½ **1965** The gunslinger and Frankenstein's granddaughter, Maria, meet up in the Old West in this wacky combination of western and horror genres. **95m/C VHS.** John Lupton, Cal Bolder, Narda Onyx, Steven Geray, Estelita, Jim Davis, William "Bill" Fawcett, Nestor Paiva, Rayford Barnes, Roger Creed; ***D:*** William Beaudine; ***W:*** Carl K. Hittleman; ***C:*** Lothrop Worth; ***M:*** Raoul Kraushaar.

Jesse James Rides Again **1947** Originally a serial, this feature depicts the further adventures of the West's most notorious outlaw. **181m/B VHS.** Clayton Moore, Linda Stirling, Roy Barcroft, Tristram Coffin; ***D:*** Fred Brannon, Thomas Carr.

Jesse James Under the Black Flag 🦴🦴½ **1921** An interesting western/pseudo biography/flashback in which Coates and James Jr. (the outlaw's son) play themselves. As Coates attempts to gather information from Jesse's decendants, a stranger appears and falls for Jesse's granddaughter, who shuns him. He proceeds to read the Coates biography and the flashback begins, in the Jesse was really a good guy forced off the straight and narrow vein. **59m/B VHS.** Jesse James Jr., Franklin Coates, Diana Reed, Marguerite Hungerford; ***D:*** Franklin Coates.

The Jesse Owens Story 🦴🦴 **1984** The moving story of the four-time Olympic Gold medal winner's triumphs and misfortunes. **174m/C VHS.** Dorian Harewood, Debbi (Deborah) Morgan, Georg Stanford Brown, LeVar Burton, George Kennedy, Tom Bosley, Ben Vereen; ***D:*** Richard Irving. **TV**

The Jesse Ventura Story 🦴½ **1999** Cheap quickie TV movie capitalizes on Ventura's unlikely career path. Small-town boy Ventura becomes a Navy SEAL, a professional wrestler known as "The Body" (among other jobs), and eventually winds up in an upset victory as the governor of Minnesota. A dull, unauthorized whitewash that would probably bore even Ventura himself. **95m/C VHS, DVD.** Nils Allen Stewart, Nancy Sakovich, Thomas Brandise, Christopher Bondy, Nola Auguston; ***D:*** David S. Jackson; ***W:*** Patricia Jones, Donald Reiker; ***C:*** John Holosko; ***M:*** Richard Gibbs. **TV**

Jessi's Girls 🦴½ *Wanted Women* **1975 (R)** In retaliation for the murder of her husband, an angry young woman frees three female prisoners, and they embark on a bloody course of revenge. Together, they track down the killers, and one by one, they fight to even the score. **86m/C VHS.** Sondra Currie, Regina Carrol, Jennifer Bishop, Rigg Kennedy; ***D:*** Al Adamson.

Jesus 🦴🦴 **1979 (G)** A supposedly authenticated life of Christ, using real artifacts. **118m/C VHS.** Brian Deacon; ***D:*** Peter Sykes, John Kirsh.

Jesus 🦴🦴½ **2000** Not completely reverential look at the life and teachings of Jesus (Sisto) from a historical, political, and religious viewpoint. Jesus is kind of a fun-loving 30-year-old who knows he has a destiny to fulfill. He and his parents (Bissett and Mueller-Stahl) struggle to deal with that as his followers seek the best course of resistance to Roman oppression, embodied by the political savvy Pontius Pilate (Oldman). The only truly disconcerting note is a slick Satan (Krabbe), who dresses like a contemporary wiseguy, and his temptation of Jesus in the wilderness. **174m/C VHS, DVD.** Jeremy Sisto, Jacqueline Bisset, Armin Mueller-Stahl, Debra Messing, Gary Oldman, Jeroen Krabbe, David O'Hara, G.W. Bailey, Thomas Lockyer, Luca Zingaretti, Stefania Rocca, Claudio Amendola; ***D:*** Roger Young; ***W:*** Suzette Couture; ***C:*** Raffaele Mertes; ***M:*** Patrick Williams. **TV**

Jesus Christ, Superstar 🦴🦴🦴 **1973 (G)** A rock opera that portrays, in music, the last seven days in the earthly life of Christ, as reenacted by young tourists in Israel. Outstanding musical score was the key to the success of the film, although Elliman and Anderson are standouts as, respectively, Mary Magdalene and Judas. Based on the stage play by Tim Rice and Andrew Lloyd Webber, film is sometimes stirring while exhibiting the usual heavy-handed Jewison approach. ♫Jesus Christ, Superstar; I Don't Know How To Love Him; What's The Buzz?; Herod's Song; Heaven On Their Minds; Strange Thing, Mystifying; Then We Are Decided; Everything's Alright; This Jesus Must Die. **108m/C VHS, DVD, Wide.** Ted Neeley, Carl Anderson, Yvonne Elliman, Josh Mostel, Barry Dennen, Bob Bingham, Larry T. Marshall; ***D:*** Norman Jewison; ***W:*** Melvyn Bragg; ***C:*** Douglas Slocombe; ***M:*** Andrew Lloyd Webber, Andre Previn, Herbert W. Spencer.

Jesus Christ Superstar 🦴🦴½ **2000** This new version updates the Tim Rice-Andrew Lloyd Webber rock opera for the MTV generation. The musical numbers have a rock video look and feel. The production is based on a stage version and so it doesn't feel or look like a real film. **112m/C DVD, Wide.** Glenn Carter, Jerome Pradon, Renee Castle, Rik Mayall; ***D:*** Nick Morris, Gale Edwards; ***W:*** Tim Rice, Andrew Lloyd Webber; ***C:*** Nicholas D. Knowland, Anthony Van Laast; ***M:*** Simon Lee, Tim Rice, Andrew Lloyd Webber.

Jesus of Montreal 🦴🦴🦴½ *Jesus de Montreal* **1989 (R)** A vagrant young actor (stage-trained Canadian star Bluteau) is hired by a Montreal priest to produce a fresh interpretation of an Easter passion play. Taking the good book at its word, he produces a contemporized literal telling that captivates audiences, inflames the men of the cloth, and eventually wins the players' faith. Quebecois director Arcand (keep an eye out for him as the judge) tells a compelling, acerbically satirical and haunting story that never forces its Biblical parallels. In French with English subtitles. **119m/C VHS.** *FR CA* Gilles Pelletier, Lothaire Bluteau, Catherine Wilkening, Robert Lepage, Johanne-Marie Tremblay, Remy Girard, Marie-Christine Barrault; ***D:*** Denys Arcand; ***W:*** Denys Arcand; ***C:*** Guy Dufaux; ***M:*** Jean-Marie Benoit, Francois Dompierre, Yves Laferriere. Cannes '89: Special Jury Prize; Genie '90: Actor (Girard), Director (Arcand), Film, Support. Actor (Girard).

Jesus of Nazareth 🦴🦴½ **1928** A dramatic recreation of the life of Christ from the Annunciation through the Ascension. The film titles are taken from descriptive Biblical passages. **85m/B VHS, 8mm.** Philip Van Loan, Anna Lehr, Charles McCaffrey.

Jesus of Nazareth 🦴🦴🦴 **1977** An all-star cast vividly portrays the life of Christ in this miniseries. Wonderfully directed and sensitively acted. **371m/C VHS.** Robert Powell, Anne Bancroft, Ernest Borgnine, Claudia Cardinale, James Mason, Laurence Olivier, Anthony Quinn; ***D:*** Franco Zeffirelli; ***M:*** Maurice Jarre. **TV**

Jesus' Son 🦴🦴 **1999 (R)** Crudup gives a fine performance as a sweet, passive, bungling druggie known only as FH (which stands for F***head). He falls for reckless heroin-addict Michelle (Morton), ODs, gets saved, gets dumped, gets in a car wreck, and eventually cleans up and finds some kind of peace working in an Arizona nursing home. There's really not much plot; it's the characters that carry things along. Film is set in the seventies and based on Dennis Johnson's 1992 collection of short stories. **109m/C VHS, DVD, Wide.** Billy Crudup, Samantha Morton, Denis Leary, Holly Hunter, Dennis Hopper, Jack Black, Will Patton, Greg Germann; ***D:*** Alison Maclean; ***W:*** Elizabeth Cuthrell, David Urrutia, Oren Moverman; ***C:*** Adam Kimmel; ***M:*** Joe Henry.

The Jesus Trip 🦴½ **1971** Hunted motorcyclists take a young nun hostage in the desert. **86m/C VHS.** Robert Porter, Tippy Walker; ***D:*** Russ Mayberry.

Jet Benny Show **1986** A Buck Rogers/Star Wars-style spoof of Jack Benny's classic TV show. **76m/C VHS.** Steve Norman, Kevin Dees, Polly MacIntyre, Ted Luedemann; ***D:*** Roger Evans.

Jet Li's The Enforcer 🦴🦴½ *The Enforcer; My Father Is a Hero; Letter to Daddy; Gei Ba Ba de Xin* **1995** Chinese cop Li goes undercover to infiltrate a Hong Kong gang. His son (Miu) has been told dad is a crook but he has faith. When Li's wife dies, cop Mui brings the boy to Hong Kong and the kid (a fighting fiend just like his father) winds up helping dad with his police work. Dubbed from Cantonese. **100m/C VHS, DVD, Wide.** *HK* Jet Li, Anita (Yim-Fong) Mui, Damian Lau, Tse Miu, Rongguang Yu, Ngai Sing; ***D:*** Corey Yuen.

Jet Over the Atlantic 🦴½ **1959** Dangerous situation arises as a bomb is discovered aboard a plane en route from Spain to New York. **92m/B VHS.** Guy Madison, George Raft, Virginia Mayo, Brett Halsey; ***D:*** Byron Haskin.

Jet Pilot 🦴🦴 **1957** An American Air Force colonel (Wayne) in charge of an Alaskan Air Force base falls in love with a defecting Russian jet pilot (Leigh). They marry, but Wayne suspects Leigh is a spy planted to find out top U.S. secrets. He pretends to defect with her back to Russia to see what he can find out, but they again flee. Ludicrous plot is saved only by spectacular flying scenes, some performed by Chuck Yeager. Although this was filmed in 1950, it took seven more years to be released because producer Hughes couldn't keep his hands off it. **112m/B VHS, DVD.** John Wayne, Janet Leigh, Jay C. Flippen, Paul Fix, Richard Rober, Roland Winters, Hans Conried, Ivan Triesault; ***D:*** Josef von Sternberg; ***C:*** Winton C. Hoch.

Jetsons: The Movie 🦴🦴 **1990 (G)** The famous outer space family of '60s TV is given a new silver-screened life. George gets a promotion that puts him in charge of an asteroid populated by furry creatures. Ecological concerns are expressed; while this is rare for a cartoon, the story is overall typical. **82m/C VHS.** ***D:*** William Hanna, Joseph Barbera; ***M:*** John Debney; ***V:*** George O'Hanlon, Mel Blanc, Penny Singleton, Tiffany, Patric Zimmerman, Donald E. Messick, Jean Vander Pyl, Ronnie Schell, Patti Deutsch, Dana Hill, Russi Taylor, Paul Kreppel, Rick Dees.

The Jew 🦴🦴 **1996** Portrait of 18th century playwright Antonio Jose da Silva (Pinheiro), whose family was forcibly converted from their Jewish faith by the Catholic Church. Living in Lisbon, da Silva founded a puppet theatre for which he wrote comic operas. Eventually condemned for heresy, he was executed by the Inquisition in 1739. Explicit torture scenes. Portuguese with subtitles. **85m/C VHS.** *PT* Felipe Pinheiro, Dina Sfat, Mario Viegas, Edwin Luisi, Jose Neto; ***D:*** Jom Tob Azulay; ***W:*** Millor Fernandes, Billy Eckstine, Gilvan Pereira; ***C:*** Eduardo Serra.

Jew-boy Levi 🦴🦴 *Viehjud Levi* **1998** When Levi, the Jewish cattle dealer, makes his annual trip to a remote farming village hoping to conduct his business and win the hand of farmer Horger's lovely daughter, Lisbeth, he finds that Nazism has polluted the town. Based on the stage play by Thomas Strittmatter. **90m/C VHS, DVD, Wide.** *GE SI AT* Bruno Cathomas, Caroline Eber, Ulrich Noethen, Martina Gedeck, Bernd Michael Lade, Georg Olschewski, Eva Mattes; ***D:*** Didi Danquart; ***W:*** Didi Danquart, Martina Docker; ***C:*** Johann Feindt; ***M:*** Cornelius Schwehr.

The Jewel in the Crown 🦴🦴🦴 **1984** Epic saga of the last years of British rule in India from 1942-47 concentrating on a controversial love affair between the Indian Hari Kumar and the English Daphne Manners, which profoundly affects the lives of many. Based on "The Raj Quartet" by Paul Scott. Originally shown on British TV, it aired in the U.S. on the PBS series "Masterpiece Theatre." An excellent miniseries that was shown in 14 segments. **750m/C VHS.** *GB* Charles Dance, Susan Wooldridge, Art Malik, Tim Pigott-Smith, Geraldine James, Peggy Ashcroft, Judy Parfitt; ***D:*** Christopher Morahan, Jim O'Brien; ***M:*** George Fenton. **TV**

The Jewel of the Nile 🦴🦴½ **1985 (PG)** Sequel to "Romancing the Stone" with the same cast but new director. Romance novelist Joan thought she found her true love in Jack but finds that life doesn't always end happily ever. After they part ways, Jack realizes that she may be in trouble and endeavors to rescue her from the criminal hands of a charming North African president. Of course, he can always check out this "jewel" at the same time. Chemistry is still there, but the rest of the film isn't quite up to the "Stone's" charm. **106m/C VHS, DVD.** Michael Douglas, Kathleen Turner, Danny DeVito, Avner Eisenberg, The Flying Karamazov Brothers, Spiros Focas, Holland Taylor; ***D:*** Lewis Teague; ***W:*** Mark Rosenthal, Larry Konner; ***C:*** Jan De Bont; ***M:*** Jack Nitzsche.

The Jeweller's Shop 🦴🦴 **1990** A highly spiritual tale of two married couples in Poland whose children meet and fall in love much later in Canada. Based on a play by Karol Wojtyla—who later became Pope Jean-Paul II. Adapted under strict Vatican supervision. **90m/C VHS.** Burt Lancaster, Ben Cross, Olivia Hussey.

Jezebel 🦴🦴🦴½ **1938** Davis is a willful Southern belle who loses fiance Fonda through her selfish and spiteful ways in this pre-Civil War drama. When he becomes ill, she realizes her cruelty and rushes to nurse him back to health. Davis' role won her an Oscar for Best Actress, and certainly provided Scarlett O'Hara with a rival for most memorable female character of all time. **105m/B VHS, DVD.** Bette Davis, George Brent, Henry Fonda, Margaret Lindsay, Fay Bainter, Donald Crisp, Spring Byington, Eddie Anderson; ***D:*** William Wyler; ***W:*** Clements Ripley, Abem Finkel, John Huston, Robert Buckner; ***C:*** Ernest Haller; ***M:*** Max Steiner. Oscars '38: Actress (Davis), Support. Actress (Bainter).

Jezebel's Kiss 🦴🦴 **1990 (R)** A sizzling young beauty returns to the town where she grew up and proceeds to destroy any man she pleases. **96m/C VHS.** Meg Foster, Malcolm McDowell, Meredith Baxter, Everett McGill, Katherine Barrese; ***D:*** Harvey Keith; ***W:*** Harvey Keith.

JFK 🦴🦴🦴½ **1991 (R)** Highly controversial examination of President John F. Kennedy's 1963 assassination, from the viewpoint of New Orleans district attorney Jim Garrison. Hotly debated because of Stone's conspiracy theory, it sparked new calls to open the sealed government records from the 1977 House Select Committee on Assassinations investigation. Outstanding performances from all-star principal and supporting casts, stunning cinematography, and excellent editing. Even Garrison himself shows up as Chief Justice Earl Warren. Considered by some to be a cinematic masterpiece, others see it as revisionist history that should be taken with a grain of salt. Extended version adds 17 minutes. **189m/C VHS, DVD, Wide.** Dale Dye, Kevin Costner, Sissy Spacek, Kevin Bacon, Tommy Lee Jones, Laurie Metcalf, Gary Oldman, Michael Rooker, Jay O. Sanders, Beata Pozniak, Joe Pesci, Donald Sutherland, John Candy, Jack Lemmon, Walter Matthau, Ed Asner, Vincent D'Onofrio, Sally Kirkland, Brian Doyle-Murray, Wayne Knight, Tony Plana, Tomas Milian, Sean Stone; ***Cameos:*** Lolita (David) Davidovich, Frank Whaley, Jim Garrison; ***D:*** Oliver Stone; ***W:*** Oliver Stone, Zachary Sklar; ***C:*** Robert Richardson; ***M:*** John Williams. Oscars '91: Cinematog., Film Editing; Golden Globes '92: Director (Stone).

The JFK Conspiracy **1991** Did Lee Harvey Oswald act alone? Opinions of government officials, eyewitnesses, and director Oliver Stone, in addition to testimony, photographs, documents, and other evidence, address the perennial American question. Includes footage from the House Select Committee on Assassination. **98m/C VHS. TV**

JFK: Reckless Youth 🦴🦴½ **1993** Glossy made for TV docudrama details the youthful exploits of Kennedy as both ladies man and emerging leader and comes perilously close to being a tacky soap. Follows the president-to-be from his party-hearty years at prep school, through his naval career (and PT-109 heroics), and his first forays into politics. Excellent portrayal by Dempsey details JFK's chronic ill health, his ambitions, and the family ties that provided both friction and support. Based on the controversial biography by Nigel Hamilton. **182m/C VHS.** Patrick Dempsey, Terry Kinney, Loren Dean, Diana Scarwid, Yolanda Jilot, Robin Tunney, Andrew Lowery, Stan Cahill, James Rebhorn, Malachy McCourt; ***D:*** Harry Winer; ***W:*** William Broyles Jr.; ***M:*** Cameron Allan. **TV**

Jigsaw 🦴🦴🦴 *Gun Moll* **1949** Crime drama with a smattering of cameos by Hollywood favorites. A newspaper reporter is murdered. The dead man's friend, an assistant district attorney, seeks the punks responsible. They send in a seductress to keep the D.A. busy, but she too is murdered. Action and tension in a well-made flick. Based on a story by John Roeburt. **70m/B VHS.** Franchot Tone, Jean Wallace, Myron McCormick, Marc Lawrence, Winifred Lenihan, Betty Harper, Robert Gist; ***Cameos:*** Marlene Dietrich, Henry Fonda, Burgess Meredith, John Garfield; ***D:*** Fletcher Markle.

Jigsaw 🦴🦴 *Man on the Move* **1971** Missing persons lawman is lured into a cover-up more complex than he had bargained for. A tense drama originated as the pilot for a series. **100m/C VHS.** James Wainwright, Vera Miles, Richard Kiley, Andrew Duggan, Edmond O'Brien; ***D:*** William A. Graham. **TV**

Jigsaw 🦴🦴 **1990** A developer is found dead the day after his wedding. His widow and a cop team up to find out who, what, where, and why. Lukewarm Australian mystery export. **85m/C VHS.** Rebecca Gibney, Dominic Sweeney, Michael Coard.

Jigsaw 🦴½ **1999 (R)** Convential neo-noir is weak in both plot and performances. Vicky (Ehm) asks her boyfriend, Jules (Corno), to pick up $5000 that's owed her. Vicky winds up dead and Jules is on the lam from both cops and drug dealers. **83m/C VHS, DVD.** *CA* William Corno, Erica Ehm, Edgar George; ***D:*** Paul Shoebridge. **VIDEO**

The Jigsaw Man 🦴🦴 **1984 (PG)** A British-Russian double agent is sent back to England to retrieve a list of Soviet agents which he hid there many years before. **90m/C VHS.** *GB* Michael Caine, Laurence Olivier, Susan George, Robert Powell, Charles Gray, David Patrick Kelly, Michael Medwin; ***D:*** Terence Young.

Jigsaw Murders **1989** A macho detective is out to solve a grisly murder, but the only available leads are a jigsaw puzzle and the victim's severed, tattooed lower limb. **98m/C VHS.** Chad Everett, Michelle Johnson, Yaphet Kotto; ***D:*** Jag Mundhra.

Jill the Ripper 🦴🦴 **2000 (R)** Alcoholic ex-cop Matt Wilson launches his own investigation after his brother is murdered. This takes him into a world of political corruption and kinky sex, circa 1977 in Boston. **94m/C VHS, DVD, Wide.** Dolph Lundgren, Danielle Brett; ***D:*** Anthony Hickox; ***W:*** Kevin Bernhardt, Gareth Wardell; ***C:*** David Pelletier; ***M:*** Steve Gurevitch, Thomas Barquee. **VIDEO**

Jim Thorpe: All American 🦴🦴½ *Man of Bronze* **1951** The life story of Thorpe, a Native American athlete who gained international recognition for his excellence in many different sports. A must for sports fans. **105m/B VHS.** Burt Lancaster, Phyllis Thaxter, Charles Bickford, Steve Cochran, Dick Wesson; ***D:*** Michael Curtiz; ***W:*** Douglas S. Morrow; ***M:*** Max Steiner.

Jimmy Hollywood 🦴½ **1994 (R)** Wanna-be Hollywood actor Pesci has never acted in his life but longs for stardom—which he gets after he accidentally becomes a community vigilante. Burned-out sidekick Slater helps create the videotapes that will bring Jimmy his 15 minutes of fame. Although appropriately desperate, Pesci's role comes off as mostly shtick; two dogs in a row for the usually talented Levinson (after "Toys"). **118m/C VHS.** Joe Pesci, Christian Slater, Victoria Abril; ***Cameos:*** Barry Levinson, Rob Weiss; ***D:*** Barry Levinson; ***W:*** Barry Levinson; ***C:*** Peter Sova; ***M:*** Robbie Robertson.

Jimmy Neutron: Boy Genius 🦴🦴½ **2001 (G)** Huge-brained and grease-haired Jimmy Neutron is a retro geek hero for the new millennium in this bright and flashy computer animated feature. The child-inventor is young enough to think a sugar rush is the ultimate taboo but smart enough to have created a toaster-satellite that makes contact with an alien race. When said alien race respond by stealing all the parents in Retroville, Jimmy and his band of nerds endeavor to rescue them. Though mildly targeted at adults, it prefers gas gags to pop culture reference; even the new-wave songs are covered by kiddie bands. Frenetic pacing and onslaught of images may tire older (than teenage) viewers, although the animation is pleasant enough and there are some inventive lines that will go over the young-uns' heads. Short and Stewart are amusing as a pair of egg-shaped space invaders. **90m/C VHS, DVD.** *US* ***D:*** John A. Davis; ***W:*** David N. Weiss, J. David Stem, Steve Oedekerk, John A. Davis; ***M:*** John Debney; ***V:*** Debi Derryberry, Carolyn Lawrence, Rob Paulsen, Martin Short, Patrick Stewart, Megan Cavanagh, Mark DeCarlo, Jeff Garcia, Candi Milo, Andrea Martin.

Jimmy, the Boy Wonder 🦴½ **1966** Goremeister Lewis' attempt at a "family" film turns out just as weird as expected. A young boy goes on a magical trip to find out who stopped time and meets an absent-minded astronomer, the evil Mr. Fig, and then discovers what happens at world's end. **?m/C VHS.** ***D:*** Herschell Gordon Lewis.

Jimmy the Kid 🦴🦴 **1982 (PG)** A young boy becomes the unlikely target for an improbable gang of would-be crooks on a crazy, "fool-proof" crime caper. Kiddie comic caper. **95m/C VHS.** Gary Coleman, Cleavon Little, Fay Hauser, Ruth Gordon, Dee Wallace Stone, Paul LeMat, Don Adams; ***D:*** Gary Nelson; ***W:*** Sam Bobrick.

Jimmy Zip 🦴🦴 **2000 (R)** Jimmy (Fletcher) is a pyromaniac abused runaway who gets a job working for drug dealing pimp Rick (Mulkey). He goes on a fireworks spree, which is how Jimmy meets down-and-out sculptor Horace (Gossett), who encourages him to channel his energies in more productive directions. But Jimmy fuels his new interests by stealing money from Rick, which puts him and girlfriend Sheila (Frantz) in a very dangerous position. **112m/C VHS, DVD, Wide.** *CA* Brendan Fletcher, Chris Mulkey, Robert Gossett, Adrienne Frantz, James Russo, Kim (Kimberly Dawn) Dawson; ***D:*** Robert McGinley; ***W:*** Robert McGinley; ***C:*** Christopher Tufty; ***M:*** Geoff Levin.

Jingle All the Way 🦴🦴 **1996 (PG)** Producer Chris Columbus grabs the reins of the slapstick and sentiment sleigh from mentor John Hughes in this farce of holiday capitalism. Any parent who has searched frantically for that Mighty Morphin' Cabbage Elmo will understand hapless Howard Langston (Schwarzenegger), a workaholic dad who was supposed to secure the coveted Turbo Man action figure for his son Jamie (Lloyd). Unfortunately, it slips his mind until Christmas Eve and all the Turbo Men have blasted off with more mindful parents. In his panic-stricken quest for the toy, he is confronted by a crazed postman (Sinbad) hunting Turbo Man, a pack of sleazy Santas, and a vicious reindeer attack. Meanwhile, Howard's slimy neighbor Ted (Hartman) is attempting to get into his wife Liz's (Wilson) stockings with great care. Although aimed at a younger audience, there's a definite lack of kids; which leaves it too grown-up for the kids and too childish for the adults. There is some satisfaction in seeing the Mall of America torn to shreds, however. Ho ho hum. **88m/C VHS, DVD, Wide.** Arnold Schwarzenegger, Phil Hartman, Sinbad, Rita Wilson, James Belushi, Robert Conrad, Martin Mull, Jake Lloyd, Harvey Korman, Laraine Newman; ***D:*** Brian Levant; ***W:*** Randy Kornfield; ***C:*** Victor Kemper; ***M:*** David Newman.

Jinxed 🦴🦴 **1982 (R)** Las Vegas nightclub singer tries to convince a gullible blackjack dealer to murder her crooked boyfriend, but the plan backfires when the gangster electrocutes himself while taking a shower. Offscreen cast disputes were probably much more interesting than on-screen comedy. **104m/C VHS.** Bette Midler, Ken Wahl, Rip Torn; ***D:*** Donald Siegel; ***W:*** David Newman, Frank D. Gilroy; ***M:*** Miles Goodman.

Jit 🦴🦴 **1994** Unpretentious romantic comedy finds the easy-going U.K., who runs errands for his uncle in a Zimbabwe town, falling in love with the beautiful Sofi, who already has a boyfriend. But U.K. won't be stopped by this or Sofi's greedy father. "Jit" refers to the infectious local music, a fusion of traditional African rhythms and reggae-pop. **98m/C VHS.** Dominic Makuvachuma, Sibongile Nene, Faria Sevenzo, Winnie Ndemera; ***D:*** Michael Raeburn.

The Jitters 🦴 **1988 (R)** The Chinese hopping vampire comes to America to make a bad movie on a different continent. The murdered dead turn into zombies and seek revenge on their killers. Maybe they should've sought revenge on the producers. **80m/C VHS.** Sal Viviano, Marilyn Tokuda, James Hong, Frank Dietz; ***D:*** John Fasano.

Jive Junction 🦴🦴 **1943** A group of patriotic teenagers convert a barn into a canteen for servicemen and name it "Jive Junction." **62m/B VHS.** Dickie Moore, Tina Thayer, Gerra Young, Johnny Michaels, Jan Wiley, Beverly Boyd, William (Bill) Halligan; ***D:*** Edgar G. Ulmer.

Jo Jo Dancer, Your Life Is Calling 🦴🦴½ **1986 (R)** Pryor directed and starred in this semi-autobiographical price-of-fame story of a comic, hospitalized for a drug-related accident, who must re-evaluate his life. A serious departure from Pryor's slapstick comedies that doesn't quite make it as a drama; Pryor nevertheless deserves credit for the honesty he demonstrates in dealing with his real-life problems. **97m/C VHS, DVD, Wide.** Richard Pryor, Debbie Allen, Art Evans, Fay Hauser, Barbara Williams, Paula Kelly, Wings Hauser, Carmen McRae, Diahnne Abbott, Scoey Mitchell, Billy Eckstine, Virginia Capers, Dennis Farina; ***D:*** Richard Pryor; ***W:*** Richard Pryor, Rocco Urbisci; ***C:*** John A. Alonzo; ***M:*** Herbie Hancock.

Joan of Arc 🦴🦴½ **1948** A touching and devout look at the life of Joan of Arc. Perhaps unfortunately, the film is accurately based on the play by Maxwell Anderson, and adds up to too much talk and too little action. **100m/C VHS.** Ingrid Bergman, Jose Ferrer, John Ireland, Leif Erickson; ***D:*** Victor Fleming; ***C:*** Joseph Valentine. Oscars '48: Color Cinematog., Costume Des. (C).

Joan of Arc 🦴🦴½ **1999** Earnest biopic of legendary 15th-century French heroine, Joan of Arc (Sobieski). Joan is a peasant girl, born during France's Hundred Years War with England. She hears saints' voices telling her to help the Dauphin Charles (Harris) claim the French throne and drive out the English. Charles persuades Joan to proclaim herself the legendary Maid of Lorraine and raise an army to battle the Brits. But after her success, Joan is betrayed by the King, sold to the English, and put on trial for heresy. **240m/C VHS, DVD.** Leelee Sobieski, Neil Patrick Harris, Peter O'Toole, Robert Loggia, Jacqueline Bisset, Powers Boothe, Shirley MacLaine, Olympia Dukakis, Maury Chaykin, Jonathan Hyde, Maximilian Schell, Peter Strauss; ***D:*** Christian Duguay; ***W:*** Ronald Parker, Michael Miller; ***C:*** Pierre Gill; ***M:*** Asher Ettinger, Tony Kosinec. **TV**

Joan of Paris 🦴🦴🦴½ **1942** A French resistance leader dies so that Allied pilots can escape from the Nazis. A well done, but obviously dated propaganda feature. **91m/B VHS.** Michele Morgan, Paul Henreid, Thomas Mitchell, Laird Cregar, May Robson, Alexander Granach, Alan Ladd; ***D:*** Robert Stevenson; ***W:*** Charles Bennett.

Jock Petersen 🦴 *Petersen* **1974 (R)** A light-hearted story about a blonde hunk who enrolls in college, cavorting and seducing his way to questionable fame and fortune. **97m/C VHS.** Jack Thompson, Wendy Hughes; ***D:*** Tim Burstall.

Jocks 🦴½ **1987 (R)** A whiz-kid tennis team competes in a pro meet in Las Vegas, and paints the town red. **90m/C VHS.** Christopher Lee, Perry Lang, Richard Roundtree, Scott Strader; ***D:*** Steve Carver; ***W:*** Jeff Buhai.

Joe 🦴🦴½ **1970 (R)** An odd friendship grows between a businessman and a blue-collar worker as they search together for the executive's runaway daughter. Thrust into the midst of the counter-culture, they react with an orgy of violence. **107m/C VHS, DVD, Wide.** Peter Boyle, Susan Sarandon, Dennis Patrick; ***D:*** John G. Avildsen; ***W:*** Norman Wexler; ***C:*** John G. Avildsen, Henri Decae; ***M:*** Bobby Scott.

Joe Dirt 🦴🦴 **2001 (PG-13)** Spade plays the hapless, well-meaning personification of every trailer-trash joke you've ever heard or told. He sports a robo-mullet, earns his keep with degrading, subminimum wage jobs, drives a beat-up muscle car, and grooves to '70s arena-rock. He's also searching for his parents, who bailed on him during a trip to the Grand Canyon when he was eight. Too bad he isn't funny. Co-writers Spade and Wolf spend too much time on the heart strings and not enough on the funny bone, which results in an unholy hybrid of Jerry Springer and the Lifetime Network. Miller's shock-jock and Walken's crazed janitor add some genuine laughs to the proceedings, but not enough. **91m/C VHS, DVD, Wide.** *US* David Spade, Dennis Miller, Adam Beach, Christopher Walken, Jaime Pressly, Caroline Aaron, Fred Ward, Bob (Kid Rock) Ritchie, Erik Per Sullivan, Megan Taylor Harvey; ***D:*** Dennie Gordon; ***W:*** David Spade, Fred Wolf; ***C:*** John R. Leonetti; ***M:*** Waddy Wachtel.

Joe Gould's Secret 🦴🦴½ **2000 (R)** Tucci directed, co-wrote, and stars as Joe Mitchell, famed "New Yorker" columnist who chronicled, among many others, the peculiar life of Greenwich Village eccentric Joe Gould in the 1940s. Gould (Holm) lived on the streets of New York for 26 years, regaling the intelligensia with wild stories and behavior while claiming to be writing the "Oral History of Our Time," which he said was two million words long and contained the fruits of 20,000 overheard conversations. The film quietly (except when Holm's Gould is onscreen) and effectively explores the relationship between Mitchell and Gould, and the reasons for Mitchell's fascination with his subject. **108m/C VHS, DVD, Wide.** Stanley Tucci, Ian Holm, Hope Davis, Patricia Clarkson, Steve Martin, Susan Sarandon, Celia Weston, Allan Corduner, Alice Drummond, Julie Halston, Hallee Hirsh, Ben Jones, John Tormey, David Wohl, Patrick Tovatt, Sarah Hyland; ***D:*** Stanley Tucci; ***W:*** Howard A. Rodman, Stanley Tucci; ***C:*** Maryse Alberti; ***M:*** Evan Lurie.

Joe Kidd 🦴🦴½ **1972 (PG)** A land war breaks out in New Mexico between Mexican natives and American land barons. Eastwood, once again portraying the "mysterious stranger," must decide with whom he should side, all the while falling in love with Garcia. Lackluster direction results in a surprisingly tedious western, in spite of the cast. One of Eastwood's lowest money grossers. **88m/C VHS, DVD, Wide.** Clint Eastwood, Robert Duvall, John Saxon, Don Stroud, Stella Garcia, James Wainwright, Paul Koslo, Gregory Walcott, Dick Van Patten, Lynn(e) Marta; ***D:*** John Sturges; ***W:*** Elmore Leonard; ***C:*** Bruce Surtees; ***M:*** Lalo Schifrin.

The Joe Louis Story 🦴🦴 **1953** The story of Joe Louis' rise to fame as boxing's Heavyweight Champion of the world. **88m/B VHS, DVD.** Coley Wallace, Paul Stewart, Hilda Simms, Albert "Poppy" Popwell; ***D:*** Robert Gordon; ***W:*** Robert Sylvester; ***C:*** Joseph Brun; ***M:*** George Bassman.

Joe Panther 🦴🦴🦴 **1976 (G)** Family drama about a young Seminole Indian who stakes his claim in the Anglo world by wrestling alligators. Montalban plays a wise old chieftain who helps the youth handle the conflict between Indian and white societies. **110m/C VHS.** Brian Keith, Ricardo Montalban, Alan Feinstein, Cliff Osmond, A. Martinez, Robert Hoffman; ***D:*** Paul Krasny.

Joe Somebody 🦴 **2001 (PG)** By-the-numbers dud feels like an after-school special with ten times the budget and half the brains or heart. Tim Allen again plays the allegedly likable Average Joe, only this time, his name is actually Joe. Trouble is, he doesn't look nerdy or ineffectual, even if he's wearing glasses and getting beat up in the parking lot. After Joe's daughter (Panettiere) witnesses his turn as punching bag for the office bully (Warburton), he slides into a depression. But after a visit from sure-to-be romantic interest Meg (Bowen), Joe decides he wants a rematch. He enlists the help of a faded martial arts guru (Belushi) and becomes popular, but his daughter and love interest like the old Joe better. Tries to have a moral message about rejecting violence while also giving a good dose of it. Joe's precocious, sage-like daughter makes the Olsen twins pleasant by comparison. **97m/C VHS, DVD.** *US* Tim Allen, Julie Bowen, Hayden Panettiere, Kelly Lynch, James Belushi, Patrick Warburton, Greg Germann, Robert Joy, Ken Marino; ***D:*** John Pasquin; ***W:*** John Scott Shepherd; ***C:*** Daryn Okada; ***M:*** George S. Clinton.

Joe the King 🦴🦴 **1999 (R)** Undistinguished coming of age pic, set in the mid-'70s, about a boy caught up in violence. Fourteen-year-old Joe (Fleiss) and his older brother Mike (Ligosh) are subjected to the constant drunken abuse of their father Bob (Henry) and the indifference of their overworked mother Theresa (Young). Joe begins stealing to get by but his crimes gradually becomes less than petty. A troubled student as well, Joe is befriended by guidance counselor Len (Hawke), whose attempts to help only result in a stint for Joe in a juvie center. Slow-paced and developmentally challenged. **101m/C VHS, DVD.** Noah Fleiss, Val Kilmer, Ethan Hawke, Karen Young, John Leguizamo, Austin Pendleton, Max Ligosh, James Costa; ***D:*** Frank Whaley; ***W:*** Frank Whaley; ***C:*** Mike Mayers; ***M:*** Robert Whaley, Anthony Grimaldi. Sundance '99: Screenplay.

Joe Torre: Curveballs Along the Way 🦴🦴½ **1997** Bio of manager Torre (Sorvino), who's hired by George Steinbrenner (Welsh) in 1996 to coach the New York Yankees. The Yanks actually start winning and Torre takes them all the way to the World Series (they win), but his triumph is marred by family heartbreak, as his brother Frank (Loggia) is in the hospital awaiting a heart transplant. Not bad for a quickie cable biopic, but only because the cast is outstanding. **90m/C VHS.** Paul Sorvino, Robert Loggia, Barbara Williams, Isaiah Washington IV, Gailard Sartain, Kenneth Welsh, Marilyn Chris; ***D:*** Sturla Gunnarsson; ***W:*** Philip Rosenberg; ***C:*** Mark Irwin. **CABLE**

Joe Versus the Volcano 🦴🦴 **1990 (PG)** Expressionistic goofball comedy about a dopey guy who, after finding out he has only months to live, contracts with a millionaire to leap into a volcano alive. Imaginative farce with great "Metropolis"-pastiche visuals that eventually fizzle out. Watch for Ryan in not one, but three roles, and mysterious symbolism throughout. Special effects courtesy of Industrial Light and Magic. **106m/C VHS, DVD, 8mm, Wide.** Tom Hanks, Meg Ryan, Lloyd Bridges, Robert Stack, Amanda Plummer, Abe Vigoda, Dan Hedaya, Barry McGovern, Ossie Davis; ***D:*** John Patrick Shanley; ***W:*** John Patrick Shanley; ***C:*** Stephen Goldblatt; ***M:*** Georges Delerue.

Joe's Apartment 🦴🦴 **1996 (PG-13)** Fresh-from-Iowa Joe (O'Connell) comes to New York, finds a squalid apartment, and then discovers its other occupants are hordes of singing, joking cockroaches. Lucky for Joe, his unwelcome roommates are on his side, even helping out with his love life, when necessary. Gross but interesting, throw in Vaughn as a panty-wearing politician and you've got yourself a potential cult-movie favorite. Neat freaks probably won't enjoy it much. Flick took three years to finish as computer-animated roaches had to do all the dancing and singing. Feature directorial debut for writer Payson, who created the original 1992 live-action/animation MTV short. **82m/C VHS, DVD.** Jerry O'Connell, Megan Ward, Robert Vaughn, Jim Turner, Don Ho, Sandra "Pepa" Denton, Shiek Mahmud-Bey; ***D:*** John Payson; ***W:*** John Payson; ***C:*** Peter Deming; ***V:*** Billy West, Reginald (Reggie) Hudlin.

Joe's Bed-Stuy Barbershop: We Cut Heads 🦴🦴½ **1983** Lee's first film takes place inside a neighborhood landmark, the corner barbershop. Lee displays the social awareness and urban humor that he honed in his later, bigger films. **60m/C VHS.** Leon Errol, Morris Carnovsky, Elyse Knox, Billy House, Trudy Marshall; ***D:*** Spike Lee; ***W:*** Spike Lee.

Joey 🦴½ **1985 (PG)** Daddy, a former doo-wopper, looks back on his years of musical success as a waste of time. His son takes to the world of rock guitar with blind fervor. Their argument plays against the backdrop of the "Royal Doo-Wopp Show" at New York City's Radio Music Hall. Features multi-generational rock songs. **90m/C VHS.** Neill Barry, James Quinn.

Joey 🦴🦴½ **1998 (PG)** Young Billy (Croft) rescues a baby kangaroo (known as a joey) who was left behind when an evil hunter captures a group of kangaroos and hauls them off to Sydney for nefarious purposes. So Billy puts Joey in his backpack and heads off to the city to reunite the little family—aided by the rebellious daughter (McKenna) of the newly appointed U.S. ambassador (Begley). **96m/C VHS.** *AU* Jamie Croft, Alex McKenna, Ed Begley Jr., Rebecca Gibney, Ruth Cracknell, Harold Hopkins; ***D:*** Ian Barry; ***W:*** Stuart Beattie; ***C:*** David Burr; ***M:*** Roger Mason.

Joey Breaker 🦴🦴🦴 **1993 (R)** Joey (cult-fave Edson) is a hot-shot Manhattan talent agent who's consumed by his job. A series of encounters (romantic and otherwise) expands his outlook, first among them with Cyan (Marley), a young Jamaican waitress. On his journey to possible enlightenment Joey also meets AIDS-stricken Fondren, who helps Joey see another side of life. Quirky with a reggae beat, small pic works large message with sense of humor and sincere performances. Dedicated to Fondren, who died of AIDS in 1992. Marley, daughter of late reggae superstar Bob, shares a tune on the soundtrack with brother Ziggy. Filmed in da Big Apple and St. Lucia, West Indies. **92m/C VHS.** Richard Edson, Cedella Marley, Erik King, Gina Gershon, Philip Seymour Hoffman, Fred Fondren; ***D:*** Steven Starr; ***W:*** Steven Starr; ***C:*** Joe DeSalvo; ***M:*** Paul Aston.

John and Julie 🦴🦴½ **1955** Sweet story about two young friends, living in the English countryside in 1953, who decide to run away to London in order to witness the coronation of Queen Elizabeth II. They're hoping John's Uncle, a Royal Escort guard, will help them but first they have to get to the city, which involves a lot of complicated travelling plans. **82m/C VHS.** *GB* Colin Gibson, Lesley Dudley, Noelle Middleton, Moira Lister, Constance Cummings, Wilfrid Hyde-White, Sidney James, Joseph Tomelty, Megs Jenkins, Patric Doonan, Peter Sellers, John Stuart, Vincent Ball, Colin Gordon, Peter Jones, Katie Johnson, Cyril Smith, Andrew Cruikshank, Winifred Shotter, Richard Dimbleby, Wynfold Vaughn Thomas; ***D:*** William Fairchild; ***W:*** William Fairchild; ***C:*** Arthur Grant.

John and the Missus 🦴½ **1987 (PG)** After the discovery of a copper mine threatens to destroy a nearby town, the Canadian government begins a relocation process. However, one man refuses to give up his generations-old home. Canadian Pinsent's directorial debut, adapting his own 1973 novel. **98m/C VHS.** *CA* Gordon Pinsent, Jackie Burroughs, Randy Follet, Jessica Steen; ***D:*** Gordon Pinsent. Genie '87: Actor (Pinsent).

John & Yoko: A Love Story 🦴 **1985** Appalling TV version of the rock legend's life and marriage. With original Beatles tunes. **146m/C VHS.** Mark McGann, Kim Miyori, Kenneth Price, Peter Capaldi, Richard Morant, Philip Walsh; ***D:*** Sandor Stern. **TV**

John Carpenter's Ghosts of Mars 🦴🦴 *Ghosts of Mars* **2001 (R)** John Carpenter unashamedly fires up his B-movie machine to maximum cheese factor in this tale of space babes and zombies. Henstridge is a police lieutenant on the matriarchal Mars colony in 2025 sent to retrieve murderer "Desolation" Williams (Ice Cube). The job turns from get the bad guy to simple survival when long-dormant Martian warriors begin taking over the bodies of the Earth intruders, turning them into zombies. So do you think the bad guys and the good guys have to team up to win one for the humans? At its best during the action sequences, but probably a bad choice to follow "A Room with a View" for a Saturday night double feature. **98m/C VHS, DVD, Wide.** *US* Natasha Henstridge, Ice Cube, Clea DuVall, Pam Grier, Jason Statham, Joanna Cassidy, Rosemary Forsyth, Liam Waite, Richard Cetrone; ***D:*** John Carpenter; ***W:*** John Carpenter, Larry Sulkis; ***C:*** Gary B. Kibbe; ***M:*** John Carpenter.

John Carpenter's Vampires 🦴🦴½ *Vampires* **1997 (R)** Vatican-sponsored vampire hunter Jack Crow (Woods) leads his team of mercenaries into the American Southwest to battle master bloodsucker Valek (Griffith) and his hordes. After destroying a vampire hideout, Crow and company are ambushed at a post-stake party. The only survivors are Crow, his buddy Montoya (Baldwin), and a hooker (Lee) with a psychic link to the vampires. Satisfying horror-western packs plenty of action and gore (along with just enough humor) to hold attention until the inevitable showdown. Woods does a good job of toning down from his usual bug-eyed crazy to merely borderline disturbed here. Based on the novel "Vampires" by John Steakley. **108m/C VHS, DVD.** James Woods, Thomas Ian Griffith, Sheryl Lee, Daniel Baldwin, Tim Guinee, Maximilian Schell, Cary-Hiroyuki Tagawa, Mark Boone Jr., Tom Rosales; ***D:*** John Carpenter; ***W:*** John Carpenter, Don Jacoby; ***C:*** Gary B. Kibbe; ***M:*** John Carpenter.

John Cleese on How to Irritate People *How to Irritate People* **1968** Cleese, a master at causing irritation, demonstrates how to take care of all those annoying people who irritate you, including job interviewers, bank clerks, waiters, and salesmen. Monty Python alumni Palin and Chapman also join Cleese in the "Airline Pilots" sketch about bored pilots deliberately trying to terrify their passengers. **65m/C VHS.** John Cleese, Michael Palin, Graham Chapman, Connie Booth.

John Grisham's The Rainmaker 🦴🦴½ *The Rainmaker* **1997 (PG-13)** Yet another legal drama from the successful pen of John Grisham. Baylor (Damon) is a young lawyer whose job disappears when his firm is absorbed by a giant company. He fills his time giving legal advice to indigents and mooning over Kelly (Danes), a young abused wife. Then he takes on the case of a couple whose leukemia-stricken son was denied treatment by their insurance company, coincidentally represented by the firm that booted Baylor. Pre-"Jack," Coppola probably wouldn't have gone anywhere near such formulaic franchise fare, and if he did, he could've directed it in his sleep. As it is he creates a serviceable, if not spectacular, piece of entertainment. His main allies are Voight's insurance company mouthpiece and DeVito's ambulance chaser. Damon plays the hero with much less bravado than previous Grisham protagonists. **137m/C VHS, DVD.** Sonny Shroyer, Matt Damon, Claire Danes, Danny DeVito, Jon Voight, Danny Glover, Virginia Madsen, Mary Kay Place, Mickey Rourke, Johnny Whitworth, Teresa Wright, Dean Stockwell, Red West, Roy Scheider, Randy Travis, Andrew Shue; ***D:*** Francis Ford Coppola; ***W:*** Francis Ford Coppola, Michael Herr; ***C:*** John Toll; ***M:*** Elmer Bernstein.

John Paul Jones 𝒥𝒥½ **1959** Big bio of the Revolutionary War naval hero ("I have not yet begun to fight!") who wins a lot of battles but can't convince Congress to maintain a strong navy at war's end. He's sent to win sea battles for the Empress Catherine the Great of Russia and then spends his last years in France. Great action scenes, otherwise tedious. **126m/C VHS.** Robert Stack, Charles Coburn, MacDonald Carey, Marisa Pavan, Jean-Pierre Aumont, Peter Cushing, Erin O'Brien, Bruce Cabot, David Farrar, Basil Sydney, John Crawford; ***Cameos:*** Bette Davis; ***D:*** John Farrow; ***W:*** John Farrow, Jesse Lasky Jr.; ***M:*** Max Steiner.

John Q 𝒥𝒥 **2002 (PG-13)** "Dog Day Afternoon" lite is essentially a two hour tirade against the U.S. health system (who can blame them?) which casts Washington as the title's everyman hero who's desperate and gutsy enough to bypass medical bureaucracy altogether to get his 10-year old son Mike (Smith) the heart transplant he desperately needs to live. John Quincy Archibald's plant has just cut his hours, and when his HMO gives him the run-around, he is forced to come up with the $75,000 for his son's operation. Unable to come up with it, John Q. takes over the ER and demands his son be placed at the top of the transplant list. Talented cast, including Duvall as the sympathetic police negotiator, Woods as the cynical doctor, and Liotta, as the boldly drawn police chief, is generally wasted on the sentimental and melodramatic one-note premise. **118m/C VHS, DVD.** *US* Denzel Washington, Robert Duvall, James Woods, Anne Heche, Eddie Griffin, Kimberly Elise, Shawn Hatosy, Ray Liotta, Daniel E. Smith, David Thornton, Ethan Suplee, Kevin Connolly, Paul Johansson, Troy Beyer, Obba Babatunde, Laura Harring; ***D:*** Nick Cassavetes; ***W:*** James Kearns; ***C:*** Rogier Stoffers; ***M:*** Aaron Zigman.

Johnnie Gibson F.B.I. 𝒥 *Johnnie Mae Gibson: FBI* **1987** Supposedly based on a true story, the adventures of a beautiful, black FBI agent who falls in love with a man she's investigating. **96m/C VHS.** Howard E. Rollins Jr., Lynn Whitfield, William Allen Young, Richard Lawson; ***D:*** Bill Duke; ***M:*** Billy Goldenberg.

Johnny Angel 𝒥𝒥𝒥 **1945** Merchant Marine captain unravels mystery of his father's murder aboard a ship. Tense film noir. **79m/B VHS.** George Raft, Claire Trevor, Signe Hasso, Lowell Gilmore, Hoagy Carmichael; ***D:*** Edwin L. Marin.

Johnny Apollo 𝒥𝒥½ **1940** Upright college student Power keeps his nose clean until Dad's sent to jail for playing with numbers. Scheming to free his old man (Arnold) from the big house, he decides crime will pay for the stiff price tag of freedom. Predictable and melodramatic, but well directed. **93m/B VHS.** Tyrone Power, Dorothy Lamour, Lloyd Nolan, Edward Arnold, Charley Grapewin, Lionel Atwill; ***D:*** Yves Allegret; ***C:*** Arthur C. Miller.

Johnny Appleseed **1986** True story of the legendary American who spent his life planting apple trees across the country. Comedy the entire family will enjoy from Shelly Duvall's "Tall Tales and Legends" cable series. **60m/C VHS.** Martin Short, Rob Reiner, Molly Ringwald. **CABLE**

Johnny Be Good 𝒥 **1988 (R)** A too-talented high school quarterback is torn between loyalty to his best friend and to his girlfriend amid bribery and schemings by colleges eager to sign him up. **91m/C VHS.** Anthony Michael Hall, Robert Downey Jr., Paul Gleason, Uma Thurman, John Pankow, Steve James, Seymour Cassel, Michael Greene, Marshall Bell, Deborah May; ***D:*** Bud Smith; ***W:*** Jeff Buhai; ***M:*** Jay Ferguson.

Johnny Belinda 𝒥𝒥𝒥 **1948** A compassionate physician cares for a young deaf mute woman and her illegitimate child. Tension builds as the baby's father returns to claim the boy. **103m/B VHS.** Jane Wyman, Lew Ayres, Charles Bickford, Agnes Moorehead; ***D:*** Jean Negulesco; ***M:*** Max Steiner. Oscars '48: Actress (Wyman); Golden Globes '49: Actress—Drama (Wyman), Film—Drama.

Johnny Belinda 𝒥𝒥 **1982** TV adaptation of the Elmer Harris weepie about a small town doctor who befriends an abused deaf girl. Remake of the 1948 film. **95m/C VHS.** Richard Thomas, Rosanna Arquette, Dennis Quaid, Candy Clark, Roberts Blossom, Fran Ryan; ***D:*** Anthony Page. **TV**

Johnny Come Lately 𝒥𝒥½ *Johnny Vagabond* **1943** An elderly editor helps out an ex-newspaperman with a police charge. The two then team up to expose political corruption despite threats from a rival newspaperman. **97m/B VHS.** James Cagney, Grace George, Marjorie Main, Marjorie Lord, Hattie McDaniel, Edward McNamara; ***D:*** William K. Howard.

Johnny Dangerously 𝒥𝒥 **1984 (PG-13)** A gangster spoof about Johnny Dangerously, who turned to crime in order to pay his mother's medical bills. Now, Dangerously wants to go straight, but competitive crooks would rather see him dead than law-abiding and his mother requires more and more expensive operations. Crime pays in comic ways. **90m/C VHS.** Michael Keaton, Joe Piscopo, Danny DeVito, Maureen Stapleton, Marilu Henner, Peter Boyle, Griffin Dunne, Glynnis O'Connor, Dom DeLuise, Richard Dimitri, Ray Walston, Dick Butkus, Alan Hale Jr., Bob Eubanks; ***D:*** Amy Heckerling; ***W:*** Norman Steinberg, Harry Colomby. **TV**

Johnny Eager 𝒥𝒥𝒥 **1942** Glossy crime melodrama starring Taylor as an unscrupulous racketeer and Turner as the daughter of D.A. Arnold who falls for him and ends up becoming a pawn in his schemes. Heflin won an Oscar for his outstanding performance as Taylor's alcoholic confidant. Excellent direction by LeRoy makes this a top-rate gangster film. Based on a story by James Edward Grant. **107m/B VHS.** Robert Taylor, Lana Turner, Edward Arnold, Van Heflin, Robert Sterling, Patricia Dane, Glenda Farrell, Barry Nelson, Henry O'Neill, Charles Dingle, Cy Kendall; ***D:*** Mervyn LeRoy; ***W:*** James Edward Grant, John Lee Mahin. Oscars '42: Support. Actor (Heflin).

Johnny Firecloud 𝒥 **1975** A modern Indian goes on the warpath when the persecution of his people reawakens his sense of identity. **94m/C VHS, DVD, Wide.** Victor Mohica, Ralph Meeker, Frank De Kova, Sacheen Little Feather, David Canary, Christina Hart; ***D:*** William Allen Castleman; ***W:*** Wilton Denmark; ***M:*** William Loose.

Johnny Frenchman 𝒥𝒥 **1946** Rival fishing groups battle it out, complicated by a romance across the water. Featured in the cast are real fishermen and villagers from Cornwall, as well as authentic Free French Resistance fighters from WWII. **104m/B VHS.** *GB* Francoise Rosay, Tom Walls, Patricia Roc, Ralph Michael, Frederick Piper, Pierre Richard, Carroll O'Connor; ***D:*** Charles Frend.

Johnny Got His Gun 𝒥𝒥𝒥 **1971 (R)** Dalton Trumbo's story of a young WWI veteran (Bottoms) who meets a bomb with his name on it and is rendered armless, legless, and more or less faceless, as well as deaf, dumb, and blind. Regarded as a vegetable and stuck in a lightless hospital utility room, he dreams and fantasizes about life before and after the bomb, and tries vainly to communicate with the staff. Wrenching and bleak antiwar diatribe made at the climax of the Vietnam War. **111m/C VHS.** Timothy Bottoms, Jason Robards Jr., Donald Sutherland, Diane Varsi, Kathy Fields, Donald (Don "Red") Barry, Peter Brocco, Judy Chaikin, Eric Christmas, Maurice Dallimore, Robert Easton, Eduard Franz, Anthony Geary, Edmund Gilbert, Ben Hammer, Wayne Heffley, Marsha Hunt, Joseph Kaufmann, Charles McGraw, Byron Morrow, David Soul; ***D:*** Dalton Trumbo; ***W:*** Dalton Trumbo; ***C:*** Jules Brenner; ***M:*** Jerry Fielding. Cannes '71: Grand Jury Prize.

Johnny Guitar 𝒥𝒥𝒥½ **1953** Women strap on six-guns in Nicholas Ray's unintentionally hilarious, gender-bending western. A guitar-playing loner wanders into a small town feud between lovelorn saloon owner Crawford and McCambridge, the town's resident lynch mob-leading harpy. This fascinating cult favorite has had film theorists arguing for decades: is it a parody, a political McCarthy-era allegory, or Freudian exercise? The off-screen battles of the two female stars are equally legendary. Stick around for the end credits to hear Peggy Lee sing the title song. **116m/C VHS.** Joan Crawford, Ernest Borgnine, Sterling Hayden, Mercedes McCambridge, Scott Brady, Ward Bond, Royal Dano, John Carradine, Ben Cooper, Frank Ferguson, Paul Fix, Denver Pyle; ***D:*** Nicholas Ray; ***W:*** Philip Yordan; ***C:*** Harry Stradling Sr.; ***M:*** Victor Young.

Johnny Handsome 𝒥𝒥𝒥 **1989 (R)** An ugly, deformed hood, after he's been double-crossed and sent to prison, volunteers for a reconstructive surgery experiment and is released with a new face, determined to hunt down the scum that set him up. A terrific modern B-picture based on John Godey's "The Three Worlds of Johnny Handsome." **96m/C VHS.** Mickey Rourke, Ellen Barkin, Lance Henriksen, Elizabeth McGovern, Morgan Freeman, Forest Whitaker, Scott Wilson, Blake Clark; ***D:*** Walter Hill; ***W:*** Ken Friedman; ***M:*** Ry Cooder.

Johnny Holiday 𝒥𝒥½ **1949** A heart-warming story about a fatherless boy, Johnny, who is dumped into reform school to prevent him from pursuing a life of crime with his small-time hood buddies. While there, he is befriended by Sargeant Walker, an ex-Calvary man who teaches him about life and becomes the father Johnny never had. **94m/B VHS.** Allen Martin Jr., William Bendix, Stanley Clements; ***D:*** Willis Goldbeck.

Johnny Mnemonic 𝒥𝒥 **1995 (R)** Robo-yuppie data courier Johnny (Reeves), has over extended the storage capacity in his head and must download his latest job before his brain turns to aplesauce. Aided by an implant-enhanced bodyguard (Meyer), underground hacker rebels called LoTeks, and a former doctor (Rollins) battling a technology-induced epidemic, Johnny is on the run from the corporation that wants his head (literally). Freshman director Longo can't seem to get a handle on the plot and doesn't get much help from Gibson, who combined characters and scenarios from his other books. Action sequences and computer effects are appropriately spiffy, preventing a total system crash. **98m/C VHS, DVD, 8mm, Wide.** Keanu Reeves, Dina Meyer, Ice-T, Takeshi "Beat" Kitano, Dolph Lundgren, Henry Rollins, Udo Kier, Barbara Sukowa, Denis Akiyama; ***D:*** Robert Longo; ***W:*** William Gibson; ***C:*** Francois Protat; ***M:*** Brad Fiedel.

Johnny Nobody 𝒥𝒥½ **1961** A mysterious stranger murders a writer who has been taunting the residents of a quaint Irish town. A sleeper of a thriller, especially in the treatment of the town's reaction to this murder. **88m/B VHS.** *GB* William Bendix, Aldo Ray, Nigel Patrick, Yvonne Mitchell, Cyril Cusack; ***D:*** Nigel Patrick.

Johnny 100 Pesos 𝒥𝒥 **1993** Seventeen-year-old Johnny (Araiza) walks into a video store that is a front for an illegal currency exchange operation. He's the advance man for a quartet of criminals who are planning to rob the place but before they can escape with the cash, the police show up and the crooks take the store's inhabitants hostage. Now there's a standoff, with the media shamelessly broadcasting all events and the Chilean authorities struggling to control the escalating situation. Based on a true 1990 incident. Spanish with subtitles. **90m/C VHS, DVD.** Armando Araiza, Patricia Rivera, Willy Semler, Sergio Hernandez; ***D:*** Gustavo Graef-Marino; ***W:*** Gustavo Graef-Marino, Gerardo Caceres; ***C:*** Jose Luis Arredondo; ***M:*** Andres Pollak.

Johnny Reno 𝒥½ **1966** Laughable western that has U.S. Marshal Andrews trying to save an accused killer from lynching. Of interest for star-watching only. Based on a story by Steve Fisher, A.C. Lyles, and Andrew Craddock. **83m/C VHS.** Dana Andrews, Jane Russell, Lon Chaney Jr., John Agar, Lyle Bettger, Tom Drake, Richard Arlen, Robert Lowery; ***D:*** R.G. Springsteen; ***W:*** Steve Fisher.

Johnny Shiloh 𝒥𝒥 **1963** An underage youth becomes a heroic drummer during the Civil War. Originally a two-part Disney TV show. **90m/C VHS.** Kevin Corcoran, Brian Keith, Darryl Hickman, Skip Homeier; ***D:*** James Neilson. **TV**

Johnny Skidmarks 𝒥𝒥 **1997 (R)** Johnny (Gallagher) is a burned-out freelance crime-scene photographer who moonlights for blackmailers by shooting incriminating pics of prominent citizens in seedy motels. Then the blackmailers start winding up dead and Johnny checks out his photos to see if he can figure out who's doing the crime before he becomes the next target. **96m/C VHS, DVD.** Peter Gallagher, Frances McDormand, John Lithgow, Jack Black, Charlie Spradling; ***D:*** John Raffo; ***W:*** John Raffo, William Preston Robinson; ***C:*** Bernd Heinl; ***M:*** Brian Langsbard.

Johnny Stecchino 𝒥𝒥𝒥 **1992 (R)** A breathless, charming comedy about mistaken identity, with Benigni starring as both Dante, a mild-mannered Roman bus driver, and his double, a notorious Mafioso known as "Johnny Toothpick." Dante happens to meet a lovely woman who takes exceptional interest in him, even inviting him to visit her home in Palermo. The reason she's interested is that Dante is the exact double of her husband, who has ratted on his fellow mobsters and needs a patsy to take the fall. Benigni's expressive body language and sweetness of character is well-showcased. In Italian with English subtitles. **100m/C VHS.** *IT* Roberto Benigni, Nicoletta Braschi, Paolo Bonacelli, Ignazio Pappalardo, Franco Volpi; ***D:*** Roberto Benigni; ***W:*** Roberto Benigni, Vincenzo Cerami; ***C:*** Giuseppe Lanci; ***M:*** Evan Lurie.

Johnny Suede 𝒥𝒥½ **1992 (R)** Hip kid with big hair wanders the city seeking an identity via retro black suede elevator shoes. Sleepy surreal comedy walks Pitt through two romantic entanglements and a rendezvous with his own rock idol in his quest for musical talent and pop singer nirvana (not necessarily in that order). Candidate for induction into the David Lynch Movie Musuem of the Weird. **97m/C VHS.** Brad Pitt, Calvin Levels, Nick Cave, Wilfredo Giovanni Clark, Alison Moir, Peter McRobbie, Tina Louise, Michael Mulheren, Catherine Keener, Samuel L. Jackson; ***D:*** Tom DiCillo; ***W:*** Tom DiCillo; ***M:*** Jim Farmer.

Johnny Tiger 𝒥𝒥½ **1966** A teacher has his hands full when he arrives at the Seminole Reservation in Florida to instruct the Indian children. **100m/C VHS.** Robert Taylor, Geraldine Brooks, Chad Everett, Brenda Scott; ***D:*** Paul Wendkos.

Johnny Tremain & the Sons of Liberty 𝒥𝒥 **1958** The story of the gallant American patriots who participated in the Boston Tea Party. **85m/C VHS.** Sebastian Cabot, Hal Stalmaster, Luana Patten, Richard Beymer; ***D:*** Robert Stevenson.

Johnny 2.0 𝒥½ **1999 (PG-13)** Contrived thriller about a genetic scientist, Johnny Dalton (Fahey), who awakens from a 15-year coma and discovers his memory has been transplanted into a clone, Johnny 2.0. Now Dalton has six days to find his duplicate before the Corporation, the group behind the procedure, decides on termination. **95m/C VHS, DVD.** Jeff Fahey, Michael Ironside, Tahnee Welch; ***D:*** Neill Fearnley. **CABLE**

Johnny We Hardly Knew Ye 𝒥𝒥½ **1977** Well-made biographical drama recounts John F. Kennedy's first political campaign for local office in Boston in 1946. **90m/C VHS.** Paul Rudd, Kevin Conway, William Prince, Burgess Meredith, Tom Berenger,

Brian Dennehy, Kenneth McMillan; *D:* Gilbert Cates. **TV**

Johnny's Girl 🦴🦴½ **1995** After her mom's death, a 16-year-old (Kirshner) moves to Anchorage, Alaska to live with her wayward dad (Williams). He's a kinda con man involved in shady deals, who tries to go legit in order to give his daughter a proper home. TV movie based on the novel by Kim Rich. **92m/C VHS.** Mia Kirshner, Treat Williams, Ron White, Gloria Reuben, Shirley Douglas, Janne Mortil; *D:* John Kent Harrison.

johns 🦴🦴½ **1996 (R)** A gritty, yet predictable tale of street hustling in L.A. redeemed by intense performances by its two lead actors. It's Christmas Eve and John (Arquette) has only one thing in mind: recover his stolen money and celebrate his birthday in style. On the way, he mentors crony Donnor (Haas), who's love for John blinds him to the rules of hustling, which can only lead to tragedy. Arquette's controlled performance is on target for the cynical male lead and Haas's doe-eyed look is perfect for the slightly dim-witted naivete his character revels in. Downfall comes when first-time director Silver fails to maintain actors' intensity with uneven editing and out of place symbolism. Still, not a bad first try. **96m/C VHS, DVD.** David Arquette, Lukas Haas, Arliss Howard, Keith David, Elliott Gould, Christopher Gartin, Joshua Schaefer, Wilson Cruz, Terrence DaShon Howard, Nicky Katt, Alanna Ubach; *D:* Scott Silver; *W:* Scott Silver; *C:* Tom Richmond; *M:* Charles D. Brown.

A Joke of Destiny, Lying in Wait Around the Corner Like a Bandit 🦴🦴 *A Joke of Destiny* **1984 (PG)** A irreverent satire about a Minister of the Interior (Tognazzi, of "La Cage aux Folles" fame) who becomes trapped in his high-tech limousine before a vital press conference. An exaggerated vision of Italian bureaucracy. With English subtitles. **105m/C VHS.** *IT* Ugo Tognazzi, Piera Degli Esposti, Gastone Moschin, Renzo Montagnani, Valeria Golino; *D:* Lina Wertmuller; *W:* Lina Wertmuller.

The Jolly Paupers 🦴🦴½ *Freylekhe Kabtsonim* **1938** A pre-war comedy made in Warsaw about two small-town Jews who try to achieve fame and fortune in the face of setbacks, community quarrels, and insanity. In Yiddish with English subtitles. **62m/B VHS.** Shimon Dzigan, Yisroel Shumacher, Max Bozyk, Menasha Oppenheim; *D:* Zygmund Turkow.

Jolson Sings Again 🦴🦴 **1949** This sequel to "The Jolson Story" brings back Larry Parks as the ebullient entertainer, with Jolson himself dubbing Parks's voice for the songs. Picking up where the other film ended, the movie chronicles Jolson's comeback in the 1940s and his tireless work with the USO overseas during WWII and the Korean War. ♫After You've Gone; Chinatown, My Chinatown; Give My Regards to Broadway; I Only Have Eyes For You; I'm Just Wild About Harry; You Made Me Love You; I'm Looking Over a Four-Leaf Clover; Is It True What They Say About Dixie?; Ma Blushin' Rose. **96m/C VHS.** Larry Parks, William Demarest, Barbara Hale, Bill Goodwin; *D:* Henry Levin; *M:* George Duning.

The Jolson Story 🦴🦴🦴 **1946** A smash Hollywood bio of Jolson, from his childhood to super-stardom. Features dozens of vintage songs from Jolson's parade of hits. Jolson himself dubbed the vocals for Parks, rejuvenating his own career in the process. ♫Swanee; You Made Me Love You; By the Light of the Silvery Moon; I'm Sitting On Top of the World; There's a Rainbow Round My Shoulder; My Mammy; Rock-A-Bye Your Baby With a Dixie Melody; Liza; Waiting for the Robert E. Lee. **128m/C VHS.** Larry Parks, Evelyn Keyes, William Demarest, Bill Goodwin, Tamara Shayne, John Alexander, Jimmy Lloyd, Ludwig Donath, Scotty Beckett; *D:* Alfred E. Green; *M:* Morris Stoloff. Oscars '46: Sound, Scoring/Musical.

Jon Jost's Frameup 🦴🦴 *Frameup* **1993** Cocky ex-con Ricky Lee hooks up with dizzy waitress Beth Ann and they head out on a 3000-mile nightmare road trip to California. Free-form story shot in 10 days. **91m/C VHS.** Howard Swain, Nancy Carlin; *D:* Jon Jost; *W:* Jon Jost.

Jonah Who Will Be 25 in the Year 2000 🦴🦴🦴½ *Jonas—Qui Aura 25 Ans en l'An 2000* **1976** A group of eight friends, former 60s radicals, try to adjust to growing older and coping with life in the 70s. The eccentric octet include a disillusioned journalist turned gambler, an unorthodox teacher, and a grocery store cashier who gives away food to the elderly. Wonderful performances highlight this social comedy. In French with English subtitles. **110m/C VHS.** *SI* Jean-Luc Bideau, Myriam Meziere, Miou-Miou, Jacques Denis, Rufus, Dominique Labourier, Roger Jendly, Miriam Boyer, Raymond Bussieres, Jonah; *D:* Alain Tanner; *W:* Alain Tanner; *C:* Renato Berta; *M:* Jean-Marie Senia. Natl. Soc. Film Critics '76: Screenplay.

Jonathan Livingston Seagull 🦴🦴½ **1973 (G)** Based on the best-selling novella by Richard Bach, this film quietly envisions a world of love, understanding, achievement, hope and individuality. **99m/C VHS.** James Franciscus, Juliet Mills; *D:* Hall Bartlett; *M:* Neil Diamond. Golden Globes '74: Score.

Joni 🦴🦴 **1979 (G)** An inspirational story based on the real life of Tada (playing herself) who was seriously injured in a diving accident, and her conquering of the odds. A born-again feature film based on the book by Tada. **75m/C VHS.** Joni Eareckson Tada, Bert Remsen, Katherine De Hetre, Cooper Huckabee; *D:* James F. Collier.

Jory 🦴🦴 **1972 (PG)** A young man's father is killed in a saloon fight, and he must grow up quickly to survive. **96m/C VHS.** Robby Benson, B.J. Thomas, John Marley; *D:* Jorge Fons.

Joseph 🦴🦴½ **1995** Following "Abraham" and "Jacob" comes the Old Testament story of young Joseph (Mercurio), beloved son of Jacob, who's sold into slavery by his envious older brothers. Joseph is bought by the Pharoah's chief steward, Potiphar (Kingsley), and, after a long series of tribulations, rises to become a power in Egypt, which unexpectedly leads Joseph to hold the fate of his long-lost family in his hands. Filmed in Morocco. **240m/C VHS.** Paul Mercurio, Ben Kingsley, Martin Landau, Lesley Ann Warren, Warren Clarke, Alice Krige, Dominique Sanda, Stefano Dionisi, Valeria Cavalli, Peter Eyre, Timothy Bateson, Jamie Glover, Mike Attwell; *D:* Roger Young; *W:* Lionel Chetwynd, James Carrington; *C:* Raffaele Mertes; *M:* Marco Frisina.

Joseph and the Amazing Technicolor Dreamcoat 🦴🦴🦴 **2000** Something more than a filmed stage presentation of the Webber-Rice musical, but something less than a real movie. It begins with a school assembly hall where the narrator (Friedman) bursts into song and tells the biblical story of Joseph (Osmond). Then the scene shifts to soundstages. The catchy songs often seem to be on the verge of morphing into "Cats" or "Phantom of the Opera." Overall, the production values are good and the sound is excellent. **78m/C DVD, Wide.** Donny Osmond, Richard Attenborough, Joan Collins, Maria Friedman; *D:* David Mallet, Steven Pimlott; *C:* Nicholas D. Knowland; *M:* Andrew Lloyd Webber, Tim Rice. **VIDEO**

Joseph Andrews 🦴🦴 **1977 (R)** This adaptation of a 1742 Henry Fielding novel chronicles the rise of Joseph Andrews from servant to personal footman (and fancy) of Lady Booby. **99m/C VHS.** *GB* Ann-Margret, Peter Firth, Jim Dale, Michael Hordern, Beryl Reid; *D:* Tony Richardson; *W:* Chris Bryant, Allan Scott; *C:* David Watkin; *M:* John Addison.

Josepha 🦴🦴🦴 **1982 (R)** A husband and wife, both actors, are forced to re-examine their relationship when the wife finds a new love while on a film location. In French with English subtitles. **114m/C VHS.** *FR* Miou-Miou, Claude Brasseur, Bruno Cremer; *D:* Christopher Frank.

The Josephine Baker Story 🦴🦴🦴 **1990 (R)** Biopic of exotic entertainer/activist Josephine Baker, an Afro-American woman from St. Louis who found superstardom in pre-WWII Europe, but repeated racism and rejection in the U.S. At times trite treatment turns her eventful life into a standard rise-and-fall showbiz tale, but a great cast and lavish scope pull it through. Whitfield recreates Baker's (sometimes topless) dance routines; Carol Dennis dubs her singing. Filmed on location in Budapest. **129m/C VHS, DVD, Wide.** Lynn Whitfield, Ruben Blades, David Dukes, Craig T. Nelson, Louis Gossett Jr., Kene Holliday, Vivian Bonnell; *D:* Brian Gibson; *M:* Ralph Burns. **CABLE**

Josh and S.A.M. 🦴🦴 **1993 (PG-13)** Road movie for youngsters with a twist: the driver can barely see over the dashboard. Josh and Sam are brothers whose parents are splitting. They cope by taking off on their own. Sam, meanwhile has been convinced by Josh that he's not a real boy at all, but rather a S.A.M.: Strategically Altered Mutant. Weber's directorial debut will appeal to young kids, but adults will see over the dashboard and through the transparent plot. **97m/C VHS.** Jacob Tierney, Noah Fleiss, Martha Plimpton, Joan Allen, Christopher Penn, Stephen Tobolowsky, Ronald Guttman; *D:* Billy Weber; *W:* Frank Deese; *C:* Don Burgess; *M:* Thomas Newman.

Josh Kirby...Time Warrior: Chapter 1, Planet of the Dino-Knights 🦴🦴½ **1995 (PG)** Time-traveling 14-year-old Josh Kirby is accidently zapped to the 25th-century where fierce warriors ride dinosaurs and a madman is out to destroy the universe. The first tale in a fantasy series designed as an old-fashioned movie serial, complete with cliff-hanger ending. **88m/C VHS.** Corbin Allred, Jennifer Burns, Derek Webster, John De Mita; *D:* Ernest Farino; *W:* Ethan Reiff, Cyrus Voris, Paul Callisi.

Josh Kirby...Time Warrior: Chapter 2, The Human Pets 🦴🦴½ **1995 (PG)** Josh and his friends now find themselves in the year 70,370—held hostage by the enormous Fatlings, who regard their human finds as pet-like action toys. **90m/C VHS.** Corbin Allred, Jennifer Burns; *D:* Frank Arnold; *W:* Ethan Reiff, Cyrus Voris, Paul Callisi.

Josh Kirby...Time Warrior: Chapter 3, Trapped on Toyworld 🦴🦴½ **1995 (PG)** Josh is stranded away from his friends on the strange planet of Toyworld and must rely on the lifelike creations of a toy magnate to defend himself from the villainous Dr. Zoetrope. **90m/C VHS.** Corbin Allred, Jennifer Burns, Derek Webster, Sharon Lee Jones, Buck Kartalian, Barrie Ingham; *D:* Frank Arnold; *W:* Nick Paine.

Josh Kirby...Time Warrior: Chapter 4, Eggs from 70 Million B.C. 🦴🦴½ **1995 (PG)** Josh and his pals finds themselves in a military compound that is under attack and encounter some very hungry alien worms. **93m/C VHS.** Corbin Allred, Jennifer Burns, Derek Webster, Gary Kasper, Barrie Ingham; *D:* Mark Manos.

Josh Kirby...Time Warrior: Chapter 5, Journey to the Magic Cavern 🦴🦴½ **1996 (PG)** Josh and pals find themselves in the center of a planet where they are befriended by the weird Mushroom People who are under siege by a monster known as "the Muncher." **93m/C VHS.** Corbin Allred, Jennifer Burns, Derek Webster, Michael Hagiwara, Barrie Ingham; *D:* Ernest Farino; *W:* Ethan Reiff, Cyrus Voris.

Josh Kirby...Time Warrior: Chapter 6, Last Battle for the Universe 🦴🦴½ **1996 (PG)** Josh is ready to get back to his own time but first he must survive a battle between long-feuding rivals of the timebelt. **90m/C VHS.** Corbin Allred, Jennifer Burns, Derek Webster, Barrie Ingham; *D:* Frank Arnold; *W:* Ethan Reiff, Cyrus Voris.

Joshua 🦴 *Black Rider* **1976 (R)** Western drama about a vigilante who tracks down the group of outlaws that killed his mother. **75m/C VHS.** Fred Williamson, Isela Vega; *D:* Larry Spangler.

Joshua Then and Now 🦴🦴🦴 **1985 (R)** When a Jewish-Canadian novelist (Woods) is threatened by the breakup of his marriage to his WASPy wife, compounded by a gay scandal, he re-examines his picaresque history, including his life with his gangster father (Arkin). A stirring story that is enhanced by a strong performance by Woods, as well as a picturesque Canadian backdrop. Adapted by Mordecai Richler from his own novel. **102m/C VHS.** *CA* James Woods, Gabrielle Lazure, Alan Arkin, Michael Sarrazin, Chuck Shamata, Linda Sorensen, Alan Scarfe, Alexander Knox, Robert Joy, Ken Campbell; *D:* Ted Kotcheff; *W:* Mordecai Richler; *M:* Philippe Sarde. Genie '86: Support. Actor (Arkin), Support. Actress (Sorensen).

Josie and the Pussycats 🦴🦴 **2001 (PG-13)** This Josie and company have almost as many dimensions as the cartoon from whence they came. Simple plot has Josie's band looking for their big break when record company exec Wyatt Frame, looking for a new sound, spots our heroines and remakes them as teen sensations. Wyatt is partnered with Fiona (Posey, chewing scenery like a starving dog in an Alpo factory) in a scheme to use pop music to control the minds of teens. Basically harmless parody of the pop music biz chokes on its own product-placing hypocrisy, but gets by on the obvious charms of leads Cook, Reid, and Dawson. **99m/C VHS, DVD, Wide.** *US* Rachael Leigh Cook, Tara Reid, Rosario Dawson, Parker Posey, Alan Cumming, Gabriel Mann, Paulo Costanzo, Tom Butler, Missi Pyle, Carson Daly; ***Cameos:*** Seth Green, Breckin Meyer, Donald Adeosun Faison; *D:* Deborah Kaplan, Harry Elfont; *W:* Deborah Kaplan, Harry Elfont; *C:* Matthew Libatique; *M:* John (Gianni) Frizzell.

Jour de Fete 🦴🦴🦴½ *The Big Day; Holiday* **1948** Tati's first film, dealing with a French postman's accelerated efforts at efficiency after viewing a motivational film of the American post service. Wonderful slapstick moments. In French with English subtitles. **79m/B VHS.** *FR* Jacques Tati, Guy Decomble, Paul Fankeur, Santa Relli; *D:* Jacques Tati; *W:* Henri Marquet, Jacques Tati; *C:* Jacques Mercanton; *M:* Jean Yatove.

Journey 🦴 **1977 (PG)** Violent story of a girl who is rescued from the Saguenay River and falls in love with her rescuer. Choosing to remain in the remote pioneer community of this "hero," she brings everyone bad luck and misery. **87m/C VHS.** *CA* Genevieve Bujold, John Vernon; *D:* Paul Almond.

Journey 🦴🦴½ **1995 (PG)** Eleven-year-old Journey (Pomeranc) and his teenaged sister Cat (Dushku) are abandoned by their unhappy, restless mother Min (Tilly) at the home of her parents, Marcus (Robards) and Lottie (Fricker). Marcus is an amatuer photographer and Journey searches through the family photo albums to find reasons for his mother's leaving as he and his grandfather slowly build their relationship. Based on the book by Patricia MacLachlan. **98m/C VHS.** Max Pomeranc, Jason Robards Jr., Brenda Fricker, Eliza Dushku, Meg Tilly; *D:* Tom McLoughlin; *W:* Patricia MacLachlan; *C:* Kees Van Oostrum. **TV**

Journey Back to Oz **1971** Animated special features Dorothy and Toto returning to visit their friends in the magical land of Oz. **90m/C VHS.** *V:* Liza Minnelli, Ethel Merman, Paul Lynde, Milton Berle, Mickey Rooney, Danny Thomas.

Journey Beneath the Desert 🦴🦴 *Antinea, l'Amante Della Citta Sepolta* **1961** Three engineers discover the lost-but-always-found-in-the-movies kingdom of Atlantis when their helicopter's forced down in the sunny Sahara. A poor hostess with a rotten disposition, the mean sub-saharan queen doesn't roll out the welcome mat for her grounded guests, so a beautiful slave babe helps them make a hasty exit. Dawdling Euro production with adequate visuals. **105m/C VHS.** *FR IT* Haya Harareet, Jean-Louis Trintignant, Brad Fulton, Amedeo Nazzari, George Riviere, Giulia Rubini, Gabriele Tinti, Gian Marie Volonte; *D:* Edgar G. Ulmer, Giuseppe Masini, Frank Borzage.

Journey for Margaret 🦴🦴🦴 **1942** Young and Day star as an expectant American couple living in London during WWII so Young can cover the war for a newspaper back home. After she loses her baby during an air raid, Day heads back to the States. Young stays in London where he meets two young orphans and takes them under his wing. He decides to take them back to the United States and adopt them, but problems arise. A real tearjerker and a good story that shows the war through the eyes of children. O'Brien's first film. Based on the book by William L. White. **81m/B VHS.** Robert Young, Laraine Day, Fay Bainter, Signe Hasso, Margaret O'Brien, Nigel Bruce, G.P. (Tim) Huntley Jr., William Severn, Doris Lloyd, Halliwell Hobbes, Jill Esmond; ***D:*** Woodbridge S. Van Dyke.

Journey into Fear **1942** During WWII, an American armaments expert is smuggled out of Istanbul, but Axis agents are close behind. From the novel by Eric Ambler. **71m/B VHS.** Joseph Cotten, Dolores Del Rio, Orson Welles, Agnes Moorehead, Norman Foster; ***D:*** Norman Foster; ***C:*** Karl Struss.

Journey into Fear ½ *Burn Out* **1974** A remake of the 1942 Orson Welles classic about a geologist ensnared in Turkish intrigue and murder. **96m/C VHS.** *CA* Sam Waterston, Vincent Price, Shelley Winters, Donald Pleasence, Zero Mostel, Yvette Mimieux, Ian McShane; ***D:*** Daniel Mann; ***M:*** Alex North.

The Journey of August King ½ **1995 (PG-13)** Adapted by Ehle from his own 1971 novel, set in 1815, about a runaway slave (Newton) protected by a lonely farmer against the landowner and posse tracking her down. August King (Patric), a widower on his way home from town, comes upon Annalees (Newton), prize possession of powerful slaveowner Olaf Singletary (Drake). August, a highly principled man, resists helping her at first, for fear of breaking the law and losing his farm and only remaining possessions. But he rises to higher moral ground, deciding to help her find freedom, whatever the consequences. Director Duigan ("Sirens") crafts a thoughtful, but not particularly suspenseful, period piece of early American history. Patric/Newton relationship reflects the gradual feel of the film. Drake booms as slaveowner. Includes brief brutal scene of slave torture. **91m/C VHS.** Jason Patric, Thandie Newton, Larry Drake, Sam Waterston; ***D:*** John Duigan; ***W:*** John Ehle; ***C:*** Slawomir Idziak; ***M:*** Stephen Endelman.

Journey of Honor ½ **1991 (PG-13)** During a civil war in 17th century Japan, a nearly defeated Shogun sends his son, Lord Mayeda, to Spain to buy guns from King Phillip III. Along the way he must fight shipboard spies and fierce storms, and once Mayeda arrives in Spain, he is confronted by the evil Duke Don Pedro. In defeating Don Pedro, Mayeda saves King Phillip, gets his guns, and wins the love of Lady Cecilia. To get revenge, Don Pedro plots to capture the Japanese ship and enslave everyone on board. Lots of action and fine acting. Based on a story by martial artist Sho Kosugi. **107m/C VHS, Wide.** Sho Kosugi, David Essex, Kane (Takeshi) Kosugi, Christopher Lee, Norman Lloyd, Ronald Pickup, John Rhys-Davies, Dylan Kussman, Toshiro Mifune; ***D:*** Gordon Hessler.

Journey of Hope ½ **1990 (PG)** Powerful drama about Kurdish family that sells its material possessions in hopes of emigrating legally to Switzerland, where life will surely be better. During the perilous journey, smugglers take their money and the family must attempt crossing the formidable slopes of the Swiss Mountains on foot. Based on a true story. In Turkish with English subtitles. **111m/C VHS.** *SI* Necmettin Cobanoglu, Nur Surer, Emin Sivas, Yaman Okay, Mathias Gnaedinger, Dietmar Schoenherr; ***D:*** Xavier Koller; ***W:*** Xavier Koller. Oscars '90: Foreign Film.

The Journey of Jared Price ½ **2000** Sweet-natured but predictable gay coming of age tale. 19-year-old Jared (Spears) leaves Georgia for California and self-discovery, winding up in a youth hostel where he's befriended by Robert (Jacobson), who wants to be more than buddies. Jared eventually gets a job as a caretaker to elderly, blind Mrs. Haines (Craigg) and is soon pulled into a destructive relationship with the older Matthew (Tyler), Mrs. Haines son. **96m/C VHS.** Corey Spears, Josh Jacobson, Steve Tyler, Rocki Craigg; ***D:*** Dustin Lance Black; ***W:*** Dustin Lance Black; ***C:*** Tony Croll; ***M:*** Damon Intrabartolo.

The Journey of Natty Gann ½ **1985 (PG)** With the help of a wolf (brilliantly portrayed by a dog) and a drifter, a 14-year-old girl travels across the country in search of her father in this warm and touching film. Excellent Disney representation of life during the Great Depression. **101m/C VHS, DVD.** Meredith Salenger, John Cusack, Ray Wise, Scatman Crothers, Lainie Kazan, Verna Bloom; ***D:*** Jeremy Paul Kagan; ***W:*** Jeanne Rosenberg; ***C:*** Dick Bush; ***M:*** James Horner.

Journey Through Rosebud **1972** A re-enactment of the 1970s protest at Wounded Knee by Native Americans. **93m/C VHS.** Robert Forster, Eddie Little Sky; ***D:*** Tom Giles.

Journey to Spirit Island ½ **1992 (PG)** A young Native American girl dreams of her ancestors who are buried on Spirit Island, an ancient burial ground. However, the island is now scheduled to be developed into a resort. With the help of three friends the girl tries to protect the land. Filmed in the Pacific Northwest. **93m/C VHS.** Brandon Douglas, Gabriel Damon, Tony Acierto, Nick Ramus, Marie Antoinette Rodgers, Tarek McCarthy; ***D:*** Laszlo Pal.

Journey to the Center of the Earth **1959** A scientist and student undergo a hazardous journey to find the center of the earth and along the way they find the lost city of Atlantis. Based upon the Jules Verne novel. **132m/C VHS.** James Mason, Pat Boone, Arlene Dahl, Diane Baker, Thayer David, Alan Napier, Peter Ronson; ***D:*** Henry Levin.

Journey to the Center of the Earth **1988 (PG)** A young nanny and two teenage boys discover Atlantis while exploring a volcano. **83m/C VHS.** Nicola Cowper, Paul Carafotes, Ilan Mitchell-Smith; ***D:*** Rusty Lemorande; ***W:*** Rusty Lemorande, Kitty Chalmers.

Journey to the Center of the Earth **1999** Jules Verne's 1864 fantasy made its way to cable in this adventurous retelling. Geologist Theodore Lytton (Williams) is hired by wealthy Alice Hastings (Bergen) to find her husband, Casper (Brown), who disappeared seven years earlier during an expedition to a volcano in New Zealand. Lytton and his compatriots descend into deep caverns and discover a tunnel system leading to the planet's center and a new civilization that Hastings has usurped for his own greedy purposes. There's derring-do and even babes in animal-hide bikinis. **139m/C VHS, DVD.** Treat Williams, Jeremy London, Tushka Bergen, Hugh Keays-Byrne, Bryan Brown, Sarah Chadwick, Petra Yared, Tessa Wells; ***D:*** George Miller; ***W:*** Thomas Baum; ***C:*** John Stokes; ***M:*** Bruce Rowland. **CABLE**

Journey to the Center of Time ½ **1967** A scientist and his crew are hurled into a time trap when a giant reactor explodes. **83m/C VHS.** Lyle Waggoner, Scott Brady, Gigi Perreau, Anthony Eisley; ***D:*** David L. Hewitt.

Journey to the Far Side of the Sun *Doppelganger* **1969 (G)** Chaos erupts in the Earth's scientific community when it is discovered that a second, identical Earth is on the other side of the Sun. Both planets end up sending out identical exploratory missions. The denouement is worth the journey. **92m/C VHS, DVD, Wide.** *GB* Roy Thinnes, Ian Hendry, Lynn Loring, Patrick Wymark, Loni von Friedl, Herbert Lom, Ed Bishop; ***D:*** Robert Parrish; ***W:*** Gerry Anderson; ***C:*** John Read; ***M:*** Barry Gray.

Journey to the Lost City ½ *Tiger of Bengal* **1958** Architect living in India happens upon a lost city, the rulership of which is being contested by two brothers. In the midst of fighting snakes and tigers, he falls in love with Paget, a beautiful dancer. This feature is actually a poorly edited hybrid of two Lang German adventures, "Der Tiger von Eschnapur" and "Das Indische Grabmal" merged for U.S. release. **95m/C VHS.** *FR IT GE* Debra Paget, Paul (Christian) Hubschmid, Walter Reyer, Claus Holm, Sabine Bethmann, Valeri Inkizhinov, Rene Deltgen, Luciana Paluzzi; ***D:*** Fritz Lang.

Joy House *The Love Cage; Les Felins* **1964** French playboy Marc (Delon) seduces the wife of an American mobster who sends his goons after him. Marc hides out by becoming the chauffeur to Barbara (Albright) at her chateau, which is also where he meets his employer's niece, Melinda (Fonda). Soon, Marc is part of a romantic triangle—or is it quartet since Barbara's lover, Vincent (Oumansky), is also living there. And don't forget the gangsters, who certainly haven't forgotten Marc. Complicated plot with no particular payoff. **98m/B VHS, DVD, Wide.** Jane Fonda, Alain Delon, Lola Albright, Andre Oumansky, Sorrell Booke; ***D:*** Rene Clement; ***W:*** Rene Clement; ***C:*** Henri Decae; ***M:*** Lalo Schifrin.

The Joy Luck Club **1993 (R)** Universal themes in mother/daughter relationships are explored in a context Hollywood first rejected as too narrow, but which proved to be a modest sleeper hit. Tan skillfully weaves the plot of her 1989 best-seller into a screenplay which centers around young June's (Ming-Na) going-away party. Slowly the stories of four Chinese women, who meet weekly to play mah-jongg, are unraveled. Each vignette reveals life in China for the four women and the tragedies they survived, before reaching into the present to capture the relationships between the mothers and their daughters. Powerful, relevant, and moving. **136m/C VHS, Wide.** Tsai Chin, Kieu Chinh, France Nuyen, Rosalind Chao, Tamlyn Tomita, Lisa Lu, Lauren Tom, Ming Na, Michael Paul Chan, Andrew McCarthy, Christopher Rich, Russell Wong, Victor Wong, Vivian Wu, Jack Ford, Diane Baker; ***D:*** Wayne Wang; ***W:*** Amy Tan, Ronald Bass.

The Joy of Knowledge ½ *Le Gai Savoir* **1965** Godard's experimental use of language and image in a plotless narrative. Berto and Leaud sit together on a bare sound stage and are exposed to popular culture through images, word association, and conversation. In French with English subtitles. **96m/C VHS.** *FR* Juliet Berto, Jean-Pierre Leaud; ***D:*** Jean-Luc Godard; ***W:*** Jean-Luc Godard.

Joy of Living **1938** Vintage screwball farce finds successful songstress Maggie (Dunne) the sole support of her n'er-do-well family. Maggie's aggressively courted by playboy Dan Brewster (Faribanks Jr.) and finally (after numerous silly complications) they fall in love. ♫You Couldn't Be Cuter; A Heavenly Party; What's Good About Goodnight; Just Let Me Look At You. **90m/B VHS.** Irene Dunne, Douglas Fairbanks Jr., Alice Brady, Guy Kibbee, Jean Dixon, Eric Blore, Lucille Ball, Warren Hymer, Billy Gilbert, Frank Milan; ***D:*** Tay Garnett; ***W:*** Graham Baker, Allan Scott, Gene Towne; ***C:*** Joseph Walker; ***M:*** Jerome Kern, Dorothy Fields.

Joy of Sex **1984 (R)** An undercover narcotics agent is sent to Southern California's Richard M. Nixon High School to investigate the school's extracurricular activities. Typical teen sex flick; no relation to the book. **93m/C VHS.** Cameron Dye, Michelle Meyrink, Colleen Camp, Christopher Lloyd, Ernie Hudson, Lisa Langlois; ***D:*** Martha Coolidge; ***W:*** Kathleen Rowell.

Joy Ride **2001 (R)** Released about the same time as fellow road thriller/horror entry "Jeepers Creepers," this superior outing benefits from better humor, pacing, and performances. Nice guy Lewis (Walker), a college freshman, offers to drive friend/potential squeeze Venna (Sobieski) back home from Colorado for the holidays. Unfortunately for Lewis, roguish brother Fuller (Zahn) calls Lewis to bail him out of jail in Utah and sticks around for the ride. Fuller instigates a CB radio prank in which Lewis, imitating a woman's voice, invites a trucker with the handle Rusty Nail to the hotel room next to theirs. The next day, the man in the room is found close to death in the middle of the road, and the trio has a very angry trucker on their tail. Taut countrywide chase thrills are reminiscent of Spielberg's "Duel." Great mixture of shocks and black humor. **96m/C VHS, DVD, Wide.** *US* Paul Walker, Steve Zahn, Leelee Sobieski, Jessica Bowman, Stuart Stone, Basil Wallace, Brian Leckner; ***D:*** John Dahl; ***W:*** J.J. Abrams, Clay Tarver; ***C:*** Jeffrey Jur; ***M:*** Marco Beltrami; ***V:*** Ted Levine.

Joy Ride to Nowhere **1978 (PG)** Two young women steal a Cadillac with $2 million in the trunk and ride away with the owner hot on their tail. **86m/C VHS.** Leslie Ackerman, Sandy Serrano, Len Lesser, Mel Welles, Ron Ross, Speed Stearns.

Joy Sticks woof! **1983 (R)** Joy sticks in question are down at the arcade. Businessman wants to shut down local video game palace. Inhabitants just say no. **88m/C VHS.** Joe Don Baker, Leif Green, Jim Greenleaf, Scott McGinnis, Jonathan (Jon Francis) Gries; ***D:*** Greydon Clark.

Joyful Laughter *Risate di Gioia* **1960** The dreary life of an Italian movie bit player draws strength from Magnani's powerful emotions as she repeatedly comes near to success only to find disappointment. Set in Rome. With English subtitles. **106m/B VHS.** *IT* Anna Magnani, Ben Gazzara, Carla Pisacane, Fred Clark; ***D:*** Mario Monicelli; ***W:*** Suso Cecchi D'Amico, Agenore Incrocci; ***C:*** Leonida Barboni; ***M:*** Lelio Luttazzi.

Joyless Street ½ *Street of Sorrow; Die Freudlosse Gasse* **1925** Silent film focuses on the dismal life of the middle class in Austria during an economic crisis. Lovely piano score accompanies the film. **96m/B VHS.** *GE* Greta Garbo, Werner Krauss, Asta Nielson, Jaro Furth, Loni Nest, Max Kohlhase, Silva Torf, Karl Ettlinger, Ilka Gruning, Agnes Esterhazy, Alexander Musky, Valeska Gert; ***D:*** G.W. Pabst; ***W:*** Willi Haas; ***C:*** Guido Seeber, Curt Oertel, Walter Robert Lach.

Joyride ½ **1977 (R)** Mistreated by a union official, three friends steal a car for a joy ride and plummet into a life of crime. **91m/C VHS.** Desi Arnaz Jr., Robert Carradine, Melanie Griffith, Anne Lockhart; ***D:*** Joseph Ruben.

Joyride **1997 (R)** Three friends make the mistake of stealing a car that belongs to a beautiful blonde assassin, who'll stop at nothing to get her wheels back (her latest victim is stashed in the trunk). **92m/C VHS.** Tobey Maguire, Wilson Cruz, Amy Hathaway, Chrisstina Naify, James Karen, Adam West, Benicio Del Toro, Judson Mills; ***D:*** Quinton Peeples; ***W:*** Quinton Peeples; ***C:*** S. Douglas Smith. **VIDEO**

Ju Dou **1990 (PG-13)** Breath-taking story of an aging factory owner in search of an heir. He takes a third wife, but she finds caring in the arms of another man, when her husband's brutality proves too much. Beautiful color cinematography, excellent acting, and epic story. Oscar nominee for Best Foreign Film. In Chinese with English subtitles. **98m/C VHS, DVD.** *CH* Gong Li, Li Bao-Tian, Li Wei, Zhang Yi, Zheng Jian; ***D:*** Zhang Yimou; ***W:*** Liu Heng; ***C:*** Gu Changwei, Yang Lun; ***M:*** Xia Rujin, Jiping Zhao.

Juarez **1939** A revolutionary leader overthrows the Mexican government and then becomes President of the country. Based on the true story of Benito Pablo Juarez. **132m/B VHS.** Paul Muni, John Garfield, Bette Davis, Claude Rains, Gale Sondergaard, Charles Halton; ***D:*** William Dieterle; ***C:*** Gaetano Antonio "Tony" Gaudio.

Jubal **1956** A rancher (Borgnine) seeks advice from a cowhand (Ford) about pleasing his wife, but another cowhand (Steiger) implies that Ford is "advising" Borgnine's wife, as well. A western take on "Othello." **101m/C VHS.** Glenn Ford, Rod Steiger, Ernest Borgnine, Felicia Farr, Charles Bronson, Valerie French, Noah Beery Jr.; ***D:*** Delmer Daves.

Jubilee Trail ½ **1954** Wagon trail western follows the lives of a group of pioneers from New Orleans to California. A woman goes through a marriage, a baby, and her husband's death. Ralston has some good tunes in this lush picture. **103m/C VHS.** Vera (Hruba) Ralston, Joan Leslie, Forrest Tucker, John Russell, Ray Middleton, Pat O'Brien; ***D:*** Joseph Kane.

Jud ½ **1971 (PG)** Society's refusal to understand a young soldier returning from the Vietnam conflict leads him to violence and tragedy. Jennings' first film; music by Phillips of Creedence Clearwater Revival. **80m/C VHS.** Joseph Kaufmann, Robert Deman, Alix Wyeth, Norman Burton, Claudia Jennings,

Maurice Sherbanee, Vic Dunlop, Bonnie Bittner; ***D:*** Gunther Collins; ***M:*** Stu Phillips.

Jud Suess 🦴🦴🦴 **1940** Classic, scandalous Nazi anti-Semitic tract about a Jew who rises to power under the duchy of Wuerttemberg by stepping on, abusing, and raping Aryans. A film that caused riots at its screenings and tragedy for its cast and crew, and the Third Reich's most notorious fictional expression of policy. In German with English subtitles. **100m/B VHS.** *GE* Ferdinand Marian, Werner Krauss, Heinrich George, Kristina Soderbaum, Eugene Klopfer; ***D:*** Veit Harlan.

Judas Kiss 🦴🦴½ **1998 (R)** Coco (Gugino) and her lover Junior (Baker-Denny) kidnap New Orleans exec Ben Dyson (Wise), but during the crime Coco shoots a woman who turns out to be Patty Hornbeck (Penberthy), the wife of a powerful Senator (Holbrook). Assigned to the case are detective David Friedman (Rickman) and FBI agent Sadie Hawkins (Thompson) and their investigation uncovers some secrets, including the fact that Patty and the kidnapped Dyson were having an affair. Uneven crime drama with an interesting cast. **108m/C VHS.** Emma Thompson, Alan Rickman, Carla Gugino, Simon Baker, Hal Holbrook, Gil Bellows, Til Schweiger, Greg Wise, Lisa Eichhorn, Beverly Penberthy; ***D:*** Sebastian Gutierrez; ***W:*** Sebastian Gutierrez; ***C:*** James Chressanthis; ***M:*** Christopher Young.

The Judas Project: The Ultimate Encounter 🦴½ **1994 (PG-13)** Religious fantasy finds Jesse battling corruption and pseudo-religious figures in a fight to save a violent and decaying world. But Jesse's destroyed by his own disciple, Jude. Sound familiar? (There's even a cruxifixion scene.) **98m/C VHS.** John O'Bannion, Ramy Zada, Richard Herd; ***D:*** James H. Barden; ***C:*** Bryan England.

Jude 🦴🦴🦴 *Jude the Obscure* **1996 (R)** Engrossing retelling of Thomas Hardy's depressing 1896 novel "Jude the Obscure," set in his fictional Wessex. Country stonemason Jude (Eccleston) hopes to improve his impoverished lot in life by becoming a student at Christminister University. But first he's distracted into an unwise marriage with lively Arabella (Griffiths), who soon leaves him, and then into an ill-fated romance with his capricious cousin Sue Brideshead (Winslet). Class and societal barriers prove impossible for the couple to overcome and lead to a shocking tragedy. Hardy's book was so badly received by critics that he never wrote another novel and stuck to poetry for the rest of his life. **123m/C VHS.** *GB* Christopher Eccleston, Kate Winslet, Liam Cunningham, Rachel Griffiths; ***D:*** Michael Winterbottom; ***W:*** Hossein Amini; ***C:*** Eduardo Serra; ***M:*** Adrian Johnston.

Jude the Obscure 🦴🦴½ **1971** Thomas Hardy's last novel is a tragic, bleak story of mismatched lovers and blighted ambitions. Jude is a poor stonemason whose dream is to get a proper education and marry his beloved cousin. Failing to get into Oxford he is seduced by a farm girl, whom he marries and fathers a child by (a gnome-like creature named "Father Time"). Meanwhile, his cousin marries a schoolteacher who disgusts her. Finally, the two thwarted lovers marry, only to find themselves living in poverty and hopelessness. After this novel (said to be Hardy's favorite), he devoted the rest of his long life to poetry. On three cassettes. **262m/C VHS.** *GB* Robert Powell, Daphne Heard, Alex Marshall, John Franklyn-Robbins, Fiona Walker; ***D:*** Hugh David; ***W:*** Harry Green. **TV**

Judex 🦴🦴½ **1964** Judex, a sensitive cloaked hero-avenger, fights master criminal gangs. In French with English subtitles. Remake of the silent French serial. **103m/B VHS.** *FR IT* Channing Pollock, Francine Berge, Jacques Jouanneau; ***D:*** Georges Franju; ***M:*** Maurice Jarre.

The Judge 🦴½ **1949** A courtroom crime-drama about the consequences of infidelity. A lawyer sends an acquitted hit man to kill his wife and her lover. Things go amiss and the lawyer winds up dead. **69m/B VHS.** Milburn Stone, Katherine DeMille, Paul Guilfoyle, Jonathan Hale; ***D:*** Elmer Clifton.

Judge & Jury 🦴½ **1996 (R)** Convicted killer Joseph Miller (Keith) dies in the electric chair but then manages to return from the dead to get revenge. So how do you kill someone who's already dead? Well, Michael Silvano (Kove) will have to find a way to send Miller back where he belongs. **98m/C VHS, DVD.** David Keith, Martin Kove, Laura Johnson, Thomas Ian Nicholas, Paul Koslo; ***D:*** John Eyres; ***W:*** John Eyres, John Cianetti, Amanda I. Kirpaul; ***C:*** Bob Paone; ***M:*** Johnathon Flood. **VIDEO**

The Judge and the Assassin 🦴🦴🦴½ *Le Juge et L'assassin* **1975** Intriguing courtroom drama. A prejudiced judge has his values challenged when he must decide if a child-killer is insane or not. The relationship that develops between the judge and the killer is the film's focus. Excellent direction by Tavernier. In French with English subtitles. **130m/C VHS, Wide.** *FR* Philippe Noiret, Michel Galabru, Isabelle Huppert, Jean-Claude Brialy, Yves Robert, Rene Faure; ***D:*** Bertrand Tavernier; ***W:*** Bertrand Tavernier, Jean Aurenche, Pierre Bost; ***C:*** Pierre William Glenn; ***M:*** Philippe Sarde. Cesar '77: Writing, Score.

Judge Dredd 🦴½ **1995 (R)** Futuristic lawman Dredd (Stallone), who acts as cop, judge, jury, and executioner, is framed for murder by his "brother" Rico (Assante), a renegade misfit. With the help of a female Judge (Lane) and an ex-con (Schneider), Dredd fights to clear his name and save the people of Mega City One. Big names, big bangs, big budget—big disappointment. Dialogue makes "Rambo" sound like Shakespeare, and the choppy, convoluted plot doesn't help. Schneider provides a rare bright spot while acting circles around Sly, who hoped (in vain) that the project would provide him with another profitable action franchise. The source comic book has been a cult favorite in England for 20 years. **96m/C VHS, DVD, Wide.** Sylvester Stallone, Armand Assante, Diane Lane, Rob Schneider, Joan Chen, Juergen Prochnow, Max von Sydow; ***D:*** Danny Cannon; ***W:*** Steven E. de Souza, Michael De Luca, William Wisher; ***C:*** Adrian Biddle; ***M:*** Alan Silvestri.

Judge Horton and the Scottsboro Boys 🦴🦴½ **1976** A courtroom drama focusing on a famous 1931 trial. A courageous judge must battle the South in the case of nine black men charged with gang-raping two white women. **100m/C VHS.** Arthur Hill, Vera Miles, Ken Kercheval, Suzanne Lederer, Tom Ligon; ***D:*** Fielder Cook. **TV**

Judge Priest 🦴🦴🦴 **1934** Small-town judge in the old South stirs up the place with stinging humor and commonsense observances as he tangles with prejudices and civil injustices. Funny, warm slice-of-life is occasionally defeated by racist characterizations. Ford remade it later as "The Sun Shines Bright." Taken from the Irvin S. Cobb stories. **80m/B VHS.** Will Rogers, Stepin Fetchit, Anita Louise, Henry B. Walthall; ***D:*** John Ford.

The Judge Steps Out 🦴🦴½ **1949** Pleasant, light comedy about a henpecked, Bostonian judge who decides he's had enough and heads for balmy California. There he finds a job in a restaurant and, more importantly, a sympathetic friend in its female owner. He soon finds himself falling for the woman, and realizes he faces an important decision. **91m/B VHS.** Alexander Knox, Ann Sothern, George Tobias, Sharyn Moffett, Florence Bates, Frieda Inescort, Myrna Dell, Ian Wolfe, H.B. Warner; ***D:*** Boris Ingster.

Judgment 🦴🦴🦴 **1990 (PG-13)** A devout Catholic couple are shocked to learn that their young son has been molested by the popular priest of their small Louisiana parish. When they find out their son is not the first victim, and other families have been coerced into silence, they vow to fight back. Tasteful treatment of a real court case. **89m/C VHS, DVD.** Keith Carradine, Blythe Danner, Jack Warden, David Strathairn, Bob Gunton, Mitchell Ryan, Michael Faustino; ***D:*** Tom Topor; ***W:*** Tom Topor. **CABLE**

Judgment at Nuremberg 🦴🦴🦴🦴 **1961** It's 1948 and a group of high-level Nazis are on trial for war crimes. Chief Justice Tracy must resist political pressures as he presides over the trials. Excellent performances throughout, especially by Dietrich and Garland. Considers to what extent an individual may be held accountable for actions committed under orders of a superior officer. Consuming account of the Holocaust and WWII; deeply moving and powerful. Based on a "Playhouse 90" TV program. **178m/B VHS.** Spencer Tracy, Burt Lancaster, Richard Widmark, Montgomery Clift, Maximilian Schell, Judy Garland, Marlene Dietrich, William Shatner, Edward Binns, Werner Klemperer, Torben Meyer, Martin Brandt, Kenneth MacKenna, Alan Baxter, Ray Teal, Karl Swenson; ***D:*** Stanley Kramer; ***W:*** Abby Mann; ***C:*** Ernest Laszlo; ***M:*** Ernest Gold. Oscars '61: Actor (Schell), Adapt. Screenplay; Golden Globes '62: Actor—Drama (Schell), Director (Kramer); N.Y. Film Critics '61: Actor (Schell), Screenplay.

Judgment Day 🦴 **1988 (PG-13)** Four college buddies pick the wrong New England town for their vacation. It seems that the town made a deal with the Devil in 1689 to save themselves from the plague, and now the Dark Master is here to collect. **93m/C VHS.** Kenneth McLeod, David Anthony Smith, Monte Markham, Gloria Hayes, Peter Mark Richman, Cesar Romero; ***D:*** Ferde Grofe Jr.

Judgment Day 🦴🦴 **1999 (R)** A meteor collides with an asteroid in deep space and if fragments from the mishap should hit Earth, it's goodbye planet. One scientist has an idea how to prevent disaster but he's kidnapped by a cult leader who thinks the planet's doom is foretold. Now the government has to get the scientist back before it's too late. **90m/C VHS, DVD.** Mario Van Peebles, Ice-T, Suzy Amis, Tommy (Tiny) Lister, Coolio; ***D:*** John Terlesky; ***W:*** William Carson; ***C:*** Maximo Munzi; ***M:*** Joseph Williams. **VIDEO**

Judgment in Berlin 🦴🦴½ *Escape to Freedom* **1988 (PG)** East German family hijacks a U.S. airliner into West Germany, and then must stand trial in Berlin before a troubled American judge. Based on a true 1978 incident and the book by Herbert J. Stern. **92m/C VHS.** Martin Sheen, Sam Wanamaker, Max Gail, Sean Penn, Heinz Hoenig, Carl Lumbly, Max Volkert Martens, Harris Yulin, Jutta Speidel, Juerger Heinrich; ***D:*** Leonard Penn; ***W:*** Joshua Sinclair; ***M:*** Peter Goldfoot.

Judgment Night 🦴🦴 **1993 (R)** Four macho buddies on their way to a boxing match detour a highway traffic jam via surface streets and find themselves witnesses to a murder. The rest of their guys-night-out is spent trying to escape a gloomy ghetto and determined killer (played convincingly by Leary). All of the action takes place after dark on the streets and in the sewers and, subsequently, the scenes are extremely dark with only a burnt orange lighting. Lots of action and a little oomph. Based on a story by Lewis Colick and Jere Cunningham. **109m/C VHS, DVD.** Emilio Estevez, Cuba Gooding Jr., Stephen Dorff, Denis Leary, Jeremy Piven, Peter Greene; ***D:*** Stephen Hopkins; ***W:*** Lewis Colick; ***C:*** Peter Levy; ***M:*** Alan Silvestri.

Judicial Consent 🦴🦴½ **1994** Gwen Warwick (Bedelia) is an accomplished criminal court judge with a bland husband (Patton) and a lot of unfulfilled desires. At least one desire is taken care of when Gwen succumbs to the charms of handsome law clerk Martin (Wirth). Then her colleague Charles (Coleman) is murdered and all the evidence points to Gwen. She knows she's been set up but can Gwen prove her innocence? Familiar plot, good performances although Patton gets stuck in an underwritten role. **101m/C VHS.** Bonnie Bedelia, Dabney Coleman, Billy Wirth, Will Patton, Lisa Blount; ***D:*** William Bindley; ***W:*** William Bindley; ***M:*** Christopher Young.

Judith of Bethulia 🦴🦴🦴 **1914** A young widow uses her charm and wits to save her city from attack by the Assyrians. Based on the Apocrypha, this is the last film Griffith directed for Biograph. It was re-released as "Her Condoned Sin" in 1971, including two reels of Griffith's outtakes. **65m/B VHS.** Blanche Sweet, Henry B. Walthall, Mae Marsh, Robert "Bobbie" Harron, Lillian Gish, Dorothy Gish, Kate Bruce, Harry Carey Sr.; ***D:*** D.W. Griffith; ***W:*** D.W. Griffith.

Judy Berlin 🦴🦴½ **1999** It's a school day in the placid suburb of Babylon, Long Island. Teacher Sue (Barrie) likes to flirt with weary principal Arthur (Dishy) who has a high-maintenance wife, Alice (Kahn), and a mopey grown son, David (Harnick), whose homecoming visit has gone on too long. Sue has her own offspring problems with sunnily ditsy, aspiring actress daughter Judy (Falco). Then Judy and David meet cute and a solar eclipse seems to inspire strange behavior. **97m/B VHS.** Barbara Barrie, Bob (Robert) Dishy, Edie Falco, Aaron Harnick, Madeline Kahn, Carlin Glynn, Julie Kavner, Anne Meara; ***D:*** Eric Mendelsohn; ***W:*** Eric Mendelsohn; ***C:*** Jeffrey Seckendorf; ***M:*** Michael Nicholas. Sundance '99: Director (Mendelsohn).

Juggernaut 🦴½ **1937** Not the classic disaster film of the '70s. A young woman hires a sinister doctor (Karloff) to murder her wealthy husband. The doctor, who happens to be insane, does away with the husband and then goes on a poisoning spree. Seems to drag on forever. **64m/B VHS.** Boris Karloff, Mona Goya, Arthur Margetson.

Juggernaut 🦴🦴🦴 **1974 (PG-13)** Well-done drama about a doomed luxury liner. A madman plants bombs aboard a cruise ship and mocks the crew about his plan over the wireless. The countdown ensues, while the bomb experts struggle to find the explosives. Suspenseful with good direction. **109m/C VHS.** *GB* Richard Harris, Omar Sharif, David Hemmings, Anthony Hopkins, Shirley Knight, Ian Holm, Roy Kinnear, Freddie Jones; ***D:*** Richard Lester; ***W:*** Richard DeKoker; ***C:*** Gerry Fisher; ***M:*** Ken Thorne.

The Juggler of Notre Dame 🦴🦴½ **1984** A hobo and a street juggler embark on an unusual journey that will change the lives of the people they meet. Based on a medieval folktale about the special gift given to the Virgin Mary on Christmas morning. **110m/C VHS.** Carl Carlson, Patrick Collins, Melinda Dillon, Merlin Olsen, Gene Roche.

Juice 🦴🦴½ **1992 (R)** Day-to-day street life of four Harlem youths as they try to earn respect ("juice") in their neighborhood. Q, an aspiring deejay, is talked into a robbery by his friends but everything takes a turn for the worse when one of the others, Bishop, gets hold of a gun. The gritty look and feel of the drama comes naturally to Dickerson in his directorial debut. Prior to his first film, Dickerson served as cinematographer for Spike Lee's "Do the Right Thing" and "Jungle Fever." **95m/C VHS, DVD, Wide.** Omar Epps, Jermaine "Huggy" Hopkins, Tupac Shakur, Khalil Kain, Cindy Herron, Vincent Laresca, Samuel L. Jackson; ***D:*** Ernest R. Dickerson; ***W:*** Gerard Brown, Ernest R. Dickerson; ***C:*** Larry Banks.

Juke Joint 🦴½ **1947** "Amos 'n Andy" star Spencer Williams acted in and directed this tale of two men who arrive in Hollywood with only 25 cents between them. Features an all-black cast and musical numbers. **60m/B VHS.** Spencer Williams Jr., Judy Jones, Mantan Moreland; ***D:*** Spencer Williams Jr.

Jules and Jim 🦴🦴🦴🦴 *Jules et Jim* **1962** Beautiful film with perfect casting, particularly Moreau. Spanning from 1912 to 1932, it is the story of a friendship between two men and their 20-year love for the same woman. Werner is the shy German Jew and Serre the fun-loving Frenchman, who meet as students. The two men discover and woo the bohemian, destructive Moreau, although it is Werner she marries. After WWI, the friends are reunited but the marriage of Moreau and Werner is in trouble and she has an affair with Serre, which leads to tragedy for all three. Adapted from the novel by Henri-Pierre Roche. In French with English subtitles. **104m/B VHS, DVD, Wide.** *FR* Jeanne Moreau, Oskar Werner, Henri Serre, Marie DuBois, Vanna Urbino; ***D:*** Francois Truffaut; ***W:*** Jean Gruault, Francois Truffaut; ***C:*** Raoul Coutard; ***M:*** Georges Delerue.

Julia ½ **1977 (PG)** The story recounted in Lillian Hellman's fictional memoir "Pentimento." Fonda plays Hellman as she risks her life smuggling money into Germany during WWII for the sake of Julia, her beloved childhood friend (Redgrave), who is working in the Resistance. All cast members shine in their performances; watch for Streep in her screen debut. **118m/C VHS.** Jane Fonda, Jason Robards Jr., Vanessa Redgrave, Maximilian Schell, Hal Holbrook, Rosemary Murphy, Meryl Streep, Lisa Pelikan; ***D:*** Fred Zinnemann; ***W:*** Alvin Sargent; ***M:*** Georges Delerue. Oscars '77: Adapt. Screenplay, Support. Actor (Robards), Support. Actress (Redgrave); British Acad. '78: Actress (Fonda), Film, Screenplay, Support. Actress (Redgrave); Golden Globes '78: Actress—Drama (Fonda), Support. Actress (Redgrave); L.A. Film Critics '77: Cinematog., Support. Actor (Robards), Support. Actress (Redgrave); N.Y. Film Critics '77: Support. Actor (Schell); Writers Guild '77: Adapt. Screenplay.

Julia and Julia ½ **1987 (R)** A beautiful American woman in Trieste is tossed between two seemingly parallel dimensions, one in which her husband died six years earlier in a car crash, and the other in which he didn't. A purposefully obscure Italian-made psychological thriller, filmed in high-definition video and then transferred to film stock, it has a very different look and feel from other films of the genre. Intriguing and engaging most of the time, slow moving and confusing some of the time, it ultimately challenges but fails adequately to reward the viewer. **98m/C VHS.** Kathleen Turner, Sting, Gabriel Byrne, Gabriele Ferzetti, Angela Goodwin; ***D:*** Peter Del Monte; ***W:*** Joe Minion, Sandro Petraglia, Silvia Napolitano, Peter Del Monte; ***C:*** Giuseppe Rotunno; ***M:*** Maurice Jarre.

Julia Has Two Lovers **1991 (R)** Minimalist comedy-drama about a woman torn between two men—her dull fiance and a mysterious phone caller. Mostly a long phone conversation; don't expect blistering action. **87m/C VHS.** Daphna Kastner, David Duchovny, David Charles; ***D:*** Bashar Shbib.

Julia Misbehaves **1948** Charming comedy that has Garson returning to ex-husband Pidgeon and daughter Taylor after an 18-year absence. Taylor is about to be married at a chateau in France and wants Garson to be there. While traveling to France from England, Garson encounters a bunch of colorful circus characters who are taking their act to Paris. Wonderful slapstick scenes give the stars a chance to have some real fun. Based on the novel "The Nutmeg Tree" by Margery Sharp. **99m/B VHS.** Greer Garson, Walter Pidgeon, Peter Lawford, Cesar Romero, Elizabeth Taylor, Lucile Watson, Nigel Bruce, Mary Boland, Reginald Owen, Veda Ann Borg, Joi Lansing; ***D:*** Jack Conway.

Julian Po ½ *The Tears of Julian Po* **1997 (PG-13)** Nondescript bookkeeper Julian Po (Slater) has his car break down near an isolated mountain community and immediately comes under suspicion when he checks into the local boarding house, which never gets any guests. And the next day Julian's car has vanished, stranding him in nowherestown. The locals become convinced he's a hit man and demand explanations. Julian unexpectedly blurts out that the only person he's planning to kill is himself. Immediately the center of attention, Julian becomes confessor to everyone's darkest secrets and a recipient of their constant kindnesses but since he really doesn't intend to off himself, he's also got some unexpected problems. **82m/C VHS.** Christian Slater, Robin Tunney, Michael Parks, Frankie Faison, Harve Presnell, Allison Janney, Cherry Jones, Latanya Richardson, Dina Spybey, Zeljko Ivanek; ***D:*** Alan Wade; ***W:*** Alan Wade; ***C:*** Bernd Heinl; ***M:*** Patrick Williams.

Julien Donkey-boy ½ **1999 (R)** Harmony Korine's story of a schizophrenic young man and his disturbed family is the first American movie to be filmed using the principles of the restrictive Danish filmmaking method known as Dogma '95. Apparently, there must be some kind of restriction on the plot and narrative as well, because the audience is merely shown disturbing images of the mentally ill Julien (Bremner), his pregnant sister Pearl (Sevigny), his jock brother Chris (Neumann) and their abusive father (Herzog). Largely improvised and shot using hand-held digital video cameras, this unsettling project is for the cinematically adventurous only. **101m/C VHS, DVD, Wide.** Ewen Bremner, Chloe Sevigny, Werner Herzog, Evan Neumann, Joyce Korine, Chrissy Kobylak, Alvin Law; ***D:*** Harmony Korine; ***W:*** Harmony Korine; ***C:*** Anthony Dod Mantle.

Juliet of the Spirits *Giulietta Degli Spiriti* **1965** Fellini uses the sparse story of a woman (Fellini's real-life wife) deliberating over her husband's possible infidelity to create a wild, often senseless surrealistic film. With a highly symbolic internal logic and complex imagery, Fellini's fantasy ostensibly elucidates the inner life of a modern woman. In Italian with English subtitles. **142m/C VHS, DVD, Wide.** *IT* Giulietta Masina, Valentina Cortese, Sylva Koscina, Mario Pisu, Sandra Milo, Caterina Boratto, Valeska Gert; ***D:*** Federico Fellini; ***W:*** Federico Fellini, Tullio Pinelli, Ennio Flaiano, Brunello Rondi; ***C:*** Gianni Di Venanzo; ***M:*** Nino Rota. N.Y. Film Critics '65: Foreign Film.

Julius Caesar ½ **1953** All-star version of the Shakespearean tragedy, heavily acclaimed and deservedly so. Working directly from the original Shakespeare, director Mankiewicz produced a lifelike, yet poetic production. **121m/B VHS.** James Mason, Marlon Brando, John Gielgud, Greer Garson, Deborah Kerr, Louis Calhern, Edmond O'Brien, George Macready, John Hoyt, Michael Pate; ***D:*** Joseph L. Mankiewicz; ***W:*** Joseph L. Mankiewicz; ***C:*** Joseph Ruttenberg; ***M:*** Miklos Rozsa. Oscars '53: Art Dir./Set Dec., B&W; British Acad. '53: Actor (Brando), Actor (Gielgud); Natl. Bd. of Review '53: Actor (Mason).

Julius Caesar **1970** Subpar adaptation of the Shakespeare play about political greed and corruption within the Roman Empire. **116m/C VHS.** *GB* Charlton Heston, John Gielgud, Jason Robards Jr., Richard Chamberlain, Robert Vaughn, Diana Rigg; ***D:*** Stuart Burge.

July Group ½ **197?** A Quaker family's peaceful existence is threatened when kidnappers invade their home and hold them for ransom. **75m/C VHS.** Nicholas (Nick) Campbell, Calvin Butler, Maury Chaykin.

Jumanji ½ **1995 (PG)** For the past 26 years Alan Parish (Williams) has been stuck in the netherworld of Jumanji, a jungle-themed board game that sucks players into its alternate universe. When unsuspecting youngsters Judy (Dunst) and Peter (Pierce) happen upon the game and begin to play, they release Williams and a jungle full of rampaging beasts from the game and into the present. Loosely based on Chris Van Allsburg's children's book, the film version relies too heavily on cutting-edge special effects to make up for a thin story. Many of the creatures and effects are utterly too bizarre and unsettling for younger audiences. With a $65 million pricetag, Jumanji is definitely a roll of the dice. **104m/C VHS, DVD.** Robin Williams, Kirsten Dunst, Bonnie Hunt, Bradley Michael Pierce, Bebe Neuwirth, Jonathan Hyde, David Alan Grier, Adam Hann-Byrd; ***D:*** Joe Johnston; ***W:*** Jonathan Hensleigh; ***C:*** Thomas Ackerman; ***M:*** James Horner.

Jumpin' at the Boneyard **1992 (R)** Gritty family drama about the trials of two dispossessed brothers, set on the streets of New York. Deeply depressed, out-of-work, divorced Manny hates his recently deceased father, adores his mother, and is estranged from his younger brother, Danny. Danny is a scared crack addict who's supported by a hooker/girlfriend. The two brothers reunite for a trip into their scarred past when Danny tries to rob his brother's apartment to get dope money. Manny starts to believe that the only way to redeem his own life is to get his brother into a rehab program. Good acting helps to overcome some script weaknesses but this is one depressing movie. **107m/C VHS.** Tim Roth, Alexis Arquette, Danitra Vance, Samuel L. Jackson, Kathleen Chalfant, Luis Guzman; ***D:*** Jeff Stanzler; ***W:*** Jeff Stanzler.

Jumpin' Jack Flash ½ **1986 (R)** A bank worker is humorously embroiled in international espionage when her computer terminal picks up distress signals from a British agent in Russia. Marshall's directing debut. Good performances from a fun cast and a particularly energetic effort by Goldberg are held back by an average and predictable script. **98m/C VHS.** Whoopi Goldberg, Stephen Collins, Carol Kane, Annie Potts, Jonathan Pryce, James Belushi, Jon Lovitz, John Wood; ***Cameos:*** Michael McKean, Tracey Ullman, Roscoe Lee Browne, Sara Botsford, Jeroen Krabbe, Phil Hartman, Tracy Reiner, Paxton Whitehead, Jamey Sheridan, Garry Marshall, Peter Michael Goetz; ***D:*** Penny Marshall; ***W:*** David Franzoni; ***C:*** Jan De Bont; ***M:*** Thomas Newman.

Jumping Jacks **1952** Martin and Lewis are a couple of nightclub performers who wind up in the paratroop corps instead of performing their act for the soldiers. Martin gets to sing and Lewis gets to parachute into enemy territory and capture a general. **96m/B VHS.** Dean Martin, Jerry Lewis, Mona Freeman, Don DeFore, Robert Strauss, Ray Teal; ***D:*** Norman Taurog; ***C:*** Daniel F. Fapp.

Junction 88 **1940** Early all-black musical chock full of great dancing and hot music. **60m/B VHS.** Noble Sissle, Bob Howard.

June Bride **1948** Fast-paced and entertaining comedy in which Davis and Montgomery are teamed up as magazine writers. A hilarious battle of the sexes erupts as they're sent to Indiana to do a feature story on June brides. Look for Debbie Reynolds in her film debut. **97m/B VHS.** Bette Davis, Robert Montgomery, Fay Bainter, Betty Lynn, Tom Tully, Barbara Bates, Jerome Cowan, Mary Wickes; ***D:*** Bretaigne Windust; ***W:*** Ranald MacDougall.

June Night *Juninatten* **1940** A woman who was victimized by a shooting incident cannot escape the public eye due to her former promiscuous behavior. In Swedish with English subtitles. **90m/C VHS, DVD.** *SW* Ingrid Bergman, Marianne Lofgren, Gunnar Sjoberg, Olaf Widgren; ***D:*** Per Lindberg; ***W:*** Ragnar Hylten-Cavalius; ***C:*** Ake Dahlqvist; ***M:*** Jules Sylvain.

Jungle **1952** A princess and an American adventurer lead an expedition into the Indian wilds to discover the source of recent elephant attacks. **74m/B VHS.** Rod Cameron, Cesar Romero, Marie Windsor; ***D:*** William Berke; ***C:*** Clyde De Vinna.

Jungle Assault **1989** Two Vietnam vets with nothing left to lose are called back into the bloodiest action of their lives. Their assignment is to locate and destroy a terrorist base and bring back an American general's brainwashed daughter. **86m/C VHS.** William Smith, Ted Prior, William Zipp; ***D:*** David A. Prior.

The Jungle Book *Rudyard Kipling's Jungle Book* **1942** A lavish version of Rudyard Kipling's stories about Mowgli, the boy raised by wolves in the jungles of India. **109m/C VHS, DVD.** Sabu, Joseph Calleia, Rosemary DeCamp, Ralph Byrd, John Qualen; ***D:*** Zoltan Korda; ***W:*** Laurence Stallings; ***C:*** Lee Garmes; ***M:*** Miklos Rozsa.

The Jungle Book **1967** Based on Kipling's classic, a young boy raised by wolves must choose between his jungle friends and human "civilization." Along the way he meets a variety of jungle characters including zany King Louie, kind-hearted Baloo, wise Bagherra and the evil Shere Khan. Great, classic songs including "Trust in Me," "I Wanna Be Like You," and Oscar-nominated "Bare Necessities." Last Disney feature overseen by Uncle Walt himself and a must for kids of all ages. **78m/C VHS, DVD.** ***D:*** Wolfgang Reitherman; ***M:*** George Bruns; ***V:*** Phil Harris, Sebastian Cabot, Louis Prima, George Sanders, Sterling Holloway, J. Pat O'Malley, Verna Felton, Darlene Carr.

Jungle Boy **1996 (PG)** After being lost in the jungles of India, Manling (Seth) is raised by a monkey and an elephant. Able to communicate with the animals, Manling uses his talents to defeat the evil poacher, Hook (Roberts), who's out to steal a sacred statue. **88m/C VHS, DVD.** Asif Mohammed Seth, Jeremy Roberts, Lea Moreno; ***D:*** Allan Goldstein; ***W:*** Allan Goldstein, John Howard Lawson, Damian Lee; ***C:*** Nicholas Josef von Sternberg.

Jungle Bride ½ **1933** Three people are shipwrecked and one of them is a suspected murderer. **66m/B VHS.** Anita Page, Charles Starrett.

Jungle Captive ½ **1945** Second campy sequel to "Captive Wild Woman" following "Jungle Woman." Mad scientist Dr. Stendahl (Kruger) has been experimenting on bringing dead animals back to life and then attempting to make them human. He steals the body of an female ape (Lane) to practice on and kidnaps his human assistant, Ann (Ward), so she can "donate" her blood. The ape becomes a woman but still has the brain of an animal. This leads to violence. **64m/B VHS.** Otto Kruger, Vicky Lane, Amelita Ward, Rondo Hatton, Phil Brown, Jerome Cowan; ***D:*** Harold Young; ***W:*** M. Coates Webster, Dwight V. Babcock; ***C:*** Maury Gertsman.

Jungle Drums of Africa *U-238 and the Witch Doctor* **1953** Jungle adventures abound as Moore and Coates encounter lions, wind tunnels, voodoo and enemy agents in deepest Africa. A 12-episode serial re-edited onto two cassettes. **167m/B VHS.** Clayton Moore, Phyllis Coates, Roy Glenn, John Cason; ***D:*** Fred Brannon.

Jungle Fever **1991 (R)** Married black architect's affair with his white secretary provides the backdrop for a cold look at interracial love. Focuses more on the discomfort of friends and families than with the intense world created by the lovers for themselves. Provides the quota of humor and fresh insight we expect from Lee, but none of the joyous sexuality experienced by the lovers in "She's Gotta Have It." In fact, Lee tells viewers that interracial love is unnatural, never more than skin deep, never more than a blind obsession with the allure of the opposite race. Very fine cast but if you don't agree with Lee, a real disappointment as well. **131m/C VHS, DVD.** Wesley Snipes, Annabella Sciorra, John Turturro, Samuel L. Jackson, Ossie Davis, Ruby Dee, Lonette McKee, Anthony Quinn, Spike Lee, Halle Berry, Tyra Ferrell, Veronica Webb, Frank Vincent, Tim Robbins, Brad Dourif, Richard Edson; ***D:*** Spike Lee; ***W:*** Spike Lee; ***C:*** Ernest R. Dickerson; ***M:*** Terence Blanchard. N.Y. Film Critics '91: Support. Actor (Jackson).

Jungle Goddess ½ **1949** Two mercenaries set out for the reward offered for finding a wealthy heiress last seen in the jungles of Africa. **61m/B VHS.** George Reeves, Wanda McKay, Ralph Byrd, Armida; ***D:*** Lewis D. Collins.

Jungle Heat ½ *Dance of the Dwarfs* **1984 (PG)** While searching for a pygmy tribe, an anthropologist and her pilot run into a pack of anthropoid mutants. **93m/C VHS.** Peter Fonda, Deborah Raffin; ***D:*** Gus Trikonis.

Jungle Hell **1955** Sabu comes to the rescue of an Indian tribe being harassed by flying saucers, death rays and radioactive debris. **?m/B VHS.** Sabu, David Bruce, George E. Stone, K.T. Stevens; ***D:*** Norman A. Cerf.

Jungle Inferno **197?** Nature boy, a fugitive from the government, fights lions, tigers and pursuing feds in this story of escape and survival. **90m/C VHS.** Brad Harris.

Jungle Master **1956** Noble British types hunt for Karzan, the jungle's number one guy, with the aid of a tribal priestess and a lovely photo-journalist. Must see for trash movie fans. **90m/C VHS.** John Kitzmiller, Simone Blondell; ***D:*** Miles Deem.

Jungle Patrol ½ **1948** In 1943 New Guinea, a squadron of entrapped fliers are confronted with a beautiful USO entertainer. Romance and show tunes follow. **72m/B VHS.** Kristine Miller, Arthur Franz, Richard Jaeckel, Ross Ford, Tommy Noonan, Gene Reynolds; ***D:*** Joseph M. Newman.

Jungle Raiders ½ *Legenda Del Rudio Malese; Captain Yankee* **1985 (PG-13)** An Indiana Jones-esque mercenary searches the steamy jungles of Malaysia for a valuable jewel, the Ruby of Gloom. **102m/C VHS.** Lee Van Cleef, Christopher Connelly, Marina Costa; ***D:*** Anthony (Antonio Margheriti) Dawson.

Jungle Siren 🦴🦴 **1942** Nazis in Africa try to foment rebellion amongst the black natives against the white residents. Crabbe and a white woman raised in the jungle set things right. **68m/B VHS.** Ann Corio, Buster Crabbe, Evelyn Wahl, Milton Kibbee; ***D:*** Sam Newfield.

Jungle 2 Jungle 🦴🦴½ **1996 (PG)** Remake of French farce released as "Little Indian, Big City," changes little of the "wild child" premise. Workaholic Wall Streeter Michael Cromwell (Allen) decides to finalize the divorce from his long-estranged doctor wife, Patricia (Williams), who happens to have been ministering to a tribe in the Amazon rain forest for many years. He gets more than the divorce when he meets the 13-year-old son, Mimi-Siku (Huntington), he never knew he had. Although the boy speaks English, he's been raised as a tribal native, which causes quite a culture shock when he returns with Michael to the jungles of Manhattan. Of course the kid's more than a match for any situation. **105m/C VHS.** Tim Allen, Sam Huntington, Martin Short, JoBeth Williams, Lolita (David) Davidovich, David Ogden Stiers, Bob (Robert) Dishy, Valerie Mahaffey, Leelee Sobieski, Luis Avalos, Frankie J. Galasso; ***D:*** John Pasquin; ***W:*** Bruce A. Evans, Raynold Gideon; ***C:*** Tony Pierce-Roberts; ***M:*** Michael Convertino.

Jungle Warriors 🦴½ **1984 (R)** Seven fashion models are abducted by a Peruvian cocaine dealer. To escape him, they must become Jungle Warriors. **96m/C VHS.** *GE MX* Sybil Danning, Marjoe Gortner, Nina Van Pallandt, Paul Smith, John Vernon, Alex Cord, Woody Strode, Kai Wulff; ***D:*** Ernst R. von Theumer.

Jungle Woman 🦴½ **1944** Scientist Dr. Fletcher (Naish) is being tried for murder and relates his story in court. He does research on apes and has a female simian currently in his lab. The ape disappears and a young woman, Paula (Acquanetta), mysteriously appears. As you might guess, Paula and the ape are the same creature and a dangerous one at that. Follows "Captive Wild Woman" and is followed by "Jungle Captive." **61m/B VHS.** J. Carrol Naish, Acquanetta, Richard Davis, Evelyn Ankers, Samuel S. Hinds, Lois Collier, Milburn Stone, Douglass Dumbrille; ***D:*** Reginald LeBorg; ***W:*** Bernard Schubert, Henry Sucher, Edward Dein; ***C:*** Jack MacKenzie.

Jungleground 🦴½ **1995 (R)** Jungleground is a urban wasteland controlled by rival gangs. Lt. Jake Cornel (Piper) gets caught in a shoot-out when a sting operation goes bad and winds up before psychotic gang leader Odin. Odin offers him one chance—Cornel's going to be hunted in Jungleground's abandoned streets and if he can escape before dawn, he gets to live. **90m/C VHS, DVD.** *CA* Roddy Piper, Torri Higginson, Peter Williams; ***D:*** Don Allan; ***W:*** Michael Stokes; ***C:*** Gilles Corbeil; ***M:*** Varouje.

Junior woof! **1986** A raving, drooling lunatic cuts up girls with a chainsaw. **80m/C VHS.** Suzanne DeLaurentis, Linda Singer, Jeremy Ruthford, Michael McKeever.

Junior 🦴🦴 **1994 (PG-13)** Out of the way women! Schwarzenegger trades the war room for the delivery room to experience the miracle of birth. As scientists, he and DeVito take a dip in the gene pool once again to test an anti-miscarriage drug. Thompson provides the egg and some surprisingly good physical comedy as the klutzy cryogenics expert who moves into their university digs. Every pregnancy cliche is explored as Schwarzenegger and DeVito bring the concept to term. Sorry, action fans...nothing blows up except Arnold. **109m/C VHS, DVD, Wide.** Arnold Schwarzenegger, Danny DeVito, Emma Thompson, Frank Langella, Pamela Reed, Judy Collins, James Eckhouse, Aida Turturro; ***D:*** Ivan Reitman; ***W:*** Kevin Wade, Chris Conrad; ***C:*** Adam Greenberg; ***M:*** James Newton Howard.

Junior Bonner 🦴🦴🦴 **1972 (PG)** A rowdy modern-day western about a young drifting rodeo star who decides to raise money for his father's new ranch by challenging a formidable bull. **100m/C VHS, DVD, Wide.** Steve McQueen, Robert Preston, Ida Lupino, Ben Johnson, Joe Don Baker, Barbara Leigh; ***D:*** Sam Peckinpah; ***W:*** Jeb Rosebrook; ***C:*** Lucien Ballard; ***M:*** Jerry Fielding.

Junior G-Men **1940** The Dead End Kids fight Fifth Columnists who are trying to sabotage America's war effort. Twelve episodes. **237m/B VHS.** Billy Halop, Huntz Hall.

Junior G-Men of the Air 🦴½ **1942** The Dead End Kids become teenage flyboys in this 12-episode serial adventure. **215m/B VHS.** Billy Halop, Huntz Hall.

Junior's Groove 🦴🦴 *The Planet of Junior Brown* **1997 (R)** Young piano prodigy grows up in a tough neighbor with a caring mom, eccentric piano teacher, and a group of street-smart friends. Based on the novel by Virginia Hamilton. **91m/C VHS, DVD.** Lynn Whitfield, Clark Johnson, Margot Kidder, Sarah Polley, Martin Villafana; ***D:*** Clement Virgo; ***W:*** Clement Virgo, Cameron Bailey; ***C:*** Jonathan Freeman; ***M:*** Christopher Dedrick. **VIDEO**

The Juniper Tree 🦴½ **1987** Based on a tale by the Brothers Grimm, this Icelandic curio finds sisters Margit (Bjork) and Katla (Bragadottir) fleeing across the medieval countryside after their mother is burned at the stake for witchcraft. The sisters have their own special powers, which they turn on each other when they become romantic rivals over a young widower (Flygenring). **78m/B VHS.** *IC* Bjork, Bryndis Petra Bragadottir, Vladimar Orn Flygenring; ***D:*** Nietzchka Keene.

Junk Mail 🦴🦴½ *Budbringeren* **1997** Grimy Oslo postman Roy (Skjaerstad) enjoys reading other people's mail, stalking Line, a deaf girl (Saether) on his route, and not washing. One day the girl leaves her keys in the mailbox, so Roy decides to have a look around, later saving her from a suicide attempt. During another of his "visits," Roy learns that Line is involved in a violent crime, along with a thug named Georg (Aske). Through a series of mistaken identities and coicidences, he becomes deeply involved in the proceedings. Sletaune's promising debut is quirky and painstaking in its attention to detail. Skjaerstad does a fine job as the slovenly, slothful, though ultimately sympathetic, mailman. **83m/C VHS.** *NO* Robert Skjaerstad, Andrine Saether, Per Egil Aske, Eli Anne Linnestad; ***D:*** Pal Sletaune; ***W:*** Pal Sletaune, Jonny Halberg; ***C:*** Kjell Vassdal; ***M:*** Joachim Holbek.

The Junkman 🦴½ **1982 (R)** Movie maker whose new film is about to be premiered is being chased by a mysterious killer. Promoted as "the ultimate car chase film" since the production used and destroyed over 150 automobiles. From the makers of "Gone in 60 Seconds." **97m/C VHS.** H.B. Halicki, Christopher Stone, Susan Shaw, Hoyt Axton, Lynda Day George; ***D:*** H.B. Halicki.

Juno and the Paycock 🦴🦴½ **1930** Perhaps if Hitchcock hadn't been so faithful to O'Casey this early effort would have been less stagey and more entertaining. In Dublin during the civil uprising, a poor family is torn apart when they receive news of an imminent fortune. Hitchcock's reported to have said that "drama is life with the dull bits left out," though here too many dull bits remain. **96m/B VHS, DVD.** Sara Allgood, Edward Chapman, John Longden, John Laurie, Maire O'Neill; ***D:*** Alfred Hitchcock; ***W:*** Alfred Hitchcock; ***Nar:*** Barry Fitzgerald.

Jupiter's Darling 🦴🦴 **1955** This spoof of Hannibal (Keel) and Amytis (Williams) gravely misses the mark in making funny the world of the Roman Empire. Amytis has the job of distracting Hannibal from attacking the Eternal City, and does so through musical interludes and unfunny jokes. ♫I Have A Dream; If This Be Slav'ry; I Never Trust A Woman; Hannibal's Victory March; Don't Let This Night Get Away; The Life Of An Elephant; Horatio's Narration. **96m/C Wide.** Esther Williams, Howard Keel, George Sanders, Gower Champion, Marge Champion, Norma Varden, Richard Haydn, William Demarest, Douglass Dumbrille, Michael Ansara, Martha Wentworth, Chris Alcaide, William Tannen; ***D:*** George Sidney; ***C:*** Charles Rosher.

Jupiter's Thigh 🦴🦴½ **1981** A madcap married pair of treasure-hunters honeymoon in Greece in search of an ancient statue's lost thigh. Available in French with English subtitles, or dubbed into English. **96m/C VHS.** *FR* Annie Girardot, Philippe Noiret; ***D:*** Philippe de Broca.

Jurassic Park 🦴🦴🦴½ **1993 (PG-13)** Crichton's spine-tingling thriller translates well (but not faithfully) due to its main attraction: realistic, rampaging dinosaurs. Genetically cloned from prehistoric DNA, all is well until they escape from their pens—smarter and less predictable than expected. Contrived plot and thin characters (except Goldblum), but who cares? The true stars are the dinos, an incredible combination of models and computer animation. Violent, suspenseful, and realistic with gory attack scenes. Not for small kids, though much of the marketing is aimed at them. Spielberg knocked his own "E.T." out of first place as "JP" became the highest grossing movie of all time. Also available in a letterbox version. **127m/C VHS, DVD, Wide.** Sam Neill, Laura Dern, Jeff Goldblum, Richard Attenborough, Bob Peck, Martin Ferrero, B.D. Wong, Joseph Mazzello, Ariana Richards, Samuel L. Jackson, Wayne Knight; ***D:*** Steven Spielberg; ***W:*** David Koepp, Michael Crichton; ***C:*** Dean Cundey; ***M:*** John Williams; ***V:*** Richard Kiley. Oscars '93: Sound, Sound FX Editing, Visual FX.

Jurassic Park 3 🦴🦴 **2001 (PG-13)** Neill (who skipped JP2) is back as Dr. Alan Grant, reluctantly leading a seach-and-rescue mission when a plane crash-lands on an island populated by his old nemeses, the dinos. Another new dinosaur species, the Spinosaurus, shows up and to make some more humans into snack food. The talented, and probably over-qualified, group of writers mercifully makes this trip a short one, making sure that any dialogue is mostly expository or in-joke amusing while glossing over the dumb-as-a-box-of-fossils plot and characters. The dinosaurs are, once again, impressive, if you haven't gotten enough of the computer-generated ferocity in the first two outings. Warning: Just because this franchise is getting progressively worse doesn't mean they didn't set up JP4. **90m/C VHS, DVD, Wide.** *US* Sam Neill, William H. Macy, Tea Leoni, Alessandro Nivola, Michael Jeter, Trevor Morgan, John Diehl, Bruce A. Young, Taylor Nichols, Mark Harelik, Julio Mechoso, Laura Dern; ***D:*** Joe Johnston; ***W:*** Peter Buchman, Alexander Payne, Jim Taylor; ***C:*** Shelly Johnson; ***M:*** Don Davis.

The Juror 🦴½ **1996 (R)** Plucky single mom (Moore) ends up on the jury in the trial of a powerful mobster and draws the attention of the smooth enforcer (Baldwin) who muscles her into providing a certain verdict. The usual good-vs.-evil, family-in-danger action ensues. Despite boasting a fine cast and impressive attention to detail, flick is guilty of ludicrous situations, a mechanical plot and a dopey ending. Based on the novel by George Dawes Green. **107m/C VHS, DVD.** Demi Moore, Alec Baldwin, Joseph Gordon-Levitt, Anne Heche, James Gandolfini, Lindsay Crouse, Tony LoBianco, Michael Constantine, Matt Craven; ***D:*** Brian Gibson; ***W:*** Ted Tally; ***C:*** Jamie Anderson; ***M:*** James Newton Howard.

Jury Duty 🦴 **1995 (PG-13)** Mama's boy loser Tommy Collins (Shore) gets jury duty on a serial-killer case and tries to keep what seems to be an open-and-shut case going so he can continue to get free room and board. He falls for babe juror Monica (Carrere) and really drags the trial (and the film) out in a pathetic attempt to woo her. Shore is even more annoying and unfunny than ever. Low-rent bastardization of "Twelve Angry Men" tries to pass off lame O.J. references and Shore falling out of chairs as humor. Creates reasonable doubt as to Shore's talent and movie execs' judgment. **88m/C VHS.** Pauly Shore, Tia Carrere, Shelley Winters, Brian Doyle-Murray, Abe Vigoda, Stanley Tucci, Charles Napier, Richard Edson; ***Cameos:*** Andrew (Dice Clay) Silverstein; ***D:*** John Fortenberry; ***W:*** Fax Bahr, Barbara Williams. Golden Raspberries '95: Worst Actor (Shore).

Just a Gigolo 🦴🦴½ **1979 (R)** Bowie stars in this unusual melodrama about a Prussian war vet turned male prostitute. He spends most of his time working for the sexiest of women. Splendid cast, but a bit incoherent. **105m/C VHS.** *GE* David Bowie, Sydne Rome, Kim Novak, David Hemmings, Maria Schell, Curt Jurgens, Marlene Dietrich; ***D:*** David Hemmings.

Just a Little Harmless Sex 🦴🦴 **1999 (R)** Alan (Mailhouse) has spent the evening with his buddies, Danny (Silverman) and Brent (Ragsdale), at a topless bar. Driving home, he offers help to a stranded motorist (who turns out to be a hooker) and winds up getting arrested. Alan's wife, Laura (Eastwood), is, naturally, not happy about the situation and discusses her plight with her gal pals while Alan and his buddies discuss his fractured marriage. Angsty but not particularly novel. **98m/C VHS, DVD.** Robert Mailhouse, Alison Eastwood, Jonathan Silverman, William Ragsdale, Lauren Hutton, Kimberly Williams, Jessica Lundy, Rachel Hunter, Michael Ontkean, Tito Larriva; ***D:*** Rick Rosenthal; ***W:*** Roger Miller, Marti Noxon; ***C:*** Bruce Surtees; ***M:*** Tito Larriva.

Just Another Girl on the I.R.T. 🦴🦴½ **1993 (R)** Double debut from two African American women, writer/director Harris, and actress Johnson, captures the sass and wit of a girl from the projects. Seventeen-year-old Chantal has a plan for her life and challenges authority with assurance, even after an unexpected pregnancy puts a twist into her plan. Strong initial statement tends to become weak and cloudy as Chantal loses her focus. This doesn't dismiss the remarkable realism and raw talent portrayed in a picture filmed in just seventeen days for $130,000. Winner of a special jury prize at the Sundance Film Festival. **96m/C VHS.** Ariyan Johnson, Kevin Thigpen, Ebony Jerido, Jerard Washington, Chequita Jackson, William Badget; ***D:*** Leslie Harris; ***W:*** Leslie Harris; ***C:*** Richard Conners. Sundance '93: Special Jury Prize.

Just Another Pretty Face 🦴🦴½ *Be Beautiful but Shut Up* **1958** An aging detective catches a gang of jewel smugglers, and gets involved with their young moll. In French with English subtitles. **110m/B VHS.** *FR* Henri Vidal, Mylene Demongeot, Isa Miranda; ***D:*** Henri Verneuil.

Just Around the Corner 🦴½ **1938 (G)** Temple helps her Depression-poor father get a job after she befriends a cantankerous millionaire. Temple duets with Bill "Bojangles" Robinson with the fourth time. Also available colorized. ♫This Is A Happy Little Ditty; I'm Not Myself Today; I'll Be Lucky With You; Just Around the Corner; I Love To Walk in the Rain; Brass Buttons and Epaulets. **71m/B VHS.** Shirley Temple, Charles Farrell, Bert Lahr, Joan Davis, Bill Robinson, Cora Witherspoon, Franklin Pangborn; ***D:*** Irving Cummings.

Just Before Dawn 🦴🦴 **1980 (R)** Another murderers stalk campers story; humans resort to their animal instincts in their struggle for survival. Not to be confused with the William Castle film (1946) from the "Crime Doctor" series. **90m/C VHS.** Chris Lemmon, Deborah Benson, Gregg Henry, George Kennedy; ***D:*** Jeff Lieberman; ***M:*** Brad Fiedel.

Just Between Friends 🦴🦴 **1986 (PG-13)** Two women become friends, not knowing that one is having an affair with the husband of the other. Allan Burns directorial debut. **110m/C VHS.** Mary Tyler Moore, Christine Lahti, Sam Waterston, Ted Danson, Jim MacKrell, Jane Greer; ***D:*** Allan Burns; ***W:*** Allan Burns; ***C:*** Jordan Cronenweth.

Just Cause 🦴🦴 **1994 (R)** Incoherent mystery/thriller set in the Florida Everglades. Retired attorney, Paul Armstrong, now a Harvard law professor, decides to defend Bobby Earl (Underwood), on death row for the murder of a white girl. As Armstrong investigates the case, he discovers that the arresting officer Tanny Brown, (Fishburne) is corrupt and tortured the confession out of Bobby. Starts off promising with the electricity of Connery's and Fishburne's presence and a frigthening cameo by Ed Harris as an incarcerated serial killer, but once the barrage of plot twists start, creating gator size holes in the plot, the movie drifts into a murkey swamp of absurdity. Adapted from the legal thriller by John Katzenbach. **102m/C VHS, DVD, Wide.** Sean Connery, Laurence "Larry" Fishburne, Kate Capshaw, Blair Underwood, Ruby Dee, Daniel J. Travanti, Ned Beatty, Lynne Thigpen, George

Plimpton, Chris Sarandon, Kevin McCarthy, Ed Harris; *D:* Arne Glimcher; *W:* Jeb Stuart, Robert Stone; *C:* Lajos Koltai; *M:* James Newton Howard.

Just for the Hell of It woof! *Destruction, Inc* **1968** A quartet of teenage punks ruthlessly terrorize their suburban Miami 'hood while an innocent kid gets blamed. More exploitation from schlock king Lewis, who also wrote the theme song, "Destruction, Inc." (pic's alternate title). Essentially the same cast as the director's "She Devils on Wheels," filmed simultaneously. **85m/C VHS, DVD.** Rodney Bedell, Ray Sager, Nancy Lee Noble, Agi Gyenes, Steve White; *D:* Herschell Gordon Lewis; *W:* Allison Louise Downe; *C:* Roy Collodi; *M:* Larry Wellington.

Just for You ♪♪½ **1952** Entertaining musical about producer Crosby who doesn't have time for his kids until Wyman steps in and shows him the way. Based on Stephen Vincent Benet's novel "Famous." ♫Zing A Little Zong; He's Just Crazy For Me; The Live Oak Tree; A Flight of Fancy; I'll Si-Si Ya In Bahia; On the 10:10; Just for You. **95m/C VHS.** Bing Crosby, Jane Wyman, Ethel Barrymore, Robert Arthur, Natalie Wood, Cora Witherspoon; *D:* Elliott Nugent; *W:* Robert Carson.

Just Like a Woman ♪♪ **1995 (R)** Sweet-natured film about an unlikely romance with some decided quirks. Young American Gerald (Pasdar) is working for a London bank and renting a flat from lonely older divorcee Monica (Walters). Ideal tenant Gerald is also recently divorced and a mutual attraction develops, in fact Gerald trusts Monica enough to confess his darkest secret—seems his marriage broke up over women's lingerie—the ones Gerald likes to wear when he cross-dresses in his female persona of Geraldine. Does this put Monica off? Well, she turns out to be very understanding indeed. Based on the memoir "Geraldine" by Monica Jay. **102m/C VHS.** *GB* Adrian Pasdar, Julie Walters, Paul Freeman, Susan Wooldridge, Gordon Kennedy, Ian Redford, Shelley Thompson; *D:* Christopher Monger; *W:* Nick Evans; *C:* Alan Hume; *M:* Michael Storey.

Just Like Weather ♪♪♪ **1986** Contemporary Hong Kong and the city's looming return to control by mainland China provide the backdrop for the troubled marriage of a young couple. Couple endure abortion, arrest, and veterinarian episodes before departing for on U.S. trip with high hopes. **98m/C VHS.** *HK* Christine Lee, Lee Chi-Keung, Allen Fong; *D:* Allen Fong.

Just Looking ♪♪½ *Cherry Pink* **1999 (R)** A comedy about teenaged voyeurism set in 1955. 14-year-old Lenny (Merriman) has only one thing on his mind for summer vacation in his Bronx neighborhood. He's determined to figure out what sex is all about by watching some adults "do it." Well, Lenny's mom decides to send him to stay in suburban Queens with her sister but that doesn't change his plans. Predictable coming of age comedy with Alexander making his directorial debut. **97m/C VHS, DVD, Wide.** *US* Ryan Merriman, Gretchen Mol, Patti LuPone, Peter Onorati, Ilana Levine, Richard V. Licata, John Bolger, Joey Franquinha; *D:* Jason Alexander; *W:* Marshall Karp; *C:* Fred Schuler; *M:* Michael Skloff.

Just Me & You ♪½ **1978** An "It Happened One Night" tale of an unlikely couple who fall in love with each other when chance brings them together on a cross-country drive. **100m/C VHS.** Louise Lasser, Charles Grodin; *D:* Charles Erman; *W:* Louise Lasser. **TV**

Just One Night ♪♪½ **2000 (PG-13)** College professor Isaac Adler (Hutton) is spending the night before his wedding in San Francisco. His taxi collides with that of beautiful, married Aurora (Cucinotta) and maybe the collision shook them up more than they thought, since they decide to spend the evening getting to know each other better. **90m/C VHS, DVD.** Timothy Hutton, Maria Grazia Cucinotta, Udo Kier, Michael O'Keefe, Robert Easton, Don Novello, Seymour Cassel, Natalie Shaw; *D:* Alan Jacobs; *W:* Alan Jacobs; *C:* John Campbell; *M:* Anthony Marinelli.

Just One of the Girls ♪½ **1993 (R)** Teen star Haim transfers to a new high school where he dresses in drag in order to avoid the itinerant leader of the school's toughest gang whom he has unwittingly enraged. Palling around with Eggert becomes one of his costume's unexpected perks. Sort of a cross between "Some Like It Hot" and "90210." **94m/C VHS.** Corey Haim, Nicole Eggert, Cameron Bancroft; *D:* Michael Keusch; *M:* Amin Bhatia.

Just One of the Guys ♪♪ **1985 (PG-13)** When the school newspaper refuses to accept the work of an attractive young girl, she goes undercover as a boy to prove that her work is good. She goes on to befriend the school's nerd, and even helps him grow out of his awkward stage, falling for him in the process. Very cute, but predictable. **100m/C VHS.** Joyce Hyser, Clayton Rohner, Billy Jacoby, Toni Hudson, Leigh McCloskey, Sherilyn Fenn, William Zabka; *D:* Lisa Gottlieb.

Just One Time ♪♪ **2000 (R)** New York-set romantic comedy about fulfilling fantasies. Fireman Anthony (Janger) is about to marry lawyer Amy (Carter) but can't resist telling her about his sexual dream to see her make out with another woman—just once—before the wedding. Distraught, Amy confides in their gay neighbor, Victor (Diaz), who admits to a crush on Anthony. So she offers a quid pro quo to her beau—she'll indulge him with sultry lesbian Michelle (Esposito) if Anthony will do the same for her with Victor, and he has to go first. **94m/C VHS, DVD.** *US* Lane Janger, Joelle Carter, Guillermo Diaz, Jennifer Esposito, Vincent Laresca, David Lee Russek, Domenick Lombardozzi; *D:* Lane Janger; *W:* Jennifer Vandever, Lane Janger; *C:* Michael St. Hilaire; *M:* Edward Bilous.

Just Suppose ♪♪½ **1926** Prince in waiting decides he'd prefer the simple life, travels to the land of the free in search of honest work and is felled by cupid's arrow. All's well 'til duty calls, and his princely presence is expected back in the royal fold. Features beautiful boy Barthelmess, whom Lillian Gish described as having "the most beautiful face of any man who ever went before a camera." Silent. **90m/B VHS.** Richard Barthelmess, Lois Moran, Geoffrey Kerr, Henry Vibart, George Spelvin; *D:* Kenneth Webb.

Just Tell Me What You Want ♪♪½ **1980 (R)** A wealthy, self-made married man finally drives his long-time mistress away when he refuses to let her take over the operation of a failing movie studio he has acquired. After she falls for another man, the tycoon does everything he can to win her back. The department store battle between MacGraw and King is priceless. **112m/C VHS.** Alan King, Ali MacGraw, Myrna Loy, Keenan Wynn, Tony Roberts; *D:* Sidney Lumet; *W:* Jay Presson Allen; *C:* Oswald Morris.

Just Tell Me You Love Me ♪ **1980 (PG)** Three budding con artists plot to make easy money in this Hawaiian romp. **90m/C VHS.** Robert Hegyes, Debralee Scott, Lisa Hartman Black, Ricci Martin, June Lockhart; *D:* Tony Mordente.

Just the Ticket ♪♪ *The Scalper* **1998 (R)** Romantic comedy set in the seedy world of ticket scalpers should have skipped the trite love story and centered on the ducat slingers. Gary (Garcia) is a fast talking huckster is trying to win back ex-girlfriend Linda (MacDowell). He's also hoping for the ever-popular last big score before he goes legit. His opportunity arrives when the Pope announces a visit to Yankee Stadium, but he must out-hustle competitor Casino (Blake). Garcia wrote many of the Salsa-flavored songs used in the movie. **115m/C VHS, DVD.** Andy Garcia, Andie MacDowell, Richard Bradford, Laura Harris, Andre B. Blake, Elizabeth Ashley, Patrick Breen, Ron Leibman, Chris Lemmon, Don Novello, Abe Vigoda, Bill Irwin, Ronald Guttman, Donna Hanover, Irene Worth, Fred Asparagus, Louis Mustillo, Paunita Nichols, Joe Frazier; *D:* Richard Wenk; *W:* Richard Wenk; *C:* Ellen Kuras; *M:* Rick Marotta.

Just the Way You Are ♪ **1984 (PG)** An attractive musician struggles to overcome a physical handicap and winds up falling in love while on vacation in the French Alps. **96m/C VHS.** Kristy McNichol, Robert Carradine, Kaki Hunter, Michael Ontkean, Alexandra Paul, Lance Guest, Timothy Daly, Patrick Cassidy; *D:* Edouard Molinaro; *W:* Allan Burns; *M:* Vladimir Cosma.

Just Visiting ♪♪ **2001 (PG-13)** Remake of the 1993 French flick "Les Visiteurs" has Reno and Clavier reprising their roles as a medieval knight and his servant who find themselves in modern-day Chicago. Original was a huge hit in France, but bombed here. This one should do much better here, since there's much less reading of subtitles involved, and this one makes good use of the excellent leads and the transplanted Chicago locales. **88m/C VHS, DVD, Wide.** *US* Jean Reno, Christian Clavier, Christina Applegate, Tara Reid, Matt Ross, Bridgette Wilson, John Aylward, George Plimpton, Malcolm McDowell, Sarah Badel, Richard Bremmer, Robert Glenister; *D:* Jean-Marie Poire; *W:* Christian Clavier, Jean-Marie Poire, John Hughes; *C:* Ueli Steiger; *M:* John Powell.

Just William's Luck ♪♪ **1947** A precocious English brat sneaks into an old mansion, which just happens to be the headquarters for a gang of thieves. Based on British series of children's books. **87m/B VHS.** *GB* William A. Graham, Garry Marsh; *D:* Val Guest.

Just Write ♪♪½ **1997 (PG-13)** Sweet and slight romantic comedy about making your dreams come true. Harold (Piven) is a Hollywood tour bus driver who works for his well-meaning but overbearing father (Rocco). He meets cute with rising star Amanda (Fenn), who is mistakenly lead to believe Harold is a screenwriter. And Amanda just happens to have a script that needs some work. They begin to fall in love but sooner or later the truth is bound to come out. Leads play well together and the supporting cast is fine, especially Williams as a hard-charging agent. **95m/C VHS, DVD, Wide.** Jeremy Piven, Sherilyn Fenn, JoBeth Williams, Alex Rocco, Jeffrey D. Sams, Wallace Shawn, Costas Mandylor, Yeardley Smith, Holland Taylor; *Cameos:* Nancy McKeon, Ed McMahon; *D:* Andrew Gallerani; *W:* Stan Williamson; *C:* Michael Brown; *M:* Leland Bond.

Just Your Luck ♪½ **1996 (R)** The New Sudka Cafe II, owned by the high strung Nick (Polito), is the setting for one wild night. An old man promptly keels over dead upon learning that his lottery ticket is a $6 million prize-winner. Customer Kim (Madsen) tries to convince Nick and her fellow diners that they should keep the ticket and split the winnings. **86m/C VHS.** Virginia Madsen, Sean Patrick Flanery, Ernie Hudson, Jon Polito, Alanna Ubach, Jon Favreau, Mike Starr, Carroll Baker; *D:* Gary Auerbach; *W:* Gary Auerbach.

Justice ♪♪ *Flight from Fear* **1955** A crusading attorney tries to keep a waterfront kangaroo court from applying its harsh justice to an admitted killer in this crime-drama. **26m/B VHS.** William Prince, Jack Klugman, Biff McGuire, Jack Warden. **TV**

Justice of the West ♪ **1961** The Lone Ranger and his sidekick, Tonto, perform good deeds in the Old West, including helping to retrieve stolen gold, helping to build an Indian school, and giving a blind man a fresh perspective on life. **71m/C VHS.** Clayton Moore, Jay Silverheels; *D:* Earl Bellamy.

Justice Rides Again ♪½ **193?** Mix tries to uphold law and order, but he's up against some very tough outlaws. **55m/B VHS.** Tom Mix.

Justin Morgan Had a Horse ♪♪ **1981** The true story of a colonial school teacher in post-Revolutionary War Vermont who first bred the Morgan horse, the first and most versatile American breed. **91m/C VHS.** Don Murray, Lana Wood, Gary Crosby; *D:* Hollingsworth Morse.

Justine ♪♪ **1969** In the 1930s, a prostitute who marries an Egyptian banker becomes involved with a variety of men and a plot to arm Palestinian Jews in their revolt against English rule. A condensed film version of Lawrence Durrell's "The Alexandria Quartet." **115m/C VHS.** *IS* Anouk Aimee, Michael York, Dirk Bogarde, Philippe Noiret, Michael Constantine, John Vernon, Jack Albertson; *D:* George Cukor; *W:* Lawrence B. Marcus; *C:* Leon Shamroy; *M:* Jerry Goldsmith.

K-9 ♪♪½ **1989 (PG-13)** After having his car destroyed by a drug dealer, "I work alone" Belushi is forced to take on a partner—a German Shepherd. Together they work to round up the bad guys and maybe chew on their shoes a little. Sometimes amusing one-joke comedy done in by a paper-thin script. Both the dog and Belushi are good, however. **111m/C VHS, DVD, Wide.** James Belushi, Mel Harris, Kevin Tighe, Ed O'Neill, Cotter Smith, James Handy, Jerry Lee; *D:* Rod Daniel; *W:* Steven Siegel, Scott Myers; *C:* Dean Semler; *M:* Miles Goodman.

K-911 ♪♪½ **1999 (PG-13)** Ten years after the original film, Belushi returns to his role of LAPD Detective Dooley, along with his German Sheperd partner, Jerry Lee. The aging duo are now reluctantly partnered with a younger K-9 unit—no-nonsense detective Welles (Tucci) and her partner, a Doberman named Zeus. But Dooley has some other things on his mind—some kook is trying to kill him. **91m/C VHS, DVD, Wide.** James Belushi, James Handy, Christine Tucci, Wade Andrew Williams, J.J. Johnston, Vincent Castellanos; *D:* Charles Kanganis; *W:* Gary Scott Thompson; *C:* George Mooradian; *M:* Steve Edwards. **VIDEO**

K-9000 ♪♪ **1989** The Hound salutes the idea behind this standard sci-fi crime-fighter; a cyberdog fights the forces of evil with the aid of a cop, a lady reporter, and the usual cliches. **96m/C VHS.** Chris Mulkey, Catherine Oxenberg; *D:* Kim Manners; *M:* Jan Hammer. **TV**

K-19: The Widowmaker **2002 (PG-13)** Based on a military incident that happened in 1961 but wasn't publicly revealed until the 1990s. The Soviet Union's first nuclear ballistic submarine has a reactor malfunction during a sea trial in the North Atlantic. Ford plays the tough Russian captain, who takes command from the more-popular Neeson, and must deal with rebellion in the ranks in order to save his sub and its crew. Cold War tensions abound. Bigelow shot on a set built to scale, with parts salvaged from an old diesel sub. Not yet reviewed. **?m/C VHS, DVD.** Harrison Ford, Liam Neeson, Peter Sarsgaard, Joss Ackland, Shaun Benson, J.J. Field; *D:* Kathryn Bigelow; *W:* Christopher Kyle.

K-PAX ♪♪½ **2001 (PG-13)** Spacey plays his patented "smirky guy with a secret" again in this tale of aliens and the humans who love them. Prot (Spacey) is admitted to a psychiatric hospital when he claims to be from outer space. Dr. Powell (Bridges) is assigned his case and soon finds himself intrigued by Prot. It seems that he's going around helping the patients in the hospital to actually get better. His other quirks include an astounding knowledge of astrophysics and an amazing tolerance to Thorazine. After Powell hypnotizes Prot, a deeply hidden personality is unmasked, but the actual truth about his identity is left open to interpretation. Bridges and Spacey work well together, and they save this sentimental E.T. tale from turning to schmaltzy mush. **120m/C VHS, DVD, Wide.** *US* Kevin Spacey, Jeff Bridges, Mary McCormack, Alfre Woodard, David Patrick Kelly, Saul Williams, Peter Gerety, Celia Weston, Ajay Naidu, John Toles-Bey, Kimberly Scott, Mary Mara, Aaron Paul, William Lucking; *D:* Iain Softley; *W:* Charles Leavitt; *C:* John Mathieson; *M:* Ed Shearmur.

Kadosh ♪♪ **1999** Meir (Hattab) and his wife Rivka (Abecassis) are ultra-Orthodox Jews living in the Mea Shearim quarter of Jerusalem. They have been married for 10 years and are still childless, so Meir is being pressured by his rabbi father to divorce his wife (though they love each other) and remarry. Rivka learns the fertility problem is with her husband but can do nothing because of religious tenets and she leaves their home. Meanwhile, Rivka's younger sister, Malka (Barda), contemplates abandoning her unhappy arranged marriage to be with the man she loves. Hebrew with subtitles. **110m/C VHS,**

DVD, Wide. *IS* Yael Abecassis, Yoram Hattab, Meital Barda, Sami Hori, Uri Klauzner, Yussef Abu-Warda; *D:* Amos Gitai; *W:* Amos Gitai, Eliette Abecassis; *C:* Renato Berta; *M:* Louis Sclavis.

Kafka ♪½ 1991 (PG-13) Disappointing and gloomy Soderbergh film that serves no purpose whatsoever. Irons plays Kafka, an insurance workers by day and a writer by night. The movie exists largely without interest until Kafka uncovers an office conspiracy and makes his way to the enemy's castle headquarters. From then on, "Kafka" is nothing but a conventional horror film. Irons is wasted in a role that requires nothing but an impeccable British accent. On the plus side, the film is exquisitely shot in black and white until the castle scenes, when the cinematography is switched to color. **100m/C VHS, Wide.** Jeremy Irons, Theresa Russell, Joel Grey, Ian Holm, Jeroen Krabbe, Armin Mueller-Stahl, Alec Guinness, Brian Glover, Robert Flemyng, Keith Allen, Simon McBurney; *D:* Steven Soderbergh; *W:* Lem Dobbs; *C:* Walt Lloyd; *M:* Cliff Martinez. Ind. Spirit '92: Cinematog.

Kagemusha ♪♪♪½ *The Shadow Warrior; The Double* 1980 (PG) A thief is rescued from the gallows because of his striking resemblance to a warlord in 16th Century Japan. When the ambitious warlord is fatally wounded, the thief is required to pose as the warlord. In Japanese with English subtitles. **160m/C VHS, Wide.** *JP* Tatsuya Nakadai, Tsutomu Yamazaki, Kenichi Hagiwara, Hideji Otaki; *D:* Akira Kurosawa; *W:* Akira Kurosawa, Masato Ide; *C:* Kazuo Miyagawa, Masaharu Ueda; *M:* Shinichiro Ikebe. British Acad. '80: Director (Kurosawa); Cannes '80: Film; Cesar '81: Foreign Film.

The Kaiser's Lackey ♪♪ *Der Untertan* 1951 Cowardly-but-ambitious Diedrich Hessling has learned his lesson—in order to gain power, you must bow to those who have it and ignore those who don't. Diedrich thinks he's finally achieved his goal when he's chosen to give the keynote speech at the dedication of an Emperor's monument. Based on the novel by Heinrich Mann. German with subitles. **105m/B VHS.** *GE* Werner Peters, Paul Esser; *D:* Wolfgang Staudte; *W:* Wolfgang Staudte.

Kalifornia ♪♪½ 1993 (R) "Badlands" meets the '90s in a road trip with the hitchhikers from hell. Early Grayce (Pitt) is your average slimeball who murders his landlord and hops a ride with his waifish girlfriend Adele (Lewis) from Kentucky to California with Brian (Duchovny), a yuppie writer interested in mass murderers, and his sultry photographer girlfriend Carrie (Forbes). Pitt and Lewis were still an item when they made this. Pitt reportedly wanted to play against type, and as pretty boy gone homicidal, he succeeds. Extremely violent and disturbing. Also available in an unrated version. **117m/C VHS, DVD, Wide.** Brad Pitt, Juliette Lewis, David Duchovny, Michelle Forbes, Sierra Pecheur, Lois Hall, Gregory Mars Martin; *D:* Dominic Sena; *W:* Tim Metcalfe; *C:* Bojan Bazelli; *M:* Carter Burwell.

Kama Sutra: A Tale of Love ♪♪ 1996 Erotic but flawed fantasy covering the sexual and political wiles of palace life in 16th-century India. Princess Tara (Choudhury) and girlhood friend/servant Maya (Varma) are close until the Princess becomes jealous of the even-more beautiful Maya. In revenge for a public humiliation, Maya seduces Tara's dissolute fiance, Raj Singh (Andrews), and is banished from the palace after the wedding. She becomes involved with handsome royal sculptor Jai Kumar (Tikaram) and later learns the sexual arts of the Kama Sutra, becoming the chief courtesan to the Raj. Messy, somewhat overwrought plot, extremely attractive cast. Also available in an R-rated version. **117m/C VHS, DVD.** *IN* Indira Varma, Sarita Choudhury, Ramon Tikaram, Naveen Andrews, Devi Rekha; *D:* Mira Nair; *W:* Mira Nair, Helena Kriel; *C:* Declan Quinn; *M:* Mychael Danna. Ind. Spirit '98: Cinematog.

Kameradschaft ♪♪♪½ *La Tragedie de la Mine; Comradeship* 1931 A great, early German sound film about Germans struggling to free themselves and French miners trapped underground on the countries' border. In German and French with English subtitles. **80m/B VHS.** *GE* Ernst Busch, Alexander Granach, Fritz Kampers, Gustav Puttjer, Daniel Mendaille, Elizabeth Wenst; *D:* G.W. Pabst; *W:* Laszlo Wajda, Karl Otten, Peter Martin Lampel; *C:* Fritz Arno Wagner, Robert Barberske.

Kamikaze '89 ♪♪♪ 1983 German director Fassbinder has the lead acting role (his last) in this offbeat story of a police lieutenant in Berlin, circa 1989, who investigates a puzzling series of bombings. In German with English subtitles. **90m/C VHS.** *GE* Rainer Werner Fassbinder, Gunther Kaufman, Boy Gobert; *D:* Wolf Gremm; *M:* Tangerine Dream.

Kamikaze Hearts ♪♪ 1991 A quasi-documentary set in the world of two lesbian-junkies (Sharon the actress and Tina the director/producer) making underground X-rated movies. **80m/C VHS.** Sharon Mitchell, Tina "Tigr" Mennett; *D:* Juliet Bashore; *W:* Tina "Tigr" Mennett.

Kanal ♪♪♪½ *They Loved Life* 1956 Wajda's first major success, a grueling account of Warsaw patriots, upon the onset of the Nazis toward the end of the war, fleeing through the ruined city's sewers. Highly acclaimed. Part 2 of Wajda's "War Trilogy," preceded by "A Generation" and followed by "Ashes and Diamonds." In Polish with English subtitles or dubbed. **96m/B VHS.** *PL* Teresa Izewska, Tadeusz Janczar, Vladek Sheybal, Emil Kariewicz, Wienczylaw Glinski; *D:* Andrzej Wajda; *W:* Jerzy Stefan Stawinski; *C:* Jerzy Lipman; *M:* Jan Krenz. Cannes '57: Grand Jury Prize.

Kandahar ♪♪ 2001 Nafas (Pazira) and her family emigrated to Canda from Afghanistan, although they were forced to leave behind Nafas's crippled sister. Now, the sister has vowed to commit suicide rather than live any long under Taliban rule and Nafas returns to try and save her. But journeying to Kandahar is a maze of obstacles and restrictions. Farsi and English. **85m/C VHS.** *IA* Nelofer Pazira, Hassan Tantai, Sadou Teymouri; *D:* Mohsen Makhmalbaf; *W:* Mohsen Makhmalbaf; *C:* Ebraheem Ghafouri; *M:* Mohammad Reza Darvishi.

Kandyland ♪ 1987 (R) An over-the-hill stripper takes a young innocent stripper under her wing. **94m/C VHS.** Sandahl Bergman, Kimberly Evenson, Charles Laulette, Bruce Baum; *D:* Robert Allen Schnitzer; *C:* Robert Brinkmann.

Kangaroo ♪♪♪ 1986 (R) An Australian adaptation of the semi-autobiographical D.H. Lawrence novel. A controversial English novelist and his wife move to the Outback in 1922, and are confronted with all manner of prejudice and temptation. **115m/C VHS.** *AU* Judy Davis, Colin Friels, John Walton, Hugh Keays-Byrne, Julie Nihill; *D:* Tim Burstall; *W:* Evan Jones; *C:* Dan Burstall; *M:* Nathan Waks. Australian Film Inst. '86: Actress (Davis).

The Kansan ♪♪ 1943 The marshall in a Kansas town won't rest until he's stamped out all traces of corruption. **79m/B VHS.** Richard Dix, Victor Jory, Albert Dekker; *D:* George Archainbaud.

Kansas ♪ 1988 (R) Two young men, one a lawless rebel, the other a rational loner, stage a bank heist, and then go on the lam. Lame plot and very weak acting combine to make this film a dud. **111m/C VHS, DVD, Wide.** Matt Dillon, Andrew McCarthy, Leslie Hope, Kyra Sedgwick; *D:* David Stevens; *W:* Spencer Eastman; *C:* David Eggby; *M:* Pino Donaggio.

Kansas City ♪♪♪ 1995 (R) Altman mixes music, politics, crime and the movies in this bittersweet homage to his hometown, set in the jazz-driven 1930s. Star-struck, tough-talking Blondie (Leigh) kidnaps Carolyn Stilton (Richardson), a self-sedating wife of a political shaker (Murphy), in a hair-brained scheme to save her husband from a local mobster (Belafonte). Styled to imitate the brilliant jazz scores played by the likes of Joshua Redman and James Carter, the action can become a bit confusing and Leigh is beyond irritating with her derivative dame routine. Belafonte, however, is brilliant, relishing the part of the legendary Seldom Seen, a real-life K.C. gangster. **110m/C VHS.** Jennifer Jason Leigh, Miranda Richardson, Harry Belafonte, Michael Murphy, Dermot Mulroney, Steve Buscemi, Brooke Smith, Jane Adams; *D:* Robert Altman; *W:* Frank Barhydt, Robert Altman; *C:* Oliver Stapleton; *M:* Hal Willner. N.Y. Film Critics '96: Support. Actor (Belafonte).

Kansas City Confidential ♪♪♪ 1952 An ex-cop on the wrong side of the law launches a sophisticated armored car heist. A disgruntled ex-con gets arrested for the crime on circumstantial evidence. When released, he scours the underworld for the real thieves. **98m/B VHS.** John Payne, Coleen Gray, Preston Foster, Neville Brand, Lee Van Cleef, Jack Elam; *D:* Phil Karlson.

Kansas Pacific ♪♪ 1953 A group of Confederate sympathizers try to stop the Kansas Pacific Railroad from reaching the West Coast in the 1860s. **73m/C VHS.** Sterling Hayden, Eve Miller, Barton MacLane, Reed Hadley, Douglas Hadley; *D:* Ray Nazarro.

The Kansas Terrors ♪♪ 1939 The "Three Mesquiteers" head for the Caribbean to deliver a herd of horses and wind up in a battle against local despot. **57m/B VHS.** Robert "Bob" Livingston, Raymond Hatton, Duncan Renaldo, Julie (Jacqueline Wells) Bishop, Yakima Canutt, Richard Alexander, Maureen McCormack; *D:* George Sherman.

Kaos ♪♪♪ *Chaos* 1985 (R) The Taviani brothers adaptation of four stories by Luigi Pirandello ("The Other Son," "Moonstruck," "The Jar," and "Requiem"), which look at peasant life in Sicily, ranging from the comic to the tragic. A fictional epilog, "Conversing with Mother," has Pirandello talking with the spirit of his dead mother. As with any anthology some stories are stronger than others but all possess the Taviani's great visual style and some fine acting. In Italian with English subtitles. **188m/C VHS.** *IT* Margarita Lozano, Claudio Bigagli, Massimo Bonetti, Omero Antonutti, Enrica Maria Modugno, Ciccio Ingrassia, Franco Franchi, Biagio Barone, Salvatore Rossi, Franco Scaldati, Pasquale Spadola, Regina Bianchi; *D:* Paolo Taviani, Vittorio Taviani; *W:* Paolo Taviani, Vittorio Taviani; *C:* Giuseppe Lanci; *M:* Nicola Piovani.

Kapo ♪♪♪ 1959 A 14-year-old Jewish girl and her family are imprisoned by the Nazis in a concentration camp. There, the girl changes identities with the help of the camp doctor, and rises to the position of camp guard. She proceeds to become taken with her power until a friend commits suicide and jolts the girl back into harsh reality. An Academy Award nominee for Best Foreign Film (lost to "The Virgin Spring"). Primarily English dialogue, with subtitles for foreign language. **116m/B VHS.** *IT FR YU* Susan Strasberg, Laurent Terzieff, Emmanuelle Riva, Gianni "John" Garko; *D:* Gillo Pontecorvo; *W:* Gillo Pontecorvo.

Karate Cop ♪½ 1993 (R) In a future without law or order John Travis (Marchini) is the last cop on earth. He saves Rachel, a beautiful scientist, from a band of scavengers and together they hunt for a hidden crystal with mysterious powers. Only first John has to defeat a gladiator in a martial arts fight to the death. **?m/C VHS.** Ron Marchini, Carrie Chambers, David Carradine, Michael Bristow, D.W. Landingham, Michael Foley, Dana Bentley; *D:* Alan Roberts.

The Karate Kid ♪♪♪½ 1984 (PG) A teenage boy finds out that Karate involves using more than your fists when a handyman agrees to teach him martial arts. The friendship that they develop is deep and sincere; the Karate is only an afterthought. From the director of the original "Rocky," this movie is easy to like. **126m/C VHS, DVD, 8mm.** Ralph Macchio, Noriyuki "Pat" Morita, Elisabeth Shue, Randee Heller, Martin Kove, Chad McQueen, William Zabka; *D:* John G. Avildsen; *W:* Robert Mark Kamen; *M:* Bill Conti.

The Karate Kid: Part 2 ♪♪½ 1986 (PG) Sequel to the first film wherein our high-kicking hero tests his mettle in real-life karate exchanges in Okinawa, and settles a long-standing score. Followed by a second sequel. **95m/C VHS, DVD, 8mm, Wide.** Ralph Macchio, Noriyuki "Pat" Morita, Danny Kamekona, Martin Kove, Tamlyn Tomita, Nobu McCarthy, Yuji Okumoto, William Zabka; *D:* John G. Avildsen; *W:* Robert Mark Kamen; *C:* James A. Crabe; *M:* Bill Conti.

The Karate Kid: Part 3 ♪½ 1989 (PG) Second sequel takes a tired plot and doesn't do much to perk it up. Macchio again battles an evil nemesis and learns about himself, but this time Morita refuses to be a part of his training until, of course, Macchio desperately needs his help. Followed by "The Next Karate Kid," which introduces a new kid—a girl. **105m/C VHS, DVD, 8mm, Wide.** Ralph Macchio, Noriyuki "Pat" Morita, John G. Avildsen, Thomas Ian Griffith, Martin Kove, Sean Kanan, Robin (Robyn) Lively; *D:* John G. Avildsen; *W:* Robert Mark Kamen; *C:* Steve Yaconelli; *M:* Bill Conti.

Karate Warrior ♪½ 1988 Young martial artist is beaten and left for dead by Filipino crime syndicate. Bones mended, he prescribes a dose of their medicine. Plenty of rest and retaliation. **90m/C VHS.** Jared Martin, Ken(saku) Watanabe.

Karmina ♪♪ 1996 Unusual French-Canadian vampire parody finds 140-year-old vamp Karmina (Cyr) fighting with her Transylvanian parents over their insistence that she marry nerdy Vlad (Pelletier). Karmina flees her home and heads to Montreal in search of her aunt, Esmeralda (Castel), who has managed to regain her humanity and now runs a dating service. A magic potion also makes Karmina human (it's a difficult transition) and she falls in love with Philippe (Brouillette) but Vlad's not out of the picture. He also turns up in Montreal, and begins adding to the vampire population. **109m/C VHS.** *CA* Isabelle Cyr, Yves Pelletier, Robert Brouillette, France Castel, Gildor Roy, Raymond Cloutier, Sylvie Potvin; *D:* Gabriel Pelletier; *W:* Gabriel Pelletier, Andree Pelletier, Ann Burke, Yves Pelletier; *C:* Eric Cayla; *M:* Patrick Bourgeois. Genie '97: Art Dir./Set Dec., Costume Des.

Kashmiri Run ♪♪ 1969 (R) Action adventure about trio on the lam from Chinese communists chasing them through Tibet. **101m/C VHS.** *SP* Pernell Roberts, Alexandra Bastedo, Julian Mateos, Gloria Gamata; *D:* John Peyser.

Kaspar Hauser ♪♪ 1993 Historical epic based on the true story of Kaspar Hauser (Eisermann), a 16-year-old found abandoned in Nuremberg, Germany in 1828, who was unable to walk, write, or speak. Entrusted to the scientific concerns of Professor Daumer (Samel), rumors begin to circulate that the boy is actually the Crown Prince of Baden. Supposedly, Kaspar was abducted as a baby and substituted for a child who died so his Uncle Ludwig (Oscsenknecht) could become Grand Duke. Court intrigue and threats abound as Kaspar struggles to survive. German with subtitles. **137m/C VHS.** *GE* Andre Eisermann, Jeremy Clyde, Katharina Thalbach, Udo Samel, Uwe Ochsenknecht; *D:* Peter Sehr; *W:* Peter Sehr; *C:* Gernot Roll; *M:* Nikos Mamangakis.

Kate & Leopold ♪♪½ 2001 (PG-13) Cute but underwhelming romantic comedy involving time travel. Eccentric scientist Stuart (Schreiber) finds a portal that allows him to visit New York City in 1876. But his presence is noticed by dashing Leopold, the Duke of Albany (Jackman), who unwittingly follows Stuart to present-day Manhattan. The Duke manages the adjustment quite well, especially after meeting business exec Kay McKay (Ryan), Stuart's ex-girlfriend. Kate's more interested in a big promotion than romance, though she finds Leopold charming if strange. Too bad Leopold can't hang around, he has to go back to 1876 but can Kate be persuaded to go with him? This is familiar territory for Ryan (who's more brittle than perky) but Jackman does chivalry with the best of them. **121m/C VHS, DVD, Wide.** *US* Meg Ryan, Hugh Jackman, Liev Schreiber, Breckin Meyer, Natasha Lyonne, Bradley Whitford, Paxton Whitehead, Spalding Gray, Philip Bosco, David Aaron Baker; *D:* James Mangold; *W:* James Mangold, Steven Rogers; *C:* Stuart Dryburgh; *M:* Rolfe Kent. Golden Globes '02: Song ("Until").

Kate's Addiction ♪♪ 1999 (R) Kate (Wuhrer) comes to L.A. in search of an old friend (Forke) but she's really interested in more than hanging around. And anyone who gets in her way may not live to regret it. **95m/C VHS, DVD.** Kari Wuhrer, Farrah Forke, Matt Borlenghi; *D:* Eric De La Barre. **VIDEO**

Katherine 🦴 *The Radical* **1975** A young heiress rejects her pampered lifestyle and becomes a violent revolutionary, rebelling against social injustices and the system that spawned them. **98m/C VHS, DVD.** Sissy Spacek, Art Carney, Jane Wyatt, Henry Winkler, Julie Kavner, Hector Elias, Jenny Sullivan; *D:* Jeremy Paul Kagan. **TV**

Katie Tippel 🦴🦴 *Katie's Passion; Cathy Tippel; Hot Sweat; Keetje Tippel* **1975 (R)** In 1881 Amsterdam, a young Dutch prostitute works her way out of poverty and enters a world of education and wealth. A Victorian tale of exploitation with a tough and intelligent Cinderella heroine. In Dutch with English subtitles. **104m/C VHS, DVD, Wide.** *NL* Monique Van De Ven, Rutger Hauer, Eddie Brugman, Hannah De Leeuwe, Andrea Domburg; *D:* Paul Verhoeven; *W:* Gerard Soeteman; *C:* Jan De Bont; *M:* Roger van Otterloo.

Kavik the Wolf Dog 🦴½ *The Courage of Kavik, the Wolf Dog* **1984** Heart-warming story of a courageous dog's love and suffering for the boy he loves. **99m/C VHS.** Ronny Cox, Linda Sorensen, Andrew Ian McMillian, Chris Wiggins, John Ireland; *D:* Peter Carter. **TV**

Kazaam 🦴½ **1996 (PG)** Twelve-year-old Max (Capra) is having problems—bullies are chasing him and his single mom's just found a new boyfriend. But his luck seems ready to change when a battered boombox reveals a seven-foot rappin' genie named Kazaam (O'Neal). The kid's beyond obnoxious and Shaq shouldn't plan to give up b-ball anytime soon (at least for an acting career), even though director Glaser did think up the part for the tall guy just before he met him at an NBA All-Star Game. **93m/C VHS.** Francis Capra, Shaquille O'Neal, Ally Walker, John A. Costelloe, Marshall Manesh, James Acheson; *D:* Paul Michael Glaser; *W:* Christian Ford, Roger Soffer; *C:* Charles Minsky; *M:* Christopher Tyng.

Keaton's Cop 🦴 **1990 (R)** Another cheap cop comedy involving the mistaken identity of an important mob witness. **95m/C VHS.** Lee Majors, Abe Vigoda, Don Rickles; *D:* Robert Burge.

The Keep 🦴🦴 **1983 (R)** At the height of the Nazi onslaught, several German soldiers unleash an unknown power from a medieval stone fortress. Technically impressive but lacking in all other aspects. From a novel by F. Paul Wilson. **96m/C VHS, Wide.** Scott Glenn, Alberta Watson, Juergen Prochnow, Robert Prosky, Gabriel Byrne, Ian McKellen; *D:* Michael Mann; *W:* Michael Mann, Dennis Lynton Clark; *C:* Alex Thomson; *M:* Tangerine Dream.

Keep 'Em Flying 🦴🦴 **1941** Bud and Lou star in this wartime morale-booster that hasn't aged well. The duo follow their barnstorming friend into flight academy; a not-too-taxing plot includes five musical numbers and two Martha Rayes (she plays twins). ♫Pig Foot Pete; Together; I'm Looking for the Boy with the Wistful Eyes; Let's Keep 'Em Flying; I'm Getting Sentimental Over You. **86m/B VHS.** Bud Abbott, Lou Costello, Martha Raye; *D:* Arthur Lubin.

Keep My Grave Open 🦴🦴 *The House Where Hell Froze Over* **1980 (R)** A woman lives in an isolated house where a series of strange murders take place. She attributes them to her brother, but does he really exist? Made cheaply, but not without style; filmed in Harrison County, Texas. **85m/C VHS.** Camilla Carr, Gene Ross, Stephen Tobolowsky, Ann Stafford, Sharon Bunn, Chelcie Ross; *D:* S.F. Brownrigg.

Keep Punching 🦴🦴 **1939** A gambler/boxer is almost destroyed by life in the fast lane, as well as by a seductive woman. **80m/C VHS.** Henry Armstrong, Mae Johnson; *Cameos:* Canada Lee; *D:* John Clein.

Keep Talking Baby 🦴🦴 **1961** Action-packed thriller that finds Eddie in prison after being framed for murder. He escapes and is out for revenge on the organization that put him there. **?m/C VHS.** Eddie Constantine.

Keep the Change 🦴🦴 **1992 (PG-13)** Joe Starling is an artist with painter's block, living in California with his girlfriend Astrid. He decides to revisit the family ranch in Deadrock, Montana, and his crackpot Uncle Smitty and saintly Aunt Lureen. The family ranch is coveted by the evil Overstreet (typecasting for Palance), whose daughter was once loved by Joe but is now married to his ex-best friend. Character more than plot rules this moody, low-key story based on a novel by Thomas McGuane. **95m/C VHS.** William L. Petersen, Lolita (David) Davidovich, Rachel Ticotin, Buck Henry, Jack Palance, Fred Dalton Thompson, Jeff Kober, Lois Smith; *D:* Andy Tennant. **CABLE**

Keeper 🦴🦴 **1984** Wealthy patients at Underwood Asylum suffer unspeakable horrors while under the care of Lee. Detective Dick Driver investigates. Obscure horror spoof. **96m/C VHS.** *CA* Christopher Lee, Tell Schreiber, Sally Gray; *D:* Tom Drake; *W:* Tom Drake.

The Keeper 🦴🦴½ **1996** Disillusioned Paul Lamott (Esposito) is a corrections officer at the King's County House of Detention in Brooklyn. Nevertheless, Paul, who's earning a law degree, is moved by the pleas of Haitian prisoner Jean Baptiste (de Bankole), who swears he's been wrongly accused of rape. Paul, who's father was Haitian, manages to help Jean make bail and then invites him home—to the strong dismay of Paul's teacher wife Angela (Taylor). However, Angela begins warming to Jean's charm—but beware the stranger. **97m/C VHS.** Giancarlo Esposito, Regina Taylor, Isaach de Bankole; *D:* Joe Brewster; *W:* Joe Brewster; *C:* Igor Sunara; *M:* John Petersen.

Keeper of the City 🦴🦴½ **1992 (R)** Gossett stars as a tough detective out to get a vigilante (LaPaglia) who is roaming the streets of Chicago. LaPaglia turns in a good performance as the son of a Mafia operative who wants to rid himself of the Mafia ties that have controlled him. As he pursues his deadly course of action, a newspaper journalist tags him "The Gangster Killer." Coyote plays the crusading journalist who is always interfering in Gossett's business. Good performances and an intriguing storyline combine to make this action-packed thriller worthwhile, although the script isn't as good as Di Pega's novel, which he adapted himself. **95m/C VHS.** Louis Gossett Jr., Peter Coyote, Anthony LaPaglia, Renee Soutendijk, Aeryk Egan, Tony Todd, Peter J. D'Noto; *D:* Bobby Roth; *W:* Gerald Di Pego.

Keeper of the Flame 🦴🦴½ **1942** Tracy and Hepburn manage to keep the murk of this story at bay as war correspondent Steven O'Malley (Tracy) is assigned to write about super patriot Robert V. Forrest, who's just died in an accident. Reclusive widow Christine Forrest (Hepburn) finally agrees to help O'Malley out but what our intrepid reporter discovers is that the hero was really a heel—something Christine still doesn't want known. Based on the novel by I.A.R. Wylie. **100m/B VHS.** Spencer Tracy, Katharine Hepburn, Richard Whorf, Margaret Wycherly, Donald Meek, Stephen McNally, Audrey Christie, Frank Craven, Forrest Tucker, Percy Kilbride, Howard da Silva, Darryl Hickman; *D:* George Cukor; *W:* Donald Ogden Stewart; *C:* William H. Daniels; *M:* Bronislau Kaper.

Keeping On 🦴🦴½ **1981** TV movie with a pro-union stance. A preacher, who is also a millworker, teams up with an organizer to try to unionize the mill. Originally produced for the PBS "American Playhouse" series. **75m/C VHS.** Dick Anthony Williams, Carol Kane, James Broderick, Marcia Rodd, Rosalind Cash, Carl Lee, Danny Glover, Guy Boyd; *D:* Barbara Kopple. **TV**

Keeping the Faith 🦴🦴½ **2000 (PG-13)** Norton's directorial debut sounds like a bad bar joke but turns out to be a slick, if meandering, romantic comedy. He's a priest, Brian, whose longtime best friend Jake (Stiller) is a rabbi with a congregation that wants him married to a nice Jewish girl. As kids, their mutual best pal was Anna, who returns to New York as a workaholic corporate exec (Elfman). The friendship is re-established but so is something more—both men fall for the lady and, unbeknownst to Brian, Anna and Jake begin an affair. More than sparks fly. **127m/C VHS, DVD, Wide.** Edward Norton, Ben Stiller, Jenna Elfman, Anne Bancroft, Eli Wallach, Milos Forman, Ron Rifkin, Holland Taylor, Rena Sofer, Lisa Edelstein, Bodhi (Pine) Elfman; *D:* Edward Norton; *W:* Stuart Blumberg; *C:* Anastas Michos; *M:* Elmer Bernstein.

Keeping Track 🦴 **1986 (R)** Two tourists witness a murder and robbery and find the stolen $5 million on a New York-bound train. The two are relentlessly pursued by everyone, including the CIA and Russian spies. **102m/C VHS.** Michael Sarrazin, Margot Kidder, Alan Scarfe, Ken Pogue, Vlasta Vrana, Donald Pilon; *D:* Robin Spry.

Kelly of the Secret Service 🦴🦴 **1936** Agent tries to find out who stole the plans for a guided missile system. Fast-pace rides over the silliness of the plot. **69m/B VHS.** Lloyd Hughes, Sheila (Manors) Mannors, Fuzzy Knight, Syd Saylor, Jack Mulhall, Forrest Taylor; *D:* Robert F. "Bob" Hill; *W:* Al Martin.

Kelly the Second 🦴½ **1936** Slow-moving boxing comedy about a punch-drunk fighter trying to win again with the encouragement of his trainer and manager. **70m/B VHS.** Guinn "Big Boy" Williams, Patsy Kelly, Charley Chase, Pert Kelton, Edward Brophy, Maxie "Slapsie" Rosenbloom, Harold Huber, DeWitt Jennings, Billy Gilbert, Syd Saylor; *D:* Gus Meins.

Kelly's Heroes 🦴🦴½ **1970 (PG)** A misfit band of crooks are led by Eastwood on a daring mission: to steal a fortune in gold from behind enemy lines. In the process, they almost win WWII. Sutherland is superb, as is McLeod, in his pre-Love Boat days. **145m/C VHS, Wide.** Clint Eastwood, Donald Sutherland, Telly Savalas, Gavin MacLeod, Don Rickles, Carroll O'Connor, Stuart Margolin, Harry Dean Stanton, Jeff Morris, Richard (Dick) Davalos, Perry Lopez, Tom Troupe, Len Lesser, David Hurst, George Savalas, Tom Signorelli; *D:* Brian G. Hutton; *W:* Troy Kennedy Martin; *C:* Gabriel Figueroa; *M:* Lalo Schifrin.

Kemek 🦴 **1988 (R)** An eccentric chemical company owner has his mistress push a new mind-control drug on an American writer, and has them killed after discovering their subsequent affair. Unfortunately, he didn't count on the woman's ex-husband seeking revenge. **82m/C VHS.** David Hedison, Helmut Snider, Mary Woronov, Alexandra Stewart, Cal Haynes.

Kennedy 🦴🦴 **1983** Miniseries biography of JFK from his inauguration to assassination. **278m/C VHS, DVD.** Martin Sheen, Blair Brown, Vincent Gardenia, Geraldine Fitzgerald, E.G. Marshall, John Shea; *D:* Richard Hartley. **TV**

The Kennedys of Massachusetts 🦴🦴½ **1995** Three cassette TV miniseries chronicles six decades of Kennedy life, from Joe Kennedy's (Petersen) courtship of Rose (O'Toole) to the presidential election of JFK and all the various scandals and tragedies. Adapted from the book "The Fitzgeralds and the Kennedys" by Doris Kearns Godwin. **278m/C VHS.** William L. Petersen, Annette O'Toole, Charles Durning, Steven Weber, Tracy Pollan, Campbell Scott. **TV**

The Kennel Murder Case 🦴🦴 **1933** Debonair detective Philo Vance suspects that a clear-cut case of suicide is actually murder. Fourth Vance mystery starring Powell. Remade as "Calling Philo Vance" in 1940. **73m/B VHS.** William Powell, Mary Astor, Jack LaRue, Ralph Morgan, Eugene Pallette; *D:* Michael Curtiz.

Kenny Rogers as the Gambler 🦴🦴½ **1980** Rogers stars as Brady Hawkes, debonair gambler searching for a son he never knew he had. Based on the Rogers song of the same name. One of the highest rated TV movies ever. Followed by several sequels. **94m/C VHS.** Kenny Rogers, Christine Belford, Bruce Boxleitner, Harold Gould, Clu Gulager, Lance LeGault, Lee Purcell, Noble Willingham; *D:* Dick Lowry. **TV**

Kenny Rogers as the Gambler, Part 2: The Adventure Continues 🦴½ **1983** The surprise success of the made-for-TV western based on the popular Kenny Rogers' song spawned this equally popular sequel. Rogers returns as Brady Hawkes, this time searching for his kidnapped son. Followed by two more sequels. **195m/C VHS, 8mm.** Kenny Rogers, Bruce Boxleitner, Linda Evans, Harold Gould, David Hedison, Clu Gulager, Johnny Crawford; *D:* Dick Lowry. **TV**

Kenny Rogers as the Gambler, Part 3: The Legend Continues 🦴🦴 **1987** Roger's third attempt at humanizing the gambler from his hit '70s song. This time, the Gambler gives a hand with the mediating between the warring U.S. government and the Sioux nation. Sitting Bull and Buffalo Bill add credibility to this average undertaking. Made for TV. **190m/C VHS.** Kenny Rogers, Bruce Boxleitner, Linda Gray, Melanie Chartoff, Matt Clark, George Kennedy, Dean Stockwell, Charles Durning, Jeffrey Jones, George American Horse; *D:* Dick Lowry. **TV**

Kent State 🦴🦴 **1981** Recounts the tragic events that took place at Kent State University in 1970, when student demonstrators faced National Guardsmen. Goldstone won an Emmy for Outstanding Direction. **120m/C VHS.** Talia Balsam, Ellen Barkin, Jane Fleiss, John Getz, Keith Gordon; *D:* James Goldstone. **TV**

The Kentuckian 🦴🦴½ **1955** Burt Lancaster stars as a rugged frontiersman who leaves with his son to go to Texas. On their journey the two are harassed by fighting mountaineers. **104m/C VHS, DVD, Wide.** Burt Lancaster, Walter Matthau, Diana Lynn, John McIntire, Dianne Foster, Una Merkel, John Carradine; *D:* Burt Lancaster; *C:* Ernest Laszlo.

Kentucky Blue Streak 🦴½ **1935** Young jockey is framed for murder while riding at an "illegal" racetrack. Later, almost eligible for parole, he escapes from jail to ride "Blue Streak" in the Kentucky Derby. **61m/B VHS.** Eddie Nugent, Frank "Junior" Coghlan, Patricia Scott, Ben Carter.

Kentucky Fried Movie 🦴🦴🦴 **1977 (R)** A zany potpourri of satire about movies, TV, commercials, and contemporary society. Written by Abrahams and the Zuckers, who later gave us "Airplane!" **85m/C VHS, DVD.** Bill Bixby, Jerry Zucker, Jim Abrahams, David Zucker, Donald Sutherland, Henry Gibson, George Lazenby, Tony Dow, Uschi Digart, Rick Baker, Marilyn Joi, Forrest J Ackerman; *D:* John Landis; *W:* Jerry Zucker, Jim Abrahams, David Zucker; *C:* Stephen M. Katz.

Kentucky Jubilee 🦴½ **1951** At the jubilee, a movie director is kidnapped and the master of ceremonies, among others, decides to find him. **67m/B VHS.** Jerry Colonna, Jean Porter, James Ellison, Raymond Hatton, Fritz Feld.

Kentucky Kernels 🦴🦴 *Triple Trouble* **1934** A pair of down and out magicians ('30s comic duo Wheeler and Woolsey) happen upon a young boy (Little Rascal Spanky) who happens to be heir to a fortune. The three head for the rascal's Kentucky home, where they're welcomed with southern inhospitality. Much feuding and slapsticking. **75m/B VHS.** Bert Wheeler, Robert Woolsey, Mary Carlisle, George "Spanky" McFarland, Noah Beery Sr., Lucille LaVerne, Willie Best; *D:* George Stevens; *M:* Max Steiner.

Kentucky Rifle 🦴½ **1955** A Comanche Indian tribe will let a group of stranded pioneers through their territory only if they agree to sell the Kentucky rifles aboard their wagon. **80m/C VHS.** Chill Wills, Lance Fuller, Cathy Downs, Jess Barker, Sterling Holloway, Jeanne Cagney; *D:* Carl K. Hittleman.

Kept 🦴🦴 **2001 (R)** Struggling architectural student Kyle Griffin thinks his worries are over when he lands a job at the firm owned by Barbara Weldon and her husband. But Barbara is a very hands-on employer and soon Kyle is involved in an affair and is a suspect in a murder. Now he has to save himself from being the fall guy. **98m/C VHS, DVD, Wide.** Ice-T, Yvette Nipar, Christian Oliver, Paul Michael Robinson, Michelle Von Flotow, Laura Rose, Art Hingle; *D:* Fred Olen Ray; *W:* Richard Uhug, Kimberly A. Ray; *C:* Theo Angell; *M:* Herman Jackson, Michael van Blum, Barry Taylor. **VIDEO**

Kept Husbands 🦴🦴 **1931** A factory worker saves two lives in an industrial accident, and the boss invites him home to dinner. When he meets the boss' daughter, romance blooms. But their different backgrounds cause difficulties. A bit dull, and dated by its chauvinism. **76m/B VHS.** Dorothy Mackaill, Joel McCrea, Robert McWade, Florence Roberts, Clara Kimball Young, Mary Carr, Ned Sparks, Bryant Washburn; ***D:*** Lloyd Bacon; ***M:*** Max Steiner.

The Kettles in the Ozarks 🦴🦴½ **1956** Since Kilbride retired after the seventh comedy, Hunnicutt played a new male character, Uncle Sledge, in the eighth film. Ma (Main) takes the young'uns to visit their uncle in the Ozarks and finds she must help him and fiancee Bedelia (Merkel) save the failing farm from bootleggers. **81m/B VHS.** Marjorie Main, Arthur Hunnicutt, Una Merkel, Ted de Corsia, Richard Eyer, Joseph (Joe) Sawyer, Richard Deacon; ***D:*** Charles Lamont; ***W:*** Kay Lenard.

The Kettles on Old MacDonald's Farm 🦴🦴½ **1957** The ninth and last in the series finds Ma (Main in her final film) and Pa (Kennelly replacing the retired Kilbride) playing matchmakers for humble lumberman Brad (Smith). Seems he wants to marry the boss' spoiled daughter, Sally (Talbott), whom Ma decides needs a little backwoods seasoning before she'll make the proper wife. **82m/B VHS.** Marjorie Main, Parker Fennelly, John Smith, Gloria Talbott, Claude Akins, Roy Barcroft, Patricia Morrow, George Dunn; ***D:*** Virgil W. Vogel; ***W:*** Herbert Margolis, William Raynor.

Kevin & Perry Go Large 🦴½ **2000 (R)** The Brits can make bad teen sex comedies adapted from TV shows just as easily as Americans can. Kevin (Enfield) and Perry (Burke in drag) are a couple of gormless teenage boys who have only one thing on their teeny brains. And since the Brits all seem to go to Spain to be naughty, the boys decide to take their summer holidays in party capital Ibiza and get some chicks. Only problem is Kevin's parents decide to accompany them. Bummer (or whatever the Brit equivalent would be). May make more sense if you've seen the characters on TV. **83m/C VHS, DVD.** *GB* Harry Enfield, Kathy Burke, Rhys Ifans, Laura Fraser, Tabitha Wady, James Fleet, Louisa Rix; ***D:*** Ed Bye; ***W:*** David Cummings, Harry Enfield; ***C:*** Alan Almond.

The Key 🦴🦴½ **1958** A long, slow WWII drama about the key to an Italian girl's apartment that gets passed from tugboat skipper to tugboat skipper before dangerous missions. Ultimately she finds true love, or does she? Based on the novel "Stella" by Jan de Hartog. **134m/B VHS.** *GB* William Holden, Sophia Loren, Trevor Howard, Oscar Homolka, Kieron Moore; ***D:*** Carol Reed; ***W:*** Carl Foreman; ***C:*** Oswald Morris; ***M:*** Malcolm Arnold. British Acad. '58: Actor (Howard).

Key Exchange 🦴🦴½ **1985 (R)** Kevin Scott and Paul Kurta based this contemporary look at love and commitments on Kevin Wade's popular play. Two New York City "yuppies" have reached a point in their relationship where an exchange of apartment keys commonly occurs—but they are hesitant. **96m/C VHS.** Brooke Adams, Ben Masters, Daniel Stern, Tony Roberts, Danny Aiello, Annie Golden, Nancy Mette; ***D:*** Barnet Kellman; ***W:*** Kevin Scott, Paul Kurta; ***M:*** Jonathan Elias.

Key Largo 🦴🦴🦴½ **1948** WWII vet Bogart travels to the run-down Florida hotel owned by Barrymore and Bacall who are, respectively, the father and widow of a war buddy. Bogart notes the other guests are of a decidedly criminal bent, but as a hurricane threatens, no one can leave. One-time mob kingpin Robinson lords it over the others while Bogart keeps his usual cynical cool. Trevor, who plays Robinson's alcoholic ex-singer moll, deservedly won an Oscar for her role. Based on a play by Maxwell Anderson. **101m/B VHS, DVD.** Humphrey Bogart, Lauren Bacall, Claire Trevor, Edward G. Robinson, Lionel Barrymore, Thomas Gomez, Dan Seymour; ***D:*** John Huston; ***W:*** Richard Brooks, John Huston; ***C:*** Karl Freund; ***M:*** Max Steiner. Oscars '48: Support. Actress (Trevor).

The Key Man 🦴½ *Life at Stake* **1957** A radio show host manages to get mixed up with gangsters after recreating a crime on the air. He uses his knowledge of crime to thwart the crooks. **63m/B VHS.** *GB* Lee Patterson, Hy Hazell, Colin Gordon, Philip Leaver, Paula Byrne; ***D:*** Montgomery Tully; ***M:*** Les Baxter.

The Key to Rebecca 🦴🦴½ **1985** The Nazis and the British go head-to-head in war torn North Africa. As the Germans push their way across Egypt, they find an unexpected ally in a half-German/half-Arab killer behind the British lines. Tense, well-made thriller; originally a miniseries. **190m/C VHS.** David Soul, Cliff Robertson, Robert Culp, Season Hubley, Lina Raymond, Anthony Quayle, David Hemmings; ***D:*** David Hemmings. **TV**

Key to the City 🦴🦴½ **1950** Light comedy featuring Gable and Young as two small town mayors who meet and fall in love at a convention in San Francisco. Throw in some sharp lines, a little slapstick, and a bit of satire for an amusing picture. Based on the story by Albert Beich. **99m/B VHS.** Clark Gable, Loretta Young, Frank Morgan, Marilyn Maxwell, Raymond Burr, James Gleason, Lewis Stone, Raymond Walburn; ***D:*** George Sidney; ***W:*** Robert Riley Crutcher.

The Keys of the Kingdom 🦴🦴🦴 **1944** An earnest adaptation of A.J. Cronin's novel about a young Scottish missionary spreading God's word in 19th Century China. **137m/B VHS.** Gregory Peck, Thomas Mitchell, Edmund Gwenn, Vincent Price, Roddy McDowall, Cedric Hardwicke, Peggy Ann Garner, James Gleason, Anne Revere, Rose Stradner, Sara Allgood, Abner Biberman, Arthur Shields; ***D:*** John M. Stahl; ***W:*** Joseph L. Mankiewicz, Nunnally Johnson; ***C:*** Arthur C. Miller.

Keys to Tulsa 🦴🦴½ **1996 (R)** After losing his job as a lowly movie reviewer (gasp!), Richter Bourdreau (Stoltz), the black-sheep son of a wealthy Tulsa family, is lured into a blackmail scheme by his ex-flame Vicky (Unger) and her perpetually stoned husband Ronnie (Spader). When the tables are turned on him, Richter finally gets up off of his slacker butt for some revenge. Excellent cast includes Moore as his flinty mother and Coburn as a wealthy redneck patriarch. Stoltz's performance holds the spiraling story of class distinction, murder and deceit together, and Spader's Elvis-helmeted loser is fun to watch. Based on the novel by Brian Fair Berkey. **112m/C VHS, DVD.** Eric Stoltz, James Spader, Mary Tyler Moore, Joanna Going, Cameron Diaz, James Coburn, Michael Rooker, Peter Strauss, Deborah Kara Unger; ***D:*** Leslie Greif; ***W:*** Harley Peyton; ***C:*** Robert Fraisse; ***M:*** Stephen Endelman.

The KGB: The Secret War 🦴½ *Lethal* **1986 (PG-13)** Reheated Cold War fare. **90m/C VHS.** Sally Kellerman, Michael Ansara, Michael Billington; ***W:*** Sandra K. Bailey; ***C:*** Peter Collister.

Khartoum 🦴🦴½ **1966** A sweeping but talky adventure epic detailing the last days of General "Chinese" Gordon as the title city is besieged by Arab tribes in 1884. **134m/C VHS, DVD, Wide.** Charlton Heston, Laurence Olivier, Ralph Richardson, Richard Johnson, Alexander Knox, Hugh Williams, Nigel Green, Michael Hordern, Johnny Sekka; ***D:*** Basil Dearden; ***W:*** Robert Ardrey; ***C:*** Edward Scaife; ***M:*** Frank Cordell.

The Kick Fighter 🦴 **1991** Would you believe the hero has to kickbox to finance his kid sister's operation? Grungy, Bangkok-set chopsocky cheapie leaves no cliche untouched, but fights are well-staged. A strange end credit lauds real-life champ Urquidez, here a bad guy. **92m/C VHS.** Richard Norton, Benny "The Jet" Urquidez, Glen Ruehland, Franco Guerrero, Erica Van Wagener, Steve Rackman; ***D:*** Anthony Maharaj.

Kick of Death: The Prodigal Boxer 🦴 **198? (R)** A young boxer is accused of a murder he didn't commit, and fights a battle to the death to prove it. **90m/C VHS.** Mang Sei, Suma Wah Lung, Pa Hung; ***D:*** Chai Yang Min.

Kickboxer 🦴½ **1989 (R)** The brother of a permanently crippled kickboxing champ trains for a revenge match. **97m/C VHS, DVD.** Jean-Claude Van Damme, Rochelle Ashana, Dennis Chan, Dennis Alexio; ***D:*** Mark DiSalle; ***W:*** Jean-Claude Van Damme, Mark DiSalle, Glenn A. Bruce; ***C:*** Jon Kranhouse; ***M:*** Paul Hertzog.

Kickboxer 2: The Road Back 🦴½ **1990 (R)** Mitchell takes over for Van Damme in this action sequel which finds our athletic hero seeking revenge on the kickboxer who murdered his brother. **90m/C VHS.** Sasha Mitchell, Peter Boyle, John Diehl; ***D:*** Albert Pyun.

Kickboxer 3: The Art of War 🦴½ **1992 (R)** Mitchell returns in this second sequel. This time the American kickboxing champ flies to Rio for a big match which turns out to be fixed by a local mobster. For a little more fun our hero saves a kidnapped girl and fights a hired killer. **92m/C VHS.** Sasha Mitchell, Dennis Chan, Richard Comar, Noah Verduzco, Althea Miranda, Ian Jacklin; ***D:*** Rick King.

Kickboxer 4: The Aggressor 🦴🦴½ **1994 (R)** Martial arts expert David Sloan (Mitchell) was framed by sworn enemy Tong Po but now he's back and looking for revenge. **90m/C VHS.** Sasha Mitchell, Kamal Krifia, Nicholas Guest, Deborah Mansy, Brad Thornton; ***D:*** Albert Pyun.

Kickboxer the Champion 🦴 **1991** The opium trade is in for a kick to the stomach when Archer challenges the big man in charge to a deathly duel. **?m/C VHS.** Don Murray, Wayne Archer; ***D:*** Alton Cheung.

Kicked in the Head 🦴🦴 **1997 (R)** Redmond, a loser who dreams of the Hindenburg disaster, is newly jobless, homeless and loveless. He decides to go on a "spiritual quest", which unfortunately consists of bad poetry and worse trouble, through Manhattan's Lower East Side. His Uncle Sam (Woods) wants him to deliver a package, his buddy Stretch (Rapaport) wants him to work for his shady (and sometimes violent) beer business and stewardess Megan (Fiorentino) wants him to leave her alone. It's all settled in a hail of gunfire and car chases, because that's how things are solved in the movies. Director Harrison did more with much less in debut "Rhythym Thief." **97m/C VHS, DVD.** Kevin Corrigan, Linda Fiorentino, James Woods, Lili Taylor, Michael Rapaport, Burt Young, Olek Krupa; ***D:*** Matthew Harrison; ***W:*** Matthew Harrison, Kevin Corrigan; ***C:*** John Thomas, Howard Krupa; ***M:*** Stephen Endelman.

Kicking and Screaming 🦴🦴🦴 **1995 (R)** Baumbach's deft, though slightly self-conscious directorial debut examines the post-college grad angst of Grover (Hamilton) and his three other slacker roomies. In denial of their recently achieved non-student status, the four bond together in pursuit of the inane and trivial, while their various girlfriends slip more easily into adulthood. Funny and tender flashback scenes of Grover and girlfriend Jane (D'Abo) add depth without all the dialogue, well-written though it is. Hilarious highlight occurs as roommate Otis interviews for that most popular of low-budget, Gen-X movie jobs—video store clerk. **96m/C VHS.** Josh Hamilton, Olivia D'Abo, Carlos Jacott, Christopher Eigeman, Eric Stoltz, Jason Wiles, Parker Posey, Cara Buono, Elliott Gould; ***D:*** Noah Baumbach; ***W:*** Oliver Berkman, Noah Baumbach; ***C:*** Steven Bernstein; ***M:*** Phil Marshall.

Kicks 🦴½ **1985** Two well-off San Francisco professionals play high-risk games with each other, culminating in a life-or-death hunt. **97m/C VHS.** Anthony Geary, Shelley Hack, Tom Mason, Ian Abercrombie, James Avery; ***D:*** William Wiard; ***M:*** Peter Bernstein. **TV**

The Kid 🦴🦴🦴 **1921** Sensitive and sassy film about a tramp who takes home an orphan. Chaplin's first feature. Also launched Coogan as the first child superstar. **60m/B VHS, DVD.** Charlie Chaplin, Jackie Coogan, Edna Purviance; ***D:*** Charlie Chaplin; ***W:*** Charlie Chaplin.

Kid 🦴🦴½ **1990 (R)** Young guy carries grudge for the murder of his parents and seeks pound of flesh. Enter mysterious beautiful woman and copious complications. Good sound FX. **94m/C VHS.** C. Thomas Howell, R. Lee Ermey, Brian Austin Green, Sarah Trigger, Dale Dye; ***D:*** John Mark Robinson.

The Kid 🦴🦴½ **1997 (PG)** High schooler Jimmy Albright (Saumier) is secretly taking boxing lessons from trainer Harry Sloan (Steiger) since his parents don't approve. Jimmy is a natural and is ready to compete in the amateur championship match. Then Harry dies and fellow boxer Trey (Brochu) schemes to have Jimmy's parents find out about his secret life and forbid him to box. **89m/C VHS, DVD, Wide.** *CA* Jeff Saumier, Rod Steiger, Ray Aranha, Mark Camacho, Jane Wheeler, Tod Fennell, Daniel Brochu, Jason Tremblay; ***D:*** John Hamilton; ***W:*** Seymour Blicker; ***M:*** Normand Corbeil.

Kid and the Killers 🦴 **198? (PG)** Young orphan and a hardened criminal band together to pursue a villain. **90m/C VHS.** Jon Cypher.

The Kid Brother 🦴🦴🦴½ **1927** The shy, weak son of a tough sheriff, Harold fantasizes about being a hero like his father and big brothers, falls in love with a carnival lady, and somehow saves the day. Classic silent comedy. **84m/B VHS.** Harold Lloyd, Walter James, Jobyna Ralston; ***D:*** Ted Wilde.

Kid Colter 🦴🦴½ **1985** Enjoyable family film about a city kid who goes to visit his dad in a remote wilderness area of the Pacific Northwest. While there he is abducted by two grizzly mountain men and left for dead, but survives and pursues his abductors relentlessly. Received the Film Advisory Board Award of Excellence and the Award of Merit from the Academy of Family Films. **101m/C VHS.** Jim Stafford, Jeremy Shamos, Hal Terrance, Greg Ward, Jim Turner; ***D:*** David O'Malley; ***W:*** David O'Malley.

Kid Courageous 🦴 **1935** An athlete goes west, tracks ore mine thieves and prevents a hot-blooded spitfire from marrying the wrong man. **53m/B VHS.** Bob Steele.

Kid Dynamite *Queen of Broadway* **1943** A Bowery Boys series episode. Gorcey is a boxer who is kidnapped to prevent his participation in a major fight. The real fighting occurs when his brother is substituted, and Gorcey is smitten. **73m/B VHS.** Leo Gorcey, Huntz Hall, Bobby Jordan, Gabriel Dell, Pamela Blake; ***D:*** Wallace Fox.

A Kid for Two Farthings 🦴🦴½ **1955** An episodic, sentimental portrait of the Jewish quarter in London's East End, centered on a boy with a malformed goat he thinks is a magic unicorn capable of granting wishes and bringing happiness to his impoverished 'hood. Acclaimed adaptation of a novel by screenwriter Wolf Mankowitz, also on tape in a shorter rehash as "The Unicorn." **96m/C VHS.** Jonathan Ashmore.

Kid from Brooklyn 🦴🦴 **1946** A shy, musically inclined milkman becomes a middleweight boxer by knocking out the champ in a street brawl. Remake of "The Milky Way" by Harold Lloyd. Available with digitally remastered stereo and original movie trailer. ♫Sunflower Song; Hey, What's Your Name; You're the Cause Of It All; Welcome, Burleigh; I Love An Old-Fashioned Song; Josie. **113m/C VHS.** Danny Kaye, Virginia Mayo, Eve Arden, Fay Bainter, Walter Abel; ***D:*** Norman Z. McLeod; ***C:*** Gregg Toland.

Kid from Gower Gulch 🦴 **1947** A singing, non-horse-riding cowboy enters a rodeo through a clever ruse. **56m/B VHS.** Spade Cooley.

The Kid from Left Field 🦴🦴 **1979** Bat boy for the San Diego Padres transforms the team from losers to champions when he passes on the advice of his father, a "has-been" ballplayer, to the team members. TV remake of the 1953 classic. **80m/C VHS.** Gary Coleman, Robert Guillaume, Ed McMahon, Tab Hunter; ***D:*** Adell Aldrich. **TV**

Kid from Not-So-Big 🦴🦴 **1978 (G)** A family film that tells the story of Jenny, a young girl left to carry on her grandfather's frontier-town newspaper. When two con-men come to town, Jenny sets out to expose them. **87m/C VHS.** Jennifer

McAllister, Veronica Cartwright, Robert Viharo, Paul Tulley; *D:* William Crain.

Kid from Spain 🦴🦴½ **1932** Early Busby Berkeley choreography highlights this fun, if nonsensical, musical. Thanks to the usual mixups, college boy Eddie (Cantor) witnesses a bank robbery and flees to his friend Ricardo's (Young) home in Mexico, with the crooks on his trail. Then he gets mistaken for a famous bullfighter and is even forced into the ring. Oh, and there's some romantic complications as well. ♫The College Song; Look What You've Done; In the Moonlight; What a Perfect Combination. **96m/B VHS.** Eddie Cantor, Robert Young, Lyda Roberti, Ruth Hall, John Miljan, Noah Beery Sr., J. Carrol Naish, Robert Emmett O'Connor; *D:* Leo McCarey; *W:* William Anthony McGuire, Bert Kalmar, Harry Ruby; *C:* Gregg Toland.

Kid Galahad 🦴🦴🦴 *The Battling Bellhop* **1937** Well-acted boxing drama with Robinson playing an honest promoter who wants to make Morris into a prize fighter. Davis plays the girl they both want. Remade as "The Wagons Roll at Night" and then made again as an Elvis Presley vehicle. **101m/B VHS.** Edward G. Robinson, Bette Davis, Humphrey Bogart, Wayne Morris, Jane Bryan, Harry Carey Sr., Veda Ann Borg; *D:* Michael Curtiz; *W:* Seton I. Miller; *C:* Gaetano Antonio "Tony" Gaudio; *M:* Max Steiner.

Kid Galahad 🦴🦴 **1962** The King plays a young boxer who weathers the fight game, singing seven songs along the way. ♫King of the Whole Wide World; This Is Living; I Got Lucky; A Whistling Tune; Home Is Where The Heart Is; Riding the Rainbow; Love Is For Loves. **95m/C VHS, Wide.** Elvis Presley, Lola Albright, Charles Bronson, Ned Glass, Joan Blackman, Ed Asner, Gig Young; *D:* Phil Karlson; *C:* Burnett Guffey.

A Kid in Aladdin's Palace 🦴🦴½ **1997 (PG)** Burger flipper Calvin (Nicholas) time travels to anicent Arabia thanks to a mischief-making genie (Negron). He meets Princess Scheherazade (Mitra), who wants Calvin's help in fighting evil Luxor (Faulkner), who's overthrown her father, King Aladdin (Ipale). **89m/C VHS, DVD.** Thomas Ian Nicholas, Rhona Mitra, Taylor Negron, James Faulkner, Aharon Ipale; *D:* Robert L. Levy; *W:* Michael Part; *C:* Wally Pfister; *M:* David Michael Frank.

A Kid in King Arthur's Court 🦴½ **1995 (PG)** Lame adaptation of Mark Twain's "A Connecticut Yankee in King Arthur's Court" finds insecure California teen Calvin Fuller (Nicholas), falling down a hole created by an earthquake and landing in Camelot. Arthur's (Ackland) a doddering old man with a cute teen daughter, Princess Katey (Baeza), who needs some help in defeating the evil Lord Belasco (Malik). Naturally, Calvin helps out and gains confidence in himself. Okay time-waster for the kids. **91m/C VHS.** Thomas Ian Nicholas, Joss Ackland, Art Malik, Paloma Baeza, Kate Winslet, Ron Moody, Daniel Craig; *D:* Michael Gottlieb; *W:* Michael Part, Robert L. Levy; *C:* Elemer Ragalyi; *M:* J.A.C. Redford.

Kid Millions 🦴🦴½ **1934** Vintage musical comedy in which a dull-witted Brooklyn boy must travel to exotic Egypt to collect an inherited fortune. The finale is filmed in early three-strip Technicolor. Lucille Ball appears as a Goldwyn Girl. ♫Your Head on My Shoulder; Ice Cream Fantasy; An Earful of Music; When My Ship Comes In; Okay Toots; I Want to be a Minstrel Man; Mandy. **90m/B VHS.** Eddie Cantor, Ethel Merman, Ann Sothern, George Murphy; *D:* Roy Del Ruth.

Kid Monk Baroni 🦴🦴½ **1952** Street punk Baroni (Nimoy) leaves his gang behind when a good-guy priest (Rober) introduces him to boxing. The kid rises to success thanks to a cagey manager (Cabot) and despite the presence of organized crime. Typical B-movie melodrama. **80m/B VHS.** Leonard Nimoy, Bruce Cabot, Richard Rober, Kathleen Freeman; *D:* Harold Schuster.

Kid 'n' Hollywood and Polly Tix in Washington **1933** These two "Baby Burlesks" shorts star a cast of toddlers, featuring the most famous moppet of all time, Shirley Temple, in her earliest screen appearances. **20m/B VHS.** Shirley Temple.

Kid Ranger 🦴 **1936** A ranger shoots an innocent man, but later sets things straight by bringing the real culprit to justice. **57m/B VHS.** Bob Steele, William Farnum; *D:* Robert North Bradbury.

Kid Sister 🦴½ **1945** A young girl is determined to grab her sister's boyfriend for herself, and enlists the aid of a burglar to do it. **56m/B VHS.** Roger Pryor, Judy Clark, Frank Jenks, Constance Worth.

Kid Vengeance 🦴½ **1975 (R)** After witnessing the brutal slaying of his family, a boy carries out a personal vendetta against the outlaws. **90m/C VHS.** Leif Garrett, Jim Brown, Lee Van Cleef, John Marley, Glynnis O'Connor; *D:* Joseph Manduke.

The Kid Who Loved Christmas 🦴🦴 **1990** After his adoptive mother is killed in a car accident, a young boy is taken from his adoptive father. The boy, upset about being removed from his new family, writes to Santa Claus for help. A touching yuletide drama. This was Sammy Davis Jr.'s last film. **118m/C VHS.** Cicely Tyson, Michael Warren, Sammy Davis Jr., Gilbert Lewis, Ken Page, Della Reese, Esther Rolle, Ben Vereen, Vanessa L(ynne) Williams, John Beal, Trent Cameron; *D:* Arthur Seidelman; *C:* Hanania Baer. **TV**

The Kid with the Broken Halo 🦴🦴 **1982** Coleman and Guillaume are paired again in this unsuccessful pilot for a TV series. A young angel, out to earn his wings, must try to help three desperate families, with the help of an experienced angel. **100m/C VHS.** Gary Coleman, Robert Guillaume, June Allyson, Mason Adams, Ray Walston, John Pleshette, Kim Fields, Georg Stanford Brown, Telma Hopkins; *D:* Leslie Martinson. **TV**

The Kid with the 200 I.Q. 🦴🦴 **1983** When an earnest boy genius enters college at age 13, predictable comic situations arise that involve his attempts at impressing his idolized astronomy professor (Guillaume), as well as an equally unrequited bout of first love. Harmless comedy, one of a series of squeaky-clean family fare starring Coleman. **96m/C VHS.** Gary Coleman, Robert Guillaume, Harriet Hilliard Nelson, Dean Butler, Karli Michaelson, Christina Murrull, Mel Stewart; *D:* Leslie Martinson. **TV**

The Kid with the X-Ray Eyes 🦴🦴 **1999 (PG)** Twelve-year-old Bobby wants to be a spy when he grows up. Then he finds a strange pair of glasses that allow him to see through anything. He attracts the attentions of the C.I.A., the police, and a pair of theives who all want his special specs. **84m/C VHS, DVD.** Justin Berfield, Robert Carradine, Mark Collie, Diane Salinger, Griffin (Griffen) Drew, Brinke Stevens; *D:* Sherman Scott; *W:* Sean O'Bannon; *C:* Theo Angell; *M:* Jay Bolton. **VIDEO**

Kidco 🦴🦴 **1983 (PG)** The true story of a money-making corporation headed and run by a group of children ranging in age from 9 to 16. **104m/C VHS.** Scott Schwartz, Elizabeth Gorcey, Cinnamon Idles, Tristen Skylar; *D:* Ronald F. Maxwell.

Kidnap Syndicate 🦴½ **1976 (R)** Kidnappers swipe two boys, releasing one—the son of a wealthy industrialist who meets their ransom demands. When they kill the other boy, a mechanic's son, the father goes on a revengeful killing spree. **105m/C VHS.** *IT* James Mason, Valentina Cortese; *D:* Fernando Di Leo.

Kidnapped 🦴🦴½ **1960** A young boy is sold by his wicked uncle as a slave, and is helped by an outlaw. A Disney film based on the Robert Louis Stevenson classic. **94m/C VHS.** Peter Finch, James MacArthur, Peter O'Toole; *D:* Robert Stevenson.

Kidnapped woof! **1987 (R)** When a teenage girl is kidnapped by pornographers, her sister seeks help from a tough cop and together they go undercover to find her. Plot is flimsy cover for what is actually an exploitative piece. **100m/C VHS.** David Naughton, Barbara Crampton, Lance LeGault, Chick Vennera, Charles Napier; *D:* Howard (Hikmet) Avedis; *W:* Howard (Hikmet) Avedis.

Kidnapped 🦴🦴½ **1995** Cable adaptation of Robert Louis Stevenson's 1886 novel. In 1751 shanghaied young David Balfour (McCardie) and Highland patriot Aln Breck Stewart (Assante) escape from a slave ship and return to Scotland to battle the British. **?m/C VHS.** Armand Assante, Brian McCardie, Michael Kitchen, Brian Blessed, Patrick Malahide; *D:* Ivan Passer; *W:* John Goldsmith. **CABLE**

Kidnapped in Paradise 🦴🦴 **1998 (PG-13)** Spoiled beauty Megan (Ross), her fiance Jack, and her practical sister, Beth (Fisher), are sailing in the Caribbean when their yacht is boarded by Renard, who's obsessed with Megan. He kills Jack, kidnaps Megan, and leaves Beth in the sinking vessel. She's rescued by Matt, who agrees to help her find her sister, which leads them to Renard's private island. **91m/C VHS.** Joely Fisher, Charlotte Ross, Rob Knepper, David Beecroft; *D:* Rob Hedden; *W:* David Chisholm. **CABLE**

Kidnapping of Baby John Doe **1988** Tragedy strikes a family's newborn, and they must make the terrifying decision between life and death. A doctor and nurse, however, take matters into their own hands to save the baby. **90m/C VHS.** Helen Hughes, Jayne (Jane) Eastwood, Janet-Laine Green, Geoffery Boues, Peter Gerretsen.

The Kidnapping of the President 🦴🦴½ **1980 (R)** The U.S. president is taken hostage by Third World terrorists. The Secret Service is on the ball trying to recover the nation's leader. Well-integrated subplot involves the vice president in a scandal. Engrossing political thriller. Based on novel by Charles Templeton. **113m/C VHS, DVD.** *CA* William Shatner, Hal Holbrook, Van Johnson, Ava Gardner, Miguel Fernandes; *D:* George Mendeluk.

Kids 🦴🦴 **1995** Very controversial docudrama about 24 hours in the lives of some aimless New York teenagers. The sullen Telly (Fitzpatrick) enjoys bragging about his skill in deflowering virgins but his promiscuity has lead Jennie (Sevigny) to test H.I.V. positive—something Telly is as yet unaware of. Telly'd rather hang around with best friend Casper (Pierce) anyway, out on the streets, being generally profane and obnoxious. Can either be regarded as a brutally realistic look at teen life today or a lot of fuss about nothing. Korine was 19 when he wrote the screenplay. The MPAA rated the film NC-17, after a protest the distributors chose to release it unrated. **90m/C VHS, DVD, Wide.** Jon Abrahams, Leo Fitzpatrick, Justin Pierce, Chloe Sevigny, Rosario Dawson, Sarah Henderson, Harold Hunter, Yakira Peguero, Joseph Knafelmacher; *D:* Larry Clark; *W:* Harmony Korine; *C:* Eric Alan Edwards; *M:* Louis Barlow. Ind. Spirit '96: Debut Perf. (Pierce).

The Kids Are Alright 🦴🦴🦴½ **1979 (PG)** A feature-length compilation of performances and interviews spanning the first 15 years of the rock group, The Who. Includes rare footage from the "Rolling Stones Rock and Roll Circus" film. Songs include: "My Generation," "I Can't Explain," "Young Man's Blues," "Won't Get Fooled Again," "Baba O' Reilly," and excerpts from "Tommy." **106m/C VHS.** Roger Daltrey, Pete Townshend, Keith Moon, John Entwhistle, Ringo Starr, Keith Richards, Steve Martin, Tom Smothers, Rick Danko.

Kids in the Hall: Brain Candy 🦴🦴 *The Drug* **1996 (R)** The Canadian Kids bring their Monty Python-meets-SCTV humor to the big screen with moderate success. Dr. Cooper (McDonald), facing corporate downsizing, allows his new, untested anti-depressant to be released to the public after it shows promise. The drug, Gleemonex, sweeps the country by forcing the user's mind to focus on a favorite memory. As befits the troupe's twisted vision, these happy memories aren't always pleasant to the "Family Values" crowd. The easily offended should be warned—there's a character named "Cancer Boy." The story wanders a bit, giving everyone a chance to show their versatility (these Kids collectively play 32 different roles). Sophomore director Makin served the same duty on many of the TV episodes. **88m/C VHS.** Dave Foley, Bruce McCulloch, Kevin McDonald, Scott Thompson, Mark McKinney, Janeane Garofalo; *D:* Kelly Makin; *W:* Bruce McCulloch, Kevin McDonald, Scott Thompson, Mark McKinney, Norm Hiscock; *C:* David Makin; *M:* Craig Northey.

Kid's Last Ride 🦴 **1941** Three tough guys come into town to settle a feud. **55m/B VHS.** Ray Corrigan, John "Dusty" King, Max Terhune, Luana Walters, Edwin Brian; *D:* S. Roy Luby.

Kids of the Round Table 🦴🦴½ **1996** Eleven-year-old Alex (Morina) and his buddies like to have mock sword battles, pretending to be King Arthur and his knights. When their games are broken up by the local bully, Alex takes off into the woods where he discovers a sword in a stone. It's the legendary Excalibur and when Alex removes it, Merlin (McDowell) appears, explaining the sword will give the boy special powers. Of course, Alex abuses his newfound strength until he comes to the rescue of his friends. **89m/C VHS.** *CA* Johnny Morina, Michael Ironside, Malcolm McDowell, Peter Aykroyd, Rene Simard; *D:* Robert Tinnell; *W:* David Sherman; *C:* Roxanne Di Santo; *M:* Normand Corbeil.

Kika 🦴🦴 **1994** Another flamboyant comedy from Almodovar finds irrepressible beautician Kika (Forque) involved with kinky photographer Ramon (Casanovas) and his stepfather Nicholas (Coyote), a sinister American pulp novelist. There's also Andrea Scarface (Jean-Paul Gaultier-costumed Abril), the host of a vile tabloid TV show called "Today's Worst," and Kika's lesbian maid Juana (de Palma) whose brother happens to be an escaped con/porn star, leading to an outlandish rape and...well, it's all pretty nonsensical, anyway. Spanish with subtitles. **115m/C VHS, DVD.** *SP* Veronica Forque, Peter Coyote, Victoria Abril, Alex Casanovas, Rossy de Palma; *D:* Pedro Almodovar; *W:* Pedro Almodovar; *C:* Alfredo Mayo; *M:* Enrique Granados.

Kikujiro 🦴🦴 **1999 (PG-13)** Eight-year-old Masao (Sekiguchi) lives with his grandmother. His father is dead and his mother lives in a distant town due to her job. Bored on his summer vacation, the boy decides to visit his mother—accompanied by the tough-guy husband, Kikujiro (Kitano), of a neighbor. Only this guy doesn't have much of an idea about kids and their travels lead to some unpredictable adventures. Clumsy and protracted; Japanese with subtitles. **116m/C VHS, DVD.** *JP* Takeshi "Beat" Kitano, Yusuke Sekiguchi; *D:* Takeshi "Beat" Kitano; *W:* Takeshi "Beat" Kitano; *C:* Katsumi Yanagishima; *M:* Joe Hisaishi.

The Kill 🦴🦴½ **1973** A rough, cynical, hard-boiled, womanizing detective tracks down stolen cash in downtown Macao. **81m/C VHS.** Richard Jaeckel, Henry Duval, Judy Washington.

Kill Alex Kill woof! **1983** A Vietnam POW returns to find his family murdered, and uses the crime underworld to take revenge. **88m/C VHS.** Tony Zarindast, Tina Bowmann, Chris Ponti.

Kill and Kill Again 🦴🦴½ **1981 (PG)** A martial arts champion attempts to rescue a kidnapped Nobel Prize-winning chemist who has developed a high-yield synthetic fuel. Colorful, tongue-in-cheek, and fun even for those unfamiliar with the genre. **100m/C VHS, DVD.** James Ryan, Anneline Kriel, Stan Schmidt, Bill Flynn, Norman Robinson, Ken Gampu, John Ramsbottom; *D:* Ivan Hall; *W:* John Crowther; *C:* Tai Krige.

Kill, Baby, Kill 🦴🦴🦴 *Curse of the Living Dead; Operacione Paura* **1966** A small Transylvania town is haunted by the ghost of a seven-year-old witchcraft victim, and the town's suicide victims all seem to have hearts of gold (coins, that is). Lots of style and atmosphere in this Transylvanian tale from horror tongue in cheekster Bava. Considered by many genre connoisseurs to be the B man's finest, except that it bears early symptoms of the director's late onset infatuation with the zoom shot. **83m/C VHS, DVD.** *IT* Erika Blanc, Giacomo "Jack" Rossi-Stuart, Fabienne Dali, Giana Vivaldi; *D:* Mario Bava; *W:* Mario Bava; *C:* Antonio Rinaldi; *M:* Carlo Rustichelli.

Kill by Inches 1999 Strange and stylized story follows traumatized tailor Thomas Klamm (Salinger) who, as a child, was forced by his authortarian father (Powell) to literally eat a tape measure as punishment for a dispute with his sister. Since then, Tom finds a sexual thrill in the measurement of human bodies. Sister Vera (Cyr), also a tailor, suddenly shows up at Thomas' Brooklyn shop with her own special gifts and they play out their odd sibling rivalry. **85m/C VHS, DVD, Wide.** *FR* Emmanuel Salinger, Myriam Cyr, Marcus Powell, Peter McRobbie; ***D:*** Diane Doniol-Valcroze, Arthur Flam; ***W:*** Diane Doniol-Valcroze, Arthur Flam; ***C:*** Richard Rutkowski; ***M:*** Geir Jenssen.

Kill Castro 1980 (R) Ever hear the one about the exploding cigar? Key West boat skipper is forced to carry a CIA agent to Cuba on a mission to assassinate Castro. Low-budget adventure that's deadly dull. **90m/C VHS.** Sybil Danning, Albert Salmi, Michael V. Gazzo, Raymond St. Jacques, Woody Strode, Stuart Whitman, Robert Vaughn, Caren Kaye; ***D:*** Chuck Workman.

Kill Cruise 1990 (R) The depressed and alcoholic skipper of the yacht Bella Donna gives up sailing until he meets two beautiful young women who want to sail to Bermuda for a taste of the good life. The calm of the Atlantic is disturbed when they are plagued by bad weather and fierce storms, and tensions rise as the two women's jealousies erupt. Will it set the climate for murder? **99m/C VHS, DVD.** Juergen Prochnow, Patsy Kensit, Elizabeth Hurley; ***D:*** Peter Keglevic; ***W:*** Peter Keglevic; ***C:*** Edward Klosinski; ***M:*** Brynmor Jones.

Kill Factor woof! *Death Dimension; Black Eliminator; The Freeze Bomb* 1978 (R) Something stupid about a killer bomb tht could freeze the planet. So inept your brain cells will also be frozen if you watch it. **91m/C VHS.** Jim Kelly, George Lazenby, Aldo Ray, Harold Sakata, Terry Moore; ***D:*** Al Adamson.

Kill Line 1991 (R) Kim stars as Joe, a street fighter who seeks to clear his name after serving a 10-year prison sentence for a crime he didn't commit. When he finds his brother's family has been murdered by criminals looking for the millions he supposedly stole, Joe wages a one-man martial arts war against a corrupt police force and the gang of thugs who are looking for the money. **93m/C VHS.** Bobby Kim, Michael Parker, Marlene Zimmerman, H. Wayne Lowery, C.R. Valdez, Mark Williams, Ben Pfeifer; ***D:*** Richard H. Kim; ***W:*** Richard H. Kim.

Kill Me Again ½ 1989 (R) Director Dahl does the contemporary noir thing through the Nevada desert with Whalley as a beautiful femme fatale. She asks a detective (then husband Kilmer) to fake her death, which gets him targeted not only by the police, but also the mob and her psycho-boyfriend (Madsen). Fun and full of plot twists that will satisfy fans of the noir persuasion. **93m/C VHS, DVD.** Val Kilmer, Joanne Whalley, Michael Madsen, Jonathan (Jon Francis) Gries, Bibi Besch; ***D:*** John Dahl; ***W:*** John Dahl, David Warfield; ***C:*** Jacques Steyn.

Kill Me Later 2001 (R) Loan officer Shawn (Blair) has just broken up with her married lover/boss (Moffett) and decides to kill herself by jumping off the bank's roof. However, she's just in time to become the hostage of British thief Charlie (Beesley) whose robbery of the bank has gone wrong. Shawn agrees to help Charlie escape if he will agree to kill her later. An unlikely romance blossoms as the on the lam duo are tracked by a couple of FBI agents. **89m/C VHS, DVD, Wide.** *US* Selma Blair, Max Beesley, Lochlyn Munro, O'Neal Compton, Brendan Fehr, D.W. Moffett; ***D:*** Dana Lustig; ***W:*** Annette Goliti Gutierrez; ***C:*** David Ferrara; ***M:*** Tal Bergman, Renato Nero.

Kill Me Tomorrow ½ 1999 Teenaged witch Holly (Vamshon) sets her sights on hunk Russell (Sheppard), which doesn't sit well with his present girlfriend Tricia (Shafia). So Holly decides to get even by stealing his soul. The inexperience of the cast shows up bigtime but they're very earnest. **80m/C VHS, DVD.** Louisa Shafia, Gregory Sheppard, Lyndee Yamshon; ***D:*** Patrick McGuinn; ***W:*** Patrick McGuinn. VIDEO

Kill My Wife...Please! 19?? Comic adventure of a despicable husband trying to bump off his wife in order to cash in on her insurance policy. **90m/C VHS.** Bob (Robert) Dishy, Joanna Barnes, Bill Dana; ***D:*** Steven Hilliard Stern.

The Kill-Off 1990 (R) Bedridden Luanne (Gross), married to janitor Ralph (Monroe), manages to cause dissension in her isolated New Jersey community with her vicious gossip. But when Luanne learns Ralph's involved with a stripper (Haase), it puts her own life in danger. Based on a story by Jim Thompson. **100m/C VHS.** Loretta Gross, Steve Monroe, Cathy Haase, Jackson Sims; ***D:*** Maggie Greenwald.

Kill or Be Killed 1980 (PG) Martial arts champion is lured to a phony martial arts contest by a madman bent on revenge. **90m/C VHS.** James Ryan, Charlotte Michelle, Norman Combes; ***D:*** Ivan Hall.

Kill or Be Killed ½ 1993 Michael Julian just spent eight years in jail for saving his brother Charlie's life. He must wonder why he bothered since Charlie has stolen his girl Beth and set up a drug empire. Michael ambushes Charlie's men and steals $1 million to use as leverage but Charlie thinks rival drug lords are out to get him and starts a street war. **97m/C VHS.** David Heavener, Joseph Nuzzolo, Paulo Tocha, Lynn Levand; ***D:*** Joe Straw; ***W:*** Joseph Nuzzolo.

The Kill Reflex 1989 (R) A tough black cop and his beautiful rookie partner battle the mob and corruption. **90m/C VHS.** Maud Adams, Fred Williamson, Bo Svenson, Phyllis Hyman; ***D:*** Fred Williamson.

Kill Shot 2001 (R) Beautiful hard bodies live a life of sun and fun in an apartment complex on the Malibu shores. Tenant Stacy (Richards) is a model with an volatile ex-husband (Scalia) while Randy (Van Dien) is her new volleyball partner. But when Stacy decides to get involved in a local beach tournament, violent things begin to happen. **92m/C VHS, DVD.** Denise Richards, Casper Van Dien, Jack Scalia, Sally Kellerman, Elliott Gould, Ernie Reyes Jr., Gianni Russo; ***D:*** Nelson McCormick; ***W:*** Gianni Russo; ***C:*** Larry Blanford. VIDEO

Kill Slade 1989 (PG-13) When a United Nations food-aid diversion conspiracy is uncovered by a beautiful journalist, a plan to kidnap her is put into action. Romance follows. **90m/C VHS.** *SA* Patrick Dollaghan, Lisa Brady, Anthony Fridjhon, Danny Keogh, Alfred Nowke; ***D:*** Bruce McFarlane.

Kill Squad 1981 (R) Squad of martial arts masters follow a trail of violence and bloodshed to a vengeful, deadly battle of skills. **85m/C VHS.** Jean Claude, Jeff Risk, Jerry Johnson, Bill Cambra, Cameron Mitchell.

Kill the Golden Goose 1979 (R) Two martial arts masters work on opposite sides of a government corruption and corporate influence peddling case. **91m/C VHS.** Brad von Beltz, Ed Parker, Master Bong Soo Han; ***D:*** Elliot Hong.

Killcrazy 1989 (R) On the way to a weekend camping trip, five Vietnam vets released from a mental hospital are slowly massacred by a group of dangerous killers until one of the vets decides to fight back. **94m/C VHS.** David Heavener, Danielle Brisebois, Burt Ward, Lawrence-Hilton Jacobs, Bruce Glover, Gary Owens, Rachelle Carson; ***D:*** David Heavener; ***W:*** David Heavener.

Killer 197? An ex-convict sets up an ingenious bank robbery, and gets double-crossed himself. **87m/C VHS.** Henry Silva.

The Killer ½ *Die Xue Shuang Xiong* 1990 (R) Jeffrey Chow is a gangster gunman who wants out. He's hired by his best friend to perform one last killing, but it doesn't go as smoothly as he wanted. He's almost caught by "Eagle" Lee, a detective who vows to hunt him down using Jennie, a singer blinded by Chow in crossfire. Lots of action and gunfights, but also pretty corny and sentimental. Very similar to American action movies, but using Chinese and Asian cultural conventions. A good introduction to the Chinese gangster-flick genre. Available with subtitles or dubbed in English. **110m/C VHS, DVD, Wide.** *HK* Chow Yun-Fat, Sally Yeh, Danny Lee, Kenneth Tsang, Chu Kong, Fui-On Shing; ***D:*** John Woo; ***W:*** John Woo; ***C:*** Wing-hang Wong, Peter Pau; ***M:*** Lowell Lo.

Killer: A Journal of Murder 1995 (R) Young, idealistic Jewish guard Henry Lesser (Leonard) befriends prisoner Carl Panzram (Woods) and encourages the man to write his life story. Then he must deal with the consequences of discovering the brutality behind Panzram's murderous crimes. The leads do fine but there's nothing new here. Inspired by true events and set in the 1920s. **91m/C VHS, DVD, Wide.** James Woods, Robert Sean Leonard, Ellen Greene, Cara Buono, Robert John Burke, Steve Forrest, John Bedford Lloyd, Harold Gould; ***D:*** Tim Metcalfe; ***W:*** Tim Metcalfe; ***C:*** Ken Kelsch; ***M:*** Graeme Revell.

Killer Bud ½ 2000 (R) Best buds Waylon (Nemec) and Buzz (Faustino) get fired and decide to to go on a road trip to score babes and marijuana. They're incredibly dumb—as is the movie—but it's funny in a stupid, I can't believe I'm watching this, kinda way. **92m/C VHS.** Corin "Corky" Nemec, David Faustino, Robert Stack, Danielle Harris, Caroline Keenan; ***D:*** Karl T. Hirsch; ***W:*** Greg DePaul, Hank Nelken; ***C:*** David Lewis; ***M:*** Russ Landau.

Killer Commandos 19?? Mercenaries go to the rescue of an oppressed African nation to overthrow the sinister white supremacy dictator. **87m/C VHS.** Cameron Mitchell, Anthony Eisley.

Killer Condom *Kondom des Grauens* 1995 Deadpan humor, gore, and severed flesh—all based on a Ralf Konig comic book that's definitely for adults. The killer condoms are jellyfish-like creatures with piranha-like teeth who have taken to feeding on the male sexual organs of the unfortunates who frequent Times Square's sleazy Hotel Quickie. Gay cop Luigi Macaroni (Semel) is determined to prevent any more emasculations. German with subtitles. **108m/C VHS, DVD.** *GE* Udo Semel, Peter Lohmeyer, Marc Richter, Leonard Lansink, Iris Bergen, Hella Von Sinnen; ***D:*** Martin Walz; ***W:*** Martin Walz, Ralf Konig; ***C:*** Alexander Honisch; ***M:*** Emil Viklicky.

Killer Dill ½ 1947 Also killer dull. A meek salesman is misidentified as a death-dealing gangster, and the comic mixups begin. **71m/B VHS.** Stuart Erwin, Anne Gwynne, Frank Albertson, Mike Mazurki, Milburn Stone, Dorothy Granger; ***D:*** Lewis D. Collins.

Killer Diller ½ 1948 All-black musical revue featuring Nat King Cole and his Trio. **70m/B VHS.** Dusty Fletcher, Nat King Cole, Butterfly McQueen, Moms (Jackie) Mabley, George Wiltshire; ***D:*** Josh Binney.

Killer Elephants 1976 A Thai man struggles to save his plantation, his wife, and his baby from the terrorists hired by a land baron to drive him away from his property. **83m/C VHS.** Sung Pa, Alan Yen, Nai Yen Ne, Yu Chien.

The Killer Elite ½ 1975 (PG) Straight-ahead Peckinpah fare examining friendship and betrayal. Two professional assassins begin as friends but end up stalking each other when they are double-crossed. This minor Peckinpah effort is murky and doesn't have a clear resolution, but is plenty bloody. Lots of Dobermans roam through this picture too. **120m/C VHS, DVD, Wide.** James Caan, Robert Duvall, Arthur Hill, Gig Young, Burt Young, Mako, Bo Hopkins, Helmut Dantine; ***D:*** Sam Peckinpah; ***W:*** Marc Norman, Stirling Silliphant; ***C:*** Peter Lathrop; ***M:*** Jerry Fielding.

Killer Fish *Deadly Treasure of the Piranha* 1979 (PG) A scheme to steal and then hide a fortune in emeralds at the bottom of a tank full of piranhas backfires as the criminals find it impossible to retrieve them...as if that took a lot of foresight. Director Dawson is AKA Antonio Margheriti. Filmed in Brazil. **101m/C VHS.** *BR GB* Lee Majors, James Franciscus, Margaux Hemingway, Karen Black, Roy Brocksmith, Marisa Berenson; ***D:*** Anthony (Antonio Margheriti) Dawson.

Killer Force ½ 1975 (R) Predictable adventure involving international diamond smuggling. **100m/C VHS.** Telly Savalas, Peter Fonda, Maud Adams, Hugh O'Brian; ***D:*** Val Guest.

Killer Image 1992 (R) A photographer unwittingly sees more than he should and becomes involved in a lethal political coverup. At the same time a wealthy senator targets him and he must fight for his life. Viewers might feel they have to fight their boredom. **97m/C VHS.** John Pyper-Ferguson, Michael Ironside, M. Emmet Walsh, Krista Errickson; ***D:*** David Winning.

A Killer in Every Corner 1974 Three psychology students visit a loony professor and succumb to his hair-raising shenanigans. **80m/C VHS.** Joanna Pettet, Patrick Magee, Max Wall, Eric Flynn.

The Killer Inside Me 1976 (R) The inhabitants of a small Western town are unaware that their mild-mannered deputy sheriff is actually becoming a crazed psychotic murderer. From the novel by Jim Thompson. **99m/C VHS, DVD.** Stacy Keach, Susan Tyrrell, Tisha Sterling, Keenan Wynn, John Dehner, John Carradine, Don Stroud, Charles McGraw, Julie Adams, Royal Dano; ***D:*** Burt Kennedy; ***W:*** Robert Chandlee; ***C:*** William A. Fraker; ***M:*** Tim McIntire, John Rubinstein.

Killer Instinct 1992 (R) Two brothers do bloody warfare with notorious mobster kingpins in prohibition-era New York City. **101m/C VHS.** Christopher Bradley, Bruce Nozick, Rachel York; ***D:*** Greydon Clark, Ken Stein.

Killer Klowns from Outer Space ½ 1988 (PG-13) Bozo-like aliens resembling demented clowns land on earth and set up circus tents to lure Earthlings in. Visually striking, campy but slick horror flick that'll make you think twice about your next visit to the big top. Mood is heightened by a cool title tune by the Dickies. Definitely has cult potential! **90m/C VHS, DVD, Wide.** Grant Cramer, Suzanne Snyder, John Allen Nelson, Royal Dano, John Vernon, Peter Licassi, Michael Siegel, Charles Chiodo; ***D:*** Stephen Chiodo; ***W:*** Stephen Chiodo, Charles Chiodo; ***C:*** Alfred Taylor; ***M:*** John Massari.

Killer Likes Candy 1978 An assassin stalks the King of Kafiristan, and a CIA operative tries to stop him. **86m/C VHS.** Kerwin Mathews, Marilu Tolo; ***D:*** Richard Owens.

Killer Looks ½ 1994 (R) Phil likes to watch his wife Diane seduce strangers. Then they meet Mickey, a charmer with ideas of his own. Soon Diane and Phil find their kinky world threatened. Unrated version contains 13 minutes of additional footage. **87m/C VHS.** Michael Artura, Sara Suzanne Brown, Len Donato; ***D:*** Toby Phillips.

Killer on Board 1977 Folks spending their holiday on a cruise ship are afflicted by a fatal virus and subsequently quarantined. Typical made-for-TV disaster flick. **100m/C VHS.** Claude Akins, Beatrice Straight, George Hamilton, Patty Duke, Frank Converse, Jane Seymour, William Daniels; ***D:*** Philip Leacock.

Killer Party woof! 1986 (R) Three coeds pledge a sorority and are subjected to a hazing that involves a haunted fraternity house. Standard horror plot; Paul Bartel ("Eating Raoul"; "Lust in the Dust") is the only significant element. **91m/C VHS.** Elaine Wilkes, Sherry Willis-Burch, Joanna Johnson, Paul Bartel, Martin Hewitt, Ralph Seymour, Woody Brown, Alicia Fleer; ***D:*** William Fruet; ***W:*** Barney Cohen; ***C:*** John Lindley; ***M:*** John Beal.

The Killer Shrews *Attack of the Killer Shrews* 1959 Lumet (Sidney's father) creates a serum that causes the humble shrew to take on killer proportions. The creatures are actually dogs in make-up. Goude was 1957's Miss Universe. **70m/B VHS.** James Best, Ingrid Goude, Baruch Lumet, Ken Curtis, Alfredo DeSoto, Gordon McLendon; ***D:*** Ray Kellogg; ***W:*** Jay Simms; ***C:*** Wilfrid M. Cline; ***M:*** Emil Cadkin, Harry Bluestone.

Killer Tomatoes Eat France ½ 1991 Professor Gangrene takes his tomato fetish to France, where the giant vegetables try to take over the streets. The fourth in the killer-vegetable series. **94m/C VHS.** John Astin, Marc Price, Steve Lundquist, John DeBello, Rick Rockwell, Angela Visser, Kevin West, Tom Ashworth, Suzanne Dean, Mary Egan, Debra Fares, Arnie Miller, J.R. Morley; ***D:*** John DeBello; ***W:*** John DeBello, Steve Peace, Constantine Dillon; *C:* Kevin Morrisey.

Killer Tomatoes Strike Back 🦴🦴 **1990** The third "Killer Tomatoes" movie isn't in the league of "The Naked Gun" satires, but it's still bright parody for the Mad Magazine crowd, as tomato-mad scientist Astin harnesses the powers of trash-TV in a planned vegetable invasion. Perhaps due to a 'Killer Tomatoes' cartoon series at the time, this isn't as saucy as its predecessors and is acceptable for family audiences. Followed by "Killer Tomatoes Eat France." **87m/C VHS.** John Astin, Rick Rockwell, Crystal Carson, Steve Lundquist, John Witherspoon, John DeBello, Tom Ashworth, Frank Davis, Debra Fares, Rock Peace, Constantine Dillon, Kevin West, Spike Sorrentino, D.J. Sullivan; *D:* John DeBello; *W:* Rick Rockwell, John DeBello, Constantine Dillon; *C:* Stephen F. Andrich; *M:* Neal Fox.

Killer Tongue 🦴 *La Lengua Asesina* **1996 (R)** Okay, now here's a story (but not a good story, mind): Candy (Clarke) and Johnny (Durr) pull off a heist but Johnny winds up in jail while Candy hides out with the loot. She winds up in a desert hotel, near where a meteorite has landed. Somehow, Candy ingests a piece of the meteorite and an alien parasite (in the form of the titular killer tongue) takes over. The tongue is big on human sacrifices and Candy can't seem to do anything to stop it. Oh, and Candy's four poodles also get a meteorite taste and turn into drag queens. Just as gross as you may imagine it to be. **98m/C VHS, DVD.** *GB SP* Melinda (Mindy) Clarke, Jason Durr, Robert Englund, Mapi Golan, Doug Bradley, Jonathan Rhys Meyers; *D:* Albert Sciamma; *W:* Albert Sciamma; *C:* Denis Crossan.

Killer with Two Faces 🦴 **1974** A woman is terrorized by the evil twin of her boyfriend. **70m/C VHS.** Donna Mills, Ian Hendry, David Lodge, Roddy McMillian. **TV**

Killer Workout 🦴 *Aerobicide* **1986 (R)** A murderer stalks the clients of a sweat/sex/muscle-filled gym. **89m/C VHS.** David James Campbell, Ted Prior; *D:* David A. Prior.

The Killers 🦴🦴🦴🦴 **1946** Classic film noir based on a Hemingway story. Lancaster's film debut comes as an ex-boxer, "The Swede," who's murdered in a contract hit. Insurance investigator Jim Reardon (O'Brien) reconstructs the young man's life, discovering his involvement with crime boss Big Jim Colfax (Dekker) and double-crossing femme fatale Kitty Collins (Gardner). So Reardon sets out to set up Colfax and Kitty. Rosza's musical score may sound familiar—it was later used on the TV series "Dragnet." **105m/B VHS.** Edmond O'Brien, Albert Dekker, Ava Gardner, Burt Lancaster, Sam Levene, William Conrad, Charles McGraw, Virginia Christine; *D:* Robert Siodmak; *W:* Anthony Veiller, John Huston; *C:* Elwood "Woody" Bredell; *M:* Miklos Rozsa.

The Killers 🦴🦴 *Ernest Hemingway's the Killers* **1964** After two hired assassins kill a teacher, they look into his past and try to find leads to a $1,000,000 robbery. Reagan's last film. Remake of 1946 film of the same name, which was loosely based on a short story by Ernest Hemingway. Originally intended for TV, but released to theatres instead due to its violence. **95m/C VHS.** Lee Marvin, Angie Dickinson, John Cassavetes, Ronald Reagan, Clu Gulager, Claude Akins, Norman Fell, Don Haggerty, Seymour Cassel; *D:* Donald Siegel; *W:* Gene L. Coon; *C:* Richard Rawlings; *M:* John Williams.

Killers 🦴 **1988** Remote jungles of southern Africa are the scene of a military coup. **83m/C VHS, DVD.** Cameron Mitchell, Alicia Hammond, Robert Dix; *D:* Ewing Miles Brown.

The Killer's Edge 🦴½ *Blood Money* **1990 (R)** Cop is caught between rock and hard place in L.A. when he's forced to confront criminal who once saved his life in 'Nam. Plenty of gut busting and soul wrenching. **90m/C VHS.** Wings Hauser, Robert Z'Dar, Karen Black.

Killers from Space woof! **1954** Cheap sci-fi flick in which big-eyed men from beyond Earth bring scientist Graves back to life to assist them with their evil plan for world domination. **80m/B VHS.** Peter Graves, Barbara Bestar, James Scay; *D:* W. Lee Wilder.

Killer's Kiss 🦴🦴½ **1955** A boxer and a dancer set out to start a new life together when he saves the woman from an attempted rape. Gritty, second feature from Kubrick was financed by friends and family and shows signs of his budding talent. **67m/C VHS, DVD.** Frank Silvera, Jamie Smith, Irene Kane, Jerry Jarrett; *D:* Stanley Kubrick; *W:* Stanley Kubrick; *C:* Stanley Kubrick; *M:* Gerald Fried.

The Killing 🦴🦴🦴 **1956** The dirty, harsh, street-level big heist epic that established Kubrick and presented its genre with a new and vivid existentialist aura, as an ex-con engineers the rip-off of a racetrack with disastrous results. Displays characteristic nonsentimental sharp-edged Kubrick vision. Based on the novel "Clean Break" by Lionel White. **83m/B VHS, DVD.** Sterling Hayden, Marie Windsor, Elisha Cook Jr., Jay C. Flippen, Vince Edwards, Timothy Carey, Coleen Gray, Joseph (Joe) Sawyer, Ted de Corsia, James Edwards, Jay Adler, Kola Kwarian, Joe Turkel; *D:* Stanley Kubrick; *W:* Stanley Kubrick, Jim Thompson; *C:* Lucien Ballard; *M:* Gerald Fried.

A Killing Affair 🦴 **1985 (R)** Set in West Virginia, 1943, this is the story of a widow who takes in a drifter who she believes is the man who killed her husband. She begins to fall for him, but cannot be sure if she should trust him. Vague and melodramatic. From the novel "Monday, Tuesday, Wednesday" by Robert Houston. Saperstein's directorial debut. **100m/C VHS.** Peter Weller, Kathy Baker, John Glover, Bill Smitrovich; *D:* David Saperstein; *M:* John Barry.

Killing at Hell's Gate 🦴½ **1981** A group of white-water rafters are being picked off by snipers as they travel down river. **96m/C VHS.** Robert Urich, Deborah Raffin, Lee Purcell; *D:* Jerry Jameson; *M:* David Bell. **TV**

The Killing Beach 🦴🦴 *Turtle Beach* **1992 (R)** Australian photojournalist Judith Wilkes (Scacchi) travels to Malaysia in the late 1970s to report on the plight of the Vietnamese boat people seeking refuge there. She befriends the wife of the Australian ambassador, a former callgirl from Saigon, who hopes to find her own children among the refugees. But the native Malays resent the foreign intrusion and are determined to stop the boat people—no matter what the cost in blood. Based on the novel "Turtle Beach" by Blanche D'Alpuget. **105m/C VHS.** *AU* Greta Scacchi, Joan Chen, Jack Thompson, Art Malik, Norman Kaye; *D:* Stephen Wallace; *W:* Ann Turner; *C:* Russell Boyd.

The Killing Device 🦴½ **1992** Two government scientists lose their funding on a covert political assassination project and decide to eliminate the government officials responsible. When two journalists attempt to solve the murders they become the next targets. **93m/C VHS.** Clu Gulager, Antony Alda, Gig Rauch.

The Killing Edge 🦴½ **1986** In post-nuclear holocaust Earth, a lone warrior seeks justice, and his family, in a lawless land. **85m/C VHS.** Bill French, Marv Spencer; *D:* Lindsay Shonteff.

Killing 'Em Softly 🦴 **1985** Segal portrays a down-on-his-luck musician who accidentally murders a music manager during an argument. Cara's boyfriend is accused and to clear his name, the singer moonlights as a detective. She and Segal end up falling in love. Disappointing. **90m/C VHS.** *CA* George Segal, Irene Cara; *D:* Max Fischer.

The Killing Fields 🦴🦴🦴½ **1984 (R)** Based on the New York Times' Sydney Schanberg's account of his friendship with Cambodian interpreter Dith Pran. They separated during the fall of Saigon, when Western journalists fled, leaving behind countless assistants who were later accused of collusion with the enemy by the Khmer Rouge and killed or sent to re-education camps during the bloodbath known as "Year Zero." Schanberg searched for Pran through the Red Cross and U.S. government, while Pran struggled to survive, finally escaping and walking miles to freedom. Ngor's own experiences echoed those of his character Pran. Malkovich's debut is intense. Joffe's directorial debut shows a generally sure hand, with only a bit of melodrama at the end. **142m/C VHS, Wide.** *GB* Sam Waterston, Haing S. Ngor, John Malkovich, Athol Fugard, Craig T. Nelson, Julian Sands, Spalding Gray, Bill Paterson; *D:* Roland Joffe; *W:* Bruce Robinson; *C:* Chris Menges. Oscars '84: Cinematog., Film Editing, Support. Actor (Ngor); British Acad. '84: Actor (Ngor), Adapt. Screenplay, Film; Golden Globes '85: Support. Actor (Ngor); L.A. Film Critics '84: Cinematog.; N.Y. Film Critics '84: Cinematog.; Natl. Soc. Film Critics '84: Cinematog.; Writers Guild '84: Adapt. Screenplay.

Killing Floor 🦴🦴 **1985 (PG)** During WWI, black sharecropper Frank Custer (Leake) travels to Chicago to get work in the stockyards and becomes a voice in the growing labor movement. The tensions in the factories lead to to bloody race riots of 1919. **118m/C VHS.** Damien Leake, Alfre Woodard, Moses Gunn, Clarence Felder, Mary Alice; ***Cameos:*** Peter J. D'Noto; *D:* Bill Duke; *W:* Leslie Lee; *M:* Elizabeth Swados. **TV**

Killing for Love 🦴½ **1995 (R)** Sleazy producer invites several couples for a weekend retreat at his mountain cabin. The unrated version is 90 minutes. **81m/C VHS.** Jay Richardson, Alex Demir, Lisa Haslehurst, Brandy (Jisel, Brandy Ledford) Sanders; *D:* Mike Kesey; *W:* H.M. Johnson.

The Killing Game 🦴🦴½ *All Weekend Lovers; Jeu de Massacre* **1967** A husband-wife cartoonist team link up with an unhinged playboy and act out a murder-mystery comic they produce together. In French with subtitles. **95m/C VHS.** *FR* Jean-Pierre Cassel, Claudine Auger, Michael Duchaussoy, Anna Gaylor; *D:* Alain Jessua.

The Killing Game 🦴 **1987** A slew of Californians kill and betray each other for lustful reasons. **90m/C VHS.** Chad Hayward, Cynthia Killion, Geoffrey Sadwith; *D:* Joseph Merhi.

Killing Grandpa 🦴🦴 *Matar al Abuelito* **1991** Wealthy family patriarch Don Mariano Aguero (Luppi) has lost the will to live and attempted suicide, which has left him comatose. His three greedy chldren are anxious for their inheritance but the Don's loyal handyman enlists the aid of his half-sister Rosita (Esteves), who possesses healing powers, to give his aged employer the strength to recover. Spanish with subtitles. **114m/C VHS.** *SP AR* Federico Luppi, Ines Estevez; *D:* Luis Cesar D'Angiolillo; *W:* Luis Cesar D'Angiolillo, Ariel Sienra; *C:* Miguel Abal.

The Killing Grounds 🦴½ **1997 (R)** Killers Vince (Gains) and Art (Hall) are searching in the mountains for a missing plane that carried $3 million in gold. But it's already been found by a group of hikers, who think finders keepers. Boy, are they wrong. **93m/C VHS, DVD.** Anthony Michael Hall, Courtney Gains, Priscilla Barnes, Charles Rocket, Rodney A. Grant, Cynthia Geary; *D:* Kurt Anderson; *W:* Thomas Ritz. **VIDEO**

Killing Heat 🦴½ *The Grass is Singing* **1984 (R)** An independent career woman living in South Africa decides to abandon her career to marry a struggling jungle farmer. Based on Doris Lessing's novel "The Grass is Singing." **104m/C VHS.** *GB SW* Karen Black, John Thaw, John Kani, John Moulder-Brown; *D:* Michael Raeburn.

Killing Hour 🦴🦴 *The Clairvoyant* **1984 (R)** A psychic painter finds that the visions she paints come true in a string of grisly murders. Her ability interests a TV reporter and a homicide detective. **97m/C VHS, DVD.** Elizabeth Kemp, Perry King, Norman Parker, Kenneth McMillan; *D:* Armand Mastroianni; *W:* Armand Mastroianni; *M:* Alexander Peskanov.

A Killing in a Small Town 🦴🦴🦴 **1990 (R)** Candy Morrison seems like the perfect member of her small Texas community—but appearances can be deceiving, particularly after she's charged with killing a fellow churchgoer by striking her 41 times with an axe (shades of Lizzie Borden)! Dennehy is her skeptical lawyer who isn't sure if it was self-defense or a peculiar sort of revenge. Good performances by Hershey and Dennehy lift this above the usual tawdry made-for-TV level. Based on a true story. **95m/C VHS.** Barbara Hershey, Brian Dennehy, Hal Holbrook, Richard Gilliland, John Terry, Lee Garlington; *D:* Stephen Gyllenhaal; *C:* Robert Elswit; *M:* Richard Gibbs. **TV**

Killing in the Sun 🦴 **19?? (R)** Gripping struggle for prosperous smuggling in the Mediterranean consume mobsters from three countries. **90m/C VHS.** Henry Silva, Michael Constantine.

The Killing Jar 🦴🦴½ **1996 (R)** Michael Sanford (Cullen) has taken his pregnant wife Diane (Tomita) back to the California wine country to take over the failing family vineyard. A series of vicious murders occur in the area, one of which Michael may have witnessed. Hypnosis brings up a lot of Michael's repressed childhood memories, he begins to unravel, and becomes the prime suspect in the killings. **101m/C VHS, DVD.** Brett Cullen, Tamlyn Tomita, Wes Studi, Brion James, M. Emmet Walsh, Tom Bower, Xander Berkeley; *D:* Evan Crooke; *W:* Mark Mullin; *C:* Michael G. Wojciechowski; *M:* David Williams.

The Killing Kind 🦴🦴½ **1973** Man released from prison is obsessed with wreaking vengeance on his daft lawyer and his accuser. His vendetta eventually draws his mother into the fray as well. Fine performance by Savage. **95m/C VHS.** Ann Sothern, John Savage, Ruth Roman, Luana Anders, Cindy Williams; *D:* Curtis Harrington; *M:* Andrew Belling.

The Killing Man 🦴🦴 **1994 (R)** Former mobster tries going legit by changing his identity and working for the government. **91m/C VHS, DVD.** Jeff Wincott, Terri Hawkes, Michael Ironside, David Bolt, Jeff Pustil; *D:* David Mitchell; *W:* David Mitchell, Damian Lee; *C:* David Pelletier.

The Killing Mind **1990** A young girl witnesses a grisly murder that is never solved. Twenty years later she (Zimbalist) becomes a cop who specializes in trapping psychos. Haunted by her memories, she and a reporter (Bill) team up to find the killer, never suspecting that she is his next victim. **96m/C VHS.** Stephanie Zimbalist, Tony Bill, Daniel Roebuck; *D:* Michael Rhodes. **CABLE**

Killing Mr. Griffin 🦴🦴½ **1997** If this sounds suspiciously akin to the plot for 1999's "Teaching Mrs. Tingle," it's not just your imagination. However, this TV movie is based on the novel by Lois Duncan. Evil high school teacher Mr. Griffin antagonizes all his students, who wind up kidnapping and humiliating him—leaving him tied up in the woods. But when Mr. G turns up dead, the students are all suspects unless they can point the cops in another direction. **108m/C VHS, DVD.** Scott Bairstow, Amy Jo Johnson, Mario Lopez, Chris Young, Michelle Williams, Jay Thomas, Scott Jaeck, Denise Dowse; *D:* Jack Bender; *W:* Michael Angeli, Kathleen Rowell; *C:* David Geddes; *M:* Christophe Beck. **TV**

Killing Obsession 🦴½ **1994** Albert (Savage) has been locked in the Parkview State Psychiatric Facility for 20 years, ever since he murdered 11-year-old Annie's mother. Annie is Albert's obsession and in his mind she's always remained a young girl. So when Albert is released, he goes looking for Annie—murdering along the way. Now that the real Annie is an adult will Albert finally accept the passage of time or will she be just another victim? **95m/C VHS, DVD.** Bobby Di-Cicco, John Savage, Kimberly Chase, John Saxon, Bernie White; *D:* Paul Leder; *W:* Paul Leder; *C:* Francis Grumman; *M:* Dana Walden.

The Killing of a Chinese Bookie 🦴🦴 **1976 (R)** Gazzara runs a Sunset Strip nightclub and is in hock to loan sharks. When he can't come up with the cash, he's offered a deal—get rid of a troublesome Chinese bookie and all debts will be forgiven. But it turns out the bookie is highly connected in the Asian mob and nothing goes as planned. Cassavette's improv technique makes for a self-indulgent and endless film. **109m/C VHS, DVD.** Ben Gazzara, Jean-Pierre Cassel, Zizi Johari, Soto Joe Hugh, Robert Phillips, Timothy Carey, Morgan Woodward; *D:* John Cassavetes; *W:* John Cassavetes; *C:* Frederick Elmes.

Killing of Angel Street 🦴🦴 **1981 (PG)** A courageous young woman unwittingly becomes the central character in an escalating nightmare about saving a community from corrupt politicians and organized crime. **101m/C VHS.** *AU* Liz Alexander, John Hargreaves; *D:* Donald Crombie; *W:* Evan Jones; *M:* Brian May.

Killing of Randy Webster 🦴½ **1981** A father attempts to prove that his son did not die as a criminal when Texas policemen shot him after transporting a stolen van across state lines. **90m/C VHS.** Hal Holbrook, Dixie Carter, Sean Penn, Jennifer Jason Leigh; *D:* Sam Wanamaker.

The Killing of Sister George 🦴🦴 **1969 (R)** Racy, sensationalized film based on the Frank Marcus black comedy/melodrama about a lesbian love triangle between a television executive and two soap opera stars. Things get a little uncomfortable when they learn one of their characters is to be written out of the show. Shot in England. **138m/C VHS, DVD.** Beryl Reid, Susannah York, Coral Browne, Ronald Fraser, Patricia Medina, Hugh Paddick, Cyril Delevanti, Brandan Dillon, Sivi Aberg, William Beckley, Elaine Church, Mike Freeman, Maggie Paige, Jack Raine, Dolly Taylor; *D:* Robert Aldrich; *W:* Lukas Heller, Frank Marcus; *C:* Joseph Biroc; *M:* Gerald Fried.

Killing Stone 🦴🦴 **1978** A freelance writer uncovers a small town sheriff's plot to cover up a scandalous homicide. **120m/C VHS.** Gil Gerard, J.D. Cannon, Jim Davis, Nehemiah Persoff; *D:* Michael Landon; *W:* Michael Landon. **TV**

Killing Streets 🦴🦴 **1991** A commando learns that his twin brother is being held hostage in Lebanon and plans a rescue mission. A standard farfetched actioner; noteworthy for a real sense of despair over the endless carnage in the Mideast. Some dialogue in Arabic with subtitles. **109m/C VHS.** Michael Pare, Lorenzo Lamas; *D:* Stephen Cornwell; *W:* Stephen Cornwell.

The Killing Time 🦴🦴 **1987 (R)** A minor, effective murder thriller about a quiet small resort town suddenly beset by a web of murder, double-crossings, blackmail, and infidelity. They seem to coincide with the appearance of a mysterious stranger posing as the town's deputy sheriff just as the new sheriff is about to take up the badge. **94m/C VHS.** Kiefer Sutherland, Beau Bridges, Joe Don Baker, Wayne Rogers; *D:* Rick King; *W:* Don Bohlinger.

Killing Time 🦴🦴 **1997 (R)** Twisted little English thriller about a day in the life of Italian hitwoman Maria (Torgan), who's working in Northern England. Gangland boss Reilly (Leach) has killed a police officer and revenge is wanted by the cop's mate, fellow officer Bryant (Fairbass). Only Bryant can't really afford Maria so after she does the job, Bryant wants her killed by a cheaper hitman, Charlie (Thirkeld). But Reilly won't be back in town until the evening train—so Maria decides to take out a few of Reilly's henchmen to kill some time, leading to a police investigation (by Bryant), and leaving Charlie itching to carry out his part of the killing spree. **91m/C VHS.** *GB* Kendra Torgan, Craig Fairbrass, Nigel Leach, Stephen D. Thirkeld; *D:* Bharat Nalluri; *W:* Neil Marshall, Fleur Costello, Caspar Berry.

Killing Zoe 🦴🦴 **1994 (R)** American safecracker travels to Paris for a little rest, recreation, and robbery. At the request of a childhood friend, he involves himself in an ill-conceived daytime bank heist, but not before enjoying a night with a local call girl and participating in some good ol' fashioned heroin-induced debauchery with the other bank robbers on the night before the job. Surprising no one (except maybe the still-stoned crooks), things don't go exactly as planned. Visually impressive debut for Tarantino collaborator Avary, who had his actors read "Beowulf" for its portrayal of Viking excess. **97m/C VHS, DVD, Wide.** Eric Stoltz, Julie Delpy, Jean-Hugues Anglade, Gary Kemp, Bruce Ramsay, Kario Salem, Carlo Scandiuzzi; *D:* Roger Roberts Avary; *W:* Roger Roberts Avary; *C:* Tom Richmond.

The Killing Zone 🦴½ **1990** Convict nephew of onetime Drug Enforcement agent rewrites zoning ordinances to hunt for Mexican drug lord south of the border. **90m/C VHS.** Daron McBee, James Dalesandro, Melissa Moore, Armando Silvestre, Augustine Beral, Sydne Squire, Debra (Deborah Dutch) Dare; *D:* Addison Randall.

Killings at Outpost Zeta 🦴 **1980** Earthmen investigate a barren planet where previous expeditions have disappeared, and find hordes of aliens. **92m/C VHS.** Gordon Devol, Jackie Ray, James A. Watson Jr.

Killjoy 🦴🦴½ *Who Murdered Joy Morgan?* **1981** A sleazy surgeon's daughter is the prey in this TV thriller. The plot twists are led by the array of people who become involved. A clever suspense mystery. **100m/C VHS, DVD.** Kim Basinger, Robert Culp, Stephen Macht, Nancy Marchand, John Rubinstein, Ann Dusenberry, Ann Wedgeworth; *D:* John Llewellyn Moxey; *M:* Bruce Broughton. **TV**

Killpoint 🦴½ **1984 (R)** Special task force is assembled to catch the criminals who robbed a National Guard armory for its weapons. **89m/C VHS.** Leo Fong, Richard Roundtree, Cameron Mitchell; *D:* Frank Harris.

Killzone 🦴 **1985** A brainwashed Vietnam vet breaks down during a training exercise and embarks on a psychotic killing spree. **86m/C VHS.** Ted Prior, David James Campbell, Richard Massery; *D:* David A. Prior.

Kilma, Queen of the Amazons woof! **1986** A shipwrecked sailor finds himself on an island populated by man-hating Amazons. When a shipload of lusty sailors arrive to rescue him, carnage ensues. **90m/C VHS.**

Kim 🦴🦴🦴 **1950** A colorful Hollywood adaptation of the Rudyard Kipling classic about an English boy disguised as a native in 19th Century India, and his various adventures. **113m/C VHS.** Errol Flynn, Dean Stockwell, Paul Lukas, Cecil Kellaway; *D:* Victor Saville; *M:* Andre Previn.

Kim 🦴🦴½ **1984** Kim (Sheth) is a 15-year-old boy living by his wits on the streets of 1890s India. Trying to discover his true identity, Kim's befriended by a Buddhist monk who wishes the boy to be his disciple and a British spy, who trains him for a daring mission against the Russians. Rousing TV adaptation of the Rudyard Kipling novel. **135m/C VHS.** Ravi Sheth, Peter O'Toole, Bryan Brown, John Rhys-Davies, Julian Glover; *D:* John Davies.

Kind Hearts and Coronets 🦴🦴🦴½ **1949** Black comedy, set in 1900, in which ambitious young Louis (Price) sets out to bump off eight relatives in an effort to claim a family title. Guinness is wonderful in his role as all eight (male and female) of the fated relations. There are a number of clever twists and turns and it proves that writing one's memoirs can be fatal. Very loosely based on Roy Horiman's novel "Israel Rank." **104m/B VHS.** *GB* Alec Guinness, Dennis Price, Valerie Hobson, Joan Greenwood, Audrey Fildes, Miles Malleson, Clive Morton, Cecil Ramage, John Penrose, Hugh Griffith, John Salew, Eric Messiter, Anne Valery, Arthur Lowe, Jeremy Spenser; *D:* Robert Hamer; *W:* Robert Hamer, John Dighton; *C:* Douglas Slocombe; *M:* Ernest Irving.

A Kind of Loving 🦴🦴🦴 **1962** Two North English young people marry rashly as a result of pregnancy, find they really didn't like each other all that much, but manage to adjust. **107m/B VHS.** *GB* Alan Bates, Thora Hird, June Ritchie, Pat Keen, James Bolam; *D:* John Schlesinger; *W:* Willis Hall, Keith Waterhouse; *C:* Denys Coop; *M:* Ron Grainer.

Kindergarten 🦴🦴🦴 **1984** Endearing tale based on a true story of a young Russian street violinist. During WWII, the boy meets a variety of interesting people as he travels throughout the Soviet Union. In Russian with English subtitles. **143m/C VHS.** *RU* Klaus Maria Brandauer; *D:* Yevgeny Yevtushenko.

Kindergarten Cop 🦴🦴½ **1990 (PG-13)** Pectoral perfect cop Kimble (Schwarzenegger) stalks mama's boy/criminal Crisp (Tyson) by locating the drug lord's ex and his six-year-old son. When the pec man's female partner succumbs to a nasty bout of food poisoning, he's forced to take her place as an undercover kindergarten teacher in the drowsy Pacific northwest community where mother and son reside incognito. A cover all the bases Christmas release, it's got romance, action, comedy and cute. And boxoffice earnings to match Arnie's chest measurements. A bit violent for the milk and cookie set. **111m/C VHS, DVD.** Arnold Schwarzenegger, Penelope Ann Miller, Pamela Reed, Linda Hunt, Richard Tyson, Carroll Baker, Cathy Moriarty, Park Overall, Richard Portnow, Jayne Brook; *D:* Ivan Reitman; *W:* Murray Salem, Herschel Weingrod, Timothy Harris; *C:* Michael Chapman; *M:* Randy Edelman.

The Kindred 🦴🦴½ **1987 (R)** A young student discovers that his mother the biologist has created a hybrid creature using his body tissue. Naturally, he is horrified and begins to search for his test-tube brother; the problem is, this brother likes eating people. Not too bad; boasts some good acting. **92m/C VHS.** Rod Steiger, Kim Hunter, David Allan Brooks, Timothy Gibbs, Amanda Pays, Talia Balsam, Jeffrey Obrow, Peter Frechette, Julia Montgomery; *D:* Stephen Carpenter, Jeffrey Obrow; *W:* Stephen Carpenter, Joseph Stefano, John Penney, Earl Ghaffari, Jeffrey Obrow; *M:* David Newman.

King 🦴🦴🦴 **1978** Docudrama with terrific cast follows the life and career of one of the greatest non-violent civil rights leaders of all time, Martin Luther King. **272m/C VHS.** Paul Winfield, Cicely Tyson, Roscoe Lee Browne, Ossie Davis, Art Evans, Ernie Banks, Howard E. Rollins Jr., William Jordan, Cliff DeYoung; *D:* Abby Mann; *W:* Abby Mann; *M:* Billy Goldenberg. **TV**

King and Country 🦴🦴🦴 **1964** Aristocratic army officer, Capt. Hargreaves (Bogarde), serves as the defense lawyer for troubled Private Arthur Hamp (Courtenay), whose wartime experiences have caused him to desert. Hargreaves at first ignores the uneducated Hamp's obvious shell-shock but soon begins to feel sympathy for his confused client. Director Losey shows the effects of war rather than the war itself and provides a sincere and bitter condemnation of military mentality. Based on the play "Hamp" by John Wilson. **86m/B VHS, DVD.** *GB* Dirk Bogarde, Tom Courtenay, Leo McKern, Barry Foster, James Villiers, Peter Copley; *D:* Joseph Losey; *W:* Evan Jones; *C:* Denys Coop; *M:* Larry Adler. British Acad. '64: Film.

The King and Four Queens 🦴🦴½ **1956** Gable, on the run from the law, happens upon a deserted town, deserted, that is, except for a woman and her three daughters. Clark soon discovers that the women are looking for $100,000 in gold that one of their missing husbands had stolen. True to form, conniving Clark wastes no time putting the moves on each of them to find the whereabouts of the loot. **86m/C VHS.** Clark Gable, Eleanor Parker, Jo Van Fleet, Jean Wiles, Barbara Nichols, Sara Shane, Roy Roberts, Arthur Shields, Jay C. Flippen; *D:* Raoul Walsh; *M:* Alex North.

The King and I 🦴🦴🦴🦴 **1956** Wonderful adaptation of Rodgers and Hammerstein's Broadway play based on the novel "Anna and the King of Siam" by Margaret Landon. English governess Kerr is hired to teach the King of Siam's many children and bring them into the 20th century. She has more of a job than she realizes, for this is a king, a country, and a people who value tradition above all else. Features one of Rodgers and Hammerstein's best-loved scores. Brynner made this role his, playing it over 4,000 times on stage and screen before his death. Kerr's voice was dubbed when she sang; the voice you hear is Marni Nixon, who also dubbed the star's singing voices in "West Side Story" and "My Fair Lady." ♫Shall We Dance?; Getting To Know You; Hello, Young Lovers; We Kiss in a Shadow; I Whistle a Happy Tune; March of the Siamese Children; I Have Dreamed; A Puzzlement; Something Wonderful. **133m/C VHS, DVD, Wide.** Deborah Kerr, Yul Brynner, Rita Moreno, Martin Benson, Terry Saunders, Rex Thompson, Alan Mowbray, Carlos Rivas, Patrick Adiate; *D:* Walter Lang; *W:* Ernest Lehman; *C:* Leon Shamroy; *M:* Richard Rodgers, Oscar Hammerstein. Oscars '56: Actor (Brynner), Art Dir./Set Dec., Color, Costume Des. (C), Sound, Scoring/Musical; Golden Globes '57: Actress—Mus./Comedy (Kerr), Film—Mus./Comedy.

The King and I 🦴🦴 **1999 (G)** Animated musical tries, but fails, to split the difference between faithfulness to the Broadway version and the action needed to entertain kids. Tells the story of Anna (Richardson), an English woman who travels to Siam in order to tutor the children of the King (Vidnovic). The evil Kralahome and stereotypical comic relief sidekick Master Little (Hammond) plan to use Anna to capture the throne. The ending is given a kid-friendly twist, but eight of the original twenty Broadway songs were slashed to keep it brief for the short attention span set. **87m/C VHS, DVD.** *D:* Richard Rich; *W:* Jacqueline Feather, David Seidler, Peter Bakalian; *V:* Miranda Richardson, Martin Vidnovic, Ian Richardson, Darrell Hammond, Allen D. Hong, Armi Arabe, Adam Wylie, Sean Smith.

King Arthur, the Young Warlord 🦴🦴 **1975 (PG)** The struggle that was the other side of Camelot—the campaign against the Saxon hordes. The early, somewhat violent years of King Art. **90m/C VHS.** Oliver Tobias, Michael Gothard, Jack Watson, Brian Blessed, Peter Firth; *D:* Sidney Hayers, Pat Jackson, Peter Sasdy.

King Cobra 🦴½ **1998 (PG-13)** If you like big snakes, this low-budgeter is for you! A mutant cobra/rattlesnake hybrid, having escaped its lab environment, threatens the populace of a small California town. **93m/C VHS, DVD.** Noriyuki "Pat" Morita, Hoyt Axton, Kasey Fallo, Scott Brandon, Joseph Ruskin, Courtney Gains; *D:* David Hillenbrand, Scott Hillenbrand; *W:* David Hillenbrand, Scott Hillenbrand; *C:* Philip D. Schwartz. **VIDEO**

King Creole 🦴🦴½ **1958 (PG)** The King goes film noir as a teenager with a criminal record who becomes a successful pop singer in New Orleans but is threatened by his ties to crime, represented by Walter Matthau. One of the better Elvis films, based on Harold Robbins' "A Stone for Danny Fisher." Features Elvis's last film appearance before his service in the Army. ♫King Creole; Banana; New Orleans; Turtles, Berries and Gumbo; Crawfish; Don't Ask Me Why; As Long As I Have You; Trouble; Hard-Headed Woman. **115m/B VHS, DVD.** Elvis Presley, Carolyn Jones, Walter Matthau, Dean Jagger, Dolores Hart, Vic Morrow, Paul Stewart, Brian G. Hutton, Liliane Montevecchi, Jan Shepard, Jack Grinnage; *D:* Michael Curtiz; *W:* Herbert Baker, Michael V. Gazzo; *C:* Russell Harlan; *M:* Walter Scharf.

King David 🦴½ **1985 (PG-13)** The story of David, the legendary Biblical hero whose acts of bravery paved the way for him to become king of Israel. **114m/C VHS.** Richard Gere, Alice Krige, Cherie Lunghi, Hurd Hatfield, Edward Woodward; *D:* Bruce Beresford; *W:* Andrew Birkin, James Costigan; *M:* Carl Davis.

King Dinosaur 🦴½ **1955** A new planet arrives in the solar system, and a scientific team checks out its giant iguana-ridden terrain. **63m/B VHS.** Bill Bryant, Wanda Curtis, Patti Gallagher, Doug(las) Henderson.

A King in New York 🦴🦴 **1957** Chaplin plays the deposed king of a European mini-monarchy who comes to the United States in hope of making a new life. Looks critically at 1950s-era America, including Cold War paranoia and over reliance on technology. Containing Chaplin's last starring performance, this film wasn't released in the U.S. until 1973. Uneven but interesting. **105m/B VHS, DVD.** *GB* Charlie Chaplin, Dawn Addams, Michael Chaplin, Oliver Johnston, Maxine Audley, Harry Green; *D:* Charlie Chaplin; *W:* Charlie Chaplin; *C:* Georges Perinal; *M:* Charlie Chaplin.

King Kelly of the U.S.A. 🦴 **1934** Robertson carries on a forgettable romance with a princess aboard a trans-Atlantic line. **64m/B VHS.** Guy Robertson, Irene Ware, Edgar Kennedy, Franklin Pangborn, Joyce Compton, Ferdinand Gottschalk, Wilhelm von Brinken, Otis Harlan; *D:* Leonard Fields.

King Kong 🦴🦴🦴🦴 **1933** The original beauty and the beast film classic tells the story of Kong, a giant ape captured in Africa by filmmaker Carl Denham (Armstrong) and brought to New York as a sideshow attraction. Kong falls for starlet Ann (Wray), escapes from his captors, and rampages through the city, ending up on top of the newly built Empire State Building. Moody Steiner score adds color, and Willis O'Brien's stop-motion animation still holds up well. Scenes were cut during the 1938 re-release because of the Hays production code, including one where a curious Kong strips Wray of her clothes. Remade numerous times with various theme derivations. **105m/B VHS, 8mm.** Fay Wray, Bruce Cabot, Robert Armstrong, Frank Reicher, Noble Johnson, Sam Hardy, James Flavin, Ernest B. Schoedsack, Merian C. Cooper; *D:* Ernest B. Schoedsack, Merian C. Cooper; *W:* James A. Creelman, Ruth Rose, Edgar Wallace; *C:* Edward Linden, J.O. Taylor, Vernon Walker; *M:* Max Steiner. AFI '98: Top 100, Natl. Film Reg. '91.

King Kong 🦴🦴 **1976 (PG)** Oil company official travels to a remote island to discover it inhabited by a huge gorilla. The transplanted beast suffers unrequited love in classic fashion: monkey meets girl, monkey gets girl and brandishes her while atop the World Trade Center. An updated remake of the 1933 movie classic that also marks the screen debut of Lange. Impressive sets and a believable King Kong romp around New York City in this film. Watch for Joe Piscopo, and quickly for Corbin Bernsen as a reporter. **135m/C VHS, DVD, 8mm.** Jeff Bridges, Charles Grodin, Jessica Lange, Rene Auberjonois, John Randolph, Ed Lauter, Jack O'Halloran, Dennis Fimple, John Agar, Rick Baker, Joe Piscopo, Corbin Bernsen; *D:* John Guillermin; *W:* Lorenzo Semple Jr.; *C:* Richard H. Kline; *M:* John Barry. Oscars '76: Visual FX.

King Kong Lives 🦴 **1986 (PG-13)** Unnecessary sequel to the 1976 remake of "King Kong," in which two scientists get the big ape, now restored after his asphalt-upsetting fall, together with a lady ape his size and type. **105m/C VHS.** Brian Kerwin, Linda Hamilton, John Ashton, Peter Michael Goetz; *D:* John Guillermin; *W:* Steven Pressfield, Ronald Shusett.

King Kong vs. Godzilla 🦴🦴½ *King Kong tai Godzilla; KinguKongu tai Gojira* **1963** The planet issues a collective shudder as the two mightiest monsters slug it out for reasons known only to themselves. Humankind can only stand by and watch in impotent horror as the tide of the battle sways to and fro, until one monster stands alone and victorious. **105m/C VHS, DVD.** *JP* Michael Keith, Tadao Takashima, Mie Hama, Kenji Sahara, Yu Fujiki, Akihiko Hirata, Jun Tazaki, Akiko Wakabayashi, Ichiro Arishima, Haruo Nakajima, Katsumi Tezuka; *D:* Inoshiro Honda; *W:* Shinichi Sekizawa; *C:* Hajime Koizumi; *M:* Akira Ifukube, Robert Emmett Dolan, Henry Mancini, Herman Stein, Milton Rosen; *Nar:* Les Tremayne.

King Kung Fu 🦴 **1987 (G)** A karate master raises a gorilla, and sends it from Asia to the U.S. There, two out-of-work reporters decide to release it from captivity and then recapture it so they can get the story and some needed recognition. The background they don't have on the gorilla is that its master taught it kung fu. **90m/C VHS.** John Balee, Tom Leahy, Maxine Gray, Bill Schwartz; *D:* Bill Hayes.

King Lear 🦴🦴🦴½ **1971** Brook's version of Shakespeare tragedy. The king drives away the only decent daughter he has, and when he realizes this, it is too late. Powerful performances and interesting effort at updating the bard. **137m/B VHS.** *GB* Paul Scofield, Irene Worth, Jack MacGowran, Alan Webb, Cyril Cusack, Patrick Magee; *D:* Peter Brook.

King Lear 🦴½ **1987** Loosely adapted from Shakespeare's tragedy of a king who loses everything. A fragmented French existential reading with gangster undercurrent. This updated version is dark, ominous, wandering, strange, and quite unlike the other 1984 remake. Or any other remake, for that matter. **91m/C VHS.** *SI* Peter Sellers, Burgess Meredith, Molly Ringwald, Jean-Luc Godard, Woody Allen; *D:* Jean-Luc Godard; *W:* Norman Mailer.

King Lear 🦴🦴🦴 **1998** Holm gives a powerful performance as the deluded monarch. The King comes to rue the day he banished faithful daughter Cordelia (Hamilton) in favor of dividing his kingdom between her manipulative siblings Goneril (Flynn) and Regan (Redman). As war engulfs his country, Lear descends into despair and madness. **150m/C VHS.** Ian Holm, Victoria Hamilton, Barbara Flynn, Amanda Redman, Michael Bryant, Paul Rhys, Timothy West, Finbar Lynch, David Burke; *D:* Richard Eyre; *W:* Richard Eyre; *C:* Roger Pratt; *M:* Dominic Muldowney. **TV**

The King Murder 🦴🦴 **1932** High-society sleuth Tearle tries to solve the mysterious death of a beautiful, yet dangerous extortionist. Looks a lot like murder, although no weapon can be found. **67m/B VHS.** Conway Tearle, Natalie Moorhead, Marceline Day, Dorothy Revier; *D:* Richard Thorpe; *W:* Charles Reed Jones.

King of America 🦴 **1980** A Greek sailor and a local labor agent battle over who will become King of America. **90m/C VHS.** *D:* Dezso Magyar.

King of Comedy 🦴🦴🦴 **1982 (PG)** An unhinged would-be comedian haunts and eventually kidnaps a massively popular Johnny Carson-type TV personality. A cold, cynical farce devised by Scorsese seemingly in reaction to John Hinckley's obsession with his film "Taxi Driver." Controlled, hard-hitting performances, especially by De Niro and Lewis. **101m/C VHS.** Robert De Niro, Jerry Lewis, Sandra Bernhard, Tony Randall, Diahnne Abbott, Shelley Hack, Liza Minnelli; *D:* Martin Scorsese. British Acad. '83: Orig. Screenplay; Natl. Soc. Film Critics '83: Support. Actress (Bernhard).

The King of Hearts 🦴🦴🦴 *Le Roi de Coeur* **1966** In WWI, a Scottish soldier finds a battle-torn French town evacuated of all occupants except a colorful collection of escaped lunatics from a nearby asylum. The lunatics want to make him their king, which is not a bad alternative to the insanity of war. Bujold is cute as ballerina wanna-be; look for Serrault ("La Cage aux Folles") as, not surprisingly, a effeminate would-be hairdresser. Light-hearted comedy with a serious message; definitely worthwhile. **101m/C VHS, Wide.** *FR GB IT* Alan Bates, Genevieve Bujold, Adolfo Celi, Francoise Christophe, Micheline Presle, Michel Serrault, Julien Guiomar, Pierre Brasseur, Jean-Claude Brialy, Pier Paola Capponi, Jacques Balutin, Marc Dudicourt, Daniel Boulanger; *D:* Philippe de Broca; *W:* Daniel Boulanger; *C:* Pierre Lhomme; *M:* Georges Delerue.

King of Jazz 🦴🦴½ **1930** A lavish revue built around the Paul Whiteman Orchestra with comedy sketches and songs by the stars on Universal Pictures' talent roster. (Though billed as the King of Jazz, Whiteman was never as good as jazz's real royalty.) Filmed in two-color Technicolor with a cartoon segment by Walter Lantz. ♫Rhapsody in Blue; So the Bluebirds and the Blackbirds Got Together; Mississippi Mud; It Happened in Monterey; Ragamuffin Romeo; Happy Feet; Song of the Dawn; A Bench in the Park. **93m/C VHS.** Paul Whiteman, John Boles, Jeanette Loff, Bing Crosby; *D:* John Murray Anderson.

King of Kings 🦴🦴½ **1927** DeMille depicts the life of Jesus Christ in this highly regarded silent epic. The resurrection scene appears in color. Remade by Nicholas Ray in 1961. **115m/B VHS.** H.B. Warner, Dorothy (Dorothy G. Cummings) Cumming, Ernest Torrence, Joseph Schildkraut, Jacqueline Logan, Victor Varconi, William Boyd; *D:* Cecil B. DeMille.

The King of Kings 🦴🦴🦴 **1961** The life of Christ is intelligently told, with an attractive visual sense and a memorable score. Remake of Cecil B. DeMille's silent film, released in 1927. **170m/C VHS, Wide.** Jeffrey Hunter, Siobhan McKenna, Hurd Hatfield, Robert Ryan, Rita Gam, Viveca Lindfors, Rip Torn; *D:* Nicholas Ray; *W:* Philip Yordan; *C:* Milton Krasner; *M:* Miklos Rozsa; *Nar:* Orson Welles.

King of Kong Island woof! **1978** Intent on world domination, a group of mad scientists implant receptors in the brains of gorillas on Kong Island, and the monster apes run amok. **92m/C VHS.** *SP* Brad Harris, Marc Lawrence; *D:* Robert Morris.

The King of Marvin Gardens 🦴🦴½ **1972 (R)** Nicholson stars as a Midwest radio jock who prefers to reminisce about his life and family back in Atlantic City, New Jersey to playing records. When Nicholson returns for a visit he finds brother Dern, king of the get-rich-quick schemers, working for a black crime syndicate. Dern is involved in another scheme which means embezzling money from his boss—not a smart idea although Nicholson can't disuade him. Talky drama also features Burstyn as Dern's neglected girlfriend. **104m/C VHS, DVD.** Jack Nicholson, Bruce Dern, Ellen Burstyn, Scatman Crothers, Julia Anne Robinson, Charles Lavine, Arnold Williams, Josh Mostel; *D:* Bob Rafelson; *W:* Jacob Brackman.

The King of Masks 🦴🦴🦴 **1999** Wang (Xu) is an elderly street performer in 1930s China who practices the ancient art of face-changing with masks. Tradition has it that he pass his secrets to a male heir, which Wang doesn't have. So, he decides to purchase a boy child on the black market, only to later discover that his clever protege (Ren-ying) is actually a little girl. Chinese with subtitles. **101m/C VHS, DVD.** *CH* Zhu Xu, Zhou Ren-ying; *D:* Wu Tianming; *W:* Wei Minglung; *C:* Mu Dayuan; *M:* Zhao Jiping.

King of New York 🦴🦴🦴 **1990 (R)** Drug czar Frank White (Walken), recently returned from a prison sabbatical, regains control of his New York drug empire with the aid of a loyal network of black dealers. How? Call it dangerous charisma, an inexplicable sympatico. Headquartered in Manhattan's chic Plaza hotel, he ruthlessly orchestrates the drug machine, while funneling the profits into a Bronx hospital for the poor. As inscrutable as White himself, Walken makes the drug czar's power tangible, believable, yet never fathomable. **106m/C VHS, DVD, Wide.** Christopher Walken, Laurence "Larry" Fishburne, David Caruso, Victor Argo, Wesley Snipes, Janet (Johnson) Julian, Joey Chin, Giancarlo Esposito, Steve Buscemi; *D:* Abel Ferrara; *W:* Nicholas St. John; *C:* Bojan Bazelli; *M:* Joe Delia.

King of the Airwaves 🦴🦴½ *Louis 19, le Roi des Ondes* **1994** Louis (Drainville) is a dull salesman who spends his days working in an electronics store and his nights in front of the TV. This leads Louis to enter (and win) a contest sponsored by the local TV station, which promises to provide 24-hour-a-day coverage of the winner's every move. Now, ordinary Louis is a media celebrity who must deal with constant intrusion and the soap opera-ish changes wrought upon his life. **93m/C VHS.** *CA FR* Martin Drainville, Agathe de la Fontaine, Dominique Michel, Patricia Tulasne, Gilbert Lachance; *D:* Michel Poulette; *W:* Michael Michaud, Emile Gaudreault, Sylvie Bouchard; *M:* Jean-Marie Benoit.

King of the Bullwhip 🦴½ **1951** Two undercover U.S. Marshals are sent to Tioga City to stop the killing and looting of a masked bandit, whose whip is as dangerous as his gun. **59m/B VHS.** Lash LaRue, Al "Fuzzy" St. John, Anne Gwynne, Tom Neal, Jack Holt, Dennis Moore, Michael Whalen, George Lewis; *D:* Ron Ormond.

King of the Congo 🦴½ **1952** Crabbe, in his last serial, as a pilot who is frantically searching for an important piece of film. In 15 parts. **?m/B VHS.** Buster Crabbe, Gloria Dee; *D:* Spencer Gordon Bennet, Wallace Grissell.

King of the Cowboys 🦴🦴 **1943** Roy fights a gang of saboteurs and saves a defense installation. **54m/B VHS.** Roy Rogers, Smiley Burnette, James Bush.

King of the Damned 🦴 **1936** On an island prison Veidt leads a convict's revolt against the cruel administrator (Hallard), who gets killed. Before he dies, Hallard alerts a convenient warship, which begins shelling the island. Hallard's daughter, who has fallen for Veidt, pleads for the men and everyone is given a fair trial. Miscast and ineptly performed, although Veidt retains some dignity. **81m/B VHS.** *GB* Conrad Veidt, Helen Vinson, C.M. Hallard, Noah Beery Sr., Percy Walsh, Raymond Lovell, Cecil Ramage, Peter Croft; *D:* Walter Forde; *W:* Charles Bennett, Sidney Gilliat, Noel Langley.

King of the Forest Rangers **1946** Ranger Steve King must stop an evil archaeologist from finding a treasure whose secret lies within an ancient Indian rug pattern. Edited from an original, 12 episode serial on two cassettes. **167m/B VHS.** Larry Thompson, Helen Talbot, Stuart Hamblen, Anthony Warde, Scott Elliott.

King of the Grizzlies 🦴½ **1969 (G)** The mystical relationship between a Cree Indian and a grizzly cub is put to the test when the full grown bear attacks a ranch at which the Indian is foreman. **93m/C VHS.** Chris Wiggins, John Yesno; *D:* Ron Kelly.

King of the Gypsies 🦴🦴½ **1978 (R)** Interesting drama. A young man, scornful of his gypsy heritage, runs away from the tribe and tries to make a life of his own. He is summoned home to his grandfather's deathbed where he is proclaimed the new king of the gypsies, thus incurring the wrath of his scorned father. From Peter Maas's best-selling novel. **112m/C VHS.** Sterling Hayden, Eric Roberts, Susan Sarandon, Brooke Shields, Shelley Winters, Annie Potts, Annette O'Toole, Judd Hirsch, Michael V. Gazzo, Roy Brocksmith; *D:* Frank Pierson; *W:* Frank Pierson; *C:* Sven Nykvist.

King of the Hill 🦴🦴🦴½ **1993 (PG-13)** Quiet depression-era drama focuses on Aaron, a 12-year-old who lives in a seedy hotel in St. Louis. The family is barely scraping by: his mother is in a tuberculosis sanitarium, his younger brother has been sent away to live with relatives, and Aaron must fend for himself when his father gets work as a traveling salesman. Aaron excels at school and his efforts there, as well as his hotel friends, manage to provide him with some semblance of a regular life. Soderberg's third directorial effort is unsentimental but admiring of his character's resourcefulness and imagination during difficult times. Based on the book by A.E. Hochner describing his own childhood. **102m/C VHS, Wide.** Jesse Bradford, Jeroen Krabbe, Lisa Eichhorn, Karen Allen, Spalding Gray, Elizabeth McGovern, Joseph Chrest, Adrien Brody, Cameron Boyd, Chris Samples, Katherine Heigl, Amber Benson, John McConnell, Ron Vawter, John Durbin, Lauryn Hill, David Jensen; *D:* Steven Soderbergh; *W:* Steven Soderbergh; *M:* Cliff Martinez.

King of the Jungle 🦴🦴 **2001 (R)** Contrived story with an energized performance by Leguizamo. He's Seymour, a mentally-challenged man with the intellectual and emotional capacity of a preadolescent. He lives with his long-divorced Puerto Rican mother Mona (Carmen) and her lover Joanne (Perez). His dad, Jack (Gorman), is a deadbeat poet who has never accepted his son's limitations. Seymour spends his time on the streets playing basketball until his mother is fatally shot and he wants revenge. **87m/C VHS, DVD.** John Leguizamo, Cliff Gorman, Julie Carmen, Rosie Perez, Michael Rapaport, Rosario Dawson, Marisa Tomei, Annabella Sciorra; *D:* Seth Zvi Rosenfeld; *W:* Seth Zvi Rosenfeld; *C:* Fortunato Procopio; *M:* Harry Gregson-Williams.

The King of the Kickboxers woof! **1991 (R)** The villains make kung-fu snuff movies with unwitting actors killed on camera. Otherwise, same old junk about a karate cop back in Bangkok to get the dude who squashed his brother. Pretty racist at times. **90m/C VHS.** Loren Avedon, Richard Jaeckel, Billy Blanks, Don Stroud, Keith Cooke; *D:* Lucas Lowe.

King of the Kongo 🦴🦴 **1929** A handsome young man is sent by the government to Nuhalla, deep in the jungle, to break up a gang of ivory thieves. Serial was made in silent and sound versions. **213m/B VHS.** Jacqueline Logan, Boris Karloff, Richard Tucker; *D:* Richard Thorpe.

King of the Mountain 🦴½ **1981 (PG)** The "Old King" and the "New King" must square off in this tale of daredevil road racers who zoom through the streets of Hollywood. Interesting cast trapped by tired script. **92m/C VHS.** Richard Cox, Harry Hamlin, Dennis Hopper, Joseph Bottoms, Deborah

Van Valkenburgh, Dan Haggerty; *D:* Noel Nosseck; *W:* Roger Christian.

King of the Pecos 🦴🦴½ **1936** A young lawyer (who's also adept at the shootin' iron) exacts revenge on his parents' killers in the courtroom. Well made early Wayne outing, with good character development, taut pacing and beautiful photography. **54m/B VHS, DVD.** John Wayne, Muriel Evans, Cy Kendall, Jack Clifford, John Beck, Yakima Canutt; *D:* Joseph Kane; *W:* Dorrell McGowan, Stuart E. McGowan, Bernard McConville; *C:* Jack Marta.

The King of the Roaring '20s: The Story of Arnold Rothstein 🦴🦴½ *The Big Bankroll* **1961** "True" story of infamous gangster, Arnold Rothstein, a brilliant and ruthless gambler who practically ran New York in the '20s. This version of his life focuses on his rise to power, the dealings with his enemies, and his crumbling personal life. Superficial due mostly to the weak screenplay. Adapted from the book "The Big Bankroll" by Leo Katcher. **106m/B VHS.** David Janssen, Dianne Foster, Mickey Rooney, Jack Carson, Diana Dors, Dan O'Herlihy, Mickey Shaughnessy, Keenan Wynn; *D:* Joseph M. Newman.

King of the Rocketmen *Lost Planet Airmen* **1949** Jeff King thwarts an attempt by traitors to steal government scientific secrets. Serial in 12 episodes. Later released as a feature titled "Lost Planet Airmen." **156m/B VHS.** Tristram Coffin, Mae Clarke, I. Stanford Jolley; *D:* Fred Brannon.

King of the Rodeo 🦴🦴 **1928** Cowpoke Hoot wins a rodeo and catches a thief in the Windy City. Hoot's final silent ride into the sunset. **54m/B VHS.** Hoot Gibson, Kathryn Crawford, Slim Summerville, Charles French, Monte Montague, Joseph Girard; *D:* Henry MacRae.

King of the Sierras 🦴½ **1938** Bosworth tells his nephew the story of a white horse that protected his mares from a black stallion. The acting of the horses is better than that of the humans. **58m/B VHS.** Hobart Bosworth, Harry Harvey, Harry Harvey Jr., Jim Campeau; *D:* Samuel Diege; *W:* W. Scott Darling.

King of the Stallions 🦴½ **1942** A dangerous stallion is a menacing threat to the herd and the cowboys and Indians and other scattered wildlife. Chief Thundercloud is the only one capable of tackling the matter. Largely Indian cast, including Iron Eyes Cody, famed for the anti-litter campaign. **63m/B VHS.** Chief Thundercloud, Princess Bluebird, Chief Yowlachie, Rick Vallin, Dave O'Brien, Barbara Felker, Iron Eyes Cody; *D:* Edward Finney.

King of the Texas Rangers **1941** Tom King, Texas Ranger, finds that his father's killers are a group of saboteurs who have destroyed American oil fields. This 12-episode serial comes on two tapes. **195m/B VHS.** Sammy Baugh, Neil Hamilton; *D:* William Witney, John English.

King of the Wild Horses 🦴🦴🦴 **1924** Engaging children's story about a wild stallion that comes to the rescue. Terrific action photography of Rex going through his paces. Look for Chase in a rare dramatic role. Silent. **50m/B VHS.** Rex, Edna Murphy, Leon Bary, Pat Hartigan, Frank Butler, Charley Chase; *D:* Fred Jackman.

King of the Wind 🦴🦴½ **1993 (PG)** An epic adventure featuring the true story of a legendary Arabian horse and a poor stable boy who gave the most precious gift of all: love. **101m/C VHS.** Richard Harris, Glenda Jackson.

King of the Zombies woof! **1941** Mad scientist creates his own zombies without souls, to be used as the evil tools of a foreign government. Zombie nonsense. **67m/B VHS, DVD.** John Archer, Dick Purcell, Mantan Moreland, Henry Victor, Joan Woodbury; *D:* Jean Yarbrough; *W:* Edmond Kelso; *C:* Mack Stengler; *M:* Edward Kay.

The King on Main Street 🦴🦴½ **1925** A king on vacation in America finds romance. **?m/B VHS.** Adolphe Menjou, Bessie Love.

King, Queen, Knave 🦴🦴🦴 *Herzbube* **1972** Sexy black comedy about a shy, awkward 19-year-old boy, keenly aware that his interest in girls is not reciprocated. He has to go live with his prosperous uncle and his much younger wife when his parents are killed. Based on the Vladimir Nabokov novel. **94m/C VHS.** *GE* Gina Lollobrigida, David Niven, John Moulder-Brown; *D:* Jerzy Skolimowski; *W:* David Seltzer.

King Ralph 🦴🦴 **1991 (PG)** When the rest of the royal family passes away in a freak accident, lounge lizard Ralph finds himself the only heir to the throne. O'Toole is the long-suffering valet who tries to train him for the job. Funny in spots and Goodman is the quintessential good sport, making the whole outing pleasant. Sometimes too forced. **96m/C VHS, DVD.** John Goodman, Peter O'Toole, Camille Coduri, Joely Richardson, John Hurt; *D:* David S. Ward; *W:* David S. Ward; *C:* Kenneth Macmillan; *M:* James Newton Howard.

King Rat 🦴🦴🦴 **1965** Drama set in a WWII Japanese prisoner-of-war camp. Focuses on the effect of captivity on the English, Australian, and American prisoners. An American officer bribes his Japanese captors to live more comfortably than the rest. Based on James Clavell's novel. **134m/B VHS.** George Segal, Tom Courtenay, James Fox, James Donald, Denholm Elliott, Patrick O'Neal, John Mills, Todd Armstrong, Gerald Sim, Leonard Rossiter, John Standing, Alan Webb, Sam Reese, Wright King, Joe Turkel, Geoffrey Bayldon, Reg Lye, Arthur Malet, Richard Dawson, William "Bill" Fawcett, John Warburton, John Ronane, Michael Lees, Hamilton Dyce, Hedley Mattingly, Dale Ishimoto; *D:* Bryan Forbes; *W:* Bryan Forbes, James Clavell; *C:* Burnett Guffey; *M:* John Barry.

King Richard and the Crusaders 🦴½ **1954** Laughable costume epic with Sanders as Richard the Lionheart, who survives an assassination attempt during the Crusades. Harvey is a loyal knight sworn to find the traitors with Harrison as the noble leader of the Arab forces. Mayo plays Harvey's object of affection. Even the battle scenes are boring. Based on "The Talisman" by Sir Walter Scott. **113m/C VHS.** George Sanders, Rex Harrison, Laurence Harvey, Virginia Mayo, Robert Douglas, Michael Pate, Paula Raymond, Lester Matthews; *D:* David Butler; *W:* John Twist; *M:* Max Steiner.

King Solomon's Mines 🦴🦴🦴 **1937** The search for King Solomon's Mines leads a safari through the treacherous terrain of the desert, fending off sandstorms, Zulus, and a volcanic eruption. Adapted from the novel by H. Rider Haggard and remade twice. **80m/B VHS, DVD.** Cedric Hardwicke, Paul Robeson, Roland Young, John Loder, Anna Lee; *D:* Robert Stevenson; *W:* Michael Hogan, Roland Pertwee; *C:* Cyril Knowles, Glen MacWilliams; *M:* Mischa Spoliansky.

King Solomon's Mines 🦴🦴🦴 **1950** Hunter Allan Quartermain (Granger) is hired by Elizabeth Curtis (Kerr) and her brother John (Carlson) to find Elizabeth's missing husband who was searching for the legendary diamond mines of King Solomon. Naturally, there are numerous adventures during their expedition. Filmed on location in Nairobi, Tanganyika and the Belgian Congo. A lavish version of the classic H. Rider Haggard novel; remake of the 1937 classic and remade again in 1985. **102m/C VHS.** Stewart Granger, Deborah Kerr, Richard Carlson, Hugo Haas, Lowell Gilmore; *D:* Compton Bennett; *W:* Helen Deutsch; *C:* Robert L. Surtees. Oscars '50: Color Cinematog., Film Editing.

King Solomon's Mines 🦴½ **1985 (PG-13)** The third remake of the classic H. Rider Haggard novel about a safari deep into Africa in search of an explorer who disappeared while searching for the legendary diamond mines of King Solomon. Updated but lacking the style of the previous two films. Somewhat imperialistic, racist point of view. **101m/C VHS.** Richard Chamberlain, John Rhys-Davies, Sharon Stone, Herbert Lom; *D:* J. Lee Thompson; *W:* Gene Quintano; *M:* Jerry Goldsmith.

King Solomon's Treasure 🦴 **1976** The great white adventurer takes on the African jungle, hunting for hidden treasure in the Forbidden City. Ekland stars as a Phoenician Queen—need we say more?? **90m/C VHS.** *CA GB* David McCallum, Britt Ekland, Patrick Macnee, Wilfrid Hyde-White; *D:* Alvin Rakoff.

The Kingdom 🦴🦴🦴½ *Riget* **1995** Danish director von Trier serves up what must be the first four-and-a- half-hour long hospital soap opera/ghost story/comedy/satire. Elderly Mrs. Drusse checks herself into a hospital known as the Kingdom, which is inhabited by the usual medical suspects: Pompous surgeons, incompetent buraucrats, and quirky residents. She hears the ghostly call of a child from an elevator shaft and sticks around to investigate. Made for Danish TV but released theatrically there and in the States, film owes a great deal to "Twin Peaks" and B-movie horror flicks. Doesn't take itself too seriously, but probably can't be watched all in one sitting. Danish and Swedish with subtitles. **279m/C VHS, DVD.** *DK* Kirsten Rolffes, Ghita Norby, Udo Kier, Ernst Hugo Jarogard, Soren Pilmark, Holger Juul Hansen, Baard Owe, Birgitte Raabjerg, Peter Mygind, Solbjorg Hojfeldt; *D:* Lars von Trier; *W:* Lars von Trier, Tomas Gislason, Niels Vorsel; *C:* Eric Kress; *M:* Joachim Holbek.

The Kingdom 2 🦴🦴🦴½ *Riget II* **1997** In the continuation of Von Trier's hospital soap/supernatural/satire, madness runs rampant through Copenhagen's Kingdom hospital. Spiritualist Mrs. Drosse comes back to life after dying during surgery. A baby, sired by a demon, grows at a monstrous rate. Pompous Swedish neurosurgeon Helmer returns from Haiti with voodoo potions and is beseiged by his unbalanced lover and on and on it goes in its quirky, bizarre way. Swedish and Danish with subtitles. **286m/C VHS, DVD.** *DK* Kirsten Rolffes, Ghita Norby, Udo Kier, Ernst Hugo Jarogard, Soren Pilmark, Holger Juul Hansen, Baard Owe, Birgitte Raabjerg, Peter Mygind, Solbjorg Hojfeldt; *D:* Lars von Trier; *W:* Lars von Trier, Niels Vorsel; *C:* Eric Kress; *M:* Joachim Holbek.

Kingdom Come 🦴🦴 **2001 (PG)** The death of an African-American family's patriarch brings archetypical relatives from near and far for the funeral. There's the wise, saintly widow (Goldberg), the stoic, hardworking son (LL Cool J) and his eager-to-please wife (Fox), the ne'er-do-well son (Anderson) and his shrewish wife (Pinkettt-Smith), the Bible-thumper (Devine), and the gold-digger (Braxton). Throw in an over-officious and unfortunately flatulent preacher (Cedric), let simmer, and bring to a boil. Most of the humor comes from the over-the-top renditions of the characters, as well as the aforementioned gastrointestinal distress, but it keeps getting in the way of the serious, and well-done drama between the at-odds family members. The swings in tone and mood are jarring, but the ride is made easier by the stellar performances, highlighted by LL Cool J's breakout as the eldest son. **89m/C VHS, DVD, Wide.** *US* L.L. Cool J., Jada Pinkett Smith, Vivica A. Fox, Loretta Devine, Anthony Anderson, Cedric the Entertainer, Darius McCrary, Whoopi Goldberg, Toni Braxton, Masasa, Clifton Davis, Richard Gant, Doug McHenry; *D:* Doug McHenry; *W:* Jessie Jones, David Bottrell; *C:* Francis Kenny; *M:* Tyler Bates.

Kingdom of the Spiders 🦴🦴½ **1977 (PG)** A desert town is invaded by swarms of killer tarantulas, which begin to consume townspeople. **90m/C VHS.** William Shatner, Tiffany Bolling, Woody Strode; *D:* John Cardos; *W:* Alan Caillou, Richard Robinson; *C:* John Morrill.

Kingfish: A Story of Huey P. Long 🦴🦴½ **1995** Charismatic political kingpin of Louisiana, Huey P. Long is brought to vivid life with Goodman's swaggering portrayal. Story is told in flashback, beginning with Long's assassination in 1935. A champion of the working man, Long parlayed charm and corruption into a Depression-era political career as governor and U.S. Senator. But naturally, the hard-drinking, hard-loving Long makes a lot of enemies along the way. Long's life was also memorably recreated in Robert Penn Warren's "All the King's Men," as was that of his younger brother, Governor Earl Long, in the film "Blaze." **97m/C VHS.** John Goodman, Matt Craven, Anne Heche, Ann Dowd, Jeffery (Jeff) Perry, Bob Gunton, Hoyt Axton, Kirk Baltz, Bill Cobbs; *D:* Thomas Schlamme; *W:* Paul Monash; *M:* Patrick Williams.

Kingfisher Caper 🦴🦴 **1976 (PG)** A power struggle between a businessman, his brother, and a divorced sister is threatening to rip a family-owned diamond empire apart. **90m/C VHS.** Hayley Mills, David McCallum; *D:* Dirk DeVilliers.

Kingfisher the Killer 🦴 **198?** Charles, the Raging Titan of Ninja skill, stalks the bad gang that killed his mother and hits them with nunchakos. **90m/C VHS.** Sho Kosugi.

Kingpin 🦴🦴½ **1996 (PG-13)** Bowling epic serves up social satire while showcasing some of the worst hair ever seen at the cinema. Roy Munson (a very bald Harrelson, reasonably subdued in relation to rest of cast) is a former bowling champ who, thanks to his sleazy ways, lost a hand and is reduced to selling bowling equipment while wearing a crude rubber prosthetic (on his hand). That is until he meets innocent Amish phenom Ishmael (Quaid), resplendent in a dutch boy wig, whom he persuades to hit the road to a big money tournament in Reno, where Roy can confront an old nemesis (Murray) and compare shampoos, while Ish attempts to win enough money to save the family farm. Claudia (Angel) is around as the highly decorative love interest of Roy. Co-written by "Dumb & Dumber" writers the brothers Farrelly. Look for Amish sensations Blues Traveler at the credit roll. **107m/C VHS, DVD.** Woody Harrelson, Randy Quaid, Vanessa Angel, Bill Murray, Chris Elliott, Mike Cerrone, William Jordan, Richard Tyson, Lin Shaye, Zen Gesner, Prudence Wright Holmes, Rob Moran; *D:* Peter Farrelly, Bobby Farrelly; *W:* Bobby Farrelly, Mort Nathan; *C:* Mark Irwin; *M:* Freedy Johnston.

Kings and Desperate Men 🦴½ **1983** Apprentice terrorists plea their case at a public forum when they take a rakish talk show host hostage. **118m/C VHS.** *GB* Patrick McGoohan, Alexis Kanner, Andrea Marcovicci, Robin Spry, Frank Moore; *D:* Alexis Kanner.

Kings Go Forth 🦴🦴½ **1958** Hormones and war rage in this love triangle set against the backdrop of WWII France. Sinatra loves Wood who loves Curtis. When Sinatra asks for her hand in marriage she refuses because she is mixed—half black, half white. He says it doesn't matter, but she still declines because she's in love with Curtis. When Sinatra tells Curtis that Wood is mixed, Curtis says that it doesn't matter to him either because he'd never planned on marrying her. Meanwhile, the war continues. Not particularly satisfying on either the war or race front. Based on a novel by Joe David Brown. **109m/B VHS, DVD.** Frank Sinatra, Tony Curtis, Natalie Wood, Leora Dana; *D:* Delmer Daves; *W:* Merle Miller; *C:* Daniel F. Fapp; *M:* Elmer Bernstein.

The King's Guard 🦴🦴½ **2001 (PG-13)** Captain Reynolds (St. John) and his men must accompany betrothed Princess Gwendolyn (Jones)—and her dowry of gold—to her intended's kingdom. But two traitors (Roberts, Perlman) seek both the princess and the treasure. Low-budget but the fast paced action helps keep things interesting. **94m/C VHS, DVD.** Ashley Jones, Eric Roberts, Ron Perlman, Trevor St. John, Lesley-Anne Down; *D:* Jonathan Tydor; *W:* Jonathan Tydor. **VIDEO**

Kings in Grass Castles 🦴🦴½ **1997** Aussie miniseries based on the memoirs of Dame Mary Durack and her immigrant family who leave famine-stricken Ireland in the 1850s for Australia. After dealing with an eight-year indenture, the family become Queensland cattle barons, lose everything, and struggle to rebuild, all the while dealing with more prejudice from the British colonials. **200m/C VHS.** *AU* Stephen (Dillon) Dillane, Essie Davis, Fionnula Flanagan, David Ngoobujarra, Susan Lynch, Ernie Dingo, James Fox, Max Cullen, Des McAleer; *D:* John Woods; *W:* Tony Morphett; *C:* Roger Lanser; *M:* Shaun Davey. **TV**

Kings of the Road—In the Course of Time ⚭⚭⚭½ *Im Lauf der Zeit* **1976** A writer and a film projectionist travel by truck across Germany. The film stands out for its simple and expressive direction, and truly captures the sense of physical and ideological freedom of being on the road. A landmark Wenders epic. In German with English subtitles. **176m/B VHS.** *GE* Ruediger Vogler, Hanns Zischler, Elisabeth (Lisa) Kreuzer; ***D:*** Wim Wenders; ***W:*** Wim Wenders; ***C:*** Robby Muller, Martin Schafer; ***M:*** Axel Linstadt.

King's Ransom woof! **1991** When the Japanese Emperor's Pearl is stolen, the underworld is abuzz with excitement. But only the wealthiest individuals are invited to bid for the jewel at Cameron King's secret casino. There, untold pleasures, and dangers, await them. **?m/C VHS.** Miles O'Keeffe, Dedee Pfeiffer, Christopher Atkins; ***D:*** Hugh Parks.

The King's Rhapsody ⚭⚭ **1955** Flynn is an heir who abdicates his throne in order to be with the woman he loves. But when the king dies, Flynn sacrifices love for honor and goes back to marry a princess. Very dated and Flynn is long past his swashbuckling-romantic days. **93m/C VHS.** *GB* Errol Flynn, Anna Neagle, Patrice Wymore, Martita Hunt, Finlay Currie, Frank Wolff, Joan Benham, Reginald Tate, Miles Malleson; ***D:*** Herbert Wilcox.

Kings Row ⚭⚭⚭ **1941** The Harry Bellamann best-selling Middle American potboiler comes to life. Childhood friends grow up with varying degrees of success, in a decidedly macabre town. All are continually dependent on and inspired by Parris (Cummings) a psychiatric doctor and genuine gentleman. Many cast members worked against type with unusual success. Warner held the film for a year after its completion, in concern for its dark subject matter, but it received wide acclaim. Shot completely within studio settings—excellent scenic design by William Cameron Menzies, and wonderful score. **127m/B VHS.** Ann Sheridan, Robert Cummings, Ronald Reagan, Betty Field, Charles Coburn, Claude Rains, Judith Anderson, Nancy Coleman, Karen Verne, Maria Ouspenskaya, Harry Davenport, Ernest Cossart, Pat Moriarity, Scotty Beckett; ***D:*** Sam Wood; ***C:*** James Wong Howe; ***M:*** Erich Wolfgang Korngold.

The King's Thief ⚭⚭½ **1955** Costume swashbuckler with Niven as the bad guy. He's a duke at the court of 17th-century English King Charles II and is involved in a plot to steal the crown jewels. **78m/C VHS.** David Niven, Edmund Purdom, George Sanders, Ann Blyth, Roger Moore, John Dehner, Sean McClory, Melville Cooper, Alan Mowbray; ***D:*** Robert Z. Leonard; ***W:*** Christopher Knopf; ***M:*** Miklos Rozsa.

The King's Whore ⚭⚭ **1990 (R)** Dalton stars as a 17th-century king who falls obsessively in love with the wife of one of his courtiers. His passions lead him to make a decision between the woman and the throne. Good-looking costume epic with obligatory sword fights. **111m/C VHS.** Timothy Dalton, Valeria Golino, Feodor Chaliapin Jr., Margaret Tyzack; ***W:*** Daniel Vigne, Frederic Raphael.

Kinjite: Forbidden Subjects ⚭⚭ **1989 (R)** A cop takes on a sleazy pimp whose specialty is recruiting teenage girls, including the daughter of a Japanese business man. Slimy, standard Bronson fare. **97m/C VHS.** Charles Bronson, Juan Fernandez, Peggy Lipton; ***D:*** J. Lee Thompson.

A Kink in the Picasso ⚭⚭ **1990** MTV personality Daddo joins a cast of criminals who chase after a Picasso artwork and a counterfeit. Artless Australian production. **84m/C VHS.** Peter O'Brien, Jon Finlayson, Jane Clifton, Andrew Daddo; ***D:*** Marc Gracie.

Kipperbang ⚭⚭ *Ptang, Yang, Kipperbang* **1982 (PG)** During the summer of 1948, a 13-year-old boy wishes he could kiss the girl of his dreams. He finally gets the chance in a school play. Not unsatisfying, but falls short of being the bittersweet coming-of-age drama it could have been. **85m/C VHS.** *GB* John Albasiny, Abigail Cruttenden, Alison Steadman; ***D:*** Michael Apted.

Kipps ⚭⚭⚭ *The Remarkable Mr. Kipps* **1941** Based on H.G. Wells's satirical novel. A young British shopkeeper inherits a fortune and tries to join high society while neglecting his working-class girlfriend. Set the stage for the musical "Half a Sixpence." **95m/B VHS.** *GB* Michael Redgrave, Phyllis Calvert, Michael Wilding; ***D:*** Carol Reed.

Kippur ⚭⚭⚭ **2000** Set during Israel's 1973 Yom Kippur War—named after the Jewish holiday on which Egypt and Syria launched a surprise attack. Director Gitai's (a veteran himself) war drama concerns friends Weinraub (Levo) and Ruso (Ruso), who are in a rush to join their reserve unit. But their unit has already left, so they wind up in the company of Klauzner (Klauzner), a medic, and join a helicoptor rescue squad in evacuating the dead and wounded. It's a striking combination of commitment, tedium, frustration, fear, and disillusionment. Hebrew with subtitles. **117m/C VHS, DVD.** *IS* Liron Levo, Tomer Ruso, Uri Klauzner; ***D:*** Amos Gitai; ***W:*** Amos Gitai, Marie-Jose Sanselme; ***C:*** Renato Berta; ***M:*** Jan Garbarek.

The Kirlian Witness ⚭ *The Plants Are Watching* **1978 (PG)** A woman uses the power of telepathic communication with house plants to solve her sister's murder. **88m/C VHS.** Nancy Snyder, Joel Colodner, Ted Leplat; ***D:*** Jonathan Sarno.

Kismet ⚭⚭⚭ **1920** Original screen version of the much filmed lavish Arabian Nights saga (remade in '30, '44 and '55). A beggar is drawn into deception and intrigue among Bagdad upper-crusters. Glorious sets and costumes; silent with original organ score. **98m/B VHS.** Otis Skinner, Elinor Fair, Herschel Mayall; ***D:*** Louis Gasnier; ***C:*** Gaetano Antonio "Tony" Gaudio.

Kismet ⚭⚭ **1955** A big-budget Arabian Nights musical drama of a Baghdad street poet who manages to infiltrate himself into the Wazir's harem. The music was adapted from Borodin by Robert Wright and George Forrest. ♫Fate; Not Since Ninevah; Baubles, Bangles, and Beads; Stranger in Paradise; Bored; Night of My Nights; The Olive Tree; And This Is My Beloved; Sands of Time. **113m/C VHS, Wide.** Howard Keel, Ann Blyth, Dolores Gray, Vic Damone; ***D:*** Vincente Minnelli; ***W:*** Charles Lederer, Luther Davis; ***C:*** Joseph Ruttenberg; ***M:*** Andre Previn.

The Kiss ⚭⚭⚭ **1929** Garbo, the married object of earnest young Ayres' lovelorn affection, innocently kisses him nighty night since a kiss is just a kiss. Or so she thought. Utterly misconstrued, the platonic peck sets the stage for disaster, and murder and courtroom anguish follow. French Feyder's direction is stylized and artsy. Garbo's last silent and Ayres' first film. **89m/B VHS.** Greta Garbo, Conrad Nagel, Holmes Herbert, Lew Ayres, Anders Randolf; ***D:*** Jacques Feyder; ***C:*** William H. Daniels.

The Kiss ⚭ **1988 (R)** A kind of "Auntie Mame from Hell" story in which a mysterious aunt visits her teenage niece in New York, and tries to apprentice her to the family business of sorcery, demon possession, and murder. Aunt Felicity's kiss will make you appreciate the harmless cheek-pinching of your own aunt; your evening would be better spent with her, rather than this movie. **98m/C VHS.** Pamela Collyer, Peter Dvorsky, Joanna Pacula, Meredith Salenger, Mimi Kuzyk, Nicholas Kilbertus, Jan Rubes; ***D:*** Pen Densham; ***W:*** Tom Ropelewski.

Kiss and Be Killed ⚭½ **1991 (R)** Crazy guy with knife cuts short couple's wedding night. Shortchanged widow is mighty miffed. Will she have to return the wedding gifts? **89m/C VHS, 8mm.** Caroline Ludvik, Crystal Carson, Tom Reilly, Chip Hall, Ken Norton, Jimmy Baio; ***D:*** Tom Milo.

Kiss and Kill ⚭⚭ *Blood of Fu Manchu; Against All Odds* **1968 (R)** Lee returns in his fourth outing as Fu Manchu. This time the evil one has injected beautiful girls with a deadly poison that reacts upon kissing. They are then sent out to seduce world leaders. Not on par with the previous movies, but still enjoyable. Sequel to "Castle of Fu Manchu." **91m/C VHS.** Christopher Lee, Richard Greene, Shirley Eaton, Tsai Chin, Maria Rohm, Howard Marion-Crawford; ***D:*** Jess (Jesus) Franco.

Kiss & Tell ⚭⚭ **1999 (R)** Self-conscious black comedy about LAPD detective Arquette who's investigating the murder (by carrot) of performance artist Bateman. Naturally, the suspects are as weird as the crime. **90m/C VHS.** Richmond Arquette; Justine Bateman, Heather Graham, Pamela Gidley; ***D:*** Jordan Alan.

A Kiss Before Dying ⚭⚭ **1991 (R)** Botched adaptation of Ira Levin's cunning thriller novel (filmed before in 1956). This flick serves up an exploded head in the first few minutes. So much for subtlety. The highlight is Dillon's chilly role as a murderous opportunist bent on marrying into a wealthy family. Young plays two roles (not very well) as lookalike sisters on his agenda. The ending was hastily reshot and it shows. **93m/C VHS.** Matt Dillon, Sean Young, Max von Sydow, Diane Ladd, James Russo, Martha Gehman, Ben Browder, Joy Lee, Adam Horovitz; ***D:*** James Dearden; ***W:*** James Dearden. Golden Raspberries '91: Worst Actress (Young), Worst Support. Actress (Young).

Kiss Daddy Goodbye ⚭½ *Revenge of the Zombie; The Vengeful Dead* **1981 (R)** A widower keeps his two children isolated in order to protect their secret telekinetic powers. When he is killed by bikers, the kids attempt to raise him from the dead. **81m/C VHS.** Fabian, Marilyn Burns, Jon Cedar, Marvin Miller; ***D:*** Patrick Regan.

Kiss Daddy Goodnight ⚭ **1987 (R)** A Danish-made thriller about a beautiful young girl who seduces men, drugs them and takes their money. One man turns the tables on her, however, and decides that she will only belong to him. **89m/C VHS.** *DK* Uma Thurman, Paul Dillon, Paul (E.) Richards, David Brisbin; ***D:*** P.I. Huemer; ***C:*** Bobby Bukowski.

A Kiss for Mary Pickford ⚭⚭½ **1927** A rare, hilarious cinematic oddity, a film formulated from Kuleshov montage techniques from footage of the famous American couple's visit to Russia in 1926, wherein a regular guy tries to win a girl through friendship with the stars. Fairbanks and Pickford didn't know of their role in this film, being spliced in later according to montage theory. **70m/B VHS.** Mary Pickford, Douglas Fairbanks Sr., Igor Ilinsky; ***D:*** Sergei Komarov.

A Kiss Goodnight ⚭⚭½ **1994 (R)** Natalie (Trickey) has a romp in the sheets with ad exec Kurt (Corley) when regular beau Michael (Moses) ignores her for work. But when Natalie decides to break things off, Kurt won't take no for an answer. **88m/C VHS.** Paula Trickey, Al Corley, Mark Moses, Lawrence Tierney, Brett Cullen, James Karen, Robert Wuhl, Sydney Walsh; ***D:*** Daniel Raskov; ***W:*** Daniel Raskov; ***C:*** Glenn Kershaw.

Kiss Me a Killer ⚭⚭ **1991 (R)** The ancient thriller plot about a young wife and her lover who scheme to kill her middle-aged husband. It's set in L.A.'s Latino community, but extensive shots of salsa music and ethnic cooking hardly raise this above the mediocre. **91m/C VHS.** Julie Carmen, Robert Beltran, Guy Boyd, Ramon Franco, Charles Boswell; ***D:*** Marcus De Leon; ***W:*** Marcus De Leon.

Kiss Me Deadly ⚭⚭⚭½ **1955** Aldrich's adaptation of Mickey Spillane's private eye tale takes pulp literature high concept. Meeker, as Mike Hammer, is a self-interested rough-and-tumble all-American dick (detective, that is). When a woman to whom he happened to give a ride is found murdered, he follows the mystery straight into a nuclear conspiracy. Aldrich, with tongue deftly in cheek, styles a message through the medium; topsy-turvy camera work and rat-a-tat-tat pacing tell volumes about Hammer, the world he orbits, and that special '50s kind of paranoia. Now a cult fave, it's considered to be the American grandaddy to French New Wave. **105m/B VHS, DVD, Wide.** Ralph Meeker, Albert Dekker, Paul Stewart, Wesley Addy, Cloris Leachman, Strother Martin, Marjorie Bennett, Jack Elam, Maxine Cooper, Gaby Rodgers, Nick Dennis, Jack Lambert, Percy Helton; ***D:*** Robert Aldrich; ***W:*** A.I. Bezzerides; ***C:*** Ernest Laszlo; ***M:*** Frank DeVol. Natl. Film Reg. '99.

Kiss Me Goodbye ⚭⚭ **1982 (PG)** Young widow Fields can't shake the memory of her first husband, a charismatic but philandering Broadway choreographer, who's the antithesis of her boring but devoted professor fiance. She struggles with the charming ghost of her first husband, as well as her domineering mother, attempting to understand her own true feelings. Harmless but two-dimensional remake of "Dona Flor and Her Two Husbands." **101m/C VHS.** Sally Field, James Caan, Jeff Bridges, Paul Dooley, Mildred Natwick, Claire Trevor; ***D:*** Robert Mulligan; ***W:*** Charlie Peters; ***M:*** Ralph Burns, Peter Allen.

Kiss Me, Guido ⚭⚭½ **1997 (R)** Heterosexual and handsome Frankie (Scotti) is a Bronx-born and -raised pizza maker and De Niro wanna-be who's not too bright. Apartment hunting in Manhattan, he thinks an ad listing "GWM" stands for "guy with money" and mistakenly moves in with gay actor Warren (Barrile). Pokes fun at both Italian-American and gay stereotypes without offending or canonizing either group. Vitale and an excellent, if largely unknown, cast inject enough energy and humor to rise above the often predictable story. Low-budget independent sex farce that offers a promising start for first-time filmmaker Vitale. **90m/C VHS, DVD, Wide.** Nick Scotti, Anthony Barrile, Craig Chester, Anthony De Sando, Christopher Lawford, Molly Price; ***D:*** Tony Vitale; ***W:*** Tony Vitale; ***C:*** Claudia Raschke; ***M:*** Randall Poster.

Kiss Me Kate ⚭⚭⚭ **1953** A married couple can't separate their real lives from their stage roles in this musical-comedy screen adaptation of Shakespeare's "Taming of the Shrew," based on Cole Porter's Broadway show. Bob Fosse bursts from the screen—particularly if you see the 3-D version—when he does his dance number. ♫Out of This World; From This Moment On; Wunderbar; So In Love; I Hate Men; Were Thine That Special Face; I've Come To Wive It Wealthily In Padua; Where Is The Life That Late I Led?; Always True To You Darling In My Fashion. **110m/C VHS.** Kathryn Grayson, Howard Keel, Ann Miller, Tommy (Thomas) Rall, Bob Fosse, Bobby Van, Keenan Wynn, James Whitmore; ***D:*** George Sidney; ***C:*** Charles Rosher; ***M:*** Andre Previn.

Kiss Me, Kill Me ⚭½ *Devil's Witch; Baba Yaga; So Sweet, So Perverse; Cosi Dolce...Cosi Perversa; Baba Yaga—Devil Witch* **1969 (R)** Confused woman is on the run after she may have murdered someone. **91m/C VHS.** Carroll Baker, George Eastman, Isabelle DeFunes, Ely Gallo; ***D:*** Corrado Farina; ***W:*** Corrado Farina.

Kiss Me, Stupid! ⚭⚭ **1964 (PG-13)** Once condemned as smut, this lesser Billy Wilder effort now seems no worse than an average TV sitcom. Martin basically plays himself as a horny Vegas crooner stranded in the boondocks. A local songwriter wants Dino to hear his tunes but knows the cad will seduce his pretty wife, so he hires a floozy to pose as the tempting spouse. It gets better as it goes along, but the whole thing suffers from staginess, being an adaptation of an Italian play "L'Ora Della Fantasia" by Anna Bonacci. **126m/B VHS, Wide.** Dean Martin, Kim Novak, Ray Walston, Felicia Farr, Cliff Osmond, Barbara Pepper, Doro Merande, Howard McNear, Henry Gibson, John Fiedler, Mel Blanc; ***D:*** Billy Wilder; ***W:*** Billy Wilder, I.A.L. Diamond; ***C:*** Joseph LaShelle; ***M:*** Andre Previn.

KISS Meets the Phantom of the Park ⚭½ *Attack of the Phantoms* **1978** The popular '70s rock band is featured in this Dr. Jekyll-esque Halloween horror tale, interspersed with musical numbers. **96m/C VHS.** Peter Criss, Ace Frehley, Gene Simmons, Paul Stanley, Anthony Zerbe, Carmine Caridi, Deborah Ryan, John Dennis Johnston, John Lisbon Wood, Lisa Jane Persky, Brion James, Bill Hudson; ***D:*** Gordon Hessler; ***W:*** J. Michael Sherman, Albert (Don) Buday; ***C:*** Robert Caramico; ***M:*** Hoyt Curtin, Fred Karlin.

Kiss My Grits 1982 (PG) A good ole boy hightails it to Mexico with his girlfriend and son, chased by mobsters and the law. **101m/C VHS.** Bruce Davison, Anthony (Tony) Franciosa, Susan George, Bruno Kirby; ***D:*** Jack Starrett.

Kiss of a Killer ½ 1993 O'Toole is a mousy miss living a dead-end life with her nagging mother. But she has a secret—she spends weekends in a hotel, dressed to entice and picking up strangers. Involved in an auto mishap she's aided by a handsome mechanic, who turns out to be a rapist. When he accidentally kills his latest victim, he realizes our mystery woman can identify him and tries to find her. Based on the novel "The Point of Murder" by Margaret Yorke. **93m/C VHS.** Annette O'Toole, Brian Wimmer, Eva Marie Saint, Gregg Henry, Vic Polizos; ***D:*** Larry Elikann; ***W:*** David Warfield. **TV**

Kiss of Death 1947 Paroled when he turns state's evidence, Mature must now watch his back constantly. Widmark, in his film debut, seeks to destroy him. Police chief Donlevy tries to help. Filmed on location in New York, this gripping and gritty film is a vision of the most terrifying sort of existence, one where nothing is certain, and everything is dangerous. Excellent. **98m/B VHS.** Victor Mature, Richard Widmark, Anne Grey, Brian Donlevy, Karl Malden, Coleen Gray; ***D:*** Henry Hathaway.

Kiss of Death 1977 Weird comedy about a shy undertaker's assistant and his attempts at first romance. **80m/C VHS.** *GB* David Threlfall, John Wheatley, Kay Adshead, Angela Curran; ***D:*** Mike Leigh; ***W:*** Mike Leigh. **TV**

Kiss of Death ½ 1994 (R) Very loose contemporary remake of the 1947 film noir classic of the same name. Jimmy Kilmartin (Caruso) is a paroled car thief turned informant. He soon finds himself trapped in a web of deceit involving corrupt district attorneys and ruthless hoodlums like Little Junior (Cage, pumped up and playing against type), with no one to trust. Crime drama keeps the far-fetched genre conventions in check until the end. Caruso makes the transition from TV cop on "NYPD Blue" by not straying far from his small screen persona. Cage's standout performance may not be as chilling as Widmark's unforgettable debut in the original, but he's able to convey a level of mercilessness and depth that'll make you wince. **100m/C VHS.** David Caruso, Nicolas Cage, Samuel L. Jackson, Helen Hunt, Stanley Tucci, Michael Rapaport, Ving Rhames, Anthony Heald, Anne Meara, Hope Davis, Kathryn Erbe, Philip Baker Hall, Kevin Corrigan, Michael Artura, Jay O. Sanders; ***D:*** Barbet Schroeder; ***W:*** Richard Price; ***M:*** Trevor Jones.

Kiss of Fire *Claudine's Return* 1998 (R) Stefano (Dionisi) gets a job as the handyman at a Georgia motel and gets involved with laundress/stripper Claudine (Applegate) in what proves to be a dangerous relationship. And despite her role, Applegate does not get naked. **92m/C VHS, DVD, Wide.** Stefano Dionisi, Christina Applegate, Matt Clark, Gabriel Mann, Perry Anzilotti, Tom Nowicki; ***D:*** Antonio Tibaldi; ***W:*** Antonio Tibaldi, Heidi A. Hall; ***C:*** Luca Bigazzi; ***M:*** Michel Colombier. **VIDEO**

Kiss of the Dragon ½ 2001 (R) Li is Chinese super-cop Liu who is sent to Paris to help stop a Chinese drug lord. Once there, he learns that the cop, Richard (Karyo), he was sent to help is actually running the drug ring, and has set Liu up for the dealer's murder. Fonda is the hooker/addict who helps Lui in order to free herself and her daughter from Richard. Spectacular action sequences, as well as Li's martial art skills and charisma more than make up for a pretty lame script which is little more than connective tissue anyway. Besson and Li co-produced the feature debut of director Nahon, who comes from the video/commercials world. **98m/C VHS, DVD, Wide.** *FR US* Jet Li, Bridget Fonda, Tcheky Karyo, Burt Kwouk; ***D:*** Chris Nahon; ***W:*** Luc Besson, Robert Mark Kamen; ***C:*** Thierry Arbogast; ***M:*** Craig Armstrong.

Kiss of the Spider Woman *O Beijo da Mulher Aranha* 1985 (R) From the novel by Manuel Puig, an acclaimed drama concerning two cell mates in a South American prison, one a revolutionary, the other a homosexual. Literate, haunting, powerful. **119m/C VHS, 8mm.** *BR* William Hurt, Raul Julia, Sonia Braga, Jose Lewgoy, Milton Goncalves, Nuno Leal Maia, Denise Dumont, Antonio Petrim, Miriam Pires, Fernando Torres; ***D:*** Hector Babenco; ***W:*** Leonard Schrader; ***C:*** Rodolfo Sanchez; ***M:*** John Neschling, Wally Badarou. Oscars '85: Actor (Hurt); British Acad. '85: Actor (Hurt); Cannes '85: Actor (Hurt); Ind. Spirit '86: Foreign Film; L.A. Film Critics '85: Actor (Hurt); Natl. Bd. of Review '85: Actor (Hurt), Actor (Julia).

Kiss of the Tarantula 1975 (PG) Teen girl who lives with her family in a mortuary battles inner torment and vents anxiety by releasing her deadly pet spiders on those whom she despises. Eight-legged "Carrie" rip-off. **85m/C VHS.** Eric Mason; ***D:*** Chris Munger; ***W:*** Warren Hamilton.

Kiss of the Vampire ½ *Kiss of Evil* 1962 Newlywed couple is stranded in Bavaria near a villa of vampires and are invited in by its charmingly evil owner. Fortunately, hubby manages to escape and finds a knowledgeable professor who unleashes a horde of bats to rout the bloodsuckers. Properly creepy; producer Hinds used the pseudonym John Elder for his screenplay. **88m/C VHS, DVD.** *GB* Clifford Evans, Noel Willman, Edward De Souza, Jennifer Daniel, Barry Warren, Jacqueline Wallis, Peter Madden, Isobel Black, Vera Cook, Olga Dickie; ***D:*** Don Sharp; ***W:*** John (Anthony Hinds) Elder; ***C:*** Alan Hume; ***M:*** James Bernard.

Kiss or Kill 1997 (R) Thieves/con artists and lovers Nikki (O'Connor) and Al (Day) head out across the Australian desert towards Perth when one of their schemes results in death. Since they've also got a videotape showing football player Zipper Doyle (Langrishe) engaged in pedophile activity, he's on their trail as are a couple of cops. But trouble also seems to follow them—everywhere the duo spend the night a dead body appears the next morning and soon the lovers begin wondering about each other. Quirky characters and fine performances from all concerned, even if the emotional core of the film is somewhat cold. **95m/C VHS.** *AU* Frances O'Connor, Matt(hew) Day, Chris Haywood, Barry Otto, Max Cullen, Andrew S. Gilbert, Barry Langrishe, Jennifer Cluff; ***D:*** Bill Bennett; ***W:*** Bill Bennett; ***C:*** Malcolm McCulloch. Australian Film Inst. '97: Director (Bennett), Film, Film Editing, Sound, Support. Actor (Gilbert); Montreal World Film Fest. '97: Actress (O'Connor).

Kiss Shot 1989 Goldberg is a struggling single mother who loses her job but still must make the mortgage payments. She takes a job as a waitress but realizes it isn't going to pay the bills so she tries her hand as a pool hustler. Frantz is the promoter who finances her bets and Harewood, the pool-shooting playboy whose romantic advances are destroying her concentration. **88m/C VHS, DVD.** Whoopi Goldberg, Dennis Franz, Dorian Harewood, David Marciano, Teddy Wilson; ***D:*** Jerry London; ***C:*** Chuy Elizondo; ***M:*** Steve Dorff.

Kiss the Girls 1997 (R) After his niece is abducted, forensic psychologist Alex Cross (Freeman) joins the hunt for a lunatic who's kidnapping and collecting successful young women. After doctor Kate McTiernan (Judd), who also happens to be a kickboxer, escapes the sicko's love dungeon, she helps Cross track him down. Borrowing heavily from "Silence of the Lambs" and "Seven," this psycho-killer thriller falls far short of both. Adapted from the novel by James Patterson. **117m/C VHS, DVD, Wide.** Morgan Freeman, Ashley Judd, Cary Elwes, Tony Goldwyn, Jay O. Sanders, Bill Nunn, Brian Cox, Alex McArthur, Richard T. Jones, Jeremy Piven, William Converse-Roberts, Gina Ravera, Roma Maffia; ***D:*** Gary Fleder; ***W:*** David Klass; ***C:*** Aaron Schneider; ***M:*** Mark Isham.

Kiss the Night 1987 (R) An unfortunate hooker falls head over heels for a man she had the pleasure of doing business with. To her chagrin, it is much harder to leave the street than she thought. A dramatic and timely presentation. **99m/C VHS.** Patsy Stephens, Warwick Moss, Gary Aron Cook; ***D:*** James Ricketson.

Kiss the Sky 1998 (R) Suffering from midlife crises, Jeff (Petersen) and Marty (Cole) head off on a business trip to the Philippines. Once there, they decide to abandon their settled lives and families in order to experiment with recapturing their lost youth. In their case, it's by becoming a menage a trois with sexy Oxford grad, Andy (Lee). Provocative but hardly gratuitous. **105m/C VHS, DVD.** William L. Petersen, Gary Cole, Sheryl Lee, Terence Stamp, Patricia Charbonneau, Season Hubley; ***D:*** Roger Young; ***W:*** Eric Lerner; ***C:*** Donald M. Morgan; ***M:*** Patrick Williams.

Kiss Toledo Goodbye 2000 (R) Young man finds out his biological dad is the local head mobster just before pops is rubbed out. The kid inherits the job (which he tries to keep a secret from his fiancee) as well as his father's enemies. **96m/C VHS, DVD.** Michael Rapaport, Christine Taylor, Christopher Walken, Robert Forster, Nancy Allen, Paul Ben-Victor, Bill Smitrovich; ***D:*** Lyndon Chubbuck; ***W:*** Robert Easter; ***C:*** Frank Byers; ***M:*** Phil Marshall. **VIDEO**

Kiss Tomorrow Goodbye 1950 A brutal, murderous escaped convict rises to crime-lord status before his inevitable downfall. Based on a novel by Horace McCoy. **102m/B VHS.** James Cagney, Barbara Payton, Ward Bond, Luther Adler, Helena Carter, Steve Brodie, Rhys Williams; ***D:*** Gordon Douglas.

Kiss Tomorrow Goodbye 2000 (R) Based on 1942's "Moontide" this updated would-be modern noir suffers from unappealing characters. Dustin Yarma (Lea) is an arrogant, hard-partying Hollywood film exec who wakes up on the beach after a night of debauchery to find that his nameless female companion is dead. Suspicious drifter Minnow (McCallany) says he saw Dustin murder the girl in a drunken rage but will take care of the matter—for a price. The price turns out to be Dustin's life as Minnow moves in on his career and his girlfriend, D'Arcy (Wuhrer). Then Dustin discovers things aren't exactly as they seem. Director Priestley plays the small role of Dustin's buddy Jarred. **90m/C VHS, DVD.** Nicholas Lea, Holt McCallany, Kari Wuhrer, Jason Priestley, Philip Casnoff, Jennifer Blanc; ***D:*** Jason Priestley; ***W:*** Ozzie Cheek; ***C:*** Bruce Logan; ***M:*** Harold Kloser. **TV**

The Kiss You Gave Me *El Beso Que Me Diste* 2000 Set in 2006, Angela is the star reporter of Teledigital TV Network in Puerto Rico. When her marriage to Armando falls apart, he kidnaps their eight-year-old son Ivan and takes the boy to the U.S. Angela enlists lawyer (and old flame) Pedro to go to the States with her and get the boy back. Based on the novel by Stella Soto. Spanish with subtitles. **90m/C VHS, DVD, Wide.** Maricarmen Aviles, Jimmy Navarro, Rene Monclova, Carola Garcia, Ernesto Concepcion, Humberto Gonzales; ***D:*** Sonia Fritz; ***W:*** Sonia Fritz; ***C:*** Augustin Cubano; ***M:*** Miguel Cubano.

Kissed 1996 (R) The subject matter (necrophilia) is sure to give one pause though debut director Stopkewich hardly dwells on the prurient. Sandra Larson (Parker) has been obsessed with death and its rituals since childhood. So as a young adult it seems natural when she gets a job in a funeral home, preparing the bodies for embalming. Only Sandra's obsession leads her to begin making love (shown through a gauzy white light) to the corpses. She does attract the attentions of a very alive medical student, Matt (Outerbridge), who becomes fascinated by Sandra's fetish and determined to make himself as appealing to her as the dead. Adapted from Barbara Gowdy's short story "We So Seldom Look on Love." **78m/C VHS.** *CA* Molly Parker, Peter Outerbridge, Jay Brazeau; ***D:*** Lynne Stopkewich; ***W:*** Lynne Stopkewich, Angus Fraser; ***C:*** Gregory Middleton; ***M:*** Don MacDonald. Genie '97: Actress (Parker).

Kisses for My President ½ 1964 Silly comedy about the first woman elected President and her trials and tribulations. MacMurray is the husband who has to adjust to the protocol of being "First Man." Bergen is miscast, but the other performances are just fine. **113m/C VHS.** Fred MacMurray, Polly Bergen, Arlene Dahl, Edward Andrews, Eli Wallach, Donald May; ***D:*** Curtis Bernhardt.

Kisses in the Dark 1997 Four short award-winning films. "Coriolis Effect" finds two daredevil tornado-chasers falling in love. "Solly's Diner" has a vagrant becoming a hero during a diner hold-up. "Looping" finds an egotistic Italian director deciding in the middle of shooting his big-budget Mafia musical that the material isn't worthy of him. "Joe" finds solace in his daily routine in a psych ward when an interloper disturbs his refuge. **75m/C VHS, DVD, Wide.** Jennifer Rubin, James Wilder, Dana Ashbrook, Corinne Bohrer, Katherine Wallach, Ronald Guttman, Quentin Tarantino; ***D:*** Larry Hankin, Louis Venosta, Roger Paradiso, Sasha Wolf; ***W:*** Louis Venosta, Roger Paradiso, Sasha Wolf.

Kissin' Cousins ½ 1964 Air Force officer on a secluded base in the South discovers a local hillbilly is his double. Presley quickie that includes country tunes such as "Smokey Mountain Boy" and "Barefoot Ballad" as well as the title song. **96m/C VHS.** Elvis Presley, Arthur O'Connell, Jack Albertson, Glenda Farrell, Pam Austin, Yvonne Craig, Cynthia Pepper, Donald Woods, Tommy Farrell, Beverly (Hills) Powers; ***D:*** Gene Nelson.

Kissing a Fool ½ 1998 (R) Movie asks the titillating question: Who will smart, pretty Sam marry? The unctuous Schwimmer character, Max, or the sensitive writer guy Max sets up with Sam to test her fidelity? Who cares. Hunt sets up the utterly lame opening premise as Sam's boss, who is throwing her a wedding and explains to guests how Sam and her intended met while the rote triangle scenario plays out in flashback. Schwimmer, as a Chicago sportscaster with a roving eye, plays nicely (and wisely) against type while Lee's novelist Jay, a supposedly close friend of Max, occupies a less gratifying role. Avital has little to do but does is well. **93m/C VHS, DVD.** David Schwimmer, Jason Lee, Mili Avital, Bonnie Hunt, Vanessa Angel, Kari Wuhrer, Frank Medrano, Bitty Schram, Judy Greer; ***D:*** Doug Ellin; ***W:*** Doug Ellin, James Frey; ***C:*** Thomas Del Ruth; ***M:*** Joseph Vitarelli.

The Kissing Place 1990 A woman who abducted her "son" years ago tracks the boy to New York City to prevent him from finding his biological family. **90m/C VHS.** Meredith Baxter, David Ogden Stiers; ***D:*** Tony Wharmby; ***W:*** Richard Altabef, Cynthia A. Cherbak.

Kissinger and Nixon ½ 1996 Intrigue, ambition, and backbiting politics consume the 18 weeks leading up to the signing of the Vietnam peace accords in Paris in January, 1973. Egotistical Kissinger (Silver) is prepared to sacrifice South Vietnam for the sake of his own ambitions (and an end to the conflict) while a distrustful Nixon (Bridges) lurks uneasily in the background. TV docudrama offers little insight; based on Walter Isaacson's biography "Kissinger." **94m/C VHS.** Ron Silver, Beau Bridges, Matt Frewer, Ron White, George Takei, Kenneth Welsh; ***D:*** Daniel Petrie; ***W:*** Lionel Chetwynd; ***M:*** Jonathan Goldsmith.

Kit Carson 1940 Frontiersman Kit Carson leads a wagon train to California, fighting off marauding Indians all the way. **97m/B VHS.** Jon Hall, Dana Andrews, Ward Bond, Lynn Bari; ***D:*** George B. Seitz.

The Kitchen Toto 1987 (PG-13) Set in 1950 Kenya as British rule was being threatened by Mau Mau terrorists. A young black boy is torn between the British for whom he works and the terrorists who want him to join them. Complex and powerful story of the Kenyan freedom crusade. **96m/C VHS.** *GB* Bob Peck, Phyllis Logan, Robert Urquhart, Edward Judd, Edwin Mahinda, Kirsten Hughes; ***D:*** Harry Hook; ***W:*** Harry Hook; ***C:*** Roger Deakins; ***M:*** John Keane.

Kitten with a Whip ½ 1964 Whatever the film's original intentions, it's now become pure camp. Jody (Ann-Margaret) is a juvenile delinquent who's broken out of a girls' reformatory and breaks into the home of wannabe politician David

Patton (Forsythe), who's separated from his wife. Jody works her considerable wiles and soon Patton's life is filled with wild parties, rampant teen lust, and violence. Too bad it wasn't filmed in the lurid color it deserved. Based on the book by Wade Miller. **84m/B VHS.** Ann-Margret, John Forsythe, Peter Brown, Patricia Barry, Richard Anderson, Diane Sayer, Ann Doran, Patrick Whyte, Audrey Dalton, Leo Gordon; ***D:*** Douglas Heyes; ***W:*** Douglas Heyes; ***C:*** Joseph Biroc.

Kitty and the Bagman 🦴🦴 **1982 (R)** A comedy about two rival madames who ruled Australia in the 1920s. **95m/C VHS.** *AU* Liddy Clark; ***D:*** Donald Crombie.

Kitty Foyle 🦴🦴🦴 **1940** From the novel by Christopher Morley, Rogers portrays the white-collar working girl whose involvement with a married man presents her with both romantic and social conflicts. **108m/B VHS.** Ginger Rogers, Dennis Morgan, James Craig, Gladys Cooper, Ernest Cossart, Eduardo Ciannelli; ***D:*** Sam Wood. Oscars '40: Actress (Rogers).

The Klansman 🦴 *Burning Cross; KKK* **1974 (R)** Race relations come out on the short end in this film about a sheriff trying to keep the lid on racial tensions in a southern town. Even the big-name cast can't save what comes off as a nighttime soaper rather than a serious drama. **112m/C VHS.** Lee Marvin, Richard Burton, Cameron Mitchell, Lola Falana, Luciana Paluzzi, Linda Evans, O.J. Simpson; ***D:*** Terence Young; ***W:*** Samuel Fuller.

Kleptomania 🦴½ **1994 (R)** Socialite meets a runaway and discoers they're both kleptomaniacs. **90m/C VHS.** Amy Irving, Patsy Kensit, Victor Garber; ***D:*** Don Boyd; ***W:*** Don Boyd.

Klondike Annie 🦴🦴½ **1936** West stars as a woman on the lam for a murder (self-defense) who heads out for the Yukon aboard McLaglen's ship. He falls for her, finds out about her problems, and helps her with a scam to pass herself off as a missionary, only she begins to take her saving souls seriously (although in her own risque style). **77m/B VHS, DVD.** Mae West, Victor McLaglen, Philip Reed, Helen Jerome Eddy, Harry Beresford, Harold Huber, Conway Tearle, Esther Howard; ***D:*** Raoul Walsh; ***W:*** Mae West; ***C:*** George T. Clemens.

Klondike Fever 🦴½ *Jack London's Klondike Fever* **1979 (PG)** Join the young Jack London as he travels from San Francisco to the Klondike fields during the Great Gold Rush of 1898. **118m/C VHS.** Rod Steiger, Angie Dickinson, Lorne Greene; ***D:*** Peter Carter; ***M:*** Hagood Hardy.

Klute 🦴🦴🦴½ **1971 (R)** A small-town policeman (Sutherland) comes to New York in search of a missing friend and gets involved with a prostitute/would-be actress (Fonda) being stalked by a killer. Intelligent, gripping drama. **114m/C VHS, DVD, Wide.** Jane Fonda, Donald Sutherland, Charles Cioffi, Roy Scheider, Rita Gam, Jean Stapleton; ***D:*** Alan J. Pakula; ***W:*** Andy Lewis, Dave Lewis; ***C:*** Gordon Willis; ***M:*** Michael Small. Oscars '71: Actress (Fonda); Golden Globes '72: Actress—Drama (Fonda); N.Y. Film Critics '71: Actress (Fonda); Natl. Soc. Film Critics '71: Actress (Fonda).

The Klutz 🦴🦴 **1973** A bumbling fool, on the way to visit his girlfriend, becomes accidentally embroiled in a bank robbery and other ridiculous mishaps. Light French comedy; dubbed. **87m/C VHS.** *FR* Claude Michaud, Louise Portal, Guy Provost; ***D:*** Pierre Rose.

The Knack 🦴🦴🦴 *The Knack...and How to Get It* **1965** Amusing, fast-paced adaptation of the play by Ann Jellicoe. Schoolteacher Crawford is baffled by his tenant Brooks' extreme luck with the ladies so Brooks decides to teach him the "knack" of picking up women. Crawford promptly falls for the first woman (Tushingham) he meets. Swinging London at its most mod. **84m/B VHS.** *GB* Michael Crawford, Ray Brooks, Rita Tushingham, Donal Donnelly; ***D:*** Richard Lester; ***W:*** Charles Wood; ***C:*** David Watkin; ***M:*** John Barry.

Knife in the Head 🦴🦴 *Messer Im Kopf* **1978** Biogeneticist Berthold Hoffman (Ganz) is meeting his wife (Winkler) at the left-wing youth centre where she works when there's a police raid and Berthold is shot in the head. He awakens in the hospital having lost both his memory and all physical co-ordination. Determined to battle his disabilities, Berthold also becomes the pawn in a political game between the police and political dissidents. In German with English subtitles. **108m/C VHS.** *GE* Bruno Ganz, Angela Winkler, Hans Honig, Hans Brenner, Udo Samel, Carla Egerer; ***D:*** Reinhard Hauff; ***W:*** Peter Schneider.

Knife in the Water 🦴🦴🦴🦴 *Noz w Wodzie* **1962** A journalist, his wife and a hitchhiker spend a day aboard a sailboat. Sex and violence can't be far off. Tense psychological drama. Served as director Polanski's debut. In Polish with English subtitles. **94m/B VHS.** *PL* Leon Niemczyk, Jolanta Umecka, Zygmunt Malandowicz; ***D:*** Roman Polanski; ***W:*** Jakub Goldberg, Jerzy Skolimowski, Roman Polanski; ***C:*** Jerzy Lipman; ***M:*** Krzysztof Komeda.

A Knight in Camelot 🦴🦴½ **1998** Oft told Mark Twain tale this time finds computer expert Vivien (Goldberg) conducting an experiment that transports her back to medieval England and the court of King Arthur (York). Lucky for Viv, she's travelling with her laptop, unluckily the kingly court think the tart-tongued woman is a witch. Bossy Vivien makes Merlin (Richardson) jealous and antagonizes everyone until lessons are learned by all. Engaging fluff. **88m/C VHS.** Whoopi Goldberg, Michael York, Amanda Donohoe, Ian Richardson, Robert Addie, Simon Fenton, Paloma Baeza, James Coombes; ***D:*** Roger Young; ***W:*** Joe Wiesenfeld; ***C:*** Elemer Ragalyi; ***M:*** Patrick Williams. **TV**

Knight Moves 🦴🦴 **1993 (R)** Suspenseful thriller about a series of murders which take place at an international resort where a championship chess match is underway. The prime suspect is a chess master who has an unlikely affair with a beautiful police psychologist called in to decipher the mind of the murderer. Filmed in the Pacific Northwest. **105m/C VHS, DVD, Wide.** Christopher Lambert, Diane Lane, Tom Skerritt, Daniel Baldwin; ***D:*** Carl Schenkel; ***W:*** Brad Mirman; ***C:*** Dietrich Lohmann; ***M:*** Anne Dudley.

Knight Without Armour 🦴🦴🦴 **1937** A journalist opposed to the Russian monarchy falls in love with the daughter of a czarist minister in this classic romantic drama. **107m/B VHS.** *GB* Marlene Dietrich, Robert Donat; ***D:*** Jacques Feyder; ***C:*** Harry Stradling Sr.; ***M:*** Miklos Rozsa.

Knightriders 🦴🦴½ **1981 (R)** The story of a troupe of motorcyclists who are members of a traveling Renaissance Fair and look and act like modern-day Knights of the Round Table. Their battles center around who is the bravest and strongest, and who deserves to be king. **145m/C VHS, DVD, Wide.** Ed Harris, Gary Lahti, Tom Savini, Amy Ingersoll; ***D:*** George A. Romero; ***W:*** George A. Romero; ***C:*** Michael Gornick; ***M:*** Donald Rubinstein.

Knights 🦴½ **1993 (R)** In a futuristic wasteland a young martial-arts warrior (Long) and a cyborg (Kristofferson) team up to battle rebel cyborgs that have discovered a new source of fuel—human blood. **89m/C VHS.** Kathy Long, Kris Kristofferson, Lance Henriksen, Scott Paulin, Gary Daniels; ***D:*** Albert Pyun; ***W:*** Albert Pyun.

Knights & Emeralds 🦴½ **1987 (PG)** Cross-cultural rivalries and romances develop between members of two high school marching bands in a British factory town as the national band championships draw near. **90m/C VHS.** *GB* Christopher Wild, Beverly (Hills) Powers, Warren Mitchell; ***D:*** Ian Emes; ***M:*** Colin Towns.

Knights of the City 🦴 **1985 (R)** Miami street gangs fight each other over their "turf." One leader decides to opt out, using music. ♫Let the Music Play; Cry of the City; Jailhouse Rap; T.K. and Jessie Rap; Kurtis Blow Rap; Bounce; My Part of Town; Can You Feel It; Love Goes Up and Down. **87m/C VHS.** Nicholas (Nick) Campbell, John Mengatti, Wendy Barry, Stoney Jackson, Janine Turner, Michael Ansara; ***D:*** Leon Isaac Kennedy, Dominic Orlando; ***W:*** Leon Isaac Kennedy.

Knights of the Range 🦴½ **1940** Vintage western. **66m/B VHS.** Russell Hayden, Victor Jory, Jean Parker, Britt Wood, J. Farrell MacDonald, Eddie Dean; ***D:*** Lesley Selander.

Knights of the Round Table 🦴🦴½ **1953** The story of the romantic triangle between King Arthur, Sir Lancelot, and Guinevere during the civil wars of 6th-century England. **106m/C VHS, Wide.** Robert Taylor, Ava Gardner, Mel Ferrer, Anne Crawford, Felix Aylmer, Stanley Baker; ***D:*** Richard Thorpe; ***C:*** Frederick A. (Freddie) Young; ***M:*** Miklos Rozsa.

A Knight's Tale 🦴🦴½ **2001 (PG-13)** Peasant squire William Thatcher (hunky Ledger) takes the identity of his recently deceased master in 14th-century France so that he may enter the jousting tournaments, which are only open to nobility. He also falls in love with Jocelyn (newcomer Sossamon), a noble lady who would be out of his league given his lowly birth. Count Adhemar (Sewell) is the bad guy rival and a young Geoffrey Chaucer (Bettany), pre-"Canterbury Tales," aids William. The soundtrack is strictly contemporary and filled with anthem rock—depending on your tolerance it's either weirdly complementary or a complete distraction. The movie's strictly popcorn entertainment for the teen set. **132m/C VHS, DVD, Wide.** *US* Heath Ledger, Mark Addy, Rufus Sewell, Shannyn Sossamon, Paul Bettany, Laura Fraser, Christopher Cazenove, Alan Tudyk, James Purefoy; ***D:*** Brian Helgeland; ***W:*** Brian Helgeland; ***C:*** Richard Greatrex; ***M:*** Carter Burwell.

Knives of the Avenger 🦴½ *Viking Massacre; I Coltelli Del Vendicatore* **1965** Brutal ax-bearing Vikings ruin the days of hundreds in this primitive story of courage and desperation. John Hold is the pseudonym for director Mario Bava. **85m/C VHS, DVD, Wide.** *IT* Cameron Mitchell, Elissa Pichelli, Luciano Pollentin, Fausto Tozzi, Giacomo "Jack" Rossi-Stuart; ***D:*** Mario Bava; ***W:*** Mario Bava, Alberto Liberati, Giorgio Simonelli; ***M:*** Marcello Giombini.

Knock Off 🦴🦴 **1998 (R)** As if anyone really cares whether the plot makes any sense (no) but a lot of booty is certainly kicked. Marcus Ray (Van Damme) and Tommy Hendricks (Schneider) are partners in a Hong Kong business that manufactures designer jeans. Marcus was once involved in the shady fashion "knock-off" business and still knows people in low places, where he hears about a Russian mob plot to sell bombs to terrorists. Oh yeah, seems Tommy has a little secret too—he's actually working undercover for the CIA. It's action schlock and you won't mind a bit. **91m/C VHS, DVD.** Jean-Claude Van Damme, Rob Schneider, Lela Rochon, Paul Sorvino, Michael Wong, Carmen Lee, Wyman Wong; ***D:*** Tsui Hark; ***W:*** Steven E. de Souza; ***C:*** Arthur Wong; ***M:*** Ron Mael, Russell Mael.

Knock on Any Door 🦴🦴 **1949** A young hoodlum from the slums is tried for murdering a cop. He is defended by a prominent attorney who has known him from childhood. **100m/B VHS.** Humphrey Bogart, John Derek, George Macready; ***D:*** Nicholas Ray; ***W:*** Daniel Taradash, John Monks Jr.; ***C:*** Burnett Guffey.

Knock Outs 🦴 **1992** Samantha not only loses her shirt at a sorority strip poker marathon but she loses her tuition money to a gang of biker chicks. Then Samantha and a bevy of bikini-clad friends decide to pose for a swimsuit calendar to earn some cash but are secretly videotaped in the nude by some local sleaze promoters. Tired of being taken advantage of these lovelies take up martial arts and challenge their nefarious girl biker rivals to a winner-take-all wrestling match, not forgetting about the purveyors of the not-so-secret videotape. **90m/C VHS, DVD.** Chona Jackson, Cindy Rome, Brad Zutaut; ***D:*** John Bowen.

Knocking on Death's Door 🦴🦴 **1999 (R)** Newlyweds Bloom and Rowe are students of the supernatural and head to a Maine town in order to document the ghosts haunting creepy Hillside House. Their investigation leads them to even more creepy doctor Carradine. Actually filmed in Ireland. **92m/C VHS, DVD.** David Carradine, Brian Bloom, Kimberly Rowe, John Doe; ***D:*** Mitch Marcus. **VIDEO**

Knocks at My Door 🦴🦴 *Golpes a Mi Puerta* **1993** A small Latin American town is in political turmoil, with military patrols making a brutal search for a rebel fugitive. The fugitive seeks refuge in the home of two Catholic nuns, Sister Ana (Oddo) and Sister Ursula (Escobar), who theoretically are protected by the Church. Ana knows the young man will be tortured and executed but when a neighbor betrays his presence, not only is he captured but Sister Ana is arrested. To save her own life Ana must sign a paper claiming the young man threatened her with a gun but will her religious faith transcend political expediencies? Adapted from a play by Gene; Spanish with subtitles. **105m/C VHS.** *VZ* Veronica Oddo, Elba Escobar; ***D:*** Alejandro Saderman; ***W:*** Juan Carlos Gene; ***C:*** Adriano Moreno; ***M:*** Julio D'Escrivan.

Knute Rockne: All American 🦴🦴🦴 *A Modern Hero* **1940** Life story of Notre Dame football coach Knute Rockne, who inspired many victories with his powerful speeches. Reagan, as the dying George Gipp, utters that now-famous line, "Tell the boys to win one for the Gipper." **96m/B VHS.** Ronald Reagan, Pat O'Brien, Gale Page, Donald Crisp, John Qualen; ***D:*** Lloyd Bacon. Natl. Film Reg. '97.

Kojak: The Belarus File 🦴🦴 **1985** The bald-headed detective of prime-time TV fame searches for a neo-Nazi who is killing Holocaust survivors in New York. **95m/C VHS.** Telly Savalas, Suzanne Pleshette, Max von Sydow, George Savalas; ***D:*** Robert Markowitz. **TV**

Kojiro 🦴🦴🦴 **1967** A sprawling epic by prolific Japanese director Inagaki about a dashing rogue's bid for power in feudal times. With English subtitles. **152m/C VHS.** *JP* Kikunosuke Onoe, Tatsuya Nakadai; ***D:*** Hiroshi Inagaki.

Kolberg 🦴🦴 *Burning Hearts* **1945** The true story of a Prussian town heroically withstanding Napoleon. Produced by Joseph Goebbels in the last days of the Third Reich, it is best remembered as the film whose expensive production and momentous use of real German soldiers, supplies, and ammunition eventually helped to fell the Axis war machine. In German with English subtitles. **118m/C VHS.** *GE* Kristina Soderbaum, Heinrich George, Horst Caspar, Paul Wegener; ***D:*** Veit Harlan.

Kolobos 🦴 **1999** Kyra and her fellow actors report to a remote filming location only to discover it's all a set-up. They've been lured into a fight for survival by a mutilated maniac—or have they? Low-budget hard-core gore. **87m/C VHS, DVD.** Amy Weber, Promise LeMarco, Linnea Quigley; ***D:*** Daniel Liatowitsch, David Todd Ocvirk. **VIDEO**

Kolya 🦴🦴🦴 **1996 (PG-13)** Set in the late '80s, just before the Velvet Revolution ended Soviet domination of Czechoslovakia, womanizing Prague cellist Louka (Sverak) agrees to marry (for money) the Russian Klara (Safrankova) who wants Czech papers. She soon clears out to join her lover in Berlin and Louka finds himself saddled with her five-year-old son, Kolya (Chaliman). Grumpy Louka isn't obvious dad material and they don't even speak the same language but the kid (who's adorable without being cloying) manages to worm his way into his new life. Czech with subtitles or dubbed. **105m/C VHS.** *CZ* Zdenek Sverak, Andrej Chalimon, Libuse Safrankova; ***D:*** Jan Sverak; ***W:*** Zdenek Sverak; ***C:*** Vladimir Smutny; ***M:*** Ondrej Soukup. Oscars '96: Foreign Film; Golden Globes '97: Foreign Film.

Komodo 🦴½ **1999 (PG-13)** Komodo dragons are pretty impressive in the wild but are they really scary? This low-budgeter tries to assure you that at least these animatronic/computer-generated versions are. The displaced lizards are breeding on an island off the North Carolina coast where teen Patrick (Zegers) and his aunt (Landis) have unwisely ventured. **85m/C VHS, DVD, Wide.** *AU* Kevin Zegers, Nina Landis, Jill(ian) Hennessey, Paul Gleeson, Billy Burke; ***D:*** Michael Lantieri; ***W:*** Hans Bauer, Craig Mitchell; ***C:*** David Burr; ***M:*** John Debney.

Konrad 199? Konrad, an "instant" child made in a factory, is accidentally delivered to an eccentric woman. The factory wants him back when the mistake is discovered, but Konrad stands up against it. Includes a viewers' guide. Part of the "Wonderworks" series. **110m/C VHS.** Ned Beatty, Polly Holliday, Max Wright, Huckleberry Fox; ***D:*** Neil Cox; ***W:*** Malcolm Marmorstein.

Korczak 1990 Based on the life of Dr. Janusz Korczak, an outspoken critic of the Nazis, who ran the Jewish orphanage in Warsaw, Poland, and accompanied 200 children to to the Treblinka concentration camp. Harshly poetic film quietly details Polish resistance to the Nazi terror. Criticized for end scenes of the children romping in the countryside, implying that they were somehow freed—since the director did not want to show the children actually entering the gas chambers, he used this allegory to imply that their souls were freed. In Polish with English subtitles. **118m/C VHS.** *PL* Wojtek Pszoniak, Ewa Dalkowska, Piotr Kozlowski, Marzena Trybala, Wojciech Klata, Adam Siemion; ***D:*** Andrzej Wajda; ***W:*** Agnieszka Holland.

Koroshi 1967 Secret Agent John Drake is dispatched to Hong Kong to disband a secret society who is killing off international political figures. **100m/C VHS.** Patrick McGoohan, Kenneth Griffith, Yoko Tani; ***D:*** Michael Truman, Peter Yates.

Kostas 1979 **(R)** A migrant Greek taxi driver romantically pursues a wealthy Australian divorcee in England. **88m/C VHS.** Takis Emmanuel, Wendy Hughes; ***D:*** Paul Cox.

Kotch 1971 **(PG)** An elderly man resists his children's attempts to retire him. Warm detailing of old age with a splendid performance by Matthau. Lemmon's directorial debut. **113m/C VHS.** Walter Matthau, Deborah Winters, Felicia Farr; ***D:*** Jack Lemmon; ***M:*** Marvin Hamlisch. Golden Globes '72: Song ("Life Is What You Make It"); Writers Guild '71: Adapt. Screenplay.

Kounterfeit 1996 **(R)** Hopscotch (Hawkes) finds three million in counterfeit cash and tries to get some real cash for the fake stuff with his topless-bar owner buddy Frankie (Payne) serving as muscle. But things go bad. Bernsen has little more than a cameo role as Hopscotch's brother. **87m/C VHS.** Andrew Hawkes, Bruce Payne, Hilary Swank, Michael Gross, Mark Paul Gosselaar, Corbin Bernsen; ***D:*** John Mallory Asher; ***W:*** Jay Irwin, David Chase; ***C:*** Karl Herrmann. **VIDEO**

Koyaanisqatsi 1983 A mesmerizing film that takes an intense look at modern life (the movie's title is the Hopi word for "life out of balance"). Without dialogue or narration, it brings traditional background elements, landscapes and cityscapes, up front to produce a unique view of the structure and mechanics of our daily lives. Riveting and immensely powerful. A critically acclaimed score by Glass, and Reggio's cinematography prove to be the perfect match to this brilliant film. Followed by "Powaqqatsi." **87m/C VHS.** ***D:*** Godfrey Reggio; ***W:*** Godfrey Reggio, Ron Fricke, Michael Hoenig; ***C:*** Godfrey Reggio, Ron Fricke; ***M:*** Philip Glass, Michael Hoenig. L.A. Film Critics '83: Score, Natl. Film Reg. '00.

Kramer vs. Kramer 1979 **(PG)** Highly acclaimed family drama about an advertising executive husband and child left behind when their wife and mother leaves on a quest to find herself, and the subsequent courtroom battle for custody when she returns. Hoffman and Streep give exacting performances as does young Henry. Successfully moves you from tears to laughter and back again. Based on the novel by Avery Corman. **105m/C VHS, DVD, Wide.** Dustin Hoffman, Meryl Streep, Jane Alexander, Justin Henry, Howard Duff, JoBeth Williams; ***D:*** Robert Benton; ***W:*** Robert Benton; ***C:*** Nestor Almendros. Oscars '79: Actor (Hoffman), Adapt. Screenplay, Director (Benton), Picture, Support. Actress (Streep); Directors Guild '79: Director (Benton); Golden Globes '80: Actor—Drama (Hoffman), Film—Drama, Screenplay, Support. Actress (Streep); L.A. Film Critics '79: Actor (Hoffman), Director (Benton), Film, Screenplay, Support. Actress (Streep); Natl. Bd. of Review '79: Support. Actress (Streep); N.Y. Film Critics '79: Actor (Hoffman), Film, Support. Actress (Streep); Natl. Soc. Film Critics '79: Actor (Hoffman), Director (Benton), Support. Actress (Streep); Writers Guild '79: Adapt. Screenplay.

The Krays 1990 **(R)** An account of British gangsters Reggie and Ronnie Kray, the brothers who ruled London's East End with brutality and violence, making them bizarre celebrities of the '60s. The leads are portrayed by Gary and Martin Kemp, founders of the British pop group Spandau Ballet. **119m/C VHS, 8mm, Wide.** *GB* Gary Kemp, Martin Kemp, Billie Whitelaw, Steven Berkoff, Susan Fleetwood, Charlotte Cornwell, Jimmy Jewel, Avis Bunnage, Kate Hardie, Alfred Lynch, Tom Bell, Victor Spinetti, Barbara Ferris, Julia Migenes-Johnson, John McEnery, Sadie Frost, Norman Rossington, Murray Melvin; ***D:*** Peter Medak; ***W:*** Philip Ridley; ***C:*** Alex Thomson; ***M:*** Michael Kamen.

Kriemhilde's Revenge *Die Nibelungen* 1924 The second film, following "Siegfried," of Lang's "Die Nibelungen," a lavish silent version of the Teutonic legends Wagner's "Ring of the Nibelungen" was based upon. In this episode, Kriemhilde avenges Siegfried's death by her marriage to the Kings of the Huns, thus fulfilling a prophecy of destruction. **95m/B VHS.** *GE* Paul Richter, Margareta Schoen, Theodore Loos, Hanna Ralph, Rudolf Klein-Rogge; ***D:*** Fritz Lang.

Krippendorf's Tribe 1998 **(PG-13)** James Krippendorf (Dreyfuss), a widowed anthropology professor, returns from an expedition to New Guinea after squandering all his grant money on his kids. Since he didn't find the rare tribe he was sent there for, he makes up tribal stories based on his own kids. When skeptic Tomlin demands proof of his amazing discoveries, the Krippendorf clan and an over-eager colleague (Elfman) go native in front of the camera. Works best when at its silliest, and in fact, could have been a fun family film. Unfortunately, most of the humor is of the smutty variety, involving mating rituals, tribal sex toys, circumcision jokes, and so on. **94m/C VHS.** Richard Dreyfuss, Jenna Elfman, Natasha Lyonne, Gregory Edward Smith, Stephen (Steve) Root, Elaine Stritch, Tom Poston, David Ogden Stiers, Lily Tomlin, Doris Belack, Julio Mechoso, Barbara Williams, Zakes Mokae, Carl Michael Linder, Siobhan Fallon; ***D:*** Todd Holland; ***W:*** Charlie Peters; ***C:*** Dean Cundey; ***M:*** Bruce Broughton.

Kristin Lavransdatter 1995 Slow and tedious romance, set in 14th-century Norway, and based on the novel "Kransen" by Sigrid Undset. Teenaged Kristin causes much grief for her family when she rejects an arranged marriage to a decent man her father has chosen for the more exciting but morally dubious nobleman Erland. Norwegian with subtitles. **144m/C VHS.** *NO* Elisabeth Matheson, Bjorn Skagestad, Henry Moan, Rut Tellefsen, Sverre Anker Ousdal; ***W:*** Liv Ullmann; ***C:*** Sven Nykvist; ***M:*** Henryk Nikolai Gorecki.

Kronos 1957 A giant robot from space drains the Earth of all its energy resources. A good example of this genre from the 50s. Includes previews of coming attractions from classic science fiction films. **78m/B VHS, DVD, Wide.** Jeff Morrow, Barbara Lawrence, John Emery; ***D:*** Kurt Neumann; ***W:*** Lawrence Louis Goldman; ***C:*** Karl Struss; ***M:*** Paul Sawtell, Bert Shefter.

Krull 1983 **(PG)** Likeable fantasy adventure set in a world peopled by creatures of myth and magic. A prince embarks on a quest to find the Glaive (a magical weapon) and then rescues his young bride, taken by the Beast of the Black Fortress. **121m/C VHS, DVD, Wide.** *GB* Ken Marshall, Lysette Anthony, Freddie Jones, Francesca Annis, Liam Neeson; ***D:*** Peter Yates; ***W:*** Stafford Sherman; ***C:*** Peter Suschitzky; ***M:*** James Horner.

Krush Groove 1985 **(R)** The world of rap music is highlighted in this movie, the first all-rap musical. ♫King of Rock; Don't You Dog Me; A Love Bizarre; Pick Up the Pace; If I Ruled the World; Holly Rock; It's Like That; Feel the Spin; I Can't Live Without My Radio. **95m/C VHS.** Blair Underwood, Eron Tabor, Kurtis Blow, Sheila E; ***D:*** Michael A. Schultz.

K2: The Ultimate High 1992 **(R)** Two men, one a skirt-chasing lawyer, the other a happily married physicist, tackle the world's second largest mountain—the K-2 in Kashmir, northern Pakistan. They encounter a number of dangers, including an ascent of sheer rock face, an avalanche, and a fall down perpendicular mountain ice, but even the exciting mountain-climbing scenes can't hold up this watered down movie. The film was actually shot on Canada's Mount Waddington. Based on the play by Patrick Meyers. **104m/C VHS.** Michael Biehn, Matt Craven, Raymond J. Barry, Luca Bercovici, Patricia Charbonneau, Julia Nickson-Soul, Hiroshi Fujioka, Jamal Shah; ***D:*** Franc Roddam; ***W:*** Patrick Meyers, Scott Roberts.

Kuffs 1992 **(PG-13)** Slater stars as George Kuffs, a young guy who reluctantly joins his brother's highly respected private security team in this original action comedy. After his brother is gunned down in the line of duty, George finds himself the new owner of the business. Out to avenge his brother, George pursues a crooked art dealer as he battles crime on the streets of San Francisco. Worthwhile premise is hampered by a predictable plot and mediocre acting. **102m/C VHS.** Mary Ellen Trainor, Christian Slater, Tony Goldwyn, Milla Jovovich, Bruce Boxleitner, Troy Evans, George de la Pena, Leon Rippy; ***D:*** Bruce A. Evans; ***W:*** Bruce A. Evans, Raynold Gideon; ***M:*** Harold Faltermeyer.

Kull the Conqueror 1997 **(PG-13)** Sorbo goes from TV's heroic Hercules to action-fantasy hero Kull, a slave who becomes the warrior king of a mythic land. Overthrown by a corrupt nobility, Kull begins a perilous journey to find the one weapon that will destroy the she-demon Akivasha (Carrere) and save the land of Valusia. Lots of action, although the PG-13 rating keeps some of the mayhem less bloody than might be expected for this genre. Based on the '30s character created by pulp writer Robert E. Howard, who also originated "Conan the Barbarian." **96m/C VHS, DVD, Wide.** Kevin Sorbo, Tia Carrere, Thomas Ian Griffith, Karina Lombard, Litefoot, Harvey Fierstein, Roy Brocksmith, Douglas Henshall, Sven-Ole Thorsen, Terry O'Neill; ***D:*** John Nicolella; ***W:*** Charles Edward Pogue; ***C:*** Rodney Charters; ***M:*** Joel Goldsmith.

Kundun 1997 **(PG-13)** Scorsese's cinematic portrait of the life of the young 14th Dalai Lama from 1937 through 1959, when he was forced to flee Chinese-occupied Tibet and live in exile in India. The incredibly detailed and sumptuous Tibetan journey begins with the discovery of the young boy as the Buddha reborn and uses different actors to portray him through young adulthood. Dramatic depiction of the Chairman Mao-ordered slaughter of Tibetan nuns and monks around the young Kundun illustrates theme of the dilemmas facing a nonviolent man in an increasingly violent world. The adult Dalai Lama's (Tsarong) meeting with cartoonishly evil incarnate Chairman Mao Zedong (Lin) mars an otherwise realistic and honest portrayal. Made with the cooperation of the 14th Dalai Lama, the story reflects the director's yen for accuracy and integrity. Scorsese's gamble on using a cast of non-professional Tibetan refugees pays off. Beautiful scenery and dreamy Philip Glass score set the proper mood. **134m/C VHS, DVD, Wide.** Tenzin Thuthob Tsarong, Robert Lin; ***D:*** Martin Scorsese; ***W:*** Melissa Mathison; ***C:*** Roger Deakins; ***M:*** Philip Glass. N.Y. Film Critics '97: Cinematog.; Natl. Soc. Film Critics '97: Cinematog.

Kung Fu 1972 A fugitive Buddhist quasi-Asian martial arts master accused of murder in his native land, roams across the Old West fighting injustice. Pilot for the successful TV series; was reincarnated 14 years later in the sequel, "Kung Fu: The Movie." **75m/C VHS.** Keith Carradine, David Carradine, Barry Sullivan, Keye Luke; ***D:*** Jerry Thorpe. **TV**

Kung Fu: The Movie 1986 Carradine reprises his role as Kwai Chang Caine from the TV show of the '70s. Now, he's hunted by evil warlord Mako, who's involved in the California opium trade. Mako sends assassin Lee (son of martial-arts star Bruce) after Caine. Luke appears in flashbacks as the young Grasshopper's blind mentor, Master Po. **93m/C VHS.** David Carradine, Mako, Brandon Lee, Keye Luke, Kerrie Keane, Martin Landau, William Lucking, Luke Askew, Benson Fong; ***D:*** Richard Lang. **TV**

Kuni Lemel in Tel Aviv 1977 The bungling folk-hero of the shtetl of 100 years ago is updated to the present. Grandpa Kuni is now 80 and living in Brooklyn. Anxious to see the family line continue, he offers $5 million to the first of his twin grandsons to marry a nice Jewish girl and settle in Israel. However, the grandsons have plans of their own which conflict with Grandpa's. In Hebrew with English subtitles. **90m/C VHS.** *IS* Mike Burstyn, Mandy Rice-Davies; ***D:*** Joel Silberg.

Kurt Vonnegut's Harrison Bergeron *Harrison Bergeron* 1995 **(R)** In the year 2053 the American government has gone to absurd lengths to ensure equality. Mediocrity is championed and everyone is forced to wear metallic headbands that stifle intellect through electronic impulses. Too bad for Harrison Bergeron (Astin), a smart young man being punished for his intelligence. But there's a secret undeground elite offering Harrison the chance to think freely, though this power comes with a price. Adapted from Vonnegut's 1961 short story. **99m/C VHS.** Sean Astin, Christopher Plummer, Miranda de Pencier, Nigel Bennett, Buck Henry, Eugene Levy, Howie Mandel, Andrea Martin; ***D:*** Bruce Pittman; ***W:*** Arthur Crimm. **CABLE**

Kurt Vonnegut's Monkey House 199? Dramatization of four short stories from Vonnegut's "Welcome to the Monkey House" collection, including a twist on the familiar Frankenstein tale. **100m/C VHS.** Frank Langella. **CABLE**

Kwaidan 1964 A haunting, stylized quartet of supernatural stories, each with a surprise ending. Adapted from the stories of Lafcadio Hearn, an American author who lived in Japan just before the turn of the century. The visual effects are splendid. In Japanese with English subtitles. **164m/C VHS, DVD, Wide.** *JP* Michiyo Aratama, Rentaro Mikuni, Katsuo Nakamura, Keiko Kishi, Tatsuya Nakadai, Takashi Shimura; ***D:*** Masaki Kobayashi; ***W:*** Yoko Mizuki; ***C:*** Yoshio Miyajima; ***M:*** Toru Takemitsu. Cannes '65: Grand Jury Prize.

The L-Shaped Room 1962 Young Frenchwoman Jane (Caron) is living in London and has an affair that leaves her pregnant. She winds up moving to a tacky boarding house, into the small room of the title. Soon, Jane has fallen for fellow tenant, out-of-work writer Toby (Bell), without disclosing her situation. However, when Toby's jealous best friend, jazz musician Johnny (Peters), learns of Jane's pregnancy, he uses his knowledge to break the twosome up. In the kitchen-sink tradition of British films that doesn't expect a happy ending. Based on the novel by Lynne Reid Banks. **89m/B VHS.** *GB* Leslie Caron, Tom Bell, Brock Peters, Mark Eden, Cicely Courtneidge, Emlyn Williams, Bernard Lee, Avis Bunnage; ***D:*** Bryan Forbes; ***W:*** Bryan Forbes; ***C:*** Douglas Slocombe; ***M:*** John Barry.

L.627 1992 Melancholy police procedural about dedicated veteran narcotics cop Lulu (Bezace) who works with a small and ill-equipped Parisian drug squad prone to taking the law into their own hands. Lulu constantly finds himself thwarted by obtuse bureaucrats while his life is disturbed by an informant—a young, drug-addicted prostitute who has disappeared and whom Lulu desires to protect. Film title refers to the French anti-drug statute. French with subtitles. **145m/C VHS.** *FR* Didier Bezace, Jean-Paul Comart, Cecile Garcia-Fogel, Lara Guirao, Charlotte Kady, Jean-Roger Milo, Philippe Torreton, Nils (Niels) Tavernier; ***D:*** Bertrand Tavernier; ***W:*** Bertrand Tavernier, Michel Alexandre; ***C:*** Alain Choquart; ***M:*** Philippe Sarde.

L.A. Bad 1985 (R) A Puerto Rican street thug learns he has cancer, and must come to terms with his own impending death. **101m/C VHS.** Esai Morales, Janice Rule, John Phillip Law, Charles "Chuck" Bail, Carrie Snodgress.

La Balance 1982 (R) An underworld stool pigeon is recruited by the Parisian police to blow the whistle on a murderous mob. Baye, as a prostitute in love with the pimp-stoolie, is a standout. Critically acclaimed; French with subtitles. **103m/C VHS.** *FR* Philippe LePlotard, Nathalie Baye, Bob Swaim; *D:* Reymond LePlont; *M:* Roland Bocquet. Cesar '83: Actor (Leotard), Actress (Baye), Film.

La Bamba 1987 (PG-13) A romantic biography of the late 1950s pop idol Ritchie Valens, concentrating on his stormy relationship with his half-brother Bob (Morales), his love for his WASP girlfriend Donna (Von Zerneck) for whom he wrote a hit song, and his tragic, sudden death in the famed plane crash that also took the lives of Buddy Holly and the Big Bopper. Soundtrack features Setzer, Huntsberry, Crenshaw, and Los Lobos as, respectively, Eddie Cochran, the Big Bopper, Buddy Holly, and a Mexican bordello band. **99m/C VHS, DVD.** Lou Diamond Phillips, Esai Morales, Danielle von Zerneck, Joe Pantoliano, Brian Setzer, Marshall Crenshaw, Howard Huntsberry, Rosana De Soto, Elizabeth Pena, Rick Dees; *D:* Luis Valdez; *W:* Luis Valdez; *C:* Adam Greenberg; *M:* Miles Goodman, Carlos Santana.

La Belle Noiseuse ½ *Divertimento; The Beautiful Troublemaker* 1990 The connections between art and life are explored in this beautiful (and long) drama. Creatively crippled, an aging painter has left unfinished a masterpiece work, entitled "La Belle Noiseuse," for ten years. When an admiring younger artist and his beautiful lover arrive for a visit, the painter is newly inspired by the young woman and makes her the model and muse for his masterwork. The film details every nuance of the work from the first to the last brushstroke and the battle of wills between artist and model over the symbiotic creative process. Based on a novella by Honore Balzac. French with subtitles. "Divertimento" is actually a recut and shortened version (126 minutes) of the original film. **240m/C VHS.** *FR* Michel Piccoli, Emmanuelle Beart, Jane Birkin, David Bursztein, Marianne (Cuau) Denicourt; *D:* Jacques Rivette; *W:* Jacques Rivette, Christine Laurent, Pascal Bonitzer; *C:* William Lubtchansky. Cannes '91: Grand Jury Prize; L.A. Film Critics '91: Foreign Film.

La Bete Humaine ½ *The Human Beast* 1938 A dark, psychological melodrama about human passion and duplicity, as an unhinged trainman plots with a married woman to kill her husband. Wonderful performances and stunning photography. Based on the Emile Zola novel. In French with English subtitles. 1954 Hollywood remake, "Human Desire," was directed by Fritz Lang. **90m/B VHS, 8mm.** *FR* Jean Gabin, Simone Simon, Julien Carette, Fernand Ledoux; *D:* Jean Renoir; *W:* Jean Renoir; *C:* Curt Courant; *M:* Joseph Cosma.

La Boca del Lobo *The Lion's Den* 1989 Peru's civil strife inspired this sluggish drama about government troops occupying a jungle village. Tormented by unseen communist guerillas, the stressed-out soldiers reach the breaking point. Spanish with subtitles. **111m/C VHS.** *AR* Gustavo Bueno, Tono Vega, Jose Tejada; *D:* Francisco J. Lombardi.

La Boum ½ 1981 A teenager's adjustment to the changes brought about by a move to Paris is compounded by her parents' marital problems. Followed by "La Boum 2." **90m/C VHS.** *FR* Sophie Marceau, Claude Brasseur, Brigitte Fossey, Denise Grey, Bernard Giraudeau; *D:* Claude Pinoteau; *M:* Vladimir Cosma.

L.A. Bounty ½ 1989 (R) A beautiful cop and a bounty hunter go after the same murderer. Hauser steals the show as a psychopath who has completely blown a gasket. **85m/C VHS.** Sybil Danning, Wings Hauser, Henry Darrow, Lenore Kasdorf, Robert Hanley; *D:* Worth Keeter.

La Buche 2000 The title refers to a special Christmas cake, fashioned in the shape of a yule log. The holiday season is proving to be particularly tiresome for three sisters: nightclub singer Louba (Azema) who's pregnant with her married lover's child; homemaker Sonia (Beart) whose husband is leaving her for a younger woman; and career-driven Milla (Gainsbourg) who becomes intrigued by melancholy Joseph (Thompson, the director's son). Family crises start with the funeral of the sisters' stepfather, leading to a reunion between their parents who haven't spoken in 25 years, and get more complicated from there. French with subtitles. **106m/C VHS, DVD.** *FR* Sabine Azema, Emmanuelle Beart, Charlotte Gainsbourg, Francoise Fabian, Claude Rich, Christopher Thompson, Jean-Pierre Darroussin; *D:* Daniele Thompson; *W:* Christopher Thompson, Daniele Thompson; *C:* Robert Fraisse; *M:* Michel Legrand.

La Cage aux Folles ½ *Birds of a Feather* 1978 (R) Adaption of the popular French play. Gay Saint-Tropez nightclub owner Renato (Tognazzi) and his drag queen lover Albin (Serrault) try to play it straight when Renato's son (Laurent) from a long-ago liaison brings his fiancee and her conservative parents home for dinner. Charming music and lots of fun. So successful, it was followed by two sequels in 1980 and 1985, a Broadway musical, and a 1995 American remake, "The Birdcage." French with subtitles. **91m/C VHS, DVD, Wide.** *FR* Ugo Tognazzi, Michel Serrault, Michel Galabru, Claire Maurier, Remy Laurent, Benny Luke, Carmen Scarpitta, Luisa Maneri; *D:* Edouard Molinaro; *W:* Edouard Molinaro, Francis Veber, Jean Poiret, Marcello Danon; *C:* Armando Nannuzzi; *M:* Ennio Morricone. Cesar '79: Actor (Serrault); Golden Globes '80: Foreign Film.

La Cage aux Folles 2 ½ 1981 (R) Albin sets out to prove to his companion that he still has sex appeal, and gets mixed up in some espionage antics. This sequel to the highly successful "La Cage aux Folles" loses some steam, but is still worth seeing. Followed by "La Cage Aux Folles 3: The Wedding." **101m/C VHS, DVD, Wide.** *FR* Ugo Tognazzi, Michel Serrault, Marcel Bozzuffi, Michel Galabru, Benny Luke; *D:* Edouard Molinaro; *W:* Francis Veber; *C:* Armando Nannuzzi; *M:* Ennio Morricone.

La Cage aux Folles 3: The Wedding ½ 1986 (PG-13) The flamboyant drag queen Albin must feign normalcy by marrying and fathering a child in order to collect a weighty inheritance. Final segment of the trilogy; inferior to the previous films. In French with English subtitles. **88m/C VHS.** *FR* Michel Serrault, Ugo Tognazzi, Michel Galabru, Benny Luke, Stephane Audran; *D:* Georges Lautner; *M:* Ennio Morricone.

La Ceremonie *A Judgment in Stone* 1995 Sullen maid Sophie (Bonnaire) is hired by the rich Lelievre family to work at their country estate. She's befriended by independent postmistress Jeanne (Huppert), who's disliked by Sophie's employers, and who encourages Sophie into small defiant actions. Something's off about the entire situation and there's violence beneath the seemingly calm surface. Based on Ruth Rendell's chiller "Judgment in Stone." French with subtitles. **109m/C VHS.** *FR GE* Sandrine Bonnaire, Isabelle Huppert, Jacqueline Bisset, Jean-Pierre Cassel, Virginie Ledoyen, Valentine Merlet, Julien Rochefort, Dominique Frot, Jean-Francois Perrier; *D:* Claude Chabrol; *W:* Claude Chabrol, Caroline Eliacheff; *C:* Bernard Zitzermann; *M:* Matthieu Chabrol. Cesar '96: Actress (Huppert); L.A. Film Critics '96: Foreign Film; Natl. Soc. Film Critics '96: Foreign Film.

La Chartreuse de Parme ½ *Charterhouse at Parma* 1948 Nineteenth century period piece featuring an Archbishop willing to break his vows for the woman he loves, and the aunt who will make sure that if she can't have him only God will. French adaptation of the novel by Stendahl. Available dubbed. **?m/C VHS.** *FR* Gerard Philipe, Maria Casares, Rene Faure.

La Chevre ½ *The Goat* 1981 A screwball French comedy about two policemen (Richard and Depardieu—picture Nick Nolte and Gene Wilder with accents) stumbling along the path of a missing heiress who suffers from chronic bad luck. Contains a hilarious scene with chairs used to test the luck of the investigative team; based on one partner's ability to sit on the only broken chair in a rather large collection, he is judged to be sufficiently jinxed to allow them to recreate the same outrageous misfortunes that befell the heiress in her plight. In French with English subtitles. **91m/C VHS.** *FR* Gerard Depardieu, Pierre Richard, Corynne Charbit, Michel Robin, Pedro Armendariz Jr.; *D:* Francis Veber; *M:* Vladimir Cosma.

La Chienne *Isn't Life A Bitch?; The Bitch* 1931 Dark, troubling tale of a bedraggled husband whose only excitement is his painting hobby until he becomes consumed by the ever-tempting prostitute Lulu. Director Renoir broke ground with his use of direct sound and Paris shooting locations, and the experiment was a hit. Portrays marriage with acidity; Renoir's own marriage broke up as a result of this film's casting. Mareze died shortly after the filming was complete in a car crash. Based on the novel by Georges de la Fouchardiere. Produced in 1931, but didn't reach American theatres until 1975. In French with English subtitles. Remade in 1945 as "Scarlet Street." **93m/B VHS.** *FR* Michel Simon, Janie Mareze, Georges Flament, Madeleine Berubet; *D:* Jean Renoir; *W:* Andre Girard, Jean Renoir.

La Chute de la Maison Usher ½ *The Fall of the House of Usher* 1928 An expressionistic, abstracted adaptation of the Poe story "The Fall of the House of Usher" about an evil mansion and its ruined denizens. Epstein used slow motion, superimpressions, and weird camera angles to obtain the proper atmosphere. **48m/B VHS, DVD.** *FR* Marguerite Gance, Jean Debucourt, Charles Lamy; *D:* Jean Epstein; *W:* Jean Epstein; *C:* Georges Lucas, Jean Lucas. Natl. Film Reg. '00.

La Cicada ½ *The Cricket* 1983 The sparks fly when a woman and her 17-year-old daughter become rivals for the affections of the same man. **90m/C VHS.** *IT* Clio Goldsmith, Virna Lisi, Anthony (Tony) Franciosa, Renato Salvatori; *D:* Alberto Lattuada.

La Collectionneuse *The Gentleman Tramp* 1967 The third of Rohmer's "Moral Tales" finds an artist (Bachau) and an antiques dealer (Pommereulle) vacationing in St. Tropez and sharing a villa with a young woman (Politoff) who picks a different man to sleep with each night. Both try to resist the sexual temptations of being added to her collection of lovers. French with subtitles. **88m/C VHS, DVD.** *FR* Patrick Bauchau, Daniel Pommereulle, Haydee Politoff, Alain Jouffroy; *D:* Eric Rohmer; *W:* Eric Rohmer; *C:* Nestor Almendros.

L.A. Confidential 1997 (R) Hard-boiled, complicated crime drama based on James Ellroy's even more complex novel. Fifties Hollywood is ripe with corruption in many forms—politics, police, business, gangsters, racial tensions, and journalistic sleaze in the persona of Sid Hudgens (DeVito), editor of tabloid rag Hush-Hush. Sid's police contact is celebrity Sgt. Jack Vincennes (Spacey), who serves as an advisor to a TV cop show (think "Dragnet"). There's a bloodbath murder case that involves brutal-yet-tender cop Bud White (Crowe); the ruthlessly ambitious, college-educated neophyte Ed Exley (Pearce); and their veteran boss, Capt. Dudley Smith (Cromwell). There's also wealthy pimp/businessman Pierce Patchett (Strathairn) and his movie-star look-alike hookers, including world-weary Lynn (Basinger), who gets involved with Bud, who... Well, lets just say that Hanson does a masterful job tying up all the loose ends and still leaving you wanting more. **136m/C VHS, DVD, Wide.** Kevin Spacey, Russell Crowe, Guy Pearce, Danny DeVito, Kim Basinger, James Cromwell, David Strathairn, Ron Rifkin, Graham Beckel, Matt McCoy, Simon Baker, Paul Guilfoyle, Amber Smith, John Mahon, Paolo Seganti, Gwenda Deacon; *D:* Curtis Hanson; *W:* Curtis Hanson, Brian Helgeland; *C:* Dante Spinotti; *M:* Jerry Goldsmith. Oscars '97: Adapt. Screenplay, Support. Actress (Basinger); Australian Film Inst. '98: Foreign Film; British Acad. '97: Film Editing, Sound; Golden Globes '98: Support. Actress (Basinger); L.A. Film Critics '97: Cinematog., Director (Hanson), Film, Screenplay; Natl. Bd. of Review '97: Director (Hanson), Film; N.Y. Film Critics '97: Director (Hanson), Film, Screenplay; Natl. Soc. Film Critics '97: Director (Hanson), Film, Screenplay; Screen Actors Guild '97: Support. Actress (Basinger); Writers Guild '97: Adapt. Screenplay; Broadcast Film Critics '97: Adapt. Screenplay, Film.

L.A. Crackdown 1987 A ruthless yet compassionate policewoman goes after crack dealers and pimps who are exploiting women. Pretty trashy fare; followed by "L.A. Crackdown 2." Made for video. **90m/C VHS.** Pamela Dixon, Tricia Parks, Kita Harrison, Jeffrey Olson, Michael Coon; *D:* Joseph Merhi. VIDEO

L.A. Crackdown 2 1988 A woman cop goes undercover as a dancer in a dance hall to try to catch a psychotic killer who stalks hookers in this silly sequel to "L.A. Crackdown." **90m/C VHS.** Pamela Dixon, Anthony Gates, Joe Vance, Cynthia Miguel, Lisa Anderson, Bo Sabato; *D:* Joseph Merhi.

La Cucaracha 1999 (R) Ex-office worker Walter (Roberts) has hightailed it to Mexico to become a writer—or so he says. Instead, he's a drunk practically immobilized by night terrors. Then the local big shot (de Almeida) suddenly offers Walter money to kill someone. Things don't go as expected. **95m/C VHS, DVD.** Eric Roberts, Joaquim de Almeida, Tara Crespo, James McManus; *D:* Jack Perez; *W:* James McManus; *C:* Shawn Maurer; *M:* Martin Davich.

La Deroute 1998 Joe Aiello has made a successful life for himself and his family since emigrating from Sicily to Canada 30 years before. Since his son Nuccio is mentally handicapped, Joe rests his hopes on his 23-year-old daughter Bennie, who only wants freedom from her possessive father. And she takes it by impulsively marrying Diego, a South American refugee about to be deported. Feeling rejected and betrayed, Joe finds himself falling into despair. French with subtitles. **111m/C VHS.** *CA* Tony Nardi, Michelle-Barbara Pelletier, Hugolin Chevrette, John Dunn-Hill, Richard Lemire; *D:* Paul Tana; *W:* Tony Nardi, Paul Tana, Bruno Ramirez; *C:* Michel Caron; *M:* Pierre Desrochers.

La Discrete *The Discreet* 1990 Antoine (Luchini) is a cocky writer who is not the lothario he imagines himself to be—in fact his girlfriend has just dumped him. He and his publisher plan a sexist revenge with Antoine advertising for a young female typist whom he will seduce and abandon—all the while keeping a diary of the experience which will be published. The self-possessed Catherine (Henry) answers the ad and even though Antoine protests that she is not his type he finds himself falling in love. Then Catherine discovers Antoine's original scheme. Vincent's directorial debut. In French with English subtitles. **95m/C VHS.** *FR* Fabrice Luchini, Judith Henry, Maurice Garrel, Marie Bunel, Francois Toumarkine; *D:* Christian Vincent; *W:* Jean-Pierre Ronssin, Christian Vincent; *M:* Jay Gottlieb. Cesar '91: Writing.

La Dolce Vita 1960 In this influential and popular work a successful, sensationalistic Italian journalist covers the show-biz life in Rome, and alternately covets and disdains its glitzy shallowness. The film follows his dealings with the "sweet life" over a pivotal week. A surreal, comic tableaux with award-winning costuming; one of Fellini's most acclaimed films. In this film Fellini called his hungry celebrity photographers the Paparazzo—and it is as the paparazzi they have been ever since. In Italian with English subtitles. **174m/B VHS, Wide.** *IT* Marcello Mastroianni, Anita Ekberg, Anouk Aimee, Alain Cuny, Lex Barker, Yvonne Furneaux, Barbara Steele, Nadia Gray, Magali Noel, Walter Santesso, Jacques Sernas, Annibale Ninchi; *D:* Federico Fellini; *W:* Tullio Pinelli, Ennio Flaiano, Brunello Rondi, Federico Fellini; *M:* Nino Rota. Oscars '61: Costume Des. (B&W); Cannes '60: Film; N.Y. Film Critics '61: Foreign Film.

La Femme Nikita 🦴🦴🦴 **1991 (R)** Stylish French noir version of Pygmalion. Having killed a cop during a drugstore theft gone awry, young French sociopath Nikita (Parillaud) is reprieved from a death sentence in order to enroll in a government finishing school, of sorts. Trained in etiquette (by Moreau) and assasination (by Karyo), she's released after three years, and starts a new life with a new beau (Anglade), all the while carrying out agency-mandated assassinations. Parillaud is excellent as the once-amoral street urchin transformed into a woman of depth and sensitivity—a bitterly ironic moral evolution for a contract killer. Remade as "Point of No Return." **117m/C VHS, DVD, Wide.** *FR* Anne Parillaud, Jean-Hugues Anglade, Tcheky Karyo, Jeanne Moreau, Jean Reno, Jean Bouise; ***D:*** Luc Besson; ***W:*** Luc Besson; ***C:*** Thierry Arbogast; ***M:*** Eric Serra. Cesar '91: Actress (Parillaud).

L.A. Gangs Rising 🦴🦴 **1989** The streets of Los Angeles run red with blood as a gang war explodes into bloody fury. **87m/C VHS.** David Kyle, Steve Bond, John Ashton; ***D:*** John Bushelman.

L.A. Goddess 🦴½ **1992 (R)** A hard-living, and drinking, movie star and her beautiful stunt double both fall for a studio head. Both of these women know what they want and the man in the middle hasn't got a clue. Also available in an unrated version. **92m/C VHS.** Kathy Shower, Jeff Conaway, David Heavener, Wendy McDonald, Joe Estevez, James Hong; ***D:*** Jag Mundhra; ***W:*** Jerry Davis.

La Grande Bouffe 🦴🦴🦴 *The Blow-Out* **1973** Four middle-aged men, bored with life, meet at a secluded mansion for one last excessive fling and to literally eat themselves to death. Four very fine actors in a vulgar feast. French with subtitles. **125m/C VHS, DVD.** *FR* Marcello Mastroianni, Philippe Noiret, Michel Piccoli, Ugo Tognazzi, Andrea Ferreol; ***D:*** Marco Ferreri; ***W:*** Marco Ferreri, Rafael Azcona; ***C:*** Mario Vulpiani; ***M:*** Philippe Sarde.

La Grande Bourgeoise 🦴🦴½ *The Murri Affair* **1974** Historical romance about the clash of aristocratic society and the new bourgeoisie in 1897 Italy. Great cast tries to save the true tale of murder and political intrigue from film's slow pacing, but in the end it's the movie's visual polish that shines forth. In Italian with subtitles. **115m/C VHS.** *IT* Catherine Deneuve, Giancarlo Giannini, Fernando Rey, Tina Aumont; ***D:*** Mauro Bolognini; ***M:*** Ennio Morricone.

La Grande Vadrouille 🦴🦴🦴 *Don't Look Now, We've Been Shot At* **1966** In 1943 German-occupied France, three Allied parachutists drop in on a Paris Opera conductor and a house painter. If the pair wish to find some peace, they must help the trio get to the free zone. France's number one boxoffice hit for almost 30 years. Also available dubbed. **122m/C VHS.** *FR* Louis de Funes, Bourvil, Terry-Thomas; ***D:*** Gerard Oury.

La Guerre Est Finie 🦴🦴🦴½ *The War Is Over; Kriget ar Slut* **1966** Alain Resnais's understated suspense film makes a belated debut on home video. It's the story of Diego (Montand), a revolutionary who comes to wonder if he can still fight the good fight against the fascists who control Spain. Montand, one of the most deceptively effortless actors ever to appear on screen, is a commanding presence in this low-keyed exercise. **121m/C DVD, Wide.** *FR SW* Yves Montand, Michel Piccoli, Ingrid Thulin, Genevieve Bujold, Jean Daste, Dominique Rozan, Jean-Francois Remi; ***D:*** Alain Resnais; ***W:*** Jorge Semprun; ***C:*** Sacha Vierny; ***M:*** Giovanni Fusco; ***Nar:*** Jorge Semprun.

L.A. Heat 🦴½ **1988** When a vice cop's partner is killed, he seeks revenge on the murderers, only to find that his own department may have been involved. Followed by "L.A. Vice." **90m/C VHS.** Jim Brown, Lawrence-Hilton Jacobs; ***D:*** Joseph Merhi.

L.A. Law 🦴🦴🦴 **1986** The pilot episode of the acclaimed dramatic series, in which the staff of a Los Angeles law firm tries a variety of cases. **97m/C VHS.** Michael Tucker, Jill Eikenberry, Harry Hamlin, Richard Dysart, Jimmy Smits, Alan Rachins, Susan Ruttan, Susan Dey, Corbin Bernsen; ***D:*** Gregory Hoblit. **TV**

La Lectrice 🦴🦴½ *The Reader* **1988 (R)** Artesian landscapes, Beethoven sonatas, and a Raymond Jean novel titled "La Lectrice" provide the backdrop for Constance (Miou-Miou) to read aloud to her boyfriend in bed, and from there she imagines herself the novel's heroine, who hires out her services as a reader to various odd characters. She reads from "L'Amant," "Alice," "War and Peace," and "Les Fleurs du Mal." Richly textured and not overly intellectual. In French with English subtitles. **98m/C VHS.** *FR* Miou-Miou, Christian Ruche, Sylvie Laporte, Michael Raskine, Brigitte Catillon, Regis Royer, Maria Casares, Pierre Dux, Patrick Chesnais; ***D:*** Michel DeVille; ***W:*** Rosalinde DeVille, Michel DeVille. Cesar '89: Support. Actor (Chesnais); Montreal World Film Fest. '88: Film.

La Marseillaise 🦴🦴🦴½ **1937** Sweeping epic by Renoir made before he hit his stride with "Grand Illusion." It details the events of the French Revolution in the summer of 1789 using a cast of thousands. The opulent lifestyle of the French nobility is starkly contrasted with the peasant lifestyle of poverty and despair. The focus is on two new recruits who have joined the Marseilles division of the revolutionary army as they begin their long march to Paris, the heart of France. As they travel, they adopt a stirring and passionate song that embodies the spirit and ideals of the revolution known as "La Marseillaise," now France's national anthem. In French with English subtitles. **130m/B VHS.** *FR* Pierre Renoir, Lisa (Lise) Delamare, Louis Jouvet, Aime Clariond, Andrex Andrisson, Paul Dullac; ***D:*** Jean Renoir; ***W:*** Jean Renoir; ***C:*** Jean (Yves, Georges) Bourgoin.

La Merveilleuse Visite 🦴🦴½ *The Marvelous Visit* **1974** Bittersweet fantasy about an angel that falls from the sky and is found unconcious by a priest. He's nursed back to health but causes problems for his host when he wanders into the nearby village and his curiosity is misunderstood. Adapted from a short story by H.G. Wells. In French with English subtitles. **102m/C VHS.** *FR* Gilles Kohler, Deborah Berger, Jean-Pierre Castaldi; ***D:*** Marcel Carne; ***W:*** Marcel Carne.

La Nuit de Varennes 🦴🦴🦴 **1982 (R)** This semi-historical romp is based on an actual chapter in French history when King Louis XVI and Marie Antoinette fled from revolutionary Paris to Varennes in 1791. On the way they meet an unlikely group of characters, including Cassanova and Thomas Paine. At times witty and charming, the melange of history and fiction is full of talk, sometimes profane, punctuated by sex and nudity. Director Scola's imagination stretches to light up this night. In French with English subtitles. **133m/C VHS.** *FR IT* Marcello Mastroianni, Harvey Keitel, Jean-Louis Barrault, Hanna Schygulla, Jean-Claude Brialy, Michel Piccoli, Jean-Louis Trintignant; ***D:*** Ettore Scola; ***W:*** Ettore Scola.

La Passante 🦴🦴🦴 *La Passante du Sans Souci; The Passerby* **1983** An otherwise peace-loving man murders the Paraguayan ambassador to France. In somewhat clumsy flashback style the murderer's orphaned childhood and other memories provide motives for the murder. Though posed more slowly than typical intrigue plots, the movie blends love and the legacy of Nazism, passion and politics in an engaging way, spiced with nudity and some violence. In her last screen appearance Schneider movingly portrays dual roles. In French with English subtitles. **106m/C VHS.** *FR GE* Romy Schneider, Michel Piccoli, Helmut Griem, Gerard Klein, Matthieu Carriere, Maria Schell; ***D:*** Jacques Rouffio; ***M:*** Georges Delerue. Cesar '83: Sound.

La Petite Sirene 🦴🦴 *The Little Mermaid* **1980** Isabelle is a 14-year-old schoolgirl, obsessed with the story of the Little Mermaid, who tries to ingratiate herself to Georges, a 40-year-old garage mechanic. Seeing him as her prince charming, she persists in trying to make him a part of her life, in spite of his resistance. In French with English subtitles. **104m/C VHS.** *FR* Laura Alexis, Philippe Leotard, Evelyne Dress, Marie DuBois; ***D:*** Roger Andrieux; ***W:*** Roger Andrieux.

La Promesse 🦴🦴 *The Promise* **1996** Fifteen-year-old Igor (Renier) helps his disreputable father Roger (Gourmet) run an illegal immigrant operation in the Beligan town of Liege. African immigrant Amidou (Ouedraogo) has just been joined by his wife Assita (Ouedraogo) and their baby. When Amidou dies in an accident, Roger forces Igor to help him bury the body secretly and tells the bewildered wife that her husband has left her. But Igor is caught in the middle—he'd promised the dying Amidou to look after Assita and he still has enough conscience to want to help—but it also puts Igor into a dangerous conflict with his father. French with subtitles. **93m/C VHS, DVD, Wide.** *FR BE* Jeremie Renier, Olivier Gourmet, Assita Ouedraogo, Rasmane Ouedraogo; ***D:*** Jean-Pierre Dardenne, Luc Dardenne; ***W:*** Jean-Pierre Dardenne, Luc Dardenne; ***C:*** Alain Marcoen; ***M:*** Jean-Marie Billy. L.A. Film Critics '97: Foreign Film; Natl. Soc. Film Critics '97: Foreign Film.

La Puritaine 🦴🦴½ **1986** Before his planned reconciliation with his daughter, the artistic manager of a theatre has young actresses portray different sides of the daughter's personality. In French with English subtitles. **90m/C VHS.** Michel Piccoli, Sandrine Bonnaire; ***D:*** Lou Doillon.

La Ronde 🦴🦴🦴½ **1951** A classic comedy of manners and sharply witty tour-de-farce in which a group of people in 1900 Vienna keep changing romantic partners until things wind up where they started. Ophuls' swirling direction creates a fast-paced farce of desire and regret with wicked yet subtle style. Based on Arthur Schnitzler's play and remade as "Circle of Love." In French with English subtitles. **97m/B VHS.** *FR* Simone Signoret, Anton Walbrook, Simone Simon, Serge Reggiani, Daniel Gelin, Danielle Darrieux, Jean-Louis Barrault, Fernand Gravet, Odette Joyeux, Isa Miranda, Gerard Philipe; ***D:*** Max Ophuls. British Acad. '51: Film.

La Rupture 🦴🦴½ *The Breakup* **1970** Thriller about a wife trying to protect her child from her husband's unsavory family. Audran and her son are attacked by her husband (Drouot), who's high on drugs. She fights back and he winds up in the hospital. Her father-in-law (Bouquet), who wants his grandson to live with him, then hires a seedy investigator (Cassel) to spy on Audran. Based on the Charlotte Armstrong novel. In French with English subtitles. **124m/C VHS.** *FR* Stephane Audran, Jean-Claude Drouot, Michel Bouquet, Jean-Pierre Cassel, Catherine Rouvel, Jean Carmet, Annie Cordy; ***D:*** Claude Chabrol; ***W:*** Claude Chabrol; ***M:*** Pierre Jansen.

La Salamandre 🦴🦴 *The Salamander* **1971** Non-conformist Rosemonde, suspected of shooting her guardian, is being interviewed by a novelist and a journalist trying to write a television script about the incident. The more they supposedly learn, the more they are both intimately drawn towards her. French with subtitles. **119m/B VHS.** *SI* Bulle Ogier, Jean-Luc Bideau, Jacques Denis; ***D:*** Alain Tanner; ***W:*** Alain Tanner, John Berger; ***M:*** Patrick Moraz.

La Scorta 🦴🦴🦴½ *The Bodyguards; The Escorts* **1994** Slick, fact-based political thriller focuses on four carabinieri (state police officers) who struggle to maintain some semblance of their normal lives after they are assigned to protect a judge investigating government corruption and a related murder in a Sicilian town. A crackling alternative to Americanized mobster melodrama, marked by taut direction, meaty characters, and coolly understated performances that seamlessly portray brotherhood, heroism, suspicion, and betrayal amid the battle for power between the Italian state and the Mafia. In Italian with English subtitles. **92m/C VHS.** *IT* Claudio Amendola, Enrico Lo Verso, Tony Sperandeo, Ricky Memphis, Carlo Cecchi, Leo Gullotta; ***D:*** Ricky Tognazzi; ***W:*** Graziano Diana, Simona Izzo; ***M:*** Ennio Morricone.

La Sentinelle 🦴🦴 *The Sentinel* **1992** Morose Mathias (Salinger)is traveling by train from Germany to France to attend medical school. The sinister Bleicher (Richard), who seems to be a customs official, grills Mathias but lets him go. In his hotel, Mathias finds a strange package in his luggage and discovers it contains the shrunken head of a man. He keeps his discovery a secret but tests samples of the head in the school laboratory on a quest to figure out who the man was. May sound like a thriller but it's too talky and paced too slowly to hold complete interest. French with subtitles. **139m/C VHS, DVD.** *FR* Emmanuel Salinger, Jean-Louis Richard, Thibault de Montalembert, Valerie Dreville, Marianne (Cuau) Denicourt, Bruno Todeschini, Jean-Luc Boutte; ***D:*** Arnaud Desplechin; ***W:*** Arnaud Desplechin; ***C:*** Caroline Champetier; ***M:*** Marc Oliver Sommer.

La Separation 🦴🦴🦴 **1998** Pierre (Auteuil) and Anne (Huppert) share a long-term relationship and a 15-month-old son. What they no longer seem to have is any passion for each other as they go through their daily routine. Anne decides to have an affair—but doesn't see any reason it should break up her household. However, the increasingly miserable Pierre doesn't share her belief. Based on the 1991 novel "Separation" by Franck. French with subtitles. **85m/C VHS, DVD, Wide.** *FR* Daniel Auteuil, Isabelle Huppert, Karin Viard, Jerome Deschamps; ***D:*** Christian Vincent; ***W:*** Christian Vincent, Dan Franck; ***C:*** Denis Lenoir.

La Signora di Tutti 🦴🦴🦴 **1934** An early Italian biography of Gaby Doriot, a movie star whose professional success is paired by personal misery. Prestigious director Ophuls, working in exile from his native Germany, was unable to complete many projects in the years leading up to and during WWII. This is one of the few. Watch for innovative camera work intended to underscore the film's mood. In Italian with English subtitles. **92m/B VHS.** *IT* Isa Miranda; ***D:*** Max Ophuls.

La Silence de la Mer 🦴🦴🦴 *The Silence of the Sea* **1947** An old French farmer (Robian) and his niece (Stephane) are forced to billet a German officer (Vernon) in their home during the Occupation. They've vowed never to speak to him but the German continues to pour out his thoughts on music, war, and his love of France into their silence. Melville's first feature; French with subtitles. **86m/B VHS.** *FR* Howard Vernon, Jean-Marie Robian, Nicole Stephane; ***D:*** Jean-Pierre Melville; ***W:*** Jean-Pierre Melville; ***C:*** Henri Decae; ***M:*** Edgar Bischoff.

L.A. Story 🦴🦴🦴 **1991 (PG-13)** Livin' ain't easy in the city of angels. Harris K. Telemacher (Martin), a weatherman in a city where the weather never changes, wrestles with the meaning of life and love while consorting with beautiful people, distancing from significant other Henner, cavorting with valley girl Parker, and falling for newswoman Tennant (Martin's real life wife). Written by the comedian, the story's full of keen insights into the everyday problems and ironies of living in the Big Tangerine. (It's no wonder the script's full of so much thoughtful detail: Martin is said to have worked on it intermittently for seven years.) Charming, fault forgiving but not fault ignoring portrait. **98m/C VHS, DVD, Wide.** Steve Martin, Victoria Tennant, Richard E. Grant, Marilu Henner, Sarah Jessica Parker, Sam McMurray, Patrick Stewart, Iman, Kevin Pollak; ***D:*** Mick Jackson; ***W:*** Steve Martin; ***C:*** Andrew Dunn; ***M:*** Peter Melnick.

La Strada 🦴🦴🦴🦴 *The Road* **1954** Simple-minded girl, played by Fellini's wife, Masina, is sold to a brutal, coarse circus strong-man and she falls in love with him despite his abuse. They tour the countryside and eventually meet up with a gentle acrobat, played by Basehart, who alters their fate. Fellini masterwork was the director's first internationally acclaimed film, and is, by turns, somber and amusing as it demonstrates the filmmaker's sensitivity to the underprivileged of the world and his belief in spiritual redemption. Subtitled in English. **107m/B VHS.** *IT* Giulietta Masina, Anthony Quinn, Richard

Basehart, Aldo Silvani; *D:* Federico Fellini; *W:* Ennio Flaiano, Brunello Rondi, Tullio Pinelli, Federico Fellini; *M:* Nino Rota. Oscars '56: Foreign Film; N.Y. Film Critics '56: Foreign Film.

La Symphonie Pastorale 🦴🦴🦴½ **1946** A Swiss pastor takes in an orphan blind girl who grows up to be beautiful. The pastor then competes for her affections with his son. Quiet drama based on the Andre Gide novel, with breathtaking mountain scenery as the backdrop for this tragedy rife with symbolism. **105m/B VHS.** *FR* Pierre Blanchar, Michele Morgan, Jean Desailly, Line Noro, Andree Clement; *D:* Jean Delannoy. Cannes '46: Actress (Morgan).

La Terra Trema 🦴🦴🦴½ *Episoda Del Mare; The Earth Will Tremble* **1948** The classic example of Italian neo-realism, about a poor Sicilian fisherman, his family and their village. A spare, slow-moving, profound and ultimately lyrical tragedy, this semi-documentary explores the economic exploitation of Sicily's fishermen. Filmed on location with the villagers playing themselves; highly acclaimed though not commercially successful. In Sicilian with English subtitles. Some radically cut versions may be available, but are to be avoided. Franco Zefferelli was one of the assistant directors. **161m/B VHS.** *IT* Antonio Pietrangeli; *D:* Luchino Visconti.

La Truite 🦴🦴🦴 *The Trout* **1983 (R)** A young woman leaves her family's rural trout farm and a loveless marriage to seek her fortune in high finance and corporate mayhem. The complicated plot, full of intrigue and sexual encounters, sometimes lacks focus. Slickly filmed. **80m/C VHS.** *FR* Isabelle Huppert, Jean-Pierre Cassel, Daniel Olbrychski, Jeanne Moreau, Jacques Spiesser, Ruggero Raimondi, Alexis Smith, Craig Stevens; *D:* Joseph Losey. Cesar '83: Cinematog.

La Vengeance d'une Femme 🦴🦴 *A Woman's Revenge* **1989** Refined Cecile and sultry Suzy are two sides of a love triangle whose third member, Cecile's husband, has just died. Cecile decides to get to know his mistress better, which naturally has Suzy worried. Is Cecile out for revenge or does she sincerely want to befriend the "other woman." Based on Dostoyevski's "The Eternal Husband." In French with English subtitles. **133m/C VHS.** *FR* Isabelle Huppert, Beatrice Dalle; *D:* Jacques Doillon; *W:* Jean-Francois Goyet, Jacques Doillon.

L.A. Vice 🦴½ **1989** A detective is transferred to the vice squad, where he must investigate a series of murders. Sequel to "L.A. Heat." **90m/C VHS.** Jim Brown, Lawrence-Hilton Jacobs, William Smith; *D:* Joseph Merhi.

La Vie Continue 🦴🦴½ **1982** A middle-aged woman suddenly finds herself widowed after 20 years of marriage and tries to build a new life for herself and her children. Girardot's performance can't quite dispel melodramatic suds. Loosely and more effectively remade as "Men Don't Leave." In French with English subtitles or dubbed. **93m/C VHS.** *IT* Annie Girardot, Jean-Pierre Cassel, Michel Aumont, Pierre Dux, Guilia Salvatori, Emmanuel Goyet, Rivera Andres; *D:* Moshe Mizrahi; *W:* Moshe Mizrahi; *M:* Georges Delerue.

La Vie de Boheme 🦴🦴🦴 *Bohemian Life* **1993** Comedy takes a mocking look at art and romantic love. A trio of hapless but dedicated comrades, Rodolfo (Pellonpaa) the painter, Marcel (Wilms) the poet, and Schaunard (Vaananen), must scrounge around the mealy edges of modern Paris because their art isn't filling their stomachs. Meanwhile, they experience the pangs of love like everyone else, although each is devoutly committed to his art as well. Starkly different from the lush, operatic version by Puccini, but based on the same source, a 19th century novel by Henri Mullet. French with subtitles. **100m/C VHS.** Matti Pellonpaa, Andre Wilms, Kari Vaananen, Jean-Pierre Leaud, Samuel Fuller, Louis Malle, Evelyne Didi, Christine Murillo, Laika, Carlos Salgado, Alexis Nitzer, Sylvie van den Elsen, Gilles Charmant, Dominique Marcas; *D:* Aki Kaurismaki; *W:* Aki Kaurismaki.

La Vie Est Belle 🦴🦴 *Life Is Rosy* **1987** The rags to riches story of a poor rural musician from Zaire who goes to the city to break into radio and TV. He uses his wit and talent to foil a greedy boss, win a beautiful wife, and make himself a singing sensation. French with subtitles. **85m/C VHS.** *D:* Nagangura Mweze, Bernard Lamy.

L.A. Wars 🦴½ **1994 (R)** A Latin American drug dealer moves into the territory of an Italian mobster, causing a turf war. When a cop rescues the mobster's daughter from the scuzzball, his boss forces him to infiltrate the mobster's organization. Abundant body count, lots of T&A. **94m/C VHS.** Vince Murdocco, Mary Zilba, A.J. Stevens, Rodrigo Obregon; *D:* Martin Morris, Tony Kandah.

Labor Pains 🦴🦴½ **1999 (R)** Sedgwick gets preggers by artist Morrow who disappears for eight months. When he returns, she's in labor and both her parents (Klein and Moore) and her best friend (Rochon) are trying to convince Sedgwick not to give the baby up for adoption. Meanwhile, the new parents decide to get reacquainted. **89m/C VHS.** Kyra Sedgwick, Rob Morrow, Lela Rochon, Mary Tyler Moore, Robert Klein, Dann Fink; *D:* Tracy Alexson; *W:* Tracy Alexson.

Laboratory 🦴 **1980** Things go awry when the earthling subjects of an alien experiment revolt against their captors. **93m/C VHS.** Camille Mitchell, Corinne Michaels, Garnett Smith.

Labyrinth 🦴🦴🦴 **1986 (PG)** While baby-sitting her baby brother Froud, Connelly is so frustrated she asks the goblins to take him away. When the Goblin King, played by Bowie, comes to answer her idle wish, she must try to rescue Froud by solving the fantastic labyrinth. If she does not find him in time, Froud will become one of the goblins forever. During her journey, Connelly is befriended by all sorts of odd creatures created by Henson, and she grows up a little along the way. A fascinating adventure movie for the whole family. **90m/C VHS, DVD, 8mm, Wide.** David Bowie, Jennifer Connelly, Toby Froud, Shelley Thompson, Dave Goetz, Karen Prell, Steve Whitmire; *D:* Jim Henson; *W:* Jim Henson, Terry Jones; *C:* Alex Thomson; *M:* Trevor Jones, David Bowie.

Labyrinth of Passion 🦴🦴½ *Laberinto de Pasiones* **1982** A screwball farce, directed by Almodovar, featuring a host of strange characters running around Madrid in search of sex and laughter. They find plenty of both. An early film by an influential director. In Spanish with English subtitles. **100m/C VHS, Wide.** *SP* Antonio Banderas, Imanol Arias, Cecilia (Celia) Roth; *D:* Pedro Almodovar; *W:* Pedro Almodovar.

The Lacemaker 🦴🦴🦴½ *La Dentielliere* **1977** Huppert's first shot at stardom, on videodisc with digital sound and a letterboxed print. A young beautician and a university student fall in love on vacation but soon begin to realize the differences in their lives. Adapted from the novel by Pascal Laine. In French with English subtitles. **107m/C Wide.** *FR SI GE* Isabelle Huppert, Yves Beneyton, Florence Giorgetti, Anna Marie Duringer; *D:* Claude Goretta.

L'Addition 🦴🦴½ *The Patsy; Caged Heart* **1985 (R)** According to some cinematic code, the male lead always gets in lots of trouble whenever he tries to help a beautiful stranger. This time, Berry, as Bruno Windler, winds up arrested for shoplifting when he attempts to help Abril. Jailed and on the verge of parole, Windler unwittingly becomes involved in a prison break and is accused of helping a crime don mastermind the escape and of shooting a guard. That's where that gallic flair for capturing the sado-masochistic underbelly of humanity comes in, as Windler is viciously pursued by the malevolent guard. **85m/C VHS.** Richard Berry, Victoria Abril, Richard Bohringer, Farid Chopel, Fabrice Eberhard; *D:* Denis Amar; *W:* Jean Curtelin; *C:* Robert Fraisse; *M:* Jean-Claude Petit.

The Ladies Club 🦴½ **1986 (R)** A group of rape victims get together and begin to victimize rapists. **86m/C VHS.** Bruce Davison, Karen Austin, Diana Scarwid, Shera Danese, Beverly Todd; *D:* A.K. Allen.

The Ladies' Man 🦴🦴 **1961** Piecemeal Lewis farce, with Jerry playing a clutzy handyman working at a girls' boarding house. Some riotous routines balanced by slow pacing. **106m/C VHS.** Jerry Lewis, Helen Traubel, Jack Kruschen, Doodles Weaver, Gloria Jean; *D:* Jerry Lewis; *W:* Jerry Lewis.

The Ladies Man 🦴½ **2000 (R)** Producer Lorne Michaels was allegedly the model for Mike Myers' Dr. Evil. It's becoming clear that his repeated abduction of SNL skits in order to stretch them out on the rack and loose them on the public is part of some nefarious plan. The victim this time is Leon Phelps (Meadows), a stuck-in-the-'70s late-night talk show host who dispenses inappropriate romantic advice. Raised by Hugh Hefner but banished for sleeping with the wrong bunny, Leon soon becomes banished from his radio gig, too. He eases the pain by seducing other men's wives, leading to the formation of an anti-Leon posse. Meanwhile, his faithful ex-producer Julie (Parsons) inexplicably sticks by his side hoping to tame Leon's wild ways. In the end, Leon is converted to a one-lady man, and the comic possibilities of this lame flick are squandered. **84m/C VHS, DVD, Wide.** Tim Meadows, Will Ferrell, Tiffani-Amber Thiessen, Billy Dee Williams, Karyn Parsons, Lee Evans, John Witherspoon, Eugene Levy, Tamala Jones, Julianne Moore, Sean Thibodeau; *D:* Reginald (Reggie) Hudlin; *W:* Tim Meadows, Dennis McNicholas, Andrew Steele; *C:* Johnny E. Jensen; *M:* Marcus Miller.

The Ladies of the Bois de Bologne 🦴🦴 *Les Dames du Bois de Bologne; Ladies of the Park* **1944** Beware the woman scorned—as Jean (Bernard) learns. He ends his longtime relationship with Helene (Casares), although they vow to stay friends, but she secretly plots revenge and finds it in the person of Agnes (Labourdette), a former prostitute. Helene introduces Agnes to Jean, hoping they'll be attracted to one another. They are but after the wedding ceremony Helene reveals the truth about Agnes' sordid past. Updated adaptation of a story in Diderot's "Jacques Le Fatalist." French with subtitles. **83m/B VHS.** *FR* Maria Casares, Paul Bernard, Elina Labourdette; *D:* Robert Bresson; *W:* Robert Bresson, Jean Cocteau.

Ladies of the Chorus 🦴🦴 **1949** Monroe stars as a burlesque chorus girl who shares the stage with her mom (Jergens) and a handful of other beauties. She meets and falls in love with a wealthy socialite (Brooks), but her mother completely disapproves of the relationship. Monroe later learns that her mother was in the same circumstances several years before. Although only her second film appearance, Monroe's talents are already quite apparent in this low-budget musical romance. ♫Every Baby Nees a Da Da Daddy; Anyone Can Tell I Love You; Crazy For You; You're Never Too Old; Ladies of the Chorus. **61m/B VHS.** Adele Jergens, Marilyn Monroe, Rand Brooks, Nana Bryant, Steven Geray, Bill Edwards; *D:* Phil Karlson.

Ladies of the Lotus 🦴 **1987** Bloodthirsty Vancouver gangsters raid Lotus, Inc., a modeling agency, and sell beautiful young women into slavery. As bad as it sounds. **120m/C VHS.** *CA* Richard Dale, Angela Read, Patrick Bermel, Darcia Carnie; *D:* Lloyd A. Simandl, Douglas C. Nicolle.

Ladies on the Rocks 🦴🦴½ *Koks I Kulissen* **1983** Aspiring comediennes Micha and Laura pack up their van and take their bizarre cabaret act on the road through rural Denmark. They find their private lives disintegrating but turn each disaster into new material for their act. In Danish with English subtitles. **100m/C VHS.** *DK* Helle Ryslinge, Anne Marie Helger, Flemming Quist Moller; *D:* Christian Braad Thomsen.

Ladies They Talk About 🦴🦴½ *Women in Prison* **1933** Stanwyck stars as a tough-talking gun moll who belongs to a gang of bank robbers. They get caught and Stanwyck is sent to the female division of San Quentin. The acting is great in this pre-Code prison movie, but the film gets a bit punchy at times. Based on the true-life experiences of actress Dorothy Mackaye, who went to jail after her husband was killed in a fight with actor Paul Kelley, who was also sent to prison. Adapted from the play "Women in Prison" by Dorothy Mackaye and Carlton Miles. **69m/B VHS.** Barbara Stanwyck, Preston Foster, Lyle Talbot, Dorothy Burgess, Lillian Roth, Maude Eburne, Harold Huber, Ruth Donnelly; *D:* Howard Bretherton, William Keighley.

Ladies Who Do 🦴🦴½ **1963** A group of cleaning ladies band together against the unscrupulous businessman who wants to tear down their homes in order to build an office tower. Along with a retired colonel, they use the stock market secrets gleaned from the rubbish they toss away to make a killing in the market and save the day. **90m/B VHS.** *GB* Peggy Mount, Robert Morley, Harry H. Corbett, Miriam Karlin, Avril Elgar, Dandy Nichols, Jon Pertwee, Nigel Davenport; *D:* C.M. Pennington-Richards; *W:* Michael Pertwee.

The Lady and the Highwayman 🦴🦴½ **1989** TV adaptation of the Barbara Cartland historical romance finds a rogue falling for the lady he's sworn to protect. Naturally, there's a happy ending. **100m/C VHS, DVD.** *GB* Hugh Grant, Emma Samms, Oliver Reed, Michael York, Robert Morley, John Mills, Lysette Anthony; *D:* John Hough; *W:* Terence Feely; *M:* Laurie Johnson.

Lady and the Tramp 🦴🦴🦴🦴 **1955 (G)** The animated Disney classic about two dogs who fall in love. Tramp is wild and carefree; Lady is a spoiled pedigree who runs away from home after her owners have a baby. They just don't make dog romances like this anymore. ♫He's a Tramp; La La Lu; Siamese Cat Song; Peace on Earth; Bella Notte. **76m/C VHS, DVD.** *D:* Hamilton Luske, Clyde Geronimi, Wilfred Jackson; *W:* Erdman Penner, Ralph Wright, Don DaGradi; *M:* Sonny Burke, Peggy Lee; *V:* Larry Roberts, Peggy Lee, Barbara Luddy, Stan Freberg, Alan Reed, Bill Thompson, Bill Baucon, Verna Felton, George Givot, Dallas McKennon, Lee Millar.

Lady Audley's Secret 🦴🦴 **2000** Old-fashioned and rather dull potboiler based on the 1862 novel by Mary Elizabeth Braddon. Governess Lucy (McIntosh) marries her employer, Sir Michael Audley (Cranham). But Lucy has a shady past, including a previous husband, George (Bamber), who turns out to be a friend of Sir Michael's nephew, Robert (Mackintosh). Then George disappears and Robert wonders just how dangerous the new Lady Audley is. **120m/C VHS.** *GB* Neve McIntosh, Steven Mackintosh, Kenneth Cranham, Jamie Bamber, Juliette Caton, Melanie Clark Pullen; *D:* Betsan Morris Evans; *W:* Donal Hounam; *C:* Julian Court; *M:* Paul Carr. **TV**

Lady Avenger 🦴 **1989 (R)** A woman is bent on getting revenge on her brother's killers. **90m/C VHS.** Peggie Sanders, Michelle (McClellan) Bauer, Daniel Hirsch; *D:* David DeCoteau; *C:* Thomas Callaway.

Lady Be Good 🦴🦴½ **1941** Adapted from the 1924 Gershwin Broadway hit, the plot's been revamped, much to the critics' distaste ("Variety" called it "molasses paced"). Sothern and Young play a tunesmith duo who excel at musical harmony and marital strife. Applauded for its music (the critics loved Hammerstein's and the Gershwins' tunes), the show's Academy Award-winning song was, ironically, written by Jerome Kern. And if that's not enough, levity man Skelton and hoofer Powell are thrown in for good measure. ♫The Last Time I Saw Paris; So Am I; Oh Lady Be Good; Fascinating Rhythm; Hang On To Me; You'll Never Know; You're Words, My Music; Saudades. **111m/B VHS.** Eleanor Powell, Ann Sothern, Robert Young, Lionel Barrymore, John Carroll, Red Skelton, Dan Dailey, Virginia O'Brien, Tom Conway, Phil Silvers, Doris Day; *D:* Norman Z. McLeod; *C:* George J. Folsey; *M:* Oscar Hammerstein, George Gershwin, Ira Gershwin, Jerome Kern, George Bassman. Oscars '41: Song ("The Last Time I Saw Paris").

Lady Beware 🦴🦴 **1987 (R)** A psychotic doctor becomes obsessed with a beautiful store-window dresser who specializes in steamy, erotic fantasies. When he wages a campaign of terror against her, she realizes that she must stop him before he kills her. **108m/C VHS.** Diane Lane, Michael Woods, Cotter Smith, Viveca Lindfors, Tyra Ferrell, Peter Nevargic, Edward Penn; ***D:*** Karen Arthur; ***W:*** Charles Zev Cohen.

Lady by Choice 🦴🦴½ **1934** Lombard stars as a beautiful young fan dancer who is arrested for a lewd public performance. Taking the advice of her press agent, she hires an old bag lady to pose as her mother on Mother's Day. Robson portrays her "mother" and comes to think of Lombard as her own daughter. Robson encourages Lombard to give up fan dancing and to strive for greater things in life. She also pushes her into romance with a wealthy young man (Pryor). Robson is excellent in her role as "mother" and Lombard shows great comic talent in this charming film. **78m/C VHS.** Carole Lombard, May Robson, Roger Pryor, Walter Connolly, Raymond Walburn, James Burke; ***D:*** David Burton; ***W:*** Jo Swerling.

Lady Caroline Lamb 🦴🦴 **1973** Lady Caroline is a passionate young lady in 19th-century England, who, although the wife of a member of Parliament, has an affair with Lord Byron and brings about her own downfall. Costume drama that never quite goes anywhere. **123m/C** *GB IT* Sarah Miles, Richard Chamberlain, Jon Finch, Laurence Olivier, John Mills, Ralph Richardson; ***D:*** Robert Bolt; ***W:*** Robert Bolt; ***C:*** Oswald Morris; ***M:*** Richard Rodney Bennett.

Lady Chatterley 🦴🦴 **1992** Oh my, Russell takes his provocative ways to D.H. Lawrence's scandalous novel about the adulterous affair between aristocratic Lady Connie Chatterley (Richardson) and her husband's gamekeeper, Oliver Mellors (Bean). Also includes material taken from two early drafts of the book "The First Lady Chatterley" and "John Thomas and Lady Jane." **210m/C VHS.** *GB* Joely Richardson, Sean Bean, James Wilby, Shirley Anne Field, Roger Hammond; ***D:*** Ken Russell; ***W:*** Ken Russell; ***C:*** Robin Vidgeon; ***M:*** Jean-Claude Petit. **TV**

Lady Chatterley's Lover 🦴½ *L'Amant de Lady Chatterley* **1955** Englishwoman has bad luck to have husband shot up during WWI and sent home paralyzed. In her quest for sexual fulfillment, she takes a new lover, the estate's earthy gamekeeper. Limp adaptation of D.H. Lawrence's novel. In French with English subtitles. **102m/B VHS.** *FR* Danielle Darrieux, Erno Crisa, Leo Genn; ***D:*** Marc Allegret.

Lady Chatterley's Lover 🦴½ **1981 (R)** Remake of the 1955 film version of D.H. Lawrence's classic novel of an English lady who has an affair with the gamekeeper of her husband's estate. Basically soft-focus soft porn. **107m/C VHS.** *GB FR* Sylvia Kristel, Nicholas Clay, Shane Briant; ***D:*** Just Jaeckin; ***C:*** Robert Fraisse.

Lady Cocoa 🦴½ **1975 (R)** Routine story of a young woman who gets released from jail for 24 hours and sets out for Las Vegas to find the man who framed her. **93m/C VHS.** Lola Falana, Joe "Mean Joe" Greene, Gene Washington, Alex Dreier; ***D:*** Matt Cimber.

The Lady Confesses 🦴🦴 **1945** Average mystery that involves Hughes trying to clear her boyfriend of murder. Independently produced. "Leave it to Beaver" fans will want to watch for "Ward Cleaver" Beaumont. **66m/B VHS.** Mary Beth Hughes, Hugh Beaumont, Edmund MacDonald, Claudia Drake, Emmett Vogan, Barbara Slater, Edward Howard, Dewey Robinson, Carol Andrews; ***D:*** Sam Newfield; ***W:*** Helen Martin, Irwin H. Franklyn; ***C:*** Jack Greenhalgh; ***M:*** Lee Zahler.

Lady Dragon 🦴🦴 **1992 (R)** A woman and her husband are viciously attacked and only she survives. Found by an old man, she learns a number of martial arts tricks and goes out to get her revenge. **89m/C VHS, DVD.** Cynthia Rothrock, Richard Norton, Robert Ginty, Bella Esperance, Hengko Tornando; ***D:*** David Worth; ***W:*** David Worth; ***C:*** David Worth; ***M:*** Jim West.

Lady Dragon 2 🦴🦴 **1993 (R)** Martial arts queen Rothrock returns in another saga of kickboxing vengeance. Susan Morgan seeks revenge on the three killers who terrorized her family. When she unleashes the power of the dragon they don't stand a chance. **?m/C VHS.** Cynthia Rothrock, Billy Drago, Sam Jones, Greg Stuart, Bella Esperance, George Rudy, Adisoerya Abdi; ***D:*** David Worth; ***W:*** Clifford Mohr; ***M:*** Jim West.

The Lady Eve 🦴🦴🦴🦴 **1941** Father/daughter (Coburn, Stanwyck) con artists, out to trip up wealthy beer tycoon Charles Pike (Fonda), instead find themselves tripped up when Jean falls in love with the mark. Ridiculous situations, but Sturges manages to keep them believable and funny. With a train scene that's every man's nightmare. Perhaps the best Sturges ever. Based on the story "The Faithful Heart" by Monckton Hoffe. Later remade as "The Birds and the Bees." **93m/B VHS, DVD.** Barbara Stanwyck, Henry Fonda, Charles Coburn, Eugene Pallette, William Demarest, Eric Blore, Melville Cooper; ***D:*** Preston Sturges; ***W:*** Preston Sturges; ***C:*** Victor Milner. Natl. Film Reg. '94.

Lady for a Day 🦴🦴🦴½ **1933** Delightful telling of the Damon Runyon story, "Madame La Gimp," about an apple peddler (Robson) down on her luck, who is transformed into a lady by a criminal with a heart. "Lady By Choice" is the sequel. **96m/B VHS, DVD.** May Robson, Warren William, Guy Kibbee, Glenda Farrell, Ned Sparks, Jean Parker, Walter Connolly; ***D:*** Frank Capra; ***W:*** Robert Riskin; ***C:*** Joseph Walker.

Lady for a Night 🦴🦴 **1942** The female owner of a gambling riverboat does her best to break into high society, when murder threatens to spoil her plans. Cast and costumes burdened by pacing. **88m/B VHS.** John Wayne, Joan Blondell, Ray Middleton, Philip Merivale, Blanche Yurka, Edith Barrett, Leonid Kinskey, Montagu Love; ***D:*** Leigh Jason.

Lady Frankenstein 🦴½ *La Figlia di Frankenstein; The Daughter of Frankenstein; Madame Frankenstein* **1972 (R)** Frankenstein's lovely daughter graduates from medical school and returns home. When she sees what her father's been up to, she gets some ideas of her own. Good fun for fans of the genre. **84m/C VHS, DVD, Wide.** *IT* Joseph Cotten, Rosalba (Sara Bay) Neri, Mickey Hargitay, Paul Muller, Herbert (Fuchs) Fux, Renate Kasche, Ada Pometti, Lorenzo Terzon, Paul Whiteman; ***D:*** Mel Welles; ***W:*** Edward Di Lorenzo; ***C:*** Riccardo (Pallton) Pallottini.

Lady from Louisiana 🦴🦴 **1942** A lawyer in old New Orleans out to rid the city of corruption falls in love with the daughter of a big-time gambler. Great storm scene. **84m/B VHS.** John Wayne, Ona Munson, Dorothy Dandridge, Ray Middleton, Henry Stephenson, Helen Westley, Jack Pennick; ***D:*** Bernard Vorhaus.

Lady from Nowhere 🦴🦴 **1936** A woman is the only witness to a gangland rub-out and is subsequently pursued by both the mob and the police. Unfortunately for her, the gangsters catch up with her first. **60m/B VHS.** Mary Astor, Charles Quigley, Thurston Hall, Victor Kilian, Spencer Charters; ***D:*** Gordon Wiles.

The Lady from Shanghai 🦴🦴🦴½ **1948** An unsuspecting seaman becomes involved in a web of intrigue when a woman hires him to work on her husband's yacht. Hayworth (a one-time Mrs. Orson Welles), in her only role as a villainess, plays a manipulative, sensual schemer. Wonderful and innovative cinematic techniques from Welles, as usual, including a tense scene in a hall of mirrors. Filmed on a yacht belonging to Errol Flynn. **87m/B VHS, DVD.** Orson Welles, Rita Hayworth, Everett Sloane, Glenn Anders, Ted de Corsia, Erskine Sanford, Gus Schilling; ***D:*** Orson Welles; ***W:*** Orson Welles; ***C:*** Charles Lawton Jr.; ***M:*** Heinz Roemheld.

Lady from Yesterday 🦴 **1985** An American couple's life is shattered by the appearance of the husband's Vietnamese mistress and her 10-year-old son. **87m/C VHS.** Wayne Rogers, Bonnie Bedelia, Pat Hingle, Barrie Youngfellow, Blue Dedeort, Tina Chen; ***D:*** Robert Day. **TV**

Lady Godiva 🦴½ **1955** The lovely O'Hara is wasted in the title role as a Saxon noblewoman married to Leofric (Nader). They're trying to stem Norman influence and Godiva vows to ride naked through the streets of Canterbury to prove the Saxon people's loyalty to King Edward (Franz). Cardboard costumer. Clint Eastwood has a bit as a Saxon soldier. **89m/C VHS.** Maureen O'Hara, George Nader, Eduard Franz, Leslie Bradley, Victor McLaglen, Torin Thatcher, Rex Reason; ***D:*** Arthur Lubin; ***W:*** Oscar Brodney, Harry Ruskin; ***C:*** Carl Guthrie.

Lady Godiva Rides *Lady Godiva Meets Tom Jones* **1968** A bad, campy version of the story of Lady Godiva. Godiva comes to the United States with a bevy of scantily clad maidens and winds up in the Old West. When the town villain threatens to compromise her, Tom Jones comes to the rescue. The film (of course) features Godiva's naked ride on horseback through the town. **88m/C VHS.** Marsha Jordan, Forman Shane, Deborah Downey, Elizabeth Knowles, James E. Myers, Jennie Jackson, Liz Rene, Vincent Barbi; ***D:*** A.C. (Stephen Apostoloff) Stephen; ***W:*** A.C. (Stephen Apostoloff) Stephen; ***C:*** R.C. Ruben; ***M:*** Jay Colonna, Robert E. Lee.

Lady Grey 🦴 **1982** A poor farmer's daughter rises to the top of the country music charts, but at a price. **111m/C VHS.** Ginger Alden, David Allen Coe; ***D:*** Worth Keeter.

Lady Ice 🦴🦴 **1973 (PG)** Sutherland, as an insurance investigator on the trail of jewel thieves, follows them to Miami Beach and the Bahamas. After stealing a diamond he enters into partnership with a crook's daughter. Worth seeing for the cast. **93m/C VHS.** Donald Sutherland, Jennifer O'Neill, Robert Duvall, Eric (Hans Gudegast) Braeden; ***D:*** Tom Gries; ***W:*** Alan R. Trustman; ***M:*** Perry Botkin.

Lady in a Cage 🦴🦴🦴 **1964** A wealthy widow is trapped in her home elevator during a power failure and becomes desperate when hoodlums break in. Shocking violence ahead of its time probably plays better than when first released. Young Caan is a standout among the star-studded cast. **95m/B VHS.** Olivia de Havilland, Ann Sothern, James Caan, Jennifer Billingsley, Jeff Corey, Scatman Crothers, Rafael Campos; ***D:*** Walter Grauman; ***W:*** Luther Davis.

Lady in Cement 🦴½ **1968 (R)** The second Tony Rome mystery, in which the seedy Miami dick finds a corpse with cement shoes while swimming. **93m/C VHS.** Frank Sinatra, Raquel Welch, Richard Conte, Martin Gabel, Lainie Kazan, Pat Henry, Steve Peck, Joe E. Lewis, Dan Blocker; ***D:*** Gordon Douglas; ***C:*** Joseph Biroc.

Lady in Distress 🦴🦴½ *A Window in London* **1939** A British drama about an unhappily married man who witnesses an apparent murder. He discovers, however, it was actually the prank of an illusionist and his flirtatious wife. He soon finds himself becoming increasingly involved with their lives. **59m/B VHS.** *GB* Michael Redgrave, Paul Lukas, Sally Gray; ***D:*** Herbert Mason.

The Lady in Question 🦴½ *It Happened in Paris* **1940** A Parisian shopkeeper, played by Aherne, sits on a jury that acquits Hayworth of murder. His interest doesn't end with the trial, however, and matters heat up when his son also becomes involved. Remake of a melodramatic French release. **81m/B VHS.** Rita Hayworth, Glenn Ford, Brian Aherne, Irene Rich, Lloyd Corrigan, George Coulouris, Evelyn Keyes, Curt Bois, Edward Norris; ***D:*** Charles Vidor; ***W:*** Ben Barzman.

The Lady in Question 🦴🦴½ **1999** Sequel to "Murder in a Small Town" finds Broadway director Larry "Cash" Carter (Wilder) pursuing his amateur gumshoe sideline once again. This time it's the poisoning death of his wealthy friend, Emma Sachs (Bloom). And there are lots of suspects. Everyone seems to be enjoying themselves in this stylish period mystery, especially Wilder. **100m/C VHS.** Gene Wilder, Mike Starr, Cherry Jones, Claire Bloom, Barbara Sukowa, John Benjamin Hickey, Michael Cumpsty, Dixie Seatle, Kerry McPherson; ***D:*** Joyce Chopra; ***W:*** Gilbert Pearlman; ***C:*** Bruce Surtees; ***M:*** John Morris. **CABLE**

Lady in Red 🦴🦴 *Guns, Sin and Bathtub Gin* **1979** A story of America in the '30s, and the progress through the underworld of the woman who was Dillinger's last lover. **90m/C VHS, DVD.** Pamela Sue Martin, Louise Fletcher, Robert Conrad, Christopher Lloyd, Dick Miller, Laurie Heineman, Robert Hogan, Glenn Withrow, Rod Gist, Mary Woronov; ***D:*** Lewis Teague; ***W:*** John Sayles; ***C:*** Daniel Lacambre; ***M:*** James Horner.

Lady in the Death House 🦴🦴 **1944** A framed woman is set to walk the last mile, as a scientist struggles to find the real killer in time. **57m/B VHS.** Jean Parker, Lionel Atwill, Marcia Mae Jones.

Lady in the Lake 🦴🦴½ **1946** Why is it everyone wants to get artsy with pulp fiction? Actor Montgomery directs himself in this Philip Marlowe go-round, using a subjective camera style to imitate Chandler's first person narrative (that means the only time we get to see Marlowe/Montgomery's mug is in a mirror. That pretty well says it all). Having decided to give up eyeing privately, Marlowe turns to the pen to tell the tangled tale of the lady in the lake: once upon a time, a detective was hired to find the wicked wife of a paying client...Some find the direction clever. Others consider MGM chief Louis B. Mayer, who made sure this was Montgomery's last project with MGM, to be a wise man. **103m/B VHS.** Robert Montgomery, Lloyd Nolan, Audrey Totter, Tom Tully, Leon Ames, Jayne Meadows; ***D:*** Robert Montgomery; ***C:*** Paul Vogel.

Lady in Waiting 🦴🦴 **1994 (R)** Detective Jimmy Scavetti (Nouri) is hunting down a serial kill preying on call girls when he meets the seductive Lori (Whirry). Then he discovers his ex-wife's new hubby was the lawyer for each of the victims—only the lawyer turns up dead and Jimmy becomes a suspect. Also available in an unrated version. **85m/C VHS.** Michael Nouri, Shannon Whirry, William Devane, Karen Kopins, Crystal Chappell, Robert Costanzo, Meg Foster, Charles Grant; ***D:*** Fred Gallo.

The Lady in White 🦴🦴🦴 **1988 (PG-13)** Small-town ghost story about murder and revenge. When young Haas is locked in school one night, he's visited by the ghost of a little girl who wants his help in discovering who murdered her. Well-developed characters, interesting style, and suspenseful plot make for a sometimes slow but overall exceptional film. **92m/C VHS, DVD, Wide.** Lukas Haas, Len Cariou, Alex Rocco, Katherine Helmond, Jason Presson, Renata Vanni, Angelo Bertolini, Jared Rushton, Joelle Jacob; ***D:*** Frank Laloggia; ***W:*** Frank Laloggia; ***C:*** Russell Carpenter; ***M:*** Frank Laloggia.

The Lady Is Willing 🦴🦴½ **1942** Dietrich is a stage star who longs for a baby and when an abandoned infant comes her way she decides to keep the child. Only she hasn't a clue about any of the practical aspects. Lucky for her MacMurray is a friendly pediatrician who gives her some advice. Dietrich finds out she can't adopt as a single parent and persuades MacMurray to marry her, in name only, but since this is a romantic comedy the two eventually fall in love. **91m/B VHS.** Marlene Dietrich, Fred MacMurray, Aline MacMahon, Stanley Ridges, Arline Judge, Roger Clark, Ruth Ford, Sterling Holloway, Harvey Stephens, Harry Shannon, Elisabeth Risdon, Charles Halton; ***D:*** Mitchell Leisen; ***W:*** James Edward Grant, Albert McCleery.

Lady Jane 🦴🦴🦴½ **1985 (PG-13)** An accurate account of the life of 15-year-old Lady Jane Grey, who secured the throne of England for nine days in 1553 as a result of political maneuvering by noblemen and the Church of England. A wonderful film even for non-history buffs. Carter's first film. **140m/C VHS.** *GB* Helena Bonham Carter, Cary Elwes, Sara Kestelman, Michael Hordern, Joss Ackland, Richard Johnson, Patrick Stewart; ***D:*** Trevor Nunn.

Lady Killer 🦴🦴🦴 **1933** Racy, pre-Code comedy with mobster Cagney hiding out in Hollywood. He gets discovered and becomes a big star, but his old gang turns up to blackmail him. Lots of movie "in" jokes and Clarke (of "Public Enemy" fame) is great as a wisecracking moll. Based on the story "The Finger Man" by Rosalind Keating Shaffer. **74m/B VHS.** James Cagney, Mae Clarke, Leslie Fenton, Margaret Lindsay, Henry O'Neill, Raymond Hatton, George Chandler; ***D:*** Roy Del Ruth; ***W:*** Ben Markson, Lillie Hayward.

Lady Killer 🦴🦴 *Ladykiller* **1997 (R)** A serial killer called the Piggyback Murderer is terrorizing a college campus. Police Lt. Jack Lasky (Gazzara) is particularly anxious since his daughter Jennifer (Allman) is a student at the school. When her new boyfriend, aspiring actor Richard Darling (McArthur), keeps turning up at the murder scenes, guess who becomes dad's prime suspect. **80m/C VHS.** Ben Gazzara, Alex McArthur, Terri Treas, Renee Allman; ***D:*** Terence H. Winkless; ***W:*** Craig J. Nevius; ***C:*** Christopher Baffa.

Lady L 🦴½ **1965** Silly turn-of-the-century farce about a sexy laundress (Loren), married to a French anarchist (Newman!), who also marries the aristocratic Niven (in name only). Elaborate sets and Paris and London backgrounds couldn't overcome the odd casting and weak script. Adapted from the novel by Romain Gary. **107m/C VHS.** *FR IT* Sophia Loren, Paul Newman, David Niven, Cecil Parker, Claude Dauphin, Marcel Dalio, Philippe Noiret, Michel Piccoli, Daniel Emilfork, Eugene Deckers; ***Cameos:*** Peter Ustinov; ***D:*** Peter Ustinov; ***W:*** Peter Ustinov.

Lady Mobster 🦴 **1988 (PG-13)** When her parents are murdered a young girl is taken in by a Mafia family. She grows up to be a shrewd lawyer but winds up working in her adoptive family's crime syndicate in order to take revenge on her parents' murderers. Exaggerated and silly but watchable for its so-bad-it's-good qualities. **94m/C VHS.** Susan Lucci, Michael Nader, Roscoe Born, Joseph Wiseman; ***D:*** John Llewellyn Moxey. **TV**

Lady of Burlesque 🦴🦴½ *Striptease Lady* **1943** Burlesque dancer is found dead, strangled with her own G-string. Clever and amusing film based on "The G-String Murders" by Gypsy Rose Lee. **91m/B VHS.** Barbara Stanwyck, Michael O'Shea, Janis Carter, Pinky Lee; ***D:*** William A. Wellman.

Lady of the Evening 🦴🦴 **1979 (PG)** A prostitute and a crook team up to seek revenge against the mob. **110m/C VHS.** *IT* Sophia Loren, Marcello Mastroianni.

Lady of the House 🦴🦴 **1978** A true story about a madame who rose from operator of a brothel to become a political force in San Francisco. **100m/C VHS.** Dyan Cannon, Susan Tyrrell, Colleen Camp, Armand Assante; ***D:*** Ralph Nelson.

Lady of the Lake 🦴🦴 **1928** Rare silent adventure film in which an exiled girl saves the king from outlaws in Scotland. Orchestra score. **47m/B VHS, DVD.** *GB* Percy Marmont, Benita Hume, Huddon Mason, Lawson Butt; ***D:*** James A. Fitzpatrick.

Lady on a Train 🦴🦴🦴 **1945** Travelling at Christmas, wealthy young Nicky Collins (Durbin) thinks she sees a murder from her train window but when she arrives in New York she can't get anyone to believe her. But not willing to give up, Nicky turns to Wayne Morgan (Bruce), a mystery writer for help. Recognizing the victim from a newspaper photo, Nicky checks out his family and gets mistaken for a nightclub singer (so Durbin can vamp a torch song). Lots of comedy amidst the mystery and romance, and some surprizes as well. Based on a story by Leslie Charteris. ♫Gimme a Little Kiss, Will You, Huh?; Night and Day; Silent Night. **95m/B VHS.** Deanna Durbin, David Bruce, Ralph Bellamy, Dan Duryea, Edward Everett Horton, Allen Jenkins, Elizabeth Patterson, William Frawley, Jacqueline DeWit, George Coulouris; ***D:*** Charles David; ***W:*** Robert O'Brien, Edmund Beloin; ***C:*** Elwood "Woody" Bredell; ***M:*** Miklos Rozsa.

Lady on the Bus 🦴🦴 **1978 (R)** Sexually frustrated newlywed bride rides the city buses looking for men to satisfy her. This bothers her husband. Shot in Rio de Janeiro. In Portuguese with English subtitles. **102m/C VHS.** *BR* Sonia Braga; ***D:*** Neville D'Almedia.

The Lady Refuses 🦴🦴 **1931** A stuffy Victorian father is disappointed in his wastrel son and decides a poor but honest young woman could be the making of him. Problems arise when the girl falls for the father instead. **70m/B VHS.** Betty Compson, John Darrow, Margaret Livingston, Gilbert Emery; ***D:*** George Archainbaud.

The Lady Says No 🦴🦴 **1951** A photographer must photograph an attractive author who has written a book uncomplimentary toward the male sex. **80m/B VHS.** Joan Caulfield, David Niven, James Robertson Justice, Frances Bavier, Henry Jones, Jeff York; ***D:*** Frank Ross.

Lady Scarface 🦴🦴 **1941** Murderous mobster queen breaks the law, bats men around, and takes the cops on a merry chase. Cheap, fast-paced action. **66m/B VHS.** Mildred Coles, Dennis O'Keefe, Frances Neal, Judith Anderson, Eric Blore, Charles Halton; ***D:*** Frank Woodruff.

Lady Sings the Blues 🦴🦴½ **1972 (R)** Jazz artist Billie Holiday's life becomes a musical drama depicting her struggle against racism and drug addiction in her pursuit of fame and romance. What could be a typical price-of-fame story is saved by Ross' inspired performance as the tragic singer. ♫My Man; Strange Fruit; God Bless the Child; Don't Explain; T'Ain't Nobody's Business If I Do; Lady Sings the Blues; All Of Me; The Man I Love; Our Love Is Here to Stay. **144m/C VHS.** Diana Ross, Billy Dee Williams, Richard Pryor, James Callahan, Paul Hampton, Sid Melton; ***D:*** Sidney J. Furie; ***C:*** John A. Alonzo.

Lady Street Fighter 🦴 **1986** A well-armed female combat fighter battles an organization of assassins to avenge her sister's murder. **73m/C VHS.** Renee Harmon, Joel McCrea Jr.

Lady Takes a Chance 🦴🦴🦴 **1943** A romantic comedy about a New York working girl with matrimonial ideas and a rope-shy rodeo rider who yearns for the wide open spaces. Fine fun on the range. **86m/B VHS.** John Wayne, Jean Arthur, Phil Silvers, Charles Winninger; ***D:*** William A. Seiter.

Lady Terminator 🦴½ **1989 (R)** A student on an anthropology expedition digs up more than she bargained for when she is possessed by an evil spirit and goes on a rampage. **83m/C VHS.** Barbara Constable, Christopher Hunt, Joseph McGlynn, Claudia Rademaker; ***D:*** Jalil Jackson.

The Lady Vanishes 🦴🦴🦴🦴 **1938** Kindly old lady, Miss Froy (Witty) seemingly disappears from a fast-moving train bound for England. But when her young friend Iris (Lockwood) investigates, she finds no one appears to believe her and she has a spiraling mystery to solve. Of course, Irish has music scholar Gilbert (Redgrave) eager to help her out. Hitchcock's first real winner, a smarmy, witdrenched British mystery that precipitated his move to Hollywood. Along with "39 Steps," considered an early Hitchcock classic. From the novel "The Wheel Spins," by Ethel Lina White. Remade in 1979. **99m/B VHS, DVD.** *GB* Margaret Lockwood, Paul Lukas, Michael Redgrave, May Whitty, Googie Withers, Basil Radford, Naunton Wayne, Cecil Parker, Linden Travers, Catherine Lacey, Alfred Hitchcock; ***D:*** Alfred Hitchcock; ***W:*** Sidney Gilliat, Frank Launder; ***C:*** Jack Cox; ***M:*** Louis Levy. N.Y. Film Critics '38: Director (Hitchcock).

The Lady Vanishes 🦴½ **1979** In this reworking of the '38 Alfred Hitchcock film, a woman on a Swiss bound train awakens from a nap to find that the elderly woman seated next to her was kidnapped. Falls short of the original movie due to the "screwball" nature of the main characters, Gould and Shepherd. Based on Ethel Lina White's novel "The Wheel Spins." **95m/C VHS, DVD.** *GB* Elliott Gould, Cybill Shepherd, Angela Lansbury, Herbert Lom; ***D:*** Anthony Page; ***W:*** George Axelrod.

Lady Windermere's Fan 🦴🦴½ **1926** The silent, Lubitsch adaptation of the Oscar Wilde tale concerning an upper-class couple's marriage being almost destroyed by suspected adultery. **66m/B VHS, 8mm.** Ronald Colman, May McAvoy, Bert Lytell; ***D:*** Ernst Lubitsch.

The Lady with the Dog 🦴🦴🦴 **1959** A bittersweet love story based on the Anton Chekhov story, about two married Russians who meet by chance in a park, fall in love, and realize they are fated to a haphazard, clandestine affair. In Russian with English titles. **86m/B VHS.** *RU* Iya Savvina, Alexei Batalov, Ala Chostakova, N. Alisova; ***D:*** Yosif Heifitz.

The Lady Without Camelias 🦴🦴½ **1953** A young woman is discovered by a film producer who casts her in a successful movie and eventually marries her. Convinced that she can sustain a career as a serious actress, the producer is dismayed by the job offers that come her way, usually of a sexually exploitive nature. What follows is a tragic decline for both. **106m/C VHS.** *IT*

Ladybird, Ladybird 🦴🦴🦴 **1993 (R)** Loach's emotionally bruising look at working-class life and family in the '90s. Maggie (Rock) is a tough unmarried mother of four who's been battered by her lovers and has come under the over-watchful eye of Britain's social services. She meets Jorge (Vega), a gentle Paraguayan, and just when things are looking up, Jorge gets immigration heat, Maggie's insecurities surface, and her baby daughter is taken into care by child welfare. Rock has a no-nonsense manner and acerbic wit that precludes any hand-wringing for her character, even as you hope she'll win out over circumstance. Based on a true story. **102m/C VHS.** *GB* Crissy Rock, Vladimir Vega, Ray Winstone, Sandie Lavelle, Mauricio Venegas, Clare Perkins, Jason Stracey, Luke Brown, Lily Farrell; ***D:*** Ken Loach; ***W:*** Rona Munro; ***C:*** Barry Ackroyd; ***M:*** George Fenton. Berlin Intl. Film Fest. '94: Actress (Rock).

Ladybugs 🦴½ **1992 (PG-13)** Hangdog salesman Dangerfield would like to move up the corporate ladder, but must first turn the company-sponsored girl's soccer team into winners. Routine Dangerfield vehicle exploits nearly everything for laughs, including dressing an athletic boy as a girl so he can play on the team. Obvious fluff. **91m/C VHS.** Rodney Dangerfield, Jackee, Jonathan Brandis, Ilene Graff, Vinessa Shaw, Tom Parks, Jeanetta Arnette, Nancy Parsons, Blake Clark, Tommy Lasorda; ***D:*** Sidney J. Furie; ***W:*** Curtis Burch; ***C:*** Dan Burstall; ***M:*** Richard Gibbs.

Ladyhawke 🦴🦴½ **1985 (PG-13)** In medieval times, a youthful pickpocket befriends a strange knight who is on a mysterious quest. This unlikely duo, accompanied by a watchful hawk, are enveloped in a magical adventure. **121m/C VHS, DVD, Wide.** Matthew Broderick, Rutger Hauer, Michelle Pfeiffer, John Wood, Leo McKern, Alfred Molina, Ken Hutchison; ***D:*** Richard Donner; ***W:*** Edward Khmara, Michael Thomas, Tom Mankiewicz; ***C:*** Vittorio Storaro; ***M:*** Andrew Powell.

Ladykiller 🦴🦴 **1992 (R)** Rogers stars as a burned-out cop who goes to a dating service to find a man who'll give her the attention she craves. When she meets wealthy professional Shea she thinks he's the one but her cop's curiosity about her lover's past may cost her her life. **92m/C VHS.** Mimi Rogers, John Shea, Alice Krige, Tom Irwin; ***D:*** Michael Scott; ***W:*** Shelley Evans.

The Ladykillers 🦴🦴🦴½ *The Lady Killers* **1955** A gang of bumbling bank robbers is foiled by a little old lady. Hilarious antics follow, especially on the part of Guinness, who plays the slightly demented-looking leader of the gang. **87m/C VHS.** *GB* Alec Guinness, Cecil Parker, Katie Johnson, Herbert Lom, Peter Sellers, Danny Green, Jack Warner, Kenneth Connor, Edie Martin, Jack Melford; ***D:*** Alexander MacKendrick; ***W:*** William Rose; ***C:*** Otto Heller; ***M:*** Tristram Cary. British Acad. '55: Actress (Johnson), Screenplay.

Ladykillers 🦴🦴 **1988** At the glitzy L.A. club Ladykillers, men strip as the women cheer. At the climax of the performance, one of the dancers is brutally murdered, live on stage. In this decadent world of glitter and sex, the women are the hunters and the men are the reward. **97m/C VHS.** Marilu Henner, Susan Blakely, Lesley-Anne Down, Thomas Calabro; ***D:*** Robert Lewis; ***W:*** Greg Dinallo.

The Lady's Not for Burning 🦴🦴½ **1987** Romantic comedy, set in a medieval English village, finds ex-soldier Thomas Mendip (Branagh) invading the home of querulous Mayor Hebble Tyson (Hepton), demanding to be hanged. He says he's murdered the local rag and bone merchant but the townspeople insist Jennet Jourdemayne (Lunghi), who's seeking refuge at the mayor's, has turned him into a dog. They demand she be burned as a witch (hence the title, since Thomas, unwillingly but strongly, objects to this action). Adapted by Fry from his play; made for TV. **90m/C VHS.** Kenneth Branagh, Cherie Lunghi, Bernard Hepton, Tim Watson, Susannah Harker, Angela Thorne, Shaun Scott; ***D:*** Julian Amyes; ***W:*** Christopher Fry. **TV**

Lafayette Escadrille 🦴🦴½ *Hell Bent for Glory* **1958** Action and romance in WWI via the famed flying unit manned by American volunteers. Hunter is banal in the lead role as is his romance with a reformed prostitute (Choreau). Director Wellman actually was a member of the squadron and his son plays him in the film but the director regarded the film as a failure because of studio interference. **92m/B VHS.** Tab Hunter, Etchika Choureau, William Wellman Jr., Joel McCrea, Dennis Devine, Marcel Dalio, David Janssen, Paul Fix, Will Hutchins, Clint Eastwood; ***D:*** William A. Wellman; ***W:*** A.S. Fleischman; ***C:*** William Clothier; ***M:*** Leonard Rosenman.

L'Age D'Or 🦴🦴🦴🦴 *Age of Gold; The Golden Age* **1930** Bunuel's first full-length film and his masterpiece of sex, repression, and of course, death. A hapless man is prevented from reaching his beloved by middle-class morality, forces of the establishment, the Church, government and every bastion of modern values. Banned for years because of its anti-religious stance. Co-scripted by Dali. A mercilessly savage, surreal satire, the purest expression of Bunuel's wry misanthropy. In French with English subtitles. **62m/B VHS.** *FR* Gaston Modot, Lya Lys, Max Ernst, Pierre Prevert, Marie Berthe Ernst, Paul Eluard; ***D:*** Luis Bunuel; ***W:*** Salvador Dali, Luis Bunuel; ***C:*** Albert Duverger; ***M:*** Claude Debussy.

Laguna Heat 🦴½ **1987** A tired LA cop investigates a series of murders that are related to an old friend of his father's. Based on a novel by T. Jefferson Parker. **110m/C VHS.** Harry Hamlin, Jason Robards Jr., Catherine Hicks, Rip Torn, Anne Francis; ***D:*** Simon Langton. **TV**

The Lair of the White Worm 🦴🦴🦴 **1988 (R)** Scottish archaeologist uncovers a strange skull, and then a bizarre religion to go with it, and then a very big worm. An unusual look at the effects of Christianity and paganism on each other, colored with sexual innuendo and, of course, giant worms. A cross between a morality play and a horror film. Adapted from Bram Stoker's last writings, done while he was going mad from Bright's disease. Everything you'd expect from Russell. **93m/C VHS, DVD.** *GB* Amanda Donohoe, Sammi Davis, Catherine Oxenberg, Hugh Grant, Peter Capaldi, Stratford Johns, Paul Brooke, Christopher Gable; ***D:*** Ken Russell; ***W:*** Ken Russell; ***C:*** Dick Bush; ***M:*** Stanislas Syrewicz.

Lake Consequence 🦴🦴 **1992 (R)** Severance plays a suburban housewife who accidentally gets locked in the camper of the tree-trimmer stud (Zane) she's been eyeing while he's been working in her neighborhood. Next thing she knows they wind up at a distant lake where the bored housewife is more than willing to give into her growing sexual fantasies. An unrated version at 90 minutes is also available. **85m/C VHS.** Joan Severance, Billy Zane, May Karasun; ***D:*** Rafael Eisenman; ***W:*** Zalman King, Melanie Finn, Henry Cobbold; ***M:*** George S. Clinton.

Lake Placid 🦴½ **1999 (R)** Hotshot TV producer David E. Kelley lures some acting careers into deadly peril in this lame comedy/horror ripoff of "Jaws." Paleontologist Fonda is sent to examine a tooth after a grisly death occurs in rural Maine. She discovers that the tooth is prehistoric, but she decides to stick around with game warden Pullman, sheriff Gleeson and eccentric professor Platt anyway. You know, just in case the crocodile that escaped through a hole in the plot is still hungry after eating the fatter (and therefore more buttery) cast members. Betty White is the lone bright spot as a foul-mouthed old woman who is rooting for the crocodile. You'll be rooting for it too, but you'll be rooting for it to devour the movie exec who green-lighted this crock. **82m/C VHS, DVD.** Bridget Fonda, Bill Pullman, Oliver Platt, Brendan Gleeson, Mariska Hargitay, Meredith Salenger, Betty White, David Lewis; *D:* Steve Miner; *W:* David E. Kelley; *C:* Daryn Okada; *M:* John Ottman.

Lakota Woman: Siege at Wounded Knee ½ 1994 Autobiography of Mary Crow Dog (Bedard) and her coming of age during the American Indian Movement's 1973 occupation of Wounded Knee. Tangled loyalties and the battle between Native Americans and U.S. troops make for strong drama. Bedard is remarkable in her film debut. Based on the book by Mary Crow Dog and Richard Erdoes. Filmed on location in South Dakota. **113m/C VHS.** Irene Bedard, August Schellenberg, Joseph Runningfox, Floyd "Red Crow" Westerman, Tantoo Cardinal, Michael Horse, Lawrence Bayne, Nancy Parsons; *D:* Frank Pierson; *W:* Bill Kerby; *C:* Toyomichi Kurita; *M:* Richard Horowitz.

The Lamb ½ 1915 Intent on proving to his sweetheart that he's not the coward people say he is, a guy heads west to engage in various manly activities, including fisticuffs, karate and Indian kidnapping. Fairbanks' debut on film (he was already an established Broadway star) set the mold for the American leading man: moral, cheerful, physical, and not hard to look at. A popular guy with the public, Fairbanks formed his own film company the following year. Story's based on D.W. Griffith's book, "The Man and the Test." **60m/B VHS.** Douglas Fairbanks Sr., Seena Owen, Lillian Langdon, Monroe Salisbury, Kate Toncray, Alfred Paget, William E. (W.E., William A., W.A.) Lowery; *D:* Christy Cabanne.

Lamb 1985 Troubled 10-year-old epileptic Owen Kane (Kane) has been dumped by his abusive mother at a Catholic-run institution for wayward boys in Ireland, run by self-righteous headmaster Brother Benedict (Bannen). Owen becomes Benedict's scapegoat—much to the dismay of Brother Michael Lamb (Neeson). When Lamb claims a small family inheritance, he decides to take Owen and head to London, posing as father and son, where they live in increasingly depressed surroundings while Michael tries painfully to make them into a real family. Based on the novel by MacLaverty, who also wrote the screenplay. **110m/C VHS.** *IR* Liam Neeson, Hugh O'Conor, Ian Bannen, Frances Tomelty; *D:* Colin Gregg; *W:* Bernard MacLaverty; *C:* Mike Garfath; *M:* Van Morrison.

Lambada 1989 (PG) By day, he's a high school teacher in Beverly Hills; by night, a Latin dirty dancer cum tutor of ghetto teens. The very first of several films based on the short-lived dance craze. **92m/C VHS.** J. Eddie Peck, Melora Hardin, Adolfo "Shabba Doo" Quinones, Ricky Paull Goldin, Basil Hoffman, Dennis Burkley; *D:* Joel Silberg.

Lamerica 1995 Two Italian hustlers, Fiore (Placido) and his younger partner Gino (Lo Verso), head for poverty-stricken Albania in 1991, the first year after the collapse of the Communist dictatorship. They intend to set up a phony corporation and scam money from government grants but they need an Albanian figurehead. The duo find simple-minded, elderly Spiro (Di Mazzarelli), who's spent most of his life in prison camps, and stash him in an orphanage for safe keeping. Only when Spiro gets away, Gino heads for the countryside to find him and discovers some secrets about Spiro's past and just how the wily Albanians have been surviving. Italian with subtitles. **116m/C VHS, Wide.** *IT* Enrico Lo Verso, Michele Placido, Carmelo Di Mazzarelli, Piro Milkani; *D:* Gianni Amelio; *W:* Gianni Amelio, Andrea Porporati, Alessandro Sermoneta; *C:* Luca Bigazzi; *M:* Franco Piersanti.

L'Amour en Herbe *Budding Love; Tender Love* 1977 His parents realize Pascal has something on his mind when he fails school. It turns out to be lovely Martine, whom he is then forbidden to see. But Pascal remains true—until betrayed. In French with subtitles. **100m/C VHS.** *FR* Pascal Meynier, Guilhaine Dubos, Bruno Raffaeli, Michel Galabru, Francoise Prevost, Alix Mahieux; *D:* Roger Andrieux; *W:* Roger Andrieux, Jean-Marie Benard; *C:* Ramon Suarez; *M:* Maxime Le Forestier.

Lamp at Midnight ½ 1966 Presentation from "George Schaefer's Showcase Theatre" deals with three critical periods in the life of Italian astronomer Galileo Galilei, from his invention of the telescope, through his appearance at the Holy Office of the Inquisition, to the publication of his "Dialogue on the Two Systems of the World." For those in a planetary state of mind. **76m/C VHS.** Melvyn Douglas, David Wayne, Michael Hordern, Hurd Hatfield, Kim Hunter; *D:* George Schaefer. **TV**

Lana in Love 1992 A lonely woman places an ad in the personal section in hopes of finding her Mr. Right. **90m/C VHS.** Daphna Kastner, Clark Gregg.

Lancelot of the Lake *Lancelot du Lac; The Grail; Le Graal* 1974 The Knights of the Round Table return to the court of King Arthur after a long, bloody, and fruitless search for the Holy Grail. Rivalries and jealousies debase the heroes as Lancelot struggles with his feelings for Arthur's Queen Guinevere. Austere acting but the film's rich visuals provide a sensuous air. French with subtitles. **85m/C VHS.** *FR* Luc Simon, Laura Duke Condominas, Vladimir Antolek-Oresek, Humbert Balsan, Patrick Bernard, Arthur De Montalembert; *D:* Robert Bresson; *W:* Robert Bresson; *C:* Pasqualino De Santis; *M:* Philippe Sarde.

Land and Freedom 1995 Earnestly talky drama focusing on idealist Liverpudlian communist David Carr (Hart), who heads to Spain in 1937 to fight against Franco's fascists. What David learns is that the Republican forces, made up of independent militia, are bitterly divided, with much infighting and betrayal from the Stalinist forces within David's own party. He falls for socialist Blanca (Pastor) and learns how terrifying and haphazard war can be (with timeout for ideological discussions). Sympathetic characters and sweeping action help to compensate for the political polemics. **109m/C VHS.** *GB SP GE* Ian Hart, Rosana Pastor, Iciar Bollain, Tom Gilroy, Frederic Pierrot, Marc Martinez, Angela Clarke, David Allen; *D:* Ken Loach; *W:* Jim Allen; *C:* Barry Ackroyd; *M:* George Fenton. Cesar '96: Foreign Film.

The Land Before Time 1988 (G) Lushly animated children's film about five orphaned baby dinosaurs who band together and try to find the Great Valley, a paradise where they might live safely. Works same parental separation theme as Bluth's "American Tail." Charming, coy, and shamelessly tearjerking; producers included Steven Spielberg and George Lucas. **67m/C VHS, DVD.** *D:* Don Bluth; *W:* Stu Krieger; *M:* James Horner; *V:* Pat Hingle, Helen Shaver, Gabriel Damon, Candice Houston, Burke Barnes, Judith Barsi, Will Ryan.

The Land Before Time 2: The Great Valley Adventure ½ 1994 (G) Sequel to 1988's animated adventure finds dinosaur pals Littlefoot, Cera, Ducky, Petrie, and Spike happily settled in the Great Valley. But their adventures don't stop as they chase two egg-stealing Struthiomimuses and retrieve an egg of unknown origin from the Mysterious Beyond. **75m/C VHS.**

The Land Before Time 3: The Time of the Great Giving ½ 1995 (G) Littlefoot and his pals try to find a new source of water when the Great Valley experiences a severe water shortage. **71m/C VHS.** *D:* Roy Allen Smith.

The Land Before Time 4: Journey Through the Mists ½ 1996 The little dinosaurs travel through the land of the mists in search of a rejuvenation flower that can save the life of Litefoot's sick grandpa. **74m/C VHS.** *D:* Roy Allen Smith.

The Land Before Time 5: The Mysterious Island ½ 1997 (G) When a swarm of insects devour all the plants in the Great Valley, the herds are forced to move. But with the adults fighting, Littlefoot and his pals go off on their own. They cross the Big Water to a mysterious island, which just happens to be the home of their old friend, the baby T-Rex, Chomper. And it's up to Chomper to protect his plant-eating friends from the island's meat-eaters, who look on the little band as dinner. **74m/C VHS.** *D:* Charles Grosvenor.

Land Before Time 7: The Stone of Cold Fire 2000 (G) In the seventh installment of the popular kid's series, the young dinosaurs Littlefoot, Cera, Spike, Ducky, and Petrie go off in search of a meteor that only Littlefoot saw. Petrie's disreputable uncle Pterano eggs them on. The moral lessons are simple; the animation is bright; the story moves quickly. In short, the movie delivers exactly what its young fans want to see. The pidgin English dialog will be hard for adults to take. **75m/C DVD.** *D:* Charles Grosvenor; *W:* Len Uhley; *V:* Jeff Bennett, Anndi McAfee, Rob Paulsen, Thomas Dekker, Aria Noelle Curzon.

The Land Girls ½ 1998 (R) Based on the real life Women's Land Army in England, which consisted of female volunteers who helped take over the duties of farmers who were fighting WWII. Stella (McCormack), Ag (Weisz) and Prue (Friel) are three city girls who come to Dorset in rural Britain to work on the farm of crusty Mr. Lawrence (Georgeson). Since the war started he has had only his submissive wife (O'Brien) and headstrong son Joe (Mackintosh) to help him. Joe, who dreams of being a fighter pilot, ends up in bed with each of the women; but on their terms, not his own. The movie is more concerned with the hard work these women did and the historical context than with the individual characters, however. The shared sacrifice and camaraderie overshadow the romantic subplots. Shot on location in western England. **110m/C VHS.** *GB* Catherine McCormack, Rachel Weisz, Anna Friel, Steven Mackintosh, Tom Georgeson, Maureen O'Brien, Paul Bettany, Lucy Akhurst; *D:* David Leland; *W:* David Leland, Keith Dewhurst; *C:* Henry Braham; *M:* Brian Lock.

Land of Doom 1984 An amazon and a warrior struggle for survival in a post-holocaust fantasy setting. **87m/C VHS.** Deborah Rennard, Garrick Dowhen; *D:* Peter Maris.

The Land of Faraway 1987 (G) A Swedish boy is whisked off to a magical land where he does battle with evil knights and flies on winged horses. Dubbed; based on a novel by Astrid Lindgren. **95m/C VHS.** Timothy Bottoms, Christian Bale, Susannah York, Christopher Lee, Nicholas Pickard; *D:* Vladimir Grammatikov.

Land of Fury *The Seekers* 1955 British naval officer Hawkins steps on New Zealand's shore and into trouble when he accidently walks on sacred Maori burial ground. Very British, very dated colonial saga, based on the novel "The Seekers" by John Guthrie. **90m/C VHS.** *GB* Jack Hawkins, Glynis Johns, Noel Purcell, Ian Fleming; *D:* Ken Annakin.

Land of Hunted Men 1943 The Range Busters are on the case as they track down the hideout of terrorizing gunmen. **58m/B VHS.** Ray Corrigan, Dennis Moore, Max Terhune.

Land of Promise ½ *Ziemia Obiecana* 1974 At the turn of the century three men build a textile factory in Lodz, Poland. They each represent a particular ethnic group: a Pole (Olbrychski), a German (Seweryn), and a Jew (Pszoniak). Class conflicts threaten to overwhelm as their overworked and underpaid workers plan a revolt. Based on the novel by Wladyslav Reymont. In Polish with English subtitles. **178m/C VHS.** *PL* Daniel Olbrychski, Wojciech (Wojtek Psoniak) Pszoniak, Andrzej Seweryn, Anna Nehrebecka; *D:* Andrzej Wajda; *W:* Andrzej Wajda; *M:* Wojciech Kilar.

Land of the Free 1998 (R) Frank Jennings (Speakman) is the campaign manager for super-patriot Senate hopeful Aidan Carvell (a deliberately hammy Shatner). Then Jennings discovers his boss has big ambitions—he wants to take over the government as the head of a terrorist organization. **96m/C VHS.** Jeff Speakman, William Shatner, Chris Lemmon, Charles Robinson; *D:* Jerry Jameson; *W:* Terry Cunningham; *C:* Ken Blakey. **VIDEO**

Land of the Lawless 1947 A group of outlaws rule over a barren wasteland. What's the point? **54m/B VHS.** Rachel Brown, Raymond Hatton, Christine McIntyre, Tristram Coffin; *D:* Lambert Hillyer.

Land of the Minotaur *The Devil's Men* 1977 (PG) Small village is the setting for horrifying ritual murders, demons, and disappearances of young terrorists. Fans of Pleasence and Cushing won't want to miss this. **88m/C VHS.** *GB* Donald Pleasence, Peter Cushing, Luan Peters; *D:* Costa Carayiannis; *M:* Brian Eno.

Land of the Pharaohs ½ 1955 Epic about the building of Egypt's Great Pyramid. Hawkins is the extremely talkative pharoah and Collins plays his sugary-sweet yet villainous wife. Sort of campy, but worth watching for the great surprise ending. **106m/C VHS, Wide.** Jack Hawkins, Joan Collins, James Robertson Justice, Dewey Martin, Alexis Minotis, Sydney Chaplin; *D:* Howard Hawks; *W:* Harold Jack Bloom; *C:* Lee Garmes.

Land Raiders 1969 Savalas plays a man who hates Apaches and wants their land, but is distracted when his brother arrives on the scene, igniting an old feud. **101m/C VHS.** Telly Savalas, George Maharis, Arlene Dahl, Janet Landgard; *D:* Nathan (Hertz) Juran.

The Land That Time Forgot 1975 (PG) A WWI veteran, a beautiful woman, and their German enemies are stranded in a land outside time filled with prehistoric creatures. Based on the 1918 novel by Edgar Rice Burroughs. Followed in 1977 by "The People that Time Forgot." **90m/C VHS.** *GB* Doug McClure, John McEnery, Susan Penhaligon, Keith Barren, Anthony Ainley, Godfrey James, Bobby Parr, Declan Mulholland, Colin Farrell, Ben Howard, Roy Holder, Andrew McCulloch, Ron Pember, Steve James; *D:* Kevin Connor; *W:* James Cawthorn, Michael Moorcock; *C:* Alan Hume; *M:* Douglas Gamley.

The Land Unknown ½ 1957 A Naval helicopter is forced down in a tropical land of prehistoric terror, complete with ferocious creatures from the Mesozoic Era. While trying to make repairs, the crew discovers the sole survivor of a previous expedition who was driven to madness by life in the primordial jungle. Good performances from cast, although monsters aren't that believable. Based on a story by Charles Palmer. **78m/B VHS.** Jock Mahoney, Shawn Smith, William Reynolds, Henry (Kleinbach) Brandon, Douglas Kennedy; *D:* Virgil W. Vogel; *W:* Laszlo Gorog; *M:* Henry Mancini.

The Landlady 1998 (R) Melanie Leroy (Shire) kills her hubby after discovering him cheating on her. When she becomes the landlady of an apartment house, she decides one of her tenants, nice-guy Patrick (Coleman), would be ideal husband material. And Melanie intends to get rid of any obstacles in her way. **98m/C VHS, DVD.** Talia Shire, Jack Coleman, Bruce Weitz, Melissa Behr, Susie Singer, Bette Ford; *D:* Rob Malenfant; *W:* Frank Rehwaldt, George Saunders; *C:* Darko Suvak; *M:* Eric Lundmark.

Landlord Blues 1987 A trashy slumlord without morals or a conscience goes one step too far, and a tenant retaliates with munitions. **96m/C VHS.** Mark Boone Jr., Raye Dowell, Richard Litt, Bill Rice, Mary Schultz, Gigi Williams; *D:* Jacob Burckhardt.

Landscape in the Mist *Topio Stin Omichli* 1988 A stark Greek landscape in a rainy winter sets the scene for a tragic search by two children for their unknown father. Relies heavily on symbolism to make its point about unfulfilled desire (including the film's imaginary German-Greek border). In Greek with English subtitles. **126m/C VHS.** *GR FR IT* Tania Palaiologou, Michalis Zeke, Stratos Tzortzoglou, Eva Kotamanidou, Alika Georgouli; *D:* Theo Angelopoulos; *W:* Thanassis Valtinos, Tonino Guerra, Theo Angelopoulos; *C:* Yorgos Arvanitis; *M:* Eleni Karaindrou.

Landslide ½ 1992 (PG-13) As a geologist, suffering from memory loss, comes closer to discovering his identity his life is endangered by a sinister plot. **95m/C VHS.** Anthony Edwards, Tom Burlinson,

Joanna Cassidy, Melody Anderson, Ronald Lacey, Ken James, Lloyd Bochner; *D:* Jean-Claude Lord.

L'Anne Sainte 🦴🦴½ *Pilgrimage to Rome* **1978** In his last film, Gabin is an escaped convict returning to his hidden loot in Rome when his plane is hijacked by international terrorists. Available dubbed. **?m/C VHS.** *FR* Jean Gabin, Jean-Claude Brialy, Paul(o) Giusti, Danielle Darrieux.

L'Annee des Meduses 🦴½ *The Year of the Jellyfish* **1986 (R)** An 18-year-old girl tries to seduce the local Monsieur Beefcake she meets on her vacation. When he doesn't return her interest, she decides to teach him a lesson. In French with English subtitles, or dubbed. **110m/C VHS.** *FR* Valerie Kaprisky, Barnard Giradeau; *D:* Christopher Frank; *C:* Renato Berta.

Lansky 🦴🦴½ **1999 (R)** Traces some 70 years in the life of Jewish mobster Meyer Lansky (Dreyfuss), which, surprisingly, doesn't make for exciting drama. Lansky grew up on New York's Lower East Side with Benjamin "Bugsy" Siegel (Roberts) and Charlie "Lucky" Luciano (LaPaglia). Th trio would mastermind a crime syndicate, with Lansky basically serving as the Mob accountant. Story is told in flashbacks as the aged Lansky awaits federal trial in Miami. **120m/C VHS, DVD.** Richard Dreyfuss, Eric Roberts, Anthony LaPaglia, Illeana Douglas, Beverly D'Angelo, Ryan Merriman, Francis Guinan, Stanley DeSantis, Nick(y) Corello; *D:* John McNaughton; *W:* David Mamet; *C:* John A. Alonzo; *M:* George S. Clinton. **CABLE**

Lantana 🦴🦴🦴 **2001 (R)** This impressive Aussie thriller starts off as a seemingly straightforward murder mystery, but that's only the jumping-off point. The burned-out cop, Leon (LaPaglia) investigating the murder, is cheating on his wife with a woman, Jane (Blke), who may know something about the case. His wife is consulting a psychiatrist, Valerie (Hershey), whose marriage to John (Rush) has been damaged by the murder of their 11-year-old daughter. John may also be having a homosexual affair with one of his wife's patients. Jane's neighbors, Nik (Colosimo) and Paula (Farinacci) seem like the only happy ones in the mix, but they, too, are touched by the mystery. LaPaglia stands out in a brilliant cast, and the deep character studies and attention to detail add dimension to what could have been a standard whodunit. **120m/C VHS, DVD, Wide.** *AU* Anthony LaPaglia, Kerry Armstrong, Geoffrey Rush, Barbara Hershey, Rachael Blake, Vince Colosimo, Peter Phelps, Daniela Farinacci, Leah Purcell, Glenn Robbins; *D:* Ray Lawrence; *W:* Andrew Bovell; *C:* Mandy Walker; *M:* Paul Kelly. Australian Film Inst. '01: Actor (LaPaglia), Actress (Armstrong), Adapt. Screenplay, Director (Lawrence), Film, Support. Actor (Colosimo), Support. Actress (Blake).

Lantern Hill 🦴🦴½ **1990 (G)** During the Depression, a 12-year-old girl attempts to fan the embers between her estranged parents. A Wonderworks production, filmed partly on Canada's Prince Edward Island. Based on a story by Lucy Maud Montgomery, whose "Anne of Green Gables" is also part of the Wonderworks series. **112m/C VHS.** *CA* Sam Waterston, Colleen Dewhurst, Sarah Polley, Marion Bennett, Zoe Caldwell; *D:* Kevin Sullivan. **CABLE**

Lap Dancing woof! **1995 (R)** What hath "Showgirls" wrought? Small town gal Angie Parker moves to Hollywood to become an actress and, when the money runs out, winds up as an exotic dancer. Also available unrated. **90m/C VHS, DVD.** Lorissa McComas, Tane McClure, C.T. Miller; *D:* Mike Sedan; *W:* K.C. Martin; *C:* Carlos Montaner; *M:* Ron Allen, Todd Schroeder. **VIDEO**

L'Appat 🦴🦴 *Fresh Bait; Live Bait; The Bait* **1994** Deglamourizing, if familiar, look at amoral teens and violence. 18-year-old salesgirl Nathalie (Gillain) supports her unemployed boyfriend Eric (Sitruk) and his dim-bulb buddy Bruno (Putzulu). The guys hang out, watch too many gangster videos, and try to be tough, deciding to get rich by dangling Nathalie as bait. She goes to a man's home (presumably for sex) but Eric and Bruno will break in and rob the mark instead. Plan goes awry when their first victim is killed. What's truly disturbing is the trio's blase attitude that crime is a viable way to obtain money or that anything would happen to them should they be caught. Based on the book by Morgan Sportes, which recounted the 1984 crime. French with subtitles. **117m/C VHS.** *FR* Marie Gillain, Olivier Sitruk, Bruno Putzulu, Philippe Duclos, Richard Berry; *D:* Bertrand Tavernier; *W:* Bertrand Tavernier, Colo Tavernier O'Hagan; *M:* Philippe Haim. Berlin Intl. Film Fest. '94: Film.

Lara Croft: Tomb Raider 🦴🦴 *Tomb Raider* **2001 (PG-13)** Laura Croft (Jolie), the daughter of a British aristocrat/adventurer (Jolie's real-life dad Voight), gives up her upper-crusty life to hunt down ancient treasures that hold the key to controlling time before they fall into the wrong hands. Sounds straightforward enough, right? Maybe it once was but too much tinkering results in a muddled story and foggy details that do, however, divert your attention away from the cheesy dialogue and flimsy characters. Stunning sets and visuals, along with Jolie's "let's have some fun" attitude go a long way toward making this disappointment more entertaining than it probably should be. **96m/C VHS, DVD, Wide.** *US* Angelina Jolie, Iain Glen, Daniel Craig, Leslie Phillips, Jon Voight, Noah Taylor, Richard Johnson, Julian Rhind-Tutt, Chris (Christopher) Barrie; *D:* Simon West; *W:* Patrick Massett, John Zinman; *C:* Peter Menzies Jr.; *M:* Graeme Revell.

Laramie Kid 🦴 **1935** A vintage Tyler sagebrush saga. **60m/B VHS.** Tom Tyler, Alberta Vaughn, Al Ferguson, Murdock McQuarrie, George Chesebro; *D:* Harry S. Webb.

The Laramie Project 🦴🦴🦴 **2002 (R)** A docudrama that explores the 1998 gay-bashing death of Matthew Shepard in Laramie, Wyoming. Shortly after the crime, Moises Kaufman (here played by Carbonell) and members of his New York Tectonic Theater Project arrived in Laramie to interview residents and others associated with the crime. Kaufman then adapted the transcripts into a stage piece, which debuted in Denver. Kaufman himself directs the film adaptation, which includes actual news footage interspersed with actor re-creations. **87m/C VHS, DVD.** Nestor Carbonell, Peter Fonda, Amy Madigan, Janeane Garofalo, Jeremy Davies, Steve Buscemi, Christina Ricci, Mark Webber, Laura Linney, Terry Kinney; *D:* Moises Kaufman; *C:* Terry Stacey; *M:* Peter Golub. **CABLE**

L'Argent 🦴🦴 *Money* **1983** When a young man's parents refuse to lend him any money a friend helps out by giving him a counterfeit 500-franc note. This sets off a chain of events, with every passing of the money leading to another lie, betrayal, and increasingly violent crime. Austere and stylized vision is not for all tastes. In French with English subtitles. **82m/C VHS.** *FR* Christian Patey, Sylvie van den Elsen, Michel Briguet, Caroline Lang; *D:* Robert Bresson; *W:* Robert Bresson; *C:* Pasqualino De Santis. Cannes '83: Director (Bresson); Natl. Soc. Film Critics '84: Director (Bresson).

Larger Than Life 🦴½ *Nickel and Dime; Large as Life* **1996 (PG)** The pitch for this movie (Murray takes an elephant on a cross-country trip) must have sounded terrific. Unfortunately, the pitch was fouled off. Murray is his usual smarmy self as cut-rate motivational speaker Jack Corcoran, who inherits the pachyderm and a pile of bills after his circus clown father dies. Following the "road movie" formula, he encounters wacky characters along the way, including a speed-freak trucker (McConaughey), a sexy animal trainer (Fiorentino) and a strait-laced zookeeper (Garofalo). In a piece of brilliant casting, Tai, the star of "Operation Dumbo Drop" appears as...the elephant. **93m/C VHS.** Bill Murray, Janeane Garofalo, Linda Fiorentino, Matthew McConaughey, Keith David, Pat Hingle, Jeremy Piven, Lois Smith, Anita Gillette, Maureen Mueller, Harve Presnell, Tracey Walter; *D:* Howard Franklin; *W:* Roy Blount Jr.; *C:* Elliot Davis; *M:* Miles Goodman.

Larks on a String 🦴🦴🦴½ **1968** Banned for 23 years, this wonderful film is Menzel's masterpiece, even better than his Oscar winning "Closely Watched Trains." Portrays the story of life in labor camps where men and women are re-educated at the whim of the government. No matter what the hardships, these people find humor, hope and love. Their individuality will not be lost, nor their humanity dissolved. Excellent performances, tellingly directed with a beautiful sense of composition and tone. Screenplay written by Menzel and Bohumil Hrabil, author of the short story on which it is based. In Czech with English subtitles. **96m/C VHS.** *CZ* Vaclav Neckar, Jitka Zelenohorska, Jaroslav Satoransky, Rudolf Hrusinsky; *D:* Jiri Menzel; *W:* Jiri Menzel.

Larry 🦴🦴 **1974** Based on the Nevada State Hospital case history of a 26-year-old man, institutionalized since infancy, who is discovered to be of normal intelligence and must learn to live the life he has always been capable of living. **80m/C VHS.** Frederic Forrest, Tyne Daly, Katherine Helmond, Michael McGuire, Robert Walden; *D:* William A. Graham. **TV**

Larry McMurtry's Dead Man's Walk 🦴🦴½ *Dead Man's Walk* **1996 (PG-13)** McMurtry's prequel to "Lonesome Dove" focuses on the teenaged Gus McCrae (Arquette) and Woodrow Call (Miller) and their first adventures as Texas Rangers in the 1840s. They're involved in the ill-fated Texas-Santa Fe Expedition, led by parrot-owning former seafarer Caleb Cobb (Abraham), to take Santa Fe and make New Mexico part of the Texas Republic. Instead, a Mexican Army detachment led by Capt. Salazar (Olmos), captures the rag-tag group, which is then forced to march across a deadly stretch of desert that few survive. Likeable leads but the supporting actors, including Carradine and Stanton as scouts, steal the show. **271m/C VHS.** Jonny Lee Miller, David Arquette, Keith Carradine, Harry Dean Stanton, F. Murray Abraham, Edward James Olmos, Eric Schweig, Patricia Childress, Jennifer Garner, Haviland (Haylie) Morris, Brian Dennehy, Joaquim de Almeida, Ray McKinnon, Akosua Busia; *D:* Yves Simoneau; *W:* Larry McMurtry, Diana Ossana; *C:* Edward Pei; *M:* David Bell. **TV**

Larry McMurtry's Streets of Laredo 🦴🦴🦴 *Streets of Laredo* **1995** Texas Ranger-turned-bounty hunter Woodrow F. Call (a splendid Garner) is hired by the railroad to track down ruthless Mexican bandit Joey Garza (Cruz), pitting an old man's skills against a young man's daring, and driving both men across Texas, deep into Mexican territory. Call's old friend Pea Eye Parker (Shepard) reluctantly comes along, with ex-prostitute Lorena (Spacek), who's Parker's wife, and Maria (Braga), Joey's tough-but-deluded mom, providing strong support. Casual cruelty and violence are the norm in the sunset days of both Call's life and that of the west itself. Third in the TV sagas, following "Return to Lonesome Dove." **227m/C VHS.** James Garner, Alexis Cruz, Sam Shepard, Sissy Spacek, Sonia Braga, Wes Studi, Randy Quaid, Charles Martin Smith, Kevin Conway, George Carlin, Ned Beatty, James Gammon, Tristan Tait, Anjanette Comer; *D:* Joseph Sargent; *W:* Larry McMurtry, Diana Ossana; *C:* Edward Pei; *M:* David Shire. **TV**

Las Vegas Hillbillys 🦴 *Country Music* **1966** A pair of country-singing hillbillies inherit a saloon in Las Vegas and enjoy wine, moonshine, and song. These two make the Clampetts look like high society. Followed, believe it or not, by "Hillbillys in a Haunted House." ♫Money Greases the Wheel. **85m/C VHS, DVD.** Mamie Van Doren, Jayne Mansfield, Ferlin Husky, Sonny James; *D:* Arthur C. Pierce.

Las Vegas Lady 🦴 **1976 (PG)** Three shrewd casino hostesses plot a multi-million dollar heist in the nation's gambling capital. Non-captivating caper. **90m/C VHS, DVD.** Stella Stevens, Stuart Whitman, George de Cecenzo, Andrew Stevens, Lynne Moody, Linda Scruggs; *D:* Noel Nosseck; *W:* Walter Dallenbach; *C:* Stephen M. Katz; *M:* Alan Silvestri.

Las Vegas Serial Killer woof! **1986** A serial killer, let out of prison on a technicality, starts killing again. **90m/C VHS.** Pierre Agostino, Ron Jason, Tara MacGowran, Kathryn Downey. **VIDEO**

The Las Vegas Story woof! **1952** Gambling, colorful sights, and a murder provide the framework for this non-compelling fictional guided-tour of the city. Save your money for the slots. **88m/B VHS.** Victor Mature, Jane Russell, Vincent Price, Hoagy Carmichael, Brad Dexter; *D:* Robert Stevenson; *W:* Paul Jarrico.

Las Vegas Weekend 🦴 **1985** A computer nerd goes to Las Vegas and discovers fun. **83m/C VHS.** Barry Hickey, Macka Foley, Ray Dennis Steckler; *D:* Dale Trevillion; *W:* Dale Trevillion.

Laser Mission 🦴🦴½ **1990** When it is discovered that the Soviets have laser weapon capabilities, an agent is given the task of destroying the weapon and kidnapping the scientist who developed it. **83m/C VHS, DVD.** Brandon Lee, Debi Monahan, Ernest Borgnine, Werner Pochath, Graham Clarke, Maureen Lahoud, Pierre Knoessen; *D:* Beau Davis; *M:* David Knopfler.

Laser Moon 🦴🦴 **1992** A serial killer uses a surgical laser beam to kill his beautiful victims, and he strikes at every full moon. When he announces his next attack on a late-night radio talk show the police call in a beautiful rookie cop (Lords) to use as bait. **90m/C VHS, DVD.** Traci Lords, Crystal Shaw, Harrison Leduke, Bruce Carter; *D:* Douglas K. Grimm.

Laserblast woof! **1978 (PG)** Standard wimp-gets-revenge story in which a frustrated young man finds a powerful and deadly laser which was left near his home by aliens; upon learning of its devastating capabilities, his personality changes and he seeks revenge against all who have taken advantage of him. **87m/C VHS, DVD, Wide.** Kim Milford, Cheryl "Rainbeaux" Smith, Keenan Wynn, Roddy McDowall; *D:* Michael Raeburn; *W:* Frank Ray Perilli, Franne Schacht; *C:* Terry Bowen; *M:* Richard Band, Joel Goldsmith.

Laserhawk 🦴½ **1999 (PG-13)** Now here's an interesting take on the origin of species—millions of years ago carnivorous aliens planted humans as a crop on earth. Now they've returned to harvest their goods and only a band of misfits may have a chance to save humanity if they can find one of the aliens' crashed spacecraft/weapons called a Laserhawk to use against them. **102m/C VHS, DVD.** Mark Hamill, Jason James Richter, Gordon Currie, Melissa Galianos; *D:* Jean Pellerin; *W:* John A. Curtis. **VIDEO**

The Laserman 🦴🦴 **1990 (R)** Exotic black comedy about a Chinese-American scientist who, when not fending off his overbearing Jewish mother or having telepathic orgasms, is contending with a band of political terrorists. **92m/C VHS.** Marc Hayashi, Peter Wang, Tony Leung Ka-Fai, Sally Yeh, Maryann Urbano, Joan Copeland; *D:* Peter Wang; *W:* Peter Wang; *M:* Mason Daring.

Lassie 🦴🦴½ **1994 (PG)** Everyone's favorite collie returns as the Turner family moves to Virginia's Shenandoah Valley to take up sheep ranching. However, because this is the '90s, Dad meets financial disaster, and junior can't stand his stepmom. Can Lassie meet the challenges of dysfunctional family living? "What is it girl? Call a therapist?" This Lassie is a direct descendant of Pal, the original 1943 star. **92m/C VHS, DVD, Wide.** Helen Slater, Jon Tenney, Tom Guiry, Brittany Boyd, Richard Farnsworth, Frederic Forrest, Michelle Williams; *D:* Daniel Petrie; *W:* Matthew Jacobs, Gary Ross, Elizabeth Anderson; *C:* Kenneth Macmillan; *M:* Basil Poledouris.

Lassie: Adventures of Neeka **1968** America's best friend joins her Native American buddy, Neeka, for a journey through a forest in the Pacific Northwest. They camp out in a deserted settlement, pull an elderly gentleman out of a frigid pond, and risk their lives to release horses from a stable during a raging wildfire. **75m/B VHS.** Jed Allan, Mark Miranda, Robert Rockwell; *D:* Richard (Dick) Moder, Jack B. Hively.

Lassie, Come Home 🦴🦴½ **1943 (G)** In first of the Lassie series, the famed collie is reluctantly sold and makes a treacherous cross-country journey back to her original family. **90m/C VHS.** Roddy McDowall, Elizabeth Taylor, Donald Crisp, Edmund Gwenn, May Whitty, Nigel Bruce, Elsa Lanchester, J. Pat O'Malley; *D:* Fred M. Wilcox. Natl. Film Reg. '93.

Lassie from Lancashire 🦴🦴 **1938** Not the famous Collie—but here, a Colleen. A pair of struggling lovebirds try to make it in show biz against all odds, including the girl's lunatic aunt, who locks her away before an audition. **67m/B VHS.** Marjorie Brown, Hal Thompson, Marjorie Sandford, Mark Daly.

Lassie: Well of Love **1990** Various installments of the classic TV series featuring the heroic collie are combined to create a movie-length presentation for home video. Lassie takes two young pups under her paw and, in the process, loses her way. As she tries to get home, she brings joy back into the lives of two despondent children. Finally, the old girl faces death when she tumbles into an abandoned well and must depend on humans for rescue. **76m/C VHS.** Mary Gregory, Robert Donner. **TV**

Lassie's Great Adventure 🦴🦴½ **1962** Lassie and her master Timmy are swept away from home by a runaway balloon. After they land in the Canadian wilderness, they learn to rely on each other through peril and adventure. **104m/C VHS.** June Lockhart, Jon(athan) Provost, Hugh Reilly; *D:* William Beaudine; *W:* Charles "Blackie" O'Neal. **TV**

Lassiter 🦴🦴½ **1984 (R)** Selleck plays a jewel thief who is asked to steal diamonds from the Nazis for the FBI. Supporting cast adds value to what is otherwise a fairly ordinary adventure drama. **100m/C VHS.** Tom Selleck, Jane Seymour, Lauren Hutton, Bob Hoskins, Joe Regalbuto, Ed Lauter, Warren Clarke; *D:* Roger Young.

Last Action Hero 🦴🦴 **1993 (PG-13)** Newcomer O'Brien finds himself in a movie starring his idol Jack Slater, the kind of guy who never loses a fight and is impervious to gunfire and explosions (and he has a really cool car and a really big gun). Disappointing action/spoof of movies within a movie (rumored to have cost $80 million) was critically maimed and never recovered. The concept isn't new and has been done better before, though Ah-nold possesses his usual self-mocking charm, which is more than can be said for the movie. Look for lots of big stars in small roles and cameos. Cluttered with inside Hollywood gags, the script was given uncredited assistance from William Goldman. **131m/C VHS, DVD.** Arnold Schwarzenegger, Austin O'Brien, Mercedes Ruehl, F. Murray Abraham, Charles Dance, Anthony Quinn, Robert Prosky, Tom Noonan, Frank McRae, Art Carney, Bridgette Wilson; ***Cameos:*** Sharon Stone, Hammer, Chevy Chase, Jean-Claude Van Damme, Tori Spelling, Joan Plowright, Adam Ant, James Belushi, James Cameron, Tony Curtis, Timothy Dalton, Tony Danza, Edward Furlong, Little Richard, Damon Wayans, Robert Patrick; *D:* John McTiernan; *W:* David Arnott, Shane Black; *C:* Dean Semler; *M:* Michael Kamen.

The Last American Hero 🦴🦴🦴 *Hard Driver* **1973 (PG)** The true story of how former moonshine runner Junior Johnson became one of the fastest race car drivers in the history of the sport. Entertaining slice of life chronicling whiskey running and stock car racing, with Bridges superb in the lead. Based on a series of articles written by Tom Wolfe. **95m/C VHS.** Jeff Bridges, Valerie Perrine, Gary Busey, Art Lund, Geraldine Fitzgerald, Ned Beatty; *D:* Lamont Johnson; *W:* William Roberts; *M:* Charles Fox.

Last American Virgin 🦴🦴 **1982 (R)** Usual brainless teen sex comedy about three school buddies who must deal with a plethora of problems in their search for girls who are willing. Music by Blondie, The Cars, The Police, The Waitresses, Devo, U2, Human League, and Quincy Jones. **92m/C VHS.** Lawrence Monoson, Diane Franklin, Steve Antin, Louisa Moritz; *D:* Boaz Davidson; *W:* Boaz Davidson.

The Last Angry Man 🦴🦴🦴½ **1959** An old, idealistic Brooklyn doctor attracts a TV producer wanting to make a documentary about his life and career, and the two conflict. Muni was Oscar-nominated for this, his last film. **100m/B VHS.** Paul Muni, David Wayne, Betsy Palmer, Luther Adler, Dan Tobin; *D:* Daniel Mann; *C:* James Wong Howe.

The Last Assassins 🦴🦴 *Dusting Cliff Seven* **1996 (R)** Ex-CIA agent Anne Bishop (Allen) is persuaded to reunite with former commander McBride (Henriksen) for another mission. Then she discovers he has his own agenda, but when Anne tries to get out, McBride kidnaps her daughter to ensure her cooperation. **90m/C VHS, DVD.** Lance Henriksen, Nancy Allen, Floyd "Red Crow" Westerman, Dean Scofield; *D:* William H. Molina; *W:* William H. Molina, Jim Menza, Charles Philip Moore, Justin Stanley; *C:* William H. Molina; *M:* David Wurst, Eric Wurst. **VIDEO**

The Last Bastion 🦴🦴 **1984** A WWII drama emphasizing the political struggle between Churchill, MacArthur, Roosevelt, and Australia's John Curtin. **160m/C VHS.** *AU* Robert Vaughn, Timothy West.

The Last Best Sunday 🦴🦴 **1998** Mexican-American Joseph (Spain) kills the two racist thugs who beat him and hides out in the isolated home of religiously brought up classmate Lolly (Bettis), whose parents are away for the weekend. Naturally, the teens bond and then they fall in love. Not quite as obvious as it all sounds. **101m/C VHS, DVD, Wide.** Douglas Spain, Angela Bettis, Kim Darby, William Lucking, Marion Ross, Craig Wasson, Daniel Beer; *D:* Donny Most; *W:* Karen Kelly; *C:* Zoran Hochstatter; *M:* Tim Westergren.

The Last Best Year 🦴🦴½ **1990 (PG)** Basic TV tearjerker has lonely psychologist Wendy (Moore) befriending patient Jane (Peters), who has a terminal illness. **88m/C VHS.** Mary Tyler Moore, Bernadette Peters, Brian Bedford, Dorothy McGuire, Kate Reid, Kenneth Welsh; *D:* John Erman; *W:* David W. Rintels.

The Last Boy Scout 🦴🦴 **1991 (R)** Are you ready for some gunplay? Formula thriller stars Willis as a private eye and Wayans as an ex-quarterback teaming up against a football team owner who will stop at nothing to get political backing for a bill promoting legalized gambling on sports. Another variation of the violent buddy-picture by "Lethal Weapon" screenwriter Black. **105m/C VHS, DVD, Wide.** Michael (Mike) Papajohn, Morris Chestnut, Eddie Griffin, Kim Coates, Joe Santos, Tony Longo, Billy Blanks, Bruce Willis, Damon Wayans, Halle Berry, Chelsea Field, Noble Willingham, Taylor Negron, Danielle Harris, Chelcie Ross, Bruce McGill; *D:* Tony Scott; *W:* Shane Black; *C:* Ward Russell; *M:* Michael Kamen.

Last Breath 🦴🦴 *Lifebreath* **1996 (R)** Martin (Perry) is obsessively devoted to his dying wife, Chrystie (Swift), who needs a double lung transplant to survive. So Martin decides to romance lovely Gail (Carides)—with murder on his mind. Twisted ending. **90m/C VHS, DVD.** Luke Perry, Gia Carides, Francie Swift, David Margulies, Lisa Gay Hamilton, Jack Gilpin, Matt McGrath, Hillary Bailey Smith; *D:* P.J. Posner; *W:* P.J. Posner, Joel Posner; *C:* Oliver Bokelberg; *M:* Michael Kessler. **VIDEO**

The Last Bridge 🦴🦴 *Die Letzte Brucke* **1954** German doctor Schell is captured by Yugoslavian partisans during WWII and forced to tend to their wounded, gradually realizing that suffering is universal. German with subtitles. **104m/B VHS.** *AT* Maria Schell, Bernhard Wicki, Barbara Rutting, Carl Mohner; *D:* Helmut Kautner; *W:* Helmut Kautner, Norbert Kunze; *C:* Fred Kollhanek; *M:* Carol De Groof. Cannes '54: Special Jury Prize, Actress (Schell).

Last Bullet 🦴🦴 **1950** A young westerner chases after a band of outlaws to avenge the cold-blooded murder of his parents. **55m/B VHS.** James Ellison, Russell Hayden, John Cason.

The Last Butterfly 🦴🦴 **1992** Quiet Holocaust movie set in Theresienstadt, the Czechoslovak ghetto city used by the Nazis to persuade the outside world of their humane treatment of the Jews. Noted French mime Antoine Moreau (Courtenay) has fallen under suspicion by the Gestapo. He's "persuaded" to give a performance in Theresienstadt for the benefit of the visiting Red Cross but decides to subvert Nazi propaganda with his own version of "Hansel and Gretel." This time the witch feeds the children into her oven. Muted performances and screenplay (adapted from the Michael Jacot novel) heightened the film's surreal calmness. **106m/C VHS.** *CZ* Tom Courtenay, Brigitte Fossey, Freddie Jones, Ingrid Held, Linda Jablonska; *D:* Karel Kachyna; *W:* Karel Kachyna, Ota Hofman; *M:* Alex North.

Last Call 🦴 **1990 (R)** Clearly, Joe Sixpack won't rent this bimbo fest for its subtle plot. Katt, a mafiosi-cheated real estate guy, decides to even the score with the assistance of gal pal/playmate of the year Tweed, who's more than willing to compromise her position. Also features the talents of playboy emerita Stevens. Available in rated and unrated versions. **90m/C VHS.** William Katt, Shannon Tweed, Joseph Campanella, Stella Stevens, Matt Roe; *D:* Jag Mundhra. **VIDEO**

The Last Castle 🦴🦴½ **2001 (R)** Redford is Gen. Irwin, a legendary army officer sent to prison on a charge that isn't clear until well into the film. The warden of the prison, Col. Winter (Gandolfini), is a dictatorial collector of military memorabilia who clearly admires his new inmate. After overhearing a remark by Irwin disparaging his collection, Winter begins to resent him. Irwin witnesses the cruelty administered by the warden and begins to win over his fellow inmates' loyalty by restoring their pride. As Winter notices control of the men slipping away, his punishments grow worse, until finally Irwin leads the inmates in an insurrection. Although driven by powerhouse performances by Redford and Gandolfini, the plot spends too much time on the battle of wills and not enough on the background of the other inmates, while a storyline about Irwin's daughter (Wright) is dropped altogether. **133m/C VHS, DVD, Wide.** *US* Robert Redford, James Gandolfini, Mark Ruffalo, Delroy Lindo, Steve (Stephen) Burton, Paul Calderon, Samuel Ball, Clifton (Gonzalez) Collins Jr., Frank Military, George W. Scott, Brian Goodman, Michael Irby, Maurice Bullard, Jeremy Childs; *D:* Rod Lurie; *W:* Graham Yost, David Scarpa; *C:* Shelly Johnson; *M:* Jerry Goldsmith.

The Last Chance 🦴🦴🦴 **1945** A realistic look at the efforts of three WWII Allied officers to help a group of refugees escape across the Alps from Italy to Switzerland. The officers are played by former pilots who were shot down over Switzerland. In spite of this—or perhaps because of it—the acting is superb. Watch for inspirational scene of refugees singing. **105m/B VHS.** E.G. Morrison, John Hoy, Ray Reagan, Odeardo Mosini, Sigfrit Steiner, Emil Gerber; *D:* Leopold Lindtberg.

Last Chase 🦴½ **1981 (PG)** Famed race car driver becomes a vocal dissenter against the sterile society that has emerged, in this drama set in the near future. Screenplay written by Christopher Crowe under the pseudonym C.R. O'Cristopher. **106m/C VHS.** *CA* Lee Majors, Burgess Meredith, Chris Makepeace, Alexandra Stewart; *D:* Martyn Burke; *W:* Martyn Burke, Christopher Crowe. **TV**

Last Command 🦴🦴🦴🦴 **1928** Famous powerful silent film by Sternberg about a expatriate Czarist general forging out a pitiful living as a silent Hollywood extra, where he is hired by his former adversary to reenact the revolution he just left. Next to "The Last Laugh," this is considered Jannings' most acclaimed performance. Deeply ironic, visually compelling film with a new score by Gaylord Carter. **88m/B VHS.** Emil Jannings, William Powell, Evelyn Brent, Nicholas Soussanin, Michael Visaroff, Jack Raymond, Fritz Feld; *D:* Josef von Sternberg; *W:* Warren Duff; *M:* Max Steiner, Gaylord Carter. Oscars '28: Actor (Jannings).

The Last Command 🦴🦴½ **1955** Jim Bowie and his followers sacrifice their lives in defending the Alamo. A good cast holds its own against a mediocre script; battle scenes are terrific. **110m/C VHS.** Sterling Hayden, Richard Carlson, Ernest Borgnine, J. Carroll Naish, Virginia Grey, Anna Maria Alberghetti; *D:* Frank Lloyd.

The Last Contract 🦴🦴 **1986 (R)** An artist who pays his bills by working as a hitman, kills the wrong man. As a result, he must fear for his life since a counterhit is inevitable. **85m/C VHS.** Jack Palance, Rod Steiger, Bo Svenson, Richard Roundtree, Ann Turkel; *D:* Allan A. Buckhantz.

Last Cry for Help 🦴½ **1979** A psychiatrist helps a 17-year-old high school coed who, fearing she has disappointed her parents, attempts suicide. Typical melodrama that attempts to make a statement, but falls short. Definitely not the "Partridge Family." **98m/C VHS.** Linda Purl, Shirley Jones, Tony LoBianco, Murray Hamilton, Grant Goodeve; *D:* Hal Sitowitz; *M:* Miles Goodman. **TV**

Last Dance 🦴½ **1991** Five scantily clad exotic dancers are ready to compete for the title of Miss Dance-TV, but trouble ensues when the dancers start turning up dead. **86m/C VHS.** Cynthia Bassinet, Elaine Hendrix, Kurt T. Williams, Allison Rhea, Erica Ringston; *D:* Anthony Markes.

The Last Dance 🦴🦴 *Sista Dansen* **1993** Two couples, Claus and Tove (Brynolfsson, Bergstrom) and best friends Lennart and Liselott (Andersson, Froling), have a shared obsession with ballroom dance competitions and some secret desires. Seems Claus and Tove have a rocky marriage and think their friends have the perfect union. Instead, Lennart is tired of his overbearing wife and longs for Tove, to whom he was once engaged. Then Liselott's body is found beneath the pier after a competition. Swedish with subtitles. **109m/C VHS.** *SW* Helena Bergstrom, Reine Brynolfsson, Ewa Froling, Peter Andersson; *D:* Colin Nutley; *W:* Colin Nutley; *C:* Jens Fischer.

Last Dance 🦴🦴 **1996 (R)** Following closely on the heels of "Dead Man Walking," this death-row drama suffered from bad timing and was dubbed by some as "Bad Hair Walking." Stone plays a convicted murderess condemned to die in an unnamed Southern state. Morrow's the rookie attorney for the state's clemency office assigned to her case. As a bond grows between the two, he uncovers errors in her trial that his bosses would rather have him ignore. The movie makes its big mistake by centering on Morrow's callow lawyer instead of Stone's embittered con. The clock-ticking countdown to the execution (which will amuse fans of "The Player") even fails to hold attention. **103m/C VHS.** Sharon Stone, Rob Morrow, Randy Quaid, Peter Gallagher, Jack Thompson, Jayne Brook, Pamela Tyson, Skeet Ulrich, Don Harvey, Diane Sellers; *D:* Bruce Beresford; *W:* Ron Koslow; *C:* Peter James; *M:* Mark Isham.

Last Day of the War 🦴½ **1969 (PG)** A German scientist is chased by Americans and Germans as WWII winds to its conclusion. Filmed in Spain. **96m/C VHS.** *SP* George Maharis, Maria Perschy, James Philbrook, Gerard Herter; *D:* Juan Antonio Bardem.

The Last Days of Chez Nous 🦴🦴½ **1992 (R)** Armstrong's dramatic comedy about a family falling apart has Ganz as a homesick Frenchman married to controlling, successful Australian writer Harrow. Trouble starts when his wayward sister-in-law Fox returns home to live with them and his wife decides to take an extended holiday with her father. Ganz suddenly finds himself only too involved in Fox's complicated life. Self-involved characters with messy emotional lives leave viewers feeling rather distant, though cast, and particularly Ganz, strive for intimacy. **96m/C VHS.** *AU* Bruno Ganz, Lisa Harrow, Kerry Fox, Kiri Paramore, Bill Hunter, Miranda Otto; *D:* Gillian Armstrong; *W:* Helen Garner; *M:* Paul Grabowsky. Australian Film Inst. '92: Actress (Harrow).

The Last Days of Disco 🦴🦴🦴 **1998 (R)** It's the early 80s and the disco scene is still alive, although it's beginning to develop a wet, hacking cough. Oblivious to this fact are brash Charlotte (Beckinsale) and reserved Alice (Sevigny), recent college grads who work as low-level corporate drones by day and party at an exclusive Studio 54-like club by night. The girls mingle with a group of Harvard educated proto-yuppie clones that include hot shot assistant D.A. Josh (Keeslar), environmental lawyer Tom (Leonard) and ad man Jimmy (Astin). Also populating the club are assistant club manager Des (Eigeman) and shady club owner Bernie (Thornton). Sharp, funny dialogue (and plenty of it) help ease the fact that the characters are merely poor little rich kids who need to shut up and dance. **113m/C VHS, DVD.** Chloe Sevigny, Kate Beckinsale, Christopher Eigeman, MacKenzie Astin, Robert Sean Leonard, Matt Keeslar, Tara Subkoff, Jennifer Beals, David Thornton, Michael Weatherly, Burr Steers; ***D:*** Whit Stillman; ***W:*** Whit Stillman; ***C:*** John Thomas; ***M:*** Mark Suozzo.

The Last Days of Dolwyn 🦴🦴½ *Woman of Dolwyn; Dolwyn* **1949** A man banned for thievery from his Welsh village returns bent upon revenge. He plans to buy the entire district when it is designated part of a water reservoir project, but finds plans thwarted by a dowager and her stepson. Burton's first film was based on a true story. **95m/B VHS.** *GB* Edith Evans, Emlyn Williams, Richard Burton, Anthony James, Barbara Couper, Alan Aynesworth, Hugh Griffith, Roddy Hughes, Tom Jones; ***D:*** Emlyn Williams; ***W:*** Emlyn Williams.

Last Days of Frank & Jesse James 🦴½ **1986** A tired TV rehash of the well-known western legend in which the famous brothers try to be like others after their personal war against society ends. **100m/C VHS.** Johnny Cash, Kris Kristofferson, June Carter Cash, Willie Nelson, Margaret Gibson, Gail Youngs; ***D:*** William A. Graham. **TV**

The Last Days of Frankie the Fly 🦴🦴 **1996 (R)** It's gonna seem familiar because it's yet another criminal lowlife story set in L.A. but at least Hopper's presence makes this slightly more than routine. He's Frankie, a semi-pathetic petty thief with big dreams and not much talent. He works for vicious gangster Sal (Madsen) and becomes smitten with ex-junkie Margaret (Hannah), who would like to be a legit actress but is instead working in porn. When Frankie decides to impress Margaret, he naturally gets into trouble. **96m/C VHS.** Dennis Hopper, Daryl Hannah, Michael Madsen, Kiefer Sutherland, Dayton Callie, Jack McGee; ***D:*** Peter Markle; ***W:*** Dayton Callie; ***C:*** Phil Parmet; ***M:*** George S. Clinton.

The Last Days of Patton 🦴½ **1986** Depicts the aging general's autumn years as a controversial ex-Nazi defender and desk-bound WWII historian. Scott reprises his feature-film role. **146m/C VHS.** George C. Scott, Ed Lauter, Eva Marie Saint, Richard Dysart, Murray Hamilton, Kathryn Leigh Scott; ***D:*** Delbert Mann. **TV**

Last Days of Planet Earth woof! *Prophecies of Nostradamus; Catastrophe 1999; Nostradamus No Daiyogen* **1974** Really stinky Japanese doomsday movie about a scientist who charges that a build-up of pollution is responsible for giant mutant sea slugs and other environmental disasters. Dubbed. **88m/C VHS.** *JP* Tetsuro Tamba, So Yamamura, Takashi Shimura; ***D:*** Toshio Masuda.

Last Days of Pompeii 🦴🦴½ **1935** Vintage DeMille-style epic based on Lord Lytton's book, where the eruption of Vesuvius threatens noblemen and slaves alike. State-of-the-art special effects still look fantastic today. Remade in 1960; available colorized. **96m/B VHS.** Preston Foster, Alan Hale, Basil Rathbone, George L. Baxt, Louis Calhern, David Holt, Dorothy Wilson, Wryley Birch, Gloria Shea; ***D:*** Ernest B. Schoedsack; ***C:*** Jack Cardiff.

The Last Days of Pompeii 🦴🦴 *Ultimi Giorni di Pompeii* **1960** Superman Reeves plays a gladiator trying to clean up the doomed town of Pompeii in this remake of the 1935 classic. Some spectacular scenes, including the explosive climax when the mountain blows its top. **105m/C VHS.** *IT* Steve Reeves, Christine Kaufmann, Barbara Carroll, Anne Marie Baumann, Mimmo Palmara; ***D:*** Mario Bonnard; ***W:*** Sergio Leone.

The Last Detail 🦴🦴🦴🦴 **1973 (R)** Two hard-boiled career petty officers (Nicholson and Young) are commissioned to transfer a young sailor facing an eight-year sentence for petty theft from one brig to another. In an act of compassion, they attempt to show the prisoner a final good time. Nicholson shines in both the complexity and completeness of his character. Adapted from a Daryl Ponicsan novel. **104m/C VHS, DVD.** Jack Nicholson, Otis Young, Randy Quaid, Clifton James, Michael Moriarty, Carol Kane, Nancy Allen, Gilda Radner; ***D:*** Hal Ashby; ***W:*** Robert Towne; ***C:*** Michael Chapman; ***M:*** Johnny Mandel. British Acad. '74: Actor (Nicholson), Screenplay; Cannes '74: Actor (Nicholson); N.Y. Film Critics '74: Actor (Nicholson); Natl. Soc. Film Critics '74: Actor (Nicholson).

The Last Don 🦴🦴½ *Mario Puzo's The Last Don* **1997 (R)** Re-edited version of the TV miniseries finds author Puzo, of "Godfather" fame, sticking to what he knows best. The Don in question is Domenico Clericuzo (Aiello), a ruthless patriarch who wipes out the rival family his pregnant daughter Rose Marie marries into (and doesn't spare her hubby). Carrying out the Don's orders is nephew Pippi (Mantegna), an enforcer who weds Vegas showgirl Nalene (Miller) and who gets involved in the casino business. The years pass with the Don manipulating the next generation, as bloodthirsty grandchild Dante (Cochrane) fights for control with Pippi's cool-headed son Cross (Gedrick). Divided loyalties abound. A complete five-hour version of the saga is also available. **150m/C VHS, DVD.** Nick(y) Corello, Danny Aiello, Joe Mantegna, Jason Gedrick, Rory Cochrane, Penelope Ann Miller, Daryl Hannah, Kirstie Alley, Michelle Rene Thomas, David Marciano, Robert Wuhl, k.d. lang, John Colicos, Cliff DeYoung, Michael Massee; ***D:*** Graeme Clifford; ***W:*** Joyce Eliason; ***C:*** Gordon C. Lonsdale; ***M:*** Angelo Badalamenti, Roger Bellon.

The Last Don 2 🦴🦴½ *Mario Puzo's The Last Don 2* **1998 (R)** Since Don Clericuzio (Aiello) has died there's a power vacuum that forces widower Cross De Lena (Gedrick) back into the family business. The family is besieged by traitors, even as Cross gets involved in a tentative romance with his autistic stepdaughter's teacher, Josie (Kensit). Then there's crazy, vindictive Aunt Rose Marie (Alley) who falls in love with her conflicted priest (Isaacs), problems with the Hollywood studio headed by Cross's sister Claudia (Thomas), and ambitious mobster Billy D'Angelo (Wilder) for Cross to deal with. Unwittingly campy but slower moving than the first installment. **127m/C VHS, DVD.** Jason Gedrick, Kirstie Alley, Patsy Kensit, James Wilder, David Marciano, Jason Isaacs, Michelle Rene Thomas, Conrad Dunn, Robert Wuhl, Andrew Jackson, Joe Mantegna; ***Cameos:*** Danny Aiello; ***D:*** Graeme Clifford; ***W:*** Joyce Eliason; ***C:*** David Franco; ***M:*** Roger Bellon. **TV**

The Last Dragon 🦴½ *Berry Gordy's The Last Dragon* **1985 (PG-13)** It's time for a Motown kung fu showdown on the streets of Harlem, for there is scarcely enough room for even one dragon. **108m/C VHS, DVD, Wide.** Taimak, Vanity, Christopher Murney, Julius J. Carry III, Faith Prince; ***D:*** Michael A. Schultz; ***W:*** Louis Venosta; ***C:*** James A. Contner; ***M:*** Misha Segal.

Last Embrace 🦴🦴🦴 **1979 (R)** A feverish thriller in the Hitchcock style dealing with an ex-secret serviceman who is convinced someone is trying to kill him. **102m/C VHS.** Roy Scheider, Janet Margolin, Christopher Walken, John Glover, Charles Napier, Mandy Patinkin; ***D:*** Jonathan Demme; ***M:*** Miklos Rozsa.

The Last Emperor 🦴🦴🦴🦴 **1987 (PG-13)** Deeply ironic epic detailing life of Pu Yi, crowned at the age of three as the last emperor of China before the onset of communism. Follows Pu Yi from childhood to manhood (sequestered away in the Forbidden City) to fugitive to puppet-ruler to party proletariat. O'Toole portrays the sympathetic Scot tutor who educates the adult Pu Yi (Lone) in the ways of the western world after Pu Yi abdicates power in 1912. Shot on location inside the People's Republic of China with a cast of thousands; authentic costumes. Rich, visually stunning movie. The Talking Heads' David Byrne contributed to the score. **140m/C VHS, DVD, 8mm, Wide.** *IT* John Lone, Peter O'Toole, Joan Chen, Victor Wong, Ryuichi Sakamoto, Dennis Dun, Maggie Han, Ying Ruocheng, Ric Young; ***D:*** Bernardo Bertolucci; ***W:*** Mark Peploe, Bernardo Bertolucci; ***C:*** Vittorio Storaro; ***M:*** Ryuichi Sakamoto, David Byrne. Oscars '87: Adapt. Screenplay, Art Dir./Set Dec., Cinematog., Costume Des., Director (Bertolucci), Film Editing, Picture, Sound, Orig. Score; British Acad. '88: Film; Cesar '88: Foreign Film; Directors Guild '87: Director (Bertolucci); Golden Globes '88: Director (Bertolucci), Film—Drama, Screenplay, Score; L.A. Film Critics '87: Cinematog.; N.Y. Film Critics '87: Cinematog.

Last Exit to Brooklyn 🦴🦴🦴½ **1990 (R)** Hubert Selby Jr.'s shocking book comes to the screen in a vivid film. Leigh gives a stunning performance as a young Brooklyn girl caught between the Mafia, union men, and friends struggling for something better. Set in the 1950s. Fine supporting cast; excellent pacing. **102m/C VHS, Wide.** Jennifer Jason Leigh, Burt Young, Stephen Lang, Ricki Lake, Jerry Orbach, Maia Danzinger, Stephen Baldwin; ***D:*** Uli Edel; ***C:*** Stefan Czapsky. N.Y. Film Critics '89: Support. Actress (Leigh).

Last Exit to Earth 🦴🦴 *Roger Corman Presents Last Exit to Earth* **1996 (R)** Your basic male fantasy. Lusty alien babes from dying world need to find some fertile males, since the men of their home planet shoot blanks. They plan to hijack a male-inhabited spaceship that's stuck in a time-warp and has (unbeknownst to the femmes) already been taken over by hijackers. Anyway, the guys get to the planet and being aggressive male pigs decide they want to run things. **80m/C VHS.** Costas Mandylor, Kim Greist, David Groh, Hilary Shepard, Michael Cudlitz, Lisa Banes, Zoe Trilling; ***D:*** Katt Shea; ***W:*** Katt Shea. **CABLE**

The Last Fight 🦴½ **1982 (R)** Boxer risks his life and his girlfriend for a shot at the championship title. Watch and see if he could've been a contender. **85m/C VHS.** Fred Williamson, Willie Colon, Ruben Blades, Joe Spinell, Darlanne Fluegel; ***D:*** Fred Williamson.

The Last Five Days 🦴🦴 **1982** Based on the true story of a girl and her brother who, in 1943 Munich, were arrested for distributing anti-Nazi propaganda. The film covers the five days between their capture and execution. In German with English subtitles. **112m/C VHS.** *GE* Lena Stolze, Irm Hermann; ***D:*** Percy Adlon.

The Last Flight of Noah's Ark 🦴🦴½ **1980 (G)** Disney adventure concerns a high-living pilot, a prim missionary, and two stowaway orphans who must plot their way off a deserted island following the crash landing of their broken-down plane. **97m/C VHS, DVD.** Elliott Gould, Genevieve Bujold, Rick Schroder, Vincent Gardenia, Tammy Lauren; ***D:*** Charles Jarrott; ***W:*** Steven W. Carabatsos, George Arthur Bloom; ***C:*** Charles F. Wheeler; ***M:*** Maurice Jarre.

Last Flight Out: A True Story 🦴🦴 **1990** Hours before Saigon fell to the Vietcong in 1975, Vietnamese and Americans rushed to board the last commercial flight out of Vietnam. Lukewarm account of a true story. **99m/C VHS, 8mm.** James Earl Jones, Richard Crenna, Haing S. Ngor, Eric Bogosian.

Last Flight to Hell 🦴🦴 **19??** When a drug lord is kidnapped, Brown is sent to South America to rescue the slimeball. His interest in the job picks up when the drug lord's 11-on-a-scale-of-ten daughter joins him for the chase. **94m/C VHS.** Reb Brown, Chuck Connors; ***D:*** Paul D. Robinson.

The Last Fling 🦴½ **1986** When Selleca has her mind set on a romantic fling, Ritter is headed for trouble. She wants love for one night, he wants it forever. Will they solve this difference of opinion? Will true love prevail? Will Ritter consent to being used as a one-night stand? Weakly plotted and poorly acted comedy. **95m/C VHS.** John Ritter, Connie Sellecca, Scott Bakula, Shannon Tweed, Paul Sand, John Bennett Perry; ***D:*** Corey Allen; ***M:*** Charles Bernstein. **TV**

Last Four Days 🦴🦴 **1977 (PG)** A chronicle of the final days of Benito Mussolini. **91m/C VHS.** Rod Steiger, Henry Fonda, Franco Nero; ***D:*** Carlo Lizzani.

Last Frontier 🦴🦴½ **1932** Serial of 12 chapters contains shades of spectacular figures in Western history: Custer, Hickok, and others in a background of grazing buffalo, boom towns, and covered wagon trails. **216m/B VHS.** Lon Chaney Jr., Yakima Canutt, Francis X. Bushman; ***D:*** Spencer Gordon Bennet, Thomas L. Story.

Last Game 🦴🦴 **1980** A college student is torn between his devotion to his blind father and going out for the college's football team. **107m/C VHS, DVD.** Howard Segal, Ed L. Grady, Terry Alden; ***D:*** Martin Beck.

The Last Gasp 🦴½ **1994 (R)** Contractor Patrick murders the Mexican Indian who's interfering with his project and is cursed. He turns into a wild killer who must satisfy his blood lust every 20 days. Only Pacula tries to save him. Gory and predictable. **90m/C VHS.** Robert Patrick, Joanna Pacula, Vyto Ruginis, Mimi (Meyer) Craven; ***D:*** Scott McGinnis.

The Last Good Time 🦴🦴½ **1994 (R)** Old-world violinist Joseph Kopple (Mueller-Stahl), retired and living in a small Brooklyn apartment, has his world turned upside down when his street-smart neighbor Charlotte (d'Abo) seeks refuge from her abusive boyfriend Eddie (Pasdar). An unsentimental friendship develops between the two in spite of the differences in their ages, educations, and lifestyles. Terrific performance from Mueller-Stahl as the lonely but dignified old man. Based on the novel by Richard Bausch. **90m/C VHS.** Armin Mueller-Stahl, Olivia D'Abo, Maureen Stapleton, Lionel Stander, Adrian Pasdar; ***D:*** Bob Balaban; ***W:*** Bob Balaban, John McLaughlin; ***C:*** Claudia Raschke.

Last Gun **1964** A legendary gunman on the verge of retirement has to save his town from a reign of terror before turning his gun in. **98m/C VHS.** Cameron Mitchell.

The Last Hit 🦴🦴½ **1993 (R)** Michael Grant (Brown) is a professional assassin, working for the CIA, who's very good at his job. But now he's burned out and ready to retire to New Mexico for some peace and quiet. He buys a house from the widowed Anna (Adams), naturally falling in love with her. Then one last assignment comes along and, wouldn't you know, his target turns out to be Anna's father (Yulin). Based on the novel "The Large Kill" by Patrick Ruell. **93m/C VHS.** Bryan Brown, Brooke Adams, Harris Yulin; ***D:*** Jan Egleson; ***W:*** Walter Klenhard, Alan Sharp; ***M:*** Gary Chang.

Last Holiday 🦴🦴🦴 **1950** A man who is told he has a few weeks to live decides to spend them in a posh resort where people assume he is important. **89m/B VHS.** *GB* Alec Guinness, Kay Walsh, Beatrice Campbell, Wilfrid Hyde-White, Bernard Lee; ***D:*** Henry Cass; ***W:*** J.B. Priestley.

The Last Hour 🦴 **1991 (R)** A Wall Street crook crosses a Mafia punk, so the latter holds the former's wife hostage in an unfinished skyscraper. Fortunately the lady's first husband is a gung-ho cop eager to commence the DIE HARD-esque action. Undistinguished fare that gives away the climax in an opening flash-forward. **85m/C VHS.** Michael Pare, Shannon Tweed, Bobby DiCicco, Robert Pucci; ***D:*** William Sachs.

Last House on Dead End Street woof! *The Fun House* **1977 (R)** Gore galore as actors die for their art in this splatter flick about snuff films. **90m/C VHS.** Steven Morrison, Dennis Crawford, Lawrence Bornman, Janet Sorley; ***D:*** Victor Janos.

Last House on the Left 🦴🦴 *Krug and Company; Sex Crime of the Century* **1972 (R)** Two girls are kidnapped from a rock concert by a gang of escaped convicts; the girls' parents exact bloody revenge when the guilty parties pay an intended housecall. Controversial and grim low-budget shocker; loosely based on Bergman's "The Virgin Spring." **83m/C VHS.** David A(lexander) Hess, Lucy Grantham, Sandra Cassel, Mark Sheffler, Fred J. Lincoln, Jeramie Rain, Gaylord St. James, Cynthia Carr, Ada Washington, Martin Kove; ***D:*** Wes Craven; ***W:*** Wes Craven; ***C:*** Victor Hurwitz; ***M:*** David A(lexander) Hess.

The Last Hunt 🦴🦴½ **1956** Well-performed western starring Taylor as a seedy buffalo hunter who gains his identity from senseless acts of murder. When personalities clash, he seeks revenge on fellow buffalo hunter Granger. Shot in Custer National Park, the buffalo scenes were real-life attempts at keeping the animals controlled. Based on the novel by Milton Lott. **108m/C VHS.** Robert Taylor, Stewart Granger, Lloyd Nolan, Debra Paget, Russ Tamblyn, Constance Ford, Ainslie Pryor, Ralph Moody, Fred Graham, Dan(iel) White, Bill Phillips, Roy Barcroft; ***D:*** Richard Brooks; ***W:*** Richard Brooks; ***M:*** Daniele Amfitheatrof.

The Last Hunter 🦴 *Hunter of the Apocalypse* **1980 (R)** A soldier fights for his life behind enemy lines during the Vietnam War. **97m/C VHS.** *IT* Tisa Farrow, David Warbeck, Tony King, Bobby Rhodes, Margit Evelyn Newton, John Steiner, Alan Collins; ***D:*** Anthony (Antonio Margheriti) Dawson.

Last Hurrah 🦴🦴½ **1958** An aging Irish-American mayor battles corruption and political backbiting in his effort to get re-elected for the last time. Semi-acclaimed heart warmer, based on the novel by Edwin O'Connor. **121m/B VHS, DVD.** Spencer Tracy, Basil Rathbone, John Carradine, Jeffrey Hunter, Dianne Foster, Pat O'Brien, Edward Brophy, James Gleason, Donald Crisp, Ricardo Cortez, Wallace Ford, Frank McHugh, Jane Darwell; ***D:*** John Ford; ***W:*** Frank Nugent; ***C:*** Charles Lawton Jr. Natl. Bd. of Review '58: Actor (Tracy), Director (Ford).

Last Hurrah for Chivalry 🦴🦴 *Hao xia* **1978** An honorable man cannot defend his family from a ruthless enemy and turns to two swordsmen-for-hire for help. Chinese with subtitles or dubbed. **108m/C VHS, DVD, Wide.** *HK* Damian Lau, Wei Pei, San Lee Hoi; ***D:*** John Woo; ***W:*** John Woo; ***C:*** Ching Yu, Yao Chu Chang.

The Last Innocent Man 🦴🦴½ **1987** An attorney who quit law due to a guilty conscience is lured into defending a suspected murderer. Things become even more complicated when he begins having an affair with his client's seductive wife. A well-acted and suspense-filled flick. **113m/C VHS.** Ed Harris, Roxanne Hart, Bruce McGill, Clarence Williams III, Rose Gregorio, David Suchet, Darrell Larson; ***D:*** Roger Spottiswoode; ***W:*** Dan Bronson; ***M:*** Brad Fiedel. **CABLE**

The Last Laugh 🦴🦴🦴½ *Der Letzte Mann* **1924** An elderly man, who as the doorman of a great hotel was looked upon as a symbol of "upper class," is demoted to washroom attendant due to his age. Important due to camera technique and consuming performance by Jannings. Silent with music score. A 91-minute version is also available. **88m/B VHS, DVD.** *GE* Emil Jannings, Maly Delshaft, Max Hiller; ***D:*** F.W. Murnau; ***W:*** Carl Mayer; ***C:*** Karl Freund; ***M:*** Giuseppe Becce.

The Last Lieutenant 🦴🦴½ *The Second Lieutenant; Secondloitnanten* **1994** Aging Thor Espedal (Skjonberg) is a one-time second lieutenant who has just retired from the Merchant Marines and returned home to his beloved wife, Anna (Tellefsen). But since the year is 1940, his retirement is interrupted by the German Army invading his country. Espedal enlists in the resistance effort but finds the army in complete disarray. Still the old man and a group of volunteers become determined to hold a key mountain pass. Norwegian with subtitles. **102m/C VHS, DVD, Wide.** *NO* Espen Skjonberg, Bjorn Sundquist, Rut Tellefsen, Gard B. Eidsvold, Lars Andreas Larssen; ***D:*** Hans Petter Moland; ***W:*** Hans Petter Moland, Axel Hellstenius; ***C:*** Harald Gunnar Paalgard; ***M:*** Randall Meyers.

Last Light 🦴🦴 **1993 (R)** A prison guard (Whitaker) on death row forms a tenuous bond with an incorrigible inmate (Sutherland) who's about to be executed. Disturbing, especially the execution scene. Filmed on location at California's Soledad Prison. Sutherland's directorial debut. **95m/C VHS.** Kiefer Sutherland, Forest Whitaker, Clancy Brown, Lynne Moody, Kathleen Quinlan, Amanda Plummer; ***D:*** Kiefer Sutherland. **CABLE**

Last Lives 🦴🦴 **1998 (R)** Confusing parallel universe story has Malakai (Wirth) traveling to an alternate world to search for his lost wife. He discovers Adrienne (Rubin) about to marry Aaron (Howell) and Malakai kidnaps her to take her back to his world. **99m/C VHS.** C. Thomas Howell, Jennifer Rubin, Billy Wirth, Judge Reinhold; ***D:*** Worth Keeter; ***W:*** Dan Duling; ***C:*** Kent Wakeford; ***M:*** Greg Edmonson. **VIDEO**

The Last Man on Earth 🦴🦴 *L'Ultimo Uomo Della Terra* **1964** Price is the sole survivor of a plague which has turned the rest of the world into vampires, who constantly harass him. Uneven U.S./Italian production manages to convey a creepy atmosphere of dismay. **86m/B VHS, DVD, Wide.** *IT* Vincent Price, Franca Bettoya, Giacomo "Jack" Rossi-Stuart, Emma Danieli; ***D:*** Ubaldo Ragona, Sidney Salkow; ***W:*** Richard Matheson, William P. Leicester, Furio M. Menotti; ***C:*** Franco Delli Colli; ***M:*** Paul Sawtell, Bert Shefter.

Last Man Standing 🦴 **1987 (R)** A cheap, gritty drama about bare-knuckle fist fighting. Wells stars as a down-on-his-luck prizefighter trying to find work that doesn't involve pugilism. **89m/C VHS.** William Sanderson, Vernon Wells, Franco (Columbo) Columbu; ***D:*** Damian Lee.

Last Man Standing 🦴🦴 **1995 (R)** L.A. police officer Wincott discovers corruption after his partner Banks is murdered. **96m/C VHS.** Jeff Wincott, Jillian McWhirter, Jonathan Banks, Steve Eastin, Jonathan Fuller, Michael Greene, Ava Fabian; ***D:*** Joseph Merhi; ***W:*** Joseph Merhi; ***M:*** Louis Febre.

Last Man Standing 🦴🦴½ *Welcome to Jericho* **1996 (R)** Engaging, but not terribly original gangster/western features a plot taken from Clint Eastwood's career-making "Fistful of Dollars" (in turn, an adaptation of Akira Kurosawa's "Yojimbo"). The producers and credits claim lineage directly from the Kurosawa film, but this story's been around for a while, folks. In the small 1930s border town of Jericho Texas, Willis, under the pseudonym John Smith, hires himself out to both sides of a bootlegging war in an effort to make some quick cash. Bigger roles for Walken, the flinty trigger man for Irish boss Doyle (Kelly), and Dern, the town sheriff on the mob payroll, could have perked things up a little. Willis nicely injects his smirking brand of wit into a film that may have benefitted from more of the dark "Yojimbo" humor. Hill provides his trademark visually exciting action sequences. **101m/C VHS, DVD, Wide.** Bruce Willis, Bruce Dern, Christopher Walken, Karina Lombard, William Sanderson, David Patrick Kelly, Alexandra Powers, Leslie Mann, Michael Imperioli, R.D. Call, Ken Jenkins, Ned Eisenberg; ***D:*** Walter Hill; ***W:*** Walter Hill; ***C:*** Lloyd Ahern; ***M:*** Ry Cooder.

The Last Married Couple in America 🦴🦴 **1980 (R)** A couple fight to stay happily married amidst the rampant divorce epidemic engulfing their friends. **103m/C VHS.** George Segal, Natalie Wood, Richard Benjamin, Valerie Harper, Dom DeLuise, Priscilla Barnes; ***D:*** Gilbert Cates; ***M:*** Charles Fox.

The Last Marshal 🦴🦴 **1999 (R)** Tough Texas lawman Glenn is mighty riled when some no-account prisoners manage to escape from his jail. So he trails them to Miami to get them back. **102m/C VHS, DVD.** Scott Glenn, Constance Marie, Randall Batinkoff, Vincent Castellanos, John Ortiz, Raymond Cruz, William Forsythe, Lisa Boyle; ***D:*** Mike Kirton. **VIDEO**

Last Mercenary woof! **1984** An angry ex-soldier kills everyone who makes him mad. **90m/C VHS.** Tony Marsina, Malcolm Duff, Kitty Nichols, Louis Walser.

The Last Metro 🦴🦴🦴 *Le Dernier Metro* **1980 (PG)** Truffaut's alternately gripping and touching drama about a theatre company in Nazi-occupied Paris. In 1942, Lucas Steiner (Bennent) is a successful Jewish theatre director who is forced into hiding. He turns the running of the theatre over to his wife, Marion (the always exquisite Deneuve), who must contend with a pro-Nazi theatre critic (Richard) and her growing attraction to the company's leading man (Depardieu), who is secretly working with the Resistance. In French with English subtitles. **135m/C VHS, DVD.** *FR* Catherine Deneuve, Gerard Depardieu, Heinz Bennent, Jean-Louis Richard, Jean Poiret, Andrea Ferreol, Paulette Dubost, Sabine Haudepin, Maurice Risch, Jean-Pierre Klein, Martine Simonet, Franck Pasquier, Jean-Jose Richer, Laszlo Szabo, Jessica Zucman; ***D:*** Francois Truffaut; ***W:*** Francois Truffaut, Suzanne Schiffman, Jean-Claude Grumberg; ***C:*** Nestor Almendros; ***M:*** Georges Delerue. Cesar '81: Actor (Depardieu), Actress (Deneuve), Art Dir./Set Dec., Cinematog., Director (Truffaut), Film, Sound, Writing, Score.

The Last Mile 🦴🦴 **1932** The staff of a prison prepares for the execution of a celebrated murderer. **70m/B VHS.** Preston Foster, Howard Phillips, George E. Stone; ***D:*** Sam Bischoff.

The Last Movie 🦴½ *Chinchero* **1971 (R)** A movie stunt man stays in a small Peruvian town after his filming stint is over. Hopper's confused, pretentious follow-up to "Easy Rider," has a multitude of cameos but little else. Given an award by the Italians; nobody else understood it. Kristofferson's film debut; he also wrote the music. Based on a story by Hopper and Stern. **108m/C VHS.** Dennis Hopper, Julie Adams, Peter Fonda, Kris Kristofferson, Sylvia Miles, John Phillip Law, Russ Tamblyn, Rod Cameron; ***D:*** Dennis Hopper; ***W:*** Stewart Stern; ***M:*** Kris Kristofferson.

Last Night 🦴🦴🦴 **1998 (R)** It's 6 p.m. in the city of Toronto and the world will come to an end in six hours. And no one's going to save the day. So all the characters are deciding how they'd like to spend their last few hours. Patrick (McKellar) is attending a family dinner and then wants to spend his last hours alone—instead he's drawn into Sandra's (Oh) drama. She's stuck in traffic across town from her husband and Patrick tries to help her get to her rendezvous. Meanwhile, his best friend Craig (Rennie) has a few sexual conquests he still wants to make, including one with their high school French teacher, Mrs. Carlton (Bujold). Mordant humor; appealing performances. **94m/C VHS, DVD.** *CA* Don McKellar, Sandra Oh, Callum Keith Rennie, Sarah Polley, David Cronenberg, Genevieve Bujold, Tracy Wright, Roberta Maxwell, Robin Gammell, Karen Glave, Jackie Burroughs; ***D:*** Don McKellar; ***W:*** Don McKellar; ***C:*** Douglas Koch; ***M:*** Alexina Louie, Alex Pauk. Genie '98: Actress (Oh), Support. Actor (Rennie).

Last Night at the Alamo 🦴🦴🦴 **1983** Patrons fight to stop the destruction of their Houston bar, the Alamo, which is about to be razed to make room for a modern skyscraper. Insightful comedy written by the author of "The Texas Chainsaw Massacre." **80m/B VHS.** Sonny Carl Davis, Lou Perry, Steve Matilla, Tina Hubbard, Doris Hargrave; ***D:*** Eagle Pennell; ***W:*** Ken Henkel; ***M:*** Wayne Bell.

The Last of England 🦴🦴🦴½ **1987** A furious non-narrative film by avant-garde filmmaker Jarman, depicting the modern British landscape as a funereal, waste-filled rubble-heap—as depleted morally as it is environmentally. **87m/C VHS.** *GB* Tilda Swinton, Spencer Leigh, Spring, Gerrard McArthur; ***D:*** Derek Jarman; ***W:*** Derek Jarman; ***C:*** Derek Jarman, Richard Helsop, Christopher Hughes; ***M:*** Simon Fisher Turner.

The Last of His Tribe 🦴🦴 **1992 (PG-13)** In 1911 an anthropologist befriends an Indian and discovers that Ishi is the last surviving member of California's Yahi tribe. Ishi then becomes a media and scientific society darling, spending the remainder of his remaining life in captivity to academia. A good portrayal of the Native American plight. Based on a true story. **90m/C VHS.** Jon Voight, Graham Greene, David Ogden Stiers, Jack Blessing, Anne Archer, Daniel Benzali; ***D:*** Harry Hook. **CABLE**

The Last of Mrs. Cheyney 🦴🦴🦴 **1937** Remake of Norma Shearer's 1929 hit, based on the play by Frederick Lonsdale, about a sophisticated jewel thief in England. Crawford stars as the jewel thief who poses as a wealthy woman to get into parties hosted by London bluebloods. Dripping with charm, she works her way into Lord Drilling's mansion where she plans a huge heist. The film is handled well, and the cast gives solid performances throughout. This chic comedy of high society proved to be one of Crawford's most popular films of the '30s. **98m/B VHS.** Joan Crawford, Robert Montgomery, William Powell, Frank Morgan, Nigel Bruce, Jessie Ralph; ***D:*** Richard Boleslawski, George Fitzmaurice; ***C:*** George J. Folsey.

The Last of Mrs. Lincoln 🦴🦴½ **1976** Intimate made for TV portrayal of the famous first lady. Film focuses on Mary Todd Lincoln's life from the assassination of her husband, through her autumn years, and her untimely downfall. **118m/C VHS.** Julie Harris, Robby Benson, Patrick Duffy. **TV**

The Last of Philip Banter 🦴½ **1987 (R)** An alcoholic writer is terrified to learn events in his life exactly match a mysterious manuscript. **105m/C VHS.** Tony Curtis, Gregg Henry, Irene Miracle, Scott Paulin, Kate Vernon; ***D:*** Herve Hachuel.

The Last of Sheila 🦴🦴½ **1973 (PG)** A movie producer invites six big-star friends for a cruise aboard his yacht, the "Sheila." He then stages an elaborate "Whodunnit" parlor game to discover which one of them murdered his wife. **119m/C VHS.** Richard Benjamin, James Coburn, James Mason, Dyan Cannon, Joan Hackett, Raquel Welch, Ian McShane; ***D:*** Herbert Ross; ***W:*** Anthony Perkins, Stephen Sondheim; ***M:*** Billy Goldenberg.

The Last of the Blonde Bombshells 🦴🦴½ **2000 (PG-13)** Elizabeth (Dench) played sax with the all-girl swing band, The Blonde Bombshells, during WWII. With the urgings of granddaughter Joan (Findlay) and drummer Patrick (Holm)—who played in drag—Elizabeth is encouraged to reunite the band members. If they can find them and get them to agree. Good cast but the charm is on the low-burner and rather than swinging, it's more a sedate fox-trot. **80m/C VHS, DVD, Wide.** Judi Dench, Ian Holm, Olympia Dukakis, Leslie Caron, Cleo Laine, Joan Sims, Billie Whitelaw, June Whitfield, Felicity Dean, Valentine Pelka, Millie Findlay; ***D:*** Gilles Mackinnon; ***W:*** Alan Plater; ***C:*** Richard Greatrex; ***M:*** John Keane. **CABLE**

Last of the Clintons 🦴½ **1935** A range detective tracks an outlaw gang amid spur jinglin', sharp shootin' and cow punchin'. **64m/B VHS.** Harry Carey Sr.

Last of the Comanches 🦴🦴 *The Sabre and the Arrow* **1952** Cavalry and Indians fight for water when both are dying of thirst in the desert. **85m/C VHS.** Broderick Crawford, Barbara Hale, John Stewart, Lloyd Bridges, Mickey Shaughnessy, George Mathews; ***D:*** Andre de Toth.

The Last of the Dogmen 🦴🦴½ **1995 (PG)** Cliched modern western with an intriguing premise and good actors. Montana bounty hunter Lewis Gates (Berenger) is recruited to nab three escaped cons but finds them dead and a Cheyenne arrow nearby. Gates does some investigating (in a library no less!) and discovers that maybe some descendants of the 1864 Sand Creek massacre are existing in the woods. He gets anthropologist Lillian Sloan (Hershey) involved, discovers a tribe of modern-day dog soldiers, and finds a very angry sheriff (Smith) on their trail. Alberta, Canada passes for Big Sky country. **117m/C VHS, DVD, Wide.** Tom Berenger, Barbara Hershey, Kurtwood Smith, Steve Reevis, Andrew Miller, Gregory Scott Cummins; ***D:*** Tab Murphy; ***W:*** Tab Murphy; ***C:*** Karl Walter Lindenlaub; ***M:*** David Arnold; ***Nar:*** Wilford Brimley.

The Last of the Finest 🦴½ *Street Legal; Blue Heat* **1990 (R)** Overzealous anti-drug task force cops break the rules in trying to put dealer-drug lords in prison; ostensibly a parallel on the Iran-Contra affair. **106m/C VHS.** Brian Dennehy, Joe Pantoliano, Jeff Fahey, Bill Paxton, Deborra-Lee Furness, Guy Boyd, Henry Darrow, Lisa Jane Persky, Michael C. Gwynne; ***D:*** John MacKenzie; ***W:*** George Armitage, Jere P. Cunningham; ***M:*** Jack Nitzsche.

The Last of the High Kings 🦴🦴½ *Summer Fling* **1996 (R)** Underachieving Irish Frankie (Leto) decides to forget about his university entrance exams and enjoy his summer (it's 1977) by cutting loose and fantasizing about various girls he knows. What he doesn't realize is that young American Erin (Ricci), who's staying with his crazy family, has fallen for him. Pleasant romance with a talented cast. Based on the novel "The Last of the High Kings" by Ferdia Mac Anna. **103m/C VHS.** *IR GB DK* Catherine O'Hara, Jared Leto, Christina Ricci, Gabriel Byrne, Stephen Rea, Colm Meaney, Lorraine Pilkington, Jason Barry, Emily Mortimer, Karl Hayden, Ciaran Fitzgerald, Darren Monks, Peter Keating, Alexandra Haughey, Renee Weldon, Amanda Shun; ***D:*** David Keating; ***W:*** David Keating, Gabriel Byrne; ***C:*** Bernd Heinl; ***M:*** Michael Convertino.

The Last of the Mohicans 1920 Color tints enhance this silent version of the James Fenimore Cooper rouser. Beery is the villanious Magua, with Bedford memorable as the lovely Cora and Roscoe as the brave Uncas. Fine action sequences, including the Huron massacre at Fort Henry. Director credit was shared when Tourneur suffered an on-set injury and was off for three months. **75m/B VHS, DVD.** Wallace Beery, Barbara Bedford, Albert Roscoe, Lillian Hall-Davis, Henry Woodward, James Gordon, George Hackathorne, Harry Lorraine, Nelson McDowell, Theodore Lorch, Boris Karloff; ***D:*** Maurice Tourneur, Clarence Brown; ***W:*** Robert Dillon; ***C:*** Charles Van Enger. Natl. Film Reg. '95.

The Last of the Mohicans 1932 Serial based on James Fenimore Cooper's novel of the life-and-death struggle of the Mohican Indians during the French and Indian War. Twelve chapters, 13 minutes each. Remade as a movie in 1936 and 1992 and as a TV movie in 1977. **230m/B VHS.** Edwina Booth, Harry Carey Sr., Hobart Bosworth, Frank "Junior" Coghlan; ***D:*** Ford Beebe, B. Reeves Eason.

The Last of the Mohicans ½ 1936 James Fenimore Cooper's classic about the French and Indian War in colonial America is brought to the screen. Remake of the 1932 serial. **91m/B VHS.** Randolph Scott, Binnie Barnes, Bruce Cabot, Henry Wilcoxon, Heather Angel, Hugh Buckler; ***D:*** George B. Seitz.

The Last of the Mohicans 1985 The classic novel by James Fenimore Cooper about the scout Hawkeye and his Mohican companions, Chingachgook and Uncas, during the French and Indian War, comes to life in this TV film. **97m/C VHS.** Steve Forrest, Ned Romero, Andrew Prine, Don Shanks, Robert Tessier, Jane Actman; ***D:*** James L. Conway. **TV**

The Last of the Mohicans 1992 (R) It's 1757, at the height of the French and English war in the American colonies, with various Native American tribes allied to each side. Hawkeye (Day-Lewis), a white frontiersman raised by the Mohicans, wants nothing to do with either "civilized" side, until he rescues the beautiful Cora (Stowe) from the revenge-minded Huron Magua (Studi in a powerful performance). Graphically violent battle scenes are realistic, but not gratuitous. The real pleasure in this adaptation, which draws from both the James Fenimore Cooper novel and the 1936 film, is in its lush look and attractive stars. Means is terrific in his film debut as Hawkeye's foster-father. Released in a letterbox format to preserve the original integrity of the film. **114m/C VHS, DVD, Wide.** Daniel Day-Lewis, Madeleine Stowe, Wes Studi, Russell Means, Eric Schweig, Jodhi May, Steven Waddington, Maurice Roeves, Colm Meaney, Patrice Chereau, Pete Postlethwaite, Terry Kinney, Tracey Ellis, Dennis Banks, Dylan Baker; ***D:*** Michael Mann; ***W:*** Christopher Crowe, Michael Mann; ***C:*** Dante Spinotti; ***M:*** Trevor Jones, Randy Edelman. Oscars '92: Sound.

Last of the Pony Riders ½ 1953 When the telegraph lines linking the East and West Coasts are completed, Gene and the other Pony Express riders find themselves out of a job. Autry's final feature film. **59m/B VHS.** Gene Autry, Smiley Burnette, Kathleen Case; ***D:*** George Archainbaud.

Last of the Red Hot Lovers ½ 1972 (PG) Not so funny adaptation of Neil Simon's Broadway hit. Middle-aged man decides to have a fling and uses his mother's apartment to seduce three very strange women. **98m/C VHS.** Alan Arkin, Paula Prentiss, Sally Kellerman, Renee Taylor; ***D:*** Gene Saks; ***W:*** Neil Simon.

The Last of the Redmen ½ 1947 An adaptation of James Fenimore Cooper's "The Last of the Mohicans" geared toward youngsters. Hall must lead three children of a British general through dangerous Indian territory. They have a number of adventures including meeting up with Uncas, the last of the Mohicans, who's a villain in this mangled version. **79m/B VHS.** Jon Hall, Michael O'Shea, Evelyn Ankers, Julie (Jacqueline Wells) Bishop, Buster Crabbe, Rick Vallin, Frederick Worlock, Guy Hedlund; ***D:*** George Sherman; ***W:*** Herbert Dalmas.

Last of the Warrens 1936 A cowboy returns home after WWI to discover that an unscrupulous storekeeper has stolen his property. **56m/C VHS.** Bob Steele, Charles "Blackie" King, Lafe (Lafayette) McKee, Margaret Marquis, Horace Murphy; ***D:*** Robert North Bradbury.

Last of the Wild Horses ½ 1949 Range war almost starts when ranch owner is accused of trying to force the small ranchers out of business. **86m/B VHS.** Mary Beth Hughes, James Ellison, Jane Frazee.

The Last Outlaw 1927 Action-packed western with Cooper following his success of "Wings" with Paramount. Most excellent equine stunts. **61m/B VHS.** Gary Cooper, Jack Luden, Betty Jewel; ***D:*** Arthur Rosson.

Last Outlaw 1936 The last of the famous badmen of the old West is released from jail and returns home to find that times have changed. The action climaxes in an old-time blazing shoot-out. **79m/B VHS.** Harry Carey Sr., Hoot Gibson, Henry B. Walthall, Tom Tyler, Russell Hopton, Alan Curtis, Harry Woods, Barbara Pepper; ***D:*** Christy Cabanne.

The Last Outlaw ½ 1993 (R) Rourke stars as an ex-Confederate officer who leads a gang of outlaws until his violent excesses leave even them disgusted. The gang shoots Rourke but of course he doesn't die and then he sets out for revenge. **90m/C VHS.** Mickey Rourke, Dermot Mulroney, Ted Levine, John C. McGinley, Steve Buscemi, Keith David; ***D:*** Geoff Murphy; ***W:*** Eric Red. **CABLE**

The Last Picture Show 1971 (R) Slice of life/ nostalgic farewell to an innocent age, based on Larry McMurtry's novel. Set in Archer City, a backwater Texas town, most of the story plays out at the local hangout run by ex-cowboy Sam the Lion (Johnson). Duane (Bridges) is hooked up with spoiled pretty girl Jacy (Shepherd), while Sonny (Bottoms), a sensitive guy, is having an affair with the coach's neglected wife, Ruth (Leachman). Loss of innocence, disillusionment and confusion are played out against the backdrop of a town about to close its cinema. Shepherd's and Bottoms' film debut. Stunningly photographed in black and white (Bogdanovich claimed he didn't want to "prettify" the picture by shooting in color) by Robert Surtees. Followed by a weak sequel, "Texasville." **118m/B VHS, DVD, Wide.** Jeff Bridges, Timothy Bottoms, Ben Johnson, Cloris Leachman, Cybill Shepherd, Ellen Burstyn, Eileen Brennan, Clu Gulager, Sharon Taggart, Randy Quaid, Sam Bottoms, Bill (Billy) Thurman, John Hillerman; ***D:*** Peter Bogdanovich; ***W:*** Peter Bogdanovich, Larry McMurtry; ***C:*** Robert L. Surtees. Oscars '71: Support. Actor (Johnson), Support. Actress (Leachman); British Acad. '72: Screenplay, Support. Actor (Johnson), Support. Actress (Leachman); Golden Globes '72: Support. Actor (Johnson); Natl. Bd. of Review '71: Support. Actor (Johnson), Support. Actress (Leachman), Natl. Film Reg. '98;; N.Y. Film Critics '71: Screenplay, Support. Actor (Johnson), Support. Actress (Burstyn); Natl. Soc. Film Critics '71: Support. Actress (Burstyn).

The Last Place on Earth 1994 Saga of bitter hardship and ambition depicting the 1911 race between the British Antarctic Expedition, led by Captain Robert Falcon (Shaw), and his Norwegian rival Roald Amundsen (Ousdal) to conquer the South Pole. On seven cassettes. **385m/C VHS, DVD.** *CA* Martin Shaw, Sverre Anker Ousdal, Max von Sydow, Susan Wooldridge; ***D:*** Ferdinand Fairfax; ***W:*** Trevor Griffiths; ***C:*** John Coquillon; ***M:*** Trevor Jones.

Last Plane Out ½ 1983 (R) A Texas journalist sent out on assignment to Nicaragua falls in love with a Sandanista rebel. Based on producer Jack Cox's real-life experiences as a journalist during the last days of the Samosa regime. Low-budget propaganda. **90m/C VHS.** Jan-Michael Vincent, Lloyd Batista, Julie Carmen, Mary Crosby, David Huffman, William Windom; ***D:*** David Nelson.

The Last Polka 1984 SCTV vets Candy and Levy are Yosh and Stan Schmenge, polka kings interviewed for a "documentary" on their years in the spotlight and on the road. Hilarious spoof on Martin Scorsese's "The Last Waltz," about The Band's last concert. Several fellow Second City-ers keep the laughs coming. If you liked SCTV or "This Is Spinal Tap," you'll like this. **54m/C VHS.** John Candy, Eugene Levy, Rick Moranis, Robin Duke, Catherine O'Hara; ***D:*** John Blanchard. **CABLE**

The Last Porno Flick 1974 (PG) A pornographic movie script winds up in the hands of a couple of goofy cab drivers. The twosome sneak the movie's genre past the producers, families, and police. **90m/C VHS.** Michael Pataki, Marianna Hill, Carmen Zapata, Mike Kellin, Colleen Camp, Tom Signorelli, Antony Carbone; ***D:*** Ray Marsh.

The Last Prostitute 1991 (PG-13) Two teenage boys search for a legendary prostitute to initiate them into manhood, only to discover that she has retired. They hire on as laborers on her horse farm, and one of them discovers the meaning of love. **93m/C VHS.** Sonia Braga, Wil Wheaton, David Kaufman, Woody Watson, Dennis Letts, Cotter Smith; ***D:*** Lou Antonio; ***W:*** Carmen Culver. **CABLE**

The Last Remake of Beau Geste 1977 (PG) A slapstick parody of the familiar Foreign Legion story from the Mel Brooks-ish school of loud genre farce. Gary Cooper makes an appearance by way of inserted footage from the 1939 straight version. **85m/C VHS.** Marty Feldman, Ann-Margret, Michael York, Peter Ustinov, James Earl Jones; ***D:*** Marty Feldman; ***W:*** Marty Feldman, Chris Allen.

Last Resort *She Knew No Other Way* 1986 (R) A married furniture executive unknowingly takes his family on vacation to a sex-saturated, Club Med-type holiday spot, and gets more than he anticipated. **80m/C VHS, DVD.** Charles Grodin, Robin Pearson Rose, John Aston, Ellen Blake, Megan Mullally, Christopher Ames, Jon Lovitz, Scott Nemes, Gerrit Graham, Mario Van Peebles, Phil Hartman, Mimi Lieber, Steve Levitt; ***D:*** Zane Buzby; ***W:*** Jeff Buhai; ***C:*** Stephen M. Katz, Alex Nepomniaschy; ***M:*** Steven Nelson, Thom Sharp.

The Last Reunion ½ 1980 The only witness to a brutal killing of a Japanese official and his wife during WWII seeks revenge on the guilty American platoon, 33 years later. Violent. **98m/C VHS.** Cameron Mitchell, Leo Fong, Chanda Romero, Vic Silayan, Hal Bokar, Philip Baker Hall; ***D:*** Jay Wertz.

The Last Ride 1991 Another movie probing the dark side of hitchhiking. This time our hero thumbs a ride with a truck driver who plans to bypass the next city...for hell. **84m/C VHS.** Dan Ranger, Michael Hilow.

The Last Ride *F.T.W* 1994 (R) Frank T. Wells (Rourke) is out of prison after 10 years and free to try to recapture his former rodeo glory. Hellcat Scarlett Stuart's on the run from a botched bank job/murder perpetrated by her vicious brother Clem (Berg). Scarlett manages to hook up with Frank and decides to help him out financially by robbing convenience stores. Frank's not too happy when he finds out. Rourke is surprisingly subdued and Singer's properly unsympathetic but they don't seem to be working in the same movie. Nice Montana scenery though. **102m/C VHS, DVD.** Mickey Rourke, Lori Singer, Brion James, Peter Berg, Rodney A. Grant, Aaron Neville; ***D:*** Michael Karbelnikoff; ***W:*** Mari Kornhauser; ***C:*** James L. Carter; ***M:*** Gary Chang.

The Last Ride of the Dalton Gang 1979 A long-winded retelling of the wild adventures that made the Dalton gang legendary among outlaws. **146m/C VHS.** Larry Wilcox, Jack Palance, Randy Quaid, Cliff (Potter) Potts, Dale Robertson, Don Collier; ***D:*** Dan Curtis.

The Last Riders 1990 (R) Motorcycle centaur Estrada revs a few motors fleeing from cycle club cronies and crooked cops. Full throttle foolishness. **90m/C VHS.** Erik Estrada, William Smith, Armando Silvestre, Kathrin Lautner; ***D:*** Joseph Merhi.

Last Rites 1988 (R) A priest at St. Patrick's Cathedral in New York allows a young Mexican woman to seek sanctuary from the Mob, who soon come after both of them. **103m/C VHS.** Tom Berenger, Daphne Zuniga, Chick Vennera, Dane Clark, Carlo Pacchi, Anne Twomey, Paul Dooley, Vassili Lambrinos; ***D:*** Donald P. Bellisario; ***W:*** Donald P. Bellisario; ***C:*** David Watkin; ***M:*** Bruce Broughton.

Last Rites 1998 (R) Dillon (Quaid) is a Florida Death Row serial killer, whose execution goes awry when the electric chair blows the generator and Dillon is left with amnesia. Oh, and he's suddenly gained psychic powers that allow him to solve crimes. A shrink (Davidtz) is brought in to see if he's faking, while the warden just wants to try fying Dillon again. **88m/C VHS.** Randy Quaid, Embeth Davidtz, A. Martinez; ***D:*** Kevin Dowling; ***W:*** Richard Outten, Tim Frost. **CABLE**

The Last Safari ½ 1967 A young man on professional safari in Africa befriends a bitter professional guide in a drama hampered by a poor script. Granger and Garas set out to hunt the rampaging elephant which killed Granger's friend. Granger thinks killing the beast will restore his courage and help him overcome the guilt he feels. Based on the novel "Gilligan's Last Elephant" by Gerald Hanley. **111m/C VHS.** Stewart Granger, Kaz Garas, Gabriella Licudi, Johnny Sekka, Liam Redmond; ***D:*** Henry Hathaway; ***W:*** John Gay; ***C:*** Ted Moore.

The Last Samurai 1990 (R) Arab arms dealer Saxon arranges a fake kidnapping by rebel military leader Cele in order to keep their weapons deal a secret. But among the other hostages is mercenary Hendricksen, who escapes and wrecks havoc on their plotting. **94m/C VHS.** Lance Henriksen, John Saxon, Henry Cele, Arabella Holzbog, John Fujioka, James Ryan, Duncan Regehr, Lisa Eilbacher; ***D:*** Paul Mayersberg.

The Last Season woof! 1987 Shoot 'em up involving a bunch of hunters. Their aimless destruction provokes the good guy to save the forest they are demolishing. A battle ensues. **90m/C VHS.** Christopher Gosch, Louise Dorsey, David Cox; ***D:*** Raja Zahr.

The Last Seduction 1994 (R) Dahl, the master of modern noir, delivers another stylish hit exploring the darker side of urban life. Fiorentino gives the performance of her life as the most evil, rotten femme fatale to ever hit the big screen. Bridget (Fiorentino) rips off the money her husband Clay (Pullman) made in a pharmaceutical drug deal and leaves Manhattan for a small town in Upstate New York. Once there, she takes nice, naive Mike (Berg) as her lover, while Clay tries to ferret her out and get his money back. Lots of dry humor and a wickedly amusing heroine make for a devilishly entertaining film. **110m/C VHS.** Linda Fiorentino, Peter Berg, J.T. Walsh, Bill Nunn, Bill Pullman; ***D:*** John Dahl; ***W:*** Steve Barancik; ***C:*** Jeffrey Jur; ***M:*** Joseph Vitarelli. Ind. Spirit '95: Actress (Fiorentino); N.Y. Film Critics '94: Actress (Fiorentino).

The Last Seduction 2 1998 (R) Low-rent sequel finds Bridget Gregory (Severance) enjoying her spoils in Barcelona where she runs a scam on a phone sex service to get even more cash. But a detective, Murphy (Goddard), has been hired to track Bridget down—only the femme fatale has no intention of getting caught. Severance looks sexy but can't match predecessor Fiorentino's cold-blooded wiles. **96m/C VHS.** Joan Severance, Beth Goddard, Con O'Neill, Rocky Taylor, Dave Atkins; ***D:*** Terry Marcel; ***W:*** David Cummings; ***C:*** Geza Sinkovics; ***M:*** Jon Mellor. **VIDEO**

The Last September 1999 (R) Danielstown is an Anglo-Irish estate located in County Cork in 1920—just four years after the Irish rebellion of 1916. Sir Richard (Gambon) and his wife, Lady

Myra (Smith), have a houseful of guests, including Richard's overly-romantic young niece Lois (Hawes), who's flirting with British officer, Gerald Colthurst (Tennant). But Lois has also taken to frequently visiting an old mill—where Irish guerilla fighter Peter (Lydon) is hiding out. Based on the novel by Elizabeth Bowen; first-time film director Warner is best known for her long career in the theatre. **103m/C VHS, DVD, Wide.** *IR GB FR* Maggie Smith, Michael Gambon, Keeley Hawes, David Tennant, Gary Lydon, Fiona Shaw, Lambert Wilson, Jane Birkin, Jonathan Slinger, Richard Roxburgh; ***D:*** Deborah Warner; ***W:*** John Banville; ***C:*** Slawomir Idziak; ***M:*** Zbigniew Preisner.

The Last Slumber Party woof! **1987** A slumber party is beset by a homicidal maniac. Heavy metal soundtrack. **89m/C VHS.** Jan Jensen, Nancy Meyer.

Last Song 🦴½ **1980 (PG)** A singer's husband discovers a plot to cover up a fatal toxic-waste accident, and is killed because of it. It's up to her to warn the authorities before becoming the next victim. **96m/C VHS.** Lynda Carter, Ronny Cox, Nicholas Pryor, Paul Rudd, Jenny O'Hara; ***D:*** Alan J. Levi.

Last Stand at Saber River 🦴🦴½ **1996** Adaptation of Elmore Leonard's 1959 western novel finds Confederate Civil War vet Paul Cable (Selleck) coming home to his wife Martha's (Amis) family in Texas, having been wounded in the fighting. However, Martha was informed he was dead, so imagine her surprise. What Cable wants to do now is return to his pre-war life—a horse ranch in Arizona—but after making the journey the family discovers their ranch has been taken over by Union sympathizer Duane Kidston (Carradine) and he's not intending to let it go. Selleck was born to ride tall in the saddle. **95m/C VHS.** Tom Selleck, Suzy Amis, David Carradine, Keith Carradine, David Dukes, Tracey Needham, Rachel Duncan, Haley Joel Osment, Harry Carey Jr., Lumi Cavazos, Patrick Kilpatrick; ***D:*** Dick Lowry; ***W:*** Ronald M. Cohen; ***C:*** Ric Waite; ***M:*** David Shire. **CABLE**

The Last Starfighter 🦴🦴 **1984 (PG)** A young man who becomes an expert at a video game is recruited to fight in an inter-galactic war. Listless adventure which explains where all those video games come from. Watch for O'Herlihy disguised as a lizard. **100m/C VHS, DVD, Wide.** Lance Guest, Robert Preston, Barbara Bosson, Dan O'Herlihy, Catherine Mary Stewart, Cameron Dye, Kimberly Ross, Wil Wheaton; ***D:*** Nick Castle; ***W:*** Jonathan Betuel; ***C:*** King Baggot; ***M:*** Craig Safan.

The Last Stop 🦴🦴½ **1999 (R)** Colorado State Trooper Jason (Beach) gets stranded because of a snowstorm at the remote "The Last Stop Cafe and Motel." He greets the other stranded souls who include his ex-girlfriend Nancy (McGowan) and soon finds out that owner Fritz (Prochnow) has stumbled on a murder and a bag of cash that's probably the loot from a recent bank robbery. So just who's guilty? **94m/C VHS, DVD, Wide.** *CA* Adam Beach, Juergen Prochnow, Rose McGowan, Callum Keith Rennie, Winston Rekert; ***D:*** Mark Malone; ***W:*** Bart Sumner; ***C:*** Tony Westman; ***M:*** Terry Frewer.

Last Summer 🦴🦴½ **1969 (R)** Three teenagers discover love, sex, and friendship on the white sands of Fire Island, N.Y. The summer vacation fantasy world they create shatters when a sweet but homely female teenager joins their group. Based on a novel by Evan Hunter. **97m/C VHS.** Barbara Hershey, Richard Thomas, Bruce Davison, Cathy Burns; ***D:*** Frank Perry.

Last Summer In the Hamptons 🦴🦴🦴 **1996 (R)** In her last film, Lindfors stars as Helena Mora, the matriarch of a charming three generation theatrical clan that gets together one weekend a year at her spacious, slightly run-down estate to participate in drama workshops and perform plays. When Helena is forced to sell the estate, the family reunites for one last weekend of bickering and performing. Featuring fine performances from the entire ensemble (including Lindfors' son and Jaglom's wife), Jaglom's touching and engaging tribute to his family gives nepotism a good name. **105m/C VHS.** Victoria Foyt, Viveca Lindfors, Jon Robin Baitz, Andre Gregory, Melissa Leo, Martha Plimpton, Roddy McDowall, Nick Gregory, Savannah Smith Boucher, Roscoe Lee Browne, Ron Rifkin, Diane Salinger, Brooke Smith, Kristopher Tabori, Holland Taylor, Henry Jaglom; ***D:*** Henry Jaglom; ***W:*** Victoria Foyt, Henry Jaglom; ***C:*** Hanania Baer; ***M:*** Johnny Mercer, Harold Arlen.

The Last Supper 🦴🦴🦴 **1976** A repentant Cuban slave-owner in the 18th-century decides to cleanse his soul and convert his slaves to Christianity by having 12 of them reenact the Last Supper. Based on a true story. In Spanish with English subtitles. **110m/C VHS.** *CU* Nelson Villagra, Silvano Rey, Lamberto Garcia, Jose Antonio Rodriguez, Samuel Claxton, Mario Balmasada; ***D:*** Tomas Gutierrez Alea.

The Last Supper 🦴🦴½ **1996 (R)** First-time feature director Title dishes out an extremely black comedy about a group of liberal roommates who accidentally kill a racist marine they've invited to dinner. This leads to the devious plan of inviting more right wingers over, baiting them into arguments about controversial topics, then killing and burying them in a vegetable garden. Somehow manages to avoid excessive preachiness despite taking on all political comers. Not exactly a great feast, but there's enough tasty snacks to be satisfying. Performances are good and the victims (led by Perlman's Limbaugh turn) really shine. Too bad their characters aren't on screen very long before they become tomato fertilizer. **91m/C VHS.** Cameron Diaz, Annabeth Gish, Ron Eldard, Jonathan Penner, Courtney B. Vance, Nora Dunn; ***Cameos:*** Ron Perlman, Jason Alexander, Charles Durning, Mark Harmon, Bill Paxton; ***D:*** Stacy Title; ***W:*** Dan Rosen; ***C:*** Paul Cameron; ***M:*** Mark Mothersbaugh.

Last Tango in Paris 🦴🦴🦴½ *L'Ultimo Tango a Parigi; Le Dernier Tango a Paris* **1973 (R)** Brando plays a middle-aged American who meets a French girl and tries to forget his wife's suicide with a short, extremely steamy affair. Bertolucci proves to be a master; Brando gives one of his best performances. Very controversial when made, still quite explicit. Visually stunning. The X-rated version, at 130 minutes, is also available. **126m/C VHS, DVD, Wide.** *IT FR* Marlon Brando, Maria Schneider, Jean-Pierre Leaud, Maria Michi, Massimo Girotti, Catherine Allegret; ***D:*** Bernardo Bertolucci; ***W:*** Bernardo Bertolucci; ***C:*** Vittorio Storaro; ***M:*** Gato Barbieri. N.Y. Film Critics '73: Actor (Brando); Natl. Soc. Film Critics '73: Actor (Brando).

The Last Temptation of Christ 🦴🦴🦴½ **1988 (R)** Scorsese's controversial adaptation of the Nikos Kazantzakis novel, portraying Christ in his last year as an ordinary Israelite tormented by divine doubt, human desires and the voice of God. The controversy engulfing the film, as it was heavily protested and widely banned, tended to divert attention from what is an exceptional statement of religious and artistic vision. Excellent score by Peter Gabriel. **164m/C VHS, DVD, Wide.** *CA* Willem Dafoe, Harvey Keitel, Barbara Hershey, Harry Dean Stanton, Andre Gregory, David Bowie, Verna Bloom, Juliette Caton, John Lurie, Roberts Blossom, Irvin Kershner, Barry Miller, Tomas Arana, Nehemiah Persoff, Paul Herman, Illeana Douglas; ***D:*** Martin Scorsese; ***W:*** Paul Schrader; ***C:*** Michael Ballhaus; ***M:*** Peter Gabriel.

The Last Time I Committed Suicide 🦴🦴 **1996 (R)** Based on a Beat-era letter from Neal Cassady to Jack Kerouac and set in the late '40s, this insubstantial pic follows a 20-year-old Cassady (Jane) as he drifts into Denver's bars, and a friendship with poolhall regular Harry (Reeves), in order to escape dealing with girlfriend Joan's (Forlani) attempted suicide. Joan's eventual recovery leads Neal to consider settling down but he blows a job interview thanks to a drunken Harry and decides to take off instead. No background is provided on the characters so their actions are inexplicable although Jane offers some appeal. **93m/C VHS.** Thomas Jane, Keanu Reeves, Tom Bower, Adrien Brody, Claire Forlani, Marg Helgenberger, Gretchen Mol; ***D:*** Stephen Kay; ***W:*** Stephen Kay; ***C:*** Bobby Bukowski.

The Last Time I Saw Paris 🦴🦴½ **1954** A successful writer reminisces about his love affair with a wealthy American girl in post-WWII Paris. **116m/C VHS, DVD.** Elizabeth Taylor, Van Johnson, Walter Pidgeon, Roger Moore, Donna Reed, Eva Gabor; ***D:*** Richard Brooks; ***W:*** Richard Brooks, Julius J. Epstein, Philip G. Epstein; ***C:*** Joseph Ruttenberg; ***M:*** Conrad Salinger.

Last Time Out 🦴🦴½ **1994 (PG-13)** Danny Dolan (Conrad) is a hard-partying college wide receiver who gets a shock when the father who abandoned him enrolls at his school to finish a college degree. Seems Joe (Beck) had his pro quarterback career cut short by a drinking problem and he's worried his son will follow in his unsteady footsteps. **92m/C VHS.** John Beck, Christian Conrad, Lori Werner, Gail Strickland, Betty Buckley; ***D:*** Don Fox Greene.

The Last Tomahawk 🦴🦴 **1965** Colorful and action packed reworking of Cooper's "Last of the Mohicans." **?m/C VHS.** *GE IT* Anthony Steffen, Karin Dor, Dan Martin, Joachim Fuchsberger.

The Last Train 🦴🦴 **1974** Romance most hopeless in the heart of France during zee beeg war. During the 1940 invasion of Paris a man and woman turn to each other for comfort when separated from their families while trying to escape the city. French, very French. **101m/C VHS, DVD.** *FR* Romy Schneider, Jean-Louis Trintignant, Maurice Biraud; ***D:*** Pierre Granier-Deferre; ***W:*** Pierre Granier-Deferre; ***C:*** Walter Wottitz; ***M:*** Philippe Sarde.

Last Train from Gun Hill 🦴🦴🦴 **1959** An all-star cast highlights this suspenseful story of a U.S. marshall determined to catch the man who raped and murdered his wife. Excellent action packed western. **94m/C VHS.** Kirk Douglas, Anthony Quinn, Carolyn Jones, Earl Holliman, Brad Dexter, Brian Hutton, Ziva Rodann; ***D:*** John Sturges; ***C:*** Charles B(ryant) Lang Jr.

The Last Tycoon 🦴🦴🦴 **1976 (PG)** An adaptation of the unfinished F. Scott Fitzgerald novel about the life and times of a Hollywood movie executive of the 1920s. Confusing and slow moving despite a blockbuster conglomeration of talent. Joan Collins introduces the film. **123m/C VHS.** Robert De Niro, Tony Curtis, Ingrid Boulting, Jack Nicholson, Jeanne Moreau, Peter Strauss, Robert Mitchum, Theresa Russell, Donald Pleasence, Ray Milland, Dana Andrews, John Carradine, Anjelica Huston; ***D:*** Elia Kazan; ***W:*** Harold Pinter; ***M:*** Maurice Jarre.

The Last Unicorn 🦴🦴½ **1982 (G)** Peter Beagle's popular tale of a beautiful unicorn who goes in search of her lost, mythical "family." **95m/C VHS.** ***D:*** Jules Bass; ***W:*** Peter S. Beagle; ***M:*** Jim Webb; ***V:*** Alan Arkin, Jeff Bridges, Tammy Grimes, Angela Lansbury, Mia Farrow, Robert Klein, Christopher Lee, Keenan Wynn.

The Last Valley 🦴🦴 **1971 (PG)** A scholar tries to protect a pristine 17th century Swiss valley, untouched by the Thirty Years War, from marauding soldiers. Historical action with an intellectual twist. **128m/C VHS, DVD, Wide.** Michael Caine, Omar Sharif, Florinda Bolkan, Nigel Davenport, Per Oscarsson, Arthur O'Connell; ***D:*** James Clavell; ***W:*** James Clavell; ***C:*** John Wilcox; ***M:*** John Barry.

The Last Voyage 🦴🦴½ **1960** Suspenseful disaster film in which Stack and Malone play a married couple in jeopardy while on an ocean cruise. To make the film more realistic, the French liner Ile de France was actually used in the sinking scenes. Although a bit farfetched, film is made watchable because of fine performances and excellent camera work. **91m/C VHS.** Robert Stack, Dorothy Malone, George Sanders, Edmond O'Brien, Woody Strode, Jack Kruschen; ***D:*** Andrew L. Stone; ***W:*** Andrew L. Stone; ***C:*** Hal Mohr.

The Last Waltz 🦴🦴🦴½ **1978 (PG)** Martin Scorsese filmed this rock documentary featuring the farewell performance of The Band, joined by a host of musical guests that they have been associated with over the years. Songs include: "Up On Cripple Creek," "Don't Do It," "The Night They Drove Old Dixie Down," "Stage Fright" (The Band), "Helpless" (Neil Young), "Coyote" (Joni Mitchell), "Caravan" (Van Morrison), "Further On Up the Road" (Eric Clapton), "Who Do You Love" (Ronnie Hawkins), "Mannish Boy" (Muddy Waters), "Evangeline" (Emmylou Harris), "Baby, Let Me Follow You Down" (Bob Dylan). **117m/C VHS, DVD, Wide.** ***D:*** Martin Scorsese; ***C:*** Michael Chapman.

Last War 🦴 **1968** A nuclear war between the United States and Russia triggers Armageddon. **79m/C VHS.** Frankie Sakai, Nobuko Otowa, Akira Takarada, Yuriko Hoshi; ***D:*** Shue Matsubayashi.

The Last Warrior 🦴½ *Coastwatcher* **1989 (R)** A good-looking but exploitive "Hell in the Pacific" rip-off, as an American and a Japanese soldier battle it out alone on a remote island during WWII. **94m/C VHS.** Gary (Rand) Graham, Cary-Hiroyuki Tagawa, Maria Holvoe; ***D:*** Martin Wragge.

The Last Warrior 🦴🦴 **1999 (PG-13)** A devastating earthquake has turned Southern California into an island and Green Beret Nick Preston (Lundgren) takes it upon himself to help a group of survivors finds civilization. Of course there's a villain—a murderer (Mer) who has taken over a maximum security prison and has his own ideas. **95m/C VHS, DVD.** Dolph Lundgren, Rebecca Cross, Julino Mer, Sherrie Alexander, Joe Michael Burke; ***D:*** Sheldon Lettich; ***W:*** Stephen J. Brackely, Pamela K. Long; ***C:*** David Garfinkel; ***M:*** David Michael Frank. **VIDEO**

The Last Wave 🦴🦴🦴 **1977 (PG)** An Australian attorney takes on a murder case involving an aborigine and he finds himself becoming distracted by apocalyptic visions concerning tidal waves and drownings that seem to foretell the future. Weir's masterful creation and communication of time and place are marred by a somewhat pat ending. **109m/C VHS, DVD, Wide.** *AU* Richard Chamberlain, Olivia Hamnett, David Gulpilil, Frederick Parslow, Vivean Gray, Nadjiwarra Amagula, Roy Bara, Walter Amagula, Cedric Lalara, Morris Lalara, Peter Carroll; ***D:*** Peter Weir; ***W:*** Peter Weir, Tony Morphett, Petru Popescu; ***C:*** Russell Boyd.

The Last Winter 🦴🦴 **1984 (R)** An American woman fights to find her Israeli husband who has disappeared in the 1973 Yom Kippur War. Trouble is, an Israeli woman thinks the man she's looking for is really her husband too. **92m/C VHS.** *IS* Kathleen Quinlan, Yona Elian, Zipora Peled, Michael Schnider; ***D:*** Riki Shelach.

The Last Winter 🦴🦴½ **1989 (PG)** Ten-year-old Will (Murray) has always lived in the country and finds it hard to accept his parents' decision to move to the city. But with the help of his grandfather (Parkes), Will begins to understand about change and growing up. **103m/C VHS.** *CA* Joshua Murray, Gerard Parkes, David Ferry, Wanda Cannon, Marsha Moreau, Nathaniel Moreau, Katie Murray; ***D:*** Aaron Kim Johnston; ***W:*** Aaron Kim Johnston; ***C:*** Ian Elkin; ***M:*** Victor Davies.

The Last Winters 🦴🦴½ **1971** From Jean Charles Tacchella, writer-producer-director of "Cousin Cousine," comes his first short film about an old couple's bittersweet romance. In French with English subtitles. **23m/C VHS.** *FR* ***D:*** Jean-Charles Tacchella.

Last Witness 🦴 **1988** A man on the run from the government claims that he is innocent and was unjustly persecuted, but the government sees him as a dangerous threat. Nothing will stop the hunt for the escaped man, no matter what it costs. **85m/C VHS.** Jeff Henderson.

The Last Woman on Earth woof! **1961** Two men vie for the affections of the sole surviving woman after a vague and unexplained disaster of vast proportions. Robert Towne, who appears herein under the pseudonym Edward Wain, wrote the script (his first screenwriting effort). You might want to watch this if it were the last movie on earth, although Corman fans will probably love it. **71m/C VHS.** Antony Carbone, Edward (Robert Towne) Wain, Betsy Jones-Moreland; ***D:*** Roger Corman; ***W:*** Robert Towne.

The Last Word 🦴🦴 *Danny Travis* **1980 (PG)** Comedy drama about struggling inventor Harris fighting to protect his home, family, and neighbors from a corrupt real estate deal involving shady politicians, angry policemen, and a beautiful TV reporter. **103m/C VHS.** Richard Harris, Karen Black, Martin Landau, Dennis Christopher, Bill McGuire, Christopher Guest, Penelope Milford, Michael Pataki; ***W:*** Michael Varhol, L.M. Kit Carson.

The Last Word 🦴🦴 **1995 (R)** Journalist Martin (Hutton) writes a newspaper column, often featuring characters based on hometown Detroit mob figures, with info supplied to him by his friend, Doc (Pantoliano), who owes the gangsters some big bucks. Doc also introduces Martin to his latest column subject—stripper Caprice (Burke)—and, thanks again to Doc, a Hollywood studio gets interested in filming her story but wants more sex and violence, which means Martin will be betraying her deepest secrets. Now, he must choose between love, success, or friendship. **95m/C VHS, DVD.** Timothy Hutton, Joe Pantoliano, Michelle Rene Thomas, Chazz Palminteri, Tony Goldwyn, Richard Dreyfuss, Cybill Shepherd, Jimmy Smits; ***D:*** Tony Spiridakis; ***W:*** Tony Spiridakis; ***C:*** Zoltan David; ***M:*** Paul Buckmaster.

Last Year at Marienbad 🦴🦴🦴 *L'Anee Derniere a Marienbad* **1961** A young man tries to lure a mysterious woman to run away with him from a hotel in France. Once a hit on the artsy circuit, it's most interesting for its beautiful photography. In French with English subtitles. **93m/B VHS, DVD, 8mm, Wide.** *FR IT* Delphine Seyrig, Giorgio Albertazzi, Sacha (Sascha) Pitoeff, Luce Garcia-Ville; ***D:*** Alain Resnais; ***W:*** Alain Resnais, Alain Robbe-Grillet; ***C:*** Sacha Vierny; ***M:*** Francis Seyrig.

L'Atalante 🦴🦴🦴½ *Le Chaland qui Passe* **1934** Vigo's great masterpiece, a slight story about a husband and wife quarreling, splitting, and reuniting around which has been fashioned one of the cinema's greatest poetic films. In French with English subtitles. **82m/B VHS.** *FR* Dita Parlo, Jean Daste, Michel Simon; ***D:*** Jean Vigo; ***W:*** Jean Vigo, Jean Guinee, Albert Riera; ***C:*** Boris Kaufman, Louis Berger; ***M:*** Maurice Jaubert.

Late August, Early September 🦴🦴½ *Fin Aout Debut Septembre* **1998** Self-absorbed group of friends and lovers find their relationships in flux and their mortality in question over the course of a year (from August of one year to the September of the next). Adrien (Cluzet) is a serious writer whose work elicits critical but not commercial acclaim. His indecisive friend Gabriel (Amalric) is an editor at a publishing house who has split with long-time love, Jenny (Balibar), for the young Anne (Ledoyen). Meanwhile, Adrien, who's learned he has a terminal illness, plunges into a reckless affair with the teenaged Vera (Hansen-Love). French with subtitles. **112m/C VHS, Wide.** *FR* Mathieu Amalric, Virginie Ledoyen, Francois Cluzet, Jeanne Balibar, Alex Descas, Arsinee Khanjian, Mia Hansen-Love; ***D:*** Olivier Assayas; ***W:*** Olivier Assayas; ***C:*** Denis Lenoir; ***M:*** Ali Sarka Toure.

Late Bloomers 🦴🦴 **1995** Romantic comedy focuses on what happens when two Midwestern women fall in love. Math teacher/basketball coach Dinah (Nelson) is friendly with fellow teacher Rom (Carter) and his wife, Carly (Hennigan), the high school secretary. A misinterpreted note, an impulsive kiss, and Carly's soon out of door and living with Dinah, which leads to a community uproar. The two leads are likeable but the other characters and the situation are heavily cliched. **105m/C VHS.** Connie Nelson, Dee Hennigan, Gary Carter, Lisa Peterson; ***D:*** Julia Dyer; ***W:*** Gretchen Dyer; ***C:*** Bill Schwarz; ***M:*** Ted Pine.

Late Chrysanthemums 🦴🦴 *Bangiku* **1954** A middle-aged geisha has settled into comfortable retirement as a money lender. When she hears a former lover wants to visit her, she tries to recapture her old glamour only to be disillusioned. Based on a short story by Fumiko Hayashi. In Japanese with English subtitles. **101m/B VHS.** *JP* Haruko Sugimura, Chikako Hosokawa, Sadako Sawahura; ***D:*** Mikio Naruse.

Late Extra 🦴🦴 **1935** A novice reporter attempts to track down a notorious bank robber and gets some help from a savvy female journalist. Mason's first role of substance. **69m/B VHS.** *GB* Virginia Cherrill, James Mason, Alastair Sim, Ian Colin, Clifford McLaglen, Cyril Cusack, David Horne, Antoinette Cellier, Donald Wolfit, Michael Wilding; ***D:*** Albert Parker.

Late for Dinner 🦴🦴 **1991 (PG)** In 1962 Willie, a young, married man, and his best friend Frank are framed by a sleazy land developer. On the run, the two decide to become guinea pigs in a cryonics experiment and wind up frozen for 29 years. It's now 1991 and Willie wants to find his family—only his wife is middle-aged and his daughter is all grown-up. Can he make a life with them again or has time indeed passed him by? **93m/C VHS.** Brian Wimmer, Peter Berg, Marcia Gay Harden, Peter Gallagher, Ross Malinger; ***D:*** W.D. Richter; ***W:*** Mark Andrus.

Late Last Night 🦴🦴 **1999 (R)** After a big fight with his wife, Dan (Estevez) hooks up with best pal, Jeff (Weber), who proposes they cut loose for the evening. So they pick up a couple of women and proceed to party, which eventually lands them in the slammer. **90m/C VHS, DVD.** Emilio Estevez, Steven Weber, Catherine O'Hara, Leah Lail, Lisa Robin Kelly; ***D:*** Steven Brill.

The Late Shift 🦴🦴½ **1996 (R)** Cable adaptation of Bill Carter's book chronicling the follies surrounding NBC's "The Tonight Show" succession battle between Jay Leno (Roebuck) and Dave Letterman (Higgins). It's the behind-the-scenes dealmakers that really steal the show, however, including Jay's profane manager Helen Kushnick (Bates) and superagent Michael Ovitz (Williams), who ultimately orchestrated Dave's move to rival CBS. Both Letterman and Leno made the movie/book fodder for their opening monlogues. **96m/C VHS.** Daniel Roebuck, John Michael Higgins, Kathy Bates, Treat Williams, Bob Balaban, Ed Begley Jr., Rich Little, Sandra Bernhard, Peter Jurasik, Reni Santoni, John Kapelos, John Getz, Lawrence Pressman; ***D:*** Betty Thomas; ***W:*** Bill Carter, George Armitage; ***C:*** Mac Ahlberg; ***M:*** Ira Newborn. CABLE

The Late Show 🦴🦴🦴 **1977 (PG)** A veteran private detective finds his world turned upside down when his ex-partner comes to visit and winds up dead, and a flaky woman whose cat is missing decides to become his sidekick. Carney and Tomlin are fun to watch in this sleeper, a tribute to the classic detective film noirs. **93m/C VHS.** Art Carney, Lily Tomlin, Bill Macy, Eugene Roche, Joanna Cassidy, John Considine; ***D:*** Robert Benton; ***W:*** Robert Benton. Natl. Soc. Film Critics '77: Actor (Carney).

Late Spring 🦴🦴🦴🦴 **1949** An exquisite Ozu masterpiece. A young woman lives with her widowed father for years. He decides to remarry so that she can begin life for herself. Highly acclaimed, in Japanese with English subtitles. Reworked in 1960 as "Late Autumn." **107m/B VHS.** *JP* Setsuko Hara, Chishu Ryu, Jun Usami, Haruko Sugimura; ***D:*** Yasujiro Ozu.

Late Summer Blues 🦴🦴 *Blues La-Chofesh Ha-Godol* **1987** Experience the life and death decisions of seven teenagers who have finished their finals and face now a more difficult test: serving in the Israeli Armed Forces in the Suez Canal. In Hebrew with English subtitles. **101m/C VHS.** *IS* Dor Zweigenbom, Shahar Segal, Yoav Zafir; ***D:*** Renen Schorr.

The Lathe of Heaven 🦴🦴½ **1980** In a late 20th century world suffocating from pollution, George Orr (Davison) visits a dream specialist because he can dream things into being. The specialist wants George to dream of a world free from war, pestilence, and overpopulation, but these dreams have disastrous side effects. Based on the futuristic novel by Ursula K. LeGuin. **100m/C VHS, DVD.** Bruce Davison, Kevin Conway, Margaret Avery, Peyton E. Park; ***D:*** David Loxton, Fred Barzyk; ***W:*** Roger E. Swaybill, Diane English; ***C:*** Robbie Greenberg; ***M:*** Michael Small. TV

Latin Lovers 🦴🦴½ **1953** Turner plays a wealthy heiress who can't decide if men love her for herself or her money in this festive Brazilian romp. Lund and Montalban portray the suitors vying for her affection. Although not one of MGM's best musicals, the music is good because of the Brodszky-Robin tunes. ♫Night and You; Carlotta, You Gotta Be Mine; A Little More of Your Armor; Come To My Arms; I Had To Kiss You. **104m/C VHS.** Lana Turner, Ricardo Montalban, John Lund, Louis Calhern, Jean Hagen, Eduard Franz, Beulah Bondi; ***D:*** Mervyn LeRoy; ***W:*** Isobel Lennart.

Latino 🦴🦴½ **1985** The self-tortured adventures of a Chicano Green Beret who, while fighting a covert U.S. military action in war-torn Nicaragua, begins to rebel against the senselessness of the war. **108m/C VHS.** Robert Beltran, Annette Cardona, Tony Plana, James Karen, Ricardo Lopez, Luis Torrentes, Juan Carlos Ortiz, Julio Medina; ***D:*** Haskell Wexler; ***W:*** Haskell Wexler; ***M:*** Diane Louie.

Lauderdale woof! *Spring Fever USA; Spring Break USA* **1989 (R)** Two college schmoes hit the beach looking for beer and babes. Few laughs for the sober and mature. Surf's down in this woofer. **91m/C VHS, DVD.** Darrel Gilbeau, Michelle Kemp, Jeff Greenman, Lara Belmonte; ***D:*** Bill Milling; ***W:*** Bill Milling.

Laughing at Danger 🦴🦴½ **1924** Talmadge is the supposedly playboy son of a Washington politician. In reality, he's the dashing "Mr. Pep" who comes to the rescue of a scientist who has invented a death ray and is being stalked by agents of a sinister foreign power. Talmadge was a fine silent-screen action star, though his heavy German action proved a barrier with sound films. **45m/B VHS.** Richard Talmadge, Joseph Girard, Eva Novak, Joe Harrington, Stanhope Wheatcroft; ***D:*** James W. Horne.

Laughing at Life 🦴½ **1933** A mercenary leaves his family to fight in South America. Years later, when he is the leader of said country, he meets a man who turns out to be his son. Rehashed plot has been done better. **72m/B VHS.** Victor McLaglen, William "Stage" Boyd, Lois Wilson, Henry B. Walthall, Regis Toomey; ***D:*** Ford Beebe.

The Laughing Policeman 🦴🦴½ *An Investigation of Murder* **1974 (R)** Two antagonistic cops embark on a vengeful hunt for a mass murderer through the seamy underbelly of San Francisco. Adapted from the Swedish novel by Per Wahloo and Maj Sjowallo. **111m/C VHS.** Walter Matthau, Bruce Dern, Louis Gossett Jr.; ***D:*** Stuart Rosenberg; ***M:*** Charles Fox.

Laughing Sinners 🦴🦴 **1931** Society girl Crawford attempts suicide after Hamilton dumps her and is rescued by Gable—a Salvation Army worker! Predictable drama with some unintentionally funny moments. Gable and Crawford were having an off-screen romance at the time which accounts for the sparks generated on-screen. Based on the play "Torch Song" by Kenyon Nicholson. **71m/B VHS.** Joan Crawford, Neil Hamilton, Clark Gable, Marjorie Rambeau, Guy Kibbee, Cliff Edwards, Roscoe Karns; ***D:*** Harry Beaumont; ***C:*** Charles Rosher.

Laura 🦴🦴🦴🦴 **1944** Detective Mark McPherson (Andrews) assigned to the murder investigation of the late Laura Hunt (Tierney) finds himself falling in love with her painted portrait and discovering some surprising facts. Superb collaboration by excellent cast and fine director. Superior suspense yarn, enhanced by a love story. Based on the novel by Vera Caspary. Rouben Mamoulian was the original director, then Preminger finished the film. **85m/B VHS.** Gene Tierney, Dana Andrews, Clifton Webb, Lane Chandler, Vincent Price, Judith Anderson, Grant Mitchell, Dorothy Adams, Ron Dunn, Clyde Fillmore, James Flavin; ***D:*** Otto Preminger; ***W:*** Elizabeth Reinhardt, Jay Dratler, Samuel Hoffenstein, Ring Lardner Jr.; ***C:*** Joseph LaShelle; ***M:*** David Raksin. Oscars '44: B&W Cinematog., Natl. Film Reg. '99.

Laurel & Hardy and the Family **1933** Four zany comedies seeing the boys in all kinds of trouble involving homelife. Includes "Brats," "Perfect Day," "Their First Mistake" and "Twice Two." **85m/B VHS.** Stan Laurel, Oliver Hardy.

Laurel & Hardy: Another Fine Mess **1930** The boys find themselves the owners of a magnificent Beverly Hills mansion. Yeah right. Lots of physical comedy and hilarious dialogue with a "special appearance" by Laurel in drag as a maid. Based on a sketch written by Laurel's father. Colorized. **25m/C VHS.** Stan Laurel, Oliver Hardy.

Laurel & Hardy: At Work **1932** Three short films collected here. Includes "Towed in a Hole," "Busy Bodies," and "The Music Box." **70m/B VHS.** Oliver Hardy, Stan Laurel.

Laurel & Hardy: Be Big **1931** Stan and Ollie ditch their wives to go to a swinging stag party at their club. Of course everything goes wrong in their quest for lascivious fun. Filled with tons of sight gags. Colorized. **25m/C VHS.** Stan Laurel, Oliver Hardy.

Laurel & Hardy: Below Zero **1930** It's the Great Depression of 1929, and Laurel and Hardy are about as depressed as you can get, working for pennies as street musicians. Their luck changes when they find a full wallet lying in the snow. But, as the saying goes, a fool and his money are soon parted. Colorized. **25m/C VHS.** Stan Laurel, Oliver Hardy.

Laurel & Hardy: Berth Marks **1929** Laurel & Hardy take a hilarious train trip to Pottsville for a vaudeville performance. Colorized. **25m/C VHS.** Stan Laurel, Oliver Hardy.

Laurel & Hardy: Blotto **1930** Laurel and Hardy want to get drunk, but they can't get any alcohol and their wives won't let them get away. When they finally do escape, they wind up at the swanky Rainbow Club, where they're drastically out of their element. Colorized. **25m/C VHS.** Stan Laurel, Oliver Hardy.

Laurel & Hardy: Brats **1930** Stan and Ollie play not only themselves but also their children when their wives go away and they have to babysit. The children, of course, wreak havoc wherever they go, playing on the hilariously oversized props and sets. One of the few films in which only Laurel and Hardy appear. Colorized. **25m/C VHS.** Stan Laurel, Oliver Hardy.

Laurel & Hardy: Chickens Come Home **1931** Ollie is running for mayor, but things go crazy when an ex-girlfriend shows up and blackmails him with a compromising photo. Stan, acting as Ollie's campaign manager, tries to help, but things just get worse. A remake of their own film "Love 'Em and Weep." Colorized. **25m/C VHS.** Stan Laurel, Oliver Hardy, James Finlayson.

Laurel & Hardy: Hog Wild **1930** Hilarity ensues when Laurel and Hardy try to fix the radio antenna on Hardy's roof. It may sound easy, but come on, this is Laurel and Hardy. Colorized. **25m/C VHS.** Stan Laurel, Oliver Hardy.

Laurel & Hardy: Laughing Gravy **1931** The boys' pet dog, oddly named Laughing Gravy, gets them into trouble with their landlord who keeps trying to evict them. So funny even the mashed potatos will laugh. Colorized. **25m/C VHS.** Stan Laurel, Oliver Hardy.

Laurel & Hardy: Men O'War **1929** Laurel & Hardy star as two sailors on shore leave trying to impress the ladies. Things go from bad to worse when they take two ladies out on a date. Features the memorable soda fountain and canoe scenes. Colorized. **25m/C VHS.** Stan Laurel, Oliver Hardy, Gloria Greer, Anne Cornwall.

Laurel & Hardy: Night Owls **1930** When a cop needs to capture some crooks to save his job, he sets up a fake break-in and catches two bungling burglars—Laurel and Hardy. Lots of sight gags and slapstick. Colorized. **25m/C VHS.** Stan Laurel, Oliver Hardy, Edgar Kennedy.

Laurel & Hardy On the Lam **1930** Four Laurel & Hardy classics are collected, including "Scram," "Another Fine Mess," "One Good Turn," and "Going

Bye-Bye." **90m/B VHS.** Oliver Hardy, Stan Laurel.

Laurel & Hardy: Perfect Day **1929** Laurel & Hardy plan a quiet picnic with their wives, but car trouble turns their day into a disaster. Colorized. **25m/C VHS.** Stan Laurel, Oliver Hardy, Edgar Kennedy.

Laurel & Hardy Spooktacular **1934** Stan and Ollie scream through four spooky comedies, including "The Live Ghost," "The Laurel-Hardy Murder Case," "Oliver the Eighth" and "Dirty Work." **95m/B VHS.**

Laurel & Hardy: Stan "Helps" Ollie **1933** Four Stan and Ollie classics including "County Hospital," "Me and My Pal," "Hog Wild" and "Helpmates." **85m/B VHS.** Stan Laurel, Oliver Hardy.

Laurel & Hardy: The Hoose-Gow **1929** Laurel and Hardy are mistakenly picked up by the police and sent to prison to do hard labor. Hilarity ensues when they try to convince the warden that they're innocent. Colorized. **25m/C VHS.**

Laurel Avenue 🦴🦴½ **1993** Looks at the life of an extended working-class black family in St. Paul, Minnesota, over a busy weekend. Large cast includes family heads Jake and Maggie who live with their basketball coach son, teenage daughter, and elderly uncle. Other children include fraternal twin Yolanda, a cop married to a white man, who knows sister Rolanda's (a recovering drug addict) son is a dealer. Their brother Marcus manages a Mafia-controlled clothing store and is involved in some shady deals while brother Woody is an aspiring musician. The four households are all united at a disastrous Sunday afternoon party. **156m/C VHS.** Mary Alice, Mel Winkler, Scott Lawrence, Malinda Williams, Jay Brooks, Juanita Jennings, Rhonda Stubbins White, Monte Russell, Vonte Sweet; ***D:*** Carl Franklin; ***W:*** Michael Henry Brown, Paul Aaron. **CABLE**

The Lavender Hill Mob 🦴🦴🦴½ **1951** A prim and prissy bank clerk schemes to melt the bank's gold down and re-mold it into miniature Eiffel Tower paper-weights for later resale. The foolproof plan appears to succeed, but then develops a snag. An excellent comedy that is still a delight to watch. **78m/B VHS.** *GB* Alec Guinness, Stanley Holloway, Sidney James, Alfie Bass, Marjorie Fielding, John Gregson; ***Cameos:*** Audrey Hepburn; ***D:*** Charles Crichton; ***W:*** T.E.B. Clarke. Oscars '52: Story & Screenplay; British Acad. '51: Film.

L'Avventura 🦴🦴🦴½ *The Adventure* **1960** A stark, dry and minimalist exercise in narrative by Antonioni, dealing with the search for a girl on an Italian island by her lethargic socialite friends who eventually forget her in favor of their own preoccupations. A highly acclaimed, innovative film; somewhat less effective now, in the wake of many film treatments of angst and amorality. Subtitled in English. Laser edition features the original trailer, commentary and a collection of still photographs from Antonioni's work. **145m/C VHS, DVD, Wide.** *IT* Monica Vitti, Gabriele Ferzetti, Lea Massari, Dominique Blanchar, James Addams; ***D:*** Michelangelo Antonioni; ***W:*** Tonino Guerra, Michelangelo Antonioni; ***C:*** Aldo Scavarda; ***M:*** Giovanni Fusco. Cannes '60: Special Jury Prize.

Law and Disorder 🦴🦴🦴 **1974** **(R)** Two average Joes, fed up with the rate of rising crime, start their own auxiliary police group. Alternately funny and serious with good performances from the leads. **103m/C VHS, DVD, Wide.** Carroll O'Connor, Ernest Borgnine, Ann Wedgeworth, Anita Dangler, Leslie Ackerman, Karen Black, Jack Kehoe; ***D:*** Ivan Passer; ***W:*** Ivan Passer, William Richert, Kenneth Harris Fishman; ***C:*** Arthur Ornitz; ***M:*** Angelo Badalamenti.

The Law and Jake Wade 🦴🦴½ **1958** Gripping western starring Taylor as a former bank robber turned marshal. His old partner (Widmark) turns up and forces Taylor to lead him to buried loot. **86m/C VHS.** Robert Taylor, Richard Widmark, Patricia Owens, Robert Middleton, Henry Silva, DeForest Kelley, Burt Douglas, Eddie Firestone; ***D:*** John Sturges.

Law and Lawless 🦴 **1933** A roving cowboy brings justice to a gang of cattle thieves in this film. **58m/B VHS.** Jack Hoxie.

Law and Order 🦴🦴 *Billy the Kid's Law and Order* **1942** Billy the Kid impersonates a Cavalry lieutenant in order to swindle his aunt out of her money. **58m/B VHS.** Buster Crabbe, Al "Fuzzy" St. John.

Law for Tombstone **1935** Alamo Bowie (Jones) must protect the Wells Fargo stagecoach from outlaw Twin Gun Jack. Includes chapter 1 of the serial "Gordon of Ghost City," which features Jones as retired ranch hand Buck Gordon who's on the trail of rustlers and meets a mysterious girl. **81m/B VHS.** Buck Jones, Muriel Evans, Harvey Clark, Carl Stockdale, Earle Hodgins, Madge Bellamy, Walter Miller; ***D:*** Ray Taylor, Buck Jones.

Law of Desire 🦴🦴🦴½ *La Ley del Deseo* **1986** A wicked, Almodovarian attack-on-decency farce about a promiscuous gay filmmaker, Pablo (Pancela), who becomes the object of desire for obsessive Antonio (Banderas), whom Pablo treats too casually for his own safety. Also in the mix is Pablo's sister, the transsexual Tina (Maura), and his current lover Juan (Molina). Romantic complications and violence abound. Unlike the work of any other director; Spanish with subtitles. **100m/C VHS.** *SP* Carmen Maura, Eusebio Poncela, Antonio Banderas, Bibi Andersson, Miguel Molina, Manuela Valasco, Nacho Martinez; ***D:*** Pedro Almodovar; ***W:*** Pedro Almodovar; ***C:*** Angel Luis Fernandez.

Law of the Jungle 🦴½ **1942** A lady scientist and a fugitive team up to uncover a secret Nazi radio base in the jungle. **61m/B VHS.** Arline Judge, John "Dusty" King, Mantan Moreland, Martin Wilkins, Arthur O'Connell; ***D:*** Jean Yarbrough.

Law of the Land 🦴 **1976** Sagebrush epic with the author/artist of "Garfield" portraying an accused but innocent man searching for a murderer. **100m/C VHS.** Jim Davis, Don Johnson, Barbara Parkins, Charles Martin Smith. **TV**

Law of the Lash 🦴 **1947** Cowboys and rustlers battle it out. **54m/B VHS.** Lash LaRue, Al "Fuzzy" St. John.

Law of the Pampas 🦴🦴 **1939** Boyd and Hayden ride off to South America to deliver some cattle, but the bad guys intervene. This is Toler's first outing as Hoppy's sidekick, briefly replacing "Gabby" Hayes. **72m/B VHS.** William Boyd, Russell Hayden, Steffi Duna, Sidney Toler, Sidney Blackmer, Pedro de Cordoba, Eddie Dean, Glenn Strange; ***D:*** Nate Watt.

Law of the Saddle 🦴½ **1945** The Lone Rider pits himself against a gang of outlaws. **60m/B VHS.** Robert "Bob" Livingston.

Law of the Sea 🦴 **1938** A family on a sinking ship is rescued by a lecherous sea captain who makes advances on the wife and blinds the husband in a fight. Twenty years later, the husband meets him again, recognizes his laugh, and exacts revenge. **63m/B VHS.** Priscilla Dean, Sally Blane, Ralph Ince, Rex Bell, William Farnum.

Law of the Texan 🦴½ **1938** Jones goes undercover to stop Harlan and his gang from stealing a town's store of silver bullion. **54m/B VHS.** Buck Jones, Dorothy Fay, Kenneth Harlan, Don Douglas, Matty Kemp, Robert F. (Bob) Kortman, Dave O'Brien; ***D:*** Elmer Clifton.

Law of the Underworld 🦴½ **1938** An innocent couple is framed for the robbery of a jewelry store which resulted in the death of a clerk. When they are arrested, their fate lies in the hands of the gangster responsible for the crime. Will he let them fry in the electric chair, or will his conscience get the better of him? **58m/B VHS.** Chester Morris, Anne Shirley, Eduardo Ciannelli, Walter Abel, Richard Bond, Lee Patrick, Paul Guilfoyle, Frank M. Thomas Sr., Eddie Acuff, Jack Arnold; ***D:*** Lew (Louis Friedlander) Landers.

Law of the Wild **1934** The search for a magnificent stallion that was hijacked by race racketeers before a big sweepstakes race is shown in this 12 chapter serial. **230m/B VHS.** Bob Custer, Ben Turpin, Lucille Browne, Lafe (Lafayette) McKee; ***D:*** B. Reeves Eason, Armand Schaefer.

The Law Rides 🦴 **1936** Rush of gold claims causes an outbreak of murder and robbery. **57m/B VHS.** Bob Steele.

The Law Rides Again 🦴 **1943** Prairie lawmen bring a cheating Indian agent to justice. **56m/B VHS.** Ken Maynard, Hoot Gibson, Betty Miles, Jack LaRue; ***D:*** William Castle.

Law West of Tombstone 🦴🦴½ **1938** A former outlaw moves to a dangerous frontier town in order to restore the peace. **73m/B VHS.** Tim Holt, Harry Carey Sr., Evelyn Brent; ***D:*** Glenn Tryon.

The Lawless Breed 🦴🦴🦴 **1952** Episodic saga based on the autobiography of outlaw John Wesley Hardin, published after his release from prison in 1896. Hardin's (Hudson) life of crime begins with a killing in self-defense that escalates into further bloodshed and flights from the law. Along the way Hardin marries (Adams) and has a son, whom he fears will follow in his violent footsteps. Walsh directs with plenty of brio. **83m/C VHS.** Rock Hudson, Julie Adams, John McIntire, Hugh O'Brian, Lee Van Cleef, Dennis Weaver, Glenn Strange, Michael Ansara; ***D:*** Raoul Walsh; ***W:*** Bernard Gordon; ***C:*** Irving Glassberg; ***M:*** Joseph Gershenson.

Lawless Frontier 🦴½ **1935** In the early West, the Duke fights for law and order. **53m/B VHS, DVD.** John Wayne, George "Gabby" Hayes, Sheila Terry, Earl Dwire; ***D:*** Robert North Bradbury.

The Lawless Land 🦴🦴 **1988 (R)** Post-holocaust America is ruled by a tyrant. Two young lovers who can't take it anymore go on the lam to escape the despotic rule. **81m/C VHS.** Leon Berkeley, Xander Berkeley, Nick Corri, Amanda Peterson; ***D:*** Jon Hess; ***W:*** Tony Cinciripini, Larry Leahy.

The Lawless Nineties 🦴🦴 **1936** Wayne plays a government agent sent to guarantee honest elections in the Wyoming territory. Hayes is exceptional as the newspaper editor who backs him up. Remade in 1940 as "The Dark Command." **55m/B VHS.** John Wayne, Ann Rutherford, Lane Chandler, Harry Woods, George "Gabby" Hayes, Charles "Blackie" King, Sam Flint; ***D:*** Joseph Kane.

Lawless Range 🦴½ **1935** Wayne and the marshal's posse save the ranchers from trouble. **56m/B VHS.** John Wayne, Sheila (Manors) Mannors, Jack Curtis, Earl Dwire; ***D:*** Robert North Bradbury.

A Lawless Street 🦴🦴½ **1955** Scott portrays a sheriff who rides the Colorado Territory cleaning up lawless towns. His dedication to duty has caused his wife to leave him and she won't come back until he lays downs his guns forever, which may come sooner than they think after he rides into the corrupt town of Medicine Bend. Based on the novel "Marshal of Medicine Bend" by Brad Ward. **78m/B VHS.** Randolph Scott, Angela Lansbury, Warner Anderson, Jean Parker, Wallace Ford, John Emery, James Bell, Ruth Donnelly, Michael Pate, Don Megowan, Jeanette Nolan; ***D:*** Joseph H. Lewis; ***W:*** Kenneth Gamet; ***C:*** Ray Rennahan.

Lawman 🦴🦴🦴 **1971 (PG)** Brutal western about a fanatical U.S. marshall (Lancaster) who rides into town after Cobb and his six ranch hands. The cowboys have accidentally killed a man and Lancaster is determined to bring them to justice no matter what the cost. Though the entire town is against him that doesn't stop his mission. Brooding and relentless with fine performances, particularly by Ryan as the local marshall living on past glories. **95m/C VHS, DVD, Wide.** Burt Lancaster, Robert Ryan, Lee J. Cobb, Sheree North, Joseph Wiseman, Robert Duvall, Albert Salmi, J.D. Cannon, John McGiver, Richard Jordan, John Beck, Ralph Waite, John Hillerman, Richard Bull; ***D:*** Michael Winner; ***W:*** Gerald Wilson; ***C:*** Robert Paynter; ***M:*** Jerry Fielding.

A Lawman Is Born 🦴🦴🦴 **1937** A tough-as-nails marshal goes gunning for a pack of no-good, land-stealing varmits in this installment of the Johnny Mack Brown movie serials. Be sure to count the number of bullets each cowboy can fire from a six-shooter before being forced to reload; you may be surprised. **58m/B VHS.** Johnny Mack Brown, Iris Meredith, Warner Richmond, Mary MacLaren, Dick Curtis, Earle Hodgins, Charles "Blackie" King, Frank LaRue; ***D:*** Sam Newfield.

Lawmen 🦴½ **1944** Government agents fight to enforce the law in the badlands. **55m/B VHS.** Johnny Mack Brown, Raymond Hatton.

Lawn Dogs 🦴🦴½ **1996** After moving into an overly manicured suburban complex for the financially secure but morally bankrupt, Morton (McDonald) and Clare (Quinlan) want their daughter to mix with the social elite. Instead, the imaginative Devon (Barton) strikes up a friendship with Trent (Rockwell), an outsider who cuts lawns in the sterile burb. At first Trent, fearing the repercussions of such a friendship, pushes Devon away. The two eventually bond over their mutual dislike for the lifeless complex. After a conflict with a couple of dim college boys, events take a turn for the worse; and Trent is forced to escape from the community with Devon's help. Interweaved with the Russian fairy tale of Baba Yaga, the climax is visually stunning. Excellent performances from both Rockwell and Barton as the unlikely friends. **101m/C VHS, DVD.** *GB* Sam Rockwell, Mischa Barton, Kathleen Quinlan, Christopher McDonald, Bruce McGill, David Barry Gray, Eric Mabius, Tom Aldredge, Beth Grant; ***D:*** John Duigan; ***W:*** Naomi Wallace; ***C:*** Elliot Davis; ***M:*** Trevor Jones.

The Lawnmower Man 🦴🦴 **1992 (R)** Brosnan is a scientist who uses Fahey, a dim-witted gardener, as a guinea pig to test his experiments in "virtual reality," an artificial computer environment. With the use of drugs and high-tech equipment, Brosnan is able to increase Fahey's mental powers—but not necessarily for the better. Fantastic special effects and a memorable "virtual reality" sex scene. Available in an unrated version which contains 32 more minutes of footage. So minimally based on a short story by Stephen King that the author sued (and won) to have his name removed from the film. **108m/C VHS, DVD.** Jeff Fahey, Pierce Brosnan, Jenny Wright, Mark Bringleson, Geoffrey Lewis, Jeremy Slate, Dean Norris, Troy Evans, John Laughlin; ***D:*** Brett Leonard; ***W:*** Brett Leonard, Gimel Everett; ***C:*** Russell Carpenter; ***M:*** Danny Wyman.

Lawnmower Man 2: Beyond Cyberspace 🦴🦴 *Lawnmower Man 2: Jobe's War* **1995 (PG-13)** Resurrecting Jobe (the title character from number one) was easy. So was blowing off his face to explain the new actor (Frewer in for Fahey) playing him. The hard part was tring to make an original movie with a decent script and believable characters. Better luck next time. Corporate baddie Walker (Conway) enlists Jobe to (what else?) take over the world using Virtual Reality. To the rescue comes one burned-out computer expert (Bergin) and a group of VR-addicted kids living in an abandoned subway. Techno-babble abounds but nothing interesting ever happens. Mann and Frewer must've raided their old "Max Headroom" set for the dreary near-future L.A. landscape scenes. **93m/C VHS.** Patrick Bergin, Matt Frewer, Austin O'Brien, Kevin Conway, Ely Pouget, Camille (Cami) Cooper; ***D:*** Farhad Mann; ***W:*** Farhad Mann; ***C:*** Ward Russell; ***M:*** Robert Folk.

Lawrence of Arabia 🦴🦴🦴🦴 **1962 (PG)** Exceptional biography of T.E. Lawrence, a British military "observer" who strategically aids the Bedouins battle the Turks during WWI. Lawrence, played masterfully by O'Toole in his first major film, is a hero consumed more by a need to reject British tradition than to save the Arab population. He takes on Arab costume and a larger-than-life persona. Stunning photography of the desert in all its harsh reality. Blacklisted co-writer Wilson had his screen credit restored by the Writers Guild of America in 1995. Laser edition contains 20 minutes of restored footage and a short documentary about the making of the film. Available in letterboxed format. **221m/C VHS, DVD, Wide.** *GB* Peter

O'Toole, Omar Sharif, Anthony Quinn, Alec Guinness, Jack Hawkins, Claude Rains, Anthony Quayle, Arthur Kennedy, Jose Ferrer, Michel Ray, Norman Rossington, John Ruddock, Donald Wolfit; ***D:*** David Lean; ***W:*** Robert Bolt, Michael Wilson; ***C:*** Frederick A. (Freddie) Young; ***M:*** Maurice Jarre. Oscars '62: Art Dir./Set Dec., Color, Color Cinematog., Director (Lean), Film Editing, Picture, Sound, Orig. Score; AFI '98: Top 100; British Acad. '62: Actor (O'Toole), Film, Screenplay; Directors Guild '62: Director (Lean); Golden Globes '63: Director (Lean), Film—Drama, Support. Actor (Sharif); Natl. Bd. of Review '62: Director (Lean), Natl. Film Reg. '91.

The Lawrenceville Stories ✌✌½ **1988** Chronicles the life and times of a group of young men at the prestigious Lawrenceville prep school in 1905. Galligan plays William Hicks, alias "The Prodigious Hickey," the ringleader of their obnoxious stunts. Based on the stories of Owen Johnson, which originally ran in the Saturday Evening Post. Shown on "American Playhouse" and The Disney Channel. Tapes are available separately or as a set. **180m/C VHS.** Zach Galligan, Edward Herrmann, Nicholas (Nick) Rowe, Allan Goldstein, Robert Joy, Stephen Baldwin; ***D:*** Robert Iscove.

Laws of Deception ✌½ **1997** As a child, Evan Marino (Howell) witnessed the murder of his parents by mobster Gino Carlucci (Russo). After becoming a ruthlessly successful criminal attorney in Miami, Evan gets drawn back into the life of former flame Elise (Smith), who happens to be Mrs. Carlucci and is accused of murdering her scummy husband. She says she didn't do it. You'll figure out all the would-be twists in this wanna-be thriller without any problem. **98m/C VHS.** C. Thomas Howell, Amber Smith, Brian Austin Green, James Russo, Nick Mancuso, Robert Miano; ***Cameos:*** John Landis; ***D:*** Joey Travolta; ***W:*** Rollin Jarrett; ***C:*** Dan Heigh; ***M:*** Jeff Lass. **VIDEO**

Laws of Gravity ✌✌✌ **1992 (R)** Critically acclaimed debut film from 29-year-old writer/director Gomez is a three day slice of life set in Brooklyn. Hotheaded Jon (Trese) and married friend Jimmy (Greene) channel violent energy into their relationships and illegal activities. Camera follows "cinema verite" style and captures urban tension as it trails them through a gun heist and subsequent arrest. **100m/C VHS.** Peter Greene, Edie Falco, Adam Trese, Arabella Field, Paul Schulzie; ***D:*** Nick Gomez; ***W:*** Nick Gomez; ***C:*** Jean De Segonzac.

Lazarillo ✌✌ *El Lazarillo de Tormes* **1959** In 17th-century Castille, a fatherless boy, abandoned by his mother, finds work with a strange succession of employers, including a blind beggar, fake nobleman, and traveling band of performers. They all teach him lessons in survival as well as cunning and deception. Spanish with subtitles. **109m/B VHS.** *SP* Marco Paoletti, Juan Jose Menendez, Carlos Casaravilla, Margarita Lozano; ***D:*** Cesar Ardavin; ***W:*** Cesar Ardavin; ***M:*** Ruiz De Luna. Berlin Intl. Film Fest. '60: Film.

The Lazarus Man ✌✌½ **1996** Pilot episode of the TV series finds the amnesiac Urich discovering he's linked to the assassination of President Lincoln. In 1865 Texas he literally claws his way out of the grave and is taken in by a farming family. This back from the dead Lazarus may not remember who he is but a trip to town demonstrates his gunslinger skills and images from his dreams may provide clues to his past. Now, he has to stay alive long enough to figure them out. **90m/C VHS.** Robert Urich, Elizabeth Dennehy, David Marshall Grant, John Diehl, Wayne Grace, Brion James; ***D:*** Johnny E. Jensen; ***W:*** Dick Beebe; ***C:*** Gary Holt; ***M:*** John Debney. **TV**

The Lazarus Syndrome **1979** Astute doctor teams up with an ex-patient of the chief of surgery in an effort to expose the chief's unethical surgical procedures. **90m/C VHS.** Louis Gossett Jr., E.G. Marshall.

LBJ: A Biography **1991** Produced for the PBS series "The American Experience," this four-hour revisionist look at LBJ is one of the most critically acclaimed political documentaries of our time. Divided into four segments. "Beautiful Texas" chronicles Johnson's rise to power. "My Fellow Americans" focuses on his years as an unelected president. The Great Society and the escalation of war in Vietnam are covered in "We Shall Overcome." "The Last Believer" highlights events leading to Johnson's withdrawal from politics. **240m/C VHS.** ***D:*** David Grubin; ***W:*** David Grubin.

LBJ: The Early Years ✌✌✌ **1988** The early years of President Lyndon Baines Johnson's political career are dramatized. Winning performances hoist this above other biographies. **144m/C VHS.** Randy Quaid, Patti LuPone, Morgan Brittany, Pat Hingle, Kevin McCarthy, Barry Corbin, Charles Frank; ***D:*** Peter Werner. **TV**

Le Bal ✌✌✌ **1982** You won't find many films with the music of Paul McCartney and Chopin in the credits, and even fewer without dialogue. With only music and dancing the film uses a French dance hall to illustrate the changes in French society over a 50-year period. Based on a French play. ♫La Vie en Rose; In the Mood; Michelle; Top Hat White Tie and Tails; Let's Face the Music and Dance; Harlem Nocturne; Shuffle Blues; Tutti Frutti; Only You. **112m/C VHS.** *IT FR* ***D:*** Ettore Scola; ***M:*** Irving Berlin, Paul McCartney, John Lennon, Vladimir Cosma. Cesar '84: Director (Scola), Film, Score.

Le Beau Mariage ✌✌✌ *A Good Marriage; The Well-Made Marriage* **1982 (R)** An award-winning comedy from the great French director about a zealous woman trying to find a husband and the unsuspecting man she chooses to marry. The second in Rohmer's Comedies and Proverbs series. French with subtitles. **97m/C VHS, DVD.** *FR* Beatrice Romand, Arielle Dombasle, Andre Dussollier, Feodor Atkine, Pascal Greggory, Sophie Renoir; ***D:*** Eric Rohmer; ***W:*** Eric Rohmer; ***C:*** Bernard Lutic; ***M:*** Ronan Girre, Simon des Innocents. Venice Film Fest. '82: Actress (Romand).

Le Beau Serge ✌✌✌ *Handsome Serge* **1958** Young theology student Francois returns to his home village and discovers his friend Serge, in despair of ever changing his life, has become a hopeless drunk. So Francois meddles in his life (with the best of intentions) and only causes Serge further disaster. Chabrol's first film, and a major forerunner of the nouvelle vague. In French with English subtitles. **97m/B VHS.** *FR* Gerard Blain, Jean-Claude Brialy, Michele Meritz, Bernadette LaFont; ***D:*** Claude Chabrol; ***W:*** Claude Chabrol.

Le Bonheur ✌✌½ *Happiness* **1965** A seemingly happily married carpenter (Drouot) takes a vacation with his wife and children where he meets the local postal clerk and the two begin a passionate affair. Unwilling to leave his family, Drouot believes the two women can share him but when his wife discovers his infidelity she kills herself. His grief does not cause Drouot to stop the affair, instead he moves in with his mistress. An uninvolving, unbelievable tale with a lovely Mozart score. In French with English subtitles. **87m/C VHS.** *FR* Jean-Claude Drouot, Claire Drouot, Marie-France Boyer; ***D:*** Agnes Varda; ***W:*** Agnes Varda; ***C:*** Jean Rabier, Claude Beausoleil.

Le Bonheur Est Dans le Pre ✌✌ *Happiness Is In the Fields; Happiness* **1995** Francis (Serrault) is the harried owner of a toilet brush-making business that is about to undergo a tax audit and is threatened by a workers strike. His wife and daughter are never happy and Francis' one relief is to have lunch with his macho, easy-going friend, Gerard (Mitchell). One day, he watches a TV show about missing persons and sees that a woman is looking for her husband who disappeared 28 years before—a man who looks suspiciously like Francis. The plot's convoluted and the comedy's flat. French with subtitles. **105m/C VHS.** *FR* Michel Serrault, Sabine Azema, Eddy Mitchell, Carmen Maura, Alexandra London; ***D:*** Etienne Chatiliez; ***W:*** Florence Quentin; ***C:*** Philippe Welt; ***M:*** Pascal Andreacchio. Cesar '95: Support. Actor (Mitchell).

Le Boucher ✌✌✌ *The Butcher* **1969** In a provincial French town a sophisticated schoolmistress is courted by the shy local butcher—who turns out to be a sex murderer. A well-played thriller that looks at sexual frustration. French with subtitles. **94m/C VHS.** *FR* Stephane Audran, Jean Yanne, Antonio Passalia; ***D:*** Claude Chabrol; ***W:*** Claude Chabrol.

Le Cas du Dr. Laurent ✌✌✌ **1957** A country doctor in a small French town tries to introduce methods of natural childbirth to the native women, but meets opposition from the superstitious villagers. Fine performance by Gabin. **88m/B VHS.** *FR* Jean Gabin, Nicole Courcel; ***D:*** Jean-Paul LeChanois.

Le Cavaleur ✌✌ *Practice Makes Perfect* **1978** A light hearted comedy about a philandering concert pianist. **90m/C VHS.** *FR* Jean Rochefort, Lila Kedrova, Nicole Garcia, Annie Girardot, Danielle Darrieux; ***D:*** Philippe de Broca; ***M:*** Georges Delerue.

Le Chat ✌✌✌½ *The Cat* **1975** A middle-aged couple's marriage dissolves into a hate-filled battle of wits, centering around the husband's love for their cat. In French with English subtitles. **88m/C VHS.** *FR* Jean Gabin, Simone Signoret, Annie Cordy, Jacques Rispal; ***D:*** Pierre Granier-Deferre. Berlin Intl. Film Fest. '71: Actor (Gabin).

Le Complot ✌✌✌ *The Conspiracy* **1973** When de Gaulle announces his intention to abandon Algeria, several army officers, feeling that their service has been in vain, stage a coup. There's suspense aplenty as the Gaulists, the leftists, and the police spy and are spied upon. In French with English subtitles. **120m/C VHS, Wide.** *FR* Michel Bouquet, Jean Rochefort; ***D:*** Rene Gainville.

Le Corbeau ✌✌✌ *The Raven* **1943** A great, notorious drama about a small French village whose everyday serenity is ruptured by a series of poison pen letters that lead to suicide and despair. The film was made within Nazi-occupied France, sponsored by the Nazis, and has been subjected to much misdirected malice because of it. In French with English subtitles. **92m/B VHS.** *FR* Pierre Fresnay, Noel Roquevert, Ginette LeClerc, Pierre Larquey, Antoine Belpetre; ***D:*** Henri-Georges Clouzot.

Le Crabe Tambour ✌✌✌ **1977** Rochefort plays a dying naval captain remembering his relationship with his first officer. Revealed via flashbacks, the recollections concern the adventures which transpired on a North Atlantic supply ship. Great performances from all and award-winning cinematography by Raoul Coutard. Winner of several French Cesars. A French script booklet is available. **120m/C VHS, Wide.** *FR* Jean Rochefort, Claude Rich, Jacques Dufilho, Jacques Perrin, Odile Versois, Aurore Clement; ***D:*** Pierre Schoendoerffer; ***C:*** Raoul Coutard. Cesar '78: Actor (Rochefort), Cinematog., Support. Actor (Dufilho).

Le Dernier Combat ✌✌✌ *The Last Battle* **1984 (R)** A stark film about life after a devastating nuclear war marks the directorial debut of Besson. The characters fight to survive in a now speechless world by staking territorial claims and forming new relationships with other survivors. An original and expressive film made without dialogue. **93m/B VHS, DVD, Wide.** *FR* Pierre Jolivet, Fritz Wepper, Jean Reno, Jean Bouise, Christiane Kruger; ***D:*** Luc Besson; ***W:*** Luc Besson; ***C:*** Carlo Varini; ***M:*** Eric Serra.

Le Doulos ✌✌✌ *Doulos—The Finger Man* **1961** Compelling story of an ex-convict and his buddy, a man who may be a police informant. Chronicles the efforts of the snitch (the "doulos" of the title) to bring the criminal element before the law. Melville blends in several plot twists and breathes a new-French life into the cliche-ridden genre. **108m/B VHS.** *FR* Serge Reggiani, Jean-Paul Belmondo, Michel Piccoli; ***D:*** Jean-Pierre Melville.

Le Gendarme de Saint-Tropez ✌✌½ **1967** Officer Ludovic Cruchot's plans for career advancement are on shaky ground after he is transferred to St. Tropez where his daughter has a little too much fun at the beach. Also available dubbed. **?m/C VHS.** *FR* Louis de Funes, Michel Galabru, Genevieve Grad, Jean (Lefevre) Lefebvre, Christian Marin.

Le Gentleman D'Epsom ✌✌ **1962** A French comedy about a breezy con man who scams everyone around him in order to keep up his upwardly mobile appearance and to put his bets down at the racetrack. Subtitled in English. **83m/B VHS.** *FR* Jean Gabin, Paul Frankeur.

Le Grand Chemin ✌✌✌ *The Grand Highway* **1987** A sweet, slice-of-life French film about a young boy's idyllic summer on a family friend's farm while his mother is having a baby. Hubert's son plays the boy Louis in this retelling of the director's own childhood. In French with English subtitles. Remade with an American setting in 1991 as "Paradise." **107m/C VHS.** *FR* Anemone, Richard Bohringer, Antoine Hubert, Vanessa Guedj, Christine Pascal, Raoul Billerey, Pascale Roberts; ***D:*** Jean-Loup Hubert; ***W:*** Jean-Loup Hubert; ***C:*** Claude Lecomte; ***M:*** Georges Granier. Cesar '88: Actor (Bohringer), Actress (Anemone).

Le Joli Mai **1962** A famous documentary that established Marker, depicting the everyday life of Paris denizens on the occasion of the end of the Algerian War, May 1962, when France was at peace for the first time since 1939. In French with English subtitles. **180m/B VHS.** *FR* ***D:*** Chris Marker; ***Nar:*** Yves Montand, Simone Signoret.

Le Jour Se Leve ✌✌✌½ *Daybreak* **1939** The dark, expressionist film about a sordid and destined murder/love triangle that starts with a police stand-off and evolves into a series of flashbacks. The film that put Carne and Gabin on the cinematic map. Highly acclaimed. French with English subtitles. Remade in 1947 as "The Long Night." **89m/B VHS.** *FR* Jean Gabin, Jules Berry, Arletty, Jacqueline Laurent; ***D:*** Marcel Carne.

Le Jupon Rouge ✌✌ *Manuela's Loves* **1987** Bacha (Valli) is a human rights activist and concentration camp survivor who is involved with younger fashion designer Manuela (Barrault). But when Manuela becomes drawn to the even younger Claude (Grobon), Bracha's overwhelmed with jealousy and Manuela is torn by her feelings for both women. French with subtitles. **90m/C VHS.** *FR* Alida Valli, Marie-Christine Barrault, Guillemette Grobon; ***D:*** Genevieve Lefebvre.

Le Magnifique ✌✌ *The Magnificent One* **1976** Belmondo is a master spy and novelist who mixes fantasy with reality when he chases women and solves cases. **84m/C VHS, DVD, Wide.** *FR* Jean-Paul Belmondo, Jacqueline Bisset, Hans Meyer, Vittorio Caprioli; ***D:*** Philippe de Broca; ***W:*** Francis Veber, Philippe de Broca; ***C:*** Rene Mathelin; ***M:*** Claude Bolling.

Le Mans ✌✌✌ **1971 (G)** The famous 24-hour sports car race sets the stage for this tale of love and speed. McQueen (who did his own driving) is the leading race driver, a man who battles competition, fear of death by accident, and emotional involvement. Excellent documentary-style race footage almost makes up for weak plot and minimal acting. **106m/C VHS, Wide.** Steve McQueen, Elga Andersen, Ronald Leigh-Hunt, Luc Merenda; ***D:*** Lee H. Katzin; ***C:*** Robert B. Hauser.

Le Million ✌✌✌½ **1931** A comedy/musical masterpiece of the early sound era which centers on an artist's adventures in searching for a winning lottery ticket throughout Paris. Highly acclaimed member of the Clair school of subtle French farce. In French with English subtitles. **89m/B VHS, DVD.** *FR* Annabella, Rene Lefevre, Paul Olivier, Louis Allibert; ***D:*** Rene Clair.

Le Petit Amour ✌✌✌ *Kung Fu Master* **1987 (R)** A popular French comedy about the fateful romance between a 40-year-old divorced woman and a 15-year-old boy obsessed with a kung fu video game. In French with English subtitles. **80m/C VHS.** *FR* Jane Birkin, Mathieu Demy, Charlotte Gainsbourg, Lou Doillon; ***D:*** Agnes Varda.

Le Petit Soldat ✌✌✌ **1960** The passage of time has softened the controversy that swirled about Godard's second film (after "Breathless") in the initial release. It's the story of photographer Bruno

Forestier (Subor), who joins the French nationalist movement against Algeria. While he tries to decide whether to follow orders to kill one of the opposition, he falls in love with a model (the lovely Karina, in her debut), unaware of her political beliefs. Godard's once-revolutionary on-the-fly filmmaking techniques seem completely contemporary and natural now. For serious students of film, this one makes a long-overdue debut on home video. **88m/B VHS, DVD.** *FR* Michel Subor, Anna Karina, Henri-Jacques Huet, Paul Beauvais, Georges De Beauregard, Jean-Luc Godard, Laszlo Szabo; ***D:*** Jean-Luc Godard; ***W:*** Jean-Luc Godard; ***C:*** Raoul Coutard; ***M:*** Maurice Leroux.

Le Plaisir 🦴🦴½ *House of Pleasure* **1952** An anthology of three Guy de Maupassant stories, "Le Masque," "Le Modele," and "La Maison Teillier," about the search for pleasure. In French with English subtitles. **97m/B VHS.** *FR* Claude Dauphin, Simone Simon, Jean Gabin, Danielle Darrieux, Madeleine Renaud, Gaby Morlay; ***D:*** Max Ophuls; ***Nar:*** Peter Ustinov.

Le Polygraphe 🦴🦴 *The Lie Detector* **1996** Francois (Goyette) is still a suspect in the murder of his girlfriend, Marie-Claire, two years after her death. The murder has so affected her friend Judith (Descenes) that she's written a screenplay about the unsolved crime (blaming the crime on a rogue cop). Meanwhile, actress Lucie (Brassard), who auditions for the role of Marie-Claire, gets involved with mystery man Christof (Stormare). English and French with subtitles. **97m/C VHS.** *CA* Patrick Goyette, Jose Descenes, Marie Brassard, Peter Stormare, Maria De Medeiros; ***D:*** Robert Lepage; ***W:*** Marie Brassard, Robert Lepage; ***C:*** Georges Dufaux.

Le Professionnel 🦴🦴🦴½ *The Professional* **1981** French assassin Joss Beaumont (Belmondo) returns from the African republic of Malagasy, where he's been imprisoned for two years because his own superiors turned him in to the authorities when they decided to abort his mission. Instantly his old department is mobilized to eliminate him, but Beaumont is faster and smarter than all of them put together. Fast, clever, and beholden to nothing done before, the film is a slick package, a spy thriller that relies on brains instead of guns. There's a constant flow of fistfights and combat encounters in the picture, none of which are hyped with cutting or music. Belmondo makes them all credible. A surprise picture for people who like intelligent thrillers. **109m/C DVD, Wide.** *FR* Jean-Paul Belmondo, Jean Desailly, Robert Hossein, Michel Beaune, Cyrielle Claire, Jean-Louis Richard, Sidiki Bakaba; ***D:*** Georges Lautner; ***W:*** Georges Lautner, Michel Audiard; ***C:*** Henri Decae; ***M:*** Ennio Morricone.

Le Repos du Guerrier 🦴🦴 *Warrior's Rest* **1962** Star vehicle for Bardot in which she plays a respectable woman who abandons societal norms to pursue an unbalanced lover. In French with English subtitles. **100m/C VHS.** *FR* Brigitte Bardot, Robert Hossein, James Robertson Justice, Jean-Mark Bory; ***D:*** Roger Vadim.

Le Samourai 🦴🦴🦴½ *The Samurai* **1967** Cold, precise professional killer Jef Costello (Delon) lives by his version of the code of the Japanese samurai. Hired to kill a nightclub owner, he establishes an alibi with the help of his lover Jane (Nathalie Delon, Alain's then-wife) and, unexpectedly, by Valerie (Rosier), the club's black piano-player. Jef finds Valerie's aid suspicious and begins to dig deeper, finding himself betrayed by his employers, and the subject of a police chase throughout Paris. The icy Delon was perfect for the anti-hero role and Melville's stylized filming heightens the tension and inevitable tragedy. A film much-admired, and copied, by contemporary filmmakers. French with subtitles. **95m/C VHS.** *FR* Alain Delon, Francois Perier, Cathy Rosier, Nathalie Delon, Jacques Leroy, Jean-Pierre Posier; ***D:*** Jean-Pierre Melville; ***W:*** Jean-Pierre Melville; ***C:*** Henri Decae; ***M:*** Francois de Roubaix.

Le Schpountz 🦴🦴 *Heartbeat* **1938** Satire on filmmaking and film-loving fans finds a small town grocer (Fernandel) in southern France becoming the victim of a practical joke when a visiting film crew promises to make him a star (signing him to a phony contract) if he'll come to Paris. Naturally, the joke's on them when the naive grocer arrives in the City of Light and becomes a successful movie comic. French with subtitles. **135m/B VHS.** *FR* Fernandel, Charpin, Orane Demazis, Odette Roger, Jean Castan, Leon Belieres; ***D:*** Marcel Pagnol; ***W:*** Marcel Pagnol; ***C:*** Willy; ***M:*** Casimir Oberfeld.

Le Secret 🦴🦴🦴 **1974** This classic French thriller with a shocking ending finds an escaped convict seeking shelter with a reclusive couple in the mountains. His tales of abuse and torture create tension for the pair as one believes the woeful story and the other doesn't. Dubbed in English. **103m/C VHS.** *FR* Jean-Louis Trintignant, Philippe Noiret, Jean-Francois Adam; ***D:*** Robert Enrico; ***M:*** Ennio Morricone.

Le Sex Shop 🦴🦴🦴 **1973 (R)** A man turns his little book store into a porn equipment palace, to make ends meet. When his relationship with his wife gets boring, they begin to use their erotic merchandise and adopt a swinging lifestyle. **92m/C VHS.** *FR* Claude Berri, Juliet Berto, Daniel Auteuil, Nathalie Delon; ***D:*** Claude Berri; ***M:*** Serge Gainsbourg.

Le Sexe des Etoiles 🦴🦴 *The Sex of the Stars* **1993** Curiously uninvolving film about 12-year-old Camille who discovers that the father who abandoned her is now a transsexual. Pierre walked out years before and Camille has always dreamed of his return but though they reach a tentative relationship, it's not what Camille hoped for. Title refers to Camille's obsession with astronomy because stars have no sex. Based on the novel by Proulx (who also wrote the screenplay). In French with English subtitles. **100m/C VHS.** *CA* Marianne-Coquelicot Mercier, Denis Mercier, Tobie Pelletier, Sylvie Drapeau; ***D:*** Paule Baillargeon; ***W:*** Monique Proulx; ***C:*** Eric Cayla. Genie '93: Sound.

Le Trou 🦴🦴🦴🦴 *The Hole; The Night Watch; Il Buco* **1959** Four long-term convicts in a Paris prison cell are planning to escape by tunneling to freedom. Then, a fifth prisoner joins them—is he going to betray them? Or is there already a Judas amongst the men? Based on a true story, the film has no musical score in order to heighten the tension and the actors were all nonprofessionals. Becker died in 1960; this is his final film. French with subtitles. **123m/B VHS, DVD, Wide.** *FR* Phillippe LeRoy, Marc Michel, Catherine Spaak, Andre Bervil, Michel Constantin, Jean-Paul Coquelin, Jean Keraudy, Raymond Meunier, Eddy Rasimi, Dominique Zardi; ***D:*** Jacques Becker; ***W:*** Jacques Becker, Jose Giovanni, Jean Aurel; ***C:*** Ghislan Cloquet.

Lea 🦴🦴 **1996** Lea (Vlasakova) becomes mute after witnessing her abusive father kill her mother but writes the dead woman poems and letters to express her motions. However, Lea becomes even more withdrawn from the world when she's given in an arranged marriage to the much-older Herbert (Redl). Herbert marries Lea because she resembles his dead wife but Lea finds he has disturbing similarities to her father. German with subtitles. **100m/C VHS.** *GE* Lenka Vlasakov, Christian Redl, Hanna Schygulla; ***D:*** Ivan Fila; ***W:*** Ivan Fila.

Leader of the Band 🦴🦴 **1987 (PG)** An out-of-work musician tries to train the world's worst high school band. Landesberg helps this attempted comedy along. **90m/C VHS.** Steve Landesberg, Gailard Sartain, Mercedes Ruehl, James Martinez, Calvert Deforest; ***D:*** Nessa Hyams; ***M:*** Dick Hyman.

The Leading Man 🦴🦴½ **1996 (R)** Bon Jovi's charming in the title role as American movie star Robin Grange. Grange has come to London to work in the prestige stage production by playwright Felix Webb (Wilson) and he's also become aware of Webb's complex romantic situation. Although married to Elena (Galiena), Felix is having an affair with young leading lady, Hilary Rule (Newton). So the studly Robin proposes that he seduce Elena, thus leaving Felix free to carry on with his own affair. Except Felix gets jealous when Robin succeeds and soon realizes that the actor has his own agenda. **96m/C VHS, DVD.** *GB* Lambert Wilson, Jon Bon Jovi, Anna Galiena, Thandie Newton, David Warner, Barry Humphries, Patricia Hodge, Diana Quick, Nicole Kidman; ***D:*** John Duigan; ***W:*** John Duigan; ***C:*** Jean-Francois Robin; ***M:*** Ed Shearmur.

The League of Gentlemen 🦴🦴🦴½ **1960** An ex-Army officer plots a daring bank robbery using specially skilled military personnel and irreproachable panache. Hilarious British humor fills the screen. **115m/B VHS, DVD.** *GB* Jack Hawkins, Nigel Patrick, Richard Attenborough, Roger Livesey, Bryan Forbes; ***D:*** Basil Dearden.

A League of Their Own 🦴🦴🦴 **1992 (PG)** Charming look at sports history and the Rockford Peaches, one of the teams in the real-life All American Girls Professional Baseball League, formed in the 40s when the men were off at war. Main focus is on sibling rivalry between Dottie Hinson (Davis), the beautiful, crackerjack catcher, and Kit Keller (Petty), her younger, insecure sister and team pitcher. Boozy coach Jimmy Dugan (Hanks) is wonderful as he reluctantly leads the team; he also gets credit for the classic "There's no crying in baseball" scene. Great cast of supporting characters, including sarcastic talent scout Ernie (Lovitz), opinionated, sleazy taxi dancer Mae (Madonna), loud-mouthed Doris (O'Donnell), and shy, homely Marla (Cavanagh). Lots of baseball for the sports fan. **127m/C VHS, DVD, Wide.** Geena Davis, Tom Hanks, Lori Petty, Madonna, Rosie O'Donnell, Megan Cavanagh, Tracy Reiner, Bitty Schram, Jon Lovitz, David Strathairn, Garry Marshall, Bill Pullman, Ann Cusack, Anne Elizabeth Ramsay, Freddie Simpson, Renee Coleman, Tea Leoni, Joey Slotnick, Mark Holton, Gregory Sporleder, David Lander; ***D:*** Penny Marshall; ***W:*** Lowell Ganz, Babaloo Mandel; ***C:*** Miroslav Ondricek; ***M:*** Hans Zimmer; ***V:*** Harry Shearer.

Lean on Me 🦴🦴🦴 **1989 (PG-13)** The romanticized version of the career of Joe Clark, a tough New Jersey teacher who became the principal of the state's toughest, worst school and, through controversial hard-line tactics, turned it around. **109m/C VHS, DVD, 8mm.** Morgan Freeman, Robert Guillaume, Beverly Todd, Alan North, Lynne Thigpen, Robin Bartlett, Michael Beach, Ethan Phillips, Regina Taylor; ***D:*** John G. Avildsen; ***W:*** Michael Schiffer; ***C:*** Victor Hammer; ***M:*** Bill Conti.

Leap of Faith 🦴🦴½ **1992 (PG-13)** Jonas Nightengale (Martin) is a traveling evangelist/scam artist whose tour bus is stranded in an impoverished farm town. Nevertheless he sets up his show and goes to work, aided by the technology utilized by accomplice Winger. Both Martin and Winger begin to have a change of heart after experiencing love—Winger with local sheriff Neeson and Martin after befriending a waitress (Davidovich) and her crippled brother (Haas). Martin is in his element as the slick revivalist with the hidden heart but the film is soft-headed as well as soft-hearted. **110m/C VHS, Wide.** Steve Martin, Debra Winger, Lolita (David) Davidovich, Liam Neeson, Lukas Haas, Meat Loaf Aday, Philip Seymour Hoffman, M.C. Gainey, La Chanze, Delores Hall, John Toles-Bey, Albertina Walker, Ricky Dillard; ***D:*** Richard Pearce; ***W:*** Janus Cercone; ***M:*** Cliff Eidelman.

Leap Year 🦴🦴½ **1921** Made at the apex of the 300-pound comedian's career, "Leap Year" wasn't released in the States until the '60s. Tried for manslaughter in 1921 (with two hung juries), Fatty was forced off camera and his films were taken out of circulation (although he did return to cinema behind the camera using the pseudonym William Goodrich). **60m/B VHS.** Fatty Arbuckle.

Leapin' Leprechauns 🦴🦴½ **1995 (PG)** John Dennehy's dad Michael has arrived from Ireland for a visit, accompanied by some "wee folk" who are invisible to all non-believers. Seems the little leprechauns are just in time to rescue their ancestral home from a plot by John to turn their Irish land into a theme park and make believers out of a family of skeptics. **84m/C VHS.** Grant Cramer, John Bluthal, Sharon Lee Jones, Gregory Edward Smith, Sylvester McCoy, James Ellis, Godfrey James, Tina Martin, Erica Nicole Hess; ***D:*** Ted Nicolaou; ***W:*** Ted Nicolaou, Michael McGann.

The Learning Curve 🦴🦴 **2001 (R)** Hospital orderly Paul (Giovinazzo) comes to the rescue of Georgia (Mazur) and gets involved in a shady sex scam. These small-timers are in for trouble when they target Marshal (Ventresca) who turns out to be a ruthless L.A. record producer with a lot of clout. Marshal's amused by their chutzpah and decides to bring them into his own shady deals where they are in over their heads. **97m/C VHS, DVD, Wide.** Carmine D. Giovinazzo, Monet Mazur, Vincent Ventresca, Steven Bauer, Majandra Delfino, Richard Erdman, Jack Laufer; ***D:*** Eric Schwab; ***W:*** Eric Schwab; ***C:*** Michael Hofstein; ***M:*** Zoran Boris.

The Learning Tree 🦴🦴 **1969 (PG)** A beautifully photographed adaptation of Parks' biographical novel about a 14-year-old black boy in the 1920s South, living on the verge of manhood, maturity, love, and wisdom. **107m/C VHS.** Kyle Johnson, Alex Clarke, Estelle Evans, Dana Elcar; ***D:*** Gordon Parks; ***C:*** Burnett Guffey. Natl. Film Reg. '89.

The Leather Boys 🦴🦴 *The Leatherboys* **1963** Teenaged Dot (Tushingham) marries mechanic Reggie (Campbell) and soon both begin to look beyond the boundaries of marriage. Dot enjoys her freedom from parental supervision by staying out and coming home drunk while Reggie takes up his friendship with biker pal, Pete (Sutton). Then Dot begins wondering just how close her husband and his best pal really are. Considered very controversial in the '60s, but looks staid now. **110m/B VHS, Wide.** *GB* Rita Tushingham, Colin Campbell, Dudley Sutton, Gladys Henson, Avice Landon, Betty Marsden, Dandy Nichols, Johnny Briggs, Geoffrey Dunn, Lockwood West, Denholm Elliott; ***D:*** Sidney J. Furie; ***W:*** Gillian Freeman; ***C:*** Gerald Gibbs.

Leather Burners 🦴🦴 **1943** Hoppy goes under cover to get the goods on a suspected rustler. When his cover is blown, the bad guys frame him for murder. Look for Robert Mitchum in his third bit part in this series. **66m/B VHS.** William Boyd, Andy Clyde, Jay Kirby, Victor Jory, George Givot, Bobby Larson, George Reeves, Hal Taliaferro, Forbes Murray, Robert Mitchum; ***D:*** Joseph Henabery.

Leather Jacket Love Story 🦴🦴 **1998** Remarkably sweet, campy, and raunchy romance finds 18-year-old Valley boy Kyle (Tataryn) taking a summer rental in bohemian Silver Lake in order to get the proper inspiration for his poetry. The local coffee shop is the preferred hangout and that's where Kyle spots leather-jacketed motorcycle man Mike (Bradley). Some 12 years older than Kyle, easygoing carpenter Mike is not adverse to some sexual fun, but both men are suprised when their feelings for each other start turning serious. **85m/B VHS.** Sean Tataryn, Christopher Bradley, Hector Mercado, Geoffrey Moody; ***Cameos:*** Mink Stole; ***D:*** David DeCoteau; ***W:*** Rondo Mieczkowski; ***C:*** Howard Wexler; ***M:*** Jeremy Jordan.

Leather Jackets 🦴🦴 **1990 (R)** Sweeney plays a nice guy who lets involvement with a childhood pal destroy his life. Elwes is the friend, now gang member, in trouble with both the cops and members of a rival gang, who needs Sweeney's help to escape. Fonda plays Sweeney's girlfriend caught between the two men. Essentially a routine fugitive pic with an attractive cast. **90m/C VHS.** D.B. Sweeney, Bridget Fonda, Cary Elwes, Christopher Penn, Marshall Bell, James LeGros, Jon Polito, Craig Ng, Ginger Lynn Allen; ***D:*** Lee Drysdale; ***W:*** Lee Drysdale.

Leatherface: The Texas Chainsaw Massacre 3 🦴 *Texas Chainsaw Massacre 3: Leatherface* **1989 (R)** The human-skin-wearing cannibal is at it again in this, the second sequel to the Tobe Hooper proto-mess. This one sports a bit more humor and is worth seeing for that reason. **81m/C VHS.** Kate Hodge, William Butler, Ken Foree, Tom Hudson, R.A. Mihailoff, Miriam Byrd-Nethery, Tom Everett, Joe Unger, Viggo Mortensen, David Cloud, Beth de Patie; ***D:*** Jeff Burr; ***W:*** David J. Schow; ***C:*** James L. Carter; ***M:*** Jim Manzie.

The Leatherneck **1928** Love unrequited in a faraway place starring soon to be cowboy (Hopalong Cassidy) matinee idol Boyd and Hale, the real life dad of Gilligan Island's skipper. **65m/B VHS.** William Boyd, Alan Hale, Diane Ellis.

Leave 'Em Laughing **1981** Rooney plays Chicago clown Jack Thum in this based-on-real-life TV movie. Thum takes in orphans even though he cannot find steady work, and then discovers he has cancer. **103m/C VHS.** Mickey Rooney, Anne Jackson, Allen (Goorwitz) Garfield, Elisha Cook Jr., William Windom, Red Buttons, Michael Le Clair; ***D:*** Jackie Cooper.

Leave Her to Heaven **1945** Beautiful neurotic Tierney takes drastic measures to keep hubby all to herself and will do anything to get what she wants. Tierney, in a departure from her usual roles, is excellent as this pathologically possessive creature. Oscar-winner Leon Shamroy's photography (in Technicolor) is breathtaking. Based on the novel by Ben Ames Williams. **110m/C VHS.** Gene Tierney, Cornel Wilde, Jeanne Crain, Vincent Price, Mary (Phillips) Philips, Ray Collins, Darryl Hickman, Gene Lockhart; ***D:*** John M. Stahl; ***W:*** Jo Swerling; ***C:*** Leon Shamroy; ***M:*** Alfred Newman. Oscars '45: Color Cinematog.

Leave It to Beaver **1997 (PG)** Gee, Mrs. Cleaver, that's an awful nice updating of an old TV favorite you have there. Cut the crap, Eddie. The "let's plop a lovable sitcom family into the dysfunctional 90s" bit has had its run. This time the victims are the Cleavers: wise dad Ward (McDonald), perfect mom June (Turner), popular older brother Wally (von Detten)...and newcomer Cameron Finley as the Beaver. Unlike the Bradys, the modern world has made some impact here. Beav has an African American friend while Mom wears jeans and owns a business. Gosh Wally, do you really think America was anxiously awaiting the return of the impossible-to-live-up-to clan? Don't be such a little dope. **88m/C VHS, DVD.** Christopher McDonald, Janine Turner, Erik von Detten, Cameron Finley, Barbara Billingsley, Ken Osmond, Adam Zolotin, Alan Rachins; ***D:*** Andy Cardiff; ***W:*** Brian Levant; ***C:*** Thomas Del Ruth; ***M:*** Randy Edelman.

Leave It to the Marines ½ **1951** A jerky guy wanders into a recruiting office instead of a marriage license bureau and unwittingly signs on for military service. **66m/B VHS.** Sid Melton, Mara Lynn.

Leaves from Satan's Book ½ **1919** Impressionistic episodes of Satan's fiddling with man through the ages, from Christ to the Russian Revolution. An early cinematic film by Dreyer, with ample indications of his later brilliance. Silent. **165m/B VHS.** *DK* Helge Milsen, Halvart Hoft, Jacob Texiere; ***D:*** Carl Theodor Dreyer.

Leaving Las Vegas ½ **1995 (R)** Ben Sanderson (Cage) is a hopeless alcoholic who goes to Vegas to drink himself to death, which is where he meets Sera (Shue), a lonely hooker who loves him enough not to stop him. Definitely as depressing as it sounds, but still manages to have both a subtle sense of humor and compassion. Cage tops his best work and Shue proves she deserves better than the lightweight roles she's had in the past. Not for everyone, but worth the effort for people who like to see honest emotion and hate Hollywood's insistence on happy endings. Based on the semi-autobiographical novel by John O'Brien, who committed suicide shortly before pre-production on the film began. **120m/C VHS, DVD.** Nicolas Cage, Elisabeth Shue, Julian Sands, Laurie Metcalf, David Brisbin, Richard Lewis, Valeria Golino, Steven Weber, Mariska Hargitay, Julian Lennon, Carey Lowell, Lucinda Jenney, Ed Lauter, R. Lee Ermey; ***D:*** Mike Figgis; ***W:*** Mike Figgis; ***C:*** Declan Quinn; ***M:*** Mike Figgis. Oscars '95: Actor (Cage); Golden Globes '96: Actor—Drama (Cage); Ind. Spirit '96: Actress (Shue), Cinematog., Director (Figgis), Film; L.A. Film Critics '95: Actor (Cage), Actress (Shue), Director (Figgis), Film; Natl. Bd. of Review '95: Actor (Cage); N.Y. Film Critics '95: Actor (Cage), Film; Natl. Soc. Film Critics '95: Actor (Cage), Actress (Shue), Director (Figgis); Screen Actors Guild '95: Actor (Cage).

Leaving Normal ½ **1992 (R)** Darly, a fed-up waitress, and Marianne, an abused housewife, meet at a bus stop in Normal, Wyoming and decide to blow town. They travel across the American West, through Canada, and up to Alaska, where Lahti's ex-boyfriend has left her a house. Because both women have made bad choices all their lives, they decide to leave their futures to chance, and end up finding their nirvana. Plot is similar to "Thelma & Louise," but "Leaving Normal" doesn't come close to the innovativeness of the former. Sappy and sentimental to the point of annoyance at times. **110m/C VHS.** Christine Lahti, Meg Tilly, Lenny Von Dohlen, Maury Chaykin, James Gammon, Patrika Darbo, Eve Gordon, James Eckhouse, Brett Cullen, Rutanya Alda; ***D:*** Edward Zwick; ***W:*** Edward Solomon; ***C:*** Ralf Bode.

The Leech Woman **1959** While in Africa, an older woman (Gray) discovers how to restore her youth through a tribal ritual. The only problem is it requires the pineal gland of males, which causes her to go on a killing spree to keep that youthful look. Based on a story by Ben Pivar and Francis Rosenwald. **77m/B VHS.** Coleen Gray, Grant Williams, Gloria Talbot, Phillip Terry; ***D:*** Edward Dein; ***W:*** David Duncan.

Left Behind: The Movie **2000** Ace TV newsman Buck Williams (Cameron) is on hand for a sneak attack on Israel. Right after it, devout Christians and innocent children mysteriously vanish. The film is a dramatization of the novels based on a conservative Christian interpretation of the Book of Revelation. As entertainment, it's heavy handed at every level—plotting, acting, writing, directing. **95m/C VHS, DVD.** Kirk Cameron, Brad Johnson, Chelsea Noble, Clarence Gilyard Jr., Colin Fox, Gordon Currie, Daniel Pilon, Jack Langedijk; ***D:*** Vic Sarin; ***W:*** Alan B. McElroy, Joe Goodman; ***C:*** George Tirl.

Left for Dead ½ **1978** A millionaire is accused of brutally killing his wife, and discovers in his search for an alibi that he is the victim of a conspiracy. **82m/C VHS.** Elke Sommer, Donald Pilon; ***D:*** Murray Markowitz.

The Left Hand of God **1955** After an American pilot escapes from a Chinese warlord in post-WWII, he disguises himself as a Catholic priest and takes refuge in a missionary hospital. Bogie is great as the flyboy/cleric. **87m/C VHS.** Humphrey Bogart, E.G. Marshall, Lee J. Cobb, Agnes Moorehead, Gene Tierney; ***D:*** Edward Dmytryk.

The Left-Handed Gun **1958** An offbeat version of the exploits of Billy the Kid, which portrays him as a 19th-century Wild West juvenile delinquent. Newman's role, which he method-acted, was originally intended for James Dean. Based on a 1955 Philco teleplay by Gore Vidal. **102m/B VHS.** Paul Newman, Lita Milan, John Dehner; ***D:*** Arthur Penn.

Left Luggage ½ **1998** Sticky family saga set in Antwerp, Belgium in 1972. Nonreligious college student Chaja (Fraser) is the daughter of Holocaust survivors (Sagebrecht and Schell), but has never sought to understand their ordeal or her religion. But that doesn't prevent her from taking a job as a nanny to a strict Hasidic family, the Kalmans. Carefree Chaja even manages to coax her mute four-year-old charge into speaking. She learns some lessons, the families learn some lessons (there's the prerequisite tragedy), and it's all so much unfortunate overkill. **100m/C VHS, DVD.** Laura Fraser, Isabella Rossellini, Jeroen Krabbe, Maximilian Schell, Marianne Saegebrecht, Chaim Topol; ***D:*** Jeroen Krabbe; ***W:*** Edwin de Vries; ***C:*** Walther Vanden Ende; ***M:*** Henry Vrienten.

The Legacy ½ *The Legacy of Maggie Walsh* **1979 (R)** An American couple become privy to the dark secrets of an English family gathering in a creepy mansion to inherit an eccentric millionaire's fortune. Death and demons abound. **100m/C VHS.** *GB* Katharine Ross, Sam Elliott, John Standing, Roger Daltrey, Ian Hogg; ***D:*** Richard Marquand; ***C:*** Dick Bush.

A Legacy for Leonette woof! **1985** A girl is led into a web of murder and love in this torrid romance novel brought to video. **90m/C** Loyita Chapel, Michael Anderson Jr., Dinah Anne Rogers.

Legacy of Horror woof! **1978 (R)** A weekend at the family's island mansion with two unfriendly siblings sounds bad enough, but when terror, death, and a few family skeletons pop out of the closets, things go from bad to weird. All-round poor effort with substantial gore. A remake of the director's own "The Ghastly Ones." **83m/C VHS.** Elaine Boies, Chris Broderick, Marilee Troncone, Jeannie Cusik; ***D:*** Andy Milligan.

Legacy of Lies ½ **1992 (R)** Zack Resnick is a serious, honest Chicago cop assigned to a murder investigation. He first discovers the killers got the wrong man and then finds out a lot of family secrets he wishes he didn't know. His cop-father is on the take to the Mob, which is really no surprise since Zack's grandfather turns out to be a retired gangland boss, all of which leaves Zack wondering where his loyalties lie. Too intricate plot hampers the story's flow but the cast performances are well worth watching. **94m/C VHS.** Michael Ontkean, Martin Landau, Eli Wallach, Joe Morton, Patricia Clarkson, Gerry Becker, Chelcie Ross, Ron Dean; ***D:*** Jason Meshover-Iorg; ***W:*** David Black. CABLE

Legacy of Rage **1986** Brandon (Lee), a waiter, befriends young mobster Michael (Wong), who turns out to be in love with Brandon's fiancee, May (Kent). In fact, Michael frames Brandon on a murder charge and gets him thrown in prison in order to get the girl. And what's Brandon's first thought when he gets out of the slammer? Revenge. Lee's first feature film. Chinese with subtitles or dubbed. **86m/C VHS, DVD, Wide.** *HK* Brandon Lee, Michael Wong, Bolo Yeung, Regina Kent; ***D:*** Ronny Yu.

Legal Deceit ½ *The Promised Land* **1995 (R)** Ambitious new lawyer Sydney Banks (Rochone) is taken under the wing of corporate hotshot Todd Hunter (Morgan). Then she learns his success is based on blackmail and murder, so she and boyfriend Derek (Morris) work to save her life as well as her career. **93m/C VHS.** Lela Rochon, Jeffrey Dean Morgan, Phil Morris, John Stockwell, Cheryl Francis Harrington, Jeff Marcus; ***D:*** Monika Harris; ***W:*** Monika Harris; ***C:*** Stan McClain; ***M:*** Michael Giacchino.

Legal Eagles ½ **1986 (PG)** An assistant D.A. faces murder, mayhem, and romance while prosecuting a girl accused of stealing a portrait painted by her father. Redford sparkles in this otherwise convoluted tale from Reitman, while Hannah lacks depth as the daffy thief. **116m/C VHS, DVD.** Robert Redford, Debra Winger, Daryl Hannah, Brian Dennehy, Terence Stamp, Steven Hill, David Clennon, Roscoe Lee Browne, John McMartin, Jennifer (Jennie) Dundas Lowe, Ivan Reitman; ***D:*** Ivan Reitman; ***W:*** Jack Epps Jr., Jim Cash; ***C:*** Laszlo Kovacs; ***M:*** Elmer Bernstein.

Legal Tender ½ **1990 (R)** Rude talk-show host Downey as a corrupt S & L chief? Big, menacing Davi as a romantic hero? Give this often-inept thriller credit for creative casting, if little else. Roberts adds steamy sex appeal as a lovely saloon-keeper imperiled by deadly bank fraud. **93m/C VHS.** Robert Davi, Tanya Roberts, Morton Downey Jr.; ***D:*** Jag Mundhra.

Legalese ½ **1998 (R)** Solid cast provides solid enjoyment in this skewering of tabloid journalists and the legal system. Celeb lawyer Norman Keane (Garner) doesn't take the case of actress Angela Beale (Gershon), who's accused of killing her brother-in-law. But he does recommend new kid attorney, Roy Guyton (Kerr), to take the heat while Keane works behind the scenes. This raises the antennae of tabloid TV anchorwoman Brenda Whitlass (Turner) who winds up with a video of Guyton getting up close and personal with fellow lawyer Rica Martin (Parker). Needless to say, ethics have very little to do with anything. **?m/C VHS.** James Garner, Edward Kerr, Kathleen Turner, Mary-Louise Parker, Gina Gershon; ***D:*** Glenn Jordan; ***W:*** Billy Ray; ***C:*** Tobias Schliessler; ***M:*** Stewart Copeland. CABLE

Legally Blonde ½ **2001 (PG-13)** Beverly Hills blonde Elle Woods (Witherspoon) is a sorority babe who dresses in pink and has her Chihuahua Bruiser as a constant companion. After getting dumped by frat boyfriend Warner (Davis), who's on his way to Harvard Law School, Elle wallows in chocolate-fueled misery. But determined to show him that's she more than the sum of her pretty parts, Elle also gets accepted and shows all those pasty-faced easterners, including Warner's new fiancee, brunette Vivian (Blair), that she has brains as well as blonde roots when she gets involved in a big murder case. Witherspoon is a delight in a very lightweight comedy. **95m/C VHS, DVD, Wide.** *US* Reese Witherspoon, Matthew Davis, Selma Blair, Luke Wilson, Ali Larter, Holland Taylor, Victor Garber, Jessica Cauffiel, Jennifer Coolidge, Osgood Perkins II, Alanna Ubach, Raquel Welch, Linda Cardellini, Meredith Scott Lynn; ***D:*** Robert Luketic; ***W:*** Karen McCullah Lutz, Kirsten Smith; ***C:*** Anthony B. Richmond; ***M:*** Rolfe Kent.

Legend **1986 (PG)** A colorful, unabashedly Tolkien-esque fantasy about the struggle to save an innocent waif from the Prince of Darkness. Set in a land packed with unicorns, magic swamps, bumbling dwarves and rainbows. Produced in Great Britain. **89m/C VHS, DVD, Wide.** *GB* Tom Cruise, Mia Sara, Tim Curry, David Bennent, Billy Barty, Alice Playten; ***D:*** Ridley Scott; ***M:*** Jerry Goldsmith.

Legend of Alfred Packer ½ **1980** The true story of how a guide taking five men searching for gold in Colorado managed to be the sole survivor of a blizzard. **87m/C VHS.** Patrick Dray, Ron Haines, Bob Damon, Dave Ellingson; ***D:*** Jim Roberson.

The Legend of Bagger Vance ½ **2000 (PG-13)** Director Redford misses the cut by presenting golf as a mystical experience instead of a bunch of guys in funny pants torturing a lawn. Rannulph Junuh (Damon) returns from WWI a vastly changed man. The former golf golden boy seems content to squander the rest of his life drinking at the 19th hole. His former girlfriend Adele (Theron), facing a pile of debts, convinces him to participate in an exhibition against golf giants Bobby Jones (Gretsch) and Walter Hagen (McGill) to showcase her new course. As he's shanking practice shots in every direction, the mysterious Bagger (Smith) appears, offering him guidance about golf and life in Eastern philosophy sound bites. Junuh finds his "Authentic Swing" with the help of Bagger, but it may be too late to catch his competition. Beautiful scenery, but the pace is a little too slow (just like golf!). Fits in well with the flawed American hero theme that has run through Redford's work since his turn as Jay Gatsby. Based on the novel by Steven Pressfield. Once upon a time director Redford wanted to star himself before deciding he was too mature for the part. **127m/C VHS, DVD, Wide.** Matt Damon, Will Smith, Charlize Theron, Jack Lemmon, Bruce McGill, Lane Smith, Harve Presnell, Peter Gerety, Michael O'Neill, Thomas Jay Ryan, Joel Gretsch, J. Michael Moncrief; ***D:*** Robert Redford; ***W:*** Jeremy Leven; ***C:*** Michael Ballhaus; ***M:*** Rachel Portman.

Legend of Big Foot **1982** Facing a spree of killings, a local town mobilizes to stop the legendary beast. **92m/C VHS.** Stafford Morgan, Katherine Hopkins.

Legend of Billie Jean **1985 (PG-13)** Billie Jean believed in justice for all. When the law and its bureaucracy landed hard on her, she took her cause to the masses and inspired a generation. **92m/C VHS.** Helen Slater, Peter Coyote, Keith Gordon, Christian Slater, Richard Bradford, Yeardley Smith, Dean Stockwell; ***D:*** Matthew Robbins; ***W:*** Mark Rosenthal.

The Legend of Black Thunder Mountain ½ **1979 (G)** A children's adventure in the mold of "Grizzly Adams" and "The Wilderness Family." **90m/C VHS.** Holly Beeman, Steve Beeman, Ron Brown, F.A. Milovich; ***D:*** Tom Beeman.

The Legend of Blood Castle *The Female Butcher; Blood Ceremony; Ceremonia Sangrienta* **1972 (R)** Another version of the Countess of Bathory legend, in which an evil woman bathes in the blood of virgins in an attempt to keep the wrinkles away. Released hot on the heels of Hammer's "Countess Dracula." **87m/C VHS.** *IT SP* Lucia Bose, Ewa Aulin; ***D:*** Jorge Grau.

Legend of Boggy Creek ½ **1975 (G)** A dramatized version of various Arkansas Bigfoot sightings. **87m/C VHS.** Willie E. Smith, John P. Nixon, John W. Gates, Jeff Crabtree, Buddy Crabtree; ***D:*** Charles B. Pierce; ***W:*** Earl E. Smith; ***C:*** Charles B. Pierce; ***Nar:*** Vern Stierman.

The Legend of Drunken Master *Drunken Master 2; Jui Kun 2* **1994 (R)** Jackie Chan shows the moves that made him the Charlie Chaplin of chopsocky in this sequel to the original "Drunken Master," the movie that made him a star in Hong Kong. Chan plays legendary Chinese folk hero Wong Fei-hong as a rowdy young man (although Chan was nearly forty when it was filmed) whose martial arts moves get better as he gets drunker. While traveling by train with his father Wong Kei-ying (Lung), he mistakenly takes a package that contains a priceless imperial Chinese artifact that is in the process of being smuggled out of the country by a corrupt British official. Evil henchmen are then sent to be pummeled by Fei-hong's inebriated fists. Director Lau Kar-leung performs double duty by playing Fu Min-chi, a grizzled old man also on the trail of the stolen artifact. If you're a fan of the kung-fu genre, the finale between Chan and Low Houi-kang (also known as Ken Lo, Chan's bodyguard) is not to be missed. Re-released in America six years after its original Asian release complete with classic "bad Chinese accent" dubbing. **102m/C VHS, DVD, Wide.** *HK* Jackie Chan, Lau Kar Leung, Anita (Yim-Fong) Mui, Ti Lung, Andy Lau; ***D:*** Lau Kar Leung; ***W:*** Edward Tang; ***C:*** Yiu-tsou Cheung, Tong-Leung Cheung, Jingle Ma, Man-Wan Wong; ***M:*** Michael Wandmacher.

Legend of Earl Durand ½ **1974** In Wyoming 1939, a man spends his life searching for freedom and justice. His Robin Hood actions cause a manhunt of massive proportions. **90m/C VHS.** Martin Sheen, Peter Haskell, Keenan Wynn, Slim Pickens, Anthony Caruso; ***D:*** John D. Patterson.

The Legend of Frank Woods **1977** Gunslinger returns to the land of the free after an extended holiday south of the border. Mistaken for an expected preacher in a small town, he poses as the padre and signs on the dotted line to take out a new lease on life. **88m/C VHS.** Troy Donahue, Brad Steward, Kitty Vallacher, Michael Christian; ***D:*** Deno Paoli.

Legend of Frenchie King ½ *Petroleum Girls* **1971** When prospectors discover oil on disputed land, two families feud over their conflicting claims to the property. Adult western still working out the kinks has Bardot heading a band of female outlaws. **96m/C VHS.** Brigitte Bardot, Claudia Cardinale, Michael J. Pollard, Micheline Presle; ***D:*** Christian-Jaque.

The Legend of Gator Face ½ **1996 (PG)** Hermit Winfield fills three youngsters in on their small community's legend of Gator Face—half-man, half-alligator. Kids being kids, they decide to wade through the swamps in search of the creature, which they find and also realize is harmless. Too bad the local folk don't believe the same thing and call out the national guard to destroy it. **100m/C VHS.** Paul Winfield, John White, Dan Warry-Smith, C. David Johnson, Gordon Michael Woolvett; ***D:*** Vic Sarin.

The Legend of Hell House **1973 (PG)** A multi-millionaire hires a team of scientists and mediums to investigate his newly acquired haunted mansion. It seems that the creepy house has been the site of a number of deaths and may hold clues to the afterlife. A suspenseful, scary screamfest. Matheson wrote the screenplay from his novel "Hell House." **94m/C VHS, DVD, Wide.** Roddy McDowall, Pamela Franklin, Clive Revill, Gayle Hunnicutt, Peter Bowles, Roland Culver, Michael Gough; ***D:*** John Hough; ***W:*** Richard Matheson; ***C:*** Alan Hume; ***M:*** Brian Hodgson, Delia Derbyshire.

The Legend of Hillbilly John *Who Fears the Devil; My Name is John* **1973 (G)** Hillbilly John holds off the devil with a strum of his six-string. While demons plague the residents of rural America, the hayseed messiah wanders about saving the day. **86m/C VHS.** Severn Darden, Denver Pyle, Susan Strasberg, Hedge Capers; ***D:*** John Newland.

The Legend of Jedediah Carver **197?** A rancher battles desert elements and hostile Indians in a desperate bid for survival. **90m/C VHS.** DeWitt Lee, Joshua Hoffman, Val Chapman, Richard Montgomery, David Terril; ***D:*** DeWitt Lee.

Legend of Lobo ½ **1962** The story of Lobo, a crafty wolf who seeks to free his mate from the clutches of greedy hunters. A Disney wildlife adventure. **67m/C VHS, DVD.** ***D:*** James Nelson Algar; ***W:*** James Nelson Algar; ***Nar:*** Rex Allen.

The Legend of 1900 *The Legend of the Pianist on the Ocean; La Leggenda del Pianista Sull'Oceano* **1998 (R)** Originally released under a different title and at 170 minutes, this re-cut English-language debut feature for Italian director Tornatore still has its problems. An abandoned infant is discovered aboard the luxury liner Virginian in 1900 and reared by the engine crew. As an adult, the nicknamed 1900 (Roth), has become a virtuoso pianist in the ship's orchestra and has superstitiously never set foot off the boat. His best friend is trumpet player Max (Vince), who tells the story in flashback after learning the ship has been condemned. But since 1900 remains an enigma, you won't really care what happens to him. **116m/C VHS, DVD, Wide.** Tim Roth, Pruitt Taylor Vince, Clarence Williams III, Bill Nunn, Melanie Thierry; ***D:*** Giuseppe Tornatore; ***W:*** Giuseppe Tornatore; ***C:*** Lajos Koltai; ***M:*** Ennio Morricone. Golden Globes '00: Score.

The Legend of Paul and Paula *Die Legende von Paul und Paula* **1973** East German censors tried to ban Carow's film, which focuses on personal freedoms, but it proved to be so popular with audiences that the ban never worked. Paula (Domrose) is a free-spirited unmarried salesclerk with two children while Paul (Glatzeder) is a conservative bureaucrat in a loveless marriage. They met by accident and fall in love while Paula tries to liberate Paul from his dull existence. But Paul finds it difficult to let go—until tragedy beset them. German with subtitles. **106m/C VHS, DVD.** *GE* Angelica Domrose, Winifried Glatzeder; ***D:*** Heiner Carow; ***W:*** Heiner Carow, Ulrich Plenzdorf; ***C:*** Jurgen Brauer; ***M:*** Peter Gotthardt.

The Legend of Rita *Die Stille Nach Dem Schuss; The Silence After the Shot* **1999** Rita (Beglau) is part of a West German left-wing terrorist group in the 1970s. She's caught attempting to enter East Germany by Stasi officer Erwin Hull (Wuttke), who lets her go but slyly offers to come to her aid when needed. After some trouble, Rita agrees to Hull's offer to assume a new identity and live a worker's life in East Germany. Then Rita discovers that her political ideals are at odds with ordinary, everyday life and people disenchanted by socialism. But she faces a greater change when the Berlin Wall comes down and Rita's terrorist past is exposed. German with subtitles. **101m/C VHS, DVD, Wide.** *GE* Bibiana Beglau, Martin Wuttke, Nadja Uhl, Harald Schrott, Alexander Beyer, Jenny Schily; ***D:*** Volker Schlondorff; ***W:*** Volker Schlondorff, Wolfgang Kohlhaase; ***C:*** Andreas Hofer.

The Legend of Sea Wolf *Wolf Larsen* **1975 (PG)** A sadistic sea captain forcefully rules his crew in this weak version of Jack London's novel. **90m/C VHS.** Chuck Connors, Barbara Bach, Joseph Palmer.

The Legend of Sleepy Hollow **1949** The story of Ichabod Crane and the legendary ride of the headless horseman by Washington Irving; narrated by Crosby. Also includes two classic short cartoons, "Lonesome Ghosts" (1932) with Mickey Mouse and "Trick or Treat" (1952) with Donald Duck. **45m/C VHS.** ***D:*** Jack Kinney, Clyde Geronimi, James Nelson Algar; ***Nar:*** Bing Crosby.

The Legend of Sleepy Hollow ½ **1979 (G)** Washington Irving's classic tale of the Headless Horseman of Sleepy Hollow is brought to life on the screen. **100m/C VHS.** Jeff Goldblum, Dick Butkus, Paul Sand, Meg Foster, James Griffith, John S. White. **TV**

The Legend of Sleepy Hollow **1986** Classic Washington Irving tale is given the Shelly Duvall treatment in her "Tall Tales and Legends" series. When a snooty teacher goes too far, the town blacksmith decides to play the ultimate Halloween trick on him. **51m/C VHS.** Ed Begley Jr., Beverly D'Angelo, Charles Durning, Tim Thomerson. **CABLE**

The Legend of Suram Fortress *Legenda Suramskoi Kreposti* **1985** Based on a Georgian folktale about a medieval fortress that collapses as soon as it is built. The village soothsayer tells a young man he must sacrifice himself, by bricking himself up alive within the fortress walls, if the building is every to stand. In Russian with English subtitles. **89m/C VHS, DVD.** *RU* Levan Outchanechvili, Zourab Kipchidze; ***D:*** Sergei Paradjanov; ***W:*** Vaja Gigashvili; ***C:*** Yuri Klimenko.

Legend of the Lone Ranger ½ **1981 (PG)** The fabled Lone Ranger (whose voice is dubbed throughout the entire movie) and the story of his first meeting with his Indian companion, Tonto, are brought to life in this weak and vapid version of the famous legend. The narration by Merle Haggard leaves something to be desired as do most of the performances. **98m/C VHS.** Klinton Spilsbury, Michael Horse, Jason Robards Jr., Richard Farnsworth, Christopher Lloyd, Matt Clark; ***D:*** William A. Fraker; ***W:*** William Roberts, Ivan Goff, Michael Kane; ***M:*** John Barry. Golden Raspberries '81: Worst Actor (Spilsbury), Worst New Star (Spilsbury).

Legend of the Lost **1957** Two men vie for desert treasure and desert women. Interesting only because of Wayne, but certainly not one of his more memorable films. **109m/C VHS.** John Wayne, Sophia Loren, Rossano Brazzi, Kurt Kasznar, Sonia Moser; ***D:*** Henry Hathaway; ***C:*** Jack Cardiff.

Legend of the Lost Tomb ½ **1997 (PG)** Adventure finds Egyptologist Dr. Leonhardt (Rossovich) discovering half of an ancient papyrus that could lead to the riches of the desert tomb of pharaoh Ramses II. But Leonhardt is ambused by his rival Dr. Bent (Keach), who demands the rest of the document, which just happens to be in the hands of Leonhardt's son (Pierce) and his archaeologist associate Karen (Peterson). **90m/C VHS.** Rick Rossovich, Stacy Keach, Kimberlee Peterson, Brock Pierce; ***D:*** Jonathan Winfrey. **CABLE**

Legend of the Northwest **1978 (G)** The loyalty of a dog is evidenced in the fierce revenge he has for the drunken hunter who shot and killed his master. **83m/C VHS.** Denver Pyle.

The Legend of the Sea Wolf ½ *Wolf Larsen; Larsen, Wolf of the Seven Seas* **1958** Adaptation of Jack London's dramatic adventure novel, "The Sea Wolf." A slave driving ship captain rescues a shipwreck victim and sets to abusing him along with the rest of his crew. A rebellion ensues. Superb musical score benefits the strong acting and good pace. **83m/B VHS.** Barry Sullivan, Peter Graves, Gita Hall, Thayer David; ***D:*** Harmon Jones; ***W:*** Jack DeWitt.

The Legend of the 7 Golden Vampires *The Seven Brothers Meet Dracula; Dracula and the Seven Golden Vampires* **1973** It's kung-fu meets horror as Van Helsing pursues Dracula to 19th-century China and is assisted by martial artists. One of the last Hammer coproductions. The Anchor Bay release also contains the 75-minute "Seven Brothers Meet Dracula," which was the U.S. version of the movie. **89m/C VHS, DVD, Wide.** *GB* Peter Cushing, David Chang, Robin Stewart, Julie Ege, John Forbes-Robertson; ***D:*** Roy Ward Baker; ***W:*** Don Houghton; ***C:*** Roy Ford, John Wilcox; ***M:*** James Bernard.

Legend of the Werewolf **1975 (R)** A child who once ran with the wolves has forgotten his past, except when the moon is full. **90m/C VHS.** *GB* Peter Cushing, Hugh Griffith, Ron Moody, David Rintoul, Lynn Dalby, Stefan Gryff, Renee Houston, Norman Mitchell, Marjorie Yates, Roy Castle; ***D:*** Freddie Francis; ***W:*** Renee Houston.

The Legend of the Wolf Woman ½ *Daughter of the Werewolf; Werewolf Woman; She-Wolf* **1977 (R)** The beautiful Daniella assumes the personality of the legendary wolfwoman, leaving a trail of gruesome killings across the countryside. Genre fans will find this one surprisingly entertaining. Also on video as "Werewolf Woman." **84m/C VHS.** *IT* Anne Borel, Frederick Stafford, Tino Carey, Elliot Zamuto, Ollie Reynolds, Andrea Scotti, Karen Carter, Howard (Red) Ross; ***D:*** Rino Di Silvestro; ***W:*** Rino Di Silvestro, Howard (Red) Ross.

Legend of Tom Dooley **1959** Somber western about three Confederate soldiers who rob a Union stagecoach and kill two soldiers, not knowing that the Civil War has ended. Landon turns in a good performance as the Rebel soldier turned outlaw. Based on the hit song by the Kingston trio. **79m/B VHS.** Michael Landon, Jo Morrow, Jack Hogan, Richard Rust, Dee Pollock, Ken Lynch; ***D:*** Ted Post; ***M:*** Ronald Stein.

Legend of Valentino **1975** Docudrama traces the legendary exploits of one of the silver screen's greatest lovers, Rudolph Valentino. Typical TV-movie fare that lacks the power of the legend's life. **96m/C VHS.** Franco Nero, Suzanne Pleshette, Lesley Ann Warren, Yvette Mimieux, Judd Hirsch, Milton Berle, Harold J. Stone; ***D:*** Melville Shavelson. **TV**

Legend of Walks Far Woman **1982** A proud Sioux woman fights for survival and her tribe during the American-Indian Wars. Welch is miscast. From Colin Stuart's novel. **120m/C VHS.** Raquel Welch, Nick Mancuso, Bradford Dillman; ***D:*** Mel Damski. **TV**

The Legend of Wolf Mountain ½ **1992 (PG)** Three children are held hostage by two prison escapees in the Utah mountains. They are aided in their escape by a Native American "wolf spirit." With the criminals on their trail will the three be able to survive in the wilderness until a search party can find them? **91m/C VHS.** Mickey Rooney, Bo Hopkins, Don Shanks, Vivian Schilling, Robert Z'Dar, David Shark, Nicole Lund, Natalie Lund, Matthew Lewis, Jonathan Best; ***D:*** Craig Clyde; ***W:*** Craig Clyde.

Legends of the Fall **1994 (R)** Sweeping, meandering, melodramatic family saga set in Montana (though filmed in Alberta, Canada). Patriarch William Ludlow (Hopkins), a retired Army colonel, is raising three sons: reserved Alfred (Quinn), idealistic Samuel (Thomas), and wild middle son Tristan (Pitt). In 1913, Samuel returns from Boston with a fiancee, the lovely and refined Susannah (Ormond). Only problem is Alfred and Tristan take one look and also desire her—a passion that will carry them through some 20 years of heartbreak. Film loses the spare toughness of the Jim Harrison novella but is a visual feast (and not just because the camera seems to drool every time Pitt appears on screen.) **134m/C VHS, DVD, 8mm, Wide.** Brad Pitt, Aidan Quinn, Julia Ormond, Anthony Hopkins, Henry Thomas, Gordon Tootoosis, Tantoo Cardinal, Karina Lombard, Paul Desmond, Kenneth Welsh; ***D:*** Edward Zwick; ***W:*** Susan Shilliday, William D. Wittliff; ***C:*** John Toll; ***M:*** James Horner. Oscars '94: Cinematog.

Legends of the North ½ **1995 (PG)** Crusty prospector Whip Gorman (Quaid) and partner Paul Bel Air are searching for a mythical lake of gold when Paul takes a fall off a mountain. Whip sends for Paul's son Charles so that he can translate his father's diary (it's in French) and get the clues to the gold's whereabouts. Naturally, some rival prospectors, some Indians, and even a feisty gal or two help or hinder our treasure seekers. Based on a story by Jack London. **95m/C VHS.** Randy Quaid.

Legion 🦴🦴 **1998 (R)** Major Agatha Doyle (Farrell) is given a group of convicts to lead on a mission to destroy The Legion, a genetically engineered killing machine. But first she has to keep them from killing each other—or her. **97m/C VHS.** Terry Farrell, Corey Feldman, Rick Springfield, Parker Stevenson, Audie England; ***D:*** Jon Hess. **CABLE**

Legion of Iron 🦴 **1990 (R)** Adventures in a computer-run, neo-Roman civilization where men and women battle for supremacy. **85m/C VHS.** Kevin T. Walsh, Erica Nann, Regie De Morton, Camille Carrigan; ***D:*** Yakov Bentsvi.

Legion of Missing Men 🦴½ **1937** Professional soldiers of fortune, the French Foreign Legion, fight the evil sheik Ahmed in the Sahara. **62m/B VHS.** Ralph Forbes, Ben Alexander, Hala Linda, Roy D'Arcy, Paul Hurst, Jimmy Aubrey; ***D:*** Hamilton MacFadden.

Legion of the Lawless 🦴½ **1940** Group of outlaws band together in order to spread terror and confusion among the populace. **59m/B VHS.** George O'Brien, Virginia Vale.

Legionnaire 🦴🦴 **1998 (R)** In the 1920s, Alain Lefevre (Van Damme) enlists in the French Foreign Legion and is stationed in Morocco with other new recruits. After rigorous training, the men find themselves being sent into battle at a remote outpost, where they'll learn about war and survival. **99m/C VHS, DVD, Wide.** Jean-Claude Van Damme, Nicholas Farrell, Steven Berkoff, Jim Carter, Adewale Akinnuoye-Agbaje; ***D:*** Peter Macdonald; ***W:*** Sheldon Lettich, Rebecca Morrison; ***C:*** Doug Milsome; ***M:*** John Altman.

Legs 🦴🦴 **1983** Backstage story of three girls who are competing for a job with Radio City Music Hall's Rockettes. **91m/C VHS.** Gwen Verdon, John Heard, Sheree North, Shanna Reed, Maureen Teefy; ***D:*** Jerrold Freedman; ***C:*** Allen Daviau. **TV**

Leila 🦴🦴 **1997** Leila, an Iranian woman, finds that she cannot have children shortly after she is married. Although her husband does not mind, Leila's mother-in-law convinces her to let her son take another wife in order to produce an heir. Farsi with subtitles. **129m/C VHS, DVD.** *IA* Leila Hatami, Ali Mosaffa, Jamileh Sheikhi; ***D:*** Dariush Mehrjui.

L'Eleve 🦴🦴 *The Pupil* **1995** In 1897 Europe, an aristocratic family hires inexperienced 25-year-old Julien (Cassel) to tutor their precocious teenaged son, Morgan (Salmon). After a tentative battle for control, the two establish a strong emotional rapport and Julien learns that the family is not only in financial difficulty but is part of an empty, amoral social class only concerned with appearance. Based on a story by Henry James; French with subtitles. **92m/C VHS.** *FR* Vincent Cassel, Caspar Solmon, Caroline Cellier, Jean-Pierre Marielle, Sabine Destailleur, Sandrine Le Berre; ***D:*** Olivier Schatzky; ***W:*** Eve Deboise, Olivier Schatzky; ***C:*** Carlo Varini; ***M:*** Romano Musumarra. Montreal World Film Fest. '95: Director (Schatzky).

The Lemon Drop Kid 🦴🦴½ **1951** Second version of the Damon Runyon chestnut about a racetrack bookie who must recover the gangster's money he lost on a bet. As the fast-talking bookie, Hope sparkles. ♫Silver Bells; It Doesn't Cost a Dime to Dream; They Obviously Want Me to Sing. **91m/B VHS, DVD.** Bob Hope, Lloyd Nolan, Fred Clark, Marilyn Maxwell, Jane Darwell, Andrea King, William Frawley, Jay C. Flippen, Harry Bellaver; ***D:*** Sidney Lanfield; ***W:*** Frank Tashlin, Edmund Hartmann, Robert O'Brien; ***C:*** Daniel F. Fapp; ***M:*** Ray Evans, Jay Livingston, Victor Young.

The Lemon Sisters 🦴🦴 **1990 (PG-13)** Three women, friends and performance partners since childhood, struggle to buy their own club. They juggle the men in their lives with less success. Great actresses like these should have done more with this interesting premise, and the excellent male cast has much more potential. **93m/C VHS, DVD, Wide.** Diane Keaton, Carol Kane, Kathryn Grody, Elliott Gould, Ruben Blades, Aidan Quinn; ***D:*** Joyce Chopra; ***W:*** Jeremy Pikser; ***C:*** Bobby Byrne; ***M:*** Dick Hyman.

Lemonade Joe 🦴🦴 *Limonadovy Joe aneb Konska Opera* **1964** The Czech New Wave does a broad spoof of the American western complete with good guys in white hats, bad guys in black hats, and a saloon gal with a heart of gold. Doug Badman (Kopecky) runs the Trigger Whiskey Saloon, along with his hotsie singer Tornado Lou (Fialova). The hard-drinking bar flies harass sweet temperance worker Winifred (Schoberova) until clean-living soft drink salesman Lemonade Joe (Fiala) shows up to save the day. Czech with subtitles. **87m/B VHS.** *CZ* Milos Kopecky, Karel Fiala, Kveta Fialova, Olga Schoberova; ***D:*** Oldrich Lipsky; ***W:*** Oldrich Lipsky, Jiri Brdecka; ***C:*** Vladimir Novotny; ***M:*** Vlastimil Hala, Jan Rychlik.

Lemora, Lady Dracula 🦴 *The Lady Dracula; The Legendary Curse of Lemora; Lemora: A Child's Tale of the Supernatural* **1973 (PG)** A pretty young church singer is drawn into the lair of the evil Lady Dracula, whose desires include her body as well as her blood. Horror fans will enjoy some excellent atmosphere, particularly in a scene where the girl's church bus is attacked by zombie-like creatures; Smith remains a '70s "B" movie favorite. Perhaps a double feature with "Lady Frankenstein"...? **80m/C VHS.** Leslie Gilb, Cheryl "Rainbeaux" Smith, William Whitton, Steve Johnson, Hy Pyke, Maxine Ballantyne, Parker West, Richard Blackburn; ***D:*** Richard Blackburn; ***W:*** Robert Fern, Richard Blackburn; ***C:*** Robert Caramico.

Lena's Holiday 🦴🦴 **1990 (PG-13)** Fluffy comedy about a winsome East German girl visiting L.A. for the first time, and the culture-shock that ensues. Sharp script and performances. **97m/C VHS, DVD, Wide.** Felicity Waterman, Chris Lemmon, Noriyuki "Pat" Morita, Susan Anton, Michael Sarrazin, Nick Mancuso, Bill Dana, Liz Torres; ***D:*** Michael Keusch; ***W:*** Michael Keusch, Deborah Tilton; ***C:*** Louis DiCesare.

L'Enfant d'Eau 🦴🦴 *Water Child; Behind the Blue* **1995** Mentally handicapped 20-something Emile (La Haye) and precocious 12-year-old Cedrine (Monette) must learn to work together to survive after a plane crash strands them on an island in the Bahamas. Familiar story offers no surprises and the script shies away from any sexual implications, negating two excellent performances. French with subtitles. **103m/C VHS.** *CA* David La Haye, Marie-France Monette; ***D:*** Robert Menard; ***W:*** Claire Wojas. Genie '95: Actor (La Haye).

L'Enfer 🦴🦴🦴 *Jealousy; Torment* **1993** Claustrophobic thriller chronicles the descent into madness of an unstable hotel owner (Cluzet) convinced that his beautiful wife (Beart) is having an affair. Intriguing plot points that blur appearances and reality lead to ambiguous and unsatisfying ending. Clouzot himself began filming his screenplay in 1964, but a heart attack forced him to abandon the project. In French with English subtitles. **103m/C VHS, DVD.** *FR* Emmanuelle Beart, Francois Cluzet, Nathalie Cardone, Andre Wilms, Marc Lavoine; ***D:*** Claude Chabrol; ***W:*** Claude Chabrol, Henri-Georges Clouzot, Jose-Andre Lacour; ***C:*** Bernard Zitzermann; ***M:*** Matthieu Chabrol.

Leningrad Cowboys Go America 🦴🦴½ **1989 (PG-13)** An outlandish Finnish band, the Leningrad Cowboys, pack up their electric accordians and their one dead member and go on tour in America. With matching front-swept pompadours and pointy shoes, the group's appearance is the picture's best joke—and one of its only jokes, as the road trip plods in deadpan fashion that may bore viewers. It's best appreciated by fans of comic minimalist Jim Jarmusch (who has a guest role). In Finnish with English subtitles. **78m/C VHS, Wide.** *FI* Matti Pellonpaa, Kari Vaananen, Sakke Jarvenpaa, Silu Seppala, Mauri Sumen, Mato Valtonen, Nicky Tesco, Jim Jarmusch; ***D:*** Aki Kaurismaki; ***W:*** Aki Kaurismaki; ***C:*** Timo Salminen; ***M:*** Mauri Sumen.

L'Ennui 🦴🦴 **1998** Detached rather than titillating look at sexual obsession. Middleaged, middle-class philosophy prof Martin (Berling) has recently separated from his wife and is dealing (or rather not dealing) with his midlife crisis. Until he meets teenaged artist's model Cecilia (Guillemin) and the two begin a very carnal affair, though Martin thinks his paramour is shallow and stupid. Then he discovers Cecilia also has a lover her own age and she wants to keep them both. In response, Martin turns obsessively jealous. Based on the novel "La Noia" by Alberto Moravia. French with subtitles. **120m/C VHS, DVD, Wide.** *FR* Charles Berling, Sophie Guillemin, Arielle Dombasle, Robert Kramer, Tom Ouedraoge; ***D:*** Cedric Kahn; ***W:*** Cedric Kahn, Laurence Ferreira Barbosa; ***C:*** Pascal Marti.

Lenny 🦴🦴🦴 **1974 (R)** Smoky nightclubs, drug abuse, and obscenities abound in Hoffman's portrayal of the controversial comedian Lenny Bruce, whose use of street language led to his eventual blacklisting. Perrine is a gem as his stripper wife. Adapted from the Julian Barry play, this is a visually compelling piece that sharply divided critics upon release. **111m/B VHS, DVD, Wide.** Dustin Hoffman, Valerie Perrine, Jan Miner, Stanley Beck; ***D:*** Bob Fosse; ***W:*** Julian Barry; ***C:*** Bruce Surtees; ***M:*** Ralph Burns. Cannes '75: Actress (Perrine); Natl. Bd. of Review '74: Support. Actress (Perrine); N.Y. Film Critics '74: Support. Actress (Perrine).

Lensman **1984** In the 25th century space pirates known as the Boskande are threatening the civilized universe. Young Kimall Kenison is chosen by a higher power to become a lensman—and live or die for freedom. Based on the E.E. "Doc" Smith novels, this production is a combination of animation and computer graphics. Dubbed in English. **107m/C VHS.** *JP*

Leo Tolstoy's Anna Karenina 🦴🦴½ *Leo Tolstoy's Anna Karenina* **1996 (PG-13)** Well, the third film version of Tolstoy's tempestuous, tragic romance certainly looks good, even if the performances don't engender the passion the story demands. Beautiful married Anna (Marceau) leaves stuffy husband Karenin (Fox) and their son to travel to 1880 Moscow and mend the marriage of her philandering brother Stiva (Huston). But she meets dashing soldier, Count Alexei Vronsky (Bean), who immediately decides to pursue the beauty and the two begin an all-encompassing affair that leads to tragedy. This version also includes the secondary, contrasting romance between young Kitty (Kirshner) and Tolstoy's alter ego, questioning aristo Levin (Molina). Filmed on location in St. Petersburg, Russia. The classical score includes selections from Tschaikovsky, Rachmaninoff and Prokofiev, under the direction of Georg Solti. **120m/C VHS.** Sophie Marceau, Sean Bean, Alfred Molina, Mia Kirshner, James Fox, Danny Huston, Fiona Shaw, Phyllida Law, David Schofield, Saskia Wickham; ***D:*** Bernard Rose; ***W:*** Bernard Rose; ***C:*** Daryn Okada.

Leolo 🦴🦴🦴 **1992** Deeply disturbing black comedy about one of the screen's most dysfunctional families. Leo is a 12-year-old French Canadian from Montreal who is determined to remake himself. He's decided to be a Sicilian lad named Leolo, escaping from his horrific family into his fantasies (and potential madness). "I dream, therefore I am not," he thinks. His parents are obsessed with toilet training, his cowardly brother with body-building, his sisters are demented, and his grandfather is a sadistic, dirty old man. Striking cinematography and great soundtrack, but not for the faint of heart (or stomach). In French with English subtitles. **107m/C VHS.** *CA* Maxime Collin, Julien Guiomar, Ginette Reno, Pierre Bourgault, Yves Montmarquette, Roland Blouin, Giuditta del Vecchio; ***D:*** Jean-Claude Lauzon; ***W:*** Jean-Claude Lauzon. Genie '92: Costume Des., Film Editing, Orig. Screenplay.

Leon Morin, Priest 🦴🦴½ **1961** A young priest and a widow, who happens to be a Communist, fall in love during the WWII German occupation of France. Based on the novel by Beatrix Beck. In French with English subtitles. **118m/B VHS.** *IT FR* Jean-Paul Belmondo, Emmanuelle Riva; ***D:*** Jean-Pierre Melville.

Leon the Pig Farmer 🦴🦴½ **1993** Dry comedic satire about identity. Leon Geller has never quite fitted into his parents' comfortable Jewish society and no wonder—Leon accidentally discovers he is the product of artificial insemination. And what's more, the lab made a mistake and Leon isn't a true Geller after all. His father is actually a genial (and Gentile) Yorkshire pig farmer named Brian Chadwick, who cheerfully welcomes Leon as his long-lost son. All four parents try to cope while Leon moves bewilderedly amongst them. Film tends to be too timid in its satire but still has its witty moments. **98m/C VHS.** *GB* Mark Frankel, Janet Suzman, Brian Glover, Connie Booth, David DeKeyser, Maryam D'Abo, Gina Bellman; ***D:*** Vadim Jean, Gary Sinyor; ***W:*** Gary Sinyor, Michael Normand.

Leonard Part 6 🦴 **1987 (PG)** A former secret agent comes out of retirement to save the world from a crime queen using animals to kill agents. In the meantime, he tries to patch up his collapsing personal life. Wooden and disappointing; produced and co-written by Cosby, who himself panned the film. **83m/C VHS.** Bill Cosby, Gloria Foster, Tom Courtenay, Joe Don Baker; ***D:*** Paul Weiland; ***W:*** Bill Cosby, Jonathan Reynolds; ***C:*** Jan De Bont; ***M:*** Elmer Bernstein. Golden Raspberries '87: Worst Picture, Worst Actor (Cosby), Worst Screenplay.

Leonor 🦴 **1975** Idiotic medieval drivel with Ullmann rising from the dead after husband Piccoli seals her in a tomb. Directed by the son of Luis Bunuel. **90m/C VHS.** *FR SP IT* Liv Ullmann, Michel Piccoli, Ornella Muti; ***D:*** Juan Bunuel; ***M:*** Ennio Morricone.

Leopard in the Snow 🦴🦴 **1978 (PG)** The romance between a race car driver allegedly killed in a crash and a young woman is the premise of this film. **89m/C VHS.** Keir Dullea, Susan Penhaligon, Kenneth More, Billie Whitelaw; ***D:*** Gerry O'Hara.

The Leopard Man 🦴🦴½ **1943** An escaped leopard terrorizes a small town in New Mexico. After a search, the big cat is found dead, but the killings continue. Minor but effective Jacques Tourneur creepie. Based on Cornell Woolrich's novel "Black Alibi." Another Val Lewton Horror production. **66m/B VHS.** Jean Brooks, Isabel Jewell, James Bell, Margaret Landry, Dennis O'Keefe, Margo, Rita (Paula) Corday, Abner Biberman; ***D:*** Jacques Tourneur; ***W:*** Ardel Wray; ***C:*** Robert De Grasse.

The Leopard Son **1996 (G)** Beautiful documentary follows the birth and first two years of life for a leopard cub born on Africa's Serengeti plain. Mom leopard shows him how to survive and then he's out into the harsh world on his own. Parents should be forewarned that the hunt-and-kill scenes may upset the little ones. **87m/C VHS.** ***D:*** Hugo Van Lawick; ***W:*** Michael Olmert; ***C:*** Hugo Van Lawick, Matthew Aeberhard; ***M:*** Stewart Copeland; ***Nar:*** John Gielgud.

The Leopard Woman 🦴🦴 **1920** Long before the cat lady cut her first claws, there was the leopard woman. Vamp Glaum finds much trouble to meow about on the Equator. **66m/B VHS.** Louise Glaum.

Leper 🦴🦴 *Tredowata* **1976** A melodrama of forbidden love between a wealthy nobleman and a beautiful high school teacher. The townspeople try to destroy the love between the two because of their different social classes. In Polish with English subtitles. **100m/C VHS.** *PL* Elzbieta Starostecka, Leszek Teleszynski; ***D:*** Jerzy Hoffman.

Lepke 🦴🦴½ **1975 (R)** The life and fast times of Louis "Lepke" Buchalter from his days in reform school to his days as head of Murder, Inc. and his execution in 1944. **110m/C VHS.** Tony Curtis, Milton Berle, Gianni Russo, Vic Tayback, Michael Callan; ***D:*** Menahem Golan.

Leprechaun WOOF! **1993 (R)** A sadistic 600-year-old leprechaun winds up wreaking havoc in North Dakota. If this makes no particular sense, neither does the film which is basic horror story excess. A man goes to Ireland for his mother's funeral, steals the gold belonging to the leprechaun, locks the creature up, and winds up accidentally taking the evil imp back to the States with him. When the leprechaun gets free, he wants a bloodthirsty revenge—and shoes. One of the so-called humorous bits is the leprechaun's shoe fetish. Irish eyes will not be smiling watching this mess. **92m/C VHS, DVD.** Warwick Davis, Jennifer Aniston, Ken Olandt, Mark Holton, John Sanderford, Robert Gorman, Shay Duffin, John Voldstad; ***D:*** Mark Jones; ***W:*** Mark Jones; ***C:*** Levie Isaacks. **VIDEO**

Leprechaun 2 🦴🦴 **1994 (R)** Sequel to the horror flick about a malevolent Irish gnome. It seems one of his fairy entitlements is that he can possess any woman he wants if she sneezes three times. Thwarted in his attempt to snare a comely lass one thousand years earlier, he returns to present-day California to exact revenge on her descendant Durkin. Contrary to the popular legend that leprechauns are benign kind-hearted sprites, this nasty combines the treachery of a Gestapo officer with the firepower of Rambo in his attempt to harass the unimpressed Durkin into his clutches. **85m/C VHS, DVD, Wide.** Warwick Davis, Sandy Baron, Adam Biesk, James Lancaster, Clint Howard, Kimmy Robertson, Charlie Heath, Shevonne Durkin; ***D:*** Rodman Flender; ***W:*** Turi Meyer, Al Septien; ***C:*** Jane Castle; ***M:*** Jonathan Elias.

Leprechaun 3 🦴 **1995 (R)** A student steals the nasty little beastie's gold and he's off to Las Vegas to get it back and to kill the gamblers, also after his magic money, in decidedly disgusting ways. **93m/C VHS, DVD.** Warwick Davis, John Gatins, Michael Callan, Caroline Williams, Lee Armstrong; ***D:*** Brian Trenchard-Smith; ***W:*** Brian Dubos; ***C:*** David Lewis; ***M:*** Dennis Michael Tenney.

Leprechaun 4: In Space **woof!** **1996 (R)** Who knows how the little imp got there but now our old friend the Leprechaun (Davis) is busy terrorizing an alien princess (Carlton) on a distant planet. He wants to marry the babe and rule the universe but its the Marines to the rescue! Yes, an Earth platoon arrives to foil his plans. **98m/C VHS, DVD.** Warwick Davis, Rebekah Carlton, Brent Jasmer, Debbe Dunning, Rebecca Cross, Tim Colceri; ***D:*** Brian Trenchard-Smith; ***W:*** Dennis Pratt; ***C:*** David Lewis; ***M:*** Dennis Michael Tenney.

Leprechaun 5: In the Hood **woof!** **1999 (R)** This time around the bloodthirsty leprechaun wants revenge on a group of wannabe rap artists who use his magic (and steal his gold) in order to become successful. If you've seen any of the others in this series, you know what to expect. **91m/C VHS, DVD.** Warwick Davis, Ice-T; ***D:*** Robert Spera. **VIDEO**

Les Assassins de L'Ordre 🦴🦴 *Law Breakers* **1971** A righteous French judge faces the case of an innocent man killed by police brutality. Subtitled in English. **100m/C VHS.** *FR* Jacques Brel, Catherine Rouvel, Michael (Michel) Lonsdale, Charles Denner; ***D:*** Marcel Carne; ***M:*** Michel Colombier.

Les Aventuriers 🦴🦴½ *The Last Adventure* **1977** Two friends find themselves swindled in an insurance scam and set out after the perpetrator who sent them off to Africa in search of a treasure. Available dubbed. **?m/C VHS.** *FR* Alain Delon, Lino Ventura, Joanna Shimkus.

Les Biches 🦴🦴🦴½ *The Heterosexuals* **1968 (R)** An exquisite film that became a landmark in film history with its theme of bisexuality and upper class decadence. A rich socialite picks up a young artist drawing on the streets of Paris, seduces her, and then takes her to St. Tropez. Conflict arises when a suave architect shows up and threatens to come between the two lovers. In French with English subtitles. **95m/C VHS.** *FR* Stephane Audran, Jean-Louis Trintignant, Jacqueline Sassard; ***D:*** Claude Chabrol; ***W:*** Claude Chabrol.

Les Bonnes Femmes 🦴🦴🦴 *The Good Girls; The Girls* **1960** Four Paris shopgirls dream of escaping the monotony of their lives and finding romance but instead discover broken dreams and danger. Chabrol's New Wave thriller focuses more on character and irony than suspense. French with subtitles. **105m/B VHS, DVD, Wide.** *FR* Bernadette LaFont, Stephane Audran, Clothilde Joano, Lucile Saint-Simon; ***D:*** Claude Chabrol; ***W:*** Paul Geoauff; ***C:*** Henri Decae; ***M:*** Pierre Jansen, Paul Misraki.

Les Bons Debarras 🦴🦴½ **1981** In French with English subtitles, this Canadian film follows a lonely 13-year-old's effort to win her mother's exclusive love. **114m/C VHS.** *CA* Marie Tifo, Charlotte Laurier, German Houde; ***D:*** Francis Mankiewicz. Genie '81: Actress (Tifo), Director (Mankiewicz), Film, Support. Actor (Houde).

Les Carabiniers 🦴🦴🦴 *The Soldiers* **1963** A cynical, grim anti-war tract, detailing the pathetic adventures of two young bums lured into enlisting with promises of rape, looting, torture and battle without justification. Controversial in its day, and typically elliptical and non-narrative. In French with English subtitles. **80m/B VHS, DVD.** *GB IT FR* Albert Juross, Marino (Martin) Mase, Catherine Ribeiro, Genevieva Galea, Anna Karina; ***D:*** Jean-Luc Godard; ***W:*** Jean-Luc Godard; ***C:*** Raoul Coutard; ***M:*** Philippe Arthuys.

Les Comperes 🦴🦴🦴 **1983** A woman suckers two former lovers into finding her wayward son by secretly telling each ex he is the natural father of the punk. Depardieu is a streetwise journalist who teams up with a suicidal hypochondriac/wimp (Richard) to find the little brat. Humorous story full of bumbling misadventures. In French with English subtitles. **92m/C VHS.** *FR* Pierre Richard, Gerard Depardieu, Anny (Annie Legras) Duperey, Michel Aumont; ***D:*** Francis Veber; ***W:*** Francis Veber; ***M:*** Vladimir Cosma.

Les Enfants Terrible 🦴🦴🦴 *The Strange Ones* **1950** The classic, lyrical treatment of adolescent deviance adapted by Cocteau from his own play, wherein a brother and sister born into extreme wealth eventually enter into casual crime, self-destruction, and incest. In French with English subtitles. **105m/B VHS.** *FR* Edouard Dermithe, Nicole Stephane; ***D:*** Jean-Pierre Melville; ***W:*** Jean Cocteau, Jean-Pierre Melville.

Les Girls 🦴🦴½ **1957** When one member of a performing troupe writes her memoirs, the other girls sue for libel. Told through a series of flashbacks, this story traces the girls' recollections of their relationships to American dancer Kelly. Cole Porter wrote the score for this enjoyable "Rashomon"-styled musical. ♫Les Girls; Flower Song; You're Just Too, Too; Ca C'est L'Amour; Ladies In Waiting; La Habanera; Why Am I So Gone (About That Gal?). **114m/C VHS, Wide.** Gene Kelly, Mitzi Gaynor, Kay Kendall, Taina Elg, Henry Daniell, Patrick Macnee; ***D:*** George Cukor; ***C:*** Robert L. Surtees. Oscars '57: Costume Des.; Golden Globes '58: Actress—Mus./Comedy (Kendall), Film—Mus./Comedy.

Les Grandes Manoeuvres 🦴🦴🦴 *Summer Manoeuvers; The Grand Maneuvers* **1955** Clair's first film in color depicts the romance between a seductive soldier (Philipe) and a divorcee (Morgan) in a pre-WWI garrison town. Gentle comedy has Philipe falling in love but his reputation as a Don Juan comes between them. French with subtitles. **106m/C VHS.** *FR* Gerard Philipe, Michele Morgan, Yves Robert, Brigitte Bardot, Jean Desailly, Pierre Dux; ***D:*** Rene Clair; ***W:*** Rene Clair; ***M:*** Georges Van Parys.

Les Miserables 🦴🦴🦴🦴 **1935** Victor Hugo's classic novel about small-time criminal Jean Valjean and 18th-century France. After facing poverty and prison, escape and torture, Valjean is redeemed by the kindness of a bishop. As he tries to mend his ways, he is continually hounded by the policeman Javert, who is determined to lock him away. The final act is set during a student uprising in the 1730s. This version is the best of many, finely detailed and well-paced with excellent cinematography by Gregg Toland. **108m/B VHS.** Fredric March, Charles Laughton, Cedric Hardwicke, Rochelle Hudson, John Beal, Frances Drake, Florence Eldridge, John Carradine, Jessie Ralph, Leonid Kinskey; ***D:*** Richard Boleslawski; ***W:*** W.P. Lipscomb; ***C:*** Gregg Toland; ***M:*** Alfred Newman.

Les Miserables 🦴🦴½ **1952** Hugo's classic novel done up Italian style with lavish sets and spectacle. Dubbed in English. **119m/B VHS.** *IT* Gino Cervi, Valentina Cortese; ***D:*** Riccardo (Robert Hampton) Freda; ***C:*** Joseph LaShelle; ***M:*** Alex North.

Les Miserables 🦴🦴🦴 **1957** An epic French adaptation of the Victor Hugo standard about Valjean, Javert, and injustice. Although this doesn't reach the level of the 1935 classic, it is still worth watching. Dubbed in English. **210m/C VHS.** *FR GE* Jean Gabin, Daniele Delorme, Bernard Blier, Bourvil, Gianni Esposito, Serge Reggiani; ***D:*** Jean-Paul LeChanois.

Les Miserables 🦴🦴🦴½ **1978** An excellent made-for-TV version of the Victor Hugo classic about the criminal Valjean and the policeman Javert playing cat-and-mouse in 18th-century France. Dauphin's last film role. **150m/C VHS.** Richard Jordan, Anthony Perkins, John Gielgud, Cyril Cusack, Flora Robson, Celia Johnson, Claude Dauphin; ***D:*** Glenn Jordan. **TV**

Les Miserables 🦴🦴½ **1995 (R)** Clever, modern rendering of the famous Victor Hugo novel, set in WWII. Humble furniture mover Fortin (Belmondo), nicknamed Valjean for displaying the same brutish strength as his Hugo counterpart, helps a Jewish family escape German occupation. The family becomes separated in the attempt, with lawyer Monsieur Ziman (Boujenah) being hidden by farmers in the country, Madame Ziman (Martines) relegated to a Polish concentration camp, and their daughter Salome (Lelouch, daughter of the director) protected by a nun at a Catholic school. Gump-like, the unusually strong but illiterate Fortin becomes involved with the French resistance and joins in D-Day. Events, though obviously updated, mirror experiences of Hugo's characters. In one sequence, the Ziman's even teach Fortin to read Hugo's "Les Miserables," with actors playing their counterparts in dramatizations. Reportedly France's most expensive film ever. **174m/C VHS.** Jean-Paul Belmondo, Michel Boujenah, Annie Girardot, Philippe Leotard, Clementine Celarie, Rufus, Alessandra Martines, Salome, Philippe Khorsand; ***D:*** Claude Lelouch; ***W:*** Claude Lelouch; ***C:*** Claude Lelouch; ***M:*** Francis Lai. Cesar '96: Support. Actress (Girardot); Golden Globes '96: Foreign Film.

Les Miserables 🦴🦴🦴 **1997 (PG-13)** Yet another adaptation of the Victor Hugo novel. Paroled convict Jean Valjean (Neeson) gets chased by police inspector Javert (Rush) while factory worker Fantine (Thurman) turns to prostitution to survive. August chose to begin this tale after Valjean's trial and imprisonment for petty theft, and until the final third of the film, doesn't really deal with the political upheaval of the time. Not as sweeping or grand as other versions, but what this adaptation lacks in scope, it makes up for with top-notch performances (especially by Neeson and Rush) and more careful study of the characters themselves. **134m/C DVD, Wide.** Liam Neeson, Geoffrey Rush, Uma Thurman, Claire Danes, Paris Vaughan, Reine Brynolfsson, Hans Matheson, Mimi Newman; ***D:*** Bille August; ***W:*** Rafael Yglesias; ***C:*** Jorgen Persson; ***M:*** Basil Poledouris.

Les Mistons 🦴🦴🦴 *The Mischief-Makers* **1957** This study of male adolescence finds five teenage boys worshiping a beautiful girl from afar, following her everywhere, spoiling her dates, and finally reaching maturity in light of their mistakes. **18m/C VHS.** *FR* ***D:*** Francois Truffaut.

Les Nuits Fauves 🦴🦴🦴 *Savage Nights* **1992** Collard's semi-autobiographical film about the emotional and physical havoc an H.I.V.-positive filmmaker visits on the two objects of his violent affections—an innocent 18-year-old girl and a sadomasochistic 20-year-old boy. As Jean displays increasing desperation with his situation, the life around him shows an equally arbitrary violence and humor. In French with English subtitles. Collard died of AIDS shortly before his film won both best first film and best French film at the 1993 Cesars—a first in the ceremony's history. **129m/C VHS.** *FR* Cyril Collard, Romane Bohringer, Carlos Lopez, Maria Schneider; ***D:*** Cyril Collard; ***W:*** Cyril Collard. Cesar '93: Film.

Les Patterson Saves the World 🦴½ **1990 (R)** An obnoxious ambassador to an anonymous Middle Eastern country teams up with the singularly distastefully named Dr. Herpes to stop a new killer disease about to engulf the world. **105m/C VHS.** Barry Humphries, Pamela Stephenson, Thaao Penghlis, Andrew Clarke, Joan Rivers; ***D:*** George Miller; ***C:*** David Connell.

Les Rendez-vous D'Anna 🦴🦴 *The Meetings of Anna* **1978** An independent woman travels through Europe and comes face to face with its post-war modernism. In French with English subtitles. **120m/C VHS.** *FR BE GE* Aurore Clement, Helmut Griem, Magali Noel, Hanns Zischler, Lea Massari, Jean-Pierre Cassel; ***D:*** Chantal Akerman; ***W:*** Chantal Akerman.

Les Vampires **1915** Irma Vep (an anagram for vampire) leads a bloodthirsty gang of thieves in Paris. She and her cohorts will use kidnapping, gas, sexual domination, and murder to gain power over the city's elite. Fueillade's 10-part serial has been restored with color-tinting and title cards in English. **420m/B VHS, DVD.** *FR* Musidora, Jean Ayme, Marcel Levesque, Edouard Mathe; ***D:*** Louis Feuillade; ***W:*** Louis Feuillade.

Les Violons du Bal 🦴🦴 **1974** Follows the story of a young Jewish boy and his family's attempted escape from Nazi-occupied France during WWII. The boy grows up to be a filmmaker obsessed with making a movie about his childhood experiences. In French with English subtitles. **110m/C VHS.** *FR* Marie-Jose Nat, Jean-Louis Trintignant; ***D:*** Michael Drach. Cannes '74: Actress (Nat).

Les Visiteurs du Soir 🦴🦴🦴½ *The Devil's Envoys* **1942** A beautiful, charming fairy tale about the devil's intrepid interference with a particular love affair in 15th-century France, which he cannot squelch. Purportedly a parable about Hitler's invasion of France. Interestingly, this was released after the Nazi occupation of France, so one assumes that the Germans didn't make the connection. In French with English subtitles. **120m/B VHS.** *FR* Arletty, Jules Berry, Marie Dea, Alain Cuny, Fernand Ledoux, Marcel Herrand; ***D:*** Marcel Carne; ***W:*** Jacques Prevert, Pierre Laroche.

Les Voleurs 🦴🦴🦴 *Thieves* **1996 (R)** Unexpected romantic triangle among desperate, lonely people, set against a crime backdrop and told from a variety of viewpoints. Edgy cop Alex (Auteuil) is from a family of thieves, including his older brother Ivan (Bezace) who's been murdered. Alex gets involved with sullen Juliette (Cote) without realizing, at first, that her brother Jimmy (Magimel) is a member of Ivan's gang or that she has another lover, her philosophy teacher, Marie (Deneuve). Events finally force a meeting between Marie and Alex over the unstable Juliette (the scenes between Auteuil and Deneuve being the most interesting in the film). French with subtitles. **116m/C VHS.** *FR* Catherine Deneuve, Daniel Auteuil, Laurence Cote, Benoit Magimel, Didier Bezace, Fabienne Babe, Ivan Desny, Julien Riviere; ***D:*** Andre Techine; ***W:*** Andre Techine, Gilles Taurand; ***C:*** Jeanne Lapoirie; ***M:*** Philippe Sarde.

L'Escorte 🦴🦴 *The Escort* **1996** Thirty-years-old and long-term lovers, Jean-Marc and Philippe find their relationship in crisis thanks to both the stress caused by their failing Montreal restaurant and the intrusion of a third party. Free-spirited Steve works as an escort and soon becomes an object of desire for both men as well as a catalyst for the revelation of long-held secrets. French with subtitles. **91m/C VHS.** *CA* Eric Cabana, Paul-Antoine Taillefer, Robin Aubert, Marie Lefebvre; ***D:*** Denis Langlois; ***W:*** Denis Langlois, Bertrand Lachance; ***C:*** Yves Beaudoin; ***M:*** Bertrand Chenier.

Less Than Zero 🦴 **1987 (R)** An adaptation of Bret Easton Ellis' popular, controversial novel about a group of affluent, drug-abusing youth in Los Angeles. McCarthy and Gertz play friends of Downey who try to get him off his self-destructive path—to no avail. Although it tries, the film fails to inspire any sort of sympathy for this self-absorbed and hedonistic group. Mirrors the shallowness of the characters although Downey manages to rise above this somewhat. Music by the Bangles, David Lee Roth, Poison, Roy Orbison, Aerosmith and more. **98m/C VHS, DVD, Wide.** Andrew McCarthy, Jami Gertz, Robert Downey Jr., James Spader; ***D:*** Marek Kanievska; ***W:*** Harley Peyton; ***C:*** Edward Lachman; ***M:*** Thomas Newman.

The Lesser Evil ½ **1997 (R)** Derek (Feore), the struggling owner of a lumber business, has invited three former high school buddies to his cabin in the Missouri woods. Ivan (Howard) is now a priest, Frank (Goldwyn) is a police officer, and George (Paymer) is a big-shot attorney. As teens they got mixed up with two deaths and a coverup that has now come back to haunt them. Now, just what kind of justice will prevail? Good cast, nice mix of flashbacks, and a satisfying final twist. **97m/C VHS.** Colm Feore, Tony Goldwyn, Arliss Howard, David Paymer, Jonathan Scarfe, Steven Petrarca, Adam Scott, Marc Worden, Jack Kehler, Richard Riehle, Mason Adams, Anne Haney; ***D:*** David Mackay; ***W:*** David Mackay, Jeremy Levine; ***C:*** Stephan Schultze; ***M:*** Don Davis.

A Lesson Before Dying **1999 (PG-13)** Cheadle's impressive as idealistic teacher Grant Wiggins, who has a one-room school for black children in 1948 Louisiana. He's reluctantly pressed into service by his formidable Aunt Lou (Tyson) and her friend Miss Emma (Hall), who want him to bring some dignity to the life of Jefferson (Phifer). This is no easy task since the young man is awaiting execution for a crime he didn't commit. Based on the 1993 novel by Ernest J. Gaines. **100m/C VHS, DVD.** Don Cheadle, Cicely Tyson, Mekhi Phifer, Irma P. Hall, Brent Jennings, Lisa Arrindell Anderson, Frank Hoyt Taylor; ***D:*** Joseph Sargent; ***W:*** Ann Peacock; ***C:*** Donald M. Morgan; ***M:*** Ernest Troost. **CABLE**

Lesson in Love ½ *En Lekiton i Karlek* **1954** A gynecologist's philandering is discovered by his wife, who then starts an affair of her own. Change of pace for Bergman as he does this modest comedy. In Swedish with English subtitles. **95m/B VHS.** *SW* Gunnar Bjornstrand, Eva Dahlbeck, Harriet Andersson; ***D:*** Ingmar Bergman; ***W:*** Ingmar Bergman.

Let 'Em Have It ½ *False Faces* **1935** Exciting action saga loosely based on the newly formed FBI and its bouts with John Dillinger. Car chases and tommy guns abound in this fairly ordinary film. **90m/B VHS.** Richard Arlen, Virginia Bruce, Bruce Cabot, Harvey Stephens, Eric Linden, Joyce Compton, Gordon Jones; ***D:*** Sam Wood.

Let 'er Go Gallegher **1928** A youngster sees a murder, tells his newspaper buddy about it, and the guy writes an article about the crime. It's a big hit, the guy's ego starts to overinflate, and his life starts to head downwind until he decides its time for him and the little guy to rope themselves a miscreant. **57m/B VHS.** Frank "Junior" Coghlan, Elinor Fair, Wade Boteler; ***D:*** Elmer Clifton.

Let Freedom Ring ½ **1939** Sappy, yet enjoyable patriotism that has lawyer Eddy returning to small hometown and fighting corruption. Hokey, but it works largely due to Hecht's fine script. ♫Dusty Road; Love Serenade; Home Sweet Home; When Irish Eyes Are Smiling; America; Pat Sez He; Where Else But Here; Funiculi Funicula; Ten Thousand Cattle Straying. **100m/B VHS.** Nelson Eddy, Virginia Bruce, Victor McLaglen, Lionel Barrymore, Edward Arnold, Guy Kibbee, Charles Butterworth, H.B. Warner, Raymond Walburn; ***D:*** Jack Conway; ***W:*** Ben Hecht.

Let Him Have It ½ **1991 (R)** Compelling, controversial film about a miscarriage of British justice. In 1952 Christopher Craig, 16, and Derek Bentley, 19, climbed onto the roof of a warehouse in an apparent burglary attempt. The police arrived and captured Bentley; Craig shot and wounded one policeman and killed another. According to testimony Bentley shouted "Let him have it" but did he mean shoot or give the officer the gun? Bentley, whose IQ was 66, was sentenced to death by the British courts—though he didn't commit the murder. The uproar over the sentence was reignited by this release, leading to a request for a reexamination of evidence and sentencing by the British Home Office. **115m/C VHS.** *GB* Christopher Eccleston, Paul Reynolds, Tom Bell, Eileen Atkins, Clare Holman, Michael Elphick, Mark McGann, Tom Courtenay, Ronald Fraser, Michael Gough, Murray Melvin, Clive Revill, Norman Rossington, James Villiers; ***D:*** Peter Medak; ***W:*** Oliver Stapleton, Neal Purvis, Robert Wade.

Let It Be **1970** Documentary look at a Beatles recording session, giving glimpses of the conflicts which led to their breakup. Features appearances by Yoko Ono and Billy Preston. **80m/C VHS.** John Lennon, Paul McCartney, George Harrison, Ringo Starr, Billy Preston, Yoko Ono; ***D:*** Michael Lindsay-Hogg; ***M:*** John Lennon, Paul McCartney, George Harrison, Ringo Starr. Oscars '70: Orig. Song Score and/or Adapt.

Let It Ride **1989 (PG-13)** Dreyfuss is a small-time gambler who finally hits it big at the track. Some funny moments but generally a lame script cripples the cast, although the horses seem unaffected. Garr is okay as his wife who slips further into alcoholism with each race. **91m/C VHS, DVD, 8mm, Wide.** Richard Dreyfuss, Teri Garr, David Johansen, Jennifer Tilly, Allen (Goorwitz) Garfield, Ed Walsh, Michelle Phillips, Mary Woronov, Robbie Coltrane, Richard Edson, Cynthia Nixon; ***D:*** Joe Pytka; ***W:*** Nancy Dowd; ***C:*** Curtis J. Wehr; ***M:*** Giorgio Moroder.

Let It Rock **1986** A maniacal promoter makes superstars out of his new band by staging publicity stunts. Not one of Hopper's better efforts. Filmed in Germany, but Roger Corman bought the U.S. rights and added clips from other movies before it was released here. **75m/C VHS.** *GE* Dennis Hopper, David A(lexander) Hess; ***D:*** Roland Klick.

Let It Snow ½ *Snow Days* **1999 (R)** Appealing romantic comedy centers on the emotional insecurity of James Ellis (scripter Marcus, whose brother, Adam, directs), who witnessed his mother Elise's (Peters) post-divorce series of loser boyfriends. His best friend is Sarah (Dylan) and the two dance around the romantic possibilities until a sudden kiss throws their relationship into turmoil. Some miscommunication has Sarah leaving to study in England and James becoming determined to win her love. **90m/C VHS, DVD.** Kipp Marcus, Alice Dylan, Bernadette Peters, Judith Malina, Henry Simmons, Miriam Shor, Larry Pine, Debra Sullivan; ***D:*** Adam Marcus; ***W:*** Kipp Marcus; ***C:*** Ben Weinstein; ***M:*** Sean McCourt.

Let No Man Write My Epitaph **1960** Winters emotes theatrically as Nellie, a southside Chicago junkie mom who is trying to raise her son, Nick (Darren), to live a better life. Based on the novel by Willard Motley. **105m/B VHS.** Shelley Winters, James Darren, Burl Ives, Ricardo Montalban, Jean Seberg, Ella Fitzgerald, Rodolfo Acosta, Jeanne Cooper; ***D:*** Philip Leacock; ***W:*** Robert Presnell; ***C:*** Burnett Guffey; ***M:*** George Duning.

Let Sleeping Corpses Lie ½ *The Living Dead at Manchester Morgue* **1974** England's answer to "Night of the Living Dead" is more polished and has a more pronounced environmental edge. George (Lovelock) and Edna (Galbo) are the heroes who must confront the cannibalistic animated corpses. If the film lacks the single-mindedness and originality of Romero's work, it's an accurate snapshot of the early 1970s with appropriately gruesome special effects. **93m/C VHS, DVD, Wide.** *GB* Ray Lovelock, Christine Galbo, Arthur Kennedy; ***D:*** Jorge Grau; ***W:*** Alessandro Continenza, Marcello Coscia; ***C:*** Francisco Sempere; ***M:*** Giuliano Sorgini.

Let the Devil Wear Black ½ **1999 (R)** A "Hamlet" update gets the noir treatment. Jack (Penner) is suspicious about his dad's murder, especially when his mom (Bisset) suddenly marries his uncle (Sheridan). Jack becomes obsessed with linking his uncle to some shady business dealings also involving dear old dad, while his girlfriend, Julia (Parker), goes a little crazy from Jack's neglect. Cleverly done. **89m/C VHS, DVD.** Jonathan Penner, Jacqueline Bisset, Jamey Sheridan, Mary-Louise Parker, Philip Baker Hall, Jonathan Banks, Maury Chaykin, Chris Sarandon, Randall Batinkoff, Norman Reedus; ***D:*** Stacy Title; ***W:*** Jonathan Penner, Stacy Title; ***C:*** James Whitaker.

L'Etat Sauvage ½ *The Savage State* **1978** This French political thriller finds its heart in the middle of racism. The story unfolds around a newly independent African republic and a love affair between a black cabinet minister and a white Frenchwoman. Corruption abounds in this film based on George Conchon's award-winning novel. In French with English subtitles. **111m/C VHS, Wide.** *FR* Marie-Christine Barrault, Claude Brasseur, Jacques Dutronc, Doura Mane, Michel Piccoli; ***D:*** Francis Girod. Cesar '79: Sound.

Lethal Charm **1990** Two power-hungry journalists go head-to-head in the high stakes arena of Washington D.C. **92m/C VHS.** Barbara Eden, Heather Locklear.

Lethal Games **1990** Stallone and Vaccaro lead a small community against a blood-thirsty band of criminals. **83m/C VHS.** Frank Stallone, Brenda Vaccaro, Dave Adams, Christopher Whalley, Heidi Paine, Karen Russell; ***D:*** John Bowen.

Lethal Lolita—Amy Fisher: My Story *Amy Fisher: My Story* **1992** The only made-for-TV Amy Fisher story out of three whose cast members even remotely resemble the real people—except of course actress Parker is actually pretty. Minor details aside, this account is Amy's story, purchased by NBC for an undisclosed amount, portraying her as an incest victim who gets involved with an opportunistic married jerk who drags her into prostitution, leading her to take out her frustration on his wife. If this is true, the obvious question is "why?"...to which she answers, "He loves me. We have great sex. And he fixes my car." Oh. See also: "The Amy Fisher Story" and "Casualties of Love: The 'Long Island Lolita' Story." **93m/C VHS.** Noelle Parker, Ed Marinaro, Kathleen Lasky, Boyd Kestner, Mary Ann Pascal, Lawrence Dane, Kate Lynch; ***D:*** Bradford May. **TV**

Lethal Ninja **1993 (R)** Kickboxers Joe and Pete set out to rescue Joe's wife from some third-world country overrun by ninjas. Hackneyed but lots of action for martial arts fans. **97m/C VHS.** Ross Kettle, David Webb, Karyn Hill, Frank Notaro.

Lethal Obsession ½ *Der Joker* **1987 (R)** Two cops battle street crime and a powerful drug ring. Filmed in Germany. **100m/C VHS.** *GE* Michael York, Elliott Gould, Tahnee Welch, Peter Maffay, Armin Mueller-Stahl; ***D:*** Peter Patzak; ***M:*** Tony Carey.

Lethal Panther **1990** A film where the female is indeed deadlier than the male. Japanese hit woman Ling (Miyamoto) gets involved with drug-smuggling gangsters operating out of the Philippines and is opposed by CIA agent Betty Lee (Hu). Dubbed. **120m/C VHS.** *HK* Yoko Miyamoto, Sibelle Hu, Lawrence Ng; ***D:*** Godfrey Ho.

Lethal Pursuit **1988** A popular singer who returns to the town where she grew up is tormented by her ex-boyfriend, a criminal. **90m/C VHS.** Mitzi Donahue, Blake Gahner, John Wildman; ***D:*** Donald M. Jones.

Lethal Seduction ½ **1997** Local crime boss Gus Gruman (Estevez) is rapidly losing friends and associates to a sexually oriented serial killer. And there's obsessed cop Trent Jacobson (Mitchum) who's determined to solve the crimes. The one clue is a mystery brunette seen leaving a crime scene. **110m/C VHS, DVD.** Julie Strain, Chris Mitchum, Joe Estevez; ***D:*** Frederick P. Watkins; ***C:*** Robert Dracup.

Lethal Tender **1996 (R)** A tour group is held hostage by a gang of terrorists as part of a plot to steal $400 million and it's up to a lone Chicago cop to save the day. Fahey does equally well in both bad and good guy roles and here he's in hero mode. **93m/C VHS.** Jeff Fahey, Kim Coates, Gary Busey, Carrie-Anne Moss; ***D:*** John Bradshaw.

Lethal Weapon **1987 (R)** In Los Angeles, a cop nearing retirement (Glover) unwillingly begins work with a new partner (Gibson), a suicidal, semi-crazed risk-taker who seems determined to get the duo killed. Both Vietnam vets, the pair uncover a vicious heroin smuggling ring run by ruthless ex-Special Forces personnel. Packed with plenty of action, violence, and humorous undertones. Clapton's contributions to the musical score are an added bonus. Gibson and Glover work well together and give this movie extra punch. Followed by three sequels. **110m/C VHS, DVD, Wide.** Mel Gibson, Danny Glover, Gary Busey, Mitchell Ryan, Tom Atkins, Darlene Love, Traci Wolfe, Steve Kahan, Jackie Swanson, Damon Hines, Lycia Naff, Mary Ellen Trainor, Jack Thibeau, Ed O'Ross, Gustav Vintas, Al Leong, Joan Severance; ***D:*** Richard Donner; ***W:*** Shane Black; ***C:*** Stephen Goldblatt; ***M:*** Michael Kamen, Eric Clapton.

Lethal Weapon 2 **1989 (R)** This sequel to the popular cop adventure finds Gibson and Glover taking on a variety of blond South African "diplomats" who try to use their diplomatic immunity status to thwart the duo's efforts to crack their smuggling ring. Gibson finally finds romance, and viewers learn the truth about his late wife's accident. Also features the introduction of obnoxious, fast-talking con artist Leo ("OK, OK") Getz, adeptly played by Pesci, who becomes a third wheel to the crime-fighting team. Followed by a second sequel. **114m/C VHS, DVD, Wide.** Mel Gibson, Danny Glover, Joe Pesci, Joss Ackland, Derrick O'Connor, Patsy Kensit, Darlene Love, Traci Wolfe, Steve Kahan, Mary Ellen Trainor; ***D:*** Richard Donner; ***W:*** Jeffrey Boam; ***C:*** Stephen Goldblatt; ***M:*** Michael Kamen, Eric Clapton, David Sanborn.

Lethal Weapon 3 ½ **1992 (R)** Murtaugh and Riggs return for more action in another slam-bang adventure. Murtaugh hopes his last week before retirement will be a peaceful one, but partner Riggs isn't about to let him go quietly. Not many changes from the successful formula with bickering buddies, lots of adventure, exploding buildings, a little comic relief from Pesci, and the addition of Russo as an Internal Affairs cop who proves to be more than a match for Riggs. **118m/C VHS, DVD, 8mm.** Mary Ellen Trainor, Mel Gibson, Danny Glover, Joe Pesci, Rene Russo, Stuart Wilson, Steve Kahan, Darlene Love, Traci Wolfe, Gregory Millar, Jason Meshover-Iorg, Delores Hall; ***D:*** Richard Donner; ***W:*** Jeffrey Boam, Robert Mark Kamen; ***C:*** Jan De Bont; ***M:*** Michael Kamen, Eric Clapton, David Sanborn. MTV Movie Awards '93: On-Screen Duo (Mel Gibson/Danny Glover), Action Seq.

Lethal Weapon 4 ½ **1998 (R)** It's old home week as Gibson, Glover, Pesci, and Russo all reunite for one more escapade, six years after 1992's "Lethal Weapon 3." Rock joins the veterans as junior detective Lee Butters, who has some unexpected ties to Murtaugh. They're investigating Asian crimelord Wah Sing Ku (Chinese action star Li) who's involved in smuggling and counterfeiting and has no problem with violence, including kicking the bejeezus out of Riggs on more than one occasion. Russo had to do her action sequences with a prosthetic belly since her character, Lorna Cole, and Riggs are about to become parents. It's the same old-same old but it's still a good time. **125m/C VHS, DVD, Wide.** Mary Ellen Trainor, Mel Gibson, Danny Glover, Joe Pesci, Rene Russo, Chris Rock, Jet Li, Steve Kahan, Darlene Love; ***D:*** Richard Donner; ***W:*** Channing Gibson; ***C:*** Andrzej Bartkowiak; ***M:*** Michael Kamen, Eric Clapton, David Sanborn.

Lethal Woman ½ **1988** A group of beautiful women, all once victimized by rapes, is recruited to an island by the "Lethal Woman," who plots revenge on any man who dares to vacation on the island. **96m/C VHS.** Shannon Tweed, Merete Van Kamp.

Let's Dance ½ **1950** A young widow tries to protect her son from his wealthy, paternal grandmother, while Fred dances his way into her heart. More obscure Astaire vehicle, but as charming as the rest. Needless to say, great dancing. ♫Tunnel of Love; The Hyacinth; Piano

Dance; Jack and the Beanstalk; Can't Stop Talking; Oh, Them Dudes; Why Fight the Feeling?. **112m/C VHS.** Betty Hutton, Fred Astaire, Roland Young, Ruth Warrick, Shepperd Strudwick, Lucile Watson, Barton MacLane, Gregory Moffett, Melville Cooper; ***D:*** Norman Z. McLeod.

Let's Do It Again 🦴½ **1975 (PG)** Atlanta milkman and his pal, a factory worker, milk two big-time gamblers out of a large sum of money in order to build a meeting hall for their fraternal lodge. Lesser sequel to "Uptown Saturday Night." **113m/C VHS.** Sidney Poitier, Bill Cosby, John Amos, Jimmie Walker, Ossie Davis, Denise Nicholas, Calvin Lockhart; ***D:*** Sidney Poitier; ***W:*** Richard Wesley.

Let's Get Harry 🦴½ *The Rescue* **1987 (R)** Americans led by mercenaries mix it up with a Columbian cocaine franchise in an attempt to rescue their friend, Harry. Never released theatrically, for good reason. **107m/C VHS.** Robert Duvall, Gary Busey, Michael Schoeffling, Thomas F. Wilson, Glenn Frey, Rick Rossovich, Ben Johnson, Matt Clark, Mark Harmon, Gregory Sierra, Elpidia Carrillo; ***D:*** Alan Smithee; ***W:*** Samuel Fuller, Charles Robert Carner; ***M:*** Brad Fiedel.

Let's Get Lost **1988** Absorbing documentary of Chet Baker, the prominent '50s "cool" jazz trumpeter (and occasional vocalist) who succumbed, like many of his peers, to drug addiction. Weber's black-and-white, fashion photography style well suits his subject. Downbeat, but rarely less than worthy. **125m/B VHS.** Chet Baker; ***D:*** Bruce Weber.

Let's Get Married 🦴 **1963** A young doctor's weakness under pressure brings him to the brink of babbling idiocy when his wife goes into early labor. **90m/B VHS.** Anthony Newley, Ann Aubrey.

Let's Get Tough 🦴 **1942** The East Side Kids, unable to enlist because of their age, harass local Oriental shopkeepers and eventually get involved with a murder. **52m/B VHS, 8mm.** Leo Gorcey, Bobby Jordan, Huntz Hall, Gabriel Dell, Sammy (Earnest) Morrison; ***D:*** Wallace Fox.

Let's Go! 🦴½ **1923** The son of a cement company president sets out to prove his worth to the firm by landing a contract with the town of Hillsboro. For some unknown reason, he sets off on an amazing set of stunts. Silent with original organ music. **79m/B VHS, 8mm.** Richard Talmadge, Hal Clements, Eileen (Elaine Persey) Percy, Tully Marshall; ***D:*** William K. Howard.

Let's Go Collegiate 🦴½ **1941** Two college rowers promise their girlfriends that they'll win the big race, but their plans are almost frustrated when their best oarsman is drafted. Their only hope lies in replacing him with a truck driver. ♫Look What You've Done To Me; Sweet 16; Let's Do A Little Dreaming. **62m/B VHS.** Frankie Darro, Marcia Mae Jones, Jackie Moran, Keye Luke, Mantan Moreland, Gale Storm; ***D:*** Jean Yarbrough.

Let's Kill All the Lawyers 🦴🦴½ **1993 (R)** Low-budget satire about one man's angst over whether to become a lawyer is witty, entertaining, and not just for legal eagles. Law-firm intern Foster Merkul (Frederick) is apprenticed to a sleazeball (Vezina) who teaches him that money—not justice—is the name of the game in the law biz. Growing increasingly disillusioned, Foster sets out to reform the system with the help of Satori, a beautiful and mysterious creature of his imagination. Shot at sites in and around Detroit, this independent production features lots of cameos by local media celebrities. **103m/C VHS.** Rick Frederick, James Vezina, Michelle De Vuono, Maggie Patton, Marty Smith; ***D:*** Ron Senkowski; ***W:*** Ron Senkowski.

Let's Make It Legal 🦴🦴½ **1951** Amusing comedy of a married couple who decide to get a divorce after 20 years of marriage. Colbert stars as the woman who decides to leave her husband, Carey, because he's a chronic gambler. They part as friends, but soon Colbert's old flame, Scott, is back in town and things get rather complicated. A solid cast serves as the main strength in this film. **77m/B VHS.** Claudette Colbert, MacDonald Carey, Zachary Scott, Barbara Bates, Robert Wagner, Marilyn Monroe; ***D:*** Richard Sale; ***W:*** F. Hugh Herbert.

Let's Make Love 🦴🦴½ **1960** An urbane millionaire discovers he is to be parodied in an off-Broadway play, and vows to stop it—until he falls in love with the star of the show. He then ends up acting in the play. ♫My Heart Belongs to Daddy; Let's Make Love; Specialization; Incurably Romantic; Sing Me a Song That Sells; You With the Crazy Eyes; Give Me the Simple Life. **118m/C VHS, DVD, Wide.** Yves Montand, Marilyn Monroe, Tony Randall, Frankie Vaughan, Bing Crosby, Gene Kelly, Milton Berle; ***D:*** George Cukor; ***W:*** Norman Krasna; ***C:*** Daniel F. Fapp; ***M:*** Lionel Newman.

Let's Make Up 🦴🦴 *Lilacs in the Spring* **1955** When it comes to giving her heart, Neagle can't decide between two dashing men. **94m/C VHS.** *GB* Errol Flynn, Anna Neagle, David Farrar, Kathleen Harrison, Peter Graves; ***D:*** Herbert Wilcox.

Let's Scare Jessica to Death 🦴🦴 **1971 (PG)** A young woman who was recently released from a mental hospital is subjected to unspeakable happenings at a country home with her friends. She encounters murder, vampires, and corpses coming out of nowhere. A supernatural thriller with quite a few genuine scares. **89m/C VHS.** Zohra Lampert, Barton Heyman, Kevin J. O'Connor, Gretchen Corbett, Alan Manson; ***D:*** John Hancock.

Let's Sing Again 🦴🦴 **1936** Eight-year-old singing sensation Bobby Breen made his debut in this dusty musical vehicle, as a runaway orphan who becomes the pal of a washed-up opera star in a traveling show. ♫Let's Sing Again; Lullaby; Farmer in the Dell; La Donna e Mobile. **70m/B VHS.** Bobby Breen, Henry Armetta, George Houston, Vivienne Osborne, Grant Withers, Inez Courtney, Lucien Littlefield; ***D:*** Kurt Neumann.

Let's Talk About Sex 🦴½ **1998 (R)** Miami magazine columnist Jazz (Beyer) pitches her idea for a TV show about women who candidly discuss sex (more accurately, their complaints about men), but is told she has the weekend to create a sample video. Jazz enlists the help of her equally frustrated and unhappy friends, Michelle and Lena (Brewster and Ingerman), and armed with a video camera, the three comb the steamy streets of Miami asking random women personal questions about their sex lives and baiting them into complaining about men. Tries to be a hip sorta-documentary blending hand-held shots with staged scenes, but comes across as a soft-core sex farce/soap opera. Beyer also wrote and directed. **82m/C VHS.** Troy Beyer, Randi Ingerman, Joseph C. Phillips, Paget Brewster, Michaline Babich, Tina Nguyen; ***D:*** Troy Beyer; ***W:*** Troy Beyer; ***C:*** Kelly Evans; ***M:*** Michael Carpenter.

The Letter 🦴🦴🦴🦴 **1940** When a man is shot and killed on a Malaysian plantation, the woman who committed the murder pleads self-defense. Her husband and his lawyer attempt to free her, but find more than they expected in this tightly paced film noir. Based on the novel by W. Somerset Maugham. Davis emulated the originator of her role, Jeanne Eagels, in her mannerisms and line readings, although Eagels later went mad from drug abuse and overwork. **96m/B VHS.** Bette Davis, Herbert Marshall, James Stephenson, Gale Sondergaard, Bruce Lester, Cecil Kellaway, Victor Sen Yung, Frieda Inescort; ***D:*** William Wyler; ***W:*** Howard Koch; ***C:*** Gaetano Antonio "Tony" Gaudio; ***M:*** Max Steiner.

Letter from an Unknown Woman 🦴🦴🦴 **1948** A woman falls in love with a concert pianist on the eve of his departure. He promises to return but never does. The story is told in flashbacks as the pianist reads a letter from the woman. A great romantic melodrama. **90m/B VHS.** Joan Fontaine, Louis Jourdan, Mady Christians, Marcel Journet, Art Smith; ***D:*** Max Ophuls. Natl. Film Reg. '92.

Letter of Introduction 🦴🦴½ **1938** A struggling young actress learns that her father is really a well known screen star and agrees not to reveal the news to the public. **104m/B VHS.** Adolphe Menjou, Edgar Bergen, George Murphy, Eve Arden, Ann Sheridan, Andrea Leeds; ***D:*** John M. Stahl; ***C:*** Karl Freund.

Letter to Brezhnev 🦴🦴🦴 **1986 (R)** Acclaimed independent film about two working-class Liverpool girls who fall in love with two furloughed Russian sailors. When the men eventually return to the USSR, one of the girls contacts the Russian Secretary General in an effort to rejoin her lover. Amusing tale of different relationships. **94m/C VHS.** *GB* Margi Clarke, Alexandra Pigg, Peter Firth, Ken Campbell, Tracy Lea, Alfred Molina, Angela Clarke; ***D:*** Chris Bernard; ***W:*** Frank Clarke; ***M:*** Alan Gill.

Letter to My Killer 🦴🦴½ **1995 (PG-13)** Construction worker Nick Parma (Chinlund) finds an unmailed letter in a demolished building, which he and wife Judy (Winningham) discover is 30 years old. The woman letter writer is describing major fraud and when Judy learns that she was murdered, she and Nick decide to blackmail the probable suspects—a powerful business cartel. But if they killed once.... **92m/C VHS.** Mare Winningham, Nicholas Chinlund, Rip Torn, Josef Sommer, Eddie Jones, Dey Young; ***D:*** Janet Meyers; ***W:*** Norman Strum; ***C:*** Stephen M. Katz; ***M:*** Mason Daring. **CABLE**

A Letter to Three Wives 🦴🦴🦴🦴 **1949** Crain, Darnell, and Sothern star as three friends who, shortly before embarking on a Hudson River boat trip, each receive a letter from Holm (who's never shown), the fourth member in their set. The letter tells them that she has run off with one of their husbands but does not specify his identity. The women spend the rest of the trip reviewing their sometimes shaky unions which provides some of the funniest and most caustic scenes, including Douglas (as Sothern's husband) ranting against the advertising business which supports his wife's radio soap opera. Sharp dialogue, moving performances. Based on the novel by John Klempner. Remade for TV in 1985. **103m/B VHS.** Jeanne Crain, Linda Darnell, Ann Sothern, Kirk Douglas, Paul Douglas, Jeffrey Lynn, Thelma Ritter, Barbara Lawrence, Connie Gilchrist, Florence Bates; ***D:*** Joseph L. Mankiewicz; ***W:*** Joseph L. Mankiewicz; ***C:*** Arthur C. Miller; ***M:*** Alfred Newman; ***V:*** Celeste Holm. Oscars '49: Director (Mankiewicz), Screenplay; Directors Guild '48: Director (Mankiewicz).

Letters from a Killer 🦴🦴 **1998 (R)** Death-row con Race Darnell (Swayze) has been corresponding with four women every since writing a best-seller about his life in prison. After a new trial overturns his conviction and sets him free, Race discovers that one of his correspondents—who believed she was his only love—is framing him for murder in revenge for his "betrayal" of her. **103m/C VHS, DVD, Wide.** Patrick Swayze, Gia Carides, Kim Myers, Olivia Birkelund, Tina Lifford, Elizabeth Ruscio, Roger E. Mosley, Bruce McGill, Mark Rolston; ***D:*** David Carson; ***W:*** Nicholas Hicks-Beach; ***C:*** John A. Alonzo; ***M:*** Dennis McCarthy.

Letters from Alou 🦴🦴 *Las Cartas de Alou* **1990** African immigrant Alou is trying to get to Barcelona to meet up with a friend but faces much exploitation and discrimination along the way. Spanish with subtitles. **100m/C VHS.** *SP* Mulie Jarju, Eulalia Ramon; ***D:*** Montxo Armendariz; ***W:*** Montxo Armendariz.

Letters from My Windmill 🦴🦴🦴½ **1954** A series of three short stories: "The Three Low Masses," "The Elixir of Father Gaucher," and "The Secret of Master Cornille" from respected director Pagnol. The unique format only enhances this film. In French with English subtitles. **116m/B VHS.** *FR* Henri Velbert, Yvonne Gamy, Robert Vattier, Roger Crouzet; ***D:*** Marcel Pagnol.

Letters from the Park 🦴🦴🦴 *Cartas del Parque* **1988** In Cuba, 1913, two taciturn would-be lovers hire a poet, Victor La Place, to write love letters to each other. Normal proboscis aside, the poet follows the fate of Cyrano, and finds himself the unhappy hypotenuse in a triangular romance. Based on an original story by Marquez; made for Spanish TV. Subtitled. **85m/C VHS.** *CU* Victor Laplace, Ivonne Lopez, Miguel Paneque; ***D:*** Tomas Gutierrez Alea; ***W:*** Tomas Gutierrez Alea, Gabriel Garcia Marquez; ***C:*** Mario Garcia Joya. **TV**

Letters to an Unknown Lover 🦴🦴½ *Les Louves* **1984** During WWII, a man and woman engage in sexual and emotional combat. **101m/C VHS.** *GB FR* Cherie Lunghi, Mathilda May, Yves Beneyton, Ralph Bates; ***D:*** Peter Duffell.

Letting Go 🦴🦴 **1985 (PG)** Comedy-drama about a broken-hearted career woman and a young widower who fall in love. **94m/C VHS.** John Ritter, Sharon Gless, Joe Cortese; ***D:*** Jack Bender. **TV**

Letting the Birds Go Free **1986** When a stranger is caught stealing from a farmer's barn, the farmer and his son decide to let the villain work off his crime. Some very interesting relationships develop from this arrangement. **60m/C VHS.** Lionel Jeffries.

Leviathan 🦴🦴 **1989 (R)** A motley crew of ocean-floor miners are trapped when they are accidentally exposed to a failed Soviet experiment that turns humans into insatiable, regenerating fish-creatures. **98m/C VHS, DVD, Wide.** Peter Weller, Ernie Hudson, Hector Elizondo, Amanda Pays, Richard Crenna, Daniel Stern, Lisa Eilbacher, Michael Carmine, Meg Foster; ***D:*** George P. Cosmatos; ***W:*** David Peoples, Jeb Stuart; ***C:*** Alex Thomson; ***M:*** Jerry Goldsmith.

Levitation 🦴½ **1997** Pregnant teenager, Acey (Paulson), decides to leave her unhappy adoptive parents and search for her birth mother. She has an imaginary friend (possibly her guardian angel) she calls Bob (London) and a real friend, DJ Downtime (Hudson), to help her out but her quest doesn't end in happiness. Title refers to Acey's weird uncontrollable ability to levitate, unfortunately the film doesn't—it's a muddled mess. **99m/C VHS, DVD.** Sarah Paulson, Ernie Hudson, Jeremy London, Ann Magnuson, Brett Cullen, Christopher Boyer; ***D:*** Scott Goldstein; ***W:*** Scott Goldstein; ***C:*** Michael G. Wojciechowski; ***M:*** Leonard Roseman.

Lewis and Clark and George 🦴🦴 **1997 (R)** Lewis (Xuereb) is a dim-witted killer and Clark (Gunther) is a computer nerd. Both are prison escapees in possession of what is supposed to be a map to a gold mine. Lewis happens to be illiterate and needs Clark, who's afraid of Lewis's trigger-happy ways. George (McGowan) is a sexy mute thief who takes both men for quite a wild ride. Filmed in rural New Mexico. **84m/C VHS, DVD, Wide.** Salvator Xuereb, Dan Gunther, Rose McGowan, Art LaFleur, Aki Aleong, James Brolin, Paul Bartel; ***D:*** Rod McCall; ***W:*** Rod McCall; ***C:*** Mike Mayers; ***M:*** Ben Vaughn.

L'Homme Blesse 🦴🦴🦴 *The Wounded Man* **1983** A serious erotic film about 18-year-old Henri (Anglade), cloistered by an overbearing family, and his sudden awakening to his own homosexuality. Anglade's film debut. In French with English subtitles. **90m/C VHS.** *FR* Jean-Hugues Anglade, Roland Bertin, Vittorio Mezzogiorno; ***D:*** Patrice Chereau; ***C:*** Renato Berta. Cesar '84: Writing.

Liam 🦴🦴 **2000 (R)** Stuttering, 7-year-old Liam (Borrows) is an Irish Catholic living in Liverpool in the 1930s. His hard-working mother is determined that Liam will look presentable for his first Communion no matter what the sacrifice but his family's struggles worsen when his father (Hart) loses his job and becomes increasingly bitter, blaming his woes on others and turning to violence as a solution. **90m/C VHS, DVD, Wide.** *GE GB* Ian Hart, Claire Hackett, David Hart, Anthony Borrows, Megan Burns, Anne Reid, Russell Dixon, Julia Deakin, Andrew Schofield, Bernadette Shortt, David Corey; ***D:*** Stephen Frears; ***W:*** Jimmy McGovern; ***C:*** Andrew Dunn; ***M:*** John Murphy.

Liana, Jungle Goddess 🦴🦴 **1956** A variation on the Greystoke legend featuring a beautiful (and topless) jungle goddess who is discovered living in the wilds of Africa. Thinking that she may be the lost granddaughter of a wealthy English nobleman, she's brought back to London for a reunion. Will civilization prove to be as dangerous as the jungle? **?m/C VHS.** Marion Michael, Hardy Kruger.

Lianna 1983 (R) Acclaimed screenwriter/director John Sayles wrote and directed this story of a woman's romantic involvement with another woman. Chronicles an unhappy homemaker's awakening to the feelings of love that she develops for a female professor. Sayles makes an appearance as a family friend. **110m/C VHS.** Jon (John) DeVries, Linda Griffiths, Jane Hallaren, Jo Henderson, Jessica Wright MacDonald; ***Cameos:*** John Sayles; ***D:*** John Sayles; ***W:*** John Sayles; ***M:*** Mason Daring.

Liar Liar ½ 1996 (PG-13) Carrey takes on one of his less manic but still appealing personas as compulsive liar and attorney Fletcher Reid. A constant disappointment to his ex-wife Audrey (Tierney) and young son Max (Cooper), Fletcher is forced to tell nothing but the truth for 24 hours, thanks to his son's supernatural birthday wish. This puts a crimp in his legal practice, especially as he tries to defend brazen would-be divorcee Samantha Cole (Tilly). Gets kinda sappy but Carrey can carry almost any situation. **87m/C VHS, DVD.** Jim Carrey, Jennifer Tilly, Maura Tierney, Amanda Donohoe, Swoosie Kurtz, Justin Cooper, Jason Bernard, Mitchell Ryan, Anne Haney, Chip Mayer, Randall "Tex" Cobb, Cary Elwes; ***D:*** Tom Shadyac; ***W:*** Paul Guay, Steve Mazur; ***C:*** Russell Boyd; ***M:*** John Debney. MTV Movie Awards '98: Comedic Perf. (Carrey).

The Liars 1964 Mystery in which a Frenchman strikes it rich in Africa, then returns home to Paris in search of a wife. He advertisies for a mate, but is set up by con artists instead. In French with English subtitles. **92m/C VHS.** Dawn Addams, Jean Servais; ***D:*** Edmond T. Greville.

The Liar's Club ½ 1993 (R) High-school football teammates try to cover up a rape and wind up involved in murder. **100m/C VHS.** Wil Wheaton, Brian Krause, Soleil Moon Frye, Jennifer Burns, Michael Cudlitz, Bruce Weitz; ***D:*** Jeffrey Porter.

Liar's Edge 1992 (R) Tweed portrays a single mother whose teenaged son, Mark, is plagued by violent fantasies. When she remarries and her new husband and sleazy brother-in-law move in, Mark's hallucinations become stronger until he believes he's witnessed a murder. The murder turns out to be a fact and his new stepfather is involved but can Mark prove it. Filmed on location in Niagra Falls. **97m/C VHS.** Shannon Tweed, Nicholas Shields, David Keith, Joseph Bottoms, Christopher Plummer; ***D:*** Ron Oliver; ***W:*** Ron Oliver.

Liar's Moon 1982 (PG) A local boy woos and weds the town's wealthiest young lady, only to be trapped in family intrigue. **106m/C VHS, DVD.** Cindy Fisher, Matt Dillon, Christopher Connelly, Susan Tyrrell; ***D:*** David Fisher.

Libeled Lady ½ 1936 A fast, complicated screwball masterwork. Newspaper editor Warren Haggerty (Tracy) prints an erroneous story that heiress Connie Allenbury (Loy) is after a married man. Connie sues and in order to defuse the lawsuit, Warren comes up with an elaborate scheme (certain to backfire) that involves his own fiancee Galdys (Harlow) and recently fired reporter Bill (Powell). Remade in 1946 as "Easy to Wed." **98m/B VHS.** Myrna Loy, Spencer Tracy, Jean Harlow, William Powell, Walter Connolly, Charley Grapewin, Cora Witherspoon, E.E. Clive, Charles Trowbridge, Dennis O'Keefe, Hattie McDaniel; ***D:*** Jack Conway; ***W:*** George Oppenheimer, Howard Emmett Rogers, Maurine Watkins; ***C:*** Norbert Brodine; ***M:*** William Axt.

The Liberation of L.B. Jones 1970 (R) A wealthy black undertaker wants a divorce from his wife, who is having an affair with a white policeman. Wyler's final film. **101m/C VHS.** Lee J. Cobb, Lola Falana, Barbara Hershey, Anthony Zerbe, Roscoe Lee Browne; ***D:*** William Wyler; ***W:*** Stirling Silliphant; ***M:*** Elmer Bernstein.

Liberators 1977 Kinski stars as a criminal soldier battling with the American authorities, German troops, and his fugitive partner. **91m/C VHS.** Klaus Kinski.

The Libertine *La Matriarca* 1969 Mimi (Spaak) is a young widow who's just discovered her late husband kept a separate apartment equipped to satisfy his more unusual sexual desires. Intrigued, Mimi decides to keep the apartment and do her own sexual exploring. Dubbed. **90m/C VHS, DVD, Wide.** *IT* Catherine Spaak, Jean-Louis Trintignant, Luigi Pistilli, Luigi Proietti, Renzo Montagnani; ***D:*** Pasquale Festa Campanile; ***C:*** Alfio Contini; ***M:*** Armando Trovajoli.

Liberty & Bash 1990 (R) Two boyhood friends who served together in Vietnam reunite to rid their neighborhood of drug pushers and save the life of a friend. **92m/C VHS.** Miles O'Keeffe, Lou Ferrigno, Mitzi Kapture, Richard Eden, Cheryl Paris, Gary Conway; ***D:*** Myrl A. Schreibman.

Liberty Heights ½ 1999 (R) Levinson heads back to Baltimore (for the fourth time) for his 1954 coming of age/family drama with his focus on the city's Jewish community and the Kurtzman family in particular. Nate (Mantegna) has a two-bit numbers racket and a failing burlesque house, college son Van (Brody) falls for a shiksa (Murphy), while high schooler Ben (Foster) is captivated by Sylvia (Johnson), the first black student in his class. It may be too early for Bob Dylan but the times were a-changin' indeed and Levinson takes an unsentimental, if heartfelt, look at his past. **127m/C VHS, DVD, Wide.** Adrien Brody, Joe Mantegna, Ben Foster, Bebe Neuwirth, Rebekah Johnson, Orlando Jones, Frania Rubinek, David Krumholtz, Richard Kline, Vincent Guastaferro, Carolyn Murphy, Justin Chambers, James Pickens Jr., Anthony Anderson, Kiersten Warren; ***D:*** Barry Levinson; ***W:*** Barry Levinson; ***C:*** Christopher Doyle; ***M:*** Andrea Morricone.

License to Drive 1988 (PG-13) When teen Haim fails the road test for his all-important driver's license, he steals the family car for a hot date with the girl of his dreams. The evening starts out quietly enough, but things soon go awry. If Haim survives the weekend, he'll definitely be able to pass his driving test on Monday morning. Semi-funny in a demolition derby sort of way. **90m/C VHS.** Corey Feldman, Corey Haim, Carol Kane, Richard Masur, Michael Manasseri; ***D:*** Greg Beeman; ***C:*** Bruce Surtees; ***M:*** Jay Ferguson.

License to Kill 1964 Constantine stars as Agent Nick Carter involved with Oriental spies and a new secret weapon. **100m/C VHS.** *FR* Eddie Constantine, Yvonne Monlaur, Paul Frankeur; ***D:*** Henri Decoin.

License to Kill 1984 A young girl is killed by a drunk driver, devastating both families. Offers a strong message against drinking and driving. **96m/C VHS.** James Farentino, Don Murray, Penny Fuller, Millie Perkins, Donald Moffat, Denzel Washington, Ari Meyers; ***D:*** Jud Taylor. **TV**

License to Kill 1989 (PG-13) Dalton's second Bond effort, in which drug lords try to kill 007's best friend and former CIA agent. Disobeying orders for the first time and operating without his infamous "license to kill," Bond goes after the fiends. Fine outing for Dalton (and Bond, too). **133m/C VHS, DVD, Wide.** *GB* Tom Adams, Timothy Dalton, Carey Lowell, Robert Davi, Frank McRae, Talisa Soto, David Hedison, Anthony Zerbe, Everett McGill, Wayne Newton, Benicio Del Toro, Desmond Llewelyn, Priscilla Barnes; ***D:*** John Glen; ***W:*** Michael G. Wilson, Richard Maibaum; ***C:*** Alec Mills; ***M:*** Michael Kamen.

The Lickerish Quartet 1970 (R) A bored, aristocratic couple live with their teenaged son in a secluded castle in Italy's Abruzzi mountains. Traveling to a nearby carnival, they think they recognize the female daredevil as the same actress they've just seen in a home-viewed porno film. So they invite her back to the castle for a little family fun—only she may not be the same woman at all. **90m/C VHS, DVD.** Silvana Venturelli, Frank Wolff, Erika Remberg, Paolo Turco; ***D:*** Radley Metzger; ***W:*** Michael DeForrest; ***C:*** Hans Jura.

L'Idiot *The Idiot* 1946 Smooth adaptation of Dostoevsky's novel about noble Prince Mishkin's (Philipe) attempts to bring peace to the life of tormented Nastasia Filipovna (Feuillere). First feature for Lampin; French with subtitles. **98m/B VHS.** *FR* Gerard Philipe, Edwige Feuillere, Lucien Coedel, Nathalie Nattier, Marguerite Moreno; ***D:*** Georges Lampin; ***W:*** Charles Spaak; ***C:*** Christian Matras; ***M:*** Maurice Thiriet.

L.I.E. 2001 (NC-17) Can you say "controversial"? 15-year-old Howie's (Dano) mother has recently died in a car accident on the Long Island Expressway (hence the title) and his world is falling apart. His dad, Marty (Blitzer), brings his bimbo girlfriend to stay and has some very shady business dealings. Meanwhile, Howie is hanging out with teen troublemaker Gary (Kay), who is both a thief and a hustler. Gary and Howie break into the home of ex-Marine, Big John Harrigan (Cox), who as it turns out, is a pedophile who discovers and confronts the boys and takes a purient interest in Howie's charms. At least at first, since the complex Harrigan realizes Howie really needs some friendly guidance and not a sex partner. Cuesta offers no apologies or explanations for the behavior he depicts and Cox is both commanding and subtle. **97m/C VHS, DVD, Wide.** *US* Brian Cox, Paul Franklin Dano, Billy Kay, Bruce Altman, James Costa, Tony Donnelly, Walter Masterson, Marcia DeBonis, Adam LeFevre; ***D:*** Michael Cuesta; ***W:*** Michael Cuesta, Stephen M. Ryder, Gerald Cuesta; ***C:*** Romeo Tirone; ***M:*** Pierre Foldes. Ind. Spirit '02: Debut Perf. (Dano).

Lie Down with Dogs 1995 (R) You will wake up with fleas if you watch this dull, very low-budget comedy about young Tommie (White), who heads out of New York for some summer fun in the gay-friendly resort of Provincetown, Massachusetts. There's lots of temporary (discreetly filmed) encounters but no lasting romance and Tommie heads back to the Big Apple at season's end satisfied but no wiser. White's debut film. **85m/C VHS.** Wally White, Randy Becker, Darren Dryden; ***D:*** Wally White; ***W:*** Wally White; ***C:*** George Mitas.

Lie Down with Lions ½ 1994 Long and dull TV adaptation of the Ken Follett spy novel. American nurse Kate Neeson (Helgenberger) is aghast when she discovers her lover, Jack Carver (Dalton), is a CIA agent. She marries Czech doctor Peter Husak (Havers) on the rebound and the newleyweds travel to Azerbijan to run a clinic, where Kate has a baby. But Jack's not out of the picture since his current assignment takes him into the war-torn region—and back into Kate's life, especially when he discovers Peter is not what he seems. On three cassettes. **136m/C VHS.** Timothy Dalton, Marg Helgenberger, Nigel Havers, Omar Sharif, Kabir Bedi, Juergen Prochnow; ***D:*** Jim Goddard; ***W:*** Guy Andrews, Julian Bond; ***C:*** Eddy van der Enden.

Liebelei 1932 Fritz (Liebeneiner), a handsome lieutenant, has broken off his romance with a married baroness and fallen for young opera singer Christine (Schneider) in turn-of-the-century Vienna. However, when the jealous baron (Grundgens) learns of his wife's infidelity, he challenges Fritz to a duel. Remade as "Christine" in 1967, with Romy Schneider in her mother's role. In German with English subtitles. **82m/B VHS.** *GE* Magda Schneider, Wolfgang Liebeneiner, Gustav Grundgens; ***D:*** Max Ophuls.

Liebestraum 1991 (R) An architectural expert, his old college friend, and the friend's wife form a dangerous triangle of passion and lust that strangely duplicates a situation that led to a double murder 40 years earlier. The unrated version clocks in at 116 minutes. **109m/C VHS, DVD, Wide.** Kevin Anderson, Bill Pullman, Pamela Gidley, Kim Novak; ***D:*** Mike Figgis; ***W:*** Mike Figgis; ***C:*** Juan Ruiz-Anchia; ***M:*** Mike Figgis.

Lies ½ 1983 (PG) Complicated mystery about a murder/thriller movie plot becoming reality as it is being filmed, revolving around a scam to collect an inheritance from a rich guy in a mental hospital. **93m/C VHS.** *GB* Ann Dusenberry, Gail Strickland, Bruce Davison, Clu Gulager, Bert Remsen, Dick Miller; ***D:*** Ken Wheat, Jim Wheat; ***C:*** Robert Ebinger; ***M:*** Marc Donahue.

Lies Before Kisses 1992 (PG-13) A woman finds out her loving husband has been spending time with a beautiful call girl. When the call girl is murdered the husband is accused. His wife decides to help him clear his name but she just may have her own type of revenge in mind. **93m/C VHS.** Jaclyn Smith, Ben Gazzara, Nick Mancuso, Greg Evigan, Penny Fuller, James Karen; ***D:*** Lou Antonio; ***W:*** Ellen Weston.

Lies My Father Told Me 1975 (PG) Simple drama about growing up in the 1920s in a Jewish ghetto. The story revolves around a young boy's relationship with his immigrant grandfather. Quiet and moving. **102m/C VHS.** *CA* Yossi Yadin, Len Birman, Marilyn Lightstone, Jeffery Lynas; ***D:*** Jan Kadar; ***W:*** Ted Allan. Golden Globes '76: Foreign Film.

Lies of the Twins 1991 A beautiful model becomes involved with her therapist and his identical, and irresponsible, twin brother. **93m/C VHS.** Isabella Rossellini, Aidan Quinn, Iman, John Pleshette; ***D:*** Tim Hunter.

Lt. Robin Crusoe, U.S.N. 1966 (G) A lighthearted navy pilot crash lands amusingly on a tropical island, falls hard for an island babe and schemes intensely against the local evil ruler. Lackluster Disney debacle. **113m/C VHS.** Dick Van Dyke, Nancy Kwan, Akim Tamiroff; ***D:*** Byron Paul; ***M:*** Robert F. Brunner.

Life 1995 Explores the relationships between a group of prisoners doing time in a prison unit for HIV-positive inmates and what it means to be a man. Stylized production was developed from Brumpton's 1991 play "Containment." Feature film debut for director Johnston. **?m/C VHS.** *AU* John Brumpton, David Tredinnick, Robert Morgan, Noel Jordan, Luke Elliot, Jeff Kovski; ***D:*** Lawrence Johnston; ***W:*** John Brumpton, Lawrence Johnston.

Life ½ 1999 (R) New Yorkers Ray (Murphy) and Claude (Lawrence) head south on a moonshine run to pay off a debt to a bootlegger (James). Along the way, ther're framed for murder and sentenced to life on a Mississippi prison farm. Through the years, the two develop a deep, but insult-filled friendship while adjusting to prison life and harboring dreams of freedom. Murphy and Lawrence click well as a comic team, and the movie is best when it stays out of their way. The institutionalized racism of the setting is treated superficially, with the prison appearing to be, despite the slave-like work and gun-toting guards, not an entirely horrible place to live. **108m/C VHS, DVD.** Eddie Murphy, Martin Lawrence, Ned Beatty, Cicely Tyson, Clarence Williams III, Obba Babatunde, Bernie Mac, Michael "Bear" Taliferro, Miguel Nunez, Bokeem Woodbine, Barry (Shabaka) Henley, Brent Jennings, Guy Torry, Lisa Nicole Carson, O'Neal Compton, Poppy Montgomery, Ned Vaughn, R. Lee Ermey, Nick Cassavetes, Noah Emmerich, Anthony Anderson, Rick James; ***D:*** Ted (Edward) Demme; ***W:*** Robert Ramsey, Matthew Stone; ***C:*** Geoffrey Simpson; ***M:*** Wyclef Jean.

Life According to Muriel *La Vida Segun Muriel* 1997 After her husband abandons her, Laura takes 9-year-old daughter Muriel and leaves Buenos Aires for the peace of the countryside. Only they lose all their stuff in an accident and are forced to rely on Mirta—another single mom who owns a run-down hotel. The women bond and start to fix up the place when Muriel's dad shows up wanting a second chance. Spanish with subtitles. **97m/C VHS, DVD.** *AR* Ines Estevez, Jorge Perugorria, Florencia Camiletti, Federico Olivera, Soledad Villamil; ***D:*** Eduardo Milewicz; ***W:*** Eduardo Milewicz, Susana Silvestre; ***C:*** Estaban Sapir; ***M:*** Bob Telson.

The Life and Adventures of Nicholas Nickleby ½ *Nicholas Nickleby* 1981 Nine-hour performance of the 1838 Dickens' tale by the Royal Shakespeare Company, featuring the work of 39 actors portraying 150 characters. Wonderful performances are characterized by frantic action and smoothly meshing intertwining plots, focusing on the trials and tribulations of the Nickleby family, amidst wealth, poverty, and injustice in Victorian England. Nine cassettes. **540m/C VHS.** *GB* Roger Rees, David Threlfis, Emily Richard, John Woodvine; ***D:*** Jim Goddard; ***W:*** David Edgar; ***M:*** Stephen Oliver.

The Life and Assassination of the Kingfish **1976** Recommended by the NEA, this story of Louisiana politician Huey Long is riveting. Asner gives a profound performance. **96m/C VHS.** Ed Asner, Nicholas Pryor, Diane Kagan; ***D:*** Robert E. Collins.

The Life and Death of Colonel Blimp 🦴🦴🦴🦴 *Colonel Blimp* **1943** Chronicles the life of a British soldier who survives three wars (Boer, WWI, and WWII), falls in love with three women (all portrayed by Kerr), and dances a fine waltz. Fine direction and performance abound. **115m/C VHS.** *GB* Roger Livesey, Deborah Kerr, Anton Walbrook, Ursula Jeans, Albert Lieven; ***D:*** Michael Powell, Emeric Pressburger; ***C:*** Georges Perinal.

The Life and Loves of Mozart 🦴🦴½ **1959** Despite the title, this is really about the great composer's later life at the time of the premiere of "Die Zauberfloete" ("The Magic Flute"). This is only partly saved by a stellar performance from Werner, as well as the music. Other than that, it gets bogged down in titillation about W.A.M.'s romantic life. In German with English subtitles. **87m/C VHS.** Oskar Werner, Johanna (Hannerl) Matz, Angelika Hauff; ***D:*** Karl Hartl; ***V:*** Anton Dermota.

Life and Nothing But 🦴🦴🦴½ *La Vie est Rien d'Autre* **1989 (PG)** Two young women search for their lovers at the end of WWI. They're helped by a French officer brutalized by the war and driven to find all of France's casualties. Romantic, evocative, and saddening. In French with English subtitles. **135m/C VHS.** *FR* Philippe Noiret, Sabine Azema, Francois Perrot; ***D:*** Bertrand Tavernier; ***W:*** Bertrand Tavernier; ***C:*** Bruno de Keyzer. British Acad. '89: Foreign Film; Cesar '90: Actor (Noiret), Score; L.A. Film Critics '90: Foreign Film.

Life and Nothing More ... 🦴🦴 *And Life Goes On ...; Zendegi Va Digar Hich ...* **1992** Following Iran's devastating 1990 earthquake, a filmmaker and his son search for the young actors who previously worked with him to see if they've survived, meeting various villagers trying to rebuild their lives. Sequel to Kiarostami's film "Where Is My Friend's House?" and followed by "Through the Olive Trees." Farsi with subtitles. **91m/C VHS.** *IA* Farhad Kheradmand, Pooya Payvar; ***D:*** Abbas Kiarostami; ***W:*** Abbas Kiarostami; ***C:*** Homayun Payvar.

Life & Times of Grizzly Adams 🦴🦴 **1974 (G)** Lightweight family adventure film based on the rugged life of legendary frontiersman, Grizzly Adams, that served as the launching pad for the TV series. Grizzly is mistakenly chased for a crime he didn't commit and along the way befriends a big bear. **93m/C VHS.** Dan Haggerty, Denver Pyle, Lisa Jones, Marjorie Harper, Don Shanks; ***D:*** Richard Friedenberg.

The Life and Times of Hank Greenberg 🦴🦴🦴🦴 **1999 (PG)** Excellent documentary tells the story of Detroit Tiger Hall of Fame first baseman Hank Greenberg though interviews with sportswriters, teammates, other players of the era, and fans (many of them which were young Jewish boys who later became famous themselves), and archival footagefrom on and off the field. Details Greenberg's struggles as a high-profile Jew in a very anti-Semitic era and as a hero and source of inspiration to the Jewish community. Also does a fine job of exploring the settings (New York and Detroit during the '20s and '30s) in which Greenberg grew up and rose to stardom. **95m/C VHS, DVD.** ***D:*** Aviva Kempner; ***W:*** Aviva Kempner.

Life & Times of Judge Roy Bean 🦴🦴½ **1972 (PG)** Based on the life of the famed Texas "hanging judge," the film features Newman as the legendary Bean who dispenses frontier justice in the days of the Wild West. Filled with gallows humor. Gardner sparkles as actress Lily Langtry. **124m/C VHS, Wide.** Paul Newman, Stacy Keach, Ava Gardner, Jacqueline Bisset, Anthony Perkins, Roddy McDowall, Victoria Principal; ***D:*** John Huston; ***W:*** John Milius; ***M:*** Maurice Jarre.

The Life & Times of the Chocolate Killer 🦴½ **1988** Police turn against the hand that's helped them save property and lives, by framing a good samaritan with deeds done by the "Chocolate Killer." **75m/C VHS.** Michael Adrian, Rod Browning, Tabi Cooper.

Life as a House 🦴🦴½ **2001 (R)** George (Kline) is an architect who lives in a broken down shack surrounded by ritzy homes on California's Pacific shore. His ex-wife Robin (Thomas) is raising their drugged-out Goth son Sam (Christensen) with her emotionally unavailable husband Peter (Sheridan). In quick succession, he is fired from his job and learns he has a fatal disease. He examines his life and decides to use his remaining time to tear down the old house and build a new one. He forces Sam to help him, intending to use the project as a means to repair his relationship with his son. Robin's feelings for George also rekindle, and they become more than friends once again. The performances of the excellent ensemble cast, especially Kline and Thomas, save this from being called "Sappy Symbolism as a Movie." **124m/C VHS, DVD, Wide.** Kevin Kline, Hayden Christensen, Kristin Scott Thomas, Jena Malone, Mary Steenburgen, Jamey Sheridan, Scott Bakula, Sam Robards, Mike Weinberg, Scotty Leavenworth, Ian Somerhalder, Sandra Nelson; ***D:*** Irwin Winkler; ***W:*** Mark Andrus; ***C:*** Vilmos Zsigmond; ***M:*** Mark Isham. Natl. Bd. of Review '01: Breakthrough Perf. (Christensen).

The Life Before This 🦴🦴 **1999** Complicated tale has six overlapping stories and 44 characters that follow the lives of a group of Torontonians for 12 hours and ends in a casino heist and a related cafe shootout. Film begins and ends with the shooting and takes place in flashbacks that show how each person came to be in the wrong place at the wrong time. Very loosely based on a true incident. **92m/C VHS, DVD.** *CA* Leslie Hope, David Hewlett, Joel S. Keller, Jacob Tierney, Alberta Watson, Jennifer Dale, Dan Lett, Catherine O'Hara, Martha Burns, Joe Pantoliano, Sarah Polley, Stephen Rea, Callum Keith Rennie; ***D:*** Gerard Ciccoritti; ***W:*** Semi Chellas; ***C:*** Norayr Kasper; ***M:*** Ron Sures. Genie '99: Support. Actress (O'Hara).

Life Begins for Andy Hardy 🦴🦴🦴 **1941** Andy gets a job in New York before entering college and finds the working world to be a sobering experience. Surprisingly downbeat and hard-hitting for an Andy Hardy film. Garland's last appearance in the series. **100m/B VHS.** Mickey Rooney, Judy Garland, Lewis Stone, Ann Rutherford, Fay Holden, Gene Reynolds, Ralph Byrd; ***D:*** George B. Seitz.

Life in the Fast Lane 🦴🦴 **2000 (R)** Mona has accidentally killed her boyfriend. And when his ghost starts to follow her everywhere, Mona realizes how much she still loves him. So just how do you make a romance between a live girl and a dead guy work? **92m/C VHS, DVD.** Fairuza Balk, Patrick Dempsey, Tea Leoni, Debi Mazar, Noah Taylor, Udo Kier.

A Life in the Theater 🦴🦴½ **1993** Life in the theatre as a hammy stage veteran (Lemmon) shares his experiences (and his dressing room) with a callow newcomer (Broderick). Petty squabbles, missed cues, and rare candor are displayed as the two stage scenes from their various repertory. Gentle, slight Mamet play, written when he was 25. **78m/C VHS.** Jack Lemmon, Matthew Broderick; ***D:*** Gregory Mosher; ***W:*** David Mamet. **TV**

Life Is a Long Quiet River 🦴🦴🦴 *La Vie Est Une Longue Fleuve Tranquille* **1988** Social comedy about a nurse who, infuriated with her married doctor employer/lover, switches two babies at birth. Twelve years later, after her lover's wife has died and he still refuses to marry her, she reveals the swap. The children are returned to their rightful families causing a multitude of confusion and adjustment. Directorial debut of Chatiliez. In French with English subtitles. **89m/C VHS.** *FR* Benoit Magimel, Helene Vincent, Andre Wilms, Daniel Gelin, Catherine Hiegel, Christine Pignet, Patrick Bouchitey, Valerie Lalande, Tara Romer, Jerome Floch, Sylvie Cubertafon; ***D:*** Etienne Chatiliez; ***W:*** Florence Quentin, Etienne Chatiliez; ***M:*** Gerard Kawczynski. Cesar '89: Support. Actress (Vincent), Writing.

Life Is Beautiful 🦴🦴🦴½ **1979** A politically neutral man is arrested and tortured in pre-revolutionary Lisbon, and forced to make, and act on, a political commitment. Dubbed. **102m/C VHS.** *PT* Giancarlo Giannini, Ornella Muti; ***D:*** Grigori Chukhraj.

Life Is Beautiful 🦴🦴🦴🦴 *La Vita E Bella* **1998 (PG-13)** At first consideration, the notion of a "feel-good Holocaust comedy" was not up the Hound's alley. But Roberto Benigni's stunning "Life Is Beautiful" is not, first and foremost, a Holocaust movie, but rather a story of endurance of family love. Benigni's Guido is so intent on *believing* that life is—and should be—beautiful, he goes to great lengths to ensure that vision for his wife and, particularly, his son. The first half of the movie is an amusing boy-meets-girl story, Italian-comedy style, with Benigni chasing and winning his real-life wife, actress Braschi. The second half shifts to the concentration camp where Guido, his son, and—because she would not be parted from him—his wife are imprisoned. Guido fabricates an elaborate game to convince his son that the whole ordeal—the "trip"—is an endurance test to be won, with prizes forthcoming. In a particularly humorous scene, Guido "translates" a guard's barking at the prisoners as further clarification of the "rules" of the game. If the movie depicts the horrors of the concentration camps as less than horrifying, it should be forgiven; Benigni's focus is on the love between father, son, and wife. When the film played at the Toronto International Film Festival, this Hound sobbed uncontrollably while the crowd rose to their feet to cheer the Italian director, writer, and star; do light-weight comedies usually have that effect on veteran movie reviewers? Italian with subtitles. **122m/C VHS, DVD.** *IT* Roberto Benigni, Nicoletta Braschi, Giustino Durano, Sergio Bustric, Horst Buchholz, Giorgio Cantarini, Marisa Paredes, Lidia Alfonsi, Giuliana Lojodice; ***D:*** Roberto Benigni; ***W:*** Vincenzo Cerami, Roberto Benigni; ***C:*** Tonino Delli Colli; ***M:*** Nicola Piovani. Oscars '98: Actor (Benigni), Foreign Film, Orig. Dramatic Score; Australian Film Inst. '99: Foreign Film; British Acad. '98: Actor (Benigni); Cannes '98: Grand Jury Prize; Cesar '99: Foreign Film; Screen Actors Guild '98: Actor (Benigni); Broadcast Film Critics '98: Foreign Film.

Life Is Sweet 🦴🦴🦴½ **1990 (R)** The consuming passions of food and drink focus the lives of an oddball English working-class family beset by hopeless dreams and passions. Mother is always fixing family meals—in between helping her friend open a gourmet restaurant which features such revolting dishes as pork cyst and prune quiche. Dad is a chef who buys a snack truck and dreams of life on the road. Natalie and Nicola, the grown twins, eat their meals in front of the television but Nicola is also a bulimic who binges and purges on chocolate bars behind her bedroom door. (Note the chocolate scene between Nicola and her boyfriend). An affectionate, if sometimes unattractive, look at a chaotic family. **103m/C VHS.** *GB* Alison Steadman, Jane Horrocks, Jim Broadbent, Claire Skinner, Timothy Spall, Stephen Rea, David Thewlis; ***D:*** Mike Leigh; ***W:*** Mike Leigh. L.A. Film Critics '91: Support. Actress (Horrocks); Natl. Soc. Film Critics '91: Actress (Steadman), Film, Support. Actress (Horrocks).

A Life Less Ordinary 🦴🦴½ **1997 (R)** Third outing from U.K. team of Boyle/Hodge/Macdonald, who made "Shallow Grave" and "Trainspotting," has hapless janitor Robert (MacGrgor) lose his job, girlfriend, and home. He reacts by kidnapping the boss's daughter Celine (Diaz), who's more upset at Robert's ineptness than anything else. Meanwhile two angels (Hunter and Lindo) are sent to make these two kids fall in love. Confused? You should be. Hodge's script looks like someone threw "It Happened One Night," "Stairway to Heaven," outtakes from a Tarantino movie, and a Road Runner cartoon into a blender and hit frappe. Some of the surreal set pieces work, and the MacGregor/Diaz chemistry clicks sporadically, but the overall effect is overkill. Producer MacDonald is the grandson of Emeric Pressberger, co-director of "Stairway to Heaven." **103m/C VHS, DVD.** Ewan McGregor, Cameron Diaz, Holly Hunter, Delroy Lindo, Ian Holm, Ian McNeice, Stanley Tucci, Dan Hedaya, Tony Shalhoub, Maury Chaykin, Judith Ivey, K.K. Dodds; ***D:*** Danny Boyle; ***W:*** John Hodge; ***C:*** Brian Tufano; ***M:*** David Arnold.

The Life of Emile Zola 🦴🦴🦴½ **1937** Writer Emile Zola intervenes in the case of Alfred Dreyfus who was sent to Devil's Island for a crime he did not commit. Well-crafted production featuring a handsome performance from Muni. **117m/B VHS.** Paul Muni, Gale Sondergaard, Gloria Holden, Joseph Schildkraut; ***D:*** William Dieterle; ***W:*** Norman Reilly Raine; ***C:*** Gaetano Antonio "Tony" Gaudio; ***M:*** Max Steiner. Oscars '37: Picture, Screenplay, Support. Actor (Schildkraut), Natl. Film Reg. '00;; N.Y. Film Critics '37: Actor (Muni), Film.

A Life of Her Own 🦴🦴½ **1950** Turner stars as a farm girl who takes her dream of becoming a top model to the Big Apple. She signs with an agency and is befriended by Dvorak, an aging model, who acts as her mentor. Turner finds success and is soon the toast of the town until she gets involved with a married man (Milland) and her life starts to crumble. Average soap opera with flimsy script. Turner is good, but Dvorak steals the show in her role as an over-the-hill fashion plate. **108m/B VHS.** Lana Turner, Ray Milland, Tom Ewell, Louis Calhern, Ann Dvorak, Barry Sullivan, Jean Hagen, Phyllis Kirk, Sara Haden; ***D:*** George Cukor; ***W:*** Isobel Lennart; ***C:*** George J. Folsey.

The Life of Jesus 🦴🦴 *La Vie de Jesus* **1996** Small town boredom and despair—French style. Twenty-year-old Freddy (Douche) is an unemployed epileptic, who lives with his mother. He spends his time with girlfriend Marie (Cottreel) or riding his moped with his equally disenfranchised buddies. When a young Arab, Kader (Chaatouf), shows an interest in Marie (that's reciprocated), Freddy and his friends beat him up. Apparently the title is a reference to the spiritual suffering Freddy feels, even if he doesn't know exactly how to articulate his emotions. French with subtitles. **96m/C VHS, DVD, Wide.** *FR* David Douche, Marjorie Cottreel, Kader Chaatouf, Samuel Boidin, Genevieve Cottreel; ***D:*** Bruno Dumont; ***W:*** Bruno Dumont; ***C:*** Philippe Van Leeuw; ***M:*** Richard Cuvillier.

Life of Oharu 🦴🦴🦴½ *Diary of Oharu; Saikaku Ichidai Onna* **1952** A near masterpiece rivaled only by "Ugetsu" in the Mizoguchi canon, this film details the slow and agonizing moral decline of a woman in feudal Japan, from wife to concubine to prostitute. A scathing portrait of social predestination based on a novel by Ibara Saikaku. In Japanese with English subtitles. **136m/B VHS.** *JP* Kinuyo Tanaka, Toshiro Mifune; ***D:*** Kenji Mizoguchi.

A Life of Sin 🦴🦴 **1992 (R)** Scandalous drama about an impoverished Caribbean girl who rises to wealth and power as a world-famous madame. Colon stars as the beautiful Isabel, who is betrayed by her childhood friend Paulo (Julia) and rejected by the Catholic bishop (Ferrer) in this tragic story of passion and greed. **112m/C VHS.** Raul Julia, Miriam Colon, Jose Ferrer; ***D:*** Efrain Lopez Neris; ***W:*** Emilio Diaz Valcarcel.

Life of Verdi **1984** Epic miniseries biography of the famous composer, with many excerpts of his music sung by Luciano Pavarotti, Renata Telbaldi, and Maria Callas. **600m/B VHS.** *IT* Ronald Pickup, Carla Fracci. **TV**

Life on a String 🦴🦴 **1990** Set in the distant past, this is a lyrical story of a young boy searching for a cure for his blindness. His possible cure involves a myth which requires him to devote his life to music and the breaking of 1000 strings on a banjo. Adapted from a story by Shi Tiesheng. In Chinese with English subtitles. **110m/C VHS, DVD, Wide.** *CH* Xu Qing; ***D:***

Chen Kaige; *W:* Chen Kaige; *C:* Gu Changwei; *M:* Xiao-Song Qu.

Life 101 ½ **1995** Innocent freshman Haim tries to adjust to college life in the '60s, aided by his hippie roommate Coogan, who introduces Haim to the pleasures of life. Innocuous coming-of-age comedy. **95m/C VHS.** Corey Haim, Keith Coogan, Ami Dolenz; *D:* Redge Mahaffey; *W:* Redge Mahaffey.

Life or Something Like It ½ **2002 (PG-13)** Disappointing fluff bunny blonde role for Jolie, who's best when she's edgy. Instead, she plays shallow Seattle newscaster Lanie Kerigan who has a fab life and a fab famous boyfriend in Seattle Mariners player Cal (Kane). Then she interviews street prophet Jack (Shalhoub) who tells Lanie that she's going to die next week—and since all his other predictions have come true, Lanie gets stressed and decides she needs to get in touch with her regular-gal roots again. Of course it doesn't hurt that her cameraman, sexy Pete (Burns), is willingly to do all he can to make things better. **104m/C VHS, DVD.** *US* Angelina Jolie, Edward Burns, Tony Shalhoub, Christian Kane, Melissa Errico, Stockard Channing, James Gammon, Gregory Itzin; *D:* Stephen Herek; *W:* John Scott Shepherd, Dana Stevens; *C:* Stephen Burum; *M:* David Newman.

Life-Size ½ **2000** Twelve-year-old tomboy, Casey (Lohan), desperately misses her recently deceased mother but her dad, Ben (Burns), is dealing with his own grief by becoming a workaholic. Casey tries out a magic spell to resurrect her mom and instead makes her beauty pageant doll, Eve (Banks), come to life. Casey's horrified and wants to send Eve back to her doll world but Eve loves becoming a human and wants to stay. **89m/C VHS, DVD.** Lindsay Lohan, Tyra Banks, Jere Burns, Anne Marie Loder, Garwin Sanford, Tom Butler; *D:* Mark Rosman; *W:* Mark Rosman, Stephanie Moore; *C:* Philip Linzey; *M:* Eric Colvin. **TV**

Life Stinks **1991 (PG-13)** So does the film. A grasping tycoon bets he can spend a month living on the street without money, resulting in cheap laughs, heavy-handed sentiment and one musical number. Those expecting the innovative, hilarious Brooks of "Young Frankenstein" or "Blazing Saddles" will be very disappointed—these jokes are stale and the timing is tedious. Those looking for a Chaplinesque tale for modern times should stick with Chaplin. **93m/C VHS.** Mel Brooks, Jeffrey Tambor, Lesley Ann Warren, Stuart Pankin, Howard Morris, Teddy Wilson, Michael Ensign, Billy Barty, Carmine Caridi, Rudy DeLuca; *D:* Mel Brooks; *W:* Mel Brooks, Rudy DeLuca; *C:* Steven Poster.

Life Upside Down *La Vie a L'Envers* **1964** Ordinary Paris worker (Denner) decides to withdraw from his seemingly perfect life, including his wife and friends. He ends staring at a blank wall in a mental institution. French with subtitles. **115m/B VHS.** *FR* Charles Denner, Anna Gaylor, Jean Yanne; *D:* Alain Jessua; *W:* Alain Jessua; *C:* Jacques Robin; *M:* Jacques Loussier.

Life with Father ½ **1947** Based on the writings of the late Clarence Day Jr., this is the story of his childhood in NYC during the 1880s. A delightful saga about a stern but loving father and his relationship with his knowing wife and four red-headed sons. **118m/C VHS, DVD.** William Powell, Irene Dunne, Elizabeth Taylor, Edmund Gwenn, ZaSu Pitts, Jimmy Lydon, Martin Milner; *D:* Michael Curtiz; *W:* Donald Ogden Stewart; *C:* William V. Skall, J. Peverell Marley; *M:* Max Steiner. Golden Globes '48: Score; N.Y. Film Critics '47: Actor (Powell).

Life with Judy Garland—Me and My Shadows ½ **2001 (PG)** Sharp direction, a solid script that goes beyond the cliches, plus excellent performances (especially by Davis and Blanchard) prevent this telling of the tortured life of Judy Garland from slipping into made-for-TV docudrama hell. Garland's life is followed, from her insecure early teens, through the movie success and the many marriages and the drug addiction that brought her downfall. Based on the book "Me and My Shadows: A Family Memoir" by daughter Lorna Luft, who participated in the production. **107m/C VHS, DVD.** Judy Davis, Victor Garber, Hugh Laurie, Tammy Blanchard, Stewart Bick, John Benjamin Hickey, Sonja Smits, Tammy Blanchard, Al Waxman, Jayne (Jane) Eastwood, Marsha Mason, Daniel Kash, Aidan Devine; ***Cameos:*** Lorna Luft; *D:* Robert Ackerman; *W:* Robert Freedman, Lorna Luft; *C:* James Chressanthis; *M:* William Ross; ***Nar:*** Cynthia Gibb. **TV**

Life with Mikey ½ **1993 (PG-13)** Michael "Mikey" Chapman (Fox) is a washed-up former child star who now half-heartedly runs a minor talent agency for other pint-sized would-be thespians. Ever mindful of his previous glory, he believes he is doomed to obscurity when a 10-year-old Brooklyn pickpocket reanimates his taste for life. Light, sweet comedy is generally predictable, a typical Fox effort. Unbilled cameo from Reuben Blades as Vidal's father. **92m/C VHS, Wide.** Michael J. Fox, Christina Vidal, Cyndi Lauper, Nathan Lane, David Huddleston, Victor Garber, David Krumholtz, Tony Hendra; ***Cameos:*** Ruben Blades; *D:* James Lapine; *W:* Marc Lawrence; *M:* Alan Menken.

Life Without Dick ½ **2001 (PG-13)** Would-be romantic comedy that does passably on the romance and fails completely at the comedy. Ditzy Colleen (Parker) is devastated when she discovers sleazy boyfriend Dick (Knoxville) is cheating on her. She threatens him with a gun and accidentally kills him. Then Daniel (Connick Jr.) shows up. He works for the Irish mob as a hitman only he can't actually kill anyone. (He really wants to be a professional singer.) Dick was his assignment and he's pleased that everything is already taken care of. Colleen thinks Daniel is just grand and decides she will help him out by taking on his hitman duties herself. **96m/C VHS, DVD, Wide.** Sarah Jessica Parker, Harry Connick Jr., Teri Garr, Johnny Knoxville, Craig Ferguson, Geoffrey Blake, Brigid Conley Walsh, Ever Carradine, Erik Palladino, Claudia Schiffer; *D:* Bix Skahill; *W:* Bix Skahill; *C:* James Glennon; *M:* David Lawrence.

Lifeboat ½ **1944** When a German U-boat sinks a freighter during WWII, the eight survivors seek refuge in a tiny lifeboat. Tension peaks after the drifting passengers take in a stranded Nazi. Hitchcock saw a great challenge in having the entire story take place in a lifeboat and pulled it off with his usual flourish. In 1989, the film "Dead Calm" replicated the technique. From a story by John Steinbeck. Bankhead shines. **96m/B VHS.** Tallulah Bankhead, John Hodiak, William Bendix, Canada Lee, Walter Slezak, Hume Cronyn, Henry Hull, Mary Anderson, Heather Angel, William Yetter Jr.; *D:* Alfred Hitchcock; *W:* Jo Swerling; *C:* Glen MacWilliams; *M:* Hugo Friedhofer. N.Y. Film Critics '44: Actress (Bankhead).

Lifeforce ½ **1985 (R)** A beautiful female vampire from outer space drains Londoners and before long the city is filled with disintegrating zombies in this hi-tech thriller. Sex was never stranger. Screenwriters O'Bannon and Jakoby adapted the story from Colin Wilson's novel, "The Space Vampires." **100m/C VHS, DVD.** Steve Railsback, Peter Firth, Frank Finlay, Patrick Stewart, Michael Gothard, Nicholas Ball, Aubrey Morris, Nancy Paul, Mathilda May, John Hallam; *D:* Tobe Hooper; *W:* Dan O'Bannon, Don Jakoby; *C:* Alan Hume; *M:* Henry Mancini, Michael Kamen.

Lifeform ½ **1996 (R)** Human beings may believe they're tops in the universe but when a Viking spaceship suddenly returns to Earth from a mission to Mars, NASA scientists discover a lifeform that thinks differently. **90m/C VHS.** Cotter Smith, Deirdre O'Connell, Ryan Phillippe, Raoul O'Connell, Leland Orser; *D:* Mark H. Baker; *W:* Mark H. Baker; *C:* James Glennon; *M:* Kevin Kiner.

Lifeguard **1976 (PG)** The lifeguard lives by the credo that work is for people who cannot surf. But 30ish Rick (Elliott) is wondering if it's time to give up beach life and get a "real" job, especially after his 15th year high school reunion where he hooks up with old flame Cathy (Archer), who's now a divorcee with a young child, and a buddy offers him a job selling Porsches. **96m/C VHS.** Sam Elliott, Anne Archer, Stephen Young, Parker Stevenson, Kathleen Quinlan; *D:* Daniel Petrie; *W:* Ron Koslow.

Lifepod **1980** A group of intergalactic travelers is forced to evacuate a luxury space liner when a mad computer sabotages the ship. **94m/C VHS.** Joe Penny, Jordan Michaels, Kristine DeBell.

Lifepod ½ **1993** Trapped on a ship with a killer—only this time it's a space ship. In the year 2169 an interplanetary liner is sabotaged. Nine people escape in a damaged lifepod emergency craft. The survivors are perilously short of food and water and cannot contact Earth. They also face frightening evidence that the terrorist is among their group and is determined to kill the remaining survivors. Very loose adaptation of Alfred Hitchcock's 1944 film "Lifeboat." **120m/C VHS.** Ron Silver, Robert Loggia, CCH Pounder, Stan Shaw, Adam Storke, Jessica Tuck, Kelli Williams, Ed Gate; *D:* Ron Silver; *W:* M. Jay Roach, Pen Densham. **TV**

Lifespan **1975** A young American scientist visiting Amsterdam discovers experiments involving a drug that halts aging. **85m/C VHS.** *GB* Klaus Kinski, Hiram Keller, Tina Aumont; *D:* Alexander Whitelaw.

The Lifetaker woof! **1989** A woman lures an unsuspecting young man into her home where she seduces him. Violence and sex ensue. **97m/C VHS.** Lea Dregorn, Peter Duncan, Terence Morgan; *D:* Michael Papas.

The Lift **1985 (R)** Unsuspecting passengers meet an unfortunate fate when they take a ride in a demonic elevator in a highrise. In this film the last stop isn't ladies' lingerie, but death. In Dutch with English subtitles. **95m/C VHS.** *NL* Huub Stapel, Willeke Van Ammelrooy; *D:* Dick Maas.

The Light Ahead ½ **1939** Lovers Fishke and Hodel dream of escaping the poverty and prejudices of their shtetl for the possibilities of big city life in Odessa. They're aided in their quest by enlightened bookseller Mendele who turns the town's superstitions to their advantage. Based on the stories of social satirist Mendele Mokher Seforim. In Yiddish with English subtitles. **94m/B VHS.** David Opatoshu, Isadore Cashier, Helen Beverly; *D:* Edgar G. Ulmer.

Light at the Edge of the World **1971 (PG)** A band of pirates torments a lighthouse keeper near Cape Horn after he sees a shipwreck they caused. **126m/C VHS, DVD, Wide.** Kirk Douglas, Yul Brynner, Samantha Eggar; *D:* Kevin Billington; *W:* Tom Rowe; *C:* Henri Decae; *M:* Piero Piccioni.

The Light in the Forest ½ **1958** Disney adaptation of the classic Conrad Richter novel about a young man, kidnapped by Indians when he was young, who is forcibly returned to his white family. **92m/C VHS.** James MacArthur, Fess Parker, Carol Lynley, Wendell Corey, Joanne Dru, Jessica Tandy, Joseph Calleia, John McIntire; *D:* Herschel Daugherty; *C:* Ellsworth Fredericks.

The Light in the Jungle ½ **1991 (PG)** The biography of Nobel Peace Prize winner Dr. Albert Schweitzer. He established a hospital in Africa and had to overcome many obstacles, including tribal superstitions and European bureaucracy to make it successful and bring health care to the area. **91m/C VHS.** Malcolm McDowell, Susan Strasberg, Andrew Davis; *D:* Gray Hofmeyr.

Light It Up ½ **1999 (R)** Tedious hostage flick plays like a humorless "Breakfast Club" with guns. When their favorite high school teacher (Nelson) gets unfairly suspended, a group of fed-up students led by jock Lester (Raymond) stage a sit-in. After a confrontational security guard (Whitaker) is shot, the students take him and the crumbling school building hostage. The usual hostage situation mind games are played until the arrival of a police negotiator (Williams). The youngsters then appeal to the public through the use of the Internet, giving their side of the story and asking for public school reform. The young cast does a good job, but they can't make us believe the wildly inane chain of events. **99m/C VHS, DVD, Wide.** Forest Whitaker, Judd Nelson, Sara Gilbert, Rosario Dawson, Usher Raymond, Robert Ri'chard, Fredro Starr, Glynn Turman, Clifton (Gonzalez) Collins Jr., Vic Polizos, Vanessa L(ynne) Williams; *D:* Craig Bolotin; *W:* Craig Bolotin; *C:* Elliot Davis; *M:* Harry Gregson-Williams.

Light of Day **1987 (PG-13)** A rock 'n' roll semi-musical about a working-class brother and sister who escape from their parents and aimless lives through their bar band. Script tends to fall flat, although both Fox and Jett are believable. Title song written by Bruce Springsteen. **107m/C VHS.** Michael J. Fox, Joan Jett, Gena Rowlands, Jason Miller, Michael McKean, Michael Rooker, Michael Dolan; *D:* Paul Schrader; *W:* Paul Schrader; *C:* John Bailey; *M:* Thomas Newman.

The Light of Faith **1922** A sick young woman is cured when she touches the Holy Grail, which a man stole from her former lover in order to help her. Silent. **33m/C VHS.** Lon Chaney Sr., Hope Hampton; *D:* Clarence Brown.

The Light of Western Stars ½ **1930** Brian plays a young woman from the east who comes to claim her late brother's ranch. She meets her murdered brother's best friend (Arlen) who is a drunken cowboy, and he falls madly in love with her. Wanting to impress her, he quickly sobers up and prevents a gang from taking over the ranch. This was Paramount's first talking adaptation of a Grey novel and the third version of this particular Grey novel; silent versions were made in 1918 and 1925. **70m/B VHS.** Richard Arlen, Mary Brian, Regis Toomey, Harry Green, Syd Saylor, George Chandler; *D:* Otto Brower, Edwin H. Knopf.

The Light of Western Stars **1940** A proper Eastern woman goes West and falls in love with a drunken lout. **67m/B VHS.** Victor Jory, Jo Ann Sayers, Russell Hayden, Morris Ankrum; *D:* Lesley Selander.

Light Sleeper **1992 (R)** Schrader's moody look at upscale drug dealers in New York. Dafoe is John LaTour, a 40 year-old drug courier to the club scene. Since his boss (Sarandon) is giving up the drug business for the safer world of natural cosmetics, John must look to his own future. His life becomes even more complicated when he runs into a bitter exflame (Delany) and finds the attraction is still overpowering. Cynical, contemplative, and menacing. **103m/C VHS, DVD.** Willem Dafoe, Susan Sarandon, Dana Delany, David Clennon, Mary Beth Hurt; *D:* Paul Schrader; *W:* Paul Schrader; *C:* Edward Lachman; *M:* Michael Been.

Light Years ½ **1988 (PG)** Garish animated fantasy epic about an idyllic land suddenly beset by evil mutations and death rays. Based on the novel "Robots Against Gondohar" by Jean-Pierre Andrevan. **83m/C VHS.** *D:* Harvey Weinstein; *W:* Isaac Asimov, Raphael Cluzel; *M:* Gabriel Yared; *V:* Glenn Close, Jennifer Grey, Christopher Plummer, Penn Jillette, John Shea, David Johansen, Bridget Fonda, Paul Shaffer, Terrence Mann, Teller.

Lightblast **1985** A San Francisco policeman tries to stop a deadly explosive-wielding mad scientist from blowing the city to kingdom come. **89m/C VHS.** Erik Estrada, Michael Pritchard; *D:* Enzo G. Castellari.

The Lighthorsemen **1987 (PG-13)** Compelling WWI drama follows several battle-hardened men of the Australian Light-Horse mounted infantry stationed in the Middle Eastern desert and the new recruit who joins their ranks and craves acceptance. Superbly filmed, particularly the final battle scene which pits the Aussies against the Turks for control of the wells at Beersheba. Fine performance by Andrews in this epic which contains the essential elements of a good war movie—horses, guns, and more horses. Originally filmed at 140 minutes. Good companion film for another Aussie WWI saga: "Gallipoli." **110m/C VHS.** *AU* Jon Blake, Peter Phelps, Tony Bonner, Bill Kerr, Nick Waters, John Walton, Tim McKenzie, Sigrid Thornton, Anthony Andrews, Shane Briant, Gary Sweet, Gerard Kennedy; *D:* Simon Wincer; *W:* Ian Jones; *C:* Dean Semler; *M:* Mario Millo.

Lightnin' Carson Rides Again 🦴½ **1938** A tough frontier lawman tracks down his payroll-carrying nephew who's been accused of murder and thievery. **58m/B VHS, 8mm.** Tim McCoy, Joan Barclay, Ted Adams, Forrest Taylor; *D:* Sam Newfield.

Lightning Bill 🦴 **1935** Bill champions good in battling rustlers. **46m/B VHS.** Buffalo Bill Jr.

Lightning Bill Crandall 🦴½ **1937** Gunman heads south for the quiet life. Unfortunately, Arizona proves the scene of a fierce battle between various factions of cattlemen. The gunman aids the good guys, and tries to win the daughter's heart. **60m/B VHS.** Bob Steele, Lois January, Charles "Blackie" King, Frank LaRue, Ernie Adams, Earl Dwire, Dave O'Brien; *D:* Sam Newfield.

Lightning Bolt 🦴 *Operazione Goldman* **1967** Someone is stealing moon rockets from Cape Kennedy, and secret agent Harry Sennet must find out who is doing this devilish deed. It leads him to an evil madman who plots to destroy the world from his underwater hideout. Cheap and unintentionally funny. **96m/C VHS.** *IT SP* Anthony Eisley, Wandisa Leigh, Folco Lulli, Diana Lorys, Ursula Parker; *D:* Anthony (Antonio Margheriti) Dawson.

The Lightning Incident 🦴 **1991 (R)** McKeon plays a young Santa Fe sculptor whose worst nightmares come true when her baby is kidnapped by a devil-worshipping cult. Discovering she has a powerful psychic gift, she pursues the kidnappers across the country in a race to save her baby. Almost as bad as it sounds. **90m/C VHS.** Nancy McKeon, Polly Bergen, Tantoo Cardinal, Elpidia Carrillo, Tim Ryan; *D:* Michael Switzer; *W:* Michael J. Murray.

Lightning Jack 🦴½ **1994 (PG-13)** Western comedy about Lightning Jack Kane (Hogan), an aging second-rate outlaw who desperately wants to become a western legend. Mute store clerk Ben (Gooding) winds up as his partner in crime, while barely eluding criticisms of Stepin Fetchitism. Cliches galore, the running gags (including Kane's surreptitious use of his eyeglasses so he can see his shooting targets) fall flat. **93m/C VHS, DVD, Wide.** Paul Hogan, Cuba Gooding Jr., Beverly D'Angelo, Kamala Dawson, Pat Hingle, Richard Riehle, Frank McRae, Roger Daltrey, L.Q. (Justus E. McQueen) Jones, Max Cullen; *D:* Simon Wincer; *W:* Paul Hogan; *C:* David Eggby; *M:* Bruce Rowland.

Lightning Raiders 🦴🦴 **1945** When a stage coach filled with mail gets robbed, Billy Carson (Crabbe) and Fuzzy (St. John) set off to avenge the postal system. One of the last Crabbe/St. John efforts; perhaps they should have called it quits a few films earlier. **61m/C VHS.** Buster Crabbe, Al "Fuzzy" St. John, Mady Lawrence, Henry Hall, Steve Darrell, I. Stanford Jolley, Karl Hackett, Roy Brent, Marin Sais, Al Ferguson; *D:* Sam Newfield; *W:* Elmer Clifton.

Lightning Range 🦴 **1933** Roosevelt stars as a U.S. Deputy Marshal who continually foils the nefarious plots of a gang of outlaws. **50m/B VHS.** Buddy Roosevelt, Lafe (Lafayette) McKee.

Lightning Strikes West 🦴½ **1940** U.S. Marshal trails an escaped convict, eventually catches him, and brings him in to finish paying his debt to society. **57m/B VHS.** Ken Maynard.

Lightning: The White Stallion 🦴½ **1986 (PG)** An old gambler and his two young friends enter a horse race in order to win their beloved white stallion back from thieves. **93m/C VHS.** Mickey Rooney, Susan George, Isabel Lorca; *D:* William A. Levey.

Lightning Warrior **1931** Western suspense about pioneer life and the unraveling of a baffling mystery. Twelve chapters, 13 minutes each. **156m/B VHS.** George Brent, Frankie Darro; *D:* Armand Schaefer, Benjamin (Ben H.) Kline.

Lights! Camera! Murder! 🦴🦴 **1989** When a 12-year-old boy witnesses a filmed murder, he becomes the next target. **89m/C VHS.** John Barrett; *D:* Frans Nel.

Lights of Old Santa Fe 🦴½ **1947** A cowboy rescues a beautiful rodeo owner from bankruptcy. The original, unedited version of the film. **78m/B VHS.** Roy Rogers, Dale Evans, George "Gabby" Hayes, Bob Nolan.

The Lightship 🦴🦴 **1986 (PG-13)** On a stationary lightship off the Carolina coast, the crew rescues three men from a disabled boat, only to find they are murderous criminals. Duvall as a flamboyant homosexual psychopath is memorable, but the tale is pretentious, overdone, and hackneyed. Based on Siegfried Lenz's story. **87m/C VHS.** Robert Duvall, Klaus Maria Brandauer, Tom Bower, William Forsythe, Arliss Howard; *D:* Jerzy Skolimowski.

Like Father, Like Son 🦴 **1987 (PG-13)** First and worst of a barrage of interchangeable switcheroo movies that came out in '87-'88. Moore is in top form, but the plot is contrived. **101m/C VHS.** Dudley Moore, Kirk Cameron, Catherine Hicks, Margaret Colin, Sean Astin; *D:* Rod Daniel; *W:* Steven L. Bloom, Lorne Cameron; *M:* Miles Goodman.

Like It Is 🦴🦴🦴 **1998** Young Craig (Bell) makes his living in illegal bareknuckles fighting matches in the old British beach resort town of Blackpool. After one win, he heads for a local disco where he meets ambitious London record producer, Matt (Rose), who's accompanying his roommate, singer Paula (Behr), to a gig. Uncertain of his sexual feelings, Craig can't follow through on his attraction to the willing Matt but does soon turn up on his London doorstep. However, not only is jealous Paula a problem for their budding romance but so is Kelvin (Daltry), Matt's manipulative gay boss. Appealing lead performances but vet Daltry steals scenes with smarmy charm. Accents and slang will be a challenge to American ears. **95m/C VHS, DVD.** *GB* Steve Bell, Ian Rose, Dani Behr, Roger Daltrey; *D:* Paul Oremland; *W:* Robert Cray; *C:* Alistair Cameron; *M:* Don McGlashan.

Like It Never Was Before 🦴🦴 *Pensionat Oskar* **1995** Conventional, middle-aged marrieds Rune (Falkman) and Gunnel (Ekblad) Runeberg travel to a seaside hotel for their annual vacation with their three children. Ordinary family man Rune, though dissatisfied, is expecting little until he meets, and falls in love with, young handyman Petrus (Norrthon), and suddenly decides to break free. Swedish with subtitles. **108m/B VHS.** *SW* Loa Falkman, Stina Ekblad, Simon Norrthon, Philip Zanden, Sif Ruud, Ghita Norby; *D:* Suzanne (Susanne) Bier; *W:* Jonas Gardell; *C:* Kjell Lagerros; *M:* Johan Soderqvist.

Like Mike **2002** That's "Mike" as in Michael Jordan—or at least his basketball shoes. A pair of old shoes, supposedly once belonging to Jordan, is donated to an orphanage and become the property of tiny teen Lil'Bow Wow, whose dreams of playing in the NBA don't seem so far-fetched anymore. Philly hoopsters Gary Payton, Alonzo Mourning, Rasheed Wallace, and Jason Kidd make appearances. Not yet reviewed. **?m/C VHS, DVD.** Lil' Bow Wow, Jonathan Lipnicki, Morris Chestnut, Eugene Levy, Crispin Glover, Reggie Theus; *D:* John Schultz; *W:* Jordan Moffet, Mike Elliot.

Like Water for Chocolate 🦴🦴🦴½ *Como Agua para Chocolate* **1993 (R)** Magical Mexican fairytale set in the early 1900s about family, love, and the power of food. Formidable Mama Elena is left a widow with three daughters. The youngest, Tita, grows up in the kitchen surrounded by all the magic. Nacha, the housekeeper, can impart to her about food. Doomed by tradition to spend her days caring for her mother, Tita escapes by cooking, releasing her sorrows and longings into the food, infecting all who eat it. Wonderfully sensuous and slyly exaggerated. Based on the novel by Esquival, who also wrote the screenplay and whose husband, Arau, directed. In Spanish with English subtitles; also available dubbed. **105m/C VHS, DVD.** *MX* Lumi Cavazos, Marco Leonardi, Regina Torne, Mario Ivan Martinez, Ada Carrasco, Yareli Arizmendi, Caludette Maille, Pilar Aranda; *D:* Alfonso Arau; *W:* Laura Esquivel; *C:* Steven Bernstein; *M:* Leo Brower.

Li'l Abner 🦴½ *Trouble Chaser* **1940** Al Capp's famed comic strip comes somewhat to life in this low-budget comedy featuring all of the Dogpatch favorites. **78m/C VHS.** Cranville Owen, Martha Driscoll, Buster Keaton; *D:* Albert Rogell.

Li'l Abner 🦴🦴½ **1959** High color Dogpatch drama adapted from the Broadway play (with most of the original cast) based on the Al Capp comic strip. When Abner's berg is considered as a site for atomic bomb testing, the natives have to come up with a reason why they should be allowed to exist. Choreography by Michael Kidd and Dee Dee Wood. ♫Jubilation T. Cornpone; Don't Take That Rag Off'n the Bush; A Typical Day; If I Had My Druthers; Room Enuff for Us; Namely You; The Country's in the Very Best of Hands; Unnecessary Town; I'm Past My Prime. **114m/C VHS.** Peter Palmer, Leslie Parrish, Stubby Kaye, Julie Newmar, Howard St. John, Stella Stevens, Billie Hayes, Joe E. Marks; *D:* Melvin Frank; *W:* Norman Panama; *C:* Daniel F. Fapp; *M:* Johnny Mercer, Jean De Paul.

Lili 🦴🦴🦴 **1953** Delightful musical romance about a 16-year-old orphan who joins a traveling carnival and falls in love with a crippled, embittered puppeteer. Heartwarming and charming, if occasionally cloying. Leslie Caron sings the films's song hit, "Hi-Lili, Hi-Lo." **81m/C VHS.** Leslie Caron, Jean-Pierre Aumont, Mel Ferrer, Kurt Kasznar, Zsa Zsa Gabor; *D:* Charles Walters; *M:* Bronislau Kaper. Oscars '53: Orig. Dramatic Score; British Acad. '53: Actress (Caron); Golden Globes '54: Screenplay.

Lilian's Story 🦴🦴½ **1995** Aging Lilian (Cracknell) has just been released after spending 40 years in a mental institution, placed there as an adolescent by her controlling, possessive father. The haunted Lilian is given a room at a residential hotel in Sydney's red-light district where the local prostitutes look out for her and she spends her days wandering the streets. Flashbacks reveal what lead the high-strung young Lilian (Collette) to her incarceration. Based on Kate Greville's 1984 novel, which was a fictional account of real-life Sydney eccentric Bea Miles. **94m/C VHS, DVD, Wide.** *AU* Ruth Cracknell, Barry Otto, Toni Collette, John Flaus, Essie Davis, Susie Lindemann, Anne Louise Lambert, Iris Shand; *D:* Jerzy Domaradzki; *W:* Steve Wright; *C:* Slawomir Idziak; *M:* Cezary Skubiszewski. Australian Film Inst. '95: Support. Actress (Collette).

Lilies 🦴🦴 *Les Feluettes* **1996 (R)** Strange revenge fantasy set in a northern Quebec men's prison in 1952. A bishop (Sabourin) goes to the prison to hear the confession of a dying convict and is taken hostage in the chapel by the prison's homosexual population. There, he's forced to watch a play that recreates a 40-year-old incident in his own life. As the prison walls fade away, the actor/prisoners turn into students Simon (Cadieux) and Vallier (Gilmore), who take the lovers' roles in a pageant about the martyrdom of St. Sebastien too seriously for comfort. The female roles in the flashbacks (which include Vallier's crazy mother and Simon's would-be fiance) are played by men. Adapted from Bouchard's play "Les Feluettes out La Repetition d'un Drame Romantique." **95m/C VHS, DVD.** *CA* Marcel Sabourin, Jason Cadieux, Danny Gilmore, Brent Carver, Matthew Ferguson, Alexander Chapman, Aubert Pallascio; *D:* John Greyson; *W:* Michel Marc Bouchard; *C:* Daniel Jobin; *M:* Mychael Danna. Genie '96: Art Dir./Set Dec., Costume Des., Film, Sound.

Lilies of the Field 🦴🦴🦴 **1963** Five former East German nuns, living on a small farm in the Southwest U.S., enlist the aid of a free-spirited Army veteran Homer Smith (Poitier) to build a chapel for them and teach them English. Poitier is excellent as the itinerant laborer, holding the saccharine to an acceptable level, bringing honesty and strength to his role. Actress Skala, as Mother Maria, had been struggling to make ends meet in a variety of day jobs until this opportunity. Poitier was the first African American man to win an Oscar, and the first African American nominated since Hattie MacDaniel in 1939. Followed by "Christmas Lilies of the Field" (1979). **94m/B VHS, DVD, Wide.** Sidney Poitier, Lilia Skala, Lisa Mann, Isa Crino, Stanley Adams, Francesca Jarvis, Pamela Branch, Dan Frazer, Ralph Nelson; *D:* Ralph Nelson; *W:* James Poe; *C:* Ernest Haller; *M:* Jerry Goldsmith. Oscars '63: Actor (Poitier); Berlin Intl. Film Fest. '63: Actor (Poitier); Golden Globes '64: Actor—Drama (Poitier).

Liliom 🦴🦴🦴 **1935** Boyer goes to heaven and is put on trial to see if he is deserving of his wings. Lang's first film after leaving Nazi Germany is filled with wonderful ethereal imagery, surprising coming from the man responsible for such grim visions as "Metropolis." In French only. **85m/B VHS.** *FR* Charles Boyer, Madeleine Ozeray, Florelle, Roland Toutain; *D:* Fritz Lang.

Lilith 🦴🦴🦴 **1964** Therapist-in-training Beatty falls in love with beautiful mental patient Seberg and approaches madness himself. A look at the doctor-patient relationship among the mentally ill and at the nature of madness and love. Doesn't always satisfy, but intrigues. Rossen's swan song. **114m/B VHS.** Warren Beatty, Jean Seberg, Peter Fonda, Gene Hackman, Kim Hunter; *D:* Robert Rossen; *C:* Eugene (Eugen Shufftan) Shuftan.

Lillie 🦴🦴🦴 **1979** The life of Edwardian beauty Lillie Langtry, known as "The Jersey Lily," is portrayed in this British drama. Defying the morals of the times, Lillie was the first publicly acknowledged mistress of the Prince of Wales, only one of her numerous lovers. Shown on "Masterpiece Theatre" on PBS. **690m/C VHS, DVD.** *GB* Francesca Annis, Cheryl Campbell, John Castle, Dennis (Denis) Lill, Peter Egan, Anton Rodgers, Ann(e) Firbank. **TV**

Lilo & Stitch **2002 (PG)** Hawaiian problem child Lilo has an alien pet named Stitch, with socially unacceptable behavior (including naughty words, drooling, and spitting food). Parents may be a little concerned but the kiddies will love the gross-out behavior. Not yet reviewed. **?m/C VHS, DVD.** *D:* Dean DeBlois, Christopher Sanders; *W:* Dean DeBlois, Christopher Sanders; *V:* Daveigh Chase, Jason Scott Lee, Tia Carrere, David Ogden Stiers, Christopher Sanders.

Lily Dale 🦴🦴½ **1996 (PG)** Nineteen-year-old Horace Robedaux (Guinee) is in Houston to visit his estranged mother Corella (Channing) and sister Lily Dale (Masterson) while his taciturn stepfather Pete Davenport (Shepard) is supposed to be away. Pete dislikes Horace and left the boy behind with relatives when he married Corella and they moved away. Self-centered Lily Dale resents Horace taking away attention from herself and matters only get worse when Pete comes home early and Horace becomes so ill that he can't leave. Set in 1910; Foote wrote the play as a memoir to his father, Horace. Made for TV. **95m/C VHS, DVD.** Tim Guinee, Stockard Channing, Mary Stuart Masterson, Sam Shepard, John Slattery, Jean Stapleton; *D:* Peter Masterson; *W:* Horton Foote; *C:* Don E. Fauntleroy; *M:* Peter Melnick.

Lily in Love 🦴🦴½ *Playing for Keeps; Jatszani Kell* **1985 (PG-13)** An aging stage star disguises himself as a suave Italian to star in his playwright wife's new play, and woos her to test her fidelity. Charming, warm, and sophisticated. Loosely based on Molnar's "The Guardsman." **100m/C VHS.** *HU* Maggie Smith, Christopher Plummer, Elke Sommer, Adolph Green; *D:* Karoly Makk; *W:* Frank Cucci. **TV**

Lily in Winter 🦴🦴½ **1994 (PG)** Christmas story about families and the ties that bind, set in 1957. Black nanny Lily (Cole in her film debut) works for busy showbiz New Yorkers, the Towlers (Hoffmann and Brown), looking after their neglected 10-year-old son Michael (Bonsall). But Lily thinks she's in trouble, thanks to her no-account brother Booker (Russell), and takes off to her rural Alabama roots without realizing Michael has followed her. His parents, however, think Lily has kidnapped him. **120m/C VHS.** Natalie Cole, Brian Bonsall, Dwier Brown, Cecil Hoffmann, Marla Gibbs, Monte Russell, Rae'ven (Alyia Larrymore) Kelly, Salli Richardson, James Pickens Jr., Matthew Faison; *D:* Delbert Mann; *W:* Robert Eisele; *C:* Charles Mills; *M:* David Shire. **CABLE**

Lily of Killarney *The Bride of the Lake* **1934** A musical comedy romance about a British lord who arranges to pay his debts via horse-races, arranged marriages and inheritances. **82m/B VHS, 8mm.** *GB* Gina Malo, John Garrick, Stanley Holloway; ***D:*** Maurice Elvey.

Lily Was Here **1989 (R)** After her fiancee is senselessly murdered, a young woman named Lily is forced to turn to a life of crime in order to survive. A series of petty thefts evolves into a huge crime wave and Lily soon finds herself the object of a massive manhunt. Lily must make the ultimate choice between freedom and motherhood in this shocking thriller. Soundtrack by Dave Stewart features hit instrumental theme "Lily was Here" by saxophonist Candy Dulfur. **110m/C VHS.** Marion Van Thijn, Thom Hoffman, Adrian Brine, Dennis Rudge; ***D:*** Ben Verbong; ***W:*** Ben Verbong, Sytze Van Der Laan, Willem Jan Otten.

The Limbic Region **1996** Terminally ill police detective Jon Lucca (Olmos) has spent 20 years tracking a serial killer known as "The Scorekeeper," who likes to shotgun the young inhabitants of small-town lovers' lanes. His most likely suspect is Lloyd Warden (Dzundza) and the duo engage in a deadly cat-and-mouse battle that may destroy them both. **96m/C VHS.** Edward James Olmos, George Dzundza, Gwynyth Walsh; ***D:*** Michael Pattinson; ***W:*** Patrick Ranahan, Todd Johnson; ***C:*** Tobias Schliessler. **CABLE**

Limbo **1999 (R)** Ambivalent family saga that leaves the viewers deliberately in limbo for good or ill. Alaskan Joe Gastineau (Strathairn) is a former fisherman traumatized by an accident at sea years before. Into his life comes smalltime singer Donna de Angelo (Mastrantonio) and her depressed teen daughter Noelle (Martinez). Joe and Donna start a tentative romance and Joe even goes back to fishing. Then Joe's fast-talking half-brother Bobby (Siemaszko) shows up, precipitating a crisis that leaves Bobby dead and Joe, Donna, and Noelle stranded on a deserted island. **126m/C VHS, DVD.** David Strathairn, Mary Elizabeth Mastrantonio, Vanessa Martinez, Casey Siemaszko, Kris Kristofferson, Kathryn Grody, Rita Taggart, Leo Burmester, Michael Laskin; ***D:*** John Sayles; ***W:*** John Sayles; ***C:*** Haskell Wexler; ***M:*** Mason Daring.

Limelight **1952** A nearly washed-up music hall comedian is stimulated by a young ballerina to a final hour of glory. A subtle if self-indulgent portrait of Chaplin's own life, featuring an historic pairing of Chaplin and Keaton. **120m/B VHS, DVD.** Charlie Chaplin, Claire Bloom, Buster Keaton, Nigel Bruce, Sydney Chaplin; ***D:*** Charlie Chaplin; ***W:*** Charlie Chaplin; ***C:*** Karl Struss; ***M:*** Charlie Chaplin.

The Limey **1999 (R)** Sixties icons Stamp and Fonda show that age has not withered their acting chops in Soderbergh's revenge thriller. Wilson (Stamp) is a Cockney career criminal who gets out of a Brit prison and immediately flies to L.A. to investigate the death of his daughter Jenny. She was involved with self-important record producer Valentine (Fonda), who has an obvious fondness for young women. Wilson may be out-of-touch with California culture but he's definitely in control of any situation. Soderbergh's flashback sequences make use of footage from Ken Loach's 1967 film "Poor Cow," which featured Stamp as a young thief named Wilson. **90m/C VHS, DVD, Wide.** Terence Stamp, Peter Fonda, Lesley Ann Warren, Luis Guzman, Barry Newman, Joe Dallesandro, Nicky Katt, Amelia Heinle, Melissa George; ***D:*** Steven Soderbergh; ***W:*** Lem Dobbs; ***C:*** Edward Lachman; ***M:*** Cliff Martinez.

Limit Up **1989 (PG-13)** An ambitious Chicago Trade Exchange employee makes a deal with the devil to corner the market in soybeans. Turgid attempt at supernatural comedy, featuring Charles as God. Catch Sally Kellerman in a cameo as a nightclub singer. **88m/C VHS.** Nancy Allen, Dean Stockwell, Brad Hall, Danitra Vance, Ray Charles, Luana Anders; ***Cameos:*** Sally Kellerman; ***D:*** Richard Martini; ***C:*** Peter Collister.

The Limping Man **1953** Bridges returns to post-WWII London to renew a wartime romance. On the way, he gets caught up in solving a murder. Unexceptional of-its-era thriller. **76m/B VHS.** *GB* Lloyd Bridges, Moira Lister, Leslie Phillips, Helene Cordet, Alan Wheatley; ***D:*** Charles De Latour.

Linda **1929** Linda, a young mountain girl, is forced to marry a much older man though her heart belongs to a young doctor. Her kind husband tries to make the best of the situation. **75m/B VHS.** Helen Foster, Warner Baxter, Noah Beery Sr., Mitchell Lewis, Kate Price, Alan Connor; ***D:*** Dorothy Davenport Reid.

Linda **1993 (PG-13)** Madsen in her femme fatale mode as treacherous wife Linda who wants to frame her schlump husband (Thomas) for murder. Whose murder? Why the inconvenient wife (Harrington) of her boyfriend (McGinley). The two homicidal lovebirds want to take the insurance money and run—leaving hubby to face the consequences. Based on the novella "Linda" by John D. MacDonald. **88m/C VHS.** Virginia Madsen, Richard Thomas, Ted McGinley, Laura Harrington; ***D:*** Nathaniel Gutman; ***W:*** Nevin Schreiner; ***M:*** David Michael Frank.

The Lindbergh Kidnapping Case **1976** The famous Lindbergh baby kidnapping in 1932 and the trial and execution of Bruno Hauptmann, convincingly portrayed by Hopkins. DeYoung as Lindbergh is blah, but the script is quite good. Made for TV. **150m/C VHS.** Anthony Hopkins, Joseph Cotten, Cliff DeYoung, Walter Pidgeon, Dean Jagger, Martin Balsam, Laurence Luckinbill, Tony Roberts; ***D:*** Buzz Kulik; ***W:*** J(ames) P(inckney) Miller; ***M:*** Billy Goldenberg. **TV**

The Line **1980 (R)** Not-so-hot anti-war drama about a sit-down strike at a military installation by Vietnam veteran prison inmates. Leans heavily on recycled footage from director Siegel's own "Parade" (1971). **94m/C VHS.** Russ Thacker, David Doyle, Erik Estrada; ***D:*** Robert Siegel.

The Linguini Incident **1992 (R)** An inept escape artist, a pathological liar, a lingerie designer, a deaf restaurant hostess who throws out one-liners in sign language, and two sinister, yet chic, restaurant owners get together in this marginal comedy about magic and adventure. **99m/C VHS.** Rosanna Arquette, David Bowie, Eszter Balint, Andre Gregory, Buck Henry, Viveca Lindfors, Marlee Matlin, Lewis Arquette, Andrea King; ***Cameos:*** Julian Lennon, Iman; ***D:*** Richard Shepard; ***W:*** Tamar Brott, Richard Shepard; ***C:*** Robert Yeoman; ***M:*** Thomas Newman.

Link woof! **1986 (R)** A primatologist and his nubile assistant find their experiment has gone—you guessed it—awry, and their hairy charges are running—yep, that's right—amok. Run for your life! **103m/C VHS, DVD, Wide.** *GB* Elisabeth Shue, Terence Stamp, Steven Pinner, Richard Garnett; ***D:*** Richard Franklin; ***W:*** Everett DeRoche; ***C:*** Mike Molloy; ***M:*** Jerry Goldsmith.

The Lion Has Wings **1940** The story of how Britain's Air Defense was set up to meet the challenge of Hitler's Luftwaffe during their "finest hour." Dated, now-quaint but stirring wartime period piece. "Docudrama" style was original at the time. **75m/B VHS.** Merle Oberon, Ralph Richardson, Flora Robson, June Duprez; ***D:*** Michael Powell, Brian Desmond Hurst; ***C:*** Harry Stradling Sr.

The Lion in Winter **1968 (PG)** Medieval monarch Henry II and his wife, Eleanor of Aquitaine, match wits over the succession to the English throne and much else in this fast-paced film version of James Goldman's play. The family, including three grown sons, and visiting royalty are united for the Christmas holidays fraught with tension, rapidly shifting allegiances, and layers of psychological manipulation. Superb dialogue and perfectly realized characterizations. O'Toole and Hepburn are triumphant. Screen debuts for Hopkins and Dalton. Shot on location, this literate costume drama surprised the experts with its boxoffice success. **134m/C VHS, DVD, Wide.** Peter O'Toole, Katharine Hepburn, Jane Merrow, Nigel Terry, Timothy Dalton, Anthony Hopkins, John Castle, Nigel Stock; ***D:*** Anthony Harvey; ***W:*** James Goldman; ***M:*** John Barry. Oscars '68: Actress (Hepburn), Adapt. Screenplay, Orig. Score; Directors Guild '68: Director (Harvey); Golden Globes '69: Actor—Drama (O'Toole), Film—Drama; N.Y. Film Critics '68: Film.

A Lion Is in the Streets **1953** Cagney stars as a backwoods politician in a southern state who fights on the side of the sharecroppers and wins their support when he exposes the corrupt practices of a powerful businessman. On his way up the political ladder, however, Cagney betrays and exploits the very people who support him. Although this is a familiar storyline, Cagney is riveting as the corrupt politician, and Hale is wonderful as his patient wife. **88m/C VHS.** James Cagney, Barbara Hale, Anne Francis, Warner Anderson, John McIntire, Jeanne Cagney, Lon Chaney Jr., Frank McHugh, Larry Keating, Onslow Stevens; ***D:*** Raoul Walsh.

The Lion King **1994 (G)** Highest grossing film in Disney history (likely a temporary title) is a winner for kids and their folks. Like his dad Mufasa (Jones), Lion cub Simba (Taylor) is destined to be king of the beasts, until evil uncle Scar (Irons) plots against him and makes him an outcast. Growing up in the jungles of Africa, Simba (now Broderick) learns about life and responsibility, before facing his uncle once again. Supporting characters frequently steal the show, with Sabella's Pumba the warthog and Lane's Timon the meerkat heading the procession (though Chong and Goldberg as hyenas give them a run). Disney epic features heartwarming combo of crowd-pleasing songs, a story with depth, emotion, and politically correct multiculturalism, and stunning animation. The sound quality is equally spectacular; during the two and a half-minute wildebeest stampede scene, you'll swear the animals are running amuck in the house. Thirty-second Disney animated feature is the first without human characters, the first based on an original story, and the first to use the voices of a well known, ethnically diverse cast. Scenes of violence in the animal kingdom may be too much for younger viewers. ♫Can You Feel the Love Tonight; The Circle of Life; I Just Can't Wait to Be King; Be Prepared; Hakuna Matata. **88m/C VHS.** ***D:*** Rob Minkoff, Roger Allers; ***W:*** Jonathan Roberts, Irene Mecchi; ***M:*** Elton John, Hans Zimmer, Tim Rice; ***V:*** Matthew Broderick, Jeremy Irons, James Earl Jones, Madge Sinclair, Robert Guillaume, Jonathan Taylor Thomas, Richard "Cheech" Marin, Whoopi Goldberg, Rowan Atkinson, Nathan Lane, Ernie Sabella, Niketa Calame, Moira Kelly, Jim (Jonah) Cummings. Oscars '94: Song ("Can You Feel the Love Tonight"), Orig. Score; Golden Globes '95: Film—Mus./Comedy, Song ("Can You Feel the Love Tonight?"), Score; Blockbuster '95: Family Movie, T., Soundtrack.

The Lion King: Simba's Pride **1998** Simba's heir comes of age and must be prepared to assume the responsibility of leadership. **75m/C VHS, DVD.** ***D:*** Darrell Rooney, Rob LaDuca; ***W:*** Flip Kobler, Cindy Marcus; ***V:*** Matthew Broderick, James Earl Jones, Nathan Lane, Ernie Sabella, Robert Guillaume, Andy Dick, Neve Campbell, Suzanne Pleshette, Jason Marsden. **VIDEO**

The Lion Man **1936** Arabian tale of a boy raised by lions. **?m/B VHS.** Jon Hall, Ted Adams.

Lion Man **1979** Raised by wild animals, the son of King Solomon returns to his father's kingdom and roars his way to the throne. **91m/C VHS.** Steve Arkin.

The Lion of Africa **1987** A down-to-earth woman doctor and an abrasive diamond dealer share a truck ride across Kenya. Filmed on location in East Africa. Fine lead performances in otherwise nothing-special adventure. **115m/C VHS.** Brian Dennehy, Brooke Adams, Joseph Shiloah; ***D:*** Kevin Connor; ***M:*** George S. Clinton. **CABLE**

Lion of the Desert *Omar Mukhtar* **1981 (PG)** Bedouin horse militias face-off against Mussolini's armored terror in this epic historical drama. Omar Muktar (Quinn as the "Desert Lion") and his Libyan guerrilla patriots kept the Italian troops of Mussolini (Steiger) at bay for 20 years. Outstanding performances enhanced by the desert backdrop. A British-Libyan coproduction. **162m/C VHS, DVD, Wide.** *GB* Anthony Quinn, Oliver Reed, Irene Papas, Rod Steiger, Raf Vallone, John Gielgud; ***D:*** Moustapha Akkad; ***W:*** H.A.L. Craig; ***C:*** Jack Hildyard; ***M:*** Maurice Jarre.

The Lion of Thebes **1964** A muscleman unhesitatingly jumps into the thick of things when Helen of Troy is kidnapped. A superior sword and sandal entry. **87m/C VHS.** *IT* Mark Forest, Yvonne Furneaux.

Lionheart **1987 (PG)** A romantic portrayal of the famous English King Richard the Lionheart's early years. Meant for kids, but no Ninja turtles herein—and this is just as silly, and slow to boot. **105m/C VHS.** Eric Stoltz, Talia Shire, Nicola Cowper, Dexter Fletcher, Nicholas Clay, Deborah Maria Moore, Gabriel Byrne; ***D:*** Franklin J. Schaffner; ***W:*** Richard Outten; ***M:*** Jerry Goldsmith.

Lionheart *A.W.O.L.; Wrong Bet* **1990 (R)** Van Damme deserts the foreign legion and hits the streets when he learns his brother has been hassled. Many fights ensue, until you fall asleep. **105m/C VHS, DVD.** Jean-Claude Van Damme, Harrison Page, Deborah Rennard, Lisa Pelikan, Brian Thompson; ***D:*** Sheldon Lettich; ***W:*** Sheldon Lettich, Jean-Claude Van Damme; ***C:*** Robert New; ***M:*** John Scott.

Lion's Den **1936** A night club performer and a detective head west to fight crime in this film. **59m/B VHS.** Tim McCoy, Dave O'Brien.

The Lion's Share **1979** A gang of bank robbers have their loot stolen and go after the guy who ripped them off. **105m/C VHS.** *SP* Julio de Grazia, Luisina Brando, Fernanda Mistral, Ulises Dumont, Julio Chavez.

Lip Service **1988** Satirical comedy-drama about the TV news industry. An ambitious young newscaster befriends a veteran reporter. He then manipulates his way to replace him on the reporter's morning program. Dooley as the veteran and Dunne as the upstart are fun to watch in this well-done cable rip-off of "Broadcast News." **67m/C VHS.** Griffin Dunne, Paul Dooley; ***D:*** William H. Macy. **CABLE**

Lip Service *Kat and Allison* **2000 (R)** Allison (Temchen) is a conservative, successful, furniture designer with a successful lawyer boyfriend, Stuart (Camargo). She reunites with her old college roommate, Kat (Gertz), a high-strung free spirit who moves into Allison's home. Then Kat discovers that Allison's success is predicated on selling copies of a chair that Kat herself designed and gave to Allison as a gift. So Kat decides to get revenge. **95m/C VHS, DVD.** Jami Gertz, Sybil Temchen, Jonathan Silverman, Christian Camargo, Adewale Akinnuoye-Agbaje, Jenna Byrne; ***D:*** Shawn Schepps; ***W:*** Shawn Schepps; ***C:*** Feliks Parnell.

Lips of Blood *Levres de Sang* **1975** Rollin whips up a typically festive mix of sex, horror, and hallucination in what some have dubbed his best film. A young man (Philippe) has visions of a woman (Briand, AKA Annie Belle) he met as a child in an abandoned castle. When he sees her again, she persuades him to unleash a couple of female vampires. Do not expect anything more in the way of narrative, but it is a well-made low-budget French horror movie. French with subtitles. **88m/C DVD.** *FR* Jean-Loup Philippe, Annie Belle; ***D:*** Jean Rollin.

Lipstick woof! **1976 (R)** Fashion model Margaux seeks revenge on the man who brutally attacked and raped her, after he preys on her kid sister (real-life sis Mariel, in her debut). Exquisitely exploitative excuse for entertainment. **90m/C VHS.** Margaux Hemingway, Anne Bancroft, Perry King, Chris Sarandon, Mariel Hemingway; ***D:*** Lamont Johnson; ***W:*** David Rayfiel; ***C:*** Bill Butler, William A. Fraker.

Lipstick Camera **1993 (R)** Keats wants a career in TV news and seeks out a successful freelance cameraman (Wimmer) to help her out. She also asks to borrow her techno-friend Feldman's mini-camera and then goes after a story on an ex-spy and his sexy companion. Only no one expects what the camera captures. Weak plot but strong cast and high-end production. **93m/C VHS, DVD.** Ele Keats, Brian Wimmer, Corey Feldman, Sandahl Bergman, Terry O'Quinn; ***D:*** Mike Bonifer; ***W:*** Mike Bonifer; ***C:*** M. David Mullen; ***M:*** Jeff Rona.

Lipstick on Your Collar **1994** British TV fantasy/drama set in the stuffy confines of the British War Offices during the Suez Crisis of 1956. Two army clerks fantasize about the world outside through daydreams set to original tunes. Last series for the innovative Potter; on three cassettes. **360m/C VHS.** *GB* Ewan McGregor, Giles Thomas, Louise Germaine; ***D:*** Renny Rye; ***W:*** Dennis Potter. **TV**

Liquid Dreams 🦴🦴 **1992 (R)** In this fast-paced, futuristic thriller, Daly goes undercover as an erotic dancer in a glitzy strip joint to try and solve her sister's murder. She finds that the owner and clientele deal not only in sexual thrills, but also in a strange brain-sucking ritual that provides the ultimate rush. Also available in an unrated version. **92m/C VHS.** Richard Steinmetz, Candice Daly, Barry Dennen, Juan Fernandez, Tracey Walter, Frankie Thorn, Paul Bartel, Mink Stole, John Doe, Mark Manos; ***D:*** Mark Manos; ***W:*** Zach Davis, Mark Manos; ***C:*** Ed Tomney, Alexandre Magno.

Liquid Sky 🦴🦴🦴 **1983 (R)** An androgynous bisexual model living in Manhattan is the primary attraction for a UFO, which lands atop her penthouse in search of the chemical nourishment that her sexual encounters provide. Low-budget, highly creative film may not be for everyone, but the audience for which it was made will love it. Look for Carlisle also playing a gay male. **112m/C VHS, DVD.** Anne Carlisle, Paula Sheppard, Bob Brady, Susan Doukas, Otto von Wernherr, Elaine C. Grove, Stanley Knap, Jack Adalist, Lloyd Ziff; ***D:*** Slava Tsukerman; ***W:*** Slava Tsukerman, Anne Carlisle; ***C:*** Yuri Neyman; ***M:*** Slava Tsukerman, Brenda Hutchinson.

Lisa 🦴 **1990 (PG-13)** A young girl develops a crush on the new guy in town and arranges a meeting with him in which she pretends to be her mother. Little does she realize he's a psychotic serial killer. Lock your doors! Don't let anyone in if they have this video! **95m/C VHS.** Staci Keanan, Cheryl Ladd, D.W. Moffett, Tanya Fenmore, Jeffrey Tambor, Julie Cobb; ***D:*** Gary Sherman; ***W:*** Karen Clark; ***C:*** Alex Nepomniaschy.

Lisa and the Devil woof! *The House of Exorcism; La Casa Dell'Exorcismo; The Devil and the Dead; The Devil in the House of Exorcism; El Diablo se Lleva a los Muertos; Il Diavolo e i Morti; Lisa e il Diavolo* **1975 (R)** An unfortunate outing for Savalas and Sommer, about devil worship. Poor quality leaves little room for redemption. Just like on the telly, Telly's sucking on a sucker. A shortened version of the director's original 1972 release, re-edited and with additional footage added by producer Alfred Leone. **93m/C VHS, DVD.** *IT SP* Telly Savalas, Elke Sommer, Sylva Koscina, Robert Alda, Alessio Orano, Gabriele Tinti, Eduardo Fajardo, Espartaco (Spartaco) Santoni, Alida Valli; ***D:*** Mario Bava; ***W:*** Mario Bava, Alfred Leone; ***C:*** Cecilio Paniagua; ***M:*** Carlo Savina.

Lisa Picard Is Famous 🦴🦴½ **2001** Well, New Yorker Lisa (Wolf) would like to be famous but right now, she's best known for a cereal commercial. Neurotic, self-absorbed Lisa just can't catch that one big break—unlike her gay pal Tate (DeWolf) whose one-man confessional show becomes a hit. So Lisa agrees to let a filmmaker (Dunne) document her struggling career in the hopes it will help her would-be career. **87m/C VHS, DVD.** Laura Kirk, Nat DeWolf, Griffin Dunne; ***Cameos:*** Sandra Bullock, Charlie Sheen, Spike Lee; ***D:*** Griffin Dunne; ***W:*** Laura Kirk, Nat DeWolf; ***C:*** William Rexer; ***M:*** Evan Lurie.

Lisboa 🦴🦴 *Lisbon* **1999** Joao (Lopez) is a salesman who travels between Portugal and Spain. One day he picks up Berta (Maura) who is on her way to Lisbon and who refuses to tell him anything about herself. If he knew what was good for him, Joao would have made Berta get out of the car since her nasty husband Jose Luis (Luppi) and psychotic family are soon after them. Spanish with subtitles. **100m/C VHS, DVD.** *SP* Sergei Lopez, Carmen Maura, Federico Luppi; ***D:*** Antonio Hernandez; ***W:*** Antonio Hernandez, Enrique Braso; ***C:*** Aiter Mantxola; ***M:*** Victor Reyes.

Lisbon 🦴🦴 **1956** First film directed by Milland, shot in Portugal, details the adventures of a sea captain entangled in international espionage and crime while attempting to rescue damsel O'Hara's husband from communist doings. A familiar plot told with less-than-average panache. **90m/C VHS.** Ray Milland, Claude Rains, Maureen O'Hara, Francis Lederer, Percy Marmont; ***D:*** Ray Milland.

Lisbon Story 🦴🦴 **1994** Director Friedrich Monroe (Bauchau) calls his friend, sound engineer Phillip Winter (Vogler), to come to Lisbon to help him finish his film on the city. By the time Winter arrives in Portugal, Monroe has vanished, leaving the unfinished silent film behind. While waiting for his friend to return, Winter starts work, wandering through the city streets in search of inspiring sounds. English, German, and Portuguese with subtitles. **100m/C VHS, Wide.** *GE* Ruediger Vogler, Patrick Bauchau; ***D:*** Wim Wenders; ***W:*** Wim Wenders; ***C:*** Lisa Renzler.

The List 🦴🦴 **1999 (R)** When prostitute Gabrielle (Amick) gets herself arrested and tried for solicitation, she attempts to use her client book to barter for her freedom. Judge Miller (O'Neal) has to decide whether to make the list public and embarass many of his wealthy and powerful friends, but when Gabrielle's clients start turning up dead, the judge is forced to take action. **93m/C VHS, DVD.** Madchen Amick, Ryan O'Neal, Roc Lafortune, Ben Gazzara; ***D:*** Sylvain Guy; ***W:*** Sylvain Guy; ***C:*** Yves Belanger; ***M:*** Louis Babin. **VIDEO**

The List of Adrian Messenger 🦴🦴🦴 **1963** A crafty murderer resorts to a variety of disguises to eliminate potential heirs to a family fortune. Solid Huston-directed thriller with a twist: you won't recognize any of the name stars. **98m/B VHS.** Kirk Douglas, George C. Scott, Robert Mitchum, Dana Wynter, Burt Lancaster, Frank Sinatra; ***D:*** John Huston; ***M:*** Jerry Goldsmith.

Listen 🦴½ **1996 (R)** Sex and violence and a faulty cordless telephone. Krista's (Buxton) suffered a nervous breakdown after her breakup with Sarah (Langton). But now they're friends again and Krista's even encouraging Sarah's new romance with weirdo boyfriend Jake (Currie) who likes phone sex. Then there's the obscene phone caller who seems to live in Sarah's apartment building and a serial killer who preys on women. Lots of nastiness and it's easy to figure out who the real killer is. **104m/C VHS.** Brooke Langton, Sarah Buxton, Gordon Currie, Andy Romano, Joel Wyner; ***D:*** Gavin Wilding; ***W:*** Jonas Quastel, Michael Bafaro; ***C:*** Brian Pearson; ***M:*** David Davidson.

Listen, Darling 🦴🦴½ **1938** Garland is appealing in her first big screen role as Pinky Wingate, who decides to find the perfect husband for her widowed mother (Astor). Pinky and her friend Buzz (Bartholomew) manage to find Pidgeon and have him become the engaging objection of everyone's affections. ♫Zing! Went the Strings of My Heart; Ten Pins in the Sky; On the Bumpy Road to Love. **70m/C VHS.** Judy Garland, Freddie Bartholomew, Mary Astor, Walter Pidgeon, Alan Hale, Scotty Beckett; ***D:*** Edwin L. Marin.

Listen to Me 🦴½ **1989 (PG-13)** A small-town college debate team heads for the big time when they go to a national debate tournament. The usual mutual-distaste-turns-to-romance thing. Cheesy-as-all-get-out climactic abortion debate, in front of supposed real-life Supreme Court justices—yeah, right. And Kirk Cameron: get an accent, will ya? **109m/C VHS.** Kirk Cameron, Jami Gertz, Roy Scheider, Amanda Peterson, Tim Quill, Christopher Atkins; ***D:*** Douglas Day Stewart; ***C:*** Fred W. Koenekamp; ***M:*** David Foster. Golden Raspberries '89: Worst Support. Actor (Atkins).

Listen to Your Heart 🦴½ **1983** Office romance in the '80s! Sounds like a mediocre, forgettable made-for-TV comedy-drama—which is exactly what it is. If Jackson was the brainy one on "Charlie's Angels," why wasn't she smart enough to avoid this one? **90m/C VHS.** Tim Matheson, Kate Jackson; ***D:*** Don Taylor.

Lisztomania woof! **1975 (R)** Russell's excessive vision of what it must have been like to be classical composer/musician Franz Liszt, who is depicted as the first pop star. Rock opera in the tradition of "Tommy" with none of the sense or music. **106m/C VHS, Wide.** *GB* Roger Daltrey, Sara Kestelman, Paul Nicholas, Fiona Lewis, Ringo Starr, Veronica Quilligan, Nell Campbell, John Justin, Andrew Reilly, Anulka Dziubinska, Rick Wakeman, Rikki Howard, Felicity Devonshire, Aubrey Morris, Kenneth Colley, Ken Parry, Otto Diamont, Murray Melvin, Andrew Faulds, Oliver Reed; ***D:*** Ken Russell; ***W:*** Ken Russell; ***C:*** Peter Suschitzsky; ***M:*** Rick Wakeman.

The Little American 🦴🦴½ **1917** German-American Karl Von Austreim leaves behind sweetheart Angela Moore, returning to Germany to fight in WWI. Angela travels to France to care for her dying aunt and discovers her aunt's chateau has been turned into a hospital. She remains in the face of a German advance and is naturally reunited with her much-changed beau. **80m/B VHS.** Mary Pickford, Jack Holt, Raymond Hatton, Walter Long, Hobart Bosworth, Ben Alexander, DeWitt Jennings.

Little Annie Rooney 🦴🦴 **1925** A policeman's tomboy daughter spends her time mothering her father and brother while getting into mischief with street punks. Minor melodrama. Silent. **60m/B VHS.** Mary Pickford, William Haines, Walter James, Gordon Griffith, Vola Vale; ***D:*** William Beaudine; ***C:*** Charles Rosher.

Little Ballerina 🦴🦴 **1947** A young dancer struggles against misfortune and jealousy to succeed in the world of ballet, under the auspices of Fonteyn. **62m/B VHS.** Margot Fonteyn, Anthony Newley, Martita Hunt, Yvonne Marsh.

Little Big Horn 🦴🦴½ *The Fighting Seventh* **1951** Low-budget depiction of Custer et al. at Little Big Horn actually has its gripping moments; solid acting all around helps. **88m/B VHS.** Marie Windsor, John Ireland, Lloyd Bridges, Reed Hadley, Hugh O'Brian, Jim Davis; ***D:*** Charles Marquis Warren.

Little Big League 🦴🦴½ **1994 (PG)** 12-year-old inherits the Minnesota Twins baseball team from his grandfather, appoints himself manager when everyone else declines, and becomes the youngest owner-manager in history. Nothing new about the premise, but kids and America's favorite pastime add up to good clean family fun. Features real-life baseball players, including the Ken Griffey, Jr. and Paul O'Neill. Good cast features TV's Busfield at first base. Screenwriting debut from Pincus, and directorial debut from the executive producer of "Seinfeld," Scheinman. **120m/C VHS.** Michael (Mike) Papajohn, Luke Edwards, Jason Robards Jr., Kevin Dunn, Dennis Farina, John Ashton, Jonathan Silverman, Wolfgang Bodison, Timothy Busfield, Ashley Crow, Scott Patterson, Billy L. Sullivan, Miles Feulner, Kevin Elster, Leon "Bull" Durham, Brad "The Animal" Lesley; ***Cameos:*** Don Mattingly, Ken Griffey Jr., Paul O'Neill; ***D:*** Andrew Scheinman; ***W:*** Gregory Pincus, Adam Scheinman.

Little Big Man 🦴🦴🦴½ **1970 (PG)** Based on Thomas Berger's picaresque novel, this is the story of 121-year-old Jack Crabb and his quixotic life as gunslinger, charlatan, Indian, ally to George Custer, and the only white survivor of Little Big Horn. Told mainly through flashbacks. Hoffman provides a classic portrayal of Crabb, as fact and myth are jumbled and reshaped. **135m/C VHS, Wide.** Dustin Hoffman, Faye Dunaway, Chief Dan George, Richard Mulligan, Martin Balsam, Jeff Corey, Aimee (Amy) Eccles; ***D:*** Arthur Penn; ***W:*** Calder Willingham; ***C:*** Harry Stradling Jr. N.Y. Film Critics '70: Support. Actor (George); Natl. Soc. Film Critics '70: Support. Actor (George).

Little Bigfoot 🦴🦴½ **1996 (PG)** The Shoemaker family are taking a camping vacation when the kids discover a baby bigfoot in the wilderness. They find out the hairy little guy and his mom are threatened by the owner of a logging company, who's hired a group of hunters to get rid of the critters. **99m/C VHS.** Ross Malinger, P.J. Soles, Ken Tigar, Kelly Packard, Don Stroud, Matt McCoy; ***D:*** Art Camacho; ***W:*** Richard Preston Jr.; ***C:*** Ken Blakey; ***M:*** Louis Febre. **VIDEO**

A Little Bit of Soul 🦴🦴½ **1997 (R)** Godfrey Usher (Rush) is an ambitious politician whose present position is that of federal treasurer, a job he has no clue about. Usher is married to Grace Michael (Mitchell) the head of a philanthropic foundation. Scientist Richard Shorkinghorm (Wenham) and rival, ex-lover Kate Haslett (O'Connor), have both applied for funding from the foundation and are invited to the Usher/Michael home for a weekend. Surprises abound for Richard and Kate when they discover their kinky hosts are Satanists. Amusing comedy does falter but its not the fault of the performers. **83m/C VHS, DVD, Wide.** *AU* Geoffrey Rush, David Wenham, Frances O'Connor, Heather Mitchell, John Gaden, Kerry Walker; ***D:*** Peter Duncan; ***W:*** Peter Duncan; ***C:*** Martin McGrath; ***M:*** Nigel Westlake.

Little Boy Blue 🦴🦴 **1997** You want dysfunction? This movie has got it. Controlling husbands, impotence, uncontrollable rage, incest, family secrets, alcoholics... Southern Gothic family drama focuses on Jimmy (Phillipe), the son of paranoid and impotent Vietnam vet Ray West (Savage). He decides not to go to college because he's afraid to leave his younger brothers with dear ol' abusive alcoholic Dad. Ray runs a bar with his timid wife Kate (Kinski), who he also forces to sleep with son Jimmy to satisfy his own twisted sexual kicks. After a man comes snooping around and ends up dead in the bathroom of the bar, secrets from the past are dredged up. A mysterious woman (Knight) arrives bringing revenge on Ray for ruining her life and the possibility of freedom for the tormented family. Excellent performances (especially Kinski and Phillippe) save the twisted ball of loose strings that make up the farfetched plot. **107m/C VHS.** Ryan Phillippe, John Savage, Nastassia Kinski, Shirley Knight, Jenny Lewis, Tyrin Turner; ***D:*** Antonio Tibaldi; ***W:*** Michael Boston; ***C:*** Ron Hagen; ***M:*** Stewart Copeland.

Little Boy Lost 🦴🦴 **1978 (G)** The true story of the disappearance of a young boy in Australia. **92m/C VHS.** *AU* John Hargreaves, Tony Barry, Lorna Lesley; ***D:*** Alan Spires.

Little Buddha 🦴🦴 **1993 (PG)** Tibetan Lama Norbu informs the Seattle Konrad family that their 10-year-old son Jesse may be the reincarnation of a respected monk. He wants to take the boy back to Tibet to find out and, with some apparently minor doubts, the family head off on their spiritual quest. In an effort to instruct Jesse in Buddhism, this journey is interspersed with the story of Prince Siddhartha, who will leave behind his worldly ways to follow the path towards enlightenment and become the Buddha. The two stories are an ill-fit, the acting awkward (with the exception of Ruocheng as the wise Norbu), but boy, does the film look good (from cinematographer Vittorio Storaro). Filmed on location in Nepal and Bhutan. **123m/C VHS, DVD, Wide.** Keanu Reeves, Alex Wiesendanger, Ying Ruocheng, Chris Isaak, Bridget Fonda; ***D:*** Bernardo Bertolucci; ***W:*** Mark Peploe, Rudy Wurlitzer; ***C:*** Vittorio Storaro; ***M:*** Ryuichi Sakamoto.

Little Caesar 🦴🦴🦴 **1930** A small-time hood rises to become a gangland czar, but his downfall is as rapid as his rise. Still thrilling. The role of Rico made Robinson a star and typecast him as a crook for all time. **80m/B VHS.** Edward G. Robinson, Glenda Farrell, Sidney Blackmer, Douglas Fairbanks Jr.; ***D:*** Mervyn LeRoy; ***C:*** Gaetano Antonio "Tony" Gaudio. Natl. Film Reg. '00.

Little Church Around the Corner 🦴🦴½ **1923** Silent small town melodrama about a preacher who falls in love with a mine owner's daughter, but finds he isn't dad's favorite fella when he confronts him about poor mining conditions. When the mine caves in, the preacher man's caught between a rock and hard place when his sweetie's family needs protection from an angry mob. **70m/B VHS.** Kenneth Harlan, Hobart Bosworth, Walter Long, Pauline Starke, Alec B. Francis, Margaret Seddon, George Cooper; ***D:*** William A. Seiter.

Little City 🦴🦴½ **1997 (R)** Best friends Kevin (Bon Jovi) and Adam (Charles) discover sex can screw up the best relationship. Adam's current girlfriend Nina (Sciorra) is having an affair with Kevin, while his ex-girlfriend Kate (Going) is having problems with her girlfriend Ann (Williams), who broke up Adam and Kate. Now Kate is having a fling with Rebecca (Miller), who's just flirting with lesbianism, and Rebecca then gets involved with Adam. Meanwhile, Kevin decides he's in love with Nina (she's not reciprocating that emotion) and Kate begins thinking about going back to Adam. San Francisco turns out to be a very small town. **90m/C VHS, DVD, Wide.** Jon Bon Jovi, Penelope Ann Miller, Annabella Sciorra, Josh Charles, Joanna Going, JoBeth Williams; ***D:*** Roberto Benabib; ***W:*** Roberto Benabib; ***C:*** Randall Love.

The Little Colonel 🦴🦴🦴 **1935 (PG)** After the Civil War, an embittered Southern patriarch turns his back on his family, until his dimple-cheeked granddaughter softens his heart. Hokey and heartwarming. Shirley's first teaming with Bill "Bojangles" Robinson features the famous dance scene. Adapted by William Conselman from the Annie Fellows Johnston best-seller. **80m/B VHS.** Shirley Temple, Lionel Barrymore, Evelyn Venable, John Lodge, Hattie McDaniel, Bill Robinson, Sidney Blackmer; ***D:*** David Butler; ***C:*** Arthur C. Miller.

Little Darlings woof! **1980 (R)** Distasteful premise has summer campers Kristy and Tatum in a race to lose their virginity. Kristy is better (at acting, that is); but who cares? And just who is meant to be the market for this movie, anyway? **95m/C VHS.** Tatum O'Neal, Kristy McNichol, Matt Dillon, Armand Assante, Margaret Blye; ***D:*** Ronald F. Maxwell; ***M:*** Charles Fox.

The Little Death 🦴🦴 **1995** Struggling musician Nick Hannon (Fraser) is forced to work for wealthy dad Ted (Walsh), who's married to young trophy wife Kelly (Gridley). She's being stalked by weirdo Bobby (Yoakam), who kills Ted but manages to get off by claiming self-defense. Kelly's no lonely widow since she's now beding Nick but he soon has suspicions of his former stepmom's involvement in her hubby's death. **91m/C VHS.** Brent Fraser, Pamela Gidley, Dwight Yoakam, J.T. Walsh, Troy Beyer, D.W. Moffett, Richard Beymer; ***D:*** Jan Verheyen; ***W:*** Nicholas Bogner, Michael Holden; ***C:*** David Phillips; ***M:*** Christopher Tyng.

Little Dorrit, Film 1: Nobody's Fault 🦴🦴🦴 **1988** The mammoth version of the Dickens tome, about a father and daughter trapped interminably in the dreaded Marshalsea debtors' prison, and the good samaritan who works to free them. Told in two parts (on four tapes), "Nobody's Fault," and "Little Dorrit's Story." **180m/C VHS.** *GB* Alec Guinness, Derek Jacobi, Cyril Cusack, Sarah Pickering, Joan Greenwood, Max Wall, Amelda Brown, Daniel Chatto, Miriam Margolyes, Bill Fraser, Roshan Seth, Michael Elphick, Eleanor Bron, Patricia Hayes, Robert Morley, Sophie Ward; ***D:*** Christine Edzard; ***W:*** Christine Edzard; ***C:*** Bruno de Keyzer; ***M:*** Giuseppe Verdi. L.A. Film Critics '88: Film, Support. Actor (Guinness). **TV**

Little Dorrit, Film 2: Little Dorrit's Story 🦴🦴🦴 **1988** The second half of the monumental adaptation of Dickens' most popular novel during his lifetime tells of Amy Dorrit's rise from debtor's prison to happiness. **189m/C VHS.** *GB* Alec Guinness, Derek Jacobi, Cyril Cusack, Sarah Pickering, Joan Greenwood, Max Wall, Amelda Brown, Daniel Chatto, Miriam Margolyes, Bill Fraser, Roshan Seth, Michael Elphick, Patricia Hayes, Robert Morley, Sophie Ward, Eleanor Bron; ***D:*** Christine Edzard; ***W:*** Christine Edzard; ***C:*** Bruno de Keyzer; ***M:*** Giuseppe Verdi. L.A. Film Critics '88: Film, Support. Actor (Guinness). **TV**

Little Dragons 🦴 **1980** A grandfather and two young karate students rescue a family held captive by a backwoods gang. **90m/C VHS.** Ann Sothern, Joe Spinell, Charles Lane, Chris Petersen, Pat Petersen, Sally Boyden, Rick Lenz, Sharon Weber, Tony Bill; ***D:*** Curtis Hanson; ***W:*** Alan Ormsby.

The Little Drummer Girl 🦴🦴🦴 **1984 (R)** An Israeli counterintelligence agent recruits an actress sympathetic to the Palestinian cause to trap a fanatical terrorist leader. Solid performances from Keaton as the actress and Kinski as the Israeli counter-intelligence office sustain interest through a puzzling, sometimes boring and frustrating, cinematic maze of espionage. Keaton is at or near her very best. Based on the bestselling novel by John Le Carre. **130m/C VHS.** Diane Keaton, Klaus Kinski, Yorgo Voyagis, Sami Frey, Michael Cristofer, Anna Massey, Thorley Walters; ***D:*** George Roy Hill; ***M:*** Dave Grusin.

The Little Foxes 🦴🦴🦴½ **1941** A vicious southern woman will destroy everyone around her to satisfy her desire for wealth and power. Filled with corrupt characters who commit numerous revolting deeds. The vicious matriarch is a part made to fit for Davis, and she makes the most of it. Script by Lillian Hellman from her own play. **116m/B VHS, DVD.** Bette Davis, Herbert Marshall, Dan Duryea, Teresa Wright, Charles Dingle, Richard Carlson, Carl Benton Reid; ***D:*** William Wyler; ***W:*** Lillian Hellman; ***C:*** Gregg Toland; ***M:*** Meredith Willson.

Little Fugitive 🦴🦴🦴 **1953** Seven-year-old Joey (Andrusco) is convinced by his Brooklyn pals that he's murdered his brother. So the tyke takes off and winds up wandering lost around Coney Island. Independent feature made on a miniscule budget features endearing performances from non-pros. **80m/C VHS, DVD.** Richie Andrusco, Ricky Brewster, Winnifred Cushing, Jay Williams; ***D:*** Morris Engel, Ruth Orkin, Ray Ashley; ***W:*** Ray Ashley; ***C:*** Morris Engel; ***M:*** Eddy Manson. Natl. Film Reg. '97.

Little Giant 🦴🦴½ **1946** The duo fly separately in this entry, which highlights Costello's comic talents and leaves Abbott in the supporting role. Costello is a country bumpkin come to the big city to get enough money to marry his sweetheart. He's hired to sell vacuum cleaners by Abbott and becomes the butt of everyone's jokes but the joke's on them when Lou becomes the company's top-selling salesman. **92m/B VHS.** Bud Abbott, Lou Costello, Brenda Joyce, Jacqueline De Wit, George Cleveland, Elena Verdugo, Mary Gordon, Pierre Watkin; ***D:*** William A. Seiter; ***W:*** Walter DeLeon.

Little Giants 🦴🦴½ **1994 (PG)** Familiar kids/sport movie about the klutzy coach (Moranis) of an equally woeful peewee football team. Coach Danny is up against his overbearing big brother Kevin (O'Neill), former local football hero and the coach of the best team in town. Naturally, there's the big game between the misfit underdogs and the stars. Predictable, of course, but not without some amusing moments. **106m/C VHS.** Rick Moranis, Ed O'Neill, Shawna Waldron, Mary Ellen Trainor, Devon Sawa, Susanna Thompson, John Madden; ***D:*** Duwayne Dunham; ***W:*** Tommy Swerdlow, Michael Goldberg, James Ferguson, Robert Shallcross; ***C:*** Janusz Kaminski; ***M:*** John Debney.

Little Girl ... Big Tease 🦴 **1975 (R)** Teen society girl is kidnapped and exploited (along with the viewer) by a group which includes her teacher. **86m/C VHS.** Jody Ray, Rebecca Brooke; ***D:*** Roberto Mitrotti.

The Little Girl Who Lives down the Lane 🦴🦴½ **1976 (PG)** Engrossing, offbeat thriller about a strange 13-year-old girl whose father is never home, and who hides something—we won't say what—in her basement. Very young Foster is excellent, as are her supporters, including Sheen as the child molester who knows what she's hiding. Based on the novel by Koenig, who also penned the script. **90m/C VHS.** *CA FR* Jodie Foster, Martin Sheen, Alexis Smith, Scott Jacoby, Mort Shuman, Dorothy Davis, Hubert Noel, Jacques Famery, Mary Morter, Judie Wildman; ***D:*** Nicolas Gessner; ***W:*** Laird Koenig; ***C:*** Rene Verzier; ***M:*** Christian Gaubert.

Little Gloria... Happy at Last 🦴🦴½ **1984** Miniseries based on the best-selling book about the custody battle over child heiress Gloria Vanderbilt, and her tumultuous youth. Lansbury leads a fine cast as the poor little rich girl's aunt Gertrude, the matriarchal family power broker. **180m/C VHS.** Bette Davis, Angela Lansbury, Christopher Plummer, Maureen Stapleton, Martin Balsam, Barnard Hughes, John Hillerman; ***D:*** Waris Hussein. **TV**

Little Heroes 🦴🦴½ **1991 (G)** An impoverished little girl gets through hard times with the aid of her loyal dog (the Hound can relate). A low-budget family tearjerker that nonetheless works, it claims to be based on a true story. **78m/C VHS.** Raeanin Simpson, Katherine Willis, Keith Christensen; ***D:*** Craig Clyde; ***W:*** Craig Clyde; ***M:*** John McCallum.

Little House on the Prairie 🦴🦴🦴 **1974** Pilot for the TV series based on the life of Laura Ingalls Wilder and her family's struggles on the American plains in the 1860s. Other episodes are also available on tape, including one in which Patricia Neal guest stars as a terminally ill widow seeking a home for her children. Neal's performance earned her a best actress Emmy in 1975. **98m/C VHS.** Michael Landon, Karen Grassle, Victor French, Melissa Gilbert, Melissa Sue Anderson; ***D:*** Michael Landon. **TV**

Little Indian, Big City 🦴🦴½ *An Indian in the City; Un Indien dans la Ville* **1995 (PG)** French blockbuster dubbed over with "Americanized" English to give U.S. audiences an appetite for upcoming Disney remake. Lhermitte travels to the Amazon to finalize the divorce of a long-dead marriage, only to find he has a 12-year-old son, Mimi-Siku (Briand). Father and son bond and Dad decides to bring the jungle-bred boy to his home in Paris. Dubbing process unfortunately tomahawks this charming story as loin cloth meets Eiffel Tower, but Lhermitte, Briand and Miou-Miou (as estranged wife Patricia) shine through. Subplot of Russian mobsters who cut the fingers off their victims gives an indication of the French definition of "family fare." **90m/C VHS.** *FR* Thierry Lhermitte, Miou-Miou, Patrick Timsit, Arielle Dombasle, Ludwig Briand; ***D:*** Herve Palud; ***W:*** Thierry Lhermitte, Herve Palud, Philippe Bruneau, Igor Aptekman; ***C:*** Pierre Lorraine; ***M:*** Manu Katche.

Little John 🦴🦴½ **2002** Natalie Britain (Reuben) is a Family Court judge with a secret of her own. Twelve years ago, she gave birth to a baby boy that she thought was put up for adoption. Instead, Little John (Bailey, Jr.), known as L.J., was raised on a Texas farm by Natalie's estranged father John (Rhames). When John's health begins to fail, it's time for his daughter to learn the truth and for L.J. to get to know his mom. **98m/C VHS.** Gloria Reuben, Ving Rhames, Robert Bailey Jr., Patty Duke; ***D:*** Dick Lowry. **TV**

The Little Kidnappers 🦴🦴½ **1990 (G)** Embittered man (Heston) is forced to take in his Scottish grandsons when the two boys are orphaned. They settle in with gramps in Nova Scotia but when the duo decide to adopt the abandoned baby they've found, they are accused of being kidnappers. Cable remake of 1953 British film. **100m/C VHS.** *CA* Charlton Heston, Bruce Greenwood, Leah K. Pinsent, Charles Miller, Leo Wheatley, Patricia Gage; ***D:*** Donald Shebib. **CABLE**

Little Ladies of the Night 🦴 *Diamond Alley* **1977** Former pimp tries to save Purl and other teenagers from the world of prostitution. Exploitation posing as "significant drama." **96m/C VHS.** Linda Purl, David Soul, Clifton Davis, Carolyn Jones, Louis Gossett Jr.; ***D:*** Marvin J. Chomsky.

Little Laura & Big John 🦴🦴 **1973** The true-life exploits of the small-time Ashley Gang in the Florida everglades around the turn of the century. Fabian's comeback vehicle, for what it's worth. **82m/C VHS.** Fabian, Karen Black; ***D:*** Luke Moberly.

Little Lord Fauntleroy 🦴🦴🦴½ **1936** The vintage Hollywood version of the Frances Hodgson Burnett story of a fatherless American boy who discovers he's heir to a British dukedom. Also available in computer-colorized version. Well cast, charming, remade for TV in 1980. Smith is loveable as the noble tyke's crusty old guardian. **102m/B VHS, DVD.** Freddie Bartholomew, Sir C. Aubrey Smith, Mickey Rooney, Dolores Costello, Jessie Ralph, Guy Kibbee; ***D:*** John Cromwell; ***W:*** Hugh Walpole; ***C:*** Charles Rosher; ***M:*** Max Steiner.

Little Lord Fauntleroy 🦴🦴½ **1980** A poor boy in New York suddenly finds himself the heir to his grandfather's estate in England. Lavish remake of the 1936 classic, adapted from Frances Hodgson Burnett's novel. Well-deserved Emmy winner for photography; Guinness is his usual old-pro self. **98m/C VHS.** Rick Schroder, Alec Guinness, Victoria Tennant, Eric Porter, Colin Blakely, Connie Booth, Rachel Kempson; ***D:*** Jack Gold. **TV**

Little Lord Fauntleroy 🦴🦴½ **1995 (G)** British TV adaptation of the Frances Hodgson Burnett classic finds Cedric Erroll's life changing forever when he's discovered to be the only heir to the Earl of Dorincourt. But the Earl turns out to be a bitter miser and it's up to the innocent child to get grandpa to enjoy life. **100m/C VHS.** *GB* Michael Benz, Betsy Brantley, George Baker, Bernice Stegers; ***D:*** Andrew Morgan.

Little Man Tate 🦴🦴🦴 **1991 (PG)** A seven-year-old genius is the prize in a tug of war between his mother, who wants him to lead a normal life, and a domineering school director who loves him for his intellect. An acclaimed directorial debut for Foster, with overtones of her own extraordinary life as a child prodigy. **99m/C VHS, DVD.** Jodie Foster, Dianne Wiest, Harry Connick Jr., Adam Hann-Byrd, George Plimpton, Debi Mazar, Celia Weston, David Hyde Pierce, Danitra Vance, Josh Mostel, P.J. Ochlan; ***D:*** Jodie Foster; ***W:*** Scott Frank; ***C:*** Mike Southon; ***M:*** Mark Isham.

Little Marines **1990** Three young boys journey into the wilderness for three days of fun and instead embark on an incredible adventure. **90m/C VHS.** Stephen Baker, Steve Landers Jr., Noah Williams; ***D:*** A.J. Hixon.

The Little Match Girl 🦴🦴 **1984** A musical version of the Hans Christian Andersen classic about a girl whose dying grandmother tells her of the magic in the matches she sells. **54m/C VHS.** Monica McSwain, Nancy Duncan, Matt McKim, Don Hays; ***D:*** Mark Hoeger.

The Little Match Girl 🦴🦴 **1987** The Hans Christian Andersen Yuletide classic about an orphan selling magical matches, this time set in the 1920s, with the littlest "Cosby" kid in the title role. Ain't she cute? **96m/C VHS.** *GB* Keisha Knight Pulliam, Maryedith Burrell, William Daniels, Hallie Foote, Bill Davis, Rue McClanahan, John Rhys-Davies, Jim Metzler; ***D:*** Michael Lindsay-Hogg; ***W:*** Maryedith Burrell.

Little Men 🦴½ **1940** A modern version of the classic juvenile story by Louisa May Alcott is too cute for words. **86m/B VHS.** Jack Oakie, Jimmy Lydon, Kay Francis, George Bancroft; ***D:*** Norman Z. McLeod.

Little Men 🦴🦴½ **1998 (PG)** Louisa May Alcott's sequel to "Little Women" hits the screen with a lot less hoopla than its 1994 predecessor. Jo March (Hemingway) has grown up, married Fritz Bhaer (Sarandon), and opened an idyllic, wholesome school for troubled boys. The house is immaculate, the grounds are beautiful, and the boys are little angels. That is, until streetwise 14-year-old Dan (Cook) shows up. He soon has the boys smoking, drinking, and stealing, until they almost burn the place down. Since this is a family movie, with moral lessons to be learned, all's well by the end. Adults may find the syrupy sweetness too much to take, and the characters are barely two-dimensional, but young kids should enjoy it. **98m/C VHS.** Mariel Hemingway, Chris Sarandon, Michael Caloz, Ben Cook, Michael Yarmush, Gabrielle Boni, Ricky Mabe, Julia Garland, B.J. McLellan, Tyler Hines, Kathleen Fee; ***D:*** Rodney Gibbons; ***W:*** Mark Evan Schwartz; ***C:*** Arch Archambault; ***M:*** Milan Kymlicka.

The Little Mermaid 🦴🦴½ **1978 (G)** An animated version of Hans Christian Andersen's tale about a little mermaid who rescues a prince whose boat has capsized. She immediately falls in love and wishes that she could become a human girl. Not to be confused with the 1989 Disney version. **71m/C VHS.** ***D:*** Tim Reid.

The Little Mermaid ½ **1989 (G)** Headstrong teenage mermaid falls in love with a human prince and longs to be human too. She makes a pact with the evil Sea Witch to trade her voice for a pair of legs; based on the famous Hans Christian Andersen tale. Charming family musical, which harks back to the days of classic Disney animation, and hails a new era of superb Disney animated musicals. Sebastian the Crab nearly steals the show with his wit and showstopping number "Under the Sea." ♫Under the Sea; Kiss the Girl; Daughters of Triton; Part of Your World; Poor Unfortunate Souls; Les Poissons. **82m/C VHS, DVD.** ***D:*** John Musker, Ron Clements; ***W:*** John Musker, Ron Clements; ***M:*** Alan Menken, Howard Ashman; ***V:*** Jodi Benson, Christopher Daniel Barnes, Pat Carroll, Rene Auberjonois, Samuel E. Wright, Buddy Hackett, Jason Marin, Edie McClurg, Kenneth Mars, Nancy Cartwright. Oscars '89: Song ("Under the Sea"), Orig. Score; Golden Globes '90: Song ("Under the Sea"), Score.

Little Minister **1934** An adaptation of the James Barrie novel about a prissy Scottish pastor who falls in love with a free-spirited gypsy...he thinks she is, in fact, the local earl's daughter, played to perfection by the young Hepburn. **101m/B VHS.** Katharine Hepburn, John Beal, Alan Hale, Donald Crisp; ***D:*** Richard Wallace; ***W:*** Victor Heerman; ***M:*** Max Steiner.

Little Miss Broadway **1938** Orphan Temple brings the residents of a theatrical boarding house together in hopes of getting them into show business. She and Durante give worthwhile performances. Also available in computer-colorized version. ♫Be Optimistic; How Can I Thank You; I'll Build a Broadway For You; If All the World Were Paper; Thank You For the Use of the Hall; We Should Be Together; Swing Me an Old-Fashioned Song; When You Were Sweet Sixteen; Happy Birthday to You. **70m/B VHS.** Shirley Temple, George Murphy, Jimmy Durante, Phyllis Brooks, Edna May Oliver, George Barbier, Donald Meek, Jane Darwell; ***D:*** Irving Cummings; ***C:*** Arthur C. Miller.

Little Miss Innocence **1973** Recording executive tries to survive the amorous advances of the two attractive female hitchhikers that he drove home. **79m/C VHS.** John Alderman, Sandy Dempsey, Judy Medford; ***D:*** Chris Warfield.

Little Miss Marker *Girl in Pawn* **1934** Heartwarming story starring Temple as the title character, who is left with bookie Sorrowful Jones (Menjou) as the IOU for a gambling debt. But when her father doesn't return, it's up to Jones and his racetrack friends to make little Marky a home. Naturally, Temple steals her way into everyone's heart. Based on a story by Damon Runyon; remade three times as "Sorrowful Jones," as "40 Pounds of Trouble," and in 1980 with the original title. **88m/B VHS.** Adolphe Menjou, Shirley Temple, Dorothy Dell, Charles Bickford, Lynne Overman; ***D:*** Alexander Hall. Natl. Film Reg. '98.

Little Miss Marker ½ **1980 (PG)** Mediocre remake of the often retold story of a bookie who accepts a little girl as a security marker for a $10 bet. Disappointing performance from Curtis adds to an already dull film. **103m/C VHS.** Walter Matthau, Julie Andrews, Tony Curtis, Bob Newhart, Lee Grant, Sara Stimson, Brian Dennehy; ***D:*** Walter Bernstein; ***W:*** Walter Bernstein; ***M:*** Henry Mancini.

Little Monsters **1989 (PG)** A young boy (Savage) discovers a monster (Mandel) under his bed and eventually befriends it. The pair embark on adventures that land them in trouble. Hardworking, talented cast hurdles the weak script, but can't save the film. **100m/C VHS.** Fred Savage, Howie Mandel, Margaret Whitton, Ben Savage, Daniel Stern, Ric(k) Ducommun, Frank Whaley; ***D:*** Richard Alan Greenberg; ***W:*** Ted Elliott, Terry Rossio; ***C:*** Dick Bush; ***M:*** David Newman.

Little Moon & Jud McGraw ½ **1978** A wronged Indian woman and a framed cowpoke take their revenge on a small, corrupt town, razing it overnight. Already-weak plot is disabled by too many flashbacks. **92m/C VHS.** James Caan, Sammy Davis Jr., Stefanie Powers, Aldo Ray; ***D:*** Bernard Girard.

Little Mother **1971** Metzger's take on Argentina's Eva Peron highlights her sexual powers (of course) as it tells of Eva's climb out of poverty and into the heights of political power. Filmed in Yugoslavia. **95m/C VHS, DVD.** Christiane Kruger, Ivan Desny, Anton Diffring; ***D:*** Radley Metzger; ***W:*** Brian Phelan; ***C:*** Hans Jura.

Little Murders **1971 (PG)** Black comedy set in NYC. A woman convinces a passive photographer to marry her. Gardenia gives an excellent performance as the woman's father. A shadow of crime, depression, and strife seem to hangs over the funny parts of this film; more often depressing than anything else. Adapted by Jules Feiffer from his own play. **108m/C VHS.** Elliott Gould, Marcia Rodd, Vincent Gardenia, Elizabeth Wilson, Jon Korkes, Donald Sutherland, Alan Arkin, Lou Jacobi; ***D:*** Alan Arkin; ***W:*** Jules Feiffer; ***C:*** Gordon Willis.

Little Nellie Kelly ½ **1940** Garland plays both mother and daughter in a film based on a musical comedy by George M. Cohan. Garland is married to Irish cop Murphy but dies in childbirth. The film then advances 20 years to daughter Garland who is trying to make good on the stage and have a romance with a young man her father disapproves of. ♫Nellie Kelly I Love You; Nellie is a Darling; It's a Great Day For the Irish; A Pretty Girl Milking Her Cow; Danny Boy; Singing in the Rain. **100m/B VHS.** Judy Garland, George Murphy, Charles Winninger, Douglas McPhail; ***D:*** Norman Taurog.

Little Nemo: Adventures in Slumberland ½ **1992 (G)** A bland animated tale of a young boy whose dreams take him to Slumberland. There, Nemo unwittingly unleashes a monster from Nightmare Land who kidnaps Slumberland's king. Nemo must then rescue the king—aided by the king's daughter, a comic squirrel sidekick, and a mischievous con-frog. Based on Winsor McCay's 1900 comic strip. Has some cute comic moments for the kiddies and, while the animation is better than Saturday-morning cartoon quality, it's not Disney. **85m/C VHS, Wide.** ***D:*** William T. Hurtz, Masami Hata; ***W:*** Chris Columbus, Richard Outten; ***M:*** Tom Chase, Steve Rucker; ***V:*** Gabriel Damon, Mickey Rooney, Rene Auberjonois, Daniel Mann, Laura Mooney, Bernard Erhard, William E. Martin.

Little Nicky **2000 (PG-13)** All hail Adam Sandler, King of the Idiot Boys! Notoriously bashed by critics, Sandler doesn't seem too worried about their opinions as he rolls around on the giant pile of money his crude but funny movies make. This time his underdog hero is Nicky (Sandler), the son of Satan (Keitel) and an angel (Witherspoon), who hangs out in a very cartoony hell. When Satan calls his sons together to name his heir, he instead declares that he will rule for another 10,000 years, causing brothers Adrian and Cassius to stage a rebellion by bringing hell to New York City. Nicky and his talking dog sidekick Mr. Beefy (voice of Smigel) are then sent to capture them. Along the way, he gains the standard Hollywood-issued love interest (Arquette). Broader and more satirical than most of Sandler's work, it's also the first that has him surrounded by top-line talent (not that it helps any). **93m/C VHS, DVD, Wide.** Adam Sandler, Rhys Ifans, Tommy (Tiny) Lister, Harvey Keitel, Patricia Arquette, Allen Covert, Blake Clark, Rodney Dangerfield, Kevin Nealon, Reese Witherspoon, Lewis Arquette, Dana Carvey, Jon Lovitz, Michael McKean, Quentin Tarantino, Carl Weathers, Rob Schneider, Clint Howard, Ellen Cleghorne, Fred Wolf; ***Cameos:*** Dan Marino, Henry Winkler, Regis Philbin, Ozzy Osbourne, Bill Walton; ***D:*** Steven Brill; ***W:*** Adam Sandler, Steven Brill, Tim Herlihy; ***C:*** Theo van de Sande; ***M:*** Teddy Castellucci; ***V:*** Robert Smigel.

A Little Night Music ½ **1977 (PG)** Features four interwoven, contemporary love stories adapted from the Broadway play, and based loosely on Bergman's "Smiles of a Summer Night." Taylor's pathetic rendition of "Send in the Clowns" should be banned. Filmed on location in Austria. **110m/C VHS.** Elizabeth Taylor, Diana Rigg, Hermione Gingold, Len Cariou, Lesley-Anne Down; ***D:*** Harold Prince. Oscars '77: Orig. Song Score and/or Adapt.

Little Nikita **1988 (PG)** A California boy (Phoenix) discovers that his parents are actually Soviet spies planted as American citizens for eventual call to duty. Poitier's performance as the FBI agent tracking the spies is about the only spark in this somewhat incoherent thriller. **98m/C VHS.** River Phoenix, Sidney Poitier, Richard Bradford, Richard Lynch, Caroline Kava, Lucy Deakins; ***D:*** Richard Benjamin; ***W:*** Bo Goldman, John Hill; ***M:*** Marvin Hamlisch.

Little Ninjas ½ **1992** Three top-notch ninja kids go up against the Sarak to rescue their friend who is being held hostage. **85m/C VHS.** Steven Nelson, Jon Anzaldo, Alan Godshaw; ***D:*** Emmett Alston.

Little Noises **1991** Glover stars as an artist who seeks not only fame and fortune, but also the love of his best friend (O'Neal). He finally creates a piece that his agent loves, but problems arise. **91m/C VHS.** Crispin Glover, Tatum O'Neal, Rik Mayall, Tate Donovan, John C. McGinley; ***D:*** Jane Spencer; ***W:*** Jane Spencer.

Little Odessa ½ **1994 (R)** Working for the stateside Russian mafia, hitman Joshua Shapira (Roth) returns to his childhood neighborhood to carry out his next assignment. Set in the Russian-Jewish emigre community of Brooklyn's Brighton Beach, Gray's directorial debut explores Joshua's relationship with his family—especially kid brother Reuben (Furlong). Not your typical mob opera, this one focuses more on characters than killing. Relationships between family members are explored to the hilt, but the audience is left with too many unanswered questions. Dimly lit and entirely too ambiguous, this family tragedy could spawn a serious case of depression. **98m/C VHS, DVD.** Tim Roth, Edward Furlong, Moira Kelly, Vanessa Redgrave, Maximilian Schell, Paul Guilfoyle, Natasha Andreichenko, David Vadim, Mina Bern, Boris McGiver, Mohammed Ghaffari, Michael Khumrov, Dmitry Preyers, David Ross, Ron Brice, Jace Kent, Marianna Lead, Gene Ruffini; ***D:*** James Gray; ***W:*** James Gray; ***C:*** Tom Richmond; ***M:*** Dana Sano.

Little Orphan Annie **1918** Surrounded by a group of children, poet James Whitcomb Riley narrates the story of Little Orphant Annie, who loses her mother at an early age and is sent to an orphanage where she charms the other children with her stories of ghosts and elves. **57m/B VHS.** Thomas Santschi, Eugenie Besserer, Ben Alexander, Lillie Hayward, Lafe (Lafayette) McKee, Colleen Moore, Harry Lonsdale, Doris Baker, Lillian Wade, Billy Jacobs, James Whitcomb Riley; ***D:*** Colin Campbell.

Little Orphan Annie ½ **1932** The unjustly forgotten first sound adaptation of the comic strip. Fun score adds a lot, as does the good cast. **60m/B VHS.** May Robson, Buster Phelps, Mitzie Green, Edgar Kennedy; ***D:*** John S. Robertson; ***M:*** Max Steiner.

The Little Prince **1974 (G)** Disappointing adaptation of the classic children's story by Antoine de Saint-Exupery, about a little boy from asteroid B-612. Lousy Lerner and Loewe score underscores a general lack of magic or spontaneity. ♫It's a Hat; I Need Air; I'm On Your Side; Be Happy; You're a Child; I Never Met a Rose; Why Is the Desert (Lovely to See)?; Closer and Closer and Closer; Little Prince (From Who Knows Where). **88m/C VHS.** *GB* Richard Kiley, Bob Fosse, Steven Warner, Gene Wilder, Joss Ackland, Clive Revill, Victor Spinetti, Graham Crowden, Donna McKechnie; ***D:*** Stanley Donen; ***W:*** Alan Jay Lerner; ***C:*** Christopher Challis; ***M:*** Frederick Loewe, Alan Jay Lerner. Golden Globes '75: Score.

The Little Princess ½ **1939 (G)** Based on the Frances Hodgson Burnett children's classic; perhaps the best of the moppet's films. Shirley is a young schoolgirl in Victorian London sent to a harsh boarding school when her Army officer father is posted abroad. When her father is declared missing, the penniless girl must work as a servant at the school to pay her keep, all the while haunting the hospitals, never believing her father has died. A classic tearjerker. **91m/B VHS, DVD.** Shirley Temple, Richard Greene, Anita Louise, Ian Hunter, Cesar Romero, Arthur Treacher, Sybil Jason, Miles Mander, Marcia Mae Jones, E.E. Clive; ***D:*** Walter Lang; ***W:*** Ethel Hill, Walter Ferris; ***C:*** Arthur C. Miller; ***M:*** Walter Bullock.

The Little Princess **1987** A three-cassette adaptation of Frances Hodgson Burnett's book. In Victorian England, kind-hearted Sara is forced into poverty when her father suddenly dies. Can his longtime friend find her and restore her happiness? Originally aired on PBS as part of the "Wonderworks" family movie series. **180m/C VHS.** *GB* Amelia Shankley, Nigel Havers, Maureen Lipman; ***D:*** Carol Wiseman. **TV**

A Little Princess ½ **1995 (G)** Compelling fantasy, based on the children's book by Frances Hodgson Burnett, and previously best known for the 1939 Shirley Temple incarnation. Sara (Mathews) has been raised in India by her widowed father (Cunningham). When he's called up to fight in WWI, Sara is taken to New York to be educated at stern Miss Michin's (Bron) school, where her money makes her a favored boarder. However, the irrepressible Sara suffers a severe reversal of fortune when her father is reported killed and Miss Michin promptly makes her a servant to pay her way. But Sara's charm has made her some true friends who become her allies under trying circumstances. Lively script, dazzling visuals, and a welcome lack of sappiness create a classic-in-the-making. **97m/C VHS, DVD, Wide.** Liesl Matthews, Eleanor Bron, Liam Cunningham, Rusty Schwimmer, Arthur Malet, Vanessa Lee Chester, Errol Sitahal, Heather DeLoach, Taylor Fry; ***D:*** Alfonso Cuaron; ***W:*** Richard LaGravenese, Elizabeth Chandler; ***C:*** Emmanuel Lubezki; ***M:*** Patrick Doyle.

The Little Rascals ½ **1994 (PG)** Alfalfa runs afoul of the membership requirements for the "He-Man Womun Haters Club" when he starts to fall for Darla. Charming remake of the short film series, now set in suburban L.A., from Spheeris, who also redid another TV favorite, "The Beverly Hillbillies." **83m/C VHS, DVD, Wide.** Daryl Hannah, Courtland Mead, Travis Tedford, Brittany Ashton Holmes, Bug Hall, Zachary Mabry, Kevin Jamal Woods, Ross Bagley, Sam Saletta, Blake Collins, Jordan Warkol, Blake Ewing, Juliette Brewer, Heather Karasek; ***Cameos:*** Whoopi Goldberg; ***D:*** Penelope Spheeris; ***W:*** Penelope Spheeris, Paul Guay, Steve Mazur; ***C:*** Richard Bowen; ***M:*** David Foster, Linda Thompson.

Little Red Riding Hood **1983** From "Faerie Tale Theatre" comes the retelling of the story about a girl (Mary Steenburgen) off to give her grandmother a picnic basket, only to get stopped by a wicked wolf McDowell. Not particularly faithful, but fun and scary. **60m/C VHS.** Mary Steenburgen, Malcolm McDowell; ***D:*** Graeme Clifford. **CABLE**

Little Red Schoolhouse **1936** A hard-nosed schoolteacher hunts for a truant lad and both of them land in jail. **64m/C VHS.** Frank "Junior" Coghlan, Dickie Moore, Ann Doran.

A Little Romance **1979 (PG)** An American girl living in Paris falls in love with a French boy; eventually they run away, to seal their love with a kiss beneath a bridge. Olivier gives a wonderful, if not hammy, performance as the old pickpocket who encourages her. Gentle, agile comedy based on the novel by Patrick Cauvin. **110m/C VHS, Wide.** Laurence Olivier, Diane Lane, Thelonious Bernard, Sally Kellerman, Broderick Crawford; ***D:*** George Roy Hill; ***W:*** Allan Burns; ***M:*** Georges Delerue. Oscars '79: Orig. Score.

A Little Sex **1982 (R)** Capshaw, in her screen debut, finds herself the wife of womanizer Matheson. Harmless, but pointless, with a TV-style plot. **94m/C VHS.** Tim Matheson, Kate Capshaw, Edward Herrmann, Wallace Shawn, John Glover; ***D:*** Bruce Paltrow; ***W:*** Robert De Laurentis; ***C:*** Ralf Bode; ***M:*** Georges Delerue.

Little Shop of Horrors ½ **1960** The landmark cheapie classic, which Roger Corman reputedly filmed in three days, about a nebbish working in a city florist shop who unknowingly cultivates an intelligent plant that demands human meat for sustenance. Notable for then-unknown Nicholson's appearance as a masochistic dental patient. Hilarious, unpretentious farce—if you liked this one, check out Corman's "Bucket of Blood" for more of the same. Inspired a musical of the same name; remade as a movie again in 1986. Available colorized. **70m/B VHS, DVD.** Jonathan Haze, Jackie Joseph, Mel Welles, Jack Nicholson, Dick Miller, Myrtle Vail; ***D:*** Roger Corman; ***W:*** Charles B. Griffith; ***C:*** Arch R. Dalzell.

Little Shop of Horrors 🦴🦴🦴 **1986 (PG-13)** During a solar eclipse, Seymour buys an unusual plant and takes it back to the flower shop where he works. The plant, Audrey 2, becomes a town attraction as it grows at an unusual rate, but Seymour learns that he must feed Audrey fresh human blood to keep her growing. Soon, Audrey is giving the orders ("Feed me") and timid Seymour must find "deserving" victims. Martin's performance as the masochistic dentist is alone worth the price. Song, dance, gore, and more prevail in this outrageous musical comedy. Four Tops Levi Stubbs is the commanding voice of Audrey 2. Based on the Off-Broadway play, which was based on Roger Corman's 1960 horror spoof. ♫Mean Green Mother From Outer Space; Some Fun Now; Your Day Begins Tonight. **94m/C VHS, DVD, Wide.** Rick Moranis, Ellen Greene, Vincent Gardenia, Steve Martin, James Belushi, Christopher Guest, Bill Murray, John Candy, Tisha Campbell, Tichina Arnold, Michelle Weeks; ***D:*** Frank Oz; ***W:*** Howard Ashman; ***C:*** Robert Paynter; ***M:*** Miles Goodman, Alan Menken, Howard Ashman; ***V:*** Levi Stubbs Jr.

Little Shots of Happiness 🦴🦴 **1997 (R)** Prim Frances leaves her unstable husband and, unbeknownst to her co-workers, is living out of her office. In the evenings, she creates a wild new identity for herself and hits the Boston nightclubs where she picks up a different man each night. Of course, Frances discovers there's a price to pay for her new liberation. **85m/C VHS, DVD.** Bonnie Dickenson, Todd Verow, Linda Ekoian, Rita Gavelis, P.J. Marino, Castalia Jason, Leanne Whitney, Bill Dwyer, Eric Sapp, Maureen Picard, Eric Romley; ***D:*** Todd Verow; ***W:*** Jim Dwyer, Todd Verow; ***C:*** Todd Verow.

Little Sister 🦴½ **1992 (PG-13)** Prankster Silverman, on a dare, dresses up as a girl and joins a sorority. Problems arise when he falls in love with his "big sister" (Milano) in the sorority. What will happen when she finds out the truth? Will we care? **94m/C VHS.** Jonathan Silverman, Alyssa Milano; ***W:*** Sergio D. Altieri.

A Little Stiff 🦴🦴 **1991** Slacker romantic comedy about the unrequited romance between filmmaker Caveh and fellow UCLA student McKim from first meeting, through angst, and grand final gestures. **85m/C VHS.** Erin McKim, Caveh Zahedi; ***D:*** Caveh Zahedi, Greg Watkins; ***M:*** Kath Bloom.

Little Sweetheart 🦴½ **1990 (R)** A reworking of "The Bad Seed," with a nine-year-old girl engaging in murder, burglary, and blackmail, ruining the adults around her. Based on "The Naughty Girls" by Arthur Wise. **93m/C VHS, 8mm.** John Hurt, Karen Young, Barbara Bosson, John McMartin, Cassie Barasch; ***D:*** Anthony Simmons.

The Little Theatre of Jean Renoir 🦴🦴🦴 **1971** A farewell by director Jean Renoir featuring three short films. In the first, Renoir's humanist beliefs are apparent in "The Last Christmas Dinner," a Hans Christian Andersen-inspired story. Next, "The Electric Floor Waxer" is a comic opera. The third piece is called "A Tribute to Tolerance." Slight but important late statement by a great director. In French with English subtitles. **100m/C VHS.** Jean Renoir, Fernand Sardou, Jean Carmet, Francoise Arnoul, Jeanne Moreau; ***D:*** Jean Renoir; ***W:*** Jean Renoir.

The Little Thief 🦴🦴🦴 **1989 (PG-13)** Touted as Francois Truffaut's final legacy, this trite minidrama is actually based on a story he co-wrote with Claude de Givray about a post-WWII adolescent girl who reacts to the world around her by stealing and petty crime. Truffaut's hand is markedly absent, but this film is a testament to his abruptly and sadly truncated career. Director Miller was Truffaut's long-time assistant. French with subtitles. **108m/C VHS.** *FR* Charlotte Gainsbourg, Simon de la Brosse, Didier Bezace, Raoul Billerey, Nathalie Cardone; ***D:*** Claude Miller; ***W:*** Annie Miller, Claude Miller; ***C:*** Dominique Chapuis; ***M:*** Alain Jomy.

Little Tough Guys 🦴🦴 **1938** The Little Tough Guys (a.k.a. Dead End Kids) come to the rescue of Halop, a young tough guy gone bad to avenge his father's unjust imprisonment. First of the "Little Tough Guys" series for the former Dead End Kids, who later became the East Side Kids before eventually evolving into the Bowery Boys. **84m/B VHS.** Helen Parrish, Billy Halop, Leo Gorcey, Marjorie Main, Gabriel Dell, Huntz Hall; ***D:*** Harold Young.

Little Treasure 🦴½ **1985 (R)** A stripper heads for Mexico to search for her long-lost father, but ends up looking for treasure with an American guy. Disappointing effort of director Sharp. **95m/C VHS.** Burt Lancaster, Margot Kidder, Ted Danson, Joseph Hacker, Malena Doria; ***D:*** Alan Sharp; ***W:*** Alan Sharp.

The Little Valentino 🦴🦴 **1979** One day in the aimless life of a young punk who gets by on his wits and petty theft. Jeles' directorial debut. In Hungarian with English subtitles. **102m/B VHS.** *HU* ***D:*** Andras Jeles.

The Little Vampire 🦴🦴 **2000 (PG)** A cluttered storyline and wandering direction help put a stake in the heart of this tale of a lonely boy and a family of vegetarian vampires. Tony (Lipnicki) is forced to move from sunny California to gloomy Scotland when his father gets a job building a golf course for crusty Lord Ashton (Wood). After being bullied by the local kids at school, Tony starts daydreaming about vampires to take his mind off his loneliness. As if summoned by magic, soon a young vampire named Rudolph (Weeks) appears at his window, befriending Tony and taking him on a flight through the countryside. After he introduces Rudolph to American slang and Nintendo, Tony is introduced to Rudolph's family. Rudolph's father Frederick (Grant) and mother Freda (Krige) explain to Tony that they are trying to become human once again, but need the other half of a magic amulet held by Lord Ashton to complete the spell. Meanwhile, crazed vampire hunter Rookery (Carter) stalks the family. Some scenes are visually stunning (especially those vampire cows) but the convoluted plot puts this one six feet under. **91m/C VHS, DVD, Wide.** Jonathan Lipnicki, Richard E. Grant, Alice Krige, Jim Carter, John Wood, Pamela Gidley, Tommy Hinkley, Rollo Weeks, Anna Popplewell, Dean Cook; ***D:*** Uli Edel; ***W:*** Karey Kirkpatrick, Larry Wilson; ***C:*** Bernd Heinl; ***M:*** Nigel Clarke, Michael Csanyi-Wills.

Little Vegas 🦴🦴½ **1990 (R)** Looks like easy street for a young man who inherits a bundle from his girlfriend, but he's forced to wake up and smell the cappuccino when her family and the other residents of the tiny desert berg think there's a gigolo in the woodpile. Much strife with siblings as he wages a battle for the bucks with the son while wooing the woman's daughter, with a measure of mob inflicted plot twists. Mildly amusing, cut from vein of you can't get rich quick and get away with it. **90m/C VHS.** Michael Nouri, Jerry Stiller, John Sayles, Anthony John (Tony) Denison, Catherine O'Hara, Bruce McGill, Anne Francis, Bob(cat) Goldthwait, Jay Thomas, Perry Lang; ***D:*** Perry Lang; ***W:*** Perry Lang; ***M:*** Mason Daring.

Little Vera 🦴🦴🦴 *Malenkaya Vera* **1988** Extremely well-done Soviet film chronicles the life of a young working-class woman who loves rock music and who has been profoundly affected by Western civilization. Post-glasnost Soviet production gives Westerners a glimpse into the Russian way of life. A boxoffice bonanza back home. Russian with subtitles. **130m/C VHS, DVD.** *RU* Natalia (Natalya) Negoda, Andrei Sokolov, Yuri Nazarov, Ludmila Zaisova, Alexander Niegreva; ***D:*** Vassili Pitchul.

Little Voice 🦴🦴🦴 **1998 (R)** Little Voice (Horrocks) misses her dead father so much that she withdraws from the world, communicating only by singing along with the records Dad loved. Whether it's Judy Garland, Shirley Bassey, or Edith Piaf, "LV" can match the voice exactly. When her mom's (Blethyn) sleazy talent-agent boyfriend (Caine) hears her, he knows she's the ticket to fame and fortune. Little Voice has no desire to be a star, so she clams up whenever there's an audience. Club owner and weasel Mr. Boo (Broadbent) books her for several shows, including one with a London talent scout on hand, and everyone wonders if she'll sing. Caine and Broadbent do their best to out-slime each other and deliver most of the comedy. Horrocks gives a showcase performance, re-creating her role from the stage play "The Rise and Fall of Little Voice." The play was written specifically to take advantage of her spectacular impersonation talents. **97m/C VHS, DVD.** *GB* Jane Horrocks, Michael Caine, Ewan McGregor, Brenda Blethyn, Jim Broadbent, Annette Badland, Philip Jackson; ***D:*** Mark Herman; ***W:*** Mark Herman; ***C:*** Andy Collins; ***M:*** John Altman. Golden Globes '99: Actor—Mus./Comedy (Caine).

Little White Lies 🦴🦴 **1989** Jillian and Matheson meet and fall in love during an exotic vacation. But both are traveling under assumed identities—she's a policewoman tracking a jewel thief and he's an incognito doctor. When they reunite stateside they try to stick to their ruses in humdrum comedic fashion. Made for network TV. **88m/C VHS.** Ann Jillian, Tim Matheson; ***D:*** Anson Williams. **TV**

Little Witches 🦴🦴 **1996 (R)** Rejected group of seniors at Catholic girls' high school are transformed into a witches coven, thanks to a book of spells. A rip-off of "The Craft." **91m/C VHS, DVD.** Mimi Reichmeister, Jack Nance, Jennifer Rubin, Sheeri Rappaport, Melissa Taub, Zoe Alexander, Zelda Rubinstein, Eric Pierpont; ***D:*** Jane Simpson; ***W:*** Brian DiMuccio, Dino Vindeni; ***C:*** Ron Turowski; ***M:*** Nicholas Rivera.

Little Women 🦴🦴🦴🦴 **1933** Louisa May Alcott's Civil War story of the four March sisters—Jo, Beth, Amy, and Meg—who share their loves, their joys, and their sorrows. Everything about this classic film is wonderful, from the lavish period costumes to the excellent script, and particularly the captivating performances by the cast. A must-see for fans of Alcott and Hepburn, and others will find it enjoyable. **107m/B VHS, DVD, 8mm.** Katharine Hepburn, Joan Bennett, Paul Lukas, Edna May Oliver, Frances Dee, Spring Byington, Jean Parker, Douglass Montgomery; ***D:*** George Cukor; ***W:*** Victor Heerman, Sarah Y. Mason; ***C:*** Henry W. Gerrard; ***M:*** Max Steiner. Oscars '33: Adapt. Screenplay; Venice Film Fest. '34: Actress (Hepburn).

Little Women 🦴🦴🦴 **1949** Stylized color remake of the George Cukor 1933 classic. Top-notch if too obvious cast portrays Louisa May Alcott's story of teenage girls growing up against the backdrop of the Civil War. **121m/C VHS.** June Allyson, Peter Lawford, Margaret O'Brien, Elizabeth Taylor, Janet Leigh, Mary Astor; ***D:*** Mervyn LeRoy; ***W:*** Andrew Solt; ***M:*** Adolph Deutsch. Oscars '49: Art Dir./Set Dec., Color.

Little Women 🦴🦴 **1978** The third screen version of Louisa May Alcott's classic story. Lackluster compared to the previous attempts, particularly the sterling 1933 film, but still worthwhile. During the Civil War, four sisters share their lives as they grow up and find romance. Garson's TV debut. Followed by a TV series. **200m/C VHS.** Meredith Baxter, Susan Dey, Ann Dusenberry, Eve Plumb, Dorothy McGuire, Robert Young, Greer Garson, Cliff (Potter) Potts, William Shatner; ***D:*** David Lowell Rich; ***M:*** Elmer Bernstein. **TV**

Little Women 🦴🦴🦴🦴 **1994 (PG)** Beloved story of the March women is beautifully portrayed in a solid production that blends a seamless screenplay with an excellent cast, authentic period costumes, and lovely cinematography and music. Ryder, perfectly cast as the unconventional Jo, is also the strongest of the sisters: domestically inclined Meg (Alvarado), the fragile Beth (Danes), and the youngest, mischevious Amy (the delightful Dunst) who grows up into a sedate young lady (Mathis). Charming adaptation remains faithful to the spirit of the Alcott classic while adding contemporary touches. Fittingly brought to the big screen by producer Denise Di Novi, writer/co-producer Swicord, and director Armstrong. **118m/C VHS, DVD, 8mm, Wide.** Winona Ryder, Gabriel Byrne, Trini Alvarado, Samantha Mathis, Kirsten Dunst, Claire Danes, Christian Bale, Eric Stoltz, John Neville, Mary Wickes, Susan Sarandon; ***D:*** Gillian Armstrong; ***W:*** Robin Swicord; ***C:*** Geoffrey Simpson; ***M:*** Thomas Newman.

Little World of Don Camillo 🦴🦴🦴 *Le Petit Monde de Don Camillo* **1951** A French-made farce based on the beloved novels of Giovanni Guareschi. Earthy priest Don Camillo clashes repeatedly with his friendly enemy, the communist mayor of a tiny Italian village. The hero talks directly to God, whose voice is provided by Orson Welles, also narrator of the English version. Charming, good-natured approach. **106m/B VHS, 8mm.** *FR IT* Fernandel, Gino Cervi, Sylvia, Vera Talqui; ***D:*** Julien Duvivier; ***Nar:*** Orson Welles.

The Littlest Angel 🦴🦴 **1969** Musical about a shepherd boy who dies falling off a cliff and wants to become an angel. He learns a valuable lesson in the spirit of giving. Made for TV. **77m/C VHS.** Johnny Whitaker, Fred Gwynne, E.G. Marshall, Cab Calloway, Connie Stevens, Tony Randall. **TV**

The Littlest Horse Thieves 🦴🦴½ *Escape from the Dark* **1976 (G)** Good Disney film about three children and their efforts to save some ponies who work in mines. The children take it upon themselves to see that the animals escape the abuse and neglect they are put through. Filmed on location in England with excellent photography. **109m/C VHS, DVD.** Maurice Colbourne, Susan Tebbs, Andrew Harrison, Chloe Franks, Alastair Sim, Peter Barkworth; ***D:*** Charles Jarrott; ***W:*** Rosemary Anne Sisson; ***C:*** Paul Beeson; ***M:*** Ronald Goodwin.

The Littlest Outlaw 🦴🦴½ **1954** A Mexican peasant boy steals a beautiful stallion to save it from being destroyed. Together, they ride off on a series of adventures. Disney movie filmed on location in Mexico. **73m/C VHS.** Pedro Armendariz Sr., Joseph Calleia, Andres Velasquez; ***D:*** Roberto Gavaldon.

The Littlest Rebel 🦴🦴½ **1935 (PG)** Temple stars in this well-done piece set during the Civil War in the Old South. She befriends a Union officer while protecting her father at the same time. She even goes to Washington to talk with President Lincoln. Nice dance sequences by Temple and Robinson. Available in computer-colored version. **70m/B VHS.** Shirley Temple, John Boles, Jack Holt, Bill Robinson, Karen Morley, Willie Best; ***D:*** David Butler.

The Littlest Viking 🦴🦴½ **1994 (PG)** Twelve-year-old Sigurd finds archery practice and mock battles an exciting way to learn to be a Viking. But when his older brother is killed in battle, Sigurd's father expects him to avenge the death, and Sigurd must decide just what being a Viking prince means. Scenic Scandinavian settings; obvious dubbing. **85m/C VHS.** Kristian Tonby, Per Jansen, Terje Stromdahl; ***D:*** Knut W. Jorfald, Lars Rasmussen, Paul Trevor Bale.

Live a Little, Love a Little 🦴🦴 **1968 (PG)** Itinerant photographer Elvis juggles two different jobs by running around a lot. Sexually more frank than earlier King vehicles. ♫Almost in Love; A Little Less Conversation; Edge of Reality; Wonderful World. **90m/C VHS.** Elvis Presley, Michele Carey, Rudy Vallee, Don Porter, Dick Sargent, Sterling Holloway, Eddie Hodges; ***D:*** Norman Taurog.

Live and Let Die 🦴🦴 **1973 (PG)** Agent 007 (Moore) is out to thwart the villainous Dr. Kananga (Kotto), a black mastermind who plans to control western powers with voodoo and hard drugs. He's aided by psychic tarot-reading virgin Solitaire (Seymour), who falls prey to Bond's charms. Moore's first appearance as Bond in the 8th film in the series. Can't we have the real Bond back? Title song by Paul McCartney and Wings. **131m/C VHS, DVD,**

Wide. *GB* Roger Moore, Jane Seymour, Yaphet Kotto, Clifton James, Julius W. Harris, Geoffrey Holder, David Hedison, Gloria Hendry, Bernard Lee, Lois Maxwell, Madeleine Smith; ***D:*** Guy Hamilton; ***W:*** Tom Mankiewicz; ***C:*** Ted Moore; ***M:*** George Martin.

Live Bait 🦴🦴½ **1995** Canadian-flavored Gen-X comedy features suburban 23-year-old virgin Trevor MacIntosh (Scholte) trying for a little romance (or at least sex) but seemingly doomed to failure. At least until he meets much older artist Charlotte (Maunsell). Sweeney handles his debut writing, directing, and producing skills with equal aplomb. **84m/B VHS.** *CA* Tom Scholte, Micki Maunsell, Kevin McNulty, Babz Chula, David Lovgren, Laara Sadiq, Michelle Beaudoin, Kelly Aisenstat; ***D:*** Bruce Sweeney; ***W:*** Bruce Sweeney; ***C:*** David Pelletier. Toronto-City '95: Canadian Feature Film.

Live Flesh 🦴🦴🦴½ *Carne Tremula* **1997 (R)** The courses of five lives in Madrid are forever altered when naive, young Victor (Rabal) accidentally shoots cop David (Bardem) and is sent to prison after an argument with Elena (Neri), a one-night stand he falls for. When he gets out he discovers Elena has transformed from junkie to model wife who runs a home for children and has married David, now a paraplegic. Still, Victor both wants and resents Elena, who he blames for the accident. While apparently stalking Elena, Victor enters into a relationship with Clara, the wife of David's former partner, Sancho (Sancho) which dramatically draws all five back together. Complex, noirish drama shows a new, more serious side for director Almadovar, who still manages some of his patented brand of humor. Highly original plot and unexpected twists delivered by a talented and attractive cast. Adapted from a British novel by Ruth Rendell. **100m/C VHS, DVD, Wide.** *FR SP* Javier Bardem, Francesca Neri, Angela Molina, Liberto Rabal, Jose Sancho, Penelope Cruz, Pilar Bardem, Alex Angulo; ***D:*** Pedro Almodovar; ***W:*** Pedro Almodovar, Ray Loriga, Jorge Guerricaechevarria; ***C:*** Alfonso Beato; ***M:*** Alberto Iglesias.

Live! From Death Row 🦴🦴 **1992** Cassidy plays a tabloid TV host who'll do anything to get ratings. She's set to do a live interview with a condemned serial killer (Davison) shortly before his execution. But Davison and his fellow death-row inmates take Cassidy and her crew hostage as he decides to use the show for his own media message. **94m/C VHS.** Joanna Cassidy, Bruce Davison, Art LaFleur, Calvin Levels, Michael D. Roberts; ***D:*** Patrick Sheane Duncan; ***W:*** Patrick Sheane Duncan.

Live Nude Girls 🦴🦴 **1995 (R)** Group of 30-something girlfriends get together to throw a bachelorette party for one of their number and sit around gossiping about sex, relationships, family, and friends. Not much plot but nice ensemble work. **92m/C VHS.** Dana Delany, Kim Cattrall, Cynthia Stevenson, Laila Robins, Olivia D'Abo, Lora Zane, Glenn Quinn, Tim Choate; ***D:*** Julianna Lavin; ***W:*** Julianna Lavin; ***C:*** Christopher Taylor; ***M:*** Anton Sanko.

The Live Wire 🦴🦴 **1934** Stunt-ridden action fare featuring Talmadge at his most daring. This adventure is complete with desert island, lost treasure, stowaways, evil-doers, and a race against the clock. **57m/B VHS.** Richard Talmadge, George Walsh, Charles French, Alberta Vaughn; ***D:*** Harry S. Webb.

Live Wire 🦴🦴½ **1992 (R)** Brosnan is an FBI bomb expert who needs a new line of work. He's up against a terrorist psychopath who has his greedy hands on a new type of explosive. It's liquid, undetectable, looks as innocent as a glass of water, and is capable of blowing up Washington, D.C. Also available in an unrated version. **85m/C VHS.** Pierce Brosnan, Ben Cross, Ron Silver, Lisa Eilbacher; ***D:*** Christian Duguay; ***W:*** Bart Baker. **CABLE**

Live Wire: Human Timebomb 🦴½ **1995 (R)** FBI agent Jim Parker is captured by a Cuban general who implants a computer chip into his neck—turning Parker into a human timebomb. **98m/C VHS.** Bryan Genesse, Joe Lara, Frantz Dobrowsky, J. Cynthia Brooks; ***D:*** Mark Roper; ***W:*** Jeff Albert; ***C:*** Rod Stewart; ***M:*** Itai Haber.

The Lives of a Bengal Lancer 🦴🦴🦴🦴 **1935** One of Hollywood's greatest rousing adventures. Based in northwest India, Lt. McGregor (Cooper) is a seasoned frontier fighter in the Bengals Lancers who befriends new officer Lt. Forsythe (Tone). Also new to the regiment is Donald Stone (Cromwell), the son of the current commanding officer (Standing). All three will soon test their courage when the Brits encounter a vicious local revolution against colonial rule. Swell plot, lotsa action, great comraderie. Based on the novel by Major Francis Yeats-Brown, and remade in 1939 as "Geronimo." **110m/B VHS.** Gary Cooper, Franchot Tone, Richard Cromwell, Guy Standing, Sir C. Aubrey Smith, Douglass Dumbrille, Kathleen Burke, Noble Johnson, Lumsden Hare, Akim Tamiroff, J. Carrol Naish, Monte Blue, Ray Cooper, Leonid Kinskey, George Regas, Reginald (Reggie, Reggy) Sheffield, Mischa Auer, Charles Stevens, James Warwick, Clive Morgan, Colin Tapley, Rollo Lloyd, Maj. Sam Harris; ***D:*** Henry Hathaway; ***W:*** Waldemar Young, John Lloyd Balderston, Grover Jones, William Slavens McNutt; ***C:*** Charles B(ryant) Lang Jr.; ***M:*** Milan Roder.

Livin' for Love: The Natalie Cole Story 🦴🦴 **2000** Singer Natalie Cole plays herself (at least in her adult years), telling the harrowing story of her slide into drug addiction after growing up the adored daughter of the legendary Nat King Cole. Based on her autobiography. **?m/C VHS.** Natalie Cole, Theresa Randle, James McDaniel, Diahann Carroll; ***D:*** Robert Townsend. **TV**

Livin' Large 🦴🦴 **1991 (R)** An African-American delivery boy gets the break of his life when a nearby newscaster is shot dead. Grabbing the microphone and continuing the story, he soon finds himself hired by an Atlanta news station as an anchorman, fulfilling a life-long dream. But problems arise when he finds himself losing touch with his friends, his old neighborhood and his roots. Comedy "deals" with the compelling issue of blacks finding success in a white world by trivializing the issue at every turn and resorting to racial stereotypes. **96m/C VHS.** Terrence "T.C." Carson, Lisa Arrindell Anderson, Blanche Baker, Nathaniel "Afrika" Hall, Julia Campbell; ***D:*** Michael A. Schultz; ***C:*** Peter Collister; ***M:*** Herbie Hancock.

The Living Coffin 🦴½ *El Grito de la Muerte* **1958** Woman has alarm rigged on her coffin in case she's buried alive. And they called her paranoid. Loosely based on Poe's "Premature Burial." **72m/C VHS.** *MX* Gaston Santos, Maria Duval, Pedro de Aguillon; ***D:*** Fernando Mendez.

The Living Daylights 🦴🦴🦴 **1987 (PG)** After being used as a pawn in a fake Russian defector plot, our intrepid spy tracks down an international arms and opium smuggling ring. Fine debut by Dalton, who takes his role as 007 in a more serious vein, in a rousing, refreshing cosmopolitan shoot-em-up. Let's be frank: we were all getting a little fatigued by Roger Moore. The 15th film in the series. **130m/C VHS, DVD, Wide.** Timothy Dalton, Maryam D'Abo, Jeroen Krabbe, John Rhys-Davies, Robert Brown, Joe Don Baker, Desmond Llewelyn, Art Malik, Geoffrey Keen, Walter Gotell, Andreas Wisniewski; ***D:*** John Glen; ***W:*** Richard Maibaum, Michael G. Wilson; ***C:*** Alec Mills; ***M:*** John Barry.

The Living Dead 🦴🦴 *The Scotland Yard Mystery* **1936** An English film about a mad, re-animating scientist. **76m/B VHS.** *GB* Gerald du Maurier, George Curzon.

The Living Dead Girl 🦴🦴½ *La Morte Vivante* **1982** Workers illegally trying to dispose of hazardous chemical wastes in a cellar make the mistake of indulging in a bit of grave robbing at the next-door crypt. A 55-gallon drum cracks open; the stuff hits an open coffin and a blonde (Blanchard) with long sharp fingernails and a taste for blood is reanimated. It's another sex-and-gore fest from the prolific Rollin, though this is one of his more polished productions. French with subtitles. **91m/C DVD.** *FR* Marina Pierro, Francoise Blanchard, Mike Marshall, Carina Barone, Fanny Magier; ***D:*** Jean Rollin; ***W:*** Jean Rollin.

The Living End 🦴🦴 **1992** Director Araki's radical lovers-on-the-lam story concerns freelance L.A. writer Jon (Gilmore) who has just learned he is H.I.V.-positive. He meets a handsome, violent, hustler named Luke (Dytri) and the two begin a desperate road trip along the California coast which can only end in tragedy. Araki not only wrote and directed the film but also served as cinematographer and editor—all on a $23,000 budget. Stylish, tragic, and filled with black humor and frank homoeroticism. **92m/C VHS.** Craig Gilmore, Mike Dytri, Darcy Marta; ***D:*** Gregg Araki; ***W:*** Gregg Araki; ***C:*** Gregg Araki.

Living Free 🦴🦴½ **1972 (G)** Sequel to "Born Free," based on the nonfictional books by Joy Adamson. Recounts the travails of Elsa the lioness, who is now dying, with three young cubs that need care. Nice and pleasant, but could you pick up the pace? **91m/C VHS.** Susan Hampshire, Nigel Davenport; ***D:*** Jack Couffer.

The Living Head 🦴½ *La Cabeza Viviente* **1959** Archaeologists discover the ancient sepulcher of the great Aztec warrior, Acatl. Ignoring a curse, they steal his severed head and incur the fury of Xitsliapoli. They should have known better. Dubbed in English. **75m/B VHS.** *MX* Mauricio Garces, Ana Luisa Peluffo, German Robles, Abel Salazar; ***D:*** Chano Urueto.

Living in Oblivion 🦴🦴🦴 **1994 (R)** Humorous tri-part story is an insiders joke on the problems of low-budget filmmaking, including talent, libido, ego, and pervasive chaos. First, director Nick Reve (Buscemi) tries to film an emotional scene with leading lady Nicole (Keener) only to have everything go wrong; then star Chad (LeGros), a dimwit but a "name," arrives to throw his weight around (and seduce Nicole); and finally the leading lady must deal with an overly sensitive dwarf and Nick's mother. A sleeper. **92m/C VHS.** Steve Buscemi, Catherine Keener, James LeGros, Dermot Mulroney, Danielle von Zerneck, Robert Wightman, Rica Martens, Hilary Gilford, Peter Dinklage, Kevin Corrigan, Matthew Grace, Michael Griffiths, Ryna Bowker, Francesca DiMauro; ***D:*** Tom DiCillo; ***W:*** Tom DiCillo; ***C:*** Frank Prinzi; ***M:*** Jim Farmer. Sundance '95: Screenplay.

Living in Peril 🦴🦴 **1997 (R)** Ambitious architect Walter Woods (Lowe) is in L.A. to design a mansion for an eccentric client (Belushi). But a series of accidents threaten to ruin his reputation, if not provoke something more deadly. **95m/C VHS.** Rob Lowe, James Belushi, Dean Stockwell, Dana Wheeler-Nicholson, Richard Moll, Alex Meneses, Patrick Ersgard; ***D:*** Joakim (Jack) Ersgard; ***W:*** Joakim (Jack) Ersgard, Patrick Ersgard; ***C:*** Ross Berryman; ***M:*** Randy Miller. **VIDEO**

Living on Tokyo Time 🦴🦴½ **1987** Interesting but often dull, low budget independent comedy about a young Japanese woman who hitches up with a boorish Japanese-American man in order to stay in the United States. An Asian view of Asian-America, filmed on location in San Francisco. **83m/C VHS.** Minako Ohashi, Ken Nakagawa, Kate Connell, Mitzi Abe, Bill Bonham, Brenda Aoki; ***D:*** Steven Okazaki; ***W:*** Steven Okazaki, John McCormick.

Living Out Loud 🦴🦴 **1998 (R)** Judith (Hunter) is dumped by her cardiologist husband for a younger women and spirals downward into depression. Of course, this leads to dramatic self-discovery, and Judith opens her eyes to the world around her, including the nice-guy elevator operator (DeVito) in her building. The two wallow in their respective personal loss and form an unlikely friendship, which teeters on becoming something more. Screenwriter LaGravanese tries his hand at directing but delivers a choppy, hard-to-believe tale of female independence and self-fulfillment. The reliable Hunter seems miscast; she's just too intense and jittery to appear sullen and reflective. DeVito gives his usual excellent performance, but also appears miscast as the debt-ridden gambler who catches Judith's refined eye. Significant events take place off-screen and the audience is left to fill in the blanks. **102m/C VHS, DVD.** Holly Hunter, Danny DeVito, Queen Latifah, Martin Donovan, Elias Koteas, Richard Schiff; ***D:*** Richard LaGravenese; ***W:*** Richard LaGravenese; ***C:*** John Bailey; ***M:*** George Fenton.

Living Proof: The Hank Williams Jr. Story 🦴🦴½ **1983** TV biopic focusing on the country singer's hell-raising ways as he seeks to get out from under the shadow of his famous father and into the spotlight on his own right. Based on Williams Jr.'s autobiography; includes 10 songs by Sr. and Jr. **97m/C VHS.** Richard Thomas, Clu Gulager, Allyn Ann McLerie, Naomi Judd, Christian Slater; ***D:*** Dick Lowry; ***W:*** I.C. Rapoport, Stephen Kandel. **TV**

Living to Die 🦴½ **1991 (R)** Vegas gumshoe is assigned to investigate a blackmailed official, and discovers a woman believed to be dead is alive and beautiful and living incognito. This mystifies him. **84m/C VHS.** Wings Hauser, Darcy Demoss, Asher Brauner, Arnold Vosloo, Jim Williams; ***D:*** Wings Hauser.

Lloyd 🦴🦴 **2000 (PG)** Goofy 11-year-old Lloyd is the class clown always getting in trouble in school. In fact, he gets demoted to a class of losers where Lloyd gets a crush on pretty Tracy. But how can he compare with junior high rebel Storm for her affections? **72m/C VHS, DVD.** Brendon Ryan Barrett, Mary Mara, Taylor Negron, Todd Bosley, Tom Arnold; ***D:*** Hector Barron; ***W:*** Hector Barron. **VIDEO**

Lloyds of London 🦴🦴🦴 **1936** If you wonder how the story of a British insurance company can be exciting, just watch this lavish spectacular (which, of course, lacks historical accuracy). Jonathan Blake (Power) has risen in the ranks of the firm, thanks in part to his lifelong friendship with Lord Horatio Nelson (Burton), much to the disgust of haughty Lord Everett Stacy (an ever-supercilious Sanders). As Bonaparte comes to power, Blake travels to France to rescue some friends and saves Elizabeth (Carroll), who turns out to be Stacy's wife. Stacy is also spreading rumors about Lloyds' solvency and Nelson's heroics at Trafalgar and his machinations lead to further trouble with Blake. **115m/B VHS, Wide.** Tyrone Power, George Sanders, Madeleine Carroll, John Burton, Guy Standing, Sir C. Aubrey Smith, Freddie Bartholomew, Virginia Field, Montagu Love, Una O'Connor; ***D:*** Henry King; ***W:*** Ernest Pascal, Walter Ferris; ***C:*** Bert Glennon.

Loaded 🦴🦴 *Bloody Weekend* **1994 (R)** Writer-director Campion (sister of director Jane) follows a group of teens to an abandoned English mansion as they try to film an amateur horror movie. While there, the group decides to have some fun, with the help of LSD. This leads to some therapeutic and angst-ridden discussions about each of their problems, as well as a tragic accident, which changes the lives of all involved. There's some nice character sketches, unfortunately they're more interesting than the loose plot, which leaves too many questions unanswered. Retitled and recut since its original '94 release. **95m/C VHS.** *NZ GB* Thandie Newton, Catherine McCormack, Oliver Milburn, Nick Patrick, Danny Cunningham, Mathew Eggleton, Biddy Hodson; ***D:*** Anna Campion; ***W:*** Anna Campion; ***C:*** Alan Almond; ***M:*** Simon Fisher Turner.

Loaded Guns woof! **1975** Airline stewardess-cum-double agent must totally immobilize a top drug trafficking ring. Pathetic spy tale with plenty of unintended laughs. **90m/C VHS.** Ursula Andress, Woody Strode; ***D:*** Fernando Di Leo.

Loaded Pistols 🦴 **1948** Story set in the old West starring Gene Autry. **80m/B VHS.** Gene Autry, Jack Holt, Barbara Britton; ***D:*** John English.

Loan Shark 🦴🦴 **1952** An ex-convict gets a job at a tire company, working undercover to expose a loan shark ring. Hackneyed plot moves quickly. **79m/B VHS.** George Raft, John Hoyt; ***D:*** Seymour Friedman.

Lobster for Breakfast 🦴🦴½ **1982 (R)** An Italian gag-fest about a toilet salesman infiltrating his friend's confused marital existence just to make a sale. With English subtitles; also available in a dubbed version. **96m/C VHS.** *IT* Enrico Montesano, Claude Brasseur, Claudine Auger; ***D:*** Giorgio Capitani.

Lobster Man from Mars **1989 (PG)** When rich movie producer (Curtis) learns from his accountant that he must produce a flop or be taken to the cleaners by the IRS, he buys a homemade horror movie from a young filmmaker. The film is an ultra-low budget production featuring a kooky lobster man and a screaming damsel. The premise peters out about halfway through, but there are enough yuks to keep you going. **84m/C VHS.** Tony Curtis, Deborah Foreman, Patrick Macnee, Tommy Sledge, Billy Barty, Phil(ip) Proctor, Anthony Hickox, Bobby "Boris" Pickett, Stanley Sheff; ***D:*** Stanley Sheff; ***W:*** Bob Greenberg; ***C:*** Gerry Lively; ***M:*** Sasha Matson.

Local Badman **1932** A dim-witted cowhand saves the day in this rip-roaring tale of the old west. **60m/B VHS.** Hoot Gibson.

Local Hero **1983 (PG)** Riegert is a yuppie representative of a huge oil company who endeavors to buy a sleepy Scottish fishing village for excavation, and finds himself hypnotized by the place and its crusty denizens. Back in Texas at company headquarters, tycoon Lancaster deals with a psycho therapist and gazes at the stars looking for clues. A low-key, charmingly offbeat Scottish comedy with its own sense of logic and quiet humor, poetic landscapes, and unique characters, epitomizing Forsyth's original style. **112m/C VHS, DVD, Wide.** *GB* Peter Riegert, Denis Lawson, Burt Lancaster, Fulton Mackay, Jenny Seagrove, Peter Capaldi, Norman Chancer; ***D:*** Bill Forsyth; ***W:*** Bill Forsyth; ***C:*** Chris Menges; ***M:*** Mark Knopfler. British Acad. '83: Director (Forsyth); N.Y. Film Critics '83: Screenplay; Natl. Soc. Film Critics '83: Screenplay.

Loch Ness ½ **1995 (PG)** American zoologist Jonathan Dempsey (Danson) specializes in hunting legendary animals and his latest assignment is to head for the Scottish highlands and take on the Nessie legend. He gets an assistant (Frain), a potential romance with single mom Laura (Richardson), and a lot of grief from some hostile locals before Laura's young daughter Isabel (Graham) decides to help him out. Jim Henson's Creature Shop takes care of the monster's animatronics. **101m/C VHS.** *GB* Ted Danson, Ian Holm, Joely Richardson, Kirsty Graham, James Frain, Harris Yulin, Keith Allen, Nick Brimble; ***D:*** John Henderson; ***W:*** John Fusco; ***C:*** Clive Tickner; ***M:*** Trevor Jones.

The Loch Ness Horror woof! **1982** The famed monster surfaces and chomps on the local poachers—and with good reason. Would that it had munched this movie's producer in, say, 1981. **93m/C VHS.** Barry Buchanan, Miki McKenzie, Sandy Kenyon; ***D:*** Larry Buchanan.

Lock 'n' Load **1990 (R)** Why are all the soldiers in the 82nd Airborne stealing vast sums, then committing suicide? One of the guys involved wants to know. **89m/C VHS.** Jack Vogel; ***D:*** David A. Prior.

Lock, Stock and 2 Smoking Barrels **1998 (R)** Plot twist-laden British caper comedy plays like Tarantino and crumpets. Four dim hoods, Bacon (Statham), Soap (Fletcher), Eddy (Moran) and Tom (Flemyng), pool their ill-gotten gains so that Eddy can play in a high stakes card game. They don't know that the game is fixed, however, and they end up owing gambler Hatchet Harry (Moriarty) 500,000 pounds. The bumbling band plan to rob their drug dealing neighbor Dog (Harper), who's planning on robbing an upper class rival of his own. Throw in a wandering pair of antique shotguns and you have the recipe for a cap-poppin' good time. Rock star Sting appears as the pub-owning father of one of the lads. **105m/C VHS, DVD, Wide.** *GB* Jason Flemyng, Dexter Fletcher, Nick Moran, Jason Statham, Steven Mackintosh, Vinnie Jones, Sting, Lenny McLean, P. H. Moriarty, Steve Sweeney, Frank Harper, Stephen Marcus; ***D:*** Guy Ritchie; ***W:*** Guy Ritchie; ***C:*** Tim Maurice-Jones; ***M:*** David A. Hughes, John Murphy. MTV Movie Awards '99: New Filmmaker (Ritchie).

Lock Up ½ **1989 (R)** Peaceful con Stallone, with only six months to go, is harassed and tortured by vicious prison warden Sutherland in retribution for an unexplained past conflict. Lackluster and moronic; semi-color; surely Sutherland can find better roles. **115m/C VHS, DVD.** Sylvester Stallone, Donald Sutherland, Sonny Landham, John Amos, Darlanne Fluegel, Frank McRae; ***D:*** John Flynn; ***W:*** Jeb Stuart; ***C:*** Donald E. Thorin; ***M:*** Bill Conti.

Lockdown ½ **1990** Charged with his partner's murder, a detective is forced to ponder the perennial puzzle of life. Not a pretty sight. **90m/C VHS, DVD.** Joe Estevez, Mike Farrell, Richard Lynch; ***D:*** Frank Harris. **VIDEO**

Locked in Silence **1999** Young boy becomes electively mute after believing he saw his older brother kill another boy. His farm family nearly goes bankrupt trying to find a cure until a psychologist is able to help the child deal with reality. Based on a true story. **94m/C VHS.** Bonnie Bedelia, Bruce Davison, Dan Hedaya, Marc Donato, Ron White, Steven McCarthy; ***D:*** Bruce Pittman; ***W:*** Dalene Young; ***C:*** Michael Storey; ***M:*** Gary Chang. **CABLE**

The Locusts ½ **1997 (R)** Backwater beefcake Clay Hewitt (Vaughn) swaggers into a small Kansas town where everyone has a lit cigarette and a secret and no one is safe from hopeless cliches and corny dialogue. Clay's sweaty, sleeveless t-shirts and choir-boy face soon have the women swarming, but he's only interested in helping a mentally and emotionally challenged kid named Flyboy (Davies) get out from under his emasculating and abusive mother Delilah (Capshaw), also Clay's boss and overly ardent admirer. Judd is barely used as Clay's spunky squeeze in this slow-paced, small-town drama by first-time director Kelley. Any high school freshman with an English lit class under his belt won't miss the not-so-subtle metaphors at play—Delilah has workers castrating bulls a lot. **123m/C VHS, DVD, Wide.** Kate Capshaw, Jeremy Davies, Vince Vaughn, Ashley Judd, Paul Rudd, Daniel Meyer, Jessica Capshaw; ***D:*** John Patrick Kelley; ***W:*** John Patrick Kelley; ***C:*** Phedon Papamichael; ***M:*** Carter Burwell.

L'Odeur des Fauves **1966** One of a cynical reporter's scandalous stories gets an innocent man killed, compelling the reporter somehow to make restitution. Subtitled in English. **86m/C VHS.** *FR* Maurice Ronet, Josephine Chaplin, Vittorio De Sica; ***D:*** Richard Balducci.

The Lodger *The Case of Jonathan Drew; The Lodger: A Case of London Fog* **1926** A mysterious lodger is thought to be a rampaging mass murderer of young women. First Hitchcock film to explore the themes and ideas that would become his trademarks. Silent. Climactic chase is memorable. Remade three times. Look closely for the Master in his first cameo. **91m/B VHS, DVD.** *GB* Ivor Novello, Marie Ault, Arthur Chesney, Malcolm Keen, June; ***Cameos:*** Alfred Hitchcock; ***D:*** Alfred Hitchcock; ***W:*** Alfred Hitchcock, Eliot Stannard.

Logan's Run ½ **1976** In the 23rd century, a hedonistic society exists in a huge bubble and people are only allowed to live to the age of 30. Intriguing concepts and great futuristic sets prevail here. Based on the novel by William Nolan and George Clayton Johnson. **120m/C VHS, DVD, Wide.** Michael York, Jenny Agutter, Richard Jordan, Roscoe Lee Browne, Farrah Fawcett, Peter Ustinov, Camilla Carr, Ann Ford; ***D:*** Michael Anderson Sr.; ***W:*** David Zelag Goodman; ***C:*** Ernest Laszlo; ***M:*** Jerry Goldsmith. Oscars '76: Visual FX.

Lois Gibbs and the Love Canal **1982** Mason's TV movie debut as Lois Gibbs, a housewife turned activist, fighting the authorities over chemical-dumping in the Love Canal area of Niagara Falls, New York. The script doesn't convey the seriousness of developments in that region. **100m/C VHS.** Marsha Mason, Bob Gunton, Penny Fuller, Roberta Maxwell, Jeremy Licht, Louise Latham; ***D:*** Glenn Jordan. **TV**

Lola **1961** A wonderful tale of a nightclub dancer and her amorous adventures. Innovative film that marked the beginning of French New Wave. In French with English subtitles. **90m/B VHS.** *FR* Anouk Aimee, Marc Michel, Elina Labourdette, Jacques Harden; ***D:*** Jacques Demy.

Lola ½ *The Statutory Affair; Twinky* **1969 (PG)** A teenaged girl links up romantically with a considerably older writer of pornographic books. One would expect more from such a good cast, but the film never follows through. British release was originally 98 minutes. **88m/C VHS.** *GB IT* Charles Bronson, Susan George, Trevor Howard, Michael Craig, Honor Blackman, Lionel Jeffries, Robert Morley, Jack Hawkins, Orson Bean, Kay Medford, Paul Ford; ***D:*** Richard Donner.

Lola and Billy the Kid *Lola + Bilikid* **1998** Murat (Davrak) is a closeted gay Turkish teenager living in Berlin with his widowed mother and homophobic brother Osman (Mete). Lola (Mukli) is a travestite dancer at a nightclub who lives with hustler Bili (Yildiz). When Lola tries to contact Murat's family, the boy discovers that Lola is his brother, who was thrown out by Osman. Murat meets Lola, who is later killed—apparently by neo-Nazi thugs. Bili vows revenge but Murat learns that the situation isn't as clear as it seems. German and Turkish with subtitles. **95m/C VHS, DVD.** *GE* Baki Darrak, Gandi Mukli, Erdal Yildiz, Hasan Ali Mete, Michael Gerber, Murat Yilmaz, Inge Keller; ***D:*** Kutlug Ataman; ***W:*** Kutlug Ataman; ***C:*** Chris Squires; ***M:*** Arpad Bondy.

Lola Montes **1955** Ophuls' final masterpiece (and his only film in color) recounts the life and sins of the famous courtesan, mistress of Franz Liszt and the King of Bavaria. Ignored upon release, but hailed later by the French as a cinematic landmark. Adapted from an unpublished novel by Cecil Saint-Laurent. French with subtitles. The original widescreen release clocked in at 140 minutes. **110m/C DVD, Wide.** *FR* Martine Carol, Peter Ustinov, Anton Walbrook, Ivan Desny, Oskar Werner; ***D:*** Max Ophuls; ***W:*** Max Ophuls; ***C:*** Christian Matras; ***M:*** Georges Auric.

Lolida 2000 ½ *Lolita 2000* **1997** In the future all sexual activity is prohibited (bummer). Lolita's working for an organization that destroys sexual material but three particular stories arouse feelings in her that she just has to act on. **90m/C VHS, DVD.** Jacqueline Lovell, Gabriella Hall, Eric Acsell; ***D:*** Sybil Richards.

Lolita **1962** A middle-aged professor is consumed by his lust for a teenage nymphet in this strange film considered daring in its time. Based on Vladimir Nabokov's novel. Watch for Winters' terrific portrayal as Lolita's sex-starved mother. **152m/B VHS, DVD, Wide.** *GB* James Mason, Shelley Winters, Peter Sellers, Sue Lyon, Gary Cockrell, Jerry Stovin, Diana Decker, Lois Maxwell, Cec Linder, Bill Greene, Shirley Douglas, Marianne Stone, Marion Mathie, James Dyrenforth, C. Denier Warren, Terence (Terry) Kilburn, John Harrison; ***D:*** Stanley Kubrick; ***W:*** Vladimir Nabokov; ***C:*** Oswald Morris; ***M:*** Nelson Riddle.

Lolita **1997 (R)** Middle-aged college professor Humbert Humbert (Irons) becomes obsessed with nymphet Lolita (Swain), even to the point of marrying her mother Charlotte (Griffith) so he can always be close by. Then Charlotte dies, and the unlikely duo begin an aimless road trip that eventually leads Lolita to a fateful meeting with yet another older man, Quilty (Langella). Director Lyne's no stranger to controversy but his reverential take on the Vladimir Nabokov novel turns out to be much ado about nothing. Then 14-year-old Swain (in a fetchingly flirty performance) debuts as Lolita (along with a body-double). **137m/C VHS, DVD, Wide.** Jeremy Irons, Melanie Griffith, Frank Langella, Dominique Swain, Suzanne Shepherd, Keith Reddin, Erin J. Dean, Ben Silverstone; ***D:*** Adrian Lyne; ***W:*** Stephen Schiff; ***C:*** Howard Atherton; ***M:*** Ennio Morricone.

Lolo **1992** Outcast Lolo loses his job in Mexico City and then accidentally kills the local moneylender. The only one who will help him is his girlfriend Sonia, who gets the money for them to flee the city by prostituting herself. Spanish with subtitles. **88m/C VHS, DVD.** *MX* Roberto Sosa, Lucha Villa; ***D:*** Francisco Athie; ***W:*** Francisco Athie; ***C:*** Jorge Medina; ***M:*** Juan Cristobal Perez Grobert.

London Kills Me **1991 (R)** A slice-of-life story London-style. Set at the end of the Thatcher era, Clint is a homeless drifter dealing drugs to get by. He's trying to get enough money for a new pair of shoes which will enable him to get a job in a fancy restaurant and away from his aimless life. His friend Muffdiver leads the group of drug pushers and is obsessed with money and power. Sylvie is the sultry junkie who drifts between Clint, Muffdiver, and her drug needs. The directorial debut of Kureishi is more a collection of characters and situations than a complete film but there are moments of disturbing intensity and odd sweetness. **105m/C VHS.** *GB* Justin Chadwick, Steven Mackintosh, Emer McCourt, Roshan Seth, Fiona Shaw, Brad Dourif, Gordon Warnecke, Dave Atkins; ***D:*** Hanif Kureishi; ***W:*** Hanif Kureishi; ***C:*** Edward Lachman.

London Melody ½ *Girl in the Street* **1937** Neagle is a spirited Cockney busker who meets a kindly Italian diplomat who decides to finance her musical education. He promptly also falls in love with her. **71m/B VHS, 8mm.** *GB* Anna Neagle, Tullio Carminati, Robert Douglas, Horace Hodgers; ***D:*** Herbert Wilcox.

The Lone Avenger **1933** Average oater centers around a bank panic, with two-gun Maynard clearing up the trouble. **60m/B VHS.** Ken Maynard, Muriel Gordon, James A. Marcus.

Lone Bandit ½ **1933** Vintage western starring Chandler. **57m/B VHS.** Lane Chandler, Doris Brook, Wally Wales; ***D:*** J(ohn) P(aterson) McGowan.

The Lone Defender **1932** A dozen episodes of the western serial starring the canine crusader, Rin Tin Tin. **235m/B VHS.** Walter Miller, June Marlowe, Buzz Barton, Josef Swickard, Frank Lanning, Robert F. (Bob) Kortman; ***D:*** Richard Thorpe.

Lone Hero **2002 (R)** You can tell by the video box that Phillips is not the titular hero—in fact, he's Bart (Phillips), a psycho biker gang leader who terrorizes a small town. Flanery is the somewhat goofball hero, John, who plays a gunfighter in the local Wild West show and who is the only one willing to stand up to the violent menace. **91m/C VHS, DVD.** Lou Diamond Phillips, Sean Patrick Flanery, Robert Forster, Tanya Allen, Garry Chalk; ***D:*** Ken Sanzel; ***W:*** Ken Sanzel; ***C:*** David Pelletier; ***M:*** Anthony Marinelli.

Lone Justice ½ **1993 (R)** Cowboy Ned Blessing has seen and done it all (from outlaw to sheriff) but his wild ways have caught up with him. Now, he's relating his exploits from a jail cell as he awaits his fate at the end of a rope. Beware—this looks like the first chapter of a series and there's no real ending. **94m/C VHS.** Daniel Baldwin, Luis Avalos, Chris Cooper, Sean Baca, Taylor Fry, Julia Campbell, Rene Auberjonois, Timothy Scott, Bob Gunton, Miguel (Michael) Sandoval, Jeff Kober; ***D:*** Peter Werner; ***W:*** William D. Wittliff; ***M:*** Basil Poledouris.

Lone Justice 2 ½ *Ned Blessing: The Story of My Life and Times* **1993 (PG-13)** Laconic hero Ned Blessing (Johnson), along with Mexican sidekick Crecencio (Avalos), return to Blessing's hometown after a six-year absence and find it ruled by six-shooters and fists. The despicable Borgers clan has murdered the local sheriff (who happens to be Blessing's daddy) and rules by intimidation—until Ned gets involved. Cliched but amusing. **93m/C VHS, DVD.** Brad Johnson, Luis Avalos, Wes Studi, Bill McKinney, Brenda Bakke, Julius Tennon, Richard Riehle, Gregory Scott Cummins, Rob Campbell, Rusty Schwimmer; ***D:*** Jack Bender; ***W:*** William D. Wittliff; ***C:*** Neil Roach; ***M:*** David Bell. **TV**

Lone Justice 3: Showdown at Plum Creek ½ **1996 (PG)** Ex-outlaw-turned-sheriff Ned Blessing (Johnson) discovers the body of the previous sheriff has disappeared from its grave, Big Emma has taken over the saloon and wants Blessing out of the way, and Oscar Wilde comes to town. Three re-edited stories from the TV miniseries. **94m/C VHS,**

DVD. Brad Johnson, Wes Studi, Brenda Bakke, William Sanderson, Luis Avalos, Rusty Schwimmer, Stephen Fry; ***D:*** Jack Bender, Dan Lerner, David Hemmings; ***W:*** Stephen Harrigan; ***C:*** Neil Roach. **TV**

The Lone Ranger **1938** Western serial about the masked man and his faithful Indian sidekick. From a long-sought print found in Mexico, this program is burdened by a noisy sound track, two completely missing chapters, an abridged episode #15, and Spanish subtitles. **234m/B VHS.** Lee Powell; ***D:*** William Witney, John English.

Lone Ranger **1956** Tonto and that strange masked man must prevent a war between ranchers and Indians in the first of the "Lone Ranger" series. "Hi-ho Silver!" **87m/C VHS, DVD, Wide.** Clayton Moore, Jay Silverheels, Lyle Bettger, Bonita Granville; ***D:*** Stuart Heisler; ***W:*** Herb Meadow; ***C:*** Edwin DuPar; ***M:*** David Buttolph.

The Lone Rider in Cheyenne 🦴½ **1942** One of the last in the "Lone Rider" series. The Lone Rider is out to clear the name of an innocent man accused of murder. **59m/B VHS.** George Houston, Al "Fuzzy" St. John; ***D:*** Sam Newfield.

The Lone Rider in Ghost Town 🦴½ **1941** Outlaws "haunt" a ghost town to protect their hidden mine and the Lone Rider and his pal, Fuzzy, are out to solve the mystery. Installment in the short-lived "Lone Rider" series. **64m/B VHS.** George Houston, Al "Fuzzy" St. John, Budd Buster; ***D:*** Sam Newfield.

The Lone Runner woof! **1988 (PG)** An adventurer rescues a beautiful heiress from Arab kidnappers in this dud. **90m/C VHS.** Miles O'Keeffe, Ronald Lacey, Michael J. Aronin, John Steiner, Al Yamanouchi; ***D:*** Ruggero Deodato.

Lone Star 🦴🦴½ **1952** Big stars, big budget western in which Texas fights for independence as good guy Gable and badman Crawford fight each other. Gardner plays a fiery newspaper editor as well as Gable's love interest. Script is chock full of holes, but great action scenes make up for it. Based on the story by Borden Chase. **94m/B VHS.** Clark Gable, Ava Gardner, Broderick Crawford, Lionel Barrymore, Beulah Bondi, Ed Begley Sr., William Farnum, Lowell Gilmore; ***D:*** Vincent Sherman; ***W:*** Howard Estabrook, Borden Chase.

Lone Star 🦴🦴🦴½ **1995 (R)** Terrific contemporary western set in the border town Frontera, Texas. Sheriff Sam Deeds (Cooper) is still dealing with the legacy of his father, legendary lawman Buddy Deeds (McConaughey) who, 40 years before, wrestled control of the town from his racist, corrupt predecessor Charlie Wade (Kristofferson) and supposedly sent him packing. But when skeletal remains and a sheriff's badge turn up on an abandoned Army rifle range, guess whose bones they turn out to be. Buddy's friends would like Sam to just leave the past lie but he can't, and learns some hard home truths. This is only one of the town's stories that Sayles gracefully tells and, as always, his ensemble cast all offer outstanding performances. **137m/C VHS, DVD.** Gabriel Casseus, Chris Cooper, Matthew McConaughey, Kris Kristofferson, Elizabeth Pena, Joe Morton, Ron Canada, Clifton James, Miriam Colon, Frances McDormand, Richard Jones; ***D:*** John Sayles; ***W:*** John Sayles; ***C:*** Stuart Dryburgh; ***M:*** Mason Daring. Ind. Spirit '97: Support. Actress (Pena).

Lone Star Kid **1988** 11-year-old Brian Zimmerman lives in Crabb, Texas—population 400. After he witnesses a car accident death because there's no adequate emergency service, he decides to run for mayor and help modernize the town. Based on a true story. Includes a viewers' guide. Presented as part of the "Wonderworks" series. **55m/C VHS.** James Earl Jones, Chad Sheets; ***M:*** Charlie Daniels.

Lone Star Law Men 🦴 **1942** A U.S. marshal has his hands full in a border town overrun with bandits. Keene stars as the deputy marshall who goes undercover and joins the gang in an attempt to foil their crooked plans. **58m/B VHS.** Tom (George Duryea) Keene, Frank Yaconelli, Sugar Dawn, Betty Miles; ***D:*** Robert Emmett Tansey.

The Lone Star Ranger 🦴½ **1930** Former outlaw O'Brien is trying to go straight by helping to bring a gang of rustlers to justice. Interesting plot twist in the link between his girlfriend and the head of the gang. **64m/B VHS.** George O'Brien, Sue Carol, Walter McGrail, Warren Hymer, Russell Simpson; ***D:*** A.F. Erickson.

Lone Wolf 🦴 **1988** A werewolf terrorizes a high school, and a few computerniks track it down. **97m/C VHS.** Dyann Brown, Kevin Hart, Jamie Newcomb, Ann Douglas; ***D:*** John Callas.

Lone Wolf McQuade 🦴🦴½ **1983** Martial arts action abounds in this modern-day Western which pits unorthodox Texas Ranger Norris against a band of gun-running mercenaries led by Carradine. Oh, and there's a conflict-ridden love interest as well. Violent (and not particularly literary) but worthy entry in chopsocky genre. **107m/C VHS, DVD, Wide.** Chuck Norris, Leon Isaac Kennedy, David Carradine, L.Q. (Justus E. McQueen) Jones, Barbara Carrera; ***D:*** Steve Carver; ***W:*** H. Kaye Dyal; ***C:*** Roger Shearman; ***M:*** Francesco De Masi.

The Loneliest Runner 🦴🦴 **1976** Based on the true story of an Olympic track star who, as a teenager, suffered humiliation as a bed-wetter. The real-life experiences of producer-director Landon are presented in a touching and sensitive manner. **74m/C VHS.** Michael Landon, Lance Kerwin, DeAnn Mears, Brian Keith, Melissa Sue Anderson; ***D:*** Michael Landon. **TV**

The Loneliness of the Long Distance Runner 🦴🦴🦴 *Rebel with a Cause* **1962** Courtenay, in his film debut, turns in a powerful performance as an angry young man infected by the poverty and hopelessness of the British slums. His first attempt at crime is a bust and lands him in a boys reformatory where he is recruited for the running team. While training for the big event with a rival school, Redgrave's obsession with winning the race and Courtenay's continued indifference to the outcome lock the two in an intriguing, seemingly one-sided power struggle. Though widely overlooked when first released, it has since been praised as one of the finest teenage angst films of the '60s. Riveting depiction on a boy's rite of passage into manhood. **104m/B VHS.** *GB* Tom Courtenay, Michael Redgrave, Avis Bunnage, Peter Madden, James Bolam, Julia Foster, Topsy Jane, Frank Finlay, Christopher Parker; ***D:*** Tony Richardson; ***C:*** Walter Lassally; ***M:*** John Addison.

Lonely Are the Brave 🦴🦴🦴 **1962** A free-spirited cowboy out of sync with the modern age tries to rescue a buddy from a local jail, and in his eventual escape is tracked relentlessly by modern law enforcement. A compelling, sorrowful essay on civilized progress and exploitation of nature. Adapted from the novel "Brave Cowboy" by Edward Abbey. **107m/B VHS.** Kirk Douglas, Walter Matthau, Gena Rowlands, Carroll O'Connor, George Kennedy; ***D:*** David Miller; ***M:*** Jerry Goldsmith.

The Lonely Guy 🦴🦴½ **1984 (R)** Romantic comedy with Martin as a jilted writer who writes a best-selling book about being a lonely guy and finds stardom does have its rewards. Based on "The Lonely Guy's Book of Life" by Bruce Jay Friedman. **91m/C VHS, DVD, Wide.** Steve Martin, Charles Grodin, Judith Ivey, Steve Lawrence, Robyn Douglass, Merv Griffin, Dr. Joyce Brothers; ***D:*** Arthur Hiller; ***W:*** Stan Daniels; ***C:*** Victor Kemper; ***M:*** Jerry Goldsmith.

Lonely Hearts 🦴🦴🦴 **1982 (R)** An endearing Australian romantic comedy about a piano tuner, who at 50 finds himself alone after years of caring for his mother, and a sexually insecure spinster, whom he meets through a dating service. Wonderful performances and a good script make this a delightful film that touches the human heart. **95m/C VHS, DVD, Wide.** *AU* Wendy Hughes, Norman Kaye, Jon Finlayson, Julia Blake, Jonathan Hardy; ***D:*** Paul Cox; ***W:*** Paul Cox, John Clarke; ***C:*** Yuri Sokol; ***M:*** Norman Kaye. Australian Film Inst. '82: Film.

Lonely Hearts 🦴½ **1991 (R)** A handsome con man works his wiles on a lonely woman in this erotic thriller. Standard plot wastes a good cast. **109m/C VHS.** Eric Roberts, Beverly D'Angelo, Joanna Cassidy; ***W:*** R.E. Daniels.

Lonely in America 🦴🦴½ **1990** Charming romantic comedy of a newcomer in New York City. Arun (Chowdhry) has just arrived from India and has quite a few things to learn about life in the Big Apple. **96m/C VHS.** Ranjit (Chaudry) Chowdhry, Adelaide Miller, Robert Kessler, Melissa Christopher, David Toney, Tirlok Malik; ***D:*** Barry Alexander Brown; ***W:*** Barry Alexander Brown, Satyajit Joy Palit.

The Lonely Lady woof! **1983 (R)** Young writer comes to Hollywood with dreams of success, gets involved with the seamy side of movie-making, and is driven to a nervous breakdown. Pia needs acting lessons, yet it probably wouldn't have helped this trash. Adapted from the novel by Harold Robbins. **92m/C VHS.** Pia Zadora, Lloyd Bochner, Bibi Besch, Joseph Cali, Ray Liotta, Jared Martin, Anthony Holland, Carla Romanelli, Olivier Pierre; ***D:*** Peter Sasdy; ***W:*** John Kershaw, Shawn Randall; ***C:*** Brian West; ***M:*** Charlie Calello. Golden Raspberries '83: Worst Picture, Worst Actress (Zadora), Worst Director (Sasdy), Worst Screenplay, Worst Song ("The Way You Do It").

Lonely Man 🦴🦴½ **1957** A gunfighter tries to end his career, but is urged into one last battle. Strong performances and tight direction make up for weak plot. **87m/B VHS.** Jack Palance, Anthony Perkins, Neville Brand, Elaine Aiken; ***D:*** Henry Levin; ***C:*** Lionel Lindon.

The Lonely Passion of Judith Hearne 🦴🦴🦴 **1987 (R)** A self-effacing Dublin spinster meets a man who gives her his attention, but she must overcome her own self-doubt and crisis of faith. Adapted from Brian Moore's 1955 novel. Excellent performances from both Hoskins and Smith. **116m/C VHS.** *GB* Maggie Smith, Bob Hoskins, Wendy Hiller, Marie Kean, Ian McNeice, Alan Devlin, Rudi Davies, Prunella Scales; ***D:*** Jack Clayton; ***W:*** Peter Nelson; ***C:*** Peter Hannan; ***M:*** Georges Delerue. British Acad. '88: Actress (Smith).

The Lonely Sex 🦴½ **1959** Creepy and bizarre film in which a maniac kidnaps a young girl and is then harassed by her psychotic housemate. **?m/C VHS.** Jean Evans, Karl Light, Mary Gonzales.

Lonely Wives 🦴🦴 **1931** A lawyer hires an entertainer to serve as his double because of his marital problems. **86m/B VHS, DVD.** Edward Everett Horton, Patsy Ruth Miller, Laura La Plante, Esther Ralston; ***D:*** Russell Mack; ***W:*** Walter DeLeon; ***C:*** Edward Snyder.

Lonelyhearts 🦴🦴½ **1958** Clift plays a reporter who is assigned the lovelorn column of his paper and gets too immersed in the problems of his readers. Given the superior cast and excellent material, this is a somewhat disappointing adaptation of the brilliant Nathanael West novel "Miss Lonelyhearts." Film debuts of both Stapleton and director Donehue. **101m/B VHS.** Montgomery Clift, Robert Ryan, Myrna Loy, Dolores Hart, Maureen Stapleton, Frank Maxwell, Jackie Coogan, Mike Kellin; ***D:*** Vincent J. Donehue.

Loners 🦴🦴 **1972 (R)** Three teenagers run from the Southwest police after they are accused of murdering a highway patrolman. **80m/C VHS.** Dean Stockwell, Gloria Grahame, Scott Brady, Alex Dreier, Pat Stich; ***D:*** Sutton Roley; ***W:*** Barry Sandler.

Lonesome Dove 🦴🦴🦴½ **1989** Classic western saga with Duvall and Jones in outstanding roles as two aging ex-Texas Rangers who decide to leave their quiet lives for a last adventure—a cattle drive from Texas to Montana. Along the way they encounter a new love (Lane), a lost love (Huston), and a savage renegade Indian (well-played by Forrest). Based on Pulitzer prize-winner Larry McMurtry's novel, this handsome TV miniseries is a finely detailed evocation of the Old West, with a wonderful cast and an equally fine production. Followed by "Return to Lonesome Dove." **480m/C VHS, DVD.** Robert Duvall, Tommy Lee Jones, Anjelica Huston, Danny Glover, Diane Lane, Rick Schroder, Robert Urich, D.B. Sweeney, Frederic Forrest; ***D:*** Simon Wincer; ***W:*** William D. Wittliff; ***M:*** Basil Poledouris. **TV**

Lonesome Trail 🦴½ **1955** Routine Western that differs from the average oater by having the good guys use bows and arrows to fight their battles. **73m/B VHS.** Buster Crabbe, Buster Crabbe, Jimmy Wakely, Lee White, Lorraine Miller, John James; ***D:*** Richard Bartlett.

Long Ago Tomorrow 🦴🦴 *The Raging Moon* **1971 (PG)** A paralyzed athlete enters a church-run home for the disabled rather than return to his family as the object of their pity. A love affair with a woman, who shares the same disability, helps the athlete to adapt. **90m/C VHS.** *GB* Malcolm McDowell, Nanette Newman, Bernard Lee, Georgia Brown, Gerald Sim; ***D:*** Bryan Forbes.

The Long Dark Hall 🦴🦴½ **1951** Courtroom drama in which an innocent man is brought to trial when his showgirl mistress is found dead. **86m/B VHS.** *GB* Rex Harrison, Lilli Palmer, Denis O'Dea, Raymond Huntley, Patricia Wayne, Anthony Dawson; ***D:*** Anthony Bushell, Reginald Beck.

The Long Day Closes 🦴🦴🦴 **1992 (PG)** It's 1956 Liverpool and 11-year-old Bud (McCormack) is part of a working-class Catholic family who longs to escape from his humdrum life. And how? By going to the movies of course and filling his head with pop songs. Nostalgic view of family life filled with sweet, small everyday moments set in a dreary postwar England. Sequel to Davies's also autobiographical film "Distant Voices, Still Lives." **84m/C VHS.** *GB* Leigh McCormack, Marjorie Yates, Anthony Watson, Ayse Owens; ***D:*** Terence Davies; ***W:*** Terence Davies; ***C:*** Michael Coulter.

Long Day's Journey into Night 🦴🦴🦴🦴 **1962** A brooding, devastating film based on Eugene O'Neill's most powerful and autobiographical play. Depicts a day in the life of a family deteriorating under drug addiction, alcoholism, and imminent death. Hepburn's performance is outstanding. In 1988, the Broadway version was taped and released on video. **174m/B VHS.** Ralph Richardson, Katharine Hepburn, Dean Stockwell, Jeanne Barr, Jason Robards Jr.; ***D:*** Sidney Lumet; ***W:*** Eugene O'Neill; ***C:*** Boris Kaufman; ***M:*** Andre Previn. Cannes '62: Actress (Hepburn); Natl. Bd. of Review '62: Support. Actor (Robards).

Long Day's Journey into Night 🦴🦴 **1988** A taped version of the Broadway production of the epic Eugene O'Neill play about a Southern family deteriorating under the weight of terminal illness, alcoholism and drug abuse. In 1962 a movie adaptation of the play was released with outstanding performances from its cast. **169m/C VHS.** Jack Lemmon, Bethel Leslie, Peter Gallagher, Kevin Spacey, Jodie Lynne McLintock; ***D:*** Jonathan Miller.

Long Day's Journey Into Night 🦴🦴🦴 **1996** Eugene O'Neill's autobiographical play about his family is adapted from Canada's Stratford Festival production. The Tyrones are a troubled Irish-American family: bullying James (Hutt) was a once-great Shakespearean actor who has been typecast in a popular stage potboiler; wife Mary (Henry) is a morphine addict; elder son James Jr. (Donaldson) is an alcoholic; and O'Neill's alter-ego is Edmund (McCamus), an overly sensitive, consumptive writer. Fine performances, excellent production. **174m/C VHS.** *CA* William Hutt, Martha Henry, Tom McCamus, Peter Donaldson, Martha Burns; ***D:*** David Wellington; ***W:*** Eugene O'Neill; ***C:*** David Franco; ***M:*** Ron Sures. Genie '96: Actor (Hutt), Actress (Henry), Support. Actor (Donaldson), Support. Actress (Burns); Toronto-City '96: Canadian Feature Film.

The Long Days of Summer 🦴🦴 **1980** Set in pre-WWII America, this film portrays a Jewish attorney's struggle against the prejudices of the New England town where he lives. Sequel to "When Every Day Is the Fourth of July." **105m/C VHS.** Dean Jones, Joan Hackett, Louanne, Donald Moffat, Andrew Duggan, Michael McGuire; ***D:*** Dan Curtis. **TV**

Long Gone 🦴🦴½ **1987** In the '50s, an over-the-hill minor-league player/manager is given a last lease on life and the pennant with two talented rookies and a sexy baseball groupie. **113m/C VHS.** William L. Petersen, Henry Gibson, Katy Boyer, Virginia

Madsen, Dermot Mulroney, Larry Riley, Teller; *D:* Martin Davidson. **CABLE**

The Long Good Friday 🦴🦴🦴½ **1980** Set in London's dockland, this is a violent story of a crime boss who meets his match. Hoskin's world crumbles over an Easter weekend when his buildings are bombed and his men murdered. He thinks its the work of rival gangsters only to discover an even deadlier threat is behind his troubles. One of the best of the crime genre, with an exquisitely charismatic performance by Hoskins. **109m/C VHS, DVD, Wide.** *GB* Bob Hoskins, Helen Mirren, Dave King, Bryan Marshall, George Coulouris, Pierce Brosnan, Derek Thompson, Eddie Constantine, Brian Hall, Stephen Davies, P. H. Moriarty, Paul Freeman, Charles Cork, Paul Barber, Patti Love, Ruby Head, Dexter Fletcher, Roy Alon; *D:* John MacKenzie; *W:* Barrie Keefe; *C:* Phil Meheux; *M:* Francis Monkman.

The Long Goodbye 🦴🦴🦴 **1973 (R)** Raymond Chandler's penultimate novel with the unmistakable Altman touch—which is to say that some of the changes to the story have pushed purist noses out of joint. Gould is cast as an insouciant anti-Marlowe, the film noir atmosphere has been transmuted into a Hollywood film neon, genre jibing abounds, and the ending has been rewritten. But the revamping serves a purpose, which is to make Marlowe a viable character in a contemporary world. Handsomely photographed by Vilmos Zsigmond. Don't miss bulky boy Arnold's cameo (his second film appearance). **112m/C VHS, Wide.** Elliott Gould, Nina Van Pallandt, Sterling Hayden, Henry Gibson, Mark Rydell, David Arkin, Warren Berlinger; ***Cameos:*** Arnold Schwarzenegger, David Carradine; *D:* Robert Altman; *W:* Leigh Brackett; *C:* Vilmos Zsigmond; *M:* John Williams. Natl. Soc. Film Critics '73: Cinematog.

The Long Gray Line 🦴🦴🦴 **1955** Power gives an outstanding performance as Marty Maher, a humble Irish immigrant who became an institution at West Point. This is the inspiring story of his rise from an unruly cadet to one of the academy's most beloved instructors. O'Hara does a fine job of playing his wife, who like her husband, adopts the young cadets as her own. Director Ford gracefully captures the spirit and honor associated with West Point in this affectionate drama. **138m/C VHS, DVD, Wide.** Tyrone Power, Maureen O'Hara, Robert Francis, Donald Crisp, Ward Bond, Betsy Palmer, Phil Carey; *D:* John Ford; *W:* Edward Hope; *C:* Charles Lawton Jr.

The Long Haul 🦴🦴 **1957** A truck driver becomes involved with crooks as his marriage sours. **88m/C VHS.** Victor Mature, Diana Dors, Patrick Allen, Gene Anderson; *D:* Ken Hughes.

The Long, Hot Summer 🦴🦴🦴½ **1958** A tense, well-played adaptation of the William Faulkner story about drifter Ben Quick (Newman), who latches himself onto a tyrannical Mississippi family, the Varners, led by larger-than-life Will Varner (Welles). The first on-screen pairing of Newman and Woodward (who plays spinster daughter Clara), and one of the best. Remade for TV in 1986. **117m/C VHS.** Paul Newman, Orson Welles, Joanne Woodward, Lee Remick, Anthony (Tony) Franciosa, Angela Lansbury, Richard Anderson; *D:* Martin Ritt; *W:* Harriet Frank Jr., Irving Ravetch; *C:* Joseph LaShelle; *M:* Alex North. Cannes '58: Actor (Newman).

The Long, Hot Summer 🦴🦴🦴½ **1986** TV version of the William Faulkner story, "The Hamlet," about a drifter taken under a Southern patriarch's wing. He's bribed into courting the man's unmarried daughter. Wonderful performances from the entire cast, especially Ivey and surprisingly, Johnson. Remake of the 1958 film with Paul Newman and Joanne Woodward that is on par with the original. **172m/C VHS.** Don Johnson, Cybill Shepherd, Judith Ivey, Jason Robards Jr., Ava Gardner, William Russ, Wings Hauser, William Forsythe, Albert Hall; *D:* Stuart Cooper; *M:* Charles Bernstein. **TV**

Long John Silver 🦴½ *Long John Silver Returns to Treasure Island* **1954** Famed pirate John Silver plans a return trip to Treasure Island to search for the elusive treasure; unofficial sequel to "Treasure Island" by Disney. **103m/C VHS, DVD.** *AU* Robert Newton, Connie Gilchrist, Kit Taylor, Grant Taylor, Rod Taylor; *D:* Byron Haskin; *W:* Martin Rackin; *C:* Carl Guthrie; *M:* David Buttolph.

Long Journey Back 🦴🦴 **1978** The biographical story of a young woman's rehabilitation after her injury in a school bus accident. **100m/C VHS.** Mike Connors, Cloris Leachman, Stephanie Zimbalist, Katy Kurtzman; *D:* Mel Damski. **TV**

The Long Kiss Goodnight 🦴🦴½ **1996 (R)** Audience-pleasing, blood-soaked, foul-mouthed, and action-packed. Davis obviously has a career as a '90s action star (female division), displaying the proper bravado, and muscles, necessary for her dual role. As mild-mannered, brown-haired Samantha Caine, she's a schoolteacher with an eight-year-old daughter, Caitlin (Zima), a nice boyfriend, Hal (Amandes), and amnesia. Sam begins having flashbacks to her past—and what a past it turns out to be. With the help of seedy PI Mitch Henessey (Jackson), she discovers her name is Charly Baltimore and she's a highly trained and very deadly CIA assassin. And the now bleached-blonde, beyond-tough Charly must match her quickly regained lethal abilities with ruthless former nemesis Timothy (Bierko). The body count's high, the blood flows freely, and there's some spectacular stunts. If you're not squeamish it's a guaranteed wild ride. Black got $4 million for his script. **120m/C VHS, DVD, Wide.** Geena Davis, Samuel L. Jackson, Craig Bierko, Patrick Malahide, Brian Cox, David Morse, Yvonne Zima, Tom Amandes, Melina Kanakaredes, G.D. Spradlin; *D:* Renny Harlin; *W:* Shane Black; *C:* Guillermo Navarro; *M:* Alan Silvestri.

The Long, Long Trailer 🦴🦴½ **1954** A couple on their honeymoon find that trailer life is more than they bargained for. Lots of fun with charming direction from Minelli, and Ball's incredible slapstick style. **97m/C VHS.** Desi Arnaz Sr., Lucille Ball, Marjorie Main, Keenan Wynn; *D:* Vincente Minnelli.

The Long Night 🦴🦴½ **1947** Remake of Marcel Carne's "Le Journe Se Leve/Daybreak" (1939). WWII vet Joe Adams (Fonda) is having a hard time with civilian life. In fact, he's just killed con man/magician Maximilian (Price) and has barricaded himself from the cops in his apartment. Flashbacks serve to show how Joe got into his present situation (women are involved, naturally). Not too involving. **101m/B VHS, DVD.** Henry Fonda, Vincent Price, Barbara Bel Geddes, Ann Dvorak, Howard Freeman, Moroni Olsen, Elisha Cook Jr.; *D:* Anatole Litvak; *W:* John Wexley; *C:* Sol Polito; *M:* Dimitri Tiomkin.

Long Pants 🦴🦴🦴 **1927** Langdon, in a typical man/child role, plays a naive young man who gets his first pair of long pants, which officially ushers him into adulthood. He immediately falls for the wrong gal (Bonner), a drug runner who winds up in jail. So he breaks her out and they go on the lam. **58m/B VHS.** Harry Langdon, Priscilla Bonner, Alma Bennett; *D:* Frank Capra.

The Long Riders 🦴🦴🦴 **1980 (R)** Excellent mythic western in which the Jesse James and Cole Younger gangs raid banks, trains, and stagecoaches in post-Civil War Missouri. Stylish, meticulous and a violent look back, with one of the better slow-motion shootouts in Hollywood history. Notable for the portrayal of four sets of outlaw brothers (James, Younger, Miller, Ford) by four Hollywood brother (Keach, Carradine, Quaid, Guest) sets. Complimented by excellent Cooder score. **100m/C VHS, DVD, Wide.** Stacy Keach, James Keach, Randy Quaid, Dennis Quaid, David Carradine, Keith Carradine, Robert Carradine, Christopher Guest, Nicholas Guest, Pamela Reed, Savannah Smith, James Whitmore Jr., Harry Carey Jr.; *D:* Walter Hill; *W:* Stacy Keach, James Keach, Bill Bryden; *C:* Ric Waite; *M:* Ry Cooder.

Long Road Home 🦴🦴½ **1991 (PG)** Migrant family must decide between working under inhumane conditions or risk losing everything by joining the labor movement during the depression. TV movie. **88m/C VHS.** Mark Harmon, John Evans, Adam Horovitz, Lee Purcell, Leon Russom, Donald Sutherland, Morgan Weisser; *D:* John Korty; *C:* Kees Van Oostrum.

Long Shadows 🦴½ **1986** An analysis of how the resonating effects of the Civil War can still be felt on society, via interviews with a number of noted writers, historians, civil rights activists and politicians. **88m/C VHS, DVD.** Robert Penn Warren, Studs Terkel, Jimmy Carter, Robert Coles, Tom Wicker.

The Long Ships 🦴 **1964** Silly Viking saga finds brothers Rolfe (Widmark) and Orm (Tamblyn) stealing a ship and heading off in search of a solid-gold bell. Among their trials are a mutinous crew and battling Moorish Prince El Mansuh (Poitier). Something to be left off the resume. **125m/C VHS.** Richard Widmark, Russ Tamblyn, Sidney Poitier, Oscar Homolka, Rosanna Schiaffino, Beba Loncar, Lionel Jeffries, Edward Judd; *D:* Jack Cardiff; *W:* Beverley Cross, Berkely Mather; *C:* Christopher Challis; *M:* Dusan Radic.

Long Shot **1981** Two foosball enthusiasts work their way through local tournaments to make enough money to make it to the World Championships in Tahoe. **100m/C VHS.** Ian Giatti.

Long Time Gone 🦴 **1986** An over-the-hill detective tries to solve a murder while dealing with his bratty, alienated 11-year-old son. **97m/C VHS.** Paul Le-Mat, Wil Wheaton, Ann Dusenberry, Barbara Stock; *D:* Robert Butler. **TV**

The Long Voyage Home 🦴🦴🦴½ **1940** A talented cast performs this must-see screen adaptation of Eugene O'Neill's play about crew members aboard a merchant steamer in 1939. Wayne plays a young lad from Sweden who is trying to get home and stay out of trouble as he and the other seaman get shore leave. **105m/B VHS.** John Wayne, Thomas Mitchell, Ian Hunter, Barry Fitzgerald, Mildred Natwick, John Qualen; *D:* John Ford; *C:* Gregg Toland. N.Y. Film Critics '40: Director (Ford).

The Long Walk Home 🦴🦴🦴 **1989 (PG)** In Montgomery Alabama, in the mid 1950s, sometime after Rosa Parks refused to sit in the black-designated back of the bus, Martin Luther King Jr. led a bus boycott. Spacek is the affluent wife of a narrow-minded businessman while Goldberg is their struggling maid. When Spacek discovers that Goldberg is supporting the boycott by walking the nine-mile trek to work, she sympathizes and tries to help, antagonizing her husband. The plot marches inevitably toward a white-on-white showdown on racism while quietly exploring gender equality between the women. Outstanding performances by Spacek and Goldberg, and a great 50s feel. **95m/C VHS.** Sissy Spacek, Whoopi Goldberg, Dwight Schultz, Ving Rhames, Dylan Baker; *D:* Richard Pearce; *W:* John Cork; *C:* Roger Deakins; *M:* George Fenton; ***Nar:*** Mary Steenburgen.

A Long Way Home 🦴🦴 **1981** A grown man searches for his long-lost siblings, after the three of them were given up for adoption after birth. **97m/C VHS.** Timothy Hutton, Brenda Vaccaro, Rosanna Arquette, Paul Regina, George Dzundza, John Lehne, Bonnie Bartlett; *D:* Robert Markowitz; *C:* Ralf Bode; *M:* William Goldstein. **TV**

The Longest Day 🦴🦴🦴½ **1962** The complete story of the D-Day landings at Normandy on June 6, 1944, as seen through the eyes of American, French, British, and German participants. Exhaustively accurate details and extremely talented cast make this one of the all-time great Hollywood epic productions. The first of the big budget, all-star war productions; based on the book by Cornelius Ryan. Three directors share credit. Also available in a colorized version. **179m/C VHS, DVD, Wide.** John Wayne, Richard Burton, Red Buttons, Robert Mitchum, Henry Fonda, Robert Ryan, Paul Anka, Mel Ferrer, Edmond O'Brien, Fabian, Sean Connery, Roddy McDowall, Arletty, Curt Jurgens, Rod Steiger, Jean-Louis Barrault, Peter Lawford, Robert Wagner, Sal Mineo, Leo Genn, Richard Beymer, Jeffrey Hunter, Stuart Whitman, Eddie Albert, Tom Tryon, Alexander Knox, Ray Danton, Kenneth More, Richard Todd, Gert Frobe, Christopher Lee; *D:* Bernhard Wicki, Ken Annakin, Andrew Marton; *W:* James Jones, David Pursall, Jack Seddon, Romain Gary; *C:* Jean (Yves, Georges) Bourgoin, Pierre Levent, Henri Persin, Walter Wottitz; *M:* Maurice Jarre. Oscars '62: B&W Cinematog.

The Longest Drive 🦴🦴 *The Quest* **1976** Two brothers comb the wildest parts of the West for their sister, whom they believe is living with Indians. TV movie originally titled "The Quest," which became a brief television series. Highlights include colorful performances from the veteran actors and a unique horse/camel race. A continuation of the series is available on video as "The Captive: The Longest Drive 2." **92m/C VHS, DVD.** Kurt Russell, Tim Matheson, Brian Keith, Keenan Wynn, Neville Brand, Cameron Mitchell, Morgan Woodward, Iron Eyes Cody, Luke Askew; *D:* Lee H. Katzin. **TV**

The Longest Yard 🦴🦴🦴 **1974 (R)** A one-time pro football quarterback, now an inmate, organizes his fellow convicts into a football team to play against the prison guards. Of course, he's being pressured by the evil warden to throw the game. One of the all-time classic football movies. Filmed on location at Georgia State Prison. **121m/C VHS, DVD, Wide.** Sonny Shroyer, Michael Conrad, James Hampton, Harry Caesar, Charles Tyner, Mike Henry, Anitra Ford, Michael Fox, Joe Kapp, Pepper Martin, Robert Tessier, Burt Reynolds, Eddie Albert, Bernadette Peters, Ed Lauter, Richard Kiel; *D:* Robert Aldrich; *W:* Tracy Keenan Wynn; *C:* Joseph Biroc; *M:* Frank DeVol. Golden Globes '75: Film—Mus./Comedy.

Longitude 🦴🦴🦴 **2000** In 1714, England's Parliament offered a large reward to anyone who could discover a way to accurately measure longitude at sea to prevent nautical disasters. Carpenter John Harrison (Gambon) decided on a mechanical solution in the form of a clock (now known as the marine chronometer) and strove to have his ideas excepted (for 40 years). His story is paralleled with that of shellshocked ex-WWI soldier Rupert Gould (Irons), who discovered Harrison's neglected originals and became equally obsessed with restoring them to working order. The performances carry the somewhat diffuse plot. Based on the book by Dava Sobel. **200m/C VHS, DVD.** *GB* Jeremy Irons, Michael Gambon, Anna Chancellor, Ian Hart, Peter Vaughan, Gemma Jones, John Wood, Stephen Fry, Alec McCowen, Frank Finlay, John Standing, Samuel West, Bill Nighy, Brian Cox, Barbara Leigh-Hunt, Clive Francis, Daragh O'Malley, Tim (McInnerny) McInnery, Nicholas (Nick) Rowe; *D:* Charles Sturridge; *W:* Charles Sturridge; *C:* Peter Hannan; *M:* Geoffrey Burgon. **TV**

The Longshot woof! **1986 (PG-13)** Four bumblers try to raise cash to put on a sure-bet racetrack tip in this sorry comedy. Mike Nichols is the executive producer. **89m/C VHS.** Tim Conway, Harvey Korman, Jack Weston, Ted Wass, Jonathan Winters, Stella Stevens, Anne Meara; *D:* Paul Bartel; *W:* Tim Conway, John Myhers; *M:* Charles Fox.

Longtime Companion 🦴🦴🦴½ **1990 (R)** Critically acclaimed film follows a group of gay men and their friends during the 1980s. The closely knit group monitors the progression of the AIDS virus from early news reports until it finally hits home and begins to take the lives of their loved ones. One of the first films to look at the situation in an intelligent and touching manner. Produced by the PBS "American Playhouse" company. **100m/C VHS, DVD, Wide.** Stephen Caffrey, Patrick Cassidy, Brian Cousins, Bruce Davison, John Dossett, Mark Lamos, Dermot Mulroney, Mary-Louise Parker, Michael Schoeffling, Campbell Scott, Robert Joy, Brad O'Hara; *D:* Norman Rene; *W:* Craig Lucas; *C:* Tony Jennelli. Golden Globes '91: Support. Actor (Davison); Ind. Spirit '91: Support. Actor (Davison); N.Y. Film Critics '90: Support. Actor (Davison); Natl. Soc. Film Critics '90: Support. Actor (Davison); Sundance '90: Aud. Award.

Look Back in Anger 🦴🦴🦴½ **1958** Based on John Osbourne's famous play, the first British "angry young man" film, in which a squalor-living lad takes out his anger on the world by seducing his friend's wife. **99m/B VHS, DVD, Wide.** *GB* Richard Burton, Claire Bloom, Mary Ure, Edith Evans, Gary Raymond, Glen Byam Shaw, George Devine, Donald Pleasence, Phyllis Neilson-Terry; *D:* Tony

Richardson; *W:* John Osborne, Nigel Kneale; *C:* Oswald Morris; *M:* John Addison.

Look Back in Anger && **1980** A working class man angered by society's hypocrisy lashes out at his upper class wife, his mistress, and the world. Inferior remake of 1958 film version starring Richard Burton, based on '50s stage hit. **100m/C VHS.** Malcolm McDowell, Lisa Banes, Fran Brill, Raymond Hardie, Lindsay Anderson.

Look Back in Anger &&& **1989** There's something about John Osborne's play that brings out the angry young man in British leads. Richard Burton played Osborne's irascible guy in 1958, Malcom McDowell looked back angrily in '80, and now Branagh convincingly vents his spleen on wife and mistress in this made for British TV production. Director Jones earlier filmed "84 Charing Cross Road" and "Jackknife." **114m/C VHS.** *GB* Kenneth Branagh, Emma Thompson, Gerard Horan, Siobhan Redmond; *D:* David Hugh Jones. **TV**

Look for the Silver Lining &&½ **1949** Insipid musical biography of Broadway star Marilyn Miller (Haver). Bolger is the highlight as Miller's mentor from vaudeville to the Great White Way. ♫Look for the Silver Lining; Whip-Poor-Will; A Kiss in the Dark; Pirouette; Just a Memory; Time On My Hands; Wild Rose; Shine On Harvest Moon; Back, Back, Back to Baltimore. **100m/C VHS.** June Haver, Ray Bolger, Gordon MacRae, Charlie Ruggles, Rosemary DeCamp, S.Z. Sakall; *D:* David Butler; *W:* Phoebe Ephron, Henry Ephron, Marian Spitzer.

Look Out Sister &&& **1948** Jordan and an all-black cast star in this musical satire of westerns. "Two Gun" Jordan saves a dude ranch from foreclosure and wins the girl. Lots of black culture, slang and music from the '40s. Broad but enjoyable humor. ♫Caldonia; Don't Burn the Candle at Both Ends. **64m/B VHS.** Louis Jordan, Suzette Harbin, Monte Hawley, Maceo B. Sheffield; *D:* Bud Pollard.

Look Who's Laughing && **1941** Bergen's plane lands in a town conveniently populated by radio stars. Not much plot here, but it might be worth a look to fans of the stars including Jim and Marion Jordan, better known as Fibber McGee and Molly. **79m/B VHS.** Edgar Bergen, Jim Jordan, Marian Jordan, Lucille Ball, Harold (Hal) Peary, Lee Bonnell, Charles Halton; *D:* Allan Dwan.

Look Who's Talking &&& **1989 (PG-13)** When Alley bears the child of a married, and quite fickle man, she sets her sights elsewhere in search of the perfect father; Travolta is the cabbie with more on his mind than driving Alley around and babysitting. All the while, the baby gives us his views via the voice of Bruce Willis. A very light comedy with laughs for the whole family. **90m/C VHS, DVD.** John Travolta, Kirstie Alley, Olympia Dukakis, George Segal, Abe Vigoda; *D:* Amy Heckerling; *W:* Amy Heckerling; *M:* David Kitay; *V:* Bruce Willis.

Look Who's Talking Now &½ **1993 (PG-13)** Continuing to wring revenue from a tired premise, the family dogs throw in their two cents in the second sequel to "Look Who's Talking." For anyone who thinks Diane Keaton's hair makes her look a little like a hound dog, here's a chance to visualize her as a similarly long-eared poodle with an attitude. DeVito is also cast in character as the voice of a rough street-smart mutt, who happens to get thrown into the same household as the bosses' pure-bred poodle. Sparks, Alpo, and butt jokes fly as the dogs mark their territory. Meanwhile, dimwit wife Alley is worried that husband Travolta is having an affair, and is determined to get him back. **95m/C VHS, DVD.** John Travolta, Kirstie Alley, Olympia Dukakis, George Segal, Lysette Anthony; *D:* Tom Ropelewski; *W:* Leslie Dixon, Tom Ropelewski; *C:* Oliver Stapleton; *M:* William Ross; *V:* Diane Keaton, Danny DeVito.

Look Who's Talking, Too & **1990 (PG-13)** If Academy Awards for Stupidest Sequel and Lamest Dialogue existed, this diaper drama would have cleaned up. The second go-round throws the now married accountant-cabbie duo into a marital tailspin when Alley's babysitting brother moves in and the Saturday Night dancer moves out. Meanwhile, Willis cum baby smartasses incessantly. A once-clever gimmick now unencumbered by plot; not advised for linear thinkers. The voice of Arnold, though, is a guarantee you'll get one laugh for your rental. **81m/C VHS, DVD, 8mm, Wide.** Kirstie Alley, John Travolta, Olympia Dukakis, Elias Koteas; *D:* Amy Heckerling; *W:* Amy Heckerling, Neal Israel; *C:* Thomas Del Ruth; *M:* David Kitay; *V:* Bruce Willis, Mel Brooks, Damon Wayans, Roseanne.

The Lookalike && **1990 (PG-13)** Cable adaptation of Kate Wilhelm's novel. Bereaved mother Gilbert questions her sanity when she thinks she sees her daughter after she was killed in an automobile accident. Could this girl provide answers to questions about her past? **88m/C VHS.** Melissa Gilbert, Diane Ladd, Frances Lee McCain, Jason Scott Lee, Thaao Penghlis; *D:* Gary Nelson; *W:* Linda J. Bergman. **CABLE**

Looker &½ **1981 (PG)** Stunning models are made even more beautiful by a plastic surgeon, but one by one they begin to die. Finney plays the Beverly Hills surgeon who decides to investigate when he starts losing all his clients. **94m/C VHS.** Albert Finney, James Coburn, Susan Dey, Leigh Taylor-Young; *D:* Michael Crichton; *W:* Michael Crichton.

Lookin' to Get Out &&½ **1982 (R)** Comedy about two gamblers running from their debts. They wind up at the MGM Grand in Las Vegas trying to get out of a mess. **70m/C VHS.** Ann-Margret, Jon Voight, Burt Young; *D:* Hal Ashby; *M:* John Beal, Miles Goodman.

Looking for an Echo &&½ **1999 (R)** Vince (Assante) is a widower pushing 50 who had some teen success in a do-wop group and then put his singing aside to marry and raise his kids. His middle son, Anthony (Balerini), is now bringing up dad's old dreams (and some regrets) by being in his own rock band. But Vince's main concerns are for youngest child, Tina (Romano), who's in the hospital battling leukemia. This puts Vince in the flirty orbit of brassy nurse Joanne (Venora), who would like to offer the guy some personal care. Assante supplies lots of charm in a glossy, sentimental tearjerker. **97m/C VHS, DVD.** Armand Assante, Diane Venora, Joe Grifasi, Tom Mason, Anthony John (Tony) Denison, Edoardo Ballerini, David Margulies, Christy Romano; *D:* Martin Davidson; *W:* Martin Davidson, Jeffrey Goldenberg, Robert Held; *C:* Charles Minsky.

Looking for Miracles &&½ **1990 (G)** Two brothers, separated during the Depression because of poverty, get a chance to cultivate brotherly love when they're reunited in 1935. A Wonderworks production based on the A.E. Hochner novel. **104m/C VHS.** Zachary Bennett, Greg Spottiswood, Joe Flaherty.

Looking for Mr. Goodbar && **1977 (R)** Young teacher Keaton seeks companionship and love by frequenting single's bars and furthers her self-destruction by her aimless intake of drugs and alcohol. In need of a father figure, she makes herself available to numerous men and eventually regrets her hedonistic behavior. Unpleasant, aimless characters do little for this dreary film, whose sexual theme sparked a bit of public conversation when first released. Based on the bestselling novel by Judith Rossner. Oscar nominations for supporting actress Weld, and cinematography. **136m/C VHS.** Diane Keaton, Tuesday Weld, Richard Gere, Tom Berenger, William Atherton, Richard Kiley; *D:* Richard Brooks; *W:* Richard Brooks; *C:* William A. Fraker.

Looking for Richard &&& **1996 (PG-13)** A Shakespearean "Vanya on 42nd Street," "Richard" is the first semi-documentary addition to the barrage of Bard adaptations. Pacino's protracted pic dwells on a filmmaker's struggles to understand the play. Punctuated with comic relief, Pacino makes a pilgrimage to the Globe Theatre, taps Brit theatre heavyweights Gielgud and Redgrave for thoughts on interpreting Shakespeare, and combs New York for candid "man in the street" impressions in a quest to bring his subject to a wider public. Over the course of four years, Pacino, in various stages of facial hair growth, plays the deformed usurper with a cast of worthy Americans (Spacey, Kline, Ryder, Baldwin, and Quinn), illustrating key scenes of the play. **108m/C VHS.** Dominic Chianese, Paul Guilfoyle, Alec Baldwin, Winona Ryder, Kevin Spacey, Aidan Quinn, F. Murray Abraham, Kenneth Branagh, Kevin Conway, John Gielgud, James Earl Jones, Kevin Kline, Estelle Parsons, Vanessa Redgrave, Harris Yulin, Penelope Allen, Al Pacino; *D:* Al Pacino; *C:* Robert Leacock; *M:* Howard Shore. Directors Guild '96: Feature Doc. (Pacino).

Looking for Trouble & **1996 (PG)** Lame kid-friendly movie finds young Jaime (Butler) befriending a baby circus elephant she names Trouble, who has an abusive owner. When the circus leaves town, worried Jaime follows along. **73m/C VHS.** Holly Butler, Shawn McAllister, Art Turk; *D:* Peter Tors, Jay Aubrey; *W:* Peter Tors, Jay Aubrey.

The Looking Glass War && **1969 (PG)** Polish defector is sent behind the Iron Curtain on a final mission to photograph a rocket in East Berlin. He's guided by frustrated British security officers Rogers and Richardson, who both offer sly turns. An otherwise slow-moving adaptation of John Le Carre's bestselling spy novel. **108m/C VHS.** *GB* Christopher Jones, Ralph Richardson, Pia Degermark, Anthony Hopkins, Susan George, Paul Rogers; *D:* Frank Pierson; *W:* Frank Pierson.

Looney Looney Looney Bugs Bunny Movie &&& *Friz Freleng's Looney Looney Looney Bugs Bunny Movie* **1981 (G)** A feature-length compilation of classic Warner Bros. cartoons tied together with new animation. Cartoon stars featured include Bugs Bunny, Elmer Fudd, Porky Pig, Yosemite Sam, Duffy Duck, and Foghorn Leghorn. **80m/C VHS.** *D:* Isadore "Friz" Freleng, Chuck Jones, Bob Clampett; *V:* Mel Blanc, June Foray.

Loophole && *Break In* **1983** An out-of-work architect, hard pressed for money, joins forces with an elite team of expert criminals, in a scheme to make off with millions from the most established holding bank's vault. **105m/C VHS.** *GB* Albert Finney, Martin Sheen, Susannah York, Robert Morley, Colin Blakely, Jonathan Pryce; *D:* John Quested.

Loose Cannons & **1990 (R)** Yet another mismatched-cop-partner comedy, wherein a mystery is ostensibly solved by a veteran cop and a schizophrenic detective. **95m/C VHS.** Gene Hackman, Dan Aykroyd, Dom DeLuise, Ronny Cox, Nancy Travis, David Alan Grier; *D:* Bob (Benjamin) Clark; *W:* Bob (Benjamin) Clark, Richard Matheson.

Loose Connections && **1987** A feminist driving to a convention in Europe advertises for a travelmate, and gets a hopeless chauvinist who is masquerading as a gay man in this offbeat cult comedy. **90m/C VHS.** *GB* Lindsay Duncan, Stephen Rea, Robbie Coltrane; *D:* Richard Eyre.

Loose in New York && **198?** Much to her surprise, a cynical socialite begins to fall for her computer-arranged mate. **91m/C VHS.** Rita Tushingham, Aldo Maccione; *D:* Gian Luigi Polidoro.

Loose Screws & **1985 (R)** Four perverted teenagers are sent to a restrictive academy where they continue their lewd ways in this stupid sequel to "Screwballs." **75m/C VHS.** *CA* Bryan Genesse, Karen Wood, Alan Deveau, Jason Warren; *D:* Rafal Zielinski; *W:* Michael Cory.

Loot ... Give Me Money, Honey! &&½ **1970** Black comedy about a motley crew of greed-driven gold-diggers who chase after a heisted fortune in jewels, which is hidden in a coffin belonging to one of the thieves' mother. From Joe Orton's play. **101m/C VHS.** *GB* Richard Attenborough, Lee Remick, Hywel Bennett, Milo O'Shea, Roy Holder; *D:* Silvio Narizzano.

Lord Jim &&& **1965** A ship officer (O'Toole) commits an act of cowardice that results in his dismissal and disgrace, which leads him to the Far East in search of self-respect. Excellent supporting cast. Based on Joseph Conrad's novel. **154m/C VHS.** Peter O'Toole, James Mason, Curt Jurgens, Eli Wallach, Jack Hawkins, Paul Lukas, Akim Tamiroff, Daliah Lavi, Andrew Keir, Jack MacGowran, Walter Gotell; *D:* Richard Brooks; *W:* Richard Brooks; *C:* Frederick A. (Freddie) Young.

Lord of Illusions &&½ *Clive Barker's Lord of Illusions* **1995 (R)** New York P.I. Harry D'Amour (Bakula), who has an affinity for the occult, becomes involved with Dorothea (Janssen), the supposed widow of magician Philip Swann (O'Connor). As Harry investigates he discovers some terrifying secrets, including resurrected cult leader Nix (Von Bargen). Gruesome effects rather than excessive gore but you'll feel like you've been dropped in the middle of a plot without a clear idea what's happening. Bakula's Harry obviously has more stories to tell but Janssen's Dorothea, while attractive, is just around to cower. Barker directs from his own short story "The Last Illusion." The unrated director's cut clocks in at 120 minutes. **109m/C VHS, DVD.** Scott Bakula, Famke Janssen, Kevin J. O'Connor, Daniel von Bargen, Joel Swetow, Barry Sherman, Jordan Marder, Joseph Latimore, Vincent Schiavelli; *D:* Clive Barker; *W:* Clive Barker; *C:* Ronn Schmidt; *M:* Simon Boswell.

Lord of the Flies &&&½ **1963** Proper English schoolboys stranded on a desert island during a nuclear war are transformed into savages. A study in greed, power, and the innate animalistic/survivalistic instincts of human nature. Based on William Golding's novel, which he described as a "journey to the darkness of the human heart." **91m/B VHS, DVD.** *GB* James Aubrey, Tom Chapin, Hugh Edwards, Roger Elwin, Tom Gamen; *D:* Peter Brook; *W:* Peter Brook; *C:* Tom Hollyman; *M:* Raymond Leppard.

Lord of the Flies && **1990 (R)** Inferior second filming of the famed William Golding novel about schoolboys marooned on a desert island who gradually degenerate into savages. Lushly photographed, yet redundant and poorly acted. **90m/C VHS, DVD, 8mm, Wide.** Balthazar Getty, Danuel Pipoly, Chris Furrh, Badgett Dale, Edward Taft, Andrew Taft; *D:* Harry Hook; *W:* Sara Schiff; *C:* Martin Fuhrer; *M:* Philippe Sarde.

The Lord of the Rings && **1978 (PG)** An animated interpretation of Tolkien's classic tale of the hobbits, wizards, elves, and dwarfs who inhabit Middle Earth. Animator Ralph Bakshi used live motion animation (roto-scoping) to give his characters more life-like and human motion. Well done in spite of the difficulty of adapting from Tolkien's highly detailed and lengthy works. **128m/C VHS, DVD, Wide.** *D:* Ralph Bakshi; *W:* J.C. (Chris) Conkling, Peter S. Beagle; *V:* Christopher Guard, John Hurt.

Lord of the Rings 1: The Fellowship of the Rings &&&½ **2001 (PG-13)** The first in Jackson's trilogy of films based on the books by J.R.R. Tolkein. Young hobbit Frodo Baggins, after inheriting a mysterious ring from his uncle Bilbo, must leave his home in order to keep it from falling into the hands of its evil creator. Along the way, a fellowship is formed to protect the ringbearer and make sure that the ring arrives at its final destination: Mt. Doom, the only place where it can be destroyed. Jackson's amazing visuals bring the imaginary world and mythology of Tolkein to life. The three and a half hour pic stays closer to the original novel than any of the previous efforts (all animated), while still managing to keep a quick enough pace for those unfamiliar with the lengthy literary work. Should get repeated viewing in parents' basements for years to come. **178m/C VHS, DVD.** Elijah Wood, Ian McKellen, Liv Tyler, Viggo Mortensen, Sean Astin, Cate Blanchett, John Rhys-Davies, Dominic Monaghan, Billy Boyd, Orlando Bloom, Christopher Lee, Hugo Weaving, Sean Bean, Ian Holm, Andy Serkis, Marton Csokas; *D:* Peter Jackson; *W:* Peter Jackson, Fran Walsh, Philippa Boyens; *C:* Andrew Lesnie; *M:* Howard Shore. Oscars '01: Cinematog.; British Acad. '01: Director (Jackson), Film, Visual FX; L.A. Film Critics '01: Score; Natl. Bd. of Review '01: Support. Actress (Blanchett); Screen Actors Guild '01: Support. Actor (McKellen); Broadcast Film Critics '01: Song ("May It Be"), Score.

The Lords of Discipline ♪♪½ 1983 (R) A military academy cadet is given the unenviable task of protecting a black freshman from racist factions at a southern school circa 1964. Based on Pat Conroy's autobiographical novel. **103m/C VHS.** David Keith, Robert Prosky, Barbara Babcock, Judge Reinhold, G.D. Spradlin, Rick Rossovich, Michael Biehn, Bill Paxton, Matt Frewer; *D:* Franc Roddam; *C:* Brian Tufano; *M:* Howard Blake.

The Lords of Flatbush ♪♪½ 1974 (PG) Four street toughs battle against their own maturation and responsibilities in 1950s Brooklyn. Winkler introduces the leather-clad hood he's made a career of and Stallone introduces a character not unlike Rocky. Interesting slice of life. **88m/C VHS, DVD, Wide.** Sylvester Stallone, Perry King, Henry Winkler, Susan Blakely, Armand Assante, Paul Mace; *D:* Stephen Verona, Martin Davidson; *M:* Joseph Brooks.

Lords of Magick ♪ 1988 (PG-13) Two warriors chase an evil sorcerer and the princess he's kidnapped across time to the 20th century. **98m/C VHS.** Jarrett Parker, Matt Gauthier, Brendan Dillon Jr.; *D:* David Marsh.

Lords of the Deep woof! 1989 (PG-13) A Roger Corman cheapie about underwater technicians trapped on the ocean floor with a race of aliens. A film rushed out to capitalize on the undersea sci-fi subgenre highlighted by "The Abyss." **95m/C VHS.** Bradford Dillman, Priscilla Barnes, Melody Ryane, Eb Lottimer, Daryl Haney; *Cameos:* Roger Corman; *D:* Mary Ann Fisher; *W:* Howard R. Cohen, Daryl Haney.

Lorenzo's Oil ♪♪♪ 1992 (PG-13) Based on the true story of Augusto and Michaela Odone's efforts to find a cure for their five-year-old, Lorenzo, diagnosed with the rare and incurable disease ALD (Adrenoleukodystrophy). Confronted by a slow-moving and clinically cold medical community, the Odones embark on their own quest for a cure. Sarandon delivers an outstanding and emotionally charged performance as Lorenzo's determined mother. Nolte is his equally devoted Italian father, complete with black hair and hand gestures. They are a powerful presence in a film which could have easily degenerated into a made-for-TV movie, but is instead a tribute to what love and hope can accomplish. **135m/C VHS, Wide.** Nick Nolte, Susan Sarandon, Zach O'Malley-Greenberg, Peter Ustinov, Kathleen Wilhoite, Gerry Bamman, Margo Martindale, James Rebhorn, Ann Hearn, Elizabeth (E.G. Dailey) Daily; *D:* George Miller; *W:* George Miller, Nick Enright; *C:* John Seale.

The Loretta Claiborne Story ♪♪½ 2000 Your basic inspirational TV movie based on a true story. Loretta (Elise) is black, poor, partially blind, and mildly retarded. She's mercilessly teased until a grade-school teacher (Palk) interests the young Loretta in running. But it's not until she's a teenager that Loretta finds her own cheerleader—social worker Janet McFarland (Manheim) who signs the girl up to participate in the Special Olympics. **90m/C VHS.** Kimberly Elise, Camryn Manheim, Tina Lifford, Nancy Palk, Damon Gupton, Nicole Ari Parker; *D:* Lee Grant; *W:* Grace McKeaney; *C:* Laszlo George; *M:* Stanley Clarke. **TV**

Lorna Doone ♪♪½ 1922 A young girl of royal descent is kidnapped and raised by the bandit Doone family in the highlands of Scotland. Adapted from the novel by R.D. Blackmore. **79m/B VHS.** Madge Bellamy, John Bowers; *D:* Maurice Tourneur.

Lorna Doone ♪♪½ 1934 Early version of the R.D. Blackmore novel about an English farmer who falls in love with the daughter of an outlaw family. Set in rural England in the 1600s; remade in 1951 and 1990. **90m/B VHS.** *GB* Victoria Hopper, John Loder, Margaret Lockwood, Roy Emerton, Mary Clare, Edward Rigby, Roger Livesey; *D:* Basil Dean; *W:* Miles Malleson.

Lorna Doone ♪♪½ 1990 (PG) Classic romance set in 17th-century England and based on the novel by R.D. Blackmore. John Ridd (Bean) vows to destroy the land-grabbing Doone family, whom he blames for the death of his parents. Then he meets, and immediately falls in love with, the beautiful and innocent Lorna Doone (Walker). **90m/C VHS.** *GB* Sean Bean, Polly Walker, Clive Owen, Billie Whitelaw; *D:* Andrew Grieve; *W:* Matthew Jacobs. **TV**

Lorna Doone ♪♪♪ 2001 Based on R.D. Blackmore's novel, which is set in the west country of 17th-century Britain, this swashbuckler is a star-crossed romance with an ultimately happy ending. John Ridd (Coyle) is a common farmer who discovers that Lorna (Warner), the young beauty he loves, is a member of the infamous Doone clan—a once aristocratic family that has turned outlaw. To make things worse for John, Lorna is already betrothed to the violent Carver Doone (Gillen) who will do anything to keep her. **150m/C VHS, DVD.** *GB* Richard Coyle, Amelia Warner, Aidan Gillen, Martin Clunes, Michael Kitchen, Martin Jarvis, Barbara Flynn, Peter Vaughan, Anton Lesser, Jack Shepherd; *D:* Mike Barker; *W:* Adrian Hodges; *C:* Chris Seager; *M:* John Lunn. **TV**

Los Locos Posse ♪♪ 1997 (R) Uneven would-be sequel to 1993's "Posse." Chance (Van Peebles) is a black military scout who is found, injured, by one of the unhinged denizens of a nearby mission. The Mother Superior enlists Chance to lead the nuns and their "Los Locos" charges to another mission some hundred miles away. The trip doesn't go smoothly and their arrival only leads to more problems. First English-language feature for Montreal director Vallee. **100m/C VHS.** Mario Van Peebles, Rene Auberjonois, Paul Lazar, Danny Trejo, Melora Walters, Rusty Schwimmer; *D:* Jean-Marc Vallee; *W:* Mario Van Peebles; *C:* Pierre Gill; *M:* Lesley Barber.

Los Olvidados ♪♪♪½ *The Young and the Damned* 1950 From surrealist Bunuel, a powerful story of the poverty and violence of young people's lives in Mexico's slums. In Spanish with English subtitles. **88m/B VHS.** *MX* Alfonso Mejias, Roberto Cobo; *D:* Luis Bunuel. Cannes '51: Director (Bunuel), Film.

Loser ♪½ 1997 (R) Very low-budget street drama concerns young small-time drug dealer James Dean Ray (Harris) and his self-destruction slide towards oblivion. **90m/C VHS, DVD.** Kirk Harris, Jonathon Chaus, Peta Wilson, Norman Salect, Jack Rubio; *D:* Kirk Harris; *W:* Kirk Harris; *C:* Kent Wakeford.

Loser ♪♪ 2000 (PG-13) College comedy finds nerdy midwesterner Biggs branded a loser by his dorm mates at New York University. He's also pining over beauty Suvari, who's having an affair with heartless prof Kinnear. Writer-director Heckerling's trademark sympathy for the adolescent outcast is intact, but this outing is missing the insight, subtlety, and (most importantly) the fun of her earlier efforts. Biggs and Suvari give passable performances, but Kinnear is the bright spot. **95m/C VHS, DVD, Wide.** Jason Biggs, Mena Suvari, Greg Kinnear, Zak Orth, Dan Aykroyd, Tom Sadoski, Jimmi Simpson, Colleen Camp, Robert Miano, Andy Dick, David Spade, Steven Wright, Taylor Negron, Andrea Martin, Scott Thompson; *D:* Amy Heckerling; *W:* Amy Heckerling; *C:* Rob Hahn; *M:* David Kitay.

The Losers ♪½ 1970 (R) Four motorcyclists are hired by the U.S. Army to rescue a presidential advisor who is being held captive by Asian bad guys. **96m/C VHS.** William Smith, Bernie Hamilton, Adam Roarke, Houston Savage, Brad Johnson, Vernon Wells; *D:* Jack Starrett.

Losin' It ♪♪ 1982 (R) Four teens travel across the Mexican border to Tijuana on a journey to lose their virginity. Cruise meets a married woman who says she is in town for a divorce, while the others become caught up in frenzied undertakings of their own. **104m/C VHS, DVD.** Tom Cruise, John Stockwell, Shelley Long, Jackie Earle Haley, John P. Navin Jr.; *D:* Curtis Hanson; *W:* Bill W.L. Norton; *C:* Gilbert Taylor; *M:* Kenneth Wannberg.

Losing Chase ♪♪½ 1996 (R) Bacon makes his directorial debut in this drama that features wife Sedgwick as Elizabeth, mother's helper to Chase (Mirren) and Richard Philips (Bridges) at their summer home on Martha's Vineyard. Chase is still recovering from a mental breakdown, having spent several months in an institution, and she resents Elizabeth's presence, constantly criticizing her. But when the two women are alone together a confusing and emotional bond gradually begins to form between them. **95m/C VHS.** Helen Mirren, Kyra Sedgwick, Beau Bridges; *D:* Kevin Bacon; *W:* Anne Meredith; *C:* Dick Quinlan; *M:* Michael Bacon. **CABLE**

Losing Isaiah ♪♪♪ 1994 (R) "Kramer vs. Kramer" meets the movie-of-the-week in this controversial and emotionally moving story of a social worker (Lange) who adopts the title character, an African American baby abandoned by his drug-addicted mother (Berry). Courtroom battle ensues when four years later mom, now clean and sober, discovers Isaiah is alive. She enlists the aid of a lawyer (Jackson) known for his high-profile, racially charged cases. Lange and Berry lead the parade of fine performances. Taking on some volatile issues, director Gyllenhaal manages (for the most part) to refrain from melodrama. Based on the novel by Seth Margolis. **108m/C VHS.** Jessica Lange, Halle Berry, David Strathairn, Samuel L. Jackson, Cuba Gooding Jr., Latanya Richardson; *D:* Stephen Gyllenhaal; *W:* Naomi Foner; *C:* Andrzej Bartkowiak; *M:* Mark Isham.

The Loss of Sexual Innocence ♪½ 1998 (R) Figgis' ambitious film follows the fall from grace (literally of Adam and Eve), and the nature of sex, love, jealousy, and violence. Unfortunately, this turns out to be less than scintillating material. Interspered with scenes from the Garden of Eden story is that of dissatisfied filmmaker Nic (Sands), as he relives his past and ponders his unhappy present. **101m/C VHS, DVD, Wide.** Julian Sands, Saffron Burrows, Stefano Dionisi, Jonathan Rhys Meyers, Kelly Macdonald, Femi Ogumbanjo, Hanne Klintoe, Johanna Torrel, George Moktar, John Cowey; *D:* Mike Figgis; *W:* Mike Figgis; *C:* Benoit Delhomme; *M:* Mike Figgis.

Lost ♪½ 1983 A young girl runs away into the wilderness because of the resentment she feels toward her new stepfather. **92m/C VHS.** Sandra Dee, Don Stewart, Ken Curtis, Jack Elam, Sheila Newhouse.

Lost ♪♪ 1986 When their boat capsizes in the Pacific, three sailors desperately cling to life, drifting aimlessly for 74 days. Based on a true story, this film is adult-fare. **93m/C VHS.** *CA* Michael Hogan, Helen Shaver, Kenneth Welsh; *D:* Peter Rowe.

Lost and Delirious ♪♪ 2001 Teen angst, romance, and sexuality taken to extremes. Shy Mouse (Barton) is trying to settle in at her exclusive girls' boarding school with new roomies, wealthy Tory (Pare) and wild Paulie (Perabo). When Mouse realizes that the girls are lovers she takes it in stride but Tory gets anxious and denies the relationship. Mouse watches helplessly as Paulie gets increasingly desperate to win Tory back and matters take a turn for the baroque. Based on the novel "The Wives of Bath" by Susan Swan. **100m/C VHS, DVD, Wide.** *CA* Mischa Barton, Piper Perabo, Jessica Pare, Jackie Burroughs, Graham Greene, Mimi Kuzyk, Luke Kirby; *D:* Lea Pool; *W:* Judith Thompson; *C:* Pierre Gill; *M:* Yves Chamberland. Genie '01: Cinematog.

Lost and Found ♪♪½ 1979 (PG) An American professor of English and an English film production secretary fall in love on a skiing vacation. Good cast but Segal and Jackson did romance better in "A Touch of Class." **104m/C VHS.** George Segal, Glenda Jackson, Maureen Stapleton, Hollis McLaren, John Cunningham, Paul Sorvino, John Candy, Martin Short; *D:* Melvin Frank; *W:* Jack Rose.

Lost and Found ♪ 1999 (PG-13) The only, repeat ONLY, reason to see this movie is Sophie Marceau. Spade, in a bold bit of casting, plays Dylan, a sniveling pipsqueak taken with his French neighbor Lila (the aforementioned Marceau). In a sick attempt to win her love, he kidnaps her dog in order to "find" him a few days later. When the dog swallows an anniversary ring Dylan's holding for a friend, many tasteless dog poo jokes ensue. Wants to be "There's Something About Mary," but doesn't have its winking sense of absurdity. Spade should stick to the snarky sidekick roles and Marceau should fire whoever told her that this would be a good career move. **97m/C VHS, DVD.** David Spade, Sophie Marceau, Artie Lange, Martin Sheen, Patrick Bruel, Jon Lovitz, Mitchell Whitfield, Carole Cook, Estelle Harris, Marla Gibbs, Natalie Barish, Phil Leeds, Christian Clemenson, Daphnee Lynn Duplaix; *D:* Jeff Pollack; *W:* J.B. Cook, Marc Meeks, David Spade; *C:* Paul Elliott; *M:* John Debney.

Lost Angels ♪♪½ 1989 (R) A glossy "Rebel Without a Cause" '80s reprise providing a no-holds-barred portrait of life in the fast lane. A wealthy, disaffected San Fernando Valley youth immerses himself in sex, drugs and rock 'n' roll. Ultimately he is arrested and sent by his parents to a youth home, where a dedicated therapist assists his tortuous road back to reality. **116m/C VHS.** Donald Sutherland, Adam Horovitz, Amy Locane, Kevin Tighe, John C. McGinley, Graham Beckel, Park Overall, Don Bloomfield, Celia Weston; *D:* Hugh Hudson; *W:* Michael Weller; *M:* Philippe Sarde.

Lost Battalion ♪♪½ 2001 True story based on the heroism of U.S. Major Charles Whittlesey (Schroder), who won the Congressional Medal of Honor during the closing days of WWI. Part of the Army's 77th Division, Whittlesey and his troops find themselves separated from their allies and surrounded by German forces in the Argonne Forest. Whittlesey led his men on a five-day defensive back to Allied lines despite limited supplies and constant battle. **100m/C VHS, DVD.** Rick Schroder, Jamie Harris, Phil McKee, Jay Rodan, Adam James; *D:* Russell Mulcahy; *W:* James (Jim) Carabatsos; *C:* Jonathan Freeman; *M:* Rick Marvin. **CABLE**

Lost Boundaries ♪♪½ 1949 Respected physician Scott Carter (debut role for Ferrer) and his family live and work in a small New Hampshire town, hiding the fact that they are black, passing for white, in their segregated society. But then the truth becomes known. Strong, if slow-moving, and based on a true story; the use of white leads for black roles was common casting. **99m/B VHS.** Mel Ferrer, Beatrice Pearson, Richard Hylton, Susan Douglas, Canada Lee, Carleton Carpenter, Seth Arnold, Wendell Holmes; *D:* Alfred Werker; *W:* Virginia Shaler, Eugene Ling, Charles A. Palmer, Furland de Kay; *C:* William J. Miller; *M:* Louis Applebaum.

The Lost Boys ♪♪ 1987 (R) Santa Cruz seems like a dull town when Michael, his younger brother, and their divorced mom move into their eccentric grandfather's home. But when Michael falls for a pretty girl with some hard-living friends he takes on more than he imagines—these partying teens are actually a group of vampires. Some humor, some bloodletting violence, and an attractive cast help out this updated vampire tale. Rock-filled soundtrack. **97m/C VHS, DVD, 8mm, Wide.** Jason Patric, Kiefer Sutherland, Corey Haim, Jami Gertz, Dianne Wiest, Corey Feldman, Barnard Hughes, Edward Herrmann, Billy Wirth, Jamison Newlander, Brooke McCarter, Alex Winter; *D:* Joel Schumacher; *W:* Jeffrey Boam, Janice Fischer, James Jeremias; *C:* Michael Chapman; *M:* Thomas Newman.

Lost Canyon ♪♪ 1943 Hoppy tries to help a fugitive who's been framed for bank robbery. This is the second installment distributed by United Artists. The song "Jingle, Jangle, Jingle" is sung by the Sportsman Quartet. **61m/B VHS.** William Boyd, Jay Kirby, Andy Clyde, Lola Lane, Douglas Fowley, Herbert Rawlinson; *D:* Lesley Selander.

The Lost Capone ♪♪♪ 1990 (PG-13) Cable TV version of the story of Al Capone's youngest brother, a clean living small town sheriff who struggles with his sibling's reputation at every turn. **93m/C VHS.** Dominic Chianese, Ally Sheedy, Eric Roberts, Adrian Pasdar, Titus Welliver, Jimmie F. Skaggs, Maria Pitillo, Anthony Crivello; *D:* John Gray; *W:* John Gray; *C:* Paul Elliott. **CABLE**

The Lost Child ♪♪½ 2000 Remarkable true story about a search for identity. Rebecca (Ruehl) always knew she was adopted, being raised Jewish in Pennsylvania. After her adoptive parents are both dead, Rebecca decides to search for her birth parents and discovers that she is a full-blooded Navaho who was taken from her family on the reservation. She immediately decides to take her children to meet her relatives in Arizona, where they are welcomed into the community. But it isn't so simple for Rebecca's husband, Jack (Sheridan), to deal with his outsider status. Based on the autobiography "Looking for Lost Bird" by Yvette Melanson and Claire Safran. **100m/C VHS.** Mercedes Ruehl, Jamey Sheridan, Irene Bedard, Dinah Manoff, Ned Romero, Tantoo Cardinal, Michael Greyeyes, Julia McIlvaine; ***D:*** Karen Arthur; ***W:*** Sally Robinson; ***C:*** Thomas Neuwirth; ***M:*** Mark McKenzie. **TV**

The Lost City 🦴🦴 **1934** A feature version of the rollicking vintage movie serial about a lost jungle city, adventurers and mad scientists. **74m/B VHS.** William "Stage" Boyd, Kane Richmond, George "Gabby" Hayes, Claudia Dell; ***D:*** Harry Revier.

Lost City of the Jungle **1945** 13-chapter serial focusing on a crazed Atwill, in his last screen role, believing that he can rule the world from the heart of a deep, dark jungle by utilizing a special mineral. The final Universal serial. **169m/B VHS.** Russell Hayden, Lionel Atwill, Jane Adams; ***D:*** Ray Taylor, Lewis D. Collins.

The Lost Command 🦴🦴½ **1966** A French colonel, relieved of his command, endeavors to regain power by battling a powerful Arab terrorist with his own specially trained platoon of soldiers. Crisp adventure set in post-WWII North Africa. Based on "The Centurions" by Jean Larteguy. **129m/C** Anthony Quinn, Michele Morgan, George Segal, Alain Delon, Maurice Ronet, Claudia Cardinale; ***D:*** Mark Robson; ***C:*** Robert L. Surtees.

The Lost Continent 🦴½ **1951** An expedition searching for a lost rocket on a jungle island discovers dinosaurs and other extinct creatures. **82m/B VHS, DVD.** Cesar Romero, Hillary Brooke, Chick Chandler, John Hoyt, Acquanetta, Sid Melton, Whit Bissell, Hugh Beaumont; ***D:*** Sam Newfield; ***W:*** Richard H. Landau; ***C:*** Jack Greenhalgh; ***M:*** Paul Dunlap.

Lost Diamond 🦴 **1974** Bumbling spies search for a smuggled gem. **83m/C VHS.** Juan Ramon, Sonia Rivas, Ricardo Bauleo.

The Lost Empire 🦴 **1983 (R)** Three bountiful and powerful women team up to battle the evil Dr. Syn Do. **86m/C VHS.** Melanie Vincz, Raven De La Croix, Angela Aames, Paul Coufos, Robert Tessier, Angus Scrimm, Angelique Pettyjohn, Kenneth Tobey; ***D:*** Jim Wynorski; ***W:*** Jim Wynorski.

The Lost Empire 🦴½ **2001** Lavish but muddled (and ultimately dull) story originally broadcast as a four-hour miniseries. American businessman Nicholas Orton (Gibson), who once studied Chinese literature and history, meets cute with a mystery woman who turns out to be Kwan Ying (Ling), the Goddess of Mercy. She tells Nick he has 3 days to save the human world from slavery by saving the classic Chinese manuscript "The Journey to the West" from falling into the wrong hands. Helping Nick are characters from the story, including the anarchic Monkey King (Wong). **134m/C VHS, DVD.** Thomas Gibson, Bai Ling, Russell Wong, Ric Young, Kabir Bedi, Henry O; ***D:*** Peter Macdonald; ***W:*** David Henry Hwang; ***C:*** David Connell; ***M:*** John Altman. **TV**

Lost for Words 🦴🦴🦴 **1999** Aging and the parent/child bond has never been more bittersweet and amusing as in this British production, which is based on the memoirs of Deric Longden (he also wrote the teleplay). Elderly Annie (88-year-old Hird in a touchingly tart performance) lives alone, with her middleaged son Deric (Postlethwaite) and his blind wife Aileen (Downie) popping in to offer support and company. But then a series of strokes rob Annie of her ability to speak coherently and of her cherished independence. **90m/C VHS.** *GB* Thora Hird, Pete Postlethwaite, Penny Downie, Tom Higgins; ***D:*** Alan J.W. Bell; ***W:*** Deric Longden. **TV**

Lost Highway 🦴🦴 **1996 (R)** Welcome once again to Lynch-world—that parallel universe understood only by master David. Jazz musician Fred Madison (Pullman) is on Death Row—supposedly for the murder of his wife Renee (Arquette). Only why does young mechanic Pete Dayton (Getty) wind up in Fred's cell (with Fred missing)? Oh, and why does gangster Mr. Eddy (Loggia) have a girlfriend named Alice (Arquette again) who looks just like Renee? And is she real—or did Fred conjure her up? Who's the Mystery Man (Blake), who literally looks like death warmed over. And.....well, you get the idea. Or maybe you're not supposed to. **135m/C VHS.** Bill Pullman, Patricia Arquette, Balthazar Getty, Robert Loggia, Robert (Bobby) Blake, Gary Busey, Jack Nance, Richard Pryor, Natasha Gregson Wagner, Lisa Boyle, Michael Massee, Jack Kehler, Henry Rollins, Gene Ross, Scott Coffey; ***D:*** David Lynch; ***W:*** David Lynch, Barry Gifford; ***C:*** Peter Deming; ***M:*** Angelo Badalamenti.

Lost Honeymoon 🦴🦴 **1947** Monkeyshines abound as a soldier marries a girl while in a state of amnesia, and then wakes up to find twin daughters. **70m/B VHS.** Franchot Tone, Ann Richards; ***D:*** Leigh Jason.

The Lost Honor of Katharina Blum 🦴🦴🦴 *Die Verlorene Ehre Der Katharina Blum* **1975 (R)** A woman becomes involved with a man who's under police surveillance and finds her life open to public scrutiny and abuse from the media and the government. Based on Heinrich Boll's prize-winning novel. In German with English subtitles. Remade for TV as "The Lost Honor of Kathryn Beck." **97m/C VHS.** *GE* Angela Winkler, Mario Adorf, Dieter Laser, Juergen Prochnow; ***D:*** Volker Schlondorff, Margarethe von Trotta.

Lost Horizon 🦴🦴🦴🦴 **1937** A group of strangers fleeing revolution in China are lost in the Tibetan Himalayas and stumble across the valley of Shangri La. The inhabitants of this Utopian community have lived for hundreds of years in kindness and peace—but what will the intrusion of these strangers bring? The classic romantic role for Colman. Capra's directorial style meshed perfectly with the pacifist theme of James Hilton's classic novel, resulting in one of the most memorable films of the 1930s. This version restores more than 20 minutes of footage which had been cut from the movie through the years. **132m/B VHS, DVD, Wide.** Ronald Colman, Jane Wyatt, H.B. Warner, Sam Jaffe, Thomas Mitchell, Edward Everett Horton, Isabel Jewell, John Howard, Margo; ***D:*** Frank Capra; ***W:*** Robert Riskin; ***C:*** Joseph Walker; ***M:*** Dimitri Tiomkin. Oscars '37: Film Editing.

Lost in a Harem 🦴🦴½ **1944** Abbott & Costello play magicians in a theatrical troupe stranded in a desert kingdom ruled by an evil sheik. The sheik's nephew (and rightful heir) hires the two to steal some magic rings and the pretty Maxwell to play footsie with his susceptible uncle in an attempt to regain his kingdom. Average comedy with musical numbers by Jimmy Dorsey and His Orchestra. **89m/B VHS.** Bud Abbott, Lou Costello, Marilyn Maxwell, John Conte, Douglass Dumbrille, Lottie Harrison; ***D:*** Charles Reisner.

Lost in Alaska 🦴🦴½ **1952** Up in the Alaskan wilderness, Abbott & Costello save Ewell from a greedy saloon owner and his cohorts who are trying to get their hands on Ewell's fortune. **87m/B VHS.** Bud Abbott, Lou Costello, Tom Ewell, Mitzie Green, Bruce Cabot, Emory Parnell, Jack Ingram, Rex Lease; ***D:*** Jean Yarbrough; ***W:*** Martin Ragaway, Leonard Stern; ***M:*** Henry Mancini.

Lost in America 🦴🦴🦴 **1985 (R)** After deciding that he can't "find himself" at his current job, ad exec David Howard and his wife sell everything they own and buy a Winnebago to travel across the country. This Albert Brooks comedy is a must-see for everyone who thinks that there is more in life than pushing papers at your desk and sitting on "Mercedes leather." **91m/C VHS, DVD, Wide.** Albert Brooks, Julie Hagerty, Michael Greene, Tom Tarpey, Garry Marshall, Art Frankel; ***D:*** Albert Brooks; ***W:*** Albert Brooks, Monica Johnson; ***M:*** Arthur B. Rubinstein. Natl. Soc. Film Critics '85: Screenplay.

Lost in Space 🦴🦴½ **1998 (PG-13)** Big-screen remake of the cheesy 60s sci-fi TV show retains the basic plot and premise, but jettisons the camp. in 2058, the Robinsons and pilot Don West (LeBlanc) are chosen to pioneer the colonization of a far-off world because Earth has become nearly uninhabitable. The evil Dr. Smith (Oldman) sabotages the mission but gets stuck on board. Once the family is appropriately lost, the story veers into familiar sci-fi territory of apparently-deserted spaceships, marauding aliens, and time warps. It's visually impressive, but writer Goldsman can't resist turning the Robinsons into an annoying collection of 1990s dysfunction. The plot pretty much hinges on Dad's lousy parenting skills, and the kids are disaffected and resentful. Eye-candy effects, the occasionally witty inside joke for fans of the show, and Oldman's deliciously oily Smith provide plenty of fun, but where's the giant carrot? **131m/C VHS, DVD.** William Hurt, Mimi Rogers, Gary Oldman, Heather Graham, Matt LeBlanc, Lacey Chabert, Jack Johnson, Lennie James, Jared Harris, Mark Goddard, Edward Fox, Adam Sims; ***Cameos:*** June Lockhart, Marta Kristen, Angela Cartwright; ***D:*** Stephen Hopkins; ***W:*** Akiva Goldsman; ***C:*** Peter Levy; ***M:*** Bruce Broughton; ***V:*** Dick Tufeld.

Lost in the Barrens 🦴🦴 **1991** Two young boys, one a Canadian Indian and the other a rich white boy, get lost in the wilderness of the Canadian north. Out of necessity and common need they become close and form a lifelong friendship. Based on the book by Farley Mowat. **95m/C VHS.** *CA* Graham Greene, Nicholas Shields.

Lost in the Bermuda Triangle 🦴½ **1998 (PG)** Brian (Verica) searches for his wife Mary (Haag), who was lost at sea, and gets sucked into the same parallel universe she was transported to after they entered the Bermuda Triangle. Dumb and dull. **88m/C VHS.** Tom Verica, Graham Beckel, Ron Canada, Charlotte d'Amboise, Christina Haag; ***D:*** Norberto Barba; ***M:*** Christopher Franke. **TV**

Lost in Yonkers 🦴🦴½ *Neil Simon's Lost in Yonkers* **1993 (PG)** Arty and Jay are two teenage brothers who, while their widowed father looks for work, are sent to live with their stern grandmother, small-time gangster uncle, and childlike aunt in 1942 New York. Ruehl reprises her Tony award-winning performance as Aunt Bella, who loses herself in the movies while trying to find a love of her own, out from under the oppressive thumb of her domineering mother (Worth). Performances by the adults are more theatrical than necessary but the teenagers do well in their observer roles. Based on the play by Neil Simon, which again chronicles his boyhood. **114m/C VHS, DVD, Wide.** Mercedes Ruehl, Irene Worth, Richard Dreyfuss, Brad Stoll, Mike Damus, David Strathairn, Robert Miranda, Jack Laufer, Susan Merson; ***D:*** Martha Coolidge; ***W:*** Neil Simon; ***M:*** Elmer Bernstein.

The Lost Jungle **1934** Circus legend Beatty searches for his girl and her dad in the jungle. Animal stunts keep it interesting. Serial in 12 chapters, 13 minutes each. **156m/B VHS.** Clyde Beatty, Cecilia Parker, Syd Saylor, Warner Richmond, Wheeler Oakman; ***D:*** Armand Schaefer, David Howard.

The Lost Language of Cranes 🦴🦴🦴 **1992** David Leavitt's novel is transported from New York to present-day London but the wrenching emotional drama remains the same. A family is in crisis as long-hidden secrets concerning homosexuality and infidelity are finally revealed. The title refers to one character's social worker's thesis on a young boy from a dysfunctional family who imitates the movements of the building cranes he sees. Fine performances by all. Adult sexual situations. **90m/C VHS.** *GB* Brian Cox, Eileen Atkins, Angus Macfadyen, Corey Parker, Cathy Tyson; ***Cameos:*** John Schlesinger, Rene Auberjonois; ***D:*** Nigel Finch; ***C:*** Remi Adefarasin.

Lost Legacy: A Girl Called Hatter Fox 🦴🦴½ **1977** Tradition and technology are at odds in the life of a young Indian girl. Strong cast makes this work. **100m/C VHS.** Ronny Cox, Joanelle Romero, Conchata Ferrell; ***D:*** George Schaefer. **TV**

Lost, Lonely, and Vicious 🦴 **1959** Clayton is a suicidal Hollywood actor who spends much of his time indulging his penchant for women, figuring he may as well enjoy what little time he has left. Then he meets Wilson, a drugstore clerk who moves him to reconsider his self-destructive ways. **73m/B VHS.** Ken Clayton, Barbara Wilson, Lilyan Chauvin, Richard Gilden, Carole Nugent, Sandra Giles, Allen Fife, Frank Stallworth, Johnny Erben, Clint Quigley, T. Earl Johnson; ***D:*** Frank Myers; ***W:*** Norman Graham; ***C:*** Ted Saizis, Vincent Saizis; ***M:*** Frederick David.

The Lost Man 🦴🦴½ **1969 (PG-13)** Odd, updated remake of 1947's "Odd Man Out," which was based on the novel by F.L. Green. Jason (Poitier) leads a group of black militants in robbing a factory in order to provide money for some civil rights organizations. Two are killed during the crime, which leads to various police shootouts. Meanwhile, Jason enlists the help of white social worker Cathy (Shimkus) to help him escape the country. **122m/C VHS.** Sidney Poitier, Joanna Shimkus, Al Freeman Jr., Michael (Lawrence) Tolan, Richard Dysart, Paul Winfield, Bernie Hamilton, Dolph Sweet, David Steinberg; ***D:*** Robert Arthur; ***W:*** Robert Arthur; ***C:*** Gerald Perry Finnerman; ***M:*** Quincy Jones.

The Lost Missile 🦴🦴 **1958** A lost, alien missile circles the Earth, causing overheating and destruction on the planet's surface. A scientist works to find a way to save the planet before it explodes into a gigantic fireball. Director Burke's last film. **70m/B VHS.** Robert Loggia, Ellen Parker, Larry Kerr, Phillip Pine, Marilee Earle; ***D:*** William Berke.

Lost Moment 🦴🦴 **1947** A publisher travels to Italy to search for a valuable collection of a celebrated author's love letters, but finds a neurotic woman in his way. Based on Henry James' "Aspern Papers." **89m/B VHS.** Robert Cummings, Agnes Moorehead, Susan Hayward; ***D:*** Martin Gabel; ***C:*** Hal Mohr.

The Lost One 🦴🦴 *Der Verlone* **1951** A German scientist's lover is suspected of selling his findings to England during WWII. Based on a true story; Lorre's only directorial outing. **97m/B VHS.** *GE* Peter Lorre, Karl John, Renate Mannhardt; ***D:*** Peter Lorre.

The Lost Patrol 🦴🦴🦴½ **1934** WWI British soldiers lost in the desert are shot down one by one by Arab marauders as Karloff portrays a religious soldier convinced he's going to die. The usual spiffy Ford exteriors peopled by great characters with a stirring score. Based on the story, "Patrol" by Philip MacDonald. **66m/B VHS.** Victor McLaglen, Boris Karloff, Reginald Denny, Wallace Ford, Alan Hale, J.M. Kerrigan, Billy Bevan, Brandon Hurst, Douglas Walton; ***D:*** John Ford; ***W:*** Dudley Nichols, Garrett Fort; ***C:*** Harold Wenstrom; ***M:*** Max Steiner.

Lost Planet Airmen 🦴½ **1949** A feature-length condensation of the 12-part sci-fi serial "King of the Rocket Men." Rocket Man is pitted against the sinister Dr. Vulcan in this intergalactic battle of good and evil. **65m/B VHS.** Tristram Coffin, Mae Clarke, Dale Van Sickel; ***D:*** Fred Brannon.

The Lost Platoon **1989 (R)** A troop of soldiers are transformed into vampires. **120m/C VHS.** David Parry, William Knight, Sean Heyman; ***D:*** David A. Prior.

The Lost Son 🦴🦴 **1998 (R)** Former French narcotics cop Xavier Lombard (Auteuil) has relocated to London where he works as a P.I. An ex-colleague, Carlos (Hinds), asks Lombard to locate his wife Deborah's (Kinski) missing brother Leon, a photographer who has somehow gotten involved with a pedophile ring. Lombard eventually tracks the supposed leader of the ring to Mexico but finds his ultimate answer lies closer to home. A serious topic undone by a one-dimensional script. **102m/C VHS.** *GB FR* Daniel Auteuil, Katrin Cartlidge, Ciaran Hinds, Nastassia Kinski, Bruce Greenwood, Marianne (Cuau) Denicourt, Billie Whitelaw; ***D:*** Chris Menges; ***W:*** Eric Leclere, Margaret Leclere, Mark Mills; ***C:*** Barry Ackroyd; ***M:*** Goran Bregovic.

Lost Souls 🦴½ **2000 (R)** If the devil keeps showing up in second-rate horror flicks like this, he should get himself an agent. Although in all likelihood he probably is an agent. At any rate, he's back and trying to take over the world again by possessing the body of atheistic New York crime journalist Peter Kelson (Chaplin). Maya (Ryder), a former possession victim herself, is one of a group of New York exorcists who become aware of the conspiracy. She tries to convince the cynical Peter, but he scoffs at the idea until he begins to experience creepy hallucinations. Rent "The Exorcist" instead. Directorial debut of "Saving Private Ryan" and "Schindler's List" cinematographer Kaminski, who offers up some beautiful scenes in the midst of an ugly movie. **98m/C VHS, DVD, Wide.** Winona Ryder, Ben Chaplin, John Hurt, Elias Koteas, John Diehl, W. Earl Brown, Sarah Wynter, Philip Baker Hall, Brian Reddy, John Beasley, Victor Slezak, Brad Greenquist; ***D:*** Janusz Kaminski; ***W:*** Pierce Gardner, Betsy Stahl; ***C:*** Mauro Fiore; ***M:*** Jan A.P. Kaczmarek.

Lost Squadron 🦴🦴½ **1932** A look at the dangers stuntmen go through in movie-making. **79m/B VHS.** Richard Dix, Erich von Stroheim; ***D:*** George Archainbaud; ***M:*** Max Steiner.

The Lost Stooges **1933** From the trio's one year at MGM, rare clips of them performing their famous slaptick gags. In black and white and color. **68m/B VHS.** Moe Howard, Curly Howard, Larry Fine, Clark Gable, Joan Crawford, Jimmy Durante, Robert Montgomery; ***Nar:*** Leonard Maltin.

The Lost Tribe 🦴 **1989** A man takes his wife on a trek through the jungle to find his lost brother. **96m/C VHS.** John Bach, Darien Teakle; ***D:*** John Laing.

The Lost Weekend 🦴🦴🦴🦴 **1945** The heartrending Hollywood masterpiece about alcoholism, depicting a single weekend in the life of struggling writer Don Birnam (Milland), who cannot believe he's addicted until he finally hits bottom. Except for its pat ending, it is an uncompromising, startlingly harsh treatment, with Milland giving one of the industry's bravest lead performances ever. Acclaimed then and now. **100m/B VHS, DVD.** Ray Milland, Jane Wyman, Phillip Terry, Howard da Silva, Doris Dowling, Frank Faylen, Mary (Marsden) Young; ***D:*** Billy Wilder; ***W:*** Charles Brackett, Billy Wilder; ***C:*** John Seitz; ***M:*** Miklos Rozsa. Oscars '45: Actor (Milland), Director (Wilder), Picture, Screenplay; Cannes '46: Actor (Milland), Film; Golden Globes '46: Actor—Drama (Milland), Director (Wilder), Film—Drama; Natl. Bd. of Review '45: Actor (Milland); N.Y. Film Critics '45: Actor (Milland), Director (Wilder), Film.

The Lost World 🦴🦴½ **1925** A zoology professor leads a group on a South American expedition in search of the "lost world," where dinosaurs roam in this silent film. Based on a story by Sir Arthur Conan Doyle. A 90-minute version includes the film's original trailer and a recreation of some of the missing footage (the film was released at 108 minutes). **93m/B VHS, DVD.** Wallace Beery, Lewis Stone, Bessie Love, Lloyd Hughes; ***D:*** Harry Hoyt; ***W:*** Marion Fairfax; ***C:*** Arthur Edeson. Natl. Film Reg. '98.

The Lost World 🦴🦴½ **1992** "Land of the Lost"/"Jurassic Park" themes, based on the story by Sir Arthur Conan Doyle. A scientific team ventures deep into uncharted African jungles where they find themselves confronted by dinosaurs and other dangers. **99m/C VHS.** John Rhys-Davies, David Warner; ***D:*** Timothy Bond.

The Lost World: Jurassic Park 2 🦴🦴½ *Jurassic Park 2* **1997 (PG-13)** Sequel to "Jurassic Park," proves only that Spielberg has tapped this well one too many times. It's four years after the first adventure and the surviving dinos have peacefully set up house on a deserted island near Costa Rica. Mathematician Ian Malcolm (Goldblum, reprising his role) reluctantly becomes part of an expedition to monitor the beasts, only because his paleontologist girlfriend (Moore) is so gung-ho. Other characters exist, but are reduced to the role of entrees. More dinos (two T-Rexs, a clan of Raptors, and bite-sized newcomers Compsognathus), thrilling special effects, and more gore make up for thin subplots involving a rich businessman who wants to use the dinosaurs for a new zoo and another who hunts them for sport. Ironically, Spielberg's predictablity owes much to better films such as "King Kong," "Aliens" and "Godzilla." Still, T-Rex and buddies, the true stars, rise to the occasion to entertain in an otherwise lackluster sequel. Based on Michael Crichton's book. **129m/C VHS, DVD, Wide.** Jeff Goldblum, Julianne Moore, Vince Vaughn, Richard Attenborough, Arliss Howard, Pete Postlethwaite, Peter Stormare, Vanessa Lee Chester, Richard Schiff, Harvey Jason, Thomas F. Duffy, Ariana Richards, Joseph Mazzello; ***D:*** Steven Spielberg; ***W:*** David Koepp; ***C:*** Janusz Kaminski; ***M:*** John Williams.

Lost Zeppelin 🦴🦴 **1929** A dirigible becomes lost in the wastes of Antarctica, forcing its passengers to combat the elements. Impressive special effects and miniatures for its time. **73m/B VHS.** Conway Tearle, Virginia Valli, Ricardo Cortez, Duke Martin, Kathryn McGuire; ***D:*** Edward Sloman.

Lotna 🦴🦴½ **1964** Wadja's first color film serves as a tribute to the Polish calvary who fought against the Germans in WWII. The story is told through the trials of a horse that passes to various military officials until it breaks a leg and must be shot. Wadja himself is the son of a cavalryman killed in the war. Polish with subtitles. **89m/C VHS.** *PL* Bozena Kurowska, Jerzy Pichelski, Jerzy Moes, Adam Pawlikowski; ***D:*** Andrzej Wajda; ***W:*** Andrzej Wajda, Wojciech Zukrowski; ***C:*** Jerzy Lipman; ***M:*** Tadeusz Baird.

Lots of Luck 🦴🦴 **1985** A knee-slapping comedy about a family that wins the million-dollar lottery and sees that money doesn't solve all problems. **88m/C VHS.** Martin Mull, Annette Funicello, Fred Willard, Polly Holliday, Hamilton Camp, Vincent Schiavelli; ***D:*** Peter Baldwin; ***M:*** William Goldstein. **CABLE**

Lottery Bride 🦴🦴½ **1930** In this charming musical, Jeanette MacDonald is the lottery bride who is won by the brother of the man she really loves. A fine outing for all involved, particularly the supporting cast. ♫You're an Angel; My Northern Lights; Come Drink to the Girl That You Love; Yubla; Round She Whirls; Shoulder to Shoulder; High and Low; Napoli; Two Strong Men. **85m/B VHS.** Jeanette MacDonald, Joe E. Brown, ZaSu Pitts, John Garrick, Carroll Nye; ***D:*** Paul Stein.

Lotto Land 🦴🦴½ **1995** Looks at the lives of black and Hispanic characters from the same Brooklyn neighborhood. Ambitious high school grad Hank (Gilliard, Jr.) works stocking shelves at the local liquor store for manager Flo (Costallos), who's raised Hank's girlfriend, the college-bound Joy (Gonzalez). The neighborhood's abuzz when someone in their area holds the winning ticket for a $27 million lottery, which was sold from Flo's store, but just who it is and what happens when the money is claimed leads to a dramatic twist. Debut for Rubino, who shows real affection for his characters. **90m/C VHS, DVD.** Larry Gilliard Jr., Barbara Gonzalez, Suzanne Costallos, Wendell Holmes, Jamie Tirelli, Luis Guzman, Paul Calderon; ***D:*** John Rubino; ***W:*** John Rubino; ***C:*** Rufus Standefer; ***M:*** Sherman Holmes, Wendell Holmes.

The Lotus Eaters 🦴🦴 **1993 (PG-13)** Sensitive family drama set in British Columbia in the 1960s about a wife who discovers her husband has fallen in love with their childrens' new teacher. Domestic angst done with naturalism and not without humor. **100m/C VHS.** *CA* Sheila McCarthy, R.H. Thomson, Michelle-Barbara Pelletier, Frances Hyland, Paul Soles; ***D:*** Paul Shapiro; ***W:*** Peggy Thompson. Genie '93: Actress (McCarthy), Orig. Screenplay, Sound.

Louisiana 🦴 **1987** A belle of the Old South tries to get back the family plantation by romancing the new owner, even though she loves someone else. Oh, and then the Civil War breaks out. **130m/C VHS.** Ian Charleson, Margot Kidder, Victor Lanoux, Len Cariou, Lloyd Bochner; ***D:*** Philippe de Broca. **TV**

Louisiana Purchase 🦴🦴½ **1941** Successful screen adaptation of the Broadway musical features several performers from the original cast, lavish costumes, and great musical numbers. As usual, Hope's comedy is extremely funny, especially his famous filibuster scene in Congress. Based on the stage musical by Morrie Ryskind and B. G. DeSylva. **95m/C VHS.** Bob Hope, Vera Zorina, Victor Moore, Dona Drake, Irene Bordoni, Raymond Walburn, Maxie "Slapsie" Rosenbloom, Frank Albertson, Barbara Britton; ***D:*** Irving Cummings.

Louisiana Story 🦴🦴🦴 **1948** The final effort by the master filmmaker, depicting the effects of oil industrialization on the southern Bayou country as seen through the eyes of a young boy. One of Flaherty's greatest, widely considered a premiere achievement. **77m/B VHS.** ***D:*** Robert Flaherty; ***M:*** Virgil Thomson. Natl. Film Reg. '94.

Loulou 🦴🦴🦴½ **1980 (R)** A woman leaves her middle-class husband for a leather-clad, uneducated jock who is more attentive. Romantic and erotic. In French with English subtitles. **110m/C VHS, DVD, Wide.** *FR* Isabelle Huppert, Gerard Depardieu, Guy Marchand; ***D:*** Maurice Pialat; ***W:*** Maurice Pialat, Arlette Langmann; ***C:*** Pierre William Glenn; ***M:*** Philippe Sarde.

The Lovable Cheat 🦴🦴 **1949** Pretty lame adapatation of Balzac's play "Mercadet Le Falseur," about a father who cons money from his friends in order to line up a marriage suitable for his daughter. **75m/B VHS.** Charlie Ruggles, Peggy Ann Garner, Richard Ney, Alan Mowbray, Iris Adrian, Ludwig Donath, Fritz Feld; ***D:*** Richard Oswald.

Love 🦴🦴½ *Szerelem* **1971** Torocsik, touted as Hungary's leading actress in the '70s, plays a young woman whose husband has been imprisoned for political crimes. Living in a cramped apartment with her mother-in-law, she keeps the news from the aged and dying woman (Darvas) by reading letters she's fabricated to keep alive the woman's belief that her son is a successful movie director in America. The story is punctuated by the older woman's dreamy remembrances of things past. Exceptional performances by both women, it was Darvas' final film. Based on two novellas by Tibor Dery. Hungarian with subtitles. **92m/B VHS.** *HU* Lili Darvas, Mari Torocsik, Ivan Darvas; ***D:*** Karoly Makk.

Love Affair 🦴🦴🦴½ **1939** Multi-kleenex weepie inspired countless romantic dreams of true love atop the Empire State Building. Dunn and Boyer fall in love on a ship bound for NYC, but they're both involved. They agree to meet later at, guess where, to see if their feelings hold true, but tragedy intevenes. Excellent comedy-drama is witty at first, more subdued later, with plenty of romance and melodrama. Remade in 1957 (by McCarey) as "An Affair to Remember," a lesser version whose popularity overshadows the original. Look for fleeting glimpses of Leslie, Beckett, and Mohr. Ignore the public domain video, which replaces the original music. Remade again in 1994 as "Love Affair." **87m/B VHS, DVD.** Irene Dunne, Charles Boyer, Maria Ouspenskaya, Lee Bowman, Astrid Allwyn, Maurice (Moscovitch) Moscovich, Scotty Beckett, Joan Leslie, Gerald Mohr, Dell Henderson, Carol Hughes; ***D:*** Leo McCarey; ***W:*** Leo McCarey, Delmer Daves, Donald Ogden Stewart; ***C:*** Rudolph Mate; ***M:*** Roy Webb.

Love Affair 🦴🦴 **1994 (PG-13)** Second remake of the timeless classic has a contemporary look and feel but doesn't justify a new version. The photogenic leads may meet on a plane, but never fear, the Empire State Building and a tragedy are still the main plot devices. The problem is viewers never feel drawn into their lives. Hepburn has a small but moving role as Beatty's aunt. Superb cinematography makes it easy on the eyes and Morricone's lush romantic score makes it easy on the ears, but ultimately, it's all gloss with little substance. Watch this one, but then set aside time to see the superior original (made in 1939) or the better known 1957 attempt "An Affair to Remember." **108m/C VHS, DVD.** Warren Beatty, Annette Bening, Katharine Hepburn, Garry Shandling, Chloe Webb, Pierce Brosnan, Kate Capshaw, Paul Mazursky, Brenda Vaccaro, Glenn Shadix, Barry Miller, Harold Ramis; ***D:*** Glenn Gordon Caron; ***W:*** Warren Beatty, Robert Towne; ***M:*** Ennio Morricone.

The Love Affair, or The Case of the Missing Switchboard Operator 🦴🦴🦴 *Switchboard Operator; Case of the Missing Switchboard Operator; Ljubarni Slucaj; An Affair of the Heart* **1967** Makavejev's second film, a dissertation on the relationship between sex and politics, involving an affair between a switchboard operator and a middle-aged ex-revolutionary, is told in the director's unique, farcically disjointed manner. In Serbian with English subtitles. **73m/B VHS.** *YU* Eva Ras, Slobodan Aligrudic, Ruzica Sokic; ***D:*** Dusan Makavejev; ***W:*** Dusan Makavejev.

Love Affair: The Eleanor & Lou Gehrig Story 🦴🦴🦴 **1977** The true story, told from Mrs. Gehrig's point of view, of the love affair between baseball great Lou Gehrig and his wife Eleanor from his glory days as a New York Yankee, to his battle with an incurable disease. Drama supported by Herrmann and Danner's convincing portrayals. **96m/C VHS.** Blythe Danner, Edward Herrmann, Patricia Neal, Ramon Bieri, Lainie Kazan; ***D:*** Fielder Cook. **TV**

Love After Love 🦴🦴 *Apres l'Amour* **1994** A look at sex and relationships among 30-something professionals in Paris. Lola (Huppert), a successful romance novelist, is suffering a crisis in both her career and, ironically, her love life. She is involved with two men who, in turn, are involved with different women who happen to have borne them children. The movie starts off with so much mate switching and secret sexual rendezvous, that by the second half, you really don't care who Lola ends up with. French with English subtitles. **104m/C VHS, DVD.** *FR* Isabelle Huppert, Hippolyte Girardot, Lio; ***D:*** Diane Kurys; ***W:*** Diane Kurys, Antoine Lacomblez; ***C:*** Fabio Conversi; ***M:*** Yves Simon, Serge Perathone, Jannick Top.

Love Among the Ruins 🦴🦴🦴 **1975** Romance about an aging, wealthy widow who, after being scandalously sued for breach of promise by her very young lover, turns for aid to an old lawyer friend who has loved her silently for more than 40 years. **100m/C VHS.** Laurence Olivier, Katharine Hepburn, Leigh Lawson, Colin Blakely; ***D:*** George Cukor; ***M:*** John Barry. **TV**

Love and a.45 🦴🦴 **1994 (R)** Satirical and violent road movie finds petty career criminal Watty Watts (Bellows) living in a Texas trailer park with gal Starlene (Zellweger), for whom he's just purchased an expensive engagement ring. But he's borrowed the money from some crazed gangster types who want the loan repaid in a timely fashion. Soon, the dippy duo are on the run to Mexico with a trail of dead bodies behind them and the media just delighted to make them the next tabloid darlings. **101m/C VHS, DVD.** Gil Bellows, Renee Zellweger, Rory Cochrane, Ann Wedgeworth, Peter Fonda, Jeffrey Combs, Jace Alexander; ***D:*** C.M. Talkington; ***W:*** C.M. Talkington; ***C:*** Tom Richmond; ***M:*** Tom Verlaine.

Love and Action in Chicago 🦴🦴 **1999 (R)** Eddie Jones (Vance) works for the State Department's Eliminator Corps, getting rid of anyone the government doesn't want around. Eddie wants to leave and make a new life with girlfriend Lois (King) but his bosses are pressing him to take one more job. And if he doesn't, he could become number one on the Corps hit parade. Although there's action, this one is of the black comedy variety with Vance particularly good as the reluctant hitman. **97m/C VHS, DVD.** Courtney B. Vance, Regina King, Jason Alexander, Kathleen Turner, Ed Asner; ***D:*** Dwayne Johnson-Cochran; ***W:*** Dwayne Johnson-Cochran; ***C:*** Phil Parmet; ***M:*** Russ Landau.

Love and Anarchy 🦴🦴🦴 *Film d'Amore et d'Anarchia* **1973** An oppressed peasant vows to assassinate Mussolini after a close friend is murdered. Powerful drama about the rise of Italian facism. In Italian with English subtitles. **108m/C VHS, DVD, Wide.** *IT* Giancarlo Giannini, Mariangela Melato; *D:* Lina Wertmuller; *W:* Lina Wertmuller; *C:* Giuseppe Rotunno; *M:* Nino Rota. Cannes '73: Actor (Giannini).

Love and Basketball **2000 (R)** Childhood friends and high school sweethearts Monica (Lathan) and Quincy (Epps) pursue their dreams of pro basketball careers and try to sort out their feelings for each other over a 12-year period. First-time director Prince-Bythewood avoids the cliches of most sports movies by removing the Big Game climax and replacing it with thoughtful character study and the understanding of the sacrifices athletes make to excel at their chosen profession. Leads Lathan and Epps are impressive. **124m/C VHS, DVD, Wide.** Omar Epps, Sanaa Lathan, Alfre Woodard, Dennis Haysbert, Debbi (Deborah) Morgan, Harry J. Lennix, Kyla Pratt, Glenndon Chatman; *D:* Gina Prince-Bythewood; *W:* Gina Prince-Bythewood; *C:* Reynaldo Villalobos; *M:* Terence Blanchard.

Love and Bullets ½ **1979 (PG)** An Arizona homicide detective is sent on a special assignment to Switzerland to bring a mobster's girlfriend back to the United States to testify against him in court. **95m/C VHS.** *GB* Charles Bronson, Jill Ireland, Rod Steiger, Strother Martin, Bradford Dillman, Henry Silva, Michael V. Gazzo; *D:* Stuart Rosenberg; *W:* Wendell Mayes; *C:* Fred W. Koenekamp; *M:* Lalo Schifrin.

Love and Death **1975 (PG)** In 1812 Russia, a condemned man reviews the follies of his life. Woody Allen's satire on "War and Peace," and every other major Russian novel. **89m/C VHS, DVD, Wide.** Woody Allen, Diane Keaton, Georges Adel, Despo Diamantidou, Frank Adu, Harold Gould; *D:* Woody Allen; *W:* Woody Allen; *C:* Ghislan Cloquet.

Love and Death on Long Island ½ **1997 (PG-13)** Stuffy English author Giles De'Ath (Hurt), barely on speaking terms with the 20th century, wanders into the wrong theatre, encounters a teen exploitation flick and becomes obsessed with Ronnie Bostock (Priestley), one of the movie's "stars." De'Ath's obsession leads to his discovery of fan magazines, TV, and video, which provide some moments of amusement as he comes to grips with the technology. It also leads Giles to seek out Bostock at his home on Long Island, where Hurt shines as Giles tries to reconcile his dignity and increasingly irrational behavior. Priestley does a fine job lampooning his own image (while not exactly dispelling it), and the supporting characters (especially Chaykin's diner owner) are appropriately quirky. Subtle reworking of "Death in Venice," based on a novel by Gilbert Adair, has its moments, but is probably best enjoyed by the same type of people who would like De'Ath's books. **93m/C VHS, DVD.** *GB CA* John Hurt, Jason Priestley, Fiona Loewi, Sheila Hancock, Maury Chaykin, Gawn Grainger, Elizabeth Quinn; *D:* Richard Kwietniowski; *W:* Richard Kwietniowski; *C:* Oliver Curtis; *M:* Richard Grassby-Lewis.

Love and Faith **1978** Two lovers are torn between their love for each other and their faiths during 16th-century Japan. English subtitles. **154m/C VHS.** *JP* Toshiro Mifune, Takashi Shimura, Yoshiko Nakana; *D:* Kei Kumai.

Love and Hate: A Marriage Made in Hell ½ *Love and Hate: The Story of Colin and Joanne Thatcher* **1990** Marital murder mystery based on a true Canadian case. Joanne (Nelligan), the wife of wealthy rancher-politico Colin (Walsh), leaves her publicly charismatic and privately abusive husband with two thirds of their brood. A bitter battle for custody is waged, and Joanne is soon found savagely slain. The number one suspect: philandering ex-spouse Colin. Based on Maggie Siggins' "A Canadian Tragedy," the faux biography originally aired in two parts on Canadian TV. **156m/C VHS.** Kate Nelligan, Ken Walsh, Leon Pownall, John Colicos, Noam Zylberman, Victoria Snow, Cedric Smith, R.H. Thomson, Victoria Wauchope, Doris Petrie, Duncan Ollenenshaw; *D:* Francis Mankiewicz; *W:* Suzette Couture.

Love and Human Remains **1993 (R)** Director Arcand's first English-language film features a group of late 20ish urbanites trying to come to grips with their place in the world (and their sexuality). David (Gibson) is an ammoral Lothario who doesn't believe in love and can only manage casual gay relationships. He hangs out with a variety of friends, all of whom are trying to cope with their varying sexual natures. Melodramatic framing story about a serial murderer who may, or may not, be one of the principal characters proves somewhat of a distraction. Lots of caustically witty dialogue and some fine performances (particularly Gibson's); filmed in Montreal. Adaptation of the play "Unidentified Human Remains and the True Nature of Love" by Fraser, who also did the screenplay. **100m/C VHS.** *CA* Thomas Gibson, Ruth Marshall, Cameron Bancroft, Mia Kirshner, Joanne Vannicola, Matthew Ferguson, Rick Roberts; *D:* Denys Arcand; *W:* Brad Fraser; *C:* Paul Sarossy. Genie '94: Adapt. Screenplay.

Love & Murder ½ **1991 (R)** Poorly developed tale of a photographer and his bevy of with beautiful models involved with murder and love, not necessarily in that order. **87m/C VHS.** Todd Waring, Kathleen Lasky, Ron White, Wayne Robson; *D:* Steven Hilliard Stern.

Love and Other Catastrophes **1995 (R)** Short, low-budget first feature from 23-year-old Croghan engagingly focuses on 24 hours in the lives of five confused college students. Film students Alice (Garner) and Mia (O'Connor) need a third roommate for their new apartment. Danni (Mitchell), Mia's girlfriend, is upset that Mia doesn't want them living together, while Alice is eyeing potential boyfriends, including shy med student Michael (Day) and womanizing Ari (Dyktynski). Meanwhile, both Alice and Mia try to cope with various academic frustrations. **76m/C VHS.** *AU* Frances O'Connor, Alice Garner, Matt(hew) Day, Radha Mitchell, Matthew Dyktynski, Suzi Dougherty, Kim Gyngell; *D:* Emma-Kate Croghan; *W:* Emma-Kate Croghan, Yael Bergman, Helen Bandis; *C:* Justin Brickle; *M:* Oleh Witer.

Love and Rage **1999 (R)** James Lynchehaun (Craig) turns up on the remote island of Achill in 1896 and soon gets a job looking after the estate of wealthy widow Agnes MacDonnell (Scacchi). He also becomes her lover and the two engage in some unnerving psychosexual games that lead to Agnes' being brutalized by James. Based on a true story; adapted from the novel "The Playboy and the Yellow Lady" by James Carney. **100m/C VHS, DVD.** *IR GE GB* Daniel Craig, Greta Scacchi, Stephen (Dillon) Dillane, Donal Donnelly, Valerie Edmond; *D:* Cathal Black; *W:* Brian Lynch; *C:* Slawomir Idziak; *M:* Ralf Wienrich.

Love & Sex ½ **2000** Famke Janssen shines in her role as Kate, a manic L.A. magazine writer who nearly gets fired due to her inability to write about good relationships because she hasn't had many. She begins to remember fondly her relationship with Adam (Favreau), a doughy artist whose fast talk made up for his slow looks. Their relationship is traced from its initial spark to its last gasp, when Adam breaks up with Kate due to a feeling of complacency. Kate then attempts to make Adam jealous by dating a string of pretty-boy losers, including his favorite actor. Kate becomes increasingly depressed and Adam becomes increasingly obsessed, setting the stage for the inevitable happy ending. Good performances and chemistry between the lead actors saves this indie effort from feeling like a really long sitcom episode. **82m/C VHS, DVD.** Famke Janssen, Jon Favreau, Noah Emmerich, Ann Magnuson, Cheri Oteri, Josh Hopkins, Rob Knepper, Vincent Ventresca; *D:* Valerie Breiman; *W:* Valerie Breiman; *C:* Adam Kane.

Love and the Frenchwoman *La Francaise et L'Amour* **1960** A French tale tracing the nature of love through stages. Deals with a story about where babies come from, puppy love, saving sex for marriage, and the way some men treat women. **135m/B VHS.** *FR* Jean-Paul Belmondo, Pierre-Jean Vaillard, Marie-Jose Nat, Annie Girardot; *D:* Jean Delannoy; *M:* Georges Delerue.

Love at First Bite ½ **1979 (PG)** Intentionally campy spoof of the vampire film. Dracula is forced to leave his Transylvanian home as the Rumanian government has designated his castle a training center for young gymnasts. Once in New York, the Count takes in the night life and falls in love with a woman whose boyfriend embarks on a campaign to warn the city of Dracula's presence. Hamilton of the never-fading tan is appropriately tongue-in-cheek in a role which resurrected his career. **93m/C VHS.** George Hamilton, Susan St. James, Richard Benjamin, Dick Shawn, Arte Johnson, Sherman Hemsley, Isabel Sanford, Barry J. Gordon, Michael Pataki, Basil Hoffman, Eric Laneuville; *D:* Stan Dragoti; *W:* Robert Kaufman; *M:* Charles Bernstein.

Love at First Sight *Love is Blind; At First Sight* **1976** A pre-"Saturday Night Live" hack job for Aykroyd, playing a blind man who falls in love with a girl he bumps into. ♫Love at First Sight. **86m/C VHS.** Dan Aykroyd, Mary Ann McDonald, George Murray, Barry Morse; *D:* Rex Bromfield.

Love at Large **1989 (R)** Hired by a beautiful woman, a private detective accidentally follows the wrong man and winds up being followed himself. He vies with a female detective in solving this case of mistaken identity. **90m/C VHS.** Tom Berenger, Elizabeth Perkins, Anne Archer, Ann Magnuson, Annette O'Toole, Kate Capshaw, Ted Levine, Kevin J. O'Connor, Ruby Dee, Neil Young, Barry Miller; *D:* Alan Rudolph; *W:* Alan Rudolph; *C:* Elliot Davis.

Love at Stake ½ **1987 (R)** It's condo owners versus the witches in this charming parody that features a hilarious cameo by Dr. Joyce Brothers and a very sexy performance from Carrera. **83m/C VHS.** Patrick Cassidy, Kelly Preston, Bud Cort, Barbara Carrera, Stuart Pankin, Dave Thomas, Georgia Brown, Annie Golden; ***Cameos:*** Dr. Joyce Brothers; *D:* John Moffitt; *M:* Charles Fox.

Love at the Top ½ **1986** Ladies' foundation designer falls in love with her boss's son-in-law, jeopardizing her career. **90m/C** Janis Paige, Richard Young, Jim MacKrell; *D:* John Bowab.

The Love Bug ½ **1968 (G)** A race car driver (Jones) is followed home by Herbie, a white Volkswagen with a mind of its own. Eventually, Jones follows the "Love Bug" to a life of madcap fun. Followed by several sequels. **110m/C VHS.** Dean Jones, Michele Lee, Hope Lange, Robert Reed, Bert Convy; *D:* Robert Stevenson; *C:* Edward Colman; *M:* George Bruns.

The Love Bug ½ **1997** Herbie, the magical Volkswagen Beetle, is now owned by egotistical English nobleman Simon Moore III (Hannah), who junks him after he loses a race. Then Herbie gets a new owner, down-on-his-luck mechanic Hank (Campbell), who decides the little guy can make a comeback. And when Herbie sees Hank and his ex-girlfriend Alex (Wentworth) together, the car decides he should live up to his nickname and get the two back together. **88m/C VHS.** Bruce Campbell, John Hannah, Alexandra Wentworth, Kevin J. O'Connor, Mickey Dolenz, Dean Jones, Clarence Williams III, Harold Gould; *D:* Peyton Reed. **TV**

Love Butcher **1982 (R)** A crippled old gardener kills his female employers with his garden tools and cleans up neatly afterward. **84m/C VHS.** Erik Stern, Kay Neer, Robin Sherwood; *D:* Mikel Angel, Donald M. Jones.

Love by Appointment **1976** An unlikely romantic comedy with a very unlikely cast has two businessmen meeting up with European prostitutes. **96m/C VHS, DVD, Wide.** *IT* Ernest Borgnine, Robert Alda, Francoise Fabian, Corinne Clery; *D:* Armando Nannuzzi; *M:* Riz Ortolani. **TV**

Love Camp **1976** A woman is invited to a swinger's holiday camp, frolics for a while, then is told she can never leave. Suspenseful hijinks ensue. **100m/C VHS.** Laura Gemser, Christian Anders, Gabriele Tinti.

Love Can Seriously Damage Your Health ½ *Amor Perjudica Seriamente la Salud* **1996** At a gala dinner Santi (Puigcorbe) and Diana (Belen) are reunited. Thirty years before, young Beatles fan Diana (Cruz) hides out in John Lennon's room when the group comes to Madrid, reluctantly aided by young hotel bellman Santi (Diego). It's love at first sight and they spend the intervening years falling in and out of a crazy romance. Spanish with subtitles. **118m/C VHS, DVD.** *SP* Ana Belen, Penelope Cruz, Gabino Diego, Juanjo Puigcorbe, Carles Sans, Lola Herrera; *D:* Manuel Gomez Pereira; *W:* Manuel Gomez Pereira; *C:* Juan Amoros.

Love, Cheat & Steal **1993 (R)** Convicted murderer Reno Adams (Roberts) breaks out of prison when he hears that his luscious ex (Amick) has just married another man (Lithgow). He turns up on her door, threatening to destroy her new life, but things aren't exactly what they seem. Faux noir. **95m/C VHS.** Eric Roberts, Madchen Amick, John Lithgow, Richard Edson, Donald Moffat, David Ackroyd, Dan O'Herlihy; *D:* William Curran; *W:* William Curran.

Love Child **1982 (R)** The story of a young woman in prison who becomes pregnant by a guard and fights to have and keep her baby. **97m/C VHS.** Amy Madigan, Beau Bridges, MacKenzie Phillips, Albert Salmi; *D:* Larry Peerce; *M:* Charles Fox.

Love Come Down **2000 (R)** Matthew (Cummins) is white; his half-brother Neville (Tate) is black. Their mother is in prison for killing Neville's abusive father but there's a definite question about her guilt. Both boys have been hugely affected by their pasts—Matthew puts his anger into his boxing career while Neville has become a drug addicted stand-up comic. Neville tries to stay clean when he falls for a singer (Cox) with her own family issues but the brothers also have to lay their traumatic past to rest. **102m/C VHS, DVD.** *CA* Larenz Tate, Martin Cummins, Sarah Polley, Deborah Cox, Travis Davis, Jake Le Doux, Rainbow Sun Francks, Barbara Williams, Peter Williams, Clark Johnson, Kenneth Welsh, Jennifer Dale, Naomi Gaskin; *D:* Clement Virgo; *W:* Clement Virgo; *C:* Dylan Mcleod; *M:* Aaron Davis, John Lang. Genie '01: Sound, Support. Actor (Cummins).

Love Crazy ½ **1941** Powell and Loy team once again for a non-"Thin Man" romp through a married-people farce. Via a nosy mother-in-law and a series of misunderstandings, Powell and Loy squabble almost to the point of divorce. Not the wry wit the team was known for, but zany, high-action comedy at its best. **99m/B VHS.** William Powell, Myrna Loy, Gail Patrick, Jack Carson, Florence Bates, Sidney Blackmer, Sig Rumann; *D:* Jack Conway.

Love Crimes **1992 (R)** A con man (Bergin) poses as a photographer who sexually intimidates women while playing on their erotic fantasies. Young is the Atlanta district attorney who sets out to nail him when none of his victims will testify against him, only she may be enjoying her undercover work more than she realizes. Implausible and sleazy. Also available in an unrated version. **84m/C VHS.** Sonny Shroyer, Sean Young, Patrick Bergin, Arnetia Walker, James Read; *D:* Lizzie Borden; *W:* Laurie Frank, Allan Moyle; *C:* Phedon Papamichael; *M:* Graeme Revell.

Love Desperados **1986** Cowboys and ranchers' wives mix it up in a lot of softcore hay. **99m/C VHS.** Virginia Gordon, James Arena.

Love 'Em and Leave 'Em **1926** Two sisters, with opposite personalities, are department store sales clerks. Brent is the "good" girl and Brooks the "bad" flirt who, under the influence of Perkins, bets the store's welfare benefit money on the horses and loses it all. Brent manages to make things right, while keeping boyfriend Gray from her sister's clutches. Brooks' baby vamp (the actress was 19) stole the picture. Introduced the "Black Bottom" shimmy dance to the screen. Remade in 1929 as "The Saturday Night Kid" with Clara Bow and Jean Arthur. **70m/B VHS.** Louise Brooks, Evelyn

Brent, Lawrence Gray, Osgood Perkins; **D:** Frank Tuttle.

Love, etc. 🦴🦴 **1996** Another messy romantic triangle played for both comedy and tragedy. Shy, thirtysomething bank employee Benoit (Attal) takes out a personal ad, but supplies a picture of his egocentric best friend Pierre (Berling) instead of his own. He meets twentysomething art restorer Marie (Gainsbourg) and, despite the deception and the fact that she's not swept away by romantic passion, Marie marries him. Then Benoit discovers that Pierre thinks he's in love with Marie and has decided to win her away—and she's torn by the attention. Based on the novel "Taking It Over" by Julian Barnes. French with subtitles. **105m/C VHS, DVD, Wide.** *FR* Charlotte Gainsbourg, Yvan Attal, Charles Berling; **D:** Marion Vernoux; **W:** Marion Vernoux, Dodine Herry; **C:** Eric Gautier; **M:** Leonard Cohen, Alexandre Desplat.

The Love Factor 🦴 *Zeta One* **1969** A secret agent tries to foil the plans of a race of topless female aliens in this sleazy softcore sci-fi film. **?m/C VHS.** *GB* Robin Hawdon, James Robertson Justice, Yutte Stensgaard.

Love Field 🦴🦴½ **1991 (PG-13)** Pfeiffer is a Jackie Kennedy-obsessed hairdresser who decides to travel by bus to D.C. when she hears about President Kennedy's assassination. Along the way she gets involved in an interracial friendship with the secretive Haysbert, who's traveling with his young daughter. Pfeiffer's Lurene is basically a sweet dim bulb and Haysbert has an unfortunately written one-note character (mainly exasperation). The six-year-old McFadden (in her debut) makes the most impact. **104m/C VHS, DVD, Wide.** Michelle Pfeiffer, Dennis Haysbert, Stephanie McFadden, Brian Kerwin, Louise Latham, Peggy Rea, Beth Grant, Cooper Huckabee, Mark Miller, Johnny Rae McGhee; **D:** Jonathan Kaplan; **W:** Don Roos; **C:** Ralf Bode; **M:** Jerry Goldsmith.

Love Film 🦴🦴 *Szerelmesfilm; A Film about Love* **1970** A train trip from Budapest, Hungary to Lyon, France leads a young man to recall his past as he journeys to visit a childhood sweetheart. Jancsi and Kata's friendship has been disrupted by the 1956 uprising and Jancsi wonders if the love once developing between them has been broken by distance and time. In Hungarian with English subtitles. **123m/C VHS, DVD, Wide.** *HU* Andras Balint, Judit Halasz, Edit Kelemen, Andras Szamosfalvi; **D:** Istvan Szabo; **W:** Istvan Szabo; **C:** Josef Lorinc.

Love Finds Andy Hardy 🦴🦴🦴 **1938** Young Andy Hardy finds himself torn between three girls before returning to the girl next door. Garland's first appearance in the acclaimed Andy Hardy series features her singing "In Between" and "Meet the Best of my Heart." **90m/B VHS.** Mickey Rooney, Judy Garland, Lana Turner, Ann Rutherford, Fay Holden, Lewis Stone, Marie Blake, Cecilia Parker, Gene Reynolds; **D:** George B. Seitz. Natl. Film Reg. '00.

The Love Flower 🦴🦴½ **1920** A man kills his second wife's lover and escapes with his daughter to a tropical island, pursued by a detective and a young adventurer. Interesting ending wraps things up nicely. Silent. **70m/B VHS.** Carol Dempster, Richard Barthelmess, George MacQuarrie, Anders Randolf, Florence Short; **D:** D.W. Griffith; **W:** D.W. Griffith.

Love for Lydia 🦴🦴🦴 **1979** British TV miniseries following wayward beauty Lydia, orphaned heiress to a manufacturing fortune, through the high-spirited 1920s. Set in the industrial Midlands and farming communities of England, Lydia dazzles every man she meets, often to an unhappy end. Based on the novel by H.E. Bates. Available as a boxed set. **657m/C VHS.** *GB* Mel Martin, Christopher Blake, Peter Davison, Jeremy Irons, Michael Aldridge, Rachel Kempson, Beatrix Lehmmann. **TV**

Love from a Stranger 🦴🦴 **1937** Thriller about a working woman who wins a lottery. Soon she is charmed by and marries a man whom she later suspects may be trying to kill her. Remade in 1947. **90m/B VHS.** *GB* Ann Harding, Basil Rathbone, Binnie Hale, Bruce Seton, Bryan Powley, Jean Cadell; **D:** Rowland V. Lee.

Love from a Stranger 🦴🦴½ *A Stranger Walked In* **1947** In this remake of the 1937 film, a young newlywed bride fears that the honeymoon is over when she suspects that her husband is a notorious killer and that she will be his next victim. **81m/B VHS.** Sylvia Sidney, John Hodiak, John Howard, Ann Richards, Isobel Elsom, Ernest Cossart; **D:** Richard Whorf.

The Love God? 🦴½ **1970 (PG-13)** Very silly comedy finds mild-mannered Abner Peacock (Knotts) trying on Hugh Hefner's mantle. With his bird-watcher's magazine in financial trouble, Abner takes on a couple of shifty partners who change it into a different kind of bird watching magazine (the nude female kind) that gets Abner charged with pornography and finds him becoming a (very) unlikely sex symbol. **103m/C VHS.** Don Knotts, Edmond O'Brien, Anne Francis, Maureen Arthur, James Gregory, Margaret (Maggie) Peterson, Marjorie Bennett; **D:** Nat Hiken; **W:** Nat Hiken; **C:** William Margulies; **M:** Vic Mizzy.

The Love Goddesses **1965** A 60-year examination of some of the most beautiful women on the silver screen, reflecting with extraordinary accuracy the customs, manners and mores of the times. Released theatrically in 1972. **83m/B VHS, DVD.** Marlene Dietrich, Greta Garbo, Jean Harlow, Gloria Swanson, Mae West, Betty Grable, Rita Hayworth, Elizabeth Taylor, Marilyn Monroe, Theda Bara, Claudette Colbert, Dorothy Lamour, Lillian Gish, Sophia Loren; **D:** Saul J. Turell; **W:** Saul J. Turell, Graeme Ferguson; **Nar:** Carl King.

Love Happy 🦴🦴½ **1950** A group of impoverished actors accidentally gain possession of valuable diamonds. Unfortunately for them, detective Groucho is assigned to recover them! **85m/B VHS.** Groucho Marx, Harpo Marx, Chico Marx, Vera-Ellen, Ilona Massey, Marion Hutton, Raymond Burr, Marilyn Monroe, Eric Blore; **D:** David Miller; **W:** Frank Tashlin, Mac Benoff; **C:** William Mellor; **M:** Ann Ronell.

Love Has Many Faces 🦴½ **1965** Judith Crist was too kind when she said this was for connoisseurs of truly awful movies. Playgal Turner marries beach-boy Robertson and many faces come between them. Much melodrama. Filmed on location. **104m/C VHS.** Lana Turner, Cliff Robertson, Hugh O'Brian, Ruth Roman, Stefanie Powers, Virginia Grey, Ron Husmann; **D:** Alexander Singer.

Love, Honour & Obey 🦴🦴 **2000** Lowlife London bad boys and a karaoke bar. Jonny (Miller) wants his best bud Jude (Law) to get him a job with Jude's gangster uncle, Ray (Winstone), who loves to croon a tune at the local karaoke club. But Jonny loves his new life too much and can't resist stirring up local gangland rivalries—to the grief of everyone. Low-budget, sometime puerile comedy. **95m/C VHS, DVD, Wide.** *GB* Jonny Lee Miller, Jude Law, Ray Winstone, Sadie Frost, Sean Pertwee, Kathy Burke, Rhys Ifans, Laila Morse, Dominic Anciano, Ray Burdis; **D:** Dominic Anciano, Ray Burdis; **W:** Dominic Anciano, Ray Burdis; **C:** John Ward.

Love Hurts 🦴🦴 **1991 (R)** A guy looking for romance finds his hands full with a number of beautiful women. Will he find the love he craves, or will the pain be too much to bear? **110m/C VHS.** Jeff Daniels, Judith Ivey, John Mahoney, Cynthia Sikes, Amy Wright; **D:** Bud Yorkin; **W:** Ron Nyswaner.

Love in Bloom 🦴🦴 **1935** Predictable romance, with Burns and Allen providing some much-needed comic relief. Carnival gal Violet Downey (Lee) falls for struggling songwriter Larry Deane (Morrison) but thinks her tawdry background will ruin his chances and takes off. After Larry becomes successful he searches for Violet, still determined to marry her. **75m/B VHS.** George Burns, Gracie Allen, Joe Morrison, Dixie Lee, Lee Kohlmar, Richard Carle; **D:** Elliott Nugent; **W:** J.P. McEvoy, Keene Thompson; **C:** Leo Tover.

A Love in Germany 🦴🦴½ *Un Amour En Allemagne; Eine Liebe in Deutschland* **1984 (R)** A tragic love affair develops between a German shopkeeper's wife and a Polish prisoner-of-war in a small German village during WWII. In German with English subtitles. **110m/C VHS.** *FR GE* Hanna Schygulla, Piotr Lysak, Elisabeth Trissenaar, Armin Mueller-Stahl; **D:** Andrzej Wajda; **W:** Andrzej Wajda, Agnieszka Holland, Boleslaw Michalek.

Love in the Afternoon 🦴🦴½ **1957** A Parisian private eye's daughter (Hepburn) decides to investigate a philandering American millionaire (Cooper) and winds up falling in love with him. Cooper's a little old for the Casanova role but Hepburn is always enchanting. **126m/B VHS.** Gary Cooper, Audrey Hepburn, John McGiver, Maurice Chevalier; **D:** Billy Wilder; **W:** Billy Wilder, I.A.L. Diamond; **C:** William Mellor.

Love in the City 🦴🦴🦴 *Amore in Citta* **1953** Five stories of life, love and tears in Rome. In Italian with English subtitles and narration. **90m/B VHS.** *IT* Ugo Tognazzi, Maresa Gallo, Caterina Rigoglioso, Silvia Lillo; **D:** Michelangelo Antonioni, Federico Fellini, Dino Risi, Carlo Lizzani, Alberto Lattuada, Francesco Maselli, Cesare Zavattini; **W:** Aldo Buzzi, Luigi Malerba, Luigi Chiarini, Tullio Pinelli, Vittorio Vettreni; **C:** Gianni Di Venanzo; **M:** Mario Nascimbene.

Love Is a Gun 🦴½ **1994 (R)** A police photographer (Roberts) begins having violent and erotic hallucinations that begin to affect his fiancee (Garrett). Things get even weirder when a femme fatale model (Preston) enters the picture. **92m/C VHS.** Eric Roberts, Kelly Preston, Eliza (Simons) Garrett, R. Lee Ermey; **D:** David Hartwell.

Love Is a Many-Splendored Thing 🦴🦴½ **1955** A married American war correspondent and a beautiful Eurasian doctor fall in love in post-WWII Hong Kong. They struggle with racism and unhappiness, until he's sent to Korea to observe the Army's activities there. Based on the novel by Han Suyin. The extensive L.A. Asian acting community got some work out of this film, although the leads are played by Caucasians. Oscar-winning song was a very big popular hit. ♫Love is a Many-Splendored Thing. **102m/C VHS, DVD, Wide.** William Holden, Jennifer Jones, Torin Thatcher, Isobel Elsom, Jorja Curtright, Virginia Gregg, Richard Loo; **D:** Henry King; **W:** John Patrick; **C:** Leon Shamroy; **M:** Alfred Newman. Oscars '55: Costume Des. (C), Song ("Love Is a Many-Splendored Thing"), Orig. Dramatic Score.

Love Is All There Is 🦴🦴½ **1996 (R)** It's a kind of comedic (happy-ending) version of "Romeo and Juliet," set in the Bronx, about rival restaurant families. Beautiful Gina's (Jolie) a finishing-school grad and Rosario's (Marston) the local boy too handsome for his own good. Both sets of parents are crazy. Oddly enough, Sorvino also plays the heroine's dad in the '96 "William Shakespeare's Romeo & Juliet." **98m/C VHS.** Dominic Chianese, Angelina Jolie, Nathaniel Marston, Paul Sorvino, Renee Taylor, Joseph Bologna, Lainie Kazan, Barbara Carrera, William Hickey, Abe Vigoda, Dick Van Patten, Connie Stevens; **D:** Renee Taylor, Joseph Bologna; **W:** Renee Taylor, Joseph Bologna; **C:** Alan Jones; **M:** Jeff Beal.

Love Is Better Than Ever 🦴🦴½ *The Light Fantastic* **1952** Lightweight romantic-comedy casts Taylor as a dancing instructor who travels to the Big Apple for a convention. Once there, she meets and falls for talent agent Parks. Carefree, bachelor Parks is too busy to be bothered by small town Taylor, but Liz is determined to land her man. Release of this picture was held back because of Parks' blacklisting by the McCarthy committee. **81m/B VHS.** Larry Parks, Elizabeth Taylor, Josephine Hutchinson, Tom Tully, Ann Doran, Elinor Donahue, Kathleen Freeman; **Cameos:** Gene Kelly; **D:** Stanley Donen; **W:** Ruth Brooks Flippen.

Love Is the Devil 🦴🦴🦴½ **1998** British painter Francis Bacon (Jacobi), at the height of his career, takes on petty thief George Dyer (Craig) as his model, lover, and whipping-post. Bacon exposes his dim lover to a world of high-brow drunks and addicts who entertain themselves by humiliating others, with Bacon viciously leading the verbal and emotional attacks. Although the estate refused director/writer Maybury permission to use Bacon's actual paintings, he captures the painful emotions expressed in the art in different ways. The incredible lead performances by Jacobi and Craig are as brilliant but ferocious as the artist himself. While at times tender and moving, their destructive relationship is difficult to watch, but worth it you do. Appeal is definitely art-house niche, but those who see it will be rewarded. **90m/C VHS, DVD.** *GB* Derek Jacobi, Daniel Craig, Tilda Swinton, Karl Johnson, Anne Lambton; **D:** John Maybury; **W:** John Maybury; **C:** John Mathieson; **M:** Ryuichi Sakamoto.

Love Jones 🦴🦴🦴 **1996 (R)** A contemporary Chicago nightclub, the Sanctuary, is the gathering spot for middle-class black urbanites looking for romance. Would-be writer/poet Darius (Tate) spouts provocative verse to beautiful photographer Nina (Long), who's not too happy with men at the moment (she's just been dumped). But they make a connection, with both protesting a little too much that's it just a "sex thing." Funny what happens when love clearly enters the picture. Witcher's directorial debut features fine lead performances. **105m/C VHS, DVD.** Larenz Tate, Nia Long, Isaiah Washington IV, Lisa Nicole Carson, Khalil Kain, Bill Bellamy, Leonard Roberts, Bernardette L. Clarke; **D:** Theodore Witcher; **W:** Theodore Witcher; **C:** Ernest Holzman; **M:** Darryl Jones. Sundance '97: Aud. Award.

Love Kills 🦴🦴 **1991 (PG-13)** Is the man a beautiful heiress falls in love with actually an assassin hired by her husband to kill her? Find out in this steamy suspenser. **92m/C VHS.** Virginia Madsen, Lenny Von Dohlen, Erich Anderson, Kate Hodge, Jim Metzler; **D:** Brian Grant.

Love Kills 🦴½ **1998 (R)** Good cast can't hold this messy film together. New Age masseur Poe Finklestein (Van Peebles) arrives at the Beverly Hills estate of wealthy widow Evelyn Heiss (Warren). Also living with Evelyn are her no-account, gay stepson Dominique (Leitch) and her voyeurish sister-in-law Alena (Fletcher). There's shots fired, and drugs, and a cop (Baldwin) and various other hijinks but not much of it makes sense. **97m/C VHS, DVD, Wide.** Mario Van Peebles, Lesley Ann Warren, Daniel Baldwin, Donovan Leitch, Louise Fletcher, Loretta Devine, Melvin Van Peebles, Susan Ruttan, Alexis Arquette; **D:** Mario Van Peebles; **W:** Mario Van Peebles; **C:** George Mooradian.

Love Laughs at Andy Hardy 🦴🦴 **1946** Andy Hardy, college boy, is in love and in trouble. Financial and romantic problems come to a head when Andy is paired with a six-foot tall blind date. One in the series. **93m/B VHS.** Mickey Rooney, Lewis Stone, Sara Haden, Lina Romay, Bonita Granville, Fay Holden; **D:** Willis Goldbeck.

Love Leads the Way 🦴🦴 **1984** The true story of how Morris Frank established the seeing-eye dog system in the 1930s. **99m/C VHS.** Richard Speight Jr., Timothy Bottoms, Eva Marie Saint, Arthur Hill, Susan Dey, Ralph Bellamy, Ernest Borgnine, Patricia Neal; **D:** Delbert Mann.

The Love Letter 🦴🦴½ **1998** Scotty Corrigan (Scott) discovers a love letter in the antique desk he's purchased, written by Lizzie Whitcomb (Leigh) who lived during the Civil War. Haunted, Scotty decides to reply to the missive and, magically, Lizzie receives his letter. Soon, they not only have a regular correspondence but a romance that transcends time. Based on a story by Jack Finney. **99m/C VHS, DVD.** Campbell Scott, Jennifer Jason Leigh, David Dukes, Estelle Parsons, Daphne Ashbrook, Gerrit Graham, Irma P. Hall; **D:** Dan Curtis; **W:** James Henerson; **M:** Robert Cobert. **TV**

The Love Letter 🦴½ **1999 (PG-13)** Disappointingly loose adaptation of the novel by Cathleen Schine feels the need to take the focus off the unexpected love story developing between 40-something bookstore owner Helen MacFarquhar (Capshaw) and college student Johnny (Scott), with too many peripheral characters. (Yeah, Tom Selleck's charming but his character's a goofy distraction.) Anyway, the love letter in question is an anonymous missive Helen receives at her bookstore. She's not certain it's meant for her, and if it is, just who the secret admirer might be. Then Johnny finds the letter and thinks it's meant for him—or maybe it was for Helen's cynical partner, Janet (DeGeneres). The biggest mystery is why the lovely Danner is playing Capshaw's MOTHER (under a ton of rubber makeup) for heaven's sake! **88m/C VHS, DVD.** Kate Capshaw, Tom Everett Scott, Tom Selleck, Ellen DeGeneres, Blythe Danner, Gloria Stuart, Geraldine McEwan, Alice Drummond; ***D:*** Peter Chan; ***W:*** Maria Maggenti; ***C:*** Tami Reiker; ***M:*** Luis Bacalov.

Love Letters 🦴🦴½ **1945** Typical forties weepie finds Victoria (Jones) marrying soldier Roger Morland (Sully) because of the beautiful letters he wrote her. Only he didn't write them, his best bud Alan Quinton (Cotten) did. Roger's actually a wife-beater and winds up dead. Victoria becomes an amnesiac from the shock but when Alan comes to check out the situation he falls immediately in love with her anyway. Based on the novel "Pity My Simplicity" by Chris Massie. **101m/B VHS.** Jennifer Jones, Joseph Cotten, Robert Sully, Ann Richards, Anita Louise, Cecil Kellaway, Gladys Cooper, Byron Barr, Reginald Denny; ***D:*** William Dieterle; ***W:*** Ayn Rand; ***C:*** Lee Garmes; ***M:*** Victor Young.

Love Letters 🦴🦴🦴 *Passion Play; My Love Letters* **1983 (R)** A young disc jockey falls under the spell of a box of love letters that her mother left behind which detailed her double life. She, in turn, begins an affair with a married man. Thoughtful treatment of the psychology of infidelity. **102m/C VHS, DVD.** Jamie Lee Curtis, Amy Madigan, Bud Cort, Matt Clark, Bonnie Bartlett, Sally Kirkland, James Keach; ***D:*** Amy Holden Jones; ***W:*** Amy Holden Jones; ***C:*** Alec Hirschfeld; ***M:*** Ralph Jones.

Love, Lies and Murder 🦴🦴½ **1991 (PG-13)** Shocking psychological thriller in which a businessman convinces his daughter and sister-in-law to murder his wife and then sends his daughter to prison for the crime. The "perfect murder" is not so perfect, however, when the daughter learns that her father has remarried and is now living an insurance-rich lifestyle. She decides to fight back in this true story of bizarre murder and deception. **190m/C VHS.** Clancy Brown, John Ashton, Sheryl Lee, Moira Kelly, Ramon Bieri, Ken Walsh, Tom Bower, John M. Jackson; ***D:*** Robert Markowitz. **TV**

The Love Light 🦴🦴½ **1921** Angela (Pickford) is a lighthouse keeper in Italy who's awaiting her soldier brother's return from war. Instead, she learns of his death. When a wounded soldier is washed ashore, Angela rescues him and nurses him back to health, thinking he's an American sailor. They fall in love and marry before she learns that he's really a German spy and may have killed her brother. There's a lot more tragedy before Angela finds happiness. One of Pickford's rare adult roles. **75m/B VHS.** Mary Pickford, Raymond Bloomer, Jean De Briac, Evelyn Dumo, Eddie (Edward) Phillips, Albert Priscoe, George Regas, Fred Thomson; ***D:*** Frances Marion; ***W:*** Frances Marion; ***C:*** Henry Cronjager, Charles Rosher.

The Love Machine 🦴½ **1971 (R)** A power-hungry newscaster climbs the corporate ladder by sleeping with many, including the president's wife. An adaptation of Jacqueline Susann's novel. **108m/C VHS.** John Phillip Law, Dyan Cannon, Robert Ryan, Jackie Cooper, David Hemmings, Jodi Wexler, William Roerick, Maureen Arthur, Shecky Greene, Clinton Greyn, Sharon Farrell, Alexandra Hay, Eve Bruce, Greg Mullavey, Edith Atwater, Gene Baylos, Claudia Jennings, Mary Collinson, Madeleine Collinson, Ann Ford, Gayle Hunnicutt; ***D:*** Jack Haley Jr.; ***W:*** Samuel A. Taylor; ***C:*** Charles B(ryant) Lang Jr.; ***M:*** Artie Butler.

Love Matters 🦴🦴 **1993 (R)** Tom and Julie's fast-track marriage is hovering on the brink when Tom's best friend Geoff, who's also married, shows up on their doorstep with his sexy mistress and announces he's getting a divorce. Reluctantly, Tom and Julie allow the X-rated lovebirds to stay the night but all that heat only shows up the flaws in their own marriage even more. An unrated version at 103 minutes is also available. **97m/C VHS.** Griffin Dunne, Tony Goldwyn, Annette O'Toole, Gina Gershon, Kate Burton; ***D:*** Eb Lottimer; ***W:*** Eb Lottimer; ***M:*** Simon Boswell.

Love Me Deadly 🦴 **1976 (R)** A young woman tries to get her husband interested in her new hobby—necrophilia. **95m/C VHS.** Mary Wilcox, Lyle Waggoner, Christopher Stone, Timothy Scott.

Love Me or Leave Me 🦴🦴🦴 **1955** A hard-hitting biography of '20s torch singer Ruth Etting and her rise and fall at the hand of her abusive, gangster husband, a part just made for Cagney. Day emotes and sings expressively in one of the best performances of her career. ♫I'll Never Stop Loving You; Never Look Back; Shaking the Blues Away; Mean to Me; Love Me or Leave Me; Sam, the Old Accordian Man; At Sundown; Everybody Loves My Baby; Five Foot Two. **122m/C VHS, Wide.** Doris Day, James Cagney, Cameron Mitchell, Robert Keith, Tom Tully, Veda Ann Borg; ***D:*** Charles Vidor. Oscars '55: Story.

Love Me Tender 🦴🦴 **1956** A Civil War-torn family is divided by in-fighting between two brothers who both seek the affections of the same woman. Presley's first film. Songs include "Poor Boy," "We're Gonna Move," and the title tune. **89m/B VHS.** Richard Egan, Debra Paget, Elvis Presley, Neville Brand, Mildred Dunnock, James Drury, Barry Coe, Robert Middleton, William Campbell, Russ Conway, L.Q. (Justus E. McQueen) Jones; ***D:*** Robert D. Webb; ***W:*** Robert Buckner; ***C:*** Leo Tover; ***M:*** Lionel Newman.

Love Meetings *Comizi d'Amore* **1964** Pasolini acts as director and interviewer to query a wide-range of individuals on their experiences at love, including homosexuality, prostitution, marital and non-marital interludes. In Italian with English subtitles. **90m/B VHS, Wide.** *IT* ***D:*** Pier Paolo Pasolini.

Love Nest 🦴🦴 **1951** Lundigan stars as Jim Scott, the landlord of an apartment building brimming with wacky tenants, including Monroe, Paar, and Fay. He dreams of becoming a famous writer, but his time is always filled with fixing up the building and trying to pay the mortgage. When one of the tenants ends up in jail because he was living off wealthy widows, Scott's luck changes. This moderately funny film is a good look at the early careers of Monroe and Paar. **84m/B VHS.** William Lundigan, June Haver, Frank Fay, Marilyn Monroe, Jack Paar; ***D:*** Joseph M. Newman.

Love Notes **1988** Three short vignettes of soft core fantasy, in the life of an ordinary guy. **60m/C VHS.** Jeff Daniels, Christine Veronica.

The Love of Jeanne Ney 🦴🦴½ **1927** Wildly convoluted silent film begins in Russia where Jeanne's (Jehanne) Bolshevik lover (Henning) kills her father for betraying the cause, and then shifts to Paris where the pair face even more daunting obstacles. The new score by Timothy Brock is engaging and effective. **113m/B VHS, DVD.** *GE* Edith Jehanne, Brigitte Helm, Uno Henning, Eugen Jenson, Fritz Rasp; ***D:*** G.W. Pabst; ***W:*** Ilya Ehrenburg, Ladislaus Vayda.

The Love of Three Queens 🦴½ **1954** The loves, on and off stage, of a beautiful actress in a European traveling theatre group. **80m/C VHS.** Gerard Oury, Massimo Serato, Robert Beatty, Cathy O'Donnell, Terence Morgan, Hedy Lamarr; ***D:*** Marc Allegret.

Love on the Dole 🦴🦴🦴 **1941** In a gloomy industrial section of England during the early '30s a family struggles to survive and maintain dignity. Grim Depression drama salvaged by great acting. **89m/B VHS.** *GB* Deborah Kerr, Clifford Evans, George Carney; ***D:*** John Baxter.

Love on the Run 🦴🦴½ **1936** Enjoyable romantic comedy starring Crawford as a rich American heiress and Gable and Tone (Crawford's real husband at the time) as journalists stationed in Europe. Gable and Tone are assigned to cover an international aviator, who turns out to be an evil spy, as well as the upcoming wedding of flighty Crawford. When Crawford asks for help in getting out of her marriage, Gable and Tone steal a plane and the trio is chased across Europe by spies. Wild and farfetched plot, but the stars make it worthwhile. Based on the story "Beauty and the Beast" by Alan Green and Julian Brodie. **80m/B VHS.** Joan Crawford, Clark Gable, Franchot Tone, Reginald Owen, Mona Maris, Ivan Lebedeff, Charles (Judel, Judells) Judels, William Demarest; ***D:*** Woodbridge S. Van Dyke; ***W:*** John Lee Mahin, Manuel Seff, Gladys Hurlbut.

Love on the Run 🦴🦴🦴 *L'Amour en Fuite* **1978 (PG)** The further amorous adventures of Antoine Doinel, hero of "The 400 Blows," "Stolen Kisses," and "Bed and Board." Doinel is now in his 30s and newly divorced. He renews affairs with several women from his past but, after his mother's death, must contend with his emotional immaturity and his inability to sustain a relationship. In French with English subtitles. **95m/C VHS, DVD.** *FR* Jean-Pierre Leaud, Marie-France Pisier, Claude Jade; ***D:*** Francois Truffaut; ***C:*** Nestor Almendros; ***M:*** Georges Delerue. Cesar '80: Score.

Love on the Run 🦴½ **1985** A beautiful lawyer helps a wrongly accused convict escape from prison, then they both evade the law. **102m/C VHS.** Stephanie Zimbalist, Alec Baldwin, Constance McCashin, Howard Duff; ***D:*** Gus Trikonis; ***M:*** Billy Goldenberg. **TV**

Love or Money? 🦴½ **1988 (PG-13)** A small comedy about a yuppie who must choose between a woman and a real estate deal. **90m/C VHS.** Timothy Daly, Haviland (Haylie) Morris, Kevin McCarthy, Shelley Fabares, David Doyle, Allen Havey; ***D:*** Todd Hallowell; ***W:*** Bart Davis.

Love Play 🦴🦴 *Playtime; La Recreation* **1960** Debut film for Moreuil, who was married to leading lady Seberg at the time, is a bland drama based on a story by Francoise Sagan (who also wrote the much better "Bonjour Tristesse" that Seberg starred in). Young American Kate Hudson (Seberg), enrolled in a Paris school, becomes obsessed with her next-door neighbors—sculptor Philippe (Marquand) and his wealthy older mistress and patron (Prevost). Soon Kate's involved in a triangle that's even more complicated than it first appears. **87m/B VHS.** *FR* Jean Seberg, Christian Marquand, Francoise Prevost, Evelyne Ker; ***D:*** Francois Moreuil; ***W:*** Francois Moreuil, Daniel Boulanger; ***C:*** Jean Penzer; ***M:*** Georges Delerue.

Love Potion #9 🦴½ **1992 (PG-13)** Two nerdy biochemists procure a love potion that they test on animals. Meeting with success they agree to test it on themselves. Predictably, the scientists are transformed and fall in love with each other. Features a talented young cast, with an amusing cameo by Bancroft, but the script is a real disappointment because of its shallow characters and lame gags. Inspired by the song by Jerry Leiber and Mike Stoller. **96m/C VHS, DVD, Wide.** Tate Donovan, Sandra Bullock, Mary Mara, Dale Midkiff, Hillary Bailey Smith, Dylan Baker, Anne Bancroft; ***D:*** Dale Launer; ***W:*** Dale Launer; ***C:*** William Wages; ***M:*** Jed Leiber.

Love Serenade 🦴🦴 **1996 (R)** Former big-time Brisbane DJ and 70s refugee Ken Sherry (Shevtsov) arrives in a sleepy Australian backwater town, setting off a rivalry between two bored sisters, Dimity (Otto) and Vicki-Ann (Frith). Fishing is one of their hobbies and metaphorically, Ken is the big fish in a very little pond. To them, his pretentious disco-era schmooze comes off as sophistication, mostly because he uses Barry White lyrics and his pillow-talk DJ voice to sell it. Critically speaking, director/writer Barrett's debut demonstrates a keen ear for dialogue and comic timing. To the average viewer though, this one's a dog, boring and very strange. If you're looking for a good Aussie comedy rent "Strictly Ballroom" or "Muriel's Wedding" instead. **101m/C VHS.** *AU* Miranda Otto, Rebecca Frith, George Shevtsov, John Alansu, Jessica Napier; ***D:*** Shirley Barrett; ***W:*** Shirley Barrett; ***C:*** Mandy Walker.

Love Song 🦴🦴½ **2000** Camille (Arnold) is a college student from an upper-crust African-American family whose surgeon father expects her to follow him into the medical field. She's also expected to marry earnest but dull Calvin (Francks). Then Camille meets white blues musician/singer Billy Ryan (Kane) and begins to question just whose dreams she's following as she discovers unexpected romance. Appealing story with sexy leads. **120m/C VHS.** Monica Arnold, Christian Kane, Rainbow Sun Francks, Peter Francis James, Vanessa Bell Calloway, Rachel True, Essence Atkins, Teck Holmes, Tyrese Gibson; ***D:*** Julie Dash; ***W:*** Josslyn Luckett; ***C:*** David Claessen; ***M:*** Frank Fitzpatrick. **CABLE**

Love Songs 🦴🦴 **1985 (R)** A mother of two is confronted with her husband's abandonment and a subsequent romance with a younger man. In French with English subtitles or dubbed. ♫Leave It to Me; Psychic Flash; I Am With You Now; Human Race; We Can Dance; One More Moment; From the Heart; This Must Be Heaven. **107m/C VHS.** *FR CA* Catherine Deneuve, Christopher Lambert; ***D:*** Elie Chouraqui; ***C:*** Robert Alazraki.

Love Songs 🦴🦴½ **1999** Trilogy of stories all set in the same black neighborhood. "A Love Song for a Champ" concerns boxer Townsend who agrees to throw a fight. "A Love Song for Jean and Ellis" concerns the would-be romance between grocer Braugher and the haughty Whitfield. "A Love Song for Dad" follows bartender Grossett who comes to the aid of his abused sister-in-law. **101m/C VHS, DVD.** Robert Townsend, Andre Braugher, Louis Gossett Jr., Rachael Crawford, Carl Gordon, Lynn Whitfield, Brent Jennings, Dule Hill, Sandra Caldwell; ***D:*** Robert Townsend, Andre Braugher, Louis Gossett Jr.; ***W:*** Charles Fuller; ***C:*** James R. Bagdonas; ***M:*** Pete Anthony, Ronnie Laws. **CABLE**

Love Stinks 🦴½ **1999 (R)** Apparently designed as an antidote to the date movie, this joyless "unromantic" comedy gives off a few rank fumes of its own. Writer Seth Winnick (Stewart) meets Chelsea (Wilson) at the wedding of his pals Larry (Bellamy) and Holly (Banks). After he's lured into Chelsea's clutches, she begins to take over his life while dropping hints that he should pop the big question. After he promises to marry her in a year but doesn't follow through, Chelsea decides to sue him for palimony. The non-couple then inexplicably live together until the trial so that further "funny comedy jokes" can be inflicted on the audience. Stewart attempts to rise above the material with his excellent comedic timing, but he's unable to escape this misogynistic mess. **94m/C VHS, DVD, Wide.** French Stewart, Bridgette Wilson, Tyra Banks, Bill Bellamy, Steve Hytner, Jason Bateman, Tiffani-Amber Thiessen; ***D:*** Jeff Franklin; ***W:*** Jeff Franklin; ***C:*** Uta Briesewitz; ***M:*** Bennett Salvay.

Love Story 🦴🦴🦴 **1970 (PG)** Melodrama had enormous popular appeal. O'Neal is the son of Boston's upper crust at Harvard; McGraw's the daughter of a poor Italian on scholarship to study music at Radcliffe. They find happiness, but only for a brief period. Timeless story, simply told, with artful direction from Hiller pulling exceptional performances from the young duo (who have never done as well since). The end result is perhaps better than Segal's simplistic novel, which was produced after he sold the screenplay and became a best-seller before the picture's release—great publicity for any film. Remember: "Love means never having to say you're sorry." **100m/C VHS, DVD, Wide.** Ryan O'Neal, Ali MacGraw, Ray Milland, John Marley, Tommy Lee Jones; ***D:*** Arthur Hiller; ***W:*** Erich Segal; ***C:*** Richard Kratina; ***M:*** Francis Lai. Oscars '70: Orig. Score; Golden Globes '71: Actress—Drama (MacGraw), Director (Hiller), Film—Drama, Screenplay, Score.

Love Strange Love 🦴½ **1982** A young boy develops a bizarre relationship with his mother who works in a luxurious bordello. Also available in an unedited 120-minute version. **97m/C VHS.** Vera Fischer, Mauro Mendonca.

Love Streams 🦴🦴½ **1984 (PG-13)** A quirky character drama about a writer and his sister who struggle to find love despite their personal problems. **122m/C VHS.** Gena Rowlands, John Cassavetes, Diahnne Abbott, Seymour Cassel; ***D:*** John Cassavetes; ***W:*** Ted Allan. Berlin Intl. Film Fest. '84: Golden Berlin Bear.

Love Thrill Murders woof! **1971 (R)** A film about a Mansonesque lunatic who is worshipped and obeyed by a mob of runaways and dropouts. **89m/C VHS.** Troy Donahue.

Love to Kill *The Girl Gets Moe* **1997 (R)** Moe (Danza) is a low-level arms dealer who falls for Elizabeth (Barondes), a gal who happens to like guns. But things go wrong thanks to dead bodies, double-crosses, and dirty cops. **102m/C VHS, DVD.** Tony Danza, Michael Madsen, James Russo, Elizabeth Barondes, Louise Fletcher, Amy Locane, Richmond Arquette, Rustam Branaman; ***D:*** James Bruce; ***W:*** Monica Clemens, Rustam Branaman; ***C:*** Keith L. Smith; ***M:*** Barry Coffing. CABLE

Love Under Pressure **198? **Man and woman's marriage starts to evaporate when they realize their son is seriously disturbed. **92m/C VHS.** Karen Black, Keir Dullea.

Love! Valour! Compassion! **1996 (R)** Follows eight gay men, longtime friends, who spend summer holiday weekends together at a beach house. Excellent cast features Alexander as Buzz, who has a severe show tune fixation, and Glover playing a pair of twins with very different personalities (and they're actually named Jeckyll). Together they wander through the turmoil of AIDS, infidelity, rage and impromptu ballet practice. Excellent cast only occasionally swerves from humor and genuine pathos into maudlin. Intermittent periods of stagy claustrophobia betray pic's Broadway origin. Based on the play by Terrence McNally. **120m/C VHS.** Jason Alexander, John Glover, Randy Becker, John Benjamin Hickey, Stephen Bogardus, Stephen Spinella, Justin Kirk; ***D:*** Joe Mantello; ***W:*** Terrance McNally; ***C:*** Alik Sakharov; ***M:*** Harold Wheeler.

Love Walked In *The Bitter End* **1997 (R)** Hardly an original story but this B-movie has a standout performance from the edgy Leary. He's Jack Hanaway, a lounge piano player with a sultry singer/wife, Vicky (Sanchez-Gijon). Jack's old P.I. friend Eddie (Badalucco) shows up with a scheme to make them all rich. He's been hired by a wealthy woman (Dusay) who suspects her husband Fred (Stamp) of infidelity. Fred's faithful (he likes his wife's money) but he's a patron of Jack's and is naturally appreciative of Vicky's charms. So they try to set Fred up. Scenes of would-be writer Jack's pulp novel intrude into the action and provide an unneeded distraction. Adapted from the novel by Jose Pable Feinmann. **90m/C VHS.** J.K. Simmons, Denis Leary, Aitana Sanchez-Gijon, Terence Stamp, Michael Badalucco, Marj Dusay, Danny Nucci, Moira Kelly, Neal Huff; ***D:*** Juan J. Campanella; ***W:*** Larry Golin, Juan J. Campanella; ***C:*** Daniel Shulman; ***M:*** Wendy Blackstone.

Love with a Perfect Stranger **1986** This Harlequin Romance takes place in Italy where a young widow meets a dashing Englishman. He changes her life forever. **102m/C VHS.** Marilu Henner, Daniel Massey; ***M:*** John Du Prez.

Love with the Proper Stranger **1963** A quiet, gritty romance about an itinerant musician and a young working girl in Manhattan awkwardly living through the consequences of their one-night stand. Moved Wood well into the realm of adult roles, after years playing teenagers and innocents. Although the story is about an Italian neighborhood and family, an exceptional number of the cast members were Jewish, as was the screenwriter. Story does not conclude strongly, although this did not hamper the boxoffice returns. **102m/B VHS.** Natalie Wood, Steve McQueen, Edie Adams, Herschel Bernardi, Tom Bosley, Harvey Lembeck, Penny Santon, Virginia Vincent, Nick Alexander, Augusta Ciolli; ***D:*** Robert Mulligan; ***W:*** Arnold Schulman; ***C:*** Milton Krasner; ***M:*** Elmer Bernstein.

Love Without Fear **1990** A dramatic, heart-rendering look at children with AIDS. Story focuses on the lives of three women from completely different backgrounds who adopt babies with AIDS and develop a special love for these children. Also shows their confrontations with a society which fears the disease and the women's strength to reach out and make a difference. **?m/C VHS.**

Love Without Pity **1991** Rochant's theatrical debut is a modern romance, with more distance and alienation than joy. A lovely, successful grad student loses her heart to a jobless, unambitious layabout who wants total commitment from her. Untypical, sardonic love story may be too cynical for sentimental types. In French with English subtitles. **95m/C VHS.** *FR* Hippolyte Girardot, Mireille Perrier, Jean Marie Rollin; ***D:*** Eric Rochant; ***W:*** Eric Rochant; ***M:*** Gerard Torikian.

Love Your Mama **1989 (PG-13)** An urban black drama about the strong Dorothy whose faith helps her cope with her many family complications, including her drunken husband, car thief son, and pregnant teenage daughter. Believable role models and good performances help out this amatuer filmmaking effort. **93m/C VHS.** Audrey Morgan, Carol E. Hall, Andre Robinson, Ernest Rayford, Kearo Johnson, Jacqueline Williams; ***D:*** Ruby L. Oliver; ***W:*** Ruby L. Oliver.

Loved **1997 (PG-13)** Hedda's (Wright Penn) obsessively and destructively in love with the nameless ex-boyfriend (Lucero) who left her scarred after a suspicious fall out a window. The loser's being arraigned for the murder of his latest girlfriend and prosecutor Dietrickson (Hurt) wants Hedda to testify. But what no one counts on, and what no one can understand, is Hedda's justification of her ex's abuse. Pic and performances are vague. **109m/C VHS.** Robin Wright Penn, William Hurt, Amy Madigan, Anthony Lucero, Lucinda Jenney, Joanna Cassidy, Paul Dooley, Jennifer Rubin; ***Cameos:*** Sean Penn; ***D:*** Erin Dignam; ***W:*** Erin Dignam; ***C:*** Reynaldo Villalobos; ***M:*** David Baerwald.

The Loved One **1965** A famously outlandish, death-mocking farce based on Evelyn Waugh's satire about a particularly horrendous California funeral parlor/cemetery and how its denizens do business. A shrill, protracted spearing of American capitalism. **118m/B VHS.** Robert Morse, John Gielgud, Rod Steiger, Liberace, Anjanette Comer, Jonathan Winters, James Coburn, Dana Andrews, Milton Berle, Tab Hunter, Robert Morley, Lionel Stander, Margaret Leighton, Roddy McDowall, Bernie Kopell, Alan Napier, Paul Williams; ***D:*** Tony Richardson; ***W:*** Terry Southern, Christopher Isherwood; ***C:*** Haskell Wexler; ***M:*** John Addison.

Loveless **1983 (R)** A menacing glance into the exploits of an outcast motorcycle gang. In the 50s, a group of bikers on their way to the Florida Cycle Races stop for lunch in a small-town diner. While repairs are being made on their motorcycles, they decide to take full advantage of their situation. **85m/C VHS.** Robert Gordon, Willem Dafoe, J. Don Ferguson; ***D:*** Kathryn Bigelow; ***W:*** Kathryn Bigelow.

Lovelife **1997 (R)** Yet another romantic saga about a group of disenchanted boomer friends who can't seem to make that love connection work. Maybe they should stop serial dating within their same small circle and take advantage of the outside world. **97m/C VHS.** Sherilyn Fenn, Bruce Davison, Saffron Burrows, Jon Tenney, Carla Gugino, Matt Letscher, Tushka Bergen, Peter Krause; ***D:*** John Harmon Feldman; ***W:*** John Harmon Feldman; ***C:*** Anthony C. "Tony" Jannelli; ***M:*** Adam Fields. VIDEO

Lovelines **1984 (R)** Two rock singers from rival high schools meet and fall in love during a panty raid. Laughs uncounted ensue. **93m/C VHS.** Greg Bradford, Michael Winslow, Mary Beth Evans, Don Michael Paul, Tammy Taylor, Stacey Toten, Miguel Ferrer, Shecky Greene, Aimee (Amy) Eccles, Sherri Stoner; ***D:*** Rod Amateau.

Lovely & Amazing **2002 (R)** Mom Blethyn watches over her three unhappy daughters: Michelle (Keener), who's bored by her marriage; insecure wannabe actress Elizabeth (Mortimer) and adopted eight-year-old African-American Annie (Goodwin), who's preoccupied by her looks. Not yet reviewed. **?m/C VHS, DVD.** Brenda Blethyn, Catherine Keener, Emily Mortimer, Raven Goodwin, Dermot Mulroney, Jake Gyllenhaal; ***D:*** Nicole Holofcener; ***W:*** Nicole Holofcener.

Lovely ... But Deadly **1982 (R)** Young girl wages a war against the drug dealers in her school after her brother dies of an overdose. **95m/C VHS.** Lucinda Dooling, John Randolph, Richard Herd, Susan Mechsner, Mel Novak; ***D:*** David Sheldon.

Lovely to Look At **1952** Three wanna-be Broadway producers (Skelton, Keel, Champion) go to gay Paree to peddle Skelton's half interest in Madame Roberta's, a chi chi dress shop. There, they meet the shop's other half interest, two sisters (Champion and Miller), and together they stage a fashion show to finance the floundering hospice of haute couture. Lavish production, light plot. Filmed in Technicolor based on Kern's 1933 Broadway hit (inspired by Alice Duer Miller's "Gowns by Roberta"). Vincent Minelli staged the fashion show, with gowns by Adrian (watch for cop-beater Zsa Zsa as a model). ♫Opening Night; Smoke Gets in Your Eyes; Lovely to Look At; The Touch of Your Hand; Yesterdays; I Won't Dance; You're Devastating; The Most Exciting Night; I'll Be Hard to Handle. **105m/C VHS.** Kathryn Grayson, Red Skelton, Howard Keel, Gower Champion, Marge Champion, Ann Miller, Zsa Zsa Gabor, Kurt Kasznar, Marcel Dalio, Diane Cassidy; ***D:*** Mervyn LeRoy; ***C:*** George J. Folsey; ***M:*** Jerome Kern.

The Lover *L'Amant* **1992 (R)** Portrays the sexual awakening of a French teenager and her older Chinese lover in Indochina in 1929. The characters, who remain nameless, meet on a ferry where the man is smitten by the girl's beauty. Detached, determined, and unromantic (the opposite of her indolent lover), she allows herself to be seduced for the experience, and money, he offers. The film is equally detached, including the beautifully photographed but uninvolving sex scenes. Moreau narrates as an adult looking back on her life. March's debut; filmed on location in Vietnam. Based on the semi-autobiographical novel by Marguerite Duras who repudiated director Annuad's film when it was released in France. Also available in an unrated, letterbox version at 115 minutes. **103m/C VHS, DVD, Wide.** *FR* Jane March, Tony Leung Ka-Fai, Frederique Meininger, Arnaud Giovanietti, Melvil Poupaud, Lisa Faulkner, Xiem Mang; ***D:*** Jean-Jacques Annaud; ***W:*** Gerard Brach, Jean-Jacques Annaud; ***C:*** Robert Fraisse; ***M:*** Gabriel Yared; ***Nar:*** Jeanne Moreau. Cesar '93: Score.

Lover Come Back **1961** More Day-Hudson antics in which an advertising executive falls in love with his competitor but that doesn't stop him from stealing her clients. Is there no shame? **107m/C VHS.** Rock Hudson, Doris Day, Tony Randall, Edie Adams, Joe Flynn, Ann B. Davis, Jack Oakie, Jack Albertson, Jack Kruschen, Howard St. John; ***D:*** Delbert Mann.

Lover Girl **1997 (R)** When teenager Jake Ferrari (Subkoff) is abandoned by her mother, she decides to track down long-gone sister, Darlene (Swanson). But when Darlene doesn't want her either, Jake is at a loss until she's reluctantly befriended by Marci (Bernhard), manager of a massage parlor. Underage Jake even badgers tough Marci into giving her a job, although the film is skittish about just how far Jake goes with her clients. Still, given the sleazy and potentially exploitative premise, the film is surprizing cheerful and light. **87m/C VHS.** Tara Subkoff, Sandra Bernhard, Kristy Swanson, Loretta Devine, Renee Humphrey, Susan Barnes, Sahara Lotti, Tim Griffin; ***D:*** Lisa Addario, Joe Syracuse; ***W:*** Lisa Addario, Joe Syracuse; ***C:*** Dean Lent; ***M:*** Mark Kilian.

Loverboy **1989 (PG-13)** A college schnook takes a summer job as a Beverly Hills pizza delivery boy and is preyed upon by many rich and sex-hungry housewives. **105m/C VHS.** Patrick Dempsey, Kate Jackson, Barbara Carrera, Kirstie Alley, Carrie Fisher, Robert Ginty, Elizabeth (E.G. Dailey) Daily; ***D:*** Joan Micklin Silver; ***W:*** Tom Ropelewski, Leslie Dixon; ***M:*** Michel Colombier.

The Lovers **1959** Chic tale of French adultery with Moreau starring as a provincial wife whose shallow life changes overnight when she meets a young man. Had a controversial American debut because of the film's tender eroticism and innocent view of adultery. In French with English subtitles. **90m/B VHS.** *FR* Jeanne Moreau, Alain Cuny, Jose-Luis De Villalonga, Jean-Mark Bory; ***D:*** Louis Malle; ***W:*** Louis Malle. Venice Film Fest. '59: Special Jury Prize.

Lovers: A True Story *Amantes* **1990 (R)** Erotic love triangle in 1950s Madrid, while Spain is under the suffocating dictatorship of Franco. Naive, young Paco has a virginal, hardworking fiancee named Trini. Things would seem to be headed for an average life until Paco rents a room from young widow Luisa and they embark on a sexual affair bordering on obsession. When Trini discovers what's going on she turns out to have a more passionate, and violent, nature than even Paco could imagine. Steamy and highly dramatic with excellent performances. Based on a true story. In Spanish with English subtitles. An unrated version is also available. **105m/C VHS.** *SP* Victoria Abril, Jorge Sanz, Maribel Verdu; ***D:*** Vicente Aranda; ***W:*** Vicente Aranda, Alvaro del Amo; ***C:*** Jose Luis Alcaine; ***M:*** Jose Nieto. Berlin Intl. Film Fest. '91: Actress (Abril).

Lovers and Liars *Travels with Anita; A Trip with Anita* **1981 (R)** A romantic adventure in Rome turns into a symphony of zany mishaps when the man forgets to tell the woman that he is married!! **93m/C VHS, DVD.** *IT* Goldie Hawn, Giancarlo Giannini, Laura Betti; ***D:*** Mario Monicelli; ***W:*** Mario Monicelli, Paul Zimmerman; ***C:*** Tonino Delli Colli; ***M:*** Ennio Morricone.

Lovers and Other Strangers **1970 (R)** Two young people decide to marry after living together for a year and a half. Various tensions surface between them and among their families as the wedding day approaches. Good comedy features some charming performances. Keaton's first film. ♫For All We Know. **106m/C VHS.** Gig Young, Beatrice Arthur, Bonnie Bedelia, Anne Jackson, Harry Guardino, Michael Brandon, Richard S. Castellano, Bob (Robert) Dishy, Marian Hailey, Cloris Leachman, Anne Meara, Diane Keaton; ***D:*** Cy Howard; ***W:*** Renee Taylor, Joseph Bologna, David Zelag Goodman. Oscars '70: Song ("For All We Know").

Lover's Knot **1996 (R)** Cutesy romantic comedy has Curry as an angel whose heavenly mission is to get the proper romantic couples together. His current pair are poetic college English prof Steve (Campbell) and practical pediatrician Megan (Grey). Steve's imaginative courtship wins Megan but day-to-day living takes its toll and the duo separate, leaving their angelic guide to get them back together. **82m/C VHS.** Billy Campbell, Jennifer Grey, Tim Curry, Adam Baldwin; ***Cameos:*** Adam Ant, Anne Francis; ***D:*** Peter Shaner; ***W:*** Peter Shaner; ***C:*** Garett Griffin; ***M:*** Laura Karpman.

Lovers Like Us *Le Sauvage; The Savage* **1975** Two people each leave their spouses, meet one another, and fall in love. **103m/C VHS.** *FR* Catherine Deneuve, Yves Montand, Luigi Vannucchi, Tony Roberts, Dana Wynter; ***D:*** Jean-Paul Rappeneau; ***W:*** Jean-Paul Rappeneau.

Lovers' Lovers **1994** All sorts of bizarre and erotic adventures ensue when Blaire the jilted narcissist meets Michael, who doesn't want to commit to girlfriend Teri. Michael plans an affair with Blaire without realizing that Teri is already having a fling with Ray, Blaire's ex. Some funny situations but too many talky scenes stop the film cold. **90m/C VHS.** Serge Rodnunsky, Jennifer Ciesar, Cindy Parker, Ray Bennett; ***D:*** Serge Rodnunsky; ***W:*** Serge Rodnunsky; ***M:*** Pierre Rodnunsky.

Lovers of the Arctic Circle *Los Amantes del Circulo Polar* **1998 (R)** Complex romantic drama set in Spain and Finland. Otto and Ana meet as children and instantly recognized each other as soul mates—their first kiss occurring over a geography book describing the

Arctic Circle. When Otto's divorced father takes up with Ana's widowed mother, the now-adolescent pair wind up sharing the same house, and secretly become lovers. When Otto's mother dies, he blames himself for abandoning her and leaves Ana to become a pilot. She, in turn, becomes obsessed with being where the Arctic sun never sets, and fate, eventually, brings the adult duo together in Finland. Spanish with subtitles. **112m/C VHS.** *SP* Fele Martinez, Najwa Nimi, Nancho Novo, Maru Valdivielso, Beate Jensen; ***D:*** Julio Medem; ***W:*** Julio Medem; ***C:*** Gonzalo F. Berridi; ***M:*** Alberto Iglesias.

Lovers of Their Time 🦴 **1985** A romantic novel on tape, about forbidden love and other problems. **60m/C** Edward Petherbridge, Cheryl Prime, Lynn Farleigh; ***D:*** Robert Knights.

The Lovers on the Bridge 🦴🦴 *Les Amants du Pont-Neuf* **1991 (R)** Overblown, extravagent romantic drama about two homeless lovers who live on Paris' Pont-Neuf bridge, which is closed for repairs. Michele (Binoche) is a disoriented artist losing her eyesight to a degenerative eye disease. She has left her home and stumbles upon the bridge squatters who include Alex (Lavant), a disturbed and alcoholic street performer. Alex rescues her and becomes Michele's protector and lover. He also becomes obsessive—fearing Michele will leave him and desperate to stop her. Set in 1989, the bicentennial of the French Revolution. The Alex character also appears in the Carax films "Boy Meets Girl" (1984) and "Bad Blood" (1986). French with subtitles. **125m/C VHS.** *FR* Juliette Binoche, Denis Lavant, Klaus-Michael Gruber, Marion Stalens; ***D:*** Leos Carax; ***W:*** Leos Carax; ***C:*** Jean-Yves Escoffier.

Lover's Prayer 🦴🦴½ *All Forgotten* **1999 (PG-13)** Wealthy, innocent young man (Stahl) becomes infatuated with a mysterious young woman (Dunst) who has moved next door for the summer. Then he learns that romance isn't what he had fantasized it to be. **106m/C VHS, DVD, Wide.** Nick Stahl, Kirsten Dunst, Julie Walters, Geraldine James, Nathaniel Parker, James Fox; ***D:*** Reverge Anselmo; ***W:*** Reverge Anselmo; ***C:*** David Watkin; ***M:*** Joel McNeely.

Loves & Times of Scaramouche 🦴½ *Scaramouche* **1976** Eighteenth-century rogue becomes involved in a plot to assassinate Napoleon and winds up seducing Josephine in the process. Dubbed. **92m/C VHS.** *IT* Michael Sarrazin, Ursula Andress, Aldo Maccione; ***D:*** Enzo G. Castellari.

Love's Labour's Lost 🦴🦴 **2000 (PG)** Branagh's latest dip into the Bard is moved into the 1930s and accompanied by the music of Cole Porter, the Gershwins, and Jerome Kern. Just as four men vow to swear off women and concentrate on their studies along comes a French princess and her three companions. Guess what happens. As with the 1996 Woody Allen film, "Everyone Says I Love You," the actors try their best to be singing/dancing fools but most just end up looking foolish. As for Shakespeare, well about two-thirds of the text is actually gone and even lesser Will shouldn't be treated like that. **93m/C VHS, DVD, Wide.** *GB* Kenneth Branagh, Alicia Silverstone, Natascha (Natasha) McElhone, Alessandro Nivola, Matthew Lillard, Nathan Lane, Timothy Spall, Geraldine McEwan, Carmen Ejogo, Adrian Lester, Emily Mortimer, Richard Briers, Stefania Rocca, Jimmy Yuill; ***D:*** Kenneth Branagh; ***W:*** Kenneth Branagh; ***C:*** Alex Thomson; ***M:*** Patrick Doyle.

Loves of a Blonde 🦴🦴🦴½ *A Blonde in Love; Lasky Jedne Plavovlasky* **1965** A shy teenage factory girl falls in love with a visiting piano player when the reservist army comes to her small town. But when she goes to visit his family, she discovers things aren't as she imagined. Touching look at the complications of love and our expectations. Czech with subtitles. **88m/B VHS, DVD.** *CZ* Hana Brejchova, Josef Sebanek, Vladimir Pucholt, Milada Jezkova; ***D:*** Milos Forman; ***W:*** Milos Forman, Vaclav Sasek, Ivan Passer, Jaroslav Papousek; ***C:*** Miroslav Ondricek; ***M:*** Evsen Illin.

The Loves of Carmen 🦴🦴½ **1948** Film version of the classic Prosper Merrimee novel about a tempestuous Spanish gypsy and the soldier who loves her. Hayworth is great to look at and the film's main selling point. **98m/C VHS, DVD.** Rita Hayworth, Glenn Ford, Ron Randell, Victor Jory, Arnold Moss, Luther Adler, Joseph Buloff; ***D:*** Charles Vidor; ***W:*** Helen Deutsch; ***C:*** William E. Snyder; ***M:*** Mario Castelnuovo-Tedesco.

The Loves of Edgar Allen Poe 🦴🦴 **1942** A bland biographical drama about young Poe's adoption, his treatment at the hands of his foster father, his rejection by a woman for a more well-off man, his marriage to his first cousin, and his early death from alcoholism. **67m/B VHS.** Linda Darnell, Shepperd Strudwick, Virginia Gilmore, Jane Darwell, Mary Howard; ***D:*** Harry Lachman.

The Loves of Hercules woof! *Hercules and the Hydra; Hercules vs. the Hydra; Gli Amori di Ercole* **1960** The mythic mesomorph finds a mate with equiponderant chest measurements, and must save her from an evil queen. Somehow it eludes him that both queen and maiden are Miss Jayne in red and black wigs. Kudos for worst dubbing and special effects; a must see for connoisseurs of kitsch. **94m/C VHS.** *IT FR* Jayne Mansfield, Mickey Hargitay; ***D:*** Carlo L. Bragaglia; ***W:*** Alessandro Continenza.

Love's Savage Fury woof! **1979** Two escapees from a Union prison camp seek out a hidden treasure that could determine the outcome of the Civil War. Bad ripoff of "Gone with the Wind." **100m/C VHS.** Jennifer O'Neill, Perry King, Robert Reed, Raymond Burr, Connie Stevens, Ed Lauter; ***D:*** Joseph Hardy; ***M:*** John Addison. **TV**

Lovesick 🦴🦴 **1983 (PG)** A very-married New York psychiatrist goes against his own best judgment when he falls in love with one of his patients. **98m/C VHS, DVD.** Dudley Moore, Elizabeth McGovern, Alec Guinness, John Huston, Ron Silver; ***D:*** Marshall Brickman; ***W:*** Marshall Brickman; ***C:*** Gerry Fisher; ***M:*** Philippe Sarde.

Lovespell 🦴 *Tristan and Isolde* **1979** A retelling of the legend of Isolde and Tristan. Stilted direction and writing, but another chance to reminisce on Richard Burton. **91m/C VHS.** Richard Burton, Kate Mulgrew, Nicholas Clay, Cyril Cusack, Geraldine Fitzgerald, Niall Toibin, Diana Van Der Vlis, Niall O'Brien; ***D:*** Tom Donovan.

Lovey: A Circle of Children 2 🦴🦴 **1982** Teacher for special children takes in a terrified girl diagnosed as brain damaged or schizophrenic, and discovers love and intelligence in the girl as well as finding some important insights into her own life. **120m/C VHS.** Jane Alexander, Kris McKeon, Karen Allen; ***D:*** Jud Taylor.

Loving 🦴🦴½ **1984** The full-length, shot-on-video pilot for the daytime TV soap opera, with various guest stars. Exteriors shot at C.W. Post Center on Long Island. **120m/C VHS.** Lloyd Bridges, Geraldine Page. **TV**

Loving Couples 🦴🦴 **1980 (PG)** Two happily married couples meet at a weekend resort...and switch partners. Tired and predictable but it has its moments. **120m/C VHS.** Shirley MacLaine, James Coburn, Susan Sarandon, Stephen Collins, Sally Kellerman; ***D:*** Jack Smight.

Loving Jezebel 🦴🦴 **1999 (R)** If anything, writer/director Kwyn Bader's "Loving Jezebel" proves that Hill Harper ("The Skulls," "In Too Deep," etc.) is a terrific talent. The problem is, even at a mere 88 minutes, Bader's film seems long and even Harper can't act his way out of a weak and contrived script. The gist of the story is that he, Hill Harper, has a track record for falling in love with his friends' and other men's girlfriends—the theme of many a sit-com—with consistently bad results. Of course you have to give Harper credit for one thing, he has excellent taste in women as all of his "girlfriends" are "eye-candy" super models. **88m/C DVD, Wide.** Hill Harper, Laurel Holloman, Nicole Ari Parker, Sandrine Holt, David Moscow, Elisa Donovan, Phylicia Rashad; ***D:*** Kwyn Bader; ***W:*** Kwyn Bader; ***C:*** Horacio Marquinez; ***M:*** Tony Prendatt.

Loving You 🦴🦴 **1957** A small town boy with a musical style all his own becomes a big success thanks to the help of a female press agent. Features many early Elvis hits. ♫Loving You; Teddy Bear; Lonesome Cowboy; Got a Lot of Livin' To Do; Party; Mean Woman Blues; Hot Dog. **101m/C VHS.** Elvis Presley, Wendell Corey, Lizabeth Scott, Dolores Hart, James Gleason; ***D:*** Hal Kanter; ***W:*** Hal Kanter.

The Low Down 🦴🦴 **2000** Not much happens in this sketchy tale of London gameshow worker Frank (Gillen), who dreams of maybe becoming a sculptor while running the prop business with his less-than-eager roommates. Tiring of their layabout ways, he moves out, facilitating his hook-up with Ruby (Ashfield), the real estate agent. Film then follows, but not too closely or attentively, their budding romance and his passive-agressiveness and growing dissatisfaction with his own life. Thraves's directorial debut is laid-back to the point of being comatose, but some interesting scenes do occur between Gillen and Ashfield. **96m/C VHS.** *GB* Aidan Gillen, Kate Ashfield, Dean Lennox Kelly, Tobias Menzies, Rupert Proctor, Samantha Powers; ***D:*** Jamie Thraves; ***W:*** Jamie Thraves; ***C:*** Igor Jadue-Lillo; ***M:*** Nick Currie, Fred Thomas.

A Low Down Dirty Shame 🦴🦴 **1994 (R)** Shame (Wayans) is a down-on-his-luck private eye, with the obligatory wisecracking secretary, Peaches (Pinkett), who's hired by an old friend to find a vicious drug lord, a sultry ex-girlfriend, and $20 million. Lots of fun stunts and one liners can't make up for major plot holes. **100m/C VHS.** Keenen Ivory Wayans, Jada Pinkett Smith, Salli Richardson, Charles S. Dutton, Andrew Divoff, Corwin Hawkins; ***D:*** Keenen Ivory Wayans; ***W:*** Keenen Ivory Wayans.

The Low Life 🦴🦴½ **1995 (R)** A "day in the life" sort of story about aspiring writer John (Cochrane) who comes to L.A. with high hopes but instead gets stuck in the low life of awful temp jobs, a lousy landlord (LeGros), and now, his newly arrived loser cousin Andrew (Astin). He tries to cozy up to looker Sedgwick but she doesn't seem too interested—so what's a would-be cool guy to do? **96m/C VHS.** Rory Cochrane, Kyra Sedgwick, Sean Astin, James LeGros, Christian Meoli, Shawnee Smith, J.T. Walsh, Renee Zellweger; ***D:*** George Hickenlooper; ***W:*** George Hickenlooper, John Enbom; ***C:*** Richard Crudo; ***M:*** Bill Boll.

The Lower Depths 🦴🦴🦴½ *Les Bas Fonds; Underground* **1936** Renoir's adaptation of the Maxim Gorky play about a thief and a financially ruined baron learning about life from one another. In French with English subtitles. **92m/B VHS.** *FR* Jean Gabin, Louis Jouvet, Vladimir Sokoloff, Robert Le Vigan, Suzy Prim; ***D:*** Jean Renoir; ***W:*** Jean Renoir, Charles Spaak; ***C:*** Jean Bachelet; ***M:*** Jean Wiener.

The Lower Depths 🦴🦴🦴½ *Donzoko* **1957** Kurosawa sets the Maxim Gorky play in Edo during the final Tokugawa period, using Noh theatre elements in depicting the lowly denizens of a low-rent hovel. In Japanese with English subtitles. **125m/B VHS.** *JP* Toshiro Mifune, Isuzu Yamada, Ganjiro Nakamura, Kyoko Kagawa, Bokuzen Hidari; ***D:*** Akira Kurosawa; ***W:*** Akira Kurosawa, Hideo Oguni; ***C:*** Kazuo Yamazaki; ***M:*** Masaru Sato.

Lower Level 🦴 **1991 (R)** While working late, an attractive business woman becomes trapped in an office building by her psychotic secret admirer. **88m/C VHS, DVD.** David Bradley, Elizabeth (Ward) Gracen, Jeff Yagher; ***D:*** Kristine Peterson; ***W:*** Joel Soisson; ***C:*** Wally Pfister; ***M:*** Terry Plumeri.

Loyalties 🦴🦴½ **1986 (R)** A strong treatment of the issue of sexual abuse of girls by men, and of an upper-class woman's willingness to establish a true friendship with a woman of a so-called lower economic class. **98m/C VHS.** *CA* Kenneth Welsh, Tantoo Cardinal, Susan Wooldridge, Vera Martin, Christopher Barrington-Leigh; ***D:*** Anne Wheeler; ***W:*** Sharon Riis; ***M:*** Michael Conway Baker.

Loyola, the Soldier Saint **1952** A biography of the founder of the Jesuits from his years as a page in the Spanish court to his daring exploits on the battle field and, finally, his spiritual awakening at the University of Paris. Narrated by Father Alfred J. Barrett. **93m/B VHS.** Rafael Duran, Maria Rosa Jiminez; ***D:*** Jose Diaz Morales.

Lucas 🦴🦴🦴 **1986 (PG-13)** A high school brain falls in love with the new girl in town, and tries to win her by trying out for the football team. Genuine film about the perils of coming of age. Thoughtful, non-condescending, and humorous. **100m/C VHS.** Corey Haim, Kerri Green, Charlie Sheen, Winona Ryder, Courtney Thorne-Smith, Tom (Thomas E.) Hodges; ***D:*** David Seltzer; ***W:*** David Seltzer; ***M:*** Dave Grusin.

Lucie Aubrac 🦴🦴 **1998 (R)** In 1943, having freed her Resistance fighter husband, Raymond Samuel (Auteuil), from the Vichy police, Lucie Aubrac (Bouquet), is not about to let the Germans execute him. Even if it means using her pregnancy and tricking Gestapo commander Klaus Barbie (Ferch). Noble but rather emotionless. Based on a true story and Aubrac's novel "Ils Partiront Dans l'Ivresse." French with subtitles. **116m/C VHS.** *FR* Daniel Auteuil, Carole Bouquet, Patrice Chereau, Heino Ferch, Jean-Roger Milo, Jean Martin, Bernard Verley, Andrzej Seweryn, Hubert Saint Macary, Eric Boucher, Gregoire Oestermann; ***D:*** Claude Berri; ***W:*** Claude Berri; ***C:*** Vincenzo Marano; ***M:*** Philippe Sarde.

The Lucifer Complex 🦴 **1978** Nazi doctors are cloning exact duplicates of such world leaders as the Pope and the President of the United States on a remote South American island in the year 1996. **91m/C VHS.** Robert Vaughn, Merrie Lynn Ross, Keenan Wynn, Aldo Ray; ***D:*** David L. Hewitt, Kenneth Hartford.

Luck of the Draw 🦴🦴 **2000 (R)** Ex-con Marshall, who finds going straight to be very dull, finds some unexpected excitement when a couple of counterfeit printing plates come into his possession. He soon realizes that a lot of unsavory types are after the plates, including mob boss Hopper. Run-of-the-mill. **108m/C VHS, DVD.** James Marshall, Michael Madsen, Ice-T, Frank Gorshin, Eric Roberts, Dennis Hopper, Wendy Benson, William Forsythe, Sasha Mitchell, Richard Ruccolo; ***D:*** Luca Bercovici; ***W:*** Namon Ami, Rick Bloggs, Kandice King; ***C:*** Keith L. Smith; ***M:*** Stephen Edwards. **VIDEO**

Lucky Cisco Kid 🦴🦴½ **1940** Romero takes over from Warner Baxter in the fourth entry in the series, with Martin as his loyal sidekick. This time a rustler and his gang are stealing cattle and using the Kid's name to place the blame. Fast-paced with Romero appropriately debonair. Andrews screen debut. **67m/B VHS.** Cesar Romero, Chris-Pin (Ethier Crispin Martini) Martin, Mary Beth Hughes, Dana Andrews, Evelyn Venable, Joseph (Joe) Sawyer, Francis Ford; ***D:*** H. Bruce Humberstone; ***W:*** Robert Ellis, Helen Logan.

Lucky Devil 🦴½ **1925** Lucky devil wins car and motors around the country to the tune of organ music. **63m/B VHS.** Richard Dix, Esther Ralston, Edna May Oliver, Tom Findley; ***D:*** Frank Tuttle.

Lucky Jim 🦴🦴½ **1958** A junior lecturer in history at a small university tries to get himself in good graces with the head of his department, but is doomed from the start by doing the wrong things at the worst possible times. Minus the social satire of the Kingsley Amis novel on which it was based; what's left is a cheerful comedy. **91m/B VHS.** *GB* Ian Carmichael, Terry-Thomas, Hugh Griffith, Sharon Acker, Jean Anderson, Maureen Connell, Clive Morton, John Welsh, Reginald Beckwith, Kenneth Griffith, Jeremy Hawk, Harry Fowler; ***D:*** John Boulting, Roy Boulting; ***W:*** Jeffrey Dell, Patrick Campbell; ***C:*** Mutz Greenbaum; ***M:*** John Addison.

Lucky Luciano 🦴🦴 *A Proposito Luciano; RE: Lucky Luciano* **1974 (R)** A violent depiction of the final years of Lucky Luciano, gangster kingpin. **108m/C VHS.** *IT FR* Edmond O'Brien, Rod Steiger, Vincent Gardenia, Gian Marie Volonte; ***D:*** Francesco Rosi; ***C:*** Pasqualino De Santis.

Lucky Luke 🦴🦴½ **1994 (PG)** Fastest gun in the west brings the law to Daisy Town, aided by his horse, Jolly Jumper—who can talk. Not exactly John Wayne material but amusing. **91m/C VHS, DVD.** Terence Hill, Nancy Morgan, Ron Carey; ***D:*** Terence Hill; ***W:*** Rene Goscinny; ***C:*** Carlo Tafani, Gianfranco

Transunto; **M:** David Grover, Aaron Schroeder; **V:** Roger Miller.

Lucky Me ☙☙ **1954** A group of theatre entertainers are stranded in Miami and are forced to work in a hotel kitchen. They soon acquire the support of a wealthy oilman (Goodwin) who invests in their show, but not before his spoiled daughter tries to thwart all plans. ♫Lucky Me; Superstition Song; I Speak to the Stars; Take a Memo to the Moon; Love You Dearly; Bluebells of Broadway; Parisian Pretties; Wanna Sing Like an Angel; High Hopes. **100m/C VHS, Wide.** Doris Day, Robert Cummings, Phil Silvers, Eddie Foy Jr., Nancy Walker, Martha Hyer, Bill Goodwin, Marcel Dalio, James Burke, Jack Shea, William "Billy" Bakewell, Charles Cane, Ray Teal, Tom Powers, Angie Dickinson, Dolores Dorn; **D:** Jack Donohue.

Lucky Numbers ☙½ **2000 (R)** Here's a lucky number for you: Zero. That's the amount of time you should spend on this unfortunate comedy. TV weatherman Russ (Travolta) is caught up in a lavish lifestyle he can't afford because unseasonably warm weather is ruining his on-the-side snowmobile business. He schemes with the station's morally lax lotto ball girl Crystal (Kudrow) to fix a jackpot lottery, with her oafish cousin Walter (Moore) as the front man with the ticket. Their plan slips out, so they're hounded by a host of greedy dimwits hoping to get in on the action. Resnick, who hails from Harrisburg PA, where the movie is set, apparently has no qualms painting his fellow townspeople as amoral losers. Loosely based on a 1980 attempt to fix the Pennsylvania State Lottery. **105m/C VHS, DVD, Wide.** John Travolta, Lisa Kudrow, Tim Roth, Ed O'Neill, Michael Rapaport, Darryl (Chill) Mitchell, Bill Pullman, Richard Schiff, Michael Moore, Michael Weston, Sam McMurray; **D:** Nora Ephron; **W:** Adam Resnick; **C:** John Lindley; **M:** George Fenton.

Lucky Partners ☙☙ **1940** When an artist and an errand girl share a winning lottery ticket, funny complications arise as they embark on a fantasy honeymoon. Although Rogers' innocence and Coleman's savoir faire provide an interesting contrast, the script isn't equal to the status of its stars. **101m/B VHS.** Ronald Colman, Ginger Rogers, Jack Carson, Spring Byington, Harry Davenport; **D:** Lewis Milestone.

Lucky Stiff ☙☙ **1988 (PG)** A fat, unpopular dweeb has the shock of his life when a radiant woman falls in love with him, the strangeness of which becomes evident when he meets her very weird family. **93m/C VHS.** Donna Dixon, Joe Alaskey, Jeff Kober, Elizabeth Arlen, Charles Frank, Barbara Howard; **D:** Anthony Perkins; **W:** Pat Proft.

Lucky Terror ☙ **1936** Routine Hoot cowboy drama. **60m/B VHS.** Hoot Gibson, Lona Andre, Charles "Blackie" King; **D:** Alan James.

Lucky Texan ☙½ **1934** Wayne plays a tough easterner who goes West and finds himself involved with miners and claim jumpers. **61m/B VHS, DVD.** John Wayne, George "Gabby" Hayes, Yakima Canutt; **D:** Robert North Bradbury; **W:** Robert North Bradbury; **C:** Archie Stout.

Luckytown ☙½ **2000 (R)** Part road movie, part Vegas movie, part family ties, and none of the parts turn out to fit together. Oklahoman Lidda (Dusnt) gets a check on her 18th birthday from her long-gone dad, gambler Charlie (Caan), so she decides to track him down in Vegas. Along for the ride is store clerk and potential beau Colonel (Kartheiser), who happens to know his way around the cards himself. Only it turns out dad is in big trouble with club owner Tony (Miano) and the kids are soon caught in the middle. **101m/C VHS, DVD, Wide.** Kirsten Dunst, Vincent Kartheiser, James Caan, Robert Miano, Luis Guzman, Jennifer Gareis, Theresa Russell; **D:** Paul Nicholas; **W:** Brendon Beseth; **C:** Denis Maloney; **M:** Greg Edmonson.

Lucy and Desi: Before the Laughter ☙☙½ **1991 (PG-13)** The meeting and early married life of actress/comedian Lucille Ball and Cuban bandleader Desi Arnaz is depicted in this routine biopic. Film depicts Desi's womanizing, their struggles with fame, and their efforts to get their show on the air. Fisher does well as TV's favorite redhead but this effort is melodramatic. Daughter Lucy Arnaz vehemently opposed this depiction of her parents life. **95m/C VHS.** Frances Fisher, Maurice Benard, John Wheeler, Robin Pearson Rose; **D:** Charles Jarrott; **W:** William Luce. **TV**

L'Udienza ☙☙½ **1971** A bizarre black comedy about a guy who does anything he can, at any criminal cost, to obtain an audience with the Pope. In Italian with subtitles. **111m/C VHS.** *IT* Claudia Cardinale, Ugo Tognazzi; **D:** Marco Ferreri.

Ludwig ☙☙ **1972 (PG)** Lavish-but-slow epic bio of Bavaria's mad monarch, Ludwig II (Berger), who built extravagent fantasy castles and sponsored composer Richard Wagner (Howard), whom the king became obsessed with. Italian with subtitles. **231m/C VHS, Wide.** *IT GE* Helmut Berger, Trevor Howard, Romy Schneider, Silvana Mangano, Helmut Griem, Gert Frobe; **D:** Luchino Visconti; **W:** Luchino Visconti; **C:** Armando Nannuzzi.

Luggage of the Gods ☙☙ **1987 (G)** A lost tribe of cave people are confronted with civilization when suitcases fall from an airplane. Low-budget comedy reminiscent of "The Gods Must Be Crazy." **78m/C VHS.** Mark Stolzenberg, Gabriel Barre, Gwen Ellison; **D:** David Kendall.

Lullaby of Broadway ☙☙½ **1951** Many songs highlight this flimsy musical about a girl (Day) who ventures from England to the Big Apple in search of an acting career. She soon discovers that her mom has become a has-been actress now performing in a Greenwich Village dive. Day struggles to gain her own success while coping with her mother's downfall. ♫Lullaby of Broadway; You're Getting to Be a Habit With Me; Just One of Those Things; Somebody Loves Me; I Love the Way You Say Goodnight; Fine and Dandy; Please Don't Talk About Me When I'm Gone; A Shanty in Old Shanty Town; We'd Like to Go On A Trip. **93m/C VHS.** Doris Day, Gene Nelson, S.Z. Sakall, Billy De-Wolfe, Gladys George, Florence Bates; **D:** David Butler.

Lulu on the Bridge ☙☙½ **1998 (PG-13)** Jazz saxman Izzy Maurer (Keitel) sinks into depression when he can no longer perform. Walking one night, Izzy stumbles across a dead body and finds no ID—only a phone number and a mysterious stone that emits a blue light. Izzy calls the number, which belongs to actress/waitress Celia (Sorvino), and their first meeting finds them instantly in love (or some variation). Meanwhile, the mysterious Dr. Van Horn (Dafoe) questions Iggy about finding the stone. And things don't get much clearer. First solo directorial effort for Auster, who co-directed Keitel in "Blue in the Face," the spinoff to his screenplay "Smoke." **104m/C VHS, DVD.** Harvey Keitel, Mira Sorvino, Willem Dafoe, Gina Gershon, Mandy Patinkin, Vanessa Redgrave, Victor Argo, Kevin Corrigan, Richard Edson; **D:** Paul Auster; **W:** Paul Auster; **C:** Alik Sakharov; **M:** Graeme Revell.

Lumiere ☙☙½ **1976 (R)** An acclaimed drama about four actresses who, during the course of one night together, make pivotal decisions about their lives and relationships. Moreau's first directorial effort; dubbed. **101m/C VHS.** *FR* Jeanne Moreau, Lucia Bose, Francine Racette, Caroline Cartier, Keith Carradine, Francois Simon, Francis Huster, Bruno Ganz, Rene Feret, Niels Arestrup, Jerome Lapperrousaz; **D:** Jeanne Moreau; **W:** Jeanne Moreau; **C:** Ricardo Aronovich; **M:** Astor Piazzolla.

Luminarias ☙☙ **1999 (R)** Romantic comedy about four Hispanic friends looking for love in East L.A. and meeting to console each other at the Luminarias restaurant. Lawyer Andrea (Fernandez), who's divorcing her philandering husband (Beltran), finds herself attracted to anglo Joseph (Bakula). Therapist Sofia (DuBois) has always tried to distance herself from her roots but gets is surprised by her feelings for cute Mexican waiter Pablo (Lopez). Artist Lilly (Moya) is hoping to change her luck in love with Korean Lu (Lim) only to run into prejudice from his parents and sexy designer Irene (Ortelli) has sworn off sex for Lent and is trying to accept her cross-dressing gay brother (Rivas). The friendships are believable even if there's too much going on with the plot. **101m/C VHS, DVD.** Evelina Fernandez, Marta DuBois, Dyana Ortelli, Angela Moya, Scott Bakula, Robert Beltran, Sal Lopez, Andrew C. Lim, Geoffrey Rivas, Richard "Cheech" Marin; **D:** Jose Luis Valenzuela; **W:** Evelina Fernandez; **C:** Alex Phillips Jr.; **M:** Eric Allaman.

Luminous Motion ☙☙ **2000** Phillip (Lloyd) is an introspective 10-year-old who spends his life on the road travelling in a red Impala with his mother (Unger), a beautiful, depressed lush who drifts from man to man. But the only male she's really close to is her son—until Phillip's father (Sheridan) finds them and wants to reclaim his family. Except the boundaries between Phillip's reality and his imagination aren't very clear at all. Based on Bradfield's novel "The History of Luminous Motion." **94m/C VHS, DVD, Wide.** Eric Lloyd, Deborah Kara Unger, Jamey Sheridan, Terry Kinney, Paz de la Huerta, James Berland; **D:** Bette Gordon; **W:** Scott Bradfield, Robert Roth; **C:** Teodoro Maniaci; **M:** Lesley Barber.

Luna e L'Altra ☙☙ **1996** Dizzy schoolteacher Luna (Forte) is the butt of practical jokes by her students and ignored by the other faculty. Dutiful and self-effacing, she's also the secret crush of school custodian Angelo (Nichetti). But Luna has a hidden side that comes to the surface thanks to magician Igor's magic latern and it turns out to be a sexy one. Italian with subtitles. **92m/C VHS.** *IT* Iaia Forte, Maurizio Nichetti, Aurelio Fierro, Luigi Burruano; **D:** Maurizio Nichetti; **W:** Maurizio Nichetti; **C:** Luca Bigazzi; **M:** Carlo Siliotto.

Luna Park ☙☙ **1991** In contemporary Russia, Andrei (Goutine) is the leader of a gang of body-builder, right-wing skinheads who beat up Jews, foreigners, and anyone else they dislike. Then the anti-Semitic Andrei learns his father is Jewish and he frantically searches through Moscow to find him and discover his past. In Russian with subtitles. **105m/C VHS.** *RU* Oleg Borisov, Andrei Goutine, Natalya Yegorova; **D:** Pavel (Lungin) Lounguine; **W:** Pavel (Lungin) Lounguine.

Lunatic ☙ **1991** "Some minds should be wasted" according to the film promo and if you're in the mood for an amateur mind (and time) waster, this is for you. High schoolers in the woods encounter mayhem in the best horror tradition as the innocents are slaughtered by an escapee from the local lunatic asylum. **90m/C VHS.** Rocky Tucker, Ondrea Tucker, Brian D'Lawrence, Keith Vallot, Bronwyn St. John, Cameron Derrick, Ernest Jackson, Rookie Macpherson, Susan Spain; **D:** James Tucker; **W:** James Tucker.

The Lunatic ☙☙ **1992 (R)** A robust, oversexed, and scheming German tourist travels to Jamaica where she meets the village idiot, a man who regularly holds conversations with the local plants. The two hook up with a butcher, and the three live happily in the hills, that is until the money is gone. The Jamaican scenery, a few bawdy laughs, and a great reggae soundtrack make this one worthwhile. **93m/C VHS.** *GB* Julie Wallace, Paul Campbell, Reggie Carter, Carl Bradshaw; **D:** Lol Creme; **M:** Wally Badarou.

Lunatics: A Love Story ☙☙☙ **1992 (PG-13)** Hank (Raimi) is an ex-mental patient poet suffering from hallucinations and afraid to leave his Los Angeles apartment. For companionship he dials a party-line until, one day, he misdials and insteads gets the number of a local pay telephone, which is answered by a naive woman dumped by her boyfriend. When Nancy (Foreman) decides to visit Hank you learn she's as crazy as he is—so it only makes sense they would fall in love. A well-acted fable of how love fragilely connects even the most unlikely of people. **87m/C VHS.** Theodore (Ted) Raimi, Deborah Foreman, Bruce Campbell, Brian McCree, Eddie Rosmaya, Michele Stacey, George Aguilar; **D:** Josh Becker; **W:** Josh Becker; **C:** Jeffrey Dougherty; **M:** Joseph LoDuca.

Lunatics & Lovers ☙½ **1976 (PG)** Musician meets a bizarre nobleman who is in love with an imaginary woman. **92m/C VHS.** *IT* Marcello Mastroianni, Lino Toffalo; **D:** Flavio Mogherini.

Lunch Wagon ☙☙ *Come 'n' Get It; Lunch Wagon Girls* **1981 (R)** Two co-eds are given a restaurant to manage during summer vacation and wind up involved in a hilarious diamond chase and sex romp. **88m/C VHS.** Rick Podell, Candy Moore, Pamela Bryant, Rosanne Katon; **D:** Ernest Pintoff.

Lupo ☙☙ **1970 (G)** When threatened with the loss of his home and the separation of his family, an exuberant Greek man challenges the modern world. **99m/C VHS.** Yehuda Barkan, Gabi Armoni, Esther Greenberg; **D:** Menahem Golan.

Lure of the Islands ☙ **1942** Federal agents track wanted criminals to an island retreat in this highly predictable low-budget thriller. **61m/B VHS.** Margie Hart, Robert Lowery, Guinn "Big Boy" Williams, Warren Hymer, Gale Storm; **D:** Jean Yarbrough.

Lure of the Sila ☙☙½ **1949** Italian melodrama about a young peasant girl infiltrating a landowner's home in order to avenge the death of her brother and mother. Dubbed and more interesting than it sounds. **72m/B VHS, 8mm.** *IT* Silvana Mangano, Amedeo Nazzari, Vittorio Gassman; **D:** Duilio Coletti.

Lured ☙☙½ **1947** Ball gives a fine dramatic performance in Sirk's glossy thriller. Sandra (Ball) is an American dancer in London whose friend falls victim to a lonelyhearts killer. She agrees to act as a decoy for Scotland Yard even while getting involved with nightclub owner Robert Fleming (Sanders), who turns out to be one of the suspects. **103m/B VHS, DVD.** Lucille Ball, George Sanders, Charles Coburn, Cedric Hardwicke, Boris Karloff, Alan Mowbray, George Zucco, Joseph Calleia, Tanis Chandler, Alan Napier, Robert Coote; **D:** Douglas Sirk; **W:** Leo Rosten; **C:** William H. Daniels; **M:** Michel Michelet.

Lured Innocence ☙☙ **1997 (R)** Steamy romance in a small town leads to murderous impulses. Elsie (Shelton) is having an affair with older, married Rick (Hopper). Then his ailing wife (Shire) finds out and threatens the twosome. The lovers aren't pleased and there's an eventual murder trial where one of the key witnesses is a newspaper reporter (Gummersall), who was also Elsie's lover. **97m/C VHS, DVD.** Dennis Hopper, Marley Shelton, Devon Gummersall, Talia Shire; **D:** Kikuo Kawasaki; **W:** Kikuo Kawasaki; **C:** Irek Hartowicz.

Lurkers woof! **1988 (R)** An unappealing metaphysical morass about a woman who has been haunted throughout her life by...something. **90m/C VHS.** Christine Moore, Gary Warner, Marina Taylor, Carissa Channing, Tom Billett; **D:** Roberta Findlay; **W:** Ed Kelleher, Hariette Vidal; **C:** Roberta Findlay.

Lurking Fear ☙☙ **1994 (R)** The town of Lefferts Corner has suffered from generations of horror thanks to man-eating ghouls that dwell beneath the local graveyard and arise whenever a storm breaks out. The inhabitants prepare to fight back but their plan is hindered by the arrival of a group of criminals who are after a fortune supposedly hidden in one of the graves. Based on a story by H.P. Lovecraft. **78m/C VHS.** Jon Finch, Blake Bailey, Ashley Lauren, Jeffrey Combs, Paul Mantee, Allison Mackie, Joe Leavengood, Vincent Schiavelli; **D:** C. Courtney Joyner; **W:** C. Courtney Joyner; **M:** Jim Manzie.

Luscious ☙½ *Vivid* **1997 (R)** It's about sex. Cole (Shellan) is a painter having inspiration problems. Then he splashes girlfriend Billie (Wuhrer) with paint and they have sex on the canvas. Suddenly his art is selling like hotcakes but Billie gets a little tired being a literal paint brush. An unrated version has three more minutes of sex and nudity. **83m/C VHS, DVD.** Stephen Shellen, Kari Wuhrer; **D:** Evan Georgiades. **VIDEO**

Lush ☙☙ **2001 (R)** The New Orleans setting is the best thing about this limp drama. Alcoholic golf pro Lionel Exley (Scott) is friends with alcoholic lawyer Carter (Harris), who names his buddy his beneficiary in an insurance policy. The lawyer promptly gets murdered and Exley decides to go on the lam from the suspicious cops, winding up taking refuge with two upper-crusty sisters Ahley (Holloman) and Rachel (Linney). **94m/C VHS, DVD.** Campbell Scott, Laura Linney, Jared Harris, Laurel Holloman; ***D:*** Mark Gibson; ***W:*** Mark Gibson; ***C:*** Caroline Champetier; ***M:*** Barrett Martin.

Lush Life 🦴🦴🦴 **1994 (R)** New York jazz session musicians Al (Goldblum) and Buddy (Whitaker) roam the city's musical scene until dawn, on the prowl for food, women, and ever more music. When trumpeter Buddy is diagnosed with an inoperable brain tumor, saxophonist Al decides on a grand final gesture—a Park Avenue farewell bash, though no one is to know just how final the farewell is to be. Great jazz soundtrack, fine acting, and atmospheric use of the Big Apple. And it avoids overt tearjerking. **96m/C VHS.** Jeff Goldblum, Forest Whitaker, Kathy Baker, Lois Chiles, Don Cheadle; ***D:*** Michael Elias; ***W:*** Michael Elias. CABLE

Lust and Revenge 🦴🦴 **1995** When wealthy George Oliphant (Haywood) needs a tax break, he commissions a statue (to be donated to the National Gallery) and gets daughter Georgina (Karvan) to choose the subject and artist. Flirty Georgina hires lesbian sculptress Lily (Eagger) and decides on the depiction of a male nude, for which Karl-Heniz Applebaum (Hope) is hired to pose. Applebaum's religious wife Cecilia (Dobrowolska) is not pleased, especially when hubby begins an affair. But she's also not above plotting a suitable revenge. Last role for Hargreaves (a cameo as a gallery habitue) while Hughes, who also worked for director Cox in "My First Wife," plays a male financial adviser. **95m/C VHS.** *AU* Claudia Karvan, Chris Haywood, Nicholas Hope, Gosia Dobrowolska, Victoria Eagger, Norman Kaye; ***Cameos:*** Wendy Hughes, John Hargreaves; ***D:*** Paul Cox; ***W:*** Paul Cox, John Clarke; ***C:*** Nino Martinetti; ***M:*** Paul Grabowsky.

Lust for a Vampire 🦴🦴 *To Love a Vampire* **1971 (R)** The sanguine tale of a deadly vampire who indiscriminately preys on pupils and teachers when she enrolls at a British finishing school. Moody and erotically charged, with an impressive ending. Quasi-sequel to "The Vampire Lovers." **95m/C VHS, DVD, Wide.** *GB* Ralph Bates, Barbara Jefford, Suzanna Leigh, Michael Johnson, Yutte Stensgaard, Pippa Steele, Helen Christie, David Healy, Mike Raven; ***D:*** Jimmy Sangster; ***W:*** Tudor Gates; ***C:*** David Muir.

Lust for Freedom 🦴 **1987** An undercover cop decides to hit the road after she sees her partner gunned down. She winds up near the California-Mexico border, where she is wrongly imprisoned with a number of other young women in a white slavery business. This low-budget film includes lots of steamy women-behind-bars sex scenes. **92m/C VHS.** Melanie Coll, William J. Kulzer; ***D:*** Eric Louzil.

Lust for Gold 🦴🦴 **1949** Ford battles against greedy former lover Lupino and her husband for control of the Lost Dutchman gold mine. **90m/B VHS.** Ida Lupino, Glenn Ford, Gig Young, William Prince, Edgar Buchanan, Will Geer, Paul Ford, Jay Silverheels; ***D:*** Sylvan Simon; ***M:*** George Duning.

Lust for Life 🦴🦴🦴½ **1956** Absorbing, serious biography of Vincent Van Gogh, from his first paintings to his death. Remarkable for Douglas' furiously convincing portrayal. Featuring dozens of actual Van Gogh works from private collections. Based on an Irving Stone novel, produced by John Houseman. **122m/C VHS, Wide.** Kirk Douglas, Anthony Quinn, James Donald, Pamela Brown, Everett Sloane, Henry Daniell, Niall MacGinnis, Noel Purcell, Lionel Jeffries, Jill Bennett; ***D:*** Vincente Minnelli; ***M:*** Miklos Rozsa. Oscars '56: Support. Actor (Quinn); Golden Globes '57: Actor—Drama (Douglas); N.Y. Film Critics '56: Actor (Douglas).

Lust in the Dust 🦴🦴🦴 **1985 (R)** When part of a treasure map is found on the derriere of none other than Divine, the hunt is on for the other half. This comedy western travels to a sleepy town called Chile Verde (green chili for those who don't speak Spanish) and the utterly ridiculous turns comically corrupt. Deliciously distasteful fun. Features Divine singing a bawdy love song in his/her break from John Waters. **85m/C VHS, DVD, Wide.** Tab Hunter, Divine, Lainie Kazan, Geoffrey Lewis, Henry Silva, Cesar Romero, Gina Gallego, Courtney Gains, Woody Strode, Pedro Gonzalez-Gonzalez; ***D:*** Paul Bartel; ***W:*** Philip John Taylor; ***C:*** Paul Lohmann; ***M:*** Peter Matz.

The Lusty Men 🦴🦴🦴 **1952** Two rival rodeo champions, both in love with the same woman, work the rodeo circuit until a tragic accident occurs. Mitchum turns in a fine performance as the has-been rodeo star trying to make it big again. **113m/B VHS.** Robert Mitchum, Susan Hayward, Arthur Kennedy, Arthur Hunnicutt; ***D:*** Nicholas Ray; ***C:*** Lee Garmes.

Luther 🦴🦴½ **1974 (G)** A well-acted characterization of Martin Luther's development from a young seminarian to his leadership of the Reformation Movement. **112m/C VHS.** Stacy Keach, Patrick Magee, Hugh Griffith, Robert Stephens, Alan Badel, Julian Glover, Judi Dench, Leonard Rossiter, Maurice Denham, Peter Cellier, Thomas Heathcote, Malcolm Stoddard, Bruce Carstairs; ***D:*** Guy Green; ***W:*** Edward Anhalt, John Osborne; ***C:*** Frederick A. (Freddie) Young; ***M:*** John Addison.

Luther the Geek woof! **1990** Little Luther's visit to the circus is dramatically changed when he sees the geek, a sideshow freak. Since then Luther has taken to biting off chicken's heads and drinking their blood in his small Illinois town; the town will never be the same. (And neither will you if you watch this stupid film.) **90m/C VHS.** Edward Terry, Joan Roth, J. Jerome Clarke, Tom Mills, Stacy Haiduk; ***D:*** Carlton J. Albright; ***W:*** Whitey Styles; ***C:*** David Knox.

Luv 🦴½ **1967 (PG)** Although good cast tries hard, they can't do much with this comic farce. Three intellectuals, including one that's suicidal, discuss the trials and tribulations of their middle-class New York existence. **95m/C VHS.** Jack Lemmon, Peter Falk, Elaine May; ***D:*** Clive Donner; ***W:*** Murray Schisgal; ***C:*** Ernest Laszlo.

The Luzhin Defence 🦴🦴 **2000 (PG-13)** Luzhin (Turturro) is an eccentric Russian chess genius who is staying at an Italian lakeside resort in 1929 preparing for an important match. Also preparing for a match—the marital kind—is Russian emigre Natalia (Watson) and her aristocratic mother Vera (James). And Luzhin is not the man Vera has in mind for her daughter, no matter what Natalia thinks. But as the stress of the match takes its toll on Luzhin, he believes he cannot have both love and the game. Based on the 1930 novel by Vladimir Nabokov. **106m/C VHS, DVD, Wide.** *FR GB* John Turturro, Emily Watson, Geraldine James, Stuart Wilson, Christopher Thompson, Peter Blythe, Orla Brady, Fabio Sartor; ***D:*** Marleen Gorris; ***W:*** Peter Berry; ***C:*** Bernard Lutic; ***M:*** Alexandre Desplat.

Luzia 🦴🦴½ **1988** Ohana stars as a tough and sexy Brazilian cowgirl who is caught in the middle of a class struggle where the personal is definitely political. Her horseriding skills and beauty give her options in both lifestyles. Will she choose to side with the squatters or the wealthy landowners? In Portuguese with English subtitles. **112m/C VHS.** *BR* Claudia Ohana, Thales Pan Chacon, Jose de Abreu, Luiza Falcao; ***D:*** Fabio Barreto.

Lydia 🦴🦴🦴 **1941** Sentimental drama in which an elderly lady (Oberon) gets to relive her romantic past when she has a reunion with four of her lost loves. Well acted and directed, Oberon gives one of her best performances ever. Adapted from the highly regarded French film "Un Carnet de Bal." **98m/B VHS.** Merle Oberon, Joseph Cotten, Alan Marshal, George Reeves; ***D:*** Julien Duvivier; ***C:*** Lee Garmes; ***M:*** Miklos Rozsa.

Lying Lips 🦴½ **1939** All-black detective mystery about a young nightclub singer framed for murder. Her boyfriend then turns detective to clear her name. **60m/B VHS.** Edna Mae Harris, Carmen Newsome, Earl Jones, Amanda Randolph; ***D:*** Oscar Micheaux.

M 🦴🦴🦴🦴 **1931** The great Lang dissection of criminal deviance, following the tortured last days of a child murderer, and the efforts of both the police and the underground to bring him to justice. Poetic, compassionate, and chilling. Inspired by real-life serial killer Peter Kurten, known as "Vampire of Dusseldorf," Lang also borrowed story elements from Jack the Ripper's killing spree. Lorre's screen debut. Lang's personal favorite among his own films. In German with English subtitles. Remade in 1951. **111m/B VHS, DVD.** *GE* Peter Lorre, Ellen Widmann, Inge Landgut, Gustav Grundgens, Otto Wernicke, Ernest Stahl-Nachbaur, Franz Stein, Theodore Loos, Fritz Gnass, Fritz Odemar, Paul Kemp, Theo Lingen, Georg John, Karl Platen, Rosa Valetti, Hertha von Walther, Rudolf Blumner; ***D:*** Fritz Lang; ***W:*** Fritz Lang, Thea von Harbou; ***C:*** Fritz Arno Wagner, Gustav Rathje; ***M:*** Edvard Grieg.

M. Butterfly 🦴🦴 **1993 (R)** Disappointing adaptation of Hwang's award-winning play, which was based on a true story. Irons is Rene Gallimard, a minor French diplomat sent to China in 1964. Taken in by the exoticism of the mysterious east, he falls for a Chinese opera performer, Song Liling (Lone). Only she's no lady and the oblivious diplomat turns out to be a patsy as Song Liling uses him to gather information. The story only works if the passion, however deceptive, between Gallimard and Song Liling is believable, passion which is noticeably lacking between Irons and Lone. Irons comes across as too intelligent to be gullibile and the usually excellent Lone does not make his role believable. **101m/C VHS, Wide.** Jeremy Irons, John Lone, Ian Richardson, Barbara Sukowa, Vernon Dobtcheff, Annabel Leventon, Shizuko Hoshi, Richard McMillan; ***D:*** David Cronenberg; ***W:*** David Henry Hwang; ***M:*** Howard Shore.

Ma and Pa Kettle 🦴🦴½ *The Further Adventures of Ma and Pa Kettle* **1949** The hillbilly couple were supporting characters in "The Egg and I" but their popularity found them spun off into their own cornpone series. This first feature finds the couple and their 15 children about to be evicted only to have Pa win a tobacco slogan contest. The prize is a brand-new fully automated house whose futuristic contraptions get the better of Pa. **76m/B VHS.** Marjorie Main, Percy Kilbride, Richard Long, Meg Randall, Esther Dale, Barry Kelley, Patricia Alphin; ***D:*** Charles Lamont; ***W:*** Al Lewis, Herbert Margolis, Louis Morheim.

Ma and Pa Kettle at Home 🦴🦴½ **1954** Elwin, one of the Kettle's 15 children, is a finalist in an essay contest that could win him a college scholarship. Then Pa Kettle hears the two judges plan to visit each of the finalists' homes so he tries to spruce-up the family's tumbled-down farm. **80m/B VHS.** Marjorie Main, Percy Kilbride, Alan Mowbray, Ross Elliott, Brett Halsey, Mary Wickes, Irving Bacon, Emory Parnell; ***D:*** Charles Lamont; ***W:*** Kay Lenard.

Ma and Pa Kettle at the Fair 🦴🦴½ **1952** The Kettle's eldest daughter Rosie wants to go to college so Ma enters the county fair baking contest to win some money and Pa buys a decrepit old nag to enter in the fair's horse race. Somehow things just have a way of working out for the Kettles. **79m/B VHS.** Marjorie Main, Percy Kilbride, Lori Nelson, James Best, Esther Dale, Russell Simpson, Emory Parnell; ***D:*** Charles T. Barton; ***W:*** John Grant, Richard Morris.

Ma and Pa Kettle at Waikiki 🦴🦴½ **1955** Ma (Main) and Pa (Kilbride), as well as oldest daughter Rosie (Nelson), head for Hawaii to help out cousin Rodney's (Smith) pineapple factory. Seems he's ill and about to go bankrupt and he thinks Pa is some kind of financial whiz who can bail him out. Pa accidentally does help the business and then gets kidnapped by some sleazy competitors. But it's Ma to the rescue (and the bad guys don't stand a chance). Kilbride retired after his seventh take as Pa in the comedy series. **79m/B VHS.** Marjorie Main, Percy Kilbride, Lori Nelson, Loring Smith, Russell Johnson, Byron Palmer, Mabel Albertson, Hilo Hattie, Fay Roope, Oliver Blake, Lowell Gilmore, Teddy Hart; ***D:*** Lee Sholem; ***W:*** Jack Henley, Harry Clork, Elwood Ullman.

Ma and Pa Kettle Back On the Farm 🦴🦴½ **1951** First-time grandparents, the Kettles have to deal with their daughter-in-law's snobby Bostonian parents and their parenting ideas. The family's also moved back to their ramshackle farm where Pa thinks he's found uranium, leading to all sorts of problems. **81m/B VHS.** Marjorie Main, Percy Kilbride, Richard Long, Meg Randall, Ray Collins, Barbara Brown, Emory Parnell; ***D:*** Edward Sedgwick; ***W:*** Jack Henley.

Ma and Pa Kettle Go to Town 🦴🦴½ **1950** Ma and Pa head off for New York City when Pa wins a jingle-writing contest, unknowingly leaving their brood in the care of on the lam mobster Mike, who asks the Kettles to deliver a package to his brother. This gets both the crooks and the cops trailing the hillbilly couple, whose backwoods ways are more than a match for any city slicker. **80m/B VHS.** Marjorie Main, Percy Kilbride, Richard Long, Meg Randall, Charles McGraw, Ray Collins, Esther Dale, Ellen Corby, Barbara Brown; ***D:*** Charles Lamont; ***W:*** Martin Ragaway, Leonard Stern.

Ma and Pa Kettle on Vacation 🦴🦴½ *Ma and Pa Kettle Go to Paris* **1953** Ma and Pa visit Paris as guests of their son's wealthy in-laws and Pa unwittingly gets involved with spies and shady ladies. **79m/B VHS.** Marjorie Main, Percy Kilbride, Ray Collins, Sig Rumann, Bodil Miller, Barbara Brown, Peter Brocco, Jay Novello; ***D:*** Charles Lamont; ***W:*** Jack Henley.

Ma Barker's Killer Brood 🦴🦴 **1960** Biography of the infamous American criminal and her four sons, edited together from a TV serial. The shoot-'em-up scenes and Tuttle's performance keep the pace from slackening. **82m/B VHS.** Lurene Tuttle, Tristram Coffin, Paul Dubov, Nelson Leigh, Myrna Dell, Vic Lundin, Donald Spruance; ***D:*** Bill Karn.

Ma Saison Preferee 🦴🦴🦴 *My Favorite Season* **1993** Focuses on the intense relationship between a middleaged brother (Auteuil) and sister (Deneuve). When the elderly Berthe (Villalonga) collapses, she goes to stay with daughter Emilie and her family, which provides Emilie with an excuse to invite her estranged brother Antoine for Christmas. It's a disaster with numerous family fights, that leads Emilie to declare her marriage over and to an eventual reapproachmont with Antoine. Film is divided into four parts, to coincide with the four seasons, beginning with autumn and ending with summer. French with subtitles. Deneuve and Auteuil reteamed for Techine's "Les Voleurs." **124m/C VHS, DVD, Wide.** *FR* Daniel Auteuil, Catherine Deneuve, Marthe Villalonga, Jean-Pierre Bouvier, Chiara Mastroianni, Anthony Prada, Carmen Chaplin; ***D:*** Andre Techine; ***W:*** Andre Techine; ***C:*** Thierry Arbogast; ***M:*** Philippe Sarde.

Ma Vie en Rose 🦴🦴🦴 *My Life in Pink* **1997 (R)** Berliner's debut portrays seven-year-old misfit Ludovic (du Fresne), who is convinced he's really a girl and likes to dress in girls' clothes. His close-knit family merely regards this as a childhood eccentricity Ludovic will grow out of. But when the child decides he's going to marry Jerome (Rivere), the boy next door, and stages a mock wedding ceremony, things get a bit dicey. Jerome's father is the straitlaced Albert (Hanssens), who happens to be the boss of Ludovic's father, Pierre (Ecoffey), and he's not nearly so understanding (neither are the other neighbors in the conservative Parisian suburb). Poignant and funny look at a child's search for identity. Convincing turn by pre-pubescent performer du Fresne. **90m/C VHS, DVD, Wide.** *BE FR GB* Georges Du-Fresne, Jean-Philippe Ecoffey, Michele Laroque, Daniel Hanssens, Julien Riviere, Helene Vincent, Laurence Bibot, Jean-Francois Galotte, Caroline Baehr, Marie Bunuel; ***D:*** Alain Berliner; ***W:*** Alain Berliner, Chris Vander Stappen; ***C:*** Yves Cape; ***M:*** Dominique Dalcan. Golden Globes '98: Foreign Film.

Mabel & Fatty **1916** Three silent shorts featuring the two stars, made with Mack Sennett: "He Did and He Didn't," "Mabel and Fatty Viewing The World's Fair at San Francisco" (with scenes of the actual 1914 World's Fair) and "Mabel's Blunder." **61m/B VHS, 8mm.** Mabel Normand, Fatty Arbuckle, Al "Fuzzy" St. John.

Maborosi 🦴🦴🦴 *Mirage; Maboroshi no Hikari* **1995** Yumiko (Esumi) has a contented life in Osaka with her husband Ikuo (Asano) and their newborn son. Yet, inexplicably, her husband commits suicide one night. Later, a neighbor of Yumiko's helps her with an arranged marriage to prosperous widower Tamio (Naitoh), who lives in a remote fishing village, and once again things seem to be happy. But her first husband's death still haunts her and Yumiko seeks an explanation that will allow her to have some peace in her life. Adapted from a story by Teru Miyamoto. Japanese with subtitles. **110m/C VHS, DVD, Wide.** *JP* Makiko Esumi, Takashi Naito, Tadanobu Asano, Gohki Kashiyama; ***D:*** Hirokazu Kore-eda; ***W:*** Yoshihisa Ogita; ***C:*** Masao Nakabori; ***M:*** Chen Ming-Chang.

Mac 🦴🦴🦴 **1993 (R)** It's a family affair. Immigrant carpenter's funeral is the starting point for the story of his three sons, construction workers who live in Queens, New York in the 1950s. The passionate bros battle, bitch, and build, with Turturro as the eldest summing up the prevailing philosophy: "It's the doing, that's the thing." Turturro's directorial debut is a labor of love and a tribute to his own dad. Filmed on location in New York City. Fine performances from newcomers Badalucco and Capotorto are complemented by smaller roles from Amos, Barkin, and Turturro's real-life wife Borowitz and brother Nick. **118m/C VHS, Wide.** John Turturro, Carl Capotorto, Michael Badalucco, Katherine Borowitz, John Amos, Olek Krupa, Ellen Barkin, Joe Paparone, Nicholas Turturro, Dennis Farina, Steven Randazzo; ***D:*** John Turturro; ***W:*** Brandon Cole, John Turturro; ***C:*** Ron Fortunato; ***M:*** Richard Termini, Vin Tese.

Mac and Me 🦴 **1988 (PG)** Lost E.T.-like alien stranded on Earth befriends a wheelchair-bound boy. Aimed at young kids, it's full of continual product plugs, most notably for McDonald's. Make the kids happy and stick to the real thing. **94m/C VHS.** Christine Ebersole, Jonathan Ward, Katrina Caspary, Lauren Stanley, Jade Calegory; ***D:*** Stewart Raffill; ***W:*** Stewart Raffill; ***M:*** Alan Silvestri. Golden Raspberries '88: Worst Director (Raffill).

Macabre 🦴🦴 **1977** A beautiful woman, lustful and precocious, kills her husband and his twin brother. **89m/C VHS.** Larry Ward, Teresa Gimpera, Giacomo "Jack" Rossi-Stuart.

Macabre 🦴 *Frozen Terror* **1980** A madman resembling both Jack Frost and Jack the Ripper claims victims at random. **90m/C VHS, DVD, Wide.** Bernice Stegers, Stanko Molnar, Veronica Zinny, Roberto Posse; ***D:*** Lamberto Bava; ***W:*** Lamberto Bava, Antonio Avati; ***C:*** Franco Delli Colli.

Macao 🦴🦴🦴 **1952** On the lam for a crime he didn't commit, an adventurer sails to the exotic Far East, meets a buxom cafe singer, and helps Interpol catch a notorious crime boss. A strong film noir entry. Russell sneers, Mitchum wise cracks. Director von Sternberg's last film for RKO. **81m/B VHS.** Robert Mitchum, Jane Russell, William Bendix, Gloria Grahame; ***D:*** Josef von Sternberg.

Macaroni 🦴½ *Maccheroni* **1985 (PG)** An uptight American businessman returns to Naples 40 years after being stationed there in WWII. Comedic situations abound when he is reunited with his Italian war buddy, brother of his lover. Pleasant acting can't save irritating script. **104m/C VHS.** *IT* Jack Lemmon, Marcello Mastroianni, Daria Nicolodi, Isa Danieli; ***D:*** Ettore Scola; ***W:*** Ettore Scola.

MacArthur 🦴🦴 **1977 (PG)** General Douglas MacArthur's life from Corregidor in 1942 to his dismissal a decade later in the midst of the Korean conflict. Episodic sage with forceful Peck but weak supporting characters. Fourteen minutes were cut from the original version; intended to be Peck's "Patton," it falls short of the mark. **130m/C VHS, DVD, Wide.** Gregory Peck, Ivan Bonar, Ward (Edward) Costello, Nicolas Coster, Dan O'Herlihy; ***D:*** Joseph Sargent; ***W:*** Hal Barwood, Matthew Robbins; ***C:*** Mario Tosi; ***M:*** Jerry Goldsmith.

MacArthur's Children 🦴🦴🦴 **1985** A poignant evocation of life in a Japanese fishing village as it faces the end of WWII and American occupation. Not as good as some of the other Japanese films, but it is an interesting look at the changes in culture caused by their defeat in the war. In Japanese with English subtitles. **115m/C VHS.** *JP* Masako Natsume, Shima Iwashita, Hiromi Go, Takaya Yamamauchi, Shiori Sakura, Ken(saku) Watanabe, Juzo Itami, Yoshiyuka Omori; ***D:*** Masahiro Shinoda; ***W:*** Takeski Tamura.

Macbeth 🦴🦴🦴½ **1948** Shakespeare's classic tragedy is performed with a celebrated lead performance by Welles, who plays the tragic king as a demonic leader of a barbaric society. A low budget adaptation with cheap sets, a three-week shooting schedule, lots of mood, and an attempt at Scottish accents. After making this film, Welles took a 10-year break from Hollywood. **111m/B VHS.** Orson Welles, Jeanette Nolan, Dan O'Herlihy, Roddy McDowall, Robert Coote; ***D:*** Orson Welles.

Macbeth 🦴🦴🦴 **1971 (R)** Polanski's notorious adaptation of the Shakespearean classic, marked by realistic design, unflinching violence, and fatalistic atmosphere. Finch and Annis star as Macbeth and his equally murderous lady (who appears nude in the sleepwalking scene). Polanski's first film following the grisly murder of his pregnant wife, actress Sharon Tate, was torn apart by critics but it contains stunning fight scenes and fine acting. It is in fact a worthy continuation of his work in the horror genre. Very well made. First film made by Playboy Enterprises. Originally rated X. **139m/C VHS, DVD, Wide.** Jon Finch, Nicholas Selby, Martin Shaw, Francesca Annis, Terence Baylor, John Stride, Stephan Chase, Noelle Rimmington, Maisie Farquhar, Elsie Taylor; ***D:*** Roman Polanski; ***W:*** Roman Polanski, Kenneth Tynan; ***C:*** Gilbert Taylor.

Macbeth 🦴🦴🦴 **1976** An extraordinary version of Shakespeare's "Macbeth" in which all the fire, ambition and doom of his text come brilliantly to life. **137m/C** Eric Porter, Janet Suzman.

Macbeth 🦴🦴 **1990** Another production of the classic tragedy by Shakespeare. Produced as part of HBO's Thames Collection. **110m/C VHS.** Michael Jayston, Leigh Hunt.

Mach 2 🦴🦴½ **2000 (R)** A senator, who's running for president, has gotten hold of a computer disk that reveals treachery by the current vice president. White House Secret Service agents are sent to retrieve the disk from the Senator (who's boarded the Concorde) and set it up so that the plane will be destroyed. Bosworth is the Air Force hero who won't let that happen. **94m/C VHS, DVD, Wide.** Brian Bosworth, Michael Dorn, Shannon Whirry, Cliff Robertson, Lance Guest, Bruce Weitz; ***D:*** Ed Raymond; ***W:*** Steve Latshaw; ***C:*** Thomas Callaway; ***M:*** Eric Wurst, David Wurst. **VIDEO**

The Machine 🦴🦴 **1996** Psychiatrist and inventor Marc Lacroix (Depardieu) is obsessed with the brain. He develops a brain transfer machine and decides to test it on himself (naturally) by fusing his psyche with that of his patient, cold-blooded killer Michael Zyto (does this sound like a good idea to you?). Naturally, the experiment causes terrifying consequences for Lacroix and his family. **96m/C VHS.** Gerard Depardieu, Nathalie Baye, Didier Boundon, Natalia Woerner, Erwan Baynaud; ***D:*** Francois Dupeyron; ***W:*** Francois Dupeyron; ***C:*** Dietrich Lohmann; ***M:*** Michel Portal.

Machine Gun Blues 🦴🦴 *Black Rose of Harlem; Pistol Blues* **1995 (R)** 1930s jazz singer Georgia (Williams) sings at a black-owned club that mobster Constanza (Viterelli) wants to take over. Right-hand man Johnny Verona (Cassavettes) is sent to help things along and makes the mistake of falling for the chanteuse amidst a scene of moonshine, gunrunning and racketeering. **80m/C VHS.** Cynda Williams, Nick Cassavetes, Joe (Johnny) Viterelli, Maria Ford, Lawrence Monoson, Garrett Morris, Richard Brooks; ***D:*** Fred Gallo; ***W:*** Charles Philip Moore; ***C:*** John Aronson; ***M:*** David Wurst, Eric Wurst.

Machine Gun Kelly 🦴🦴½ **1958** Corman found Euro-appeal with this '30s style gangster bio. Bronson, who was just gaining a reputation as an action lead, stars as criminal Kelly, who's convinced by his moll to give up bank robbery for kidnapping. Amsterdam, the wisecracking writer from "The Dick Van Dyke Show," is the fink who turns him in. **80m/B VHS.** Charles Bronson, Susan Cabot, Morey Amsterdam, Barboura Morris, Frank De Kova, Jack Lambert, Wally Campo, Richard Devon, Bob Griffin; ***D:*** Roger Corman; ***W:*** Mike Werb, Robert W(right) Campbell; ***C:*** Floyd Crosby; ***M:*** Gerald Fried.

Machine to Kill Bad People 🦴🦴 *La Macchina Ammazzacattivi* **1948** In a small Italian village, a photographer receives a magical camera that has the power to terrify and kill anyone it photographs. The photographer decides to get rid of all the village's evil people but soon learns the difficulty of distinguishing between the grey areas of good and bad. Italian with subtitles. **80m/B VHS.** *IT* Gennaro Pisano, Giovanni Amato, Marilyn Buferd; ***D:*** Roberto Rossellini; ***W:*** Roberto Rossellini.

Macho Callahan 🦴🦴 **1970 (R)** A Civil War convict escapes from a frontier jail bent on tracking down the man who imprisoned him. (The escaped prisoner bit is a recurring theme in Janssen's oeuvre.) Confused script even has a one-armed Carradine! **99m/C VHS.** David Janssen, Jean Seberg, David Carradine, Lee J. Cobb; ***D:*** Bernard L. Kowalski.

Maciste in Hell 🦴½ *Witch's Curse* **1960** Inexplicably living in 17th century Scotland, Italian hero Maciste pursues a witch into the depths of Hell. She's placed a curse on the world and he wants her to remove it. **78m/C VHS.** *IT* Kirk Morris, Helene Chanel, Vira (Vera) Silenti, Andrea Bosic, Angelo Zanolli, John Karlsen; ***D:*** Riccardo (Robert Hampton) Freda.

The Mack 🦴½ **1973 (R)** The Mack is a pimp who comes out of retirement to reclaim a piece of the action in Oakland, California. Violent blaxploitation flick was boxoffice dynamite at time of release. Early Pryor appearance. **110m/C VHS.** Max Julien, Richard Pryor, Don Gordon, Roger E. Mosley, Carol Speed; ***D:*** Michael Campus.

Mack & Carole **1928** Lombard began her screen career, in earnest, as a Mack Sennett comedienne. These three shorts represent her earliest screen work. **60m/B VHS.** Carole Lombard.

Mack the Knife woof! *The Threepenny Opera* **1989 (PG-13)** Terrible adaptation of Brecht and Weill's "Threepenny Opera," detailing the adventures of a master thief in love with an innocent girl. Too much music, too much dancing, too much emoting. **121m/C VHS.** Raul Julia, Roger Daltrey, Richard Harris, Julie Walters, Clive Revill, Erin Donovan, Rachel Robertson, Julia Migenes-Johnson; ***D:*** Menahem Golan.

MacKenna's Gold 🦴🦴½ **1969 (PG)** Grim desperados trek through Apache territory to uncover legendary cache of gold in this somewhat inflated epic. Subdued stars Peck and Shariff vie for attention here with such overactors as Cobb, Meredith, and Wallach. Meanwhile, Newmar (Catwoman of TV's Batman) swims nude. A must for all earthquake buffs. **128m/C VHS, DVD, Wide.** Gregory Peck, Omar Sharif, Telly Savalas, Julie Newmar, Edward G. Robinson, Keenan Wynn, Ted Cassidy, Eduardo Ciannelli, Eli Wallach, Raymond Massey, Lee J. Cobb, Burgess Meredith, Anthony Quayle, John David Garfield; ***D:*** J. Lee Thompson; ***W:*** Carl Foreman; ***C:*** Joe MacDonald; ***M:*** Quincy Jones.

Mackintosh Man 🦴🦴½ **1973 (PG)** An intelligence agent must undo a communist who has infiltrated the free world's network in this solid but somewhat subdued thriller. Good cast keeps narrative rolling, but don't look here for nudity-profanity-violence fix. **100m/C VHS.** Paul Newman, Dominique Sanda, James Mason, Ian Bannen, Nigel Patrick, Harry Andrews, Leo Genn, Peter Vaughan, Michael Hordern; ***D:*** John Huston; ***W:*** Walter Hill; ***M:*** Maurice Jarre.

Macon County Line 🦴🦴½ **1974 (R)** A series of deadly mistakes and misfortunes lead to a sudden turn-around in the lives of three young people when they enter a small Georgia town and find themselves accused of brutally slaying the sheriff's wife. Sequelled by "Return to Macon County" in 1975, starring Don Johnson and Nick Nolte. **89m/C VHS, DVD.** Alan Vint, Jesse Vint, Cheryl Waters, Geoffrey Lewis, Joan Blackman, Max Baer Jr.; ***D:*** Richard Compton.

Macumba Love 🦴 **1960** An author journeys to Brazil to prove a connection between mysterious murders and voodoo. A tedious suspense exploitation travelogue with generous servings of cheesecake and calypso music. **86m/C VHS.** Walter Reed, Ziva Rodann, William Wellman Jr., June Wilkinson, Ruth de Souza; ***D:*** Douglas Fowley.

Mad About Mambo 🦴🦴½ **2000 (PG-13)** Lucy McLoughlin (Russell) is an upper-class student in Belfast who's determined to prove herself as a Latin dancer. So she teams up with a working-class athlete, Danny Mitchell (Ash), who wants to play pro soccer and who needs to improve his timing, and the duo polish their moves on the dance floor. Appealing wrong-side-of-the-tracks dance/romance that doesn't ignore its setting but doesn't dwell on religious differences and soldiers either. **92m/C VHS.** Keri Russell, William Ash, Brian Cox, Rosaleen Linehan, Theo Fraser Steele; ***D:*** John Forte; ***W:*** John Forte; ***C:*** Ashley Rowe; ***M:*** Richard Hartley.

Mad About Money 🦴🦴 *He Loved an Actress; Stardust* **1937** Comedy about a bespectacled mild-mannered fellow who runs up against a Mexican spitfire. ♫Oh So Beautiful; Perpetual Motion; Little Lost Tune; Dustin' The Stars. **80m/B VHS.** *GB* Lupe Velez, Wallace Ford, Ben Lyon, Harry Langdon, Jean Colin; ***D:*** Melville Brown.

Mad About Music 🦴🦴🦴 **1938** On the advice of her publicist, film star Gwen Taylor (Patrick) sends her teenaged daughter Gloria (Durbin) off to a Swiss boarding school and keeps her identity a secret. So Gloria invents an exciting world-traveler father that envious schoolmate Felice (Parrish) insists upon meeting. Gloria manages to persuade a complete stranger, composer Richard Todd (Marshall), into playing the role (he's charmed by her singing). Naturally, there's lots of confusion, especially when mother and "father" finally meet. ♫I Love to Whistle; Chapel Bells; Serenade to the Stars; There Isn't a Day Goes By. **92m/B VHS.** Deanna Durbin, Herbert Marshall, Gail Patrick, Arthur Treacher, Helen Parrish, William Frawley, Marcia Mae Jones, Jackie Moran; ***D:*** Norman Taurog; ***W:*** Bruce Manning, Felix Jackson; ***C:*** Joseph Valentine.

Mad About You woof! **1990 (PG)** Millionaire helps his daughter measure prospective suitors. Adam West is not the fourth man in the Montgomery Clift-James Dean-Marlon Brando chain of American acting greats. **92m/C VHS.** Claudia Christian, Joseph Gian, Adam West, Shari Shattuck; ***D:*** Lorenzo Doumani.

Mad at the Moon 🦴🦴 **1992 (R)** Western thriller in which a young bride (Masterson) discovers that the man she married is less than human with the rising of the full moon. The only one who can protect her is her husband's half-brother played by Bochner. Masterson gives a great performance as a woman torn apart by a terrifying family secret out on the American plains. **98m/C VHS.** Mary Stuart Masterson, Hart Bochner, Fionnula Flanagan, Cec Verrell, Stephen Blake; ***D:*** Martin Donovan; ***W:*** Martin Donovan, Richard Pelusi.

The Mad Bomber woof! *Police Connection; Detective Geronimo* **1972** Grim lawman Edwards tracks deranged bomber Connors, who is determined to blow up anyone who ever offended him. A must for all connoisseurs of acting that is simultaneously overblown and flat. **80m/C VHS.** Vince Edwards, Chuck Connors, Neville Brand; ***D:*** Bert I. Gordon.

Mad Bull 🦴 **1977** Sensitive wrestler finds meaning in life when he falls in love. If you ever cared about Karras, then you probably already saw this. If you never cared about Karras, then you probably never heard of this. If you ever cared about Anspach, rent "Five Easy Pieces" instead. **96m/C VHS.** Alex Karras, Susan Anspach, Nicholas Colasanto, Tracey Walter; ***D:*** Walter Doniger.

The Mad Butcher *The Mad Butcher of Vienna; The Strangler of Vienna; The Vienna Strangler; Der Wurger kommt auf leisen Socken; Lo Strangolatore di Vienna; Meat Is Meat* **1972 (R)** Typically unhinged mental patient seeks teenage flesh for his various instruments of torture and death. Buono has never been more imposing. **82m/C VHS, DVD, Wide.** *IT* Victor Buono, Karin (Karen) Field, Brad Harris; ***D:*** Guido Zurli.

Mad City ½ **1997 (PG-13)** Out-of-work security guard Sam Baily (Travolta) goes postal, taking hostages in a museum while has-been journalist Max Brackett (Hoffman) manages to exploit Baily and hype the situation into a massive broadcast news event. The media circus that ensues provides social commentary on the questionable state of journalism. Drawing from famously explored material in numerous older films ("Network" and "All the President's Men") the subject is also enjoying a revival in current films ("Primary Colors" and "Wag the Dog"). Relationship between Max and Sam carries most interest in Costa-Gravas' intense drama, while uneven tone and script inadequacies hold back satisfying story development. Talented supporting cast (Alda, Danner, Kirshner, Prosky) have little to do. **114m/C VHS, DVD, Wide.** John Travolta, Dustin Hoffman, Mia Kirshner, Alan Alda, Blythe Danner, Robert Prosky, William Atherton, Ted Levine, Bill Nunn; ***D:*** Constantin Costa-Gavras; ***W:*** Tom Matthews; ***C:*** Patrick Blossier; ***M:*** Thomas Newman.

Mad Death **1985** The British Isles take extreme steps to quarantine themselves against rabies from the European continent. This condensed TV miniseries preys on fears of the worst, as an outbreak of the virus spreads from dogs and other pets to humans, and special commandoes are mobilized. **120m/C VHS.** *GB*

Mad Doctor of Blood Island woof! *Tomb of the Living Dead; Blood Doctor* **1969** Dull band of travelers arrive on mysterious tropical island and encounter bloodthirsty creature. Warning: This film is not recognized for outstanding achievements in acting, dialogue, or cinematography. **110m/C VHS.** *PH* John Ashley, Angelique Pettyjohn, Ronald Remy, Alicia Alonzo, Alfonso Carvajal, Johnny Long, Nadja, Bruno Punzalan; ***D:*** Gerardo (Gerry) De Leon, Eddie Romero; ***W:*** Reuben Candy; ***C:*** Justo Paulino; ***M:*** Tito Arevalo.

Mad Dog woof! **1984** An escaped convict seeks revenge on the cop responsible for his imprisonment. **90m/C VHS.** Helmut Berger, Marisa Mell; ***D:*** Sergio Grieco.

Mad Dog and Glory **1993 (R)** Cast against type, Murray and De Niro play each other's straight man in this dark romantic comedy. Meek "Mad Dog" (De Niro) is an off-duty police photographer who happens upon a convenience store robbery and manages to save the life of Frank (Murray), obnoxious gangster by day, obnoxious stand-up comic by night. To settle up, Frank offers him Glory (Thurman), for a week. Eventually, Frank wants Glory back, forcing wimpy Mad Dog to either confront or surrender. Directed by McNaughton, who established himself with "Henry: Portrait of a Serial Killer." Uneven and not of the knee-slapper ilk, but the performances are tight, including "NYPD Blue" Caruso as a cop buddy of De Niro's. **97m/C VHS, DVD, Wide.** Robert De Niro, Uma Thurman, Bill Murray, David Caruso, Mike Starr, Tom Towles, Kathy Baker, Derek Anunciation, J.J. Johnston, Richard Belzer; ***D:*** John McNaughton; ***W:*** Richard Price; ***C:*** Robby Muller; ***M:*** Elmer Bernstein.

Mad Dog Morgan ½ *Mad Dog* **1976 (R)** Hopper delivers as engaging outlaw roaming outlands of 19th-century Australia. Quirky and violent G'day man. Based on a true story. **93m/C VHS.** *AU* Dennis Hopper, David Gulpilil; ***D:*** Philippe Mora.

The Mad Executioners *Der Henker Von London* **1965** Scotland Yard inspector searches for a sex maniac who decapitates women. In the meantime, a group of vigilantes capture criminals and sentence them without a trial. Confusing film with a predictable ending. Based on the book "White Carpet" by Bryan Edgar Wallace. **92m/B VHS.** *GE* Hansjorg Felmy, Maria Perschy, Dieter Borsche, Rudolph Forster, Chris Howland, Wolfgang Preiss; ***D:*** Edwin Zbonek.

The Mad Ghoul ½ **1943** Mad scientist (is there any other kind?) Dr. Morris (Zucco) is researching an ancient Egyptian gas that causes paralysis, turning victims into obedient zombies. Morris exposes his innocent assistant Ted (Bruce) to the gas, making Ted dependent on the antidote serum made from newly dead hearts. Poor Ted's fiance Isabel (Ankers) just can't understand what's the matter. **66m/B VHS.** George Zucco, David Bruce, Evelyn Ankers, Turhan Bey, Robert Armstrong, Milburn Stone, Charles McGraw, Rose Hobart; ***D:*** James Hogan; ***W:*** Brenda Weisberg, Paul Gangelin.

Mad Love *The Hands of Orlac* **1935** Brilliant surgeon Gogol (Lorre) falls madly in love with actress Yvonne Orlac (Drake), but she rebuffs him. When her pianist husband Stephen's (Clive) hands are cut off in a train accident, Gogol agrees to attach new hands, using those of a recently executed knife-wielding murderer, Reagan (Brophy). Gogol then kills Stephen's stepfather and uses psychological terror to make the pianist think he killed him. There's also an appearance by the supposedly dead murderer who shows up to reclaim his hands. A real chiller about obsessive love and psychological fear. The only downfall to this one is the unnecessary comic relief by Healy. Lorre's first American film. **70m/B VHS.** Peter Lorre, Colin Clive, Frances Drake, Ted Healy, Edward Brophy, Sara Haden, Henry Kolker, Keye Luke, May Beatty; ***D:*** Karl Freund; ***W:*** P.J. Wolfson, John Lloyd Balderston, Guy Endore; ***C:*** Gregg Toland, Chester Lyons; ***M:*** Dimitri Tiomkin.

Mad Love ½ **1995 (PG-13)** Teen love has rarely been so insipid. Impulsive, fragile, and annoyingly melodramatic Casey (Barrymore) bewitches responsible, straightlaced Matt (O'Donnell) with her kewpie-doll charm and penchant for mischief. When Casey's bipolar ways land her in a mental hospital, Matt breaks her out and the unconvincing duo hit the road, where their supposedly free-spirited, passion-filled escapades grow increasingly inconsistent and silly, eventually halted by Casey's clinical crash. Slightly redeemed by a cool soundtrack and decent acting, but otherwise dull and insignificant, with an ending that may induce involuntary eyerolling. You've been warned. **95m/C VHS, DVD.** Chris O'Donnell, Drew Barrymore, Joan Allen, Kevin Dunn, Jude Ciccolella, Amy Sakasitz, T.J. Lowther; ***D:*** Antonia Bird; ***W:*** Paula Milne; ***C:*** Fred Tammes.

Mad Max ½ **1980 (R)** Set on the stark highways of the post-nuclear future, an ex-cop seeks personal revenge against a rovin' band of vicious outlaw bikers who killed his wife and child. Futuristic scenery and excellent stunt work make for an exceptionally entertaining action-packed adventure. Followed by "The Road Warrior" (also known as "Mad Max 2") in 1981 and "Mad Max Beyond Thunderdome" in 1985. **93m/C VHS, DVD, Wide.** *AU* Mel Gibson, Joanne Samuel, Hugh Keays-Byrne, Steve Bisley, Tim Burns, Roger Ward, Vincent (Vince Gill) Gil; ***D:*** George Miller; ***W:*** George Miller; ***C:*** David Eggby; ***M:*** Brian May.

Mad Max: Beyond Thunderdome ½ **1985 (PG-13)** Max drifts into evil town ruled by Turner and becomes gladiator, then gets dumped in desert and is rescued by band of feral orphans. Third in a bleak, extremely violent, often exhilirating series. **107m/C VHS, DVD, Wide.** *AU* Mel Gibson, Tina Turner, Helen Buday, Frank Thring Jr., Bruce Spence, Robert Grubb, Angelo Rossitto, Angry Anderson, George Spartels, Rod Zuanic; ***D:*** George Miller, George Ogilvie; ***W:*** Terry Hayes, George Miller; ***C:*** Dean Semler; ***M:*** Maurice Jarre.

Mad Miss Manton **1938** A socialite turns detective to solve murder. Pleasant comedy-mystery provides occasional laughs and suspense. **80m/B VHS.** Barbara Stanwyck, Henry Fonda, Hattie McDaniel, Sam Levene, Miles Mander, Charles Halton; ***D:*** Leigh Jason.

Mad Mission 3 ½ **1984** Chinese man vacationing in Paris becomes involved in plot to recover precious jewels stolen from England's royal crown. Has there already been "Mad Mission" and "Mad Mission 2"? **81m/C VHS.** Richard Kiel, Sam Kui, Karl Muka, Sylvia Chang, Tsuneharu Sugiyama.

The Mad Monster ½ **1942** This "Wolf Man"-inspired cheapie looks like a misty relic today. A mad scientist furthers the war effort by injecting wolf's blood into a handyman, who becomes hairy and anti-social. **77m/B VHS.** Johnny Downs, George Zucco, Anne Nagel, Sarah Padden, Glenn Strange, Gordon DeMain, Mae Busch; ***D:*** Sam Newfield.

Mad Monster Party ½ **1968** Frankenstein is getting older and wants to retire from the responsibilities of being senior monster, so he calls a convention of creepy creatures to decide who should take his place—The Wolfman, Dracula, the Mummy, the Creature, It, the Invisible Man, or Dr. Jekyll and Mr. Hyde. Animated feature using the process of "Animagic." **94m/C VHS.** ***D:*** Jules Bass; ***V:*** Boris Karloff, Ethel Ennis, Phyllis Diller.

Mad Wax: The Surf Movie **1990** A flimsy plot about a window-cleaner who discovers a magical surfing wax serves as a framework for lots and lots of scenes of surfin' dudes. **45m/C VHS.** Richard Cram, Marvin Foster, Aaron Napolean, Tom Carroll, Bryce Andrews, Ross Clarke-Jones; ***D:*** Michael Hohensee.

The Mad Whirl ½ **1925** The Roarin' '20s are a mad mad whirl in this silent silent period piece. **80m/B VHS.** Myrtle Stedman, Barbara Bedford, Alec B. Francis, George Fawcett, Joseph Singleton.

Mad Youth woof! **1940** A teenage girl falls in love with a man whom her slutty, alcoholic mother had been chasing. Bottom of the barrel production provides many unintentional laughs. Extraneous South American dance sequences included as character development. **61m/B VHS, DVD.** Mary Ainslee, Betty Atkinson, Willy Castello, Betty Compson, Tommy Wonder; ***D:*** Melville Shyer; ***W:*** Willis Kent.

Madagascar Skin **1995 (R)** Harry (Hannah) is a young gay man who's disfigured by a large port-wine birthmark on one side of his face (in the shape of Madagascar). Suicidally depressed he drives to a deserted beach on the Welsh coast but before making any final decisions, he picks up an overturned bucket lying on the sand. To his shock, it's covering the head of the very much alive middle-aged Flint (Hill), who's been buried up to his neck in sand and left to drown by some fellow crooks. Flint knows of a deserted beach shack, the oddly matched duo move in, and Harry falls in love. Deliberately dreamlike in some respects, the leads provide a bittersweet, adult romance. **95m/C VHS.** *GB* John Hannah, Bernard Hill; ***D:*** Chris Newby; ***W:*** Chris Newby; ***C:*** Oliver Curtis.

Madam Satan ½ **1930** Extremely bizarre DeMille film highlighted by lavish musical numbers and outrageous costumes. Wealthy socialite realizes she's losing her husband to a young showgirl, so she disguises herself as a sultry French tramp and entices her husband at a masquerade party aboard a zeppelin—surely one of the wildest party scenes ever captured on film. Chorus girls perform several exotic dance numbers inside the airship that are nothing short of fantastic. A storm breaks out and the floating dirigible is struck by lightning—leading viewers to wonder if the mad party-goers will make it to safety or crash and burn like this pic did at the boxoffice. **115m/B VHS.** Kay Johnson, Reginald Denny, Lillian Roth, Roland Young, Boyd Irwin, Elsa Peterson; ***D:*** Cecil B. DeMille.

Madame Bovary **1934** A young adultress with delusions of romantic love finds only despair in this offbeat adaptation of Flaubert's masterpiece. In French with English subtitles. **102m/B VHS.** *FR* Pierre Renoir, Valentine Tessier, Max Dearly; ***D:*** Jean Renoir.

Madame Bovary **1949** Young adultress with delusions of romantic love finds only despair, even in this Hollywood version of Flaubert's classic. Mason/Flaubert is put on trial for indecency following publication of the novel, with the story told from the witness stand. While this device occasionally slows the narrative, astute direction helps the plot along. Minnelli's handling of the celebrated ball sequence is superb. **115m/B VHS.** Jennifer Jones, Van Heflin, Louis Jourdan, James Mason, Gene Lockhart, Gladys Cooper, George Zucco; ***D:*** Vincente Minnelli; ***M:*** Miklos Rozsa.

Madame Bovary ½ **1991 (PG-13)** Provincial 19th century France is the setting for the tragedy of a romantic woman. Emma Bovary is bored by her marriage to an unsuccessful country doctor and longs for passion and excitement. She allows herself to be seduced (and abandoned) by a local aristocrat and herself seduces a young banker. She also struggles with an increasing burden of debt as she continues her quest for luxury. Realizing she will never find the passion she desires, Emma takes drastic, and tragic, measures. Sumptuous-looking film, with an extraordinary performance by Huppert. In French with English subtitles. Based on the novel by Gustave Flaubert. **130m/C VHS.** *FR* Isabelle Huppert, Jean-Francois Balmer, Christophe MaLavoy, Jean Yanne; ***D:*** Claude Chabrol; ***W:*** Claude Chabrol; ***M:*** Matthieu Chabrol.

Madame Bovary ½ **2000** British adaptation of Gustave Flaubert's scandalous novel, which is set in rural Normandy in the 1830s and 40s. Emma (O'Connor) is the convent-educated daughter of a farmer, who makes an unwise marriage to country doctor Charles Bovary (Bonneville), whom she doesn't love. Indeed, Emma has some overly-romantic notions about love that lead to infidelity and despair. But it's Emma's extravagence and her borrowing from the usurious Lheureux (Barron) that bring her to disaster. None of the characters are particularly bright (or likeable) so your sympathy is at a minimum. **140m/C VHS.** *GB* Frances O'Connor, Hugh Bonneville, Greg Wise, Hugh Dancy, Keith Barron, Trevor Peacock; ***D:*** Tim Fywell; ***W:*** Heidi Thomas. **TV**

Madame Butterfly **1995** A French production, filmed in Tunisia, with a Chinese soprano, and Italian subtitles. Mitterrand takes on Puccini's opera, setting it in 1904 Nagasaki, but playing most of the story straight (he adds some documentary footage of old Japan between the acts). 15-year-old Butterfly (Huang) is a geisha who makes the mistake of falling in love and marrying deceitful American naval officer Pinkerton (Troxell). She's disowned by her family, he eventually sails away, and when he does return, it's with an American bride. Tragedy ensues. Newcomer Huang's fine but the handsome Troxell's a little stiff. **129m/C VHS, DVD, Wide.** *FR* Ying Huang, Richard Troxell, Ning Liang, Richard Cowan; ***D:*** Frederic Mitterrand; ***W:*** Frederic Mitterrand; ***C:*** Philippe Welt.

Madame Curie **1943** The film biography of Madame Marie Curie, the woman who discovered Radium. A deft portrayal by Garson, who is reteamed with her "Mrs. Miniver" co-star, Pidgeon. Certainly better than most biographies from this time period and more truthful as well. **124m/B VHS.** Greer Garson, Walter Pidgeon, Robert Walker, May Whitty, Henry Travers, Sir C. Aubrey Smith, Albert Bassermann, Victor Francen, Reginald Owen, Van Johnson; ***D:*** Mervyn LeRoy; ***C:*** Joseph Ruttenberg.

Madame Rosa *La Vie Devant Soi* **1977 (PG)** An aging Jewish prostitute tends prostitutes' offspring in this warmhearted work. A survivor of the Holocaust, the old woman finds her spirit revived by one of her charges—an abandoned Arab boy. In French with English subtitles. **105m/C VHS.** *FR IS* Simone Signoret, Claude Dauphin, Samy Ben Youb, Michal Bat-Adam; ***D:*** Moshe Mizrahi; ***W:*** Moshe Mizrahi; ***C:*** Nestor Almendros; ***M:*** Philippe Sarde. Oscars '77: Foreign Film; Cesar '78: Actress (Signoret); L.A. Film Critics '78: Foreign Film.

Madame Sin 🦴🦴½ **1971** Aspiring world dominator enlists former CIA agent in scheme to obtain nuclear submarine. Davis is appealing as evil personified, in her first TV movie. **91m/C VHS.** Bette Davis, Robert Wagner; ***D:*** David Greene; ***M:*** Michael Gibbs. **TV**

Madame Sousatzka 🦴🦴🦴 **1988 (PG-13)** Eccentric, extroverted piano teacher helps students develop spiritually as well as musically. When she engages a teenage Indian student, however, she finds herself considerably challenged. MacLaine is perfectly cast in this powerful, winning film. **113m/C VHS.** Shirley MacLaine, Peggy Ashcroft, Shabana Azmi, Twiggy, Leigh Lawson, Geoffrey Bayldon, Navin Chowdhry, Lee Montague; ***D:*** John Schlesinger; ***W:*** Ruth Prawer Jhabvala, John Schlesinger; ***M:*** Gerald Gouriet. Golden Globes '89: Actress—Drama (MacLaine); Venice Film Fest. '88: Actress (MacLaine).

Madame X 🦴🦴½ **1937** Fourth version of this classic tearjerker finds diplomat's wife George having a fling with a playboy. There's a murder and she turns to her nasty mother-in-law for aid. She arranges for daughter-in-law-dearest's "death" in order to prevent a scandal. Then George is on the slippery path to alcoholism and prostitution. Adapted from the play by Alexandre Bisson. Run-of-the-mill; Lana Turner's 1966 version is still the one to watch. **96m/B VHS.** Gladys George, John Beal, Warren William, Reginald Owen, William Henry, Henry Daniell, Philip Reed, Lynne Carver, Emma Dunn, Ruth Hussey; ***D:*** Sam Wood; ***W:*** John Meehan.

Madame X 🦴🦴 *Absinthe* **1966** Turner is perfectly cast in this oft-filmed melodrama about a social outcast who is tried for murder and defended by her unknowing son, who believes her long dead. Bennett's last film. **100m/C VHS.** Lana Turner, John Forsythe, Ricardo Montalban, Burgess Meredith, Virginia Grey, Constance Bennett, Keir Dullea; ***D:*** David Lowell Rich; ***C:*** Russell Metty.

M.A.D.D.: Mothers Against Drunk Driving 🦴🦴½ **1983** Emotionally gripping movie recounts the story of Candy Lightner, who, after her daughter was killed in a drunk driving accident, founded M.A.D.D. and built it into a nationwide organization. Similar to "License to Kill," which dramatized the effect that a drunk driving accident can have on the families of those involved. **97m/C VHS.** Mariette Hartley, Paula Prentiss, Bert Remsen; ***D:*** William A. Graham; ***C:*** Dean Cundey; ***M:*** Bruce Broughton. **TV**

The Maddening 🦴½ **1995 (R)** When their car breaks down in a remote area, Cassie (Sara) and daughter Samantha find refuge at the home of Roy Scudder (Reynolds) and his wife Georgina (Dickinson). At least Cassie thought it was a refuge—until she realizes the Scudders are crazy killers. **97m/C VHS.** Burt Reynolds, Angie Dickinson, Mia Sara, Brian Wimmer, Josh Mostel, William Hickey; ***D:*** Danny Huston; ***W:*** Leslie Greif.

Made 🦴🦴½ **2001 (R)** Favreau, who also wrote and directed, teams up again with "Swingers" buddy Vaughn in this tale of two-bit losers trying to weasel their way into the mob. Bobby (Favreau), a past-his-prime boxer and construction worker, chauffeurs his stripper girlfriend Jessica (Janssen) to her gigs at night. Ricky (Vaughn), his irritating, motor-mouthed friend, wants to get mobbed up with crime boss Max (Falk). Hoping to earn enough money to "save" Jessica, Bobby reluctantly agrees. Max sends them to New York with cryptic instructions to follow the orders of slick gangsta Ruiz (Puff Da...um...P. Did...er...Sean Combs). While Bobby tries to follow orders, Ricky's rash behavior lands them in constant trouble. Vaughn's comic riffing occasionally crosses the line into excess, but the chemistry between the two leads is excellent and the laughs are plentiful. **94m/C VHS, DVD, Wide.** *US* Jon Favreau, Vince Vaughn, Famke Janssen, Faizon Love, David O'Hara, Vincent Pastore, Peter Falk, Sean (Puffy, Puff Daddy, P. Diddy) Combs, Drea De Matteo; ***D:*** Jon Favreau; ***W:*** Jon Favreau; ***C:*** Christopher Doyle; ***M:*** John O'Brien, Lyle Workman.

Made for Each Other 🦴🦴🦴 **1939** Newlyweds John (Stewart) and Jane (Lombard) Mason must overcome meddlesome in-laws, poverty, and even the arrival of a baby in this classic melodrama. Things become so serious, they decide to separate but their child's serious illness brings them together for a second chance. Dated but appealing. **94m/B VHS, DVD.** James Stewart, Carole Lombard, Charles Coburn, Lucile Watson; ***D:*** John Cromwell; ***W:*** Jo Swerling; ***C:*** Leon Shamroy; ***M:*** Louis Forbes.

Made for Love 🦴½ **1926** Couple journeys romantically in Egypt until disaster strikes: they fall into a tomb and can't get out. **65m/B VHS.** Leatrice Joy, Edmund Burns, Ethel Wales, Brandon Hurst, Frank Butler; ***D:*** Paul Sloane.

Made in America 🦴🦴 **1993 (PG-13)** High-energy, lightweight comedy stars Whoopi as a single mom whose daughter Long discovers her birth was the result of artifical insemination. More surprising is her biological dad: white, obnoxious, country-western car dealer Danson. Overwrought with obvious gags, basically a one-joke movie. Nonetheless, Goldberg and Danson chemically connect onscreen (and for a short time offscreen as well) while supporting actor Smith grabs comedic attention as Teacake, Long's best friend. Both Goldberg and Danson deserve better material. **111m/C VHS, DVD, Wide.** Whoopi Goldberg, Ted Danson, Will Smith, Nia Long, Paul Rodriguez, Jennifer Tilly, Peggy Rea, Clyde Kusatsu; ***D:*** Richard Benjamin; ***W:*** Holly Goldberg Sloan; ***C:*** Ralf Bode; ***M:*** Mark Isham.

Made in Argentina 🦴🦴 **1986** An Argentinean couple living in New York decide to return for a visit. Having left for political reasons, they still harbor bitterness. **90m/C VHS.** *AR* Luis Brandoni, Marta Bianchi, Leonor Manso; ***D:*** Juan Jose Jusid.

Made in Heaven 🦴🦴 **1952** Arid comedy in which British newlyweds try to sustain honeymoon for entire year. The bride, however, eventually suspects her husband of shenanigans with the maid. If this sounds good, then you may like it. **90m/C VHS.** *GB* Petula Clark, David Tomlinson, Sonja Ziemann, A.E. Matthews; ***D:*** John Paddy Carstairs.

Made in Heaven 🦴🦴½ **1987 (PG)** Two souls in heaven fall in love and must find each other after being reborn on Earth if they are to remain eternal lovers. Contains ethereal interpretations of heaven and several cameo appearances by famous actors and musicians. **105m/C VHS.** Timothy Hutton, Kelly McGillis, Maureen Stapleton, Mare Winningham, Ann Wedgeworth, Don Murray, Amanda Plummer, Timothy Daly, Marj Dusay; ***Cameos:*** Ellen Barkin, Neil Young, Tom Petty, Ric Ocasek, Tom Robbins, Debra Winger, Gary Larsen, David Rasche; ***D:*** Alan Rudolph; ***W:*** Raynold Gideon, Bruce A. Evans; ***M:*** Mark Isham.

Made in USA 🦴½ **1988 (R)** Wayward dudes engage vixen while cruising Midwest. Trouble, however, awaits. Note: This is not Godard's mid-'60s classic. **82m/C VHS.** Adrian Pasdar, Lori Singer, Christopher Penn; ***D:*** Ken Friedman; ***W:*** Ken Friedman.

Made Men 🦴🦴 **1999 (R)** Former hitman, now in the witness protection program, gets caught stealing 12 million from the mob. If he wants to save his life, he's got to outwit four mobsters sent to get the money. **90m/C VHS, DVD.** James Belushi, Michael Beach, Timothy Dalton, Vanessa Angel, Steve Railsback; ***D:*** Louis Morneau; ***C:*** George Mooradian; ***M:*** Stewart Copeland. **VIDEO**

Madeleine 🦴🦴½ *The Strange Case of Madeleine* **1950** Courtroom drama of woman charged with poisoning her French lover in 1850s Scotland. Directed by the same David Lean who made "Bridge on the River Kwai" and "Lawrence of Arabia." Here, though, he was merely trying to provide a vehicle for his wife, actress Todd. Intrigued? **114m/B VHS.** Ann Todd, Leslie Banks, Ivan Desny, Norman Wooland, Barbara Everest, Susan Stranks, Patricia Raine, Elizabeth Sellars, Edward Chapman, Jean Cadell, Eugene Deckers, Amy Veness, John Laurie, Henry Edwards, Ivor Barnard, Barry Jones, David Morne, Andre Morell; ***D:*** David Lean; ***W:*** Nicholas Phipps, Stanley Haynes; ***C:*** Guy Green; ***M:*** William Alwyn.

Madeline 🦴🦴 **1998 (PG)** Adaptation of Ludwig Bemelmans' classic 1939 children's book about the trouble-finding orphan Madeline (Jones), her schoolmates, and their patient teacher Miss Clavel (McDormand). As the credits open, Bemelmans' familiar paintings are animated. After the live action starts, you'll wish that the producers had animated the entire film. Travelling through the plots of four of the six Madeline books, the acting seems a little flat, even for kids. McDormand and Hawthorne as Lord "Cucuface" Covington are unable to act to their fullest, and the child actors are mostly forgettable. If you liked the books as a kid, you may be disappointed; but it's a good way to introduce your own children to the series. **90m/C VHS, DVD, Wide.** Hatty Jones, Frances McDormand, Nigel Hawthorne, Ben Daniels, Arturo Venegas, Stephane Audran, Katia Caballero; ***D:*** Daisy von Scherler Mayer; ***W:*** Marc Levin, Jennifer Flacket, Chris Weitz, Paul Weitz; ***C:*** Pierre Aim; ***M:*** Michel Legrand.

Mademoiselle 🦴🦴 **1966** Moreau is a psychotic, sexually repressed schoolteacher in a small village who manages to keep herself under control until studly woodcutter Manni and his son take up residence. The locals distrust the stranger but Moreau can't wait to get her hands on him. Suddenly, the village is battered by a rash of poisonings, fires, and floods, all of which are blamed on Manni, leading the locals to exact a terrible vengeance. In French with English subtitles. **105m/B VHS, DVD, Wide.** *FR GB* Jeanne Moreau, Ettore Manni, Umberto Orsini, Keith Skinner, Jane Berretta, Mony Rey; ***D:*** Tony Richardson; ***W:*** Jean Genet; ***C:*** David Watkin.

Mademoiselle Fifi 🦴½ **1944** Simon stars as a French laundress in 1870 France who refuses to give in to her small town's Prussian oppressors. The film title is the nickname of the most brutal of the Prussian officers, played by Kreuger. An unsucessful attempt at political allegory for the devastation of WWII. **69m/B VHS.** Simone Simon, John Emery, Kurt Kreuger, Alan Napier, Jason Robards Sr.; ***D:*** Robert Wise.

Madhouse 🦴🦴 **1974** A troubled horror film star tries to bring his "Dr. Death" character to TV, but during production people begin dying in ways remarkably similar to the script. A strong genre cast should hold the fans' attention during this mild adaptation of Angus Hall's novel "Devilday." **92m/C VHS.** *GB* Vincent Price, Peter Cushing, Robert Quarry, Adrienne Corri, Natasha Pyne, Linda Hayden, Michael Parkinson; ***D:*** Jim Clark.

Madhouse 🦴🦴 **1987** A woman has bizarre recollections of her twin sister whom she finally meets when she escapes from a mental hospital. Lots of violence and gore, has definite cult potential. **90m/C VHS.** Trish Everly, Michael MacRae, Dennis Robertson, Morgan Hart; ***D:*** Ovidio G. Assonitis.

Madhouse 🦴🦴 **1990 (PG-13)** New homeowners find themselves unable to expel loathsome, boorish guests. Presumably, a comedy cashing in on two of sitcom's brightest lights. **90m/C VHS.** John Larroquette, Kirstie Alley, Alison La Placa, John Diehl, Jessica Lundy, Bradley Gregg, Dennis Miller, Robert Ginty; ***D:*** Tom Ropelewski; ***W:*** Tom Ropelewski; ***M:*** David Newman.

Madhouse Mansion 🦴🦴½ *Ghost Story* **1974 (PG)** A horror actor revives his career and becomes embroiled in murder. Plenty of in-jokes and clips from older movies. **86m/C VHS.** *GB* Marianne Faithfull, Leigh Lawson, Anthony Bate, Larry Dann, Sally Grace, Penelope Keith, Vivian Mackerell, Murray Melvin, Barbara Shelley; ***D:*** Stephen Weeks; ***C:*** Peter Hurst.

Madigan 🦴🦴🦴 **1968** Realistic and exciting and among the best of the behind-the-scenes urban police thrillers. Hardened NYC detectives (Widmark and Guardino) lose their guns to a sadistic killer and are given 72 hours to track him down. Fonda is the police chief none too pleased with their performance. Adapted by Howard Rodman, Abraham Polonsky, and Harry Kleiner from Richard Dougherty's "The Commissioner." **101m/C VHS, DVD, Wide.** Richard Widmark, Henry Fonda, Inger Stevens, Harry Guardino, James Whitmore, Susan Clark, Michael Dunn, Don Stroud; ***D:*** Donald Siegel; ***W:*** Abraham Polonsky; ***C:*** Russell Metty; ***M:*** Don Costa.

Madigan's Millions woof! **1967 (G)** Incompetent Treasury agent treks to Italy to recover funds swiped from deceased gangster. This is Hoffman's first film, and is to his career what "The Last Chalice" was to Paul Newman's and "Studs and Kitty" was Sylvester Stallone. Recommended only to the terminally foolhardy. **89m/C VHS.** Dustin Hoffman, Elsa Martinelli, Cesar Romero; ***D:*** Stanley Prager.

Madman 🦴 **1979 (R)** Deranged Soviet Jew joins Israeli army to more effectively fulfill his desire to kill loathsome Soviets. Good date movie for those nights when you're home alone. Weaver's first starring role. **95m/C VHS.** *IS* Sigourney Weaver, Michael Beck, F. Murray Abraham; ***D:*** Dan Cohen.

Madman 🦴 **1982 (R)** Camp leader prompts terror when he revives legend regarding ax murderer. Seems that when you call his name, he appears. Buffoon does not believe story and calls out madman's name. Madman hears the call and emerges from forest, says hi, and hacks everyone to death. Lesson learned, case closed. Filmed on Long Island. **89m/C VHS, DVD, Wide.** Carl Fredericks, Alexis Dubin, Tony Fish, Paul Ehlers; ***D:*** Joe Giannone; ***W:*** Joe Giannone, Gary Sales; ***C:*** James (Momel) Lemmo; ***M:*** Gary Sales, Stephen Horelick.

The Madness of King George 🦴🦴🦴½ **1994 (R)** Poor King George is a monarch with problems—his 30 years of royal authority are being usurped by Parliament, his American colonies have been lost, and, in 1788, he's begun to periodically lose his mind. So what do you do when a ruler becomes irrational? The royal physicians are baffled, his loving Queen Charlotte (Mirren) is in despair, but the noxious Prince of Wales (Everett) can barely contain his glee at finally having a chance at the throne. A last resort is offered by Dr. Willis (Holm), a former clergyman with some unusual and sadistic ideas about treating the mentally ill (even if they do have royal blood). Brilliant performance by Hawthorne (who originated the stage role in Bennett's 1991 play "The Madness of George III"). Screen note explains that King George suffered from the metabolic disorder known as porphyria. A Tony Award-winner for his Broadway productions of "Miss Saigon" and "Carousel," Hytner makes his feature-film directing debut. **110m/C VHS, DVD, Wide.** *GB* Nigel Hawthorne, Helen Mirren, Ian Holm, Rupert Everett, Amanda Donohoe, Rupert Graves, Julian Wadham, John Wood, Julian Rhind-Tutt, Jim Carter; ***D:*** Nicholas Hytner; ***W:*** Alan Bennett; ***C:*** Andrew Dunn; ***M:*** George Fenton. Oscars '94: Art Dir./Set Dec.; British Acad. '95: Actor (Hawthorne); Cannes '95: Actress (Mirren).

Mado 🦴🦴🦴 **1976** A middle-aged businessman's life is undone when he falls for a mysterious woman. Piccoli and Schneider are, as usual, convincing. Another of underrated director Sautet's effective, low-key works. In French with subtitles. **130m/C VHS.** Romy Schneider, Michel Piccoli, Charles Denner; ***D:*** Claude Sautet. Cesar '77: Sound.

Madonna: Innocence Lost 🦴½ **1995** Tacky TV movie focusing on the ambitious singer and would-be actress who made wearing underwear as outerwear almost acceptable. Tawdry gossip highlights this laughfest as the trash talker hustles her way to the top of the heap, uncaring of whom she steps on along the way. Toronto substitutes for New York City grit. **90m/C VHS.** Terumi Matthews, Wendie Malick, Jeff Yagher, Dean Stockwell, Nigel Bennett, Don Francks, Rod Wilson, Tom Melissis; ***D:*** Bradford May; ***W:*** Michael J. Murray.

Madron 🦴½ **1970 (PG)** Road western filmed in the Israel desert, complete with menacing Apaches, wagon train massacre, a nun and a gunslinger. **93m/C VHS, DVD.** Richard Boone, Leslie Caron, Paul Smith; ***D:*** Jerry Hopper; ***W:*** Edward Chappell, Lee McMahon; ***C:*** Marcel Grignon, Adam Greenberg; ***M:*** Riz Ortolani.

The Madwoman of Chaillot 🦴½ **1969 (G)** Four men conspire to drill for oil which they believe lurks under Paris. Hepburn finds out about their plot and tells each man that oil is bubbling up through her basement. Before the men can arrive at her house to confirm this, she and her three cronies hold a mock trial and sentence the men to death. Features a stellar cast, but this modern-day adaptation of Jean Giraudoux's play "La Folle de Chaillot" falls flat. **142m/C VHS, Wide.** Katharine Hepburn, Charles Boyer, Claude Dauphin, Edith Evans, John Gavin, Paul Henreid, Oscar Homolka, Margaret Leighton, Giulietta Masina, Nanette Newman, Richard Chamberlain, Yul Brynner, Donald Pleasence, Danny Kaye, Fernand Gravet; ***D:*** Bryan Forbes; ***W:*** Edward Anhalt.

Mae West 🦴🦴½ **1984** Details West's life from her humble beginnings to her racy film stardom. Jillian does a good job bringing the buxom legend back to life. **97m/C VHS.** Ann Jillian, James Brolin, Piper Laurie, Roddy McDowall; ***D:*** Lee Philips; ***M:*** Brad Fiedel. **TV**

Maedchen in Uniform 🦴🦴🦴½ *Girls in Uniform* **1931** A scandalous early German talkie about a rebellious schoolgirl who falls in love with a female teacher and commits suicide when the teacher is punished for the relationship. A controversial criticism of lesbianism and militarism that impelled the Nazis, rising to power two years later, to exile its director. It was also banned in the United States. In German with English subtitles. Remade in 1965. **90m/B VHS.** *GE* Dorothea Wieck, Ellen Schwanecke, Hertha Thiele; ***D:*** Leontine Sagan.

Mafia! 🦴🦴 *Jane Austen's Mafia!* **1998 (PG-13)** Director Abrahams returns to the "Airplane" well once again as he takes aim at the Mafia movies of Coppola and Scorcese. As usual, the results are hit and miss, with the joke machine gun set on full automatic. Plot follows that of the Godfather trilogy most closely, with Bridges (in his last film) as klutzy patriarch Vincenzo Cortino. His sons, sensitive war hero Anthony (Mohr) and hot tempered Joey (Burke), wrestle for control of the keystone kriminal empire after pop takes the dirt nap. Basically, the actors' jobs are to remain deadpan while all manner of shenanigans and hijinks take place and hilarity allegedly ensues. This genre is quickly running out of ammo. It's time for someone to administer the kiss of death. **87m/C VHS, Wide.** Lloyd Bridges, Jay Mohr, Billy Burke, Olympia Dukakis, Christina Applegate, Pamela Gidley, Tony LoBianco, Joe (Johnny) Viterelli, Vincent Pastore, Jason Fuchs; ***D:*** Jim Abrahams; ***W:*** Jim Abrahams, Michael McManus, Greg Norberg; ***C:*** Pierre Letarte; ***M:*** John (Gianni) Frizzell.

Mafia Princess 🦴🦴 **1986** The daughter of a Mafia boss tries to discover her own identity despite her father's involvement in crime. Based on a best-selling autobiography by a real-life member of a Mob family, Antoinette Giancana. **100m/C VHS.** Tony Curtis, Susan Lucci, Kathleen Widdoes, Chuck Shamata, Louie Dibianco; ***D:*** Robert E. Collins. **TV**

Mafia vs. Ninja 🦴½ **1984** The mob wants to control the city, but the Ninja has other ideas. **90m/C VHS.** Alexander Lou, Silvio Azzolini, Wang Hsia, Charlema Hsu, Eugene Trammel.

Magdalene 🦴½ **1988 (PG)** Somewhere in medieval Europe, a violent Baron seeks revenge on a beautiful whore that spurned him. Small-budget costumer. **89m/C VHS.** Steve Bond, Nastassia Kinski, David Warner, Gunter Meisner, Ferdinand "Ferdy" Mayne, Anthony Quayle, Franco Nero, Janet Agren; ***D:*** Monica Teuber.

Magee and the Lady 🦴🦴 *She'll Be Sweet* **1978 (PG)** The crusty captain of a rusty ship must warm up to a spoiled debutante or lose his ship to a foreclosure firm. Could be better. Made for TV. **92m/C VHS.** *AU* Tony LoBianco, Sally Kellerman; ***D:*** Gene Levitt. **TV**

Magenta 🦴🦴 **1996 (R)** Don't mess around with your teenaged sister-in-law! You'd think guys would've learned that lesson by now. Handsome Dr. Michael Walsh (McMahon) and his lovely wife, Helen (Storry), have a seemingly happy life with their daughter Brittany. Then Helen's sister Magenta (Atkins) comes to stay and she and Michael are soon exchanging more than eye contact. Naturally, all this leads to betrayal, lies, and even more problems. **94m/C VHS.** Julian McMahon, Crystal Atkins, Alison Storry, Marklen Kennedy; ***D:*** Gregory C. Haynes; ***W:*** Gregory C. Haynes; ***C:*** Mark Anthony Galluzzo; ***M:*** Harold Kloser. **VIDEO**

Magic 🦴🦴½ **1978 (R)** Ventriloquist Hopkins and his dummy, an all-too-human counterpart, get involved with a beautiful but impressionable woman lost between reality and the irresistible world of illusion. Spine-chilling psycho-drama with a less-than-believable premise. Screenplay by Goldman from his novel. **106m/C VHS.** Anthony Hopkins, Ann-Margret, Burgess Meredith, Ed Lauter, Jerry Houser, David Ogden Stiers, Lillian Randolph; ***D:*** Richard Attenborough; ***W:*** William Goldman; ***C:*** Victor Kemper; ***M:*** Jerry Goldsmith.

The Magic Bow 🦴½ **1947** Typically ridiculous musical bio—this time of violinist Nicolo Paganini (Granger). He's the talented poor boy who falls for the wealthy Jeanne (Calvert) but his one true love is for his Stradivarius. Yehudi Menuhim plays the solos. Based on the novel by Manuel Komroff. **105m/B VHS.** *GB* Stewart Granger, Phyllis Calvert, Jean Kent, Dennis Price, Cecil Parker, Felix Aylmer, Frank Cellier, Marie Lohr; ***D:*** Bernard Knowles; ***W:*** Roland Pertwee, Norman Ginsburg; ***C:*** Jack Asher, Jack Cox.

The Magic Bubble 🦴🦴½ **1993 (PG-13)** On her 40th birthday, Julia Cole finds the fountain of youth...inside a bottle of enchanted bubbles. Ageless and timeless, she begins to know the meaning of true happiness. **90m/C VHS.** Diane Salinger, John Calvin, Priscilla Pointer, Colleen Camp, Tony Peck, Wallace Shawn, George Clooney; ***D:*** Alfredo Ringel, Deborah Taper Ringel; ***W:*** Meridith Baer, Geof Pryssir.

The Magic Christian 🦴🦴🦴 **1969 (PG)** A series of related skits about a rich man (Sellers) and his son (Starr) who try to prove that anyone can be bought. Raucous, now somewhat dated comedy; music by Badfinger, including Paul McCartney's "Come and Get It." **101m/C VHS.** *GB* Peter Sellers, Ringo Starr, Isabel Jeans, Wilfrid Hyde-White, Graham Chapman, John Cleese, Peter Graves, John Lennon, Yoko Ono, Richard Attenborough, Leonard Frey, Laurence Harvey, Christopher Lee, Spike Milligan, Yul Brynner, Roman Polanski, Raquel Welch, Caroline Blakiston, Ferdinand "Ferdy" Mayne; ***D:*** Joseph McGrath; ***W:*** Terry Southern, Peter Sellers, Graham Chapman, John Cleese; ***C:*** Geoffrey Unsworth; ***M:*** Ken Thorne.

The Magic Flute 🦴🦴🦴½ **1973 (G)** Bergman's acclaimed version of Mozart's famous comic opera, universally considered one of the greatest adaptations of opera to film ever made. Staged before a live audience for Swedish TV. Subtitled. **134m/C VHS, DVD.** *SW* Josef Kostlinger, Irma Urrila, Hakan Hagegard, Elisabeth Erikson; ***D:*** Ingmar Bergman.

The Magic Fountain 🦴🦴 **1961** Three princes search for a magic fountain whose waters will cure their ailing father. Two of them, however, take the evil course and are turned into ravens by a wicked dwarf. Based on the fairy tale "Das Wasser des Lebens" by the Brothers Grimm. **82m/C VHS.** Peter Nestler, Helmo Kinderman, Josef Marz, Catherine Hansen, Cedric Hardwicke; ***D:*** Allan David.

Magic Hunter 🦴🦴 **1996** Max (Kemp) is supposed to be the best sharpshooter on the Budapest police force, but his skill deserts him and he accidentally shoots the woman he was assigned to protect. A sinister colleague gives him seven magic bullets guaranteed to hit their target but what Max doesn't realize is that he's made a bargain with the Devil, and the Devil gets to choose the seventh target. Hungarian with subtitles. **106m/C VHS.** *HU* Gary Kemp, Alexander Kaidanovsky, Sadie Frost; ***D:*** Ildiko Enyedi.

Magic in the Mirror: Fowl Play 🦴🦴½ **1996 (G)** Young Mary Margaret (Smith) does an "Alice Through the Looking Glass" when she steps through an antique mirror bequeathed to her by her grandmother and discovers an enchanted kingdom run by giant ducks. But just how will MM find her way back? **86m/C VHS.** Jamie Renee Smith, Kevin Wixted, Saxon Trainor, David Brooks, Godfrey James; ***D:*** Ted Nicolaou; ***W:*** Frank Dietz, Ken Carter Jr.; ***C:*** Adolfo Bartoli; ***M:*** Richard Kosinski.

Magic in the Water 🦴½ **1995 (PG)** Divorced, obnoxious radio shrink and neglectful dad Dr. Jack Black (Harmon) takes the kiddies on a summer jaunt to a Canadian lake, where they begin to explore the legend of Orky, Canada's answer to the Loch Ness monster. Dad becomes a believer when Orky possesses his body and (New Age Alert!) releases his inner child. Harmless fun for the kids, but parents will gag at the attempt to provide a meaningful and symbolic message, which arrives with all the subtlety of an Oliver Stone history lesson. Sort of an "E.T." meets "Free Willy" with Orky shilling for the EPA. Beautiful cinematography showcasing the British Columbia landscape helps, but not enough. **100m/C VHS.** Mark Harmon, Joshua Jackson, Harley Jane Kozak, Sarah Wayne, Willie Nark-Orn, Frank S. Salsedo; ***D:*** Rick Stevenson; ***W:*** Icel Dobell Massey, Rick Stevenson; ***C:*** Thomas Burstyn; ***M:*** David Schwartz. Genie '95: Cinematog., Sound.

Magic Island 🦴🦴½ **1995 (PG)** Thirteen-year-old Jack (Bryan) gets sucked into the pages of a pirate book and finds himself with Blackbeard and his scurvy crew. They're on a treasure hunt and figure Jack's book contains some missing clues. Naturally, Jack finds himself in lots of trouble. **88m/C VHS.** Zachery Ty Bryan, Edward Kerr, Lee Armstrong, French Stewart, Abraham Benrubi, Jessie-Ann Friend, Oscar Dillon, Sean O'Kane, Schae Harrison, Ja'net DuBois, Andrew Divoff; ***D:*** Sam Irvin; ***W:*** Neil Ruttenberg, Brent Friedman; ***C:*** James Lawrence Spencer; ***M:*** Richard Band.

Magic Kid 🦴🦴½ *Ninja Dragons* **1992 (PG)** Thirteen-year-old martial-arts champ Kevin and his older sister vacation in L.A., staying with their shady Uncle Bob, a second-rate talent agent. Kevin wants to meet his martial arts movie idol and his sister her favorite soap opera hunk. But they wind up being chased by the mobsters Uncle Bob owes money to. **91m/C VHS.** Ted Jan Roberts, Shonda Whipple, Stephen Furst, Joseph Campanella, Billy Hufsey, Sondra Kerns, Pamela Dixon, Lauren Tewes, Don "The Dragon" Wilson; ***D:*** Joseph Merhi; ***W:*** Stephen Smoke; ***M:*** Jim Halfpenny.

Magic Kid 2 🦴🦴½ **1994 (PG)** The young star of a popular martial arts program wants to quit and go to high school like a normal teenager. But the studio execs have other ideas. **90m/C VHS.** Ted Jan Roberts, Stephen Furst, Donald Gibb, Jennifer Savidge; ***D:*** Stephen Furst.

Magic Moments 🦴🦴½ **199?** Ambitious British TV exec Melanie James (Seagrove) is about to score the coup of her career. She's persuaded charismatic American illusionist Troy Gardner (Shea) to recreate his death-defying act on TV—but only if Melanie will produce the show herself. Too bad her power-hungry boss is out to cause trouble. Made for British TV. **103m/C VHS.** *GB* Jenny Seagrove, John Shea. **TV**

Magic of Lassie 🦴🦴 **1978 (G)** Stewart is engaging as the nice grandpa who refuses to sell his land to mean rich guy Roberts. Innocuous, pleasant remake of "Lassie Come Home." Stewart sings, as do Pat Boone and daughter Debby. **100m/C VHS.** James Stewart, Mickey Rooney, Stephanie Zimbalist, Alice Faye, Pernell Roberts; ***D:*** Don Chaffey.

Magic on Love Island 🦴 **1980** Romantic misadventures ensue when eight ladies go on vacation to Love Island, a tropical paradise. **96m/C VHS.** Adrienne Barbeau, Bill Daily, Howard Duff, Dody Goodman, Dominique Dunne, Lisa Hartman Black, Janis Paige; ***D:*** Earl Bellamy.

Magic Serpent 🦴🦴🦴 **1966** Fantasy set in medieval Japan features a grand duel in magic between a good hero and evil sorcerer who transform into a giant dragon and a giant frog to do battle. **?m/C VHS.** Hiroki Matsukata, Tomoko Ogawa, Ryutaro Otomo, Bin Amatsu; ***D:*** Tetsuya Yamauchi.

The Magic Stone 🦴🦴½ *Kilian's Chronicle* **1995** Kilian is the 10th-century Irish slave of brutish Viking Ivar, who decides to sacrifice him to the Norse god Thor when the Vikings become lost while sailing off the North American coast. Kilian manages to escape and make it to shore where he's rescued by a Native American tribe and falls in love with local beauty, Turtle. But Ivar goes after Kilian to steal his magic stone, which can navigate a ship through the worst weather, and begins a Viking war with the tribe. **95m/C VHS.** Christopher Johnson, Robert McDonough, Eva Kim, Jonah Ming Lee; ***D:*** Pamela Berger; ***W:*** Pamela Berger; ***C:*** John Hoover; ***M:*** R. Carlos Nakai, Bevan Manson.

The Magic Sword 🦴🦴 *St. George and the Seven Curses; St. George and the Dragon* **1962** A family-oriented adventure film about a young knight who sets out to rescue a beautiful princess who is being held captive by an evil sorcerer and his dragon. **80m/C VHS.** Basil Rathbone, Estelle Winwood, Gary Lockwood; ***D:*** Bert I. Gordon.

Magic Town 🦴🦴½ **1947** An opinion pollster investigates a small town which exactly reflects the views of the entire nation, making his job a cinch. The publicity causes much ado in the town with ensuing laughs. Uneven but entertaining. **103m/B VHS.** Jane Wyman, James Stewart, Kent Smith, Regis Toomey, Donald Meek; ***D:*** William A. Wellman; ***C:*** Joseph Biroc.

The Magic Voyage 🦴🦴½ **1993 (G)** Animated tale of a friendly woodworm named Pico who voyages with Columbus to the new world and convinces him that the world is indeed round. He then comes to the aid of a magical firefly named Marilyn who helps Columbus find gold to bring back to Spain. **82m/C VHS, DVD.** ***D:*** Michael Schoemann; ***V:*** Dom DeLuise, Mickey Rooney, Corey Feldman, Irene Cara, Dan Haggerty, Samantha Eggar.

The Magic Voyage of Sinbad 🦴🦴 *Sadko* **1952** Sinbad embarks on a fantastic journey after promising the people of his Covasian home that he will find the elusive Phoenix, the bird of happiness. Unreleased in the U.S. until 1962; rewritten for the American screen by a young Coppola. **79m/C VHS.** *RU* Sergey Stolyarov, Alla Larionova, Mark Troyanovsky; ***D:*** Alexander Ptushko; ***W:*** Francis Ford Coppola.

The Magical Legend of the Leprechauns 🦴½ **1999** Goofy fantasy finds American businessman Jack Woods (Quaid) sent to a remote part of Ireland where he happens to save the life of leprechaun, Seamus Muldoon (Meaney), which puts the "little person" in his debt. While Jack tries to romance neighbor Kathleen (Brady), the leprechauns are getting into a fracas with their enemies, the Trooping Fairies, leading to a battle and Jack's involvement. **139m/C VHS, DVD.** Randy Quaid, Colm Meaney, Orla Brady, Whoopi Goldberg, Roger Daltrey, Daniel Betts, Zoe Wanamaker, Caroline Carver, Kieran Culkin, Frank Finlay, Phyllida Law; ***D:*** John Henderson; ***W:*** Peter Barnes; ***C:*** Clive Tickner; ***M:*** Richard Harvey. **TV**

Magical Mystery Tour **1967** On the road with an oddball assortment of people, the Beatles experience a number of strange incidents around the English countryside. ♫Magical Mystery Tour; Blue Jay Way; Your Mother Should Know; The Fool on the Hill. **55m/C VHS, DVD.** *GB* John Lennon, George Harrison, Ringo Starr, Paul McCartney, Victor Spinetti, Neil Innes, Jessie Robbins; ***D:*** John Lennon, George Harrison, Ringo Starr, Paul McCartney; ***C:*** Daniel Lacambre; ***M:*** John Lennon, George Harrison, Ringo Starr, Paul McCartney. **TV**

The Magician 🦴🦴🦴 **1958** A master magician in 19th century Sweden (von Sydow) wreaks ill in this darkly comical, supernatural parable. Dark, well photographed early Bergman effort. In Swedish with English subtitles. **101m/B VHS.** *SW* Max von Sydow, Ingrid Thulin, Gunnar Bjornstrand, Bibi Andersson, Naima Wifstrand; *D:* Ingmar Bergman; *W:* Ingmar Bergman. Venice Film Fest. '59: Special Jury Prize.

The Magician of Lublin **1979 (R)** Based on an unusual story by Issac Bashevis Singer. Follows the exploits of a magician/con man in turn-of-the-century Poland whose personal flaws kill his career, until a chance emerges for one last trick. A good example of movie not as good as book; this rendering is superficial, badly acted and unsatisfying. Made soon after Singer won the Nobel Prize for literature in 1978. **105m/C VHS.** Alan Arkin, Valerie Perrine, Louise Fletcher, Lou Jacobi, Shelley Winters, Elspeth March; *D:* Menahem Golan; *M:* Maurice Jarre.

Magnificent Adventurer **1976** Ostensibly a biography of Benvenuto Cellini, the Florentine sculptor, with a concentration on his love life and swordplay. **94m/C VHS.** Brett Halsey.

The Magnificent Ambersons **1942** Welles's second film. A fascinating, inventive translation of the Booth Tarkington novel about a wealthy turn of the century family collapsing under the changing currents of progress. Pure Welles, except the glaringly bad tacked-on ending that the studio shot (under the direction of the great Robert Wise and Fred Fleck), after taking the film from him. It seems they wanted the proverbial happy ending. **88m/B VHS.** Joseph Cotten, Anne Baxter, Tim Holt, Richard Bennett, Dolores Costello, Erskine Sanford, Ray Collins, Agnes Moorehead; *D:* Freddie Fleck, Robert Wise, Orson Welles; *W:* Orson Welles; *M:* Bernard Herrmann, Roy Webb. Natl. Film Reg. '91;; N.Y. Film Critics '42: Actress (Moorehead).

The Magnificent Ambersons **2002** George Amberson (Rhys Meyers) is the spoiled son of an upper-class, turn-of-the-century Midwestern family. When his widowed mother Isabel (Stowe) is reunited with old flame Eugene Morgan (Greenwood), George becomes obsessively jealous and schemes to break up the match even as he romances Eugene's daughter, Lucy (Mol). Stowe looks beautiful but Rhys Meyers over-emphasizes George's less-than-filial response to his mother. Adaptation of Booth Tarkington's novel that reportedly used Orson Welles original script for his 1942 film. **139m/C VHS, DVD.** Madeleine Stowe, Bruce Greenwood, Jonathan Rhys Meyers, Jennifer Tilly, Gretchen Mol, James Cromwell, William Hootkins; *D:* Alfonso Arau. **CABLE**

Magnificent Doll **1946** Boring Hollywood bio of first lady Dolly Madison (Rogers) who is wooed by dynamic Aaron Burr (Niven) before she decides on marrying quiet James Madison (Meredith) and pushing his political career to the office of the presidency. **93m/B VHS.** Ginger Rogers, David Niven, Burgess Meredith, Stephen McNally, Peggy Wood, Grandon Rhodes, Arthur Space, Robert Barrat; *D:* Frank Borzage; *W:* Irving Stone; *C:* Joseph Valentine; *M:* Hans J. Salter.

The Magnificent Dope **1942** Fonda is likeable, as usual, as the hapless yokel in the big city. A trip to New York to take a course on being successful is his prize for winning a "laziest man" contest. He falls for his teacher; she uses his crush to motivate him. Funny and entertaining. **83m/B VHS.** Henry Fonda, Lynn Bari, Don Ameche, Edward Everett Horton, Hobart Cavanaugh, Pierre Watkin; *D:* Walter Lang.

The Magnificent Matador *The Brave and the Beautiful* **1955** The story of an aging matador who faces death in the bullring to win the love of a woman. Quinn is the bullfighter on the horns of a dilemma. Lots of bull in script carried by harried bull in ring. **94m/C VHS.** Anthony Quinn, Maureen O'Hara, Thomas Gomez; *D:* Budd Boetticher.

Magnificent Obsession **1954** A drunken playboy (Hudson) kills a man and blinds his wife in an automobile accident. Plagued by guilt, he devotes his life to studying medicine in order to restore the widow's sight. Well-acted melodrama lifted Hudson to stardom. Faithful to the 1935 original, based on a novel by Lloyd C. Douglas. **108m/C VHS.** Jane Wyman, Rock Hudson, Barbara Rush, Agnes Moorehead; *D:* Douglas Sirk; *W:* Robert Blees; *C:* Russell Metty.

The Magnificent Seven **1960** Western remake of Akira Kurosawa's classic "The Seven Samurai." Mexican villagers hire gunmen to protect them from the bandits who are destroying their town. Most of the actors were relative unknowns, though not for long. Sequelled by "Return of the Seven" in 1966, "Guns of the Magnificent Seven" in 1969, and "The Magnificent Seven Ride" in 1972. Excellent score. Uncredited writing by Walter Newman and Walter Bernstein. **126m/C VHS, DVD, Wide.** Yul Brynner, Steve McQueen, Robert Vaughn, James Coburn, Charles Bronson, Horst Buchholz, Eli Wallach, Brad Dexter; *D:* John Sturges; *W:* William Roberts; *C:* Charles B(ryant) Lang Jr.; *M:* Elmer Bernstein.

The Magnificent Seven **1998** Pilot movie for the brief TV series that was loosely based on the 1960 film. An indian chief hires seven gunslingers to help defend tribal land from a gang of greedy outlaws who want the tribe's gold mine. **90m/C VHS.** Michael Biehn, Ron Perlman, Dale Midkiff, Eric Close, Anthony Starke, Laurie Holden, Andrew Kavovit, Rick Worthy, Kurtwood Smith, Ned Romero, Daragh O'Malley, Michael Greyeyes, Tony Burton; *D:* Geoff Murphy; *W:* Frank Q. Dobbs, Chris Black; *C:* Jack Conroy; *M:* Don Harper. **TV**

The Magnificent Yankee *The Man with Thirty Sons* **1950** Adaptation of Emmet Lavery's Broadway play on the life of Supreme Court Justice Oliver Wendell Holmes, starring Calhern (who also did the stage version). America's foremost legal mind was well-served by Calhern, with Harding as his ever-patient wife. **80m/B VHS.** Louis Calhern, Ann Harding, Eduard Franz, Philip Ober, Ian Wolfe, Edith Evanson, Richard Anderson, Jimmy Lydon, Robert Sherwood, Hugh Sanders; *D:* John Sturges; *W:* Emmet Lavery.

Magnolia **1999 (R)** It's a really long, frantic, and surreal look into a 24-hour series of interlocking stories, with a fine ensemble cast. Bad dads Jimmy Gator (Hall) and Earl Partridge (Robards) are both dying and estranged from their children—Jimmy's coke-addicted daughter, Claudia (Walters), and Earl's flashy motivational speaker son, Frank (Cruise). Earl's trophy wife Linda (Moore) is having a breakdown but he's being cared for by kind-hearted nurse Phil (Hoffman). And then there's a popular game show (of which Jimmy is the host) and its current and past quiz kids, and a rain of frogs, and everyone suddenly breaks into song, and, well, just watch it. **188m/C VHS, DVD, Wide.** Jason Robards Jr., Julianne Moore, Tom Cruise, Philip Seymour Hoffman, Philip Baker Hall, Melora Walters, John C. Reilly, Melinda Dillon, William H. Macy, Michael Bowen, Jeremy Blackman, Emmanuel Johnson; *D:* Paul Thomas Anderson; *W:* Paul Thomas Anderson; *C:* Robert Elswit; *M:* Jon Brion, Aimee Mann. Golden Globes '00: Support. Actor (Cruise); Natl. Bd. of Review '99: Support. Actor (Hoffman), Support. Actress (Moore).

Magnum Force **1973 (R)** Eastwood's second "Dirty Harry" movie. Harry finds a trail leading from a series of gangland killings straight back to the P.D. Less gripping than "Dirty Harry" (1971), but still effective. Holbrook is cast intriguingly against type. **124m/C VHS, DVD, Wide.** Clint Eastwood, Hal Holbrook, Mitchell Ryan, David Soul, Robert Urich, Tim Matheson, Kip Niven, Albert "Poppy" Popwell; *D:* Ted Post; *W:* Michael Cimino, John Milius; *C:* Frank Stanley; *M:* Lalo Schifrin.

Magnum Killers **1976** A young man becomes involved in a web of deadly intrigue when he sets out to find who cheated him out of a small fortune during a card game. **92m/C VHS.** Sombat Methance, Prichela Lee.

Magnum P.I.: Don't Eat the Snow in Hawaii **1980** Series pilot finds Vietnam-vet-turned-private-eye Thomas Sullivan Magnum (Selleck) living in Hawaii (in the guest house of never-seen mystery writer Robin Masters) and investigating the death of a wartime buddy. Hillerman excels as autocratic major domo Higgins. **99m/C VHS.** Tom Selleck, John Hillerman, Roger E. Mosley, Larry Manetti; *D:* Roger Young; *W:* Donald P. Bellisario, Glen Larson. **TV**

The Mahabharata **1989** Adapted from the myths and folklore of ancient India, the screen version of the original nine-hour stage play is the story of a devastating war between two powerful clans. Initially broadcast on public TV, the six-hour movie is divided into three two-hour segments: "The Game of Dice," "Exile in the Forest," and "The War." **318m/C VHS.** *GB FR* Robert Langton-Lloyd, Antonin Stahly-Vishwanadan, Bruce Myers; *D:* Peter Brook; *W:* Jean-Claude Carriere; *M:* Toshi Tsuchitori. **TV**

Mahler **1974 (PG)** Strange Russell effort on the life of the great composer Gustav Mahler. Imperfect script is rescued by fine acting. **110m/C VHS, DVD.** Robert Powell, Georgina Hale, Richard Morant, Lee Montague, Terry O'Quinn; *D:* Ken Russell; *W:* Ken Russell; *C:* Dick Bush.

Mahogany **1975 (PG)** Poor girl becomes world-famous high fashion model and designer, ditches boyfriend in the old neighborhood, gets a career boost when she daringly appears in a dress of her own creation at a Roman fashion show, and still yearns for the boy back home. Motown attempt to make mainstream hit that's glossy and predictable. **109m/C VHS.** Diana Ross, Billy Dee Williams, Jean-Pierre Aumont, Anthony Perkins, Nina Foch; *D:* Berry Gordy; *W:* John Byrum; *C:* David Watkin.

The Maid **1990 (PG)** An offbeat comedy romance with Sheen as the house husband to Bisset's female executive character. Nice acting; charming, if unoriginal, premise. **91m/C VHS.** Martin Sheen, Jacqueline Bisset, Jean-Pierre Cassel, James Faulkner, Victoria Shalet; *D:* Ian Toynton.

Maid to Order **1987 (PG)** Rich girl Sheedy's fairy godmother puts her in her place by turning her into a maid for a snooty Malibu couple. Good-natured and well-acted if rather mindless Cinderella story. **92m/C VHS.** Ally Sheedy, Beverly D'Angelo, Michael Ontkean, Dick Shawn, Tom Skerritt, Valerie Perrine, Rigg Kennedy; *D:* Amy Holden Jones; *W:* Perry Howze; *M:* Georges Delerue.

Maid's Night Out **1938** Pleasant, simple-minded mistaken-identity comedy. Fontaine is an heiress; rich-guy posing-as-milkman Lane thinks she is a maid. They fall in love, of course. **64m/B VHS.** Joan Fontaine, Allan "Rocky" Lane, Hedda Hopper, George Irving, William Brisbane, Billy Gilbert, Cecil Kellaway; *D:* Ben Holmes.

Maids of Wilko *The Young Ladies of Wilko; Panny z Wilka* **1979** Wajda's adaptation of Jaroslav Iwaszkiewicz's memoirs set in the late '20s. Viktor Ruben (Olbrychski) reexamines his life following the death of a friend. He returns to the home of his aunt and uncle in Wilko where he renews friendships with five sisters on a neighboring estate in an attempt to resurrect a happier past. Lots of fruitless romantic yearning. In French and Polish with English subtitles. **118m/C VHS.** *PL FR* Daniel Olbrychski, Christine Pascal, Maja Komorowska, Anna Seniuk, Krystyna Zachwatowicz, Stanislawa Celinska, Zofia Jaroszewska, Tadeusz Bialoszczynski; *D:* Andrzej Wajda; *W:* Zbigniew Kaminski.

The Main Event **1979 (PG)** Streisand plays a wacky—and bankrupt—cosmetic executive who must depend on the career of washed-up boxer O'Neal to rebuild her fortune. Desperate (and more than a little smitten), she badgers and bullies him back into the ring. Lame, derivative screwball comedy desperate to suggest chemistry of Streisand and O'Neal's "What's Up, Doc?" (1972). Streisand sings the title song. **109m/C VHS.** Barbra Streisand, Ryan O'Neal; *D:* Howard Zieff.

Main Street to Broadway **1953** Superficial story of a struggling playwright. Interesting mainly for abundant big-name cameos. Based on a story by Robert E. Sherwood. **102m/B VHS.** Tom Morton, Mary Murphy, Agnes Moorehead, Herb Shriner, Rosemary DeCamp, Clinton Sundberg; *Cameos:* Lionel Barrymore, Ethel Barrymore, Tallulah Bankhead, Shirley Booth, Cornel Wilde, Rex Harrison, Joshua Logan, Helen Hayes, Mary Martin; *D:* Tay Garnett.

Mainline Run **1998** Smalltime drug runner Taro (Speer) gets out of prison and immediately goes back to work for crime boss Mr. Fletcher (Ward). Taro sets up a deal, which goes bad, the drugs are lost, and one of his men is killed. Now Taro and his buddy Sean (Joseph) are looking to get out, but Mr. Fletcher has something else in mind. **96m/C VHS.** Hugo Speer, Andrew Joseph, Nelson E. Ward, Kelly Marcel; *D:* Howard Ford; *C:* Jonathan Ford.

Maitresse **1976** An examination of the sexual underworld in the same vein as "Blue Velvet" and "Crimes of Passion" as a man falls for a high-priced dominatrix. Director Scroeder also created "Reversal of Fortune." In French with English subtitles. **112m/C VHS.** *FR* Gerard Depardieu, Bulle Ogier; *D:* Barbet Schroeder; *C:* Nestor Almendros.

The Majestic **2001 (PG)** Carrey is a blacklisted writer who suffers from amnesia after a car crash. He winds up in a small town where he's mistaken for a presumed MIA soldier, who was the son of Landau, the local movie theater owner. Darabont's self-admitted ode to Frank Capra evokes the All-American innocence and decency that Capra's films revelled in, but doesn't quite match the charm. Cynics will think it's too sentimental and tries to hard, romantics and others not quick to sneer at nostalgia should enjoy themselves. Carrey does a fine job with the lead role. **152m/C VHS, DVD.** *US* Jim Carrey, Martin Landau, Laurie Holden, David Ogden Stiers, James Whitmore, Jeffrey DeMunn, Ron Rifkin, Hal Holbrook, Bob Balaban, Brent Briscoe, Gerry Black, Susan Willis, Catherine Dent, Chelcie Ross, Amanda Detmer, Allen (Goorwitz) Garfield, Daniel von Bargen, Shawn Doyle, Bruce Campbell, Clifford Curtis; *D:* Frank Darabont; *W:* Michael Sloane; *C:* David Tattersall; *M:* Mark Isham.

The Major and the Minor **1942** Very funny comedy that marked Wilder's directorial debut. Susan Applegate (Rogers) decides she's had it with New York and wants to head home to Iowa, but she only has enough money for a child's half-price train ticket. So she passes herself off as a 12-year-old (!) and then runs into problems when Army major Kirby (Milland), who's traveling to a boys military school, decides to take the child under his protective wing. Soon he's insisting Susan stay at the school until her mother (played by Rogers' mother Lela) can collect her. Potentially risque situations never cross the line into sleaze but remain bright and breezy. **101m/B VHS.** Ginger Rogers, Ray Milland, Rita Johnson, Robert Benchley, Diana Lynn, Frankie Thomas Jr.; *D:* Billy Wilder; *W:* Billy Wilder, Charles Brackett; *C:* Leo Tover; *M:* Robert Emmett Dolan.

Major Barbara **1941** A wealthy, idealistic girl joins the Salvation Army against her father's wishes. Based on the play by George Bernard Shaw. The excellent adaptation of the original and the cast make this film a winner. Deborah Kerr's film debut. **90m/B VHS.** *GB* Wendy Hiller, Rex Harrison, Robert Morley, Sybil Thorndike, Deborah Kerr; *D:* Gabriel Pascal.

Major Dundee **1965** A Union army officer (Heston) chases Apaches into Mexico with a motley collection of prisoner volunteers. Too long and flawed; would have been better had Peckinpah been allowed to finish the project. Excellent cast. **124m/C VHS.** Charlton Heston, Richard Harris, James Coburn, Jim Hutton, Ben Johnson, Slim Pickens; *D:* Sam Peckinpah; *C:* Sam Leavitt.

Major League **1989 (R)** Comedy about the Cleveland Indians, a pathetic major league baseball team whose new owner, ex-showgirl Rachel (Wilton) who inherited from her late hubby, schemes to lose the season and relocate the team to Miami. Sheen is okay as pitcher Ricky "Wild Thing" Vaughan, who suffers with control problems (both on and off the field), while Bernsen (as third baseman Roger Dorn) seems to be gazing affectionately at "L.A. Law" from a distance.

Predictable sports spoof is good for a few laughs, particularly those scenes involving Haysbert as slugger Pedro Cerrano with voodoo on his mind (and in his locker) and Snipes as base stealer Willie Mays Hayes, whose only problem is getting on base. Followed by two sequels. **107m/C VHS, 8mm.** Tom Berenger, Charlie Sheen, Corbin Bernsen, James Gammon, Margaret Whitton, Bob Uecker, Rene Russo, Wesley Snipes, Dennis Haysbert, Charles Cyphers, Chelcie Ross; ***D:*** David S. Ward; ***W:*** David S. Ward; ***C:*** Reynaldo Villalobos; ***M:*** James Newton Howard.

Major League 2 🦴½ **1994 (PG)** It's been five years since they won the series, and this plodding sequel finds the wacky championship Cleveland Indians ruined by success and once again struggling in last place. Limited charm of original is lost; dull and filled with so many lame jokes that you won't care if they manage to make it to the top again. Cast returns, with the exception of Wesley Snipes as Willie Mays Hays (now played by Epps). **105m/C VHS, DVD, Wide.** Charlie Sheen, Tom Berenger, Corbin Bernsen, James Gammon, Dennis Haysbert, Omar Epps, David Keith, Bob Uecker, Alison Doody, Michelle Rene Thomas, Margaret Whitton, Eric Bruskotter, Takaaki Ishibashi, Randy Quaid; ***D:*** David S. Ward; ***W:*** R.J. Stewart; ***C:*** Victor Hammer; ***M:*** Michel Colombier.

Major League 3: Back to the Minors 🦴½ **1998 (PG-13)** Three strikes and this franchise is out. Gus Cantrell (Bakula) is a burned-out pitcher who's offered the chance to manage the Minnesota Twins' Triple A team and finds a bunch of central casting misfits. Just when you thought they'd run out of baseball cliches, in comes a young prospect who won't take advice (Goggins), an arrogant manager (McGinley), and the "big game" showdown (twice!). We've seen this stuff done (not much better) in the first two "Major Leagues" and (very much better) elsewhere. Bakula's always solid, but it's not enough to get the save. Take an intentional pass on this one. **90m/C VHS, DVD, Wide.** Scott Bakula, Corbin Bernsen, Dennis Haysbert, Takaaki Ishibashi, Jensen Daggett, Eric Bruskotter, Walton Goggins, Ted McGinley, Kenneth Johnson, Peter M. MacKenzie, Bob Uecker, Steve Yeager, Larry Brandenburg, Judson Mills, Lobo Sebastian, Thom Barry, Tim DiFilippo, Tom DiFilippo, Ted DiFilippo; ***D:*** John Warren; ***W:*** John Warren; ***C:*** Tim Suhrstedt; ***M:*** Robert Folk.

Major Payne 🦴 **1995 (PG-13)** When the marines have no more use for killing-machine Major Payne (Wayans), he reluctantly agrees to train the inept junior ROTC cadets at academically challenged Madison Academy. The misfit brigade contains the usual assortment of stock loser-types who follow the predictable "outcasts get even" plot to the letter. Wayans shows flashes of comic genius, but not nearly enough to make up for the one-dimensional characters and indifferent writing. Most of the showcase jokes involve the humiliation and degradation of the kids, always a laugh-riot. Sub-moronic remake of 1955's "The Private War of Major Benson." **97m/C VHS, DVD, Wide.** Damon Wayans, Karyn Parsons, William Hickey, Albert Hall, Steven Martini, Andrew Harrison Leeds, Scott "Bam Bam" Bigelow; ***D:*** Nick Castle; ***W:*** Dean Lorey, Gary Rosen, Damon Wayans; ***C:*** Richard Bowen; ***M:*** Craig Safan.

The Majorettes 🦴 **1987 (R)** Eek! Someone is lurking around a high school murdering the majorettes with their own batons. A bare-bones plot lurks within this otherwise worthless pic. **93m/C VHS.** Kevin Kindlin, Terrie Godfrey, Mark V. Jevicky, Sueanne Seamans, John A. Russo, Bill (William Heinzman) Hinzman, Russell Streiner; ***D:*** Bill (William Heinzman) Hinzman; ***W:*** John A. Russo.

A Majority of One 🦴🦴½ **1956** Dated comedy about late-in-life romance and prejudice. Russell stars as Jewish Brooklyn widow Mrs. Jacoby, who tags along with her daughter and diplomat son-in-law on their shipboard trip to Japan. She meets the charming Koichi Asano (a surprisingly effective Guinness), who's with the Japanese diplomatic corp, runs into problems with her family, and decides she must give up her chance at romance. Adapted from the play by Leonard Spigelgass. **149m/C VHS.** Rosalind Russell, Alec Guinness, Ray Danton, Madlyn Rhue, Mae Questel, Frank Wilcox, Alan Mowbray; ***D:*** Mervyn LeRoy; ***W:*** Leonard Spigelgass.

Make a Million 🦴🦴 **1935** The Depression is played (successfully) for yuks in this tale of an economics professor fired from his post for advocating radical income redistribution. He doesn't get mad, he gets even: he makes a million by advertising for money. **66m/B VHS.** Charles Starrett, Pauline Brooks.

Make a Wish 🦴🦴 **1937** A noted composer goes stale in this colorful musical about backstage life. The comic relief provides the films best moments. ♫Music In My Heart; My Campfire Dreams; Make a Wish; Old Man Rip. **80m/B VHS.** Basil Rathbone, Leon Errol, Bobby Breen, Ralph Forbes; ***D:*** Kurt Neumann; ***M:*** Oscar Straus.

Make Haste to Live 🦴🦴½ **1954** Good, scary thriller. A woman survives attempted murder by her husband; moves far away to raise their infant daughter. He does time, then returns for revenge. McGuire is good as the terrorized wife. **90m/B VHS.** Dorothy McGuire, Stephen McNally, Edgar Buchanan, John Howard; ***D:*** William A. Seiter; ***M:*** Elmer Bernstein.

Make Me an Offer 🦴🦴 **1955** Somewhat slow-moving comedy centering on an antique dealer who attempts to buy an expensive vase from an old man. From the novel by Wolf Mankowitz. **88m/C VHS.** *GB* Peter Finch, Adrienne Corri, Rosalie Crutchley, Finlay Currie; ***D:*** Cyril Frankel.

Make Me an Offer 🦴½ **1980** Made-for-TV movie about selling real estate in Hollywood. Better than similar efforts. **97m/C VHS.** Susan Blakely, Stella Stevens, Patrick O'Neal; ***D:*** Jerry Paris; ***M:*** Ralph Burns.

Make Mine Mink 🦴🦴🦴 **1960** Oft-hilarious British comedy about guests at an elegant but run-down mansion who become unlikely thieves, stealing furs for charity. Good cast headed by Terry-Thomas. **100m/C VHS.** *GB* Terry-Thomas, Billie Whitelaw, Hattie Jacques; ***D:*** Robert Asher.

Make Room for Tomorrow 🦴🦴 **1981 (R)** Subtle, somewhat funny French comedy about generations in a family. A man in mid-life crisis has to cope with his father, son, and grandfather on the grandfather's 90th birthday. **106m/C VHS.** *FR* Victor Lanoux, Jane Birkin, George Wilson; ***D:*** Peter Kassovitz.

Make-Up 🦴🦴 **1937** A doctor turned circus clown uses his medical skills when an elephant renders a society girl unconscious. After she awakens the two become involved. The clown's daughter objects, but is soon caught up in an accusation that she murdered the lion tamer. Her father the clown tries to save the day. Predictable doctor/clown relationship. **72m/B VHS.** Nils Asther, June Clyde, Judy Kelly, Kenne Duncan, John Turnbull; ***D:*** Alfred Zeisler.

The Maker 🦴🦴½ **1998 (R)** Restless SoCal high-schooler Josh (Rhys Myers) indulges in petty crime with lesbian friend Bella (Balk) but isn't really in trouble until his long-missing older brother Walter (Modine) hits town. Walter soon pulls Josh into his shady schemes that turn into some very dangerous games. **98m/C VHS.** Jonathan Rhys Meyers, Matthew Modine, Mary-Louise Parker, Fairuza Balk, Michael Madsen, Jesse Borrego, Kate McGregor-Stewart, Lawrence Pressman, Jeff Kober; ***D:*** Tim Hunter; ***W:*** Rand Ravich; ***C:*** Hubert Taczanowski; ***M:*** Paul Buckmaster.

Maker of Men 🦴½ **1931** Melodrama finds tough college football coach Dudley pushing son Bob to play. Only the kid's inexperience causes the team's defeat in the big game. Humiliated, Bob transfers to a rival school and gives football another try, going up against his old man. **71m/B VHS.** Jack Holt, Richard Cromwell, Joan Marsh, John Wayne, Walter Catlett; ***D:*** Edward Sedgwick; ***W:*** Howard J. Green; ***C:*** L.W. O'Connell.

Making Contact 🦴½ **1986 (PG)** A small boy's telekinetic powers enable him to bring to life his favorite toys. The ridicule he endures because of this leads him to set off on terrifying adventures with only his toys and a friend for company. **83m/C VHS.** Joshua Morrell, Eve Kryll; ***D:*** Roland Emmerich.

Making Love 🦴🦴 **1982 (R)** A closet homosexual risks his eight-year marriage by getting involved with a carefree writer. What could be a powerful subject gets only bland treatment. **112m/C VHS.** Kate Jackson, Harry Hamlin, Michael Ontkean, Wendy Hiller, Arthur Hill, Nancy Olson, Terry Kiser, Camilla Carr, Michael Dudikoff; ***D:*** Arthur Hiller; ***W:*** Barry Sandler.

Making Mr. Right 🦴🦴½ **1986 (PG-13)** Under-rated satire about a high-powered marketing and image consultant who falls in love with the android that she's supposed to be promoting. Unbelievable comedy is shaky at times, but Magnuson and Malkovich create some magic. **95m/C VHS.** John Malkovich, Ann Magnuson, Glenne Headly, Ben Masters, Laurie Metcalf, Polly Bergen, Hart Bochner, Polly Draper, Susan Anton; ***D:*** Susan Seidelman; ***W:*** Laurie Frank, Floyd Byars.

Making the Grade 🦴🦴 *Preppies* **1984 (PG)** Jersey tough kid owes the mob; attends prep school in place of a rich kid who can't be bothered. Better than similar '80s teen flicks, but not by much. **105m/C VHS, DVD, Wide.** Judd Nelson, Joanna Lee, Dana Olsen, Ronald Lacey, Scott McGinnis, Gordon Jump, Carey Scott, Andrew (Dice Clay) Silverstein; ***D:*** Dorian Walker; ***W:*** Gene Quintano; ***C:*** Jacques Haitkin; ***M:*** Basil Poledouris.

The Makioka Sisters 🦴🦴🦴 **1983** Much praised drama centering around the lives of four Japanese sisters who are heiresses to the family fortune and, hence, must be found proper husbands. The efforts of the older sisters to "match" their younger siblings are entwined with a gradual realization on the part of the elders that the quiet way of life representative of their own formative years is passing away with the advent of WWII. The movie is as visually stunning as it is poignant. In Japanese with English subtitles. **140m/C VHS.** *JP* Keiko Kishi, Yoshiko Sakuma, Sayuri Yoshinaga; ***D:*** Kon Ichikawa.

Malarek 🦴🦴 **1989 (R)** Tough Montreal journalist Victor Malarek exposed abuse in that city's teen detention center in his book "Hey, Malarek." Compelling lead performance from Koteas in decent though not great screen adaptation. **95m/C VHS.** Michael Sarrazin, Elias Koteas, Al Waxman, Kerrie Keane; ***D:*** Roger Cardinal.

Malaya 🦴🦴½ *East of the Rising Sun* **1949** Hokey adventure tale set in WWII that's based on a true story. Stewart and Tracy are hired to smuggle a huge shipment of rubber out of Malaya to waiting U.S. ships without the Japanese finding out. Greenstreet does his usual shifty role. **98m/B VHS.** Spencer Tracy, James Stewart, Sydney Greenstreet, Valentina Cortese, John Hodiak, Lionel Barrymore, Gilbert Roland, Richard Loo, Roland Winters; ***D:*** Richard Thorpe; ***W:*** Frank Fenton; ***C:*** George J. Folsey; ***M:*** Bronislau Kaper.

Malcolm 🦴🦴½ **1986 (PG-13)** An offbeat comedy about a slightly retarded young man who is mechanically inclined and his unusual entry into a life of crime. Directorial debut for actress Tass, whose husband Parker wrote the screenplay (and designed the Tinkertoys). Music score performed by The Penguin Cafe Orchestra. **86m/C VHS.** *AU* Colin Friels, John Hargreaves, Lindy Davies, Chris Haywood, Charles Tingwell, Beverly Phillips, Judith Stratford; ***D:*** Nadia Tass; ***W:*** David Parker; ***C:*** David Parker; ***M:*** Simon Jeffes. Australian Film Inst. '86: Actor (Friels), Film.

Malcolm X 🦴🦴🦴 **1992 (PG-13)** Stirring tribute to the controversial black activist, a leader in the struggle for black liberation. Hitting bottom during his imprisonment in the '50s, he became a Black Muslim and then a leader in the Nation of Islam. His assassination in 1965 left a legacy of black nationalism, self-determination, and racial pride. Marked by strong direction from Lee and good performances (notably Freeman Jr. as Elijah Muhammad), it is Washington's convincing performance in the title role that truly brings the film alive. Based on "The Autobiography of Malcolm X" by Malcolm X and Alex Haley. **201m/C VHS, DVD, 8mm.** Denzel Washington, Angela Bassett, Albert Hall, Al Freeman Jr., Delroy Lindo, Spike Lee, Theresa Randle, Kate Vernon, Lonette McKee, Tommy Hollis, James McDaniel, Ernest Thompson, Jean LaMarre, Giancarlo Esposito, Craig Wasson, John Ottavino, David Patrick Kelly, Shirley Stoler; ***Cameos:*** Christopher Plummer, Karen Allen, Peter Boyle, William Kunstler, Bobby Seale, Al Sharpton; ***D:*** Spike Lee; ***W:*** Spike Lee, Arnold Perl, James Baldwin; ***M:*** Terence Blanchard. MTV Movie Awards '93: Male Perf. (Washington); N.Y. Film Critics '92: Actor (Washington).

Malcolm X: Make It Plain **1995** In-depth portrait of the life of Malcolm X as told through the memories of many of Malcolm's close personal friends and individuals who had worked closely with him. Contains footage of Malcolm X speaking at rallies, meetings, and interviews with Maya Angelou, Ossie Davis, Alex Haley, Mike Wallace, and his family. **136m/C VHS.** ***Nar:*** Alfre Woodard.

Male and Female 🦴🦴🦴🦴 **1919** A group of British aristocrats is shipwrecked on an island and must allow their efficient butler (Meighan) to take command for their survival. Swanson is the spoiled rich girl who falls for her social inferior. Their rescue provides a return to the rigid British class system. Based on the play "The Admirable Crichton" by James M. Barrie. **110m/B VHS, DVD.** Gloria Swanson, Thomas Meighan, Lila Lee, Raymond Hatton, Bebe Daniels; ***D:*** Cecil B. DeMille; ***W:*** Jeanie Macpherson; ***C:*** Alvin Wyckoff.

Malena 🦴🦴 **2000** Nostalgic coming of age story centered on a fantasy woman. The beautiful Malena (Bellucci) inspires lust in the men and jealousy in the women of her Sicilian village in 1940. Her husband is away fighting and, because of unjustified gossip, Malena loses her teaching job and eventually turns to prostitution to support herself. Only puberty-struck 13-year-old Renato (Sulfaro) shows any interest in her plight, which becomes worse as the war drags on. Italian with subtitles. **106m/C VHS, DVD.** *IT* Monica Bellucci, Giuseppe Sulfaro, Luciano Federico, Matilde Piana, Pietro Notarianni, Gaetano Aronica; ***D:*** Giuseppe Tornatore; ***W:*** Giuseppe Tornatore; ***C:*** Lajos Koltai; ***M:*** Ennio Morricone.

Malevolence 🦴🦴 **1998 (R)** Billy Bob Jones (Cortese) was unjustly imprisoned as a boy and has now spent half his life in jail. Shortly after his release, he drifts into petty crime and is suddenly the prime suspect in the murder of a black politician. The only thing is, Billy Bob is being framed. **95m/C VHS.** Joe Cortese, Michael McGrady, Tom Bower, Lou Rawls.

Malibu Beach 🦴½ **1978 (R)** The California beach scene is the setting for this movie filled with bikini clad girls, tanned young men, and instant romances. For connoisseurs of the empty-headed teen beach movie. **93m/C VHS.** Kim Lankford, James Daughton; ***D:*** Robert J. Rosenthal; ***C:*** Jamie Anderson.

The Malibu Beach Vampires **1991 (R)** Three unscrupulous yuppies, Congressman Teri Upstart, Col. Ollie West and Rev. Timmy Fakker, keep beautiful mistresses in their Malibu beach house. What they don't know is, the girls are all really vampires who have injected them with a serum that compels them to tell the truth! Will our "heroes" continue to dupe the American Public, or will the sexy blood suckers cause their downfall? **90m/C VHS.** Angelyne, Becky Le Beau, Joan Rudelstein, Marcus A. Frishman, Rod Sweitzer, Francis Creighton, Anet Anatelle, Yvette Buchanan, Cherie Romaors, Kelly Galindo; ***D:*** Francis Creighton.

Malibu Bikini Shop 🦴 **1986 (R)** Two brothers manage a beachfront bikini shop in Malibu, and spend their time ogling the customers and arguing about running the "business." Just another excuse for parading babes in bathing suits across the naked screen. **90m/C VHS.** Michael David Wright, Bruce Greenwood, Barbara Horan, Debra Blee, Jay Robinson, Galyn Gorg, Ami Julius, Frank Nelson, Kathleen Freeman, Rita Jenrette; ***D:*** David Wechter; ***W:*** David Wechter.

Malibu Express 🦴 1985 (R) Mystery/adventure plot about a P.I. is the excuse; babes in swimsuits is the reason for this waste of time. **101m/C VHS.** Darby Hinton, Sybil Danning, Art Metrano, Shelley Taylor Morgan, Niki Dantine, Barbara (Lee) Edwards; ***D:*** Andy Sidaris.

Malibu High 🦴 1979 (R) The accidental death of a young prostitute's client leads her to a new series of illegal activities of the "sex and hit" variety. Dark, sleazy, and antisocial; belies Beach Boys-esque title. **92m/C VHS.** Jill Lansing, Stuart Taylor; ***D:*** Irvin Berwick.

Malice 🦴🦴½ 1993 (R) In a sleepy little college town, strange things sure do happen. Too bad rumpled college dean Andy Safian (Pullman) didn't see "Pacific Heights." If he did, he would know that sometimes roommates are more trouble than they're worth, even if renovation on that old Victorian is getting expensive. Routine thriller throws out an inventive twist to keep things moving, but manages to be fairly predictable anyway. **107m/C VHS, DVD.** Alec Baldwin, Nicole Kidman, Bill Pullman, Bebe Neuwirth, Anne Bancroft, George C. Scott, Peter Gallagher, Josef Sommer, Gwyneth Paltrow; ***D:*** Harold Becker; ***W:*** Aaron Sorkin, Scott Frank; ***C:*** Gordon Willis; ***M:*** Jerry Goldsmith.

Malicious 🦴🦴 *Malizia* 1974 (R) A housekeeper hired for a widower and his three sons becomes the object of lusty affection of all four men. As Papa makes plans to court and marry her, his 14-year-old son plots to have her as a companion on his road to sensual maturity. Dubbed in English. **98m/C VHS.** *IT* Laura Antonelli, Turi Ferro, Alessandro Momo, Tina Aumont; ***D:*** Salvatore Samperi.

Malicious 🦴🦴 1995 (R) College athlete Doug Gordon (McGaw) impulsively has what he thinks is a one-nighter with mystery lady, Melissa (Ringwald). Only she's not willing to give him up and his rejection sends her on the road to revenge. **92m/C VHS.** Molly Ringwald, Patrick McGaw, Sarah Lassez, John Vernon, Mimi Kuzyk, Rick Henrickson; ***D:*** Ian Corson; ***W:*** George Saunders; ***C:*** Michael Slovis; ***M:*** Graeme Coleman.

Mallrats 🦴🦴½ 1995 (R) Smith's better-financed follow-up to the legendary "Clerks" (the second in the "Lord of the Rings" trilogy) follows Jersey slackers T.S. (London) and Brodie (Lee) to the mall, where they intend to wallow in food-court cookies and reclaim their girlfriends, who recently dumped them. While wandering the mall in low-key and confused pursuit of their women and self respect, they encounter the usual band of bizarre inhabitants, including Ivannah, the topless psychic, and Silent Bob (Smith) and stoner Jay (Mewes), the guys who hung out in front of the video shop during "Clerks." Dialogue and sightgags are director/writer Smith's strong point; moving the plot forward is not high on the priority list. The ensemble cast, featuring Doherty as the boring babe who spurns Brodie, is up to the often funny sidebits and gen-x references. Ribald humor is not for young teens with virgin ears, unless mom and dad are out for the evening. Slick packaging with alternative soundtrack insures return on investment. **95m/C VHS, DVD.** Priscilla Barnes, Stan Lee, Art James, Shannen Doherty, Jeremy London, Jason Lee, Claire Forlani, Michael Rooker, Renee Humphrey, Ben Affleck, Joey Lauren Adams, Jason Mewes, Brian O'Halloran, David Brinkley, Kevin Smith; ***D:*** Kevin Smith; ***W:*** Kevin Smith; ***C:*** David Klein; ***M:*** Ira Newborn.

Malone 🦴½ 1987 (R) A burnt-out secret agent stumbles into a real-estate swindle/murder plot in Oregon and sets out to stop it. Film tries hard but doesn't succeed in being believable. **92m/C VHS.** Burt Reynolds, Lauren Hutton, Cliff Robertson, Kenneth McMillan, Scott Wilson, Cynthia Gibb; ***D:*** Harley Cokliss; ***M:*** David Newman.

Malou 🦴🦴 1983 (R) A young French woman tries to uncover the truth about her late mother's life, sifting through wildly contradictory evidence in the desire to discover her own identity and avoid her mother's mistakes. A feminist story. In German with English subtitles. **95m/C VHS.** *GE* Grischa Huber, Ingrid Caven, Helmut Griem; ***D:*** Jeanine Meerapfel; ***C:*** Michael Ballhaus.

Malta Story 🦴🦴½ 1953 A British WWII flier becomes involved with the defense of Malta. **103m/B VHS.** Alec Guinness, Jack Hawkins, Anthony Steel, Flora Robson, Muriel Pavlow; ***D:*** Brian Desmond Hurst.

The Maltese Falcon 🦴🦴🦴 *Dangerous Female* 1931 A good first screen version of the Dashiell Hammett story about private detective Sam Spade's search for the elusive Black Bird. Remade five years later as "Satan Met a Lady" with Bette Davis. Its most famous remake, however, occurred in 1941 with Humphrey Bogart in the lead. **80m/B VHS.** Bebe Daniels, Ricardo Cortez, Dudley Digges, Thelma Todd, Una Merkel, Dwight Frye, Robert Elliott; ***D:*** Roy Del Ruth.

The Maltese Falcon 🦴🦴🦴🦴 1941 After the death of his partner, detective Sam Spade (Bogart) finds himself enmeshed in a complicated, intriguing search for a priceless statuette. "It's the stuff dreams are made of," says Bogart of the Falcon. Excellent, fast-paced film noir with outstanding performances, great dialogue, and concentrated attention to details. Director Huston's first film and Greenstreet's talky debut. First of several films starring Bogart and Astor. Based on the novel by Dashiell Hammett. Also available colorized. **101m/B VHS, DVD.** Humphrey Bogart, Mary Astor, Peter Lorre, Sydney Greenstreet, Ward Bond, Barton MacLane, Gladys George, Lee Patrick, Elisha Cook Jr., Jerome Cowan, Walter Huston; ***D:*** John Huston; ***W:*** John Huston; ***C:*** Arthur Edeson; ***M:*** Adolph Deutsch. AFI '98: Top 100, Natl. Film Reg. '89.

Mama Dracula woof! 1980 Fletcher stars in this poor satire of the horror genre. She's a vampire who needs the blood of virgins to stay young. Her son helps out—what good son wouldn't? **90m/C VHS.** *FR* Louise Fletcher, Bonnie Schneider, Maria Schneider, Marc-Henri Wajnberg, Alexander Wajnberg, Jess Hahn; ***D:*** Boris Szulzinger.

Mama Flora's Family 🦴🦴½ 1998 Based on the novel by Alex Haley, which was finished by co-author Stevens after Haley's 1992 death. Loosely based on Haley's mother, Mama Flora (Tyson) endures one tragedy after another while raising her family. First, as a teenaged servant, Flora gets pregnant and is forced to give the child up. Then when she does marry, her husband is killed and their property burned. Meanwhile, her other children and grandchildren struggle with discrimination and grow up angry and resentful. Holds together because of the force of Tyson's portrayal. **175m/C VHS, DVD.** Cicely Tyson, Mario Van Peebles, Blair Underwood, Queen Latifah, Hill Harper, Shemar Moore, Della Reese; ***D:*** Peter Werner; ***W:*** David Stevens, Carol Schreder; ***C:*** Neil Roach. **TV**

Mama, There's a Man in Your Bed 🦴🦴🦴 *Romauld et Juliet* 1989 (PG) When a powerful executive is framed for insider trading, the only witness to the crime and his only hope is an earthy cleaning woman named Juliette. Together they plot revenge and takeovers in her tiny apartment, filled with children. Soon, he regains his former position of power but realizes his life isn't complete without his co-conspirator. In French with English subtitles. **111m/C VHS.** *FR* Daniel Auteuil, Firmine Richard, Pierre Vernier, Maxime LeRoux, Gilles Privat, Muriel Combeau, Catherine Salviat, Sambou Tati; ***D:*** Coline Serreau; ***W:*** Coline Serreau.

Mama Turns a Hundred 🦴🦴🦴 1979 (R) A baronial family (a bizarre set of characters) is celebrating their mother's 100th birthday at her estate. One of the daughter's seduces her brother-in-law, another has a uniform fetish, a religious zealot is desperate to hang-glide, and several of them are trying to kill poor Mama. But of course she prevails, although sick and ailing. Slow-paced yet uproarious film full of inept characters who bumble along. In Spanish with English subtitles. **100m/C VHS.** *SP* Geraldine Chaplin, Fernando Gomez, Amparo Munoz; ***D:*** Carlos Saura.

Mama's Dirty Girls 1974 (R) A gangster mom's daughters take over where their mother left off and have the time of their lives. **82m/C VHS.** Gloria Grahame, Paul Lambert, Sondra Currie, Candice Rialson, Mary Stoddard; ***D:*** John Hayes; ***M:*** Don Bagley.

Mambo 🦴🦴½ 1955 A poor young dancer inspires patronage and lust by dancing the Mambo. Although attracted to Gassman, she marries Rennie for his money. Technically weak but artistically interesting, though Rennie and Mangano have done their roles somewhat better elsewhere. **94m/B VHS.** Silvana Mangano, Michael Rennie, Vittorio Gassman, Shelley Winters, Katherine Dunham, Mary Clare, Eduardo Ciannelli; ***D:*** Robert Rossen; ***M:*** Nino Rota.

Mambo Cafe 🦴🦴 2000 (PG-13) Low-budget mob comedy with a quirky premise. The Mambo Cafe is a Spanish Harlem restaurant in dire need of some business. So the owners invite a local mobster to dine at their establishment in hopes he'll be murdered and they'll get a boost from the publicity. He is, business improves, but the restaurant and the family also draw unwelcome Mob scrutiny. **98m/C VHS, DVD.** Paul Rodriguez, Rosana Desoto, Danny Aiello, Thalia; ***D:*** Reuben Gonzalez; ***W:*** Reuben Gonzalez. **VIDEO**

The Mambo Kings 🦴🦴🦴 1992 (R) Armand and Banderas (in his first English speaking role) are Cesar and Nestor Castillo, two brothers who flee Cuba for New York City with dreams of hitting it big with their mambo music. Desi Arnaz Jr. gets to play his own dad in a funny and technical scene that leads to a climactic confrontation between the brothers. Good cast and great music make this one worthwhile. Based on the Pulitzer prizewinning novel "The Mambo Kings Play Songs of Love" by Oscar Hijuelos. **100m/C VHS, 8mm.** Armand Assante, Antonio Banderas, Cathy Moriarty, Maruschka Detmers, Desi Arnaz Jr., Celia Cruz, Roscoe Lee Browne, Vondie Curtis-Hall, Tito Puente, Talisa Soto; ***D:*** Arne Glimcher; ***W:*** Cynthia Cidre; ***C:*** Michael Ballhaus; ***M:*** Robert Kraft, Carlos Franzetti.

Mame 🦴🦴 1974 (PG) In an adaptation of the Broadway musical "Auntie Mame" by Jerry Herman, Ball plays a dynamic woman who takes it upon herself to teach a group of eccentrics how to live life to the fullest. Arthur plays Mame's friend just as splendidly as she did in the Broadway version, but Ball in her last feature film is a lame Mame. Overly ambitious production avoids reaching goal. ♫Mame; We Need a Little Christmas; If He Walked Into My Life; Bosom Buddies; It's Today; Loving You; My Best Girl; What Do I Do Now? (Gooch's Sont); Open a New Window. **132m/C VHS, Wide.** Lucille Ball, Beatrice Arthur, Robert Preston, Joyce Van Patten, Bruce Davison; ***D:*** Gene Saks.

Mamele 🦴½ *Little Mother* 1938 Picon prematurely becomes the "mother" of her seven siblings when their mother dies. Quintessential Yiddish musical with the usual shimmering performance from Picon. In Yiddish with English subtitles. **95m/B VHS.** *PL* Molly Picon, Max Bozyk, Edmund Zayenda; ***D:*** Joseph Green.

Mamma Roma 🦴🦴🦴½ 1962 Pasolini's second film is a heartbreaking story of family ties, escaping the past, and dreams of the future. The title character (Magnani) is a former prostitute who attempts respectability for herself and her teenaged son (Garofolo). But her ex-pimp (Citti) threatens her new life and Rome's big-city temptations prove to be a pathway to crime and tragedy for the boy. Magnani gives one of her finest performances. Italian with subtitles. **110m/B VHS.** *IT* Anna Magnani, Ettore Garofolo, Franco Citti, Silvana Corsini, Luisa Loiano; ***D:*** Pier Paolo Pasolini; ***W:*** Pier Paolo Pasolini; ***C:*** Tonino Delli Colli.

Mam'zelle Pigalle 🦴½ *Naughty Girl* 1958 Bardot portrays a songstress involved with criminals. French with subtitles. **77m/C VHS, DVD.** *FR* Brigitte Bardot, Jean Bretonniere, Francoise Fabian, Bernard Lancret; ***D:*** Michel Boisrond.

A Man, a Woman, and a Bank 🦴🦴½ *A Very Big Weekend* 1979 (PG) Two con-men plan to rob a bank by posing as workers during the bank's construction. An advertising agency woman snaps their picture for a billboard to show how nice the builders have been, then becomes romantically involved with one of the would-be thieves. Nice performances, but wacky touches aren't plentiful enough or well timed to sustain comedy. **100m/C VHS.** *CA* Donald Sutherland, Brooke Adams, Paul Mazursky; ***D:*** Noel Black; ***W:*** Bruce A. Evans, Raynold Gideon; ***C:*** Jack Cardiff; ***M:*** Bill Conti.

A Man, a Woman and a Killer 🦴🦴½ 19?? Unusual film within a film shows the actual making of a movie while unfolding a story of a hired killer. A joint project from the directors of the well-received "Emerald Cities" and "Chan is Missing." **75m/C VHS.** ***D:*** Rick Schmidt, Wayne Wang.

A Man About the House 🦴🦴½ 1947 Two unmarried English sisters move into the Italian villa they have inherited. There, one marries the caretaker, who secretly plans to regain the property that once belonged to his family. When the newly married sister is found dead, her sibling sets out to solve the murder. **83m/B VHS.** *GB* Kieron Moore, Margaret Johnston, Dulcie Gray, Guy Middleton, Felix Aylmer; ***D:*** Leslie Arliss.

A Man Alone 🦴🦴 1955 Man falsely accused of robbing a stagecoach hides not alone but with comely sheriff's daughter. Milland's debut behind the camera. **96m/C VHS.** Ray Milland, Ward Bond, Mary Murphy, Raymond Burr, Lee Van Cleef; ***D:*** Ray Milland; ***C:*** Lionel Lindon.

A Man and a Woman 🦴🦴🦴 *Un Homme et Un Femme* 1966 When a man and a woman, both widowed, meet and become interested in one another but experience difficulties in putting their past loves behind them. Intelligently handled emotional conflicts within a well-acted romantic drama, acclaimed for excellent visual detail. Remade in 1977 as "Another Man, Another Chance." Followed in 1986 with "A Man and A Woman: 20 Years Later." Dubbed. **102m/C VHS.** *FR* Anouk Aimee, Jean-Louis Trintignant, Pierre Barouh, Valerie Lagrange; ***D:*** Claude Lelouch; ***W:*** Claude Lelouch, Pierre Uytterhoeven; ***C:*** Claude Lelouch; ***M:*** Francis Lai. Oscars '66: Foreign Film, Story & Screenplay; British Acad. '67: Actress (Aimee); Cannes '66: Film; Golden Globes '67: Actress—Drama (Aimee), Foreign Film.

A Man and a Woman: 20 Years Later 🦴½ *Un Homme Et Une Femme: Vingt Ans Deja* 1986 (PG) Slouchy sequel to the highly praised "A Man and a Woman" that catches up with a couple after a long separation. The sad romantic complications of the original are more mundane in this sequel, which is burdened by a film-within-a-film script as well as shots from the original. In French with English subtitles. **112m/C VHS.** *FR* Jean-Louis Trintignant, Anouk Aimee, Richard Berry; ***D:*** Claude Lelouch; ***W:*** Claude Lelouch.

Man & Boy 🦴🦴 *Ride a Dark Horse* 1971 (G) A black Civil War veteran, played by Bill Cosby, encounters bigotry and prejudice when he tries to set up a homestead in Arizona. An acceptable family film, some might be disappointed that Cosby is not playing this one for laughs. **98m/C VHS.** Bill Cosby, Gloria Foster, George Spell, Henry Silva, Yaphet Kotto; ***D:*** E.W. Swackhamer; ***M:*** Quincy Jones.

The Man and the Monster 🦴½ 1965 When a concert pianist sells his soul to the devil, he fails to realize that part of the deal has him turning into a hideous beast every time he hears a certain piece of music. Maybe it was "Stairway to Heaven." **78m/B VHS.** *MX* Enrique Rambal, Abel Salazar, Martha Roth; ***D:*** Rafael Baledon Sr.

Man Bait 🦴🦴½ *The Last Page* 1952 A complex web of intrigue and mystery surrounds a blackmailed book dealer when he allows a blonde woman to catch his eye. A competently made film. **78m/B VHS.** *GB* George Brent, Marguerite Chapman, Diana Dors; ***D:*** Terence Fisher.

Man Beast 🦴 **1955** The abominable snowman is sought and found in this grade-Z '50s monster movie. **65m/B VHS.** Rock Madison, Virginia Maynor, George Skaff, Lloyd Nelson, Tom Maruzzi; ***D:*** Jerry Warren.

Man Bites Dog 🦴🦴 *C'est Arrive pres de Chez Vous* **1991 (NC-17)** A pseudo-documentary about a serial killer, filled with ever-mounting violence. Ben is the killer being followed by a two-man camera/sound crew (which he's hired), who record his casual carnage without lifting a finger to stop him. Indeed his continued killing and robbing is to pay for financing the documentary about himself. This satire on film violence, as well as reality-based TV shows, is both appalling and humorous in a sick way. French with English subtitles. Also available in an unrated edited version. **95m/B VHS.** *BE* Benoit Poelvoorde, Remy Belvaux, Andre Bonzel, Vincent Tavier, Jean-Marc Chenut; ***D:*** Benoit Poelvoorde, Remy Belvaux, Andre Bonzel; ***W:*** Benoit Poelvoorde, Remy Belvaux, Andre Bonzel, Vincent Tavier; ***C:*** Andre Bonzel; ***M:*** Laurence Dufrene, Jean-Marc Chenut.

A Man Called Adam 🦴½ **1966** A jazz musician is tortured by prejudice and the guilt created by his having accidentally killed his wife and baby years before. Davis is appropriately haunted, but the film is poorly produced. **103m/B VHS.** Sammy Davis Jr., Louis Armstrong, Ossie Davis, Cicely Tyson, Frank Sinatra Jr., Lola Falana, Mel Torme, Peter Lawford; ***D:*** Leonard Penn; ***C:*** Jack Priestley.

A Man Called Horse 🦴🦴🦴 **1970 (PG)** After a wealthy Britisher is captured and tortured by the Sioux Indians in the Dakotas, he abandons his formal ways and discovers his own strength. As he passes their torture tests, he is embraced by the tribe. In this very realistic and gripping portrayal of American Indian life, Harris provides a strong performance. Sequelled by "Return of a Man Called Horse" (1976) and "Triumphs of a Man Called Horse" (1983). **114m/C VHS, Wide.** Richard Harris, Judith Anderson, Jean Gascon, Stanford Howard, Manu Tupou, Dub Taylor; ***D:*** Elliot Silverstein; ***W:*** Jack DeWitt; ***C:*** Robert B. Hauser.

A Man Called Peter 🦴🦴🦴 **1955** A biographical epic about Peter Marshall, a Scottish chaplain who served the U.S. Senate. Todd does his subject justice by sensitively showing all that was human in Marshall, and a talented supporting cast makes for a thoroughly watchable film. **119m/C VHS.** Richard Todd, Jean Peters, Marjorie Rambeau, Jill Esmond, Les Tremayne, Robert Burton; ***D:*** Henry Koster.

A Man Called Rage woof! **1984** Rage is the only man capable of safely escorting a group of pioneers through a nuclear wasteland infested with mutants and cannibals. **90m/C VHS.** *IT* Stelio Candelli, Conrad Nichols; ***D:*** Anthony Richmond.

A Man Called Sarge 🦴½ **1990 (PG-13)** Sophomoric comedy about a daffy WWII sergeant leading his squad against the Germans at Tobruk. **88m/C VHS.** Bobby DiCicco, Gary Kroeger, Marc Singer, Gretchen German, Jennifer Runyon; ***D:*** Stuart Gillard.

A Man Called Sledge 🦴🦴 **1971** Garner fans might be surprised to see the star play a villain in this violent story of a gang of outlaws who wind up fighting each over a cache of gold. This is mainstream Western entertainment. **93m/C VHS.** James Garner, Dennis Weaver, Claude Akins, John Marley, Laura Antonelli; ***D:*** Vic Morrow.

A Man Escaped 🦴🦴🦴½ *Un Condamne a Mort s'est Echappe, Ou le Vent Souffle ou il Vent; A Man Escaped, or the Wind Bloweth Where It Listeth; A Condemned Man Has Escaped* **1957** There's an excruciating realism about Bresson's account of a WWII Resistance fighter's escape from a Nazi prison just before he was to be executed by the Gestapo. It's the sounds and lingering camera shots, not the wham bam variety of action, that create and sustain the film's suspense. Bresson, who had been a Nazi prisoner, solicited the supervision of Andre Devigny, whose true story the film tells. Contributing to the realistic feel was the use of non professional actors. An award-wiining film that fellow director Truffaut lauded as the most crucial French film of the previous ten years. In French with English subtitles. **102m/B VHS.** Francois Leterrier, Charles Le Clainche, Roland Monod, Maurice Beerblock, Jacques Ertaud, Jean-Paul Delhumeau, Roger Treherne, Jean-Philippe Delamarre, Cesar Gattegno, Jacques Oerlemans, Klaus Detlef Grevenhorst, Leonard Schmidt; ***D:*** Robert Bresson; ***W:*** Robert Bresson; ***C:*** Leonce-Henri Burel. Cannes '57: Director (Bresson).

Man Facing Southeast 🦴🦴🦴½ *Hombre Mirando Al Sudeste; Man Looking Southeast* **1986 (R)** The acclaimed Argentinean film about the sudden appearance of a strange man in an asylum who claims to be an extraterrestrial, and a psychologist's attempts to discover his true identity. The sense of mystery intensifies when the new patient indeed seems to have some remarkable powers. Although the pace at times lags, the story intriguingly keeps one guessing about the stranger right to the end. In Spanish, with English subtitles. **105m/C VHS.** *AR* Lorenzo Quinteros, Hugo Soto, Ines Vernengo; ***D:*** Eliseo Subiela; ***C:*** Ricardo De Angelis; ***M:*** Pedro Aznar.

A Man for All Seasons 🦴🦴🦴🦴 **1966 (G)** Sterling, heavily Oscar-honored biographical drama concerning the life and subsequent martyrdom of 16th-century Chancellor of England, Sir Thomas More (Scofield). Story revolves around his personal conflict when King Henry VIII (Shaw) seeks a divorce from his wife, Catherine of Aragon, so he can wed his mistress, Anne Boleyn—events that ultimately lead the King to bolt from the Pope and declare himself head of the Church of England. Remade for TV in 1988 with Charlton Heston in the lead role. **120m/C VHS, DVD.** *GB* Paul Scofield, Robert Shaw, Orson Welles, Wendy Hiller, Susannah York, John Hurt, Nigel Davenport, Vanessa Redgrave; ***D:*** Fred Zinnemann; ***W:*** Constance Willis, Robert Bolt; ***C:*** Ted Moore; ***M:*** Georges Delerue. Oscars '66: Actor (Scofield), Adapt. Screenplay, Color Cinematog., Costume Des. (C), Director (Zinnemann), Picture; British Acad. '67: Actor (Scofield), Film, Screenplay; Directors Guild '66: Director (Zinnemann); Golden Globes '67: Actor—Drama (Scofield), Director (Zinnemann), Film—Drama, Screenplay; Natl. Bd. of Review '66: Actor (Scofield), Director (Zinnemann), Support. Actor (Shaw); N.Y. Film Critics '66: Actor (Scofield), Director (Zinnemann), Film, Screenplay.

A Man for All Seasons 🦴🦴🦴 **1988** Fresh from the London stage, Heston directs and stars in this version of Robert Bolt's play depicting the conflict between Henry VIII and his chief advisor, Sir Thomas More. Strong supporting cast. **150m/C VHS.** Charlton Heston, Vanessa Redgrave, John Gielgud, Richard Johnson, Roy Kinnear, Martin Chamberlain; ***D:*** Charlton Heston. **CABLE**

Man Friday 🦴🦴 **1975 (PG)** Stranded on a deserted island, a man forces a native from a neighboring island to be his slave. Based on the classic story "Robinson Crusoe" by Daniel Defoe, this adaptation charts the often-brutal treatment the native receives as his captor tries to civilize him. Through his intelligence, the enslaved man regains his freedom and returns home with his former captor, who then seeks acceptance from the native's tribe. A sometimes confusing storyline and excessive blood and guts detract from this message-laden effort. **115m/C VHS.** *GB* Peter O'Toole, Richard Roundtree, Peter Cellier, Christopher Cabot, Joel Fluellen; ***D:*** Jack Gold; ***M:*** Carl Davis.

The Man from Atlantis 🦴🦴 **1977** Patrick Duffy stars as the water-breathing alien who emerges from his undersea home, the Lost City of Atlantis. Led to a brief TV series. **60m/C VHS.** Patrick Duffy, Belinda J. Montgomery, Victor Buono; ***D:*** Lee H. Katzin. **TV**

The Man from Beyond 🦴🦴½ **1922** Frozen alive, a man returns 100 years later to try and find his lost love. Silent. **50m/B VHS.** Harry Houdini, Arthur Maude, Nita Naldi; ***D:*** Burton King.

Man from Button Willow 🦴🦴 **1965 (G)** Classic animated adventure is the story of Justin Eagle, a man who leads a double life. He is a respected rancher and a shrewd secret agent for the government, but in 1869 he suddenly finds himself the guardian of a four-year-old Oriental girl, leading him into a whole new series of adventures. Strictly for younger audiences. **79m/C VHS.** ***M:*** George Bruns; ***V:*** Dale Robertson, Edgar Buchanan, Barbara Jean Wong, Howard Keel.

Man from Cairo 🦴🦴 **1954** An American in Algiers is mistaken for a detective in search of gold lost during WWII and decides to play along. **82m/B VHS.** *IT* George Raft, Gianna Maria Canale; ***D:*** Ray Enright.

Man from Cheyenne 🦴 **1942** Cowboy comes home to find his town under a siege of terror from a lawless gang of cattle rustlers. He gets mad and seeks some frontier justice. **54m/B VHS.** Roy Rogers, Gale Storm, George "Gabby" Hayes, Sally Payne.

Man from Colorado 🦴🦴½ **1949** An odd Technicolor western about two Civil War vets at odds, one an honest marshall, the other a sadistic judge. Solid Western fare with a quirky performance by Ford. **99m/C VHS.** William Holden, Glenn Ford, Ellen Drew, Ray Collins, Edgar Buchanan, Jerome Courtland, James Millican, Jim Bannon; ***D:*** Henry Levin; ***M:*** George Duning.

Man from Deep River woof! **1977 (R)** A photographer is captured by a savage tribe in Thailand and forced to undergo a series of grueling initiation rites. Full of very violent and sickening tortures inflicted on both human and animal victims. **90m/C VHS.** *IT* Ivan Rassimov; ***D:*** Umberto Lenzi.

The Man from Gun Town 🦴½ **1936** McCoy comes to the rescue of a woman who has been framed by an evil gang for the murder of her brother. **58m/B VHS.** Tim McCoy, Billie Seward, Rex Lease, Jack Clifford, Wheeler Oakman, Bob McKenzie; ***D:*** Ford Beebe.

Man from Headquarters 🦴🦴 **1928** Good silent mystery in which a U.S. agent takes on a gang of foreign operatives. **?m/B VHS.** Cornelius Keefe, Edith Roberts.

The Man from Hell 🦴 **1934** Sheriff Russell goes undercover to expose the head of a gang of outlaws. Low-budget fare. **55m/B VHS.** Reb Russell, Fred Kohler Jr., Ann Darcy, George "Gabby" Hayes, Jack Rockwell, Charles French, Charles "Slim" Whitaker, Yakima Canutt; ***D:*** Lewis D. Collins.

Man from Hell's Edges 🦴½ **1932** An innocent cowpoke escapes from jail and brings the real baddy to justice. **63m/B VHS.** Bob Steele, Nancy Drexel, Julian Rivero, Robert E. Homans, George "Gabby" Hayes; ***D:*** Robert North Bradbury.

The Man from Laramie 🦴🦴🦴½ **1955** Aging ranch baron Alec Waggoman (Crisp), who is going blind, worries about which of his two sons he will leave the ranch to. Into this tension-filled familial atmosphere rides Lockhart (Stewart), a cow-herder obsessed with hunting down the men who sold guns to the Indians that killed his brother. Needless to say, the tension increases. Tough, surprisingly brutal western, the best of the classic Stewart-Mann films. **104m/B VHS, DVD, Wide.** James Stewart, Arthur Kennedy, Donald Crisp, Alex Nicol, Cathy O'Donnell, Aline MacMahon, Wallace Ford, Jack Elam; ***D:*** Anthony Mann; ***W:*** Philip Yordan; ***C:*** Charles B(ryant) Lang Jr.; ***M:*** George Duning.

The Man from Left Field 🦴½ **1993** Homeless man winds up coaching a little league baseball team, inspiring the kids, and turning his life around. Made for TV. **96m/C VHS.** Burt Reynolds, Reba McEntire; ***D:*** Burt Reynolds; ***M:*** Bobby Goldsboro. **TV**

Man from Mallorca 🦴🦴 *Mannen fran Mallorca* **1984** Sgts. Jarnebring (Wollter) and Johansson (von Bromssen) are in pursuit of a gunman who robbed a Stockholm post office. The robber gets away and the investigation stalls until two witnesses are murdered. The detectives begin to suspect an official cover-up and think that senior police officer Hedberg (Hellberg) has something to hide. When they're taken off the case, the duo forge ahead on their own time with some disturbing results. Swedish with subtitles. **104m/C VHS.** *SW* Sven Wollter, Tomas von Bromssen, Thomas Hellberg; ***D:*** Bo Widerberg; ***W:*** Bo Widerberg; ***C:*** Thomas Wahlberg.

Man from Montana 🦴½ *Montana Justice* **1941** Brown is a sheriff who battles outlaws trying to stir up trouble between ranchers and homesteaders. **56m/B VHS.** Johnny Mack Brown, Fuzzy Knight, William (Bill) Gould, Kermit Maynard, Nell O'Day, Billy Lenhart, Kenneth Brown, Murdock McQuarrie, Ray Taylor.

Man from Monterey 🦴🦴 **1933** South-of-the-border Western has U.S. Army captain Wayne trying to get Mexican landowners to register their property under Spanish land grants or lose them to public domain. Wayne's last series western for Warner Bros. **59m/B VHS.** John Wayne, Ruth Hall, Luis Alberni, Francis Ford, Lafe (Lafayette) McKee, Lillian (Lillianne, Lyllian) Leighton, Charles "Slim" Whitaker; ***D:*** Mack V. Wright; ***W:*** Lesley Mason.

The Man from Music Mountain 🦴🦴 **1938** Worthless mining stock is sold in a desert mining town, but Gene and Smiley clear that up, with a little singing as well. **54m/B VHS.** Gene Autry, Smiley Burnette, Carol Hughes, Polly Jenkins.

Man from Nowhere 🦴🦴½ **1937** A henpecked man gets the break of his life when his domineering wife and mother-in-law believe he's dead. Based on the novel by Luigi Pirandello. In French with English subtitles. **98m/B VHS.** *FR* Pierre Blanchar, Ginette LeClerc; ***D:*** Pierre Chenal.

The Man from Painted Post 🦴 **1917** Fairbanks plays a Cattlemen's Association detective who comes to the range to stop the cattle rustlers as well as to find the man who murdered his sister. **?m/B VHS.** Douglas Fairbanks Sr., Eileen (Elaine Persey) Percy, Frank Campeau, Monte Blue; ***D:*** Joseph Henabery.

The Man from Planet X 🦴🦴 **1951** Making a belated arrival on home video is this prototypical low-budget first-contact tale. All the elements are there—reporter, aging scientist, his nubile daughter, crafty associate—but the setting is Scotland. Not that it matters, because virtually all of the action takes place on sets. **71m/B DVD.** Robert Clarke, Margaret Field, William Schallert; ***D:*** Edgar G. Ulmer; ***W:*** Aubrey Wisberg, Jack Pollexfen; ***C:*** John L. "Jack" Russell; ***M:*** Charles Koff.

The Man from Snowy River 🦴🦴½ **1982 (PG)** Stunning cinematography highlights this otherwise fairly ordinary adventure story set in 1880s Australia. Jim Craig (Burlinson) is an orphaned young man coming of age in the mountains while seeking a life of his own and falling in love with the well-brought up Jessica (Thornton). In a dual role, Douglas portrays battling brothers, one a rich landowner and the other a one-legged prospector. A wild horse roundup is a stunning highlight. Based on the epic poem by A.B. "Banjo" Paterson and followed by "Return to Snowy River." A big hit in Australia and not directed by "Mad Max's" Miller, but another Miller named George. **104m/C VHS, Wide.** *AU* Kirk Douglas, Tom Burlinson, Sigrid Thornton, Terence Donovan, Tommy Dysart, Jack Thompson, Bruce Kerr; ***D:*** George Miller; ***W:*** Fred Cullen, John Dixon; ***C:*** Keith Wagstaff; ***M:*** Bruce Rowland.

Man from Texas 🦴🦴 **1939** Singing and gun-slinging Tex defends a kid accused of horse thieving until the kid turns bad and Tex must bring him in. **55m/B VHS.** Tex Ritter, Hal Price, Charles B. Wood, Vic Demourelle Sr.; ***D:*** Al(bert) Herman.

Man from the Alamo 🦴🦴🦴 **1953** A soldier sent from the Alamo during its last hours to get help is branded as a deserter, and struggles to clear his name. Well acted, this film will satisfy those with a taste for action. **79m/C VHS.** Glenn Ford, Julie Adams, Chill Wills, Victor Jory, Hugh O'Brian; ***D:*** Budd Boetticher.

The Man from the Pru 🦴🦴½ **1989** Shocking 1931 murder case follows insurance agent William Wallace (Pryce) who was sentenced to hang for the murder of his wife, Julia. Wallace insisted he was called from home on a possible insurance sale and returned home to find his wife dead. His case made British legal history when the appeals court overturned the verdict. Made for TV. **90m/C VHS.** *GB* Jonathan Pryce, Anna Massey, Susannah York; ***D:*** Rob Rohrer. **TV**

Man from Thunder River **1943** A group of cowboys uncover a plot to steal gold ore and wind up saving a young girl's life in the process. Standard western with lots of action. **55m/B VHS.** Wild Bill Elliott, George "Gabby" Hayes, Anne Jeffreys, Ian Keith, John James; ***D:*** John English.

Man from Utah ½ **1934** The Duke tangles with the crooked sponsor of some rodeo events who has killed several of the participants. **55m/B VHS, DVD.** John Wayne, George "Gabby" Hayes, Polly Ann Young, Yakima Canutt, Lafe (Lafayette) McKee; ***D:*** Robert North Bradbury; ***W:*** Lindsley Parsons; ***C:*** Archie Stout.

The Man I Love **1946** Slick drama about nightclub singer Lupino falling for no-good mobster Alda. Enjoyable and well-acted, although script doesn't make sense. Great selection of tunes. This film inspired Scorsese's "New York, New York." Based on the novel "Night Shift" by Maritta Wolff. ♫Body and Soul; Why Was I Born; Bill; The Man I Love; Liza; If I Could Be With You. **96m/B VHS.** Ida Lupino, Robert Alda, Andrea King, Martha Vickers, Bruce (Herman Brix) Bennett, Alan Hale, Dolores Moran, John Ridgely, Don McGuire, Warren Douglas, Craig Stevens; ***D:*** Raoul Walsh, John Maxwell; ***W:*** Catherine Turney, Jo Pagano; ***M:*** Max Steiner.

The Man in Grey **1945** In a story of romantic intrigue set in 19th-century England, a Marquis's wife is betrayed by her vile husband and the schoolmate she once befriended who has an affair with him. Stunning costumes and fine performances compensate for the overly extravagant production values in a work that helped bring stardom to Mason. **116m/B VHS.** *GB* James Mason, Margaret Lockwood, Stewart Granger, Phyllis Calvert; ***D:*** Leslie Arliss.

A Man in Love *Un Homme Amoureux* **1987 (R)** An international romantic melodrama set during the Italian filming of a biography of suicidal author Cesar Pavese. The self-important lead actor and a beautiful supporting actress (Coyote and Scacchi) become immersed in the roles and fall madly in love, oblivious to the fact that Coyote is married and Scacchi's engaged. The two make a steamy pair, to the detriment of friends, family, and the movie they're making. Kurys' first English-language film is visually appealing with a lush, romantic score, seamlessly weaving the storylines among vivid characters. **110m/C VHS.** *FR* Peter Coyote, Greta Scacchi, Jamie Lee Curtis, Peter Riegert, Jean Pigozzi, John Berry, Claudia Cardinale, Vincent Lindon; ***D:*** Diane Kurys; ***W:*** Diane Kurys, Olivier Schatzky, Israel Horovitz; ***M:*** Georges Delerue.

The Man in the Attic ½ **1994 (R)** Harris certainly leaves his "Doogie Howser" past behind as he takes a grown-up turn in an erotic thriller based on a true case history from the early 20th century, gathered from the book "Sex and the Criminal Mind." Teenaged Edward (Harris) has a blazing affair with married, mature Krista (Archer), who does indeed hide her young lover in the family attic when her clueless husband (Cariou) returns home at night. But such consuming passion can hardly be kept a secret for long—and takes a decidedly deadly turn. **97m/C VHS.** Anne Archer, Neil Patrick Harris, Len Cariou, Alex Carter; ***D:*** Graeme Campbell; ***W:*** Duane Poole, Tom Swale; ***C:*** Dick Bush; ***M:*** Lou Natale. **CABLE**

The Man in the Glass Booth **1975 (PG)** In this adaptation of a play written by actor Robert Shaw, a successful Jewish businessman is suspected of being a Nazi war criminal. Loosely based on the life of death camp commandant Otto Adolf Eichmann, the film depicts the arrest and subsequent trial of the former Nazi by the Israelis. The film's title is derived from the fact that Eichmann sat in a glass booth during his trial. Schell's performance is outstanding. **117m/C VHS.** Maximilian Schell, Lois Nettleton, Luther Adler, Lawrence Pressman, Henry Brown, Richard Rasof; ***D:*** Arthur Hiller; ***W:*** Edward Anhalt; ***C:*** Sam Leavitt.

The Man in the Gray Flannel Suit ½ **1956** A very long and serious adaptation of the Sloan Wilson novel about a Madison Avenue advertising exec trying to balance his life between work and family. The Hollywood treatment falls short of the adaptation potential of the original story. **152m/C VHS.** Gregory Peck, Fredric March, Jennifer Jones, Ann Harding, Arthur O'Connell, Henry Daniell, Lee J. Cobb, Marisa Pavan, Gene Lockhart, Keenan Wynn, Gigi Perreau, Joseph Sweeney, Kenneth Tobey, DeForest Kelley; ***D:*** Nunnally Johnson.

The Man in the Iron Mask **1939** Swashbuckling tale about twin brothers (played by Hayward) separated at birth. One turns out to be King Louis XIV of France, and the other is imprisoned and forced to wear an iron mask that hides his identity. Philippe is eventually rescued by musketeer D'Artagnan (William) and the musketeers join forces for action-packed adventure and royal revenge. Remake of the "The Iron Mask" (1929) with Douglas Fairbanks and subsequently remade several times for both TV and the big screen. **110m/B VHS.** Louis Hayward, Alan Hale, Joan Bennett, Warren William, Joseph Schildkraut, Walter Kingsford, Marion Martin; ***D:*** James Whale; ***W:*** George Bruce; ***C:*** Robert Planck; ***M:*** Lucien Moraweck.

The Man in the Iron Mask **1977** A tyrannical French king kidnaps his twin brother and imprisons him on a remote island. Chamberlain, the king of the miniseries, is excellent in a dual role in this big production swashbuckler. Adapted from the Dumas classic. **105m/C VHS.** Richard Chamberlain, Patrick McGoohan, Louis Jourdan, Jenny Agutter, Ian Holm, Ralph Richardson; ***D:*** Mike Newell. **TV**

The Man in the Iron Mask ½ **1997** Low-budget, personalized version of the Dumas swashbuckler from director Richert, which he filmed at the historic Mission Inn in Riverside, CA. Prologue establishes the birth of twin royals to the French Queen (Foster) and the fate of Philippe (Richert's son Nick) as the man in the iron mask. A deathbed confession to Count Aramis (the director himself) alerts the Musketeers, who decide to set things right. Well-intentioned but not a lot of fun. **85m/C VHS.** William Richert, Edward Albert, Rex Ryon, Timothy Bottoms, Dennis Hayden, Nick Richert, Meg Foster, James Gammon, Dana Barron, Brigid Brannah, Fannie Brett; ***D:*** William Richert; ***W:*** William Richert; ***C:*** William Barber; ***M:*** Jim Ervin.

The Man in the Iron Mask **1998 (PG-13)** Lavish retelling of Alexandre Dumas's classic story boasts a stellar cast with teen heartthrob DiCaprio in a dual role. Snotty tyrant King Louis XIV's (DiCaprio) lust for women inadvertently leads to the reunion of the retired Musketeers, bent on replacing cold Louis with his more sensitive twin brother Phillippe (DiCaprio, again), an inmate of the Bastille and hidden behind a ghastly mask. Irons, Malkovich, Depardieu, and Byrne bring a welcome seriousness and style to the often-told story as the older, jaded Musketeers, while DiCaprio holds his own in the presence of such formidable company. Although first-time director Wallace doesn't balance the star power with enough swordplay, the high gloss production provides old-fashioned escapist entertainment. **132m/C VHS, DVD.** Leonardo DiCaprio, Gabriel Byrne, Jeremy Irons, John Malkovich, Gerard Depardieu, Anne Parillaud, Judith Godreche, Edward Atterton, Peter Sarsgaard, Hugh Laurie; ***D:*** Randall Wallace; ***W:*** Randall Wallace; ***C:*** Peter Suschitzsky; ***M:*** Nick Glennie-Smith.

The Man in the Moon ½ **1991 (PG-13)** Beautifully rendered coming-of-age tale. On a farm outside a small Louisiana town in the 1950s, 14-year-old Dani wonders if she will ever be as pretty and popular as her 17-year-old sister Maureen. This becomes especially important as Dani is beginning to notice boys, particularly Court, the 17-year-old young man she meets when swimming. Although Dani and Maureen have always been especially close, a rift develops between the sisters after Court meets Maureen. Intelligently written, excellent direction, lovely cinematography, and exceptional acting make this a particularly worthwhile and entertaining film. **100m/C VHS, DVD.** Reese Witherspoon, Emily Warfield, Jason London, Tess Harper, Sam Waterston, Gail Strickland; ***D:*** Robert Mulligan.

The Man in the Raincoat **1957** French film about a bumbling clarinet player who is erroneously tracked down as a murderer. Strenuous efforts to evoke laughter usually fail. Dubbed. **97m/B VHS, 8mm.** *FR* Fernandel, John McGiver, Bernard Blier; ***D:*** Julien Duvivier.

Man in the Saddle ½ *The Outcast* **1951** Western star Scott gets roped in a romantic triangle out on the range, leading to some exciting gunplay. As usual, justice triumphs in this above average oater. Based on the novel by Ernest Haycox. **87m/C VHS.** Randolph Scott, Joan Leslie, Ellen Drew, Alexander Knox, Richard Rober, John Russell; ***D:*** Andre de Toth; ***W:*** Kenneth Gamet.

The Man in the Santa Claus Suit **1979** A costume shop owner has an effect on three people who rent Santa Claus costumes from him. Astaire plays seven different roles in this average holiday feel-good movie. **96m/C VHS.** Fred Astaire, Gary Burghoff, John Byner, Nanette Fabray, Bert Convy; ***D:*** Corey Allen. **TV**

Man in the Shadow ½ **1957** Sheriff Ben Sadler (Chandler) is the only man in the county willing to stand up to wealthy Texas rancher Virgil Renchler (Welles). Sadler suspects Renchler is behind the brutal death of a Mexican laborer but gets no support when he tries to find justice. **80m/C VHS.** Jeff Chandler, Orson Welles, Ben Alexander, Colleen Miller, John Larch, James Gleason, Barbara Lawrence, Royal Dano, Paul Fix, William Schallert; ***D:*** Jack Arnold; ***W:*** Gene L. Coon; ***C:*** Arthur E. Arling; ***M:*** Joseph Gershenson.

Man in the Silk Hat **1915** A collection of the nearly forgotten French comic's early silent comedy shorts, made in France before his resettlement in America. **96m/B VHS.** *FR* Max Linder; ***D:*** Maud Linder.

Man in the Silk Hat **1983** Gabriel-Maximilien Leuvielle, known in films as Max Linder, is now credited with developing the style of silent-movie slapstick comedy that Mack Sennett, Charlie Chaplin, and others became more famous for in their time. Here, Linder's daughter has done a fine job writing and directing a film full of historic footage of her father's work. **99m/B VHS.** Mack Sennett, Buster Keaton, Charlie Chaplin, Max Linder.

The Man in the White Suit ½ **1951** A humble laboratory assistant in a textile mill invents a white cloth that won't stain, tear, or wear out, and can't be dyed. The panicked garment industry sets out to destroy him and the fabric, resulting in some sublimely comic situations and a variety of inventive chases. **82m/B VHS.** *GB* Alec Guinness, Joan Greenwood; ***D:*** Alexander MacKendrick.

Man in the Wilderness ½ **1971 (PG)** Harris is part of an expedition traveling through the Northwest Territory. He's mauled by a grizzly and left for dead by leader Huston. While Harris fights for survival, he also plots revenge. Blood and violence is somewhat offset by good lead performances. **108m/C VHS.** Richard Harris, John Huston, Henry Wilcoxon, Percy Herbert, Dennis Waterman, Prunella Ransome, Norman Rossington, James Doohan; ***D:*** Richard Sarafian; ***W:*** Jack DeWitt; ***M:*** Johnny Harris.

A Man in Uniform *I Love a Man in Uniform* **1993 (R)** A look at the making of a sociopath. Henry (McCamus) is a quiet bank employee who moonlights as an actor. Then he gets his big break in the role of a self-righteous cop in a TV series. Only the lines between his make-believe cop and the real world begin to blur and Henry's intensity turns to violence. Fine performances lead to an unsatisfying film conclusion. **99m/C VHS, DVD.** *CA* Tom McCamus, Brigitte Bako, Kevin Tighe, David Hemblen, Alex Karzis, Graham McPherson, Richard Blackburn; ***D:*** David Wellington; ***W:*** David Wellington; ***C:*** David Franco; ***M:*** Ron Sures. Genie '93: Actor (McCamus), Support. Actor (Tighe).

The Man Inside ½ **1976** Undercover agent infiltrates a powerful underworld narcotics ring and finds his honesty tested when $2 million is at stake. **96m/C VHS.** *CA* James Franciscus, Stefanie Powers, Jacques Godin; ***D:*** Gerald Mayer.

The Man Inside **1990 (PG)** Lukewarm Cold War saga based on the true story of Gunther Wallraff, a West German journalist who risked all to expose the corruption behind a large European newspaper. **93m/C VHS.** *NL GE* Juergen Prochnow, Peter Coyote, Nathalie Baye, Dieter Laser, Monique Van De Ven, Sylvie Granotier; ***D:*** Bobby Roth; ***W:*** Bobby Roth.

Man Is Not a Bird ½ *Covek Nije Tica* **1965** Follows the destructive love of a factory engineer and a hairdresser in a small Yugoslavian mining town. In Serbian with English subtitles. **80m/B VHS.** *YU* Eva Ras, Milena Dravic, Janez Urhovec; ***D:*** Dusan Makavejev; ***W:*** Dusan Makavejev; ***C:*** Aleksandar Petkovic; ***M:*** Petar Bergamo.

A Man Like Eva *Ein Mann wie Eva* **1983** A weird, morbid homage to and portrait of Rainer Werner Fassbinder after his inevitable death, detailing his work-obsessed self-destruction. Mattes, one of Fassbinder's favorite actresses, plays him in drag, in an eerie gender-crossing transformation. In German with English subtitles. **92m/C VHS.** *GE* Eva Mattes, Elisabeth (Lisa) Kreuzer, Charles Regnier, Werner Stocker; ***D:*** Radu Gabrea.

Man Made Monster ½ *Atomic Monster; The Electric Man* **1941** Chaney stars as carnival performer "Dynamo" Dan McCormick, whose act has caused Dan to build up an immunity to electrical charges. Dan falls prey to the mad Dr. Rigas (Atwill) who seeks to create a race of electro-men who'll do his bidding. Experiments on the hapless Dan turn him into a glowing monster whose very touch can kill. Chaney's first role in the horror genre led to Universal's casting him in "The Wolf Man" and "The Ghost of Frankenstein." **61m/B VHS.** Lon Chaney Jr., Lionel Atwill, Anne Nagel, Frank Albertson, Samuel S. Hinds; ***D:*** George Waggner; ***W:*** Joseph West; ***C:*** Elwood "Woody" Bredell.

Man of a Thousand Faces ½ **1957** A tasteful and touching portrayal of Lon Chaney, from his childhood with his deaf and mute parents to his success as a screen star. Recreates some of Chaney's most famous roles, including the Phantom of the Opera and Quasimodo in "Notre Dame." Cagney is magnificent as the long-suffering film star who was a genius with makeup and mime. **122m/B VHS, DVD, Wide.** James Cagney, Dorothy Malone, Jane Greer, Marjorie Rambeau, Jim Backus, Roger Smith, Robert Evans; ***D:*** Joseph Pevney; ***W:*** Ivan Goff; ***C:*** Russell Metty; ***M:*** Frank Skinner.

Man of Action ½ **1933** Texas Ranger McCoy is out to solve the mystery of what happened to money, recovered from a robbery, which has vanished once again. **56m/B VHS.** Tim McCoy, Wheeler Oakman, Walter Brennan, Stanley Blystone, Charles French; ***D:*** George Melford.

Man of Aran **1934** Celebrated account of a fisherman's struggle for survival on a barren island near the west coast of Ireland, featuring amateur actors. Three years in the making, it's the last word in man against nature cinema, and a visual marvel. A former explorer, Flaherty became an influential documentarian. Having first gained fame with "Nanook of the North," he compiled an opus of documentaries made for commercial release. **132m/B VHS.** ***D:*** Robert Flaherty. **TV**

Man of Ashes *Rih Essed* **1986** Hachemi is terrified of women though he is a bridegroom-to-be. He and his friend Farfat have kept hidden the fact that they were molested by their male employer. They try to overcome their insecurities by visiting a prostitute but this experience is only successful for one of the men, leading the other to more torment. Arabic with subtitles. **109m/C VHS, DVD.** Imad Maalal, Khalid Ksouri; ***D:*** Nouri Bouzid; ***W:*** Nouri Bouzid; ***C:*** Youssef Ben Youssef; ***M:*** Salah Mahdi.

Man of Destiny 🦴🦴½ **1973** Bonaparte (Keach) and a mysterious woman battle good-humoredly over a collection of love letters. From a Bernard Shaw story. Charming and well-acted. **60m/C VHS.** Stacy Keach, Samantha Eggar.

Man of Evil 🦴🦴 *Fanny by Gaslight* **1948** The hard times of the illegitimate daughter of a member of the British Parliament in the early 1900s, told with an astonishing number of plot twists and a plodding melodramtic style. Based on the novel "Fanny by Gaslight." **108m/B VHS.** *GB* Phyllis Calvert, James Mason, Wilfred Lawson, Stewart Granger, Margaretta Scott, Jean Kent, John Laurie, Stuart Lindsell, Nora Swinburne, Amy Veness, Ann Wilton, Helen Haye, Cathleen Nesbitt, Guy Le Feuvre, John Turnbull, Peter Jones; ***D:*** Anthony Asquith.

Man of Flowers 🦴🦴½ **1984** Because of his puritan upbringing, a reclusive art collector has trouble coping with his feelings of sexuality. He pays a woman to disrobe in front of him, but is never able to bring himself to see her naked. A moody piece with overtones of black humor, this work has limited audience appeal. **91m/C VHS.** *AU* Norman Kaye, Alyson Best, Chris Haywood, Sarah Walker, Julia Blake, Bob Ellis, Werner Herzog; ***D:*** Paul Cox; ***W:*** Bob Ellis, Paul Cox; ***C:*** Yuri Sokol; ***M:*** Gaetano Donizetti. Australian Film Inst. '83: Actor (Kaye).

Man of Iron 🦴🦴🦴 *Czlowiek z Zelaza* **1981 (PG)** Director Wajda's follow-up to "Man of Marble" deals with a reporter (Odania) who is expected to tow the government line when writing about the Gdansk shipyard strike of 1980. He meets the harassed laborer son (Radziwilowicz) of worker-hero Birkut, against whom Odania is expected to conduct a smear campaign, and finds his loyalties tested. In Polish with English subtitles. **116m/C VHS.** *PL* Jerzy Radziwilowicz, Marian Opania, Krystyna Janda; ***D:*** Andrzej Wajda; ***W:*** Aleksander Scibor-Rylski; ***C:*** Edward Klosinski; ***M:*** Andrezej Korzynski. Cannes '81: Film.

Man of La Mancha 🦴½ **1972 (PG)** Arrested by the Inquisition and thrown into prison, Miguel de Cervantes relates the story of Don Quixote. Not nearly as good as the Broadway musical it is based on. ♫It's All the Same; The Impossible Dream; Barber's Song; Man of La Mancha; Dulcinea; I'm Only Thinking of Him; Little Bird, Little Bird; Life as It Really Is; The Dubbing. **129m/C VHS.** Peter O'Toole, Sophia Loren, James Coco, Harry Andrews, John Castle, Brian Blessed; ***D:*** Arthur Hiller. Natl. Bd. of Review '72: Actor (O'Toole).

Man of Legend 🦴🦴 **1971 (PG)** An adventure-romance filmed in Morocco; a WWI German soldier flees to the Foreign Legion and fights with nomadic rebels, ultimately falling in love with their chief's beautiful daughter. An unoriginal desert saga. **95m/C VHS.** *IT SP* Peter Strauss, Tina Aumont, Pier Paola Capponi; ***D:*** Sergio Grieco.

Man of Marble 🦴🦴🦴 **1976** A satire on life in post-WWII Poland. A young filmmaker sets out to tell the story of a bricklayer who, because of his exceptional skill, once gained popularity with other workers. He became a champion for worker rights, only to then find himself being persecuted by the government. The conclusion was censored by the Polish government. Highly acclaimed and followed by "Man of Iron" in 1981. In Polish with English subtitles. **160m/C VHS.** *PL* Krystyna Janda, Jerzy Radziwilowicz, Tadeusz Lomnicki, Jacek Lomnicki, Krystyna Zachwatowicz; ***D:*** Andrzej Wajda; ***W:*** Aleksander Scibor-Rylski; ***M:*** Andrezej Korzynski.

A Man of No Importance 🦴🦴🦴 **1994 (R)** Touching and entertaining saga of lovable Alfie Byrne (Finney), a 1960s Dublin bus conductor with a passion for the work of Oscar Wilde, who successfully represses his own homosexuality. He also moonlights as director of a community theatre, where he sets out to produce Wilde's controversial play "Salome" starring fetching new bus passenger Adele (Fitzgerald), who further confuses Alfie's take on his identity. Finney is both delightful and heartbreaking in this character study of an innocent soul whose life is tested by the social code of his day. Equally affecting and charming supporting performances round out this witty but sad tale. **98m/C VHS.** *GB* Albert Finney, Brenda Fricker, Michael Gambon, Tara Fitzgerald, Rufus Sewell, Patrick Malahide, David Kelly; ***D:*** Suri Krishnamma; ***W:*** Barry Devlin; ***M:*** Julian Nott.

A Man of Passion 🦴🦴 **1988 (R)** Quinn plays an aging artist living pleasurably on a Mediterranean isle. His summer guest is his uptight grandson, a classical pianist. Naturally, Gramps is about to teach the kid to loosen up, including appreciating one of his lovely artist's models. Another variation for Quinn on his "Zorba" personality but it works. **90m/C VHS.** Anthony Quinn, Ramon Sheen, Maud Adams, Elizabeth Ashley, R.J. Williams, Ray Walston, Victoria Vera; ***D:*** J. Anthony (Jose Antonio de la Loma) Loma; ***W:*** J. Anthony (Jose Antonio de la Loma) Loma.

Man of the Century 🦴½ **1999 (R)** Journalist Johnny Twennies (Fraser) is an anachronism living in 1990s Manhattan. He dresses, talks, and acts as if it were the 1920s. But Johnny doesn't seem to find anything strange in this and nor does anyone else. **77m/C VHS.** Gibson Frazier, Susan Egan, Anthony Rapp, Cara Buono, Dwight Ewell, Brian Davies, Frank Gorshin; ***D:*** Adam Abramham; ***W:*** Adam Abramham, Gibson Frazier; ***C:*** Matthew Jensen; ***M:*** Michael Weiner.

Man of the Forest 🦴🦴 **1933** A cowboy goes to the aid of a damsel in distress and he winds up being framed for murder for his efforts. Based on Zane Grey's novel. **59m/B VHS.** Randolph Scott, Verna Hillie, Harry Carey Sr., Noah Beery Sr., Barton MacLane; ***D:*** Henry Hathaway.

Man of the House 🦴🦴 **1995 (PG)** Kids' comedy about a boy's scheme to sabotage his mother's new love interest. Ben (Thomas) concocts a plan to join the YMCA Indian Guides to discourage daddy wanna-be Jack (Chase), while mom (Fawcett) stands idly by tolerating her son's bratty behavior. Subplot involves a screwy gangster theme that deteriorates into a "Home Alone-ish" ending. Film attempts to play off of Chase's knack for physical comedy, but falls short. And what's with the mime? Wendt is amusing as the Indian Guide leader. Will probably appeal more to younger crowds as Thomas's scheming teen upstages Chase's deadpan dad-to-be. **97m/C VHS.** Chevy Chase, Farrah Fawcett, Jonathan Taylor Thomas, George Wendt, David Shiner, Art LaFleur, Richard Portnow, Richard Foronjy, Spencer Vrooman, John Disanti, Chief Leonard George, Peter Appel, George Greif, Chris Miranda, Ron Canada, Zachary Browne, Nicholas Garrett; ***D:*** James Orr; ***W:*** James Orr, Jim Cruickshank; ***C:*** Jamie Anderson; ***M:*** Mark Mancina.

Man of the West 🦴🦴½ **1958** Reformed bad guy Cooper is asked to deliver a tidy hunk of cash to another city to recruit a school marm. Ambushed en route by his former partners in crime (who are led by his wacko uncle) he's forced to revert to his wanton ways in order to survive and save innocent hostages. There's a raging debate among Cooper fans whether this late effort has been unduly overlooked or duly ignored. A number of things conspire to give it a bad rap: Cooper does little but look mournful until the very end; there's no hiding the fact that he's older than Cobb, who plays his uncle; and the acting is in general more befitting of a B-grade slice and dicer. You be the judge. **100m/C VHS.** Gary Cooper, Julie London, Lee J. Cobb, Arthur O'Connell, Jack Lord, John Dehner, Royal Dano, Guy Wilkerson, Emory Parnell; ***D:*** Anthony Mann; ***W:*** Reginald Rose.

Man of Violence 🦴 *The Sex Racketeers* **1971** A vulgar, tasteless man spends the worthless hours of his wasted life lurking about the more wretched entranceways of his native land. **107m/C VHS.** Michael Latimer, Luan Peters; ***D:*** Pete Walker.

Man on a String 🦴🦴½ **1971 (PG)** In order to bring down a Mob boss the feds first frame cop Peter King and send him to the pen. When he gets out, King uses his prison contacts to get in with the Mob and winds up pitting two rival gangs against each other in order to destroy them both. **73m/C VHS.** Christopher George, Jack Warden, Keith Carradine, Joel Grey, William Schallert, Kitty Winn; ***D:*** Joseph Sargent. **TV**

Man on Fire 🦴 **1987 (R)** Told via flashback, a cynical ex-CIA man is hired as a bodyguard for the daughter of a wealthy Italian couple, who is soon thereafter kidnapped by terrorists. He goes to her rescue with all the subtlety of a wrecking ball. Decent cast goes down the tubes in this botched thriller. **92m/C VHS.** *FR* Scott Glenn, Brooke Adams, Danny Aiello, Joe Pesci, Paul Shenar, Jonathan Pryce, Jade Malle; ***D:*** Elie Chouraqui.

The Man on the Box 🦴🦴½ **1925** Chaplin is a wealthy bachelor who takes a job as a gardener to be near his girl. He overhears a plot by the butler, who's an enemy agent, to steal the secret plans for a helicopter from his sweetie's father. In order to thwart the dastardedly scheme Chaplin dresses as a maid to infiltrate the household. **58m/B VHS.** Sydney Chaplin, David Butler, Alice Calhoun, Kathleen Calhoun, Helene Costello, Theodore Lorch; ***D:*** Charles Reisner.

Man on the Eiffel Tower 🦴🦴🦴 **1948** Laughton plays Inspector Maigret, the detective created by novelist Georges Simenon, in a highly suspenseful and cerebral mystery about a crazed killer who defies the police to discover his identity. This is the first film Meredith directed. **82m/C VHS.** Charles Laughton, Burgess Meredith, Franchot Tone, Patricia Roc; ***D:*** Burgess Meredith.

Man on the Moon 🦴🦴 **1999 (R)** Clunky bio of bizarro comedian Andy Kaufman (Carrey) who died of cancer at age 35 in 1984. The problem is that Kaufman is opaque—he doesn't seem to have a true personality but assumes bizarre alter-egos, including obnoxious lounge singer Tony Clifton. Kaufman turned out to be most appealing as innocent Latka on the sitcom "Taxi," which he professes to despise. For all Carrey's expertise, you won't care too much about what's onscreen. Title comes from R.E.M.'s song about Kaufman; they also supplied the film's music. **118m/C VHS, DVD, Wide.** Jim Carrey, Courtney Love, Danny DeVito, Paul Giamatti, Vincent Schiavelli, Peter Bonerz, Marilu Henner, Judd Hirsch; ***D:*** Milos Forman; ***W:*** Scott M. Alexander, Larry Karaszewski; ***C:*** Terry Michos. Golden Globes '00: Actor—Mus./Comedy (Carrey).

The Man on the Roof 🦴🦴 *Manen Pa Taket* **1976** A police officer, who's been accused of brutality, is murdered and Martin Beck (Lindstedt) and his colleagues are called in to investigate. Then someone climbs a roof in central Stockholm and begins killing policemen with a rifle. Turns out the cases are related and involve an ex-cop named Eriksson (Hirdwall). Based on the novel "The Abominable Man" by Maj Sjowall and Per Wahloo. Swedish with subtitles. **110m/C VHS.** *SW* Carl Gustav Lindstedt, Ingvar Hirdwall, Sven Wollter, Thomas Heelberg; ***D:*** Bo Widerberg; ***W:*** Bo Widerberg; ***C:*** Odd Geir Saether, Per Kallberg.

Man on the Run 🦴🦴 **1949** A robbery takes place in the store where an Army deserter is trying to sell his gun, and he ends up taking the rap. It's up to a lovely lady lawyer to prove his innocence. Efficiently told "B" crime drama. **82m/B VHS.** *GB* Derek Farr, Joan Hopkins, Edward Chapman, Laurence Harvey, Howard Marion-Crawford, Alfie Bass, John Bailey, John Stuart, Edward Underdown, Leslie Perrins, Kenneth More, Martin Miller, Eleanor Summerfield; ***D:*** Lawrence Huntington; ***W:*** Lawrence Huntington.

Man on the Run 🦴½ **1974 (R)** After an unwitting involvement with a small robbery, a teenager finds himself the object of a police manhunt for a murder suspect. **90m/C VHS.** Kyle Johnson, James B. Sikking, Terry Carter; ***D:*** Herbert L. Strock.

Man or Gun 🦴½ **1958** Standard western yarn involving a drifter who rides into a town operated by a powerful family and liberates the cowardly townsfolk. **79m/B VHS.** MacDonald Carey, Audrey Totter, James Craig, James Gleason, Warren Stevens, Harry Shannon; ***D:*** Albert C. Gannaway; ***W:*** Vance Skarstedt, James C. Cassity.

The Man Outside 🦴🦴 **1968 (R)** After a CIA agent is fired for allegedly assisting another agent in defecting to the East, he becomes involved in further intrigue. A Russian spy is looking to defect. In the process, the ex-agent is framed for murder. Straightforward espionage tale taken from Gene Stackleborg's novel "Double Agent." **98m/C VHS.** *GB* Van Heflin, Heidelinde Weis, Pinkas Braun, Peter Vaughan, Charles Gray, Ronnie Barker; ***D:*** Samuel Gallu.

Man Outside 🦴 **1988 (PG-13)** Logan is an ex-lawyer who takes to the Arkansas outback after his wife dies. Anthropologist/teacher Quinlan takes a shine to him. He seems like an okay guy, but bad guy Dillman has made it look like he's a child snatcher. Slick on the outside but empty inside independent effort. Look for former members of The Band in supporting roles. **109m/C VHS.** Robert F. Logan, Kathleen Quinlan, Bradford Dillman, Rick Danko, Levon Helm; ***D:*** Mark Stouffer.

The Man They Could Not Hang 🦴🦴½ **1939** A good doctor tinkering with artificial hearts is caught by police while experimenting on a willing student. When the doctor is convicted and hanged for a murder, his assistant uses the heart to bring him back to life. No longer a nice guy, he vows revenge against the jurors that sentenced him. Karloff repeated the same storyline in several films, and this one is representative of the type. **70m/B VHS.** Boris Karloff, Adrian (Lorna Gray) Booth, Roger Pryor, Robert Wilcox; ***D:*** Nick Grinde.

Man Trouble 🦴🦴 **1992 (PG-13)** A divorcing opera singer (Barkin) seeks the help of a sleazy attack-dog trainer (Nicholson) when she becomes the victim of a stalker. Nicholson hits on her, first because that's one of his habits, and then because he is being paid to by a billionaire who wants him to steal the manuscript of a tell-all book about him written by Barkin's sister. Although both Nicholson and Barkin are excellent actors, they lack the electricity to make the romance credible, and the jokes are weak. Supporting cast, including D'Angelo, Stanton, and McKean, provide the funny parts in this otherwise dull film. **100m/C VHS, Wide.** Jack Nicholson, Ellen Barkin, Harry Dean Stanton, Beverly D'Angelo, Michael McKean, Saul Rubinek, Viveka Davis, Veronica Cartwright, David Clennon, John Kapelos, Paul Mazursky; ***D:*** Bob Rafelson; ***W:*** Adrien (Carole Eastman) Joyce; ***C:*** Stephen Burum; ***M:*** Georges Delerue.

The Man Upstairs 🦴🦴½ **1993** Escaped con Moony Polaski (O'Neal) hides out in the home of crotchety spinster Victoria Brown (Hepburn). When she finds the crook in her attic, instead of turning him in, Victoria befriends the slob and soon the two are sharing dinner and secrets. Meanwhile, the manhunt for Moony is intensifying and, oh yes, Christmas is coming as well. TV cornpone barely saved by some professional performances. Executive producer Burt Reynolds was hoping for a part until scheduling made it impossible. **95m/C VHS.** Katharine Hepburn, Ryan O'Neal, Henry Beckman, Helen Carroll, Brenda Forbes; ***D:*** George Schaefer; ***W:*** James Prideaux. **TV**

The Man Who Broke 1,000 Chains 🦴🦴 **1987** Tells the story of a man who is committed to a chain gang after WWII for a petty crime, and his efforts, after escaping, in making a new life for himself. An unimaginative plot is occasionally highlighted by a good scene or two. **113m/C VHS.** Val Kilmer, Charles Durning, Sonia Braga; ***D:*** Daniel Mann; ***M:*** Charles Bernstein. **TV**

The Man Who Came to Dinner 🦴🦴🦴½ **1941** Based on the Moss Hart-George S. Kaufman play, this comedy is about a bitter radio celebrity (Woolley) on a lecture tour (a character based on Alexander Woolcott). He breaks his hip and must stay in a quiet suburban home for the winter. While there, he occupies his time by barking orders, being obnoxious and generally just driving the other residents nuts. Woolley reprises his Broadway role in this film that succeeds at every turn, loaded with plenty of satiric jabs at the Algonquin Hotel Roundtable regulars. **112m/B VHS.** Monty Woolley, Bette Davis, Ann Sheridan, Jimmy Durante, Reginald Gardiner, Richard Travis, Billie Burke, Grant Mitchell, Mary Wickes, George Barbier, Ruth Vivian, Elisabeth Fraser; ***D:*** William Keighley; ***W:*** Julius J. Epstein, Philip G. Epstein; ***C:*** Gaetano Antonio "Tony" Gaudio.

The Man Who Captured Eichmann 🦴🦴½ **1996** In 1960 Israeli Mossad agents prepare to capture Adolf Eichmann (Duvall), who organized the transport of millions of Jews to the concentration camps, from his home in Argentina. Peter Malkin (Howard), the agent responsible for the kidnapping, holds Eichmann in a Buenos Aires safe house before smuggling him into Israel as Eichmann tries to ingratiate himself with Malkin, refusing to accept responsiblity and constantly maintaining his innocence. Based on the book "Eichmann In My Hands" by Peter Z. Malkin and Harry Stein. **96m/C VHS.** Robert Duvall, Arliss Howard, Jeffrey Tambor, Jack Laufer, Nicolas Surovy, Joel Brooks, Sam Robards, Michael Tucci; ***D:*** William A. Graham; ***W:*** Lionel Chetwynd; ***C:*** Robert Steadman; ***M:*** Laurence Rosenthal. CABLE

The Man Who Could Work Miracles 🦴🦴🦴½ **1937** A mild-mannered draper's assistant becomes suddenly endowed with supernatural powers to perform any feat he wishes. Great special effects (for an early film) and fine performances result in a classic piece of science fiction. **82m/B VHS.** Ralph Richardson, Joan Gardner, Roland Young; ***D:*** Lothar Mendes.

The Man Who Cried 🦴🦴 **2000 (R)** In 1927 Russia, young Jewish Fegele is separated from her father (who manages to emigrate to America) and instead winds up in England, where she's adopted and renamed Suzie. An adult Suzie (Ricci) heads to Paris in the late '30s and finds bit work in an opera company, sharing a garret with gold-digging Russian Lola (a lively Blanchett) and a romance with gypsy Cesar (Depp). Lola has set her sights on hammy opera singer, Dante (Turturro). Then the Nazis invade Paris. The film's surprisingly plodding and the characters either stereotypical and/or underwritten. **97m/C VHS, DVD, Wide.** *GB FR* Christina Ricci, Johnny Depp, Cate Blanchett, John Turturro, Harry Dean Stanton, Oleg Yankovsky; ***D:*** Sally Potter; ***W:*** Sally Potter; ***C:*** Sacha Vierny; ***M:*** Osvaldo Golijoy. Natl. Bd. of Review '01: Support. Actress (Blanchett).

The Man Who Envied Women 🦴½ **1985** The non-narrative feminist story of a smug womanizer: the man "who knows almost too much about women." **125m/C VHS.** Bill Raymond, Larry Loonin, Trisha Brown; ***D:*** Yvonne Rainer; ***W:*** Yvonne Rainer.

The Man Who Fell to Earth 🦴🦴🦴½ **1976 (R)** Entertaining and technically adept cult classic about a man from another planet (Bowie, in a bit of typecasting) who ventures to earth in hopes of finding water to save his family and drought-stricken planet. Instead he becomes a successful inventor and businessman, along the way discovering the human vices of booze, sex, and television. Also available in a restored version at 138 minutes. Remade for TV in 1987 and based on Walter Tevis's novel. **118m/C VHS, DVD, Wide.** *GB* David Bowie, Candy Clark, Rip Torn, Buck Henry, Bernie Casey, Jackson D. Kane, Rick Riccardo, Tony Mascia; ***D:*** Nicolas Roeg; ***W:*** Paul Mayersberg; ***C:*** Anthony B. Richmond; ***M:*** John Phillips.

The Man Who Guards the Greenhouse **1988** Tracy must come to terms with her attraction for Jeff as well as once again trying to write a meaningful novel. **150m/C VHS.** Christopher Cazenove, Rebecca Dewey.

Man Who Had Power Over Women 🦴🦴 **1970 (R)** Disappointing sex farce about the exploits of a carnally insatiable (and married) talent executive (Taylor) who has an affair with every woman he meets and creates problems aplenty. Adapted from a novel by Gordon Williams. **89m/C VHS.** *GB* Rod Taylor, James Booth, Carol White, Penelope Horner, Clive Francis; ***D:*** John Krish; ***W:*** Chris Bryant, Allan Scott.

The Man Who Haunted Himself 🦴🦴 **1970** While a man lies in critical condition on the operating table after a car accident, his alter-ego emerges and turns his ideal life into a nightmare until the man recovers and moves toward a fateful encounter. An expanded version of an episode of the TV series "Alfred Hitchcock Presents," this was Moore's first movie after having starred in the TV series "The Saint," and it was Dearden's last film; he died in a car accident the following year. Appeals primarily to those fascinated by "Hitchcock" or "The Twilight Zone"—where mystery matters most. Filmed in London. **94m/C VHS, DVD, Wide.** *GB* Roger Moore, Hildegard(e) Neil, Olga Georges-Picot; ***D:*** Basil Dearden; ***W:*** Bryan Forbes; ***C:*** Tony Spratling; ***M:*** Michael Lewis.

The Man Who Knew Too Little 🦴🦴½ *Watch That Man* **1997 (PG)** Wallace (Murray), a video store clerk from Iowa, travels to London in order to surprise his yuppie brother James (Gallagher) on his birthday. James is hosting an important dinner party, however, so he sends his less than upper-crusty brother to the Theater of Life, where the patrons take part in scenes with actors in real-life settings. Unbeknownst to Wallace, the designated call to start the play is intended for a real hit man, and he is thrown into a plot to rekindle the Cold War. Totally oblivious to the danger he is in, he treats every threat and tense situation with a sly smile and a smart-aleck remark. Joanne Whalley is the call girl/spy who turns into the sidekick/love interest. Although it's mainly a stretched out one-joke premise, that joke is delivered by comedy maestro Bill Murray. If you like his previous work, you'll love him as he messes with snooty Europeans. If you don't, seek professional help immediately. **94m/C VHS, DVD.** Bill Murray, Peter Gallagher, Joanne Whalley, Alfred Molina, Richard Wilson, Geraldine James, John Standing, Anna Chancellor, Nicholas Woodeson, Simon Chandler; ***D:*** Jon Amiel; ***W:*** Howard Franklin, Robert Harrar; ***C:*** Robert Stevens; ***M:*** Chris Young.

The Man Who Knew Too Much 🦴🦴🦴 **1934** Hitchcock's first international success. A British family man on vacation in Switzerland is told of an assassination plot by a dying agent. His daughter is kidnapped to force his silence. In typical Hitchcock fashion, the innocent person becomes caught in a web of intrigue; the sticky situation culminates with surprising events during the famous shootout in the final scenes. Remade by Hitchcock in 1956. **75m/B VHS, DVD.** *GB* Leslie Banks, Edna Best, Peter Lorre, Nova Pilbeam, Pierre Fresnay, Frank Vosper, Hugh Wakefield, Cicely Oates, D. A. Clarke-Smith, George Curzon, Henry Oscar, Wilfrid Hyde-White; ***D:*** Alfred Hitchcock; ***W:*** Emlyn Williams, Charles Bennett, A.H. Rawlinson, Edwin Greenwood, D. B. Wyndham-Lewis; ***C:*** Curt Courant.

The Man Who Knew Too Much 🦴🦴½ **1956 (PG)** Hitchcock's remake of his 1934 film, this time about an American doctor and his family vacationing in Marrakech. They become involved in a complicated international plot involving kidnapping and murder. While Doris tries to save the day by singing "Que Sera, Sera," Stewart tries to locate his abducted son. More lavish settings and forms of intrigue make this a less focused and, to some, inferior version. ♫Que Sera, Sera. **120m/C VHS, DVD, Wide.** James Stewart, Doris Day, Brenda de Banzie, Bernard Miles, Ralph Truman, Daniel Gelin, Alan Mowbray, Carolyn Jones, Hillary Brooke; ***D:*** Alfred Hitchcock; ***W:*** John Michael Hayes; ***C:*** Robert Burks; ***M:*** Bernard Herrmann. Oscars '56: Song ("Que Sera, Sera").

The Man Who Laughs 🦴🦴🦴½ **1927** Veidt's sensitive performance highlights this silent classic. He plays a young man whose features are surgically altered into a permanent smile because his family are political enemies of the current ruler. The man is befriended by the owner of a sideshow who first exhibits him as a freak but later finds Veidt gaining fame as a clown. A beautiful blind girl in the show loves Veidt for who he is and the two find happiness. **110m/B VHS.** Conrad Veidt, Mary Philbin, Olga Baclanova, Josephine Crowell, George Siegmann, Brandon Hurst; ***D:*** Paul Leni.

The Man Who Lived Again 🦴🦴½ *The Man Who Changed His Mind; The Brainsnatchers; Dr. Maniac* **1936** Boris strives to be a brain-switcher, and suspense builds around the question of whether or not he will change his mind. Shot in England with fine sets and a definite Anglo feel to the proceedings, with Karloff doing one of his better mad scientist routines. **61m/B VHS, 8mm.** *GB* Boris Karloff, Anna Lee, John Loder, Frank Cellier, Lyn Harding, Cecil Parker; ***D:*** Robert Stevenson.

Man Who Loved Cat Dancing 🦴🦴 **1973 (PG)** Reynolds is an outlaw on the run after avenging his wife's murder and robbing a safe with pals Hopkins and Warden, and Miles has recently escaped from her abusive husband. It's love on the run as Burt and Sarah are pursued by bounty hunters and their tragic pasts—coming close to making us care, but close doesn't mean as much in movies as it does in dancing. Based on Marilyn Durham's novel. **114m/C VHS.** Burt Reynolds, Sarah Miles, Jack Warden, Lee J. Cobb, Jay Silverheels, Robert Donner; ***D:*** Richard Sarafian; ***C:*** Harry Stradling Jr.; ***M:*** John Williams.

The Man Who Loved Women 🦴🦴🦴 *L'Homme Qui Aimait les Femmes* **1977** An intelligent, sensitive bachelor writes his memoirs and recalls the many, many, many women he has loved. Truffaut couples sophistication and lightheartedness, the thrill of the chase and, when it leads to an accidental death, the wondering what-it's-all-about in the mourning after. In French with English subtitles. Remade in 1983. **119m/C VHS, DVD, Wide.** *FR* Charles Denner, Brigitte Fossey, Leslie Caron, Nelly Borgeaud, Genevieve Fontanel, Nathalie Baye, Sabine Glaser; ***D:*** Francois Truffaut; ***W:*** Francois Truffaut, Suzanne Schiffman, Michel Fermaud; ***C:*** Nestor Almendros; ***M:*** Maurice Jaubert.

The Man Who Loved Women 🦴🦴 **1983 (R)** A remake of the 1977 French film, this is slower, tries to be funnier, and is less subtle than the original. Reynolds is a Los Angeles sculptor whose reputation as a playboy leads him to a psychoanalyst's couch, where a lot of talk slows the action—though Burt & Julie (the shrink) do share the couch. **110m/C VHS, DVD, Wide.** Burt Reynolds, Julie Andrews, Kim Basinger, Marilu Henner, Cynthia Sikes, Jennifer Edwards; ***D:*** Blake Edwards; ***W:*** Blake Edwards; ***C:*** Haskell Wexler; ***M:*** Henry Mancini.

The Man Who Made Husbands Jealous 🦴🦴½ *Jilly Cooper's The Man Who Made Husbands Jealous* **1998** Young, handsome ne'er-do-well Lysander Hawkley (Billington) is broke. He has few prospects but one undeniable talent—women love him. So his friend Ferdie (Bonneville) looks around at the unhappily married women he knows (and their cheating spouses) and comes up with a plan. The wives will hire Lysander to make their neglectful husbands jealous. And the plan is very enjoyable for both Lysander and the ladies, until he falls in love. Based on the naughty novel by Jilly Cooper. **150m/C VHS.** *GB* Stephen Billington, Hugh Bonneville, Kate Byers, Gilly Coman, Kim Criswell, Derek De Lint; ***D:*** Robert Knights; ***W:*** Andrew Maclear, Harvey Bamburg. TV

The Man Who Never Was 🦴🦴🦴 **1955** Tense true story (with melodramatic embroidery) from WWII shows in step-by-step detail how Britain duped the Axis by letting them find an Allied corpse bearing phony invasion plans. Based on the book by the scheme's mastermind Ewen Montagu, played by Webb; Peter Sellers provides the voice of an offscreen Winston Churchill. **102m/C VHS.** *GB* Clifton Webb, Gloria Grahame, Robert Flemyng, Josephine Griffin, Stephen Boyd, Andre Morell, Laurence Naismith, Geoffrey Keen, Michael Hordern; ***D:*** Ronald Neame; ***C:*** Oswald Morris. British Acad. '56: Screenplay.

The Man Who Shot Liberty Valance 🦴🦴🦴½ **1962** Tough cowboy Wayne and idealistic lawyer Stewart join forces against dreaded gunfighter Liberty Valance, played leatherly by Marvin. While Stewart rides to Senatorial success on his reputation as the man who shot the villain, he suffers moral crises about the act, but is toughened up by Wayne. Wayne's use of the word "pilgrim" became a standard for his impersonators. Strong character acting, great Western scenes, and value judgments to ponder over make this last of Ford's black-and-white westerns among his best. **123m/B VHS, DVD, Wide.** James Stewart, John Wayne, Vera Miles, Lee Marvin, Edmond O'Brien, Andy Devine, Woody Strode, Ken Murray, Jeanette Nolan, John Qualen, Strother Martin, Lee Van Cleef, John Carradine, Carleton Young, Willis Bouchey, Denver Pyle, Robert F. Simon, O.Z. Whitehead, Paul Birch, Joseph Hoover, Earle Hodgins, Jack Pennick; ***D:*** John Ford; ***W:*** James Warner Bellah, Willis Goldbeck; ***C:*** William Clothier; ***M:*** Cyril Mockridge, Alfred Newman.

The Man Who Wagged His Tail 🦴🦴½ *An Angel Passed Over Brooklyn; Un Angelo e Sceso a Brooklyn* **1957** A mean slumlord is turned into a dog as the result of a curse cast upon him. In order to return to his human form, he must be loved by someone. Despite his attempts to be loved, the dog alienates his only friend and must try to redeem himself. Played for fun, this is a mildly amusing fantasy filmed in Spain and Brooklyn. Not released in the U. S. until 1961. **91m/B VHS.** *IT SP* Peter Ustinov, Pablito Calvo, Aroldo Tieri, Silvia Marco; ***D:*** Ladislao Vajda.

The Man Who Wasn't There 🦴 **1983 (R)** A member of the State department receives a formula from a dying spy that can render him invisible, see? He has to use the formula to protect himself from the police and other spies, becoming a comic "Invisible Man," see? Generally chaotic tale that's bad, but not so bad that it's worth seeing, though you might want to see what invisibility looks like in 3-D. **111m/C VHS.** Steve Guttenberg, Jeffrey Tambor, Art Hindle, Lisa Langlois; ***D:*** Bruce Malmuth; ***M:*** Miles Goodman. Natl. Bd. of Review '01: Actor (Thornton).

The Man Who Wasn't There 🦴🦴🦴 **2001 (R)** Ed Crane (Thornton, in a masterfully underplayed performance) is a small-town barber who goes unnoticed by many. He suspects that his wife Doris (McDormand) is cheating on him with Dave (Gandolfini), who owns the store where she works. When Ed decides that he wants to invest in the new "dry cleaning" process that a stranger tells him about, he decides to try blackmail. What follows is a series of stately paced twists and complications. **116m/B VHS, DVD, Wide.** *US* Billy Bob Thornton, Frances McDormand, Michael Badalucco, James Gandolfini, Katherine Borowitz, Jon Polito, Scarlett Johansson, Richard Jenkins, Tony Shalhoub; ***D:*** Joel Coen; ***W:*** Joel Coen, Ethan Coen; ***C:*** Roger Deakins; ***M:*** Carter Burwell. L.A. Film Critics '01: Cinematog.

The Man Who Would Be King 🦴🦴🦴🦴 **1975 (PG)** A grand, old-fashioned adventure based on the classic story by Rudyard Kipling about two mercenary soldiers who travel from India to Kafiristan in order to conquer it and set themselves up as kings. Splendid characterizations by Connery and Caine, and Huston's royal directorial treatment provides it with adventure, majestic sweep, and well-developed characters. **129m/C VHS, DVD, Wide.** Sean Connery, Michael Caine, Christopher Plummer, Saeed Jaffrey, Shakira Caine; ***D:*** John Huston; ***W:*** Gladys Hill, John Huston; ***C:*** Oswald Morris; ***M:*** Maurice Jarre.

The Man Who Would Not Die 🦴🦴 *Target in the Sun* **1975 (PG)** During his investigation of several deaths, a man discovers that all of the deceased were actually the same man. It seems the deaths were part of a intricate scheme to cover up a $1 million heist. Two of the top three actors are killed early on; it's not very suspenseful. It's more like the mystery that would not die. From Charles Williams's novel "The Sailcloth Shroud." **83m/**

C VHS. Dorothy Malone, Keenan Wynn, Aldo Ray; *D:* Robert Arkless.

Man with a Cross 1943 Archaeologists of the cinema may want to unearth this early Rossellini, made by the future father of neo-realist cinema as a propaganda piece for the fascist war effort. A heroic Italian chaplain on the Russian front ministers to foe and friend alike, and even converts a few commies to Christ. Not as awful as it sounds—but never forget where this came from. **88m/B VHS.** *IT D:* Roberto Rossellini.

Man with a Gun 1995 (R) Hitman John Hardin (Madsen) is asked by mobster employer Jack Rushton (Busey) to kill his ex-girlfriend Rena (Tilly) and get a CD-ROM filled with info he doesn't want to get out. Rena now happens to be John's gal pal but isn't too upset since she figures they'll substitute Rena's goody two-shoes twin sister Kathy for the needed corpse. Too bad John starts to fall for the intended victim, leaving the plan to unravel. It's a connect-the-dots plot with a creditable cast. Based on the novel "The Shroud Society" by Hugh C. Rae. **100m/C VHS.** Michael Madsen, Jennifer Tilly, Gary Busey, Robert Loggia, Ian Tracey, Bill Cobbs; *D:* David Wyles; *W:* Laurie Finstad-Knizhik; *C:* Jan Kiesser; *M:* George Blondheim.

A Man with a Maid *The Groove Room; What the Swedish Butler Saw* 1973 A bizarre British exploitation pic mixes spookhouse cliches and sex, as a young man finds his new bachelor pad haunted by Jack the Ripper. Originally shot in 3-D. **83m/C VHS.** Sue Longhurst, Martin Long, Diana Dors; *D:* Vernon Becker.

The Man with Bogart's Face *Sam Marlowe, Private Eye* 1980 (PG) Sacchi is no Bogart, but he does imitate him well. Bogart fans will enjoy this fond tribute to the late great actor, but the story uncertainly wavers between genuine detective story and detective spoof. **106m/C VHS.** Robert Sacchi, Misty Rowe, Sybil Danning, Franco Nero, Herbert Lom, Victor Buono, Olivia Hussey; *D:* Robert Day; *W:* Andrew J. Fenady; *M:* John Beal, George Duning. Golden Raspberries '80: Worst Song ("The Man with Bogart's Face").

The Man with One Red Shoe 1985 (PG) Hanks is a lovable clod of a violinist who ensnares himself in a web of intrigue when CIA agents, both good and evil, mistake him for a contact by his wearing one red shoe. Sporadically funny remake of the French "The Tall Blond Man with One Black Shoe." **92m/C VHS.** Tom Hanks, Dabney Coleman, Lori Singer, Carrie Fisher, James Belushi, Charles Durning, Edward Herrmann, Tom Noonan, Gerrit Graham, David Lander, David Ogden Stiers; *D:* Stan Dragoti; *M:* Thomas Newman.

The Man with the Golden Arm 1955 A gripping film version of the Nelson Algren junkie melodrama, about an ex-addict who returns to town only to get mixed up with drugs again. Crooked card dealer Frankie Machine (Sinatra in a standout performance) returns after a stint in rehab, hoping to pursue new dreams. But his crippled wife Zosch (Parker) wants him to stick with what he knows while drug dealer Louie (McGavin) makes Frankie offers he finds harder and harder to refuse, even with blonde beauty Molly (Novak) to offer Frankie comfort. Considered controversial in its depiction of addiction when released. **119m/B VHS.** Frank Sinatra, Kim Novak, Eleanor Parker, Arnold Stang, Darren McGavin, Robert Strauss, George Mathews, John Conte, Doro Merande; *D:* Otto Preminger; *W:* Lewis Meltzer, Walter Newman; *C:* Sam Leavitt; *M:* Elmer Bernstein.

The Man with the Golden Gun 1974 (PG) Roger Moore is the debonair secret agent 007 in this ninth James Bond flick. Assigned to recover a small piece of equipment which can be utilized to harness the sun's energy, Bond engages the usual bevy of villains and beauties. **134m/C VHS, DVD, Wide.** *GB* Roger Moore, Christopher Lee, Britt Ekland, Maud Adams, Herve Villechaize, Clifton James, Soon-Teck Oh, Richard Loo, Marc Lawrence, Bernard Lee, Lois Maxwell, Desmond Llewelyn; *D:* Guy Hamilton; *W:* Tom Mankiewicz; *C:* Ted Moore; *M:* John Barry.

The Man with the Movie Camera *Chelovek s Kinoapparatom* 1929 A plotless, experimental view of Moscow through the creative eye of the cameraman Dziga Vertov, founder of the Kino Eye. The editing methods and camera techniques used in this silent film were very influential and still stand up to scrutiny today. **69m/B VHS, DVD.** *RU D:* Dziga Vertov; *W:* Dziga Vertov; *C:* Mikhail Kaufman; *M:* Pierre Henry.

The Man with the Perfect Swing 1995 Middle-aged ex-baseball player-turned-business entrepreneur Anthony "Babe" Lombardo (Black) is deep in debt and having trouble with the IRS even as he schemes to find success with his latest endeavor—designing specialty golf equipment. But Babe's latest design is a radically new golf swing (combining putting with his baseball expertise) featured in a how-to video with a budding PGA star. Naturally, given Babe's woeful record, the money just doesn't seem to be coming his way. **94m/C VHS.** James Black, Suzanne Savoy, Marco Perella, James Belcher, Richard Bradshaw; *D:* Michael Hovis; *W:* Michael Hovis; *C:* Jim Barham; *M:* Paul English.

The Man with Two Brains 1983 (R) Did you hear the one about the brilliant neurosurgeon who falls in love with a woman's diembodied brain in his laboratory? Dr. Michael Hfuhruhurr (Martin) only has two problems: dealing with his frigid, covetous wife (Turner) and finding a body for his cerebral lover. Isn't it nice that a serial murderer, known as the Elevator Killer, is on the loose. Plenty of laughs in this spoof of mad scientist movies that is redeemed from potential idiocy by the cast's titillating performances. Listen closely and you'll recognize the voice of Spacek as the brain-in-the-jar of Martin's dreams. **91m/C VHS, DVD.** Steve Martin, Kathleen Turner, David Warner, Paul Benedict, James Cromwell, Frank McCarthy, George Furth, Randi Brooks, Bernard Behrens, Stephanie Kramer; *Cameos:* Merv Griffin; *D:* Carl Reiner; *W:* Carl Reiner, George Gipe, Steve Martin; *C:* Michael Chapman; *M:* Joel Goldsmith; *V:* Sissy Spacek.

Man with Two Heads 1972 (R) Doctor Jekyll gets in touch with his innermost feelings when his muffed experiments turn him into, gasp, Mr. Blood. Another forlorn addition to the Dr. Jekyll retread collection. **80m/C VHS.** *D:* Andy Milligan; *W:* Andy Milligan.

The Man with Two Lives 1942 Well done horror thriller about a wealthy young man who's killed in a car accident, then brought back to life by a mad scientist. At precisely the moment his life is restored, a murderous gangster is executed and his soul enters the young man's body. **?m/C VHS.** Edward Norris, Addison Richards, Marlo Dwyer.

The Man Without a Country 1973 Faithful adaptation of Everett Edward Hale's short story features a sparkling performance by Robertson as Lt. Philip Nolan, who is court-martialed for treason and denounces his country, proclaiming that he never wishes to see or hear of the United Stats again. He gets his wish when his sentence is to spend the rest of his life aboard a ship sailing the U.S. coast but never docking. The crew of the ship is forbidden from giving him news of America. Beautifully illustates the old warning "Be careful what you wish for." **90m/C VHS.** Cliff Robertson, Beau Bridges, Peter Strauss, Robert Ryan, Walter Abel, Geoffrey Holder, Shepperd Strudwick, John Cullum, Peter Coffield, Addison Powell, Peter Weller; *D:* Delbert Mann; *W:* Sidney Carroll; *C:* Andrew Laszlo; *M:* Jack Elliott, Allyn Ferguson. **TV**

The Man Without a Face 1993 (PG-13) Gibson plays a badly scarred recluse in Maine who develops a mentor relationship with a lonely, fatherless boy. Chuck (Stahl) wants to go away to military school, but flunks the entrance exam, and enlists former teacher McLeod as a tutor. First foray for Gibson into the director's chair tends to be overly melodramatic. Adapted from a novel by Isabelle Holland. **115m/C VHS.** Mel Gibson, Nick Stahl, Margaret Whitton, Fay Masterson, Richard Masur, Gaby Hoffman, Geoffrey Lewis, Jack DeMave; *D:* Mel Gibson; *W:* Malcolm MacRury; *M:* James Horner.

Man Without a Star 1955 A cowboy helps ranchers stop a ruthless cattle owner from taking over their land. The conflict between freedom in the wild west and the need for order and settlements is powerfully internalized in Douglas, whose fight for justice will tame the cowboy code he lives by. You'll shed a tear for the fading frontier. **89m/B VHS.** Kirk Douglas, Jeanne Crain, Claire Trevor, William Campbell; *D:* King Vidor.

Man, Woman & Child 1983 (PG) A close, upscale California family is shocked when a child from the husband's long-ago affair with a Frenchwoman appears at their door. Pure sentimentalism, as the family confronts this unexpected development. Two hankies—one each for fine performances by Sheen and Danner. Based on a sentimental novel by Erich Segal of "Love Story" fame, who co-wrote the script. **99m/C VHS.** Martin Sheen, Blythe Danner, Craig T. Nelson, David Hemmings; *D:* Dick Richards; *W:* Erich Segal; *M:* Georges Delerue.

Managua 1997 (R) Paul Gleason (Gossett Jr.) goes to Nicaragua to claim the body of old friend Dennis Rice (Savage) but gets stonewalled by the authorities. Rice was working undercover, going after drug cartels and supposedly crossed over to the bad guys. Gleason decides to find out the truth and, of course, discovers Rice is alive. **108m/C VHS.** Louis Gossett Jr., Assumpta Serna, John Savage, Robert Beltran, Michael Moriarty, John Diehl; *D:* Michele Taverna.

Manchurian Avenger 1984 (R) Desperados have wrested control of a Colorado gold rush town from Joe Kim's family, but he'll put an end to that, chop chop. **87m/C VHS.** Bobby Kim, Bill Wallace; *D:* Ed Warnick.

The Manchurian Candidate 1962 Political thriller about an American Korean War vet who suspects that he and his platoon may have been brainwashed during the war, with his highly decorated, heroic friend programmed by commies to be an operational assassin. Loaded with shocks, conspiracy, inventive visual imagery, and bitter political satire of naivete and machinations of the left and right. Excellent performances by an all-star cast, with Lansbury and Gregory particularly frightening. Based on the Richard Condon novel. Featuring a special interview with Sinatra and Frankenheimer in which Sinatra is deified. **126m/B VHS, DVD, Wide.** Frank Sinatra, Laurence Harvey, Angela Lansbury, Janet Leigh, James Gregory, Leslie Parrish, John McGiver, Henry Silva, Khigh (Kaie Deei) Deigh, James Edwards, Doug(las) Henderson, Albert Paulsen, Barry Kelley, Lloyd Corrigan, Whit Bissell, Joe Adams, Madame Spivy, Mimi Dillard, John Lawrence, Tom Lowell; *D:* John Frankenheimer; *W:* John Frankenheimer, George Axelrod; *C:* Lionel Lindon; *M:* David Amram. AFI '98: Top 100; Golden Globes '63: Support. Actress (Lansbury); Natl. Bd. of Review '62: Support. Actress (Lansbury), Natl. Film Reg. '94.

The Mandarin Mystery 1937 In the process of trying to retrieve a stolen Mandarin stamp, detective Ellery Queen uncovers a counterfeiting ring. Some fine performances, but a muddled script creates a mystery as to whether or not the action is played for laughs. **65m/B VHS.** Eddie Quillan, Charlotte Henry, Rita La Roy, Wade Boteler, Franklin Pangborn, George Irving, Kay Hughes, William "Billy" Newell; *D:* Ralph Staub.

Mandela 1987 A gripping, powerful drama about human rights and dignity, tracing the real-life trials of Nelson and Winnie Mandela. The story focuses on the couple's early opposition to South African apartheid, as well as the events leading up to Nelson's life-imprisonment sentencing in 1964. Excellent, restrained performances from Glover and Woodard. **135m/C VHS, DVD.** Danny Glover, Alfre Woodard, John Matshikiza, Warren Clarke, Allan Corduner, Julian Glover; *D:* Philip Saville. **CABLE**

Mandela and de Klerk 1997 (PG) Docudrama about the two men who changed South Africa. White Afrikaaner president F.W. de Klerk (Caine) declared an end to apartheid in 1992 and two years later was succeeded as the country's president by Nelson Mandela (Poitier), a black activist imprisioned on treason charges for 27 years before his release. Both men shared the Nobel Peace Prize for their efforts to unite South Africa. **114m/C VHS.** Sidney Poitier, Michael Caine, Tina Lifford, Ian Roberts, Gerry Maritz, Jerry Mofokeng; *D:* Joseph Sargent; *W:* Richard Wesley; *C:* Tobias Schliessler; *M:* Cedric Gradus-Samson. **CABLE**

Mandinga 1977 A plantation owner develops an obsession for one of his female slaves. Made to cash in on the already exploitive "Mandingo"; two wrongs don't make a right. **100m/C VHS.** Anthony Gismond; *D:* Mario Pinzauti.

Mandingo 1975 (R) Overheated Southern-fried tale of slavery in the Deep South, circa 1840, dealing with the tangled loves and hates of a family and their slaves. Heavyweight boxer Norton made his screen debut in the title role as the slave who makes his master money with his boxing prowess. King is the wastrel son who makes Norton's wife, another slave, his mistress. Followed by 1975's "Drum." Based on the novel by Kyle Onstott. **127m/C VHS.** James Mason, Susan George, Perry King, Richard Ward, Ken Norton, Ben Masters, Brenda Sykes, Paul Benedict, Ji-Tu Cumbuka; *D:* Richard Fleischer; *W:* Richard H. Kline, Norman Wexler; *M:* Maurice Jarre.

Mandragora 1997 Marek (Caslavka) is a 16-year-old small town boy who takes off for the bright lights of post-Communist Prague. He's soon selling his body on the streets and makes friends with fellow hustler, David (Svec), but the duo sink into the usual morass of drugs and self-destruction. Czech with subtitles. **133m/C VHS, DVD, Wide.** *CZ* Miroslav Caslavka, David Svec, Miroslav Breu, Pavel Skripaz; *D:* Wiktor Grodecki; *W:* Wiktor Grodecki, David Svec; *C:* Vladimir Holomek; *M:* Wolfgang Hammerschmid.

Mandroid 1993 (R) Two scientists design a high-tech robot, Mandroid, to handle a powerful new element they've discovered. Dr. Zimmer and daughter Zanna want to use their creation to help mankind while mad scientist Dr. Drago wants the power Mandroid can give him. When a laboratory accident leaves Drago horribly disfigured it also gives him the chance to steal Mandroid and put his evil plan into action. Filmed on location in Romania. **81m/C VHS.** Brian Cousins, Jane Caldwell, Michael DellaFemina, Curt Lowens, Patrick Ersgard, Robert Symonds; *D:* Joakim (Jack) Ersgard; *W:* Jackson Barr, Earl Kenton.

Mandy *Crash of Silence* 1953 Poignant drama of a deaf child and the family who must come to terms with her deafness. Well-developed plot and well performed; an intelligent treatment in all. **93m/B VHS.** *GB* Phyllis Calvert, Jack Hawkins, Mandy Miller; *D:* Alexander MacKendrick.

Manfish 1956 Two men venture out in a boat, the Manfish, to hunt for sunken treasure in the Caribbean. Only one survives the trip, as his greed destroys the other. The scenes off the Jamaican coast are lovely, but the story fails to take hold. Though there is a star aboard in Chaney, you'll look astern and bow out with a sinking feeling. Derived from two Edgar Allan Poe stories, "The Gold Bug" and "The Tell-Tale Heart." **76m/C VHS.** John Bromfield, Lon Chaney Jr., Victor Jory, Barbara Nichols; *D:* W. Lee Wilder.

The Mangler 1994 (R) Laundry machine munches workers in a small-town Maine industrial plant. Bossman Englund's only concern (besides huge workman's comp premiums) is keeping the machine well-fed. Weak attempt at horror by veteran Tobe "If it's worth doing, it's worth overdoing" Hooper ("The Texas Chainsaw Massacre") that tries to capitalize on the popularity of story originator Stephen King. Offers little in plot or scare, but fans of the gore genre will enjoy the overuse of chunky-style blood and guts spewed from the monstrous steam ironer and folder that is apparently possessed by the devil. About 45 minutes too long for anybody to suspend their disbelief. **106m/C VHS.** Robert Englund, Ted Levine, Daniel Matmor, Vanessa Pike, Demetre Phillips, Lisa Morris, Ashley Hayden, Vera Blacker; ***D:*** Tobe Hooper; ***W:*** Tobe Hooper, Peter Welbeck, Stephen Brooks; ***C:*** Amnon Salomon; ***M:*** Barrington Pheloung.

The Mango Tree ½ **1977** A young man comes of age in a small Australian town during the 1920s. Everything is well done, if not dramatic or fascinating. **93m/C VHS.** *AU* Geraldine Fitzgerald, Robert Helpmann, Diane Craig, Gerald Kennedy, Christopher Pate; ***D:*** Kevin James Dobson.

Manhandled ½ **1924** Department store clerk Swanson is the hit of an artist's party with her impersonations and is asked by Morgan to impersonate a Russian countess to lend some class to his store. She winds up with lots of suitors. **67m/B VHS.** Gloria Swanson, Frank Morgan, Tom Moore, Lilyan Tashman, Ian Keith, Arthur Houseman; ***D:*** Allan Dwan.

The Manhandlers **1973 (R)** After the uncle of a young woman is killed by the mob, she goes after them for revenge. For your entertainment pleasure, best stick with the soup commercial of the same name. **87m/C VHS.** Cara Burgess, Judy Brown, Vince Cannon, Rosalind Miles; ***D:*** Lee Madden.

Manhattan **1979 (R)** Successful TV writer Isaac Davis (Allen) yearns to be a serious writer. He struggles through a series of ill-fated romances, including one with high school senior Tracy (Hemingway) and another with Mary (Keaton), who's also having an on-again, off-again affair with Yale (Murphy), Isaac's best friend. Streep does very well with her role of Jill, Isaac's ex-wife who's come out as a lesbian and written a withering (and successful) account of their marriage. Scathingly serious and comic view of modern relationships in urban America and of the modern intellectual neuroses. Shot in black-and-white to capture the mood of Manhattan and mated with an excellent Gershwin soundtrack. **96m/B VHS, DVD, Wide.** Woody Allen, Diane Keaton, Meryl Streep, Mariel Hemingway, Michael Murphy, Wallace Shawn, Anne Byrne, Tisa Farrow, Mark Linn-Baker, David Rasche, Karen Allen; ***D:*** Woody Allen; ***W:*** Woody Allen, Marshall Brickman; ***C:*** Gordon Willis; ***M:*** George Gershwin. British Acad. '79: Film, Screenplay; Cesar '80: Foreign Film; L.A. Film Critics '79: Support. Actress (Streep), Natl. Film Reg. '01;; N.Y. Film Critics '79: Director (Allen), Support. Actress (Streep); Natl. Soc. Film Critics '79: Director (Allen), Support. Actress (Streep).

Manhattan Baby **1982** Unscary horror film about an archaeologist who digs up a relic that draws evil into the world and infects an American girl with powers that lead to many deaths. Advice to you that might have saved the archaeologist: don't dig this. **90m/C VHS, DVD, Wide.** *IT* Christopher Connelly, Martha Taylor, Brigitta Boccoli, Giovanni Frezza, Lucio Fulci; ***D:*** Lucio Fulci; ***W:*** Elisa Briganti, Dardano Sacchetti; ***C:*** Guglielmo Mancori; ***M:*** Fabio Frizzi.

Manhattan Melodrama ½ **1934** Powell and Gable are best friends from childhood, growing up together in an orphanage. Their adult lives take different paths, however, as Powell becomes a respected prosecuting attorney while Gable becomes a notorious gambler/racketeer. Lovely Loy is Gable's girl who comes between the two. Eventually, Powell must prosecute his life-long friend for murder in order to win the governorship. One of Gable's toughest roles; Powell's character, however, is a bit unbelievable as his ethics seem to extend beyond love and friendship. This is the first film to team Powell and Loy, who would go on to make 13 more films together, including the "Thin Man" series. **93m/B VHS.** Clark Gable, William Powell, Myrna Loy, Leo Carrillo, Nat Pendleton, George Sidney, Isabel Jewell, Muriel Evans, Claudelle Kaye, Frank Conroy, Jimmy Butler, Mickey Rooney, Edward Van Sloan; ***D:*** Woodbridge S. Van Dyke; ***C:*** James Wong Howe. Oscars '34: Story.

Manhattan Merenque! ½ *Rice, Beans and Ketchup* **1995 (R)** Young mambo dancer Miguel (Perez) has been unable to get a visa to come to the U.S. from the Dominican Republic so he stows away and eventually makes it to New York with new friend Carmello (Leonardi), who's searching for an old girlfriend and their son. While Miguel tries for dance work on Broadway, he makes a friend in dance instructor Susan (Reed) and locates long-lost girlfriend Rosita (Cavazos). Too bad Carmello's luck isn't as good. Sweetly cornball and romantic. **100m/C VHS, DVD.** George Perez, Lumi Cavazos, Marco Leonardi, Alyson Reed; ***D:*** Joseph B. Vasquez; ***W:*** Joseph B. Vasquez, Rue Kent Wildman; ***C:*** David Castillo; ***M:*** Lalo Schifrin.

Manhattan Merry-Go-Round **1937** One of the movies where a corrupt boss—in this case a record producer—threatens a bunch of good people as a pretense for a plot when the movie simply serves as a showcase for stars. Features many singing stars of the '30s ("where have you gone Cab Calloway?") plus Joltin' Joe, who ended up having a hit-streak in another genre. ♫Mama I Wanna Make Rhythm; Manhattan Merry-Go-Round; Heaven?; I Owe You; It's Round Up Time in Reno. **89m/B VHS.** Cab Calloway, Louis Prima, Ted Lewis, Ann Dvorak, Phil Regan, Kay Thompson, Gene Autry, Joe DiMaggio; ***D:*** Charles Reisner.

Manhattan Murder Mystery **1993 (PG)** Keaton and Allen team up again as two New Yorkers who get involved in a mystery when their neighbor dies under strange circumstances. Light, entertaining comedy steers clear of some of Allen's heavier themes and should keep audiences laughing till the end. Allen, writing with Brickman for the first time since "Annie Hall" and "Manhattan," makes viewers fall in love with the magic of NYC all over again. **105m/C VHS, DVD, 8mm, Wide.** Woody Allen, Diane Keaton, Anjelica Huston, Alan Alda, Jerry Adler, Ron Rifkin, Joy Behar, Lynn Cohen, Melanie Norris; ***D:*** Woody Allen; ***W:*** Woody Allen, Marshall Brickman; ***C:*** Carlo Di Palma.

The Manhattan Project *Manhattan Project: The Deadly Game* **1986 (PG-13)** An exceptionally bright teenager decides to build a nuclear bomb for his project at the New York City science fair. He's out to prove how dangerously easy it is to build big bombs. When he steals plutonium from a local government installation, the feds attempt to nab the precocious youngster. Light moral overtones abound. Director Brickman co-wrote similarly titled "Manhattan." **112m/C VHS, DVD, Wide.** John Lithgow, Christopher Collet, Cynthia Nixon, Jill Eikenberry, John Mahoney, Sully Boyer, Richard Council, Robert Schenkkan, Paul Austin; ***D:*** Marshall Brickman; ***W:*** Marshall Brickman, Thomas Baum; ***C:*** Billy Williams.

Manhunt *The Italian Connection; La Mala Ordina* **1973 (R)** A man marked for execution by the mob launches his own assault on the organization's headquarters. Action and Italian food, but not much else. Dubbed. **93m/C VHS.** *IT* Henry Silva, Mario Adorf, Woody Strode, Luciana Paluzzi; ***D:*** Fernando Di Leo. **TV**

The Manhunt **1986** A framed cowhand escapes from prison to prove his innocence. De Angelis used the pseudonym Larry Ludman. **89m/C VHS.** Ernest Borgnine, Bo Svenson, John Ethan Wayne; ***D:*** Fabrizio de Angelis. **TV**

Manhunt ½ **1995 (R)** Fugitive Jim Trudell (Wilson) rescues a woman from a gang of thugs and winds up in a net of police corruption. Now he needs to survive long enough to figure out what's going on. **95m/C VHS.** Don "The Dragon" Wilson, Jillian McWhirter, Jonathan Penner; ***D:*** Jonathan Winfrey.

Manhunt for Claude Dallas **1986** Mountain man uses game wardens for firing practice, ticks off local sheriff Torn, is tossed behind bars, checks out ahead of schedule and becomes a legend in his own time. Mediocre made-for-TV macho man melodrama. From the novel "Outlaw" by Jeff Long. **93m/C VHS.** Matt Salinger, Rip Torn, Claude Akins, Pat Hingle, Lois Nettleton, Beau Starr, Frederick Coffin; ***D:*** Jerry London; ***W:*** John Gay; ***M:*** Steve Dorff.

Manhunt in the African Jungle **1954** An American undercover agent battles Nazi forces in Africa. A serial in 15 episodes. **240m/B VHS.** Rod Cameron, Joan Marsh, Duncan Renaldo.

Manhunt of Mystery Island *Captain Mephisto and the Transformation Machine* **1945** Serial about the super-powered Captain Mephisto. **100m/C VHS.** Linda Stirling, Roy Barcroft, Richard Bailey, Kenne Duncan; ***D:*** Spencer Gordon Bennet.

Manhunter **1974** A WWI Marine returns home from China in 1933 to track down a bunch of gangsters headed by his sister. **78m/C VHS.** Ken Howard, Stefanie Powers, Gary Lockwood, Tim O'Connor, L.Q. (Justus E. McQueen) Jones; ***D:*** Walter Grauman. **TV**

Manhunter ½ **1983** A mercenary sets out to disengage organized crime from high-level politics. Produced by Owensby. **92m/C VHS.** Earl Owensby, Johnny Popwell, Doug Hale, Elizabeth Upton; ***D:*** Earl Owensby.

Manhunter *Red Dragon* **1986 (R)** Will Graham (Petersen) was the FBI's top guy in their Behavioral Science Unit who retired after a harrowing pursuit of a serial killer. Now, he's called back to duty to find a psychotic family killer by colleague Jack (Farina). Will's technique: to match the thought processes of serial killers and thus anticipate their moves. Intense thriller, based on the Thomas Harris novel "Red Dragon." Harris also wrote "The Silence of the Lambs," whose most notorious character Hannibal ("The Cannibal") Lecter, appears in this movie as well (spelled Lektor and played by Cox). Graham visits the prisoner to get fresh insights into his new case and Lektor plays his usual nasty mind games. Director Mann applies the slick techniques he introduced in the popular TV series "Miami Vice," creating a quiet, moody intensity broken by sudden onslaughts of violence. **100m/C VHS, DVD, Wide.** William L. Petersen, Kim Greist, Joan Allen, Brian Cox, Dennis Farina, Stephen Lang, Tom Noonan, Benjamin Hendrickson, David Seaman; ***D:*** Michael Mann; ***W:*** Michael Mann; ***C:*** Dante Spinotti; ***M:*** Michel Rubini.

Maniac woof! **1934** A scientist has designs on raising the dead and searches for victims on which to experiment. Bizarre "adults only" exploitation feature was considered very risque for its time, and includes eaten eyeballs, a cat fight with syringes, and a rapist who thinks he's an orangutan. A must for genre aficionados. **67m/B VHS, DVD.** Bill Woods, Horace Carpenter, Ted Edwards, Thea Ramsey, Jennie Dark, Marcel Andre, Celia McGann; ***D:*** Dwain Esper; ***W:*** Hildegarde Stadie; ***C:*** William C. Thompson.

Maniac **1963** An American artist living in France becomes involved with the daughter of a cafe owner, not suspecting that murder will follow. Seems that her old man is locked up in an insane asylum for torching the daughter's rapist several years earlier. **86m/B VHS.** *GB* Kerwin Mathews, Nadia Gray, Donald Houston, Liliane Brousse; ***D:*** Michael Carreras; ***W:*** Jimmy Sangster; ***C:*** Wilkie Cooper; ***M:*** Stanley Black.

Maniac *Ransom; Assault on Paradise; The Town That Cried Terror* **1977 (PG)** A New York cop hunts down an arrow-shooting and obviously crazed Vietnam veteran who endeavors to hold an entire Arizona town for ransom. Which is entirely appropriate, since the cast is in it only for the money. **87m/C VHS.** Bill Allen, Oliver Reed, Deborah Raffin, Stuart Whitman, Jim Mitchum, Edward Brett, John Ireland, Paul Koslo; ***D:*** Richard Compton.

Maniac woof! **1980** A psycho murderer slaughters and scalps his victims, adding the "trophies" to his collection. Carries a self-imposed equivalent "X" rating due to its highly graphic gore quotient. For extremely strong stomachs only. **91m/C VHS, DVD, Wide.** Joe Spinell, Caroline Munro, Gail Lawrence, Kelly Piper, Tom Savini, Rita Montone, Hyla Marrow, William Lustig, Sharon Mitchell; ***D:*** William Lustig; ***W:*** C.A. Rosenberg, Joe Spinell; ***C:*** Robert Lindsay; ***M:*** Jay Chattaway.

Maniac Cop **1988 (R)** In New York city, a cop goes beyond the realm of sanity and turns vigilante. Low-budget slasher/thriller that too often sags. **92m/C VHS, DVD.** Tom Atkins, Bruce Campbell, Laurene Landon, Richard Roundtree, William Smith, Robert Z'Dar, Sheree North, Sam Raimi; ***D:*** William Lustig; ***W:*** Larry Cohen; ***C:*** Vincent Rabe, James (Momel) Lemmo; ***M:*** Jay Chattaway.

Maniac Cop 2 **1990 (R)** Everyone thought he was dead but you can't keep a bad guy down so this grossly disfigured policeman forms a one-man vigilante squad, seeking revenge (why never matters—just the body count). Blood and guts fly as any plot shortcomings are cleverly disguised by an array of violent video deaths. Sequel to "Maniac Cop." **90m/C VHS, Wide.** Robert Davi, Claudia Christian, Michael Lerner, Bruce Campbell, Laurene Landon, Robert Z'Dar, Clarence Williams III, Leo Rossi, James Dixon; ***D:*** William Lustig; ***W:*** Larry Cohen; ***C:*** James (Momel) Lemmo.

Maniac Cop 3: Badge of Silence **1993 (R)** The grossly disfigured policeman returns yet again to exact gory vengeance as the good guys try to get rid of him once and for all. **85m/C VHS.** Bobby DiCicco, Robert Z'Dar, Robert Davi, Gretchen Becker, Paul Gleason, Doug Savant, Caitlin Dulany, Jackie Earle Haley, Robert Forster; ***D:*** William Lustig, Joel Soisson; ***W:*** Larry Cohen; ***M:*** Jerry Goldsmith.

Maniac Nurses Find Ecstasy woof! **1994** Even by Troma standards, this one's scraping the bottom of the barrel. The nearly non-existent plot is an excuse to present several young women dressed in nurse uniforms and underwear while holding various weapons. The sense of energy that's needed for good exploitation is lacking. **80m/C VHS, DVD.** Susanna Makay, Hajni Brown, Nicole A. Gyony, Csilia Farago; ***D:*** Harry M. (Leon P. Howard) Love; ***W:*** Harry M. (Leon P. Howard) Love.

Maniac Warriors **1992** A nuclear apocalypse has caused some strange changes in the population—and not for the better. Blood-crazed mutants attack the heavily armed inhabitants of New State Idaho and there's lots of mayhem in store. **91m/C VHS.** Tom Schioler, John Wood, Melanie Kilgour.

The Manions of America ½ **1981** The long and sometimes interesting rags-to-riches tale of Rory O'Manion, a feisty Irish patriot who leaves his native land during the potato famine of 1845 to settle in America. Originally a TV miniseries. **290m/C VHS.** Pierce Brosnan, Kate Mulgrew, Linda Purl, David Soul, Kathleen Beller, Simon MacCorkindale; ***D:*** Joseph Sargent, Charles S. Dubin. **TV**

Manipulator **1971 (R)** A deranged ex-movie makeup man (Rooney, playing to type) kidnaps a young actress and holds her prisoner in a deserted Hollywood sound stage. **91m/C VHS.** Mickey Rooney, Luana Anders, Keenan Wynn; ***D:*** Yabo Yablonsky.

The Manitou **1978 (PG)** A San Francisco woman suffers from a rapidly growing neck tumor which eventually grows into a 400-year-old Indian witch doctor. (I hate when that happens.) Redeemed only by good special effects, especially those that kept Curtis, Strasberg, and Meredith from laughing. **104m/C VHS.** Susan Strasberg, Tony Curtis, Stella Stevens, Ann Sothern, Burgess Meredith, Michael Ansara, Jon Cedar, Paul Mantee, Lurene Tuttle, Jeanette Nolan; ***D:*** William Girdler; ***W:*** William Girdler, Tom Pope, Jon Cedar; ***C:*** Michael Hugo; ***M:*** Lalo Schifrin.

Mankillers **1987** A group of tough female convicts are enlisted to hunt down and rub out a psycho drug dealer, all the while displaying their feminine charms. **90m/C VHS.** Edd Byrnes, Gail Fisher, Edy Williams, Lynda Aldon, William Zipp, Christopher Lunde, Susanne Tegman, Marilyn Stafford, Paul Bruno, Byron Clark; ***D:*** David A. Prior.

Mannequin ½ **1937** Tracy and Crawford star in this romantic story of a poor girl who finds temporary happiness by marrying a wealthy man after ditching her con-artist husband. Somewhat predictable, the movie reads like a "People" magazine story on The Donald and Ivana. Tracy and Crawford keep the story afloat (in their only film together), with an able assist from Curtis. **95m/B VHS.** Joan Crawford, Spencer Tracy, Alan Curtis, Ralph Morgan, Leo Gorcey, Elisabeth Risdon, Paul Fix; ***D:*** Frank Borzage; ***W:*** Lawrence Hazard; ***C:*** George J. Folsey.

Mannequin 🦴🦴 **1987 (PG)** A young artist creates a store window display using various mannequins, one of which contains the spirit of an ancient Egyptian woman. She comes to life when he is around, and naturally none of his co-workers believe him. Very light comedy, featuring two pretty stars and music by Jefferson Starship. **90m/C VHS, DVD, Wide.** Andrew McCarthy, Kim Cattrall, Estelle Getty, James Spader, Meshach Taylor, Carole (Raphaelle) Davis, G.W. Bailey; ***D:*** Michael Gottlieb; ***W:*** Ed Rugoff; ***C:*** Tim Suhrstedt; ***M:*** Sylvester Levay.

Mannequin 2: On the Move woof! **1991 (PG)** Less of a sequel, more of a lame rehash proving that the first "Mannequin" could have been even dumber. At this rate part three will be off the scale. Now it's a lovesick Teutonic princess frozen for 1,000 years who revives in a department store. Taylor reprises his grotesque gay role. **95m/C VHS.** Kristy Swanson, William Ragsdale, Meshach Taylor, Terry Kiser, Stuart Pankin; ***D:*** Stewart Raffill; ***W:*** Ed Rugoff.

Manny & Lo 🦴🦴🦴 **1996 (R)** Krueger's directorial debut features fine performances in a story about three misfits forming a unique family bond. Surly 16-year-old Lo (Palladino) and her serious 11-year-old sister Manny (Johansson) have run away from their foster homes and hit the road together. Living hand-to-mouth, it's Manny who persuades her irresponsible pregnant sister that they need a home and they settle into an isolated cabin. When the sisters visit a baby store, eccentric clerk Elaine (Place) seems such a font of wisdom that the girls kidnap her and hold her as a hostage to help with the pregnancy. But Elaine's not trying to escape and has an agenda of her own. **90m/C VHS.** Mary Kay Place, Scarlett Johansson, Aleksa Palladino, Paul Guilfoyle, Glenn Fitzgerald, Cameron Boyd, Novella Nelson, Angie Phillips; ***D:*** Lisa Krueger; ***W:*** Lisa Krueger; ***C:*** Tom Krueger; ***M:*** John Lurie.

Manny's Orphans 🦴 *Here Come the Tigers* **1978 (PG)** An out-of-work teacher takes on a lovable home for orphaned boys. Dull remake of "Bad News Bears." **92m/C VHS.** Richard Lincoln, Malachy McCourt, Sel Skolnick; ***D:*** Sean S. Cunningham.

Manon 🦴🦴 **1950** Tragic tale of a French woman condemned for her affair with a Resistance fighter. They flee to Paris, where her brother forces her into prostitution. Based on the novel "Manon Lescaut" by Abbe Antoine-Francois Prevost. In French with English subtitles. **91m/B VHS.** Cecile Aubry, Michel Auclair, Serge Reggiani, Henri Vilbert, Daniel Ivernel; ***D:*** Henri-Georges Clouzot.

Manon of the Spring 🦴🦴🦴½ *Manon des Sources; Jean de Florette 2* **1987 (PG)** In this excellent sequel to "Jean de Florette," the adult daughter of the dead hunchback, Jean, discovers who blocked up the spring on her father's land. She plots her revenge, which proves greater than she could ever imagine. Montand is astonishing. Based on a Marcel Pagnol novel. In French with English subtitles. **113m/C VHS, DVD, Wide.** *FR* Yves Montand, Daniel Auteuil, Emmanuelle Beart, Hippolyte Girardot, Margarita Lozano, Elisabeth Depardieu, Yvonne Gamy, Armand Meffre, Gabriel Bacquier; ***D:*** Claude Berri; ***W:*** Claude Berri, Gerard Brach; ***C:*** Bruno Nuytten; ***M:*** Jean-Claude Petit, Roger Legrand.

Manos, the Hands of Fate woof! **1966** Horrible acting and laughable special effects elevate this story of a family ensnared by a satanic cult a notch above your average bad horror film. Highlights include a Satan-like character who can't stop laughing; the dreaded "hounds of hell" (or are those mangy dogs with big ears glued on?); and Torgo the monstrous henchman, who you know is evil because he has giant kneecaps (a sure sign of the devil's work). Notable as the one of the most often requested movies on Comedy Central's satiric "Mystery Science Theatre 3000," this one is good for a laugh. **74m/C VHS, DVD.** Tom Nayman, Diane Mahree, Hal P. Warren, John Reynolds; ***D:*** Hal P. Warren; ***W:*** Hal P. Warren.

Man's Best Friend 🦴½ **1993 (R)** A guard dog is the object of a genetic experiment that has given him the agressiveness of other creatures, including a cobra and a leopard. Since Max is an enormous Tibetan mastiff this means big trouble for everyone but the reporter (Sheedy) who rescued him—and even she better watch out. **87m/C VHS.** Ally Sheedy, Lance Henriksen, Frederic Lehne, Robert Costanzo, John Cassisi, J.D. Daniels; ***D:*** John Lafia; ***W:*** John Lafia; ***M:*** Joel Goldsmith.

Man's Country 🦴🦴 **1938** A rip-roarin' western saga filled with the usual action and danger, as ranger Randall leads the fight against a band of nasties headed by Long, in a dual role as twin brothers. **55m/B VHS.** Addison "Jack" Randall, Ralph Peters, Marjorie Reynolds, Walter Long; ***D:*** Robert F. "Bob" Hill.

Man's Favorite Sport? 🦴🦴½ **1963** A slapstick comedy about a renowned fishing expert author who actually hates fishing, but is forced to compete in a major tournament by a romantically inclined publicity agent. Very funny in spots. **121m/C VHS.** Rock Hudson, Paula Prentiss, Charlene Holt, Maria Perschy, John McGiver; ***D:*** Howard Hawks; ***M:*** Henry Mancini.

Man's Land 🦴½ **1932** A ranch needs savin', and Hoot's the guy to do it in this formulaic Gibson epic. **65m/B VHS.** Hoot Gibson, Marion Shilling, Skeeter Bill Robbins, Alan Bridge; ***D:*** Phil Rosen.

Mansfield Park 🦴🦴½ **1985** Fanny is an impoverished young woman, snubbed by society, who earns the respect and love of her cousin in a BBC miniseries adaptation of the Jane Austen classic set in 19th-century England. **261m/C VHS.** *GB* Sylvestria Le Touzel, Bernard Hepton, Anna Massey, Donald Pleasence; ***D:*** David Giles. **TV**

Mansfield Park 🦴🦴½ **1999 (PG-13)** Fanny Price (O'Connor) is a poor relation, who has grown up with her wealthy cousins at their elegant home, Mansfield Park. While some of the Bertrams have been civil, others have treated Fanny as little better than a servant. However, cousin Edmund (Miller) has been very kind indeed and Fanny develops very warm feelings towards him. Then the entire family is thrown into chaos by the arrival of Henry Crawford (Nivola) and his sister Mary (Davidtz) and scandal seems about to break. Jane Austen's 3rd novel has been given a feminist slant and some belabored relevancy by Rozema. **110m/C VHS, DVD, Wide.** Frances O'Connor, Jonny Lee Miller, Alessandro Nivola, Embeth Davidtz, Harold Pinter, Lindsay Duncan, Sheila Gish, Justine Waddell, Victoria Hamilton, James Purefoy, Hugh Bonneville; ***D:*** Patricia Rozema; ***W:*** Patricia Rozema; ***C:*** Michael Coulter; ***M:*** Lesley Barber.

The Manster 🦴 *The Manster—Half Man, Half Monster; The Split; The Two-Headed Monster* **1959** Another masterpiece from the director who brought us "Monster from Green Hell." Womanizing, whiskey swilling American journalist receives mysterious injection from crazed scientist and sprouts unsightly hair and extra head. Although shot in the land of the rising sun, lips move in sync with dialogue. **72m/B VHS.** *JP* Peter Dyneley, Jane Hylton, Satoshi Nakamura, Terri Zimmern, Tetsu Nakamura, Jerry Ito, Toyoko Takechi; ***D:*** Kenneth Crane, George Breakston; ***W:*** William J. Sheldon; ***C:*** David Mason; ***M:*** Hirooki Ogawa.

Mantis in Lace 🦴½ *Lila* **1968 (R)** A go-go dancer slaughters men while tripping on LSD. Watch it for the "hep" dialogue. **68m/C VHS, DVD.** Susan Stewart, Steve Vincent, M.K. Evans, Vic Lance, Pat (Barringer) Barrington, Janu Wine, Stuart Lancaster, John Carrol, Judith Crane, Cheryl Trepton; ***D:*** William Rotsler; ***W:*** Sanford White; ***C:*** Laszlo Kovacs; ***M:*** Frank A. Coe.

Mantrap 🦴🦴½ **1926** Early silent success by Fleming, who later directed "Gone with the Wind" and "The Wizard of Oz." Fabled flapper Bow tempts a lawyer on retreat in the woods. **66m/B VHS.** Clara Bow, Ernest Torrence, Percy Marmont, Eugene Pallette, Tom Kennedy; ***D:*** Victor Fleming.

The Manxman 🦴🦴½ **1929** Hitchcock's last silent film, a romantic melodrama about ambition and infidelity on the Isle of Man. **129m/B VHS, DVD.** *GB* Carl Brisson, Anny Ondra, Malcolm Keen, Randle Ayrton; ***D:*** Alfred Hitchcock; ***W:*** Hall Caine, Eliot Stannard; ***C:*** Jack Cox.

The Many Adventures of Winnie the Pooh **1977 (G)** Disney's 22nd animated feature offers A.A. Milne's beloved characters and their adventures in the Hundred Acre Wood. Includes a behind-the-scenes featurette with the original creators, animators, and voices. **83m/C VHS, DVD.**

Many Faces of Sherlock Holmes **1986** A documentary look at the various incarnations of the famous sleuth from A. Conan Doyle's stories to various film portrayals. **58m/C VHS.** Christopher Plummer, Basil Rathbone, Christopher Lee.

Map of the Human Heart 🦴🦴 **1993 (R)** Thirty-year saga told in flashback. Young Eskimo Avik (Lee) and his Metis love interest Albertine (Parillaud) struggle with racism in a white world. They meet and become friends as children and years later meet again in Dresden during WWII, but now Albertine is married to Avik's once close friend, denying her heritage and living in the white world that he has been fighting for so long. Mediocre movie with extraordinary Arctic scenery. Cusack has a small role as a mapmaker. **109m/C VHS.** Jason Scott Lee, Anne Parillaud, Patrick Bergin, Robert Joamie, Annie Galipeau, John Cusack, Jeanne Moreau; ***D:*** Vincent Ward; ***W:*** Vincent Ward, Louis Nowra.

A Map of the World 🦴🦴 **1999 (R)** Excellent cast; tough story, based on the novel by Jane Hamilton. Flinty would-be farm wife/mom Alice Goodwin (Weaver) hasn't endeared herself to her Wisconsin community. But she's a good deal more vulnerable than anyone suspects as Alice finds her life falling apart. Her neighbor Theresa's (Moore) daughter accidentally drowns while in Alice's care and soon after Alice is shockingly accused of sexual abuse in her role as school nurse, which lands her jail. Uneven script is part family drama, part prison drama, part courtroom drama, part melodrama, and all the drama doesn't necessarily make for a coherent movie. **125m/C VHS, DVD, Wide.** Sigourney Weaver, David Strathairn, Julianne Moore, Ron Lea, Arliss Howard, Chloe Sevigny, Louise Fletcher; ***D:*** Scott Elliott; ***W:*** Peter Hedges, Polly Platt; ***C:*** Seamus McGarvey; ***M:*** Pat Metheny. Natl. Bd. of Review '99: Support. Actress (Moore).

Mapp & Lucia 🦴🦴½ **1985** British TV adaptation of H.E. Benson's stories of provincial English society in the fictional village of Tilling-on-Sea in the 1920s. Miss Mapp (Scales) holds local court but finds a potential usurper when elegant widow Lucia (McEwan) comes to town. Battle lines are formed between the two women in this sharp-tongued satire. On five cassettes; followed by a second series of five episodes. **270m/C VHS.** *GB* Prunella Scales, Geraldine McEwan, Nigel Hawthorne.

Mararia 🦴🦴 **1998** Romantic triangle set amidst the heat and beauty of 1940s island life on Lanzarote in the Canary Islands. The newly arrived Dr. Fermin (Gomez) falls under the spell of enticing local beauty Mararia (Toledo), who returns his affections. At least until British surveyor Bertrand (Glen) comes to the island and she changes her mind. This might be a woman's perogative but in Mararia's case, it leads to tragedy for all. Spanish with subtitles. **109m/C VHS, DVD, Wide.** *SP* Goya Toledo, Carmelo Gomez, Iain Glen, Mirta Ibarra; ***D:*** Antonio J. Betancor; ***W:*** Antonio J. Betancor, Carlos Alvarez; ***C:*** Juan Ruiz-Anchia; ***M:*** Pedro Guerra.

Marathon 🦴🦴 **1980** When a middle-aged jogger's ego gets a boost through the attention of a beautiful young woman, he takes up marathon running. Light comedy. **100m/C VHS.** Bob Newhart, Leigh Taylor-Young, Herb Edelman, Dick Gautier, Anita Gillette, John Hillerman; ***D:*** Jackie Cooper. **TV**

Marathon Man 🦴🦴🦴 **1976 (R)** Nightmarish chase-thriller in which a graduate student becomes entangled in a plot involving a murderous Nazi fugitive. As student Hoffman is preparing for the Olympic marathon, he is reunited with his secret-agent brother, setting the intricate plot in motion. Courtesy of his brother, Hoffman becomes involved with Olivier, an old crazed Nazi seeking jewels taken from concentration camp victims. Non-stop action throughout, including a torture scene sure to set your teeth on edge. Goldman adapted the screenplay from his novel. **125m/C VHS.** Dustin Hoffman, Laurence Olivier, Marthe Keller, Roy Scheider, William Devane, Fritz Weaver; ***D:*** John Schlesinger; ***W:*** William Goldman; ***C:*** Conrad L. Hall. Golden Globes '77: Support. Actor (Olivier).

Marauder 🦴🦴 **1965** The prince of Venice leads a sea-faring onslaught against ransacking pirates and enemy fleets. **90m/C VHS.** *IT* Gordon Scott, Gianna Maria Canale, Franca Bettoya; ***D:*** Luigi Capuano.

Marbella 🦴½ **1985** A luxury resort in Spain is the setting for a big caper heist of $3 million from a monarchical tycoon. **96m/C VHS.** Rod Taylor, Britt Ekland; ***D:*** Miguel Hermoso.

March of the Wooden Soldiers 🦴🦴🦴 *Babes in Toyland* **1934** The classic Mother Goose tale about the secret life of Christmas toys, with Laurel and Hardy as Santa's helpers who must save Toyland from the wicked Barnaby. A Yuletide "must see." Also available in a colorized version. **73m/B VHS, DVD.** Stan Laurel, Oliver Hardy, Charlotte Henry, Henry (Kleinbach) Brandon, Felix Knight, Jean Darling, Johnny Downs, Marie Wilson; ***D:*** Charles R. Rogers, Gus Meins; ***W:*** Frank Butler, Nick Grinde; ***C:*** Art Lloyd, Francis Corby.

March or Die 🦴🦴½ **1977 (PG)** Great potential, unrealized. An American joins the French Foreign Legion during WWI after his dismissal from West Point. Following the brutality of training, he is assigned to guard an archeological expedition in Morocco, where he pulls together a rag-tag outfit for the mission. Hackman proves once again the wide range of his acting abilities, surmounting the cliched and fairly sadistic plot. Shot on location in the Sahara Desert. **104m/C VHS.** *GB* Gene Hackman, Terence Hill, Max von Sydow, Catherine Deneuve, Ian Holm; ***D:*** Dick Richards; ***W:*** David Zelag Goodman; ***M:*** Maurice Jarre.

Marciano 🦴🦴 **1979** Average fight movie chronicling the great boxer's life. **97m/C VHS.** Tony LoBianco, Vincent Gardenia; ***D:*** Bernard L. Kowalski; ***M:*** Ernest Gold. **TV**

Marco 🦴🦴 **1973** Entertaining musical adventure of Marco Polo's life casts Arnaz as Marco Polo and Mostel as Kublai Khan. A couple of cut-ups, right? One of the first films to combine animation with live action. Shot partially on location in the Orient. ♫By Damn; Walls; A Family Man; Spaghetti. **109m/C VHS.** Desi Arnaz Jr., Zero Mostel, Jack Weston, Cie Cie Win; ***D:*** Seymour Robbie.

Marco Polo, Jr. 🦴 **1972** Marco Polo Jr., the daring descendant of the legendary explorer, travels the world in search of his destiny in this song-filled, feature-length, but poorly animated, fantasy. **82m/C VHS.** ***D:*** Eric Porter; ***V:*** Bobby Rydell.

Mardi Gras for the Devil 🦴🦴 *Night Trap* **1993 (R)** Black magic and the occult combine as a New Orleans cop tries to catch a killer who strikes only at Mardi Gras. The cop's got his work cut out for him since the killer is no mere mortal but a demon who believes in human sacrifice. **95m/C VHS.** Robert Davi, Michael Ironside, Lesley-Anne Down, Lydie Denier, Mike Starr, Margaret Avery, John Amos; ***D:*** David A. Prior; ***W:*** David A. Prior.

Mardi Gras Massacre woof! *Crypt of Dark Secrets* **1978** Aztec priest arrives in New Orleans during Mardi Gras to revive the blood ritual of human sacrifice to an Aztec god. A police detective relentlessly pursues him. Much gore and gut-slicing, with no redeeming social value. **92m/C VHS.** Curt Dawson, Gwen Arment, Wayne Mack, Laura Misch; ***D:*** Jack Weis.

Margaret's Museum ½ **1995 (R)** The museum of the title is the bizarre shrine Margaret (Bonham Carter) dedicates to the family members who have been killed in the coal mines that dominate her small (1940s) Cape Breton, Nova Scotia town. Both Margaret and her mother, Catherine (Nelligan), are embittered by their tragedies and when Margaret finds romance with eccentric bagpiper Neil (Russell), she makes him promise he'll never return to mine work. But with a bad economy, Neil is forced back to the pits and inevitable disaster. It's Bonham Carter's picture all the way and she shows a wide (and welcome) range of emotions and strength. Adapted from a story by Sheldon Currie. **114m/C VHS.** *CA GB* Helena Bonham Carter, Clive Russell, Kate Nelligan, Kenneth Welsh, Craig Olejnik; ***D:*** Mort Ransen; ***W:*** Mort Ransen, Gerald Wexler; ***C:*** Vic Sarin; ***M:*** Milan Kymlicka. Genie '95: Actress (Bonham Carter), Adapt. Screenplay, Costume Des., Support. Actor (Welsh), Support. Actress (Nelligan), Score.

Margin for Murder *Mickey Spillane's Margin for Murder* **1981** Mike Hammer investigates a mysterious accident that killed his best friend. **98m/C VHS.** Kevin Dobson, Cindy Pickett, Donna Dixon, Charles Hallahan; ***D:*** Daniel Haller. **TV**

Maria Candelaria *Portrait of Maria; Xochimilco* **1946** Society rejects a woman because people don't like her mother. (She posed nude for an artist, and the town responds by stoning her to death, proving that going against small-town morals can be lethal). Eventually, time and circumstance push daughter onto mother's path in this tragic soaper. Del Rio portrays the scorned young woman, although she was 40 years old. **96m/B VHS.** *MX* Dolores Del Rio, Pedro Armendariz Sr., Margarita Cortes; ***D:*** Emilio Fernandez.

Maria Chapdelaine **1934** An early film from the renowned French director, in which a brutish trapper and a sophisticate battle for the love of a girl in the Canadian wilderness. English subtitles. Remade in 1984. **75m/B VHS.** *FR* Jean Gabin, Jean-Pierre Aumont, Madeleine Renaud; ***D:*** Julien Duvivier.

Maria Chapdelaine ½ **1984** Around the turn of the century, a young girl in the Northern Canadian wilderness endures a year of passion, doomed love, and tragedy. In French with subtitles. Remake of a 1935 French film. **108m/C VHS.** *FR CA* Nick Mancuso, Carole Laure, Claude Rich, Pierre Curzi; ***D:*** Gilles Carle.

Marianne and Juliane ½ *The German Sisters; Die Bleierne Zeit* **1982** Powerful combination of relationships and politics in West Germany as experienced through the lives of two sisters—Juliane, a feminist editor, and Marianne, a political terrorist. Based on the lives of Gudrun and Christiane Ensslin. German with subtitles. **106m/C VHS.** *GE* Jutta Lampe, Barbara Sukowa, Ruediger Vogler, Doris Schade, Franz Rudnick; ***D:*** Margarethe von Trotta; ***W:*** Margarethe von Trotta; ***C:*** Franz Rath; ***M:*** Nicolas Economou.

Maria's Child ½ **1993** Light comedy about a dancer who becomes pregnant and must decide whether or not to keep the baby. When her live-in boyfriend (not the father) admits he cheated on her, she kicks him out. Unable to make up her mind, she imagines a dialogue with the fetus. Second of a trilogy by British TV screenwriter Malcolm McKay on the subject of forgiveness. **97m/C VHS.** *GB* Yolanda Vasquez, David O'Hara, Fiona Shaw, Alec McCowen, Sophie Okenado, Linda Davidson, Rudi Davies, Nicholas Woodeson, Anita Zagaria; ***D:*** Malcolm McKay; ***W:*** Malcolm McKay; ***M:*** Philip Appleby.

Maria's Day *Maria-nap* **1984** Chronicles the plague-riddled downfall of a formerly aristocratic and wealthy Hungarian family in the years following the failed 1849 Revolution. In Hungarian with English subtitles. **113m/C VHS.** Sandor Szabo, Lajos Kovacs, Edit Handel, Eva Igo, Imre Csiszar, Tamas Fodor; ***D:*** Judit Elek; ***W:*** Luca Karall, Gyorgy Petho; ***C:*** Emil Novak; ***M:*** Gabor Csalog.

Maria's Lovers ½ **1984 (R)** The wife (Kinski) of an impotent WWII veteran (Savage) succumbs to the charms of a rakish lady-killer (Spano). Savage turns to the charms of an older woman, finds love again with Kinski, but is still impotent; she gets pregnant by a wandering minstrel (Carradine) and on we go to film climax. Offbeat and uneven, representing Russian director Konchalovsky's first American film and one of Kinski's better roles. **103m/C VHS, DVD, Wide.** Nastassia Kinski, John Savage, Robert Mitchum, Keith Carradine, Anita Morris, Bud Cort, Karen Young, Tracy Nelson, John Goodman, Vincent Spano; ***D:*** Andrei Konchalovsky; ***W:*** Gerard Brach, Marjorie David, Andrei Konchalovsky; ***C:*** Juan Ruiz-Anchia; ***M:*** Gary S. Remal.

Maricela **1988** Young Maricela Flores and her mother have come to the U.S. from El Salvador to escape the fighting. Living with a Southern Californian family, Maricela has a hard time adjusting to American life and, in particular, dealing with prejudice. An entry in the PBS "Wonderworks" series. **55m/C VHS.** Linda Lavin, Carlina Cruz.

Marie **1985 (PG-13)** In this true story, a divorced (and battered) mother works her way through school and the system to become the first woman to head the Parole Board in Tennessee. Finding rampant corruption, she blows the whistle on her bosses, who put her life in jeopardy. Spacek gives a powerful performance, as does first-time actor Thompson, portraying himself as the abused woman's attorney. Based on the book by Peter Maas. **113m/C VHS.** Sissy Spacek, Jeff Daniels, Keith Szarabajka, John Cullum, Morgan Freeman, Fred Dalton Thompson, Don Hood, Lisa Banes, Vincent Irizarry; ***D:*** Roger Donaldson; ***W:*** John Briley; ***C:*** Chris Menges; ***M:*** Francis Lai.

Marie Antoinette ½ **1938** An elephantine costume drama chronicling the French queen's life from princesshood to her final days before the Revolution. A Shearer festival all the way, and a late example of MGM's overstuffed period style and star-power. Overlong, but engrossing for the wrong reasons. Morley, in his first film, plays Louis XVI. Power's only MGM loan-out casts him as a Swedish count and Marie's romantic dalliance. Based on a book by Stephan Zweig, with script assistance from (among others) F. Scott Fitzgerald. **160m/B VHS.** Norma Shearer, Tyrone Power, John Barrymore, Robert Morley, Gladys George, Anita Louise, Joseph Schildkraut, Henry Stephenson, Reginald Gardiner, Peter Bull, Albert Dekker, Joseph Calleia, George Zucco, Cora Witherspoon, Barry Fitzgerald, Mae Busch, Harry Davenport, Scotty Beckett; ***D:*** Woodbridge S. Van Dyke; ***W:*** F. Scott Fitzgerald; ***C:*** William H. Daniels.

Marie Baie des Anges *Angel Sharks; Marie, Bay of Angels* **1997 (R)** Although Nice's harbor is known as "The Bay of Angels," Pradal sets his film in a sort of mythic French port, filled with French teens, gang members, American sailors, and tourists. Pretty gypsy Marie (Giocante) likes to flirt with the Americans but after getting dumped goes back to the local toughs, including petty criminal Orso (Malgras). They manage a brief idyll, then Orso begins pressuring Marie to steal a gun for him. She does, and you can imagine how things turn out. French with subtitles. **90m/C VHS.** *FR* Vahina Giocante, Frederic Malgras; ***D:*** Manuel Pradal; ***W:*** Manuel Pradal; ***C:*** Christophe Pollock; ***M:*** Carlo Crivelli.

Marie Galante **1934** Fine spy drama has Tracy running into Gallian in Panama (years earlier she had been left there after a kidnapping). He finds her most helpful in his attempt to thwart the bombing of the Panama Canal. It's the performances that raise this otherwise standard thriller up a few notches. **88m/B VHS, DVD.** Spencer Tracy, Ketti Gallian, Ned Sparks, Helen Morgan, Sig Rumann, Leslie Fenton, Jay C. Flippen; ***D:*** Henry King.

Marihuana *Marijuana: The Devil's Weed; Marijuana, Weed with Roots in Hell* **1936** An unintentionally hilarious, "Reefer Madness"-type cautionary film about the exaggerated evils of pot smoking. A real dopey film favored by right-winger zealots. **57m/B VHS, DVD.** Harley Wood, Hugh McArthur, Pat Carlyle, Dorothy Dehn, Paul Ellis, Richard Erskine; ***D:*** Dwain Esper; ***W:*** Rex Elgin, Hildegarde Stadie; ***C:*** Roland Price.

Marilyn & Bobby: Her Final Affair ½ **1994** Sordid account of the alleged romance between movie star Monroe (Anderson) and Attorney General Robert Kennedy (Kelly). Culminates in a silly scene at Marilyn's home, on the night of her death, where various men all try to find her tell-all diary while keeping out of sight of each other. **95m/C VHS.** Melody Anderson, James F. Kelly, Richard Dysart, Thomas Wagner, Raymond Serra, Kristopher Tabori, Jonathan Banks, Geoffrey Blake, Ian Buchanan; ***D:*** Bradford May. **CABLE**

Marilyn: The Untold Story **1980** Nominated for an Emmy, Hicks elevates what could easily have been a dull made-for-TV movie with her remarkable performance as Marilyn Monroe. Based on the book by Norman Mailer. **156m/C VHS.** Catherine Hicks, Richard Basehart, Frank Converse, John Ireland, Sheree North, Anne Ramsey, Viveca Lindfors, Jason Miller, Bill Vint; ***D:*** Jack Arnold, John Flynn, Lawrence Schiller; ***M:*** William Goldstein.

Marine Raiders **1943** Marines train and then fight at Guadalcanal. A typical flag-waver, watchable but not particularly engaging. **90m/B VHS.** Pat O'Brien, Robert Ryan, Ruth Hussey, Frank McHugh, Barton MacLane; ***D:*** Harold Schuster.

Marius **1931** This is the first of Marcel Pagnol's trilogy ("Fanny" and "Cesar" followed), about the lives and adventures of the people of Provence, France. Marius is a young man who dreams of going away to sea. When he acts on those dreams, he leaves behind his girlfriend, Fanny. Realistic dialogue and vivid characterizations. Adapted by Pagnol from his play. The musical play and film "Fanny" (1961) were adapted from this trilogy. **125m/B VHS.** *FR* Raimu, Pierre Fresnay, Charpin, Orane Demazis; ***D:*** Alexander Korda; ***W:*** Marcel Pagnol; ***M:*** Francis Gromon.

Marius and Jeannette ½ *Marius et Jeannette: Un Conte de L'Estaque* **1997** Single mother of two, Jeannette (Ascaride), works as a checkout clerk in a poor Marseilles neighborhood. Marius (Meylan) works as a security guard at a closed cement factory and meets Jeannette when he catches her stealing paint cans from the property. He offers to help her paint her apartment and the two begin a tentative romance. But something spooks Marius and he begins to drink heavily, abandoning Jeannette. Two of Jeannette's male neighbors decide to find out what Marius' problem is and get the twosome back together. Very sweet and sentimental. **101m/C VHS.** *FR* Ariane Ascaride, Gerard Meylan, Pascale Roberts, Jacques Boudet, Jean-Pierre Darroussin, Frederique Bonnal; ***D:*** Robert Guediguian; ***W:*** Robert Guediguian, Jean-Louis Milesi; ***C:*** Bernard Cavile. Cesar '98: Actress (Ascaride).

Marjoe **1972 (PG)** Documentary follows the career of rock-style evangelist Marjoe Gortner, who spent 25 years of his life touring the country as a professional preacher. Marjoe later went on to become an actor and professional fundraiser. **88m/C VHS.** Marjoe Gortner; ***D:*** Howard Smith, Sarah Kernochan. Oscars '72: Feature Doc.

Marjorie Morningstar **1958** A temperate Hollywood adaptation of the Herman Wouk story of a young actress who fails to achieve stardom and settles on being a housewife. Wood slipped a bit in this story. **123m/C VHS.** Natalie Wood, Gene Kelly, Martin Balsam, Claire Trevor, Ed Wynn, Everett Sloane, Carolyn Jones; ***D:*** Irving Rapper; ***C:*** Harry Stradling Sr.; ***M:*** Max Steiner.

The Mark ½ **1961** Story of a convicted child molester who cannot escape his past upon his release from prison. Whitman gives a riveting performance as the convict. **127m/B VHS, DVD, Wide.** *GB* Stuart Whitman, Maria Schell, Rod Steiger, Brenda de Banzie, Maurice Denham, Donald Wolfit, Paul Rogers, Donald Houston, Amanda Black, Russell Napier, Marie Devereux; ***D:*** Guy Green; ***W:*** Sidney Buchman, Raymond Stross; ***C:*** Dudley Lovell; ***M:*** Richard Rodney Bennett.

Mark of Cain ½ **1984** Twin brothers, one normal, the other a raving lunatic with murderous tendencies, confuse the authorities who imprison the nice guy, allowing the nutcase to chase after his beautiful sister-in-law. **90m/C VHS.** Robin Ward, Wendy Crewson, August Schellenberg; ***D:*** Bruce Pittman; ***W:*** Peter Colley.

Mark of the Beast **19??** Two students inadvertently videotape an assassination, and are then relentlessly pursued by the killer. **90m/C VHS.** Carolyn Guillet, David Smulker; ***D:*** Robert Stewart.

Mark of the Devil *Burn, Witch, Burn; Brenn, Hexe, Brenn; Austria 1700; Satan; Hexen bis aufs Blut Gequaelt* **1969 (R)** Witchcraft and romance don't mix, as a Medieval witch hunter and a sexy girl accused of witchery discover. Notoriously graphic torture scenes add to the mayhem but the weird part is that this is based on true stories. **96m/C VHS, DVD.** *GB GE* Herbert Lom, Olivera Vuco, Udo Kier, Reggie Nalder, Herbert (Fuchs) Fux, Michael Maien, Ingeborg (Inge) Schoener, Johannes Buzalski, Gaby Fuchs, Adrian Hoven; ***D:*** Michael Armstrong; ***W:*** Sergio Casstner, Adrian Hoven; ***C:*** Ernst W. Kalinke; ***M:*** Michael Holm.

Mark of the Devil 2 **1972 (R)** Sadistic witchhunters torture satan's servants and torch sisters of mercy, whilst trying to horn in on a nobleman's fortune. It's just not as gross without the vomit bags. **90m/C VHS.** *GB GE* Erika Blanc, Anton Diffring, Reggie Nalder; ***D:*** Adrian Hoven.

The Mark of the Hawk *The Accused* **1957** A uniquely told story of African nations struggling to achieve racial equality after gaining independence. Songs include "This Man Is Mine," sung by Kitt. **83m/C VHS.** *GB* Sidney Poitier, Eartha Kitt, Juano Hernandez, John McIntire; ***D:*** Michael Audley.

Mark of the Spur ½ **1932** The mark on an injured man's face is used to track down his attacker. **60m/B VHS.** Bob Custer, Lillian Rich, Franklyn Farnum, Bud Osborne; ***D:*** J(ohn) P(aterson) McGowan.

Mark of the Vampire *Vampires of Prague* **1935** A murder in a small town is solved through the use of vaudeville actors who pose as vampires. Great cast, surprise ending. **61m/B VHS.** Lionel Barrymore, Bela Lugosi, Elizabeth Allan, Lionel Atwill, Jean Hersholt, Donald Meek, Carroll Borland; ***D:*** Tod Browning; ***W:*** Tod Browning, Guy Endore, Bernard Schubert; ***C:*** James Wong Howe.

Mark of Zorro **1920** Fairbanks plays a dual role as the hapless Don Diego and his dashing counterpart, Zorro, the hero of the oppressed. Silent film. **80m/B VHS, DVD.** Douglas Fairbanks Sr., Marguerite de la Motte, Noah Beery Sr., Mary Astor, Noah Beery Jr., Milton Berle, Charles Stevens; ***D:*** Fred Niblo; ***W:*** Douglas Fairbanks Sr.; ***C:*** William McGann, Harris (Harry) Thorpe.

The Mark of Zorro ½ **1940** The dashing Power swashbuckles his way through this wonderfully acted and directed romp. He plays the foppish son of a 19th-century California aristocrat who is secretly the masked avenger of the oppressed peons. Bromberg plays the wicked governor, with the beautiful niece (Darnell) beloved by Power, and Rathbone is supremely evil as his cruel minion. Lots of swordplay with a particularly exciting duel to the death between Rathbone and Power. Based on the novel "The Curse of Capistrano" by Johnston McCulley. Remake of the 1921 silent film and followed by a number of other Zorro incarnations. **93m/B VHS.** Tyrone Power, Linda Darnell, Basil Rathbone, Gale Sondergaard, Eugene Pallette, J. Edward Bromberg, Montagu Love, Janet Beecher; ***D:*** Rouben Mamoulian; ***W:*** John Taintor Foote; ***C:*** Arthur C. Miller; ***M:*** Alfred Newman.

Mark Twain and Me 🦴🦴½ **1991** Robards portrays the aging and irascible Mark Twain, attended by a neglected but devoted daughter, and befriended by 11-year-old Dorothy Quick, as they travel on the same ship. Based on a true story. **93m/C VHS.** Jason Robards Jr., Talia Shire, Amy Stewart, Chris Wiggins, R.H. Thomson, Fiona Reid; ***D:*** Daniel Petrie. **TV**

Marked for Death 🦴½ *Screwface* **1990 (R)** Having killed a prostitute, DEA agent Seagal decides it's time to roll out the white picket fence in the 'burbs with the little woman and brood. Trouble is, a bunch of guys with dreadlocks don't approve of his early retirement, and the Jamaican gangsters plan to send him and his family to the great Rasta playground in the sky. Whereupon the Stevester kicks and punches and wags his ponytail. Much blood flows, mon. Tunes by Jimmy Cliff. **93m/C VHS, DVD, Wide.** Steven Seagal, Joanna Pacula, Basil Wallace, Keith David, Danielle Harris, Arlen Dean Snyder, Teri Weigel; ***D:*** Dwight Little; ***W:*** Mark Victor, Michael Grais; ***C:*** Ric Waite; ***M:*** James Newton Howard.

Marked for Murder 🦴½ **1945** Another in the Texas Ranger series. In this entry, the Rangers come to the rescue when a rancher war appears inevitable. **58m/B VHS.** Tex Ritter, Dave O'Brien, Guy Wilkerson; ***D:*** Elmer Clifton; ***W:*** Elmer Clifton.

Marked for Murder 🦴½ **1989 (R)** Two TV station employees are framed for murder after being sent out to find a missing videocassette. Renee Estevez is part of the Sheen/Estevez dynasty. **88m/C VHS.** Renee Estevez, Wings Hauser, Jim Mitchum, Ross Hagen, Ken Abraham; ***D:*** Rick Sloane.

Marked Man 🦴🦴 **1996 (R)** After auto mechanic Frank Stanton (Piper) witnesses a murder he finds himself accused of the crime and on the run, trying to prove his innocence. **94m/C VHS.** Roddy Piper, Jane Wheeler, Alina Thompson, Miles O'Keeffe; ***D:*** Marc Voizard; ***W:*** Thomas Ritz; ***C:*** Stephen Reizes; ***M:*** Marty Simon. **VIDEO**

Marked Money 🦴🦴 **1928** Amiable captain takes in boy who'll soon roll in the dough and swindlers show up on the scene. The captain's courageous girl and her pilot beau step in to right the rookery. **61m/B VHS.** Frank "Junior" Coghlan, Tom (George Duryea) Keene, Tom Kennedy, Bert Woodruff, Virginia Bradford, Maurice Black, Jack (H.) Richardson; ***D:*** Spencer Gordon Bennet.

Marked Trails 🦴 **1944** One clue stamps out the guilty parties in this wild west saga. **59m/B VHS.** Hoot Gibson, Bob Steele, Veda Ann Borg.

Marked Woman 🦴🦴🦴 **1937** Gangster drama about crusading District Attorney who persuades a group of clip-joint hostesses to testify against their gangster boss. A gritty studio melodrama loosely based on a true story. **97m/B VHS.** Bette Davis, Humphrey Bogart, Eduardo Ciannelli, Isabel Jewell, Jane Bryan, Mayo Methot, Allen Jenkins, Lola Lane; ***D:*** Lloyd Bacon; ***C:*** George Barnes. Venice Film Fest. '37: Actress (Davis).

Marlowe 🦴🦴½ **1969 (PG)** Updated telling by Stirling Silliphant of Chandler's "The Little Sister" sports retro guy Garner as Philip Marlowe, gumshoe. Hired by a mystery blonde to find her misplaced brother, rumpled sleuth Marlowe encounters kicking Bruce Lee in his first film. Slick looking, but the story's a bit slippery. **95m/C VHS.** James Garner, Gayle Hunnicutt, Carroll O'Connor, Rita Moreno, Sharon Farrell, William Daniels, Bruce Lee; ***D:*** Paul Bogart; ***W:*** Stirling Silliphant; ***C:*** William H. Daniels.

Marnie 🦴🦴🦴½ **1964** A lovely blonde with a mysterious past robs her employers and then changes her identity. When her current boss catches her in the act and forces her to marry him, he soon learns the puzzling aspects of Marnie's background. Criticized at the time of its release, the movie has since been accepted as a Hitchcock classic. **130m/C VHS, DVD, Wide.** Tippi Hedren, Sean Connery, Diane Baker, Bruce Dern, Louise Latham, Martin Gabel, Henry Beckman, Mariette Hartley, Alan Napier; ***D:*** Alfred Hitchcock; ***W:*** Jay Presson Allen; ***C:*** Robert Burks; ***M:*** Bernard Herrmann.

Maroc 7 🦴 **1967** Slow story of a secret agent after a thief suffering from a split personality. **92m/C VHS.** Gene Barry, Elsa Martinelli, Cyd Charisse, Leslie Phillips; ***D:*** Gerry O'Hara.

Marooned 🦴½ *Space Travellers* **1969 (G)** Tense thriller casts Crenna, Hackman, and Franciscus as astronauts stranded in space after a retro-rocket misfires and their craft is unable to return to earth. Amazingly inept despite an Academy Award for effects and an excellent cast. Story bears a striking resemblance to 1995's "Apollo 13." **134m/C VHS.** Gregory Peck, David Janssen, Richard Crenna, James Franciscus, Gene Hackman, Lee Grant; ***D:*** John Sturges; ***C:*** Daniel F. Fapp. Oscars '69: Visual FX.

Marquis 🦴🦴 **1990** A bizarre satire combining sex, lust, and the French Revolution, based on the writings of the Marquis de Sade. Amusing, decadent, and not for the prudish. In French with English subtitles. **88m/C VHS.** *FR* ***D:*** Henri Xhonneux.

Marquis de Sade 🦴½ *Dark Prince: Intimate Tales of Marquis de Sade* **1996 (R)** Justine searches for her sister Juliette in 17th-century Paris and is drawn into the sexually deviant world of the Marquis de Sade. Also available unrated. **88m/C VHS, DVD.** Nick Mancuso, Janet Gunn, John Rhys-Davies; ***D:*** Gwyneth Gibby; ***W:*** Craig J. Nevius; ***C:*** Eugeny Guslinsky. **CABLE**

The Marquise of O 🦴🦴 *Die Marquise Von O* **1976 (PG)** In the early 18th century, the Russian army is invading Lombardy. The widowed Marquise (Clever) is drugged and raped by Count F (Ganz), an officer with the Russians. When the Marquise discovers she's pregnant, she forces the Count to marry her, although they separate immediately after the ceremony. Adaptation of Heinrich Von Kleist's novella. German with subtitles. **102m/C VHS, DVD.** *FR GE* Edith Clever, Bruno Ganz, Peter Luhr, Edda Seipel, Otto Sander, Ruth Drexel; ***D:*** Eric Rohmer; ***W:*** Eric Rohmer; ***C:*** Nestor Almendros.

The Marriage Circle 🦴🦴🦴 **1924** A pivotal silent comedy depicting the infidelity of several married couples in Vienna. Director Lubitsch's first American comedy. Remade as a musical, "One Hour With You," in 1932. Silent. **90m/B VHS, DVD.** Florence Vidor, Monte Blue, Marie Prevost, Creighton Hale, Adolphe Menjou, Harry C. (Henry) Myers, Dale Fuller; ***D:*** Ernst Lubitsch; ***W:*** Paul Bern; ***C:*** Charles Van Enger.

Marriage Is Alive and Well 🦴 **1980** A wedding photographer reflects on the institution of marriage from his unique perspective. **100m/C VHS.** Joe Namath, Jack Albertson, Melinda Dillon, Judd Hirsch, Susan Sullivan, Fred McCarren, Swoosie Kurtz; ***D:*** Russ Mayberry. **TV**

Marriage Italian Style 🦴🦴🦴 **1964** When an engaged man hears that his mistress is on her death bed, he goes to her side and, in an emotional gesture, promises to marry her if she survives. She does, and holds him to his promise. After they're married, however, she gives him a big surprise—three grown sons. A silly film, but DeSica's direction keeps it from being too fluffy. Lots of fun. Based on the play "Filumena Marturano" by Eduardo De Filippo. **102m/C VHS.** *IT* Sophia Loren, Marcello Mastroianni, Aldo Puglisi, Tecla Scarano, Marilu Tolo; ***D:*** Vittorio De Sica. Golden Globes '65: Foreign Film.

The Marriage of Figaro 🦴🦴 *Figaros Hochzeit* **1949** DEFA studio's lavish adaptation of Mozart's opera. Count Almaviva's valet, Figaro, plans to marry the Countess's chambermaid, Susanna. But since the Count also fancies Susanna, he keeps coming up with plans to postpone the wedding and the lovestuck duo must use their own trickery to forge ahead. German with subtitles. **109m/B VHS.** *GE* Angelika Hauff, Willi Domgraf-Fassbaender, Sabine Peters, Mathieu Ahlersmeyer; ***D:*** Georg Wildhagen; ***W:*** Georg Wildhagen; ***C:*** Eugen Klagemann, Karl Plintzner.

The Marriage of Maria Braun 🦴🦴🦴🦴 *Die Ehe Der Maria Braun* **1979 (R)** In post-WWII Germany, a young woman uses guile and sexuality to survive as the nation rebuilds itself into an industrial power. The first movie in Fassbinder's trilogy about German women in Germany during the post war years, it is considered one of the director's finest films, and an indispensable example of the New German Cinema. In German with English subtitles. **120m/C VHS.** *GE* Hanna Schygulla, Klaus Lowitsch, Ivan Desny, Gottfried John, Gisela Uhlen; ***D:*** Rainer Werner Fassbinder; ***W:*** Rainer Werner Fassbinder, Peter Marthesheimer, Pea Frolich; ***C:*** Michael Ballhaus; ***M:*** Peer Raben. Berlin Intl. Film Fest. '79: Actress (Schygulla).

Married? 🦴½ **1926** Couple endures 365 days of marital bliss in order to inherit big bucks. Some do it for less. **65m/B VHS.** Owen Moore, Constance Bennett; ***D:*** George Terwilliger.

A Married Man 🦴🦴 **1984** Story focusing on a bored British lawyer who begins cheating on his wife. Amid the affair, someone gets murdered. **200m/C VHS.** *GB* Anthony Hopkins, Ciaran Madden, Lise Hilboldt, Yvonne Coulette, John Le Mesurier, Sophie Ashton; ***D:*** John Davies. **TV**

Married People, Single Sex 🦴🦴½ **1993 (R)** Three couples decide to spread their sexual wings. Shelly takes a new lover; Artie makes obscene phone calls; and Beth and Mike, who end their relationship, still can't keep out of bed. An unrated version is also available. **110m/C VHS.** Chase Masterson, Joe Pilato, Darla Slavens, Shelley Michelle, Wendi Westbrook, Robert Zachar, Samuel Mongiello, Teri Thompson; ***D:*** Mike Sedan; ***W:*** Catherine Tavel.

Married People, Single Sex 2: For Better or Worse 🦴½ **1994 (R)** Three women are faced with sexual unhappiness: Carol's hubby had an affair, Valerie wants a baby but her spouse doesn't, and Karen's husband is just too darn nice (she wants some spice in her life). So, there's lots of sexual encounters to solve their problems. Also available unrated. **93m/C VHS.** Kathy Shower, Monique Parent, Liza Smith, Craig Stepp, Doug Jeffery; ***D:*** Mike Sedan.

Married to It 🦴🦴 **1993 (R)** Three vastly different couples work together to plan a pageant at a private school. The oil and water group includes struggling hippie leftovers Bridges and Channing, '80s-era corporate cutthroats Shepherd and Silver, and starry-eyed newlyweds Masterson and Leonard. Contrived plot offers few humourous moments, with the main focus revolving around coping rather than comedy. And the coping is slow business, done by characters you don't really care about with problems that don't really matter. **112m/C VHS.** Beau Bridges, Stockard Channing, Robert Sean Leonard, Mary Stuart Masterson, Cybill Shepherd, Ron Silver; ***D:*** Arthur Hiller; ***W:*** Janet Kovalcik; ***M:*** Henry Mancini.

Married to the Mob 🦴🦴🦴 **1988 (R)** After the murder of her husband, an attractive Mafia widow tries to escape "mob" life, but ends up fighting off amorous advances from the current mob boss while being wooed by an undercover cop. A snappy script and a spry performance by Pfeiffer pepper this easy-to-watch film. **102m/C VHS, DVD, Wide.** Michelle Pfeiffer, Dean Stockwell, Alec Baldwin, Matthew Modine, Mercedes Ruehl, Anthony J. Nici, Joan Cusack, Ellen Foley, Chris Isaak, Trey Wilson, Charles Napier, Tracey Walter, Al Lewis, Nancy Travis, David Johansen, Jonathan Demme; ***D:*** Jonathan Demme; ***W:*** Mark Burns, Barry Strugatz; ***C:*** Tak Fujimoto; ***M:*** David Byrne. N.Y. Film Critics '88: Support. Actor (Stockwell); Natl. Soc. Film Critics '88: Support. Actor (Stockwell), Support. Actress (Ruehl).

Married Too Young 🦴🦴 *I Married Too Young* **1962** High school honeys elope, despite disapproval from the parental units. When the boy groom trades his med school plans for a monkey wrench in order to support the little missus, he finds much trouble with the hot rod heavies. **76m/B VHS.** Harold Lloyd Jr., Jana Lund, Anthony Dexter, Marianna Hill, Trudy Marshall, Brian O'Hara, Nita Loveless; ***D:*** George Moskov; ***W:*** Nat Tanchuck; ***C:*** Ernest Haller.

The Married Virgin 🦴🦴 **1918** One of the earliest films in which Valentino appeared in a featured role prior to "The Four Horsemen of the Apocalypse" and "The Sheik." Count Roberto di Fraccini (Valentino) is a fortune hunter having an affair with Ethel Spencer McMillan (Kirkham), wife of wealthy older businessman Fiske McMillan (Jobson). After the couple unsuccessfully plot to blackmail McMillan, the Count tells his lover's daughter, Mary (Sisson), that in return for her hand in marriage (and her dowry), he will save her father from a life in prison. **71m/B DVD.** Rudolph Valentino, Kathleen Kirkham, Edward Jobson, Vera Sisson, Frank Newburg; ***D:*** Joe Maxwell; ***W:*** Hayden Talbott.

A Married Woman 🦴🦴🦴 *La Femme Mariee* **1965** Dramatizes a day in the life of a woman who has both a husband and a lover. One of Godard's more mainstream efforts. **94m/B VHS, 8mm.** *FR* Macha Meril, Phillippe LeRoy, Bernard Noel; ***D:*** Jean-Luc Godard; ***W:*** Jean-Luc Godard; ***C:*** Raoul Coutard.

Marry Me, Marry Me 🦴🦴🦴 *Mazel Tov Ou le Mariage* **1969 (R)** While in Paris, a Jewish encyclopedia salesman falls in love with a pregnant Belgian woman. A sensitive story about European Jewish families. Berri wrote, produced, directed, and starred in this romantic comedy. **87m/C VHS.** *FR* Elisabeth Wiener, Regine, Claude Berri, Louisa Colpeyn; ***D:*** Claude Berri; ***C:*** Ghislan Cloquet.

The Marrying Kind 🦴🦴½ **1952** Marrieds Florence (Holliday) and Chet (Ray) Keefer are in the chambers of Judge Carroll (Kennedy) talking about why they want a divorce. They flashback to their courtship and marriage and the bumps they've endured along the way, and then realize they still love each other. Holliday reunited with Cukor and scriptwriters Gordon and Kanin after their triumph with "Born Yesterday." **92m/B VHS.** Judy Holliday, Aldo Ray, Madge Kennedy, Sheila Bond, John Alexander, Peggy Cass, Rex Williams; ***D:*** George Cukor; ***W:*** Ruth Gordon, Garson Kanin; ***C:*** Joseph Walker; ***M:*** Hugo Friedhofer.

The Marrying Man 🦴½ **1991 (R)** Young man meets his match when his buddies take him to Las Vegas for his bachelor party. He falls like a ton of bricks for the singer, not knowing she belongs to the local crime lord, who catches them together and forces them to marry. They immediately divorce, can't forget each other and eventually re-marry, again and again and again. Silly story supposedly based on the story of Harry Karl (eventual husband of Debbie Reynolds) and Marie MacDonald. Basinger and Baldwin's off-stage romance created quite a stir but their chemistry onscreen is zilch. Ineffective, not funny, poorly paced and acted: a good example of what happens when egotistical stars get their way. **116m/C VHS.** Alec Baldwin, Kim Basinger, Robert Loggia, Armand Assante, Elisabeth Shue, Paul Reiser, Fisher Stevens, Peter Dobson, Gretchen Wyler; ***D:*** Jerry Rees; ***W:*** Neil Simon; ***M:*** David Newman.

Mars 🦴½ **1996** Fast-paced space western finds independent lawman Caution Templar (Gruner) receiving a frantic message from his brother to return to the wild mining town of Alpha City, Mars. Only by the time he arrives his brother is dead and Templar is determined to find out what happened. **92m/C VHS.** Olivier Gruner, Shari Belafonte, Scott Valentine, Amber Smith, Alex Hyde-White, Lee DeBroux, Gabriel Dell; ***D:*** Jon Hess; ***W:*** Patrick Highsmith, Steven Hartov. **VIDEO**

Mars Attacks! 🦴🦴½ **1996 (PG-13)** Only director Burton could make a movie based on a series of 1960s trading cards. Intentionally tacky, this huge scale epic spoof of monster, sci-fi, and disaster flicks finds moronic President Dale (Nicholson), his frigid wife (Close) and a cast of thousands battling the green-skinned invaders. Jack's back for a second role as Vegas hotel developer Art Land, who tries to cash in on the opportunities the invasion brings. Plot is relatively nonexistent and zig-zags wildly throughout, but the gist is that the aliens are bent on destroying the population, and have little trouble battling the bumbling humans. Brosnan is the hilariously deluded alien-hugger, Professor Kessler. A semi-lampoon of fellow alien flick competitor "Independence Day," this film goes all out for the camp laugh, but its big budget effects, way over-the-top style and all-star cast can't conquer the audience. **106m/C VHS, DVD, Wide.** Jack Nicholson, Glenn Close, Martin Short, Pierce Brosnan, Lukas Haas, Sarah Jessica Parker, Michael J. Fox, Natalie Portman, Rod Steiger, Paul Winfield, Annette Bening, Sylvia Sidney, Danny DeVito, Joe Don Baker, Pam Grier, Jim Brown, Lisa Marie; ***Cameos:*** Tom Jones; ***D:*** Tim Burton; ***W:*** Jonathan Gems; ***C:*** Peter Suschitzsky; ***M:*** Danny Elfman.

Mars Needs Women 🦴 **1966** When the Martian singles scene starts to drag, Mars boys cross the galaxy in search of fertile earth babes to help them repopulate the planet. Seems Batgirl Craig, the go-go dancing lady scientist, is at the top of their dance cards. **80m/C VHS, DVD.** Tommy Kirk, Yvonne Craig, Warren Hammack, Tony Houston, Larry Tanner, Cal Duggan; ***D:*** Larry Buchanan; ***W:*** Larry Buchanan; ***C:*** Robert C. Jessup.

Marshal Law 🦴🦴 **1996 (R)** Highland Glen is a gated community in L.A. that seems very secure, especially to ex-Texas Marshal Jack Coleman (Smits) and his family. But an earthquake leaves the neighborhood prey to a vicious gang unless Coleman can find a way to outwit them. **96m/C VHS.** Jimmy Smits, James LeGros, Vonte Sweet, Scott Plank, Kristy Swanson, Channon Roe, Michael Cavalieri, Rodney Rowland, Tai Thai; ***D:*** Stephen Cornwell; ***W:*** Stephen Cornwell, Nick Gregory; ***C:*** Levie Isaacks; ***M:*** Tim Truman.

Marshal of Cedar Rock 🦴🦴 **1953** Marshal Rocky Lane sets a prisoner free, thinking the guy will lead him to a stash of stolen bank funds. Seems he miscalculates, but by way of consolation, he routs a rotten railroad agent who's rooking innocent people. Features the equine talent of Black Jack. **54m/B VHS.** Allan "Rocky" Lane, Phyllis Coates, Roy Barcroft, William Henry, Robert Shayne, Eddy (Eddie, Ed) Waller; ***D:*** Harry Keller.

Marshal of Heldorado 🦴 **1950** An outlaw-infested town needs an injection of law and order. **53m/B VHS.** James Ellison, Russell Hayden, Raymond Hatton, Fuzzy Knight; ***D:*** Thomas Carr.

The Marshal's Daughter 🦴½ **1953** A father and daughter team up to outwit an outlaw. Features many cowboy songs, including the title track by Tex Ritter. **71m/B VHS.** Tex Ritter, Ken Murray, Laurie Anders, Preston Foster, Hoot Gibson; ***D:*** William Berke.

Martha and I 🦴🦴🦴 **1991** In 1934 Czechoslovakia, distinguished Jewish doctor Ernest Paul Fuchs (Piccoli), having divorced his unfaithful wife, impulsively marries his lower-class gentile German maid Martha (Sagebrecht). What turns out to be a true love match is witnessed through the adolescent eyes of nephew Emil (Chalupa), who comes to live with the couple. With the rise of Nazism and increased Jewish persecution the devoted Martha begins to fear for her husband and makes a futile attempt to find a safe haven. Stirring drama based on the director's childhood (he's the semi-fictionalized Emil). German with subtitles. **107m/C VHS.** *GE* Marianne Saegebrecht, Michel Piccoli, Vaclov Chalupa, Ondrej Vetchy; ***D:*** Jiri Weiss; ***W:*** Jiri Weiss; ***C:*** Viktor Ruzicka; ***M:*** Jiri Stivin.

Martial Law 🦴½ **1990 (R)** A film solely for martial arts fans. Two cops use their hands, feet, and other body parts to fight crime. **90m/C VHS.** Chad McQueen, Cynthia Rothrock, David Carradine, Andy McCutcheon; ***D:*** S.E. Cohen; ***W:*** Richard Brandes.

Martial Law 2: Undercover 🦴½ **1991 (R)** Two cops, martial arts experts and part of an elite police force called Martial Law, go undercover to investigate the murder of a colleague. They uncover a fast-growing crime ring headed by a bad cop and a nightclub owner. The nightclub is host to the city's rich and powerful, who are treated to a bevy of beautiful women, protected by martial arts experts, and entertained by martial arts fights to the death. Lots of high-kicking action. **92m/C VHS.** Jeff Wincott, Cynthia Rothrock, Paul Johansson, Evan Lurie, L. Charles Taylor, Sherrie Rose, Billy Drago; ***D:*** Kurt Anderson; ***W:*** Richard Brandes, Jiles Fitzgerald.

Martial Outlaw 🦴🦴 **1993 (R)** DEA man Kevin White (Wincott) has been following a drug-dealing ex-KGB kingpin from Moscow to San Francisco. The Russian's latest move takes him to Los Angeles where Kevin meets up with his older brother Jack (Hudson), a maverick LA cop. Jack persuades Kevin to let him in on the action but Kevin begins to suspect Jack is playing both sides and their sibling rivalry could lead to death. **89m/C VHS.** Jeff Wincott, Gary Hudson, Richard Jaeckel, Krista Errickson, Vladimir Skomarovsky, Liliana Komorowska, Gary Wood; ***D:*** Kurt Anderson; ***W:*** Thomas Ritz.

The Martian Chronicles: Part 1 **1979** Series episode "The Explorers." Adapted from Ray Bradbury's critically acclaimed novel. Futuristic explorations of the planet Mars. Strange fates of the discovery teams make everything more curious. **120m/C VHS.** Rock Hudson, Bernie Casey, Nicholas Hammond, Darren McGavin; ***D:*** Michael Anderson Sr. **TV**

The Martian Chronicles: Part 2 🦴½ **1979** Episode following the television movie. This part is called "The Settlers." The planet Mars meets with its first colonization and the settlers watch the Earth explode. **97m/C VHS.** Rock Hudson, Fritz Weaver, Roddy McDowall, Bernie Casey, Darren McGavin, Gayle Hunnicutt, Barry Morse, Bernadette Peters; ***D:*** Michael Anderson Sr. **TV**

The Martian Chronicles: Part 3 🦴🦴½ **1979** In the final chapter of this space saga, the Martian's secrets become known and will forever change man's destiny. Adapted from Ray Bradbury's classic novel. **97m/C VHS.** Rock Hudson, Bernadette Peters, Christopher Connelly, Fritz Weaver, Roddy McDowall, Bernie Casey, Nicholas Hammond, Darren McGavin, Gayle Hunnicutt, Barry Morse; ***D:*** Michael Anderson Sr. **TV**

Martians Go Home! 🦴½ **1990 (PG-13)** Joke-loving Martians come to earth and pester a nerdy composer. **89m/C VHS.** Randy Quaid, Margaret Colin, Anita Morris, John Philbin, Ronny Cox, Gerrit Graham, Barry Sobel, Vic Dunlop; ***D:*** David Odell.

Martin 🦴🦴🦴 **1977 (R)** Martin is a charming young man, though slightly mad. He freely admits of the need to drink blood. Contemporary vampire has found a new abhorrent means of killing his victims. **96m/C VHS, DVD.** John Amplas, Lincoln Maazel, Christine Forrest, Elayne Nadeau, Tom Savini, Sarah Venable, George A. Romero, Fran Middleton; ***D:*** George A. Romero; ***W:*** George A. Romero; ***C:*** Michael Gornick; ***M:*** Donald Rubinstein.

Martin Chuzzlewit 🦴🦴½ **1994** Martin Chuzzlewit (Scofield) is a rich and elderly man with a lot of greedy relatives just waiting for him to die so they can get their hands on his money. The only exceptions being his already disinherited namesake grandson and his young orphaned nurse, Mary Graham. Adapted from the Charles Dickens novel. On three cassettes. **288m/C VHS.** Paul Scofield, John Mills, Pete Postlethwaite, Tom Wilkinson, Julia Sawalha, David Bradley; ***D:*** Pedr James. **TV**

Martin Luther 🦴½ **1953** French-made biography of the 16th century reformer who began the Protestant Reformation. **105m/B VHS.** *FR* Niall MacGinnis, John Ruddock, Pierre Leeavre, Guy Verney.

Martin's Day 🦴🦴 **1985 (PG)** An unusual friendship develops between an escaped convict and the young boy he kidnaps. **99m/C VHS.** *CA* Richard Harris, Lindsay Wagner, James Coburn, Justin Henry, Karen Black, John Ireland; ***D:*** Alan Gibson; ***W:*** Chris Bryant, Allan Scott.

Marty 🦴🦴🦴½ **1955** Marty is a painfully shy bachelor who feels trapped in a pointless life of family squabbles. When he finds love, he also finds the strength to break out of what he feels is a meaningless existence. A sensitive and poignant film from the writer of "Altered States." Remake of a TV version that originally aired in 1953. Notable for Borgnine's sensitive portrayal, one of his last quality jobs before sinking into the B-movie sludge pit. **91m/B VHS, DVD.** Ernest Borgnine, Betsy Blair, Joe Mantell, Esther Minciotti, Jerry Paris, Karen Steele, Augusta Ciolli, Frank Sutton, Walter Kelley, Robin Morse; ***D:*** Delbert Mann; ***W:*** Paddy Chayefsky; ***C:*** Joseph LaShelle; ***M:*** Roy Webb, Harry Warren. Oscars '55: Actor (Borgnine), Director (Mann), Picture, Screenplay; British Acad. '55: Actor (Borgnine), Actress (Blair); Directors Guild '55: Director (Mann); Golden Globes '56: Actor—Drama (Borgnine); Natl. Bd. of Review '55: Actor (Borgnine), Natl. Film Reg. '94;; N.Y. Film Critics '55: Actor (Borgnine), Film.

Marvin & Tige 🦴🦴½ **1984 (PG)** A deep friendship develops between an aging alcoholic and a street-wise 11-year-old boy after they meet one night in an Atlanta park. **104m/C VHS.** John Cassavetes, Gibran Brown, Billy Dee Williams, Fay Hauser, Denise Nicholas-Hill; ***D:*** Eric Weston; ***W:*** Eric Weston, Wanda Dell.

Marvin's Room 🦴🦴½ **1996 (PG-13)** Guaranteed sobfest with a gifted set of performers. Sensitive spinster Bessie (Keaton) is living in Orlando where she's been caring for her bedridden father, Marvin (Cronyn), who's been dying for the last 20 years, and her eccentric aunt Ruth (Verdon). When she's stricken with leukemia and needs a bone marrow donor, Bessie must rely on tough, estranged sister Lee (Streep) to help out. But divorcee Lee's got her hands full with rebellious teenaged son Hank (DiCaprio) and his geeky younger bro Charlie (Scardino) and is none too eager to renew the family ties. Based on Scott McPherson's 1991 Off-Broadway play. **98m/C VHS, DVD.** Diane Keaton, Meryl Streep, Leonardo DiCaprio, Hume Cronyn, Gwen Verdon, Hal Scardino, Robert De Niro, Dan Hedaya, Margo Martindale, Cynthia Nixon; ***D:*** Jerry Zaks; ***W:*** Scott McPherson; ***C:*** Piotr Sobocinski; ***M:*** Rachel Portman.

The Marx Brothers in a Nutshell 🦴🦴🦴½ **1990** A tribute to the Marx Brothers, narrated by Gene Kelly. Contains clips from "Duck Soup," "Horse Feathers," "Animal Crackers," "Cocoanuts," and "Room Service." Also contains rare outtakes and interviews with the brothers, plus guest appearances by Dick Cavett, Robert Klein, David Steinberg, and others. Indispensable. **100m/B VHS.** Groucho Marx, Chico Marx, Harpo Marx, Zeppo Marx, Robert Klein, David Steinberg, George Fenneman, Dick Cavett; ***Nar:*** Gene Kelly.

Mary and Joseph: A Story of Faith 🦴½ **1979** A speculative look at the experiences and courtship of Mary and Joseph before the birth of Jesus. **100m/C VHS.** Blanche Baker, Jeff East, Colleen Dewhurst, Stephen McHattie, Lloyd Bochner, Paul Hecht; ***D:*** Eric Till. **TV**

Mary, Mary, Bloody Mary 🦴 **1976 (R)** Young beautiful artist ravages Mexico with her penchant for drinking blood. Turns out she's a bisexual vampire. When even her friends become victims, her father steps in to end the bloodbath. **85m/C VHS.** Christina Ferrare, David Young, Helena Rojo, John Carradine; ***D:*** Juan Lopez Moctezuma; ***W:*** Malcolm Marmorstein; ***M:*** Tom Bahler.

Mary, Mother of Jesus 🦴🦴½ **1999** The life of Jesus (Bale) is retold through the eyes of his mother (August), as her faith is tested by her son's ultimate sacrifice. The production stays close to the Biblical scripts of Matthew, Mark, Luke, and John and the characters are pretty much reverential cardboard. **94m/C VHS.** Christian Bale, Pernilla August, Geraldine Chaplin, David Threlfall, Hywel Bennett, Christopher Lawford; ***D:*** Kevin Connor; ***W:*** Albert Ross; ***C:*** Elemer Ragalyi; ***M:*** Mario Klemens. **TV**

Mary, My Dearest 🦴🦴 *Maria di Mi Corazon* **1983** Maria (Rojo) persuades her smalltime crook boyfriend Hector (Bonilla) to join her in a traveling magic show. When the van breaks down while they're touring, Maria goes in search of a telephone and winds up in a mental institution. Mixture of styles—from an everyday look at the bourgeoise to magic realism and terror—may confuse. Spanish with subtitles. **100m/C VHS.** *MX* Maria Rojo, Hector Bonilla, Salvador Sanchez; ***D:*** Jaime Humberto Hermosillo; ***W:*** Gabriel Garcia Marquez, Jaime Humberto Hermosillo; ***C:*** Angel Goded; ***M:*** Joaquin Gutierrez Heras.

Mary of Scotland 🦴🦴🦴 **1936** The historical tragedy of Mary, Queen of Scots and her cousin, Queen Elizabeth I of England is enacted in this classic film. Traces Mary's claims to the throne of England which ultimately led to her execution. Based on the Maxwell Anderson play. **123m/B VHS.** Katharine Hepburn, Fredric March, Florence Eldridge, Douglas Walton, John Carradine, Robert Barrat, Gavin Muir, Ian Keith, Moroni Olsen, William Stack, Alan Mowbray; ***D:*** John Ford.

Mary Poppins 🦴🦴🦴½ **1964** Magical English nanny arrives one day on the East Wind and takes over the household of a very proper London banker. She introduces her two charges to her friends and family, including Bert, the chimney sweep (Van Dyke), and eccentric Uncle Albert (Wynn). She also changes the lives of everyone in the family. From her they learn that life can always be happy and joyous if you take the proper perspective. Film debut of Andrews. Based on the books by P.L. Travers. A Disney classic that hasn't lost any of its magic. Look for the wonderful sequence where Van Dyke dances with animated penguins. ♫Chim Chim Cheree; A Spoonful of Sugar; The Perfect Nanny; Sister Suffragette; The Life I Lead; Stay Awake; Feed the Birds; Fidelity Feduciary Bank; Let's Go Fly a Kite. **139m/C VHS, DVD, Wide.** Julie Andrews, Dick Van Dyke, Ed Wynn, Hermione Baddeley, David Tomlinson, Glynis Johns, Karen Dotrice, Matthew Garber; ***D:*** Robert Stevenson; ***W:*** Bill Walsh, Whip Wilson; ***C:*** Edward Colman; ***M:*** Richard M. Sherman, Robert B. Sherman. Oscars '64: Actress (Andrews), Film Editing, Song ("Chim Chim Cher-ee"), Visual FX, Orig. Score; Golden Globes '65: Actress—Mus./Comedy (Andrews).

Mary, Queen of Scots 🦴🦴½ **1971 (PG-13)** Redgrave does a spirited job in the title role as the headstrong and romantic queen who came to an unfortunate end. Mary is raised in France by her mother's Catholic family, from whom she inherits the Scottish title after her mother's death. She claims the throne much to the dismay of her Protestant half-brother James Stuart (McGoohan) and England's equally Protestant Queen Elizabeth (Jackson), who does not want her own Catholic subjects to get any ideas. Mary makes two unfortunate marriages and winds up being betrayed, eventually forcing Elizabeth to eliminate her dangerous cousin. **128m/C VHS.** Vanessa Redgrave, Glenda Jackson, Patrick McGoohan, Timothy Dalton, Nigel Davenport, Trevor Howard, Daniel Massey, Ian Holm; ***D:*** Charles Jarrott; ***W:*** John Hale; ***C:*** Christopher Challis; ***M:*** John Barry.

Mary Reilly 🦴🦴 **1995 (R)** Mary (Roberts) is an innocent maid whose employer happens to be the infamous Dr. Jekyll (Malkovich). They both seem to be employed by Dr. Freud in this dank, dreary psychosexual thriller. Mary is torn between the repressed affection of the doctor and the oily sexuality of his alter ego, who conjures up images of her abusive father. Reuniting the crew and some of the cast of "Dangerous Liaisons" (Glenn Close also appears as a bawdy brothel owner), they fail to reach their previous heights. Most of the gloomy sets will make you wish you were wearing galoshes. Release date was bumped several times as the ending of the film was reshot (more than once). Based on the novel by Valerie Martin. **108m/C VHS, DVD, Wide.** Julia Roberts, John Malkovich, George Cole, Michael Gambon, Kathy Staff, Glenn Close, Michael Sheen, Bronagh Gallagher, Linda Bassett, Henry Goodman, Ciaran Hinds, Sasha Hanav; ***D:*** Stephen Frears; ***W:*** Christopher Hampton; ***C:*** Philippe Rousselot; ***M:*** George Fenton.

Mary Shelley's Frankenstein 🦴🦴½ *Frankenstein* **1994 (R)** Branagh turns from Shakespeare to another form of literary classic with his operatic (and loose) adaptation of the Shelley novel. He also plays Victor, the overwrought medical student who decides that death can be vanquished and sets out to prove his theories by making a man. De Niro is suffecently grisly (though lacking in pathos) as the reanimated corpse with Bonham Carter alternately suffering and excitable as Victor's fiancee Elizabeth. Visually arresting—particularly the Creature's birth scene—pic doesn't engender audience sympathy for the characters' trials and final fates. **123m/C VHS, DVD.** Kenneth Branagh, Robert De Niro, Helena Bonham Carter, Tom Hulce, Aidan Quinn, John Cleese, Ian Holm, Richard Briers, Robert Hardy, Cherie Lunghi, Celia Imrie, Trevyn McDowell; ***D:*** Kenneth Branagh; ***W:*** Frank Darabont, Steph Lady; ***C:*** Roger Pratt; ***M:*** Patrick Doyle.

Mary White **1977** The true story of Mary White, the 16-year-old daughter of a newspaper editor who rejects her life of wealth and sets out to find her own identity. **102m/C VHS.** Ed Flanders, Kathleen Beller, Tim Matheson, Donald Moffat, Fionnula Flanagan; ***D:*** Jud Taylor; ***C:*** Bill Butler.

Masada **1981** Based on Ernest K. Gann's novel "The Antagonists," this dramatization re-creates the 1st-century A.D. Roman siege of the fortress Masada, headquarters for a group of Jewish freedom fighters. Abridged from the original TV presentation. **131m/C VHS.** Peter O'Toole, Peter Strauss, Barbara Carrera, Anthony Quayle, Giulia Pagano, David Warner; ***D:*** Boris Sagal; ***M:*** Jerry Goldsmith.

Masala **1991** An experiment in a variety of genres, including glitzy musical-comedy numbers, erotic fantasy sequences, and all manner of kitsch. Krishna (who both stars and directs in his feature film debut) is a violence-prone, ex-junkie still trying to recover from the deaths of his family in a plane crash as they travelled from their home in Toronto to a vacation in India. Jaffrey has multi-roles as Krishna's unscrupulous uncle and cousin as well as the blue-skinned Indian deity, Lord Krishna, who appears to an Indian grandmother on her TV set. Multicultural confusion. **105m/C VHS.** *CA* Srinivas Krishna, Saeed Jaffrey, Zohra Segal, Sakina Jaffrey; ***D:*** Srinivas Krishna; ***W:*** Srinivas Krishna.

Mascara **1987 (R)** A group inspecting a transvestite's death are led into the seedy underground world of Belgian nightlife. **99m/C VHS.** *BE* Derek De Lint, Charlotte Rampling, Michael Sarrazin; ***D:*** Patrick Conrad.

Masculine Feminine ½ *Masculin Feminin* **1966** A young Parisian just out of the Army engages in some anarchistic activities when he has an affair with a radical woman singer. Hailed as one of the best French New Wave films. In French with English subtitles. **103m/B VHS.** *FR* Jean-Pierre Leaud, Chantal Goya, Marlene Jobert; ***D:*** Jean-Luc Godard. Berlin Intl. Film Fest. '66: Actor (Leaud).

M*A*S*H **1970 (R)** Hilarious, irreverent, and well-cast black comedy about a group of surgeons and nurses at a Mobile Army Surgical Hospital in Korea. The horror of war is set in counterpoint to their need to create havoc with episodic late-night parties, practical jokes, and sexual antics. An all-out anti-war festival, highlighted by scenes that starkly uncover the chaos and irony of war, and establish Altman's influential style. Watch for real-life football players Fran Tarkenton, Ben Davidson, and Buck Buchanan in the game. Loosely adapted from the novel by the pseudonymous Richard Hooker (Dr. H. Richard Hornberger and William Heinz). Subsequent hit TV series moved even further from the source novel. **116m/C VHS, DVD, Wide.** Franz Gottlieb, Donald Sutherland, Elliott Gould, Tom Skerritt, Sally Kellerman, JoAnn Pflug, Robert Duvall, Rene Auberjonois, Roger Bowen, Gary Burghoff, Fred Williamson, John Schuck, Bud Cort, G(eorge) Wood, David Arkin, Michael Murphy, Indus Arthur, Ken Prymus, Bobby Troup, Kim Atwood, Timothy Brown; ***D:*** Robert Altman; ***W:*** Ring Lardner Jr.; ***C:*** Harold E. Stine; ***M:*** Johnny Mandel; ***V:*** Sal Viscuso. Oscars '70: Adapt. Screenplay; AFI '98: Top 100; Cannes '70: Film; Golden Globes '71: Film—Mus./Comedy, Natl. Film Reg. '96;; Natl. Soc. Film Critics '70: Film; Writers Guild '70: Adapt. Screenplay.

M*A*S*H: Goodbye, Farewell & Amen ½ **1983** The final two-hour special episode of the TV series "M*A*S*H" follows Hawkeye, B.J., Colonel Potter, Charles, Margaret, Klinger, Father Mulcahy, and the rest of the men and women of the 4077th through the last days of the Korean War, the declaration of peace, the dismantling of the camp, and the fond and tearful farewells. **120m/C VHS.** Alan Alda, Mike Farrell, Harry (Henry) Morgan, David Ogden Stiers, Loretta Swit, Jamie Farr, William (Bill) Christopher, Allan Arbus. **TV**

The Mask *Eyes of Hell; The Spooky Movie Show* **1961** A deservedly obscure gory horror film about a masked killer, filmed mostly in 3-D. With special 3-D packaging and limited edition 3-D glasses. **85m/B VHS.** *CA* Paul Stevens, Claudette Nevins, Bill Walker, Anne Collings, Martin Lavut, Leo Leyden, Bill Bryden, Eleanor Beecroft, Steven Appleby; ***D:*** Julian Roffman; ***W:*** Slavko Vorkapich, Franklin Delessert, Sandy Haver, Frank Taubes; ***C:*** Herbert S. Alpert; ***M:*** Louis Applebaum.

Mask **1985 (PG-13)** A dramatization of the true story of a young boy afflicted with craniodiaphyseal dysplasia (elephantiasis). The boy overcomes his appearance and revels in the joys of life in the California bikers' community. Well acted, particularly the performances of Stoltz and Cher. A touching film, well-directed by Bogdanovich, that only occasionally slips into maudlin territory. **120m/C VHS, DVD.** Cher, Sam Elliott, Eric Stoltz, Estelle Getty, Richard Dysart, Laura Dern, Harry Carey Jr., Lawrence Monoson, Marsha Warfield, Barry Tubb, Andrew (Andy) Robinson, Alexandra Powers; ***D:*** Peter Bogdanovich; ***W:*** Anna Hamilton Phelan; ***C:*** Laszlo Kovacs. Oscars '85: Makeup; Cannes '85: Actress (Cher).

The Mask **1994 (PG-13)** Adolescent supernatural comedy with lollapalooza special effects is Carrey's follow-up to "Ace Ventura." Mild-mannered bank clerk Carrey discovers an ancient mask that has supernatural powers. Upon putting on the mask, he turns into one truly animated guy. He falls for a dame mixed up with gangsters and from there on, our hero deals not only with the incredible powers of the mask, but with hormones and bad guys as well. Based on the Dark Horse comic book series and originally conceived as a horror flick, director Russell, who gave Freddy Krueger a sense of humor, recast this one as a hellzapoppin' cartoon-action black comedy. Carrey's rubber face is an asset magnified by the breakthrough special effects courtesy of Industrial Light and Magic. **100m/C VHS, DVD, Wide.** Jim Carrey, Cameron Diaz, Peter Greene, Peter Riegert, Amy Yasbeck, Orestes Matacena, Richard Jeni, Ben Stein; ***D:*** Chuck Russell; ***W:*** Mike Werb; ***C:*** John R. Leonetti; ***M:*** Randy Edelman. Blockbuster '95: Comedy Actor, T. (Carrey), Female Newcomer, T. (Diaz); Blockbuster '96: Comedy Actor, V. (Carrey).

Mask of Death **1997 (R)** Detective Dan McKenna's (Lamas) wife is killed by Frank Dallio (Dunn) during the criminal's escape from the FBI and he's shot in the face by Dallio's buddy Mason, who happens to be a ringer for McKenna and conveniently dies in a car crash. Since the FBI want Dallio, Agent Jeffries (Williams) persuades McKenna to pose as Mason, which he does in order to get revenge. **125m/C VHS.** Lorenzo Lamas, Billy Dee Williams, Rae Dawn Chong, Conrad Dunn; ***D:*** David Mitchell; ***C:*** David Pelletier; ***M:*** Norman Orenstein.

The Mask of Diijon ½ **1946** A mad magician suspects that his wife is cheating on him and tries to hypnotize her into killing her supposed paramour. The plan goes awry when the wife uses a gun loaded with blanks. Von Stroheim's performance makes it worthwhile. **73m/B VHS, DVD.** Erich von Stroheim, Jeanne Bates, William Wright, Edward Van Sloan, Denise Vernac; ***D:*** Lew (Louis Friedlander) Landers; ***W:*** Griffin Jay, Arthur St. Claire; ***C:*** Jack Greenhalgh; ***M:*** Lee Zahler.

The Mask of Dimitrios **1944** Dutch mystery writer Leyden (Lorre) is vacationing in Instanbul, where he meets a fan, Col. Haki (Katch), at a party. Haki, the head of the secret police, informs Leyden that the body of arch criminal Dimitrios Makropoulous (Scott) has washed ashore and the man was stabbed to death. Leyden decides to write a novel about the criminal and delves into a dark world of intrigue and danger. Adapted from Eric Ambler's novel "A Coffin for Dimitrios." **96m/B VHS.** Peter Lorre, Kurt Katch, Zachary Scott, Sydney Greenstreet, Faye Emerson, George Tobias, Victor Francen, Steven Geray, Florence Bates, Eduardo Ciannelli, George Metaxa, Monte Blue; ***D:*** Jean Negulesco; ***W:*** Frank Gruber; ***C:*** Arthur Edeson; ***M:*** Adolph Deutsch.

The Mask of Fu Manchu ½ **1932** The evil Dr. Fu Manchu and his equally evil daughter set out to capture the scimitar and golden mask of Genghis Khan. With them, they will be able to destroy all white men and rule the world. Although a detective from Scotland Yard tries to stop them, the pair obtain the treasures and begin sadistically torturing their victims to death. Can they be stopped before they destroy the earth? One of the creepiest entries in the Fu Manchu series, and Loy's last oriental role. Based on the novel by Sam Rohmer. **72m/B VHS.** Boris Karloff, Lewis Stone, Karen Morley, Charles Starrett, Myrna Loy, Jean Hersholt, Lawrence Grant, David Torrence; ***D:*** Charles Brabin; ***C:*** Gaetano Antonio "Tony" Gaudio.

Mask of the Dragon **1951** A soldier's friend and girlfriend track down his killer after he delivers a golden curio to a shop in Los Angeles. **54m/B VHS.** Richard Travis, Sheila Ryan, Richard Emory, Jack Reitzen.

The Mask of Zorro *Zorro* **1998 (PG-13)** The dashing masked swordsman, who first made an appearance in a 1919 newspaper comic, returns to the big screen. Aging Zorro (Hopkins) escapes from 20 years in prison when he discovers his mortal enemy Montero (Wilson) is looking to establish an independent republic of California. But he needs some help and picks bandit Alejandro (Banderas), who needs a lot of training. Caught in the middle is Elena (Zeta Jones), a spirited beauty who was raised by Montero (Wilson) and doesn't know she's really Zorro's daughter. She wields quite a mean sword herself as Alejandro learns before any romancing can begin. A little long but offering swashbuckling fun. **136m/C VHS, DVD, Wide.** Antonio Banderas, Anthony Hopkins, Catherine Zeta-Jones, Stuart Wilson, Matt Letscher, Maury Chaykin, Tony Amendola, Pedro Armendariz Jr., L.Q. (Justus E. McQueen) Jones; ***D:*** Martin Campbell; ***W:*** Ted Elliott, Terry Rossio, John Eskow; ***C:*** Phil Meheux; ***M:*** James Horner.

The Masked Marvel *Sakima and the Masked Marvel* **1943** The Masked Marvel saves America's war industries from sabotage. Serial in 12 episodes. **195m/B VHS.** William Forrest, Louise Currie, Johnny Arthur; ***D:*** Spencer Gordon Bennet.

The Masked Rider ½ **1941** Drifters Brown and Knight head south of the border and find themselves trying to solve crimes committed by a mysterious masked rider. Latin American dancers and singers provide a nice change of pace from the usual cowpoke musical relief. Based on a story by Sam Robins. **57m/B VHS.** Johnny Mack Brown, Fuzzy Knight, Nell O'Day, Grant Withers; ***D:*** Ford Beebe; ***W:*** Sherman Lowe, Victor McLeod.

Masks of Death **1986** New adventure for Sherlock Holmes, as he is pulled from retirement to find the murderer of three unidentified corpses found in London's East End. **80m/C VHS.** Peter Cushing, John Mills, Anne Baxter, Ray Milland; ***D:*** Roy Ward Baker.

Mason of the Mounted **1932** Harmless enough western in which a Canadian Mountie tracks down a murderer in the U.S. **58m/B VHS.** Bill Cody, Nancy Drexel, Art Mix, Nelson McDowell; ***D:*** Harry Fraser.

Masque of the Red Death **1965** An integral selection in the famous Edgar Allan Poe/Roger Corman canon, it deals with an evil prince who traffics with the devil and playfully murders any of his subjects not already dead of the plague. Remade in 1989 with Corman as producer. **88m/C VHS.** *GB* Vincent Price, Hazel Court, Jane Asher, Patrick Magee, David Weston, Nigel Green, Julian Burton, Skip Martin, Gaye Brown, John Westbrook; ***D:*** Roger Corman; ***W:*** Charles Beaumont, Robert W(right) Campbell; ***C:*** Nicolas Roeg; ***M:*** David Lee.

Masque of the Red Death **1989 (R)** Roger Corman's second attempt at Edgar Allan Poe's horror tale pales compared to his Vincent Price version made 25 years earlier. Under-aged cast adds youth appeal but subtracts credibility from the fable of a sadistic prince and his sycophants trying to ignore the plague outside castle walls. Only late in the plot does veteran actor Macnee add proper note of doom. **90m/C VHS.** Patrick Macnee, Jeffery Osterhage, Adrian Paul, Tracy Reiner, Maria Ford, Clare Hoak; ***D:*** Larry Brand; ***W:*** Larry Brand, Daryl Haney; ***C:*** Edward Pei; ***M:*** Mark Governor.

Masque of the Red Death ½ **1990 (R)** Unrecognizable Poe mutation has guests invited to the mansion of a dying millionaire, only to be murdered by an unknown stalker. One scene features a pendulum, and that's it for literary faithfulness. **94m/C VHS.** Frank Stallone, Brenda Vaccaro, Herbert Lom, Michelle McBride, Christine Lunde; ***D:*** Alan Birkinshaw.

Masquerade **1988 (R)** A lonely young heiress meets a handsome "nobody" with a mysterious background and it is love at first sight. The romance distresses everyone in the circle of the elite because they assume that he is after her money and not her love. At first it seems decidedly so, then definitely not, and then nothing is certain. A real romantic thriller, with wonderful scenes of the Hamptons. **91m/C VHS.** Rob Lowe, Meg Tilly, John Glover, Kim Cattrall, Doug Savant, Dana Delany, Eric Holland; ***D:*** Bob Swaim; ***W:*** Dick Wolf; ***C:*** David Watkin; ***M:*** John Barry.

Mass Appeal **1984 (PG)** An adaptation of the Bill C. Davis play about the ideological debate between a young seminarian and a complacent but successful parish pastor. Lemmon has had better roles and done better acting. **99m/C VHS.** Jack Lemmon, Zeljko Ivanek, Charles Durning, Louise Latham, James Ray, Sharee Gregory, Talia Balsam; ***D:*** Glenn Jordan; ***W:*** Bill Davis; ***M:*** Bill Conti.

Massacre at Central High ½ *Blackboard Massacre* **1976 (R)** A new student takes matters into his own hands when gang members harass other students at a local high school. Other than some silly dialogue, this low-budget production is above average. **85m/C VHS.** Derrel Maury, Andrew Stevens, Kimberly Beck, Robert Carradine, Roy Underwood, Steve Bond, Steve Sikes, Lani O'Grady, Damon Douglas, Cheryl "Rainbeaux" Smith; ***D:*** Renee Daalder; ***W:*** Renee Daalder; ***C:*** Bert Van Munster.

Massacre in Dinosaur Valley ½ **1985** A dashing young paleontologist and his fellow explorers go on a perilous journey down the Amazon in search of the Valley of the Dinosaur. **98m/C VHS.** Michael Sopkiw, Suzanne Carvall.

Massacre in Rome ½ **1973 (PG)** A priest opposes a Nazi colonel's plan to execute Italian civilians in retaliation for the deaths of 33 German soldiers. Strong drama based on a real event. **110m/C VHS.** Richard Burton, Marcello Mastroianni, Leo McKern, John Steiner, Anthony Steel; ***D:*** George P. Cosmatos; ***W:*** George P. Cosmatos; ***M:*** Ennio Morricone.

Masseuse **1995 (R)** Kristy (Drew) decides to get back at cheating fiance Jack (Abell), who's out of town on a business trip, by turning their house into a massage parlor. **90m/C VHS, DVD.** Griffin (Griffen) Drew, Monique Parent, Tim Abell, Brinke Stevens; ***D:*** Daniel Peters; ***W:*** Steve Armogida; ***C:*** Gary Graver; ***M:*** Paul Di Franco.

Massive Retaliation **1985** Hordes of pesky villagers seek refuge within the secluded safety of a family's country house as WWIII approaches. **90m/C VHS.** Tom Bower, Peter Donat, Karlene Crockett, Jason Gedrick, Michael Pritchard; ***D:*** Thomas A. Cohen.

Master Blaster ½ **1985 (R)** Friendly game of survival with paintball guns goes awry when one of the contestants exchanges the play guns for deadly weapons. **94m/C VHS.** Jeff Moldovan, Donna Rosae, Joe Hess, Peter Lunblad, Robert Goodman, Richard St. George, George Gill, Jim Reynolds; ***D:*** Glenn Wilder; ***W:*** Glenn Wilder, Randy Grinter Jr., Jeff Moldovan; ***C:*** F. Pershing Flynn; ***M:*** Alain Salvati.

Master Harold and the Boys **1984** Stagey cable presentation of South African Athol Fugard's play about relationship between white man and two black servants. Occasionally provocative. **90m/C VHS.** Matthew Broderick; ***D:*** Michael Lindsay-Hogg. CABLE

Master Key 🦴½ **1944** Federal agents battle Nazis in this action-packed 12-chapter serial. **169m/B VHS.** Jan Wiley, Milburn Stone, Lash LaRue, Dennis Moore; ***D:*** Ray Taylor, Lewis D. Collins.

Master Mind 🦴🦴 **1973** A renowned Japanese super sleuth attempts to solve the theft of a sophisticated midget android. **86m/C VHS.** Zero Mostel, Keiko Kishi, Bradford Dillman, Herbert Berghof, Frankie Sakai; ***D:*** Alex March.

Master Minds 🦴½ **1949** The Bowery Boys run into trouble when Hall gets a toothache and can suddenly predict the future. He takes a job at a carnival where a mad scientist wants to transplant his brain into that of a monster ape man. **64m/B VHS.** Leo Gorcey, Huntz Hall, Glenn Strange, Gabriel Dell, Alan Napier, William Benedict, Bennie Bartlett, David Gorcey; ***D:*** Jean Yarbrough.

The Master of Ballantrae 🦴🦴 **1953** Flynn plays James Durrisdear, the heir to a Scottish title, who gets involved in a rebellion with Bonnie Prince Charlie against the English crown. When the rebellion fails, Flynn heads for the West Indies where he and his partner amass quite a fortune through piracy. Flynn eventually returns to Scotland where he finds that his brother has taken over his title as well as his longtime love. Based on the novel by Robert Louis Stevenson. Flynn's riotous life had put him long past his peak swashbuckling days, as this film unfortunately demonstrates. **89m/C VHS.** Errol Flynn, Roger Livesey, Anthony Steel, Beatrice Campbell, Yvonne Furneaux, Jacques Berthier, Felix Aylmer, Mervyn Johns; ***D:*** William Keighley; ***C:*** Jack Cardiff.

Master of Disguise **2002 (PG)** Pistachio Disguisey (Carvey) is a waiter at his father Fabbrizio's (Brolin) restaurant, where he displays a talent for mimicing all the customers. Turns out this is a family legacy, coveted by criminal Devlin Bowman (Spiner) who kidnaps Fabbrizio. So Pistachio has to get his act together, rescue dad, and defeat Devlin. Not yet reviewed. **?m/C VHS, DVD.** Dana Carvey, Jennifer Esposito, Brent Spiner, James Brolin, Edie McClurg, Harold Gould; ***D:*** Perry Andelin Blake; ***W:*** Dana Carvey, Harris Goldberg.

Master of Dragonard Hill 🦴½ **1989** A low-rent swashbuckling romance-novel pastiche. **92m/C VHS.** Oliver Reed, Eartha Kitt; ***W:*** R.J. Marx.

Master of the House 🦴🦴🦴 *Thou Shalt Honour Thy Wife* **1925** Story of a spoiled husband, a type extinct in this country but still in existence abroad. Silent with titles in English. **118m/B VHS.** ***D:*** Carl Theodor Dreyer.

Master of the World 🦴🦴½ **1961** Visionary tale of a fanatical 19th century inventor who uses his wonderous flying fortress as an antiwar weapon. Adapted from "Robur, the Conqueror" and "Master of the World," both by Jules Verne. **95m/C VHS.** Vincent Price, Charles Bronson, Henry Hull; ***D:*** William Witney; ***W:*** Richard Matheson; ***M:*** Les Baxter.

Master Race 🦴🦴½ **1944** Absorbing cautionary tale of a German officer who escapes retribution when the Nazis collapse, continuing to hold control over the inhabitants of a small town through intimidation. **98m/B VHS.** George Coulouris, Lloyd Bridges, Osa Massen, Nancy Gates, Stanley Ridges; ***D:*** Herbert Biberman; ***C:*** Russell Metty.

Master Touch 🦴½ *Hearts and Minds; Un Uomo da Rispettare* **1974 (PG)** When a legendary safecracker is released from prison, he attempts one last heist at a Hamburg insurance company. **96m/C VHS.** *GE IT* Kirk Douglas, Florinda Bolkan, Giuliano Gemma; ***D:*** Michele Lupo; ***M:*** Ennio Morricone.

Master with Cracked Fingers 🦴🦴 *Snake Fist Fighter* **1971 (R)** In one of the highest-grossing martial arts movies of all time, Jackie Chan uses the deadly "snake fist" technique against the bad guys. Chan's first feature is an abominable low-budget flick which, h, reportedly, sat on a shelf until he became a star. Then it was re-edited and footage of a double was inserted. **83m/C VHS, DVD, Wide.** *HK* Jackie Chan; ***D:*** Chin Hsin.

Masterminds 🦴🦴½ **1996 (PG-13)** Mildly diverting actioner has teen troublemaker Ozzie (Kartheiser) once again on the outs with his workaholic father Jake (Craven) and stepmom Helen (Hurwitch). Forced to take bratty stepsister Melissa (Stuart) to the private school he's been expelled from, Ozzie plans one more prank on officious principal Claire Maloney (Fricker). But the joke's on everyone when security analyst Ralph Bentley (Stewart) puts his plan in motion, taking control of the school and asking a ransom for a group of the wealthiest children. But the ingenious Ozzie's lurking about to get the best of the adults. **105m/C VHS.** Vincent Kartheiser, Patrick Stewart, Brenda Fricker, Matt Craven, Bradley Whitford, Annabelle Gurwitch, Katie Stuart, Callum Keith Rennie, Michael MacRae, Earl Pastko, Michael Simms, Jon Abrahams; ***D:*** Roger Christian; ***W:*** Floyd Byars; ***C:*** Nic Morris; ***M:*** Anthony Marinelli.

The Masters of Menace 🦴½ **1990 (PG-13)** The men in blue are mighty miffed when a bunch of bikers break parole to pay their last respects to a comrade in leather. Comic bits by Candy, Belushi, Aykroyd and Wendt provide little relief. **97m/C VHS.** David Rasche, Catherine Bach, Dan Aykroyd, James Belushi, John Candy, George Wendt, Tino Insana; ***D:*** Daniel Raskov; ***W:*** Tino Insana.

Masters of the Universe 🦴🦴 **1987 (PG)** A big-budget live-action version of the cartoon character's adventures, with He-Man battling Skeletor for the sake of the universe. **109m/C VHS, DVD, Wide.** Dolph Lundgren, Frank Langella, Billy Barty, Courteney Cox Arquette, Meg Foster; ***D:*** Gary Goddard; ***W:*** David Odell; ***C:*** Hanania Baer; ***M:*** Bill Conti.

Masters of Venus 🦴½ **1959** Eight-part serial about spaceships, space maidens and the like. **121m/B VHS.** Ferdinand "Ferdy" Mayne.

Master's Revenge 🦴½ **1971** When a girl is kidnapped by a violent motorcycle gang, martial artists are called in to rescue her. Originally released as "Devil Rider." **78m/C VHS.** Sharon Mahon, Ridgely Abele, Johnny Pachivas.

Mata Hari 🦴🦴🦴 **1932** During WWI, a lovely German spy steals secrets from the French through her involvement with two military officers. Lavish production and exquisite direction truly make this one of Garbo's best. Watch for her exotic pseudo-strip tease. **90m/B VHS.** Greta Garbo, Ramon Novarro, Lionel Barrymore, Lewis Stone, C. Henry Gordon, Karen Morley, Alec B. Francis; ***D:*** George Fitzmaurice; ***C:*** William H. Daniels.

Mata Hari 🦴🦴 **1985 (R)** Racy, adventure-prone story of WWI's most notorious spy, Mata Hari, who uses her seductive beauty to seduce the leaders of Europe. Stars "Emmanuelle" Kristel. **105m/C VHS.** Sylvia Kristel, Christopher Cazenove, Oliver Tobias, Gaye Brown, Gottfried John; ***D:*** Curtis Cunningham.

Matador 🦴🦴½ **1986** Bizarre, entertaining black comedy about a retired matador who finds a new way to satiate his desire to kill. He meets his match in an equally deadly woman and the two are drawn closer together by a young bullfighting student who confesses to a series of murders. Not for all tastes, but fine for those who like the outrageous. In Spanish with English subtitles. **90m/C VHS, Wide.** *SP* Assumpta Serna, Antonio Banderas, Nacho Martinez, Eva Cobo, Carmen Maura, Julieta Serrano, Chus (Maria Jesus) Lampreave, Eusebio Poncela; ***D:*** Pedro Almodovar; ***W:*** Pedro Almodovar, Jesus Ferrere; ***C:*** Angel Luis Fernandez; ***M:*** Bernardo Bonazzi.

The Match 🦴🦴½ **1999 (PG-13)** The small Scottish Highland village of Inverdoune has a very important soccer match on its collective minds. It's the annual grudge match with Le Bistro against rival pub Benny's Bar. Benny's has lost all previous 99 matches and, according to an ancient wager, if they lose the 100th match, Le Bisto can shut them down for good. So it's up to eccentric milkman Wullie (Beesley) to save the day. Predictable but filled with eccentric characters and a lot of heart. **96m/C VHS.** *GB* Max Beesley, James Cosmo, Laura Fraser, Isla Blair, Richard E. Grant, Ian Holm, Neil Morrissey, David Hayman, Bill Paterson, David O'Hara, Iain Robertson, Tom Sizemore; ***Cameos:*** Pierce Brosnan; ***D:*** Mick Davis; ***W:*** Mick Davis; ***C:*** Witold Stok; ***M:*** Harry Gregson-Williams.

The Match Factory Girl 🦴🦴🦴 *Tulitkkutehtaan Tytto* **1990** Kaurismak's final segment of his "working class" trilogy. Iris, a plain, shy outsider shares a drab dwelling with her one-dimensional mother and stepfather, works in a match factory, and hopes desperately for romantic love. Her world is transformed when the extraordinary occurs—she spots a brightly colored party dress in a shop window, buys it, wears it to a bar, and meets the Scandinavian creep who will soon get her pregnant and dump her. Angry at the world, Iris seeks revenge, and in so doing the audience learns that she has become very real and human. Kaurismaki makes his point that beauty can exist in ugly places. In Finnish with English subtitles. **70m/C VHS.** *SW FI* Kati Outinen, Elina Salo, Esko Nikkari, Vesa Vierikko; ***D:*** Aki Kaurismaki; ***W:*** Aki Kaurismaki.

The Matchmaker 🦴🦴🦴 **1958** An adaptation of the Thornton Wilder play concerning two young men in search of romance in 1884 New York. Later adapted as "Hello Dolly." An amusing diversion. **101m/B VHS.** Shirley Booth, Anthony Perkins, Shirley MacLaine, Paul Ford, Robert Morse, Perry Wilson, Wallace Ford, Russell Collins, Rex Evans, Gavin Gordon, Torben Meyer; ***D:*** Joseph Anthony; ***W:*** John Michael Hayes; ***C:*** Charles B(ryant) Lang Jr.

The Matchmaker 🦴🦴½ **1997 (R)** Big city girl Marcy (Garofalo) heads to a wee quaint Ireland burgh where she finds love and humanity amid the beer-guzzling, blarney-slinging locals. Jaded aide to a politico spin doctor (Leary), Marcy is there to track down some McGlory's, the Irish relatives of an American senator, in order to help his re-election campaign but hits town during the annual matchmaking festival and becomes the target of Irish marriage broker O'Shea. O'Hara is Sean, Marcy's laconic and appealing local suitor. Entertaining enough, with Garofalo and O'Hara more than filling the bill in a romantic comedy that heavily flirts with cliche. Sweeping vistas and a soundtrack appropriately filled with Irish favorites, old and new. Filmed in the village of Roundstone, Ireland. **97m/C VHS, DVD.** Janeane Garofalo, Milo O'Shea, David O'Hara, Denis Leary, Jay O. Sanders, Rosaleen Linehan, Maria Doyle Kennedy, Saffron Burrows, Paul Hickey, Jimmy Keogh; ***D:*** Mark Joffe; ***W:*** Louis Nowra, Karen Janszen, Graham Linehan, Greg Dinner; ***C:*** Ellery Ryan; ***M:*** John Altman.

Maternal Instincts 🦴🦴½ **1996 (PG-13)** Tracy (Burke) is a childless woman who undergoes an emergency hysterectomy without her consent. But she badly wants a baby and decides to get revenge on anyone thwarting her plans. **92m/C VHS.** Delta Burke, Beth Broderick, Garwin Sanford, Sandra Nelson, Gillian Barber, Kevin McNulty, Tom Butler, Tom Mason; ***D:*** George Kaczender. CABLE

Matewan 🦴🦴🦴½ **1987 (PG-13)** An acclaimed dramatization of the famous Matewan massacre in the 1920s, in which coal miners in West Virginia, reluctantly influenced by union organizer Joe Kenehan (Cooper), rebelled against terrible working conditions. Complex and imbued with myth, the film is a gritty, moving, and powerful drama with typically superb Sayles dialogue and Haskell Wexler's beautiful and poetic cinematography. Jones delivers an economical yet intense portrayal of the black leader of the miners. Sayles makes his usual onscreen appearance, this time as an establishment-backed reactionary minister. Partially based on the Sayles novel "Union Dues." **130m/C VHS, DVD.** John Sayles, Chris Cooper, James Earl Jones, Mary McDonnell, William Oldham, Kevin Tighe, David Strathairn, Jace Alexander, Gordon Clapp, Mason Daring, Jo Grifasi, Bob Gunton, Jo Henderson, Jason Jenkins, Ken Jenkins, Nancy Mette, Josh Mostel, Michael B. Preston, Maggie Renzi, Frank Hoyt Taylor; ***D:*** John Sayles; ***W:*** John Sayles; ***C:*** Haskell Wexler; ***M:*** Mason Daring. Ind. Spirit '88: Cinematog.

Matilda 🦴🦴 **1978 (PG)** Family fare about a entrepreneur who decides to manage a boxing kangaroo, which nearly succeeds in defeating the world heavyweight champion. Uneven and occasionally engaging. Based on Paul Gallico's novel. **103m/C VHS.** Elliott Gould, Robert Mitchum, Harry Guardino, Clive Revill; ***D:*** Daniel Mann.

Matilda 🦴🦴🦴 **1996 (PG)** Intelligent child Matilda Wormwood (Wilson) is oppressed by both her monstrous parents (DeVito and Perlman) and awful school principal, Trunchbull (Ferris). However, her first grade teacher, appropriately named Miss Honey (Davidtz), believes in her, which is enough to make Matilda plot an appropriate fate for the miserable people in her life. Excellent adaptation of a typically subversive book by Roald Dahl. Director DeVito, who wanted to create the illusion of a live-action cartoon, built among other things a "Carrot-cam" to capture the flying food of a food fight. **93m/C VHS, DVD.** Mara Wilson, Danny DeVito, Rhea Perlman, Embeth Davidtz, Pam Ferris, Paul (Peewee Herman) Reubens, Tracey Walter; ***D:*** Danny DeVito; ***W:*** Robin Swicord, Nicholas Kazan; ***C:*** Stefan Czapsky; ***M:*** David Newman.

Matinee 🦴🦴½ **1992 (PG)** "MANT: Half-man, Half-ant, All Terror!" screams from the movie marquee after Lawrence Woolsey, promoter extraordinare, and Ruth Corday, his leading lady, roll into Key West circa 1962. Meanwhile, teen Gene Loomis listens to his health teacher push the benefits of red meat and his girlfriend question life, while worrying about his dad, stationed in Cuba. Builds sly parallels between real life and movie horror by juxtaposing Woolsey (modeled after B-movie king William Castle) hyping his schlock, shown in "Atomo-Vision," against JFK solemnly announcing the Russian's approach. Fun, nostalgic look at days gone by—and the matinees that died with them. **98m/C VHS, DVD.** John Goodman, Cathy Moriarty, Simon Fenton, Omri Katz, Lisa Jakub, Kellie Martin, Jesse Lee, Lucinda Jenney, James Villemaire, Robert Picardo, Dick Miller, John Sayles, Mark McCracken, Jesse White, David Clennon, Luke Halpin, Robert Cornthwaite, Kevin McCarthy, William Schallert; ***D:*** Joe Dante; ***W:*** Charles Haas, Jerico (Weingrod) Stone; ***C:*** John Hora; ***M:*** Jerry Goldsmith.

The Mating Game 🦴🦴🦴 **1959** A fast-paced comedy about a tax collector, a beautiful girl, and a wily farm couple. Randall is the straitlaced IRS agent who finds out that the farming Larkins have never paid taxes and use a complicated barter system to get along. Randall falls for farm daughter Reynolds, gets drunk with her Pa, and decides to help the family out of their government dilemma—to the dismay of his superiors. Randall has a terrific drunk scene among his many comedic capers and Reynolds is a highlight. **96m/C VHS.** Tony Randall, Debbie Reynolds, Paul Douglas, Una Merkel, Fred Clark, Philip Ober, Charles Lane; ***D:*** George Marshall; ***W:*** William Roberts.

The Mating Habits of the Earthbound Human 🦴🦴 **1999 (R)** One-joke premise has an alien narrator (Pierce) making a nature doumentary about humans, focusing on the mating habits of nebbishy accountant Bill (Astin) and babe Jenny (Electra). The actors do what they can but the humor and situations are predictable. **90m/C VHS.** MacKenzie Astin, Carmen Electra, Markus Redmond, Lucy Alexis Liu; ***D:*** Jeff Abugov; ***W:*** Jeff Abugov; ***C:*** Michael Bucher; ***M:*** Michel McCarty; ***Nar:*** David Hyde Pierce.

Mating Season 🦴🦴½ **1981** Successful female attorney Arnaz meets good-natured laundromat owner Luckinbill at a bird-watching retreat. Romance ensues. **96m/C VHS.** Lucie Arnaz, Laurence Luckinbill; ***D:*** John Llewellyn Moxey. TV

Matrimaniac 🦴🦴 **1916** A man goes to great lengths to marry a woman against her father's wishes. Silent with music score. **48m/B VHS.** Douglas Fairbanks Sr., Constance Talmadge.

The Matrix 🦴🦴🦴 **1999 (R)** Visually wild ride (and rather complicated plot), courtesy of the brothers Wachowski. Mild-mannered computer programmer Thomas Anderson (Reeves) turns into hacker Neo by night. Neo thinks something is off about his world and he's right. Seems everything around him is just a computer-generated illusion, fostered by machines who use human beings as an electrical energy source. Neo is shown the truth by the mysterious Morpheus (Fishburne) and his renegade team, including capable and beautiful Trinity (Moss). Is Neo the chosen one, who'll make the world safe for humanity once again? Spectacular action sequences, a hissably evil villain (Weaving), a magisterial mentor, and a reluctant hero. What more could you ask for? **136m/C VHS, DVD.** Keanu Reeves, Carrie-Anne Moss, Laurence "Larry" Fishburne, Joe Pantoliano, Hugo Weaving, Gloria Foster, Marcus Chong, Paul Goddard, Robert Taylor, Julian (Sonny) Arahanga, Matt Doran, Belinda McClory, Anthony Ray Parker; ***D:*** Andy Wachowski, Larry Wachowski; ***W:*** Andy Wachowski, Larry Wachowski; ***C:*** Bill Pope; ***M:*** Don Davis. Oscars '99: Film Editing, Sound, Visual FX; British Acad. '99: Sound, Visual FX; MTV Movie Awards '00: Film, Male Perf. (Reeves), Fight (Keanu Reeves/Laurence Fishburne).

A Matter of Degrees 🦴🦴 **1990 (R)** Weeks before his graduation, a beatnik-type college senior finally acquires a goal: romancing a mystery girl...or maybe saving the student radio station...or not. The hero's aimlessness permeates the script, which never goes anywhere in its exploration of campus ennui. Good photography and a great stratum of alternative music groups on the soundtrack: Dream Syndicate, Pere Ubu, Schooly D, Pixies, Poi Dog Pondering, Minutemen, and Throwing Muses. **89m/C VHS.** Arye Gross, Judith Hoag, Tom Sizemore, John Doe; ***Cameos:*** John F. Kennedy Jr., Fred Schneider, Kate Pierson; ***D:*** W.T. Morgan.

A Matter of Dignity 🦴🦴 *To Telefteo Psemma* **1957** Chloe (Lambetti), whose family is on the brink of financial ruin, agrees to marriage with an incredibly boring millionaire to try and save them. She has to make a painful journey of self-discovery in order to escape the shallowness of how she was raised and the life she doesn't want to lead. Greek with subtitles. **104m/B VHS, DVD.** *GR* Georges Pappas, Ellie Lambetti, Athena Michaelidou, Eleni Zafirou; ***D:*** Michael Cacoyannis; ***W:*** Michael Cacoyannis; ***C:*** Walter Lassally; ***M:*** Manos Hadjidakis.

A Matter of Honor 🦴🦴 **1995 (PG)** Rugby player is killed during match and his coach gets blamed. So, to clear his name, said coach takes up an unusual challenge with the captain of the opposing team. **95m/C VHS.** Jackson Bostwick, Allen Arkus, Rebecca Gray, David Michie; ***D:*** Frederick P. Watkins.

A Matter of Life and Death 🦴🦴 **1981** True story follows the real-life experiences of nurse Joy Ufema who has devoted her life to helping terminally ill patients. Exceptional work from Lavin. **98m/C VHS.** Linda Lavin, Salome Jens, Gail Strickland, Gerald S. O'Loughlin, Ramon Bieri, Tyne Daly, Larry Breeding, John Bennett Perry; ***D:*** Russ Mayberry. **TV**

A Matter of Love 🦴 **1978 (R)** Two couples indulge in spouse swapping while vacationing at the beach. **89m/C VHS.** Michelle Harris, Mark Anderson, Christy Neal, Jeff Alin; ***D:*** Chuck Vincent.

A Matter of Principle **1983** The perennial Christmas special about a Scrooge-like character's yuletide change of heart. He decides it's time to shape up when he realizes he may lose his family permanently. **60m/C VHS.** Alan Arkin, Barbara Dana, Tony Arkin; ***D:*** Gwen Arner.

A Matter of Taste 🦴🦴 *Un Affaire de Gout* **2000** Actress/writer Jaoui's directorial debut finds married, boorish businessman Castella (Bacri) falling for 40-year-old actress Clara (Alvaro), who's fretting about aging and her uncertain prospects, and who has been hired to teach Castella English. He pursues, she resists—at first. Meanwhile, Castella's tough bodyguard Moreno (Lanvin) is involved with Clara's friend, free-spirited barmaid Manie (Jaoui). French with subtitles. **95m/C VHS, DVD.** *FR* Bernard Giraudeau, Jean-Pierre Lorit, Florence Thomassin, Charles Berling, Jean-Pierre Leaud, Laurent Spielvogel, Artus de Penguern, Anne-Marie Philipe; ***D:*** Barnard Rapp; ***W:*** Gilles Taurand, Barnard Rapp; ***C:*** Gerard de Battista; ***M:*** Jean-Philippe Goude.

A Matter of Time woof! **1976 (PG)** Maid is taught to enjoy life by an eccentric, flamboyant contessa, then finds the determination to become an aspiring actress. Often depressing and uneven, arguably Minnelli's worst directing job and his last film. Also Boyer's last appearance and first bit for Bergman's daughter Rossellini, in a small part as a nun. **97m/C VHS.** Liza Minnelli, Ingrid Bergman, Charles Boyer, Tina Aumont, Spiros Andros, Anna Proclemer, Isabella Rossellini; ***D:*** Vincente Minnelli; ***C:*** Geoffrey Unsworth.

Matter of Trust 🦴🦴 **1998 (R)** Mike D'Angelo (Howell) is an alcoholic L.A. cop barely hanging onto his job. The woman he loves, Theresa (Severance), is not only an Assistant D.A. but is married to a prominent doctor, Peter (Mancuso). But their paths aren't as separate as Mike might believe. **90m/C VHS, DVD.** C. Thomas Howell, Joan Severance, Nick Mancuso, Robert Miano, Jennifer Leigh Warren, Randee Heller; ***D:*** Joey Travolta; ***W:*** John Penney; ***C:*** Dan Heigh; ***M:*** Jeff Lass. **VIDEO**

A Matter of WHO 🦴🦴 **1962** A detective for the World Health Organization, or WHO, investigates the disease related deaths of several oil men. Travelling to the Middle East, he uncovers a plot by an unscrupulous businessman to control the oil industry by killing off its most powerful members. Although intended as a comedy, the subject matter is too grim to be taken lightly. **92m/B VHS.** *GB* Terry-Thomas, Alex Nicol, Sonja Ziemann, Richard Briers, Clive Morton, Vincent Ball, Honor Blackman, Carol White, Martin Benson, Geoffrey Keen; ***D:*** Don Chaffey; ***M:*** Edwin Astley.

Matters of the Heart 🦴🦴 **1990** Young pianist searches for an opportunity to display his talents, much to the disapproval of his veteran father. He meets a successful but embittered musician who takes him under her wing and passion between the two soon flares. Based on "The Country of the Heart" by Barbara Wersba. **94m/C VHS.** Jane Seymour, Christopher Gartin, James Stacy, Geoffrey Lewis, Nan Martin, Allan Rich, Clifford David, Katherine (Kathy) Cannon; ***D:*** Michael Rhodes; ***W:*** Linda J. Bergman. **CABLE**

Maurice 🦴🦴🦴 **1987 (R)** Based on E.M. Forster's novel about a pair of Edwardian-era Cambridge undergraduates who fall in love, but must deny their attraction and abide by British society's strict norms regarding homosexuality. Maurice finds, however, that he cannot deny his nature, and must come to a decision regarding family, friends, and social structures. A beautiful and stately film of struggle and courage. **139m/C VHS.** *GB* James Wilby, Hugh Grant, Rupert Graves, Mark Tandy, Ben Kingsley, Denholm Elliott, Simon Callow, Judy Parfitt, Helena Bonham Carter, Billie Whitelaw, Phoebe Nicholls, Barry Foster; ***D:*** James Ivory; ***W:*** James Ivory, Kit Hesketh-Harvey; ***C:*** Pierre Lhomme; ***M:*** Richard Robbins.

Mausoleum 🦴🦴 **1983 (R)** Only one man can save a woman from eternal damnation. **96m/C VHS.** Marjoe Gortner, Bobbie Bresee, Norman Burton, LaWanda Page, Shari Mann, Julie Christy Murray, Laura Hippe, Maurice Sherbanee; ***D:*** Michael Dugan; ***W:*** Robert Madero, Robert Barich; ***C:*** Robert Barich.

Mauvais Sang 🦴🦴 *Bad Blood* **1986** Carax's second film tells the story of rival gangsters who are searching for a serum that cures a devastating disease. Streetwise Alex (Lavant) from "Boy Meets Girl" (1984) also returns as the thief who is supposed to steal the serum (his character is again seen in 1991's "The Lovers on the Bridge."). French with subtitles. **125m/C VHS, DVD, Wide.** *FR* Michel Piccoli, Denis Lavant, Juliette Binoche, Hans Meyer, Julie Delpy, Carroll Brooks, Serge Reggiani, Hugo Pratt, Mireille Perrier; ***D:*** Leos Carax; ***W:*** Leos Carax; ***C:*** Jean-Yves Escoffier; ***M:*** Serge Reggiani, Charles Aznavour.

Mauvaise Graine 🦴🦴 *Bad Seed* **1933** Wilder (in his debut) filmed this comedy-drama (along with Esway) before heading off to Hollywood. Parisian wastrel Henri Pasquier (Mingand) impulsively steals a car when his disgusted wealthy father cuts him off. This lands Henri in with a professional gang of thieves, headed by Jean (Galle), who uses his pretty teenaged sister Jeannette (Darrieux) as a decoy. Henri enjoys his new career (and Jeannette) until jealousy gets in the way. French with subtitles. **76m/B VHS.** *FR* Pierre Mingand, Danielle Darrieux, Raymond Galle, Jean Wall; ***D:*** Billy Wilder, Alexander Esway; ***W:*** Billy Wilder, Alexander Esway; ***C:*** Paul Cotteret, Maurice Delattre; ***M:*** Franz Waxman, Walter Gray.

Maverick 🦴🦴½ **1994 (PG)** Entertaining remake of the popular ABC series is fresh and funny, with sharp dialogue and a good cast. Everybody looks like they're having a great time, not difficult for the charming Gibson, but a refreshing change of pace for the usually serious Foster and Greene. In a fun bit of casting, Garner, the original Maverick, shows up as Marshal Zane Cooper. Lightweight, fast-paced comedy was reportedly highly improvised, though Donner retained enough control to keep it coherent. The end is left wide open so a sequel seems likely. Keep your eyes peeled for cameos from country stars, old time Western actors, and an unbilled appearance from Glover. **127m/C VHS, DVD, Wide.** Mel Gibson, Jodie Foster, James Garner, Graham Greene, James Coburn, Alfred Molina, Paul Smith, Geoffrey Lewis, Max Perlich; ***Cameos:*** Dub Taylor, Dan Hedaya, Robert Fuller, Doug McClure, Bert Remsen, Denver Pyle, Will Hutchins, Waylon Jennings, Kathy Mattea, Danny Glover, Clint Black; ***D:*** Richard Donner; ***W:*** William Goldman; ***C:*** Vilmos Zsigmond; ***M:*** Randy Newman. Blockbuster '95: Comedy Actress, T. (Foster).

The Maverick Queen 🦴🦴½ **1955** Barbara Stanwyck, owner of a gambling casino and a member of the "Wild Bunch" outlaw gang, is torn between going straight for the love of a lawman or sticking with the criminals. Stanwyck is perfectly cast in this interesting Western. **90m/C VHS.** Barbara Stanwyck, Barry Sullivan, Wallace Ford, Scott Brady, Jim Davis, Mary Murphy; ***D:*** Joseph Kane.

Max 🦴🦴 **1979** A night watchman watches an aspiring actress who is working on her performance in a Broadway play. He tells her she would be better off marrying a doctor. **20m/C VHS.** Jack Gilford, Lynn Lipton; ***D:*** Joseph Gilford, Jennifer Lax.

Max and Helen 🦴🦴½ **1990** Uneven, but sensitive and at times highly moving made for TV story of two lovers who are victims of the holocaust. Max (Williams) survives both Nazi and Stalinist camps out of both love for his fiancee and guilt for having lived while she did not. **94m/C VHS.** *GB* Treat Williams, Alice Krige, Martin Landau, Jodhi May, John Phillips, Adam Kotz; ***D:*** Philip Saville; ***W:*** Corey Blechman. **TV**

Max Dugan Returns 🦴🦴 **1983 (PG)** A Simon comedy about an ex-con trying to make up with his daughter by showering her with presents bought with stolen money. Sweet and light, with a good cast. **98m/C VHS.** Jason Robards Jr., Marsha Mason, Donald Sutherland, Matthew Broderick, Kiefer Sutherland; ***D:*** Herbert Ross; ***W:*** Neil Simon; ***M:*** David Shire.

Max Is Missing 🦴🦴½ **1995 (PG)** Twelve-year-old Max (Caudell) gets separated from his father, is given a priceless Incan artifact by a dying man, and joins with a local lad to guard it from fortune hunters. Set in the ruins of Machu Picchu in the Peruvian Andes. **95m/C VHS.** Toran Caudell, Victor Rojas, Matthew Sullivan, Rick Dean, Charles Napier; ***D:*** Mark Griffiths. **CABLE**

Max Keeble's Big Move 🦴🦴 **2001 (PG)** Max (Linz), a kid on the verge of entering seventh grade, decides that he must change his image to be a little cooler, much to the dismay of his pals Megan (Grey) and Robe (Peck). On the first day of school, however, he is confronted with two bullies, a fussy principal (Miller) who wants to tear down an animal shelter that Max loves, and a renegade ice cream man. Max's dad comes home and announces that the family is moving to Chicago. Thinking that he can avoid the consequences by moving out of town, Max hatches numerous messy plots to get back at everyone who's tormenting him. After Max has taken revenge, dad reveals that the family is staying put after all, leaving Max to face the music. Not very original, but the kids will get a kick out of the food fight scene. **101m/C VHS, DVD.** *US* Alex D. Linz, Larry Miller, Jamie Kennedy, Zena Grey, Josh Peck, Orlando Brown, Noel Fisher, Nora Dunn, Robert Carradine, Clifton Davis, Amy Hill, Amber Valletta, Justin Berfield; ***D:*** Timothy Hill; ***W:*** Jon Bernstein, Mark Blackwell, James Greer; ***C:*** Arthur Albert; ***M:*** Michael Wandmacher.

Max, Mon Amour 🦴🦴 *Max, My Love* **1986** A very refined British diplomat in Paris discovers his bored wife has become involved with Max, who happens to be a chimpanzee. Instead of being upset, the husband decides Max should live with them. Very strange menage a trois manages to avoid the obvious vulgarities. In French with English subtitles. **97m/C VHS.** *FR* Anthony (Corlan) Higgins, Charlotte Rampling, Victoria Abril, Christopher Hovik, Anne-Marie Besse, Pierre Etaix; ***D:*** Nagisa Oshima; ***W:*** Jean-Claude Carriere, Nagisa Oshima; ***C:*** Raoul Coutard; ***M:*** Michel Portal.

Maxie 🦴🦴 **1985 (PG)** Highly predictable, and forgettable, comedy where a ghost of a flamboyant flapper inhabits the body of a modern-day secretary, and her husband is both delighted and befuddled with the transformations in his spouse. Close is okay, but the film is pretty flaky. **98m/C VHS.** Glenn Close, Ruth Gordon, Mandy Patinkin, Barnard Hughes, Valerie Curtin, Harry Hamlin; ***D:*** Paul Aaron; ***W:*** Patricia Resnick; ***M:*** Georges Delerue.

Maxim Xul woof! **1991** A professor of the occult is forced to tangle with a beast from Hell that possesses enormous strength and an insatiable appetite for human blood. **90m/C VHS.** Adam West, Jefferson Leinberger, Hal Strieb, Mary Schaeffer; ***D:*** Arthur Egeli.

Maximum Breakout 🦴½ **1991** A beautiful and wealthy girl is kidnapped, her boyfriend left for dead. But he recovers and leads a posse of mercenaries to the rescue. **93m/C VHS.** Sydney Coale Phillips; ***D:*** Tracy Lynch Britton.

Maximum Force 🦴½ **1992 (R)** Three renegade cops join together to infiltrate the underworld and bring to justice both the city's leading crime king and their own corrupt chief of police. **90m/C VHS.** Sam Jones, Sherrie Rose, Jason Lively, John Saxon, Richard Lynch, Mickey Rooney, Jeff Langton; ***D:*** Joseph Merhi.

Maximum Overdrive 🦴 **1986 (R)** Based upon King's story "Trucks," recounts what happens when a meteor hits Earth and machines run by themselves, wanting only to kill people. Score by AC/DC. **97m/C VHS, DVD, Wide.** Emilio Estevéz, Pat Hingle, Laura Harrington, Christopher Murney, Yeardley Smith, Stephen King; ***D:*** Stephen King; ***W:*** Stephen King; ***C:*** Armando Nannuzzi; ***M:*** AC/DC.

Maximum Risk 🦴🦴½ **1996 (R)** Like we need two of them? Van Damme, in a deja vu storyline (see "Double Impact") plays identical twins—a good French guy and a bad Russian guy—and when the bad guy gets killed, his brother takes over his life to find out whodunit. Risk and danger aside, the ruse is not all that bad, what with Henstridge as his sib's squeeze, unaware that the man she has in a lip lock is not her beloved. Has all the action you'd expect from a pic with "The Muscles from Brussels" and more guns, fists, and car chases is, of course, the major reason to invest your entertainment dollars here. Hong Kong action auteur Lam's stateside debut ensures that fast-paced chases and full-throttle combat is well done and visually appealing. **100m/C VHS, DVD, Wide.** Jean-Claude Van Damme, Natasha Henstridge, Jean-Hugues Anglade, Stephane Audran, Paul Ben-Victor, Zach Grenier, Frank Senger; ***D:*** Ringo Lam; ***W:*** Larry Ferguson; ***C:*** Alexander Grusynski; ***M:*** Robert Folk.

Maximum Security 1987 A small-budget prison film detailing the tribulations of a model prisoner struggling to resist mental collapse. **113m/C VHS.** Geoffrey Lewis, Jean Smart, Robert Desiderio; ***D:*** Bill Duke.

Maximum Thrust woof! *Waldo Warren: Private Dick Without a Brain* **1988** A few white men confront a deadly Caribbean voodoo tribe. **80m/C** Rick Gianasi, Joe Derrig, Jennifer Kanter, Mizan Nunes; ***D:*** Tim Kincaid.

May Fools *Milou en Mai; Milou in May* **1990 (R)** Malle portrays individuals collectively experiencing personal upheaval against the backdrop of unrelated social upheaval. An upper-crust family gathers at a country estate for the funeral of the clan's matriarch, while the May of '68 Parisian riots unfold. Few among the family members mourn the woman's passing, save her son Milou (Piccoli) who leads a pastoral existence tending grapes on the estate. Milou's daughter (Miou-Miou), like the others, is more concerned with her personal gain, suggesting, to her father's horror, that they divide the estate in three. Touching, slow, keenly observed. In French with English subtitles. **105m/C VHS.** *FR* Michel Piccoli, Miou-Miou, Michael Duchaussoy, Dominique Blanc, Harriet Walter, Francois Berleand, Paulette Dubost, Bruno Carette, Martine Gautier; ***D:*** Louis Malle; ***W:*** Jean-Claude Carriere, Louis Malle; ***C:*** Renato Berta; ***M:*** Stephane Grappelli. Cesar '91: Support. Actress (Blanc).

May Wine **1990 (R)** A sexy, romantic comedy starring "Twin Peaks" alumna, Boyle. **85m/C VHS.** Guy Marchand, Lara Flynn Boyle, Joanna Cassidy.

Maya **1966** After the death of his mother, young Terry (North) goes to join his big-game hunting father in India. After a quarrel Terry runs off and meets an Indian boy who has promised his dying father he will deliver a sacred white elephant to a jungle temple. The two lads join forces for the trek and have all sorts of adventures along the way. Basis for a short-lived TV series. **91m/C VHS.** Jay North, Clint Walker, Sajid Kahn, I.S. Johar; ***D:*** John Berry; ***W:*** John Fante.

Maya woof! **1982** A teacher of fashion in a high school becomes the object of a student's devotion and another teacher's insane jealousy. **114m/C VHS.** Berta Dominguez, Joseph D. Rosevich; ***D:*** Agust Agustsson.

Mayalunta **1986** A young artist is emotionally tortured by a dying older couple. **90m/C VHS.** *SP* Federico Luppi, Miguel Angel Sola, Barbara Mujica.

Maybe Baby **1999 (R)** Sam (Laurie) and Lucy (Richardson) Bell are a happily married couple trying to have a baby. She's a talent agent and he works for the BBC. Dissatisfied at work, Sam tries his hand at scriptwriting and decides his subject will be a comic look at the couple's infertility problems. Naturally, he keeps this a secret from Lucy, although she finds out when his script is accepted and walks out on Sam. Tends towards the smug and the leads don't particularly click as a couple, which makes the supporting players the most interesting to watch onscreen. **93m/C VHS, DVD.** *GB FR* Hugh Laurie, Joely Richardson, Adrian Lester, James Purefoy, Tom Hollander, Joanna Lumley, Rowan Atkinson, Dawn French, Emma Thompson, Rachael Stirling; ***D:*** Ben Elton; ***W:*** Ben Elton; ***C:*** Roger Lanser; ***M:*** Colin Towns.

Maybe I'll Be Home in the Spring *Deadly Desire* **1970 (PG)** Denise (Field) is estranged from her family and decides to leave home for life on a commune where she becomes involved with drugs. When she decides to return home everyone finds it hard to adjust. **90m/C VHS.** Sally Field, Jackie Cooper, Eleanor Parker, David Carradine, Lane Bradbury; ***D:*** Joseph Sargent. **TV**

Maybe ... Maybe Not *Der Bewegte Mann; The Most Desired Man* **1994 (R)** The German title refers to a man who moves between both sexual preferences although the film takes a straighter line. Hunky-but-dumb Axel (Schweiger) has cheated on girlfriend Dorothy (Riemann) once too often and she kicks him out. Axel winds up staying with gay pal Norbert (Krol), who would like to go from friendship to lovers, which Axel doesn't pick up on. Dorothy does, however, and wonders if Axel is really gay, but when she discovers she's pregnant, Dorothy decides to marry him anyway. Warm-hearted and campy, with some blatantly sexual dialogue. Based on two gay comic books by Ralf Koenig. German with subtitles or dubbed. **93m/C VHS.** *GE* Til Schweiger, Katja Riemann, Joachim Krol, Rufus Beck; ***D:*** Soenke Wortmann; ***W:*** Soenke Wortmann; ***C:*** Gernot Roll; ***M:*** Torsten Breuer.

Mayerling **1936** Considered one of the greatest films about doomed love. Story of the tragic and hopeless affair between Crown Prince Rudolf of Hapsburg and young Baroness Marie Vetsera. Heart wrenching and beautiful, with stupendous acting. Remade in 1968. In French with English subtitles. **95m/B VHS.** Charles Boyer, Danielle Darrieux; ***D:*** Anatole Litvak. N.Y. Film Critics '37: Foreign Film.

Mayerling **1968 (PG-13)** Based on the tragic romance between Crown Prince Rudolf of Hapsburg (Sharif) and the teenaged Baroness Maria Vetsera (Deneuve). Set in 1888, the royal Rudolf defies his father, the Emperor Franz Josef (Mason), to take part in a student revolt for the liberation of Hungary and to fall for the common-born Maria (despite his political marriage). No doubt meant to be a sweeping combo of politics and love ala "Doctor Zhivago," it's mostly tedious; see the 1936 version instead. **140m/C VHS.** *GB FR* Omar Sharif, Catherine Deneuve, James Mason, Ava Gardner, James Robertson Justice, Genevieve Page, Ivan Desny, Fabienne Dali; ***D:*** Terence Young; ***W:*** Terence Young; ***C:*** Henri Alekan; ***M:*** Francis Lai.

Mayflower Madam **1987 (R)** Fairly unsexy and uninteresting TV movie recounting the business dealings and court battles of the real-life Sydney Biddle Barrows. Barrows/Bergen is a prominent New York socialite and madam of an exclusive escort service whose clientele includes businessmen and dignitaries. **93m/C VHS.** Candice Bergen, Chris Sarandon, Chita Rivera; ***D:*** Lou Antonio; ***M:*** David Shire. **TV**

Mayflower: The Pilgrims' Adventure **1979** The Pilgrims flee religious persecution in England in 1620 and sail to America on the Mayflower, which is captained by Hopkins. Crenna plays the leader of the Puritans, the Rev. William Brewster. **96m/C VHS.** Anthony Hopkins, Richard Crenna, Jenny Agutter, Michael Beck, David Dukes, Trish Van Devere, Guy Sorel, Paul Sparer; ***D:*** George Schaefer; ***W:*** James Lee Barrett. **TV**

Mayhem **1987** Two loners in Hollywood confront all types of urban low-life murderers, drug pushers, and child molesters. **90m/C VHS.** Raymond Martino, Pamela Dixon, Robert Gallo, Wendy MacDonald.

Maytime **1937** Lovely story of an opera star (MacDonald) and penniless singer (Eddy) who fall in love in Paris, but her husband/teacher (Barrymore) interferes. One of the best films the singing duo ever made. ♫Maytime Finale; Virginia Ham and Eggs; Vive l'Opera; Student Drinking Song; Carry Me Back to Old Virginny; Reverie; Jump Jim Crow; Road to Paradise; Page's Aria. **132m/B VHS.** Jeanette MacDonald, Nelson Eddy, John Barrymore, Herman Bing, Tom Brown, Lynne Carver; ***D:*** Robert Z. Leonard; ***W:*** Noel Langley.

Maytime in Mayfair **1952** A dress shop owner's rival is getting all the goodies first, for which he takes the heat from his partner. When he finds out how the rival is doing it, the partners up and head for a vacation in the south of France. Overly simplistic but charming kitsch, helped along by Technicolor shots of the fashions and sets. **94m/C VHS.** Anna Neagle, Michael Wilding, Peter Graves, Nicholas Phipps, Tom Walls, Tom Walls Jr.; ***D:*** Herbert Wilcox.

The Maze **1985** Mystery about a young girl who meets the ghost of her mother's first love in her garden estate. **60m/C VHS.** *GB* Francesca Annis, James Bolam, Sky McCatskill. **TV**

Maze **2001 (R)** Introverted New York artist Lyle Maze (Morrow) is a sculptor afflicted with Tourette's syndrome, which makes him romantically hesitant. Lyle's best friend is a doctor named Mike (Sheffer), whose devotion is to his career rather than his girlfriend Callie (Linney). Mike leaves Callie for a months-long tour with Doctors Without Borders in Africa and when Callie discovers she is pregnant, she turns to Lyle for emotional support. Unsurprisingly, the needy duo fall in love before they have to explain what's happened on Mike's return. **98m/C VHS, DVD.** Rob Morrow, Laura Linney, Craig Sheffer, Gia Carides, Rose Gregorio, Robert Hogan; ***D:*** Rob Morrow; ***W:*** Rob Morrow, Bradley White; ***C:*** Wolfgang Held; ***M:*** Bobby Previte.

Mazes and Monsters *Rona Jaffe's Mazes and Monsters; Dungeons and Dragons* **1982** A group of university students becomes obsessed with playing a real life version of the fantasy role-playing game, Dungeons and Dragons (known in the film as Mazes & Monsters since D&D is trademarked). Early Hanks appearance is among the film's assets. Adapted from the book by Rona Jaffe. **100m/C VHS.** *CA* Tom Hanks, Wendy Crewson, David Wallace, Chris Makepeace, Lloyd Bochner, Peter Donat, Murray Hamilton, Vera Miles, Louise Sorel, Susan Strasberg, Anne Francis; ***D:*** Steven Hilliard Stern; ***M:*** Hagood Hardy. **TV**

McBain **1991 (R)** In this exciting fast-paced action-thriller, POW Robert McBain (Walken) leads a group of veterans into battle against the Columbian drug cartel. Stunning cinematography and superb performances combine to make this a riveting action film you won't soon forget. **104m/C VHS.** Christopher Walken, Maria Conchita Alonso, Michael Ironside, Steve James, Jay Patterson, Thomas G. Waites; ***D:*** James Glickenhaus; ***W:*** James Glickenhaus.

McCabe & Mrs. Miller **1971 (R)** Altman's characteristically quirky take on the Western casts Beatty as a self-inflated entrepreneur who opens a brothel in the Great North. Christie is the madame who helps stabilize the haphazard operation. Unfortunately, success comes at a high price, and when gunmen arrive to enforce a business proposition, Beatty must become the man he has, presumably, merely pretended to be. A poetic, moving work, and a likely classic of the genre. Based on the novel by Edmund Naughton. **121m/C VHS, Wide.** Warren Beatty, Julie Christie, William Devane, Keith Carradine, John Schuck, Rene Auberjonois, Shelley Duvall, Bert Remsen, Michael Murphy, Hugh Millais, Jack Riley; ***D:*** Robert Altman; ***W:*** Robert Altman; ***C:*** Vilmos Zsigmond; ***M:*** Leonard Cohen.

The McConnell Story *Tiger in the Sky* **1955** True story of ace flyer McConnell, his heroism during WWII and the Korean conflict, and his postwar aviation pioneer efforts. Fine acting from Allyson and Ladd, with good support from Whitmore and Faylen. **107m/C VHS.** Alan Ladd, June Allyson, James Whitmore, Frank Faylen; ***D:*** Gordon Douglas; ***M:*** Max Steiner.

The McCullochs *The Wild McCullochs* **1975 (PG)** Texas millionaire J.J. McCulloch (Tucker) is the kind of domineering patriarch whose kids wind up hating him and destroying their own lives. Stereotypical family saga set in 1949. **93m/C VHS, DVD, Wide.** Forrest Tucker, Julie Adams, Janice Heiden, Max Baer Jr., Don Grady, Chip Hand, Dennis Redfield, William Demarest, Harold J. Stone, Vito Scotti, James Gammon, Mike Mazurki; ***D:*** Max Baer Jr.; ***W:*** Max Baer Jr.; ***C:*** Fred W. Koenekamp; ***M:*** Ernest Gold.

The McGuffin **1985** A film critic's inquisitiveness about the activities of his neighbors gets him caught up in murder and a host of other problems. A takeoff of Alfred Hitchcock's 1954 classic "Rear Window." **95m/C VHS.** *GB* Charles Dance, Ritza Brown, Francis Matthews, Brian Glover, Phyllis Logan, Jerry Stiller, Anna Massey; ***D:*** Colin Bucksey.

McHale's Navy **1964** The TV sitcom came to the big screen with its silly humor intact as Lt. Commander Quinton McHale (Borgnine) and the reprobate crew of PT-73 get into debt gambling with a bunch of marines, which they try to get out of in a variety of unorthodox ways. **93m/C VHS.** Ernest Borgnine, Tim Conway, Joe Flynn, Bob Hastings, Billy (Billie) Sands, Gavin MacLeod, George Kennedy; ***D:*** Edward Montagne; ***W:*** Frank Gill Jr., George Carleton Brown; ***C:*** William Margulies.

McHale's Navy **1997 (PG)** Yet another (unsuccessful) attempt to take a TV series and let it loose on the big screen. Retired Navy skipper McHale (Arnold) has set up his scheming ways on the Caribbean island of San Ysidro, where he can be a thorn in the side of Capt. Binghampton (Stockwell), the newly transferred commanding officer of the island's sleepy naval base. McHale's former cronies aid their leader when he's reluctantly reunited with the Navy in order to prevent the terrorist threats of his former Soviet nemesis Vladakov (Curry). A shining example of "why bother?" moviemaking. TV's original McHale, Borgnine, has a cameo (and gets a promotion to admiral). **108m/C VHS.** Tom Arnold, Tim Curry, Dean Stockwell, David Alan Grier, Debra Messing, Thomas Chong, Bruce Campbell, French Stewart, Brian Haley, Danton Stone; ***Cameos:*** Ernest Borgnine; ***D:*** Bryan Spicer; ***W:*** Peter Crabbe; ***C:*** Buzz Feitshans IV; ***M:*** Dennis McCarthy.

McHale's Navy Joins the Air Force **1965** McHale is conspicuously missing from this sequel (Borgnine had a contract dispute) so second banana Conway, as Ensign Charles Parker, gets to shine in slapstick gags. A drunken Parker winds up in an Air Force uniform and is mistaken for a hot-shot flier, gets involved with some Russians, and is even cited for bravery by President Franklin D. Roosevelt. **91m/C VHS.** Tim Conway, Joe Flynn, Tom Tully, Ted Bessell, Bob Hastings, Gavin MacLeod, Billy (Billie) Sands; ***D:*** Edward Montagne; ***W:*** John Fenton Murray; ***C:*** Lionel Lindon.

McKenzie Break **1970** Irish intelligence agent John Connor (Keith) is sent to Scotland to Camp McKenzie, a prison for German POWs during WWII. Captured U-boat commander Schluetter (Griem) is suspected of planning a mass escape and Connor is supposed to stop the action. The battle of wills between the hard-headed Connor and wily Schluetter provides taut, suspenseful drama. Adapted from "The Bowmanville Break" by Sidney Shelley. **106m/C VHS, DVD, Wide.** Brian Keith, Helmut Griem, Ian Hendry, Jack Watson, Horst Janson, Patrick O'Connell; ***D:*** Lamont Johnson; ***W:*** William W. Norton Sr.; ***C:*** Michael Reed; ***M:*** Riz Ortolani.

McLintock! **1963** Rowdy western starring Wayne as a tough cattle baron whose refined wife (O'Hara) returns from the east after a two-year separation. She wants a divorce and custody of their 17-year-old daughter (Powers), who's been away at school. In the meantime, he's hired a housekeeper (De Carlo), whose teenage son (real-life son Patrick) promptly falls for Powers. It's a battle royal between the feisty wife and cantankerous husband but no one out-dukes the Duke. Other Wayne family members involved in the production include daughter Aissa (as the housekeeper's daughter) and son Michael who produced the film. **127m/C VHS, DVD.** John Wayne, Maureen O'Hara, Yvonne De Carlo, Patrick Wayne, Stefanie Powers, Jack Kruschen, Chill Wills, Jerry Van Dyke, Edgar Buchanan, Bruce Cabot, Perry Lopez, Michael Pate, Strother Martin, Gordon Jones; ***D:*** Andrew V. McLaglen; ***W:*** James Edward Grant; ***C:*** William Clothier.

The McMasters *The Blood Crowd; The McMasters...Tougher Than the West Itself* **1970 (PG)** Set shortly after the Civil War, the film tells the story of the prejudice faced by a black soldier who returns to the southern ranch on which he was raised. Once there, the rancher gives him half of the property, but the ex-soldier has difficulty finding men who will work for him. When a group of Native Americans assist him, a band of bigoted men do their best to stop it. The movie was released in two versions with different endings: in one, prejudice prevails; in the other, bigotry is defeated. **89m/C VHS.** Burl Ives, Brock Peters, David Carradine, Nancy Kwan, Jack Palance,

Dane Clark, L.Q. (Justus E. McQueen) Jones, Alan Vint, John Carradine; *D:* Alf Kjellin.

McQ ½ **1974 (PG)** After several big dope dealers kill two police officers, a lieutenant resigns to track them down. Dirty Harry done with an aging Big Duke. **116m/C VHS.** John Wayne, Eddie Albert, Diana Muldaur, Clu Gulager, Colleen Dewhurst, Al Lettieri, Julie Adams, David Huddleston; *D:* John Sturges; *C:* Harry Stradling Jr.; *M:* Elmer Bernstein.

McVicar ½ **1980 (R)** A brutish and realistic depiction of crime and punishment based on the life of John McVicar, who plotted to escape from prison. From the book by McVicar. **90m/C VHS.** *GB* Roger Daltrey, Adam Faith, Cheryl Campbell; *D:* Tom Clegg; *W:* Tom Clegg.

Me and Him ½ *Ich und Er* **1989 (R)** An unsuspecting New Yorker finds himself jockeying for position with his own instincts when his libido decides it wants a life of its own. **94m/C VHS.** *GE* Griffin Dunne, Carey Lowell, Ellen Greene, Craig T. Nelson; *D:* Doris Dorrie; *M:* Klaus Doldinger; *V:* Mark Linn-Baker.

Me and the Colonel ½ **1958** Average satire finds Jewish refugee S.L. Jacobowsky (Kaye) trying to get out of Paris to Spain before the Nazis occupy the city. He gets stuck travelling with anti-Semitic Polish colonel Prokoszny (Jurgens), who's also not eager to fall into German hands. If the trip went smoothly, there wouldn't be a story, so naturally the men are forced to put aside their differences to survive. Adapted from Franz Werfel's play "Jacobowsky and the Colonel." **110m/B VHS.** Danny Kaye, Curt Jurgens, Akim Tamiroff, Nicole Maurey, Francoise Rosay, Martita Hunt, Alexander Scourby, Liliane Montevecchi; *D:* Peter Glenville; *W:* S.N. Behrman, George Froeschel; *C:* Burnett Guffey; *M:* George Duning.

Me and the Kid ½ **1993 (PG)** Minor career criminals Aiello and Pantoliano try a robbery on a ruthless financier's (Dukes) home and wind up kidnapping his 10-year-old son instead. But dad doesn't want to pay the ransom and Aiello dumps his partner (who wants to kill the kid) and heads out on the road with the boy. **97m/C VHS.** Danny Aiello, Joe Pantoliano, Alex Zuckerman, Cathy Moriarty, David Dukes, Anita Morris; *D:* Dan Curtis.

Me and the Mob ½ *Wo Do I Gotta Kill?* **1994 (R)** Writer Jimmy Corona (Lorinz) thinks the way to get some colorful stories is to join up with his mobster uncle (Darrow). But Jimmy's no tough guy and the feds coerce him into wearing a wire to bust the local godfather. Low-budget comedy is a lesson in tedium. **85m/C VHS.** James Lorinz, Tony Darrow, John A. Costelloe, Sandra Bullock, Anthony Michael Hall, Stephen Lee, Ted (Theodore) Sorel; *Cameos:* Steve Buscemi; *D:* Frank Rainone; *W:* James Lorinz, Frank Rainone.

Me & Veronica **1993 (R)** Two estranged sisters try to come to terms with each other and their dead end lives. Good sister Fanny (McGovern) is a divorced waitress living in a run-down seaside town in New Jersey. One day bad sister Veronica (Wettig) shows up, announcing she's about to be sent to jail for welfare fraud. Veronica asks Fanny to look after her two kids while she's in jail and it is while visiting Veronica in prison that Fanny comes to realize her seemingly flamboyant sister is actually mentally ill and possibly suicidal. Grim little film with good lead performances. **97m/C VHS.** Elizabeth McGovern, Patricia Wettig, Michael O'Keefe, John Heard; *D:* Don Scardino; *W:* Leslie Lyles; *M:* David Mansfield.

Me & Will ½ **1999 (R)** Babes on bikes take to the road. Aspiring writer Jane (Rose) and artist Will (Behr) both have bad luck with men and drug problems, as well as a liking for chopper-riding. They meet in rehab and decide a road trip in search of the cycle ridden by Peter Fonda in "Easy Rider" is just the kind of quest they need. Uneven quality but a lot of recognizable faces in supporting roles. **93m/C VHS, DVD.** Sherrie Rose, Melissa Behr, Patrick Dempsey, Seymour Cassel, Grace Zabriskie, M. Emmet Walsh, Steve Railsback, Traci Lords, Billy Wirth; *D:* Sherrie Rose, Melissa Behr; *W:* Sherrie Rose, Melissa Behr; *C:* Joey Forsyte. **VIDEO**

Me, Myself & I ½ **1992 (R)** Segal is a successful New York writer who falls in love with next-door neighbor Williams. But the road to romance is never smooth—particularly when your paranoid gal suffers from multiple personality disorder. Fun leads, dumb movie. **97m/C VHS.** George Segal, JoBeth Williams, Shelley Hack, Don Calfa, Bill Macy, Betsey Lynn George, Sharon McNight, Ruth Gilbert; *D:* Pablo Fero; *W:* Julian Barry.

Me, Myself, and Irene **2000 (R)** Carrey is Charlie, a Rhode Island state trooper whose split personality (one meek and mild-mannered, the other an out-of-control sociopath) is controlled by medication, which he loses when transporting crime suspect Irene (Zellweger). Both sides fall for the girl and declare war on each other. Carrey's verbal and physical acrobatics, along with the Farrellys' patented gross-out scenes are as hilarious, and joyfully disgusting, as you'd imagine. And if you're into that kind of thing, you'll not be disappointed, but the movie shares the lead character's ailment: it has another side. The romance between Charlie and Irene can't keep up with the energy of the comedic scenes, especially the ones involving Charlie's three Mensa-candidate, African-American sons, who almost steal the movie right out from under him (who'd a thunk it?) **117m/C VHS, DVD, Wide.** Jim Carrey, Renee Zellweger, Robert Forster, Chris Cooper, Richard Jenkins, Traylor Howard, Daniel Greene, Zen Gesner, Tony Cox, Anthony Anderson, Lenny Clarke, Shannon Whirry, Rob Moran, Mongo Brownlee, Jerod Mixon, Michael Bowman, Mike Cerrone; *Cameos:* Anna Kournikova, Cam Neely, Brendan Shanahan; *D:* Bobby Farrelly, Peter Farrelly; *W:* Bobby Farrelly, Peter Farrelly, Mike Cerrone; *C:* Mark Irwin; *M:* Peter Yorn, Lee Scott; *V:* Rex Allen.

Me Myself I **1999 (R)** Pamela Drury (Griffiths) is a successful Sydney journalist who's also single, in her late thirties, and depressed by both situations. She moans about not marrying her long-ago beau Robert Dickson (Roberts) and, lo and behold, Pam's whisked into the life she could have had—marriage and mother of three in the suburbs. Of course, this Pam doesn't have a clue as to how her new life runs, which makes for some comic mileage. But it's the appealing Griffiths that holds all the unlikely yet cliched situations together. **104m/C VHS, DVD, Wide.** *AU* Rachel Griffiths, David Roberts, Sandy Winton; *D:* Pip Karmel; *W:* Pip Karmel; *C:* Graeme Lind; *M:* Charlie Chan.

Me You Them *Eu Tu Eles* **2000 (PG-13)** Hard-working Darlene (Case) returns to her dusty Brazilian village with a young son (and no husband) upon the death of her mother. She marries elderly Osias (Duarte) basically because he has a new house and has another son, whose father is probably not Osias. Then Osias's younger cousin Zezinho (Garcia) moves in and takes over household management while Darlene works in the fields. Yep, there's another baby. Finally, Darlene meets younger Ciro (Vasconcelos), a migrant worker, and invites him to stay around. You can guess what happens next. There's a little squabbling but soon everyone settles into a big, contented family. Portuguese with subtitles. **107m/C VHS, DVD, Wide.** *BR PT* Regina Case, Lima Duarte, Stenio Garcia, Luiz Carlos Vasconcelos, Nilda Spencer; *D:* Andrucha Waddington; *W:* Elena Soarez; *C:* Breno Silveira; *M:* Gilberto Gil.

The Meal *Deadly Encounter* **1975 (R)** During a dinner party held by a wealthy woman, the rich and powerful guests divulge each others' secrets with reckless disregard for the consequences. **90m/C VHS.** Dina Merrill, Carl Betz, Leon Ames, Susan Logan, Vicki Powers, Steve Potter; *D:* R. John Hugh.

Mean Dog Blues ½ **1978 (PG)** A musician is convicted of hit-and-run driving after hitching a ride with an inebriated politician. **108m/C VHS.** George Kennedy, Kay Lenz, Scatman Crothers, Gregg Henry, Gregory Sierra, Tina Louise, William Windom; *D:* Mel Stuart; *C:* Robert B. Hauser.

Mean Frank and Crazy Tony **1975 (R)** A mobster and the man who idolizes him attempt a prison breakout in this fun, action-packed production. **92m/C VHS.** *IT* Lee Van Cleef, Tony LoBianco, Jean Rochefort, Jess Hahn; *D:* Michele Lupo.

Mean Guns ½ **1997 (R)** Lots of mayhem will redeem this silly plot for the action fan. Moon (Ice-T) lures 100 assassins to an abandoned prison with the promise of $10 million for the last three men standing. Lou (Lambert) and Marcus (Halsey) are Moon's rivals. **90m/C VHS, DVD.** Ice-T, Christopher Lambert, Michael Halsey, Deborah Van Valkenburgh, Tina Cote, Yuji Okumoto; *D:* Albert Pyun; *W:* Andrew Witham, Nat Whitcomb; *C:* George Mooradian; *M:* Tony Riparetti. **VIDEO**

Mean Johnny Barrows ½ **1975** When Johnny Barrows returns to his home town after being dishonorably discharged from the Army he is offered a job as a gang hitman. **83m/C VHS.** Fred Williamson, Roddy McDowall, Stuart Whitman, Luther Adler, Jenny Sherman, Elliott Gould; *D:* Fred Williamson.

Mean Machine **1973 (R)** A man and his beautiful cohort plot revenge on organized crime for the murder of his father. **89m/C VHS.** Chris Mitchum, Barbara Bouchet, Arthur Kennedy.

Mean Machine **2001 (R)** British remake of Robert Aldrich's 1974 film, "The Longest Yard," that stresses comedy and crazies. Danny Meechan (former soccer star Jones) is a disgraced pro player who winds up in prison on assault charges. The warden (Hemmings) wants Danny to coach the guards' soccer team instead of chief guard Burton (Brown), who will make Danny's life very difficult if he accepts. So Danny proposes a compromise—he'll train and coach an inmate team in a match against the guards. You can guess where this one is going but Jones and Statham (who plays a violent con) are worth watching. **98m/C VHS, DVD.** *US GB* Vinnie Jones, Jason Statham, David Hemmings, Ralph Brown, David Kelly, Jason Flemyng, Danny Dyer, Vas Blackwood, John Forgeham, Robbie Gee; *D:* Barry Skolnick; *W:* Charlie Fletcher, Chris Baker, Andrew Day; *C:* John Murphy; *M:* Alex Barber.

Mean Season **1985 (R)** A vicious mass murderer makes a Miami crime reporter his confidante in his quest for publicity during his killing spree. In time, the madman's intentions become clear as the tensions and headlines grow with each gruesome slaying. Then the reporter must come to terms with the idea that he is letting himself be used due to the success that the association is bringing him. Suspenseful story with a tense ending. Good performance from Russell as the reporter. Screenplay written by Christopher Crowe under the pseudonym Leon Piedmont. **106m/C VHS, DVD, Wide.** Kurt Russell, Mariel Hemingway, Richard Jordan, Richard Masur, Andy Garcia, Joe Pantoliano, Richard Bradford, William Smith; *D:* Phillip Borsos; *W:* Christopher Crowe; *M:* Lalo Schifrin.

Mean Streak **1999 (R)** White supremacist serial killer goes after black baseball player Cash Manley (Dell), who's about to break Joe DiMaggio's hitting streak record of 56 baseball games. White cop Lou Mattoni (Bakula) and black FBI agent Altman Rogers (Leon) are out to stop him if their own prejudices don't derail the investigation. **97m/C VHS.** Scott Bakula, Leon, Howard G.H. Dell, Wayne Best, Ron McLarty, Beau Starr, Brigid Coulter, Michael Filipowich; *D:* Tim Hunter; *W:* David Ryan, John Fasano; *C:* Denis Lenoir; *M:* Paul Buckmaster. **CABLE**

Mean Streets **1973 (R)** A grimy slice of street life in Little Italy among lower echelon Mafiosos, unbalanced punks, and petty criminals. Charlie (Keitel), the nephew of mob boss Giovanni (Danova), struggles to keep his crazy friend Johnny Boy (De Niro) out of serious trouble. A riveting, free-form feature film, marking the formal debut by Scorsese (five years earlier he had completed a student film, "Who's That Knocking At My Door?"). Unorthodox camera movement and gritty performances by De Niro and Keitel, with underlying Catholic guilt providing the moral conflict. Excellent early '60s soundtrack. **112m/C VHS, DVD, Wide.** Harvey Keitel, Robert De Niro, David Proval, Amy Robinson, Richard Romanus, David Carradine, Robert Carradine, Cesare Danova, George Memmoli; *D:* Martin Scorsese; *W:* Martin Scorsese, Mardik Martin; *C:* Kent Wakeford. Natl. Film Reg. '97;; Natl. Soc. Film Critics '73: Support. Actor (De Niro).

The Meanest Men in the West **1976 (PG)** Two criminal half-brothers battle frontier law and each other. **92m/C VHS, DVD.** Charles Bronson, Lee Marvin, Lee J. Cobb, James Drury, Albert Salmi, Charles Grodin; *D:* Samuel Fuller; *W:* Charles S. Dubin; *C:* Lionel Lindon, Alric Edens; *M:* Hal Mooney. **TV**

Meantime **1981** British TV comedy/drama about the working class finds brothers Mark (Daniels) and Colin (Roth) living with their unemployed dad in a depressing East London flat. Colin, who's looking to escape his dreary life, befriends skinhead Coxy (Oldman) to the dismay of the rest of the family. **90m/C VHS, DVD.** *GB* Tim Roth, Gary Oldman, Phil Daniels, Alfred Molina, Pam Ferris; *D:* Mike Leigh; *C:* Roger Pratt; *M:* Andrew Dickson.

Meat Loaf: To Hell and Back **2000 (PG-13)** Saga of rock singer Meat Loaf (Brown), born Marvin Lee Aday, from his dysfunctional family life to his early musical start and his first success in the '70s with the Top 10 hits from "Bat Out of Hell." Of course, there's also the inevitable decline and resurrection. Brown's a Meat Loaf lookalike and Pfeiffer is good as his loyal wife, Leslie, but this is a very familiar story. **90m/C VHS.** W. Earl Brown, Dedee Pfeiffer, Zachary Throne, Jesse Lenat, Lisa Jane Persky; *D:* Jim McBride; *W:* Ron McGee; *C:* Denis Lenoir; *M:* Hummie Mann. **CABLE**

Meatballs **1979 (PG)** The Activities Director at a summer camp who is supposed to organize fun for everyone prefers his own style of "fun." If you enjoy watching Murray blow through a movie, you'll like this one even as it lapses into boxoffice sentimentality. **92m/C VHS, DVD, Wide.** *CA* Bill Murray, Harvey Atkin, Kate Lynch; *D:* Ivan Reitman; *W:* Len Blum, Harold Ramis, Janis Allen; *C:* Donald Wilder; *M:* Elmer Bernstein. Genie '80: Actress (Lynch).

Meatballs 2 ½ **1984 (PG)** The future of Camp Sasquatch is in danger unless the camp's best fighter can beat Camp Patton's champ in a boxing match. The saving grace of Bill Murray is absent in this one. **87m/C VHS, 8mm.** Archie Hahn, John Mengatti, Tammy Taylor, Kim Richards, Ralph Seymour, Richard Mulligan, Hamilton Camp, John Larroquette, Paul (Pee-wee Herman) Reubens, Misty Rowe, Elayne Boosler; *D:* Ken Wiederhorn.

Meatballs 3 woof! **1987 (R)** Second sequel to the teenage sex/summer camp comedy. Enough is enough! **95m/C VHS.** Sally Kellerman, Shannon Tweed, George Buza, Isabelle Mejias, Al Waxman, Patrick Dempsey; *D:* George Mendeluk.

Meatballs 4 ½ **1992 (R)** Feldman stars as a water skier hired to serve as recreation director of Lakeside Water Ski Camp. His enemy is Monica (Douglas) of a nearby rival camp who wants to buy out Lakeside's owner and use the land for real estate development. Lame plot only serves to showcase some good water skiing stunts. **87m/C VHS.** Corey Feldman, Jack Nance, Sarah Douglas, Bojesse Christopher; *D:* Bob Logan.

The Meateater woof! **1979** Disgusting horror flick of a disfigured hermit who inhabits a closed-up movie house. When it is reopened he turns into a stereotypical slasher. Vegetarians beware: references throughout about eating meat. **84m/C VHS.** Arch Jaboulian, Diane Davis, Emily Spendler; *D:* Derek Savage.

The Mechanic *Killer of Killers* **1972 (R)** Bronson stars as Arthur Bishop, a wealthy professional killer for a powerful organization. He has innumerable ways to kill. **100m/C VHS.** Charles Bronson, Jan-Michael Vincent, Keenan Wynn, Jill Ireland, Linda Ridgeway; *D:* Michael Winner; *W:* Lewis John Carlino.

Medea 1970 Cinema poet Pasolini directs opera diva Callas in this straightforward adaptation of Euripides's classic about a sorceress whose escapades range from assisting in the theft of the Golden Fleece to murdering her own children. Not Pasolini at his best, but still better than most if what you're looking for is something arty. In Italian with English subtitles. **118m/C VHS.** *IT* Maria Callas, Guiseppi Gentile, Laurent Terzieff; ***D:*** Pier Paolo Pasolini.

Medicine Man 🦴½ 1930 Benny stars as a con-man who fronts a medicine show in this early talkie comedy. **57m/B VHS.** Jack Benny, Betty Bronson, E. Alyn Warren, George E. Stone, Tom Dugan; ***D:*** Scott Pembroke.

Medicine Man 🦴🦴 1992 (PG-13) Connery's usual commanding presence and the beautiful scenery are the only things to recommend in this lame effort. Dr. Robert Campbell (Connery) is a biochemist working in the Amazon rain forest on a cancer cure. Bracco is Dr. Rae Crane, a fellow researcher sent by the institute sponsoring Campbell to see how things are going. Although Crane is uptight and Campbell is gruff, they fall in love (supposedly), but they're sorely lacking in chemistry. Oh, Campbell's cancer cure is made from a rare flower being eradicated by the destruction of the rain forest. This politically correct cause meets romance falls short of ever being truly entertaining. **105m/C VHS, DVD.** Sean Connery, Lorraine Bracco, Jose Wilker, Rodolfo de Alexandra, Francisco Tsirene Tsere Rereme, Elias Monteiro da Silva; ***D:*** John McTiernan; ***W:*** Tom Schulman; ***C:*** Donald McAlpine; ***M:*** Jerry Goldsmith.

Medicine River 🦴🦴½ 1994 (PG) A Native American photojournalist returns to his hometown after a 20-year absence and winds up in hot water with newfound friend Harlen Bigbear. **96m/C VHS.** *CA* Graham Greene, Tom Jackson, Sheila Tousey, Jimmy Herman, Raoul Trujillo, Byron Chief-Moon, Janet-Laine Green; ***D:*** Stuart Margolin.

The Mediterranean in Flames 🦴½ 1972 In Nazi-occupied Greece, a small but brave resistance is formed to fight its captors. One of the women within the group is forced to seduce a Nazi officer in an attempt to learn enemy secrets. **85m/C VHS.** *GR* Costas Karras, Costas Precas; ***D:*** Dimis Dadiras.

Mediterraneo 🦴🦴🦴 1991 (R) Languid, charming comedy based on the premise that love does make the world go 'round—especially in wartime. In 1941, eight misfit Italian soldiers are stranded on a tiny Greek island and are absorbed into the life of the island, finding love and liberty in the idyllic setting. Lighthearted fun. In Italian with English subtitles. **90m/C VHS.** *IT* Diego Abatantuono, Giuseppe Cederna, Claudio Bigagli, Vanna Barba, Claudio Bisio, Luigi Alberti, Ugo Conti, Memo Dini, Vasco Mirandola, Luigi Montini, Irene Grazioli, Antonio Catania; ***D:*** Gabriele Salvatores. Oscars '91: Foreign Film.

The Medium 🦴🦴 1951 A phony medium is done in by her own trickery in this filmed version of the Menotti opera. **80m/B VHS.** Marie Powers, Anna Maria Alberghetti, Leo Coleman; ***D:*** Gian-Carlo Menotti; ***W:*** Gian-Carlo Menotti.

Medium Cool 🦴🦴🦴½ 1969 Commentary on life in the '60s focuses on a TV news cameraman and his growing apathy with the events around him. His involvement with a Appalachian woman and her young son reawakens his conscience, leading to the three getting caught up in the turbulence of the 1968 Chicago Democratic convention. A frightening depiction of detachment in modern society. **111m/C VHS, DVD, Wide.** Robert Forster, Verna Bloom, Peter Bonerz, Marianna Hill, Peter Boyle, Harold Blankenship, Charles Geary, Sid McCoy, Christine Bergstrom, William Sickingen; ***D:*** Haskell Wexler; ***W:*** Haskell Wexler; ***C:*** Haskell Wexler; ***M:*** Michael Bloomfield.

Medusa 🦴 *Twisted* 1974 A bizarre series of events occur when an abandoned yacht containing two lifeless bodies is found on the Aegean Sea. **103m/C VHS.** George Hamilton, Cameron Mitchell, Luciana Paluzzi, Theodore Roubanis; ***D:*** Gordon Hessler.

Medusa Against the Son of Hercules 🦴 *Perseus the Invincible; Perseo l'Invincibile; Medusa vs. the Son of Hercules* 1962 This time the strongman takes on the evil Medusa and her deadly army of rock men. **90m/C VHS.** *IT* Richard Harrison.

The Medusa Touch 🦴 1978 (R) A man is struck over the head and is admitted to a hospital. Meanwhile, strange disasters befall the surrounding city. It seems that despite his unconscious state, the man is using his telekinetic powers to will things to happen.... **110m/C VHS.** *GB* Richard Burton, Lino Ventura, Lee Remick, Harry Andrews, Alan Badel, Marie-Christine Barrault, Michael Hordern, Derek Jacobi, Jeremy Brett; ***D:*** Jack Gold; ***W:*** Jack Gold, John Briley.

Meet Danny Wilson 🦴🦴½ 1952 Talented New York singer Wilson (Sinatra) and his pianist buddy Mike Ryan (Nicol) head out to Hollywood to try their luck. Danny meets club singer Joy Carroll (Winters) who introduces him to gangster owner Nick Driscoll (Burr). Nick manages Danny for a hefty percentage and makes him a star at his club but Danny's lovelife goes south when Joy picks Mike over him. Then Driscoll demands his money. Sinatra gets to croon some great tunes. ♫I've Got a Crush on You; How Deep Is the Ocean; When You're Smiling; All of Me; She's Funny That Way; That Old Black Magic; You're a Sweetheart; Lonesome Man Blues; A Good Man Is Hard to Find. **88m/B VHS.** Frank Sinatra, Alex Nicol, Shelley Winters, Raymond Burr, Tommy Farrell, Vaughn Taylor, Jack Kruschen, Donald MacBride; ***D:*** Joseph Pevney; ***W:*** Don McGuire.

Meet Dr. Christian 🦴½ 1939 The good old doctor settles some problems. Part of a series. **72m/B VHS.** Jean Hersholt, Robert Baldwin, Paul Harvey; ***D:*** Bernard Vorhaus.

Meet Joe Black 🦴🦴 1998 (PG-13) It's too long. And it's unremittingly hokey. But, it does have the savvy Hopkins and Pitt in full desirable object mode. In this reworking of 1934's "Death Takes a Holiday," Pitt plays a not-so-Grim Reaper who decides to see what living is all about by inhabiting the body of a recently-deceased man. He grants some extra time to wealthy businessman William Parrish (Hopkins), if he'll serve as Death's guide. Now named Joe Black, Death takes to his new life but causes problems in Parrish's household, especially when he falls in love with Parrish's doctor daughter, Susan (a weak Forlani). **180m/C VHS, DVD.** Brad Pitt, Anthony Hopkins, Claire Forlani, Marcia Gay Harden, Jeffrey Tambor, Jake Weber; ***D:*** Martin Brest; ***W:*** Ron Osborn, Jeff Reno, Kevin Wade, Bo Goldman; ***C:*** Emmanuel Lubezki; ***M:*** Thomas Newman.

Meet John Doe 🦴🦴🦴 1941 A social commentary about an unemployed, down-and-out man selected to be the face of a political goodwill campaign. Honest and trusting, he eventually realizes that he is being used to further the careers of corrupt politicians. Available in colorized version. **123m/B VHS, DVD.** Gary Cooper, Barbara Stanwyck, Edward Arnold, James Gleason, Walter Brennan, Spring Byington, Gene Lockhart, Regis Toomey, Ann Doran, Rod La Rocque; ***D:*** Frank Capra; ***W:*** Robert Riskin; ***C:*** George Barnes; ***M:*** Dimitri Tiomkin.

Meet Me in Las Vegas 🦴🦴 1956 Compulsive gambler/cowboy Dailey betters his luck when he hooks up with hoofer girlfriend Charisse. Much frolicking and dancing and cameo appearances by a truckload of stars. A little more entertaining than a game of solitaire. ♫The Girl With the Yaller Shoes; If You Can Dream; Hell Hath No Fury; Lucky Charm; I Refuse to Rock 'n Roll; Rehearsal Ballet; Sleeping Beauty Ballet; Frankie and Johnny. **112m/C VHS, Wide.** Dan Dailey, Cyd Charisse, Agnes Moorehead, Lili Darvas, Jim Backus, Cara Williams, Betty Lynn, Oscar Karlweis, Liliane Montevecchi, Jerry Colonna, Frankie Laine; ***Cameos:*** Debbie Reynolds, Frank Sinatra, Peter Lorre, Vic Damone, Tony Martin, Elaine Stewart; ***D:*** Roy Rowland; ***W:*** Isobel Lennart.

Meet Me in St. Louis 🦴🦴🦴½ 1944 Wonderful music in this charming tale of a St. Louis family during the 1903 World's Fair. One of Garland's better musical performances. ♫You and I; Skip to My Lou; Over the Bannister; Meet Me In St. Louis; Brighten the Corner; Summer In St. Louis; All Hallow's Eve; Ah, Love; The Horrible One. **113m/C VHS, 8mm.** Judy Garland, Margaret O'Brien, Mary Astor, Lucille Bremer, Tom Drake, June Lockhart, Harry Davenport; ***D:*** Vincente Minnelli; ***C:*** George J. Folsey. Natl. Film Reg. '94.

Meet Sexton Blake 🦴🦴 1944 A detective is hired to find a ring and some secret papers that were stolen from the corpse of a man killed in an air raid. He discovers that the papers contained the plans for a new metal alloy to be used in planes. Entertaining for its melodramatic elements. **80m/B VHS.** *GB* David Farrar, John Varley, Magda Kun, Gordon McLeod, Manning Whiley; ***D:*** John Harlow; ***W:*** John Harlow.

Meet the Deedles 🦴½ 1998 (PG) The answer to the question, "What would happen if Bill and Ted or Wayne and Garth were even dumber?" Hard to believe? No, just hard to watch. Phil and Stew Deedle (Walker and Van Wormer) are two rich surfer airheads who just wanna have fun, dude. Facing expulsion from school, the twins are forced to attend the bogus Camp Broken Spirit by their father. The boys slip and fall on a plot device and wake up in the hospital, mistaken for rookie Yellowstone park rangers there to fight a mounting prarie dog problem. It seems that bitter ex-ranger Slater (Hopper, phoning in his patented mondo-weirdo) has enslaved the rodents and is trying to redirect the geyser Old Faithful. Features heinous dialogue and stunts lifted from Mountain Dew commercials. **94m/C VHS.** Steve Van Wormer, Paul Walker, A.J. (Allison Joy) Langer, John Ashton, Dennis Hopper, Eric (Hans Gudegast) Braeden, Richard Lineback, Robert Englund, Ana Gasteyer, Megan Cavanagh; ***D:*** Steve Boyum; ***W:*** Jim Herzfeld, Dale Pollock; ***C:*** David Hennings; ***M:*** Steve Bartek.

Meet the Feebles 🦴🦴 1989 Sex and violence gorefest perpetuated by puppets—and the dementia of director Jackson. A TV variety show, populated by animal puppets and humans in costume, is the setting for backstage mayhem, including sex, drugs, and a shooting spree. Among the characters are a sleazy walrus producer, his slinky Siamese cat mistress, a junkie frog, and a manic-depressive elephant. There's also several musical production numbers, if things aren't strange enough for you already. **94m/C VHS, DVD.** *NZ* ***D:*** Peter Jackson; ***W:*** Peter Jackson, Danny Mulheron, Frances Walsh, Stephen Sinclair; ***C:*** Murray Milne; ***M:*** Peter Dasent; ***V:*** Peter Vere-Jones, Mark Hadlow, Stuart Devine, Donna Atkinson, Mark Wright, Brian Sergent.

Meet the Hollowheads 🦴½ 1989 (PG-13) Family situation comedy set in a futuristic society. **89m/C VHS.** John Glover, Nancy Mette, Richard Portnow, Matt Shakman, Juliette Lewis, Anne Ramsey; ***D:*** Tom Burman; ***W:*** Tom Burman.

Meet the Mob 🦴🦴 1942 A country spinster visits her son in the big city and is mistaken for a notorious murderess. Complications arise when she tries to keep the boy honest. Could have worked better. **62m/B VHS.** ZaSu Pitts, Roger Pryor, Warren Hymer, Gwen Kenyon, Douglas Fowley, Elizabeth Russell, Tristram Coffin, Lester Dorr, Wheeler Oakman, Bud McTaggart; ***D:*** Jean Yarbrough.

Meet the Navy 🦴🦴 1946 Post-war musical revue about a pianist and a dancer. **81m/B VHS.** Joan Pratt, Margaret Hurst, Lionel Murton.

Meet the Parents 🦴🦴 1991 A young man visits his fiance's parents and every nightmare, every tragedy that can possibly happen, does. From the minds of "National Lampoon," with an appearance by beyond-bizarre comedian Emo Phillips. **?m/C VHS.** Greg Glionna, Jacqueline Cahill, Dick Galloway, Carol Wheeler, Mary Ruth Clarke, Emo Phillips; ***D:*** Greg Glionna; ***W:*** Mary Ruth Clarke.

Meet the Parents 🦴🦴🦴 2000 (PG-13) If you have any sense of empathy at all, you'll be squirming uncomfortably for Greg (Stiller), a nice Jewish boy who suffers an extended brainlock when he meets his girlfriend Pam's (Polo) WASPy parents during her sister's wedding weekend. It doesn't help that one of those parents is Jack (De Niro), an ex-CIA psychological profiler who takes an immediate dislike to his prospective son-in-law. Greg starts off on the wrong foot by accidentally smashing the urn holding the ashes of Jack's mother with a champagne cork, and his luck goes down from there. The rest of the cast performs well, especially Danner as Pam's mother, and De Niro plays off of his tough guy image for a brilliant comedic performance. **108m/C VHS, DVD, Wide.** Ben Stiller, Robert De Niro, Teri Polo, Blythe Danner, James Rebhorn, Jon Abrahams, Owen C. Wilson, Phyllis George, Kali Rocha, Tom McCarthy, Nicole DeHuff; ***D:*** Jay Roach; ***W:*** Jim Herzfeld, John Hamburg; ***C:*** Peter James; ***M:*** Randy Newman.

Meet Wally Sparks 🦴🦴 1997 (R) No-brow "Man Who Came to Dinner." Smutty TV shock-talk host Sparks (Dangerfield) is given one week to save his failing show when producer Reynolds (with a noticeably bad rug) puts him on notice. Opportunity knocks when he is invited to a party at the governor's mansion to interview the conservative head honcho (Stiers). Once there, a freak accident with a drunken horse prevents Sparks from leaving, and the new guest makes himself right at home by turning the fancy digs into a broadcast studio. Dangerfield's machine gun spray of one liners occasionally hits, as do his sometimes lengthy and elaborately set up jokes that do little to propel the plot along but are pure Dangerfield. Not much beyond Rodney makes lackluster "Sparks" fly. **107m/C VHS, DVD.** Rodney Dangerfield, David Ogden Stiers, Burt Reynolds, Debi Mazar, Cindy Williams, Alan Rachins; ***D:*** Peter Baldwin; ***W:*** Rodney Dangerfield, Harry Basil; ***C:*** Richard H. Kline; ***M:*** Michel Colombier.

Meeting at Midnight 🦴🦴 1944 Charlie Chan is invited to a seance to solve a perplexing mystery. Chan discovers that they use mechanical figures and from there on solving the murder is easy. **67m/B VHS.** Sidney Toler, Joseph Crehan, Mantan Moreland, Frances Chan, Ralph Peters, Helen Beverly; ***D:*** Phil Rosen.

Meeting Daddy 🦴🦴½ 1998 (R) Neurotic New Yorker Peter (Charles) falls in love with Georgia peach Melanie (Wentworth) and then he travels to Savannah to meet her southern-fried family, including her eccentric, irascible father, The Colonel (Bridges). **91m/C VHS.** Lloyd Bridges, Josh Charles, Alexandra Wentworth, Beau Bridges, Walter Olkewicz, Kristy Swanson; ***D:*** Peter Gould; ***W:*** Peter Gould; ***C:*** Mike Mayers; ***M:*** Adam Fields.

VIDEO

Meeting Venus 🦴🦴½ 1991 (PG-13) Backstage drama featuring Close as Karin Anderson, a world-famous Swedish opera diva. An international cast of characters adds to this sophisticated film of romance, rivalry and political confrontation set amidst a newly unified Europe. **121m/C VHS.** Glenn Close, Niels Arestrup, Erland Josephson, Johanna Ter Steege, Maria De Medeiros, Ildiko Bansagi, Macha Meril, Dorottya Udvaros, Jay O. Sanders, Victor Poletti; ***D:*** Istvan Szabo; ***W:*** Istvan Szabo, Michael Hirst; ***C:*** Lajos Koltai; ***V:*** Kiri Te Kanawa.

Meetings with Remarkable Men 🦴🦴½ 1979 An acclaimed, visually awesome film version of the memoir by Gurdjieff, about his wanderings through Asia and the Middle East searching for answers and developing his own spiritual code. Mildly entertaining but only of true interest to those familiar with the subject. **108m/C VHS.** Terence Stamp, Dragan Maksimovic, Mikica Dmitrijevic; ***D:*** Peter Brook.

Megaforce woof! 1982 (PG) Futuristic thriller directed by stuntman Needham follows the adventures of the military task force, Megaforce, on its mission to save a small democratic nation from attack. Bostwick leads the attack. 'Nuff said. **99m/C VHS.** Barry Bostwick, Persis Khambatta, Edward Mulhare, Henry Silva, Michael Beck, Ralph Wilcox; ***D:*** Hal Needham.

Megaville 🦴🦴 1991 (R) Set in the not too distant future, corrupt politician Travanti struggles to corner the market on the evil technology "Dream-a-Life," which aims to control the rebellious "riff-raff" of Megaville. He does all of his dealings while up against a hitman who has a defective memory chip in his brain. **96m/C VHS.** Billy Zane, Daniel J. Travanti, J.C. Quinn, Grace Zabriskie; *D:* Peter Lehner; *W:* Peter Lehner.

Melanie ♪♪½ **1982 (PG)** Drama tells the tale of one poor woman's courage, determination, and optimism, as she tries to regain her child from her ex-husband. She befriends musician Cummings (a founding member of "Guess Who" rock band) who helps. Usual cliches balanced by good performances. **109m/C VHS.** *CA* Glynnis O'Connor, Paul Sorvino, Don Johnson, Burton Cummings; *D:* Rex Bromfield.

Melanie Darrow ♪½ **1997 (PG-13)** Routine drama finds relentless attorney Melanie Darrow (Burke) defending the younger husband of a socialite friend for the woman's murder, much to the dismay of Melanie's homicide cop brother (Bloom). **88m/C VHS.** Delta Burke, Brian Bloom, Daniel Birt, Jonathan Banks, Bruce Abbott, Shawn Ashmore, Wendel Meldrum; *D:* Gary Nelson. **CABLE**

Melody ♪♪ **1971 (G)** Sensitive but slow study of a special friendship which enables two pre-teens to survive in a regimented and impersonal world. Features music by the Bee Gees. **106m/C VHS.** *GB* Tracy Hyde, Jack Wild, Mark Lester, Colin Barrie, Roy Kinnear; *D:* Waris Hussein; *W:* Alan Parker.

Melody Cruise ♪♪ **1932** Boring musical romantic comedy that can't stay with any one of those three things for more than a minute without careening into one of the other two. ♫I Met Her at a Party; He's Not the Marrying Kind; Isn't This a Night For Love; This is the Hour. **75m/B VHS.** Phil Harris, Charlie Ruggles, Greta Nissen, Helen Mack, Chick Chandler; *D:* Mark Sandrich; *M:* Max Steiner.

Melody for Three ♪♪ **1941** In the tradition of matchmaker, Doctor Christian aids in the reuniting of music-teacher mother and great-conductor father, who have been divorced for years, in order to help the couple's son, a violin prodigy. **69m/B VHS, 8mm.** Jean Hersholt, Fay Wray; *D:* Erle C. Kenton.

Melody in Love ♪ **1978** A young girl visits her cousin and her swinging friends on a tropical island. Dubbed. **90m/C VHS.** Melody O'Bryan, Sasha Hehn; *D:* Hubert Frank.

Melody Master ♪♪ *New Wine* **1941** Romanticized biography of composer Franz Schubert, chronicling his personal life and loves, along with performances of his compositions. If you just have to know what drove the composer of "Ave Maria" it may hold your interest, but otherwise not very compelling. **80m/B VHS.** Alan Curtis, Ilona Massey, Binnie Barnes, Albert Bassermann, Billy Gilbert, Sterling Holloway; *M:* Miklos Rozsa.

Melody of the Plains ♪ **1937** Singing cowpoke teams up with a young girl for some cattle-rustlin' adventure. Substandard horse opry due to poor direction and haphazard lensing. **53m/B VHS.** Fred Scott, Louise Small, Al "Fuzzy" St. John, David Sharpe, Lafe (Lafayette) McKee, Charles "Slim" Whitaker, Hal Price, Lew Meehan; *D:* Sam Newfield; *W:* Bennett Cohen.

Melody Ranch ♪½ **1940** Gene returns to his home town as an honored guest and appointed sheriff. But gangster MacLane is determined to drive him out of town. ♫Melody Ranch; Call of the Canyon; We Never Dream the Same Dream Twice; Vote for Autry; My Gal Sal; Torpedo Joe; What Are Cowboys Made Of?; Rodeo Rose; Back in the Saddle Again. **84m/C VHS.** Gene Autry, Jimmy Durante, George "Gabby" Hayes, Ann Miller, Barton MacLane, Joseph (Joe) Sawyer, Horace McMahon, Veda Ann Borg; *D:* Joseph Santley.

Melody Time **1948** Seven animated/musical tales from the Disney studios, including "Blame It On the Samba" with Donald Duck; "Once Upon a Wintertime;" "Bumble Boogie;" "Johnny Appleseed;" "Little Toot" with musical narration provided by the Andrews Sisters; Fred Waring and the Pennsylvanians singing "Trees," the Joyce Kilmer poem; and Roy Rogers narrating the story of "Pecos Bill." **75m/C VHS, DVD.** Roy Rogers; *D:* Clyde Geronimi, Wilfred Jackson, Jack Kinney, Hamilton Luske; *C:* Winton C. Hoch; *V:* Dennis Day, Ethel Smith, Buddy Clark, Bob Nolan, The Andrews Sisters, Frances Langford.

Melody Trail ♪ **1935** Autry wins $1000 in a rodeo, loses the money to a gypsy, gets a job, falls for his employer's daughter...and in the end captures a kidnapper and cattle rustlers. ♫Hold On, Little Doggie, Hold On; On the Prairie; Lookin for the Lost Chord; The Hurdy Gurdy Man; My Prayer For Tonight; End of the Trail; I'd Love a Home in the Mountains. **60m/B VHS.** Gene Autry, Smiley Burnette, Ann Rutherford; *D:* Joseph Kane.

Meltdown ♪♪ *High Risk; Shu Dan Long Wei* **1995** Apparently producer/director Wong Jing has a score to settle with Jackie Chan. This action/comedy revolves around a drunken action star called Frankie (Cheung) who claims to do all of his own stunts but uses a team of stuntmen, including former cop Kit Li (Li), whose wife and son were killed (in a particularly ridiculous opening sequence) by an evil criminal mastermind (Wong). Who, with his gang, turns up to steal the Russian crown jewels that are being exhibited in a Hong Kong hotel. Think slapstick "Die Hard," although it's virtually impossible for western audiences to figure out where the action ends and the comedy begins. **100m/C VHS, DVD.** *HK* Jet Li, Jacky Cheung, Chingmy Yau, Valerie Chow, Charlie Yoeh, Kelvin Wong; *D:* Wong Jing; *W:* Wong Jing.

Melvin and Howard ♪♪♪½ **1980 (R)** Story of Melvin Dummar, who once gave Howard Hughes a ride. Dummar later claimed a share of Hughes's will. Significant for Demme's direction and fine acting from Steenburgen/LeMat, and Robards in a small role as Hughes. Offbeat and very funny. **95m/C VHS, DVD.** Paul LeMat, Jason Robards Jr., Mary Steenburgen, Michael J. Pollard, Dabney Coleman, Elizabeth Cheshire, Pamela Reed, Cheryl "Rainbeaux" Smith; *D:* Jonathan Demme; *W:* Bo Goldman; *C:* Tak Fujimoto; *M:* Bruce Langhorne. Oscars '80: Orig. Screenplay, Support. Actress (Steenburgen); Golden Globes '81: Support. Actress (Steenburgen); L.A. Film Critics '80: Support. Actress (Steenburgen); N.Y. Film Critics '80: Director (Demme), Screenplay, Support. Actress (Steenburgen); Natl. Soc. Film Critics '80: Film, Screenplay, Support. Actress (Steenburgen); Writers Guild '80: Orig. Screenplay.

Melvin Purvis: G-Man ♪♪ *The Legend of Machine Gun Kelly; Kansas City Massacre* **1974** Mediocre action film has dedicated federal agent tracking killer Machine Gun Kelly across American Midwest during Depression. **78m/C VHS.** Dale Robertson, Harris Yulin, Margaret Blye, Matt Clark, Elliot Street, Dick Sargent, John Karlen, David Canary; *D:* Dan Curtis. **TV**

The Member of the Wedding ♪♪♪ **1952** While struggling through her adolescence, 12-year-old tomboy Frankie (played by 26-year-old Harris) is growing up in 1945 Georgia and seeking solace from her family's cook, Berenice (Waters) and her cousin, John Henry (de Wilde). Based on Carson McCullers's play, this story of family, belonging, and growth is well acted and touching. **90m/C VHS.** Ethel Waters, Julie Harris, Brandon de Wilde, Arthur Franz, William Hansen, Nancy Gates, James Edwards, Harry Bolden; *D:* Fred Zinnemann; *W:* Edward Anhalt; *C:* Hal Mohr; *M:* Alex North.

The Member of the Wedding ♪♪ **1983** TV rehash of Carson McCuller's play about a young girl who finds she's got some growing up to do when big brother marries. No match for Zinnemann's '52 version, or for Mann's earlier "All Quiet on the Western Front" and "Marty." **90m/C VHS.** Dana Hill, Pearl Bailey, Howard E. Rollins Jr.; *D:* Delbert Mann.

The Member of the Wedding ♪♪½ **1997 (PG)** The second TV remake of Carson's McCuller's 1946 novel follows the adolescent struggles of 12-year-old Frankie Adams (Paquin). It's the summer of 1944 in Georgia and desperate for a change, Frankie decides the wedding of her brother Jarvis (McGrath) will give her the opportunity to leave her troubles behind. Woodard is the family's gentle but no-nonsense housekeeper Berenice. **93m/C VHS.** Anna Paquin, Alfre Woodard, Matt McGrath, Corey Dunn, Anne Tremko, Enrico Colantoni; *D:* Fielder Cook; *W:* David W. Rintels; *C:* Paul LaMastra; *M:* Laurence Rosenthal.

Memento ♪♪♪½ **2000 (R)** Twisty and engaging noir thriller of a man searching for his wife's killer in Los Angeles. Only problem is, Leonard Shelby (Pearce) lost his short-term memory after the attack and forgets all current events every 15 minutes, or so. Problem solved as Shelby tattoos the most vital info all over his body and leaves less permanent "clues" for himself on Post-Its and Polaroids of the usual suspects. Shelby meets Natalie (Moss) and Teddy (Pantoliano) who may want to help him, but like his own memory, definitely can't be trusted. Ingeniously constructed story is told backwards, from Pearce's shooting of the killer to his puzzle-like construction of events and renders the audience as clueless as the impaired hero. Clever use of flashbacks and black-and-white segs help define events in time. More than normally required mental exercise is more than worth the effort. Director Nolan adapted the film from short story by brother Jonathan. **116m/C VHS, DVD, Wide.** *US* Guy Pearce, Carrie-Anne Moss, Joe Pantoliano, Mark Boone Jr., Stephen Tobolowsky, Callum Keith Rennie, Harriet Harris, Jorja Fox; *D:* Christopher Nolan; *W:* Christopher Nolan; *C:* Wally Pfister; *M:* David Julyan. Ind. Spirit '01: Director (Nolan), Screenplay; Ind. Spirit '02: Film, Support. Actress (Moss); L.A. Film Critics '01: Screenplay; Broadcast Film Critics '01: Screenplay.

Memoirs of an Invisible Man ♪½ **1992 (PG-13)** Nick Halloway, a slick and shallow stock analyst, is rendered invisible by a freak accident. When he is pursued by a CIA agent-hit man who wants to exploit him, Nick turns for help to Alice, a documentary filmmaker he has just met. Naturally, they fall in love along the way. Effective sight gags, hardworking cast can't overcome pitfalls in script, which indecisively meanders between comedy and thrills. **99m/C VHS.** Chevy Chase, Daryl Hannah, Sam Neill, Michael McKean, Stephen Tobolowsky, Jim Norton, Patricia Heaton, Rosalind Chao; *D:* John Carpenter; *W:* Robert Collector.

Memorial Day ♪♪ **1983** Good cast highlights this TV outing covering a Vietnam veterans reunion. With the old memories come new problems for the men and their families. **120m/C VHS.** Mike Farrell, Shelley Fabares, Keith Mitchell, Bonnie Bedelia, Robert Walden, Edward Herrmann, Danny Glover; *D:* Joseph Sargent; *M:* Billy Goldenberg. **TV**

Memorial Day ♪½ **1998 (R)** Routine to the point of boredom. Downey (Speakman) is an ex-Marine/government operative who's just been released from a mental ward. He's needed to stop a terrorist group that's stolen a Russian satellite. **95m/C VHS.** Jeff Speakman, Bruce Weitz, Paul Mantee, Stephanie Niznik; *D:* Worth Keeter. **VIDEO**

Memorial Valley Massacre ♪ **1988 (R)** When campers settle for a weekend in a new, unfinished campground, they're slaughtered in turn by a nutty hermit. **93m/C VHS.** Cameron Mitchell, William Smith, John Kerry, Mark Mears, Lesa Lee, John Caso; *D:* Robert C. Hughes.

Memories of a Marriage ♪♪♪ **1990** A nostalgic look at a couple's many years of marriage, from the husband's point of view, as they face their most trying times. Touchingly reminiscent as it spans the youthful years of new love and marriage to the more quiet, solid years of matured love. In Danish with English subtitles. **90m/C VHS.** *DK* Ghita Norby, Frits Helmuth, Rikke Bendsen, Henning Moritzen; *D:* Kaspar Rostrup.

Memories of Hell **1987** Examines the special bonds of friendship that have been maintained among the New Mexicans who survived one of WWII's most brutal battles and subsequent prisoner experiences. **57m/C VHS.**

Memories of Me ♪♪ **1988 (PG-13)** A distraught doctor travels to L.A. to see his ailing father and make up for lost time. Both the doctor and his father learn about themselves and each other. Story of child/parent relationships attempts to pull at the heartstrings but only gets as far as the liver. Co-written and co-produced by Crystal, this film never quite reaches the potential of its cast. **103m/C VHS.** Billy Crystal, Alan King, JoBeth Williams, David Ackroyd, Sean Connery, Janet Carroll; *D:* Henry Winkler; *W:* Billy Crystal, Eric Roth; *M:* Georges Delerue.

Memories of Murder **1990** A woman suffering from amnesia is stalked by a merciless killer, apparently seeking revenge. Can she regain her memory and understand why she is being hunted, before it's too late? **104m/C VHS.** Vanity, Nancy Allen, Robin Thomas; *D:* Robert Lewis; *W:* John Kent Harrison, Nevin Schreiner.

Memories of Underdevelopment ♪♪½ *Memorias del Subdesarrollo* **1968** Set in the early 1960s. An anti-revolutionary, Europeanized intellectual takes a stand against the new government in Cuba. In Spanish with English subtitles. **97m/B VHS.** *CU* Sergio Corrieri, Daisy Granados, Eslinda Nunez, Beatriz Ponchora; *D:* Tomas Gutierrez Alea; *W:* Tomas Gutierrez Alea, Edmundo Desnoes; *C:* Ramon Suarez; *M:* Leo Bower.

Memory of Us ♪♪ **1974 (PG)** Still-relevant story of a married, middle-aged woman who starts to question her happiness as a wife and mother. Written by its star Geer, whose father, Will, plays a bit part. **93m/C VHS.** Ellen Geer, Jon Cypher, Barbara Colby, Peter Brown, Robert Hogan, Rose Marie, Will Geer; *D:* H. Kaye Dyal.

Memphis ♪♪½ **1991 (PG-13)** In 1957 three white drifters (two men and a woman) decide to secure some easy money by kidnapping the young grandson of the richest black businessman in Memphis. They think it's an easy job since, given the prejudice of the times, the police will do little or nothing but they reckon without the resources of the black community itself. Based on the novel "September, September" by Shelby Foote. **92m/C VHS.** Cybill Shepherd, John Laughlin, J.E. Freeman, Richard Brooks, Moses Gunn, Vanessa Bell Calloway, Martin C. Gardner; *D:* Yves Simoneau; *W:* Cybill Shepherd, Larry McMurtry; *M:* David Bell. **CABLE**

Memphis Belle ♪♪♪ **1990 (PG-13)** Satisfying Hollywood version of the documentary of the same name captures the true story of the final mission of a WWII bomber crew stationed in England. The boys of the Memphis Belle were the first group of B-17 crewmen to complete a 25 mission tour—no small feat in an air war that claimed many lives. Good ensemble cast of up and coming young actors; Lithgow has a nice turn as an army PR guy determined to exploit their boyish good looks on the homefront. Caton-Jones effectively uses 1940s film techniques and some original footage, making up for a rather hokey script. Film debut of singer Connick. Produced by Catherine Wyler, whose father made the original. **107m/C VHS, DVD, 8mm.** Matthew Modine, John Lithgow, Eric Stoltz, Sean Astin, Harry Connick Jr., Reed Edward Diamond, Tate Donovan, D.B. Sweeney, Billy Zane, David Strathairn, Jane Horrocks, Courtney Gains, Neil Giuntoli; *D:* Michael Caton-Jones; *W:* Monte Merrick; *C:* David Watkin; *M:* George Fenton.

The Men ♪♪♪½ *Battle Stripe* **1950** A paraplegic WWII veteran sinks into depression until his former girlfriend manages to bring him out of it. Marlon Brando's first film. A thoughtful story that relies on subtle acting and direction. **85m/B VHS.** Marlon Brando, Teresa Wright, Everett Sloane, Jack Webb; *D:* Fred Zinnemann.

Men... ♪♪♪½ **1985** A funny and insightful satire about a man who discovers his loving wife has been having an affair with a young artist. In a unique course of revenge, the husband ingratiates himself with the artist and gradually turns him into a carbon copy of himself. In German with English subtitles or dubbed. **96m/C VHS.** *GE* Heiner Lauterbach, Uwe Ochsenknecht, Ulrike Kriener, Janna Marangosoff; *D:* Doris Dorrie.

Men 🦴🦴 **1997 (R)** Aspiring chef Stella James (Young) is encouraged by best friend Teo (Dylan Walsh) to move from New York to L.A. in search of romance. Stella promptly lands a job and gets involved with George (Heard), the restaurant's owner. However, a new man, photographer Frank (Hillman), comes onto the scene and Stella decides she likes him too. But what she thinks will be another casual encounter becomes unexpectedly serious. Based on the novel by Margaret Diehl. **93m/C VHS, DVD.** Sean Young, John Heard, Dylan Walsh, Richard Hillman, Karen Black; ***D:*** Zoe Clarke-Williams; ***W:*** Zoe Clarke-Williams, Karen Black; ***C:*** Susan Emerson; ***M:*** Mark Mothersbaugh.

Men Are Not Gods 🦴🦴½ **1937** Verbose film (precursor to "A Double Life") about an actor playing Othello who nearly kills his wife during Desdemona's death scene. **90m/B VHS.** *GB* Rex Harrison, Miriam Hopkins, Gertrude Lawrence; ***D:*** Walter Reisch.

Men at Work 🦴🦴 **1990 (PG-13)** Garbage collectors Sheen and Estevez may not love their work, but at least it's consistent from day to day. That is, until they get wrapped up in a very dirty politically motivated murder. And who will clean up the mess when the politicians are through trashing each other? A semi-thrilling semi-comedy that may leave you semi-satisfied. **98m/C VHS, DVD, Wide.** Charlie Sheen, Emilio Estevez, Leslie Hope, Keith David; ***D:*** Emilio Estevez; ***W:*** Emilio Estevez; ***C:*** Tim Suhrstedt; ***M:*** Stewart Copeland.

Men Cry Bullets 🦴🦴 **2000** Low-budget weird comedy has midnight movie potential. Billy (Nelson) is a naive performance artist who falls for hard-drinking writer Gloria (Lauren), who introduces him to the world of rough sex. And Gloria's unhappy when her debutante cousin Lydia (Ryan) comes to pay a visit and Billy starts looking her way. **106m/C VHS.** Steven Nelson, Jeri Ryan, Honey Lauren; ***D:*** Tamara Hernandez; ***W:*** Tamara Hernandez.

Men Don't Leave 🦴🦴½ **1989 (PG-13)** A recent widow tries to raise her kids single-handedly, suffers big city life, and takes a chance at a second love. Good performances by all, especially Cusack as the sweet seducer of teenaged O'Donnell. By the director of "Risky Business." **115m/C VHS, 8mm.** Jessica Lange, Arliss Howard, Joan Cusack, Kathy Bates, Charlie Korsmo, Corey Carrier, Chris O'Donnell, Tom Mason, Jim Haynie; ***D:*** Paul Brickman; ***W:*** Barbara Benedek, Paul Brickman; ***C:*** Bruce Surtees; ***M:*** Thomas Newman.

Men in Black 🦴🦴🦴 *MIB* **1997 (PG-13)** Charm, wit and some outrageous insect-type aliens make a winning cosmic combination. K (Jones) and J (Smith) are top-secret government operatives, investigating alien visitations on Earth, who must stop terrorist extraterrestrial D'Onofrio from causing a galactic disaster. Excellent chemistry between deadpan Jones and hip-hop Smith is strengthened by a very funny script. Director Sonnenfeld tops it off with just enough detail and human element to keep the special effects from stealing the show, and with Rick Baker around, that's not easy to do. Boxoffice hit that should spawn a sequel or two. Adapted from the Marvel comic book. **98m/C VHS, DVD, Wide.** Tommy Lee Jones, Will Smith, Linda Fiorentino, Rip Torn, Vincent D'Onofrio, Tony Shalhoub, Carel Struycken, Sergio Calderon, Siobhan Fallon; ***D:*** Barry Sonnenfeld; ***W:*** Edward Solomon; ***C:*** Don Peterman; ***M:*** Danny Elfman. Oscars '97: Makeup; MTV Movie Awards '98: Song ("Men in Black"), Fight (Will Smith/alien).

Men in Black 2 **2002 (PG-13)** Kay (Jones) had returned to civilian life at the end of the first film (with no memory of his past life), while Jay (Smith) went on with the men in black. When evil alien Serleena (Boyle) takes the entire MiB hostage, lone escapee Jay must convince Kay to help him save the galaxy. Not yet reviewed. **?m/C VHS, DVD.** Tommy Lee Jones, Will Smith, Lara Flynn Boyle, Johnny Knoxville, Rosario Dawson, Rip Torn; ***D:*** Barry Sonnenfeld; ***W:*** Robert Gordon, Barry Fanaro.

Men in Love 🦴🦴 **1990** A young San Franciscan travels to Hawaii with the cremated remains of his lover, who has succumbed to AIDS. There he encounters a supportive group of men who nurse him back to sexual and spiritual wholeness. **93m/C VHS.** Doug Self, Joe Tolbe, Emerald Starr, Kutira Decosterd, Scott Catamas; ***D:*** Marc Huestis; ***W:*** Emerald Starr, Scott Catamas; ***C:*** Fawn Yacker.

Men in War 🦴🦴½ **1957** Korean War drama about a small platoon trying to take an enemy hill by themselves. A worthwhile effort with some good action sequences. **100m/B VHS, DVD.** Robert Ryan, Robert Keith, Aldo Ray, Vic Morrow, Phillip Pine, Nehemiah Persoff, James Edwards, L.Q. (Justus E. McQueen) Jones, Scott Marlowe, Adam Kennedy, Race Gentry, Walter Kelley, Anthony Ray, Robert Normand, Michael Miller, Victor Sen Yung; ***D:*** Anthony Mann; ***W:*** Philip Yordan, Ben Maddow; ***C:*** Ernest Haller; ***M:*** Elmer Bernstein.

Men Men Men 🦴🦴 *Uomini Uomini Uomini* **1995** Quartet of gay friends are permanent Peter Pans. Never having grown up, they extend their adolescence in a series of increasingly vicious pranks at the expense of both strangers and friends. But eventually they're forced to re-examine their behavior. Very funny, if certainly non-pc, comedy. Italian with subtitles. **84m/C VHS, DVD, Wide.** *IT* Christian de Sica, Massimo Ghini, Leo Gullotta, Alessandro Haber, Monica Scattini, Paco Reconti; ***D:*** Christian de Sica; ***W:*** Christian de Sica; ***C:*** Gianlorenzo Battaglia; ***M:*** Manuel De Sica.

Men of Boys Town 🦴🦴½ **1941** Sequel to 1938's "Boys Town" has the same sentimentality, even more if that's possible. Father Flanagan's reformatory faces closure, while the kids reach out to an embittered new inmate. Worth seeing for the ace cast reprising their roles. **106m/B VHS.** Spencer Tracy, Mickey Rooney, Darryl Hickman, Henry O'Neill, Lee J. Cobb, Sidney Miller; ***D:*** Norman Taurog.

Men of Honor 🦴🦴½ *Navy Diver* **2000 (R)** Based on the true story of Carl Brashear, the first African-American to break the color barrier in the U.S. Navy's diving program, this biography is a straightforward no-frills tribute. Played by Gooding, Brashear comes across as the very embodiment of perseverence, as shown in his rise from sharecropper's son to military man. De Niro plays Billy Sunday, a racist training officer whose discrimination nearly kills Brashear on several occasions before Brashear earns Sunday's respect. As Brashear's career advances, Sunday's declines due to drunkenness and insubordination. When Brashear loses his leg in the line of duty, the now-recovered Sunday helps him retrain using a prosthetic leg. The character of Billy Sunday is actually a composite drawn from many men in Carl Brashear's military career. **129m/C VHS, DVD, Wide.** Cuba Gooding Jr., Robert De Niro, Charlize Theron, David Keith, Michael Rapaport, Hal Holbrook, Powers Boothe, Aunjanue Ellis, Joshua Leonard, David Conrad, Glynn Turman, Holt McCallany, Lonette McKee, Carl Lumbly; ***D:*** George Tillman Jr.; ***W:*** Scott Marshall Smith; ***C:*** Anthony B. Richmond; ***M:*** Mark Isham.

Men of Ireland 🦴🦴 **1938** A Dublin medical student cavorts with islanders off the Irish coast. Uninspired programmer with authentic native folk of the Blasket Islands, plus their songs and dances. **62m/B VHS, 8mm.** *IR* Cecil Ford, Eileen Curran, Brian O'Sullivan, Gabriel Fallon; ***D:*** Richard Bird.

Men of Means 🦴🦴 **1999 (R)** Mob goon Rico Burke (Pare) decides it's time to get out when he sees his boss (Serra) becoming increasingly psychotic. Only he gets doublecrossed. Lots of action and avoids most mob movie cliches. **80m/C VHS.** Michael Pare, Raymond Serra, Austin Pendleton, Kaela Dobkin; ***D:*** George Mendeluk. **VIDEO**

Men of Respect 🦴🦴 **1991 (R)** Shakespeare meets the mafia in this misbegotten gangster yarn. Turturro, a gangster MacBeth, is prodded by wife and psychic to butcher his way to the top o' the mob. Well acted but ill conceived, causing Bard's partial roll over in grave. **113m/C VHS, 8mm, Wide.** John Turturro, Katherine Borowitz, Peter Boyle, Dennis Farina, Chris Stein, Steven Wright, Stanley Tucci; ***D:*** William Reilly; ***W:*** William Reilly; ***C:*** Bobby Bukowski.

Men of Sherwood Forest 🦴🦴½ **1957** Robin Hood and his band take it to the sheriff et al in this colorful Hammer version of the timeless legend. **77m/C VHS.** *GB* Don Taylor, Reginald Beckwith, Eileen Moore, Davis King-Wood, Patrick Holt, John Van Eyssen, Douglas Wilmer; ***D:*** Val Guest.

Men of Steel 🦴 **1988 (PG)** Two Canadian military officers, one French and one English, must struggle to survive when their plane crashes in the wilderness. Besides contending with the surroundings, they must deal with one another's instilled bitterness and underlying prejudices. **91m/C VHS.** Allan Royal, Robert Lalonde, David Ferry, Mavor Moore, Yvan Ponton; ***D:*** Donald Shebib.

Men of the Fighting Lady 🦴🦴🦴½ *Panther Squadron* **1954** Action-adventure offers plenty of exciting battle footage. Features the stories of selected pilots stationed on a U.S. aircraft carrier in the Pacific during the Korean War. The stories, told to Calhern as writer James A. Michener, center around the lead pilot Johnson. Dramatic airflights include a scene in which Johnson helps a blinded Martin land his plane safely on the carrier deck. Gene Ruggerio's editing of the war footage was so expertly done that he was questioned by the Pentagon when they had a hard time believing the scenes were achieved by skillful editing and painted backdrops. Look for "Beaver" Mathers as one of Wynn's sons. **81m/C VHS.** Van Johnson, Walter Pidgeon, Louis Calhern, Dewey Martin, Keenan Wynn, Frank Lovejoy, Robert Horton, Bert Freed, Lewis Martin, Dick Simmons, Paul Smith, George Cooper, Ann Baker, Jonathan Hale, Dorothy Patrick, Jerry Mathers, Sarah Selby; ***D:*** Andrew Marton; ***W:*** Art Cohn; ***C:*** George J. Folsey; ***M:*** Miklos Rozsa.

Men of Two Worlds 🦴🦴 *Witch Doctor; Kisenga, Man of Africa* **1946** Classical musician raised in Africa is the toast of Europe until he finds out he's got a voodoo curse, and suddenly he's got the heebie jeebies too bad to play chopsticks. **90m/C VHS.** *GB* Robert Adams, Eric Portman, Orlando Martins, Phyllis Calvert, Arnold Marle, Cathleen Nesbitt, David Horne, Cyril Raymond; ***D:*** Thorold Dickinson.

Men of War 🦴½ **1994 (R)** Ex-Special Forces mercenaries decide to defend, rather than destroy, the inhabitants of an exotic island, whose land is wanted by a suspicious company interested in mining rights. **102m/C VHS, DVD, Wide.** Dolph Lundgren, Charlotte Lewis, B.D. Wong, Anthony John (Tony) Denison, Tim Guinee, Don Harvey, Tommy (Tiny) Lister, Trevor Goddard, Kevin Tighe; ***D:*** Perry Lang; ***W:*** John Sayles, Ethan Reiff, Cyrus Voris; ***C:*** Ronn Schmidt; ***M:*** Gerald Gouriet.

The Men Who Tread on the Tiger's Tail 🦴🦴½ *Tora No O Wo Fumu Otokotachi; They Who Step on the Tiger's Tail; Walkers on the Tiger's Tail* **1945** Twelfth-century Japan is the setting for this struggle of power between two brothers, one a reigning shogun, the other on the run. English subtitles. **60m/B VHS.** *JP* Denjiro Okochi, Susumu Fujita, Masayuki Mori, Takashi Shimura, Yoshio Kosugi; ***D:*** Akira Kurosawa; ***W:*** Akira Kurosawa; ***C:*** Takeo Ito; ***M:*** Tadashi Hattori.

Menace on the Mountain 🦴🦴 **1970 (G)** Family-oriented drama about a father and son who battle carpetbagging Confederate deserters during the Civil War. **89m/C VHS.** Pat(ricia) Crowley, Albert Salmi, Charles Aidman; ***D:*** Vincent McEveety.

Menace II Society 🦴🦴🦴½ **1993 (R)** Portrayal of black teens lost in inner-city hell is realistically captured by 21-year-old twin directors, in their big-screen debut. Caine (Turner) lives with his grandparents and peddles drugs for spending money, from the eve of his high school graduation to his decision to escape south-central Los Angeles for Atlanta. Bleak and haunting, with some of the most unsettling, bloodiest violence ever shown in a commercial film. Disturbing to watch, but critcally acclaimed. The Hughes' make their mark on contemporary black cinema with intensity, enhanced by an action-comics visual flair. Based on a story by the Hughes' and Tyger Williams. **104m/C VHS, DVD.** Tyrin Turner, Larenz Tate, Samuel L. Jackson, Glenn Plummer, Julian Roy Doster, Bill Duke, Charles S. Dutton, Jada Pinkett Smith, Vonte Sweet, Ryan Williams; ***D:*** Allen Hughes, Albert Hughes; ***W:*** Tyger Williams; ***C:*** Lisa Rinzler. Ind. Spirit '94: Cinematog.; MTV Movie Awards '94: Film.

Menage 🦴🦴🦴 *Tenue de Soiree* **1986** Depardieu is the homosexual crook who breaks into the home of an impoverished couple—the dominating Miou-Miou and her submissive husband, Blanc. An unrepentant thief, he begins to take over their lives, introducing them to the wonderful world of crime, among other, more kinky, pastimes. Gender-bending farce that doesn't hold up to the end but is worth watching for sheer outrageousness. In French with English subtitles. **84m/C VHS.** *FR* Gerard Depardieu, Michel Blanc, Miou-Miou, Bruno Cremer, Jean-Pierre Marielle; ***D:*** Bertrand Blier; ***W:*** Bertrand Blier; ***M:*** Serge Gainsbourg. Cannes '86: Actor (Blanc).

Mendel 🦴🦴🦴 **1998** Mendel (Sorenson) is the nine-year-old son of German-Jewish concentration camp survivors and displaced persons, who are relocated to Norway in 1954. Mendal is too young to know about the horrors that befell his family and that still cause them all nightmares. His parents are determined to shield him from their past while Mendel is equally determined to discover the family secrets. German and Norwegian with subtitles. **98m/C VHS.** *NO* Thomas Jungling Sorensen, Teresa Harder, Hans Kremer, Martin Meingast; ***D:*** Alexander Rosler; ***W:*** Alexander Rosler; ***C:*** Helge Sembe; ***M:*** Geir Bohren, Bent Aserud.

Menno's Mind 🦴🦴½ **1996** Rebel leader Bruce Campbell downloads his brain into a computer before being killed. Now his associates force computer techie Menno (Bill Campbell) to upload the material into his own mind in order to thwart presidential candidate Bernsen, who wants to use his online skills to influence the outcome of the election. **95m/C VHS, DVD.** Billy Campbell, Corbin Bernsen, Bruce Campbell, Michael Dorn, Robert Picardo, Robert Vaughn, Richard Speight Jr.; ***D:*** Jon Kroll; ***W:*** Mark Valenti; ***C:*** Gary Tieche; ***M:*** Christopher Franke. **CABLE**

The Men's Club 🦴½ **1986 (R)** Seven middle-aged buddies get together for a single night, and bare their respective souls and personal traumas, talking about women and eating and drinking. Banal. Based on novel by Leonard Michael. **100m/C VHS.** Harvey Keitel, Roy Scheider, Craig Wasson, Frank Langella, David Dukes, Richard Jordan, Treat Williams, Stockard Channing, Jennifer Jason Leigh, Ann Dusenberry, Cindy Pickett, Gwen Welles; ***D:*** Peter Medak.

Mephisto 🦴🦴🦴½ **1981** Egomaniacal stage actor Hendrik Hofgren (compellingly played by Brandauer) sides with the Nazis to further his career, with disastrous results. An updated version of the Faust legend and the first of three brilliant films by Szabo and Brandauer exploring the price of power and personal sublimation in German history. Klaus Mann based his 1936 novel on the career of German stage actor Gustaf Grundgens who became the director and star of Berlin's Prussian State Theater during WWII. German with subtitles. Followed by "Colonel Redl" and "Hanussen." **144m/C VHS, DVD, Wide.** *HU* Klaus Maria Brandauer, Krystyna Janda, Ildiko Bansagi, Karin Boyd, Rolf Hoppe, Christine Harbort, Gyorgy Cserhalmi, Christiane Graskoff, Peter Andorai, Ildiko Kishonti; ***D:*** Istvan Szabo; ***W:*** Istvan Szabo, Peter Dobai; ***C:*** Lajos Koltai; ***M:*** Zdenko Tamassy. Oscars '81: Foreign Film.

The Mephisto Waltz 🦴🦴🦴 **1971 (R)** Journalist gets more than a story when he is granted an interview with a dying pianist. It turns out that he is a satanist and the cult he is a part of wants the journalist. Chilling adaptation of the Fred Mustard Stewart novel features a haunting musical score. **108m/C VHS.** Alan Alda, Jacqueline Bisset, Barbara Parkins, Curt Jurgens, Bradford Dillman, William Windom, Kathleen Widdoes; ***D:*** Paul Wendkos; ***M:*** Jerry Goldsmith.

The Mercenaries 🦴½ **1965** Romantic warrior fights to save the lives and honor of his people who are under attack from mercenaries murdering and raping their way across Europe. **98m/C** Debra Paget.

The Mercenaries 🦴 *Cuba Crossing; Kill Castro; Assignment: Kill Castro; Key West Crossing; Sweet Dirty Tony* **1980** A tough guy, given the assignment to kill Fidel Castro, encounters all sorts of adversity along the way. Key West scenery is the only thing of interest. **92m/C VHS.** Stuart Whitman, Robert Vaughn, Caren Kaye, Raymond St. Jacques, Woody Strode, Sybil Danning, Albert Salmi, Michael V. Gazzo; ***D:*** Chuck Workman.

Mercenary 🦴🦴 **1996** Ex-Commando-turned-mercenary Alex Hawks (Gruner) is hired by wealthy businessman Jonas Ambler (Ritter) to avenge his wife's death at the hands of terrorists. Only Ambler's desk jockey doesn't want to stay on the sidelines and watch—he wants to do. So, Hawks is forced to take him along to Iraq when he goes after the bad guys. **97m/C VHS.** Olivier Gruner, John Ritter, Robert Culp, Ed Lauter, Martin Kove; ***D:*** Avi Nesher; ***W:*** Avi Nesher, Steven Hartov; ***C:*** Irek Hartowicz; ***M:*** Roger Neill.

Mercenary 2: Thick and Thin 🦴½ **1997 (R)** Mercenaries Hawk (Gruner) and Ray (Turturro) are hired to rescue a businessman (Townsend) who's apparently been kidnapped by a druglord and who's being held in a Central America jungle. Turns out it's all a set-up. **100m/C VHS.** Robert Townsend, Olivier Gruner, Nicholas Turturro, Claudia Christian, John Dennis Johnston, Tom Towles, Sam Bottoms; ***D:*** Philippe Mora. **VIDEO**

Mercenary Fighters 🦴½ **1988 (R)** An American soldier-of-fortune fights for both sides of an African revolution. Shot in South Africa. **90m/C VHS.** Peter Fonda, Reb Brown, Ron O'Neal, Jim Mitchum; ***D:*** Riki Shelach.

The Merchant of Four Seasons 🦴🦴🦴 **1971** Story focuses on the depression and unfulfilled dreams of an average street merchant. Direction from Fassbinder is slow, deliberate, and mesmerizing. In German with English subtitles. **88m/C VHS, DVD.** Hans Hirschmuller, Irm Hermann, Hanna Schygulla, Andrea Schober, Gusti Kreissl; ***D:*** Rainer Werner Fassbinder; ***W:*** Rainer Werner Fassbinder.

The Merchant of Venice 🦴🦴🦴 **1973** Shakespeare's tragedy of prejudice, vengeance, and sacrifice stars Olivier as the persecuted money lender Shylock, who demands his payment of a pound of flesh for a defaulted loan. **131m/C VHS.** *GB* Laurence Olivier, Joan Plowright, Jeremy Brett.

Merchants of War 🦴 **1990 (R)** Sent out by the CIA on a mission, two best friends are soon the target of one of the most dangerous terrorists in the world. The fanatical Islamic terrorist soon casts his wrath upon the two men. **100m/C VHS.** Asher Brauner, Jesse Vint, Bonnie Beck; ***D:*** Peter M. MacKenzie.

Mercury Rising 🦴🦴½ **1998 (R)** Renegade FBI agent Art Jeffries (Willis) must protect an autistic child who has inadvertently cracked a secret government code. Together, they dodge bullets from evil government forces headed by Nicholas Kudrow (Baldwin), who insist on having the innocent boy killed rather than change the code. That glaring logic aside, Willis does more than grunt here, showing moments of tenderness as he bonds with the oprhaned boy in between nailing bad guys and amassing an assortment of cuts and bruises. Baldwin is effective as the snake who truly believes killing a child will benefit national security. When action time isn't being sacrificed for Jeffries' paternal aspirations, film rises slightly above tepid to provide substantial thrills. **112m/C VHS, DVD, Wide.** Bruce Willis, Alec Baldwin, Miko Hughes, Kim Dickens, Chi McBride, Robert Stanton, Peter Stormare, Kevin Conway; ***D:*** Harold Becker; ***W:*** Larry Konner, Mark Rosenthal; ***C:*** Michael Seresin; ***M:*** John Barry. Golden Raspberries '98: Worst Actor (Willis).

Mercy 🦴🦴 **1996 (R)** When New York lawyer Frank Kramer's (Rubenstein) daughter is kidnapped he comes to realize it wasn't for ransom but for revenge. **82m/C VHS.** John Rubinstein, Sam Rockwell, Phil Brock, Novella Nelson, Amber Kain, Jane Lanier; ***D:*** Richard Shepard; ***W:*** Richard Shepard; ***C:*** Sarah Cawley.

Mercy 🦴🦴 **2000 (R)** Glossy sleaze based on the book by David L. Lindsey. Catherine Barker (Barkin) is a hard-drinking homicide detective investigating a serial killer with sexual kinks. Bombshell Vickie Kittrie (Wilson) reveals that each female victim belonged to an exclusive club that liked to experiment with the wilder side of life. All the victims also turn out to be patients of psychotherapist Dominick Broussard (Sands), who may be more psycho than anyone knows. **94m/C VHS, DVD, Wide.** Ellen Barkin, Peta Wilson, Julian Sands, Wendy Crewson, Karen Young, Marshall Bell, Stephen Baldwin, Beau Starr, Bill MacDonald, Stewart Bick; ***D:*** Damian Harris; ***W:*** Damian Harris; ***C:*** Manuel Teran; ***M:*** B.C. Smith.

Mercy Mission 🦴🦴½ **1993** Young pilot Bakula runs into trouble over the Pacific with his small plane and it's upto Air New Zealand airline pilot Loggia, who risks the lives of his passengers and crew, to come to his rescue. **92m/C VHS.** Scott Bakula, Robert Loggia; ***D:*** Roger Young.

Meridian: Kiss of the Beast 🦴½ **1990 (R)** A beautiful heiress is courted, kidnapped and loved by a demonic man-beast. **90m/C VHS.** Sherilyn Fenn, Malcom Jamieson, Hilary Mason, Alex Daniels, Phil Fondacaro, Charlie Spradling; ***D:*** Charles Band; ***W:*** Dennis Paoli; ***M:*** Pino Donaggio.

Merlin 🦴🦴½ **1992 (PG-13)** In a remote California town reporter Christy Lake is stunned to discover her ancient heritage. Turns out she's the reincarnated daughter of legendary Merlin the magician and it is her duty to protect the Sword of Power from the evil sorcerer Pendragon. And aided by a handsome warrior and an ancient sage, that's just what she intends to do. **112m/C VHS.** Nadia Cameron, Peter Phelps, Richard Lynch, James Hong, Ted Markland, Desmond Llewelyn; ***D:*** Paul Hunt; ***W:*** Nick McCarty.

Merlin 🦴🦴🦴 **1998** Legend of Camelot and Arthur's mentor is brought to the small screen with fine performances and equally impressive special effects. Merlin is conceived through the magic of evil Queen Mab (Richardson) to bring Britain back to its pagan roots. But Merlin doesn't really like magic and grows up to be (in the commanding persona of Neill) a most reluctant sorcerer. Still, he mentors Arthur (Curran) and continues to battle Mab, who works with Arthur's half sister Morgan Le Fey (Bonham Carter) to destroy Camelot. Merlin also pursues a long-time romance with Nimue (Rossellini), who falls victim to Mab's treachery. **140m/C VHS, DVD.** Sam Neill, Miranda Richardson, Isabella Rossellini, Martin Short, Helena Bonham Carter, Rutger Hauer, Paul Curran, Billie Whitelaw, Lena Headey, Jason Done, Mark Jax, John McEnery, Nicholas Clay, Sebastien Roche, Jeremy Sheffield; ***Cameos:*** John Gielgud; ***D:*** Steven Barron; ***W:*** David Stevens, Edward Khmara; ***C:*** Sergei Koslov; ***M:*** Trevor Jones; ***V:*** James Earl Jones. **TV**

Merlin and the Sword 🦴 *Arthur the King* **1985** Poor use of a good cast in this treatment of the legend of Merlin, Arthur and Excalibur. **94m/C VHS.** Malcolm McDowell, Edward Woodward, Candice Bergen, Dyan Cannon; ***D:*** Clive Donner.

Mermaid 🦴🦴½ **2000** Young Desi is mourning her father's death. She writes a letter to him and ties it to a balloon, hoping that it will fly to heaven so he can read it. Instead, the winds blow the balloon to Canada's St. Edward's Island and the small town of Mermaid. When the letter is found, the islanders decide to respond to Desi's message. **94m/C VHS, DVD.** Samantha Mathis, Ellen Burstyn, David Kaye, Jodelle Ferland, Blu Mankuma, Tom Heaton; ***D:*** Peter Masterson; ***W:*** Todd Robinson; ***C:*** Jon Joffin; ***M:*** Peter Melnick. **CABLE**

Mermaids 🦴🦴🦴 **1990 (PG-13)** Mrs. Flax (Cher) is the flamboyant mother of two who hightails out of town every time a relationship threatens to turn serious. Having moved some 18 times, her daughters, Charlotte (Ryder), 15, and Kate (Ricci), 8, are a little worse for the wear, psychologically speaking. One aspires to be a nun though not Catholic, and the other holds her breath under water. Now living in Massachusetts, Mrs. Flax starts having those "I got you, babe" feelings for Hoskins, a shoestore owner. Amusing, well-acted multi-generational coming of ager based on a novel by Patty Dann. **110m/C VHS, DVD, Wide.** Cher, Winona Ryder, Bob Hoskins, Christina Ricci, Michael Schoeffling, Caroline McWilliams, Jan Miner; ***D:*** Richard Benjamin; ***W:*** June Roberts; ***C:*** Howard Atherton; ***M:*** Jack Nitzsche. Natl. Bd. of Review '90: Support. Actress (Ryder).

The Mermaids of Tiburon 🦴 *The Aqua Sex* **1962** A marine biologist and a criminal travel to a remote island off Mexico in search of elusive, expensive "fire pearls." There they encounter a kingdom of lovely mermaids who promptly liven things up. Filmed in "Aquascope" for your viewing pleasure. **77m/C VHS.** Diane Webber, George Rowe, Timothy Carey, Jose Gonzalez-Gonzalez, John (Jack) Mylong, Gil Baretto, Vicki Kantenwine, Nani Morrissey, Judy Edwards, Jean Carroll, Diana Cook, Karen Goodman, Nancy Burns; ***D:*** John Lamb; ***W:*** John Lamb.

Merrill's Marauders 🦴🦴½ **1962** Chandler is the commander of a battle-hardened regiment fighting in the jungles of Burma in 1944. The exhausted unit gains their latest objective and expects to be relieved, only to be continuously pushed into more fighting down the line. Director Fuller excels at showing the confusion of battle; Chandler's last film role (he died before the film was released). **98m/C VHS.** Jeff Chandler, Ty Hardin, Peter Brown, Andrew Duggan, Will Hutchins, Claude Akins, John Hoyt, Chuck Hicks, Charles Briggs, Vaughan Wilson, Pancho Magalona; ***D:*** Samuel Fuller; ***W:*** Samuel Fuller, Milton Sperling, Charlton Ogburn Jr.; ***C:*** William Clothier; ***M:*** Howard Jackson.

Merry Christmas, Mr. Lawrence 🦴🦴🦴 **1983 (R)** An often overlooked drama about a WWII Japanese POW camp. Taut psychological drama about clashing cultures and physical and emotional survival focusing on the tensions between Bowie as a British POW and camp commander Sakamato, who also composed the outstanding score. A haunting and intense film about the horrors of war. Based on the novel by Laurens van der Post. **124m/C VHS.** *JP GB* David Bowie, Tom Conti, Ryuichi Sakamoto, Takeshi "Beat" Kitano, Jack Thompson, Takashi Naito, Alistair Browning, Johnny Okura, Yuya Uchida, Ryunosuke Kaneda, Kan Mikami, Yuji Honma, Diasuke Iijima; ***D:*** Nagisa Oshima; ***W:*** Nagisa Oshima, Paul Mayersberg; ***C:*** Toichiro Narushima. Natl. Bd. of Review '83: Actor (Conti).

Merry-Go-Round 🦴🦴🦴 **1923** A handsome Austrian count is engaged to a woman of his class when he meets the beautiful Agnes, who works as an organ grinder for the local merry-go-round. He disguises himself to woo her but finally decides to marry his fiance, although Agnes continues to love him. But the story doesn't end for the two lovers who are destined to be together. Producer Thalberg and director von Stroheim battled over the expense and length of the film until Thalberg had the director replaced. However, much of the film still shows the von Stroheim brillance and attention to lavish detail. **110m/B VHS.** Norman Kerry, Mary Philbin, Cesare Gravina, Edith Yorke, George Hackathorne; ***D:*** Rupert Julian, Erich von Stroheim.

A Merry War 🦴🦴🦴 *Keep the Aspidistra Flying* **1997** Gordon Comstock (Grant) is a frustrated ad-man in London, circa 1935. He believes that his comfortable middle-class lifestyle is stifling his creativity (he is mistakenly lead to believe that he is a poet when he gets published). Convinced that slumming is the only way to tap into his supposed talent, he quits his advertising job and moves into a shabby little apartment to augment his misery, despite the doubts of girlfriend Rosemary (Bonham Carter). Based on George Orwell's only comedy, which fictionalizes his own experiences in London and Paris. In spite of being a comedy (and a funny one at that), story has that Orwellian feel of political commentary and, naturally, makes a statement on social classes. Performances are solid, with the beautiful Bonham Carter showing her comedic chops. Very British pic will appeal to fans of '30s era dialogue. **101m/C VHS, DVD, Wide.** Richard E. Grant, Helena Bonham Carter, Julian Wadham, Jim Carter, Harriet Walter, Liz Smith, Barbara Leigh-Hunt; ***D:*** Robert Bierman; ***W:*** Alan Plater; ***C:*** Giles Nuttgens; ***M:*** Mike Batt.

The Merry Widow 🦴🦴🦴½ *The Lady Dances* **1934** The first sound version of the famous Franz Lehar operetta, dealing with a playboy from a bankrupt kingdom who must woo and marry the land's wealthy widow or be tried for treason. A delightful musical comedy, with a sterling cast and patented Lubitschian gaiety. Made as a silent in 1912 and 1925; remade in color in 1952. ♫Girls, Girls, Girls; Vilia; Tonight Will Teach Me to Forget; Melody of Laughter; Maxim's; The Girls at Maxim's; The Merry Widow Waltz; If Widows are Rich; Russian Dance. **99m/B VHS.** Maurice Chevalier, Jeanette MacDonald, Edward Everett Horton, Una Merkel, George Barbier, Minna Gombell, Ruth Channing, Sterling Holloway, Henry Armetta, Barbara Leanard, Donald Meek, Akim Tamiroff, Herman Bing; ***D:*** Ernst Lubitsch; ***M:*** Franz Lehar, Lorenz Hart.

The Merry Widow 🦴🦴½ **1952** Rich widow Turner travels to her husband's homeland of Marshovia to dedicate a statue to his memory. The country is deeply in debt and the king would like the widow to marry a local count and remain (along with her fortune). Lamas is charming as the intended bridegroom but Turner, though lovely looking, is miscast; her singing was dubbed by Erwin. Uninspired remake of the 1934 film only benefits from being shot in color and the lavish production values. Based on the operetta by Lehar. ♫The Merry Widow Waltz; Can-Can; Girls, Girls, Girls; I'm Going to Maxim's. **105m/C VHS.** Lana Turner, Fernando Lamas, Una Merkel, Richard Haydn, Thomas Gomez, John Abbott, Marcel Dalio, King Donovan, Robert Coote, Joi Lansing; ***Cameos:*** Gwen Verdon; ***D:*** Curtis Bernhardt; ***W:*** Sonya Levien, William Ludwig; ***C:*** Robert L. Surtees; ***M:*** Franz Lehar; ***V:*** Trudy Erwin.

The Merry Wives of Windsor 🦴🦴 *Die Lustigen Weiber von Windsor* **1950** Fat, ribald, and boastful Sir John Falstaff indulges in excess at his favorite Windsor tavern. He also likes the ladies and has taken to flattering both Mistress Reich and Fluth. The ladies and the townspeople eventually decide that Falstaff needs to be taught a lesson. German with subtitles. **96m/B VHS.** *GE* Paul Esser, Sonja Ziemann, Camilla Spira; ***D:*** Georg Wildhagen; ***W:*** Georg Wildhagen, Wolff von Gordon; ***C:*** Karl Plintzner, Eugen Klagemann; ***M:*** Otto Nikolai.

Merton of the Movies 🦴🦴½ **1947** Skelton stars as star-struck, small town theatre usher Merton Gill who wins a trip to Hollywood. He's befriended by stunt double Phyllis (O'Brien) who recognizes his comedic talents and works to get him that big break. Based on the play by George S. Kaufman and Marc Connelly and previously filmed in 1924 and 1932 (as "Make Me a Star"). **82m/B VHS.** Red Skelton, Virginia O'Brien, Gloria Grahame, Leon Ames, Alan Mowbray, Charles D. Brown, Hugo Haas, Harry Hayden; ***D:*** Robert Alton; ***W:*** George Wells, Lou Breslow.

Mesa of Lost Women woof! *Lost Women; Lost Women of Zarpa* **1952** Mad scientist creates brave new race of vicious women with long fingernails. So bad it's a wanna-B. Addams Family buffs will spot the Fester in Coogan. **70m/B VHS, DVD.** Jackie Coogan, Richard Travis, Allan Nixon, Mary Hill, Robert Knapp, Tandra Quinn, Lyle Talbot, Katherine Victor, Angelo Rossitto, Dolores Fuller; ***D:*** Ron Ormond, Herbert Tevos; ***W:*** Herbert Tevos; ***C:*** Gilbert Warrenton, Karl Struss; ***M:*** Hoyt Curtin.

Mesmer 🦴🦴 **1994** Rickman gives a bravura performance in the title role of controversial 18th-century Austrian doctor Franz Anton Mesmer, who put the term "mesmerize" in the dictionary. This court (in Vienna and Paris) physician's unorthodox healing practices were concerned with filtering out negative magnetism through hypnotism and positive thinking. Was he a charlatan or merely a man ahead of his time? **107m/C VHS, DVD.** *GB* Alan Rickman, Donal Donnelly, Peter Dvorsky, David Hemblen, Simon McBurney, Gillian Barge, Jan Rubes; ***D:*** Roger Spottiswoode; ***W:*** Dennis Potter; ***C:*** Elemer Ragalyi; ***M:*** Michael Nyman.

Mesmerized 🦴🦴 *Shocked* **1984** Based on the work by Jerzy Skolimowski, the film is a dramatization of the Victoria Thompson murder case in 1880s New Zealand. A teenaged orphaned girl marries an older man and decides after years of abuse to kill him through hypnosis. An unengaging drama, though the lovely New Zealand landscape serves as a fitting contrast to the film's ominous tone. **90m/C VHS, DVD.** *GB NZ AU* John Lithgow, Jodie Foster, Michael Murphy, Dan Shor, Harry Andrews; ***D:*** Michael Laughlin; ***W:*** Michael Laughlin; ***C:*** Louis Horvath; ***M:*** Georges Delerue.

Mesquite Buckaroo 🦴 **1939** Two cowboys bet over who is the better bronco buster, but one of them gets kidnapped. **59m/B VHS.** Bob Steele, Carolyn Curtis, Frank LaRue, Juanita Fletcher, Charles "Blackie" King; ***D:*** Harry S. Webb.

The Message 🦴🦴 *Mohammad: Messenger of God; Al-Ris-Alah* **1977 (PG)** Sprawling saga of the genesis of the religion of Islam, with Quinn portraying Mohammad's uncle, Hamza, an honored warrior. The story behind the movie might prove much more successful as a sequel than did the movie itself. The filming itself created a religious controversy. **220m/C VHS, DVD.** *GB* Damien Thomas, Anthony Quinn, Irene Papas, Michael Ansara, Johnny Sekka, Michael Forest, Neville Jason; ***D:*** Moustapha Akkad; ***W:*** H.A.L. Craig; ***C:*** Jack Hildyard; ***M:*** Maurice Jarre.

Message in a Bottle 🦴🦴 **1998 (PG-13)** Romantic drama that's paced slower than the method of mail delivery in the title. Wright Penn is a divorced mother who finds a love note written to a mystery man's lost love floating in the Atlantic. She tracks the note to strong silent guy Costner, still grieving for his dead wife. She tries to get him to open up and move on with his life (with her preferably), but this takes a mind-numbingly long time. The two are destined to be together, but half of those watching are destined to be asleep by the time it happens. The sole reason to watch this movie is to see old pro Paul Newman steal every scene he's in as Costner's father. **132m/C VHS, DVD, Wide.** Kevin Costner, Robin Wright Penn, Paul Newman, John Savage, Illeana Douglas, Robbie Coltrane, Jesse James Jr., Bethel Leslie, Tom Aldredge, Viveka Davis, Raphael Sbarge, Richard Hamilton, Rosemary Murphy, Stephen Eckholdt; ***D:*** Luis Mandoki; ***W:*** Gerald Di Pego; ***C:*** Caleb Deschanel; ***M:*** Gabriel Yared.

Messalina vs. the Son of Hercules 🦴 **1964** A Roman slave leads a rebellion against the emperor Messalina. Italian; dubbed into English. **105m/C VHS.** *IT* Richard Harrison, Marilu Tolo, Lisa Gastoni; ***D:*** Umberto Lenzi.

The Messenger 🦴 **1987 (R)** A man right out of prison sets out to avenge his wife's murder by an Italian drug syndicate. **95m/C VHS.** Fred Williamson, Sandy Cummings, Christopher Connelly, Cameron Mitchell.

Messenger of Death 🦴🦴½ **1988 (R)** A tough detective investigates the slaughter of a Mormon family, and uncovers a conspiracy centering around oil-rich real estate. **90m/C VHS.** Charles Bronson, Trish Van Devere, Laurence Luckinbill, Daniel Benzali, Marilyn Hassett, Jeff Corey, John Ireland, Penny Peyser, Gene Davis; ***D:*** J. Lee Thompson; ***W:*** Paul Jarrico; ***M:*** Robert O. Ragland.

The Messenger: The Story of Joan of Arc 🦴🦴 **1999 (R)** Besson's take on the legendary 15th-century French teen martyr Joan of Arc (Jovovich) leans heavily on gory battle scenes, stilted dialogue, and spectacle to tell her story. After seeing her sister murdered and raped (actually in that order) by English soldiers, Joan begins to hear heavenly voices that tell her that she must free her country and king from the invaders. After a visit with the Dauphin, several bloody battles ensue, and Joan is eventually captured, she and put on trial for sorcery and heresy. Awaiting her fate, she has conversations with a character that is actually billed as her Conscience (Hoffman), which brings up questions in her mind whether she was really divinely inspired or merely a cake du fruit. Jovovich's pop-eyed, semi-intelligible performance helps this poor effort go up in flames. **148m/C VHS, DVD.** Milla Jovovich, John Malkovich, Faye Dunaway, Dustin Hoffman, Pascal Greggory, Vincent Cassel, Tcheky Karyo, Richard Ridings, Desmond Harrington; ***D:*** Luc Besson; ***W:*** Luc Besson, Andrew Birkin; ***C:*** Thierry Arbogast; ***M:*** Eric Serra.

The Messiah 🦴🦴🦴½ *Il Messia* **1975** Rossellini's final film, a rarely seen version of the life of Christ, completely passed over any notions of divinity to portray him as a morally perfect man. In Italian with subtitles. **145m/C VHS.** *IT* Tina Aumont, Flora Carabella, Vernon Dobtcheff, Jean Martin; ***D:*** Roberto Rossellini; ***W:*** Roberto Rossellini; ***C:*** Mario Montuori; ***M:*** Mario Nascimbene.

Messiah of Evil 🦴 *Dead People; Return of the Living Dead; Revenge of the Screaming Dead; The Second Coming* **1974 (R)** California coastal town is invaded by zombies. Confusing low-rent production from the writers of "American Graffiti." **90m/C VHS.** Marianna Hill, Joy Bang, Royal Dano, Elisha Cook Jr., Michael Greer; ***D:*** Gloria Katz, Willard Huyck; ***W:*** Gloria Katz, Willard Huyck.

Messidor 🦴🦴 **1977** Bored university student Jeanne (Amouroux) and shop assistant Marie (Retore) meet while hitchhiking and decide to travel together through Europe—committing robberies when they run out of money. French with subtitles. **118m/C VHS.** *SI* Clementine Amouroux, Catherine Retore, Franziskus Abgottspon, Gerald Battiaz, Hansjorg Bedschard; ***D:*** Alain Tanner; ***W:*** Alain Tanner; ***C:*** Renato Berta; ***M:*** Arie Dzierlatka.

Metallica 🦴 **1985** Alien warmongers endeavor to conquer Earth and scientists try to stop them. **90m/C VHS.** Anthony Newcastle, Sharon Baker; ***D:*** Al (Alfonso Brescia) Bradley.

Metalstorm: The Destruction of Jared Syn 🦴 **1983 (PG)** It's the science fiction battle of the ages with giant cyclopes and intergalactic magicians on the desert planet of Lemuria. **84m/C VHS.** Jeffrey Byron, Mike (Michael) Preston, Tim Thomerson, Kelly Preston, Richard Moll; ***D:*** Charles Band; ***W:*** Alan J. Adler; ***C:*** Mac Ahlberg; ***M:*** Richard Band.

Metamorphosis 🦴 **1990 (R)** Novice scientist foolishly uses himself as the guinea pig for his anti-aging experiments. He quickly loses control of the project. **90m/C VHS.** Gene Le Brock, Catherine Baranov, Stephen Brown, Harry Cason, Jason Arnold; ***D:*** G.L. Eastman.

Metamorphosis: The Alien Factor 🦴🦴½ **1993 (R)** Gerard is a genetic engineer who is bitten by a frog injected with a mutation sample from outer space. He turns into a slimy virus that infects everything he touches. **92m/C VHS.** George Gerard, Tony Gigante, Katharine Romaine; ***D:*** Glen Takakjian.

Meteor woof! **1979 (PG)** American and Soviet scientists attempt to save the Earth from a fast-approaching barrage of meteors from space in this disaster dud. Destruction ravages parts of Hong Kong and the Big Apple. **107m/C VHS, DVD, Wide.** Sean Connery, Natalie Wood, Karl Malden, Brian Keith, Martin Landau, Trevor Howard, Henry Fonda, Joseph Campanella, Richard Dysart; ***D:*** Ronald Neame; ***W:*** Stanley Mann; ***C:*** Paul Lohmann; ***M:*** Laurence Rosenthal.

Meteor & Shadow 🦴🦴 *Meteoro Kai Skia* **1985** Based on the life of esteemed Greek poet Napoleon Lapathiotis (1888-1944), whose openly gay lifestyle shocked conservative Athenian society. A leftist charmer, Lapathiotis indulged in the bohemian life until it finally destroyed him. Greek with subtitles. **101m/C VHS, DVD.** *GR* Takis Moschos; ***D:*** Takis Spetsiotis; ***W:*** Takis Spetsiotis.

The Meteor Man 🦴🦴½ **1993 (PG)** Townsend is a school teacher who reluctantly becomes a hero when he acquires semi-super powers after being hit by a meteor. Meteor Man flies only four feet off the ground (because he's afraid of heights) and wears costumes fashioned by his mother. Funny premise satires "superhero" movies, but is inconsistent with some hilarious gags and others that fall flat. Includes interesting cameos by Cosby, Sinbad, Vandross, and Page. **100m/C VHS, Wide.** Robert Townsend, Robert Guillaume, Marla Gibbs, James Earl Jones, Frank Gorshin; ***Cameos:*** Bill Cosby, Sinbad, Luther Vandross, LaWanda Page; ***D:*** Robert Townsend; ***W:*** Robert Townsend; ***C:*** John A. Alonzo.

Metro 🦴½ **1996 (R)** Murphy has now officially made this exact movie one kajillion times. He plays fast-talking, fast-shooting cop Axel Fo... er... Scott Roper, who's forced to accept a partner that he doesn't want, played by Nick... um... Judge... uh... Michael Rapaport! When a villain kills his best friend, he vows revenge. He and his sidekick are involved in car chases, shoot-outs and a tense situation where his girlfriend is taken hostage. Any of this ring a bell? Maybe it was in that "Another 48 Beverly Hills Cop Movies." **117m/C VHS, DVD, Wide.** Eddie Murphy, Michael Rapaport, Michael Wincott, Carmen Ejogo, Denis Arndt, Art Evans, Donal Logue, Paul Ben-Victor, Kim Miyori, David Michael Silverman; ***D:*** Thomas Carter; ***W:*** Randy Feldman; ***C:*** Fred Murphy; ***M:*** Steve Porcaro.

Metroland 🦴🦴 **1997 (R)** Marital ennui and male friendship is explored in this adaptation of Julian Barnes' 1980 novel. In 1977, advertising exec Chris Lloyd (Bale) is settled in a London suburb with his wife, Marion (Watson), and their baby. His predictable existence is blasted when old chum, Toni (Ross), arrives. The duo once shared a dream of living a bohemian life and Chris is reminded of a time he spent in Paris in the late-'60s and his wild French lover. Toni increasingly tries to undermine Chris' marriage as he struggles to decide what he expects from life. **105m/C VHS, DVD.** *GB FR* Christian Bale, Emily Watson, Lee Ross, Elsa Zylberstein, Ifan Meredith, Rufus, Amanda Ryan; ***D:*** Philip Saville; ***W:*** Adrian Hodges; ***C:*** Jean-Francois Robin; ***M:*** Mark Knopfler.

Metropolis 🦴🦴🦴🦴 **1926** Now a classic meditation on futurist technology and mass mentality, this fantasy concerns mechanized society. Original set design and special effects made this an innovative and influential film in its day. Is now considered one of the hippest films of the sci-fi genre. Silent, with musical score. The 1984 re-release features some color tinting, reconstruction, and a digital score with songs by Pat Benatar, Bonnie Tyler, Giorgio Moroder, and Queen. **115m/B VHS, DVD.** *GE* Brigitte Helm, Alfred Abel, Gustav Froehlich, Rudolf Klein-Rogge, Fritz Rasp, Heinrich George, Theodore Loos, Erwin Biswanger, Olaf Storm, Hans Leo Reich, Heinrich Gotho, Fritz Alberti, Max Dietze; ***D:*** Fritz Lang; ***W:*** Fritz Lang, Thea von Harbou; ***C:*** Karl Freund, Gunther Rittau, Eugene Schufftan; ***M:*** Gottfried Huppertz.

Metropolitan 🦴🦴🦴 **1990 (PG-13)** The Izod set comes of age on Park Avenue during Christmas break. Tom Townsend (Clements), a member of the middle class, finds himself drawn into a circle of self-proclaimed urban haute bourgeoisie types. They're embarrassingly short on male escorts for the holiday season's parties so he stands in and gets an inside look at life with the brat pack. Intelligently written and carefully made, it transcends the flirting-with-adulthood genre. **98m/C VHS.** Carolyn Farina, Edward Clements, Taylor Nichols, Christopher Eigeman, Allison Rutledge-Parisi, Dylan Hundley, Isabel Gillies, Bryan Leder, Will Kempe, Elizabeth Thompson; ***D:*** Whit Stillman; ***W:*** Whit Stillman; ***C:*** John Thomas; ***M:*** Mark Suozzo. Ind. Spirit '91: First Feature; N.Y. Film Critics '90: Director (Stillman).

The Mexican 🦴🦴 **2001 (R)** South-of-the-border snorer has Jerry (Pitt), an inept go-fer for mobster Margolese (Hackman), on a mission for a priceless antique gun with a name which gives the movie its title. Jerry's quirky girlfriend Samantha (Roberts) wants him to go straight and, when he refuses, heads to Vegas to pursue her dreams of becoming a croupier. Sam's dreams are temporarily sidetracked when she's kidnapped as leverage for the supposedly cursed gun by homosexual hitman Leroy (Gandolfini). Gandolfini is far-and-away the standout as the sensitive hood with whom Samantha bonds during her captivity. Screwball romantic comedy is neither, as the few but much-anticipated scenes with Pitt and Roberts are easily outshone by Roberts' chemistry with Gandolfini. Pitt does his part, providing some comic moments in Mexico but can't save cliched tale. **123m/C VHS, DVD, Wide.** *US* Brad Pitt, Julia Roberts, James Gandolfini, Bob Balaban, Gene Hackman, J.K. Simmons, David Krumholtz, Michael Ceveris; ***D:*** Gore Verbinski; ***W:*** J.H. Wyman; ***C:*** Darius Wolski; ***M:*** Alan Silvestri.

Mexican Bus Ride 🦴🦴½ *Ascent to Heaven; Subida Al Cielo* **1951** A good-natured Bunuel effort about a newlywed peasant who travels to the big city to attend to his mother's will. While en route, he encounters a diversity of people on the bus and some temptation. In Spanish with English subtitles. **85m/B VHS.** *MX* Lilia Prado, Esteban Marquez, Carmelita Gonzalez; ***D:*** Luis Bunuel.

Mexican Hayride 🦴🦴 **1948** Bud heads a gang of swindlers and Lou is the fall guy. When things up north get too hot, the boys head south of the border to cool off and start a mining scam. Watch for the hilarious bullfighting scene. Believe it or not, this is based on a Cole Porter musical—minus the music. **77m/B VHS.** Bud Abbott, Lou Costello, Virginia Grey, Luba Malina, John Hubbard, Pedro de Cordoba, Fritz Feld, Tom Powers, Pat Costello, Frank Fenton; ***D:*** Charles T. Barton; ***W:*** Oscar Brodney.

Mexican Spitfire at Sea 🦴½ **1942** The feisty wife from South of the Border heads for Hawaii to close a deal for her husband. He goes along to help her, impersonating nobility. The thin storyline keeps it from being quite as good as the first "Mexican Spitfire" film. Most of the action takes place aboard ship. **73m/B VHS.** Lupe Velez, Leon Errol, Charles "Buddy" Rogers, ZaSu Pitts, Elisabeth Risdon, Florence Bates, Marion Martin, Eddie Dunn, Harry Holman; ***D:*** Leslie Goodwins.

Mexico City 🦴🦴½ **2000 (R)** This one gets points for having a strong heroine in Edwards. She plays Mitch who takes a holiday in Mexico with photographer brother Sam (Zander). Only Sam disappears and Mitch enlists the help of a local taxi driver (Robles) to help her find him. Shows the seedy underworld side of Mexico City—not exactly a tourist mecca. **88m/C VHS, DVD, Wide.** Stacy Edwards, Jorge Robles, Johnny Zander, Robert Patrick; ***D:*** Richard Shepard; ***W:*** Richard Shepard, Jonathan Stern. **VIDEO**

Mi Vida Loca 🦴🦴 *My Crazy Life* **1994 (R)** Looks at the lives of Latina gang members from L.A.'s Echo Park. The women talk about their romantic dreams, friendships, families, and raising children amidst the pervasive violence and despair of their tough neighborhood. Small budget and some unpolished performances don't lessen film's impact—about the stupidity of violence and how "average" the hopes and dreams of these women are. **92m/C VHS.** Angel Aviles, Jacob Vargas, Jesse Borrego, Seidy Lopez, Marlo Marron, Neilida Lopez, Bertilla Damas, Art Esquer, Christina Solis, Salma Hayek, Magali Alvarado, Julian Reyes, Panchito Gomez; ***D:*** Allison Anders; ***W:*** Allison Anders; ***M:*** John Taylor.

Miami Beach Cops 🦴½ **1993** Two vets return home expecting life to be routine when they become sheriff's deputies. But when bad guys murder a local merchant things heat up fast. **97m/C VHS.** Frank Maldonatti, Salvatore Rendino, William Childers, Joyce Geier, Raff Baker, Dan Preston, Deborah Daniels; ***D:*** James R. Winburn.

Miami Blues 🦴🦴½ **1990 (R)** Cold-blooded killer plays cat-and-mouse with bleary cop while diddling with an unflappable prostitute. Violent and cynical, with appropriate performances from three leads. Based on the novel by Charles Willeford. **97m/C VHS.** Fred Ward, Alec Baldwin, Jennifer Jason Leigh, Nora Dunn, Charles Napier, Jose Perez, Paul Gleason, Obba Babatunde, Martine Beswick, Shirley Stoler; ***D:*** George Armitage; ***W:*** George Armitage; ***C:*** Tak Fujimoto; ***M:*** Gary Chang. N.Y. Film Critics '90: Support. Actress (Leigh).

Miami Cops 🦴 1989 When a cop's father is killed by a drug smuggler, he and his partner pursue the murderer over two continents. Italian-made adventure is a bit drawn-out. **103m/C VHS.** *IT* Richard Roundtree, Harrison Muller, Dawn Baker, Michael J. Aronin; ***D:*** Al (Alfonso Brescia) Bradley.

Miami Horror 🦴 1987 A Florida scientist is experimenting with bacteria from space, trying to recreate a human only to have his efforts stolen by a crook. His intentions for the use of the experiment are not exactly for the furtherance of science. De martino used the pseudonym Martin Herbert. **85m/C VHS.** *IT* David Warbeck, Laura Trotter, Lawrence Loddi, John Ireland; ***D:*** Alberto De Martino.

Miami Hustle 🦴½ 1995 (R) Con artist Marsha (Ireland) is forced by a sleazy lawyer to impersonate a bar waitress (England) who's about to inherit a fortune. But when things turn sour, she gets a computer mogul (Enos) to figure out who's setting her up. **81m/C VHS.** Kathy Ireland, John Enos, Audie England, Richard Sarafian; ***D:*** Lawrence Lanoff. **CABLE**

Miami Rhapsody 🦴🦴 1995 (PG-13) Woody Allen-ish romantic comedy about a young, neurotic copywriter who becomes disillusioned with the idea of marriage as she discovers every member of her family is having an affair. Parker plays the newly engaged Gwyn who is not entirely sure if she wants to marry her cute, zoologist boyfriend. Most of the characters come across as annoying, self-absorbed whiners, except for Banderas, who charms as a sexy Cuban nurse. Film moves along with its light-hearted narrative, but never reaches the comic or emotional depth of Allen's work. Director/writer Frankel shows promise, but should come out from behind the Woodman's shadow. Filmed on location in Miami. **95m/C VHS, DVD.** Sarah Jessica Parker, Gil Bellows, Antonio Banderas, Mia Farrow, Paul Mazursky, Kevin Pollak, Barbara Garrick, Carla Gugino, Bo Eason, Naomi Campbell, Jeremy Piven, Kelly Bishop, Ben Stein; ***D:*** David Frankel; ***W:*** David Frankel; ***C:*** Jack Wallner; ***M:*** Mark Isham.

Miami Supercops 🦴½ 1985 Two goofy policemen strike out against such threats as a gang that hassles buses, the attempted kidnapping of an Orange Bowl quarterback, and a multi-million-dollar robbery. **97m/C VHS.** Terence Hill, Bud Spencer, Jackie Castellano, C.V. Wood Jr.; ***D:*** Bruno Corbucci.

Miami Vendetta 🦴 1987 L.A. vice cop risks it all to avenge his friend's death at the hands of Cuban drug smugglers. **90m/C VHS.** Sandy Brooke, Frank Gargani, Maarten Goslins, Barbara Pilavin; ***D:*** Steven Seemayer.

Miami Vice 🦴🦴½ 1984 Pilot for the popular TV series paired Crockett and Tubbs for the first time on the trail of a killer in Miami's sleazy underground. Music by Jan Hammer and other pop notables. **99m/C VHS.** Don Johnson, Philip Michael Thomas, Saundra Santiago, Michael Talbott, John Diehl, Gregory Sierra; ***D:*** Thomas Carter. **TV**

Michael 🦴🦴½ 1996 (PG) Following up "Phenomenon" with another celestial storyline, Travolta tries on the giant, molting wings of Michael, an atypical archangel with an amazing joie de vive and an appetite for alcohol, women, and sugar. Residing in Iowa with the elderly Pansy (Stapleton), Michael is being tracked by a cynical tabloid reporter (Hurt) and an angel expert (MacDowell), so he figures he might as well play cupid. The now standard dance sequence in Travolta movies takes place in a bar to the tune of "Chain of Fools" and is one of the movie's standouts. While Travolta gives another stellar performance, Hurt and MacDowell have little to do but play out their tired romantic subplot in a script that could've used some inspiration from its lead character. **105m/C VHS, DVD.** John Travolta, William Hurt, Andie MacDowell, Bob Hoskins, Robert Pastorelli, Jean Stapleton, Teri Garr; ***D:*** Nora Ephron; ***W:*** Nora Ephron, Delia Ephron, Pete Dexter; ***C:*** John Lindley; ***M:*** Randy Newman.

Michael Collins 🦴🦴🦴 1996 (R) Collins (Neeson) was a revolutionary leader with the Irish Volunteers, a guerilla force (an early version of the IRA) dedicated to freeing Ireland from British rule by any means necessary. After a number of successful moves against British intelligence, Collins is unwillingly drawn into a statesman's role as negotiations for an Anglo-Irish Treaty begin in 1921, ultimately dividing the country in two and leading to Collins' own assassination. Controversy surrounded the film as historians, politicians, and the media took potshots at director Jordan's admittedly personal look at the complexities of Irish life and one of its equally complicated heroes. **117m/C VHS, DVD.** Liam Neeson, Aidan Quinn, Alan Rickman, Stephen Rea, Julia Roberts, Ian Hart, Sean McGinley, Gerard McSorley, Stuart Graham, Brendan Gleeson, Charles Dance, Jonathan Rhys Meyers; ***D:*** Neil Jordan; ***W:*** Neil Jordan; ***C:*** Chris Menges; ***M:*** Elliot Goldenthal. L.A. Film Critics '96: Cinematog.; Venice Film Fest. '96: Golden Lion, Actor (Neeson).

The Michigan Kid 🦴🦴 1928 Two boys fight for the same girl in this silent love triangle set in Alaska. Film's most notable scene is of a raging forest fire, considered a classic even today. **62m/B VHS.** Conrad Nagel, Renee Adoree, Fred Esmelton, Virginia Grey, Adolph Milar, Lloyd Whitlock; ***D:*** Irvin Willat.

Mickey 🦴🦴 1917 Spoof on high society as a penniless young woman moves in with relatives and works as the family's maid. Silent film. **105m/B VHS.** Mabel Normand, Lew Cody, Minta Durfee; ***D:*** Mack Sennett.

Mickey 🦴 1948 A tomboy becomes a woman even as she plays matchmaker for her own father and sings a few songs. Not too exciting; you may fall alseep if you're slipped this "Mickey." Based on the novel "Clementine," by Peggy Goodin. **87m/C VHS.** Lois Butler, Bill Goodwin, Irene Hervey, John Sutton, Hattie McDaniel; ***D:*** Ralph Murphy.

Mickey Blue Eyes 🦴🦴½ 1999 (PG-13) Grant reprises his role as the maddeningly polite, apologetic British guy for about the bazillionth time. This time he plays Michael Felgate, an art auctioneer who proposes to schoolteacher Gina (Tripplehorn). Her father Frank (Caan) turns out to be a mobster, whose boss wants to use his auction house as a front for money laundering. After Michael tells a string of lies to hide his involvement from Gina, a series of wild events and misunderstandings leads to Michael posing as mobster Little Big Mickey Blue Eyes from Kansas City. Listening to tea-and-crumpety Grant trying to pronounce "fuhgeddaboudit" briefly brings the movie to life, but the premise is quickly abandoned and he sinks back into his droopy British bit again. All is wrapped up in your standard issue romantic comedy ending. **103m/C VHS, DVD, Wide.** Hugh Grant, Jeanne Tripplehorn, James Caan, Burt Young, Gerry Becker, James Fox, Joe (Johnny) Viterelli, Maddie Corman, Tony Darrow, Paul Lazar, Vincent Pastore, Frank Pellegrino, Scott Thompson, John Ventimiglia; ***D:*** Kelly Makin; ***W:*** Robert Kuhn, Adam Scheinman; ***C:*** Donald E. Thorin; ***M:*** Wolfgang Hammerschmid.

Mickey One 🦴🦴½ 1965 Nightclub comic Mickey (Beatty) gets into trouble when he can't pay his gambling debts. So he hides out in Chicago under an assumed name, working as a janitor, but can't live without the applause. His agent finds him a club job but Mickey panics, thinking the place is under mob control, and spends a lot of time running around, trying to clear his debts. Finally, returning to the club, Mickey resigns himself to a bleak fate. Beatty's jumpy character is an acquired taste—as is the film. **93m/B** Warren Beatty, Hurd Hatfield, Alexandra Stewart, Franchot Tone, Teddy Hart, Jeff Corey; ***D:*** Arthur Penn; ***W:*** Alan M. Surgal; ***C:*** Ghislan Cloquet; ***M:*** Jack Shaindlin, Eddie Sauter.

Mickey the Great 1939 Stitched together from several late '20s Mickey McGuire shorts, starring 10-year-old Rooney. **70m/B VHS.** Billy Barty, Mickey Rooney.

Micki & Maude 🦴🦴 1984 (PG-13) When a man longs for a baby, he finds that his wife, Micki, is too busy for motherhood. Out of frustration, he has an affair with Maude that leads to her pregnancy. Still shocked by the news of his upcoming fatherhood, the man learns that his wife is also expecting. **117m/C VHS.** Dudley Moore, Amy Irving, Ann Reinking, Richard Mulligan, Wallace Shawn, George Gaynes, Andre the Giant; ***D:*** Blake Edwards; ***W:*** Jonathan Reynolds; ***C:*** Harry Stradling Jr. Golden Globes '85: Actor—Mus./Comedy (Moore).

Microcosmos 🦴🦴🦴 1996 (G) Warning: Do not attempt to smash the bugs on the screen with your shoe. They're supposed to be there. This French documentary uses special cameras and sound recording devices to explore the world of insects like never before. The editing and score also add a human dimension to the creepy-crawly world under the lawn, making amorous snails and workaholic beetles seem like people you know (well, if they had an extra set of legs and a shell-like carapace). Of course, if you don't like bugs, then this is just a 77-minute gross out. Cameo appearances by some birds and frogs. **77m/C VHS.** *FR* ***D:*** Claude Nuridsany, Marie Perennou; ***C:*** Claude Nuridsany, Marie Perennou, Hughes Ryffel, Thierry Machado; ***M:*** Bruno Coulais. Cesar '97: Art Dir./Set Dec., Cinematog., Film Editing, Sound, Score.

Microwave Massacre 🦴 1983 (R) Killer kitchen appliances strike again as late lounge comic Vernon murders nagging wife and 'waves her. Overcome by that Betty Crocker feeling, he goes on a microwave murdering/feeding spree of the local ladies. Lots of Roger Corman copying. **80m/C VHS.** Jackie Vernon, Loren Schein, Al Troupe, Claire Ginsberg, Lou Ann Webber, Sarah Alt; ***D:*** Wayne Berwick; ***W:*** Thomas Singer; ***C:*** Karen Grossman; ***M:*** Leif Horvath.

Mid-Channel 🦴🦴½ 1920 A married couple become bored with each other and the wife seeks diversion with other men. Surprise ending. **70m/B VHS.** Clara Kimball Young, J. Frank Glendon, Edward M. Kimball, Bertram Grassby, Eileen Robinson, Helen Sullivan, Katherine Griffith, Jack Livingston; ***D:*** Harry Garson.

Mid Knight Rider 🦴 1984 Penniless actor becomes a male prostitute at the service of bored, rich women. At an all-night orgy, he suddenly goes on a rampage, nearly killing one of his customers. **76m/C VHS.** Michael Christian, Keenan Wynn.

Midaq Alley 🦴🦴🦴 *The Alley of Miracles; El Callejon de los Milagros* 1995 Amusing melodrama based on the 1947 novel by Egyptian Naguib Mahfouz and transported from Cairo's backstreets to those of a rundown, modern-day Mexico City neighborhood known as "The Alley of Miracles." Four segments all begin on the same Sunday afternoon and follow a variety of the Alley's inhabitants, including a married man who becomes attracted to a young male clerk, a beauty who falls prey to a suave pimp, and a homely woman looking for love and finding Mr. Wrong. Spanish with subtitles. **140m/C DVD.** *MX* Ernesto Cruz, Maria Rojo, Salma Hayek, Bruno Bichir, Claudio Obregon, Delia Casanova, Margarita Sanz, Juan Manuel Bernal, Luis Felipe Tovar, Daniel Gimenez Cacho; ***D:*** Jorge Fons; ***W:*** Vicente Lenero; ***C:*** Carlos Marcovich; ***M:*** Lucia Alvarez.

The Midas Touch 🦴🦴 1989 A flea market merchant in 1956 Budapest has the ability to turn items into gold. In Hungarian with English subtitles. **100m/C VHS.** *HU* ***D:*** Geza Beremenyi; ***W:*** Geza Beremenyi.

Middle Age Crazy 🦴½ 1980 (R) Story of a Texas building contractor who takes life pretty lightly until his own father dies. Then he becomes immersed in a mid-life crisis and has an affair with a Dallas Cowboys' cheerleader. Ann-Margaret plays the victim wife of the middle aged swingin' guy. **95m/C VHS.** *CA* Bruce Dern, Ann-Margret, Graham Jarvis, Eric Christmas, Deborah Wakeham; ***D:*** John Trent.

The Middleman 🦴🦴 *Jana Aranya* 1976 Recent college graduate Somnath has struggled to find a job and eventually enters the business world as a middleman, where he soons discovers that success will depend on his willingness to break the rules. Bengali with subtitles. **131m/B VHS.** *IN* Pradip Mukherjee; ***D:*** Satyajit Ray; ***W:*** Satyajit Ray; ***C:*** Soumendu Roy.

Middlemarch 🦴🦴🦴 1993 Stylish British TV costume drama, adapted from George Eliot's 1872 novel, finds idealistic Dorothea Brooke (Aubrey) determined to be a helpmate to the older scholar, the Rev. Edward Casaubon (Malahide), whom she marries. Too bad that he takes so little interest in her ability (or in Dorothea herself). This leads Casaubon's distant cousin, young and handsome Will Ladislaw (Sewell), to discreetly make his interest clear. Naturally, Eliot has a number of other plots (some dealing with the impact of the Industrial Revolution on 19th-century life) and romances worked into the mix. Filmed in Stamford, England. On three cassettes. **360m/C VHS.** *GB* Juliet Aubrey, Patrick Malahide, Rufus Sewell, Douglas Hodge, Trevyn McDowell, Michael Hordern, Robert Hardy, John Savident, Jonathan Firth, Peter Jeffrey, Simon Chandler, Julian Wadham; ***D:*** Anthony Page; ***W:*** Andrew Davies, Stanley Myers; ***C:*** Brian Tufano.

Midnight 🦴🦴½ *Call It Murder* 1934 A jury foreman's daughter is romantically involved with a gangster who is interested in a particular case before it appears in court. The foreman, who sentenced a girl to death, faces a dilemma when his own daughter is arrested for the same crime. An early Bogart appearance in a supporting role led to a re-release of the film as "Call it Murder" after Bogart made it big. Weak melodrama. **74m/B VHS, DVD.** Humphrey Bogart, Sidney (Sydney) Fox, O.P. Heggie, Henry Hull, Richard Whorf, Margaret Wycherly, Lynne Overman; ***D:*** Chester Erskine; ***W:*** Chester Erskine.

Midnight 🦴🦴🦴½ 1939 Struggling showgirl Colbert masquerades as Hungarian countess in sophisticated comedy of marital conflicts. Near-classic film scripted by Wilder and Brackett. Based on a story by Edwin Justus Mayer and Franz Schulz. Remade as "Masquerade in Mexico." **94m/B VHS.** Claudette Colbert, Don Ameche, John Barrymore, Francis Lederer, Mary Astor, Hedda Hopper, Rex O'Malley; ***D:*** Mitchell Leisen; ***W:*** Billy Wilder, Charles Brackett; ***C:*** Charles B(ryant) Lang Jr.

Midnight 🦴 *Backwoods Massacre* 1981 (R) Russo, who cowrote the original "Night of the Living Dead," wrote and directed this film about a runaway girl who is driven out of her home by a lecherous stepfather and meets two young thieves and then a family of cultists. Russo adapted his own novel. He also attains some of "Night of the Living Dead's" low-budget ambience. **88m/C VHS.** Lawrence Tierney, Melanie Verliin, John Hall, John Amplas; ***D:*** John A. Russo.

Midnight 🦴 1989 (R) Murder-thriller involving the vampirish hostess of a TV horror movie showcase and a fanatical fan. **90m/C VHS.** Lynn Redgrave, Tony Curtis, Steve Parrish, Rita Gam, Gustav Vintas, Karen Witter, Frank Gorshin, Wolfman Jack; ***D:*** Norman Thaddeus Vane.

Midnight 2: Sex, Death, and Videotape 🦴 1993 Sequel to "Midnight" finds the sole surviving member of the crazed family stalking a beautiful unsuspecting teller with a video camera. Only she's teamed up with a detective to solve the murder of her best friend—even if it means she's bait for a psycho. **70m/C VHS.** Matthew Jason Walsh, Jo Norcia; ***D:*** John A. Russo.

Midnight at the Wax Museum 🦴 *Midnight at Madame Tussaud's* 1936 A man attempts to spend an evening in a wax museum's chamber of horrors, only to find that he is the target of a murder plot. **66m/B VHS.** Lucille Lisle, James Carew, Charles Oliver, Kim Peacock; ***D:*** George Pearson.

Midnight Auto Supply 🦴½ *Love and the Midnight Auto Supply* 1978 Dealers in hot car parts, working out of the garage behind the local brothel, become persuaded to donate some of their profits to the cause of Mexican farm workers. **91m/C VHS.** Michael Parks, Rory Calhoun, Scott Jacoby,

Rod Cameron, Colleen Camp, Linda Cristal, John Ireland; *D:* James Polakof.

Midnight Blue 🦴🦴 **1996 (R)** Martin Blake (Chapa) is a lonely banker on a trip to Atlanta where he meets prostitute Martine (Schofield). They have a one-nighter and Martin later decides he loves her and hires a detective (Stockwell) to find her—only Martine has disappeared. After Martin has moved to L.A., he discovers his new boss' wife, Georgine, just happens to be a double for Martine. Naturally, Martin becomes obessed and this leads to big trouble. **95m/C VHS.** Damian Chapa, Annabel Schofield, Steve Kanaly, Dean Stockwell, Harry Dean Stanton, Jennifer Jostyn; *D:* Skott Snider; *W:* Douglas Brode; *C:* Mark Vicente; *M:* Eric Allaman.

Midnight Cabaret woof! **1990 (R)** A New York nightclub-based Satanic cult selects a child actress to bear Satan's child. **94m/C VHS.** Michael Des Barres, Thom Mathews, Carolyn Seymour, Leonard Termo, Norbert Weisser, Lydie Denier; *D:* Pece Dingo; *W:* Pece Dingo; *M:* Michel Colombier.

A Midnight Clear 🦴🦴🦴 **1992 (PG)** Sensitive war drama that takes place in the Ardennes Forest, near the French-German border in December 1944. It's Christmastime and six of the remaining members of a 12-member squad are sent on a dangerous mission to an abandoned house to locate the enemy. Filmed in a dreamy surreal style, the setting is somewhat reminiscent of a fairytale, although a sense of anguish filtrates throughout the picture. A solid script, excellent direction, and a good cast make this a worthwhile film that pits the message of peace against the stupidity of war. Adapted from the novel by William Wharton. **107m/C VHS, DVD.** Peter Berg, Kevin Dillon, Arye Gross, Ethan Hawke, Gary Sinise, Frank Whaley, John C. McGinley, Larry Joshua, Curt Lowens, David Jensen, Rachel Griffin, Tim Shoemaker; *D:* Keith Gordon; *W:* Keith Gordon; *C:* Tom Richmond; *M:* Mark Isham.

Midnight Confessions 🦴 **1995 (R)** Provocative night-time DJ Vannesse (Hoyt) lures her listeners into revealing their sexual fantasies. But when an obessed fan begins killing women just how deeply is she involved? **98m/C VHS, DVD.** Carol Hoyt, Julie Strain, Monique Parent, Richard Lynch; *D:* Allan Shustak; *W:* Jake Jacobs, Allan Shustak, Marc Cushman, Timothy O'Rawe; *C:* Tom Frazier; *M:* Scott Singer.

Midnight Cop 🦴 **1988 (R)** A young woman gets tangled up in a web of murder, intrigue, prostitution and drugs, and she enlists the aid of a cop to help get her out of it. **100m/C VHS.** Michael York, Morgan Fairchild, Frank Stallone, Armin Mueller-Stahl; *D:* Peter Patzak.

Midnight Cowboy 🦴🦴🦴½ **1969 (R)** Drama about the relationship between a naive Texan hustler and a seedy derelict, set in the underbelly of NYC. Graphic and emotional character study is brilliantly acted and engaging. Shocking and considered quite risque at the time of its release, this film now carries an "R" rating. It was the only "X"-rated film ever ever to win the Best Picture Oscar. From James Leo Herlihy's novel. **113m/C VHS, DVD, Wide.** Dustin Hoffman, Jon Voight, Sylvia Miles, Brenda Vaccaro, John McGiver, Bob Balaban, Barnard Hughes; *D:* John Schlesinger; *W:* Waldo Salt; *C:* Adam Holender; *M:* John Barry. Oscars '69: Adapt. Screenplay, Director (Schlesinger), Picture; AFI '98: Top 100; British Acad. '69: Actor (Hoffman), Director (Schlesinger), Film, Screenplay; Directors Guild '69: Director (Schlesinger), Natl. Film Reg. '94;; N.Y. Film Critics '69: Actor (Voight); Natl. Soc. Film Critics '69: Actor (Voight); Writers Guild '69: Adapt. Screenplay.

Midnight Crossing 🦴🦴 **1987 (R)** Two married couples are subjected to jealousy, betrayal and uncloseted-skeletons as their pleasure cruise on a yacht turns into a ruthless search for sunken treasure. **96m/C VHS.** Faye Dunaway, Daniel J. Travanti, Kim Cattrall, John Laughlin, Ned Beatty; *D:* Roger Holzberg.

Midnight Dancer 🦴🦴 **1987** A young ballerina is forced to work as an erotic dancer. **97m/C VHS.** *AU* Deanne Jeffs, Mary Regan; *D:* Pamela Gibbons.

Midnight Dancers 🦴🦴 **1994** Seamy look at Manila's gay subculture and male prostitution. Sonny and his older brothers Dennis and Joel work as dancers at a sleazy club whose upstairs apartments are used for prostitution. The boys need the money to help their impoverished family survive in the slums but the emotional wear and tear (not to mention police raids and assorted brutalities) provide lots of melodrama. Filipino with subtitles. **115m/C VHS, DVD.** *PH* Alex Del Rosario, Gandong Cervantes, Laurence David, Perla Bautista, Soxy Topacio; *D:* Mel Chionglo; *W:* Ricardo Lee; *C:* George Tutanes; *M:* Nonong Buenoamino.

Midnight Edition 🦴🦴 **1993 (R)** Investigative reporter Jack Travers (Patton) returns to his Georgia hometown newspaper just in time to write the story of his life. Nineteen-year-old Darryl Weston (DeLuise) massacres a local family for no apparent reason, is tried, convicted, and sentenced to die. Jack's death row interviews with Darryl become hot news but his reporter's objectivity is lost and he becomes a pawn in an escape plan. Good interplay between the charming sociopath and the self-deluded reporter in a sometimes confusing thriller. Based on the autobiography "Escape of My Dead Men" by Charles Postell. **98m/C VHS.** Will Patton, Michael DeLuise, Clare Wren, Nancy Moore Atchison, Sarabeth Tucek, Judson Vaughn, Ji-Tu Cumbuka, Jay Bernard; *D:* Howard Libov; *W:* Howard Libov, Yuri Zeltser, Michael Stewart; *M:* Murray Attaway.

Midnight Express 🦴🦴🦴 **1978 (R)** Gripping and powerful film based on the true story of Billy Hayes (Davis), a young American busted in Turkey wfor trying to smuggle hashish. He is sentenced to a brutal and nightmarish prison for life as an example to other potential smugglers. After enduring tremendous mental and physical torture, Billy seeks the "Midnight Express," his chance at escape. Not always easy to watch, but the overall effect is riveting and unforgettable. Adapted from the book by Hayes and William Hoffer. **120m/C VHS, DVD, 8mm, Wide.** John Hurt, Randy Quaid, Brad Davis, Paul Smith, Bo Hopkins, Oliver Stone; *D:* Alan Parker; *W:* Oliver Stone; *C:* Michael Seresin; *M:* Giorgio Moroder. Oscars '78: Adapt. Screenplay, Orig. Score; British Acad. '78: Director (Parker), Support. Actor (Hurt); Golden Globes '79: Film—Drama, Screenplay, Support. Actor (Hurt), Score; Writers Guild '78: Adapt. Screenplay.

Midnight Faces 🦴🦴 **1926** Mysterious doings abound in a house in the Florida bayous, recently inherited by Bushman. Silent, with original organ music. **72m/B VHS, 8mm.** Francis X. Bushman, Jack Perrin, Kathryn McGuire.

Midnight Fear 🦴½ **1990** When a sexually demented killer skins a woman alive, Sheriff Hanley sets out to find whodunit. He suspects two weird brothers, who turn out to be holding a woman hostage, but the situation may not be so simple. Carradine plays the good-guy sheriff in this creeper. **90m/C VHS.** David Carradine, Craig Wasson; *D:* William Crain.

Midnight Girl 🦴½ **1925** A fading opera impresario plots to steal a family's fortune. Lugosi before he became Dracula. Silent. **84m/B VHS, 8mm.** Bela Lugosi, Lila Lee.

Midnight Heat 🦴🦴½ **1995 (R)** Football player is the prime suspect when his lover's husband (who happens to be the team owner) is murdered. **97m/C VHS.** Tim Matheson, Stephen Mendel, Mimi (Meyer) Craven; *D:* Harvey Frost.

The Midnight Hour 🦴½ **1986** A group of high schoolers stumbles upon a vintage curse that wakes up the dead. More humor than horror. **97m/C VHS, DVD.** Shari Belafonte, LeVar Burton, Lee Montgomery, Dick Van Patten, Kevin McCarthy, Jonelle Allen, Peter DeLuise, Dedee Pfeiffer, Mark Blankfield; *D:* Jack Bender; *C:* Rexford Metz; *M:* Brad Fiedel. **TV**

Midnight in Saint Petersburg 🦴🦴½ **1997 (R)** Caine once again returns to his role of super spy Harry Palmer, who's after terrorists buying stolen plutonium to use in nuclear weapons. Harry's aided by Nikolai (Connery), whose girlfriend Tatiana is kidnapped, leading the men to a link between the kidnapping, the terrorists, and recent art thefts from the Hermitage Museum. Adapted from stories by Len Deighton. **90m/C VHS.** Michael Caine, Jason Connery, Michael Gambon, Michael Sarrazin, Michelle Rene Thomas. **CABLE**

Midnight in the Garden of Good and Evil 🦴🦴 **1997 (R)** An all-star cast can't save Eastwood's grossly mishandled adaptation of John Berendt's best-selling novel on the eccentric citizens and lush scenery of Savannah. New York journalist John Kelso (Cusack) is sent on assignment to report on the glamourous Christmas parties of famed citizen and ham Jim Williams (Spacey, oozing his usual silky charm), only to be detoured by Williams shooting his male, live-in companion. Was it cold-blooded murder or self defense? With Eastwood's clumsy direction, a dragging running time, an overabundance of characters taken verbatim from the book (including drag queen Lady Chablis playing herself, unfortunately), and a dull romance between Kelso and local flower Mandy (Eastwood's daughter), the rich subject which made the book a top-seller for four years is all but lost and the answer to the above question moot. "Midnight" has the star power for greatness, but looks certainly are deceiving. **155m/C VHS, DVD, Wide.** Kevin Spacey, John Cusack, Jack Thompson, Alison Eastwood, The Lady Chablis, Irma P. Hall, Paul Hipp, Jude Law, Dorothy Loudon, Anne Haney, Kim Hunter, Geoffrey Lewis; *D:* Clint Eastwood; *W:* John Lee Hancock; *C:* Jack N. Green; *M:* Lennie Niehaus.

Midnight Kiss 🦴🦴½ **1993 (R)** When a woman police detective investigates a mysterious series of deaths—women whose blood has been drained—she gets more than she bargains for. She's attacked by a vampire and is herself turned into a reluctant bloodsucker. Quick moving and some gross special effects. Also available in an unrated version. **85m/C VHS.** Michelle Owens, Gregory A. Greer, Celeste Yarnall; *D:* Joel Bender; *W:* John Weidner, Ken Lamplugh.

Midnight Lace 🦴🦴½ **1960** Acceptable thriller about a woman in London who is being harassed by a telephone creep. Day is at her frantic best, and Harrrison is suitably charming. Handsome Gavin later became American ambassador to Mexico. Adapted from the play "Matilda Shouted Fire." **108m/C VHS.** Doris Day, Rex Harrison, John Gavin, Myrna Loy, Roddy McDowall, Elspeth March; *D:* David Miller; *W:* Ivan Goff; *C:* Russell Metty.

Midnight Limited 🦴🦴 **1940** A detective sets out to thwart the criminals who would rob the "Midnight Limited" train on its route from New York to Montreal. **61m/B VHS.** John "Dusty" King, Marjorie Reynolds, George Cleveland, Edward (Ed Kean, Keene) Keane, Pat Flaherty, Monty Collins, I. Stanford Jolley; *D:* Howard Bretherton.

Midnight Madness 🦴 **1980 (PG)** Five teams of college stereotypes search the city of Los Angeles for clues as part of a wacky scavenger hunt designed by a fellow student. Features the big-screen debut of Michael J. Fox as the little brother of David "I'm a Pepper" Naughton (look closely to see the former Pepper pitchman drinking a bottle of the stuff; it's the only near-witty moment). Also casts Stephen "Flounder" Dorf, making this flick somewhat of an "It's a Mad, Mad, Mad, Mad Animal House," but to say that is an insult to both of those films. Even the presence of arch-geek Eddie Deezen can't save the outing. **110m/C VHS, DVD.** David Naughton, Stephen Furst, Debra Clinger, Eddie Deezen, Michael J. Fox, Maggie Roswell; *D:* David Wechter; *W:* David Wechter; *C:* Frank Phillips; *M:* Julius Wechter.

Midnight Murders 🦴🦴½ *Manhunt in the Dakotas; In the Line of Duty: Manhunt in the Dakotas* **1991 (R)** Steiger stars as a farmer and Posse Commitatus member whose paramilitary pretensions lead to a bloody confrontation with federal marshals. Gross is the FBI agent sent to hunt him down. Made for TV. **95m/C VHS.** Rod Steiger, Michael Gross, Gary Basaraba, Christopher Rich, Henderson Forsythe; *D:* Dick Lowry. **TV**

The Midnight Phantom 🦴🦴 **1935** Incredibly rare horror film featuring a bizarre murder at a midnight lecture. **?m/B VHS.** Reginald Denny.

Midnight Ride 🦴½ **1992** Lots of silly action fails to save this slight tale of a cop (Dudikoff) chasing after his runaway wife (Gersak), who has made the mistake of picking up a psycho hitchhiker (Hamill, gleefully overacting). **95m/C VHS.** Michael Dudikoff, Mark Hamill, Savina Gersak; *Cameos:* Robert Mitchum; *D:* Robert Bralver.

Midnight Run 🦴🦴🦴 **1988 (R)** An ex-cop, bounty hunter must bring in an ex-mob accountant who has embezzled big bucks from his former boss. After he catches up with the thief, the hunter finds that bringing his prisoner from New York to Los Angeles will be very trying, especially when it is apparent that the Mafia and FBI are out to stop them. The friction between the two leads—De Niro and Grodin—is fun to watch, while the action and comic moments are enjoyable. **125m/C VHS, DVD.** Robert De Niro, Charles Grodin, Yaphet Kotto, John Ashton, Dennis Farina, Joe Pantoliano, Richard Foronjy, Wendy Phillips; *D:* Martin Brest; *W:* George Gallo; *C:* Donald E. Thorin; *M:* Danny Elfman.

Midnight Tease 🦴½ **1994** Strip bar, the Club Fugazi, is having trouble with its help—the dancers keep getting murdered. Dancer Samantha (Leigh) actually dreams about the murders before they occur, so naturally she becomes the prime suspect. Leigh can actually do more than look fetching but plot is barely apparent. **87m/C VHS, DVD.** Cassandra Leigh, Rachel Reed, Edmund Halley, Ashlie Rhey, Todd Joseph; *D:* Scott Levy; *W:* Daniella Purcell; *C:* Dan E. Toback; *M:* Christopher Lennertz.

Midnight Tease 2 🦴 **1995 (R)** Jen Brennan (Kelly) goes undercover at an L.A. strip club to find out who's been murdering the dancers, including her sister. **93m/C VHS, DVD.** Kimberly Kelley, Tane McClure, Ross Hagen; *D:* Richard Styles; *W:* Richard Styles; *C:* Gary Graver.

Midnight Warning 🦴🦴½ **1932** A woman thinks she's going off the deep-end when her brother and all records of his existence disappear. Based on an urban legend that appeared somewhere around the time of the 1893 World's Fair. Remade in 1952 as "So Long at the Fair." **63m/B VHS.** William Boyd, Claudia Dell, Henry Hall, John Harron, Hooper Atchley; *D:* Spencer Gordon Bennet.

Midnight Warrior 🦴 **1989** A reporter strikes it big when he investigates the underside of L.A. nightlife, but things go terribly wrong when he becomes wrapped up in the sleaze. **90m/C VHS.** Bernie Angel, Michelle Berger, Kevin Bernhardt, Lilly Melgar; *D:* Joseph Merhi.

Midnight Witness 🦴½ **1993 (R)** Guy finds himself on the run when after he videotapes the beating of a young drug dealer by corrupt cops. Plot bears more than a little resemblance to the Rodney King incident, but according to writer Foldy it was written before it took place. Low-budget thriller went direct to video. **90m/C VHS.** Maxwell Caulfield, Jan-Michael Vincent, Paul Johansson, Karen Moncrieff, Mark Pellegrino, Virginia Mayo; *D:* Peter Foldy; *W:* Peter Foldy; *M:* Graydon Hillock. **VIDEO**

Midnight's Child 🦴½ **1993** Another Nanny-from-Hell story, only this time it's literal. D'Abo is the Nanny in question, who belongs to a Satanic cult. Her mission is to select the young daughter in her care as a bride for the devil, even if the girl's parents don't approve of the match. **89m/C VHS.** Olivia D'Abo, Marcy Walker, Cotter Smith, Elissabeth (Elisabeth, Elizabeth, Liz) Moss, Jim Norton, Judy Parfitt, Roxann Biggs-Dawson, Mary Larkin; *D:* Colin Bucksey; *W:* David Chaskin.

Midnite Spares 🦴🦴 **1985** A young man's search for the men who kidnapped his father leads him into the world of car thieves and chop-shops. **90m/C VHS.** Bruce Spence, Gia Carides, James Laurie; *C:* Geoff Burton; *M:* Cameron Allan.

A Midsummer Night's Dream 🦴🦴🦴 **1935** Famed Reinhardt version of the Shakespeare classic, featuring nearly every star on the Warner Bros. lot. The plot revolves around the amorous battle between the king (Jory) and queen (Louise) of a fairy kingdom, and the humans who are drawn into their sport. Features de Havilland's first film role (as Hermia), althogh Rooney, as the fairy Puck, seems to be having the most fun. Classic credit line: Dialogue by William Shakespeare. **117m/B VHS.** James Cagney, Dick Powell, Joe E. Brown, Hugh Herbert, Olivia de Havilland, Ian Hunter, Mickey Rooney, Victor Jory, Arthur Treacher, Billy Barty; ***D:*** Max Reinhardt, William Dieterle; ***W:*** Mary C. McCall, Charles Kenyon; ***C:*** Hal Mohr. Oscars '35: Cinematog., Film Editing.

A Midsummer Night's Dream 🦴🦴½ **1968** Fine acting from the Royal Shakespeare Company cast in this filmed version of the play. Makes very little use of the Athens, Greece scenery. **124m/C VHS.** *GB* David Warner, Diana Rigg, Ian Richardson, Judi Dench, Ian Holm, Barbara Jefford, Nicholas Selby, Helen Mirren, Michael Jayston, Derek Godfrey, Hugh Sullivan, Paul Rogers, Sebastian Shaw, Bill Travers; ***D:*** Peter Hall.

A Midsummer Night's Dream 🦴🦴½ **1996 (PG-13)** The Royal Shakespeare Company offers their version of the Shakespeare classic in which a spat between Oberon and Titania, the king and queen of the fairies, leads to a romantic and comedic woodland fantasy for a quartet of would-be lovers who get caught up in their spells, as well as a group of rustics rehearsing their own play. **103m/C VHS.** *GB* Lindsay Duncan, Alex Jennings, Desmond Barrit, Barry Lynch, Monica Dolan, Emily Raymond; ***D:*** Adrian Noble; ***C:*** Ian Wilson; ***M:*** Howard Blake.

A Midsummer Night's Sex Comedy 🦴🦴🦴½ **1982 (PG)** Allen's homage to Shakespeare, Renoir, Chekhov, Bergman, and who knows who else is an engaging ensemble piece about hijinks among friends and acquaintances gathered at a country house at the turn of the century. Standouts include Ferrer as pompous professor and Steenburgen as Allen's sexually repressed wife. Mia's first for the Woodman. **88m/C VHS, DVD, Wide.** Woody Allen, Mia Farrow, Mary Steenburgen, Tony Roberts, Julie Hagerty, Jose Ferrer; ***D:*** Woody Allen; ***W:*** Woody Allen; ***C:*** Gordon Willis.

Midway 🦴🦴 **1976 (PG)** The epic WWII battle of Midway, the turning point in the war, is retold through Allied and Japanese viewpoints by a big all-star cast saddled with dumpy dialogue and enough weaponry to seize Hollywood on any given Wednesday. **132m/C VHS, DVD, Wide.** Charlton Heston, Henry Fonda, James Coburn, Glenn Ford, Hal Holbrook, Robert Mitchum, Cliff Robertson, Robert Wagner, Kevin Dobson, Christopher George, Toshiro Mifune, Tom Selleck; ***D:*** Jack Smight; ***W:*** Donald S. Sanford; ***C:*** Harry Stradling Jr.; ***M:*** John Williams.

A Midwinter's Tale 🦴🦴½ *In the Bleak Midwinter* **1995 (R)** Branagh assembles a largely unknown cast in this low-budget backstage saga about an out-of-work thesp, Joe Harper (Maloney), who assembles a shaggy crew of actors to stage an alternative "Hamlet" in a small English country church. The diverse cast squabble, stumble, and emote their way through rehearsals, finally pulling together for the big show. Funny and interesting performances manage to show through the dense and somewhat cliched script. Maloney's Joe, who exhibits the proper frustration of being forced to deal with amateurs and Sessions as a camp queen playing the Queen (Gertrude, that is) stand out. **98m/B VHS.** *GB* Michael Maloney, Richard Briers, Mark Hadfield, Nicholas Farrell, Gerard Horan, John Sessions, Celia Imrie, Hetta Charnley, Julia Sawalha, Joan Collins, Jennifer Saunders; ***D:*** Kenneth Branagh; ***W:*** Kenneth Branagh; ***C:*** Roger Lanser; ***M:*** Jimmy Yuill.

Mifune 🦴🦴 *Mifunes Sidste Sang; Mifune's Last Song* **1999 (R)** Third release for the Danish film collective Dogma 95 (following "The Idiots" and "The Celebration") is a comedy/romance with a couple of twists. Yuppie Kresten (Berthelsen) travels to the family's run-down farm to check on his mentally handicapped brother, Rud (Asholt), after their father's death. Kresten needs a housekeeper and winds up with attractive Livia (Hjeljle), who neglects to tell him she is a hooker on the lam from her threatening pimp and also shows up with her younger brother (Tarding). Kresten and Livia soon share a mutual attraction and lots of obstacles. Title refers to Rud's hero worship of actor Toshiro Mifune. Danish with subtitles. **102m/C VHS, DVD.** *DK* Iben Hjejle, Anders W. Berthelsen, Jesper Asholt, Emil Tarding, Anders (Tofting) Hove, Sofie Graboel, Paprika Steen, Mette Bratlann; ***D:*** Soeren Kragh-Jacobsen; ***W:*** Soeren Kragh-Jacobsen, Anders Thomas Jensen; ***C:*** Anthony Dod Mantle; ***M:*** Karl Bille, Christian Sievert.

The Mighty 🦴🦴🦴 **1998 (PG-13)** Like "Simon Birch," this one also features a central character, Kevin (Culkin), who's smart and brave despite suffering from Morquio's syndrome. His new neighbor, Max (Henson), is just the opposite: large in size, not too bright, and afraid of everything. The two quickly find they're much stronger as a team than individually. When Kevin is made Max's reading tutor, he brings along a book on the legend of King Arthur. Kevin rides Max's shoulders and, dubbing themselves "Freak the Mighty" (the title of Rodman Philbrick's novel, on which the film is based), the inspired boys embark on knightly neighborhood quests, even facing the evil Black Knight—in the form of Max's ex-con father. Henson is amazing as the at-first introverted Max, and Culkin does a good job as Kevin. Stone's understated performance as Kevin's mom shows she's more than a sexpot. **100m/C VHS, DVD.** Kieran Culkin, Elden (Ratliff) Henson, Sharon Stone, Gillian Anderson, Harry Dean Stanton, Gena Rowlands, James Gandolfini, Joe Perrino, Meat Loaf Aday, Jenifer Lewis; ***D:*** Peter Chelsom; ***W:*** Charles Leavitt; ***C:*** John de Borman; ***M:*** Trevor Jones.

Mighty Aphrodite 🦴🦴½ **1995 (R)** Neurotic (Surprise!) New York sportswriter Lenny Weinrib (Allen) is trapped in an unhappy marriage to art dealer Amanda (Bonham Carter), who talks him into adopting a child. Film comes alive when Lenny tracks down his son's biological mother, consummate dumb blond and hooker/porno actress Linda, played with over-the-top (in a good way) gusto by Sorvino. Lenny attempts to reform his son's real mother while a Greek chorus (including Abraham and Dukakis) provide a running commentary on the tragedy/comedy of Lenny's predicaments. Allen's 31st film treads into familiar Woodman waters but falls short of his past comic genius. **95m/C VHS, DVD, Wide.** Woody Allen, Helena Bonham Carter, Mira Sorvino, F. Murray Abraham, Michael Rapaport, Jack Warden, Olympia Dukakis, Peter Weller, Claire Bloom, David Ogden Stiers; ***D:*** Woody Allen; ***W:*** Woody Allen; ***C:*** Carlo Di Palma; ***M:*** Dick Hyman. Oscars '95: Support. Actress (Sorvino); Golden Globes '96: Support. Actress (Sorvino); Natl. Bd. of Review '95: Support. Actress (Sorvino); N.Y. Film Critics '95: Support. Actress (Sorvino); Broadcast Film Critics '95: Support. Actress (Sorvino).

The Mighty Ducks 🦴🦴½ **1992 (PG)** Bad News Bears on skates. Selfish yuppie lawyer is arrested for drunk driving and as part of his community service sentence, he is forced to coach an inner-city hockey team full of the usual misfits and underachievers. Although sarcastic and skeptical, Coach Gordon Bombay (Estevez) eventually bonds with the Ducks and learns to treat them with respect. Dual themes of teamwork and redemption are repeated constantly, and it gets a bit hokey at times, but the kids won't mind with this fun Disney film, while adults will appreciate the sarcasm. Followed by "D2: The Mighty Ducks." **114m/C VHS, DVD, Wide.** Emilio Estevez, Joss Ackland, Lane Smith, Heidi Kling, Josef Sommer, Matt Doherty, Steven Brill, Joshua Jackson, Elden (Ratliff) Henson, Shaun Weiss; ***D:*** Stephen Herek; ***W:*** Brian Hohlfield, Steven Brill; ***C:*** Thomas Del Ruth; ***M:*** David Newman.

Mighty Joe Young 🦴🦴½ **1949** Tongue-in-cheek King Kong variation features giant ape brought to civilization and exploited in a nightclub act, whereupon things get darned ugly. Bullied and given the key to the liquor cabinet, mild-mannered Joe goes on a drunken rampage, but eventually redeems himself by rescuing orphans from a fire. Special effects (courtesy of Willis O'Brien and the great Ray Harryhausen) are probably the film's greatest asset. Also available colorized. **94m/B VHS.** Terry Moore, Ben Johnson, Robert Armstrong, Frank McHugh; ***D:*** Ernest B. Schoedsack.

Mighty Joe Young 🦴🦴 **1998 (PG)** Loose adaptation of the 1949 film has special effects wizard Rick Baker creating a very life-like model of the fifteen-foot, 2,000-lb. gorilla. With his elaborate features, including a pair of huge brown eyes, this Joe has more personality than his human allies Jill (Theron) and O'Hara (Paxton) who, in between saving Joe from evil South African poachers, spend most of the film giving each other the goo-goo eyes. Wholesome, harmless, lightweight (the movie, not the gorilla) family entertainment. **114m/C VHS, DVD.** Bill Paxton, Charlize Theron, David Paymer, Regina King, Rade Serbedzija, Peter Firth, Lawrence Pressman, Linda Purl, Ray Harryhausen; ***D:*** Ron Underwood; ***W:*** Mark Rosenthal, Larry Konner; ***C:*** Don Peterman, Oliver Wood; ***M:*** James Horner.

Mighty Jungle 🦴🦴 **1964** Lost in the Amazon jungle, a hunter must fight off killer iguanas, man-eating crocodiles and bloodthirsty natives who perform human sacrifices. **90m/C VHS.** Marshall Thompson, David DaLie.

Mighty Morphin Power Rangers: The Movie 🦴🦴 **1995 (PG)** From the living room onto the big screen, these six surburban teenagers with super powers battle the evil Ivan Ooze to save Earth. Offers more special effects, new Zord animals, more ooze and more growth to the retail toy industry than the small screen could provide. A child's dream come true, but a parent's nightmare. **93m/C VHS.** Paul Freeman, Jason Harold Yost, Amy Jo Johnson, Jason David Frank, John Yong Bosch, Stephen Antonio Cardenas; ***D:*** Bryan Spicer; ***W:*** Arne Olsen, John Camps; ***C:*** Paul Murphy; ***M:*** Graeme Revell.

The Mighty Pawns **1987** Inner-city kids turn to chess when their teacher inspires them to stay off the streets. Originally aired on PBS as part of the "Wonderworks" family movie series. **58m/C VHS.** Paul Winfield, Alfonso Ribeiro, Terence Knox, Rosalind Cash, Teddy Wilson; ***D:*** Eric Laneuville.

The Mighty Peking Man woof! *Goliathon* **1977 (PG-13)** A ten-story-tall gorilla resides in the jungle and is sought by a group of Hong Kong businessman who want to display the creature. Johnny, the hunter hired to find the beast, discovers both the gorilla and a beautiful jungle goddess. Incredibly campy, with badly dubbed and hilariously awful dialogue. **91m/C VHS, DVD, Wide.** *HK* Evelyn Kraft, Danny Lee, Chen Cheng-Fen; ***D:*** Ho Meng-Hua; ***W:*** Yi Kuang; ***C:*** Tsao Hui-Chi, Wu Cho-Hua; ***M:*** De Wolfe, Chuen Yung-Yu.

The Mighty Quinn 🦴🦴½ **1989 (R)** While investigating the local murder of a rich white guy, the black Jamaican head of police becomes convinced that the prime suspect, a childhood friend, is innocent. As the police chief, Denzel is good in this off-beat comedy mystery. **98m/C VHS, DVD, Wide.** Denzel Washington, Robert Townsend, James Fox, Mimi Rogers, M. Emmet Walsh, Sheryl Lee Ralph, Esther Rolle, Art Evans, Norman Beaton, Keye Luke; ***D:*** Carl Schenkel; ***W:*** Hampton Fancher; ***C:*** Jacques Steyn; ***M:*** Anne Dudley.

The Migrants 🦴🦴🦴 **1974** Adaptation of the Tennessee Williams play about the hard-scrabble world of a migrant family yearning for a better life. Made for TV. **83m/C VHS.** Cloris Leachman, Ron Howard, Sissy Spacek, Cindy Williams, Ed Lauter, Lisa Lucas, Mills Watson, Claudia McNeil, Dolph Sweet; ***D:*** Tom Gries; ***W:*** Lanford Wilson. **TV**

Mike's Murder 🦴½ **1984 (R)** Disjointed drama about a shy bank teller who falls for a slick tennis player. When he is murdered, she investigates the circumstances, placing herself in dangerously close contact with his seedy, drug-involved buddies. The twists and confused plot leave the viewer bewildered. **109m/C VHS.** Debra Winger, Mark Keyloun, Paul Winfield, Darrell Larson, Dan Shor, William Ostrander; ***D:*** James Bridges; ***W:*** James Bridges; ***M:*** John Barry.

Mikey 🦴½ **1992 (R)** Mikey seems like such a sweet little boy—but these awful things keep happening all around him. At every foster home and every school people have such dreadful, and deadly, accidents. But innocent Mikey couldn't be to blame—or could he. **92m/C VHS, DVD.** Brian Bonsall, John Diehl, Lyman Ward, Josie Bissett, Ashley Laurence, Mimi (Meyer) Craven, Whitby Hertford; ***D:*** Dennis Dimster; ***W:*** Jonathan Glassner; ***C:*** Thomas Jewett; ***M:*** Tim Truman.

Mikey & Nicky 🦴🦴½ **1976 (R)** Quirky, uneven film about longtime friends dodging a hit man during one long night. Bears little evidence of time and money invested. Cassavetes and Falk, however, provide some salvation. **105m/C VHS.** John Cassavetes, Peter Falk, Ned Beatty, Oliver Clark, William Hickey; ***D:*** Elaine May; ***W:*** Elaine May.

The Milagro Beanfield War 🦴🦴🦴½ **1988 (R)** Redford's endearing adaptation of John Nichols's novel about New Mexican townfolk opposing development. Seemingly simple tale provides plenty of insight into human spirit. Fine cast, with especially stellar turns from Blades, Braga, and Vennera. **118m/C VHS.** Chick Vennera, John Heard, Ruben Blades, Sonia Braga, Daniel Stern, Julie Carmen, Christopher Walken, Richard Bradford, Carlos Riqueline, James Gammon, Melanie Griffith, Freddy Fender, M. Emmet Walsh; ***D:*** Robert Redford; ***W:*** David S. Ward; ***C:*** Robbie Greenberg; ***M:*** Dave Grusin. Oscars '88: Orig. Score.

Mildred Pierce 🦴🦴🦴½ **1945** Gripping melodrama features Crawford as hard-working divorcee rivaling daughter for man's love. Things, one might say, eventually get ugly. Adaptation of James M. Cain novel is classic of its kind. **113m/B VHS.** Joan Crawford, Jack Carson, Zachary Scott, Eve Arden, Ann Blyth, Bruce (Herman Brix) Bennett; ***D:*** Michael Curtiz; ***W:*** Ranald MacDougall; ***M:*** Max Steiner. Oscars '45: Actress (Crawford), Natl. Film Reg. '96.

Miles from Home 🦴🦴 *Farm of the Year* **1988 (R)** Times are tough for farmers Frank and Terry Roberts. The brothers are about to have another bad harvest and the bank is threatening to foreclose. In a symbolic last ditch effort to save their pride, they decide to burn the farm and leave. On their journey, they meet strangers who recognize the pair and help them escape the police. A melodrama with many members of Chicago's Steppenwolf Theater. **113m/C VHS.** Richard Gere, Kevin Anderson, John Malkovich, Brian Dennehy, Judith Ivey, Penelope Ann Miller, Laurie Metcalf, Laura San Giacomo, Daniel Roebuck, Helen Hunt; ***D:*** Gary Sinise; ***W:*** Chris Gerolmo; ***C:*** Elliot Davis; ***M:*** Robert Folk.

Miles to Go 🦴½ **1986** A successful businesswoman tries to enjoy her last days after learning she has terminal cancer. **88m/C VHS.** Mimi Kuzyk, Tom Skerritt, Jill Clayburgh; ***D:*** David Greene.

Miles to Go Before I Sleep 🦴🦴½ **1974** A retired, lonely man and a delinquent girl distrust each other but eventually reach out in mutual need. **78m/C VHS.** Martin Balsam, MacKenzie Phillips, Kitty Winn, Elizabeth Wilson; ***D:*** Fielder Cook. **TV**

Militia 🦴🦴 **1999 (R)** ATF agents Ethan Carter (Cain) and Julie Sanders (Beals) must enlist the help of William Fain (Forrest), an imprisoned member of a radical militia group, in order to stop the deployment of three stolen missiles and an assassination attempt on the President. **97m/C VHS, DVD.** Dean Cain, Jennifer Beals, Frederic Forrest, Stacy Keach, John Beck, Jeff Kober, Brett Butler; ***D:*** Jim Wynorski; ***W:*** Steve Latshaw, William Carson; ***C:*** Mario D'Ayala; ***M:*** Neal Acree. **VIDEO**

Milk Money 🦴½ **1994 (PG-13)** Twelve year-old Frank (Carter) talks his pals into pooling their milk money and heading to the big city so they can get a look at a naked woman. They find a prostitute (Griffith) for the job, whom Frank decides would be perfect to bring home to his widower dad (Harris). Although Griffith is generally adorable and the movie is actually less salacious than the premise might suggest, overall, it's sappy and another in the long line of cute-hooker/Cinderella fairytales. **110m/C VHS.** Michael Patrick Carter, Melanie Griffith, Ed Harris, Malcolm McDowell, Casey Siemaszko, Anne Heche, Philip Bosco; ***D:*** Richard Benjamin; ***W:*** John Mattson; ***M:*** Michael Convertino.

Milky Way 🦴🦴½ **1936** Loopy comedy about milkman who finds unhappiness after accidentally knocking out champion boxer. Adequate, but not equal to Lloyd's fine silent productions. **89m/B VHS.** Harold Lloyd, Adolphe Menjou, Verree Teasdale, Helen Mack, William Gargan; ***D:*** Leo McCarey.

The Milky Way 🦴🦴🦴 **1968** Wicked anti-clerical farce. Two bums team on religious pilgrimage and encounter seemingly all manner of strangeness and sacrilege in this typically peculiar Bunuel work. Perhaps the only film in which Jesus is encouraged to shave. In French with English subtitles. **102m/C VHS.** *FR* Laurent Terzieff, Paul Frankeur, Delphine Seyrig, Alain Cuny, Bernard Verley, Michel Piccoli, Edith Scob; ***D:*** Luis Bunuel; ***W:*** Jean-Claude Carriere.

The Milky Way 🦴🦴 *Shvil Hahalav* **1997** The Palestinian occupants of a small village in the Galilee try to balance their traditions against the Israeli military occupation in 1964. Many of the villagers were traumatized as children by the 1948 war and old fears and resentments linger as the village's mukhtar (Khoury) tries to placate the occupiers. Meanwhile, the Israelis are investigating forged work passes and a village murder leads to trouble for everyone. Arabic and Hebrew with subtitles. **104m/C VHS.** *IS* Muhamad Bakri, Suheil Haddad, Makram Khoury, Yussef Abu-Warda; ***D:*** Ali Nassar; ***W:*** Ali Nassar, Ghalib Shaath; ***C:*** Amnon Salomon; ***M:*** Nachum Heiman.

Mill of the Stone Women 🦴🦴½ *Il Mulino delle Donne di Pietra; Horror of the Stone Women; The Horrible Mill Women; Drops of Blood* **1960** Sculpture-studying art student encounters strange carousel with beautiful babes rather than horsies, and soon finds out that the statues contain shocking secrets. Filmed in Holland, it's offbeat and creepy. **94m/C VHS.** *FR IT* Pierre Brice, Scilla Gabel, Danny Carrel, Wolfgang Preiss, Herbert Boenne, Liana Orfei, Marco Guglielmi, Olga Solbelli; ***D:*** Giorgio Ferroni; ***W:*** Giorgio Ferroni, Giorgio Stegani, Remigio del Grosso, Ugo Liberatore; ***C:*** Pier Ludovico Pavoni; ***M:*** Carlo Innocenzi.

The Mill on the Floss 🦴🦴 **1937** Based on George Eliot's classic novel, this film follows the course of an ill-fated romance and family hatred in rural England. Underwhelming, considering the source. **77m/B VHS.** *GB* James Mason, Geraldine Fitzgerald, Frank Lawton, Victoria Hopper, Fay Compton, Griffith Jones, Mary Clare; ***D:*** Tim Whelan.

The Mill on the Floss 🦴🦴½ **1997** Maggie Tulliver (Watson) is a smart, emotional young woman painfully at odds with her conventional times. She adores her intolerant older brother Tom (Meredith) but when Maggie becomes involved with Philip Wakeum (Frain), the son of their father Edward's (Hill) greatest enemy, she reluctantly acquieses when Tom forbids the romance. When Stephen Guest (Weber-Brown), the fiance of Maggie's cousin Lucy (Whybrow), falls in love with her, his attentions bring scandal and tragedy to both Maggie and Tom. Watson is fine as the harried heroine but Meredith seems too young for his role, upsetting the sibling balance between the two. Based on the novel by George Eliot. **90m/C VHS.** *GB* Emily Watson, Ifan Meredith, James Frain, Bernard Hill, James Weber-Brown, Lucy Whybrow, Nicholas Gecks, Cheryl Campbell; ***D:*** Graham Theakston; ***W:*** Hugh Stoddart; ***C:*** David Johnson; ***M:*** John Scott.

Mille Bolle Blu 🦴🦴 **1993** Follows the lives of the inhabitants of a single block in 1961 Rome, on the eve of a solar eclipse. The neighborhood children take the opportunity to spy on their elders, including the engaged Elvira, whose old boyfriend Antonio wants her back, escaped convict Caligiuri who returns to his loving wife, and blind Guido, who's undergone an operation to restore his sight. Italian with subtitles. **83m/C VHS.** *IT* Stefano Dionisi, Claudio Bigagli, Paolo Bonacelli, Nicoletta Boris; ***D:*** Leone Pompucci; ***W:*** Leone Pompucci; ***M:*** Franco Piersanti.

Millennium 🦴🦴½ **1989 (PG-13)** The Earth of the future is running out of time. The people are sterile and the air is terrible. To keep the planet viable, Ladd and company must go back in time and yank people off planes that are doomed to crash. Great special effects and well-thought out script make this a ball of fun. **108m/C VHS, DVD.** Kris Kristofferson, Cheryl Ladd, Daniel J. Travanti, Lloyd Bochner, Robert Joy, Brent Carver, Maury Chaykin, David McIlwraith, Al Waxman; ***D:*** Michael Anderson Sr.; ***W:*** John Varley; ***C:*** Rene Ohashi; ***M:*** Eric N. Robertson.

Miller's Crossing 🦴🦴🦴½ **1990 (R)** From the Coen brothers (makers of "Blood Simple" and "Raising Arizona") comes this extremely dark entry in the gangster movie sweepstakes of 1990. Jewish, Italian, and Irish mobsters spin webs of deceit, protection, and revenge over themselves and their families. Byrne is the protagonist, but no hero, being as deeply flawed as the men he battles. Harden stuns as the woman who sleeps with Byrne and his boss, Finney, in hopes of a better life and protection for her small-time crook brother. Visually exhilarating, excellently acted and perfectly paced. **115m/C VHS.** Albert Finney, Gabriel Byrne, Marcia Gay Harden, John Turturro, Jon Polito, J.E. Freeman; ***D:*** Joel Coen; ***W:*** Ethan Coen, Joel Coen; ***M:*** Carter Burwell.

Millie 🦴½ **1931** Creaky melodrama about a divorcee who wants every man but one. He pursues her teenage daughter instead, leading to tragedy and courtroom hand-wringing. Twelvetrees still stands out in this hokum, based on a Donald Henderson novel considered daring in its day. **85m/B VHS.** Helen Twelvetrees, Robert Ames, Lilyan Tashman, Joan Blondell, John Halliday, James Hall, Anita Louise, Frank McHugh; ***D:*** John Francis Dillon.

Million Dollar Duck 🦴½ **1971 (G)** A family duck is doused with radiation and begins to lay gold eggs. Okay Disney family fare, especially for youngsters. **92m/C VHS.** Dean Jones, Sandy Duncan, Joe Flynn, Tony Roberts; ***D:*** Vincent McEveety; ***M:*** Buddy (Norman Dale) Baker.

Million Dollar Haul 🦴 **1935** Tarzan sniffs out a ring of warehouse thieves. **60m/B VHS.** Reed Howes, Janet Chandler, William Farnum.

The Million Dollar Hotel 🦴🦴 **1999 (R)** Director Wenders displays his obsession with disposable Americana in this tale of the murder of an entertainment mogul's son in a sleazy, run-down hotel. FBI special agent Skinner (Gibson) is sent to investigate and discovers a group of oddballs and losers inhabit the hotel, including mildly retarded narrator Tom Tom (Davies), intellectual hooker Eloise (Jovovich), creepy artist Geronimo (Smits), and self-proclaimed "fifth Beatle" Dixie (Stormare). Skinner carries on the investigation by spying on the tenants and making life even more miserable for them. The scattered storyline is countered somewhat by Wenders always brilliant visual style, but the performances are mixed, with Gibson giving the only notable performance. Bono, lead singer for the rock group U2, allegedly came up with the original idea for the film, as the hotel used in the movie was the one on which U2 performed in the video for "Where the Streets Have No Name." **122m/C VHS, DVD, Wide.** *US* Conrad Roberts, Mel Gibson, Jeremy Davies, Milla Jovovich, Jimmy Smits, Peter Stormare, Amanda Plummer, Gloria Stuart, Tom Bower, Donal Logue, Bud Cort, Julian Sands, Tim Roth, Richard Edson, Harris Yulin, Charlaine Woodard; ***D:*** Wim Wenders; ***W:*** Nicholas Klein; ***C:*** Phedon Papamichael; ***M:*** Brian Eno, Bono, Daniel Lanois, John Hassell.

Million Dollar Kid 🦴🦴 **1944** When a group of thugs wreak havoc in the neighborhood, the East Side Kids try to help a wealthy man put a stop to it. They face an even greater dilemma when they discover that the man's son is part of the gang. Part of the "Bowery Boys" series. **65m/B VHS, DVD.** Leo Gorcey, Huntz Hall, Gabriel Dell, Louise Currie, Noah Beery Jr., Iris Adrian, Mary Gordon; ***D:*** Wallace Fox.

The Million Dollar Kid 🦴🦴½ **1999 (PG)** A $50 million lottery jackpot is up for grabs when the winning ticket goes missing. Now Shane and his family must find their lost prize before someone else does. **92m/C VHS, DVD.** Richard Thomas, Maureen McCormick, John Ritter, C. Thomas Howell, Corey Feldman, Clint Howard, Randy Travis, Andrew Sandler; ***D:*** Neil Mandt. **VIDEO**

Million Dollar Mermaid 🦴🦴 **1952** The prototypical Williams aquashow, with the requisite awesome Berkeley dance numbers. As a biography of swimmer Annette Kellerman it isn't much, but as an MGM extravaganza, it fits the bill. **115m/C VHS.** Esther Williams, Victor Mature, Walter Pidgeon, Jesse White, David Brian, Maria Tallchief, Howard Freeman, Busby Berkeley; ***D:*** Mervyn LeRoy; ***C:*** George J. Folsey.

Million Dollar Mystery 🦴½ **1987 (PG)** A dying man's last words indicate that several million dollars have been stashed near a diner. Chaos breaks out as nearly everyone in town tries to dig up the loot. **95m/C VHS.** Eddie Deezen, Penny Baker, Tom Bosley, Rich Hall, Wendy Sherman, Rick Overton, Mona Lyden; ***D:*** Richard Fleischer; ***W:*** Rudy DeLuca, Tim Metcalfe; ***C:*** Jack Cardiff.

A Million to Juan 🦴🦴½ **1994 (PG)** Familiar rags-to-riches tale, this time set in a L.A. barrio, centers on Juan Lopez (Rodriguez), an uneducated good guy struggling to raise his son. Juan gets his lucky break when a stranger hands him a check for $1 million, explains it's a loan, and if Juan can use the money properly for a month, he'll get a reward. Juan remains incredibly noble; the movie remains mushy. Loose adaptation of the Mark Twain story "The Million Pound Bank Note." Directorial debut for Rodriguez. **97m/C VHS.** Paul Rodriguez, Polly Draper, Pepe Serna, Bert Rosario, Jonathan Hernandez, Gerardo Mejia, Victor Rivers, Edward James Olmos, Paul Williams; ***Cameos:*** Tony Plana, Ruben Blades, Richard "Cheech" Marin, David Rasche, Liz Torres; ***D:*** Paul Rodriguez; ***W:*** Francisca Matos, Robert Grasmere.

A Million to One 🦴½ **1937** An athlete trains for the Olympic decathlon, and catches the eye of an upper-class woman in the process. The lead Bennett was actually a shot-putter in the 1932 Olympic Games. **60m/B VHS.** Bruce (Herman Brix) Bennett, Joan Fontaine, Monte Blue, Kenneth Harlan, Reed Howes; ***D:*** Lynn Shores.

The Millionaire's Express 🦴🦴 *Shanghai Express; Fu Gui Lie Che* **1986** Hung returns to his village with a plan to derail the local train, which carries a number of wealthy passengers, in hopes of saving his poor hometown. Chinese with subtitles or dubbed. **107m/C VHS, DVD, Wide.** *HK* Sammo Hung, Yuen Biao, Cynthia Rothrock, Richard Norton, Yukari Oshima; ***D:*** Sammo Hung; ***W:*** Sammo Hung.

The Millionairess 🦴🦴½ **1960** Loren is an incredibly rich woman who has ended a bad marriage, and feels that the only thing she still needs to fulfill her life is a good husband. She meets a humble doctor from India, in the person of Sellers, and finds he evades her every effort to snare him. In the process she learns that money can't buy everything. From a play by George Bernard Shaw. **90m/C VHS, DVD.** *GB* Sophia Loren, Peter Sellers, Alastair Sim, Vittorio De Sica, Dennis Price; ***D:*** Anthony Asquith; ***C:*** Jack Hildyard.

Millions 🦴½ **1990 (R)** To a family of millionaires, money is everything, and the heir to the family fortune is willing to do anything to get his hands on all that money. Even if it means sleeping with his sister-in-law and cousin! Lucky for him they happen to be beautiful models. **118m/C VHS.** *IT* Billy Zane, Lauren Hutton, Carol Alt, Alexandra Paul, Catherine Hickland, Donald Pleasence; ***D:*** Carlo Vanzina.

Milo 🦴🦴 **1998 (R)** Four young girls are lured to the home of creepy kid Milo where they witness the murder of one of their friends. Sixteen years later, the girls are reunited for a wedding and Milo returns as well. **94m/C VHS, DVD.** Jennifer Jostyn, Maya McLaughlin, Asher Metchik, Paula Cale, Vincent Schiavelli, Antonio Fargas, Rae'ven (Alyia Larrymore) Kelly, Walter Olkewicz; ***D:*** Pascal Franchot; ***W:*** Craig Mitchell; ***C:*** Yuri Neyman; ***M:*** Kevin Manthei. **VIDEO**

Milo & Otis 🦴🦴½ **1989 (G)** Charming tale of a kitten named Milo and his best friend, a puppy named Otis. The two live on a farm and, when exploring the countryside, Milo is swept down a rushing river. Otis goes after to rescue his friend and the two begin a series of adventures as they try to return home. **76m/C VHS.**

Milo Milo 🦴🦴 **196?** Comedy about some very silly French people who propose to steal the Venus de Milo from the Louvre. **110m/C VHS.** Antonio Fargas, Joe Higgins.

The Milpitas Monster 🦴 **1975 (PG)** Creature spawned in a Milpitas, California, waste dump terrorizes the town residents. **80m/C VHS.** Doug Hagdahl, Scott A. Henderson, Scott Parker; ***D:*** Robert L. Burrill; ***Nar:*** Paul Frees.

Mimi 🦴🦴 **1935** Melodrama with a down-on-his-luck playwright falling for a poor lass who provides him with the needed inspiration to be a winner. The question is, will she die before he hits the big time? Loosely based on "La Vie de Boheme" by Henri Murger. **98m/B VHS.** *GB* Douglas Fairbanks Jr., Gertrude Lawrence, Diana Napier, Harold Warrender, Carol Goodner, Richard Bird, Austin Trevor, Lawrence Hanray, Paul Graetz, Martin Walker; ***D:*** Paul Stein.

Mimic 🦴🦴½ **1997 (R)** Married biotech scientists Sorvino and Northam upset the balance of nature when they cure a plague only to have their insectoid concoction unleashed in the New York subways. This causes giant cockroaches to mimic—and kill—humans. Far-fetched story is forgiven with a unique script (both John Sayles and Steven Soderbergh made additions) and original kills and thrills. Plenty of gore also makes it a worthy addition to the horror genre. **105m/C VHS, DVD, Wide.** Jeremy Northam, Mira Sorvino, Josh Brolin, Charles S. Dutton, Giancarlo Giannini, F. Murray Abraham, Alexander Goodwin; ***D:*** Guillermo del Toro; ***W:*** John Sayles, Steven Soderbergh, Matthew Robbins; ***C:*** Dan Laustsen; ***M:*** Marco Beltrami.

Mimic 2 🦴🦴½ **2001 (R)** If you like squishy giant bug movies, this direct-to-video sequel is for you. New York detective Campos and entomologist Koromzay discover that a mutant six-foot cockroach is responsible for three murders where the victims' face has been ripped off. And now it wants to mate. **82m/C VHS, DVD, Wide.** Alix Koromzay, Bruno Campos, Will Estes, Edward Albert, Jon Polito, Gaven Eugene Lucas; ***D:*** Jean De Segonzac; ***W:*** Joel Soisson; ***C:*** Nathan Hope. **VIDEO**

Min & Bill 🦴🦴 **1930** Patchy early talkie about two houseboat dwellers fighting to preserve their waterfront lifestyle and keep their daughter from being taken to a "proper" home. **66m/B VHS.** Marie Dressler, Wallace Beery, Marjorie Rambeau, Dorothy Jordan; ***D:*** George Hill. Oscars '31: Actress (Dressler).

Mina Tannenbaum 🦴🦴 **1993** Touching but unsentimental look at the 25-year friendship between two Jewish women in Paris. Mina (Bohringer) and Ethel (Zylberstein) meet as seven-year-olds and go through various childhood and teenage tramas together, including the desperate pangs of first love. Mina becomes an intense artist while flirty Ethel works as a freelance journalist. And, naturally, their friendship undergoes its own relentless changes. Pacing problems cause something of a letdown. Directorial debut for cinematographer Dugowson. French with subtitles. **128m/C VHS.** *FR* Romane Bohringer, Elsa Zylberstein, Nils (Niels) Tavernier, Florence Thomassin, Jean-Philippe Ecoffey, Stephane Slima; ***D:*** Martine Dugowson; ***W:*** Martine

Dugowson; **C:** Dominique Chapuis; **M:** Peter Chase.

Minbo—Or the Gentle Art of Japanese Extortion ♂♂ *Minbo No Onna; The Gangster's Moll; The Anti-Extortion Woman* **1992** Satire on Japanese mobsters, known as the Yakuza, focusing on the blackmail and intimidation that gives these criminals a great deal of their power. The ill-mannered group like to congregate at a local hotel—much to the detriment of business—and hotel management finally hire a hardball-playing female lawyer to solve their problems with the thugs. Japanese with subtitles. **123m/C VHS.** *JP* Nobuko Miyamoto, Akira Takarada, Takehiro Murata, Yasuo Daichi, Hideji Otaki; **D:** Juzo Itami; **W:** Juzo Itami; **C:** Yonezo Maeda; **M:** Toshiyuki Honda.

Mind, Body & Soul ♂♂ **1992 (R)** When a woman witnesses a human sacrifice performed by her boyfriend's satanic cult, she goes to the police. The cops, however, believe she is part of the cult, so she is forced to rely on the public defender to protect her from angry cult members. Pretty dull, but Hauser and Allen add some spice to this hokey thriller. **93m/C VHS, DVD.** Wings Hauser, Ginger Lynn Allen, Jay Richardson, Ken Hill, Jesse Kaye, Tami Bakke; **D:** Rick Sloane; **W:** Rick Sloane; **C:** Robert Hayes; **M:** Alan Der Marderosian.

Mind Games ♂½ **1989 (R)** A young couple and their ten-year-old son pick up a hitcher in their mobile home, never suspecting that he's a deranged psychology student ready to pit the family against each other as an experiment. **93m/C VHS.** Edward Albert, Shawn Weatherly, Matt Norero, Maxwell Caulfield; **D:** Bob Yari.

Mind Snatchers ♂♂½ **1972 (PG)** An American G.I. becomes involved in U.S. Army experimental psychological brain operations when he is brought into a western European hospital for treatment. Also know as "The Happiness Cage." **94m/C VHS.** Christopher Walken, Ronny Cox, Ralph Meeker, Joss Ackland; **D:** Bernard Girard.

A Mind to Kill ♂♂ **1995** When a murdered girl is found in a small English seaside town, the crime is linked to a previous death. Police call on a university professor for help but then a new victim, with ties to the professor, is discovered and the police detective in charge finds that his own loved ones are now in danger. **95m/C VHS.** *GB* Hywel Bennett, Philip Madoc, Sue Jones-Davies, Nicola Beddoe; **D:** Peter Edwards.

A Mind to Murder ♂♂½ *P.D. James: A Mind to Murder* **1996** Scotland Yard Commander Adam Dalgliesh (Marsden) is still depressed over the murder of a colleague some months earlier when he's discreetly called in to investigate the stabbing death of the administrator of the Steen Clinic, located in East Anglia. The exclusive psychiatric facility is home to some politically sensitive patients and Dalgleish is under pressure to solve the crime quickly and quietly. His work would go a lot easier if people cooperated, but naturally the investigation doesn't go smoothly at all. Based on the 1963 novel by P.D. James and updated for the TV movie. **100m/C VHS.** *GB* Roy Marsden, Sean Scanlan, Robert Pugh, Mairead Carty, Frank Finlay, Cal Macaninch, Ann-Gisel Glass, Sian Thomas, Jerome Flynn, Suzanne Burden, Donald Douglas, Christopher Ravenscroft; **Cameos:** David Hemmings; **D:** Gareth Davies; **C:** Bill Broomfield. **TV**

Mind Trap ♂½ **1991** A beautiful movie star's family is killed due to her father's involvement with naval research. The government wants no part of her troubles so she is forced to take the law into her own hands. **90m/C VHS.** Dan Haggerty, Lyle Waggoner, Martha Kincare, Thomas Elliot, Samuel Steven; **D:** Eames Demetrios.

Mind Twister ♂½ **1993 (R)** Erotic thriller finds a tough police detective on the trail of a sadistic killer with a twist. An unrated version is available at 94 minutes. **87m/C VHS.** Telly Savalas, Gary Hudson, Richard Roundtree, Erica Nann, Suzanne Slater; **D:** Fred Olen Ray.

Mind Warp ♂½ *Grey Matter; The Brain Machine* **1972 (R)** A future society exercises mental control and torture over its citizens. **92m/C VHS.** James Best, Barbara Burgess, Gil Peterson, Gerald McRaney, Marcus J. Grapes, Doug Collins, Anne Latham; **D:** Joy Houck Jr.

Mindfield ♂½ **1989 (R)** An innocent man gets trapped by the CIA and is used by them in mind control experiments. **91m/C VHS.** *CA* Michael Ironside, Lisa Langlois, Christopher Plummer, Stefan Wodoslowsky, Sean McCann; **D:** Jean-Claude Lord.

Mindkiller ♂½ **1987** A tongue-in-cheek gore-fest about a shy young guy who develops his brain in an effort to be socially accepted. Unfortunately, he overdoes it and his brain mutates, bursts from his head, and runs around on its own. **84m/C VHS.** Joe McDonald, Christopher Wade, Shirley Ross, Kevin Hart; **D:** Michael Krueger.

Mindstorm ♂♂½ **2001 (R)** The plot has holes big enough to fly a helicopter through but the action keeps things from being boring. Psychic private eye Tracy Wellman (Vaugier) is hired to free Senator Armitage's (Ironside) daughter from the clutches of cult leader David Mendez (a prototypically evil Roberts) and is aided by FBI hunk Dan Oliver (Sabato). Turns out that Mendez and Wellman have a past together—they're both telepaths as the result of a government mind control experiment when they were children—a project headed by Armitage. **106m/C VHS, DVD.** *CA* Emmanuelle Vaugier, Antonio Sabato Jr., Eric Roberts, Michael Ironside, Clarence Williams III, Michael Moriarty, Ed O'Ross, William B. Davis; **D:** Richard Pepin; **W:** Paul A. Berkitt; **C:** Adam Sliwinski; **M:** John Sereda. **CABLE**

Mindwalk: A Film for Passionate Thinkers ♂♂♂ **1991 (PG)** A feature-length intellectual workout; a physicist, poet and politician stroll the ancient grounds of Mont St. Michel monastery in France and discuss the need to change mankind's view of the universe. Uncinematic? Perhaps, but it entertainingly conveys the epochal ideas of scientist/author Fritjof Capra (whose book was adapted for the screen by younger brother Bernt). **111m/C VHS.** Liv Ullmann, Sam Waterston, John Heard, Ione Skye; **D:** Bernt Capra; **W:** Fritjof Capra, Floyd Byars; **M:** Philip Glass.

Mindwarp ♂♂ **1991 (R)** After an ecological disaster, residents of Earth move to a sterile haven known as "Inworld." When survivor Judy (Alicia) seeks answers about her missing father (accidentally killing her mother in the process), she is cast from "Inworld" into Earth's wasteland, where she and human compatriot Stover (Campbell) are left to fight the elements and learn the awful truth about Judy's father. **91m/C VHS.** Marta Alicia, Bruce Campbell, Angus Scrimm, Elizabeth Kent, Mary Becker; **D:** Steve Barnett; **W:** Henry Dominick.

Mine Own Executioner ♂♂♂ **1947** Determined but unstable psychologist in postwar London struggles to treat schizophrenic who suffered torture by Japanese while wartime prisoner. Strong, visually engrossing fare. **102m/B VHS.** *GB* Burgess Meredith, Kieron Moore, Dulcie Gray, Christine Norden, Barbara White, John Laurie, Michael Shepley; **D:** Anthony Kimmins.

Mines of Kilimanjaro ♂½ **1987 (PG-13)** An archaeology student heads for Africa to investigate his professor's murder and comes up with a heap of trouble. **88m/C VHS.** Christopher Connelly, Tobias Hoels, Gordon Mitchell, Elena Pompei; **D:** Mino Guerrini.

The Minion ♂♂ *Fallen Knight* **1998 (R)** Lucas (Lundgren) is a modern-day Knights Templar, the emissary of an ancient religious order that guards a temple door, which is the gateway to the antichrist. When the key to the door is discovered, Lucas must battle an ancient demon who has risen from hell to claim possession. But since the demon can inhabit anyone, how's Lucas going to know who to fight? **97m/C VHS, DVD.** *CA* Dolph Lundgren, Francoise Robertson, Roc Lafortune, Michael Greyeyes, David Nerman, Karen Goodleaf; **D:** Jean-Marc Piche; **W:** Matt Roe, Ripley Highsmith; **C:** Barry Parrell.

Ministry of Fear ♂♂♂ **1944** Creepy noir based on the novel by Graham Greene. Stephen Neale (Milland) has just been released from two years in an insane asylum. As he waits for a train, he decides to visit a nearby carnival that turns out to be fronted by a Nazi organization, where Neale's mistaken for an agent. After finally reaching London, he's later accused of murder, escapes the police, and is aided by the sympathetic Carla (Reynolds). No one and nothing is as it seems, however, and soon the unwitting Neale is deeply involved in espionage. Since the viewer sees only what Neale does, it's just as puzzling for the audience as it is for the character. **85m/B VHS.** Ray Milland, Marjorie Reynolds, Percy Waram, Dan Duryea, Carl Esmond, Hillary Brooke, Alan Napier, Erskine Sanford; **D:** Fritz Lang; **W:** Seton I. Miller; **C:** Henry Sharp; **M:** Victor Young.

Ministry of Vengeance ♂ **1989 (R)** A psychotic murderer who hates grapes of any kind finds the woman of his dreams—she's a psychotic murderer who hates grapes! Together they find bliss—until the plumber discovers their secret! **90m/C VHS.** John Schneider, Ned Beatty, George Kennedy, Yaphet Kotto, James Tolkan, Apollonia.

The Miniver Story ♂♂ **1950** Weepy sequel to "Mrs. Miniver" reunites the family in post-WWII England, but clearly lacks the inspiration of the original. Garson is again Mrs. Miniver and she's secretly suffering from a never-named fatal disease. She decides to straighten out the family troubles before her time is up, including her daughter's love life and her husband's plan to move to Brazil. Depressing and glum. **104m/B VHS.** *GB* Greer Garson, Walter Pidgeon, John Hodiak, Leo Genn, Cathy O'Donnell, Reginald Owen, Anthony Bushell; **D:** H.C. Potter; **W:** Ronald Millar, George Froeschel; **C:** Joseph Ruttenberg; **M:** Miklos Rozsa.

Minna von Barnhelm or The Soldier's Fortune ♂♂ *Minna von Barnhelm oder das Soldatengluck* **1962** Prussian nobleman Major von Tellheim becomes engaged to noblewoman Minna von Barnhelm during the Seven Year's War. But after the war has ended, the King inexplicably deprives von Tellheim of his title, leaving him humiliated and impoverished, and causing him to break his engagement. But Minna loves her man and refuses to let him go. Based on the drama by Gotthold Ephraim Lessing. German with subtitles. **103m/C VHS.** *GE* Marita Bohme, Otto Mellies, Manfred Krug; **D:** Martin Hellberg.

Minnesota Clay ♂½ *L'Homme du Minnesota* **1965** A blind gunman, who aims by sound and smell, is marked by two rival gangs and a tempestuous tramp. **89m/C VHS.** *FR IT* Cameron Mitchell, Diana Martin; **D:** Sergio Corbucci.

Minnie and Moskowitz ♂♂½ **1971** Minnie's (Rowlands) about to turn 40 and wants out of her affair with married man, Jim (Cassavetes). She accepts a blind date with Zelmo (Avery) and when he turns out to be a nut, Minnie's rescued by parking attendant Moskowitz (Cassel). Through the opposites attract ploy, Minnie and Moskowitz start dating and soon decide to get married. It's basically a Cassavetes home movie, featuring a number of family and friends who probably had a better time making it than you'll have watching it. **114m/C VHS, DVD.** Gena Rowlands, Seymour Cassel, Val Avery, Timothy Carey, Holly Near, Katherine Cassavetes, Mary Allen "Lady" Rowlands, David Rowlands, Elizabeth Deering, Elsie Adams, John Cassavetes; **D:** John Cassavetes; **W:** John Cassavetes; **C:** Arthur Ornitz.

A Minor Miracle ♂♂ **1983 (G)** Tender family fare about a group of orphaned children who band together under the loving guidance of their guardian (Huston) to save St. Francis School for boys from the town planners. Warms the cockles. **100m/C VHS.** John Huston, Pele, Peter Fox; **D:** Terrell Tannen.

Minority Report **2002** Spielberg and Cruise in a sci-fi adventure. In a futuristic Washington, D.C., a law enforcement agency employs seers to anticipate homicides. Cruise plays one of the cops who go after the potential murderers until he becomes a suspect himself and has to go on the lam. **?m/C VHS, DVD.** Tom Cruise, Samantha Morton, Colin Farrell, Max von Sydow, Neal McDonough; **D:** Steven Spielberg; **W:** Scott Frank, Jon Cohen.

The Minus Man ♂♂ **1999 (R)** Vann Siegert (Wilson) is the blandest, nicest serial killer you are ever likely to meet. A drifter, Vann has settled into a small California town where he boards with a troubled married couple, Doug (Cox) and Jane (Ruehl), who come to think of ever-smiling Vann as a surrogate son. Vann gets a job at the post office (!), befriends lonely co-worker Ferrin (Garofalo), and calmly proceeds to off the locals. Eerie thriller offers no explanations for Vann's behavior, which makes it all the creepier. Adapted from the 1990 novel by Lew McCreary, who has a cameo as a victim. **112m/C VHS, DVD, Wide.** Owen C. Wilson, Brian Cox, Mercedes Ruehl, Janeane Garofalo, Dwight Yoakam, Dennis Haysbert, Eric Mabius, Sheryl Crow, Larry Miller; **D:** Hampton Fancher; **W:** Hampton Fancher; **C:** Bobby Bukowski; **M:** Marco Beltrami.

A Minute to Pray, a Second to Die ♂♂ *Un Minuto Per Pregare, Un Istante Per Morire; Dead or Alive; Outlaw Gun* **1967** A notorious, wanted-dead-or-alive gunman retreats to the amnesty of the New Mexico Territory, but finds he cannot shake his past. **100m/C VHS.** *IT* Robert Ryan, Arthur Kennedy, Alex Cord; **D:** Franco Giraldi.

The Miracle ♂♂♂ *Ways of Love* **1948** An innocent peasant woman is seduced by a shepherd and becomes convinced that her pregnancy will produce a second Christ. Controversial, compelling film derived from a story by Federico Fellini. In Italian with English subtitles. **43m/B VHS.** *IT* Anna Magnani, Federico Fellini; **D:** Roberto Rossellini; **W:** Federico Fellini; **C:** Aldo Tonti.

The Miracle ♂♂½ **1991 (PG)** Irish teens, whose strong friendship is based upon their equally unhappy home lives, find both tested when a secretive American woman turns up in town. Excellent debuts from Byrne and Pilkington but tedious pacing in a dreamy script that tells too much too soon. Worth watching just for D'Angelo's smouldering rendition of "Stardust." **97m/C VHS.** *GB* Beverly D'Angelo, Donal McCann, Niall Byrne, Lorraine Pilkington, J.G. Devlin; **D:** Neil Jordan; **W:** Neil Jordan; **C:** Philippe Rousselot; **M:** Anne Dudley.

Miracle at Midnight ♂♂½ **1998** Having occupied Denmark for several years, the Nazis decide to round up all Danish Jews on October 1, 1943. Word is leaked and a number of citizens risk their lives to warn and hide the Jews, spiriting more than 7,000 to safety in Sweden. This Disney version focuses on the non-Jewish Kloster family and how each of them become involved in the rescue. **89m/C VHS.** Sam Waterston, Mia Farrow, Justin Whalin, Nicola Mycroft, Barry McGovern, Patrick Malahide; **D:** Ken Cameron; **W:** Chris Bryant, Monte Merrick. **TV**

Miracle at Moreaux **1986** Three Jewish children fleeing from Nazis find sanctuary with a nun and her wards. Based on Clare Huchet Bishop's book "Twenty and Ten." Originally aired on PBS as part of the "Wonderworks" family movie series. **58m/C VHS.** Loretta Swit, Marsha Moreau, Robert Joy, Ken Pogue, Robert Kosoy, Talya Rubin; **D:** Paul Shapiro; **M:** Jonathan Goldsmith.

Miracle Beach ♂½ **1992 (PG-13)** Scotty McKay has lost his job, his apartment, and his girl. Then he gets rejected by Dana, the super model he's secretly adored. Can things get any worse? Scotty decides to take a walk along the beach and sort things out when he stumbles across a girl genie, named Jeanie, who has been sent to Earth on a good will mission. Scotty gets Jeanie to grant his every material wish in order to dazzle model Dana. But when Jeanie falls in love with Scotty can she get him to recognize the difference between true love and fantasy? **88m/C VHS.** Dean Cameron, Felicity Waterman, Ami Dolenz, Alexis Arquette, Martin Mull, Noriyuki "Pat" Morita, Vincent Schiavelli; **D:** Skott Snider.

Miracle Down Under 1987 A family endures arduous times in 1890s Australia before a Christmas miracle changes their fortunes. Inoffensive Disney-produced drama. Australia has two directors named George Miller—one directs Mad Max movies; the other directs family fare such as "The Man from Snowy River." This Miller is the latter. **101m/C VHS.** *AU* Dee Wallace Stone, John Waters, Charles Tingwell, Bill Kerr, Andrew Ferguson; ***D:*** George Miller.

Miracle in Harlem 1948 A gang tries to take over a candy shop and when the gang leader is killed, the evidence points to the foster daughter of the shop owner. The script suffers from cliched dialog and less-than-believable situations, but the all-black cast turns in good performances. **69m/B VHS.** Sheila Guyse, Stepin Fetchit, Hilda Offley, Lawrence Criner, Monte Hawley; ***D:*** Jack Kemp.

Miracle in Lane Two 2000 Based on the true story of 12-year-old Justin Yoder (Muniz) who's confined to a wheelchair but still wins a national soap box derby championship. **89m/C VHS.** Frankie Muniz, Roger Aaron Brown, Molly Hagan, Rick Rossovich, Tuc Watkins; ***D:*** Greg Beeman. **CABLE**

Miracle in Milan *Miracolo a Milano* **1951** An innocent, child-like fantasy about heavenly intervention driving capitalists out of a Milanese ghetto and helping the poor to fly to a new Utopia. Happy mixture of whimsy and neo-realism. In Italian with English subtitles. **95m/B VHS.** *IT* Francesco Golisano, Brunella Bova, Emma Gramatica, Paolo Stoppa; ***D:*** Vittorio De Sica; ***W:*** Cesare Zavattini. Cannes '51: Film; N.Y. Film Critics '51: Foreign Film.

Miracle in Rome ½ *Milagro en Roma* **1988** Margarito Duarte digs up his dead daughter and finds her body in perfect condition despite 12-year internment. Attempting to convince the local clergy that she's miracle material, he finds them less than eager to elect her to sainthood. Based on a story by Gabriel Garcia marquez; made for Spanish TV. In Spanish with English subtitles. **76m/C VHS.** *SP* Frank Ramirez, Gerardo Arellano, Amalia Duque Garcia, Lisandro Duque, Daniel Priolett; ***D:*** Lisandro Duque Naranjo; ***W:*** Lisandro Duque Naranjo, Gabriel Garcia Marquez. **TV**

Miracle in the Wilderness ½ 1991 A Christmas western based on Paul Gallico's novella, "The Snow Goose." Kristofferson stars as Jericho Adams, a former Indian fighter, who turns to farming to support his wife and child. When they are captured by a raiding party of Blackfeet, Adams discovers they have never heard the story of the Nativity. **88m/C VHS.** Kris Kristofferson, Kim Cattrall, John Dennis Johnston, Joanelle Romero, Dennis Olvers, Sheldon Peters Wolfchild; ***D:*** Kevin James Dobson; ***W:*** Jim Byrnes.

Miracle Kid 1942 Standard story of a young boxer who'd rather be something else. His romance is interrupted when he becomes successful in the ring. **66m/B VHS.** Tom Neal, Carol Hughes, Betty Blythe, Minta Durfee, Gertrude Messinger; ***D:*** William Beaudine.

The Miracle Maker: The Story of Jesus ½ 2000 Elaborate 3-D claymation is surprisingly effective in telling the story of Jesus, based on the Gospel of St. Luke. Christ's ministry is seen through the eyes of sickly child, Tamar, who is healed by one of his miracles. **87m/C VHS, DVD.** ***V:*** Ralph Fiennes, Rebecca Callard, Michael Bryant, Julie Christie, James Frain, Richard E. Grant, Ian Holm, William Hurt, Daniel Massey, Alfred Molina, Bob Peck, Miranda Richardson, Anthony Sher, Ken Stott, David Thewlis. **TV**

Miracle Mile 1989 (R) A riveting, apocalyptic thriller about a mild-mannered misfit who, while inadvertently standing on a street corner at 2 a.m., answers a ringing pay phone. The caller is a panicked missile-silo worker who announces that the bombs have been launched for an all-out nuclear war. With about an hour left before the end, he decides to head into the city and rendezvous with his new girlfriend. A surreal, wicked farce sadly overlooked in theatrical release. Music by Tangerine Dream. **87m/C VHS.** Edward (Eddie) Bunker, Anthony Edwards, Mare Winningham, John Agar, Denise Crosby, Lou Hancock, Mykelti Williamson, Kelly Jo Minter, Kurt Fuller, Robert DoQui, Danny De La Paz, O-lan Jones, Alan Rosenberg, Claude Earl Jones; ***D:*** Steve DeJarnatt; ***W:*** Steve DeJarnatt; ***C:*** Theo van de Sande; ***M:*** Tangerine Dream.

The Miracle of Marcelino ½ *Marcelino, Pan y Vino; Marcelino* **1955** Marcelino (Calvo) was left at birth on a monastery doorstep and raised by the Franciscan friars. The high-spirited young boy finds a life-sized crucifix in the church attic and, believing the figure of Christ to be real, befriends the image, bringing it food and wine. Then, one day, the image of Jesus comes to life. Spanish with subtitles. **88m/B VHS.** *SP* Pablito Calvo, Fernando Rey, Rafael Rivelles; ***D:*** Ladislao Vajda; ***W:*** Ladislao Vajda; ***C:*** Enrique Guerner; ***M:*** Pablo Sarosabal.

Miracle of Morgan's Creek 1944 Sturges's breakneck comedy details the misadventures of wartime floozy Trudy Kockenlocker (Hutton) who gets drunk at a party, thinks she marries a soldier on leave, gets pregnant, forgets the whole thing, and then tries to evade scandal by getting local schnook and sometimes boyfriend Norval (Bracken) to take responsibility. Oh yeah, and it turns out Trudy's expecting sextuplets. Hilarious, out-to-make-trouble farce that shouldn't have, by all rights, made it past the censors of the time. The director's most scathing assault on American values. Loosely remade as 1958's "Rock-A-Bye Baby" starring Jerry Lewis. **98m/B VHS.** Eddie Bracken, Betty Hutton, Diana Lynn, Brian Donlevy, Akim Tamiroff, Porter Hall, Emory Parnell, Alan Bridge, Julius Tannen, Victor Potel, Almira Sessions, Chester Conklin, William Demarest, Jimmy Conlin; ***D:*** Preston Sturges; ***W:*** Preston Sturges; ***M:*** Leo Shuken, Charles Bradshaw. Natl. Film Reg. '01.

Miracle of Our Lady of Fatima *The Miracle of Fatima* **1952** Slick cold-war version of the supposedly true events surrounding the sighting of a holy vision by three children in Portugal during WWI. **102m/C VHS.** Gilbert Roland, Susan Whitney, Sherry Jackson, Sammy Ogg, Angela Clark, Frank Silvera, Jay Novello; ***D:*** John Brahm; ***M:*** Max Steiner.

The Miracle of the Bells 1948 A miracle occurs after a dead movie star is buried in the cemetary of her modest hometown. Given the premise, the casting is all the more peculiar. Adapted by Ben Hecht from Russell Janney's novel. **120m/B VHS.** Fred MacMurray, Alida Valli, Frank Sinatra, Lee J. Cobb; ***D:*** Irving Pichel.

Miracle of the Heart: A Boys Town Story 1986 Based on the story of Boys Town, and an old priest who sticks up for Boys Town's principles in the face of a younger priest with rigid ideas. **100m/C VHS.** Art Carney, Casey Siemaszko, Jack Bannon; ***D:*** Georg Stanford Brown. **TV**

The Miracle of the White Stallions ½ *The Flight of the White Stallions* **1963** A disappointing Disney adventure about the director of a Viennese riding academy who guides his prized Lipizzan stallions to safety when the Nazis occupy Austria in WWII. **92m/C VHS.** Robert Taylor, Lilli Palmer, Eddie Albert, Curt Jurgens; ***D:*** Arthur Hiller; ***W:*** A.J. Carothers.

Miracle on Ice ½ 1981 Occasionally stirring TV film recounts the surprise triumph of the American hockey team over the touted Soviet squad during the 1980 Winter Olympics at Lake Placid. **150m/C VHS.** Karl Malden, Steve Guttenberg, Andrew Stevens, Lucinda Dooling, Jessica Walter; ***D:*** Steven Hilliard Stern. **TV**

Miracle on 34th Street *The Big Heart* **1947** The actual Kris Kringle is hired as Santa Claus for the Macy's Thanksgiving parade but finds difficulty in proving himself to the cynical parade sponsor. When the boss's daughter also refuses to acknowledge Kringle, he goes to extraordinary lengths to convince her. Holiday classic equal to "It's a Wonderful Life," with Gwenn and Wood particularly engaging. Also available colorized. **97m/B VHS, DVD.** Maureen O'Hara, John Payne, Edmund Gwenn, Natalie Wood, William Frawley, Porter Hall, Gene Lockhart, Thelma Ritter, Jack Albertson; ***D:*** George Seaton; ***W:*** George Seaton; ***C:*** Lloyd Ahern, Charles Clarke; ***M:*** Cyril Mockridge. Oscars '47: Screenplay, Story, Support. Actor (Gwenn); Golden Globes '48: Screenplay, Support. Actor (Gwenn).

Miracle on 34th Street ½ 1994 (PG) Updated remake of the 1947 Christmas classic in which a jolly, bearded gent (Attenborough) claiming to be Santa Claus brings happiness to a doubting girl (Wilson) and her jaded mother (Perkins). Before he can prove himself to the precocious child, he must prove himself in a court of law with the help of Perkins's impossibly perfect neighbor (McDermott), a lawyer with a heart of gold (talk about your Christmas miracles!). This version can't compete with the original's "classic" status, but Attenborough and Wilson bring soul and substance to this otherwise average adaptation. **114m/C VHS, DVD.** Richard Attenborough, Elizabeth Perkins, Dylan McDermott, J.T. Walsh, Mara Wilson, Joss Ackland, James Remar, Jane Leeves, Simon Jones, Robert Prosky, William Windom; ***D:*** Les Mayfield; ***W:*** John Hughes, George Seaton; ***M:*** Bruce Broughton.

The Miracle Rider 1935 A 15-chapter serial finds the bad guys trying to run the Indians off their lands in this saga of the old west. **295m/B VHS.** Tom Mix, Joan Gale, Charles Middleton, Jason Robards Sr., Pat O'Malley, Robert Frazer, Wally Wales, Tom London, George Chesebro, Lafe (Lafayette) McKee; ***D:*** B. Reeves Eason, Armand Schaefer.

The Miracle Woman ½ 1931 Stanwyck's particularly fine as evangelist Florence "Faith" Fallon, who becomes very successful thanks to her way with words, some fake miracles, and the talents of shady promoter Hornsby (Hardy). After blind ex-pilot John Carson (Manners) hears her on the radio, he decides Faith might be able to cure him. Florence winds up falling in love with John but Hornsby starts to worry she's going soft and will end their scam. Even Capra apparently thought this film was corny but it still works. Based on the play "Bless You Sister" by John Meehan and Robert Riskin. **90m/B VHS.** Barbara Stanwyck, David Manners, Sam Hardy, Beryl Mercer, Russell Hopton, Charles Middleton, Eddie Boland; ***D:*** Frank Capra; ***W:*** Dorothy Howell, Jo Swerling; ***C:*** Joseph Walker.

The Miracle Worker ½ 1962 Depicts the unconventional methods that teacher Anne Sullivan used to help the deaf and blind Helen Keller adjust to the world around her and shows the relationship that built between the two courageous women. An intense, moving experience. William Gibson adapted his own play for the screen. **107m/B VHS, DVD, Wide.** Anne Bancroft, Patty Duke, Victor Jory, Inga Swenson, Andrew Prine, Beah Richards; ***D:*** Arthur Penn; ***W:*** William Gibson; ***C:*** Ernesto Caparros; ***M:*** Laurence Rosenthal. Oscars '62: Actress (Bancroft), Support. Actress (Duke); British Acad. '62: Actress (Bancroft); Natl. Bd. of Review '62: Actress (Bancroft).

The Miracle Worker 1979 Remade for TV story of blind, deaf and mute Helen Keller and her teacher, Annie Sullivan, whose patience and perseverance finally enable Helen to learn to communicate with the world. Duke was Keller in the 1962 original, but plays the teacher in this version. **98m/C VHS.** Patty Duke, Melissa Gilbert; ***D:*** Paul Aaron; ***M:*** Billy Goldenberg. **TV**

The Miracle Worker ½ 2000 Yet another remake of William Gibson's Tony award-winning play, following the 1962 movie and the 1979 TV version. This time around precocious Eisenberg is young Helen Keller and Elliott (particularly good) is her dedicated teacher Annie Sullivan. Rather a genteel retelling although Annie's breakthrough with Helen still carries a strong emotional power. **90m/C VHS, DVD.** Hallie Kate Eisenberg, Alison Elliott, David Strathairn, Lucas Black, Kate Greenhouse; ***D:*** Nadia Tass; ***W:*** Monte Merrick; ***C:*** David Parker; ***M:*** William Goldstein. **TV**

Miracles ½ 1986 (PG) Comedic misfire pairs a recently divorced couple as reluctant adventurers dodging jewel thieves and peculiar tribes in South America. In a desperate move to create a plot, Mexican jewel thieves, strange tribal rites, and some outrageously unlikely coincidences reunite the family. If this sounds good, see "Romancing the Stone" instead. **90m/C VHS.** Tom Conti, Teri Garr, Paul Rodriguez, Christopher Lloyd, Jorge Russek, Charles Rocket, Bob Nelson; ***D:*** Jim Kouf; ***M:*** Peter Bernstein.

Miracles ½ *Qiji; Black Dragon* **1989 (PG-13)** Chan stars (and writes and directs) as a bumpkin who saves the life of a mob boss and is thrust into the world of crime in 1930s Hong Kong. He gets some social help from a mysterious woman that gives him the confidence to romance nightclub singer Mui. But when his mob patron is murdered, Chan decides he has to show his loyalty by seeking justice. Humor and action turn out to be a winning combo. **106m/C VHS, DVD.** *HK* Jackie Chan, Anita (Yim-Fong) Mui, Richard Ng, Yuen Biao; ***D:*** Jackie Chan; ***W:*** Jackie Chan.

Mirage 1966 An amnesiac finds himself the target of a dangerous manhunt in New York City in this offbeat thriller. Peck is particularly sympathetic in the lead, and McCarthy, Matthau, and Kennedy all shine in supporting roles. Worth it just to hear thug Kennedy grunt, "I owe this man some pain!" **108m/B VHS.** Gregory Peck, Diane Baker, Walter Matthau, Jack Weston, Kevin McCarthy, Walter Abel, George Kennedy; ***D:*** Edward Dmytryk; ***M:*** Quincy Jones.

Mirage ½ 1994 (R) Neo-noir with plot problems has former Palm Springs cop Matteo Juarez (Olmos) hired to protect Jennifer (Young), the wife of wealthy environmentalist Donald Gale (Williams). But Jennifer just happens to suffer from multiple personality disorder, leading a not-so-secret second life as a stripper and having trouble always on her heels. **106m/C VHS.** Edward James Olmos, Sean Young, James Andronica, Paul W. Williams; ***D:*** Paul W. Williams; ***W:*** James Andronica.

Mirele Efros ½ 1938 A widowed but successful businesswoman finds herself at odds with her daughter-in-law in this film set in the turn of the century. In Yiddish with English subtitles. **80m/B VHS.** Berta Gersten, Michael Rosenberg, Ruth Elbaum, Albert Lipton, Sarah Krohner, Moishe Feder; ***D:*** Joseph Berne.

The Mirror *Zerkalo; A White White Boy* **1975** Wonderful child's view of life in Russia during WWII. Black and white flashbacks of important events in the country's history are interspersed with scenes of day-to-day family life. In Russian with English subtitles. **106m/C VHS, DVD.** *RU* Margarita Terekhova, Philip Yankovsky, Ignat Daniltsev, Oleg (Yankovsky) Jankowsky; ***D:*** Andrei Tarkovsky; ***W:*** Andrei Tarkovsky; ***C:*** Georgy Rerberg; ***M:*** Eduard Artemyev.

The Mirror Crack'd 1980 (PG) While filming a movie in the English countryside, an American actress is murdered and Miss Marple must discover who the killer is. Based on the substantially better Agatha Christie novel. **105m/C VHS, DVD, Wide.** *GB* Angela Lansbury, Wendy Morgan, Margaret Courtenay, Charles Gray, Maureen Bennett, Carolyn Pickles, Elizabeth Taylor, Rock Hudson, Kim Novak, Tony Curtis, Edward Fox, Geraldine Chaplin, Pierce Brosnan; ***D:*** Guy Hamilton; ***W:*** Barry Sandler; ***C:*** Christopher Challis; ***M:*** John Cameron.

The Mirror Has Two Faces 1996 (PG-13) Gregory (Bridges) is a hunky, but flustered, professor (hunky professor?) looking for romance without all that complicated sex, which shortly leads him to plain but soulful Rose (Streisand), the ugly duckling of her family. Rose's mother (Bacall) seems more happy with her much married sister (Rogers), who is headed down the aisle again with gorgeous Alex (Brosnan). Rose decides it's her turn, despite Gregory's protests, and she weds the bow-tied (and perhaps hog-tied?) educator anyway. When Gregory leaves her on a promotional book tour, frumpy Babs decides a big makeover is in order. Her newfound outer beauty, however, becomes the beast on the inside. Premise is marred by Streisand's unwillingness to look bad, and there's a too-subtle transformation between the "ugly" Rose and the updated version. Bacall gives a memorable, Oscar-nominated performance. Remake of 1959 French film. La Streisand added to her reputation for being a "difficult" perfectionist with her constant reshoots and personnel firings that extended the film's schedule. **127m/C VHS, DVD.** Barbra Streisand, Jeff Bridges, Pierce Brosnan, Mimi Rogers, Lauren Bacall, Brenda Vaccaro, Austin Pendleton, George Segal, Elle Macpherson; ***D:*** Barbra Streisand; ***W:*** Richard LaGravenese; ***C:*** Dante Spinotti, Andrzej Bartkowiak; ***M:*** Barbra Streisand, Marvin Hamlisch. Golden Globes '97: Support. Actress (Bacall); Screen Actors Guild '96: Support. Actress (Bacall).

Mirror Images 🦴½ **1991 (R)** Although sexy twins Kaitlin and Shauna may look alike, they couldn't have more diverse personalities. Yet the gorgeous twins find their lives thrown together in a mad tornado of passion and danger when they each encounter a handsome, mysterious stranger. Could it be that this guy has something more on his mind than love, something like... murder? Also available in an even steamier unrated version. **94m/C VHS.** Delia Sheppard, Jeff Conaway, Richard Arbolino, John O'Hurley, Korey Mall, Julie Strain, Nels Van Patten; ***D:*** Alexander Gregory (Gregory Dark) Hippolyte.

Mirror Images 2 🦴🦴 **1993** Direct-to-video erotic thriller features identical twins Carrie and Terrie (Whirry in a dual role). Carrie's Miss Goody Two-Shoes and Terrie's a murderous nympho who likes Carrie's guys. Terrie dies in a mysterious fire and Carrie sets out to investigate. Sex and nudity sells. **92m/C VHS.** Shannon Whirry, Luca Bercovici, Tom Reilly; ***D:*** Alexander Gregory (Gregory Dark) Hippolyte.

Mirror, Mirror 🦴🦴 **1990 (R)** The prolific Ms. Black turns on the ol' black magic when her daughter's classmates decide it's open season for taunting shrinking violets. Thanks to a magical mirror on the wall, the cheerleading classmates are willed to the great pep rally in the sky. **105m/C VHS, DVD.** Karen Black, Rainbow Harvest, Kristin Dattilo-Hayward, Ricky Paull Goldin, Yvonne De Carlo, William Sanderson, Charlie Spradling, Ann Hearn, Stephen Tobolowsky; ***D:*** Marina Sargenti; ***W:*** Marina Sargenti; ***C:*** Robert Brinkmann; ***M:*** Jimmy Lifton.

Mirror, Mirror 2: Raven Dance 🦴½ **1994 (R)** Teenaged Marlee (Wells) and her brother are temporarily housed in a convent after the death of their parents. The mystery mirror is discovered and looking into it causes Marlee to become partially blind. Meanwhile, her inheritance is threatened and a mysterious stranger, living in the convent's basement, may be Marlee's only hope. **91m/C VHS, DVD.** Tracy Wells, Roddy McDowall, Sally Kellerman, Veronica Cartwright, William Sanderson, Lois Nettleton; ***D:*** Jimmy Lifton; ***W:*** Jimmy Lifton, Virginia Perfili; ***C:*** Troy Cook; ***M:*** Jimmy Lifton.

Mirror, Mirror 3: The Voyeur 🦴½ **1996** Artist discovers a mirror in an abandoned mansion and sees that it reflects the presence of his lost lover, who is now able to manipulate his dreams. **91m/C VHS, DVD.** Billy Drago, Monique Parent, David Naughton, Mark Ruffalo, Elizabeth Baldwin, Richard Cansino; ***D:*** Rachel Gordon, Virginia Perfili; ***W:*** Steve Tymon; ***C:*** Nils Erickson.

Mirror of Death 🦴 **1987** A woman subject to physical abuse gets more than she bargains for when she seeks revenge by unleashing the gruesome Queen of Hell. Watch this if you dare! **85m/C VHS.** Julie Merrill, Kuri Browne, John Reno, Deryn Warren.

Mirrors 🦴 **1978** Woman finds that her dreams lead to death and destruction in New Orleans. **83m/C VHS.** Kitty Winn, Peter Donat, William Swetland, Mary-Robin Redd, William Burns; ***D:*** Noel Black.

Mirrors 🦴🦴½ **1985** A Detroit-born ballerina goes to the Big Apple in search of fame and glory, leaving behind her journalist boyfriend. This upbeat love story features some spectacular dance routines and a behind-the-scenes look at a Broadway dancer's lifestyle. **99m/C VHS.** Timothy Daly, Marguerite Hickey, Antony Hamilton; ***D:*** Harry Winer. **TV**

The Misadventures of Merlin Jones 🦴½ **1963 (G)** A pair of college sweethearts become embroiled in a rollicking chimp-napping scandal. Disney pap done appropriately. A sequel, "The Monkey's Uncle," followed. **90m/C VHS.** Tommy Kirk, Annette Funicello, Leon Ames, Stuart Erwin, Connie Gilchrist; ***D:*** Robert Stevenson; ***W:*** Alfred Lewis Levitt, Helen Levitt; ***C:*** Edward Colman; ***M:*** Buddy (Norman Dale) Baker.

The Misadventures of Mr. Wilt 🦴🦴 *Wilt* **1990 (R)** Bumbling college lecturer has to convince inept inspector that he murdered a blowup doll, not his mean missing wife. Based on Tom Sharpe's bestseller. **84m/C VHS.** *GB* Griff Rhys Jones, Mel Smith, Alison Steadman, Diana Quick; ***D:*** Michael Tuchner; ***M:*** Anne Dudley.

Misbegotten 🦴🦴 **1998 (R)** Infertile couple Paul (Mancuso) and Caitlin (Anthony) are able to have their bundle of joy thanks to artifical insemination. Only psycho donor daddy Billy Crapshoot (Dillon) finds out who they are and decides to come for his soon-to-be-born offspring. **97m/C VHS.** Kevin Dillon, Nick Mancuso, Lysette Anthony, Robert Lewis, Matthew (Matt) Walker, Stefan Arngrim; ***D:*** Mark L. Lester; ***W:*** Larry Cohen; ***C:*** Mark Irwin. **CABLE**

Misbehaving Husbands 🦴½ **1941** Weak story finds store-owner Langton suspected of being untrue by wife Blythe—thanks to rumors spread by a shyster lawyer only too happy to console the lady after the divorce. **65m/B VHS.** Harry Langdon, Betty Blythe, Ralph Byrd, Esther Muir, Luana Walters; ***D:*** William Beaudine.

Mischief 🦴🦴 **1985 (R)** Alienated youths form a friendship during James Dean's heydey. Warning: this film offers a fairly convincing recreation of the 1950s. **97m/C VHS.** Doug McKeon, Catherine Mary Stewart, Kelly Preston, Chris Nash, D.W. Brown, Jami Gertz, Margaret Blye, Graham Jarvis, Terry O'Quinn; ***D:*** Mel Damski; ***W:*** Noel Black.

Misery 🦴🦴🦴 **1990 (R)** Author Caan decides to chuck his lucrative but unfulfilling pulp novels and write seriously by finishing off his most popular character, Misery Chastain. However, fate intervenes when he crashes his car near the home of Bates, his "biggest fan ever," who saves his life, but then tortures him into resurrecting her favorite character. Bates is chillingly glib and and calmly brutal—watch your ankles. Based on the novel by Stephen King. **107m/C VHS, DVD, Wide.** James Caan, Kathy Bates, Lauren Bacall, Richard Farnsworth, Frances Sternhagen, Graham Jarvis; ***D:*** Rob Reiner; ***W:*** William Goldman; ***C:*** Barry Sonnenfeld; ***M:*** Marc Shaiman. Oscars '90: Actress (Bates); Golden Globes '91: Actress—Drama (Bates).

The Misfit Brigade 🦴🦴 *Wheels of Terror* **1987 (R)** Variation on the "Dirty Dozen" finds German misfits recruited for warfare by desperate Nazis during WWII. **99m/C VHS.** Bruce Davison, Oliver Reed, David Carradine, David Patrick Kelly, D.W. Moffett, Keith Szarabajka; ***D:*** Gordon Hessler.

The Misfits 🦴🦴🦴 **1961** A cynical floozy befriends grim cowboys in this downbeat drama. Compelling performances from leads Clift, Monroe (screenwriter Miller's wife), and Gable. Last film for the latter two performers, and nearly the end for Clift. **124m/B VHS, DVD, Wide.** Clark Gable, Marilyn Monroe, Montgomery Clift, Thelma Ritter, Eli Wallach, James Barton, Estelle Winwood; ***D:*** John Huston; ***W:*** Arthur Miller; ***C:*** Russell Metty; ***M:*** Alex North.

Misfits of Science 🦴 **1985** Pilot for a failed TV series about a group of teens with special powers who fight to save the world. **96m/C VHS.** Dean Paul (Dino Martin Jr.) Martin, Kevin Peter Hall, Mark Thomas Miller, Kenneth Mars, Courteney Cox Arquette; ***D:*** Philip DeGuere. **TV**

Mishima: A Life in Four Chapters 🦴🦴🦴 **1985 (R)** Somewhat detached account and indulgent portrayal of the narcissistic Japanese author (and actor, filmmaker, and militarist) alternates between stylized interpretations of his books and a straightforward account of his life. Culminates in a pseudo-military operation that, in turn, resulted in Mishima's ritualistic suicide. A U.S./Japanese production. Innovative design by Eiko Ishioka. In Japanese with English subtitles. **121m/C VHS, DVD, Wide.** Ken Ogata, Kenji Sawada, Yasosuke Bando; ***D:*** Paul Schrader; ***W:*** Leonard Schrader, Paul Schrader; ***C:*** John Bailey; ***M:*** Philip Glass; ***Nar:*** Roy Scheider.

Miss A & Miss M **1986** A young girl is shocked when she realizes that two teachers she has befriended also live together. **60m/C VHS.** Kika Markham, Jennifer Hilary.

Miss All-American Beauty 🦴½ **1982** A behind-the-scenes look at a small-time Texas beauty pageant. Lane stars as a contestant who comes to realize her self-respect is more important than winning an award. Meadows's mean pageant director adds an ironic edge that the movie as a whole lacks. **96m/C VHS.** Diane Lane, Cloris Leachman, David Dukes, Jayne Meadows, Alice Hirson, Brian Kerwin; ***D:*** Gus Trikonis. **TV**

Miss Annie Rooney 🦴🦴 **1942 (G)** Intended to bill the child star in a more mature role, Temple receives her first screen kiss in this story about a poor Irish girl who falls in love with a wealthy young man. The well-worn plot is weighed down by lifeless dialogue. **86m/B VHS.** Shirley Temple, Dickie Moore, William Gargan, Guy Kibbee, Peggy Ryan, June Lockhart; ***D:*** Edwin L. Marin.

Ms. Bear 🦴🦴½ **1997 (G)** Logging operations in a Canadian forest have disturbed the local bear population and down-on-his-luck Barney decides to make some money by tranquilizing the animals and selling them to a zoo importer. A cub escapes and wanders into the yard of lonely, seven-year-old Emily, who befriends the cute critter. Then, with Emily's help, Barney learns the importer is actually killing the bears and only selling their paws to the overseas market. So a rescue is in order. **95m/C VHS.** Ed Begley Jr., Kaitlyn Burke, Shawn Johnston; ***D:*** Paul Ziller.

Miss Congeniality 🦴🦴 **2000 (PG-13)** Tough FBI agent Gracie Hart (Bullock) must go undercover at the Miss USA Pageant after the event is threatened by terrorists. Eric (Bratt) is a helpful fellow agent (and potential beau) while down-on-his-luck consultant Victor Melling (Caine) is hired to girly-up Gracie and make her pageant material. Predictable comedy shows flashes of witty satire but lives up to its name by easing up on intended targets at the moment of truth. Bullock, as always, is game and both Bergen as a former beauty queen turned pageant manager and Shatner as unctuous pageant host add a spark to the proceedings. **111m/C VHS, DVD, Wide.** Sandra Bullock, Benjamin Bratt, Michael Caine, William Shatner, Ernie Hudson, Candice Bergen, Heather Burns, Melissa De Sousa, Steve Monroe, John DiResta, Jennifer Gareis, Wendy Raquel Robinson; ***D:*** Donald Petrie; ***W:*** Donald Petrie, Marc Lawrence; ***C:*** Laszlo Kovacs; ***M:*** Ed Shearmur.

Miss Evers' Boys 🦴🦴½ **1997 (PG)** Wrenching docudrama covers a 40-year U.S. Public Health Service study in which black men suffering from syphillis were monitored but not treated for the disease. Eunice Evers (Woodard) is a nurse at Alabama's Tuskegee Hospital in 1932, assisting Dr. Brodus (Morton) in the care of the afflicted men. White Dr. Douglas (Sheffer) first has a funded government program for treatment but when the program is cut, he's offered funding only for the study of syphilitic black men and establishing whether the disease affects blacks and whites differently. Brodus and Evers both lie to their patients as each comes to realize that treatment will never be re-established and only the deaths of their patients will provide the final information for the study. Based on the play by David Feldshuh. **120m/C VHS.** Alfre Woodard, Laurence "Larry" Fishburne, Joe Morton, Craig Sheffer, Obba Babatunde, Ossie Davis, E.G. Marshall; ***D:*** Joseph Sargent; ***W:*** Walter Bernstein; ***C:*** Donald M. Morgan; ***M:*** Charles Bernstein. **CABLE**

Miss Firecracker 🦴🦴🦴 **1989 (PG)** Hunter, longing for love and self-respect, decides to change her promiscuous image by entering the local beauty pageant in her conservative southern hometown. The somewhat drippy premise is transformed by a super script and cast into an engaging and upbeat film. Henley's script was adapted from her own Off-Broadway play where Hunter created the role. Actress Lahti, wife of director Schlamme, makes a brief appearance. **102m/C VHS.** Holly Hunter, Scott Glenn, Mary Steenburgen, Tim Robbins, Alfre Woodard, Trey Wilson, Bert Remsen, Ann Wedgeworth, Christine Lahti, Amy Wright; ***D:*** Thomas Schlamme; ***W:*** Beth Henley; ***C:*** Arthur Albert; ***M:*** David Mansfield.

Ms. 45 🦴🦴🦴 *Angel of Vengeance* **1981 (R)** Rough, bristling cult favorite about a mute girl who, in response to being raped and beaten twice in one night, goes on a man-killing murder spree. Wild ending. **84m/C VHS, DVD, Wide.** Abel Ferrara, Zoe Tamerlis, Steve Singer, Jack Thibeau, Peter Yellen, Darlene Stuto, Editta Sherman, Albert Sinkys; ***D:*** Abel Ferrara; ***W:*** Nicholas St. John; ***C:*** James (Momel) Lemmo; ***M:*** Joe Delia.

Miss Grant Takes Richmond 🦴🦴 *Innocence is Bliss* **1949** Zipperhead secretary finds herself in hot water a la Lucy when she finds out the company she's been working for is really the front for a gambling getup. Only Lucy fans need apply. **87m/B VHS.** Lucille Ball, William Holden, Janis Carter, James Gleason, Gloria Henry, Frank McHugh, George Cleveland, Arthur Space, William Wright, Jimmy Lloyd; ***D:*** Lloyd Bacon.

Miss Julie 🦴🦴 *Froken Julie* **1950** Melodramatic stew adapted from from the August Strindberg play about a confused noblewoman who disgraces herself when she allows a servant to seduce her. In Swedish with English subtitles. **90m/B VHS.** *SW* Anita Bjork, Ulf Palme, Anders Henrikson, Max von Sydow; ***D:*** Alf Sjoberg; ***W:*** Alf Sjoberg; ***C:*** Goran Strindberg; ***M:*** Dag Wiren. Cannes '51: Film.

Miss Julie 🦴🦴 **1999 (R)** Dry adaptation of August Strindberg's 1889 banned-in-Sweden play about the turbulent relationship between an imperious young noblewoman and an ambitious servant. Neurotic Miss Julie (Burrows), restless and bored, strides into the servants' kitchen and begin ordering about her father's footman, Jean (Mullan). Their upstairs/downstairs division deteriorates into a series of psycho/sexual clashes over an evening where mutual loathing, humiliation, and self-destruction are the only means of communication. **101m/C VHS, DVD.** *GB* Saffron Burrows, Peter Mullan, Maria Doyle Kennedy; ***D:*** Mike Figgis; ***W:*** Helen Cooper; ***C:*** Benoit Delhomme; ***M:*** Mike Figgis.

Miss Mary 🦴🦴½ **1986 (R)** A compassionate English governess in Buenos Aires conflicts with the honor-obsessed family she works for and Argentina's tumultuous history. Christie gives a wonderful performance. **100m/C VHS.** *AR* Julie Christie, Donald McIntire, Sofia Viruboff, Luisina Brando; ***D:*** Maria-Luisa Bemberg; ***W:*** Jorge Goldenberg, Maria-Luisa Bemberg.

Miss Melody Jones 🦴 **1973** A beautiful young black woman's dreams of stardom unravel as she is forced to pander to prurient men by disrobing publicly for financial recompense. **86m/C VHS.** Philomena Nowlin, Ronald Warren, Jacqueline Dalya, Peter Jacob; ***D:*** Bill Brame; ***W:*** Bill Brame.

Miss Right 🦴 **1981 (R)** A young man determines to find the ideal woman for himself and casts aside his other romantic interests. Sputtering lightweight comedy. **98m/C VHS.** William Tepper, Karen Black, Virna Lisi, Margot Kidder, Marie-France Pisier; ***D:*** Paul Williams.

Miss Rose White 🦴🦴🦴 **1992 (PG)** Sedgwick is Rose, a modern young career woman in post-WWII New York, as American as apple pie, who lives two very separate lives. Born Rayzel Weiss, a Polish Jew, she immigrated to the U.S. with her father as a very young girl, before the holocaust devastated her remaining family in Poland. After the war her older sister, thought dead, comes to America. The haunted Luisa causes Rose to question whether she can ever leave her past behind. Above average Hallmark Hall of Fame presentation has a good cast, particularly Plummer as Luisa. Based on the play "A Shayna Maidel" by Barbara Lebow. **95m/C VHS.** Kyra Sedgwick, Amanda Plummer, Maximilian Schell, D.B. Sweeney, Penny Fuller, Milton Selzer, Maureen Stapleton; ***D:*** Joseph Sargent; ***W:*** Anna Sandor. **TV**

Miss Sadie Thompson 🦴🦴🦴 **1953** Based on the novel "Rain" by W. Somerset Maugham. Promiscuous tart Hayworth arrives on a Pacific island occupied by a unit of Marines and a sanctimonious preacher played by Ferrer While Hayworth parties with the Marines and becomes involved with Ray's Sgt. O'Hara, Ferrer moralizes and insists she return to the mainland to face moral charges. Quasi-musical with a scattering of dubbed songs by Hayworth includes a memorable erotic dance scene complete with tight dress and dripping sweat. Hayworth's strong performance carries the picture with Ferrer and Ray turning in cardboard versions of their Maugham characters. Originally filmed in 3-D. **91m/C VHS.** Rita Hayworth, Jose Ferrer, Aldo Ray, Charles Bronson; ***D:*** Curtis Bernhardt.

Missile to the Moon 🦴½ **1959** First expedition to the moon encounters not acres of dead rock but a race of gorgeous women in lingerie and high heels. A bad but entertaining remake of "Cat Women of the Moon," featuring a bevy of beauty contest winners from New Hampshire to Yugoslavia. Who says truth is stranger than fiction. **78m/B VHS, DVD.** Gary Clarke, Cathy Downs, K.T. Stevens, Laurie Mitchell, Michael Whalen, Nina Bara, Richard Travis, Tommy Cook, Marjorie Hellen; ***D:*** Richard Cunha; ***W:*** Vincent Fotre, H.E. Barrie; ***C:*** Meredith Nicholson; ***M:*** Nicholas Carras.

Missiles of October 🦴🦴🦴 **1974** Telling the story of the October 1962 Cuban Missile crisis, this TV drama keeps you on the edge of your seat while unfolding the sequence of events within the U.S. government. Well written, with a strong cast including Devane, who turns in a convincing performance as—guess who—J.F.K. **155m/C VHS.** William Devane, Ralph Bellamy, Martin Sheen, Howard da Silva; ***D:*** Anthony Page. **TV**

Missing 🦴🦴🦴½ **1982 (PG)** At the height of a military coup in Chile (never named in the movie), a young American writer (Shea) disappears. His right-wing father Lemmon tries to get to the bottom of his disappearance while bickering with Shea's wife, played by Spacek, a bohemian who is the political opposite of her father-in-law. Outstanding performances by Spacek and Lemmon along with excellent writing and direction result in a gripping and thought-provoking thriller. Based on the book by Thomas Hauser from the true story of Charles Horman. **122m/C VHS.** Jack Lemmon, Sissy Spacek, John Shea, Melanie Mayron, David Clennon, Charles Cioffi, Joe Regalbuto, Richard Venture, Janice Rule; ***D:*** Constantin Costa-Gavras; ***W:*** Constantin Costa-Gavras, Donald Stewart; ***M:*** Vangelis. Oscars '82: Adapt. Screenplay; British Acad. '82: Screenplay; Cannes '82: Actor (Lemmon), Film; Writers Guild '82: Adapt. Screenplay.

The Missing Corpse 🦴🦴 **1945** When a newspaper publisher's worst rival is murdered, he fears that he will be implicated. He decides the only thing to do is hide the body to prevent its being discovered. Enjoyable, light comedy/mystery. **62m/B VHS.** J. Edward Bromberg, Eric Sinclair, Frank Jenks, Isabelle Randolph, Paul Guilfoyle, John Shay, Lorell Sheldon; ***D:*** Al(bert) Herman.

Missing in Action 🦴½ **1984 (R)** An army colonel returns to the Vietnam jungle to settle some old scores and rescue some POWs while on an MIA fact-finding mission. Box office smash. **101m/C VHS, DVD, Wide.** Chuck Norris, M. Emmet Walsh; ***D:*** Joseph Zito; ***W:*** James Bruner; ***C:*** Joao Fernandes; ***M:*** Jay Chattaway.

Missing in Action 2: The Beginning 🦴 **1985 (R)** Set in Vietnam, this prequel to the original "Missing in Action" provides some interesting background on Norris's rocky relationship with communism. Packed with violence, bloodshed and torture. **96m/C VHS.** Chuck Norris, Soon-Teck Oh, Cosie Costa, Steven Williams; ***D:*** Lance Hool; ***W:*** Steve Bing.

Missing Link 🦴🦴½ **1988 (PG)** A strange, meditative quasi-documentary depicting the singular adventures of a humanoid silently transversing the African wilderness and confronting various natural phenomena. Beautifully photographed. Make-up by Rick Baker. **92m/C VHS.** Peter Elliott, Michael Gambon; ***D:*** David Hughes.

Missing Pieces 🦴🦴½ **1983** A woman takes a job as a private investigator in order to find her journalist husband's killer. Effective mystery taken from the novel "A Private Investigation" by Karl Alexander. **96m/C VHS.** Elizabeth Montgomery, Louanne, John C. Reilly, Ron Karabatsos, Robin Gammell, Julius W. Harris; ***D:*** Mike Hodges. **TV**

Missing Pieces 🦴🦴½ **1991 (PG)** Goof-ups Wuhl and Idle find out about a potential inheritance thanks to a fortune cookie. Now if they can jut figure out what the riddle means. **93m/C VHS.** Eric Idle, Robert Wuhl, Lauren Hutton; ***D:*** Leonard Stern; ***W:*** Leonard Stern.

Missing Pieces 🦴🦴 **2000** Rancher Atticus Cody (Coburn) leaves his home in Colorado to investigate his estranged artist son Scott's (Kersey) supposed suicide in a remote part of Mexico. And what he finds are more questions and lots of lies. Unfortunately lame script filled with cliches. Based on the Ron Hansen novel "Atticus." **90m/C VHS.** James Coburn, Lisa Zane, Paul Kersey, Finn Carter, William R. Moses, Julio Mechoso, Maxwell Caulfield; ***D:*** Carl Schenkel; ***W:*** Philip Rosenberg, Richard Kletter, D.W. Owen, Peachy Markowitz; ***C:*** Karl Herrmann; ***M:*** Lawrence Shragge. **TV**

The Mission 🦴🦴🦴 **1986 (PG)** Sweeping, cinematically beautiful historical drama about an 18th-century Jesuit mission in the Brazilian jungle. The missionaries struggle against the legalized slave trade of Portugal and political factions within the church. Written by Bolt (of "A Man for All Seasons" fame), its visual intensity is marred by length and so much overt symbolism that an emotional coolness surfaces when the action slows. Nonetheless, epic in ambition and nearly in quality. Magnificent musical score. **125m/C VHS, 8mm, Wide.** Robert De Niro, Jeremy Irons, Ray McAnally, Aidan Quinn, Liam Neeson, Cherie Lunghi, Rev. Daniel Berrigan, Ronald Pickup; ***D:*** Roland Joffe; ***W:*** Robert Bolt; ***C:*** Chris Menges; ***M:*** Ennio Morricone. Oscars '86: Cinematog.; British Acad. '86: Support. Actor (McAnally); Cannes '86: Film; Golden Globes '87: Screenplay, Score; L.A. Film Critics '86: Cinematog.

The Mission 🦴🦴½ *Cheung Fo* **1999** A Hong Kong mobster hires five gunmen to be his bodyguards. Everything's cool until one of them has an affair with the boss's wife. Director To revisits Tarantino-Woo territory. Most of the guys have bad haircuts and all of them have big pistols. **84m/C DVD, Wide.** *HK* Anthony Wong, Frances Ng, Roy Cheung, Simon Yam, Jackie Lui, Lam Suet; ***D:*** Johnny To; ***W:*** Nai-Hoi Yau.

Mission Batangas 🦴½ **1969** Unremarkable adventure-war-heist movie tells the story of a shallow American WWII pilot (Weaver) and a missionary nurse (Miles), who team up to steal the Philippine government's entire stock of gold bullion from the Japanese who captured it. Beautiful scenery, shot in the Philippines, adds something to an otherwise vacant effort. **100m/C VHS.** Dennis Weaver, Vera Miles, Keith Larsen; ***D:*** Keith Larsen.

Mission Galactica: The Cylon Attack 🦴🦴 **1979** Spaceship Battlestar Galactica is stranded in space without fuel and open to attack from the chrome-plated Cylons. Adama (Greene) is forced to stop Commander Cain's (Bridges) efforts to launch an attack against the Cylons, while countering the attacks of the Cylon leader. Warmed over TV sci-fi. **108m/C VHS.** Lorne Greene, Lloyd Bridges, Richard Hatch, Dirk Benedict. **TV**

Mission: Impossible 🦴🦴🦴 **1996 (PG-13)** Cruise and director DePalma did not completely succeed or fail in their mission to create a blockbuster hit based on the popular '60s TV series. Cruise (one of the film's producers) is Ethan Hunt, pointman extraordinaire of the IMF team headed by Jim Phelps (Jon Voight). Their team is sent to recover a computer disk with devastating information from a mercenary Russian spy. Smelling a double cross, Hunt confronts his conniving agency boss Kitteridge (the perfectly cast Czerny) and creates his own team of crack agents to get to the truth, mind-boggling plot twists and crazy train rides be damned. The plotline may have self-destructed two-thirds into the movie and the absence of a truly sinister villain causes some damage, but with solid acting talent, tight pacing, alluring European locales, and tension-inducing special effects, who has time to notice? $100 million gross in the first two weeks would seem to indicate a sequel is in order. **110m/C VHS, DVD.** Tom Cruise, Jon Voight, Emmanuelle Beart, Ving Rhames, Henry Czerny, Emilio Estevez, Vanessa Redgrave, Jean Reno, Dale Dye; ***D:*** Brian DePalma; ***W:*** Robert Towne, David Koepp; ***C:*** Stephen Burum; ***M:*** Danny Elfman.

Mission: Impossible 2 🦴🦴🦴 *M:I 2* **2000 (PG-13)** In this visually stunning sequel to the 1996 film, Ethan Hunt tracks a rogue IMF agent Ambrose (Scott), who threatens to release deadly virus on Sydney, Australia and corner the market on the cure. Ambrose's ex-girlfriend Nyah (Newton), a jewel theif, is recruited by Hunt to spy on Ambrose from inside. Of course Nyah and Hunt fall in love (the weakest element of the movie, by the way). Director Woo brings his trademark balletic style to the action, although it seems to take a while to actually get to it. The stunts and fights, while completely preposterous, are beautifully done. The plot is a lot less convoluted than the first 'Mission,' which is either good or bad, depending on how you feel about the original. **125m/C VHS, DVD, Wide.** Tom Cruise, Anthony Hopkins, Dougray Scott, Thandie Newton, Ving Rhames, Brendan Gleeson, John Polson, Richard Roxburgh, Rade Serbedzija; ***D:*** John Woo; ***W:*** Robert Towne; ***C:*** Jeffrey L. Kimball; ***M:*** Hans Zimmer.

Mission in Morocco 🦴 **1959** When an oilman scouting for oil fields in the Sahara is killed, his partner, Barker, hops a jet to Morocco to find the whereabouts of a microfilm that gives the location of a valuable oil deposit. The search for the secret microfilm is complicated by competing parties also interested in the black gold. Ho-hum action adventure. **79m/C VHS.** Lex Barker, Juli Reding.

Mission Kashmir 🦴🦴 **2000 (R)** Altaff (Roshan) is a young Kashmiri whose family is killed by state police hunting a rebel leader. He's adopted by Inayat Khan (Dutt), whom Altaff eventually learns was the man who lead the raid. Fleeing, Altaff seeks the tutleage of Hila Kohistani (Shroff), a militant whose only aim is the independence of Kashmir and Altaff is his weapon. But when Altaff returns to Kashmir, he unexpectedly meets his childhood girlfriend, Sufi (Zinta), and is torn between love and revenge. Hindi with subtitles or English dubbed. **157m/C VHS, DVD, Wide.** *IN* Hrithik Roshan, Sanjay Dutt, Jackie Shroff, Preity Zinta, Sonali Kulkarni; ***D:*** Vidhu Vinod Chopra; ***W:*** Vidhu Vinod Chopra, Vikram Chandra; ***C:*** Vinod Pradhan.

Mission Manila 🦴 **1987 (R)** An ex-CIA operative and Manila-based drug addict is called by his ex-lover to return to Manila to help his brother, who has gotten in much the same trouble he had. **98m/C VHS, DVD.** Larry Wilcox, Tetchie Agbayani, Sam Hennings, Al Mancini, James Wainwright, Robin Eisenman; ***D:*** Peter M. MacKenzie; ***W:*** Peter M. MacKenzie; ***C:*** Les Parrott; ***M:*** Nicholas Pike.

Mission Mars 🦴 **1967** American astronauts McGavin and Adams, on a mission to the red planet, discover the bodies of two cosmonauts floating in space. After landing on the planet's surface, they find a third cosmonaut, this one in a state of suspended animation. While putting the viewer to sleep, they proceed to revive the third cosmonaut and have at it with the sinister alien force responsible for all the trouble. **87m/C VHS.** Darren McGavin, Nick Adams, George DeVries; ***D:*** Nicholas Webster.

Mission of Justice 🦴🦴 **1992 (R)** Revel in non-stop martial arts action with this tale of a cop who goes undercover to get the goods on a corrupt female politico, who also happens to run her own ruthless private army. **?m/C VHS.** Jeff Wincott, Brigitte Nielsen, Matthias Hues, Luca Bercovici, Cyndi Pass, Billy "Sly" Williams, Tony Burton; ***D:*** Steve Barnett; ***W:*** John Bryant.

Mission of the Shark 🦴🦴🦴 **1991** A top secret naval mission leads to a scandal-ridden court martial in this true WWII saga, based on the worst sea disaster in naval history. The USS Indianapolis has just completed a secret mission when it is torpedoed by enemy subs. The survivors spend five days in shark-infested waters awaiting rescue and, when the Navy points fingers, the ship's highly decorated and well-respected Captain McVay accepts responsibility for the good of the service. Contains some harrowing scenes of sailors versus sharks. **92m/C VHS.** Stacy Keach, Richard Thomas, Steve Landesberg, Carrie Snodgress, Bob Gunton, Andrew Prine, Stacy Keach Sr., Don Harvey; ***D:*** Robert Iscove. **TV**

Mission Phantom 🦴 **1979** A group of spies on a mission in Russia plans to steal some diamonds and help a woman get to the United States. **90m/C VHS.** Andrew Ray, Ingrid Sholder, Peter Martell; ***D:*** James Reed.

Mission Stardust 🦴½ *4...3...2...1...Morte* **1968** An internationally produced but thoroughly unambitious adaptation of the once-popular Perry Rhodan sci-fi serial, in which Rhodan and his team bring ill aliens back to Earth and defend them against evil spies. Dubbed. **90m/C VHS.** *GE IT SP* Essy Persson, Gianni Rizzo, Lang Jeffries, Pinkas Braun; ***D:*** Primo Zeglio.

Mission to Death 🦴🦴 **1966** Small American patrol during WWII is beset by numerous attacks on their way to their final destination and each time more members of the unit are wounded or killed. **71m/C VHS, DVD.** Jim Brewer, James E. McLarty, Jim Westerbrook, Robert Stolper, Dudley Hafner, Jerry Lasater; ***D:*** Kenneth W. Richardson; ***C:*** Ronald Perryman; ***M:*** Emil Cadkin, William Loose.

Mission to Glory 🦴🦴 *The Father Kino Story* **1980 (PG)** This dozer tells the story of Father Francisco "Kino" Kin, a tough, 17th-century priest in California who took on the Apaches and murderous Conquistadors in defense of his people. **100m/C VHS.** Richard Egan, John Ireland, Cesar Romero, Ricardo Montalban, Rory Calhoun, Michael Ansara, Keenan Wynn, Aldo Ray; ***D:*** Ken Kennedy.

Mission to Kill 🦴½ **1985 (R)** An American demolitions expert, Ginty, joins a Latin American guerrilla force in battling tyrannical junta forces. This action-packed, fast-paced thriller is big on revenge and violence but not much else. **97m/C VHS.** Robert Ginty, Olivia D'Abo, Cameron Mitchell; ***D:*** David Winters.

Mission to Mars 🦴½ **2000 (PG)** When the first manned flight to Mars ends in disaster, leaving Commander Luke Graham (Cheadle) as the only survivor, NASA sends a rescue mission consisting of Graham's best friend Jim (Sinise), married astronauts Woody (Robbins) and Terri (Nielsen), and generic tech guy Phil (O'Connell). On the way to Mars they encounter problems you've seen in other, better-done sci-fi flicks. Once on Mars, they find the New Age-y, touchy-feely secrets of creation. DePalma is known for his visual wizardry, and on that element he doesn't disappoint, but the horrible script and indifferent performances undermine whatever it was he was trying to accomplish. **112m/C VHS, DVD, Wide.** Tim Robbins, Gary Sinise, Don Cheadle, Connie Nielsen, Jerry O'Connell, Kim Delaney, Elise Neal, Peter Outerbridge, Jill Teed, Kavan Smith; ***D:*** Brian DePalma; ***W:*** Jim Thomas, John Thomas, Graham Yost; ***C:*** Stephen Burum; ***M:*** Ennio Morricone.

Mission to Venice 🦴🦴 **1963** Flynn plays a sleuth attempting to find a missing husband when he accidentally stumbles upon a ring of spies. **?m/C VHS.** Sean Flynn, Madeleine Robinson.

The Missionary 🦴🦴½ **1982 (R)** A mild-mannered English missionary returns to London from his work in Africa and is recruited into saving the souls of a group of prostitutes. Aspiring to gentle comedy status, it's often formulaic and flat, with Palin and Smith fighting gamely to stay above script level. Still, good for some laughs, particularly during the near classic walking butler sequence. **86m/C VHS.** *GB* Michael Palin, Maggie Smith, Trevor Howard, Denholm Elliott, Michael Hordern; ***D:*** Richard Loncraine; ***W:*** Michael Palin.

Mississippi Burning 🦴🦴🦴 **1988 (R)** Hard-edged social drama centers around the civil rights movement in Mississippi in 1964. When three activists turn up missing, FBI agents Anderson (Hackman) and Ward (Dafoe) are sent to head up the investigation. Unfortunately, this is another example of a "serious" film about racial conflict in which white characters predominate and blacks provide background. **127m/C VHS, DVD, Wide.** Gene Hackman, Willem Dafoe, Frances McDormand, Brad Dourif, R. Lee Ermey, Gailard Sartain, Stephen Tobolowsky, Michael Rooker, Pruitt Taylor Vince, Badja (Medu) Djola, Kevin Dunn, Frankie Faison, Tom Mason, Park Overall; ***D:*** Alan Parker; ***W:*** Chris Gerolmo; ***C:*** Peter Biziou; ***M:*** Trevor Jones. Oscars '88: Cinematog.; Berlin Intl. Film Fest. '88: Actor (Hackman); Natl. Bd. of Review '88: Actor (Hackman), Director (Parker), Support. Actress (McDormand).

Mississippi Masala 🦴🦴🦴 **1992 (R)** "Masala" is an Indian seasoning blending different-colored spices, as this film is a blend of romance, comedy, and social conscience. An interracial romance sets off a cultural collision and escalates racial tensions in a small Southern town when Mina, a sheltered young Indian woman, falls in love with Demetrius, an ambitious black man with his own carpet-cleaning business. Washington and Choudhury are engaging as the lovers with Seth, as Mina's unhappy father, especially watchable. **118m/C VHS.** Denzel Washington, Sarita Choudhury, Roshan Seth, Sharmila Tagore, Charles S. Dutton, Joe Seneca, Ranjit (Chaudry) Chowdhry; ***Cameos:*** Mira Nair; ***D:*** Mira Nair; ***W:*** Sooni Taraporevala; ***M:*** L. Subramaniam.

Mississippi Mermaid 🦴🦴🦴 *Le Sirene du Mississippi* **1969 (PG)** Truffaut generally succeeds in merging his own directorial style with Hitchcockian suspense, but the U.S. release was cut by some 13 minutes and the restored version deserves a re-appraisal. Millionaire tobacco planter Louis (Belmondo) looks for a bride in the personals and finds Julie (Deneuve). Louis feels lucky landing this beauty until she leaves him and takes his money with her. After a breakdown, he finds his wife working in a dance-hall under another name. Louis agrees to a reconciliation, which proves to be a mistake. Look for numerous references to the movies, including Bogart, Balzac and Cocteau. Based on the Cornell Woolrich novel "Waltz into Darkness." French with subtitles. **110m/C VHS, DVD, Wide.** *FR IT* Jean-Paul Belmondo, Catherine Deneuve, Michel Bouquet, Nelly Borgeaud, Marcel Berbert, Martine Ferriere; ***D:*** Francois Truffaut; ***W:*** Francois Truffaut; ***C:*** Denys Clerval; ***M:*** Antoine Duhamel.

Missouri Breaks 🦴🦴 **1976 (PG)** Thomas McGuane wrote the screenplay for this offbeat tale of Montana ranchers and rustlers fighting over land and livestock in the 1880s. Promising combination of script, cast and director unfortunately yields rather disappointing results, though both Brando and Nicholson chew up scenery to their hearts' content. **126m/C VHS.** Jack Nicholson, Marlon Brando, Randy Quaid, Kathleen Lloyd, Frederic Forrest, Harry Dean Stanton; ***D:*** Arthur Penn; ***W:*** Thomas McGuane; ***M:*** John Williams.

Missouri Traveler 🦴🦴🦴 **1958** An orphan boy struggles to get his own farm in Missouri. Family fare based on John Buress' novel. **103m/C VHS.** Lee Marvin, Gary Merrill, Brandon de Wilde, Paul Ford.

Missourians 🦴🦴½ **1950** Small-town sheriff Hale helps a Polish rancher overcome ethnic prejudice among the townspeople. The situation worsens with the arrival in town of the rancher's outlaw brother. Strong direction and engaging storyline. **60m/B VHS.** Monte Hale, Paul Hurst.

Mrs. 'Arris Goes to Paris 🦴🦴½ **1992** Ada Harris (Lansbury) is a widowed charwoman, living in '50s London, whose one dream is to visit Paris and buy a Christian Dior gown at the designer's own salon. Naturally, her dream comes true—and she even finds a little romance too. Adapted from the Paul Gallico novel; made for TV. **90m/C VHS.** Angela Lansbury, Omar Sharif, Diana Rigg, Lothaire Bluteau, Lila Kaye, John Savident. **TV**

Mrs. Brown 🦴🦴🦴 *Her Majesty Mrs. Brown* **1997 (PG)** Unusual drama finds Queen Victoria (Dench), bereft by the death of Prince Albert, withdrawing from public life to her Scottish retreat at Balmoral. There she's looked after by coarse highlander John Brown (Connolly), who encourages her to take an interest in life. As he rises in the Queen's esteem, the brash commoner begins to become overly protective of her; leading to whispers of an affair. The powers-that-be, including the Prince of Wales (Westhead) and the oily Prime Minister Disraeli (Sher), then must persuade Brown to withdraw from her company in order to preserve her reputation. Merely hints at what may or may not have been a sexual relationship between the two, but isn't that the Victorian way? **103m/C VHS, DVD.** *GB* Judi Dench, Billy Connolly, Geoffrey Palmer, Anthony Sher, Richard Pasco, Gerard Butler, David Westhead; ***D:*** John Madden; ***W:*** Jeremy Brock; ***C:*** Richard Greatrex; ***M:*** Stephen Warbeck. British Acad. '97: Actress (Dench), Costume Des.; Golden Globes '98: Actress—Drama (Dench).

Mrs. Brown, You've Got a Lovely Daughter 🦴½ **1968 (G)** The Herman's Hermits gang inherits a greyhound and attempts to make a racer out of him while singing their songs. For the Brit group's diehard fans only. ♫It's Nice To Be Out in the Morning; Ooh, She's Done It Again; Lemon and Lime; The World is for the Young; Holiday Inn; The Most Beautiful Thing in My Life; Daisy Chain; Mrs. Brown, You've Got a Lovely Daughter; There's a King of Hush. **95m/C VHS.** Peter Noone, Stanley Holloway, Mona Washbourne; ***D:*** Saul Swimmer.

Mrs. Dalloway 🦴🦴½ **1997 (PG-13)** Mannered retelling of the Virginia Woolf novel has a radiant performance by Redgrave in the title role. Wealthy, middle-aged, and long-married to boring politician Richard (Standing), Clarissa Dalloway is making preparations for her latest soiree in 1923 London. But the past rudely intrudes when old flame Peter Walsh (Kitchen) suddenly re-enters, causing Clarissa to reflect on her youth and the choices she's made. She's also shaken out of her social ennui by the unexpected sight of a shell-shocked WWI veteran (Graves) whose tragic plight disturbs her placid life. Director Gorris' English-language debut. **97m/C VHS, DVD, Wide.** *GB* Vanessa Redgrave, Michael Kitchen, John Standing, Rupert Graves, Natascha (Natasha) McElhone, Alan Cox, Sarah Badel, Lena Headey, Robert Portal, Amelia Bullmore, Margaret Tyzack, Robert Hardy; ***D:*** Marleen Gorris; ***W:*** Eileen Atkins; ***C:*** Sue Gibson; ***M:*** Ilona Sekacz.

Mrs. Doubtfire 🦴🦴½ **1993 (PG-13)** Williams is an unemployed voiceover actor going through a messy divorce. When his wife gets custody, the distraught father decides to dress up as a woman and become a nanny to his own children. He also has to deal with the old flame who re-enters his ex-wife's life. Williams schtick extraordinaire with more than a little sugary sentimentality. Based on the British children's book "Madame Doubtfire" by Anne Fine. **120m/C VHS, DVD.** Paul Guilfoyle, Robin Williams, Sally Field, Pierce Brosnan, Harvey Fierstein, Robert Prosky, Mara Wilson; ***D:*** Chris Columbus; ***W:*** Leslie Dixon, Randi Mayem Singer; ***C:*** Donald McAlpine; ***M:*** Howard Shore. Oscars '93: Makeup; Golden Globes '94: Actor—Mus./Comedy (Williams), Film—Mus./Comedy; MTV Movie Awards '94: Comedic Perf. (Williams).

Mrs. Mike 🦴🦴½ **1949** Boston-bred Kathy O'Fallon (Keyes) falls in love with Canadian Mountie Mike Flannigan (Powell) and then finds it hard to adjust to a rural life in Northwest woods. Based on the novel by Benedict and Nancy Freedman. **98m/B VHS.** Evelyn Keyes, Dick Powell, J.M. Kerrigan, Angela Clarke, John Miljan; ***D:*** Louis King; ***W:*** Alfred Lewis Levitt, DeWitt Bodeen; ***C:*** Joseph Biroc.

Mrs. Miniver 🦴🦴🦴🦴 **1942** A moving tale of a courageous, gentle middle-class British family and its struggle to survive during WWII. A classic that garnered six Academy Awards, it's recognized for contributions to the Allied effort. Contains one of the most powerful orations in the film history, delivered by Wilcoxon, who portrayed the vicar. Followed by "The Miniver Story." Adapted from Jan Struther's book. **134m/B VHS.** Greer Garson, Walter Pidgeon, Teresa Wright, May Whitty, Richard Ney, Henry Travers, Reginald Owen, Henry Wilcoxon, Helmut Dantine, Aubrey Mather, Rhys Williams, Tom Conway, Peter Lawford, Christopher Severn, Clare Sandars, Marie De Becker, Connie Leon, Brenda Forbes, John Abbott, Billy Bevan, John Burton, Mary Field, Forrester Harvey, Arthur Wimperis, Ian Wolfe; ***D:*** William Wyler; ***W:*** George Froeschel, James Hilton, Claudine West, Arthur Wimperis; ***C:*** Joseph Ruttenberg; ***M:*** Herbert Stothart. Oscars '42: Actress (Garson), B&W Cinematog., Director (Wyler), Picture, Screenplay, Support. Actress (Wright).

Mrs. Munck 🦴🦴 **1995 (R)** Creepy cable thriller finds widowed Rose Munck (Ladd) agreeing to care for bitter father-in-law Patrick Leary (Dern, Ladd's real-life ex-hubby), who's suffered a debilitating stroke. But they share a nasty past—seems he seduced a teenaged Rose (played by Preston), she had a child, Patrick refused any responsibilty, and the child died. So whacked-out Rose is really out for revenge. Based on a novel by Ella Leffland. Ladd's debut as writer/director. **99m/C VHS.** Diane Ladd, Bruce Dern, Kelly Preston, Shelley Winters; ***D:*** Diane Ladd; ***W:*** Diane Ladd; ***C:*** James Glennon; ***M:*** Leonard Rosenman. **CABLE**

Mrs. Parker and the Vicious Circle 🦴🦴½ *Mrs. Parker and the Round Table* **1994 (R)** Bio of witty, suicidal writer Dorothy Parker and her equally witty friends, including theatre critics, playwrights, and novelists, who lunched together at New York's Algonquin Hotel for most of the 1920s. An irreverant band known as the Algonquin Round Table, their numerous bon mots were regularly reported in the papers. Their private lives were often less than happy with alcohol, drug addiction and depression prominent factors. Parker's downward spiral is depressing though compelling to watch, thanks to Leigh's performance (in spite of much criticism for her lockjawed accent) but many of the characters come and go so quickly they make little impression. **124m/C VHS.** Mina (Badiyi) Badie, Jennifer Jason Leigh, Matthew Broderick, Andrew McCarthy, Campbell Scott, Jennifer Beals, Tom McGowan, Nick Cassavetes, Sam Robards, Rebecca Miller, Wallace Shawn, Martha Plimpton, Gwyneth Paltrow, Peter Gallagher, Lili Taylor; ***D:*** Alan Rudolph; ***W:*** Rudolph Coburn, Randy Sue Coburn; ***C:*** Jan Kiesser; ***M:*** Mark Isham. Natl. Soc. Film Critics '94: Actress (Leigh).

Mrs. Parkington 🦴🦴½ **1944** Overblown epic drama spanning six decades tells the story of the rise and fall of an American dynasty made on easy money. Garson plays the woman who goes from working as a maid in a boarding house to living a life of luxury when she marries a multimillionaire. This was the fifth pairing of Garson and Pidgeon and although it's not one of their best, it proved to be a big hit with audiences. Lavish costumes and good performances by Garson and Moorehead. Based on the novel by Louis Bromfield. **124m/B VHS.** Greer Garson, Walter Pidgeon, Edward Arnold, Frances Rafferty, Agnes Moorehead, Selena Royle, Gladys Cooper, Lee Patrick; ***D:*** Tay Garnett; ***W:*** Robert Thoeren, Polly James; ***C:*** Joseph Ruttenberg. Golden Globes '45: Support. Actress (Moorehead).

Mrs. R's Daughter 🦴🦴 **1979** An outraged mother fights the judicial systems in order to bring her daughter's rapist to trial. Based on a true story. **97m/C VHS.** Cloris Leachman, Season Hubley, Donald Moffat, John McIntire, Stephen Elliott, Ron Rifkin; ***D:*** Dan Curtis. **TV**

Mrs. Santa Claus 🦴🦴½ **1996 (G)** Who better than Lansbury to star as the title character in this sweet TV musical set in 1910. Vivacious Mrs. C is tired of being left home during Santa's (Durning) annual trip and decides to borrow the sleigh for a test drive just before the big day. But bad weather and an injured reindeer force an emergency landing in New York City where she befriends the young sweatshop workers at villainous toy-maker A.P. Tavish's (Mann) factory and does a little matchmaking too. But Mrs. Claus still must make it back to the North Pole by Christmas Eve. ♫Avenue A; Almost Jolly; We Don't Go Together; Suffragette March; He Needs Me. **90m/C VHS.** Angela Lansbury, Charles Durning, Terrence Mann, David Norona, Debra Wiseman, Rosalind Harris, Bryan Murray, Lynsey Bartilson, Michael Jeter; ***D:*** Terry Hughes; ***W:*** Mark Saltzman; ***C:*** Stephen M. Katz; ***M:*** Jerry Herman.

Mrs. Silly 🦴 **1985** Romance novel on tape, following the exploits of an aging woman who in losing material wealth, gains contentment. **60m/C** Maggie Smith, James Villiers, Cyril Luckham.

Mrs. Soffel 🦴🦴½ **1984 (PG-13)** Falling in love with a convicted murderer and helping him flee confinement occupies the time of the prison warden's wife. Effectively captures the 1901 setting, yet a dark pall fairly strangles any emotion. Based on a true story. **110m/C VHS, Wide.** Diane Keaton, Mel Gibson, Matthew Modine, Edward Herrmann, Trini Alvarado, Terry O'Quinn, Jennifer (Jennie) Dundas Lowe, Danny Corkill, Maury Chaykin, Dana Wheeler-Nicholson; ***D:*** Gillian Armstrong; ***W:*** Ron Nyswaner; ***C:*** Russell Boyd; ***M:*** Mark Isham.

Mrs. Wiggs of the Cabbage Patch 🦴🦴½ **1942** A warm, funny, and altogether overdone story of a mother whose husband abandons her, leaving the woman to raise their four children alone. It's Thanksgiving, so the rich visit the poor household to deliver a turkey dinner, and in the end all live happily ever after. Not one of Fields' larger roles; he doesn't even make an appearance until midway through the schmaltz. **80m/B VHS.** Pauline Lord, ZaSu Pitts, W.C. Fields, Evelyn Venable, Donald Meek, Barbara Britton; ***D:*** Norman Taurog.

Mrs. Winterbourne 🦴🦴 **1996 (PG-13)** Pregnant loser Connie Doyle (Lake) is whisked into the lap of luxury when she's assumed to be the widowed Patricia Winterbourne after a train wreck. The grieving family (who had never met the bride) take her in and accept her and her baby as part of the household. Since her life is now going well, Connie decides to keep her true identity a secret while she falls for faux-brother-in-law Bill (Fraser). MacLaine is brilliant as the spirited matriarch of the family. Retooled as a comedy, the story is actually based on the noirish novel "I Married a Dead Man" by Cornell Woolrich and a remake of the equally dark "No Man of Her Own" from 1950. **106m/C VHS, DVD, Wide.** Ricki Lake, Brendan Fraser, Shirley MacLaine, Miguel (Michael) Sandoval, Loren Dean, Susan Haskell, Paula Prentiss; ***D:*** Richard Benjamin; ***W:*** Phoef Sutton, Lisa-Marie Rodano; ***C:*** Alex Nepomniaschy; ***M:*** Patrick Doyle.

Mistaken Identity 🦴½ **1936** A swank hotel is the setting for this so-so comedy about three con men who wind up conning each other as much as their supposed victims. A couple of light romances are also thrown in for good measure. **75m/B VHS.** Chick Chandler, Evalyn Knapp, Berton Churchill, Patricia Farr, Richard Carle, Bradley Page, Lew Kelly; ***D:*** Phil Rosen.

Mistaken Identity 🦴½ **1941** All-black mystery set against the background of a nightclub, and featuring a production number, "I'm a Bangi from Ubangi." **60m/B VHS.** Nellie Hill, George Oliver.

Mr. Accident 🦴½ **1999 (PG-13)** Australian comedian Serious returns as star/writer/director/producer. Accident-prone Roger Crumpkin (Serious) finds out his egg-processing factory boss (Fiels) is planning to produce eggs that are filled with nicotine so that people will become addicted. No, not to eggs!—to cigarettes! A lame attempt at comedy. **89m/C VHS, DVD, Wide.** *AU* Yahoo Serious, David Field, Helen Dallimore, Grant Piro, Jeanette Cronin; ***D:*** Yahoo Serious; ***W:*** Yahoo Serious; ***C:*** Steve Arnold; ***M:*** Nerida Tyson-Chew.

Mr. Ace 🦴½ **1946** A congresswoman decides to run for governor without the approval of the loyal political kingpin, Mr. Ace. **85m/B VHS, DVD.** George Raft, Sylvia Sidney, Sara Haden, Stanley Ridges; ***D:*** Edwin L. Marin; ***W:*** Fred Finklehoffe; ***C:*** Karl Struss; ***M:*** Heinz Roemheld.

Mr. & Mrs. Bridge 🦴🦴🦴🦴 **1990 (PG-13)** Set in the '30s and '40s in Kansas City, Ivory's adaptation of Evan S. Connell's novels painstakingly portrays an upper middle-class family struggling to survive within an emotional vacuum. Newman and Woodward, together for the first time in many years as Walter and Ivory Bridge, bring a wealth of experience and insight to their characterizations. Many consider this to be Newman's best, most subtle and nuanced performance. **127m/C VHS, DVD, Wide.** Joanne Woodward, Paul Newman, Kyra Sedgwick, Blythe Danner, Simon Callow, Diane Kagan, Robert Sean Leonard, Saundra McClain, Margaret Welsh, Austin Pendleton, Gale Garnett, Remak Ramsay; ***D:*** James Ivory; ***W:*** Ruth Prawer Jhabvala; ***C:*** Tony Pierce-Roberts; ***M:*** Richard Robbins. N.Y. Film Critics '90: Actress (Woodward), Screenplay.

Mr. & Mrs. Loving 🦴🦴🦴 **1996 (PG-13)** Fact-based movie, set in the 1960s, follows the romance, marriage, and struggle of Richard Loving (Hutton) and Mildred "Bean" Jeter (Rochon). Growing up in rural Virginia, their interracial relationship isn't considered uncommon. But when Bean gets pregnant, they aren't allowed to marry and live together because of Virginia's racial laws. Instead, the Lovings start a life in Washington, D.C., but desperately homesick and increasingly aware of the civil rights movement, Bean writes a letter to the Attorney General's office. What results is young ACLU lawyer Bernie Cohen (Parker) taking on their case—which eventually leads to a landmark Supreme Court decision about miscegenation laws. **95m/C VHS.** Timothy Hutton, Lela Rochon, Corey Parker, Ruby Dee, Isaiah Washington IV, Bill Nunn, Charles Gray; ***D:*** Richard Friedenberg; ***W:*** Richard Friedenberg; ***C:*** Kenneth Macmillan; ***M:*** Branford Marsalis. **CABLE**

Mr. & Mrs. Smith 🦴🦴🦴½ **1941** Hitchcock's only screwball comedy, an underrated, endearing farce about a bickering but happy modern couple who discover their marriage isn't legitimate and go through courtship all over again. Vintage of its kind, with inspired performances and crackling dialogue. **95m/B VHS.** Carole Lombard, Robert Montgomery, Gene Raymond, Jack Carson, Lucile Watson, Charles Halton; ***D:*** Alfred Hitchcock; ***W:*** Norman Krasna.

Mr. Arkadin 🦴🦴🦴 *Confidential Report* **1955** Screenwriter, director, star Welles, adapting from his own novel, gave this plot a dry run on radio during early 1950s. Welles examines the life of yet another ruthless millionaire, but this one can't seem to remember the sordid source of all that cash. Investigator Arden follows the intriguing and descending trail to a surprise ending. As in "Citizen Kane," oblique camera angles and layered dialogue prevail, but this time only serve to confuse the story. Shot over two years around Europe, required seven years of post production before finding distribution in 1962. **99m/B VHS.** *GB* Orson Welles, Akim Tamiroff, Michael Redgrave, Patricia Medina, Mischa Auer; ***D:*** Orson Welles; ***C:*** Jean (Yves, Georges) Bourgoin.

Mr. Baseball 🦴🦴 **1992 (PG-13)** Washed-up American baseball player tries to revive his career by playing in Japan and experiences cultures clashing under the ballpark lights. Semi-charmer swings and misses often enough to warrant return to minors. Film drew controversy during production when Universal was bought by the Japanese Matsushita organization and claims of both Japan- and America-bashing were thrown about. **109m/C VHS, DVD, Wide.** Tom Selleck, Ken Takakura, Toshi Shioya, Dennis Haysbert, Aya Takanashi; ***D:*** Fred Schepisi; ***W:*** Gary Ross, Kevin Wade, Monte Merrick; ***C:*** Ian Baker; ***M:*** Jerry Goldsmith.

Mr. Billion 🦴🦴 **1977 (PG)** Engaging chase adventure comedy about an Italian mechanic who stands to inherit a billion dollar fortune if he can travel from Italy to San Francisco in 20 days. Of course, things get in his way. Hill made his American debut in this film. **89m/C VHS.** Jackie Gleason, Terence Hill, Valerie Perrine, Slim Pickens, Chill Wills; ***D:*** Jonathan Kaplan; ***W:*** Jonathan Kaplan, Ken Friedman; ***M:*** Dave Grusin.

Mr. Blandings Builds His Dream House 🦴🦴🦴½ **1948** Jim Blandings (Grant), wife Muriel (Loy), and their two daughters must give up their Manhattan apartment for new digs. City boy Jim wants to become a suburbanite and the Blandings decide to build their dream house—with many complications. Timely at its release because of the post-WWII housing shortage and building boom, this classic comedy is still a humorous treat with Grant at his funniest. Loy and Douglas provide strong backup. A must for all homeowners. Based on the novel by Eric Hodgins. **93m/B VHS.** Cary Grant, Myrna Loy, Melvyn Douglas, Lex Barker, Reginald Denny, Louise Beavers, Jason Robards Sr.; ***D:*** H.C. Potter; ***W:*** Norman Panama, Melvin Frank; ***C:*** James Wong Howe; ***M:*** Leigh Harline.

Mr. Boggs Steps Out 🦴½ **1938** A pencil-pusher wins a bundle and invests it in a barrel factory. Trouble arises when a slickster tries to close it down. Even with the usual romantic entanglements, the film has trouble staying interesting. **68m/B VHS.** Stuart Erwin, Helen Chandler, Toby Wing, Tully Marshall, Spencer Charters, Otis Harlan, Walter Byron, Milburn Stone; ***D:*** Gordon Wiles.

Mr. Corbett's Ghost 🦴🦴 **1990** A young man, displeased with his boss's managerial finesse, cuts a deal with a soul collector who pink slips the guy to the great unemployment line in the sky. Once a boss always a boss, and the guy's ghost stops in to say boo, while the soul collector is hot to get his hands on his part of the bargain. Huston's final film appearance. **60m/C VHS.** John Huston, Paul Scofield, Burgess Meredith. **TV**

Mr. Deeds **2002 (PG-13)** In this loose remake of 1936's "Mr. Deeds Goes to Town," Sandler has the chutzpah to take on the role made famous by Gary Cooper. Longfellow Deeds owns a pizzeria in Mandrake Falls, New Hampshire and is about to inherit 40 billion dollars and a mammoth media company. Naturally, this inheritance brings out all the scam artists and tabloid reporters, including Babe Bennett (Ryder). Not yet reviewed. **?m/C VHS, DVD.** Adam Sandler, Winona Ryder, John Turturro, Peter Gallagher, Steve Buscemi, Jared Harris; ***D:*** Steven Brill; ***W:*** Tim Herlihy.

Mr. Deeds Goes to Town 🦴🦴🦴½ **1936** Typical Capra fare offers Cooper as small town Vermonter and philanthropic fellow Longfellow Deeds, who inherits $20 million and promptly donates it to the needy, which leads to a courtroom hearing on his sanity. He also manages to find time to fall in love with beautiful reporter and tough cookie, Babe Bennett (Arthur), who's determined to fathom the good guy's motivation. Superior entertainment. Based on Clarence Budington Kelland's story "Opera Hat." **118m/B VHS, DVD.** Gary Cooper, Jean Arthur, Raymond Walburn, Walter Catlett, Lionel Stander, George Bancroft, H.B. Warner, Ruth Donnelly, Douglass Dumbrille, Margaret Seddon, Margaret McWade; ***D:*** Frank Capra; ***W:*** Robert Riskin; ***C:*** Joseph Walker. Oscars '36: Director (Capra); N.Y. Film Critics '36: Film.

Mr. Destiny 🦴🦴 **1990 (PG-13)** Mid-level businessman Belushi has a mid-life crisis of sorts when his car dies. Wandering into an empty bar, he encounters bartender Caine who serves cocktails and acts omniscient before taking him on the ten-cent tour of life as it would've been if he hadn't struck out in a high school baseball game. Less than wonderful rehash of "It's a Wonderful Life." **110m/C VHS.** James Belushi, Michael Caine, Linda Hamilton, Jon Lovitz, Bill McCutcheon, Hart Bochner, Rene Russo, Jay O. Sanders, Maury Chaykin, Pat Corley, Douglas Seale, Courteney Cox Arquette, Kathy Ireland; ***D:*** James Orr; ***W:*** James Orr, Jim Cruickshank.

Mister Drake's Duck 🦴🦴½ **1950** American newlyweds Don (Fairbanks Jr.) and Penny (Donlan) Drake settle down on the English farm that Don has inherited. At a auction, Penny mistakenly buys five dozen ducks, one of which turns out to lay radioactive eggs. Soon the British Army has quarantined the farm and then other branches of the military turn up—all claiming the duck and turning the Drakes' life into chaos. Rather dated, but still amusing, satire on nuclear arms and the military. Based on a play by Ian Messiter. **80m/B VHS.** *GB* Douglas Fairbanks Jr., Yolande Donlan, Reginald Beckwith, Howard Marion-Crawford, Wilfrid Hyde-White, Jon Pertwee, John Boxer, A.E. Matthews; ***D:*** Val Guest; ***W:*** Val Guest; ***C:*** Jack Cox, Harry Gillam; ***M:*** Bruce Campbell.

Mr. Emmanuel 🦴🦴½ **1944** An elderly Jewish widower leaves his English home in 1935 in quest of the mother of a German refugee boy, and is subjected to shocking treatment in Germany. **97m/B VHS.** Felix Aylmer, Greta Gynt, Walter Rilla, Jean Simmons.

Mr. Frost 🦴 **1989 (R)** Goldblum feigns fascination in this lackluster tale of the devil incarnate, who is imprisoned after owning up to a series of grisly murders, and who hides his true identity until approached by a woman psychiatrist. **92m/C VHS.** Jeff Goldblum, Kathy Baker, Alan Bates, Roland Giraud, Jean-Pierre Cassel; ***D:*** Phillip Setbon; ***W:*** Phillip Setbon, Brad Lynch.

Mr. Headmistress 🦴🦴½ **1998** Smalltime con man Tucker (Williams) is trying to avoid a couple of thugs out to collect a bad debt when he assumes the identity of the headmistress of the Rawlings Academy for Girls. Seems the school is about to receive a big donation if grades improve and Tucker wants the money. But of course, he learns more than how to walk like a lady along the way. **89m/C VHS.** Harland Williams, Katey Sagal, Shawna Waldron; ***D:*** James Frawley. **TV**

Mr. Hobbs Takes a Vacation 🦴🦴🦴 **1962** Good-natured comedy in which beleaguered parents try to resolve family squabbles while the entire brood is on a seaside vacation. Stewart and O'Hara are especially fine and funny as the well-meaning parents. **116m/C VHS.** James Stewart, Maureen O'Hara, Fabian, John Saxon, Marie Wilson, John McGiver, Reginald Gardiner; ***D:*** Henry Koster; ***W:*** Nunnally Johnson; ***M:*** Henry Mancini. Berlin Intl. Film Fest. '62: Actor (Stewart).

Mr. Holland's Opus 🦴🦴🦴 **1995 (PG)** Well-done Disney tearjerker begins in 1965 as musician Glenn Holland (Dreyfuss) takes a teaching job to get himself off the wedding reception circuit and help support his wife, Iris (Headly), and their deaf son. Spanning three decades, with actual newsreel footage thrown in to highlight time passing, Holland sets aside his dream of composing a great symphony and finds his true calling—mentoring and inspiring young minds. Holland's son being deaf might have proved corny, but their rocky relationship is deeply rooted to the storyline. Dreyfuss turns in his most vibrant performance in years and, while sentimental buttons are definitely pushed, director Herek avoids falling into sappiness. **142m/C VHS, DVD, Wide.** Richard Dreyfuss, Glenne Headly, Jay Thomas, Olympia Dukakis, William H. Macy, Alicia Witt, Jean (Louisa) Kelly, Anthony Natale; ***D:*** Stephen Herek; ***W:*** Patrick Sheane Duncan; ***C:*** Oliver Wood; ***M:*** Michael Kamen.

Mr. Horn 🦴🦴 **1979** Slow-paced film about folk-hero Scott Tom Horn capturing the famous Apache warrior, Geronimo, is average at best. **200m/C VHS.** David Carradine, Richard Widmark, Karen Black, Jeremy Slate, Enrique Lucero, Jack Starrett; ***D:*** Jack Starrett; ***W:*** William Goldman.

Mr. Hulot's Holiday 🦴🦴🦴½ *Les Vacances de Monsieur Hulot; Monsieur Hulot's Holiday* **1953** Superior slapstick details the misadventures of an oblivious bachelor's seaside holiday, where disaster follows his every move. Inventive French comedian Tati at his best. Light-hearted and natural, with magical mime sequences. Followed by "Mon Oncle." French with subtitles. **86m/B VHS, 8mm.** *FR* Jacques Tati, Natalie Pascaud, Michelle Rolia; ***D:*** Jacques Tati; ***W:*** Jacques Tati, Henri Marquet, Jacques Lagrange, Pierre Aubert; ***C:*** Jacques Mercanton; ***M:*** Alain Romans.

Mr. Inside, Mr. Outside 🦴½ **1974** Two N.Y.C. cops, one undercover, one not, try to infiltrate a tough diamond-smuggling ring. **74m/C VHS.** Tony LoBianco, Hal Linden; ***D:*** William A. Graham. **TV**

Mr. Jealousy 🦴🦴½ **1998 (R)** When Lester Grimm (Stoltz) was 15, he chickened out on a good night kiss with his girl, and later spied her necking with another boy. Ever since then, he's had this thing about infidelity and he trashes every relationship because of his suspicions. It's no different when he meets the vivacious Ramona (Sciorra), who has recently broken up with arrogant author Dashiell (Eigemann). Lester joins Dashiell's therapy group to spy on his possible competition. Writer-director Baumbach stretches this thin material by making the characters interesting and the dialogue funny. Fonda's role is a cameo as Dashiell's stuttering girlfriend. **105m/C VHS, DVD, Wide.** Eric Stoltz, Annabella Sciorra, Christopher Eigeman, Carlos Jacott, Marianne Jean-Baptiste, Brian Kerwin, Peter Bogdanovich; ***Cameos:*** Bridget Fonda; ***D:*** Noah Baumbach; ***W:*** Noah Baumbach; ***C:*** Steven Bernstein; ***M:*** Robert Een, Luna.

Mister Johnson 🦴🦴🦴 **1991 (PG-13)** In 1923 Africa, an educated black man working for the British magistrate constantly finds himself in trouble, thanks to backfiring schemes. This highly enjoyable film from the director of "Driving Miss Daisy" suffers only from the underdevelopment of the intriguing lead character. Based on the novel by Joyce Cary. **105m/C VHS, DVD.** Pierce Brosnan, Edward Woodward, Maynard Eziashi, Beatie Edney, Denis Quilley, Nick Reding; ***D:*** Bruce Beresford; ***W:*** Bruce Beresford, William Boyd; ***C:*** Peter James; ***M:*** Georges Delerue.

Mr. Jones 🦴½ **1993 (R)** Psychiatrist (Olin) falls in love with her manic-depressive patient (Gere). Head case Mr. Jones (Gere) is a charmer who gets a rush from tightrope walking a high beam on a construction site, yet is prone to bad moods when he fails to remember his own name. He can't resist flirting with the seductive Dr. Bowen, who eagerly leaps past professional boundaries while trying to coax him out of his illness. Wastes the talents of its stars with Gere showy, Olin brittle, and the whole story as contrived as their prefunctory love affair. Psychiatrists are getting as bad a rep professionally as lawyers in their recent film appearances. **110m/C VHS, DVD, Wide.** Richard Gere, Lena Olin, Anne Bancroft, Tom Irwin, Delroy Lindo, Bruce Altman, Lauren Tom; ***D:*** Mike Figgis; ***W:*** Michael Cristofer, Eric Roth; ***C:*** Juan Ruiz-Anchia; ***M:*** Maurice Jarre.

Mr. Kingstreet's War 🦴🦴½ *Heroes Die Hard* **1971** An idealistic game warden and his wife defend the wildlife of Africa against the fighting Italian and British armies at the dawn of WWII. **92m/C VHS.** John Saxon, Tippi Hedren, Rossano Brazzi, Brian O'Shaughnessy; ***D:*** Percival Rubens.

Mr. Klein 🦴🦴🦴 **1976 (PG)** Cleverly plotted script and fine direction in this dark and intense film about French-Catholic art dealer Robert Klein (Delon), who buys valuables from Jews trying to escape Nazi occupied France in 1942, paying far less than what the treasures are worth. Ironically, he is mistaken for another Robert Klein, a Jew who's wanted for anti-Nazi activities. French with subtitles. **122m/C VHS.** *FR* Alain Delon, Jeanne Moreau, Suzanne Flon, Michael (Michel) Lonsdale, Juliet Berto, Louis Seigner, Francine Racette, Massimo Girotti; ***D:*** Joseph Losey; ***W:*** Franco Solinas; ***C:*** Gerry Fisher; ***M:*** Egisto Macchi. Cesar '77: Film.

Mr. Love 🦴🦴½ **1986 (PG-13)** A meek gardener is perceived by neighbors as a fool until he dies and numerous women arrive for his funeral. Is it his cologne? The radishes? **91m/C VHS.** *GB* Barry Jackson, Maurice Denham, Margaret Tyzack, Linda Marlowe; ***D:*** Roy Battersby; ***M:*** Willy Russell.

Mr. Lucky 🦴🦴🦴 **1943** Likeable wartime drama about a gambler who hopes to swindle a philanthropic organization, but then falls in love and determines to help the group in a fundraising effort. Grant is, no surprise, excellent as the seemingly cynical con artist who actually has a heart of gold. Cliched, but nonetheless worthwhile. Later developed into a TV series. **99m/B VHS.** Cary Grant, Laraine Day, Charles Bickford, Gladys Cooper, Paul Stewart, Henry Stephenson, Florence Bates; ***D:*** H.C. Potter; ***C:*** George Barnes.

Mr. Magoo 🦴 **1997 (PG)** Ah Magoo, we wish you wouldn't have done it again! Live-action version of the cartoon character popular in the 50's and 60's. Elderly myopic millionaire Quincy Magoo (Nielsen) unwittingly comes into possession of a stolen gem that he gives to his bulldog Angus as a toy. Bumbling government agents and evil arch-criminals are after the gem and Magoo, but he avoids them through luck and bad plot devices. Meanwhile, Magoo is mistaking a mummy's sarcophagus for a phone booth, a riverboat paddle wheel for an escalator and...well, you get the idea. Nielsen puts a "Naked Gun" spin on Magoo, and that routine is getting a bit stale. Although criticized by some blind groups as an inaccurate portrayal of the visually challenged, after a very brief run in the theaters, no one was able to see it. Opening and closing sequences include animated Magoo bits. **87m/C VHS, DVD, Wide.** Leslie Nielsen, Kelly Lynch, Matt Keeslar, Nicholas Chinlund, Ernie Hudson, Malcolm McDowell, Stephen Tobolowsky, Jennifer Garner, Miguel Ferrer; ***D:*** Stanley Tong; ***W:*** Pat Proft, Tom Sherohman; ***C:*** Jingle Ma; ***M:*** Michael Tavera.

Mr. Majestyk 🦴🦴½ **1974 (PG)** When a Vietnam veteran's attempt to start an honest business is thwarted by Mafia hitmen and the police, he goes after them with a vengeance. Based on Leonard's novel (he also did the screenplay). **103m/C VHS.** Charles Bronson, Al Lettieri, Linda Cristal, Lee Purcell; ***D:*** Richard Fleischer; ***W:*** Elmore Leonard; ***M:*** Charles Bernstein.

Mister Mean 🦴 **1977** A man who once worked for a mafia don is now given the task of rubbing him out. For Cosa Nostra diehards and gluttons for Roman scenery. **98m/C VHS.** *IT* Fred Williamson; ***D:*** Fred Williamson.

Mr. Mike's Mondo Video 🦴🦴 **1979 (R)** A bizarre, outrageous comedy special declared too wild for TV and conceived by the "Saturday Night Live" alumnus Mr. Mike. **75m/C VHS.** Michael O'Donoghue, Dan Aykroyd, Jane Curtin, Carrie Fisher, Teri Garr, Joan Haskett, Deborah Harry, Margot Kidder, Bill Murray, Laraine Newman, Gilda Radner, Julius LaRosa, Paul Shaffer, Sid Vicious; ***W:*** Mitch Glazer.

Mr. Mom 🦴🦴🦴 **1983 (PG)** Tireless auto exec Jack (Keaton) loses his job and stays home with the kids while his wife Caroline (Garr) becomes the breadwinner. He's forced to cope with the rigors of housework and child care, resorting to drugs, alcohol and soap operas. Keaton's hilarious as the homebound dad chased by killer appliances and poker buddy to the ladies in the neighborhood. **92m/C VHS.** Jeffrey Tambor, Michael Keaton, Teri Garr, Christopher Lloyd, Martin Mull, Ann Jillian, Edie McClurg, Valri Bromfield; ***D:*** Stan Dragoti; ***W:*** John Hughes; ***C:*** Victor Kemper; ***M:*** Lee Holdridge.

Mr. Moto's Last Warning 🦴🦴🦴 **1939** One of the better in the series of Mr. Moto, the wily detective! Lorre is convincing in the title role and gets good support from character villains Carradine and Sanders in this story of saboteurs converging on the Suez Canal plotting to blow up the French Fleet. **71m/B VHS.** Peter Lorre, George Sanders, Ricardo Cortez, John Carradine, Virginia Field, Robert Coote; ***D:*** Norman Foster.

Mr. Music 🦴🦴½ **1950** Crosby is a successful songwriter who would rather enjoy life on the golf course than pen any more tunes. He's persuaded by his secretary to help out an old-time producer who's fallen on hard times by writing a new Broadway show. Light-hearted fluff. Based on the play "Accent on Youth" by Samson Raphaelson which had been filmed in 1935. ♫Life is So Precious; Accidents Will Happen; High on the List; Wouldn't It Be Funny; Wasn't I There?; Mr. Music; Once More the Blue and White; Milady; Then You'll Be Home. **113m/B VHS.** Bing Crosby, Nancy Olson, Charles Coburn, Robert Stack, Tom Ewell, Ruth Hussey, Charles Kemper, Donald Woods, Gower Champion, Marge Champion; ***Cameos:*** Groucho Marx, Peggy Lee; ***D:*** Richard Haydn.

Mr. Nanny 🦴🦴 **1993 (PG)** For those who fear change, this predictable plot should serve as comforting assurance that Hollywood will still sacrifice substance for the quick buck. Basic storyline has the child-hating Hulkster playing nanny/bodyguard to a couple of bratty kids. Meanwhile, his arch rival (Johansen) hatches a scheme to gain world dominance by kidnapping the kids for the ransom of their father's top secret computer chip. Never fear—in this world, the good guys kick butt, naturally, and everyone learns a lesson. **85m/C VHS.** Hulk Hogan, Sherman Hemsley, Austin Pendleton, Robert Gorman, Madeline Zima, Mother Love, David Johansen; ***D:*** Michael Gottlieb; ***W:*** Ed Rugoff, Michael Gottlieb; ***M:*** David Johansen, Brian Koonin.

Mr. Nice Guy 🦴 **1986 (PG-13)** In the near future, a hired gun strives for national recognition as the best of his now legitimate profession. Comedy with few laughs. **92m/C VHS.** Michael MacDonald, Jan Smithers, Joe Silver.

Mr. Nice Guy 🦴🦴½ *Yatgo Ho Yan* **1998 (PG-13)** Jackie Chan brings another installment of his Bruce Lee-meets-Charlie Chaplin action adventure shenanigans to the screen. This time he plays a TV cooking show host who gets into boiling water when he saves a female reporter (Fitzpatrick) who has videotaped a drug deal. He ends up with the videotape, so reptilian bad guy Giancarlo (Norton) sends his lackeys out to chop-suey Jackie, though they turn out to be boneless chickens. The high action/low talk meter is cranked up in this outing, due to the fact that it's Chan's first movie filmed primarily in English (although it was still produced in Hong Kong). The plot seems to have been chopped up a bit while travelling over the Pacific, but Chan fans are well aware that the whirling dervish stunts are more important than a silly old story anyway. **90m/C VHS, DVD.** *HK* Jackie Chan, Richard Norton, Gabrielle Fitzpatrick, Miki Lee, Karen McLymont, Vince Poletto, Barry Otto, Sammo Hung; ***D:*** Sammo Hung; ***W:*** Edward Tang, Fibe Ma; ***C:*** Raymond Lam; ***M:*** J. Peter Robinson.

Mr. North 🦴🦴½ **1988 (PG)** Capracorn fable about a charming, bright Yale graduate who encounters admiration and disdain from upper-crust Rhode Island residents when news of his miraculous "cures" spreads. Marks the directorial debut of Danny Huston, son of John Huston, who co-wrote the script and served as executive producer before dying several weeks into shooting. Set in the 1920s and adapted from Thornton Wilder's "Theophilus North." **90m/C VHS.** Anthony Edwards, Robert Mitchum, Lauren Bacall, Harry Dean Stanton, Anjelica Huston, Mary Stuart Masterson, Virginia Madsen, Tammy Grimes, David Warner, Hunter Carson, Christopher Durang, Mark Metcalf, Katharine Houghton, Christopher Lawford; ***D:*** Danny Huston; ***W:*** John Huston, Janet Roach, James Costigan; ***C:*** Robin Vidgeon; ***M:*** David McHugh.

Mr. Peabody & the Mermaid 🦴🦴½ **1948** Lightweight fish story about a middle-aged married man who hooks a beautiful mermaid while fishing in the Caribbean and eventually falls in love with her. Powell is smooth as always, though hampered by the unrestrained absurdity of it all. Based on the novel by Guy and Constance Jones. Also available colorized. **89m/B VHS.** William Powell, Ann Blyth, Irene Hervey, Andrea King, Clinton Sundberg, Art Smith; ***D:*** Irving Pichel; ***W:*** Nunnally Johnson.

Mr. Peek-A-Boo 🦴🦴½ *Garou Garou le Passe Muraille* **1950** A French clerk discovers he has the ability to walk through walls. Although friends try to coax him into a life of crime, he instead comes to the aid of an English girl who is being blackmailed. Good-natured French comedy was shot with English dialogue for the American market. **74m/B VHS.** *FR* Joan Greenwood, Bourvil, Marcel Arnold, Roger Treville; ***D:*** Jean Boyer.

Mr. Reeder in Room 13 🦴🦴 **1938** Based on the mystery stories created by Edgar Wallace, Mr. Reeder (a cultured English gentleman who fights crime) enlists the aid of a young man to get evidence on a gang of counterfeiters. **66m/B VHS.** Gibb McLaughlin.

Mr. Reliable: A True Story 🦴🦴 **1995 (R)** A "truth is stranger than fiction" comedy about Australia's first hostage situation. During the summer of 1968, recently released car thief Wally Mellish (Friels) rents a rundown cottage in a Sydney suburb. He finds a girlfriend in Beryl Muddle (McKenzie), who moves in with her two-year-old daughter. When Wally steals some trifles to brighten up the place, the cops come 'round and Wally, who's still on probation, pulls a gun. The authorities think Beryl and the baby are hostages and are afraid to storm the cottage while the standoff becomes hot media news. Wally and Beryl are thrilled with the attention but there's increasing political pressure to put an end to the farcical situation. **112m/C VHS.** *AU* Colin Friels, Jacqueline McKenzie, Paul Sonkkila, Frank Gallacher, Barry Otto, Lisa Hensley, Ken Radley, Neil Fitzpatrick; ***D:*** Nadia Tass; ***W:*** Terry Hayes, Don Catchlove; ***C:*** David Parker; ***M:*** Phil Judd.

Mr. Rice's Secret 🦴🦴 **2000 (PG)** Mysterious Englishman Mr. Rice (Bowie) lives next door to 13-year-old Owen (Switzer), who has cancer. He's struggling but Mr. Rice offers words of wisdom (that come from the fact he's lived hundreds of years). When Mr. Rice suddenly does die, it's not before letting Owen in on some posthumous life-saving secrets. **113m/C VHS, DVD, Wide.** *CA* David Bowie, Garwin Sanford, Bill Switzer, Teryl Rothery; ***D:*** Nicholas (Nick) Kendall; ***W:*** J.H. Wyman; ***C:*** Gregory Middleton; ***M:*** Simon Kendall, Al Rodger.

Mister Roberts 🦴🦴🦴🦴 **1955** Crew of a Navy cargo freighter in the South Pacific during WWII relieves the boredom of duty with a series of elaborate practical jokes, mostly at the expense of their long-suffering and slightly crazy captain, who then determines that he will get even. The ship's cargo officer, Mr. Roberts, longs to be transferred to a fighting vessel and see some action. Originally a hit Broadway play (based on the novel by Thomas Heggen) which also featured Fonda in the title role. Great performance from Lemmon as Ensign Pulver. Powell's last film. Sequelled in 1964 by "Ensign Pulver," and later a short-lived TV series as well as a live TV special. Newly transferred in 1988 from a pristine stereo print. **120m/C VHS, DVD.** Henry Fonda, James Cagney, Jack Lemmon, William Powell, Betsy Palmer, Ward Bond, Harry Carey Jr., Nick Adams, Phil Carey, Ken Curtis, Martin Milner, Jack Pennick, Perry Lopez, Patrick Wayne, Tige Andrews, William Henry; ***D:*** John Ford, Mervyn LeRoy; ***W:*** Frank Nugent, Joshua Logan, Thomas Heggen; ***C:*** Winton C. Hoch; ***M:*** Franz Waxman. Oscars '55: Support. Actor (Lemmon).

Mr. Robinson Crusoe 🦴🦴½ **1932** Rollicking adventure in the South Seas as Fairbanks makes a bet that he can live on a desert island for a year without being left any refinements of civilization. Lucky for him, a woman arrives. Also written by Fairbanks. **76m/B VHS.** Douglas Fairbanks Sr., William Farnum, Maria Alba, Earle Brown; ***D:*** Edward Sutherland; ***W:*** Douglas Fairbanks Sr.; ***M:*** Alfred Newman.

Mr. Rock 'n' Roll: The Alan Freed Story 🦴🦴½ **1999** In the early 1950s, Cleveland disc jockey Alan Freed (Nelson) decides to play the new-fangled rock 'n' roll on his station, where it becomes an immediate hit and an immediate controversy. Freed's success takes him to New York and further celebrity but career missteps lead to the payola scandal and his eventual disgrace. Original recordings are used and they turn out to be the most exciting thing about this TV movie. Based on the book by John A. Jackson. **91m/C VHS.** Judd Nelson, Madchen Amick, Leon, Paula Abdul; ***Cameos:*** Bobby Rydell, Fabian; ***D:*** Andy Wolk; ***W:*** Matt Dorff; ***C:*** Derick Underschultz. **TV**

Mr. Sardonicus 🦴🦴 *Sardonicus* **1961** Tidy little horror film finds the title character's (Rolfe) face frozen in a hideous grin after being cursed for stealing a winning lottery ticket from his father's corpse. Sardonicus has been experimenting with solutions to his problem (each more disgusting than the last) and finally forces neurosurgeon, Sir Robert Cargrave (Lewis), to assist him with his dilemma. **89m/B VHS, DVD, Wide.** Guy Rolfe, Ronald Lewis, Oscar Homolka, Audrey Dalton, Vladimir Sokoloff; ***D:*** William Castle; ***W:*** Ray Russell; ***C:*** Burnett Guffey; ***M:*** Von Dexter.

Mr. Saturday Night 🦴🦴½ **1992 (R)** Crystal, in his directorial debut, stars as Buddy Young Jr., a self-destructive comedian whose career spans five decades. His nasty one-liners and witty jokes combine with poignancy in this satisfying comedy/drama. Paymer is excellent as Young's long-suffering, faithful brother and manager. Watch for Lewis in a cameo role. Expectations were very high and the boxoffice results were disappointing, but fans of Crystal shouldn't miss this one. **118m/C VHS, DVD, Wide.** Billy Crystal, David Paymer, Julie Warner, Helen Hunt, Mary Mara, Jerry Orbach, Ron Silver, Sage Allen, Jackie Gayle, Carl Ballantine, Slappy (Melvin) White, Conrad Janis, Jerry Lewis; ***D:*** Billy Crystal; ***W:*** Babaloo Mandel, Lowell Ganz, Billy Crystal; ***C:*** Don Peterman; ***M:*** Marc Shaiman.

Mr. Scarface 🦴½ **1977 (R)** A young man searches for the man who murdered his father years earlier in a dark alley. **85m/C VHS.** Jack Palance, Edmund Purdom, Al Cliver, Harry Baer, Gisela Hahn; ***D:*** Fernando Di Leo.

Mr. Skeffington 🦴🦴🦴 **1944** A super-grade soap opera spanning 26 years in the life of a ravishing, spoiled New York socialite. The beauty with a fondness for bedrooms marries for convenience, abuses her husband, then enjoys a highly equitable divorce settlement. Years later when diphtheria leaves her totally deformed and no man will have her, she is saved by her former husband. Based on the novel by "Elizabeth" (Mary Annette Beauchamp Russell) and adapted by "Casablanca's" Julius and Philip Epstein. **147m/B VHS.** Bette Davis, Claude Rains, Walter Abel, Richard Waring, George Coulouris, John Alexander; ***D:*** Vincent Sherman.

Mr. Skitch 🦴🦴 **1933** Weak Rogers offering. Couple loses their farm and begins cross country jaunt with mishaps at every turn. All ends well when their daughter meets an Army cadet, but few laughs and lots of loose ends. **70m/B VHS.** Will Rogers, ZaSu Pitts, Rochelle Hudson, Charles Starrett; ***D:*** James Cruze.

Mr. Smith Goes to Washington 🦴🦴🦴🦴 **1939** Another classic from Hollywood's golden year of 1939. Jimmy Stewart is an idealistic and naive young man selected to fill in for an ailing Senator. Upon his arrival in the Capitol, he is inundated by a multitude of corrupt politicians. He takes a stand for his beliefs and tries to denounce many of those he feels are unfit for their positions, meeting with opposition from all sides. Great cast is highlighted by Stewart in one of his most endearing performances. Quintessential Capra tale sharply adapted from Lewis Foster's story. Outstanding in every regard. **130m/B VHS.** James Stewart, Jean Arthur, Edward Arnold, Claude Rains, Thomas Mitchell, Beulah Bondi, Eugene Pallette, Guy Kibbee, Harry Carey Sr., H.B. Warner, Porter Hall, Jack Carson, Charles Lane; ***D:*** Frank Capra; ***W:*** Sidney Buchman; ***M:*** Dimitri Tiomkin. Oscars '39: Story; AFI '98: Top 100, Natl. Film Reg. '89;; N.Y. Film Critics '39: Actor (Stewart).

Mr. Stitch ♂ 1995 (R) Demented scientist (Hauer) plays Frankenstein and makes a creature, named Lazarus (Wheaton), from the body parts of more than 80 men and women. Unfortunately, the sensitive Lazarus has retained the collective memories of all these people and becomes obsessed with finding the reason for his existence. He receives compassion from a shrink (Peeples) but his maker has less-than-honorable plans for Lazarus. **98m/C VHS.** Rutger Hauer, Wil Wheaton, Nia Peeples, Taylor Negron, Ron Perlman, Michael (M.K.) Harris; ***Cameos:*** Tom Savini; ***D:*** Roger Roberts Avary; ***W:*** Roger Roberts Avary.

Mr. Superinvisible ♂♂ *Mr. Invisible; L'Inafferrabile Invincibile* **1973 (G)** Searching to cure the common cold, a bumbling scientist invents a bizarre virus, then strives with his loyal (of course) sheepdog to keep it from falling into the wrong hands. The Disney-like plot, featuring enemy agents and invisibility, may appeal to youngsters. **90m/C VHS.** *IT GE SP* Dean Jones, Ingeborg (Inge) Schoener, Gastone Moschin; ***D:*** Anthony (Antonio Margheriti) Dawson.

Mr. Sycamore ♂½ 1974 A sappy mail carrier escapes his badgering wife by sprouting into a tree. A potentially whimsical piece that wilts. **90m/C VHS.** Jason Robards Jr., Jean Simmons, Sandy Dennis; ***D:*** Pancho Kohner; ***M:*** Maurice Jarre.

Mr. Toad's Wild Ride ♂♂ *The Wind in the Willows* **1996 (PG)** Kenneth Grahame's 1908 children's book gets the Monty Python treatment. Set in Edwardian England, but with a definitely modern slant, Jones' adaptation removes much of the gentle whimsy and replaces it with Pythonesque skits. Mole (Coogan) wakes up one day to find his home being bulldozed by the industrialist weasels who have purchased the property from the motorcar-infatuated Mr. Toad (Jones). Toad keeps selling more land to buy more cars as the weasels take over the area and Toad is sent to jail for reckless driving. Mole, along with friends Rat (Idle) and Badger (Williamson) must help him escape and reclaim his land. Grahame's early 20th century fable railing against modern industralism's encroachment on the countryside becomes a satire on '90s consumerism and corporate greed. Mighty heady stuff for a kid's movie. **88m/C VHS.** *GB* Terry Jones, Steve Coogan, Eric Idle, Anthony Sher, Nicol Williamson, John Cleese, Stephen Fry, Bernard Hill, Michael Palin, Nigel Planer, Julia Sawalha, Victoria Wood, Richard James; ***D:*** Terry Jones; ***W:*** Terry Jones; ***C:*** David Tattersall; ***M:*** John Du Prez, Terry Jones.

Mr. Vampire ♂♂ 1986 Undertaker Uncle Kau (Ying) is also a master vampire hunter—necessary when your town is under siege from a vampire army who can make new converts with a single bite. Vampire movie with a Chinese twist combines elements of both comedy and horror, presenting a vampire who comes closer to resembling a corpse, who, when not levitating, hops like a bunny. Chinese with subtitles or dubbed. **99m/C VHS, DVD.** *CH* Moon Lee, Lam Ching Ying, Ricky Hui, Pauline Wong; ***D:*** Ricky Lau; ***W:*** Roy Szeto; ***C:*** Peter Ngor.

Mr. Walkie Talkie ♂♂ 1952 Tired of a sargeant's jabber-jaws, a soldier requests to be relocated to the front lines, only to find his catty comrade has followed. Set during the Korean War and featuring some truly amusing escapades set between the lulls in the war. **65m/B VHS.** William Tracy, Joseph (Joe) Sawyer; ***D:*** Fred Guiol.

Mr. Winkle Goes to War ♂♂ *Arms and the Woman* **1944** A weak, nerdy former banker is drafted for service during WWII and proves himself a hero by bulldozing a Japanese foxhole. Bits of genuine war footage add a measure of realism to an otherwise banal flag-waving comedy that is based on a novel by Theodore Pratt. **80m/B VHS.** Edward G. Robinson, Ruth Warrick, Richard Lane, Robert Armstrong, Ted Donaldson, Richard Gaines, Bob Haymes, Hugh Beaumont, Walter Baldwin, Howard Freeman; ***D:*** Alfred E. Green; ***W:*** Waldo Salt, Louis Solomon; ***C:*** Joseph Walker; ***M:*** Paul Sawtell, Carmen Dragon.

Mr. Wise Guy ♂♂ 1942 The East Side Kids break out of reform school to clear one of the Kids' brother of a murder charge. Typical pre-Bowery Boys vehicle. **70m/B VHS.** Leo Gorcey, Huntz Hall, Billy Gilbert, Guinn "Big Boy" Williams, Benny Rubin, Douglas Fowley, Ann Doran, Jack Mulhall, Warren Hymer, David Gorcey; ***D:*** William Nigh.

Mr. Wonderful ♂♂½ 1993 (PG-13) Bittersweet (rather than purely romantic) look at love and romance. Divorced Con Ed worker Gus (Dillon) is hard up for cash and tries to marry off ex-wife Lee (Sciorra) so he can use her alimony to invest in a bowling alley with his buddies. Routine flick's saved by the cast, who manage to bring a small measure of believability to a transparent plot. This was director Minghella's sophomore effort, between "Truly, Madly, Deeply" and "The English Patient." **99m/C VHS, DVD, Wide.** James Gandolfini, Bruce Kirby, Jessica Harper, Bruce Altman, Paul Bates, Matt Dillon, Annabella Sciorra, William Hurt, Mary-Louise Parker, Luis Guzman, Dan Hedaya, Vincent D'Onofrio; ***D:*** Anthony Minghella; ***W:*** Amy Schor, Vicki Polon; ***C:*** Geoffrey Simpson; ***M:*** Michael Gore.

Mr. Wong, Detective ♂♂ 1938 The first in the Mr. Wong series, the cunning detective traps a killer who feigns guilt to throw suspicion away from himself. The plot is loaded with the usual twists and villains. However, Karloff is a standout. **69m/B VHS, DVD.** Boris Karloff, Grant Withers; ***D:*** William Nigh; ***W:*** Houston Branch; ***C:*** Harry Neumann.

Mr. Wong in Chinatown ♂½ 1939 Third of the Mr. Wong series finds James Lee Wong investigating the murder of a wealthy Chinese woman. She had been helping to fund the purchase of airplanes to equip China in its 1930s' struggle with Japan. **70m/B VHS.** Boris Karloff, Grant Withers, William Royle, Marjorie Reynolds, Peter George Lynn, Lotus Long, Richard Loo; ***D:*** William Nigh.

Mr. Write ♂♂ 1992 (PG-13) Modest advertising satire mixed with romance. Aspiring writer Charlie (Reiser) decides to make some money by acting in commercials. He falls for ad exec Nicole (Tuck) but there are some complications to be overcome first, including her dim bulb boyfriend and obnoxious father. Adapted from the play by Howard J. Morris. **89m/C VHS.** Paul Reiser, Jessica Tuck, Doug Davidson, Martin Mull, Wendie Jo Sperber, Eddie Barth, Darryl M. Bell, Thomas F. Wilson, Jane Leeves, Calvert Deforest, Ben Stein; ***D:*** Charles Loventhal; ***W:*** Howard J. Morris; ***C:*** Elliot Davis.

Mr. Wrong ♂♂ 1995 (PG-13) In her feature film debut, DeGeneres plays Martha, a 30-something single woman with wacky friends who's being pressured by parents toward marriage while having little luck in the dating scene. Hmm...sounds familiar. Pullman plays Whitman, her dreamboat who quickly turns into the Titanic. Along the relationship road to ruin she is forced to deal with bad poetry, charades and...gum in her hair!! The usually entertaining DeGeneres is given little to do but react lamely to the wild events going on around her. Those that have had an experience with "the ex that would not go away" might want to rent something more calming, such as "Psycho." **97m/C VHS.** Ellen DeGeneres, Bill Pullman, Joan Cusack, Dean Stockwell, Joan Plowright, John Livingston, Robert Goulet, Ellen Cleghorne, Brad Henke, Polly Holliday, Briant Wells; ***D:*** Nick Castle; ***W:*** Chris Matheson, Kerry Ehrin, Craig Munson; ***C:*** John Schwartzman; ***M:*** Craig Safan.

Mistral's Daughter ♂½ 1984 Frothy miniseries, based on the Judith Krantz novel, about a French artist and his relationship with three beautiful women. Formulaic TV melodrama offers sexual scenes and revealing glimpses. Produced, like other Krantz miniseries, by author's hubby, Steve. **390m/C VHS.** Stefanie Powers, Lee Remick, Stacy Keach, Robert Urich, Timothy Dalton; ***D:*** Douglas Hickox; ***M:*** Vladimir Cosma. **TV**

Mistress ♂♂♂ *Wild Geese* **1953** A classic Japanese period piece about an innocent woman who believes she's married to a ruthless industrialist, only to find he is already married and she is but his mistress. Her love for a medical student unleashes tragedy. Subtly moving in a low-key way; starkly beautiful in black and white. In Japanese, with English subtitles. **106m/B VHS.** *JP* Hideko Takamine, Hiroshi Akutagawa; ***D:*** Shiro Toyoda.

Mistress ♂½ 1987 Weepy melodrama about a woman who makes a living as a mistress. When her lover dies, she must learn to stand on her own two feet. **96m/C VHS.** Victoria Principal, Alan Rachins, Don Murray; ***D:*** Michael Tuchner; ***M:*** Michael Convertino. **TV**

Mistress ♂♂ 1991 (R) A weak script does in a formidable cast in a behind-the-scenes look at movie making. Wuhl plays Marvin Landisman, a failed director/screenwriter, who's approached by has-been producer Jack Roth (Landau) who says he's found a backer to finance a movie from one of Marvin's old scripts. It turns out Roth has three men (De Niro, Aiello, and Wallach) ready to finance the film as long as each of their mistresses, who all have acting ambitions, gets the starring role. Double-dealing at a bargain basement level sets up the rest of this lifeless comedy. **100m/C VHS, DVD.** Robert Wuhl, Martin Landau, Robert De Niro, Eli Wallach, Danny Aiello, Sheryl Lee Ralph, Jean Smart, Tuesday Weld, Jace Alexander, Laurie Metcalf, Christopher Walken, Ernest Borgnine; ***D:*** Barry Primus; ***W:*** J.F. Lawton, Barry Primus; ***C:*** Sven Kirsten; ***M:*** Galt MacDermot.

Mistress of the Apes woof! 1979 (R) A woman searches for her missing husband in Africa with a group of scientists and discovers a tribe of near-men, who may be the missing link in evolution (or perhaps, a professional football team). Into their little group she is accepted, becoming their queen. Buchanan earned his reputation as a maker of horrible films honestly. Includes the songs "Mistress of the Apes" and "Ape Lady." **88m/C VHS.** Jenny Neumann, Barbara Leigh, Garth Pillsbury, Walt Robin, Stuart Lancaster, Suzy Mandel; ***D:*** Larry Buchanan; ***W:*** Larry Buchanan.

Mistress of the World ♂♂ 1959 A scientist, aided by Swedish Intelligence agent Ventura, works to protect his gravity-altering invention from Chinese agents. Partly based on a German serial from the silent film era, but not up to director Dieterle's usual fare. A must-see for Ventura fans and Mabuse mavens. **107m/C VHS.** Martha Hyer, Micheline Presle, Gino Cervi, Lino Ventura, Sabu, Wolfgang Preiss; ***D:*** William Dieterle.

Mistress Pamela ♂½ 1974 (R) When young Pamela goes to work in the household of handsome Lord Devonish, he sets about in wild pursuit of her virginity. Loosely based on the 1740 work "Pamela" by Samuel Richardson, considered the first modern English novel. Read the book unless you only have 95 minutes to spend finding out who gets what. **95m/C VHS.** Anne Michelle, Julian Barnes, Anna Quayle, Rosemary Dunham; ***D:*** Jim O'Connor.

Mistrial ♂♂ 1996 (R) NYC cop Steve Donohue (Pullman) is incensed when accused cop killer Eddie Rios (Seda) is acquited and Donohue himself is about to be charged in the wrongful deaths of the suspect's wife and brother, which occurred during his pursuit. So he takes the entire courtroom hostage. **90m/C VHS.** Bill Pullman, Robert Loggia, Jon Seda, Blair Underwood, Casey Siemaszko, Josef Sommer, Roberta Maxwell, James Rebhorn, Leo Burmester, Roma Maffia, Kate Burton; ***D:*** Heywood Gould; ***W:*** Heywood Gould; ***C:*** Paul Sarossy; ***M:*** Brad Fiedel. **CABLE**

Mists of Avalon ♂♂♂ 2001 A womancentric version of the story of Camelot based on Marion Zimmer Bradley's 1982 bestseller. Morgaine (Margulies) is the niece of the Lady of the Lake, Viviane (Huston), who raises her in the mother/goddess religion even as Christianity takes hold of the land. Morgaine is reunited with her half-brother Arthur (Atterton), who is betrothed to the Christian Gwenhwyfer (Mathis), who falls for Arthur's best friend and knight, Lancelot (Vartan). But as the years pass, Viking invasions and familial circumstances threaten to tear Arthur's kingdom apart and Morgaine can only watch as the vision of Avalon disappears as well. **180m/C VHS, DVD, Wide.** Julianna Margulies, Anjelica Huston, Samantha Mathis, Edward Atterton, Joan Allen, Michael Vartan, Hans Matheson, Caroline Goodall, Michael Byrne, Clive Russell, Mark Lewis Jones; ***D:*** Uli Edel; ***W:*** Gavin Scott; ***C:*** Vilmos Zsigmond; ***M:*** Lee Holdridge. **CABLE**

Misty ♂♂½ 1961 Ladd and Smith are two kids who capture a wild pony and teach it to run around in circles and step over things. Based on Marguerite Henry's bestselling "Misty of Chincoteague," and filmed on an island off the coast of Virginia. **92m/C VHS.** David Ladd, Arthur O'Connell, Pam Smith; ***D:*** James B. Clark.

Misunderstood ♂♂½ 1984 (PG) A former black market merchant has to learn how to relate to his sons after his wife dies. The father, now a legitimate businessman, is more concerned with running his shipping business than growing closer to his boys. Fine acting can't overcome a transparent plot. **92m/C VHS.** Gene Hackman, Susan Anspach, Henry Thomas, Rip Torn, Huckleberry Fox; ***D:*** Jerry Schatzberg; ***C:*** Pasqualino De Santis.

Misunderstood 1987 A father learns his lonely son is full of love and sensitivity when a tragedy reveals that it is this son who takes the blame for all the wrongs his brother commits. **101m/C VHS.** Anthony Quayle, Stefano Colagrande, Simone Gianozzi, John Sharp; ***D:*** Luigi Comencini.

Mitchell ♂ 1975 (R) Tough cop battles drug traffic and insipid script. Big screen release with that certain TV look. **90m/C VHS, DVD.** Joe Don Baker, Linda Evans, Martin Balsam, John Saxon, Merlin Olsen, Harold J. Stone; ***D:*** Andrew V. McLaglen; ***W:*** Ian Kennedy Martin; ***C:*** Harry Stradling Jr.; ***M:*** Jerry Styner.

Mixed Blood ♂♂½ 1984 (R) From the renowned underground film-maker, a dark comedy that examines the seedy drug subculture in New York. Violent, fast, and funny. **98m/C VHS.** Marilia Pera, Richard Vlacia, Linda Kerridge, Geraldine Smith, Angel David; ***D:*** Paul Morrissey; ***W:*** Paul Morrissey.

Mixed Nuts ♂ *Lifesavers* **1994 (PG-13)** Misfits man a suicide hotline on Christmas Eve in this unfunny, pathetic comedy that's a real downer. Director/writer Ephron (along with her co-writer sister Delia) try way too hard to fashion a hip, racy, madcap farce reminiscent of the screwball comedies that Hollywood churned out in the 1930s and '40s. Film never finds its style and the storyline is very weak. Most of the performances are over the top, although Martin, Shandling, and Kahn are good for a few amusing scenes. Ephron and the cast are capable of doing so much better, it's a shame their talents are virtually wasted here. Adapted from the French film "Le Pere Noel Est une Ordure." **97m/C VHS.** Steve Martin, Madeline Kahn, Robert Klein, Anthony LaPaglia, Juliette Lewis, Rob Reiner, Adam Sandler, Rita Wilson, Garry Shandling, Liev Schreiber; ***D:*** Nora Ephron; ***W:*** Nora Ephron, Delia Ephron; ***M:*** George Fenton.

Mixing Nia ♂♂½ 1998 (R) Biracial ad exec Nia (Parsons) becomes upset when she is asked to head a new beer campaign aimed at black youth. She quits, and decides to write a novel about the black experience and then realizes that she's lost touch with that part of her heritage. So, Nia decides to regain her roots and finds a real culture clash. **93m/C VHS, DVD.** Karyn Parsons, Isaiah Washington IV, Eric Thal, Diego Serrano, Heidi Schanz, Rosalyn Coleman; ***D:*** Alison Swan.

M'Lady's Court ♂ 198? A lawyer searching for an heiress in a convent of lusty maidens has loads of fun. None too captivating. **92m/C VHS.** Sonia Jeanine, Maja Hoppe.

Mo' Better Blues ♂♂½ 1990 (R) Not one of his more cohesive or compelling works, Lee's fourth feature is on the surface a backstage jazz biopic. But all Lee features are vitally concerned with complicated racial issues, and though subtle, this is no exception. Bleek Gilliam is a handsome, accomplished jazz trumpeter who divides his limited extra-curricular time between Clarke (newcomer Williams) and Indigo (junior Lee sibling Joie).

What's interesting is not so much the story of self-interested musician and ladies' man Gilliam, but the subtle racial issues his life draws into focus. The Branford Marsalis Quartet provides the music for Bleek's group, scored by Lee's dad Bill (on whose life the script is loosely based). **129m/C VHS, DVD, Wide.** Denzel Washington, Spike Lee, Joie Lee, Wesley Snipes, Cynda Williams, Giancarlo Esposito, Robin Harris, Bill Nunn, John Turturro, Dick Anthony Williams, Ruben Blades, Nicholas Turturro, Samuel L. Jackson, Abbey Lincoln, Tracy C. Johns, Joe Seneca; ***D:*** Spike Lee; ***W:*** Spike Lee; ***C:*** Ernest R. Dickerson; ***M:*** Bill Lee, Branford Marsalis.

Mo' Money && ½ **1992 (R)** Damon Wayans is a small-time con-artist who is inspired to go straight by a beautiful woman (Dash). He lands a job at the credit card company she works for, but temptation overcomes him, he swipes some plastic, and the scamming begins anew. With the help of his younger brother (played by real-life younger brother Marlon), they get involved in an even bigger, more dangerous scam being operated by the credit card company's head of security. Crude formula comedy driven by energetic, inventive performances by the brothers Wayans. Needless to say, will be especially enjoyed by fans of TV's "In Living Color." **97m/C VHS, DVD, Wide.** Damon Wayans, Marlon Wayans, Stacey Dash, Joe Santos, John Diehl, Harry J. Lennix, Mark Beltzman, Quincy Wong, Larry Brandenburg, Almayvonne; ***D:*** Peter Macdonald; ***W:*** Damon Wayans; ***C:*** Don Burgess; ***M:*** Jay Gruska.

Moana, a Romance of the Golden Age &&& ½ **1926** An early look through American eyes at the society of the people of Samoa, in the Pacific Islands. Picturesque successor to Flaherty's "Nanook of the North." **76m/B VHS.** Ta'avale, Fa'amgase, Moana; ***D:*** Robert Flaherty.

Mob Boss & **1990 (R)** Gangster films spoof starring Hickey as the head of a successful California crime ring. When his beautiful wife conspires to have him killed, he is left just breaths away from his demise. He calls his nerdy son to his bedside to ask him to take over the family business. But this kid thinks that money laundering requires detergent! Take this one down for a walk by the river in its new cement shoes. **93m/C VHS.** Eddie Deezen, Morgan Fairchild, William Hickey, Stuart Whitman; ***D:*** Fred Olen Ray.

Mob Queen && ½ **1998** Dim low-level Brooklyn mobsters George (Proval) and Dip (Moran) want to impress their boss, Joey "The Heart" Aorta (Sirico), by giving him a memorable birthday present. So George sets up a "date" with sexy new prostitute on the docks, Glorice (Cayne). And it works—Joey's smitten by the tough babe and George and Dip figure they're in clover. Until they find out that Glorice is actually a he—and they decide the safest thing would be to end the budding romance before Joey finds out too. Set in 1957. **87m/C VHS.** David Proval, Dan Moran, G. Anthony "Tony" Sirico, Candis Cayne, Marlene Forte, Jerry Grayson, Gerry Cooney; ***D:*** Jon Carnoy; ***W:*** Mike Horelick; ***C:*** Nils Kenaston; ***M:*** Jonathan Cossu.

Mob Story & ½ **1990 (R)** Vernon stars as a big-wig mob boss on the run from the government and a few of his "closest" friends. He plans to disappear into Canada, but if his girl (Kidder) and best friend (Waxman) find him first he'll be traveling in a body-bag. Very silly, but fun. **98m/C VHS, DVD.** John Vernon, Margot Kidder, Al Waxman, Kate Vernon; ***D:*** Gabriel Markiw, Jancarlo Markiw.

Mob War & ½ **1988 (R)** A war breaks out between the head of New York's underworld and a media genius. After deciding to become partners, the "family" tries to take over. For fun, count how many times the word "respect" pops up in the script. Tries hard but fails. **96m/C VHS, DVD.** John Christian, David Henry Keller, Jake La Motta, Johnny Stumper; ***D:*** J. Christian Ingvordsen; ***W:*** J. Christian Ingvordsen, John Weiner; ***C:*** Steven Kaman.

Mobsters & ½ **1991 (R)** It sounded like a great idea, casting the hottest young actors of the '90s as youthful racketeers "Lucky" Luciano, Meyer Lansky, Bugsy Siegel, and Frank Costello. But it would take an FBI probe to straighten out the blood-choked plot, as the pals' loyalties get tested the hard way in a dismembered narrative. Sicker than the violence is a seeming endorsement of the glamorous hoods. **104m/C VHS.** Joe (Johnny) Viterelli, Christian Slater, Patrick Dempsey, Richard Grieco, Costas Mandylor, Anthony Quinn, F. Murray Abraham, Lara Flynn Boyle, Michael Gambon, Christopher Penn; ***D:*** Michael Karbelnikoff; ***W:*** Nicholas Kazan; ***C:*** Lajos Koltai.

Moby Dick &&& **1956** This adaptation of Herman Melville's high seas saga features Peck as Captain Ahab. His obsession with desire for revenge upon the great white whale, Moby Dick, isn't always believable, but the moments that click, however, make the film more than worthwhile. **116m/C VHS, DVD.** Gregory Peck, Richard Basehart, Orson Welles, Leo Genn, Harry Andrews, Friedrich Ledebur; ***D:*** John Huston; ***W:*** Ray Bradbury, John Huston; ***C:*** Oswald Morris. Natl. Bd. of Review '56: Director (Huston); N.Y. Film Critics '56: Director (Huston).

Moby Dick && ½ **1998 (PG)** TV adaptation of Herman Melville's 1851 novel, starring a mesmerizing Stewart as the obsessive peg-legged Captain Ahab. Novice seaman Ishmael (Thomas) signs aboard the whaling ship Pequod, making friends with Polynesian native, harpooner Queequeg (Waretini). Soon enough Ishmael learns about the great white whale who claimed the captain's leg and Ahab's determination to seek revenge on the beast, no matter what the cost to himself, his crew, or the ship. Peck, who starred as Ahab in the 1956 movie version, takes on the role of Jonah-and-the-whale sermonizing Father Mapple. **145m/C VHS, DVD.** Patrick Stewart, Henry Thomas, Ted Levine, Piripi Waretini, Gregory Peck, Bill Hunter, Hugh Keays-Byrne, Norman D. Golden II, Bruce Spence; ***D:*** Franc Roddam; ***W:*** Franc Roddam, Anton Diether; ***C:*** David Connell; ***M:*** Christopher Gordon. **TV**

Mockery && ½ **1927** Chaney plays a peasant working for a Russian countess. He becomes involved in a peasant revolution against the rich and threatens the countess but eventually saves her from the mob. **75m/B VHS.** Lon Chaney Sr., Barbara Bedford, Ricardo Cortez, Emily Fitzroy; ***D:*** Benjamin Christiansen.

The Mod Squad & **1999 (R)** Tangled rehash of the '60s series tries very hard to be cool, but ends up as hip as a $2 haircut. Attempts to update the premise, but teen criminals-turned-cops Pete (Ribisi), Linc (Epps), and Julie (Danes) merely look like they're guilty of shoplifting from The Gap and making unwise acting career decisions. They all glower sullenly as they try to crack a convoluted case involving drugs, prostitution and their dead boss Capt. Greer (Farina). Director Silver manages to crush what little dramatic tension was left in the stale script into a bland pulp. This shameless attempt to highjack youth culture in order to sell jeans is just another case of the man trying to keep you down. **94m/C VHS, DVD.** Bodhi (Pine) Elfman, Holmes Osborne, Dey Young, Eddie Griffin, Claire Danes, Giovanni Ribisi, Omar Epps, Dennis Farina, Josh Brolin, Richard Jenkins, Larry Brandenburg, Steve Harris, Sam McMurray, Michael Lerner; ***D:*** Scott Silver; ***W:*** Scott Silver, Stephen Kay, Kate Lanier; ***C:*** Ellen Kuras; ***M:*** B.C. Smith.

Model Behavior & ½ **1982** Fresh from college, an aspiring photographer pines for a glamorous model. **86m/C VHS.** Richard Bekins, Bruce Lyons, Cindy Harrel; ***D:*** Bud Gardner.

Model Behavior && **2000** Shy, boyfriendless, 16-year-old Alex (Lawson) is your typically anguished teen. She wishes she had the life of teen supermodel Janine and gets her chance when the girls accidentally meet and realize they are lookalikes. So they decide to trade places for a week—Alex gets to do fashion shoots, go to parties, and hang-out with fellow model Jason (played by 'N Sync's Timberlake) and Janine gets to go to high school, eat stuff that's bad for her, and laze around. It's kind of a "The Prince and the Pauper" for girls with no one threatening their lives. Based on the book by Michael Levin. **90m/C VHS.** Maggie Lawson, Justin Timberlake, Kathie Lee Gifford, Cody Gifford, Jim Abele, Daniel Clark, Karen Hines, Jesse Nilsson; ***Cameos:*** Vendela Thommessen; ***D:*** Mark Rosman; ***W:*** David Kukoff, Matt Roshkow; ***C:*** Laszlo George; ***M:*** Eric Colvin. **TV**

Model by Day & ½ **1994 (R)** When New York model Janssen's father is murdered, she takes up martial arts training and becomes the vengeful "Lady X." Then she becomes the prime suspect in a murder and finds herself falling for a plainsclothes cop. Fair amount of action, somewhat less exploitive than usual for the genre. **89m/C VHS.** Famke Janssen, Stephen Shellen, Shannon Tweed, Sean Young; ***D:*** Christian Duguay.

A Modern Affair & ½ *Mr. 247* **1994 (R)** Single executive Grace Rhodes' (Eichhorn) biological clock is ringing and without Mr. Right in sight, she decides to visit a sperm bank. Grace gets pregnant and also very curious about her anonymous donor—who of course doesn't stay anonymous. Grace even manages to fall for photographer Peter Kessler (Tucci) but how does she tell him she's carrying his baby when they haven't even had sex yet? **91m/C VHS.** Lisa Eichhorn, Stanley Tucci, Caroline Aaron, Tammy Grimes, Robert Joy, Wesley Addy, Cynthia Martells, Mary Jo Salerno; ***D:*** Vern Oakley; ***W:*** Paul Zimmerman; ***C:*** Rex Nicholson; ***M:*** Jan Hammer.

Modern Girls & ½ **1986 (PG-13)** Teen comedy about three bubble-headed LA rock groupies and their various wild adventures during a single night on the town. Surprising in that the three lead actresses waste their talents in this lesson in exploitation. Bruce Springsteen's younger sister portrays a drug user. **82m/C VHS.** Cynthia Gibb, Daphne Zuniga, Virginia Madsen; ***D:*** Jerry Kramer; ***W:*** Laurie Craig; ***M:*** Eddie Arkin.

Modern Love & **1990 (R)** An average slob realizes that marriage, fatherhood and in-law-ship isn't quite what he expected. Benson stars, directs and produces as well as co-starring with real-life wife DeVito. A plotless hodgepodge of bits that were more successful in "Look Who's Talking" and "Parenthood." **89m/C VHS, DVD.** Robby Benson, Karla DeVito, Rue McClanahan, Kaye Ballard, Frankie Valli, Cliff Bemis, Louise Lasser, Burt Reynolds, Lyric Benson; ***D:*** Robby Benson; ***W:*** Robby Benson.

Modern Problems && **1981 (PG)** A man involved in a nuclear accident discovers he has acquired telekinetic powers, which he uses to turn the tables on his professional and romantic rivals. A fine cast but an unsuccessful fission trip. **93m/C VHS.** Chevy Chase, Patti D'Arbanville, Mary Kay Place, Brian Doyle-Murray, Nell Carter, Dabney Coleman; ***D:*** Ken Shapiro.

Modern Romance &&& **1981 (R)** The romantic misadventures of a neurotic film editor who is hopelessly in love with his girlfriend but can't seem to maintain a normal relationship with her. Smart and hilarious at times and always simmering with anxiety. Offers an honest look at relationships as well as an accurate portrait of filmmaking. **102m/C VHS.** Albert Brooks, Kathryn Harrold, Bruno Kirby, George Kennedy, James L. Brooks, Bob Einstein; ***D:*** Albert Brooks; ***W:*** Albert Brooks, Monica Johnson.

Modern Times &&&& **1936** This "mostly" silent film finds Chaplin playing a factory worker who goes crazy from his repetitious job on an assembly line and his boss's demands for greater speed and efficiency. Ultimately encompassing the tyranny of machine over man, this cinematic masterpiece has more relevance today than ever. Chaplin wrote the musical score which incorporates the tune "Smile." Look for a young Gloria De Haven as one of Goddard's sisters; she's the real-life daughter of Chaplin's assistant director. **87m/B VHS, DVD.** Charlie Chaplin, Paulette Goddard, Henry Bergman, Stanley Sandford, Gloria De Haven, Chester Conklin; ***D:*** Charlie Chaplin; ***W:*** Charlie Chaplin; ***C:*** Ira Morgan, Roland H. Totheroh; ***M:*** Charlie Chaplin. AFI '98: Top 100, Natl. Film Reg. '89.

Modern Vampires & ½ *Revenant* **1998 (R)** Think vampire-lite. A community of European vamps have moved to L.A., where the beautiful Nico (Wagner) is threatening their anonymity by her bloody kills. Dallas (Van Dien), Nico's vampire boyfriend, tries to protect her from Dracula (Pasortelli), who wants her destroyed. Meanwhile, vampire hunter Van Helsing (Steiger) seeks to get rid of the entire community. **95m/C VHS, DVD.** Casper Van Dien, Natasha Gregson Wagner, Rod Steiger, Robert Pastorelli, Kim Cattrall, Natasha Andreichenko, Gabriel Casseus, Udo Kier, Natasha Lyonne; ***D:*** Richard Elfman; ***W:*** Matthew Bright; ***M:*** Danny Elfman, Michael Wandmacher.

The Moderns &&& **1988 (R)** One of the quirkier directors around, this time Rudolph tries a comedic period piece about the avant-garde art society of 1920s Paris. Fleshed out with some familiar characters (Ernest Hemingway, Gertrude Stein) and some strange art-world types. The tone is not consistently funny but, instead, romantic as the main characters clash over art and love. **126m/C VHS, 8mm.** Keith Carradine, Linda Fiorentino, John Lone, Genevieve Bujold, Geraldine Chaplin, Wallace Shawn, Kevin J. O'Connor; ***D:*** Alan Rudolph; ***W:*** Alan Rudolph; ***M:*** Mark Isham. L.A. Film Critics '88: Support. Actress (Bujold).

Modesty Blaise && ½ **1966** Adaptation of Peter O'Donnell's comic strip finds his tough British babe spy embodied by Italian beauty Vitti, aided by her right-hand man Willie Garvin (Stamp). The secret agent is watching out for a diamond shipment, which is the target of her archrival Gabriel (Bogarde). Very campy and sixties pop-arty, with everyone having fun and not taking any situation seriously. O'Donnell retired himself and Modesty in 2001. **118m/C VHS, DVD.** *GB* Monica Vitti, Terence Stamp, Dirk Bogarde, Harry Andrews, Michael Craig, Clive Revill, Alexander Knox, Rossella Falk; ***D:*** Joseph Losey; ***W:*** Evan Jones; ***C:*** Jack Hildyard; ***M:*** John Dankworth.

Modigliani && ½ *Montparnasse 19; The Lovers of Montparnasse; Modigliani of Montparnasse* **1958** Life of dissolute 19th-century painter Modigliani (Philipe), which tracks his affairs with British poet Beatrice Hastings (Palmer) and later mistress Jeanne (Aimee), who commits suicide shortly before his death. Female performances make up for the lackluster lead. Becker inherited the film from director Max Ophuls, who co-wrote the screenplay but who died before the start of production. In French with English subtitles. **110m/B VHS.** *FR* Gerard Philipe, Lilli Palmer, Anouk Aimee, Gerard Sety, Lino Ventura, Lila Kedrova, Lea Padovani; ***D:*** Jacques Becker; ***W:*** Max Ophuls, Henri Jeanson, Jacques Becker.

Mogambo &&& **1953** Remake of "Red Dust," this is the steamy story of a love triangle between an African game hunter, a proper British lady, and an American showgirl in the jungles of Kenya. **115m/C VHS.** Clark Gable, Ava Gardner, Grace Kelly; ***D:*** John Ford; ***C:*** Robert L. Surtees. Golden Globes '54: Support. Actress (Kelly).

Mohawk & ½ **1956** A cowboy and his Indian maiden try to stop a war between Indian tribes and fanatical landowners. **80m/C VHS, DVD.** Rita Gam, Neville Brand, Scott Brady, Lori Nelson; ***D:*** Kurt Neumann; ***W:*** Maurice Geraghty, Milton Krims; ***C:*** Karl Struss; ***M:*** Edward L. Alperson Jr.

Mojave Moon && ½ **1996 (R)** Middle-aged car dealer Al (Aiello) is asked by nymphet Ellie (Jolie) to drive her home—a trailer in the desert where Al meets her perky-yet-kinky mom Julie (Archer) and Julie's violent boyfriend Boyd (Biehn). A series of strange happenings finds Al tied to the trio and discovering both adventure and romance. **95m/C VHS.** Danny Aiello, Anne Archer, Angelina Jolie, Michael Biehn, Alfred Molina; ***D:*** Kevin Dowling; ***W:*** Leonard Glasser; ***C:*** James Glennon.

Mole Men Against the Son of Hercules & **1961** Italian muscleman Maciste battles the pale-skinned denizens of an underground city. **?m/C VHS.** *IT* Mark Forest.

The Mole People 1956 A really bad '50s creature feature which finds two archeologists accidentally discovering an underground civilization of albinos who shun all forms of light. They've also enslaved the local populace of half-human, half-mole creatures who decide to help the good guys escape by rising up in a revolt against their evil masters. When the weapon of choice is a flashlight you know not to expect much. **78m/B VHS.** John Agar, Cynthia Patrick, Hugh Beaumont, Alan Napier, Nestor Paiva, Phil Chambers; ***D:*** Virgil W. Vogel; ***W:*** Laszlo Gorog.

Moll Flanders ½ *The Fortunes and Misfortunes of Moll Flanders* **1996** Rousing, bawdy retelling of Daniel Defoe's 1722 novel about the wickedly seductive Moll (Kingston). Born in London's Newgate prison, Moll becomes a house servant, embarks on her first marriage, is soon widowed, and decides to make her own way (and fortune). She becomes a thief, a whore, marries several more times, and eventually winds up back in prison and a likely candidate for the gallows. But the ever-enterprising Moll always finds her way. TV miniseries on two cassettes. **210m/C VHS, DVD.** *GB* Alex Kingston, Daniel Craig, Diana Rigg, Colin Buchanan, Christopher Fulford, James Fleet, Ian Driver, Tom Ward; ***D:*** David Attwood; ***W:*** Andrew Davies; ***C:*** Ivan Strasburg; ***M:*** Jim Parker. **TV**

Moll Flanders ½ **1996 (PG-13)** Writer/director Densham takes only the title character and the 18th-century London setting from Daniel Defoe's 1722 novel in telling of spirited heroine Moll Flanders' (Wright) life. Orphaned Moll eventually finds herself working at the brothel of greedy, scheming Mrs. Allworthy (Channing). Her life as a prostitute leads her to drink and near suicide—despite the unwavering friendship of Hibble (Freeman), Allworthy's dignified servant—until she falls for an impoverished artist (Lynch) and briefly finds happiness. Wright's heartfelt performance holds everything together (with help from a talented supporting cast) but things get dreary. **120m/C VHS, DVD.** Robin Wright Penn, Morgan Freeman, Stockard Channing, John Lynch, Brenda Fricker, Aisling Corcoran, Geraldine James, Jim Sheridan, Jeremy Brett, Britta Smith, Ger Ryan; ***D:*** Pen Densham; ***W:*** Pen Densham; ***C:*** David Tattersall; ***M:*** Mark Mancina.

Molly **1999 (PG-13)** Sounds like a ripoff of 1968's "Charly," which was more successful and sensitive. Molly (Shue) is a mentally challenged woman who undergoes experimental surgery which leaves her functionally normal—temporarily. She begins to gain overly-powerful senses and sex drive, leading her to have an affair with fellow patient Sam (Jane). As her brain rejects the cells from the operation, she sinks back into the fog of her previous illness. Her brother Buck (Eckhart) goes from apathetic to overprotective seemingly overnight. He also begins a relationship with Molly's surgeon Susan (Hennessy) without any initial romantic foundations being shown. While Shue's performance is fairly good, the horrible editing and ill-conceived storyline doom this would-be drama. **87m/C VHS, DVD, Wide.** Elisabeth Shue, Aaron Eckhart, Jill(ian) Hennessey, Thomas Jane, D.W. Moffett, Elizabeth Mitchell, Robert Harper, Elaine Hendrix, Michael Paul Chan, Lucy Alexis Liu; ***D:*** John Duigan; ***W:*** Dick Christie; ***C:*** Gabriel Beristain; ***M:*** Trevor Jones.

Molly and Gina **1994 (R)** The very different lives of Molly and Gina intersect suddenly when their boyfriends are killed in the street by gunfire. They are drawn into the underworld of gun-runners and violence, as they seek justice for the men they loved. **90m/C VHS.** Frances Fisher, Natasha Gregson Wagner, Bruce Weitz, Stella Stevens, Peter Fonda; ***D:*** Paul Leder; ***W:*** Reuben Leder; ***M:*** Dana Walden.

Molly & Lawless John **1972** Average western, with Miles the wife of a sadistic sheriff who helps a prisoner escape the gallows so they can run away together. Enough cliches for the whole family to enjoy. **90m/C VHS.** Sam Elliott, Vera Miles; ***D:*** Gary Nelson.

Molly Maguires ½ **1970 (PG)** Dramatization based on a true story, concerns a group of miners called the Molly Maguires who resort to using terrorist tactics in their fight for better working conditions during the Pennsylvania Irish coal mining rebellion in the 1870s. During their reign of terror, the Mollies are infiltrated by a Pinkerton detective who they mistakenly believe is a new recruit. It has its moments but never fully succeeds. Returned less than 15% of its initial $11 million investment. **123m/C VHS.** Sean Connery, Richard Harris, Samantha Eggar, Frank Finlay; ***D:*** Martin Ritt; ***W:*** Walter Bernstein; ***C:*** James Wong Howe; ***M:*** Henry Mancini.

The Mollycoddle **1920** Fairbanks is a British-educated American whom everyone thinks is less-than-manly until he brings a smuggler to justice. **?m/B VHS.** Douglas Fairbanks Sr., Wallace Beery, Ruth Renick; ***D:*** Victor Fleming; ***W:*** Douglas Fairbanks Sr.

Molokai: The Story of Father Damien ½ **1999** In the 19th century, the government sent suspected lepers to the island of Molokai in an effort to stop the spread of infection. The inhabitants were dependant on the efforts of the church to ease their suffering. Father Damien (Wenham) volunteers to go to the island to provide spiritual and physical comfort and care, even at the risk of contracting the disease himself. Based on a true story. **112m/C VHS, DVD.** Jan Decleir, David Wenham, Derek Jacobi, Alice Krige, Kris Kristofferson, Peter O'Toole, Sam Neill, Leo McKern, Tom Wilkinson; ***D:*** Paul Cox; ***W:*** John Briley; ***M:*** Wim Mertens. **VIDEO**

Mom woof! **1989 (R)** When his mother is bitten by a flesh-eater, Clay Dwyer is at a loss as to what to do. How do you tell your own mother that she must be destroyed, lest she continue to devour human flesh? A campy horror/comedy. **95m/C VHS.** Mark Thomas Miller, Art Evans, Mary (Elizabeth) McDonough, Jeanne Bates, Brion James, Stella Stevens, Claudia Christian; ***D:*** Patrick Rand.

Mom & Dad **1947** An innocent young girl's one night of passion leads to an unwanted pregnancy. Stock footage of childbirth and a lecture on the evils of syphilis concludes this campy schlock that features the national anthem. Banned or denied release for years, this movie is now a cult favorite for its time-capsule glimpse at conventional 1940s sexual attitudes. **97m/B VHS.** Hardie Albright, Sarah Blake, George Eldredge, June Carlson, Jimmy Clark, Bob Lowell; ***D:*** William Beaudine; ***W:*** Mildred Horn; ***C:*** Barney A. Sarecky.

Mom and Dad Save the World ½ **1992 (PG)** A suburban housewife (Garr) is transported along with her husband in the family station wagon to the planet Spengo, ruled by King Tod Spengo (Lovitz), who has fallen in love with her and wants to save her from his plans to blow up Earth. While trying to prevent the king from marrying her and killing him, Garr and Jones wind up in many goofy situations and wind up saving the Earth from its imminent doom. Uninspired comedy just isn't funny, and the excellent cast is misused, especially Idle and Shawn. Save this one for the kiddies. **87m/C VHS.** Teri Garr, Jeffrey Jones, Jon Lovitz, Eric Idle, Wallace Shawn, Dwier Brown, Kathy Ireland, Thalmus Rasulala; ***D:*** Greg Beeman; ***M:*** Jerry Goldsmith.

Mom, Can I Keep Her? ½ **1998 (PG)** Goofy family film features 12-year-old Timmy who's having problems at school and at home with a too-busy father and a new stepmom. But that's nothing compared to the new friend that follows Timmy home—a 500 lb. gorilla. **?m/C VHS, DVD.** Gil Gerard, Kevin Dobson, Terry Funk, Justin Berfield, Alana Stewart, Henry Darrow, Don Mcleod; ***D:*** Fred Olen Ray; ***W:*** Sean O'Bannon; ***C:*** Jesse Weathington. **VIDEO**

Mom, the Wolfman and Me ½ **1980** An 11-year-old girl arranges and manages the love affair of her mother, an ultra-liberated photographer, and an unemployed teacher, who is also the owner of an Irish wolfhound. Charming adaptation of a novel by Norma Klein. **100m/C VHS.** Patty Duke, David Birney, Danielle Brisebois, Keenan Wynn, Viveca Lindfors, John Lithgow; ***D:*** Edmond Levy. **TV**

Moment to Moment ½ **1966** Standard romantic suspenser set on the French Riviera. Kay Stanton (Seberg) is being neglected by her shrink hubby Neil (Hill). So she decides to fool around with young Navy stud Mark (Garrison). Only she accidentally shoots him during a quarrel and then asks her best pal, Daphne (Blackman), to help her get rid of the body. Only Mark isn't so dead after all. **108m/C VHS.** Jean Seberg, Arthur Hill, Honor Blackman, Sean Garrison, Gregoire Aslan; ***D:*** Mervyn LeRoy; ***W:*** John Lee Mahin, Alec Coppel; ***C:*** Harry Stradling Sr.; ***M:*** Henry Mancini.

Mommie Dearest **1981 (PG)** Film based on Christina Crawford's memoirs of her incredibly abusive and violent childhood at the hands of her adoptive mother, actress Joan Crawford. The story is controversial and sometimes trashy, but fairly well done nevertheless. However, it is also so campy and the immortal Crawford/Dunaway screech "No wire hangers—ever!" became so associated with Dunaway's over-the-top performance that it was thought by some to have damaged the actress's career. **129m/C VHS, DVD, Wide.** Faye Dunaway, Diana Scarwid, Steve Forrest, Mara Hobel, Rutanya Alda, Harry Goz, Howard da Silva; ***D:*** Frank Perry; ***W:*** Frank Perry, Robert Getchell, Frank Yablans; ***C:*** Paul Lohmann; ***M:*** Henry Mancini. Golden Raspberries '81: Worst Picture, Worst Actress (Dunaway), Worst Support. Actor (Forrest), Worst Support. Actress (Scarwid), Worst Screenplay.

Mommy ½ **1995** Schoolteacher is stalked by murderous mom who'll do anything for her daughter. Mommy McCormack was the original "Bad Seed" child. Filmed in Muscatine, Iowa. **89m/C VHS, DVD.** Patty McCormack, Majel Barrett, Jason Miller, Brinke Stevens, Rachel Lemieux, Mickey Spillane, Michael Cornelison, Sarah Jane Miller; ***D:*** Max Allan Collins; ***W:*** Max Allan Collins; ***C:*** Phillip W. Dingeldein; ***M:*** Richard Lowry.

Mommy 2: Mommy's Day ½ **1996** Murderous Mommy (McCormack) returns as does her beloved daughter (now rebellious teenager), Jessica Ann (Lemieux). Mommy's on Death Row, awaiting execution after her murder spree but the Mommy-style killings continue. Shot on location in Iowa. **89m/C VHS, DVD.** Patty McCormack, Rachel Lemieux, Brinke Stevens, Michael Cornelison, Sarah Jane Miller, Mickey Spillane, Gary Sandy, Paul Petersen, Arlen Dean Snyder, Todd Eastland, Del Close; ***D:*** Max Allan Collins; ***W:*** Max Allan Collins; ***C:*** Phillip W. Dingeldein; ***M:*** Richard Lowry.

Mom's Outta Sight **2001 (PG)** Substandard kiddie SF comedy exudes cheapness. Special effects and props are bargain-basement material. The story has something to do with a matter transmission machine that turns a sexy woman into a mincing man and makes another (Williamson) invisible. The only redeeming feature is an all-too-brief cameo by Brinke Stevens. **89m/C VHS, DVD.** Hannes Jaenicke, Melissa Williamson, Steve Scionti, Ariauna Albright, Brinke Stevens; ***D:*** Peter Stewart; ***W:*** Sean O'Bannon; ***C:*** Theo Angell; ***M:*** Jay Bolton. **VIDEO**

Mon Amie Max **1994** Marie-Alexandrine (Max) Babant (Bujold) is a middle-aged former pianist who returns to her native Quebec City after 25 years of self-imposed exile. Pregnant at 15, Max was forced to give her son up for adoption and ran away from friends and family. Now, she's meet former best friend Catherine (Keller), who's had the concert career Max never did, who's also agreed to help Max find her son. Slow-going melodrama with little emotional impact. **107m/C VHS.** *CA FR* Genevieve Bujold, Marthe Keller, Michel Rivard, Johanne McKay; ***D:*** Michel Brault; ***W:*** Jefferson Lewis.

Mon Homme *My Man* **1996** Marie's (Grinberg) a very happy hooker (think male fantasy) whose kindly impulses wind up getting her into difficulty. She picks up the homeless Jeannot (Lanvin), invites him in for a meal, offers him sex, and is enthralled by his unexpected prowess. Marie decides Jeannot should become her pimp but, unfortunately for her, he takes to his new job with great zeal, seducing manicurist Sanguine (Bruni-Tedeschi) as another lover/prostitute. But when Jeannot gets arrested, his two women decide to abandon him and turn respectable. Nothing exactly works out. French with subtitles. **95m/C VHS, Wide.** *FR* Anouk Grinberg, Gerard Lanvin, Valeria Bruni-Tedeschi, Olivier Martinez; ***Cameos:*** Mathieu Kassovitz, Jean-Pierre Leaud; ***D:*** Bertrand Blier; ***W:*** Bertrand Blier; ***C:*** Pierre Lhomme.

Mon Oncle *My Uncle; My Uncle, Mr. Hulot* **1958** Tati's celebrated comedy contrasts the simple life of Monsieur Hulot with the technologically complicated life of his family when he aids his nephew in war against his parents' ultramodern, push-button home. An easygoing, delightful comedy, this is the director's first piece in color. Sequel to "Mr. Hulot's Holiday," followed by "Playtime." In French with English subtitles. **110m/C VHS, DVD, 8mm.** *FR* Jacques Tati, Jean-Pierre Zola, Adrienne Serrantie, Alain Bacourt; ***D:*** Jacques Tati; ***W:*** Jacques Lagrange, Jacques Tati; ***C:*** Jean (Yves, Georges) Bourgoin; ***M:*** Alain Romans, AMG. Oscars '58: Foreign Film; Cannes '58: Grand Jury Prize; N.Y. Film Critics '58: Foreign Film.

Mon Oncle Antoine ½ **1971** A splendid tale of young Benoit, who learns about life from a surprisingly compassionate uncle, who works as everything from undertaker to grocer in the depressed area where they live. **104m/C VHS.** *CA* Jean Duceppe, Olivette Thibault; ***D:*** Claude Jutra.

Mon Oncle d'Amerique ½ *Les Somnambules* **1980 (PG)** Three French characters are followed as they try to find success of varying kinds in Paris, interspersed with ironic lectures by Prof. Henri Laborit about the biology that impels human behavior. Their disappointments lead them to dream of a legendary American uncle, who could make their desires come true. An acclaimed, witty comedy by former Nouvelle Vague filmmaker, dubbed into English. **123m/C VHS, DVD.** *FR* Gerard Depardieu, Nicole Garcia, Roger-Pierre, Marie DuBois; ***D:*** Alain Resnais; ***W:*** Jean Gruault; ***C:*** Sacha Vierny; ***M:*** Arie Dzierlatka. Cannes '80: Grand Jury Prize; N.Y. Film Critics '80: Foreign Film.

Mona Lisa ½ **1986 (R)** Jordan's wonderful, sad, sensitive story of a romantic, small-time hood who gets personally involved with the welfare and bad company of the high-priced whore he's been hired to chauffeur. Hoskins is especially touching and Caine is chilling as a suave gangster. Fine film debut for Tyson. Brilliantly filmed and critically lauded. **104m/C VHS, DVD.** *GB* Bob Hoskins, Cathy Tyson, Michael Caine, Clarke Peters, Kate Hardie, Robbie Coltrane, Zoe Nathenson, Sammi Davis, Rod Bedall, Joe Brown, Pauline Melville; ***D:*** Neil Jordan; ***W:*** David Leland, Neil Jordan; ***C:*** Roger Pratt; ***M:*** Michael Kamen. British Acad. '86: Actor (Hoskins); Cannes '86: Actor (Hoskins); Golden Globes '87: Actor—Drama (Hoskins); L.A. Film Critics '86: Actor (Hoskins), Support. Actress (Tyson); N.Y. Film Critics '86: Actor (Hoskins); Natl. Soc. Film Critics '86: Actor (Hoskins).

Monaco Forever **1983** An enigmatic American meets a mysterious Frenchwoman and they set off on a string of unusual romantic adventures. Set around the 1956 marriage of Grace Kelly to Prince Rainier of Monaco. Film debut of Van Damme. **79m/C VHS.** Charles Pitt, Martha Farris, Sydney Lassick, Jean-Claude Van Damme; ***D:*** William A. Levey; ***W:*** C. William Pitt, William A. Levey.

Mondo **1996** Orphaned gypsy boy Mondo (Balan) winds up living on the streets of Nice looking for a new family. He's befriended and sheltered by various street people as he hides from the police who want to place him in care. Based on the novel "Ed. Gallinard" by J.M.G. Le Clezio. French with subtitles. **80m/C VHS.** *FR* Ovidiu Balan, Philippe Petit, Pierrette Fesch, Jerry Smith; ***D:*** Tony Gatlif; ***W:*** Tony Gatlif; ***C:*** Eric Guichard.

Mondo Balordo **1964** Translated as "Crazy World," this is crude sensationalism masked as a horror story. Karloff guides the viewer through a curious mixture of society's fringe elements. A loosely connected series of sketches includes portraits of a reincarnated Rudolph Valentino, practitioners of transvestism, Roman coke whores, and an Italian-Japanese rock 'n roll midget (Drago) in director Montero's unusual vision of an anti-paradise. Includes standard lesbian club scene. Volume 11 of Frank Henenlotter's Sexy Shockers. **86m/C VHS, DVD.** Franz Drago; ***D:*** Robert Montero; ***W:*** Albert T. Viola; ***Nar:*** Boris Karloff.

Mondo Cane *A Dog's Life* **1963 (R)** A documentary showcasing the eccentricities of human behavior around the world, including cannibalism, pig killing and more. Dubbed in English. Inspired a rash of "shockumentaries" over the next several years. The song "More" made its debut in this film. **105m/C VHS, DVD.** *IT* ***D:*** Gualtiero Jacopetti; ***W:*** Gualtiero Jacopetti; ***C:*** Antonio Climati, Benito Frattari; ***M:*** Riz Ortolani, Nino Oliviero; ***Nar:*** Stefano Sibaldi.

Mondo Cane 2 *Mondo Pazzo; Mondo Insanity; Crazy World; Insane World* **1964 (R)** More documentary-like views of the oddities of mankind and ethnic rituals around the world. Enough, already. **94m/C VHS.** *IT* ***D:*** Gualtiero Jacopetti, Franco Prosperi.

Mondo Trasho woof! **1969** A major trasho film of the last day in the life of a most unfortunate woman, complete with sex and violence. First full length effort from cult filmmaker Waters, who was also writer, producer, and editor. **95m/B VHS.** Mary Vivian Pearce, Divine, John Leisenring, Mink Stole, David Lochary, Chris Atkinson, Mark Isherwood; ***D:*** John Waters; ***W:*** John Waters; ***C:*** John Waters.

The Money **1975 (R)** The quest for money drives a young man to kidnap the child that his girlfriend is baby-sitting. Average but Workman's direction is right on the money. **88m/C VHS.** Laurence Luckinbill, Elizabeth Richards, Danny DeVito, Graham Beckel; ***D:*** Chuck Workman.

Money Buys Happiness **1999** Money (Weatherford) and Georgia (Murphy) are on the verge of divorce when a friend commits suicide and leaves them an upright piano. Their problems crystallize as they attempt to transport the instrument 50 blocks across town. That's a curious premise for a comedy but this one manages to generate some genuine wit. **104m/C DVD, Wide.** Megan Murphy, Jeff Weatherford, Michael Chick, Cynthia Whalen, Caveh Zahedi; ***D:*** Gregg Lachow; ***W:*** Gregg Lachow; ***C:*** Jamie Hook; ***M:*** Jim Ragland.

Money for Nothing **1993 (R)** $1.2 million falls off a truck in the warehouse district of Philadelphia where a simple-minded unemployed longshoreman (Cusack) finds the chance of a lifetime. Indiscreetly leaving behind a trail of spending, he soon has a detective (Madsen) snooping around dangerously close. But he only digs himself deeper by enlisting the assistance of the mob to help him launder the money. At this point the film disintegrates into a limp diatribe on the injustice of capitalism on society's downtrodden. Mazar plays Joey's ex-girlfriend who double-times it back to the fold after his find. Based on a true story. **100m/C VHS.** John Cusack, Michael Madsen, Benicio Del Toro, Michael Rapaport, Debi Mazar, Fionnula Flanagan, Maury Chaykin, James Gandolfini, Elizabeth Bracco, Ashleigh Dejon, Lenny Venito; ***D:*** Ramon Menendez; ***W:*** Ramon Menendez, Carol Sobieski, Tom Musca; ***M:*** Craig Safan.

Money Kings *Vig* **1998 (R)** Slow-starter is worth the time it takes to get the story moving. Soft-hearted Vinnie Glenn (Falk) runs a Boston bar and serves as a small-time bookie for some backroom gambling. Then the local mob decide Vinnie needs an assistant to help him collect on the bad debts and send in a young hothead, Anthony (Prinze). Vinnie would like to restore the status quo before he heads to a Florida vacation with loyal wife Ellen (Daly), if only Anthony will listen. **96m/C VHS, DVD.** Peter Falk, Freddie Prinze Jr., Lauren Holly, Timothy Hutton, Tyne Daly; ***D:*** Graham Theakston.

Money Madness **1947** Beaumont (Ward Cleaver) plays a taxi driver turned thief in this curiosity. **?m/C VHS.** Hugh Beaumont, Frances Rafferty, Harlan Warde, Cecil Weston, Ida Moore, Danny Morton, Joel Friedkin, Lane Chandler; ***D:*** Peter Stewart, Sam Newfield; ***W:*** Al Martin; ***C:*** Jack Greenhalgh.

Money Movers **1978** Aussie thieves plan megabuck bank robbery but heist and plot go sour. An oft told tale based on a true story. Features early appearance from burly boy Brown. **94m/C VHS.** *AU* Terence Donovan, Ed Devereaux, Tony Bonner, Lucky Grills, Charles Tingwell, Candy (Candida) Raymond, Bryan Brown, Alan Cassell; ***D:*** Bruce Beresford; ***W:*** Bruce Beresford.

The Money Pit **1986 (PG)** A young yuppie couple encounter sundry problems when they attempt to renovate their newly purchased, seemingly self-destructive, Long Island home. However, the collapse of their home leads directly to the collapse of their relationship as well. Somewhat modeled after "Mr. Blandings Builds His Dream House." Hanks and Long fail to jell as partners and the many sight gags are on the predictable side. A Spielberg production. **91m/C VHS.** Tom Hanks, Shelley Long, Alexander Godunov, Maureen Stapleton, Philip Bosco, Joe Mantegna, Josh Mostel; ***D:*** Richard Benjamin; ***C:*** Gordon Willis; ***M:*** Michel Colombier.

Money Talks **1997 (R)** Hustler Franklin Hatchett (Tucker) is falsely accused of orchestrating a violent jail break. Ratings-hungry TV reporter James Russell (Sheen) agrees to help Franklin clear his name in return for exclusive rights to his story. The mismatched pair search for stolen jewels, dodge bullets and endure explosive escapes, but this being an action-comedy, there needs to be some laughs. These are provided (intermittently) by the frenzied comic style of Tucker, who easily eclipses Sheen's straight man demeanor (which could be mistaken for acting if you've never seen any of Sheen's previous films). Tucker shows flashes of deserving better material than he has to work with here. **92m/C VHS, DVD, Wide.** Chris Tucker, Charlie Sheen, Heather Locklear, Paul Sorvino, Veronica Cartwright, Elise Neal, Paul Gleason, Larry Hankin, Daniel Roebuck, David Warner, Michael Wright, Gerard Ismael; ***D:*** Brett Ratner; ***W:*** Joel Cohen, Alec Sokolow; ***C:*** Russell Carpenter, Robert Primes; ***M:*** Lalo Schifrin.

Money to Burn **1983** Aging high school counselor and two senior citizens develop a plan to steal $50 million from the Federal Reserve Bank. Harmless bit of fun. **90m/C VHS.** Jack Kruschen, Meegan King, David Wallace, Phillip Pine; ***D:*** Virginia Lively Stone.

Money to Burn **1994 (R)** Two buddies go off on a wild spending spree when $2 million in cash falls into their laps. Only one problem—a crazy cop who's determined to stop them squandering the money. **96m/C VHS.** Chad McQueen, Don Swayze, Joe Estevez, Julie Strain, Sydney Lassick; ***D:*** John Sjogren; ***W:*** John Sjogren, Scott Ziehl.

Money Train **1995 (R)** Snipes and Harrelson team up again, this time as New York City transit cops (and foster brothers) who decide to rob the money train—a subway car that collects all the cash accrued from the transit system each day. To complicate matters, they're both in love with their new Latina partner (Lopez). Lame attempt to cash in on the Snipes and Harrelson chemistry leaves out one important ingredient—a competent script. The movie is almost over before the train actually becomes part of the plotline. Film came under criticism when it was blamed for a series of "copycat" arsons in which a New York City subway clerk was killed. **110m/C VHS, DVD, 8mm, Wide.** Skipp (Robert L.) Sudduth, Vincent Laresca, Aida Turturro, Vincent Pastore, Enrico Colantoni, Jose Zuniga, Bill Nunn, Larry Gilliard Jr., Michael Artura, Woody Harrelson, Wesley Snipes, Jennifer Lopez, Robert (Bobby) Blake, Chris Cooper, Joe Grifasi; ***D:*** Joseph Ruben; ***W:*** Doug Richardson, David Loughery; ***C:*** John Lindley; ***M:*** Mark Mancina.

The Moneytree **1993** A carefree would-be actor decides to make some money by harvesting a huge marijuana crop in the California hills, all the while fending off his girlfriend, the cops, and some wild boars. **92m/C VHS.** Christopher Dienstag; ***D:*** Alan Dienstag.

A Mongolian Tale *Hei Ma* **1994** Nai Nai has raised her granddaughter Somiya and the abandoned Bayingbulag among the Mongolian steppes. Eventually, Bayingbulag leaves to get an education but promises to return and marry Somiya. Away three years, he comes back only to discover Somiya pregnant, so he takes off, finds success as a folk singer, and doesn't return for 12 years. Somiya now has a drunken husband, four sons, and an illegitimate 12-year-old daughter who is desperate for a father. Mongolian dialogue. Adapted by Chengzhi from his story "A Song of the Grassland." **105m/C VHS.** *CH HK* Narenhua, Tengger; ***D:*** Xie Fei; ***W:*** Zhang Chengzhi; ***C:*** Jing Sheng Fu; ***M:*** Tengger. Montreal World Film Fest. '95: Director (Fei).

The Mongols *Les Mongols* **1960** Splashy Italian production has Genghis Khan's son repelling invading hordes while courting buxom princess. Pairing of Palance and Ekberg makes this one worthy of consideration. **105m/C VHS.** *IT FR* Jack Palance, Anita Ekberg, Antonella Lualdi, Franco Silva, Gianni "John" Garko, Roldano Lupi, Gabriella Pallotta; ***D:*** Andre de Toth, Leopoldo Savona, Riccardo (Robert Hampton) Freda.

Mongrel woof! **1983** El-cheapo kennel horror about a man who dreams he's a wild murderous mutt. His relief upon waking up is short-lived, however, when he discovers the people he killed in his dreams are actually dead. Flick will make you want to gnaw on a bone. **90m/C VHS.** Aldo Ray, Terry Evans; ***D:*** Robert Burns.

Monika *Summer with Monika* **1952** Two teenagers who run away together for the summer find the winter brings more responsibility than they can handle when the girl becomes pregnant and gives birth. Lesser, early Bergman, sensitively directed, but dull. Adapted by Bergman from a Per Anders Fogelstrom novel. In Swedish with English subtitles. **96m/B VHS.** *SW* Harriet Andersson, Lars Ekborg, John Harryson, Georg Skarstedt, Dagmar Ebbesen, Ake Gronberg; ***D:*** Ingmar Bergman; ***W:*** Ingmar Bergman; ***M:*** Les Baxter.

Monique **1983** A sophisticated career woman is about to unleash a terrifying secret on her new husband. **96m/C VHS.** Florence Giorgetti, John Ferris.

Monkey Boy **1990** Decent sci-fi horror from Britain, about a cunning human-ape hybrid that escapes from a genetics lab after massacring the staff. Not excessively gruesome or vulgar, and some sympathy is aroused for the killer mutant. Based on the novel "Chimera." **104m/C VHS.** John Lynch, Christine Kavanagh, Kenneth Cranham; ***D:*** Lawrence Gordon Clark.

Monkey Business **1931** Marx Brothers run amok as stowaways on ocean liner. Fast-paced comedy provides seemingly endless amount of gags, quips, and pratfalls, including the fab four imitating Maurice Chevalier at Immigration. This film, incidentally, was the group's first to be written—by noted humorist Perelman—directly for the screen. **77m/B VHS, DVD.** Groucho Marx, Harpo Marx, Chico Marx, Zeppo Marx, Thelma Todd, Ruth Hall, Harry Woods, Tom Kennedy, Rockliffe Fellowes, Maxine Castle; ***D:*** Norman Z. McLeod; ***W:*** S.J. Perelman, Arthur Sheekman; ***C:*** Arthur L. Todd.

Monkey Business **1952** A scientist invents a fountain-of-youth potion, a lab chimpanzee mistakenly dumps it into a water cooler, and then grown-ups start turning into adolescents. Top-flight crew occasionally labors in this screwball comedy, though comic moments shine. Monroe is the secretary sans skills, while absent-minded Grant and sexy wife Rogers race hormonally as teens. **97m/B VHS, DVD.** Cary Grant, Ginger Rogers, Charles Coburn, Marilyn Monroe, Hugh Marlowe, Larry Keating, George Winslow; ***D:*** Howard Hawks; ***W:*** Ben Hecht, Charles Lederer, I.A.L. Diamond; ***C:*** Milton Krasner; ***M:*** Leigh Harline.

Monkey Grip **1982** An unmarried woman copes with parenthood and a drug-addicted boyfriend while working on the fringe of Australia's music business. Grim but provocative, based on Helen Graham's novel. **101m/C VHS.** *AU* Noni Hazlehurst, Colin Friels, Alice Garner, Harold Hopkins, Candy (Candida) Raymond; ***D:*** Ken Cameron; ***W:*** Ken Cameron. Australian Film Inst. '82: Actress (Hazlehurst).

Monkey Hustle **1977 (PG)** Vintage blaxploitation has trouble hustling laffs. The Man plans a super freeway through the ghetto, and law abiding do gooders join forces with territorial lords of vice to fight the project. Shot in the Windy City. **90m/C VHS.** Yaphet Kotto, Rudy Ray Moore, Rosalind Cash, Debbi (Deborah) Morgan, Thomas Carter; ***D:*** Arthur Marks.

Monkey Shines *Monkey Shines: An Experiment in Fear; Ella* **1988 (R)** Based on the novel by Michael Stuart, this is a sick, scary yarn about a quadriplegic who is given a specially trained capuchin monkey as a helpmate. However, he soon finds that the beast is assuming and acting on his subconscious rages. **108m/C VHS, DVD, Wide.** Jason Beghe, John Pankow, Kate McNeil, Christine Forrest, Stephen (Steve) Root, Joyce Van Patten, Stanley Tucci, Janine Turner; ***D:*** George A. Romero; ***W:*** George A. Romero; ***C:*** James A. Contner; ***M:*** David Shire.

Monkey Trouble **1994 (PG)** Lonely schoolgirl Birch is feeling abandoned when mom and stepdad shower attention on her new baby brother. Then a monkey trained as a pickpocket enters her life. Keitel is the organ grinder turned bad who must answer to the mob when the monkey scampers off to suburbia. Stakes a lot of its entertainment wallop on the considerable talents of the slippery-fingered monkey, who steals the show. Birch is amusing as the youngster caught in all sorts of uncomfortable situations. Formula abounds, but the milk and cookies set won't notice; fine family fare. **95m/C VHS.** Thora Birch, Harvey Keitel, Mimi Rogers, Christopher McDonald; ***D:*** Franco Amurri; ***W:*** Franco Amurri, Stu Krieger; ***M:*** Mark Mancina.

Monkeybone **2001 (PG-13)** Weird comedy about comatose cartoonist Stu Miley (Fraser), who must escape from his own comic fantasy world in order to return to consciousness after an accident. Monkeybone, a chimp embodiment of a teenager's libido from his "Show Me the Monkey" animated pilot is the focus of the rest of the film as he escapes from the underworld and "steals" Stu's body to romance his awaiting girlfriend (Fonda). Kattan is funny as the organ donor and Turturro, who puts his considerable talent to voicing a monkey, is successful, but one-note libidinous simian humor makes flimsy material for a film. Based on the graphic novel "Dark Town" by Kaja Blackley. **92m/C VHS, DVD, Wide.** *US* Brendan Fraser, Bridget Fonda, Whoopi Goldberg, Chris Kattan, Dave Foley, Giancarlo Esposito, Rose McGowan, Megan Mullally, Lisa Zane; ***D:*** Henry Selick; ***W:*** Sam Hamm; ***C:*** Andrew Dunn; ***M:*** Anne Dudley; ***V:*** John Turturro.

Monkeys, Go Home! **1966** Dumb Disney yarn about young American who inherits a badly neglected French olive farm. When he brings in four chimpanzees to pick the olives, the local townspeople go on strike. People can be so sensitive. Based on "The Monkeys" by G. K. Wilkinson. Chevalier's last film appearance. **89m/C VHS.** Dean Jones, Yvette Mimieux, Maurice Chevalier, Clement Harari, Yvonne Constant; ***D:*** Andrew V. McLaglen; ***M:*** Robert F. Brunner.

The Monkey's Mask **2000** Lesbian private detective Jill Fitzpatrick (Porter) is hired by the parents of missing student Mickey Norris (Cornish). Jill meets Mickey's married poetry professor Diana (McGillis) and the two soon embark on a torrid affair. Then Mickey is found strangled and Jill searches (rather ineptyly) for the killer and nearly becomes a victim herself. Who knew poetry could be so dangerous? Based on the 1994 nonrhyming verse thriller by Dorothy Porter. **94m/C VHS, DVD.** *AU* Susie Porter, Kelly McGillis, Marton Csokas, Abbie Cornish, Caroline Gillmer, Jean-Pierre Mignon, Jim Holt, John Noble, Linden Wilkinson; *D:* Samantha Lang; *W:* Anne Kennedy; *C:* Garry Philips.

Monkey's Uncle 🦴½ **1965** A sequel to Disney's "The Misadventures of Merlin Jones" and featuring more bizarre antics and scientific hoopla, including chimps and a flying machine. **90m/C VHS.** Tommy Kirk, Annette Funicello, Leon Ames, Arthur O'Connell; *D:* Robert Stevenson; *W:* Alfred Lewis Levitt, Helen Levitt; *C:* Edward Colman; *M:* Buddy (Norman Dale) Baker.

The Monocle 🦴🦴 **1964** Steele plays a seductive villainess in this rare, spy/comedy thriller. **?m/C VHS.** *FR* Paul Meurisse, Barbara Steele, Marcel Dalio.

Monolith 🦴🦴½ **1993 (R)** Tucker (Paxton) and Flynn (Frost) are unlikely partners on the LAPD. But they're teamed up on an unlikely case: a Russian scientist commits a seemingly senseless murder and is taken away by a mystery man (Hurt) before she can be interrogated. What the curious duo discover is a lethal alien force capable of posessing any living creature and whose objective is the destruction of the planet. **96m/C VHS.** Bill Paxton, Lindsay Frost, John Hurt, Louis Gossett Jr.; *D:* John Eyres; *W:* Stephen Lister.

The Monolith Monsters 🦴🦴 **1957** A geologist investigates a meteor shower in Arizona and discovers strange crystals. The crystals attack humans and absorb their silicone, causing them to grow into monsters. Good "B" movie fun. **76m/B VHS.** Grant Williams, Lola Albright, Les Tremayne, Trevor Bardette; *D:* John Sherwood; *W:* Norman Jolley, Robert M. Fresco; *M:* Joseph Gershenson.

Monsieur Beaucaire 🦴½ **1924** The Duke of Chartres ditches France posing as a barber, and once in Britain, becomes a lawman. Not a classic Valentino vehicle. **100m/B VHS.** Rudolph Valentino, Bebe Daniels, Lois Wilson, Doris Kenyon, Lowell Sherman, John Davidson; *D:* Sidney Olcott.

Monsieur Beaucaire 🦴🦴🦴 **1946** Entertaining Hope vehicle that casts him as a barber impersonating a French nobleman in the court of Louis XV. He's set to wed a Spanish princess in order to prevent a full-scale war from taking place. However, he really wants to marry social-climber chambermaid Caulfield. Director Marshall was at his best here. Based on the novel by Booth Tarkington. **93m/B VHS.** Bob Hope, Joan Caulfield, Patric Knowles, Marjorie Reynolds, Cecil Kellaway, Joseph Schildkraut, Reginald Owen, Constance Collier; *D:* George Marshall; *W:* Melvin Frank, Norman Panama; *C:* Lionel Lindon.

Monsieur Hire 🦴🦴🦴½ *M. Hire* **1989 (PG-13)** The usual tale of sexual obsesssion and suspense. Mr. Hire spends much of his time trying to spy on his beautiful young neighbor woman, alternately alienated and engaged by her love affairs. The voyeur soon finds his secret desires have entangled him in a vicious intrigue. Political rally set-piece is brilliant. Excellent acting, intense pace, elegant photography. Based on "Les Fiancailles de M. Hire" by Georges Simenone and adapted by Leconte and Patrick Dewolf. In French with English subtitles. **81m/C VHS.** *FR* Michel Blanc, Sandrine Bonnaire, Luc Thuillier, Eric Berenger, Andre Wilms; *D:* Patrice Leconte; *W:* Patrice Leconte. Cesar '90: Sound.

Monsieur Verdoux 🦴🦴🦴 **1947** A thorough Chaplin effort, as he produced, directed, wrote, scored and starred. A prim and proper bank cashier in Paris marries and murders rich women in order to support his real wife and family. A mild scandal in its day, though second-thought pacifism and stale humor date it. A bomb upon release (leading Chaplin to shelve it for 17 years) and a cult item today, admired for both its flaws and complexity. Raye fearlessly chews scenery and croissants. Initially based upon a suggestion from Orson Welles. **123m/B VHS, DVD.** Charlie Chaplin, Martha Raye, Isobel Elsom, Mady Correll, Marilyn Nash, Irving Bacon, William Frawley, Allison Roddan, Robert Lewis; *D:* Charlie Chaplin; *W:* Charlie Chaplin; *C:* Curt Courant, Roland H. Totheroh; *M:* Charlie Chaplin.

Monsieur Vincent 🦴🦴🦴 **1947** True story of 17th century French priest who became St. Vincent de Paul (Fresnay). He forsakes worldly possessions and convinces members of the aristocracy to finance his charities for the less fortunate. Inspirational. French with subtitles. **112m/B VHS.** *FR* Pierre Fresnay, Lisa (Lise) Delamare, Aime Clariond, Jean Debucourt, Pierre Dux, Gabrielle Dorziat, Jean Carmet, Michel Bouquet; *D:* Maurice Cloche; *W:* Jean Anouilh, Jean-Bernard Luc; *C:* Claude Renoir; *M:* Jean Jacques Grunenwald. Oscars '48: Foreign Film.

Monsignor woof! **1982 (R)** Callow, ambitious priest befriends mobsters and even seduces a nun while managing Vatican's business affairs. No sparks generated by Reeve and Bujold (who appears nude in one scene), and no real conviction related by most other performers. Absurd, ludicrous melodrama best enjoyed as unintentional comedy. Based on Jack Alain Leger's book. **121m/C VHS.** Christopher Reeve, Fernando Rey, Genevieve Bujold, Jason Miller; *D:* Frank Perry; *W:* Abraham Polonsky, Wendell Mayes; *C:* Billy Williams; *M:* John Williams.

Monsignor Quixote 🦴🦴½ **1991** A small town priest takes on the persona of his ancestor, Don Quixote, and prepares to battle the evil he sees around him. Based on the novel by Graham Greene. **118m/C VHS.** Alec Guinness, Ian Richardson, Graham Crowden, Maurice Denham, Philip Stone, Rosalie Crutchley, Valentine Pelka, Don Fellows, Leo McKern; *D:* Rodney Bennett.

Monsoon 🦴🦴 **1997** Ambitious project from director Mundhra (known best for his erotic thrillers) is set in Goa, India. That's where Kenneth Blake (Tyson) and his fiancee Sally Stephens (McShane) go to visit his friend (McCoy). But in a previous incarnation Kenneth was a lover of Leela (Brodie), who's now married to the local drug lord Miranda (Grover). Their centuries-spanning affair causes the usual complications. Local color is actually much more interesting and the film looks very sharp. **96m/C DVD.** Richard Tyson, Matt McCoy, Gulsham Grover, Jenny McShane, Doug Jeffery, Helen Brodie; *D:* Jag Mundhra; *C:* Blain Brown; *M:* Alan Dermot Derosian.

Monsoon Wedding 🦴🦴🦴 **2001 (R)** Outlines the clash of India's traditional culture with the growing modern sensibilities of the new Delhi. Aditi Vermas (Das) is promised in marriage to Hemant (Dabas) an Indian computer programmer living in Houston, whom she has yet to meet. The problem is, Aditi has a life of her own, including a married TV host for a boyfriend. When the couple eventually meet, tensions and attraction arises as a bevy of romantic subplots swirl like the title's monsoon around them. Film's large, Altman-esque cast of characters include both sides of the intendeds' family. Anir's engaging storylines, fresh premise and lush cinematography succeed in depicting the turbulent modern life in Delhi. In English, and Hindi, and Punjabi (with English subtitles). **113m/C VHS, DVD.** *IN US* Naseeruddin Shah, Lillete Dubey, Shefali Shetty, Vasundhara Das, Parvin Dabas, Vijay Raaz, Tilotama Shome, Rajat Kapoor; *D:* Mira Nair; *W:* Sabrina Dhawan; *C:* Declan Quinn; *M:* Mychael Danna.

The Monster 🦴🦴🦴 **1925** This silent horror film has all the elements that would become genre standards. Mad scientist Dr. Ziska (Chaney), working in an asylum filled with lunatics, abducts strangers to use in his fiendish experiments to bring the dead back to life. There's the obligatory dungeon and even a lovely heroine (Olmsted) that needs rescuing. Great atmosphere and Chaney's usual spine-tingling performance. Based on the play by Crane Wilbur. **86m/B VHS.** Lon Chaney Sr., Gertrude (Olmstead) Olmsted, Johnny Arthur, Charles Sellon, Walter James, Hallam Cooley; *D:* Roland West; *W:* Albert Kenyon, Willard Mack; *C:* Hal Mohr.

Monster 🦴 **1978 (R)** Bloodthirsty alien indiscriminately preys on gaggle of teens in wilds of civilization. Performers struggle with dialogue and their own self-esteem. **98m/C VHS.** Jim Mitchum, Diane McBain, Roger Clark, John Carradine, Phil Carey, Anthony Eisley, Keenan Wynn; *D:* Herbert L. Strock.

The Monster 🦴🦴½ *Il Monstro; Le Monstre* **1996 (R)** Italian impresario of comedy Benigni co-wrote, directed and starred in this film that has become the highest grossing film in Italian history to date. Jaded American audiences, however, may find the broad comedy of errors all too familiar territory with Loris (Benigni) as a criminal Clouseau, an incompetent petty thief whom police mistake for a serial murderer on the loose. Cops install an attractive female detective (Braschi, Benigni's wife) in the sexually strained shyster's apartment to tempt him into striking again. Sight gags aplenty populate Benigni's highly physical performance, including: being pulled wildly around a garage attached to an out-of-control chainsaw; contending with a lit cigarette down his pants; and scores of pratfalls, all of which garner comparisons to comedy phenom, Jim Carrey. French director and actor Blanc ("Dead Tired") is great as the loony police psychiatrist. **110m/C VHS, DVD.** *IT* Roberto Benigni, Nicoletta Braschi, Michel Blanc, Dominque Lavanant, Jean-Claude Brialy, Ivano Marescotti, Laurent Spielvogel, Massimo Girotti, Franco Mescolini; *D:* Roberto Benigni; *W:* Roberto Benigni, Vincenzo Cerami; *C:* Carlo Di Palma; *M:* Evan Lurie.

Monster a Go-Go! woof! **1965** Team of go-go dancers battle a ten-foot monster from outerspace whose mass is due to a radiation mishap. He can't dance, either. **70m/B VHS.** Phil Morton, June Travis, Bill Rebane, Herschell Gordon Lewis, Lois Brooks, George Perry; *D:* Bill Rebane, Herschell Gordon Lewis; *W:* Herschell Gordon Lewis.

The Monster and the Girl 🦴🦴½ **1941** It's the mob vs. the ape in this tale of revenge. Scott (Terry) discovers innocent sister Susan (Drew) is being lead down the path to prostitution by suave mobster Reed (Paige). But Reed manages to frame Scott for murder and he's executed, although not before donating his brain to science. Then scientist Parry (Zucco) decides to transplant the brain into the body of an ape who goes on a rampage aimed at the mobster. **65m/B VHS.** Ellen Drew, Robert Paige, Phillip Terry, Paul Lukas, Joseph Calleia, Onslow Stevens, Rod Cameron, George Zucco, Marc Lawrence, Gerald Mohr; *D:* Stuart Heisler; *W:* Stuart Anthony; *C:* Victor Milner.

The Monster Club 🦴🦴 **1985** Price and Carradine star in this music-horror compilation, featuring songs by Night, B.A. Robertson, The Pretty Things and The Viewers. Soundtrack music by John Williams, UB 40 and The Expressos. **104m/C VHS.** *GB* Vincent Price, Donald Pleasence, John Carradine, Stuart Whitman, Britt Ekland, Simon Ward, Patrick Magee; *D:* Roy Ward Baker.

The Monster Demolisher 🦴🦴 **1960** Nostradamus' descendent shares the family penchant for sanguine cocktails, and threatens a professor who protects himself with an electronic wonder of modern technology. Edited from a sombrero serial; if you make it through this one, look up its Mexican siblings, "Curse of Nostradamus" and "Genie of Darkness." **?m/B VHS.** *MX* German Robles; *D:* Frederick Curiel.

Monster Dog woof! **1982** A rock band is mauled, threatened, and drooled upon by an untrainable mutant canine. Rock star Cooper plays the leader of the band. No plot, but the German shepherd is worth watching. **88m/C VHS.** Alice Cooper, Victoria Vera; *D:* Clyde (Claudio Fragasso) Anderson.

Monster from Green Hell 🦴 **1958** An experimental rocket containing radiation-contaminated wasps crashes in Africa, making giant killer wasps that run amok. Stinging big bug horror. **71m/B VHS, DVD.** Jim Davis, Robert E. (Bob) Griffin, Barbara Turner, Eduardo Ciannelli; *D:* Kenneth Crane; *W:* Endre Bohem, Louis Vittes; *C:* Ray Flin; *M:* Albert Glasser.

Monster from the Ocean Floor 🦴 *It Stalked the Ocean Floor; Monster Maker* **1954** An oceanographer in a deep-sea diving bell is threatened by a multi-tentacled creature. Roger Corman's first production. **66m/C VHS, DVD.** Anne Kimball, Stuart Wade, Jonathan Haze, Wyott Ordung, David Garcia, Dick Pinner; *D:* Wyott Ordung; *W:* William Danch; *C:* Floyd Crosby; *M:* Andre Brummer.

Monster High 🦴 **1989 (R)** Bloodthirsty alien indiscriminately preys on gaggle of teens in wilds of civilization. Even the people who made this one may not have seen it all the way through. **89m/C VHS.** David Marriott, Dean Iandoli, Diana Frank, D.J. Kerzner; *D:* Rudiger Poe.

Monster in a Box 🦴🦴🦴 **1992 (PG-13)** Master storyteller Gray spins a wonderful tale about his life, including stories about his adventures at a Moscow film festival, a trip to Nicaragua, and his first experience with California earthquakes. Filled with wit, satire, and hilarity. Filmed before an audience, this is based on Gray's Broadway show of the same title. By the way, the monster in the box is a 1,900-page manuscript of his autobiography and the box in which he lugs it around. **88m/C VHS.** Spalding Gray; *D:* Nick Broomfield; *W:* Spalding Gray; *C:* Michael Coulter; *M:* Laurie Anderson.

Monster in the Closet 🦴🦴 **1986 (PG)** A gory horror spoof about a rash of San Francisco murders that all take place inside closets. A news reporter and his scientist friend decide they will be the ones to protect California from the evil but shy creatures. From the producers of "The Toxic Avenger." **87m/C VHS, DVD.** Paul Dooley, Donald Grant, Claude Akins, Denise DuBarry, Stella Stevens, Howard Duff, Henry Gibson, Jesse White, John Carradine; *D:* Bob Dahlin; *W:* Bob Dahlin; *C:* Ronald W. McLeish; *M:* Barrie Guard.

The Monster Maker 🦴🦴 **1944** Low-budget gland fest in which deranged scientist develops serum that inflates heads, feet, and hands. He recklessly inflicts others with this potion, then must contend with deformed victims while courting a comely gal. **65m/B VHS, DVD.** J. Carrol Naish, Ralph Morgan, Wanda McKay, Terry Frost; *D:* Sam Newfield; *W:* Martin Mooney, Pierre Gendron; *C:* Robert C. Cline; *M:* Albert Glasser.

The Monster of London City 🦴½ *Das Ungeheuer von London City* **1964** During a stage play about Jack the Ripper, murders occur paralleling those in the production. The lead actor finds himself to be the prime suspect. Lightweight horror from Germany. **87m/B VHS.** *GE* Hansjorg Felmy, Marianne Koch, Dietmar Schoenherr, Hans Nielsen; *D:* Edwin Zbonek.

The Monster of Piedras Blancas woof! **1957** During a seaside festival, two fisherman are killed by a bloodthirsty oceanic critter with no respect for holidays. The fishing village is determined to find it and kill it. Low-budget, with amateurish effects and poor acting. **72m/B VHS.** Les Tremayne, Jeanne Carmen, Forrest Lewis, John Harmon, Don Sullivan; *D:* Irvin Berwick; *W:* H. Haile Chace; *C:* Philip Lathrop.

Monster on the Campus 🦴🦴½ **1959** Science-fiction thriller about the blood of a prehistoric fish turning college professor into murderous beast. Will the halls of Dunsfield University ever be safe again? **76m/B VHS.** Arthur Franz, Joanna Moore, Judson Pratt, Nancy Walters, Troy Donahue; *D:* Jack Arnold; *W:* David Duncan.

The Monster Squad 🦴½ **1987 (PG-13)** Youthful monster enthusiasts find their community inundated by Dracula, Frankenstein creature, Wolf Man, Mummy, and Gill Man(!?!), who are all searching for a life-sustaining amulet. Somewhat different, but still somewhat mediocre. **82m/C VHS.** Mary Ellen Trainor, Andre Gower, Stephen Macht, Tom Noonan, Duncan Regehr; *D:* Fred Dekker; *W:* Fred Dekker, Shane Black; *M:* Bruce Broughton.

The Monster That Challenged the World 🦴🦴½ **1957** Huge, ancient eggs are discovered in the Salton Sea and eventually hatch into killer, crustaceous caterpillars. Superior monster action. **83m/B VHS, DVD.** Tim Holt, Audrey Dalton, Hans Conried, Harlen Ward, Max (Casey Adams) Showalter, Mimi Gibson, Gordon Jones; *D:* Arnold Laven; *W:* Pat Fielder; *C:* Lester White; *M:* Heinz Roemheld.

The Monster Walks && *The Monster Walked* **1932** A whodunit thriller, complete with stormy nights, suspicious cripples, weird servants, a screaming gorilla, and a spooky house. Not unique but entertaining. **60m/B VHS.** Rex Lease, Vera Reynolds, Mischa Auer, Willie Best; ***D:*** Frank Strayer.

Monster's Ball &&&& **2001 (R)** Georgia death-row prison guard Hank (Thornton) is following in his father Buck's (Boyle) footsteps as a guard, and as a bigot. His son (Ledger) also has joined the family business, but doesn't seem to have the heart or stomach for it. When his son throws up during the execution of Lawrence Musgrove (Combs), Hank flies into a rage that makes him reexamine his life. Soon after, he helps the waitress, Leticia (Berry) from the diner he frequents after an auto accident. Leticia is Musgrove's widow, unbeknownst to Hank, who begins what at first is a desperate, sexual relationship with her that changes both of them. Director Forster and scripters Addica and Rokos provide a well-done, raw, and unflinching story that the excellent cast, especially Berry (who won the Best Actress Oscar) and Thornton inhabit perfectly. Boyle is also powerful as the malevolent patriarch. Everything comes together to announce Forster's arrival as a directorial force. **111m/C VHS, DVD.** *US* Billy Bob Thornton, Halle Berry, Heath Ledger, Peter Boyle, Sean (Puffy, Puff Daddy, P. Diddy) Combs, Coronji Calhoun, Dante "Mos Def" Beze, Will Rokos, Milo Addica; ***D:*** Marc Forster; ***W:*** Will Rokos, Milo Addica; ***C:*** Roberto Schaefer. Oscars '01: Actress (Berry); Natl. Bd. of Review '01: Actor (Thornton), Actress (Berry); Screen Actors Guild '01: Actress (Berry).

Monsters Crash the Pajama Party && **1965** Mad scientist is discovered conducting weird experiments by a group of teens who enter a supposedly haunted house. This one was much better in the theatre, because "monsters" would run through the audience and select a victim. Then the monsters and the victim would magically appear on the screen. Weird. **31m/C VHS, DVD.** Peter J. D'Noto, Vic McGee, James Reason, Pauline Hilcurt, Charles Egan, Joseph Ormond; ***D:*** David L. Hewitt; ***W:*** David L. Hewitt, Jay Lister; ***C:*** David L. Hewitt, Austin McKay.

Monsters, Inc. &&& **2001 (G)** Sweet-natured animated film from Pixar that's geared more towards the younger end of the family spectrum than films like "Toy Story." Monstropolis is a town that is powered by the screams of children, which are captured in tanks thanks to "scarers" who invade the kids' bedrooms via their closet doors. Sulley (Goodman) is the best there is, with the help of buddy Mike (Crystal), but he has a problem when human toddler Boo (Gibbs) accidentally gets loose in monster town, which is a big no-no, and Sulley has to get her safely home. There's also some sinister goingson at a company level causing problems for our boys. Very colorful and more silly than scary (what's scary is the familiar toddler behavior). **92m/C VHS, DVD.** *US* ***D:*** Pete Docter; ***W:*** Andrew Stanton, Daniel Gerson; ***M:*** Randy Newman; ***V:*** John Goodman, Billy Crystal, Steve Buscemi, Mary Gibbs, James Coburn, Jennifer Tilly, John Ratzenberger, Frank Oz, Bob Peterson, Bonnie Hunt. Oscars '01: Song ("If I Didn't Have You").

Montana &&½ **1990 (PG)** Hoyce and Bess Guthrie are long-married and strong-willed ranchers who are at odds over the family ranch in Montana. He wants to sell the land to a power company for oil drilling but she wants to keep the land in the family. **91m/C VHS.** Gena Rowlands, Richard Crenna, Lea Thompson, Justin Deas, Elizabeth Berridge, Scott Coffey, Darren Dalton; ***D:*** William A. Graham; ***W:*** Larry McMurtry. **CABLE**

Montana && **1997 (R)** Claire (Sedgwick) is a professional killer, who works with partner Nick (Tucci) for the eccentric Boss (Coltrane). When Boss' drug addict mistress Kitty (Tunney) runs away, Claire and Nick are given the thankless task of retrieving her and have to also endure the presence of the man's imbecilic son, Jimmy (Embry). Then Kitty kills Jimmy and Claire and Nick are also accused of embezzling from the organization—so the lethal trio are now being hunted by their own syndicate. Good cast is hampered by a not particularly memorable story. **96m/C VHS.** Kyra Sedgwick, Stanley Tucci, Robbie Coltrane, Robin Tunney, Philip Seymour Hoffman, John Ritter, Ethan (Randall) Embry; ***D:*** Jennifer Leitzes; ***W:*** Erich Hoeber, Jon Hoeber; ***C:*** Ken Kelsch; ***M:*** Cliff Eidelman.

Montana Belle && **1952** A buxom bandit teams with the notorious Dalton Brothers before embarking on a life of reform. In the cardgame of life, Russell is always holding a pair. **81m/C VHS.** Jane Russell, George Brent, Scott Brady, Forrest Tucker, Andy Devine, Jack Lambert, John Litel, Ray Teal; ***D:*** Allan Dwan.

Monte Carlo && **1986** A sexy Russian woman aids the Allies by relaying important messages during WWII. Fun TV production featuring Collins at her seductive best. **200m/C VHS.** Joan Collins, George Hamilton, Lisa Eilbacher, Lauren Hutton, Robert Carradine, Malcolm McDowell; ***D:*** Anthony Page. **TV**

Monte Carlo Nights &½ **1934** Wrongly convicted murderer determines to prove his innocence even as he is tracked by police. **60m/B VHS.** Mary Brian, John Darrow, Kate Campbell, Robert Frazer, Astrid Allwyn, George "Gabby" Hayes, George Cleveland; ***D:*** William Nigh.

Monte Walsh &&& **1970 (PG)** Aging cowboy sees declining of Old West, embarks on mission to avenge best friend's death. Subdued, moving western worthy of genre greats Marvin and Palance. Cinematographer Fraker proves himself a proficient director in this, his first venture. Based on Jack Schaefer's novel. **100m/C VHS.** Lee Marvin, Jack Palance, Jeanne Moreau, Jim Davis, Mitchell Ryan; ***D:*** William A. Fraker; ***W:*** David Zelag Goodman; ***M:*** John Barry.

Montenegro &&&½ *Montenegro—Or Pigs and Pearls* **1981** Offbeat, bawdy comedy details experiences of bored, possibly mad housewife who lands in a coarse, uninhibited ethnic community. To its credit, this film remains unpredictable to the end. And Anspach, an intriguing, resourceful—and attractive—actress, delivers what is perhaps her greatest performance. **97m/C VHS, DVD, Wide.** *SW* Susan Anspach, Erland Josephson; ***D:*** Dusan Makavejev; ***W:*** Dusan Makavejev; ***C:*** Tomislav Pinter; ***M:*** Kornell Kovac.

Monterey Pop &&&½ **1968** This pre-Woodstock rock 'n' roll festival in Monterey, California, features landmark performances by some of the most popular '60s rockers. Compelling for the performances, and historically important as the first significant rock concert film. Appearances by Jefferson Airplane, Janis Joplin, Jimi Hendrix, Simon and Garfunkel, The Who, and Otis Redding. **72m/C VHS, 8mm.** ***D:*** James Desmond, Richard Leacock, D.A. Pennebaker.

A Month by the Lake &&½ **1995 (PG)** Redgrave takes the plunge into highly familiar romantic comedy of the Proper English sort and glides effortlessly through this slow-moving but often charming adaptation of an H. E. Bates short story. Set in pre-WWII northern Italy, Miss Bentley (Redgrave) sets her spinster's eye on the somewhat wooden, but gradually warming, English Major Wilshaw (Fox). Petulant American nanny Thurman arrives to provide an arresting diversion for Wilshaw, while Gassman proves an unwitting pawn for Miss Bentley's game of "get the major." Touching and lighthearted performances, especially by heavyweight Redgrave, are complemented by glorious cinematography. **92m/C VHS.** Vanessa Redgrave, Edward Fox, Uma Thurman, Alida Valli, Alessandro Gassman, Carlo Cartier; ***D:*** John Irvin; ***W:*** Trevor Bentham; ***C:*** Pasqualino De Santis; ***M:*** Nicola Piovani.

A Month in the Country &&& **1987** The reverently quiet story of two British WWI veterans, one an archaeologist and the other a church painting restorer, who are working in a tiny village while trying to heal their emotional wounds. Based on the novel by J.L. Carr. **92m/C VHS.** *GB* Colin Firth, Natasha Richardson, Kenneth Branagh, Patrick Malahide, Tony Haygarth, Jim Carter; ***D:*** Pat O'Connor; ***W:*** Simon Gray; ***C:*** Kenneth Macmillan; ***M:*** Howard Blake.

Monty Python and the Holy Grail &&&½ **1975 (PG)** Britain's famed comedy band assaults the Arthurian legend in a cult classic replete with a Trojan rabbit and an utterly dismembered, but inevitably pugnacious, knight. Fans of manic comedy—and graphic violence—should get more than their fill here. **90m/C VHS, DVD, 8mm, Wide.** *GB* Graham Chapman, John Cleese, Terry Gilliam, Eric Idle, Terry Jones, Michael Palin, Carol Cleveland, Connie Booth, Neil Innes, Patsy Kensit; ***D:*** Terry Gilliam, Terry Jones; ***W:*** Graham Chapman, John Cleese, Terry Gilliam, Eric Idle, Terry Jones, Michael Palin; ***C:*** Terry Bedford; ***M:*** De Wolfe, Neil Innes.

Monty Python's Life of Brian &&&½ *Life of Brian* **1979 (R)** Often riotous spoof of Christianity tracks hapless peasant mistaken for the messiah in A.D. 32. Film reels from routine to routine, and only the most pious will remain unmoved by a chorus of crucifixion victims. Probably the group's most daring, controversial venture. **94m/C VHS, DVD, Wide.** *GB* Graham Chapman, John Cleese, Terry Gilliam, Eric Idle, Michael Palin, George Harrison, Terry Jones, Kenneth Colley, Spike Milligan, Carol Cleveland, Neil Innes, Andrew MacLachlan; ***D:*** Terry Jones; ***W:*** Graham Chapman, John Cleese, Terry Gilliam, Eric Idle, Michael Palin, Terry Jones; ***C:*** Peter Biziou; ***M:*** Geoffrey Burgon.

Monty Python's The Meaning of Life &&& **1983 (R)** Funny, technically impressive film conducts various inquiries into the most profound questions confronting humanity. Notable among the sketches here are a live sex enactment performed before bored schoolboys, a student-faculty rugby game that turns quite violent, and an encounter between a physician and a reluctant, untimely organ donor. Another sketch provides a memorable portrait of a glutton prone to nausea. And at film's end, the meaning of life is actually revealed. **107m/C VHS, DVD, Wide.** *GB* Graham Chapman, John Cleese, Terry Gilliam, Eric Idle, Terry Jones, Michael Palin, Carol Cleveland, Matt Frewer, Simon Jones, Patricia Quinn, Andrew MacLachlan; ***D:*** Terry Gilliam, Terry Jones; ***W:*** Graham Chapman, John Cleese, Terry Gilliam, Eric Idle, Terry Jones, Michael Palin; ***C:*** Peter Hannan; ***M:*** John Du Prez, Graham Chapman, John Cleese, Eric Idle, Terry Jones, Michael Palin. Cannes '83: Grand Jury Prize.

Monument Ave. &&½ *Snitch* **1998** Updated, Irish-American version of Martin Scorsese's "Mean Streets" focuses on a group of petty thieves from Boston's mostly Irish Charleston neighborhood. The hoods, lead by Bobby O'Grady (Leary), pass time stealing cars, snorting cocaine, and waxing poetic about their dead-end lives. But when a recently paroled member of their gang is murdered by the neighborhood kingpin Jackie O' (Meaney), Bobby must decide between upholding the gang's code of silence and avenging his pal's death. Excellent performances all around, especially from Leary, who grew up in this neighborhood. Originality, however, is not the film's strong suit. In addition to borrowing from Scorsese, script is full of Tarantinoesque banter. Worthy effort, just don't expect anything you haven't seen before. **90m/C VHS, DVD.** Denis Leary, Billy Crudup, Famke Janssen, Colm Meaney, Martin Sheen, Jeanne Tripplehorn, Ian Hart, Jason Barry, John Diehl, Noah Emmerich, Greg Dulli; ***D:*** Ted (Edward) Demme; ***W:*** Mike Armstrong; ***C:*** Adam Kimmel; ***M:*** Amanda Scheer-Demme.

The Moon and Sixpence &&& **1943** Stockbroker turns ambitious painter in this adaptation of W. Somerset Maugham's novel that was, in turn, inspired by the life of artist Paul Gauguin. Fine performance from Sanders. Filmed mainly in black and white, but uses color sparingly to great advantage. Compare this one to "Wolf at the Door," in which Gauguin is played by Donald Sutherland. **89m/B VHS.** George Sanders, Herbert Marshall, Steven Geray, Doris Dudley, Eric Blore, Elena Verdugo, Florence Bates, Albert Bassermann, Heather Thatcher; ***D:*** Albert Lewin.

Moon 44 &&½ **1990 (R)** A space prison is overrun by thugs who terrorize their fellow inmates. Fine cast, taut pacing. Filmed in Germany. **102m/C VHS.** *GE* Malcolm McDowell, Lisa Eichhorn, Michael Pare, Stephen Geoffreys, Roscoe Lee Browne, Brian Thompson, Dean Devlin, Mechmed Yilmaz, Leon Rippy; ***D:*** Roland Emmerich.

Moon in Scorpio &½ **1986** Three Vietnam-vet buddies go sailing and are attacked by the back-from-the-dead victims of a bloody war crime. **90m/C VHS.** John Phillip Law, Britt Ekland, William Smith; ***D:*** Gary Graver.

Moon in the Gutter &½ *La Lune Dans le Caniveau* **1983 (R)** In a ramshackle harbor town, a man searches despondently for the person who killed his sister years before. Various sexual liaisons and stevedore fights intermittently spice up the action. Nasty story that doesn't make much sense on film; adapted from a book by American pulp writer David Goodis. In French with English subtitles. **109m/C VHS.** *IT FR* Gerard Depardieu, Nastassia Kinski, Victoria Abril, Vittorio Mezzogiorno, Dominique Pinon; ***D:*** Jean-Jacques Beineix; ***W:*** Jean-Jacques Beineix; ***C:*** Philippe Rousselot; ***M:*** Gabriel Yared. Cesar '84: Art Dir./Set Dec.

The Moon Is Blue &&½ **1953** A young woman flaunts her virginity in this stilted adaptation of F. Hugh Herbert's play. Hard to believe that this film was once considered risque. Good performances, though, from Holden and Niven. **100m/B** William Holden, David Niven, Maggie McNamara, Tom Tully; ***D:*** Otto Preminger; ***C:*** Ernest Laszlo. Golden Globes '54: Actor—Mus./Comedy (Niven).

Moon of the Wolf & **1972** A small town in bayou country is terrorized by a modern-day werewolf that rips its victims to shreds. **74m/C VHS, DVD.** David Janssen, Barbara Rush, Bradford Dillman, John Beradino, Geoffrey Lewis, Royal Dano; ***D:*** Daniel Petrie; ***W:*** Alvin Sapinsley; ***C:*** Richard C. Glouner; ***M:*** Bernardo Segal. **TV**

Moon over Broadway **1998** Filmmakers (and spouses) Pennebaker and Hegedus follow the Broadway-bound comedy "Moon over Buffalo" in its evolution from pen to premiere—a lot like "Waiting for Guffman," but for real. Along the way we see how a bunch of professionals try to fine-tune a very average script into a funny comedy, and all the rewrites, conflicts, and jealousies that entails. As the celebrity of the cast, Burnett is at first resented (this isn't TV and she hasn't been on Broadway in 30 years), but winds up the life of the party, injecting most of the humor, and shows herself to be the real trouper among them. All in all an interestingly tense, and sometimes funny, behind-the-scenes look—with the biggest disappointment being the play itself, which did manage to run for nine months, probably thanks to Burnett. **92m/C VHS, DVD.** Carol Burnett, Philip Bosco; ***D:*** D.A. Pennebaker, Chris Hegedus; ***C:*** D.A. Pennebaker, James Desmond.

Moon over Harlem &½ **1939** A musical melodrama about a widow who unwittingly marries a fast-talking gangster involved in the numbers racket. The film features 20 chorus girls, a choir, and a 60-piece orchestra. **67m/B VHS, DVD.** Bud Harris, Cora Green, Alec Lovejoy, Sidney Bechet; ***D:*** Edgar G. Ulmer.

Moon over Miami &&& **1941** Manhunting trio meet their match in this engaging musical. A remake of 1938's "Three Blind Mice," this was later remade in 1946 as "Three Little Girls in Blue." ♫Moon Over Miami; I've Got You All To Myself; What Can I Do For You?; Kindergarten Congo; You Started Something; Oh Me Oh Mi-Am-Mi; Solitary Seminole; Is That Good?; Loveliness and Love. **91m/C VHS.** Don Ameche, Betty Grable, Robert Cummings, Carole Landis, Charlotte Greenwood, Jack Haley; ***D:*** Walter Lang; ***W:*** Mitch Glazer; ***C:*** Leon Shamroy.

Moon over Parador &&½ **1988 (PG-13)** An uneven comedy about a reluctant American actor who gets the role of his life when he gets the chance to pass himself off as the recently deceased dictator of a Latin American country. A political strongman wants to continue the charade until he can take over, but the actor begins to enjoy the benefits of dictatorship. Look for a cameo by director/writer Mazursky in drag. **103m/C VHS.** Richard Dreyfuss, Sonia Braga, Raul Julia, Jonathan Winters, Fernando Rey, Ed Asner, Dick Cavett, Michael Greene, Sammy Davis Jr., Polly Holliday, Charo, Marianne Saegebrecht, Dana Delany, Ike Pappas, Paul Mazursky; ***D:*** Paul Mazursky; ***W:*** Leon Capetanos, Paul Mazursky; ***M:*** Maurice Jarre.

Moon Pilot **1962** An astronaut on his way to the moon encounters a mysterious alien woman who claims to know his future. **98m/C VHS.** Tom Tryon, Brian Keith, Edmond O'Brien, Dany Saval, Tommy Kirk; ***D:*** James Neilson.

The Moon-Spinners **1964 (PG)** Lightweight Disney drama featuring Mills as a young tourist traveling through Crete who meets up with a young man, accused of being a jewel thief, and the two work together to find the real jewel thieves. Watch for silent film star Pola Negri. **118m/C VHS.** Hayley Mills, Peter McEnery, Eli Wallach, Pola Negri; ***D:*** James Neilson.

The Moon Stallion ½ **1985** A charming tale of mystery and fantasy for children and adults. Professor Purwell is researching King Arthur. His blind daughter soon becomes involved with supernatural events and a white horse that appears to lead her into adventures not of this age. **95m/C VHS.** *GB* Sarah Sutton, David Haig, James Greene, John Abineri, Caroline Goodall; ***D:*** Dorothea Brooking.

Moonbase **1997 (R)** In the year 2045, John Russell, manager of the Moonbase Waste Disposal Plant, has his hands full with more than garbage when a group of prison escapees take over the facility. **89m/C VHS.** Scott Plank, Jocelyn Seagrave, Kurt Fuller, Robert O'Reilly; ***D:*** Paolo Mazzucato; ***W:*** Brian DiMuccio, Dino Vindeni; ***M:*** Michael Sherwood. **VIDEO**

Mooncussers ½ **1962** A children's film detailing the exploits of a precocious 12-year-old determined to exact revenge upon a band of ruthless pirates. **85m/C VHS.** Kevin Corcoran, Rian Garrick, Oscar Homolka; ***D:*** James Neilson.

Moondance **1995 (R)** When lovely young German tourist Anya (Brendler) comes to an Irish fishing village on a summer holiday, two young brothers, Patrick (Shaw) and Dominic (Conroy), vie for her affections causing a family rift. Adapted from the novel "The White Hare" by Francis Stuart. **96m/C VHS.** *GB* Ruaidhri Conroy, Ian Shaw, Julia Brendler, Marianne Faithfull, Gerard McSorley, Kate Flynn, Brendan Grace; ***D:*** Dagmar Hirtz; ***W:*** Burt Weinshanker, Matt Watters; ***C:*** Steven Bernstein; ***M:*** Van Morrison, Fiancha Trench.

Moonfleet ½ **1955** Follows the adventures of an 18th century buccaneer who tries to swindle a young lad in his charge of a valuable diamond. From J. Meade Falkner's novel. **89m/C VHS.** Stewart Granger, Jon Whiteley, George Sanders, Viveca Lindfors, Joan Greenwood, Ian Wolfe; ***D:*** Fritz Lang; ***M:*** Miklos Rozsa.

Moonlight and Valentino **1995 (R)** To help her recover from the death of her husband, Rebecca turns to the comfort of flaky neighbor Sylvie (Goldberg), self-destructive sis Lucy (Paltrow), and overbearing ex-stepmother Alberta (Turner). Together they sit around and talk some of the more contrived and cliched "women talk" ("Chicken soup is the most womanly thing on the face of the planet") in recent film history. The finale, a hokey ritual in a cemetery, will have you pulling out hair rather than hankies. Rock star Bon Jovi makes his screen debut as the beefcake (discussion of his butt takes up about two-thirds of the dialogue) who puts the fire back into Rebecca's life. Not for the estrogen impaired. **104m/C VHS, DVD, Wide.** Elizabeth Perkins, Whoopi Goldberg, Gwyneth Paltrow, Kathleen Turner, Jon Bon Jovi, Jeremy Sisto, Josef Sommer, Peter Coyote; ***D:*** David Anspaugh; ***W:*** Ellen Simon; ***C:*** Julio Macat; ***M:*** Howard Shore.

Moonlight Sonata ½ **1938** Professional concert pianist Paderewski performs his way through a confusing soap-opera of a film. Includes performances of Franz Liszt's "Second Hungarian Rhapsody" and Frederic Chopin's "Polonaise." **80m/B VHS.** *GB* Ignace Jan Paderewski, Charles Farrell, Marie Tempest, Barbara Greene, Eric Portman; ***D:*** Lothar Mendes.

Moonlighting ½ **1982 (PG)** Compelling drama about Polish laborers illegally hired to renovate London flat. When their country falls under martial law, the foreman conceals the event and pushes workers to complete project. Unlikely casting of Irons as foreman is utterly successful. **97m/C VHS.** *PL GB* Jeremy Irons, Eugene Lipinski, Jiri Stanislay, Eugeniusz Haczkiewicz; ***D:*** Jerzy Skolimowski; ***C:*** Tony Pierce-Roberts; ***M:*** Hans Zimmer.

Moonlighting ½ **1985** Pilot for the popular detective show, where Maddie and David, the daffy pair of impetuous private eyes, meet for the first time and solve an irrationally complex case. **93m/C VHS, DVD.** Cybill Shepherd, Bruce Willis, Allyce Beasley; ***D:*** Robert Butler; ***W:*** Glenn Gordon Caron; ***C:*** Michael D. Margulies; ***M:*** Lee Holdridge. **TV**

The Moonraker ½ **1958** Compelling action scenes highlight this tale set at the end of the English Civil War, as the Royalists attempt to sneak the king out of England and into France. **82m/C VHS.** *GB* George Baker, Sylvia Syms, Peter Arne, Marius Goring, Clive Morton, Gary Raymond, Richard Leech, Patrick Troughton; ***D:*** David MacDonald.

Moonraker **1979 (PG)** Uninspired Bond fare has 007 unraveling intergalactic hijinks. Bond is aided by a female CIA agent, assaulted by a giant with jaws of steel, and captured by Amazons when he sets out to protect the human race. Moore, Chiles, and Lonsdale all seem to be going through the motions only. **136m/C VHS, DVD, Wide.** *GB* Roger Moore, Lois Chiles, Richard Kiel, Michael (Michel) Lonsdale, Corinne Clery, Geoffrey Keen, Emily Bolton, Walter Gotell, Bernard Lee, Lois Maxwell, Desmond Llewelyn; ***D:*** Lewis Gilbert; ***W:*** Christopher Wood; ***C:*** Jean Tournier; ***M:*** John Barry.

Moonrise **1948** A melodramatic tale about the son of an executed murderer who becomes the object of derision in the small town where he lives. One tormentor finally attacks him, and the young man must make a split-second decision that may affect his own mortality. **90m/B VHS.** Dane Clark, Gail Russell, Ethel Barrymore, Allyn Joslyn, Harry (Henry) Morgan, Lloyd Bridges, Selena Royle, Rex Ingram, Harry Carey Jr.; ***D:*** Frank Borzage.

The Moon's Our Home ½ **1936** A fast-paced, breezy, screwball comedy about an actress and adventurer impulsively marrying and then bickering through the honeymoon. Silliness at its height. Fonda and Sullavan were both married and then divorced before filming this movie. **80m/B VHS.** Margaret Sullavan, Henry Fonda, Beulah Bondi, Charles Butterworth, Margaret Hamilton, Walter Brennan; ***D:*** William A. Seiter; ***C:*** Joseph Valentine.

Moonshine County Express ½ **1977 (PG)** Three sexy daughters of a hillbilly moonshiner set out to run the still and avenge their father's murder. **97m/C VHS.** John Saxon, Susan Howard, William Conrad, Morgan Woodward, Claudia Jennings, Jeff Corey, Dub Taylor, Maureen McCormick, Albert Salmi, Candice Rialson; ***D:*** Gus Trikonis.

Moonshine Highway **1996 (PG-13)** Redneck alert! '50s Tennessee moonshiner Jed Muldoon (MacLachlan) clashes with Sheriff Miller (Quaid), who's not only aggrieved about Jed's illegal liquor running but is not happy that his estranged wife Ethel (Del Mar) has taken up with the miscreant. Lots of backwoods car chases. **96m/C VHS.** Kyle MacLachlan, Randy Quaid, Maria Del Mar, Gary Farmer, Jeremy Ratchford; ***D:*** Andy Armstrong; ***W:*** Andy Armstrong; ***C:*** Dick Quinlan. **CABLE**

Moonshine Mountain woof! *White Trash on Moonshine Mountain* **1964** A country-western star travels with his girlfriend to the singer's home in backwoods Carolina. When the girl is killed by a lusting resident, all hell breaks loose. One of gore-meister Lewis' excursions into the dramatic. **90m/C VHS.** Chuck Scott, Adam Sorg, Jeffrey Allen, Bonnie Hinson, Carmen Sotir, Ben Moore, Pat Patterson, Mark Douglas; ***D:*** Herschell Gordon Lewis; ***W:*** Herschell Gordon Lewis; ***C:*** Herschell Gordon Lewis; ***M:*** Herschell Gordon Lewis.

The Moonstone **1997** In the mid-19th century, the Moonstone, a sacred Hindu diamond, is stolen from a shrine in India. The jewel, which carries a curse, winds up in the hands of heiress Rachel Verinder (Hawes), thanks to her suitor Franklin Blake (Wise). But when the diamond is stolen from Rachel, police Sergeant Cuff (Sher) investigates and uncovers deception and a variety of villains. Based on the novel by Wilkie Collins and considered the first detective story, some 20 years before Conan Doyle's Sherlock Holmes. **120m/C VHS.** Greg Wise, Anthony Sher, Keeley Hawes, Patricia Hodge; ***D:*** Robert Bierman. **TV**

Moonstruck ½ **1987 (PG-13)** Winning romantic comedy about widow engaged to one man but falling in love with his younger brother in Little Italy. Excellent performances all around, with Cher particularly fetching as attractive, hapless widow. Unlikely casting of usually dominating Aiello, as unassuming mama's boy also works well, and Cage is at his best as a tormented one-handed opera lover/baker. **103m/C VHS, DVD, Wide.** Cher, Nicolas Cage, Olympia Dukakis, Danny Aiello, Vincent Gardenia, Julie Bovasso, Louis Guss, Anita Gillette, Feodor Chaliapin Jr., John Mahoney; ***D:*** Norman Jewison; ***W:*** John Patrick Shanley; ***C:*** David Watkin; ***M:*** Dick Hyman. Oscars '87: Actress (Cher), Orig. Screenplay, Support. Actress (Dukakis); Berlin Intl. Film Fest. '87: Director (Jewison); Golden Globes '88: Actress—Mus./Comedy (Cher), Support. Actress (Dukakis); L.A. Film Critics '87: Support. Actress (Dukakis); Natl. Bd. of Review '87: Support. Actress (Dukakis); Writers Guild '87: Orig. Screenplay.

Moontrap **1989** An astronaut discovers an alien frozen in space and returns to Earth with it. Once thawed, the creature reveals its horrible secret. **92m/C VHS.** Walter Koenig, Bruce Campbell, Leigh Lombardi; ***D:*** Robert Dyke.

Morals for Women ½ **1931** This soap-opera's so old it almost predates soap. A secretary becomes the Kept Woman of her boss in the Big Bad City. She escapes, but not for long. **65m/B VHS.** Bessie Love, Conway Tearle, John Holland, Natalie Moorhead, Emma Dunn, June Clyde; ***D:*** Mort Blumenstock.

Moran of the Lady Letty ½ **1922** Seaweed saga of Ramon Laredo (Valentino), a high society guy who's kidnapped aboard a pirate barge. When the salty dogs rescue/capture Moran (a theme ahead of its time?) from a ship fuming with burning coal, Ramon is smitten in a big way with the boyish girl and battles contagiously to prevent the pirates from selling her as a slave. Excellent fight scenes with much hotstepping over gangplanks and swinging from masts, with a 60-foot death dive from above. Little known Dalton was a celluloid fave in the 'teens and twenties, and Valentino is atypically cast as a man's man. The sheik himself is said not to have like this one because it undermined his image as a ladies' man. **71m/B VHS.** Dorothy Dalton, Rudolph Valentino, Charles Brinley, Walter Long, Emil Jorgenson; ***D:*** George Melford.

More ½ **1969** Smells like teen angst in the '60s when a German college grad falls for an American in Paris, to the tune of sex, drugs, and Pink Floyd. Schroeder's first effort as director, it's definitely a '60s pic. In French with English subtitles. **110m/C VHS.** Mimsy Farmer, Klaus Grunberg, Heinz Engelmann, Michel Chanderli; ***D:*** Barbet Schroeder; ***C:*** Nestor Almendros.

More about the Children of Noisy Village ½ *More About the Children of Bullerby Village; Mem om oss barn i Bullerby* **1987** The six adventurous children, who live in an idyllic Swedish village before WWII, return. This time they're ready to start a new school year, including playing pranks on the teacher, getting stranded during a blizzard, and enjoying a memorable New Year's Eve. Based on stories by Astrid Lindgren. Dubbed. **85m/C VHS.** *SW* ***D:*** Lasse Hallstrom.

More American Graffiti ½ **1979 (PG)** Sequel to 1973's acclaimed '50s homage "American Graffiti" charts various characters' experiences in the more radical '60s. George Lucas didn't direct, Richard Dreyfuss didn't reprise. Ron Howard doesn't direct, he acts. B.W.L. Norton doesn't direct either, though he's credited. Pass on this one and have that root canal done instead. **111m/C VHS.** Delroy Lindo, James Houghton, John Lansing, Mary Kay Place, Rosanna Arquette, Jonathan (Jon Francis) Gries, Naomi Judd, Harrison Ford, Candy Clark, Bo Hopkins, Ron Howard, Paul LeMat, MacKenzie Phillips, Charles Martin Smith, Anna Bjorn, Richard Bradford, Cindy Williams, Scott Glenn; ***D:*** Bill W.L. Norton; ***W:*** Gloria Katz, Willard Huyck; ***C:*** Caleb Deschanel.

The More the Merrier **1943** Likeable romantic comedy in which working girl must share apartment with two bachelors in Washington, D.C., during WWII. Arthur is especially endearing as a young woman in male company. **104m/B VHS.** Joel McCrea, Jean Arthur, Charles Coburn, Richard Gaines, Bruce (Herman Brix) Bennett, Ann Savage, Ann Doran, Frank Tully, Grady Sutton; ***D:*** George Stevens. Oscars '43: Support. Actor (Coburn); N.Y. Film Critics '43: Director (Stevens).

More Wild, Wild West **1980** Another feature-length continuation of the satirical TV western series, with Winters taking on Conrad and Martin. **94m/C VHS.** Robert Conrad, Ross Martin, Jonathan Winters, Victor Buono; ***D:*** Burt Kennedy. **TV**

Morgan: A Suitable Case for Treatment ½ *Morgan!; A Suitable Case for Treatment* **1966** Offbeat comedy in which deranged artist copes with divorce by donning ape suit. Some laughs ensue. Based on David Mercer's play. **93m/B VHS, DVD, Wide.** *GB* Vanessa Redgrave, David Warner, Robert Stephens, Irene Handl, Bernard Bresslaw, Arthur Mullard, Newton Blick, Nan Munro, Graham Crowden, John Rae, Peter Collingwood, Edward Fox; ***D:*** Karel Reisz; ***W:*** David Mercer; ***C:*** Larry Pizer; ***M:*** John Dankworth. British Acad. '66: Screenplay; Cannes '66: Actress (Redgrave).

Morgan Stewart's Coming Home *Home Front* **1987 (PG-13)** When Dad needs a good family image in his political race, he brings Morgan home from boarding school. Fortunately, Morgan can see how his parents are using him and he doesn't approve at all. He decides to turn his family's life upside down while pursuing the love of his life. **96m/C VHS.** Jon Cryer, Lynn Redgrave, Nicholas Pryor, Viveka Davis, Paul Gleason, Andrew Duncan, Savely Kramorov, John David (J.D.) Cullum, Robert Sedgwick, Waweru Njenga, Sudhir Rad; ***D:*** Alan Smithee; ***M:*** Peter Bernstein.

Morgan the Pirate *Capitaine Morgan; Morgan il Pirata* **1960** Steve Reeves is at his finest as Morgan, an escaped slave who becomes a notorious pirate in the Caribbean and is wrongly condemned to death in this brisk, sea-going adventure. **93m/C VHS.** *FR IT* Steve Reeves, Valerie Lagrange; ***D:*** Andre de Toth.

Morituri *Saboteur: Code Name Morituri; The Saboteur* **1965** Gripping wartime drama in which an Allied spy tries to persuade German gunboat captain to surrender his vessel. Brando is—no surprise—excellent. **123m/C VHS.** Marlon Brando, Yul Brynner, Trevor Howard, Janet Margolin, Wally Cox, William Redfield; ***D:*** Bernhard Wicki; ***W:*** Daniel Taradash; ***C:*** Conrad L. Hall; ***M:*** Jerry Goldsmith.

A Mormon Maid ½ **1917** Young woman and her family, after being saved from an Indian attack by a Mormon group, come to live among them without converting to their beliefs. Considered a shocking expose of controversial Mormon practices, including polygamy. **78m/B VHS.** Mae Murray, Frank Borzage, Hobart Bosworth, Noah Beery Sr.; ***D:*** Robert Z. Leonard.

The Morning After **1986 (R)** A predictable suspense-thriller about an alcoholic actress who wakes up one morning with a corpse in bed next to her, but cannot remember anything about the night before. She evades the police, accidentally meets up with an ex-cop, and works with him to unravel an increasingly complicated mystery. **103m/C VHS.** Jane Fonda, Jeff Bridges, Raul Julia, Diane Salinger, Richard Foronjy, Geoffrey Scott, Kathleen Wilhoite, Frances Bergen, Rick Rossovich, Kathy Bates; ***D:*** Sidney Lumet; ***W:*** James Cresson; ***C:*** Andrzej Bartkowiak.

Morning Glory 🦴🦴½ **1933** Small-town girl finds love and fame in the big city. Predictable fare nonetheless boasts fine performances from Hepburn and Fairbanks. Adapted from Zoe Atkins' stage play. **74m/B VHS.** Katharine Hepburn, Douglas Fairbanks Jr., Adolphe Menjou, Mary Duncan; ***D:*** Lowell Sherman; ***M:*** Max Steiner. Oscars '33: Actress (Hepburn).

Morning Glory 🦴🦴½ **1993 (PG-13)** Sappy romance, set during the Depression, about a pregnant widow (Raffin) trying to survive on her hardscrabble farm in Georgia. Elly Dinsmore advertises for a husband, not for romance but to help with the work, and is answered by Will Parker (Reeve), an ex-con trying to live down his past. When a local floozy who has been eyeing Will is killed the sheriff (Walsh) is only too happy to go after the stranger in town. Light-weight with some unbelievable plot twists. Based on the novel "Morning Glory" by LaVyrle Spencer. **90m/C VHS.** Deborah Raffin, Christopher Reeve, Lloyd Bochner, Nina Foch, Helen Shaver, J.T. Walsh; ***D:*** Steven Hilliard Stern; ***W:*** Deborah Raffin, Charles Jarrott; ***M:*** Jonathan Elias.

Morocco 🦴🦴🦴½ **1930** A foreign legion soldier falls for a world-weary chanteuse along the desert sands. Cooper has never been more earnest, and Dietrich has never been more blase and exotic. In her American film debut, Dietrich sings "What Am I Bid?" A must for anyone drawn to improbable, gloriously well-done kitsch. Based on Benno Vigny's novel, "Amy Jolly." **92m/B VHS.** Marlene Dietrich, Gary Cooper, Adolphe Menjou, Ullrich Haupt, Francis McDonald, Eve Southern, Paul Porcasi; ***D:*** Josef von Sternberg; ***C:*** Lee Garmes. Natl. Film Reg. '92.

Morons from Outer Space 🦴🦴 **1985 (PG)** Slow-witted aliens from elsewhere in the universe crash onto Earth, but unlike other sci-fis, these morons become internationally famous, despite them acting like intergalactic stooges. Plenty of sight gags. **87m/C VHS, DVD, Wide.** *GB* Griff Rhys Jones, Mel Smith, James B. Sikking, Dinsdale Landen, Jimmy Nail, Joanne Pearce, Paul Brown; ***D:*** Mike Hodges; ***W:*** Griff Rhys Jones, Mel Smith; ***C:*** Phil Meheux; ***M:*** Peter Brewis.

Mortal Challenge 🦴½ **1997 (R)** A corrupt police force, known as the Centurions, guard a futuristic L.A., which is divided into rich and poor sectors. When wealthy Tori is captured visiting her wrong-side-of-the-sectors boyfriend, the Centurions decide to have some fun by matching her with a cyborg in a death game. **77m/C VHS.** Timothy Bottoms, David McCallum, Evan Lurie, Nick (Nicholas, Niko) Hill; ***D:*** Randolph Cheveldare. **VIDEO**

Mortal Danger 🦴🦴½ *Turn Your Pony Around* **1994 (PG-13)** Kathy and Phil are suicidal teens finding different solutions to their difficulties over the same weekend. Comes across like a TV movie but does maintain an honest message with affecting performances. **86m/C VHS.** Ami Dolenz, Noah Hathaway, Paul Coufos, Larry Gatlin, Charles Napier; ***D:*** Brianne Murphy.

Mortal Kombat 1: The Movie 🦴🦴 **1995 (PG-13)** Inevitable film version of mega popular arcade game intended to cash in fast on the game's popularity. Shameless nirvana for youngin's with permanent joystick scars on their hands. Grown-ups forced to sit through it may get into some of the eye-popping special effects and nifty martial arts sequences if they can block out the contrived plot, lame acting, and Lambert's presence as Thunder God. **101m/C VHS, DVD, Wide.** Christopher Lambert, Talisa Soto, Cary-Hiroyuki Tagawa, Bridgette Wilson; ***D:*** Paul Anderson; ***W:*** Kevin Droney; ***C:*** John R. Leonetti; ***M:*** George S. Clinton.

Mortal Kombat 2: Annihilation 🦴½ **1997 (PG-13)** The treacherous Shao-Khan brings his evil horde of video-game villians through a portal ripped in the universe and threatens to destroy the Earth in this highly unnecessary sequel. Liu Kang and his buds are on the scene to once again do battle to save humanity. Moves from one badly staged fight scene to another with little story or acting (except for Remar in the role of Rayden, replacing Christopher Lambert in the first "Kombat"), and adults should quickly tire of the non-stop back flips and somersaulting that combine with computer graphics to give each character their own special abilities. Kids and gamers, however, should enjoy the new characters, the same-sounding pulse-pounding techno music, and the non-stop, but fairly bloodless, violence. **98m/C VHS, DVD.** James Remar, Robin Shou, Talisa Soto, Daron McBee, Sandra Hess, Brian Thompson, Reiner Schoene, Musetta Vander, Marjean Holden, Litefoot, Lynn Red Williams, Irina Pantaeva; ***D:*** John R. Leonetti; ***W:*** Brent Friedman, Bruce Zabel; ***C:*** Matthew F. Leonetti; ***M:*** George S. Clinton.

Mortal Passions 🦴½ **1990 (R)** Another "Double Indemnity" rip-off, with a scheming tramp manipulating everyone around her with betrayal, sex, and murder. Her dead husband's brother eventually ignites old flames to steer her away from his money. **96m/C VHS.** Zach Galligan, Krista Errickson, Michael Bowen, Luca Bercovici, Sheila Kelley, David Warner; ***D:*** Andrew Lane.

Mortal Sins 🦴 **1990 (R)** A TV evangelist finds more than salvation at the altar, when bodies begin to turn up. The detective he hires is close-mouthed, but more than a little interested in the preacher's daughter. A tense psycho-sexual thriller. **85m/C VHS.** Brian Benben, Anthony LaPaglia, Debrah Farentino; ***D:*** Yuri Sivo.

Mortal Sins 🦴🦴 **1992 (PG-13)** Reeve stars as parish priest Thomas Cusack, who hears the confession of a serial killer. What's worse is that the killer is preying on the women of Cusack's parish. Since he can't break the seal of the confessional, the good Father tries to stop the killer himself before another murder takes place. **93m/C VHS.** Christopher Reeve; ***D:*** Bradford May.

The Mortal Storm 🦴🦴🦴½ **1940** Phyllis Bottome's famous novel comes to life in this extremely well acted film about the rise of the Nazi regime. Stewart and Sullavan are young lovers who risk everything to escape the country after their families are torn apart by the Nazi takeover. Although Germany is never identified as the country, it is obvious in this story about the early days of WWII. Hitler took one look at this and promptly banned all MGM movies in Nazi Germany. **100m/B VHS.** Margaret Sullavan, James Stewart, Robert Young, Frank Morgan, Robert Stack, Bonita Granville, Irene Rich; ***D:*** Frank Borzage; ***W:*** Claudine West, George Froeschel, Anderson Ellis; ***C:*** William H. Daniels.

Mortal Thoughts 🦴🦴½ **1991 (R)** Best friends find their relationship tested when the brutal husband of one of them is murdered. Moore and Headly are exceptional, capturing the perfect inflections and attitudes of the hard-working New Jersey beauticians sure of their friendship. Excellent pacing, fine supporting cast, with Keitel and Willis stand-outs. **104m/C VHS, DVD, 8mm, Wide.** Demi Moore, Bruce Willis, Glenne Headly, Harvey Keitel, John Pankow, Billie Neal; ***D:*** Alan Rudolph; ***W:*** William Reilly, Claude Kerven; ***C:*** Elliot Davis; ***M:*** Mark Isham. Natl. Soc. Film Critics '91: Support. Actor (Keitel).

Mortuary 🦴 **1981 (R)** Young woman's nightmares come startlingly close to reality. **91m/C VHS.** Christopher George, Lynda Day George, Paul Smith; ***D:*** Howard (Hikmet) Avedis; ***W:*** Howard (Hikmet) Avedis.

Mortuary Academy 🦴 **1991 (R)** To win an inheritance two brothers must attend the family mortician school, a situation paving the way for aggressively tasteless jokes on necrophilia. An attempt to recapture the successful black humor of the earlier Bartel/Woronov teaming "Eating Raoul," this one's dead on arrival. **86m/C VHS.** Christopher Atkins, Perry Lang, Paul Bartel, Mary Woronov, Tracey Walter, Lynn Danielson, Cesar Romero, Wolfman Jack; ***D:*** Michael Schroeder; ***W:*** William Kelman; ***C:*** Roy Wagner, Ronald Vidor; ***M:*** David Spear.

The Mosaic Project 🦴½ **1995 (R)** Action junkies should be happy with the chases, explosions, and other mayhem engendered by this story of two buddies who find themselves the victims of a mad scientist. Now they have experimental computer chips implanted in their brains that make them skilled in 25 martial arts forms (and some other stuff that doesn't matter much). **89m/C VHS.** Jon Tabler, Ben Marley, Joe Estevez, Julie Strain, Colleen T. Coffey, Robert Z'Dar; ***D:*** John Sjogren; ***W:*** John Sjogren.

Mosby's Marauders 🦴🦴 **1966** A young boy joins a Confederate raiding company during the Civil War and learns about bravery, war, and love. **79m/C VHS.** Kurt Russell, James MacArthur, Jack Ging, Peggy Lipton, Nick Adams; ***D:*** Michael O'Herlihy.

Moscow Does Not Believe in Tears 🦴🦴🦴 *Moscow Distrusts Tears; Moskwa Sljesam Nje Jerit* **1980** Three provincial girls—Lyuda (Muravyova), Tonya (Ryazanova), and Katya (Alentova)—realize very different fates when they pursue their dreams in 1958 Moscow. The film picks up 20 years later to see what became of the women. Bittersweet, moving fare that seems a somewhat surprising production from pre-Glasnost USSR. In Russian with English subtitles. A 150-minute version has also been released. **115m/C VHS.** *RU* Vera Alentova, Irina Muravyova, Raisa Ryazanova, Natalie Vavilova, Alexei Batalov, Alexander Fatyushin, Yuri Vasilyev; ***D:*** Vladimir Menshov; ***W:*** Valentin Chernykh; ***C:*** Igor Slabnevich; ***M:*** Sergei Nikitin. Oscars '80: Foreign Film.

Moscow on the Hudson 🦴🦴🦴 **1984 (R)** Good-natured comedy has Williams as Soviet defector trying to cope with new life of freedom in fast-paced, freewheeling melting pot of New York City. Williams is particularly winning as naive jazzman, though Alonso also scores as his Hispanic love interest. Be warned though, it's not just played for laughs. **115m/C VHS, DVD, Wide.** Robin Williams, Maria Conchita Alonso, Cleavant Derricks, Alejandro Rey, Elya Baskin; ***D:*** Paul Mazursky; ***W:*** Paul Mazursky, Leon Capetanos; ***C:*** Donald McAlpine; ***M:*** David McHugh.

Moscow Parade 🦴🦴 *Prorva* **1992** Sexy cabaret singer gets caught up in the shifting alliances caused by war. Set in Russia before the Nazi invasion. Russian with subtitles. **103m/C VHS.** *RU* Ute Lemper, Vladimir Simonov; ***D:*** Ivan Dykhovichny.

Moses woof! **1976 (PG)** Lancaster goes biblical as Moses, the man with the tablets. Edited from the 360-minute British TV series, with no improvement obvious from the economy, except that the bad parts are shorter. Poor chatter and scattered bouts of acting are surpassed in inadequacy only by special effects. **141m/C VHS.** Burt Lancaster, Anthony Quayle, Ingrid Thulin, Irene Papas, William Lancaster; ***D:*** Gianfranco DeBosio; ***W:*** Anthony Burgess, Vittorio Bonicelli; ***M:*** Ennio Morricone.

Moses 🦴🦴½ **1996** Another entry in TNT's series of Bible stories finds a humble Moses (Kingsley), raised in the Egyptian court, finding his way to his own people, the Israelites. Chosen by God to be his messenger and lead his people out of bondage, Moses must unleash a series of plagues upon Egypt before pharaoh Merneftа (Langella) will let them go. If you want action, look to "The Ten Commandments," since this is a faithful but tedious retelling. Filmed on location in Morocco; on two cassettes. **185m/C VHS.** Ben Kingsley, Frank Langella, David Suchet, Christopher Lee, Anna Galiena, Enrico Lo Verso, Geraldine McEwan, Maurice Roeves, Anthony (Corlan) Higgins, Anton Lesser; ***D:*** Roger Young; ***W:*** Lionel Chetwynd; ***C:*** Raffaele Mertes; ***M:*** Marco Frisina.

Mosley 🦴🦴 **1998** Looks at the life and political career of Oswald "Tom" Mosley (Cake), the leader of the British Fascist Movement from the end of WWI to his rise to prominence and eventual imprisonment during WWII. **240m/C VHS.** *GB* Jonathan Cake, Hugh Bonneville, Jeremy Child, Eric Allan, Caroline Langrishe, Jemma Redgrave, Windsor Davies; ***D:*** Robert Knights. **TV**

Mosquito 🦴 **1995 (R)** Alien forces transform the annoying insects into monstrous mutants. Schlocky special effects are good for laughs. **92m/C VHS, DVD.** Gunnar Hansen, Ron Asheton, Steve Dixon, Rachel Loiselle, Tim Loveface; ***D:*** Gary Jones; ***W:*** Gary Jones, Steve Hodge, Tom Chaney; ***C:*** Tom Chaney; ***M:*** Allen Lynch, Randall Lynch.

The Mosquito Coast 🦴🦴½ **1986 (PG)** Ambitious adaptation of Paul Theroux's novel about an asocial inventor who transplants his family to a rainforest to realize his utopian dream. A nightmare ensues. Ford tries hard, but supporters Mirren and Phoenix are main appeal of only intermittently successful drama. **119m/C VHS, DVD, Wide.** Harrison Ford, Helen Mirren, River Phoenix, Andre Gregory, Martha Plimpton, Conrad Roberts, Butterfly McQueen, Jadrien Steele, Hilary Gordon, Rebecca Gordon, Dick O'Neill, Jason Alexander; ***D:*** Peter Weir; ***W:*** Paul Schrader; ***C:*** John Seale; ***M:*** Maurice Jarre.

The Most Dangerous Game 🦴🦴🦴 *The Hounds of Zaroff* **1932** Shipwrecked McRae washed ashore on the island of Banks's Count Zaroff, a deranged sportsman with a flair for tracking humans. Guess who becomes the mad count's next target. Oft-told tale is compellingly related in this, the first of many using Richard Connell's famous short story. If deja vu sets in, don't worry. This production uses most of the scenery, staff, and cast from its studio cousin, "King Kong." Remade in 1945 as "A Game of Death" and in 1956 as "Run for the Sun." **78m/B VHS, DVD.** Joel McCrea, Fay Wray, Leslie Banks, Robert Armstrong, Noble Johnson; ***D:*** Ernest B. Schoedsack, Irving Pichel; ***W:*** James A. Creelman; ***C:*** Henry W. Gerrard; ***M:*** Max Steiner.

Most Wanted 🦴½ **1976** A psychopath with a penchant for raping nuns and collecting crucifixes is tracked down by a special police unit in this successful TV pilot. **78m/C VHS.** Robert Stack, Shelly Novack, Leslie Charleson, Tom Selleck, Sheree North; ***D:*** Walter Grauman. **TV**

Most Wanted 🦴🦴½ **1997 (R)** Marine Sgt. James Dunn (Wayans), framed for the assassination of the first lady, is on the run from the CIA, FBI, LAPD, and the covert team he was working with, which is led by Voight, the gung-ho general who set up the whole scam. Wayans, who wrote and produced, seems convinced that an action hero must be of the strong-silent-superhero mold, and appears at a loss without a joke to crack. Voight, however, is right at home in the bad-guy role, employing an overdone but effective southern drawl. Plenty of elaborate stunts, oversized fireballs, shootings, and chases provide the expected wild ride, including the film's funniest sequence as thousands of L.A. natives spontaneously become wild-in-the-street bounty hunters. **99m/C VHS, DVD.** Keenen Ivory Wayans, Jon Voight, Jill(ian) Hennessey, Eric Roberts, Paul Sorvino, Robert Culp, Wolfgang Bodison, Simon Baker; ***D:*** David Hogan; ***W:*** Keenen Ivory Wayans; ***C:*** Marc Reshovsky; ***M:*** Paul Bruckmaster.

Motel Blue 🦴½ **1998 (R)** Kyle Rivers (Frye) is an agent with the Department of Defense, who's doing a security clearance check on scientist Lana Hawking (Young). Lana maintains an expensive lifestyle that suggests she may be selling government secrets. But when Lana finds out about Kyle's suspicions, she frames her and Kyle gets suspended. But she decides to continue the investigation on her own terms. No particular surprises but there are a number of sleazy sex scenes. **96m/C VHS, DVD.** Sean Young, Soleil Moon Frye, Seymour Cassel, Robert Vaughn, Robert Stewart, Lou Rawls, Spencer Rochfort; ***D:*** Sam Firstenberg; ***W:*** Marianne S. Wibberly, Cormac Wibberly; ***C:*** Moshe Levin. **VIDEO**

Motel Hell 🦴½ **1980 (R)** A completely tongue-in-cheek gore-fest about a farmer who kidnaps tourists, buries them in his garden, and reaps a human harvest to grind into his distinctive brand of smoked, preservative-free sausage. **102m/C VHS.** Rory Calhoun, Nancy Parsons, Paul (Link) Linke, Nina Axelrod, Wolfman Jack, Elaine Joyce, Dick

Curtis, Rosanne Katon, Monique St. Pierre, John Ratzenberger; *D:* Kevin Connor; *W:* Robert Jaffe, Steven-Charles Jaffe; *C:* Thomas Del Ruth; *M:* Lance Rubin.

Mother 𝒟𝒟𝒟½ **1926** Pudovkin's innovative classic about a Russian family shattered by the uprising in 1905. A masterpiece of Russian cinema that established Pudovkin, and rivaled only Eisenstein for supremacy in montage, poetic imagery, and propagandistic ideals. Based on Maxim Gorky's great novel, it's one of cinematic history's seminal works. Striking cinematography, stunning use of montage make this one important. Silent with English subtitles. **70m/B VHS, DVD.** *RU* Vera Baranovskaya, Nikolai Batalov; *D:* Vsevolod Pudovkin.

Mother 𝒟𝒟𝒟½ *Okasan* **1952** A Japanese family is undone after the devastation of WWII. An uncharacteristically dramatic, and thus more accessible, film from one of the Japanese cinema's greatest masters. In Japanese with English subtitles. **98m/B VHS.** *JP* Kinuyo Tanaka, Kyoko Kagawa, Eiji Okada, Akihiko Katayama; *D:* Mikio Naruse.

Mother 𝒟𝒟½ **1994 (R)** Olivia Hendrix (Ladd) is a very over-protective mom—even though son Tom (Weisser) is nineteen and anxious to untie the apron strings. But Mom thinks she knows best and she's willing to kill to made certain Tom stays home where he belongs. **90m/C VHS.** Diane Ladd, Olympia Dukakis, Morgan Weisser, Ele Keats; *D:* Frank Laloggia.

Mother 𝒟𝒟½ **1996 (PG-13)** Yes, you will shake your head in recognition of that parent-child bond. Twice-divorced writer John Henderson (Brooks) decides it's all Mom's fault he has problems with women, so he decides to move back home and figure out what went wrong. Mom Beatrice (Reynolds) is exasperated and married younger brother Jeff (Morrow) winds up jealous of mom's attentions to his sibling. Reynolds' first feature film in 25 years. **104m/C VHS, DVD, Wide.** Albert Brooks, Debbie Reynolds, Rob Morrow, Lisa Kudrow, John C. McGinley, Isabel Glasser, Peter White; *D:* Albert Brooks; *W:* Albert Brooks, Monica Johnson; *C:* Lajos Koltai; *M:* Marc Shaiman. N.Y. Film Critics '96: Screenplay; Natl. Soc. Film Critics '96: Screenplay.

Mother & Daughter: A Loving War 𝒟½ **1980** Three women experience motherhood. Special appearance by Harry Chapin as himself. **96m/C VHS.** Tuesday Weld, Frances Sternhagen, Kathleen Beller, Jeanne Lang, Edward Winter; *D:* Burt Brinckerhoff. **TV**

Mother and Son 𝒟𝒟 **1931** Melodrama finds the wayward Young shielding her son from the fact that she runs a gambling hall. He grows up to be a society lad before discovering the devastating truth. **67m/B VHS.** Clara Kimball Young, Bruce Warren, Mildred Golden, John Elliott, Gordon Wood, Ernest Hilliard; *D:* John P. McCarthy.

Mother and Son 𝒟𝒟 *Mat i Syn; Mutter und Sohn* **1997** Slow-paced, dreamlike story about a dedicated son's (Ananishnov) caring for his dying mother (Geyer) in their old house in the country. She wishes to go outside—he carries her along a path in the woods and they recall his childhood. She eventually goes back to her bed where they discuss death and she falls asleep, never to waken. Russian with subtitles. **73m/C VHS, DVD.** *RU GE* Gudrun Geyer, Alexi Ananishnov; *D:* Alexander Sokurov; *W:* Yuri Arabov; *C:* Aleksei Federov; *M:* Otmar Nussio.

The Mother and the Whore 𝒟𝒟𝒟𝒟 *La Maman et la Putain* **1973** Alexander (Leaud) lives with slightly older Marie (Lafont) but still can't resist picking up sexy Veronika (Lebrun). Their menage works for a while but then tensions between the sexual threesome force them to discuss their situation. Talky, witty, provocative example of French New Wave, which Eustache shot in his own apartment and local bistros. French with subtitles. **210m/B VHS.** *FR* Jean-Pierre Leaud, Bernadette LaFont, Francoise Lebrun, Isabelle Weingarten, Jean-Noel Picq, Jessa Darrieux, Genevieve Mnich, Marinka Matuszewski; *D:* Jean Eustache; *W:* Jean Eustache; *C:* Pierre Lhomme.

Mother Doesn't Always Know Best 𝒟½ **196?** A strange relationship between a young count and his widowed mother initiates a strange series of events. **95m/C VHS.** Senta Berger; *D:* Alfredo Gianelli.

Mother Goose Rock 'n' Rhyme **1990** Duvall follows the success of her "Faerie Tale Theatre" series with a new comedic fable, starring some of Hollywood's top names. Great fun for the whole family. **96m/C VHS.** Shelley Duvall, Teri Garr, Howie Mandel, Jean Stapleton, Ben Vereen, Bobby Brown, Art Garfunkel, Dan Gilroy, Deborah Harry, Cyndi Lauper, Little Richard, Paul Simon, Harry Anderson, Elayne Boosler, Woody Harrelson, Richard "Cheech" Marin, Garry Shandling.

Mother Joan of the Angels 𝒟𝒟𝒟 *The Devil and the Nun; Matka Joanna Od Aniolow* **1960** A priest investigating demonic possession among nuns in a 17th-century Polish convent becomes involved in a mutual attraction with the Mother Superior. A powerful allegory complemented by the stylized narrative and performances. Polish with subtitles. Based on actual events at Loudun and also the subject of a play by John Whiting, an opera by Krzysztof Penderecki, "The Devils of Loudon" novel by Aldous Huxley, and Ken Russell's movie "The Devils." **108m/B VHS.** *PL* Lucyna Winnicka, Mieczyslaw Voit, Anna Ciepielewska, Maria Chwalibog; *D:* Jerzy Kawalerowicz; *W:* Jerzy Kawalerowicz, Tadeusz Konwicki; *M:* Adam Walacinski. Cannes '61: Grand Jury Prize.

Mother, Jugs and Speed 𝒟½ **1976 (PG)** Black comedy about the day-to-day tragedies encountered by a group of ambulance drivers. Interesting mix of stars. **95m/C VHS.** Bill Cosby, Raquel Welch, Harvey Keitel, Allen (Goorwitz) Garfield, Larry Hagman, Bruce Davison, Dick Butkus, L.Q. (Justus E. McQueen) Jones, Toni Basil; *D:* Peter Yates; *W:* Tom Mankiewicz.

Mother Kusters Goes to Heaven 𝒟𝒟𝒟 *Mutter Kusters Fahrt Zum Himmel* **1976** Mrs. Kusters's husband is a frustrated factory worker who goes over the edge and kills the factory owner's son and himself. Left alone, she learns that everyone is using her husband's death to further their own needs, including her daughter, who uses the publicity to enhance her singing career. A statement that you should trust no one, not even your family and friends. This film was banned from the Berlin Film Festival because of its political overtones. In German with English subtitles. **108m/C VHS.** *GE* Brigitte Mira, Ingrid Caven, Armin Meier, Irm Hermann, Gottfried John, Margit Carstensen, Karl-Heinz Boehm; *D:* Rainer Werner Fassbinder; *W:* Rainer Werner Fassbinder; *C:* Michael Ballhaus.

Mother Lode 𝒟½ *Search for the Mother Lode; The Last Great Treasure* **1982 (PG)** The violent conflict between twin brothers (played by Heston) is intensified by greed, near madness, and the all-consuming lust for gold in this action-adventure. Heston's son, Fraser Clarke Heston, wrote as well as produced the film. **101m/C VHS.** Charlton Heston, Nick Mancuso, Kim Basinger; *D:* Charlton Heston.

Mother Night 𝒟𝒟𝒟 **1996 (R)** American writer Howard Campbell (Nolte) is recruited as a spy in pre-WWII Germany in this adaptation of Kurt Vonnegut's 1962 novel. He poses as a Nazi sympathizer in broadcasts to American troops, but his anti-semitic diatribes are actually coded information crucial to the Allies. After the war, Campbell's life unravels as he loses his young wife (Lee) and the U.S. government refuses to acknowledge his efforts. He is smuggled back to the U.S., where both Israeli Nazi-hunters and twisted neo-Nazis search for him. After being captured, imprisoned in Israel, and conversing with fellow prisoner Adolf Eichmann (Gibson), Campbell realizes the moral of this dark comedy: "We are what we pretend to be." Arkin is excellent as his Greenwich Village neighbor who also has some secrets. If you look closely, you can see author Vonnegut in a cameo. **113m/C VHS, DVD, Wide.** Nick Nolte, Sheryl Lee, Alan Arkin, John Goodman, Kirsten Dunst, David Strathairn, Arye Gross, Frankie Faison, Bernard Behrens; *D:* Keith Gordon; *W:* Robert B. Weide; *C:* Tom Richmond; *M:* Michael Convertino; *V:* Henry Gibson.

Mother of Kings 𝒟𝒟 **1982** Livin' ain't easy for a widowed charwoman thanks to WWII and Stalinism. Innovative use of newsreel scenes. In Polish with English subtitles. **126m/C VHS.** *PL* Magda Teresa Wojcik.

Mother Teresa: In the Name of God's Poor 𝒟𝒟 **1997** Bio of the missionary begins when the 36-year-old cloistered nun (Chaplin) starts her work in the Calcutta slums and founds the Missionaries of Charity, and culminates with her 1979 Nobel Peace Prize acceptance speech. This drama was unauthorized and reportedly did not receive the approval of Mother Teresa when she learned of the project. **93m/C VHS.** Geraldine Chaplin, Keene Curtis, William Katt, Alan Shearman, Cornelia Hayes O'Herlihy; *D:* Kevin Connor; *W:* Dominique Lapierre, Carol Kaplan. **CABLE**

Mother Wore Tights 𝒟𝒟𝒟 **1947** Colorful nostalgic musical stars Grable as married turn-of-the-century vaudevillian Myrtle McKinley Burt, who leaves the stage to raise her two daughters. Once they're grown, Myrtle decides to rejoin husband Frank (Dailey) in the theater again, thus embarassing daughter Iris (Freeman) who's at a snotty finishing school. Of course, Iris learns what's really important in life. **107m/C VHS.** Betty Grable, Dan Dailey, Mona Freeman, Connie Marshall, Vanessa Brown, Robert Arthur, Sara Allgood, William Frawley; *D:* Walter Lang; *W:* Lamar Trotti; *C:* Harry Jackson; *M:* Josef Myrow, Alfred Newman, Mack Gordon. Oscars '47: Scoring/Musical.

Mother's Boys 𝒟𝒟 **1994 (R)** Estranged mother Curtis attempts to reunite with the family she abandoned only to be snubbed, inspiring in her a ruthless effort to win back the children and oust father Gallagher's new live-in girlfriend Whalley-Kilmer. With an almost psychotic devotion, she terrorizes everyone in the family, including enticing her 12-year-old son Edwards into a nude bathtub game of peek-a-boo. Film lacks the tension necessary to carry suspense. Based on the novel by Bernard Taylor. **96m/C VHS, DVD, Wide.** Jamie Lee Curtis, Peter Gallagher, Joanne Whalley, Luke Edwards, Vanessa Redgrave, Colin Ward, Joss Ackland, Paul Guilfoyle, John C. McGinley, J.E. Freeman, Ken Lerner, Lorraine Toussaint, Joey Zimmerman, Jill Freedman; *D:* Yves Simoneau; *W:* Richard Hawley, Barry Schneider; *C:* Elliot Davis; *M:* George S. Clinton.

Mother's Day 𝒟½ **1980** Three women who were former college roommates plan a reunion together in the wilderness. All goes well until they are dragged into an isolated house by two insane boys who constantly watch TV, ardently consume the products advertised, and then terrorize and torture people to please their mom. Sanitized gore with black satiric intentions. **98m/C VHS, DVD.** Tiana Pierce, Nancy Hendrickson, Deborah Luce, Holden McGuire, Billy Ray McQuade, Rose Ross; *D:* Charles Kaufman; *W:* Charles Kaufman, Warren Leight; *C:* Joseph Mangine; *M:* Phil Gallo, Clem Vicari Jr.

A Mother's Prayer 𝒟𝒟½ **1995 (PG-13)** Fact-based story about young mom Rosemary Holmstrom (Hamilton), who has AIDS, and is determined to find a home for her eight-year-old son T.J. (Fleiss) before she dies. Guaranteed to make the tear ducts flow, with a determined performance from Hamilton that lessens the sentimentality. Holmstrom died at the age of 36 in 1994. **94m/C VHS.** Linda Hamilton, Noah Fleiss, Bruce Dern, Kate Nelligan, S. Epatha Merkerson, Corey Parker, Jenny O'Hara, RuPaul Charles; *D:* Larry Elikann; *W:* Lee Rose; *C:* Eric Van Haren Noman; *M:* Tom Scott. **CABLE**

The Mothman Prophecies 𝒟𝒟 **2002 (PG-13)** Supernatural thriller based on true events occurring in Point Pleasant, WV in the mid-1960s. John and Mary Klein (Gere and Messing) are happily-married, until a car crash with a moth-like creature only seen by Mary, who later dies, but not before making some preliminary sketches of the insect-like beast. John, a "Washington Post" reporter, mysteriously ends up in the town of Point Pleasant, where things get weird. The town, which is actually far from pleasant, boasts cop Connie (Linney) the sole voice of reason in the superstitious bunch of locals, some of whom have seen the same creature Mary did, and John and Connie team to solve the Mothman mystery. Gere and Linney are fine actors wasted in this ho-hum story. Movie does have an aptly creepy tone, however, and Bates is good as the hermit-ish psychic phenomena expert. **119m/C VHS, DVD, Wide.** *US* Richard Gere, Laura Linney, Will Patton, Debra Messing, Lucinda Jenney, Alan Bates, David Eigenberg, Nesbitt Blaisdell; *D:* Mark Pellington; *W:* Richard Hatem; *C:* Fred Murphy; *M:* Tomandandy.

Mothra 𝒟𝒟𝒟 *Mosura; Daikaiju Masura* **1962** Classic Japanese monster shenanigans about an enraged giant caterpillar that invades Tokyo while searching for the Alilenas, a set of very tiny, twin princesses who've been kidnapped by an evil nightclub owner in the pursuit of big profits. After tiring of crushing buildings and wreaking incidental havoc, the enormous crawly thing zips up into a cocoon and emerges as Mothra, a moth distinguished by both its size and bad attitude. Mothra and the wee babes make appearances in later Godzilla epics. **101m/C VHS.** *JP* Frankie Sakai, Hiroshi Koizumi, Kyoko Kagawa, Yumi Ito, Emi Ito, Lee Kresel, Ken Uehara, Akihiko Hirata, Kenji Sahara, Takashi Shimura; *D:* Inoshiro Honda; *W:* Shinichi Sekizawa; *C:* Hajime Koizumi; *M:* Yuji Koseki.

Motor Patrol 𝒟½ **1950** A cop poses as a racketeer to infiltrate a car-stealing ring. **66m/B VHS.** Don Castle, Jane Nigh, Charles Victor.

Motor Psycho woof! *Motor Rods and Rockers; Rio Vengeance* **1965** When a motorcycle gang rapes a woman, she and her husband pursue them into the desert to seek their brutal revenge. **73m/B VHS.** Haji, Alex Rocco, Stephen Oliver, Holle K. Winters, Joseph Cellini, Thomas Scott, Coleman Francis, Sharon Lee, Russ Meyer; *D:* Russ Meyer; *W:* William E. Sprague, Russ Meyer; *C:* Russ Meyer.

Motorama 𝒟𝒟 **1991 (R)** A 10-year-old juvenile delinquent becomes obsessed with winning a gas station contest which involves collecting game cards. So he steals a car and hits the road where he gets his first tattoo and encounters a beautiful "older" woman (Barrymore) and lots of trouble. **89m/C VHS, DVD.** Jordan Christopher Michael, Martha Quinn, Flea, Michael J. Pollard, Meat Loaf Aday, Drew Barrymore, Garrett Morris, Robin Duke, Sandy Baron, Mary Woronov, Susan Tyrrell, John Laughlin, John Diehl, Robert Picardo, Jack Nance, Vince Edwards, Dick Miller, Allyce Beasley, Shelley Berman; *D:* Barry Shils; *W:* Joe Minion; *C:* Joseph Yacoe; *M:* Andy Summers.

Motorcycle Gang 𝒟 **1957** It's the summer of '57, and Randy plans to bring home the title at the Pacific Motorcycle Championships for his club, the "Skyriders." But first his old rival Nick, who's just out of jail, turns up and challenges Randy to an illegal street race. Will Randy succumb to peer pressure and race? Lame plot + lame acting = lame movie. **78m/B VHS.** Steven Terrell, John Ashley, Anne Neyland, Carl "Alfalfa" Switzer, Raymond Hatton; *D:* Edward L. Cahn; *W:* Lou Rusoff.

Motorcycle Squad 𝒟½ **1937** A policeman is dishonorably discharged so he can get the "inside" dope on a gang of crooks in this 'B' thriller. **?m/C VHS.** Kane Richmond, Wynne Gibson.

Mouchette 𝒟𝒟𝒟½ **1967** A lonely 14-year-old French girl, daughter of a drunk father and dying mother, eventually finds spiritual release by committing suicide. Typically somber, spiritual fare from unique master filmmaker Bresson. Perhaps the most complete expression of Bresson's austere, Catholic vision. In French with English subtitles. **80m/B VHS.** *FR* Nadine Nortier, Maria Cardinal, Paul Hebert; *D:* Robert Bresson; *C:* Ghislan Cloquet.

Moulin Rouge 𝒟𝒟𝒟½ **1952** Colorful, entertaining portrait of acclaimed Impressionist painter Toulouse-Lautrec, more famous for its production stories than on-screen drama, Ferrer delivers one of his most impressive performances as the physically stunted, cynical artist who basked in the seamy Montmartre nightlife. **119m/C VHS.** Jose Ferrer, Zsa Zsa Gabor, Christopher Lee, Peter Cushing, Colette Marchand, Katherine Kath, Michael Balfour, Eric Pohlmann, Suzanne Flon, Claude Nollier, Muriel Smith, Mary Clare, Walter Crisham, Harold Kasket, Jim Gerald, George Lannes, Lee Montague, Maureen Swanson, Tutte Lemkow, Jill Bennett, Theodore Bikel; ***D:*** John Huston; ***W:*** John Huston, Anthony Veiller; ***C:*** Oswald Morris. Oscars '52: Art Dir./Set Dec., Color, Costume Des. (C).

Moulin Rouge ½ **2001 (PG-13)** Luhrmann resurrects the famed Parisian/Montmartre nightclub decadence in his surreal quasi 1899-set movie musical that stars Kidman as the club's star singer/dancer/courtesan Satine, who entrances McGregor's naive poet, Christian. Naturally, their love is doomed—in part because she has this nasty cough. Leguizamo shows up as artist Toulouse Lautrec. Luhrmann likes to shake up staid genres (witness "Strictly Ballroom" and "Romeo + Juliet") and in this case he married pop music (uneasily) with extraordinary elaborate visuals. This doesn't always work but the director deserves points for sheer chutzpah and Kidman has never looked more stunning. **126m/C VHS, DVD, Wide.** *AU US* Nicole Kidman, Ewan McGregor, John Leguizamo, Jim Broadbent, Garry McDonald, Kylie Minogue, Richard Roxburgh, David Wenham, Natalie Mendoza; ***D:*** Baz Luhrmann; ***W:*** Baz Luhrmann, Craig Pearce; ***C:*** Donald McAlpine; ***M:*** Craig Armstrong. Oscars '01: Art Dir./Set Dec., Costume Des.; Australian Film Inst. '01: Cinematog., Costume Des., Film Editing, Sound; British Acad. '01: Sound, Support. Actor (Broadbent), Score; Golden Globes '02: Actor—Mus./Comedy, Actress—Mus./Comedy (Kidman), Score; L.A. Film Critics '01: Support. Actor (Broadbent); Natl. Bd. of Review '01: Film, Support. Actor (Broadbent).

The Mountain **1956** A man and his shady younger brother set out to inspect a Paris-routed plane that crashed in the French Alps. After some harrowing experiences in climbing the peak, it becomes evident that one brother has designs to save whatever he can, while the other intends to loot it. Many real, as well as staged, climbing scenes. Based on Henri Troyat's novel. **105m/C VHS.** Spencer Tracy, Robert Wagner, Claire Trevor, William Demarest, Richard Arlen, E.G. Marshall; ***D:*** Edward Dmytryk.

Mountain Charlie ½ **1980** Mountain girl's life is destroyed by three drifters. **96m/C VHS.** Denise Neilson, Dick Robinson, Rick Guinn, Lynn Seus; ***D:*** George Stapleford.

Mountain Family Robinson **1979 (G)** An urban family, seeking escape from the hassles of city life, moves to the Rockies, determined to get back to nature. They soon find that nature may be more harsh than rush-hour traffic and nasty bosses when a bear comes calling. More "Wilderness Family"-type adventures. **102m/C VHS.** Robert F. Logan, Susan Damante Shaw, Heather Rattray, Ham Larsen, William Bryant, George "Buck" Flower; ***D:*** John Cotter.

Mountain Justice ½ *Kettle Creek* **1930** Maynard's first all-talkie western finds our hero in search of his father's murderer. Good action sequences (with stunts performed by Maynard), including those aboard a moving train and a buckboard. **73m/B VHS.** Ken Maynard, Otis Harlan, Kathryn Crawford, Paul Hurst; ***D:*** Harry Joe Brown.

Mountain Man ½ *Guardian of the Wilderness* **1977** Historically accurate drama about Galen Clark's successful fight in the 1860s to save the magnificent wilderness area that is now Yosemite National Park. Together with naturalist John Muir, he fought a battle against the lumber companies who wanted the timber and won President Lincoln's support for his cause. **96m/C VHS.** Denver Pyle, John Dehner, Ken Berry, Cheryl Miller, Don Shanks, Cliff Osmond, Jack Kruschen, Ford Rainey; ***D:*** David O'Malley; ***W:*** David O'Malley.

The Mountain Men ½ **1980 (R)** Dull adventure drama set in the American West of the 1880s. Two trappers argue about life and have trouble with Indians. **102m/C VHS, DVD.** Charlton Heston, Brian Keith, John Glover, Seymour Cassel, Victor Jory; ***D:*** Richard Lang; ***W:*** Fraser Heston; ***C:*** Michael Hugo; ***M:*** Michel Legrand.

Mountain of the Cannibal God woof! *Il Montagna di Dio Cannibale; Slave of the Cannibal God* **1979** Beautiful Andress is captured by "native" cannibals; Keach must save her. **103m/C VHS, DVD, Wide.** *IT* Stacy Keach, Ursula Andress, Claudio Cassinelli, Franco Fantasia; ***D:*** Sergio Martino; ***M:*** Guido de Angelis, Maurizio de Angelis.

The Mountain Road ½ **1960** Listless drama of an American squadron stationed in China during the last days of WWII. Only Stewart makes this drab film worthwile. **102m/B VHS.** James Stewart, Harry (Henry) Morgan, Glenn Corbett, Mike Kellin; ***D:*** Daniel Mann.

Mountains of the Moon ½ **1990 (R)** Sprawling adventure detailing the obsessive search for the source of the Nile conducted by famed Victorian rogue/explorer Sir Richard Burton and cohort John Hanning Speke in the late 1800s. Spectacular scenery and images. Director Rafelson, better known for overtly personal films such as "Five Easy Pieces" and "The King of Marvin Gardens," shows considerable skill with this epic. From William Harrison's novel "Burton and Speke." **140m/C VHS, DVD, Wide.** Patrick Bergin, Iain Glen, Fiona Shaw, Richard E. Grant, Peter Vaughan, Roger Rees, Bernard Hill, Anna Massey, Leslie Phillips, John Savident, James Villiers, Delroy Lindo, Roshan Seth; ***D:*** Bob Rafelson; ***W:*** Bob Rafelson; ***C:*** Roger Deakins; ***M:*** Michael Small.

Mountaintop Motel Massacre woof! **1986 (R)** A resort motel's hostess is a raving lunatic who regularly slaughters her guests. **95m/C VHS, DVD, Wide.** Bill (Billy) Thurman, Anna Chappell, Will Mitchell; ***D:*** Jim McCullough; ***W:*** Jim McCullough Jr.; ***C:*** Joseph M. Wilcots; ***M:*** Ron Di Lulio.

Mountbatten: The Last Viceroy ½ *Lord Mountbatten: The Last Viceroy* **1986** Originally a British TV miniseries detailing English viceroy Lord Mountbatten's (Williamson) turning over ruling power from Great Britain to India in 1947 and the birth of Pakistan. **107m/C VHS.** *GB* Nicol Williamson, Janet Suzman, Sam Dastor, Nigel Davenport, Wendy Hiller, Ian Richardson, Julian Wadham; ***D:*** Tom Clegg; ***W:*** David Butler; ***C:*** Peter Jessop; ***M:*** John Scott.

Mouse and His Child **1977** A gentle animated fantasy adventure about a toy wind-up mouse and his child who fall into the clutches of a villainous rat when they venture into the outside world. **83m/C VHS.** ***D:*** Fred Wolf; ***V:*** Peter Ustinov, Cloris Leachman, Andy Devine.

Mouse Hunt **1997 (PG)** The Smuntz brothers (Lane and Evans) inherit a run-down mansion from their wealthy string magnate father (Hickey, in his last role). Since the boys are involved in a bitter long-standing argument over cord versus twine, they're happy to learn about an offer from a preservation society for a small fortune. The boys try to fix up the house, only to be foiled by the mouse who had been the sole occupant. There are plenty of new mouse traps and tricks thanks to the 65 trained mice (along with 3-D animation) who play the hero. The plucky rodent must also battle a psychotic cat and an obsessed exterminator (Walken, or Lord High King Psycho). If you've ever laughed at a cartoon character taking an anvil to the head, you'll like this. The cartoon-like action livens up the otherwise dismal setting of the mansion and it's surroundings. Directorial debut by Verbinski, the man who brought you the Bud frogs. **97m/C VHS, DVD.** Nathan Lane, Lee Evans, Christopher Walken, William Hickey, Vicki Lewis, Maury Chaykin, Eric Christmas, Michael Jeter, Debra Christofferson, Camilla Soeberg; ***D:*** Gore Verbinski; ***W:*** Adam Rifkin; ***C:*** Phedon Papamichael; ***M:*** Alan Silvestri.

The Mouse on the Moon **1962** Sort-of sequel to "The Mouse That Roared" lacks the presence of Peter Sellers but maintains the whimsical tone of the original. The prime minister (Moody) of the Duchy of Grand Fenwick asks for American aid in setting up a space program. (Actually, he wants the money for indoor plumbing.) When it turns out that the local wine is actually rocket fuel, his amiable goof of a son (Cribbins) fulfills his lifelong dream of becoming an astronaut. The mild spoof of cold war politics lacks the anarchic spirit that director Lester has brought to "Help!" and his "Musketeer" films. **85m/C DVD, Wide.** *GB* Margaret Rutherford, Ron Moody, Bernard Cribbins, Terry-Thomas, June Ritchie, David Kosoff; ***D:*** Richard Lester; ***W:*** Michael Pertwee; ***C:*** Wilkie Cooper; ***M:*** Ron Grainer.

The Mouse That Roared **1959** With its wine export business going down the drain, a tiny, desperate country decides to declare war on the United States in hopes that the U.S., after its inevitable triumph, will revive the conquered nation. So off to New York go 20 chain-mail clad warriors armed with bow and arrow. Featured in three roles, Sellers is great as the duchess, less effective (though still funny) as the prime minister, and a military leader. A must for Sellers' fans; maintains a sharp satiric edge throughout. Based on the novel by Leonard Wibberley. **83m/C VHS.** *GB* Peter Sellers, Jean Seberg, Leo McKern, David Kossoff, William Hartnell, Timothy Bateson, MacDonald Parke, Monte Landis; ***D:*** Jack Arnold; ***W:*** Roger MacDougall, Stanley Mann; ***M:*** Edwin Astley.

Mouth to Mouth *Boca a Boca* **1995 (R)** Budding actor Victor (Bardem) is working in Madrid as a phone sex operator while waiting to hear about his big break on an American picture. Victor's regularly called by repressed gay surgeon Ricardo (Flotats) and Amanda (Sanchez-Gijon), who says she's Ricardo's wife. Naive Victor falls for Amanda—who of course isn't Ricardo's wife but seems to be involved in a plot to kill Ricardo masterminded by his real wife Angela (Barranco) and her lover David (Gutierrez Caba). The plot's a little tangled but there's lots of visual gags and bedroom farce and the virile Bardem turns out to be a gifted comedian. Spanish with subtitles. **97m/C VHS.** *SP* Javier Bardem, Aitana Sanchez-Gijon, Josep Maria Flotats, Maria Barranco, Emilio Gutierrez-Caba, Fernando Guillen, Myriam Meziere; ***D:*** Manuel Gomez Pereira; ***W:*** Manuel Gomez Pereira, Joaquin Oristrell, Naomi Wise, Juan Luis Iborra; ***C:*** Juan Amoros; ***M:*** Bernardo Bonazzi.

Mouvements du Desir *Desire in Motion* **1994** Sex-on-a-train sequences add more than a little steam to this romantic drama. Catherine (Kaprisky) is travelling with her young daughter on the Montreal to Vancouver train in order to forget a failed relationship. She meets shy Vincent (Pichette), who is supposed to be on his way to meet his lover, but somewhere on the journey the sexual sparks start igniting. There are some eccentric fellow passengers to contend with (and director Pool drops in some surreal dream sequences as well) but the heat generated by the leads is genuine enough. **94m/C VHS.** *CA SI* Valerie Kaprisky, Jean-Francois Pichette, Jolianne L'Allier-Matteau, Matthew Mackay, William Jacques; ***D:*** Lea Pool; ***W:*** Lea Pool; ***C:*** Pierre Mignot; ***M:*** Zbigniew Preisner.

Movers and Shakers ½ **1985 (PG)** An irreverent spoof of Hollywood depicting a filmmaker's attempt to render a best-selling sex manual into a blockbuster film. Fails to live up to its potential and wastes a star-studded cast. **100m/C VHS.** Walter Matthau, Charles Grodin, Gilda Radner, Vincent Gardenia, Bill Macy, Tyne Daly, Steve Martin, Penny Marshall, Luana Anders; ***D:*** William Asher; ***W:*** Charles Grodin.

The Movie House Massacre **1978** A psychopath runs rampant in a theatre killing and maiming moviegoers. No refunds are given. **80m/C VHS.** Mary Woronov.

Movie ... In Your Face **1990** Japanese mobsters want to take over a movie studio. This supposed comedy comes with a "PU-13" rating—"Stinks to anyone with an I.Q. over 13," make of that what you will and be forewarned that it's also sophomoric and tasteless. **85m/C VHS.** Tommy Sledge.

Movie Maker *Smart Alec* **1986** A young filmmaker ineptly raises money for his next film. **87m/C VHS.** Zsa Zsa Gabor, Antony Alda, Orson Bean, Bill Henderson; ***D:*** Jim Wilson.

Movie, Movie ½ **1978 (PG)** Acceptable spoof of 1930s films features Scott in twin-bill of black and white "Dynamite Hands," which lampoons boxing dramas, and "Baxter's Beauties," a color send-up of Busby Berkeley musicals. There's even a parody of coming attractions. Wholesome, mildly entertaining. **107m/B VHS.** Stanley Donen, George C. Scott, Trish Van Devere, Eli Wallach, Red Buttons, Barbara Harris, Barry Bostwick, Harry Hamlin, Art Carney; ***D:*** Stanley Donen; ***W:*** Larry Gelbart; ***M:*** Ralph Burns. Writers Guild '78: Orig. Screenplay.

A Movie Star's Daughter **1979** The daughter of a famous movie star moves to a new town and school. She is afraid her popularity is due to her famous father. She must make choices and learn the real meaning of friendship. Also available in a 33-minute edited version. **46m/C VHS.** Frank Converse, Trini Alvarado; ***D:*** Robert Fuest.

Movie Stuntmen *Hollywood Thrillmakers; Hollywood Stunt Man* **1953** A retired Hollywood stunt man takes a job for a dead friend so that the friend's widow can receive the fee. Good stunt work taken mostly from old Richard Taldmadge movies almost makes up for poor production. **56m/B VHS.** James Gleason, William Henry; ***D:*** Bernard B. Ray.

Movies Money Murder **1996** Ruthless actress Lee McNight (Purcell) seduces Dr. Jim (Mull) into helping her produce a movie and then invites the moviemakers, including the writer (Black), to his beach house. Too bad the doc's wife (Kazan) shows up unexpectedly and the doc kills her. And when Dr. Jim hears the plot of the movie (about a murder in a doctor's house), he figures he's being blackmailed and decides to get rid of the suspects. **?m/C VHS.** Martin Mull, Lee Purcell, Karen Black, Lainie Kazan; ***D:*** Arthur Webb.

Moving **1988 (R)** An engineer must relocate his family from New Jersey to Idaho in order to get his dream job. Predictable calamities ensue. Not apt to move you. **89m/C VHS, 8mm.** Richard Pryor, Randy Quaid, Dana Carvey, Dave Thomas, Rodney Dangerfield, Stacey Dash; ***D:*** Alan Metter; ***W:*** Andy Breckman; ***M:*** Howard Shore.

Moving Out **1983** Adolescent migrant Italian boy finds it difficult to adjust to his new surroundings in Melbourne, Australia. **91m/C VHS.** Vince Colosimo, Sally Cooper, Maurice Devincentis, Tibor Gyapjas; ***D:*** Michael Pattinson.

Moving Target ½ **1989 (R)** A young woman witnesses the brutal murder of her boyfriend by mobsters and flees to Florida. Unbeknownst to her, the thugs are still after her. Although top-billed, Blair's role is actually a supporting one. **85m/C VHS.** *IT* Linda Blair, Ernest Borgnine, Stuart Whitman, Charles Pitt, Jainine Linde, Kurt Woodruff; ***D:*** Marius Mattei.

Moving Target **1996 (R)** Sonny McClean (Dudikoff) is a bounty hunter. But his latest job has him framed for murder and caught up in the middle of mob rivalries. So in order to clear his name, Sonny has to avoid getting killed by violent gangs and quick-draw cops. **106m/C VHS, DVD.** *CA* Michael Dudikoff, Billy Dee Williams, Michelle Johnson, Aaron Bess, Tom Harvey, Len Doncheff, Noam Jenkins; ***D:*** Damian Lee; ***W:*** Mark Sevi, Kevin McCarthy; ***C:*** David Pelletier; ***M:*** David Lawrence.

Moving Target **2000 (R)** Martial arts expert Wilson is framed for murder and must battle the mob to clear his name. **86m/C VHS, DVD.** Don "The Dragon" Wilson, Bill Murphy, Hilary Kavanagh, Terry McMahon, Eileen McCloskey, Lisa Duane; ***D:*** Paul Ziller; ***W:*** Paul Ziller; ***C:*** Yoram Astrakhan; ***M:*** Derek Gleeson. VIDEO

Moving Targets **1987** A young girl and her mother find themselves tracked by a homicidal maniac. **95m/C VHS.** *AU* Michael Aitkens, Carmen Duncan, Annie Jones, Shane Briant; ***D:*** Chris Langman.

Moving Violation 🦴🦴 **1976 (PG)** Crooked cops chase two young drifters who have witnessed the local sheriff commit a murder. Corman car chase epic. **91m/C VHS.** Eddie Albert, Kay Lenz, Stephen McHattie, Will Geer, Lonny (Loni) Chapman; ***D:*** Charles S. Dubin; ***W:*** William W. Norton Sr.

Moving Violations 🦴 **1985 (PG-13)** This could be entitled "Adventures in Traffic Violations School." A wise-cracking tree planter is sent to traffic school after accumulating several moving violations issued to him by a morose traffic cop. Bill Murray's little brother in feature role. **90m/C VHS.** John Murray, Jennifer Tilly, James Keach, Brian Backer, Sally Kellerman, Fred Willard, Clara Peller, Wendie Jo Sperber; ***D:*** Neal Israel; ***W:*** Pat Proft; ***C:*** Robert Elswit; ***M:*** Ralph Burns.

Mozart: A Childhood Chronicle 🦴🦴🦴 **1976** An experimental, semi-narrative portrait of the immortal composer, from the ages of seven to twenty, filmed on authentic locations and with the original instruments of the era. Entire soundtrack is composed of Mozart's music. In German with English subtitles. **224m/B VHS.** *GE* ***D:*** Klaus Kirschner.

The Mozart Brothers 🦴🦴🦴 **1986** An angst-ridden Swedish opera director decides to break all the rules while doing an innovative production of Mozart's "Don Giovanni." At first he horrifies his conservative opera company but as his vision is gradually realized their resistance breaks down. A wonderful look at behind-the-scenes chaos and not just for opera aficionados. In Swedish with English subtitles. **111m/C VHS.** *SW* Etienne Glaser, Philip Zanden, Henry Bronett; ***D:*** Suzanne Osten.

The Mozart Story 🦴🦴 **1948** After Mozart's death, music minister to the Emperor, Antonio Salieri, reflects on how his jealousy and hatred of the musical genius held the great composer back and contributed to his death. Originally filmed in Austria in 1937, scenes were added for the U.S. release in 1948. **91m/B VHS.** Hans Holt, Winnie Markus, Irene von Meyendorf, Rene Deltgen, Edward Vedder, Wilton Graff, Walther Jansson, Curt Jurgens, Paul Hoerbiger; ***D:*** Karl Hartl.

Ms. Scrooge 🦴🦴½ **1997 (G)** Modern-day distaff version of the Dickens Christmas saga. Ebenita Scrooge (Tyson) is a miserly banker but you get the same familiar characters with the Crachits and Tiny Tim as well as the various ghosts to show Ebenita the errors of her ways. **87m/C VHS.** Cicely Tyson, Katherine Helmond, Michael Beach, John Bourgeois, Arsinee Khanjian, William Greenblatt, Rae'ven (Alyia Larrymore) Kelly, Michael J. Reynolds; ***D:*** John Korty; ***W:*** John McGreevey; ***C:*** Elemer Ragalyi; ***M:*** David Shire. CABLE

Much Ado about Nothing 🦴🦴🦴½ **1993 (PG-13)** Shakespeare for the masses details romance between two sets of would-be lovers—the battling Beatrice and Benedick (Thompson and Branagh) and the ingenuous Hero and Claudio (Beckinsale and Leonard). Washington is the noble warrior leader, Reeves his evil half-dressed half-brother, and Keaton serves comic relief as the officious, bumbling Dogberry. Sunlit, lusty, and revealing about all the vagaries of love, Branagh brings passion to his quest of making Shakespeare more approachable. His second attempt after "Henry V" at breaking the stuffy Shakespearean tradition. Filmed on location in Tuscany, Italy. **110m/C VHS, DVD.** *GB* Kenneth Branagh, Emma Thompson, Robert Sean Leonard, Kate Beckinsale, Denzel Washington, Keanu Reeves, Michael Keaton, Brian Blessed, Phyllida Law, Imelda Staunton, Gerard Horan, Jimmy Yuill, Richard Clifford, Ben Elton, Richard Briers; ***D:*** Kenneth Branagh; ***W:*** Kenneth Branagh; ***C:*** Roger Lanser; ***M:*** Patrick Doyle.

Mugsy's Girls 🦴 *Delta Pi* **1985 (R)** A messy comedy about six sorority women, educated in the refined skills of bar mud wrestling, who wallow in a Las Vegas championship tournament. Features pop singer Laura Branigan. **87m/C VHS.** Ruth Gordon, Laura Branigan, Eddie Deezen; ***D:*** Kevin Brodie.

Mulan 🦴🦴½ **1998 (G)** Disney's 36th animated tale is taken from a Chinese fable. The Emperor (Morita) sends out an order that one man from every family must become a soldier in order to repel the advances of Shan-Yu (Ferrer) and his army of Huns. But Mulan's (Wen) father (Oh) is ill and she's afraid he won't return, so she decides to take his place and disguises herself as a warrior. The family's ancestral spirits enlist a guardian—the pint-sized dragon, Mushu (Murphy)—as Mulan goes off to war. The two mainstays of Disney's previous animated features—the songs and the comedy-relief sidekicks—turn out to be the weak links in this story. While Murphy's Mushu does have the funniest lines, he doesn't quite fit the more serious tone. Impressive visuals, and careful characterization by the voice actors make up for any formulaic missteps so that adults, as well as kids, should enjoy the show. **87m/C VHS, DVD.** ***D:*** Barry Cook, Tony Bancroft; ***W:*** Philip LaZebnik, Raymond Singer, Rita Hsaio, Christopher Sanders, Eugenia Bostwick-Singer; ***M:*** Matthew Wilder, Jerry Goldsmith, David Zippel; ***V:*** Matthew Wilder, Ming Na, Eddie Murphy, B.D. Wong, Miguel Ferrer, Soon-Teck Oh, Noriyuki "Pat" Morita, Harvey Fierstein, Gedde Watanabe, James Hong, Freda Foh Shen, June Foray, Marni Nixon, George Takei, Miriam Margolyes, James Shigeta, Frank Welker, Lea Salonga, Donny Osmond, Jerry S. Tondo.

Mulholland Drive 🦴🦴🦴 **2001 (R)** David Lynch is back to his old trippy surrealistic tricks again, folks. Lush visuals and atmospheric Badalamenti music are once again the key ingredients in this hypnotic look at Hollywood through a kaleidoscope. Betty (Watts), an aspiring actress staying at her aunt's vacant apartment, comes home to find mystery girl Rita (Harring) taking a shower there. Rita, who has taken her name from a movie poster, has amnesia, and Betty tries to help her piece her life together. Meanwhile, successful young director Adam (Theroux) is threatened with death unless he casts a certain actress favored by a wheelchair-bound dwarf who issues orders over a cell phone. Then (if you can believe it) things get even weirder. Originally conceived as a pilot for ABC television, but reshot as a feature. Execs must have guessed the public wasn't ready for "Laverne and Shirley Drop Acid." **146m/C VHS, DVD, Wide.** *US* Naomi Watts, Laura Harring, Justin Theroux, Ann Miller, Dan Hedaya, Lafayette Montgomery, Michael J. Anderson, Scott Coffey, Chad Everett, Melissa George, James Karen, Katharine Towne, Billy Ray Cyrus, Angelo Badalamenti, Mark Pellegrino, Lee Grant, Kathrine (Kate) Forster, Missy (Melissa) Crider, Brent Briscoe, Marcus Graham, Vincent Castellanos, Michael Des Barres, Robert Forster; ***D:*** David Lynch; ***W:*** David Lynch; ***C:*** Peter Deming; ***M:*** Angelo Badalamenti. Cesar '01: Foreign Film; Ind. Spirit '02: Cinematog.; L.A. Film Critics '01: Director (Lynch); Natl. Bd. of Review '01: Breakthrough Perf. (Watts); N.Y. Film Critics '01: Film; Natl. Soc. Film Critics '01: Actress (Watts), Film.

Mulholland Falls 🦴🦴½ **1995 (R)** Noir meets the nuclear age in this stylish period piece from New Zealand director Tamahori. Nolte plays the leader of the Hat Squad, a vicious group of fedora-sporting detectives assigned to bust organized crime in '50s L.A. at all costs. While investigating the murder of his ex-mistress, Nolte and cohorts Madsen, Palminteri and Penn discover evidence linking the murder to a general (Malkovich) in charge of the top secret nuclear program. Although the cast is dripping with big name stars, the best performance is put in by the glossy set design of Richard Sylbert, who probably had a strong case of deja vu, having previously done "Chinatown." **107m/C VHS.** Nick Nolte, Melanie Griffith, Chazz Palminteri, Michael Madsen, Christopher Penn, Treat Williams, Jennifer Connelly, Andrew McCarthy, John Malkovich, Daniel Baldwin, Bruce Dern, Ed Lauter; ***Cameos:*** William L. Petersen, Rob Lowe; ***D:*** Lee Tamahori; ***W:*** Pete Dexter; ***C:*** Haskell Wexler; ***M:*** Dave Grusin. Golden Raspberries '96: Worst Support. Actress (Griffith).

Multiple Maniacs 🦴 **1970** Waters at his most perverse. Divine's travelling freak show, filled with disgusting sideshow sex acts, is the vehicle used for robbing and killing hapless spectators. One of the best scenes of a sordid lot is Divine being raped by Lobstora, a 15-foot broiled lobster. **90m/B VHS.** Divine, David Lochary, Mary Vivian Pearce, Edith Massey, Mink Stole, Susan Lowe, Cookie Mueller, Pat Moran, Paul Swift, Jack Walsh, Susan Walsh, Ed Peranio, George Figgs; ***D:*** John Waters; ***W:*** John Waters; ***C:*** John Waters.

Multiplicity 🦴🦴½ **1996 (PG-13)** With too many business and personal responsibilities, construction supervisor Doug Kinney (Keaton) is a prime candidate for the cloning experiments of Dr. Leeds (Yulin). Since the cloning process isn't exactly perfect, each clone (Doug winds up with three) has a different dominant personality trait—a hard-charger, a "Mister Mom," and a dopey slacker. Confusion reigns as wife Laura (MacDowell) deals with separation anxiety on a grand scale. Pleasant comedy shows Keaton can still be funny given the chance. Keaton had his choice of cloning comedies and chose this one over Chris Columbus's "More." **117m/C VHS, DVD.** Michael Keaton, Andie MacDowell, Harris Yulin, Richard Masur, Eugene Levy, Obba Babatunde, Ann Cusack, Brian Doyle-Murray, Julie Bowen; ***D:*** Harold Ramis; ***W:*** Harold Ramis, Chris Miller, Lowell Ganz, Babaloo Mandel, Mary Hale; ***C:*** Laszlo Kovacs; ***M:*** George Fenton.

Mumford 🦴🦴🦴 **1999 (R)** Writer/director Lawrence Kasdan creates another ensemble gem in this story of small town psychologist Mumford (Dean), who uses unusual methods to help the quirky townsfolk deal with their problems. His ability to actually listen to people helps out the young skateboarding millionaire (Lee) who employs most of the town, a shopaholic wife (McDonnell), her loutish husband (Danson), and nearly everyone else in town whose screws are a bit loose. Everyone except a slimy lawyer (Short) who the good doctor fires as a patient. He begins to dig up facts that may prove that Mumford isn't even a doctor. Since there's no big plot payoff or mind-boggling twists, some viewers may find it a bit boring. Those who enjoy deeper character development will love it, however. **112m/C VHS, DVD.** Loren Dean, Alfre Woodard, Hope Davis, Jason Lee, Mary McDonnell, Pruitt Taylor Vince, Zooey Deschanel, Martin Short, David Paymer, Jane Adams, Dana Ivey, Kevin Tighe, Ted Danson, Jason Ritter, Elissabeth (Elisabeth, Elizabeth, Liz) Moss, Robert Stack; ***D:*** Lawrence Kasdan; ***W:*** Lawrence Kasdan; ***C:*** Ericson Core; ***M:*** James Newton Howard.

The Mummy 🦴🦴🦴½ **1932** A group of scientists examine a sarcophagus taken from an unmarked grave at an archeological dig in 1921 Egypt. There is a warning on the box that it should not be opened. Does this stop anyone? Of course not! So Im-Ho-Tep (Karloff), a 4000-year-old priest who was disgraced and buried alive, is now revived. Then, of course, ther's his objective—heroine Helen (Johann) whom the wrapped one believes is the reincarnation of his long-gone love Anck-es-en-Amon. Eerie chills mark this classic horror tale that found Karloff undergoing eight hours of extraordinary makeup (by Jack Pierce) to transform him into the macabre mummy. Marked the directing debut of famed German cinematographer Freund. The first in the Universal series. **72m/B VHS, DVD.** Boris Karloff, Zita Johann, David Manners, Edward Van Sloan, Arthur Byron, Bramwell Fletcher, Noble Johnson, Leonard Mudie, Henry Victor; ***D:*** Karl Freund; ***W:*** John Lloyd Balderston; ***C:*** Charles Stumar.

The Mummy 🦴🦴🦴 **1959** A group of British archaeologists discover they have made a grave mistake when a mummy kills off those who have violated his princess' tomb. A summation of all the previous "mummy" films, this one has a more frightening mummy (6'4" Lee) who is on screen much of the time. Additionally, there is pathos in this monster, not merely murder and revenge. An effective remake of the 1932 classic. **88m/C VHS, DVD, Wide.** *GB* Peter Cushing, Christopher Lee, Felix Aylmer, Yvonne Furneaux, Eddie Byrne, Raymond Huntley, George Pastell, Michael Ripper, John Stuart; ***D:*** Terence Fisher; ***W:*** Jimmy Sangster; ***C:*** Jack Asher.

The Mummy 🦴🦴½ **1999 (PG-13)** Cheesy fun in the Saturday matinee tradition, this horror tale is a loose remake of the 1932 Boris Karloff-starrer. In the 1920s, American adventurer Rick O'Connell (Fraser) is hired by British librarian Evelyn (Weisz) and her Egyptologist brother Jonathan (Hannah) to escort them to the ancient Egyptian city of the dead. Unfortunately, their meddling results in the release of cursed mummified priest Imhotep (Vosloo), who manages to regenerate into living flesh and who wants to use Evelyn to resurrect his dead girlfriend. Lots of zombies, mummies, skeletons, and flesh-eating beetles as well as spooky tombs. **124m/C VHS, DVD, Wide.** Brendan Fraser, Rachel Weisz, Arnold Vosloo, John Hannah, Kevin J. O'Connor, Jonathan Hyde, Oded Fehr, Erik Avari, Tuc Watkins, Stephen Dunham, Corey Johnson, Bernard Fox, Aharon Ipale, Omid Djalili, Patricia Velasquez; ***D:*** Stephen Sommers; ***W:*** Stephen Sommers; ***C:*** Adrian Biddle; ***M:*** Jerry Goldsmith.

Mummy & Curse of the Jackal woof! **1967** Upon opening the tomb of female mummy, a man is cursed to roam the streets of Las Vegas as a werejackal. Impossibly inept. **86m/C VHS.** Anthony Eisley, Martina Pons, John Carradine, Saul Goldsmith; ***D:*** Oliver Drake.

The Mummy Returns 🦴🦴½ **2001 (PG-13)** Bombastic sequel to the 1999 hit is set a decade later and finds marrieds Rick (Fraser) and Evelyn (Weisz) living in London with their 8-year-old son, Alex (Boath). Unfortunately, a reincarnated Anck-Su-Namun (Velasquez) manages to bring crispy Inhotep (Vosloo) back again to rule the world. Fehr returns as desert warrior Ardeth Bay, as does Hannah as Evelyn's ne'er-do-well brother. Wrestler Dwayne "The Rock" Johnson briefly shows up as a new villain—The Scorpion King, who's already going to have his own film. As usual there's too much going on—it's loud and crowded, sacrificing the original's unexpected charm for visual overkill. **129m/C VHS, DVD.** *US* Brendan Fraser, Rachel Weisz, Oded Fehr, John Hannah, Patricia Velasquez, Dwayne "The Rock" Johnson, Arnold Vosloo, Freddie Boath, Adewale Akinnuoye-Agbaje, Shaun Parkes, Alun Armstrong; ***D:*** Stephen Sommers; ***W:*** Stephen Sommers; ***C:*** Adrian Biddle; ***M:*** Alan Silvestri.

The Mummy's Curse 🦴🦴 **1944** Sequel to "The Mummy's Ghost" and Chaney's last outing as Kharis. Construction by a government order causes Kharis and Ananka (Christine) to be dug up in a Louisiana bayou (how they got there from a New England swamp is anyone's guess) and taken to Cajun country for study by archaeologists. The usual havoc ensues. Includes lots of stock footage from earlier mummy movies. Based on a story by Leon Abrams and Dwight V. Babcock. **61m/B VHS, DVD.** Lon Chaney Jr., Peter Coe, Virginia Christine, Kay Harding, Dennis Moore, Martin Kosleck, Kurt Katch; ***D:*** Leslie Goodwins; ***W:*** Bernard Schubert; ***C:*** Virgil Miller.

The Mummy's Ghost 🦴🦴 **1944** The fourth in the Universal series and the sequel to "The Mummy's Tomb" has Kharis (Chaney Jr.) searching for the reincarnation of his ancient love, Princess Ananka, who just happens to be New England college coed Amina (Ames). The high priest (Zucco) sends fellow priest Yousef Bey (Carradine) along to assist but he makes the mistake of declaring his own love for Amina and the mummy gets very, very mad. Oh, and both Kharis and Amina sink into a swamp, thus setting up the next (and last) film in the series. **61m/B VHS, DVD.** Lon Chaney Jr., John Carradine, Ramsay Ames, Robert Lowery, Barton MacLane, George Zucco; ***D:*** Reginald LeBorg; ***W:*** Griffin Jay, Henry Sucher, Brenda Weisberg; ***C:*** William Sickner; ***M:*** Hans J. Salter.

The Mummy's Hand 🦴🦴½ **1940** Although this is the followup to 1932's "The Mummy," it actually has little to do with the original film. Archaeologists Steve Banning (Foran) and Babe Jensen (Ford) are searching for the tomb of ancient Egyptian Princess Ananka. Crazy high priest Andoheb (Zucco) sends mummy Kharis (Tyler), who is the tomb's guardian, to kill anyone who defiles her rest. So Kharis shuffles off but finds Marta (Moran) instead. And being a guy, albeit a long-dead guy, wants to make the beauty his bride. Low-budget but the mix of scares and comedy make this worth watching. **70m/B VHS, DVD.** Dick Foran, Wallace Ford, Peggy Moran, Cecil Kellaway, George Zucco, Tom Tyler, Eduardo Ciannelli, Charles Trowbridge; ***D:*** Christy Cabanne; ***W:*** Griffin Jay, Maxwell Shane; ***C:*** Elwood "Woody" Bredell; ***M:*** Hans J. Salter.

The Mummy's Revenge 🦴 *La Venganza de la Momia* **1973** A fanatic revives a mummy with virgin blood. The first mummy movie to feature open gore. **91m/C VHS.** *SP* Paul (Jacinto Molina) Naschy, Jacinto (Jack) Molina, Jack Taylor, Maria Silva, Helga Line, Luis Davila, Eduardo Calvo; ***D:*** Carlos Aured; ***W:*** Jacinto (Jack) Molina.

The Mummy's Shroud 🦴🦴 **1967** Hammer's next-to-last Mummy horror is a handsomely produced but tepid affair. The plot trots out the familiar elements—British archeological dig led by Sr. Basil Walden (Morell) discovers the remains of Pharaoh Kah-to-Bey; hieroglyphics from the shroud are read aloud...you know the drill. Lots of talk, comparatively little action. **90m/C DVD, Wide.** *GB* Andre Morell, John Phillips, David Buck, Elizabeth Sellars; ***D:*** John Gilling; ***W:*** John Gilling; ***C:*** Arthur Grant; ***M:*** Don Banks.

The Mummy's Tomb 🦴🦴 **1942** Chaney Jr. is in wraps for the first time in this sequel to "The Mummy's Hand." Kharis is transported to America by a crazed Egyptian high priest to kill off surviving members of the expedition. Weakened by a lame script and too much stock footage. Based on a story by Neil P. Varnick. **71m/B VHS, DVD.** Lon Chaney Jr., Dick Foran, John Hubbard, Elyse Knox, George Zucco, Wallace Ford, Turhan Bey; ***D:*** Harold Young; ***W:*** Griffin Jay, Henry Sucher; ***C:*** George Robinson.

Munchie 🦴½ **1992 (PG)** A forgotten alien critter is discovered in a mine shaft by young Gage. Munchie turns out to be a good friend, protecting Gage from bullies and granting other wishes. Frequent sight gags help keep the film moving but it's still awfully slow. Sequel to "Munchies" (1987). **80m/C VHS.** Loni Anderson, Andrew Stevens, Arte Johnson, Jamie McEnnan; ***D:*** Jim Wynorski; ***V:*** Dom DeLuise.

Munchies 🦴 **1987 (PG)** "Gremlins" rip-off about tiny aliens who love beer and fast food, and invade a small town. Lewd and ribald. **83m/C VHS.** Harvey Korman, Charles Stratton, Nadine Van Der Velde, Alix Elias, Jon Stafford, Charlie Phillips, Hardy Rawls, Robert Picardo, Wendy Schaal, Paul Bartel; ***D:*** Bettina Hirsch; ***W:*** Lance Smith; ***C:*** Jonathan West.

Munster, Go Home! 🦴🦴½ **1966** Herman learns he's inherited the stately manor Munster Hall so he and the family head for jolly old England to claim their family history. Will the Brits ever recover? **96m/C VHS, DVD.** Fred Gwynne, Yvonne De Carlo, Al Lewis, Butch Patrick, Debbie Watson, Terry-Thomas, Hermione Gingold, Robert Pine, John Carradine, Bernard Fox, Richard Dawson, Arthur Malet; ***D:*** Earl Bellamy; ***W:*** Joe Connelly, Bob Mosher, George Tibbles; ***C:*** Benjamin (Ben H.) Kline; ***M:*** Jack Marshall.

The Munsters' Revenge 🦴🦴 **1981** Based on the continuing adventures of the 1960s comedy series characters. Herman, Lily, and Grandpa have to contend with robot replicas of themselves that were created by a flaky scientist. **96m/C VHS, DVD.** Fred Gwynne, Yvonne De Carlo, Al Lewis, Jo McDonnel, Sid Caesar, Ezra Stone, Howard Morris, Bob Hastings, K.C. Martel; ***D:*** Don Weis; ***M:*** Vic Mizzy. **TV**

The Muppet Christmas Carol 🦴🦴½ **1992 (G)** Christmas classic features all the muppet favorites together and in Victorian garb. Storyline is more or less faithful to Dickens original, with pleasant special effects. Gonzo the Great as Dickens narrates the tale as Scrooge (Caine) takes his legendary Christmas Eve journey escorted by three (flannel) spirits. The Cratchits are led by Kermit and Miss Piggy. Directed by Brian Henson, Jim's son, the film is as heartwarming as the Cratchit's crackling fire, but doesn't quite achieve the former muppet magic. Also features some sappy songs by Williams, including "Love is Like a Heatwave" and "Island in the Sun." **120m/C VHS.** Michael Caine; ***D:*** Brian Henson; ***C:*** John Fenner; ***M:*** Paul Williams, Miles Goodman; ***V:*** Dave Goetz, Steve Whitmire, Jerry Nelson, Frank Oz.

The Muppet Movie 🦴🦴🦴½ **1979 (G)** Seeking fame and footlights, Kermit the Frog and his pal Fozzie Bear travel to Hollywood, and along the way are joined by sundry human and muppet characters, including the lovely Miss Piggy. A delightful cult favorite filled with entertaining cameos, memorable (though somewhat pedestrian) songs and crafty special effects—Kermit rides a bike and rows a boat! A success for the late Jim Henson. ♫The Rainbow Connection; Frog's Legs So Fine; Movin Right Along; Can You Picture That?; Never Before; Something Better; This Looks Familiar; I'm Going Back There Someday. **94m/C VHS, DVD, Wide.** *GB* ***Cameos:*** Edgar Bergen, Milton Berle, Mel Brooks, Madeline Kahn, Steve Martin, Carol Kane, Paul Williams, Charles Durning, Bob Hope, James Coburn, Dom DeLuise, Elliott Gould, Cloris Leachman, Telly Savalas, Orson Welles; ***D:*** James Frawley; ***W:*** Jack Burns, Jerry Juhl; ***C:*** Isidore Mankofsky; ***M:*** Paul Williams; ***V:*** Jim Henson, Frank Oz, Jerry Nelson, Richard Hunt, Dave Goetz.

Muppet Treasure Island 🦴🦴½ **1996 (G)** Literary classic gets its first coat of felt as Kermit the Frog, Miss Piggy and the entire Muppet gang hit the high seas in an adaptation of Robert Louis Stevenson's 1883 well-worn adventure tale. Delightful settings, from an old English tavern to an exotic south sea island, frame the journey of young Jim Hawkins (flesh and blood Bishop), who along with tavern owners Rizzo the Rat (Whitmire) and the Great Gonzo (Goelz) search for buried treasure. Long John Silver is played to the hilt by Curry, master of the over-the-top villain. Helmer Henson steers a steady ship, with over 400 Muppet critters making an appearance. **99m/C VHS.** Tim Curry, Kevin Bishop, Billy Connolly, Jennifer Saunders; ***D:*** Brian Henson; ***W:*** Jerry Juhl, Jim V. Hart, Kirk R. Thatcher; ***C:*** John Fenner; ***M:*** Hans Zimmer; ***V:*** Steve Whitmire, Frank Oz, Dave Goetz.

Muppets from Space 🦴🦴½ **1999 (G)** The sixth full-length movie featuring Jim Henson's uberpuppets centers on Gonzo and his search for his real family. He discovers that he is an alien from a distant planet and announces his findings on Miss Piggy's talk show. Soon, government bad guy K. Edgar Singer (Tambor) is after him. After escaping Singer, Gonzo must decide whether to stay on earth with his friends or leave on the family spaceship. Features cameos by Ray Liotta, F. Murray Abraham, Andie MacDowell and Hulk Hogan. Perfect for the sippy-cup set. **88m/C VHS, DVD.** Jeffrey Tambor, F. Murray Abraham, David Arquette, Ray Liotta, Andie MacDowell, Rob Schneider, Josh Charles, Kathy Griffin, Pat Hingle; ***D:*** Timothy Hill; ***W:*** Jerry Juhl, Joseph Mazzarino; ***C:*** Alan Caso; ***V:*** Frank Oz, Dave Goetz, Steve Whitmire.

The Muppets Take Manhattan 🦴🦴🦴 **1984 (G)** Following a smashing success with a college musical, the Muppets take their show and talents to Broadway, only to face misfortune in the form of an unscrupulous producer. A less imaginative script than the first two Muppet movies, yet an enjoyable experience with numerous major stars making cameo appearances. **94m/C VHS, DVD, Wide.** ***Cameos:*** Dabney Coleman, James Coco, Art Carney, Joan Rivers, Gregory Hines, Linda Lavin, Liza Minnelli, Brooke Shields, John Landis; ***D:*** Frank Oz; ***W:*** Frank Oz; ***C:*** Robert Paynter; ***M:*** Ralph Burns; ***V:*** Frank Oz, Tom Patchett, Jim Henson.

Murder 🦴🦴🦴 **1930** Believing in a young woman's innocence, one jurist begins to organize the pieces of the crime in order to save her. Fine early effort by Hitchcock based on play "Enter Sir John," by Clemense Dane and Helen Simpson. **92m/B VHS, DVD.** *GB* Herbert Marshall, Nora Baring, Phyllis Konstam, Miles Mander; ***D:*** Alfred Hitchcock; ***W:*** Alfred Hitchcock; ***C:*** Jack Cox; ***M:*** John Reynders.

Murder Ahoy 🦴🦴½ **1964** Miss Marple looks perplexed when dead bodies surface on a naval cadet training ship. Dame Marge is the dottie detective in the final, and least appealing, of her four Agatha Christie films of the '60s (although it was released in the States prior to "Murder Most Foul"). **74m/B VHS.** Margaret Rutherford, Lionel Jeffries, Charles Tingwell, William Mervyn, Francis Matthews; ***D:*** George Pollock.

Murder at 45 R.P.M. 🦴🦴 *Meurtre en 45 Tours* **1965** A singer and her lover suspect each other of her husband's murder. Things become sticky when she receives a recorded message from her dead husband. Average. **98m/C VHS.** *FR* Danielle Darrieux, Michel Auclair, Jean Servais, Henri Guisol; ***D:*** Etienne Perier.

Murder at Midnight 🦴🦴 **1931** The killings begin with a game of charades in which the gun wasn't supposed to be loaded, and continue as members of English high society die one by one. "Blondie" director Strayer still working on his change of pace. **69m/B VHS, 8mm.** Alice White, Leslie Fenton, Aileen Pringle, Hale Hamilton, Robert Elliott, Clara Blandick, Brandon Hurst; ***D:*** Frank Strayer.

Murder at 1600 🦴🦴 **1997 (R)** Jaded D.C. detective Harlan Regis (Snipes) is called to investigate the murder of Carla Town (Moore), a secretary found dead in a White House bathroom. He's reluctantly assisted by hard-boiled Secret Service agent Chance (Lane), while head of security Nick Spikings (Benzali) wants the whole matter wrapped up quickly and quietly—justice not being his main concern. Cliche-fest script gives stereotypical characters a little more development than you may be used to seeing, but doesn't give them anything new or interesting to say or do. Snipes and Lane make a good team, however, and Miller fulfills his usual wise-cracking sidekick role effortlessly. **107m/C VHS, DVD.** Wesley Snipes, Diane Lane, Daniel Benzali, Dennis Miller, Alan Alda, Ronny Cox, Tate Donovan, Diane Baker, Mary Moore, Harris Yulin, Richard Blackburn; ***D:*** Dwight Little; ***W:*** Wayne Beach, David Hodgin; ***C:*** Steven Bernstein; ***M:*** Christopher Young.

Murder at the Baskervilles 🦴🦴 *Silver Blaze; Sherlock Holmes: The Silver Blaze* **1937** Sherlock Holmes is invited to visit Sir Henry Baskerville at his estate, but then finds that Baskerville's daughter's fiance is accused of stealing a race horse and murdering its keeper. Based on Sir Arthur Conan Doyle's story "Silver Blaze." Remade in 1977. **67m/B VHS.** *GB* Arthur Wontner, Ian Fleming, Lyn Harding; ***D:*** Thomas Bentley.

Murder at the Gallop 🦴🦴🦴½ **1963** Snooping Miss Marple doesn't believe a filthy rich old-timer died of natural causes, despite the dissenting police point of view. Wheedling her way into the police investigation, she discovers the secret of the Gallop club, a place where people bounce up and down on top of horses. Much mugging between Dame Margaret and Morley. Marple's assistant, Mr. Stringer, is the real life Mr. Dame Margaret. Based on Christie's Poirot mystery "After the Funeral." **81m/B VHS.** Margaret Rutherford, Robert Morley, Flora Robson, Charles Tingwell, Duncan Lamont; ***D:*** George Pollock.

Murder at the Vanities 🦴🦴½ **1934** Vintage murder mystery set against a musical revue format, in which a tough detective must find a killer before the Earl Carroll-based cabaret ends and he or she will escape with the exiting crowd. Also featured is a mind-boggling production number based on the song "Marijuana." ♫Marijuana; Lovely One; Where Do They Come From Now; Live and Love Tonight; Cokctails for Two; Ebony Rhapsody. **91m/B VHS.** Victor McLaglen, Kitty Carlisle Hart, Jack Oakie, Duke Ellington, Carl Brisson; ***D:*** Mitchell Leisen.

Murder by Death 🦴🦴½ **1976 (PG)** Capote is an eccentric millionaire who invites the world's greatest detectives to dinner, offering $1 million to the one who can solve the evening's murder. Entertaining and hammy spoof of Agatha Christie's "And Then There Were None" and the earlier "Ten Little Indians." **95m/C VHS, DVD, Wide.** Peter Falk, Alec Guinness, David Niven, Maggie Smith, Peter Sellers, Eileen Brennan, Elsa Lanchester, Nancy Walker, Estelle Winwood, Truman Capote, James Coco; ***D:*** Robert Moore; ***W:*** Neil Simon; ***C:*** David M. Walsh; ***M:*** Dave Grusin.

Murder by Decree 🦴🦴🦴 **1979 (PG)** Realistic and convincing version of the Jack the Ripper story. Sherlock Holmes and Dr. Watson find a vast web of conspiracy when they investigate the murders of Whitechapel prostitutes. Based partially on facts, it's a highly detailed suspenser with interesting camera work and fine performances. **120m/C VHS.** *CA* Christopher Plummer, James Mason, Donald Sutherland, Genevieve Bujold, Susan Clark, David Hemmings, Frank Finlay, John Gielgud, Anthony Quayle; ***D:*** Bob (Benjamin) Clark; ***W:*** John Hopkins. Genie '80: Actor (Plummer), Director (Clark), Support. Actress (Bujold).

Murder by Moonlight 🦴🦴 **1991 (PG-13)** Rival agents investigate a mysterious murder in a prosperous mining colony on the moon. Not only do they discover a dastardly trail that leads all the way back to Earth, but a strange romantic attraction for each other. Originally broadcast on British TV. **94m/C VHS.** *GB* Julian Sands, Brigitte Nielsen, Gerald McRaney, Jane Lapotaire, Brian Cox; ***D:*** Michael Lindsay-Hogg; ***M:*** Trevor Jones.

Murder by Natural Causes 🦴🦴🦴 **1979** A made-for-TV brain teaser in which a woman and her lover plot to kill her mind-reader husband. Lots of twists make this fun for viewers who enjoy a challenge. **96m/C VHS.** Hal Holbrook, Barry Bostwick, Katharine Ross, Richard Anderson; ***D:*** Robert Day.

Murder by Night 🦴🦴½ **1989 (PG-13)** Amnesia victim Urich is found next to a dead body, the result of a gruesome murder. Urich is the only witness and thinks he may be the next victim. Others think he's the killer. Mystery with enough twists to make it worthwhile. **95m/C VHS.** Robert Urich, Kay Lenz, Jim Metzler, Richard Monette, Michael Ironside, Michael Williams; ***D:*** Paul Lynch. **CABLE**

Murder by Numbers 🦴½ **1989 (PG-13)** Murder in the art world stumps a detective. What might have been a good suspense story is ruined by bad editing and a lack of continuity, resulting in confusion rather than suspense. **91m/C VHS.** Sam Behrens, Shari Belafonte, Ronee Blakley, Stanley Kamel, Jayne Meadows, Debra Sandlund, Dick Sargent, Cleavon Little; ***D:*** Paul Leder; ***W:*** Paul Leder.

Murder by Numbers 🦴🦴½ **2002 (R)** Homicide detective Cassie Mayweather (Bullock) is a crime scene specialist who is saddled with a by-the-book new partner, Sam Kennedy (Chaplin). This isn't good since she has to prove that two wealthy young men (Gosling, Pitt) have committed what they think is the perfect murder (shades of Leopold and Loeb and with nods to Hitchcock). Naturally, Cassie has baggage and must come to terms with her past in order to solve the crime. Gosling's downright scary while Pitt well-plays his weaker partner; Bullock works against being likeable as a loner toughie. **120m/C VHS, DVD.** *US* Sandra Bullock, Ben Chaplin, Ryan Gosling, Michael Pitt, Christopher Penn, R.D. Call, Agnes Bruckner; ***D:*** Barbet Schroeder; ***W:*** Tony Gayton; ***C:*** Luciano Tovoli; ***M:*** Clint Mansell.

Murder by Phone 🦴🦴 *Bells; The Calling* **1982 (R)** A deranged technician has turned his phone into an instrument of electronic death. Chamberlain is the visiting professor trying to discover who's permanently disconnecting the numbers of his students. Good cast decides to test schlock meter. **79m/C VHS.** *CA* Richard Chamberlain, John Houseman, Sara Botsford; ***D:*** Michael Anderson Sr.; ***W:*** Michael Butler, John Kent Harrison; ***M:*** John Barry.

Murder by Television 🦴½ *The Houghland Murder Case* **1935** Low-budget murder mystery with Lugosi in a dual role as twins—one good, one not so. When a professor and the evil twin are murdered, the instrument of death suspected is...television. Still an exotic and misunderstood invention when this was made, TV sometimes invoked fear and suspicion in the general public. Historically interesting and Lugosi fans will appreciate seeing him in a non-vampiric role. **55m/B VHS.** Bela Lugosi, George Meeker; *D:* Clifford Sanforth.

Murder by the Book 🦴🦴½ *Alter Ego* **1987** A mystery writer finds that his fictional character, a hard-boiled private eye, has taken control of his life. With his new macho persona the writer solves a crime and saves the obligatory dame. Based on the novel "Alter Ego" by Mel Arrighi. **100m/C VHS.** Robert Hays, Catherine Mary Stewart, Celeste Holm, Fred Gwynne, Christopher Murney; *D:* Mel Damski. **TV**

Murder Czech Style 🦴🦴 *Vrazda Po Cesky* **1966** Chubby and boring office clerk Frantisek (Hrusinsky) is amazed when a colleague, the beautiful Alice (Fialova), agrees to marry him. He can't believe his good fortune—and he's right—Frantisek soon discovers his wife has a married lover. So, he plots to murder her in several increasingly silly fantasies. Czech with subtitles. **87m/C VHS.** *CZ* Rudolf Hrusinsky, Kveta Fialova, Vaclav Voska, Vladimir Mensik; *D:* Jiri Weiss; *W:* Jiri Weiss, Jan Otcenasek; *C:* Jan Nemecek; *M:* Zdenek Liska.

Murder Elite 🦴½ **1986** A murdering maniac terrorizes the rural English countryside, where MacGraw has returned after losing all her money in America. Poor acting and direction make this one a dust-gatherer. **98m/C VHS.** Ali MacGraw, Billie Whitelaw, Hywel Bennett; *D:* Claude Whatham.

Murder for Sale 🦴 **1970** Secret Agent 117 stages an elaborate scam in order to infiltrate a ring of terrorists and criminals. Ask for Bond next time. **90m/C VHS.** John Gavin, Margaret Lee, Curt Jurgens.

Murder, He Says 🦴🦴½ **1945** Sinister comedy finds insurance salesman Peter Marshall (MacMurray) sent to gather statistics in the Ozarks and encountering the murderous hillbilly Fleagle family and various other looney characters. Naturally, the prettiest girl in the area, Claire (Walker), also happens to be the only sane person, which is lucky for Peter. **91m/B VHS.** Fred MacMurray, Helen Walker, Marjorie Main, Peter Whitney, Barbara Pepper, Jean Heather, Mabel Paige, Porter Hall; *D:* George Marshall; *W:* Lou Breslow; *C:* Theodor Sparkuhl; *M:* Robert Emmett Dolan.

Murder in a Small Town 🦴🦴½ **1999** It's the 1930s and Broadway director Wilder has moved to Connecticut after his wife's murder and runs the community theater. But soon he finds himself surrounded by dead bodies and, with the aid of an opera-loving cop (Starr), Wilder decides to do some detecting. **100m/C VHS.** Gene Wilder, Mike Starr, Cherry Jones, Frances Conroy, Deirdre O'Connell, Terry O'Quinn; *D:* Joyce Chopra; *W:* Gene Wilder; *C:* Bruce Surtees; *M:* John Morris. **CABLE**

Murder in Coweta County 🦴🦴½ **1983** Griffith and Cash are strong in this true-crime drama based on the book by Margaret Anne Barnes. Griffith is a Georgia businessman who thinks he's gotten away with murder; Cash is the lawman who tenaciously pursues him. Based on an actual 1948 case. **100m/C VHS, DVD.** Johnny Cash, Andy Griffith, Earl Hindman, June Carter Cash, Cindi Knight, Ed Van Nuys; *D:* Gary Nelson; *W:* Dennis Nemec; *C:* Larry Pizer; *M:* Brad Fiedel. **TV**

Murder-in-Law 🦴 **1992 (R)** Graphic slasher flick about a mother-in-law from hell who escapes from an insane asylum and terrorizes her son-in-law (Estevez) and his family in a series of gruesome killings. **97m/C VHS.** Marilyn Adams, Joe Estevez, Sandy Snyder, Darrel Guilbeau; *D:* Tony Jiti Gill.

Murder in Mind 🦴🦴½ **1997 (R)** Caroline Walker's (Parker) accused of murdering her husband (Smits) but can't remember doing so. She tries to figure out the truth by undergoing regression therapy with a hynotherapist (Hawthorne). But what she supposedly uncovers are a lot of ugly secrets that were better left hidden. Adapted by Cooney from his play. **89m/C VHS.** *GB* Nigel Hawthorne, Mary-Louise Parker, Jimmy Smits, Jason Scott Lee, Gailard Sartain; *D:* Andrew Morahan; *W:* Michael Cooney; *C:* John Aronson; *M:* Paul Buckmaster.

Murder in New Hampshire: The Pamela Smart Story 🦴🦴½ **1991 (PG-13)** A sleazy true story about a young high school teacher who seduces an impressionable student into murdering her husband. Hunt's fine as the seductress but this TV fare is just average. **93m/C VHS, DVD.** Helen Hunt, Chad Allen, Larry Drake, Howard Hesseman, Ken Howard, Michael Learned; *D:* Joyce Chopra; *M:* Gary Chang. **TV**

Murder in Space 🦴½ **1985** Nine multinational astronauts are stranded aboard a space station when they discover one of them is a murderer. This creates anxiety, particularly since the killer's identity is unknown. Oatmeal salesman Brimley is the earth-bound mission control chief trying desperately to finger a spaceman while the bodies pile up. **95m/C VHS.** Wilford Brimley, Martin Balsam, Michael Ironside; *D:* Steven Hilliard Stern. **TV**

Murder in Texas 🦴🦴🦴 **1981** Docudrama looks at the strange but true events surrounding the death of society woman Joan Robinson Hill, first wife of prominent plastic surgeon, Dr. John Hill, and daughter of wealthy oilman Ash Robinson. Well-crafted script and effective performances keep your interest. Griffith was Emmy nominated. From the book "Prescription Murder," written by the doctor's second wife. **200m/C VHS.** Farrah Fawcett, Katharine Ross, Andy Griffith, Sam Elliott, Craig T. Nelson, Barbara Sammeth; *D:* William Hale. **TV**

Murder in the Doll House 🦴½ **1979** Private detective must find out who is systematically killing off the family of a Japanese toy executive. With English subtitles. **92m/C VHS.** *JP* Yusaku Matsuda, Hiroko Shino, Yoko Nosaki.

Murder in the First 🦴🦴½ **1995 (R)** Hours after leaving a three-year stint in solitary confinement at Alcatraz, petty thief Henri Young (Bacon) kills the inmate he thinks ratted him out. Young, eager-puppy lawyer James Stamphill (Slater) defends Young by claiming that inhumane and brutal prison treatment turned him into a murderer. Heavy-handed and uneven despite excellent performances by top-notch cast. Oldman does his usual fine job with yet another unsympathetic character, the sadistic warden. Major professional landmark for both Slater and Bacon. Loosely based on a true story that led to the closing of Alcatraz. **123m/C VHS, DVD, Wide.** Christian Slater, Kevin Bacon, Gary Oldman, Embeth Davidtz, William H. Macy, Stephen Tobolowsky, Brad Dourif, R. Lee Ermey, Mia Kirshner, Stefan Gierasch, Kyra Sedgwick; *D:* Marc Rocco; *W:* Dan Gordon; *C:* Fred Murphy; *M:* Christopher Young. Broadcast Film Critics '95: Actor (Bacon).

Murder in the Footlights 🦴🦴 **1951** Murder drama involving a socialite and a vaudeville team. **?m/C VHS.** *GB* Lesley Brook, David Hutcheson.

Murder in the Old Red Barn 🦴 *Maria Marten* **1936** Based on the real murder of an unassuming girl by a randy squire. Stiff, melodramatic performances are bad enough, but the play-style production, unfamiliar to modern viewers, is the last nail in this one's coffin. **67m/B VHS.** *GB* Tod Slaughter, Sophie Stewart, D.J. Williams, Eric Portman; *D:* Milton Rosmer.

A Murder Is Announced 🦴🦴 *Agatha Christie's Miss Marple: A Murder Is Announced* **1987** From the critically acclaimed BBC series. While on holiday, super-sleuth Marple encounters a murder that was advertised in the local newspaper one week prior to its occurrence. Based on the 1952 Agatha Christie novel, Hickson shines once again as Christie's detective extraordinaire. **155m/C VHS.** *GB* Joan Hickson; *D:* David Giles. **TV**

Murder Mansion 🦴½ **1970** Some decent scares ensue when a group of travelers is stranded in an old haunted mansion. **84m/C VHS.** *SP* Evelyn Stewart, Analia Gade; *D:* Francisco Lara Polop.

Murder Most Foul 🦴🦴🦴 **1965** Erstwhile school marm Dame Margaret is excellent as the only jury member to believe in the accused's innocence. Posing as a wealthy actress to insinuate herself into the local acting troupe, she sniffs out the true culprit. Based on the Poirot mystery "Mr. McGinty's Dead." **90m/B VHS.** Margaret Rutherford, Ron Moody, Charles Tingwell, Megs Jenkins, Dennis Price, Ralph Michael; *D:* George Pollock.

Murder Motel 🦴 **1974** Inept spine-tingler about a motel keeper who makes a practice of killing his customers. There's always a vacancy at the Murder Motel, at least until the fiancee of one of his victims decides to look into the matter. **80m/C VHS.** Robyn Millan, Derek Francis, Ralph Bates, Edward Judd. **TV**

Murder, My Sweet 🦴🦴🦴½ *Farewell, My Love* **1944** Down-on-his-luck private detective Philip Marlowe (Powell) searches for an ex-convict's missing girlfriend through a dark world of murder, mayhem, and ever-twisting directions. Classic film noir screen version of Raymond Chandler's tense novel "Farewell, My Lovely," which employs flashback fashion using that crisp Chandler narrative. A breakthrough dramatically for singer Powell; Chandler's favorite version. Remade using the novel's title in 1975. **95m/B VHS.** Dick Powell, Claire Trevor, Mike Mazurki, Otto Kruger, Anne Shirley, Miles Mander; *D:* Edward Dmytryk; *W:* John Paxton.

Murder of a Moderate Man 🦴½ **197?** An Interpol agent sets out for the Alps to apprehend an assassin gunning down political leaders. A British-made effort based on a novel by John Howlett. **165m/C VHS.** *GB* Denis Quilley, Susan Fleetwood.

A Murder of Crows 🦴🦴½ **1999 (R)** Alcoholic, disbarred New Orleans attorney Lawson Russell (Gooding Jr.) decides to write a book. He happens to meet an elderly man who lets him read his own murder mystery manuscript and when the man unexpectedly dies, Lawson gets the book published as his own. It's a success—only it seems the the story about five lawyers being murdered is real and a detective (Berenger) thinks that since Russell knows so much about the crimes, he must be the killer. **102m/C VHS, DVD, Wide.** Cuba Gooding Jr., Tom Berenger, Marianne Jean-Baptiste, Eric Stoltz; *D:* Rowdy Herrington; *W:* Rowdy Herrington.

The Murder of Mary Phagan 🦴🦴🦴½ **1987 (PG)** Lemmon stars as John Slaton, governor of Georgia during one of America's most notorious miscarriages of justice. In 1913, timid, Jewish factory manager Leo Frank is accused of the brutal murder of a female worker. Prejudice and a power hungry prosecuting attorney conspire to seal the man's fate at the end of the hangman's noose. Sensing the injustice, Slaton reopens the case, causing riots in Atlanta. Top-notch TV drama, featuring a superb re-creation of turn-of-the-century atmosphere and a compelling, true story which was not finally resolved until the 1970s. **251m/C VHS.** Jack Lemmon, Peter Gallagher, Richard Jordan, Robert Prosky, Paul Dooley, Rebecca Miller, Kathryn Walker, Charles S. Dutton, Kevin Spacey, Wendy J. Cooke; *D:* Billy Hale; *M:* Maurice Jarre. **TV**

A Murder of Quality 🦴🦴½ **1990** Spymaster George Smiley (Elliott) comes to aid of colleague Ailsa Brimley (Jackson) when he agrees to investigate the nefarious goings-on at the Carne School for boys. It seems a schoolmaster's wife predicted her murder and named her husband as the killer. Now she's dead but her husband has a very solid alibi. Based on the novel by John Le Carre. **103m/C VHS.** *GB* Denholm Elliott, Glenda Jackson, Joss Ackland, Billie Whitelaw, David Threlfall, Ronald Pickup, Christian Bale, Matthew Scurfield; *D:* Gavin Millar; *C:* Denis Crossan; *M:* Stanley Myers. **TV**

The Murder of Stephen Lawrence 🦴🦴🦴 **2001** Institutional racism is explored in this fact-based drama about the 1993 murder of black teenager Stephen Lawrence (Black) in London. Lawrence is waiting at a bus stop when he is attacked by five teenaged neo-Nazis. His Jamaican-born parents (Baptiste and Quarshie) seek justice but are treated indifferently by the police. Then the charges against the suspects are thrown out for lack of evidence and the Lawrences insist on a private prosecution (civil suit) that studies the incompetent police investigation. **?m/C VHS.** *GB* Marianne Jean-Baptiste, Hugh Quarshie, Leon Black, Joseph Kpobie, Kenneth Cranham, David Calder; *D:* Paul Greengrass; *W:* Paul Greengrass; *C:* Ivan Strasburg. **TV**

Murder on Approval 🦴 *Barbados Quest* **1956** Conway is a carbon-copy Sherlock Holmes, called in to verify the authenticity of a stamp and finds himself involved in murder. Slow-paced, weak and transparent. **70m/B VHS.** Tom Conway, Delphi Lawrence, Brian Worth, Michael Balfour, John Colicos; *D:* Bernard Knowles.

Murder on Flight 502 🦴🦴 **1975** A crisis arises on a 747 flight from New York to London when a terrorist runs amuck. Big cast of TV stars and Stack as the pilot keep this stale flick from getting lost in the ozone. **97m/C VHS.** Farrah Fawcett, Sonny Bono, Ralph Bellamy, Theodore Bikel, Dane Clark, Polly Bergen, Laraine Day, Fernando Lamas, George Maharis, Hugh O'Brian, Molly Picon, Walter Pidgeon, Robert Stack; *D:* George McCowan. **TV**

Murder on Lenox Avenue 🦴🦴½ **1941** When the leader of the Harlem Better Business Bureau is overthrown, he swears revenge. **60m/C VHS.** Alec Lovejoy.

Murder on Line One 🦴🦴 **1990** A London murderer films his crimes for his later viewing pleasure. The police arrest a suspect, but the killings continue. Both the police and viewer are soon aware that they've made a mistake. **103m/C VHS.** Emma Jacobs, Peter Blake, Simon Shepherd, Allan Surtees, Andrew Wilde, Dirkan Tulane, Neil Duncan, Brett Forrest; *D:* Anders Palm; *W:* Anders Palm.

Murder on the Bayou 🦴🦴🦴 *A Gathering of Old Men* **1991 (PG)** Down on the L'siana bayou, a white guy who thinks civil rights are color coded is murdered, and an elderly black man is accused of the crime. Made for TV, well performed, engaging. From the novel by Ernest J. Gaines. **91m/C VHS.** Louis Gossett Jr., Richard Widmark, Holly Hunter, Woody Strode, Joe Seneca, Papa John Creach, Julius W. Harris, Will Patton; *D:* Volker Schlondorff. **TV**

Murder on the Campus 🦴🦴 *Out of the Shadow* **1952** A reporter investigates the apparant suicide of his brother at Cambridge University. He discovers that a number of other mysterious deaths have occurred as well. Interesting characterizations hampered by predictability. **61m/B VHS.** *GB* Terence Longdon, Donald Gray, Diane Clare, Robertson Hare, Dermot Walsh; *D:* Michael Winner; *W:* Michael Winner.

Murder on the High Seas 🦴🦴 **1932** Infidelity and murder aboard a cruise ship. **?m/C VHS.** Natalie Moorhead, Jack Mulhall.

Murder on the Midnight Express 🦴½ **1974** Mystery about spies, thieves, honeymooners, and a corpse aboard an all-night train. All aboard. **70m/C VHS.** Judy Geeson, James Smilie, Charles Gray. **TV**

Murder on the Orient Express 🦴🦴🦴 **1974 (PG)** An Agatha Christie mystery lavishly produced with an all-star cast. In 1934, a trainful of suspects and one murder victim make the trip from Istanbul to Calais especially interesting. Super-sleuth Hercule Poirot sets out to solve the mystery. An entertaining whodunit, ably supported by the remarkable cast. Followed by "Death on the Nile." **128m/C VHS.** *GB* Albert Finney, Martin Balsam, Ingrid Bergman, Lauren Bacall, Sean Connery, Richard Widmark, Anthony Perkins, John Gielgud, Jacqueline Bisset, Jean-Pierre Cassel, Wendy Hiller, Rachel Roberts, Vanessa Redgrave, Michael York, Colin Blakely, George Coulouris, Denis Quilley, Vernon Dobtcheff, Jeremy Lloyd; *D:* Sidney Lumet; *W:* Paul Dehn; *C:* Geoffrey Unsworth; *M:* Richard Rodney Bennett. Oscars '74: Support. Actress (Bergman); British Acad. '74: Support. Actor (Gielgud), Support. Actress (Bergman).

Murder on the Yukon ✂½ 1940 An installment in the "Renfrew of the Royal Mounted" series. Newill and O'Brien's vacation plans are ruined when they find a corpse in a canoe and must investigate. Lots of action, but a somewhat threadbare production. Based on "Renfrew Rides North" by Lauri York Erskine. **57m/B VHS.** James Newill, Dave O'Brien, Polly Ann Young; *D:* Louis Gasnier.

Murder Once Removed ✂½ 1971 A private eye discovers that a respectable doctor has a bedside manner that women are dying for. **74m/C VHS, DVD.** John Forsythe, Richard Kiley, Barbara Bain, Joseph Campanella; *D:* Charles S. Dubin; *M:* Robert Jackson Drasnin. **TV**

Murder One ✂ 1988 (R) Two half-brothers escape from a Maryland prison and go on a killing spree, dragging their younger brother with them. Low-budget and it shows. Based on a true story. **83m/C VHS.** Henry Thomas, James Wilder, Stephen Shellen, Errol Slue; *D:* Graeme Campbell.

Murder 101 ✂✂ 1991 (PG-13) Brosnan plays Charles Lattimore, an author and English professor who specializes in murder mysteries. He gives his students a rather unique assignment of planning the perfect murder. When a student is killed right before his eyes and a fellow teacher turns up dead, Lattimore realizes he's being framed for murder. Surprising twists abound in this stylish thriller. **93m/C VHS, DVD.** Pierce Brosnan, Dey Young, Raphael Sbarge, Kim Thomson; *D:* Bill Condon; *W:* Bill Condon.

Murder or Mercy ✂✂½ 1974 Still timely story of a famous doctor accused of killing his terminally ill wife. Focuses on the morality of mercy killing. **78m/C VHS.** Melvyn Douglas, Bradford Dillman, David Birney, Denver Pyle, Mildred Dunnock; *D:* Harvey Hart. **TV**

Murder Ordained ✂✂½ 1987 Yet another true-crime network miniseries, this time about a Kansas minister and her lover plotting the demise of their spouses. Good acting for this sort of thing. In two-cassette package. **183m/C VHS.** Keith Carradine, JoBeth Williams, Terry Kinney, Guy Boyd, Terence Knox, Darrell Larson, M. Emmet Walsh, Kathy Bates; *D:* Mike Robe.

Murder over New York ✂✂ 1940 Episode in the Charlie Chan mystery series. Chan visits New York City and becomes involved in an investigation at the airport. With the aid of his klutzy son, he sleuths his way through a slew of suspects until the mystery is solved. Standard fare for the Chan fan. **65m/B VHS.** Sidney Toler, Marjorie Weaver, Robert Lowery, Ricardo Cortez, Donald MacBride, Melville Cooper, Victor Sen Yung; *D:* Harry Lachman.

Murder Rap ✂ 1987 An aspiring musician/sound technologist becomes involved with a mysterious woman and her plot to kill her husband. Complications galore, especially for the viewer. **90m/C VHS.** John Hawkes, Seita Kathleen Feigny; *D:* Kliff Keuhl.

Murder She Purred: A Mrs. Murphy Mystery ✂✂½ 1998 Mrs. Murphy is a cat, who along with her doggie housemate Tucker, a Welsh Corgi who complains about his short legs, assists their human owner, postmistress Mary "Harry" Haristeen (Lake), in investigating a murder in their small Virginia town. Based on the mystery series by Rita Mae Brown. **88m/C VHS.** Ricki Lake, Linden Ashby, Bruce McGill, Ed Begley Jr., Christina Pickles, Judith Scott, Wayne Robson, Edie McClurg; *D:* Simon Wincer; *W:* Jim Cox; *V:* Blythe Danner, Anthony Clark. **TV**

Murder She Said ✂✂½ *Meet Miss Marple* 1962 Dame Margaret, playing the benign Miss M for the first time, witnesses a murder on board a train, but the authorities don't seem inclined to believe her. Posing as a maid at an estate near where she thought the body was dropped, she solves the murder and lands three more Miss Marple movies. Based on Christy's "4:50 From Paddington," it features Marple-to-be Hickson as the cook. **87m/B VHS.** Margaret Rutherford, Arthur Kennedy, Muriel Pavlow, James Robertson Justice, Thorley Walters, Charles Tingwell, Conrad Phillips; *D:* George Pollock.

Murder So Sweet ✂✂½ *Poisoned by Love: The Kern County Murders* 1993 Hamlin stars as a slick small-town loser, with an apparently limitless appeal to women. He marries five of them but two wives and his mother mysteriously die of poisoning. Then an ex gets suspicious and tries to make certain it'll never happen again. Based on a true story. **94m/C VHS.** Harry Hamlin, Helen Shaver, Faith Ford, Daphne Ashbrook, Eileen Brennan, K.T. Oslin, Terence Knox, Ed Lauter. **TV**

Murder Story ✂✂½ 1989 (PG) An aspiring mystery writer finds himself mixed up in a real murder and winds up involving his mentor as well. An overdone story, but a reasonably enjoyable film. **90m/C VHS.** Christopher Lee, Bruce Boa; *D:* Eddie Arno, Markus Innocenti; *W:* Eddie Arno.

Murder: Ultimate Grounds for Divorce ✂ 1985 A quiet weekend of camping turns into a night of horror for two couples when one of them plans an elaborate murder scheme. **90m/C VHS.** Roger Daltrey, Toyah Wilcox, Leslie Ash, Terry Raven.

Murder with Music ✂✂ 1945 A musical drama featuring an all-black cast. **60m/B VHS.** Bob Howard, Noble Sissle, Nellie Hill; *D:* George P. Quigley.

Murder Without Motive ✂✂½ 1992 When two African American teenagers harrass an undercover cop, a struggle ensues and one teen ends up dead. Was the struggle racially motivated, or did the police act justifiably? **93m/C VHS.** Curtis McClaren, Anna Maria Horsford, Carla Gugino, Christopher Daniel Barnes, Cuba Gooding Jr., Georg Stanford Brown; *D:* Kevin Hooks.

Murdered Innocence ✂✂ 1994 (R) In 1972, a rookie New York cop is called to a crime scene where a woman has been stabbed to death. Her young son is hysterical and her husband is holding the knife. When the husband panics and tries to flee, the cop shoots him in the back. Now, it's 1992, the convicted killer is out of prison and out for revenge (seems the son said his mother's lover committed the crime but there was a police coverup). **88m/C VHS.** Jason Miller, Ellen Greene, Fred Carpenter; *D:* Frank Coraci; *W:* Frank Coraci, Diego Matamoros.

Murderers Among Us: The Simon Wiesenthal Story ✂✂✂ 1989 Powerful re-enactment of concentration camp survivor Simon Wiesenthal's search for war criminals. Kingsley's gripping performance drives this cable film. Be prepared for disturbing death camp scenes. **157m/C VHS.** Ben Kingsley, Renee Soutendijk, Craig T. Nelson, Paul Freeman, Louisa Haigh, Jack Shepherd; *D:* Brian Gibson; *W:* Abby Mann; *M:* Bill Conti. **CABLE**

The Murderers Are Among Us ✂✂ *Die Morder Sind Unter Uns* 1946 In post WWII Germany, Suzanne Wallner (Knef) returns from a concentration camp to her apartment in Berlin only to find it occupied by Dr. Hans Mertens (Borchert). Haunted by his wartime experiences, Mertens has turned to women and alcohol. Suzanne refuses to give up her claim and moves in with Hans, eventually falling in love with him. In turn, Hans decides to face his demons by going after his former superior, Colonel Otto Bruckner (Paulsen), who's living an untroubled life despite the war crimes he committed. German with subtitles. **84m/B VHS.** *GE* Hildegarde Knef, Ernst Borchert, Arno Paulsen; *D:* Wolfgang Staudte; *W:* Wolfgang Staudte; *C:* Friedl Behn-Grund, Eugen Klagemann; *M:* Ernst Roters.

The Murderers are Among Us ✂✂ *Die Morder sind Unter Uns* 1946 First film produced amidst the rubble of what would become East Germany after WWII. Susanne Wallner (Knef) is a concentration camp survivor who wants to return to some semblance of her previous life in Berlin by moving back into her old apartment. It's now occupied by Dr. Hans Mertens (Borchert), a former surgeon who cannot return to his medical practice because of his war experiences. Susanne and Hans decide to share the apartment as she tries to help him come to terms with his role as an army officer. But in order to heal, Hans decides he needs to confront his one-time commanding officer, who committed a wartime atrocity, and demand justice. German with subtitles. **81m/B VHS, DVD.** *GE* Hildegarde Knef, Ernst Borchert, Arno Paulsen; *D:* Wolfgang Staudte; *W:* Wolfgang Staudte; *C:* Friedl Behn-Grund, Eugen Klagemann; *M:* Ernst Roters.

Murderer's Keep woof! 1988 Secret ingredients used in the Central Meat Market's hamburger are discovered by a young, deaf girl. Beware of filler, she learns, particularly if it's someone you know. **89m/C VHS.** Vic Tayback, Talia Shire, Robert Walden; *D:* Paulmichel Miekhe.

Murderers' Row ✂½ 1966 Daredevil bachelor and former counter-espionage agent Matt Helm is summoned from his life of leisure to ensure the safety of an important scientist. Martin's attempt as a super-spy doesn't wash, and Margret is implausible as the kidnapped scientist's daughter. Unless you want to hear Martin sing "I'm Not the Marrying Kind," don't bother. Second in the "Matt Helm" series. **108m/C VHS.** Dean Martin, Ann-Margret, Karl Malden, Beverly Adams, James Gregory, Camilla Sparv; *D:* Henry Levin; *W:* Herbert Baker; *C:* Sam Leavitt; *M:* Lalo Schifrin, Lalo Schifrin.

Murderlust woof! 1986 Employers in search of a security guard make a poor choice in offering the position to a sexually frustrated man whose hobbies include strangling prostitutes. Poor hiring decisions come into play later when he secures a job at an adolescent crisis center. **90m/C VHS.** Eli Rich, Rochelle Taylor, Dennis Gannon, Bonnie Schneider, Lisa Nichols; *D:* Donald M. Jones.

Murderous Vision ✂✂ 1991 (R) Television fixture Boxleitner is a bored detective in this outing. But one day, while tracking a young mother in the missing persons bureau, he stumbles upon the trail of a serial killer. Enter a beautiful psychic who wants to help, add a race to catch the murderer, and Bruce suddenly has his hands full. **93m/C VHS.** Bruce Boxleitner, Laura Johnson, Robert Culp; *D:* Gary Sherman. **TV**

Murders at Lynch Cross 1985 Mystery about a weird, isolated hotel on the Yorkshire moors. **60m/C VHS.** *GB* Jill Bennett, Joanna David, Barbara Jefford, Sylvia Syms. **TV**

Murders in the Rue Morgue ✂✂½ 1932 Lugosi stars as a deranged scientist (what a stretch) who wants to find a female companion for his pet gorilla. He kidnaps a beautiful woman and prepares to make her the gorilla's bride. Very loosely based on the story by Edgar Allan Poe, which has been remade several times. **61m/B VHS.** Bela Lugosi, Sidney (Sydney) Fox, Leon Ames, Brandon Hurst, Arlene Francis, Noble Johnson; *D:* Robert Florey; *W:* John Huston, Tom Reed, Dale Van Every; *C:* Karl Freund.

Murders in the Rue Morgue ✂✂½ 1971 (PG) A young woman has frightening dreams inspired by a play that her father is producing in Paris at the turn of the century. After many people associated with the production become murder victims, the girl becomes involved with one of her father's former associates, a man who killed her mother years ago and then faked his own suicide. The fourth film based on Edgar Allan Poe's classic horror story. **87m/C VHS.** Jason Robards Jr., Lilli Palmer, Herbert Lom, Michael Dunn, Christine Kaufmann, Adolfo Celi; *D:* Gordon Hessler.

The Murders in the Rue Morgue ✂✂✂ 1986 (PG) The fifth filmed version of the Edgar Allan Poe story. Set in 19th-century Paris; actors in a mystery play find their roles coming to life. Scott is terrific, with good supporting help. **92m/C VHS.** George C. Scott, Rebecca DeMornay, Val Kilmer, Ian McShane, Neil Dickson; *D:* Jeannot Szwarc; *C:* Bruno de Keyzer. **TV**

Murders in the Zoo ✂✂½ 1933 Zoologist Atwill has a reason to be insanely jealous since his wife (Burke) has been having lots of extramarital affairs. But his way of dealing with these other men is certainly unique—he feeds them to various zoo animals (after first sewing the victims' lips shut). Censors were outraged and the film underwent various edits for its theatrical release. **62m/B VHS.** Lionel Atwill, Kathleen Burke, Charlie Ruggles, Randolph Scott, Gail Patrick, John Lodge, Harry Beresford; *D:* Edward Sutherland; *W:* Philip Wylie, Seton I. Miller.

Muriel ✂✂✂½ *Muriel, Ou le Temps d'Un Retour; The Time of Return; Muriel, Or the Time of Return* 1963 A complex, mosaic drama about a middle-aged woman who meets an old lover at Boulogne, and her stepson who cannot forget the needless suffering he caused a young woman named Muriel while he was a soldier at war. Throughout, director Alain Resnais plumbs the essential meanings of memory, age, and the anxieties created from the tension between personal and public actions. Acclaimed; in French with subtitles. **115m/C VHS.** *FR IT* Delphine Seyrig, Jean-Pierre Kerien, Nita Klein, Jean-Baptiste Thierree; *D:* Alain Resnais; *W:* Jean Cayrol; *C:* Sacha Vierny; *M:* Georges Delerue. Venice Film Fest. '63: Actress (Seyrig).

Muriel's Wedding ✂✂✂ 1994 (R) Muriel (Collette) can catch a bridal bouquet, but can she catch a husband? Her blonde, bitch-goddess friends don't think so. But dowdy, pathetic, overweight Muriel dreams of a fairy tale wedding anyway. How she fulfills her obsessive fantasy is the basis for this quirky, hilarious, and often touchingly poignant ugly duckling tale with the occasional over-the-top satiric moment. Strong cast is led by sympathetic and engaging performances from Collette (who gained 40-plus pounds for the role) and Griffiths as her best friend, Rhonda. '70s pop supergroup ABBA lends its kitschy but catchy tunes to the plot and soundtrack. Not released in the U.S. until 1995. **105m/C VHS, DVD.** *AU* Toni Collette, Bill Hunter, Rachel Griffiths, Jeanie Drynan, Gennie Nevinson Brice, Matt(hew) Day, Daniel Lapaine, Sophie Lee, Rosalind Hammond, Belinda Jarrett; *D:* P.J. Hogan; *W:* P.J. Hogan; *C:* Martin McGrath; *M:* Peter Best. Australian Film Inst. '94: Actress (Collette), Film, Sound, Support. Actress (Griffiths).

Murmur of the Heart ✂✂✂½ *Dearest Love; La Souffle au Coeur* 1971 (R) Honest treatment of a 14-year-old's coming of age. After his older brothers take him to a prostitute for his first sexual experience, he comes down with scarlet fever. He then travels to a health spa with his mom to recover. There they find that their mother-son bond is stronger than most. Music by Charlie Parker is featured in the score. In French with English subtitles. **118m/C VHS.** *FR* Benoit Ferreux, Daniel Gelin, Lea Massari, Corinne Kersten, Jacqueline Chauveau, Marc Wincourt, Michael (Michel) Lonsdale; *D:* Louis Malle; *W:* Louis Malle; *C:* Ricardo Aronovich; *M:* Charlie Parker.

Murph the Surf ✂✂½ *Live a Little, Steal a Lot; You Can't Steal Love* 1975 (PG) Fact-based, engrossing story of two beach bums turned burglars who grow bored with small-time robbery and plan a trip to New York City to steal the Star of Africa sapphire. Notable among the many action scenes is a boat chase through the inland waterways of Miami, Florida. **102m/C VHS.** Robert Conrad, Don Stroud, Donna Mills, Luther Adler, Robyn Millan, Paul Stewart; *D:* Marvin J. Chomsky.

Murphy's Fault ✂✂ 1988 (PG-13) Dark comedy about a night watchman/writer plagued by a series of bad luck incidents. **94m/C VHS.** Patrick Dollaghan, Anne Curry, Stack Pierce; *D:* Robert J. Smawley.

Murphy's Law ✂ 1986 (R) A hard-headed cop gets framed for his ex-wife's murder and embarks on a mission to find the actual killer. He is slowed down by a smart-mouthed prostitute who is handcuffed to him during his search. Casting a female in the role of a psycho-killer is unique to the genre. **101m/C VHS.** Charles Bronson, Carrie Snodgress, Kathleen Wilhoite, Robert F. Lyons, Richard Romanus, Angel Tompkins, Bill Henderson, James Luisi, Janet MacLachlan, Lawrence Tierney; *D:* J. Lee Thompson; *C:* Alex Phillips Jr.; *M:* Marc Donahue.

Murphy's Romance 1985 (PG-13) A young divorced mother with an urge to train horses pulls up the stakes and heads for Arizona with her son. There she meets a pharmacist who may be just what the doctor ordered to help her build a new life. **107m/C VHS, DVD.** James Garner, Sally Field, Brian Kerwin, Corey Haim, Dennis Burkley, Charles Lane, Georgann Johnson; *D:* Martin Ritt; *W:* Harriet Frank Jr., Irving Ravetch; *M:* Carole King.

Murphy's War 1971 (PG) In WWII, the Germans sink an English ship and gun down most of its crew. An Irishman, however, survives and returns to health with the help of a nurse. He then seeks revenge on those who killed his crewmates, even after he learns the war has ended. O'Toole is interesting as the revenge-minded seaman though saddled with a mediocre script. **106m/C VHS.** *GB* Peter O'Toole, Sian Phillips, Philippe Noiret; *D:* Peter Yates; *W:* Stirling Silliphant; *M:* John Barry.

Murrow ½ 1986 Biography of the renowned chain-smoking journalist who changed broadcasting history by fearlessly voicing his liberal ideas on the air waves. His life was more interesting though Travanti does his best to breathe some life into the script. **114m/C VHS.** Daniel J. Travanti, Dabney Coleman, Edward Herrmann, David Suchet, John McMartin, Robert Vaughn, Kathryn Leigh Scott; *D:* Jack Gold; *W:* Ernest Kinoy; *M:* Carl Davis. **CABLE**

Muscle Beach Party 1964 Sequel to "Beach Party" finds Frankie and Annette romping in the sand again. Trouble invades teen nirvana when a new gym opens and the hardbodies try to muscle in on surfer turf. Meanwhile, Paluzzi tries to muscle in on Funicello's turf. Good clean corny fun, with the usual lack of script and plot. Lorre appeals in a cameo, his final screen appearance. Watch for "Little" Stevie Wonder in his debut. Rickles' first appearance in the "BP" series; Lupus was credited as Rock Stevens. Followed by "Bikini Beach." ♫Muscle Beach Party; Runnin' Wild; Muscle Bustle; My First Love; Surfin' Woodie; Surfer's Holiday; Happy Street; A Girl Needs a Boy; A Boy Needs a Girl. **94m/C VHS.** Frankie Avalon, Annette Funicello, Buddy Hackett, Luciana Paluzzi, Don Rickles, John Ashley, Jody McCrea, Morey Amsterdam, Peter Lupus, Candy Johnson, Dolores Wells, Peter Lorre, Stevie Wonder, Donna Loren, Amadee Chabot, Dick Dale; *D:* William Asher; *W:* William Asher, Robert Dillon; *C:* Harold E. Wellman; *M:* Les Baxter.

The Muse ½ 1999 (PG-13) Brooks plays Steven, a screenwriter who finds he's unable to get a job when his creative well runs dry. He is introduced by fellow scribe Jack (Bridges) to Sarah (Stone, showing off some surprising comedy chops), who may actually be one of the Greek goddesses of inspiration. Of course, she may be a total lunatic too. After he discovers that some of the biggest names in Hollywood swear by her mojo, Steven is thrilled when he's deemed worthy of her service. Unfortunately for him, Sarah's inspiration requires a fancy hotel room, expensive gifts, and boatloads of cash, which draws the suspicion of his wife Laura (MacDowell). As he begins writing, Steven discovers that Sarah has also inspired his wife to start a career of her own and kick him out of bed. Lots of movie in-jokes and cameos from big shots like Rob Reiner, James Cameron and Martin Scorsese. **97m/C VHS, DVD.** Albert Brooks, Sharon Stone, Jeff Bridges, Andie MacDowell, Steven Wright, Mark Feuerstein, Bradley Whitford, Dakin Matthews, Concetta Tomei; *Cameos:* James Cameron, Rob Reiner, Martin Scorsese, Jennifer Tilly, Lorenzo Lamas; *D:* Albert Brooks; *W:* Albert Brooks, Monica Johnson; *C:* Thomas Ackerman; *M:* Elton John.

Music Box ½ 1989 (R) An attorney defends her father against accusations that he has committed inhumane Nazi war crimes. If she loses, her father faces deportation. As the case progresses, she must struggle to remain objective in the courtroom and come to terms with the possibility that her father is guilty. Lange's portrayal of an ethnic character is highly convincing. **126m/C VHS, Wide.** Jessica Lange, Frederic Forrest, Lukas Haas, Armin Mueller-Stahl, Michael Rooker, Donald Moffat, Cheryl Lynn Bruce; *D:* Constantin Costa-Gavras; *W:* Joe Eszterhas; *C:* Patrick Blossier; *M:* Philippe Sarde.

Music from Another Room ½ 1997 (PG-13) Danny (Law) is a hopeless romantic who decided, at five, to marry Anna, whose birth he assisted. But the icy adult Anna's (Mol) doesn't seem to be Danny's ideal when he happens to meet her again—and she's got a fiance. **104m/C VHS.** Jude Law, Gretchen Mol, Brenda Blethyn, Jennifer Tilly, Martha Plimpton, Jon Tenney, Jeremy Piven, Vincent Laresca, Jane Adams, Kevin Kilner, Jan Rubes, Judith Malina, Jon Polito; *D:* Charlie Peters; *W:* Charlie Peters; *C:* Richard Crudo; *M:* Richard Gibbs.

Music in My Heart ½ 1940 Two taxi cabs crash and spur the love of Martin and Hayworth. She proceeds to break off her engagement to save Martin from deportation. Hayworth's last low-budget film before becoming a Hollywood goddess. **69m/B VHS.** Rita Hayworth, Tony Martin, Edith Fellows, Alan Mowbray, Eric Blore, George Tobias, Joseph Crehan, George Humbert, Phil Tead; *D:* Joseph Santley; *M:* Robert Wright, Chet Forrest.

The Music Lovers ½ 1971 (R) Russell's version of Tchaikovsky's tormented life and glorious achievements is a shocker, a movie that infuriates professed music lovers but, nonetheless, has introduced many a neophyte to the world of classical music via its sensationalism. Homosexual Tchaikovsky marries an admirer to appease the Russian government and his financial benefactor. Stunned when he discovers his wife is a nymphomaniac, he banishes her to a netherworld of prostitution and eventual insanity which Russell mercilessly explores. Tchaikovsky's own squalid life is hardly better, though he does enjoy success before the bottom falls out. **122m/C VHS, Wide.** *GB* Richard Chamberlain, Glenda Jackson, Max Adrian, Christopher Gable, Kenneth Colley, Izabella Telezynska, Maureen Pryor; *D:* Ken Russell; *W:* Melvyn Bragg; *C:* Douglas Slocombe; *M:* Andre Previn.

The Music Man 1962 (G) Con man in the guise of a traveling salesman gets off the train in River City, Iowa. After hearing about plans to build a pool hall, he argues it would be the gateway to hell for the young, impressionable males of the town. He then convinces the River Cityzens to look toward the future of the community and finance a wholesome children's marching band. Although the huckster plans to take their money and run before the instruments arrive, his feelings for the town librarian cause him to think twice about fleeing the Heartland. This isn't just a slice of Americana; it's a whole pie. Acting and singing are terrific "with a capital 'T' and that rhymes with 'P' and that stands for" Preston, who epitomizes the charismatic pitchman. ♫Seventy-six Trombones; Trouble; Till There Was You; The Wells Fargo Wagon; Being in Love; Goodnight, My Someone; Rock Island; Iowa Stubborn. **151m/C VHS, DVD, Wide.** Robert Preston, Shirley Jones, Buddy Hackett, Hermione Gingold, Paul Ford, Pert Kelton, Ron Howard; *D:* Morton DaCosta; *W:* Marion Hargrove; *C:* Robert Burks; *M:* Meredith Willson, Ray Heindorf. Oscars '62: Adapt. Score; Golden Globes '63: Film—Mus./Comedy.

The Music of Chance ½ 1993 (R) Convoluted story about a small-time gambler (Spader) and a drifter (Patinkin) who wind up involved in a bizarre high stakes poker game with a Laurel and Hardyish pair (Durning and Grey) who live in an isolated mansion. When Spader and Patinkin lose, their debt forces them into an indentured servitude where they must construct a brick wall around their new masters' estate. Bloated with symbolism, this adaptation from cult fave novelist Auster (who has a small part), loses its eclectic significance in the translation to the big screen. Nonetheless, valiant effort by rookie director Haas. **98m/C VHS.** James Spader, Mandy Patinkin, Joel Grey, Charles Durning, M. Emmet Walsh, Samantha Mathis, Christopher Penn, Pearl Jones, Paul Auster; *D:* Philip Haas; *W:* Philip Haas, Belinda Haas; *C:* Bernard Zitzermann; *M:* Philip Johnston.

Music of the Heart ½ *50 Violins* 1999 (PG) Based on the true story of violin teacher Roberta Guaspari, who was also the subject of the 1996 documentary, "Small Wonders." A divorced Guaspari (Streep) leaves suburbia with her two young sons and a dream to teach music to children, using the 50 violins she had purchased. Roberta finds herself working with a group of Harlem students on what will become the landmark East Harlem Violin Program. Despite numerous obstacles, their determination eventually leads to a performance at Carnegie Hall. Streep gives her usual professionally winning performance in this sentimental heart-tugger. **124m/C VHS, DVD, Wide.** Meryl Streep, Angela Bassett, Aidan Quinn, Gloria Estefan, Cloris Leachman, Kieran Culkin, Charlie Hofheimer, Jay O. Sanders, Josh Pais; *D:* Wes Craven; *W:* Pamela Gray; *C:* Peter Deming; *M:* Mason Daring.

Music Shoppe 1982 (G) Four teenagers form a rock band with the assistance of the local music store proprietor. Interesting cast. **93m/C VHS.** Gary Crosby, Nia Peeples, Benny Medina, Stephen Schwartz, David Jackson, Jesse White, Doug Kershaw, Giselle MacKenzie.

The Music Teacher ½ *Le Maitre de Musique* 1988 (PG) A Belgian costume drama dealing with a famed singer who retires to devote himself to teaching two students exclusively. In time, he sees his prized pupils lured into an international competition by an old rival of his. Although the singing is sharp, the story is flat. In French with yellow English subtitles. **95m/C VHS.** *BE* Patrick Bauchau, Sylvie Fennec, Phillipe Volter, Jose Van Dam, Johan Leysen, Anne Roussel; *D:* Gerard Corbiau.

Musica Proibita ½ 1943 A serious opera-spiced drama about a young romance crushed by adultery in the teenage couple's ancestry. In Italian with English subtitles. **93m/B VHS.** Tito Gobbi, Maria Mercader.

The Musketeer 2001 (PG-13) Very, very loose adaptation of Dumas's "The Three Musketeers" features fight choreography from Hong Kong stunt master Xin-Xin Xiong. Unfortunately, the direction is murky and the action sequences are too cramped to be effective. In this version of the musketeer-go-round, D'Artagnan (Chambers) is motivated to join the famed battalion to avenge the murder of his parents by the evil Febre (Roth). He is disappointed to find that the musketeers have been decommissioned by the scheming Cardinal Richelieu (Rea), so he forms an alliance with Athos (Gregor), Porthos (Speirs) and Aramis (Moran) to set things aright. Along the way he falls for Francesca (Suvari), a close confidant of the queen (Deneuve). Despite the shortcomings of the fight scenes, the scenic French countryside is filmed beautifully and the actors do their best with the garbled yet overly familiar material. **105m/C VHS, DVD, Wide.** *US* Justin Chambers, Mena Suvari, Tim Roth, Catherine Deneuve, Stephen Rea, Daniel Mesguich, David Schofield, Nick Moran, Jeremy Clyde, Michael Byrne, Steve Spiers, Jan Gregor Kremp, Jean-Pierre Castaldi; *D:* Peter Hyams; *W:* Gene Quintano; *C:* Peter Hyams; *M:* David Arnold.

Mussolini & I ½ *Mussolini: The Decline and Fall of Il Duce* 1985 Docudramatization of the struggle for power between Italy's Benito Mussolini and his son-in-law, Galeazzo Ciano. Narrated by Sarandon in the role of Il Duce's daughter. **130m/C VHS.** Bob Hoskins, Anthony Hopkins, Susan Sarandon, Annie Girardot, Barbara DeRossi, Fabio Testi, Kurt Raab; *D:* Alberto Negrin. **CABLE**

Must Be Santa ½ 1999 (G) Santa is about to retire (three days before Christmas!) and Tuttle (Coleman), the CEO of the North Pole, is in desperate need of a replacement. And who does he find? Why classic loser Floyd (Pinnock), who decides that having the job will certainly get him his daughter's attention. **92m/C VHS.** *CA* Dabney Coleman, Arnold Pinnock, Deanna Milligan; *D:* Brad Turner; *W:* Douglas Bowie; *C:* Albert J. Dunk; *M:* Jonathan Goldsmith. **VIDEO**

Mutant ½ *Night Shadows* 1983 (R) Another argument for the proper disposal of toxic waste. Hazardous materials transform the people of a southern town into monsters. **100m/C VHS, DVD, Wide.** Wings Hauser, Bo Hopkins, Jennifer Warren, Lee Montgomery; *D:* John Cardos; *W:* Michael Jones; *C:* Alfred Taylor; *M:* Richard Band.

Mutant Hunt woof! *Matt Riker* 1987 Story of a battle between robots gone haywire and an all-American hero. The detective cyborgs are set free while high on a sexual stimulant called Euphoron to wreak their technological havoc on a rampage in Manhattan. **90m/C VHS.** Rick Gianasi, Mary-Anne Fahey; *D:* Tim Kincaid; *W:* Tim Kincaid. **VIDEO**

Mutant on the Bounty ½ 1989 A musician, lost in space as a beam of light for 23 years, is transported aboard a spaceship. Once he materializes, it becomes apparent that he has undergone some incredible physical changes. As if that's not enough, the crew then must flee from a couple of thugs who are trying to steal a vial of serum they have on board. A space spoof that never gets into orbit. **93m/C VHS.** John Roarke, Deborah Benson, John Furey, Victoria Catlin, John Fleck, Kyle T. Heffner; *D:* Robert Torrance.

Mutant Species *Bio-Force I* 1995 (R) Soldier is accidentally exposed to altered DNA and begins to mutate into a remorseless and terrifying killer. **100m/C VHS.** Leo Rossi, Ted Prior, Grant Gelt, Denise Crosby, Powers Boothe, Wilford Brimley; *D:* David A. Prior; *W:* David A. Prior, William Vigil; *C:* Carlos Gonzalez.

Mutants In Paradise woof! 1988 Comedy about a human guinea-pig who always gets involved in some sort of mishap. **78m/C VHS.** Brad Greenquist, Robert Ingham, Anna Nicholas.

Mutator *Time of the Beast* 1990 (R) A corporation makes a tiny genetic mistake and winds up creating a new life form...a demonic pussycat who preys on humans. **91m/C VHS.** Brion James, Carolyn Ann Clark, Milton Raphiel Murrill; *D:* John R. Bowey; *W:* Lynn Rose Higgins.

Mute Witness ½ 1995 (R) Low-budget British thriller, lensed in Moscow film studio, about U.S. filmers making a cheap thriller in Moscow film studio. Billy (Sudina) is the mute make-up artist of the title who, returning to the studio for a forgotten item, witnesses some of the crew shooting a snuff film with a real-life stabbing. First-timer Waller mocks both thriller genre and film biz, sometimes relying on, rather than spoofing, cliched elements. Highlight is 20-minute long chase scene with the killers pursuing Billy in the cavernous studio. Guinness makes a surprise appearance in a cameo. **100m/C VHS.** *GB* Marina Sudina, Fay Ripley, Evan Richards, Oleg (Yankovsky) Jankowsky, Igor Volkow, Sergei Karlenkov; *Cameos:* Alec Guinness; *D:* Anthony Waller; *W:* Anthony Waller; *C:* Egon Werdin; *M:* Wilbert Hirsch.

The Muthers 1976 (R) Women prisoners escape from their confinement in a South American jungle. **101m/C VHS.** Jeannie Bell, Rosanne Katon, Jayne Kennedy, Trina Parks; *D:* Cirio H. Santiago.

The Mutilator woof! *Fall Break* 1985 (R) After accidentally bumping off his mother, a young man stalks five high school students wanting to cut them up into tiny bits. An unedited version is also available. Bloody boredom. **85m/C VHS.** Jack Chatham, Trace Cooper, Frances Raines, Bill Hitchcock; *D:* Buddy Cooper.

Mutiny 1952 In the War of 1812, the crew of an American ship carrying $10 million in gold fight among themselves for a part of France's donation to the war effort. The beautiful photography doesn't make up for the predictability of the storyline. **76m/C VHS.** Mark Stevens, Gene Evans, Angela Lansbury, Patric Knowles; *D:* Edward Dmytryk; *W:* Philip Yordan.

Mutiny ½ 1999 (PG-13) On July 17, 1944, a Victory ship anchored near San Francisco exploded, killing 323 sailors and injuring 390 (most of them black) in the worst homefront disaster of WWII. Three weeks later, 50 of the primarily untrained munition loaders who refused to continue working without safety equipment and proper training were charged with mutiny by the Navy. The men were defended by a young Thurgood Marshall (Morton) in a controversial case. **90m/C VHS.** Michael Jai White, Duane Martin, Joe Morton, Matthew Glave, Adrian Pasdar, James B. Sikking, Troy Winbush, David Ramsey; ***D:*** Kevin Hooks; ***W:*** James Henerson; ***C:*** Ron Garcia; ***M:*** Lee Holdridge. **TV**

Mutiny in the Big House ½ **1939** A man is sent to prison for writing a bad $10 check and must choose between seeking salvation with the prison chaplain or toughing it out with a hardened convict. Suprisingly good low-budget programmer. **83m/B VHS.** Charles Bickford, Barton MacLane, Pat Moriarity, Dennis Moore, William Royle, Charles Foy, George Cleveland; ***D:*** William Nigh.

The Mutiny of the Elsinore **1939** A writer on board an old sailing ship fights mutineers and wins back both the helm and the captain's daughter. Tedious British flotsam that made hash of an oft-filmed Jack London tale, and made news even in 1939 for its use of modern-day slang and clothing in the period setting. **74m/B VHS.** Paul Lukas, Lyn Harding, Kathleen Kelly, Clifford Evans, Ben Soutten, Jiro Soneya; ***D:*** Roy Lockwood.

Mutiny on the Bounty **1935** Compelling adaptation of the true story of sadistic Captain Bligh, Fletcher Christian and their turbulent journey aboard the HMS Bounty and the subsequent mutiny in 1788. No gray here: Laughton's Bligh is truly a despicable character and extremely memorable in this MGM extravaganza. Remade twice, in 1962 and again in 1984 as "The Bounty." Much, much better than the 1962 remake. **132m/B VHS, 8mm.** Clark Gable, Franchot Tone, Charles Laughton, Donald Crisp, Dudley Digges, Spring Byington, Henry Stephenson, Eddie Quillan, Herbert Mundin, Movita, Ian Wolfe; ***D:*** Frank Lloyd; ***W:*** Talbot Jennings, Jules Furthman, Carey Wilson; ***M:*** Herbert Stothart. Oscars '35: Picture; AFI '98: Top 100; N.Y. Film Critics '35: Actor (Laughton).

Mutiny on the Bounty ½ **1962** Based on the novel by Charles Nordhoff and James Norman Hall, this account of the 1789 mutiny led by Fletcher Christian against Captain Bligh of the Bounty is highlighted by lavish photography and an eccentric, though interesting, portrayal of the mutiny leader by Brando. Though overshadowed by Laughton's compelling performance in the original 1935 masterpiece, Howard's Bligh is shipshape as the cold-hearted, single-minded captain determined to reach Tahati and return with a hold full of breadfruit trees. Brando is all knickers and attitude as the peeved Mr. Christian, who finally can take no more of Bligh's social criticism. The other actors, especially Harris, join in the slightly over the top spirit of things. **177m/C VHS, Wide.** Marlon Brando, Trevor Howard, Richard Harris, Hugh Griffith, Richard Haydn, Percy Herbert, Noel Purcell; ***D:*** Lewis Milestone; ***W:*** Charles Lederer; ***C:*** Robert L. Surtees.

Mutual Respect ½ **1977 (PG)** A dying wealthy man sets out to find the son he never knew. **88m/C VHS.** Lloyd Bridges, Beau Bridges.

MVP (Most Valuable Primate) ½ **2000 (PG)** Predictable and lackluster tale about a hockey-playing chimp and the team of lovable losers that he helps to the inevitable "big game." Jack is a chimp with very human characteristics thanks to training from animal behavior professor Dr. Kendall (Study). After Dr. Kendall dies, Jack mistakenly ends up in Nelson, British Columbia. He then makes contact with Tara (Smith), a deaf girl who is picked on by her classmates, and her older brother Steven, a hockey player on the worst team in the league. They discover that Jack has natural hockey skills, and recruit him for Steven's team. Unfortunately, the slimy Dr. Peabody (Muirhead) is searching for Jack due to his value as a lab animal, setting up a showdown between the kids and the evil grown-up. Hockey footage of the chimp was actually shot using three honest-to-God skating chimps named Mac, Bernie, and Louie. **91m/C VHS, DVD.** Kevin Zegers, Ric(k) Ducommun, Oliver Muirhead, Jamie Renee Smith; ***D:*** Robert Vince; ***W:*** Robert Vince, Anne Vince; ***C:*** Glen Winter; ***M:*** Brahm Wenger.

MVP2: Most Vertical Primate ½ **2001** Takes up where those "Air Bud" movies left off. In this equally dumb sequel, Jack the chimp is thrown out of the ZHL hockey league and goes on the lam from authorities. He meets homeless boy Ben (Goodman), who introduces the hairy one to amateur skateboarding. Of course, the chimp is a natural and many monkeyshines ensue. **97m/C VHS, DVD.** Richard Karn, Cameron Bancroft, Scott Goodman, Bob Burnquist; ***D:*** Robert Vince; ***W:*** Robert Vince, Anne Vince, Elan Mastai. **VIDEO**

My African Adventure woof! **1987** Silly tale of an ambassador's son discovering a talking monkey in Africa and meeting a slew of opportunistic misfits in his travels. A comedy unfortunately short on laughs. Based on Tamar Burnstein's book. **93m/C VHS.** Dom DeLuise, Jimmie Walker; ***D:*** Sam Firstenberg.

My American Cousin **1985 (PG)** Award-winning autobiographical Canadian coming-of-age comedy set in 1959 on a British Columbia farm. 12-year-old Sandy (Langrick) exasperates her parents and has just discovered the appeal of boys when her rebellious, fun-loving, runaway 17-year-old American cousin Butch (Wildman) shows up (in a red Cadillac convertible) over summer vacation. Followed by "American Boyfriends" (1989) **94m/C VHS.** *CA* Margaret Langrick, John Wildman, Richard Donat, Jane Mortifee; ***D:*** Sandy Wilson; ***W:*** Sandy Wilson. Genie '86: Actor (Wildman), Actress (Langrick), Director (Wilson), Film.

My Antonia ½ **1994 (PG)** Orphaned teenaged farm boy Jim Burden (Harris) discovers first romance with poor immigrant girl Antonia (Lowensohn) in 1886 Nebraska. They fall in love, separate, but maintain a 30-year friendship. Based on the book by Willa Cather. **92m/C VHS.** Neil Patrick Harris, Jason Robards Jr., Eva Marie Saint, Elina Lowensohn, Norbert Weisser, Travis Fine, Jan Triska, Anne Tremko, Mira Furlan, Boris Krutonog; ***D:*** Joseph Sargent; ***C:*** Robert Primes.

My Apprenticeship **1939** The second film of Donskoi's trilogy on Maxim Gorky has the writer earning his living, at the age of eight, as an apprentice to a bourgeois family. Although they promise him an education, Gorky is forced to learn to read on his own and eventually sets off on a series of land and sea voyages. He recognizes that the poverty and abuse he has suffered is typical of the lives of most Russians and he encounters the beginnings of revolution. In Russian with English subtitles. Preceded by "My Childhood" and followed by "My Universities." **100m/C VHS.** *RU* ***D:*** Mark Donskoi.

My Beautiful Laundrette **1985 (R)** Omar (Warnecke), the nephew of a Pakistani businessman, is given the opportunity to better himself by turning his uncle's run-down laundry into a profitable business. He reunites with Johnny (Day Lewis), a childhood friend and a working-class street punk, and they go into the business together. They find themselves battling the prejudice of each other's families and friends in order to succeed. An intelligent look at the sexuality, race relations and economic problems of Thatcher's London. Great performances by a relatively unknown cast (for contrast, note Day Lewis' performance in "Room with a View," released in the same year.) **93m/C VHS.** Gordon Warnecke, Daniel Day-Lewis, Saeed Jaffrey, Roshan Seth, Shirley Anne Field, Derrick Branche, Rita Wolf, Souad Faress, Richard Graham, Dudley Thomas, Garry Cooper, Charu Bala Choksi, Neil Cunningham, Walter Donohue, Stephen Marcus, Badi Uzzaman; ***D:*** Stephen Frears; ***W:*** Hanif Kureishi; ***C:*** Oliver Stapleton; ***M:*** Ludus Tonalis, Stanley Myers. Natl. Bd. of Review '86: Support. Actor (Day-Lewis); N.Y. Film Critics '86: Screenplay, Support. Actor (Day-Lewis); Natl. Soc. Film Critics '86: Screenplay.

My Best Friend Is a Vampire **1988 (PG)** Another teenage vampire story, about trying to cope with certain changes that adolescence and bloodsucking bring. Good supporting cast. **90m/C VHS.** Robert Sean Leonard, Evan Mirand, Cheryl Pollak, Rene Auberjonois, Cecilia Peck, Fannie Flagg, Kenneth Kimmins, David Warner, Paul Willson, Kathy Bates; ***D:*** Jimmy Huston; ***W:*** Tab Murphy; ***C:*** James Bartle; ***M:*** Steve Dorff.

My Best Friend's Girl ½ *La Femme De Mon Pote* **1984** Coy, sardonic French romance about a woman who slaloms between two buddies working at a ski resort. Despite fine performances from all, it never quite makes it to the top of the hill. In French with English subtitles. **99m/C VHS.** *FR* Isabelle Huppert, Thierry Lhermitte, Coluche, Francois Perrot; ***D:*** Bertrand Blier; ***W:*** Bertrand Blier, Gerard Brach.

My Best Friend's Wedding ½ **1997 (PG-13)** Yes, it's a romantic comedy, but like director Hogan's previous effort, "Muriel's Wedding," there's some snap among the smiles. Restaurant critic Julianne (Roberts) and sports writer Michael (Mulroney) are best friends who have a pact that they'll marry each other if neither has found someone else by the age of 28. Michael finds sweet, wealthy Kimmy (Diaz) and invites Julianne to his nuptials. Naturally, Julianne realizes she's in love with Michael and she'll stop at nothing to break up the wedding, even enlisting gay friend George (Everett) to pose as her new beau. Roberts appears as the critics prefer her (long hair and smiling) while she extends her range of physical comedy. Diaz gets to be nice, Everett gets to steal every scene he's in, and Mulroney gets to be the lucky object of two lovely women's affections. Shot on location in Chicago. **105m/C VHS, DVD, Wide.** Julia Roberts, Dermot Mulroney, Cameron Diaz, Rupert Everett, Philip Bosco, M. Emmet Walsh, Rachel Griffiths, Susan Sullivan, Paul Giamatti; ***D:*** P.J. Hogan; ***W:*** Ronald Bass; ***C:*** Laszlo Kovacs; ***M:*** James Newton Howard.

My Best Girl **1927** Plucky Maggie (Pickford) is a store clerk who is the main support for her eccentric family. She falls in love with the store owner's son (future hubby Rogers) but his father is skeptical of the match. A gentle satire on middle-American life in the 1920s. **88m/B VHS, DVD.** Mary Pickford, Charles "Buddy" Rogers, Lucien Littlefield, Carmelita Geraghty, Sunshine Hart, Hobart Bosworth; ***D:*** Sam Taylor; ***W:*** Hope Loring, Tim Whelan, Allen McNeil; ***C:*** Charles Rosher, David Keeson.

My Big Fat Greek Wedding ½ **2002 (PG)** This is a big fat wet smooch of a movie—the kind you get from an enthusiastic older relative at a spare-no-expense wedding. Toula (Nardalos) is a frumpy 30-year-old waitress at her Greek parents' Chicago restaurant. They expect her to marry a Greek boy, have babies, and feed everyone. Then she meets handsome Ian Miller (Corbett), a non-Greek vegetarian schoolteacher who really, really likes her. Enough to want to marry her—if Toula's family can ever recover from the shock of her marrying outside their heritage. Every cliche imaginable is trotted out and you won't care as you'll laugh and groan at the too-recognizable family behavior (no matter what your ethnicity). Based on Vardalos' stage monologue. **95m/C VHS, DVD.** *US* Nia Vardalos, John Corbett, Lainie Kazan, Michael Constantine, Gia Carides, Louis Mandylor, Andrea Martin, Joey Fatone, Bruce Gray, Fiona Reid, Bess Meisler, Ian Gomez; ***D:*** Joel Zwick; ***W:*** Nia Vardalos; ***C:*** Jeffrey Jur; ***M:*** Chris Wilson, Alexander Janko.

My Bloody Valentine **1981 (R)** Psychotic coal miner visits the peaceful little town of Valentine Bluffs on the night of the yearly Valentine Ball. Many of the townspeople have their hearts removed with a pick axe and sent to the sheriff in candy boxes. The bloodiest scenes were cut out to avoid an X-rating. **91m/C VHS.** *CA* Paul Kelman, Lori Hallier, Neil Affleck, Keith Knight, Alf Humphreys, Cynthia Dale, Terry Waterland, Peter Cowper, Don Francks, Jack Van Evera; ***D:*** George Mihalka; ***W:*** John Beaird; ***C:*** Rodney Gibbons.

My Blue Heaven **1990 (PG-13)** After agreeing to rat on the Mafia, Martin is dropped into suburbia as part of the witness protection program. Moranis plays the FBI agent assigned to help the former mobster become an upstanding citizen. Adjusting to life in the slow lane isn't easy for an ex con who has grown accustomed to the big time. Not the typical role for Martin, who plays a brunette with a New York accent and is handcuffed by bad writing. **96m/C VHS, DVD.** Steve Martin, Rick Moranis, Joan Cusack, Melanie Mayron, Carol Kane, Bill Irwin, William Hickey, Daniel Stern; ***D:*** Herbert Ross; ***W:*** Nora Ephron; ***C:*** John Bailey; ***M:*** Ira Newborn.

My Bodyguard **1980 (PG)** An undersized high school student fends off attacking bullies by hiring a king-sized, withdrawn lad as his bodyguard. Their "business" relationship, however, develops into true friendship. An adolescent coming of age with more intelligence and sensitivity than most of its ilk, and a pack of up and coming stars as well as old stand-bys Houseman and Gordon. **96m/C VHS, DVD, Wide.** Chris Makepeace, Adam Baldwin, Martin Mull, Ruth Gordon, Matt Dillon, John Houseman, Joan Cusack, Craig Richard Nelson, Tim Kazurinsky, George Wendt, Jennifer Beals; ***D:*** Tony Bill; ***W:*** Alan Ormsby; ***C:*** Michael D. Margulies; ***M:*** Dave Grusin.

My Boy ½ **1921** Coogan stars as a foreign orphan who faces deportation. Instead he escapes and follows an old man home. This rare film includes an organ score. **56m/B VHS.** Jackie Coogan, Claude Gillingwater, Mathilde Brundage; ***D:*** Albert Austin; ***W:*** Victor Heerman.

My Boyfriend's Back *Johnny Zombie* **1993 (PG-13)** Embarassingly dumb flick about a teenage boy who wants to take the prettiest girl in the school to the prom. The only problem is that he's become a zombie. Bits of him keep falling off (his girl thoughtfully glues them back on) and if he wants to stay "alive" long enough to get to the dance he has to munch on human flesh. Yuck. **85m/C VHS.** Andrew Lowery, Traci Lind, Edward Herrmann, Mary Beth Hurt, Danny Zorn, Austin Pendleton, Jay O. Sanders, Paul Dooley, Bob (Robert) Dishy, Cloris Leachman, Matthew Fox, Paxton Whitehead; ***D:*** Bob Balaban; ***W:*** Dean Lorey; ***C:*** Mac Ahlberg.

My Boys Are Good Boys **1978 (PG)** A young foursome steal from an armored car and have to face the consequences. Quirky with an implausible storyline. **90m/C VHS.** Ralph Meeker, Ida Lupino, Lloyd Nolan, David Doyle; ***D:*** Bethel Buckalew.

My Brilliant Career ½ **1979 (G)** Sybella (Davis) is a poor, headstrong young woman spurns the social expectations of turn-of-the-century Australia and pursues opportunities to broaden her intellect and preserve her independence. This despite the fact that she loves Harry (Neill), a handsome, wealthy farmer. Davis is wonderful as the energetic and charismatic community trendsetter, especially in the scenes transforming her from a tomboy to a "lady." Has an excellent supporting cast. Based on an autobiographical novel by Miles Franklin which has been marvelously transferred to the screen. Armstrong deserves credit for her fine direction. **101m/C VHS.** *AU* Judy Davis, Sam Neill, Wendy Hughes, Robert Grubb, Patricia Kennedy, Aileen Britton, Peter Whitford, Alan Hopgood, Julia Blake; ***D:*** Gillian Armstrong; ***W:*** Eleanor Witcombe; ***C:*** Donald McAlpine; ***M:*** Nathan Waks. Australian Film Inst. '79: Film; British Acad. '80: Actress (Davis).

My Brother Has Bad Dreams **1988** Young man with sibling tosses and turns in bed. **97m/C VHS.** Nick Kleinholz, Marlena Lustic.

My Brother Tom ½ **1986** The rural village of St. Helens is scarcely disturbed by WWII. But a burgeoning love affair between young Peggy MacGibbon and Tom Quayle, and the conflict between their two religions, does threaten to tear their country town apart. Based on the novel by James Aldridge. On three cassettes. **200m/C VHS.** Gordon Jackson, Keith Michell, Catherine McClements, Tom Jennings, Christopher Mayer, Christopher Cummings; *D:* Pino Amenta. **TV**

My Brother's War 🦴🦴½ **1997 (R)** Brothers Gerry (Foy) and Liam (Xuereb) find themselves on opposite sides of the troubles in Ireland. Then, CIA operative Hall (Brolin) arrives to prevent Liam kidnapping three politicians who are trying to reach a peace accord. Some plot twists help out this standard actioner. **85m/C VHS.** Salvator Xuereb, Patrick Foy, James Brolin, Josh Brolin, Jennie Garth, Cristi Conaway; *D:* James Brolin; *W:* Alex Simon; *C:* Michael Bucher; *M:* John Graham.

My Brother's Wife 🦴🦴½ **1989 (PG)** Barney (Ritter), the black sheep of a wealthy family, spends two decades pursuing Eleanor (Harris), the woman of his dreams. Unfortunately, she's already married—to the brother he despises. Adapted from the play "The Middle Ages" by A.R. Gurney. **94m/C VHS.** John Ritter, Mel Harris, Polly Bergen, Dakin Matthews, David Byron, Lee Weaver; *D:* Jack Bender; *W:* Percy Granger. **TV**

My Champion 🦴 **1984** Chance meeting propels Mike Gorman and Miki Tsuwa into a relationship based on the strong bonds of love and athletic competition. **101m/C VHS.** Yoko Shimada, Chris Mitchum.

My Chauffeur 🦴🦴½ **1986 (R)** When a wise-cracking female is hired on as a chauffeur at an all-male chauffeur service, sparks fly. And when the owner takes a definite liking to her work, things take a turn for the worse. As these sort of sexploitation flicks go, this is one of the better ones. **94m/C VHS, DVD.** Deborah Foreman, Sam Jones, Howard Hesseman, E.G. Marshall, Sean McClory; *D:* David Beaird; *W:* David Beaird.

My Childhood 🦴🦴🦴 **1938** The first of director Donskoi's trilogy on the life of Maxim Gorky, based on Gorky's autobiographical stories. In this first film, Donskoi depicts Gorky's childhood of abuse and poverty with his grandparents in the 1870s. Eventually, Gorky is forced into the streets and he becomes a wandering beggar. In Russian with English subtitles. Followed by "My Apprenticeship" and "My Universities." **100m/C VHS.** *RU* *D:* Mark Donskoi.

My Cousin Vinny 🦴🦴🦴 **1992 (R)** Vinny Gambini (Pesci), a lawyer who took the bar exam six times before passing, goes to Wahzoo City, Alabama to get his cousin and a friend off the hook when they're accused of killing a store clerk. Leather jackets, gold chains, Brooklyn accents, and his fiancee Tomei's penchant for big hair and bold clothing don't go over well with conservative judge Gwynne, causing plenty of misunderstandings. Surprising hit with simplistic story reaches popular heights via entertaining performances by the entire cast. Tomei in particular steals every scene she's in and has an Oscar to prove it. **120m/C VHS, DVD, Wide.** Joe Pesci, Ralph Macchio, Marisa Tomei, Mitchell Whitfield, Fred Gwynne, Lane Smith, Austin Pendleton, Bruce McGill; *D:* Jonathan Lynn; *W:* Dale Launer; *C:* Peter Deming; *M:* Randy Edelman. Oscars '92: Support. Actress (Tomei); MTV Movie Awards '93: Breakthrough Perf. (Tomei).

My Darling Clementine 🦴🦴🦴½ **1946** One of the best Hollywood westerns ever made, this recounts the precise events leading up to and including the gunfight at the O.K. Corral. Fonda's the lawman, with Bond, Holt, and Garner as his brothers, and Mature co-stars as best friend, Doc Holliday. Schoolteacher Clementine (Downs) is Earp's gal, but the real revelation should be Brennan as old man Clanton—he's chilling not folksy. Ford allegedly knew Wyatt Earp and used his stories to recount the details vividly, though not always accurately. Remake of 1939's "Frontier Marshal." **97m/B VHS.** Henry Fonda, Victor Mature, Walter Brennan, Linda Darnell, Tim Holt, Ward Bond, John Ireland, Cathy Downs, Alan Mowbray, Don Garner, Jane Darwell, Grant Withers; *D:* John Ford; *W:* Sam Hellman, Winston Miller, Samuel G. Engel; *C:* Joe MacDonald; *M:* David Buttolph, Cyril Mockridge. Natl. Film Reg. '91.

My Date with the President's Daughter 🦴🦴½ **1998** Hallie, the President's sheltered daughter, just wants to go out with a boy and have a little fun. But between her father's re-election campaign and those darn Secret Service agents, what's a teen to do? **89m/C VHS.** Will Friedle, Dabney Coleman, Elisabeth Harnois, Ron Reagan; *D:* Alex Zamm. **TV**

My Daughter's Keeper 🦴🦴 **1993 (R)** The apparently perfect nanny of an unsuspecting family reveals her deadly agenda of murder, adultery, and more. **94m/C VHS.** Nicholas Guest, Jocelyn Broderick, Ana Padrao.

My Dear Secretary 🦴🦴½ **1949** After she marries her boss, a woman grows jealous of the secretary that replaces her. Comedic dialogue and antics result. **94m/B VHS.** Kirk Douglas, Laraine Day, Keenan Wynn, Rudy Vallee, Florence Bates, Alan Mowbray, Charles Halton; *D:* Charles Martin; *W:* Charles Martin.

My Demon Lover 🦴🦴 **1987 (PG-13)** This sex comedy is complicated by the hero's transformation into a demon whenever he is aroused. Saved from complete mediocrity by Family Ties's Valentine in a likable performance. **90m/C VHS.** Scott Valentine, Michelle Little, Arnold Johnson, Gina Gallego; *D:* Charles Loventhal; *M:* David Newman, Ed Alton.

My Dinner with Andre 🦴🦴🦴½ **1981** Two friends talk about their lives and philosophies for two hours over dinner one night. A wonderful exploration into storytelling, the conversation juxtaposes the experiences and philosophies of nerdish, bumbling Shawn and the globe-trotting spiritual pilgrimage of Gregory, in this sometimes poignant, sometimes comic little movie that starts you thinking. **110m/C VHS, DVD.** Andre Gregory, Wallace Shawn, Roy Butler, Jean Lenauer; *D:* Louis Malle; *W:* Andre Gregory, Wallace Shawn; *C:* Jeri Sopanen; *M:* Allen Shawn.

My Dog Shep 🦴½ **1946** An orphan and his dog run away and are pursued diligently when it is discovered that he is a wealthy heir. **71m/B VHS.** Tom Neal, William Farnum, Lannie Rees; *D:* Ford Beebe.

My Dog Skip 🦴🦴🦴 **1999 (PG)** This is just the kind of movie people are talking about when they complain that there's no family friendly movies being made anymore. In 1940's Mississippi, awkward only child Willie (Muniz) sees his life change when, over the protests of his overprotective father (Bacon), he gets a puppy, Skip, for his ninth birthday. Amid much nostalgia and sentiment, Willie learns to be more outgoing and has many coming-of-age moments. Even if some of the plot elements are weak, the look and feel of the period is captured well, and Muniz does a fine job, although no human is likely to compete with the pooch, anyway. Kids will love the antics of Skip, and adults will enjoy having their hearts, and memories, tugged. Based on the book by Willie Morris. **95m/C VHS, DVD, Wide.** Frankie Muniz, Diane Lane, Kevin Bacon, Luke Wilson, Caitlin Wachs, Bradley Coryell, Daylan Honeycutt, Cody Linley; *D:* Jay Russell; *W:* Gail Gilchriest; *C:* James L. Carter; *M:* William Ross; *Nar:* Harry Connick Jr.

My Dog, the Thief 🦴 **1969** A helicopter weatherman is unaware that the lovable St. Bernard he has adopted is a kleptomaniac. When the dog steals a valuable necklace from a team of professional jewel thieves, the fun begins. **88m/C VHS.** Joe Flynn, Elsa Lanchester, Roger C. Carmel, Mickey Shaughnessy, Dwayne Hickman, Mary Ann Mobley; *D:* Robert Stevenson.

My Dream Is Yours 🦴🦴½ **1949** Day plays an up-and-coming radio star in this Warner Bros. musical comedy with a cameo from Bugs Bunny in a dream sequence. This fresh, fun remake of "Twenty Million Sweethearts" is often underrated, but is well worth a look. ♫My Dream is Yours; Some Like You; Tic, Tic, Tic; Love Finds a Way; I'll String Along with You; Canadian Capers; Freddie Get Ready; You Must Have Been a Beautiful Baby; Jeepers, Creepers. **101m/C VHS.** Jack Carson, Doris Day, Lee Bowman, Adolphe Menjou, Eve Arden, S.Z. Sakall, Selena Royle, Edgar Kennedy; *D:* Michael Curtiz.

My Fair Lady 🦴🦴🦴½ **1964 (G)** Colorful production of Lerner and Loewe's musical version of "Pygmalion," about ill-mannered cockney Eliza (Hepburn) who is plucked from her job as a flower girl by Professor Henry Higgins (Harrison). Higgins makes a bet with a colleague that he can turn this rough diamond into a "lady." Winner of eight Academy Awards. Hepburn's singing voice is dubbed by Marni Nixon, who was also responsible for the singing in "The King and I" and "West Side Story"; the dubbing may have undermined Hepburn's chance at an Oscar nomination. Typecasting role for Harrison as the crusty, egocentric Higgins. A timeless classic. ♫Why Can't the English?; Wouldn't It Be Loverly?; I'm an Ordinary Man; With a Little Bit of Luck; Just You Wait, 'Enry 'Iggins; The Servant's Chorus; The Rain in Spain; I Could Have Danced all Night; Ascot Gavotte. **170m/C VHS, DVD, Wide.** Audrey Hepburn, Rex Harrison, Stanley Holloway, Wilfrid Hyde-White, Theodore Bikel, Mona Washbourne, Jeremy Brett, Robert Coote, Gladys Cooper; *D:* George Cukor; *W:* Alan Jay Lerner; *C:* Harry Stradling Sr.; *M:* Frederick Loewe, Alan Jay Lerner. Oscars '64: Actor (Harrison), Adapt. Score, Art Dir./Set Dec., Color, Color Cinematog., Costume Des. (C), Director (Cukor), Picture, Sound; AFI '98: Top 100; British Acad. '65: Film; Directors Guild '64: Director (Cukor); Golden Globes '65: Actor—Mus./Comedy (Harrison), Director (Cukor), Film—Mus./Comedy; N.Y. Film Critics '64: Actor (Harrison), Film.

My Family 🦴🦴🦴½ *Mi Familia* **1994 (R)** Patriarch Jose Sanchez (Rojas) comes to America in the early 1900s from Mexico and soon finds that the grass is not always greener on the other side. Thus begins the multigenerational saga of the Sanchez family in L.A., which chronicles their struggles and hopes over a time span of 60 years. Overlooked in the glut of Hispanic-themed movies released, featuring soulful performances from the ensemble cast, especially Smits and Morales as troubled men from separate generations. Their deep-seated need to assimilate matched by a disdain for authority provide most of the family's heartaches. English and Spanish dialogue. **126m/C VHS.** Jimmy Smits, Esai Morales, Eduardo Lopez Rojas, Jenny Gago, Elpidia Carrillo, Lupe Ontiveros, Jacob Vargas, Jennifer Lopez, Scott Bakula, Edward James Olmos, Michael De Lorenzo, Maria Canals, Leon Singer, Jonathan Hernandez, Constance Marie, Enrique Castillo, Mary Steenburgen; *D:* Gregory Nava; *W:* Gregory Nava, Anna Thomas; *C:* Edward Lachman; *M:* Pepe Avila, Mark McKenzie; *Nar:* Edward James Olmos.

My Family Treasure 🦴🦴½ **1993** Mother tells her children about her dangerous trip into Russia to recover a family legacy—a priceless Faberge egg. **95m/C VHS.** Dee Wallace Stone, Theodore Bikel, Alex Vincent, Bitty Schram; *D:* Rolfe Kanefsky, Edward Staroselsky.

My Father Is Coming 🦴🦴 **1991** German immigrant, Vicky, is trying to get an acting career off the ground in New York. She shares her apartment with Ben, a gay man, and generally does more work as a waitress than actress. Vicky's alarmed when her father, Hans, arrives for a visit. She's told him she's married (Vicky's also gay), so Ben agrees to pose as her husband. The rest of the film details Vicky's complicated love life, unsuccessful career tryouts, and her father's increasing bewilderment. It's meant as a sort of reverse, and perverse, innocents abroad, with the two Germans adrift in zany New York but this only works fitfully. **82m/C VHS.** *GE* Shelley Kastner, Alfred Edel, David Bronstein, Mary Lou Graulau, Michael Massee, Annie Sprinkle, Bruce Benderson; *D:* Monika Treut; *W:* Monika Treut.

My Father, My Rival 🦴 **1985** A high school student's crush on his teacher leads to emotional complications when his widowed father becomes romantically involved with her. **60m/C VHS.** Lance Guest.

My Father the Hero 🦴🦴 **1993 (PG)** Another adaptation of a French film ("Mon Pere, Ce Heroes") finds 14-year-old Heigl on an island paradise with divorced dad Depardieu, passing him off as her boyfriend (without his knowledge) to impress a cute boy, causing obvious misunderstandings. Depardieu shows a flair for physical comedy, but his talent is wasted in a role that's vaguely disturbing; one of the few funny moments finds him unwittingly singing "Thank Heaven For Little Girls" to a horrified audience. For the preteen set only, others will probably find it a waste of time. Top notch actress Thompson's surprising (uncredited) cameo is due to her friendship with Depardieu. **90m/C VHS.** Gerard Depardieu, Katherine Heigl, Dalton James, Lauren Hutton, Faith Prince; ***Cameos:*** Emma Thompson; *D:* Steve Miner; *W:* Francis Veber, Charlie Peters; *M:* David Newman.

My Father's Glory 🦴🦴🦴 *La Gloire de Mon Pere* **1991 (G)** Based on Marcel Pagnol's tales of his childhood, this is a sweet, beautiful memory of a young boy's favorite summer in the French countryside of the early 1900s. Not much happens, yet the film is such a perfect evocation of the milieu that one is carried swiftly into the dreams and thoughts of all the characters. One half of a duo, followed by "My Mother's Castle." In French with English subtitles. **110m/C VHS.** *FR* Julien Ciamaca, Philippe Caubere, Nathalie Roussel, Therese Liotard, Didier Pain; *D:* Yves Robert; *W:* Lucette Andrei; *C:* Robert Alazraki; *M:* Vladimir Cosma.

My Father's House 🦴🦴 **1975** Magazine editor recounts his youth while recovering from a heart attack. He measures his own quality of life against the life that his father led and begins to question his own choices with regard to his family. **96m/C VHS.** Cliff Robertson, Robert Preston, Eileen Brennan, Rosemary Forsyth.

My Favorite Blonde 🦴🦴🦴 **1942** Beautiful British spy Carroll convinces Hope to aid her in carrying out a secret mission. Lots of fun as Hope and his trained penguin, along with Carroll, embark on a cross-country chase to elude the Nazis. Hope's behavior is hilarious and the pacing of the film is excellent. Based on a story by Melvin Frank and Norman Panama. **78m/B VHS, DVD.** Bob Hope, Madeleine Carroll, Gale Sondergaard, George Zucco, Lionel Royce, Walter Kingsford, Victor Varconi, Bing Crosby; *D:* Sidney Lanfield; *W:* Frank Butler, Don Hartman; *C:* William Mellor; *M:* David Buttolph.

My Favorite Brunette 🦴🦴½ **1947** Detective parody starring Hope as a photographer turned grumbling private eye. He becomes involved with a murder, a spy caper, and a dangerous brunette (Lamour). **85m/B VHS, DVD.** Bob Hope, Dorothy Lamour, Peter Lorre, Lon Chaney Jr., Alan Ladd, Reginald Denny, Bing Crosby; *D:* Elliott Nugent; *W:* Edmund Beloin, Jack Rose; *C:* Lionel Lindon; *M:* Robert Emmett Dolan.

My Favorite Martian 🦴½ **1998 (PG)** This retread of the semi-successful;60s TV sitcom adds to the growing pile of evidence that the words "original" and "thought" are not used in the same sentence in Hollywood anymore. Tim (Daniels) is a TV producer cajoled into hiding his "Uncle Martin." Martin (Lloyd) is actually an alien whose spaceship has crashed, and he's on the run from a government agency and the prying press. Tim must throw racy reporter Hurley off the trail as well, although he has a crush on her. Numerous animated and computer morphed sight gags, including a horny wisecracking spacesuit named Zoot (who brings new meaning to the term "skirt chasing"), take the place of a plot. Sets new standards for mediocrity, but the kiddies might enjoy it. **93m/C VHS, DVD.** Jeff Daniels, Christopher Lloyd, Elizabeth Hurley, Daryl Hannah, Wallace Shawn, Christine Ebersole, Ray Walston, Michael Lerner; *D:* Donald Petrie; *W:* Sherri Stoner, Deanna Oliver; *C:* Thomas Ackerman; *M:* John Debney.

My Favorite Wife 🦴🦴🦴 **1940** Handsome widower Nick (Grant) has just married Bianca (Patrick) only to discover that first wife Ellen (Dunne), shipwrecked seven years earlier and presumed dead, has reappeared. Ellen wants Nick back and makes him jealous by revealing that she spent her island sojourn with fellow survivor, Stephen (Scott). Eventually, a judge must decide what to do about their most unusual situation. Farcical and hilarious story filled with a clever cast. The 1963 remake "Move Over Darling" lacks the style and wit of this presentation. **88m/B VHS.** Ann Shoemaker, Granville Bates, Irene Dunne, Cary Grant, Randolph Scott, Gail Patrick, Scotty Beckett; ***D:*** Garson Kanin; ***W:*** Samuel Spewack, Bella Spewack, Leo McCarey; ***C:*** Rudolph Mate; ***M:*** Roy Webb.

My Favorite Year ♪♪♪ *My Favourite Year* **1982 (PG)** A young writer on a popular live TV show in the 1950s is asked to keep a watchful eye on the week's guest star—his favorite swashbuckling movie hero. Through a series of misadventures, he discovers his matinee idol is actually a drunkard and womanizer who has trouble living up to his cinematic standards. Sterling performance from O'Toole, with memorable portrayal from Bologna as the show's host, King Kaiser (a take-off of Sid Caesar from "Your Show of Shows"). **92m/C VHS, Wide.** Peter O'Toole, Mark Linn-Baker, Joseph Bologna, Jessica Harper, Lainie Kazan, Bill Macy, Anne DeSalvo, Lou Jacobi, Adolph Green, Cameron Mitchell, Gloria Stuart; ***D:*** Richard Benjamin; ***W:*** Norman Steinberg; ***M:*** Ralph Burns.

My Fellow Americans ♪♪ **1996 (PG-13)** Political "Odd Couple" pits cantankerous conservative Kramer (Lemmon) against womanizing liberal Douglas (Garner) when current President Aykroyd frames his two predecessors for a White House scandal. The age-old adversaries must set aside their differences long enough to clear their names by reaching Kramer's presidential library, where he has vindicating papers. Along the way, they encounter adventure, danger and "the people," the average Americans they used to work for. "Grumpy Old Men" veteran Lemmon is plenty cranky while Garner's charisma is a suitable foil. The ironic "charm" of course banter from the mouths of two ex-Presidents is supposed to carry much of the humor, but instead wears thin. Supporting characters (Aykroyd, Bacall) aren't as well used as the two main characters. Mainly for Lemmon, Garner, and "Grumpy" fans. **96m/C VHS, DVD.** Dan Aykroyd, James Garner, Jack Lemmon, John Heard, Sela Ward, Wilford Brimley, Everett McGill, Bradley Whitford, Lauren Bacall, James Rebhorn, Esther Rolle, Conchata Ferrell, Jack Kehler, Tom Everett, Jeff Yagher; ***D:*** Peter Segal; ***W:*** E. Jack Kaplan, Richard Chapman, Peter Tolan; ***C:*** Julio Macat; ***M:*** William Ross.

My First Mister ♪♪½ **2001 (R)** Explores the delicate friendship between two lost and lonely souls. Teenaged Jennifer (Sobieski) is a goth girl whose look and attitude alienates both school and family members. Looking for a job, she is unexpectedly hired as a stock clerk by men's clothing salesman, Randall (Brooks), a middle-aged conservative in both dress and manner. They discover they have a number of feelings in common, although Randall is careful never to let their relationship get out of control. Film does take an unfortunate turn towards the maudlin when we learn that Randall is dying but the leads keep sentimentality fairly well-checked. **109m/C VHS, DVD, Wide.** *US* Albert Brooks, Leelee Sobieski, Desmond Harrington, Carol Kane, Michael McKean, Mary Kay Place, John Goodman, Lisa Jane Persky; ***D:*** Christine Lahti; ***W:*** Jill Franklyn; ***C:*** Jeffrey Jur; ***M:*** Steve Porcaro.

My First Wife ♪♪½ **1984 (PG)** Strong drama about a self-indulgent man's devastation when his wife abruptly leaves him after ten years of marriage. Realistic and well-acted. **95m/C VHS.** *AU* John Hargreaves, Wendy Hughes, Lucy Angwin, Anna Jemison, David Cameron; ***D:*** Paul Cox; ***W:*** Paul Cox, Bob Ellis. Australian Film Inst. '84: Actor (Hargreaves).

My 5 Wives ♪♪ **2000 (R)** Dangerfield is a thrice-divorced real estate tycoon who discovers the Utah land he's invested in comes complete with five wives. **100m/C VHS, DVD, Wide.** Rodney Dangerfield, Andrew (Dice Clay) Silverstein, John Byner, Molly Shannon, Jerry Stiller, John Pinette, Emmanuelle Vaugier, Fred Keating, Kate Luyben, Judy Tylor, Angelika Baran, Anita Brown; ***D:*** Sidney J. Furie; ***W:*** Rodney Dangerfield, Harry Basil; ***C:*** Curtis Petersen; ***M:*** Robert Carli. **VIDEO**

My Forbidden Past ♪♪½ **1951** Melodrama set in 1890 New Orleans centers on a young woman (Gardner) with an unsavory past who unexpectedly inherits a fortune and vows to break up the marriage of the man (Mitchum) she loves. His wife is murdered and he is charged with doing the deed until Gardner, exposing her past, wins his love and helps to extricate him. **81m/B VHS.** Ava Gardner, Melvyn Douglas, Robert Mitchum; ***D:*** Robert Stevenson.

My Friend Flicka ♪♪♪ **1943** Boy makes friends with four-legged beast. Dad thinks the horse is full of wild oats, but young Roddy trains it to be the best gosh darned horse in pre-Disney family faredom. Based on Mary O'Hara book, followed by "Thunderhead, Son of Flicka," and TV series. **89m/C VHS.** Roddy McDowall, Preston Foster, Rita Johnson, James Bell, Jeff Corey; ***D:*** Harold Schuster.

My Friend Irma ♪½ **1949** An adaptation of the radio series, featuring Wilson as the dumb blonde with boyfriend trouble and Lynn as her sensible pal. The film debut of Martin (singing) and Lewis (mugging) as juice-bar operators. Followed by a sequel, "My Friend Irma Goes West," and later by a TV series. **103m/B VHS.** Marie Wilson, Diana Lynn, John Lund, Don DeFore, Dean Martin, Jerry Lewis, Hans Conried; ***D:*** George Marshall.

My Friend Walter ♪♪½ **1993** Bess Throckmorten attends a family reunion in London with her Aunt Ellie and discovers one of her ancestors is Sir Walter Raleigh. Visiting the Tower of London, Bess finds Sir Walter's ghost who wants to follow her home to Devon to see how the family is doing. He finds that the Throckmorten's are about to lose the family farm but Sir Walter comes up with a plan to restore their fortunes. Shot on location in England and based on the book by Michael Morpurgo. **87m/C VHS.** *GB* Polly Grant, Ronald Pickup, Prunella Scales, Louise Jameson, James Hazeldine, Lawrence Cooper, Constance Chapman; ***D:*** Gavin Millar.

My Geisha ♪♪½ **1962** MacLaine and husband experience bad karma because she wants to be in his new film. In pancake makeup and funny shoes, she poses as a geisha girl and is cast as Madame Butterfly. Her husband, however, is one sharp cookie. Filmed in Japan. **120m/C VHS.** Shirley MacLaine, Yves Montand, Edward G. Robinson, Robert Cummings; ***D:*** Jack Cardiff.

My Giant ♪♪ **1998 (PG)** Billy Crystal plays a short, annoying, Hollywood-type guy and Romanian-born NBA player Gheorghe Muresan plays a really tall Romanian guy, so you know there's not exactly an Olivier thing happening here. Crystal is the brutish showbiz agent Sammy, who accidently stumbles onto Muresan's Max. The gentle Max is at peace in his monastery; but Sammy, being an agent, quickly finds a way to make money off of him. Max is talked into a movie career so he can be reunited with his childhood crush Lillianna (Pacula). The odd couple schtick is milked until bone dry, and then the sentimentality floodgates open when it's discovered that Max has a serious medical condition. Warning: although presented as a family film, unless you want to recreate that whole "Why did Bambi's mom have to die?" scene (with you as the parent this time), you might want to reconsider renting this movie for small children. **103m/C VHS, DVD.** Michael (Mike) Papajohn, Billy Crystal, Gheorghe Muresan, Kathleen Quinlan, Joanna Pacula, Rider Strong, Harold Gould, Doris Roberts, Philip Sterling, Heather Thomas, Zane Carney; ***Cameos:*** Steven Seagal; ***D:*** Michael Lehmann; ***W:*** David Seltzer; ***C:*** Michael Coulter; ***M:*** Marc Shaiman.

My Girl ♪♪½ **1991 (PG)** Chlumsky is delightful in her film debut as an 11-year-old tomboy who must come to grips with the realities of life. Culkin plays her best friend Thomas, who understands her better than anyone else, including her father, a mortician, and his girlfriend, the makeup artist at the funeral parlor. Some reviewers questioned whether young children would be able to deal with some unhappy occurrences in the film, but most seemed to classify it as a movie the whole family would enjoy. **102m/C VHS, DVD, 8mm.** Dan Aykroyd, Jamie Lee Curtis, Macaulay Culkin, Anna Chlumsky, Griffin Dunne, Raymond Buktenica, Richard Masur, Ann Nelson, Peter Michael Goetz, Tom Villard; ***D:*** Howard Zieff; ***W:*** Laurice Elehwany; ***C:*** Paul Elliott; ***M:*** James Newton Howard. MTV Movie Awards '92: Kiss (Macaulay Culkin/ Anna Chlumsky).

My Girl 2 ♪♪½ **1994 (PG)** It's 1974 and Chlumsky is back as Vada (this time without Culkin, given the killer bee attack in MG1) in this innocent coming-of-ager. Portly Aykroyd and flaky Curtis return as parental window dressing who encourage Vada's search for information on her long-dead mother. She tracks down old friends of her mom's (Masur and Rose) who are having difficulties with their obnoxious adolescent son (O'Brien). Predictable, but enjoyable. Certain to fail the credibility test of nit-pickers who may wonder why the only thing Aykroyd can remember of his first wife is that she left behind a paper bag with a date scribbled on it. **99m/C VHS, 8mm.** Anna Chlumsky, Dan Aykroyd, Jamie Lee Curtis, Austin O'Brien, Richard Masur, Christine Ebersole, Ben Stein; ***D:*** Howard Zieff; ***W:*** Janet Kovalcik; ***C:*** Paul Elliott; ***M:*** Cliff Eidelman.

My Girl Tisa ♪♪½ **1948** Chronicles the experiences of a young immigrant woman who struggles to survive in the U.S. at the turn of the century and hopes to bring her father over from their home country. Based on a play by Lucille S. Prumbs and Sara B. Smith. **95m/B VHS.** Lilli Palmer, Sam Wanamaker, Akim Tamiroff, Alan Hale, Hugo Haas, Gale Robbins, Stella Adler; ***D:*** Elliott Nugent; ***M:*** Max Steiner.

My Grandpa Is a Vampire ♪½ **1992 (PG)** When 12 year-old Lonny and his pal visit Grandpa Cooger in New Zealand Lonny discovers a long-hidden family secret—Grandpa's a vampire! This doesn't stop either boy from joining with Grandpa in lots of scary adventures. **90m/C VHS.** Al Lewis, Justin Gocke, Milan Borich, Noel Appleby; ***D:*** David Blyth.

My Heroes Have Always Been Cowboys ♪♪½ **1991 (PG)** An aging rodeo rider returns to his hometown to recuperate and finds himself forced to confront his past. His ex-girlfriend, his dad and his sister all expect something from him. He learns how to give it, and gains the strength of purpose to get back on the bull that stomped him. Excellent rodeo footage, solid performances, but the story has been around the barn too many times to hold much interest. **106m/C VHS.** Scott Glenn, Kate Capshaw, Ben Johnson, Balthazar Getty, Mickey Rooney, Gary Busey, Tess Harper, Clarence Williams III, Dub Taylor, Clu Gulager, Dennis Fimple; ***D:*** Stuart Rosenberg; ***W:*** Joel Don Humphreys; ***M:*** James Horner.

My Husband's Double Life ♪♪½ *The Familiar Stranger* **2001** Men are scum. Cable drama based on a true story finds Elizabeth Welsh (Sanders) trying to cope with the apparent suicide of her embezzling husband Patrick (Sanders). She has to sell the house and get a job to support their kids. Then, 10 years later, the Social Security Department informs Elizabeth that the weasel is alive and living in Maine. Naturally, Elizabeth heads off to confront the two-timer. **96m/C VHS, DVD.** Margaret Colin, Jay O. Sanders, Will Estes, Aaron Ashmore, Gary Hudson, Victoria Snow; ***D:*** Alan Metzger; ***W:*** Alan Hines. **CABLE**

My Husband's Secret Life ♪♪ **1998 (PG-13)** Nonsensical thriller about cop's widow Archer who discovers her late hubby had a mistress (Alonso). Unlikely as it seems, the two pair up to investigate police corruption after it seems their mutual honey was also taking payoffs from the mob. The two actresses are much classier than their material. Based on the novel "Tin Wife" by Joe Flaherty. **93m/C VHS.** Anne Archer, Maria Conchita Alonso, Garry Chalk, James Russo, Gerard Plunkett; ***D:*** Graeme Clifford; ***W:*** Georgia Jeffries; ***C:*** David Geddes; ***M:*** Roger Bellon. **CABLE**

My Lady of Whims ♪ **1925** Clara Bow's dad disapproves of debutante daughter's desire to hang out with the girls who just want to have fun. **42m/B VHS.** Clara Bow, Betty Baker, Carmelita Geraghty, Donald Keith, Lee Moran.

My Left Foot ♪♪♪♪ **1989 (R)** A gritty, unsentimental drama based on the life and autobiography of cerebral-palsy victim Christy Brown. Considered an imbecile by everyone but his mother (Fricker, in a stunning award-winning performance) until he teaches himself to write. He survives his impoverished Irish roots to become a painter and writer using his left foot, the only appendage over which he has control. He also falls in love and finds some heartaches along the way. Day-Lewis is astounding; the supporting cast, especially Shaw and Cusack, match him measure for measure. **103m/C VHS, DVD.** *IR* Daniel Day-Lewis, Brenda Fricker, Ray McAnally, Cyril Cusack, Fiona Shaw, Hugh O'Conor, Adrian Dunbar, Ruth McCabe, Alison Whelan; ***D:*** Jim Sheridan; ***W:*** Shane Connaughton, Jim Sheridan; ***C:*** Jack Conroy; ***M:*** Elmer Bernstein. Oscars '89: Actor (Day-Lewis), Support. Actress (Fricker); British Acad. '89: Actor (Day-Lewis), Support. Actor (McAnally); Ind. Spirit '90: Foreign Film; L.A. Film Critics '89: Actor (Day-Lewis), Support. Actress (Fricker); Montreal World Film Fest. '89: Actor (Day-Lewis); N.Y. Film Critics '89: Actor (Day-Lewis), Film; Natl. Soc. Film Critics '89: Actor (Day-Lewis).

My Life ♪♪½ **1993 (PG-13)** Maudlin, sometimes depressing production preaches the power of a well-examined life. Public relations exec Keaton is diagnosed with cancer and the doctors predict he will most likely die before the birth of his first child. Film follows his transition from uncommunicative and angry to acceptance, a role to which Keaton brings a sentimental strength. Kidman is window dressing as the ever-patient, nobly suffering wife, a cardboard character notable mainly for her beauty. **114m/C VHS, DVD, 8mm, Wide.** Michael Keaton, Nicole Kidman, Haing S. Ngor, Bradley Whitford, Queen Latifah, Michael Constantine, Toni Sawyer, Rebecca Schull, Lee Garlington; ***D:*** Bruce Joel Rubin; ***W:*** Bruce Joel Rubin; ***C:*** Peter James; ***M:*** John Barry.

My Life and Times with Antonin Artaud ♪♪♪ *En Compagnie d'Antonin Artaud* **1993** Postwar Parisian bohemia is depicted in the obsessive friendship between ambitious young poet Jacques Prevel (Barbe) and famed intellectual/poet/impressario Antonin Artaud (Frey), who founded the Theatre of Cruelty. Artaud has returned to Paris after spending nine years in an asylum and is suffering from terminal cancer, the misery of which is partially alleviated by the opiates that Prevel can provide. Delusional and paranoid, Artaud makes his self-destruction into genius while Prevel documents Artaud's last two years in diaries, hoping to gain some measure of fame for himself. French with subtitles. Based on Prevel's "En Compagnie d'Antonin Artaud." **93m/B VHS.** *FR* Sami Frey, Marc Barbe, Valerie Jeannet, Julie Jezequel, Charlotte Valandrey; ***D:*** Gerard Mordillat; ***W:*** Gerard Mordillat, Jerome Prieur; ***C:*** Francois Catonne; ***M:*** Jean-Claude Petit.

My Life As a Dog ♪♪♪♪ *Mitt Liv Som Hund* **1985** A troublesome boy is separated from his brother and is sent to live with relatives in the country when his mother is taken ill. Unhappy and confused, he struggles to understand sexuality and love and tries to find security and acceptance. Remarkable Swedish film available with English subtitles or dubbed. **101m/C VHS, DVD.** *SW* Anton Glanzelius, Tomas Van Bromssen, Anki Liden, Melinda Kinnaman, Kicki Rundgren, Ing-mari Carlsson; ***D:*** Lasse Hallstrom; ***W:*** Lasse Hallstrom, Per (Pelle) Berglund, Brasse Brannstrom; ***C:*** Jorgen Persson, Rolf Lindstrom; ***M:*** Bjorn Isfalt. Golden Globes '88: Foreign Film; Ind. Spirit '88: Foreign Film; N.Y. Film Critics '87: Foreign Film.

My Life So Far ♪♪½ **1998 (PG-13)** In the 1920's, the Pettigrews live on the family estate of Gamma Macintosh (Harris) in the Scottish Highlands. Eccentric would-be inventor Edward (Firth) ineffectually manages the property, with wife

Moira (Mastrantonio) and his children, including mischievious 10-year-old Fraser (Norman). Fraser's safe world is rocked by the arrival of his businessman Uncle Morris (McDowell) and his uncle's seductive French fiancee, Heloise (Jacob), who draws the immediate and overly-attentive gaze of Edward. Based on the autobiographical book "Son of Adam" by Sir Denis Forman. **93m/C VHS, DVD.** *GB* Colin Firth, Mary Elizabeth Mastrantonio, Irene Jacob, Malcolm McDowell, Rosemary Harris, Tcheky Karyo, Robert Norman, Kelly Macdonald; ***D:*** Hugh Hudson; ***W:*** Simon Donald; ***C:*** Bernard Lutic; ***M:*** Howard Blake.

My Life to Live 🦴🦴🦴🦴 *Vivre Sa Vie; It's My Life* **1962** A woman turns to prostitution in this probing examination of sexual, and social, relations. Idiosyncratic Godard has never been more starstruck than in this vehicle for the endearing Karina, his wife at the time. A classic. In French with English subtitles. **85m/B VHS, DVD.** *FR* Anna Karina, Sady Rebbot, Andre S. Labarthe, Guylaine Schlumberger; ***D:*** Jean-Luc Godard; ***W:*** Jean-Luc Godard; ***C:*** Raoul Coutard; ***M:*** Michel Legrand. Venice Film Fest. '62: Special Jury Prize.

My Life's in Turnaround 🦴🦴 **1994 (R)** Amusing low-budget comedy takes a behind-the-scenes, semi-autobiographical look at the lives of two would-be filmmakers. They try for cool but manage only goofy. **84m/C VHS.** Eric Schaeffer, Donal Lardner Ward, Lisa Gerstein, Dana Wheeler-Nicholson, Debra Clein, Sheila Jaffe; ***Cameos:*** Casey Siemaszko, John Sayles, Martha Plimpton, Phoebe Cates; ***D:*** Eric Schaeffer, Donal Lardner Ward; ***W:*** Eric Schaeffer, Donal Lardner Ward; ***M:*** Reed Hays.

My Little Assassin 🦴🦴 **1999** In 1959, idealistic 19-year-old Marita Lorenz is in Cuba with her CIA operative mother (Clayburgh), when she falls for revolutionary leader Fidel Castro (Mantegna). She winds up pregnant and alone in New York, where the CIA tries to convince her that Fidel's a bad guy. So, she decides to return to Cuba and assassinate him. In 1993, Lorenz wrote a book detailing her affair, the birth of their daughter, and Lorenz's involved in a failed plot to poison the dictator in 1960. If you can suspend your credulity, you'll discover a watchable potboiler with Mantegna as a charismatic Cuban leader. **90m/C VHS, DVD.** Joe Mantegna, Gabrielle Anwar, Jill Clayburgh, Robert Davi, Scott Paulin, Tony Plana, Reiner Schone, Mike Moroff, Glenn Morshower, Dean Norris; ***D:*** Jack Bender; ***W:*** Howard Korder; ***M:*** David Schwartz. **CABLE**

My Little Chickadee 🦴🦴🦴 **1940** Classic comedy about a gambler and a fallen woman who marry for convenience so they can respectably enter an unsuspecting town. Sparks fly in their adventures together. Fields and West are both at their best playing their larger-than-life selves. **91m/B VHS.** W.C. Fields, Mae West, Joseph Calleia, Dick Foran, Margaret Hamilton, Donald Meek, Ruth Donnelly, Fuzzy Knight; ***D:*** Edward F. (Eddie) Cline; ***W:*** W.C. Fields, Mae West; ***C:*** Joseph Valentine; ***M:*** Frank Skinner.

My Little Girl 🦴🦴 **1987 (R)** A rich Philadelphia girl idealistically volunteers her time to help local institutionalized orphans, but meets with opposition. **118m/C VHS.** Mary Stuart Masterson, James Earl Jones, Geraldine Page, Anne Meara, Peter Gallagher, George Newbern; ***D:*** Connie Kaiserman.

My Louisiana Sky 🦴🦴½ **2002** Twelve-year-old Tiger Ann (Keel) lives with her grandma Jewel (Knight) and her "slow" parents in Saitler, Louisiana. She's looking forward to the summer when her glamorous aunt, Dorie Kay (Lewis), will visit but Jewel's unexpected death has Tiger Ann re-thinking what matters to her. Based on the book by Kimberly Willis Holt. **99m/C VHS, DVD.** Kelsey Keel, Shirley Knight, Juliette Lewis; ***D:*** Adam Arkin. **CABLE**

My Love For Yours 🦴🦴½ *Honeymoon in Bali* **1939** The romantic tale of a young man hoping to win the love of a beautiful but icy girl. A tad silly in parts, but the clever dialogue moves the story along. **99m/B VHS.** Fred MacMurray, Madeleine Carroll; ***D:*** Edward H. Griffith.

My Lucky Star 🦴🦴½ **1938** Skating star Henie plays a department store clerk that gets sent off to college to model clothes from the store's sports line. She somehow manages to convince school officials to stage their winter ice show in the department store, where she gets to show off her stuff. Don't miss the grand finale, a performance of "Alice in Wonderland Ice Ballet." Based on the story "They Met in Chicago" by Karl Tunberg and Don Ettlinger. ♪I've Got a Date With a Dream; Could You Pass in Love; This May Be the Night; The All-American Swing; Plymouth University Song. **81m/B VHS.** Sonja Henie, Richard Greene, Joan Davis, Cesar Romero, Buddy Ebsen, Arthur Treacher, George Barbier, Gypsy Rose Lee; ***D:*** Roy Del Ruth; ***W:*** Harry Tugend, Jack Yellen.

My Magic Dog 🦴🦴½ **1997** Lucky is eight-year-old Toby's dog. Lucky happens to be invisible. Which turns out to be a good thing when evil Aunt Violet tries to steal Toby's inheritance. **98m/C VHS.** Leo Millbrook, Russ Tamblyn, John Phillip Law; ***D:*** John Putch. **VIDEO**

My Man Adam 🦴🦴 **1986 (R)** A dreamy, Mitty-esque high schooler falls in love with a girl (Daryl's auburn-haired sister, Page Hannah), and becomes ensnared in a real life crime, leaving his friend to bail him out. Typical boy-meets-girl, boy-gets-in-trouble yarn. **84m/C VHS.** Raphael Sbarge, Veronica Cartwright, Page Hannah, Larry B. Scott, Charlie Barnett, Arthur Pendleton, Dave Thomas; ***D:*** Roger L. Simon.

My Man Godfrey 🦴🦴🦴🦴 **1936** Spoiled rich girl Irene Bullock (Lombard) picks up someone she assumes is a bum (Powell) as part of a scavenger hunt and decides to keep him on as her family's butler. In the process, Godfrey teaches her about life, money, and happiness—and that everything is not as it seems. Top-notch screwball comedy defines the genre. Lombard is a stunner alongside the equally charming Powell. Watch for Jane Wyman as an extra in the party scene. From the novel by Eric Hatch. Remade in 1957 with June Allyson and David Niven. **95m/B VHS, DVD.** William Powell, Carole Lombard, Gail Patrick, Alice Brady, Mischa Auer, Eugene Pallette, Alan Mowbray, Franklin Pangborn, Jane Wyman; ***D:*** Gregory La Cava; ***W:*** Gregory La Cava, Morrie Ryskind; ***C:*** Ted Tetzlaff; ***M:*** Charles Previn. Natl. Film Reg. '99.

My Man Godfrey 🦴🦴½ **1957** Inferior remake of the sophisticated screwball comedy of the '30s about a butler who brings a touch of the common man to the filthy rich. Niven stars as the butler and Allyson plays the rich girl, but nothing compares to the original roles created by Powell and Lombard. **92m/C VHS, DVD.** June Allyson, David Niven, Martha Hyer, Jessie Royce Landis, Robert Keith, Eva Gabor, Jay Robinson, Jeff Donnell; ***D:*** Henry Koster; ***W:*** Everett Freeman, Peter Berneis, William Bowers; ***C:*** William H. Daniels.

My Michael 🦴🦴🦴 **1975** Sensitive adaptation of Amos Oz's novel set in Jerasalem in the late 1950s. A young woman is stifled by marriage and the conventions of her bourgeois life and her fantasies begin to take over. In Hebrew with English subtitles. **90m/C VHS.** *IS* Efrat Lavie, Oded Kotler; ***D:*** Dan Wolman.

My Mom's a Werewolf 🦴½ **1989 (PG)** An average suburban mother gets involved with a dashing stranger and soon, to her terror, begins to turn into a werewolf. Her daughter and companion must come up with a plan to regain dear, sweet mom. **90m/C VHS, DVD.** Susan Blakely, John Saxon, John Schuck, Katrina Caspary, Ruth Buzzi, Marilyn McCoo, Marcia Wallace, Diana Barrows; ***D:*** Michael Fischa; ***W:*** Mark Pirro; ***C:*** Bryan England; ***M:*** Dana Walden, Barry Fasman.

My Mother's Castle 🦴🦴🦴½ *Le Chateau de Ma Mere* **1991 (PG)** The second half of the two part film series based on the autobiography of Marcel Pagnol. Picking up where "My Father's Glory" left off, the family begins a series of vacations in a beautiful country home. Dynamically acted and tenderly directed, charming and suitable for the entire family. In French with English subtitles. **98m/C VHS.** *FR* Philippe Caubere, Nathalie Roussel, Didier Pain, Therese Liotard, Julien Ciamaca, Victorien Delmare; ***D:*** Yves Robert; ***M:*** Vladimir Cosma.

My Mother's Courage 🦴🦴 *Mutters Courage* **1995** Based on writer George Tabori's memoir of his Jewish mother, Elsa (Collins), who managed to escape deportation from Budapest in 1944. Her husband is in prison, her sons have left the country, but an unwavering Elsa remains to care for her asthmatic sister. Finally, she is detained and sent to the railyard to be deported—until she confronts a Nazi official and manages to obtain her release. German with subtitles. **88m/C VHS.** *GE GB* Pauline Collins, Ulrich Tukur, Natalie Morse; ***D:*** Michael Verhoeven; ***W:*** Michael Verhoeven; ***C:*** Michael Epp, Theo Bierkes; ***M:*** Julian Nott, Simon Verhoeven.

My Mother's Secret Life 🦴½ **1984** Dull drama focusing on a long-forgotten daughter who suddenly appears on her mother's doorstep and discovers that mom makes a living as a high-priced hooker. **100m/C VHS.** Loni Anderson, Paul Sorvino, Amanda Wyss, James Sutorius, Sandy McPeak; ***D:*** Robert Markowitz; ***M:*** Brad Fiedel.

My Name Is Ivan 🦴🦴🦴½ *Ivan's Childhood; The Youngest Spy* **1962** Tarkovsky's first feature film is a vivid, wrenching portrait of a young Soviet boy surviving as a spy behind enemy lines during WWII. Technically stunning, heralding the coming of modern cinema's greatest formalist. In Russian with English subtitles. **84m/B VHS.** *RU* Kolya Burlyayev, Valentin Zubkov, Ye Zharikov, S. Krylov; ***D:*** Andrei Tarkovsky. Venice Film Fest. '62: Film.

My Name Is Joe 🦴🦴 **1998 (R)** Set in Glasgow, the Scots accents prove a distinct challenge in this story of working-class romance. Unemployed alcoholic Joe Kavanagh (Mullan) is 10 months sober and does odd jobs to get by, while coaching the local no-hoper football team. By chance he meets community health worker Sarah (Goodall) and the two are drawn together by their similar outlooks on life and begin a cautious romance. But Joe's loyalty to his mates and his efforts to get his friend Liam (McKay) out of trouble, helps to put a strain on the relationship. **105m/C VHS.** *GB* Peter Mullan, Louise Goodall, David McKay, Annemarie Kennedy, David Hayman, Gary Lewis, Lorraine McIntosh; ***D:*** Ken Loach; ***W:*** Paul Laverty; ***C:*** Barry Ackroyd; ***M:*** George Fenton. Cannes '98: Actor (Mullan).

My Name Is Nobody 🦴🦴½ *Il Mio Nome e Nessuno* **1974 (PG)** Fast-paced spaghetti-western wherein a cocky, softhearted gunfighter is sent to kill the famous, retired outlaw he reveres, but instead they band together. **115m/C VHS.** *IT* Henry Fonda, Terence Hill, R.G. Armstrong; ***D:*** Tonino Valerii; ***M:*** Ennio Morricone.

My Neighbor Totoro 🦴🦴½ **1993 (G)** Rather gooey Japanese animated movie about Satsuki and her younger sister Lucy, whose new house in the country is filled with magic, including a friendly creature named Totoro. Totoro is a cuddly, if weird, mix of bear, owl, and seal, with whiskers and a gentle roar. He can fly, has a magic bus, and can only be seen by children. Naturally, every time the two girls get into mischief Totoro is there to rescue them. Dubbed into English. **76m/C VHS.** *JP* ***D:*** Hayao Miyazaki; ***W:*** Hayao Miyazaki.

My New Gun 🦴🦴½ **1992 (R)** Uneven, restless dark comedy about Debbie and Gerald Bender, yuppified suburban couple whose lives are disrupted by a gun. When their newly engaged friends get a gun, Gerry decides they need a gun as well. Debbie is very uncomfortable about having a weapon in the house and doesn't want anything to do with it. When mysterious neighbor LeGros steals the gun, it sets off a bizarre chain of events that culminate at the wedding of their friends. Impressive first effort for writer/director Cochran. **99m/C VHS, Wide.** Diane Lane, Stephen Collins, James LeGros, Tess Harper, Bill Raymond, Bruce Altman, Maddie Corman; ***D:*** Stacy Cochran; ***W:*** Stacy Cochran; ***M:*** Pat Irwin. Cannes '92: Film.

My New Partner 🦴🦴½ *Les Ripoux* **1984 (R)** Amiable French comedy in which cynical veteran cop is saddled with straight arrow rookie partner. French Cesars for best film and best director, but remember: They like Jerry Lewis too. In French with English subtitles. **106m/C VHS.** *FR* Philippe Noiret, Thierry Lhermitte, Regine, Grace de Capitani, Claude Brosset, Julien Guiomar; ***D:*** Claude Zidi; ***W:*** Claude Zidi; ***C:*** Jean-Jacques Tarbes; ***M:*** Francis Lai.

My Night at Maud's 🦴🦴🦴 *My Night with Maud; Ma Nuit Chez Maud* **1969** Typically subtle Rohmer entry concerns quandary of upright fellow who finds himself drawn to comparatively carefree woman. Talky, somewhat arid film is one of director's Six Moral Tales. You'll either find it fascinating or wish you were watching "Rocky XXIV" instead. In French with English subtitles. **111m/B VHS, DVD.** *FR* Jean-Louis Trintignant, Francoise Fabian, Marie-Christine Barrault, Antoine Vitez; ***D:*** Eric Rohmer; ***W:*** Eric Rohmer; ***C:*** Nestor Almendros. N.Y. Film Critics '70: Screenplay; Natl. Soc. Film Critics '70: Cinematog., Screenplay.

My Old Man 🦴🦴½ **1979** Plucky teen and her seedy horsetrainer father come together over important horse race. Oates makes this one worth watching on a slow evening. Based on a Hemingway story. **102m/C VHS.** Kristy McNichol, Warren Oates, Eileen Brennan; ***D:*** John Erman. **TV**

My Old Man's Place 🦴½ **1971 (R)** A veteran, with two war buddies and a girl, returns to his father's run-down farm, hoping to fix it up. Sexual tensions arise and violence erupts. **93m/C VHS.** Arthur Kennedy, Michael Moriarty, Mitchell Ryan, William Devane, Topo Swope; ***D:*** Edwin Sherin.

My Other Husband 🦴🦴½ *Attention! Une Femme Peut en Cacher une Autre* **1985 (PG-13)** A woman has two husbands and families, one in Paris and one in Trouville, who eventually meet each other. Seems silly but grows into a sensitive and sad portrait of married life. In French with English subtitles. **110m/C VHS.** *FR* Miou-Miou, Rachid Ferrache, Roger Hanin; ***D:*** Georges Lautner.

My Outlaw Brother 🦴🦴 *My Brother, the Outlaw* **1951** A man travelling West to visit his brother in Mexico meets a Texas Ranger on the train. The man discovers that his brother is an outlaw, and teams up with the Ranger to capture him. **82m/B VHS.** Mickey Rooney, Wanda Hendrix, Robert Preston, Robert Stack, Jose Torvay; ***D:*** Elliott Nugent.

My Own Country 🦴🦴½ **1998 (R)** Abraham Verghese (Andrews) is an Indian immigrant who becomes the head of infectious diseases at the rural Johnson City, Tennessee hospital, where he had interned, in 1985. Considered an outsider, the doctor also finds himself dealing with the area's first AIDS cases, and his patients who are discriminated against. In fact, Verghese becomes so obsessed with their care that he neglects his own wife and children. Based on Verghese's memoirs. **106m/C VHS, DVD.** Naveen Andrews, Glenne Headly, Marisa Tomei, Hal Holbrook, Swoosie Kurtz, Sean Hewitt, William Webster; ***D:*** Mira Nair; ***W:*** Sooni Taraporevala, Jim Leonard Jr. **CABLE**

My Own Private Idaho 🦴🦴🦴 **1991 (R)** Director Van Sant of "Drugstore Cowboy" returns to the underworld to examine another group of outsiders, this time young, homosexual hustlers. On the streets of Seattle, narcoleptic hustler Mike meets slumming rich boy Scott, and together they begin a search for Mike's lost mother, which leads them to Idaho and Italy. Stunning visuals, an elliptical plot, and a terrific performance by Phoenix highlight this search for love, the meaning of life, and power. Van Sant couples these activities with scenes from Shakespeare's "Henry IV" for a sometimes inscrutable, but always memorable film. Look for director Richert's Falstaff role as an aging chickenhawk. **105m/C VHS, Wide.** River Phoenix, Keanu Reeves, James Russo, William Richert, Rodney Harvey, Michael Parker, Flea, Chiara Caselli, Udo Kier, Grace Zabriskie, Tom Troupe; ***D:*** Gus Van Sant; ***W:*** Gus Van Sant; ***C:*** John Campbell, Eric Alan Edwards. Ind. Spirit '92: Actor

(Phoenix), Screenplay; Natl. Soc. Film Critics '91: Actor (Phoenix).

My Pal, the King 🦴🦴½ 1932 Amusing western with Rooney as the boy king of Ruritania, who's bored with his official duties. He meets Mix, the proprietor of a traveling wild west show which just happens to be performing in the country. Good thing too because Rooney has an evil prime minister who wants the throne for himself and kidnaps the kid. Naturally, Mix and his friends arrive to save him in the nick of time. **62m/B VHS.** Tom Mix, Mickey Rooney, Stuart Holmes, Paul Hurst, Noel Francis, James Kirkwood, Jim Thorpe; ***D:*** Kurt Neumann.

My Pal Trigger 🦴🦴 1946 Roy is unjustly imprisoned in this high adventure on the plains. Better than usual script and direction makes this is one of the more entertaining of the singing cowboy's films. **79m/B VHS.** Roy Rogers, George "Gabby" Hayes, Dale Evans, Jack Holt; ***D:*** Frank McDonald.

My Pleasure Is My Business 1974 **(R)** Cinematic autobiography of Xaveria Hollander, the world's most renowned prostitute of the '70s, and the zany occurrences which abound in her profession. **85m/C VHS.** *CA* Xaviera Hollander, Henry Ramer, Colin Fox, Ken Lynch, Jayne (Jane) Eastwood; ***D:*** Al Waxman.

My Samurai 🦴½ 1992 **(R)** When young Peter McCrea witnesses a gang murder he turns to his martial-arts expert friend Young Park to help him. On the run from both the gang and the police Peter learns self-defense and the courage to face his fears. **87m/C VHS.** Julian Lee, Mako, Terry O'Quinn, Bubba Smith, Jim Turner, Carlos Palomino, John Kallo; ***D:*** Fred Dresch.

My Science Project 🦴½ 1985 **(PG)** Teenager Stockwell stumbles across a crystal sphere with a funky light. Unaware that it is an alien time-travel device, he takes it to school to use as a science project in a last-ditch effort to avoid failing his class. Chaos follows and Stockwell and his chums find themselves battling gladiators, mutants, and dinosaurs. Plenty of special effects and a likeable enough, dumb teenage flick. **94m/C VHS, DVD.** John Stockwell, Danielle von Zerneck, Fisher Stevens, Raphael Sbarge, Richard Masur, Barry Corbin, Ann Wedgeworth, Dennis Hopper, Candace Silvers, Beau Dremann, Pat Simmons, Pamela Springsteen; ***D:*** Jonathan Betuel; ***W:*** Jonathan Betuel; ***C:*** David M. Walsh; ***M:*** Peter Bernstein.

My Sex Life...Or How I Got into an Argument 🦴🦴 *Ma Vie Sexuelle...Comment Je Me Suis Dispute* 1996 Paul (Amalric) is unhappy personally and professionally. He's a bored grad student/assistant professor of philosophy and breaking up with lover of ten years, Esther (Devos). Soon Paul's romancing other women, one of whom, Sylvia (Denicourt), is already involved with Paul's best friend Nathan (Salinger). Very talky and Frenchly intellectual. French with subtitles. **178m/C VHS, DVD, Wide.** *FR* Mathieu Amalric, Marianne (Cuau) Denicourt, Emmanuelle Devos, Emmanuel Salinger, Jeanne Balibar, Michel Vuillermoz; ***D:*** Arnaud Desplechin; ***W:*** Arnaud Desplechin, Emmanuel Bourdieu; ***C:*** Eric Gautier; ***M:*** Krishna Levy.

My Side of the Mountain 🦴🦴½ 1969 **(G)** A 13-year-old boy decides to emulate his idol, Henry David Thoreau, and gives up his home and his family to live in the Canadian mountains. **100m/C VHS.** *CA* Teddy Eccles, Theodore Bikel; ***D:*** James B. Clark.

My Sister Eileen 🦴🦴🦴 1955 Ruth and Eileen are two small-town Ohio sisters who move to Manhattan seeking excitement. They live in a basement apartment in Greenwich Village with an assortment of oddball tenants as they pursue success and romance. Everyone is daffy and charming, as is the film. Fun, but unmemorable songs, however the terrific choreography is by Fosse, who also appears as one sister's suitor. Remake of a 1942 film which was based on a Broadway play, which was based on a series of autobiographical stories published in the New Yorker. The play was later turned into a Broadway musical known as "Wonderful Town," which has nothing to do with this version of the original stories. ♫Give Me a Band and My Baby; It's Bigger Than You and Me; There's Nothing Like Love; As Soon As They See Eileen; I'm Great; Conga; Atmosphere. **108m/C VHS.** Janet Leigh, Betty Garrett, Jack Lemmon, Bob Fosse, Kurt Kasznar, Dick York, Lucy Marlow, Tommy (Thomas) Rall, Barbara Brown, Horace McMahon; ***D:*** Richard Quine; ***W:*** Blake Edwards, Richard Quine; ***M:*** Jule Styne.

My Sister, My Love 🦴½ *The Cage; The Mafu Cage* 1978 **(R)** Odd tale of two sisters' incestuous relationship and what happens when one of them takes another lover. The cage of the alternate titles refers to the place where their pet apes are kept and seems to symbolize the confining nature of their life together. **102m/C VHS.** Lee Grant, Carol Kane, Will Geer, James Olson; ***D:*** Karen Arthur.

My Sister's Keeper 🦴🦴½ 2002 Christina (Bates) and her sister Judy (Perkins) couldn't have more different lives. Christina struggles to cope with her schizophrenia and her dependence on others while Judy is a work-obsessed art editor in New York. When their mother Helen (Redgrave) dies, Judy is suddenly responsible for Christina's care and they must struggle to accept and support one another. Based on the memoir by Margaret Moorman. **98m/C VHS.** Kathy Bates, Elizabeth Perkins, Lynn Redgrave, Bobby Harwell, Kimberly J. Brown, Hallee Hirsh, Kathleen Wilhoite, Jascha Washington; ***D:*** Ron Lagomarsino; ***W:*** Susan Tarr; ***C:*** Lloyd Ahern II; ***M:*** Lawrence Shragge. **TV**

My Son, My Son 🦴🦴½ 1940 The spoiled son (Hayward) of a successful businessman (Aherne) doesn't think twice about making everyone miserable in his quest to get everything he wants. He even goes as far as trying to steal his dad's new bride. When world war comes, he has a chance to redeem himself. Melodrama is kept from sinking to overwrought soap opera by Hayward and Aherne. **115m/B VHS.** Louis Hayward, Brian Aherne, Scotty Beckett, Lionel Belmore, Laraine Day, Madeleine Carroll, Henry Hull, Howard Davies, Pat Flaherty, Leyland Hodgson, Josephine Hutchinson, Sophie Stewart, Stanley Logan; ***D:*** Charles Vidor; ***W:*** Lenore Coffee; ***C:*** Harry Stradling Sr.

My Son the Fanatic 🦴🦴🦴 1997 **(R)** Pakistani immigrant Parvez (Puri) has been driving a cab in Bradford, England and trying to fit in his new country for 25 years. He ekes out a living driving prostitutes around town, which leads to a relationship with hooker Bettina (Griffiths). His working-class life is disrupted when Parvez realizes his son, Farid (Kurtha) is exploring his cultural roots by turning to Islamic fundamentalism. Moral and religious tensions lead to a climactic conflict between father and son. **86m/C VHS, DVD.** *GB* Om Puri, Rachel Griffiths, Stellan Skarsgard, Akbar Kurtha; ***D:*** Udayan Prasad; ***W:*** Hanif Kureishi; ***C:*** Alan Almond; ***M:*** Stephen Warbeck.

My Son, the Vampire 🦴½ *Old Mother Riley Meets the Vampire; The Vampire and the Robot; Vampire Over London; Mother Riley Meets the Vampire* 1952 Last of Britain's Old Mother Riley series in which Lucan plays the Irish housekeeper in drag. Lugosi is a crazed scientist who thinks he's a vampire and wants to take over the world with his giant robot. Mother Riley interferes. Theme song by Alan Sherman. **72m/B VHS, DVD.** *GB* Bela Lugosi, Arthur Lucan, Dora Bryan, Richard Wattis; ***D:*** John Gilling; ***W:*** Val Valentine; ***C:*** Stanley Pavey.

My Song Goes Round the World 🦴½ 1934 Chronicles the romantic foibles of a singing trio and the one girl they decide they all love. **68m/B VHS.** Joseph Schmidt, John Loder, Charlotte Ander; ***D:*** Richard Oswald.

My Stepmother Is an Alien 🦴🦴 1988 **(PG-13)** When eccentric physicist Aykroyd sends a message beam to another galaxy on a stormy night, the last thing he expects is a visit from beautiful alien Basinger. Unfortunately, he does not realize that this gorgeous blonde is an alien and he continues to court her despite her rather odd habits. Only the daughter seems to notice the strange goings on, and her dad ignores her warnings, enabling Basinger's evil sidekick to continue in its plot to take over the Earth. **108m/C VHS, DVD.** Dan Aykroyd, Kim Basinger, Jon Lovitz, Alyson Hannigan, Joseph Maher, Seth Green, Wesley Mann, Adrian Sparks, Juliette Lewis, Tanya Fenmore; ***D:*** Richard Benjamin; ***W:*** Jerico (Weingrod) Stone, Herschel Weingrod, Timothy Harris, Jonathan Reynolds; ***C:*** Richard H. Kline; ***M:*** Alan Silvestri.

My Summer Story 🦴🦴½ *It Runs in the Family* 1994 **(PG)** Humorist Shepherd and director Clark re-team for another period family comedy in the tradition of their first collaboration, "A Christmas Story," now a video classic. This time the Parkers find themselves battling their crazy new neighbors, the Bumpus family, Ralphie (Kieran Culkin) has troubles with a neighborhood bully and tries to bond with his dad (Grodin) while fishing, and mom (Steenburgen) goes loopy over gravy boats. Charming family fun. Based on Shepherd's novels "In God We Trust, All Others Pay Cash" and "Wanda Hickey's Night of Golden Memories and Other Disasters." **85m/C VHS.** Charles Grodin, Mary Steenburgen, Kieran Culkin, Chris Culkin, Al Mancini, Troy Evans, Glenn Shadix, Dick O'Neill, Wayne Grace; ***D:*** Bob (Benjamin) Clark; ***W:*** Jean Shepherd, Bob (Benjamin) Clark, Leigh Brown; ***C:*** Stephen M. Katz; ***M:*** Paul Zaza; ***Nar:*** Jean Shepherd.

My Sweet Charlie 🦴🦴½ 1970 Unwed, pregnant white woman hides out with black lawyer in backwater Texas. Better than it sounds, with nice performances by Duke and Freeman. **97m/C VHS.** Patty Duke, Al Freeman Jr., Ford Rainey, William Hardy, Chris Wilson, Archie Moore, Noble Willingham; ***D:*** Lamont Johnson. **TV**

My Sweet Little Village 🦴🦴½ *Vesnicko Ma Strediskova* 1986 Gentle comedy set in a rural village and dealing with everyday events, including a romantic teenager who develops a crush on a schoolteacher, an adulterous wife and her boyfriend, the accident-prone doctor, a Laurel and Hardy duo of truck drivers, and others. Czech with subtitles. **100m/C VHS.** *CZ* Rudolf Hrusinsky, Janos Ban, Marian Labuda, Milena Dvorska, Ladislav Zupanic, Petr Cepek; ***D:*** Jiri Menzel; ***W:*** Zdenek Sverak; ***C:*** Jaromir Sofr; ***M:*** Jiri Sust.

My Sweet Suicide 🦴🦴 1998 Very low-budget comedy about staging the perfect suicide. Depressed Kevin (Aldrich) can't even manage to kill himself. He confides his dilemma to eccentric bookstore clerk Thompson, who agrees to help him out. **78m/C VHS.** Matthew Aldrich, Michelle Leigh Thompson, Eric Wheeler; ***D:*** David Michael Flanagan; ***W:*** David Michael Flanagan.

My Sweet Victim 🦴🦴 1985 A young couple who recently moved to the United States from Poland try to make a go of their own business. The business fails, and so does their marriage. Will it end in murder? **92m/C VHS.** Candice Bergen, Juergen Prochnow.

My Teacher's Wife 🦴🦴½ 1995 **(R)** High-schooler London has big college plans, which won't get anywhere if he doesn't pass math. So he asks Carrere to tutor him, only the problems they study become more personal. **90m/C VHS, DVD.** Tia Carrere, Jason London, Christopher McDonald, Leslie Lyles, Zak Orth, Jeffrey Tambor, Randy Pearlstein; ***D:*** Bruce Leddy; ***W:*** Bruce Leddy, Seth Greenland; ***C:*** Zoltan David; ***M:*** Kevin Gilbert. **VIDEO**

My Therapist woof! 1984 A sex therapist's boyfriend cannot bear the thought of her having intercourse with other men as part of her work. Soft core. **81m/C VHS.** Marilyn Chambers; ***D:*** Gary Legon.

My Tutor 🦴½ 1982 **(R)** When a high school student is in danger of flunking French, his parents hire a private tutor to help him learn the lessons. It becomes clear that his studies will involve many more subjects, however. Standard teen sex comedy. **97m/C VHS, DVD.** Caren Kaye, Matt Lattanzi, Kevin McCarthy, Clark Brandon, Bruce Bauer, Arlene Golonka, Crispin Glover, Shelley Taylor Morgan, Amber Denyse Austin, Francesca "Kitten" Natividad, Jewel Shepard, Marilyn Tokuda; ***D:*** George Bowers; ***W:*** Joe Roberts; ***C:*** Mac Ahlberg; ***M:*** Webster Lewis.

My Twentieth Century 🦴🦴🦴 *Az en XX. Szazadom* 1990 This quirky gem of a movie is a charming, sentimental journey through the early 1900s. Twins Dora and Lili are separated in early childhood. They reunite as grown, very different women on the Orient Express after they both (unknowingly) have sex with the same man. Dora is a sex kitten, while Lili is a radical equipped with explosives. When the two sisters come together, they both lose their destructive, dependent selves (Dora on men, Lili on politics) and become independent women. Lots of sidelights and subplots that are sure to amuse the viewer. In Hungarian with English subtitles. **104m/B VHS.** *HU CA* Dortha Segda, Oleg (Yankovsky) Jankowsky, Peter Andorai, Gabor Mate, Paulus Manker, Laszlo Vidovszky; ***D:*** Ildiko Enyedi; ***W:*** Ildiko Enyedi.

My Uncle Silas 🦴🦴🦴 2001 Finney certainly has fun in the title role as an aging reprobate (with an eye for the ladies) who teaches his 10-year-old grandnephew Edward (Prospero) how to enjoy life. Based on five short stories by H.E. Bates and set during a rural English summer in the early 1900s. **120m/C VHS.** *GB* Albert Finney, Charlotte Rampling, Joe Prospero, Annabelle Apsion; ***D:*** Philip Saville; ***C:*** John Kenway. **TV**

My Uncle: The Alien 🦴🦴½ 1996 **(PG)** Kelly, President Sullivan's teenaged daughter, travels to L.A. to visit a children's shelter at Christmas. When she finds out the shelter needs money to stay open, she eludes the Secret Service and hatches a plan to raise the funds. But she does have someone watching out for her—no, not a guardian angel, a guardian alien! **90m/C VHS.** Hailey Foster; ***D:*** Henri Charr.

My Universities 🦴🦴🦴 1940 In the final part of Donskoi's trilogy on Maxim Gorky, Gorky is a young man at university who is introduced to radical politics by several liberal intellectuals. He makes his first attempts at writing and joins the revolution as he leaves his painful past behind. In Russian with English subtitles. Preceded by "My Childhood" and "My Apprenticeship." **100m/C VHS.** *RU* ***D:*** Mark Donskoi.

My Very Best Friend 🦴🦴 1996 **(PG)** Former model Dana Griffin (Smith) likes the good life and seems to have latch onto the prize when a multi-millionaire (Mason) proposes marriage. But Dana has a nasty habit of lying and when things fall, she turns to her oldest friend, Barbara (Eikenberry), to help rebuild her life. But instead of rebuilding her own life, Dana decides she'd just rather take over Barbara's. TV movie. **92m/C VHS.** Jaclyn Smith, Jill Eikenberry, Tom Mason, Tom Irwin, Mary Kay Place, Garwin Sanford, Robert Lewis, Beverley Elliott; ***D:*** Joyce Chopra; ***W:*** John Robert Bensink; ***C:*** James Glennon; ***M:*** Patrick Williams. **TV**

My Wicked, Wicked Ways 🦴🦴½ 1984 Cleverly cast, low-budget drama based on the autobiography of Errol Flynn. **95m/C VHS.** Duncan Regehr, Barbara Hershey, Hal Linden, Darren McGavin; ***D:*** Don Taylor. **TV**

My Wonderful Life 🦴 1990 **(R)** Softcore gristle about a beautiful tramp climbing the social ladder via the boudoir. **107m/C VHS.** *IT* Pierre Cosso, Jean Rochefort, Massimo Venturiello, Carol Alt, Elliott Gould; ***D:*** Carlo Vanzina.

Myra Breckinridge woof! 1970 **(R)** A tasteless version of the Gore Vidal novel. An alleged satire of a film critic who undergoes a sex change operation and then plots the destruction of the American male movie star stereotype. Created an outcry from all sides, and hung out to dry by studio where it's reportedly still blowing in the wind. **94m/C VHS.** Mae West, John Huston, Raquel Welch, Rex Reed, Farrah Fawcett, Jim Backus, John Carradine, Andy Devine, Tom Selleck; ***D:*** Michael Sarne; ***W:*** Michael Sarne, David Giler; ***C:*** Richard Moore; ***M:*** Lionel Newman.

The Mysterians 🦴🦴½ *Earth Defense Forces; Chikyu Boelgun* 1958 A race of gigantic scientific intellects from a doomed planet attempts to conquer Earth. They want to rebuild their race by reproducing with earth women. Earth fights back. From the director of "Godzilla." Dubbed in English from Japanese. **85m/C VHS.** *JP* Kenji Sahara, Yumi Shirakawa, Takashi Shimura; ***D:*** Inoshiro Honda.

Mysteries 🦴½ **1984** A rich tourist becomes obsessed by a beautiful local girl. As his obsession grows, his behavior becomes stranger. Interesting and well-acted. The film is an adaptation of the famous love story by Nobel-laureate Knut Hamsun. Suffers from poor dubbing. **100m/C VHS.** Rutger Hauer, Sylvia Kristel, David Rappaport, Rita Tushingham; ***D:*** Paul de Lussanet.

Mysterious Desperado 🦴½ **1949** Young man, about to inherit a large estate, is framed on a murder charge by land grabbers. **61m/B VHS.** Tim Holt, Richard Martin.

Mysterious Doctor Satan 🦴🦴 **1940** A mad satanic scientist builds an army of mechanical robots to rob and terrorize the nation. In 15 episodes. **250m/B VHS.** Eduardo Ciannelli, Robert Wilcox, Ella Neal; ***D:*** William Witney.

Mysterious Island 🦴🦴🦴½ **1961** Exhilirating sci-fi classic adapted from Jules Verne's novel about escaping Civil War soldiers who go up in Verne balloon and come down on a Pacific island populated by giant animals. They also encounter two shipwrecked English ladies, pirates, and Captain Nemo (and his sub). Top-rate special effects by master Ray Harryhausen. **101m/C VHS.** *GB* Michael Craig, Joan Greenwood, Michael Callan, Gary Merrill, Herbert Lom, Beth Rogan, Percy Herbert, Dan Jackson, Nigel Green; ***D:*** Cy Endfield; ***W:*** John Prebble, Daniel Ullman, Crane Wilbur; ***C:*** Wilkie Cooper; ***M:*** Bernard Herrmann.

Mysterious Island of Beautiful Women 🦴 **1979** A male sextet is stranded on a South Sea island, where they must endure the trials of an angry tribe of conveniently bikini-clad women. **100m/C VHS.** Jamie Lyn Bauer, Jayne Kennedy, Kathryn Davis, Deborah Shelton, Susie Coelho, Peter Lawford, Steven Keats, Clint Walker; ***D:*** Joseph Pevney.

Mysterious Jane 🦴 **198?** Amid soft-focus nudity, a husband and his lover conspire to institutionalize his wife. **90m/C VHS.** Amber Lee, Sandy Carey.

The Mysterious Lady 🦴🦴½ **1928** Pre-Ninotchka Garbo plays Russian spy who betrays her mother country because she does not want to be alone. **99m/B VHS.** Greta Garbo, Conrad Nagel, Gustav von Seyffertitz, Richard Alexander, Albert Pollet, Edward Connelly; ***C:*** William H. Daniels.

The Mysterious Magician 🦴🦴½ **1965** Entertaining suspense story of the mad murderer known as "The Wizard," who was thought by Scotland Yard to be dead, but the current murderwave in London suggests otherwise. Based on an Edgar Wallace story. **95m/C VHS.** *GE* Joachim Fuchsberger, Eddi Arent, Sophie Hardy, Karl John, Heinz Drache; ***D:*** Alfred Vohrer.

Mysterious Mr. Wong 🦴½ **1935** The Thirteen Coins of Confucius put San Francisco's Chinatown in a state of terror until Mr. Wong arrives. **56m/B VHS, DVD.** Bela Lugosi, Arline Judge, Wallace Ford, Fred Warren, Lotus Long; ***D:*** William Nigh; ***W:*** Nina Howatt; ***C:*** Harry Neumann.

The Mysterious Rider 🦴🦴½ *The Fighting Phantom* **1933** A cowboy tries to prevent unscrupulous homesteaders from cheating farmers out of their land. **59m/B VHS.** Kent Taylor, Lona Andre, Gail Patrick, Warren Hymer, Berton Churchill; ***D:*** Fred Allen.

The Mysterious Rider 🦴½ *Mark of the Avenger* **1938** A man framed for murder must help innocent homesteaders from being cheated out of their land. **75m/B VHS.** Douglass Dumbrille, Sidney Toler, Russell Hayden, Charlotte Field; ***D:*** Lesley Selander.

The Mysterious Rider 🦴🦴 **1942** Routine oater has Crabbe and St. John helping a couple of kids protect their inheritance. **56m/B VHS.** Buster Crabbe, Al "Fuzzy" St. John, Caroline Burke, John Merton, Kermit Maynard, Jack Ingram, Charles "Slim" Whitaker; ***D:*** Sam Newfield.

The Mysterious Stranger 🦴🦴 **1982** Printer's apprentice is given to bouts of daydreaming about a magic castle in Austria. Based on Twain tale. **89m/C VHS.** Chris Makepeace, Lance Kerwin, Fred Gwynne; ***D:*** Peter H. Hunt.

Mysterious Two 🦴🦴½ **1982** Two aliens visit the Earth in an effort to enlist converts to travel the universe with them. **100m/C VHS.** John Forsythe, Priscilla Pointer, Noah Beery Jr., Vic Tayback, James Stephens, Karen Werner, Robert Englund, Robert Pine; ***D:*** Gary Sherman.

Mystery, Alaska 🦴🦴½ **1999 (R)** Amiable sports comedy that plays like a TV movie (with a little more sex and language). Journalist and ex-local Charles Danner (Azaria) does a Sports Illustrated feature on his hometown's weekly cuthtroat hockey game. Danner's story draws NHL interest and, for a publicity stunt, the New York Rangers fly in for an exhibition game. This leads to hurt feelings since aging team captain (and local sheriff) John Biebe (Crowe) is asked to step aside for young phenom Stevie Weeks (Northcott). Expect cliches. **118m/C VHS, DVD, Wide.** Russell Crowe, Hank Azaria, Mary McCormack, Burt Reynolds, Ron Eldard, Lolita (David) Davidovich, Colm Meaney, Maury Chaykin, Ryan Northcott, Scott Grimes, Judith Ivey, Rachel Wilson, Mike Myers; ***Cameos:*** Little Richard; ***D:*** Jay Roach; ***W:*** David E. Kelley, Sean O'Byrne; ***C:*** Peter Deming; ***M:*** Carter Burwell.

Mystery at Fire Island 🦴 **1981** A clever young girl and her cousin encounter some strange people as they try to find out why their fisherman friend mysteriously vanished. **52m/C VHS.** Frank Converse, Barbara Byrne, Beth Ehlers, Eric Gurry.

Mystery Date 🦴🦴 **1991 (PG-13)** A sort of teen version of "After Hours," in which a shy college guy gets a date with the girl of his dreams, only to be mistaken for a master criminal and pursued by gangsters, police and a crazed florist. Not terrible, but if you're old enough to drive you're probably too old to watch with amusement. **98m/C VHS.** Ethan Hawke, Teri Polo, Brian McNamara, Fisher Stevens, B.D. Wong; ***D:*** Jonathan Wacks; ***W:*** Terry Runte, Parker Bennett; ***M:*** John Du Prez.

Mystery in Swing 🦴🦴 **1940** An all-black mystery with music, about a trumpet player who has snake venom put on his mouthpiece. **66m/B VHS.** F.E. (Flourney) Miller, Monte Hawley, Marguerite Whitten, Tommie Moore, Ceepee Johnson; ***D:*** Arthur Dreifuss.

Mystery Island 🦴🦴½ **1981** Beautifully filmed underwater scenes in this children's film about four youths who discover a deserted island which they name Mystery Island, and a retired pirate who lives there. When the children find counterfeit money and the bad guys return for it, the old pirate's clever plans keep the kids safe. **75m/C VHS.** *AU* Jayson Duncan, Niklas Juhlin, Michael McGlinchey, Melissa Woodhams; ***D:*** Gene W. Scott; ***W:*** Clifford Green, Geoff Beak; ***C:*** Phil Pike.

Mystery Kids 🦴🦴½ **1999 (PG)** Preteens Herford and Baltes spend their summer snooping into the disappearance of high school girl Lakin in order to claim a reward. They first think her boyfriend killed her but then discover Lakin has just run away and is working as a singer in a local bar. So the kids decide to try and reconcile the troubled teen with her family. Innocuous family fare but the two would-be sleuths are good. **88m/C VHS, DVD.** Brighton Hertford, Jameson Baltes, Christine Lakin; ***D:*** Lynn Hamrick. **VIDEO**

Mystery Liner 🦴🦴½ *The Ghost of John Holling* **1934** Dead bodies are found aboard ocean liner and passengers are concerned about it. Slow-moving sea cruise. **62m/B VHS, DVD.** Noah Beery Sr., Astrid Allwyn, Cornelius Keefe, Gustav von Seyffertitz, Edwin Maxwell, Boothe Howard, George "Gabby" Hayes; ***D:*** William Nigh.

The Mystery Man 🦴🦴½ **1935** A Chicago reporter goes on a drinking binge and ends up in St. Louis. There he stumbles upon a mystery which may involve the paper for which he works. He teams up with a beautiful woman to try to crack the case. **65m/B VHS.** Robert Armstrong, Maxine Doyle, Henry Kolker, Leroy Mason, James Burke; ***D:*** Ray McCarey.

Mystery Man 🦴½ **1944** Below-average episode has rancher Hoppy being bothered by rustlers. Boyd solves things in the usual way, while Clyde provides the laughs. **58m/B VHS.** William Boyd, Andy Clyde, Jimmy Rogers, Don Costello, Francis McDonald, Forrest Taylor, Eleanor Stewart; ***D:*** George Archainbaud.

Mystery Mansion 🦴🦴 **1983 (PG)** Fortune in gold and a hundred-year-old mystery lead three children into an exciting treasure hunt. Family fare. **95m/C VHS.** Dallas McKennon, Greg Wynne, Jane Ferguson.

Mystery Men 🦴🦴½ **1999 (PG-13)** A cast of quirky comedy all-stars, including Garafalo, Stiller and Macy, help deflate the superhero genre by playing a team of bush league crimefighters. The superhero washouts use their dubious powers to save Champion City from party monster villain Casanova Frankenstein (Rush), who has kidnapped real superhero Captain Amazing (Kinnear). Great concept and dialogue are stretched a bit thin over the long running time. Based on the Dark Horse comic book. **120m/C VHS, DVD.** Ben Stiller, Hank Azaria, William H. Macy, Paul (Peewee Herman) Reubens, Claire Forlani, Wes Studi, Janeane Garofalo, Kel Mitchell, Geoffrey Rush, Lena Olin, Greg Kinnear, Tom Waits, Eddie Izzard, Ricky Jay, Louise Lasser; ***D:*** Kinka Usher; ***W:*** Neil Cuthbert; ***C:*** Stephen Burum; ***M:*** Stephen Warbeck.

Mystery Mountain 🦴½ **1934** Twelve episodes depict the villain known as the "Rattler" attempting to stop the construction of a railroad over Mystery Mountain. **156m/B VHS.** Ken Maynard, Gene Autry, Smiley Burnette; ***D:*** Otto Brower, B. Reeves Eason.

The Mystery of Alexina 🦴🦴½ *Mystere Alexina* **1986** True story of Herculine Adelaide Barbin, a 19th-century French hermaphrodite, who, after growing up a woman, fell in love with another woman and was actually revealed to be a man. Subtitled. **86m/C VHS.** *FR* Vuillemin, Valeri Stroh; ***D:*** Rene Feret; ***W:*** Jean Gruault.

The Mystery of Edwin Drood 🦴🦴½ **1935** Nicely creepy gothic atmosphere highlights this version of Charles Dickens' final novel, which was unfinished at the time of his death. English choirmaster and opium addict John Jasper (Rains) is visited by his nephew Edwin Drood (Manners), who's soon to enter into an arranged marriage with Rosa (Angel). Unbeknownst to anyone, Jasper has long desired Rosa for himself and kills his nephew in a jealous rage. Now that Drood's disappeared, will Jasper have Rosa to himself? **85m/B VHS.** Claude Rains, Heather Angel, Douglass Montgomery, Valerie Hobson, David Manners, Francis L. Sullivan, Ethel Griffies, E.E. Clive; ***D:*** Stuart Walker; ***W:*** John Lloyd Balderston, Gladys Unger; ***C:*** George Robinson; ***M:*** Edward Ward.

The Mystery of Edwin Drood 🦴🦴½ **1993** When Edwin Drood vanishes on Christmas Eve, his disappearance leads to a terrifying mystery that unfolds amidst the slums of Victorian England. Adapted from Charles Dickens' last novel, which was left unfinished at his death. **98m/C VHS.** *GB* Robert Powell, Michelle Evans, Jonathan Phillips, Finty Williams, Rupert Rainsford, Nanette Newman, Freddie Jones, Rosemary Leach, Ronald Fraser; ***D:*** Timothy Forder; ***W:*** Timothy Forder.

Mystery of Mr. Wong 🦴½ **1939** The largest star sapphire in the world, the "Eye of the Daughter of the Moon," is stolen from a museum in its home country of China. Mr. Wong becomes involved in trying to trace its trail and the perpetrator of the murders that follow in its wake. One in the series of detective films. **67m/B VHS.** Boris Karloff, Grant Withers, Dorothy Tree, Lotus Long; ***D:*** William Nigh.

The Mystery of Rampo 🦴🦴🦴 **1994 (R)** Visually dazzling fantasy that propels mystery writer Edogawa Rampo (Takenaka) into his own stories. Set just before WWII, Rampo is despondent when his latest novel (about a woman suffocating her husband in a trunk) is censored by the government and then amazed when a newspaper story reveals a similar crime. So Rampo decides to meet the widow Shizuko (Hada) and discovers she's a double for his fictional character. He then writes a sequel, again featuring Shizuko, and once again finds reality and fiction blending into the bizarre. Rampo was the pseudonym for renowned writer Hirai Taro, regarded as the Japanese Edgar Allan Poe. The film had its own complications when the version filmed by original director Rentaro Mayusumi was rejected by producer Okuyama, who then reshot much of the film himself. Japanese with subtitles. **96m/C VHS.** *JP* Naoto Takenaka, Michiko Hada, Masahiro Motoki, Teruyuki Kagawa, Mikijiro Hira; ***D:*** Kazuyoshi Okuyama; ***W:*** Kazuyoshi Okuyama, Yuhei Enoki; ***C:*** Yasushi Sasakibara; ***M:*** Akira Senju.

Mystery of the Hooded Horseman 🦴🦴 **1937** Tex finds himself pitted against a very strange adversary. **61m/B VHS.** Tex Ritter, Iris Meredith, Charles "Blackie" King, Joseph Girard, Lafe (Lafayette) McKee; ***D:*** Ray Taylor.

The Mystery of the Mary Celeste 🦴🦴 *The Phantom Ship; The Mystery of the Marie Celeste* **1937** Tale of terror based on the bizarre case of the "Marie Celeste," an American ship found adrift off the coast of England with her sails set but minus any of her crew on December 5, 1872. **64m/B VHS.** Bela Lugosi, Shirley Grey, Edmund Willard, Arthur Margetson.

Mystery of the Million Dollar Hockey Puck 🦴½ **198?** Sinister diamond smugglers learn a lesson on ice from a pair of orphan lads. Features the National Hockey League's Montreal Canadians in one of their few film appearances. **88m/C VHS.** Michael MacDonald, Angele Knight; ***D:*** Jean LaFleur, Peter Svatek.

Mystery of the Riverboat 🦴🦴½ **1944** Louisiana and the Mississippi River are the background for these 13 episodes of mystery and murder. **90m/B VHS.** Robert Lowery, Eddie Quillan, Lyle Talbot, Francis McDonald, Arthur Hohl; ***D:*** Ray Taylor, Lewis D. Collins.

Mystery of the Wax Museum 🦴🦴🦴 **1933** Rarely seen, vintage horror classic about a wax-dummy maker who, after a disfiguring fire, resorts to murder and installs the wax-covered bodies of his victims in his museum. Famous for its pioneering use of two-strip Technicolor. Remade in 1953 in 3-D as "House of Wax." **77m/C VHS.** Lionel Atwill, Fay Wray, Glenda Farrell, Frank McHugh, Allen Vincent, Holmes Herbert; ***D:*** Michael Curtiz; ***W:*** Carl Erickson, Don Mullaly; ***C:*** Ray Rennahan.

Mystery Plane 🦴½ **1939** An inventor devises a new bomb-dropping mechanism, and must evade secret agents on his way to deliver it to the government. **60m/B VHS.** John Trent, Marjorie Reynolds, Milburn Stone, Peter George Lynn, Polly Ann Young; ***D:*** George Waggner.

Mystery Ranch 🦴½ **1934** A cowboy finds himself in strange predicaments out on the range. **52m/B VHS.** George O'Brien, Charles Middleton, Cecilia Parker; ***D:*** David Howard.

Mystery Science Theater 3000: The Movie 🦴🦴½ **1996 (PG-13)** Mad scientist Dr. Clayton Forrester (Beaulieu) maroons Mike Nelson on the Satellite of Love, forces him to watch bad movies, and monitors his reactions. Mike and his robotic pals, Tom Servo and Crow T. Robot, save their sanity by wisecracking their way through the movies. Today's experiment is "This Island Earth," an uncharacteristically semi-respectable flick. As regular viewers know, the jokes and snide remarks come fast and in bunches. Not all of them work, but the ones that do will be remembered and repeated often. Audience participation is inevitable. Weekend theme-party status is virtually assured. **73m/C VHS, DVD, Wide.** Trace Beaulieu, James Mallon, Michael J. Nelson, Kevin Murphy, John Brady; ***D:*** James Mallon; ***W:*** Trace Beaulieu, James Mallon, Michael J. Nelson, Kevin Murphy, Mary Jo Pehl, Paul Chaplin, Bridget Jones; ***C:*** Jeff Stonehouse; ***M:*** Billy Barber.

Mystery Squadron 1933 Twelve chapters, 13 minutes each. Daredevil air action in flight against the masked pilots of the Black Ace. **240m/B VHS.** Bob Steele, Guinn "Big Boy" Williams, Lucille Browne, Jack Mulhall, J. Carrol Naish, Jack Mower; ***D:*** Colbert Clark.

Mystery Train 1989 (R) A run down hotel in Memphis is the scene for three vignettes concerning the visit of foreigners to the U.S. Themes of mythic Americana, Elvis, and life on the fringe pervade this hip and quirky film. The three vignettes all tie together in clever and funny overlaps. Waits fans should listen for his performance as a DJ. **110m/C VHS, DVD, Wide.** Masatoshi Nagase, Youki Kudoh, Screamin' Jay Hawkins, Cinque Lee, Joe Strummer, Nicoletta Braschi, Elizabeth Bracco, Steve Buscemi, Tom Noonan, Rockets Redglare, Rick Aviles, Rufus Thomas, Vondie Curtis-Hall; ***D:*** Jim Jarmusch; ***W:*** Jim Jarmusch; ***C:*** Robby Muller; ***M:*** John Lurie; ***V:*** Tom Waits.

Mystery Trooper *Trail of the Royal Mounted* 1932 Adventures in the great wilderness full of prospecting, greed, and Indians all being observed by the Royal Mounties. Ten chapters of the serial at 20 minutes each. **200m/B VHS.** Robert Frazer, Buzz Barton.

Mystic Circle Murder *Religious Racketeers* 1939 Reporter sets out to uncover phony mediums, particularly the Great La Gagge, whose fake apparitions are so convincing that it caused one of his clients to have a heart attack. Cheaply made, and it's obvious. Watch for a cameo by Harry Houdini's wife, who talks about life after death. Based on a story by director O'Connor. **69m/B VHS.** Betty Compson, Robert (Fisk) Fiske, Helene Le Berthon, Arthur Gardner; ***D:*** Frank O'Connor.

Mystic Pizza 1988 (R) Intelligent coming of age drama centers on two sisters and their best friend as they struggle with their hopes, loves, and family rivalries in the small town of Mystic, Connecticut. At times predictable, there are enough unexpected moments to keep interest high; definite appeal to young women, but others may not relate. The relatively unknown Roberts got most of the attention, but is the weakest of the three leads, so watch this one for the strong performances from Gish and Taylor. **101m/C VHS, DVD, Wide.** Annabeth Gish, Julia Roberts, Lili Taylor, Vincent D'Onofrio, William R. Moses, Adam Storke, Conchata Ferrell, Joanna Merlin, Matt Damon; ***D:*** Donald Petrie; ***W:*** Amy Holden Jones, Perry Howze, Alfred Uhry; ***C:*** Tim Suhrstedt; ***M:*** David McHugh. Ind. Spirit '89: First Feature.

The Myth of Fingerprints ½ 1997 (R) Four adult siblings and their various partners return to their New England home to spend Thanksgiving with their parents. As with most movie families of upper-middle class status, old resentments and issues abound. Dad (Scheider), a sullen, misanthropic near-recluse, isn't thrilled about the reunion. Younger son Warren (Wyle) hopes to reconcile with his high school sweetheart, a relationship mostly done in by his father's indescretion. Another brother can't commit. Older sister Mia (Moore) can't think of anything nice to say about anyone, and her tomboy sister Leigh (Holloman) does the sibling rivalry dance with her. Subdued and interesting, Freundlich's debut doesn't go for a grand conclusion or startling revelation. Depending on your taste for pat endings and easy answers, that could be it's greatest asset or a reason not to bother. Excellent performances by a great cast should have a bearing on the decision. **91m/C VHS, DVD, Wide.** Blythe Danner, Roy Scheider, Julianne Moore, Noah Wyle, Michael Vartan, Laurel Holloman, Hope Davis, Brian Kerwin, James LeGros; ***D:*** Bart Freundlich; ***W:*** Bart Freundlich; ***C:*** Stephen Kazmierski; ***M:*** David Bridie, John Phillips.

Nabonga *Gorilla; Jungle Woman* 1944 The daughter of an embezzler, whose plane crashes in the jungle, befriends a gorilla who protects her. Soon a young man comes looking for the embezzler's cash, meets the woman and the ape, and together they go on a wonderful journey. **72m/B VHS, DVD.** Buster Crabbe, Fifi d'Orsay, Barton MacLane, Julie London, Herbert Rawlinson; ***D:*** Sam Newfield.

Nadia ½ 1984 Entertaining account of the life of Nadia Comaneci, the Romanian gymnast who earned six perfect tens with her stunning performance at the 1976 Olympic Games. **100m/C VHS.** Talia Balsam, Jonathan Banks, Simone Blue, Johann Carlo, Carrie Snodgress; ***D:*** Alan Cooke. **TV**

Nadine ½ 1987 (PG) In Austin circa 1954, an almost divorced beautician witnesses a murder and goes undercover with her estranged husband to track down the murderer, before he finds her. Plenty of low-key humor. Well-paced fun; Basinger is terrific. **83m/C VHS.** Jeff Bridges, Kim Basinger, Rip Torn, Gwen Verdon, Glenne Headly, Jerry Stiller, Jay Patterson; ***D:*** Robert Benton; ***W:*** Robert Benton; ***C:*** Nestor Almendros; ***M:*** Howard Shore.

Nadja 1995 (R) Fresh, modern comic take on the vampire tale is about family ties and the power of home, with the required AIDS analogy and lesbian sex scenes. Tired of nightly blood-letting, the daughter of the now-deceased Count, Nadja (Lowensohn), lives in New York's East Village, hoping to change her life. She seduces and falls in love with Lucy (Craze), whose husband is the nephew of old family nemesis Van Helsing (Fonda, in a surprisingly comedic role). Manic Fonda Van Helsing sets out to save Lucy and steal the film. Meanwhile, Nadja finds her long lost twin brother (Harris, son of Richard) and Lucy discovers sex with Nadja is draining. Innovative camera work (vampire point-of-view scenes shot with a toy Pixelvision camera and blown up to 35mm for a moody, grainy look) and a great score keep "Nadja" very watchable despite some missteps in the plot. (Director Almereyda pioneered use of the Pixel-vision camera in "Another Girl, Another Planet.") Executive producer David Lynch contributes a cameo as a guard at the morgue where Nadja claims her father's body. **92m/B VHS, DVD, Wide.** Elina Lowensohn, Suzy Amis, Galaxy Craze, Martin Donovan, Peter Fonda, Karl Geary, Jared Harris; ***Cameos:*** David Lynch; ***D:*** Michael Almereyda; ***W:*** Michael Almereyda; ***C:*** Jim Denault; ***M:*** Simon Fisher Turner.

Nail Gun Massacre woof! 1986 A crazed killer with a penchant for nailing bodies to just about anything goes on a hammering spree. In horrific, vivid color. **90m/C VHS.** Rocky Patterson, Ron Queen, Beau Leland, Michelle Meyer; ***D:*** Bill Lesley.

Nails ½ 1992 (R) Harry "Nails" Niles (Hopper) is a tough, experienced cop whose partner has been killed by drug dealers. Harry doesn't take this well and decides to go on a violent search for revenge. Archer is wasted as Harry's estranged wife and Hopper can sleepwalk through this type of cliched wildman role. **96m/C VHS.** Dennis Hopper, Anne Archer, Tomas Milian, Cliff DeYoung; ***D:*** John Flynn. **CABLE**

Nairobi Affair 1988 (PG) Savage and Heston fight poachers and each other in Kenya, when the father has an affair with his son's ex-wife. Mediocre, derivative script, but beautiful scenery. **95m/C VHS.** Charlton Heston, John Savage, Maud Adams, John Rhys-Davies, Connie Booth; ***D:*** Marvin J. Chomsky. **TV**

Nais 1945 Vintage Pagnolian peasant drama. A hunchback sacrifices himself for the girl he loves. She escapes to another man's arms. Adapted from the Emile Zola novel "Nais Micoulin." In French with English subtitles. **105m/B VHS, 8mm.** *FR* Fernandel; ***D:*** Fernand Lauterier; ***W:*** Marcel Pagnol.

Naked *Mike Leigh's Naked* 1993 (R) Existential angst in a '90s London filled with Leigh's usual eccentrics. The unemployed Johnny (Thewlis) comes to London and bunks with former girlfriend Louise (Sharp). After seducing her flatmate Sophie (Cartlidge), Johnny leaves to wander the streets, exchanging philosophical, if foul-mouthed, dialogues with a variety of odd characters. Thewlis gives an explosive performance as the calculatingly brutal and desolate Johnny. Chaotic shifts in mood from comedy to violence to love prove a challenge and the pervasive abuse of all the women characters is very disturbing. Critically acclaimed; see it as a reflection on the mess of modern England. **131m/C VHS.** *GB* David Thewlis, Lesley Sharp, Katrin Cartlidge, Greg Cruttwell, Claire Skinner, Peter Wight, Ewen Bremner, Susan Vidler, Deborah MacLaren, Gina McKee; ***D:*** Mike Leigh; ***W:*** Mike Leigh; ***C:*** Dick Pope; ***M:*** Andrew Dickson. Cannes '93: Actor (Thewlis), Director (Leigh); N.Y. Film Critics '93: Actor (Thewlis); Natl. Soc. Film Critics '93: Actor (Thewlis).

The Naked and the Dead ½ 1958 Sanitized adaptation of Norman Mailer's bestselling novel about army life in the Pacific during WWII. Resentment between officers and enlisted men proves to be almost as dangerous as the Japanese. Uneven acting and cliched characterizations make this an average outing. Don't expect to hear the profane language that sensationalized the book, because most of it was edited out of the screenplay. **131m/C VHS.** Aldo Ray, Cliff Robertson, Joey Bishop, Raymond Massey, Lili St. Cyr, James Best; ***D:*** Raoul Walsh; ***C:*** Joseph LaShelle.

The Naked Angels 1969 (R) Rape, mayhem, beatings, and road-hogging streetbikes highlight this biker film, acted, in part, by actual bikers, and in part by others who were actually (almost) actors. The gang war rages from Los Angeles to Las Vegas. Roger Corman was the executive producer. **83m/C VHS.** Michael Greene, Richard Rust, Felicia Guy; ***D:*** Bruce (B.D.) Clark; ***W:*** Bruce (B.D.) Clark.

Naked Cage woof! 1986 (R) Brutal women's prison film that is borderline softcore, about an innocent country woman, a horseriding fanatic, who is framed for a robbery and sent to the slammer. There, she contends with lesbian wardens and inmates. Disgusting. **97m/C VHS.** Shari Shattuck, Angel Tompkins, Lucinda Crosby, Christina Whitaker; ***D:*** Paul Nicholas.

The Naked City ½ 1948 Film noir classic makes spectacular use of its NYC locations. Beautiful playgirl is murdered and police detectives Fitzgerald and Taylor are left without clues. They spend most of their time running down weak leads and interviewing various suspects and witnesses. When they finally get a break, it leads to playboy Duff. Spectacular ending on the Brooklyn Bridge between cops and killer. Producer Hellinger provided the hard-boiled narration, patterned after the tabloid newspaper stories he once wrote. Served as the impetus for the TV show of the same name, where Hellinger's film postscript also became the show's noted tagline: "There are eight million stories in the naked city, this has been one of them." **96m/B VHS, DVD.** Barry Fitzgerald, Don Taylor, Howard Duff, Ted de Corsia, Dorothy Hart; ***D:*** Jules Dassin; ***W:*** Albert (John B. Sherry) Maltz; ***C:*** William H. Daniels; ***M:*** Miklos Rozsa; ***Nar:*** Mark Hellinger. Oscars '48: B&W Cinematog., Film Editing.

Naked City: A Killer Christmas ½ 1998 Cops Muldoon (Glenn) and Halloran (Vance) are on the case of a serial killer who's sent New York into a panic, thanks to the media efforts of an ambitious newscaster. **92m/C VHS.** Scott Glenn, Courtney B. Vance, Laura Leighton, Barbara Williams, Nigel Bennett, Lisa Vidal, Al Waxman, Jason Blicker, Richard McMillan; ***D:*** Peter Bogdanovich; ***W:*** Christopher Trumbo, Jeff Freilich; ***C:*** James Gardner; ***M:*** Hummie Mann. **CABLE**

Naked City: Justice with a Bullet 1998 Undercover NYC detectives Scott Muldoon (Glenn) and James Halloran (Vance) come to the rescue of naive tourists Sarah (Erbe) and Merri (Tunney) who unwittingly become involved in a drug dealer's murder. And then Halloran has to deal with a boyhood pal from the 'hood who isn't the friend he seems. Based on the 1948 film "The Naked City." **107m/C VHS.** Scott Glenn, Courtney B. Vance, Giancarlo Esposito, Robin Tunney, Kathryn Erbe, Eli Wallach, Tony Bill, Sebastien Roche, Barbara Williams; ***D:*** Jeff Freilich; ***W:*** Jeff Freilich; ***C:*** Miroslaw Baszak; ***M:*** Ashley Irwin. **CABLE**

The Naked Civil Servant ½ 1975 Remarkable film, based on the life of flamboyant homosexual Quentin Crisp, who came out of the closet in his native England, long before his lifestyle would be tolerated by Britains. For mature audiences. **80m/C VHS.** John Hurt; ***D:*** Jack Gold; ***M:*** Carl Davis.

The Naked Country ½ 1985 (R) In the untamed frontier of Australia rancher bigoted Lance Dillion and his sensual wife Mary are determined to make their way. But when Lance finds out that the neglected Mary is fooling around with a local cop, he goes on a killing spree on land sacred to the Aborigines. Plodding plot. **90m/C VHS.** *AU* John Stanton, Rebecca Gilling, Ivar Kants; ***D:*** Tim Burstall; ***C:*** David Eggby; ***M:*** Bruce Smeaton.

The Naked Edge 1961 Cooper stars as a middle-aged businessman whose wife suspects him of murder after she begins snooping into his business affairs. Cooper's last film and far from his best. Poor direction and holes in the screenplay divert from what could have been a tight thriller. **99m/C VHS.** *GB* Gary Cooper, Deborah Kerr, Eric Portman, Diane Cilento, Hermione Gingold, Peter Cushing, Michael Wilding, Ronald Howard; ***D:*** Michael Anderson Sr.; ***W:*** Joseph Stefano.

The Naked Face 1984 (R) A psychiatrist tries to find out why his patients are being killed. He gets no help from police, who suspect he is the murderer. A dull affair featuring unusual casting of Moore, while Steiger's suspicious police captain character provides spark. From the novel by Sidney Sheldon. **105m/C VHS.** Roger Moore, Rod Steiger, Elliott Gould, Art Carney, Anne Archer, David Hedison; ***D:*** Bryan Forbes.

The Naked Flame woof! 1968 (R) O'Keefe plays an investigator in a strange town inhabited by weird, religious fanatics. After he arrives, the womenfolk shed their clothes in this pitiful, pathetic hilarity. **90m/C VHS.** *CA* Dennis O'Keefe, Kasey Rogers, Al Ruscio, Linda Bennett, Tracey Roberts, Barton Heyman, Robert Howay; ***D:*** Larry Matanski; ***W:*** Al Everett Dennis; ***C:*** Paul Ivano.

The Naked Gun: From the Files of Police Squad 1988 (PG-13) More hysterical satire from the creators of "Airplane!" The short-lived TV cop spoof "Police Squad" moves to the big screen and has Lt. Drebin uncover a plot to assassinate Queen Elizabeth while she is visiting Los Angeles. Nearly nonstop gags and pratfalls provide lots of laughs. Nielsen is perfect as Drebin and the supporting cast is strong; cameos abound. **85m/C VHS, DVD, 8mm, Wide.** Leslie Nielsen, Ricardo Montalban, Priscilla Presley, George Kennedy, O.J. Simpson, Nancy Marchand, John Houseman; ***Cameos:*** Weird Al Yankovic, Reggie Jackson, Dr. Joyce Brothers; ***D:*** David Zucker; ***W:*** Jerry Zucker, Jim Abrahams, Pat Proft, David Zucker; ***M:*** Ira Newborn.

Naked Gun 33 1/3: The Final Insult 1994 (PG-13) Ever dumb, crass, and crude, Lt. Drebin returns to the force from retirement to lead an investigation into terrorist activities in Hollywood. Lots of current events jokes—dated as soon as they hit the screen. Sure to satisfy genre fans with a taste for bad puns. Watch for the cameos, especially at the "Oscars." **90m/C VHS, DVD, Wide.** Leslie Nielsen, Priscilla Presley, O.J. Simpson, Fred Ward, George Kennedy, Gary Cooper, Kathleen Freeman, Raquel Welch; ***Cameos:*** Pia Zadora, James Earl Jones, Weird Al Yankovic, Ann B. Davis; ***D:*** Peter Segal; ***W:*** Robert Locash, David Zucker, Pat Proft; ***M:*** Ira Newborn. Golden Raspberries '94: Worst Support. Actor (Simpson), Worst New Star (Smith).

Naked Gun 2 1/2: The Smell of Fear ½ 1991 (PG-13) Lt. Drebin returns to rescue the world from a faulty energy policy devised by the White House and oil-lords. A notch down from the previous entry but still hilarious cop parody. Nielsen has this character down to a tee, and there's a laugh every minute. **85m/C VHS, DVD, 8mm, Wide.** Leslie Nielsen, Priscilla Presley, George Kennedy, O.J. Simpson, Robert Goulet, Richard Griffiths, Jacqueline Brookes, Lloyd Bochner, Tim O'Connor, Peter Mark Richman; ***Cameos:*** Mel Torme, Eva Gabor, Weird Al Yankovic; ***D:*** David Zucker; ***W:*** David Zucker, Pat Proft; ***M:*** Ira Newborn.

Naked Hills 🦴½ **1956** Meandering tale about a man (Wayne) who, suffering from gold fever, searches for 40 years in 19th Century California and ends up out of luck, losing his wife and family. **72m/C VHS.** David Wayne, Keenan Wynn, James Barton, Marcia Henderson, Jim Backus, Denver Pyle, Myrna Dell, Frank Fenton, Fuzzy Knight; ***D:*** Josef Shaftel; ***W:*** Josef Shaftel.

Naked in New York 🦴🦴½ **1993 (R)** Aspiring New York playwright Jake Briggs (Stoltz) and his girlfriend Joanne (Parker), an aspiring photographer, find their relationship in jeopardy when their respective careers start to take off. Offspring from the "Annie Hall" school of neurotic romance examines a number of issues, including ambition, commitment, and the societal dynamics of theatre and art. Celebrity appearances abound, including Styron as himself and Goldberg as a tragedy mask on a wall. Directorial debut of Scorsese protege Algrant is uneven but charming. Parker is particularly strong, and Turner's a riot as a sexpot soap star on the prowl for Jake. **89m/C VHS.** Eric Stoltz, Mary-Louise Parker, Ralph Macchio, Jill Clayburgh, Tony Curtis, Kathleen Turner, Timothy Dalton, Lynne Thigpen, Roscoe Lee Browne; ***Cameos:*** Whoopi Goldberg, William Styron, Eric Bogosian, Quentin Crisp; ***D:*** Dan Algrant; ***W:*** Dan Algrant, John Warren; ***M:*** Angelo Badalamenti; ***V:*** David Johansen.

Naked in the Night 🦴 **1958** Cheap German exploitation film about the dangers of promiscuous women. Dubbed in English. **?m/C VHS.** *GE* Eva Bartok, Alexander Kerst.

Naked in the Sun 🦴🦴 **1957** The true story of events leading to the war between the Osceola and Seminole Indians and a slave trader. Somewhat slow. **95m/C VHS.** James Craig, Lita Milan, Barton MacLane, Tony Hunter; ***D:*** R. John Hugh.

Naked Is Better 🦴 **1973** A couple of buffoons pose as hospital workers so they can play doctor with a hospitalized actress. **93m/C VHS.** Alberto Olmedo, Jorge Porcel, Jorge Barreiro, Maria Casan.

Naked Jungle 🦴🦴🦴 **1954** Suspenseful, well-done jungle adventure of a plantation owner (Heston) in South America and his North American mail-order bride (Parker), who do battle with a deadly, miles-long siege of red army ants. Realistic and worth watching. Produced by George Pal, shot by Ernest Laszlo and based on the story "Leiningen vs. the Ants" by Carl Stephenson. **95m/C VHS.** Charlton Heston, Eleanor Parker, Abraham Sofaer, William Conrad; ***D:*** Byron Haskin; ***W:*** Philip Yordan; ***C:*** Ernest Laszlo.

Naked Killer 🦴 *Chiklo Gouyeung* **1992** Kitty (Ching) turns to a female assassin to learn the art of killing so that she may avenge her father's death. When her teacher is herself unceremoniously murdered, Kitty and her policeman boyfriend (Yam) have two scores to settle. Sex and violence. Subtitled in English. **86m/C VHS, DVD, Wide.** *HK* Chingmy Yau, Simon Yam, Carrie Ng, Kelly Yao, Svenvara Madoka; ***D:*** Clarence Fok Yiu Leung; ***W:*** Jing Wong; ***C:*** Peter Pau, William Yim; ***M:*** Lowell Lo.

Naked Kiss 🦴🦴½ *The Iron Kiss* **1964** Fuller's most savage, hysterical film noir. A brutalized prostitute escapes her pimp and tries to enter respectable small-town society. She finds even more perversion and sickness there. **92m/B VHS, DVD, Wide.** Constance Towers, Anthony Eisley, Michael Dante, Virginia Grey, Patsy Kelly, Betty Bronson, Edy Williams, Marie Devereux, Karen Conrad, Linda Francis, Barbara Perry, Walter Matthews, Betty Robinson; ***D:*** Samuel Fuller; ***W:*** Samuel Fuller; ***C:*** Stanley Cortez; ***M:*** Paul Dunlap.

Naked Lie 🦴🦴 **1989** A District Attorney and a judge engage in an ultra-steamy affair and inevitably clash when she is assigned as a prosecutor on the politically explosive case over which he is presiding. **89m/C VHS.** Victoria Principal, James Farentino, Glenn Withrow, William Lucking, Dakin Matthews; ***D:*** Richard A. Colla; ***M:*** Robert Alcivar.

Naked Lies 🦴🦴 **1998 (R)** FBI agent Cara Landry (Tweed) gets transferred to treasury after a drug bust goes bad and is assigned to work an undercover operation that reunites Cara with ex-lover Mitch Kendall (Baker). Kendall has been trying to bust international counterfeiter Damian Medina (Allende) and sends Cara in to work one of Medina's casinos. But Cara finds herself drawn to the bad guy, putting both her career and her life in jeopardy. **93m/C VHS.** Shannon Tweed, Jay Baker, Fernando Allende, Steven Bauer, Hugo Stiglitz; ***D:*** Ralph Portillo. **VIDEO**

Naked Lunch 🦴🦴🦴 **1991 (R)** Whacked-out movie based on William S. Burroughs's autobiographical account of drug abuse, homosexuality, violence, and weirdness set in the drug-inspired land called Interzone. Hallucinogenic images are carried to the extreme: typewriters metamorphose into beetles, bloblike creatures with sex organs scurry about, and characters mainline insecticide. Some of the characters are clearly based on writers of the Beat generation, including Jane and Paul Bowles, Allen Ginsberg, and Jack Kerouac. **117m/C VHS.** *CA GB* Peter Weller, Judy Davis, Ian Holm, Julian Sands, Roy Scheider, Monique Mercure, Nicholas (Nick) Campbell, Michael Zelniker; Robert A. Silverman, Joseph Scorsiani; ***D:*** David Cronenberg; ***W:*** David Cronenberg; ***C:*** Peter Suschitzky; ***M:*** Howard Shore. Genie '92: Adapt. Screenplay, Art Dir./Set Dec., Cinematog., Director (Cronenberg), Film, Sound, Support. Actress (Mercure); N.Y. Film Critics '91: Screenplay, Support. Actress (Davis); Natl. Soc. Film Critics '91: Director (Cronenberg), Screenplay.

The Naked Maja 🦴🦴 **1959** Elaborate, yet dull drama about the tumultous romance between a Spanish duchess and the legendary painter Francisco Goya. Even the gorgeous costumes and spectacular sets can't overcome the weak script and poor direction that plague the film. Based on a story by Oscar Saul and Talbot Jennings. **111m/C VHS.** Ava Gardner, Anthony (Tony) Franciosa, Amedeo Nazzari, Gino Cervi, Lea Padovani, Massimo Serato, Carlo Rizzo, Renzo Cesana; ***D:*** Henry Koster, Mario Russo; ***W:*** Norman Corwin, Giorgio Prosperi.

The Naked Man 🦴🦴 **1998 (R)** When a pharmaceutical conglomerate muscles into his small town, chiropractor Rapaport decides to take action to save the livelihood of his family's drugstore—by becoming a professional wrestler. **98m/C VHS.** Michael Rapaport, Michael Jeter, Rachael Leigh Cook, Joe Grifasi, John Slattery; ***D:*** J. Todd Anderson; ***W:*** J. Todd Anderson, Ethan Coen.

Naked Massacre 🦴 **198?** A maniac kills nurses, leaving no clues for the police to follow. **90m/C VHS.** Matthieu Carriere, Carol Laurie; ***D:*** Denis Heroux.

Naked Obsession 🦴½ **1991 (R)** A city councilman running for mayor is mugged in one of the seedier parts of the city. He's found by a homeless man who takes him to a kinky nightclub where the councilman is promptly seduced by a topless bar hostess with secrets of her own. Also available in an unrated version. **93m/C VHS.** William Katt, Maria Ford, Rick Dean; ***D:*** Dan Golden.

Naked Paradise **1978 (R)** A young woman moves in with her mother and step-sister and finds difficulty in adjusting. **86m/C VHS.** Laura Gemser, Annie Belle.

The Naked Prey 🦴🦴🦴 **1966** Unnerving African adventure which contains some unforgettably brutal scenes. A safari guide (Wilde), leading a hunting party, must watch as an indigenous tribe murders all his companions, and according to their customs, allows him to be set free, sans clothes or weapons, to be hunted by the best of the tribe. **96m/C VHS.** Cornel Wilde, Gertrude Van Der Berger, Ken Gampu; ***D:*** Cornel Wilde.

Naked Souls 🦴 **1995 (R)** Artist Brit Clark (Anderson) must save scientist fiance Edward (Krause) from the evil experiments of murderous scientist Longstreet (Warner). Like you'll care as long as the Anderson bod is on display. **90m/C VHS.** Michael (Mike) Papajohn, Pamela Anderson, Brian Krause, Clayton Rohner, Justina Vail, David Warner; ***Cameos:*** Dean Stockwell; ***D:*** Lyndon Chubbuck; ***W:*** Frank Dietz; ***C:*** Eric Goldstein; ***M:*** Nigel Holton.

The Naked Spur 🦴🦴🦴½ **1953** A compulsive bounty hunter tracks down a vicious outlaw and his beautiful girlfriend. An exciting film from the Mann-Stewart team and considered one of their best, infusing the traditional western with psychological confusion. Wonderful use of Rockies locations. **93m/C VHS.** James Stewart, Robert Ryan, Janet Leigh, Millard Mitchell; ***D:*** Anthony Mann; ***C:*** William Mellor. Natl. Film Reg. '97.

The Naked Sword of Zorro 🦴 **1969** Deadly Don Luis taxes the town by day and violates the women by night, but Zorro takes a stand and saves the town. When he's not dressed as Zorro, he is Don Diego, an inept fool, but when he puts that suit on, look out. The ladies can't keep their hands off of him. There are more lusty females than villains, but there's still lots of swordplay and action. **94m/C VHS.**

Naked Tango 🦴½ **1991 (R)** A lurid recreation of the Argentinian underworld in 1924. Stephanie is a bored wife with an older husband who, while traveling with her husband on a cruise ship, pretends to fall overboard in order to establish a new identity. The problem is she becomes the supposed mail-order bride of a young man who promptly sells her into white slavery. One of her customers is a charismatic killer named Cholo who isn't interested in Stephanie for sex, he just wants to dance the tango with her. This is meant to be taken seriously but is one of the many pretensions, erotic and otherwise, that hamper the film. **90m/C VHS.** Mathilda May, Vincent D'Onofrio, Esai Morales, Fernando Rey; ***D:*** Leonard Schrader; ***W:*** Leonard Schrader; ***M:*** Thomas Newman.

The Naked Truth 🦴🦴½ *Your Past is Showing* **1958** A greedy publisher tries to get rich quick by publishing a scandal magazine about the "lurid" lives of prominent citizens. Well-drawn characters in an appealing offbeat comedy. **92m/C VHS, DVD.** *GB* Peter Sellers, Terry-Thomas, Shirley Eaton, Dennis Price; ***D:*** Mario Zampi.

Naked Vengeance woof! *Satin Vengeance* **1985 (R)** A woman's husband is murdered, she is beaten and raped, and she becomes a vengeful, vicious killing machine. Gratuitous violence, distasteful to the max. **97m/C VHS.** Deborah Tranelli, Kaz Garas, Bill McLaughlin; ***D:*** Cirio H. Santiago.

Naked Venus 🦴½ **1958** Ulmer's last film is a slow-paced tale about an American artist, married to a model who poses in the nude and belongs to a nudist camp, whose wealthy mother tries to tear the marriage apart. Discrimination and intolerance of nudist camps is explored. **80m/B VHS.** Patricia Conelle; ***D:*** Edgar G. Ulmer.

Naked Wishes 🦴🦴 **2000** Sex therapist Taj inherits a trunk from his uncle that contains only a dusty old bottle. When he cleans it up, very sexy genie Samathia is released and she lets Taj knows that they were lovers in a previous life and she's ready to resume their affair, besides granting his every wish. Taj, silly guy, wavers because he's engaged but then Samthia disturbs his therapy sessions by having his patients act out their deepest sexual fantasies. **99m/C VHS.** Jennifer Marks, Jeff Kueppers, Chanda Marie, Lance Moseley; ***D:*** Mike Sedan. **VIDEO**

The Naked Witch 🦴 **1964** College students researching witchcraft dig up the grave of a long-dead witch. She comes back to life to take revenge on the descendants of the villagers who killed her. Nude shots feature a finger over the camera lens to cover up the witch's, uh, vital organs. **60m/C VHS.** Jack Herman, Libby Hall, Robert Short, Jo Maryman, Denis Adams, Charles West, Marilyn Pope; ***D:*** Larry Buchanan, Claude Alexander; ***W:*** Larry Buchanan, Claude Alexander.

Naked Youth woof! *Wild Youth* **1959** Seedy drive-in cheapie about two punks breaking out of juvenile prison and heading south of the border on a trail filled with crime, drugs, and loose women. **80m/B VHS.** Robert Hutton, John Goddard, Carol Ohmart, Jan Brooks, Robert Arthur, Steve Rowland, Clancy Cooper; ***D:*** John F. Schreyer.

Nam Angels 🦴 **1988 (R)** Hell's Angels enter Southeast Asia and rescue POWs. **91m/C VHS.** *PH US* Brad Johnson, Vernon Wells, Kevin Duffis, Fred Bailey, Archie Adamos, Rick Dean, Jeff Griffith, Eric Hahn, Ken Metcalfe, Tonichi Fructuoso, Leah Navarro, Ruben Ramos; ***D:*** Cirio H. Santiago; ***C:*** Ricardo Remias, Chris Squires; ***M:*** Jaime Fabregas.

A Name for Evil 🦴🦴 **1970 (R)** Having grown tired of city living, a couple moves to an old family estate out in the country near the Great Lakes. Strange sounds in the night are the first signs of the terror to come. **74m/C VHS.** Robert Culp, Samantha Eggar, Sheila Sullivan, Mike Lane; ***D:*** Bernard Girard.

The Name of the Rose 🦴🦴½ **1986 (R)** An exhaustive, off-center adaptation of the bestselling Umberto Eco novel about violent murders in a 14th-century Italian abbey. An English monk struggles against religious fervor in his quest to uncover the truth. **128m/C VHS.** *IT GE FR* Sean Connery, F. Murray Abraham, Christian Slater, Ron Perlman, William Hickey, Feodor Chaliapin Jr., Elya Baskin, Michael (Michel) Lonsdale; ***D:*** Jean-Jacques Annaud; ***W:*** Andrew Birkin, Gerard Brach, Howard Franklin; ***C:*** Tonino Delli Colli; ***M:*** James Horner. British Acad. '87: Actor (Connery); Cesar '87: Foreign Film.

Namu, the Killer Whale 🦴🦴½ **1966** Based on the true story of a marine biologist (Lansing) who gets the perfect opportunity to study killer whales when one is confined to a small cove. The local fisherman want to kill the creature because it feeds on the salmon they catch but they are persuaded against their baser instincts. Filmed on location in the San Juan Islands of Puget Sound. The real Namu lived at the Seattle Public Aquarium. **89m/C VHS.** Robert Lansing, John Anderson, Robin Mattson, Richard Erdman, Lee Meriwether, Joe Higgins; ***D:*** Laslo Benedek.

Nana 🦴🦴🦴 **1955** French version of Emile Zola's novel about an actress-prostitute who seduces the high society of Paris in the late 1880s, and suffers a heart-breaking downfall and death. Film has three remakes of the original 1926 version. **118m/C VHS.** *FR* Charles Boyer, Martine Carol.

Nana 🦴🦴½ **1982** A lavishly photographed, graphic adaptation of the Emile Zola novel about a Parisian whore who acquires power by seducing the richest and politically formidable men. Dubbed. **92m/C VHS.** *IT* Katya Berger, Jean-Pierre Aumont; ***D:*** Dan Wolman; ***W:*** Marc Behm; ***M:*** Ennio Morricone.

Nancy Drew, Reporter 🦴🦴 **1939** The young sleuth gets to play reporter after winning a newspaper contest. In no time at all, she's involved in a murder mystery. **68m/B VHS.** Bonita Granville, John Litel, Frankie Thomas Jr., Mary Lee, Sheila (Manors) Mannors, Betty Amann, Dick(ie) Jones, Olin Howlin, Charles Halton; ***D:*** William Clemens.

Nancy Goes to Rio 🦴🦴½ **1950** Actresses Powell and Sothern compete for the same part in a play and for the same man. Catch is, they're mother and daughter. Zany consequences ensue. Sothern's last film for MGM. ♫Time and Time Again; Shine On Harvest Moon; Cha Bomm Pa Pa; Yipsee-I-O; Magic is the Moonlight; Musetta's Waltz; Love is Like This; Nancy Goes to Rio. **99m/C VHS.** Ann Sothern, Jane Powell, Barry Sullivan, Carmen Miranda, Louis Calhern, Scotty Beckett, Hans Conried, Glenn Anders; ***D:*** Robert Z. Leonard; ***W:*** Sidney Sheldon.

The Nanny 🦴🦴½ **1965** Creepfest stars Davis as a seemingly proper nameless nanny who's been accused by her young charge Joey (Dix) of drowning his sister in the bathtub. But it's Joey who's sent away to a home for disturbed children and when he returns two years later (and just why is the nanny still around a childless home?) it's a battle of wills between the duo over who's responsible for some evil goings-on. Based on a novel by Evelyn Piper. **93m/B VHS.** *GB* Bette Davis, William Dix, Wendy Craig, Jill Bennett, James Villiers, Pamela Franklin, Jack Watling, Alfred Burke, Maurice Denham; *D:* Seth Holt; *W:* Jimmy Sangster; *C:* Henry Waxman; *M:* Richard Rodney Bennett.

Napoleon 1927 A vivid, near-complete restoration of Gance's epic silent masterpiece about the famed conqueror's early years, from his youth through the Italian Campaign. An innovative, spectacular achievement with its use of multiple split screens, montage, color, and triptychs. Given a gala theatrical re-release in 1981. Remade in 1955. **235m/B VHS.** *FR* Albert Dieudonne, Antonin Artaud, Pierre Batcheff, Gina Manes, Armand Bernard, Harry Krimer, Albert Bras, Abel Gance, Georges Cahuzac, Annabella, Georges Lampin, Max Maxudian, Maurice Schutz, Marguerite Gance, Conrad Veidt, Edmond Van Daele, Alexandre Koubitzky, W. Percy Day, Yvette Dieudonne, Nicolas Koline, Vladimir Roudenko, Suzy Vernon, Robert Vidalin, Paul Amiot, Suzanne Bianchetti, Louis Sance; *D:* Abel Gance; *W:* Abel Gance; *C:* Leonce-Henri Burel, Roger Hubert, Jules Kruger; *M:* Carmine Coppola, Arthur Honegger, Carl Davis.

Napoleon 1955 Depicts life story of Napoleon from his days as a soldier in the French army to his exile on the Island of Elba. Falls short of the fantastic 1927 silent classic as it attempts to delve into Napoleon the man, as opposed to his conquests. Some might find it too slow for their tastes. **123m/C VHS.** *FR* Raymond Pellegrin, Orson Welles, Maria Schell, Yves Montand, Erich von Stroheim, Jean Gabin, Jean-Pierre Aumont; *D:* Sacha Guitry.

Napoleon ½ 1996 (G) Cute pic for young kiddies who like animals. A very curious golden retriever puppy named Muffin manages to slip into a balloon-covered basket and finds himself airborne across Australia. Deciding he likes the idea of adventuring, Muffin renames himself Napoleon because it sounds braver. He lands unexpectedly near Sydney Harbor and is befriended by Birdo, who becomes his guide when Napoleon decides he wants to meet his wild dog cousins, the dingoes. And it's off into the bush, with kangaroos, koalas, snakes, and lizards to help or hinder along the way. **81m/C VHS, DVD.** *AU JP* *D:* Mario Andreacchio; *W:* Mario Andreacchio, Mark Saltzman; *C:* Roger Dowling; *M:* Bill Conti; *V:* Jamie Croft, Philip Quast, Carole Skinner, Anne Louise Lambert, David Argue, Joan Rivers, Steven Vidler, Susan Lyons.

Napoleon and Samantha 1972 Disney adventure about Napoleon, an orphan (Whitaker), who is befriended by Danny, a college student (Douglas). After the death of his grandfather, Napoleon decides to take Major, his elderly pet lion, and follow Danny, who is herding goats for the summer, across the American northwest mountains and they are joined by Samantha (Foster in her film debut). Worth watching. **91m/C VHS, DVD.** Jodie Foster, Johnny Whitaker, Michael Douglas, Will Geer, Henry Jones; *D:* Bernard McEveety; *W:* Stewart Raffill; *C:* Monroe Askins; *M:* Buddy (Norman Dale) Baker.

The Narcotics Story woof! *The Dreaded Persuasion* 1958 Bad film on the same vein as "Reefer Madness." Originally intended as a police training film, this shows the evils and destruction of heroin addiction. Portrayals of drug addicts are hilarious. **75m/C VHS.** Sharon Strand, Darlene Hendricks, Herbert Crisp, Fred Marratto; *D:* Robert W. Larsen; *Nar:* Art Gilmore.

The Narrow Margin 1952 Well-made, harrowing adventure about a cop who is in charge of transporting a gangster's widow to a trial where she is to testify. On the train he must try to keep her safe from the hit-men who would murder her. A real cat and mouse game—one of the best suspense movies of the '50s. **71m/B VHS, DVD.** Charles McGraw, Marie Windsor, Jacqueline White, Queenie Leonard, Gordon Gebert, Don Beddoe, Harry Harvey; *D:* Richard Fleischer.

Narrow Margin 1990 (R) Archer reluctantly agrees to testify against the mob after witnessing a murder, and Los Angeles D.A. Hackman is assigned to protect her on the train through the Rockies back to L.A. Bad idea, she finds out. No match for its '52 predecessor. **99m/C VHS, DVD, Wide.** Gene Hackman, Anne Archer, James B. Sikking, J.T. Walsh, M. Emmet Walsh; *D:* Peter Hyams; *W:* Peter Hyams; *M:* Bruce Broughton.

Narrow Trail ½ 1917 A silent classic that still stands as one of the best Westerns ever made. A tough cowboy with a troubled past hopes a good woman can save him. But she's seen trouble, too. They meet up again in San Francisco's Barbary Coast. A horse race might hold the answer. **56m/B VHS.** William S. Hart, Sylvia Bremer, Milton Ross; *D:* William S. Hart.

Nashville 1975 (R) Altman's stunning, brilliant film tapestry that follows the lives of 24 people during a political campaign/music festival in Nashville. Seemingly extemporaneous vignettes, actors playing themselves (Elliott Gould and Julie Christie), funny, touching, poignant character studies concerning affairs of the heart and despairs of the mind. Repeatedly blurs reality and fantasy. ♫I'm Easy; Two Hundred Years; Keep A'Goin'; One, I Love You; Let Me Be the One; The Day I Looked Jesus in the Eye; For the Sake of the Children; I Never Get Enough; It Don't Worry Me. **159m/C VHS, DVD, Wide.** Keith Carradine, Lily Tomlin, Henry Gibson, Ronee Blakley, Keenan Wynn, David Arkin, Geraldine Chaplin, Lauren Hutton, Shelley Duvall, Barbara Harris, Allen (Goorwitz) Garfield, Karen Black, Christina Raines, Michael Murphy, Ned Beatty, Barbara Baxley, Scott Glenn, Jeff Goldblum, Gwen Welles, Bert Remsen, Robert DoQui, Elliott Gould, Julie Christie; *D:* Robert Altman; *W:* Joan Tewkesbury; *C:* Paul Lohmann; *M:* Richard Baskin. Oscars '75: Song ("I'm Easy"); Golden Globes '76: Song ("I'm Easy"); Natl. Bd. of Review '75: Director (Altman), Support. Actress (Blakley), Natl. Film Reg. '92;; N.Y. Film Critics '75: Director (Altman), Film, Support. Actress (Tomlin); Natl. Soc. Film Critics '75: Director (Altman), Film, Support. Actor (Gibson), Support. Actress (Tomlin).

Nashville Beat 1989 Gang targets the citizens of Nashville, Tennessee, until two tough cops stomp the gang's delusion that Southern folk are easy marks. **110m/C VHS.** Kent McCord, Martin Milner; *D:* Bernard L. Kowalski.

Nashville Girl *Country Music Daughter; New Girl in Town* 1976 (R) Innocent country girl who wants to make good in the country music scene, rises to the top of the Nashville success ladder, by compromising everything and hanging out with stereotyped no-goods in the show biz world. It's as good as a yawn. **90m/C VHS.** Monica Gayle, Johnny Rodriguez; *D:* Gus Trikonis.

The Nasty Girl ½ *Das Schreckliche Madchen* 1990 (PG-13) A bright young German model plans to enter a national essay contest on the topic of her hometown's history during the Third Reich. While researching the paper, she's harassed and even brutalized, but refuses to cease her sleuthing. Excellent performances, tight direction, with comedic touches that charmingly imparts an important message. Based on a true story. In German with English subtitles. **93m/C VHS.** *GE* Lena Stolze, Monika Baumgartner, Michael Gahr; *D:* Michael Verhoeven; *W:* Michael Verhoeven; *C:* Axel de Roche. British Acad. '91: Foreign Film; N.Y. Film Critics '90: Foreign Film.

Nasty Habits 1977 (PG) Broad farce depicting a corrupt Philadelphia convent as a satiric parallel to Watergate, with nuns modeled on Nixon, Dean and Mitchell. Includes cameo appearances by various media personalities. Based on the British novel "The Abbess of Crewe" by Muriel Spark. **92m/C VHS.** *GB* Glenda Jackson, Geraldine Page, Anne Jackson, Melina Mercouri, Sandy Dennis, Susan Penhaligon, Anne Meara, Edith Evans, Rip Torn, Eli Wallach, Jerry Stiller; *Cameos:* Mike Douglas, Bill Jorgensen, Jessica Savitch, Howard K. Smith; *D:* Michael Lindsay-Hogg.

Nasty Hero ½ 1989 (PG-13) Hard-boiled ex-con comes to Miami to avenge the car thieves who framed him and got him sent to the slammer. This is car-chase scene heaven—little plot or drama. **79m/C VHS.** Robert Sedgwick, Carlos Palomino, Scott Feraco, Mike Starr, Rosanna DaVon; *D:* Nick Barwood.

Nasty Rabbit *Spies-A-Go-Go* 1964 Ridiculous spoof about Soviet spies intent on releasing a rabbit with a hideous Communist disease into the U.S. Everyone gets in on the chase: Nazi forces, cowboys and Indians, sideshow freaks, banditos—what is the point? **88m/C VHS.** Arch Hall Jr., Micha Terr, Melissa Morgan, John Akana; *D:* James Landis.

Natas ... The Reflection 1983 (PG) A reporter persists in validating an Indian demon myth. **90m/C VHS.** Randy Mulkey, Pat Bolt, Craig Hensley, Kelli Kuhn.

Nate and Hayes ½ 1983 (PG) Set during the mid-1800s in the South Pacific, the notorious real-life swashbuckler Captain "Bully" Hayes ("good pirate") helps young missionary Nate recapture his fiancee from a cutthroat gang of evil slave traders. Entertaining "jolly rogers" film. **100m/C VHS.** *NZ* Tommy Lee Jones, Michael O'Keefe, Max Phipps, Jenny Seagrove; *D:* Ferdinand Fairfax; *M:* Trevor Jones.

A Nation Aflame ½ 1937 Anti-Klan film is based on a story by Thomas L. Dixon, the author of "The Clansman," from which D.W. Griffith made "The Birth of a Nation." In this story, a con man gains control of the state's government through an ultra-nationalistic secret society, and eventually pays for his corruption. **70m/B VHS.** Lila Lee, Noel Madison, Snub Pollard, Norma Trelvar; *D:* Victor Halperin.

National Lampoon Goes to the Movies 1981 Parodies of popular Hollywood genres, including cop thrillers, melodramas, and inspirational biographies, done in goofy "Lampoon" style. **89m/C VHS.** Robby Benson, Candy Clark, Diane Lane, Christopher Lloyd, Peter Riegert, Richard Widmark, Henny Youngman, Bobby DiCicco; *D:* Henry Jaglom.

National Lampoon's Animal House ½ *Animal House* 1978 (R) Classic Belushi vehicle running amuck. Set in 1962 and responsible for launching Otis Day and the Knights and defining cinematic food fights. Every college tradition from fraternity rush week to the homecoming pageant is irreverently and relentlessly mocked in this wild comedy about Delta House, a fraternity on the edge. Climaxes with the homecoming parade from hell. Sophomoric, but very funny, with a host of young stars who went on to more serious work. Remember: "Knowledge is good." **109m/C VHS, DVD.** John Belushi, Tim Matheson, John Vernon, Donald Sutherland, Peter Riegert, Stephen Furst, Bruce McGill, Mark Metcalf, Verna Bloom, Karen Allen, Tom Hulce, Mary Louise Weller, James Widdoes, Kevin Bacon, Doug Kenney, Martha Smith, Cesare Danova, Stephen Bishop, Sarah Holcomb; *D:* John Landis; *W:* Harold Ramis, Chris Miller, Doug Kenney; *C:* Charles Correll; *M:* Elmer Bernstein. Natl. Film Reg. '01.

National Lampoon's Attack of the 5 Ft. 2 Women *Attack of the 5 Ft. 2 Women* 1994 (R) Brown parodies two of 1994's most notorious tabloid queens in "Tonya: The Battle of Wounded Knee" and "He Never Give Me Orgasm: The Lenora Babbitt Story." **82m/C VHS.** Julie Brown, Sam McMurray, Adam Storke, Priscilla Barnes, Lauren Tewes, Dick Miller, Rick Overton, Stanley DeSantis, Anne DeSalvo, Liz Torres, Vicki Lawrence, Stella Stevens, Peter DeLuise; *D:* Julie Brown, Richard Wenk; *W:* Julie Brown, Charlie Coffey; *M:* Christopher Tyng. CABLE

National Lampoon's Christmas Vacation ½ *Christmas Vacation* 1989 (PG-13) The third vacation for the Griswold family finds them hosting repulsive relatives for Yuletide. The sight gags, although predictable, are sometimes on the mark. Quaid is a standout as the slovenly cousin. **93m/C VHS, DVD, 8mm.** Chevy Chase, Beverly D'Angelo, Randy Quaid, Diane Ladd, John Randolph, E.G. Marshall, Doris Roberts, Julia Louis-Dreyfus, Mae Questel, William Hickey, Brian Doyle-Murray, Juliette Lewis, Johnny Galecki, Nicholas Guest, Miriam Flynn; *D:* Jeremiah S. Chechik; *W:* John Hughes; *C:* Thomas Ackerman; *M:* Angelo Badalamenti.

National Lampoon's Class of '86 *Class of '86* 1986 This is a live stage comedy show written and sponsored by the infamous adult humor magazine, featuring a new cast of comics. **86m/C VHS.** Rodger Bumpass, Veanne Cox, Annie Golden, John Michael Higgins, Tommy Koenig.

National Lampoon's Class Reunion woof! *Class Reunion* 1982 (R) Class reunion with some very wacky guests and a decided lack of plot or purpose. Things go from bad to worse when a crazed killer decides to join in on the festivities. Disappointing with very few laughs. **85m/C VHS, DVD.** Shelley Smith, Gerrit Graham, Michael Lerner; *D:* Michael Miller; *W:* John Hughes; *C:* Philip Lathrop; *M:* Peter Bernstein.

National Lampoon's Dad's Week Off *Dad's Week Off* 1997 (R) Jack (Winkler) is a stressed-out salesman who decides he needs time away from both his job and his family. His wife agrees to take their kids camping while Jack spends a week peacefully at home. But before he knows it, Jack's bud (Jeni) has introduced him to kooky Cherice (d'Abo) and it's party-time at Jack's place. **92m/C VHS.** Henry Winkler, Olivia D'Abo, Richard Jeni, Justin Louis, Ken Pogue, Wendel Meldrum; *D:* Neal Israel; *W:* Neal Israel; *C:* Jan Kiesser; *M:* Marc Bonilla. CABLE

National Lampoon's European Vacation ½ *European Vacation* 1985 (PG-13) Sappy sequel to "Vacation" that has witless Chase and his family bumbling around in the land "across the pond." The Griswolds nearly redefine the term "ugly American." Stonehenge will never be the same. **94m/C VHS, DVD, 8mm, Wide.** Chevy Chase, Beverly D'Angelo, Dana Hill, Jason Lively, Victor Lanoux, John Astin, William Zabka; *D:* Amy Heckerling; *W:* John Hughes, Robert Klane, Eric Idle; *M:* Charles Fox.

National Lampoon's Favorite Deadly Sins ½ 1995 (R) Three sketches about greed, anger, and lust. In "Lust," Leary plays a security guard who spies on a neighbor; "Anger" finds Clay as an irate convenience store shopper; and Mantegna, in "Greed," stars as a sleazoid producer who helps a young woman kill her wicked stepmother and stepsisters in order to make a movie about it. **99m/C VHS.** Joe Mantegna, Denis Leary, Annabella Sciorra, Andrew (Dice Clay) Silverstein, Cassidy Rae, Brian Keith, William Ragsdale, Farrah Forke, Tanya Pohlkotte; *D:* Denis Leary, David Jablin; *W:* Michael Barrie, Jim Mulholland, Lee Biondi, Ann Lembeck.

National Lampoon's Golf Punks ½ 1999 (PG-13) Innocuous comedy finds luckless former golf pro Al Oliver (Arnold) in desperate need of cash to pay off his gambling debts. So, he becomes an instructor to a bunch of teen misfits and decides to enter the uncoordinated group in a prestigious tournament. **95m/C VHS, DVD.** *CA* Tom Arnold, James Kirk, Rene Tardif; *D:* Harvey Frost; *W:* Jill Mazursky; *C:* Patrick Williams; *M:* Richard Bronskill. VIDEO

National Lampoon's Last Resort ½ 1994 (PG-13) Retired film actor finds his long-time movie nemesis can't separate screen life from the real thing anymore and is planning an invasion of the actor's private island. So, he calls on his nephew (who brings along a friend) to help him out. **91m/C VHS, DVD.** Corey Feldman, Corey Haim, Geoffrey Lewis, Robert Mandan; *D:* Rafal Zielinski.

National Lampoon's Loaded Weapon 1 ½ *Loaded Weapon 1* 1993 (PG-13) Cop Jack Colt (Estevez) and partner Wes Luger (Jackson) attempt to recover a microfilm which contains a formula for turning cocaine into cookies. Essentially a sendup of the popular "Lethal Weapon" series, although other movies and themes make an appearance, well sort of. Short on plot and long on slapstick, but that's the whole point. Tired formula creates nostalgia for the granddaddy of them all, "Airplane." Lots of cameos, including one from sibling spoof star Sheen. The magazine folded while the movie was in production, an ominous sign. **83m/C VHS, DVD.** Emilio Estevez, Samuel L. Jackson, Jon Lovitz, Tim Curry, Kathy Ireland, William Shatner, Dr. Joyce Brothers, James Doohan, Richard Moll, F. Murray Abraham, Denis Leary, Corey Feldman, Phil Hartman, J.T. Walsh, Erik Estrada, Larry Wilcox, Allyce Beasley, Charlie Sheen; *D:* Gene Quintano; *W:* Don Holley, Gene Quintano; *C:* Peter Deming; *M:* Robert Folk.

National Lampoon's Senior Trip 🦴 *Senior Trip* **1995 (R)** According to the promotion, "they came, they saw, they passed out." Good dumb fun is hard to come by, particularly here. Latest lesser "Lampoon" effort in a long line of lesser Lampoons is about midwestern high school seniors who take a bus trip to Washington to meet the President. Along the way they have hijinks, including manipulation by a stereotypically corrupt senator out to embarrass his politcal opponent. Frewer is the inept principal who leads the hopelessly cliched group of misfits through the dopey corridors of power. Somehow, even the Coreys avoided this one. **91m/C VHS.** Matt Frewer, Valerie Mahaffey, Lawrence Dane, Thomas Chong, Kevin McDonald; ***D:*** Kelly Makin; ***W:*** I. Marlene King, Roger Kumble.

National Lampoon's The Don's Analyst 🦴🦴 *The Don's Analyst* **1997 (R)** Don Vito (Loggia) has lots of problems—his wife has left him, his sons are too stupid to take over the business, and his mob rival wants both his business and his wife. The Don's so upset he's thinking of going legit. Instead, his sons kidnap therapist Dr. Riceputo (Pollak) to straighten the Don out. **103m/C VHS.** Robert Loggia, Kevin Pollak, Joseph Bologna, Angie Dickinson, Sherilyn Fenn; ***D:*** David Jablin. **CABLE**

National Lampoon's Vacation 🦴🦴🦴 *Vacation* **1983 (R)** The Clark Griswold (Chase) family of suburban Chicago embarks on a westward cross-country vacation via car to the renowned "Wally World." Ridiculous and hysterical misadventures, including a falling asleep at the wheel sequence and the untimely death of Aunt Edna. **98m/C VHS, DVD.** Chevy Chase, Beverly D'Angelo, Imogene Coca, Randy Quaid, Christie Brinkley, James Keach, Anthony Michael Hall, John Candy, Eddie Bracken, Brian Doyle-Murray, Eugene Levy, Dana Barron, Jane Krakowski, Miriam Flynn, Frank McRae, John Diehl, Mickey Jones; ***D:*** Harold Ramis; ***W:*** John Hughes, Harold Ramis; ***C:*** Victor Kemper; ***M:*** Ralph Burns.

National Lampoon's Van Wilder 🦴 *Van Wilder* **2002 (R)** Cliched and crass college comedy of suave coed Van Wilder (Reynolds) who gets cut off by his dad (Matheson, in a nice bit of ironic casting), who realizes his son's seven college years have not yielded a degree. The universally adored, high-profile, frat house toastmaster then uses his charm to helps fund his education by helping the underprivileged undergrads meet women and have fun—for a price, of course. A circus of gross-out jokes and sight gags that would make the Farrelly brothers blush ensue. Reid is typically vapid as the lackluster Lois Lane college reporter and love interest. An unrated version is also available. **92m/C VHS, DVD.** Ryan Reynolds, Tara Reid, Tim Matheson, Kal Penn, Teck Holmes, Daniel Cosgrove, Deon Richmond, Alex Burns, Paul Gleason, Tom Everett Scott, Chris Owen, Curtis Armstrong, Kim Smith, Erik Estrada, Michelle Rene Thomas; ***D:*** Walt Becker; ***W:*** Brent Goldberg, David T. Wagner; ***C:*** James R. Bagdonas; ***M:*** David Lawrence.

National Velvet 🦴🦴🦴🦴 **1944 (G)** Velvet Brown (Taylor) wins a horse in a raffle and is determined to train it to compete in the famed Grand National race with the help of her best friend, Mi (Rooney). Taylor, only 12 at the time, is superb in her first starring role. Rooney also gives a fine performance. Filmed with a loving eye on lushly decorated sets, this is a masterpiece version of the story of affection between a girl and her pet. Based on the novel by Enid Bagnold and followed by the dismal "International Velvet" in 1978. **124m/C VHS, DVD.** Elizabeth Taylor, Mickey Rooney, Arthur Treacher, Donald Crisp, Anne Revere, Angela Lansbury, Reginald Owen, Norma Varden, Jackie "Butch" Jenkins, Terence (Terry) Kilburn; ***D:*** Clarence Brown; ***W:*** Theodore Reeves, Helen Deutsch; ***C:*** Leonard Smith; ***M:*** Herbert Stothart. Oscars '45: Film Editing, Support. Actress (Revere).

Native Son 🦴🦴½ **1951** A young black man from the ghettos of Chicago is hired as a chauffeur by an affluent white family. His job is to drive their head-strong daughter anywhere she wants to go. Unintentionally, he kills her, tries to hide, and is ultimately found guilty. Based on the classic novel by Richard Wright, who also stars. Remade in 1986. Unprofessional direction and low budget work against the strong story. **91m/B VHS.** Richard Wright, Jean Wallace, Nicholas Joy, Gloria Madison, Charles Cane; ***D:*** Pierre Chenal.

Native Son 🦴🦴½ **1986 (R)** This second film adaptation of the classic Richard Wright novel is chock full of stars and tells the story of a poor black man who accidentally kills a white woman and then hides the body. Changes in the script soft-soap some of the novel's disturbing truths and themes—so-so drama for those who have not read the book. **111m/C VHS.** Geraldine Page, Oprah Winfrey, Matt Dillon, John Karlen, Elizabeth McGovern, Akosua Busia, Carroll Baker, Victor Love, John McMartin, Art Evans, Willard Pugh, David Rasche; ***D:*** Jerrold Freedman; ***W:*** Richard Wesley; ***C:*** Thomas Burstyn; ***M:*** James Mtume.

Nativity 🦴🦴 **1978** Unmemorable, made-for-TV portrayal of the romance between Mary and Joseph (of the Bible story), Joseph's response to Mary's pregnancy, and the birthing of Jesus. Not exactly a Bible epic, the direction and acting are uninspired. **97m/C VHS.** John Shea, Madeleine Stowe, Jane Wyatt, John Rhys-Davies, Kate O'Mara; ***D:*** Bernard L. Kowalski.

The Natural 🦴🦴🦴 **1984 (PG)** A beautifully filmed movie about baseball as myth. A young man, whose gift for baseball sets him apart, finds that trouble dogs him, particularly with a woman. In time, as an aging rookie, he must fight against his past to lead his team to the World Series, and win the woman who is meant for him. From the Bernard Malamud story. **134m/C VHS, DVD, Wide.** Robert Redford, Glenn Close, Robert Duvall, Kim Basinger, Wilford Brimley, Barbara Hershey, Richard Farnsworth, Robert Prosky, Darren McGavin, Joe Don Baker, Michael Madsen; ***D:*** Barry Levinson; ***W:*** Roger Towne, Phil Dusenberry; ***C:*** Caleb Deschanel; ***M:*** Randy Newman.

Natural Born Killers 🦴🦴 **1994 (R)** An old script by (Graphic Screen Violence) Tarantino is resurrected by (Damn the Torpedoes) Stone and invested with its own unique subtle nuance and style. Controversial (natch, considering the director and writer) look at the way the media portrays criminals. Harrelson and Lewis are the lovestruck, white-trash serial killers who become tabloid-TV darlings, thanks to a sensationalistic press led by Downey Jr. Stone's dark and manic comment on America's fascination and revulsion with violence is strictly of the love it or leave it variety. Bloodshed galore, dazzling photography, and a dynamite soundtrack (with over 75 selections) add up to sensory overload. **119m/C VHS, DVD, Wide.** Louis Lombardi, Woody Harrelson, Robert Downey Jr., Juliette Lewis, Tommy Lee Jones, Ashley Judd, Tom Sizemore, Rodney Dangerfield, Rachel Ticotin, Arliss Howard, Russell Means, Denis Leary, Steven Wright, Pruitt Taylor Vince, Dale Dye; ***D:*** Oliver Stone; ***W:*** Oliver Stone; ***C:*** Robert Richardson; ***M:*** Trent Reznor.

Natural Causes 🦴½ **1994 (PG-13)** Muddled political thriller finds Dr. Jessie McCarthy (Purl) traveling to Thailand to visit her estranged mother Rachel (Paige), only to discover she's just been murdered. Then Jessie learns Rachel had a secret life aiding Vietnamese refugees and a scheme is afoot to sabotage a reconciliation treaty between the U.S. and Vietnam. However, none of this makes much sense, though the Bangkok settings provide a pleasant distraction. **90m/C VHS.** Linda Purl, Cary-Hiroyuki Tagawa, Will Patton, Tim Thomerson, Janis Paige, Ali MacGraw; ***D:*** James Becket; ***W:*** Jake Raymond Needham; ***C:*** Denis Maloney; ***M:*** Nathan Wang.

Natural Enemies 🦴🦴½ **1979 (R)** A successful publisher begins to consider suicide and murder as the cure for his family's increasing alienation and despair. Dark and depressing drama. **100m/C VHS.** Hal Holbrook, Louise Fletcher, Jose Ferrer, Viveca Lindfors; ***D:*** Jeff Kanew; ***W:*** Jeff Kanew.

Natural Enemy 🦴🦴 **1996 (R)** Unsuspecting married couple become the target of a disturbed man with a big secret. **?m/C VHS.** Donald Sutherland, William McNamara, Lesley Ann Warren, Joe Pantoliano, Tia Carrere; ***D:*** Douglas Jackson; ***W:*** Kevin Bernhardt; ***C:*** Rodney Gibbons; ***M:*** Alan Reeves. **CABLE**

The Natural History of Parking Lots 🦴🦴 **1994** What's a rich L.A. father to do when his teenage son hot-wires antique cars for kicks? Why pay his gun-running older brother to keep an eye on him. And the whackiness is just beginning. **92m/C VHS.** ***D:*** Everet Lewis.

Nature of the Beast 🦴🦴 **1994 (R)** A businessman and a drifter are both hiding deadly secrets as police search for both a serial killer and the $1 million missing in a Vegas casino robbery. Just which man is involved in which crime? **91m/C VHS.** Eric Roberts, Lance Henriksen, Brion James; ***D:*** Victor Salva; ***W:*** Victor Salva.

Nature's Playmates 🦴 **1962** A beautiful private eye tours Florida nudist camps in search of a missing man with a distinctive tattoo on his posterior. One of H.G. Lewis' obscure "nudie" flicks, sexually tame by modern standards, awful by any standards. **56m/B VHS.** Vicki (Allison Louise Downe) Miles, Allison Louise Downe, Scott Osborne, Terry Stevens, Peter Lathrop, Fred Gordon, Al Glick; ***D:*** Herschell Gordon Lewis; ***W:*** Ben T. Williams; ***C:*** William R. Johnson.

Naughty Knights 🦴 *Up the Chastity Belt* **1971 (PG)** Soft-core romp in a medieval setting. Toss it in the moat. **94m/C VHS.** Frankie Howerd, Graham Crowden, Bill Fraser, Roy Hudd, Hugh Paddick, Anna Quayle, Eartha Kitt, Dave King, Fred Emney; ***D:*** Bob Kellett; ***M:*** Carl Davis.

Naughty Marietta 🦴🦴½ **1935** A French princess switches identities with a mail-order bride to escape from her arranged marriage, and is captured by pirates. When she's saved by a dashing Indian scout, it's love at first sight. The first MacDonald-Eddy match-up and very popular in its day. ♫Italian Street Song; Chansonette; Antoinette and Anatole; Prayer; Tramp, Tramp, Tramp; The Owl and the Bobcat; Neath the Southern Moon; Mon Ami Pierrot; Ship Ahoy. **106m/B VHS.** Jeanette MacDonald, Nelson Eddy, Frank Morgan, Elsa Lanchester, Douglass Dumbrille, Cecilia Parker; ***D:*** Woodbridge S. Van Dyke; ***C:*** William H. Daniels. Oscars '35: Sound.

The Naughty Nineties 🦴🦴 **1945** Bud and Lou help a showboat owner fend off crooks in the 1890s. Usual slapstick shenanigans, but highlighted by verbal banter. Includes the first on-screen rendition of the classic "Who's on First?" routine. ♫Rolling Down the River; Uncle Tom's Cabin; I Can't Get You Out of My Mind; On a Sunday Afternoon; I'd Leave My Happy Home for You; Nora Malone; Ma Blushin' Rosie; The Showboat's Comin' to Town; A Blarney from Killarney. **72m/B VHS.** Bud Abbott, Lou Costello, Henry Travers, Alan Curtis, Joseph (Joe) Sawyer, Rita Johnson, Joe (Joseph) Kirk, Lois Collier; ***D:*** Jean Yarbrough.

Navajo Blues 🦴🦴 **1997 (R)** Police detective Nicholas Epps is installed in the federal witness protection program after seeing a mob hit on his partner. He's sent to a Native American reservation to hide out until the trial but can't resist investigating a series of local murders. **99m/C VHS.** Steven Bauer, Irene Bedard, Charlotte Lewis, Ed O'Ross, Michael Horse, Tom Fridley; ***D:*** Joey Travolta; ***C:*** Dan Heigh.

Navajo Joe 🦴½ **1967** The sole survivor of a massacre single-handedly kills each person involved in the atrocity, and aids a terrorized, though unappreciative, town in the process. Low-budget Spanish-Italian western only worth watching because of Reynolds. Filmed in Spain. **89m/C VHS.** *IT SP* Burt Reynolds, Aldo Sambrel, Tanya Lopert, Fernando Rey; ***D:*** Sergio Corbucci; ***M:*** Ennio Morricone.

The Navigator 🦴🦴🦴 **1924** Ever the quick thinker, Keaton actually bought a steamer headed for the scrap heap and used it to film an almost endless string of sight gags. Rejected by a socialite, millionaire Keaton finds himself alone with her on the abandoned boat. As he saves her from various and sundry perils, the gags and thrills abound—including one stunt that was inspired by a near-accident on the set. Too bad they don't make 'em like this anymore. Silent. **60m/B VHS, DVD.** Buster Keaton, Kathryn McGuire, Frederick Vroom, Noble Johnson, Clarence Burton, H. M. Clugston; ***D:*** Donald Crisp, Buster Keaton; ***W:*** Clyde Bruckman, Jean C. Havez, Joseph A. Mitchell; ***C:*** Byron Houck, Elgin Lessley.

The Navigator 🦴🦴🦴 **1988 (PG)** A creative time-travel story of a 14th-century boy with visionary powers who leads the residents of his medieval English village away from a plague by burrowing through the earth's core and into late-20th-century New Zealand. Quite original and refreshing. **92m/C VHS, DVD.** *NZ* Hamish McFarlane, Bruce Lyons, Chris Haywood, Marshall Napier, Noel Appleby, Paul Livingston, Sarah Pierse; ***D:*** Vincent Ward; ***W:*** Vincent Ward. Australian Film Inst. '88: Cinematog., Director (Ward), Film.

Navy Blue and Gold 🦴🦴½ **1937** Three football-playing midshipmen (Young, Stewart, and Brown) at Annapolis share a friendship. Stewart has registered under a false name since his dad was unfairly cashiered from the service. When he hears some slander about his old man he stands up and tells the truth and gets suspended, just before the big game with Army. Naturally, he's reinstated just in time to make the big play and carry the team to victory. Well-done, old-fashioned hokum. **94m/B VHS.** James Stewart, Robert Young, Tom Brown, Lionel Barrymore, Florence Rice, Billie Burke, Samuel S. Hinds, Paul Kelly, Frank Albertson, Minor Watson; ***D:*** Sam Wood; ***W:*** George Bruce.

The Navy Comes Through 🦴🦴 **1942** Salty sailors aboard a mangy freighter beat the odds and sink Nazi warships and subs with the greatest of ease. Boy meets girl subplot is added for good measure. Morale booster includes newsreel footage. **81m/B VHS.** Pat O'Brien, George Murphy, Jane Wyatt, Jackie Cooper, Carl Esmond, Max Baer Sr., Desi Arnaz Sr., Ray Collins, Lee Bonnell, Frank Jenks, Helmut Dantine; ***D:*** Edward Sutherland.

Navy SEALS 🦴½ **1990 (R)** A group of macho Navy commandos, whose regular work is to rescue hostages from Middle Eastern underground organizations, finds a stash of deadly weapons. They spend the balance of the movie attempting to destroy the arsenal. Sheen chews the scenery as a crazy member of the commando team. Lots of action and violence, but simplistic good guys-bad guys philosophy and plot weaknesses keep this from being more than below average. **113m/C VHS, DVD, Wide.** Charlie Sheen, Michael Biehn, Joanne Whalley, Rick Rossovich, Cyril O'Reilly, Bill Paxton, Dennis Haysbert, Paul Sanchez, Ron Joseph, Nicholas Kadi; ***D:*** Lewis Teague; ***W:*** Gary Goldman; ***C:*** John A. Alonzo; ***M:*** Sylvester Levay.

Navy vs. the Night Monsters woof! *Monsters of the Night* **1966** When horrifying, acid-secreting plant monsters try to take over the world, Van Doren and the Navy must come to the rescue, with the action taking place in a tropical South Pole setting. Amazing deployment of talents. **87m/C VHS.** Mamie Van Doren, Anthony Eisley, Pamela Mason, Bobby Van, Russ Bender; ***D:*** Michael Hoey; ***W:*** Michael Hoey.

Navy Way 🦴 **1944** Hurriedly produced war propaganda film in which a boxer gets inducted into the Navy just before his title shot. **74m/B VHS.** Robert Lowery, Jean Parker; ***D:*** William Berke, William C. Thomas.

Nazarin 🦴🦴🦴 **1958** Bunuel's scathing indictment of Christianity finds its perfect vehicle in the adventures of a defrocked priest attempting to relive Christ's life. Gathering a group of disciples, he wanders into the Mexican desert as a cross between Christ and Don Quixote. Filmed in Mexico, this is Bunuel at his grimmest. Based on a novel by Benito Perez Galdos; Spanish with subtitles. **92m/B VHS.** *MX* Francesco Rabal, Rita Macedo, Margo Lopez, Rita McLedo, Ignacio Lopez Tarso, Jesus Fernandez; ***D:*** Luis Bunuel.

Nea 🦴🦴½ **1978 (R)** Comic drama about a young girl from a privileged home who writes a best selling pornographic novel anonymously. When her book writing talents are made public through betrayal, she gets even in a most unique way. Subtitled "A Young Emmanuelle." Kaplan also performs. Appealing and sophisticated. **101m/C VHS.** Sami Frey, Ann Zacharias, Heinz Bennent; ***D:*** Nelly Kaplan.

Near Dark ✌✌✌ **1987 (R)** Southwestern farm boy Caleb (Pasdar) is attracted to the pretty Mae (Wright) and falls in unwillingly with a family of thirsty, outlaw-fringe vampires who roam the West in a van. The first mainstream effort by Bigelow, and a rollicking, blood-saturated, slaughterhouse of a movie, with enough laughs and stunning imagery to revive the genre. **95m/C VHS.** Adrian Pasdar, Jenny Wright, Bill Paxton, Jenette Goldstein, Lance Henriksen, Tim Thomerson, Joshua John Miller; ***D:*** Kathryn Bigelow; ***W:*** Kathryn Bigelow, Eric Red; ***C:*** Adam Greenberg; ***M:*** Tangerine Dream.

Near Misses ✌½ **1991** Missable farce with Reinhold as a bigamist in the foreign service. To make time for a mistress he swaps identities with a young Marine in Paris, but then the KGB kidnaps the imposter. Doors slam in hallways all over the place as the performers crank up the mixups to maximum frenzy, but with little effect since you really don't care much about these fools. **93m/C VHS.** Judge Reinhold, Casey Siemaszko, Kasia (Katarzyna) Figura, Muriel Combeau; ***D:*** Baz Taylor; ***W:*** Peter Baloff, Dave Wollert.

Near the Rainbow's End ✌½ **1930** Cattle rancher Steele (in his first talking western) finds out that rustlers are aggravating the trouble between the cattlemen and the sheep herders. So he goes after the bad guys and then settles the feud by marrying a sheep herder's daughter. **57m/B VHS.** Bob Steele, Lafe (Lafayette) McKee, Louise Lorraine, Al Ferguson, Al Hewston; ***D:*** J(ohn) P(aterson) McGowan.

'Neath Brooklyn Bridge ✌✌ **1942** The Boys from the Bowery get tangled up in crime when they try to help a young girl whose guardian was murdered. **61m/B VHS.** Leo Gorcey, Huntz Hall, Bobby Jordan, Sammy (Earnest) Morrison, Ann Gillis, Noah Beery Jr., Marc Lawrence, Gabriel Dell; ***D:*** Wallace Fox.

'Neath Canadian Skies ✌ **1946** Mounted lawman who says "eh" a lot tracks murdering gang of mine looters. **41m/B VHS, 8mm.** *CA* Russell Hayden, Inez Cooper, Cliff Nazarro, Kermit Maynard, Jack Mulhall.

'Neath the Arizona Skies ✌✌ **1934** Low budget oater epic about a cowhand who finds all the action he and his friends can handle as they try to rescue a young Indian girl (and oil heiress) who has been kidnapped. 'Nuff said. **54m/B VHS.** John Wayne, George "Gabby" Hayes, Sheila Terry; ***D:*** Harry Fraser.

Necessary Parties **1988** Based on Barbara Dana's book that has a 15-year-old boy filing a lawsuit to stop his parents' divorce. Originally aired on PBS as part of the "Wonderworks" family movie series. **120m/C VHS.** Alan Arkin, Mark Paul Gosselaar, Barbara Dana, Adam Arkin, Donald Moffat, Julie Hagerty, Geoffrey Pierson, Taylor Fry; ***D:*** Gwen Arner.

Necessary Roughness ✌✌ **1991 (PG-13)** After losing their NCAA standing, the Texas Southern University (passing for the real Texas State) Armadillos football team looks like it's headed for disaster. The once proud football factory is now composed of assorted goofballs instead of stud players. But hope arrives in the form of a 34-year-old farmer with a golden arm, ready to recapture some lost dreams as quarterback. Can this unlikey team rise above itself and win a game, or will their hopes be squashed all over the field? **108m/C VHS, DVD, Wide.** Scott Bakula, Robert Loggia, Harley Jane Kozak, Sinbad, Hector Elizondo, Kathy Ireland, Jason Bateman; ***D:*** Stan Dragoti; ***W:*** Rick Natkin, David Fuller; ***C:*** Peter Stein; ***M:*** Bill Conti.

Necromancer: Satan's Servant ✌✌ **1988 (R)** After a woman is brutally raped, she contacts a sorceress and makes a pact with the devil to ensure her successful revenge. Plenty of graphic violence and nudity. **90m/C VHS, DVD.** Elizabeth (Kaitan) Cayton, Russ Tamblyn, Rhonda Dorton; ***D:*** Dusty Nelson; ***W:*** William T. Naud; ***C:*** Eric Cayla, Richard Clabaugh; ***M:*** Kevin Klinger, Bob Mamet, Gary Stockdale.

Necropolis ✌ **1987 (R)** A witch burned at the stake 300 years ago is brought back to life as a motorcycle punkette in New York searching for a sacrificial virgin (in New York?). New wave horror should have been watchable. **77m/C VHS.** Leeanne Baker, Michael Conte, Jacquie Fritz, William Reed, Paul Ruben; ***D:*** Tim Kincaid.

Ned Kelly ✌✌½ *Ned Kelly, Outlaw* **1970 (PG)** Dramatizes the life of Australia's most notorious outlaw. Kelly (Jagger) and his family start off as horse thieves and proceed from there. A manhunt results in death and the eventual capture and execution of Kelly. The very contemporary British Jagger was miscast as a period Australian and British director Richardson seems to have lacked an empathy for the material, given his lethargic direction. **100m/C VHS.** *GB* Mick Jagger, Allen Bickford, Geoff Gilmour, Mark McManus, Serge Lazareff, Peter Sumner, Ken Shorter, James Elliott, Diane Craig, Sue Lloyd, Clarissa Kaye; ***D:*** Tony Richardson; ***W:*** Ian Jones, Tony Richardson; ***M:*** Shel Silverstein.

Needful Things ✌✌½ **1993 (R)** Stephen King film adaptations are becoming as prolific as his novels, though few seem to improve in the transition from page to screen. This time a scheming Maine shopkeeper (Von Sydow) sells unsuspecting small towners peculiar items that, not surprisingly, begin to cause horror and mayhem. Harris is the town sheriff who tries to warn everyone that he's the devil in disguise. Big screen directorial debut for Heston (yes, Charlton's son). **120m/C VHS, DVD.** Ed Harris, Bonnie Bedelia, Max von Sydow, Amanda Plummer, J.T. Walsh; ***D:*** Fraser Heston; ***W:*** W.D. Richter; ***C:*** Tony Westman; ***M:*** Patrick Doyle.

Nefertiti, Queen of the Nile ✌✌ **1964** Woman, married against her will, turns into Nefertiti. For fans of Italo-Biblical epics only. **97m/C VHS.** *IT* Jeanne Crain, Vincent Price, Edmund Purdom, Amedeo Nazzari, Liana Orfei; ***D:*** Fernando Cerchio.

Negatives ✌✌ **1968** A couple indulge in sexual fantasies to dangerous extremes, with the man first impersonating Dr. Crippen, the early 1900s murderer, and later a WWI flying ace. When a photographer friend joins the fun, the action careens off the deep end. **90m/C VHS.** *GB* Peter McEnery, Diane Cilento, Glenda Jackson, Maurice Denham, Norman Rossington; ***D:*** Peter Medak.

The Negotiator ✌✌½ **1998 (R)** Police hostage negotiator Danny Roman (Jackson) has had his life destroyed by false accusations of theft and murder. So he decides to go after his accusers by taking the Chicago Internal Affairs Bureau staff (what else?) hostage. Chris Sabian (Spacey), a negotiator from another precinct, is Roman's only hope to save himself and find the real culprits. Jackson and Spacey are excellent in their scenes together, and the supporting cast does a fine job. Nice action sequences and suspenseful storyline make for a thrilling ride, as long as you don't contemplate the details for too long. **115m/C VHS, DVD, Wide.** Samuel L. Jackson, Kevin Spacey, David Morse, Ron Rifkin, John Spencer, Regina Taylor, J.T. Walsh, Siobhan Fallon, Paul Giamatti, Paul Guilfoyle, Carlos Gomez, Nestor Serrano; ***D:*** F. Gary Gray; ***W:*** James DeMonaco, Kevin Fox; ***C:*** Russell Carpenter; ***M:*** Graeme Revell.

The Neighbor ✌✌½ **1993 (R)** See nice city couple John and Mary move to small town Vermont. See their nice retired obstetrician neighbor Myron welcome them. See Mary get pregnant and Myron take an obsessional interest. See John arrested for murder. See Mary left alone—except for Myron's tender care. **93m/C VHS.** Linda Kozlowski, Ron Lea, Rod Steiger, Frances Bay, Bruce Boa, Jane Wheeler; ***D:*** Rodney Gibbons; ***W:*** Kurt Wimmer.

Neighbors ✌✌ **1981 (R)** The Keeses (Belushi and Walker) live in a quiet, middle-class suburban neighborhood where life is calm and sweet. But their new neighbors, Ramona and Vic (Aykroyd and Moriarty), prove to be loud, obnoxious, crazy, and freeloading. Will Earl and Enid Keese mind their manners as their neighborhood disintegrates? Some funny moments, but as the script fades, so do the laughs. Belushi's last waltz is based on Thomas Berger's novel. **90m/C VHS.** John Belushi, Dan Aykroyd, Kathryn Walker, Cathy Moriarty; ***D:*** John G. Avildsen; ***W:*** Larry Gelbart; ***M:*** Bill Conti.

Neil Simon's The Odd Couple 2 ✌½ *The Odd Couple 2* **1998 (PG-13)** In the not-too-grand tradition of "Caddyshack II," "Son of the Pink Panther," and "Blues Brothers 2000" they waited too long. And like the others, they shouldn't have even bothered. Oscar (Matthau) and Felix (Lemmon) reunite when their respective kids (Silverman as Oscar's son, Waltz as Felix's daughter) marry. Meeting at LAX, the duo immediately falls into the old routine of annoying each other and, this time out, the audience. Simon fills his script with leftover road movie cliches and vaudeville jokes, leaving Lemmon and Matthau nothing to do but mug and yell. Since almost everything these two have done together since the original has been a de facto sequel, it's a shame that the real thing falls so flat. **96m/C VHS, DVD.** Jack Lemmon, Walter Matthau, Jonathan Silverman, Lisa Waltz, Christine Baranski, Jean Smart, Barnard Hughes, Doris Belack, Ellen Geer, Jay O. Sanders, Rex Linn, Mary Beth Peil, Alice Ghostley, Rebecca Schull, Florence Stanley, Lou (Cutel) Cutell; ***D:*** Howard Deutch; ***W:*** Neil Simon; ***C:*** Jamie Anderson; ***M:*** Alan Silvestri.

Nell ✌✌½ **1994 (R)** "Wild child" story—adult version. When illiterate, barely verbal backwoods Nell (Foster) is discovered after her stroke-afflicted mother's death, she's placed in the care of a doctor (Neeson) and psychologist (Richardson) who have different ideas about how to bring her into society. Unfairly dismissed by some as self-indulgent, Foster's raw, physical performance is truly mesmerizing; dull script, unconvincingly tidy ending, and gross over-sentimentality are what disappoint. From the play "Idioglossia" by Mark Handley. **114m/C VHS.** Jodie Foster, Liam Neeson, Natasha Richardson, Richard Libertini; ***D:*** Michael Apted; ***W:*** William Nicholson. Screen Actors Guild '94: Actress (Foster).

Nelly et Monsieur Arnaud ✌✌✌ *Nelly and Mr. Arnaud* **1995** Chatty adult May/December would-be romance between 25-year-old secretary Nelly (Beart) and Pierre Arnaud (Serrault), the mid-60s retired magistrate for whom she's working. The arrogant divorced Arnaud is intrigued by the independent Nelly, whom he finds he can't control, while she comes to appreciate their emotional ties (altogether different from the selfishness of the younger men she knows). Conclusion avoids a neat resolution to a situation beset by bad timing. French with subtitles. **105m/C VHS, DVD, Wide.** *IT GE FR* Emmanuelle Beart, Michel Serrault, Jean-Hugues Anglade, Francoise Brion, Claire Nadeau, Michael (Michel) Lonsdale, Charles Berling, Michele Laroque; ***D:*** Claude Sautet; ***W:*** Jacques Fieschi, Claude Sautet; ***C:*** Jean-Francois Robin; ***M:*** Philippe Sarde. Cesar '96: Actor (Serrault), Director (Sautet).

Nemesis ✌½ **1993 (R)** Futuristic thriller that combines cybernetics and cyborgs in post-nuclear Los Angeles. Gruner plays a human (although he's mostly composed of mechanical replacement parts) in a world overwrought with system cowboys, information terrorists, bio-enhanced gangsters, and cyborg outlaws. Film's biggest flaw is the extremely confusing script that makes no attempt at logic whatsoever. Special visual effects are good despite the obviously low f/x budget. **95m/C VHS, DVD, Wide.** Olivier Gruner, Tim Thomerson, Cary-Hiroyuki Tagawa, Merle Kennedy, Yuji Okumoto, Marjorie Monaghan, Nicholas Guest, Vincent Klyn; ***D:*** Albert Pyun; ***W:*** Rebecca Charles; ***C:*** George Mooradian; ***M:*** Michel Rubini.

Nemesis 2: Nebula ✌½ **1994 (R)** Cyborg goes on a rampage across time with a superhuman in pursuit. **83m/C VHS.** Sue Price, Tina Cote, Earl White, Jahi JJ Zuri, Tracy Davis; ***D:*** Albert Pyun.

Nemesis 3: Time Lapse ✌½ *Nemesis 3: Prey Harder* **1996 (R)** Superhuman mutant Alex is the last hope for mankind as the cyborgs once again prepare to destroy civilization. **90m/C VHS.** Sue Price, Tim Thomerson, Norbert Weisser, Xavier DeClie, Sharon Bruneau, Debbie Muggli; ***D:*** Albert Pyun; ***W:*** Albert Pyun; ***C:*** George Mooradian; ***M:*** Tony Riparetti.

Nemesis 4: Cry of Angels ✌ **1997 (R)** Alex (Price) is an assassin in the year 2082. When she mistakenly kills the son of crimelord Bernardo (Divoff), a bounty is placed on her head. Cartoonish dreck. **80m/C VHS.** Sue Price, Norbert Weisser, Andrew Divoff, Simon Poland, Nicholas Guest; ***D:*** Albert Pyun; ***W:*** Albert Pyun; ***C:*** George Mooradian. **VIDEO**

Nenette and Boni ✌✌✌ **1996** Boni (Colin) is a 19-year-old pizza chef in Marseilles who likes to have sexual fantasies about the local baker's sensuous wife (Bruni-Tedeschi). His life is basically carefree until his pregnant, rebellious 15-year-old sister Nenette (Houri) shows up at his door, having run away from school. Nenette really doesn't want to deal with the pregnancy until Boni forces her to do so and, just to make the teens lives more complicated, their estranged small-time gangster dad (Nolot) has learned about Nenette's condition and wants to help her out. Fine performances. French with subtitles. **103m/C VHS, Wide.** *FR* Gregoire Colin, Alice Houri, Valeria Bruni-Tedeschi, Jacques Nolot, Vincent Gallo, Gerard Meylan, Alex Descas, Jamila Farah, Christine Gaya; ***D:*** Claire Denis; ***W:*** Claire Denis, Jean-Pol Fargeau; ***C:*** Agnes Godard.

The Neon Bible ✌✌ **1995** Beautifully crafted, yet thin telling of the struggles of a rural family in 1940s Georgia. The stories unfold in a series of flashbacks, as a 15-year-old boy travels alone on a train, reflecting on his dysfunctional early adolescence. An abusive father (Leary) who dies in the war, suicidal mom (Scarwid), and ex-showgirl visiting aunt (Rowlands) provide plenty of opportunities for familial angst. Starts out strong, with some stunning scenes sprinkled throughout, but director Davies never ventures far from the narrative territory he's covered thoroughly in his other films ("Distant Voices, Still Lives" and "The Long Day Closes"). Adapted from the novel by Pulitzer Prize winning author John Kennedy Toole. **92m/C VHS, DVD.** Gena Rowlands, Jacob Tierney, Diana Scarwid, Drake Bell, Denis Leary, Leo Burmester, Frances Conroy, Peter McRobbie, Joan Glover, Dana Dick, Virgil Graham Hopkins; ***D:*** Terence Davies; ***W:*** Terence Davies; ***C:*** Michael Coulter.

Neon City ✌✌ **1991 (R)** Title refers to a rumored city of refuge in the year 2053, where eight misfit adventurers in an armored transport seek safety from the Earth's toxic environment and "Mad Max" cliches. **99m/C VHS.** Michael Ironside, Vanity, Lyle Alzado, Valerie Wildman, Nick Klar, Juliet Landau, Arsenio "Sonny" Trinidad, Richard Sanders; ***D:*** Monte Markham.

The Neon Empire ✌½ **1989 (R)** Tepid tale of two gangsters battling inner mob opposition and backstabbing to build Las Vegas. Ostensibly based on the story of Bugsy Siegel and Meyer Lansky. **120m/C VHS.** Martin Landau, Ray Sharkey, Gary Busey, Harry Guardino, Julie Carmen, Linda Fiorentino, Dylan McDermott; ***D:*** Larry Peerce; ***W:*** Pete Hamill. **CABLE**

Neon Maniacs woof! **1986 (R)** An even half-dozen fetish-ridden zombies stalk the streets at night, tearing their victims into teensy weensy bits. Brave teenagers try to stop the killing. Brave viewers will stop the tape. **90m/C VHS.** Allan Hayes, Leilani Sarelle Ferrer, Bo Sabato, Donna Locke, Victor Elliot Brandt; ***D:*** Joseph Mangine.

The Nephew ✌✌ **1997** Part culture clash, part melodrama. Teenager Chad (Harper) heads to Inis Dora, a small island off the Irish coast, in order to fulfill his mother Karen's last request—that her ashes be scattered in her homeland. Karen was long estranged from her family and they're shocked to discover that Chad's father is black. Everyone tries to make the best of the situation but Chad's would-be romance with Aislin (McGuckin), whose father Joe (Brosnan) once loved Karen, causes a lot of friction. **104m/C VHS.** *IR* Hill Harper, Aislin McGuckin, Pierce Brosnan, Donal McCann, Sinead Cusack, Lorraine Pilkington; ***D:*** Eugene Brady; ***W:*** Jacqueline O'Neill, Sean P. Steele; ***C:*** Jack Conroy; ***M:*** Stephen McKeon.

Neptune Factor 🦴 *The Neptune Disaster; An Underwater Odyssey* **1973 (G)** Scientists board a special new deep-sea sub to search for their colleagues lost in an undersea earthquake. Diving ever deeper into the abyss that swallowed their friend's Ocean Lab II, they end up trapped themselves. The plot's many holes sink it. **94m/C VHS.** Ben Gazzara, Yvette Mimieux, Walter Pidgeon, Ernest Borgnine; ***D:*** Daniel Petrie; ***W:*** Jack DeWitt.

Neptune's Daughter 🦴🦴 **1949** A swim-happy bathing suit designer finds romance and deep pools of studio water to dive into. Typically lavish and ridiculous Williams aqua-parade. ♫Baby It's Cold Outside; I Love Those Men; My Heart Beats Faster. **92m/C VHS.** Esther Williams, Red Skelton, Ricardo Montalban, Betty Garrett, Keenan Wynn, Xavier Cugat, Ted de Corsia, Mike Mazurki, Mel Blanc, Juan Duvall, George Mann, Joi Lansing; ***D:*** Edward Buzzell; ***C:*** Charles Rosher. Oscars '49: Song ("Baby It's Cold Outside").

Nerolio 🦴🦴 **1996** Three imagined episodes depicting the final months of an unnamed poet/director (Cavicchioli), who is actually based on homosexual writer/filmmaker Pier Paolo Pasolini. The contradictory, hypocritical, aging Poet is shown buying sex, while extolling the virtues of male beauty in voiceover, and as the maker of his own doom (Pasolini was murdered in 1975). "Nerolio" is a contraction of "nero" (black) and "Petrolio" (oil), which refers to Pasolini's posthumous novel "Petrolio." Italian with subtitles. **82m/B VHS.** *IT* Marco Cavicchioli, Vincenzo Crivello, Salvatore Lazzaro; ***D:*** Aurelio Grimaldi; ***W:*** Aurelio Grimaldi; ***C:*** Maurizio Calvesi; ***M:*** Maria Soldatini.

Nervous Ticks 🦴🦴½ **1993 (R)** Ninety minutes in the life of airline employee York Daley. All he needs to do is get off work, go home, grab his luggage, pick up his married girfriend, and get back to the airport for a flight to Rio De Janeiro. Simple, right? Not in this movie. **95m/C VHS.** Bill Pullman, Julie Brown, Peter Boyle, James LeGros, Brent Jennings; ***D:*** Rocky Lang; ***W:*** David Frankel.

The Nervous Wreck 🦴🦴🦴 **1926** Harrison Ford (not the one from "Indiana Jones") heads West, seeking a cure for what he believes is a terminal illness. Once there, he becomes romantically entangled with the sheriff's fiancee, uses a wrench to hold up a gas station, and gets involved in other shenanigans. And then he discovers he's going to live after all. **70m/B VHS.** Harrison Ford, Phyllis Haver, Chester Conklin, Mack Swain, Hobart Bosworth, Charles Gerrard; ***D:*** Scott Sidney.

The Nest 🦴🦴½ *El Nido* **1980** Tragic romance of an elderly man and a 13-year-old girl is helped along by superior script and directing. **109m/C VHS.** *SP* Ana Torrent, Hector Alterio, Patricia Adriani, Luis Politti, Agustin Gonzalez; ***D:*** Jaime de Arminan; ***W:*** Jaime de Arminan; ***C:*** Teodoro Escamilla.

The Nest 🦴🦴½ **1988 (R)** A small island is overcome by giant cockroaches created by, you guessed it, a scientific experiment gone wrong. Special effects make it watchable. **89m/C VHS, DVD.** Robert Lansing, Lisa Langlois, Franc Luz, Terri Treas, Stephen Davies, Diana Bellamy, Nancy Morgan; ***D:*** Terence H. Winkless; ***W:*** Robert King; ***C:*** Ricardo Jacques Gale; ***M:*** Rick Conrad.

The Nesting 🦴½ **1980 (R)** Too-long tale of a neurotic author who rents a haunted Victorian manor and finds herself a pawn in a ghostly plan for revenge. Features Grahame's last performance. **104m/C VHS.** Robin Groves, John Carradine, Gloria Grahame, Christopher Loomis, Michael Lally; ***D:*** Armand Weston; ***C:*** Joao Fernandes.

The Net 🦴🦴½ **1995 (PG-13)** The ever-spunky Bullock gets stuck behind a computer screen rather than the wheel of a bus as reclusive computer systems analyst Angela Bennett. She's puzzled by a mysterious Internet program, which Angela finds can easily access highly classified databases. It's soon apparent that someone knows she knows because every record of her identity has been erased and the conspirators decide to take care of one last detail by eliminating her as well. Miller's the ex she turns to for help and Northam's a seductive British hacker. Techno paranoia. **114m/C VHS, DVD, 8mm, Wide.** Sandra Bullock, Jeremy Northam, Dennis Miller, Diane Baker, Ken Howard, Wendy Gazelle, Ray McKinnon; ***D:*** Irwin Winkler; ***W:*** John Brancato, Michael Ferris; ***C:*** Jack N. Green; ***M:*** Mark Isham.

Netherworld 🦴½ **1990 (R)** A young man investigating his mysterious, dead father travels to his ancestral plantation in the bayou. To his horror, he discovers that his father was involved in the black arts. Now two beautiful young witches are after him. Can he possibly survive this madness? **87m/C VHS, DVD.** Michael C. Bendetti, Denise Gentile, Anjanette Comer, Holly Floria, Robert Burr, Robert Sampson; ***D:*** David Schmoeller; ***W:*** Billy Chicago; ***C:*** Adolfo Bartoli; ***M:*** Edgar Winter.

Network 🦴🦴🦴½ **1976 (R)** As timely now as it was then; a scathing indictment of the TV industry and its propensity towards self-prostitution. A television newscaster's mental breakdown turns him into a celebrity when the network tries to profit from his illness. The individual characters are startlingly realistic and the acting is excellent. **121m/C VHS, DVD, Wide.** Faye Dunaway, Peter Finch, William Holden, Robert Duvall, Wesley Addy, Ned Beatty, Beatrice Straight; ***D:*** Sidney Lumet; ***W:*** Paddy Chayefsky; ***C:*** Owen Roizman. Oscars '76: Actor (Finch), Actress (Dunaway), Orig. Screenplay, Support. Actress (Straight); AFI '98: Top 100; British Acad. '77: Actor (Finch); Golden Globes '77: Actor—Drama (Finch), Actress—Drama (Dunaway), Director (Lumet), Screenplay; L.A. Film Critics '76: Director (Lumet), Film, Natl. Film Reg. '00;; N.Y. Film Critics '76: Screenplay; Writers Guild '76: Orig. Screenplay.

Neurotic Cabaret 🦴½ **1990** Would-be actress dances exotically and finds more exotic ways to roll in dough. **90m/C VHS.** Edwin Neal, Tammy Stone.

Neutron and the Black Mask 🦴 **1961** Man wears mask with lightning bolts and gains comic book style powers to do deathly battle with a scientist with a neutron bomb up his sleeve. First Neutron feature. **80m/B VHS.** *MX* Wolf Ruvinskis, Julio Aleman, Armando Silvestre, Rosita (Rosa) Arenas, Claudio Brook; ***D:*** Frederick Curiel.

Neutron vs. the Amazing Dr. Caronte 🦴 **1961** Dr. Caronte from "Neutron and the Black Mask" just won't give up that neutron bomb and let the series die. **80m/B VHS.** *MX* Wolf Ruvinskis, Julio Aleman, Armando Silvestre, Rosita (Rosa) Arenas, Rodolfo Landa; ***D:*** Frederick Curiel.

Neutron vs. the Death Robots 🦴 **1962** Guy with a mask takes on army of killer robots and neutron bomb to protect the world from future sequels. **80m/B VHS.** *MX* Wolf Ruvinskis, Julio Aleman, Armando Silvestre, Rosita (Rosa) Arenas; ***D:*** Frederick Curiel.

Neutron vs. the Maniac 🦴 **1962** Man in mask hunts guys who kill people. **80m/B VHS.** *MX* Wolf Ruvinskis.

Nevada 🦴🦴½ **1927** Entertaining silent western with a great cast finds gunslinger Cooper running from the law and winding up on a ranch where he falls for Todd, the rancher's daughter. Naturally, Cooper redeems himself by going after a gang of cattle rustlers, led by Powell. Based on a novel by Zane Grey. **67m/B VHS.** Gary Cooper, Thelma Todd, William Powell, Ernie Adams, Philip Strange, Christian J. Frank, Ivan Christy, Guy Oliver; ***D:*** John S. Waters; ***W:*** Jon Stone, L.G. Rigby; ***C:*** Charles E. Schoenbaum.

Nevada 🦴🦴½ **1944** Cowpoke Mitchum is mistaken for the killer of a homesteader and narrowly escapes the rope by finding the real killer. First leading role for Mitchum as the tough but laconic hero. Based on a story by Zane Grey. **62m/B VHS.** Robert Mitchum, Anne Jeffreys, Nancy Gates, Craig Reynolds, Guinn "Big Boy" Williams, Richard Martin, Harry Woods; ***D:*** Edward Killy.

Nevada 🦴🦴½ **1997 (R)** Women run a small Nevada town Monday through Friday while their men work at a dam several hours away, returning only on the weekends. When stranger Chrysty (Brenneman) shows up, the townswomen become curiously unsettled in their normally placid lives—accusing her of being a troublemaker or seeing her as a hopeful sign of change. **108m/C VHS.** Amy Brenneman, Kirstie Alley, Gabrielle Anwar, Saffron Burrows, Angus Macfadyen, Kathy Najimy, Dee Wallace Stone, James Wilder, Bridgette Wilson; ***D:*** Gary Tieche; ***W:*** Gary Tieche; ***C:*** Nancy Schreiber; ***M:*** Robert Perry.

Nevada City 🦴½ **1941** Roy outwits a financier who is trying to monopolize transportation in California. **54m/B VHS.** Roy Rogers.

Nevada Smith 🦴🦴 **1966** The half-breed Nevada Smith (previously introduced in Harold Robbins' story "The Carpetbaggers" and film of same name) seeks the outlaws who killed his parents. Standard western plot, characters. Later remade as a TV movie. **135m/C VHS.** Steve McQueen, Karl Malden, Brian Keith, Arthur Kennedy, Raf Vallone, Suzanne Pleshette, Paul Fix, Pat Hingle, Janet Margolin, Howard da Silva, John Doucette, Gene Evans, Val Avery, Lyle Bettger; ***D:*** Henry Hathaway; ***W:*** John Michael Hayes; ***C:*** Lucien Ballard; ***M:*** Alfred Newman.

The Nevadan 🦴½ *The Man From Nevada* **1950** A marshal goes in search of an outlaw's gold cache, only to be opposed by a crooked rancher. Good scenery and action, but not one of Scott's best. **81m/C VHS.** Randolph Scott, Dorothy Malone, Forrest Tucker, Frank Faylen, George Macready, Charles Kemper, Jeff Corey, Tom Powers, Jock Mahoney; ***D:*** Gordon Douglas.

Never a Dull Moment 🦴🦴 **1950** New York songwriter falls for rodeo Romeo, moves out West, and finds welcome wagon deficient. Mediocre songs; many dull moments. ♫Once You Find Your Guy; Sagebrush Lullaby; The Man With the Big Felt Hat. **89m/B VHS.** Irene Dunne, Fred MacMurray, William Demarest, Andy Devine, Gigi Perreau, Natalie Wood, Philip Ober, Jack Kirkwood, Ann Doran, Margaret Gibson; ***D:*** George Marshall.

Never a Dull Moment 🦴🦴 **1968 (G)** Mobsters mistake an actor for an assassin in this gag-filled adventure. They threaten the thespian into thievery, before the trouble really starts when Ace, the actual assassin, arrives. **90m/C VHS.** Dick Van Dyke, Edward G. Robinson, Dorothy Provine, Henry Silva, Joanna Moore, Tony Bill, Slim Pickens, Jack Elam; ***D:*** Jerry Paris; ***W:*** A.J. Carothers; ***M:*** Robert F. Brunner.

Never Been Kissed 🦴🦴 **1999 (PG-13)** Lightweight and logic-defying, Barrymore's producing debut hypothesizes that the people who were unpopular in high school want another chance at it. Not. Still-nerdy newspaper copy editor Josie is assigned to go undercover as a student and write about high school life. She see it as a chance to be a big-time journalist and one of the "cool kids." When it turns that not much has changed for her, she enlists the help of her brother (Arquette) and a coworker (Shannon), and eventually falls for sensitive teacher Sam (Vartan). Barrymore is sweet, but doesn't exactly stretch here, and the script sounds a lot like the John Hughes comedies of the '80s. Probably more enjoyable if you're actually high school age. **107m/C VHS, DVD, Wide.** Drew Barrymore, David Arquette, Leelee Sobieski, Michael Vartan, Molly Shannon, John C. Reilly, Garry Marshall, Sean M. Whalen, Jeremy Jordan, Marley Shelton, Jordan Ladd, Jessica Alba; ***D:*** Raja Gosnell; ***W:*** Abby Kohn, Marc Silverstein; ***C:*** Alex Nepomniaschy; ***M:*** David Newman.

Never Cry Wolf 🦴🦴🦴½ **1983 (PG)** A young biologist is sent to the Arctic to study the behavior and habitation of wolves, then becomes deeply involved with their sub-society. Based on Farley Mowat's book. Beautifully photographed. **105m/C VHS, DVD, Wide.** Charles Martin Smith, Brian Dennehy, Samson Jorah; ***D:*** Carroll Ballard; ***W:*** Curtis Hanson, Sam Hamm; ***C:*** Hiro Narita; ***M:*** Mark Isham. Natl. Soc. Film Critics '83: Cinematog.

Never Forget 🦴🦴 **1991** True story of California resident Mel Mermelstein (played by Nimoy), a survivor of Hitler's death camps who accepted a pro-Nazi group's challenge to prove in court that the Holocaust of six million Jews really happened. A sincere, well-meaning courtroom drama that just can't surmount the uncinematic nature of the source material. **94m/C VHS.** Leonard Nimoy, Blythe Danner, Dabney Coleman; ***D:*** Joseph Sargent; ***M:*** Henry Mancini. CABLE

Never Give a Sucker an Even Break 🦴🦴🦴½ *What a Man* **1941** An almost plotless comedy, based on an idea reputedly written on a napkin by Fields (he took screenplay credit as Otis Criblecoblis), and features Fields at his most unleashed. It's something of a cult favorite, but not for all tastes. Classic chase scene ends it. Fields' last role in a feature-length film. **71m/B VHS.** W.C. Fields, Gloria Jean, Franklin Pangborn, Leon Errol, Margaret Dumont, Susan Miller; ***D:*** Edward F. (Eddie) Cline; ***W:*** John Thomas Neville, Prescott Chaplin, W.C. Fields; ***C:*** Charles Van Enger; ***M:*** Frank Skinner.

Never Let Go 🦴🦴 **1960** A man unwittingly tracks down the mastermind of a gang of racketeers. Sellers sheds his comedic image to play the ruthless and brutal gang boss, something he shouldn't have done. **91m/C VHS.** *GB* Peter Sellers, Richard Todd, Elizabeth Sellars, Carol White; ***D:*** John Guillermin; ***M:*** John Barry.

Never Let Me Go 🦴🦴½ **1953** Implausible yet entertaining account of American newsman Gable trying to smuggle ballerina wife Tierney out of Russia. Hard to believe Gable as a one-man assault force infiltrating Russia, but enjoyable nonetheless. Based on the novel "Came the Dawn" by Roger Bax. **94m/B VHS.** Clark Gable, Gene Tierney, Richard Haydn, Bernard Miles, Kenneth More, Karel Stepanek, Theodore Bikel; ***D:*** Delmer Daves; ***W:*** Ronald Millar, George Froeschel.

Never Love a Stranger 🦴🦴 **1958** A young man becomes a numbers runner for a mobster and ultimately winds up heading his own racket. Later he finds himself in conflict with his old boss and the district attorney. No surprises here. Based on the Harold Robbins' novel. **93m/B VHS.** John Blythe Barrymore Jr., Steve McQueen, Lita Milan, Robert Bray; ***D:*** Robert Stevens.

Never Met Picasso 🦴🦴½ **1996** Thirty-year-old artist Andrew (Arquette) lives with self-absorbed actress/mom Genna (Kidder) in Boston, struggling with both his lack of work and romantic prospects. Andrew's one consolation is gay Uncle Alfred (Epstein), who serves as a role model. Until, unexpectedly, Andrew meets confident Jerry (McKellar) at his mother's dreadful opening night bash. After Alfred dies suddenly, Andrew discovers some hidden photos of his uncle's lover and seeks to make connections between the past and the present. **97m/C VHS.** Alexis Arquette, Margot Kidder, Don McKellar, Alvin Epstein, Georgia Ringsdale; ***D:*** Stephen Kijak; ***W:*** Stephen Kijak; ***C:*** David Tames; ***M:*** Kristen Hersh.

Never on Sunday 🦴🦴🦴 **1960** An American intellectual tries to turn a Greek prostitute into a refined woman. Fine performances and exhilarating Greek photography. Fun all around. ♫Never on Sunday. **91m/B VHS.** *GR* Melina Mercouri, Titos Vandis, Jules Dassin, Mitsos Liguisos; ***D:*** Jules Dassin; ***W:*** Jules Dassin; ***M:*** Manos Hadjidakis. Oscars '60: Song ("Never on Sunday"); Cannes '60: Actress (Mercouri).

Never on Tuesday 🦴½ **1988 (R)** Two jerks from Ohio head to California and find themselves stuck midway in the desert with a beautiful girl, who has plans of her own. **90m/C VHS.** Claudia Christian, Andrew Lauer, Peter Berg; ***Cameos:*** Charlie Sheen, Emilio Estevez; ***D:*** Adam Rifkin; ***W:*** Adam Rifkin.

Never Pick Up a Stranger 🦴½ *Bloodrage* **1979** When a local hooker is murdered, her cop boyfriend, who never gives up on a case, hunts her killer with a vengeance. Extremely graphic. **82m/C VHS.** Ian Scott, Judith-Marie Bergan, James Johnston, Lawrence Tierney; ***D:*** Joseph Bigwood.

Never Say Die 🦴🦴½ **1939** Wealthy John Kidley (Hope) is at the Swiss spa of Bad Gasswasser, thinking he only has a few weeks to live. So he marries Mickey Hawkins (Raye) to save her from a crazy Russian, Prince Smirnov (Mowbray), and ends up fighting a duel! Oh, and Mickey thinks she's in love with bus driver Henry Munch (Devine), who accompanies the duo on their honeymoon. Much silliness. Based on the play by William H. Post. **82m/B VHS.** Bob Hope, Martha Raye, Alan Mowbray, Andy Devine, Gale Sondergaard, Monty Woolley, Sig Rumann; ***D:*** Elliott Nugent; ***W:*** Preston Sturges, Don Hartman, Frank Butler; ***C:*** Leo Tover.

Never Say Die 🦴½ **1990** Two innocents are thrown into a web of international intrigue and acquit themselves rather well. Lots of explosions and car crashes for a film shot in New Zealand. **98m/C VHS.** *NZ* George Wendt, Lisa Eilbacher; ***D:*** Geoff Murphy.

Never Say Die 🦴🦴 **1994 (R)** Ex-Special Forces soldier John Blake (Zagarino), ambushed and left to die, returns to seek vengeance on the renegade commander who betrayed him. And he has the perfect opportunity when his nemesis kidnaps a general's daughter. **99m/C VHS.** Frank Zagarino, Billy Drago, Todd Jensen, Jennifer Miller, Robin Smith; ***D:*** Yossi Wein; ***W:*** Jeff Albert; ***M:*** Wendy Oldfield, Adrian Levy.

Never Say Goodbye 🦴🦴 **1946** Cliche-ridden story about a man trying to win back his divorce-bound wife. Flynn tries hard, but the material just isn't up to par. Based on the story "Don't Ever Leave Me" by Ben and Norma Barzman. Co-screenwriter Diamond later became famous when he teamed up with Billy Wilder to script "Some Like it Hot" and "The Apartment." **97m/B VHS.** Errol Flynn, Eleanor Parker, Lucile Watson, S.Z. Sakall, Forrest Tucker, Donald Woods, Peggy Knudsen, Tom D'Andrea, Hattie McDaniel; ***D:*** James V. Kern; ***W:*** James V. Kern, I.A.L. Diamond, Lewis R. Foster.

Never Say Never Again 🦴🦴½ **1983 (PG)** James Bond matches wits with a charming but sinister tycoon who is holding the world nuclear hostage as part of a diabolical plot by SPECTRE. Connery's return to the world of Bond after 12 years is smooth in this remake of "Thunderball" hampered by an atrocious musical score. Carrera is stunning as Fatima Blush. Although Connery is back, purists will have qualms considering this part of the "official" Bond series since longtime Bond producer, Albert "Cubby" Broccoli, had nothing to do with this endeavor. **134m/C VHS, DVD, Wide.** Sean Connery, Klaus Maria Brandauer, Max von Sydow, Barbara Carrera, Kim Basinger, Edward Fox, Bernie Casey, Pamela Salem, Rowan Atkinson, Valerie Leon, Prunella Gee, Saskia Cohen Tanugi; ***D:*** Irvin Kershner; ***W:*** Lorenzo Semple Jr.; ***C:*** Douglas Slocombe; ***M:*** Michel Legrand.

Never So Few 🦴🦴½ **1959** A military commander and his outnumbered troops overcome incredible odds against the Japanese. There is a lot of focus on romance, but the script and acting make a strong impression nonetheless. Based on the novel by Tom T. Chamales. **124m/C VHS, Wide.** Frank Sinatra, Gina Lollobrigida, Peter Lawford, Steve McQueen, Richard Johnson, Paul Henreid, Charles Bronson; ***D:*** John Sturges; ***C:*** William H. Daniels.

Never Steal Anything Small 🦴½ **1959** A tough union boss pushes everyone as he battles the mob for control of the waterfront. A strange musical-drama combination that will be of interest only to the most ardent Cagney and Jones fans. Based on the Maxwell Anderson/Rouben Mamoulian play "The Devil's Hornpipe." Largely forgettable songs. ♫I'm Sorry, I Want a Ferrari; I Haven't Got a Thing to Wear; It Takes Love to Make a Home; Never Steal Anything Small; Helping Out Friends. **94m/C VHS.** James Cagney, Shirley Jones, Cara Williams; ***D:*** Charles Lederer; ***M:*** Henry Mancini.

Never Talk to Strangers 🦴🦴 **1995 (R)** Sarah Taylor (DeMornay) is an uptight criminal psychologist who gets involved with handsome stranger Tony Ramirez (Banderas) while working on the case of a serial killer (Stanton). Then Sarah finds herself the target of an increasingly malevolent stalker—and she has lots of suspects to choose from. Typical woman-in-peril film with easily standard frights but the leads certainly look good (and Banderas is a fine sex object in a bit of role reversal). Filmed in Toronto. **86m/C VHS, DVD.** Rebecca DeMornay, Antonio Banderas, Harry Dean Stanton, Dennis Miller, Len Cariou, Beau Starr; ***D:*** Peter Hall; ***W:*** Lewis Green, Jordan Rush; ***C:*** Elemer Ragalyi; ***M:*** Pino Donaggio.

Never Too Late to Mend 🦴🦴 **1937** Victorian British play about the abuses of the penal system which had, upon its initial London West End run, caused Queen Victoria to institute a sweeping program of prison reform. The movie caused considerably less stir. **67m/B VHS, 8mm.** *GB* Tod Slaughter, Marjorie Taylor, Jack Livesey, Ian Colin; ***D:*** David MacDonald.

Never Too Young to Die 🦴 **1986 (R)** A young man is drawn into a provocative espionage adventure by his late father's spy associates. Together they try to discover who killed the young man's father. High point may be Simmons as a crazed hermaphrodite plotting to poison L.A. **97m/C VHS.** John Stamos, Vanity, Gene Simmons, George Lazenby; ***D:*** Gil Bettman; ***W:*** Gil Bettman; ***M:*** James Newton Howard, Lennie Niehaus.

Never 2 Big 🦴🦴 **1998 (R)** A young record company exec wants to prove that someone at the company murdered his singer sister in order to prevent her from leaving and signing with another label. Only he's been framed for the crime and has to stay out of jail and prove his own innocence. **100m/C VHS, DVD.** Ernie Hudson, Nia Long, Tony Todd, Donnie Wahlberg, Terrence DaShon Howard, Donald Adeosun Faison, Tommy (Tiny) Lister, Salli Richardson, Shemar Moore; ***D:*** Peter Gathings Bunche; ***W:*** Peter Gathings Bunche; ***C:*** Nancy Schreiber; ***M:*** Joseph Williams. VIDEO

Never Wave at a WAC 🦴🦴½ *The Private Wore Skirts* **1952** A Washington socialite joins the Women's Army Corps hoping for a commission that never comes. She has to tough it out as an ordinary private. A reasonably fun ancestor of "Private Benjamin," with a cameo by Gen. Omar Bradley as himself. **87m/B VHS.** Rosalind Russell, Paul Douglas, Marie Wilson, William Ching, Arleen Whelan, Leif Erickson, Hillary Brooke, Regis Toomey; ***Cameos:*** Omar Bradley; ***D:*** Norman Z. McLeod; ***M:*** Elmer Bernstein.

The NeverEnding Story 🦴🦴🦴½ **1984 (PG)** A lonely young boy helps a warrior save the fantasy world in his book from destruction by the Nothing. A wonderful, intelligent family movie about imagination, with swell effects and a sweet but not overly sentimental script. Petersen's first English-language film, based on the novel by Michael Ende. **94m/C VHS, DVD, 8mm, Wide.** Barret Oliver, Noah Hathaway, Gerald McRaney, Moses Gunn, Tami Stronach, Patricia Hayes, Sydney Bromley, Thomas Hill; ***D:*** Wolfgang Petersen; ***W:*** Wolfgang Petersen; ***C:*** Jost Vacano; ***M:*** Klaus Doldinger, Giorgio Moroder.

NeverEnding Story 2: The Next Chapter 🦴🦴 **1991 (PG)** Disappointing sequel to the first story that didn't end. Bastian (Brandis) must again save Fantasia, this time from the evil sorceress Xayride (Burt). So dull, the kids may wander away. But wait: contains the first Bugs Bunny theatrical cartoon in 26 years, "Box Office Bunny." **90m/C VHS, DVD, 8mm, Wide.** Jonathan Brandis, Kenny Morrison, Clarissa Burt, John Wesley Shipp, Martin Umbach; ***D:*** George Miller; ***W:*** Karin Howard; ***C:*** David Connell; ***M:*** Robert Folk.

The NeverEnding Story 3: Escape from Fantasia 🦴🦴 **1994 (G)** The third time was not the charm in this case. Bastian, on the edge of puberty, is being bullied by a group at school called the Nasties. He seeks refuge in the library and enters the world of Fantasia through the "Neverending Story" tome. When the book is stolen by the Nasties, it is up to Bastian to return it. Unfortunately, the story does not have the charm of the original, trying to incorporate too much reality and not enough of dreamland. **95m/C VHS.** Jason James Richter, Melody Kay, Freddie Jones, Jack Black, Ryan Bollman, Tracey Ellis, Kevin McNulty; ***D:*** Peter Macdonald; ***C:*** Robin Vidgeon; ***M:*** Peter Wolf.

Nevil Shute's The Far Country 🦴🦴½ *The Far Country* **1985** Carl Zlintner (York), once a doctor in Hitler's army, escapes to Australia from postwar Europe to begin a new life with a new identity. Falling in love with the beautiful Jennifer Morton (Thornton), Carl hopes he's left his past behind. But nothing is every that simple. Adaptation of the Shute novel. **200m/C VHS.** *AU* Michael York, Sigrid Thornton; ***D:*** George Miller. TV

The New Adventures of Pippi Longstocking 🦴½ **1988 (G)** Decent cast is trapped in another musical rehashing of the Astrid Lindgren children's books about a precocious red-headed girl and her fantastic adventures with horses, criminals, and pirates. **101m/C VHS, DVD.** Tami Erin, Eileen Brennan, Dennis Dugan, Dianne Hull, George DiCenzo, John Schuck, Dick Van Patten; ***D:*** Ken Annakin; ***W:*** Ken Annakin; ***C:*** Roland Smith; ***M:*** Misha Segal.

The New Adventures of Tarzan *Tarzan and the Green Goddess* **1935** Twelve episodes, each 22 minutes long, depict the adventures of Edgar Rice Burrough's tree-swinging character—Tarzan. **260m/B VHS.** Bruce (Herman Brix) Bennett, Ula Holt, Frank Baker, Dale Walsh, Lewis Sargent; ***D:*** Edward Kull.

The New Age 🦴🦴 **1994 (R)** Illusions in L.A. centering on talent agent Peter (Weller) and art designer Katherine (Davis) Witner. Katherine loses her job the same day Peter decides to quit his and suddenly the caustic duo are dependent upon each other. The trendy couple decide to open a boutique and quickly find themselves in a fiscal sinkhole and on a downhill slide. The acting is fine but the story is empty. **106m/C VHS.** Peter Weller, Judy Davis, Adam West, Patrick Bauchau, Corbin Bernsen, Jonathan Hadary, Samuel L. Jackson, Patricia Heaton, Audra Lindley, Paula Marshall, Maureen Mueller, Bruce Ramsay, Sandra Seacat, Susan Traylor; ***D:*** Michael Tolkin; ***W:*** Michael Tolkin, Mark Mothersbaugh.

New Best Friend 🦴½ **2002 (R)** Obvious and sleazy whodunnit wastes its cast. Alicia (Kirshner) is in a cocaine-induced coma after getting in with the wrong college crowd. Working-class mom Connie (O'Connor) raises a stink with new sheriff Bonner (Diggs) to investigate, though the school wants all the sordid details swept under the rug since it involves some wild partying by rich and vapid students. **91m/C VHS, DVD.** Mia Kirshner, Dominique Swain, Rachel True, Meredith Monroe, Scott Bairstow, Taye Diggs, Glynnis O'Connor, Eric Michael Cole; ***D:*** Zoe Clarke-Williams; ***W:*** Victoria Strouse; ***C:*** Tom Priestley; ***M:*** David A. Hughes, John Murphy.

New Blood 🦴🦴 **1999 (R)** Violent thriller that has a few nifty twists. After seven years, Danny White (Moran) turns up on the doorstep of his estranged father, Alan (Hurt). Danny is bleeding from a gunshot wound and makes the devil's own deal with dad: Danny's twin sister needs a heart transplant and Danny offers his own organ if dad will participate in a mob ordered kidnapping that's gone wrong once already. Solid performances are an asset. **92m/C VHS, DVD.** *GB* Nick Moran, John Hurt, Carrie-Anne Moss, Shawn Wayans, Joe Pantoliano, Eugene Glazer, Richard Fitzpatrick, Rob Freeman; ***D:*** Michael Hurst; ***W:*** Michael Hurst; ***C:*** David Pelletier; ***M:*** Jeff Danna.

The New Centurions 🦴🦴½ **1972 (R)** Rookies training for the Los Angeles Police Department get the inside info from retiring cops. Gritty and realistic drama based on the novel by former cop Joseph Wambaugh. Tends to be disjointed at times, but overall is a good adaptation of the bestseller. Scott, excellent as the retiring beat-walker, is supported well by the other performers. **103m/C VHS.** George C. Scott, Stacy Keach, Jane Alexander, Scott Wilson, Erik Estrada, James B. Sikking; ***D:*** Richard Fleischer; ***W:*** Stirling Silliphant; ***M:*** Quincy Jones.

New Crime City: Los Angeles 2020 🦴½ **1994 (R)** Prisoner Tony Ricks (Rossovich) is executed and then revived thanks to technology. But there's a price to pay for his life and freedom—he must retrieve a biowarfare weapon from a prison gang and he only has 24 hours to do it. **95m/C VHS.** Rick Rossovich, Stacy Keach, Sherrie Rose; ***W:*** Rick Rossovich.

New Eden 🦴🦴 **1994 (R)** In the year 2237 wartime prisoners are condemned to a desert planet where they are preyed upon by brutal Sand Pirates. An idealistic engineer falls in love and seeks to protect his new family from a deadly confrontation. **89m/C VHS.** Stephen Baldwin, Lisa Bonet, Tobin Bell, Michael Bowen, Janet Hubert-Whitten; ***D:*** Alan Metzger; ***W:*** Dan Gordon.

The New Eve 🦴🦴🦴 *La Nouvelle Eve* **1998 (R)** Camille (Viard in an astonishing performance) is a hard-partying Parisienne whose hedonistic life is changed when she meets Alexis (Rajot). He's a political activist, married with a couple of kids—not at all the sort of drugged-up playboy she is used to. Their rocky relationship is both sexual and emotional. French with subtitles. **90m/C VHS, DVD, Wide.** *FR* Karin Viard, Pierre-Loup Rajot, Catherine Frot, Sergei Lopez, Mireille Roussel, Nozha Khouadra; ***D:*** Catherine Corsini; ***W:*** Catherine Corsini, Marc Syrigas; ***C:*** Agnes Godard.

New Faces of 1952 🦴🦴½ **1954** Based on the hit Broadway revue. The plot revolves around a Broadway show that is about to be closed down, and the performers who fight to keep it open. Lots of hit songs. Mel Brooks is credited as a writer, under the name Melvin Brooks. ♫C'est Si Bon; Santa Baby; Uskadara; Monotonous; Bal Petit Bal; Boston Beguine; I'm in Love with Miss Logan; Penny Candy; Time for Tea. **98m/C VHS.** Ronny Graham, Eartha Kitt, Robert Clary, Alice Ghostley, June Carroll, Carol Lawrence, Paul Lynde; ***D:*** Harry Horner.

New Fist of Fury 🦴 *Xin Ching-wu Men* **1976** During WWII, a former pickpocket becomes a martial arts whiz with the assistance of his fiancee, and fights the entire Imperial Army. **120m/C VHS, DVD.** Jackie Chan; ***D:*** Lo Wei; ***W:*** Lo Wei.

The New Frontier 🦴½ **1935** Wayne is a small-town sheriff whose predecessor, his father, was murdered. The local saloon-keeper and his gang do everything they can to prevent Wayne from bringing the culprit to justice. **59m/B VHS.** John Wayne, Muriel Evans, Murdock McQuarrie, Mary MacLaren, Warner Richmond; ***D:*** Carl Pierson.

The New Gladiators woof! **1983** In the future, criminals try to kill each other on TV for public entertainment. Two such gladiators discover that the network's computer is using the games in order to take over mankind, and they attempt to stop it. Even if the special effects were any good, they couldn't save this one. **90m/C VHS, DVD.** *IT* Jared Martin, Fred Williamson, Eleanor Gold, Howard (Red) Ross, Claudio Cassinelli; ***D:*** Lucio Fulci; ***W:*** Elisa Briganti, Dardano Sacchetti; ***C:*** Guiseppe Pinori; ***M:*** Riz Ortolani.

The New Guy 🦴½ **2002 (PG-13)** Dorky high school senior Dizzy (Qualls) wants to transform himself into a cool guy—by getting expelled and transferring to another school. Instead, he winds up in prison where he meets Luther (Griffin), who gives him an attitude makeover. Once he hits the new school, his newfound popularity has him winning a hottie cheerleader (Dushku) and uniting the school. Long (but not quite long enough)-delayed high school flick shows a certain lack of effort on most everyone's part, most notably the director, writer, and cinematographer. Qualls is likable, Deschanel is better than flick deserves, and Dushku supplies the expected sexual spark. **88m/C VHS, DVD.** *US* DJ Qualls, Eddie Griffin, Eliza Dushku, Zooey Deschanel, Lyle Lovett, Jerod Mixon, Parry Shen, Sunny Mabrey, Ross Patterson, Matt Gogin, Illeana Douglas, Kurt Fuller, M.C. Gainey, Julius J. Carry III, Horatio Sanz, Geoffrey Lewis; ***Cameos:*** Henry Rollins, Gene Simmons, Vanilla Ice, Tommy Lee; ***D:*** Edward Decter; ***W:***

David Kendall; **C:** Michael D. O'Shea; **M:** Ralph Sall.

The New Invisible Man 🦴🦴 *H.G. Wells' New Invisible Man* **1958** A so-so Mexican adaptation of the popular H.G. Wells novel has a prisoner receiving a vanishing drug from his brother, who created it—perhaps to aid an escape attempt. **95m/B VHS.** *MX* Arturo de Cordova, Ana Luisa Peluffo, Jorge Mondragon; **D:** Alfredo B. Crevenna.

New Jack City 🦴🦴½ **1991 (R)** Just say no ghetto-melodrama. Powerful performance by Snipes as wealthy Harlem drug lord sought by rebel cops Ice-T and Nelson. Music by Johnny Gill, 2 Live Crew, Ice-T and others. **101m/C VHS, DVD.** Wesley Snipes, Ice-T, Mario Van Peebles, Chris Rock, Judd Nelson, Tracy C. Johns, Allen Payne, Kim Park, Vanessa Williams, Nick Ashford, Thalmus Rasulala, Michael Michele, Bill Nunn, Russell Wong; **D:** Mario Van Peebles; **W:** Keith Critchlow, Barry Michael Cooper; **C:** Francis Kenny; **M:** Roger Bourland, Michel Colombier.

New Jersey Drive 🦴🦴½ **1995 (R)** Jason (Corley) has dreams of life outside the mean streets of Newark, but he jeopardizes his future by stealing cars and joyriding around the neighborhood with his friends. Unblinking realism, provided by credible actors (especially Corley, a former gang member), dialogue, and filming in the projects of Brooklyn and Queens, is nuetralized by stereotypical characters (especially the lily-white, sadistically brutal cops) and lack of a sympathetic point of view. Loosely based on a series of articles by Michel Mariott, a reporter for the "New York Times." **98m/C VHS, DVD.** Sharron Corley, Gabriel Casseus, Saul Stein, Andre Moore, Donald Adeosun Faison, Conrad Meertin Jr., Deven Eggleston, Gwen McGee, Koran C. Thomas, Samantha Brown, Christine Baranski, Robert Jason Jackson, Roscoe Orman, Dwight Errington Myers, Gary DeWitt Marshall; **D:** Nick Gomez; **W:** Nick Gomez, Michel Marriott; **C:** Adam Kimmel; **M:** Wendy Blackstone.

The New Kids 🦴🦴 **1985 (R)** An orphaned brother and sister find out the limitations of the good neighbor policy. A sadistic gang terrorizes them after their move to a relatives' home in Florida. They go after expected revenge. **90m/C VHS.** Shannon Presby, Lori Loughlin, James Spader, Eric Stoltz; **D:** Sean S. Cunningham; **W:** Brian Taggert, Stephen Gyllenhaal.

A New Kind of Love 🦴🦴½ **1963** Romantic fluff starring real-life couple Newman and Woodward who meet en route to Paris and end up falling in love. Newman plays a reporter and Woodward is a fashion designer in this light comedy set amidst the sights of Paris. **110m/C VHS.** Paul Newman, Joanne Woodward, Thelma Ritter, Eva Gabor, Maurice Chevalier, George Tobias; **D:** Melville Shavelson; **W:** Melville Shavelson; **C:** Daniel F. Fapp.

The New Land 🦴🦴🦴 *Nybyggarna* **1973 (PG)** Sequel to "The Emigrants" follows Von Sydow and his family as they struggle to make their new home in the new world. Hardships include severe weather which devastates the farm, a Sioux indian uprising, and a disastrous trek to the Southwest to search for gold. Sensitive performances and direction. Based on the novels by Vilhelm Moberg. Dubbed into English. **161m/C VHS.** *SW* Max von Sydow, Liv Ullmann, Allan Edwall, Eddie Axberg, Hans Alfredson, Halvar Bjork, Peter Lindgren, Monica Zetterlund, Pierre Lindstedt, Per Oscarsson; **D:** Jan Troell; **W:** Jan Troell, Bengt Forslund; **C:** Jan Troell; **M:** Bengt Ernryd, George Oddner. Natl. Bd. of Review '73: Actress (Ullmann); Natl. Soc. Film Critics '73: Actress (Ullmann).

A New Leaf 🦴🦴½ **1971 (G)** A playboy who has depleted his financial resources tries to win the hand of a clumsy heiress. May was the first woman to write, direct and star in a movie. She was unhappy with the cuts that were made by the studio, but that didn't seem to affect its impact with the public. Even with the cuts, the film is still funny and May's performance is worth watching. **102m/C VHS.** Walter Matthau, Elaine May, Jack Weston, George Rose, William Redfield, James Coco; **D:** Elaine May; **W:** Elaine May.

A New Life 🦴🦴½ **1988 (PG-13)** An uptight stockbroker is abandoned by his wife. The New York singles scene beckons both of them to a new chance at life. Appealing performances cannot completely mask the old storyline, but it's definitely worth a look. **104m/C VHS.** Alan Alda, Ann-Margret, Hal Linden, Veronica Hamel, John Shea, Mary Kay Place, Cynthia Belliveau, Beatrice Alda; **D:** Alan Alda; **W:** Alan Alda; **M:** Joseph Turrin.

New Mafia Boss 🦴½ *Crime Boss* **1972 (PG)** Italian-made plodder has Savalas taking over a huge Mafia family and all hell breaking loose. **90m/C VHS.** *IT* Telly Savalas, Lee Van Cleef, Antonio (Tony) Sabato, Paolo Tedesco; **D:** Alberto De Martino.

New Moon 🦴🦴½ **1940** An adaptation of the operetta by Sigmund Romberg and Oscar Hammerstein II. A French heiress traveling on a boat that is captured by pirates falls in love with their leader. Remake of the 1930 film. Includes the 1935 Robert Benchley MGM short "How to Sleep." ♫Dance Your Cares Away; Stranger in Paris; The Way They Do It in Paris; Lover Come Back; Shoes; Softly as in a Morning Sunrise; One Kiss; Troubles of the World; No More Weeping. **106m/B VHS.** Jeanette MacDonald, Nelson Eddy, Buster Keaton, Joe Yule, Jack Perrin, Mary Boland; **D:** Robert Z. Leonard.

New Orleans 🦴🦴½ **1947** The great legends of jazz re-enact its birth in this song-filled tribute to the town where it all began. When the proprietor (de Cordova) of a Bourbon Street gambling joint (and haven for musicians) falls for an opera-singing socialite, he realizes that only through music will he gain responsibility. He begins a campaign to bring jazz to the highbrow American stage. **90m/B VHS, DVD.** Arturo de Cordova, Dorothy Patrick, Louis Armstrong, Billie Holiday, Woody Herman, Richard Hageman; **D:** Arthur Lubin; **W:** Elliot Paul, Dick Irving Hyland; **C:** Lucien N. Andriot.

New Orleans After Dark 🦴🦴 **1958** A pair of New Orleans detectives tour the city, crime-buster style, and bag a dope ring. Average crime tale, shot on location in the Big Easy. **69m/B VHS.** Stacy Harris, Louis Sirgo, Ellen Moore; **D:** John Sledge.

New Pastures 🦴🦴½ **1962** Three ex-convicts run into some humorous situations when they go back to their small hometown. A semi-acclaimed Czech comedy, with subtitles. **92m/B VHS.** *CZ* **D:** Vladimir Cech.

New Rose Hotel 🦴½ **1998 (R)** Corporate raider Fox (Walken) and his assistant X (Dafoe) are hired to get scientific genius Hiroshi (Amano) into working for another company. Slinky Sandii (Argento) is the lure. She succeeds but double-crosses her employers who now expect to be killed for not fulfilling their contract. (Industrial espionage is apparently quite hazardous.) Frustrating as director Ferrara repeats scenes with minor variations, leaving viewers bewildered if nothing else. Based on a story by William Gibson. **92m/C VHS, DVD.** Christopher Walken, Willem Dafoe, Asia Argento, Yoshitaka Amano, Annabella Sciorra, Gretchen Mol, John Lurie, Ryuichi Sakamoto; **D:** Abel Ferrara; **W:** Abel Ferrara, Chris Zois; **C:** Ken Kelsch.

New Waterford Girl 🦴🦴½ **1999** Mooney Pottie (Balaban) is a 15-year-old stuck in a small coal-mining community in Nova Scotia in the 1970s. Mooney has won a scholarship to a prestigious arts school and is desperate to attend but her parents refuse to let her. But careful observation has shown Mooney that girls who get themselves into "trouble" leave the community to have their babies in secret and she decides to transform herself into a slut (while keeping her virginity) and get out of town. Sweetly amusing with a compelling debut performance from Balaban. **97m/C VHS, DVD.** *CA* Liane Balaban, Tara Spencer-Nairn, Andrew McCarthy, Nicholas (Nick) Campbell, Mary Walsh, Cathy Moriarty; **D:** Allan Moyle; **W:** Tricia Fish; **C:** Derek Rogers.

New World Disorder 🦴🦴 **1999 (R)** Action thriller combines familiar elements of the formula with high-tech computer jargon. A gang of thieves led by the bestudded Bishop (McCarthy) blasts into a computer chip company and steals the Rosetta encryption program. Young computer-savvy FBI agent Paddock (Fitzgerald) winds up working with old-fashioned local cop Marx (Hauer) to catch the bad guys. The action scenes are fairly ambitious for a video premiere. **94m/C VHS, DVD.** Rutger Hauer, Andrew McCarthy, Tara Fitzgerald; **D:** Richard Spence; **W:** Ehren Kruger, Jeffrey Smith; **C:** Ivan Strasburg; **M:** Gast Waltzing. **VIDEO**

New Year's Day 🦴🦴🦴 **1989 (R)** Jaglom continues his look at modern relationships in this story of a man reclaiming his house from three female tenants. Introspective character study lightened by humor and insight. **90m/C VHS.** Maggie Jakobson, Gwen Welles, Melanie Winter, Milos Forman, Michael Emil, David Duchovny, Tracy Reiner, Henry Jaglom; **D:** Henry Jaglom; **W:** Henry Jaglom.

New Year's Evil woof! **1978 (R)** Every hour during a New Year's Eve concert, a madman kills an unsuspecting victim. After each killing, the murderer informs a local disc jockey of his deed. Little does the disc jockey know that she will soon be next on his list. No suspense, bad music makes this slash and crash a holiday wrecker. **88m/C VHS.** Roz Kelly, Kip Niven, Chris Wallace, Louisa Moritz, Grant Kramer, Jed Mills; **D:** Emmett Alston; **W:** Emmett Alston; **M:** Michael W. Lewis.

New York Cop 🦴½ **1994 (R)** Japanese martial arts expert Toshi (Nakamura) joins the NYPD and is given an undercover assignment to infiltrate a gun-running gang that supplies both drug lords and Japanese mobsters. But internal rivalries force Toshi to bond with gang leader Hawk (McQueen) and the duo to do battle together. **88m/C VHS.** Toru Nakamura, Chad McQueen, Mira Sorvino; **D:** Toru Murakawa.

New York, New York 🦴🦴🦴 **1977 (PG)** Tragic romance evolves between a saxophonist and an aspiring singer/actress in this salute to the big-band era. A love of music isn't enough to hold them together through career rivalries and life on the road. Fine performances by De Niro and Minnelli and the supporting cast. Re-released in 1981 with the "Happy Endings" number, which was cut from the original. Look for "Big Man" Clarence Clemons on sax. ♫New York, New York; There Goes the Ball Game; Happy Endings; But the World Goes 'Round; Night in Tunisia; Opus One; Avalon; You Brought a New Kind of Love to Me; I'm Getting Sentimental Over You. **163m/C VHS, Wide.** Robert De Niro, Liza Minnelli, Lionel Stander, Barry Primus, Mary Kay Place, Dick Miller, Diahnne Abbott; **D:** Martin Scorsese; **W:** Mardik Martin; **M:** Ralph Burns.

New York Nights 🦴 **1984 (R)** The lives of nine New Yorkers intertwine in a treacherous game of passion and seduction. Liberal borrowing from plot of "La Ronde." **104m/C VHS.** Corinne Alphen, George Auyer, Bobbi Burns, Peter Matthey, Cynthia Lee, Willem Dafoe; **D:** Simon Nuchtern.

New York Ripper woof! *Lo Squartatore de New York; The Ripper* **1982** A New York cop tracks down a rampaging murderer in this dull, mindless slasher flick. **88m/C VHS, DVD.** *IT* Jack Hedley, Antonella Interlenghi, Howard (Red) Ross, Andrea Occhipinti, Alessandra Delli Colli, Paolo Malco; **D:** Lucio Fulci; **W:** Lucio Fulci, Gianfranco Clerici, Vincenzo Mannino, Dardano Sacchetti; **C:** Luigi Kuveiller; **M:** Francesco De Masi.

New York Stories 🦴🦴🦴 **1989 (PG)** Entertaining anthology of three separate short films by three esteemed directors, all set in New York. In "Life Lessons" by Scorsese, an impulsive artist tries to prevent his live-in girlfriend from leaving him. "Life Without Zoe" by Coppola involves a youngster's fantasy about a wealthy 12-year-old who lives mostly without her parents. Allen's "Oedipus Wrecks," generally considered the best short, is about a 50-year-old man who is tormented by the specter of his mother. **124m/C VHS.** Nick Nolte, Rosanna Arquette, Woody Allen, Mia Farrow, Mae Questel, Julie Kavner, Talia Shire, Giancarlo Giannini, Don Novello, Patrick O'Neal, Peter Gabriel, Paul Herman, Deborah Harry, Steve Buscemi, Heather McComb, Chris Elliott, Carole Bouquet, Edward I. Koch; **D:** Woody Allen, Martin Scorsese, Francis Ford Coppola; **W:** Woody Allen, Francis Ford Coppola, Richard Price, Sofia Coppola; **C:** Sven Nykvist, Nestor Almendros; **M:** Carmine Coppola.

New York's Finest 🦴 **1987 (R)** Three prostitutes are determined to leave their calling and marry very eligible millonaires. But becoming society ladies is more difficult than they thought. Would-be sophisticated comedy misfires. **80m/C VHS.** Ruth (Coreen) Collins, Jennifer Delora, Scott Thompson Baker, Heidi Paine, Jane (Veronica Hart) Hamilton, Alan Naggar, John Altamura, Alan Fisler, Josey Duval; **D:** Chuck Vincent.

The Newlydeads 🦴½ **1987** An uptight, conservative, honeymoon resort owner murders one of his guests and finds out that "she" is really a he. Fifteen years later, on his wedding night, all of his guests are violently murdered by the transvestite's vengeful ghost. Oddball twist to the usual slasher nonsense. **84m/C VHS.** Scott Kaske, Jim Williams, Jean Levine, Jay Richardson; **D:** Joseph Merhi.

Newman's Law 🦴🦴 **1974 (PG)** A city detective is implicated in a corruption investigation. While on suspension, he continues with his own investigation of a large drug ring and finds corruption is closer than he thought. Director Heffron's first feature film. **98m/C VHS.** George Peppard, Roger Robinson, Eugene Roche, Gordon Pinsent, Louis Zorich, Abe Vigoda; **D:** Richard T. Heffron.

News at Eleven 🦴🦴 **1986** A fading news anchorman is pressured by his ambitious young boss to expose a touchy local sex scandal, forcing him to consider the public's right to know versus the rights of the individual. About average for TV drama. **95m/C VHS.** Martin Sheen, Peter Riegert, Barbara Babcock, Sheree J. Wilson, Sydney Penny, David S. Sheiner, Christopher Allport; **D:** Mike Robe. **TV**

News from Home 🦴🦴 **1976** Scenes of life in New York are juxtaposed with voiceover from the letters of a mother to her young daughter. Plotless narrative deals with the small details of life. **85m/C VHS.** **D:** Chantal Akerman; **W:** Chantal Akerman; **Nar:** Chantal Akerman.

Newsbreak 🦴🦴 **2000 (R)** Reckless and arrogant reporter John McNamara (Rooker) has made a lot of enemies. When he decides to investigate the disappearance of a fellow journalist, John uncovers citywide corruption that involves the president of a construction company (Reinhold) and his own father (Culp), a judge with a sterling reputation. **95m/C VHS, DVD.** Michael Rooker, Judge Reinhold, Robert Culp, Kelly Miller, Kim Darby, Noelle Parker; **D:** Serge Rodnunsky; **W:** Serge Rodnunsky, Paul Tarantino; **C:** Howard Wexler; **M:** Evan Evans. **VIDEO**

Newsfront 🦴🦴🦴 **1978** A story about two brothers, both newsreel filmmakers, and their differing approaches to life and their craft in the 1940s and '50s. Tribute to the days of newsreel film combines real stories and fictionalized accounts with color and black and white photography. Noyce's feature film debut. **110m/C VHS.** *AU* Bill Hunter, Gerard Kennedy, Angela Punch McGregor, Wendy Hughes, Chris Haywood, John Ewart, Bryan Brown; **D:** Phillip Noyce. Australian Film Inst. '78: Actor (Hunter), Film.

Newsies 🦴½ **1992 (PG)** An unfortunate attempt at an old-fashioned musical with a lot of cute kids and cardboard characters and settings. The plot, such as it is, concerns the 1899 New York newsboys strike against penny-pinching publisher Joseph Pulitzer. Bale plays the newsboy's leader and at least shows some charisma in a strictly cartoon setting. The songs are mediocre but the dancing is lively. However, none of it moves the story along. Add a bone for viewers under 12. Choreographer Ortega's feature-film directorial debut. **121m/C VHS, DVD, Wide.** Christian Bale, Bill Pullman, Robert Duvall, Ann-Margret, Michael Lerner, Kevin Tighe, Charles Cioffi, Luke Edwards, Max Casella, David Moscow; **D:** Kenny Ortega; **W:** Bob Tzudiker; **C:** Noni White; **M:** Alan Menken, Jack Feldman. Golden Raspberries '92: Worst Song ("High Times, Hard Times").

The Newton Boys 🦴🦴½ **1997 (PG-13)** Fact-based drama chronicling the careers and love lives of the bank robbing Newton brothers, who robbed their way from Texas to Toronto during the '20s and '30s. They lived and worked by a romantic credo: no killing, stealing from women or children, and no ratting each other out. McConaughey and Ulrich lead the group as Willis and Joe, respectively, and both prove likeable gangsters. Hawke and D'Onfrio do their best in less developed roles. Highlight is the great train robbery, which garnered the outlaws $3 million and eventually landed the boys in court. Though well-acted with interesting material, Linklater's departure lacks precise angle, which keeps the story from really humming. Stealing the show is the real-life footage of a 1980 "Tonight Show" where Johnny Carson interviews the personable Joe. **122m/C VHS, DVD, Wide.** Matthew McConaughey, Skeet Ulrich, Ethan Hawke, Vincent D'Onofrio, Julianna Margulies, Dwight Yoakam, Gail Cronauer, Chloe Webb, Charles Gunning, Becket Gremmels, Richard Jones; ***D:*** Richard Linklater; ***W:*** Claude Stanush, Clark Lee Walker; ***C:*** Peter James; ***M:*** Edward D. Barnes.

The Next Best Thing 🦴½ **2000 (PG-13)** L.A. yoga instructor Abbie (Madonna) manages to get preggers thanks to a drunken one-nighter with gay best friend, Robert (Everett). She has the kid, they decide to live together and share parental responsibilities (but nothing more), and for six years things just go along swimmingly. Then Abbie meets the perfect guy—investment banker Ben (Bratt). But Ben is planning to relocate to New York and suddenly sole custody is all that matters to Abbie—even it means a court case. Sappy, predictable story falls prey to Madonna's limited acting ability though both Everett and Bratt supply charm galore. **108m/C VHS, DVD, Wide.** Madonna, Rupert Everett, Benjamin Bratt, Michael Vartan, Josef Sommer, Lynn Redgrave, Malcolm Stumpf, Neil Patrick Harris, Illeana Douglas, Mark Valley, Stacy Edwards; ***D:*** John Schlesinger; ***W:*** Tom Ropelewski; ***C:*** Elliot Davis; ***M:*** Gabriel Yared. Golden Raspberries '00: Worst Actress (Madonna).

Next Door 🦴🦴½ **1994 (R)** College professors Matt (Woods) and Karen (Capshaw) have the perfect suburban home—complete with the perfect suburban garden. Then their boorish blue-collar neighbor Lenny (Quaid) takes to enthusiastic lawn watering and ruins their flowers. One thing leads to a full-scale feud. **95m/C VHS.** James Woods, Randy Quaid, Kate Capshaw, Lucinda Jenney; ***D:*** Tony Bill; ***W:*** Barney Cohen; ***C:*** Thomas Del Ruth. CABLE

Next Friday 🦴🦴 **2000 (R)** Amiable, meandering sequel to 1995's surprise hit "Friday" finds Craig (Ice Cube) fleeing to the suburbs to escape Debo (Lister), who's out of prison and looking for payback. Uncle Elroy (Curry) has hit the lotto and moved to the 'burbs, giving Craig, and a whole new bunch of central casting characters a new place to hang out and cause some mischief. The original's biggest success came on home video and cable, and this one's likely to duplicate that pattern. **93m/C VHS, DVD, Wide.** Ice Cube, Tommy (Tiny) Lister, John Witherspoon, Justin Pierce, Jacob Vargas, Lobo Sebastian, Rolando Molina, Tamala Jones, Mike Epps, Don "DC" Curry, Lisa Rodriguez, Kym E. Whitley, Amy Hill, Robin Allen; ***D:*** Steve Carr; ***W:*** Ice Cube; ***C:*** Christopher Baffa; ***M:*** Terence Blanchard.

The Next Karate Kid 🦴🦴½ **1994 (PG)** Fourth installment in the "Kid" series finds martial arts expert Miyagi (Morita) training Julie Pierce (Swank), the orphaned tomboy daughter of an old war buddy who saved his life 50 years earlier. He even teaches her the waltz, just in time for the prom, but she's still tough enough to scrap with a guy. A must-see for "Karate Kid" fans, if there are any left. **107m/C VHS.** Noriyuki "Pat" Morita, Hilary Swank; ***D:*** Christopher Cain; ***W:*** Mark Lee; ***M:*** Bill Conti.

Next of Kin 🦴 **1982** A daughter moves into her dead mother's retirement home and discovers an unspeakable evil that lurks there. Typical horror stuff has some very creepy moments; filmed in New Zealand. **90m/C VHS, 8mm.** *AU* Jackie Kerin, John Jarratt, Gerida Nicholson, Alex Scott; ***D:*** Tony Williams.

Next of Kin 🦴🦴 **1984** A young man experiencing familial difficulties undergoes experimental video therapy where he views a videotape of an Armenian family who gave their son up for adoption. When he discovers the actual family he insinuates himself into their life, determined to be their long-lost son. **72m/C VHS, DVD.** *CA* Patrick Tierney; ***D:*** Atom Egoyan; ***W:*** Atom Egoyan.

Next of Kin 🦴🦴 **1989 (R)** A Chicago cop returns to his Kentucky home to avenge his brother's brutal murder. Swayze's return to action films after his success in "Dirty Dancing" is unimpressive. **108m/C VHS, DVD, 8mm.** Patrick Swayze, Adam Baldwin, Bill Paxton, Helen Hunt, Andreas Katsulas, Ben Stiller, Michael J. Pollard, Liam Neeson; ***D:*** John Irvin; ***C:*** Steven Poster; ***M:*** Jack Nitzsche.

Next One 🦴½ **1984** Mysterious visitor from another time winds up on an isolated Greek island as the result of a magnetic storm. The local inhabitants are amazed when the visitor displays some Christ-like characteristics. **105m/C VHS.** Keir Dullea, Adrienne Barbeau, Jeremy Licht, Peter Hobbs; ***D:*** Nico Mastorakis.

The Next Step 🦴🦴½ **1995** Nick Mendez (Negron) is a 35-year-old Broadway dancer who's feeling the wear and tear of his profession. A practiced seducer, Nick does have a devoted girlfriend in ex-dancer turned physical therapist, Amy (Moreu). Amy gets a job offer in Connecticut just as Nick's confidence is shaken when he's rejected for a dance role he originated in favor of a younger performer. Amy wants Nick to retire and move away with her but life away from Broadway leaves Nick wondering what he'd do. Negron is a former Broadway dancer and offers a compelling performance in a film that's ripe with showbiz cliches. **97m/C VHS, DVD, Wide.** Rick Negron, Kristin Moreu, Denise Faye, Taylor Nichols; ***D:*** Christian Faber; ***W:*** Aaron Reed; ***C:*** Zack Winestine; ***M:*** Mio Morales, Brian Otto, Roni Skies.

Next Stop, Greenwich Village 🦴🦴🦴 **1976 (R)** An affectionate, autobiographical look by Mazursky at a Brooklyn boy with acting aspirations, who moves to Greenwich Village in 1953. Good performances, especially by Winters as the overbearing mother. **109m/C VHS.** Lenny Baker, Christopher Walken, Ellen Greene, Shelley Winters, Lou Jacobi, Mike Kellin; ***D:*** Paul Mazursky; ***W:*** Paul Mazursky; ***M:*** Bill Conti.

Next Stop, Wonderland 🦴🦴½ **1998 (R)** Charming romance, set in Boston, about a couple of odd ducks who are totally right for each other. Waifish Eric (Davis) is a nurse whose boyfriend Sean (Hoffman) has just left her. So her meddling mom Piper (Taylor) secretly places a personal ad to get her daughter some dates. They're a bunch of losers but plumber/marine-biology student Alan (Gelfant), whom Erin keeps seeing on the subway is Mr. Right. If only the duo could get together. Intelligent characters and a terrific bossa nova soundtrack. Title refers to the name of an actual subway stop. **96m/C VHS, DVD, Wide.** Hope Davis, Alan Gelfant, Holland Taylor, Robert Klein, Cara Buono, Jose Zuniga, Phil Hoffman, Lyn Vaus, Larry Gilliard Jr., Victor Argo, Roger Rees, Robert Stanton; ***D:*** Brad Anderson; ***W:*** Brad Anderson, Lyn Vaus; ***C:*** Uta Briesewitz; ***M:*** Claudio Ragazzi.

Next Summer 🦴🦴🦴 *L'Ete Prochain* **1984** A large, character-studded French family pursues power, love and beauty. Excellent performances. In French with English subtitles. **120m/C VHS.** *FR* Jean-Louis Trintignant, Claudia Cardinale, Fanny Ardant, Philippe Noiret, Marie Trintignant; ***D:*** Nadine Trintignant.

Next Time I Marry 🦴½ **1938** Lucy fraternizes with ditch digger Ellison because she needs to hitch a Yankee in order to inherit $20 mill. Seems she really loves a foreigner, though. Not much to bobaloo about. Director Kanin's second effort. **65m/B VHS.** Lucille Ball, James Ellison, Lee Bowman, Granville Bates, Mantan Moreland, Florence Lake; ***D:*** Garson Kanin.

The Next Victim 🦴 *Lo Strano Vizio Della Signora Wardh* **1971 (PG)** The unfaithful wife of an Austrian diplomat attempts to find out who has been slicing up beautiful jet-setters. Tepid mystery. **87m/C VHS.** George Hilton, Edwige Fenech, Christina Airoldi, Ivan Rassimov; ***D:*** Sergio Martino.

Next Victim 🦴 **1974** A beautiful woman confined to a wheelchair is stalked by a lunatic killer. You've seen it before, and done better. **80m/C VHS.** *GB* Carroll Baker, T.P. McKenna, Ronald Lacey, Maurice Kaufmann; ***D:*** James Ormerod.

The Next Voice You Hear 🦴🦴½ **1950** Lives are changed forever when a group of people hear the voice of God on the radio. Interesting premise presented seriously. **84m/B VHS.** James Whitmore, Nancy Davis, Gary Gray, Lillian Bronson, Art Smith, Tom D'Andrea, Jeff Corey, George Chandler; ***D:*** William A. Wellman.

Next Year If All Goes Well 🦴🦴½ **1983** Two young lovers struggle to overcome insecurities while establishing a relationship. Dubbed. **95m/C VHS.** *FR* Isabelle Adjani, Thierry Lhermitte, Mariann (Marie-Anne) Chazel; ***D:*** Jean-Loup Hubert.

Next Year in Jerusalem 🦴🦴 **1998** Charlie is openly gay—but what he's hiding is his Orthodox Jewish background. Pressured by his mother, Charlie shows up at the family Passover seder, where he meets Manny. Devout Manny is supposed to marry the Rabbi's daughter, only he's got a secret too. The duo soon begin a relationship they keep from their families but it becomes clear that Charlie and Manny need to be honest about who they truly are. **103m/C VHS.** Peter J. Byrnes, Reed McGowan, Georgina Spelvin, Louis Edmonds; ***D:*** David Nahmod; ***W:*** David Nahmod; ***C:*** Kelvin Walker; ***M:*** Richard Barone.

Niagara 🦴🦴½ **1952** During their honeymoon in Niagara Falls, a scheming wife (Monroe) plans to kill her crazed war-vet husband (Cotten). Little does she know that he is plotting to double-cross her. Steamy, quasi-Hitchcockian mystery ably directed, with interesting performances. Monroes sings "Kiss." **89m/B VHS, DVD.** Joseph Cotten, Jean Peters, Marilyn Monroe, Max (Casey Adams) Showalter, Don Wilson; ***D:*** Henry Hathaway; ***W:*** Charles Brackett, Walter Reisch; ***C:*** Joe MacDonald; ***M:*** Sol Kaplan.

Niagara, Niagara 🦴🦴 **1997 (R)** Marcy (Tunney) is a victim of Tourette's Syndrome, which causes the sufferer to twitch and unleash strings of profanity that would make a longshoreman blush. She meets shy, introverted Seth (Thomas) while they're both shoplifting, and it's love at first sight. They hit the road, supposedly for a doll that Marcy believes can be found in Toronto, but in reality because they are already outcasts at home. When Seth is injured in a botched pharmacy robbery, they're taken in by fellow oddball Walter, a tow truck driver who dotes on a pet chicken named after his dead wife. All of these lost characters are on a road to nowhere, and are pulled apart by Marcy's bourbon-fueled tics and tantrums. Compelling performance by Tunney carries the rest of this dull, flat movie on its back. **96m/C VHS.** Robin Tunney, Henry Thomas, Michael Parks, Stephen Lang, John MacKay; ***D:*** Bob Gosse; ***W:*** Matthew Weiss; ***C:*** Michael Spiller; ***M:*** Michael Timmins, Jeff Bird.

Nice Girl? 🦴🦴½ **1941** Jane (Durbin) develops a crush on visiting professor Richard Calvert (Tone), much to his embarassment. But her steady beau Don (Stack) sticks around to provide support while Calvert seeks a way to let Jane down easy. The video includes a 3-minute alternate ending. **96m/B VHS.** Deanna Durbin, Franchot Tone, Robert Stack, Robert Benchley, Walter Brennan, Ann Gillis, Helen Broderick, Anne Gwynne; ***D:*** William A. Seiter; ***W:*** Richard Connell, Gladys Lehman; ***C:*** Joseph Valentine.

Nice Girl Like Me 🦴🦴 **1969 (PG)** An orphaned young girl roams Europe, getting pregnant twice by two different men. She eventually finds love in the form of a kind caretaker. Harmless fluff. Based on Anne Piper's novel "Marry At Leisure." **91m/C VHS.** *GB* Harry Andrews, Barbara Ferris, Gladys Cooper, Bill Hinnant, James Villiers; ***D:*** Desmond Davis.

Nice Girls Don't Explode 🦴🦴 **1987 (PG)** A girl telekinetically starts fires when sexually aroused. This puts a bit of a damper on her relationship with O'Leary, much to her mother's delight. Matchless entertainment. **92m/C VHS.** Barbara Harris, Wallace Shawn, Michelle Meyrink, William O'Leary; ***D:*** Chuck Martinez; ***M:*** Brian Banks.

Nice Guys Sleep Alone 🦴🦴🦴 **1999 (R)** Overachieving independent romantic comedy finds nice guy Carter (O'Bryan) hearing those three dreaded words "let's be friends" at the end of each date. He has resolved to take a new approach when he meets Maggie (Temchen), a vet recently arrived in Louisville from New York. The complications that keep the plot moving are familiar, and Carter's rival Robert (Murray) is such a swine that it's impossible any intelligent woman would pay attention to him, no matter how rich he is. But the characters are engaging, especially Carter's stepsister Erin (Marcil), and the film has its heart in the right place. **92m/C DVD, Wide.** Sean O'Bryan, Sybil Temchen, Vanessa Marcil, Blake Steury, Christopher Murray, Morgan Fairchild, William Sanderson; ***D:*** Stu Pollard; ***W:*** Stu Pollard; ***C:*** Nathan Hope.

Nice Neighbor 🦴🦴🦴 **1979** An acclaimed film about an outwardly self-sacrificing neighbor who cold-bloodedly manipulates his fellow rooming house tenants for his own ends. In Hungarian with English subtitles. **90m/C VHS.** *HU* Laszlo Szabo, Margit Dayka, Agi Margittay; ***D:*** Zsolt Kedzi-Kovacs.

Nicholas and Alexandra 🦴🦴½ **1971 (PG)** Epic chronicling the final years of Tsar Nicholas II, Empress Alexandra, and their children. Their lavish royal lifestyle gives way to imprisonment and eventual execution under the new Lenin government. Beautiful, but overlong costume epic that loses steam in the second half. Based on the biography by Robert Massie. **183m/C VHS, DVD, Wide.** Michael Jayston, Janet Suzman, Tom Baker, Laurence Olivier, Michael Redgrave, Harry Andrews, Jack Hawkins, Alexander Knox, Curt Jurgens; ***D:*** Franklin J. Schaffner; ***W:*** James Goldman; ***C:*** Frederick A. (Freddie) Young; ***M:*** Richard Rodney Bennett. Oscars '71: Art Dir./Set Dec., Costume Des.

Nicholas Nickleby 🦴🦴🦴 *The Life and Adventures of Nicholas Nickleby* **1946** An ensemble cast works hard to bring to life Charles Dickens' novel about an impoverished family dependent on their wealthy but villainous uncle. Young Nicholas is an apprentice at a school for boys, and he and a student run away to a series of exciting adventures. An enjoyable film, though it is hard to tell the entire story in such a small amount of time. **108m/B VHS.** *GB* Cedric Hardwicke, Stanley Holloway, Derek Bond, Alfred Drayton, Sybil Thorndike, Sally Ann Howes, Bernard Miles, Mary Merrall, Cathleen Nesbitt; ***D:*** Alberto Cavalcanti; ***C:*** Georges Perinal.

Nick and Jane 🦴🦴 **1996 (R)** See John sleep with another woman. See Jane see John sleep with another woman. See Jane run out of the building to catch a cab. See Nick pick her up in the cab. This is just a glimpse of all the hilarious fun you'll see when New Yorker Jane (Wheeler-Nicholson) gets a fake boyfriend, Nick (McCaffrey), to upset two-timing John (Dossett). Predictable romantic comedy does have something to offer in sparks between the leads, but they're buried amid the bizarre subplots and off-beat supports. The opening scene where Jane catches her boyfriend cheating is the lone unique and funny segment. Cost-saving camera work, devoid of close-ups and reaction shots, shows. **94m/C VHS.** Dana Wheeler-Nicholson, James McCaffrey, Lisa Gay Hamilton, John Dossett, David Johansen, Gedde Watanabe, Saundra Santiago, George Coe, Clinton Leupp; ***D:*** Rich Mauro; ***W:*** Rich Mauro, Peter Quigley, Neil Alumkal; ***C:*** Chris Norr; ***M:*** Mark Suozzo.

Nick Knight 🦴🦴 **1989** An L.A. cop on the night beat is really a good-guy vampire, who quaffs cattle blood as he tracks down another killer who's draining humans of their plasma. A gimmicky pilot for a would-be TV series that never bit. **92m/C VHS.** Rick Springfield, Michael Nader, Laura Johnson. **TV**

Nick of Time 🦴½ **1995 (R)** A malicious stranger (Walken) and his cohort give ordinary accountant Gene Watson (Depp) 90 minutes to assassinate the governor of California (Mason) or his little girl will be killed. Walken as an evil psycho...now there's a stretch. On the other hand, Depp as a button-down, conservative widower is a bit of a switch after his usually quirky roles of the recent past. This may be the first time Depp's picked up a gun since "21 Jump Street." Illogical scenarios (even for an action flick) and curiously uneven pacing do this one in. Shot almost entirely in L.A's Bonaventure Hotel in real time with a handheld camera. **98m/C VHS, DVD, Wide.** Johnny Depp, Christopher Walken, Charles S. Dutton, Peter Strauss, Roma Maffia, Gloria Reuben, Marsha Mason, Courtney Chase, Bill Smitrovich, G.D. Spradlin; ***D:*** John Badham; ***W:*** Patrick Duncan; ***C:*** Roy Wagner; ***M:*** Arthur B. Rubinstein.

Nickel & Dime 🦴🦴 **1992 (PG)** A con artist's luck turns bad when the IRS catches up with him, impounds all his worldly goods, and sticks him with an officious auditor. But if Jack can find the heiress to a fortune, within 48 hours, he can claim a hefty finder's fee and his money worries will be a thing of the past. **96m/C VHS.** C. Thomas Howell, Wallace Shawn, Lise Cutter, Lynn Danielson, Roy Brocksmith; ***D:*** Ben Moses; ***W:*** Seth Front, Eddy Polon, Ben Moses.

Nickel Mountain 🦴🦴½ **1985** Heartwarming story of a suicidal 40-year-old man who finds a new reason to live when he falls in love with a pregnant 16-year-old girl who works at his diner. Langenkamp particularly appealing. Based on a John Gardner novel. **88m/C VHS.** Michael Cole, Heather Langenkamp, Ed Lauter, Brian Kerwin, Patrick Cassidy, Grace Zabriskie, Don Beddoe; ***D:*** Drew Denbaum.

Nico and Dani 🦴🦴½ *Krampack* **2000** Best buddies Nico (Vilches) and Dani (Ramallo) are 17-year-old virgins who hope to change that situtaion while on a Spanish beach vacation. Nico has the hots for pretty Elena (Orozco), who returns his interest, which leaves her cousin Berta (Nubiola) pining for Dani. Too bad Dani realizes that he not only loves Nico, he's IN love with him and that Nico doesn't share his sexual feelings. Dani finds a mentor in an older gay man (Amado) but the situation remains tangled in an all-too realistic (if somewhat overly sunny) way. Based on the play "Krampack" by Jordi Sanchez. Spanish with subtitles. **90m/C VHS, DVD, Wide.** *SP* Fernando Ramallo, Jordi Vilches, Marieta Orozco, Esther Nubiola, Chisco Amado, Ana Gracia; ***D:*** Cesc Gay; ***W:*** Cesc Gay, Tomas Aragay; ***C:*** Andreu Rebes; ***M:*** Riqui Sabates, Joan Diaz, Jordi Prats.

Nico Icon 🦴🦴🦴 **1995 (R)** Documentary probes the life of Velvet Underground sensation and Warhol superstar Nico. A pastiche showing V.U. concert footage and movie clips from Nico's most famous film appearances: Fellini's "La Dolce Vita" and Warhol's "The Chelsea Girls." Also features interviews from Warhol's Factory inhabitants, band members, and Nico's grown son Ari. Visually as interesting as the subject herself, film manages to bring the viewer closer to the untouchable Teutonic figure without being sensational or overly flashy. Director Paul Morrissey and musician Jackson Browne make appearances. Some French and German language; subtitled. **75m/C VHS, DVD.** *GE* ***D:*** Susanne Ofteringer; ***W:*** Susanne Ofteringer; ***C:*** Judith Kaufmann.

Nicole 🦴 **1972 (R)** The downfall of a wealthy woman who is able to buy everything she wants except love. **91m/C VHS.** Leslie Caron, Catherine Bach, Ramon Bieri; ***D:*** Istvan Ventilla.

The Night After Halloween 🦴 **1983 (R)** A young woman gets the shock of her life when she discovers that her boyfriend is a crazed killer. **90m/C VHS.** *IT* Chantal Contouri, Robert Bruning, Sigrid Thornton.

Night After Night 🦴🦴½ **1932** West's screen debut finds her in an unaccustomed secondary role, although a prime scene-stealer. In Raft's first starring role, he's a monied low-life who opens a fancy nightclub and becomes infatuated with Park Avenue beauty Cummings. His problems are compounded by the arrival of raucous ex-flames West and Gleason. When a hatcheck girl cries "Goodness!" over West's diamonds, she replies, in suggestive West-style, "Goodness had nothing to do with it, dearie." Adapted from the novel "Single Night" by Louis Bromfield. **73m/B VHS.** George Raft, Constance Cummings, Mae West, Wynne Gibson, Alison Skipworth, Roscoe Karns, Louis Calhern; ***D:*** Archie Mayo; ***W:*** Mae West, Kathryn Scola, Vincent Lawrence.

Night Ambush 🦴🦴½ *Ill Met By Moonlight* **1957** A Nazi general is kidnapped on Crete by British agents, who embark on a dangerous trip to the coast where a ship awaits to take them to Cairo. The general tries to thwart their plans, but they outwit him at every turn. Based on a novel by W. Stanley Moss that details a similar real-life event. **100m/B VHS.** *GB* Dirk Bogarde, Marius Goring, David Oxley, Cyril Cusack, Christopher Lee; ***D:*** Michael Powell, Emeric Pressburger.

Night and Day 🦴🦴½ **1946** Sentimental musical about the life of bon-vivant composer-extraordinaire Cole Porter. His intensity and the motivations for his music are dramatized, but this film succeeds best as a fabulous showcase for Porter's songs. ♫Begin the Beguine; My Heart Belongs to Daddy; You're the Top; I've Got You Under My Skin; Just One of Those Things; I Get a Kick Out of You; Night and Day; What Is This Thing Called Love; Do I Love You. **128m/C VHS.** Cary Grant, Alexis Smith, Jane Wyman, Eve Arden, Mary Martin, Alan Hale, Monty Woolley, Ginny Simms, Dorothy Malone; ***D:*** Michael Curtiz; ***M:*** Max Steiner.

Night and Day 🦴🦴🦴 *Nuit et Jour* **1991** Charming adult romance about Jack and Julie, young lovers newly arrived in Paris. When Jack gets a night job driving a cab, Julie finds her evenings lonely. But not for long. She meets Joseph, a cab driver on the day shift. Soon, Julie is juggling sexual affairs with both men and everything gets increasingly complicated. Her lovers find out about each other but Julie doesn't want to fully commit to either of them. In French with English subtitles. **90m/C VHS.** *FR BE SI* Guilaine Londez, Thomas Langmann, Francois Negret; ***D:*** Chantal Akerman; ***W:*** Pascal Bonitzer, Chantal Akerman; ***M:*** Marc Herouet.

Night and the City 🦴🦴🦴½ **1950** A film noir classic about a hustler's money-making schemes. Widmark is Harry Fabian, a small-time promoter working for slimy nightclub owner Sullivan, whose job is to hustle the marks into the club where his girlfriend Tierney is the singer. Widmark also happens to be romancing Sullivan's wife, Withers, and wants her to back his latest con. But his schemes go awry and Fabian's on the run for his life. Widmark gives a riveting performance of a lowlife whose brains don't match his ambitions. Filmed in London with appropriate brooding tawdriness. Adapted from the novel by Gerald Kersh; remade in 1992. **95m/B VHS.** *GB* Richard Widmark, Gene Tierney, Googie Withers, Francis L. Sullivan, Hugh Marlowe, Herbert Lom, Mike Mazurki, Charles Farrell; ***D:*** Jules Dassin; ***W:*** Jo Eisinger; ***M:*** Franz Waxman.

Night and the City 🦴🦴🦴 **1992 (R)** Harry Fabian (De Niro), a con-artist/ambulance-chaser, concocts a scheme to make it big, and approaches an old boxing great (Warden) to come out of retirement and revive a local boxing night. Problem is, although Harry has energy and ambition, he also has a talent for making enemies out of the wrong people, like the boxer's brother (King), a neighborhood mobster. Filled with details more interesting than the plot; more about fast-living, fast-talking New Yorkers, a fine showcase for De Niro's talent. Winkler's remake of the 1950 Jules Dassin film. **98m/C VHS.** Robert De Niro, Jessica Lange, Cliff Gorman, Alan King, Jack Warden, Eli Wallach, Barry Primus, Gene Kirkwood, Pedro Sanchez; ***Cameos:*** Regis Philbin, Joy Philbin, Richard Price; ***D:*** Irwin Winkler; ***W:*** Richard Price; ***C:*** Tak Fujimoto; ***M:*** James Newton Howard.

The Night and the Moment 🦴½ **1994 (R)** Dull, mishmashy costume drama (set in the 17th century) about an imprisoned author (Dafoe) who became intrigued with the mystery woman who had occupied the next cell. They exchanged notes, and he vows to find her when he's released from prison. But first he spends a seductive night, exchanging stories about past conquests, at the chateau of the Marquise (Olin), who, of course, turns out to be the mystery lady. Based on the novel "La Nuit er le Moment" by Claude-Prosper de Jolyot Crebillon. **89m/C VHS.** *GB FR IT* Willem Dafoe, Lena Olin, Miranda Richardson, Jean-Claude Carriere, Carole Richert; ***D:*** Anna Maria Tato; ***W:*** Anna Maria Tato, Jean-Claude Carriere; ***C:*** Giuseppe Rotunno; ***M:*** Ennio Morricone.

Night Angel 🦴 **1990 (R)** A beautiful seductress lures men into a deadly trap from which only true love can free them. **90m/C VHS.** Isa Anderson, Linda Ashby, Debra Feuer, Helen Martin, Karen Black, Doug Jones, Gary Hudson, Sam Hennings; ***D:*** Dominique Othenin-Girard; ***W:*** Joe Augustyn.

A Night at the Opera 🦴🦴🦴🦴 **1935** The Marx Brothers get mixed up with grand opera in their first MGM-produced epic and their first without Zeppo. Jones, as a budding opera singer warbles "Alone" and "Cosi Cosa." One of their best films, blessed with a big budget—used to reach epic anarchic heights. Some scenes were tested on live audiences before inclusion, including the Groucho/Chico paper-tearing contract negotiation and the celebrated stateroom scene, in which the boys are joined in a small closet by two maids, the ship's engineer, his assistant, a manicurist, a young woman, a cleaning lady, and four food-laden waiters. **92m/B VHS, DVD, Wide.** Groucho Marx, Chico Marx, Harpo Marx, Allan Jones, Kitty Carlisle Hart, Sig Rumann, Margaret Dumont, Walter Woolf King, Edward (Ed Kean, Keene) Keane, Robert Emmett O'Connor; ***D:*** Sam Wood; ***W:*** George S. Kaufman, Morrie Ryskind, Bert Kalmar, Harry Ruby, Al Boasberg; ***C:*** Merritt B. Gerstad; ***M:*** Herbert Stothart. Natl. Film Reg. '93.

A Night at the Roxbury 🦴½ **1998 (PG-13)** The Bubati brothers, like so many Saturday Night Live veterans before them, make the leap to the big screen with limited success. Steve and Doug (Ferrell and Kattan) continue their fruitless quest to gain entrance into the hallowed Roxbury night club. Their luck changes when they get into a fender bender with former "21 Jump Street" star Richard Grieco (playing himself), who gets them in. Typical of the SNL skits-to-big-screen formula, the bit works as a three-minute sketch but isn't funny or interesting enough to sustain even its meager 82 minute running time. **83m/C VHS, DVD.** Will Ferrell, Chris Kattan, Molly Shannon, Dan Hedaya, Loni Anderson, Richard Grieco, Elisa Donovan, Lochlyn Munro, Dwayne Hickman, Mark McKinney; ***D:*** John Fortenberry; ***W:*** Steve Koren, Will Ferrell, Chris Kattan; ***C:*** Francis Kenny; ***M:*** David Kitay.

Night Beast 🦴 **1983** Alien creature lands his spaceship near a small town and begins a bloody killing spree. Recycled plot. **90m/C VHS.** Tom Griffith, Dick Dyszel, Jaimie Zemarel, George Stover; ***D:*** Donald M. Dohler.

Night Beat 🦴½ **1948** A labored crime drama from postwar Britain. Two army pals pursue diverging careers. One becomes a cop, the other a crook. Want to bet that they meet again? **95m/B VHS.** *GB* Anne Crawford, Maxwell Reed, Ronald Howard, Christine Norden; ***D:*** Harold Huth.

The Night Before 🦴🦴½ **1988 (PG-13)** Snobby high school beauty Loughlin loses a bet and has to go to the prom with the school geek Reeves. On the way, they get lost on the wrong side of the tracks, and become involved with pimps, crime, and the police. A drunken Reeves loses Loughlin as well as his father's car. Typical teen farce. **90m/C VHS.** Keanu Reeves, Lori Loughlin, Trinidad Silva, Michael Greene, Theresa Saldana, Suzanne Snyder, Morgan Lofting, Gwil Richards; ***D:*** Thom Eberhardt; ***W:*** Gregory Scherick, Thom Eberhardt.

Night Birds 🦴 **1931** Early British thriller about a notorious crook named "Flash Jack," who heads a gang of top-hatted criminals that rob the wealthy. Poor production quality and Raine's standoffish screen presence contribute to this below-average film. **76m/B VHS.** *GB* Jameson Thomas, Jack Raine, Muriel Angelus, Eve Gray; ***D:*** Richard Eichberg; ***W:*** Miles Malleson.

The Night Brings Charlie 🦴½ **1990** A disfigured tree surgeon is the prime suspect in some grisly murders committed with a tree trimming saw. Obviously, everyone in the town fears him as a result. Not a sequel to "Roots." **90m/C VHS.** Kerry Knight, Joe Fishback, Aimee Tenalia, Monica Simmons; ***D:*** Tom Logan.

Night Call Nurses 🦴🦴 *Young L.A. Nurses 2* **1972 (R)** Three gorgeous nurses find danger and intrigue on the night shift at a psychiatric hospital. Third in the "nurse" quintet is back on target, shrugging off the previous film's attempts at "serious" social commentary. Miller provides comic relief. Preceded by "The Student Nurses" and "Private Duty Nurses," and followed by "The Young Nurses" and "Candy Stripe Nurses." **85m/C VHS.** Patricia T. Byrne, Alana Collins, Mittie Lawrence, Clinton Kimbrough, Felton Perry, Stack Pierce, Richard Young, Dennis Dugan, Dick Miller; ***D:*** Jonathan Kaplan; ***W:*** George Armitage.

The Night Caller 🦴🦴 **1997 (R)** Radio psychologist attracts the attentions of a deranged listener. **94m/C VHS.** Shanna Reed, Tracy Nelson, Mary Crosby, Cyndi Pass; ***D:*** Rob Malenfant; ***W:*** Frank Rehwaldt; ***C:*** M. David Mullen.

Night Caller from Outer Space 🦴½ *Blood Beast from Outer Space; The Night Caller* **1966** When a woman-hunting alien arrives in London, women begin to disappear. At first, incredibly, no one makes the connection, but then the horrible truth comes to light. **84m/B VHS, DVD.** *GB* John Saxon, Maurice Denham, Patricia Haines, Alfred Burke, Jack Watson, Aubrey Morris; ***D:*** John Gilling; ***W:*** James O'Connolly; ***C:*** Stephen Dade; ***M:*** Johnny Gregory.

Night Children 🦴 **1989 (R)** Tough L.A. cop teams with a parole officer to battle a nasty gang leader. The battle is quite violent and senseless. **90m/C VHS.** David Carradine, Nancy Kwan, Griffin O'Neal, Tawny (Ellis) Fere; ***D:*** Norbert Meisel.

The Night Club 🦴🦴½ **1925** Swinging single stands to gain fortune if he weds a certain girl, and, as luck would have it, he falls for her. When the usual hearts and roses don't convince her he's earnest, he tries to prove his love is true by attempting suicide and hiring a hit man. **62m/B VHS.** Raymond Griffith, Vera Reynolds, Wallace Beery, Louise Fazenda; ***D:*** Frank Urson.

Night Creature 🦴 *Out of the Darkness; Fear* **1979 (PG)** A tough, Hemingway-type writer is determined to destroy the man-eating black leopard which nearly killed him once before. Filmed in Thailand. **83m/C VHS.** Donald Pleasence, Nancy Kwan, Ross Hagen; ***D:*** Lee Madden.

Night Cries 🦴🦴½ **1978** After a woman's baby dies at birth, she has persistent dreams that he is alive and in trouble. No one will believe her when she tells them that something is wrong. **100m/C VHS.** Susan St. James, Michael Parks, William Conrad; ***D:*** Richard Lang. **TV**

Night Crossing 🦴🦴½ **1981 (PG)** The fact-based story of two East German families who launch a daring escape to the West in a homemade hot air balloon. Exciting action for the whole family. **106m/C VHS.** John Hurt, Jane Alexander, Glynnis O'Connor, Doug McKeon, Beau Bridges; ***D:*** Delbert Mann; ***W:*** John McGreevey; ***M:*** Jerry Goldsmith.

The Night Cry 🦴🦴 **1926** Silent canine melodrama has sheep-murdering dog sentenced to death row until he saves little girl from unbelievably big bird. **65m/B VHS.** John Harron, June Marlowe, Mary Louise Miller; ***D:*** Herman C. Raymaker.

The Night Evelyn Came Out of the Grave 🦴½ *La Notte Che Evelyn Usca Dalla Tomba* **1971 (R)** A wealthy Italian playboy, obsessed with his dead, flame-haired wife, lures living redheads into his castle, where he tortures and kills them. Standard '70s Euro/horror/sex stuff enlivened by the presence of the incredible Erika Blanc as a stripper who works out of a coffin. **99m/C VHS.** *IT* Anthony Steffen, Marina Malfatti, Rod Murdock, Erika Blanc, Giacomo "Jack" Rossi-Stuart, Umberto Raho; ***D:*** Emilio P. Miraglio.

Night Eyes 🦴 *Hidden Vision* **1990 (R)** Surveillance can be a dangerous profession, especially when your boss happens to be the jealous husband of a very sexy woman. Watching turns to yearning for this professional peeper, but he may just get more than he bargained for. Roberts is worth watching. **95m/C VHS.** Andrew Stevens, Tanya Roberts, Warwick Sims, Cooper Huckabee; ***D:*** Emilio P. Miraglio; ***W:*** Tom Citrano.

Night Eyes 2 🦴½ **1991 (R)** A security expert assigned to protect the sultry wife of a foreign diplomat finds himself spending a little too much time eyeing her through his hidden cameras. Soon he can no longer control his desire and he makes a move on her that may have international implications. Also available in an unrated version. **97m/C VHS.** Andrew Stevens, Shannon Tweed, Tim Russ, Richard Chaves, Geno Silva; ***D:*** Rodney McDonald.

Night Eyes 3 🦴🦴 **1993 (R)** Night Eyes Security boss Stevens' latest assignment is to protect the superstar lead (Shannon Tweed) of a top TV cop show from a stalker. They wind up in very close contact but someone is videotaping their private moments which don't stay private for long. Maybe on-screen partner Tracy (Shannon's sister) has something to do with it. Also available in an unrated version. **97m/C VHS.** Andrew Stevens, Shannon Tweed, Tracy Tweed, Tristan Rogers; ***D:*** Andrew Stevens; ***W:*** Andrew Stevens, Michael W. Potts.

Night Eyes 4: Fatal Passion 🦴½ **1995 (R)** Beverly Hills shrink Angela Cross (Barbieri) gets involved with bodyguard Steve Caldwell (Trachta), who's been hired to protect her from a stalker, who may also be the same person who stole some sexual explosive patient files. Also available unrated. **101m/C VHS.** Casper Van Dien, Chick Vennera, Paula Barbieri, Jeff Trachta, Andrew Stevens; ***D:*** Rodney McDonald; ***W:*** John Eubanks, Henry Krinkle; ***C:*** Gary Graver; ***M:*** Patrick Seymour.

Night Falls on Manhattan 🦴🦴🦴 **1996 (R)** One man's search for truth runs into serious problems in this adaptation of "Tainted Evidence" by Robert Daley. Former cop turned junior DA, Sean Casey (Garcia), is chosen to lead the prosecution in a sensational NY trial involving a drug dealer/cop killer, who also seriously wounded Sean's long-time cop father, Liam (Holm). He wins but allegations of police corruption dog the trial, thanks to liberal defense lawyer Vigoda (Dreyfuss), and when Sean rather unexpectedly becomes the new district attorney, the issue becomes a full-blown scandal, leading the naive Sean very close to home. Veteran director Lumet knows this scandal-ridden territory very well and is aided by fine performances from his leads. **114m/C VHS, DVD, Wide.** Dominic Chianese, Andy Garcia, Ian Holm, Richard Dreyfuss, Lena Olin, James Gandolfini, Ron Leibman, Colm Feore, Shiek Mahmud-Bey, Paul Guilfoyle; ***D:*** Sidney Lumet; ***W:*** Sidney Lumet; ***C:*** David Watkin; ***M:*** Mark Isham.

Night Fire 🦴½ **1994 (R)** Barry wants wife Lydia to try to rekindle the passion in their marriage by getting away for the weekend at their remote ranch. But they're interrupted in their leisure by the stranded Cal and Gwen. Only it turns out Barry has hired the duo, who like kinky games, to peak Lydia's interest. She's merely disgusted and Barry gets nasty. Also available unrated. **93m/C VHS, DVD.** Shannon Tweed, John Laughlin, Martin Hewitt, Rochelle Swanson; ***D:*** Mike Sedan; ***W:*** Catherine Tavel, Helen Haxton; ***C:*** Zoran Hochstatter; ***M:*** Miriam Cutler.

Night Flight from Moscow 🦴🦴½ *The Serpent* **1973 (PG)** A Soviet spy defects with a fistful of secret documents that implicate every free government. Then the CIA must decide if he's telling the truth. Complex espionage thriller. **113m/C VHS.** *FR IT GE* Yul Brynner, Henry Fonda, Dirk Bogarde, Virna Lisi, Philippe Noiret, Farley Granger, Robert Alda, Marie DuBois, Elga Andersen; ***D:*** Henri Verneuil; ***M:*** Ennio Morricone.

A Night for Crime 🦴🦴 **1942** A movie star disappears during the filming of a movie. When she turns up dead, a bumbling cop suspects everyone on the set. **75m/B VHS.** Glenda Farrell, Lyle Talbot, Lena Basquette, Donald Kirke, Ralph Sanford; ***D:*** Alexis Thurn-Taxis.

Night Friend 🦴 **1987 (R)** A priest sets out to help a young woman caught up in a world of drug abuse and prostitution. Exploitation morality flick. **94m/C VHS.** Art Carney, Chuck Shamata, Jayne (Jane) Eastwood, Heather Kjollesdal; ***D:*** Peter Gerretsen.

A Night Full of Rain 🦴½ *End of the World (in Our Usual Bed in a Night Full of Rain)* **1978 (R)** Italian communist tries unsuccessfully to seduce vacationing American feminist. They meet again in San Francisco and wedding bells chime. They argue. They argue more. They put all but rabid Wertmuller fans to sleep. The director's first English-language film. **104m/C VHS.** *IT* Giancarlo Giannini, Candice Bergen, Anne Byrne, Flora Carabella; ***D:*** Lina Wertmuller; ***W:*** Lina Wertmuller.

Night Gallery 🦴🦴🦴 **1969** Serling is the tour guide through an unusual art gallery consisting of portraits that reflect people's greed, desire, and guilt. Pilot for the 1969-1973 TV series. Three stories, including "Eyes," which saw novice Spielberg directing veteran Crawford. **95m/C VHS.** Joan Crawford, Roddy McDowall, Tom Bosley, Barry Sullivan, Ossie Davis, Sam Jaffe, Kate Greenfield, Richard Kiley, George Macready, Norma Crane, Barry Atwater; ***D:*** Steven Spielberg, Boris Sagal, Boris Shear; ***W:*** Rod Serling; ***C:*** Richard Batcheller; ***M:*** Billy Goldenberg. **TV**

Night Game 🦴½ **1989 (R)** A cop links a string of serial killings to the night games won by the Houston Astros. Brave cast tries hard, but is retired without a hit. **95m/C VHS.** Roy Scheider, Karen Young, Paul Gleason, Lane Smith, Carlin Glynn; ***D:*** Peter Masterson; ***M:*** Pino Donaggio.

Night Games 🦴 **1980 (R)** Raped as a child, California girl Pickett has trouble relating to her husband. To overcome her sexual anxieties, she engages in a number of bizarre fantasies. **100m/C VHS.** Cindy Pickett, Joanna Cassidy, Barry Primus, Gene Davis; ***D:*** Roger Vadim; ***M:*** John Barry.

The Night God Screamed woof! *Scream* **198? (PG)** A fanatical cult leader is convicted of murder and the cult goes wild. **85m/C VHS.** Michael Sugich, Jeanne Crain, James B. Sikking; ***D:*** Lee Madden.

The Night Has Eyes 🦴🦴½ *Terror House* **1942** Tense melodrama concerns a young teacher who disappears on the Yorkshire moors at the same spot where her girlfriend had vanished the previous year. Early film appearance for Mason. **79m/B VHS.** *GB* James Mason, Joyce Howard, Wilfred Lawson, Mary Clare; ***D:*** Leslie Arliss.

The Night Heaven Fell 🦴🦴½ *Les Bijoutiers du Clair de Lune* **1957** Ursula (Bardot) returns from the convent to the Spanish town where her Aunt Florentine (Valli) lives unhappily with Count Ribera (Nieto), a macho brute and womanizer. A local malcontent, Lambert (Boyd) has returned from political exile to find his sister dead by suicide over the Count; and a deadly feud is reignited. Complicating matters is Aunt Florentine's unwillingness to admit her love for Lambert, and virgin Ursula's instantaneous attraction to him. It's serious, overheated melodrama in a commercial package that reveals Vadim to be basically the sex merchant everyone accuses him of being. **95m/C DVD, Wide.** *FR IT* Brigitte Bardot, Stephen Boyd, Alida Valli, Pepe Nieto; ***D:*** Roger Vadim; ***W:*** Roger Vadim, Peter Viertel, Jacques Remy; ***C:*** Armand Thirard; ***M:*** Georges Auric.

Night Hunter 🦴🦴 **1995 (R)** Jack Cutter's (Wilson) vampire-hunting parents were killed by a group of bloodsuckers so he teams up with a tabloid reporter (Smith) to eliminate the last nine vampires who have gathered together in Los Angeles and plan to multiply. **86m/C VHS.** Don "The Dragon" Wilson, Melanie Smith, Nicholas Guest, Maria Ford; ***D:*** Rick Jacobson.

A Night in Casablanca 🦴🦴🦴 **1946** Groucho, Harpo and Chico find themselves in the luxurious Hotel Casablanca, going after some leftover Nazis searching for treasure. One of the later Marx Brothers' films, but still loaded with the familiar wisecracks and mayhem. **85m/B VHS.** Groucho Marx, Harpo Marx, Chico Marx, Charles Drake, Dan Seymour, Sig Rumann, Lisette Verea, Lois Collier, Paul Harvey, Lewis L. Russell; ***D:*** Archie Mayo; ***W:*** Roland Kibbee, Frank Tashlin, Joseph Fields; ***C:*** James Van Trees; ***M:*** Werner Janssen.

A Night in Heaven woof! **1983 (R)** A college teacher gets involved with one of her students, who moonlights as a male stripper. Will he earn that extra credit he needs to pass? Uninspired, overly explicit. Look for Denny Terrio of "Dance Fever" fame. **85m/C VHS.** Christopher Atkins, Lesley Ann Warren, Carrie Snodgress, Andy Garcia; ***D:*** John G. Avildsen; ***W:*** Joan Tewkesbury. Golden Raspberries '83: Worst Actor (Atkins).

A Night in the Life of Jimmy Reardon 🦴½ **1988 (R)** A high school Casanova watches his friends leave for expensive schools while he contemplates a trip to Hawaii with his rich girlfriend, a ruse to avoid the dull business school his father has picked out. Well photographed, but acting leaves something to be desired. Based on Richert's novel "Aren't You Even Going to Kiss Me Good-bye?" **95m/C VHS, DVD, Wide.** River Phoenix, Meredith Salenger, Matthew Perry, Louanne, Ione Skye, Ann Magnuson, Paul Koslo, Jane Hallaren, Jason Court; ***D:*** William Richert; ***W:*** William Richert; ***C:*** John J. Connor; ***M:*** Elmer Bernstein, Bill Conti.

Night Is My Future 🦴🦴½ *Music in Darkness* **1947** A young musician, blinded in an accident, meets a girl who tries to bring him happiness. Usual somber Bergman, but unimportant story. In Swedish with English subtitles. **89m/B VHS.** *SW* Mai Zetterling, Birger Malmsten, Naima Wifstrand, Olof Winnerstrand, Hilda Borgstrom; ***D:*** Ingmar Bergman.

Night Life 🦴🦴 **1990 (R)** A teenager gets the all-out, high-stakes ride of his life when four cadavers are re-animated in his uncle's mortuary. **92m/C VHS.** Scott Grimes, John Astin, Cheryl Pollak, Alan Blumenfeld; ***D:*** David Acomba; ***W:*** Keith Critchlow; ***M:*** Roger Bourland.

Night Life in Reno 🦴🦴 **1931** When a man leaves his wife, she sets out for Reno and falls in love with a married man. When her new love is killed by his jealous wife, the woman returns to her husband and they begin their marriage anew. Watchable melodrama. **58m/B VHS.** Jameson Thomas, Dorothy Christy, Virginia Valli, Carmelita Geraghty.

Night Master 🦴 **1987** A handful of karate students practice their homework with much higher stakes away from the classroom. For them, deadly Ninja games are the only way to study. **87m/C VHS.** Tom Jennings, Nicole Kidman, Vince Martin; ***D:*** Mark Joffe.

Night Monster 🦴🦴½ *House of Mystery* **1942** A maniac wears artifical limbs to hunt down and murder the doctors responsible for amputating his legs. Picture was shot in 11 days. Fire scene was stock footage from "The Ghost of Frankenstein." **80m/B VHS.** Bela Lugosi, Ralph Morgan, Lionel Atwill, Leif Erickson, Don Porter, Irene Hervey, Nils Asther; ***D:*** Ford Beebe; ***W:*** Clarence Upson Young; ***C:*** Charles Van Enger.

'night, Mother 🦴🦴½ **1986 (PG-13)** A depressed woman, living with her mother, announces one evening that she is going to kill herself. Her mother spends the evening reliving their lives and trying to talk her out of it, but the outcome seems inevitable. Well acted, though depressing. Based on Marsha Norman's Pulitzer Prize-winning novel. **97m/C VHS.** Sissy Spacek, Anne Bancroft, Ed Berke, Carol Robbins, Jennifer Roosendahl; ***D:*** Tom (Thomas R.) Moore; ***W:*** Marsha Norman; ***M:*** David Shire.

Night Moves 🦴🦴🦴½ **1975 (R)** Smalltime L.A. detective Harry Moseby (Hackman) is hired by fading actress Arlene Iverson (Ward) to find her wild teenaged daughter Delly (Griffith) who has taken off for the Florida Keys. Delly winds up dead and Harry uncovers a bizarre smuggling ring. Hackman is realistic as the detective whose own life is unraveling and Penn and screenwriter Sharp tweaked the detective convention by Harry being ultimately ineffectual. Underrated when released and worth a view. **100m/C VHS.** Gene Hackman, Susan Clark, Jennifer Warren, Melanie Griffith, Harris Yulin, Edward Binns, Kenneth Mars, James Woods, Dennis Dugan, Max Gail; ***D:*** Arthur Penn; ***W:*** Alan Sharp; ***C:*** Bruce Surtees; ***M:*** Michael Small.

Night Must Fall 🦴🦴🦴 **1937** Effective thriller based on the play by Emlyn Williams. Wheelchair-bound grand dame Mrs. Branson (Whitty) hires personable Danny (Montgomery) as a handyman for the cottage she lives in with niece, Olivia (Russell). Danny is, of course, too good to be true. He's a creepy killer after moolah, which Olivia discerns but does nothing about until he strikes again. Oh yeah, he also keeps a suspicious hatbox in his room. Remade in 1964 with Albert Finney as the killer. **101m/B VHS.** Robert Montgomery, May Whitty, Rosalind Russell, Merle Tottenham, Alan Marshal, Kathleen Harrison, Matthew Boulton; ***D:*** Richard Thorpe; ***W:*** John Van Druten; ***C:*** Ray June; ***M:*** Edward Ward.

Night Nurse 🦴🦴🦴 **1931** Stanwyck is a nurse who uncovers a sordid plot involving the murder of two young children for an inheritance. An entertaining, overlooked crime-drama, initially notorious for Stanwyck and roommate Blondell's continual onscreen dressings and undressings. Gable is compelling in an early, villainous role. **72m/B VHS.** Barbara Stanwyck, Ben Lyon, Joan Blondell, Charles Winninger, Charlotte Merriam, Eddie Nugent, Blanche Frederici, Allan "Rocky" Lane, Walter McGrail, Ralf Harolde, Clark Gable; ***D:*** William A. Wellman.

Night Nurse 🦴 **1977** Young nurse signs on to care for an aging, wheelchair-ridden opera star, only to find that the house is haunted. **80m/C VHS.** Davina Whitehouse, Kay Taylor, Gary Day, Kate Fitzpatrick; ***D:*** Igor Auzins.

Night of a Thousand Cats 🦴🦴 *La Noche de los Mil Gatos; Blood Feast; Cats* **1972 (R)** A reclusive playboy cruises Mexico City in his helicopter, searching for beautiful women. It seems he needs their bodies for his cats who, for some reason, eat only human flesh. He keeps the heads, for some reason, for his private collection. A really odd '70s cannibal cat entry, but it moves along nicely and features some truly groovy fashions (floppy hats, translucent blouses, etc.). Not to be confused with the 1963 film of the same name. From the director of "Night of the Bloody Apes" and "Survive!" **83m/C VHS.** *MX* Anjanette Comer, Zulma Faiad, Hugo Stiglitz, Christa Linder, Teresa Velasquez, Barbara Ange; ***D:*** Rene Cardona Jr.

Night of Bloody Horror 🦴½ **1976 (R)** Tale of a former mental patient who is believed to be responsible for the brutal murders of his ex-girlfriends. A night of bloody horror indeed, as the gore is liberally spread. **89m/C VHS.** Gaye Yellen, Evelyn Hendricks, Gerald McRaney.

Night of Dark Shadows 🦴🦴🦴 *Curse of Dark Shadows* **1971 (PG)** Underrated, atmospheric follow-up to "House of Dark Shadows." When newlyweds Quentin (Selby) and Tracy Collins (Jackson) move into the family mansion, they find the place haunted by a ghostly woman named Angelique (Parker). As Quentin is disturbed by visissss of the past, he finds himself possessed by the spirit of Angelique's lover (also Selby) and Tracy's life in danger from the vengeful specter. Though occasionally muddled due to last-minute cuts ordered by the studio, the film still delivers a surplus of chills and is beautifully photographed. **94m/C VHS.** David Selby,

Kate Jackson, Lara Parker, Grayson Hall, John Karlen, Nancy Barrett, James Storm, Thayer David; *D:* Dan Curtis; *W:* Sam Hall; *C:* Richard Shore. **TV**

Night of Evil 🦴½ **1962** Girl is released from reform school and promptly wins a beauty contest. Her bid to win the Miss America title is blown to smithereens however, when it is discovered that she has been secretly married all along. From there she resorts to working in strip joints and attempts to pull off an armed robbery. As exploitation fare goes, a winner. **88m/B VHS.** Lisa Gaye, William Campbell; *D:* Richard Galbreath; *Nar:* Earl Wilson.

Night of Horror 🦴½ **198? (R)** Zombies attack four young people stranded in the wilderness. **76m/C VHS.** Steve Sandkuhler, Gae Schmitt, Rebecca Bach, Jeff Canfield.

A Night of Love 🦴🦴½ *Manifesto* **1987 (R)** Because of an assassination threat on the new king, Inspector Avanti (Molina) is charged with rounding up the town's troublemakers. Among them is a beguiling debutante (Soeberg) whose sexual appetites are matched only by her passion to kill the king. Based on a story by Emile Zola. **97m/C VHS.** Alfred Molina, Camilla Soeberg, Eric Stoltz, Gabrielle Anwar; *D:* Dusan Makavejev.

Night of Terror 🦴½ *He Lived to Kill* **1933** A swami, a couple of Hindu servants, a pretty heroine, a reporter, and all stalked by a killer who's after a formula that can put people in a state of suspended animation. Lame chiller. **64m/B VHS.** Bela Lugosi, Sally Blane, Wallace Ford, Tully Marshall, George Meeker, Edwin Maxwell; *D:* Ben Stoloff; *C:* Joseph Valentine.

Night of Terror **1987** A bizarre family conducts brain experiments on themselves and then begins to kill each other. Bloodshed for the whole family. **105m/C VHS.** Renee Harmon, Henry Lewis.

Night of the Assassin 🦴 **1977** Priest leaves his pulpit to become a terrorist. He plans a surprise for a U.N. secretary visiting Greece that would put the U.S. and Greek governments in the palm of his hand. Hard to believe. **98m/C VHS.** Klaus Kinski, Michael Craig, Eva Renzi; *D:* Robert McMahon.

Night of the Blood Beast 🦴½ *Creature from Galaxy 27* **1958** An astronaut comes back from space with an alien growing inside his body. The low-budget defeats a valiant attempt at a story. **65m/B VHS.** Michael Emmet, Angela Greene, John Baer, Ed Nelson, Georgianna Carter, Tyler McVey; *D:* Bernard L. Kowalski; *W:* Martin Varno; *C:* John M. Nickolaus Jr.; *M:* Alexander Laszlo.

Night of the Bloody Apes woof! *Gomar the Human Gorilla; La Horriplante Bestia Humana* **1968 (R)** When a doctor transplants an ape's heart into his dying son's body, the son goes berserk. Gory Mexican-made horror at its finest. **84m/C VHS.** *MX* Jose Elias Moreno, Armando Silvestre, Norma Lazarendo, Augustin Martinez Solares, Gina Moret, Noelia Noel, Gerard Zepeda, Carlos Lopez Moctezuma; *D:* Rene Cardona Jr.; *W:* Rene Cardona Jr.; *C:* Raul Martinez Solares; *M:* Antonio Diaz Conde.

Night of the Bloody Transplant woof! **1986 (R)** A lunatic scientist switches hearts from one person to another in this bloody gorefest. Footage of real surgery adds authenticity, but not believeability. **90m/C VHS.** Dick Grimm; *D:* David W. Hanson.

Night of the Cobra Woman 🦴 **1972 (R)** A woman who can turn herself into a cobra needs constant sex and snake venom to keep her eternally young. Shot on location in the Philippines. One-time underground filmmaker Meyer co-wrote the script, for the Corman factory. **85m/C VHS.** *PH* Joy Bang, Marlene Clark, Roger Garrett, Slash Marks, Vic Diaz; *D:* Andrew Meyer; *W:* Andrew Meyer.

Night of the Comet 🦴🦴½ **1984 (PG-13)** After surviving the explosion of a deadly comet, two California girls discover that they are the last people on Earth. When zombies begin to chase them, things begin to lose their charm. Cute and funny, but the script runs out before the movie does. **90m/C VHS.** Catherine Mary Stewart, Kelli Maroney, Robert Beltran, Geoffrey Lewis, Mary Woronov, Sharon Farrell, Michael Bowen; *D:* Thom Eberhardt; *W:* Thom Eberhardt; *C:* Arthur Albert.

Night of the Creeps 🦴🦴½ *Creeps; Homecoming Night* **1986 (R)** In 1958 an alien organism lands on earth and infects a person who is then frozen. Thirty years later he is accidentally unfrozen and starts spreading the infection throughout a college town. B-movie homage contains every horror cliche there is. Director Dekker's first film. **89m/C VHS.** Jason Lively, Jill Whitlow, Tom Atkins, Steve Marshall, Wally Taylor, Bruce Solomon, Kenneth Tobey, Dick Miller; *D:* Fred Dekker; *W:* Fred Dekker; *C:* Robert New; *M:* Barry de Vorzon.

Night of the Cyclone 🦴🦴 **1990 (R)** A complex but not overly interesting thriller about a big city cop who goes to an island paradise in search of his missing daughter and finds murder. **90m/C VHS.** Kris Kristofferson, Jeffrey Meek, Marisa Berenson, Winston Ntshona, Gerrit Graham; *D:* David Irving.

Night of the Death Cult 🦴🦴 *Night of the Seagulls* **1975** After moving to a quiet seaside community, a young couple is plagued by cult practising human sacrifice in order to appease the Templars, a zombie-like pack of ancient clergymen who rise from the dead and torture the living. Last in a four film series about the Templars. **90m/C VHS.** *SP* Victor Petit, Julie James, Maria Kosti, Sandra Mozarowsky; *D:* Armando de Ossorio.

Night of the Demon woof! **1980** Anthropology students are attacked by the legendary Bigfoot. Later they discover that he has raped and impregnated a young woman. Gore and sex prevail. **97m/C VHS.** Jay Allen, Michael J. Cutt, Bob Collins, Jodi Lazarus; *D:* James C. Watson.

Night of the Demons 🦴🦴 **1988 (R)** A gory, special-effects-laden horror farce about teenagers calling up demons in a haunted mortuary. On Halloween, of course. **92m/C VHS.** Linnea Quigley, Cathy Podewell, Alvin Alexis, William Gallo, Mimi Kinkade, Lance Fenton; *D:* Kevin S. Tenney; *W:* Joe Augustyn.

Night of the Demons 2 🦴🦴 **1994 (R)** Some humor and reasonable special effects help this rise above the usual teen-slasher horror sequels. The demonic Angela (complete with her skull-shaped lollipops) lives on in legend, handily haunting her creepy old house where a group of dumb teens end up on Halloween (and soon wind up dead). With each casualty, a new victim also joins the ranks of the undead. Funniest parts come with heroic rescuer, yardstick-wielding Sister Gloria, who's not about to let any of Satan's helpers get the better of her. **96m/C VHS.** Amelia Kinkade, Jennifer Rhodes, Merle Kennedy, Bobby Jacoby, Rod McCary, Zoe Trilling, Cristi Harris, Johnny Moran, Rick Peters, Christine Taylor, Ladd York, Darin Heames; *D:* Brian Trenchard-Smith; *W:* Joe Augustyn; *M:* Jim Manzie.

Night of the Demons 3 woof! **1997 (R)** Yet another bunch of moronic teenagers take refuge in Hull House funeral home on Halloween. Don't they know the mansion houses a bloodthirsty demon by now? May the demon win. **85m/C VHS.** Amelia Kinkade, Kris Holdenried, Vlasta Vrana; *D:* Jim Kaufman.

The Night of the Following Day 🦴🦴 **1969 (R)** Four professional criminals kidnap a young girl at France's Orly airport, demanding a large ransom from her wealthy father. Each kidnapper turns out to be beset by personal demons, hindering their plans and leading to a bloody climax. Then, there's a final twist to the entire story. Brando and Boone are properly chilling but the plot is muddled and melodramatic. From the novel "The Snatchers" by Lionel White. **93m/C VHS.** Marlon Brando, Richard Boone, Rita Moreno, Pamela Franklin, Jess Hahn, Jacques Marin, Gerard Buhr, Hughes Wanner; *D:* Hubert Cornfield; *W:* Robert Phippeny, Hubert Cornfield.

Night of the Fox 🦴🦴 **1990 (R)** An American officer with top secret knowledge is captured by Germans on the brink of D-Day. His home team plans to kill him if he cannot be rescued before spilling the beans. On-location filming adds much. **95m/C VHS.** Michael York, Deborah Raffin, George Peppard; *D:* Charles Jarrott. **CABLE**

Night of the Generals 🦴🦴🦴 *La Nuit de Generaux* **1967 (R)** A Nazi intelligence officer is pursuing three Nazi generals who may be involved in the brutal murder of a Warsaw prostitute. Dark and sinister, may be too slow for some tastes. Based on Hans Helmut Kirst's novel. **148m/C VHS.** Peter O'Toole, Omar Sharif, Tom Courtenay, Joanna Pettet, Donald Pleasence, Christopher Plummer, Philippe Noiret, John Gregson, Charles Gray; *D:* Anatole Litvak; *M:* Maurice Jarre.

Night of the Ghouls woof! *Revenge of the Dead* **1959** Second to last in Wood's celebrated series of inept horror films that began with "Bride of the Monster" and "Plan 9 from Outer Space." This one tells of a phony spiritualist who swindles the grieving by pretending to raise the dead. To his great surprise he actually does enliven some cadavers, who then go after him. Unreleased for over 20 years because Wood couldn't pay the film lab. Not quite as classically bad as his other films, but still a laugh riot. **69m/B VHS, DVD.** Paul Marco, Tor Johnson, Duke Moore, Kenne Duncan, John Carpenter, Criswell, Bud Osborne, Anthony Cardoza, Vampira, Valda Hansen, Tom Mason; *D:* Edward D. Wood Jr.; *W:* Edward D. Wood Jr.; *C:* William C. Thompson.

Night of the Grizzly 🦴🦴 **1966** An ex-lawman's peaceful life as a rancher is threatened when a killer grizzly bear goes on a murderous rampage terrorizing the residents of the Wyoming countryside. **99m/C VHS.** Clint Walker, Martha Hyer; *D:* Joseph Pevney.

Night of the Howling Beast 🦴 *La Maldicion de la Bestia; The Werewolf and the Yeti* **1975 (R)** The selling point of this one is an epic, first-time battle between a werewolf and a Yeti. Unfortunately it lasts about 15 seconds. Naschy's eighth stint as the wolfman. **87m/C VHS.** *SP* Paul (Jacinto Molina) Naschy, Grace Mills, Castillo Escalona, Silvia Solar, Gil Vidal, Luis Induni, Jacinto (Jack) Molina; *D:* Miguel Iglesias Bonns; *W:* Jacinto (Jack) Molina; *C:* Tomas Pladevall.

The Night of the Hunter 🦴🦴🦴🦴 **1955** The nightmarish story of psychotic bogus preacher Harry Powell (Mitchum) who has the words H-A-T-E tattooed on the knuckles of his left hand and L-O-V-E on his right. He marries lonely widow Willa Harper (Winters), who has two children, in the hopes of finding the cache of money her thieving husband (Graves) had stashed. Gish plays Rachel, the shotgun-wielding, Bible-reading old lady who defends the kids when Harry threatens them. A dark, terrifying tale, completely unique in Hollywood's history. Mitchum is terrific. From novel by Davis Grubb and, sadly, Laughton's only directorial effort. **93m/B VHS, DVD.** Robert Mitchum, Shelley Winters, Lillian Gish, Don Beddoe, Evelyn Varden, Peter Graves, James Gleason, Billy Chapin, Sally Jane Bruce, Gloria Castillo, Mary Ellen Clemons, Cheryl Callaway, Corey Allen, Paul Bryar; *D:* Charles Laughton; *W:* James Agee; *C:* Stanley Cortez; *M:* Walter Schumann. Natl. Film Reg. '92.

The Night of the Iguana 🦴🦴🦴 **1964** An alcoholic ex-minister acts as a tour guide in Mexico, becoming involved with a spinster and a hotel owner. Based on Tennessee Williams' play. Excellent performances from Burton and Gardner. **125m/B VHS, Wide.** Richard Burton, Deborah Kerr, Ava Gardner, Grayson Hall, Sue Lyon, Emilio Fernandez; *D:* John Huston. Oscars '64: Costume Des. (B&W).

Night of the Juggler 🦴🦴½ **1980 (R)** An ex-cop encounters countless obstacles in trying to track down his daughter's kidnapper in NYC. Just a tad too complicated for some tastes. **101m/C VHS.** James Brolin, Cliff Gorman, Richard S. Castellano, Mandy Patinkin, Julie Carmen; *D:* Robert Butler; *W:* William W. Norton Sr.

Night of the Kickfighters 🦴 **1991** A mighty band of martial artists takes on a terrorist group that has in their possession a secret weapon that could destroy the world. **87m/C VHS.** Andy Bauman, Adam West, Marcia Karr; *D:* Buddy Reyes.

Night of the Laughing Dead 🦴½ *Crazy House; House in Nightmare Park* **1975** Veteran British comedy cast perform unthinkable spoof. Man stands to inherit lotsa money as his family members kick the bucket one by one. **90m/C VHS.** *GB* Ray Milland, Frankie Howerd, Rosalie Crutchley, Kenneth Griffith; *D:* Peter Sykes.

Night of the Living Babes woof! **1987** Two yuppie men go looking for fun at a brothel. They get their just deserts in the form of sex-seeking female zombies. **60m/C VHS.** Michelle (McClellan) Bauer, Connie Woods, Andrew Nichols, Louie Bonanno; *D:* Jon Valentine.

Night of the Living Dead 🦴🦴🦴½ *Night of the Flesh Eaters; Night of the Anubis* **1968** Cult favorite is low budget but powerfully frightening. Space experiments set off a high level of radiation that makes the newly dead return to life, with a taste for human flesh. Handful of holdouts find shelter in a farmhouse. Claustrophobic, terrifying, gruesome, extreme, and yes, humorous. Followed by "Dawn of the Dead" (1979) and "Day of the Dead" (1985). Romero's directorial debut. Available in a colorized version. **90m/B VHS, DVD.** Judith O'Dea, Duane Jones, Karl Hardman, Marilyn Eastman, Keith Wayne, Judith Ridley, Russell Streiner, Bill "Chilly Billy" Cardille, John A. Russo, Kyra Schon, Bill (William Heinzman) Hinzman, John Simpson, Vincent Survinski, George A. Romero; *D:* George A. Romero; *W:* John A. Russo, George A. Romero; *C:* George A. Romero. Natl. Film Reg. '99.

Night of the Living Dead 🦴🦴 **1990 (R)** A bunch of people are trapped in a farmhouse and attacked by ghouls with eating disorders. Remake of the '68 classic substitutes high tech blood 'n' guts for bona fide frights. **92m/C VHS, DVD, Wide.** Tony Todd, Patricia Tallman, Tom Towles, William Butler, Bill Moseley, McKee Anderson, Kate Finneran, Bill "Chilly Billy" Cardille; *D:* Tom Savini; *W:* George A. Romero, John A. Russo; *C:* Frank Prinzi; *M:* Paul McCollough.

Night of the Living Dead, 25th Anniversary Documentary **1993** Features behind the scenes look at low-budget 1968 classic film about legions of dead people who stalk the earth looking for live humans to feed on. **83m/C VHS.**

Night of the Running Man 🦴½ **1994 (R)** Las Vegas cab driver McCarthy finds $1 million stolen from a casino and goes on the run from hit man Glenn, who's been hired to recover the loot. **93m/C VHS.** Scott Glenn, Andrew McCarthy, John Glover; *D:* Mark L. Lester.

Night of the Scarecrow 🦴🦴½ **1995 (R)** Hundreds of years before a small town makes a pact with a warlock (Lazar) to ensure prosperity. After regretting the deal, the townspeople kill him and bury the body in a field where it's eventually uncovered. Now the warlock's ghost inhabits the frame of a scarecrow and is off on a murderous rampage. Formula horror with some decent production values. Based on a comic book. **90m/C VHS.** Elizabeth Barondes, John Mese, Stephen (Steve) Root, Bruce Glover, Dirk Blocker, Howard Swain, Gary Lockwood, John Lazar, John Hawkes, Martine Beswick; *D:* Jeff Burr; *W:* Reed Steiner, Dan Mazur; *C:* Thomas Callaway; *M:* Jim Manzie.

Night of the Sharks woof! **1987** Mercenaries in a downed plane go after a jewel-ridden shipwreck despite a plethora of sharks. **87m/C VHS.** Treat Williams, Christopher Connelly, Antonio Fargas, Janet Agren; *D:* Anthony Richmond.

The Night of the Shooting Stars 🦴🦴🦴🦴 *The Night of San Lorenzo; La Notte di San Lorenzo* **1982 (R)** Set in an Italian village during the last days of WWII, this film highlights the schism in the village between those who support the fascists and those who sympathize with the Allies. This division comes to a head in the stunning final scene. A poignant, deeply moving film. **106m/C VHS.** *IT* Omero Antonutti, Margarita Lozano, Claudio Bigagli, Massimo Bonetti, Norma Martel; *D:* Paolo Taviani, Vittorio Taviani; *W:* Tonino Guerra, Giuliani G. De Negri, Paolo Taviani, Vittorio Taviani; *C:* Franco Di Giacomo; *M:* Nicola Piovani. Cannes '82: Grand Jury Prize; Natl. Soc. Film Critics '83: Director (Taviani), Director (Taviani), Film.

Night of the Sorcerers woof! **1970** An expedition to the Congo uncovers a bizarre tribe of vampire leopard women who lure young girls to their deaths. **85m/C VHS.** Jack Taylor, Simon Andrew, Kali Hansa; *D:* Armando de Ossorio.

Night of the Strangler **1973 (R)** A love affair between a white society girl and a young black man causes a chain of events that end with brutal murders in New Orleans. **88m/C VHS.** Mickey Dolenz, James Ralston, Susan McCullough; *D:* Joy Houck Jr.

Night of the Twisters ½ **1995** Teenager Dan (Sawa) and his new stepfather Jack (Schneider) must work together to protect the family when tornadoes rip through their small Nebraska town. Based on the book by Ivy Ruckman. **91m/C VHS.** John Schneider, Devon Sawa, Lori Hallier, Helen Hughes; *D:* Timothy Bond; *M:* Lawrence Shragge. **CABLE**

Night of the Warrior **1991 (R)** Music videos and martial arts don't mix...not here, anyway. A hunky exotic-dance-club owner pays his disco bills by fighting in illegal, underground blood matches, but not enough to make it exciting. Lamas stars with real life wife Kinmont and mom Dahl. **96m/C VHS, DVD.** Lorenzo Lamas, Anthony Geary, Kathleen Kinmont, Arlene Dahl; *D:* Rafal Zielinski; *W:* Thomas Ian Griffith; *C:* Edward Pei; *M:* Ed Tomney.

Night of the Wilding **1990** Very, very loosely based on the story of the female jogger who was gang-raped and left for dead in New York's Central Park. Made soon after the actual incident occurred. **90m/C VHS.** Erik Estrada, Kathrin Lautner; *D:* Joseph Merhi. **TV**

Night of the Zombies *Gamma 693; Night of the Wehrmacht Zombies* **1981 (R)** WWII soldiers with eating disorders shuffle through 88 minutes of gratuitous gore, while pursued by porn star cum intelligence agent. From the director of "Bloodsucking Freaks." **88m/C VHS.** James Gillis, Ryan Hilliard, Samantha Grey, Joel M. Reed; *D:* Joel M. Reed; *W:* Joel M. Reed.

Night on Earth **1991 (R)** Jarmusch's "road" movie comprises five different stories taking place on the same night in five different cities—Los Angeles, New York, Paris, Rome, and Helsinki—between cabbies and their passengers. As with any anthology some stories work better than others but all have their moments in this ambitious film with its outstanding international cast. Subtitled in English for the three foreign segments. **125m/C VHS, Wide.** Winona Ryder, Gena Rowlands, Giancarlo Esposito, Armin Mueller-Stahl, Rosie Perez, Beatrice Dalle, Roberto Benigni, Paolo Bonacelli, Matti Pellonpaa, Kari Vaananen, Sakari Kuosmanen, Tomi Salmela, Lisanne Falk, Isaach de Bankole, Alan Randolph Scott, Anthony Portillo, Richard Boes, Pascal Nzonzi, Emile Abossolo-M'Bo; *D:* Jim Jarmusch; *W:* Jim Jarmusch; *C:* Frederick Elmes; *M:* Tom Waits, Kathleen Brennan. Ind. Spirit '93: Cinematog.

Night Orchid **1997 (R)** Filmmaker Mark Atkins heads for Stephen King territory with the story of a young psychic (Paris) who arrives in a rural hamlet and has visions of murders. For a low-budget video premiere, this one looks very good. It's made with a degree of style and originality. Fans have seen worse. **93m/C DVD, Wide.** Dale Paris, Alyssa Simon, Mary Ellen O'Brien; *D:* Mark Atkins; *C:* Paul Atkins; *M:* C.C. Adcock.

Night Partners ½ **1983** Bored housewives assist the police to patrol the streets after the kids have gone to bed. Originally a TV pilot, but the script doesn't hold water. **100m/C VHS.** Yvette Mimieux, Diana Canova, Arlen Dean Snyder, M. Emmet Walsh, Patricia Davis, Larry Linville; *D:* Noel Nosseck. **TV**

The Night Patrol ½ **1926** Talmadge is a cop who winds up arresting his girlfriend's brother for murder. Convinced the boy is innocent, Talmadge disguises himself in order to infiltrate the gang he thinks is actually responsible for the crime. Lots of derring-do and a last-minute rescue from the electric chair. **53m/B VHS.** Richard Talmadge, Mary Carr, Rose Blossom, Josef Swickard, Gardner James; *D:* Noel Mason Smith.

Night Patrol woof! **1985 (R)** The streets of Hollywood will never be the same after the night patrol runs amuck in the town. Crude imitation of "Police Academy." **87m/C VHS.** Linda Blair, Pat Paulsen, Jaye P. Morgan, Jack Riley, Murray Langston, Billy Barty, Noriyuki "Pat" Morita, Sydney Lassick, Andrew (Dice Clay) Silverstein; *D:* Jackie Kong; *C:* Hanania Baer. Golden Raspberries '85: Worst Actress (Blair).

The Night Porter *Il Portiere de Notte* **1974 (R)** Max, an ex-SS concentration camp officer, unexpectedly meets his former lover-victim at the Viennese hotel where he works as the night porter. After they get reacquainted, the couple must hide from the porter's ex-Nazi friends who want the women dead because they fear she will disclose their past. A sado-masochistic voyage not for the faint-hearted. **115m/C VHS, DVD.** *IT* Dirk Bogarde, Charlotte Rampling, Phillippe LeRoy, Gabriele Ferzetti, Isa Miranda; *D:* Liliana Cavani; *W:* Liliana Cavani; *C:* Alfio Contino; *M:* Daniele Paris.

Night Rhythms ½ **1992 (R)** Nick West is a radio talk show host with a sexy voice that causes his women listeners to reveal their most intimate fantasies and problems to him on the air. When one listener goes too far, it's murder, and Nick must work to prove his innocence in the crime if he intends to save his career—and his life. Also available in an unrated version. **?m/C VHS.** Martin Hewitt, Delia Sheppard, David Carradine, Terry Tweed, Sam Jones, Deborah Driggs, Julie Strain; *D:* Alexander Gregory (Gregory Dark) Hippolyte.

Night Ride Home ½ **1999** Nora Mahler (DeMornay) loves running the family ranch with her teenaged children Clea (Birch) and Simon (Brower) and her somewhat indifferent husband, Neil (Carradine). Then Simon is killed in a riding accident and Nora falls apart. Neil thinks the family needs to make a fresh start but Nora's too shattered to make decisions until her mother, Maggie (Burstyn), comes to visit and help her daughter cope with the family's tragedy—and failing marriage. **?m/C VHS.** Rebecca DeMornay, Keith Carradine, Ellen Burstyn, Thora Birch, Lynne Thigpen, Jordan Brower; *D:* Glenn Jordan. **TV**

Night Rider **1932** A cowboy posing as a gunman ends a trail of murder and violence in a small western town. **54m/B VHS.** Harry Carey Sr., George "Gabby" Hayes.

Night Riders of Montana **1950** A state ranger helps a group of ranchers to fight off a band of rustlers. **60m/B VHS.** Allan "Rocky" Lane.

Night Ripper **1986** A psychopathic killer stalks high fashion models and kills them by carving them up. Lots of violence. **88m/C VHS.** James Hansen, April Anne, Larry Thomas; *D:* Jeff Hathcock.

Night School *Terror Eyes* **1981 (R)** A police detective must find out who has been decapitating the women attending night school at Wendell College. Ward's first film. **89m/C VHS.** Leonard Mann, Rachel Ward, Drew Snyder, Joseph R. Sicari, Nicholas Cairis, Bill McCann, Margo Skinner; *D:* Ken Hughes; *W:* Ruth Avergon; *C:* Mark Irwin; *M:* Brad Fiedel.

Night Screams **1987** Violent scare-monger about two escaped convicts who crash a high school house party. Kids and convicts start getting killed, one by one. **85m/C VHS, DVD.** Joe Manno, Ron Thomas, Randy Lundsford, Megan Wyss; *D:* Allen Plone.

Night Shade **1997 (R)** Recent widower Scott Travers (Abell) is still grieving over the death of his wife, although his friends are persistent that he should get out and mingle. So he goes to a club and notices one of the dancers looks very familiar—yep, it's the missus, and she's only kinda dead: she's become a vampire. **90m/C VHS.** Tim Abell, Tane McClure, Teresa Langley; *D:* Fred Olen Ray; *W:* Sean O'Bannon; *C:* James Lawrence Spencer.

Night Shadow **1990 (R)** A woman, returning home after being away for years, picks up a hitchhiker. Soon after her arrival, terrible serial killings begin, and only she has the nerve to track down the killer. **90m/C VHS.** Brenda Vance, Dana Chan, Tom Boylan; *D:* Randolph Cohlan; *W:* Randolph Cohlan.

Night Shift **1982 (R)** Two morgue attendants, dull Winkler and manic Keaton, decide to spice up their latenight shift by running a call-girl service on the side. Keaton turns in a fine performance in his film debut, and Howard's sure-handed direction almost overcomes the silly premise. Watch closely for Costner in the morgue frat party scene. **106m/C VHS, DVD.** Henry Winkler, Michael Keaton, Shelley Long, Kevin Costner, Pat Corley, Bobby DiCicco, Nita Talbot, Richard Belzer, Shannen Doherty, Clint Howard, Joe Spinell; *D:* Ron Howard; *W:* Babaloo Mandel, Lowell Ganz; *C:* James A. Crabe; *M:* Burt Bacharach; *V:* Vincent Schiavelli.

Night Siege Project: Shadowchaser 2 ½ *Project Shadowchaser 2* **1994 (R)** Smooth actioner finds a terrorist android taking over a nuclear arsenal and threatening to make Washington, D.C. a mushroom cloud. Naturally, there's a hero (and a heroine) to take care of the evildoers. **97m/C VHS.** Bryan Genesse, Frank Zagarino, Beth Toussaint; *D:* John Eyres; *W:* Nick Davis; *M:* Steve Edwards.

Night Slasher **1984** A madman enjoys spilling the innards of London prostitutes with his dagger. **87m/C VHS.** Jack May, Linda Marlowe.

Night Stage to Galveston ½ **1952** Autry leads his Texas Rangers on a mission to uncover corruption in the Texas State Police during the turbulent post-Civil War era. **61m/B VHS.** Gene Autry, Pat Buttram, Virginia Huston, Thurston Hall; *D:* George Archainbaud.

The Night Stalker ½ **1971** Pilot movie for the TV series finds veteran reporter Carl Kolchak (McGavin) investigating a series of murders that lead him to believe a modern-day vampire is stalking the streets of Vegas. **73m/C VHS, DVD.** Darren McGavin, Carol Lynley, Simon Oakland, Ralph Meeker, Claude Akins, Kent Smith, Larry Linville, Barry Atwater; *D:* John Llewellyn Moxey; *W:* Richard Matheson; *M:* Robert Cobert. **TV**

Night Stalker **1987 (R)** A bloodthirsty serial killer is tracked by a detective through the streets in New York. The usual rigamarole of fisticuffes, gunplay, and car chases ensure. Impressive acting from Napier raises the film from the run-of-the-mill. **91m/C VHS.** Charles Napier, John Goff, Robert Viharo, Robert Z'Dar, Joseph Gian, Gary Crosby, Joan Chen, Michelle Reese; *D:* Max Cleven; *C:* Don Burgess.

The Night Strangler ½ **1972** Still creepy sequel to 1971's "The Night Stalker" finds reporter Carl Kolchak (McGavin) investigating of series of murders with female victims. He discovers that similar crimes have been committed in Seattle every 21 years for more than a century and the killer's description is always the same. **90m/C VHS, DVD.** Darren McGavin, Richard Anderson, Simon Oakland, Wally Cox, Margaret Hamilton, John Carradine, Al Lewis; *D:* Dan Curtis; *W:* Richard Matheson; *M:* Robert Cobert. **TV**

Night Sun ½ *Il Sole Anche di Notte; Sunshine Even by Night* **1990** Sergio (Sands) is an 18th-century nobleman who discovers his fiance was once the king's mistress. He abandons worldly pursuits to become a monk and find some peace but temptation follow him. Based on the Tolstoy story "Father Sergius." Sands' voice was dubbed by Italian actor Giancarlo Giannini. Italian with subtitles. **112m/C VHS.** *IT* Julian Sands, Charlotte Gainsbourg, Massimo Bonetti, Margarita Lozano, Ruediger Vogler; *D:* Paolo Taviani, Vittorio Taviani; *W:* Tonino Guerra, Paolo Taviani, Vittorio Taviani; *C:* Giuseppe Lanci; *M:* Nicola Piovani.

Night Terror **1976** Everyone's after a hausfrau who saw a highway patrolman murdered on an expressway...including the psychotic murderer. Pretty standard fare. **73m/C VHS.** Valerie Harper, Richard Romanus, Michael (Lawrence) Tolan, Beatrice Manley, John Quade, Quinn Cummings, Nicholas Pryor; *D:* E.W. Swackhamer. **TV**

Night Terror **1989** A man wakes up from a nightmare only to find that his terrors are still present. **90m/C VHS.** Lloyd B. Mote, Jeff Keel, Guy Ecker, Jon Hoffman, Michael Coopet; *D:* Michael Weaver, Paul Howard.

The Night the City Screamed ½ **1980 (PG)** It's the hottest day of the year, the city experiences a massive blackout, and nighttime brings out less-than-noble emotions amongst the citizenry. **96m/C VHS.** Raymond Burr, Georg Stanford Brown, Linda Purl, Robert Culp, Clifton Davis, David Cassidy, George DiCenzo, Gary Frank, Don Meredith, Shelley Smith, Vic Tayback, Dick Anthony Williams; *D:* Harry Falk; *W:* Larry Brody. **TV**

The Night the Lights Went Out in Georgia **1981 (PG)** Loosely based on the popular hit song, the film follows a brother and sister as they try to cash in on the country music scene in Nashville. McNichol is engaging. **112m/C VHS.** Kristy McNichol, Dennis Quaid, Mark Hamill, Don Stroud; *D:* Ronald F. Maxwell; *W:* Bob Bonney; *C:* Bill Butler; *M:* David Shire.

The Night They Raided Minsky's *The Night They Invented Striptease* **1969 (PG)** Chaotic but interesting period comedy about a young Amish girl who leaves her tyrannical father to come to New York City in the 1920s. She winds up at Minsky's Burlesque and accidentally invents the striptease. Lahr's last performance—he died during filming. ♫The Night They Raided Minsky's; Take Ten Terrific Girls But Only 9 Costumes; How I Love Her; Perfect Gentleman; You Rat, You; Penny Arcade; Wait For Me. **97m/C VHS.** Jason Robards Jr., Britt Ekland, Elliott Gould, Bert Lahr, Norman Wisdom, Denholm Elliott; *D:* William Friedkin; *W:* Norman Lear, Arnold Schulman.

The Night They Robbed Big Bertha's **1983** Bungling burglar attempts to knock off Big Bertha's massage parlor. **83m/C VHS.** Robert Nichols.

The Night They Saved Christmas ½ **1987** A Christmas special in which Santa's North Pole headquarters are endangered by the progress of an expanding oil company. Will the attempts of three children be enough to save the day? **94m/C VHS.** Art Carney, Jaclyn Smith, Paul Williams, Paul LeMat; *D:* Jackie Cooper.

Night Tide ½ **1963** Hopper in another off the wall character study, this time as a lonely sailor. He falls for a mermaid (Lawson) who works at the dock. She may be a descendent of the man-killing Sirens. Interesting and different little love story, sometimes advertised as horror, which it is not. **84m/B VHS, DVD, Wide.** Dennis Hopper, Gavin Muir, Linda Lawson, Luana Anders, Marjorie Eaton, Tom Dillon, Bruno VeSota; *D:* Curtis Harrington; *W:* Curtis Harrington; *C:* Vilis Lapenieks; *M:* David Raksin.

Night Time in Nevada ½ **1948** Young woman heads West to claim $50,000 trust left by dear old dad, but his crooked lawyer and associate have their hands in the pot. Cowboy Roy rides horse and flexes dimples while helping helpless girl. **67m/B VHS, 8mm.** Roy Rogers, Adele Mara, Andy Devine, Grant Withers, Joseph Crehan; *D:* William Witney.

A Night to Remember **1942** A murder-mystery writer's wife convinces him to move to a new apartment because she thinks the change might help him finish a novel he started long ago. When they find a dead body behind their new building, they try their hands at sleuthing. A clever and witty mystery, indeed, supported by likeable performances. **91m/B VHS.** Loretta Young, Brian Aherne, Sidney Toler, Gale Sondergaard, William Wright, Donald MacBride, Blanche Yurka; *D:* Richard Wallace.

A Night to Remember **1958** Gripping tale of the voyage of the Titanic with an interesting account of action in the face of danger and courage amid despair. Large cast is effectively used. Adapted by Eric Ambler from the book by Walter Lord. **119m/B VHS, DVD.** Kenneth More, David McCallum, Anthony Bushell, Honor Blackman, Michael Goodliffe, George Rose, Laurence Naismith, Frank Lawton, Alec McCowen, Jill Dixon, John Cairney, Joseph Tomelty, Jack Watling, Richard Clarke, Ralph Michael, Kenneth Griffith; ***D:*** Roy Ward Baker; ***W:*** Eric Ambler; ***C:*** Geoffrey Unsworth. Golden Globes '59: Foreign Film.

The Night Train to Kathmandu 𝒹𝒹 **1988** A young girl accompanies her parents on a research expedition to Nepal, where her head is turned by an exotically handsome young Sherpa. Old story without much help from actors or director. **102m/C VHS.** Milla Jovovich, Pernell Roberts, Eddie Castrodad; ***D:*** Robert Wiemer. **CABLE**

Night Train to Munich 𝒹𝒹𝒹 *Night Train; Gestapo* **1940** There's Nazi intrigue galore aboard a big train when a scientist's daughter joins allied intelligence agents in retrieving some secret documents. From the book "Report on a Fugitive" by Gordon Wellesley. **93m/B VHS.** *GB* Margaret Lockwood, Rex Harrison, Paul Henreid, Basil Radford, Naunton Wayne, James Harcourt, Felix Aylmer, Roland Culver, Raymond Huntley, Austin Trevor, Kenneth Kent, C.V. France, Frederick Valk, Morland Graham, Wally Patch, Irene Handl, Albert Lieven, David Horne; ***D:*** Carol Reed; ***W:*** Frank Launder, Sidney Gilliat; ***C:*** Otto Kanturek.

Night Train to Terror woof! *Shiver* **1984 (R)** Strange things start happening on the train where a rock band makes its last appearance. Clips from other horror flicks were pieced together to make this film that's so bad it's almost good. **98m/C VHS, DVD.** John Phillip Law, Cameron Mitchell, Marc Lawrence, Charles Moll, Ferdinand "Ferdy" Mayne; ***D:*** Jay Schlossberg-Cohen; ***W:*** Philip Yordan.

Night Train to Venice 𝒹½ **1993 (R)** Martin (Grant) is aboard the Orient Express on his way to Venice to deliver his book about the rise of neo-Nazism. He meets a mystery man (McDowell) and an actress (Welch) with ties to a neo-Nazi group, who also happen to be aboard the train and anxious to stop Martin from delivering his expose. Extended dream sequences and flashbacks tend to stop the story cold but Grant is a draw (and probably the only reason this mishmash has been released to video). **98m/C VHS.** Hugh Grant, Malcolm McDowell, Tahnee Welch, Kristina Soderbaum; ***D:*** Carlo U. Quinterio; ***W:*** Leo Tichat, Toni Hirtreiter; ***M:*** Alexander Bubenheim.

Night Vision 𝒹 **1987** A young writer in the big city is given a video monitor by a street thief which is equipped with some remarkable features, including the ability to present scenes of future murders and demon worship. **102m/C VHS.** Ellie Martins, Stacy Carson, Shirley Ross, Tony Carpenter; ***D:*** Michael Krueger.

Night Vision 𝒹𝒹 **1997 (R)** Burned-out detective Dak Smith (Williamson) has been demoted to motorcycle cop on the graveyard shift. But he unexpectedly becomes involved with the case of a serial killer who likes to stalk and videotape his victims. Now Dak and his new partner Kristen O'Conner (Rothrock) are working to capture this psychopath. **95m/C VHS.** Fred Williamson, Cynthia Rothrock, Robert Forster, Frank Pesce, Willie Gault, Amanda Welles, Nina Richardson; ***D:*** Gil Bettman; ***W:*** Michael Thomas Montgomery; ***C:*** Trey Smith. **VIDEO**

The Night Visitor 𝒹𝒹½ **1970 (PG)** A man in a prison for the criminally insane seeks violent vengeance on those he believes have set him up. Heavily detailed, slow moving. Ullman and von Sydow can do better. **106m/C VHS.** *GB DK* Max von Sydow, Liv Ullmann, Trevor Howard, Per Oscarsson, Andrew Keir; ***D:*** Laslo Benedek; ***M:*** Henry Mancini.

Night Visitor 𝒹 *Never Cry Devil* **1989 (R)** A retired police detective teams up with a teenage peeping tom to disclose the identity of a satanic serial killer. The killer, of course, is one of the youth's teachers. **95m/C VHS, DVD.** Derek Rydell, Shannon Tweed, Elliott Gould, Allen (Goorwitz) Garfield, Michael J. Pollard, Richard Roundtree, Henry Gibson; ***D:*** Rupert Hitzig; ***W:*** Randal Viscovich.

The Night Walker 𝒹𝒹½ **1964** Stanwyck is always worth watching and she has the best moments in this psycho-thriller which suffers from a low-budget and confused script. The basic story has Stanwyck as a rich widow with a recurring nightmare featuring a faceless lover. There's also a too-helpful lawyer (Taylor), a suspicious private detective (Bochner)—and maybe her husband isn't so dead after all. Taylor and Stanwyck, who had once been married, worked together for the first time in 27 years. **86m/B VHS.** Barbara Stanwyck, Robert Taylor, Lloyd Bochner, Hayden Rorke, Judith Meredith, Rochelle Hudson; ***D:*** William Castle; ***W:*** Robert Bloch.

Night Warning 𝒹𝒹 *Nightmare Maker; Butcher Baker (Nightmare Maker)* **1982 (R)** A slasher gorefest redeemed by Tyrrell's go-for-broke performance. She plays a sexually repressed aunt who makes up for her problems by going on murderous rampages. Hide the kitchen knives! **96m/C VHS.** Bo Svenson, Jimmy (James Vincent) McNichol, Susan Tyrrell, Julia Duffy; ***D:*** William Asher; ***W:*** Stephen Breimer.

Night Wars 𝒹½ **1988** Two ex-POWs who are plagued by their memories turn to dream therapy to relive their escape. Eventually, they rescue a buddy they left behind. **90m/C VHS.** Dan Haggerty, Brian O'Connor, Cameron Smith; ***D:*** David A. Prior.

Night Watch 𝒹½ *Le Trou; Il Buco* **1972** A woman recovering from a nervous breakdown witnesses a murder, but no one will believe her. **100m/C VHS.** *GB* Elizabeth Taylor, Laurence Harvey, Billie Whitelaw; ***D:*** Brian G. Hutton; ***C:*** Billy Williams.

The Night We Never Met 𝒹𝒹½ **1993 (R)** Three yuppies bring different visions of romance and a case of mistaken identity to a time-share apartment in New York's Greenwich Village. Sam (Broderick) needs a quiet space to get over being dumped by a flaky performance artist (Tripplehorn). Ellen (Sciorra) is looking for space to paint away from the confines of her thick-headed spouse (Mantell). Brian, the organizer of the living arrangement, wants a space where he can be one of the boys and escape from his cloying fiancee (Bateman). Fairly predictable but enjoyable romantic comedy. **98m/C VHS.** Paul Guilfoyle, Matthew Broderick, Jeanne Tripplehorn, Kevin Anderson, Justine Bateman, Annabella Sciorra, Christine Baranski, Doris Roberts, Dominic Chianese, Michael Mantell, Tim Guinee, Greg Germann, Dana Wheeler-Nicholson, Louise Lasser, Billy Campbell, Ranjit (Chaudry) Chowdhry, Garry Shandling, Katharine Houghton, Brooke Smith; ***D:*** Warren Leight; ***W:*** Warren Leight; ***M:*** Evan Lurie.

Night Zoo 𝒹𝒹 *Un Zoo, La Nuit* **1987** A confusing story about a father/son reconciliation and the lurid underworld of drugs and sex in Montreal. The graphic sex and violence undermines the sensitive aspects of the film. **115m/C VHS.** *CA* Gilles Maheu, Roger Le Bel, Lynne Adams, German Houde; ***D:*** Jean-Claude Lauzon. Genie '88: Actor (Le Bel), Director (Lauzon), Film, Support. Actor (Houde).

Nightbreaker 𝒹𝒹𝒹 **1989** Revelation of the U.S. government's deliberate exposure of servicemen to atomic bomb tests and the resulting radiation, in order to observe the effects on humans. Sheen and his son, Estevez, portray a U.S. doctor in the 1980s and the 1950s, respectively. **100m/C VHS.** Martin Sheen, Emilio Estevez, Lea Thompson, Melinda Dillon, Nicholas Pryor, Joe Pantoliano; ***D:*** Peter Markle; ***W:*** T.S. Cook; ***M:*** Peter Bernstein.

Nightbreed 𝒹½ **1990 (R)** A teenager flees a chaotic past to slowly become a member of a bizarre race of demons that live in a huge, abandoned Canadian graveyard; a place where every sin is forgiven. Based on Barker's novel "Cabal," and appropriately gross, nonsensical and strange. Good special effects almost save this one. **102m/C VHS, DVD, Wide.** *CA* Craig Sheffer, Anne Bobby, David Cronenberg, Charles Haid; ***D:*** Clive Barker; ***W:*** Clive Barker; ***C:*** Robin Vidgeon; ***M:*** Danny Elfman.

The Nightcomers 𝒹 **1972 (R)** A pretend "prequel" to Henry James's "The Turn of the Screw," wherein an Irish gardener trysts with the nanny of two watchful children who believe that lovers unite in death. Don't be fooled: stick to the original. **96m/C VHS.** *GB* Marlon Brando, Stephanie Beacham, Thora Hird, Harry Andrews, Christopher Ellis, Verna Harvey, Anna Palk; ***D:*** Michael Winner; ***W:*** Michael Hastings; ***C:*** Robert Paynter; ***M:*** Jerry Fielding.

Nightfall 𝒹𝒹𝒹 **1956** Ray, accused of a crime he didn't commit, is forced to flee from both the law and the underworld. Classic example of film noir, brilliantly filmed by Tourneur. **78m/B VHS.** Aldo Ray, Brian Keith, Anne Bancroft, Jocelyn Brando, James Gregory, Frank Albertson; ***D:*** Jacques Tourneur; ***W:*** Stirling Silliphant.

Nightfall 𝒹𝒹 **1988 (PG-13)** Adaptation of the classic Isaac Asimov short story. A planet that has two suns (and therefore no night) experiences an eclipse and its inhabitants go mad. **87m/C VHS.** David Birney, Sarah Douglas, Alexis Kanner, Andra Millian; ***D:*** Paul Mayersberg; ***C:*** Darius Wolski. **TV**

Nightflyers 𝒹½ **1987 (R)** Aboard a weathered space freighter, the crew experience a series of deadly accidents caused by an unknown evil presence. From a novella by George R.R. Martin; T.C. Blake is better known as Robert Collector. **88m/C VHS.** Michael Praed, Michael Des Barres, Catherine Mary Stewart, John Standing, Lisa Blount; ***D:*** T.C. Blake.

Nightforce 𝒹 **1986 (R)** Five buddies plunge into Central American jungles to rescue a young girl held by terrorists. **87m/C VHS.** Linda Blair, James Van Patten, Chad McQueen, Richard Lynch, Cameron Mitchell; ***D:*** Lawrence Foldes.

Nighthawks 𝒹𝒹 **1978** Jim (Robertson) is a geography teacher in London who lives a closeted life. His quiet daily routine is separate from his cruising of the city's gay pleasure spots until his two worlds converge when he's confronted by his students. **113m/C VHS.** *GB* Ken Robertson; ***D:*** Ron Peck; ***W:*** Ron Peck, Paul Hallam; ***C:*** Johanna Davis; ***M:*** David Graham Ellis.

Nighthawks 𝒹𝒹½ **1981 (R)** NYC cops scour Manhattan to hunt down an international terrorist on the loose. They race from disco to subway to an airborne tramway. Exciting and well paced. Hauer's American film debut. **100m/C VHS, DVD.** Sylvester Stallone, Billy Dee Williams, Rutger Hauer, Lindsay Wagner, Nigel Davenport, Persis Khambatta, Catherine Mary Stewart, Joe Spinell; ***D:*** Bruce Malmuth; ***W:*** David Shaber; ***C:*** James A. Contner; ***M:*** Keith Emerson.

The Nightingale **1983** From "Faerie Tale Theatre" comes the story of an Emperor who discovers the value of true friendship and loyalty from his palace kitchen maid who gives him a nightingale. **60m/C VHS.** Mick Jagger, Barbara Hershey, Bud Cort, Mako; ***D:*** Ivan Passer. **CABLE**

Nightjohn 𝒹𝒹½ **1996 (PG-13)** Nightjohn (Lumbly) is the new slave purchased by Southern plantation owner Clel Walker (Bridges). He moves into the cabin shared by 12-year-old Sarny (Jones) and Delie (Toussaint). When Sarny finds out that Nightjohn can read and write (illegal for slaves), she's determined to learn from him. And with her new knowledge, Sarny looks for ways to help her fellow slaves. Based on Gary Paulsen's 1993 novel; filmed on location at Rip Raps Plantation in Sumter, South Carolina. **96m/C VHS.** Carl Lumbly, Allison Jones, Beau Bridges, Lorraine Toussaint, Bill Cobbs, Kathleen York, Gabriel Casseus, Tom Nowicki, Monica Ford, Joel Thomas Traywick; ***D:*** Charles Burnett; ***W:*** Bill Cain; ***C:*** Elliot Davis; ***M:*** Stephen James Taylor. **CABLE**

Nightkill 𝒹𝒹½ **1980 (R)** Simple love affair turns into a deadly game of cat and mouse when a bored wife plots to do away with her wealthy, powerful husband with the aid of her attractive lover. Mitchum is the reluctant investigator pulled into the game. **104m/C VHS.** Jaclyn Smith, Mike Connors, James Franciscus, Robert Mitchum, Sybil Danning; ***D:*** Ted Post.

Nightlife 𝒹𝒹½ **1990** An ancient vampiress who rises from the dead spends her time haunting a blood clinic, where the Jewish hematologist starts to fall for her. **93m/C VHS.** Ben Cross, Maryam D'Abo, Keith Szarabajka, Jesse Corti, Oliver Clark, Glenn Shadix, Camille Saviola; ***D:*** Daniel Taplitz. **CABLE**

The Nightman 𝒹𝒹 **1993 (R)** Ex-soldier Marcoux becomes the night manager of a failing southern resort, run by sexy, and lonely, Kerns. They begin an affair, which turns sour when Robertson, Kerns's teenaged daughter, also falls for the stud. Then mom is murdered and Marcoux goes to prison. But 18 years later Robertson's past comes back to haunt her. Just what did happen all those years ago? Made-for-TV thriller with additional footage. **96m/C VHS.** Ted Marcoux, Jenny Robertson, Joanna (Joanna DeVarona) Kerns; ***D:*** Charles Haid; ***W:*** James Poe; ***M:*** Gary Chang. **TV**

Nightmare 𝒹𝒹½ **1963** As a child, Janet sees her insane mother stab her father to death. Left in the care of two guardians, the now-grown Janet has recurring nightmares and fears she's inherited her mother's madness. Routine, with red herrings galore. **83m/B VHS.** *GB* Jennie Linden, David Knight, Moira Redmond, Brenda Bruce; ***D:*** Freddie Francis; ***W:*** Jimmy Sangster; ***C:*** John Wilcox; ***M:*** Don Banks.

Nightmare woof! *Blood Splash; Nightmare in a Damaged Brain* **1982 (R)** Boring splatterthon has a young boy hacking his father and his aggressive mistress to pieces when he discovers them in bed. He grows up to be a psycho who continues along the same lines. Humorless and dreadful, the original ads claimed Tom Savini did the special effects. He had nothing to do with it. **97m/C VHS.** Baird Stafford, Sharon Smith, C.J. Cooke, Mik Cribben, Kathleen Ferguson, Danny Ronan; ***D:*** Romano Scavolini; ***W:*** Romano Scavolini; ***C:*** Gianni Fiore; ***M:*** Jack Eric Williams.

Nightmare 𝒹𝒹 **1991 (PG-13)** Single mom Linda Hemmings (Principal) takes matters into her own hands when her daughter Dana (Harris) is kidnapped. Though Dana escapes and her assailant, Edward Ryter (Banks), is arrested, he's soon released and threatening Dana to prevent her testifying. So mom teams up with police detective Jake Wilman (Sorvino) to get the goods on the psycho before he can do further harm. **84m/C VHS.** Victoria Principal, Jonathan Banks, Paul Sorvino, Danielle Harris; ***D:*** John Pasquin; ***W:*** Rich Husky; ***C:*** Denis Lewiston; ***M:*** Dana Kaproff.

Nightmare at Bittercreek 𝒹𝒹 **1991 (PG-13)** Four babes and a tour guide are pursued by psycho gang in the Sierra mountains. Made for TV nightmare in your living room. **92m/C VHS.** Tom Skerritt, Joanna Cassidy, Lindsay Wagner, Constance McCashin, Janne Mortil; ***D:*** Tim Burstall. **TV**

Nightmare at 43 Hillcrest **1974** A family's life becomes a living hell when the police mistakenly raid their house. Based on a true story. **72m/C VHS.** Jim Hutton, Mariette Hartley.

Nightmare at Noon 𝒹 **1987 (R)** Watered-down thriller about a small desert town beset by violent terrorists (who are really locals gone mad from a chemical experiment dumped into the water system). Only the sheriff's small staff is there to stop them. **96m/C VHS, DVD.** Wings Hauser, George Kennedy, Bo Hopkins, Brion James, Kimberly Beck, Kimberly Ross; ***D:*** Nico Mastorakis.

The Nightmare before Christmas 𝒹𝒹𝒹 *Tim Burton's The Nightmare before Christmas* **1993 (PG)** Back when he was a animator trainee at Disney, Burton came up with this adventurous idea but couldn't get it made; subsequent directorial success brought more clout. Relies on a painstaking stop-motion technique that took more than two years to film and is justifiably amazing. The story revolves around Jack Skellington, the Pumpkin King of the dangerously weird Halloweentown. Suffering from ennui, he accidentally discovers the wonders of Christmastown and decides to kidnap Santa and rule over this peaceable holiday. Fast pace is maintained by the equally breathless score. Not cuddly, best appreciated by those with a feel for the macabre. **75m/C VHS, DVD, Wide.** ***D:*** Henry Selick; ***W:*** Caroline Thompson, Tim Burton, Michael McDowell; ***C:*** Pete Kozachik; ***M:*** Danny Elfman; ***V:*** Danny Elfman, Chris Sarandon, Catherine O'Hara, William Hickey, Ken Page, Ed Ivory, Paul (Peewee Herman) Reubens, Glenn Shadix.

Nightmare Castle 🦴🦴 *Amanti d'Oltretomba; Night of the Doomed; The Faceless Monsters; Lovers from Beyond the Tomb* **1965** Jealous mad scientist murders his wife and her lover. Then he conducts a bizarre experiment, using the dead couple's blood to rejuvenate an old servant. Not quite satisfied with his revenge, he then seeks to marry his late wife's sister after realizing that she has been left the inheritance. In time, the perturbed ghosts of the late lovers appear and seek revenge. A real nightmare. **90m/B VHS.** *IT* Barbara Steele, Paul Muller, Helga Line; ***D:*** Allan Grunewald; ***M:*** Ennio Morricone.

Nightmare in Badham County 🦴 *Nightmare* **1976** Two girls get arrested on trumped-up charges in a small backwoods town. They soon discover that the prison farm is a front for a slavery ring. **100m/C VHS.** Deborah Raffin, Lynne Moody, Chuck Connors, Della Reese, Robert Reed, Ralph Bellamy, Tina Louise; ***D:*** John Llewellyn Moxey; ***M:*** Charles Bernstein. **TV**

Nightmare in Blood 🦴½ *Horror Convention* **1975** Vampires lurk in San Francisco and wreak havoc on the night life. **90m/C VHS.** Kerwin Mathews, Jerry Walter, Barrie Youngfellow; ***D:*** John Stanley.

Nightmare in Wax 🦴½ *Crimes in the Wax Museum* **1969** After suffering disfigurement in a fight with a studio boss, a former make-up man starts a wax museum. For fun, he injects movie stars with a formula that turns them into statues. **91m/C VHS.** Cameron Mitchell, Anne Helm; ***D:*** Bud Townsend.

A Nightmare on Elm Street 🦴🦴½ **1984 (R)** Feverish, genuinely frightening horror film about Freddy Krueger (Englund), a scarred maniac in a fedora and razor-fingered gloves who kills neighborhood teens in their dreams and, subsequently, in reality. Of the children-fight-back genre, in which the lead victim (Langenkamp) ingeniously goes to great lengths to destroy Freddy. In the tradition of "Friday the 13th"'s Jason and "Halloween"'s Michael Myers, "Elm Street" spawned a "Freddy" phenomenon: seven sequels (including the upcoming "Freddy Vs. Jason," linking "Elm Street, Part 8" with "Friday the 13th, Part 10"); a TV series ("Freddy's Nightmares," a horror anthology show hosted by Englund to capitalize on his character); and an army of razor-clawed trick or treaters at Halloween. **92m/C VHS, DVD.** John Saxon, Heather Langenkamp, Ronee Blakley, Robert Englund, Amanda Wyss, Nick Corri, Johnny Depp, Charles Fleischer; ***D:*** Wes Craven; ***W:*** Wes Craven; ***C:*** Jacques Haitkin; ***M:*** Charles Bernstein.

A Nightmare on Elm Street 2: Freddy's Revenge 🦴½ **1985 (R)** Mediocre sequel to the popular horror film. Freddy, the dream-haunting psychopath with the ginsu knife hands, returns to possess a teenager's body in order to kill again. Nothing new here, however praise is due for the stunning high-tech dream sequence. **87m/C VHS, DVD.** Mark Patton, Hope Lange, Clu Gulager, Robert Englund, Kim Myers, Robert Rusler, Marshall Bell, Sydney Walsh; ***D:*** Jack Sholder; ***W:*** David Chaskin; ***C:*** Jacques Haitkin.

A Nightmare on Elm Street 3: Dream Warriors 🦴🦴 **1987 (R)** Chapter three in this slice and dice series. Freddy Krueger is at it again, haunting the dreams of unsuspecting suburban teens. Langenkamp, the nightmare-freaked heroine from the first film, returns to counsel the latest victims of Freddy-infested dreams. Noted for the special effects wizardry but little else, Part Three was produced on a $4.5 million shoe string and took in more than $40 million, making it one of the most successful independently produced films in Hollywood. Followed by "A Nightmare on Elm Street 4: Dream Master." **96m/C VHS, DVD.** Patricia Arquette, Robert Englund, Heather Langenkamp, Craig Wasson, Laurence "Larry" Fishburne, Priscilla Pointer, John Saxon, Brooke Bundy, Jennifer Rubin, Rodney Eastman, Nan Martin, Dick Cavett, Zsa Zsa Gabor; ***D:*** Chuck Russell; ***W:*** Chuck Russell, Bruce Wagner, Wes Craven, Frank Darabont; ***C:*** Roy Wagner; ***M:*** Angelo Badalamenti.

A Nightmare on Elm Street 4: Dream Master 🦴🦴½ **1988 (R)** Freddy Krueger is still preying on people in their dreams, but he may have met his match as he battles for supremacy with a telepathically talented girl. What Part 4 lacks in substance, it makes up for in visual verve, including scenes of a kid drowning in his waterbed, and a pizza covered with pepperoni-like faces of Freddy's previous victims. This boxoffice bonanza set a new record as the most successful opening weekend of any independently released film. Followed by "A Nightmare on Elm Street 5: Dream Child." **99m/C VHS, DVD.** Robert Englund, Rodney Eastman, Danny Hassel, Andras Jones, Tuesday Knight, Lisa Wilcox, Ken Sagoes, Toy Newkirk, Brooke Theiss, Brooke Bundy; ***D:*** Renny Harlin; ***W:*** Brian Helgeland, Scott Pierce; ***C:*** Steven Fierberg; ***M:*** Craig Safan.

A Nightmare on Elm Street 5: Dream Child 🦴🦴 **1989 (R)** The fifth installment of Freddy Krueger's never-ending adventures. Here, America's favorite knife-wielding burn victim, unable to best the Dream Master from the previous film, haunts the dreams of her unborn fetus. Gore fans may be disappointed to discover that much of the blood and guts ended up on the cutting room floor. **90m/C VHS, DVD.** Robert Englund, Lisa Wilcox, Kelly Jo Minter, Danny Hassel, Erika Anderson, Nicholas Mele, Beatrice Boepple; ***D:*** Stephen Hopkins; ***W:*** Leslie Bohem; ***C:*** Peter Levy; ***M:*** Jay Ferguson. Golden Raspberries '89: Worst Song ("Bring Your Daughter to the Slaughter").

Nightmare on the 13th Floor 🦴 **1990 (PG-13)** A travel writer at an old hotel glimpses murder on a supposedly non-existent floor. Nasty devil-worshippers are afoot, but the chills in this mild cable throwaway seldom dip below room temperature. **85m/C VHS.** Michael Greene, John Karlen, Louise Fletcher, Alan Fudge, James Brolin; ***D:*** Walter Grauman. **CABLE**

Nightmare Sisters woof! **1987 (R)** Three sorority sisters become possessed by a demon and then sexually ravage a nearby fraternity. **83m/C VHS.** Brinke Stevens, Michelle (McClellan) Bauer, Linnea Quigley; ***D:*** David DeCoteau.

Nightmare Weekend 🦴 **1986 (R)** A professor's evil assistant lures three young women into his lab and performs cruel and vicious experiments that transform the girls and their dates into crazed zombies. **86m/C VHS.** Dale Midkiff, Debbie Laster, Debra Hunter, Lori Lewis; ***D:*** Henry Sala.

The Nightmare Years **1989** An American reporter in Nazi Germany dares to report the truth to an unbelieving world. Based on a true story. Two cassettes. **237m/C VHS.** Sam Waterston, Marthe Keller, Kurtwood Smith; ***D:*** Anthony Page; ***M:*** Vladimir Cosma.

Nightmares 🦴🦴 **1983 (PG)** A less-than-thrilling horror anthology featuring four tales in which common, everyday occurrences take on the ingredients of a nightmare. In the same vein as "Twilight Zone" and "Creepshow." **99m/C VHS, DVD.** Christina Raines, Emilio Estevez, Moon Zappa, Lance Henriksen, Richard Masur, Veronica Cartwright; ***D:*** Joseph Sargent; ***W:*** Christopher Crowe, Jeffrey Bloom; ***C:*** Mario DiLeo, Gerald Perry Finnerman; ***M:*** Craig Safan.

Nights and Days 🦴🦴½ **1976** Adaptation of writer Maria Dabrowska's tale about a Polish family chronicles the persecution, expulsions, and land grabbing that occurred after the unsuccessful Uprising of 1864. In Polish with English subtitles. **255m/C VHS.** *PL* Jadwiga Baranska, Jerzy Binczycki; ***D:*** Jerzy Antczak.

Nights in White Satin 🦴½ **1987** A made-for-video Cinderella story about the growing love between a fashion photographer and a young model whose boyfriend has just been murdered. **96m/C VHS.** Kenneth Gilman, Priscilla Harris; ***D:*** Michael Bernard.

Nights of Cabiria 🦴🦴🦴½ *Le Notti de Cabiria; Cabiria* **1957** Fellini classic which details the personal decline of a naive prostitute who thinks she's found true love. In Italian with English subtitles or dubbed. Basis for the musical "Sweet Charity." **117m/B VHS, DVD.** *IT* Giulietta Masina, Amedeo Nazzari, Francois Perier, Franca Marzi, Dorian Gray, Aldo Silvani, Ennio Girolami; ***D:*** Federico Fellini; ***W:*** Federico Fellini, Tullio Pinelli, Ennio Flaiano; ***C:*** Aldo Tonti; ***M:*** Nino Rota. Oscars '57: Foreign Film; Cannes '57: Actress (Masina).

Nightscare 🦴🦴 *Night Scare; Beyond Bedlam* **1993 (R)** When Dr. Stephanie Lyell's (Hurley) drug behavior-modification experiment goes wrong it allows serial killer Marc Gilmour (Allen) to get to his victims through their dreams. The doc tries to prove to Detective Inspector Terry Hamilton (Fairbrass) that the drug is safe by injecting them both but things get out of hand. Adapted from the novel by Harry Adam Knight. **89m/C VHS.** *GB* Craig Fairbrass, Elizabeth Hurley, Keith Allen, Jesse Birdsall, Craig Kelly; ***D:*** Vadim Jean; ***W:*** Vadim Jean.

Nightstalker woof! **1979** A brother and sister who were condemned to eternal death 12,000 years ago must eat virgins to keep their bodies from rotting. Trouble is, while they search for dinner, the movie decomposes. For mature audiences with no fantasies of celluloid nirvana. **90m/C VHS.** Aldo Ray.

Nightstick 🦴½ *Calhoun* **1987 (R)** New York vigilante cop fights nasties who threaten to blow the lid off the city. Worse, they kidnap super cop's girl forcing him to save her along with the city. Lots of violence, predictable plot, and mediocre acting leave this one without much bang. **90m/C VHS.** Bruce Fairbairn, Kerrie Keane, John Vernon, Robert Vaughn, Isaac Hayes, Leslie Nielsen; ***D:*** Joseph L. Scanlan.

Nightwatch 🦴🦴 **1996 (R)** Law student Martin (McGregor) takes a job as a night watchman in a morgue at the same time a serial killer is killing prostitutes and gouging out their eyes. As if that weren't enough, he has to deal with a cop (Nolte) who suspects him, a sadistic best friend (Brolin) who likes to scare him on the job, and a creepy boss (Dourif) who doesn't like him. Adapted by director Bornedal from his Dutch film "Nattevagten," this one's effectively creepy, but disjointed. Excellent cast is misused, as hardly any of the characters are developed beyond simple types. If you enjoyed the murky, depressing atmosphere of "Seven," you'll probably like this. **101m/C VHS, DVD, Wide.** Ewan McGregor, Nick Nolte, Patricia Arquette, Josh Brolin, John C. Reilly, Brad Dourif, Lonny (Loni) Chapman, Alix Koromzay, Lauren Graham; ***D:*** Ole Bornedal; ***W:*** Ole Bornedal, Steven Soderbergh; ***C:*** Dan Laustsen; ***M:*** Joachim Holbek.

Nightwing 🦴½ **1979 (PG)** Suspense drama about three people who risk their lives to exterminate a colony of plague-carrying vampire bats in New Mexican Indian community. From the novel by Martin Cruz Smith and adapted by Smith, Steve Shagan, and Bud Shrake. O.K. viewing for those who aren't choosy about their rabid bat movies. **103m/C VHS.** Nick Mancuso, David Warner, Kathryn Harrold, Strother Martin, Stephen Macht, Pat Corley, Charles Hallahan, Ben Piazza, George Clutesi; ***D:*** Arthur Hiller; ***W:*** Steve Shagan, Bud Shrake, Martin Cruz Smith; ***C:*** Charles Rosher Jr.; ***M:*** Henry Mancini.

Nightwish 🦴½ **1989 (R)** Students do more than homework when a professor leads them into their own horrifying dreams. Soon it becomes impossible to distinguish dreams from reality. **96m/C VHS.** Jack Starrett, Robert Tessier, Clayton Rohner, Elizabeth Kaitan, Alisha Das, Tom Dugan, Brian Thompson, Artur Cybulski; ***D:*** Bruce Cook Jr.; ***W:*** Bruce Cook Jr.

Nijinsky 🦴🦴 **1980 (R)** An opulent biography of the famous ballet dancer. His exciting and innovative choreography gets little attention. The film concentrates on his infamous homosexual lifestyle and his relationship with impresario Sergei Diaghilev (Bates, in a tour-de-force performance). Lovely to look at, but slow and unconvincing. **125m/C VHS.** Alan Bates, George de la Pena, Leslie Browne, Alan Badel, Carla Fracci, Colin Blakely, Ronald Pickup, Ronald Lacey, Vernon Dobtcheff, Jeremy Irons, Frederick Jaeger, Janet Suzman, Sian Phillips; ***D:*** Herbert Ross.

Nikki, the Wild Dog of the North 🦴½ **1961 (G)** When a Malemute pup is separated from his Canadian trapper master, he teams up with a bear cub for a series of adventures. Later the pup is reunited with his former master for still more adventures. Adapted from a novel by James Oliver Curwood for Disney. **73m/C VHS, DVD.** *CA* Jean Coutu, Emile Genest, Uriel Luft, Robert Rivard; ***D:*** Jack Couffer, Don Haldane; ***W:*** Winston Hibler, Ralph Wright; ***C:*** Lloyd Beebe; ***M:*** Oliver Wallace.

Nil by Mouth 🦴🦴 **1996 (R)** Oldman draws on his own dysfunctional working-class London background for his impressive writer/director debut, which casually puts you into the middle of one Cockney family's life. There's brutal Ray (Winstone), husband to Val (Burke) and brother-in-law to young addict Billy (Creed-Miles), as well as his tough mother-in-law Janet (Morse) and her mother, Kath (Dore). Billy gets kicked out of the house by Ray and struggles to survive outside his family while a drunken Ray beats the pregnant Val, prompting a display of female solidarity. Formless pic drops into characters' lives at random, showcasing family loyalty and generosity amidst the violence. **128m/C VHS.** *GB* Ray Winstone, Kathy Burke, Charlie Creed-Miles, Laila Morse, Edna Dore, Steve Sweeney, Chrissie Cotterill, Jon Morrison, Jamie Forman; ***D:*** Gary Oldman; ***W:*** Gary Oldman; ***C:*** Ron Fortunato; ***M:*** Eric Clapton. British Acad. '97: Film, Orig. Screenplay; Cannes '97: Actress (Burke).

Nina Takes a Lover 🦴🦴 **1994 (R)** Romantic comedy finds Nina (San Giacomo) deciding that the passion is gone from her three-year marriage so, while her husband is out of town, she picks up a nameless Welsh photographer (Rhys) and begins an affair. The affair is over as the movie begins but Nina tells her story to a tabloid journalist (O'Keefe) who's writing about adultery. Gimmicky, with shallow if attractive characters and an equally attractive San Francisco setting. **100m/C VHS.** Laura San Giacomo, Paul Rhys, Michael O'Keefe, Cristi Conaway, Fisher Stevens; ***D:*** Alan Jacobs; ***W:*** Alan Jacobs; ***C:*** Phil Parmet; ***M:*** Todd Boekelheide.

Nine Ages of Nakedness 🦴 **1969** The story of a man whose ancestors have been plagued by a strange problem: beautiful, naked women who create carnal chaos. **88m/C VHS.** Harrison Marks; ***Nar:*** Charles Gray.

9 1/2 Ninjas 🦴🦴½ **1990 (R)** A cautious and disciplined martial artist trains a young and flirtatious woman in the ways of the ninja. His life becomes exciting in more ways than one, when he realizes she's being followed by ninjas with more on their minds than her training—they want to assassinate her! Crazy mixture of sex, kung fu and humor make this film one surprise after another. **88m/C VHS.** Michael Phenicie, Andee Gray, Tommy (Tiny) Lister; ***D:*** Aaron Worth; ***W:*** Bill Crounse.

9 1/2 Weeks 🦴🦴½ **1986 (R)** Chance meeting between a Wall Street exec and an art gallery employee evolves into an experimental sexual relationship bordering on sado-masochism. Video version is more explicit than the theatrical release, but not by much. Strong characterizations by both actors prevent this from being strictly pornography. Well-written, with strength of male and female personalities nicely balanced. Intriguing, but not for all tastes. **114m/C VHS, DVD, Wide.** Mickey Rourke, Kim Basinger, Margaret Whitton, Karen Young, David Margulies, Christine Baranski, Roderick Cook, Dwight Weist; ***D:*** Adrian Lyne; ***W:*** Patricia Louisianna Knop, Zalman King; ***C:*** Peter Biziou; ***M:*** Jack Nitzsche.

Nine Days a Queen 🦴🦴🦴 *Lady Jane Grey; Tudor Rose* **1936** An historical drama based on the life of Lady Jane Grey, proclaimed Queen of England after the death of Henry VIII of England and summarily executed for treason by Mary Tudor after a nine-day reign. An obscure tragedy with good performances and absorbing storyline. Remade as "Lady Jane" (1985). **80m/B VHS.** *GB* John Mills, Cedric Hardwicke, Nova Pilbeam, Sybil Thorndike, Leslie Perrins, Felix Aylmer, Miles Malleson, Frank Cellier, Desmond Tester, Gwen Francon-Davies, Martita Hunt, John Laurie, Roy Emerton, John Turnbull, J.H. Roberts; ***D:*** Robert Stevenson; ***W:*** Robert Stevenson, Miles Malleson; ***C:*** Mutz Greenbaum.

Nine Deaths of the Ninja woof! **1985 (R)** Faceless ninja warrior Kosugi leads a team of commandos on a mission to rescue a group of political prisoners held captive in the Philippine jungles. Features Ozone-depleted plot, incongruous performances, and inane dialogue, not to mention two main villains—a neurotic Nazi in a wheelchair and a black lesbian amazon—who chew jungle and bring bad art to a new level of appreciation. Amazing in its total badness. Produced by Cannon. **93m/C VHS, DVD.** Sho Kosugi, Brent Huff, Emelia Lesniak, Regina Richardson, Kane (Takeshi) Kosugi, Vijay Amritraj, Blackie Dammett, Sonny Erang, Bruce Fanger; ***D:*** Emmett Alston; ***W:*** Emmett Alston; ***M:*** Cecile Calayco.

The Nine Lives of Elfego Baca && **1958** Venerable Western hero Loggia faces a veritable army of gunfighters and bandits. Action-packed but not too violent; family fun. **78m/C VHS.** Robert Loggia, Robert F. Simon, Lisa Montell, Nestor Paiva; ***D:*** Norman Foster.

Nine Lives of Fritz the Cat && **1974** Fritz feels that life's too square in the '70s, so he takes off into some of his other lives for more adventure. Cleaner but still naughty sequel to the X-rated "Fritz the Cat," featuring neither the original's writer/director Ralph Bakshi nor cartoonist Robert Crumb. Tame and lame. Animated. **77m/C VHS, DVD, Wide.** ***D:*** Robert Taylor; ***W:*** Robert Taylor, Eric Monte; ***V:*** Skip Hinnant.

Nine Months &&½ **1995 (PG-13)** Happily single Samuel (Grant) gets girlfriend Rebecca (Moore) pregnant and promptly wigs out. He makes amends to the lovely Rebecca, they marry, and true to writer/director Columbus' style, live happily ever after. Bachelor pal Sean (Goldblum) and an expectant couple (Arnold and Cusack) with three kids round out the cast, with Williams offering his usual manic flair as a Russian obstetrician, improvising his scenes with glee. Grant's knack for clumsy befuddlement fits well with the warm, fuzzy style of Columbus. "Nine" doesn't go out on any limbs, but is a pleasant diversion anyway. Remake of the French film "Neuf Mois." **103m/C VHS, DVD, Wide.** Hugh Grant, Julianne Moore, Tom Arnold, Joan Cusack, Jeff Goldblum, Robin Williams; ***D:*** Chris Columbus; ***W:*** Chris Columbus; ***C:*** Donald McAlpine; ***M:*** Hans Zimmer.

9 to 5 &&½ **1980 (PG)** In this caricature of large corporations and women in the working world, Coleman plays the male chauvinist boss who calls the shots and keeps his employees, all female, under his thumb. Three of the office secretaries daydream of Coleman's disposal and rashly kidnap him after a silly set of occurrences threaten their jobs. While they have him under lock and key, the trio take office matters into their own hands and take a stab at running things their own way, with amusing results. Basis for a TV series. **111m/C VHS, DVD, Wide.** Jane Fonda, Lily Tomlin, Dolly Parton, Dabney Coleman, Sterling Hayden, Norma Donaldson; ***D:*** Colin Higgins; ***W:*** Patricia Resnick; ***C:*** Reynaldo Villalobos; ***M:*** Charles Fox.

976-EVIL && **1988 (R)** Englund (the infamous Freddy from the Nightmare on Elm Street epics) directs this horror movie where a lonely teenager dials direct to demons from hell. **102m/C VHS.** Stephen Geoffreys, Jim Metzler, Maria Rubell, Sandy Dennis, Robert Picardo, Lezlie (Dean) Deane, Pat O'Bryan, J.J. (Jeffrey Jay) Cohen; ***D:*** Robert Englund; ***W:*** Brian Helgeland, Rhet Topham; ***C:*** Paul Elliott; ***M:*** Tom Chase, Steve Rucker.

976-EVIL 2: The Astral Factor &½ **1991 (R)** Satan returns the call in this supernatural thriller that sequels the original film. **93m/C VHS.** Pat O'Bryan, Rene Assa, Debbie James; ***D:*** Jim Wynorski; ***W:*** Erik Anjou.

984: Prisoner of the Future *The Tomorrow Man* **1984** A shocking, futuristic tale of human self-destruction. **70m/C VHS.** Don Francks, Stephen Markle; ***D:*** Tibor Takacs.

1900 &&& *Novecento* **1976 (R)** Bertolucci's impassioned epic about two Italian families, one land-owning, the other, peasant. Shows the sweeping changes of the 20th century begun by the trauma of WWI and the onslaught of Italian socialism. Edited down from its original 360-minute length and dubbed in English from three other languages, the film suffers somewhat from editing and from its nebulous lack of commitment to any genre. **255m/C VHS.** *FR IT GE* Robert De Niro, Gerard Depardieu, Burt Lancaster, Donald Sutherland, Dominique Sanda, Sterling Hayden, Laura Betti, Francesca Bertini, Werner Bruhns, Stefania Sandrelli, Anna Henkel, Alida Valli; ***D:*** Bernardo Bertolucci; ***W:*** Giuseppe Bertolucci, Bernardo Bertolucci; ***C:*** Vittorio Storaro.

1918 &&½ **1985** An adaptation of the Horton Foote play about the effects of WWI and an influenza epidemic on a small Texas town. Slow-moving but satisfying. Score by Willie Nelson. Originally produced for PBS's "American Playhouse." Prequelled by "On Valentine's Day." **89m/C VHS.** Matthew Broderick, Hallie Foote, William Converse-Roberts, Rochelle Oliver, Michael Higgins, Horton Foote Jr., William Bill McGhee, Jeannie McCarthy; ***D:*** Ken Harrison; ***W:*** Horton Foote; ***M:*** Willie Nelson.

1931: Once Upon a Time in New York && **1972** Prohibition-era gangsters war, beat each other up, make headlines, and drink bathtub gin. **90m/C VHS.** Richard Conte, Adolfo Celi, Lionel Stander, Irene Papas.

1941 &&½ **1979 (PG)** Proved to be the most expensive comedy of all time with a budget exceeding $35 million. The depiction of Los Angeles in the chaotic days after the bombing of Pearl Harbor combines elements of fantasy and black humor. **120m/C VHS, DVD, Wide.** John Belushi, Dan Aykroyd, Patti LuPone, Ned Beatty, Slim Pickens, Murray Hamilton, Christopher Lee, Tim Matheson, Toshiro Mifune, Warren Oates, Robert Stack, Nancy Allen, Elisha Cook Jr., Lorraine Gary, Treat Williams, Mickey Rourke, John Candy, Wendie Jo Sperber, Lucille Benson, Eddie Deezen, Bobby DiCicco, Dianne Kay, Perry Lang, Frank McRae, Lionel Stander, Dub Taylor, Joe Flaherty, David Lander, Michael McKean, Samuel Fuller, Audrey Landers, John Landis, Walter Olkewicz, Donovan Scott, Penny Marshall; ***D:*** Steven Spielberg; ***W:*** Robert Zemeckis, Bob Gale, John Milius; ***C:*** William A. Fraker; ***M:*** John Williams.

1969 &&&½ **1989 (R)** Three teenage friends during the 1960s become radicalized by the return of one of their friends from Vietnam in a coffin. Critically lambasted directorial debut for "On Golden Pond" author Ernest Thompson. **96m/C VHS, DVD, Wide.** Kiefer Sutherland, Robert Downey Jr., Winona Ryder, Bruce Dern, Joanna Cassidy, Mariette Hartley, Christopher Wynne; ***D:*** Ernest Thompson; ***W:*** Ernest Thompson; ***C:*** Jules Brenner; ***M:*** Michael Small.

1984 &&&½ **1984 (R)** A very fine adaptation of George Orwell's infamous novel, this version differs from the overly simplistic and cautionary 1954 film because of fine casting and production design. The illegal love affair of a government official becomes his attempt to defy the crushing inhumanity and lack of simple pleasures of an omniscient government. Filmed in London, it skillfully visualizes our time's most central prophetic nightmare. **117m/C VHS.** *GB* John Hurt, Richard Burton, Suzanna Hamilton, Cyril Cusack, Gregory Fisher, Andrew Wilde, Rupert Baderman; ***D:*** Michael Radford; ***C:*** Roger Deakins.

1990: The Bronx Warriors woof! *1990 I Guerrieri del Bronx; Bronx Warriors* **1983 (R)** Good street gang members combat evil corporate powers in a semi-futuristic South Bronx. Lame copy of "Escape from New York." **86m/C VHS.** *IT* Vic Morrow, Christopher Connelly, Fred Williamson; ***D:*** Enzo G. Castellari.

1991: The Year Punk Broke **1992** Documents a grunge rock tour of European festivals in 1991 when the alternative bands were largely unknown to all but hardcore fans. Follows Sonic Youth, Nirvana, Dinosaur Jr., Babes in Toyland, Gumball, and grandaddy punk idols, The Ramones, behind-the-scenes and through their performances. **95m/C VHS.** ***D:*** David Markey.

1999 && **1998 (R)** On New Year's Eve, Rufus King (Futterman) is partying like it's 1999 (which it is), deciding it's the perfect opportunity to make some life-changing decisions. Like dumping his sweet girlfriend for the office sexpot (Peet). **93m/C VHS, DVD, Wide.** Dan Futterman, Jennifer Garner, Matt McGrath, Amanda Peet, Steven Wright, Sandrine Holt, Buck Henry, Margaret Devine, Daniel Lapaine, David Gelb, Nick Davis; ***D:*** Nick Davis; ***W:*** Nick Davis; ***C:*** Howard Krupa; ***M:*** Sue Jacobs, Lynne Geller.

90 Days &&& **1986** Charming independently made Canadian comedy about two young men handling their respective romantic dilemmas—one awaiting an oriental fiancee he's never met, the other who is being kicked out of his house by his wife. **99m/C VHS.** *CA* Stefan Wodoslowsky, Sam Grana, Christine Pak; ***D:*** Giles Walker.

92 in the Shade &&& **1976 (R)** Based upon McGuane's novel, the film deals with a bored, wealthy rogue who becomes a fishing guide in the Florida Keys, and battles against the competition of two crusty, half-mad codgers. Sloppy, irreverent comedy as only a first-time writer-turned-director can fashion. **91m/C VHS.** Peter Fonda, Warren Oates, Margot Kidder, Burgess Meredith, Harry Dean Stanton; ***D:*** Thomas McGuane; ***W:*** Thomas McGuane.

99 & 44/100 Dead & *Call Harry Crown* **1974 (PG)** Frankenheimer falters with this silly gangster flick. Harris is hired to kill Dillman, by local godfather O'Brien. Originally written as a satirical look at gangster movies, but it doesn't stick to satire, and as a result is disappointing. **98m/C VHS.** Richard Harris, Chuck Connors, Edmond O'Brien, Bradford Dillman, Ann Turkel; ***D:*** John Frankenheimer; ***W:*** Robert Dillon; ***M:*** Henry Mancini.

99 Women &½ *Isle of Lost Women* **1969 (R)** Sympathetic prison warden attempts to investigate conditions at a women's prison camp. Thin and exploitative view of lesbianism behind bars that sensationalizes the subject. **90m/C VHS.** *GB SP GE IT* Maria Schell, Herbert Lom, Mercedes McCambridge, Luciana Paluzzi; ***D:*** Jess (Jesus) Franco.

Ninja 3: The Domination && **1984 (R)** Ninja master must remove the spirit of a deadly ninja assassin from a young woman intent on wreaking havoc among the Phoenix police department. Extremely silly super ninja epic utterly uninhibited by the usual plot conventions. **92m/C VHS.** Lucinda Dickey, Sho Kosugi; ***D:*** Sam Firstenberg; ***W:*** James R. Silke; ***C:*** Hanania Baer.

Ninja Academy &½ **1990 (R)** Seven wimps, losers, and spoiled brats come to the Ninja Academy to learn the art. Will they make it? **93m/C VHS.** Will Egan, Kelly Randall, Gerald Okomura, Michael David, Robert Factor, Jeff Robinson; ***D:*** Nico Mastorakis.

Ninja: American Warrior &½ **1990** An evil ninja takes on the U.S. Drug Enforcement Agency when the authorities threaten to shut him down. **90m/C VHS.** Joff Houston, John Wilford; ***D:*** Tommy Cheung.

Ninja Brothers of Blood & **1989** A guy falls for a rival gang member's girl. Neither the gang nor the guy's former girlfriend take kindly to this! **90m/C VHS.** Marcus Gibson, Fonda Lynn, Brian McClave, Jonathan Soper; ***D:*** Raymond Woo.

Ninja Champion woof! **198?** White-clad and masked ninja heros come to the aid of some Interpol agents tracking down a sleazy diamond smuggler. Invisible storyline features very little actual ninja. Extremely unconvincing and poorly dubbed. **90m/C VHS.** *HK* Bruce Baron, Richard Harrison; ***D:*** Godfrey Ho; ***W:*** Godfrey Ho.

Ninja Commandments & **1987** Everything is at stake when an evil warrior takes on the greatest fighter in the land: the winner will rule the empire! **90m/C VHS.** Richard Harrison, Dave Wheeler; ***D:*** Joseph Lai.

Ninja Condors & **1987** A young man grows up to avenge the murder of his father. **85m/C VHS.** Alexander Lou, Stuart Hugh; ***D:*** James Wu.

Ninja Connection & **1990** Ninja terrorism is employed as a scare tactic to deter a group who wants to break up an international drug ring. **90m/C VHS.** Patricia Greenford, Jane Kingsly, Joe Nelson, Louis Roth, Henry Steele, Stuart Steen; ***D:*** York Lam.

Ninja Death Squad & **1987** A team specializing in political assassinations is hunted down by a special agent. **89m/C VHS.** Glen Carson, Patricia Goodman, Joff Houston, Billy Jones, Wallace Jones, John Wilford; ***D:*** Tommy Cheung.

Ninja Destroyer & **197? (R)** Ninja warriors battle over an emerald mine. **92m/C VHS.** *HK* Bruce Baron, Stuart Smith; ***D:*** Godfrey Ho; ***W:*** Godfrey Ho.

Ninja Fantasy woof! **1986** Ninja drug smugglers and government officials battle over a large drug shipment. Everybody go chop socky. Not much in way of ninja fantasy. Dubbed. **95m/C VHS.** *HK* Adam Nell, Ian Frank, Jordan Heller, Ken Ashley, Jenny Mills, Jack Rodman; ***D:*** Bruce Lambert; ***W:*** Anthony Green.

Ninja Hunt woof! **198?** This time, ninjas kick international terrorists in the head while searching for secret formula. Poorly dubbed pseudo ninja developed by Godfrey Ho. **92m/C VHS.** *HK* Bruce Baron, Stuart Smith; ***D:*** Joseph Lai; ***W:*** Stephen Saul.

Ninja in the U.S.A. &½ **1988** Evil drug kingpin Tyger McFerson (Albergo) is acquitted of murder charges because all witnesses against him have been killed by his ninja army. Cops Rodney Kuen and Jerry Wong (Lou) give McFerson the benefit of the doubt because he saved their lives in Viet Nam. But when Jerry's reporter wife is kidnapped by Tyger's ninjas to suppress evidence against him, Jerry suits up with all his ninja gear and storms McFerson's compound. Despite the video release title, there's no reason to believe any of this takes place anywhere in the United States. **93m/C VHS, DVD.** *TW* Alexander Lou, George Nicholas Albergo, Eugene Thomas, Alex Yip; ***D:*** Dennis Wu; ***W:*** Ed Jones; ***C:*** Owen Casey; ***M:*** Sherman Chow.

Ninja Masters of Death & **1985** Terrorists reign supreme until the white ninja saves the city. **90m/C VHS.** Mick Jones, Chris Petersen, Daniel Wells, Richard Young; ***D:*** Bruce Lambert.

Ninja Mission &½ **1984 (R)** First Scandinavian ninja epic follows CIA agent and his group of ninja fighters as they embark on a hazardous mission to rescue two people from a Soviet prison. They use their fighting skills (Swedish ninjas favor guns more than ninjutsu) against Russian soldiers. Dubbed. **95m/C VHS.** *SW* Christopher Kohlberg, Curt Brober, Hanna Pola; ***D:*** Mats Helge.

Ninja of the Magnificence &½ **1989** When the ninja master is killed, factions within his group battle for control. **90m/C VHS.** Sam Baker, Patrick Frbezar, Clive Hadwen, Tim Michael, Renato Sala; ***D:*** Charles Lee.

Ninja Operation: Licensed to Terminate & **1987** Two warriors risk broken noses and twisted limbs to take on the Black Ninja Empire. **89m/C VHS.** Richard Harrison, Paul Marshall, Jack McPeat, Grant Temple; ***D:*** Joseph Lai.

Ninja Phantom Heroes & **1987** Two Vietnam vets are imprisoned for war crimes. One escapes and forms his own secret ninja society. **90m/C VHS.** Glen Carson, George Dickson, Allen Leung, Christine Wells; ***D:*** Bruce Lambert.

Ninja Powerforce &½ **1990** Two childhood friends end up as members of rival ninja gangs in the midst of a bloody war. Usual assortment of ninja-inflicted injuries result. **90m/C VHS.** Jonathan Bould, Richard Harrison; ***D:*** Joseph Lai.

Ninja Showdown 🦴 **1990** A warrior must take on a number of vicious bandits in order to defend his small town. He vows revenge on anyone who threatens his people. **92m/C VHS.** Richard Harrison; ***D:*** Joseph Lai.

Ninja Strike Force 🦴½ **1988** The Black Ninjas steal the powerful "spirit sword," and go on a bloody rampage. **89m/C VHS.** Richard Harrison, Gary Carter; ***D:*** Joseph Lai.

Ninja the Battalion 🦴 **1990** Agents from America, the Soviet Union, and China try to recover germ warfare secrets stolen by the Japanese secret service. **90m/C VHS.** Roger Crawford, Sam Huxley, Alexander Lou, Dickson Warn; ***D:*** Victor Sears.

Ninja, the Violent Sorcerer 🦴½ **1986** Murderer, with the help of Chinese vampires, does battle with the ghost of a dead gambling lord's wife and the gambling lord's living brother. Often tedious even with above average production and incredible plot. **90m/C VHS.** ***D:*** Bruce Lambert; ***W:*** Daniel Clough.

Ninja Vengeance 🦴½ **1993 (R)** The corrupt sheriff of a small Texas town, who also leads the KKK, is terrorizing a young African-American local. Then our lone hero rides into town on his trusty motorcycle to save the day. Only this time instead of your average gunman, he's a ninja. **87m/C VHS.** Stephen K. Hayes, Janet K. Pawlak, Craig Boyett, David Paul Lord; ***D:*** Karl Armstrong; ***W:*** Carrie Armstrong, Karl Armstrong.

Ninotchka 🦴🦴🦴½ **1939 (R)** Delightful romantic comedy. Garbo is a cold Russian agent sent to Paris to check up on her comrades, who are being seduced by capitalism. She inadvertently falls in love with a playboy, who melts her communist heart. Garbo talks and laughs. Satirical, energetic, and witty. Later a Broadway musical called "Silk Stockings." **110m/B VHS, 8mm.** Greta Garbo, Melvyn Douglas, Ina Claire, Sig Rumann, Felix Bressart, Bela Lugosi; ***D:*** Ernst Lubitsch; ***W:*** Billy Wilder; ***C:*** William H. Daniels. Natl. Film Reg. '90.

The Ninth Configuration 🦴🦴🦴 *Twinkle, Twinkle, Killer Kane* **1979 (R)** Based on Blatty's novel "Twinkle, Twinkle, Killer Kane" (also the film's alternate title), this is a weird and surreal tale of a mock rebellion of high-ranking military men held in a secret base hospital for the mentally ill. Keach is good as the commander who is just as insane as the patients. Available in many different lengths, this is generally considered to be the best. **115m/C VHS.** Stacy Keach, Scott Wilson, Jason Miller, Ed Flanders, Neville Brand, Alejandro Rey, Robert Loggia, George DiCenzo; ***D:*** William Peter Blatty; ***W:*** William Peter Blatty. Golden Globes '81: Screenplay.

The Ninth Gate 🦴🦴 **1999 (R)** Less-than-scrupulous rare-book dealer Dean Corso (Depp) is hired by wealthy publishing mogul Balkan (Langella) to find and authenticate three copies of a 17th-century book that supposedly holds the secrets to conjuring up the devil. Naturally, he encounters many spooky and deadly people along the way. Depp is perfectly cast as the sleazy bookworm and every scene is appropriately atmospheric, but Polanski's glacial pace and lack of any dramatic tension keeps this flick from getting its due. **127m/C VHS, DVD, Wide.** *FR SP* Johnny Depp, Frank Langella, Lena Olin, Emmanuelle Seigner, Barbara Jefford, Jack Taylor, James Russo, Jose Lopez Rodero; ***D:*** Roman Polanski; ***W:*** Roman Polanski, John Brownjohn, Enrique Urbizu; ***C:*** Darius Khondji; ***M:*** Wojciech Kilar.

Nitti: The Enforcer 🦴🦴 **1988 (PG-13)** Made-for-TV saga about Al Capone's brutal enforcer and right-hand man, Frank Nitti. Diversified cast (Moriarty in particular) do their best to keep things moving along, and the atmosphere is consistently and appropriately violent. Made to capitalize on the success of 1987's "The Untouchables." **94m/C VHS.** Anthony LaPaglia, Vincent Guastaferro, Trini Alvarado, Michael Moriarty, Michael Russo, Louis Guss, Bruno Kirby; ***D:*** Michael Switzer.

Nixon 🦴🦴🦴 **1995 (R)** Stone again "interprets" historical events of the '60s and '70s with a sprawling, bold bio of Richard Nixon. Covering all the highlights of Nixon's public life, and speculating on his private one, Hopkins convincingly portrays "Tricky Dick" as an embattled, lonely political genius. Gigantic all-star cast is lead by Oscar-caliber performance of Joan Allen as Pat Nixon. Even at over three hours, there isn't nearly enough time to explore the significance of all the events covered here. As usual, Stone has taken some creative license, which lead to the Nixon daughters publicly trashing the film, and Walt Disney's daughter expressing "shame" at being affiliated with it. **192m/C VHS, DVD, Wide.** Anthony Hopkins, Joan Allen, Ed Harris, Bob Hoskins, David Paymer, Paul Sorvino, J.T. Walsh, James Woods, Madeline Kahn, Brian Bedford, Mary Steenburgen, Powers Boothe, E.G. Marshall, David Hyde Pierce, Kevin Dunn, Annabeth Gish, Tony Goldwyn, Larry Hagman, Edward Herrmann, Saul Rubinek, Tony LoBianco; ***D:*** Oliver Stone; ***W:*** Christopher Wilkinson, Stephen J. Rivele, Oliver Stone; ***C:*** Robert Richardson; ***M:*** John Williams. L.A. Film Critics '95: Support. Actress (Allen); Natl. Soc. Film Critics '95: Support. Actress (Allen).

No 🦴🦴 **1998** Based on a segment of writer-director Lepage's play "The Seven Branches of the River Ota," which juxtaposes events at the 1970 World's Fair in Osaka, Japan with an infamous event in Canadian history, as separatist terrorists in Quebec kidnap a British diplomat and a Quebec cabinet minister. Montreal actress Sophie (Cadieux) is performing in Osaka while her boyfriend Michel (Martin) is back home watching the political upheaval on TV. Sophie has a number of personal crises to contend with, while Michel gets so wrapped up in politics he contemplates taking radical actions of his own. The cultural and political differences won't necessarily travel well outside French-speaking Canada. **85m/C VHS.** *CA* Anne-Marie Cadieux, Alexis Martin, Marie Brassard, Richard Frechette, Marie Gignac, Eric Bernier; ***D:*** Robert Lepage; ***W:*** Robert Lepage, Andre Morency; ***C:*** Pierre Mignot; ***M:*** Michael F. Cote, Bernard Falaise. Toronto-City '98: Canadian Feature Film.

No Alibi 🦴🦴½ **2000 (R)** Upstanding businessman Bob Valenz (Cain) becomes involved with beautiful Camille (Doig), who also has something kinky going on with Bob's smalltime crook brother, Phil (Stebbings). Phil gets dead and it leads back not only to Camille but to the third man in her life, criminal slickster Vic (Roberts). But by then Bob and Camille are married and she's pregnant. But Bob won't stop investigating his brother's death and he's not going to like what he finds out. **94m/C VHS, DVD.** *CA* Dean Cain, Eric Roberts, Lexa Doig, Peter Stebbings, Richard Chevolleau, Frank Schorpion, Melissa Di Marco; ***D:*** Bruce Pittman; ***W:*** Ivan Kane, John Schafer; ***C:*** Michael Storey; ***M:*** Marty Simon. **VIDEO**

No Big Deal 🦴½ **1983 (PG-13)** Dillon is a streetwise teenager who makes friends at his new school. Blah promise; bad acting makes this no big deal. **86m/C VHS.** Kevin Dillon, Sylvia Miles, Tammy Grimes, Jane Krakowski, Christopher Gartin, Mary Joan Negro; ***D:*** Robert Charlton.

No Code of Conduct 🦴🦴 **1998 (R)** Veteran cop Bill Peterson (Sheen) is working with the DEA on a sting operation to recover millions in heroin but when things go wrong, Bill suspects corruption within his own department. So he calls on hot-headed cop son Jake (Charlie Sheen) for help. **90m/C VHS, DVD, Wide.** Mark Dacascos, Joe Estevez, Charlie Sheen, Martin Sheen, Courtney Gains, Paul Gleason, Joe Lando, Meredith Salenger, Bret Michaels; ***D:*** Bret Michaels; ***W:*** Charlie Sheen, Bret Michaels, Bill Gucwa, Ed Masterson; ***C:*** Adam Kane; ***M:*** Bret Michaels. **VIDEO**

No Comebacks **1985** Two British mysteries from stories by Frederick Forsyth: "A Careful Man," about a dying millionaire who cheats his heirs, and "Privilege," about a clever stamp dealer who exacts revenge upon a libelous gossip columnist. **60m/C VHS.** *GB* Milo O'Shea, Cyril Cusack, Dan O'Herlihy, Gayle Hunnicutt. **TV**

No Contest 🦴🦴 **1994 (R)** International terrorists, lead by Oz (Clay), hold the TV host (Tweed) and contestants of the Ms. Galaxy beauty pageant hostage with a $10 million ransom demand. **98m/C VHS.** Andrew (Dice Clay) Silverstein, Shannon Tweed, Robert Davi, Roddy Piper, Nicholas (Nick) Campbell; ***D:*** Paul Lynch; ***W:*** Robert Cooper.

No Dead Heroes 🦴 **1987** Green Beret Vietnam war hero succumbs to Soviet scheming when they plant a computer chip in his brain. Unoriginal and unworthy. **86m/C VHS.** Max Thayer, John Dresden, Toni Nero; ***D:*** J.C. Miller.

No Deposit, No Return 🦴🦴 *Double Trouble* **1976 (G)** Tedious, silly, pointless Disney action comedy. Rich brats persuade bumbling crooks to kidnap them, offer them for ransom to millionaire grandfather. **115m/C VHS.** David Niven, Don Knotts, Darren McGavin, Barbara Feldon, Charles Martin Smith; ***D:*** Norman Tokar; ***W:*** Arthur Alsberg; ***M:*** Buddy (Norman Dale) Baker.

No Dessert Dad, 'Til You Mow the Lawn 🦴½ **1994 (PG)** Suburban parents Ken and Carol Cochran (Robert Hays and Joanna Kerns) are harassed at home by their annoying offspring, Justin, Monica, and Tyler. When they try hypnosis tapes to quit smoking, the kids discover by doctoring the tapes, they can plant suggestions resulting in parental perks. **80m/C VHS, DVD.** Robert Hays, Joanna (Joanna DeVarona) Kerns, Joshua Schaefer, Allison Meek, Jimmy Marsden, Richard Moll, Larry Linville; ***D:*** Howard McCain.

No Drums, No Bugles 🦴½ **1971 (G)** A West Virginia farmer and conscientious objector leaves his family to live alone in a cave for three years during the Civil War. Bad direction spoils Sheen's good performance. **85m/C VHS.** Martin Sheen, Davey Davidson, Denine Terry, Rod McCary; ***D:*** Clyde Ware.

No End 🦴🦴 *Bez Konca* **1984** The ghost of a dead lawyer watches as his wife and young son struggle to survive without him, including the widow getting involved in her husband's last case about a worker arrested for organizing a strike. Well-acted but overly solemn and slow; set during Poland's martial law in 1982. In Polish with English subtitles. **108m/C VHS.** *PL* Grazyna Szapolowska, Jerzy Radziwilowicz, Maria Pakulnis, Aleksander Bardini, Artur Barcis, Michal Bajor; ***D:*** Krzysztof Kieslowski; ***W:*** Krzysztof Piesiewicz, Krzysztof Kieslowski.

No Escape 🦴🦴½ **1994 (R)** In 2022, Captain Robbins (Liotta) has been banished to a prison colony island inhabited by the most dangerous criminals. With no walls and no guards, the prisoners are left to kill each other. Then Robbins discovers a relatively peaceful community of prisoners who help each other. But this group is soon bedeviled by the evil nasties on the other side of the island. Attempts at escape define the plot, so the film is filled with superhuman feats of sheer courage, determination, and guts. Adapted from the book "The Penal Colony" by Richard Herley. **118m/C VHS, DVD, Wide.** Ray Liotta, Lance Henriksen, Stuart Wilson, Kevin Dillon, Kevin J. O'Connor, Michael Lerner, Ernie Hudson, Ian McNeice, Jack Shepherd; ***D:*** Martin Campbell; ***W:*** Joel Gross; ***C:*** Phil Meheux; ***M:*** Graeme Revell.

No Escape, No Return 🦴🦴½ **1993 (R)** An FBI agent (Nouri) and a police captain (Saxon) force three renegade cops (Nguyen, Caulfield, and Loveday) to infiltrate a drug syndicate. But things go from bad to worse when a war breaks out between rival drug gangs, leaving a lot of bodies, and a large chunk of money gone missing. Now the trio is sought by both the cops and the crooks. **93m/C VHS.** Maxwell Caulfield, Dustin Nguyen, Denise Loveday, John Saxon, Michael Nouri, Kevin Benton; ***D:*** Charles Kanganis; ***W:*** Charles Kanganis; ***M:*** Jim Halfpenny.

No Fear, No Die 🦴🦴 **1990** To make some quick cash two black immigrants in France train and sell birds for illegal cockfights at a roadside restaurant. Jocelyn, who trains the cocks, pays them lavish, obsessive attention. But cultural conflicts and repressed passions are just waiting to explode. In French with English subtitles. **97m/C VHS.** *FR* Alex Descas, Isaach de Bankole, Jean-Claude Brialy, Solveig Dommartin, Christopher Buchholz; ***D:*** Claire Denis; ***W:*** Claire Denis, Jean-Pol Fargeau; ***M:*** Abdullah Ibrahim.

No Greater Love 🦴🦴½ **1943** Capraesque Soviet war movie. A peasant woman mobilizes her village against the Nazis to avenge her family's death. Dubbed into English by the Soviets for Western circulation during WWII. **74m/B VHS.** *RU* Vera Maretskaya; ***D:*** Frederic Ermler.

No Highway in the Sky 🦴🦴🦴 **1951** Eccentric scientist Theodore Honey (Stewart) works for the Royal Aircraft Establishment, which has just produced a new plane, the Reindeer. But Honey tells his boss Dennis Scott (Hawkins) that the plane has a serious defect. While flying to examine a Reindeer crash site, Honey befriends Monica (Dietrich), a musical star, and stewardess Marjorie (Johns), who support him when his company accuses him of maliciously damaging the aircraft's reputation. Dietrich steals every scene with her Christian Dior wardrobe and star attitude. Based on the novel "No Highway" by Nevil Shute. **98m/B VHS.** *GB* James Stewart, Marlene Dietrich, Glynis Johns, Jack Hawkins, Ronald Squire, Niall MacGinnis, Elizabeth Allan, Kenneth More, David Hutcheson; ***D:*** Henry Koster; ***W:*** R.C. Sherriff, Oscar Millard; ***M:*** Malcolm Arnold.

No Holds Barred 🦴½ **1989 (PG-13)** Cheesy, campy remake of cheesy, campy 1952 wrestling movie. Hulk Hogan on the big screen, at last. **98m/C VHS.** Hulk Hogan, Kurt Fuller, Joan Severance, Tommy (Tiny) Lister; ***D:*** Thomas J. Wright.

No Laughing Matter 🦴🦴½ **1997 (PG-13)** The widow of a policeman, outgoing Emma (Somers) is especially close to her teenaged son Charlie (Christ), who feels protective of his mother. And Emma needs protection since she has a long-standing drinking problem she refuses to admit to. Her ability to function becomes increasingly impaired just as Charlie needs her most—seems his girlfriend Lauren (Blair) is pregnant. Finally, Emma seeks help but as she pulls herself together, Charlie turns hostile over his own volatile situation. **90m/C VHS.** Suzanne Somers, Chad Christ, Selma Blair, Robert Desiderio; ***D:*** Michael Elias; ***W:*** Michael Elias, Ted Kristian. **TV**

No Looking Back 🦴🦴 *Long Time, Nothing New* **1998 (R)** Small-town 30ish waitress Claudia (Holly) is about to settle for a boring life with decent-but-dull Michael (Bon Jovi) when her ne'er-do-well former boyfriend Charlie (Burns) comes home looking to relive the glory days. Burns stays with the working-class, northeastern setting, but goes for drama this time. With themes that cover economic hopelessness and a yearning to escape, Burns seems to be trying for a cinematic distillation of Bruce Springsteen's (very cinematic) music. In fact, many Springsteen songs are used to set scenes. Like Bruce, Burns knows the working class vernacular, and uses it well. But this time, all traces of subtlety are gone, and the story plays out pretty much as expected. Holly doesn't help much, barely registering in the crucial role. She also looks too damn good to be a washed-up waitress with no options. **96m/C VHS, DVD, Wide.** Lauren Holly, Edward Burns, Jon Bon Jovi, Blythe Danner, Connie Britton; ***D:*** Edward Burns; ***W:*** Edward Burns; ***C:*** Frank Prinzi; ***M:*** Joe Delia.

No Love for Johnnie 🦴🦴🦴 **1960** Well acted if unoriginal political drama. Finch is a British M.P. who fails in both public and private life. Based on the novel by Wilfred Fienburgh. **105m/B VHS.** *GB* Peter Finch, Stanley Holloway, Donald Pleasence, Mary Peach, Mervyn Johns, Dennis Price, Oliver Reed, Billie Whitelaw; ***D:*** Ralph Thomas; ***W:*** Mordecai Richler; ***M:*** Malcolm Arnold. British Acad. '61: Actor (Finch).

No Man Is an Island 🦴🦴½ **1962** Wartime adventure based on the exploits (Hollywoodized) of U.S. Naval radio operator George R. Tweed (Hunter), who is stationed on Guam when the Japanese invade. He hides out in the jungle to avoid capture and is aided by the natives for nearly three years until he's able to contact some American warships. Thanks to Tweed's info, the Americans are able to recapture the island. **114m/C VHS.** Jeffrey

Hunter, Marshall Thompson, Ronald Remy, Rolf Bayer, Barbara Perez, Joseph de Cordova; *D:* John Monks Jr., Richard Goldstone; *W:* John Monks Jr., Richard Goldstone; *C:* Carl Kayser; *M:* Restie Umali.

No Man of Her Own 🦴🦴½ **1932** Gable and Lombard in their only screen pairing. Gambler Babe Stewart (Gable) marries small town librarian (Lombard) on a bet and attempts to hide his secret life from her. Neither star's best film. **81m/B VHS.** Carole Lombard, Clark Gable, Grant Mitchell, Elizabeth Patterson, Dorothy Mackaill; *D:* Wesley Ruggles.

No Man's Land 🦴🦴 **1987 (R)** Undercover cop Sweeney tails playboy car thief Sheen but is seduced by wealth and glamour. Flashy surfaces, shiny cars, little substance. **107m/C VHS.** Charlie Sheen, D.B. Sweeney, Lara Harris, Randy Quaid; *D:* Peter Werner; *W:* Dick Wolf; *M:* Basil Poledouris.

No Man's Land 🦴🦴½ **2001 (R)** Let's talk about the futility and stupidity of war. In Bosnia in 1993, Croatian soldier Ciki (Branko Djuric) and Serbian Nino (Rene Bitorajac) wind up sharing the same trench between enemy lines, which is booby-trapped by a land mine. Laying on the mine is injured Croat Cera (Filip Sovagovic) and if he moves, they all die. Reluctantly brought into the already tense situation is ineffectual U.N. officer Col. Soft (Callow) and then journalist Jane (Cartlidge) also shows up. Bosnian with subtitles. **98m/C VHS, DVD, Wide.** *BS FR IT BE GB* Branko Djuric, Rene Bitorajac, Filip Sovagovic, Georges Siatidis, Serge-Henri Valcke, Simon Callow, Katrin Cartlidge; *D:* Danis Tanovic; *W:* Danis Tanovic; *C:* Walther Vanden Ende; *M:* Danis Tanovic. Oscars '01: Foreign Film; Cannes '01: Screenplay; L.A. Film Critics '01: Foreign Film.

No Man's Law 🦴🦴½ **1927** Hardy plays the depraved villian desperate to get the goldmine owned by an old prospector and his beautiful daughter. But the mine is protected by Rex the Wonder Horse! **?m/B VHS.** Oliver Hardy, Barbara Kent, James Finlayson, Theodore von Eltz; *D:* Fred Jackman.

No Man's Range 🦴 *No Man's Land* **1935** Unremarkable, typical, predictable Western: good guys, bad guys, guns, bullets, horses. **56m/B VHS.** Bob Steele.

No Mercy 🦴🦴 **1986 (R)** A Chicago cop (Gere) plunges into the Cajun bayou in order to avenge the murder of his partner. He falls for a beautiful girl enslaved by the killer, but that doesn't stop him from using her to flush out the powerful swamp-inhabiting crime lord. Absurd story without much plot. **108m/C VHS, DVD.** Richard Gere, Kim Basinger, Jeroen Krabbe, George Dzundza, William Atherton, Ray Sharkey, Bruce McGill; *D:* Richard Pearce; *W:* James (Jim) Carabatsos; *C:* Michel Brault; *M:* Alan Silvestri.

No Name on the Bullet 🦴🦴🦴 **1959** Aloof gunman John Gant (Murphy) is seeking revenge from someone in the town of Lordsburg, only none of the inhabitants know who the intended victim is. And slowly the town's citizens begin to panic. Great final showdown. **77m/C VHS.** Audie Murphy, Charles Drake, Joan Evans, Edgar Stehli, Warren Stevens, R.G. Armstrong, Whit Bissell, Karl Swenson; *D:* Jack Arnold; *W:* Gene L. Coon; *C:* Harold Lipstein.

No, No Nanette 🦴½ **1940** Lackluster filming of the Broadway production which fared better on the stage. Stock story of a young woman (Neagle) who rescues her uncle from financial ruin and finds romance in the process. **96m/B VHS.** Anna Neagle, Richard Carlson, Victor Mature, Roland Young, ZaSu Pitts, Eve Arden, Billy Gilbert, Keye Luke; *D:* Herbert Wilcox; *C:* Russell Metty.

No One Cries Forever woof! **1985** When a prostitute breaks away from a gangster-madam after finding love, she is tracked down and disfigured. Swedish; dubbed. **96m/C** Elke Sommer, Howard Carpendale, Zoli Marks; *D:* Jans Rautenbach.

No One Sleeps 🦴🦴 **2001** Berlin medical researcher Stefan Hein (Wlaschiha) is attending an AIDS conference in San Francisco just as a serial killer is targeting men who are HIV positive. Stefan also wants to investigate his late father's theory that U.S. researchers used prisoners to test a virus that created HIV by trying to find an alleged list of the injected prisoners. Along the way Stefan meets detective Louise Tolliver (Levi) and discovers the two investigations may be linked. **108m/C VHS, DVD.** Tom Wlashchiha, Irit Levi, Jim Thalman, Kalene Parker; *D:* Jochen Hick; *W:* Jochen Hick; *C:* Thomas M. Harting, Michael Maley; *M:* James Hardway.

No Place to Hide 🦴½ **1981** A girl's father drowns and she blames herself. Her mother and psychologist try to convince the girl that her father's spirit isn't stalking her, but she doesn't believe them. **120m/C VHS.** Keir Dullea, Mariette Hartley, Kathleen Beller, Arlen Dean Snyder, Gary (Rand) Graham, John Llewellyn Moxey; *D:* John Llewellyn Moxey. **TV**

No Place to Hide 🦴🦴½ **1993 (R)** Barrymore is the target of a psycho who's already killed her sister. Kristofferson plays the hard-edged cop who's out to protect her and trap the killer. **90m/C VHS.** Drew Barrymore, Kris Kristofferson, Martin Landau, O.J. Simpson, Dey Young, Bruce Weitz; *D:* Richard Danus; *W:* Richard Danus.

No Place to Run 🦴🦴 **1972** An elderly man fights for custody of his grandson, then kidnaps him and flees with him to Canada. Made for TV. **78m/C VHS.** Herschel Bernardi, Larry Hagman, Stefanie Powers, Neville Brand; *D:* Delbert Mann. **TV**

No Prince for My Cinderella **1978** A schizophrenic girl who has turned to prostitution is sought desperately by her social worker. **100m/C VHS.** Robert Reed.

No Problem 🦴🦴 *Pas de Probleme!* **1975** A man is pursued, shot, and drops dead in the apartment of an unsuspecting man who doesn't know what to do with the body. Dubbed in English. **94m/C VHS.** *FR* Miou-Miou, Bernard Menez, Jean (Lefevre) Lefebvre, Henri Guybet, Anny (Annie Legras) Duperey, Renee (Raymonde-Renee Vittoret) Saint-Cyr; *D:* Georges Lautner; *W:* Jean-Marie Poire; *C:* Maurice Fellous; *M:* Philippe Sarde.

No Regrets for Our Youth 🦴🦴🦴 **1946** A feminist saga depicting the spiritual growth of a foolish Japanese girl during the tumultuous years of WWII. In Japanese with English subtitles. **110m/B VHS.** *JP* Setsuko Hara; *D:* Akira Kurosawa.

No Retreat, No Surrender 🦴 **1986 (PG)** A young American kick-boxer battles a formidable Russian opponent and wins, quite improbably, after having been tutored by the ghost of Bruce Lee in an abandoned house. Notable as Van Damme's debut, but little else recommends this silly "Rocky" rehash. Followed by "No Retreat, No Surrender II." **85m/C VHS.** Kurt McKinney, J.W. Fails, Jean-Claude Van Damme; *D:* Corey Yuen.

No Retreat, No Surrender 2 🦴 **1989 (R)** With help from two karate experts, a man sets out to find his girlfriend who has been kidnapped by Soviets. Has little or nothing to do with the movie to which it is ostensibly a sequel. High level kick-boxing action sequences. **92m/C VHS.** Loren Avedon, Max Thayer, Cynthia Rothrock; *D:* Corey Yuen; *W:* Maria Elene Cellino.

No Retreat, No Surrender 3: Blood Brothers 🦴 **1991 (R)** Sibling martial arts rivals decide to bond in a manly way when CIA agent dad is most heinously slain by terrorists. Answers the burning question: "Whatever became of Joseph Campanella?" **97m/C VHS.** Keith Vitali, Loren Avedon, Joseph Campanella.

No Room to Run 🦴½ **1978** Concert promoter's life turns into a nightmare of deadly corporate intrigue when he arrives in Australia. Luckily, he finds time to fall in love. **101m/C VHS.** *AU* Richard Benjamin, Paula Prentiss, Barry Sullivan; *D:* Robert Lewis. **TV**

No Safe Haven 🦴 **1987 (R)** A government agent seeks revenge for his family's death. **92m/C VHS, DVD.** Wings Hauser, Marina Rice, Robert Tessier; *D:* Ronnie Rondell; *W:* Nancy Locke, Wings Hauser; *C:* Steve McWilliams; *M:* Joel Goldsmith.

No Secrets 🦴½ **1991 (R)** A young man on the run seeks refuge with three girls in an isolated house. His dread secret isn't so dread, leaving this mild teen-oriented thriller starved for lack of menace. **92m/C VHS.** Adam Coleman Howard, Amy Locane, Heather Fairfield, Traci Lind; *D:* Dezso Magyar.

No Sex Please—We're British 🦴½ **1973** Silly—and now dated—sex farce finds a postman accidentally delivering a parcel of pornography to a conservative bank. The contents inflame the bank's stuffy employees and suddenly it's a sexual free-for-all! Based on the play by Anthony Marriott and Alistair Foot. **90m/C VHS.** *GB* Ronnie Corbett, Beryl Reid, Arthur Lowe, Ian Ogilvy, Susan Penhaligon, Michael Bates, Gerald Sim, David Swift; *D:* Cliff Owen; *W:* John Mortimer, Anthony Marriott, Brian Cooke; *C:* Ken Hodges; *M:* Eric Rogers.

No Small Affair 🦴🦴 **1984 (R)** A 16-year-old aspiring photographer becomes romantically involved with a sultry 22-year-old rock star. **102m/C VHS.** Jon Cryer, Demi Moore, George Wendt, Peter Frechette, Elizabeth (E.G. Dailey) Daily, Tim Robbins, Jennifer Tilly, Ric(k) Ducommun, Ann Wedgeworth; *D:* Jerry Schatzberg; *C:* John A. Alonzo; *M:* Rupert Holmes.

No Such Thing 🦴🦴 **2001 (R)** This "Beauty and the Beast" fairytale for grownups doesn't always work but it's at least intriguing. Burke stars as an ill-tempered, drunken, ageless, nameless monster who has been terrorizing the remote areas of Iceland. When timid Beatrice (Polley) learns that her fiance, part of a news crew, has been slaughtered by the beast, she persuades her ratings-driven TV news show boss (Mirren) to send her to follow up on the story. Monster and Beatrice develop an unexpected rapport and she brings him back to New York where he's exploited, not unknowingly, as the lastest celeb. **103m/C VHS, DVD.** *US* Sarah Polley, Robert John Burke, Helen Mirren, Julie Christie, Baltasar Kormakur; *D:* Hal Hartley; *W:* Hal Hartley; *C:* Michael Spiller; *M:* Hal Hartley.

No Surrender 🦴🦴🦴 **1986 (R)** An unpredictable, darkly charming comedy about a Liverpool nightclub newly managed by Angelis. On New Year's Eve, a small drunken war is triggered when two groups of irate senior citizens are booked into the club and clash over their beliefs. The group is made up of Protestants and Catholics and the fight resembles the ongoing conflicts in modern-day Northern Ireland, although most of the action takes place in the loo. Watch for Costello as an inept magician. **100m/C VHS.** *GB* Ray McAnally, Michael Angelis, Avis Bunnage, James Ellis, Tom Georgeson, Mark Mulholland, Joanne Whalley, Elvis Costello, Bernard Hill, Michael Ripper; *D:* Peter Smith; *W:* Alan Bleasdale; *C:* Michael Coulter; *M:* Daryl Runswick.

No Survivors, Please 🦴½ *Der Chef Wuenscht Keine Zeugen; The Chief Wants No Survivors* **1963** Aliens from Orion take over politicians in order to rule the Earth. Bizarre, obscure, based on true story. **92m/B VHS.** *GE* Maria Perschy, Uwe Friedrichsen, Robert Cunningham, Karen Blanguernon, Gustavo Rojo; *D:* Hans Albin, Peter Berneis.

No Time for Romance 🦴🦴 **1948** A sprightly musical with an all-black cast. First such film to be shot in color. **?m/C VHS.** Bill Walker.

No Time for Sergeants 🦴🦴🦴 **1958** Hilarious film version of the Broadway play by Ira Levin, which was based on the novel by Mac Hyman. Griffith is excellent as Georgia farm boy Will Stockdale, who gets drafted into the service and creates mayhem among his superiors and colleagues. Of course, Griffith had already played the role both on stage and in a TV version. McCormick was also repeating his Broadway role of Sgt. King. Note Don Knotts in a small role along with Jameel Farah who went on to star in TV's "M*A*S*H" after changing his name to Jamie Farr. **119m/B VHS.** Andy Griffith, Nick Adams, Murray Hamilton, Myron McCormick, Howard Smith, Will Hutchins, Sydney Smith, Don Knotts, Jamie Farr; *D:* Mervyn LeRoy; *W:* John Lee Mahin; *C:* Harold Rosson; *M:* Ray Heindorf.

No Time to Die 🦴 **1978** In Indonesia, two corporate pawns and a beautiful reporter battle for the possession of a new laser cannon. **87m/C VHS.** Chris Mitchum, John Phillip Law, Grazyna Dylong.

No Tomorrow 🦴½ **1999 (R)** Criminal Busey works with shipping-company employee Daniels to broker a multimillion-dollar arms deal. As word of the deal spreads, both a gangster (Master P) and an FBI agent (Grier) get involved as well. Lots of shootouts and explosions cover the threadbare plot. **99m/C VHS, DVD.** Gary Busey, Gary Daniels, Pam Grier, Jeff Fahey, Percy (Master P) Miller; *D:* Percy (Master P) Miller. **VIDEO**

No Trace 🦴🦴 **1950** A writer who broadcasts his crime stories as part of a radio show is the victim of blackmail. It seems a former associate is aware that the stories are all based in fact. A Scotland Yard detective investigates when murder rears its ugly head. **76m/B VHS.** *GB* Hugh Sinclair, Dinah Sheridan, John Laurie, Barry Morse, Michael Brennan, Dora Bryan; *D:* John Gilling.

No Way Back 🦴🦴 **1974 (R)** Way. Writer, director, and producer Williamson portrays Jess Crowder, a man-for-hire who is an expert with guns, fists, and martial arts. An angry look at the white establishment. **92m/C VHS.** Fred Williamson, Charles Woolf, Tracy Reed, Virginia Gregg, Don Cornelius; *D:* Fred Williamson.

No Way Back 🦴🦴 **1996 (R)** FBI agent Zack Grant (Crowe) has never dealt with the death of his wife in childbirth and his career has suffered. His last professional chance is a sting operation involving the Mafia and the Yakuza. But when the operation goes wrong, Grant has a vendetta on his hands. Mafia boss Serlano (Lerner) kidnaps Zack's young son so Zack will turn over his prisoner—Yuji (Toyokawa), a Yakuza whom Serlano believes is responsible for his own son's death. Zack's only interest is to rescue his son and he doesn't care who gets in his way, including his fellow feds and the gangsters. **92m/C VHS.** Kelly Hu, Russell Crowe, Helen Slater, Michael Lerner, Etsushi Toyokawa, Ian Ziering; *D:* Frank Cappello; *W:* Frank Cappello; *C:* Richard Clabaugh; *M:* David Williams.

No Way Home 🦴🦴 **1996 (R)** Joey (Roth), who's mentally a little slow, returns to his tough Staten Island neighborhood after being paroled from prison. He goes to live with his low-level drug dealer older brother Tommy (Russo) and Tommy's wife, Lorrain (Unger), who's not too happy about the situation—at first. But Joey's basically a decent guy and Lorrain begins to respond to his consideration. Meanwhile, desperate Tommy's in debt to a loan shark and his behavior may once again find Joey taking the rap for his brother's misdeeds. The story's predictable but the cast definitely rises above the material. **101m/C VHS, DVD.** Catherine Kellner, Joe Ragno, Tim Roth, James Russo, Deborah Kara Unger; *D:* Buddy Giovinazzo; *W:* Buddy Giovinazzo; *C:* Claudia Raschke; *M:* Ricky Giovinazzo.

No Way Out 🦴🦴½ **1950** When bigoted bad guy Roy Biddle (Widmark) and his brother George (Bellaver) are shot, they're taken to a small hospital run by Dr. Wharton (McNally), who believes in giving all his doctors a fair chance. So black doctor Luther Brooks (Poitier) works on George, who dies. Naturally, Roy blames the doctor and gets his hoodlum pals to cause some bloody confrontations. **105m/B VHS.** Sidney Poitier, Richard Widmark, Stephen McNally, Linda Darnell, Harry Bellaver, Stanley Ridges, Ruby Dee, Ossie Davis; *D:* Joseph L. Mankiewicz; *W:* Joseph L. Mankiewicz, Lesser Samuels; *C:* Milton Krasner; *M:* Alfred Newman.

No Way Out 🦴🦴🦴 **1987 (R)** Career Navy man Tom Farrel (Costner) is involved with a beautiful, sexy party girl, Susan (Young), who gets killed. Turns out she was also the mistress of Secretary of Defense Brice (Hackman), Tom's boss. Assigned to investigate her suspicious death, Tom suddenly finds himself set-up as the chief suspect. A tight thriller based on 1948's "The Big Clock," with a new surprise ending. Costner looks fine in his

Navy whites and there's a backseat limousine sex scene that's quite steamy. **114m/C VHS, DVD, Wide.** Kevin Costner, Sean Young, Gene Hackman, Will Patton, Howard Duff, George Dzundza, Iman, Chris D, Marshall Bell, Jason Bernard, Fred Dalton Thompson, David Paymer, Eugene Glazer; *D:* Roger Donaldson; *W:* Robert Garland; *C:* John Alcott; *M:* Maurice Jarre.

No Way to Treat a Lady ♂♂♂ **1968** Steiger is a psychotic master of disguise who stalks and kills various women in this suspenseful cat-and-mouse game. Segal, as the detective assigned to the case, uncovers clues, falls in love, and discovers that his new girl may be the killer's next victim. **108m/C VHS.** Rod Steiger, Lee Remick, George Segal, Eileen Heckart, Murray Hamilton; *D:* Jack Smight; *W:* John Gay; *C:* Jack Priestley.

Noa at Seventeen ♂♂♂ **1982** The political/social turmoil of Israel in 1951 is allegorically depicted by the school vs. kibbutz debate within a young girl's middle-class family. In Hebrew with English subtitles. **86m/C VHS.** *IS* Dalia Shimko, Idit Zur, Shmuel Shilo, Moshe Havazelet; *D:* Isaac Yeshurun.

Noah ♂♂ **1998** Contemporary update of the biblical story of Noah and his ark, retold for laughs (and morals). Busy widowed contractor Norman Waters (Danza) has three sons to provide for and can't spend as much time with them as he may like. Then a heavenly bureaucrat (Shawn) comes down and tells Norman to build an ark in the usual 40 days. At least it brings the family together. **90m/C VHS.** Tony Danza, Wallace Shawn, Jane Sibbett; *D:* Ken Kwapis. **TV**

Noah's Ark ♂♂ **1999** Made-for-TV biblical epic of the Old Testament story that doesn't exactly stay close to its biblical roots. It's eccentric, special effects-laden, and borders on the irreverent. Noah builds his ark, gathers the animals (and his family), watches as the world is destroyed, and survives the 40 days and nights of flooding. **178m/C VHS, DVD.** Jon Voight, Mary Steenburgen, F. Murray Abraham, Carol Kane, James Coburn, Jonathan Cake, Alexis Denisof, Emily Mortimer, Sydney Tamiia Poitier, Sonya Walger; *D:* John Irvin; *W:* Peter Barnes; *C:* Mike Molloy; *M:* Paul Grabowsky. **TV**

Noble House **1988** Continuation of James Clavell's Hong Kong series, following "Tai-Pan," and set in the present day. Ian Dunross (Brosnan) is the head of Struan and Company, Hong Kong's leading trading company, which is being undermined by the nefarious Quillan Gornt (Rhys-Davies) who plots to destroy his archrival. American businesswoman Casey Tcholok (the bland Raffin) serves as Dunross' love interest. Originally a four-part TV miniseries partially filmed on location. **350m/C VHS.** Pierce Brosnan, John Rhys-Davies, Deborah Raffin, Ben Masters, Julia Nickson-Soul, Khigh (Kaie Deei) Deigh, Tia Carrere, Gordon Jackson.

Nobody ♂♂ **1999** Three businessmen get involved in a bar fight that isn't your average brawl. In fact, the situation begins to take over their lives and they're no longer certain even who they're fighting. Japanese with subtitles. **100m/C VHS, DVD.** *JP* Masaya Kato, Jinpachi Nezu, Riki Takeuchi, Hideo Nakano; *D:* Shundo Ohkawa, Toshimichi Ohkawa; *W:* Shundo Ohkawa.

Nobody's Daughter ♂♂½ **1976** The tragedy of an eight-year-old orphan shuttled from one family to another, all of whom are only interested in the money the government will pay for her care. In Hungarian with English subtitles. **90m/C VHS.** *HU* Zsuzsi Czinkoczi; *D:* Lazlo Ranody.

Nobody's Fool ♂♂ **1986 (PG-13)** Another entry in the genre of quirky Americana, this romantic comedy concerns a hapless Midwestern waitress suffering from low-self esteem who falls in love with a traveling stage-hand. **107m/C VHS.** Rosanna Arquette, Eric Roberts, Mare Winningham, Louise Fletcher, Jim Youngs, Gwen Welles, Stephen Tobolowsky, Charlie Barnett, Lewis Arquette; *D:* Evelyn Purcell; *W:* Beth Henley; *C:* Misha (Mikhail) Suslov; *M:* James Newton Howard.

Nobody's Fool ♂♂♂½ **1994 (R)** Newman shines as 60-year-old Donald "Sully" Sullivan, a construction worker who, in spite of himself, begins mending his many broken relationships over the course of the holiday season. Seemingly plotless scenario is sprinkled with enough humor, hope, and understated inspiration to become a delightfully modest celebration of a perfectly ordinary man. Character-driven story is blessed with commendable performances by supporting players—obviously inspired by Newman's brilliant portrayal. Based on the novel by Richard Russo. **110m/C VHS.** Paul Newman, Jessica Tandy, Bruce Willis, Melanie Griffith, Dylan Walsh, Pruitt Taylor Vince, Gene Saks, Josef Sommer, Philip Seymour Hoffman, Philip Bosco, Margo Martindale, Jay Patterson; *D:* Robert Benton; *W:* Robert Benton; *C:* John Bailey; *M:* Howard Shore. Berlin Intl. Film Fest. '94: Actor (Newman); N.Y. Film Critics '94: Actor (Newman); Natl. Soc. Film Critics '94: Actor (Newman).

Nobody's Perfect ♂ **1990 (PG-13)** Where "Tootsie" and "Some Like It Hot" collide (or more likely crash and burn). A lovesick teenager masquerades as a girl and joins the tennis team to be near his dream girl. Takes its title from Joe E. Brown's famous last line in "Some Like It Hot." **90m/C VHS.** Chad Lowe, Gail O'Grady, Patrick Breen, Kim Flowers, Robert Vaughn; *D:* Robert Kaylor; *W:* Joel Block.

Nobody's Perfekt woof! **1979 (PG)** Supposed comedy about three psychiatric patients who decide to extort $650,000 from the city of Miami when their car is wrecked. Lacks laughs and generally considered a turkey. **95m/C VHS.** Gabe Kaplan, Robert Klein, Alex Karras, Susan Clark; *D:* Peter Bonerz.

Nocturna woof! *Nocturna, Granddaughter of Dracula* **1979 (R)** Hard times have fallen upon the house of Dracula. To help pay the taxes on the castle, the owners have converted it to the Hotel Transylvania. In order to increase business and the blood supply at the hotel, Nocturna books a disco group to entertain the guests. Hard times fell on this script, too. It's no wonder that director Tampa hid behind the alias Harry Hurwitz. **82m/C VHS.** Yvonne De Carlo, John Carradine, Tony Hamilton, Nai Bonet; *D:* Harry (Hurwitz) Tampa; *C:* Mac Ahlberg.

Nocturne ♂♂½ **1946** A police lieutenant investigates the supposed suicide of a famous composer and uncovers dark secrets that suggest murder is afoot. An overlooked RKO production shines thanks to Raft's inimitable tough guy performance and some offbeat direction. For film noir completists. **88m/B VHS.** George Raft, Lynn Bari, Virginia Huston, Joseph Pevney, Myrna Dell, Edward Ashley, Walter Sande, Mabel Paige; *D:* Edwin L. Marin.

Noir et Blanc ♂♂ **1986** Antoine (Frappat) is a shy accountant who takes a job in a health club and begins an increasingly sado-masochistic relationship with black masseur, Jacques (Martial). The violence is inferred not actually shown but still makes for some kinky adult fare. Based on a short story by Tennessee Williams; debut film for director Devers. French with subtitles. **82m/B VHS.** *FR* Francis Frappat, Jacques Martial, Josephine Fresson, Marc Berman, Claire Rigollier; *D:* Claire Devers; *W:* Claire Devers.

Noises Off ♂♂½ **1992 (PG-13)** An Americanization of a British farce about a group of second-rate actors touring in a sex comedy and their convoluted private lives. Wretched rehersals and equally disasterous preformances, backstage sniping, lovers' quarrels, and a beleaguered director all bumble along together. It worked better on stage, where it was a Broadway hit, but the actors at least have some fun with the material. Based on the play by Michael Frayn. **101m/C VHS, Wide.** Michael Caine, Carol Burnett, Denholm Elliott, Julie Hagerty, Marilu Henner, Mark Linn-Baker, Christopher Reeve, John Ritter, Nicolette Sheridan; *D:* Peter Bogdanovich; *W:* Marty Kaplan; *M:* Phil Marshall.

Nomad Riders ♂ **1981** A la "Mad Max," (though with an even smaller budget and a decided lack of originality) one rugged man goes after the bikers who killed his wife and daughter. **82m/C VHS.** Wayne Chema, Richard Cluck, Ron Gregg; *D:* Frank Roach.

Nomads ♂♂½ **1986 (R)** A supernatural thriller set in Los Angeles about a French anthropologist who is mysteriously killed, and the woman doctor who investigates and becomes the next target of a band of strange street people with nomadic spirits. Nomad notables include pop stars Adam Ant and Josie Cotton. **91m/C VHS, DVD, Wide.** Pierce Brosnan, Lesley-Anne Down, Adam Ant, Anna Maria Monticelli, Mary Woronov, Hector Mercado; *D:* John McTiernan; *W:* John McTiernan; *C:* Stephen Ramsey; *M:* Bill Conti.

Nomads of the North ♂½ **1920** Vintage silent melodrama set in the North Woods with the requisite young girl beset by evil villians, a climactic forest fire, and a dashing Mountie who allows a man wrongly sought by the law to be reunited with the woman he secretly loves. Also available at 75 minutes. **109m/B VHS, 8mm.** Lon Chaney Sr., Lewis Stone, Betty Blythe; *D:* David M. Hartford.

Nomugi Pass ♂♂½ **1979** A young woman working in a Japanese silk mill in the early 1900s must endure hardship and abuse. English subtitles. **154m/C VHS.** *JP* Shinobu Otake, Meiko Harada, Rentaro Mikuni, Takeo Jii.

Non-Stop New York ♂♂½ **1937** Mystery tale with interesting twist. A wealthy woman can give an alibi for a murder suspect, but no one will listen, and she is subsequently framed. Pays homage to Hitchcock with its photography and humor. Quick and charming. **71m/B VHS.** Anna Lee, John Loder, Francis L. Sullivan, Frank Cellier, Desmond Tester, Athene Seyler, William Dewhurst, Drusilla Wills, Jerry Verno, James Pirrie, Ellen Pollock, Arthur Goullet, James Carew, Alf Goddard, Danny Green; *D:* Robert Stevenson; *W:* Curt Siodmak, Roland Pertwee, Derek Twist, J.O.C. Orton, E.V.H. Emmett; *C:* Mutz Greenbaum.

None But the Brave ♂♂ **1965** During WWII, an American bomber plane crash-lands on an island already inhabited by stranded Japanese forces. After a skirmish, the two groups initiate a fragile truce, with the understanding that fighting will resume if one or the other sends for help. The Americans repair their radio unit and must decide on their next actions. Sinatra's directorial debut is a poor effort. **105m/C VHS.** Frank Sinatra, Clint Walker, Tommy Sands, Brad Dexter, Tony Bill, Tatsuya Mihashi, Takeshi Kato, Sammy Jackson; *D:* Frank Sinatra; *M:* John Williams.

None But the Lonely Heart ♂♂♂ **1944** In the days before WWII, a Cockney drifter (Grant) wanders the East End of London. When his get-rich-quick schemes fail, his dying shopkeeper-mother tries to help and lands in prison. Interesting characterization of life in the slums. Odets not only directed, but wrote the screenplay. **113m/B VHS.** Cary Grant, Ethel Barrymore, Barry Fitzgerald, Jane Wyatt, Dan Duryea, George Coulouris, June Duprez; *D:* Clifford Odets; *W:* Clifford Odets; *C:* George Barnes. Oscars '44: Support. Actress (Barrymore).

Noon Sunday ♂ **1971 (PG)** A cold war situation in the Pacific islands explodes into an orgy of death. **104m/C VHS.** Mark Lenard, John Russell, Linda Avery, Keye Luke.

Noon Wine ♂♂♂ **1984** Dramatization of Katherine Anne Porter's classic story about a Swedish worker on a Texas farm who becomes the center of a family battle. Made for PBS' American Playhouse. **60m/C VHS.** Fred Ward, Lise Hilboldt, Stellan Skarsgard, Jon Cryer; *D:* Michael Fields. **TV**

The Noose Hangs High ♂♂♂ **1948** This broad comedy has our heroes as window washers mistaken for gamblers and getting involved with a bunch of gangsters. Much physical and verbal shenanigans as only these two can do it. The bits may be a bit old, but they're done with a fresh twist. Some good word play with the phrase "You can't be here" runs in the same vein as their classic "Who's on first?" routine. Genuinely funny. **77m/B VHS.** Bud Abbott, Lou Costello, Cathy Downs, Joseph Calleia, Leon Errol, Mike Mazurki, Jack Overman, Fritz Feld, Vera Martin, Joe (Joseph) Kirk, Matt Willis, Benny Rubin; *D:* Charles T. Barton.

Nora ♂♂½ **2000 (R)** In a film about the passionate relationship between two people, there's actually little heat to be found, although the leads are effective. Ambitious would-be writer James Joyce (McGregor) and hotel maid Nora Barnacle (Lynch) meet in Dublin in 1904. Nora soon becomes his muse, common-law wife, and the mother of his children but insecure Joyce is mistrustful of her faithfulness and the two are locked in a constant battle as they travel between Italy and Ireland and Joyce seeks to find a publisher for his work. Based on the book by Brenda Maddox. **106m/C VHS, DVD.** *IR GB GE* Ewan McGregor, Susan Lynch, Peter McDonald, Roberto Citran, Andrew Scott, Vincent McCabe, Veronica Duffy, Aedin Moloney, Darragh Kelly; *D:* Pat Murphy; *W:* Gerard Stembridge, Pat Murphy; *C:* Jean-Francois Robin; *M:* Stanislas Syrewicz.

Noriega: God's Favorite ♂♂½ **2000** Hoskins is the reason to watch this cable drama about Panamanian strongman Gen. Manuel "Tony" Noriega who was deposed in 1989 after the U.S. invasion. He has a complicated private life and an even more complicated political existence that includes Castro, the CIA, Colombian drug cartels, and various rivals for power. **115m/C VHS.** Bob Hoskins, Jeffrey DeMunn, Richard Masur, Nestor Carbonell, Tony Plana, Luis Avalos, Edward Edwards, David Marshall Grant, Rosa Blasi, Denise Blasor, John Verea, Michael Sorich; *D:* Roger Spottiswoode; *W:* Lawrence Wright; *C:* Pierre Mignot. **CABLE**

Norma Jean and Marilyn ♂♂½ **1995 (R)** Blonde screen goddess Marilyn Monroe (Sorvino) is haunted by her past, literally, since she never escapes the legacy of ambitious Norma Jean Baker (Judd). As her relationships and career falter, Norma Jean is always there (thanks to drug-induced hallucinations) to remind Marilyn how worthless she is. Drama deals with Norma Jean's troubled past and how she was willing to do anything to be in the movies, although it (apparently) brought her little happiness. The dual stars work surprisingly well and director Fywell offers the proper camp flair. **133m/C VHS.** Mira Sorvino, Ashley Judd, Josh Charles, Peter Dobson, Ron Rifkin, David Dukes, Taylor Nichols, Lindsay Crouse, John Rubinstein, Steven Culp, Perry Stephens, Earl Boen; *D:* Tim Fywell; *W:* Jill Isaacs; *C:* John Thomas; *M:* Christopher Young. **CABLE**

Norma Rae ♂♂♂ **1979 (PG)** A poor, uneducated textile worker joins forces with a New York labor organizer to unionize the reluctant workers at a Southern mill. Field was a surprise with her fully developed character's strength, beauty, and humor; her Oscar was well-deserved. Ritt's direction is top-notch. Jennifer Warnes sings the theme song, "It Goes Like It Goes," which also won an Oscar. ♫It Goes Like It Goes. **114m/C VHS, DVD, Wide.** Sally Field, Ron Leibman, Beau Bridges, Pat Hingle; *D:* Martin Ritt; *W:* Harriet Frank Jr., Irving Ravetch; *C:* John A. Alonzo; *M:* David Shire. Oscars '79: Actress (Field), Song ("It Goes Like It Goes"); Cannes '79: Actress (Field); Golden Globes '80: Actress—Drama (Field); L.A. Film Critics '79: Actress (Field); Natl. Bd. of Review '79: Actress (Field); N.Y. Film Critics '79: Actress (Field); Natl. Soc. Film Critics '79: Actress (Field).

Normal Life ♂♂ **1996 (R)** Straight-arrow, smalltown Illinois rookie cop Chris Anderson (Perry) comes to the aid of sexy, impetuous biker chick Pam (Judd) and they impulsively marry. Fast forward two years and the willfully irresponsible Pam has turned their lives into a disaster but for some reason Chris (now a security guard) sticks it out, even pulling bank jobs to afford Pam's luxuries. When she finds out what Chris has been doing, Pam insists on joining in, leading to a bitter end. Based on the true story of Jeffrey and Jill Erickson, who went on a bank robbing spree and were killed in 1991. Great lead performances though character motivation is lacking. **108m/C VHS.** Luke Perry, Ashley Judd, Bruce A. Young, Jim True, Dawn Maxey, Penelope Milford, Tom Towles; ***D:*** John McNaughton; ***W:*** Bob Schneider, Peg Haller; ***C:*** Jean De Segonzac.

Norman Conquest 🦴 *Park Plaza* **1953** Conway finds himself drugged and framed for murder in this bargain-basement thriller. Bartok is the leader of a diamond-smuggling operation who may be involved. **75m/B VHS.** *GB* Tom Conway, Eva Bartok, Joy Shelton, Sidney James, Richard Wattis, Robert Adair, Ian Fleming; ***D:*** Bernard Knowles; ***W:*** Bernard Knowles.

The Norman Conquests, Part 1: Table Manners 🦴🦴🦴 **1980** Part one of playwright Alan Ayckbourn's comic trilogy of love unfulfilled, as the charmingly unreliable Norman (Conti) works his amorous wiles on three women. **108m/C VHS.** *GB* Tom Conti, Richard Briers, Penelope Keith.

The Norman Conquests, Part 2: Living Together 🦴🦴🦴 **1980** Part two concerns the happenings in the living room during Norman's disastrous weekend of unsuccessful seduction. **93m/C VHS.** *GB* Tom Conti, Penelope Keith, Richard Briers.

The Norman Conquests, Part 3: Round and Round the Garden 🦴🦴🦴 **1980** Part three concerns Norman's furtive appearance in the garden, which suggests that the weekend is going to misfire. **106m/C VHS.** *GB* Tom Conti, Penelope Keith, Richard Briers.

Norman, Is That You? 🦴½ **1976** Unsuccessful film adaptation based on the unsuccessful Broadway play about one family's sexual revolution. Revamped by a host of black stars, it's basically a one-joke affair when Foxx discovers his son is gay and living with his white lover. Shot on videotape and transferred to film. **91m/C VHS.** Redd Foxx, Pearl Bailey, Dennis Dugan, Michael Warren, Tamara Dobson, Vernee Watson-Johnson, Jayne Meadows, George Furth; ***D:*** George Schlatter; ***W:*** George Schlatter, Ron Clark, Sam Bobrick; ***M:*** William Goldstein.

Norman Loves Rose 🦴½ **1982 (R)** A precocious 13-year-old and his married sister-in-law join forces in this substandard comedy. When Rose tries to help Norman by teaching him about sex, she learns a little too—she's pregnant. **95m/C VHS.** *AU* Carol Kane, Tony Owen, Warren Mitchell, Myra de Groot; ***D:*** Henri Safran.

Norman's Awesome Experience WOOF! **1988 (PG-13)** Three adolescents are transported back in time to the Roman Empire. Bill and Ted, anyone? **90m/C VHS.** Tom McCamus, Laurie Paton, Jaques Lussier; ***D:*** Paul Donovan.

Norseman 🦴½ **1978 (PG)** Leader of a band of Norsemen sets sail for the New World in search of his missing royal father. Low-budget Viking adventure. **90m/C VHS.** Lee Majors, Cornel Wilde, Mel Ferrer, Christopher Connelly, Jack Elam; ***D:*** Charles B. Pierce; ***W:*** Charles B. Pierce.

North 🦴🦴½ **1994 (PG)** Some laughs with a message in family fare from Reiner. Eleven-year-old ace kid actor Wood divorces his workaholic parents Alexander and Louis-Dreyfus and searches the world for a functional family (good luck). Willis, who's a treat in a pink bunny suit, acts as guardian angel/narrator and shows the kid what's really important. Illustrious comedic cast inhabits story based on a book by original "Saturday Night Live" screenwriter (and "Gary Shandling Show" co-creator) Zweibel, who put things in motion ten years ago when he asked Reiner to write a book jacket quote for the novel. **87m/C VHS.** Elijah Wood, Jason Alexander, Julia Louis-Dreyfus, Bruce Willis, Jon Lovitz, Alan Arkin, Dan Aykroyd, Kathy Bates, Faith Ford, Graham Greene, Reba McEntire, John Ritter, Abe Vigoda, Kelly McGillis, Alexander Godunov, Noriyuki "Pat" Morita, Ben Stein; ***D:*** Rob Reiner; ***W:*** Andrew Scheinman, Alan Zweibel; ***M:*** Marc Shaiman.

North and South Book 1 🦴🦴🦴 **1985** Lavish spectacle about a friendship tested by the turbulent times leading up to Civil War. Orry Main (Swayze) is a South Carolina plantation owner while his best friend George Hazard (Read) comes from a Pennsylvania industrial family. Orry is also involved in a doomed romance with the beautiful Madeline (Down), who's forced to marry the odious Justin LaMotte (Carradine). Lots of intrigue and excitement. Based on the novel by John Jakes. Filmed on location in Charleston, South Carolina. Originally broadcast as a six-part TV miniseries. Available on six cassettes. **561m/C VHS.** Patrick Swayze, James Read, Lesley-Anne Down, David Carradine, Kirstie Alley, Jean Simmons, Inga Swenson, Jonathon Frakes, Genie Francis, Terri Garber, Georg Stanford Brown, Olivia Cole, David Ogden Stiers, Robert Guillaume, Hal Holbrook, Gene Kelly, Robert Mitchum, Johnny Cash, Elizabeth Taylor; ***M:*** Bill Conti.

North and South Book 2 🦴🦴🦴 **1986** Equally dramatic sequel follows the southern Main clan and the northern Hazard family into the Civil War as friendship and romance struggle to survive the fighting. Casnoff is a notable presence as the aptly named Bent, who will go to any length to settle old scores with both families. Based on the John Jakes novel "Love and War." Originally broadcast as a six-part TV miniseries; on six cassettes. The last of the Jakes trilogy, "Heaven and Hell," was finally filmed for TV in '94 but proved a major disappointment. **570m/C VHS.** Patrick Swayze, James Read, Lesley-Anne Down, Terri Garber, Genie Francis, Jean Simmons, Kirstie Alley, Philip Casnoff, Hal Holbrook, Lloyd Bridges, James Stewart, Morgan Fairchild, Nancy Marchand, Parker Stevenson, Lewis Smith; ***M:*** Bill Conti.

The North Avenue Irregulars 🦴🦴½ **1979 (G)** Slapstick Disney comedy along the same lines as some of their earlier laugh-fests. A priest and three members of the local ladies' club try to bust a crime syndicate. Though the premise is silly, there are still lots of laughs in this family film. **99m/C VHS, DVD.** Edward Herrmann, Barbara Harris, Susan Clark, Karen Valentine, Michael Constantine, Cloris Leachman, Melora Hardin, Alan Hale Jr., Ruth Buzzi, Patsy Kelly, Virginia Capers; ***D:*** Bruce Bilson; ***W:*** Don Tait; ***C:*** Leonard J. South; ***M:*** Robert F. Brunner.

North by Northwest 🦴🦴🦴🦴 **1959** Self-assured Madison Avenue ad exec Roger Thornhill (Grant) inadvertently gets involved with international spies when they mistake him for someone else. His problems are compounded when he's framed for murder and winds up on a cross-country train trip with pretty Eve Kendall (Saint) who offers her help. The movie where Grant and Saint dangle from the faces of Mount Rushmore and a plane chases Grant through farm fields. Exceptional performances, particularly Grant's. Plenty of plot twists are mixed with tongue-in-cheek humor. **136m/C VHS, DVD, Wide.** Cary Grant, Eva Marie Saint, James Mason, Leo G. Carroll, Martin Landau, Jessie Royce Landis, Philip Ober, Adam Williams, Josephine Hutchinson, Edward Platt; ***D:*** Alfred Hitchcock; ***W:*** Ernest Lehman; ***C:*** Robert Burks; ***M:*** Bernard Herrmann. AFI '98: Top 100, Natl. Film Reg. '95.

North Dallas Forty 🦴🦴🦴½ **1979 (R)** Based on the novel by former Dallas Cowboy Peter Gent, the film focuses on the labor abuses in pro-football. One of the best football movies ever made, it contains searing commentary and very good acting, although the plot is sometimes dropped behind the line of scrimmage. **119m/C VHS, DVD, Wide.** Nick Nolte, Mac Davis, Charles Durning, Bo Svenson, Brian Dennehy, John Matuszak, Dayle Haddon, Steve Forrest, Dabney Coleman, G.D. Spradlin; ***D:*** Ted Kotcheff; ***W:*** Ted Kotcheff, Frank Yablans; ***C:*** Paul Lohmann; ***M:*** John Scott.

North of the Border 🦴½ **1946** A cowboy in Canada gets involved with back-stabbing and treachery in and around Alberta. **40m/B VHS.** *CA* Russell Hayden, Lyle Talbot, Inez Cooper, Douglas Fowley, Jack Mulhall; ***D:*** B. Reeves Eason.

North of the Great Divide 🦴½ **1950** Standard Rogers programmer, with Roy as a half-breed mediator between salmon fisherman and Indians. **67m/C VHS.** Roy Rogers, Penny Edwards, Gordon Jones, Roy Barcroft, Jack Lambert, Douglas Evans, Noble Johnson; ***D:*** William Witney.

North Shore 🦴½ **1987 (PG)** A young surfer from Arizona hits the beaches of Hawaii and discovers love, sex, and adventure. Only redeeming quality is surfing footage. **96m/C VHS.** Matt Adler, Nia Peeples, John Philbin, Gregory Harrison, Christina Raines; ***D:*** Will Phelps.

North Shore Fish 🦴🦴 **1997 (R)** North Shore Fish is a failing Massachusetts fish-packing factory with various cynical managers and employees, including divorcee Flo (Ruehl), who's just found out she's pregnant by her married boss Sal (Danza); 60ish Arlyne (Baker), who regards her co-workers as family; and Josie (Schwimmer), whose husband has left her for a younger woman. It's on this one day that they realize how uncertain all their futures are. Based on the play by Israel Horovitz. **95m/C VHS.** Mercedes Ruehl, Peter Riegert, Carroll Baker, Tony Danza, Rusty Schwimmer, Wendie Malick, Cordelia Richards; ***D:*** Steve Zuckerman; ***W:*** Israel Horovitz; ***C:*** Levie Isaacks. CABLE

The North Star 🦴🦴🦴 *Armored Attack* **1943** Gripping war tale of Nazis overrunning an eastern Russian city, with courageous villagers fighting back. Colorized version available. **108m/B VHS, DVD.** Dana Andrews, Walter Huston, Anne Baxter, Farley Granger, Walter Brennan, Erich von Stroheim, Jack Perrin, Dean Jagger; ***D:*** Lewis Milestone; ***W:*** Lillian Hellman; ***C:*** James Wong Howe; ***M:*** Aaron Copland.

North Star 🦴½ **1996 (R)** Formulaic actioner where no one seems very enthusiastic. Half-breed trapper Hudson Ipsehawk (Lambert) refuses to mine the gold on his Alaskan property because the land is considered sacred. This doesn't concern greedy miner Sean McLennon (Caan) who wants the property for himself. Oh yeah, there's also a babe, Sarah (McCormack), that both men are interested in. Norway substitutes for Alaska. Based on the novel by Will Henry. **89m/C VHS.** Christopher Lambert, James Caan, Catherine McCormack, Burt Young; ***D:*** Nils Gaup; ***W:*** Paul Ohl, Sergio Donati, Lorenzo Donati; ***C:*** Bruno de Keyzer; ***M:*** Bruce Rowland.

North to Alaska 🦴🦴🦴 **1960** A gold prospector encounters many problems when he agrees to pick up his partner's fiancee in Seattle to bring her home to Nome, Alaska, in the 1890s. Overly slapstick at times, but great fun nonetheless. Loosely based on Laszlo Fodor's play "The Birthday Gift." **120m/C VHS, Wide.** John Wayne, Stewart Granger, Ernie Kovacs, Fabian, Capucine; ***D:*** Henry Hathaway; ***C:*** Leon Shamroy.

Northanger Abbey 🦴🦴½ **1987** Catherine is a young woman whose head is turned by her romance readings of dark secrets, sinister castles, dashing heroes, and helpless women. When the handsome Henry Tilney invites her to visit his ancestral home, Northanger Abbey, it seems all her fancies have come to life. A somewhat tepid adaptation of Jane Austen's parody of the popular Gothic romances of her day. **90m/C VHS, DVD.** *GB* Peter Firth, Katherine Schlesinger, Googie Withers, Robert Hardy; ***D:*** Giles Foster; ***W:*** Maggie Wadey; ***C:*** Nat Crosby; ***M:*** Ilona Sekacz.

Northeast of Seoul 🦴 **1972 (PG)** Three people will stop at nothing to steal a legendary jewel-encrusted sword out of Korea. **84m/C VHS.** Anita Ekberg, John Ireland, Victor Buono; ***D:*** David Lowell Rich.

Northern Extremes 🦴½ *Buried on Sunday* **1993 (PG)** Silly comedy about an eccentric Canadian island village whose fishing livelihood is threatened. So the town mayor captures an errant nuclear submarine and uses it as a big bargaining chip. Filmed in Nova Scotia, Canada. **80m/C VHS.** *CA* Paul Gross, Denise Virieux, Henry Czerny, Jeff Leder, Tommy Sexton, Louis Del Grande, Maury Chaykin; ***D:*** Paul Donovan; ***W:*** Bill Flemming.

Northern Lights 🦴🦴🦴 **1979** A small, black-and-white independent drama depicting the struggle of a lowly farmer combating governmental forces in the 1915 heartland. Subtitled. **85m/B VHS.** Robert Behling, Susan Lynch, Joe Spano, Rob Nilsson, Henry Martinson, Marianne Astrom-DeFina, Ray Ness, Helen Ness; ***D:*** Rob Nilsson, John Hanson; ***W:*** Rob Nilsson.

Northern Passage 🦴🦴½ **1995 (PG-13)** Cowboy tries to protect a young Native American woman from harm in the wilderness. **97m/C VHS.** Jeff Fahey, Neve Campbell.

Northern Pursuit 🦴🦴½ **1943** A Canadian Mountie disguises himself to infiltrate a Nazi spy ring in this exciting adventure film. Based on Leslie White's "Five Thousand Trojan Horses." **94m/B VHS.** Errol Flynn, Helmut Dantine, Julie (Jacqueline Wells) Bishop, Gene Lockhart, Tom Tully; ***D:*** Raoul Walsh.

Northville Cemetery Massacre 🦴 *The Northfield Cemetery Massacre* **1976 (R)** Gang of bikers comes to town and all hell breaks loose. The result is a horribly bloody war between the townsfolk and the gang. Yup, it was a massacre. **81m/C VHS.** David Hyry, Craig Collicott, Jan Sisk, Carson Jackson; ***D:*** William Dear, Thomas L. Dyke; ***C:*** William Dear, Thomas L. Dyke; ***M:*** Michael Nesmith.

Northwest Outpost 🦴½ *End of the Rainbow* **1947** Eddy is a California cavalry officer in this lightweight operetta. He helps a young woman who is trying to free her husband from jail, and after his death they are able to pursue their relationship. Eddy's last film. ♫Weary; Raindrops on a Drum; Tell Me With Your Eyes; One More Mile to Go; Russian Easter Hymn; Love is the Time; Nearer and Dearer. **91m/B VHS.** Nelson Eddy, Ilona Massey, Hugo Haas, Elsa Lanchester, Lenore Ulric; ***D:*** Allan Dwan.

Northwest Passage 🦴🦴🦴 **1940** The lavish first half of a projected two-film package based on Kenneth Roberts' popular novel, depicting the troop of Rogers' Rangers fighting the wilderness and hostile Indians. Beautifully produced; the second half was never made and the passage itself is never seen. **126m/C VHS.** Spencer Tracy, Robert Young, Ruth Hussey, Walter Brennan, Nat Pendleton, Robert Barrat, Lumsden Hare; ***D:*** King Vidor.

Northwest Trail 🦴🦴 **1946** Royal Canadian Mountie Steele's assignment is to escort Woodbury across the wilderness. She's carrying a large sum of money to save her uncle's business. Problem is, killers are on their trail. **75m/C VHS.** Bob Steele, Joan Woodbury, John Litel, Raymond Hatton, Madge Bellamy, Charles Middleton; ***D:*** Derwin Abrahams.

Nosferatu 🦴🦴🦴🦴 *Nosferatu, Eine Symphonie des Grauens; Nosferatu, A Symphony of Terror; Nosferatu, A Symphony of Horror; Nosferatu, the Vampire; Terror of Dracula; Die Zwolfte Stunde* **1922** The first film adaptation of Bram Stoker's "Dracula" remains one of the creepiest and most atmospheric versions. Murnau knew how to add just the right touches to make this one of the best vampire films ever made. All it lacks is the name of Dracula, which was changed due to copyright problems with Stoker's widow. Filmed in Bavaria. Silent with music and English titles. Remade by Werner Herzog in 1979. **63m/B VHS, DVD.** *GE* Max Schreck, Alexander Granach, Gustav von Wagenheim, Greta Schroder, John Gottowt, Ruth Landshoff, G.H. Schnell; ***D:*** F.W. Murnau; ***W:*** Henrik Galeen; ***C:*** Fritz Arno Wagner, Gunther Krampf.

Nosferatu the Vampyre 🦴🦴 *Nosferatu: Phantom der Nacht* **1979** Herzog's tribute to fellow countryman's F.W. Murnau's 1922 silent film interpretation of Bram Stoker's "Dracula" story. It features Kinski as the disgustingly rodent-like Count, with Ganz as Jonathan Harker, and Adjani as Harker's wife and the beautiful object of the Count's lust. Released in a German language version with subtitles and an English language version. **107m/C VHS, DVD.** *FR GE* Klaus Kinski, Isabelle Adjani, Bruno Ganz, Roland Topor, Walter Ladengast; ***D:*** Werner Herzog; ***W:*** Werner Herzog; ***C:*** Jorge Schmidt-Reitwein; ***M:*** Popul Vuh, Florian Fricke.

Nostalghia 🦴🦴 **1983** Russian academic Jankovsky comes to Tuscany to research the life of an 18th-century composer and meets the mysterious Josephson, who's convinced the end of the world is near. And soon the homesick Russian is in a search for himself. Filled with Christian iconography and some extraordinary images. Tarkovsky's first film outside his native Russia. Russian and Italian with subtitles; the Russian sequences are filmed in B&W. **126m/C VHS, DVD.** *IT* Oleg (Yankovsky) Jankowsky, Erland Josephson, Domiziana Giordano, Delia Boccardo; *D:* Andrei Tarkovsky; *W:* Andrei Tarkovsky, Tonino Guerra; *C:* Giuseppe Lanci.

Nostradamus 🦴🦴 **1993 (R)** Historical soap opera about unconventional 16th-century French physician and astrologer Michel de Nostradame. Persecuted by the Inquisition, he comes under the protection of Queen Catherine de Medici of France, although his visions of destruction and death continue to haunt him. Nostradamus' prophecies, first published in 1555, have continued to fascinate, being used to predicate everything from the death of historical leaders to WWI. The film, however, is slow going and fails to hold much interest. **118m/C VHS.** *FR* Tcheky Karyo, F. Murray Abraham, Julia Ormond, Rutger Hauer, Amanda Plummer, Assumpta Serna, Anthony (Corlan) Higgins, Diana Quick, Michael Gough; *D:* Roger Christian; *W:* Knut Boeser, Piers Ashworth.

The Nostradamus Kid 🦴🦴 **1992 (R)** Young man, convinced the world is about to end, decides his last goal will be to make love (for the first time) with his girlfriend. **120m/C VHS.** Noah Taylor, Miranda Otto, Arthur Dignam; *D:* Bob Ellis.

Nostromo 🦴🦴 *Joseph Conrad's Nostromo* **1996** Tediously drawn-out TV adaptation of the 1904 novel by Joseph Conrad takes place in the 1890s in the fictional South American country of Costaguana. Englishman Charles Gould (Firth) is determined to reopen his family's silver mine—a plan supported by the local regime, which is, however, soon to be overthrown. Amidst the revolution is the title character Nostromo (Amendola), a contraction of "nostro uomo" or "our man," an enigmatic Italian immigrant who organizes the dockworkers and is thrust into the role of hero. Filmed on location in Cartagena, Colombia. On three cassettes. **360m/C VHS.** Colin Firth, Albert Finney, Claudio Amendola, Serena Scott Thomas, Claudia Cardinale, Brian Dennehy, Lothaire Bluteau, Ruth Gabriel, Joaquim de Almeida; *D:* Alastair Reid; *W:* John Hale; *M:* Ennio Morricone. **TV**

Not Another Teen Movie 🦴½ **2001 (R)** Unsuccessful parody of the recent proliferation of bad teen movies and the better John Hughes films of the 80s. Teen moviedom's stereotypes are hammed up to the extreme, from the bitchy teenager to the dumb jock, nerdy beauty-in-waiting and fat guy for comic relief. Which is okay if you like really obvious, unoriginal humor. Film's self-awareness is sometimes amusing but more often sinks to the level of what it's supposed to be satirizing, and of course, there's enough bodily-function and base sexual jokes to fill three Tom Green flicks. If there was ever a genre begging to be parodied, it's teen movies, but this entry flunks. Entertaining cameos by Molly Ringwald and John Vernon, though. **90m/C VHS, DVD, Wide.** *US* Chyler Leigh, Chris Evans, Eric Jungmann, Eric Christian Olsen, Cody McMains, Sam Huntington, Ron Lester, Samm Levine, Deon Richmond, Jaime Pressly, Mia Kirshner, Riley Smith, Lacey Chabert, Cerina Vincent, Beverly Polcyn, Joanna Garcia, Randy Quaid, Ed Lauter, Mr. T, Paul Gleason, Molly Ringwald; *D:* Joel Gallen; *W:* Michael G. Bender, Adam Jay Epstein, Andrew Jacobson, Phil Beauman, Buddy Johnson; *C:* Reynaldo Villalobos; *M:* Theodore Shapiro.

Not as a Stranger 🦴🦴½ **1955** Glossy film about the medical profession and the varying degrees of dedication shown by doctors. Mitchum stars as an medical student who can't afford to pay his tuition, so he marries nurse de Havilland and continues going to school on her money, although their relationship is far from being a loving one. Producer Kramer's directorial debut. Based on the book by Morton Thompson. **135m/B VHS.** Olivia de Havilland, Robert Mitchum, Frank Sinatra, Gloria Grahame, Broderick Crawford, Charles Bickford, Myron McCormick, Lon Chaney Jr.; *D:* Stanley Kramer; *W:* Edward Anhalt.

Not for Publication 🦴🦴 **1984 (R)** A woman working as both a tabloid reporter and a mayoral campaign worker uncovers governmental corruption with the help of a shy photographer and a midget. Meant to be on par with older screwball comedies but lacking the wit and subtlety. **87m/C VHS.** Nancy Allen, David Naughton, Richard Paul, Alice Ghostley, Laurence Luckinbill; *D:* Paul Bartel; *W:* Paul Bartel.

Not in This Town 🦴🦴½ **1997 (PG-13)** Fact-based drama stars Baker as Billings, Montana, housewife Tammie Schnitzer, who is shocked when white supremacists, led by Henry Whitcomb (Begley Jr.), begin harassing religious and ethnic minorities in her town. She forms the Montana Coalition for Human Rights and begins a public appeal to rally the community but soon Tammie and her family need some protection of their own. **95m/C VHS.** Kathy Baker, Adam Arkin, Ed Begley Jr., Bradford Tatum, Max Gail; *D:* Donald Wrye; *W:* Adam Gilad; *M:* Don Davis. **CABLE**

Not Like Us 🦴½ **1996 (R)** Bored Anita's (Pacula) tired of life in her small town and glad to make a new friend in Janet (Grant). But she's shocked to discover Janet may be involved in several mysterious deaths (oh yeah, and she happens to be an alien). **87m/C VHS.** Joanna Pacula, Annabelle Gurwitch, Peter Onorati, Morgan Englund, Rainer Grant; *D:* Dave Payne; *W:* Daniella Purcelli.

Not My Kid 🦴🦴½ **1985** The 15-year-old daughter of a surgeon brings turmoil to her family when she becomes heavily involved in drugs. Producer Polson, along with Dr. Miller Newton, wrote the original book for this emotional story that is one of the better treatments of this important subject. **120m/C VHS.** George Segal, Stockard Channing, Viveka Davis, Andrew (Andy) Robinson, Gary Bayer, Nancy Cartwright, Tate Donovan; *D:* Michael Tuchner; *W:* Christopher Knopf. **TV**

Not of This Earth 🦴½ **1988 (R)** In a remake of the 1957 Roger Corman quickie, an alien wearing sunglasses makes an unfriendly trip to Earth. In order to save his dying planet he needs major blood donations from unsuspecting Earthlings. Not a match for the original version, some may nevertheless want to see exporn star Lords in her role as the nurse. **92m/C VHS, DVD.** Traci Lords, Arthur Roberts, Lenny Juliano, Rebecca Perle, Ace Mask, Roger Lodge, Michael Delano, Monique Gabrielle, Becky Le Beau; *D:* Jim Wynorski; *W:* Jim Wynorski, R.J. Robertson, Charles B. Griffith, Mark Hanna; *C:* Zoran Hochstatter; *M:* Chuck Cirino.

Not of This Earth 🦴🦴 **1996 (R)** Corman remake of his own 1957 cheapie is both camp and sexy. Sunglass-wearing mystery millionaire Paul Johnson (York) apparently suffers from a rare condition and must have constant blood transfusions, so he hires a sexy live-in nurse (Barondes) to be at his beck-and-call. Yes, he does turn out to be a vampire but of the space alien-with-telepathic-powers variety who has a particular purpose for coming to earth. **92m/C VHS.** Michael York, Elizabeth Barondes, Richard Belzer, Parker Stevenson; *D:* Terence H. Winkless; *W:* Charles Philip Moore. **CABLE**

Not One Less 🦴🦴½ *Yi Ge Dou Bu Neng Shao* **1999 (G)** Gao is teaching in a rundown rural Chinese school when he is called away to visit his dying mother. The only substitute he can find is 13-year-old Wei Minzhi, who's scarcely older than her would-be students. Because so many children are forced to leave school because of their poverty-stricken families, Gao promises the girl extra money if she will keep all the pupils in class until he returns. When Zhang Huike must go to work in the city, Wei Minzhi is stubbornly determined to find and bring him back. Mandarin with subtitles. **106m/C VHS, DVD.** *CH* Wei Minzhi, Zhang Huike, Gao Enman; *D:* Zhang Yimou; *W:* Shi Xiangsheng; *C:* Hou Yong; *M:* San Bao.

Not Quite Human 🦴🦴 **1987** When Jonas Carson builds himself an android teenage son, he must keep the technology from falling into the hands of an evil toy manufacturer with plans of his own. Humorous hijinks abound. Based on the book series "Not Quite Human" by Seth McEvoy. Followed by two sequels. **91m/C VHS.** Alan Thicke, Robin (Robyn) Lively, Robert Harper, Joseph Bologna, Jay Underwood; *D:* Steven Hilliard Stern. **CABLE**

Not Quite Human 2 🦴🦴½ **1989** In this sequel, Dr. Jonas Carson sends his cyber-son off to college where Chip meets the not-quite-human girl of his dreams. Followed by "Still Not Quite Human." **91m/C VHS.** Alan Thicke, Jay Underwood, Robin (Robyn) Lively, Greg Mullavey, Katie Barberi, Mark Arnott; *D:* Eric Luke. **CABLE**

Not Quite Paradise 🦴 *Not Quite Jerusalem* **1986 (R)** A young American medical student falls in love with a young Israeli girl living on a kibbutz. **106m/C VHS.** Sam Robards, Joanna Pacula; *D:* Lewis Gilbert.

Not Tonight Darling 🦴 **1972 (R)** A bored suburban housewife becomes involved with a fast-talking businessman who leads her into a web of deceit and blackmail. **70m/C VHS.** Luan Peters, Vincent Ball, Jason Twelvetrees.

Not Without My Daughter 🦴½ **1990 (PG-13)** Overwrought drama shot in Israel about American Field, who travels with her Arab husband and their daughter to his native Iran, where (he must have forgotten to tell her) she has no rights. He decides the family will stay, using beatings and confinement to persuade his uncooperative wife, but she risks all to escape with daughter. Based on the true story of Betty Mahmoody. **116m/C VHS, DVD, Wide.** Sally Field, Alfred Molina, Sheila Rosenthal, Roshan Seth, Sarah Badel, Mony Rey, Georges Corraface; *D:* Brian Gilbert; *W:* David W. Rintels; *C:* Peter Hannan; *M:* Jerry Goldsmith.

Notes for an African Orestes 🦴🦴 **1970** Director Pasolini's insight into how a filmmaker works and what motivates him, as the camera reveals his plans to film a modern day version of Aeschylus' "Orestes" in Africa. **75m/B VHS.** *D:* Pier Paolo Pasolini; *M:* Gato Barbieri.

Notes from Underground 🦴🦴 **1995** Modern adaptation of the Dostoevsky novella has Czerny starring as a nameless, alienated civil servant who can only find pleasure in the petty torments his job allows him to inflict on others. Everything he does to broaden his world backfires in humiliating ways. Most of the film consists of monologues that Czerny records on a homevideo camera as he recalls the worst moments in his life. Fortunately, Czerny is up to the nearly one-man task of carrying this odd film. **90m/C VHS.** Henry Czerny, Sheryl Lee, Jon Favreau, Charles Stratton; *D:* Gary Walkow; *W:* Gary Walkow; *C:* Dan Gillham; *M:* Mark Governor.

Nothin' 2 Lose 🦴½ **2000** Kwame (Brian Hooks, *3 Strikes*) can't bring him himself to commit to marriage with his girlfriend, Yasmine (Shani Bayete). He prefers to spend his time hanging with his friends, gambling on playground basketball games, and chattering illiterate gibberish about all things inane. Racist language serves for humor and women serve as objects in what proves to be a sad excuse for an urban comedy. **?m/C DVD.** Brian Hooks, Shani Bayete, Cedric Pendleton, Crystal Sessoms, Michael A. LeMelle, Martin C. Jones, Rodney J. Hobbs, Sekenia Williams, Malik Jones; *D:* Barry Bowles; *W:* Barry Bowles.

Nothing but a Man 🦴🦴½ **1964** Duff Anderson (Dixon) is a black laborer trying to make a life in a small Alabama town. He falls for the daughter of a minister, they marry, and he gets a job at a local sawmill. When he won't bend to his racist white employers, he's fired and labeled a troublemaker. Unsentimental depiction of the times. **95m/B VHS.** Ivan Dixon, Abbey Lincoln, Gloria Foster, Julius W. Harris, Martin Priest, Yaphet Kotto, Leonard Parker, Stanley Greene, Helen Lounck, Helene Arrindell; *D:* Michael Roemer; *W:* Michael Roemer, Robert M. Young; *C:* Robert M. Young. Natl. Film Reg. '93.

Nothing But the Night 🦴½ *The Devil's Undead; The Resurrection Syndicate* **1972 (PG)** Lee's company produced this convoluted story of orphans who are victims of a cult that uses them in their quest for immortality. **90m/C VHS.** *GB* Christopher Lee, Peter Cushing, Diana Dors, Georgia Brown, Keith Barron, Fulton Mackay, Gwyneth Strong; *D:* Peter Sasdy.

Nothing But Trouble 🦴🦴½ **1944** Laurel & Hardy's last film for MGM is a complicated tale of two servants who wind up protecting an exiled boy king from the machinations of his power-mad uncle. **70m/B VHS.** Stan Laurel, Oliver Hardy, Henry O'Neill, Mary Boland, David Leland, John Warburton, Connie Gilchrist, Philip Merivale; *D:* Sam Taylor.

Nothing But Trouble 🦴 **1991 (PG-13)** Yuppie couple out for weekend drive find themselves smoldering in small town hell thanks to a traffic ticket. Horror and humor mix like oil and water in Aykroyd's debut as director. **93m/C VHS, DVD, 8mm.** Dan Aykroyd, Demi Moore, Chevy Chase, John Candy, Taylor Negron, Bertila Demas, Valri Bromfield; *D:* Dan Aykroyd; *W:* Dan Aykroyd, Peter Aykroyd; *C:* Dean Cundey. Golden Raspberries '91: Worst Support. Actor (Aykroyd).

Nothing in Common 🦴🦴½ **1986 (PG)** In his last film, Gleason plays the abrasive, diabetic father of immature advertising agency worker Hanks. After his parents separate, Hanks learns to be more responsible and loving in caring for his father. Comedy and drama are blended well here with the help of satirical pokes at the ad business and Hanks turns in a fine performance, but the unorganized, lengthy plot may lose some viewers. **119m/C VHS, DVD, Wide.** Tom Hanks, Jackie Gleason, Eva Marie Saint, Bess Armstrong, Hector Elizondo, Barry Corbin, Sela Ward, John Kapelos, Jane Morris, Dan Castellaneta, Tracy Reiner; *D:* Garry Marshall; *W:* Rick Podell; *C:* John A. Alonzo; *M:* Patrick Leonard.

Nothing Personal 🦴½ **1980 (PG)** Confused mix of romantic comedy and environmental themes. Lawyer (?) Somers attempts to help college professor Sutherland prevent the slaughter of seals. Enter romance (hey, but what about the baby seals?). Enlivened by appearances of Canadian SCTV vets and Somers's first starring theatrical role. **96m/C VHS.** Donald Sutherland, Suzanne Somers, Dabney Coleman, John Dehner, Roscoe Lee Browne, Catherine O'Hara; *D:* George Bloomfield.

Nothing Personal 🦴🦴🦴 *All Our Fault* **1995 (R)** Uncompromising drama about the sectarian violence in northern Ireland that engulfs even the innocent. The IRA bombing of a Protestant pub sets a Loyalist unit, led by dedicated Kenny (Frain) and psychotic Ginger (a terrifying Hart), on an increasingly deadly 24-hour rampage through Belfast (in 1975). Catholic single father Liam Kelly (Lynch) finds himself in the wrong part of town and only wants to return to his two children but is inexorably drawn into the violence, which leads to tragedy for all. Adapted from the novel "All Our Fault" by Mornin, who wrote the screenplay. **86m/C VHS.** *GB IR* Ian Hart, John Lynch, James Frain, Michael Gambon, Ruaidhri Conroy, Jeni Courtney, Gary Lydon, Maria Doyle Kennedy, Gerard McSorley, Gareth O'Hare; *D:* Thaddeus O'Sullivan; *W:* Daniel Mornin; *C:* Dick Pope; *M:* Philip Appleby.

Nothing Sacred 🦴🦴🦴½ **1937** Slick, overzealous reporter takes advantage of a small-town girl's situation. As a publicity stunt, his newspaper brings her to the Big Apple to distract her from her supposedly imminent death in order to manipulate the public's sentiment as a means to sell more copy. Innocent young Lombard, however, is far from death's door, and deftly exploits her exploitation. Scathing indictment of the mass media and bovine mentality of the masses. Both hysterically funny and bitterly cynical; boasts Lombard's finest performance as the small-town rube who orchestrates the ruse. Remade in 1954 as "Living It Up." DVD version includes home movie footage of a Lombard-Gable hunting trip and two Mack Sennett shorts—"Campus Vamp" (1928) and "Matchmaking Mama." **75m/C VHS, DVD.** Fredric March, Carole Lombard, Walter Connolly, Sig Rumann, Charles Winninger, Margaret Hamilton; ***D:*** William A. Wellman; ***W:*** Ben Hecht; ***C:*** William Howard Greene; ***M:*** Oscar Levant.

Nothing to Lose 🦴🦴½ **1996 (R)** Ad exec Nick Beam (Robbins) is having a very bad day. He loses his job, finds his wife is having an affair, then gets carjacked by street-wise but dim-witted thief T-Paul (Lawrence). T-Paul picked the wrong day to rob Nick, who ironically takes T-Paul hostage. The unlikely pair find they have more in common than realized. Screwball buddy comedy shows its originality in casting, and not much else. Robbins and Lawrence are an inspired pair with great comedic potential but are trapped in a mundane story. Filming was delayed due, in part, to Lawrence's constant run-ins with the law. **97m/C VHS, DVD.** Tim Robbins, Martin Lawrence, John C. McGinley, Giancarlo Esposito, Kelly Preston, Michael McKean, Irma P. Hall, Susan Barnes, Rebecca Gayheart, Patrick Cranshaw; ***D:*** Steve Oedekerk; ***W:*** Steve Oedekerk; ***C:*** Donald E. Thorin; ***M:*** Robert Folk.

Nothing Underneath 🦴½ **1985** An American guy goes to Rome to search for his model twin sister, who may be one of the victims of a series of scissor killings. **95m/C VHS.** Tom Schanley, Renee Simonsen, Nicola Perring, Donald Pleasence; ***D:*** Carlo Vanzina.

Notorious 🦴🦴🦴🦴 **1946** Post-WWII story of beautiful playgirl Alicia (Bergman), who's sent by the U.S. government to marry a suspected spy (Rains) living in Brazil. Cynical agent Devlin (Grant) is assigned to watch her. Duplicity and guilt are important factors in this brooding, romantic spy thriller. Suspenseful throughout, with a surprise ending. The acting is excellent all around and Hitchcock makes certain that suspense is maintained throughout this classy and complex thriller. **101m/B VHS, DVD.** Cary Grant, Ingrid Bergman, Claude Rains, Louis Calhern, Leopoldine Konstantin, Reinhold Schunzel, Moroni Olsen; ***D:*** Alfred Hitchcock; ***W:*** Ben Hecht; ***C:*** Ted Tetzlaff; ***M:*** Roy Webb.

The Notorious Lady 🦴🦴½ **1927** Englishman Stone kills the man he finds in Bedford's room, believing him to be his wife's lover. He's mistaken but she lies to save him and Stone takes off for the diamond mines in Africa. Bedford hears he's dead and sets out, seeking the truth. **79m/B VHS.** Lewis Stone, Barbara Bedford, Earl Metcalfe, Francis McDonald; ***D:*** King Baggot; ***C:*** Gaetano Antonio "Tony" Gaudio.

Notting Hill 🦴🦴🦴 **1999 (PG-13)** Romantic comedy that can coast by on charm alone. Roberts is not playing herself (okay, so there are, possibly, some similarities). She is playing a famous and neurotic movie star, Anna Scott, who's filming on location in London. She meets cute with shy travel bookstore owner William Thacker (Grant) and the unexpected twosome are soon spending a lot of time together. Trouble immediately begins when the paparazzi find out about their affair and William finds his face splashed all over the tabloids and reporters camped out in his garden. Ifans is a scene stealer as William's grubby and crazy housemate. **123m/C VHS, DVD.** Julia Roberts, Hugh Grant, Hugh Bonneville, Rhys Ifans, Tim (McInnerny) McInnery, Gina McKee, James Dreyfus, Richard McCabe, Emma Chambers; ***D:*** Roger Michell; ***W:*** Richard Curtis; ***C:*** Michael Coulter; ***M:*** Trevor Jones.

Nous N'Irons Plus au Bois 🦴🦴 **1969** On the outskirts of a forest held by the Germans, a small group of French resistance fighters capture a German soldier during WWII. He actually wants to join forces with them, however, after falling in love with a lovely young French girl. In French; subtitled in English. **98m/C VHS.** *FR* Marie-France Pisier, Siegfried Rauch, Richard Leduc; ***D:*** Georges Dumoulin.

Nouvelle Vague 🦴🦴½ *New Wave* **1990** Delon is a philosopher king and Giordano a wealthy countess involved in Godard's usual sexual and political themes, which has society geared toward support of the rich. Dialogue is composed entirely of quotations. In French with English subtitles. **89m/C VHS.** *SI FR* Alain Delon, Domiziana Giordano, Roland Amstutz, Laurence Cote, Christophe Odent; ***D:*** Jean-Luc Godard; ***W:*** Jean-Luc Godard.

Novel Desires 🦴½ **1992 (R)** Brian Freedman is a best-selling author who teams up with his writing rival, Vicky Chance. But it isn't just their imaginations they give free reign to, it's all their desires as well. **80m/C VHS, DVD.** Tyler Gains, Caroline Monteith, Mitchell Clark, Lisa Hayland; ***D:*** Lawrence Unger.

November Conspiracy 🦴🦴½ **1996 (R)** Journalist Jenny Baron (Turco) is covering the presidential campaign of a senator (Segal) when she uncovers a conspiracy linking a number of assassinations and murder attempts. A computer disk reveals more information but when her lover (Benedict) is murdered during an attempted political assassination, Baron goes on the run to save her own life. **103m/C VHS.** Paige Turco, George Segal, Elliott Gould, Bo Hopkins, Dirk Benedict, Conrad Janis; ***D:*** Conrad Janis; ***W:*** Maria Grimm; ***M:*** Tony Humecke.

The November Men 🦴½ **1993 (PG)** In 1992, liberal Hollywood director Arthur Gwenlyn (Williams) begins filming a thriller about an assassin after a presidential candidate. But cinematographer Elizabeth (Bevis) begins to suspect that Gwenlyn's actually serious about killing off some right-wing politicos and is using the production as a cover. Doesn't make a lot of sense. **98m/C VHS.** Paul W. Williams, James Andronica, Leslie Bevis, Robert Davi; ***D:*** Paul W. Williams; ***W:*** James Andronica.

November Moon 🦴🦴 *Novembermond* **1985** On the eve of WWII, Jewish November Messing (Osburg) flees Germany for what she hopes will be safety in Paris. She meets Ferial (Millet) and the two become lovers, but Ferial must hide November when the Nazis occupy the city. Ferial also decides to take a position on a Nazi-run newspaper in order to gather information and protect them both. German with subtitles. **106m/C VHS, DVD.** *GE* Gabriele Osburg, Christiane Millet, Gerhard Olschewski, Daniele Delorme, Bruno Pradal, Werner Stocker; ***D:*** Alexandra von Grote; ***W:*** Alexandra von Grote; ***C:*** Bernard Zitzermann.

Novocaine 🦴🦴 **2001 (R)** Ambitious, occasionally successful blend of black comedy and film noir framed in toothy imagery. Frank (Martin) is a humdrum dentist with a thriving practice and perfect, if nutty, hygienist/fiancee (Dern). The normalcy is crushing and dread is palpable. Enter Susan (Carter), a seductive, if grungy, first-time patient with a need for painkillers. She appeals to Frank's latent desire for danger by allowing a cavity search of another kind right in the dentist's chair. From there, playing the classic noir role of the stooge, Frank makes a lot of really bad decisions. Story is pretty unbelievable, but the screwball quality keeps it afloat to a point. Ultimately the plot stumbles and dueling tones bump into each other. Martin has some funny moments but Carter is still in "Fight Club" mode and falls into caricature. Laughing gas would've been preferable to the numbness of the film's ending, but points given for originality. **95m/C VHS, DVD, Wide.** *US* Steve Martin, Helena Bonham Carter, Laura Dern, Elias Koteas, Scott Caan, Keith David, Lynne Thigpen, Kevin Bacon; ***D:*** David Atkins; ***W:*** David Atkins; ***C:*** Vilko Filac; ***M:*** Steve Bartek.

Now and Forever 🦴🦴½ **1934** Penny (Temple) is the young daughter of charming widower and con man Jerry Day (Cooper). Penny's been in the care of her uncle but Jerry's decided to settle down in Paris with his lady love Toni (Lombard) and figures he can give the tyke a home. But the hard-up Jerry can't resist stealing a valuable necklace and there's much trouble ahead (and not your average happy ending). Temple steals the film from her elders. Adapted from the story "Honor Bright" by Jack Kirkland and Melville Baker. Colorized. **82m/C VHS.** Gary Cooper, Carole Lombard, Shirley Temple, Guy Standing, Charlotte Granville, Gilbert Emery; ***D:*** Henry Hathaway; ***W:*** Vincent Lawrence, Sylvia Thalberg; ***C:*** Harry Fischbeck.

Now and Forever 🦴½ **1982 (R)** Young wife's life is shattered when her unfaithful husband is wrongly accused and convicted of rape. After he is sent to prison, she begins drinking and taking drugs. From the novel by Danielle Steel, it will appeal most to those who like their romances a la Harlequin. **93m/C VHS.** *AU* Cheryl Ladd, Robert Coleby, Carmen Duncan, Christine Amor, Aileen Britton; ***D:*** Adrian Carr.

Now and Then 🦴🦴 **1995 (PG-13)** Four women hold a reunion 25 years after their most eventful childhood summer to relive the good ol' days of prepubescent triumphs and tragedies. Flashback, which thankfully comprises about 85% of the movie, explores first kisses, budding breasts, death and divorce. Despite good intentions, this nostalgic coming-of-ager for the girls is a jumbled mass of borrowed formulas that just can't shake that feeling of forced sentimentality. The young actresses are talented and charming, but their less convincing adult counterparts serve mostly as big names to draw crowds and studio support. **97m/C VHS, DVD.** Rosie O'Donnell, Melanie Griffith, Demi Moore, Rita Wilson, Christina Ricci, Thora Birch, Gaby Hoffman, Ashleigh Aston Moore, Cloris Leachman, Lolita (David) Davidovich, Bonnie Hunt, Brendan Fraser; ***D:*** Leslie Linka Glatter; ***W:*** I. Marlene King; ***C:*** Ueli Steiger; ***M:*** Cliff Eidelman.

Now, Voyager 🦴🦴🦴½ **1942** Davis plays a lonely spinster who is transformed into a vibrant young woman by therapy. She comes out of her shell to have a romantic affair with a suave European (who turns out to be married) but still utters the famous phrase "Oh, Jerry, we have the stars. Let's not ask for the moon." Definitely melodramatic, but an involving story nonetheless. Based on a novel by Olive Higgins Prouty. **117m/B VHS, DVD.** Bette Davis, Gladys Cooper, Claude Rains, Paul Henreid, Bonita Granville; ***D:*** Irving Rapper; ***W:*** Casey Robinson; ***C:*** Sol Polito; ***M:*** Max Steiner. Oscars '42: Orig. Dramatic Score.

Now You See Him, Now You Don't 🦴🦴 **1972 (G)** Light Disney comedy involving a gang of crooks who want to use a college student's invisibility formula to rob a local bank. Sequel to Disney's "The Computer Wore Tennis Shoes." **85m/C VHS.** Kurt Russell, Joe Flynn, Cesar Romero, Jim Backus; ***D:*** Robert Butler; ***M:*** Robert F. Brunner.

Nowhere 🦴🦴 **1996 (R)** Third in Araki's teen trilogy, following "Totally F***ed Up" and "The Doom Generation" is a basic day-in-the-life look at alienated L.A. 18-year-old Dark Smith (Duval), adrift in a world of consumerism and looking for love. He loves Mel (True) but she's torn between Dark and girlfriend Lucifer (Robertson), so Dark turns to Montgomery (Bexton). His friends have their own trials with drugs and sex (in various combos), and violence. Angst to the Nth degree, with Araki's imagination in wild disarray. **82m/C VHS.** James Duval, Rachel True, Kathleen Robertson, Nathan Bexton, Guillermo Diaz, Alan Boyce, Christina Applegate, Jeremy Jordan, Chiara Mastroianni, Debi Mazar, Jordan Ladd, Thyme Lewis, Sarah Lassez, Ryan Phillippe, Heather Graham, Scott Caan, Jaason Simmons, Mena Suvari; ***Cameos:*** John Ritter, Beverly D'Angelo, David Leisure, Traci Lords, Shannen Doherty; ***D:*** Gregg Araki; ***W:*** Gregg Araki; ***C:*** Arturo Smith.

Nowhere in Sight 🦴🦴½ **2001** Rehash of "Wait until Dark" has little to add that masterpiece of suspense/horror. This time, Carly Bauer (Slater) is the blind woman who's tormented in her apartment by a couple of nasty thugs. The cast does credible work with familiar material. **94m/C DVD.** Helen Slater, Mark Camacho, Richard Jutras, Max Perlus, Andrew McCarthy; ***D:*** Douglas Jackson; ***W:*** James (Momel) Lemmo; ***C:*** Bruno Philip; ***M:*** Helen Slater, David Findlay.

Nowhere Land 🦴🦴 **1998 (R)** If the feds want to make a case against the mob, they need to keep their witness alive and the dangerous beauty sent to provide protection is more than anyone bargained for. **88m/C VHS, DVD.** Peter Dobson, Dina Meyer, Francesco Quinn, Jon Polito, Martin Kove; ***D:*** Rupert Hitzig; ***W:*** Dennis Manuel; ***M:*** Russ Landau.

Nowhere to Hide 🦴🦴 **1987 (R)** A widow whose Marine officer husband has been assassinated is chased by some bad guys who are after a helicopter part (say what?) and she must fight for survival for herself and her six-year-old son. **91m/C VHS.** Amy Madigan, Daniel Hugh-Kelly, Michael Ironside; ***D:*** Mario Azzopardi; ***M:*** Brad Fiedel.

Nowhere to Hide 🦴🦴 **19??** A hitman is hired to kill a young boy who witnesses a brutal murder. The hitman, however, decides he's already killed too many people and wants to get out of the business. Will he become the next murder target? **80m/C VHS.** Paul Winfield, Rod Taylor.

Nowhere to Land 🦴🦴½ **2000** Familiar plotline still manages to be suspenseful. A bomb filmed with nerve gas is stashed aboard a Boeing 747 flying from Australia to California. It's up to pilot John Prescott (Wagner) and the feds to get the situation under control. **90m/C VHS.** Jack Wagner, Christine Elise, James B. Sikking, Ernie Hudson, Mark Lee, Helen Thomson; ***D:*** Armand Mastroianni. **CABLE**

Nowhere to Run 🦴 **1988 (R)** Slipshod version of a true story about a series of murders in Caddo, Texas in 1960. Carradine, parolled from prison, murders for revenge while six high school seniors get involved in the chase and in the seedy side of politics, police, and their own puberty. **87m/C VHS.** David Carradine, Jason Priestley, Kieran Mulroney, Henry Jones; ***D:*** Carl Franklin.

Nowhere to Run 🦴½ **1993 (R)** Kickboxer with heart seeks cross-over movie to establish real acting career. Unfortunately, even if such a movie existed, Van Damme wouldn't know what to do with it. Arquette plays the damsel in distress, facing eviction from the family farm with her two small children. Fortunately for Van Damme's escaped convict character, she is also a very lonely widow (nudge, nudge). He saves the day by abusing the daylights out of the big bad bankers, yet also finds time to play surrogate dad. Whatta guy. **95m/C VHS, DVD, 8mm.** Jean-Claude Van Damme, Rosanna Arquette, Kieran Culkin, Tiffany Taubman, Joss Ackland, Ted Levine; ***D:*** Robert Harmon; ***W:*** Joe Eszterhas, Leslie Bohem, Randy Feldman; ***C:*** David Gribble, Doug Milsome, Michael A. Benson; ***M:*** Mark Isham.

Nuclear Conspiracy 🦴½ **1985** A reporter disappears while investigating a huge nuclear waste shipment, and his wife searches for him. **115m/C VHS.** Birgit Doll, Albert Fortell.

The Nude Bomb 🦴🦴½ *The Return of Maxwell Smart* **1980 (PG)** Proof that old TV shows never die—they just get made into big screen movies. Maxwell Smart from "Get Smart" (would you believe?) tries to save the world from a bomb intended to destroy clothing and leave everyone in the buff. Old hat lines. Followed by the TV movie "Get Smart, Again!" **94m/C VHS.** Don Adams, Dana Elcar, Pamela Hensley, Sylvia Kristel, Norman Lloyd, Rhonda Fleming, Joey Forman; ***D:*** Clive Donner; ***W:*** Bill Dana; ***M:*** Lalo Schifrin.

Nude on the Moon woof! **1961** Lunar expedition discovers moon inhabited by people who bare skin as hobby. Groovy theme song, "I'm Mooning Over You, My Little Moon Doll." Part of Joe Bob Brigg's "Sleaziest Movies in the History of the World" series. **83m/C VHS, DVD.** Shelby Livingston, Pat Reilly; ***D:*** Doris Wishman; ***W:*** Doris Wishman; ***C:*** Raymond Phelan; ***M:*** Daniel Hart.

Nudity Required 🦴 **1990** Two pals use the casting couch, pretending to be Hollywood producers, to seduce young women. Silly comedy with gratuitous nudity (Ms. Newmar included). Hardly a laugh to be found. **90m/C VHS.** Julie Newmar, Troy Donahue, Brad Zutaut, Billy Frank, Ty Randolph, Alvin Silver, Eli Rich, Phil Hock; ***D:*** John Bown.

Nudo di Donna 🦴🦴🦴 *Portrait of a Woman, Nude* **1983** A witty comedy about a Venetian bookseller who is becoming tired of marital struggles with his sexy wife of 16 years. He wanders into a fashion photography shop, sees a backside nude photo of a model who looks like his wife, and he takes off in fiery pursuit to find the subject of the photo. Venetian location photography is quite nice. In Italian with English subtitles. **112m/C VHS.** *IT* Nino Manfredi, Jean-Pierre Cassel, George Wilson, Elenora Giorgi; ***D:*** Nino Manfredi.

Nueba Yol 🦴🦴 **1995** Balbuena (Marti) is a recent widower with nothing much to look forward to in his native Dominican Republic, so he's easily persuaded by fast-talking friend Fellito (Carbonell) into immigrating to New York (illegally). He has trouble finding any kind of work, is confused and intimidated by the city, and finds himself at odds with more acclimated immigrants from his homeland. Spanish with subtitles. **105m/C VHS.** Luisito Marti, Caridad Ravelo, Raul Carbonell, Joel Garcia; ***D:*** Angel Muniz; ***W:*** Angel Muniz; ***C:*** Chris Norr.

Nukie 🦴🦴½ **1993 (G)** Brothers from another planet crash land on Earth. The first one is subjected to a dizzying array of scientific experiments in Florida involving electric cattle prods. The other one, Nukie, lands in Africa and is befriended by twins from a remote tribal village. They join him in his quest to free his brother from the sadistic clutches of suntanned professionals who have lost all compassion. Important message for our youth about the dangers of a runaway technocracy. **99m/C VHS.** Glynis Johns, Steve Railsback; ***D:*** Sias Odendal.

Number One Fan 🦴½ **1994 (R)** Hollywood action star Zane Barry (McQueen) is stalked by Blair (Ammann), a fan with whom he had a brief romance. Zane manages to patch things up when fiancee Holly (Stewart) finds out but Blair's determined to be the only woman in his life. **93m/C VHS.** Chad McQueen, Catherine Mary Stewart, Renee Ammann, Hoyt Axton, Paul Bartel, Eric (DaRe) Da Re, Charles Matthau; ***D:*** Jane Simpson; ***W:*** Anthony Laurence Greene.

Number 1 of the Secret Service 🦴🦴 **1977 (PG)** A handsome secret agent must foil the plans of a millionaire industrialist to destroy the economy. Spy spoof that's marginally interesting. **87m/C VHS.** *GB* Nicky Henson, Geoffrey Keen, Sue Lloyd, Aimi MacDonald, Richard Todd; ***D:*** Lindsay Shonteff.

Number One with a Bullet 🦴🦴 **1987 (R)** Two unorthodox "odd couple" detectives are demoted after losing a key witness, but still set out on their own to unearth a drug czar. Carradine and Williams are better than this standard action material. **103m/C VHS.** Bobby DiCicco, Doris Roberts, Mykelti Williamson, Jonathan (Jon Francis) Gries, Vanessa Bell Calloway, Shari Shattuck, Robert Carradine, Billy Dee Williams, Peter Graves, Valerie Bertinelli; ***D:*** Jack Smight; ***W:*** James Belushi, Andrew Kurtzman, Rob Riley; ***C:*** Alex Phillips Jr.; ***M:*** Alf Clausen.

No. 17 🦴🦴🦴 **1932** A humorous early thriller by the Master Hitchcock, filmed before the likes of "The 39 Steps." An unsuspecting hobo accidentally discovers a jewel thief's cache. The chase is on—superb final chase sequence involving a bus and a train. Based on the play by J. Jefferson Farjeon. **64m/B VHS, DVD, 8mm.** *GB* Leon M. Lion, Anne Grey, John Stuart, Donald Calthrop; ***D:*** Alfred Hitchcock; ***W:*** Alfred Hitchcock; ***C:*** Jack Cox, Bryan Langley.

Numero Deux 🦴🦴 *Number Two* **1975** Godard explores politics, sex, and the trials of the modern family. A dissatisfied wife suffers from chronic constipation, her exhausted husband is impotent, they, their children, and grandparents all try to cope with daily life. For nine-tenths of the film Godard only used small portions of the screen (the upper left and lower right corners) to manipulate his message of frustration. It's only at the end that the full-screen is used to offer some sort of relief. In French with English subtitles. **90m/C VHS.** *FR* Sandrine Battistella, Pierre Oudry, Alex(andre) Rignault, Rachel Stefanopol; ***D:*** Jean-Luc Godard; ***W:*** Anne-Marie Mieville, Jean-Luc Godard.

The Nun 🦴🦴½ **1966** A young woman, unable to meet financial obligations, is forced into a convent. Victimized by the mother superior and betrayed by a clergyman who befriends her, she escapes from the convent and eventually ends up in a bordello, despairing and suicidal. Not a cheery story. Banned in France for two years. In French with English subtitles. **155m/C VHS.** *FR* Anna Karina, Lilo (Liselotte) Pulver, Micheline Presle, Christine Lenier, Francine Berge, Francesco Rabal, Wolfgang Reichmann, Catherine Diamant, Yori Bertin; ***D:*** Jacques Rivette.

Nuns on the Run 🦴🦴 **1990 (PG-13)** Idle and Coltrane are two nonviolent members of a robbery gang who double-cross their boss during a hold-up and disguise themselves as nuns while on the run from both the Mob and the police. Catholic humor, slapstick, and much fun with habits dominate. Idle and Coltrane do their best to keep the so-so script moving with its one-joke premise. **95m/C VHS.** Eric Idle, Robbie Coltrane, Janet Suzman, Camille Coduri, Robert Patterson, Tom Hickey, Doris Hare, Lila Kaye; ***D:*** Jonathan Lynn; ***W:*** Jonathan Lynn; ***C:*** Mike Garfath.

The Nun's Story 🦴🦴🦴½ **1959** The melancholy tale of a young nun working in the Congo and Belgium during WWII, and struggling to reconcile her free spirit with the rigors of the order. Gabrielle (Hepburn) is the daughter of a Belgian doctor (Jagger), who leaves the convent as Sister Luke. Her assignment in the Congo is at a European hospital where's she influenced by dedicated surgeon, Dr. Fortunai (Finch). But Sister Luke comes to question her vocation as the Nazis rise to power and invade her homeland. Highly acclaimed; from the Kathryn Hulme novel. **152m/C VHS.** Audrey Hepburn, Peter Finch, Edith Evans, Peggy Ashcroft, Mildred Dunnock, Dean Jagger, Beatrice Straight, Colleen Dewhurst; ***D:*** Fred Zinnemann; ***W:*** Robert Anderson; ***C:*** Franz Planer; ***M:*** Franz Waxman. British Acad. '59: Actress (Hepburn); Natl. Bd. of Review '59: Director (Zinnemann), Support. Actress (Evans); N.Y. Film Critics '59: Actress (Hepburn), Director (Zinnemann).

Nuremberg 🦴🦴½ **2000** A decent but not overly compelling intro to the allied prosecution of Nazi war criminals at Nuremberg, Germany in 1945/46. Supreme Court Justice Robert H. Jackson (Baldwin) is asked to take a leave from the bench to head up the prosecution and he decides to try a representative sample of Third Reich leaders, including Hitler's No. 2 man, Hermann Goering (the always chilling Cox). The trial scenes generally work but there's also the needless byplay of a romance between Jackson and his secretary Elsie (Hennessy). Based on the book "Nuremberg: Infamy on Trial" by Joseph E. Persico. **240m/C VHS, DVD, Wide.** Alec Baldwin, Jill(ian) Hennessey, Brian Cox, Michael Ironside, Christopher Plummer, Matt Craven, Max von Sydow, Len Cariou, Len Doncheff, Herbert Knaup; ***D:*** Yves Simoneau; ***W:*** David W. Rintels; ***C:*** Alan Dostie; ***M:*** Richard Gregoire. **CABLE**

Nurse 🦴🦴½ **1980** A recently widowed woman resumes her career as a nurse in a large urban hospital, after her son leaves for college. Based on Peggy Anderson's book. Pilot for a TV series. **105m/C VHS.** Michael Learned, Robert Reed, Antonio Fargas; ***D:*** David Lowell Rich. **TV**

The Nurse 🦴½ **1997 (R)** Nurse Laura Harriman (Zane) seeks revenge from the man she holds responsible for her father's suicide by destroying his family. **94m/C VHS.** Lisa Zane, John Stockwell, Janet Gunn, William R. Moses, Nancy Dussault, Sherrie Rose, Jay Underwood, Michael Fairman; ***D:*** Rob Malenfant; ***W:*** Richard Brandes; ***C:*** Feliks Parnell; ***M:*** Richard Bowers.

Nurse Betty 🦴🦴🦴 **2000 (R)** Small-time waitress Betty (Zellweger) fantasizes about her favorite soap opera doc David Ravell (Kinnear). But she confuses fantasy and reality after witnessing the murder of her sleazoid husband (Eckhart) over a drug deal and thinks she's a character in the soap herself. So she travels to Hollywood to be reunited with her true love, trailed by her husband's two killers (Rock and Freeman). LaBute's unpredictable black comedy represents a departure from his previous claustrophobic, misanthropic work, but retains a cynical edge. Zellweger and Freeman stand out in a stellar cast that includes Kinnear at his smarmy best. **110m/C VHS, DVD, Wide.** Renee Zellweger, Morgan Freeman, Chris Rock, Greg Kinnear, Aaron Eckhart, Crispin Glover, Allison Janney, Pruitt Taylor Vince, Kathleen Wilhoite, Harriet Harris, Susan Barnes, Sheila Kelley, Steven Culp; ***D:*** Neil LaBute; ***W:*** John C. Richards; ***C:*** Jean-Yves Escoffier; ***M:*** Rolfe Kent. Golden Globes '01: Actress—Mus./Comedy (Zellweger).

Nurse Edith Cavell 🦴🦴🦴 **1939** Fine performances in this true story of Britain's famous nurse who aided the Belgian underground during WWI, transporting wounded soldiers out of the German-occupied country. Decidedly opposes war and, ironically, was released just as WWII began to heat up in 1939. **95m/B VHS.** George Sanders, Edna May Oliver, ZaSu Pitts, Robert Coote, May Robson, Anna Neagle; ***D:*** Herbert Wilcox.

Nurse Marjorie 🦴🦴 **1920** Aristocratic nurse Marjorie (Minter) falls in love and marries the leader of the Labor Party, much to her family's dismay. Based on the play by Israel Zangwill. Minter made four films with director Taylor, whose murder in 1922 has never been solved. **?m/B VHS.** Mary Miles Minter, Clyde Fillmore, George Periolat, Mollie McConnell, Frank Leigh, Vera Lewis; ***D:*** William Desmond Taylor; ***W:*** Julia Crawford Ivers.

Nurse on Call 🦴 **1988** A bevy of trampy nurses cavort throughout a big city hospital. Softcore. **80m/C VHS.** Anne Tilson, Jennie Martinez, Christopher Floyd.

The Nut 🦴🦴½ **1921** Charlie Jackson (Fairbanks) is a wacky, wealthy inventor who falls for Estrell Wynn (De La Motte), a society gal dedicated to improving the lives of underprivileged children. He tries to aid her in a variety of ways—none of which work out as he expects. The usually swashbuckling Fairbanks does get to rescue the heroine. **61m/B VHS.** Douglas Fairbanks Sr., Marguerite de la Motte, William E. (W.E., William A., W.A.) Lowery; ***D:*** Theodore Reed; ***W:*** William Parker.

Nutcase 🦴 **1983** A trio of young children in New Zealand attempt to thwart a group of terrorists who threaten to reactivate a large city's volcanoes unless they are given a large sum of money. Novel twist there. **49m/C VHS.** *NZ* Nevan Rowe, Ian Watkin, Michael Wilson; ***D:*** Roger Donaldson.

The Nutcracker Prince 🦴🦴 **1991** The classic children's Christmas tale comes alive in this feature-length animated special. **75m/C VHS, 8mm.** *CA* ***D:*** Paul Schibli; ***V:*** Kiefer Sutherland, Megan Follows, Michael MacDonald, Phyllis Diller, Peter O'Toole.

Nutcracker Sweet 🦴 **1984** Ridiculous drama about a beautiful and powerful socialite (Collins) who runs a renowned ballet company with an iron fist. A Russian ballerina defects and infiltrates Collins's company to try out her own treacherous motives. **101m/C VHS.** Joan Collins, Finola Hughes, Paul Nicholas; ***D:*** Anwar Kawadri.

Nutcracker: The Motion Picture 🦴🦴½ **1986** A lavish, stage-bound filmization of the Tchaikovsky ballet, designed by Maurice Sendak. **82m/C VHS.** ***D:*** Carroll Ballard.

Nuts 🦴🦴🦴 **1987 (R)** A high-priced prostitute attempts to prove her sanity when she's accused of manslaughter. Ashamed of her lifestyle, and afraid of her reasons for it, her parents attempt to institutionalize her. A filmed version of Tom Topor's play that manages to retain its mesmerizing qualities. Fine performances, although the funnygirl goes over the top on several occasions. **116m/C VHS, 8mm.** Barbra Streisand, Richard Dreyfuss, Maureen Stapleton, Karl Malden, James Whitmore, Robert Webber, Eli Wallach, Leslie Nielsen, William Prince, Dakin Matthews, Hayley Taylor Block; ***D:*** Martin Ritt; ***W:*** Tom Topor, Darryl Ponicsan, Alvin Sargent; ***C:*** Andrzej Bartkowiak; ***M:*** Barbra Streisand.

Nuts in May 🦴🦴 **1976** Two smug, middle-aged, middle-class vegetarians go on a camping trip and totally alienate their cynical, working-class fellow campers. **84m/C VHS.** *GB* Alison Steadman; ***D:*** Mike Leigh. **TV**

The Nutt House 🦴½ **1995 (PG-13)** Identical twins—separated at birth—grow up to be a slimy politician and a nutcase (living up to the family name) with multiple personalities. Naturally, when the two are reunited it makes for lots of outrageous complications. **90m/C VHS, DVD.** Stephen Kearney, Traci Lords, Amy Yasbeck; ***Cameos:*** Stella Stevens, Robert Mandan, Catherine Bach; ***D:*** Adam Rifkin; ***W:*** Ron Zwang, Scott Spiegel, Sam Raimi; ***C:*** Bernd Heinl; ***M:*** Cameron Allan.

The Nutty Professor 🦴🦴🦴 **1963** A mild-mannered chemistry professor creates a potion that turns him into a suave, debonair, playboy type with an irresistible attraction to women. Lewis has repeatedly denied the slick character is a Dean Martin parody, but the evidence is quite strong. Easily Lewis's best film. **107m/C VHS, DVD, Wide.** Jerry Lewis, Stella Stevens, Del Moore, Kathleen Freeman, Howard Morris, Les Brown, Med Flory, Norman Alden, Milton Frome, Buddy Lester, Henry Gibson; ***D:*** Jerry Lewis; ***W:*** Bill Richmond, Jerry Lewis; ***C:*** Wallace Kelley; ***M:*** Walter Scharf.

The Nutty Professor 🦴🦴🦴 **1996 (PG-13)** Remake of the 1963 Jerry Lewis comedy stars Murphy as Professor Sherman Klump, a severely overweight but bright man whose heft gets in the way of his love life. He takes a swig of his own secret potion and is transformed into the slim and suave Buddy Love. Only the formula isn't perfect and seems to wear off at the worst possible times. After a string of bad movies, Murphy may have stumbled upon his own formula for a comeback by relinquishing creative control and concentrating on the comedy. Reminiscent of "Coming to America," Murphy plays eight different roles. The fat and fart jokes are plentiful and so are the laughs. **96m/C VHS, DVD, Wide.** Eddie Murphy, Jada Pinkett Smith, James Coburn, Dave Chappelle; ***D:*** Tom Shadyac; ***W:*** David Sheffield, Barry W. Blaustein, Steve Oedekerk, Tom Shadyac; ***C:*** Julio Macat; ***M:*** David Newman. Oscars '96: Makeup; Natl. Soc. Film Critics '96: Actor (Murphy).

Nutty Professor 2: The Klumps 🦴🦴½ **2000 (PG-13)** Sequel to the 1996 hit finds Murphy working overtime as Sherman Klump attempts to remove the DNA of his alter ego Buddy Love from his system. Once Buddy escapes, he steals Sherman's latest experiment, a youth serum. Buddy also complicates Sherman's relationship with a beautiful colleague (Jackson) and the entire Klump clan. Expanding a one-joke scene from the original is risky, but Murphy and the writers manage to pull it off rather impressively. Yes, the humor is crude, (the more uptight may even say offensive) but the story is funny and interesting while the characters, if not always appealing, are sympathetic and genuine. **105m/C VHS, DVD, Wide.** Eddie Murphy, Janet Jackson, Anna Maria Horsford, Melinda McGraw, Richard Gant, John Ales, Larry Miller, Chris Elliott, Earl Boen, Kathleen Freeman, Charles Napier, Jamal Mixon, Nikki Cox; ***D:*** Peter Segal; ***W:*** Barry W. Blaustein, David Sheffield, Chris Weitz, Paul Weitz, Steve Oedekerk; ***C:*** Dean Semler; ***M:*** David Newman.

A Nymphoid Barbarian in Dinosaur Hell woof! **1994** Nuclear holocaust survivors, human and otherwise, vie for the affections of the last woman alive, a voluptuous nymphoid barbarian. **90m/C VHS, DVD.** Linda Corwin, Paul Guzzi; ***D:*** Bret Piper; ***W:*** Bret Piper.

Nyoka and the Tigermen *Nyoka and the Lost Secrets of Hippocrates; Perils of Nyoka* **1942** The adventures of the jungle queen Nyoka and her rival Vultura in their search for the lost tablets of Hippocrates. In 15 episodes. **250m/B VHS.** Kay Aldridge, Clayton Moore; ***D:*** William Witney.

O 🦴🦴🦴 **2001 (R)** Apparently Hollywood has discovered that this Shakespeare fella can do some writin'. An exclusive South Carolina high school serves as background for this updated teen "Othello," which substitutes basketball for battle. Odin (Phifer) is the sole black student at Palmetto Grove Academy due to his hoops prowess. He has an intimate relationship with Desi (Stiles, in her third Bard adaptation in as many years), the daughter of the school's dean. Hugo (Hartnett), the envious son of the basketball coach (Sheen), plots Odin's disgrace and destruction by poisoning his mind against

Desi. Although blasted by some critics as full of skimpy plot devices, there's not much that's not taken straight from the source material. Filmed in 1999, it was pulled by skittish studio bigwigs following the Columbine shootings and not released until 2001. **94m/C VHS, DVD, Wide.** *US* Mekhi Phifer, Josh Hartnett, Julia Stiles, Elden (Ratliff) Henson, Andrew Keegan, Rain Phoenix, John Heard, A.J. (Anthony) Johnson, Martin Sheen; ***D:*** Tim Blake Nelson; ***W:*** Brad Kaaya; ***C:*** Russell Fine; ***M:*** Jeff Danna.

O Brother Where Art Thou? 🦴🦴½ **2000 (PG-13)** Clooney stars as chain gang escapee Ulysses Everett McGill, who, along with fellow escapees Pete and Delmar (Turturro and Nelson), sets out on an "Odessey"-like journey through Depression-era Mississippi bound for home, where waits McGill's wife, Penny (Hunter). What the trio encounter along the way are a number of Coenesque situations and characters that, when all is said and done, seem like just that—individual situations that never really add up to a cohesive whole. They fit well enough to comprise a pretty enjoyable film, though. Fine performances by Clooney, Nelson, and Coen regulars Goodman and Turturro. **103m/C VHS, DVD, Wide.** George Clooney, Tim Blake Nelson, John Turturro, Holly Hunter, John Goodman, Charles Durning, Del Pentacost, Michael Badalucco, Brian Reddy, Wayne Duvall, Ed Gale, Ray McKinnon, Daniel von Bargen, Royce D. Applegate, Frank Collison, Lee Weaver, Stephen (Steve) Root, Musetta Vander, Chris Thomas King, Mia Tyler, Christy Taylor; ***D:*** Joel Coen; ***W:*** Ethan Coen, Joel Coen; ***C:*** Roger Deakins; ***M:*** T Bone Burnett, Chris Thomas King, Carter Burwell. Golden Globes '01: Actor—Mus./Comedy (Clooney).

O Lucky Man! 🦴🦴🦴🦴 **1973 (R)** Surreal, black comedy following the rise and fall and eventual rebirth of a modern British coffee salesman. Several actors play multiple roles with outstanding performances throughout. Price's excellent score combines with the hilarity for an extraordinary experience. **178m/C VHS.** *GB* Malcolm McDowell, Ralph Richardson, Rachel Roberts, Arthur Lowe, Alan Price, Helen Mirren, Mona Washbourne, Warren Clarke; ***D:*** Lindsay Anderson; ***M:*** Alan Price. British Acad. '73: Support. Actor (Lowe).

O Pioneers! 🦴🦴½ **1991 (PG)** Lange plays Alexandra Bergson, an unmarried woman at the turn of the century, who inherits her family's Nebraska homestead because her father knows how much she loves the land. Although the family has prospered through Alexandra's smart investments, her brothers come to resent her influence. When her first love returns after 15 years and the romance is rekindled, family resentments surface once again. Based on the novel by Willa Cather. A Hallmark Hall of Fame presentation. **99m/C VHS.** Jessica Lange, David Strathairn, Tom Aldredge, Reed Edward Diamond, Anne Heche, Heather Graham, Josh Hamilton, Leigh Lawson, Graham Beckel; ***D:*** Glenn Jordan; ***W:*** Glenn Jordan. **TV**

O Quatrilho 🦴🦴 **1995** Two young couples from Italy immigrate to southern Brazil in the 1910s, hoping to find their fortunes. Thrifty peasant Angelo (Paternost) marries romantic Teresa (Pillar) and goes into business with the equally romantic Massimo (Campos), who's married to the thrifty Pierina (Pires). The grain mill thrives but the romantic half of each couple delve into some illicit amore and decide to flee while their left-behind spouses discover their own attractions. A happy ending is had by all (this must be a fairytale). Lots of high-gloss gush. Based on the novel by Jose Clemente Pozenat. Portuguese and Italian with subtitles. **120m/C VHS.** *BR* Gloria Pires, Patricia Pillar, Bruno Campos, Alexandre Paternost; ***D:*** Fabio Barreto; ***W:*** Leopoldo Serran; ***C:*** Felix Monti; ***M:*** Caetano Veloso.

The Oak 🦴🦴½ **1993** Morgenstern grieves over the loss of her father until she realizes she can't get rid of the body. Her difficulties in locating adequate medical facilities reflect the nightmarish realities of pre-1990 communist Romania. Potentially farcical aspects of storyline are successfully removed by violence in following scene involving Morgenstern and a band of roaming soldiers. A tragicomic look at obstinate communist bureaucrats and the wily, willful peasants who overcome them. Based on a novel by Ion Baiesu. In Romanian with English subtitles. **105m/C VHS.** *RO* Maia Morgenstern, Razvan Vasilescu, Victor Rebengiuc, Dorel Visan, Mariana Mihut, Dan Condurache, Virgil Andriescu, Leopoldina Balanuta, Matei Alexandru, Gheorghe Visu, Magda Catone, Ionel Mahailescu; ***D:*** Lucian Pintilie; ***W:*** Lucian Pintilie.

Oasis of the Zombies 🦴 *Bloodsucking Nazi Zombies; Treasure of the Living Dead* **1982** European students set out to find buried treasure in Saharan oasis but instead find bevy of hungry Nazis with eating disorders. Franco directed under the name "A.M. Frank." **75m/C VHS, DVD, Wide.** *SP FR* Manuel Gelin, France Jordan, Jeff Montgomery, Miriam Landson, Eric Saint-Just, Caroline Audret, Henry Lambert; ***D:*** Jess (Jesus) Franco; ***W:*** A. L. Mariaux.

Oath of Vengeance 🦴½ **1944** Billy the Kid rides the West once more. **50m/B VHS.** Buster Crabbe, Al "Fuzzy" St. John, Jack Ingram, Charles "Blackie" King; ***D:*** Sam Newfield.

The Object of Beauty 🦴🦴🦴 **1991 (R)** Two Americans, trapped in Europe by their love of pleasure and their lack of money, bicker over whether to sell their one object of value—a tiny Henry Moore sculpture. When it disappears, their relationship is challenged. Excellent acting and telling direction. Forces an examination of one's own value placement. **105m/C VHS, DVD.** Andie MacDowell, John Malkovich, Joss Ackland, Lolita (David) Davidovich, Peter Riegert, Bill Paterson, Rudi Davies, Ricci Harnett; ***D:*** Michael Lindsay-Hogg; ***W:*** Michael Lindsay-Hogg; ***C:*** David Watkin; ***M:*** Tom Bahler.

The Object of My Affection 🦴🦴½ **1998 (R)** Nina (Aniston) is a Brooklyn social worker with an overbearing boyfriend, Vince (Pankow), she doesn't really love. Unfortunately, the man she does fall for is handsome gay teacher George (Rudd), who's just broken up with his pretentious boyfriend Joley (Daly), and who winds up renting Nina's spare room. When Nina discovers she's pregnant, she decides George would make a terrific father and asks him to raise the baby with her. But both turn out to have very unrealistic expectations about friendship and romance. Mix of humor and tears, with good performances, particularly by the appealing leads. Adapted from the novel by Stephen McCauley. **112m/C VHS, DVD, Wide.** Jennifer Aniston, Paul Rudd, John Pankow, Timothy Daly, Alan Alda, Nigel Hawthorne, Allison Janney, Amo Gulinello, Steve Zahn, Daniel Cosgrove; ***D:*** Nicholas Hytner; ***W:*** Wendy Wasserstein; ***C:*** Oliver Stapleton; ***M:*** George Fenton.

Object of Obsession 🦴½ **1995 (R)** One wrong phone call propels divorcee Margaret into an affair with a stranger that leads to kinky psycho/sexual games and revenge. **91m/C VHS, DVD.** Erika Anderson, Scott Valentine; ***D:*** Alexander Gregory (Gregory Dark) Hippolyte; ***W:*** Brad (Sean) Marlowe; ***C:*** Wally Pfister.

Objective, Burma! 🦴🦴🦴🦴 **1945** Deemed by many to be the greatest and most moving WWII production released during the war. American paratroopers are dropped over Burma where their mission is to destroy a Japanese radar station. The Americans led by Flynn are successful in wiping out the station, but they are spotted and descended upon by Japanese forces. Impeded from returning to Allied lines, the American soldiers must try to survive enemy encounters, exhaustion, starvation, and the elements until they are rescued. Splendid performance by Flynn and exceptional direction from Walsh; excellent performances enhanced by energetic score. **142m/B VHS.** Errol Flynn, James Brown, William Prince, George Tobias, Henry Hull, Warner Anderson, Richard Erdman, Mark Stevens, Anthony Caruso, Hugh Beaumont, John Alvin, William (Bill) Hudson, Lester Matthews, George Tyne, Erville Alderson; ***D:*** Raoul Walsh; ***W:*** Ranald MacDougall, Lester Cole; ***C:*** James Wong Howe; ***M:*** Franz Waxman.

Oblivion 🦴🦴½ **1994 (PG-13)** In this sci-fi western, set in the year 3031, its cowboys versus the aliens. A sheriff's son (Paul) returns to the town of Oblivion to avenge his father's murder and finds a reptilian extraterrestrial (Divoff) terrorizing the community. **94m/C VHS.** Richard Joseph Paul, Andrew Divoff, Jackie Swanson, Meg Foster, Isaac Hayes, Julie Newmar, Carel Struycken, George Takei; ***D:*** Sam Irvin; ***W:*** Peter David; ***M:*** Pino Donaggio.

Oblomov 🦴🦴🦴½ *A Few Days in the Life of I.I. Oblomov; Neskolko Dnei iz Zhizni I.I. Oblomov* **1981** A production of the classic Goncharov novel about a symbolically inert Russian aristocrat whose childhood friend helps him find a reason for action. Well made, with fine performances. In Russian with English subtitles. **145m/C VHS.** *RU* Oleg Tabakov, Elena Solovei; ***D:*** Nikita Mikhalkov.

The Oblong Box 🦴🦴 *Edgar Allen Poe's The Oblong Box* **1969 (PG)** Coffins, blood, and live corpses fill drawn-out and lifeless adaptation of Edgar Allan Poe story. English aristocrat Price attempts to hide his disfigured brother in an old tower. Brother predictably escapes and rampages through town before being killed. **91m/C VHS.** *GB* Vincent Price, Christopher Lee, Alastair Williamson, Hilary Dwyer, Peter Arne, Harry Baird, Carl Rigg, Sally Geeson, Maxwell Shaw; ***D:*** Gordon Hessler; ***W:*** Lawrence Huntington; ***C:*** John Coquillon.

The Obsessed 🦴🦴 *The Late Edwina Black* **1951** Uninspiring story with Farrar suspected of murdering his wife. Competent performances, but this mystery isn't developed with any sense of style and the killer's real identity will be obvious to anyone watching. Cliches and stereotyped situations don't add anything. **77m/B VHS.** *GB* David Farrar, Geraldine Fitzgerald, Roland Culver, Jean Cadell, Mary Merrall, Harcourt Williams, Charles Heslop, Ronald Adam, Sydney Monkton; ***D:*** Maurice Elvey; ***W:*** Charles Frank, David Evans; ***C:*** Stephen Dade.

Obsessed 🦴½ **1988 (PG-13)** Semi-realistic tale of a woman's exhausting desire for revenge against hit-and-run driver who killed her son. Cast acceptable but lack of psychological foundation weakens plot. **100m/C VHS.** Kerrie Keane, Alan Thicke, Colleen Dewhurst, Saul Rubinek, Daniel Pilon, Lynne Griffin; ***D:*** Robin Spry. Genie '89: Support. Actress (Dewhurst).

Obsession 🦴🦴½ **1976 (PG)** A rich, lonely businessman meets a mysterious young girl in Italy, the mirror image of his late wife who was killed by kidnappers. Intriguing suspense film that's not quite up to comparisons with Hitchcock thrillers. Music by Hitchcock-collaborator Herrmann. **98m/C VHS, DVD, Wide.** Cliff Robertson, Genevieve Bujold, John Lithgow; ***D:*** Brian DePalma; ***W:*** Paul Schrader; ***C:*** Vilmos Zsigmond; ***M:*** Bernard Herrmann.

Obsession: A Taste for Fear 🦴½ **1989 (R)** Diane's high fashion models are being killed and although there are plenty of suspects, she can't find the killer. **90m/C VHS.** Virginia Hey, Gerard Darmon, Carlo Mucari; ***D:*** Piccio Raffanini.

Obsessive Love 🦴🦴½ **1984** A lonely, mentally unstable typist (Mimieux) becomes obsessed with her soap opera hero and decides to go to Hollywood to seduce him. She transforms herself into a sleek and stunning Hollywood temptress to woo him, and at first he goes along with her—until he realizes that she is insane. An average made-for-TV movie of the older woman/younger man genre. **97m/C VHS.** Yvette Mimieux, Simon MacCorkindale, Kin Shriner, Constance McCashin, Allan Miller, Lainie Kazan; ***D:*** Steven Hilliard Stern.

O.C. and Stiggs 🦴½ **1987 (R)** Two teens spend a summer harassing a neighbor and his family. Flimsy attempts at comedy fall flat. A failed adaptation of a National Lampoon short story, it was held for three years before release. **109m/C VHS.** Daniel H. Jenkins, Neill Barry, Jane Curtin, Tina Louise, Jon Cryer, Dennis Hopper, Paul Dooley, Ray Walston, Louis Nye, Martin Mull, Melvin Van Peebles; ***D:*** Robert Altman; ***W:*** Donald Cantrell.

An Occasional Hell 🦴🦴½ **1996 (R)** Ernest DeWalt (Berenger) is an ex-cop turned writer and college professor. He investigates the death of a fellow professor (Lang) at the behest of the beautiful widow (Golino) and then learns the lady is the prime suspect. Filmed in South Carolina and based on the novel by Silvis, who wrote the screenplay. **93m/C VHS, DVD.** Tom Berenger, Valeria Golino, Kari Wuhrer, Robert Davi, Stephen Lang, Richard Edson, Geoffrey Lewis; ***D:*** Salome Breziner; ***W:*** Randall Silvis; ***C:*** Mauro Fiore; ***M:*** Anton Sanko.

The Occultist woof! **1989** Satan worshippers do the dance of death as they skin men alive for their evil purposes. **82m/C VHS.** Rick Gianasi; ***D:*** Tim Kincaid; ***W:*** Tim Kincaid.

Ocean Drive Weekend woof! **1985 (PG-13)** Several college students congregate at "Ocean Drive" for a weekend of beer, sex, and dancing. Stereotypical characters, lack of plot, and poor versions of 1960 classics combine for boring and inane comedy. **98m/C VHS.** Robert Peacock, Charles Redmond, Tony Freeman; ***D:*** Brian Thomas Jones.

Ocean's 11 🦴🦴½ **1960** A Rat Pack romp. Spyros Acebos (Tamiroff) comes up with a plan to simultaneously rob five Las Vegas casinos on New Year's Eve. Danny Ocean (Sinatra) will lead his buddies—all of whom are veterans of the 82nd Airborne Division—in the action by shutting off all the electricity. The planning's elaborate but the plan itself goes wrong (so what else is new) and the gang can't get their stolen loot out of the city. **148m/C VHS, DVD, Wide.** Frank Sinatra, Dean Martin, Sammy Davis Jr., Angie Dickinson, Peter Lawford, Richard Conte, Cesar Romero, Joey Bishop, Akim Tamiroff, Henry Silva, Buddy Lester, Norman Fell, Red Skelton, Shirley MacLaine, George Raft; ***D:*** Lewis Milestone; ***W:*** Harry Brown, Charles Lederer; ***C:*** William H. Daniels; ***M:*** Nelson Riddle.

Ocean's Eleven 🦴🦴🦴 **2001 (PG-13)** Stylish, fun remake of the 1960 Rat Pack caper flick measures up to the original in Cool Factor and surpasses it in plot and action. In this version, Danny Ocean (Clooney) is an ex-con with a taste for the grift and a grudge against powerful casino owner Benedict (Garcia). Backed by an eclectic, amusingly quirky crew, he encounters complications when his ex (Roberts) turns out to be involved with Benedict. Great cast looks like they're having a blast (especially Gould and Reiner, who make the most of small but showy roles) as Soderburgh's "Midas touch" streak continues. **116m/C VHS, DVD, Wide.** *US* George Clooney, Brad Pitt, Andy Garcia, Matt Damon, Julia Roberts, Don Cheadle, Casey Affleck, Scott Caan, Elliott Gould, Bernie Mac, Carl Reiner, Edward Jemison, Shaobo Qin; ***Cameos:*** Henry Silva, Angie Dickinson, Holly Marie Combs, Joshua Jackson, Topher Grace, Steve Lawrence, Eydie Gorme, Wayne Newton; ***D:*** Steven Soderbergh; ***W:*** Ted Griffin; ***C:*** Steven Soderbergh; ***M:*** David Holmes.

Oceans of Fire 🦴 **1986 (PG)** Average rehash of the tension-filled world of oil riggers. Lives of two ex-cons are threatened when they hire on as divers for world's deepest undersea oil rig. **100m/C VHS.** Gregory Harrison, Billy Dee Williams, Cynthia Sikes, Lyle Alzado, Tony Burton, Ray "Boom Boom" Mancini, David Carradine, Ken Norton; ***D:*** Steve Carver.

Octagon 🦴🦴 **1980 (R)** Norris protects a woman from threatening Ninja warriors in average kung-fu adventure. Enough action and violence for fans of the genre. **103m/C VHS.** Chuck Norris, Karen Carlson, Lee Van Cleef, Kim Lankford, Art Hindle, Jack Carter; ***D:*** Eric Karson; ***W:*** Paul Aaron, Leigh Chapman.

Octaman 🦴½ **1971** Comical thriller featuring non-threatening octopus-man discovered by scientists in Mexico. Rip-off of director Essex's own "Creature from the Black Lagoon." Not without its curiosity factor: young Rick Baker designed the octopus man, while actress Angeli died of a drug overdose during filming. **79m/C VHS.** Kerwin Mathews, Pier Angeli, Harry Guardino, David Essex, Jeff Morrow, Norman Fields; ***D:*** Harry Essex; ***W:*** Harry Essex; ***C:*** Robert Caramico.

Octavia 1982 (R) A contemporary fable about a blind girl who befriends a convict and learns about life and love. **93m/C VHS.** Susan Curtis; ***D:*** David Beaird; ***W:*** David Beaird.

The October Man 1948 When a model is found murdered, a stranger with mental problems must prove his innocence to others and himself. Strong characters make good, suspenseful mystery reminiscent of Hitchcock. **95m/B VHS.** *GB* John Mills, Joan Greenwood, Edward Chapman, Joyce Carey, Kay Walsh, Felix Aylmer, Juliet Mills; ***D:*** Roy Ward Baker; ***W:*** Eric Ambler.

October Sky 1999 (PG) Relates the true story of young Homer Hickam Jr. (Gyllenhaal), who rose from a gloomy West Virginia mining town to become a NASA engineer. Spurred by the launch of Sputnik and a supportive teacher (Dern), Homer and three of his friends experiment with rockets with the hope of winning college scholarships. The boys battle the skepticism of their peers and families as well as the looming possibility of a future in the mines. Entertaining and uplifting without resorting to melodrama and sentimentality. Adapted from Hickam's memoir "Rocket Boys." **108m/C VHS, DVD.** Jake Gyllenhaal, Chris Cooper, Laura Dern, Chris Owen, William Lee Scott, Chad Lindberg, Natalie Canerday, Scott Miles, Randy Stripling, Chris Ellis; ***D:*** Joe Johnston; ***W:*** Lewis Colick; ***C:*** Paul Murphy; ***M:*** Mark Isham.

Octopus 2000 (PG-13) Giant mutant octopus lurking in the ocean depths is disturbed by a U.S. Navy submarine and decides to make it lunch. This, however, is not the only bad news. Seems the sub was transporting a terrorist who escapes in the confusion, and winds up on a cruise ship. He thinks he's safe but our eight-legged horror is just getting started. Special effects are pretty lame but the film doesn't take itself serously and the humor covers a lot of holes. **99m/C VHS, DVD, Wide.** Carolyn Lowery, David Beecroft, Jay Harrington, Ravil Isyanov; ***D:*** John Eyres; ***W:*** Michael D. Weiss; ***C:*** Adolfo Bartoli; ***M:*** Marco Marinangelo. **VIDEO**

Octopussy 1983 (PG) The Bond saga continues as Agent 007 is on a mission to prevent a crazed Russian general from launching a nuclear attack against the NATO forces in Europe. Lots of special effects and gadgets keep weak plot moving. **140m/C VHS, DVD, Wide.** *GB* Roger Moore, Maud Adams, Louis Jourdan, Kristina Wayborn, Kabir Bedi, Steven Berkoff; ***D:*** John Glen; ***W:*** Michael G. Wilson; ***C:*** Alan Hume; ***M:*** John Barry.

The Odd Angry Shot ½ 1979 Australian soldiers fighting in Vietnam discover the conflict is not what they expected. Ironic perspective of men struggling with their feelings about the war. More of an unremarkable drama with comic overtones than a combat film, it will appeal to those who prefer good direction to bloodshed. **90m/C VHS.** *AU* Graham Kennedy, John Hargreaves, John Jarratt, Bryan Brown, Graeme Blundell, Richard Moir, Ian Gilmour, John Allen, Brandon Burke, Graham Rouse, Tony Barry, Max Cullen, John Fitzgerald, Ray Meagher; ***D:*** Tom Jeffrey; ***W:*** Tom Jeffrey; ***C:*** Donald McAlpine; ***M:*** Walter (Wendy) Carlos.

Odd Birds ½ 1985 Coming of age drama set in 1965 California. Shy 15-year-old Joy Chan is a Chinese-American dreaming of becoming an actress. Her widowed immigrant mother wants Joy to have a practical profession—like nursing. Longing for someone to understand Joy meets Brother Murphy, a math teacher at the local boys school. Murphy's been trying to reconcile his religious commitment with his unorthodox views. It isn't long before these two individualists recognize a fellow kindred spirit. **87m/C VHS.** Michael Moriarty, Donna Lai Ming Lew, Nancy Lee, Bruce Gray, Karen Maruyama, Scott Crawford; ***D:*** Jeanne Collachia; ***W:*** Jeanne Collachia.

The Odd Couple ½ 1968 (G) Two divorced men with completely opposite personalities move in together. Lemmon's obsession with neatness drives slob Matthau up the wall, and their inability to see eye-to-eye results in many hysterical escapades. A Hollywood rarity, it is actually better in some ways than Neil Simon's original Broadway version. Simon based the characters on brother Danny and his roommates. Basis for the hit TV series. **106m/C VHS, DVD, Wide.** Jack Lemmon, Walter Matthau, Herb Edelman, John Fiedler, Monica Evans, Carol(e) Shelley; ***D:*** Gene Saks; ***W:*** Neil Simon; ***C:*** Robert B. Hauser.

The Odd Job 1978 Insurance salesman Chapman, depressed after his wife leaves him, hires a hit man to kill him. Chapman then has a hard time shaking his stalker after deciding he wants to live. Monty Python fans will enjoy seeing extroupe member Chapman again, but the comic's heart isn't in this unoriginal story. **100m/C VHS.** *GB* Graham Chapman; ***D:*** Peter Medak; ***M:*** Howard Blake.

Odd Jobs 1985 (PG-13) When five college friends look for jobs during summer break, they wind up running their own moving business with the help of the mob. Good comic talent, but a silly slapstick script results in only a passable diversion. **89m/C VHS.** Paul Reiser, Scott McGinnis, Rick Overton, Robert Townsend; ***D:*** Mark Story; ***W:*** Robert Conte; ***C:*** Arthur Albert, Peter Collister; ***M:*** Robert Folk.

Odd Man Out ½ *Gang War* 1947 An Irish revolutionary is injured during a robbery attempt. Suffering from gunshot wounds and closely pursued by the police, he must rely on the help of others who could betray him at any moment. A gripping tale of suspense and intrigue that will keep the proverbial seat's edge warm until the final credits. Adapted from F.L. Green's novel, previously filmed as "The Last Man." **111m/B VHS, DVD.** *GB* James Mason, Robert Newton, Dan O'Herlihy, Kathleen Ryan, Cyril Cusack; ***D:*** Carol Reed; ***W:*** F.L. Green, R.C. Sherriff; ***C:*** Robert Krasker; ***M:*** William Alwyn. British Acad. '47: Film.

Odd Obsession ½ *The Key* 1960 One of Ichikawa's first films, about an elderly Japanese gentleman with a young wife whose feelings of jealousy and impotence eventually wreak havoc on the marriage. In Japanese with English subtitles. **96m/C VHS.** *JP* Machiko Kyo, Ganjiro Nakamura; ***D:*** Kon Ichikawa. Golden Globes '60: Foreign Film.

The Odd Squad 1986 (R) Five GIs in WWII defend a bridge from the enemy, and manage in doing so to have loads of laughs. **82m/C VHS.** Johnny Dorelli, Vincent Gardenia; ***D:*** E.B. (Enzo Barboni) Clucher.

Oddball Hall 1991 (PG) Two aging jewel thieves hide out in the African wilds, masquerading as powerful "wizards." When they head back to civilization, an African tribe beseeches the phony sorcerers to cure their long drought. **87m/C VHS.** Don Ameche, Burgess Meredith; ***D:*** Jackson Hunsicker; ***W:*** Jackson Hunsicker.

Oddballs woof! 1984 (PG-13) In another attempt to capitalize on the success of Bill Murray's "Meatballs," this summer camp story follows three campers and their pathetic attempts to lose their virginity. Brooks has his moments, but there is little else to recommend here. **92m/C VHS.** Foster Brooks, Jason Sorokin, Wally Wodchis, Konnie Krome; ***D:*** Miklos Lente.

Odds Against Tomorrow 1959 Compulsive gambler/nightclub singer Johnny Ingram (Belafonte) owes big money to gangster Bacco (Kuluva). He hooks up with racist ex-con Earl Slater (Ryan) and former policeman Dave Burke (Begley) to rob a bank but everything goes wrong. Ingram and Slater manage to escape to a nearby oil storage area but the racial tensions between the two are proving deadlier than the cops on their trail. Based on the novel by William P. McGivern; because of the blacklist screenwriter Polonsky was "fronted" by John O. Killens. Polonsky officially received credit for his work in 1996. **120m/B VHS.** Harry Belafonte, Robert Ryan, Shelley Winters, Ed Begley Sr., Gloria Grahame, Will Kuluva, Richard Bright; ***D:*** Robert Wise; ***W:*** Abraham Polonsky, Nelson Gidding; ***C:*** Joseph Brun; ***M:*** John Lewis.

Odds and Evens ½ 1978 (PG) Italian supercops pretend they don't have badges in order to clean up illegal betting and gambling rings in sunny Miami. Odds are this spaghetti cop-o-rama won't keep Morpheus at bay. **109m/C VHS.** *IT* Terence Hill, Bud Spencer; ***D:*** Sergio Corbucci.

Ode to Billy Joe 1976 (PG) The 1967 Bobby Gentry hit song of the same title is expanded to tell why a young man jumped to his death off the Tallahatchie Bridge. The problems of growing up in the rural South and teenage romance do not match the appeal of the theme song. Benson and O'Connor, however, work well together. **106m/C VHS.** Robby Benson, Glynnis O'Connor, Joan Hotchkis, Sandy McPeak, James Best; ***D:*** Max Baer Jr.

The Odessa File ½ 1974 (PG) During 1963, a German journalist attempts to track down some SS war criminals who have formed a secret organization called ODESSA. The story, from Frederick Forsyth's novel, drags in some places, but the scene where bad guy Schell and reporter Voight finally confront each other is a high point. **128m/C VHS, DVD.** *GB GE* Jon Voight, Mary Tamm, Maximilian Schell, Maria Schell, Derek Jacobi, Peter Jeffrey, Klaus Lowitsch, Kurt Meisel, Hannes Meesember, Garfield Morgan, Shmuel Rodensku, Ernst Schroder, Noel Willman, Hans Canineberg, Towje Kleiner, Gunnar Moiler; ***D:*** Ronald Neame; ***W:*** Kenneth Ross, George Markstein; ***C:*** Oswald Morris; ***M:*** Andrew Lloyd Webber.

The Odyssey ½ 1997 (PG-13) Lavish TV miniseries based on Homer's 2,700-year-old epic poem, relating the adventures of King Odysseus of Ithaca. On the day his son is born to faithful wife Penelope (Scacchi), Odysseus (Assante) is commanded by the goddess Athena (Rossellini) to leave his home and travel to battle the Trojans. Little does he realize that this is the beginning of a 20-year sojourn, where additional trials include sea monsters, the Cyclops, the Kingdom of the Dead, enchantress Circe (Peters), and getting shipwrecked on the isle of Calypso (Williams), who wants to keep the hunk around. But even Odysseus realizes there's no place like home. **203m/C VHS, DVD.** Armand Assante, Greta Scacchi, Geraldine Chaplin, Eric Roberts, Bernadette Peters, Irene Papas, Vanessa L(ynne) Williams, Christopher Lee, Isabella Rossellini, Jeroen Krabbe, Nicholas Clay, Ron Cook, Michael J. Pollard, Paloma Baeza, Alan Cox, Heathcote Williams; ***D:*** Andrei Konchalovsky; ***W:*** Andrei Konchalovsky, Chris Solimine; ***C:*** Sergei Koslov; ***M:*** Eduard Artemyev. **TV**

The Odyssey of the Pacific ½ *The Emperor of Peru* 1982 Three young Cambodian refugees encounter retired train engineer Rooney living in the woods where a railway station once thrived. Together they work to restore an old locomotive. The ordinary, inoffensive script will not endanger quality family time. **82m/C VHS.** *CA* Mickey Rooney, Monique Mercure; ***D:*** Fernando Arrabal.

Oedipus Rex *Edipo Re* 1967 A new twist on the famous tragedy as Pasolini gives the story a modern prologue and epilogue. The classic plot has Oedipus spiraling downward into moral horror as he tries to avoid fulfulling the prophecy that he will murder his father and sleep with his mother. Cross-cultural curiosities include Japanese music and Lenin-inspired songs, some written by Pasolini, who also stars as the high priest. In Italian with English subtitles. **110m/C VHS.** *IT* Franco Citti, Silvana Mangano, Alida Valli, Julian Beck, Pier Paolo Pasolini; ***D:*** Pier Paolo Pasolini.

Of Freaks and Men *Pro Urodov i Lyudej* 1998 Kinky Russian melodrama set in pre-revolutionary St. Petersburg. Pornographer Johann and his assistant Viktor specialize in selling photos and films featuring half-naked women getting flogged. They manage to insinuate themselves into two upper class Russian households and involve the families in some secret sadomasochistic games. Russian with subtitles. **93m/C VHS, DVD.** *RU* Tatiana Polonskaia, Sergei Makovetsky, Dinara Drukarova, Anzhelika Nevolina, Viktor Sukhorukov, Aleksei De, Chingiz Tsydendabayev, Vadim Prokhorov, Aleksandr Mezentsev, Igor Shibanov, Darya Lesnikova; ***D:*** Alexei Balabanov; ***W:*** Alexei Balabanov; ***C:*** Sergei Astakhov; ***M:*** Eric Neveux.

Of Human Bondage 1934 The first movie version of W. Somerset Maugham's classic novel in which a young, handicapped medical student falls in love with a crude cockney waitress, in a mutually destructive affair. Established Davis's role as the tough, domineering woman. Remade in 1946 and 1964. **84m/B VHS, DVD.** Bette Davis, Leslie Howard, Frances Dee, Reginald Owen, Reginald Denny, Alan Hale; ***D:*** John Cromwell; ***W:*** Lester Cohen; ***C:*** Henry W. Gerrard; ***M:*** Max Steiner.

Of Human Bondage 1964 An essentially decent man falls fatally in love with an alluring but heartless waitress, who subtly destroys him. Based on the W. Somerset Maugham novel. Miscast and least interesting of the three film versions, although Novak gives a good performance. **100m/B VHS.** *GB* Kim Novak, Laurence Harvey, Robert Morley, Roger Livesey, Siobhan McKenna; ***D:*** Henry Hathaway, Ken Hughes; ***W:*** Bryan Forbes; ***C:*** Oswald Morris.

Of Human Hearts ½ 1938 Rural life just before the Civil War sets up this cornpone tale of family strife. Huston is a stern preacher who has his family living in near poverty as an example of sacrifice to his flock. Son Stewart wants to study medicine and Bondi, defying her husband, manages to fund his dream. Only Stewart becomes so engrossed by his ambitions that he ignores the family, even after his father dies and his mother is left poor and alone. Then Stewart joins the Civil War as a doctor where he meets President Lincoln (Carradine), who tells him he should never neglect his mother. Oy. Well, the cast is good. Adapted from the story "Benefits Forgot" by Honore Morrow. **100m/B VHS.** James Stewart, Beulah Bondi, Walter Huston, John Carradine, Guy Kibbee, Charles Coburn, Ann Rutherford, Charley Grapewin, Gene Lockhart; ***D:*** Clarence Brown; ***W:*** Bradbury Foote; ***C:*** Clyde De Vinna.

Of Love and Shadows 1994 (R) Political photojournalist Francisco (Banderas) begins investigating the disappearance of a self-proclaimed saint after the bloody 1973 coup in Chile. He's aided by aristocratic Chilean Irene (Connelly), who's engaged to her Army captain cousin Gustavo (Gallardo) but can't resist Francisco's ever-smoldering charms. The intrepid duo naturally find lots of corruption. Based on the novel by Isabel Allende; shot on location in Argentina. **103m/C VHS.** Antonio Banderas, Jennifer Connelly, Stefania Sandrelli, Camillo Gallardo, Patricio Contreras; ***D:*** Betty Kaplan; ***W:*** Donald Freed; ***C:*** Felix Monti; ***M:*** Jose Nieto.

Of Mice and Men 1939 A powerful adaptation of the classic Steinbeck tragedy about the friendship between two itinerant Southern ranch hands during the Great Depression. Chaney is wonderful as the gentle giant and mentally retarded Lenny, cared for by migrant worker Meredith. They both get into an irreversible situation when a woman is accidentally killed. **107m/C VHS, DVD.** Lon Chaney Jr., Burgess Meredith, Betty Field, Bob Steele, Noah Beery Jr., Charles Bickford; ***D:*** Lewis Milestone; ***W:*** Eugene Solow; ***C:*** Norbert Brodine; ***M:*** Aaron Copland.

Of Mice and Men 1981 TV remake of the classic Steinbeck tale, casting TV's Baretta (Blake) as George and Quaid as Lenny. Worth watching. **150m/C VHS.** Robert (Bobby) Blake, Randy Quaid, Lew Ayres, Mitchell Ryan, Ted Neeley, Cassie Yates, Pat Hingle, Whitman Mayo, Dennis Fimple, Pat Corley; ***D:*** Reza Badiyi. **TV**

Of Mice and Men ½ 1992 (PG-13) Set on the migratory farms of California, John Steinbeck's novel covers the friendship of the simple-minded Lenny, his protector George, and a flirtatious farm wife who doesn't know Lenny's strength. Director Sinise got permission from Steinbeck's widow to film the novel (actually the third adaptation). **110m/C VHS, DVD, Wide.** John Malkovich, Sherilyn Fenn, Casey Siemaszko, Joe Morton, Ray Walston, Gary Sinise, John Terry, Richard Riehle; ***D:*** Gary Sinise; ***W:*** Horton Foote; ***C:*** Kenneth Macmillan; ***M:*** Mark Isham.

Of Unknown Origin ♂♂½ 1983 (R) Weller encounters a mutated rampaging rat in his New York townhouse while his family is away on vacation. His house becomes the battleground in a terror-tinged duel of survival. A well-done rat thriller not for those with a delicate stomach. Based on the novel "The Visitor." **88m/C VHS.** *CA* Peter Weller, Jennifer Dale, Lawrence Dane, Kenneth Welsh, Louis Del Grande, Shannon Tweed; *D:* George P. Cosmatos; *W:* Brian Taggert; *C:* Rene Verzier.

Off and Running ♂½ 1990 (PG-13) Struggling actress Cyd (Lauper) is working as a mermaid at a Miami hotel lounge when her horse trainer boyfriend Woody is suddenly murdered by a psycho thug (Belzer). Turns out he's after a key hidden in a necklace now in Cyd's possession. Cyd goes on the run and gets some help from failed golf pro Jack (Keith) as they try to stay one step ahead of the killer and discover what the key unlocks. **91m/C VHS.** Cyndi Lauper, David Keith, Richard Belzer, David Thornton, Anita Morris; *D:* Edward Bianchi; *W:* Eugene Glazer; *C:* Andrzej Bartkowiak; *M:* Mason Daring.

Off Beat ♂½ 1986 (PG) A shy librarian unluckily wins a spot in a police benefit dance troupe, and then falls in love with a tough police woman. With a screenplay by playwright Medoff, and a good supporting cast, it still manages to miss the mark. **92m/C VHS.** Judge Reinhold, Meg Tilly, Cleavant Derricks, Fred Gwynne, John Turturro, Jacques D'Amboise, James Tolkan, Joe Mantegna, Harvey Keitel, Amy Wright, Christopher Noth; *D:* Michael Dinner; *W:* Mark Medoff; *C:* Carlo Di Palma; *M:* James Horner.

Off Limits ♂♂½ 1953 When a boxing manager is drafted into the Army, he freely breaks regulations in order to train a fighter as he sees fit. Hope and Rooney, while not in peak form, make a snappy duo in this amusing romp. **89m/B VHS.** Bob Hope, Mickey Rooney, Marilyn Maxwell, Marvin Miller; *D:* George Marshall.

Off Limits ♂½ 1987 (R) A spree of murders involving Vietnamese hookers draws two cops from the Army's Criminal Investigation Department into the sleazy backstreets of 1968 Saigon. There is little mystery as to who the killer is in this tale that seems written more for the sake of foul language and gratuitous gunfights than actual plot. **102m/C VHS.** Willem Dafoe, Gregory Hines, Fred Ward, Scott Glenn, Amanda Pays, Keith David, David Alan Grier; *D:* Christopher Crowe; *W:* Christopher Crowe, Jack Thibeau; *M:* James Newton Howard.

Off the Mark ♂♂ 1987 (R) Neely is a young athlete suffering from a childhood affliction that causes spasms in his legs. Facing the ultimate challenge, he must overcome his handicap and defeat a talented woman athlete and a Russian student in a triathalon competition. An unremarkable effort, it had a limited one-week run in theatres. **89m/C VHS.** Mark Neely, Terry Farrell, Jon Cypher, Clarence Gilyard Jr.; *D:* Bill Berry; *C:* Arledge Armenaki.

Off the Wall ♂ 1982 (R) Two hitchhikers wind up in a southern maximum security prison after being accused of a crime they did not commit. What follows is a series of shenanigans as they try to escape. This supposed comedy falls flat in every way with the possible exception of Arquette's portrayal of the governor's daughter. **86m/C VHS.** Paul Sorvino, Rosanna Arquette, Patrick Cassidy, Billy Hufsey, Monte Markham, Mickey Gilley; *D:* Rick Friedberg.

Off Your Rocker ♂½ 1980 Representatives of a corporate conglomerate find that the residents of Flo Adler's Mapleview Nursing Home can still muster stiff resistance to a threatened takeover. **99m/C VHS.** Milton Berle, Red Buttons, Lou Jacobi, Dorothy Malone, Helen Shaver, Sharon Acker, Helen Hughes; *D:* Morley Markson, Larry Pall.

The Offence ♂♂♂ *Something Like the Truth* 1973 (R) Connery plays a London detective who beats a suspected child molester to death during a police interrogation. Turns out he's reacting to a long-buried molestation incident from his own childhood. A chilling psycho-drama highlighted by a strong lead performance by Connery. **108m/C VHS.** *GB* Sean Connery, Trevor Howard, Vivien Merchant, Ian Bannen, Derek Newark, John Hallam, Peter Bowles; *D:* Sidney Lumet; *W:* John Hopkins.

Offerings ♂ 1989 (R) After a boy is tormented by a gang of children who cause him to fall down a well, his resulting brain injuries turn him into a psychopathic killer. Seeking revenge ten years later, he systematically murders his oppressors, offering bits of their anatomy to the one girl who treated him kindly. A typical slasher movie, the plot is only slightly better than the worst examples of the genre. **96m/C VHS.** G. Michael Smith, Loretta L. Bowman; *D:* Christopher Reynolds.

Office Killer ♂ 1997 (R) Just when you thought it was safe to run with scissors! Dorine (Kane) is a meek copy editor who is in danger of losing her job. After securing her position by accidentally electrocuting a fellow employee, Dorine begins some downsizing of her own. Pent up frustrations cause her sanity to take a personal leave of absence, and she begins to streamline her department by folding, spindling and mutilating her co-workers. Office tramp Kim (Ringwald) suspects the truth, but no one believes her. Stab at horror-black comedy isn't very scary or very funny. First directorial effort by still photographer Cindy Sherman, who didn't adapt very well to people moving around. **83m/C VHS.** Carol Kane, Molly Ringwald, Jeanne Tripplehorn, Barbara Sukowa, Michael Imperioli, David Thornton, Alice Drummond, Mike Hodge; ***Cameos:*** Eric Bogosian; *D:* Cindy Sherman; *W:* Tom Kalin, Todd Haynes, Elise MacAdam; *C:* Russell Fine; *M:* Evan Lurie.

Office Romances ♂♂ 1986 A woman who has moved to London from the country is seduced by her employer. Because of her plain appearance, she is flattered by his attention even though he is married and has no real feelings for her. Competently made, nonetheless hard to watch because of the slow pace. **60m/C VHS.** *GB* Judy Parfitt, Ray Brooks, Suzanne Burden.

Office Space ♂♂½ 1998 (R) Cartoon bigwig Mike Judge tries his hand at live action in this satire of white collar corporate drudgery. Peter (Livingston) is a drone for a software company well on his way to a nervous breakdown when a hypnosis mishap opens his eyes. He becomes so apathetic toward his job that he can't even muster up the energy to quit. His new no-work ethic is mistaken by a pair of corporate headhunters as "middle-management potential," and he is promoted as his pals Michael (Herman) and Samir (Naidu) are laid off. Frustrated in his attempts to be down-sized, Peter hatches a plot to embezzle the company. Stephen Root, as disgruntled nerd Milton, steals scenes like they were office supplies in an unlocked cabinet. Adapted from animated shorts made by Judge before the Beavis and Butthead gravy train rolled into the station. **89m/C VHS, DVD.** Mike Judge, John C. McGinley, Paul Willson, Orlando Jones, Alexandra Wentworth, Michael McShane, Ron Livingston, Jennifer Aniston, David Herman, Ajay Naidu, Gary Cole, Diedrich Bader, Stephen (Steve) Root, Richard Riehle; *D:* Mike Judge; *W:* Mike Judge; *C:* Tim Suhrstedt; *M:* John (Gianni) Frizzell.

An Officer and a Gentleman ♂♂♂½ 1982 (R) Young drifter Gere, who enters Navy Officer Candidate School because he doesn't know what else to do with his life, becomes a better person almost despite himself. Winger is the love interest who sets her sights on marrying Gere, and Gossett is the sergeant who whips him into shape. Strong performances by the whole cast made this a must-see in 1982 that is still appealing, despite the standard Hollywood premise. ♪Up Where We Belong; Hungry for Your Love; An Officer and a Gentleman; Treat Me Right; Tunnel of Love. **126m/C VHS, DVD, Wide.** Richard Gere, Louis Gossett Jr., David Keith, Lisa Eilbacher, Debra Winger, David Caruso, Robert Loggia, Lisa Blount; *D:* Taylor Hackford; *W:* Douglas Day Stewart; *C:* Donald E. Thorin; *M:* Jack Nitzsche. Oscars '82: Song ("Up Where We Belong"), Support. Actor (Gossett); Golden Globes '83: Song ("Up Where We Belong"), Support. Actor (Gossett).

Official Denial ♂♂½ 1993 A victim of an alien abduction becomes the only hope for a captured space being. Can Paul help the alien escape from a special Air Force UFO group and what secrets will he uncover if he does? **86m/C VHS.** Parker Stevenson, Erin Gray, Dirk Benedict, Chad Everett; *D:* Brian Trenchard-Smith; *W:* Bruce Zabel; *M:* Garry McDonald, Laurie Stone. **TV**

The Official Story ♂♂♂½ *La Historia Oficial; The Official History; The Official Version* 1985 (R) A devastating drama about an Argentinian woman who realizes her young adopted daughter may be a child stolen from one of the thousands of citizens victimized by the country's repressive government. A powerful, important film. In Spanish with English subtitles or dubbed. **112m/C VHS, DVD.** *AR* Norma Aleandro, Hector Alterio, Chunchuna Villafane, Patricio Contreras; *D:* Luis Puenzo; *W:* Luis Puenzo, Aida Bortnik. Oscars '85: Foreign Film; Cannes '85: Actress (Aleandro); Golden Globes '86: Foreign Film; L.A. Film Critics '85: Foreign Film; N.Y. Film Critics '85: Actress (Aleandro).

The Offspring ♂♂ *From a Whisper to a Scream* 1987 (R) In four stories of past evils Price reveals his hometown can force folks to kill. Not the usual Price material: dismemberment, cannibalism, and necrophilia clash with his presence. Strong yuk factor. **99m/C VHS, DVD.** Vincent Price, Cameron Mitchell, Clu Gulager, Terry Kiser, Susan Tyrrell, Harry Caesar, Rosalind Cash, Martine Beswick, Angelo Rossitto, Lawrence Tierney; *D:* Jeff Burr; *W:* Jeff Burr, C. Courtney Joyner; *M:* John Beal.

The Ogre ♂♂ *Der Unhold* 1996 Misfit Abel (Malkovich) desperately believes in his own personal power to change the world around him. He winds up captured by the Germans in 1939 and is held in a POW camp until chance lands him in the service of a group of high-ranking Nazis, including Hermann Goring (Spengler). Goring sends Abel out to recruit young boys into becoming military conscripts and he gains the nickname of the Ogre, the mythic devourer of children. Adapted from Michael Tournier's novel "The Erl King." **117m/C VHS, DVD, Wide.** *GE FR GB* John Malkovich, Volker Spengler, Armin Mueller-Stahl, Gottfried John; *D:* Volker Schlondorff; *W:* Volker Schlondorff, Jean-Claude Carriere; *C:* Bruno de Keyzer; *M:* Michael Nyman.

Oh, Alfie ♂♂ *Alfie Darling* 1975 (R) In every man's life, there comes a time to settle down... but never when you're having as much fun as Alfie! Inadequate sequel to "Alfie." **99m/C VHS.** *GB* Joan Collins, Alan Price, Jill Townsend; *D:* Ken Hughes; *W:* Ken Hughes.

Oh, Bloody Life! ♂♂½ 1988 Young actress faces deportation during the Stalin era in Hungary because of her aristocratic family ties. In Hungarian with English subtitles. **115m/C VHS.** *HU* Udvaros Dorottya, Szacsvay Laszlo, Kern Andras, Bezeredi Zoltan, Oze Lajos, Lukacs Margit; *D:* Peter Bacso; *W:* Peter Bacso. Montreal World Film Fest. '88: Actress (Dorottya).

Oh! Calcutta! ♂½ 1972 Film version of the first nude musical to play on Broadway, which caused a sensation in the late 1960s. It's really a collection of skits, some of which were written by such notables as John Lennon, Sam Shepard, and Jules Feiffer. And it's really not that funny or erotic. **105m/C VHS.** Bill Macy, Mark Dempsey, Raina Barrett, Samantha Harper, Patricia Hawkins, Mitchell McGuire; *D:* Guillaume Martin Aucion; *W:* Robert Benton, Jules Feiffer, Dan Greenberg, John Lennon, Jacques Levy, Sam Shepard, Leonard Melfi, David Newman, Clovis Trouille, Sherman Yellen; *C:* Frank Biondo, Arnold Giordano, Jerry Sarcone; *M:* Prof. Peter Schickele, Robert Dennis.

Oh Dad, Poor Dad (Momma's Hung You in the Closet & I'm Feeling So Sad) ♂♂ 1967 Cult fave black comedy about a bizarre family on a vacation in Jamaica. The domineering mother travels with a coffin containing the stuffed body of her late husband. Additional corpses abound. Based on the play by Arthur L. Kopit. **86m/C VHS.** Rosalind Russell, Robert Morse, Barbara Harris, Hugh Griffith, Lionel Jeffries, Jonathan Winters, Cyril Delavanti, Hiram Sherman, George Kirby, Janis Hansen; *D:* Richard Quine; *W:* Herbert Baker, Pat McCormick, Ian Bernard; *C:* Geoffrey Unsworth; *M:* Neal Hefti.

Oh, God! ♂♂½ 1977 (PG) God, in the person of Burns, recruits Denver as his herald in his plan to save the world. Despite initial skepticism, Denver, in his film debut, keeps faith and is rewarded. Sincere performances and optimistic end make for satisfying story. Followed by "Oh God! Book 2" and "Oh God! You Devil." **104m/C VHS.** George Burns, John Denver, Paul Sorvino, Ralph Bellamy, Teri Garr, William Daniels, Donald Pleasence, Barnard Hughes, Barry Sullivan, Dinah Shore, Jeff Corey, David Ogden Stiers; *D:* Carl Reiner; *W:* Larry Gelbart. Writers Guild '77: Adapt. Screenplay.

Oh, God! Book 2 ♂ 1980 (PG) Burns returns as the "Almighty One" in strained sequel to "Oh God!" This time he enlists the help of a young girl to remind others of his existence. The slogan she concocts saves God's image, but not the movie. Followed by "Oh, God! You Devil." **94m/C VHS.** George Burns, Suzanne Pleshette, David Birney, Louanne, Conrad Janis, Wilfrid Hyde-White, Hans Conried, Howard Duff; *D:* Gilbert Cates; *M:* Charles Fox.

Oh, God! You Devil ♂♂ 1984 (PG) During his third trip to earth, Burns plays both the Devil and God as he first takes a struggling musician's soul, then gives it back. A few zingers and light atmosphere save unoriginal plot. The second sequel to "Oh, God!" **96m/C VHS.** George Burns, Ted Wass, Roxanne Hart, Ron Silver, Eugene Roche, Robert Desiderio; *D:* Paul Bogart; *W:* Andrew Bergman; *M:* David Shire.

Oh, Heavenly Dog! ♂♂ 1980 (PG) A private eye returns from the dead as a dog to solve his own murder. Man's best friend and intelligent to boot. The famous dog Benji's third film, and his acting improves with each one. Adults may find this movie slow, but kids will probably love it. **104m/C VHS.** Chevy Chase, Jane Seymour, Omar Sharif, Robert Morley, Susan Kellerman; *D:* Joe Camp; *W:* Joe Camp, Rod Browning.

Oh, Mr. Porter ♂♂ 1937 Billeted at an obscure railway post, the stationmaster hero renovates the place and hires a special train to transport the area soccer team. Trouble arises when the train is hijacked by gun smugglers. **85m/B VHS.** *GB* Will Hay, Moore Marriott, Graham Moffatt, Frederick Piper; *D:* Marcel Varnel.

Oh Susannah ♂½ 1938 Robbed and thrown from a train, Autry and the two drifters who rescue him follow the thieves to Mineral Springs. Their journey is plagued by too many songs and the bad guys are predictably punished in the end. **59m/B VHS.** Gene Autry, Boothe Howard, Smiley Burnette, Frances Grant, Donald Kirke, Clara Kimball Young; *D:* Joseph Kane.

Oh, What a Night ♂♂ 1992 (PG-13) Bittersweet coming of age tale about a lonely 17-year-old (Haim) who has moved with his father and stepmother to a chicken farm in 1955 Ontario. After struggling with the untimely death of his mother, Haim falls in love with an older woman who has a husband and two kids. Features a great '50s soundtrack and beautiful scenes of the Canadian countryside. **93m/C VHS.** *CA* Corey Haim, Barbara Williams, Keir Dullea, Genevieve Bujold, Robbie Coltrane; *D:* Eric Till.

O'Hara's Wife ♂½ 1982 Loving wife Harley continues to care for her family even after her untimely death. Only husband Asner, however, can see her ghost. Lightweight drama traps good cast. **87m/C VHS.** Ed Asner, Mariette Hartley, Jodie Foster, Tom Bosley, Perry Lang, Ray Walston; *D:* William S. Bartman; *W:* William S. Bartman; *M:* Artie Butler. **TV**

O.H.M.S. ♂½ 1937 Convoluted story about a New York hood (Ford) who flees to England where he joins the British Army by posing as a Canadian. He buddies up with Mills and they both fall for Lee. His regiment is sent to China, via ship, and Lee just happens to be a stowaway. In China, Ford manages to prove his worth by saving Lee from bandits. Maybe it's not supposed to make sense. **71m/B VHS.** *GB* Wallace Ford, John Mills, Anna Lee, Frank Cellier, Frederick Leister, Peter Croft; ***D:*** Raoul Walsh.

Oil **1978 (PG)** Seven men fight a raging oil fire that threatens to destroy an entire country. Unfortunately, the movie is unable to ignite any interest at all. **95m/C VHS.** Ray Milland, Woody Strode, Stuart Whitman, Tony Kendall, William Berger; ***D:*** Mircea Dragan.

The O.J. Simpson Story **1994** Tacky tabloid TV movie follows incredibly exploited story about former gridiron star Simpson (Hosea) who's accused of murdering blonde babe ex-wife Nicole (Tuck). Mainly stolid performances though Weitz is slick as Simpson lawyer Robert Shapiro. Told in flashbacks, the actual murder is never depicted. Director Jerry Friedman took his name off the credits, leaving the standard Smithee pseudonym as a replacement. **90m/C VHS.** Bobby Hosea, Jessica Tuck, James Handy, Kimberly Russell, David Roberson, Bruce Weitz; ***D:*** Alan Smithee; ***W:*** Stephen Harrigan; ***M:*** Harold Kloser.

Oklahoma! ½ **1955 (G)** Jones's film debut; a must-see for musical fans. A cowboy and country girl fall in love, but she is tormented by another unwelcomed suitor. At over two hours, cuteness wears thin for some. Actually filmed in Arizona. Adapted from Rodgers and Hammerstein's broadway hit with original score; choreography by Agnes de Mille. ♫Oh, What a Beautiful Morning; Surrey with the Fringe on Top; I Cain't Say No; Many a New Day; People Will Say We're in Love; Poor Jud Is Dead; All 'Er Nuthin'; Everything's Up to Date in Kansas City; The Farmer and the Cowman. **145m/C VHS, DVD, Wide.** Gordon MacRae, Shirley Jones, Rod Steiger, Gloria Grahame, Eddie Albert, Charlotte Greenwood, James Whitmore, Gene Nelson, Barbara Lawrence, Jay C. Flippen; ***D:*** Fred Zinnemann; ***W:*** Sonya Levien, William Ludwig; ***C:*** Robert L. Surtees; ***M:*** Richard Rodgers, Oscar Hammerstein. Oscars '55: Sound, Scoring/Musical.

Oklahoma Annie **1951** Storekeeper Canova joins the new sheriff in booting undesirables out of town, and tries to sing her way into his heart. Amazingly, it works—not for delicate ears. **90m/C VHS.** Judy Canova, Fuzzy Knight, Grant Withers, John Russell, Denver Pyle, Allen Jenkins, Almira Sessions; ***D:*** R.G. Springsteen.

Oklahoma Badlands ½ **1948** Lane and his horse outsmart a corrupt newspaper publisher trying to steal land from a female rancher. An early directorial work for veteran stuntman Canutt. **59m/B VHS.** Allan "Rocky" Lane, Mildred Coles; ***D:*** Yakima Canutt.

Oklahoma Bound **1981** A feisty farmer tries to save his failing farm through a series of ostensibly comedic, unsuccessful schemes. **92m/C VHS.** F.E. Bowling, Dan Jones; ***D:*** Patrick C. Poole.

Oklahoma Crude ½ **1973 (PG)** Sadistic oil trust rep Palence battles man-hating Dunaway for her well. Drifter Scott helps her resist on the promise of shared profits. In this 1913 setting, Dunaway tells Scott she wishes she could avoid men altogether, but later settles for him. **108m/C VHS.** George C. Scott, Faye Dunaway, John Mills, Jack Palance, Harvey Jason, Woodrow Parfrey; ***D:*** Stanley Kramer; ***W:*** Marc Norman; ***C:*** Robert L. Surtees; ***M:*** Henry Mancini.

Oklahoma Cyclone ½ **1930** A group of bronco busters find action and adventure on the prairie. Second of eight talkies in Steele series, includes his first of few singing roles. **64m/B VHS.** Bob Steele, Al "Fuzzy" St. John, Nita Ray, Charles "Blackie" King; ***D:*** John P. McCarthy.

Oklahoma Kid **1939** Offbeat, hilarious western with Bogie as the villain and gunfighter Cagney seeking revenge for his father's wrongful death. Highlight is Cagney's rendition of "I Don't Want To Play In Your Yard," complete with six-shooter accompaniment. **82m/B VHS.** James Cagney, Humphrey Bogart, Rosemary Lane, Ward Bond, Donald Crisp, Charles Middleton, Harvey Stephens; ***D:*** Lloyd Bacon; ***C:*** James Wong Howe; ***M:*** Max Steiner.

The Oklahoman **1956** A routine western with some trivia value. Town doc McCrea helps Indian Pate keep his land. Talbott plays Indian maiden in same year as her title role in Daughter of Jekyll. Continuity buffs will note Hale wears the same outfit in most scenes. **80m/C VHS.** Joel McCrea, Barbara Hale, Brad Dexter, Gloria Talbott, Verna Felton, Douglas Dick, Michael Pate, Scotty Beckett; ***D:*** Francis D. Lyon.

Okoge *Fag Hag* **1993** Rueful sexual comedy about a triangular friendship. Sayoko is a single young working woman living in a tiny Tokyo apartment. She meets the gay Noh and his older married lover Tochi and when they become friendly, Sayoko lets them use her apartment as their love nest—to the complications of all concerned. Title is a slang term used to refer to women who prefer the company of gay men. In Japanese with English subtitles. **120m/C VHS.** *JP* Misa Shimizu, Takehiro Murata, Takeo Nakahara, Masayuki Shionoya, Noriko Songoku, Kyozo Nagatsuka, Toshie Nogishi; ***D:*** Takehiro Nakajima; ***W:*** Takehiro Nakajima; ***C:*** Yoshimasa Hakata; ***M:*** Hiroshi Ariyoshi.

Old Barn Dance ½ **1938** Autry and his singing cowboys are selling horses until a crooked tractor company puts them out of business. They join a radio program, discovers that it is owned by the same company that put them out of the horse-selling business, and runs the crooks out of town. **54m/B VHS.** Gene Autry, Smiley Burnette, Roy Rogers; ***D:*** Joseph Kane.

Old Boyfriends **1979 (R)** Shire is weak as a psychologist searching for old boyfriends in order to analyze her past. Strange combination of Carradine and Belushi may draw curious fans. **103m/C VHS.** Talia Shire, Richard Jordan, John Belushi, Keith Carradine, John Houseman, Buck Henry; ***D:*** Joan Tewkesbury; ***W:*** Leonard Schrader, Paul Schrader; ***M:*** David Shire.

Old Corral *Texas Serenade* **1936** Sheriff Autry protects his love interest, a girl fleeing the Mob. **54m/B VHS.** Gene Autry, Roy Rogers, Smiley Burnette; ***D:*** Joseph Kane.

The Old Curiosity Shop ½ **1935** Webster and Benson are an old gambler and his daughter in this well-made film adaptation of the Dickens tale. Their miserly landlord tries to ruin their lives by evicting them and forcing them into a life of poverty. Remade as "Mr. Quilp" in 1957. **90m/B VHS.** Ben Webster, Elaine Benson, Hay Petrie, Beatrix Thompson, Gibb McLaughlin, Reginald Purdell; ***D:*** Thomas Bentley.

The Old Curiosity Shop *Mr. Quilp* **1975 (G)** Flat musical version of the Charles Dickens story about an evil man who wants to take over a small antique shop run by an elderly man and his granddaughter. ♫When a Felon Needs a Friend; Somewhere; Love Has the Longest Memory; Happiness Pie; The Sport of Kings; What Shouldn't Happen to a Dog; Quilp. **118m/C VHS.** *GB* Anthony Newley, David Hemmings, David Warner, Jill Bennett, Peter Duncan, Michael Hordern; ***D:*** Michael Tuchner; ***M:*** Elmer Bernstein.

The Old Curiosity Shop **1984 (G)** An animated adaptation of the classic Dickens story about a young girl and her grandfather who are evicted from their curiosity shop by an evil man. **72m/C VHS.** ***V:*** John Benton, Jason Blackwell, Wallas Easton, Penne Hackforth-Jones, Brian Harrison.

The Old Curiosity Shop ½ **1994 (PG)** Another adaptation of Charles Dickens's 1840 tale about Grandfather Trent (Ustinov), an antiques dealer who has lost his fortune through gambling and makes matters worse by borrowing money from the miserable Mr. Quilp (Courtenay). Unable to repay the debt, Trent and young granddaughter Sally (Walsh) try to escape London, which turns Quilp's wrath upon them. Fine performances and a colorful production. **280m/C VHS.** Peter Ustinov, Tom Courtenay, James Fox, Sally Walsh, William Mannering, Christopher Ettridge, Julia McKenzie, Anne White, Jean Marlow, Cornelia Hayes O'Herlihy, Michael Mears; ***D:*** Kevin Connor; ***W:*** John Goldsmith; ***C:*** Doug Milsome; ***M:*** Mason Daring. CABLE

The Old Dark House **1932** An atmospheric horror film, with more than a touch of comedy, well-directed by Whale. In an old haunted house live the bizarre Femm family: the 102 year-old patriarch (Dudgeon), an atheist son (Thesinger), a religious fanatic daughter (Moore), and a crazed pyromanic son (Wills), all watched over by the mute, scarred, and psychotic butler (Karloff's first starring role). Into this strange group wander five unsuspecting, stranded travelers who set all sorts of dastardly plots in motion. Based on the novel "Benighted" by J.B. Priestley. John Dudgeon is actually actress Elspeth Dudgeon who's playing in drag. Remade in 1963 by William Castle. **71m/B VHS, DVD.** Boris Karloff, Melvyn Douglas, Charles Laughton, Gloria Stuart, Ernest Thesiger, Raymond Massey, Lillian Bond, Eva Moore, Brember Wills, Elspeth (John) Dudgeon; ***D:*** James Whale; ***W:*** Benn W. Levy, R.C. Sherriff; ***C:*** Arthur Edeson.

Old Enough **1984 (PG)** Slow-moving coming-of-age comedy on the rich kid-poor kid friendship theme. Silver's directing debut. **91m/C VHS.** Sarah Boyd, Rainbow Harvest, Neill Barry, Danny Aiello, Susan Kingsley, Roxanne Hart, Alyssa Milano, Fran Brill, Anne Pitoniak; ***D:*** Marisa Silver; ***W:*** Marisa Silver; ***C:*** Michael Ballhaus. Sundance '84: Grand Jury Prize.

Old Explorers ½ **1990 (PG)** Two old friends refuse to let old age lessen their want for excitement, so they get together on a regular basis to set out on dangerous, imaginary adventures. They search for Atlantis, explore the Himalayan Mountains, and visit the Bermuda Triangle. After one of the men survives a stroke, the two set out on a real-life adventure on a tugboat cruising down the Mississippi River. Although the leads put in strong performances, they can't hide the slow-moving plot or the thin action sequences. Based on the play by James Cada and Mark Keller. **91m/C VHS.** Jose Ferrer, James Whitmore, Jeffrey Gadbois, Caroline Kaiser, William Warfield, Christopher Pohlad, Storm Richardson, William M. Pohlad.

Old Gringo ½ **1989 (R)** Adapted from Carlos Fuentes' novelization of writer Ambrose Bierce's mysterious disappearance in Mexico during the revolution of 1913. Features Fonda in the unlikely role of a virgin schoolteacher, Smits as her revolutionary lover, and Peck as her hero. Soggy acting by all but Peck, whose presence is wasted in a sketchy character. Technical problems and cheesy sets and costumes—look for the dusk backdrop in the dance scene and Smits' silly moustache. Better to read the book. **119m/C VHS, 8mm, Wide.** Jane Fonda, Gregory Peck, Jimmy Smits, Patricio Contreras, Jenny Gago, Gabriela Roel, Sergio Calderon, Guillermo Rios, Anne Pitoniak, Pedro Armendariz Jr., Jim Metzler; ***D:*** Luis Puenzo; ***W:*** Aida Bortnik, Luis Puenzo; ***M:*** Lee Holdridge.

Old Gun **1976** A grief-plagued doctor finds he must seek out and kill each Nazi involved in the slaughter of his wife and child to ease his pain. Excellent directing and a fully formed main character. **141m/C VHS.** Philippe Noiret, Romy Schneider, Jean Bouise; ***D:*** Robert Enrico.

Old Ironsides **1926** Silent, black-and-white version of the big budget/important director and stars action-adventure. Merchant marines aboard the famous Old Ironsides battle 19th century Barbary pirates in rousing action scenes. Home video version features an engaging organ score by Gaylord Carter. Based on the poem "Constitution" by Oliver Wendell Holmes. **111m/B VHS.** Esther Ralston, Wallace Beery, Boris Karloff, Charles Farrell, George Bancroft; ***D:*** James Cruze; ***M:*** Gaylord Carter.

The Old Lady Who Walked in the Sea *La Vieille qui Marchait dans la Mer* **1991** Eccentric Lady M (Moreau) and her equally aging ex-lover Pompilius (Serrault) have spend their lives conning the rich. Summering on the French Riviera, Lady M spots handsome beach boy/thief Lambert (Thuiller) and decides to groom him for their latest caper, a jewel heist. Meanwhile, Pompilius pursues the young Noemie (Danon) and brings her into their menage, where Lambert is instantly smitten. Their lust leads to some unexpected complications but the real drama in the film is watching old pros Moreau and Serrault at work. Based on the novel by San Antonio; French with subtitles. **95m/C VHS.** *FR* Jeanne Moreau, Michel Serrault, Luc Thuillier, Geraldine Danon; ***D:*** Laurent Heynemann; ***W:*** Dominique Roulet; ***C:*** Robert Alazraki; ***M:*** Philippe Sarde.

The Old Maid **1939** After her beau is killed in the Civil War, a woman allows her cousin to raise her illegitimate daughter, and therein begins a years-long struggle over the girl's affections. High grade soaper based on Zoe Adkin's stage adaptation of Edith Wharton's novel. **96m/B VHS.** Bette Davis, Miriam Hopkins, George Brent, Donald Crisp, Jane Bryan, Louise Fazenda, Henry Stephenson; ***D:*** Edmund Goulding; ***C:*** Gaetano Antonio "Tony" Gaudio; ***M:*** Max Steiner.

The Old Man and the Sea ½ **1958** Cuban fisherman Santiago hooks a giant marlin and battles sharks and the sea to bring his trophy home. Tracy's performance as the tough, aging fisherman garnered him his sixth Academy Award nomination and Tiomkin's beautiful score was an Oscar winner. **86m/C DVD, Wide.** Spencer Tracy, Felipe Pazos, Harry Bellaver, Don Diamond, Don Blackman, Joey Ray; ***D:*** John Sturges; ***W:*** Peter Viertel; ***C:*** James Wong Howe, Floyd Crosby; ***M:*** Dimitri Tiomkin. Oscars '59: Orig. Score (Tiomkin).

The Old Man and the Sea ½ **1990** Quinn is wonderful as Hemingway's aging Cuban fisherman, Santiago, who battles a band of marauding sharks for a giant marlin in the Gulf Stream. Unfortunately, this made-for-TV adaptation is ordinary. **97m/C VHS, DVD, Wide.** Anthony Quinn, Gary Cole, Alexis Cruz, Patricia Clarkson, Francesco Quinn; ***D:*** Jud Taylor; ***W:*** Roger O. Hirson; ***C:*** James Wong Howe; ***M:*** Bruce Broughton. TV

Old Mother Riley, Headmistress ½ **1950** Irish washerwoman Mrs. Riley (Lucan) winds up the headmistress of a girls' school that is threatened when a railroad line is planned to go through the property. **76m/B VHS.** *GB* Arthur Lucan, Kitty McShane, Enid Hewitt, Jenny Mathot, Cyril Smith; ***D:*** John Harlow; ***W:*** Jack Marks, Con West; ***C:*** Ken Talbot.

Old Mother Riley's Ghosts **1941** A group of spies "haunt" Mother Riley's castle home in a futile attempt to scare her out; she turns the tables. Some good scares and laughs. Part of the Old Mother Riley series. Look for similarities to later Monty Python films. **82m/B VHS.** *GB* Arthur Lucan, Kitty McShane, John Stuart; ***D:*** John Baxter.

Old Mother Riley's Jungle Treasure ½ **1951** Mother Riley (Lucan) and daughter Kitty (McShane) are working in an antiques shop where they discover a treasure map. So they head for the South Seas and find a pirate's ghost as well. **75m/B VHS.** *GB* Arthur Lucan, Kitty McShane, Sebastian Cabot, Garry Marsh, Roddy Hughes; ***D:*** Maclean Rogers; ***W:*** Val Valentine; ***C:*** James Wilson.

Old Mother Riley's New Venture ½ **1949** Old Mother Riley (Lucan) is hired as the manager of a hotel that's been victimized by a series of robberies. But she's soon framed for a hotel jewel heist by the real thief. **80m/B VHS.** *GB* Arthur Lucan, Kitty McShane, Chili Bouchier, Willer Neal, Sebastian Cabot; ***D:*** John Harlow; ***W:*** Jack Marks, Con West; ***C:*** James Wilson.

The Old Settler ½ **2001** Elizabeth Barney (Rashad) is middleaged and has never been married, thus making her an old settler according to sister Quilly (Allen). Quilly has been abandoned by her husband and is living with Elizabeth in her Harlem apartment because times are hard. In fact to make a little extra cash, Elizabeth rents a room to handsome country boy Husband Witherspoon (Robinson), fresh off the bus from South Carolina. Eventually Husband, who's been disappointed in love, turns his attentions to Elizabeth, much to the bitter Quilly's astonishment. Based on the play by John Henry Redwood. **90m/C VHS.** Phylicia Rashad, Debbie Allen, Bumper Robinson, Eartha D. Robinson, Crystal Fox, Randy J. Goodwin; ***D:*** Debbie Allen; ***W:*** Shauneille Perry. **TV**

Old Spanish Custom 🦴 *The Invader* **1936** Only a Keaton fan could love this comedy, set in Spain and filmed in England. One of his rarest—and poorest—sound films. He plays a bumbling rich yachtsman smitten with Tovar, a Spanish maiden who uses him to make her lover jealous. **58m/B VHS.** *GB* Buster Keaton, Lupita Tovar, Lyn Harding, Esme Percy; ***D:*** Adrian Brunel.

Old Swimmin' Hole 🦴🦴 *When Youth Conspires* **1940** Small-town friends Moran and Jones try to bring their single parents together; his mother can't afford to finance his dream to be a doctor. Dull, melodramatic ode to heartland America, reminiscent of "Our Town." **78m/B VHS.** Marcia Mae Jones, Jackie Moran, Leatrice Joy, Charles D. Brown; ***D:*** Robert McGowan.

Old Yeller 🦴🦴🦴½ **1957 (G)** Disney Studios' first and best boy-and-his-dog film, set in Texas in 1969. 15-year-old Travis Coates (Kirk) is left in charge of the family farm while dad Jim (Parker) is away on a cattle drive. When his younger brother Arliss (Corcoran) brings home a stray dog, Travis is displeased but lets him stay. Yeller saves Travis's life, but contracts rabies in the process. Keep tissue handy, especially for the kids. Strong acting, effective scenery—all good stuff. Based on the novel by Fred Gipson. Sequel "Savage Sam" released in 1963. **84m/C VHS, DVD, Wide.** Dorothy McGuire, Fess Parker, Tommy Kirk, Kevin Corcoran, Jeff York, Beverly Washburn, Chuck Connors; ***D:*** Robert Stevenson; ***W:*** Fred Gipson, William Tunberg; ***C:*** Charles P. Boyle; ***M:*** Oliver Wallace.

Oldest Confederate Widow Tells All 🦴🦴🦴 **1995** TV drama starts with the recollections of 99-year-old Lucy Marsden (Bancroft), the widow of the title, as she revisits her marriage to troubled Civil War veteran Capt. William Marsden (Sutherland, sporting an impressive set of whiskers). In 1899, the teenaged Lucy (played by Lane) marries the eccentric 50-year-old, who constantly relives battlefield horrors and the loss of his boyhood friend, while she deals with family and various domestic crises. Somewhat meandering story with fine performances and subtle details. Based on Allan Gurganus' novel. **180m/C VHS.** Diane Lane, Donald Sutherland, Anne Bancroft, Cicely Tyson, Blythe Danner, E.G. Marshall, Gwen Verdon, Maureen Mueller, Wil Horneff; ***D:*** Ken Cameron; ***W:*** Joyce Eliason; ***M:*** Mark Snow.

Oldest Living Graduate 🦴🦴🦴½ **1982** Fonda is memorable in his last stage role as the oldest graduate of a Texas military academy. He and his son clash when Fonda refuses to give up his land. Teleplay features strong performances from Leachman and other big-name cast members. **75m/C VHS.** Cloris Leachman, Henry Fonda, John Lithgow, Timothy Hutton, Harry Dean Stanton, David Ogden Stiers, George Grizzard, Penelope Milford.

Oldest Profession 🦴 *Le Plus Vieux Metier du Monde* **1967** A study of prostitution from prehistoric times to the future. Generally unexciting and unfunny. In six segments meant as vehicles for their directors. **97m/C VHS.** *FR GE IT* Raquel Welch, Jeanne Moreau, Elsa Martinelli, Michele Mercier; ***D:*** Jean-Luc Godard, Philippe de Broca, Claude Autant-Lara, Franco Indovina, Mauro Bolognini, Michael Pfleghar; ***W:*** Jean-Luc Godard.

Oleanna 🦴½ **1994** Mamet directs the big-screen version of his controversial play about political correctness, sexual harrassment, and the gender gap. Pompous, burned-out college professor (Macy) is accused of sexual harassment by dense, shrill, academically weak student (Eisenstadt) after she misconstrues a self-important speech as a come-on. Unbalanced perspective, obvious stereotyping of unsympathetic characters, and weak performances remove any hint of the intended drama. **90m/C VHS.** William H. Macy, Debra Eisenstadt; ***D:*** David Mamet; ***W:*** David Mamet; ***C:*** Andrzej Sekula; ***M:*** Rebecca Pidgeon.

Olga's Girls 🦴🦴 *Mme. Olga's Massage Parlor; Olga's Massage Parlor; Olga's Parlor* **1964** Sadistic Olga deals in narcotics and white slavery in New York's Chinatown. Her drug addicted girls turn to each other for comfort but Olga suspects there's a snitch in her outfit. She'll stop at nothing to get the informant but the girls think it's about time for revenge. Campy sexploitation. **72m/B VHS.** Audrey Campbell, Alice Linville; ***D:*** Joseph P. Mawra; ***M:*** Claude Otis.

Oliver! 🦴🦴🦴½ **1968 (G)** Splendid big-budget musical adaptation of Dickens' "Oliver Twist." An innocent orphan is dragged into a life of crime when he is befriended by a gang of pickpockets. ♫Food, Glorious Food; Oliver; Boy For Sale; Where Is Love?; Consider Yourself; Pick a Pocket or Two; I'd Do Anything; Be Back Soon; As Long As He Needs Me. **145m/C VHS, DVD, Wide.** *GB* Mark Lester, Jack Wild, Ron Moody, Shani Wallis, Oliver Reed, Hugh Griffith; ***D:*** Carol Reed; ***W:*** Vernon Harris; ***C:*** Oswald Morris; ***M:*** Lionel Bart. Oscars '68: Adapt. Score, Art Dir./Set Dec., Director (Reed), Picture, Sound; Golden Globes '69: Actor—Mus./Comedy (Moody), Film—Mus./Comedy.

Oliver & Company 🦴🦴½ **1988 (G)** Animated animal retelling of Dicken's "Oliver Twist"—Disney style. Kitten Oliver (Lawrence) is left to fend for himself on the mean streets of New York until he's taken under the paw of Dodger (Joel) the dog. Dodger heads up a gang of doggy thieves, who help down-and-out human Fagin (DeLuise), who owes money to ruthless loan shark Sykes (Loggia). Out on his first job, Oliver's found by rich little Jenny (Gregory) and happily adopted. But his pals think he's been kidnapped and are off to rescue him. ♫Once Upon a Time in New York City; Why Should I Worry?. **72m/C VHS, DVD, Wide.** ***D:*** George Scribner; ***W:*** Jim Cox, James Mangold; ***V:*** Joey Lawrence, Billy Joel, Richard "Cheech" Marin, Bette Midler, Dom DeLuise, Roscoe Lee Browne, Richard Mulligan, Sheryl Lee Ralph, Robert Loggia, Taurean Blacque, Carl Weintraub, Natalie Gregory, William Glover.

Oliver Twist 🦴🦴🦴 **1922** Silent version of the Dickens classic is a vehicle for young Jackie Coogan. As orphan Oliver Twist, he is subjected to many frightening incidents before finding love and someone to care for him. Remade numerous times, most notably in 1933 and 1948 and as the musical "Oliver!" in 1968. **77m/B VHS.** Jackie Coogan, Lon Chaney Sr., Gladys Brockwell, George Siegmann, Esther Ralston, James Marcus, Aggie Herring, Nelson McDowell, Lewis Sargent, Joan Standing, Carl Stockdale, Edouard Trebaol, Lionel Belmore; ***D:*** Frank Lloyd; ***W:*** Frank Lloyd, Henry Weil; ***C:*** Glen MacWilliams, Robert Martin.

Oliver Twist 🦴🦴 **1933** The first talking version of Dickens's classic about an ill-treated London orphan involved with youthful gang of pickpockets. Moore was too young—at seven—to be very credible in the lead role. The 1948 version is much more believable. **70m/B VHS.** Dickie Moore, Irving Pichel, William "Stage" Boyd, Barbara Kent; ***D:*** William J. Cowen.

Oliver Twist 🦴🦴🦴🦴 **1948** Charles Dickens' immortal story of a workhouse orphan who is forced into a life of crime with a gang of pickpockets. The best of many film adaptations, with excellent portrayals by the cast. **116m/C VHS, DVD.** *GB* Robert Newton, John (Howard) Davies, Alec Guinness, Francis L. Sullivan, Anthony Newley, Kay Walsh, Diana Dors, Henry Stephenson; ***D:*** David Lean; ***W:*** David Lean; ***C:*** Guy Green; ***M:*** Arnold Bax.

Oliver Twist 🦴🦴🦴 **1982** Good version of the classic Dicken's tale of a boy's rescue from a life of crime. Scott's Fagin is a treat, and period details are on the mark. **100m/C VHS.** George C. Scott, Tim Curry, Michael Hordern, Timothy West, Lysette Anthony, Eileen Atkins, Cherie Lunghi; ***D:*** Clive Donner; ***W:*** James Goldman; ***M:*** Nick Bicat. **TV**

Oliver Twist **1985** Miniseries adaptation of the Charles Dickens classic about an orphan boy plunging into the underworld of 19th-century London. **333m/C VHS.** *GB* Ben Rodska, Eric Porter, Frank Middlemass, Gillian Martell. **TV**

Oliver Twist 🦴🦴½ **1997** Lavish TV version of the Dickens tale finds orphaned Oliver (Trench) escaping to 1837's London and being befriended by the wicked Fagin (Dreyfuss) and his gang of pickpocketing youngsters, including the Artful Dodger (Wood). **92m/C VHS.** Alex Trench, Richard Dreyfuss, Elijah Wood, David O'Hara, Antoine Byrne, Olivia Caffrey; ***D:*** Tony Bill; ***W:*** Monte Merrick; ***C:*** Keith Wilson; ***M:*** Van Dyke Parks. **TV**

Oliver Twist 🦴🦴🦴 **2000** The umpteenth version of the Dickens saga is a well-done British miniseries that includes the backstory of Oliver's parents, an inheritance, scheming relatives, and finally young Oliver (Smith) himself and his adventures with Fagin (Lindsay) and the criminal elements of London. **360m/C VHS.** Sam Smith, Robert Lindsay, Andy Serkis, Emily Woof, Julie Walters, Michael Kitchen, Annette Crosbie, Alex Crowley, David Ross, Tim Dutton, Lindsay Duncan, Sophia Myles, Keira Knightley; ***D:*** Renny Rye; ***W:*** Alan Bleasdale; ***C:*** Walter McGill; ***M:*** Elvis Costello, Paul Pritchard. **TV**

Oliver's Story 🦴 **1978 (PG)** A "not so equal" sequel to "Love Story," where widower O'Neal wallows in grief untils rich heiress Bergen comes along. He falls in love again, this time with money. **90m/C VHS.** Ryan O'Neal, Candice Bergen, Ray Milland, Edward Binns, Nicola Pagett, Charles Haid; ***D:*** John Korty; ***W:*** Erich Segal.

Olivia 🦴½ **1983** Abused housewife moonlights as a prostitute and begins killing her customers. She falls in love with an American businessman and flees to America when her husband finds out about the affair. Revenge and murder are the result. **90m/C VHS.** Suzanna Love, Robert Walker Jr., Jeff Winchester; ***D:*** Ulli Lommel.

Olivier, Olivier 🦴🦴🦴 **1992 (R)** Holland's directorial follow-up to "Europa, Europa" is based on a 1984 French newspaper story and evokes "The Return of Martin Guerre" and its update, "Sommersby." Beloved nine-year-old boy disappears from his home in a small French town and his dysfunctional family falls apart. Mom obsesses and falls into trances, dad escapes to North Africa, and sister Nadine develops telekinetic powers in order to cope. Six years later a detective brings an amnesiac teenager, who has been working as a hustler in Paris, to the boy's family. Is it the missing Olivier? Spooky, provocative, and emotionally resonate. In French with English subtitles. **110m/C VHS.** *FR* Francois Cluzet, Brigitte Rouan, Gregoire Colin, Marina Golovine, Jean-Francois Stevenin, Emmanuel Morozof, Faye Gatteau, Frederic Quiring; ***D:*** Agnieszka Holland; ***W:*** Agnieszka Holland. L.A. Film Critics '93: Score.

Ollie Hopnoodle's Haven of Bliss 🦴🦴½ **1988** Humorist Jean Shepherd (of "A Christmas Story" fame) spins another tale of frantic family life with his alter ego, Ralphie. This time the family is off on a summer vacation—with all its inherent problems. **90m/C VHS.** James B. Sikking, Dorothy Lyman, Jerry O'Connell; ***D:*** Richard Bartlett. **TV**

Olly Olly Oxen Free 🦴🦴 *The Great Balloon Adventure* **1978** Junkyard owner Hepburn helps two boys fix up and fly a hot-air balloon, once piloted by McKenzie's grandfather, as a surprise for the man's birthday. Beautiful airborne scenes over California and a dramatic landing to the tune of the "1812 Overture," but not enough to make the whole film interesting. **89m/C VHS.** Katharine Hepburn, Kevin McKenzie, Dennis Dimster, Peter Kilman; ***D:*** Richard A. Colla; ***M:*** Robert Alcivar.

Olongape: The American Dream 🦴½ **1989** A young woman works in a cheap bar while waiting for the chance to come to America. **97m/C VHS.** Jacklyn Jose, Susan Africa, Chanda Romero, Joel Torre, Marilou Sadiua; ***D:*** Chito Rono.

Omaha (the movie) 🦴🦴 **1995** Gen-Xer Simon (Walkinshaw) flees his native Nebraska and eccentric, dysfunctional family for enlightenment in Tibet. He's instructed in Buddhism and returns home but doesn't find the peace he's seeking and decides to hit the road with former girlfriend Gina (Anderson). **85m/C VHS.** Hughston Walkinshaw, Jill Anderson; ***D:*** Dan Mirvish; ***W:*** Dan Mirvish; ***C:*** Oslo Anderson.

Omar Khayyam 🦴🦴 **1957** In medieval Persia, Omar (Wilde) becomes involved in a romance with the Shah of Persia's fiancee, while trying to fight off a faction of assassins trying to overthrow the Shah. Although this film has a great cast, the script is silly and juvenile, defeating the cast's fine efforts. **101m/C VHS.** Cornel Wilde, Michael Rennie, Debra Paget, Raymond Massey, John Derek, Yma Sumac, Margaret Hayes, Joan Taylor, Sebastian Cabot; ***D:*** William Dieterle.

The Omega Code 🦴½ **1999 (PG-13)** This entry in the God vs. Devil steel cage apocalypse smackdown genre was actually financed by the Christian cable network TBN. Therefore, you can be sure that it's not evil, although it's plenty bad. In this corner, representing good, is motivational speaker Gillen Lane (Van Dien), who believes that hidden truths may be discovered by applying mathematical equations to sections of the Bible or by overacting. In that corner, representing evil, is Stone Alexander (York), AKA The Antichrist, who uses the hidden codes for nefarious purposes such as taking over the world government and overacting. In the stunning climax stolen from "Raiders of the Lost Ark," evil is overthrown and we find that the whole thing was a fix from the beginning. Caused a minor stir with semi-big boxoffice numbers, but much of the business was a case of preaching to the choir of fervent TBN viewers in its opening weeks. **99m/C VHS, DVD, Wide.** Casper Van Dien, Michael York, Catherine Oxenberg, Michael Ironside, Jan Triska, William Hootkins, Robert Ito, Janet Carroll, Gregory Wagrowski, Devon Odessa, George Coe, Robert F. Lyons; ***D:*** Robert Marcarelli; ***W:*** Stephan Bliss, Hollis Barton; ***C:*** Carlos Gonzalez; ***M:*** Harry Manfredini.

Omega Cop 🦴 *John Travis, Solar Survivor* **1990 (R)** In a post-apocalyptic future, there's only one cop left. He uses his martial arts skills and tons of guns attempting to rescue three women, but the violence doesn't cover the poor acting and shoddy production. Fans of TV's Batman might enjoy this for West's presence. **89m/C VHS.** Ron Marchini, Adam West, Stuart Whitman, Troy Donahue, Meg Thayer, Jennifer Jostyn, Chrysti Jimenez, D.W. Landingham, Chuck Katzakian; ***D:*** Paul Kyriazi.

Omega Doom 🦴🦴 **1996 (PG-13)** Four hundred years after an apocalyptic war the most organic thing around are the cyborgs, who exist along with androids and robots in a world where humans no longer matter. Omega Doom (Hauer) is an android developed as a fighter who has no function except to kill. In a ruined amusement park, the Roms and Droids, two rival cyborg groups, maintain an uneasy truce and when Doom wanders in they unite to destroy the intruder. But they don't know what they're up against. **84m/C VHS, DVD.** Rutger Hauer, Anna (Katerina) Katarina, Norbert Weisser, Jahi JJ Zuri, Shannon Whirry, Earl White, Tina Cote, Jill Pierce; ***D:*** Albert Pyun; ***W:*** Ed Naha; ***C:*** George Mooradian; ***M:*** Tony Riparetti.

Omega Man 🦴🦴½ **1971 (PG)** In post-holocaust Los Angeles, Heston is immune to the effects of a biologically engineered plague and battles those who aren't—an army of albino victims bent on destroying what's left of the world. Strong suspense with considerable violence, despite the PG rating. Based on the science fiction thriller "I Am Legend" by Richard Matheson, which is also the basis for the film "The Last Man on Earth." **98m/C VHS, DVD.** Charlton Heston, Anthony Zerbe, Rosalind Cash, Paul Koslo, Eric Laneuville, Lincoln Kilpatrick, Anna Aries, John Dierkes, Monika Henreid; ***D:*** Boris Sagal; ***W:*** John W. Corrington, Joyce H. Corrington; ***C:*** Russell Metty; ***M:*** Ron Grainer.

Omega Syndrome 🦴½ **1987 (R)** Neo-Nazis kidnap Wahl's daughter. He and Vietnam buddy DiCenzo get her back. Ho hum. DiCenzo's is the best performance. Tolerable for vigilante film fans. **90m/C VHS.** Ken Wahl, Ron Kuhlman, George DiCenzo, Doug McClure; ***D:*** Joseph Manduke.

The Omen ♪♪½ *Birthmark* **1976 (R)** American diplomat's family adopts a young boy who always seems to be around when bizarre and inexplicable deaths occur. Of course, what else would you expect of Satan's son? The shock and gore prevalent in "The Exorcist" is replaced with more suspense and believable effects. Well-done horror film doesn't insult the viewer's intelligence. Followed by three sequels: "Damien: Omen 2," "The Final Conflict," and "Omen 4." **111m/C VHS, DVD, Wide.** Gregory Peck, Lee Remick, Harvey Stephens, Billie Whitelaw, David Warner, Holly Palance, Robert Rietty, Patrick Troughton, Martin Benson, Leo McKern, Richard Donner; ***D:*** Richard Donner; ***W:*** David Seltzer; ***C:*** Gilbert Taylor; ***M:*** Jerry Goldsmith. Oscars '76: Orig. Score.

Omen 3: The Final Conflict ♪½ *The Final Conflict* **1981 (R)** Unwelcomed third installment in the "Omen" series, concerning Satan's son Damien. Now 32, and the head of an international conglomerate, he is poised for world domination but fears another savior is born. Several monks and many babies meet gruesome deaths before he gets his comeuppance. The last theatrical release; the next entry was made for TV. **108m/C VHS, DVD, Wide.** Sam Neill, Lisa Harrow, Barnaby Holm, Rossano Brazzi, Don Gordon, Mason Adams, Robert Arden, Marc Boyle, Tommy Duggan, Richard Oldfield, Arwen Holm; ***D:*** Graham Baker; ***W:*** Andrew Birkin; ***C:*** Phil Meheux, Robert Paynter; ***M:*** Jerry Goldsmith.

Omen 4: The Awakening ♪♪ **1991** It turns out Damien of Omens past had a daughter, Delia, who takes up where dear old devilish Dad left off. Delia is adopted by your basic clueless couple and proceeds to wreak havoc wherever she goes, including getting rid of several interfering adults. She also plans to make her adoptive father, a U.S. senator, President, so that his delightful child anti-Christ can have him carry out all her evil plans. **97m/C VHS, DVD.** Faye Grant, Michael Woods, Michael Lerner, Asia Vieira; ***D:*** Jorge Montesi, Dominique Othenin-Girard. **TV**

Omoo Omoo, the Shark God ♪ **1949** A sea captain is cursed when he removes the black pearls from a stone shark god in this extremely cheap adventure. **58m/B VHS.** Ron Randell, Devera Burton, Trevor Bardette, Pedro de Cordoba, Richard Benedict, Rudy Robles, Michael Whalen, George Meeker; ***D:*** Leo Leonard.

On a Clear Day You Can See Forever ♪♪ **1970 (G)** A psychiatric hypnotist helps a girl stop smoking and finds that in trances she remembers previous incarnations. He falls in love with one of the women she used to be. Alan Jay Lerner of "My Fair Lady" and "Camelot" wrote the lyrics and the book. Based on a musical by Lerner and Burton Lane. ♫On a Clear Day, You Can See Forever; Come Back to Me; What Did I Have That I Don't Have?; He Isn't You; Hurry, It's Lovely Up Here; Go To Sleep; Love with All the Trimmings; Melinda. **129m/C VHS.** Barbra Streisand, Yves Montand, Bob Newhart, Jack Nicholson, Simon Oakland; ***D:*** Vincente Minnelli; ***C:*** Harry Stradling Sr.

On an Island with You ♪♪½ **1948** Williams plays a movie star who finds romance on location in Hawaii in this musical extravaganza. Contains many of Williams' famous water ballet scenes and a bevy of bathing beauties. ♫On an Island with You; If I Were You; Taking Miss Mary to the Ball; Dog Song; Buenas Noches, Buenos Aires; Wedding Samba; I Can Do Without Broadway, But Can Broadway Do Without Me?. **107m/C VHS.** Esther Williams, Peter Lawford, Ricardo Montalban, Jimmy Durante, Cyd Charisse, Leon Ames; ***D:*** Richard Thorpe.

On Approval ♪♪♪ **1944** Hilarious British farce in which two women trade boyfriends. Lillie's performace provides plenty of laughs. Brook runs the show as leading man, co-author, director, and co-producer. Based on the play by Frederick Lonsdale. **80m/B VHS, DVD.** *GB* Clive Brook, Beatrice Lillie, Googie Withers, Roland Culver, O.B. Clarence, Lawrence Hanray, Elliot Mason, Hay Petrie, Marjorie Munks, Molly Munks; ***D:*** Clive Brook; ***W:*** Terence Young, Clive Brook; ***C:*** Claude Friese-Greene; ***M:*** William Alwyn.

On Borrowed Time ♪♪♪ **1939** Engrossing tale of Death (Hardwicke) coming for an old man (Barrymore) who isn't ready to die so he traps him in his backyard apple tree. Performances are first rate in this good adaptation of the stage success (originally by Eugene O'Neill). Hardwicke is especially a standout; he gave up theatre for Hollywood after making this film. **99m/B VHS.** Lionel Barrymore, Cedric Hardwicke, Beulah Bondi, Una Merkel, Bobs Watson, Henry Travers; ***D:*** Harold Bucquet; ***C:*** Joseph Ruttenberg.

On Dangerous Ground ♪♪♪ **1951** A world-weary detective is sent to the countryside to investigate a murder. He encounters the victim's revenge-hungry father and the blind sister of the murderer. In the hateful father the detective sees a reflection of the person he has become, in the blind woman, he learns the redeeming qualities of humanity and compassion. A well-acted example of film noir that features the composer Herrman's favorite score. **82m/B VHS.** Robert Ryan, Ida Lupino, Ward Bond, Ed Begley Sr., Cleo Moore, Charles Kemper; ***D:*** Nicholas Ray; ***M:*** Bernard Herrmann.

On Deadly Ground woof! **1994 (R)** Seagal nearly destroys Alaska in an effort to save it in this inane, preachy story of an oil-rig roughneck out to protect the landscape from an evil oil company's drilling habits. Directorial debut for Seagal lumbers from scene to scene. Violence is expected, as is silly dialogue—just try to keep from laughing when stoneyfaced Steven intones "What does it take to change the essence of man?" A better script, for one. **102m/C VHS, DVD, Wide.** Steven Seagal, Michael Caine, Joan Chen, John C. McGinley, Billy Bob Thornton, R. Lee Ermey; ***D:*** Steven Seagal; ***W:*** Ed Horowitz; ***C:*** Ric Waite; ***M:*** Basil Poledouris. Golden Raspberries '94: Worst Director (Seagal).

On Golden Pond ♪♪♪½ **1981 (PG)** Henry Fonda won his first—and long overdue—Oscar for his role as the curmudgeonly patriarch of the Thayer family. He and his wife have grudgingly agreed to look after a young boy while at their summer home in Maine. Through his gradually affectionate relationship with the boy, Fonda learns to allay his fears of mortality. He also gains an understanding of his semi-estranged daughter. Jane Fonda plays his daughter and Hepburn is his loving wife in this often funny adaptation of Ernest Thompson's 1978 play. Predictable but deeply moving. Henry Fonda's final screen appearance. **109m/C VHS, DVD.** Henry Fonda, Jane Fonda, Katharine Hepburn, Dabney Coleman, Doug McKeon, William Lanteau; ***D:*** Mark Rydell; ***W:*** Ernest Thompson; ***C:*** Billy Williams; ***M:*** Dave Grusin. Oscars '81: Actor (Fonda), Actress (Hepburn), Adapt. Screenplay; British Acad. '82: Actress (Hepburn); Golden Globes '82: Actor—Drama (Fonda), Film—Drama, Screenplay; Natl. Bd. of Review '81: Actor (Fonda); Writers Guild '81: Adapt. Screenplay.

On Her Majesty's Secret Service ♪♪♪ **1969 (PG)** In the sixth 007 adventure, Bond again confronts the infamous Blofeld, who is planning a germ-warfare assault on the entire world. Australian Lazenby took a crack at playing the super spy, with mixed results. Many feel this is the best-written of the Bond films and might have been the most famous, had Sean Connery continued with the series. Includes the song "We Have All the Time In the World," sung by Louis Armstrong. **144m/C VHS, DVD, Wide.** *GB* George Lazenby, Diana Rigg, Telly Savalas, Gabriele Ferzetti, Ilse Steppat, Bernard Lee, Lois Maxwell, Desmond Llewelyn, Catherine Schell, Julie Ege, Joanna Lumley, Mona Chong, Anouska (Anoushka) Hempel, Jenny Hanley; ***D:*** Peter Hunt; ***W:*** Richard Maibaum; ***M:*** John Barry.

On Moonlight Bay ♪♪½ **1951** Set in small-town Indiana in 1917 with Day as the tomboyish Marjorie who falls for college man MacRae. Her father (Ames) doesn't approve but the trouble really begins when Marjorie's younger brother gets into trouble at school. The incorrigible Wesley (Gray) blames everything on dear old dad and MacRae feels he must come to Marjorie's rescue! Gray steals the movie as the bratty brother—otherwise its business as usual. Based on Booth Tarkington's "Penrod" stories and followed by "By the Light of the Silvery Moon." ♫Love Ya; On Moonlight Bay; Till We Meet Again; Pack Up Your Troubles In Your Old Kit Bag; I'm Forever Blowing Bubbles; Christmas Story; Tell Me Why Nights Are Lonely; Cuddle Up a Little Closer; Every Little Movement Has a Meaning All Its Own. **95m/C VHS.** Doris Day, Gordon MacRae, Leon Ames, Billy Gray, Rosemary DeCamp, Mary Wickes, Ellen Corby, Esther Dale; ***D:*** Roy Del Ruth; ***W:*** Melville Shavelson, Jack Rose; ***M:*** Max Steiner.

On My Own ♪♪ **1992** Fifteen-year-old Simon Henderson (Ferguson) struggles to cope with his life when he's sent away to school after his mother (Davis) suffers a nervous breakdown. Just as he begins to adjust and make friends, his mother pays a disturbing visit and reveals the source of her troubles. **96m/C VHS.** *CA* Judy Davis, Matthew Ferguson, David McIlwraith; ***D:*** Antonio Tibaldi.

On Our Merry Way ♪♪½ *A Miracle Can Happen* **1948** Episodic comedy with Meredith starring as Oliver Pease, a would-be newspaper reporter (he actually works on the classifieds), asking the question "How has a child changed your life?" Among those queried are a couple of jazz musicians (Fonda, Stewart), Hollywood bit players (Lamour, Moore), and con men (Demerest, MacMurray). Goddard, who was married to Meredith at the time, plays his wife in the film. **107m/B VHS, DVD.** Burgess Meredith, Paulette Goddard, Dorothy Lamour, Victor Moore, James Stewart, Henry Fonda, Fred MacMurray, William Demarest, Hugh Herbert, Eilene Janssen, Dorothy Ford, David Whorf; ***D:*** King Vidor, Leslie Fenton; ***W:*** Laurence Stallings, Lou Breslow; ***C:*** John Seitz, Ernest Laszlo, Gordon Avil, Joseph Biroc, Edward Cronjager; ***M:*** Heinz Roemheld.

On the Air Live with Captain Midnight ♪½ *Captain Midnight* **1979** Socially challenged teen finds hipness as a rebel DJ operating an illegal radio station from his van. Leading actor is the son of the director/writer/producer but nepotism does not a good film make. **90m/C VHS.** Tracy Sebastian; ***D:*** Ferd Sebastian.

On the Avenue ♪♪♪ **1937** Broadway showman Powell opens up a new musical, starring Faye as the richest girl in the world, in this musical-comedy satirizing upper-crust society. Debutante Carroll is outraged because she realizes it's mocking her actual life. Carroll tries to get Powell to change the show, they fall in love, Faye gets her nose out of joint, and after lots of fuss everything ends happily. Fine Berlin score. ♫He Ain't Got Rhythm; You're Laughing at Me; This Year's Kisses; Slumming on Park Avenue; The Girl on the Police Gazette; I've Got My Love to Keep Me Warm. **90m/B VHS.** Dick Powell, Madeleine Carroll, Alice Faye, George Barbier, Al Ritz, Harry Ritz, Jimmy Ritz, Alan Mowbray, Cora Witherspoon, Walter Catlett, Stepin Fetchit, Sig Rumann, Douglas Fowley, Joan Davis; ***D:*** Roy Del Ruth; ***W:*** Gene Markey; ***M:*** Irving Berlin.

On the Beach ♪♪♪½ **1959** A group of survivors attempt to live normal lives in post-apocalyptic Australia, waiting for the inevitable arrival of killer radiation. Astaire is strong in his first dramatic role. Though scientifically implausible, still a good anti-war vehicle. Based on the best-selling novel by Nevil Shute. **135m/B VHS, DVD, Wide.** Gregory Peck, Anthony Perkins, Donna Anderson, Ava Gardner, Fred Astaire; ***D:*** Stanley Kramer; ***W:*** John Paxton; ***C:*** Daniel F. Fapp; ***M:*** Ernest Gold. Golden Globes '60: Score.

On the Beach ♪♪½ **2000** Remake of the 1959 anti-nuke film (based on the 1957 novel by Nevil Shute) is well-acted but so low-key that it never generates real tension. In 2006, the bomb has been dropped and Australia is the current refuge and the destination of sub commander Dwight Towers (Assante). A radio transmission from Alaska offers some hope but Towers needs the help of Melbourne scientist Julian Osborne (Brown), who happens to be the ex- of Towers' sultry love, Moira (Ward). **180m/C VHS.** Armand Assante, Rachel Ward, Bryan Brown, Jacqueline McKenzie, Grant Bowler; ***D:*** Russell Mulcahy; ***W:*** David Williamson, Bill Kerby; ***C:*** Martin McGrath; ***M:*** Anna Borghesi. **CABLE**

On the Border ♪♪½ **1998 (R)** Familiar neo-noir revolves around a bank heist. Ex-bank robber Jake (Van Dien) is now a security guard. Kristin (Roos) entices him into a plot involving Brown, Baldwin, and Mitchum. The humor is intentional, and the Texas locations are well utilized. Overall, this is an overachieving video premiere. **103m/C DVD.** Casper Van Dien, Bryan Brown, Bentley Mitchum, Camilla Overbye Roos, Rochelle Swanson, Daniel Baldwin; ***D:*** Bob Misiorowski; ***W:*** Josh Olson; ***C:*** Lawrence Sher; ***M:*** Serge Colbert. **VIDEO**

On the Comet ♪♪♪ *Na Komete; Hector Servadac's Ark* **1968** Zeman's fourth fantasy based on Jules Verne stories, about a chunk of the Earth's crust suddenly becoming a comet and giving its passengers a ride through the galaxy. Complete with Zeman's signature animation fantasias. In English. **76m/C VHS.** *CZ* Emil Horvath Jr., Magda Vasarykova, Frantisek Filipovsky; ***D:*** Karel Zeman.

On the Edge ♪♪½ **1986 (PG-13)** A drama about the inevitable Rocky-esque triumph of Dern as an aging marathon runner. Simultaneous to his running endeavor, Dern is trying to make up for lost time with his father. Available in two versions, one rated, the other unrated with a racy appearance by Pam Grier as the runner's interracial lover. **86m/C VHS.** Bruce Dern, John Marley, Bill Bailey, Jim Haynie, Pam Grier; ***D:*** Rob Nilsson; ***W:*** Rob Nilsson.

On the Edge ♪♪½ **2000 (R)** Troubled 19-year-old Jonathan Breech (Murphy) deals with his depression over his father's death by stealing a car and driving it over a cliff. Surviving with very minor injuries, Jonathan is faced with prison or spending time in a mental institution. He chooses the latter, where he meets his caring therapist, Dr. Figure (Rea), and some fellow patients to bond with—Rachel (Vessey) and Toby (Jackson). Much teen angst is explored before the resolution and the material may not be fresh but it is heartfelt. **86m/C VHS, DVD, Wide.** *IR* Cillian Murphy, Tricia Vessey, Jonathan Jackson, Stephen Rea; ***D:*** John Carney; ***W:*** Daniel James, John Carney; ***C:*** Eric Alan Edwards.

On the Edge: The Survival of Dana ♪ **1979** Another entry from the world of low-quality made-for-TV films. A young girl moves with her family to a new town. When she falls in with the "bad" crowd, her ethical standards are challenged. A stinker that may appeal to those with campy tastes. Not for the discriminating palate. **92m/C VHS.** Melissa Sue Anderson, Robert Carradine, Marion Ross, Talia Balsam, Michael Pataki, Kevin Breslin, Judge Reinhold, Barbara Babcock; ***D:*** Jack Starrett. **TV**

On the Fiddle ♪♪½ *Operation Snafu; Operation Warhead* **1961** Conniving Horace Pope (Lynch) gets his mate Pedlar Pascoe (Connery) to join the Royal Air Force with him during WWII. Horace sets up a number of rackets but, despite their larcency, they become unintentional heroes. Based on the novel "Stop at a Winner" by R.F. Delderfield. **93m/B VHS.** *GB* Alfred Lynch, Sean Connery, Cecil Parker, Stanley Holloway, Wilfrid Hyde-White; ***D:*** Cyril Frankel; ***W:*** Harold Buchman; ***C:*** Edward Scaife; ***M:*** Malcolm Arnold.

On the Line ♪½ **1983** Two Mexico-US border guards, one hard-bitten, the other sympathetic to the illegal immigrants' plight, battle it out over a beautiful Mexican whore. Disjointed and confusing. **95m/C VHS.** *SP* David Carradine, Victoria Abril, Scott Wilson, Sam Jaffe, Jesse Vint; ***D:*** Jose Luis Borau; ***W:*** Jose Luis Borau.

On the Line ♪½ **2001 (PG)** Insipid romance featuring Bass and Fatone from the teenybopper group 'N Sync. Kevin (Bass) meets Abbey (Chriqui), the girl of his dreams, on a train in Chicago. How does he know she's the one for him? Well, they can both name all the presidents in order and they both like the Cubs. Gee! Ain't that sweet? Unfortunately, Kevin is too shy to ask for her number, and he lets her slip away. He laments to his friends Rod (Fatone), Eric (GQ) and Randy (Bulliard) and they decide to help him find her by posting flyers all over town. A local reporter (Montgomery) picks up the story and a gaggle of girls claiming to be "The L Girl" respond. Further plot contrivances keep the two apart. Love wins out in the end, however, much to the delight of squealing 12-year-old girls everywhere. **90m/C VHS, DVD, Wide.** *US* Lance Bass, Joey Fatone, Emmanuelle Chriqui, GQ, Al Green, Tamala Jones, Dave Foley, Dan Montgomery Jr., Jerry Stiller; ***D:*** Eric Bross; ***W:*** Paul Stanton, Eric Aronson; ***C:*** Michael Bernard; ***M:*** Stewart Copeland.

On the Nickel 🦴🦴 **1980 (R)** An ex-alcoholic returns to Fifth Street in Los Angeles to save his friend from a life of despair. Waits' musical score enhances this sentimental skid row drama. Scripted, directed, and produced by "The Waltons'" Waite. **96m/C VHS.** Ralph Waite, Donald Moffat, Hal Williams, Jack Kehoe; ***D:*** Ralph Waite; ***W:*** Ralph Waite; ***M:*** Tom Waits.

On the Night Stage 🦴🦴 **1915** Gruff bandit (legendary Hart) loses his girl-of-questionable-values to town preacher. One of the first feature length westerns. **83m/B VHS, 8mm.** William S. Hart, Robert Edeson, Rhea Mitchell, Shorty Hamilton; ***D:*** Reginald Barker.

On the Old Spanish Trail 🦴½ **1947** Rogers becomes a singing cowboy with a traveling tent show in order to pay off a note signed by the Sons of the Pioneers. **56m/B VHS.** Roy Rogers, Jane Frazee, Andy Devine, Tito Guizar; ***D:*** William Witney.

On the Right Track 🦴½ **1981 (PG)** Young orphan living in Chicago's Union Station has the gift of being able to pick winning race horses. May be appealing to fans of Coleman and "Different Strokes" TV show, but lacks the momentum to keep most viewers from switching tracks. **98m/C VHS.** Gary Coleman, Lisa Eilbacher, Michael Lembeck, Norman Fell, Maureen Stapleton, Herb Edelman; ***D:*** Lee Philips.

On the Run 🦴 **1985 (R)** An ex-con and his gal cut a law-defying swath through the Bayou. **96m/C VHS.** Jack Conrad, Rita George, Dub Taylor, David Huddleston.

On the Sunny Side 🦴🦴 *Auf der Sonnenseite* **1962** Martin, who works as a steel worker, wants to become an actor and tries his hand at drama school, where his anarchic ways eventually get him expelled. This doesn't seem to bother Martin much, probably because he's fallen in love with Ottilie, an architect who's immune to his charms. German with subtitles. **97m/B VHS.** *GE* Manfred Krug, Marita Bohme, Heinz Schubert; ***D:*** Ralf Kirsten; ***W:*** Ralf Kirsten; ***C:*** Hans Heinrich; ***M:*** Andre Asriel.

On the Third Day 🦴 **1983** A headmaster finds a mysterious stranger in his house who turns out to be his long-lost illegitimate son. **101m/C VHS.** Richard Marant, Catherine Schell, Paul Williamson.

On the Town 🦴🦴🦴½ **1949** Kelly's directorial debut features three sailors on a one day leave search for romance in the Big Apple. Filmed on location in NYC, with uncompromisingly authentic flavor. Based on the successful Broadway musical. ♫New York, New York; I Feel Like I'm Not Out of Bed Yet; Come Up to My Place; Miss Turnstiles Ballet; Main Street; You're Awful; On the Town; You Can Count on Me; Pearl of the Persian Sea. **98m/C VHS, DVD.** Gene Kelly, Frank Sinatra, Vera-Ellen, Ann Miller, Betty Garrett; ***D:*** Gene Kelly, Stanley Donen; ***W:*** Betty Comden, Adolph Green; ***M:*** Leonard Bernstein. Oscars '49: Scoring/Musical.

On the Town 🦴🦴½ **1991** Bernstein's first big Broadway success in 1944, recorded in a live performance June 1992, at London's Barbican Centre. Follows the story of three sailors on a 24-hour leave in New York City during WWII. This version includes numbers which never made it into the original Broadway show. **110m/C VHS.** Frederica von Stade, Tyne Daly, Marie McLaughlin, David Garrison, Thomas Hampson, Kurt Ollman, Evelyn Lear, Samuel Ramey, Cleo Laine; ***M:*** Leonard Bernstein, Betty Comden, Adolph Green.

On the Waterfront 🦴🦴🦴🦴 **1954** A trend-setting, gritty portrait of New York dock workers embroiled in union violence. Cobb is the gangster union boss, Steiger his crooked lawyer, and Brando, Steiger's ex-fighter brother who "could've been a contender!" Intense performances and excellent direction stand up well today. The picture was a huge financial success. **108m/B VHS, DVD.** Marlon Brando, Rod Steiger, Eva Marie Saint, Lee J. Cobb, Karl Malden, Pat Henning, Leif Erickson, Tony Galento, John Hamilton, Nehemiah Persoff; ***D:*** Elia Kazan; ***W:*** Budd Schulberg; ***C:*** Boris Kaufman; ***M:*** Leonard Bernstein. Oscars '54: Actor (Brando), Art Dir./Set Dec., B&W, B&W Cinematog., Director (Kazan), Film Editing, Picture, Story & Screenplay, Support. Actress (Saint); AFI '98: Top 100; British Acad. '54: Actor (Brando); Directors Guild '54: Director (Kazan); Golden Globes '55: Actor—Drama (Brando), Director (Kazan), Film—Drama, Natl. Film Reg. '89;; N.Y. Film Critics '54: Actor (Brando), Director (Kazan), Film.

On the Yard 🦴🦴 **1979 (R)** An attempt to realistically portray prison life. Focuses on a murderer who runs afoul of the leader of the prisoners and the system. A fairly typical prison drama with above average performances from Heard and Kellin. **102m/C VHS.** Dominic Chianese, John Heard, Thomas G. Waites, Mike Kellin, Joe Grifasi; ***D:*** Raphael D. Silver; ***W:*** Malcolm Braly.

On Top of Old Smoky 🦴½ **1953** Autry and the Cass County Boys are mistaken for Texas Rangers by a gang of land poachers. **59m/B VHS.** Gene Autry, Smiley Burnette, Gail Davis, Sheila Ryan; ***D:*** George Archainbaud.

On Top of the Whale 🦴🦴 **1982** Two scholars move onto the estate of strange but wealthy benefactor to conduct research on the few survivors of a disappearing clan of Indians. Two tribesmen speak bizarre dialect which utilizes only one word while others confound the researchers with stories of ghosts and graveyards. Dutch comedy subtitled in English. **93m/C VHS.** *NL* ***D:*** Raul Ruiz.

On Valentine's Day 🦴🦴½ *Story of a Marriage* **1986 (PG)** Author Horton Foote based this story loosely on his parents' lives. A wealthy young Southern girl marries a poor but decent young man and finds herself ostracized from her family. A prequel to the same author's "1918." Produced with PBS for "American Playhouse." **106m/C VHS.** Hallie Foote, Matthew Broderick, Michael Higgins, Steven Hill, William Converse-Roberts, Rochelle Oliver, Richard Jenkins, Horton Foote Jr., Carol Goodheart; ***D:*** Ken Harrison; ***W:*** Horton Foote; ***M:*** Jonathan Sheffer.

On Wings of Eagles 🦴🦴½ **1986** During the 1979 Iranian revolution two American executives are imprisoned by Islamic radicals. Help arrives in the form of covert agents of their boss—Texas tycoon H. Ross Perot (played by Crenna). Don't expect strict historical veracity or insight from this network miniseries (based on the "nonfiction novel" by Ken Follett), an okay but lengthy "mission impossible." It came out in a two-cassette set, just in time for Perot's 1992 presidential campaign. **221m/C VHS.** Burt Lancaster, Richard Crenna, Paul LeMat, Esai Morales, Constance Towers, Jim Metzler, James Sutorius, Lawrence Pressman, Karen Carlson, Cyril O'Reilly; ***D:*** Andrew V. McLaglen.

Onassis 🦴½ *The Richest Man in the World: The Story of Aristotle Onassis* **1988** Romanticized biography of Greek shipping magnate Aristotle Onassis, from the poverty of his youth to his later wealth and family and romantic liaisons and tragedies. Julia is adequate as the title character but English actress Annis is badly miscast as Jackie Kennedy Onassis. However, Seymour is terrific as Onassis's lover, opera star Maria Callas. Quinn, who played Onassis in "The Greek Tycoon," plays Onassis's father in this one. Miniseries based on the novel by Peter Evans. **120m/C VHS.** Raul Julia, Jane Seymour, Francesca Annis, Anthony Quinn, Anthony Zerbe, Lorenzo Quinn; ***D:*** Waris Hussein. **TV**

Once a Hero 🦴🦴 **1988** The dregs of society, the Cicero Gang, have taken Captain Justice's number one fan and his mother hostage. Is it really curtains for rosy cheeks, bubble gum, and apple pie? But wait, it's Captain Justice, the man, the myth, to the rescue! **74m/C VHS.** Jeff Lester, Robert Forster, Milo O'Shea; ***D:*** Claudia Weill.

Once a Thief 🦴🦴🦴 **1996 (R)** A fun and action-packed TV movie finds adopted children Li Ann (Holt) and Mac (Sergei) being raised along with natural son Michael (Wong) by Hong Kong crime head Tang (Ito) and trained as daring professional thieves. A falling out finds Li Ann in Vancouver, involved with ex-cop Victor (Lea), and both of them working for a covert crime-fighting agency headed by a very tough director (Dale). Then Mac is forced to join the duo in an elaborate heist to bring down Michael and his family's criminal empire. Woo's director's cut contains additional footage. **101m/C VHS, DVD.** Ivan Sergei, Sandrine Holt, Nicholas Lea, Michael Wong, Robert Ito, Jennifer Dale, Alan Scarfe; ***D:*** John Woo; ***W:*** Glenn Davis, William Laurin; ***C:*** Bill Wong; ***M:*** Amin Bhatia.

Once Around 🦴🦴½ **1991 (R)** 30ish, lonely Renata Bella (Hunter) meets boisterous, self-assured (read utterly obnoxious) Lithuanian salesman Sam Sharpe (Dreyfuss). He sweeps her off her feet, showers her with affection and gifts, and then tries hard—too hard—to please her close-knit Italian family. Casting doesn't get much better than the group assembled here and Hallstrom steers everyone to wonderful performances in his American directorial debut. The major flaw is the script, a light romantic comedy that sometimes swerves into heavy drama, so much so that you may need Kleenex. **115m/C VHS.** Richard Dreyfuss, Holly Hunter, Danny Aiello, Gena Rowlands, Laura San Giacomo, Roxanne Hart, Danton Stone, Tim Guinee, Greg Germann, Griffin Dunne; ***D:*** Lasse Hallstrom; ***W:*** Malia Scotch Marmo; ***M:*** James Horner.

Once Before I Die 🦴🦴½ **1965** Army soldiers caught in the Philippines during WWII struggle to survive and elude the Japanese. A single woman traveling with them becomes the object of their spare time considerations. A brutal, odd, and gritty war drama. Director/actor Derek was Andress' husband at the time. **97m/C VHS.** *PH* Ursula Andress, John Derek, Richard Jaeckel, Rod Lauren, Ron Ely; ***D:*** John Derek.

Once Bitten 🦴🦴 **1985 (PG-13)** Centuries-old though still remarkably youthful vampiress comes to LA to stalk male virgins. That may be the wrong city, but she needs their blood to retain her young countenance. Vampire comedy theme was more effectively explored in 1979s "Love at First Bite," notable, however for the screen debut of comic Carrey who would later gain fame for TV's "In Living Color" and "Ace Ventura, Pet Detective." **94m/C VHS.** Lauren Hutton, Jim Carrey, Cleavon Little, Karen Kopins, Thomas Balltore, Skip Lackey; ***D:*** Howard Storm; ***W:*** Jonathan Roberts, David Hines, Jeffrey Hause; ***C:*** Adam Greenberg; ***M:*** John Du Prez.

Once in Paris... 🦴🦴½ **1979 (PG)** A bittersweet romance about a scriptwriter working in Paris, the chauffeur who befriends him, and the aristocratic British woman with whom the writer falls in love. Beautiful French scenery and the engaging performance of Lenoir as the chauffeur make this film a diverting piece of entertainment. **100m/C VHS.** Wayne Rogers, Gayle Hunnicutt, Jack Lenoir; ***D:*** Frank D. Gilroy; ***W:*** Frank D. Gilroy.

Once in the Life 🦴🦴½ **2000 (R)** Fishburne transfers his 1995 Off Broadway play "Riff Raff" to the big screen but its stage antecedents are apparent. 20/20 Mike (Fishburne) has hooked up with his heroin-addicted white half-brother Torch (Welliver) and they have trouble over a drug score gone wrong that has enraged local boss Manny (Calderon). Manny has sent henchman Tony the Tiger (Walker) to take care of things, even though Tony and Mike are old prison buddies. The film basically turns into a talky, one-set triangle leading to inevitable tragedy. **107m/C VHS, DVD.** Laurence "Larry" Fishburne, Titus Welliver, Eamonn Walker, Paul Calderon, Dominic Chianese, Gregory Hines, Annabella Sciorra, Michael Paul Chan; ***D:*** Laurence "Larry" Fishburne; ***W:*** Laurence "Larry" Fishburne; ***C:*** Richard Turner; ***M:*** Branford Marsalis.

Once Is Not Enough 🦴½ *Jacqueline Susann's Once is Not Enough* **1975 (R)** Limp trash-drama concerning the young daughter of a has-been movie producer who has a tempestuous affair with a writer who reminds her of her father. Based on the novel by Jacqueline Susann. **121m/C VHS.** Kirk Douglas, Deborah Raffin, David Janssen, George Hamilton, Brenda Vaccaro, Alexis Smith, Melina Mercouri; ***D:*** Guy Green; ***W:*** Julius J. Epstein; ***C:*** John A. Alonzo; ***M:*** Henry Mancini. Golden Globes '76: Support. Actress (Vaccaro).

Once Upon a Brothers Grimm 🦴🦴 **1977** An original musical fantasy in which the Brothers Grimm meet a succession of their most famous storybook characters including Hansel and Gretel, the Gingerbread Lady, Little Red Riding Hood, and Rumpelstiltskin. **102m/C VHS.** Dean Jones, Paul Sand, Cleavon Little, Ruth Buzzi, Chita Rivera, Teri Garr.

Once Upon a Crime 🦴½ **1992 (PG)** Extremely disappointing comedy featuring a high profile cast set in Europe. The plot centers around Young and Lewis finding a dachshund and travelling from Rome to Monte Carlo to return the stray and collect a $5,000 reward. Upon arrival in Monte Carlo, they find the dog's owner dead and they end up getting implicated for the murder. Other prime suspects include Belushi, Candy, Hamilton, and Shepherd. Weak script is made bearable only by the comic genius of Candy. **94m/C VHS.** John Candy, James Belushi, Cybill Shepherd, Sean Young, Richard Lewis, Ornella Muti, Giancarlo Giannini, George Hamilton, Joss Ackland, Elsa Martinelli; ***D:*** Eugene Levy; ***M:*** Richard Gibbs.

Once Upon a Forest 🦴🦴 **1993 (G)** Animated tale of three woodland creatures in a daring race against time when their young friend's life is at stake. Ecologically correct story by "American Tail" creator David Kirschner is light on humor and heavy on gloom, as little animals encounter oppressive human society and their big, bad machines. Servicable animation, though not up to Don Bluth standards (and a long, long way from Disney). Crawford, the voice of the wise old uncle, has a song, while Vereen breaks into a fervent gospel number as a marsh bird with a yen for preaching. For an evening of anti-pollution, treat the earth kindly animation, see it with "Ferngully." **80m/C VHS.** ***D:*** Charles Grosvenor; ***W:*** Mark Young, Kelly Ward; ***V:*** Michael Crawford, Ben Vereen.

Once Upon a Honeymoon 🦴🦴½ **1942** Set in 1938, Grant is an American radio broadcaster reporting on the oncoming war. Rogers is the ex-showgirl who unknowingly marries a Nazi. In this strange, uneven comedy, Grant tries to get the goods on him and also rescue Rogers. The plot is basic and uneven with Grant attempting to expose the Nazi and save Rogers. However, the slower moments are offset by some fairly surreal pieces of comedy. **116m/B VHS.** Ginger Rogers, Cary Grant, Walter Slezak, Albert Dekker; ***D:*** Leo McCarey; ***C:*** George Barnes.

Once Upon a Midnight Scary 🦴🦴 **1990** Price narrates a collection of three tales of terror, "The Ghost Belonged to Me," "The Legend of Sleepy Hollow," and "The House with a Clock in Its Walls." Aimed at the kiddies. **50m/C VHS.** Rene Auberjonois, Severn Darden; ***D:*** Neil Cox; ***Nar:*** Vincent Price.

Once Upon a Scoundrel 🦴🦴½ **1973 (G)** A ruthless Mexican land baron arranges to have a young woman's fiance thrown in jail so he can have her all to himself. **90m/C VHS.** Zero Mostel, Katy Jurado, Titos Vandis, Priscilla Garcia, A. Martinez; ***D:*** George Schaefer; ***M:*** Alex North.

Once Upon a Time in America 🦴🦴🦴½ **1984 (R)** The uncut original version of director Leone's saga of five young men growing up in Brooklyn during the '20s who become powerful mob figures. Also available in a 143-minute version. Told from the perspective of De Niro's Noodles as an old man looking back at 50 years of crime, love, and death, told with a sweeping and violent elegance. **225m/C VHS.** Robert De Niro, James Woods, Elizabeth McGovern, Treat Williams, Tuesday Weld, Burt Young, Joe Pesci, Danny Aiello, Darlanne Fluegel, Jennifer Connelly; ***D:*** Sergio Leone; ***C:*** Tonino Delli Colli; ***M:*** Ennio Morricone.

Once Upon a Time in China 🦴🦴🦴 *Wong Fei-hung* **1991** Martial arts expert Wong Fei-hung (Li) is dismayed as his country is overrun with western influences and the slave trade that provides labor to the California gold fields. When his aunt is kidnapped by slavers, Wong is determined to get revenge. The DVD edition clocks in at 134 minutes. **100m/C VHS, DVD, Wide.** *HK* Jet Li, Yuen Biao, Jacky Cheung, Rosamund Kwan, Kent Cheng; ***D:*** Tsui Hark; ***W:*** Tsui Hark; ***C:*** Arthur Wong, David Chung; ***M:*** James Wong.

Once Upon a Time in China II 🦴🦴🦴 *Wong Fei-hung Ji Yi: Naam Yi Dong Ji Keung* **1992 (R)** Wong (Li), his assistant Foon, and his aunt arrive in the city of Canton for a medical conference at which Wong is to demonstrate the Chinese art of acupuncture. But the city is on the brink of anarchy as a crumbling dynasty threatens its stability. So Wong joins the revolutionary Sun Yat Sen when a terrorist group initiates a campaign of violence. Dubbed into English. **112m/C VHS, DVD.** *HK* Jet Li, Rosamund Kwan, Mok Siu Chung, Xiong Xin Xin, John Chiang, Zhang Tie Lin, Yen Chi Tan; ***D:*** Tsui Hark; ***W:*** Tsui Hark; ***C:*** Wong Ngok Tai; ***M:*** Richard Yuen.

Once Upon a Time in China III 🦴🦴🦴 *Wong Fei-hung Tsi Sam: Siwong Tsangba* **1993 (R)** Wong Fei-Hung, his young aunt-by-adoption Yee (to whom he is secretly engaged), and his friend Chung arrive in Peking just as the Empress announces an important martial arts contest. Wong faces rivals on two fronts: a brutal martial arts foe and a Russian diplomat who has a history with Yee. **105m/C VHS, DVD.** *HK* Jet Li, Rosamund Kwan, Mok Siu Chung, Xiong Xin Xin, Shun Lau; ***D:*** Tsui Hark; ***W:*** Tsui Hark; ***C:*** Wai Keung Lau; ***M:*** Wai Lap Wu.

Once Upon a Time in the West 🦴🦴🦴½ **1968 (PG)** The uncut version of Leone's sprawling epic about a band of ruthless gunmen who set out to murder a mysterious woman waiting for the railroad to come through. Filmed in John Ford's Monument Valley, it's a revisionist western with some of the longest opening credits in the history of the cinema. Fonda is cast against type as an extremely cold-blooded villain. Brilliant musical score. **165m/C VHS.** *IT* Henry Fonda, Jason Robards Jr., Charles Bronson, Claudia Cardinale, Keenan Wynn, Lionel Stander, Woody Strode, Jack Elam; ***D:*** Sergio Leone; ***W:*** Sergio Leone, Bernardo Bertolucci, Dario Argento; ***C:*** Tonino Delli Colli; ***M:*** Ennio Morricone.

Once Upon a Time ... When We Were Colored 🦴🦴🦴 **1995 (PG)** Actor Reid makes a fine directorial debut with the story of a black youngster growing up parentless in '50s Mississippi. His family faces the usual troubles of the time, including poor wages and white bigotry, but manages to provide a positive and loving home life for him. Nostalgic, sensitive, and heartwarming adaptation of Clifton Taulbert's autobiographical book. **112m/C VHS, DVD, Wide.** Al Freeman Jr., Paula Kelly, Phylicia Rashad, Polly Bergen, Richard Roundtree, Charles Taylor, Willie Norwood, Jr., Damon Hines, Leon; ***D:*** Tim Reid; ***W:*** Paul Cooper; ***C:*** Johnny (John W.) Simmons; ***M:*** Steve Tyrell; ***Nar:*** Phill Lewis.

Once Were Warriors 🦴🦴🦴 **1994 (R)** Violent story of the struggling Maori Heke family, who have left their rural New Zealand roots to live in the city. Feisty mom Beth (Owen) is struggling with five kids and volatile hubby Jake (Heke), who's continuously out of work, boozing, and fighting. Eldest son Nig (Arahanga) has left home and joined a street gang and the rest of the kids hate Jake for beating up on their mother. They also fall victim to his temper and his habit of bringing his brawling, drunk buddies home-leading to further tragedy. Intense drama showcases great performances, with Owen honored as best actress at the Montreal World Film Festival. Based on the novel by Alan Duff. Feature-film directorial debut of Tamahori. **102m/C VHS.** *NZ* Rena Owen, Temuera Morrison, Mamaengaroa Kerr-Bell, Julian (Sonny) Arahanga, Taungaroa Emile, Rachael Morris, Joseph Kairau, Pete Smith; ***D:*** Lee Tamahori; ***W:*** Riwia Brown; ***C:*** Stuart Dryburgh; ***M:*** Murray Grindlay, Murray McNabb. Australian Film Inst. '95: Foreign Film; Montreal World Film Fest. '94: Actress (Owen), Film.

The One 🦴🦴 **2001 (PG-13)** The premise of this action-intensive martial arts flick is that there are 125 parallel universes, and that each person has a counterpart in all of them. Gabriel Yulaw (Li) is a renegade Multiverse Bureau of Investigation agent who is killing his fellow selves in order to absorb their energy. He has fellow MBI agents Roedecker (Lindo) and Funsch (Statham) after him, but he only has one Gabe left to kill, this one a hardworking L.A. deputy sheriff. Bad Gabe kills good Gabe's wife, and the stage is set for a showdown in a grungy factory. Did you follow all of that? Well, it doesn't matter, because it's all just an excuse to have Jet Li kick Jet Li's butt on a catwalk to the sounds of grating techno/metal. Should have added a touch of humor to a completely ludicrous plot instead of concentrating on stealing special effects from "The Matrix." **80m/C VHS, DVD.** *US* Jet Li, Delroy Lindo, Carla Gugino, Jason Statham, Dylan Bruno, Richard Steinmetz, James Morrison; ***D:*** James Wong; ***W:*** Glen Morgan, James Wong; ***C:*** Robert McLachlan; ***M:*** Trevor Rabin.

One Against the Wind 🦴🦴🦴 **1991 (PG)** A true story of one woman's courage against great odds. British Mary Liddell and her children are living in Paris during the WWII Nazi occupation. Mary's secret agenda is to smuggle downed Allied pilots out of the country to safety without arousing Nazi suspicions. Great performances by Davis as the resourceful Mary and Neill as one of the pilots she rescues. A Hallmark Hall of Fame presentation. **96m/C VHS.** Judy Davis, Sam Neill, Denholm Elliott, Anthony (Corlan) Higgins, Christien Anholt, Kate Beckinsale, Frank Middlemass, Benedick Blythe, Peter Cellier, Stefan Gryff, Mark Wing-Davey, John Savident, David Ryall, Tom Hodgkins, Wolf Kahler, Michael Crossman, Terry Taplin, Mikush Alexander; ***D:*** Larry Elikann; ***W:*** Chris Bryant; ***C:*** Denis Lewiston; ***M:*** Lee Holdridge. **TV**

One A.M. **1916** Charlie is a drunk who must first battle a flight of stairs in order to get to bed. Silent with music track. **20m/B VHS.** Charlie Chaplin.

The One and Only 🦴🦴½ **1978 (PG)** An egotistical young man is determined to make it in show business. Instead, he finds himself in the world of professional wrestling. Most of the humor comes from the wrestling scenes, with Winkler and Darby's love story only serving to dilute the film. **98m/C VHS.** Henry Winkler, Kim Darby, Gene Saks, William Daniels, Harold Gould, Herve Villechaize; ***D:*** Carl Reiner.

The One and Only, Genuine, Original Family Band 🦴🦴🦴 **1968 (G)** A harmonious musical family becomes divided when various members take sides in the presidential battle between Benjamin Harrison and Grover Cleveland, a political era that has been since overlooked. **110m/C VHS.** Walter Brennan, Buddy Ebsen, Lesley Ann Warren, Kurt Russell, Goldie Hawn, Wally Cox, Richard Deacon, Janet Blair; ***D:*** Michael O'Herlihy.

One Arabian Night 🦴🦴🦴 *Sumurun* **1921** When an exotic dancer in a traveling carnival troupe is kidnapped into a harem, a dwarf acts on his unrequited love and avenges her death by murdering the sheik who killed her. Secured a place in American filmmaking for director Lubitsch. **85m/B VHS.** *GE* Pola Negri, Ernst Lubitsch, Paul Wegener; ***D:*** Ernst Lubitsch.

One Armed Executioner 🦴🦴 **1980 (R)** An Interpol agent seeks revenge on his wife's murderers. **90m/C VHS.** Franco Guerrero, Jody Kay; ***D:*** Bobby A. Auarez.

One Away 🦴 **1980 (PG)** Gypsy escapes from a South African prison and the police are in hot pursuit. **83m/C VHS.** Elke Sommer, Bradford Dillman, Dean Stockwell.

One Body Too Many 🦴🦴 **1944** A mystery spoof about a wacky insurance salesman who's mistaken for a detective. The usual comedy of errors ensues. A contrived mish-mash—but it does have Lugosi going for it. **75m/B VHS.** Jack Haley, Jean Parker, Bela Lugosi, Lyle Talbot; ***D:*** Frank McDonald.

One Brief Summer woof! **1970 (R)** Love triangles and intrigues abound on a spectacular country manor. An aging woman is mortified by her father's interest in a young seductress, who finds herself attracted to the old man, but not only him. **86m/C VHS.** Clifford Evans, Felicity Gibson, Jennifer Hilary, Jan Holden, Peter Egan; ***D:*** John MacKenzie.

One Christmas 🦴🦴½ *Truman Capote's One Christmas* **1995** Conman father uses his estranged son as a pawn to gain access to New Orleans high society. Based on the story "One Christmas" by Truman Capote. **91m/C VHS, DVD.** Katharine Hepburn, Henry Winkler, Swoosie Kurtz, T.J. Lowther, Pat Hingle, Julie Harris; ***D:*** Tony Bill; ***W:*** Duane Poole; ***M:*** Van Dyke Parks. **TV**

One Cooks, the Other Doesn't 🦴🦴 **1983** A most unlikely story of a man's ex-wife and his son moving back into his house, where he's now living with his new wife. **96m/C VHS.** Suzanne Pleshette, Joseph Bologna, Rosanna Arquette, Oliver Clark; ***D:*** Richard Michaels. **TV**

One Crazy Night 🦴🦴½ **1993 (PG-13)** In 1964, five Australian teenagers try to get into the Melbourne hotel where the Beatles are staying on tour. They wind up trapped in the basement, swapping secrets, and finding out how much they have in common. **92m/C VHS.** *AU* Noah Taylor, Beth Champion, Malcolm Kennard, Danni Minogue, Malcolm Braly; ***D:*** Michael Pattinson.

One Crazy Summer 🦴🦴½ **1986 (PG)** A group of wacky teens spends a fun-filled summer on Nantucket Island in New England. Follow-up to "Better Off Dead" is offbeat and fairly charming, led by Cusack's perplexed cartoonist and with comic moments delivered by Goldthwait. **94m/C VHS.** John Cusack, Demi Moore, William Hickey, Curtis Armstrong, Bob(cat) Goldthwait, Mark Metcalf, Joel Murray, Tom Villard, Joe Flaherty; ***D:*** Steve Holland; ***W:*** Steve Holland; ***M:*** Cory Lerios.

One Dark Night 🦴½ *Entity Force; Mausoleum* **1982 (R)** Two high school girls plan an initiation rite for one of their friends who is determined to shed her "goody-goody" image. West is the caped crusader of TV series "Batman" fame. **94m/C VHS.** Meg Tilly, Adam West, David Mason Daniels, Robin Evans, Elizabeth (E.G. Dailey) Daily; ***D:*** Tom McLoughlin.

One Day in the Life of Ivan Denisovich 🦴🦴🦴 **1971** The film version of Nobel Prize-winner Alexander Solzhenitsyn's novel about a prisoner's experiences in a Soviet labor camp. A testament to human endurance. Photography be Sven Nykvist. **105m/C VHS.** *NO GB* Tom Courtenay, Alfred Burke, Espen Skjonberg, James Maxwell, Eric Thompson; ***D:*** Casper Wrede; ***W:*** Ronald Harwood; ***C:*** Sven Nykvist.

One Deadly Owner 🦴 **1974** A possessed Rolls-Royce tortures its new owner. Quite a vehicle for the usually respectable set of wheels. **80m/C VHS.** Donna Mills, Jeremy Brett, Robert Morris, Laurence Payne. **TV**

One Deadly Summer 🦴🦴🦴 *L'Ete Meurtrier* **1983 (R)** Revenge drama about a young girl who returns to her mother's home village to ruin three men who had assaulted her mother years before. Very well acted. From the novel by Sebastien Japrisot. In French with English subtitles. **134m/C VHS.** *FR* Isabelle Adjani, Alain Souchon, Suzanne Flon; ***D:*** Jean Becker; ***M:*** Georges Delerue. Cesar '84: Actress (Adjani), Support. Actress (Flon), Writing.

One Down, Two to Go! woof! **1982 (R)** When the mob is discovered to be rigging a championship karate bout, two dynamic expert fighters join in a climactic battle against the hoods. Example of really bad "blaxploitation" that wastes talent, film, and the audience's time. **84m/C VHS.** Jim Brown, Fred Williamson, Jim Kelly, Richard Roundtree, Tom Signorelli, Joe Spinell, Paula Sills, Laura Loftus; ***D:*** Fred Williamson; ***W:*** Jeff Williamson; ***C:*** James (Momel) Lemmo; ***M:*** Herb Hetzer, Joe Trunzo.

187 🦴🦴½ **1997 (R)** Jackson's a Brooklyn high school teacher who is brutally attacked by one of his students. His physical scars are healed, but his emotional state is marred as he takes some pretty unorthodox teaching methods to a troubled L.A. school. Very dark, psychological drama with a powerful performance by Jackson. Tough film whose title refers to the California penal code number for murder. First film from director Reynolds after his "Waterworld" fiasco. **119m/C VHS, DVD, Wide.** Samuel L. Jackson, John Heard, Kelly Rowan, Clifton (Gonzalez) Collins Jr., Tony Plana, Lobo Sebastian, Jack Kehler, Demetrius Navarro, Karina Arroyave; ***D:*** Kevin Reynolds; ***W:*** Scott Yagemann; ***C:*** Ericson Core.

One-Eyed Jacks 🦴🦴🦴½ **1961** An often engaging, but lengthy, psychological western about an outlaw who seeks to settle the score with a former partner who became a sheriff. Great acting by all, particularly Brando, who triumphed both as star and director. Stanley Kubrick was the original director, but Brando took over mid-way through the filming. The photography is wonderful and reflects the effort that went into it. **141m/C VHS, DVD.** Marlon Brando, Karl Malden, Katy Jurado, Elisha Cook Jr., Slim Pickens, Ben Johnson, Pina Pellicer, Timothy Carey; ***D:*** Marlon Brando; ***W:*** Calder Willingham; ***C:*** Charles B(ryant) Lang Jr.

One-Eyed Soldiers 🦴 **1967** Young woman, criminal, and dwarf follow trail to mysterious key to unlock $15 million treasure. Much cheesy intrigue. **83m/C VHS.** *GB YU* Dale Robertson, Luciana Paluzzi; ***D:*** Jean Christopher.

One-Eyed Swordsman 🦴 **1963** A handicapped samurai battles shogun warriors. With English subtitles. **95m/C VHS.** *JP* Tetsuro Tamba, Haruko Wanibuchi; ***D:*** Seiichiro Uchikawa.

One False Move 🦴🦴🦴 **1991 (R)** Black psycho Pluto, his white-trash partner Ray, and Ray's biracial lover Fantasia are three low-level drug dealers on the streets of Los Angeles who get involved in murder. Fleeing the city for Fantasia's small hometown in Arkansas, they come up against the local sheriff and two L.A. cops sent to bring them back. Not a typical crime thriller, first-time feature director Franklin is more interested in a psychological character study of racism and small-town mores than in your average shoot 'em up action picture. Good performances, especially by Williams as the deceptive bad girl. **105m/C VHS, DVD, Wide.** Bill Paxton, Cynda Williams, Michael Beach, Jim Metzler, Earl Billings, Billy Bob Thornton, Natalie Canerday, Robert Ginnaven, Robert Anthony Bell, Kevin Hunter; ***D:*** Carl Franklin; ***W:*** Billy Bob Thornton, Tom Epperson; ***C:*** James L. Carter; ***M:*** Peter Haycock, Derek Holt. Ind. Spirit '93: Director (Franklin); MTV Movie Awards '93: New Filmmaker (Franklin).

One Fine Day 🦴🦴½ **1996 (PG)** Marshmallows. That's what this movie is like—light, fluffy, not much substance, but enjoyable when you're in the mood. Nod to the classic screwball comedies of the '40s and '50s throws harried single mom/ architect Pfeiffer and political columnist/ weekend dad Clooney together when their kids, who attend the same school, miss a class field trip. Naturally, they take an instant dislike to each other, but are forced to cooperate to solve the daycare situation. An accidental switching of cell phones provides the chance for repeated encounters, and growing mutual interest. Predictable, but pleasantly so. No matter how hard she tries, Pfeiffer always looks good, and Clooney has that cocked head, devilish grin thing working overtime. Screenplay by Neil Simon's daughter Ellen supplies all the elements for a fine date movie. **108m/C VHS, DVD, Wide.** Michelle Pfeiffer, George Clooney, Alex D. Linz, Mae Whitman, Charles Durning, Jon Robin Baitz, Ellen Greene, Joe Grifasi, Pete Hamill, Anna Maria Horsford, Sheila Kelley, Barry Kivel, Robert Klein, George Martin, Michael Massee, Amanda Peet, Bitty Schram, Holland Taylor, Rachel York; ***D:*** Michael Hoffman; ***W:*** Terrel Seltzer, Ellen Simon; ***C:*** Oliver Stapleton; ***M:*** James Newton Howard.

One Flew Over the Cuckoo's Nest 🦴🦴🦴🦴 **1975 (R)** Touching, hilarious, dramatic, and completely effective adaptation of Ken Kesey's novel. Nicholson is two-bit crook Randle Patrick McMurphy, who, facing a jail sentence, feigns insanity to be sentenced to a cushy mental hospital. The hospital is anything but cushy, with tyrannical head nurse Ratched (Fletcher) out to squash any vestige of the patients' independence. Nicholson proves to be a crazed messiah and catalyst for these mentally troubled patients and a worthy adversary for the head nurse. Classic performs superbly on numerous levels. **129m/C VHS, DVD.** Jack Nicholson, Brad Dourif, Louise Fletcher, Will Sampson, William Redfield, Danny DeVito, Christopher Lloyd, Scatman Crothers, Vincent Schiavelli, Michael Berryman, Peter Brocco, Louisa Moritz; ***D:*** Milos Forman; ***W:*** Ken Kesey, Bo Goldman; ***C:*** Haskell Wexler, Bill Butler, William A. Fraker; ***M:*** Jack Nitzsche. Oscars '75: Actor (Nicholson), Actress (Fletcher), Adapt. Screenplay, Director (Forman), Picture; AFI '98: Top 100; British Acad. '76: Actor (Nicholson), Actress (Fletcher), Director (Forman), Film, Support. Actor (Dourif); Directors Guild '75: Director (Forman); Golden Globes '76: Actor—Drama (Nicholson), Actress—Drama (Fletcher), Director (Forman), Film—Drama, Screenplay; Natl. Bd. of Review '75: Actor (Nicholson), Natl. Film Reg. '93;; N.Y. Film Critics '75: Actor (Nicholson); Natl. Soc. Film Critics '75: Actor (Nicholson); Writers Guild '75: Adapt. Screenplay.

One for the Road 🦴 *Against All Hope* **1982** Michael Madsen's screen debut is unwatchable in this atrocious movie. He plays alcoholic Cecil Moe who's trying to straighten himself out. **90m/C VHS, DVD.** Michael Madsen, Maureen McCarthy, Rex Flores, Tim Joosten, Herb Harms, Ron Schultz; ***D:*** Edward T. McDougal.

One Frightened Night 🦴🦴½ **1935** An eccentric millionaire informs his family members that he is leaving each of them $1 million...as long as his long-lost granddaughter doesn't reappear. Guess who comes to dinner. **69m/B VHS.** Mary Carlisle, Wallace Ford, Hedda Hopper, Charley Grapewin; ***D:*** Christy Cabanne.

One from the Heart 🦴🦴 **1982 (R)** The film more notable for sinking Coppola's Zoetrope Studios than for its cinematic context. Garr and Forrest are a jaded couple who seek romantic excitement with other people. An extravagant (thus Coppola's finance problems) fantasy Las Vegas set, pretty to look at but does little to enhance the weak plot. Score by Waits, a much-needed plus. **100m/C VHS.** Teri Garr, Frederic Forrest, Nastassia Kinski, Raul Julia, Lainie Kazan, Rebecca DeMornay, Harry Dean Stanton; ***D:*** Francis Ford Coppola; ***W:*** Armyan Bernstein, Francis Ford Coppola; ***M:*** Tom Waits, Robert Alcivar.

One Good Cop 🦴🦴½ **1991 (R)** A noble, inconsistent attempt to do a police thriller with a human face, as a young officer and his wife adopt the three little daughters of his slain partner from the force. But it reverts to a routine action wrapup, with 'Batman' Keaton even donning a masked-avenger getup to get revenge. **105m/C VHS.** Michael Keaton, Rene Russo, Anthony LaPaglia, Kevin Conway, Rachel Ticotin, Grace Johnston, Blair Swanson, Rhea Silver-Smith, Tony Plana, Benjamin Bratt, Charlaine Woodard; ***D:*** Heywood Gould; ***W:*** Heywood Gould; ***C:*** Ralf Bode; ***M:*** William Ross.

One Good Turn 🦴🦴 **1995 (R)** Matt Forrest (Von Dohlen) and his wife Laura (Amis) seemingly have it all only to have their fortunes take a radical turn for the worse. Matt "accidentally" runs into Simon Jury (Remar), the man who saved his life 12 years before. But the seemingly friendly Jury is actually intent on destroying everything they have. **90m/C VHS, DVD.** Lenny Von Dohlen, James Remar, Suzy Amis, John Savage; ***D:*** Tony Randel; ***W:*** Jim Piddock; ***C:*** Jacques Haitkin; ***M:*** Joel Goldsmith.

One Hour Photo **2002 (R)** Williams stars as milquetoast Seymour Parrish, Sy the Photo Guy, who mans the one-hour photo booth. But Sy turns out to be quite creepy when he discovers his favorite family (headed by Nielsen and Vartan) isn't as perfect as they seem in their pictures, of which Sy has copies, of course. Not yet rated. **?m/C VHS, DVD.** Robin Williams, Connie Nielsen, Michael Vartan, Gary Cole, Eriq La Salle, Dylan Smith; ***D:*** Mark Romanek; ***W:*** Mark Romanek.

One Hundred and One Nights 🦴🦴 *Les Cent et Une Nuits; Les Cent et Une Nuits de Simon Cinema* **1995** Simon Cinema (Piccoli) is a 100-year-old producer/director whose memory is fading. So he hires young film student Camille (Gayet) to prompt his memory. Numerous celebrities make cameo appearances to talk about film and numerous film clips are shown. **101m/C VHS, DVD.** *FR GB* Michel Piccoli, Marcello Mastroianni, Henri Garcin, Julie Gayet, Mathieu Demy, Emmanuel Salinger; ***D:*** Agnes Varda; ***W:*** Agnes Varda; ***C:*** Eric Gautier.

100 Days Before the Command 🦴🦴 *Sto Dnej Do Pri Kaza* **1990** Five young Red Army recruits struggle for survival and to preserve their humanity against the violence of their daily lives by leaning on each other. Russian with subtitles. **71m/C VHS, DVD.** *RU* Vladimir Zamansky, Armen Dzhigarkhanyan, Oleg Vasilkov, Roman Grekov, Valeri Troshinl; ***D:*** Hussein Erkenov; ***W:*** Vladimir Kholodov, Yuri Polyakov; ***C:*** Vladislav Menshikov.

100 Girls 🦴🦴 **2000 (R)** College freshman Tucker (Tucker) scores an unexpected sexual encounter with a co-ed in the girls' dorm elevator during a blackout. He can't see her face and doesn't know her name, so he spends the semester investigating the 100 possibles in search of his mystery girl. Actually funny and not as sleazy as it may sound. **95m/C VHS, DVD, Wide.** Jonathan Tucker, James DeBello, Emmanuelle Chriqui, Larisa Oleynik, Jaime Pressly, Katherine Heigl; ***D:*** Michael Davis; ***W:*** Michael Davis; ***C:*** James Lawrence Spencer; ***M:*** Kevin Bassinson.

100 Men and a Girl 🦴🦴🦴 **1937** Charming musical features Durbin as the daughter of an unemployed musician, who decides she will try to persuade Leopold Stokowski to help her launch an orchestra that will employ her father and his musician friends. Beautiful mix of classical and pop music. Based on a story by Hans Kraly. ♫Hungarian Rhapsody No. 2; Symphony No. 5; Alleluja; It's Raining Sunbeams; A Heart That's Free. **85m/B VHS.** Deanna Durbin, Leopold Stokowski, Adolphe Menjou, Alice Brady, Eugene Pallette, Mischa Auer, Billy Gilbert, Alma Kruger, Christian Rub, Jed Prouty, Jack Mulhall; ***D:*** Henry Koster; ***C:*** Joseph Valentine. Oscars '37: Score.

100 Proof 🦴🦴 **1996** Based on a 1986 murder rampage in Lexington, Kentucky. Rae (Stewart) and her compliant sidekick, Carla (Bellando), are a couple of smalltime, small-town hustlers, with drug/booze habits, who turn tricks to get by. The day begins in its usual bleak fashion until Rae encounters her degenerate father (Varney), who routinely abused her. Rae's anger grows, fueled by cocaine and alcohol, until she snaps and begins shooting people. **94m/C VHS.** Pamela Stewart, Tara Bellando, Larry Brown, Jim Varney; ***D:*** Jeremy Horton; ***W:*** Jeremy Horton; ***C:*** Harold McNeese.

100 Rifles 🦴🦴 **1969 (R)** Native American bank robber and Black American lawman join up with a female Mexican revolutionary to help save the Mexican Indians from annihilation by a despotic military governor. What it lacks in political correctness it makes up for in fits of action. Although quite racy in its day for its interracial sex sizzle of Brown and Rachel, it's tame and overblown by today's standards. **110m/C VHS.** Jim Brown, Raquel Welch, Burt Reynolds, Fernando Lamas; ***D:*** Tom Gries; ***M:*** Jerry Goldsmith.

101 Dalmatians 🦴🦴🦴½ **1961 (G)** Disney classic is one of the highest-grossing animated films in the history of Hollywood. Dogowners Roger and Anita, and their spotted pets Pongo and Perdita are shocked when their puppies are kidnapped by Cruella de Vil, villainess extraordinaire, to make a simply fabulous spotted coat. The aid of various animals including a dog named Colonel, a horse, a cat, and a goose is enlisted to rescue the doomed pups. Imagine their surprise when they find not only their own puppies, but 84 more as well. You can expect a happy ending and lots of spots—6,469,952 to be exact. Based on the children's book by Dodie Smith. Technically notable for the first time use of the Xerox process to transfer the animator's drawings onto celluloid, which made the film's opening sequence of dots evolving into 101 barking dogs possible. ♫Remember When; Cruella de Vil; Dalmation Plantation; Kanine Krunchies Kommercial. **79m/C VHS, DVD.** ***D:*** Clyde Geronimi, Wolfgang Reitherman, Hamilton Luske; ***W:*** Bill Peet; ***M:*** George Bruns; ***V:*** Rod Taylor, Betty Lou Gerson, Lisa Davis, Ben Wright, Frederick Worlock, J. Pat O'Malley.

101 Dalmatians 🦴🦴½ **1996 (G)** Yes, it's the live-action Disney version of their own 1961 animated feature (based on the book by Dodie Smith) about dognapping villainess Cruella De Vil (Close) and lots of spotted pups. They're absolutely adorable, of course, Cruella's costumes (and hair) are certainly eye-catching, and the bumbling crooks get their proper comeuppance. Daniels and Richardson have the thankless role of the dogs' human owners, Roger and Anita, and get upstaged at every opportunity. Kids familiar with the cartoon pups may be surprised that the live pups don't talk—and keep in mind that Close, while terrific, may be too scary for the little ones. The Hound is always happy to see another dog movie but still feels some classics should be left alone. **103m/C VHS, DVD.** Glenn Close, Jeff Daniels, Joely Richardson, Joan Plowright, Hugh Laurie, Mark Williams; ***D:*** Stephen Herek; ***W:*** John Hughes; ***C:*** Adrian Biddle; ***M:*** Michael Kamen.

102 Dalmatians 🦴½ **2000 (G)** Lackluster sequel to the 1996 live-action Disney film finds Cruella De Vil (Close) being released from prison and teaming up with fur designer Jean Pierre Le Pelt (Depardieu). She still wants that dalmatian fur coat (and this time a hood as well). The puppies are as cute as ever, with the addition of digitally de-spotted Oddball, but this one just seems like another excuse for Disney to print money and Close to chew scenery. Stick with the original (the 1961 cartoon version, that is). **100m/C VHS, DVD, Wide.** Glenn Close, Gerard Depardieu, Ioan Gruffudd, Tim (McInnerny) McInnery, Ian Richardson, Ben Crompton, Jim Carter, Ron Cook, David Horovitch, Timothy West, Alice Evans, Carol MacReady; ***D:*** Kevin Lima; ***W:*** Bob Tzudiker, Noni White, Kristen Buckley, Brian Regan; ***C:*** Adrian Biddle; ***M:*** David Newman; ***V:*** Eric Idle.

125 Rooms of Comfort 🦴🦴 **1983** A mental patient has bizarre fantasies that create havoc among those who stand in his way. **82m/C VHS.** Tim Henry, Jackie Burroughs, Bob Warner, Bob Silverman, Les Barker; ***D:*** Patrick Loubert; ***W:*** Patrick Loubert, Bill Freut.

One in a Million 🦴🦴🦴 **1936** Debut film of Norwegian skating star Henie centers around a Swiss girl whose father is training her for the Olympics. Features good comedy by the Ritz Brothers and Sparks, as well as the beautiful skating of Henie. ♫One in a Million; We're Back in Circulation Again; Who's Afraid of Love; Lovely Lady in White; The Moonlight Waltz. **95m/B VHS.** Sonja Henie, Adolphe Menjou, Jean Hersholt, Al Ritz, Harry Ritz, Jimmy Ritz, Arline Judge, Don Ameche, Ned Sparks, Montagu Love, Leah Ray; ***D:*** Sidney Lanfield; ***W:*** Leonard Praskins, Mark Kelly.

One in a Million: The Ron LeFlore Story 🦴🦴½ **1978** The true story of Detroit Tigers' star Ron LeFlore, who rose from the Detroit ghetto to the major leagues. Adaptation of LeFlore's autobiography, "Breakout." A well-acted and compelling drama with Burton in a standout performance. **90m/C VHS.** LeVar Burton, Madge Sinclair, Billy Martin, James Luisi; ***D:*** William A. Graham; ***C:*** Jordan Cronenweth.

One Kill 🦴🦴🦴 **2000 (PG-13)** Fact-based drama focuses on a murder and a trial. Mary Jane O'Malley (Heche) is a decorated Marine captain and divorced mom who is having an affair with her troubled senior officer, Maj. Nelson Gray (Shepard). Mary Jane breaks things off when she finds out Nelson is married but he's obsessed and when he breaks into her home, she shoots him in self-defense. At least, the D.A. says justifiable homicide but the military has other ideas and decides to try O'Malley itself. Good performances by the leads. **93m/C VHS.** Anne Heche, Sam Shepard, Eric Stoltz, Bill MacDonald, Kate McNeil, Carl Marotte; ***D:*** Christopher Menaul; ***W:*** Shelley Evans; ***C:*** Michael Storey; ***M:*** Eric Allaman. CABLE

One Last Run 🦴½ **1989** It's drama on the slopes as a variety of individuals confront their pasts/fears/personal demons via extreme skiing. Features the performances of champion skiers Franz Weber and Scot Schmidt. **82m/C VHS.** Russell Todd, Ashley Laurence, Craig Branham, Jimmy Aleck, Tracy Scoggins, Nels Van Patten, Chuck Connors; ***D:*** Peter Winograd, Glenn Gebhard; ***W:*** Peter Winograd, Glenn Gebhard.

One Little Indian 🦴🦴 **1973** AWOL cavalry man Garner and his Indian ward team up with a widow (Miles) and her daughter (Foster) in an attempt to cross the New Mexican desert. A tepid presentation from the usually high quality Disney studio. **90m/C VHS, DVD.** James Garner, Vera Miles, Jodie Foster, Clay O'Brien, Andrew Prine, Bernard McEveety; ***D:*** Bernard McEveety; ***M:*** Jerry Goldsmith.

One Magic Christmas 🦴🦴½ **1985 (G)** Disney feel-good film about a disillusioned working woman whose faith in Christmas is restored when her guardian angel descends to Earth and performs various miracles. Somewhat cliched and tiresome, but partially redeemed by Stanton and Steenburgen's presence. **88m/C VHS, DVD.** Mary Steenburgen, Harry Dean Stanton, Gary Basaraba, Michelle Meyrink, Arthur Hill, Elisabeth Harnois, Robbie Magwood; ***D:*** Phillip Borsos; ***W:*** Thomas Meehan; ***C:*** Frank Tidy; ***M:*** Michael Conway Baker.

One Man Army 🦴½ **1993 (R)** Kickboxer goes to visit gramps in small town, only to discover the old guy has been murdered and corruption and cover-ups abound. So he decides to kick some butt and set things right. **95m/C VHS.** Jerry Trimble; ***D:*** Cirio H. Santiago.

One Man Force 🦴🦴 **1989 (R)** L.A. narcotics cop Jake Swan goes on a vigilante spree. Huge in body and vengeful in spirit, he makes his partner's murderers pay! **92m/C VHS.** John Matuszak, Ronny Cox, Charles Napier, Sharon Farrell, Sam Jones, Chance Boyer, Richard Lynch, Stacey Q; ***D:*** Dale Trevillion; ***W:*** Dale Trevillion; ***M:*** Charles Fox.

One Man Jury 🦴 **1978 (R)** LAPD lieutenant, wearied by an ineffective justice system, becomes a one-man vigilante avenger. Pale Dirty Harry rip-off with over acting and an overdose of violence. **95m/C VHS.** Jack Palance, Chris Mitchum, Joe Spinell, Pamela Shoop; ***D:*** Charles Martin.

One Man Out 🦴 **1989 (R)** An ex-CIA agent diverts his psychological problems into his new job: assassin for a South American despot. His jaded view of life changes when he meets and falls in love with an American journalist. Trouble in paradise when he is ordered to kill her. One man out was not enough, they should have done away with the entire crew of this stinker. **90m/C VHS.** Stephen McHattie, Deborah Van Valkenburgh, Aharon Ipale, Ismael Carlo, Michael Champion, Dennis A. Pratt; ***D:*** Michael Kennedy.

One Man's Hero 🦴½ **1998 (R)** Heavy-handed retelling of the U.S.-Mexican war of the 1840s. Irish Catholic Army Sgt. John Riley (Berenger) is tired of the constant harassment he and his fellow Irishmen are subjected to. After disobeying an officer, Riley leads his men into Mexico where they eventually join the Mexican army as the St. Patrick's Battalion just in time to battle the U.S. troops of Gen. Zachary Taylor (Gammon). The history's confusing and isn't helped when the action stops for romantic interludes between Riley and rebel girl, Marta (Romo). **122m/C VHS, DVD.** Tom Berenger, Joaquim de Almeida, Daniela Romo, James Gammon, Mark Moses, Stuart Graham, Stephen Tobolowsky, Carlos Carrasco, Patrick Bergin; *D:* Lance Hool; *W:* Milton S. Gelman; *C:* Joao Fernandes; *M:* Ernest Troost.

One Man's Justice ☠☠½ **1995 (R)** Army drill sergeant John North (Bosworth) heads for the streets of Venice, California to get the drug-dealing, gun-running scum who killed his wife and daughter. And a streetwise 10-year-old may be his best chance for finding them. **100m/C VHS, DVD, Wide.** Brian Bosworth, Bruce Payne, Jeff Kober, DeJuan Guy, Hammer; *D:* Kurt Wimmer; *W:* Steven Selling; *C:* Jurgen Baum, John Huneck; *M:* Anthony Marinelli.

One Man's War ☠☠½ **1990 (PG-13)** A human-rights crusader in repressive Paraguay won't be silenced, even after government thugs torture and murder his son. He fights obsessively to bring the killers to justice. The true story of the Joel Filartiga family is heartfelt but ultimately a dramatic letdown; an epilogue proves that full story hasn't been told. **91m/C VHS.** Anthony Hopkins, Norma Aleandro, Fernanda Torres, Ruben Blades; *D:* Sergio Toledo.

One Man's Way ☠☠½ **1963** Murray is appropriately devout as charasmatic religious leader Norman Vincent Peale. With the support of his wife (Hyland), he survives the adulations and accusations of blasphemy for his rather unorthodox theological ideas and his book, "The Power of Positive Thinking." Based on the book "Norman Vincent Peale: Minister to Millions" by Arthur Gordon. **105m/B VHS.** Don Murray, Diana Hyland, William Windom, Virginia Christine, Carol Ohmart, Veronica Cartwright, Liam Sullivan, June Dayton, Ian Wolfe; *D:* Denis Sanders; *W:* Eleanore Griffin, John W. Bloch.

One Million B.C. ☠☠½ *The Cave Dwellers; Cave Man; Man and His Mate* **1940** The strange saga of the struggle of primitive cavemen and their battle against dinosaurs and other monsters. Curiously told in flashbacks, this film provided stock footage for countless dinosaur movies that followed. Portions of film rumored to be directed by cinematic pioneer D. W. Griffith. **80m/B VHS.** Victor Mature, Carole Landis, Lon Chaney Jr.; *D:* Hal Roach, Hal Roach Jr.

One Million Years B.C. ☠☠½ **1966 (R)** It's Welch in a fur bikini and special FX expert Ray Harryhausen doing dinosaurs so who cares about a plot (which involves Welch and her boyfriend, who's from a rival clan). Remake of the 1940 film "One Million B.C." **100m/C VHS.** *GB* Raquel Welch, John Richardson, Percy Herbert, Robert Brown, Martine Beswick; *D:* Don Chaffey.

One Minute to Zero ☠☠ **1952** Korean War action film divides its time between an army romance and war action. The lukwarm melodrama features Mitchum as a colonel in charge of evacuating American civilians but who ends up bombing refugees. **105m/B VHS.** Robert Mitchum, Ann Blyth, William Talman, Charles McGraw, Margaret Sheridan, Richard Egan, Eduard Franz, Robert Osterloh, Robert Gist; *D:* Tay Garnett.

One More Chance ☠½ **1990** While he was in jail, an ex-con's family moves away without leaving a forwarding address. When he's released he strikes up a friendship with a woman from the neighborhood who knows where they've gone. **102m/C VHS.** Kirstie Alley, John Lamotta, Logan Clarke, Michael Pataki, Hector Maisonette; *D:* Sam Firstenberg.

One More Saturday Night ☠ **1986 (R)** Franken and Davis, "Saturday Night Live" alumni, wrote this film about a small town going wild on the weekend. Dry, taxing, and unfunny. Averages about one laugh per half hour—at one-and-a-half hours, that's way too long. **96m/C VHS.** Al Franken, Tom Davis, Nan Woods, Dave Reynolds; *D:* Dennis Klein; *W:* Al Franken, Tom Davis.

One Night at McCool's ☠☠ **2001 (R)** Quirky and inventive, this poor man's "Rashomon" gets points for effort, but the execution doesn't always live up to the ambition. Easygoing bartender Randy (Dillon) is involved in a murder by aggressively materialistic con artist Jewel (Tyler) and before he knows it, he's in love. Somehow his sleazy lawyer cousin (Reiser) becomes involved, as well as Det. Dehling (Goodman) who is investigating the murder of Jewel's former partner (Clay). Of course, all three fall in love, and we see the preceding night's events through each set of love-struck eyes as they spill their guts to a hitman (Douglas), a shrink (McIntire), and a priest (Jenkins), respectively. Douglas's outlandish toupee and understated portrayal of the hitman, as well as some fine comic touches by Dillon, are highlights. **93m/C VHS, DVD, Wide.** *US* Liv Tyler, Matt Dillon, Paul Reiser, John Goodman, Michael Douglas, Reba McEntire, Richard Jenkins, Andrew (Dice Clay) Silverstein, Leo Rossi, Eric Schaeffer; *D:* Harald Zwart; *W:* Stan Seidel; *C:* Karl Walter Lindenlaub; *M:* Marc Shaiman.

One Night in the Tropics ☠☠½ **1940** The film debut of radio stars Abbott & Costello who play secondary roles to a love triangle (set to music). Jones is an insurance salesman who falls in love with Kelly, the fiance of Cummings. Based on the novel "Love Insurance" by Earl Derr Biggers. ♫Back in My Shell; Remind Me; You and Your Kiss; Your Dream is the Same as My Dream. **83m/B VHS.** Allan Jones, Robert Cummings, Nancy Kelly, Bud Abbott, Lou Costello, Mary Boland, Peggy Moran, William Frawley, Leo Carrillo; *D:* Edward Sutherland; *W:* Kathryn Scola, Gertrude Purcell, Charles Grayson, Francis Martin.

One Night of Love ☠☠☠½ **1934** Moore's best quasi-operetta, about a young American diva rebelling in response to her demanding Italian teacher. "Pygmallion"-like story has her falling in love with her maestro. Despite being nearly 60 years old, this film is still enchanting and fresh. ♫One Night of Love; Ciri-Biri-Bin; Sempre Libera; Sextet; Indian Love Call; 'Tis the Last Rose of Summer; Habanera; Un bel di; None But the Lonely Heart. **95m/B VHS.** Grace Moore, Tullio Carminati, Lyle Talbot, Jane Darwell, Nydia Westman, Mona Barrie, Jessie Ralph, Luis Alberni; *D:* Victor Schertzinger. Oscars '34: Sound, Score.

One Night Only **1984** A gorgeous law student decides to make big money by hiring herself and her friends out as hookers to the school football team. **87m/C VHS.** Lenore Zann, Jeff Braunstein, Grant Alianak; *D:* Timothy Bond.

One Night Stand ☠☠ **1977** Woman's chance encounter with a man in a singles bar leads to an evening of unexpected terror. Billed as a horror flick, it is really more of a drama. **90m/C VHS.** *CA* Chapelle Jaffe, Brent Carver. **TV**

One Night Stand ☠☠☠ **1984** Four young people attempt to amuse themselves at the empty Sydney Opera House on the New Year's Eve, that night WWIII begins. An odd commentary on nuclear war that sees the bomb as the ultimate bad joke. Features an appearance by alternative rock group Midnight Oil. **94m/C VHS.** Tyler Coppin, Cassandra Delaney, Jay Hackett, Saskia Post; *D:* John Duigan.

One Night Stand ☠☠½ **1995 (R)** Lonely Michelle (Sheedy) visits a nightclub and allows herself to be picked up by your basic handsome stranger, Jack (Martinez) in this case. She wakes up alone and learns from building owner Josslyn (Forrest) that the apartment is up for lease. Obsessed with finding her mystery man, Michelle discovers Jack's wife was murdered—possibly by him or maybe by Josslyn, who turns out to be the dead woman's father. Debut feature for director Shire covers familiar territory, with Sheedy giving a strong performance. **92m/C VHS.** Ally Sheedy, A. Martinez, Frederic Forrest, Don Novello, Diane Salinger, Millie Slavin; *D:* Talia Shire; *W:* Marty Casella; *C:* Arthur Albert; *M:* David Shire.

One Night Stand ☠☠☠ **1997 (R)** Max (Snipes) is a commercial director in New York on business. While visiting his friend Charlie (Downey), a choreographer dying of AIDS, he meets willowy beauty Karen (Kinski). This chance meeting leads to, you guessed it, a one night stand. When Max returns home to L.A., he realizes how empty and stale his life is. One year later, he and wife Mimi (Wen) return to visit the quickly fading Charlie. They meet Charlie's brother Vernon (McLachlan) and his wife...Karen. Good performances (especially by Downey) and characterization make this more than a morality play about the ramifications of a sexual fling. Although paid for his original material, Joe Eszterhas didn't take any writing credit after Figgis totally rewrote the script. **103m/C VHS, DVD.** Mike Figgis, Wesley Snipes, Nastassia Kinski, Ming Na, Robert Downey Jr., Kyle MacLachlan, Glenn Plummer, Amanda Donohoe, Thomas Haden Church, Julian Sands, John Ratzenberger, Annabelle Gurwitch, Donovan Leitch, Zoe Nathenson, Vincent Ward, Susan Barnes; ***Cameos:*** Ione Skye, Xander Berkeley; *D:* Mike Figgis; *W:* Mike Figgis; *C:* Declan Quinn; *M:* Mike Figgis.

1-900 ☠☠ **1994** Based on the play "06" by Doesburg, which refers to the Dutch exchange for phone-sex numbers. Sarah (Schluter) and Thomas (van Kempen) are both lonely professionals who "meet" when Thomas answers Sarah's personal ad. Their weekly phone chats lead to descriptions of sexual fantasies but relationship issues begin to intrude as time passes. Dutch with subtitles. **80m/C VHS, DVD.** *NL* Ariane Schluter, Ad van Kempen; *D:* Theo van Gogh; *W:* Ariane Schluter, Ad van Kempen, Johan Doesburg, Marcel Otten; *C:* Tom Erisman; *M:* Ruud Bos.

One of Her Own ☠☠½ **1997** Based on the true story of a police officer (Laughlin) who decides to press charges against the fellow cop (Evigan) who raped her, despite the consequences to her career. **91m/C VHS.** Lori Loughlin, Greg Evigan, Martin Sheen, Vel Johnson; *D:* Armand Mastroianni; *W:* Pablo F. Fenjves, Valerie West. **TV**

One of My Wives Is Missing ☠☠½ **1976** An ex-New York cop tries to solve the mysterious disappearance of a newlywed socialite. Things become strange when she reappears but is discovered as an imposter. Above-average acting in a film adapted from the play "The Trap for a Lonely Man." **97m/C VHS.** Jack Klugman, Elizabeth Ashley, James Franciscus; *D:* Glenn Jordan. **TV**

One of Our Aircraft Is Missing ☠☠☠½ **1941** The crew of an R.A.F. bomber downed in the Netherlands, struggle to escape Nazi capture. A thoughtful study of wars and the men who fight them, with an entertaining melodramatic plot. Look for the British version, which runs 106 minutes. Some of the American prints only run 82 minutes. **103m/B VHS.** *GB* Godfrey Tearle, Eric Portman, Hugh Williams, Pamela Brown, Googie Withers, Peter Ustinov; *D:* Emeric Pressburger, Michael Powell.

One of Our Dinosaurs Is Missing ☠☠ **1975 (G)** An English nanny and her cohorts help British Intelligence retrieve a microfilm—concealing dinosaur fossil from the bad guys that have stolen it. Disney film was shot on location in England. **101m/C VHS.** Peter Ustinov, Helen Hayes, Derek Nimmo, Clive Revill, Robert Stevenson, Joan Sims; *D:* Robert Stevenson.

One on One ☠☠½ **1977 (PG)** A Rocky-esque story about a high school basketball star from the country who accepts an athletic scholarship to a big city university. He encounters a demanding coach and intense competition. Light weight drama that is economically entertaining. **100m/C VHS.** Robby Benson, Annette O'Toole, G.D. Spradlin, Gail Strickland, Melanie Griffith; *D:* Lamont Johnson; *W:* Robby Benson; *M:* Charles Fox.

One Plus One ☠ *Exploring the Kinsey Report* **1961** A dramatization, believe it or not, of the Kinsey sex survey of the 1950s. Participants in a sex lecture talk about and demonstrate various "risque" practices, such as premarital sex and extramarital affairs. Despite this film, the sexual revolution went on as planned. **114m/B VHS.** *CA* Leo G. Carroll, Hilda Brawner, William Traylor, Kate Reid, Ernest Graves; *D:* Arch Oboler; *W:* Arch Oboler.

One-Punch O'Day ☠ **1926** Boxing boy tries to buy back hometown's oil livelihood by winning prizefight. Much patient waiting by his honey. **60m/B VHS.** Billy Sullivan, Jack Herrick, Charlotte Merriam; *D:* Harry Joe Brown.

One Rainy Afternoon ☠☠ **1936** A bit-player kisses the wrong girl in a Paris theatre causing a massive uproar that brands him as a notorious romantic "monster." Patterned after a German film, the story lacks depth and zest. **80m/B VHS.** Francis Lederer, Ida Lupino, Hugh Herbert, Roland Young, Donald Meek; *D:* Rowland V. Lee.

One Russian Summer woof! **1973 (R)** During the Russian Revolution, a cripple seeks revenge on the corrupt land baron who murdered his parents. An unfortunate attempt to dramatize a novel by M. Lermontov. **112m/C VHS.** Oliver Reed, Claudia Cardinale, John McEnery, Carole Andre, Ray Lovelock; *D:* Antonio Calenda.

One Shoe Makes It Murder ☠☠ **1982** A shady casino owner hires ex-cop Mitchum to investigate the disappearance of his unfaithful wife. Adapted from Eric Bercovici's novel, the story does little to enhance Mitchum's TV debut. **100m/C VHS.** Robert Mitchum, Angie Dickinson, Mel Ferrer, Howard Hesseman, Jose Perez; *D:* William Hale; *M:* Bruce Broughton.

One Sings, the Other Doesn't ☠☠½ *L'Une Chante, l'Autre Pas* **1977** Seeking contentment, a conservative widow and a liberal extrovert help each other cope in a man's world. Endearing characters, but a superficial treatment of dated feminist issues. In French with English subtitles. **105m/C VHS.** *FR BE* Valerie Mairesse, Therese Liotard, Robert Dadies, Ali Affi, Jean-Pierre Pellegrin; *D:* Agnes Varda; *W:* Agnes Varda; *C:* Charlie Van Damme; *M:* Francois Wertheimer.

One Small Hero ☠½ **1999 (PG)** Dopey family entertainment might not be a complete waste of time for easygoing viewers. Joey Cooper (Kiley) can't pass the tests to become a member of the Wilderness Club and go on their camping trip. He fails once again (he's physically too small) but can't tell his mom after she surprises Joey with camping gear. So, he trails behind the campers and is the only one who can save them from kidnappers. **90m/C VHS, DVD.** Nathan Kiley, Matthew Peters, Lindsay Lewis, Bonnie Burroughs; *D:* Jennifer Malchese; *C:* Denis Maloney; *M:* Herman Beeftink. **CABLE**

One Step to Hell ☠½ *Caccia Ai Violenti; King of Africa* **1968** Good cop rescues gold-miner's widow from three escaped convicts. Beautiful African scenery helps save an otherwise mediocre film. **90m/C VHS.** Ty Hardin, Rossano Brazzi, Pier Angeli, George Sanders, Tab Hunter, Sandy Howard.

One Summer Love ☠½ *Dragonfly* **1976** Man checks out from loony bin, searches for family ties and befriends beautiful woman who works in a moviehouse. **95m/C VHS.** Beau Bridges, Susan Sarandon, Mildred Dunnock, Ann Wedgeworth, Michael B. Miller, Linda Miller, James Noble, Frederick Coffin; *D:* Gilbert Cates; *W:* N. Richard Nash.

One That Got Away ☠☠☠ **1957** A loyal German Luftwaffe pilot captured by the British becomes obsessed with escape. Fast paced and exciting. Based on a true story. **111m/B VHS.** Hardy Kruger, Colin Gordon, Alec Gordon; *D:* Roy Ward Baker.

One Third of a Nation ☠☠½ **1939** Depression era film contrasts the conditions of slum life with those in high society. A young entrepreneur inherits a city block in ruins, only to fall in love with a young woman who lives there and help her crippled brother. Timely social criticism. **79m/B VHS.** Sylvia Sidney, Leif Erickson, Myron McCormick, Sidney Lumet; *D:* Dudley Murphy.

1001 Arabian Nights ½
1959 In this Arabian nightmare, the near-sighted Mr. Magoo is known as "Azziz" Magoo, lamp dealer and uncle of Aladdin. **76m/C VHS.** ***D:*** Jack Kinney; ***M:*** George Duning; ***V:*** Jim Backus, Kathryn Grant, Hans Conried, Herschel Bernardi.

One Too Many *The Important Story of Alcoholism; Killer With a Label* **1951** Exploitation film depicting the evils of alcoholism. Camp, but slick. **?m/C VHS.** Ruth Warrick, Richard Travis, Victor Kilian, Onslow Stevens, Lyle Talbot.

One Touch of Venus ½
1948 Love fills a department store when a window dresser kisses a statue of the goddess Venus—and she comes to life. Appealing adaptation of the Broadway musical. ♫Speak Low; The Trouble with Women; That's Him; Don't Look Now But My Heart Is Showing; My Week. **82m/B VHS.** Ava Gardner, Robert Walker, Eve Arden, Dick Haymes, Olga San Juan, Tom Conway; ***D:*** William A. Seiter; ***M:*** Kurt Weill, Ogden Nash.

One Tough Cop **1998 (R)** Baldwin proves he's more than just a goofy face in a potential breakthrough role as headstrong NYPD detective Bo Dietl. Together with partner Finnerty (Penn), Dietl investigates a brutal rape and mutilation of a nun in East Harlem. Despite Brazilian director Barreto's good eye for the mean streets of New York and Baldwin's stellar performance, this is just one more derivative police drama without distinction. Barreto's wife Irving makes an appearance as a mean-spirited federal agent. Based on the autobiography on real-life retired cop Bo Dietl. **94m/C VHS, DVD.** Stephen Baldwin, Gina Gershon, Christopher Penn, Mike McGlone, Paul Guilfoyle, Amy Irving, Victor Slezak, Luis Guzman; ***D:*** Bruno Barreto; ***W:*** Jeremy Iacone; ***C:*** Ron Fortunato; ***M:*** Bruce Broughton.

One Trick Pony ½ **1980 (R)** Once-popular rock singer/songwriter struggles to keep his head above water in a turbulent marriage and in the changing currents of popular taste. Simon wrote the autobiographical screenplay and score, but let's hope he is more sincere in real life. A good story. **100m/C VHS.** Paul Simon, Blair Brown, Rip Torn, Joan Hackett, Mare Winningham, Lou Reed, Harry Shearer, Allen (Goorwitz) Garfield, Daniel Stern; ***D:*** Robert M. Young; ***C:*** Dick Bush.

One True Thing **1998 (PG-13)** Better check for the family-sized box of tissues before you take home this tearjerker about cancer-stricken mother Kate (Streep) and her relationship with arrogant, career-oriented daughter Ellen (Zellweger). After being guilted by her stuffy college professor dad (Hurt), Ellen agrees to care for Kate as the disease progresses, and the two bridge their emotional distance. Lifted above the disease-of-the-week Lifetime TV material by the presence of stars Streep and Hurt, and by the stellar performance of Zellweger. Based on the novel by Anna Quindlen. **128m/C VHS, DVD.** Meryl Streep, Renee Zellweger, William Hurt, Tom Everett Scott, Nicky Katt, Lauren Graham, James Eckhouse, Patrick Breen, Gerrit Graham; ***D:*** Carl Franklin; ***W:*** Karen Croner; ***C:*** Declan Quinn; ***M:*** Cliff Eidelman.

One, Two, Three ½ **1961** Cagney, an American Coca-Cola exec in Germany, zealously pursues any opportunity to run Coke's European operations. He does the job too well and loses his job to a Communist hippie turned slick capitalist. Fast-paced laughs, wonderful cinematography, and a fine score. **110m/B VHS, Wide.** James Cagney, Horst Buchholz, Arlene Francis, Pamela Tiffin; ***D:*** Billy Wilder; ***W:*** Billy Wilder, I.A.L. Diamond; ***C:*** Daniel F. Fapp; ***M:*** Andre Previn.

One Way Out **1995** Frank (Gwaltney) gets out of jail, teams up with Bobby (Monahan) and his stripper girlfriend Eve (Golden), and the trio go to visit Frank's brother, Snooky (Turano). When Frank learns that Snooky's lowlife boss (Ironside) has been ripping him off, they plan to even the score. Naturally, the heist goes wrong and they wind up with a hostage (Gillies) and on the lam. **106m/C VHS.** Jack Gwaltney, Jeff Monahan, Annie Golden, Robert Turano, Michael Ironside, Isabel Gillies; ***D:*** Kevin Lynn.

One Wild Moment ½ **1978 (R)** Comic complications arise when a divorced man is seduced by his best friend's daughter while vacationing. Warm and charming. Later re-made as "Blame It on Rio." In French with English subtitles. **88m/C VHS.** *FR* Jean-Pierre Marielle, Victor Lanoux, Agnes Soral, Christine Dejoux, Martine Sarcey; ***D:*** Claude Berri; ***W:*** Claude Berri.

One Wish Too Many ½
1955 A young boy finds a marble that grants wishes. He has the time of his life with his teachers and the school bullies, but runs into trouble when he creates a giant steam roller which overruns London. Winner of Best Children's Film, 1956 Venice Film Festival, but it is hard to say why. **55m/B VHS.** *GB* Anthony Richmond, Rosalind Gourgey, John Pike; ***D:*** John Durst.

One Woman or Two ½ *Une Femme ou Deux* **1985 (PG-13)** Paleontologist Depardieu is duped by beautiful ad-exec who plans to use his findings to push perfume. Remake of "Bringing Up Baby," this screwball comedy has a few screws loose. Dubbed. **100m/C VHS.** *FR* Gerard Depardieu, Sigourney Weaver, Dr. Ruth Westheimer, Michel Aumont, Zabou; ***D:*** Daniel Vigne; ***W:*** Elisabeth Rappeneau, Daniel Vigne.

One Wonderful Sunday
Subarashiki Nichiyobi **1947** It's postwar Tokyo, so just how wonderful can things be? Well, perky Masako (Nakakita) is determined to make the day as bright as possible for her depressed fiance, Yuzo (Numasaki), despite the fact they have no money and can't afford to do much more than walk around together. More of a curiosity in Kurosawa's oeuvre than a substantial work. Japanese with subtitles. **108m/B VHS.** *JP* Chieko Nakakita, Isao Numasaki; ***D:*** Akira Kurosawa; ***W:*** Akira Kurosawa, Keinosuke Uekusa; ***C:*** Asakazu Nakai; ***M:*** Tadashi Hattori.

Onegin **1999** Fiennes family affair, with Martha assuming directorial duties, brother Magnus providing the score, and Ralph starring as the titular 18th-century Russian aristocrat. The cynical sophisticate inherits a vast country estate in the 1820s, where Onegin befriends his young neighbor Lensky (Stephens) and his featherbrained fiancee, Olga (Headey). But Onegin is intrigued by Olga's older sister, lovely innocent Tatyana (Tyler), though he rejects her impulsive romantic gestures. This isn't the only mistake that Onegin makes—all of which cost him dearly. Film looks beautiful but doesn't have much soul. Based on the Aleksandr Pushkin novel "Eugene Onegin." **106m/C VHS, DVD, Wide.** *GB* Ralph Fiennes, Liv Tyler, Toby Stephens, Lena Headey, Martin Donovan, Alun Armstrong, Harriet Walter, Irene Worth, Francesca Annis; ***D:*** Martha Fiennes; ***W:*** Peter Ettedgui, Michael Ignatieff; ***C:*** Remi Adefarasin; ***M:*** Magnus Fiennes.

Onibaba *The Demon; The Devil Woman* **1964** A brutal parable about a mother and her daughter-in-law in war-ravaged medieval Japan who subsist by murdering stray soldiers and selling their armor. One soldier beds the daughter, setting the mother-in-law on a vengeful tirade. Review of the film varied widely, hailed by some as a masterpiece and by others as below average; in Japanese with subtitles. **103m/B VHS.** *JP* Nobuko Otowa, Yitsuko Yoshimura, Kei Sato; ***D:*** Kaneto Shindo.

The Onion Field ½ **1979 (R)** True story about the mental breakdown of an ex-cop who witnessed his partner's murder. Haunted by the slow process of justice and his own feelings of insecurity, he is unable to get his life together. Based on the novel by Joseph Wambaugh, who also wrote the screenplay. Compelling script and excellent acting. **126m/C VHS.** John Savage, James Woods, Ronny Cox, Franklyn Seales, Ted Danson; ***D:*** Harold Becker.

Only Angels Have Wings **1939** Melodramatic adventure about a broken-down Peruvian air mail service. Large cast adds to the love tension between Grant, a pilot, and Arthur, a showgirl at the saloon. Nominated for special effects, a category recognized by the Academy that year for the first time. William Rankin and Eleanor Griffin are uncredited writers. **121m/B VHS, DVD.** Cary Grant, Thomas Mitchell, Richard Barthelmess, Jean Arthur, Noah Beery Jr., Rita Hayworth, Sig Rumann, John Carroll, Allyn Joslyn; ***D:*** Howard Hawks; ***W:*** Jules Furthman; ***C:*** Joseph Walker; ***M:*** Dimitri Tiomkin.

Only Love ½ *Erich Segal's Only Love* **1998** Sappy made for TV romance adapted from the Segal novel. Neurosurgeon Matthew Heller (Morrow) is shocked by the reappearance of former fiancee Silvia Rinaldi (May) some 15 years after they broke up. She's dying of a brain tumor and needs his medical help. His longtime (platonic) female friend Evie (Tomei) can't understand his obsession and you won't either. (The scenery's nice though). **130m/C VHS.** Rob Morrow, Marisa Tomei, Mathilda May, Jeroen Krabbe, Paul Freeman, Georges Corraface; ***D:*** John Erman; ***W:*** Gerald Christopher; ***M:*** John Morris. **TV**

Only Once in a Lifetime
1983 A love story about an Hispanic immigrant painter looking for success in America. **90m/C VHS.** Miguel Robelo, Estrellita Lopez, Sheree North.

Only One Night *En Enda Natt* **1942** Upon finding out that he's the illegitimate son of an aristocrat, a happy-go-lucky carousel operator in a circus joins high society and is promptly matched with a beautiful but repressed woman. In Swedish with English subtitles. **87m/B VHS.** *SW* Ingrid Bergman, Edvin Adolphson, Aino Taube, Olof Sandborg, Erik "Bullen" Berglund, Marianne Lofgren, Magnus Kesster; ***D:*** Gustaf Molander.

Only the Brave **1994** Gay coming-of-age story about two teenaged, working-class girls living on the seedy fringes of Melbourne. Alex (Manadalis), her wild best friend Vicki (Kaskanis), and their equally tough girlfriends seem to spend most of their time hanging out, smoking dope, and getting into trouble. But Alex slowly recognizes her feelings for Vicki are also sexual, and their friendship drastically changes. **62m/C VHS.** *AU* Elena Mandalis, Dora Kaskanis, Moudo Davey, Bob Bright; ***D:*** Ana Kokkinos; ***W:*** Ana Kokkinos, Mira Robertson.

Only the Lonely ½ **1991 (PG)** Middle-aged cop, Candy, falls in love with a shy undertaker's assistant, Sheedy, and is torn between love and dear old Mom, O'Hara, in her first role in years. Candy is an unlikely leading man and even the jokes are forced. But the restaurant scene makes the whole thing well worth seeing. **104m/C VHS, Wide.** John Candy, Ally Sheedy, Maureen O'Hara, Anthony Quinn, Kevin Dunn, James Belushi, Milo O'Shea, Bert Remsen, Macaulay Culkin, Joe V. Greco; ***D:*** Chris Columbus; ***W:*** Chris Columbus; ***M:*** Maurice Jarre.

Only the Strong ½ **1993 (PG-13)** Louis (Dacascos) is a special forces officer who has mastered capoeira, a Brazilian form of kung fu. In Miami, he works with his old teacher (Lewis) to instill discipline in the 12 toughest punks in school by teaching them his martial arts skills. A neighborhood drug lord, related to two of the students, decides to cause trouble for Louis. Dascascos displays some charm along with his physical abilities but the story's ridiculous and the movie hastily put together. **96m/C VHS.** Mark Dacascos, Stacy Travis, Todd Susman, Geoffrey Lewis, Paco Christian Prieto; ***D:*** Sheldon Lettich; ***W:*** Sheldon Lettich, Luis Esteban; ***M:*** Harvey W. Mason.

Only the Valiant **1950** Action-packed story of a cavalry officer who struggles to win his troops respect while warding off angry Apaches. Fast-paced Western fun requires little thought. **105m/B VHS.** Gregory Peck, Ward Bond, Gig Young, Lon Chaney Jr., Barbara Payton, Neville Brand; ***D:*** Gordon Douglas; ***C:*** Lionel Lindon.

The Only Thrill ½ *Tennessee Valley* **1997** Old-fashioned small town romance based on Ketron's play "The Trading Post." In 1966, Reece McHenry (Shepard) decides to open a used clothing store in his Tennessee hometown and hires widowed seamstress Carol Fitzsimmons (Keaton) to help him out. Reece is married but his wife is in an irreversible coma and soon the aw-shucks storekeeper is interested in romancing his new employee. Meanwhile, Reece's son Tom (Patrick) and Carol's daughter Katherine (Lane) have also discovered a reciprocated love. However, neither romance runs smoothly. **108m/C VHS.** Sam Shepard, Diane Keaton, Robert Patrick, Diane Lane, Tate Donovan, Sharon Lawrence, Stacy Travis; ***D:*** Peter Masterson; ***W:*** Larry Ketron; ***C:*** Don E. Fauntleroy; ***M:*** Peter Melnick.

Only Two Can Play **1962** Sellers is a hilarious Casanova librarian who puts the moves on a society lady to get a promotion. Funny, of course, and based on Kingsley Amis' novel "That Uncertain Feeling." **106m/C VHS.** *GB* Peter Sellers, Virginia Maskell, Mai Zetterling, Richard Attenborough; ***D:*** Sidney Gilliat; ***M:*** Richard Rodney Bennett.

The Only Way ½ **1970 (G)** A semi-documentary account of the plight of the Jews in Denmark during the Nazi occupation. Despite German insistence, the Danes succeeded in saving most of their Jewish population from the concentration camps. **86m/C VHS.** Jane Seymour, Martin Potter, Benjamin Christiansen; ***M:*** Carl Davis.

The Only Way Home **1972 (PG)** Two bikers end up in big trouble when one of them kills a wealthy man, and they kidnap his wife. Filmed entirely in Oklahoma. **86m/C VHS.** Bo Hopkins, Beth Brickell, Steve Sandor, G.D. Spradlin; ***D:*** G.D. Spradlin.

Only When I Laugh *It Hurts Only When I Laugh* **1981 (R)** Neil Simon reworked his Broadway flop "The Gingerbread Lady" to produce this poignant comedy about the relationship between an aging alcoholic actress and her teenage daughters. **120m/C VHS.** Marsha Mason, Kristy McNichol, James Coco, Joan Hackett, David Dukes, Kevin Bacon, John Bennett Perry; ***D:*** Glenn Jordan; ***W:*** Neil Simon; ***M:*** David Shire. Golden Globes '82: Support. Actress (Hackett).

Only with Married Men **1974** Carne's hassle-free dating routine is disrupted when a sly bachelor pretends that he's married to get a date. A middle-aged persons answer to a teenage sex comedy. Pretty bad. **74m/C VHS.** David Birney, Judy Carne, Gavin MacLeod, John Astin; ***D:*** Jerry Paris.

Only You ½ **1992 (PG-13)** A shy guy has always searched for true romance. But his cup runneth over when he meets, and must choose between, two beautiful women—your basic beach babe and a sensible beauty. What's a guy to do? **85m/C VHS.** Andrew McCarthy, Kelly Preston, Helen Hunt; ***M:*** Wendy Blackstone.

Only You ½ *Him; Just in Time* **1994 (PG)** According to her ouija board, young Faith's (Tomei) soul mate is named Damon Bradley. But as the years pass, Faith is about to settle for a podiatrist—until an old school friend of her fiance's calls from Venice, Italy, with best wishes. Guess what his name is. So Faith and best friend Kate (Hunt) hop on a plane in search of Mr. Right. Then Faith meets charming shoe salesman Peter Wright (Downey) and wonders if ouija got things wrong. Slight romantic comedy with Jewison creating satisfactory chemistry with charming Downey and the somewhat miscast Tomei (and the Venetian scenery is gorgeous). **108m/C VHS, DVD.** Marisa Tomei, Robert Downey Jr., Bonnie Hunt, Fisher Stevens, Billy Zane, Joaquim de Almeida; ***D:*** Norman Jewison; ***W:*** Diane Drake; ***C:*** Sven Nykvist; ***M:*** Rachel Portman.

Open All Hours **1983** Comedy about a small corner shop and its viciously greedy, opportunistic owner. **85m/C VHS.** *GB* Ronnie Barker, Lynda Baron, David Jason, Stephenie Cole. **TV**

Open City *Roma, Citta Aperta; Rome, Open City* **1945** A leader in the Italian underground resists Nazi control of the city. A stunning film, making Rossellini's realistic style famous. In Italian with English subtitles. **103m/B VHS, DVD.** *IT* Anna Magnani, Aldo Fabrizi, Marcel Pagliero, Maria Michi, Vito Annicchiarico, Nando (Fernando) Bruno, Harry Feist; ***D:*** Roberto Rossellini; ***W:*** Federico

Fellini, Sergio Amidei; *C:* Ubaldo Arata; *M:* Renzo Rossellini. N.Y. Film Critics '46: Foreign Film.

Open Doors 🦴🦴🦴½ *Porte Aperte* **1989 (R)** Bitter review of Fascist rule and justice. The Fascist regime promises security, safety, and tranquility. So, on the morning that a white collar criminal murders his former boss, murders the man who got his job, and then rapes and murders his wife, tensions rise and the societal structures are tested. The people rally for his death. A judge and a juror struggle to uphold justice rather than serve popular passions. Winner of four Donatello Awards, Italian Golden Globes for Best Film, Best Actor, and Best Screenplay, and many international film awards. In Italian with English subtitles. **109m/C VHS.** *IT* Gian Marie Volonte, Ennio Fantastichini, Lidia Alfonsi; *D:* Gianni Amelio; *W:* Gianni Amelio.

Open Fire 🦴🦴 **1994 (R)** Alex McNeil (Wincott) is an ex-FBI agent, haunted by the death of his partner. But when a group of terrorists threaten to release a cloud of nerve gas over L.A. and hold McNeil's father hostage, he comes back full force. **93m/C VHS.** Jeff Wincott, Patrick Kilpatrick, Lee DeBroux, Mimi (Meyer) Craven, Arthur Taxier.

Open House 🦴 **1986** Radio psychologist and beautiful real estate agent search for the killer of real estate agents and their clients. A mystery-thriller for the very patient. **95m/C VHS.** Joseph Bottoms, Adrienne Barbeau, Mary Stavin, Rudy Ramos; *D:* Jag Mundhra.

Open Season 🦴🦴 **1995 (R)** Stuart Sain (Wuhl) is an ambitious executive at Fielding, a TV ratings company (think Nielsen) whose boxes turn out to be defective. The ratings error causes public television programming to be number one, forcing the networks to counter-program culturally in order to regain their market share. Meanwhile, the public TV executives get overconfident and everything's just up for grabs. Flawed satire. **97m/C VHS.** Robert Wuhl, Rod Taylor, Gailard Sartain, Maggie Han, Joe Piscopo, Helen Shaver, Dina Merrill, Saul Rubinek, Steven C. White, Timothy Arrington, Barry Flatman, Tom Selleck, Alan Thicke, Jimmie Walker; *D:* Robert Wuhl; *W:* Robert Wuhl; *C:* Stephen Lighthill; *M:* Marvin Hamlisch.

Open Secret 🦴🦴 **1948** Jewish residents are plagued by a gang of anti-semitic thugs. Violence and destruction escalate until a fed up police lieutenant, tenaciously played by Ireland, and a victimized shop owner (Tyne) join forces to just say no more. When the gang learns the shopkeeper has caught their dastardly deeds on camera, the battle begins in earnest. Fast-paced and intriguing suspense. **70m/B VHS.** John Ireland, Jane Randolph, Roman Bohnen, Sheldon Leonard, George Tyne, Morgan Farley, Ellen Lowe, Anne O'Neal, Arthur O'Connell; *D:* John Reinhardt.

Open Your Eyes 🦴🦴🦴 *Abre Los Ojos* **1997 (R)** Reality gets taken for a mind-bending spin in this Spanish thriller. Gorgeous womanizer, Cesar (Noriega), meets equally gorgeous Sofia (Cruz) and thinks he's finally found the one. Only his crazy ex-girlfriend Nuria (Nimri) causes a car crash that kills her and disfigures Cesar. He awakens in a prison hospital wearing a mask, accused of murder, and with confused memories. But maybe he's had an operation to restore his looks and is actually back together with Sofia but then Cesar keeps seeing Nuria's ghost. So just what is going on? Spanish with subtitles. **117m/C VHS, DVD, Wide.** *SP* Eduardo Noriega, Penelope Cruz, Najwa Nimri, Chete Lera, Fele Martinez, Gerard Barray; *D:* Alejandro Amenabar; *W:* Alejandro Amenabar, Mateo Gil; *C:* Hans Burman; *M:* Alejandro Amenabar, Mariano Marin.

Opening Night 🦴🦴½ **1977 (PG-13)** Very long study about an actress (Rowlands) and the play she's about to open in on Broadway. Backstage turmoil increases her own insecurities and the bad luck persists when an adoring fan is struck by a car while the play is in try-outs in New Haven. Performances carry this neurotic epic along, including Cassavettes as Rowland's co-star and Blondell as the playwright. **144m/C VHS, DVD.** Gena Rowlands, John Cassavetes, Joan Blondell, Ben Gazzara, Paul Stewart, Zohra Lampert, Laura Johnson; *D:* John Cassavetes; *W:* John Cassavetes; *C:* Frederick Elmes; *M:* Bo Harwood.

Opera 🦴½ *Terror at the Opera* **1988 (R)** A bizarre staging of Verdi's "Macbeth" is plagued by depraved gore murders. But the show must go on, as one character chirps in badly dubbed English. Italian horrormeister Argento's ever-fluid camera achieves spectacular shots, but the lurid, ludicrous script make this one for connoisseurs only. The operatic scenes employ the voice of Maria Callas. Available in an edited "R" rated version. **107m/C VHS, DVD, Wide.** *IT* Christina Marsillach, Ian Charleson, Urbano Barberini, William McNamara, Antonella Vitale, Barbara Cupisti, Coralina Cataldi Tassoni, Daria Nicolodi; *D:* Dario Argento; *W:* Dario Argento, Franco Ferrini; *C:* Ronnie Taylor; *M:* Claudio Simonetti.

Opera do Malandro **1987** A lavish Brazilian take off of "The Threepenny Opera." Married hustler falls for a beautiful entrepreneur longing to get rich off of American goods. Based on Chico Buarque's musical play. In Portuguese, with subtitles. **106m/C VHS.** *BR* Edson Celulari, Claudia Ohana, Elba Ramalho, Ney Latorraca; *D:* Ruy Guerra.

Operation Amsterdam 🦴🦴 **1960** Four agents have 14 hours to snare $10 million in diamonds from under the noses of local Nazis. Based on a true story. Full of 1940s wartime action and suspense. **103m/B VHS.** Peter Finch, Eva Bartok, Tony Britton, Alexander Knox; *D:* Michael McCarthy.

Operation C.I.A. 🦴🦴 *Last Message From Saigon* **1965** A plot to assassinate the U.S. ambassador in Saigon inspires brave CIA agent Reynolds to wipe out the bad guys. Action-packed and somewhat exciting. **90m/C VHS.** Burt Reynolds, John Hayt, Kieu Chinh, Danielle Aubry; *D:* Christian Nyby.

Operation Condor 🦴🦴 **1991 (PG-13)** Secret agent Jackie (Chan) is sent by the United Nations to retrieve 240 tons of gold buried by the Nazis in a Moroccan desert during WWII. Naturally, he's not the only one after the treasure. Lots of typically exhuberant stunts and laughable dialogue (dubbed into English from Cantonese). **92m/C VHS, DVD.** *HK* Jackie Chan, Carol Cheng, Eva Cabo De Garcia, Ikeda Shoko; *D:* Jackie Chan; *W:* Edward Tang, Jackie Chan; *C:* Wong Ngok Tai; *M:* Stephen Endelman.

Operation Condor 2: The Armour of the Gods 🦴🦴 *Armour of God; Longxiong Hudi* **1986 (R)** Prequel to "Operation Condor" was re-released in 1997. Chan plays an adventurous treasure-hunter who is asked by his ex-girlfriend's new fiancee Alan (Tam), who used to be Jackie's best friend, to rescue her from an evil cult. The kidnappers want Jackie and Alan to deliver a priceless medieval set of armour, thought to contain mysterious powers, to them. Naturally, Chan must come up with some spectacular saves of both the armour and the girl. In Cantonese with English subtitles. **88m/C VHS, DVD.** *HK* Jackie Chan, Alan Tam, Rosamund Kwan, Lola Forner; *D:* Jackie Chan; *W:* Jackie Chan, Edward Tang, John Sheppard; *C:* Peter Ngor; *M:* Michael Lai.

Operation Cross Eagles 🦴🦴 *Unakrsna Vatra* **1969** Routine WWII military thriller with Conte and Calhoun on a mission to rescue an American general in exchange for their German prisoner. Their mission is complicated by a traitor in the group. Conte's only directorship. **90m/C VHS.** *YU* Richard Conte, Rory Calhoun, Aili King, Phil Brown; *D:* Richard Conte.

Operation Crossbow 🦴🦴🦴 *The Great Spy Mission; Code Name: Operation Crossbow* **1965** Action-packed espionage tale in which a trio of agents are assigned to destroy a Nazi munitions installation. Exciting ending and sensational pyrotechnics. **116m/C VHS.** Sophia Loren, George Peppard, Trevor Howard, John Mills, Richard Johnson, Tom Courtenay, Jeremy Kemp, Anthony Quayle, Helmut Dantine; *D:* Michael Anderson Sr.

Operation Dames 🦴½ **1959** A squadron of soldiers must go behind Korean enemy lines to locate a missing U.S.O. troupe and bring them to safety. Low budget and not very funny for a supposed comedy. **73m/B VHS.** Eve Meyer, Chuck Henderson, Don Devlin, Ed Craig, Cindy Girard; *D:* Louis Clyde Stouman.

Operation: Delta Force 🦴🦴 **1997 (R)** Nash (Lara) and his South African terrorist band have stolen two vials of the Ebola virus in order to provide some cleansing of the population. So the Delta Force, lead by Lang (Fahey), are flown into Mozambique to stop 'em. Macho guys and lots of firepower. **93m/C VHS.** Jeff Fahey, Ernie Hudson, Frank Zagarino, Joe Lara, Todd Jensen, Hal Holbrook; *D:* Sam Firstenberg; *W:* David Sparling; *C:* Yossi Wein; *M:* Serge Colbert.

Operation Delta Force 2: Mayday 🦴½ **1997 (R)** Russian terrorist Lukash (Campbell) is threatening atomic mayhem unless he's paid $25 billion and it's up to the elite combat unit, the Delta Force, to stop him. Standard actioner is less than memorable. **98m/C VHS, DVD.** Michael McGrady, J. Kenneth Campbell, Dale Dye, Simon Jones; *D:* Yossi Wein; *W:* David Sparling; *C:* Peter Belcher; *M:* Russell Stirling, Wessel Van Rensburg. **VIDEO**

Operation Delta Force 3: Clear Target 🦴½ **1998 (R)** When the Delta Force destroys a billion-dollar cocaine operation, the drug cartel is out for revenge. Drug lord Umberto Salvatore steals a submarine and programs its warheads to fire on New York City. Of course, Delta Force has to get to the sub first. **96m/C VHS, DVD.** Bryan Genesse, Danny Keogh, Jim Fitzpatrick, Greg Collins, Darcy La Pier; *D:* Mark Roper; *W:* David Sparling; *C:* John Scheepers; *M:* Serge Colbert. **VIDEO**

Operation Dumbo Drop 🦴🦴½ *Dumbo Drop* **1995 (PG)** It's 1968 and tough Green Beret captain (Glover), rescued by Vietnamese villagers, promises to replace their prized elephant, which was killed during his mission. He and a group of commandos use land, sea, and air to transport the reluctant beast, learning way more about elephant hygiene and eating habits than they ever wanted to know in the process. Wincer, who also directed "Free Willy," seems to be going for the title of "greatest large mammal director of all time." Anything with good-guy U.S. troops, a paratrooper elephant, and a family-friendly plot should be a Bob Dole favorite. **107m/C VHS.** Danny Glover, Ray Liotta, Doug E. Doug, Denis Leary, Corin "Corky" Nemec, Thein Le Dihn; *D:* Simon Wincer; *W:* Jim Kouf, Gene Quintano; *C:* Russell Boyd; *M:* David Newman.

Operation Golden Phoenix 🦴 **1994 (R)** A security specialist (Mehri) is betrayed in his assignment is to protect one half of a valuable medallion. Seems the medal reveals the location in Lebanon of a ancient mountain of gold—desired by a ruthless warlord (Hong). Martial arts fights are well done in this routine actioner. **95m/C VHS.** Jalal Merhi, James Hong, Al Waxman, Loren Avedon; *D:* Jalal Merhi.

Operation Haylift 🦴🦴 **1950** The true story of the U.S. Air Force's efforts to rescue starving cattle and sheep herds during Nevada's blizzards of 1949. The Air Force provided realism for the film with planes, equipment, and servicemen. **73m/B VHS.** Bill Williams, Tom Brown, Ann Rutherford, Jane Nigh; *D:* William Berke.

Operation Intercept 🦴½ **1995 (R)** Francesca (Andreichenko) suspects that the government is behind her father's murder after he develops technology that causes enemy planes to crash. So she threatens to destroy civilian aircraft until the killer is brought to justice. **94m/C VHS.** Natasha Andreichenko, Bruce Payne, John Stockwell, Lance Henriksen, Dennis Christopher, Michael Champion, Curt Lowens, Corbin Bernsen; *D:* Paul Levine; *W:* Paul Levine; *C:* John Newby.

Operation Julie 🦴½ **1985** A detective searches out a huge drug ring that manufactures LSD. **100m/C VHS.** Colin Blakely, Lesley Nightingale, Clare Powney; *D:* Bob Mahoney.

Operation 'Nam 🦴🦴 **1985** A group of bored Vietnam vets return to 'Nam to rescue their leader from a POW camp. Nothing special, but features John Wayne's son. De Angelis used the pseudonym Larry Ludman. **85m/C VHS.** Oliver Tobias, Christopher Connelly, Manfred Lehman, John Steiner, Ethan Wayne, Donald Pleasence; *D:* Fabrizio de Angelis.

Operation Orient 🦴½ **19??** A statue laden with drugs is stolen when an international drug smuggler tries to bring it to the U.S. **94m/C VHS.** Gianni Gori, Gordon Mitchell; *D:* Elia Milonakos.

Operation Petticoat 🦴🦴🦴½ **1959** Submarine captain Grant teams with wheeler-dealer Curtis to make his sub seaworthy. They're joined by a group of Navy women, and the gags begin. Great teamwork from Grant and Curtis keeps things rolling. Jokes may be considered sexist these days. Later remake and TV series couldn't hold a candle to the original. **120m/C VHS, DVD, Wide.** Cary Grant, Tony Curtis, Joan O'Brien, Dina Merrill, Gene Evans, Arthur O'Connell, Virginia Gregg; *D:* Blake Edwards; *W:* Stanley Shapiro, Maurice Richlin; *C:* Russell Harlan; *M:* David Rose.

Operation Sandman: Warriors in Hell 🦴🦴 **2000 (R)** Scientist Perlman develops a serum for the military that allows soldiers to remain awake for weeks with heightened senses. Only there turns out to be a disturbing side effect—the soldiers eventually begin hallucinating and turn violent. Very disturbing. **89m/C VHS.** Ron Perlman, Richard Tyson, Mary B. Ward, John Haymes Newton; *D:* Nelson McCormick; *W:* Nelson McCormick; *C:* Larry Blanford. **TV**

Operation Thunderbolt 🦴🦴½ *Entebbe: Operation Thunderbolt* **1977** Israeli-produced depiction of Israel's July 14, 1976 commando raid on Entebbe, Uganda to rescue the passengers of a hijacked plane. Better than the American versions "Raid on Entebbe" and "Victory at Entebbe" in its performances as well as the information provided, much of it unavailable to the American filmmakers. **120m/C VHS.** Yehoram Gaon, Assaf Dayan, Ori Levy, Klaus Kinski; *D:* Menahem Golan.

Operation Warzone 🦴 **1989** A platoon of soldiers uncovers a plot by corrupt officers to continue the Vietnam war and sell weapons. **86m/C VHS.** Joe Spinell, John Cianetti, Sean Holton, William Zipp, David Marriott; *D:* David A. Prior; *W:* David A. Prior, Ted Prior; *C:* Andy Parke.

The Operator 🦴🦴 **2001** Scumdog lawyer Gary Whelan (Laurence) gets his comeuppance when he insults the wrong telephone operator (Kim). Calling herself Shiva (the Hindu goddess of destruction), she decides to even the karmic balance by stripping Gary of all his worldly possessions, breaking up his marriage, and framing him for murder. Set in Dallas, Texas. **102m/C VHS, DVD.** Jacqueline Kim, Michael Laurence, Christa Miller, Stephen Tobolowsky, Brion James, Frances Bay; *D:* Jon Dichter; *W:* Jon Dichter.

The Oppermann Family 🦴🦴½ *Die Geschwister Oppermann* **1982** Long epic (made for German TV) about a family trying to survive in Berlin during the rise of Hitler. In German with subtitles. **238m/C VHS.** *GE* Peter Fitz, Wolfgang Kieling, Rosel Zech, Andrea Dahmen, Michael Degen, Til Topf; *D:* Egon Monk; *C:* Wolfgang Treu; *M:* Alexander Goehr. **TV**

The Opponent 🦴🦴 **1989 (R)** A young boxer saves a young woman's life, not realizing that she has mob connections, thus embroiling him in a world of crime. **102m/C VHS.** *IT* Daniel Greene, Ernest Borgnine, Julian Gemma, Mary Stavin, Kelly Shaye Smith; *D:* Sergio Martino.

The Opponent 🦴🦴½ **2001 (R)** After years of domestic violence, Patty (Eleniak) finds an outlet for her anger in the boxing ring of the community center. With the encouragement of her trainer (Colby), she decides to take it to the next level and go for a pro career. But when Patty embarks on a romance with the guy, she also gets distracted from her goals. **90m/C VHS, DVD, Wide.** Erika Eleniak, Aunjanue Ellis, James Colby, John Doman; *D:* Eugene Jarecki; *W:* Eugene Jarecki; *C:* Joe Di Gennaro. **VIDEO**

Opportunity Knocks 🦴🦴½ **1990 (PG-13)** Carvey's first feature film has him impersonating a friend of a rich suburbanite's family while hiding from a vengeful gangster. They buy it, and give him a job and the daughter. Not hilarious, but not a dud either. **105m/C VHS.** Dana Carvey, Robert Loggia, Todd Graff, Milo O'Shea, Julia Campbell, James Tolkan, Doris Belack, Sally Gracie, Del Close; ***D:*** Donald Petrie; ***W:*** Mitchel Katlin, Nat Bernstein; ***M:*** Miles Goodman.

Opposing Force 🦴🦴½ *Hellcamp* **1987 (R)** The commander of an Air Force camp simulates prisoner-of-war conditions for realistic training, but he goes too far, creating all too real torture situations. He preys on the only female in the experiment, raping her as part of the training. A decent thriller. **97m/C VHS.** Tom Skerritt, Lisa Eichhorn, Anthony Zerbe, Richard Roundtree, Robert Wightman, John Considine, George Kee Chueng, Paul Joynt, Jay Louden, Ken Wright, Dan Hamilton; ***D:*** Eric Karson; ***W:*** Gil Cowan; ***M:*** Marc Donahue.

Opposite Corners 🦴🦴 **1996 (R)** Bryant Donatello (Warlock) is looking for a shot at the Golden Gloves boxing championship, something his father (Dennison) has been obsessed about ever since his own chance was taken away. Then Bryant realizes just what kind of "connections" his dad has. **106m/C VHS.** Billy Warlock, Cathy Moriarty, Anthony John (Tony) Denison, Jay Acovone, Robert Miano; ***D:*** Louis D'Esposito.

The Opposite of Sex 🦴🦴½ **1998 (R)** Teenaged terror Dedee (Ricci) wreaks havoc with the life of gay half-brother Bill (Donovan). She seduces his boyfriend Matt (Sergei), gets pregnant, steals his savings, and nearly costs him his high school teacher's job. Then she takes off for L.A., with Bill, his best friend Lucia (Kudrow), and sheriff Carl (Lovett) in pursuit. Quirky black comedy isn't shy, especially when Ricci's vamping across the screen, and features fine work by Kudrow (in a welcome departure from the dumb blonde roles) and Ricci (who can definitely remove the words "child actress" from her resume). Dedee's acerbic narration is another highlight. **105m/C VHS, DVD, Wide.** Christina Ricci, Martin Donovan, Lisa Kudrow, Ivan Sergei, Lyle Lovett, Johnny Galecki, William Lee Scott, Colin Ferguson; ***D:*** Don Roos; ***W:*** Don Roos; ***C:*** Hubert Taczanowski; ***M:*** Mason Daring. Ind. Spirit '99: First Feature, Screenplay; Natl. Bd. of Review '98: Support. Actress (Ricci); N.Y. Film Critics '98: Support. Actress (Kudrow).

The Opposite Sex 🦴🦴 **1956** Bevy of women battle mediocre script in adaptation of 1939's "The Women." ♫The Opposite Sex; Dere's Yellow Gold on de Trees (De Banana); A Perfect Love; Rock and Roll Tumbleweed; Now! Baby, Now; Jungle Red; Young Man with a Horn. **115m/C VHS, Wide.** June Allyson, Joan Collins, Dolores Gray, Ann Sheridan, Ann Miller, Leslie Nielsen, Agnes Moorehead, Joan Blondell; ***D:*** David Miller; ***W:*** Fay Kanin, Michael Kanin.

The Opposite Sex and How to Live With Them 🦴 **1993 (R)** Yuppies (Gross and Cox) from different backgrounds (he's Jewish, she's a WASP) meet, fall in love, fight, break up, and reunite, inspiring yawning disinterest. All this while their two best buddies (Pollak and Brown) offer what are meant to be "candid insights" delivered directly to the camera. Flat and formulaic romantic comedy wants to sparkle, but script lacks both purpose and point, and worse, takes way too much time not getting there. Winner of the annual Grammar Police award for the worst example of a semantically incorrect title in recent years. **86m/C VHS.** Arye Gross, Courteney Cox Arquette, Kevin Pollak, Julie Brown, Mitchell Ryan, Philip Bruns, Mitzi McCall, B.J. Ward; ***D:*** Matthew Meshekoff; ***W:*** Noah Stern; ***M:*** Ira Newborn.

Options 🦴🦴 **1988 (PG)** Nerdy Hollywood agent Salinger treks to Africa to "option" a princess's life story—hence the title. He gets mixed up with her kidnapping and with her. Misplaced cameos by Roberts and Anton drag down the overall comedy content, which isn't to high to begin with. **105m/C VHS.** Matt Salinger, Joanna Pacula, John Kani, James Keach; ***Cameos:*** Susan Anton, Eric Roberts; ***D:*** Camilo Vila; ***W:*** Edward Decter.

The Oracle 🦴 **1985** A woman takes a new apartment only to find that the previous occupant's spirit is still a resident. The spirit tries to force her to take revenge on his murderers. Not bad for a low-budget thriller, but bad editing is a distraction. **94m/C VHS.** Caroline Capers Powers, Roger Neil; ***D:*** Roberta Findlay.

Orange County 🦴🦴½ **2002 (PG-13)** Pedigreed star Hanks (son of Tom) enters the world of leading men alongside character-meister Black in this pleasant buddy comedy. Equally credible Tinseltown offspring continue aplenty with love-interest Fisk (daughter of Sissy Spacek and Jake Fisk) and director Jake Kasdan (son of Lawrence). Typical Orange County, California teen Shaun Brumder trades his surf board for a pen when he accidentally discovers the joys of literature via a Marcus Skinner (an uncredited Kline) novel on the beach. Determined to study under Skinner at Stanford, Brumder is bummed when the wrong test scores are submitted to the college who summarily rejects him. Enter stoner brother Lance, to help him straighten everything out. Dynamic comedy with character development of a surprisingly sophisticated nature for this type of film. **81m/C VHS, DVD.** *US* Colin Hanks, Jack Black, Schuyler Fisk, Catherine O'Hara, John Lithgow, Harold Ramis, Jane Adams, Garry Marshall, Dana Ivey, Chevy Chase, Lily Tomlin, George Murdock, Leslie Mann, Kyle Howard, Kevin Kline; ***D:*** Jake Kasdan; ***W:*** Mike White; ***C:*** Greg Gardiner; ***M:*** Michael Andrews.

Oranges Are Not the Only Fruit 🦴🦴½ **1989** Lesbian coming of age story about young Jess (Coleman), who must escape her evangelical religious upbringing and mother (McEwan) in order to be true to herself. When the teenaged Jess gets a schoolgirl crush on her friend Melanie, the congregation finds out and condemns the girls until Jess finds the strength to break away. Based on the novel by Winsterson, who also wrote the screenplay. Made for TV. **165m/C VHS.** *GB* Charlotte Coleman, Geraldine McEwan, Cathryn Bradshaw, Kenneth Cranham, Freda Dowie, Richard Henders, Elizabeth Spriggs, Sophie Thursfield; ***D:*** Beeban Kidron; ***W:*** Jeanette Winterson; ***M:*** Rachel Portman. **TV**

Orca woof! *Orca—Killer Whale; The Killer Whale* **1977 (PG)** Ridiculous premise has a killer whale chasing bounty hunter Harris to avenge the murder of its pregnant mate. Great for gore lovers, especially when the whale chomps Derek's leg off. **92m/C VHS.** Richard Harris, Charlotte Rampling, Bo Derek, Keenan Wynn, Will Sampson, Robert Carradine; ***D:*** Michael Anderson Sr.; ***W:*** Sergio Donati, Luciano Vincenzoni; ***C:*** Ted Moore; ***M:*** Ennio Morricone.

Orchestra Rehearsal 🦴🦴 *Prova d'Orchestra* **1978** Italian orchestra musicians gather in a 13th-century chapel to film a TV documentary, protest the increasing authoritarianism of their German conductor, but are eventually persuaded to play amidst the chaos. Rota's last score. Italian with subtitles. **72m/C VHS, DVD.** *IT* Balduin Baas, Clara Colosimo, Elisabeth Labi, Ronaldo Bonacchi, Ferdinando Villella, Giovanni Javarone, David Mauhsell, Francesco Aluigi; ***D:*** Federico Fellini; ***W:*** Federico Fellini, Brunello Rondi; ***C:*** Giuseppe Rotunno; ***M:*** Nino Rota.

Orchestra Wives 🦴🦴🦴 **1942** A drama bursting with wonderful Glenn Miller music. A woman marries a musician and goes on the road with the band and the other wives. Trouble springs up with the sultry singer who desperately wants the woman's new husband. The commotion spreads throughout the group. ♫People Like You and Me; At Last; Serenade in Blue; I've Got a Gal in Kalamazoo. **98m/B VHS.** George Montgomery, Glenn Miller, Lynn Bari, Carole Landis, Jackie Gleason, Cesar Romero, Ann Rutherford, Virginia Gilmore, Mary Beth Hughes, Harry (Henry) Morgan; ***D:*** Archie Mayo.

Ordeal by Innocence 🦴½ **1984 (PG-13)** Sutherland is an amateur sleuth in 1950s England convinced he has proof that a convicted murderer is innocent, but no one wishes to reopen the case. Big-name cast is essentially wasted. Based on an Agatha Christie story. **91m/C VHS.** Donald Sutherland, Christopher Plummer, Faye Dunaway, Sarah Miles, Ian McShane, Diana Quick, Annette Crosbie, Michael Elphick; ***D:*** Desmond Davis; ***C:*** Billy Williams; ***M:*** Pino Donaggio.

Ordeal in the Arctic 🦴🦴½ **1993 (PG)** Military transport plane, piloted by Capt. John Couch (Chamberlain), crashes into the remote glaciers of the Arctic. The survivors face a blizzard and freezing to death unless a rescue team can get to them quickly. Based on the book "Death and Deliverance" by Robert Mason Lee. **93m/C VHS.** *CA* Richard Chamberlain, Melanie Mayron, Catherine Mary Stewart, Scott Hylands, Page Fletcher, Christopher Bolton, Richard McMillan; ***D:*** Mark Sobel; ***W:*** Paul F. Edwards; ***C:*** Miklos Lente; ***M:*** Amin Bhatia. **CABLE**

The Ordeal of Dr. Mudd 🦴🦴🦴 **1980** His name was Mudd—a fitting moniker after he unwittingly aided President Lincoln's assassin. Dr. Mudd set John Wilkes Boothe's leg, broken during the assassination, and was jailed for conspiracy. He became a hero in prison for his aid during yellow fever epidemics and was eventually released. A strong and intricate performance by Weaver keeps this TV drama interesting. Mudd's descendants are still trying to completely clear his name of any wrongdoing in the Lincoln assassination. **143m/C VHS.** Dennis Weaver, Susan Sullivan, Richard Dysart, Michael McGuire, Nigel Davenport, Arthur Hill; ***D:*** Paul Wendkos. **TV**

Order of the Black Eagle 🦴½ **1987 (R)** A Bond-ish spy and his sidekick, Typhoon the Baboon, battle neo-Nazis planning to bring Hitler back to life in this silly tongue-in-cheek thriller. **93m/C VHS.** *GB* Ian Hunter, Charles K. Bibby, William T. Hicks, Jill Donnellan; ***D:*** Worth Keeter.

Order of the Eagle 🦴½ **1989** An innocent scouting trip turns into a non-stop nightmare when an Eagle Scout uncovers some dangerous information. **88m/C VHS.** Frank Stallone; ***D:*** William Zipp; ***W:*** William Zipp.

Order to Kill 🦴🦴½ **1973** A gambling boss puts out a contract on a hit man. **110m/C VHS.** Jose Ferrer, Helmut Berger, Sydne Rome, Kevin McCarthy; ***D:*** Jose Maesso.

Ordet 🦴🦴🦴½ *The Word* **1955** A man who believes he is Jesus Christ is ridiculed until he begins performing miracles, which result in the rebuilding of a broken family. A statement on the nature of religious faith vs. fanaticism by the profoundly religious Dreyer, and based on the play by Kaj Munk. In Danish with English subtitles. **126m/B VHS, DVD.** *DK* Henrik Malberg, Birgitte Federspiel, Cay Kristiansen, Emil Hass Christiansen; ***D:*** Carl Theodor Dreyer; ***W:*** Carl Theodor Dreyer, Kaj Munk; ***C:*** Henning Bendtsen. Golden Globes '56: Foreign Film; Venice Film Fest. '55: Film.

Ordinary Heroes 🦴🦴½ **1985** The story is familiar but the leads make it worthwhile. Anderson is strong as a blinded Vietnam vet readjusting to life at home. Bertinelli's portrayal of his former girlfriend is eloquent. Nice work on an overdone story. **105m/C VHS.** Richard Dean Anderson, Doris Roberts, Valerie Bertinelli; ***D:*** Peter H. Cooper.

Ordinary Magic 🦴🦴½ **1993** Teenaged Jeffrey was raised in India, picking up more than a little eastern wisdom along the way. After the death of his parents Jeffrey comes to the U.S. to live with his aunt where he sticks out not only as the new kid but as a decided oddball. But he manages to make some new friends and teach a few lessons about individuality along the way. Adapted from the novel by Malcolm Bosse. **96m/C VHS.** David Fox, Glenne Headly, Heath Lamberts, Ryan Reynolds; ***Cameos:*** Paul Anka; ***D:*** Giles Walker; ***W:*** Jefferson Lewis.

Ordinary People 🦴🦴🦴½ **1980 (R)** Powerful, well-acted story of a family's struggle to deal with one son's accidental death and the other's subsequent guilt-ridden suicide attempt. Features strong performances by all, but Moore is especially believable as the cold and rigid mother. McGovern's film debut as well as Redford's directorial debut. Based on the novel by Judith Guest. **124m/C VHS, DVD, Wide.** Mary Tyler Moore, Donald Sutherland, Timothy Hutton, Judd Hirsch, M. Emmet Walsh, Elizabeth McGovern, Adam Baldwin, Dinah Manoff, James B. Sikking, Frederic Lehne; ***D:*** Robert Redford; ***W:*** Alvin Sargent; ***C:*** John Bailey; ***M:*** Marvin Hamlisch. Oscars '80: Adapt. Screenplay, Director (Redford), Picture, Support. Actor (Hutton); Directors Guild '80: Director (Redford); Golden Globes '81: Actress—Drama (Moore), Director (Redford), Film—Drama, Support. Actor (Hutton); L.A. Film Critics '80: Support. Actor (Hutton); Natl. Bd. of Review '80: Director (Redford); N.Y. Film Critics '80: Film; Writers Guild '80: Adapt. Screenplay.

Oregon Trail **1939** A western serial in 15 chapters, each 13 minutes long. **195m/B VHS.** Johnny Mack Brown, Fuzzy Knight; ***D:*** Ford Beebe.

Orfeu 🦴🦴 **1999** Diegues's musical drama is adapted from the Vinicius de Moraes play that also inspired Marcel Camus's 1959 film "Black Orpheus." The retelling of the Greek Orpheus and Eurydice tragedy is set during carnivale in Rio and features pop singer Garrido as egotistical songwriter Orfeu who becomes smitten with country girl Eurydice (Franca). Portuguese with subtitles. **112m/C VHS.** *BR* Toni Garrido, Patricia Franca, Murilo Benicio, Zeze Motta, Milton Goncalves, Isabel Fillardis; ***D:*** Carlos Diegues; ***W:*** Carlos Diegues; ***C:*** Alfonso Beato; ***M:*** Caetano Veloso.

The Organization 🦴🦴🦴 **1971 (PG)** Poitier's third and final portrayal of Detective Virgil Tibbs, first seen in "In the Heat of the Night." This time around he battles a drug smuggling ring with a vigilante group. Good action scenes and a realistic ending. **108m/C VHS, DVD, Wide.** Sidney Poitier, Barbara McNair, Sheree North, Raul Julia; ***D:*** Don Medford; ***W:*** James R. Webb; ***C:*** Joseph Biroc; ***M:*** Gil Melle.

Organized Crime & Triad Bureau 🦴🦴 *Chungon Satluk Linggei* **1993** Determined Lee and his cop team seal off crowded Hong Kong island Cheung Chai to trap mob boss Tung and his tootsie. And the bystanders better just get out of the way. Lots of action; Chinese with subtitles. **91m/C VHS, DVD.** *HK* Danny Lee, Anthony Wong, Cecilia Yip, Roy Cheung, Elizabeth Lee; ***D:*** Kirk Wong; ***W:*** Winky Wong; ***C:*** Wing-hang Wong, Kwong-Hung Chan; ***M:*** Danny Chung, Ding-Yat Tsung.

The Organizer 🦴🦴 *I Compagni; Comrades* **1964** In 19th-century Turin, impoverished aristocratic professor Mastroianni unites a group of textile workers striking against unsafe working conditions. Italian with subtitles. **127m/B VHS.** *IT* Marcello Mastroianni, Annie Girardot, Renato Salvatori, Bernard Blier, Francois Perier, Folco Lulli; ***D:*** Mario Monicelli; ***W:*** Mario Monicelli; ***C:*** Giuseppe Rotunno.

Orgazmo 🦴½ **1998 (NC-17)** "South Park" co-creator Trey Parker plays Morman porn star Joe Young in this tale of sinners and Latter Day Saints in the dirty movie biz. When his sidekick (Bachar) invents an orgasm ray gun, they become superheroes and ride the one-joke premise like a rented Ferrari. Although hung with an NC-17 rating, it's guilty of bad humor more than bad taste. Parker is likeable, however, and provides intermittent laughs. **95m/C VHS.** Trey Parker, Dian Bachar, Ron Jeremy, Matt Stone, Robyn Lynne, Michael Dean Jacobs, Andrew W. Kemler, David Dunn; ***D:*** Trey Parker; ***W:*** Trey Parker; ***C:*** Kenny Gioseffi; ***M:*** Paul Robb.

Orgy of the Dead woof! **1965** Classic anti-canon film scripted by Ed Wood Jr., from his own novel. Two innocent travelers are forced to watch an even dozen nude spirits dance in a cardboard graveyard. Hilariously bad. **90m/C VHS.** Criswell, Fawn Silver, William Bates, Pat (Barringer) Barrington, John Andrews, Colleen O'Brien; ***D:*** A.C. (Stephen Apostoloff) Stephen; ***W:*** Edward D. Wood Jr.; ***C:*** Robert Caramico.

Orgy of the Vampires 🦴 *Vampire's Night Orgy* **1973 (R)** Tourists wander into village during cocktail hour. **86m/C VHS.** *SP IT* Jack Taylor, Charo Soriano, Dianik Zurakowska, John Richard; ***D:*** Leon Klimovsky.

Oriane 🦴🦴 **1985** A troubled Venezuelan woman must leave France for her native soil when her aunt dies. Once there, in the place where she spent youthful summers, she begins to recall her incestuous past. Spanish with subtitles. **88m/C VHS.** Deniela Sliverio, Doris Wells, Philippe Rouleau, David Crotto; ***D:*** Fina Torres.

The Original Fabulous Adventures of Baron Munchausen 🦴🦴½ *The Fabulous Baron Munchausen* **1961** An adventure fantasy that takes the hero all over, from the belly of a whale, eventually landing him on the surface of the moon. **84m/C VHS.** *CZ* Milos Kopecky, Hana Brejchova, Rudolph Jelinek, Jan Werich; ***D:*** Karel Zeman.

Original Gangstas 🦴🦴 **1996 (R)** In Hollywood everything old eventually becomes new again. John Bookman (Williamson) returns to his old neighborhood in Gary, Indiana, after his father is brutally shot by a gang leader. Things have changed from Bookman's days of gang banging, with the streets swarming with young machine gun-toting lowlifes. Bent on revenge, cigar-chewing Bookman, aided by childhood friends Jake (Brown), Slick (Roundtree), and Bubba (O'Neal), decide to take back their streets with a little help from Foxy Brown herself (Grier), as a greiving mother. The nostalgia quotient is high watching these '70s blaxploitation stars together in one movie, older, more gray and a little wider, but still able to kick butt. Serious topic (gang violence) is lost in a conventional vigilante vehicle, which sacrifices a message for an all-too-familiar and bloody showdown. **98m/C VHS, DVD.** Jim Brown, Fred Williamson, Pam Grier, Ron O'Neal, Richard Roundtree, Paul Winfield; ***D:*** Larry Cohen; ***W:*** Aubrey Rattan; ***C:*** Carlos Gonzalez; ***M:*** Vladimir Horunzhy.

Original Intent 🦴🦴 **1991 (PG)** A successful lawyer, facing a mid-life crisis, jeopardizes both his family and career when he decides to defend a homeless shelter from eviction proceedings. What might have been a powerful drama about one man's crusade to help the homeless instead merely melodramtic. Actor/activist Sheen appears briefly as a homeless man. **97m/C VHS.** Jay Richardson, Candy Clark, Kris Kristofferson, Vince Edwards, Cindy Pickett, Robert DoQui, Joseph Campanella; ***Cameos:*** Martin Sheen; ***D:*** Robert Marcarelli; ***W:*** Robert Marcarelli.

Original Sin 🦴🦴 **2001 (R)** 1880s Cuban coffee-plantation owner Luis (Banderas) sends to America for a mail-order bride, seeking only someone loyal and of child-bearing years. To discourage gold diggers, he describes himself as a clerk. When his bride-to-be Julia (Jolie) shows up, Luis discovers that she's much more attractive than her picture. She claims that she wanted to be desired for something other than her beauty. With a start like that, what could go wrong? Well, betrayal, murder and theft for starters. An American private detective arrives on the scene, hired by Julia's family to report on her well-being. This fuels doubts in Luis, but a little too late. Soon he's cleaned out, shamed and on the trail of his former "wife." Banderas and Jolie torch the scenes as the couple in lust, but the ham-handed dialogue and direction derail this period potboiler. Loosely based on the Cornell Woolrich novel "Waltz Into Darkness," which was also the source for Truffaut's "Mississippi Mermaid." **112m/C VHS, DVD, Wide.** *US* Antonio Banderas, Angelina Jolie, Thomas Jane, Jack Thompson, Gregory Itzin, Joan Pringle, Allison Mackie, Cordelia Richards, Pedro Armendariz Jr.; ***D:*** Michael Cristofer; ***W:*** Michael Cristofer; ***C:*** Rodrigo Prieto; ***M:*** Terence Blanchard.

Orlando 🦴🦴🦴 **1992 (PG-13)** Potter's sumptuous film adaptation of Virginia Woolf's 1928 novel, which covers 400 years in the life of an English nobleman, who not only defies death but evolves from a man to a woman in the intervening years. Orlando (Swinton) is first seen as a young man in the court of Queen Elizabeth I (Crisp) but after a deep sleep it's suddenly 40 years later. Things like this just keep happening and by 1750 he is now a she (and remains so), finding and losing love, and eventually gaining fulfillment in the 20th century. Elaborate productions never overwhelm Swinton's serene, self-assured performance. **93m/C VHS, DVD, Wide.** *GB* Tilda Swinton, Charlotte Valandrey, Billy Zane, Lothaire Bluteau, John Wood, Quentin Crisp, Heathcote Williams, Dudley Sutton, Thom Hoffman, Peter Eyre, Jimmy Somerville; ***D:*** Sally Potter; ***W:*** Sally Potter; ***C:*** Alexei Rodionov; ***M:*** Bob Last.

Orloff and the Invisible Man 🦴 *Orloff Against the Invisible Man; The Invisible Dead; Dr. Orloff's Invisible Monster* **1970** So many invisible man movies, so little time. A scientist creates an invisible man, imprisons and tortures him. A bit miffed with his host, he who can't be seen escapes, and vents his invisible spleen. **76m/C VHS, DVD, Wide.** *IT FR* Howard Vernon, Brigitte Carva, Fernando (Fernand) Sancho, Isabel Del Rio, Paco Valladares; ***D:*** Pierre Chevalier; ***W:*** France Villon; ***M:*** Camile Sauvage.

The Orphan 🦴½ **1979** A young orphaned boy seeks revenge against his cruel aunt who is harassing him with sadistic discipline. **80m/C VHS.** Mark Evans, Joanna Miles, Peggy (Margaret) Feury; ***D:*** John Ballard.

An Orphan Boy of Vienna 🦴½ **1937** A homeless street urchin with a beautiful singing voice is accepted into the wonderful world of the Choir, but is later unjustly accused of stealing. Performances by the Vienna Boys' Choir redeem the melodramatic plot. In German with English subtitles. **87m/B VHS.** *GE* ***D:*** Max Neufeld.

Orphan Train 🦴🦴🦴 **1979** A woman realizes her New York soup kitchen can't do enough to help the neighborhood orphans, so she takes a group of children out West in hopes of finding families to adopt them. Their journey is chronicled by a newspaper photographer and a social worker. Based on the actual "orphan trains" of the mid- to late 1800s. From the novel by Dorothea G. Petrie. **150m/C VHS.** Jill Eikenberry, Kevin Dobson, Glenn Close, Linda Manz; ***D:*** William A. Graham. **TV**

The Orphans 🦴🦴🦴 *Podranki* **1977** A sensitive edge-of-glasnost portrait of a young boy's discovery of love, friendship, and literature. In Russian with English subtitles. **97m/C VHS.** *RU* Nikolai Gubenko, Y. Boudraitis, A. Tcherstvov, A. Kaliaguine, E. Bourkov, J. Bolotova, R. Bikov, E. Evstigneev; ***D:*** Nikolai Gubenko; ***W:*** Nikolai Gubenko; ***C:*** Alexander Kniajinsky.

Orphans 🦴🦴🦴 **1987 (R)** A gangster on the run is kidnapped by a tough New York orphan but soon takes control by befriending his abductor's maladjusted brother. Eventually each brother realizes his need for the older man, who has become a father figure to them. This very quirky film is salvaged by good performances. Based on the play by Lyle Kessler. **116m/C VHS.** Albert Finney, Matthew Modine, Kevin Anderson; ***D:*** Alan J. Pakula; ***W:*** Lyle Kessler; ***M:*** Michael Small.

Orphans 🦴🦴 **1997** Three brothers and their handicapped sister come unraveled in the 24-hour period following their mother's death. The four Flynn siblings head for the pub the night before the funeral where eldest brother Thomas (Lewis) takes to singing, drawing amusement from the onlookers. This upsets Michael (Henshall), who then gets stabbed in the subsequent bar fight, leading youngest brother John (McCole) to vow to get revenge. Meanwhile, angry, wheelchair-bound Sheila (Stevenson) is bored and decides to take a little roll around Glasgow on her own. Frustrated characters all lash out at one another. Feature directorial debut of actor Mullan. **102m/C VHS, DVD, Wide.** *GB* Douglas Henshall, Gary Lewis, Stephen McCole, Rosemarie Stevenson, Alex Norton, Frank Gallagher, Malcolm Shields; ***D:*** Peter Mullan; ***W:*** Peter Mullan; ***C:*** Grant Scott Cameron; ***M:*** Craig Armstrong.

Orphans of the North 🦴 **1940** The story of Bedrock Brown's search for gold and his lost partner. Filmed on location in Alaska with non-professional actors. Impressive footage of America's "last frontier," including the flora and fauna. **56m/C VHS, 8mm.** ***D:*** Norman Dawn; ***W:*** Susan Denis; ***Nar:*** Norman Dawn.

Orphans of the Storm 🦴🦴🦴½ **1921** Two sisters are separated and raised in opposite worlds—one by thieves, the other by aristocrats. Gish's poignant search for her sister is hampered by the turbulent maelstrom preceding the French Revolution. Silent. Based on the French play "The Two Orphans." **190m/B VHS, DVD.** Lillian Gish, Dorothy Gish, Monte Blue, Joseph Schildkraut; ***D:*** D.W. Griffith; ***W:*** D.W. Griffith; ***C:*** Billy (G.W.) Bitzer, Hendrik Sartov; ***M:*** Louis F. Gottschalk, William F. Peters.

Orpheus 🦴🦴½ *Orphee* **1949** Cocteau's fascinating, innovative retelling of the Orpheus legend in a modern, though slightly askew, Parisian setting. Classic visual effects and poetic imagery. In French with English subtitles. **95m/B VHS, 8mm.** Jean Marais, Francois Perier, Maria Casares, Marie Dea, Edouard Dermithe, Juliette Greco; ***D:*** Jean Cocteau; ***W:*** Jean Cocteau; ***C:*** Nicolas Hayer; ***M:*** Georges Auric.

Orpheus Descending 🦴🦴½ **1991** Lust and hatred in small Southern town. Confusing, poorly paced, but interesting for Anderson as Elvis-style drifter and Redgrave as woman addicted to love. Cable version of the 1989 Broadway revival of Tennessee Williams play. **117m/C VHS.** Vanessa Redgrave, Kevin Anderson, Anne Twomey, Miriam Margolyes, Brad Sullivan, Sloane Shelton, Patti Allison; ***D:*** Peter Hall; ***W:*** Peter Hall, Tennessee Williams. **CABLE**

Osa 🦴½ **1985** Yet another post-nuke flick with the usual devastated landscape, leather-clad survivors, and hokey dialog. It's sometimes funny, despite everyone's effort to make it dramatic. The supposed plot centers on one woman's efforts to break up a man's monopoly on clean water. **94m/C VHS.** Kelly Lynch, Daniel Grimm, Phillip Vincent, Etienne Chicot, John Forristal, Pete Walker, David Hausman, Bill Moseley; ***D:*** Oleg Egorov; ***M:*** Mason Daring.

Osaka Elegy 🦴🦴½ *Woman of Osaka* **1936** A study of Japanese cultural rules when society condemns a woman for behavior that is acceptable for a man. In Japanese with English subtitles. **71m/B VHS.** *JP* Isuzu Yamada; ***D:*** Kenji Mizoguchi.

The Oscar 🦴½ **1966 (R)** Unless you enjoy razzing bad acting, this is not for you. Meant as a comeuppance for Hollywood, by Hollywood, this story of movie star Frank Fane (Boyd), climbing the ladder of success and squashing fingers on every rung is too schlocky to succeed. The climax, when the scumbag star thinks he's won an Oscar and stands up, only to find it's for someone else, was based on Frank Capra's embarrassing experience in 1932 with the same situation. Adapted from the novel by Richard Sale. **119m/C VHS.** Stephen Boyd, Elke Sommer, Jill St. John, Tony Bennett, Milton Berle, Eleanor Parker, Joseph Cotten, Edie Adams, Ernest Borgnine, Ed Begley Sr., Walter Brennan, Broderick Crawford, James Dunn, Peter Lawford, Merle Oberon, Bob Hope, Frank Sinatra; ***D:*** Russell Rouse; ***W:*** Russell Rouse, Harlan Ellison, Clarence Green; ***C:*** Joseph Ruttenberg.

Oscar 🦴🦴 **1991 (PG)** The improbable casting of Stallone in a 1930s style crime farce (an attempt to change his image) is hard to imagine, and harder to believe. Stallone has little to do as he plays the straight man in this often ridiculous story of a crime boss who swears he'll go straight. Cameos aplenty, with Curry's the most notable. Based on a French play by Claude Magnier. **109m/C VHS.** Sylvester Stallone, Ornella Muti, Peter Riegert, Vincent Spano, Marisa Tomei, Kirk Douglas, Art LaFleur, Ken Howard, Chazz Palminteri, Tim Curry, Don Ameche, Richard Romanus; ***D:*** John Landis; ***W:*** Michael Barrie, Jim Mulholland; ***C:*** Mac Ahlberg; ***M:*** Elmer Bernstein.

Oscar and Lucinda 🦴🦴½ **1997 (R)** A priest and a glassworks heiress are united by a shared passion for gambling; together they attempt to transport a glass church through 1860s Australian wilderness. Fiennes' performance as the vulnerable and flailing Oscar is particularly good. Narrated by Geoffrey Rush. Based on the Booker Prize-winning novel by Peter Carey. **131m/C VHS.** Ralph Fiennes, Cate Blanchett, Ciaran Hinds, Tom Wilkinson, Richard Roxburgh, Clive Russell, Bille Brown, Josephine Byrnes, Barnaby Kay, Barry Otto, Linda Bassett; ***D:*** Gillian Armstrong; ***W:*** Laura Jones; ***C:*** Geoffrey Simpson; ***M:*** Thomas Newman; ***Nar:*** Geoffrey Rush. Australian Film Inst. '98: Cinematog., Score.

Osmosis Jones 🦴🦴½ **2001 (PG-13)** Combo of animation and live-action concerns a slob named Frank (Murray) who's suffering from an evil virus (Fishburne) that's taking over his body. To the rescue are white blood cell Osmosis Jones (Rock) and cold tablet Drix (Pierce). The Farrellys once again push the envelope of gross-out humor, but this time it's a PG envelope, and the live-action sequences suffer for it, especially when compared to the funny, clever, and high-energy animated sequences. Luckily, the animation comprises about two-thirds of the movie. Kids will enjoy the lively animation and the gross stuff, while the adults should have a good enough time picking out the puns and references to other movies. Murray goes to heroic lengths to portray Frank's devotion to self-degradation. **95m/C VHS, DVD, Wide.** *US* Bill Murray, Molly Shannon, Chris Elliott, Elena Franklin; ***D:*** Bobby Farrelly, Peter Farrelly, Piet Kroon, Tom Sito; ***W:*** Marc Hyman; ***C:*** Mark Irwin; ***M:*** Randy Edelman; ***V:*** Chris Rock, Laurence "Larry" Fishburne, David Hyde Pierce, Brandy Norwood, William Shatner, Ron Howard.

O.S.S. 🦴🦴🦴 **1946** John Martin (Ladd) has been recruited by Commander Brady (Knowles) as a would-be spy for the new Office of Strategic Services. Martin's teamed with Ellen Rogers (Fitzgerald) and they parachute into France with orders to obtain information on German troop movements and destroy an important railroad tunnel. A turncoat Gestapo agent sells them information but German colonel Meister (Hoyt) is after them and it's a race to see if their mission can be completed before they're caught. The O.S.S. allowed Paramount studio a look at their WWII files for story purposes and numerous ex-agents served as technical advisors. **108m/B VHS.** Alan Ladd, Geraldine Fitzgerald, Patric Knowles, John Hoyt, Richard Benedict, Gloria Saunders, Bobby Driscoll, Don Beddoe, Richard Webb, Gavin Muir, Onslow Stevens, Joseph Crehan, Leslie Denison; ***D:*** Irving Pichel; ***W:*** Richard Maibaum; ***C:*** Lionel Linden; ***M:*** Daniele Amfitheatrof.

Ossessione 🦴🦴🦴½ **1942** An adaptation of "The Postman Always Rings Twice," transferred to Fascist Italy, where a drifter and an innkeeper's wife murder her husband. Visconti's first feature, which initiated Italian neo-realism, was not released in the U.S. until 1975 due to a copyright dispute. In Italian with English subtitles. **135m/B VHS.** *IT* Massimo Girotti, Clara Calamai, Juan deLanda, Elio Marcuzzo; ***D:*** Luchino Visconti; ***W:*** Guiseppe de Santis, Mario Alicata; ***C:*** Aldo Tonti, Domenico Scala.

The Osterman Weekend 🦴🦴 **1983 (R)** Peckinpah was said to have disliked the story and the script in this, his last film, which could account for the convoluted and confusing end result. Adding to the problem is the traditional difficulty of adapting Ludlum's complex psychological thrillers for the screen. The result: cast members seem to not quite "get it" as they portray a group of friends, one of whom has been convinced by the CIA that the others are all Soviet spies. **102m/C VHS.** Burt Lancaster, Rutger Hauer, Craig T. Nelson, Dennis Hopper, John Hurt, Chris Sarandon, Meg Foster, Helen Shaver; ***D:*** Sam Peckinpah; ***M:*** Lalo Schifrin.

Otaku No Video 🦴🦴🦴 *Fan's Video* **1991** The title of this satirized bio of Gainax animation studio and its founders can be read as "Fan's Video." The tape contains two installments, one made in 1982 and one in 1985. In 1982, college freshman Kubo is reunited with his old friend Tanaka and slowly gets sucked into the world of hopelessly obsessed anime and science fiction fans or "otaku." Both the fun and social costs of his new hobby are examined (in Japan, like the U.S., the coolest guys aren't sitting inside watching TV all day). The second installment finds Kubo and Tanaka starting two different businesses that are directly related to their beloved hobby. As if the animated stories weren't hilarious enough (and, perhaps, all-too familiar to some anime fans), there are live-action, fake documentary segments. These examine different aspects of "otakudom." People less familiar with the world of anime should be able to understand the basic story which is very funny (keeping in mind that practically nothing about this video is to be taken seriously). More experienced anime fans will have the added fun of trying to spot all the anime references and in-jokes liberally woven into the script. **100m/C VHS.** *JP*

Otello ½ **1986 (PG)** An uncommon film treat for opera fans, with a stellar performance by Domingo as the troubled Moor who murders his wife in a fit of jealous rage and later finds she was never unfaithful. Be prepared, however, for changes from the Shakespeare and Verdi stories, necessitated by the film adaptation. Highly acclaimed and awarded; in Italian with English subtitles. **123m/C VHS.** *IT* Placido Domingo, Katia Ricciarelli, Justino Diaz; ***D:*** Franco Zeffirelli.

Othello ½ **1922** A silent version of Shakespeare's tragedy, featuring Jannings as the tragic Moor. Titles are in English; with musical score. **81m/B VHS, DVD.** *GE* Emil Jannings, Lya de Putti, Werner Krauss; ***D:*** Dimitri Buchowetzki.

Othello *Orson Welles's Othello; The Tragedy of Othello: The Moor of Venice* **1952** Welles's striking adaptation of the Shakespeare tragedy casts him as the self-deluding Moor, with MacLiammoir as the despicable Iago and Cloutier as innocent victim, Desdemona. Welles filmed his epic over a four-year period due to budget difficulties, which also resulted in his filming in a number of different countries and settings. The film underwent a $1 million restoration, supervised by Welles's daughter, prior to its limited theatrical re-release in 1992. **90m/B VHS, DVD.** Orson Welles, Michael MacLiammoir, Suzanne Cloutier, Robert Coote, Hilton Edwards, Michael Lawrence, Nicholas Bruce, Fay Compton, Doris Dowling, Jean Davis, Joseph Cotten, Joan Fontaine; ***D:*** Orson Welles; ***W:*** Orson Welles; ***C:*** Anchise Brizzi, George Fanto, Alberto Fusi, Aldo (G.R. Aldo) Graziatti, Oberdan Troiani; ***M:*** Alberto Barberis, Angelo Francesco Lavagnino. Cannes '52: Film.

Othello ½ **1965** Olivier (in blackface) gives another towering performance as Shakespeare's tragic Moor, led to disaster by his own jealousy. He's ably supported by Finlay's insinuating performance as Iago, Smith as a sweetly vulnerable Desdemona, and Jacobi as unwitting rival Cassio. The production, however, doesn't stray far from its stage-bound roots. **150m/C VHS.** Laurence Olivier, Frank Finlay, Maggie Smith, Derek Jacobi, Joyce Redman, Anthony Nicholls, Sheila Reid, Roy Holder; ***D:*** Stuart Burge; ***W:*** Margaret Unsworth; ***C:*** Geoffrey Unsworth; ***M:*** Richard Hampton.

Othello **1995 (R)** Fishburne stars as Shakespeare's tragic Moor, with Branagh as silken agitator Iago, and Jacob as the tragic Desdemona. First time director Oliver Parker (brother Nathaniel is also in the film) drastically cut the play, rearranging scenes (and even adding material)—purists will no doubt scream, but performances carry the production. Through the clever use of asides directed at the camera, Branagh's Iago makes the viewer feel like an accomplice in the plot. French-speaking Jacob, however, seems to have a hard time pronouncing the Shakespearean dialogue. **125m/C VHS, DVD.** Laurence "Larry" Fishburne, Irene Jacob, Kenneth Branagh, Nathaniel Parker, Michael Maloney, Anna Patrick, Nicholas Farrell, Indra Ove, Michael Sheen, Andre Oumansky, Philip Locke, John Savident, Gabriele Ferzetti, Pierre Vaneck; ***D:*** Oliver Parker; ***W:*** Oliver Parker; ***C:*** David Johnson; ***M:*** Charlie Mole.

Othello **2001** Updated version (with modern dialogue) of Shakespeare's "Othello" set in contemporary London. John Othello (Walker) is a respected police officer who has just been installed as the first black commissioner of the Metropolitan force. His promotion comes at the expense of his mentor/friend Ben Jago (Eccleston) who does not handle the slight well as he is now second-in-command. So Ben plays the race card and works on John's jealousy of his heiress white wife, Dessie (Hawley), by suggesting that she is unfaithful. Walker is convincingly impassioned but Eccleston's slimy manipulation is rather too obvious. **96m/C VHS, DVD.** *GB* Eamonn Walker, Christopher Eccleston, Keeley Hawes, Richard Coyle, Del Synnott, Christopher Fox, Allan Cutts, Patrick Myers; ***D:*** Geoffrey Sax; ***W:*** Andrew Davies; ***C:*** Daf Hobson; ***M:*** Debbie Wiseman. **TV**

The Other **1972 (PG)** Eerie, effective thriller adapted by Tyron from his supernatural novel. Twin brothers represent good and evil in a 1930s Connecticut farm town beset with gruesome murders and accidents. A good scare. **100m/C VHS.** Martin Udvarnoky, Chris Udvarnoky, Uta Hagen, Diana Muldaur, Norma Connolly, Victor French, John Ritter, Loretta Leversee, Lou Frizzell, Portia Nelson, Jenny Sullivan; ***D:*** Robert Mulligan; ***W:*** Tom Tryon; ***C:*** Robert L. Surtees; ***M:*** Jerry Goldsmith.

The Other Brother ½ **2002 (R)** Nice guy Martin (Phifer) is shocked to discover his girlfriend in bed with another woman. Uncertain about his judgement of the fair sex, he reluctantly agrees to listen to his player brother Junnie's (Blake) advice, which results in some awkward pick-up moments. Of course, Martin has already meet the perfect new girlfriend, his new upstairs neighbor Paula (Miller), if only he would listen to what his own heart says. **94m/C VHS, DVD.** Mekhi Phifer, Andre B. Blake, Michele Morgan, Tangi Miller, Ebony JoAnn, Regina Hall, Collette Wilson; ***D:*** Mandel Holland; ***W:*** Mandel Holland; ***C:*** Matthew Clark.

Other Hell **1985 (R)** Schlocky Italian-made chiller has the devil inhabiting a convent where he does his damnest to upset the nuns. Gross, but not scary—lots of cliche dark-hallway scenes and fright music. **88m/C VHS.** *IT* Carlo De Meyo, Francesca Carmeno; ***D:*** Stefan Oblowsky.

Other People's Money ½ **1991 (R)** DeVito is "Larry the Liquidator," a corporate raider with a heart of stone and a penchant for doughnuts. When he sets his sights on a post-smokestack era, family-owned cable company, he gets a taste of love for the first time in his life. He and Miller, the daughter of the company president and also its legal advisor, court one another while sparring over the fate of the company. Unbelievably clipped ending mars otherwise enterprising comedy about the triumph of greed in corporate America. Based on the off-Broadway play by Jerry Sterner. **101m/C VHS, 8mm, Wide.** Danny DeVito, Penelope Ann Miller, Dean Jones, Gregory Peck, Piper Laurie, Tom Aldredge, R.D. Call; ***D:*** Norman Jewison; ***W:*** Alvin Sargent; ***C:*** Haskell Wexler; ***M:*** David Newman.

The Other Side of Heaven **2002 (PG)** Well-meaning if heavy-handed bio-drama based on Groberg's memoir "In the Eye of the Storm." John Groberg (Gorham) is a Mormon college student at Brigham Young University in 1953, who's pining for Jean (Hathaway), the girl of his dreams. Then he receives his missionary assignment—to Tonga in the South Seas. Groberg has to struggle with native culture, the language barrier, and various hardships and natural disasters before he can accomplish his goals. Film's sincere although you never get much of an idea of how Groberg feels about all that befalls him except for his enduring faith. Picture was filmed in the Cook Islands. **113m/C VHS, DVD.** *US* Christopher Gorham, Anne Hathaway, Joe Folau, Miriama Smith, Nathaniel Lees, Whetu Fala; ***D:*** Mitch Davis; ***W:*** Mitch Davis; ***C:*** Brian J. Breheny; ***M:*** Kevin Kiner.

The Other Side of Midnight woof! **1977 (R)** The dreary, depressingly shallow life story of a poor French girl, dumped by an American GI, who sleeps her way to acting stardom and a profitable marriage, then seeks revenge for the jilt. Based on Sidney Sheldon's novel, it's not even titillating—just a real downer. **160m/C VHS, Wide.** Susan Sarandon, Marie-France Pisier, John Beck, Raf Vallone, Clu Gulager, Sorrell Booke; ***D:*** Charles Jarrott; ***W:*** Daniel Taradash; ***C:*** Fred W. Koenekamp.

The Other Side of Sunday *Sondagsengler* **1996** A small town in 1959 Norway is the setting for this coming of age comedy. Maria (Thiesen) is the eldest daughter of conservative priest Johannes (Sundquist). Fun doesn't seem to be part of their religion but puberty is hitting Maria hard and she longs to join in with the livelier crowd of her school friend Brigit (Salvesen), who listens to rock 'n' roll, wears makeup, and makes out with boys. Maria does find a compassionate listener in Mrs. Tunheim (Riise), who urges the teenager to learn how to think for herself. Based on the novel "Sunday" by Reidun Nortvedt. Norwegian with subtitles. **103m/C VHS, DVD.** *NO* Marie Theisen, Bjorn Sundquist, Hildegunn Riise, Sylvia Salvesen; ***D:*** Berit Nesheim; ***W:*** Berit Nesheim, Lasse Glomm; ***C:*** Arne Borsheim; ***M:*** Geir Bohren, Bent Aserud.

The Other Side of the Law **1995 (R)** Man makes a wilderness hideout with his son after killing his wife's murderer. But when the boy grows up, dad decides to send him back into civilization for education, leading to nothing but trouble. **96m/C VHS.** Juergen Prochnow; ***D:*** Gilles Carle.

The Other Side of the Mountain *A Window to the Sky* **1975 (PG)** Tear-jerking true story of Olympic hopeful skier Jill Kinmont, paralyzed in a fall. Bridges helps her pull her life together. A sequel followed two years later. Based on the book "A Long Way Up" by E. G. Valens. **102m/C VHS.** Marilyn Hassett, Beau Bridges, Dabney Coleman, John David Garfield, Griffin Dunne; ***D:*** Larry Peerce; ***W:*** David Seltzer; ***M:*** Charles Fox.

The Other Side of the Mountain, Part 2 **1978 (PG)** Quadriplegic Jill Kinmont, paralyzed in a skiing accident that killed her hopes for the Olympics, overcomes depression and the death of the man who helped her to recover. In this chapter, she falls in love again and finds happiness. More tears are jerked. **99m/C VHS.** Marilyn Hassett, Timothy Bottoms; ***D:*** Larry Peerce.

The Other Sister **1998 (PG-13)** Carla (Lewis) is the mentally challenged but exuberant member of the repressed Tate family. After leaving a "special school," she convinces her uptight parents Elizabeth (Keaton) and Radley (Skerritt) to let her enroll in a vocational program. She meets and falls for fellow retarded student Danny (Ribisi), much to her parents' dismay. Love wins out, but the script is so sappy that a maple syrup factory could be built on it. Lewis and Ribisi do an admirable job of rising above the material, which was co-written by schmaltz-meister director Garry Marshall. **129m/C VHS, DVD, Wide.** Juliette Lewis, Giovanni Ribisi, Diane Keaton, Tom Skerritt, Poppy Montgomery, Linda Thorson, Juliet Mills, Hector Elizondo, Sarah Paulson, Joe Flanigan; ***D:*** Garry Marshall; ***W:*** Garry Marshall, Bob Brunner; ***C:*** Dante Spinotti; ***M:*** Rachel Portman.

Other Voices, Other Rooms ½ **1995** Adaptation of Truman Capote's 1948 novel (his first) is the semi-autobiographical story of a young boy's search for his father set against the backdrop of a decaying Bayou mansion. Southern saga, narrated by Capote sound-alike Kingdom, starts when 12-year-old Joel's mother dies and he is sent by his aunts to live with his father. Instead of being greeted by his father, Joel (Speck) instead meets an odd collection of guests, including Amy (Thomson), a fragile and pretty Southern belle and her cousin Randolph (Bluteau), a sensitive, effete, and charming alcoholic. Pic deals with the secrets of the father's illness and what lies behind the unhappiness of the two cousins, who try to keep the child from fleeing the wacky "family." Lacks the danger and suspense of Capote's novel, but sets proper mood and shows off actors talents. Best known as a documentary director/producer, this is Rocksavage's feature debut. **98m/C VHS.** Lothaire Bluteau, Anna Thomson, David Speck, April Turner, Aubrey Dollar; ***D:*** David Rocksavage; ***W:*** David Rocksavage, Sara Flanigan; ***C:*** Paul Ryan; ***M:*** Chris Hajian; ***Nar:*** Bob Kingdom.

The Other Woman ½ **1992 (R)** Investigative reporter Jessica is working on a murder case when she finds incriminating sex photos showing her husband with another woman. She becomes obsessed with finding the woman in the pictures but it would be dangerous for Jessica to forget there's still a murderer on the loose. **90m/C VHS.** Adrian Zmed, Lee Ann Beaman, Daniel Moriarty, Jenna Persaud, Sam Jones; ***D:*** Jag Mundhra.

The Others **2001 (PG-13)** Twisting Gothic haunt-fest centers on Grace (Kidman) and her two children Anne (Mann) and Nicholas (Bentley), living in a mansion on Britain's remote Isle of Jersey. She waits for her husband's return from WWII, although she fears he may be dead. After her servants disappear in the middle of the night, she's surprised when a trio of domestics show up, claiming to have worked in the house before. They're hired on the spot, but the help soon discovers why their predecessors took off. Grace is demanding and high-strung to the point of mania. Because of rare allergies, the kids must be kept out of the sunlight. Maybe the solitude is preying on Grace's mind, maybe she's crazy, or maybe their house is haunted. Kidman is at her chilly best as the audience is kept guessing. **101m/C VHS, DVD, Wide.** *US* Nicole Kidman, Fionnula Flanagan, Alakina Mann, James Bentley, Christopher Eccleston, Elaine Cassidy, Eric Sykes, Renee Asherson; ***D:*** Alejandro Amenabar; ***W:*** Alejandro Amenabar; ***C:*** Javier Aguirresarobe; ***M:*** Alejandro Amenabar.

Oubliette **1914** A peripheral version of Francois Villon, in what is a recently discovered and restored film, the earliest extant Chaney film. **35m/B VHS.** Lon Chaney Sr., Murdock MacQuarrie, Pauline Bush, Doc (Harry F.) Crane, Chester Withey; ***D:*** Charles Giblyn; ***W:*** H.G. Stafford; ***C:*** Lee Bartholomew.

Our Daily Bread *Miracle of Life* **1934** Vidor's sequel to the 1928 "The Crowd." A young couple inherit a farm during the Depression and succeed in managing the land. A near-classic, with several sequences highly influenced by directors Alexander Dovshenko and Sergei Eisenstein. Director Vidor also co-scripted this film, risking bankruptcy to finance it. **80m/B VHS, DVD.** Karen Morley, Tom (George Duryea) Keene, John Qualen, Barbara Pepper, Addison Richards; ***D:*** King Vidor; ***W:*** King Vidor, Elizabeth Hill; ***C:*** Robert Planck.

Our Dancing Daughters ½ **1928** Flapper (Crawford on the brink of stardom) falls hard for millionaire who's forced into arranged marriage, but obliging little missus kicks bucket so Crawford can step in. **98m/B VHS.** Joan Crawford, Johnny Mack Brown, Nils Asther, Dorothy Sebastian, Anita Page; ***D:*** Harry Beaumont; ***C:*** George Barnes.

Our Family Business **1981** TV pilot; this generally plodding "Godfather"-type story is saved by good performances by Wanamaker and Milland. **74m/C VHS.** Sam Wanamaker, Vera Miles, Ray Milland, Ted Danson, Chip Mayer; ***D:*** Robert E. Collins. **TV**

Our Hospitality **1923** One of Keaton's finest silent films, with all the elements in place. William McKay (Keaton) travels to the American South on a quaint train (a near-exact replica of the Stephenson Rocket), to claim an inheritance as the last survivor of his family. En route, a young woman traveler informs him that her family has had a long, deadly feud with his, and that they intend to kill him. McKay resolves to get the inheritance, depending on the Southern rule of hospitality to guests to save his life until he can make his escape. Watch for the river scene where, during filming, Keaton's own life was really in danger. By the way, Keaton married his leading lady in real life. **74m/B VHS, DVD.** Buster Keaton, Natalie Talmadge, Joe Keaton, Buster Keaton Jr., Kitty Bradbury, Joe Roberts; ***D:*** John Blystone, Buster Keaton; ***W:*** Jean C. Havez, Joseph A. Mitchell, Clyde Bruckman; ***C:*** Elgin Lessley, Gordon Jennings.

Our Lady of the Assassins && *La Virgen de los Sicarios* **2001 (R)** Based on Vallejo's 1994 autobiographical novel, the film follows Fernando (Jaramillo), an older gay man and a writer who has returned to his hometown of Medellin, Colombia to die. After 30 years away, Fernando discovers a crime-ridden city with drug trafficking, gangs, and violence to be the norm. At a party, Fernando is introduced to 16-year-old street tough Alexis (Ballesteros), who soon moves in with him. But when Alexis's past catches up with him, Fernando seeks the truth in a city of lies. Not for the faint-hearted; Spanish with subtitles. **98m/C VHS, DVD, Wide.** *CL FR* German Jaramillo, Anderson Ballesteros, Juan David Restrepo, Manuel Busquets; ***D:*** Barbet Schroeder; ***W:*** Fernando Vallejo; ***C:*** Rodrigo Lalinde; ***M:*** Jorge Arrigagda.

Our Little Girl && **1935 (PG)** A precocious little tyke tries to reunite her estranged parents by running away to their favorite vacation spot. Sure to please Shirley Temple fans, despite a lackluster script. **65m/B VHS.** Shirley Temple, Joel McCrea, Rosemary Ames, Lyle Talbot, Erin O'Brien-Moore; ***D:*** John S. Robertson.

Our Man Flint && **1966** James Bond clone Derek Flint uses gadgets and his ingenuity to save the world from an evil organization, GALAXY, that seeks world domination through control of the weather. The plot moves quickly around many bikini-clad women, but still strains for effect. Spawned one sequel: "In Like Flint." **107m/C VHS, DVD, Wide.** James Coburn, Lee J. Cobb, Gila Golan, Edward Mulhare, Benson Fong, Shelby Grant, Sigrid Valdis, Gianna Serra, James Brolin, Helen Funai, Michael St. Clair; ***D:*** Daniel Mann; ***C:*** Daniel F. Fapp; ***M:*** Jerry Goldsmith.

Our Miss Brooks &&½ **1956** Quietly pleasing version of the TV series. Miss Brooks pursues the "mother's boy" biology professor. The father of the child she begins tutoring appears taken with her. The professor takes notice. **85m/B VHS.** Eve Arden, Gale Gordon, Nick Adams, Richard Crenna, Don Porter; ***D:*** Al Lewis.

Our Modern Maidens &&½ **1929** Scandalous jazz-age drama in which Crawford and Fairbanks both fall in love with other people before their wedding is to take place. This sequel to "Our Dancing Daughters" features beautiful gowns and lush, opulent Art Deco interiors. Based on a story by Josephine Lovett. **75m/B VHS.** Joan Crawford, Rod La Rocque, Douglas Fairbanks Jr., Anita Page, Josephine Dunn; ***D:*** Jack Conway; ***W:*** Josephine Lovett.

Our Mother's Murder &&½ **1997 (PG-13)** Title says it all in this drama based on the true story of publishing heiress Anne Scripps Douglas (Hart) who, in 1989, marries volatile young carpenter, Scott (Wilder), and begins an abusive four-year marriage that will end with her beating death in 1993. Scripps Douglas's two daughters by her first marriage, Alexandra and Annie (portrayed on screen by Clarke and Combs), cooperated with the production. **92m/C VHS.** Roxanne Hart, Holly Marie Combs, Sarah Chalke, James Wilder, Jonathan Scarfe; ***D:*** Bill W.L. Norton; ***W:*** Richard DeLong Adams. **CABLE**

Our Mutual Friend &&½ **1998** Charles Dickens' last completed novel follows the complicated saga of John Harmon (Mackintosh), who must consent to a prearranged marriage if he's to inherit a fortune. But when fate allows Harmon to assume a new identity, he decides to see what anonymity will bring him. Meanwhile, Harmon's life and death also brings together low-born Lizzie Hexum and wastrel lawyer Eugene Wrayburn, who develops an unexpected affection for the lovely young woman. On 3 cassettes. **339m/C VHS.** *GB* Steven Mackintosh, Anna Friel, Paul McGann, Keeley Hawes, David Morrissey, Dominic Mafham, Peter Vaughan, Pam Ferris, Kenneth Cranham, Timothy Spall, David Bradley, Margaret Tyzack; ***D:*** Julian Farino; ***W:*** Sandy Welch; ***C:*** David Odd; ***M:*** Adrian Johnston. **TV**

Our Relations &&&½ **1936** Confusion reigns when Stan and Ollie meet the twin brothers they never knew they had, a pair of happy-go-lucky sailors. Laurel directs the pair through madcap encounters with their twins' wives and the local underworld. One of the pair's best efforts, though not well-remembered. Based on a story by W.W. Jacobs. **94m/B VHS.** Stan Laurel, Oliver Hardy, Alan Hale, Sidney Toler, James Finlayson, Daphne Pollard; ***D:*** Harry Lachman.

Our Song &&& **2001 (R)** Not your average teen drama. McKay's second dramatic feature concerning the troubled lives of adolescent girls faced with tough choices is a quietly affecting, poetic and solid effort. First-time actors Washington, Simpson and Martinez bring poignancy and realism to their roles as high school friends living in the Brooklyn projects and rehearsing for a marching band competition. The expected issues are present, but the film's treatment of them is what makes it unique. Bold in its way of forgoing major plot drama in favor of finding powerful moments in small places and offering food for thought. Real-life marching band the Jackie Robinson Steppers, who were the inspiration for the film, provide a focal point for the story and punch to the mostly languid pacing. **96m/C VHS, DVD.** *US* Kerry Washington, Anna Simpson, Melissa Martinez, Marlene Forte, Rosalyn Coleman, Ray Anthony Thomas, D'Monroe, Kim Howard, Carmen Lopez; ***D:*** Jim McKay; ***W:*** Jim McKay; ***C:*** Jim Denault.

Our Sons &&½ **1991** Two middle-aged moms strike up an unlikely friendship over their gay sons in this TV weeper. Arkansas waitress Luanna (Ann Margret) hasn't talked to son Donald (Ivanek) in years—now he's dying of AIDS. Successfull career woman Audrey (Andrews in her TV-movie debut) has seemingly accepted son James' (Grant) life with Donald and it's James who urges his mother to make contact with Luanna and persuade her to see Donald one last time. **100m/C VHS.** Julie Andrews, Ann-Margret, Hugh Grant, Zeljko Ivanek, Tony Roberts; ***D:*** John Erman; ***W:*** John Erman, William Hanley.

Our Time &&½ *Death of Her Innocence* **1974** An exclusive girls finishing school in the '50s is the setting for the friendship of Abby (Martin) and Muffy (Slade) and their first stirrings of romance. But when Muffy gets pregnant, tragedy awaits. Sappy. **91m/C VHS.** Pamela Sue Martin, Betsey Slade, Parker Stevenson, George O'Hanlon Jr., Roderick Cook, Edith Atwater, Meg Wyllie, Debralee Scott, Nora Heflin, Kathryn Holcomb, Robert Walden; ***D:*** Peter Hyams; ***W:*** Jane C. Stanton.

Our Town &&& **1940** Small-town New England life in Grover's Corners in the early 1900s is celebrated in this well-performed and directed adaptation of the Pulitzer Prize-winning play by Thornton Wilder. Film debut of Scott. **90m/B VHS, DVD.** Martha Scott, William Holden, Thomas Mitchell, Fay Bainter, Guy Kibbee, Beulah Bondi, Frank Craven; ***D:*** Sam Wood; ***W:*** Harry Chandlee, Frank Craven; ***C:*** Bert Glennon; ***M:*** Aaron Copland.

Our Town &&& **1977** TV version of Thornton Wilder's classic play about everyday life in Grovers Corners, a small New England town at the turn of the century. It hews more closely to the style of the stage version than the earlier film version. **120m/C VHS.** Ned Beatty, Sada Thompson, Ronny Cox, Glynnis O'Connor, Robby Benson, Hal Holbrook, John Houseman; ***D:*** Franklin J. Schaffner. **TV**

Our Town &&½ **1989** Filmed TV version of the Tony Award-winning Lincoln Center production of the Thornton Wilder play focusing on small-town life in Grover's Corners, New Hampshire. Gray is the omniscient Stage Manager, with Stolz and Miller as the young couple brought together by the everyday cycle of happiness and hardship. **104m/C VHS.** Eric Stoltz, Penelope Ann Miller, Spalding Gray; ***D:*** Gregory Mosher.

Our Very Own && **1950** At eighteen, and about to graduate from high school, Gail (Blyth) discovers she was adopted. So she decides to find her birth mother and then comes to realize what her foster parents really mean to her. Pretty sappy all the way 'round. **93m/B VHS.** Ann Blyth, Jane Wyatt, Donald Cook, Farley Granger, Ann Dvorak, Joan Evans, Natalie Wood, Martin Milner, Phyllis Kirk; ***D:*** David Miller; ***W:*** F. Hugh Herbert; ***C:*** Lee Garmes; ***M:*** Victor Young.

Our Vines Have Tender Grapes &&&½ **1945** A change of pace role for the volatile Robinson who plays a kind Norwegian farmer, living in Wisconsin with his daughter, the spunky O'Brien. The film is made-up of small-town moments as O'Brien learns a few of life's lessons, eased by the thoughtful compassion of Robinson. Based on the novel "For Our Vines Have Tender Grapes" by George Victor Martin. **105m/B VHS.** Edward G. Robinson, Margaret O'Brien, James Craig, Agnes Moorehead, Jackie "Butch" Jenkins, Morris Carnovsky, Frances Gifford, Sara Haden, Louis Jean Heydt; ***D:*** Roy Rowland; ***W:*** Dalton Trumbo; ***C:*** Robert L. Surtees.

Out &&½ **1988** A drifter's travels throughout the U.S. from the '60s to the '80s. Successfully manages to satirize just about every conceivable situation but keeps from posturing by not taking itself too seriously. Adapted from an experimental novel by Ronald Sukenick. **88m/C VHS.** Peter Coyote, Danny Glover, O-Lan Shepard, Jim Haynie, Scott Beach, Semu Haute; ***D:*** Eli Hollander; ***W:*** Eli Hollander; ***M:*** David Cope.

Out Cold &½ **1989 (R)** Black comedy follows the misadventures of a butcher who believes he has accidentally frozen his business partner; the iced man's girlfriend, who really killed him; and the detective who tries to solve the crime. Too many poor frozen body jokes may leave the viewer cold. **91m/C VHS.** John Lithgow, Teri Garr, Randy Quaid, Bruce McGill; ***D:*** Malcolm Mowbray; ***M:*** Michel Colombier.

Out Cold &½ **2001 (PG-13)** Dumb snowboarding comedy (the snowboarding scenes are the only cool things about the movie) focuses on a ragged ski resort in Bull Mountain, Alaska that developer Jack Majors (Majors) wants to turn into a family-oriented resort. That means getting rid of the resort's raucous loser employees, including Rick (London) and his buddies. **90m/C VHS, DVD, Wide.** Jason London, Willie Garson, Lee Majors, A.J. Cook, Derek Hamilton, Zach Galifianakis, Flex Anderson, Caroline Dhavernas, Victoria Silvstedt; ***D:*** Brendan Malloy, Emmett Malloy; ***W:*** Jon Zack; ***C:*** Richard Crudo; ***M:*** Michael Andrews.

Out for Blood && **1993 (R)** Attorney John Decker is living a happy life until his family is murdered by drug dealers. He turns vigilante, dubbed "Karateman" by the press, and finds himself hunted by the cops and the criminals. **?m/C VHS.** Don "The Dragon" Wilson, Shari Shattuck, Michael Delano, Kenneth McLeod, Todd Curtis, Timothy Baker, Howard Jackson, Bob Schott, Eric Lee; ***D:*** Richard W. Munchkin; ***W:*** David S. Green.

Out for Justice &½ **1991 (R)** A psycho Brooklyn hood goes on a murder spree, and homeboy turned lone-wolf cop Seagal races other police and the mob to get at him. Bloodthirsty and profane, it does try to depict N.Y.C.'s Italian-American community—but 90 percent of them are dead by the end so what's the point? Better yet, why does it open with a quote from Arthur Miller? Better still, what's Daffy Duck doing on this tape peddling Warner Bros. T-shirts to kid viewers?! **91m/C VHS, DVD, 8mm, Wide.** Dominic Chianese, Steven Seagal, William Forsythe, Jerry Orbach, Julianna Margulies, Gina Gershon, John Leguizamo, Julie Strain; ***D:*** John Flynn; ***W:*** David Lee Henry; ***C:*** Ric Waite; ***M:*** David Michael Frank.

Out in Fifty &½ **1999 (R)** Con is released from prison only to be pursued by a psycho detective who wants him back in the slammer and a mystery babe who has her own plans for the guy. **95m/C VHS, DVD.** Mickey Rourke, Bojesse Christopher, Christina Applegate, Scott Leet, Balthazar Getty, Peter Greene; ***D:*** Bojesse Christopher, Scott Leet. **VIDEO**

Out of Africa &&& **1985 (PG)** An epic film of the years spent by Danish authoress Isak Dinesen (her true name is Karen Blixen) on a Kenya coffee plantation. She moved to Africa to marry, and later fell in love with Denys Finch-Hatten, a British adventurer. Based on several books, including biographies of the two lovers. Some critics loved the scenery and music; others despised the acting and the script. A definite "no" for those who love action. **161m/C VHS, DVD, Wide.** Meryl Streep, Robert Redford, Klaus Maria Brandauer, Michael Kitchen, Malick Bowens, Michael Gough, Suzanna Hamilton, Rachel Kempson, Graham Crowden, Shane Rimmer, Donal McCann, Iman, Joseph Thiaka, Stephen Kinyanjui; ***D:*** Sydney Pollack; ***W:*** Kurt Luedtke; ***C:*** David Watkin; ***M:*** John Barry. Oscars '85: Adapt. Screenplay, Art Dir./Set Dec., Cinematog., Director (Pollack), Picture, Sound, Orig. Score; British Acad. '86: Adapt. Screenplay; Golden Globes '86: Film—Drama, Support. Actor (Brandauer), Score; L.A. Film Critics '85: Actress (Streep), Cinematog.; Natl. Bd. of Review '85: Support. Actor (Brandauer); N.Y. Film Critics '85: Cinematog., Support. Actor (Brandauer).

Out of Annie's Past &&½ **1994 (R)** Successful career woman Annie Carver (Stewart) has managed to hide a dreadful secret from family and co-workers for some 10 years. But now the past is back to haunt her—seems Annie was once the prime suspect in a murder. **91m/C VHS.** Catherine Mary Stewart, Dennis Farina, Scott Valentine, Carsten Norgaard, Michael Flynn; ***D:*** Stuart Cooper; ***W:*** Pablo F. Fenjves. **CABLE**

Out of Bounds &½ **1986 (R)** An Iowa farmboy picks up the wrong bag at the Los Angeles airport, and is plunged into a world of crime, drugs, and murder. Plenty of action, but the fast pace can't hide huge holes in the script or the silliness of Hall playing a tough kid on the run from the law. **93m/C VHS.** Anthony Michael Hall, Jenny Wright, Jeff Kober; ***D:*** Richard Tuggle; ***C:*** Bruce Surtees; ***M:*** Stewart Copeland.

Out of Control & **1985 (R)** A plane full of rich teenagers crash on a secluded island and must battle a gang of vicious smugglers to survive. A teen sex theme keeps working its way in, leaving the viewer as confused as the actors and actresses appear to be. **78m/C VHS.** Betsy Russell, Martin Hewitt, Claudia Udy, Andrew J. Lederer; ***D:*** Allan Holzman; ***W:*** Vicangelo Bulluck; ***C:*** John A. Alonzo.

Out of Order &½ **1984** A German-made film about people stuck in an office building's malevolent, free-thinking elevator. Dubbed. **87m/C VHS.** *GE* Renee Soutendijk, Goetz George, Wolfgang Kieling, Hannes Jaenicke; ***D:*** Carl Schenkel.

Out of Season && *Winter Rates* **1975 (R)** Mother and teenage daughter compete for the attentions of the mother's mysterious ex-lover. We never know who wins the man in this enigmatic drama set in an English village, and hints of incest make the story even murkier. Had only a short run in the U.S. **90m/C VHS, DVD.** *GB* Cliff Robertson, Vanessa Redgrave, Susan George; ***D:*** Alan Bridges.

Out of Sight &&& **1998 (R)** Cerebral director Soderbergh turns up the heat in this fine adaptation (with fine performances) of the Elmore Leonard crime caper. Jack Foley (Clooney) is a charming bank robber with bad luck and three prison terms—his current one being served in a Florida pen from which he escapes with the aid of partner Buddy (Rhames). Even the escape doesn't go as planned since federal marshal Karen Sisco (Lopez) becomes an unexpected (temporary) hostage. Sparks fly between the duo but Karen's still determined to bring Jack to justice, even as he plans his next heist. A heist involving shady financier Richard Ripley (Brooks) that will take Jack and Buddy to Detroit and more complications. **122m/C VHS, DVD, Wide.** George Clooney, Jennifer Lopez, Ving Rhames, Don Cheadle, Albert Brooks, Steve Zahn, Dennis Farina, Catherine Keener, Luis Guzman, Isaiah Washington IV, Keith Loneker, Nancy Allen; ***Cameos:*** Michael Keaton, Samuel L. Jackson; ***D:*** Steven Soderbergh; ***W:*** Scott Frank; ***C:*** Elliot Davis; ***M:*** Cliff Martinez. Natl. Soc. Film Critics '98: Director (Soderbergh), Film, Screenplay; Writers Guild '98: Adapt. Screenplay.

Out of Sight, Out of Her Mind && **1989 (R)** After witnessing her daughter burned alive, Alice is released from a mental institution. She tries to start a new life, but her daughter won't let her—she keeps appearing, crying out for help. **94m/C VHS.** Susan Blakely, Eddie Albert, Wings Hauser.

Out of Sync 🦴½ **1995 (R)** Deejay Jason St. Julian gets in trouble with his bookies and L.A. detectives, one of whom forces him into an undercover job with a drug-dealing club owner. Then Jason falls for the dealer's girlfriend. Hip-hop soundtrack may provide the only interest. **105m/C VHS, DVD.** L.L. Cool J., Victoria Dillard, Howard Hesseman, Ramy Zada, Don Yesso, Yaphet Kotto; ***D:*** Debbie Allen; ***W:*** Robert E. Dorn; ***C:*** Isidore Mankofsky; ***M:*** Steve Tyrell.

Out of the Blue 🦴🦴½ **1947** There's trouble in paradise for a married man when a shady lady passes out in his apartment. Thinking she is dead, he tries to get rid of the body. The antics with his neighbor and wife provide plenty of laughs. **86m/B VHS.** George Brent, Virginia Mayo, Carole Landis, Turhan Bey, Ann Dvorak; ***D:*** Leigh Jason.

Out of the Blue 🦴🦴🦴 **1980 (R)** A harsh, violent portrait of a shattered family. When an imprisoned father's return fails to reunite this Woodstock-generation family, the troubled teenage daughter takes matters into her own hands. "Easy Rider" star Hopper seems to have reconsidered the effects of the 1960s. **94m/C VHS, DVD.** Dennis Hopper, Linda Manz, Raymond Burr; ***D:*** Dennis Hopper; ***W:*** Gary Jules Jouvenat, Brenda Nielson, Leonard Yakir; ***C:*** Marc Champion; ***M:*** Tom Lavin.

Out of the Body 🦴 **1988 (R)** A man is possessed by a spirit that likes to kill young, beautiful women. This makes him (and the viewer) uncomfortable. **91m/C VHS.** *AU* Mark Hembrow, Tessa Humphries, John Clayton, John Ley, Carrie Zivetz, Linda Newton; ***D:*** Brian Trenchard-Smith; ***W:*** Kenneth Ross; ***C:*** Kevan Lind; ***M:*** Peter Westheimer.

Out of the Cold 🦴½ **1999 (R)** Jewish tap dancer Dan Scott (Carradine) decides to take his fading cabaret act to his family's homeland of Estonia on the eve of WWII. Bad idea. Trapped between the Nazis and the Soviets, Dan still finds time to romance local beauty Deborah (Kirshner), although their love affair is cut short by tragedy. Blah film whose plot goes nowhere quickly. **111m/C VHS, DVD.** Keith Carradine, Mia Kirshner, Judd Hirsch, Brian Dennehy, Mercedes Ruehl, Bronson Pinchot, Kim Hunter, Mark Sheppard; ***D:*** Aleksandr (Sasha) Buravsky; ***W:*** Aleksandr (Sasha) Buravsky, Alex Kustanovich; ***C:*** Vladimir Klimov; ***M:*** Maksim Dunayevsky.

Out of the Dark 🦴½ **1988 (R)** The female employees of a telephone-sex service are stalked by a killer wearing a clown mask in this tongue-in-cheek thriller. A few laughs amid the slaughter. Look for Divine. **98m/C VHS.** Cameron Dye, Divine, Karen Black, Bud Cort, Lynn Danielson, Geoffrey Lewis, Paul Bartel, Tracey Walter, Silvania Gallardo, Starr Andreeff, Lainie Kazan, Tab Hunter, John DeBello; ***D:*** Michael Schroeder; ***W:*** James DeFelice, Zane W. Levitt; ***C:*** Julio Macat; ***M:*** Paul Antonelli, David Wheatley.

Out of the Darkness 🦴🦴🦴 **1985 (R)** TV movie about the personal life of the New York detective who hunted and arrested sexual killer Son of Sam. Sheen shines in a tight suspenser. **96m/C VHS.** Martin Sheen, Hector Elizondo, Matt Clark, Jennifer Salt, Eddie Egan, Robert Trebor; ***D:*** Jud Taylor; ***W:*** T.S. Cook. **TV**

Out of the Past 🦴🦴🦴½ *Build My Gallows High* **1947** A private detective gets caught in a complex web of love, murder, and money in this film noir classic. The plot is torturous but clear thanks to fine directing. Mitchum became an overnight star after this film, which was overlooked but now considered one of the best in its genre. Based on Geoffrey Homes's novel "Build My Gallows High." Remade in 1984 as "Against All Odds." **97m/B VHS, DVD.** Robert Mitchum, Kirk Douglas, Jane Greer, Rhonda Fleming, Steve Brodie, Dickie Moore, Richard Webb, Virginia Huston, Ken Niles, Paul Valentine; ***D:*** Jacques Tourneur; ***W:*** Geoffrey Homes, Daniel Mainwaring; ***C:*** Nicholas Musuraca; ***M:*** Roy Webb. Natl. Film Reg. '91.

Out of the Rain 🦴🦴½ **1990 (R)** A small town becomes a hotbed of deceit and lies due to the influence of drugs. A man and and a woman engage in a passionate struggle to free themselves from the town's grip. **91m/C VHS.** Bridget Fonda, Michael O'Keefe, John E. O'Keefe, John Seitz, Georgine Hall, Al Shannon; ***D:*** Gary Winick; ***W:*** Shem Bitterman.

Out of the Shadows 🦴🦴½ **1988** Scotland Yard Chief Inspector Michael Hayden (Dance) investigates a series of international art thefts that lead him to believe the goods are being smuggled out of the country through diplomatic channels. **95m/C VHS.** *GB* Charles Dance, Alexandra Paul, Wanda Ventham; ***D:*** Willi Patterson. **TV**

Out of Time 🦴½ **2000** Dull update of the Rip Van Winkle legend. While walking in the woods outside his small Oregon town, Jack Epson (McDaniels) takes a drink from a spring and falls asleep for 20 years. He wakes up to find his natural surroundings are under siege from developers and his now-grown daughter has a child of her own. **94m/C VHS, DVD.** James McDaniel, Mel Harris, August Schellenberg, Ken Pogue; ***D:*** Ernest Thompson; ***W:*** Ernest Thompson, Rob Gilmer; ***C:*** Stephen McNutt; ***M:*** Terry Frewer. **CABLE**

The Out-of-Towners 🦴🦴🦴 **1970 (G)** A pair of Ohio rubes travels to New York City and along the way everything that could go wrong does. Lemmon's performance is excellent and Simon's script is, as usual, both wholesome and funny. **98m/C VHS.** Jack Lemmon, Sandy Dennis, Anne Meara, Sandy Baron, Billy Dee Williams; ***D:*** Arthur Hiller; ***W:*** Neil Simon. Writers Guild '70: Orig. Screenplay.

The Out-of-Towners 🦴🦴 **1999 (PG-13)** Hawn and Martin are Nancy and Henry Clark, middle-aged Ohio empty-nesters headed for Henry's job interview in New York. Along the way, they're thwarted by every tourist nightmare obstacle imaginable: rerouting to Boston, missed trains, rental car mishaps, muggings, maxed credit cards, snooty hotel personnel, etc, etc. Martin's seen all this before (in "Planes, Trains, and Automobiles") and so have we, in any number of movies, including the original 1970 Neil Simon script. Mostly uninspired and inconsistent, with flashes of fine physical comedy from Hawn and Martin. Cleese plays a familiar role as a needlessly pompous hotel manager. **92m/C VHS, DVD.** Mark McKinney, Goldie Hawn, Steve Martin, John Cleese, Oliver Hudson; ***D:*** Sam Weisman; ***W:*** Marc Lawrence; ***C:*** John Bailey; ***M:*** Marc Shaiman.

Out on a Limb 🦴🦴 **1987** MacLaine plays herself in this miniseries based on her best-selling book by the same name. In the midst of love affairs with an unnamed British politician and a mysterious teacher, she learns about her past, present, and future through meditation and her beliefs in reincarnation. Features footage of psychics performing spiritual channeling. Beautiful scenery filmed on location in California, Hong Kong, London, Hawaii, Sweden, and Peru, but the acting is just average, and the movie is slow in some parts. **160m/C VHS.** Shirley MacLaine, Charles Dance, John Heard, Anne Jackson, Jerry Orbach; ***D:*** Robert Butler. **TV**

Out on a Limb 🦴 **1992 (PG)** Lame comedy follows the misadventures of financial whiz Bill Campbell (Broderick). His young sister is convinced their stepfather is a criminal and persuades her brother to return home. On his way, Bill is robbed and abandoned by a woman hitchhiker, then found by two moronic brothers. It also turns out his stepfather has a twin brother who wants revenge for past crimes. Frantic chase scenes and lots of noise do not a comedy make. Broderick and Jones also appeared together in "Ferris Bueller's Day Off." **82m/C VHS.** Matthew Broderick, Jeffrey Jones, Heidi Kling, John C. Reilly, Marian Mercer, Larry Hankin, David Margulies; ***D:*** Francis Veber.

Out on Bail 🦴½ **1989 (R)** A law-abiding citizen witnesses a murder, only to discover the crooked town council is behind the slaying. **102m/C VHS.** Robert Ginty, Kathy Shower, Tom Badal, Sydney Lassick; ***D:*** Gordon Hessler; ***W:*** Tom Badal, Jason Booth.

Out There 🦴🦴½ **1995 (PG-13)** Cable sci-fi comedy finds photographer Delbert Mosley (Campbell) buying a Brownie camera at a garage sale and discovering the 25-year-old film shows pictures of a UFO encounter. Mosley then tries to verify the photos with a supermarket tabloid, the military, and UFO fanatics all on his trail. Fast-paced amusement with appealing performances. **98m/C VHS.** Richard Speight Jr., Billy Campbell, Wendy Schaal, Julie Brown, David Rasche, Paul Dooley, Bill Cobbs, Bob(cat) Goldthwait, Rod Steiger, June Lockhart, Jill St. John, Carel Struycken, Billy Bob Thornton, P.J. Soles; ***D:*** Sam Irvin; ***W:*** Thomas Strelich, Alison Nigh; ***C:*** Gary Tieche; ***M:*** Deborah Holland, Frankie Blue. **CABLE**

Out to Sea 🦴🦴½ **1997 (PG-13)** Charlie (Matthau) persuades brother-in-law Herb (Lemmon) to become a dance instructor aboard a cruise ship so they can meet women and con them out of money. Charlie sets his sights on feisty socialite Liz (Cannon), while Herb romances Vivian (DeHaven), who's tagging along on her daughter's honeymoon. Both of these "salty old dogs" have to avoid the wrath of militaristic cruise director Gil (Spiner). The duo still has great comic timing, as they continue to defy the odds that this is the one that's gonna flop. Great supporting cast, which includes O'Connor in a couple of nifty dance scenes, seems to be having a great time. **109m/C VHS.** Joe (Johnny) Viterelli, Walter Matthau, Jack Lemmon, Dyan Cannon, Gloria De Haven, Brent Spiner, Elaine Stritch, Hal Linden, Donald O'Connor, Edward Mulhare, Rue McClanahan; ***D:*** Martha Coolidge; ***W:*** Robert Nelson Jacobs, Danny Jacobson; ***C:*** Lajos Koltai; ***M:*** David Newman.

Outbreak 🦴🦴🦴 **1994 (R)** Smuggled African monkey spits on someone who kisses someone else who sneezes on a bunch of people, thus initiating the spread of a highly infectious mystery disease in a northern California 'burb. Hoffman leads a team of scientists in a search for the anti-serum, but it's a secret government plot to exterminate the victims that literally sends Hoffman and crew into action movie cliche overdrive (add "helicopter" to the list of chase scene vehicles). Not that that's so bad—if the beat-the-clock tempo doesn't grab you, paranoia certainly will. But Hoffman's hardly a threat to Arnold or Sylvester as the next action hero, and the talented Russo remains suspiciously ravishing even with festering pustules. Based on two books: Richard Preston's "The Hot Zone" and Laurie Garrett's "The Coming Plague." **128m/C VHS, DVD, Wide.** Dustin Hoffman, Rene Russo, Morgan Freeman, Donald Sutherland, Cuba Gooding Jr., Kevin Spacey, J.T. Walsh, Dale Dye; ***D:*** Wolfgang Petersen; ***W:*** Laurence Dworet, Robert Roy Pool; ***C:*** Michael Ballhaus; ***M:*** James Newton Howard. N.Y. Film Critics '95: Support. Actor (Spacey).

The Outcast 🦴🦴 **1954** A young tough heads west to seize the family ranch wrongfully held by a conniving uncle. Of course he finds love as well, and enjoys gun and fistfights in this exciting though unspectacular western. **90m/C VHS.** John Derek, Jim Davis, Joan Davis; ***D:*** William Witney.

The Outcast 🦴½ **1984** Story of three brothers who live by the ax, love from the heart, hate with passion, and die violently. Trouble is they have to recite from a script written in crayon. **86m/C VHS.** Ben Dekker, Sandra Prinsloo.

The Outcasts 🦴🦴🦴 **1986** A Taiwanese film about young gay boys in an urban jungle who are given shelter and protection by an aging photographer. In Chinese with English subtitles. **102m/C VHS.** *TW* ***D:*** Yu Kan-Ping.

Outcasts of the City 🦴🦴 **1958** The sort of negligible film filler that TV killed off. An American officer in post-WWII Germany romances a German girl, then gets blamed for the death of her Boche beau. **61m/B VHS.** Osa Massen, Robert Hutton, Maria Palmer, Nestor Paiva, John Hamilton, George Neise, Norbert Schiller, George Sanders; ***D:*** Boris L. Petroff.

Outcasts of the Trail 🦴½ **1949** When Tom White (Gallaudet) is jailed for robbing the stage, his children are shunned by the town even after Tom decides to return the stolen cash after his release. So, it's up to stagecoach driver Pat Garrett (Hale) to clear up the family's trouble. **61m/B VHS.** Monte Hale, John Gallaudet, Roy Barcroft, Jeff Donnell, T.V. Tommy Ivo, Paul Hurst; ***D:*** Philip Ford; ***W:*** Olive Cooper, Stanley Wilson; ***C:*** Bud Thackery.

The Outer Limits: Sandkings 🦴🦴🦴 *Sandkings* **1995** Cable revival of the '60s sci-fi series is creepier than ever with this tale of loony scientist Simon Kress (Bridges). He discovers tiny alien eggs while doing an analysis of Martian soil samples and decides to take his research home with him when the government cuts off funding. Big mistake—the critters he successfully hatches in his barn are mean and hungry. Features both dad Lloyd and Beau's 10-year-old son, Dylan, in roles. **93m/C VHS.** Beau Bridges, Lloyd Bridges, Helen Shaver, Dylan Bridges, Kim Coates; ***D:*** Stuart Gillard; ***W:*** Melinda M. Snodgrass. **CABLE**

The Outfit 🦴🦴½ **1993 (R)** It's the 1930s and a mob war is brewing between Lucky Luciano, Legs Diamond and Dutch Schultz. A maverick FBI agent gets in good with Diamond and works to end their reign of crime—only he winds up being the spark to light a war between the rival bosses. **92m/C VHS.** John Christian, Billy Drago, Lance Henriksen, Martin Kove, Josh Moby, Rick Washburne; ***D:*** J. Christian Ingvordsen; ***W:*** J. Christian Ingvordsen, Steven Kaman, Whitney Ransick.

The Outing 🦴🦴 *The Lamp* **1987 (R)** A group of high school kids sneaks into a museum at night to party, and get hunted down by a 3,000-year-old genie-in-a-lamp. The genie idea is original enough to make things interesting. Mediocre special effects and run-of-the-mill acting. **87m/C VHS.** Deborah Winters, James Huston, Andra St. Ivanyi, Scott Bankston, Mark Mitchell, Andre Chimene, Damon Merrill, Barry Coffing; ***D:*** Tom Daley; ***W:*** Warren Chaney; ***C:*** Herbert Raditschnig.

Outland 🦴🦴 **1981 (R)** On a volcanic moon of Jupiter, miners begin suffering from spells of insanity. A single federal marshal begins an investigation that threatens the colony's survival. No more or less than a western in space, and the science is rather poor. Might make an interesting double feature with "High Noon," though. **109m/C VHS, DVD, Wide.** Kika Markham, Clarke Peters, Steven Berkoff, John Ratzenberger, Manning Redwood, Angus MacInnes, Sean Connery, Peter Boyle, Frances Sternhagen, James B. Sikking; ***D:*** Peter Hyams; ***W:*** Peter Hyams; ***C:*** Stephen Goldblatt; ***M:*** Jerry Goldsmith.

The Outlaw 🦴🦴 **1943** Hughes's variation on the saga of Billy the Kid, which spends more time on Billy's relationship with girlfriend Rio than the climactic showdown with Pat Garrett. The famous Russell vehicle isn't as steamy as it must have seemed to viewers of the day, but the brouhaha around it served to keep it on the shelf for six years. Also available colorized. **123m/B VHS, DVD.** Jane Russell, Jack Buetel, Walter Huston, Thomas Mitchell, Mimi Aguglia, Gene Rizzi, Joseph (Joe) Sawyer; ***D:*** Howard Hughes; ***W:*** Jules Furthman; ***C:*** Gregg Toland; ***M:*** Victor Young.

The Outlaw and His Wife 🦴🦴½ **1917** An early silent film about a farmer, accused of a petty crime, who flees with his wife into the mountains to escape the police. This powerful drama was a breakthrough film for the early Swedish movie industry. **73m/B VHS.** *SW* Victor Sjostrom, Edith Erastoff; ***D:*** Victor Sjostrom.

The Outlaw Bikers—Gang Wars 🦴 **1970** The original road warriors take it to the streets as rival biker gangs square off. **90m/C VHS.** Clancy Syrko, Des Roberts, John King III, Linda Jackson; ***D:*** Lawrence Merrick.

Outlaw Blues 🦴🦴 **1977 (PG)** An ex-convict becomes a national folk hero when he sets out to reclaim his stolen hit song about prison life. St. James is charming in her first major movie role. A grab bag of action, drama, and tongue-in-cheek humor. **101m/C VHS.** Peter Fonda, Susan St. James, Johnny Crawford, Michael Lerner, James Callahan; ***D:*** Richard T. Heffron; ***M:*** Charles Bernstein.

Outlaw Country 🦴🦴½ **1949** LaRue has a dual role as the marshal who is after a band of counterfeiters and an outlaw who's part of the gang. **72m/B VHS.** Lash LaRue, Al "Fuzzy" St. John, House Peters Jr., Ted Adams, Dan(iel) White, Steve Dunhill; ***D:*** Ray Taylor.

The Outlaw Deputy 🦴½ **1935** The law-abiding McCoy as an outlaw! It's really a mistake and Lane helps him clear his name. Based on the story "King of Cactusville" by Johnston McCulley. **55m/B VHS.** Tim McCoy, Nora Lane, Bud Osborne, Si Jenks, George Offerman Jr.; ***D:*** Otto Brower.

Outlaw Express 🦴½ **1938** After the annexing of California, a U.S. marshall is sent to stop a gang of outlaws who have been raiding Spanish landowners. **57m/B VHS.** Bob Baker, Cecilia Callejo, Leroy Mason, Don Barclay, Carleton Young; ***D:*** George Waggner.

Outlaw Force 🦴 **1987 (R)** A Vietnam veteran country singer tracks down the vicious rednecks that kidnapped his daughter and raped and killed his wife. Heavener did all the work in this low-budget, low-quality take-off on "Death Wish." **95m/C VHS.** David Heavener, Frank Stallone, Paul Smith, Robert Bjorklund, Devin Dunsworth; ***D:*** David Heavener.

Outlaw Fury 🦴½ **1950** Another Shamrock Ellison epic, this time dealing with a coward proving himself by killing the bad guys. **55m/B VHS.** James Ellison, Russell Hayden.

Outlaw Gang 🦴½ **1949** A marshal investigates a rash of rancher killings, leading to a conflict between Indians and local land and water companies. **59m/B VHS.** Donald (Don "Red") Barry, Robert Lowery, Betty Adams.

The Outlaw Josey Wales 🦴🦴🦴🦴 **1976 (PG)** Eastwood plays a farmer with a motive for revenge—his family was killed and for years he was betrayed and hunted. His desire to play the lone killer is, however, tempered by his need for family and friends. He kills plenty, but in the end finds happiness. Considered one of the last great Westerns, with many superb performances. Eastwood took over directorial chores during filming from Kaufman, who co-scripted. Adapted from "Gone To Texas" by Forest Carter. **135m/C VHS, DVD, Wide.** Clint Eastwood, Chief Dan George, Sondra Locke, Matt Clark, John Vernon, Bill McKinney, Sam Bottoms, Will Sampson, Woodrow Parfrey, Royal Dano, John Quade, John Russell, John Mitchum, Kyle Eastwood; ***D:*** Clint Eastwood; ***W:*** Philip Kaufman; ***C:*** Bruce Surtees; ***M:*** Jerry Fielding. Natl. Film Reg. '96.

Outlaw Justice 🦴🦴 **1932** Worn oater plot has our hero infiltrating a gang of outlaws to bring them to justice and save the heroine. **56m/C VHS.** Jack Hoxie, Dorothy Gulliver, Donald Keith, Kermit Maynard, Charles "Blackie" King, Tom London; ***D:*** Armand Schaefer.

Outlaw Justice 🦴🦴½ **1998 (R)** Aging gunslingers Nelson and Kristofferson meet up with buddy Tritt in order to avenge the death of their old partner. Nothing new storywise but the cast is certainly comfortable with the material. **94m/C VHS, DVD.** Kris Kristofferson, Willie Nelson, Sancho Gracia, Travis Tritt, Chad Willett, Waylon Jennings; ***D:*** Bill Corcoran; ***W:*** Gene Quintano; ***C:*** Federico Ribes; ***M:*** Jay Gruska. **TV**

Outlaw of Gor 🦴½ **1987 (PG)** Once again, the mild professor is transported to Gor, where he has new, improved, bloody adventures. Lots of swordplay, but no magic. Sequel to "Gor." From the novel by John Norman. **89m/C VHS.** Rebecca Ferratti, Urbano Barberini, Jack Palance, Donna Denton; ***D:*** John Cardos; ***W:*** R.J. Marx.

Outlaw of the Plains 🦴 **1946** Another of Crabbe's cowboy pictures in which he played hero Billy Carson, now bailing his trouble-prone sidekick out of a land swindle. Very plain indeed. **56m/B VHS.** Buster Crabbe, Al "Fuzzy" St. John, Patti McCarty, Charles "Blackie" King, Karl Hackett, John Cason, Bud Osborne, Budd Buster, Charles "Slim" Whitaker; ***D:*** Sam Newfield.

Outlaw Riders 🦴 **1972 (PG)** Three outlaw bikers take it on the lam after committing a series of disastrous bank robberies. **84m/C VHS.** Sonny West, Darlene Duralia, Bambi Allen, Bill Bonner; ***D:*** Tony Houston.

Outlaw Roundup 🦴 **1944** The Texas Rangers battle an outlaw gang. Guess who wins. **51m/B VHS.** Tex O'Brien, James Newill, Guy Wilkerson, Helen Chapman, Jack Ingram, I. Stanford Jolley; ***D:*** Harry Fraser.

Outlaw Rule 🦴½ **1936** Standard action-packed western adventure pitting outlaws against the law of the West. **61m/B VHS.** Reb Russell, Betty Mack, Yakima Canutt, Jack Rockwell, John McGuire, Alan Bridge; ***D:*** S. Roy Luby.

The Outlaw Tamer 🦴 **1933** Even though Chandler is on the run he still helps capture some horse thieves. **56m/B VHS.** Lane Chandler, J(ohn) P(aterson) McGowan, Janet Morgan, George "Gabby" Hayes; ***D:*** J(ohn) P(aterson) McGowan.

Outlaw Trail 🦴½ **1944** The Trail Blazers put an end to a counterfeiter's evil ways. **53m/B VHS.** Hoot Gibson, Bob Steele, Chief Thundercloud, Jennifer Holt, Cy Kendall; ***D:*** Robert Emmett Tansey.

Outlaw Women 🦴 **1952** A western town is run by a woman who won't let male outlaws in—until one wins her heart. **76m/C VHS.** Marie Windsor, Jackie Coogan, Carla Balenda; ***D:*** Sam Newfield.

The Outlaws Is Coming! 🦴🦴½ **1965** Three magazine staffers (Larry, Moe, and Curly Joe) and their editor (West) encounter Wyatt Earp, Wild Bill Hickock, Jesse James, and Annie Oakley when they journey out West to save the buffalo. Last, and one of the best, of the Three Stooges feature films. **90m/B VHS.** Moe Howard, Larry Fine, Joe DeRita, Adam West, Nancy Kovack, Emil Sitka, Henry Gibson; ***D:*** Norman Maurer.

Outlaws of Sonora 🦴½ **1938** A man transports money to a neighboring town while his outlaw double tries to steal it from him. **58m/B VHS.** Robert "Bob" Livingston, Ray Corrigan, Max Terhune, Jack Mulhall, Otis Harlan; ***D:*** George Sherman.

Outlaws of the Desert 🦴½ **1941** Having run out of bad guys in the Old West, Hoppy and his pals head to Arabia to buy some horses. Once there, they get involved in a kidnapping. Russell Hayden is replaced as Hoppy's sidekick by Brad King. Duncan ("The Cisco Kid") Renaldo plays the sheik. **66m/B VHS.** William Boyd, Brad King, Andy Clyde, Forrest Stanley, Jean Phillips, Duncan Renaldo, George Lewis; ***D:*** Howard Bretherton.

Outlaws of the Range 🦴½ **1936** Action western featuring outlaws who terrorize the countryside. **60m/B VHS.** Bill Cody, Catherine Cotter, William (Bill, Billy) McCall, Gordon Griffith; ***D:*** Al(bert) Herman.

Outlaw's Paradise 🦴🦴 **1939** Cowboy hero McCoy plays not only a lawman out to catch mail thieves, but also the chief outlaw he's hunting! That's one way to keep the budget low. **62m/B VHS.** Tim McCoy, Ben (Benny) Corbett, Joan Barclay, Ted Adams, Forrest Taylor, Bob Terry; ***D:*** Sam Newfield.

Outpost in Morocco 🦴½ **1949** A desert soldier is sent to quiet the restless natives and falls for the rebel leader's daughter. The good guys win, but the love interest is sacrificed. Glory before love boys, and damn the story. **92m/B VHS, DVD.** George Raft, Marie Windsor, Akim Tamiroff, John Litel, Eduard Franz; ***D:*** Robert Florey; ***W:*** Charles Grayson, Paul de Sainte-Colombe; ***C:*** Lucien N. Andriot; ***M:*** Michel Michelet.

Outrage! 🦴🦴½ **1986** An upstanding citizen guns down his daughter's killer and turns himself in to police. His ambitious lawyer fights an open-and-shut homicide case with both fair and foul means. Not a shootout like the cassette box suggests, but an okay courtroom drama attacking excesses of the legal system. From a novel by Henry Denker, made for TV by producer Irwin Allen. **96m/C VHS.** Robert Preston, Beau Bridges, Anthony Newley, Mel Ferrer, Burgess Meredith, Linda Purl, William Allen Young; ***D:*** Walter Grauman. **TV**

Outrage 🦴🦴 *Dispara* **1993 (R)** Journalist Marco Vallez's (Banderas) latest assignment is a story about a traveling circus. Bored with the usual acts, he's intrigued by equestrian/sharpshooter Anna (Neri) and asks her for an interview, which leads to passion. While Marco is on assignment in Barcelona, Anna is attacked and raped in her trailer. Rather than calling the police, Anna decides to take her own revenge. Spanish with subtitles or dubbed. **108m/C VHS, DVD.** *SP* Antonio Banderas, Francesca Neri, Eulalia Ramon, Walter Vidarte, Coque Malla; ***D:*** Carlos Saura; ***W:*** Carlos Saura; ***C:*** Javier Aguirresarobe; ***M:*** Alberto Iglesias.

Outrageous! 🦴🦴🦴 **1977 (R)** An offbeat, low-budget comedy about the strange relationship between a gay female impersonator and his pregnant schizophrenic friend. The pair end up in New York, where they feel right at home. Russell's impersonations of female film stars earned him the best actor prize at the Berlin Film Festival. **100m/C VHS.** *CA* Craig Russell, Hollis McLaren, Richard Easley, Allan Moyle, Helen Shaver, Martha Gibson, Helen Hughes, David McIlwraith, Andree Pelletier; ***D:*** Richard Benner; ***W:*** Richard Benner; ***C:*** James Kelly; ***M:*** Paul Hoffert.

Outrageous Fortune 🦴🦴 **1987 (R)** Two would-be actresses—one prim and innocent and one wildly trampy—chase after the same two-timing boyfriend and get involved in a dangerous CIA plot surrounding a deadly bacteria. Tired plot. Mediocre acting and formula jokes, but somehow still funny. Disney's first foray into comedy for grown-ups. **112m/C VHS, DVD.** Shelley Long, Bette Midler, George Carlin, Peter Coyote; ***D:*** Arthur Hiller; ***W:*** Leslie Dixon; ***C:*** David M. Walsh; ***M:*** Alan Silvestri.

Outside Chance 🦴 **1978** A soapy, sanitized remake of Mimieux's film, "Jackson County Jail," wherein an innocent woman is persecuted in a small Southern jail. **92m/C VHS.** Yvette Mimieux, Royce D. Applegate; ***D:*** Michael Miller. **TV**

Outside Chance of Maximillian Glick 🦴🦴 **1988 (G)** A sentimental Canadian comedy about a boy's dreams and his tradition-bound Jewish family. **94m/C VHS.** *CA* Noam Zylberman, Fairuza Balk, Saul Rubinek; ***D:*** Allan Goldstein; ***C:*** Ian Elkin. Toronto-City '88: Canadian Feature Film.

The Outside Man 🦴🦴 *Un Homme Est Mort* **1973 (PG)** A French hit man is called to Los Angeles to knock off a crime boss, which he does. But then an American hit man is hired to do in the Frenchman. The climatic showdown is set around the crime boss' body, which happens to be embalmed in a sitting position. Decidely offbeat. **104m/C VHS.** *FR* Jean-Louis Trintignant, Roy Scheider, Ann-Margret, Angie Dickinson, Georgia Engel, Carlo De Meyo, Umberto Orsini, Ted de Corsia, Felice Orlandi, John Hillerman; ***D:*** Jacques Deray.

Outside Ozona 🦴🦴 **1998 (R)** Three sets of couples listen to a ranting all-night DJ (Taj Mahal) as they drive through the desolate Southwest. Wit Roy (Pollak) is an unemployed circus clown driving with his ex-stripper girlfriend, Earlene (Miller), trucker Odell Parks (Forster) comes to the aid of stranded Reba Twosalt (Walker) and her grandmother, while feuding sisters Marcy (Fenn) and Bonnie (Styne) are driving to their father's funeral. Oh yeah, there's also a backroads serial killer on the loose. Looks good but doesn't make much of an impression. **100m/C VHS.** Robert Forster, Kevin Pollak, Penelope Ann Miller, David Paymer, Sherilyn Fenn, Beth Ann Styne, Lois Red Elk, Kateri Walker, Swoosie Kurtz, Taj Mahal, Meat Loaf Aday, Lucy Webb; ***D:*** J.S. Cardone; ***W:*** J.S. Cardone; ***C:*** Irek Hartowicz; ***M:*** Taj Mahal, Johnny Lee Schell.

Outside Providence 🦴🦴½ **1999 (R)** Although heavily promoted as created "by the makers of 'There's Something About Mary'" upon its release to draw fans of lowbrow humor, this coming-of-age comedy is actually a bit more sensitive. Based on Peter Farrelly's semi-autobiographical novel, it tells the story of Dunph (Hatosy), a stoner teen from Pawtucket who's sent to a snooty prep school by his father (Baldwin) after he and his high-on friends crash into a police car. He has immediate trouble fitting in, although he manages to hook up with coed Jane (Smart), whose book smarts help his anemic GPA. Unfortunately, his pranks put her Ivy League hopes in danger. Baldwin gives a good performance as the gruff-but-loving dad, but too many of the characters are merely skimmed over before they have a chance to develop. **103m/C VHS, DVD.** Shawn Hatosy, Alec Baldwin, George Wendt, Jonathan Brandis, Amy Smart, Gabriel Mann, Jon Abrahams, Adam LaVorgna, Mike Cerrone, Richard Jenkins; ***D:*** Michael Corrente; ***W:*** Peter Farrelly, Michael Corrente, Bobby Farrelly; ***C:*** Richard Crudo; ***M:*** Sheldon Mirowitz.

Outside the Law 🦴🦴 **1921** Lon Chaney plays dual roles of the underworld hood in "Black Mike Sylva," and a Chinese servant in "Ah Wing." Silent. **77m/B VHS, DVD.** Lon Chaney Sr., Priscilla Dean, Ralph Lewis, Wheeler Oakman; ***D:*** Tod Browning; ***W:*** Lucien Hubbard; ***C:*** William Fildew.

Outside the Law 🦴½ **1995 (R)** Maverick cop Brad Kingsbury (Bradley) crosses the line when he falls for luscious Tanya Borgman (Thomson), who's the prime suspect in a murder investigation. Also available unrated. **94m/C VHS.** David Bradley, Anna Thomson, Ashley Laurence; ***D:*** Boaz Davidson; ***W:*** Dennis Dimster Denk; ***C:*** Avi (Avraham) Karpik; ***M:*** Blake Leyh.

The Outsiders 🦴🦴½ **1983 (PG)** Based on the popular S.E. Hinton book, the story of a teen gang from the wrong side of the tracks and their conflicts with society and each other. Melodramatic and over-done, but teenagers still love the story. Good soundtrack and cast ripples with up and coming stars. Followed by a TV series. Coppola adapted another Hinton novel the same year, "Rumble Fish." **91m/C VHS, DVD, Wide.** C. Thomas Howell, Matt Dillon, Ralph Macchio, Patrick Swayze, Diane Lane, Tom Cruise, Emilio Estevez, Rob Lowe, Tom Waits, Leif Garrett; ***D:*** Francis Ford Coppola; ***W:*** Kathleen Rowell; ***C:*** Stephen Burum; ***M:*** Carmine Coppola.

Outta Time 🦴🦴 *The Courier* **2001 (R)** Tijuana native David Morales (Lopez) has gottan an athletic scholarship to the University of San Diego but loses it because of a knee injury. Needing cash to pay his tuition, David doesn't ask a lot of questions when ex-professor Darabont (Saxon) asks David to transport some sealed packages of serum for testing across the border. Naturally, this job isn't as easy as David has been told. **90m/C VHS, DVD, Wide.** Mario Lopez, John Saxon, Ali Landry, Nancy O'Dell, Tava Smiley, Tim Sitarz; ***D:*** Lorena David; ***W:*** Scott Duncan, Ned Kerwin; ***C:*** Lisa Wiegard; ***M:*** Scott Gilman.

The Oval Portrait 🦴½ **1988** An adaptation of the Edgar Allan Poe suspense tale about a Civil War-era maiden, her illicit love for a Confederate soldier and her eventual death. **89m/C VHS.** Giselle MacKenzie, Barry Coe; ***D:*** Regelio A. Gonzalez Jr.

Over Indulgence 🦴🦴 **1987 (R)** A young woman witnesses a murder in an affluent society in British East Africa. **95m/C VHS.** Denholm Elliott, Holly Aird, Michael Byrne, Kathryn Pogson; ***D:*** Ross Devenish.

Over the Brooklyn Bridge 🦴🦴 *My Darling Shiksa* **1983 (R)** A young Jewish man (Gould) must give up his Catholic girlfriend (Hemingway) in order to get his uncle (Caesar) to lend him the money he needs to buy a restaurant in Manhattan. Nowhere near as funny as it should be, and potentially offensive to boot. **100m/C VHS.** Elliott Gould, Sid Caesar, Shelley Winters, Margaux Hemingway, Carol Kane, Burt Young; ***D:*** Menahem Golan; ***M:*** Pino Donaggio.

Over the Edge 🦴🦴🦴½ **1979 (PG)** The music of Cheap Trick, The Cars, and The Ramones highlights this realistic tale of alienated suburban youth on the rampage. Dillon makes his screen debut in this updated, well-done "Rebel Without a Cause." Shelved for several years, the movie was finally released after Dillon made it big. Sleeper with excellent direction and dialogue. **91m/C VHS.** Michael Kramer, Matt Dillon, Pamela Ludwig, Vincent Spano, Tom Fergus, Harry Northrup, Andy Romano, Ellen Geer, Richard Jamison, Julia Pomeroy, Tiger Thompson; *D:* Jonathan Kaplan; *W:* Charles Haas, Tim Hunter; *C:* Andrew Davis; *M:* Sol Kaplan.

Over the Hill ☠☠½ **1993 (PG)** Dukakis stars as Alma, an eccentric widow who decides to leave her well-meaning son's restrictive home in Maine to visit her estranged daughter Elizabeth in Sydney, Australia. Embarassed by her peculiarities Elizabeth arranges a holiday away but Mom has her own plans. She wants to "loop the loop," and make a complete circuit around the Australian continent. Soon Alma is on the road, meeting fellow eccentrics and experiencing a variety of adventures. **102m/C VHS.** Olympia Dukakis, Sigrid Thornton, Derek Fowlds, Pippa Grandison; *D:* George Miller; *W:* Robert Caswell; *C:* David Connell.

Over the Hill Gang ☠☠ **1969** A quirky cast is the only real reason to watch this made-for-TV western about a retired Texas Ranger and his pals who clean up a corrupt town. **75m/C DVD.** Walter Brennan, Edgar Buchanan, Andy Devine, Jack Elam, Gypsy Rose Lee, Kristin Harmon, Ricky Nelson, Chill Wills, Edward Andrews; *D:* Jean Yarbrough; *W:* Jameson Brewer. **TV**

Over the Summer ☠☠½ **1985** Strong drama about a troubled teen who escapes the city for a summer with her grandparents. No cliches here—the grandfather lusts after the granddaughter and eventually kills himself, and problems remain at the end. Intelligent and entertaining, though marred by needless nude scenes. **97m/C VHS.** Laura Hunt, Johnson West, Catherine Williams, David Romero; *D:* Teresa Sparks.

Over the Top ☠½ **1986 (PG)** The film that started a nationwide arm-wrestling craze. A slow-witted trucker decides the only way he can retain custody of his estranged son, as well as win the boy's respect, is by winning a big arm-wrestling competition. Stallone is an expert at grinding these movies out by now, and the kid (General Hospital's Mikey) is all right, but the end result is boredom, as it should be with an arm-wrestling epic. **94m/C VHS.** Sylvester Stallone, Susan Blakely, Robert Loggia, David Mendenhall; *D:* Menahem Golan; *W:* Sylvester Stallone, Gary Conway, Stirling Silliphant. Golden Raspberries '87: Worst Support. Actor (Mendenhall), Worst New Star (Mendenhall).

Over the Wire ☠½ **1995** Telephone lineman Bruce (Christensen) accidentally overhears a conversation where a woman hires a hitman to kill her sister. He finds out that the sisters live together and tries to figure out just who the target is before it's too late (of course, he has to seduce both of them to accomplish this). Ray used the pseudonym Nicholas Medina. **90m/C VHS, DVD.** David Christensen, Shauna O'Brien, Landon Hall, Tim Abell, John Lazar, Bob Dole; *D:* Fred Olen Ray; *W:* Pete Slate; *C:* Howard Wexler.

Overboard ☠☠ **1987 (PG)** A wealthy, spoiled woman falls off of her yacht and into the arms of a low-class carpenter who picks her up and convinces her she is in fact his wife, and mother to his four brats. Just when she learns to like her life, the tables are turned again. Even though it's all been done before, you can't help but laugh at the screwy gags. **112m/C VHS, DVD, Wide.** Goldie Hawn, Kurt Russell, Katherine Helmond, Roddy McDowall, Edward Herrmann; *D:* Garry Marshall; *W:* Leslie Dixon; *C:* John A. Alonzo; *M:* Alan Silvestri.

The Overcoat ☠☠☠½ *The Cloak; Shinel* **1959** An adaptation of Nikolai Gogol's classic story about the dehumanizing life endured in 20th-century bureaucracy. All a menial civil servant wants is a new overcoat. When he finally gets one, this treasured article not only keeps him warm but makes him feel self-satisfied as well. In Russian with English subtitles. **93m/B VHS.** *RU* Rolan Bykov, Yuri Tolubeyev; *D:* Alexei Batalov; *W:* L. Solovyov; *C:* Heinrich Marandzhjan; *M:* N. Sidelnikov.

Overdrawn at the Memory Bank ☠☠ **1983** In a futuristic tyranny, a romantic rebel becomes somehow fused with the spirit of Humphrey Bogart in the milieu of "Casablanca," and lives out a cliched version of the film character's adventures. **84m/C VHS.** Raul Julia, Linda Griffiths; *D:* Douglas Williams.

Overexposed ☠☠ **1990 (R)** All the wackos love the sultry soap star Oxenburg; one is a killer. Eighty minutes and a bunch of bodies later the killer is unmasked. Plenty of suspense and some original gore. Based on the true stories of fans who stalk celebrities. **83m/C VHS.** Catherine Oxenberg, David Naughton, Jennifer Edwards, Karen Black; *D:* Larry Brand; *W:* Larry Brand.

Overkill ☠ **1986 (R)** A detective and the vengeance-minded brother of a dead Japanese-American fight back against the controlling Yakuza in Little Tokyo. **81m/C** Steve Rally, John Nishio, Laura Burkett, Roy Summerset; *D:* Ulli Lommel.

Overkill ☠☠ **1996 (R)** Burnt-out cop Jack Hazard (Norris) heads for vacation in Costa Rica and winds up being the prey for demented hunter Lloyd Wheeler (Nouri). **92m/C VHS.** Aaron Norris, Michael Nouri; *D:* Dean Ferrandini; *W:* Dean Ferrandini.

Overland Mail **1941** Fifteen episodes of the vintage serial filled with western action. **225m/B VHS.** Lon Chaney Jr., Helen Parrish.

Overland Stage Raiders ☠☠☠ **1938** The "Three Mesquiteers" ride again, this time to guard a Greyhound bus! The trio must protect a shipment of gold from hijackers. This is the last film for Brooks, who had starred in the German masterpiece "Pandora's Box" in 1929. **55m/B VHS.** John Wayne, Ray Corrigan, Max Terhune, Louise Brooks, John Archer, Frank LaRue, Yakima Canutt; *D:* George Sherman.

Overlanders ☠☠☠ **1946** The Japanese may invade, but rather than kill 1,000 head of cattle, these Aussies drive the huge herd across the continent, facing danger along the way. Beautifully photographed, featuring the "Australian Gary Cooper" and a stampede scene to challenge "Dances with Wolves." **91m/B VHS.** *AU* Chips Rafferty, Daphne Campbell, Jean Blue, John Nugent Hayward; *D:* Harry Watt.

Overnight Delivery ☠☠ **1996 (PG-13)** Convinced his girlfriend (Taylor) has been cheating on him, Wyatt (Rudd) sends her a nasty breakup letter via overnight mail. But when he realizes he's been wrong, Wyatt enlists the aid of friendly stripper Ivy (Witherspoon) to help him retrieve the letter. **87m/C VHS.** Larry Drake, Tobin Bell, Reese Witherspoon, Paul Rudd, Christine Taylor; *D:* Jason Bloom; *W:* Steven L. Bloom; *C:* Edward Pei; *M:* Andrew Gross.

Overnight Sensation ☠☠ **1983** A modern adaptation of the W. Somerset Maugham story about a traditional marriage being tested by the wife's sudden literary success. **30m/C VHS.** Louise Fletcher, Robert Loggia, Shari Belafonte.

Overseas: Three Women with Man Trouble ☠☠☠ **1990** Three beautiful sisters in French colonial Algeria surround themselves in a life of luxury to avoid the incredible social changes going on around them. Each sister has a different perspective on her life, and the perspectives are graphically revealed. Lush photography set in the Mediterranean. In French with English subtitles. **96m/C VHS.** *FR* Nicole Garcia, Marianne Basler, Philippe Galland, Pierre Doris, Brigitte Rouan; *D:* Brigitte Rouan; *W:* Brigitte Rouan. Cannes '90: Film.

Overthrow ☠½ **1982 (R)** American sportswriter finds himself caught up in violence and intrigue in Buenos Aires. De Angelis used the pseudonym Larry Ludman. **90m/C VHS.** John Phillip Law, Lewis Van Bergen, Roger Wilson; *D:* Fabrizio de Angelis.

Overture **1975** An episode of "The Persuaders." Brett and Danny are tricked into helping a retired judge. This adventure leads them to the Mediterranean and a gorgeous gal. **52m/C VHS.** *GB* Roger Moore, Tony Curtis.

Overture to Glory ☠☠½ *Der Vilner Shtot Khazn* **1940** A Jewish cantor longs for the world of opera. He leaves his wife and son to fulfill his passion, but eventually he loses his voice and humbly returns home on Yom Kippur, the Jewish Day of Atonement. He learns that his son has passed away. Grief-stricken, he goes to the synagogue. There, the cantor regains his voice as he performs Kol Nidre in a passionate and melodious rendering. In Yiddish with English subtitles. **85m/B VHS.** Helen Beverly, Florence Weiss.

The Owl and the Pussycat ☠☠☠ **1970 (PG)** Nerdy author gets the neighborhood hooker evicted from her apartment. She returns the favor, and the pair hit the street—and the sack—in Buck Henry's hilarious adaptation of the Broadway play. Streisand's first non-singing role. **96m/C VHS, DVD, Wide.** Barbra Streisand, George Segal, Robert Klein, Allen (Goorwitz) Garfield; *D:* Herbert Ross; *W:* Buck Henry; *C:* Harry Stradling Sr., Andrew Laszlo; *M:* Dick Halligan.

The Ox ☠☠½ **1991** Slow-moving, simple tale, set in rural Sweden in the 1860s during a famine. Desperate to feed his family a tenant farmer kills his employer's ox. Consumed by guilt, the man is quickly found out and sentenced to life imprisonment. Pardoned after six years, the farmer returns to his family, to find out his wife has survived by doing things he finds difficult to forgive. Based on a true story. Directorial debut of Nykvist, the longtime cinematographer for Ingmar Bergman, well displays his familiarity with composition and lighting to heighten mood. In Swedish with English subtitles. **93m/C VHS.** *SW* Stellan Skarsgard, Ewa Froling, Lennart Hjulstrom, Max von Sydow, Liv Ullmann, Bjorn Granath, Erland Josephson; *D:* Sven Nykvist; *W:* Lasse Summanen, Sven Nykvist.

The Ox-Bow Incident ☠☠☠☠ *Strange Incident* **1943** A popular rancher is murdered, and a mob of angry townspeople can't wait for the sheriff to find the killers. They hang the young man, despite the protests of Fonda, a cowboy with a conscience. Excellent study of mob mentality with strong individual characterizations. A brilliant western based on a true story by Walter Van Tilburg Clark. Also see "Twelve Angry Men"—less tragic but just as moving. **75m/B VHS.** Henry Fonda, Harry (Henry) Morgan, Dana Andrews, Anthony Quinn, Frank Conroy, Harry Davenport, Jane Darwell, William Eythe, Mary Beth Hughes; *D:* William A. Wellman; *W:* Lamar Trotti; *C:* Arthur C. Miller; *M:* Cyril Mockridge. Natl. Bd. of Review '43: Director (Wellman), Natl. Film Reg. '98.

Oxford Blues ☠☠ **1984 (PG-13)** An American finagles his way into England's Oxford University and onto the rowing team in pursuit of the girl of his dreams. Beautiful scenery, but the plot is wafer-thin. Remake of "Yank at Oxford." **98m/C VHS.** Rob Lowe, Ally Sheedy, Amanda Pays, Julian Sands, Michael Gough, Gail Strickland, Cary Elwes, Jeffery S. (Jeff) Perry; *D:* Robert Boris; *W:* Robert Boris; *M:* John Du Prez.

Oxygen ☠☠ **1999 (R)** Madeline (Tierney) is a troubled police detective who's married to another cop (Kinney) and involved in a kinky extramarital affair. Harry (Brody) is an escape artist who fancies himself the new Houdini—he kidnaps the wife (Robbins) of wealthy Clarke Hannon (Naughton) and buries her alive. Madeline's assigned to the case and Harry takes to taunting her and their dangerous game could have more than one victim. **92m/C VHS, DVD, Wide.** Adrien Brody, Maura Tierney, Terry Kinney, James Naughton, Laila Robins, Dylan Baker; *D:* Richard Shepard; *W:* Richard Shepard; *C:* Sarah Cawley; *M:* Rolfe Kent.

Pace That Kills ☠ **1928** An anti-drug cautionary drama from the Roaring '20s, one of many now marketed on cassette as campy fun. Beware, though, a little bit of this stuff goes a long way. A young man goes to the big city to find his missing sister and winds up hooked on heroin. **87m/B VHS, 8mm.** Owen Gorin, Virginia Roye, Florence Turner.

Pacific Heights ☠☠☠ **1990 (R)** Young San Francisco couple takes on mammoth mortgage assuming tenants will write their ticket to the American dream, but psychopathic tenant Keaton moves in downstairs and redecorates. He won't pay the rent and he won't leave. Creepy psycho-thriller has lapses but builds to effective climax. It's a treat to watch mother/daughter actresses Hedren and Griffith work together. Watch for D'Angelo as Keaton's lover. **103m/C VHS, DVD.** Melanie Griffith, Matthew Modine, Michael Keaton, Mako, Nobu McCarthy, Laurie Metcalf, Carl Lumbly, Dorian Harewood, Luca Bercovici, Tippi Hedren, Sheila McCarthy, Dan Hedaya, Beverly D'Angelo, Nicholas Pryor, Miriam Margolyes; *D:* John Schlesinger; *W:* Daniel Pyne; *M:* Hans Zimmer.

Pacific Inferno ☠☠ **1985** During WWII, American POWs endeavor to break out of a Japanese prison camp in the Philippines. Their goal is to prevent their captors from retrieving millions of dollars worth of sunken U.S. gold. **90m/C VHS.** Jim Brown, Richard Jaeckel, Tim Brown; *D:* Rolf Bayer. **CABLE**

The Pack ☠☠½ *The Long, Dark Night* **1977 (R)** A group of dogs become wild when left on a resort island. A marine biologist leads the humans who fight to keep the dogs from using vacationers as chew toys. Fine production valves keep it from going to the dogs. Made with the approval of the American Humane Society who helped with the treatment of stage hands. **99m/C VHS.** Joe Don Baker, Hope Alexander-Willis, R.G. Armstrong, Richard B. Shull; *D:* Robert Clouse; *W:* Robert Clouse.

The P.A.C.K. ☠☠ **1996** The P.A.C.K. are alien warriors who mistakenly land on earth, which doesn't prevent them from killing all but one of a team of government agents sent to investigate. Now lone agent Rachel (Bergman) reluctantly teams up with a second alien who's been sent to destroy the P.A.C.K. **90m/C VHS.** Sandahl Bergman, Ted Prior, Red West.

Pack Up Your Troubles ☠☠½ *We're in the Army Now* **1932** Laurel and Hardy make good on a promise to help find the grandfather of a girl whose father was killed in WWI. All they know is the grandfather's last name though—Smith. Wholesome R and R. **68m/B VHS.** Stan Laurel, Oliver Hardy, James Finlayson, Jacquie Lyn; *D:* George Marshall.

The Package ☠☠½ **1989 (R)** An espionage thriller about an army sergeant who loses the prisoner he escorts into the U.S. When he tries to track him down, he uncovers a military plot to start WWIII. Hackman is believable in his role as the sergeant. **108m/C VHS, DVD.** Gene Hackman, Tommy Lee Jones, Joanna Cassidy, Dennis Franz, Pam Grier, John Heard, Reni Santoni, Thalmus Rasulala, Ike Pappas, Kevin Crowley; *D:* Andrew Davis; *W:* John Bishop; *M:* James Newton Howard.

Packin' It In ☠☠ **1983** A Los Angeles family is in for a rude awakening when they leave the city for a quieter life in the Oregon woods. There they encounter a band of survivalists with semi-comedic results. **92m/C VHS.** Richard Benjamin, Paula Prentiss, Molly Ringwald, Tony Roberts, Andrea Marcovicci; *D:* Jud Taylor.

Paco ☠½ **1975 (G)** A young, South American boy heads for the city, where he meets his uncle. He discovers his uncle is the leader of a gang of youthful thieves. Predictable and sluggish. **89m/C VHS.** Jose Ferrer, Panchito Gomez, Allen (Goorwitz) Garfield, Pernell Roberts, Andre Marquis; *D:* Robert Vincent O'Neil.

The Pact ☠☠ *The Secret Pact* **1999 (R)** When teenager Greg (Frost) witnesses his parents' murder by the mob, he's sent to a private school in Montreal as part of the witness protection program. He makes a new best friend with a fellow student (Strong) but discovers his fellow teen is actually a hit man sent to kill him. Only they come to a strange sort of deal instead. **94m/C VHS, DVD.** *CA* Rider Strong, Adam Frost, John Heard, Nick Mancuso, Jack Langedijk, Lisa Zane; *D:* Rodney Gibbons; *W:* William Lee, Brian Cameron Fuld; *C:* Bert Tougas; *M:* Antonio Battista. **VIDEO**

Paddy 🦴🦴 *Goodbye to the Hill* **1970 (PG)** A young Irish lad realizes his sexual potential by seducing every woman he can find. Freudians will have a field day. **97m/C VHS.** *IR* Des Cave, Milo O'Shea, Darbnia Molloy, Peggy Cass; ***D:*** Daniel Haller.

Padre Nuestro 🦴🦴½ **1985** Religious satire about a dying priest who wishes to reunite his family, who include an atheist brother, a mistress from his youth, and his illegitimate daughter who's a notorious prostitute. In Spanish with English subtitles. **91m/C VHS.** *SP* Fernando Rey, Francesco Rabal, Victoria Abril; ***D:*** Francisco Regueiro.

Padre Padrone 🦴🦴🦴½ *Father Master; My Father, My Master* **1977** The much acclaimed adaptation of the Gavino Ledda autobiography about his youth in agrarian Sardinia with a brutal, tyrannical father. Eventually he overcomes his handicaps, breaks the destructive emotional ties to his father and successfully attends college. Highly regarded although low budget; in an Italian dialect (Sardinian) with English subtitles. **113m/C VHS, DVD.** *IT* Omero Antonutti, Saverio Marconi, Marcella Michelangeli, Fabrizio Forte; ***D:*** Paolo Taviani, Vittorio Taviani; ***W:*** Paolo Taviani, Vittorio Taviani; ***C:*** Mario Masini; ***M:*** Egisto Macchi. Cannes '77: Film.

Pagan Island 🦴 **1960** A man is stranded on a desert island with 30 beautiful girls who tie him up and abandon him. Maki, to be sacrificed by the rest, saves Dew and they fall in love. They go off in search of a reputed treasure, which they find, but at a deadly cost. **67m/B VHS.** Eddie Dew, Nani Maka, Yanka (Doris Keating) Mann; ***D:*** Barry Mahon; ***W:*** Clelle Mahon; ***C:*** Mark Dennis.

Pagan Love Song 🦴🦴 **1950** A dull musical which finds Keel in Tahiti taking over his uncle's coconut plantation and falling in love with Williams. Surprise! Williams performs one of her famous water ballets, which is the only saving grace in this lifeless movie. ♫The House of Singing Bamboo; Singing in the Sun; Etiquette; Why is Love So Crazy; Tahiti; The Sea of the Moon; Pagan Love Song; Coconut Milk. **76m/C VHS.** Esther Williams, Howard Keel, Minna Gombell, Rita Moreno; ***D:*** Robert Alton.

The Pagemaster 🦴½ **1994 (G)** Timid Richard (Macauley) is basically scared of his own shadow but, during a storm, he's forced to take refuge in a mysterious library with an even odder librarian, Mr. Dewey (Lloyd). Richard's intrigued by the library's mural, which turns out to be the doorway to an animated universe where the wizardlike Pagemaster (voiced by Lloyd) and other literary characters help Richard discover his strengths and overcome his fears. Mildly amusing but kids may not know who the characters refer to unless they're readers (a good intro, perhaps?) **76m/C VHS.** Macaulay Culkin, Christopher Lloyd, Ed Begley Jr., Mel Harris; ***D:*** Joe Johnston, Maurice Hunt; ***W:*** David Casci, David Kirschner, Ernie Contreras; ***M:*** James Horner; ***V:*** Christopher Lloyd, Whoopi Goldberg, Patrick Stewart, Frank Welker, Leonard Nimoy.

Paid to Kill 🦴🦴 *Five Days* **1954** A failing businessman hires a thug to kill him in order to leave his family insurance money, but when the business picks up, he can't contact the thug to cancel the contract. The actors' lack of talent is matched only by the characters' lack of motivation. **71m/B VHS.** *GB* Dane Clark, Paul Carpenter, Thea Gregory; ***D:*** Montgomery Tully.

Pain in the A— 🦴🦴🦴 **1977 (PG)** A hit man helps a suicidal shirt salesman solve his marital problems in this black comedy that was later Americanized as "Buddy, Buddy." Not for all tastes, but has acquired a reputation for its dark wit. In French with English subtitles. **90m/C VHS.** *FR IT* Lino Ventura, Jacques Brel, Caroline Cellier; ***D:*** Edouard Molinaro; ***W:*** Edouard Molinaro, Francis Veber.

Paint It Black 🦴🦴½ **1989 (R)** A violent/steamy mystery and action flick from the director of "River's Edge," in which a young man from the silver-spoon set develops a fascination for an artist. **101m/C VHS.** Sally Kirkland, Rick Rossovich, Martin Landau, Doug Savant, Peter Frechette, Jason Bernard, Julie Carmen, Monique Van De Ven; ***D:*** Tim Hunter.

The Paint Job 🦴🦴 **1993 (R)** Wesley, the lonely house painter, falls in love with his neighbor, Margaret. Unfortunately, Margaret is married—to Wesley's boss Willy. Margaret is drawn to Wesley and bored with Willy. But one of the men turns out to be a serial killer. What's a gal in love to do? **90m/C VHS.** Will Patton, Bebe Neuwirth, Robert Pastorelli; ***D:*** Micheal Taav; ***W:*** Micheal Taav; ***M:*** John Wesley Harding.

Paint Your Wagon 🦴🦴½ **1969 (PG)** Big-budget western musical-comedy about a gold mining boom town, and two prospectors sharing the same Mormon wife complete with a classic Lerner and Lowe score. Marvin chews up the sagebrush and Eastwood attempts to sing, although Seberg was mercifully dubbed. Overlong, with patches of interest, pretty songs, and plenty of panoramic scenery. Adapted from the L & L play. ♫I Talk to the Trees; I Still See Elisa; I'm on My Way; Hand Me Down That Can o' Beans; Whoop-Ti-Ay; They Call the Wind Maria; There's a Coach Comin' In; Wandrin' Star; Best Things. **164m/C VHS, DVD, Wide.** Lee Marvin, Clint Eastwood, Jean Seberg, Harve Presnell; ***D:*** Joshua Logan; ***W:*** Paddy Chayefsky; ***M:*** Frederick Loewe, Andre Previn, Alan Jay Lerner.

Painted Desert 🦴🦴 **1931** Gable's first film role of any consequence came in this early sound western. Gable plays a villain opposite "good guy" William Boyd. **80m/B VHS, DVD.** William Boyd, Helen Twelvetrees, George O'Brien, Clark Gable, William Farnum; ***D:*** Howard Higgin.

Painted Hero 🦴🦴½ **1995 (R)** Rodeo clown Virgil Kidder (Yoakum) has to watch out for more than rampaging bulls when he returns to Waco, where he's accused of murder and reunites with the mother of his now-dead son. **105m/C VHS.** Dwight Yoakam, Bo Hopkins, Cindy Pickett, Michelle Joyner; ***D:*** Terry Benedict; ***W:*** Terry Benedict; ***C:*** David Bridges; ***M:*** Rick Marotta.

The Painted Hills 🦴🦴½ **1951 (G)** Lassie outsmarts crooked miners and rescues her friends. Surprise, Surprise! Overly sentimental, but action packed and beautifully shot. Lassie's last outing with MGM. **70m/C VHS.** Paul Kelly, Bruce Cowling, Gary Gray, Art Smith, Ann Doran; ***D:*** Harold F. Kress.

The Painted Lady 🦴🦴🦴 **1997** Maggie Sheridan (Mirren) is a hard-living ex-blues singer with some destructive habits. After bottoming out some years before, she was taken in by Sir Charles Stafford (Cuthbertson), the father of childhood friend Sebastian (Glen). Sir Charles is murdered during a botched robbery, a 16th-century painting stolen, and Sebastian becomes the victim of a brutal attack, so Maggie decides to get involved. And finds herself deeply enmeshed in the illegal art trade, posing as a collector, and romancing a very dangerous man (Nero). **204m/C VHS.** *GB* Helen Mirren, Franco Nero, Iain Glen, Michael Maloney, Leslie Manville, Roland Gift, Iain Cuthbertson, Michael Liebman, Indro Montanelli; ***D:*** Julian Jarrold. **TV**

Painted Skin 🦴🦴 *Hua Pi Zhi Yinyang Fawang* **1993** Historical supernatural tale concerns a ghost (Joey Wang) who's trapped on Earth and must paint her skin to pass among humans. The evil Demon King is responsible. Sammo Hung costars as a monk. **93m/C DVD, Wide.** *HK* Adam Cheng, Joey Wang, Sammo Hung; ***D:*** King Hu; ***W:*** King Hu, Chang A. Cheng; ***C:*** Stephen Yip; ***M:*** Ng Tai Kong.

The Painted Stallion **1937** This 12-chapter serial features a mysterious figure on a painted stallion who attempts to maintain peace between Mexicans and Indians. **212m/B VHS.** Ray Corrigan, Hoot Gibson, Duncan Renaldo, Leroy Mason, Yakima Canutt; ***D:*** William Witney, Ray Taylor.

The Painted Veil 🦴🦴½ **1934** Adaptation of a W. Somerset Maugham story. Garbo, once again the disillusioned wife turning to the affections of another man, is magnificent, almost eclipsing the weak script. Lost money at the box office, but for Garbo fans, an absolute must. **83m/B VHS.** Greta Garbo, Herbert Marshall, George Brent, Warner Oland, Jean Hersholt; ***D:*** Richard Boleslawski; ***C:*** William H. Daniels.

Pair of Aces 🦴🦴½ **1990** Kristofferson is a Texas Ranger who's on the trail of a serial killer. His only other problem is being saddled with Nelson, a philosophical safecracker who's awaiting trial and in the reluctant cop's custody. Low-key western with good buddy pairing of Nelson and Kristofferson. **94m/C VHS.** Willie Nelson, Kris Kristofferson, Rip Torn, Helen Shaver, Jane Cameron, Sonny Carl Davis, Lash LaRue, Emily Warfield, Michael Marich; ***D:*** Aaron Lipstadt. **TV**

Paisan 🦴🦴🦴 **1946** Six episodic tales of life in Italy, several featuring Allied soldiers and nurses during WWII. One of the stories tells of a man who tries to develop a relationship without being able to speak Italian. Another focuses on a young street robber who is confronted by one of his victims. Strong stories that covers a wide range of emotions. In Italian with English subtitles. **115m/B VHS.** *IT* Maria Michi, Carmela Sazio, Gar Moore, William Tubbs, Harriet White, Robert Van Loon, Dale Edmonds, Carla Pisacane, Dots Johnson; ***D:*** Roberto Rossellini; ***W:*** Federico Fellini, Roberto Rossellini. Natl. Bd. of Review '48: Director (Fellini); N.Y. Film Critics '48: Foreign Film.

The Pajama Game 🦴🦴🦴½ **1957** A spritely musical about the striking workers of the Sleeptite Pajama Ffactory and their plucky negotiator, Katie (Day), who falls in love with the new foreman, Sid (Raitt). Based on the hit Broadway musical, which was based on Richard Bissell's book "Seven and a Half Cents" and adapted for the screen by Bisell and Abbott. Bob Fosse choreographed the dance numbers. ♫I'm Not at All in Love; Small Talk; There Once Was a Man; Steam Heat; Hernando's Highway; Hey There; Once-a-Year Day; Seven and a Half Cents; I'll Never Be Jealous Again. **101m/C VHS, DVD.** Doris Day, John Raitt, Eddie Foy Jr., Reta Shaw, Carol Haney; ***D:*** Stanley Donen, George Abbott; ***W:*** George Abbott, Richard Bissell; ***C:*** Harry Stradling Sr.

Pajama Party 🦴🦴 **1964** Followup to "Bikini Beach" takes the party inside in this fourth entry in the popular "Beach Party" series. Plot is up to beach party realism. Funicello is Avalon-less (although he does have a cameo) so she falls for Martian Kirk instead. He's scouting for an alien invasion, but after he falls into Annette's lap decides to save the planet instead. Typical fluff with the usual beach movie faces present; look for a young Garr as a dancer. Followed by the classic "Beach Blanket Bingo." ♫It's That Kind of Day; There Has to Be a Reason; Where Did I Go Wrong?; Pajama Party; Beach Ball; Among the Young; Stuffed Animal. **82m/C VHS, DVD.** Tommy Kirk, Annette Funicello, Elsa Lanchester, Harvey Lembeck, Jesse White, Jody McCrea, Donna Loren, Susan Hart, Bobbi Shaw, Cheryl Sweeten, Luree Holmes, Candy Johnson, Dorothy Lamour, Toni Basil, Frankie Avalon, Don Rickles, Teri Garr, Ben Lessy; ***Cameos:*** Buster Keaton; ***D:*** Don Weis; ***W:*** Louis M. Heyward; ***C:*** Floyd Crosby; ***M:*** Les Baxter.

Pajama Tops 🦴🦴½ **1983** A stage production of the classic French bedroom farce, taped live at the Music Hall Theatre in Toronto, Canada. Includes all the trials of marriage including adultery and deceit. **105m/C VHS.** Robert Klein, Susan George, Pia Zadora.

Pal Joey 🦴🦴🦴 **1957** Musical comedy about an opportunistic singer who courts a wealthy socialite in hopes that she will finance his nightclub. His play results in comedic complications. Stellar choreography, fine direction, and beautiful costumes complement performances headed by Hayworth and Sinatra. Oscar overlooked his pal Joey when awards were handed out. Songs include some of Rodgers and Hart's best. Based on John O'Hara's book and play. ♫Zip; Bewitched, Bothered and Bewildered; I Could Write a Book; That Terrific Rainbow; Whad Do I Care for a Dame?; Happy Hunting Horn; Plant You Now, Dig You Later; Do It the Hard Way; Take Him. **109m/C VHS, DVD, Wide.** Frank Sinatra, Rita Hayworth, Kim Novak, Barbara Nichols, Hank Henry, Elizabeth Patterson; ***D:*** George Sidney; ***W:*** Dorothy Kingsley; ***C:*** Harold Lipstein; ***M:*** Richard Rodgers, Lorenz Hart. Golden Globes '58: Actor—Mus./Comedy (Sinatra).

Palais Royale 🦴½ **1988** Craven plays an ad exec who gets involved in the world of gangsters in the late 50s. **100m/C VHS.** *CA* Matt Craven, Kim Cattrall, Dean Stockwell; ***D:*** Martin Lavut; ***M:*** Jonathan Goldsmith.

Pale Blood 🦴½ **1991 (R)** A serial killer in Los Angeles is leaving his victims drained of blood. Could it be that a vampire is stalking the modern American metropolis, or is this merely the workings of a bloodthirsty psychopath? **93m/C VHS.** George Chakiris, Wings Hauser, Pamela Ludwig, Diana Frank, Darcy Demoss, Earl Garnes; ***D:*** V.V. Dachin Hsu; ***W:*** V.V. Dachin Hsu, Takashi Matsuoka.

Pale Rider 🦴🦴🦴 **1985 (R)** A mysterious nameless stranger rides into a small California gold rush town to find himself in the middle of a feud between a mining syndicate and a group of independent prospectors. Christ-like Eastwood evokes comparisons to "Shane." A classical western theme treated well complemented by excellent photography and a rock-solid cast. **116m/C VHS, DVD, 8mm.** Clint Eastwood, Michael Moriarty, Carrie Snodgress, Sydney Penny, Richard Dysart, Richard Kiel, Christopher Penn, John Russell, Charles Hallahan, Douglas McGrath, Fran Ryan; ***D:*** Clint Eastwood; ***W:*** Michael Butler, Dennis Shryack; ***C:*** Bruce Surtees; ***M:*** Lennie Niehaus.

Pale Saints 🦴🦴½ **1997 (R)** Small-time hoods Louis (Flanery) and Dody (Riley) decide that they will do one last job for crime broker Quick Vic and use their share of the money to head off to California. They travel to Montreal and wind up with a botched heist, a case of mistaken identity, and a lot of double-dealing. The plot gets too convoluted, although it's so fast-paced you may not notice the holes. **98m/C VHS.** *CA* Sean Patrick Flanery, Michael Riley, Saul Rubinek, Maury Chaykin, Rachael Crawford, Gordon Pinsent; ***D:*** Joel Wyner; ***W:*** Joel Wyner; ***C:*** Barry Stone; ***M:*** Michel Theriault.

The Paleface 🦴🦴🦴 **1948** A cowardly dentist becomes a gunslinging hero when Calamity Jane starts aiming for him. A rip-roarin' good time as the conventions of the Old West are turned upside down. Includes the Oscar-winning song "Buttons and Bows." The 1952 sequel is "Son of Paleface." Remade in 1968 as "The Shakiest Gun in the West." ♫Buttons and Bows; Get a Man!; Meetcha 'Round the Corner. **91m/C VHS.** Jane Russell, Bob Hope, Robert Armstrong, Iris Adrian, Robert Watson; ***D:*** Norman Z. McLeod; ***C:*** Ray Rennahan. Oscars '48: Song ("Buttons and Bows").

The Palermo Connection 🦴🦴 **1991 (R)** Not the action-thriller the cassette box claims, but a cynical study of a crusading N.Y.C. mayoral candidate who honeymoons in Mafia-haunted Sicily and learns that the war on crime has already been lost. Remote adaptation of "To Forget Palermo" by Edmonde Charles-Roux. **100m/C VHS.** James Belushi, Mimi Rogers, Joss Ackland, Philippe Noiret, Vittorio Gassman, Caroline Rosi; ***D:*** Francesco Rosi; ***W:*** Gore Vidal.

The Pallbearer 🦴🦴½ **1995 (PG-13)** You probably liked this one better when it was called "The Graduate," as this one shares some key plot points with, but lacks the edge and cultural impact of the 1967 classic. Basset-faced Schwimmer plays Tom, who is asked to be a pallbearer for an old high school classmate whom he can't quite remember. He is then seduced by the mother (Hershey) of the deceased, while trying to kindle a romance with the fabulous Julie DeMarco (Paltrow), an old classmate who can't quite remember him. The spurned older woman then begins to exact her revenge, while Tom tries to figure out how to court Julie while living at home with his mom. Good performances make it watchable. **98m/C VHS, DVD, Wide.** David Schwimmer, Gwyneth Paltrow, Barbara Hershey, Michael Rapaport, Carol Kane, Toni Collette, Michael Vartan; ***D:*** Matt Reeves; ***W:*** Matt Reeves, Jason Katims; ***C:*** Robert Elswit; ***M:*** Stewart Copeland.

Palm Beach && **1979** The lives of two petty thieves, a runaway, and a private detective intertwine at Palm Beach Down Under. Best appreciated by fans of things Aussie. **90m/C VHS.** *AU* Bryan Brown, Nat Young, Ken Brown, Amanda Berry; ***D:*** Albie Thomas.

The Palm Beach Story &&& **1942** Young architect Tom Jeffers (McCrea) dreams of building an airport and his adoring wife Gerry (Colbert) decides to help him out—by divorcing him. That way she can head to Palm Beach, marry rich, and finance Tom's ambitions. So Gerry sets her considerable charms on catching eccentric J.D. Hackensacker (Vallee). When Tom follows, he becomes prey for J.D.'s tart-tongued sister (Astor). Takes amusing aim at the idle rich with Sturges's trademark witty, sophisticated dialogue. **88m/B VHS.** Claudette Colbert, Joel McCrea, Mary Astor, Rudy Vallee, William Demarest, Franklin Pangborn; ***D:*** Preston Sturges; ***C:*** Victor Milner.

Palm Springs Weekend &&½ **1963** A busload of love-hungry kids head south and get involved in routine hijinks. Actually shot in Palm Springs with adove average performances by a handful of stars. **100m/C VHS.** Troy Donahue, Ty Hardin, Connie Stevens, Stefanie Powers, Robert Conrad, Jack Weston, Andrew Duggan; ***D:*** Norman Taurog.

Palmetto &½ **1998 (R)** Another contempo-noir that misses the mark has bitter ex-con Harry (Harrelson) partnered with seductress Rhea (Shue) in a phony kidnapping of her step-daughter Odette (Sevigny). Newly released from the joint after a rotten frame-up job, Harry is lured back to the steamy backwater that sent him up the river in the first place by ex Nina (Gershon), where he, once again, winds up in trouble as all three women go to work on him. Originality and character development go AWOL, as the normally adept Harrelson flounders for an identity alongside Shue's broad characterization of a vamp who teeters on high heels and the brink of satire, and Gershon in an unaccustomed good girl role. Tropical, southern Florida backdrop makes this feel like Tennessee Williams as written by Joe Eszterhas. Adaptation of Rene Raymond's (a.k.a. James Hadley Chase) novel, "Just Another Sucker." **114m/C VHS, DVD.** Angela Featherstone, Woody Harrelson, Elisabeth Shue, Michael Rapaport, Gina Gershon, Chloe Sevigny, Rolf Hoppe, Tom Wright; ***D:*** Volker Schlondorff; ***W:*** E. Max Frye; ***C:*** Thomas Kloss; ***M:*** Klaus Doldinger.

Palmy Days &&½ **1931** Shy Eddie (Cantor) is involved with a phony medium, a scam involving a bakery, theft, romance, singing, and a disguise as a woman (the other bakery workers are the Goldwyn Girls, including Betty Grable). Silly fun, with choreography by Busby Berkeley. ♫Bend Down, Sister; Goose Pimples; Dunk Dunk Dunk; My Honey Said Yes, Yes; There's Nothing Too Good for My Baby. **77m/B VHS.** Eddie Cantor, Charlotte Greenwood, Charles Middleton, George Raft, Harry Woods, Spencer Charters, Barbara Weeks, Paul Page; ***D:*** Edward Sutherland; ***W:*** Morrie Ryskind, Keene Thompson, Eddie Cantor; ***C:*** Gregg Toland.

Palombella Rossa && **1989** Political comedy about the fate of Italian communism. When communist politician Michele loses his memory in a car crash, he finds himself trying to reconstruct his life during a game of water polo as well as trying to answer political questions and keep track of the people from his life who randomly appear and disappear. In Italian with English subtitles. **87m/C VHS.** *IT* ***D:*** Nanni Moretti.

Palooka &&½ *Joe Palooka; The Great Schnozzle* **1934 (G)** Based on the comic strip, this film portrays a fast-talking boxing manager and his goofy, lovable protege. The young scrapper fights James Cagney's little brother. Durante sings his classic tune, "Inka-Dinka-Doo," and packs a punch in the lead. A two-fisted comedy with a witty dialogue and fine direction. Not a part of the Palooka series of the 1940s. **86m/B VHS.** Jimmy Durante, Stuart Erwin, Lupe Velez, Robert Armstrong, Thelma Todd, William Cagney; ***D:*** Ben Stoloff.

Palookaville &&& **1995 (R)** Nostalgic comedy of three under-employed friends who take up crime, temporarily, just until they can secure legit work. Using a little-known 1950s crime movie as their tutor, the trio of criminal cretins encounter a variety of setbacks on their way to financial security. Planning an elaborate scheme to rob an armored car, they decide to use toy guns, so Jerry (Trese) rounds up a most intimidating assortment of the neon orange plastic variety. Later, while chiseling through a wall to a jewelry store, they find themselves in the bakery next door, with Jerry delighted to score some pastries instead. The other two aren't much brighter—Russ (Gallo) is the leader of the three and a small-time ladies man while Sid (Forsythe) is a devout dog lover whose dreams of a taxi service for the aged are shattered when customers are driven away by his kennel on wheels. Adapted from short stories written in the 1940s by the Italian Italo Calvino, modern adaptation manages to retain a '40s feel and charm. **92m/C VHS.** William Forsythe, Vincent Gallo, Adam Trese, Lisa Gay Hamilton, Frances McDormand, David Boulton, James David Hilton, Gareth Williams, Bridget Ryan, Kim Dickens, Suzanne Shepherd, Robert LuPone; ***D:*** Alan Taylor; ***W:*** David Epstein; ***C:*** John Thomas; ***M:*** Rachel Portman.

Pals && **1987** Old friends stumble across $3 million in cash and learn the predictable lesson that money can't buy happiness. A terribly trite TV-movie with an exceptional cast. **90m/C VHS.** Don Ameche, George C. Scott, Sylvia Sidney, Susan Rinell, James Greene; ***D:*** Lou Antonio.

Pals of the Range & **1935** A framed ranch owner breaks out of jail in order to catch the real cattle thieves. Ho hum in the Old West. **55m/B VHS.** Rex Lease.

Pals of the Saddle &&½ **1938** The intrepid trio go after enemy agents who are trying to smuggle chemicals for poisonous gas into Mexico. This is the first of the series in which the Duke played the part of Stony Brooke. Somewhat convoluted plot, but nevertheless enjoyable. **55m/B VHS.** John Wayne, Ray Corrigan, Max Terhune, Doreen McKay, Josef Forte, Ted Adams, Curly Dresden; ***D:*** George Sherman.

The Pamela Principle && **1991 (R)** A bored, middle-aged man thinks his prayers are answered when he meets a sexy 20-year-old model and begins a sordid affair with her. Soon, however, he finds himself in a tense situation when he must choose between his family or his fantasy. Also available in an unrated version. **94m/C VHS.** J.K. Dumont, Veronica Cash, Shelby Lane, Troy Donahue, Frank Pesce; ***D:*** Toby Phillips.

Panama Hattie && **1942** Screen adaptation of Cole Porter's delightful Broadway musical. Unfortunately, something (like a plot) was lost in transition. Southern runs a saloon for our boys down in Panama. Among the musical numbers and vaudevillian acts some spies show up. Several screenwriters and directors, including Vincente Minnelli, worked uncredited on this picture, to no avail. Horne's second screen appearance. ♫It Was Just One of Those Things; Fresh as a Daisy; I've Still Got My Health; Let's Be Buddies; Make It Another Old Fashioned; Hattie from Panama; Good Neighbors; I'll Do Anything for You; The Son of a Gun Who Pick on Uncle Sam. **79m/B VHS.** Ann Sothern, Dan Dailey, Red Skelton, Virginia O'Brien, Rags Ragland, Alan Mowbray, Ben Blue, Carl Esmond, Lena Horne; ***D:*** Norman Z. McLeod; ***C:*** George J. Folsey; ***M:*** George Bassman, Cole Porter.

Panama Lady &½ **1939** Ball stars as the sexy, sultry "Panama Lady" in this old-fashioned romance. She gets involved in some shady business south of the border. A lackluster remake of "Panama Flo." **65m/B VHS.** Lucille Ball, Evelyn Brent.

Panama Menace & *South of Panama* **1941** An agent heads to Panama to thwart spies who are after a special paint that makes things invisible. Poor effort all around, in spite of Beaumont's presence. **68m/B VHS.** Roger Pryor, Virginia Vale, Lionel Royce, Lucien Prival, Duncan Renaldo, Lester Dorr, Hugh Beaumont; ***D:*** Jean Yarbrough.

Panama Patrol &&½ **1939** Just as they are about to be married, two Army officers are called to duty in Panama. It seems that the Chinese have infiltrated the area with spies and something's got to be done. Too much attention to minor parts of the plot slows the story occasionally, but performances and photography compensate for some of the sluggishness. **67m/B VHS.** Leon Ames, Charlotte Wynters, Weldon Heyburn, Adrienne Ames, Abner Biberman, Hugh McArthur, Donald (Don "Red") Barry; ***D:*** Charles Lamont.

Panamint's Bad Man & **1938** Ballaw is a poor man's Gary Cooper fighting for justice against stagecoach robbers. Almost as much flavor as tumbleweed. **59m/B VHS.** Smith Ballew, Evelyn Daw, Noah Beery Sr.; ***D:*** Ray Taylor.

Pancho Barnes &&½ **1988 (PG)** Routine biography of one of the first female pilots of the 1920s. Barnes is a bored debutante who finds her challenge in life when she learns to fly, becoming a barnstormer and movie stunt pilot. Her ambitions naturally get in the way of her romantic life. Good flying scenes. **150m/C VHS.** Valerie Bertinelli, Ted Wass, Sam Robards, James Stephens, Cynthia Harris, Geoffrey Lewis; ***D:*** Richard T. Heffron; ***W:*** John Michael Hayes. **TV**

Pancho Villa &½ **1972 (PG)** Savalas has the lead in this fictional account of the famous Mexican, He leads his men in a raid on an American fort after being hoodwinked in an arms deal. Connors tries to hold the fort against him. The finale, in which two trains crash head on, is the most exciting event in the whole darn movie. **92m/C VHS, DVD, Wide.** *SP* Telly Savalas, Clint Walker, Anne Francis, Chuck Connors, Angel Del Pozo, Luis Davila; ***D:*** Eugenio (Gene) Martin; ***W:*** Julian Zimet; ***C:*** Alejandro Ulloa; ***M:*** Anton Abril.

Pancho Villa Returns && **1950** It's 1913, and noble Mexican General Pancho Villa leads his merry men against the assassins of President Madera. This Mexican production (filmed in English) paints a partisan portrait of title character as a good-hearted revolutionary folk hero, not the roving bandit later notorious north of the border. **95m/B VHS.** *MX* Leo Carrillo, Esther Fernandez, Jeanette Comber, Rodolfo Acosta; ***D:*** Miguel Contreras Torres; ***W:*** Miguel Contreras Torres.

Pandaemonium &&½ **2000 (PG-13)** Friendship, rivalry, and jealousy between 19th century English romanticists William Wordsworth (Hannah) and Samuel Taylor Coleridge (Roache). In 1813, debilitated by opium abuse, Coleridge attends a reception for the now-distant Wordsworth and flashes back to their first meeting some 20 years before. Coleridge and his wife Sara (Morton) move to a country cottage with Wordworth and his sister Dorothy (Woof) living nearby as the two men collaborate on a poetry collection. Coleridge becomes (mutually) attracted to Dorothy and finds inspiration in drugs. A rift between the two men deepens when Wordsworth marries and Coleridge dependency on drugs worsens—even as his poetry soars. **125m/C VHS, DVD.** *GB* Linus Roache, John Hannah, Samantha Morton, Emily Woof, Emma Fielding, Andy Serkis, Samuel West, Guy Lankester; ***D:*** Julien Temple; ***W:*** Frank Cottrell-Boyce; ***C:*** John Lynch; ***M:*** Dario Marianelli.

Pandemonium &&½ *Thursday the 12th* **1982 (PG)** A spoof of teen slasher films involving murder at Bambi's Cheerleading School. Seems that nationwide, cheerleaders have been brutally eliminated from their squads, leaving Bambi's as the last resort for the terminally perky. Smothers is interesting and more intelligent than his TV persona (although not by much) as the Mountie hero, assisted by Paul Reubens in a pre-Pee-Wee role. Kane steals the show as Candy, a pleasant lass with hyperkinetic powers. **82m/C VHS.** *CA* Tom Smothers, Carol Kane, Miles Chapin, Paul (Peewee Herman) Reubens, Judge Reinhold, Tab Hunter, Marc McClure, Donald O'Connor, Eve Arden, Eileen Brennan, Edie McClurg; ***D:*** Alfred Sole.

Pandora and the Flying Dutchman &&½ **1951** Feverish romantic fantasy has playgirl/nightclub singer Pandora Reynolds (Gardner) living in '30s Spain and being romanced by every man in sight. Naturally, she cares for none of them until she meets enigmatic Dutch captain Hendrick van der Zee (Mason) who is, in fact, the legendary Flying Dutchman—condemned to wander the seas forever unless a woman is willing to give up her life for him. Gardner is, as usual, exotically lovely. **123m/C VHS, DVD.** Ava Gardner, James Mason, Nigel Patrick, Sheila Sim, Harold Warrender, Mario Cabre; ***D:*** Albert Lewin; ***W:*** Albert Lewin; ***C:*** Jack Cardiff; ***M:*** Alan Rawsthorne.

Pandora's Box &&&& *Die Buechse der Pandora; Lulu* **1928** This silent classic marked the end of the German Expressionist era and established Brooks as a major screen presence. She plays the tempestuous Lulu, who destroys everyone she comes in contact with, eventually sinking to prostitution and a fateful meeting with Jack the Ripper. Silent with orchestral score. **110m/B VHS, DVD.** *GE* Louise Brooks, Fritz Kortner, Francis Lederer, Carl Goetz, Alice Roberts, Gustav Diesl; ***D:*** G.W. Pabst; ***W:*** G.W. Pabst; ***C:*** Gunther Krampf.

Panic &½ **1983** A scientist terrorizes a small town when he becomes hideously deformed by one of his bacteria experiments. He should have known better. **90m/C VHS.** David Warbeck, Janet Agren.

Panic &&½ **2000 (R)** Hangdog Macy is perfect as middle-aged Alex, who is not having your usual midlife crisis since he's a hit man. As a matter of fact, he learned his trade from his ruthless dad Michael (Sutherland), who still calls the shots. But Alex has been keeping the truth from his wife Martha (Ullman) and his beloved son Sammy (Dorfman) and he needs to talk. So he goes to shrink Josh Parks (Ritter) and, in the waiting room, Alex meets neurotic Sarah (Campbell), with whom he contemplates an affair. Alex wants to make some changes but when you're a professional killer, it's not that easy. **93m/C VHS, DVD, Wide.** William H. Macy, John Ritter, Neve Campbell, Donald Sutherland, Tracey Ullman, Barbara Bain, David Dorfman; ***D:*** Henry Bromell; ***W:*** Henry Bromell; ***C:*** Jeffrey Jur; ***M:*** Brian Tyler.

Panic Button &½ **1962** Mel Brooks took the plot from this film and made "The Producers," which was much better. Italian gangsters produce a TV show and stack the deck so that it will fail. Unbeknownst to them, the star has figured out what they are doing and works to make it a success. Shot in Italy, mainly in Venice and Rome. **90m/B VHS.** *IT* Maurice Chevalier, Eleanor Parker, Jayne Mansfield, Mike Connors, Akim Tamiroff; ***D:*** George Sherman.

Panic in Echo Park && **1977** A doctor races against time to find the cause of an epidemic that is threatening the health of a city. Good performances compensate for a predictable plot. **78m/C VHS.** Dorian Harewood, Robin Gammell, Catlin Adams, Ramon Bieri, Movita; ***D:*** John Llewellyn Moxey. **TV**

Panic in Needle Park &&& **1975 (R)** Drugs become an obsession for a young girl who goes to New York for an abortion. Her new boyfriend is imprisoned for robbery in order to support both their habits. She resorts to prostitution to continue her drug habit, and trouble occurs when her boyfriend realizes she was instrumental in his being sent to jail. Strikes a vein in presenting an uncompromising look at drug use. May be too much of a depressant for some. Pacino's first starring role. **90m/C VHS.** Al Pacino, Kitty Winn, Alan Vint, Richard Bright, Kiel Martin, Warren Finnerty, Raul Julia, Paul Sorvino; ***D:*** Jerry Schatzberg; ***W:*** Joan Didion, John Gregory Dunne; ***C:*** Adam Holender. Cannes '71: Actress (Winn).

Panic in the Skies && **1996** The cockpit of a Boeing 747 is struck by lightning in mid-flight, killing the pilot and co-pilot. Flight attendant Jackson and passenger Marinaro try to figure out a way to safely land the passenger-filled jet. **90m/C**

VHS, DVD. Kate Jackson, Ed Marinaro, Erik Estrada, Maureen McCormick, Billy Warlock, Robert Guillaume; *D:* Paul Ziller; *W:* Robert Hamilton; *C:* Rod Parkhurst; *M:* Todd Hayen. TV

Panic in the Streets ♪♪♪ 1950 The Black Death threatens New Orleans in this intense tale. When a body is found on the waterfront, a doctor (Widmark) is called upon for a diagnosis. The carrier proves to be deadly in more ways than one. Fine performances, taut direction (this was one of Kazan's favorite movies). Filmed on location in New Orleans. **96m/B VHS.** Richard Widmark, Jack Palance, Barbara Bel Geddes, Paul Douglas, Zero Mostel; *D:* Elia Kazan; *W:* Edward Anhalt. Oscars '50: Story.

Panic in the Year Zero! ♪♪½ *End of the World* 1962 Milland and family leave Los Angeles for a fishing trip just as the city is hit by a nuclear bomb. Continuing out into the wilderness for safety, the family now must try to survive as their world crumbles around them. Generally considered the best of Milland's five directorial efforts. **92m/B VHS.** Ray Milland, Jean Hagen, Frankie Avalon, Mary Mitchell, Joan Freeman, Richard Garland, Rex Holman, Richard Bakalyan, Willis Bouchey, Neil Nephew; *D:* Ray Milland; *W:* Jay Simms, John Morton; *C:* Gilbert Warrenton; *M:* Les Baxter.

Panic on the 5:22 ♪♪ 1974 Wealthy commuters are kidnapped and held hostage by terrorist hoodlums in a suburban train club car. **78m/C VHS.** Lynda Day George, Laurence Luckinbill, Ina Balin, Bernie Casey; *D:* Harvey Hart. TV

Panic Room ♪♪½ 2002 (R) Recently divorced mom Meg (Foster) moves with daughter Sarah (Stewart) into a huge, ominous four-story brownstone in New York. The house comes equipped with a "panic room" a fortress-like room the paranoid billionaire previous occupant had built. Before the night is over, the room comes into play as three intruders come looking for something. The three happen to be looking for something that's in the room, where the women have holed themselves up. And thus the cat-and-mouse game begins. Fincher's talents for visual style, creative camera work, and squirmy set pieces are well-used here as the tension mounts with each scene. The plot isn't especially original, but the twists are well-done the performers acquit themselves nicely. **112m/C VHS, DVD.** *US* Jodie Foster, Forest Whitaker, Dwight Yoakam, Jared Leto, Kristen Stewart, Ann Magnuson, Patrick Bauchau, Ian Buchanan, Paul Schulze; *D:* David Fincher; *W:* David Koepp; *C:* Conrad W. Hall, Darius Khondji; *M:* Howard Shore.

Panic Station ♪♪ *The Plains of Heaven* 1982 Two guys get lonely at remote satellite relay station. **90m/C VHS.** *AU* Richard Moir, Reg Evans, Gerard Kennedy; *D:* Ian Pringle.

Panique ♪♪♪ *Panic* 1947 A study of mob psychology in slums of post-WWII Paris. Two lovers frame a stranger for murder. Dark and tautly paced thriller taken from the novel by Georges Simenon. In French with English subtitles. **87m/B VHS.** *FR* Michel Simon, Viviane Romance; *D:* Julien Duvivier.

Pantaloons ♪♪ 1957 A man who fancies himself to be irresistible chases women for sport. A quaint and lively period film. **93m/C VHS.** *FR* Fernandel, Carmen Sevilla, Fernando Rey; *D:* John Berry.

Panther ♪♪ 1995 (R) The Van Peebles family teaches Oliver Stone History 101 with a fictionalized account of the Black Panthers' emergence as a voice for African Americans and as a fixture on the FBI's most wanted list in the late '60s. Judge (Hardison), a Vietnam vet forced by the FBI to become an informant, chronicles the activities of leaders Bobby Seale (Vance) and Huey P. Newton (Chong) and serves as witness to the Panthers' rise and subsequent fall into corruption and disintegration. Scatter-shot editing is meant to signify the chaos of the times, but instead adds to the action-flick feel and further detracts from the professed intent of being a message movie. **124m/C VHS, DVD, Wide.** Kadeem Hardison, Marcus Chong, Courtney B. Vance, Bokeem Woodbine, Joe Don Baker, Anthony Griffith, Nefertiti, James Russo, Richard Dysart, M. Emmet Walsh, Mario Van Peebles; *D:* Mario Van Peebles; *W:* Melvin Van Peebles; *C:* Edward Pei; *M:* Stanley Clarke.

Panther Squad ♪ 1984 Litter of sex kittens led by Danning get into major scraps to save world. **77m/C VHS.** Sybil Danning.

The Panther's Claw ♪♪ 1942 Murder befalls an opera troupe, but a sleuth with the memorable name of Thatcher Colt is on the case. A quick-moving mystery quickie that delivers on its own modest terms. **72m/B VHS.** Sidney Blackmer, Byron Foulger, Rick Vallin, Herbert Rawlinson; *D:* William Beaudine.

Papa's Delicate Condition ♪♪♪ 1963 Based on the autobiographical writings of silent screen star Corinne Griffith. Gleason is Papa whose "delicate condition" is a result of his drinking. His antics provide a constant headache to his family. A paean to turn-of-the-century family life. No I.D.s required as the performances are enjoyable for the whole family. Features the Academy Award-winning song "Call Me Irresponsible." ♫Call Me Irresponsible; Bill Bailey, Won't You Please Come Home?. **98m/C VHS.** Jackie Gleason, Glynis Johns, Charlie Ruggles, Laurel Goodwin, Elisha Cook Jr., Murray Hamilton; *D:* George Marshall; *W:* Jack Rose; *C:* Loyal Griggs. Oscars '63: Song ("Call Me Irresponsible").

The Paper ♪♪♪ 1994 (R) Another crowd pleaser from director Howard follows a red letter day in the life of an editor at the tabloid New York Sun (modeled on the trashy Post). Fresh, fast-moving script by the Koepp brothers (who appear as reporters) offers a fairly accurate portrayal of the business of journalism (including the "brisk" language), with a few Hollywood exceptions. Pace suffers from cutaways to life outside, while script and direction sometimes coast past targets. Propelled by a fine cast, with cola-swigging editor Keaton the focus as he juggles his personal and professional lives. As a managing editor married to her work and ready to run over anyone in her way, Close is both funny and scary. Duvall contributes salt as the old newsroom warhorse. Tons of cameos, though those outside of the business may not notice them. **112m/C VHS, DVD, Wide.** Michael Keaton, Robert Duvall, Marisa Tomei, Glenn Close, Randy Quaid, Jason Robards Jr., Jason Alexander, Spalding Gray, Catherine O'Hara, Lynne Thigpen; *D:* Ron Howard; *W:* David Koepp, Steven Koepp; *C:* John Seale; *M:* Randy Newman.

The Paper Brigade ♪♪½ 1996 (PG) Fifteen-year-old Gunther (Howard) gets a paper route to pay for the concert tickets he bought to impress a girl. Now he has to contend with his crazy neighbor (Englund) and a gang of bullies, as well as other obstacles. **89m/C VHS.** Kyle Howard, Robert Englund, Travis Wester; *D:* Blair Treu.

Paper Bullets ♪♪ 1999 (R) Cop John Rourke's son is kidnapped by a Chinese drug lord and, naturally, he'll do anything to get his boy back. Including aligning himself with a beautiful woman who has an equal obsession for revenge. **95m/C VHS, DVD.** James Russo, William McNamara, Ernie Hudson, Nicole Bilderback, Jeff Wincott, Francois Chan; *D:* Serge Rodnunsky; *W:* Serge Rodnunsky; *C:* Greg Patterson; *M:* Jeff Walton. VIDEO

The Paper Chase ♪♪♪ 1973 (PG) Students at Harvard Law School suffer and struggle through their first year. A realistic, sometimes acidly humorous look at Ivy League ambitions, with Houseman stealing the show as the tough professor. Wonderful adaptation of the John Jay Osborn novel which later became the basis for the acclaimed TV series. **111m/C VHS.** Timothy Bottoms, Lindsay Wagner, John Houseman, Graham Beckel, Edward Herrmann, James Naughton, Craig Richard Nelson, Bob Lydiard; *D:* James Bridges; *W:* James Bridges; *C:* Gordon Willis; *M:* John Williams. Oscars '73: Support. Actor (Houseman); Golden Globes '74: Support. Actor (Houseman); Natl. Bd. of Review '73: Support. Actor (Houseman).

Paper Lion ♪♪½ 1968 A comedy "documentary" about bestselling writer George Plimpton's tryout game as quarterback with the Detroit Lions. Film debut of Alan Alda. Helped Karras make the transition from the gridiron to the silver screen. Moves into field goal range but doesn't quite score. **107m/C VHS.** Alan Alda, Lauren Hutton, Alex Karras, Ann Turkel, John Gordy, Roger Brown, "Sugar Ray" Robinson, Roy Scheider, David Doyle; *D:* Alex March.

Paper Man ♪♪ 1971 A group of college students create a fictitious person in a computer for a credit card scam. The scheme snowballs, resulting in murder and hints of possible artificial intelligence. But it's just standard network TV fare, with a creepy performance by Stockwell as a computer whiz. **90m/C VHS.** Dean Stockwell, Stefanie Powers, James Stacy, Elliot Street, Tina Chen, James Olson, Ross Elliott; *D:* Walter Grauman.

Paper Marriage ♪½ 1988 In Canada, a less-than-successful Chinese boxer agrees to marry a Hong Kong girl for a promise of payment in order that she may become a citizen. The money never comes, but the nearly betrothed pair discover that they love each other, after all. In Cantonese with English subtitles. **102m/C VHS.** *CH* Sammo Hung, Maggie Cheung; *D:* Alfred Cheung.

Paper Marriage ♪♪½ 1993 Yet another variation on the marriage in order to gain citizenship but yes we're going to fall in love films. A young Polish woman has fallen for an upper-crust English doctor she's met in Warsaw. When Alicja arrives in England, she's promptly dumped by the cad. She's ambitious and wants to stay in England so Alicja arranges a marriage of convenience with small-time crook Aiden, who finds his new bride is more than he bargained for. **88m/C VHS.** *GB PL* Gary Kemp, Joanna Trepechinska, Rita Tushingham, Richard Hawley, David Horovitch, William Ilkley, Mark McKellen, Ann Mitchell, Sadie Frost; *D:* Krzysztof Lang; *W:* Marek Kreutz, Krzysztof Lang.

Paper Mask ♪♪½ 1991 (R) When a promising young doctor is killed in an auto accident, an unscrupulous, psychotic porter assumes his identity. He uses said identity to, among other things, initiate an affair with a sultry co-worker. How long will this madman play his unholy game, and at what cost? **105m/C VHS.** *GB* Paul McGann, Amanda Donohoe, Frederick Treves, Barbara Leigh-Hunt, Jimmy Yuill, Tom Wilkinson; *D:* Christopher Morahan; *W:* John Collee; *C:* Nat Crosby; *M:* Richard Harvey.

Paper Moon ♪♪♪½ 1973 (PG) Award-winning story set in depression-era Kansas with Ryan O'Neal as a Bible-wielding con who meets up with a nine-year-old orphan. During their travels together, he discovers that the orphan (his daughter, Tatum) is better at "his" game than he is. Irresistible chemistry between the O'Neals, leading to Tatum's Oscar win (she is the youngest actor ever to take home a statue). Cinematically picturesque and cynical enough to keep overt sentimentalism at bay. Based on Joe David Brown's novel, "Addie Pray." The director's version contains a prologue by director Bogdanovich. **102m/B VHS.** Ryan O'Neal, Tatum O'Neal, Madeline Kahn, John Hillerman, Randy Quaid; *D:* Peter Bogdanovich; *W:* Alvin Sargent. Oscars '73: Support. Actress (O'Neal); Writers Guild '73: Adapt. Screenplay.

Paper Tiger ♪♪ 1974 Niven plays an imaginative English tutor who fabricates fantastic yarns fictionalizing his past in order to impress his student, the son of the Japanese ambassador to a Southeast Asian country. Poorly executed karate, misdirection, and a simplistic storyline work against it. **104m/C VHS.** *GB* David Niven, Toshiro Mifune, Eiko Ando, Hardy Kruger; *D:* Ken Annakin; *W:* Jack Davies.

A Paper Wedding ♪♪♪ *Les Noces de Papier* 1989 A middle-aged literature professor with a dead-end career and equally dead-end romance with a married man is persuaded by her lawyer sister to marry a Chilean political refugee to avoid his deportation. Of course, they must fool an immigration official and their fake marriage does turn into romance, but this is no light-hearted "Green Card." Bujold shines. In French and Spanish with English subtitles. **90m/C VHS, DVD.** *CA* Genevieve Bujold, Manuel Aranguiz, Dorothee Berryman; *D:* Michel Brault; *C:* Sylvain Brault.

Paperback Hero ♪♪ 1973 A hotshot hockey player turns to crime when his team loses its financial backing. Choopy storyline could use a Zamboni, while Dullea should be penalized for occasionally losing his rustic accent. Still the supporting actors skate through their roles and, for periods, it works. A slapshot that ultimately clangs off the goal post. **94m/C VHS.** *CA* Keir Dullea, Elizabeth Ashley, John Beck, Dayle Haddon; *D:* Peter Pearson.

Paperback Hero ♪♪½ 1999 Engaging leads help carry a weak story in this fluffy romantic comedy. Studly Jack (Jackman) is a long-distance trucker who makes his home in a remote outback community and is the secret author of a bodice-ripper that has become a bestseller. What Jack has neglected to tell his best friend, Ruby (karvan), is that he used her name as his nom de plume. Now the book's publisher wants Ruby to come to Sydney for a face-to-face meeting and Jack has a tough time getting her to go along with the deception. **96m/C VHS.** *AU* Hugh Jackman, Claudia Karvan, Andrew S. Gilbert, Angie Milliken, Jeanie Drynan, Tony Barry, Ritchie Singer, Bruce Venables, Charlie Little; *D:* Antony J. Bowman; *W:* Antony J. Bowman; *C:* David Burr; *M:* Burkhard Dallwitz.

Paperback Romance ♪♪½ *Lucky Break* 1996 (R) Sophie (Carides) is a writer of erotica who doesn't act on her own impulses because she's embarassed by her polio-crippled leg. But when she breaks her leg, the cast allows her to pass the injury off as a skiing accident and Sophie decides to go after the man of her dreams, a charmingly shady jewelry dealer named Eddie (LaPaglia)—who just happens to be engaged. **99m/C VHS.** *AU* Gia Carides, Anthony LaPaglia, Rebecca Gibney; *D:* Ben Lewin; *W:* Ben Lewin; *C:* Vincent Monton; *M:* Paul Grabowsky.

The Paperboy ♪♪ 1994 (R) Melissa Thorpe (Paul) returns to her small hometown to settle her mother's estate, only to become the obsession of Johnny (Marut), the 12-year-old paperboy she mistakenly befriends. Seems he becomes psychotically jealous when Melissa takes up with an old flame (Katt) and dead bodies become as common as old newspapers. **93m/C VHS.** Alexandra Paul, Marc Marut, William Katt, Brigid Tierney; *D:* Douglas Jackson; *W:* David Peckinpah; *M:* Milan Kymlicka.

Paperhouse ♪♪♪ 1989 An odd fantasy about a young girl plagued by recurring dreams that begin to influence real life. Very obtuse, British-minded film with "Twilight Zone" feel that manages to capture genuine dream-ness. Not for all audiences, but intriguing nontheless. Based on the novel "Marianne Dreams" by Catherine Storr. **92m/C VHS.** *GB* Glenne Headly, Ben Cross, Charlotte Burke, Elliott Spiers, Gemma Jones, Sarah Newbold; *D:* Bernard Rose; *W:* Matthew Jacobs; *M:* Hans Zimmer, Stanley Myers.

Papillon ♪♪♪ 1973 (PG) McQueen is a criminal sent to Devil's Island in the 1930s determined to escape from the Lemote prison. Hoffman is the swindler he befriends. A series of escapes and recaptures follow. Boxoffice winner based on the autobiographical writings of French thief Henri Charriere. Excellent portrayal of prison life and fine performances from the prisoners. Certain segments would have been better left on the cutting room floor. The film's title refers to the lead's butterfly tattoo. **150m/C VHS, DVD.** Steve McQueen, Dustin Hoffman, Victor Jory, George Coulouris, Anthony Zerbe; *D:* Franklin J. Schaffner; *W:* Dalton Trumbo, Lorenzo Semple Jr.; *C:* Fred W. Koenekamp; *M:* Jerry Goldsmith.

Parade ♪♪♪ 1974 A series of vignettes in a circus, "Parade" is actually a play within a play, meshing the action with events offstage. **85m/C VHS.** *FR* Jacques Tati; *D:* Jacques Tati; *W:* Jacques Tati.

The Paradine Case ☙☙½ **1947** A passable Hitchcock romancer about a young lawyer who falls in love with the woman he's defending for murder, not knowing whether she is innocent or guilty. Script could be tighter and more cohesive. $70,000 of the $3 million budget were spent recreating the original Bailey courtroom. Based on the novel by Robert Hichens. **125m/B VHS, DVD.** Gregory Peck, Alida Valli, Ann Todd, Louis Jourdan, Charles Laughton, Charles Coburn, Ethel Barrymore, Leo G. Carroll; ***D:*** Alfred Hitchcock; ***W:*** David O. Selznick; ***C:*** Lee Garmes; ***M:*** Franz Waxman.

Paradise ☙☙ **1982 (R)** Young American boy and beautiful English girl on a 19th-century jaunt through the Middle East are the sole survivors when their caravan is massacred. Left to their own devices, they discover a magnificent oasis and the joys of frolicking naked and experience (surprise) their sexual awakening. Do a double-take: it's the "Blue Lagoon" all over, with a bit more nudity and a lot more sand. **96m/C VHS.** Phoebe Cates, Willie Aames, Richard Curnock, Tuvio Tavi; ***D:*** Stuart Gillard.

Paradise ☙☙☙ **1991 (PG-13)** Young boy is sent to the country to live with his pregnant mother's married friends (real life husband and wife Johnson and Griffith). From the outset it is clear that the couple are experiencing marital troubles, making the boy's assimilation all the more difficult. Help arrives in the form of a sprightly ten-year-old girl, with whom he forms a charming relationship. Largely predictable, this remake of the French film "Le Grand Chemin" works thanks to the surprisingly good work of its ensemble cast, and the gorgeous scenery of South Carolina, where the movie was filmed. **112m/C VHS.** Melanie Griffith, Don Johnson, Elijah Wood, Thora Birch, Sheila McCarthy, Eve Gordon, Louise Latham, Greg Travis, Sarah Trigger; ***D:*** Mary Agnes Donoghue; ***W:*** Mary Agnes Donoghue; ***M:*** David Newman.

Paradise Alley ☙☙ **1978 (PG)** Rocky tires of boxing, decides to join the WWF. Three brothers brave the world of professional wrestling in an effort to strike it rich and move out of the seedy Hell's Kitchen neighborhood of New York, circa 1946. Stallone wrote, stars in, and makes his directorial debut in addition to singing the title song. He makes a few good moves as director, but is ultimately pinned to the canvas. **109m/C VHS.** Sylvester Stallone, Anne Archer, Armand Assante, Lee Canalito, Kevin Conway; ***D:*** Sylvester Stallone; ***W:*** Sylvester Stallone; ***M:*** Bill Conti.

Paradise Canyon ☙½ **1935** Early Wayne "B" thriller, in which he plays an undercover government agent sent to track down a group of counterfeiters. **59m/B VHS, DVD.** John Wayne, Yakima Canutt, Marion Burns; ***D:*** Carl Pierson; ***W:*** Lindsley Parsons, Robert Emmett Tansey; ***C:*** Archie Stout.

Paradise, Hawaiian Style ☙½ **1966 (G)** Out-of-work pilot returns to Hawaii, where he and a buddy start a charter service with two helicopters. Plenty of gals are wooed by "the Pelvis." Filmed four years after Elvis's first Pacific piece, "Blue Hawaii." Presley, showing the first signs of slow-down, displays no surprises here. ♫Paradise, Hawaiian Style; Scratch My Back (Then I'll Scratch Yours); Stop Where You Are; This Is My Heaven; House of Sand; Queenie Wahine's Papaya; Datin'; Drums of the Islands; A Dog's Life. **91m/C VHS.** Elvis Presley, Suzanna Leigh, James Shigeta, Donna Butterworth, Irene Tsu, Julie Parrish, Philip Ahn, Mary Treen, Marianna Hill, John Doucette, Grady Sutton; ***D:*** Michael Moore; ***W:*** Anthony Lawrence, Allan Weiss; ***C:*** Wallace Kelley; ***M:*** Joseph J. Lilley.

Paradise in Harlem ☙½ **1940** All-black musical in which a cabaret performer witnesses a gangland murder, sees his sick wife die, and is pressured into leaving town by the mob. Have a nice day. **83m/B VHS.** Frank Wilson, Mamie Smith, Edna Mae Harris, Juanita Hall; ***D:*** Joseph Seiden.

Paradise Island ☙ **1930** Downscale musical romance about an ingenue on her way to join her fiance in the South Seas, only to find that he has gambled away his money. The opportunistic saloon owner tries to put the moves on her. Will the two lovers be reunited? ♫I've Got a Girl In Every Port; Drinking Song; Lazy Breezes; Just Another Dream. **68m/B VHS.** Kenneth Harlan, Marceline Day, Thomas Santschi, Paul Hurst, Victor Potel, Gladden James, Will Stanton; ***D:*** Bert Glennon.

Paradise Motel ☙½ **1984 (R)** Teen exploitation film centered around a local motel predominantly used for one-night rendezvous. High school heroes and jocks battle for the affections of a beautiful classmate. **87m/C VHS.** Bob Basso, Gary Hershberger, Jonna Leigh Stack, Robert Krantz; ***D:*** Cary Medoway; ***C:*** James L. Carter.

Paradise Park ☙☙½ **1991** A whimsical comedy about the inhabitants of a West Virginia trailer park who dream of better lives while coping with their depressing surroundings. An English teacher (Groce) wishes he was a writer, an elderly woman (Basquette) dreams of winning a TV quiz show, and a mechanic wants to be a race car driver. Director Boyd sprinkles in appearances of non-Hollywood notables Porter Waggoner, Johnny Paycheck, Webb Wilder, and wrestler Dusty Rhodes. Includes some black and white fantasy sequences. **100m/C VHS.** Lena Basquette, Larry Groce, Jennifer Gurney; ***Cameos:*** Johnny Paycheck, Webb Wilder, Dusty Rhodes, Porter Waggoner; ***D:*** Daniel Boyd.

Paradise Road ☙☙ **1997 (R)** Fleeing Singapore during WWII, a group of British, American, and Australian women straggle to the shore of Sumatra after their ship is bombed, where they're taken prisoner by the Japanese. Headed by Close, the prisoners form a vocal ensemble that crosses their collective national differences and attempts to lift the spirits of the brutalized women. Familiar ground is trod in this prisoner-of-war saga, but the music is genuinely moving, and excellent performances from the cast help sustain interest. The symphonic choral pieces were taken from actual sheet music used by a similar group of real-life WWII prisoners. **115m/C VHS, DVD, Wide.** Glenn Close, Frances McDormand, Julianna Margulies, Pauline Collins, Jennifer Ehle, Elizabeth Spriggs, Tessa Humphries, Sab Shimono, Cate Blanchett, Wendy Hughes, Johanna Ter Steege, Pamela Rabe, Clyde Kusatsu, Stan(ford) Egi, Susie Porter, Lisa Hensley, Penne Hackforth-Jones, Pauline Chan; ***D:*** Bruce Beresford; ***W:*** Bruce Beresford, David Giles, Martin Meader; ***C:*** Peter James; ***M:*** Margareth Dryburgh, Ross Edwards.

A Paradise Under the Stars ☙☙ *Un Paraiso Bajo las Estrellas* **1999** Sissy wants to perform at Cuba's Tropicana nightclub, just as her mother did, but her strict father Candido forbids it. But Sissy has more problems when she discover her new lover Sergio may also be her brother! Spanish with subtitles. **90m/C VHS, DVD, Wide.** *CU SP* Vladimir Cruz, Thais Valdes, Enrique Molina, Amparo Munoz, Daisy Granados, Litico Rodriguez, Satiago Alfonso, Jacqueline Arenal; ***D:*** Gerardo Chijona; ***W:*** Gerardo Chijona, Senel Paz; ***C:*** Raul Perez Ureta; ***M:*** Carlos Faruolo.

Paradisio ☙½ **1961 (R)** Dying inventor wills Oxford professor an authentic pair of X-ray specs. Spies come gunning for the professor, chasing him through Europe. Doc keeps forgetting he's being chased while using the special specs to see (sometimes in 3-D) through the clothing of young women. Meager plot does not get in way of 3-D nudie exploitation. **82m/C VHS.** Arthur Howard, Eva Waegner.

The Parallax View ☙☙☙½ **1974 (R)** Lee (Prentiss) was a witness to the assassination of a senator and is worried for her own safety, so she goes to newspaper reporter Joe Frady (Beatty) with her fears. He becomes suspicious after her alleged suicide and starts to investigate, discovering a mysterious corporation that hires assassins. As Joe digs deeper and deeper, he uncovers more than he bargained for and becomes a pawn in the conspirators' further plans. Beatty is excellent and the conspiracy is never less than believable. A lesser-known, compelling political thriller that deserves to be more widely seen. Based on the novel by Loren Singer. **102m/C VHS, DVD, Wide.** Warren Beatty, Hume Cronyn, William Daniels, Paula Prentiss, Kenneth Mars, Bill McKinney, Anthony Zerbe, Walter McGinn; ***D:*** Alan J. Pakula; ***W:*** David Giler, Lorenzo Semple Jr.; ***C:*** Gordon Willis; ***M:*** Michael Small. Natl. Soc. Film Critics '74: Cinematog.

Parallel Corpse ☙ **1983** A mortuary attendant finds a murder victim hidden in a coffin and blackmails the remorseless killer. **89m/C VHS.** Buster Larsen, Jorgen Kiil, Agneta Ekmanner, Masja Dessau.

Parallel Lives ☙☙½ **1994 (R)** Sorority sisters and frat brothers (and their various spouses and lovers), from the classes of both 1948 and 1973, gather for an on-campus weekend reunion and discover old and new jealousies, rivalries, and lots of lust (requited and not). There's also an unexpected death and a police investigation as well. Director Yellen had her cast improvise much of their dialogue—the same method she used in "Chantilly Lace." **105m/C VHS.** James Belushi, James Brolin, LeVar Burton, Lindsay Crouse, Jill Eikenberry, Ben Gazzara, Jack Klugman, David Lansbury, Liza Minnelli, Dudley Moore, Gena Rowlands, Ally Sheedy, Helen Slater, Mira Sorvino, Paul Sorvino, Robert Wagner, Patricia Wettig, JoBeth Williams, Treat Williams; ***D:*** Linda Yellen; ***W:*** Gisella Bernice; ***M:*** Patrick Seymour. **CABLE**

Parallel Sons ☙☙ **1995** No-budget first feature from Young has an awkward construction but a couple of fine performances. Teen Seth (Mick) lives in a conservative upstate New York farming community—exactly the wrong place for a young white man with a penchant for black culture and both artistic and homosexual desires. He's working at the local diner, which just happens to get held up by Knowledge (Mason), a black con shot during an escape from the local prison. Seth shelters Knowledge, whose hostility is gradually overcome by both Seth's concern and a mutual sexual attraction. However, more plot complications lead to melodrama. **93m/C VHS.** Heather Gottlieb, Gabriel Mick, Laurence Mason, Murphy Guyer, Graham Alex Johnson; ***D:*** John G. Young; ***W:*** John G. Young; ***C:*** Matt Howe; ***M:*** E.D. Menasche.

Paralyzed ☙☙ **197?** An unconscious journalist, mistaken for dead in a hospital emergency room, flashes back to the investigation that embroiled him in his predicament. **90m/C VHS.** Ingrid Thulin, Jean Sorel, Mario Adorf; ***D:*** Aldo Lado; ***W:*** Aldo Lado.

Paramedics ☙½ **1988 (PG-13)** A motley crew of cavorting paramedics battle their evil captain. Another parody of people in uniform. A comedy with little pulse. **91m/C VHS.** George Newbern, Christopher McDonald, John P. Ryan, Ray Walston, Lawrence-Hilton Jacobs; ***D:*** Stuart Margolin.

Paranoia ☙ *Orgasmo; A Beautiful Place to Kill; A Quiet Place to Kill* **1969** Beautiful jet-set widow is trapped in her own Italian villa by a young couple who drug her to get her to perform in various sex orgies, which are probably the most interesting part of this muddled affair. **94m/C VHS.** *IT* Carroll Baker, Lou Castel, Colette Descombes; ***D:*** Umberto Lenzi.

Paranoia ☙☙ **1998 (R)** An imprisoned killer uses a computer to harass the surviving member of the family he murdered. **86m/C VHS, DVD.** Larry Drake, Sally Kirkland, Scott Valentine, Brigitte Bako; ***D:*** Larry Brand; ***W:*** Larry Brand; ***M:*** Martin Trum. **VIDEO**

Paranoiac ☙☙½ **1962** Greed and terror set in a country mansion. Simon (Reed) wants the family inheritance all to himself even if it means driving sister Eleanor (Scott) insane. This may not be so hard—she's claiming to see their dead brother Tony. Surprise! Tony (Davion) shows up (really throwing Simon for a loop). Reed's evil is tinged with humor although the numerous plot twists can get confusing. First directorial effort for cinematographer Francis. **80m/B VHS.** *GB* Oliver Reed, Janette Scott, Alex Davion, Liliane Brousse, Sheila Burell, Maurice Denham; ***D:*** Freddie Francis; ***W:*** Jimmy Sangster; ***C:*** Arthur Grant; ***M:*** Elisabeth Lutyens.

Parasite woof! **1982 (R)** A small town is beset by giant parasites. An "Alien" rip-off originally filmed in 3-D, during that technique's brief return in the early '80s. Bad films like this killed it both the first and second times. An unpardonable mess that comes off as a stinky sixth-grade film project. **90m/C VHS, DVD.** Bob Glaudini, Demi Moore, Luca Bercovici, Cherie Currie, Gale Robbins, James Davidson, Al Fann, Cheryl "Rainbeaux" Smith, Vivian Blaine; ***D:*** Charles Band; ***W:*** Alan J. Adler, Frank Levering, Michael Shoob; ***C:*** Mac Ahlberg; ***M:*** Richard Band.

Parasite Eve ☙☙☙ **1997** Hiroshi Mikami stars as Dr. Nagashima, a scientist who has discovered that mitochondria, the organisms which provide energy for cells, appear to have their own DNA and life-cycle. Nagashima has put this theory to work in his research, as he attempts to cure diseases in lab animals, using the mitochondrian energy. When Nagashima's young wife Kiyomi (Riona Hakuzi) is killed in an auto accident, Nagashima takes her liver in order to try and clone her, once again, using the energy of the mitochondria. He doesn't realize is that her death may be the first step in an evolutionary leap, in which the mitochondria will rise up and dominate the world. **120m/C DVD, Wide.** *JP* Hiroshi Mikami, Riona Hakuzi, Tomoko Nakajima; ***D:*** Masayuki Ochiai.

Pardners ☙☙½ **1956** Spoiled New York millionaire (Lewis) becomes the sheriff of small western town, with Martin as a ranch foreman. The two team up to rid the town of bad guys and romance two local cuties. Western spoof (with music) is a remake of 1936's "Rhythm on the Range." ♫Buckskin Beauty; Pardners; The Wind! The Wind!; Me 'N You 'N the Moon. **88m/C VHS.** Jerry Lewis, Dean Martin, Lori Nelson, Jackie Loughery, Jeff Morrow, John Baragrey, Agnes Moorehead, Lon Chaney Jr., Milton Frome, Lee Van Cleef, Jack Elam, Bob Steele, Emory Parnell; ***D:*** Norman Taurog; ***W:*** Sidney Sheldon, Jerry Davis.

Pardon Mon Affaire ☙☙☙ *Un Elephant a Trompe Enormement* **1976 (PG)** When a middle-aged civil servant gets a look at a model in a parking garage, he decides it's time to cheat on his wife. Enjoyable French farce. Re-made as in the United States "The Woman in Red" and followed by "Pardon Mon Affair, Too!" Subtitled. **107m/C VHS.** *FR* Jean Rochefort, Claude Brasseur, Guy Bedos, Victor Lanoux, Daniele Delorme, Martine Sarcey, Anny (Annie Legras) Duperey; ***D:*** Yves Robert; ***M:*** Vladimir Cosma. Cesar '77: Support. Actor (Brasseur).

Pardon Mon Affaire, Too! ☙☙½ *We Will All Meet in Paradise* **1977** Pale sequel to the first popular French comedy, "Pardon Mon Affair." This time the four fantasy-minded buddies withstand the trials of marriage and middle-class life. With English subtitles or dubbed. **105m/C VHS.** *FR* Jean Rochefort, Claude Brasseur, Guy Bedos; ***D:*** Yves Robert; ***M:*** Vladimir Cosma.

Pardon My Gun ☙½ **1930** Cowpoke falls for the boss' daughter but has a rival in a wealthy rancher, who isn't above sabotage to get the girl. **64m/B VHS.** Tom (George Duryea) Keene, Harry Woods, Sally Starr, Lee Moran, Mona Ray; ***D:*** Robert De Lacy; ***W:*** Hugh Cummings.

Pardon My Sarong ☙☙½ **1942** Bud and Lou star as Chicago bus drivers who end up shipwrecked on a South Pacific island when they get involved with notorious jewel thieves. The island natives think Lou is a god! Standard Abbott & Costello fare. **83m/B VHS.** Bud Abbott, Lou Costello, Virginia Bruce, Robert Paige, Lionel Atwill, Leif Erickson, William Demarest, Samuel S. Hinds; ***D:*** Erle C. Kenton; ***C:*** Milton Krasner.

Pardon My Trunk ☙☙ *Hello Elephant; Bvongiorno, Elefante* **1952** Struggling against poverty on his teacher's salary, a man and his family receive a gift from a Hindu prince—an elephant. De Sica carries this silly premise beyond mere slapstick. Dubbed. **85m/B VHS.** *IT* Sabu, Vittorio De Sica; ***D:*** Gianni Franciolini.

Pardon Us 🦴🦴½ *Jail Birds* **1931** Laurel and Hardy are thrown into prison for bootlegging. Plot meanders along aimlessly, but the duo have some inspired moments. The first Laurel and Hardy feature. **78m/B VHS.** Stan Laurel, Oliver Hardy, June Marlowe, James Finlayson; ***D:*** James Parrott.

The Parent Trap 🦴🦴½ **1961** Mills plays a dual role in this heartwarming comedy as twin sisters Susan and Sharon, who were separated at birth by their divorcing parents Mitch (Keith) and Maggie (O'Hara), discover each other during a stay a summer camp. They decide to switch lives and when they realize that dear old dad is about to get married to just the wrong woman (Barnes), the twins conspire to bring their divorced parents back together. Well-known Disney fluff. Followed by several made-for-TV sequels featuring the now grown-up twins (Mills reprised her role). **127m/C VHS, DVD, Wide.** Hayley Mills, Maureen O'Hara, Brian Keith, Charlie Ruggles, Una Merkel, Leo G. Carroll, Joanna Barnes, Cathleen Nesbitt, Ruth McDevitt; ***D:*** David Swift; ***W:*** David Swift; ***C:*** Lucien Ballard; ***M:*** Paul J. Smith.

The Parent Trap 🦴🦴½ **1998 (PG)** Updated remake of Disney's 1961 family film about long-separated identical twins, Hallie and Annie (both played by Lohan), who meet accidentally at camp and decide to reunite their divorced parents. Quaid is Napa vineyard-owning dad while Richardson is London fashion designer mom. The twins switch places and foil gold digging publicist Meredith (Hendrix) in order to get their parents back together. Since it's both Disney and a remake, you can assume that it works. However, it's doubtful that parents that don't even tell their kid that they have a twin are going to be winning any PTA awards. "Let's Get Together," the song that the guitar strummin' Hayley Mills made popular with the original, makes a cameo in an elevator. **128m/C VHS, DVD.** Dennis Quaid, Natasha Richardson, Lindsay Lohan, Polly Holliday, Elaine Hendrix, Joanna Barnes, Ronnie Stevens, Lisa Ann Walter, Simon Kunz, Maggie Wheeler; ***D:*** Nancy Meyers; ***W:*** Nancy Meyers, Charles Shyer; ***C:*** Dean Cundey; ***M:*** Alan Silvestri.

Parental Guidance 🦴🦴 *Kinfolks* **1998 (R)** Sean (Lee) is part of a crazy extended family in South Central L.A. who is reluctant to bring his upscale girlfriend Lisa (Johnson) home for the family's Christmas dinner. **87m/C VHS, DVD.** Maia Campbell, Stacii Jae Johnson, Casey Lee; ***D:*** A.M. Cali; ***W:*** A.M. Cali; ***C:*** Scott Edelstein; ***M:*** Horace Washington.

Parenthood 🦴🦴🦴 **1989 (PG-13)** Four grown siblings and their parents struggle with various levels of parenthood. From the college drop-out, to the nervous single mother, to the yuppie couple raising an overachiever, every possibility is explored, including the perspective from the older generation, portrayed by Robards. Genuinely funny with dramatic moments that work most of the time, with an affecting performance from Martin and Wiest. Director Howard has four kids and was inspired to make this film when on a European jaunt with them. **124m/C VHS, DVD.** Steve Martin, Mary Steenburgen, Dianne Wiest, Martha Plimpton, Keanu Reeves, Tom Hulce, Jason Robards Jr., Rick Moranis, Harley Jane Kozak, Joaquin Rafael (Leaf) Phoenix, Paul (Link) Linke, Dennis Dugan; ***D:*** Ron Howard; ***W:*** Ron Howard, Lowell Ganz, Babaloo Mandel; ***C:*** Donald McAlpine; ***M:*** Randy Newman.

Parents 🦴🦴🦴 **1989 (R)** Dark satire of middle class suburban life in the '50s, centering on a young boy who discovers that his parents aren't getting their meat from the local butcher. Gives new meaning to leftovers and boasts a very disturbing barbecue scene. Balaban's debut is a strikingly visual and creative gorefest with definite cult potential. The eerie score is by Badalamenti, who also composed the music for "Blue Velvet," "Wild at Heart," and "Twin Peaks." **81m/C VHS, DVD.** Randy Quaid, Mary Beth Hurt, Bryan Madorsky, Sandy Dennis, Kathryn Grody, Deborah Rush, Graham Jarvis, Juno Mills-Cockell; ***D:*** Bob Balaban; ***W:*** Christopher Hawthorne; ***C:*** Robin Vidgeon, Ernest Day; ***M:*** Angelo Badalamenti, Jonathan Elias, Sherman Foote.

Paris Belongs to Us 🦴🦴½ *Paris Nous Appartient; Paris is Ours* **1960** An early entry in the French "new wave" of naturalistic cinema, this psychological mystery drama has a woman investigating a suicide linked to a possible worldwide conspiracy. Interesting, if somewhat dated by Cold War elements. **120m/B VHS.** *FR* Jean-Claude Brialy, Betty Schneider, Gianni Esposito, Francoise Prevost; ***D:*** Jacques Rivette; ***W:*** Jacques Rivette, Jean Grualt.

Paris Blues 🦴🦴½ **1961** Two jazz musicians, one white, one black, strive for success in Paris and become involved with American tourists who want to take them back to the States. Score by Duke Ellington and an appearance by Armstrong make it a must-see for jazz fans. **100m/B VHS.** Paul Newman, Sidney Poitier, Joanne Woodward, Diahann Carroll, Louis Armstrong, Barbara Lange; ***D:*** Martin Ritt; ***W:*** Jack Sher, Walter Bernstein; ***M:*** Duke Ellington.

Paris Express 🦴🦴½ *The Man Who Watched Trains Go By* **1953** When a man steals money from his employer, he boards the Paris Express to escape from the police. A bit convoluted, but well acted. Based on the George Simenon novel. **82m/C VHS.** Claude Rains, Herbert Lom, Felix Aylmer, Marius Goring, Anouk Aimee, Marta Toren; ***D:*** Harold French; ***W:*** Paul Jarrico.

Paris, France 🦴🦴 **1994 (NC-17)** Lucy (Hope) is a frustrated writer, living in Toronto, who decides the pursuit of sexual passion will unleash her blocked creative urges. Her main partner is poet Sloan (Outerbridge), the young man Lucy is trying to fashion in the image of a deceased Parisian lover, and also the man whose poetry her husband (and publisher) Michael (Ertmanis) is promoting. Lots of self-delusion and literary pretensions as well as erotic grappling. Adapted from the novel by Tom Walmsley. **111m/C VHS.** *CA* Leslie Hope, Peter Outerbridge, Victor Ertmanis, Raoul Trujillo, Dan Lett; ***D:*** Gerard Ciccoritti; ***W:*** Tom Walmsley; ***M:*** John McCarthy.

Paris Holiday 🦴🦴½ **1957** An actor heading for Paris to buy a noted author's latest screenplay finds mystery and romance. Entertaining chase scenes as the characters try to find the elusive script. **100m/C VHS, DVD.** Bob Hope, Fernandel, Anita Ekberg, Martha Hyer, Preston Sturges; ***D:*** Gerd Oswald; ***W:*** Edmund Beloin, Dean Reisner; ***C:*** Roger Hubert.

Paris Is Burning 🦴🦴🦴 **1991 (R)** Livingston's documentary portrayal of New York City's transvestite balls where men dress up, dance, and compete in various categories. Filmed between 1985 and 1989, this is a compelling look at a subculture of primarily black and Hispanic men and the one place they can truly be themselves. Madonna noted this look and attitude (much watered down) in her song "Vogue." **71m/C VHS.** Dorian Corey, Pepper Labeija, Venus Xtravaganza, Octavia St. Laurant, Willi Ninja, Anji Xtravaganza, Freddie Pendavis, Junior Labeija; ***D:*** Jennie Livingston; ***C:*** Paul Gibson. Natl. Soc. Film Critics '91: Feature Doc.; Sundance '91: Grand Jury Prize.

Paris, Texas 🦴🦴🦴½ **1983 (PG)** After four years a drifter returns to find his son is being raised by his brother because the boy's mother has also disappeared. He tries to reconnect with the boy. Introspective script acclaimed by many film critics, but others found it to be too slow. **145m/C VHS.** *FR GE* Harry Dean Stanton, Nastassia Kinski, Dean Stockwell, Hunter Carson, Aurore Clement; ***D:*** Wim Wenders; ***W:*** Sam Shepard, L.M. Kit Carson; ***M:*** Ry Cooder. British Acad. '84: Director (Wenders); Cannes '84: Film.

Paris Trout 🦴🦴½ **1991 (R)** Believing himself above the law, southern Trout (Hopper) shoots the mother and sister of a young black man who reneged on his IOU. Lawyer Harris is forced to defend a man he knows deserves to be punished, and wife Hershey suffers long. Adapted by Pete Dexter from his National Book Award-winning novel. **98m/C VHS.** Dennis Hopper, Barbara Hershey, Ed Harris, Tina Lifford, Darnita Henry, Eric Ware, Ray McKinnon; ***D:*** Stephen Gyllenhaal; ***W:*** Pete Dexter; ***C:*** Robert Elswit. **CABLE**

Paris When It Sizzles 🦴🦴 **1964** A screenwriter and his secretary fall in love while working on a film in Paris, confusing themselves with the script's characters. Star-studded cast deserves better than this lame script. Shot on location in Paris. Holden's drinking—he ran into a brick wall while under the influence—and some unresolved romantic tension between him and Hepburn affected shooting. Dietrich, Sinatra, Astaire, Ferrer, and Curtis show up for a party on the set. **110m/C VHS, DVD, Wide.** William Holden, Audrey Hepburn, Gregoire Aslan, Raymond Bussieres, Tony Curtis, Fred Astaire, Frank Sinatra, Noel Coward, Marlene Dietrich, Mel Ferrer; ***D:*** Richard Quine; ***W:*** George Axelrod; ***C:*** Charles B(ryant) Lang Jr.; ***M:*** Nelson Riddle.

Parisian Love 🦴🦴 **1925** Marie (Bow) is a streetwise Paris urchin who makes her living by fleecing the tourists. When her lover Armand (Keith) is shot, Marie vows revenge on the culprit, wealthy Pierre Marcel (Tellegen). With the help of some underworld friends, Marie transforms herself into a beauty in order to seduce Pierre. **62m/B VHS, DVD.** Clara Bow, Donald Keith, Lou Tellegen, Lillian (Lillianne, Lyllian) Leighton; ***D:*** Louis Gasnier; ***W:*** Lois Hutchinson; ***C:*** Allen Siegler.

Park Avenue Logger 🦴½ **1937** Silly story has blue-blood Ingraham believing son O'Brien is a panty-waist, so he sends him to a lumber camp to prove his manhood. But junior is actually a wrestling champ (known as The Masked Marvel) and manages just fine, even winning the gal. **65m/B VHS.** George O'Brien, Beatrice Roberts, Lloyd Ingraham, Ward Bond, Willard Robertson, Bert Hanlon; ***D:*** David Howard.

The Park Is Mine 🦴🦴 **1985** A deranged and desperate Vietnam vet takes hostages in Central Park. Semi-infamous film, notable for being the first movie made for HBO, and for being filmed in Toronto, before the inexpensive practice of filming in Canada became widespread. **102m/C VHS.** Tommy Lee Jones, Yaphet Kotto, Helen Shaver; ***D:*** Steven Hilliard Stern; ***M:*** Tangerine Dream. **CABLE**

Parker 🦴🦴 **1984** An executive is kidnapped, then released, but does not know why. Unable to live with the mystery, he tracks his kidnappers down into a world of blackmail, drugs, and intrigue. **100m/C VHS.** Bryan Brown, Kurt Raab.

Parlor, Bedroom and Bath 🦴🦴 *Romeo in Pyjamas* **1931** A family tries to keep a young woman from seeing that her love interest is flirting with other prospects. Doesn't live up to the standard Keaton set in his silent films. Keaton spoke French and German for foreign versions. **75m/B VHS.** Buster Keaton, Charlotte Greenwood, Cliff Edwards, Reginald Denny; ***D:*** Edward Sedgwick.

Parole, Inc. 🦴🦴 **1949** FBI takes on the underground in this early crime film. Criminals on parole have not served their sentences, and the mob is responsible. A meagerly financed yawner. **71m/B VHS.** Michael O'Shea, Evelyn Ankers, Turhan Bey, Lyle Talbot; ***D:*** Alfred Zeisler.

Paroled to Die 🦴½ **1937** A man frames a young rancher for a bank robbery and a murder he committed in this wild west saga. Predictable and bland. **66m/B VHS.** Bob Steele, Kathleen Elliott.

Parrish 🦴½ **1961** Parrish McLean (Donohue) is a very ambitious young man, determined to make it in the rich world of the tobacco growers of the Connecticut River Valley. But his ruthless tobacco king stepfather (Malden) would like to thwart his plans. As befits Donohue's teen idol status, he also gets to romance three beautiful girls. Very silly and much too long. Based on the novel by Mildred Savage. **138m/C VHS.** Troy Donahue, Claudette Colbert, Karl Malden, Dean Jagger, Diane McBain, Connie Stevens, Sharon Hugueny, Dub Taylor, Hampton Fancher, Bibi Osterwald, Madeline Sherwood, Sylvia Miles, Carroll O'Connor, Vincent Gardenia; ***D:*** Delmer Daves; ***W:*** Delmer Daves; ***C:*** Harry Stradling Sr.; ***M:*** Max Steiner.

Parting Glances 🦴🦴🦴 **1986 (R)** Low-budget but acclaimed film shows the relationship between two gay men and how they deal with a close friend's discovery of his exposure to the AIDS virus. Touching and realistic portrayals make this a must see. In 1990 Sherwood died of AIDS without completing any other films. **90m/C VHS, DVD.** John Bolger, Richard Ganoung, Steve Buscemi, Adam Nathan, Patrick Tull, Kathy Kinney; ***D:*** Bill Sherwood; ***W:*** Bill Sherwood; ***C:*** Jacek Laskus.

Partner 🦴🦴🦴 **1968** An extremely shy young man invents a strong alter ego to cope with the world but this second personality comes to dominate—with tragic results. In Italian with English subtitles. **110m/C VHS.** *IT* Pierre Clementi, Stefania Sandrelli, Tina Aumont; ***D:*** Bernardo Bertolucci; ***M:*** Ennio Morricone.

Partners 🦴🦴 **1982 (R)** A straight, macho cop must pose as the lover of a gay cop to investigate the murder of a gay man in Los Angeles' homosexual community. Sets out to parody "Cruising"; unfortunately, the only source of humor the makers could find was in ridiculous homosexual stereotypes that are somewhat offensive and often unfunny. **93m/C VHS.** Ryan O'Neal, John Hurt, Kenneth McMillan, Robyn Douglass, Jay Robinson, Rick Jason; ***D:*** James Burrows; ***W:*** Francis Veber; ***M:*** Georges Delerue.

Partners 🦴🦴 **1999 (R)** All of the usual suspects are rounded up for this action comedy. Mild-mannered Bob (Paymer) steals a super-secret computer program from his company. Then it's stolen from him by hunky thief Axel (Van Dien). A series of double-crosses and chases—involving the obligatory Caddy convertible—ensue. Toss in the sexy girlfriend (Angel) and a cheap L.A. motel with a heart-shaped bed. **90m/C VHS, DVD, Wide.** Casper Van Dien, Vanessa Angel, David Paymer, Jenifer Lewis, Yuji Okumoto, Donna Pescow; ***D:*** Joey Travolta; ***W:*** Jeff Ferrell; ***C:*** Kristian Bernier; ***M:*** Jeff Lass.

Partners in Crime 🦴🦴 **1999 (R)** Local detective Gene Reardon (Hauer) is assigned to investigate the kidnapping of a wealthy man from a small town. But soon the FBI is called in, including Reardon's ex-wife Wallis Longworth (Porizkova). Then the victim turns up dead on Reardon's property and he's suddenly suspect numero uno. Since Wallis doesn't think Gene's guilty, she decides to secretly help him prove who really done it. **90m/C VHS, DVD.** Rutger Hauer, Paulina Porizkova, Michael Flynn, Andrew Dolan; ***D:*** Jennifer Warren; ***W:*** Brett Lewis; ***C:*** Stevan Larner. **VIDEO**

Partners of the Trail 🦴½ **1944** U.S. marshals Brown and Hatton try to find out who's murdering ranchers which leads them to gunplay with Ingraham's band of outlaws. **57m/B VHS.** Johnny Mack Brown, Raymond Hatton, Lloyd Ingraham, Christine McIntyre, Robert Frazer; ***D:*** Lambert Hillyer.

The Party 🦴🦴🦴 **1968** Disaster-prone Indian actor wreaks considerable havoc at a posh Hollywood gathering. Laughs come quickly in this quirky Sellers vehicle. **99m/C VHS, DVD, Wide.** Peter Sellers, Claudine Longet, Marge Champion, Sharron Kimberly, Denny Miller, Gavin MacLeod, Carol Wayne; ***D:*** Blake Edwards; ***W:*** Blake Edwards; ***C:*** Lucien Ballard; ***M:*** Henry Mancini.

Party 🦴🦴 **1996** Leonor (Silveira) and Rogerio (Samora) are having a 10th anniversary party at their seaside villa. As the celebration continues, Leonor is pursued by aging playboy Michel (Piccoli) while her husband stands idly by. Maybe that has something to do with the secret Rogerio's about to reveal. French and Portuguese with subtitles. **91m/C VHS, DVD.** *FR PT* Leonor Silveira, Michel Piccoli, Rogerio Samora, Irene Papas; ***D:*** Manoel de Oliveira; ***W:*** Manoel de Oliveira, Augustina Bessa-Luis; ***C:*** Renato Berta.

Party Animal 🦴 **1983 (R)** A college stud teaches a shy farm boy a thing or two about the carnal aspects of campus life. **78m/C VHS.** Timothy Carhart, Matthew Causey, Robin Harlan; ***D:*** David Beaird; ***W:*** David Beaird; ***C:*** Bryan England.

Party Camp 🦴 **1987 (R)** A rowdy summer camp counselor endeavors to turn a tame backwoods camp into a non-stop party. Late entry in the "Meatballs"-spawned genre fails to do anything of even minor interest. **96m/C VHS.** Andrew Ross, Billy Jacoby, April Wayne, Kirk Cribb; ***D:*** Gary Graver.

Party Favors woof! **1989 (R)** Erotic dancing, strip tease acts, and general hilarity are featured in this party tape. **83m/C VHS.** Jeannie Winters, Marjorie Miller, Gail Thackray; ***D:*** Ed Hansen.

Party Girl 🦴🦴🦴½ **1958** A crime drama involving an attorney representing a 1920s crime boss and his henchmen when they run afoul of the law. The lawyer falls in love with a nightclub dancer who successfully encourages him to leave the mob, but not before he is wounded in a gang war attack, arrested, and forced to testify against the mob as a material witness. The mob then takes his girlfriend hostage to prevent his testifying, leading to an exciting climax. Must-see viewing for Charisse's steamy dance numbers. **99m/C VHS, Wide.** Robert Taylor, Cyd Charisse, Lee J. Cobb, John Ireland, Kent Smith, Claire Kelly, Corey Allen; ***D:*** Nicholas Ray.

Party Girl 🦴🦴½ **1994 (R)** In the "girls just wanna have fun" category comes this spritely saga of 20-something Manhattan club gal Mary (Posey), who needs some steady income after the cops bust her for throwing an illegal rent party. So, since Mary's godmother is a librarian, she gets a job as a library clerk and discovers the wonders of the Dewey Decimal system (no, I'm not joking but presumably director Mayer is). Parker's Mary is a properly flaunting poseur but a little nightlife tends to go a long way. **94m/C VHS.** Parker Posey, Omar Townsend, Anthony De Sando, Guillermo Diaz, Sasha von Scherler, Liev Schreiber; ***D:*** Daisy von Scherler Mayer; ***W:*** Harry Birckmayer, Daisy von Scherler Mayer; ***C:*** Michael Slovis; ***M:*** Anton Sanko.

Party Girls 🦴½ **1929** Escort service girls run afoul of the law in this hokey melodrama. **67m/B VHS.** Douglas Fairbanks Jr., Jeanette Loff, Judith Barrie, Marie Prevost, John St. Polis, Lucien Prival; ***D:*** Victor Halperin.

Party Girls for Sale 🦴🦴 *Violated* **1954** Mystery thriller in which a young girl's body is found on the beach in Rio de Janeiro. **?m/C VHS.** Raymond Burr, Scott Brady, Johanna (Hannerl) Matz.

Party Incorporated 🦴🦴 *Party Girls* **1989 (R)** Marilyn Chambers (of "Behind the Green Door" fame) stars as a young widow with a huge tax load who gives parties to pay it off. Also known as "Party Girls." **80m/C VHS.** Marilyn Chambers, Kurt Woodruff, Christine Veronica, Kimberly Taylor; ***D:*** Chuck Vincent.

Party Line 🦴 **1988 (R)** A veteran police captain and a district attorney team up to track down a pair of killers who find their victims through party lines. **90m/C VHS.** Richard Hatch, Shawn Weatherly, Richard Roundtree, Leif Garrett, Greta Blackburn; ***D:*** William Webb; ***W:*** Richard Brandes.

Party! Party! **1983** A bunch of kids go nuts and have a party when their parents leave. **100m/C VHS.** *GB* ***M:*** Sting, David Bowie, Joe Jackson, Elvis Costello.

Party Plane 🦴 **1990** Softcore funfest about a plane full of oversexed stewardesses. **81m/C VHS.** Kent Stoddard, Karen Annarino, John Goff; ***D:*** Ed Hansen.

Pas Tres Catholique 🦴🦴 *Something Fishy* **1993** Pleasant comedy finds 40ish, chain-smoking, unconventional P.I. Maxine (Anemone) investigating her ex-husband for an insurance scam, drawing closer to her estranged son, and trying to decide romantically between long-time friend Florence and handsome economist Jacques. French with subtitles. **100m/B VHS.** *FR* Anemone, Christine Boisson, Michel Didym, Gregoire Colin, Denis Podalydes, Roland Bertin, Bernard Verley, Michel Roux; ***Cameos:*** Micheline Presle; ***D:*** Tonie Marshall; ***W:*** Tonie Marshall; ***C:*** Dominique Chapuis.

Pascali's Island 🦴🦴🦴½ **1988 (PG-13)** A Turkish spy becomes involved with an adventurer's plot to steal rare artifacts, then finds himself ensnared in political and personal intrigue. Superior tragedy features excellent performances from Kingsley, Dance, and Mirren. **106m/C VHS.** *GB* Ben Kingsley, Helen Mirren, Charles Dance, Sheila Allen, Vernon Dobtcheff; ***D:*** James Dearden; ***W:*** James Dearden; ***C:*** Roger Deakins; ***M:*** Loek Dikker.

Pass the Ammo 🦴🦴½ **1988 (R)** Entertaining comedy about a young couple who attempt to steal back $50,000 of inheritance money that a televangelist swindled from the family. One of the more creative satires on this religious TV phenomenon. **93m/C VHS.** Bill Paxton, Tim Curry, Linda Kozlowski, Annie Potts, Anthony Geary, Dennis Burkley, Glenn Withrow, Richard Paul; ***D:*** David Beaird; ***W:*** Neil Cohen, Joel Cohen; ***M:*** Carter Burwell.

A Passage to India 🦴🦴🦴 **1984 (PG)** An ambitious adaptation of E.M. Forster's complex novel about relations between Brits and Indians in the 1920s. Drama centers on a young British woman's accusations that an Indian doctor raped her while serving as a guide in some rather ominous caves. Film occasionally flags, but is usually compelling. Features particularly strong performances from Bannerjee, Fox, and Davis. **163m/C VHS, DVD, Wide.** *GB* Peggy Ashcroft, Alec Guinness, James Fox, Judy Davis, Victor Banerjee, Nigel Havers; ***D:*** David Lean; ***W:*** David Lean; ***C:*** Ernest Day; ***M:*** Maurice Jarre. Oscars '84: Support. Actress (Ashcroft), Orig. Score; British Acad. '85: Actress (Ashcroft); Golden Globes '85: Foreign Film, Support. Actress (Ashcroft), Score; L.A. Film Critics '84: Support. Actress (Ashcroft); Natl. Bd. of Review '84: Actor (Banerjee), Actress (Ashcroft), Director (Lean); N.Y. Film Critics '84: Actress (Ashcroft), Director (Lean), Film.

Passage to Marseilles 🦴🦴🦴 **1944** Hollywood propaganda in which convicts escape from Devil's Island and help French freedom fighters combat Nazis. Routine but entertaining. What else could it be with Bogart, Raines, Greenstreet, and Lorre, who later made a pretty good film set in Casablanca? **110m/B VHS.** Humphrey Bogart, Claude Rains, Sydney Greenstreet, Peter Lorre, Helmut Dantine, George Tobias, John Loder, Eduardo Ciannelli, Michele Morgan; ***D:*** Michael Curtiz; ***C:*** James Wong Howe; ***M:*** Max Steiner.

Passed Away 🦴½ **1992 (PG-13)** Family patriarch Jack Scanlan dies and his entire family gets together for the funeral and a big Irish wake. The family, of course, is made up of a weird group of characters, good steadfast son Hoskins, dim-witted but good-looking son Petersen, rebellious daughter Reed, and a left-wing nun who works in Central America and is accompanied by an illegal alien (McDormand). Throw in a mysterious female mourner and a pregnant granddaughter who goes into labor at the graveside and you come up with a movie that manages to use every comic death cliche ever imagined. Talented cast is wasted in a movie that should have passed away. **96m/C VHS.** Bob Hoskins, Jack Warden, William L. Petersen, Helen Lloyd Breed, Maureen Stapleton, Pamela Reed, Tim Curry, Peter Riegert, Blair Brown, Patrick Breen, Nancy Travis, Teri Polo, Frances McDormand; ***D:*** Charlie Peters; ***W:*** Charlie Peters; ***C:*** Arthur Albert; ***M:*** Richard Gibbs.

Passenger 🦴🦴🦴 *Pasazerka* **1961** While on a cruise ship Lisa (Slaska), a former camp guard at Auschwitz, realizes that fellow passenger Martha (Ciepielewska) was once one of her prisoners. Their meeting triggers a series of flashbacks to the Holocaust and to domination, suffering, and resistance. Director Munk was killed in a car crash during filming, which was completed by his colleague Witold Lesiewicz. Based on the novel by Zofia Posmysz-Piasecka; Polish with subtitles. **63m/B VHS.** *PL* Aleksandra Slaska, Anna Ciepielewska, Marek Walezewski, Jan Kreczewski, Irena Malkiewicz; ***D:*** Andrzej Munk; ***W:*** Andrzej Munk, Zofia Posmysz-Piasecka; ***C:*** Krzysztof Winiewicz; ***M:*** Tadeusz Baird.

The Passenger 🦴🦴🦴½ *Profession: Reporter* **1975 (PG)** A dissatisfied TV reporter changes identities with a dead man while on assignment in Africa, then learns that he is posing as a gunrunner. Mysterious, elliptical production from Italian master Antonioni, who co-wrote. Nicholson is fine in the low-key role, and Schneider is surprisingly winning as the woman drawn to him. The object of much debate, hailed by some as quintessential cinema and by others as slow and unrewarding. **119m/C VHS.** *IT* Jack Nicholson, Maria Schneider, Ian Hendry, Jenny Runacre, Steven Berkoff; ***D:*** Michelangelo Antonioni; ***W:*** Mark Peploe, Michelangelo Antonioni; ***M:*** Claude Bolling.

Passenger 57 🦴 **1992 (R)** Classic movie-of-the-week fare. Anti-terrorist specialist John Cutter (Snipes) leaves his profession because of his wife's murder, and coincidentally boards the same plane as Charles Rane (Payne), an apprehended evil terrorist headed to trial in L.A. Somehow, Rane's thugs have also sneaked aboard with plans to hijack the plane, and it's up to Cutter to use his skills and save the day. Athletic Snipes is convincing in his role but can't make up for the plot's lack of premise. **84m/C VHS, DVD, Wide.** Wesley Snipes, Bruce Payne, Tom Sizemore, Alex Datcher, Bruce Greenwood, Robert Hooks, Elizabeth Hurley, Michael Horse; ***D:*** Kevin Hooks; ***W:*** Dan Gordon, David Loughery; ***C:*** Mark Irwin; ***M:*** Stanley Clarke.

The Passing 🦴🦴½ **1988** Two men find themselves trapped in the darker vicissitudes of life. The two lead almost parallel lives until an extraordinary event unites them. **96m/C VHS.** James Plaster, Welton Benjamin Johnson, Lynn Dunn, Albert B. Smith; ***D:*** John Huckert.

Passing Glory 🦴🦴🦴 **1999** The script may not be a three-pointer but the acting is a slam-dunk in this fact-based drama. Joseph Verrett (Braugher) is a black priest in segregationist New Orleans in the early '60s, teaching at St. Augustine High and coaching the school's unbeaten varsity basketball squad. Verrett is a go-getter who wants to integrate the league now, while his boss, Father Robert Grant (Torn) preaches patience. Despite numerous obstacles, Verrett manages to challenge white Jesuit High to an unofficial city championship game. **94m/C VHS.** Andre Braugher, Rip Torn, Bill Nunn, Sean Squire, Ruby Dee, Daniel Hugh-Kelly, Anderson Bourell, Khalil Kain; ***D:*** Steve James; ***W:*** Harold Sylvester; ***C:*** Bill Butler; ***M:*** Stephen James Taylor. **CABLE**

The Passing of Evil 🦴🦴½ *The Grasshopper; Passions* **1970 (R)** Bisset is a starstruck Canadian undone by the bright lights and big cities of America. By age 22, she's a burnt-out prostitute in Las Vegas. Cheerless but compelling. **96m/C VHS.** Jacqueline Bisset, Jim Brown, Joseph Cotten, Corbett Monica, Ramon Bieri, Christopher Stone, Roger Garrett, Stanley Adams, Dick Richards, Tim O'Kelly, Ed Flanders; ***D:*** Jerry Paris; ***C:*** Sam Leavitt; ***M:*** Billy Goldenberg.

The Passing of the Third Floor Back 🦴🦴 **1936** Boarding house tenants improve their lives after being inspired by a mysterious stranger. They revert, though, when he leaves. Now you know. Based on a Victorian morality play. **80m/B VHS.** *GB* Conrad Veidt, Rene Ray, Frank Cellier, Anna Lee, John Turnbull, Cathleen Nesbitt; ***D:*** Berthold Viertel.

Passion 🦴🦴½ **1919** Paris, and the decadent Louis XV falls for the lovely Jeanne, making her his mistress, much to the scandal of the nation. Respectable silent version of "Madame DuBarry" is a relatively realistic costume drama, but it doesn't rate with the best German films of this period. **135m/B VHS.** *GE* Pola Negri, Emil Jannings, Harry Liedtke; ***D:*** Ernst Lubitsch.

Passion 🦴🦴 **1954** When a rancher's young family falls victim to rampaging desperadoes, he enlists an outlaw's aid to avenge the murders of his loved ones. **84m/C VHS.** Raymond Burr, Cornel Wilde, Yvonne De Carlo, Lon Chaney Jr., John Qualen; ***D:*** Allan Dwan.

Passion 🦴🦴 **1982 (R)** A Polish film director (Radziwilowicz) is making a movie called "Passion" and practicing what he's filming by having an affair with the motel owner (Schygulla) where the film crew are staying. Then the money for the film begins to run out. Meanwhile, Schygulla's husband, Piccoli, is having problems at his factory because of a labor dispute called by worker Huppert. French with subtitles. **88m/C VHS.** *FR* Jerzy Radziwilowicz, Hanna Schygulla, Michel Piccoli, Isabelle Huppert, Laszlo Szabo; ***D:*** Jean-Luc Godard; ***W:*** Jean-Luc Godard; ***C:*** Raoul Coutard.

Passion 🦴½ **1992** Linda decides she married the wrong brother. So she plots to kill her husband and marry her in-law instead. **90m/C VHS.** Kristine Rose, Robert Labrosse, Kristine Frischhertz, Jack Ciolini; ***D:*** Joe D'Amato.

Passion 🦴🦴 **1999** Over-the-top bio of Aussie-born composer Percy Grainger (1882-1961). Although born in Melbourne and starting his career as a concert pianist, Grainger (Roxburgh) spent most of his life in Europe and the U.S. and was involved in recovering English and Celtic folk songs. But his home life is a twisted psychosexual drama as his devoted mother, Rose (Hershey), suffers from syphilitic fits amid rumors of their incestuous relationship and Grainger's own masochistic impulses, which are catered to by his piano student, Karen (Woof). **98m/C VHS.** *AU* Richard Roxburgh, Barbara Hershey, Emily Woof, Claudia Karvan, Simon Burke, Linda Cropper, Julia Blake; ***D:*** Peter Duncan; ***W:*** Don Watson; ***C:*** Martin McGrath. Australian Film Inst. '99: Art Dir./Set Dec., Cinematog., Costume Des.

Passion Fish 🦴🦴🦴 **1992 (R)** McDonnell plays May-Alice, a soap opera actress who is paralyzed after a taxi accident in New York. Confined to a wheelchair, the bitter woman moves back to her Louisiana home and alienates a number of live-in nurses until Chantelle (Woodard), who has her own problems, comes along. Blunt writing and directing by Sayles overcome the story's inherent sentimentality as do the spirited performances of the leads, including Curtis-Hall as the rogue romancing Chantelle and Strathairn as the Cajun bad boy McDonnell once loved. **136m/C VHS, DVD, Wide.** Mary McDonnell, Alfre Woodard, David Strathairn, Vondie Curtis-Hall, Nora Dunn, Sheila Kelley, Angela Bassett, Mary Portser, Maggie Renzi, Leo Burmester, Shauntisa Willis, John Henry, Michael Laskin; ***D:*** John Sayles; ***W:*** John Sayles; ***C:*** Roger Deakins; ***M:*** Mason Daring. Ind. Spirit '93: Support. Actress (Woodard).

Passion Flower 🦴🦴 **1986 (PG-13)** A tropical romantic melodrama made for network TV and set in Singapore, where an ambitious banker falls in love with the daughter of island's wealthiest smuggler. The mixture of high finance, low-dealing and lust only proves moderately passionate. **95m/C VHS.** Bruce Boxleitner, Barbara Hershey, Nicol Williamson; ***D:*** Joseph Sargent; ***M:*** Miles Goodman. **TV**

Passion for Life 🦴🦴½ *L'Ecole Buissonniere; I Have a New Master* **1948** A new teacher uses revolutionary methods to engage students, but draws ire from staid parents in rural France. Worthwhile drama. In French with English subtitles. **89m/B VHS.** Bernard Blier, Julliette Faber, Edouard Delmont; ***D:*** Jean-Paul LeChanois.

Passion for Power **1985** Two men involved in a drug-smuggling syndicate attempt to take over the business. Complications arise when they both fall for a beautiful, deceitful woman who turns them against one another. **94m/C VHS.** *SP* Hector Suarez, Sasha Montenegro, Manuel Capetillo, Alejandra Peniche.

Passion in Paradise 🦴🦴½ **1989** Fact-based mystery set in the Bahamas in 1943. Stewart is a spoiled rich girl who marries a handsome gigolo (Assante), much to daddy big bucks' (Steiger) displeasure. Then daddy is murdered and the son-in-law becomes the key suspect. Trashy, but Assante's fine. **100m/C VHS.** Armand Assante, Catherine Mary Stewart, Rod Steiger, Mariette Hartley, Wayne Rogers; ***D:*** Harvey Hart. **TV**

Passion in the Desert && *Simoom: A Passion in the Desert* **1997 (PG-13)** Definitely one of the stranger plots going. Augustin Roberts (Daniels) is a French officer in Napoleon's Egyptian campaign. He's escorting artist Venture de Paradis (Piccoli), who's been commissioned to record the country's monuments. The duo are lost and separated in a desert sandstorm, with Roberts eventually finding shelter in the ruins of an ancient city. But he's not alone—his dangerous companion is a female leopard, who decides to help out the two-legged interloper. Based on a novella by Honore de Balzac. **93m/C VHS.** Ben Daniels, Michel Piccoli; ***D:*** Lavinia Currier; ***W:*** Lavinia Currier, Martin Edmunds; ***C:*** Alexei Rodionov; ***M:*** Jose Nieto.

The Passion of Anna &&& **1970 (R)** A complicated psychological drama about four people on an isolated island. Von Sydow is an ex-con living a hermit's existence when he becomes involved with a crippled widow (Ullmann) and her two friends—all of whom have secrets in their pasts. Brutal and disturbing. Wonderful cinematography by Sven Nykvist. Filmed on the island of Faro. In Swedish with English subtitles. **101m/C VHS.** *SW* Max von Sydow, Liv Ullmann, Bibi Andersson, Erland Josephson, Erik Hell; ***D:*** Ingmar Bergman; ***W:*** Ingmar Bergman; ***C:*** Sven Nykvist. Natl. Soc. Film Critics '70: Director (Bergman).

The Passion of Ayn Rand &&½ **1999** Warts-and-all bio of the Russian-born novelist/philosopher that focuses on the 20-year friendship between Rand (Mirren) and psychoanalyst Nathaniel Branden (Stolz). When the pic opens in 1951, self-important Rand is already famous for "The Fountainhead" and has a longtime marriage to the overshadowed Frank (Fonda). Nathaniel and Barbara (Delpy) are college students pushed to marry by mentor Rand, who soon becomes Nathaniel's lover and encourages his ambitions—to the dismay of both spouses. Based on the 1986 memoir by Barbara Branden so there's an axe to grind. **104m/C VHS, DVD.** Helen Mirren, Eric Stoltz, Julie Delpy, Peter Fonda, Tom McCamus, Sybil Temchen, Don McKellar, David Ferry; ***D:*** Christopher Menaul; ***W:*** Howard Korder, Mary Gallagher; ***C:*** Ronald Orieux; ***M:*** Jeff Beal. CABLE

The Passion of Darkly Noon &½ **1995** Strange religious/sexual allegory. Running through the woods, Darkly Noon (Fraser) stumbles across the rural home of Callie (Judd) and Clay (Mortensen). Callie sees that the young man is ill and allows him to stay, discovering his parents have recently died and he's escaped from the ultra-religious community where he was raised. The sexy Callie is an uncomfortable attraction for the naive lad and when he meets a crazy old woman, Roxy (Zabriskie), in the woods, he's inclined to listen to her ravings against Callie, leading Darkly to believe he's been sent to punish the transgressors. **106m/C VHS.** *GB GE BE* Brendan Fraser, Ashley Judd, Viggo Mortensen, Grace Zabriskie, Loren Dean; ***D:*** Philip Ridley; ***W:*** Philip Ridley; ***C:*** John de Borman; ***M:*** Nick Bicat.

Passion of Joan of Arc &&&& **1928** Dreyer's version of the life of France's Joan of Arc ignores all the battlefield dramatics and confines itself to showing Joan in her cell and at her trial, with only one exterior shot—that of Joan (stage actress Falconetti in her only film role) on her way to the stake. The script is drawn from the Latin text of the heresy trial itself and Dreyer uses numerous close-ups (the actors wore no makeup) to show the bewilderment, fear, and anger of the participants. Dreyer refused to have his film shown with musical accompaniment but the tape includes Richard Einhron's oratoria, "Voices of Light." **114m/B VHS, DVD.** *FR* Renee (Marie) Falconetti, Eugena Sylvaw, Maurice Schultz, Antonin Artaud, Michel Simon; ***D:*** Carl Theodor Dreyer; ***W:*** Carl Theodor Dreyer, Joseph Delteil; ***C:*** Rudolph Mate.

Passion of Love &&& *Passione d'Amore* **1982** Military captain becomes the obsession of his commander's mysterious cousin when he reports to an outpost far from home. Daring and fascinating. An unrelentingly passionate historical romance guaranteed to heat up the VCR. Available dubbed or with subtitles. **117m/C VHS.** *IT FR* Laura Antonelli, Bernard Giraudeau, Valeria (Valerie Dobson) D'Obici, Jean-Louis Trintignant; ***D:*** Ettore Scola; ***W:*** Ettore Scola.

Passion of Mind &½ **2000 (PG-13)** Moore plays two roles: Marie is an American widow and mother living in France while Marty is a hard-charging single New York literary agent. Marie falls asleep and wakes up as Marty and vice versa. Marie/Marty can't tell anymore which of her two worlds is real and things get even more complicated when each persona falls for an appealing man (Skarsgard in France, Fichtner in New York). It's not really confusing since the script is so simplistic and both her lives turn out to be remarkably dull (as is Moore's performance). English-language debut for Berliner and Moore's first film since 1997's "G.I. Jane." **105m/C VHS, DVD.** Demi Moore, Stellan Skarsgard, William Fichtner, Peter Riegert, Joss Ackland, Sinead Cusack; ***D:*** Alain Berliner; ***W:*** Ronald Bass, David Field; ***C:*** Eduardo Serra; ***M:*** Randy Edelman.

A Passion to Kill &½ *Rules of Obsession* **1994 (R)** Formulaic thriller finds psychologist David (Bakula) getting sexually involved with his best friend Jerry's (Getz) wife, who has a lurid past. Seems Diana (Field) stuck a kitchen knife into her abusive first husband and now Jerry's prospects don't look too good. **93m/C VHS.** Scott Bakula, Chelsea Field, Sheila Kelly, John Getz, Rex Smith, France Nuyen, Michael Warren; ***D:*** Rick King; ***W:*** William F. Delligan.

Passionate Thief &&½ *Risate de Gioia; Joyous Laughter* **1960** Two pickpockets and a bumbling actress plan to rip off the guests at a posh New Year's Eve party with slightly comic results. Not much to recommend in this slow moving flick. **100m/C VHS.** *IT* Anna Magnani, Ben Gazzara, Fred Clark, Toto, Edy Vessel; ***D:*** Mario Monicelli; ***C:*** Leonida Barboni.

The Passover Plot && **1975 (PG)** A controversial look at the crucifixion of Christ which depicts him as a Zealot leader who, aided by his followers, faked his death and then "rose" to win new converts. **105m/C VHS.** Harry Andrews, Hugh Griffith, Zalman King, Donald Pleasence, Scott Wilson; ***D:*** Michael Campus; ***M:*** Alex North.

Passport to Pimlico &&½ **1949** Farce about a London neighborhood's residents who discover an ancient charter proclaiming their right to form their own country within city limits. Passable comedy. **81m/B VHS.** *GB* Stanley Holloway, Margaret Rutherford, Hermione Baddeley, Naunton Wayne, Basil Radford; ***D:*** Henry Cornelius.

Past Midnight && **1992 (R)** Richardson plays a social worker who believes recently paroled killer Hauer was wrongly convicted. She attempts to prove his innocence while also falling in love—a dangerous combination. Richardson's beautiful and Hauer's making a successful career out of playing handsome psychos. **100m/C VHS, Wide.** Natasha Richardson, Rutger Hauer, Clancy Brown, Guy Boyd; ***D:*** Jan Eliasberg; ***W:*** Frank Norwood; ***M:*** Steve Bartek.

Past Perfect &&½ **1998 (R)** Gun battles, car chases, and fights move this actioner right along. Cop Dylan Cooper's (Roberts) job is made harder because his city is overrun with juvenile crime. But even he's shocked when the young criminals start turning up dead. Then Cooper discovers a group of futuristic bounty hunters have been sent back in time to eliminate these violent delinquents before they become adult killers. **92m/C VHS.** Eric Roberts, Nick Mancuso, Saul Rubinek, Laurie Holden; ***D:*** Jonathan Heap; ***W:*** John Penney; ***C:*** John Houtman; ***M:*** Christophe Beck.

Past Tense &&½ **1994 (R)** Complicated thriller about a cop with a gorgeous but mysterious neighbor, a murder to solve, and problems separating reality from his nightmares. **91m/C VHS.** Scott Glenn, Lara Flynn Boyle, Anthony LaPaglia, David Ogden Stiers, Sheree J. Wilson, Marita Geraghty, Stephen Graziano; ***D:*** Graeme Clifford. CABLE

Past the Bleachers &&½ **1995 (PG)** Sentimental TV movie finds Anderson starring as Bill Parish—a man still lost by the death of his 11-year-old son. Reluctantly, he agrees to coach the Little League team his son had played on, with the help of an opinionated senior citizen (scene-stealer Hughes), and is drawn to the boy who turns out to be the team's star player. The appropriately named Lucky Diamond (Fricke) is both mute and of a mysterious family background, and bonding proves therapeutic for both Bill and the youngster. Based on a novel by Christopher A. Bohjalian. **120m/C VHS.** Richard Dean Anderson, Barnard Hughes, Grayson Fricke, Glynnis O'Connor, Ken Jenkins; ***D:*** Michael Switzer; ***W:*** Don Rhymer; ***M:*** Stewart Levin.

Pastime &&& *One Cup of Coffee* **1991 (PG)** A bittersweet baseball elegy set in the minor leagues in 1957. A boyish 41-year-old pitcher can't face his impending retirement and pals around with the team pariah, a 17-year-old black rookie. Splendidly written and acted, it's a melancholy treat whether you're a fan of the game or not, and safe for family attendance. The only drawback is a grungy, low-budget look. **94m/C VHS.** William Russ, Scott Plank, Glenn Plummer, Noble Willingham, Jeffrey Tambor, Deirdre O'Connell, Ricky Paull Goldin; ***Cameos:*** Ernie Banks, Harmon Killebrew, Duke Snider, Bob Feller, Bill Mazeroski, Don Newcombe; ***D:*** Robin B. Armstrong; ***W:*** David Eyre; ***C:*** Tom Richmond. Sundance '91: Aud. Award.

Pat and Mike &&& **1952** War of the sexes rages in this comedy about a leathery sports promoter who futilely attempts to train a woman for athletic competition. Tracy and Hepburn have fine chemistry, but supporting players contribute too. Watch for the first on-screen appearance of Bronson (then Charles Buchinski) as a crook. **95m/B VHS, DVD.** Spencer Tracy, Katharine Hepburn, Aldo Ray, Jim Backus, William Ching, Sammy White, Phyllis Povah, Charles Bronson, Chuck Connors, Mae Clarke, Carl "Alfalfa" Switzer; ***D:*** George Cukor; ***W:*** Garson Kanin, Ruth Gordon; ***C:*** William H. Daniels; ***M:*** David Raksin.

Pat Garrett & Billy the Kid &&& **1973** Coburn is Garrett, one-time partner of Billy the Kid (Kristofferson), turned sheriff. He tracks down and eventually kills the outlaw. The uncut director's version released on video is a vast improvement over the theatrical and TV versions. Dylan's soundtrack includes the now famous "Knockin' on Heaven's Door." **106m/C VHS, Wide.** Kris Kristofferson, James Coburn, Bob Dylan, Richard Jaeckel, Katy Jurado, Chill Wills, Charles Martin Smith, Slim Pickens, Harry Dean Stanton; ***D:*** Sam Peckinpah; ***W:*** Rudy Wurlitzer; ***M:*** George Duning.

Patch Adams && **1998 (PG-13)** Maverick medical student Hunter "Patch" Adams (Williams) takes the expression "laughter is the best medicine" literally and treats terminally ill patients with slapstick routines. Naturally, his stodgy old boss, not to mention the rest of the medical establishment, frown on his antics and prefer more conventional treatments (like medicine). But Patch thumbs his nose at The Man and tries to defend his unorthodox ways to fellow students, including the requisite love interest (Carter). Director Shadyac and screenwriter Oedekerk seem to let Williams unleash his rapid-fire wackiness without much direction. Ultimately, flick is brought down by sappy melodrama and emotional manipulation under the guise of sincere emotion. **115m/C VHS, DVD.** Robin Williams, Philip Seymour Hoffman, Monica Potter, Bob Gunton, Josef Sommer, Irma P. Hall, Daniel London, Frances Lee McCain, Harve Presnell, Peter Coyote, Michael Jeter, Harold Gould, Richard Kiley; ***D:*** Tom Shadyac; ***W:*** Steve Oedekerk; ***C:*** Phedon Papamichael; ***M:*** Marc Shaiman.

A Patch of Blue &&½ **1965** A kind-hearted blind girl falls in love with a black man without acknowledging racial differences. Good performances from Hartman and Poitier are film's strongest assets. **108m/C VHS.** Sidney Poitier, Elizabeth Hartman, Shelley Winters, Wallace Ford, Ivan Dixon, John Qualen, Elisabeth Fraser, Kelly Flynn; ***D:*** Guy Green; ***C:*** Robert Burks; ***M:*** Jerry Goldsmith. Oscars '65: Support. Actress (Winters).

Patchwork Girl of Oz && **1914** You wonder what Baum might have been imbibing when he wrote some of his Oz books. In this story a mysterious Emerald City doctor is working on a powder of life that his wife accidentally tests on a patchwork servant doll that suddenly comes alive. **80m/B VHS.** Frank Moore, Violet MacMillan, Raymond Russell, Leontine Dranet, Pierre Couderc, Richard Rosson, Bobbie Gould, Marie Wayne; ***D:*** J. Farrell MacDonald; ***W:*** L. Frank Baum; ***C:*** James A. Crosby.

Paternity && **1981 (PG)** Routine comedy about middle-aged manager of Madison Square Gardens (Reynolds) who sets out to find a woman to bear his child, no strings attached. The predictability of the happy ending makes this a yawner. Steinberg's directorial debut. **94m/C VHS.** Burt Reynolds, Beverly D'Angelo, Lauren Hutton, Norman Fell, Paul Dooley, Elizabeth Ashley; ***D:*** David Steinberg; ***W:*** Charlie Peters; ***M:*** David Shire. Golden Raspberries '81: Worst Song ("Baby Talk").

Path to Paradise && **1997 (R)** Based on the true story of the 1993 World Trade Center bombing, which focuses on both the terrorists and the FBI investigators. FBI agent John Anticev (Gallagher) is investigating a rabbi's murder, which leads him to Islamic extremists. An informant warns Anticev that the group are planning terrorist activities in Manhattan but the conspirators are closer to their target than the FBI imagine. **95m/C VHS.** Peter Gallagher, Art Malik, Ned Eisenberg, Marcia Gay Harden, Paul Guilfoyle, Andreas Katsulas, Shiek Mahmud-Bey, Mike Starr; ***D:*** Larry Williams, Leslie Libman; ***W:*** Ned Curren; ***C:*** Jean De Segonzac. CABLE

Pather Panchali &&&& *The Song of the Road; The Saga of the Road; The Lament of the Path* **1954** Somber, moving story of a young Bengali boy growing up in impoverished India. Stunning debut from India's master filmmaker Ray, who continued the story in "Aparajito" and "World of Apu." A truly great work. In Bengali with English subtitles. **112m/B VHS.** *IN* Kanu Banerjee, Karuna Banerjee, Uma Das Gupta, Subir Banerji, Runki Banerji, Chunibala Devi; ***D:*** Satyajit Ray; ***W:*** Satyajit Ray; ***M:*** Ravi Shankar.

Pathfinder &&&½ **1987** A young boy in Lapland of 1,000 years ago comes of age prematurely after he falls in with cutthroat nomads who already slaughtered his family and now want to wipe out the rest of the village. Gripping adventure in the ice and snow features stunning scenery. In Lappish with English subtitles and based on an old Lapp fable. **88m/C VHS.** *NO* Mikkel Gaup, Nils Utsi, Svein Scharffenberg, Helgi Skulason, Sara Marit Gaup, Sverre Porsanger; ***D:*** Nils Gaup; ***W:*** Nils Gaup.

The Pathfinder &&½ **1994 (PG-13)** TV adaptation of the 1840 James Fenimore Cooper novel that finds legendary woodsman Natty Bumppo, his adoptive Indian father Chingachgook, and lovely Mabel Dunham trying to aid a beseiged British fort during the French and Indian wars. If this sounds familiar, it's because Cooper's "Leatherstocking Tales" were also the basis for "The Last of the Mohicans." **104m/C VHS.** Kevin Dillon, Graham Greene, Jaimz Woolvett, Laurie Holden, Russell Means, Stacy Keach; ***D:*** Donald Shebib; ***W:*** James Mitchell Miller, Thomas W. Lynch; ***M:*** Reg Powell.

Paths of Glory &&&& **1957** Classic anti-war drama set in WWI France. A vain, ambitious officer imposes unlikely battle strategy on his hapless troops, and when it fails, he demands that three soldiers be selected for execution as cowards. Menjou is excellent as the bloodless French officer, with Douglas properly heroic as the French officer who knows about the whole disgraceful enterprise. Fabulous, wrenching fare from filmmaking great Kubrick, who co-wrote. Based on a true story from Humphrey Cobb's novel of the same name. **86m/B VHS, DVD.** Kirk Douglas, Adolphe Menjou, George Macready, Ralph Meeker, Richard Anderson, Wayne Morris, Timothy Carey, Susanne Christian, Bert Freed, Joe Turkel, Peter Capell; ***D:*** Stanley Kubrick; ***W:*** Stanley Kubrick, Calder Willingham, Jim Thompson; ***C:***

Georg Krause; *M:* Gerald Fried. Natl. Film Reg. '92.

Paths to Paradise 1925 Compson and Griffith share criminal past, reunite at gala event to snatch priceless necklace and head south of the border. World- class chase scene. **78m/B VHS.** Raymond Griffith, Betty Compson, Thomas Santschi, Bert Woodruff, Fred Kelsey; *D:* Clarence Badger.

Patrick ½ 1978 (PG) Coma patient suddenly develops strange powers and has a weird effect on the people he comes in contact with. **115m/C VHS.** *AU* Robert Helpmann, Susan Penhaligon, Rod Mullinar; *D:* Richard Franklin; *M:* Brian May.

The Patriot ½ 1986 (R) An action film about an ex-Navy commando who battles a band of nuclear-arms smuggling terrorists. Edited via George Lucas' electronic editor, Edit Droid. **88m/C VHS, DVD.** Jeff Conaway, Michael J. Pollard, Leslie Nielsen, Gregg Henry, Simone Griffeth; *D:* Frank Harris; *W:* Andy Ruben, Katt Shea; *M:* Jay Ferguson.

The Patriot 1999 (R) Wesley McClaren (Seagal) is a former government immunologist who's now the local doctor for a small ranching community. The peaceful community becomes a plague town when an extremist militia group take over and turn out to be carriers of a mysterious disease. McClaren might be a healer but he also can kick some extremist butt when necessary. **90m/C VHS, DVD.** Steven Seagal, Gailard Sartain, L.Q. (Justus E. McQueen) Jones; *D:* Dean Semler; *C:* Stephen Windon; *M:* Steve Edwards.

The Patriot ½ 2000 (R) Bloody, long, and melodramatic Revolutionary War revenge pic with a strong lead by Gibson and a notably hissable villain in Isaacs. Benjamin Martin (Gibson) is a former guerilla soldier in the French and Indian wars who just wants to raise his family in peace. Unfortunately, local redcoat leader, Col. Tavington (Isaacs), has other ideas and when Martin's idealistic soldier son Gabriel (Aussie heartthrob Ledger) is captured, dad gets caught up in the action. Producing partners Roland Emmerich and Dean Devlin did "Independence Day" and "Godzilla," so spectacle is their middle name. Film gave the British critics apoplexy with its inaccuracies but who won, anyway? **164m/C VHS, DVD, Wide.** Mel Gibson, Heath Ledger, Jason Isaacs, Chris Cooper, Tcheky Karyo, Joely Richardson, Tom Wilkinson, Donal Logue, Rene Auberjonois, Adam Baldwin, Leon Rippy; *D:* Roland Emmerich; *W:* Robert Rodat; *C:* Caleb Deschanel; *M:* John Williams.

Patriot Games 1992 (R) Jack Ryan, retired CIA analyst, takes his wife and daughter to England on a holiday and ends up saving a member of the Royal Family from assassination by IRA extremists. Ryan, who has killed one of the terrorists, then becomes the target of revenge by the dead man's brother. Good action sequences but otherwise predictable adaptation of the novel by Tom Clancy. Companion to "The Hunt for Red October," with Ford taking over the role of Ryan from Alec Baldwin. Since this movie did well, we can probably expect two more from Ford, who's becoming the king of trilogies. Followed by "Clear and Present Danger." **117m/C VHS, DVD, CD-I, Wide.** Harrison Ford, Anne Archer, Patrick Bergin, Thora Birch, Sean Bean, Richard Harris, James Earl Jones, James Fox, Samuel L. Jackson, Polly Walker, Theodore (Ted) Raimi; *D:* Phillip Noyce; *W:* Donald Stewart, W. Peter Iliff; *C:* Donald McAlpine; *M:* James Horner.

The Patriots 1933 A German prisoner works as a shoemaker in a small village during WWI. A lyrical drama in German and Russian with English titles. **82m/B VHS, DVD.** *RU D:* Boris Barnet.

The Patsy 1964 Shady producers attempt to transform a lowly bellboy into a comedy superstar. Not one of Lewis's better efforts; Lorre's last film. **101m/C VHS.** Jerry Lewis, Ina Balin, Everett Sloane, Phil Harris, Keenan Wynn, Peter Lorre, John Carradine, Hans Conried, Richard Deacon, Scatman Crothers, Del Moore, Neil Hamilton, Buddy Lester, Nancy Kulp, Norman Alden, Jack Albertson; *D:* Jerry Lewis; *W:* Jerry Lewis.

Pattern for Plunder ½ *The Bay of Saint Michel* 1962 Ex-commando leader rounds up his former comrades to head back to Normandy in search of buried Nazi plunder. **73m/B VHS.** *GB* Keenan Wynn, Mai Zetterling, Ronald Howard, Edward Underdown; *D:* John Ainsworth; *W:* Christopher Davis.

Patterns *Patterns of Power* 1956 Realistic depiction of big business. Heflin starts work at a huge New York office that is under the ruthless supervision of Sloane. Serling's astute screenplay (adapted from his TV play) is adept at portraying ruthless, power-struggling executives and the sundry workings of a large corporation. Film has aged slightly, but it still has some edge to it. Originally intended for television. **83m/B VHS.** Van Heflin, Everett Sloane, Ed Begley Sr., Beatrice Straight, Elizabeth Wilson; *D:* Fielder Cook; *W:* Rod Serling; *C:* Boris Kaufman.

Pattes Blanches ½ *White Paws* 1949 A reclusive aristocrat always wears white spats, causing ridicule in the small fishing village where he lives. Trouble comes when a local saloon-keeper becomes resentful of the rich man's advances on his girlfriend. Moody, sensual French melodrama exploring class, money and sex. Adaptation of a play by Jean Anouilh. In French with English subtitles. **92m/B VHS.** *FR* Suzy Delair, Fernand Ledoux, Paul Bernard, Michel Bouquet; *D:* Jean Gremillon.

Patti Rocks 1988 (R) Offbeat, realistic independent effort concerns a foul chauvinist who enlists a friend to accompany him on a visit to a pregnant girlfriend who turns out to be less than the bimbo she's portrayed as en route. Mulkey shines as the sexist. Same characters featured earlier in "Loose Ends." **86m/C VHS.** Chris Mulkey, John Jenkins, Karen Landry, David L. Turk, Stephen Yoakam; *D:* David Burton Morris; *W:* Chris Mulkey, John Jenkins, Karen Landry, David Burton Morris; *M:* Doug Maynard.

Patton ½ *Patton—Lust for Glory; Patton: A Salute to a Rebel* 1970 (PG) Lengthy but stellar bio of the vain, temperamental American general who masterminded significant combat triumphs during WWII. "Old Blood and Guts," who considered himself an 18th-century commander living in the wrong era, produced victory after victory in North Africa and Europe, but not without a decided impact upon his troops. Scott is truly magnificent in the title role, and Malden shines in the supporting role of General Omar Bradley. Not a subtle film, but neither is its subject. Interesting match-up with the 1986 TV movie "The Last Days of Patton," also starring Scott. **171m/C VHS, DVD, Wide.** George C. Scott, Karl Malden, Stephen Young, Michael Strong, Frank Latimore, James Edwards, Lawrence (Larry) Dobkin, Michael Bates, Tim Considine, Edward Binns, John Doucette, Morgan Paull, Siegfried Rauch, Paul Stevens, Richard Muench; *D:* Franklin J. Schaffner; *W:* Francis Ford Coppola, Edmund H. North; *C:* Fred W. Koenekamp; *M:* Jerry Goldsmith. Oscars '70: Actor (Scott), Art Dir./Set Dec., Director (Schaffner), Film Editing, Picture, Sound, Story & Screenplay; AFI '98: Top 100; Directors Guild '70: Director (Schaffner); Golden Globes '71: Actor—Drama (Scott); Natl. Bd. of Review '70: Actor (Scott); N.Y. Film Critics '70: Actor (Scott); Natl. Soc. Film Critics '70: Actor (Scott); Writers Guild '70: Orig. Screenplay.

Patty Hearst ½ 1988 (R) Less than fascinating, expressionistic portrait of Hearst from her kidnapping through her brainwashing and eventual criminal participation with the SLA. An enigmatic film that seems to only make Hearst's transformation into a Marxist terrorist all the more mysterious. Based on Hearst's book, "Every Secret Thing." **108m/C VHS.** Natasha Richardson, William Forsythe, Ving Rhames, Frances Fisher, Jodi Long, Dana Delany; *D:* Paul Schrader; *W:* Nicholas Kazan; *C:* Bojan Bazelli.

Paul and Michelle 1974 (R) The equally dull sequel to "Friends" finds the two lovers a little older but no wiser. Paul has graduated from his British school and returns to France to seek out Michelle and their child. They try to rekindle their romance but the stresses of everyday life cause them problems. **102m/C VHS.** *GB FR* Sean Bury, Anicee Alvina, Keir Dullea, Ronald Lewis, Catherine Allegret, Georges Beller; *D:* Lewis Gilbert; *M:* Michel Colombier.

Paul Bartel's The Secret Cinema ½ *The Secret Cinema* 1969 Long before "The Truman Show" or "Ed TV," there was this little Bartel short of a woman who can't determine whether her life is real or a film by a maniacal director. Offbeat, creative, and a little disturbing. Followed by Bartel's short "Naughty Nurse." **37m/B VHS.** Amy Vane, Gordon Felio, Connie Ellison, Phillip Carlson, Estelle Omens, Barry Dennen, Mara Lepmanis, Camille Fife, Mimi Randolph, Glenn Johnson; *D:* Paul Bartel; *W:* Paul Bartel; *C:* Fred Wellington.

Paul Robeson 1977 Major events in the life of the popular actor are recounted in this one-man performance. Originally staged by Charles Nelson Reilly. **118m/C VHS.** James Earl Jones; *D:* Lloyd Richards.

Paulie ½ 1998 (PG) Dreamworks follows up "Mouse Hunt" with this tale of a conversant parrot (voiced by Mohr) whose mouth keeps getting him in trouble. Trapped in a dingy basement, Paulie tells a lonely Russian janitor (Shalhoub) the story of his cross-country quest to return to his original owner, the little girl (Eisenberg) who raised him from a fledgling. After the girl's parents send him away, Paulie goes through a procession of owners: a smart-aleck pawn shop owner (Hackett); a kindly old woman (Rowlands) who drives him to L.A in her RV; a petty criminal (Mohr again); a taco stand owner (Marin) who manages a parrot dancing act; and a scientist (Davison) looking to cash in on the bird's talent. Not a whole lot of action for a kiddie movie, and some of the jokes may go over their heads, but fine performances all around and a charming story keep pic aloft. **91m/C VHS, DVD.** Jay Mohr, Gena Rowlands, Tony Shalhoub, Richard "Cheech" Marin, Hallie Kate Eisenberg, Bruce Davison, Trini Alvarado, Buddy Hackett, Matt Craven, Bill Cobbs, Laura Harrington, Tia Texada; *D:* John Roberts; *W:* Laurie Craig; *C:* Tony Pierce-Roberts; *M:* John Debney; *V:* Jay Mohr.

Pauline at the Beach ½ *Pauline a la Plage* 1983 (R) Fifteen-year-old Pauline (Langlet) accompanies her more experienced divorced cousin Marion (Dombasle) to the French coast for a summer of sexual hijinks. Contemplative, not coarse, though the leads look great in—and out—of their swimsuits. Breezy, typically talky fare from small-film master Rohmer. Third film in the director's Comedies & Proverbs series. French with subtitles. **95m/C VHS.** *FR* Amanda Langlet, Arielle Dombasle, Pascal Greggory, Rosette, Feodor Atkine, Simon de la Brosse; *D:* Eric Rohmer; *W:* Eric Rohmer; *C:* Nestor Almendros.

Pavilion of Women ½ 2001 (R) Dull adaptation of the 1946 Pearl S. Buck novel. As the Japanese prepare to invade Manchuria in 1938, Madame Wu (Luo), tired of her husband's brutality, decides to give him a peasant girl concubine, Chiuming (Ding), whom he promptly rejects. However, the pretty girl attracts the interest of the Wu's youngest son, Fengmo (Cho), just as Madame becomes interested in American missionary doctor, Father Andre (Dafoe), who runs the local orphanage. The film is in English and the Chinese actors do struggle with their dialogue which doesn't help the emotional balance of the production. **120m/C VHS, DVD.** Luo Yan, Willem Dafoe, John Cho, Yi Ding, Shek Sau, Amy Hill, Anita Loo, Kate McGregor-Stewart; *W:* Luo Yan, Paul R. Collins; *C:* Poon Hang-Seng; *M:* Conrad Pope.

The Pawnbroker ½ 1965 A Jewish pawnbroker in Harlem is haunted by his grueling experiences in a Nazi camp during the Holocaust. Powerful and well done. Probably Steiger's best performance. Adapted from a novel by Edward Lewis Wallant. **120m/B VHS.** Rod Steiger, Brock Peters, Geraldine Fitzgerald, Jaime Sanchez, Thelma Oliver; *D:* Sidney Lumet; *C:* Boris Kaufman; *M:* Quincy Jones. Berlin Intl. Film Fest. '65: Actor (Steiger); British Acad. '66: Actor (Steiger).

Pawnshop 1916 Charlie is employed as a pawnbroker's assistant. Silent with music track. **20m/B VHS.** Charlie Chaplin.

Pay It Forward 2000 (PG-13) Seventh-grade student Trevor (Osment) takes his social studies assignment very seriously. His teacher Eugene (Spacey) has his students think of an idea to change the world and tells them to put it into action. Trevor comes up with the idea of doing a good deed for someone who is then supposed to do a favor for someone else as a way to "pay the favor forward." Trevor's cocktail waitress/recovering alcoholic mom Arlene (Hunt) finds herself wary of both the project and the teacher. Trevor, however, has decided to use the two of them as his first "pay it forward" subjects. Cloyingly emotional and more than a little manipulative. Based on the novel by Catherine Ryan Hyde. **122m/C VHS, DVD, Wide.** Haley Joel Osment, Kevin Spacey, Helen Hunt, Jay Mohr, James Caviezel, Jon Bon Jovi, Angie Dickinson, David Ramsey, Gary Werntz; *D:* Mimi Leder; *W:* Leslie Dixon; *C:* Oliver Stapleton; *M:* Thomas Newman.

Pay Off 1989 A lunatic psychiatrist seeks murderous revenge on his ex-patient/girlfriend and her family. **87m/C VHS.** Michael Fitzpatrick, Veronika Mattson, Margareta Krook; *D:* George Tirl.

Pay or Die 1983 (R) A crime boss' men turn on him and kidnap his daughter. **92m/C VHS.** Dick Adair, Johnny Wilson; *D:* Bobby Suarez.

Payback 1989 A brawny young man uses firepower to avenge those who have wronged him. **90m/C VHS.** Jean Carol, Alex Meneses; *D:* Addison Randall.

Payback ½ 1990 (R) A convict sets out to avenge his brother's death, and creates all sorts of mayhem in the process. Produced by Bob "Newlywed Game" Eubanks and scored by Daryl "Captain and Tenille" Dragon. **94m/C VHS.** Corey Michael Eubanks, Michael Ironside, Teresa Blake, Bert Remsen, Vincent Van Patten, Don Swayze; *D:* Russell Solberg; *M:* Daryl Dragon.

Payback ½ 1994 (R) An old, dying con (Armstrong) tells fellow inmate Oscar Bonsetter (Howell) the whereabouts of a fortune if he'll promise to kill cruel jail guard Gully (Bell) who made the geezer's life a misery. Years later, the now ex-con finds the ex-guard running a diner near the spot where the money is buried and decides to carry out his plan for revenge. If Oscar doesn't get too distracted by Gully's hot-to-trot wife, Rose (Severance), first. Also available in an unrated version. **92m/C VHS.** C. Thomas Howell, Joan Severance, Marshall Bell, R.G. Armstrong; *D:* Anthony Hickox; *W:* Sam Bernard; *C:* David Bridges.

Payback 1998 (R) Mel's very, very mean. Of course, his character has every reason to be in this loose remake of 1967's "Point Blank" and the novel "The Hunter" by Richard Stark. Porter (Gibson) is doublecrossed by partner Val (Henry), who steals the loot from their latest heist as well as Porter's junkie wife, Lynn (Unger), and then leaves Porter for dead. Porter becomes obsessed with getting his money back, and he'll take on anyone who gets in his way. Very cold, violent pseudo-noir with a pro lead and interesting supporting cast. **110m/C VHS, DVD.** Mel Gibson, Gregg Henry, Maria Bello, David Paymer, Deborah Kara Unger, William Devane, Kris Kristofferson, Bill Duke, Jack Conley, John Glover, Lucy Alexis Liu, James Coburn; *D:* Brian Helgeland; *W:* Brian Helgeland, Terry Hayes; *C:* Ericson Core; *M:* Chris Boardman.

Payday ½ 1972 Torn stars as a declining country music star on tour in this portrayal of the seamy side of show business, from groupies to grimy motels. Well-written script and fine performances make this an engaging, if rather draining, drama not easily found on the big screen. **98m/C VHS.** Sonny Shroyer, Rip Torn, Ahna Capri, Michael C. Gwynne, Jeff Morris; *D:* Daryl Duke.

The Payoff ½ 1943 The old-fashioned newspaper-reporter-as-crime-fighter routine. When the city's special prosecutor is murdered a daring newshawk investigates and tracks the bad guys. But will he spell their names right? **74m/B VHS.** Lee Tracy, Tom Brown, Tina Thayer, Evelyn Brent, Jack LaRue, Ian Keith, John Maxwell; ***D:*** Arthur Dreifuss.

Payoff 🦴🦴 **1991 (R)** An ex-cop discovers the identity of gangsters who killed his parents. He traces them to a Lake Tahoe resort and plots revenge. Familiar crime story with a good cast. **111m/C VHS.** Keith Carradine, Kim Greist, Harry Dean Stanton, John Saxon, Jeff Corey; ***D:*** Stuart Cooper; ***W:*** Douglas S. Cook; ***M:*** Charles Bernstein.

P.C.U. 🦴🦴 **1994 (PG-13)** Satire on campus political correctness follows freshman Tom Lawrence's (Young) adventures as he navigates the treacherous waters of Port Chester University (PCU). He falls in with the gang from the Pit, the militantly non-PC dorm, who encourage bizarre and offensive behavior. Essentially a modern update of "National Lampoon's Animal House," but without the brilliance; add half a bone for tackling the thorny sensitivity issue in a humorous way that parodies, but shouldn't offend. Actor Bochner's directorial debut. **81m/C VHS.** Jeremy Piven, Chris Young, David Spade, Sarah Trigger, Jessica Walter, Jon Favreau, Megan Ward, Jake Busey, Alex Desert; ***Cameos:*** George Clinton; ***D:*** Hart Bochner; ***W:*** Adam Leff, Zak Penn; ***M:*** Steve Vai.

The Peacekeeper 🦴🦴 **1998 (R)** Frank Cross (Lundgren) is one unlucky man. While guarding the president (Scheider), he manages to lose the briefcase containing nuclear launch codes to a terrorist group. Now, they're blackmailing the government and Cross needs to breach the terrorist's stronghold to save the day. **98m/C VHS, DVD.** *CA* Dolph Lundgren, Roy Scheider, Michael Sarrazin, Montel Williams, Monika Schnarre; ***D:*** Frederic Forestier; ***W:*** James H. Stewart, Robert Geoffrion; ***C:*** John Berrie; ***M:*** Francois Forestier.

Peacekillers 🦴½ **1971** A mean bunch of bikers visit a commune to kidnap a young woman. The gang has a big surprise in store for them when the girl escapes. **86m/C VHS.** Michael Ontkean, Clint Ritchie, Paul Krokop; ***D:*** Douglas Schwartz.

Peacemaker 🦴 **1990 (R)** Two aliens masquerading as human cops stalk each other through a major city. **90m/C VHS, DVD.** Robert Forster, Lance Edwards, Hilary Shepard, Bert Remsen, Robert Davi; ***D:*** Kevin S. Tenney; ***W:*** Kevin S. Tenney.

The Peacemaker 🦴🦴½ **1997 (R)** First-time feature director Leder teams up with fellow "ER" vet Clooney on the first theatrical release for Dreamworks SKG (the brainchild of Steven Spielberg, Jeffrey Katzenberg, and David Geffen). Clooney's Army Intel officer Lt. Col. Thomas Devoe works with White House nuke expert Dr. Julia Kelly (Kidman) when a renegade Russian colonel diverts some nuclear warheads, scheduled for dismantling, into the hands of a Bosnian diplomat (Iures) with a grudge against the West. Plenty of well-constructed action set pieces and a reasonably plausible plot overcome a lack of snappy dialogue. Extra credit for making the terrorist human instead of the usual evil caricature, and for letting the two leads work together without having to sleep together. **123m/C VHS, DVD.** George Clooney, Nicole Kidman, Armin Mueller-Stahl, Marcel Iures, Alexander Baluyev, Randall Batinkoff, Jim Haynie, Michael Boatman, Gary Werntz, Holt McCallany, Joan Copeland, Carlos Gomez, Rene Medvesek, Alexander Strobele; ***D:*** Mimi Leder; ***W:*** Michael Schiffer; ***C:*** Dietrich Lohmann; ***M:*** Hans Zimmer.

The Peacock Fan 🦴½ **1929** The Peacock Fan is protected by a deadly curse, with certain death to anyone who possesses it. **50m/B VHS.** Lucian Preval, Dorothy Dwan, Rosemary Theby, Gladden James; ***D:*** Phil Rosen; ***W:*** Arthur Hoerl; ***C:*** M.A. Anderson.

The Peanut Butter Solution 🦴🦴½ **1985 (PG)** An imaginative 11-year-old boy investigates a strange old house which is haunted by friendly ghosts who are in possession of a magic potion. **96m/C VHS.** Matthew Mackay, Siluck Saysanasy, Alison Podbrey, Michael Maillot, Griffith Brewer, Michael Hogan, Helen Hughes; ***D:*** Michael Rubbo; ***W:*** Michael Rubbo; ***M:*** Lewis Furey.

The Pearl 🦴🦴🦴 **1948** Based on a John Steinbeck story, a Mexican fisherman, living in poverty, finds a magnificent pearl and he thinks it will improve the lives of his family. He is bewildered by what this pearl really brings—liars and thieves. Simple, yet larger-than-life film, beautifully photographed; a timeless picture capturing human nature. **77m/B VHS.** *MX* Pedro Armendariz Sr., Maria Elena Marques, Fernando Wagner, Charles Rooner; ***D:*** Emilio Fernandez.

Pearl 🦴🦴½ **1978** Sweeping miniseries covers the careers and private lives of those who live and work at the naval base at Pearl Harbor, Hawaii, from right before the Japanese attack to its aftermath. **233m/C VHS.** Robert Wagner, Dennis Weaver, Lesley Ann Warren, Brian Dennehy, Max Gail, Mary Crosby, Gregg Henry, Katherine Helmond, Angie Dickinson, Tiana Alexandra, Richard Anderson, Adam Arkin, Marion Ross, Allan Miller, David Elliott; ***D:*** Hy Averback, Alexander Singer; ***W:*** Stirling Silliphant; ***C:*** Gayne Rescher; ***M:*** John Addison; ***Nar:*** Joseph Campanella. **TV**

Pearl Harbor 🦴🦴 **2001 (PG-13)** Director Bay has also done "The Rock" and "Armageddon" so he knows his way around big-budget, action-packed event movies. The problem, besides his usual difficulties with characterization and subtlety, is that we have to wade through the trite romantic triangle between U.S. Army Air aviator Hartnett, flyboy Affleck, and Navy nurse Beckinsale before we get to the well-done spectacle of the bombing on December 7, 1941, as well as the subsequent U.S. raid on Tokyo led by James Doolittle (Baldwin). It's probably quicker, and more enjoyable, to skip to the attack sequence between a rented double feature of "From Here to Eternity" and "Thirty Seconds Over Tokyo." **183m/C VHS, DVD, Wide.** *US* Ben Affleck, Josh Hartnett, Kate Beckinsale, Alec Baldwin, Cuba Gooding Jr., Dan Aykroyd, Mako, Tom Sizemore, Jon Voight, William Lee Scott, Colm Feore, Michael Shannon, Peter Firth, Jennifer Garner, Catherine Kellner, James King, Scott Wilson, William Fichtner, Ewen Bremner, Leland Orser, Graham Beckel, Tomas Arana, Guy Torry, Brian Haley, Tony Curran, Kim Coates, Glenn Morshower, John Fujioka, Tim Choate, John Diehl, Ted McGinley, Raphael Sbarge; ***D:*** Michael Bay; ***W:*** Randall Wallace; ***C:*** John Schwartzman; ***M:*** Hans Zimmer.

The Pearl of Death 🦴🦴½ **1944** Holmes and Watson investigate the theft of a precious pearl. **69m/B VHS.** Basil Rathbone, Nigel Bruce, Dennis Hoey, Miles Mander, Rondo Hatton, Evelyn Ankers; ***D:*** Roy William Neill.

Pearl of the South Pacific 🦴🦴 *South Sea Woman* **1955** A trio of adventurers destroy a quiet and peaceful island when they ransack it for pearl treasures. **85m/C VHS, DVD.** Dennis Morgan, Virginia Mayo, David Farrar; ***D:*** Allan Dwan; ***W:*** Edwin Blum; ***C:*** John Alton; ***M:*** Louis Forbes.

Peau D'Ane 🦴🦴🦴 **1971** Charming fairy tale about a widowed king in search of a beautiful wife. Gorgeous color production. In French with English subtitles. **90m/C VHS.** *FR* Catherine Deneuve, Jacques Perrin, Jean Marais, Delphine Seyrig; ***D:*** Jacques Demy.

The Pebble and the Penguin 🦴🦴½ **1994 (G)** Animated musical about a shy, romantic penguin named Hubie (Short), who must present his lady love Marina (Golden) with a beautiful pebble to win her hand forever before the villainous Drake (Curry) can claim her. Hubie is helped along the way by a cantankerous new friend (Belushi) he meets when stranded on a boat to Tahiti. Together the two race back to Antarctica fighting enemies and the elements along the way. Based on a true mating custom of the Adeli penguins, the story is satisfying for younger viewers, but does not have the animation magic of other recents films to keep adults interested. Beware of the sugary Manilow tunes. **74m/C VHS, DVD.** ***D:*** Don Bluth; ***W:*** Rachel Koretsky, Steve Whitestone; ***M:*** Barry Manilow, Bruce Sussman, Mark Watters; ***V:*** Martin Short, Annie Golden, Tim Curry, James Belushi; ***Nar:*** Shani Wallis.

Pecker 🦴🦴½ **1998 (R)** A kinder, gentler Waters? To be sure, he doesn't laugh at, but with, his working-class Baltimoreans. Still, you've got strippers (of both sexes), a "talking" statue of the Virgin Mary, and rats having sex, so this isn't a Disney film. Pecker (Furlong), who gets his name from pecking at his food, is a sweet teenager and amateur photog, who takes pictures of what's around him. His work catches the eye of New York art dealer Rorey Wheeler (Taylor), who wants to showcase the next hot trend, and Pecker becomes an overnight superstar in the fickle art world. But his celeb status has unexpected repercussions on his hometown friends and family. **87m/C VHS, DVD, Wide.** Edward Furlong, Lili Taylor, Christina Ricci, Martha Plimpton, Mary Kay Place, Brendan Sexton III, Mark Joy, Mink Stole, Bess Armstrong, Patty (Patricia Campbell) Hearst, Mary Vivian Pearce, Lauren Hulsey, Jean Schertler; ***D:*** John Waters; ***W:*** John Waters; ***C:*** Robert Stevens; ***M:*** Stewart Copeland; ***V:*** John Waters. Natl. Bd. of Review '98: Support. Actress (Ricci).

Peck's Bad Boy 🦴🦴 **1921** Impudent, precocious brat causes his parents considerable grief. Someone should lock this kid in a room with W.C. Fields or the Alien. Silent film based on the stories by George Wilbur Peck. **51m/B VHS.** Jackie Coogan, Thomas Meighan, Raymond Hatton, Wheeler Oakman, Lillian (Lillianne, Lyllian) Leighton; ***D:*** Sam Wood.

Peck's Bad Boy 🦴🦴½ **1934** A wedge is driven between a young boy and his adoptive father when the man's sister and her son move in. The aunt wants her son to be number one, causing much discord. Cooper is excellent in his role as the adopted son. **70m/B VHS.** Thomas Meighan, Jackie Cooper, Dorothy Peterson, Jackie Searl, O.P. Heggie, Harvey Clark, Lloyd Ingraham; ***D:*** Edward F. (Eddie) Cline.

Peck's Bad Boy with the Circus 🦴🦴 **1938** The circus will never be the same after the mischievous youngster and his buddies get done with it. Gilbert and Kennedy provide the high points. **67m/B VHS.** Tommy Kelly, Ann Gillis, George "Spanky" McFarland, Edgar Kennedy, Billy Gilbert; ***D:*** Edward F. (Eddie) Cline.

Pecos Bill **1986** Meet the man who used the Grand Canyon for a swimmin' hole, dug the Rio Grande, and used the Texas panhandle for a fryin' pan. From Shelly Duvall's "Tall Tales and Legends" cable series. **50m/C VHS.** Steve Guttenberg, Martin Mull, Claude Akins, Rebecca DeMornay. **CABLE**

Pecos Kid 🦴 **1935** A child has his parents killed, and grows up embittered, vengeful and thirsty for blood. **56m/B VHS.** Fred Kohler Jr.

Pedale Douce 🦴🦴½ *What a Drag* **1996** Irreverant comedy features a romantic triangle involving content gay businessman Adrien (Timsit), whose confidante is the liberal Eva (Ardant), owner of a trendy Paris eatery with an all-gay staff and predominatly gay clientele. Adrien persuades Eva to pose as his wife in order to close a deal with conservative, married banker Alexandre (Berry). Alexandre becomes enchanted with Eva and begins to pursue her, causing a comedy of errors and unexpected jealousy for Adrien, who tries to derail their affair. French with subtitles. **102m/C VHS.** *FR* Patrick Timsit, Fanny Ardant, Richard Berry, Michele Laroque, Jacques Gamblin; ***D:*** Gabriel Aghion; ***W:*** Patrick Timsit, Gabriel Aghion, Pierre Palmade; ***C:*** Fabio Conversi; ***M:*** Herve Masini, Philippe Chopin. Cesar '97: Actress (Ardant).

Peddlin' in Society 🦴🦴 *Da Bancarella a Bancarotta* **1947** A fruit vendor makes it big on the black market and lives the good life, until poor investments force her back to her old means. Strong performances by Magnani and De Sica. In Italian with English subititles. **85m/B VHS.** *IT* Anna Magnani, Vittorio De Sica, Virgilio Riento, Laura Gore; ***D:*** Gennaro Righelli.

The Pedestrian 🦴🦴🦴½ *Der Fussgaenger* **1973 (PG)** A prominent German industrialist is exposed as a Nazi officer who supervised the wholesale devastation of a Greek village during WWII. Impressive debut for director Schell, who also appears in a supporting role. **97m/C VHS.** *GE SI* Maximilian Schell, Peggy Ashcroft, Lil Dagover, Francoise Rosay, Elisabeth Bergner; ***D:*** Maximilian Schell; ***M:*** Manos Hadjidakis. Golden Globes '74: Foreign Film.

The Pee-wee Herman Show **1982** The original HBO special which introduced Pee-wee to the world. Hilarious stuff, with help from Captain Carl (Hartman), Miss Yvonne, and other assorted pals. Warning: Not to be confused with Pee-wee's children's show. **60m/C VHS.** Paul (Pee-wee Herman) Reubens, John Moody, John Paragon, Tito Larriva, Nicole Panter, Phil Hartman, Lynne Stewart, Edie McClurg; ***D:*** Marty Callner; ***W:*** Bill Steinkellner; ***M:*** Jay Condom. **CABLE**

Pee-wee's Big Adventure 🦴🦴🦴½ **1985 (PG)** Zany, endearing comedy about an adult nerd's many adventures while attempting to recover his stolen bicycle. Chock full of classic sequences, including a barroom encounter between Pee-wee and several ornery bikers, and a tour through the Alamo. A colorful, exhilarating experience. **92m/C VHS, DVD.** Paul (Pee-wee Herman) Reubens, Elizabeth (E.G. Dailey) Daily, Mark Holton, Diane Salinger, Judd Omen, Cassandra Peterson, James Brolin, Morgan Fairchild, Tony Bill, Jan Hooks, Phil Hartman, Jason Hervey, John Paragon; ***D:*** Tim Burton; ***W:*** Michael Varhol, Paul (Pee-wee Herman) Reubens, Phil Hartman; ***C:*** Victor Kemper; ***M:*** Danny Elfman.

Peephole 🦴 **1993** Prison psychiatrist is asked by the DA to keep Rick, who committed a sex crime against a little girl, in jail any way he can. So he visits Rick's prostitute girlfriend Sheena for info but instead winds up one of her clients. Meanwhile, Rick has been released and a little girl has been found dead, but nothing's that clear cut. Based on director/writer Bitterman's play. **90m/C VHS.** Patrick Husted, Rick Dean, William Dennis Hunt, Kristen Trucksess, Peter Crook; ***D:*** Shem Bitterman; ***W:*** Shem Bitterman.

Peeping Tom 🦴🦴🦴½ *Face of Fear; The Fotographer of Panic* **1960** Controversial, unsettling thriller in which psychopath Mark Lewis (Boehm) lures women before his film camera, then records their deaths at his hand. Unnerving subject matter is rendered impressively by British master Powell, who plays the part of Mark's abusie father who's shown in home movies tormenting the boy. A classic of its kind, but definitely not for everyone. Critical brickbats effectively derailed Powell's career and the original uncut version was not released until 1979. **88m/C VHS, DVD.** *GB* Karl-Heinz Boehm, Moira Shearer, Anna Massey, Maxine Audley, Esmond Knight, Shirley Anne Field, Brenda Bruce, Pamela Green, Jack Watson, Nigel Davenport, Susan Travers, Veronica Hurst, Martin Miller, Miles Malleson, Michael Powell; ***D:*** Michael Powell; ***W:*** Leo Marks; ***C:*** Otto Heller; ***M:*** Brian Easdale.

Peg o' My Heart 🦴🦴 **1922** Taylor portrays the motherless Irish charmer sent to live with her mother's English relatives during the Irish rebellion. Of course, she must overcome their upper-class English snobbery to become a part of the family. **85m/B VHS.** Laurette Taylor, Mahlon Hamilton, Russell Simpson, Ethel Grey; ***D:*** King Vidor; ***C:*** George Barnes.

Peggy Sue Got Married 🦴🦴½ **1986 (PG-13)** Uneven but entertaining comedy about an unhappily married woman seemingly unable to relive her life when she falls unconscious at a high school reunion and awakens to find herself back in school. Turner shines, but the film flags often, and Cage isn't around enough to elevate entire work. O'Connor scores, though, as a sensitive biker. Look for musician Marshall Crenshaw as part of the reunion band. **103m/C VHS, DVD.** Kathleen Turner, Nicolas Cage, Catherine Hicks, Maureen O'Sullivan, John Carradine, Helen Hunt, Lisa Jane Persky, Barbara Harris, Joan Allen, Kevin J. O'Connor, Barry Miller, Don Murray, Leon Ames, Sofia Coppola, Sachi (MacLaine) Parker, Jim Carrey; ***D:*** Francis Ford Coppola; ***W:*** Jerry Leichtling, Arlene Sarner; ***C:*** Jordan Cronenweth; ***M:*** John Barry. Natl. Bd. of Review '86: Actress (Turner).

The Peking Blond 🦴½ *The Blonde From Peking; Le Blonde de Pekin* **1968** French-fried spyfilm boasts lousy acting unencumbered by plot. Amnesiac may or may not hold secrets coveted by Americans, Russians and Chinese. **80m/C VHS.** *FR* Mireille Darc, Claudio Brook, Edward G. Robinson, Pascale Roberts; ***D:*** Nicolas Gessner; ***W:*** Nicolas Gessner, Marc Behm.

The Pelican Brief 🦴🦴½ **1993 (PG-13)** Tulane law student Darby Shaw (Roberts) writes a speculative brief on the murders of two Supreme Court justices that results in more murder and sends her running for her life. Fairly faithful to the Grisham bestseller, but the multitude of characters is confusing. Pakula adds style and star-power, but much will depend on your tolerance for paranoid political thrillers and ability to accept Roberts as the smart cookie who hits on the right answer and then manages to keep herself alive while bodies are dropping all around her. Washington is sharp as reporter Gray Grantham, the guy Roberts looks like she falls hard for (but the book's romance is nowhere to be seen). **141m/C VHS, DVD, 8mm, Wide.** Julia Roberts, Denzel Washington, John Heard, Tony Goldwyn, Stanley Tucci, James B. Sikking, William Atherton, Robert Culp, John Lithgow, Sam Shepard, Hume Cronyn; ***D:*** Alan J. Pakula; ***W:*** Alan J. Pakula; ***C:*** Stephen Goldblatt; ***M:*** James Horner.

Pelle the Conqueror 🦴🦴🦴🦴 **1988** Overpowering tale of a Swedish boy and his widower father who serve landowners in late 19th-century Denmark. Compassionate saga of human spirit contains numerous memorable sequences. Hvenegaard is wonderful as young Pelle, but von Sydow delivers what is probably his finest performance as a sympathetic weakling. American distributors foolishly trimmed the film by some 20 minutes (140 minute version). From the novel by Martin Anderson Nexo. In Swedish with English subtitles. **160m/C VHS.** *SW DK* Max von Sydow, Pelle Hvenegaard, Erik Paaske, Bjorn Granath, Axel Strobye, Astrid Villaume, Troels Asmussen, John Wittig, Anne Lise Hirsch Bjerrum, Kristina Tornqvist, Morten Jorgensen; ***D:*** Bille August; ***W:*** Bille August. Oscars '88: Foreign Film; Cannes '88: Film; Golden Globes '89: Foreign Film.

The Penalty 🦴🦴½ **1920** Legless madman Blizzard (Chaney) is after revenge on his family, doctor, and society. Chaney's properly creepy. **93m/B VHS, DVD.** Lon Chaney Sr., Claire Adams, Kenneth Harlan, Charles Clary; ***D:*** Wallace Worsley II; ***W:*** Charles Kenyon, Philip Lonergan; ***C:*** Don Short.

Penalty Phase 🦴🦴 **1986** An up-for-election judge must decide a murder case in which his future, as well as the defendant's, is in question. **94m/C VHS.** Peter Strauss, Melissa Gilbert, Jonelle Allen; ***D:*** Tony Richardson; ***M:*** Ralph Burns. **TV**

Pendulum 🦴🦴 **1969 (PG)** A police captain struggles to prove himself innocent of his wife's—and his wife's lover's—murders. Wow. **106m/C VHS.** George Peppard, Jean Seberg, Richard Kiley, Madeline Sherwood, Charles McGraw, Marj Dusay; ***D:*** George Schaefer; ***C:*** Lionel Lindon.

The Penitent 🦴🦴 **1988 (PG-13)** A remote village's annual reenactment of the crucifixion of Christ serves as the backdrop for Assante's affair with his friend's (Julia) wife. Quirky little tale that focuses a shade too much on the romantic problems of the trio rather than the intriguing religious practices going on around them. **94m/C VHS.** Raul Julia, Armand Assante, Rona Freed, Julie Carmen; ***D:*** Cliff Osmond; ***M:*** Alex North.

Penitentiary 🦴🦴½ **1979 (R)** A realistic story of a black fighter who survives his prison incarceration by winning bouts against the other prisoners. Well-made and executed, followed by two progressively worse sequels. **99m/C VHS, DVD, Wide.** Leon Isaac Kennedy, Jamaa Fanaka, Badja (Medu) Djola, Chuck "Porky" Mitchell; ***D:*** Jamaa Fanaka; ***W:*** Jamaa Fanaka; ***C:*** Marty Ollstein.

Penitentiary 2 🦴 **1982 (R)** A welterweight fighter is after the man who murdered his girlfriend, who, luckily, is incarcerated in the same prison as Our Hero. Sometimes things just work out right. **108m/C VHS, DVD, Wide.** Leon Isaac Kennedy, Mr. T, Leif Erickson, Ernie Hudson, Glynn Turman; ***D:*** Jamaa Fanaka; ***W:*** Jamaa Fanaka; ***C:*** Stephen Posey; ***M:*** Jack Wheaton.

Penitentiary 3 🦴½ **1987 (R)** Once again, Kennedy as the inmate boxer extraordinaire punches his way out of various prison battles. Another punch-drunk sequel. **91m/C VHS.** Leon Isaac Kennedy, Anthony Geary, Steve Antin, Ric Mancini, Kessler Raymond, Jim Bailey; ***D:*** Jamaa Fanaka; ***W:*** Jamaa Fanaka.

Penn and Teller Get Killed 🦴🦴 **1990 (R)** The comedy team with a cult following are pursued by an assassin through dozens of pratfalls in this dark comedy. **91m/C VHS.** Penn Jillette, Teller, Caitlin Clarke, Leonardo Cimino, David Patrick Kelly; ***D:*** Arthur Penn.

Pennies from Heaven 🦴🦴🦴½ **1981 (R)** Underrated, one-of-a-kind musical about a horny sheet-music salesman in Chicago and his escapades during the Depression. Extraordinary musical sequences have stars lip-synching to great effect. Martin is only somewhat acceptable as the hapless salesman, but Peters and Harper deliver powerful performances as the women whose lives he ruins. Walken brings down the house in a stunning song-and-dance sequence. Adapted by Dennis Potter from his British TV series. ♫The Clouds Will Soon Roll By; Did You Ever See A Dream Walking?; Yes, Yes; Pennies From Heaven; Love Is Good for Anything That Ails You; I Want to Be Bad; Let's Misbehave; Life Is Just a Bowl of Cherries; Let's Face the Music and Dance. **107m/C VHS.** Steve Martin, Bernadette Peters, Christopher Walken, Jessica Harper, Vernel Bagneris; ***D:*** Herbert Ross; ***W:*** Dennis Potter; ***C:*** Gordon Willis; ***M:*** Ralph Burns, Marvin Hamlisch. Golden Globes '82: Actress—Mus./Comedy (Peters); Natl. Soc. Film Critics '81: Cinematog.

Penny Serenade 🦴🦴🦴 **1941** Newlyweds adopt a child, but tragedy awaits. Simplistic story nonetheless proves to be a moving experience. They don't make 'em like this anymore, and no one plays Grant better than Grant. Dunne is adequate. Also available colorized. **120m/B VHS, DVD.** Cary Grant, Irene Dunne, Beulah Bondi, Edgar Buchanan, Ann Doran, Wallis (Clarke) Clark; ***D:*** George Stevens; ***W:*** Morrie Ryskind; ***C:*** Joseph Walker; ***M:*** W. Franke Harling.

The Pentagon Wars 🦴🦴½ **1998 (R)** Based on the true story of Air Force Col. James G. Burton (Elwes) whose mandate in the 1980s was to monitor weapons testing. What he discovers is the ultimate in white elephants—the Bradley Fighting Vehicle, an armored troop transport project that cost the taxpayers $14 billion over 17 years. Grammer is the scheming and pompous Army General Patridge (a composite character) who'll brook no interference. Adapted from the book "The Pentagon Wars" by James Burton. **104m/C VHS.** Cary Elwes, Kelsey Grammer, Olympia Dukakis, Richard Benjamin, John C. McGinley, Tom Wright, Clifton Powell, Richard Schiff; ***D:*** Richard Benjamin; ***W:*** Martyn Burke, Jamie Malanowski; ***C:*** Robert Yeoman; ***M:*** Joseph Vitarelli. **CABLE**

Pentathlon 🦴🦴½ **1994 (R)** East German Olympic athlete Eric Brogar (Lundgren) defects to the U.S. a year before the crash of the Berlin Wall, causing embarassed German authorities to seek revenge on him and his family. **101m/C VHS.** Dolph Lundgren, David Soul, Roger E. Mosley, Renee Coleman; ***D:*** Bruce Malmuth.

Penthouse 🦴🦴🦴 *Crooks in Clover* **1933** Baxter is a corporation lawyer who, for a change of pace, defends a gangland boss (Pendleton). His success loses him his high-society clientele but wins him Pendleton's respect and protection. But Baxter then gets involved in a further series of gang-related crimes, which nearly cost him his life. Also aiding Baxter is Loy, playing a smart-cookie gun moll, who would take her wisecracks to "The Thin Man" the following year. Good combo of melodrama, suspense, and humor. **90m/B** Warner Baxter, Myrna Loy, Nat Pendleton, C. Henry Gordon, Mae Clarke, Charles Butterworth, Phillips Holmes; ***D:*** Woodbridge S. Van Dyke.

The Penthouse 🦴🦴 **1992** Givens stars as a wealthy young woman stalked by an old boyfriend who just happens to have escaped from a mental institution. When he traps her in her home, she has two choices—love him or die. Based on the novel by Elleston Trevor. **93m/C VHS.** Robin Givens, David Hewlett, Cedric Smith, Donnelly Rhodes, Robert Guillaume; ***D:*** David Greene.

The People 🦴🦴½ **1971** A young teacher takes a job in a small town and finds out that her students have telepathic powers and other strange qualities. Adapted from a novel by Zenna Henderson. Good atmosphere, especially for a TV movie. **74m/C VHS.** Kim Darby, Dan O'Herlihy, Diane Varsi, William Shatner; ***D:*** John Korty; ***M:*** Carmine Coppola.

People Are Funny 🦴🦴 **1946** Battling radio producers vie to land the big sponsor with an original radio idea. Comedy ensues when one of them comes up with a great idea—stolen from a local station. **94m/B VHS.** Jack Haley, Rudy Vallee, Ozzie Nelson, Art Linkletter, Helen Walker; ***D:*** Sam White.

The People Next Door 🦴🦴 **1970** Seventies attempt at exposing the drug problems of suburban youth. Typical middle-class parents Wallach and Harris are horrified to discover that daughter Winters is strung out on LSD. They fight to expose the neighborhood pusher while struggling to understand their now-alien daughter. Based on J.P. Miller's television play. **93m/C VHS.** Deborah Winters, Eli Wallach, Julie Harris, Stephen McHattie, Hal Holbrook, Cloris Leachman, Nehemiah Persoff; ***D:*** David Greene; ***W:*** J(ames) P(inckney) Miller.

The People That Time Forgot 🦴🦴½ **1977 (PG)** Sequel to "The Land That Time Forgot," based on the Edgar Rice Burroughs novel. A rescue team returns to a world of prehistoric monsters to rescue a man left there after the first film. **90m/C VHS, DVD, Wide.** *GB* Doug McClure, Patrick Wayne, Sarah Douglas, Dana Gillespie, Thorley Walters, Shane Rimmer; ***D:*** Kevin Connor; ***W:*** Patrick Tilley; ***C:*** Alan Hume; ***M:*** John Scott.

The People under the Stairs 🦴🦴½ **1991 (R)** Adams is part of a scheme to rob a house in the slums owned by a mysterious couple (Robie and McGill, both of "Twin Peaks" fame). After his friends are killed off in a gruesome fashion, he discovers that the couple aren't the house's only strange inhabitants—homicidal creatures also lurk within. **102m/C VHS.** Everett McGill, Wendy Robie, Brandon Adams, Ving Rhames, A.J. (Allison Joy) Langer, Sean M. Whalen, Kelly Jo Minter; ***D:*** Wes Craven; ***W:*** Wes Craven; ***C:*** Sandi Sissel; ***M:*** Don Peake.

The People vs. Jean Harris 🦴🦴🦴 **1981** Follows the trial of Jean Harris. Shortly before this film was released, she had been convicted of murder in the death of Dr. Herman Tarnower, the author of "The Scarsdale Diet." Harris was headmistress in a private school all the while. Burstyn was nominated for an Emmy Award for best actress. **147m/C VHS.** Ellen Burstyn, Martin Balsam, Richard Dysart, Peter Coyote, Priscilla Morrill, Sarah Marshall, Millie Slavin; ***D:*** George Schaefer; ***M:*** Brad Fiedel. **TV**

The People vs. Larry Flynt 🦴🦴🦴 **1996 (R)** Controversy surrounded director Forman's look at unrepentant pornographer and Hustler Magazine publisher, Larry Flynt (Harrelson). While feminists decried what they saw as a whitewash of Flynt's career, Forman insisted his movie was about Flynt's legal battles concerning the First Amendment and freedom of speech. If you can set aside your prejudices, you'll find a master storyteller at work and some great performances from Harrelson as Flynt, Love as his drug-addicted and ultimately tragic wife Althea, and Norton as Flynt's sometimes impatient attorney, Alan Isaacman, who does get his big moment before the U.S. Supreme Court (his speeches are taken from actual court transcripts). **130m/C VHS, DVD.** Woody Harrelson, Courtney Love, Edward Norton, James Cromwell, Crispin Glover, Brett Harrelson, James Carville, Vincent Schiavelli, Richard Paul, Donna Hanover, Norm MacDonald, Miles Chapin, Jan Triska; ***Cameos:*** Larry Flynt; ***D:*** Milos Forman; ***W:*** Larry Karaszewski, Scott M. Alexander; ***C:*** Philippe Rousselot; ***M:*** Thomas Newman. Golden Globes '97: Director (Forman), Screenplay; L.A. Film Critics '96: Support. Actor (Norton); Natl. Bd. of Review '96: Support. Actor (Norton); N.Y. Film Critics '96: Support. Actress (Love).

People Who Own the Dark woof! **1975 (R)** A group of wealthy men and a coterie of call girls are having an orgy in the basement of an old home when a nuclear war breaks out. Everyone outside is blinded by the blast but some survivors manage to make their way to the house where they try to attack the inhabitants. Don't bother. **87m/C VHS.** Paul (Jacinto Molina) Naschy, Jacinto (Jack) Molina, Tony Kendall, Maria Perschy, Terry Kemper, Tom Weyland, Anita Brock, Paul Mackey; ***D:*** Armando de Ossorio; ***W:*** Armando de Ossorio.

People Will Talk 🦴🦴🦴½ **1951** Grant plays Dr. Noah Praetorius, a doctor and educator who believes that the mind is a better healer than medicine. Archenemy Cronyn is the fellow instructor with a vengeance. Sickened by Grant's goodwill and the undying attention he receives, Cronyn reports Grant's unconventional medical practices to the higher-ups in hopes of ruining his reputation as doctor/educator. Witty and satirical, this well-crafted comedy-drama is chock-full of interesting characters and finely tuned dialogue. Adapted from the play "Dr. Praetorius" by Curt Goetz. **110m/B VHS.** Cary Grant, Jeanne Crain, Finlay Currie, Hume Cronyn, Walter Slezak, Sidney Blackmer, Basil Ruysdael, Katherine Locke, Margaret Hamilton, Carleton Young, Billy House, Stuart Holmes; ***D:*** Joseph L. Mankiewicz; ***W:*** Joseph L. Mankiewicz; ***C:*** Milton Krasner.

People's Choice 🦴🦴 **1946** A small town boy suffers laryngitis, becomes a radio personality via his new huskiness, and claims he's a notorious criminal. **68m/B VHS.** Drew Kennedy, Louise Arthur, George Meeker, Rex Lease, Fred Kelsey.

Pepe Le Moko 🦴🦴🦴 **1937** An influential French film about a notorious gangster holed up in the Casbah, emerging at his own peril out of love for a beautiful woman. Stirring film established Gabin as a matinee idol. Cinematography is particularly fine too. Based upon the D'Ashelbe novel. The basis for both "Algiers," the popular Boyer-Lamarr melodrama, and the musical "The Casbah." In French with English subtitles. **87m/B VHS, 8mm.** *FR* Jean Gabin, Mireille Balin, Gabriel Gabrio, Lucas Gridoux; ***D:*** Julien Duvivier; ***W:*** Julien Duvivier, Henri Jeanson; ***C:*** Jules Kruger; ***M:*** Vincent Scotto.

Pepi, Luci, Bom and Other Girls on the Heap 🦴½ *Pepi, Luci, Bom y Otras Chicas del Monton* **1980** Almodovar's low-budget directorial debut will be of interest primarily to the director's aficionadoes. Pepi (Maura's debut role) is a Madrid heiress who gets in trouble when her neighbor, a policeman, notices her marijuana plants. She offers sexual favors in return for silence but is raped instead. Pepi later decides on revenge by seducing Luci, the policeman's wife, aided by her girlfriend, Bom. There's lots of partying, drugs, promiscuity, and violence, none of it very involving. In Spanish with English subtitles. **80m/C VHS.** *SP* Carmen Maura, Eva Siva, Olivido Gara, Felix Rotaeta; ***D:*** Pedro Almodovar; ***W:*** Pedro Almodovar.

Pepper and His Wacky Taxi 🦴½ **1972 (G)** Father of four buys a '59 Cadillac and starts a cab company. Time-capsule fun. **79m/C VHS.** John Astin, Frank Sinatra Jr., Jackie Gayle, Alan Sherman; ***D:*** Alex Grasshof.

Peppermint Soda 🦴🦴🦴 **1977** Kurys' affecting directorial debut is a semi-autobiographical tale of two teenaged sisters set in 1963 Paris. Seen through the eyes of the 13-year-old Anne, who lives with 15-year-old sister Frederique and their divorced mother, this is the year of first loves, strict teachers, dreaded family vacations, and a general awareness of growing up. Sweet look at adolescence and all its embarassing tribulations. In French with English subtitles. **97m/C VHS.** *FR* Eleonore Klarwein, Odile Michel, Anouk Ferjac, Tsilla Chelton, Coralie Clement, Marie-Veronique Maurin, Puterflam; ***D:*** Diane Kurys; ***W:*** Diane Kurys; ***C:*** Philippe Rousselot.

Perceval ✌✌ *Perceval Le Gallois* **1978** Rohmer's extremely stylized version of Chretien de Troyes unfinished 12th century poem. Young Welsh knight Perceval (Luchini) comes to a mysterious castle where he sees a vision of the Holy Grail, although he doesn't recognize it. In the morning, the castle is deserted and Perceval resumes his wanderings. When he finally realizes what he has seen, the castle has disappeared and Perceval continues with his search for the Grail. French with subtitles. **140m/C VHS, DVD.** *FR* Fabrice Luchini, Andre Dussollier, Arielle Dombasle, Marie-Christine Barrault; ***D:*** Eric Rohmer; ***W:*** Eric Rohmer; ***C:*** Nestor Almendros.

Percy & Thunder ✌✌½ **1993** Percy Banks (Jones) is an old-school boxing trainer who believes in hard work and he sees a likely prospect in Wayne "Thunder" Carter (Vance), a middleweight with a chance to be a champ. That is, if big time boxing promotion doesn't get in the way. **90m/C VHS.** James Earl Jones, Billy Dee Williams, Courtney B. Vance, Robert Wuhl, Gloria Foster, Zakes Mokae, Gloria Reuben; ***D:*** Ivan Dixon; ***W:*** Art Washington; ***M:*** Tom Scott.

The Perez Family ✌✌½ **1994 (R)** Juan Paul Perez (Molina) has spent 20 years in Cuban jails, dreaming of being reunited with wife Carmela (Huston) and daughter Teresa (Alvarado) who successfully escaped to Miami. Part of the 1980 Mariel exodus, Juan meets exuberant Dottie (Tomei), who learns families get sponsored first at the refugee camps. She convinces Juan to pose as her husband, while Carmela, who's being wooed by cop Pirelli (Palminteri), mistakenly believes Juan has literally missed the boat. Tomei's spunky (but with a garish accent), Huston's regal, Palminteri courtly, and Molina morose. The film's inconsistently whimsical, wistful, and clunky. From the novel by Christine Bell. **135m/C VHS.** Marisa Tomei, Alfred Molina, Anjelica Huston, Chazz Palminteri, Trini Alvarado, Celia Cruz; ***D:*** Mira Nair; ***W:*** Robin Swicord; ***C:*** Stuart Dryburgh; ***M:*** Alan Silvestri.

Perfect ✌½ **1985 (R)** A "Rolling Stone" reporter goes after the shallowness of the Los Angeles health club scene, and falls in love with the aerobics instructor he is going to write about. "Rolling Stone" publisher Wenner plays himself. As bad as it sounds. **120m/C VHS.** John Travolta, Jamie Lee Curtis, Carly Simon, Marilu Henner, Laraine Newman, Jann Wenner, Anne DeSalvo; ***D:*** James Bridges; ***W:*** James Bridges, Aaron Latham; ***C:*** Gordon Willis; ***M:*** Ralph Burns.

Perfect Alibi ✌✌½ **1994** Woman's suspicions of her husband's affair leads to murder. **90m/C VHS.** Teri Garr, Hector Elizondo, Kathleen Quinlan, Anne Ramsey, Rigg Kennedy; ***D:*** Kevin Meyer.

The Perfect Bride ✌½ **1991 (R)** A pretty young nurse prepares to marry her fiance, but his sister thinks she is hiding a secret. Could the bride-to-be have murder on her mind? **95m/C VHS.** John Agar, Sammi Davis, Kelly Preston, Linden Ashby, Marilyn Rockafellow, Ashley Tillman; ***D:*** Terrence O'Hara; ***M:*** Richard Bronskill. **CABLE**

Perfect Crime ✌✌ **1978** A Scotland Yard inspector must find out who has been killing off executives of a powerful world trust. **90m/C VHS.** Joseph Cotten, Anthony Steel, Janet Agren.

Perfect Crime ✌✌ **1997 (PG-13)** Navy investigator Joanne Jensen (Kapture) is assigned to look into the disappearance of a black Marine captain (Guy) and all fingers point to her white, alcoholic, ex-Marine estranged husband (Searcy). Though Jensen doesn't have a body, murder weapon, or confession, she stills decides to take the case to trial. Based on a 1989 true story. **92m/C VHS.** Mitzi Kapture, Nick Searcy, Jasmine Guy, Andrew Masset. **CABLE**

The Perfect Daughter ✌✌½ **1996 (PG-13)** A near-fatal hit-and-run accident reintroduces Alexandra Michelson (Gold) to her family—mother, Jill (Armstrong), father, Tom (Joy), and younger brother, Josh (Shulman). They'd cut the ties to the troubled drug abuser and runaway but the accident has erased Alexandra's memory of her recent life. Unfortunately for them all, Alex's sordid and dangerous past will leave neither her nor her family alone. **90m/C VHS.** Tracey Gold, Bess Armstrong, Mark Joy, Michael Shulman, Harold P. Pruett, Jay Edward Anthony, Brian Gamble; ***D:*** Harry S. Longstreet; ***W:*** Sean Silas; ***C:*** Stephen Lighthill; ***M:*** Don Davis. **CABLE**

Perfect Family ✌✌ **1992 (R)** Standard woman-and-kids-in-peril-from-psycho tale. Maggie is a recent widow with two young daughters who's looking for a nanny and a handyman. She hires brother and sister combo Janice and Alan, who, of course, are too good to be true. One is a sociopath who has murdered a family once before. Guess along with Maggie who the nut might be. **92m/C VHS.** Jennifer O'Neill, Bruce Boxleitner, Joanna Cassidy, Juliana Hansen, Shiri Appleby; ***D:*** E.W. Swackhamer; ***W:*** Christian Stoianovich, Phoebe Dorin; ***M:*** Nicholas Pike.

The Perfect Furlough ✌✌½ *Strictly for Pleasure* **1959** Paul Hodges (Curtis) is an Army corporal who wins three weeks in Paris with a movie star (Cristal) as a publicity gimmick. It's the idea of a female Army psychologist (Leigh), who thinks the guys need a morale booster, and she accompanies Hodges on his trip. Pretty bizarre, but it works. **93m/C VHS.** Tony Curtis, Janet Leigh, Keenan Wynn, Linda Cristal, Elaine Stritch, Marcel Dalio, King Donovan; ***D:*** Blake Edwards; ***W:*** Stanley Shapiro.

Perfect Game ✌✌½ **2000** Kanin Crosby (Finley) and his equally uncoordinated friends are determined to make it into the winning park league baseball team, the Bulldogs, but they're all surprised when they're chosen by the team's arrogant coach, Bobby Geiser (Duffy). Eventually the kids learn that Geiser is only playing and coaching his best players, leaving the others to warm the bench. A confrontation leads to Kanin's mom Diane (Nelson) taking over along with grumbling retired coach Billy Hicks (Asner) and the kids are on their way once again. **99m/C VHS.** Cameron Finley, Tracy Nelson, Patrick Duffy, Ed Asner; ***D:*** Dan Guntzelman; ***W:*** Dan Guntzelman; ***M:*** David Benoit. **VIDEO**

The Perfect Gift ✌✌ **1995 (R)** Suzanne decides to fulfill her boyfriend's menage-a-trois fantasy and discovers that the partner they involve just may be the woman of her dreams. **90m/C VHS.** John McCafferty, Kim (Kimberly Dawn) Dawson, Monique Parent.

Perfect Harmony ✌✌½ **1991** Racial conflict at an exclusive Southern boys school in 1950s South Carolina is overcome through friendship and the love of music in this sentimental tale. **93m/C VHS.** Peter Scolari, Darren McGavin, Catherine Mary Stewart, Moses Gunn, Cleavon Little, Justin Whalin, David Faustino, Richie Havens, Eugene Boyd; ***D:*** Will MacKenzie. **CABLE**

The Perfect Husband ✌✌ *El Marido Perfecto* **1992** Womanizing 19th-century opera singer Milan (Roth) finally falls in love—only it's to a woman he can't have. **90m/C VHS, DVD.** *SP GB* Tim Roth, Peter Firth, Aitana Sanchez-Gijon, Ana Belen; ***D:*** Beda Docampo Feijoo; ***W:*** Beda Docampo Feijoo, Juan Bautista Stagnaro; ***C:*** Frantisek Uldrich; ***M:*** Jose Nieto.

Perfect Killer ✌½ *Satanic Mechanic* **1977 (R)** Van Cleef stars as a world weary Mafia hit-man who is double-crossed by his girl, set up by his best friend, and hunted by another hired assassin. **85m/C VHS.** Lee Van Cleef, Tita Barker, John Ireland, Robert Widmark; ***D:*** Marlon Sirko.

Perfect Lies ✌½ **1997** Trying to pull her life back together, private eye Toby Merck (Friese) winds up being blackmailed by her former lover, an FBI agent, who wants her to infilitrate a drug kingpin's operation. **94m/C VHS.** Brettanya Friese. **VIDEO**

A Perfect Little Murder ✌✌½ *A Quiet Little Neighborhood, A Perfect Little Murder* **1990** Marsha is expecting an uneventful life of barbecues and Little League when her family settles down in the suburbs. But then she overhears a murder plot and someone finds out she knows. **94m/C VHS.** Teri Garr, Robert Urich, Susan Ruttan, Jeffrey Tambor, Tom Poston, Florence Stanley, Gail Edwards, Alex Rocco; ***D:*** Anson Williams; ***W:*** Mark Stein. **TV**

Perfect Love ✌✌ *Parfait Amour* **1996** Divorced Frederique (Renauld) has an affair with volatile younger man, Christophe (Renaud). When she realizes he's also seeing other women, she's angry and the tension builds as each seeks to psychologically wound the other. The only thing they still agree upon is sex but then Christophe loses control. French with subtitles. **110m/C VHS, DVD, Wide.** *FR* Isabelle Renauld, Francis Renaud, Laura Saglio; ***D:*** Catherine Breillat; ***W:*** Catherine Breillat; ***C:*** Laurent Dailland.

The Perfect Marriage ✌✌ **1946** Tired comedy about a perfect couple who decide they can't stand each other anymore after ten years of marriage. Good cast makes the most of weak script. Based on the play by Samuel Raphaelson. **88m/B VHS.** Loretta Young, David Niven, Eddie Albert, Charlie Ruggles, ZaSu Pitts, Jerome Cowan, Rita Johnson; ***D:*** Lewis Allen; ***W:*** Leonard Spigelgass.

Perfect Match ✌✌ **1988 (PG)** A timid young woman and an unambitious young man meet each other through the personal ads and then lie to each other about who they are and what they do for a living. **93m/C VHS.** Marc McClure, Jennifer Edwards, Diane Stilwell, Rob Paulsen, Karen Witter; ***D:*** Mark Deimel.

A Perfect Murder ✌✌ **1998 (R)** Steven Taylor (Douglas), a rich commodities trader about to lose his fortune, is married to young, rich, Emily (Paltrow), who's having a torrid affair with hippie artist David (Mortensen). The love triangle gets shaken when Steven devises a solution to both his wife's infidelities and his financial woes by paying David to kill Emily. Things go a little bit astray, and the psychological cat and mouse game begins. Glossy production is only eye candy while the unsympathetic characters (led by a weak protagonist in Paltrow) march to the beat of many plot points that all come together in a rushed and dull climax. Douglas, the aged yet sturdy centerpiece of the film, shines as the pompous rich dude devoid of morals, and overpowers his youthful supporting players. Inspired by Hitchcock's 1954 film, "Dial M for Murder." **105m/C VHS, DVD.** Michael Douglas, Gwyneth Paltrow, Viggo Mortensen, David Suchet, Sarita Choudhury, Constance Towers, Novella Nelson; ***D:*** Andrew Davis; ***W:*** Patrick Smith Kelly; ***C:*** Darius Wolski; ***M:*** James Newton Howard.

The Perfect Nanny ✌✌ **2000** Andrea McBride (Nelson) gets released from a mental institution and manages to get a job as a nanny to the children of a wealthy widower (Boxleitner). But Andrea expects a fairy-tale life and will do anything to make her romantic happy ending come true. **90m/C VHS, DVD.** Tracy Nelson, Bruce Boxleitner, Dana Barron, Susan Blakely, Katherine Helmond; ***D:*** Rob Malenfant; ***W:*** Victor Schiller, Christine Conradt, Richard Gilbert Hill; ***C:*** Don E. Fauntleroy; ***M:*** Richard Bowers. **VIDEO**

A Perfect Spy ✌✌½ *John Le Carre's A Perfect Spy* **1988** In this BBC miniseries, John Le Carre takes a break from the world of George Smiley to take a look at spying from a personal view. Magnus Pym (Evan) would seem to be the perfect English gentleman; having gone to the right schools he proceeds to join the covert world of espionage. But Magnus hides the secret that his estranged father is a con man par excellence and it leads him to his own betrayals. Adapted from the novel, which Le Carre is said to have drawn from his own past. On three cassettes. **360m/C VHS.** *GB* Peter Egan, Ray McAnally, Frances Tomelty, Benedict Taylor, Tim Healy; ***W:*** Arthur Hopcraft.

The Perfect Storm ✌✌½ **2000 (PG-13)** Based on the true story of the Andrea Gail, a swordfishing boat lost at sea in 1991 during a freak storm off the coast of Newfoundland—one of the biggest storms of the century. Film briefly sets up the backgrounds of the six men who will be the captain and crew on the tragic voyage, but not even Clooney and Wahlberg can compete with the watery special effects and it turns into a stereotypical disaster flick. Adapted from Sebastian Junger's bestselling nonfiction account of the tragedy. **129m/C VHS, DVD, Wide.** George Clooney, Mark Wahlberg, Mary Elizabeth Mastrantonio, John C. Reilly, Diane Lane, William Fichtner, Allen Payne, John Hawkes, Karen Allen, Bob Gunton, Cherry Jones, Christopher McDonald, Dash Mihok, Josh Hopkins, Michael Ironside, Janet Wright, Rusty Schwimmer; ***D:*** Wolfgang Petersen; ***W:*** William D. Wittliff; ***C:*** John Seale; ***M:*** James Horner.

Perfect Strangers ✌✌ *Blind Alley* **1984 (R)** Thriller develops around a murder and the child who witnesses it. The killer attempts to kidnap the young boy, but problems arise when he falls in love with the lad's mother. **90m/C VHS.** Anne Carlisle, Brad Rijn, John Woehrle, Matthew Stockley, Ann Magnuson, Stephen Lack; ***D:*** Larry Cohen; ***W:*** Larry Cohen.

Perfect Target ✌½ **1998 (R)** An ex-CIA agent is forced to work as a mercenary, protecting the president of Santa Brava. Naturally, this assignment doesn't go well and he becomes the fall guy for the politico's murder. Only he doesn't intend to stay that way. **97m/C VHS, DVD.** Daniel Bernhardt, Robert Englund, Brian Thompson, Dara Tomanovich; ***D:*** Sheldon Lettich. **VIDEO**

Perfect Tenant ✌½ **1999 (R)** Overly familiar thriller. Because of financial problems Jessica (Purl) is forced to rent out her guesthouse. She thinks she's found the perfect tenant in Bryan (Caulfield) since he's not only handsome but polite and tidy. But it's all a facade since Bryan actually wants revenge on the woman he blames for his father's suicide. **93m/C VHS, DVD, Wide.** Linda Purl, Maxwell Caulfield, Tracy Nelson, Earl Holliman, Melissa Behr, Stacy Hogue; ***D:*** Doug Campbell; ***W:*** Jim Vines, M. Todd Bonin; ***C:*** M. David Mullen. **VIDEO**

Perfect Timing woof! **1984** Softcore film about a fledgling photographer who can't turn his orgy-like photo sessions into anything profitable. **87m/C VHS.** Stephen Markle, Michelle Scarabelli; ***D:*** Rene Bonniere.

Perfect Victims ✌ *Hidden Rage* **1987 (R)** Beautiful models are being hunted by a killer, and a police officer wants to catch the psychopath before he strikes again. **100m/C VHS.** John Agar, Deborah Shelton, Clarence Williams III, Lyman Ward; ***D:*** Shuki Levy.

The Perfect Weapon ✌✌ **1991 (R)** Kenpo karate master Speakman severs family ties and wears funny belt in order to avenge underworld murder of his teacher. **85m/C VHS.** Jeff Sanders, Jeff Speakman; ***D:*** Mark DiSalle; ***W:*** David Wilson; ***C:*** Russell Carpenter; ***M:*** Gary Chang.

The Perfect Wife ✌✌ **2000** Liza (Sturges) is another of those vengeful blondes who, in the wake of *Hand That Rocks the Cradle,* thrive on video premieres. She goes after everyone she blames for her beloved brother's death, including the doctor (King) who did not save his life after an auto accident. How does she get close to the good doctor? She marries him, of course, and sets about to ruin everyone he cares for. The pace moves along briskly while production values are strictly of the made-for-TV level. **92m/C DVD.** Shannon Sturges, Perry King, Lesley-Anne Down, William R. Moses; ***D:*** Don E. Fauntleroy; ***W:*** Frank Rehwaldt, George Saunders.

Perfect Witness ✌✌½ **1989** A restaurant owner witnesses a mob slaying and resists testifying against the culprit to save his family and himself. Filmed in New York City. **104m/C VHS.** Brian Dennehy, Aidan Quinn, Stockard Channing, Laura Harrington, Joe Grifasi; ***D:*** Robert Mandel; ***M:*** Brad Fiedel. **CABLE**

A Perfect World ½ 1993 (PG-13) Butch Haynes (Costner) is an escaped con who takes eight-year-old fatherless Phillip (Lowther) as a hostage in 1963 Texas and is pursued by Texas Ranger Red Garnett (Eastwood). Butch is a bad guy and the film never tries to make him heroic but it also allows him to grow attached to Phillip and acknowledge him as a surrogate son. Costner gives a quiet and strong performance and the remarkable Lowther never goes wrong in his role as the needy little boy. Eastwood's role is strictly secondary as the well tested lawman who understands justice without seeking vengeance. Somewhat draggy—especially the protracted final scene. **138m/C VHS, Wide.** Kevin Costner, T.J. Lowther, Clint Eastwood, Laura Dern, Keith Szarabajka, Leo Burmester, Paul Hewitt, Bradley Whitford, Ray McKinnon, Wayne Dehart, Jennifer Griffin, Linda Hart; ***D:*** Clint Eastwood; ***W:*** John Lee Hancock; ***C:*** Jack N. Green; ***M:*** Lennie Niehaus.

Perfectly Normal 1991 (R) Two friends end up in hilarious situations when one opens an eccentric restaurant with a mysterious, newly found fortune. **106m/C VHS.** Michael Riley, Robbie Coltrane, Kenneth Welsh, Eugene Lipinski; ***D:*** Yves Simoneau; ***W:*** Eugene Lipinski, Paul Quarrington.

Performance ½ 1970 (R) Grim and unsettling psychological account of a criminal who hides out in a bizarre house occupied by a peculiar rock star and his two female companions. Entire cast scores high marks, with Pallenberg especially compelling as a somewhat mysterious and attractive housemate to mincing Jagger. A cult favorite, with music by Nitzsche under the direction of Randy Newman. **104m/C VHS.** *GB* James Fox, Mick Jagger, Anita Pallenberg, Michele Breton, Ann Sidney, John Bindon, Stanley Meadows, Allan Cuthbertson, Antony Morton; ***D:*** Donald Cammell, Nicolas Roeg; ***W:*** Donald Cammell; ***C:*** Nicolas Roeg; ***M:*** Jack Nitzsche.

Perfume ½ 1991 Five beautiful, black childhood friends join together to conquer the cosmetics industry with their new perfume, Sassy. But can they resist all the temptations success brings and keep both their company and their friendship? **98m/C VHS.** Cheryl Francis Harrington, Kathleen Bradley Overton, Shy Jefferson, Lynn Marlin, Eugina Wright, Ted Lange; ***D:*** Roland S. Jefferson.

Perfume 2001 (R) Rymer worked from an outline rather than a complete script and had his actors improvise this satire on the fashion world but the film fumbles on fuzzy plots and characters. English photog Anthony (Harris) deals with professional and personal crises; gay fashion mogul Lorenzo (Sorvino) learns he has terminal cancer and draws closer to his family and lover; magazine editor Janice (Baron) is suddenly confronted by the daughter (Williams) she hasn't seen in years; and various designers (Epps, Wilson, Mann) have various problems. **106m/C VHS, DVD, Wide.** Rita Wilson, Leslie Mann, Jared Harris, Michelle Forbes, Paul Sorvino, Peter Gallagher, Sonia Braga, Omar Epps, Jeff Goldblum, Harris Yulin, Michelle Williams, Joanne Baron, Mariel Hemingway, Carmen Electra, Coolio, Harry Hamlin, Mariska Hargitay, Gaby Hoffman, Robert Joy, Chris Sarandon, Angela Bettis, Kyle MacLachlan; ***D:*** Michael Rymer; ***W:*** Michael Rymer, L.M. Kit Carson; ***C:*** Rex Nicholson; ***M:*** Adam Plack.

Perfumed Nightmare 1989 Unique, appealing fable about a Filipino youth who discovers the drawbacks of social and cultural progress when he moves to Paris. Director Tahimik also plays the lead role. Imaginative, yet remarkably economical, this film was produced for $10,000 and received the International Critics Award at the Berlin Film Festival. In Tagalog with English dialogue and subtitles. **93m/C VHS.** *PH* Kidlat Tahimik, Dolores Santamaria, Georgette Baudry, Katrin Muller, Harmut Lerch; ***D:*** Kidlat Tahimik.

Peril ½ *Peril en la Demeure* 1985 (R) From the novel "Sur La Terre Comme Au Ciel" by Rene Belletto. Deals with a music teacher's infiltration into a wealthy family and the sexually motivated, back-stabbing murder plots that ensue. DeVille does poorly with avant-garde technique. In French with English subtitles. **100m/C VHS.** *FR* Michel Piccoli, Christophe MaLavoy, Richard Bohringer, Nicole Garcia, Anais Jeanneret; ***D:*** Michel DeVille; ***W:*** Michel DeVille. Cesar '86: Director (DeVille).

Peril 2000 (R) Out-of-control plot dooms this women-in-peril saga. Terry (Fairchild) and her semi-disabled hubby Scott (James) are facing financial ruin but have one chance to save themselves. Unfortunately, Scott falls and gets trapped in a storm drain and when Terry goes for help, she gets captured by an escaped mental patient (Pare) who uses her as a hostage against the cops. Oh, and the water is rising in the storm drain, so Scott's gonna drown unless Terry can get free. Very dumb. **90m/C VHS, DVD.** Morgan Fairchild, Michael Pare, John James, Steve Eastin, Thom Christopher; ***D:*** David Giancola. **VIDEO**

The Perils of Gwendoline ½ *Gwendoline; The Perils of Gwendoline in the Land of the Yik-Yak* 1984 (R) A young woman leaves a convent to search for her long-lost father, in this adaptation of a much funnier French comic strip of the same name. What ends up on the screen is merely a very silly rip-off of the successful "Raiders of the Lost Ark," and of primary interest for its numerous scenes of amply endowed Kitaen in the buff. **88m/C VHS.** *FR* Tawny Kitaen, Brent Huff, Zabou, Bernadette LaFont, Jean Rougerie; ***D:*** Just Jaeckin; ***M:*** Pierre Bachelet.

The Perils of Pauline ½ 1934 All 12 episodes of this classic melodrama/adventure serial in one package, featuring dastardly villains, cliff-hanging predicaments, and worldwide chases. **238m/B VHS.** Evalyn Knapp, Robert "Tex" Allen, James Durkin, Sonny Ray, Pat O'Malley; ***D:*** Ray Taylor.

The Perils of Pauline 1947 A musical biography of Pearl White, the reigning belle of silent movie serials. Look for lots of silent film stars. **96m/C VHS, DVD.** Betty Hutton, John Lund, Constance Collier, William Demarest, Billy DeWolfe; ***D:*** George Marshall; ***C:*** Ray Rennahan; ***M:*** Frank Loesser.

Perils of the Darkest Jungle ½ *The Tiger Woman; Jungle Gold* 1944 Tiger Woman battles money-mad oil profiteers to protect her tribe. This 12-episode serial comes on two tapes. **180m/B VHS.** Linda Stirling, Allan "Rocky" Lane, Duncan Renaldo, George Lewis; ***D:*** Spencer Gordon Bennet.

Period of Adjustment 1962 Heartwarming comedy about young newlyweds adjusting to the pressures of domestic life and trying to help the troubled marriage of an older couple. Based on the play by Tennessee Williams. **112m/B VHS.** Anthony (Tony) Franciosa, Jane Fonda, Jim Hutton, Lois Nettleton, John McGiver, Jack Albertson; ***D:*** George Roy Hill; ***W:*** Isobel Lennart.

Permanent Midnight ½ 1998 (R) Stiller stars as TV writer Jerry Stahl in this film version of his 1995 autobiography, which follows his plunge from a guy who has it all to a loser junkie who's as unlikable as this movie itself. At its real-life peak, Stahl's heroine habit reached $6,000 a week. There are some great flashes of dark humor—Jerry is obsessed with exercising and eating right even while pumping himself full of drugs—and some truly horrific sequences (at one low point, Stahl both scores and shoots up with his baby daughter by his side). The problem is that we don't care. Stiller's comic timing makes most of the bleak jokes work, and it's the only thing that makes the movie bearable; however, his brooding performance (possibly due to writer/director Veloz) lacks any charisma. Watch for Stahl himself as a pessimistic doctor at a methadone clinic. **85m/C VHS, DVD, Wide.** Ben Stiller, Elizabeth Hurley, Maria Bello, Owen C. Wilson, Lourdes Benedicto, Peter Greene, Cheryl Ladd, Fred Willard, Charles Fleischer, Janeane Garofalo, Jerry Stahl; ***D:*** David Veloz; ***W:*** David Veloz; ***C:*** Robert Yeoman; ***M:*** Daniel Licht.

Permanent Record ½ 1988 (PG-13) Hyper-sincere drama about a popular high schooler's suicide and the emotional reactions of those he left behind. Great performance from Reeves. **92m/C VHS.** Alan Boyce, Keanu Reeves, Michelle Meyrink, Jennifer Rubin, Pamela Gidley, Michael Elgart, Richard Bradford, Barry Corbin, Kathy Baker, Dakin Matthews; ***D:*** Marisa Silver; ***W:*** Jarre Fees, Alice Liddle, Larry Ketron; ***C:*** Frederick Elmes; ***M:*** Joe Strummer.

Permanent Vacation ½ 1984 A young man disenchanted with New York City decides to escape to Europe to forget about his problems. **80m/C VHS.** John Lurie, Chris Parker; ***D:*** Jim Jarmusch; ***W:*** Jim Jarmusch; ***M:*** John Lurie.

Permission To Kill ½ 1975 (PG) Grim spy drama features Bogard as an agent determined to prevent the return of a third-world radical to a totalitarian state. **96m/C VHS.** *GB* Dirk Bogarde, Ava Gardner, Timothy Dalton, Frederic Forrest; ***D:*** Cyril Frankel; ***C:*** Frederick A. (Freddie) Young; ***M:*** Richard Rodney Bennett.

Perpetrators of the Crime 1998 (R) Dumb criminals—dumb crime. Jones (Burgess) comes up with a kidnapping scheme but his sidekicks, Phil (Strong) and Ed (Devine), kidnap the wrong girl (Spelling) and take her to the wrong hideout. That makes things difficult when Jones tries to shake down their mark (Davis) for the ransom. **85m/C VHS, DVD.** *CA* Danny Strong, Tori Spelling, Mark Burgess, Sean Devine, William B. Davis; ***D:*** John Hamilton; ***W:*** Max Sartor.

Perry Mason Returns 1985 Perry Mason returns to solve another baffling mystery. This time he must help his longtime assistant, Della Street, when she is accused of killing her new employer. **95m/C VHS.** Raymond Burr, Barbara Hale, William Katt, Patrick O'Neal, Richard Anderson, Cassie Yates, Al Freeman Jr.; ***D:*** Ron Satlof.

Perry Mason: The Case of the Lost Love ½ 1987 Super-lawyer Mason defends the husband of a former lover he hadn't seen in 30 years. The solution to the mystery may catch viewer off guard. **98m/C VHS.** Raymond Burr, Barbara Hale, William Katt, Jean Simmons, Gene Barry, Robert Walden, Stephen Elliott, Robert Mandan, David Ogden Stiers; ***D:*** Ron Satlof. **TV**

Persona 1966 A famous actress turns mute and is treated by a talkative nurse at a secluded cottage. As their relationship turns increasingly tense, the women's personalitites begin to merge. Memorable, unnerving—and atypically avant garde—fare from cinema giant Bergman. First of several collaborations between the director and leading lady Ullman. In Swedish with English subtitles. **100m/C VHS, 8mm.** *SW* Bibi Andersson, Liv Ullmann, Gunnar Bjornstrand, Margareta Krook, Jorgen Lindstrom; ***D:*** Ingmar Bergman; ***W:*** Ingmar Bergman; ***C:*** Sven Nykvist; ***M:*** Lars Johan Werle. Natl. Soc. Film Critics '67: Actress (Andersson), Director (Bergman), Film.

Personal Best 1982 (R) Lesbian lovers compete while training for the 1990 Olympics. Provocative fare often goes where few films have gone before, but overly stylized direction occasionally overwhelms characterizations. It gleefully exploits locker-room nudity, with Hemingway in her pre-implant days. Still, an ambitious, often accomplished production. Towne's directorial debut. **126m/C VHS.** Mariel Hemingway, Scott Glenn, Patrice Donnelly; ***D:*** Robert Towne; ***W:*** Robert Towne; ***C:*** Michael Chapman; ***M:*** Jack Nitzsche.

Personal Exemptions ½ 1988 (PG) In this stock comedy a frenzied IRS auditor learns that her daughter is smuggling aliens into the country, her son is brokering with some businessmen she's targeted for tax fraud, and her husband is having an affair with a high-school girl. **100m/C VHS.** Nanette Fabray, John Cotton; ***D:*** Peter Rowe.

Personal Property ½ *The Man in Possession* 1937 Taylor tries every trick in the book to win Harlow over in this MGM romantic fluff. Not that big on laughs, but plenty of good shots of Harlow and a beefcake scene of Taylor in a bathtub, who was the darling of the MGM lot and worked with every leading lady. This was the only film Harlow and Taylor made together. Remake of the 1931 film "The Man in Possession." **84m/B VHS.** Robert Taylor, Jean Harlow, Reginald Owen, Una O'Connor, E.E. Clive, Henrietta Crosman, Cora Witherspoon; ***D:*** Woodbridge S. Van Dyke; ***W:*** Hugh Mills.

Personal Services ½ 1987 (R) A bawdy satire loosely based on the life and times of Britain's modern-day madam, Cynthia Payne, and her rise to fame in the world of prostitution. Payne's earlier years were featured in the film "Wish You Were Here." **104m/C VHS.** *GB* Julie Walters, Alec McCowen, Shirley Stelfox, Tim Woodward, Dave Atkins, Danny Schiller, Victoria Hardcastle; ***D:*** Terry Jones; ***W:*** David Leland; ***C:*** Roger Deakins; ***M:*** John Du Prez.

The Personals ½ 1983 (PG) A recently divorced young man takes out a personal ad in a newspaper to find the woman of his dreams. But it isn't quite that simple in this independent comedy shot entirely in Minneapolis. **90m/C VHS.** Bill Schoppert, Karen Landry, Paul Eiding, Michael Laskin, Vickie Dakil; ***D:*** Peter Markle.

Personals 1990 Chilling drama that casts O'Neill as an unnoticed librarian, until she begins to meet (and kill) the men who answer her ads. Zimbalist is a widow who is determined to learn the truth. **93m/C VHS.** Stephanie Zimbalist, Jennifer O'Neill, Robin Thomas, Clark Johnson, Gina Gallego, Rosemary Dunsmore, Colm Feore; ***D:*** Steven Hilliard Stern. **TV**

The Personals ½ 1998 Fed up with her boring love life, Dr. Du Jia-zhen (Liu) takes out a personal ad and gets 100 responses. The body of the film is made up of the interviews she conducts with these men—well, most of them are men. Other filmmakers have made more of the same premise, but director Kuo-fu Chen keeps his camera squarely on his characters. The Taiwan setting is a bit exotic. Liu's performance is a model of restraint. Mandarin with subtitles. **104m/C VHS, DVD, Wide.** *TW* Rene Liu, Wu Bai; ***D:*** Kuo-fu Chen, Shih-chich Chen; ***W:*** Kuo-fu Chen, Shih-chich Chen; ***C:*** Nan-hong Ho.

Personals ½ 2000 New Yorker Keith (Yoba) is juggling two girlfriends and a writing job and sucking at all three endeavors. So it's no big surprise when he loses it all. Keith then decides to write an expose of personal ads but finds out more about himself then the women who answer his ad. Entertaining debut for filmmaker Sargent. **91m/C VHS, DVD.** Malik Yoba, Stacey Dash, Sheryl Lee Ralph, Rhonda Ross Kendrick, Monteria Ivey; ***D:*** Mike Sargent; ***W:*** Mike Sargent. **VIDEO**

Persons Unknown 1996 Melodramatic noir with a decent cast. Disgraced ex-cop Jim Holland (Mantegna) now runs a security firm in Long Beach, CA. He has a one-nighter with foxy Amanda (Lynch) and wakes up to discover she's stolen confidential files. So, with colleague Cake (Walsh), he tracks Amanda down and discovers that she and her wheelchair-bound sister, Molly (Watts), are planning a robbery that involves ripping off Columbian drug lords. But, as usual, nothing works out as intended. **99m/C VHS.** Joe Mantegna, Kelly Lynch, J.T. Walsh, Naomi Watts, Xander Berkeley, Jon Favreau, Channon Roe, Michael Nicolosi; ***D:*** George Hickenlooper; ***W:*** Craig Smith; ***C:*** Richard Crudo; ***M:*** Ed Tomney.

Persuasion ½ 1971 Practical Anne Elliott is always at the beck-and-call of her snobbish and helpless family. She even turned down a marriage proposal for their sake. Now Captain Wentworth has come back into Anne's life and she has a second chance. But will she be strong enough to take it? Made for BBC TV. **225m/C VHS.** *GB* Ann(e) Firbank, Basil Dignam, Valerie Gearon, Marian Spence, Charlotte Mitchell. **TV**

Persuasion ½ 1995 (PG) Charming British costume romance, based on Jane Austen's final novel, deals with the constricted life of practical, plain, put-upon Anne Elliot (Root). Thanks to well-meaning interference, Anne refused the marriage proposal of the manly Frederick Wentworth (Hinds) and instead stuck by her snobbish and demanding family. Eight years later, Anne is given a second chance at love when the now-wealthy

Wentworth happens back into her life—but she still has her obnoxious relations to contend with. It's wonderful to see Anne blossom from mouse to lioness although the swirl of supporting players (and settings) provide some confusion. **104m/C VHS, DVD.** *GB* Amanda Root, Ciaran Hinds, Susan Fleetwood, Corin Redgrave, Fiona Shaw, John Woodvine, Phoebe Nicholls, Samuel West, Sophie Thompson, Judy Cornwell, Felicity Dean, Simon Russell Beale, Victoria Hamilton, Emma Roberts; ***D:*** Roger Mitchell; ***W:*** Nick Dear, Jeremy Sams; ***C:*** John Daly; ***M:*** Jeremy Sams.

The Perverse Countess 🦴 *La Comtesse Perverse* **1973** Romay is a bored tourist who spends a free weekend on a fling with Woods, who procures human flesh for the cannibalistic Count and Countess Zaroff (Vernon and Arno). Romay accompanies her lover to the haunted castle on a delivery, not realizing she is the package. When the Countess sees what a succulent bon-bon Romay is, she faces difficult choices. Subtitled in English. **86m/C VHS.** *FR* Lina Romay, Robert Woods, Howard Vernon, Alice Arno, Caroline Riviere; ***D:*** Jess (Jesus) Franco.

The Pest 🦴 **1996 (PG-13)** Movie certainly lives up to its title. A hyperkinetic Leguizamo stars as Pestario (Pest) Vargas, a small-time Miami con man, who owes 50 large to the mob. Eccentric German businessman Gustav Shank (Jones) offers the money to Pest—the catch being that Pest will become the human prey for Gustav's private island hunting party. You'll be rooting for the hunter. **85m/C VHS, DVD.** John Leguizamo, Jeffrey Jones, Edoardo Ballerini, Freddy Rodriguez, Joe Morton, Charles Hallahan, Tammy Townsend, Aries Spears; ***D:*** Paul Miller; ***W:*** David Bar Katz; ***C:*** Roy Wagner; ***M:*** Kevin Kiner.

Pet Sematary 🦴🦴 **1989 (R)** A quirky adaptation of Stephen King's best-seller about a certain patch of woods in the Maine wilderness that rejuvenates the dead, and how a newly located college MD eventually uses it to restore his dead son. Mildly creepy. **103m/C VHS, DVD, Wide.** Dale Midkiff, Fred Gwynne, Denise Crosby, Blaze Berdahl, Brad Greenquist, Miko Hughes, Stephen King; ***D:*** Mary Lambert; ***W:*** Stephen King; ***C:*** Peter Stein; ***M:*** Elliot Goldenthal.

Pet Sematary 2 🦴½ **1992 (R)** Lame sequel to original Stephen King flick. After seeing his mother electrocuted, a teen and his veterinarian father move to the Maine town where the legendary Pet Sematary is located. Horror begins when the boy's friend's dog is shot by his stepfather, and the boys bury the dog in the "sematary." King wasn't involved with this film, so the story isn't very coherent, but shock value and special effects are great. Not recommended for those with a weak stomach. **102m/C VHS, DVD, Wide.** Anthony Edwards, Edward Furlong, Clancy Brown, Jared Rushton, Darlanne Fluegel, Lisa Waltz, Jason McGuire, Sarah Trigger; ***D:*** Mary Lambert; ***W:*** Richard Outten; ***C:*** Russell Carpenter.

Pet Shop 🦴🦴½ **1994 (PG)** Pair of evil, galaxy-travelling aliens take over the local pet store in a remote desert town and plan to abduct all the kids by bewitching them with a spaceship full of intergalactic creatures. Only Dena (aided by the good alien furballs) can stop the bad guys from making space pets of the earthlings. **88m/C VHS.** Leigh Ann Orsi, Spencer Vrooman, David Wagner, Joanne Baron, Jane Morris, Terry Kiser, Jeff Michalski, Shashawnee Hall, Sabrina Wiener, Cody Burger; ***D:*** Hope Perello; ***W:*** Mark Goldstein, Greg Suddeth, Brent Friedman; ***M:*** Reg Powell.

Pete Kelly's Blues 🦴🦴 **1955** A jazz musician in a Kansas City speakeasy is forced to stand up against a brutal racketeer. The melodramatic plot is brightened by a nonstop flow of jazz tunes sung by Lee and Fitzgerald and played by an all-star lineup that includes Dick Cathcart, Matty Matlock, Eddie Miller and George Van Eps. ♫Sugar; Sombody Loves Me; Bye Bye Blackbird; What Can I Say After I Say I'm Sorry?; He Needs Me; Sing a Rainbow; Pete Kelly's Blues. **96m/C VHS, Wide.** Jack Webb, Janet Leigh, Edmond O'Brien, Lee Marvin, Martin Milner, Peggy Lee, Ella Fitzgerald, Jayne Mansfield; ***D:*** Jack Webb.

Pete 'n' Tillie 🦴🦴½ **1972 (PG)** Amiable comedy turns to less appealing melodrama as couple meets, marries, and endures tragedy. Film contributes little to director Ritt's hitt-and-miss reputation, but Matthau and Burnett shine in leads. Adapted by Julius J. Epstein from a Peter de Vries' story. **100m/C VHS.** Walter Matthau, Carol Burnett, Geraldine Page, Barry Nelson, Rene Auberjonois, Lee Montgomery, Henry Jones, Kent Smith; ***D:*** Martin Ritt; ***W:*** Julius J. Epstein; ***C:*** John A. Alonzo; ***M:*** John Williams. British Acad. '73: Actor (Matthau).

Peter and Paul 🦴🦴½ **1981** TV miniseries follows the lives of the two apostles, Peter (Foxworth) and Paul (Hopkins), from the Crucifixion through the next three decades as they travel spreading the word of Christ, until both are executed in Rome. Tries valiantly, but falls a bit short. **194m/C VHS.** Anthony Hopkins, Robert Foxworth, Eddie Albert, Raymond Burr, Jose Ferrer, Jon Finch, David Gwillim, Herbert Lom, Jean Peters; ***D:*** Robert Day; ***W:*** Christopher Knopf.

Peter Gunn 🦴🦴 **1989** Detective Peter Gunn returns, only to find himself being hunted by both the mob and the Feds. A TV movie reprise of the vintage series that has none of the original cast members. **97m/C VHS.** Peter Strauss, Barbara Williams, Jennifer Edwards, Charles Cioffi, Pearl Bailey, Peter Jurasik, David Rappaport; ***D:*** Blake Edwards; ***M:*** Henry Mancini. **TV**

Peter Lundy and the Medicine Hat Stallion 🦴🦴½ *The Medicine Hat Stallion; Pony Express* **1977** A teenaged Pony Express rider must outrun the Indians and battle the elements in order to carry mail from the Nebraska Territory to the West Coast. Good family entertainment. **85m/C VHS.** Leif Garrett, Mitchell Ryan, Bibi Besch, John Quade, Milo O'Shea; ***D:*** Michael O'Herlihy. **TV**

Peter Pan 🦴🦴½ **1924** The first film adaptation of James M. Barrie's children's classic stars Bronson as the title character (in a performance endorsed by Barrie himself) that of an adventurous boy who refuses to grow up. Torrence is a scene-stealer as Captain Hook. A little on the stagy side but it still shines. **102m/B VHS, DVD.** Betty Bronson, Ernest Torrence, Mary Brian, Virginia Brown Faire, Anna May Wong, Esther Ralston, Cyril Chadwick, Philippe De Lacey, Jack Murphy; ***D:*** Herbert Brenon; ***W:*** Willis Goldbeck; ***C:*** James Wong Howe; ***M:*** Philip Carli. Natl. Film Reg. '00.

Peter Pan 🦴🦴🦴 **1953 (G)** Disney classic about a boy who never wants to grow up. Based on J.M. Barrie's book and play. Still stands head and shoulders above any recent competition in providing fun family entertainment. Terrific animation and lovely hummable music. **76m/C VHS, DVD.** ***D:*** Hamilton Luske; ***W:*** Milt Banta, William Cottrell, Winston Hibler, Bill Peet, Erdman Penner, Joe Rinaldi, Ted Sears, Ralph Wright; ***M:*** Edward Plumb, Oliver Wallace; ***V:*** Bobby Driscoll, Kathryn Beaumont, Hans Conried, Heather Angel, Candy Candido, Bill Thompson; ***Nar:*** Tom Conway.

Peter Pan 🦴🦴🦴½ **1960** A TV classic, this videotape of a performance of the 1954 Broadway musical adapted from the J.M. Barrie classic features Mary Martin in one of her most famous incarnations, as the adolescent Peter Pan. Songs include "I'm Flying," "Neverland," and "I Won't Grow Up." **100m/C VHS, DVD.** Mary Martin, Cyril Ritchard, Sondra Lee, Heather Halliday, Luke Halpin; ***D:*** Vincent J. Donehue. **TV**

Peter the First: Part 1 🦴🦴 **1937** The first half of Petrov's Soviet epic about the early years of Tsar Peter I's reign. Lavish, in Russian with English subtitles. **95m/B VHS.** *RU* ***D:*** Vladimir Petrov.

Peter the First: Part 2 🦴🦴 *The Conquests of Peter the Great* **1938** The second half of Petrov's epic, covering the triumphs and final years of the famous Tsar. In Russian with English subtitles. **104m/B VHS.** *RU* ***D:*** Vladimir Petrov.

Peter the Great 🦴🦴🦴 **1986** Dry but eye-pleasing TV miniseries follows the life of Russia's colorful, very tall ruler, from childhood on. Much of the interesting cast is wasted in tiny roles. **371m/C VHS.** Maximilian Schell, Laurence Olivier, Omar Sharif, Vanessa Redgrave, Ursula Andress. **TV**

Peter's Friends 🦴🦴½ **1992 (R)** Peter has recently inherited a grand manor house located outside London and invites some chums to celebrate a New Year's Eve weekend, ten years after they've been at university together. So begins another nostalgic trip down memory lane ala "The Big Chill," but unlike other clones, this one can stand on its own, with a lightweight and sly script by talented comedienne Rudner (in her film debut) and her husband Bergman. If the script sometimes falls a little flat, the fine cast will make up for it. Thompson's mother, actress Law, plays the housekeeper. **102m/C VHS.** *GB* Kenneth Branagh, Rita Rudner, Emma Thompson, Stephen Fry, Hugh Laurie, Imelda Staunton, Alphonsia Emmanuel, Tony Slattery, Alex Lowe, Alex Scott, Phyllida Law, Richard Briers; ***D:*** Kenneth Branagh; ***W:*** Rita Rudner, Martin Bergman; ***M:*** Jacques Offenbach.

Pete's Dragon 🦴🦴½ **1977 (G)** Elliot, an enormous, bumbling dragon with a penchant for clumsy heroics, becomes friends with poor orphan Pete. Combines brilliant animation with the talents of live actors for an interesting effect. **128m/C VHS, DVD, Wide.** Helen Reddy, Shelley Winters, Mickey Rooney, Jim Dale, Red Buttons, Sean Marshall, Jim Backus, Jeff Conaway; ***D:*** Don Chaffey; ***W:*** Malcolm Marmorstein; ***C:*** Frank Phillips; ***M:*** Irwin Kostal; ***V:*** Charlie Callas.

Petit Con 🦴🦴½ **1984 (R)** A live-action version of the popular French comic strip wherein a young rebel drops out of society to live with aging hippies. With English subtitles. **90m/C VHS.** *FR* Guy Marchand, Michel Choupon, Caroline Cellier, Bernard Brieux, Soudad Amidou; ***D:*** Gerard Lauzier.

Petits Freres 🦴🦴½ *Little Fellas* **2000** Troubled 13-year-old Talia (Touly) takes her pitbull Kim and runs away from her brutal stepfather. She hangs out in the projects with a group of boys her own age whom she warily befriends, only to be victimized when they steal and sell Kim to a dogfighting ring. Despite their denials, Talia knows what they did, even when they promise to help her rescue the dog. Kids, who are non-professionals, do fine but the story meanders it's way to a predictable ending. French with subtitles. **92m/C VHS, DVD.** *FR* Stephanie Touly, Ilies Sefraoui, Mustapha Goumane, Nassim Izem, Rachid Mansouri, Gerald Dantsoff; ***D:*** Jacques Doillon; ***W:*** Jacques Doillon; ***C:*** Manuel Teran.

Petrified Forest 🦴🦴🦴 **1936** Writer Alan Squier (Howard) is hitchhiking through the Arizona desert when he stops at a run-down gas station/diner run by Maple (Hall) and his daughter Gabrielle (Davis). Once an idealist, Alan now feels he has little to live for, which may explain his attitude when the diner patrons and employees are held hostage by on the lam gangster Duke Mantee (Bogart) and his boys. Often gripping, with memorable performances from Davis, Howard, and Bogart. Based on the play by Robert Sherwood with Howard and Bogart recreating their stage roles. **83m/B VHS.** Bette Davis, Leslie Howard, Humphrey Bogart, Dick Foran, Charley Grapewin, Porter Hall, Genevieve Tobin, Joseph (Joe) Sawyer; ***D:*** Archie Mayo; ***W:*** Delmer Daves; ***C:*** Sol Polito; ***M:*** Bernhard Kaun.

Petulia 🦴🦴🦴🦴 **1968 (R)** Overlooked, offbeat drama about a flighty woman who spites her husband by dallying with a sensitive, recently divorced surgeon. Classic '60s document and cult favorite offers great performance from the appealing Christie, with Scott fine as the vulnerable surgeon. On-screen performances by the Grateful Dead and Big Brother. Among idiosyncratic director Lester's best. From the novel "Me and the Arch Kook Petulia" by John Haase. **105m/C VHS.** George C. Scott, Richard Chamberlain, Julie Christie, Shirley Knight, Arthur Hill, Joseph Cotten, Pippa Scott, Richard Dysart, Kathleen Widdoes, Austin Pendleton, Rene Auberjonois; ***D:*** Richard Lester; ***W:*** Lawrence B. Marcus; ***C:*** Nicolas Roeg; ***M:*** John Barry.

Peyton Place 🦴🦴🦴 **1957** Passion, scandal, and deception in a small New England town set the standard for passion, scandal, and deception in soap operadom. Shot on location in Camden, Maine. Performances and themes now seem dated, but produced a blockbuster in its time. Adapted from Grace Metalious' popular novel and followed by "Return to Peyton Place." **157m/C VHS, Wide.** Lana Turner, Hope Lange, Lee Philips, Lloyd Nolan, Diane Varsi, Lorne Greene, Russ Tamblyn, Arthur Kennedy, Terry Moore, Barry Coe, David Nelson, Betty Field, Mildred Dunnock, Leon Ames, Alan Reed Jr.; ***D:*** Mark Robson; ***W:*** John Michael Hayes; ***C:*** William Mellor; ***M:*** Franz Waxman.

Phaedra 🦴🦴 **1961** Loose and updated adaptation of Euripides' "Hipploytus." Mercouri, the second wife of a rich Greek shipping magnate, is dispatched to London to convince her husband's adult son (Perkins) to come home to Greece. Mercouri and Perkins immediately begin a steamy affair but their return home brings problems for all. Dubbed. **116m/B VHS.** *GR FR* Melina Mercouri, Anthony Perkins, Raf Vallone, Elizabeth Ercy; ***Cameos:*** Jules Dassin; ***D:*** Jules Dassin; ***W:*** Jules Dassin, Margarita Liberaki; ***M:*** Mikis Theodorakis.

Phantasm 🦴🦴½ *The Never Dead* **1979 (R)** A small-budgeted, hallucinatory horror fantasy about two parentless brothers who discover weird goings-on at the local funeral parlor, including the infamous airborne, brain-chewing chrome ball. Creepy, unpredictable nightmare fashioned on a shoestring by young independent producer Coscarelli. Scenes were cut out of the original film to avoid "X" rating. Followed by "Phantasm II." **90m/C VHS, DVD.** Michael Baldwin, Bill Thornbury, Reggie Bannister, Kathy Lester, Terrie Kalbus, Ken Jones, Susan Harper, Lynn Eastman, David Arntzen, Angus Scrimm, Bill Cone; ***D:*** Don A. Coscarelli; ***W:*** Don A. Coscarelli; ***C:*** Don A. Coscarelli; ***M:*** Fredric Myrow, Malcolm Seagrave.

Phantasm 2 🦴🦴 **1988 (R)** Teen psychic keeps flashing on villainous Tall Man. A rehash sequel to the original, cultishly idiosyncratic fantasy, wherein more victims are fed into the inter-dimensional abyss and Mike discovers that the horror is not all in his head. Occasional inspired gore; bloodier than its predecessor. More yuck for the buck. **97m/C VHS.** James LeGros, Reggie Bannister, Angus Scrimm, Paula Irvine, Samantha (Sam) Phillips, Ken Tigar; ***D:*** Don A. Coscarelli; ***W:*** Don A. Coscarelli; ***C:*** Daryn Okada.

Phantasm 3: Lord of the Dead 🦴½ **1994 (R)** Murderous mortician The Tall Man and his killer silver spheres return once again in this continuing gore fest. Mike, whose brother Jody was one of The Tall Man's victims, teams up with the cynical Reggie and martial arts expert Rocky to try to defeat the creep. That's if they can get past his zombie cohorts and flesh-eating ghouls. **91m/C VHS.** Reggie Bannister, A. Michael Baldwin, Bill Thornbury, Gloria Henry, Kevin Connor, Angus Scrimm; ***D:*** Don A. Coscarelli; ***W:*** Don A. Coscarelli.

Phantasm 4: Oblivion 🦴½ **1998 (R)** At least this sequel can boast the original's lead actors, which allows for footage from the first movie to be used in telling a familiar story. The Tall Man (Scrimm) is still transporting corpses and Mike (Baldwin) is now becoming one of the evil guy's minions. But some time travel takes Mike back to the Tall Man's origins and he tries to take care of the problem at the source. **90m/C VHS, DVD, Wide.** Angus Scrimm, A. Michael Baldwin, Reggie Bannister, Bill Thornbury, Bob Ivy; ***D:*** Don A. Coscarelli; ***W:*** Don A. Coscarelli; ***C:*** Chris Chomyn; ***M:*** Christopher Stone. **VIDEO**

The Phantom 🦴🦴 **1931** Rare cheapie of a hooded killer terrorizing a group of people in a haunted house. **62m/C VHS.** Guinn "Big Boy" Williams, Wilfrid Lucas, Sheldon Lewis, William (Bill) Gould; ***D:*** Alan James.

The Phantom 🦴🦴½ **1996 (PG)** Based on the Lee Falk comic created in 1936. Deep in the Bengalla jungle, a mysterious costumed figure honors a 400-year-old legacy by fighting piracy, greed, and cruelty. With the help of a beautiful newspaper heiress (Swanson), the latest guardian (Zane) must keep an American industrialist (Williams) and a secret brotherhood of pirates from finding three sacred skulls that contain the power to dominate the world. Old-fashioned swashbuckling story is helped along by Zane's enthusiastic portrayal of the stalwart hero. Action set pieces, while done more dynamically elsewhere, are fun and exciting. Older kids (read: teenagers) may find the proceedings a bit hokey, but everyone seems to be having a good time. **100m/C VHS, DVD.** Billy Zane, Kristy Swanson, Treat Williams, Catherine Zeta-Jones, James Remar, Jon Tenney, Patrick McGoohan, Samantha Eggar, Cary-Hiroyuki Tagawa, Robert Coleby, David Proval; ***D:*** Simon Wincer; ***W:*** Jeffrey Boam; ***C:*** David Burr; ***M:*** David Newman.

The Phantom Broadcast 🦴🦴½ *Phantom of the Air* **1933** A popular radio crooner is murdered. The main suspect is his hunchbacked accompanist and manager, who had all along secretly pre-recorded his own velvet voice for the crooner to lip-sync along with. A tightly plotted minor thriller that holds up surprisingly well. **63m/B VHS, 8mm.** Ralph Forbes, Gail Patrick, Vivienne Osborne, Guinn "Big Boy" Williams, George "Gabby" Hayes; ***D:*** Phil Rosen.

Phantom Brother 🦴½ **1988** A semi-spoof about a teenager left orphaned by a car crash that wiped out his entire family, and who is subsequently haunted by his dead brother. Even thinner than it sounds. **92m/C VHS.** Jon Hammer, Patrick Molloy, John Gigante, Mary Beth Pelshaw; ***D:*** William Szarka.

The Phantom Bullet 🦴½ **1926** Hoot wants to holler at his father's murderers. **60m/B VHS.** Hoot Gibson.

The Phantom Chariot 🦴🦴½ **1920** A fantasy depicting the Swedish myth about how Death's coach must be driven by the last man to die each year. Silent. **89m/B VHS.** *SW* ***D:*** Victor Sjostrom.

The Phantom Creeps **1939** Evil Dr. Zorka, armed with a meteorite chunk which can bring an army to a standstill, provides the impetus for this enjoyable serial in 12 episodes. **235m/B VHS, DVD.** Bela Lugosi, Dorothy Arnold, Robert Kent, Regis Toomey; ***D:*** Ford Beebe, Saul Goodkind.

The Phantom Empire *Radio Ranch* **1935** Autry faces the futuristic "Thunder Riders" from the subterranean city of Murania, located 20,000 feet beneath his ranch. A complete serial in 12 episodes. If you only see one science-fiction western in your life, this is the one. Also available in an edited theatrical version at 80 minutes. **245m/B VHS.** Gene Autry, Frankie Darro, Betsy King Ross, Smiley Burnette; ***D:*** B. Reeves Eason, Otto Brower.

Phantom Empire 🦴🦴 **1987 (R)** A woman who rules over a lost city takes a bunch of scientists prisoner and forces them to be slaves. **85m/C VHS.** Ross Hagen, Jeffrey Combs, Dawn Wildsmith, Robert Quarry, Susan Stokey, Michelle (McClellan) Bauer, Russ Tamblyn, Sybil Danning; ***D:*** Fred Olen Ray; ***W:*** Fred Olen Ray, T.L. Lankford.

Phantom Express 🦴🦴 **1932** Experienced old engineer is dismissed from his job because no one believes his explanation that a mysterious train caused the wreck of his own train. He aims to find justice. **65m/B VHS.** J. Farrell MacDonald, Sally Blane, William "Buster" Collier Jr., Hobart Bosworth; ***D:*** Emory Johnson.

Phantom Fiend 🦴½ **1935** A gentle musician becomes a suspect when a series of Jack-the-Ripper type murders terrorize London. Is he the nice guy known by his girlfriend and the people in his lodging house, or is the musician really JTR? Based on the novel "The Lodger" by Marie Belloc-Lowndes. **70m/B VHS.** *GB* Ivor Novello, Elizabeth Allan, A.W. Baskcomb, Jack Hawkins, Barbara Everest, Peter Gawthorne, Kynaston Reeves; ***D:*** Maurice Elvey.

The Phantom Flyer 🦴½ **1928** Stunt pilot helps out a cattle-owning frontier family bedeviled by rustlers. Silent. **54m/B VHS, 8mm.** Al Wilson.

Phantom from Space 🦴½ **1953** An invisible alien lands on Earth, begins killing people, and is pursued by a pair of scientists. **72m/B VHS.** Ted Cooper, Rudolph Anders, Noreen Nash, James Seay, Harry Landers; ***D:*** W. Lee Wilder; ***C:*** William Clothier.

The Phantom from 10,000 Leagues 🦴 **1956** Slimy sea monster attacks swimmers and fishermen; investigating oceanographer pretends not to notice monster is hand puppet. Early AIP release, when still named American Releasing Company. **80m/B VHS, DVD.** Kent Taylor, Cathy Downs, Michael Whalen, Helene Stanton, Phillip Pine; ***D:*** Dan Milner; ***W:*** Lou Rusoff; ***C:*** Brydon Baker; ***M:*** Ronald Stein.

Phantom Gold 🦴½ **1938** The wicked Whitaker claims to have struck it rich but it's really a scam to lure unsuspecting miners to the claim and then rob and murder them. Luden's suspicious and proves Whitaker's a bad guy. **56m/B VHS.** Jack Luden, Charles "Slim" Whitaker, Beth Marion, Hal Taliaferro, Art Davis; ***D:*** Joseph Levering.

The Phantom in the House 🦴🦴 **1929** A woman commits a murder and has her inventor husband take the rap. While he's in prison, she gets rich off of his work. Things get hairy when he is released 15 years later and is introduced to his daughter as a friend of the family. Melodramatic film was originally made with and without sound. **64m/B VHS.** Ricardo Cortez, Nancy Welford, Henry B. Walthall, Grace Valentine; ***D:*** Phil Rosen.

Phantom Killer 🦴🦴 **1942** A district attorney tries to hang a murder rap on a most improbable suspect. When the man is aquitted, the DA quits his job to find the truth, which takes a disturbing twist. The plot is a thinly veiled rehash of "The Sphinx" (1933). **61m/B VHS.** Dick Purcell, Joan Woodbury, John Hamilton, Warren Hymer, Kenneth Harlan, J. Farrell MacDonald, Mantan Moreland; ***D:*** William Beaudine.

Phantom Lady 🦴🦴🦴 **1944** After an argument with his wife Scott Henderson (Curtis) walks into a bar and chats up a mystery woman (Helm). When he returns home, the police are there and his wife has been strangled with his necktie. Since he doesn't know his bar mate's name and no one professes to remember her, Scott is quickly convicted of the crime. Only his loyal secretary Carol (Raines) believes him and she sets out to solve the crime. Based on the novel by Cornell Woolrich. **87m/B VHS.** Ella Raines, Alan Curtis, Franchot Tone, Thomas Gomez, Elisha Cook Jr., Fay Helm, Aurora Miranda, Andrew Tombes, Regis Toomey, Joseph Crehan, Virginia Brissac, Milburn Stone; ***D:*** Robert Siodmak; ***W:*** Bernard C. Schoenfeld; ***C:*** Elwood "Woody" Bredell.

The Phantom Light 🦴🦴½ **1935** A lighthouse keeper is murdered under strange circumstances and a mysterious light keeps appearing at the scene. Detective Hale joins up with a navy man and another lighthouse keeper to solve the crime. A low-budget mystery with good atmosphere and some humor. **75m/B VHS.** *GB* Binnie Hale, Gordon Harker, Ian Hunter, Donald Calthrop; ***D:*** Michael Powell.

The Phantom Lover 🦴🦴½ *Ye Bang Ge Sheng* **1995** It's "The Phantom of the Opera" Hong Kong style, although it's a adult fairytale rather than a horror story. In 1936 a theatrical troupe hopes to restore a burned-out opera house for their performances. Legendary singer Sung Dan-Ping (Cheung) was thought to have died in the fire, instead, horribly disfigured, he hides out in the ruins and dreams of his lost love (Chein-Lien). Chinese with subtitles or dubbed. **102m/C VHS, DVD, Wide.** *HK* Leslie Cheung, Chien-Lien Wu, Philip Kwok, Roy Szeto; ***D:*** Ronny Yu; ***W:*** Roy Szeto, Raymond Wong; ***C:*** Peter Pau; ***M:*** Chris Babida.

Phantom of Chinatown 🦴 **1940** Mr. Wong is called in to solve another murder in the final entry in the series. The first to have an Asian actor portray the lead, as Luke replaced Boris Karloff. **61m/B VHS.** Keye Luke, Lotus Long, Grant Withers, Paul McVey, Charles F. Miller; ***D:*** Phil Rosen.

Phantom of Death 🦴½ **1987 (R)** A brilliant pianist, stricken by a fatal disease that causes rapid aging, goes on a murderous rampage. **95m/C VHS.** *IT* Michael York, Donald Pleasence, Edwige Fenech; ***D:*** Ruggero Deodato; ***M:*** Pino Donaggio.

The Phantom of 42nd Street 🦴🦴 **1945** An actor and a cop team up to find the killer of a wealthy uncle. **58m/B VHS.** Dave O'Brien, Kay Aldridge, Alan Mowbray, Frank Jenks; ***D:*** Al(bert) Herman.

Phantom of Liberty 🦴🦴🦴½ *Le Fantome de la Liberte; The Specter of Freedom* **1974** Master surrealist Bunuel's episodic film wanders from character to character and from event to event. Animals wander through a man's bedroom, soldiers conduct military exercises in an inhabited area, a missing girl stands before her parents even as they futilely attempt to determine her whereabouts, and an assassin is found guilty, then applauded and led to freedom. They don't get much more surreal than this. If you think you may like it, you'll probably love it. Bunuel, by the way, is among the firing squad vicitms in the film's opening enactment of Goya's May 3, 1808. In French with English subtitles. **104m/C VHS.** *FR* Adriana Asti, Jean-Claude Brialy, Michel Piccoli, Adolfo Celi, Monica Vitti, Milena Vukotic, Michael (Michel) Lonsdale, Claude Pieplu, Julien Bertheau, Paul Frankeur, Paul Leperson, Bernard Verley; ***D:*** Luis Bunuel; ***W:*** Luis Bunuel, Jean-Claude Carriere; ***C:*** Edmond Richard.

The Phantom of Soho 🦴🦴 *Das Phantom von Soho* **1964** A Scotland Yard detective investigates the murders of several prominent businessmen and is assisted by a beautiful mystery writer. **92m/B VHS.** *GE* Dieter Borsche, Barbara Rutting, Hans Sohnker, Peter Vogel, Helga Sommerfeld, Werner Peters; ***D:*** Franz Gottlieb.

Phantom of the Air **1933** Twelve chapters of high-flying adventure with Tom Tyler! **230m/B VHS.** Tom Tyler, Gloria Shea, William Desmond, Leroy Mason, Walter Brennan; ***D:*** Ray Taylor.

Phantom of the Mall: Eric's Revenge 🦴 **1989** A murderous spirit haunts the local mall. Gore flows like water. **91m/C VHS.** Morgan Fairchild, Kari Whitman, Jonathan Goldsmith, Derek Rydell, Pauly Shore, Robert Estes, Brinke Stevens; ***D:*** Richard S. Friedman; ***W:*** Robert King; ***C:*** Harry Mathias; ***M:*** Stacy Widelitz.

The Phantom of the Opera 🦴🦴🦴 **1925** Deranged, disfigured music lover haunts the sewers of a Parisian opera house and kills to further the career of an unsuspecting young soprano. First of many film versions still packs a wallop, with fine playing from Chaney Sr. Silent with two-color Technicolor "Bal Masque" sequence. Versions with different running times are also available, including 79 and 88 minutes. **101m/B VHS, DVD.** Lon Chaney Sr., Norman Kerry, Mary Philbin, Gibson Gowland, Arthur Edmund Carewe, John St. Polis, Snitz Edwards, Virginia Pearson; ***D:*** Rupert Julian, Edward Sedgwick, Lon Chaney Sr.; ***W:*** Elliot J. Clawson, Raymond L. Schrock, Frank M. McCormack; ***C:*** Virgil Miller, Charles Van Enger, Milton Bridenbecker. Natl. Film Reg. '98.

The Phantom of the Opera 🦴🦴🦴 **1943** Second Hollywood version (following the 1925 silent) of Gaston Leroux's novel, remade by the same studio (Universal), suffers by dispersing the chills with too many opera scenes (no doubt to give Eddy something to do) and weak comedy. Enrique (a sympathetic Rains) is a disfigured musician in the Paris Opera who sacrifices himself for the love of young singer Christine (DuBois), who doesn't even know he exists. Rains is only briefly seen in his horror visage. **92m/C VHS, DVD.** Nelson Eddy, Susanna Foster, Claude Rains, Edgar Barrier, Leo Carrillo, Hume Cronyn, J. Edward Bromberg; ***D:*** Arthur Lubin; ***W:*** Samuel Hoffenstein, Eric Taylor; ***C:*** Hal Mohr, William Howard Greene; ***M:*** Edward Ward. Oscars '43: Color Cinematog.

The Phantom of the Opera 🦴🦴½ **1962** Hammer version of the Gaston Leroux novel transfers the action from Paris to London but keeps the basic story of a young singer (Sears) and her masked benefactor (Lom), who lives in the sewers beneath the opera house. There's also the wimpy fiance (De Souza) to come between them. Good gothic melodrama. Sears' singing was dubbed by opera performer Pat Clark; producer Hinds used the pseudonym John Elder for his screenplay. **85m/C VHS.** Herbert Lom, Heather Sears, Edward De Souza, Thorley Walters, Michael Gough, Martin Miller, Ian Wilson; ***D:*** Terence Fisher; ***W:*** John (Anthony Hinds) Elder; ***C:*** Arthur Grant; ***M:*** Edwin Astley.

The Phantom of the Opera 🦴½ **1989 (R)** A gory, "Elm Street"-ish version of the Gaston Leroux classic, attempting to cash in on the success of the Broadway musical. **93m/C VHS.** Robert Englund, Jill Schoelen, Alex Hyde-White, Bill Nighy, Terence Harvey, Stephanie Lawrence, Nathan Lewis, Peter Clapham, Molly Shannon; ***D:*** Dwight Little; ***W:*** Duke Sandefur; ***C:*** Elemer Ragalyi; ***M:*** Misha Segal.

The Phantom of the Opera 🦴🦴½ **1990** Yet another version of the tragic tale of a disfigured mask-wearing opera lover, who lurks in the depths of the Paris Opera House, and his desire for lovely young singer, Christine. Dance plays the Phantom as doomed romantic, with Lancaster his protective father. Kopit adapted from his 1983 play. Made for TV drama, originally shown in two parts. **200m/C VHS, DVD.** *GB* Charles Dance, Burt Lancaster, Teri Polo, Ian Richardson, Andrea Ferreol, Adam Storke, Jean-Pierre Cassel; ***D:*** Tony Richardson; ***W:*** Arthur Kopit; ***C:*** Steve Yaconelli; ***M:*** John Addison. **TV**

The Phantom of the Opera 🦴½ *Dario Argento's Phantom of the Opera; Il Fantasma dell'Opera* **1998 (R)** Campy excess (and lots of gore) overwhelms Gaston Leroux's often-filmed chiller. This Phantom (Sands) doesn't have a facial disfigurement and goes unmasked but he's weird nonetheless. Abandoned as a baby, he's raised by rats (ewwww) beneath the Paris Opera where he becomes smitten by young singer, Christine (Argento), and does his best to make her his alone. **100m/C VHS, DVD.** *IT* Julian Sands, Asia Argento, Andrea Di Stefano, Nadia Rinaldi, Coralina Cataldi-Tassoni, Istvan Bubik, Zoltan Barabas; ***D:*** Dario Argento; ***W:*** Dario Argento, Gerard Brach; ***C:*** Ronnie Taylor; ***M:*** Ennio Morricone.

Phantom of the Paradise 🦴🦴 **1974 (PG)** A rock 'n' roll parody of "Phantom of the Opera." Splashy, only occasionally horrific spoof in which cruel music executive Williams, much to his everlasting regret, swindles a songwriter. Violence ensues. Not for most, or even many, tastes. Graham steals the film as rocker Beef. A failure at the boxoffice, and now a cult item (small enthusiastic cult with few outside interests) for its oddball humor and outrageous rock star parodies. Williams also wrote the turgid score. ♫Goodbye, Eddie, Goodbye; Faust; Upholstery; Special to Me; Old Souls; Somebody Super Like You; Life At Last; The Hell of It; The Phantom's Theme (Beauty and the Beast). **92m/C VHS, DVD, Wide.** Paul Williams, William Finley, Jessica Harper, Gerrit Graham, George Memmoli, Archie Hahn; ***D:*** Brian DePalma; ***W:*** Brian DePalma; ***C:*** Larry Pizer; ***M:*** George Aliceson Tipton, Paul Williams.

The Phantom of the Range 🦴½ **1938** Marion is trying to sell her grandfather's ranch only his "ghost" is scaring everyone away. She and cowpoke Tyler find out a group of evil treasure hunters are searching the property for hidden gold. **59m/B VHS.** Tom Tyler, Beth Marion, Charles "Blackie" King, Forrest Taylor, John Elliott, Soledad Jiminez, Sammy Cohen; ***D:*** Robert F. "Bob" Hill.

Phantom of the Ritz 🦴🦴 **1988 (R)** Bizarre accidents begin to take place when Ed Blake and his girlfriend start renovating the old Ritz Theatre. It seems the theatre is inhabited by a rather angry ghost and somebody's got to deal with it before the Ritz can rock and roll. Features the fabulous sounds of the '50s. **89m/C VHS.** Peter Bergman, Deborah Van Valkenburgh; ***D:*** Allen Plone.

Phantom of the West 🦴🦴 **1931** Ten-episode serial about a rancher who becomes "The Phantom of the West" in order to smoke out his father's killer. **166m/B VHS.** William Desmond, Thomas Santschi, Tom Tyler; ***D:*** David Ross Lederman.

Phantom Patrol ♪½ **1936** A mystery writer is kidnapped and someone impersonates him. Mountie Maynard must come to the rescue. **60m/B VHS.** Kermit Maynard, Joan Barclay, Paul Fix, Julian Rivero, Eddie (Edward) Phillips, Roger Williams; ***D:*** Charles (Hutchison) Hutchinson.

The Phantom Planet ♪½ **1961** An astronaut crash-lands on an asteroid and discovers a race of tiny people living there. Having breathed the atmosphere, he shrinks to their diminutive size and aids them in their war against brutal invaders. Infamously peculiar. **82m/B VHS, DVD.** Dean Fredericks, Coleen Gray, Tony Dexter, Dolores Faith, Francis X. Bushman, Richard Kiel; ***D:*** William Marshall; ***W:*** Fred De Gorter, Fred Gebhardt, William Telaak; ***C:*** Elwood J. Nicholson; ***M:*** Hayes Pagel.

Phantom Rancher ♪½ **1939** Roaring melodrama finds Maynard donning a mask to find the real Phantom, who is causing havoc. **61m/B VHS.** Ken Maynard.

Phantom Ranger ♪½ **1938** A federal agent masquerades as a crook to catch a band of counterfeiters. **54m/B VHS.** Tim McCoy, Suzanne Kaaren, Karl Hackett, John St. Polis, John Merton, Harry Strang; ***D:*** Sam Newfield.

The Phantom Rider **1937** Mystery fills the old West in this serial composed of 15 chapters. **152m/B VHS.** Buck Jones, Marla Shelton.

The Phantom Rider ♪½ **1946** The masked do-gooder rides the plains protecting the local Indians from some surly settlers. A 12-episode serial. **167m/C VHS.** Robert Kent, Peggy Stewart, Leroy Mason, Chief Thundercloud.

Phantom Stallion ♪½ **1954** Routine oater has a ranch owner believing a wild stallion is enticing away horses from his herd. But Rex thinks the answer is human and lies close to home. **54m/B VHS.** Rex Allen, Slim Pickens, Carla Balenda, Harry Shannon; ***D:*** Harry Keller; ***W:*** Gerald Geraghty; ***C:*** Bud Thackery; ***M:*** R. Dale Butts.

Phantom Thunderbolt ♪½ **1933** A man who has falsely spread the rumor that he's a gunfighter is hired to chase away some good-for-nothings. **62m/B VHS.** Ken Maynard, Frances Lee, Frank Rice, William (Bill) Gould, Robert F. (Bob) Kortman; ***D:*** Alan James.

Phantom Tollbooth ♪♪♪ **1969 (G)** A young boy drives his car into an animated world, where the numbers are at war with the letters and he has been chosen to save Rhyme and Reason, to bring stability back to the Land of Wisdom. Completely unique and typically Jonesian in its intellectual level and interests. Bright children will be interested, but this is really for adults who will understand the allegory. Based on Norman Justers' metaphorical novel. **89m/C VHS.** ***D:*** Chuck Jones; ***V:*** Mel Blanc, Hans Conried.

Phantom 2040 Movie: The Ghost Who Walks ♪♪½ **1995** Teenager Kit Walker discovers his destiny when a mysterious stranger tells him about his late father and how Kit must carry on his father's legacy as a superhero called the Phantom. A purple suit renders Kit invisible and he finds himself battling his dad's old nemesis, Rebecca Madison, who's out to destroy the Earth's resources. Based on the TV and comic book series. **97m/C VHS.** ***V:*** Scott Valentine, Margot Kidder, Ron Perlman, Carrie Snodgress, Mark Hamill.

Phantoms ♪ **1997 (R)** Dr. Jennifer Pailey (Going) and her sister Lisa (McGowan) arrive in a Colorado resort town and discover that the entire population has been wiped out by a mysterious force. They team up with local sheriff Hammond (Affleck) and his odd deputy (Schrieber) to battle the evil force thingie, which also seems to have an adverse affect on acting ability. Peter O'Toole appears as an expert on ancient plagues, and to show the rest of the cast what a real actor looks like. Schrieber plays the part of the squirmy deputy very well, but the rest of the characters are cheap plywood. Will they stop the amorphous monster who is taking over the corpses of its victims? Will they remember their lines if someone drops the cue card? Based on the novel by Dean Koontz, who also adapted it for the screen and produced. **91m/C VHS, DVD.** Peter O'Toole, Joanna Going, Rose McGowan, Ben Affleck, Liev Schreiber, Nicky Katt, Clifton Powell, Adam Nelson, John Hammil, John Scott Clough; ***D:*** Joe Chappelle; ***W:*** Dean Koontz; ***C:*** Richard Clabaugh; ***M:*** David Williams.

Phar Lap ♪♪½ *Phar Lap: Heart of a Nation* **1984 (PG)** Saga of a legendary Australian racehorse who rose from obscurity to win nearly 40 races in just three years before mysteriously dying in 1932. American version runs 10 minutes shorter than the Aussie one. **107m/C VHS.** *AU* Ron Leibman, Tom Burlinson, Judy Morris, Celia de Burgh; ***D:*** Simon Wincer; ***W:*** David Williamson; ***C:*** Russell Boyd.

Pharaoh ♪♪ **1966** An expensive Polish epic about the power plays of royalty in ancient Egypt. Dubbed. **125m/B VHS.** *PL* Jerzy Zelnick; ***D:*** Jerzy Kawalerowicz.

Pharmacist ♪♪½ **1932** A day in the life of a hapless druggist undone by disgruntled customers and robbers. Typical Fields effort. **19m/B VHS.** Elise Cavanna, Marjorie "Babe" Kane, W.C. Fields, Grady Sutton; ***D:*** Arthur Ripley.

Pharoah's Army ♪♪½ **1995 (PG-13)** Five Union soldiers are foraging for food at a small Kentucky farm when one young soldier (Fox) is badly injured and his captain, John Abston (Cooper), is forced to stay put while he treats the wounds. The farm is home to Sarah Anders (Clarkson) and her young son (Lucas), while her husband is off fighting for the Confederates. Sarah isn't happy about the arrangement but the decent Alston, a farmer himself in peacetime, begins slowly to win her over. Their friendship, however, doesn't sit well with either his men nor Sarah's son. Fine performances in a restrained drama. **90m/C VHS.** Chris Cooper, Patricia Clarkson, Kris Kristofferson, Richard Tyson, Huckleberry Fox, Will Lucas; ***D:*** Robby Henson; ***W:*** Robby Henson; ***C:*** Doron Schlair.

Phase 4 ♪♪ **1974 (PG)** A tale of killer ants retaliating against the humans attempting to exterminate them. **84m/C VHS.** Nigel Davenport, Michael Murphy, Lynne Frederick; ***D:*** Saul Bass; ***C:*** Dick Bush.

Phat Beach ♪♪½ **1996 (R)** Generic but basically harmless buddies-at-the-beach comedy with a hip-hop beat. Fast-talking, slickster Durrell (Hooks) manipulates sensitive, overweight pal Benny (Hopkins, who's real life nickname is "Huggy") into emptying his savings, "borrowing" his dad's Mercedes convertible, and taking off for some Southern California fun. Scores of scantily clad beach bunnies aren't the only ones threadbare—so's the whole premise of this flick—but that's not the point of this lighthearted romp. The likable Hopkins/Hooks comedy team is a hit with precise, lowbrow humor. Coolio, prominent in the ads, is barely window dressing with minimal screen time. Kickin' soundtrack includes E-40, Biz Markie, and SugaT featuring The Click. **99m/C VHS, DVD.** Jermaine "Huggy" Hopkins, Brian Hooks, Jennifer Lucienne, Claudia Kaleem, Gregg D. Vance, Tommy (Tiny) Lister, Erick Fleeks, Alma Collins, Candice Merideth, Sabrina De Pina, Coolio; ***D:*** Doug Ellin; ***W:*** Doug Ellin, Brian E. O'Neal, Ben Morris; ***C:*** Jurgen Baum; ***M:*** Paul Stewart.

Phedre ♪½ **1968** Jean Racine's adaptation of the Greek legend involving Phedre, Theseus, and Hippolyte. Bell is the only one worth watching in this weak and stagy picture. In French with English subtitles. **93m/C VHS.** Marie Bell; ***D:*** Pierre Jourdan.

Phenomenal and the Treasure of Tutankamen ♪♪ **197? (R)** Fiendish criminal genius steals priceless golden mask of King Tut. Superhero Phenomenal is less than dry spaghetti sci-fi. **90m/C VHS.** *IT* Mauro Parenti, Lucretia Love.

Phenomenon ♪♪½ **1996 (PG)** Average small town schmoe George Malley (Travolta) is turned into a genius when he's struck by a bright light on his 37th birthday. This development brings him to the attention of the scientific community and, of course, the military. The locals scorn him, thus fulfilling the Hollywood stereotype of rural folks fearing anything they don't understand. Good-natured weeper plays the Gump card (but turns too paranoid) and wins as Travolta gets to be the nice guy, while attractive Sedgwick is fine as romantic interest Lace. **123m/C VHS, DVD.** John Travolta, Robert Duvall, Kyra Sedgwick, Forest Whitaker, Richard Kiley, Brent Spiner; ***D:*** Jon Turteltaub; ***W:*** Gerald Di Pego; ***C:*** Phedon Papamichael; ***M:*** Thomas Newman.

Phffft! ♪♪½ **1954** Holliday and Lemmon are a bored couple who decide to divorce, date others, and take mambo lessons. By no stretch of plausibility, they constantly run into each other and compete in the same mambo contest. **91m/B VHS.** Judy Holliday, Jack Lemmon, Jack Carson, Kim Novak, Luella Gear, Merry Anders; ***D:*** Mark Robson; ***W:*** George Axelrod; ***C:*** Charles B(ryant) Lang Jr.

Philadelphia ♪♪♪½ **1993 (PG-13)** AIDS goes Hollywood as hot-shot corporate attorney Andrew Beckett (Hanks), fired because he has the disease, hires brilliant but homophobic personal injury attorney Washington as his counsel when he sues for discrimination. Boxoffice winner was criticized by some gay activists as too mainstream, which is the point. It doesn't probe deeply into the gay lifestyle, focusing instead on justice and compassion. Boasts a good script, make-up that transforms Hanks, sure direction, great soundtrack, and a strong supporting cast, but all would mean little without Hanks' superb performance, his best to date. ♫Streets of Philadelphia. **125m/C VHS, DVD, 8mm, Wide.** Tom Hanks, Denzel Washington, Antonio Banderas, Jason Robards Jr., Joanne Woodward, Mary Steenburgen, Ron Vawter, Robert Ridgely, Obba Babatunde, Robert Castle, Daniel Chapman, Roger Corman, John Bedford Lloyd, Roberta Maxwell, Warren Miller, Anna Deavere Smith, Kathryn Witt, Andre B. Blake, Ann Dowd, Bradley Whitford, Chandra Wilson, Charles Glenn, Peter Jacobs, Paul Lazar, Dan Olmstead, Joey Perillo, Lauren Roselli, Bill Rowe, Lisa Talerico, Daniel von Bargen, Tracey Walter; ***Cameos:*** Karen Finley, David Drake, Quentin Crisp; ***D:*** Jonathan Demme; ***W:*** Ron Nyswaner; ***C:*** Tak Fujimoto; ***M:*** Howard Shore. Oscars '93: Actor (Hanks), Song ("Streets of Philadelphia"); Berlin Intl. Film Fest. '94: Actor (Hanks); Golden Globes '94: Actor—Drama (Hanks), Song ("Streets of Philadelphia"); MTV Movie Awards '94: Male Perf. (Hanks); Blockbuster '95: Drama Actor, V. (Hanks).

The Philadelphia Experiment ♪♪½ **1984 (PG)** A WWII sailor falls through a hole in time and lands in the mid-1980s, whereupon he woos a gorgeous woman. Sufficient chemistry between Pare and Allen, but PG rating is an indication of the film's less-than-graphic love scenes. **101m/C VHS, DVD, Wide.** Michael Pare, Nancy Allen, Eric Christmas, Bobby DiCicco; ***D:*** Stewart Raffill; ***W:*** Don Jakoby; ***C:*** Dick Bush; ***M:*** Kenneth Wannberg.

Philadelphia Experiment 2 ♪♪½ **1993 (PG-13)** Melodramatic sci-fi what-ifer has Germany winning WWII by dropping a bomb on Washington. So southern California is now one big labor camp with an evil mad scientist (Graham) and a beleagured hero (Johnson) who must time-travel back to 1943 to prevent the Germans from dropping that bomb. **98m/C VHS.** Brad Johnson, Gerrit Graham, Marjean Holden, James Greene, Geoffrey Blake, John Christian Grass, Cyril O'Reilly; ***D:*** Stephen Cornwell; ***W:*** Kevin Rock, Nick Paine; ***M:*** Gerald Gouriet.

The Philadelphia Story ♪♪♪♪ **1940** A woman's plans to marry again go awry when her dashing ex-husband arrives on the scene. Matters are further complicated when a loopy reporter—assigned to spy on the nuptials—falls in love with the blushing bride. Classic comedy, with trio of Hepburn, Grant, and Stewart all serving aces. Based on the hit Broadway play by Philip Barry, and remade as the musical "High Society" in 1956 (stick to the original). Also available colorized. **112m/B VHS, DVD.** Katharine Hepburn, Cary Grant, James Stewart, Ruth Hussey, Roland Young, John Howard, John Halliday, Virginia Weidler, Henry Daniell, Hillary Brooke, Mary Nash; ***D:*** George Cukor; ***W:*** Donald Ogden Stewart; ***C:*** Joseph Ruttenberg; ***M:*** Franz Waxman. Oscars '40: Actor (Stewart), Screenplay; AFI '98: Top 100, Natl. Film Reg. '95;; N.Y. Film Critics '40: Actress (Hepburn).

Philby, Burgess and MacLean: Spy Scandal of the Century ♪♪½ **1984** The true story of the three infamous British officials who defected to the Soviet Union in 1951, after stealing some vital British secrets for the KGB. **83m/C VHS.** *GB* Derek Jacobi, Anthony Bate, Michael Culver; ***D:*** Gordon Flemyng.

Phobia woof! **1980 (R)** Patients at a hospital are mysteriously being murdered. Stupid and unpleasant story that lasts too long and probably should never have started. **91m/C VHS.** *CA* Paul Michael Glaser, Susan Hogan; ***D:*** John Huston; ***W:*** Peter Bellwood, Lew Lehman, Gary Sherman, Ronald Shusett, Jimmy Sangster.

Phoenix ♪½ **1978** Aging queen summons her marksman to find the Phoenix, a mythical bird that she believes will bring her eternal life. With English subtitles. **137m/C VHS, DVD.** *JP* Tatsuya Nakadai, Tomisaburo Wakayama, Raoru Yumi, Reiko Ohara.

Phoenix ♪♪ **1995** The Titus 4 deep-space outpost has problems when the creators of a killing machine are targeted for death by their creation, which has begun to think for itself. **94m/C VHS.** Stephen Nichols, Billy Drago, William Sanderson, Brad Dourif; ***D:*** Troy Cook; ***W:*** Troy Cook, Jimmy Lifton.

Phoenix ♪♪ **1998 (R)** With a cast like this, you hope for a bit more than the usual cliched crime drama. Gambling addict/ Phoenix cop Harry Collins (Liotta) is in big debt to loansharks. He decides the best way to get the money is to rob the nightclub of a local sleaze where fellow corruptible officer Mike Henshaw (LaPaglia) moonlights. But beyond the inherent stupidity of such a plan is the lurking presence of internal affairs officer Clyde Webber (Berkely). **104m/C VHS, DVD.** Ray Liotta, Anthony LaPaglia, Daniel Baldwin, Jeremy Piven, Xander Berkeley, Giancarlo Esposito, Anjelica Huston, Tom Noonan, Kari Wuhrer, Brittany Murphy; ***D:*** Danny Cannon; ***W:*** Eddie Richey; ***C:*** James L. Carter; ***M:*** Graeme Revell.

The Phoenix and the Magic Carpet ♪♪½ **1995 (PG)** Visiting England to settle her father's estate, Mrs. Wilson and her three children discover an egg from which a phoenix emerges. This mythical firebird proceeds to take the children on a magic adventure. Adapted from the book by Edith Nesbit. **80m/C VHS.** Dee Wallace Stone, Timothy Hegeman, Nick Klein, Laura Kamrath, Peter Ustinov; ***D:*** Zoran Perisic; ***W:*** Florence Fox; ***M:*** Alan Parker.

Phoenix Team ♪ **1980** Two agents discover their mutual attraction can be deadly in the spy business. **90m/C VHS.** Don Francks, Elizabeth Shepherd.

Phoenix the Warrior ♪ **1988** Sometime in the future, female savages battle each other for control of the now ravaged earth. A newcomer seeks the tribe most worthy of receiving the last man on the planet, thereby continuing the human race. **90m/C VHS.** Persis Khambatta, James H. Emery, Peggy Sands, Kathleen Kinmont; ***D:*** Robert Hayes.

The Phone Call ♪♪ **1989 (R)** 900-number morality tale about high-powered executive who calls phone sex line and is connected with escaped homicidal maniac who takes a toll on him and his family. **95m/C VHS.** Michael Sarrazin, Linda Smith, Ron Lea, Lisa Jakub; ***D:*** Allan Goldstein.

Phone Call from a Stranger ♪♪½ **1952** After a plane crash, a survivor visits the families of three of the victims whom he met during the flight. **96m/B VHS.** Bette Davis, Gary Merrill, Michael Rennie, Shelley Winters, Hugh Beaumont, Keenan Wynn, Eve Arden, Craig Stevens; ***D:*** Jean Negulesco; ***W:*** Nunnally Johnson; ***C:*** Milton Krasner.

Photographer ♪ **1975 (PG)** A photographer turns into a murderer, showing the negative side of his personality. **94m/C VHS.** Michael Callan; ***D:*** William B. Hillman.

Photographing Fairies **1997 (R)** Haunting story that's not quite as compelling as it could be. After Anne-Marie (Shelley), the bride of photographer Charles Castle (Stephens), is killed on their honeymoon, Charles shuts down emotionally, and the horrors he photographs in WWI only numb him further. After the war, Charles sets up a studio in London and becomes an expert in unmasking doctored photos. When Beatrice (Barber) shows him photos of fairies taken by her young daughters, Charles travels to her country home to expose them as fakes. Instead, Charles comes to believe that the fairies represent the "Other Side" and if he can photograph their spirit world, he can enter it and be reunited with his lost love. Based on the novel by Steve Szilagyi. The premise involving the young girls and the faked fairy photos is also the basis of the film "Fairytale: A True Story." **107m/C VHS.** *GB* Toby Stephens, Frances Barber, Ben Kingsley, Emily Woof, Philip Davis, Rachel Shelley, Edward Hardwicke, Hannah Bould, Miriam Grant, Clive Merrison; ***D:*** Nick Willing; ***W:*** Nick Willing, Chris Harrald; ***C:*** John de Borman; ***M:*** Simon Boswell.

Physical Evidence **1989 (R)** A lawyer finds herself falling for an ex-cop turned murder suspect while she tries to defend him for a crime he doesn't remember committing. **99m/C VHS.** Burt Reynolds, Theresa Russell, Ned Beatty, Kay Lenz, Ted McGinley; ***D:*** Michael Crichton; ***W:*** Bill Phillips; ***C:*** John A. Alonzo; ***M:*** Henry Mancini.

Pi **1998 (R)** Definitely a first—a religious/mathematical thriller about a man obsessed with decoding the real name of God. Max (Gullette) is a genius mathematician who believes everything can be understood in terms of numbers, so he works on his homebuilt supercomputer to unravel the stock market. Max begins to suffer hallucinations and blackouts just as his work draws the interest of both a high-powered Wall Street firm and a Hasidic cabalistic sect. **85m/B VHS, DVD, Wide.** Sean Gullette, Mark Margolis, Ben Shenkman, Pamela Hart, Stephen Perlman, Samia Shoaib, Ajay Naidu; ***D:*** Darren Aronofsky; ***W:*** Darren Aronofsky, Eric Watson, Sean Gullette; ***C:*** Matthew Libatique; ***M:*** Clint Mansell. Ind. Spirit '99: First Screenplay; Sundance '98: Director (Aronofsky).

P.I. Private Investigations **1987 (R)** Corrupt, drug-dealing cops stalk another cop who can finger them. **91m/C VHS.** Martin Balsam.

Piaf **1981 (PG)** Musical drama chronicles the life of Edith Piaf, France's legendary singer of the Roaring '20s. Her rise from the streets, bout with temporary blindness, and many self-destructive attempts at experiencing life are retold in music. **114m/C VHS.** Jane Lapotaire.

The Pianist **1991** As teenagers in Toronto, sisters Jean (Travers) and Colette (Grenon) become infatuated with Yoshi Takahashi (Okuda), a Japanese concert pianist who lived across the street. Ten years later, they have a family reunion in Vancouver and learn Yoshi is giving a concert in the city. Jean is excited to renew their ties but Colette is reluctant—and Jean reveals that she knows her sister and the pianist had a sexual relationship. Is Jean jealous? Or does she plan on establishing her own claims? Based on Ann Ireland's novel "A Certain Mr. Takahashi." **90m/C VHS, DVD.** *CA* Gail Travers, Macha Grenon, Eiji Okuda, Maury Chaykin, Dorothee Berryman, Carl Alacchi; ***D:*** Claude Gagnon; ***W:*** Claude Gagnon.

The Piano ½ **1993 (R)** In the 1850s, Ada (Hunter), a mute Scottish widow with a young daughter, agrees to an arranged marriage with Stewart (Neill), a colonial landowner in New Zealand. The way she expresses her feelings is by playing her cherished piano, left behind on the beach by her new husband. Another settler, George (Keitel), buys it, arranges for lessons with Ada, and soon the duo begin a grand passion leading to a cruelly calculated revenge. Fiercely poetic and well acted (with Keitel in a notably romantic role), though the film may be too dark and intense for some. Fine original score with Hunter doing her own piano playing. **120m/C VHS, DVD, Wide.** *AU* Holly Hunter, Harvey Keitel, Sam Neill, Anna Paquin, Kerry Walker, Genevieve Lemon; ***D:*** Jane Campion; ***W:*** Jane Campion; ***C:*** Stuart Dryburgh; ***M:*** Michael Nyman. Oscars '93: Actress (Hunter), Orig. Screenplay, Support. Actress (Paquin); Australian Film Inst. '93: Actor (Keitel), Actress (Hunter), Cinematog., Costume Des., Director (Campion), Film, Film Editing, Screenplay, Sound, Score; British Acad. '93: Actress (Hunter); Cannes '93: Actress (Hunter), Film; Golden Globes '94: Actress—Drama (Hunter); Ind. Spirit '94: Foreign Film; L.A. Film Critics '93: Actress (Hunter), Cinematog., Director (Campion), Screenplay, Support. Actress (Paquin); Natl. Bd. of Review '93: Actress (Hunter); N.Y. Film Critics '93: Actress (Hunter), Director (Campion), Screenplay; Natl. Soc. Film Critics '93: Actress (Hunter), Screenplay; Writers Guild '93: Orig. Screenplay.

A Piano for Mrs. Cimino **1982** Declared senile and incompetent, a widowed woman fights for control of her own life. Good script helps this made for TV soaper. **100m/C VHS.** Bette Davis, Keenan Wynn, Alexa Kenin, Penny Fuller, Christopher Guest, George Hearn; ***D:*** George Schaefer; ***M:*** James Horner. **TV**

The Piano Lesson **1994 (PG)** The prized heirloom of the Charles family is an 80-year-old, ornately carved upright piano, jealously guarded by widowed Berniece (Woodard), and housed in the Pittsburgh home of Uncle Doaker (Gordon). When Berniece's brother Willie Boy (Dutton) visits from Mississippi, it's to persuade her to sell the piano in order to buy some land that their grandfather had worked as a slave. But the past, carved into the piano's panels, has a strong hold—one that Berniece refuses to give up. Set in 1936. Adaptation by Wilson of his 1990 Pulitzer Prize-winning play. **99m/C VHS.** Alfre Woodard, Charles S. Dutton, Courtney B. Vance, Carl Gordon, Tommy Hollis, Zelda Harris, Lou Myers, Rosalyn Coleman, Tommy La Fitte; ***D:*** Lloyd Richards; ***W:*** August Wilson; ***M:*** Stephen James Taylor, Dwight Andrews. **TV**

Picasso Trigger **1989 (R)** An American spy tries to catch an elusive murderer. The sequel to "Hard Ticket to Hawaii" and "Malibu Express." **99m/C VHS, DVD.** Steve Bond, Dona Speir, John Aprea, Hope Marie Carlton, Guich Koock, Roberta Vasquez, Bruce Penhall, Harold Diamond, Rodrigo Obregon; ***D:*** Andy Sidaris; ***W:*** Andy Sidaris; ***C:*** Howard Wexler; ***M:*** Gary Stockdale.

Pick a Card *Afula Express* **1997 (PG-13)** David (Hadar) is an unemployed mechanic who dreams of becoming a magician while his girlfriend Batla (Zakheim) just wants to get married. So how can they reconcile their dreams with their reality? **94m/C VHS, DVD, Wide.** *IS* Zvika Hadar, Esti Zakheim, Aryeh Moskona, Orli Perl; ***D:*** Julie Shles; ***W:*** Amit Leor; ***C:*** Itzik Portal; ***M:*** Yuval Shafrir.

Pick a Star *Movie Struck* **1937** Lawrence is a small-town girl who wins a contest and is off to Hollywood. Only no one pays any attention to her except for publicity man Haley, who arranges her screen test. Naturally, she knocks the studio bosses for a loop and becomes a star. Laurel & Hardy are featured in a couple of comedy segments showing the newcomer some backstage silliness and movie business on the set of a Western they're filming (with Finlayson, better known as a director, cast as the duo's director). **70m/B VHS.** Rosina Lawrence, Jack Haley, Patsy Kelly, Mischa Auer, Stan Laurel, Oliver Hardy, Charles Halton, Tom Dugan, Russell Hicks, James Finlayson; ***D:*** Edward Sedgwick.

The Pick-Up Artist ½ **1987 (PG-13)** The adventures of a compulsive Don Juan who finds he genuinely loves the daughter of an alcoholic who's in debt to the mob. Standard story with no surprises. **81m/C VHS.** Robert Downey Jr., Molly Ringwald, Dennis Hopper, Harvey Keitel, Danny Aiello, Vanessa L(ynne) Williams, Robert Towne, Mildred Dunnock, Lorraine Bracco, Joe Spinell, Victoria Jackson, Polly Draper, Brian Hamill; ***D:*** James Toback; ***W:*** James Toback; ***C:*** Gordon Willis; ***M:*** Georges Delerue.

Pick-Up Summer *Pinball Summer; Pinball Pick-Up* **1979 (R)** Two suburban boys cruise their town after school lets out, chasing a pair of voluptuous sisters. **99m/C VHS.** *CA* Michael Zelniker, Carl Marotte; ***D:*** George Mihalka.

Picking Up the Pieces **1999 (R)** Tex (Allen) is a kosher cowboy in a New Mexico town, who's also a butcher. This trade comes in handy when he dismembers unfaithful wife, Candy (Stone), and scatters her remains in the desert. When a blind woman stumbles on Candy's severed hand and miraculously has her sight restored, she delivers the hand to the local church where it becomes a shrine for pilgrims seeking miracle cures. Meanwhile, Tex just wants to rebury the evidence. If you can buy Allen as any kind of cowboy, you can buy the rest of this would-be comedy. **95m/C VHS, DVD, Wide.** Woody Allen, David Schwimmer, Maria Grazia Cucinotta, Kiefer Sutherland, Sharon Stone, Alfonso Arau, Richard "Cheech" Marin, Lou Diamond Phillips, Danny De La Paz, Andy Dick, Fran Drescher, Joseph Gordon-Levitt, Elliott Gould, Eddie Griffin, Lupe Ontiveros; ***D:*** Alfonso Arau; ***W:*** Bill Wilson; ***C:*** Vittorio Storaro; ***M:*** Ruy Folguera.

The Pickle **1993 (R)** Self-indulgent comedy about a midlife crisis. Aiello stars as a middle-aged manic-depressive director certain that his new film is going to be an abysmal flop (as have all his recent pictures). He seeks comfort and reassurance from various ex-wives, children, lovers, and others, though he abuses them all. This dispirited tale also shows clips of the director's dreadful film about children who launch a giant pickle into space. It couldn't possibly be worse that what Mazursky actually put up on the screen. **103m/C VHS, Wide.** Danny Aiello, Dyan Cannon, Clotilde Courau, Shelley Winters, Barry Miller, Jerry Stiller, Christopher Penn, Rebecca Miller; ***Cameos:*** Ally Sheedy, Little Richard, Spalding Gray, Griffin Dunne, Isabella Rossellini, Dudley Moore; ***D:*** Paul Mazursky; ***W:*** Paul Mazursky; ***M:*** Michel Legrand.

Pickpocket ½ **1959** Slow moving, documentary-like account of a petty thief's existence is a moral tragedy inspired by "Crime and Punishment." Ending is particularly moving. Classic filmmaking from Bresson, France's master of austerity. In French with English subtitles. **75m/B VHS.** *FR* Martin LaSalle, Marika Green, Pierre Leymarie, Pierre Etaix, Jean Pelegri, Dolly Scal; ***D:*** Robert Bresson; ***W:*** Robert Bresson; ***C:*** Leonce-Henri Burel.

Pickup on South Street **1953** Petty thief Widmark lifts woman's wallet only to find it contains top secret Communist micro-film for which pinko agents will stop at nothing to get back. Intriguing look at the politics of the day. The creme of "B" movies. **80m/B VHS.** Richard Widmark, Jean Peters, Thelma Ritter, Murvyn Vye, Richard Kiley, Milburn Stone; ***D:*** Samuel Fuller; ***W:*** Samuel Fuller.

The Pickwick Papers ½ **1954** Comedy based on the Dickens classic wherein Mrs. Bardell sues the Pickwick Club for breach of promise. **109m/B VHS.** *GB* James Hayter, James Donald, Nigel Patrick, Hermione Gingold, Hermione Baddeley, Kathleen Harrison; ***D:*** Noel Langley.

Picnic ½ **1955** Drifter Hal Carter (Holden) arrives in a small town and immediately wins the love of his friend's girl, Madge (Novak). The other women in town seem interested too. Strong, romantic work, with Holden excelling in the lead. Novak provides a couple pointers too. Lavish Hollywood adaptation of the William Inge play, including the popular tune "Moonglow/Theme from Picnic." Remade for TV in 2000 with Josh Brolin in the Holden role. **113m/C VHS, DVD, Wide.** William Holden, Kim Novak, Rosalind Russell, Susan Strasberg, Arthur O'Connell, Cliff Robertson, Betty Field, Verna Felton, Reta Shaw, Nick Adams, Phyllis Newman, Raymond Bailey; ***D:*** Joshua Logan; ***W:*** Daniel Taradash; ***C:*** James Wong Howe; ***M:*** George Duning. Oscars '55: Art Dir./Set Dec., Color, Film Editing; Golden Globes '56: Director (Logan).

Picnic at Hanging Rock **1975 (PG)** School outing in 1900 into a mountainous region ends tragically when three girls disappear. Eerie film is strong on atmosphere, as befits mood master Weir. Lambert is extremely photogenic—and suitable subdued—as one of the girls to disappear. Otherwise beautifully photographed on location. From the novel by Joan Lindsey. **110m/C VHS, DVD, Wide.** *AU* Margaret Nelson, Rachel Roberts, Dominic Guard, Helen Morse, Jacki Weaver, Vivean Gray, Anne Louise Lambert; ***D:*** Peter Weir; ***W:*** Clifford Green; ***C:*** Russell Boyd; ***M:*** Bruce Smeaton.

Picnic on the Grass *Le Dejeuner sur l'Herbe; Lunch on the Grass* **1959** A strange, whimsical fantasy heavily evocative of the director's Impressionist roots; a science-minded candidate for the president of Europe throws a picnic as public example of his earthiness, and falls in love with a peasant girl. In French with English subtitles. **92m/C VHS.** *FR* Paul Meurisse, Catherine Rouvel, Fernand Sardou, Jacqueline Morane, Jean-Pierre Granval; ***D:*** Jean Renoir.

Picture Bride ½ **1994 (PG-13)** Familiar immigrant saga finds 17-year-old Japanese Riyo (Kudoh) setting off for Hawaii in 1918 as a "picture bride" to a husband she's never met but with whom she's exchanged photos (hence the title). Riyo's shocked to discover her intended, sugarcane worker Matsuji (Takayama), has deceived her with an out-of-date picture and is at least 25 years older than she. She refuses to consummate the marriage and goes to work in the fields, intending to earn money for her passage home but of course things don't work out quite as Riyo intends. Japanese with subtitles. **95m/C VHS.** *JP* Yoko Sugi, Youki Kudoh, Akira Takayama, Tamlyn Tomita, Cary-Hiroyuki Tagawa; ***Cameos:*** Toshiro Mifune; ***D:*** Kayo Hatta; ***W:*** Kayo Hatta, Mari Hatta, Diane Mark; ***C:*** Claudio Rocha; ***M:*** Cliff Eidelman. Sundance '95: Aud. Award.

Picture Mommy Dead **1966** Well acted melodrama involving a scheming shrew who struggles to drive her mentally disturbed stepdaughter insane for the sake of cold, hard cash. **85m/C VHS.** Don Ameche, Zsa Zsa Gabor, Martha Hyer, Susan Gordon; ***D:*** Bert I. Gordon; ***C:*** Ellsworth Fredericks.

Picture of Dorian Gray **1945** Hatfield plays the rake who stays young while his portrait ages in this adaptation of Oscar Wilde's classic novel. Lansbury steals this one. **110m/B VHS.** Hurd Hatfield, George Sanders, Donna Reed, Angela Lansbury, Peter Lawford, Lowell Gilmore, Miles Mander; ***D:*** Albert Lewin; ***W:*** Albert Lewin; ***C:*** Harry Stradling Sr. Oscars '45: B&W Cinematog.; Golden Globes '46: Support. Actress (Lansbury).

Picture of Dorian Gray **1974** Another version of Wilde's renowned novel about a man who retains his youthful visage while his portrait shows the physical ravages of aging. Davenport is particularly appealing in the lead. **130m/C VHS.** Shane Briant, Nigel Davenport, Charles Aidman, Fionnula Flanagan, Linda Kelsey, Vanessa Howard; ***D:*** Glenn Jordan. **TV**

Picture Perfect ½ **1996 (PG-13)** While trying to impress her new boss, ad exec Kate (Aniston) claims Nick (Mohr), the man standing with her in a photo, is her fiance. Unfortunately, the boss now wants to meet the guy (a stranger who was at the same party) and she must find him and get him to play along. The story's cliched, but Aniston's appealing screen presence perks things up a bit. **100m/C VHS, DVD.** Jennifer Aniston, Jay Mohr, Kevin Bacon, Illeana Douglas, Olympia Dukakis, Kevin Dunn, Faith Prince, Anne Twomey; ***D:*** Glenn Gordon Caron; ***W:*** Glenn Gordon Caron; ***C:*** Paul Sarossy; ***M:*** Carter Burwell.

Picture Windows **1995 (R)** Three short cable movies inspired by works of art. "Lightning," based on Frederic Remington sketches and a Zane Grey short story, finds western codger Keith striking gold with the help of his trusty mule. A David Hockney painting suggested "Armed Response," which features a confrontation between a wealthy lawyer (Loggia) and a burglar (Zahn). And an anonymous 16th-century canvas "Two Nudes Bathing" is given an imaginative history. **95m/C VHS, DVD.** Brian Keith, Robert Loggia, Steve Zahn, Charley Boorman; ***D:*** Joe Dante, Bob Rafelson, John Boorman. **CABLE**

Pictures ½ **198?** The silent-film era in England is spoofed in this look at ambitious waitress Ruby Sears, who's determined to be a film star, and writer Bill

Trench, who winds up a novice screenwriter. Bill's first movie script is based on Ruby's life and she desperately wants to star in the production, if only she can convince the producer and the drunken male lead that she has the talent. **208m/C VHS.** *GB* Wendy Morgan, Peter McEnery, Harry Towb, Anton Rodgers, Annette Badland, Malcom Jamieson, Marc Smith; ***W:*** Roy Clarke. **TV**

Pie in the Sky ½ **1995 (R)** Charles Dunlap (Charles) is a traffic geek, fascinated by the flow of cars on the nearby freeway, whose hero is local traffic reporter Alan Davenport (Goodman), with whom he eventually gets a job in L.A. Charles' other interest is dancer/waitress Amy (Heche)—their first attempt at romance goes awry but persistence pays off. Optimistic and corny. **94m/C VHS.** Josh Charles, Anne Heche, John Goodman, Christine Lahti, Peter Riegert, Christine Ebersole, Wil Wheaton, Bob Balaban, Dey Young; ***D:*** Bryan Gordon; ***W:*** Bryan Gordon; ***C:*** Bernd Heinl; ***M:*** Michael Covertino.

Piece of Cake ½ **1990** Adaptation of the Derek Robinson novel follows the flyboys of the RAF Hornet Squadron during the early years of WWII. They have trouble taking the war seriously but tangles with the Luftwaffe and increasing casualties put a strain on everyone. Great aerial photography and the British planes are vintage Spitfires not repros. Made for British TV miniseries on six cassettes. **312m/C VHS, DVD.** *GB* Tom Burlinson, Tim Woodward, Boyd Gaines, Nathaniel Parker, Neil Dudgeon, David Horovitch, Richard Hope, Jeremy Wortham, Michael Elwyn, Corinne Dacla, Helena Michell. **TV**

A Piece of Pleasure *Un Partie de Plaisir* **1974** Marriage declines due to a domineering husband in this familiar domestic study from French master Chabrol. Good, but not among the director's best efforts. In French with English subtitles. **100m/C VHS.** *FR* Paul Gegauff, Danielle Gegauff, Clemence Gegauff, Paula Moore, Michel Valette, Cecile Vassort; ***D:*** Claude Chabrol; ***W:*** Paul Gegauff; ***C:*** Jean Ralsier; ***M:*** Pierre Jansen.

Piece of the Action ½ **1977 (PG)** An ex-cop beats two con men at their own game when he convinces them to work for a Chicago community center. **135m/C VHS.** Sidney Poitier, Bill Cosby, James Earl Jones, Denise Nicholas, Hope Clarke, Tracy Reed, Titos Vandis, Ja'net DuBois; ***D:*** Sidney Poitier; ***M:*** Curtis Mayfield.

Pieces woof! **1983 (R)** Chain-saw wielding madman roams a college campus in search of human parts for a ghastly jigsaw puzzle. Gory and loathsome. **90m/C VHS.** *IT SP* Christopher George, Lynda Day George, Paul Smith; ***D:*** J(uan) Piquer Simon.

The Pied Piper of Hamelin **1957** The evergreen classic of the magical piper who rids a village of rats and then disappears with the village children into a mountain when the townspeople fail to keep a promise. **90m/C VHS.** Van Johnson, Claude Rains, Jim Backus, Kay Starr, Lori Nelson; ***D:*** Bretaigne Windust.

The Pied Piper of Hamelin **1984** From Shelley Duvall's "Faerie Tale Theatre" comes the story of how a man with a magic flute charmed the rats out of Hamelin. **60m/C VHS.** Eric Idle; ***D:*** Nicholas Meyer. **CABLE**

Pier 23 **1951** A private eye is hired to bring a lawless ex-convict to a priest's custody, but gets an imposter instead. A web of intrigue follows. **57m/B VHS.** Hugh Beaumont, Ann Savage, David Bruce, Raymond Greenleaf, Joi Lansing.

Pierrot le Fou ½ **1965** A woman fleeing a gangster joins a man leaving his wife in this stunning, occasionally confusing classic from iconoclast Godard. A hallmark in 1960s improvisational filmmaking, with rugged Belmondo and always-photogenic Karina effortlessly excelling in leads. In French with English subtitles. **110m/C VHS, DVD, Wide.** *FR IT* Samuel Fuller, Jean-Pierre Leaud, Jean-Paul Belmondo, Anna Karina, Dirk Sanders; ***D:*** Jean-Luc Godard; ***W:*** Jean-Luc Godard; ***C:*** Raoul Coutard; ***M:*** Antoine Duhamel.

Pigalle **1995** Dridi's feature debut focuses on the red light district of Paris and the company of various lowlifes, including pickpocket Fifi (Renaud), who's involved with both stripper Vera (Brile) and transvestite hooker Divine (Li). There's also an increasingly violent turf war between a couple of drug dealers that takes in everyone around. Violent and sordid melodrama. French with subtitles. **93m/C VHS.** *FR* Francis Renaud, Vera Briole, Bianca Li, Raymond Gil, Younesse Boudache, Philippe Ambrosini, Jean-Claude Grenier; ***D:*** Karim Dridi; ***W:*** Karim Dridi; ***C:*** John Mathieson.

Pigs ½ *Daddy's Deadly Darling; The Killers* **1973** Young woman who has escaped from a mental hospital teams up with an evil old man to go on a murdering spree. They complement each other beautifully. She kills them and he disposes of the bodies by making pig slop out of them. **90m/C VHS.** Toni Lawrence, Marc Lawrence, Jesse Vint, Katharine Ross; ***D:*** Marc Lawrence; ***M:*** Charles Bernstein.

A Pig's Tale ½ *Summer Camp* **1994 (PG)** Rich kids rule at Kamp Kipperman but one 13-year-old forms the Pig Pen club and the club members decide to turn the tables on their overbearing rivals. **94m/C VHS.** Joe Flaherty, Graham Sack; ***D:*** Paul Tassie.

Pigskin Parade ½ **1936** Fifteen-year-old Garland's first feature is a lighthearted musical combining college and football. Winston Winters (Haley) coaches the Texas State U team, which has been mistakenly invited to play Yale, and goes to great lengths to give his team a chance by recruiting a farmboy (Erwin) who's a natural phenom. (Garland's the boy's singing sister.) ♫Balboa; The Texas Tornado; It's Love I'm After; You're Simply Terrific; You Do the Darndest Things, Baby; T.S.U. Alma Mater; Hold That Bulldog; Down with Everything; We'd Rather Be In College. **95m/B VHS.** Jack Haley, Patsy Kelly, Stuart Erwin, Judy Garland, Johnny Downs, Betty Grable, Arline Judge, Tony Martin, Fred Kohler Jr., Elisha Cook Jr.; ***D:*** David Butler; ***W:*** Harry Tugend, Jack Yellen; ***C:*** Arthur C. Miller.

Pilgrim, Farewell ½ **1982** Dramatic story about a dying woman who needs to tie up loose ends before her death and goes looking for her estranged teenage daughter. Made for PBS's "American Playhouse." **110m/C VHS.** Elizabeth Huddle, Christopher Lloyd, Laurie Pranage, Lesley Paxton, Shelley Wyant, Robert Brown; ***D:*** Michael Roemer. **TV**

The Pillow Book **1995 (NC-17)** Greenaway's usual chilliness gives way to some true erotic heat that still keeps to arcane subjects, violence, and dazzling visuals. Japanese model Nagiko (Wu) longs for the childhood rituals enacted by her calligrapher father (Ogata) as he literally painted birthday greetings on her face with brush and ink. As an adult, Nagiko searches out calligrapher/lovers willing to use her body as their paper but she's still unsatisfied until she meets bisexual Englishman Jerome (McGregor) and he insists Nagiko write on him. When Nagiko learns Jerome's male lover is the publisher (Oida) who was once involved with her father, her jealousy triggers tragic consequences. Title refers to the 10th century diary "The Pillow Book of Sei Shonagon." Some subtitled Japanese dialogue. **126m/C VHS, DVD.** *NL FR GB* Vivian Wu, Ewan McGregor, Yoshi Oida, Ken Ogata, Hideko Yoshida, Judy Ongg, Ken Mitsuishi, Yutaka Honda, Ronald Guttman; ***D:*** Peter Greenaway; ***W:*** Peter Greenaway; ***C:*** Sacha Vierny.

Pillow Talk ½ **1959** Sex comedy in which a man woos a woman who loathes him. By the way, they share the same telephone party line. Narrative provides minimal indication of the film's strengths, which are many. Classic '50s comedy with masters Day and Hudson exhibiting considerable rapport, even when fighting. Lighthearted, constantly funny. **102m/C VHS, DVD, Wide.** Rock Hudson, Doris Day, Tony Randall, Thelma Ritter, Nick Adams, Lee Patrick; ***D:*** Michael Gordon; ***W:*** Maurice Richlin, Stanley Shapiro; ***C:*** Arthur E. Arling; ***M:*** Frank DeVol. Oscars '59: Story & Screenplay.

Pimpernel Smith ½ *Mister V* **1942** Seemingly scatterbrained archaeology professor is actually a dashing agent rescuing refugees from evil Nazis in WWII France. Howard is well cast, but the film is somewhat predictable, and it's too long. Wonderful scene, though, in which a Nazi officer champions Shakespeare as Aryan. **121m/B VHS.** *GB* Leslie Howard, Mary Morris, Francis L. Sullivan, David Tomlinson; ***D:*** Leslie Howard.

Pin... ½ **1988 (R)** A boy's imaginary friend assists in the slaying of various enemies. Horror effort could be worse. **103m/C VHS, DVD, Wide.** Cyndy Preston, David Hewlett, Terry O'Quinn, Bronwen Mantel, Helene Udy, Patricia Collins, Steven Bednarski, Katie Shingler, Jacob Tierney, Michelle Anderson; ***D:*** Sandor Stern; ***W:*** Sandor Stern; ***C:*** Guy Defaux.

Pin Down Girls *Racket Girls; Pin Down Girl* **1951** Great schlock about girl wrestlers. **81m/B VHS, DVD.** Clara Mortensen, Rita Martinez.

Pin-Up Girl **1944** Grable plays a secretary who becomes an overnight sensation during WWII. Loosely based on her famous pinup poster that was so popular at the time, the movie didn't even come close to being as successful. The songs aren't particularly memorable, although Charlie Spivak and his Orchestra perform. ♫Once Too Often; Yankee Doodle Dandy; I'll Be Marching to a Love Song; You're My Little Pin Up Girl; Story of the Very Merry Widow; Time Alone Will Tell; Don't Carry Tales Out of School; Red Robins, Bob Whites and Blue Birds. **83m/C VHS.** Betty Grable, Martha Raye, Jon Harvey, Joe E. Brown, Eugene Pallette, Mantan Moreland; ***D:*** H. Bruce Humberstone; ***C:*** Ernest Palmer.

Pinero **2001 (R)** Change of pace role for Bratt, best known for clean-cut characters on the right side of the law. Although he physically did not resemble the Puerto Rican poet/playwright/actor Miguel Pinero, Bratt gives a dynamic performance as the street smart hustler/heroin addict who died at age 40 in 1988. An ex-con who did time at Sing-Sing, Pinero put his experience to use with the Tony Award-nominated play, "Short Eyes," and was one of the founders of the Nuyorican Cafe. Film is non-chronological, which can get confusing, and few of the secondary characters have enough screen time to make strong impressions. **103m/C VHS, DVD.** Benjamin Bratt, Talisa Soto, Giancarlo Esposito, Rita Moreno, Mandy Patinkin, Michael Irby, Michael Wright, Nelson Vasquez, Jaime Sanchez, Rome Neal; ***D:*** Leon Ichaso; ***W:*** Leon Ichaso; ***C:*** Claudio Chea.

Ping Pong ½ **1987 (PG)** A Chinese patriarch drops dead in London's Chinatown, leaving a young law student to disentangle his will, and get mixed up with his cross-cultured family. **100m/C VHS.** David Yip, Lucy Sheen, Robert Lee, Lam Fung, Victor Kan, Ric Young; ***D:*** Po Chich Leong.

Pink Cadillac ½ **1989 (PG-13)** A grizzled, middle-aged bondsman is on the road, tracking down bail-jumping crooks. He helps the wife and baby of his latest target escape from her husband's more evil associates. Eastwood's performance is good and fun to watch, in this otherwise lightweight film. **121m/C VHS, 8mm.** Clint Eastwood, Bernadette Peters, Timothy Carhart, Michael Des Barres, William Hickey, John Dennis Johnston, Geoffrey Lewis, Jim Carrey, Tiffany Gail Robinson, Angela Louise Robinson; ***D:*** Buddy Van Horn; ***W:*** John Eskow; ***M:*** Steve Dorff.

The Pink Chiquitas **1986 (PG-13)** Sci-fi spoof about a detective battling a mob of meteorite-traveling Amazons. **86m/C VHS.** Frank Stallone, Eartha Kitt, Bruce Pirrie, McKinlay Robinson, Elizabeth Edwards, Claudia Udy; ***D:*** Anthony Currie.

Pink Flamingos **1972 (NC-17)** Divine, the dainty 300-pound transvestite, faces the biggest challenge of his/her career when he/she competes for the title of World's Filthiest Person. Tasteless, crude, and hysterical film; this one earned Waters his title as "Prince of Puke." If there are any doubts about this honor—or Divine's rep—watch through to the end to catch Divine chewing real dog excrement, all the time wearing a you-know-what-eating grin. **95m/C VHS, DVD, Wide.** Divine, David Lochary, Mary Vivian Pearce, Danny Mills, Mink Stole, Edith Massey, Cookie Mueller, Channing Wilroy, Paul Swift, Susan Walsh, Linda Olgierson, Elizabeth Coffey, Steve Yeager, Pat Moran, George Figgs; ***D:*** John Waters; ***W:*** John Waters; ***C:*** John Waters; ***Nar:*** John Waters.

Pink Floyd: The Wall ½ **1982 (R)** Film version of Pink Floyd's 1979 LP, "The Wall." A surreal, impressionistic tour-de-force about a boy who grows up numb from society's pressures. The concept is bombastic and overwrought, but Geldof manages to remain somewhat likeable as the cynical rock star and the Gerald Scarfe animation perfectly complements the film. **95m/C VHS, DVD, Wide.** *GB* Bob Geldof, Christine Hargreaves, Bob Hoskins, James Laurenson, Eleanor David, Kevin McKeon, David Bingham, Jenny Wright, Alex McAvoy, Nell Campbell, Joanne Whalley; ***D:*** Alan Parker; ***W:*** Roger Waters; ***C:*** Peter Biziou; ***M:*** Michael Kamen, David Gilmour, Roger Waters.

The Pink Jungle ½ **1968** Ben Morris (Garner) is a fashion photographer on assignment with model Alison (Renzi) in South America where they become entangled with eccentric Sammy Ryderbeit (Kennedy) who's searching for a lost diamond mine. Caught up in the adventure, the duo accompany Sammy and find the mine, only to discover Raul Ortega (Ansara) and his band of revolutionaries have gotten there first. Based on the novel "Snake Water" by Alan Williams. **104m/C VHS.** James Garner, Eva Renzi, George Kennedy, Michael Ansara, Nigel Green, George Rose; ***D:*** Delbert Mann; ***W:*** Charles Williams; ***C:*** Russell Metty; ***M:*** Ernie Freeman.

Pink Motel woof! *Motel* **1982 (R)** Several people spend a night meant to be romantic at a pink stucco motel which caters to couples. Comic stiff with Diller and Pickens as the owners of said pink motel. **90m/C VHS.** Phyllis Diller, Slim Pickens, Terri Berland, Squire Fridell; ***D:*** Mike MacFarland.

Pink Nights **1987 (PG)** A high school nebbish is suddenly pursued by three beautiful girls, and his life gets turned upside-down. **87m/C VHS.** Shaun Allen, Kevin Anderson, Larry King, Johnathan Jamcovic Michaels; ***D:*** Philip Koch.

The Pink Panther **1964** Bumbling, disaster-prone inspector invades a Swiss ski resort and becomes obsessed with capturing a jewel thief hoping to lift the legendary "Pink Panther" diamond. Said thief is also the inspector's wife's lover, though the inspector doesn't know it. Slick slapstick succeeds on strength of Sellers' classic portrayal of Clouseau, who accidentally destroys everything in his path while speaking in a funny French accent. Followed by "A Shot in the Dark," "Inspector Clouseau" (without Sellers), "The Return of the Pink Panther," "The Pink Panther Strikes Again," "Revenge of the Pink Panther," "Trail of the Pink Panther," and "Curse of the Pink Panther." Memorable theme supplied by Mancini. **113m/C VHS, DVD, Wide.** *GB* Peter Sellers, David Niven, Robert Wagner, Claudia Cardinale, Capucine, Brenda de Banzie; ***D:*** Blake Edwards; ***W:*** Blake Edwards; ***C:*** Philip Lathrop; ***M:*** Henry Mancini.

The Pink Panther Strikes Again **1976 (PG)** Fifth in the series has the incompetent inspector tracking his former boss, who has gone insane and has become preoccupied with destroying the entire world. A must for Sellers buffs and anyone who appreciates slapstick. **103m/C VHS, DVD.** *GB* Peter Sellers, Herbert Lom, Lesley-Anne Down, Colin Blakely, Leonard Rossiter, Burt Kwouk; ***D:*** Blake Edwards; ***W:*** Edwards Waldman, Frank Waldman; ***C:*** Harry Waxman; ***M:*** Henry Mancini. Writers Guild '76: Adapt. Screenplay.

Pink String and Sealing Wax **1945** A brutish pub owner in Victorian England is poisoned by his abused wife. She tries to involve the son of a chemist with the idea of blackmailing the father. Fine period flavor. **89m/B VHS.** *GB* Mervyn Johns, Mary Merrall, Gordon Jackson, Googie Withers, Sally Ann Howes, Catherine Lacey, Garry Marsh, Frederick Piper, Don Stannard, Valentine Dyall; ***D:*** Robert Hamer; ***W:*** Robert Hamer; ***C:*** Richard S. Pavey.

Pinky 🦴🦴🦴 **1949** Early Hollywood treatment of the tragic choice made by some black Americans to pass as white in order to attain a better life for themselves and their families. The story is still relevant today. Waters and Barrymore also star, but the lead black character is portrayed by a white actress. Based on the novel "Quality" by Cyd Ricketts Sumner. **102m/B VHS.** Jeanne Crain, Ethel Barrymore, Ethel Waters, Nina Mae McKinney, William Lundigan; ***D:*** Elia Kazan; ***W:*** Philip Dunne, Dudley Nichols; ***M:*** Alfred Newman.

Pinocchio 🦴🦴🦴🦴 **1940 (G)** Second Disney animated film featuring Pinocchio, a little wooden puppet, made with love by the old woodcarver Geppetto, and brought to life by a good fairy. Except Pinocchio isn't content to be just a puppet—he wants to become a real boy. Lured off by a sly fox, Pinocchio undergoes a number of adventures as he tries to return safely home. Has some scary scenes, including Geppetto, Pinocchio, and their friend Jiminy Cricket getting swallowed by a whale, and Pleasure Island, where naughty boys are turned into donkeys. An example of animation at its best and a Disney classic that has held up over time. ♫When You Wish Upon a Star; Give a Little Whistle; Turn on the Old Music Box; Hi-Diddle-Dee-Dee (An Actor's Life For Me); I've Got No Strings. **87m/C VHS, DVD.** ***D:*** Hamilton Luske, Ben Sharpsteen; ***W:*** Aurelius Battaglia, William Cottrell, Otto Englander, Erdman Penner, Joseph Sabo, Ted Sears, Webb Smith; ***V:*** Dick(ie) Jones, Cliff Edwards, Evelyn Venable, Walter Catlett, Frankie Darro, Charles (Judel, Judells) Judels, Don Brodie, Christian Rub. Oscars '40: Song ("When You Wish Upon a Star"), Orig. Score, Natl. Film Reg. '94.

Pinocchio **1983** Pee-wee Herman is the puppet who wants to be a real little boy in this "Faerie Tale Theatre" adaptation of this children's classic. **60m/C VHS.** Paul (Pee-wee Herman) Reubens, James Coburn, Carl Reiner, Lainie Kazan; ***D:*** Peter Medak. **CABLE**

Pinocchio's Revenge 🦴 **1996 (R)** Man murders his child and buries the body with a wooden Pinocchio puppet. Somehow before his execution, his lawyer, Jennifer Garrick (Allen), and her cute daughter Zoe (Smith) wind up with the grisly toy and Jennifer allows her daughter to keep it. Naturally, this is not a good thing. **96m/C VHS.** Rosalind Allen, Brittany Alyse Smith, Todd Allen, Lewis Van Bergen, Aaron Lustig, Ron Canada; ***D:*** Kevin S. Tenney; ***W:*** Kevin S. Tenney; ***M:*** Dennis Michael Tenney.

Pinto Canyon 🦴½ **1940** An honest sheriff does away with a band of cattle rustlers. **55m/B VHS.** Bob Steele, Louise Stanley, Kenne Duncan, Ted Adams, Steve Clark, Budd Buster; ***D:*** Raymond K. Johnson.

Pinto Rustlers 🦴½ **1936** A cowboy left orphaned by a gang of rustlers seeks revenge. **52m/C VHS.** Tom Tyler, Catherine Cotter.

Pioneer Marshal 🦴 **1949** Lawman Hale disguises himself as a criminal to track down an embezzler. **60m/B VHS.** Monte Hale, Paul Hurst.

Pioneer Woman 🦴🦴 *Pioneers* **1973** A family encounters hostility when they set up a frontier homestead in Nebraska in 1867. Told from the feminine perspective, the tale is strewn with hurdles, both personal and natural. **74m/C VHS.** Joanna Pettet, William Shatner, David Janssen, Helen Hunt; ***D:*** Buzz Kulik. **TV**

The Pioneers 🦴½ **1941** Ritter sets out to protect a wagon train. **59m/B VHS.** Tex Ritter.

Pipe Dreams 🦴🦴 **1976 (PG)** A couple tries to repair their broken marriage against the backdrop of the Alaskan pipeline's construction. **89m/C VHS.** Gladys Knight, Barry Hankerson, Bruce French, Sally Kirkland, Sherry Bain; ***D:*** Stephen Verona.

Pippi Goes on Board 🦴🦴½ **1975 (G)** The fourth and last film in the Swedish series finds Pippi's father arriving one day to take her sailing to Taka-Kuka, his island kingdom. She can't bear to leave her friends and jumps off the ship to return home. The series is poorly dubbed and technically flawed, which the kids probably won't notice. Based on the books by Astrid Lindgren. Preceded by "Pippi Longstocking," "Pippi in the South Seas," and "Pippi on the Run." **83m/C VHS.** ***SW*** Inger Nilsson; ***D:*** Olle Hellbom.

Pippi in the South Seas 🦴🦴½ *Pippi Langstrump Pa de Sju Haven* **1974 (G)** Pippi, a fun-loving, independent, red haired little girl, and her two friends decide to rescue her father, who is being held captive by a band of pirates on a South Sea island. Naturally, clever Pippi saves the day. Poorly dubbed and edited. Based on the children's book by Astrid Lindgren. Follows "Pippi Longstocking" and precedes "Pippi on the Run" and "Pippi Goes on Board." **99m/C VHS.** ***SW*** Inger Nilsson; ***D:*** Olle Hellbom.

Pippi Longstocking 🦴🦴½ **1973 (G)** This little red-headed, pigtailed terror is left alone by her sailor father as he heads out to sea. Not that Pippi minds, since it gives her the chance to create havoc in her town through the antics of her pets, a monkey and a horse. Pippi's antics may amuse the kiddies but adults will find her obnoxious. Poorly dubbed and technically somewhat shaky. Based on the children's book by Astrid Lindgren. Followed by "Pippi in the South Seas," "Pippi on the Run," and "Pippi Goes on Board." **99m/C VHS.** ***SW*** Inger Nilsson; ***D:*** Olle Hellbom.

Pippi on the Run 🦴🦴½ **1974 (G)** The third film in the series finds Pippi on the trail of two friends who have run away from home. The three have many adventures before deciding home is best. Preceded by "Pippi Longstocking" and "Pippi in the South Seas," followed by "Pippi Goes on Board." Films lacks technical and dubbing skills. Based on the children's book by Astrid Lindgren. **99m/C VHS.** ***SW***

Pippin 🦴🦴🦴 **1981** Video version of the stage musical about the adolescent son of Charlemagne finding true love. Adequate record of Bob Fosse's Broadway smash. Features Vereen recreating his original Tony Award-winning role. **120m/C VHS, DVD.** Ben Vereen, William Katt, Martha Raye, Chita Rivera.

Piranha 🦴🦴½ **1995 (R)** Genetically enhanced piranha terrorize the resort community of Lost River. Scientists Paul (Katt) and Maggie (Paul) have accidentally released the vicious fishies but everyone ignores their warnings until some swimmers become din-din. Remake of Roger Corman's 1978 cult item and based on John Sayles' original screenplay. **81m/C VHS, DVD.** Alexandra Paul, William Katt, Soleil Moon Frye, Monte Markham, Darlene Carr, James Karen, Lincoln Kilpatrick; ***D:*** Scott Levy; ***W:*** Alex Simon; ***C:*** Christopher Baffa; ***M:*** Christopher Lennertz.

Piranha 🦴🦴½ **1978 (R)** A rural Texas resort area is plagued by attacks from ferocious man-eating fish which a scientist created to be used as a secret weapon in the Vietnam War. Spoofy horror film features the now-obligatory Dante film in-jokes in the background. **90m/C VHS, DVD.** Bradford Dillman, Heather Menzies, Kevin McCarthy, Keenan Wynn, Barbara Steele, Dick Miller, Paul Bartel, John Sayles, Richard Deacon; ***D:*** Joe Dante; ***W:*** John Sayles; ***C:*** Jamie Anderson; ***M:*** Pino Donaggio.

Piranha 2: The Spawning 🦴½ *Piranha 2: Flying Killers* **1982 (R)** Diving instructor and a biochemist seek to destroy piranha mutations that are murdering tourists at a club. Early Cameron exercise in gore tech that's a step down from original "Piranha." **88m/C VHS.** Tricia O'Neil, Steve Marachuk, Lance Henriksen, Ricky Paul; ***D:*** James Cameron; ***W:*** H.A. Milton; ***C:*** Roberto D'Ettorre Piazzoli.

The Pirate 🦴🦴🦴 **1948** A traveling actor poses as a legendary pilot to woo a lonely woman on a remote Caribbean island. Minnelli always scores with this type of fare, and both Garland and Kelly make the most of the Cole Porter score. ♫Be a Clown; Nina; Mack the Black; You Can Do No Wrong; Sweet Ices, Papayas, Berry Man; Sea Wall; Serafin; The Ring; Judy Awakens. **102m/C VHS.** Judy Garland, Gene Kelly, Walter Slezak, Gladys Cooper, George Zucco, Reginald Owen; ***D:*** Vincente Minnelli; ***C:*** Harry Stradling Sr.

Pirate Movie 🦴🦴½ **1982 (PG)** Gilbert and Sullivan's "The Pirates of Penzance" is combined with new pop songs in this tale of fantasy and romance. Feeble attempt to update a musical that was fine the way it was. **98m/C VHS.** Kristy McNichol, Christopher Atkins, Ted Hamilton, Bill Kerr, Garry McDonald; ***D:*** Ken Annakin; ***M:*** Tony Britten. Golden Raspberries '82: Worst Director (Annakin), Worst Song ("Pumpin' and Blowin'").

Pirate Ship 🦴½ *The Mutineers* **1949** Slow-moving story has sailor Hall discovering new captain Reeves is involved with a gang of gun-runners and counterfeiters. **60m/C VHS.** Jon Hall, George Reeves, Adele Jergens, Noel Cravat, Tom Kennedy, Lyle Talbot; ***D:*** Jean Yarbrough.

Pirate Warrior 🦴🦴 **1964** Grade-B pirate flick about slavery and the evil Tortuga. **86m/C VHS.** Ricardo Montalban, Vincent Price, Liana Orfei; ***D:*** Mary Costa.

Pirates 🦴½ **1986 (PG-13)** Blustery, confused effort at a big-budgeted retro-adventure, about a highly regarded pirate and his gains and losses on the high seas. Broad comedy, no story to speak of. **124m/C VHS.** Walter Matthau, Cris Campion, Damien Thomas, Richard Pearson, Charlotte Lewis, Olu Jacobs, David Patrick Kelly, Roy Kinnear, Bill Fraser, Jose Santamaria; ***D:*** Roman Polanski; ***W:*** Gerard Brach, Roman Polanski. Cesar '87: Art Dir./Set Dec., Costume Des.

The Pirates of Penzance 🦴🦴 **1983 (G)** Gilbert and Sullivan's comic operetta is the story of a band of fun-loving pirates, their reluctant young apprentice, the "very model of a modern major general," and his lovely daughters. An adaptation of Joseph Papp's award-winning Broadway play. **112m/C VHS.** Kevin Kline, Angela Lansbury, Linda Ronstadt, Rex Smith, George Rose; ***D:*** Wilford Leach.

The Pirates of Silicon Valley 🦴🦴½ **1999** Fact-based docudrama covering the early days of Apple and Microsoft. The partners in both companies tend to get the short end of the story as the telepic focuses on charismatic manipulator Steve Jobs (Wyle) and shrewd geek kingpin Bill Gates (Hall), who not only kept an eye on each other but outmanuevered industry giants such as IBM and Xerox to virtually begin the personal computer market. **95m/C VHS.** Noah Wyle, Anthony Michael Hall, Joey Slotnick, John DiMaggio, Josh Hopkins, Gema Zamprogna, Allan Royal, Bodhi (Pine) Elfman, Gailard Sartain; ***D:*** Martyn Burke; ***W:*** Martyn Burke; ***C:*** Ousama Rawi; ***M:*** Frank Fitzpatrick. **CABLE**

Pirates of the Coast 🦴½ **1961** A Spanish naval commander teams up with a group of pirates to even the score with an evil governor during the 1500s. **102m/C VHS.** Lex Barker, Estella Blain, Livio Lorenzon, Liana Orfei; ***D:*** Domenico Paolella.

Pirates of the High Seas 🦴½ **1950** Crabbe helps a friend save his shipping line from sabotage. A serial in 15 chapters. **?m/C VHS.** Buster Crabbe, Lois Hall, Tommy Farrell, Gene Roth, Tristram Coffin; ***D:*** Spencer Gordon Bennet, Thomas Carr.

Pirates of the Seven Seas 🦴½ **1962** In the further tales of "Sandokan the Great," the pirate hero helps save the heroine's father from an evil English Imperialist. **90m/C VHS.** Steve Reeves, Jacqueline Sassard, Andrea Bosic; ***D:*** Umberto Lenzi.

Pistol: The Birth of a Legend 🦴🦴½ **1990 (G)** Biography of "Pistol" Pete Maravich, the basketball star who defied age limitations in the 1960s to play on his varsity team. **104m/C VHS.** Adam Guier, Nick Benedict, Boots Garland, Millie Perkins; ***D:*** Frank C. Schroeder; ***W:*** Darrel A. Campbell.

Pistoleros Asesinos 🦴🦴 **1987** Plenty of action, plus a little romance, when a man falls in love with a crooked landowner's daughter and must battle her father's henchmen for her hand. **83m/C VHS.** ***SP*** Maria de Lourdes, Federico Villa, Victor Alcocer, Arturo Benavides, Polo Ortin, Rosa Gloria.

The Pit 🦴½ **1981 (R)** Autistic boy gets his chance for revenge. The townspeople who humiliate him are in for a surprise after he stumbles across a huge hole in the forest, at the bottom of which are strange and deadly creatures. **96m/C VHS.** Sammy Snyders, Sonja Smits, Jeannie Elias, Laura Hollingsworth; ***D:*** Lew Lehman.

The Pit and the Pendulum 🦴🦴🦴 **1961** A woman and her lover plan to drive her brother mad, and he responds by locking them in his torture chamber, which was built by his loony dad, whom he now thinks he is. Standard Corman production only remotely derived from the classic Poe tale, with the cast chewing on a loopy script. A landmark in Gothic horror. **80m/C VHS, DVD, Wide.** Vincent Price, John Kerr, Barbara Steele, Luana Anders, Antony Carbone, Charles Victor, Lynn Bernay, Patrick Westwood; ***D:*** Roger Corman; ***W:*** Richard Matheson; ***C:*** Floyd Crosby; ***M:*** Les Baxter.

The Pit & the Pendulum 🦴🦴½ **1991 (R)** Retelling of the classic Poe short story, mixed with his "A Cask of Amantillado" and set during the Spanish Inquisition. Great special effects and professional scary guy, Lance Henriksen. **97m/C VHS, DVD.** Lance Henriksen, Rona De Ricci, Jonathan Fuller, Jeffrey Combs, Tom Towles, Stephen Lee, Frances Bay, Oliver Reed; ***D:*** Stuart Gordon; ***W:*** Dennis Paoli; ***M:*** Richard Band.

Pit Stop 🦴🦴🦴 **1967** On the DVD commentary track, director Jack Hill admits that he made this movie quickly to capitalize on the short-lived phenomenon of figure-8 racing, where the shape of the track guarantees many crashes. Brian Donlevy is the promoter who involves young racers Sid Haig and Dick Davalos in his plans. **91m/B DVD, Wide.** Brian Donlevy, Richard (Dick) Davalos, Ellen Burstyn, Sid Haig, Beverly Washburn; ***D:*** Jack Hill; ***W:*** Jack Hill; ***C:*** Austin McKinney.

Pitch Black 🦴🦴🦴 **2000 (R)** Scary sci-fier with some familiar elements. Freak meteor storm causes a spaceship to make a crash landing on an unknown planet with three suns and apparently no life. Hah! In this version of "they only come out at night," the survivors discover that very nasty hunting creatures attack after dark—and the planet is in for a total eclipse. Diesel gives a hard-ass performance as a convicted murderer who has nothing to lose. Shot in Queensland, Australia. **108m/C VHS, DVD, Wide.** Vin Diesel, Radha Mitchell, Cole Hauser, Keith David, Lewis Fitz-Gerald, John Moore, Simon Burke, Claudia Black, Rhiana Griffith; ***D:*** David N. Twohy, Jim Wheat, Ken Wheat; ***W:*** David N. Twohy; ***C:*** David Eggby; ***M:*** Graeme Revell.

Pitfall 🦴🦴🦴 **1948** Gritty tale in which an insurance salesman, bored with his routine suburban life and family, follows his less noble instincts—and finds himself up to his ears in stolen goods, adultery and murder. **85m/B VHS.** Dick Powell, Jane Wyatt, Lizabeth Scott, Raymond Burr, John Litel, Byron Barr, Ann Doran, Jimmy Hunt, Selmer Jackson, Margaret Wells, Dick Wassel; ***D:*** Andre de Toth; ***W:*** Karl Kamb; ***C:*** Harry Wild; ***M:*** Louis Forbes.

Pittsburgh 🦴🦴 **1942** Slow-moving drama about a love triangle combined with class differences. Dietrich loves Wayne, but he's more interested in the coal and steel business, so rival Scott steps in. Although limited by standard plot, picture works because of excellent performances by leads. Based on a screen story by George Owen and Tom Reed. **98m/B VHS.** Marlene Dietrich, Randolph Scott, John Wayne, Frank Craven, Louise Allbritton, Shemp Howard, Thomas Gomez, Ludwig Stossel; ***D:*** Lewis Seiler; ***W:*** Kenneth Gamet, Tom Reed, John Twist.

Pixote 🦴🦴🦴🦴 *Pixote: A Lei do Mais Fraco* **1981** Wrenching, documentary-like account of an orphan-boy's life on the streets in a Brazil metropolis. Graphic and depressing, it's not for all tastes but nonetheless masterfully done. In Portuguese with English subtitles. **127m/C VHS, DVD.** ***BR*** Fernando Ramos Da Silva, Marilia Pera, Jorge Juliao, Gilberto Moura, Jose Nilson dos Santos, Edilson Lino; ***D:*** Hector Babenco; ***W:*** Hector Babenco; ***C:*** Rodolfo Sanchez; ***M:*** John Neschling. L.A. Film

Critics '81: Foreign Film; N.Y. Film Critics '81: Foreign Film; Natl. Soc. Film Critics '81: Actress (Pera).

Pizza Man 🦴½ **1991 (PG-13)** Pizza deliveryman Elmo Bunn is minding his own business, delivering an extra large with anchovies and sausage, when he finds himself mixed up in a political scandal. Lawton directed under alias "J.D. Athens." **90m/C VHS.** Bill Maher, Annabelle Gurwitch; ***D:*** J.F. Lawton; ***W:*** J.F. Lawton.

Pizzicata 🦴🦴 **1996** When an American fighter plane is shot down over southern Italy in 1943, the pilot, Italian-American Tony Marciano (Frascaro), is rescued by peasant family, the Panaleos, who nurse the wounded man despite the danger. When Tony is discovered by a neighbor, he pretends to be a family cousin and tries to fit into the community—all the while falling for young Cosima Panaleo (Torelli), even though she's engaged to Paquale (Massafra). During a community dance, everyone's feelings become dramatically clear. Italian with subtitles. **93m/C VHS.** *IT* Fabio Frascaro, Chiara Torelli, Cosimo Cinieri, Paolo Massafra; ***D:*** Edoardo Winspeare; ***W:*** Edoardo Winspeare; ***C:*** Paolo Carnera.

P.K. and the Kid 🦴🦴 **1985** A runaway kid meets up with a factory worker on his way to an arm wrestling competition and they become friends. **90m/C VHS.** Molly Ringwald, Paul LeMat, Alex Rocco, John Madden, Esther Rolle; ***D:*** Lou Lombardo; ***W:*** Neal Barbera; ***M:*** James Horner.

A Place Called Glory 🦴🦴 *Die Holle von Manitoba* **1966** Barker comes to the aid of the local townsfolk in Glory city who have their hands full with a gang of bloodthirsty outlaws. **92m/C VHS.** Lex Barker, Pierre Brice, Marianne Koch.

A Place Called Today 🦴 *City in Fear* **1972** Sordid tale of big city politics where violence and fear in the streets is at the heart of the campaign. **105m/C VHS.** Cheri Caffaro, J. Herbert Kerr Jr., Lana Wood, Richard Smedley, Tim Brown; ***D:*** Don Schain.

A Place Called Truth 🦴½ **1998 (R)** A millionaire's daughter has an affair with the hired help, which incites the jealousy of her best friend and the wrath of her father. **95m/C VHS.** Audie England, Brion James, Jacqueline Lovell, Chris Browning, Joseph Whipp, Valerie Perrine, Anthony Addabbo; ***D:*** Rafael Eisenman. **VIDEO**

A Place for Annie 🦴🦴½ **1994 (PG)** Lots of tears in this drama of devoted pediatrics nurse Susan Lansing (Spacek) who decides to become the foster mother of abandoned baby girl Annie, who's been diagnosed as HIV-positive. Then Annie's destitute birth mom (Parker), a former junkie dying of AIDS, resurfaces and decides she wants her daughter back. Sputters into melodrama but good performances by strong women, including Plowright as the nanny and Merkerson as a concerned hospital social worker. Based on a true story. **98m/C VHS.** Sissy Spacek, Mary-Louise Parker, Joan Plowright, S. Epatha Merkerson, Jack Noseworthy; ***D:*** John Gray; ***W:*** Cathleen Young, Lee Guthrie. **TV**

Place in Hell 🦴½ **1965** The Japanese armed forces camouflage a Pacific island beach which they are holding and invite the American forces to invade it during WWII. **106m/C VHS.** Guy Madison, Helene Chanel, Monty Greenwood.

A Place in the Sun 🦴🦴🦴 **1951** Melodramatic adaptation of "An American Tragedy," Theodore Dreiser's realist classic about an ambitious laborer whose aspirations to the high life with a gorgeous debutante are threatened by his lower-class lover's pregnancy. Clift is magnificent in the lead, and Taylor and Winters also shine in support. Burr, however, grossly overdoes his role of the vehement prosecutor. Still, not a bad effort from somewhat undisciplined director Stevens. **120m/B VHS, DVD.** Montgomery Clift, Elizabeth Taylor, Shelley Winters, Raymond Burr, Anne Revere; ***D:*** George Stevens; ***W:*** Harry Brown, Michael Wilson; ***C:*** William Mellor; ***M:*** Franz Waxman. Oscars '51: B&W Cinematog., Costume Des. (B&W), Director (Stevens), Film Editing, Screenplay, Orig. Dramatic Score; AFI '98: Top 100; Directors Guild '51: Director (Stevens); Golden Globes '52: Film—Drama, Natl. Film Reg. '91.

A Place in the World 🦴🦴🦴 **1992** Returning from exile to their native Argentina during a military dictatorship, Mario and Ana (Luppi and Roth) work to help the less advantaged in their society, determined to make a difference. Story is seen as a flashback from point-of-view of the couples' son Ernesto (Batyi). Well-crafted, finely acted piece exploring political, social, and interpersonal themes. 1993 Oscar bid retracted due to controversy over country of film's origin. **120m/C VHS.** *AR* Jose Sacristan, Federico Luppi, Cecilia (Celia) Roth, Leonor Benedetto, Gaston Batyi, Lorena Del Rio; ***D:*** Adolfo Aristarain; ***W:*** Alberto Lecchi, Adolfo Aristarain; ***C:*** Ricardo De Angelis; ***M:*** Emilio Kauderer.

Place of Weeping 🦴🦴½ **1986 (PG)** Early entry in the anti-apartheid sweepstakes (made in South Africa, no less). A South African woman opposes her nation's racist policies. A reporter supports her. **88m/C VHS.** *SA* James Whylie, Geini Mhlophe; ***D:*** Darrell Roodt.

Place Vendome 🦴🦴🦴 **1998** Deneuve stars as elegant alcoholic Marianne Malivert, who finds a new interest after her husband's (Fresson) suicide. A prominent jeweler with a shop on the fashionable Place Vendome, he was unable to confess that the business is bankrupt and his connections shady. Instead, he leaves Marianne with seven priceless diamonds that turn out to be stolen, which rekindles her business instincts (she's a former gem broker) and places her in danger. French with subtitles; originally released at 117 minutes. **105m/C VHS, DVD.** *FR* Catherine Deneuve, Jean-Pierre Bacri, Emmanuelle Seigner, Jacques Dutronc, Bernard Fresson, Francois Berleand, Philippe Clevenot; ***D:*** Nicole Garcia; ***W:*** Nicole Garcia, Jacques Fieschi; ***C:*** Laurent Dailland; ***M:*** Richard Robbins.

Places in the Heart 🦴🦴🦴 **1984 (PG)** A young widow determines to make the best of a bad situation on a small farm in Depression-era Texas, fighting poverty, racism, and sexism while enduring backbreaking labor. Support group includes a blind veteran and a black drifter. Hokey but nonetheless moving film is improved significantly by strong performances by virtually everyone in the cast. In his debut, Malkovich shines through this stellar group. Effective dust-bowl photography by Nestor Almendros. **113m/C VHS, DVD, Wide.** Sally Field, John Malkovich, Danny Glover, Ed Harris, Lindsay Crouse, Amy Madigan, Terry O'Quinn, Ned Dowd, Ray Baker; ***D:*** Robert Benton; ***W:*** Robert Benton; ***C:*** Nestor Almendros; ***M:*** Howard Shore. Oscars '84: Actress (Field), Orig. Screenplay; Golden Globes '85: Actress—Drama (Field); Natl. Bd. of Review '84: Support. Actor (Malkovich); N.Y. Film Critics '84: Screenplay; Natl. Soc. Film Critics '84: Support. Actor (Malkovich).

The Plague 🦴½ **1992 (R)** An outbreak of bubonic plague has turned the South American city of Oran into a prison, with no one permitted to leave until the disease has run its course. Hurt is the doctor trying to balance his duties with his own fears. Necessarily bleak adaptation of the Albert Camus novel is also slow-moving and long-winded—an equally deadly combination for the viewer. **105m/C VHS.** *FR SP* William Hurt, Robert Duvall, Raul Julia, Sandrine Bonnaire, Jean-Marc Barr; ***D:*** Luis Puenzo.

The Plague Dogs 🦴🦴½ **1982** Two dogs carrying a plague escape from a research center and are tracked down in this unlikely animated film. A bit ponderous. And yes, that is Hurt's voice. From the novel by Richard Adams, author of "Watership Down." **99m/C VHS.** ***D:*** Martin Rosen; ***W:*** Martin Rosen; ***M:*** Patrick Gleeson; ***V:*** John Hurt, Christopher Benjamin, Judy Geeson, Barbara Leigh-Hunt, Patrick Stewart.

Plague of the Zombies 🦴🦴½ **1966** The local doctor in a Cornish village gets suspicious when its inhabitants begin suddenly dying off and the local squire refuses to allow any autopsies. That's because he's learned voodoo rites while staying in Haiti and is turning the dead locals into zombies. **90m/C VHS, DVD.** *GB* Andre Morell, John Carson, Diane Clare, Alex Davion, Jacqueline Pearce, Brook Williams, Michael Ripper, Marcus Hammond, Roy Royston; ***D:*** John Gilling; ***W:*** Peter Bryan, John (Anthony Hinds) Elder; ***C:*** Arthur Grant; ***M:*** James Bernard.

Plain Clothes 🦴🦴½ **1988 (PG)** An undercover cop masquerades as a high school student to solve the murder of a teacher. He endures all the trials that made him hate high school the first time around. **98m/C VHS.** Arliss Howard, George Wendt, Suzy Amis, Diane Ladd, Seymour Cassel, Larry Pine, Jackie Gayle, Abe Vigoda, Robert Stack; ***D:*** Martha Coolidge; ***M:*** Scott Wilk.

Plain Jane 🦴🦴½ **2001** In 1911, David Bruce (Whately) has just moved to London with his wife (Manville) and baby daughter. Newly prosperous, the family can afford to hire live-in maid, Jane (Cunniffe). But David begins to take too much of an interest in Jane (and doesn't realize that his grown son is also involved with her) and sexual obsession leads to murder. **150m/C VHS, DVD.** *GB* Kevin Whately, Emma Cunniffe, Leslie Manville, Jason Hughes; ***D:*** John Woods; ***W:*** Lucy Gannon; ***M:*** Ray Russell. **TV**

The Plainsman 🦴🦴½ **1937** Western legends Wild Bill Hickock, Buffalo Bill, and Calamity Jane team up for adventure in this big, empty venture. Just about what you'd expect from splashy director DeMille. **113m/B VHS.** Gary Cooper, Jean Arthur, Charles Bickford, Anthony Quinn, George "Gabby" Hayes, Porter Hall, James Mason; ***D:*** Cecil B. DeMille; ***C:*** Victor Milner.

Plan B 🦴🦴½ **1997** Comedy, set between Halloween and New Year's Eve, about a group of 30-ish friends who realize their lives aren't going the way they'd planned. Waiter Stuart (Cryer) despairs of being a serious writer and has instead penned a lurid serial killer novel; aspiring actor Ricky (Matheison) freaks about growing older; Gina (Mornell) is successful in business but unlucky in love; while Gina's older sister Clare (Darr) is happily married to Jack (Guest) but fretting over not being a mother yet. It's pretty familiar but not a complete waste of time, thanks to the appealing cast. **102m/C VHS.** Jon Cryer, Mark Matheison, Sara Mornell, Lisa Darr, Lance Guest; ***D:*** Gary Leva; ***W:*** Gary Leva; ***C:*** Yoram Astrakhan; ***M:*** Andrew Rose.

Plan 9 from Outer Space woof! *Grave Robbers from Outer Space* **1956** Two or three aliens in silk pajamas conspire to resurrect several slow-moving zombies from a cardboard graveyard in order to conquer the Earth. Spaceships that look suspiciously like paper plates blaze across the sky. Pitiful, inadvertently hilarious fright worth a look if you're desperate to kill time since it's in the running for the "dumbest movie ever made" award. Lugosi's actual screen time is under two minutes, since he had the good sense to die before the film was complete. Enjoy the taller and younger replacement (the chiropractor of Wood's wife) they found for Lugosi, who remains hooded to protect his identity. **78m/B VHS, DVD.** Bela Lugosi, Tor Johnson, Lyle Talbot, Vampira, Gregory Walcott, Tom (George Duryea) Keene, Dudley Manlove, Mona McKinnon, Duke Moore, Joanna Lee, Bunny Breckinridge, Criswell, Carl Anthony, Paul Marco, Norma McCarty, David DeMering, Bill Ash, Conrad Brooks, Tom Mason, Edward D. Wood Jr.; ***D:*** Edward D. Wood Jr.; ***W:*** Edward D. Wood Jr.; ***C:*** William C. Thompson; ***M:*** Trevor Duncan, Van Phillips, James Stevens, Bruce Campbell.

Plan 10 from Outer Space 🦴½ **1995** The play on the infamous Ed Wood title is the only connection between the two fringe features as director Harris takes aim at his hometown of Salt Lake City, Utah. Heroine Lucinda (Russell) discovers a mysterious bronze plaque buried near the Great Salt Lake and uncovers a UFO conspiracy loosely conforming to Mormon mythology. There's a basic mass hysteria/alien invasion scene, cheesy special effects, dumb sexual humor, and not much else. **82m/C VHS.** Stefene Russell, Pat Collins, Curtis James, Karen Black; ***D:*** Trent Harris; ***W:*** Trent Harris; ***C:*** Bryan Duggan; ***M:*** Fredric Myrow.

Planes, Trains & Automobiles 🦴🦴½ **1987 (R)** One-joke Hughes comedy saved by Martin and Candy. Strait-laced businessman Neal Page (played straight by Martin) on the way home for Thanksgiving meets up with a oafish, bad-luck-ridden boor Del Griffith (Candy) who turns his efforts to get home upside down. Martin and Candy both turn in fine performances, and effectively straddle a thin line between true pathos and hilarious buffoonery. Bacon and McClurg, both Hughes alumni, have small but funny roles. **93m/C VHS, DVD, Wide.** Steve Martin, John Candy, Edie McClurg, Kevin Bacon, Michael McKean, William Windom, Laila Robins, Martin Ferrero, Charles Tyner, Dylan Baker, Ben Stein, Lyman Ward; ***D:*** John Hughes; ***W:*** John Hughes; ***C:*** Don Peterman; ***M:*** Ira Newborn.

Planet Burg 🦴🦴½ **1962** A classic Soviet sci-fi flick about a space exploration team landing on Venus. Their job becomes a rescue mission when one of the crew is stranded. Although there are some silly moments, some good plot twists and acting make up for them. In Russian with English subtitles. **90m/C VHS.** *RU* Vladimir Temelianov, Gennadi Vernov, Kyunna Ignatova; ***D:*** Pavel Klushantsev.

Planet Earth 🦴🦴½ **1974** In the year 2133, a man who has been in suspended animation for 154 years is revived to lead the troops against a violent group of women (and mutants, too!). **78m/C VHS.** John Saxon, Janet Margolin, Ted Cassidy, Diana Muldaur, Johana DeWinter, Christopher Gary; ***D:*** Marc Daniels.

Planet of Blood 🦴🦴 *Queen of Blood* **1966** Space opera about an alien vampire discovered on Mars by a rescue team. If you've ever seen the Soviet film "Niebo Zowiet," don't be surprised if some scenes look familiar; the script was written around segments cut from that film. **81m/C VHS.** John Saxon, Basil Rathbone, Judi Meredith, Dennis Hopper, Florence Marly, Forrest J Ackerman; ***D:*** Curtis Harrington; ***W:*** Curtis Harrington; ***C:*** Vilis Lapenieks; ***M:*** Leonard Morand.

Planet of the Apes 🦴🦴🦴½ **1968 (G)** Astronauts crash land on a planet where apes are masters and humans are merely brute animals. Superior science fiction with sociological implications marred only by unnecessary humor. Heston delivers one of his more plausible performances. Superb ape makeup creates realistic pseudo-simians of McDowall, Hunter, Evans, Whitmore, and Daly. Adapted from Pierre Boulle's novel "Monkey Planet." Followed by four sequels and two TV series. **112m/C VHS, DVD, Wide.** Charlton Heston, Roddy McDowall, Kim Hunter, Maurice Evans, Linda Harrison, James Whitmore, James Daly; ***D:*** Franklin J. Schaffner; ***W:*** Rod Serling, Michael Wilson; ***C:*** Leon Shamroy; ***M:*** Jerry Goldsmith. Natl. Film Reg. '01.

Planet of the Apes 🦴🦴🦴 **2001 (PG-13)** Burton's "re-imagining" of the story looks more to the original novel by Pierre Boulle than it does to the 1968 classic. Wahlberg, as generic action hero Leo Davidson, takes over the Heston role, but with nowhere near the bravado or screen presence. Roth excels as Gen. Thade, an angry militarist with a loathing for all humans and a contempt for polite ape society. Needless to say, Leo becomes the focus for his rage. Come to think of it, all of the actors in the ape makeup do a fine job. The makeup effects, courtesy of Rick Baker, are astounding (and light-years ahead of where they were in '68), and the action moves along at a satisfyingly brisk pace. The screenplay provides plenty of sly and clever references to the original, but doesn't have its sense of social commentary (this is, after all, a summer blockbuster). What it does have is a twist ending that seems tacked on for the purpose of setting up a sequel. **125m/C VHS, DVD, Wide.** *US* Mark Wahlberg, Tim Roth, Helena Bonham Carter, Michael Clarke Duncan, Paul Giamatti, Estella Warren, Cary-Hiroyuki Tagawa, David Warner, Kris Kristofferson, Erik Avari, Luke Eberl, Charlton Heston, Evan Dexter Parke, Michael Jace; ***D:*** Tim Burton; ***W:*** William Broyles Jr., Larry Konner, Mark Rosenthal; ***C:*** Philippe Rousselot; ***M:*** Danny Elfman. Golden Raspberries '01: Worst

Remake/Sequel, Worst Support. Actor (Heston), Worst Support. Actress (Warren).

Planet of the Dinosaurs 🦴½ **1980 (PG)** Survivors from a ruined spaceship combat huge savage dinosaurs on a swampy uncharted planet. **85m/C VHS, DVD.** James Whitworth, Michael Thayer, Louie Lawless, Pamela Bottaro, Charlotte Speer; ***D:*** James K. Shea; ***W:*** Ralph Lucas.

Planet of the Vampires 🦴🦴½ *The Demon Planet; The Haunted Planet; The Outlawed Planet; Planet of Blood; Planet of Terror; Planet of the Damned; Space Mutants; Terror in Space; Terrore nello Spazio; Terreur dans l'Espace* **1965** Astronauts search for missing comrades on a planet dominated by mind-bending forces. Acceptable atmospheric filmmaking from genre master Bava, but it's not among his more compelling ventures. **86m/C VHS, DVD, Wide.** *IT SP* Barry Sullivan, Norma Bengell, Angel Aranda, Evi Marandi, Stelio Candelli, Ivan Rassimov, Fernando Villena; ***D:*** Mario Bava; ***W:*** Mario Bava, Alberto Bevilacqua, Callisto Cosulich, Louis M. Heyward, Ib Melchior, Antonio Roman, Rafael J. Salvia; ***C:*** Antonio Rinaldi; ***M:*** Gino Marinuzzi Jr.

Planet on the Prowl 🦴 *War Between the Planets* **1965** A fiery planet causes earthly disasters, so a troop of wily astronauts try to destroy it with the latest technology. They fail, leading one sacrificial soul to do it himself. **80m/C VHS.** *IT* Giacomo "Jack" Rossi-Stuart, Amber Collins, Peter Martell, John Bartha, Halina Zalewska, James Weaver; ***D:*** Anthony (Antonio Margheriti) Dawson.

Planets Against Us 🦴½ *I Pianeti Contro di Noi; The Man with the Yellow Eyes; Hands of a Killer; The Monster with Green Eyes* **1961** Science fiction tale of escaped alien humanoid robots who take refuge on Earth, but whose touch is fatal. Good special effects. **85m/B VHS.** *IT FR* Michel Lemoine, Maria Pia Luzi, Jany Clair; ***D:*** Romano Ferrara.

The Plastic Age 🦴🦴½ **1925** Cynthia (Bow) is a flapper college babe who likes boys and parties. She easily manages to charm naive newcomer Hugh (Keith), who pays more attention to her than his athletic career. But Cynthia's not heartless—when she sees that Hugh is ruining his chances, she decides to give him up. **73m/B VHS, DVD.** Clara Bow, Donald Keith, Gilbert Roland, Henry B. Walthall, Mary Alden; ***D:*** Wesley Ruggles; ***W:*** Eve Unsell, Frederica Sagor; ***C:*** Gilbert Warrenton, Allen Siegler.

Platinum Blonde 🦴🦴🦴 **1931** Screwball comedy in which a newspaper journalist (Williams) marries a wealthy girl (Harlow) but finds that he doesn't like the restrictions and confinement of high society. Yearning for a creative outlet, he decides to write a play and hires a reporter (Young) to collaborate with him. The results are funny and surprising when Young shows up at the mansion flanked by a group of hard-drinking, fun-loving reporters. **86m/B VHS.** Loretta Young, Robert Williams, Jean Harlow, Louise Closser Hale; ***D:*** Frank Capra; ***W:*** Jo Swerling, Dorothy Howell.

Platinum High School 🦴½ *Trouble at 16; Rich, Young, and Deadly* **1960** Divorced father Rooney is appalled when his son is "accidentally" killed while off at an exclusive military academy. His suspicions are aroused by the prevaricating school commander and he discovers some horrible truths about his son's death and life at the school. **91m/B VHS.** Mickey Rooney, Terry Moore, Dan Duryea, Conway Twitty, Warren Berlinger, Yvette Mimieux, Jimmy Boyd, Richard Jaeckel, Harold Lloyd Jr., Elisha Cook Jr., Jimmy Murphy; ***D:*** Charles Haas; ***W:*** Robert Smith; ***M:*** Van Alexander.

Platoon 🦴🦴🦴½ **1986 (R)** A grunt's view of the Vietnam War is provided in all its horrific, inexplicable detail. Sheen is wooden in the lead, but both Dafoe and Berenger are resplendent as, respectively, good and bad soldiers. Strong, visceral filmmaking from fearless director Stone, who based the film on his own GI experiences. Highly acclaimed; considered by many to be the most realistic portrayal of the war on film. **113m/C VHS, DVD, Wide.** Charlie Sheen, Willem Dafoe, Tom Berenger, Francesco Quinn, Forest Whitaker, John C. McGinley, Kevin Dillon, Richard Edson, Reggie Johnson, Keith David, Johnny Depp, Dale Dye, Mark Moses, Chris Pederson, David Neidorf, Tony Todd, Ivan Kane, Paul Sanchez, Corey Glover, Oliver Stone; ***D:*** Oliver Stone; ***W:*** Oliver Stone; ***C:*** Robert Richardson; ***M:*** Georges Delerue. Oscars '86: Director (Stone), Film Editing, Picture, Sound; AFI '98: Top 100; British Acad. '87: Director (Stone); Directors Guild '86: Director (Stone); Golden Globes '87: Director (Stone), Film—Drama, Support. Actor (Berenger); Ind. Spirit '87: Cinematog., Director (Stone), Film, Screenplay.

Platoon Leader 🦴🦴 **1987 (R)** A battle-drenched portrait of a West Point lieutenant in Vietnam. When he first arrives, he must win the trust of his men, who have been on their tours for a much longer time. As time goes on, he slowly becomes hardened to the realities of the brutal life in the field. Made on the heels of the widely acclaimed "Platoon," but it doesn't have the same power. Norris is martial arts king Chuck Norris' brother. **97m/C VHS.** Michael Dudikoff, Brian Libby, Robert F. Lyons, Rick Fitts, Jesse Dabson, William Smith, Michael De Lorenzo; ***D:*** Aaron Norris; ***W:*** R.J. Marx; ***M:*** George S. Clinton.

Platoon the Warriors 🦴 **1988** The underworld rages with violence when two kingpins, Rex and Bill, become bitter and declare war over a botched drug deal. **90m/C VHS.** David Coley, Dick Crown, James Miller, Don Richard, Alex Sylvian; ***D:*** Philip Ko.

Plato's Run 🦴🦴 **1996 (R)** Ex-CIA agent agrees to free a Cuban who's been falsely imprisoned. But once the job is done, the agent learns he's been double-crossed and the prisoner turns out to be a professional assassin. **96m/C VHS.** Gary Busey, Roy Scheider, Steven Bauer, Jeff Speakman; ***D:*** James Becket; ***W:*** James Becket; ***C:*** Richard Clabaugh; ***M:*** Robert O. Ragland.

Platypus Cove 🦴 **1986** An adopted boy tracks down the culprits responsible for the sabotage of his family's boat, a crime for which he was suspected. Australian. **72m/C VHS.** Paul Smith; ***D:*** Peter Maxwell.

Play Dead 🦴 *Satan's Dog* **1981** Poor Yvonne De Carlo plays a psychotic woman who trains a dog to rip people to shreds. **89m/C VHS.** Yvonne De Carlo, Stephanie Dunham, David Cullinane, Glenn Kezer, Ron Jackson, Carolyn Greenwood; ***D:*** Peter Wittman.

Play for Me 🦴🦴 *Toca Para Mi* **2001** Punk rock drummer Carlos goes on a search for identity after his adoptive father dies. He travels to the town of his birth in the Argentine pampas and meets hooker Fabiana who helps him on his journey. Spanish with subtitles. **101m/C VHS, DVD.** *AR* Hermes Gaido, Maria Laura Frigerio, Alejandro Fiore, Emilio Urdapilleta; ***D:*** Rodrigo Furth; ***W:*** Rodrigo Furth, Eduardo Ruderman; ***C:*** Paula Grandio; ***M:*** Fernando Manuel Dieguez.

Play It Again, Sam 🦴🦴🦴½ **1972 (PG)** Allen is—no surprise—a nerd, and this time he's in love with his best friend's wife. Modest storyline provides a framework of endless gags, with Allen borrowing heavily from "Casablanca." Bogey even appears periodically to counsel Allen on the ways of wooing women. Superior comedy isn't hurt by Ross directing instead of Allen, who adapted the script from his own play. **86m/C VHS, DVD, Wide.** Woody Allen, Diane Keaton, Tony Roberts, Susan Anspach, Jerry Lacy, Jennifer Salt, Joy Bang, Viva, Herbert Ross; ***D:*** Herbert Ross; ***W:*** Woody Allen; ***C:*** Owen Roizman; ***M:*** Billy Goldenberg.

Play It to the Bone 🦴🦴 **1999 (R)** Harrelson and Banderas are fading boxers and best friends Vince and Cesar, who unexpectedly wind up in an undercard bout against each other. Since they need to get to Vegas, and didn't think to get travel money from the promoter, Cesar's girlfriend (and Vince's ex) Grace (Davidovich) agrees to drive them. Along the way, she uses her wiles to whip up their competitive juices to use in the fight. It works, as the excessively brutal fight sequence shows. Shelton's fifth attempt at sports movie success doesn't quite connect, as it's mostly an uninteresting road movie with boxing-movie cliches tacked onto both ends. **124m/C VHS, DVD, Wide.** Woody Harrelson, Antonio Banderas, Lolita (David) Davidovich, Lucy Alexis Liu, Tom Sizemore, Robert Wagner, Richard Masur, Willie Garson, Cylk Cozart, Jack Carter; ***D:*** Ron Shelton; ***W:*** Ron Shelton; ***C:*** Mark Vargo; ***M:*** Alex Wurman.

Play Misty for Me 🦴🦴🦴 **1971 (R)** A radio deejay obliges a psychotic woman's song request and suddenly finds himself the target of her obsessive behavior, which rapidly turns from seductive to murderous. Auspicious directorial debut for Eastwood, borrowing from the Siegel playbook (look for the director's cameo as a barkeep). Based on a story by Heims. **102m/C VHS, DVD, Wide.** Jessica Walter, Donna Mills, John Larch, Irene Hervey, Jack Ging, Clint Eastwood; ***Cameos:*** Donald Siegel; ***D:*** Clint Eastwood; ***W:*** Jo Heims, Dean Riesner; ***C:*** Bruce Surtees; ***M:*** Dee Barton.

Play Murder for Me 🦴🦴 **1991 (R)** Saxophonist performing in a seedy Buenos Aires nightclub has his world turned upside down when a former lover suddenly re-enters his life. She still has her eye on him, but she's now the woman of a notorious mobster. Soon the musician finds himself drawn into the usual deadly world of crime, deceit, and unharnessed passion. **80m/C VHS.** Jack Wagner, Tracy Scoggins; ***D:*** Hector Olivera.

Play Nice 🦴½ **1992 (R)** A detective hunts down a murderous psychopath but is shocked when he discovers his suspect is a woman—and someone he knows. Also available in an unrated version. **90m/C VHS.** Ed O'Ross.

Play Time 🦴🦴 **1994** Jeannie, Lindsay, and their husbands are on vacation in Palm Springs where they get up to some naughty sexual games that test the limits of friendship. Available in an unedited version at 95 minutes. **90m/C VHS, DVD.** Monique Parent, Craig Stepp, Jennifer Burton, Elliot David, Julie Strain, Tammy Parks, Ashlie Rhey; ***D:*** Dale Trevillion; ***W:*** Mary Ellen Hanover; ***C:*** Sven Kirsten; ***M:*** Joel Derouin.

Playback 🦴🦴½ **1995 (R)** Young couple think they've finally captured the gold ring when hubby David (Grant) gets a chance at a million dollar merger deal. But David's set-up by sexy co-worker Karen (Whirry) and his slimy boss Gil (Hamilton) tries to seduce his wife Sara (Kitaen). **91m/C VHS.** Charles Grant, Shannon Whirry, George Hamilton, Tawny Kitaen, Harry Dean Stanton; ***D:*** Oley Sassone; ***W:*** Oley Sassone, David DuBos; ***C:*** Russ Brandt.

Playboy of the Western World 🦴🦴½ **1962** An innkeeper's daughter is infatuated with a young man who says he murdered his father. Adapted from the classic play by John Millington Synge. **96m/C VHS.** *IR* Siobhan McKenna, Gary Raymond; ***D:*** Brian Desmond Hurst.

The Playboys 🦴🦴🦴 **1992 (PG-13)** In 1957 in a tiny Irish village, unmarried Tara Maguire (Wright Penn) causes a scandal by having a baby. Her beauty attracts lots of men—there's a former beau who kills himself, the obsessive, middle-aged Sergeant Hegarty (Finney), and the newest arrival, Tom Castle (Quinn), an actor with a rag-tag theatrical troupe called the Playboys. Slow-moving and simple story with particularly good performances by Wright as the strong-willed Tara and Finney as Hegarty, clinging to a last chance at love and family. The Playboys' hysterically hammy version of "Gone With the Wind" is a gem. Directorial debut of Mackinnon. Filmed in the village of Redhills, Ireland, the hometown of co-writer Connaughton. **114m/C VHS.** Albert Finney, Aidan Quinn, Robin Wright Penn, Milo O'Shea, Alan Devlin, Niamh Cusack, Ian McElhinney, Niall Buggy, Adrian Dunbar; ***D:*** Gilles Mackinnon; ***W:*** Shane Connaughton, Kerry Crabbe; ***C:*** Jack Conroy; ***M:*** Jean-Claude Petit.

The Player 🦴🦴🦴½ **1992 (R)** Clever, entertaining, and biting satire of the movie industry and the greed that controls it. Robbins is dead-on as Griffin Mill, a young studio exec who becomes the chief suspect in a murder investigation. He personifies Hollywood's ethics (or lack thereof) in a performance both cold and vulnerable, as he looks for the right buttons to push and the proper back to stab. Strong leading performances are supplemented by 65 star cameos. Some viewers may be put off by the inside-Hollywood jokes, but Altman fans will love it. **123m/C VHS, DVD, Wide.** Michael Tolkin, Louise Fletcher, Dennis Franz, Malcolm McDowell, Ray Walston, Rene Auberjonois, David Alan Grier, Jayne Meadows, Michael Bowen, Steve James, Brian Tochi, Tim Robbins, Greta Scacchi, Fred Ward, Whoopi Goldberg, Peter Gallagher, Brion James, Cynthia Stevenson, Vincent D'Onofrio, Dean Stockwell, Richard E. Grant, Dina Merrill, Sydney Pollack, Lyle Lovett, Randall Batinkoff, Gina Gershon, Burt Reynolds, Cher, Nick Nolte, Jack Lemmon, Lily Tomlin, Marlee Matlin, Julia Roberts, Bruce Willis, Anjelica Huston, Elliott Gould, Sally Kellerman, Steve Allen, Richard Anderson, Harry Belafonte, Shari Belafonte, Karen Black, Gary Busey, Robert Carradine, James Coburn, Cathy Lee Crosby, John Cusack, Brad Davis, Peter Falk, Teri Garr, Leeza Gibbons, Scott Glenn, Jeff Goldblum, Joel Grey, Buck Henry, Kathy Ireland, Sally Kirkland, Andie MacDowell, Martin Mull, Mimi Rogers, Jill St. John, Susan Sarandon, Rod Steiger, Joan Tewkesbury, Robert Wagner; ***D:*** Robert Altman; ***W:*** Michael Tolkin; ***C:*** Jean Lepine; ***M:*** Thomas Newman. British Acad. '92: Adapt. Screenplay; Cannes '92: Actor (Robbins), Director (Altman); Golden Globes '93: Actor—Mus./Comedy (Robbins), Film—Mus./Comedy; Ind. Spirit '93: Film; N.Y. Film Critics '92: Cinematog., Director (Altman), Film; Writers Guild '92: Adapt. Screenplay.

Players 🦴 **1979 (PG)** Young tennis hustler touring Mexico hooks up with beautiful and mysterious older woman. They seem to be from different worlds yet their love grows. She inspires him enough to enter Wimbledon. Several tennis pros appear, including Guillermo Vilas, John McEnroe, and Ilie Nastase. Almost as boring as watching a real tennis game. **120m/C VHS.** Ali MacGraw, Dean Paul (Dino Martin Jr.) Martin, Maximilian Schell, Pancho Gonzales; ***D:*** Anthony Harvey; ***W:*** Arnold Schulman; ***M:*** Jerry Goldsmith.

The Players Club 🦴🦴🦴 **1998 (R)** Rapper-turned-auteur Ice Cube directs this look at the seamy and steamy world of strip clubs from his own screenplay. Diana (LisaRaye) is a single mom and college student by day, and a dancer at a strip club owned by the bombastic Dollar Bill (Mac) by night. When her naive cousin Ebony (Calhoun) is lured into turning tricks by fellow stripper Ronnie (Wilson), trouble starts. Blue (Foxx) is the deejay who falls for Diana, and is persuaded to act honorably by Diana's disapproving (and target shooting) father (Williams). Ice Cube appears as a customer who inadvertently lights the fuse for the movie's climax. While not in Woody Allen territory yet, Mr. Cube brings both humor and reality to the seedy world of strip joints. **103m/C VHS, DVD.** (Lisa Ray MacCoy) LisaRaye, Bernie Mac, Monica Calhoun, A.J. (Anthony) Johnson, Jamie Foxx, Ice Cube, Dick Anthony Williams, Tommy (Tiny) Lister, John Amos, Faizon Love, Alex Thomas, Chrystale Wilson, Adele Givens, Larry McCoy; ***D:*** Ice Cube; ***W:*** Ice Cube; ***C:*** Malik Hassan Sayeed; ***M:*** Hidden Faces.

Playgirl Killer 🦴 *Decoy for Terror* **1966** After impulsively murdering a restless model, an artist continues to kill indiscriminately, keeping his spoils on ice. Sedaka croons between kills and luxuriates poolside—seemingly oblivious to the plot of the film—while a female decoy is sent to bait the killer for the police. For adult viewers. **86m/C VHS, DVD.** *CA* William Kerwin, Jean Christopher, Andree Champagne, Neil Sedaka; ***D:*** Erick Santamaria.

Playing Away 🦴 **1987** A team of Caribbean cricket players meet a team of stuffy Brits on the field in a clash of the cultures. **100m/C VHS.** *GB* Norman Beaton, Robert Urquhart; ***D:*** Horace Love.

Playing by Heart 🦴🦴 *Dancing about Architecture* **1998 (R)** Excellent ensemble cast doesn't save this episodic film about several L.A. couples falling in and out of love. Theatre director Anderson tries to avoid becoming involved with architect Stewart; loud-mouthed night-clubber Jolie won't give up on Phillippe; Quaid uses bad lines and lies on Kinski and Clarkson, while his wife, Stowe, fools around with Edwards; Connery and Rowlands (in the best-acted segments) find their 40-year marriage threatened by emotional and health problems; and Burstyn tries to comfort her son Mohr, in the last stages of AIDS. Writer/director Carroll claims he was inspired by the saying "talking about love is like dancing about architecture," and appropriately the working title was "Dancing about Architecture." **121m/C VHS, DVD, Wide.** Sean Connery, Gena Rowlands, Ryan Phillippe, Angelina Jolie, Ellen Burstyn, Gillian Anderson, Dennis Quaid, Jay Mohr, Anthony Edwards, Madeleine Stowe, Jon Stewart, Patricia Clarkson, Nastassia Kinski, Jeremy Sisto; *D:* Willard Carroll; *W:* Willard Carroll; *C:* Vilmos Zsigmond; *M:* John Barry.

Playing Dangerous 🦴½ **1995 (PG-13)** Eleven-year-old computer whiz must outsmart computer thieves with the aid of a water gun and a remote-controlled car. **86m/C VHS.** David Keith Miller; *D:* Lawrence Lanoff.

Playing Dead 🦴🦴½ **1915** Drew and his wife portray a married couple in this silent farce. The insecure husband decides to fake his death so his wife can be with the man he thinks she loves. **58m/B VHS.** Sidney Drew, Lucille Drew, Alice Lake, Donald Hall, Harry English, Isadore Marcil; *D:* Sidney Drew.

Playing for Keeps 🦴 **1986 (PG-13)** Three high school grads turn a dilapidated hotel into a rock 'n' roll resort. Music by Pete Townshend, Peter Frampton, Phil Collins, and others. **103m/C VHS.** Daniel Jordano, Matthew Penn, Leon Grant, Harold Gould, Jimmy Baio; *D:* Bob Weinstein.

Playing for Time 🦴🦴🦴 **1980** Compelling, award-winning TV drama based on actual experiences of a Holocaust prisoner who survives by leading an inmate orchestra. Strong playing from Redgrave and Mayron. Pro-Palestinian Redgrave's political beliefs made her a controversial candidate for the role of Jewish Fania Fenelon, but her stunning performance is on the mark. **148m/C VHS.** Vanessa Redgrave, Jane Alexander, Maud Adams, Verna Bloom, Melanie Mayron; *D:* Daniel Mann; *M:* Brad Fiedel. **TV**

Playing God 🦴🦴½ **1996 (R)** Eugene (Duchovny), a disgraced junkie doctor who has lost his license, saves the life of a hood in a bar while trying to score more drugs. This brings him to the attention of Raymond (Hutton), the head of a counterfeiting and smuggling ring, who hires Eugene as his own personal emergency room. While patching up crooks so they don't get arrested at the hospital, Eugene develops more than a doctor-patient relationship with Raymond's pillow-lipped girlfriend Claire (Jolie). Things begin to get a little slicey and dicey for Eugene, until he saves the life of an undercover cop. While sufficiently bloody and nasty, flick tries too hard to be offbeat and hip. **94m/C VHS, DVD.** David Duchovny, Timothy Hutton, Angelina Jolie, Michael Massee, Peter Stormare, Andrew Tiernan, John Hawkes, Gary Dourdan; *D:* Andy Wilson; *W:* Mark Haskell Smith; *C:* Anthony B. Richmond; *M:* Richard Hartley.

Playing Mona Lisa 🦴🦴½ **2000 (R)** Piano prodigy Claire (Witt) gets dumped by her boyfriend on the night of her college graduation and then is humiliated at a piano competition. So, while trying to cope with her problems, Claire decides to adopt a Mona Lisa smile and see what life has to offer. **97m/C VHS, DVD, Wide.** Alicia Witt, Ivan Sergei, Brooke Langton, Johnny Galecki, Elliott Gould, Marlo Thomas, Harvey Fierstein, Molly Hagan, Estelle Harris, Sandra Bernhard, Shannon Finn; *D:* Matthew Huffman; *W:* Marni Freedman, Carlos De Los Rios; *C:* James Glennon.

Playing with Fire 🦴 **197?** A young girl gets caught up in drugs, casual sex, and murder. **87m/C VHS.** Karen Tungay, Danny Keogh, Sam Marais; *D:* Alan Nathanson.

Playmaker 🦴½ **1994 (R)** Jaime (Rubin) is a struggling actress whose coach Talbert (Firth) guarantees success as long as she follows his bizarre training methods, which include seduction, abuse, and betrayal. Good chemistry between the leads but a mishmash of a script. **91m/C VHS.** Jennifer Rubin, Colin Firth, John Getz, Jeffery (Jeff) Perry; *D:* Yuri Zeltser; *W:* Yuri Zeltser; *C:* Ross Berryman; *M:* Mark Snow.

Playmates 🦴 **1941** Barrymore is practically wasted in his last film as a down-on-his-luck actor who agrees to turn bandleader Kyser into a Shakespearean actor. Bizarre comedy is funny at times, but leaves the audience wondering what Barrymore thought he was doing. ♫Humpty Dumpty Heart; How Long Did I Dream?; Que Chica?; Romeo Smith and Juliet Jones; Thank Your Lucky Stars and Stripes. **96m/B VHS.** Kay Kyser, John Barrymore, Ginny Simms, Lupe Velez, May Robson, Patsy Kelly, Peter Lind Hayes, George Cleveland; *D:* David Butler.

Playmates 🦴🦴½ **1972** Two divorced buddies fall in love with each other's ex-wives. Typical Alda vehicle isn't bad. **78m/C VHS.** Doug McClure, Alan Alda, Connie Stevens, Barbara Feldon, Eileen Brennan, Tiger Williams, Severn Darden; *D:* Theodore J. Flicker. **TV**

Playroom 🦴🦴 **1990 (R)** Archaeologist McDonald is completing his father's search for the tomb of a medieval boy-prince. But someone, or something, has been waiting for him for a long, long time. When he finally reaches the long-sought-after tomb, he discovers that it is a torture chamber where his worst nightmares become realities. The demonic prince who was buried in the tomb has picked Chris as his playmate, and the rest of the staff as his personal toys. **87m/C VHS.** Lisa Aliff, Aron Eisenberg, Christopher McDonald, James Purcell, Jamie Rose, Vincent Schiavelli; *D:* Manny Coto; *C:* James L. Carter.

Playtime 🦴🦴🦴 **1967** Occasionally enterprising comedy in which the bemused Frenchman Hulot tries in vain to maintain an appointment in an urban landscape of glass and steel. The theme of cold, unfeeling civilization is hardly unique, but the film is nonetheless enjoyable. The third in the Hulot trilogy, preceded by "Mr. Hulot's Holiday" and "Mon Oncle." In French with English subtitles. **108m/C VHS.** *FR* Jacques Tati, Barbara Dennek, Jacqueline Lecomte, Jack Gautier; *D:* Jacques Tati.

Plaza Suite 🦴🦴🦴 **1971 (PG)** Three alternating skits from Neil Simon's play about different couples staying at the New York hotel. Matthau shines in all three vignettes. Some of Simon's funnier stuff, with the first sketch being the best: Matthau and Stapleton are a couple celebrating their 24th anniversary. She's sentimental, while he's yearning for his mistress. Number two has producer Matthau putting the make on old flame Harris, while the finale has father Matthau coaxing his anxious daughter out of the bathroom on her wedding day. **114m/C VHS.** Walter Matthau, Maureen Stapleton, Barbara Harris, Lee Grant, Louise Sorel; *D:* Arthur Hiller; *W:* Neil Simon; *M:* Maurice Jarre.

Pleasantville 🦴🦴🦴½ **1998 (PG-13)** Nerdy David (Maguire) and his slut wanna-be sister Jennifer (Witherspoon) are sucked into the sterile and innocent world of Pleasantville, a 1950s B/W TV show in constant reruns, where they find themselves in the roles of Bud and Mary Sue, the blandly adorable children of George and Betty Parker (Macy and Allen). After Jennifer shows a classmate what lovers' lane is really for, the townspeople begin to lose their innocence; the black-and-white world becomes more colorful as each new human passion is realized. The performances are dead-on, particularly Allen as the sexually awakening mom. The transition from straight comedy to social commentary is adeptly handled. The great character actor J. T. Walsh gives his usual excellent (and sadly, last) performance as the stubborn head of the chamber of commerce bitterly fighting change. **124m/C VHS, DVD, Wide.** Tobey Maguire, Reese Witherspoon, William H. Macy, Joan Allen, Jeff Daniels, J.T. Walsh, Don Knotts, Paul Walker, Jane Kaczmarek, Marley Shelton; *D:* Gary Ross; *W:* Gary Ross; *C:* John Lindley; *M:* Randy Newman. L.A. Film Critics '98: Support. Actress (Allen); Broadcast Film Critics '98: Support. Actress (Allen).

Please Don't Eat My Mother woof! *Hungry Pets; Glump* **1972** A softcore remake of "Little Shop of Horrors" in which a lonely voyeur plays host to a human-eating plant. **95m/C VHS, DVD.** Buck Kartalian, Lynn Lundgren, Art Hedberg, Alice Fredlund, Adam Blair, Flora Wiesel, Ric Lutze, Renee Bond, Dash Fremont; *D:* Carl Monson; *W:* Eric Norden; *C:* Jack Beckett; *M:* Dan Foly.

Please Don't Eat the Daisies 🦴🦴½ **1960** City couple and kids leave the Big Apple for the country and are traumatized by flora and fauna. Goofy '60s fluff taken from Jean Kerr's book and the basis for the eventual TV series. **111m/C VHS, Wide.** Doris Day, David Niven, Janis Paige, Spring Byington, Richard Haydn, Patsy Kelly, Jack Weston, Margaret Lindsay; *D:* Charles Walters.

Please Not Now! 🦴🦴 *Only for Love; La Bride sur le Cou* **1961** Parisian model Bardot discovers her boyfriend Riberolles is cheating on her and she decides to shoot him. He's warned by Subor, who wants Bardot for himself, and takes off with new gal pal James, but Bardot and Subor are in pursuit. Then Bardot and James commiserate over the fact that men are scum and decide to team up against their lovers. French with subtitles. **74m/B VHS, DVD, Wide.** *FR IT* Brigitte Bardot, Josephine James, Michel Subor, Jacques Riberolles, Mireille Darc, Serge Marquand, Claude Brasseur, Jean Tissier, Bernard Fresson, Claude Berri; *D:* Roger Vadim, J(ack) D(unn) Trop; *W:* Roger Vadim, Claude Brule, J(ack) D(unn) Trop; *C:* Robert Lefebvre; *M:* James Campbell.

Pleasure 🦴🦴 **1931** A saga of love, treachery, and melodrama in English society where self-indulgence held priority and good manners were the rule. **53m/B VHS.** Conway Tearle, Roscoe Karns, Carmel Myers, Lena Basquette.

A Pleasure Doing Business 🦴 **1979 (R)** Three high school buddies, now in their 40s, are reunited at a stag party, where they decide to go into business as managers in "the oldest profession." **86m/C VHS.** Conrad Bain, John Byner, Alan Oppenheimer, Misty Rowe, Phyllis Diller, Tom Smothers; *D:* Steve Vagnino.

Pleasure Palace 🦴🦴 **1980** A gambling lady's-man (Sharif) meets his match when he helps a woman casino owner (Lange). **96m/C VHS.** Omar Sharif, Victoria Principal, J.D. Cannon, Gerald S. O'Loughlin, Jose Ferrer, Hope Lange, Alan King; *D:* Walter Grauman. **TV**

The Pledge 🦴🦴🦴 **2000 (R)** Retired Reno homicide detective Nicholson is obsessed with the unsolved murder of a little girl, which bares a resemblance to past unsolved child murders. Unconventional thriller's dark subject matter will no doubt dissuade some potential viewers, but Penn's third (and best) directorial outing is impressive, thanks in large part to Nicholson's subtle, intense work. **124m/C VHS, DVD, Wide.** *US* Jack Nicholson, Robin Wright Penn, Aaron Eckhart, Vanessa Redgrave, Patricia Clarkson, Benicio Del Toro, Costas Mandylor, Helen Mirren, Tom Noonan, Michael O'Keefe, Mickey Rourke, Sam Shepard, Lois Smith, Harry Dean Stanton, Dale Dickey, Pauline Roberts; *D:* Sean Penn; *W:* Jerzy Kromolowski, Mary Olson-Kromolowski; *C:* Chris Menges; *M:* Hans Zimmer.

Pledge Night 🦴🦴 **1990 (R)** Tale of horror and revenge. Killed years before in a fraternity hazing, Sid returns for the brothers who did him in. Gory and violent. **90m/C VHS.** Will Kempe, Shannon McMahon, Todd Eastland; *D:* Paul Ziller.

Plenty 🦴🦴½ **1985 (R)** Difficult but worthwhile film with Streep in top form as a former member of the French Resistance, who upon returning to England finds life at home increasingly tedious and banal and begins to fear her finest hours may be behind her. Gielgud is flawless as the aging career diplomat. Adapted by David Hare from his play, an allegory to British decline. **119m/C VHS, DVD, Wide.** Meryl Streep, Tracey Ullman, Sting, John Gielgud, Charles Dance, Ian McKellen, Sam Neill, Burt Kwouk; *D:* Fred Schepisi; *W:* David Hare; *C:* Ian Baker; *M:* Bruce Smeaton. L.A. Film Critics '85: Support. Actor (Gielgud); Natl. Soc. Film Critics '85: Support. Actor (Gielgud).

The Plot Against Harry 🦴🦴🦴 **1969** Jewish racketeer Harry Plotnik checks out of prison, and finds the outside world ain't what it used to be. Attempting to lead an honest life only makes matters worse. Completely overlooked when first released in 1969 (and quickly shelved) because it was considered to have no commercial potential, Roemer's crime comedy found an enthusiastic audience when it was rediscovered 20 years later. **81m/B VHS.** Martin Priest, Ben Lang, Maxine Woods, Henry Nemo, Jacques Taylor, Ellen Herbert, Sandra Kazan; *D:* Michael Roemer; *W:* Michael Roemer; *C:* Robert M. Young; *M:* Frank Lewin.

The Ploughman's Lunch 🦴🦴🦴 **1983** A BBC news reporter claws and lies his way to the top. He then discovers that he is the victim of a far more devious plan. Engrossing and well made, although some of the political views are simplistic. **107m/C VHS.** Jonathan Pryce, Charlie Dore, Tim Curry, Rosemary Harris, Frank Finlay, Bill Paterson; *D:* Richard Eyre.

Plucking the Daisy 🦴🦴½ *Please! Mr. Balzac; While Plucking the Daisy; En Effeuillant la Marguerite; Mademoiselle Striptease* **1956** Agnes Dumont (Bardot) anonymously writes a scandalous romantic novel that becomes a best-seller and causes her straitlaced father to send Agnes to a convent school. Only she escapes to her brother's in Paris instead, where she decides to earn some money by entering a striptease contest (which serves to put enticing Bardot's ample charms on display). French with subtitles. **100m/B VHS, DVD.** *FR* Brigitte Bardot, Robert Hirsch, Daniel Gelin, Jacques Dumesnil; *D:* Marc Allegret; *W:* Marc Allegret, Roger Vadim; *C:* Louis Page; *M:* Paul Misraki.

Plughead Rewired: Circuitry Man 2 🦴🦴 *Circuitry Man 2* **1994 (R)** Earth's atmosphere has been destroyed and survivors are forced underground, where they're terrorized by the humanoid Plughead, who likes to literally plug into the minds of his victims. Plughead wants to rule what's left of life on Earth and all that stands in his way is the android Circuitry Man and FBI agent Kyle. Special effects are strictly bargain basement level. **97m/C VHS, DVD, Wide.** Vernon Wells, Deborah Shelton, Jim Metzler, Dennis Christopher, Nicholas Worth, Traci Lords; *D:* Steven Lovy, Robert Lovy; *W:* Steven Lovy, Robert Lovy; *C:* Stephen Timberlake; *M:* Tim Kelly.

Plumber 🦴🦴½ **1979** A plumber who makes a house call extends his stay to psychologically torture the woman of the house. Originally made for Australian TV. **76m/C VHS.** *AU* Judy Morris, Ivar Kants, Robert Coleby; *D:* Peter Weir; *W:* Peter Weir. **TV**

Plump Fiction 🦴 **1997 (R)** The movie that proves beyond a doubt that when you make fun of Quentin Tarantino, you should stick to his truly horrible acting. Instead, this spoof attacks his already over-the-top characters from "Pulp Fiction" and "Natural Born Killers." Julius (Davidson) and Jimmy (Dinello) are the loser hit men, and Mimi (Brown) is the gangster's wife. You see, Mimi has a substance abuse problem, but it's not cocaine. It's food! She's fat, get it? Ha! Ha ha. Ha? Hmm. Intersecting storylines feature Nicky (Glave) and Vallory (Segall, doing a dead-on Juliette Lewis) as "Natural Blonde Killers." The only redeeming scene is that of Kane Picoy as "Christopher Walken character," doing an uncanny impersonation of the king of the psychos. **82m/C VHS, DVD.** Tommy Davidson, Julie Brown, Sandra Bernhard, Paul Dinello, Dan Castellaneta, Colleen Camp, Pamela Segall, Kevin Meaney, Matthew Glave, Jennifer Rubin, Robert Costanzo, Phillipe Bergerone; *D:* Bob Koherr; *W:* Bob Koherr; *C:* Rex Nicholson; *M:* Michael Muhlfriedel.

Plunder Road 🦴🦴½ **1957** A pair of crooks cook up a plan to rob a train bound for the San Francisco Mint that's carrying a fortune in gold bullion. Top notch B-film noir. **76m/B VHS.** Gene Raymond, Jeanne Cooper, Wayne Morris, Elisha Cook Jr.; *D:* Hubert Cornfield.

Plunge Into Darkness 🦴½ **1977** Quiet weekend in the mountains turns into a nightmare for an ex-Olympic runner and his family. **77m/C VHS.** Bruce Barry, Olivia Hamnett, Ashley Greenville, Wallace Eaton, Tom Richards; *D:* Peter Maxwell.

Plunkett & Macleane 🦴🦴 **1998 (R)** Will Plunkett (Carlyle) is a lower-class thief who teams up with wastrel aristocrat Macleane (Miller) for careers as highwaymen in 18th-century London. The rogues are aided by hedonistic Lord Rochester

(Cumming) and opposed by Lord Chief Justice Gibson (Gambon), whose vixenish niece, Lady Rebecca (Tyler), becomes Macleane's inamorata. Carlyle and Miller make a fine criminal duo but the film has lots of flaws to distract the viewer. (Son of Ridley) Scott's directorial debut. **102m/C VHS, DVD, Wide.** *GB* Robert Carlyle, Jonny Lee Miller, Liv Tyler, Michael Gambon, Alan Cumming, Ken Stott, Terence Rigby, Claire Rushbrook, Iain Robertson, Dave Atkins; ***D:*** Jake Scott; ***W:*** Robert Wade, Neal Purvis, Charles McKeown; ***C:*** John Mathieson; ***M:*** Craig Armstrong.

Plutonium Baby ℐ **1987** A mutated kid, whose mother was killed by the same radiation exposure that infected him, tracks down the guilty party in New York in this comic-book style film. **85m/C VHS.** Patrick Molloy, Danny Guerra; ***D:*** Ray Hirschman.

Plutonium Incident ℐℐ **1982** A female technician at a nuclear power plant suspects the facility to be less safe than it appears, and faces a diabolical plan of harassment when she attempts to bring attention to the hazards. **90m/C VHS.** Janet Margolin, Powers Boothe, Bo Hopkins, Joseph Campanella; ***D:*** Richard Michaels.

Pocahontas ℐℐℐ **1995 (G)** It's 1607 and spirited Powhatan maiden Pocahontas and British settler Captain John Smith strike an unlikely but doomed romance in Disney's 33rd animated feature, its first based on the life of a historical figure. Lovely Poca, a virtual post-adolescent Native American superbabe, introduces the roguish captain (spoken and sung by Gibson) to the wonders of unspoiled nature and serves as peacemaker in the clash of European and Native American cultures. Disney puts its spin on history but maintains cultural sensitivity: several characters are voiced by Native American performers, including Chief Powhatan, spoken by American Indian activist Means, who led the 1973 siege at Wounded Knee, and Bedard as Pocahantas. Just don't tell the kids the real Pocahontas married someone else, moved to England, and died of smallpox at 21. Stunningly animated, but its mediocre soundtrack and decidedly somber tone leave it lacking in typical Disney majesty and charm. Premiered at New York's Central Park, for the usual theatre crowd of 100,000 or so. **90m/C VHS, DVD, Wide.** ***D:*** Mike Gabriel, Eric Goldberg; ***W:*** Carl Binder, Susannah Grant, Philip LaZebnik; ***M:*** Alan Menken, Stephen Schwartz; ***V:*** Irene Bedard, Judy Kuhn, Mel Gibson, Joe Baker, Christian Bale, Billy Connolly, James Apaumut Fall, Linda Hunt, John Kassir, Danny Mann, Bill Cobbs, David Ogden Stiers, Michelle St. John, Gordon Tootoosis, Frank Welker. Oscars '95: Song ("Colors of the Wind"), Orig. Score; Golden Globes '96: Song ("Colors of the Wind").

Pocahontas: The Legend ℐℐ½ **1995** Live-action version of the increasingly familiar story of the Native American girl who aids Virginia settler, John Smith. **101m/C VHS.** *CA* Sandrine Holt, Miles O'Keeffe, Tony Goldwyn, Gordon Tootoosis; ***D:*** Daniele Suissa; ***W:*** Daniele Suissa.

The Pocatello Kid ℐ½ **1931** Maynard stretches in a dual role as the wrongly convicted Kid and the Kid's no-good sheriff brother. **60m/B VHS.** Ken Maynard, Marceline Day, Charles "Blackie" King, Lafe (Lafayette) McKee; ***D:*** Phil Rosen.

Pocket Money ℐℐ **1972 (PG)** Down-on-their-luck cowpokes foolishly do business with crooked rancher in attempt to make comeback in faltering acting careers. Star-powered, moderately entertaining modern western-comedy based on the novel "Jim Kane" by J.K.S. Brown. **100m/C VHS.** Paul Newman, Lee Marvin, Strother Martin, Christine Belford, Wayne Rogers, Hector Elizondo, Gregory Sierra; ***D:*** Stuart Rosenberg; ***W:*** Terrence Malick; ***M:*** Alex North.

Pocketful of Miracles ℐℐℐ **1961** Capra's final film, a remake of his 1933 "Lady for a Day," is just as corny and sentimental but doesn't work quite as well. Davis is delightful as Apple Annie, a down-on-her-luck street vendor who will go to any extreme to hide her poverty from the well-married daughter she adores. Ford is terrific as the man who transforms Annie into a lady in time for her daughter's visit. Touching. Maybe too touching. Also marks Ann-Margret's film debut. **136m/C VHS, DVD, Wide.** Bette Davis, Glenn Ford, Peter Falk, Hope Lange, Arthur O'Connell, Ann-Margret, Thomas Mitchell, Jack Elam, Edward Everett Horton, David Brian, Mickey Shaughnessy; ***D:*** Frank Capra; ***W:*** Hal Kanter, Harry Tugend; ***C:*** Robert J. Bronner; ***M:*** Walter Scharf. Golden Globes '62: Actor—Mus./Comedy (Ford).

A Pocketful of Rye ℐℐ *Agatha Christie's Miss Marple: A Pocketful of Rye* **1987** Based on Agatha Christie's novel featuring the sleuthing Miss Marple. She faces another murderous puzzle, this one based on an old nursery rhyme. **101m/C VHS.** *GB* Joan Hickson; ***D:*** Guy Slater. **TV**

Poco ℐ **1977** The story of Poco, a shaggy little dog who travels across the country to search for the young girl who owns him. **88m/C VHS.** Chill Wills, Michelle Ashburn, John Steadman.

Poetic Justice ℐℐ½ **1993 (R)** Justice (Jackson in her movie debut, for better or worse) gives up college plans to follow a career in cosmetology after her boyfriend's brutal murder. She copes with her loss by dedicating herself to poetry writing (provided by no less than poet Maya Angelou) and meets postal worker Shakur. Singleton's second directorial effort is about the girlz n the hood and boasts a lighter script (well, it is about a hairdresser) focusing less on the Boyz-style morality and more on the trials and tribulations of Justice. Production stopped on the South Central L.A. set during the '92 riots, but the aftermath provided poignant pictures for later scenes. **109m/C VHS, DVD, 8mm, Wide.** Janet Jackson, Tupac Shakur, Tyra Ferrell, Regina King, Joe Torry, Norma Donaldson; ***D:*** John Singleton; ***W:*** John Singleton; ***C:*** Peter Collister; ***M:*** Stanley Clarke. MTV Movie Awards '94: Female Perf. (Jackson), Most Desirable Female (Jackson); Golden Raspberries '93: Worst New Star (Jackson).

Pogo for President: "I Go Pogo" ℐℐ½ **1984 (PG)** Animated adventure with Walt Kelly's Pogo Possum becoming an unlikely presidential candidate when Howland Owl proclaims him the winner of a election. **120m/C VHS.** ***V:*** Jonathan Winters, Vincent Price, Ruth Buzzi, Stan Freberg, Jimmy Breslin, Arnold Stang.

Poil de Carotte ℐℐ½ *The Red Head* **1931** A semi-famous French melodrama about a young boy harassed by his overbearing mother to the point of disaster, redeemed finally by the love of his father. In French with English subtitles. **90m/B VHS.** *FR* Harry Baur, Robert Lynen, Catherine Fontenoy; ***D:*** Julien Duvivier.

The Point **1971** Charming and sincere animated feature about the rejection and isolation of a round-headed child in a world of pointy-headed people. Excellent score. **74m/C VHS.** ***D:*** Fred Wolf; ***M:*** Harry Nilsson; ***V:*** Paul Frees; ***Nar:*** Ringo Starr. **TV**

Point Blank ℐℐ½ **1967** Adapted from Stark's "The Hunter." The film's techniques are sometimes compared to those of Resnais and Godard. Double-crossed and believed dead, gangster Marvin returns to claim his share of the loot from the Organization. Hard-nosed examination of the depersonalization of a mechanized urban world. **92m/C VHS, Wide.** Lee Marvin, Angie Dickinson, Keenan Wynn, Carroll O'Connor, Lloyd Bochner, Michael Strong, James B. Sikking; ***D:*** John Boorman.

Point Blank ℐ½ **1998 (R)** A bus carrying death-row convicts is ambushed but the cons don't go their separate ways. Instead, they take over a shopping mall and begin fighting among themselves. **90m/C VHS, DVD.** Mickey Rourke, Danny Trejo, Kevin Gage, Michael Wright, Frederic Forrest, James Gammon; ***D:*** Matt Earl Beesley. **VIDEO**

Point Break ℐℐ½ **1991 (R)** If you can suspend your disbelief—and you'd need a crane—then this crime adventure is just dandy. Reeves is a young undercover FBI kid sent to infiltrate a gang of bank-robbing surfer dudes. Swayze is the leader of the beach subculture, a thrill-seeker who plays cat-and-mouse with the feds in a series of excellent action scenes. Silly brain candy. **117m/C VHS, DVD, Wide.** Patrick Swayze, Keanu Reeves, Gary Busey, Lori Petty, John C. McGinley, Chris Pederson, Bojesse Christopher, Julian Reyes, Daniel Beer, Sydney Walsh, Vincent Klyn, James LeGros, John Philbin; ***D:*** Kathryn Bigelow; ***W:*** W. Peter Iliff; ***C:*** Don Peterman; ***M:*** Mark Isham. MTV Movie Awards '92: Most Desirable Male (Reeves).

Point of Impact ℐℐ **1993 (R)** A Miami customs officer is killed in an explosion and his partner is blamed. He knows a Cuban crime boss was actually behind it and goes undercover to bring the criminal organization down. But there's also the temptation of the criminal's sexy lady-friend. Also available in an unrated version. **96m/C VHS.** Michael Pare, Barbara Carrera, Michael Ironside.

Point of No Return ℐℐ½ **1993 (R)** Fonda is Maggie, a drugged-out loser condemned to death for her part in a murder spree, but if she agrees to work as a government assassin, she'll be given a reprieve. Fonda displays a certain perkiness as the assassin and is better in her early surly scenes; Keitel is creepy as another assassin. Flashy, exacting, but ultimately innocuous remake of the 1990 French thriller "La Femme Nikita." **108m/C VHS, DVD, Wide.** Bridget Fonda, Gabriel Byrne, Dermot Mulroney, Miguel Ferrer, Anne Bancroft, Olivia D'Abo, Harvey Keitel, Richard Romanus, Lorraine Toussaint, Geoffrey Lewis, Calvin Levels; ***D:*** John Badham; ***W:*** Robert Getchell, Alexandra Seros; ***C:*** Michael Watkins; ***M:*** Hans Zimmer.

Point of Terror ℐ **1971 (R)** A handsome rock singer seduces a record company executive's wife in order to further his career. **88m/C VHS.** Peter Carpenter, Dyanne Thorne, Lory Hansen, Leslie Simms; ***D:*** Alex Nicol.

The Pointsman ℐℐ½ *De Wisselwachter* **1986 (R)** A quirky, small film based on the novel by Jean Paul Franssens. A beautiful Scandinavian woman accidentally gets off a train in Northern Scotland, where the only shelter is a small railway outpost, and the only company is a mysterious pointsman who lives by the comings and goings of the trains. The couple's increasing isolation as winter falls and their lack of a common language persists is portrayed with both humor and poignancy. **95m/C VHS.** *NL* Jim Van Der Woude, Stephane Excoffier, John Kraaykamp, Josse De Pauw, Ton Van Dort; ***D:*** Jos Stelling.

Poison ℐℐℐ **1991 (R)** A controversial, compelling drama weaving the story of a seven year-old boy's murder of his father with two other tales of obsessive, fringe behavior. From the director of the underground hit "Superstar: The Karen Carpenter Story," which was shot using only a cast of "Barbie" dolls. **85m/C VHS, DVD.** Edith Meeks, Larry Maxwell, Susan Norman, Scott Renderer, James Lyons, Millie White, Buck Smith, Anne Giotta, Al Quagliata, Michelle Sullivan, John R. Lombardi, Tony Pemberton, Andrew Harpending; ***D:*** Todd Haynes; ***W:*** Todd Haynes; ***C:*** Maryse Alberti; ***M:*** James Bennett. Sundance '91: Grand Jury Prize.

Poison Ivy ℐℐ **1985** A routine comedy about a chaotic and lusty summer camp. **97m/C VHS.** Michael J. Fox, Nancy McKeon, Robert Klein, Caren Kaye; ***D:*** Larry Elikann; ***M:*** Miles Goodman. **TV**

Poison Ivy ℐℐ **1992 (R)** Barrymore is right on target as a junior femme fatale in this trashy tale of a wayward teenager and her takeover of her best friend's family. Ivy has no discernable family life and quickly attaches herself to the lonely, neglected Cooper (Gilbert) who ends up watching as she systematically seduces both her mother (emotionally) and her father (physically). But when Ivy's homewrecking turns lethal, Cooper must fight her "friend" to save herself. Glossy, over-done pulp. An unrated version is also available. **91m/C VHS, DVD.** Drew Barrymore, Sara Gilbert, Tom Skerritt, Cheryl Ladd; ***D:*** Katt Shea; ***W:*** Katt Shea, Andy Ruben; ***C:*** Phedon Papamichael; ***M:*** David Michael Frank.

Poison Ivy 2: Lily ℐ½ **1995 (R)** Art student Lily (Milano) finds the provocative Ivy's diary and becomes intrigued enough to decide to take a walk on the wild side herself, which gets her into all sorts of trouble. Also available unrated. **110m/C VHS, DVD.** Alyssa Milano, Xander Berkeley, Johnathon Schaech, Belinda Bauer; ***D:*** Anne Goursaud; ***W:*** Chloe King; ***C:*** Suki Medencevic; ***M:*** Joseph Williams.

Poison Ivy 3: The New Seduction ℐ½ **1997 (R)** Now Ivy has a long-lost sister, appropriately named Violet (Pressly), who heads to their childhood home to get revenge on those she believes betrayed them. Naturally, it's all sex and men being led around by their...zippers. Also available unrated. **93m/C VHS, DVD.** Jaime Pressly, Megan Edwards, Michael Des Barres, Greg Vaughan; ***D:*** Kurt Voss; ***W:*** Karen Kelly; ***C:*** Feliks Parnell; ***M:*** Reg Powell.

Pokemon 3: The Movie ℐℐ **2001 (G)** As opposed to what, "Pokemon 3: The Dinner Theater?" This installment of the interminable franchise has a young girl, who's father has disappeared, turning her surroundings into a land of icy crystal. Ash, Pikachu and the other Pokemon (Pokemen?) show up to save the day with various pocket monster battles. Lessons are learned, battles are fought and won or lost, and days are saved, except for the days wasted by parents who have to sit throught it all. **88m/C VHS, Wide.** ***D:*** Kunihiko Yuyama, Michael Haigney; ***W:*** Michael Haigney, Norman Grossfeld, Takeshi Shudo, Hideki Sonoda; ***V:*** Veronica Taylor, Eric Stuart, Rachael Lillis, Maddie Blaustein, Ikue Otani.

Pokemon: The First Movie ℐℐ **1999 (G)** If your kid is saying things like "Pikachu," "Squirtle," and "Charizard," then you've already been introduced to the multimedia (and mucho dollar) world of Pokemon. In that case, you'll be forced to rent or buy this movie regardless of any criticism (unless by the time you read this the craze has gone the way of the Teenage Mutant Ninja Turtle). In this full-length version of the popular cartoon series (video game, trading card game, toy line, etc...), hero Ash and his pals Misty and Brock go to New Island to do battle with a twisted genetically engineered Pokemon called Mewtwo. Mewtwo defeats all the Pokemon trainers in battle, and is ready to clone hideous monsters from the defeated critters when he is challenged by the mysterious and rare Mew. Several new characters are introduced along with clever marketing ties, because apparently the gigantic pile of money this stuff is generating is not yet the size of Mt. Fuji. Also contains the short "Pikachu's Vacation." **75m/C VHS, DVD.** ***D:*** Kunihiko Yuyama, Michael Haigney; ***W:*** Michael Haigney, Takeshi Shudo; ***C:*** Hisao Shirai.

Pokemon the Movie 2000: The Power of One *Poketto Monsutaa: Maboroshi No Pokemon X: Lugia Bakudan* **2000 (G)** As with the first Pokemon movie, considerations such as quality, plot, characterization, or dialogue do not matter. If you have kids under ten years old, you will be forced to rent (or more likely buy) this movie and watch it repeatedly. If you don't have any kids under ten, you most likely don't know or care what a Pokemon is anyway. If you do, for some strange reason, need to know the plot, here it is: Ash must stop the Collector from capturing Pokemon. If the kiddies like the Pokemon, they'll enjoy this little exercise in media overkill. **103m/C VHS, DVD.** *JP* ***D:*** Kunihiko Yuyama, Michael Haigney; ***W:*** Michael Haigney, Takeshi Shudo; ***M:*** Ralph Schuckett, John Loeffler.

Poker Alice ℐℐ **1987** A lively Western starring Elizabeth Taylor as a sometime gambler who wins a brothel in a poker game. **100m/C VHS.** Elizabeth Taylor, George Hamilton, Tom Skerritt, Richard Mulligan, David Wayne, Susan Tyrrell, Pat Corley; ***D:*** Arthur Seidelman; ***W:*** James Lee Barrett.

Pola X ℐℐ **1999** French film continues to push the sexual envelope even when it's inspired by Herman Melville's 1852 novel, "Pierre, or, the Ambiguities." Rich boy Pierre (Depardieu) lives with his beautiful widowed mother, Marie (Deneuve), in a country chateau. He's about to marry his faithful girlfriend, Lucie (Chuillot), when a strange woman named Isabelle (Golubeva) shows up, claiming to be Pierre's half-sister. Soon Pierre is living the grunge life with Isabelle in Paris and the two are involved in an incestuous relationship (some of which is explicitly displayed). Another bizarre film from auteur Carax. French with subtitles. **134m/C VHS, DVD, Wide.** *FR* Guillaume Depardieu, Katerina Golubeva, Catherine Deneuve, Delphine Chuillot, Laurent Lucas; ***D:*** Leos Carax; ***W:*** Leos Carax, Jean-Pol Fargeau, Lauren Sedofsky; ***C:*** Eric Gautier; ***M:*** Scott Walker.

The Polar Bear King **1994 (PG)** When a handsome prince refuses to marry the evil witch of Summerland, the wicked woman uses her power to turn him into a polar bear. The polar bear prince embarks on a journey to Winterland where he meets and falls in love with a beautiful princess. Together they return to Summerland and try to break the witch's spell. Filmed on location in Norway and Sweden. **87m/C VHS.** Maria Bonnevie, Jack Fjeldstad, Tobias Hoesl, Anna-Lotta Larsson; ***D:*** Ola Solum.

Poldark **1975** Tempestuous love, political intrigue, and family struggles all set in 18th-century Cornwall, then the copper-producing center of England. Heroic Ross Poldark has just returned from fighting upstart Americans in the Revolutionary War only to discover that his father has died and the family mines are about to be sold to the scheming Warleggan family. Ross struggles to pay off family debts, reclaim his heritage, resolve his feelings for an old love, and fight his attraction to the beguiling, but completely unsuitable, Demelza. Adapted from the novels by Winston Graham. **720m/C VHS.** *GB* Robin Ellis, Angharad Rees, Jill Townsend, Judy Geeson, Ralph Bates, Richard Morant, Clive Francis, John Baskcomb, Paul Curran, Tilly Tremayne, Mary Wimbush; ***D:*** Paul Annett, Christopher Barry, Kenneth Ives; ***W:*** Paul Wheeler, Peter Draper, Jack Pulman. **TV**

Poldark **1996** Picks up the story of Ross and Demelza Poldark and their family from where the 1970's BBC series ended. It's 1810 and Ross is spending most of his time in London as a Member of Parliament while at their Cornwall home, Demelza deals with the continuing Warleggan feud. Poldark son, Jeremy, struggles to keep the mine going and daughter Clowance is in the throes of her first romance. Based on the novel "The Stranger from the Sea" by Winston Graham. **105m/C VHS, DVD.** *GB* John Bowe, Mel Martin, Ioan Gruffudd, Mike Attwell, Kelly Reilly, Hans Matheson, Amanda Ryan, Nicholas Gleaves, Gabrielle Lloyd, Sarah Carpenter; ***D:*** Richard Laxton; ***W:*** Robin Mukbarjee; ***C:*** Rex Maidment; ***M:*** Ian Hughes. **TV**

Poldark 2 **1975** The further adventures of Ross Poldark, wife Demelza, and assorted family, friends, and enemies, all set in 18th-century Cornwall. Demelza's two meddlesome younger brothers come to live at Nampara, enemy George Warleggan and Ross' old love Elizabeth move too close for comfort, and the uncertainties of the copper mining economy all bring their share of trouble. Adapted from the novels by Winston Graham. Made for British TV; six cassettes. **720m/C VHS.** *GB* Robin Ellis, Angharad Rees, Jill Townsend, Judy Geeson, Ralph Bates, Kevin McNally, Brian Stirner, Michael Cadman, Jane Wymark, David Delve, Christopher Biggins, Trudie Styler; ***D:*** Philip Dudley, Roger Jenkins; ***W:*** Alexander Baron, John Wiles, Martin Worth. **TV**

Police **1985** French police drama with the intense Depardieu as a cop hunting an Algerian drug boss. Matters grow complicated when he falls for the elusive crook's girlfriend. Sometimes gripping, but unveven; the actors were encouraged to improvise. Inspired by the novel "Bodies Are Dust" by P.J. Wolfson. In French with English subtitles. **113m/C VHS.** *FR* Gerard Depardieu, Sophie Marceau, Sandrine Bonnaire, Richard Anconina, Pascale Rocard; ***D:*** Maurice Pialat; ***W:*** Catherine Breillat. Venice Film Fest. '85: Actor (Depardieu).

Police Academy **1984 (R)** In an attempt to recruit more cops, a big-city police department does away with all its job standards. The producers probably didn't know that they were introducing bad comedy's answer to the "Friday the 13th" series, but it's hard to avoid heaping the sins of its successors on this film. Besides, it's just plain dumb. **96m/C VHS, DVD, 8mm.** Steve Guttenberg, Kim Cattrall, Bubba Smith, George Gaynes, Michael Winslow, Leslie Easterbrook, Georgina Spelvin, Debralee Scott; ***D:*** Hugh Wilson; ***W:*** Hugh Wilson, Pat Proft, Neal Israel; ***C:*** Michael D. Margulies; ***M:*** Robert Folk.

Police Academy 2: Their First Assignment **1985 (PG-13)** More predictable idiocy from the cop shop. This time they're determined to rid the precinct of some troublesome punks. No real story to speak of, just more high jinks in this mindless sequel. **87m/C VHS.** Steve Guttenberg, Bubba Smith, Michael Winslow, Art Metrano, Colleen Camp, Howard Hesseman, David Graf, George Gaynes; ***D:*** Jerry Paris; ***W:*** Barry W. Blaustein.

Police Academy 3: Back in Training **1986 (PG)** In yet another sequel, the bumbling cops find their alma mater is threatened by a budget crunch and they must compete with a rival academy to see which school survives. The "return to school" plot allowed the filmmakers to add new characters to replace those who had some scruples about picking up yet another "Police Lobotomy" check. Followed by three more sequels. **84m/C VHS.** Steve Guttenberg, Bubba Smith, David Graf, Michael Winslow, Marion Ramsey, Art Metrano, Bob(cat) Goldthwait, Leslie Easterbrook, Tim Kazurinsky, George Gaynes, Shawn Weatherly; ***D:*** Jerry Paris; ***W:*** Gene Quintano; ***M:*** Robert Folk.

Police Academy 4: Citizens on Patrol **1987 (PG)** The comic cop cutups from the first three films aid a citizen's patrol group in their unnamed, but still wacky, hometown. Moronic high jinks ensue. Fourth in the series of five (or is it six?) that began with "Police Academy." **88m/C VHS.** James Carroll, Steve Guttenberg, Bubba Smith, Michael Winslow, David Graf, Tim Kazurinsky, George Gaynes, Colleen Camp, Bob(cat) Goldthwait, Sharon Stone; ***D:*** Jim Drake; ***W:*** Gene Quintano; ***M:*** Robert Folk.

Police Academy 5: Assignment Miami Beach woof! **1988 (PG)** The fourth sequel, wherein the misfits-with-badges go to Miami and bumble about in the usual manner. It's about time these cops were retired from the force. **89m/C VHS.** Bubba Smith, David Graf, Michael Winslow, Leslie Easterbrook, Rene Auberjonois, Marion Ramsey, Janet Jones, George Gaynes, Matt McCoy; ***D:*** Alan Myerson; ***W:*** Stephen J. Curwick; ***M:*** Robert Folk.

Police Academy 6: City under Siege **1989 (PG)** In what is hoped to be the last in a series of bad comedies, the distinguished graduates pursue three goofballs responsible for a crime wave. **85m/C VHS.** Bubba Smith, David Graf, Michael Winslow, Leslie Easterbrook, Marion Ramsey, Matt McCoy, Bruce Mahler, G.W. Bailey, George Gaynes; ***D:*** Peter Bonerz; ***W:*** Stephen J. Curwick; ***M:*** Robert Folk.

Police Academy 7: Mission to Moscow **1994 (PG)** The seventh in the series is another inept comedy, which finds the chaotic crew tackling a Russian mobster on his Moscow turf—all because of a popular computer game with some sinister software. Like you'll care about the plot anyway. **83m/C VHS.** George Gaynes, Michael Winslow, David Graf, Leslie Easterbrook, G.W. Bailey, Charlie Schlatter, Ron Perlman, Christopher Lee; ***D:*** Alan Metter; ***W:*** Michele S. Chodos, Randolph Davis; ***M:*** Robert Folk.

Police Court **1937** The son of a faded, alcoholic screen star tries to bring the old fellow back to prominence. **62m/B VHS.** Nat Barry, Henry B. Walthall, Leon Janney.

Police Story *Jackie Chan's Police Force; Police Force; Jackie Chan's Police Story; Ging Chaat Goo Si* **1985 (PG-13)** Chopsocker Chan's assigned to protect a witness in a drug case. Faced by unsavory thugs, he flies through the air with the greatest of ease. Very cool stunts. **92m/C VHS.** *HK* Jackie Chan, Brigitte (Lin Chinag-hsia) Lin, Maggie Cheung, Cho Yuen, Bill Tung, Kenneth Tong; ***D:*** Jackie Chan; ***C:*** Yiu-tsou Cheung.

Policewoman Centerfold **1983** Exploitative rendering based on the true story of a cop who posed for a pornographic magazine. Anderson is appealing in the lead. **100m/C VHS.** Melody Anderson, Ed Marinaro, Donna Pescow, Bert Remsen, David Spielberg; ***D:*** Reza Badiyi. **TV**

Policewomen **1973 (R)** Female undercover agent must stop a ring of gold smugglers. **99m/C VHS.** Sondra Currie, Tony Young, Phil Hoover, Elizabeth Stuart, Jeannie Bell; ***D:*** Lee Frost.

A Polish Vampire in Burbank **1980** A shy vampire in Burbank tries again and again to find blood and love. Wacky. **84m/C VHS.** Mark Pirro, Lori Sutton, Eddie Deezen; ***D:*** Mark Pirro.

Polish Wedding **1997 (PG-13)** Strong-willed teenager Hala (Danes) throws her working-class Polish/American family into a tizzy when she becomes pregnant and the family decides she must get married. But Hala's not the only one whose life is romntically complicated—her mom Jadzia's (Olin) had a longtime affair with Roman (Serbedzja), which husband Bolek (Byrne) tolerates because he's afraid of losing her. Too slapsticky but the cast is game and it does have heart. **107m/C VHS, DVD, Wide.** Claire Danes, Lena Olin, Gabriel Byrne, Adam Trese, Rade Serbedzija, Mili Avital, Daniel Lapaine; ***D:*** Theresa Connelly; ***W:*** Theresa Connelly; ***C:*** Guy Dufaux; ***M:*** Luis Bacalov.

Pollock **2000 (R)** First-time director Harris (who also stars) scores a personal triumph with his bio of abstract expressionist artist Jackson Pollock (whom the actor resembles quite astonishingly). Pollock is a troubled soul, beset by alcoholism and insecurity, who leads himself down a self-destructive path. The film covers 1941-1956 as Pollock struggles to find his artistic breakthrough and marries fellow artist Lee Krasner (Harden), a tough New Yorker who takes his career in hand, but his success only exacerbates Pollock's problems. Solid production with a couple of great leading performances; based on the book by Steven Naifeh and Gregory White Smith. **122m/C VHS, DVD, Wide.** Ed Harris, Marcia Gay Harden, Amy Madigan, Jennifer Connelly, Jeffrey Tambor, Bud Cort, John Heard, Val Kilmer; ***D:*** Ed Harris; ***W:*** Barbara Turner, Susan J. Emshwiller; ***C:*** Lisa Rinzler; ***M:*** Jeff Beal. Oscars '00: Support. Actress (Harden); N.Y. Film Critics '00: Support. Actress (Harden).

Pollyanna **1920** A young orphan girl is adopted by her cold, embittered aunt and does her best to bring joy and gladness to all the new people she meets. Silent with music score. **60m/B VHS.** Mary Pickford; ***C:*** Charles Rosher.

Pollyanna **1960** Based on the Eleanor Porter story about an enchanting young girl whose contagious enthusiasm and zest for life touches the hearts of all she meets. Mills is perfect in the title role and was awarded a special Oscar for outstanding juvenile performance. A distinguished supporting cast is the icing on the cake in this delightful Disney confection. Original version was filmed in 1920 with Mary Pickford. **134m/C VHS, DVD, Wide.** Hayley Mills, Jane Wyman, Richard Egan, Karl Malden, Nancy Olson, Adolphe Menjou, Donald Crisp, Agnes Moorehead, Kevin Corcoran; ***D:*** David Swift; ***W:*** David Swift; ***C:*** Russell Harlan; ***M:*** Paul J. Smith.

Poltergeist **1982 (PG)** This production has Stephen Spielberg written all over it. A young family's home becomes a house of horrors when they are terrorized by menancing spirits who abduct their five-year-old daughter...through the TV screen! Roller-coaster thrills and chills, dazzling special effects, and perfectly timed humor highlight this stupendously scary ghost story. **114m/C VHS, DVD, Wide.** JoBeth Williams, Craig T. Nelson, Beatrice Straight, Heather O'Rourke, Zelda Rubinstein, Dominique Dunne, Oliver Robbins, Richard Lawson, James Karen, Michael McManus; ***D:*** Tobe Hooper; ***W:*** Steven Spielberg, Michael Grais, Mark Victor; ***C:*** Matthew F. Leonetti; ***M:*** Jerry Goldsmith.

Poltergeist 2: The Other Side **1986 (PG-13)** Adequate sequel to the Spielburg-produced venture into the supernatural, where demons follow the Freeling family in their efforts to recapture the clairvoyant young daughter Carol Anne. The film includes sojourns into Indian lore and a four-foot high agave worm designed by H.R. Giger. The movie was followed by "Poltergeist 3" in 1988. **92m/C VHS, Wide.** Craig T. Nelson, JoBeth Williams, Heather O'Rourke, Will Sampson, Julian Beck, Geraldine Fitzgerald, Oliver Robbins, Zelda Rubinstein; ***D:*** Brian Gibson; ***W:*** Mark Victor, Michael Grais; ***C:*** Andrew Laszlo; ***M:*** Jerry Goldsmith.

Poltergeist 3 **1988 (PG-13)** Wrestling with the supernatural has finally unnerved Carol Ann and she's sent to stay with her aunt and uncle in Chicago where she attends a school for gifted children with emotional disorders. Guess who follows her? Uninspired acting, threadbare premise, and one ghastly encounter too many. Oddly, O'Rourke died suddenly four months before the film's release. **97m/C VHS.** Tom Skerritt, Nancy Allen, Heather O'Rourke, Lara Flynn Boyle, Zelda Rubinstein; ***D:*** Gary Sherman; ***W:*** Gary Sherman, Brian Taggert; ***C:*** Alex Nepomniaschy.

Poltergeist: The Legacy **1996** Pilot for the cable series about a secret international society, the Legacy, which is devoted to the paranormal and to protecting mankind from supernatural evil. Derek Rayne (De Lint), the head of the San Francisco Legacy house, must find the last of five sepulchers containing the evil spirits of five fallen angels. This takes him and his cohorts to Ireland where Rachel Corrigan (Shaver) and her young psychic daughter Kat (Purvis) come into unwitting possession of the fifth box and untold danger. **86m/C VHS.** Derek De Lint, Helen Shaver, Alexandra Purvis, Martin Cummins, Robbi Chong, Patrick Fitzgerald, Jordan Bayne, William Sadler, Daniel Pilon, Chad Krowchuk; ***D:*** Stuart Gillard; ***W:*** Brad Wright; ***C:*** Manfred Guthe. **CABLE**

Polyester **1981 (R)** Amusing satire on middle-class life, described by producer, director and writer Waters as "'Father Knows Best' gone berserk." Forlorn housewife Divine pines for the man of her dreams while the rest of her life is falling apart at the seams. Filmed in "Odorama," a hilarious gimmick in which theatre goers were provided with scratch-n-sniff cards, containing specific scents corresponding to key scenes. Video watchers will have to use their imagination in experiencing a wide range of smells. The first of Waters' more mainstream films. Features songs by Murray and Harry. **86m/C VHS, DVD, Wide.** Divine, Tab Hunter, Edith Massey, Mink Stole, Stiv Bators, David Samson, Mary Garlington, Kenneth King, Joni-Ruth White, Jean Hill, Hans Kramm, Mary Vivian Pearce, Cookie Mueller, Susan Lowe, George Stover, George Figgs, Steve Yeager; ***D:*** John Waters; ***W:*** John Waters; ***C:*** David Insley; ***M:*** Deborah Harry, Michael Kamen.

Pom Pom Girls **1976 (R)** High school seniors, intent on having one last fling before graduating, get involved in crazy antics, clumsy romances, and football rivalries. **90m/C VHS, DVD.** Robert Carradine, Jennifer Ashley, Michael Mullins, Cheryl "Rainbeaux" Smith, Dianne Lee Hart, Lisa Reeves, Bill Adler; ***D:*** Joseph Ruben; ***W:*** Joseph Ruben; ***C:*** Stephen M. Katz; ***M:*** Michael Lloyd.

The Pompatus of Love **1995 (R)** Remember Steve Miller's song "The Joker"?—well, that's where the title comes from—and we still don't know what it means. But the film's about four New York guys and the mystery of women. They may be (reasonably) bright and literate but they still don't have a clue about love or how to grow-up. Naturally, the women they know—or meet—are all too smart for them. **99m/C VHS, DVD.** Jon Cryer, Tim Guinee, Adrian Pasdar, Adam Oliensis, Kristen Wilson, Dana Wheeler-Nicholson, Paige Turco, Mia Sara, Kristin Scott Thomas, Arabella Field, Jennifer Tilly, Roscoe Lee Browne; ***D:*** Richard Schenkman; ***W:*** Jon Cryer, Adam Oliensis, Richard Schenkman; ***C:*** Russell Fine; ***M:*** John Hill. **VIDEO**

The Ponder Heart **2001** Eccentric Daniel Ponder (MacNicol) wants to give all his inherited fortune away. So folks in his Mississippi community considered him a mite peculiar, especially after he suddenly marries the teenaged Bonnie Dee (Bettis). Then Bonnie disappears and Ponder is put on trial for the alleged murder of his bride. Easy-going southern charm and smalltown craziness. Based on the novel by Eudora Welty. **120m/C VHS.** Peter MacNicol, JoBeth Williams, Angela Bettis; *D:* Martha Coolidge. **TV**

Ponette 🦴🦴 **1995** Four-year-old Ponette (Thivisol) is hard-pressed to understand what's happening to her family after her mother is killed in a car accident. Her father can't seem to explain it properly, so Ponette comes to her own acceptance with the help of some school friends. Film drew some controversy when the very young Thivisol was awarded the best actress award at the Venice Film Festival—since Thivisol was thought by some critics to be too young to "act," director Doillon was accused of manipulating the youngster in order to get a performance. French with subtitles. **92m/C VHS, DVD.** *FR* Victorie Thivisol, Marie Trintignant, Claire Nebout, Xavier Beauvois; *D:* Jacques Doillon; *W:* Jacques Doillon; *C:* Caroline Champetier; *M:* Philippe Sarde. N.Y. Film Critics '97: Foreign Film; Venice Film Fest. '96: Actress (Thivisol).

Pontiac Moon 🦴½ **1994 (PG-13)** Danson plays a high school teacher who takes his son on a road trip to Spires of the Moon National Park hoping to arrive simultaneously with the astronauts' first lunar landing. His wife (Steenburgen) decides to follow them, although she's phobic about leaving the house and hasn't set foot outside in seven years. Sincere yet tedious film about father-son bonding has a few heartfelt moments, but not enough to sustain interest for entire viewing period. Best (and only) reason for watching: Monument Valley scenery. **108m/C VHS.** Ted Danson, Mary Steenburgen, Ryan Todd, Eric Schweig, Cathy Moriarty, Max Gail, Lisa Jane Persky; *D:* Peter Medak; *W:* Finn Taylor, Jeffrey Brown; *M:* Randy Edelman.

The Pony Express 🦴🦴½ **1925** Melodramatic western about an evil senator (Hart) who's out to establish his own empire. His scheme is thwarted by pony express rider Cortez. Based on the novel by Henry James Forman and Walter Woods. **67m/B VHS.** Ricardo Cortez, Al Hart, Betty Compson, Ernest Torrence, Wallace Beery, George Bancroft, Frank Lackteen; *D:* James Cruze; *W:* Walter Woods.

Pony Express 🦴🦴🦴 **1953** Buffalo Bill Cody and Wild Bill Hickok join forces to extend the Pony Express mail route west to California through rain and sleet, snow and hail. Far from a factual account but good for extending the myth of the Old West. **101m/C VHS.** Charlton Heston, Rhonda Fleming, Jan Sterling, Forrest Tucker; *D:* Jerry Hopper; *C:* Ray Rennahan.

Pony Express Rider 🦴🦴🦴 **1976 (G)** Young man with a mission joins up with the Pony Express hoping to bag the male responsible for killing his pa. The well-produced script boasts a bevy of veteran western character actors, all lending, solid, rugged performances. **100m/C VHS.** Stewart Peterson, Henry Wilcoxon, Buck Taylor, Maureen McCormick, Joan Caulfield, Ken Curtis, Slim Pickens, Dub Taylor, Jack Elam; *D:* Robert Totten.

Pony Post 🦴½ **1940** Standard horse opera has Brown running a pony express station where he battles Indians and typical villains. **59m/B VHS.** Johnny Mack Brown, Fuzzy Knight, Nell O'Day, Dorothy Short, Kermit Maynard, Lane Chandler; *D:* Ray Taylor; *W:* Sherman Lowe.

Pool Hustlers 🦴½ **1983** A romantic comedy about an amateur billiards whiz who finds love and successfully defeats the national champ. In Italian with English subtitles. **101m/C VHS.** *IT* Francesco Nuti, Guilliana de Sio, Marcello Loti; *D:* Maurizio Ponzi.

Pool Sharks 🦴🦴½ **1915** W.C. Fields' first film features the comedian's antics while playing a pool game to win the love of a woman. Silent. **10m/B VHS.** W.C. Fields; *D:* Edwin Middleton; *W:* W.C. Fields.

Poor Girl, a Ghost Story 🦴🦴 **1974** A young girl takes a job as a governess at an English mansion and is besieged by all manner of strange goings-on. **52m/C VHS.** *AU* Lynn Miller, Angela Thorne; *D:* Michael Apted.

A Poor Little Rich Girl 🦴🦴🦴 **1917** Mary Pickford received raves in this film, in which she portrayed Gwendolyn, with everything money could buy, except the attention of her family. Gwendolyn has a bizarre dream in which she sees a number of horrors and is tempted by death. Elaborate sets and special effects, as well as Pickford's delicate performance, make this one special. Organ score. **64m/B VHS.** Mary Pickford, Madeline Traverse, Charles Wellesley, Gladys Fairbanks; *D:* Maurice Tourneur. Natl. Film Reg. '91.

The Poor Little Rich Girl 🦴🦴½ **1936** A motherless rich girl wanders away from home and is "adopted" by a pair of struggling vaudevillians. With her help, they rise to the big time. ♫Oh My Goodness; Buy a Bar of Barry's; Wash Your Neck With a Cake of Peck's; Military Man; When I'm with You; But Definitely; You've Gotta Eat Your Spinach, Baby. **79m/B VHS.** Shirley Temple, Jack Haley, Alice Faye, Gloria Stuart, Michael Whalen, Sara Haden, Jane Darwell; *D:* Irving Cummings.

Poor Little Rich Girl: The Barbara Hutton Story 🦴🦴½ **1987** Bio-drama of the one-time richest woman in America, Woolworth heiress Hutton (Fawcett), and her extravagant lifestyle. She married seven times (including actor Cary Grant) until falling into self-destructive alcohol and drug addictions. Lavishly presented but superficial. Based on the book by C. David Heymann. **98m/C VHS.** Farrah Fawcett, Bruce Davison, Kevin McCarthy, Burl Ives, James Read, Stephane Audran, Anne Francis, David Ackroyd, Tony Peck, Zoe Wanamaker, Amadeus August; *D:* Charles Jarrott; *W:* Dennis Turner; *M:* Richard Rodney Bennett. **TV**

Poor Pretty Eddie 🦴½ *Black Vengeance; Heartbreak Motel; Redneck County* **1973 (R)** A young black singer gets waylaid and taken in by a twisted white Southern clan. An incredibly sleazy movie which boasts Shelly Winters performing a strip act. **90m/C** Leslie Uggams, Shelley Winters, Michael Christian, Ted Cassidy, Slim Pickens, Dub Taylor; *D:* Richard Robinson.

Poor White Trash 🦴½ *Bayou* **1957** An architect arrives in bayou country with plans to design a new building. He meets with resistance from the locals but falls for the sensual daughter of one of his staunchest detractors. **83m/B VHS.** Peter Graves, Lita Milan, Douglas Fowley, Timothy Carey, Jonathan Haze; *D:* Harold Daniels.

Poor White Trash 🦴½ **2000 (R)** One-note comedy. Buddies Mike (Denman) and Lennie's (Tierney) prank on a local store owner backfires and the boys are in bigtime trouble that could be eased if they had money for defense attorney Ron (Devane). So Mike's trailer-trash mom, Linda (Young), and her boy toy Brian (London) agree to help the dummies raise the money through some burglaries that, of course, get botched. The gags are repeated so often that they lose what humor they minimally possessed. **85m/C VHS, DVD, Wide.** Jacob Tierney, Sean Young, Jason London, Tony Denman, William Devane, Jaime Pressly, M. Emmet Walsh, Tim Kazurinsky; *D:* Michael Addis; *W:* Michael Addis; *C:* Peter Kowalski; *M:* Tree Adams.

Poor White Trash 2 🦴 *Scum of the Earth* **1975 (R)** A young couple, vacationing in Louisiana's bayou country, are introduced to an unusual brand of southern hospitality by the eponymous group of locals. **90m/C VHS.** Gene Ross, Ann Stafford, Norma Moore, Camilla Carr; *D:* S.F. Brownrigg.

Pootie Tang 🦴½ **2001 (PG-13)** The gibberish-babbling Pootie Tang (Crouther) was mildly amusing as a three-minute one-joke sketch on "The Chris Rock Show." Stretched to eighty minutes, it turns into "It's Pat II: Electric Boogaloo." The premise here is that Pootie talks so cool, no one wants to admit they don't have a clue what he's saying. He's also a role model to all the kids and fights crime with his whip-crackin' belt, which he wields like a kung-fu master. Evil captain of industry Lecter (Vaughn) tricks Pootie into endorsing his empire of cigarettes, booze and junk food by using the feminine wiles of slinky Ireenie (Coolidge). Pootie retires in disgrace to his hometown before he can come back and make everything wambly again. Or something like that. It really is hard to figure out what that dude is saying. **81m/C VHS, DVD, Wide.** *US* Lance Crouther, Jennifer Coolidge, Robert Vaughn, Chris Rock, Reg E. Cathey, Wanda Sykes, Dave Attell, Mario Joyner, JB Smoove, Cathy Trien, Andy Richter; ***Cameos:*** Bob Costas; *D:* Louis CK; *W:* Louis CK; *C:* Willy Kurant.

Pop Always Pays 🦴🦴 **1940** A father gets in a jam when he has to make good on a bet with his daughter's boyfriend. **67m/B VHS.** Walter Catlett, Dennis O'Keefe, Leon Errol, Adele Pearce; *D:* Leslie Goodwins.

Pop Goes the Cork **1922** Three films by the man Chaplin referred to as his "professor," Max Linder: "Be My Wife," "Seven Years Bad Luck," and "The Three Must-Get-Theres." Linder was the foremost film comedian in early 20th-century France, and made these three films during a stay in America. **87m/B VHS.** Max Linder.

Popcorn 🦴🦴 **1989 (R)** A killer stalks a movie audience who is unaware that his crimes are paralleling those in the very film they are watching. **93m/C VHS, DVD, Wide.** Jill Schoelen, Tom Villard, Dee Wallace Stone, Derek Rydell, Elliott Hurst, Kelly Jo Minter, Malcolm Danare, Ray Walston, Tony Roberts, Karen Witter; *D:* Mark Herrier, Alan Ormsby; *W:* Alan Ormsby; *C:* Ronnie Taylor.

Pope John Paul II 🦴🦴 **1984** Biography of the Pontiff, from childhood to world eminence. **150m/C VHS.** Albert Finney, Michael Crompton, Nigel Hawthorne, John McEnery, Brian Cox; *D:* Herbert Wise. **TV**

The Pope Must Diet 🦴½ *The Pope Must Die* **1991 (R)** Coltrane stars as a misfit who accidentally becomes Pope Dave I. Living up to the benevolence suggested by his title, Pope Dave proposes to use Vatican money to create a children's fund. But there are those in the organization who have different, less noble plans for the cash, and soon Dave finds himself the target of a mob hit. Frantic comedy caused a stir with its original title "The Pope Must Die," with many newspapers refusing to run ads for the film. This, coupled with lukewarm critical reviews, led to a very brief stint at the boxoffice. **87m/C VHS.** *GB* Robbie Coltrane, Alex Rocco, Beverly D'Angelo, Herbert Lom, Paul Bartel, Salvatore Cascio, Balthazar Getty; *D:* Peter Richardson; *M:* Anne Dudley.

The Pope of Greenwich Village 🦴🦴½ **1984 (R)** Two Italian-American cousins (Rourke and Roberts) struggle to escape the trap of poverty in New York's Greenwich Village. When a small crime goes wrong in a big way, the two must learn about deception and loyalty. Mostly character study; Page is exceptional. Inferior re-run of the "Mean Streets" idea does have its moments. **122m/C VHS, DVD, Wide.** Eric Roberts, Mickey Rourke, Daryl Hannah, Geraldine Page, Tony Musante, M. Emmet Walsh, Kenneth McMillan, Burt Young, Jack Kehoe, Philip Bosco, Val Avery, Joe Grifasi, Tony DiBenedetto; *D:* Stuart Rosenberg; *W:* Vincent Patrick; *C:* John Bailey; *M:* Dave Grusin.

Popeye 🦴🦴 **1980 (PG)** The cartoon sailor brought to life is on a search to find his long-lost father. Along the way, he meets Olive Oyl and adopts little Sweet Pea. Williams accomplishes the near-impossible feat of physically resembling the title character, and the whole movie does accomplish the maker's stated goal of "looking like a comic strip," but it isn't anywhere near as funny as it should be. **114m/C VHS.** Ned Dowd, Robin Williams, Shelley Duvall, Ray Walston, Paul Dooley, Bill Irwin, Paul Smith, Linda Hunt, Richard Libertini; *D:* Robert Altman; *W:* Jules Feiffer; *M:* Harry Nilsson.

Popi 🦴🦴🦴 **1969 (G)** Arkin is the heart and soul of this poignant charmer in his role as a Puerto Rican immigrant hell-bent on securing a better life outside the ghetto for his two sons. His zany efforts culminate in one outrageous scheme to set them adrift off the Florida coast in hopes they will be rescued and raised by a wealthy family. Far fetched, but ultimately heartwarming. **115m/C VHS.** Alan Arkin, Rita Moreno, Miguel Alejandro, Reuben Figueroa; *D:* Arthur Hiller.

The Poppy Is Also a Flower 🦴½ *Poppies Are Also Flowers; Opium Connection* **1966 (PG)** A star-laden, anti-drug drama produced by the United Nations. Filmed on location in Iran, Monaco, and Italy. Based on a drug trade thriller by Ian Fleming that explains how poppies, converted into heroin, are brought into the United States. **100m/C VHS.** E.G. Marshall, Trevor Howard, Gilbert Roland, Eli Wallach, Marcello Mastroianni, Angie Dickinson, Rita Hayworth, Yul Brynner, Trini Lopez, Bessie Love; *D:* Terence Young. **TV**

Porcile 🦴🦴 *Pigsty; Porcherie* **1969** Pasolini intertwines the story of a soldier cannibal living in a medieval age with the son of an ex-Nazi industrialist in present day Germany. Both the soldier and the young German (who prefers pigs to his fiance) become sacrificial victims of their differing societies. A grotesque fable on Pasolini's hatred of middle class mores and the 20th century. In Italian with English subtitles. **90m/C VHS.** *IT FR* Pierre Clementi, Franco Citti, Jean-Pierre Leaud, Anna Wiazemsky, Ugo Tognazzi, Alberto Lionello; *D:* Pier Paolo Pasolini; *W:* Pier Paolo Pasolini; *C:* Armando Nannuzzi, Giuseppe Ruzzolini, Tonino Delli Colli.

Pork Chop Hill 🦴🦴🦴 **1959** A powerful, hard-hitting account of the last hours of the Korean War. Peck is totally believable as the man ordered to hold his ground against the hopeless onslaught of Chinese Communist hordes. A chilling, stark look in the face of a no-win situation. Top notch cast and masterful directing. **97m/B VHS, DVD.** Gregory Peck, Harry Guardino, Rip Torn, George Peppard, James Edwards, Bob Steele, Woody Strode, Robert (Bobby) Blake, Martin Landau, Norman Fell, Bert Remsen, George Shibata, Biff (Elliott) Elliot, Barry Atwater, Martin Garth, Lew Gallo, Charles Aidman, Leonard Graves, Ken Lynch, Paul Comi, Cliff Ketchum, Abel Fernandez, Gavin MacLeod; *D:* Lewis Milestone; *W:* James R. Webb; *C:* Sam Leavitt; *M:* Leonard Rosenman.

Porky's 🦴🦴½ **1982 (R)** Investigation of teen horniness set in South Florida during the fab '50s. Irreverent comedy follows the misadventures of six youths imprisoned in Angel Beach High School who share a common interest: girls. Their main barrier to sexual success: the no-touch babes they lust after and the incredibly stupid adults who run the world. Fairly dumb and tasteless with occasional big laughs that earned mega bucks at the drive-in and created perceived popular outcry for more porky: "Porky's II: The Next Day" (1983) and "Porky's Revenge" (1985). **94m/C VHS, DVD, Wide.** *CA* Dan Monahan, Wyatt Knight, Scott Colomby, Tony Ganios, Mark Herrier, Cyril O'Reilly, Roger Wilson, Alex Karras, Kim Cattrall, Kaki Hunter, Nancy Parsons, Boyd Gaines, Douglas McGrath, Susan Clark, Art Hindle, Wayne Maunder, Chuck "Porky" Mitchell, Eric Christmas, Bob (Benjamin) Clark; *D:* Bob (Benjamin) Clark; *W:* Bob (Benjamin) Clark; *C:* Reginald Morris; *M:* Paul Zaza, Carl Zittrer.

Porky's 2: The Next Day 🦴🦴 **1983 (R)** More tame tomfoolery about teenage sex drives, Shakespeare, fat high school teachers, the Ku Klux Klan, and streaking in the Florida high school where it all began. Outright caricature shares the stage with juvenile humor, some of which may induce laughter. **100m/C VHS, DVD, Wide.** *CA* Bill Wiley, Dan Monahan, Wyatt Knight, Cyril O'Reilly, Roger Wilson, Tony Ganios, Mark Herrier, Scott Colomby, Kaki Hunter, Nancy Parsons, Eric Christmas, Art Hindle; *D:* Bob (Benjamin) Clark; *W:* Alan Ormsby, Bob (Benjamin) Clark, Roger E. Swaybill; *C:* Reginald Morris; *M:* Carl Zittrer.

Porky's Revenge 🦴 **1985 (R)** The Angel Beach High School students are out to get revenge against Porky who orders the school basketball coach to throw the championship game. The second of the "Porky's" sequels. **95m/C VHS.** *CA* Dan Monahan, Wyatt Knight, Tony Ganios, Nancy Parsons, Chuck "Porky" Mitchell, Kaki Hunter, Kimberly Evenson, Scott Colomby, Mark Herrier, Eric Christmas, Rose McVeigh; *D:* James Komack; *W:* Ziggy Steinberg; *C:* Robert C. Jessup; *M:* Dave Edmunds.

The Pornographer ☙☙ 2000 (R) In his introduction, director Atchison says that the inspiration for this story of lonely guy Paul Ryan (Degood) who becomes a porno filmmaker almost by accident came from his own situation. While trying to raise money for his own legitimate movies, Atchison briefly considered trying to make skin flicks to raise money. Instead, he came up with an intriguing little video premiere. **88m/C VHS, DVD.** Michael Degood, Craig Wasson, Monique Parent, Katheryn Cain; ***D:*** Doug Atchison; ***W:*** Doug Atchison; ***C:*** Christopher Mosio; ***M:*** Warner David Jansen.

The Pornographers ☙☙☙ 1966 Bizzare, black comedy focuses on a part-time porno filmmaker lusting after the daughter of the widow he lives with and trying to cope with his family, the world, and himself. A perversely fascinating exploration of contemporary Japanese society and the many facets of sexual emotion. In Japanese with English subtitles. **128m/B VHS.** *JP* Shoichi Ozawa, Massaomi Konda, Sumiko Sakamota, Haruo Tanaka, Keiko Sagowa; ***D:*** Shohei Imamura.

Porridge ☙☙ *Doing Time* 1991 A British comedy inspired by the popular BBC situation comedy of the title, about a habitual criminal and convict who makes the most of his time in prison. **105m/C VHS.** *GB* Ronnie Barker, Fulton Mackay, Peter Vaughan, Julian Holloway, Geoffrey Bayldon; ***D:*** Dick Clement.

Port of Call ☙☙☙ 1948 Early Bergman drama about a seaman on the docks who falls for a troubled woman whose wild, unhappy past has earned her an unsavory reputation. The hopeful, upbeat tone seems incongruous with the grim harbor/slum setting. It's minor Bergman but the seeds of his trademark themes can be seen taking shape, making it a must-see for avid fans. In Swedish with English subtitles. **100m/B VHS.** *SW* Ivine-Christine Jonsson, Bengt Eklund, Erik Hell, Berta Hall, Mimi Nelson; ***D:*** Ingmar Bergman.

The Port of Missing Girls ☙ 1938 A young woman implicated in a murder stows away on a freighter. There she becomes caught up in a waterfront world of pirates, smugglers and other assorted undesirables. **56m/B VHS, 8mm.** Harry Carey Sr., Judith Allen, Milburn Stone, Betty Compson; ***D:*** Karl Brown.

Port of New York ☙☙ 1949 A narcotics gang is smuggling large quantities of drugs into New York. A government agent poses as a gang member in order to infiltrate the mob and get the goods on them. Brynner's film debut. **82m/B VHS.** Scott Brady, Yul Brynner, K.T. Stevens; ***D:*** Laslo Benedek.

Portfolio 1988 (R) Real-life models star in this gritty drama about rising to the top of the fashion heap. Music by Eurythmics, Fun Boy Three and others. **83m/C VHS.** Paulina Porizkova, Julie Wolfe, Carol Alt, Kelly Emberg.

Portnoy's Complaint ☙½ 1972 (R) Limp screen adaptation of Philip Roth's novel follows the frustrating experiences of a sexually obsessed young man as he relates them to his psychiatrist. **101m/C VHS.** Richard Benjamin, Karen Black, Lee Grant, Jeannie Berlin, Jill Clayburgh; ***D:*** Ernest Lehman; ***W:*** Ernest Lehman.

The Portrait ☙☙☙ 1993 Longtime real-life friends Bacall and Peck on-screen together for the first time in 37 years prove they are still shining stars as they play aging parents to Peck's real-life daughter, Cecilia Peck. The younger Peck is an artist preparing for a exhibition and asks her parents to sit for a portrait. This is the pole around which their relationships and reconciliations swing in this emotional drama based loosely on Tina Howe's 1983 off-Broadway play, "Painting Churches." **89m/C VHS.** Lauren Bacall, Gregory Peck, Cecilia Peck, Paul McCrane, Joyce O'Connor, Donna Mitchell, Mitchell Laurance, William Prince, Augusta Dabney; ***D:*** Arthur Penn; ***W:*** Lynn Roth, Jack Darcus; ***M:*** Michael Conway Baker. **CABLE**

The Portrait ☙½ 1999 (R) A distaff version of "The Picture of Dorian Gray." Beautiful woman meets strange photographer whose work is weird. Nevertheless, she poses for him and, after seeing the results, unwittingly vows to remain as eternally youthful as her portrait. But the photo shows the real story as time passes by. **85m/C VHS, DVD.** Gabriella Hall, Jenna Bodnar, Avalon Anders, Christopher Johnston; ***D:*** David Goldner; ***W:*** David Goldner; ***C:*** Rocky Dijon. **VIDEO**

Portrait in Black ☙☙½ 1960 Invalid shipping magnate Matthew Cabot (Nolan) is contemptuous of second wife Sheila (Turner), who can't leave the marriage because of young son Peter (Kohler). She finds comfort in the arms of her husband's doctor, David Rivera (Quinn), and the duo decide the only way to find happiness is to kill off Cabot, which they do. Then Sheila begins to get anonymous letters accusing her of murder. Turner's glamor can't hide the gaping holes in the contrived plot. Adapted from the Goff/Roberts play. **113m/C VHS.** Lana Turner, Lloyd Nolan, Anthony Quinn, Richard Basehart, Sandra Dee, John Saxon, Ray Walston, Anna May Wong, Virginia Grey, Dennis Kohler; ***D:*** Michael Gordon; ***W:*** Ivan Goff, Ben Roberts; ***C:*** Russell Metty; ***M:*** Frank Skinner.

Portrait in Terror ☙½ 1966 A master thief and a deranged artist plan a heist of a Titian painting in an oddball suspense piece. Not a great success, but atmospheric and weird. **81m/B VHS.** Patrick Magee, William Campbell, Anna Pavane; ***D:*** Jack Hill.

Portrait of a Hitman ☙ *Jim Buck* 1977 Aspiring painter leads a double life as a professional hitman. Ragged feature feels more abandoned than finished, as if most of the movie had been shot and then the money ran out. All leads turn in paycheck performances, no more. **85m/C VHS.** Jack Palance, Rod Steiger, Richard Roundtree, Bo Svenson, Ann Turkel; ***D:*** Allan A. Buckhantz.

Portrait of a Lady ☙☙½ 1967 A spirited young American woman is taken to England and insists on complete freedom to choose her own future and make her own choices. Based on the 1881 novel by Henry James. On two cassettes. **240m/C VHS.** *GB* Richard Chamberlain, Suzanne Neve, Edward Fox.

Portrait of a Lady ☙☙☙ 1996 (PG-13) Adapted from the century-old Henry James novel, "Portrait" paints the story of independent and newly wealthy American, Isabel Archer (Kidman). Abroad in Europe, she falls under the influence of the bitter, opportunistic Madame Merle (Hershey, in a strong portrayal), who manages to steer the innocent Isabel into a disastrous marriage with Gilbert Osmond (Malkovich). From there, film deals with Isabel's efforts to flee the domineering Osmond and find herself again. Kidman plays her role with never-before-seen efficiency. Malkovich is suitably evil but plays his villain card a bit too early. Director Campion's modern voice carries the film through, but is sometimes out of place, as in the opening segment. Filmed in England and Italy. **142m/C VHS, DVD, Wide.** *GB* Nicole Kidman, John Malkovich, Barbara Hershey, Martin Donovan, Christian Bale, Shelley Winters, Shelley Duvall, Mary-Louise Parker, Richard E. Grant, John Gielgud, Viggo Mortensen; ***D:*** Jane Campion; ***W:*** Laura Jones; ***C:*** Stuart Dryburgh; ***M:*** Wojciech Kilar. L.A. Film Critics '96: Support. Actress (Hershey); Natl. Soc. Film Critics '96: Support. Actor (Donovan), Support. Actress (Hershey).

Portrait of a Rebel: Margaret Sanger ☙☙½ 1982 TV docudrama about the struggle of Margaret Sanger to repeal the Comstock Act of 1912, which prohibited the distribution of birth control information. **96m/C VHS.** Bonnie Franklin, David Dukes, Milo O'Shea; ***D:*** Virgil W. Vogel.

Portrait of a Showgirl ☙☙ 1982 Inexperienced showgirl learns the ropes of Las Vegas life from a veteran of the Vegas stages. **100m/C VHS.** Lesley Ann Warren, Rita Moreno, Tony Curtis, Dianne Kay, Howard Morris; ***D:*** Steven Hilliard Stern. **TV**

Portrait of a Stripper ☙ 1979 A widowed mother works part-time as a stripper to support her son. Trouble arises when her father-in-law attempts to prove that she is an unfit mother. **100m/C VHS.** Lesley Ann Warren, Edward Herrmann, Vic Tayback, Sheree North; ***D:*** John A. Alonzo.

Portrait of a White Marriage ☙☙½ 1988 An extended cable comedy special revamping certain old "Mary Hartman, Mary Hartman" and "Fernwood 2-Night" conventions; a moronic talk show host moves his cheap show to his hometown of Hawkins Falls in order to boost the ratings. **81m/C VHS.** Martin Mull, Mary Kay Place, Fred Willard, Michael McKean, Harry Shearer, Jack Riley, Conchata Ferrell; ***D:*** Harry Shearer. **CABLE**

Portrait of an Assassin ☙☙ 1949 Unhappy with his marriage to a nagging wife (Arletty), carnival daredevil Fabius (Brasseur) goes so far as to tell her that he killed a woman by mistake, thinking it was her. Can this marriage be saved? Before it's over, more infidelity and the paralyzed Eric (the inimitable Von Stroheim) have come into play. French with subtitles. **86m/B VHS, DVD.** *FR* Pierre Brasseur, Arletty, Maria Montez, Erich von Stroheim; ***D:*** Bernard Roland; ***W:*** Marcel Rivet; ***C:*** Roger Hubert; ***M:*** Maurice Hiriet.

Portrait of Jennie ☙☙☙½ *Jennie; Tidal Wave* 1948 In this haunting, romantic fable, a struggling artist is inspired by and smitten with a strange and beautiful girl who he also suspects may be the spirit of a dead woman. A fine cast works wonders with what could have been a forgettable story. The last reel was tinted green in the original release with the last scene shot in technicolor. Oscar-winning special effects. Based on a novella by Robert Nathan. **86m/B VHS, DVD.** Joseph Cotten, Jennifer Jones, Cecil Kellaway, Ethel Barrymore, David Wayne, Lillian Gish, Henry Hull, Florence Bates, Felix Bressart, Anne Francis; ***D:*** William Dieterle; ***W:*** Leonardo Bercovici, Peter Berneis, Paul Osborn; ***C:*** Joseph August; ***M:*** Dimitri Tiomkin. Venice Film Fest. '49: Actor (Cotten).

Portrait of Teresa ☙☙☙ 1979 Havana housewife has to balance motherhood, textile job, and cultural group activities without the cooperation of her husband. Vega skillfully portrays the lingering archaic attitudes and insulting assumptions that still confront post-revolution women. A fine eye for the revealing moments and movements of everyday life. In Spanish with English subtitles. **115m/C VHS.** Daisy Granados, Aldolfo Llaurado, Alina Sanchez, Alberto Molina; ***D:*** Pastor Vega.

Portraits Chinois ☙☙½ *Shadow Play* 1996 Uneven romantic drama finds English fashion designer Ada (Bonham Carter) living in Paris with her screenwriter boyfriend Paul (Ecoffey). They have just moved into an apartment together though dissatisfaction looms. Paul's writing partner, Guido (Castellito), has broken up with his girlfriend thus complicating their latest assignment, and Ada's fellow designer Lise (Bohringer) has not only impressed their boss Rene (Brialy) but has fallen for Paul. Various other friends interact and everything breaks apart and re-forms over the course of several months. French with subtitles. **105m/C VHS, DVD, Wide.** *FR* Helena Bonham Carter, Jean-Philippe Ecoffey, Romane Bohringer, Sergio Castellitto, Marie Trintignant, Elsa Zylberstein, Yvan Attal, Miki (Predrag) Manojlovic, Jean-Claude Brialy; ***D:*** Martine Dugowson; ***W:*** Martine Dugowson, Peter Chase; ***C:*** Vincenzo Marano; ***M:*** Peter Chase.

Portraits of a Killer ☙☙ *Portraits of Innocence* 1995 Attorney Elaine Taylor (Grey) is getting all hot and bothered by her client—photographer George Kendell (Mandylor), who's suspected in the murders of five hookers. But the detective (Ironside) on the case thinks she's just asking for trouble. **93m/C VHS.** Jennifer Grey, Costas Mandylor, Michael Ironside, Patricia Charbonneau, Kenneth Welsh, M. Emmet Walsh; ***D:*** Bill Corcoran.

Posed for Murder ☙☙ 1989 (R) A young centerfold is stalked by a psycho who wants her all for himself. **90m/C VHS.** Charlotte J. Helmkamp, Carl Fury, Rick Gianasi, Michael Merrins; ***D:*** Brian Thomas Jones.

The Poseidon Adventure ☙☙½ 1972 (PG) The cruise ship Poseidon is on its last voyage from New York to Athens on New Year's Eve when it is capsized by a tidal wave. The ten survivors struggle to escape the water-logged tomb. Oscar-winning special effects, such as Shelley Winters floating in a boiler room. Created an entirely new genre of film making—the big cast disaster flick. ♫The Morning After. **117m/C VHS, DVD, Wide.** Gene Hackman, Ernest Borgnine, Shelley Winters, Red Buttons, Jack Albertson, Carol Lynley, Roddy McDowall; ***D:*** Ronald Neame; ***W:*** Wendell Mayes, Stirling Silliphant; ***C:*** Harold E. Stine; ***M:*** John Williams. Oscars '72: Song ("The Morning After"), Visual FX; Golden Globes '73: Support. Actress (Winters).

Positive I.D. ☙☙ 1987 (R) A troubled housewife learns that the man who raped her years before is getting released on parole. She devises a second persona for herself with which to entrap him and get her revenge. **96m/C VHS, DVD, Wide.** Stephanie Rascoe, John Davies, Steve Fromholz; ***D:*** Andy Anderson; ***W:*** Andy Anderson; ***C:*** Paul Barton.

The Positively True Adventures of the Alleged Texas Cheerleader-Murdering Mom ☙☙☙½ 1993 (R) Satirical melodrama about Texas housewife Wanda Holloway (Hunter), accused of hiring a hitman to murder the mother of her daughter's chief cheerleading rival. She figures the girl will be so distraught that her own daughter can easily replace her. Ruthless and hilarious, this fact-based cable movie goes way over the top in satirizing suburban life-style excess and media overkill. Hunter, complete with whiney Texas twang, is perfect in her role as self-absorbed Wanda and Bridges is great as her loopy ex-brother-in-law and partner in planned homicide. A riot compared to the usual dramatic movies served up by the networks. **99m/C VHS.** Andy Richter, Holly Hunter, Beau Bridges, Swoosie Kurtz, Gregg Henry, Matt Frewer, Frankie Ingrassia, Elizabeth Ruscio, Megan Berwick; ***D:*** Michael Ritchie; ***W:*** Jane Anderson; ***M:*** Lucy Simon. **CABLE**

Posse ☙☙☙ 1975 (PG) There's a hidden agenda, fueled by political ambition, in a lawman's (Douglas) dauntless pursuit of an escaped bandit (Dern). An interesting contrast between the evil of corrupt politics and the honesty of traditional lawlessness. Well performed, well photographed, and almost insightful. **94m/C VHS.** Kirk Douglas, Bruce Dern, James Stacy, Bo Hopkins, Luke Askew, David Canary, Alfonso Arau, Kate Woodville, Mark Roberts; ***D:*** Kirk Douglas; ***W:*** William Roberts; ***M:*** Maurice Jarre.

Posse ☙☙☙ 1993 (R) Big, brawny western shot with MTV in mind that tells the tale in part of how more than 8,000 black cowboys helped tame the American frontier. Or, as the advertising put it, "The untold story of the wild West." Or, spaghetti western meets blaxploitation meets the magnificent seven meets the L.A. riots, with characters actually saying, "No justice, no peace" and "Can't we all get along." However categorized, the intent is to show a side of Americana seldom seen, a goal realized. Strode, perhaps the greatest black Western star, appears at both the beginning and ending, while several other veteran black performers, including Russell, appear in cameos. Hunky Van Peebles is the leader of the usual misfits in the "Dirty Dozen" tradition, infantry deserters holding a load of gold. Between them and freedom is a gang of goons led by Zane. Lots of flash and dash, but lacking soul. **113m/C VHS, DVD, Wide.** Mario Van Peebles, Stephen Baldwin, Charles Lane, Tommy (Tiny) Lister, Big Daddy Kane, Billy Zane, Blair Underwood, Tone Loc, Salli Richardson, Reginald (Reggie) Hudlin, Richard Edson, Reginald Vel Johnson, Warrington Hudlin; ***Cameos:*** Melvin Van Peebles, Pam Grier, Isaac Hayes, Robert Hooks, Richard Jordan, Paul Bartel, Nipsey Russell, Woody Strode, Aaron Neville, Stephen J. Cannell; ***D:*** Mario Van Peebles; ***W:*** Sy Richardson, Dario Scardapane; ***C:*** Peter Menzies Jr.; ***M:*** Michel Colombier.

Possessed ☙☙½ 1931 A poor factory girl becomes a wealthy Park Avenue sophisticate when she falls in love with a rich lawyer who wants to be governor. Not to be confused with Crawford's 1947 movie of the same name, but worth a look. Gable and Crawford make a great couple! **77m/B VHS.** Joan Crawford, Clark Gable, Wallace

Ford, Richard "Skeets" Gallagher, John Miljan; ***D:*** Clarence Brown.

The Possessed 🦴🦴🦴 **1947** Crawford is at her melodramatic best as a crazed gal who can't find happiness with either hunk Heflin or bland Massey. First film for Brooks. From the story "One Man's Secret" by Rita Weiman. **109m/B VHS.** Joan Crawford, Van Heflin, Raymond Massey, Geraldine Brooks, Stanley Ridges, John Ridgely, Nana Bryant, Moroni Olsen; ***D:*** Curtis Bernhardt; ***C:*** Joseph Valentine.

The Possessed 🦴½ **1977 (PG-13)** Farentino is a priest who loses his faith, but regains it after an apparently fatal auto accident. Hackett is the headmistress of a private girls' school which is in need of an exorcist, since one of her student's appears to be possessed, and Farentino seems just the man for the job. Fairly tame, since originally made for TV. **75m/C VHS.** James Farentino, Joan Hackett, Diana Scarwid, Claudette Nevins, Eugene Roche, Ann Dusenberry, Dinah Manoff, P.J. Soles; ***D:*** Jerry Thorpe. **TV**

The Possessed 🦴🦴 *Les Possedes* **1988** Based on the Dostoevsky novel which follows a young aristocrat who's torn between love and politics during the failed Russian revolution of the 1870's. French with subtitles. **124m/C VHS.** *FR* Lambert Wilson, Jean-Philippe Ecoffey, Isabelle Huppert, Jutta Lampe, Laurent Malet, Remi Martin, Omar Sharif, Bernard Blier; ***D:*** Andrzej Wajda; ***W:*** Jean-Claude Carriere, Agnieszka Holland; ***C:*** Witold Adamek; ***M:*** Zygmunt Konieczny.

Possessed 🦴🦴 **2000** William Bowdern (Dalton) is a troubled priest in 1949 St. Louis, who has taken to drink because of his WWII nightmares. He's called on to help 11-year-old Robbie (Malen) who is apparently possessed by a demon. Will reluctant Archbishop Hume (Plummer) allow Bowdern to performan an arcane exorcism and does Robbie's strange Aunt Hanna (Laurie) have anything to do with his condition? Based on the true story of the only documented exorcism performed by the Catholic Church in the U.S. **111m/C VHS, DVD, Wide.** Timothy Dalton, Christopher Plummer, Henry Czerny, Jonathan Malen, Shannon Lawson, Piper Laurie, Michael Rhoades; ***D:*** Steven E. de Souza; ***W:*** Steven E. de Souza, Michael Lazarou; ***C:*** Edward Pei; ***M:*** John (Gianni) Frizzell. **CABLE**

Possessed by the Night 🦴🦴 **1993 (R)** Kinky sex games ensue between a married writer and a sexy other woman thanks to a mysterious fetish object. Unrated version also available. **84m/C VHS.** Ted Prior, Shannon Tweed, Sandahl Bergman, Chad McQueen, Henry Silva; ***D:*** Fred Olen Ray.

Possession 🦴 **1981 (R)** Returned from a long mission, a secret agent notices that his wife is acting very strangely. She's about to give birth to a manifestation of the evil within her! Gory, hysterical, over-intellectual and often unintelligible. **123m/C VHS, DVD, Wide.** *FR GE* Johanna Hofer, Isabelle Adjani, Sam Neill, Heinz Bennent, Margit Carstensen, Shaun Lawtor; ***D:*** Andrzej Zulawski; ***W:*** Andrzej Zulawski, Frederic Tuten; ***C:*** Bruno Nuytten; ***M:*** Andrezej Korzynski, Art Phillips. Cesar '82: Actress (Adjani).

Possession **2002 (PG-13)** Two scholars (Paltrow, Eckhart) find that opposites attract both in the present and the past as they investigate an illicit romance between a pair of 19th-century poets (Northam, Ehle). Based on the 1990 novel by A.S. Byatt. Not yet reviewed. **?m/C VHS, DVD.** Gwyneth Paltrow, Aaron Eckhart, Jeremy Northam, Jennifer Ehle, Lena Headey; ***D:*** Neil LaBute; ***W:*** Neil LaBute, David Henry Hwang, Laura Jones.

The Possession of Joel Delaney 🦴🦴½ **1972 (R)** Blend of occult horror and commentary on social mores works for the most part, but some viewers may be put off by the low production values and spottiness of the script. MacLaine is a wealthy divorcee who must deal with the mysterious transformations affecting her brother. Skeptical at first, she begins to suspect he is the victim of Caribbean voodoo. **105m/C VHS.** Shirley MacLaine, Perry King, Michael Hordern, David Elliott, Robert Burr; ***D:*** Waris Hussein.

Possession: Until Death Do You Part 🦴 **1990** When one man's attraction for a beautiful young woman becomes an obsession, a bizarre series of inexplicable events unravels a terrifying account of passion and revenge. **93m/C VHS.** Monica Marko, John R. Johnston, Sharlene Martin, Cat Williamson; ***D:*** Michael Mazo, Lloyd A. Simandl.

Post Mortem 🦴🦴 **1999** Single mom Linda (Moreau) will do anything to safeguard her daughter Charlotte, which in reality means Linda robs every man she dates after whacking him with some heavy object. Then there's lonely Ghislain (Arcand), who is abruptly arrested by the cops and accused of a crime. Naturally, his life and Linda's intersect. French with subtitles. **92m/C VHS.** *CA* Gabriel Arcand, Sylvie Moreau, Helene Loiselle; ***D:*** Louis Belanger; ***W:*** Louis Belanger; ***C:*** Jean-Pierre St.-Louis; ***M:*** Guy Belanger. Genie '99: Actress (Moreau), Screenplay.

Postal Inspector 🦴🦴 **1936** An extraordinary tale of a postal inspector's life. Crime, romance, and natural disaster all overtake this civil servant. Catch the song "Let's Have Bluebirds On All Our Wallpaper." **58m/B VHS.** Carlos Cortez, Patricia Ellis, Michael Loring, Bela Lugosi, David Oliver, Wallis (Clarke) Clark; ***D:*** Otto Brower.

Postcards from America 🦴🦴 **1995 (R)** Traces the non-artistic aspects of the life of writer/artist David Wojnarowicz, who died of AIDS. Neophyte McLean concentrates on troubled childhood with an abusive father and teen years spent as a street hustler years. Choppy narrative uses little of Wojnarowicz's dialogue, save the voice-over narration by the lead character. Based on two semi-autobiographical novels by the artist. **93m/C VHS.** James Lyons, Michael Tighe, Olmo Tighe, Michael Imperioli, Michael Ringer, Maggie Low; ***D:*** Steve McLean; ***W:*** Steve McLean; ***C:*** Ellen Kuras; ***M:*** Stephen Endelman.

Postcards from the Edge 🦴🦴🦴½ **1990 (R)** Fisher adapted her best-selling novel, tamed and tempered, for the big screen with a tour-de-force of talent. Streep very fine as a delightfully harried actress struggling with her career, her drug dependence, and her competitive, overwhelming show-biz mother. Autobiographical script is bitingly clever and filled with refreshingly witty dialogue. Lots of cameos by Hollywood's hippest. **101m/C VHS, DVD, 8mm, Wide.** Meryl Streep, Shirley MacLaine, Dennis Quaid, Gene Hackman, Richard Dreyfuss, Rob Reiner, Mary Wickes, Conrad Bain, Annette Bening, Michael Ontkean, Dana Ivey, Robin Bartlett, Anthony Heald, Oliver Platt, CCH Pounder; ***D:*** Mike Nichols; ***W:*** Carrie Fisher; ***C:*** Michael Ballhaus; ***M:*** Shel Silverstein, Carly Simon, Stephen Sondheim, Howard Shore, Paul Shaffer, Gilda Radner.

The Postman 🦴🦴🦴½ *Il Postino* **1994 (PG)** Bittersweet, charming film about Mario (Troisi), a shy villager who winds up the personal postman of poet Pablo Neruda (Noiret), who is exiled from his beloved Chile in 1952, granted asylum by the Italian government, and who finds himself living in the tiny Italian community of Isla Negra. The tongue-tied Mario has fallen in love with barmaid Beatrice (Cucinotta) and asks the poet's help in wooing the dark-eyed beauty, striking up an unlikely friendship with the worldly Neruda. Based on the novel "Burning Patience" by Antonio Skarmeta. Italian with subtitles. Troisi, a beloved comic actor in his native Italy, was gravely ill, needing a heart transplant, during the making of the film (all-too apparent from his gaunt appearance) and died the day after filming was completed. **115m/C VHS, DVD.** *IT* Massimo Troisi, Philippe Noiret, Maria Grazia Cucinotta, Linda Moretti, Renato Scarpa, Anna Buonaiuto, Mariana Rigillo; ***D:*** Michael Radford; ***W:*** Massimo Troisi, Michael Radford, Furio Scarpelli, Anna Pavignano, Giacomo Scarpelli; ***C:*** Franco Di Giacomo; ***M:*** Luis Bacalov. Oscars '95: Orig. Dramatic Score; British Acad. '95: Director (Radford), Foreign Film, Score; Broadcast Film Critics '95: Foreign Film.

The Postman 🦴 **1997 (R)** It's postapocalypse time (the year's 2013), with a nameless drifter (Costner) assuming the role of a postal carrier in order to bring hope to a devasted town terrorized by marauding hooligans, led by General Bethlehem (Patton). If you fancy deadpan dialogue and can swallow the image of a mail carrier as the symbol for patriotism, then this one's for you. Overall, Costner offers nothing new to the genre of the stranger offering hope, and soon flick becomes a cornball exercise and extravagant waste of time for all involved. Costner's first directing effort since "Dances with Wolves." It's time someone told Kevin to get out of the epic business and stick to the "everyday Joe" roles. **170m/C VHS, DVD, Wide.** Kevin Costner, Larenz Tate, Will Patton, Olivia Williams, James Russo, Tom Petty, Daniel von Bargen, Scott Bairstow, Giovanni Ribisi, Roberta Maxwell, Joe Santos, Peggy Lipton, Ron McLarty, Rex Linn, Todd Allen, Shawn Hatosy; ***D:*** Kevin Costner; ***W:*** Brian Helgeland, Eric Roth; ***C:*** Stephen Windon; ***M:*** James Newton Howard. Golden Raspberries '97: Worst Picture, Worst Actor (Costner), Worst Director (Costner), Worst Screenplay, Worst Song (Entire Song Score).

The Postman Always Rings Twice 🦴🦴🦴½ **1946** Even without the brutal sexuality of the James M. Cain novel, Garfield and Turner sizzle as the lustladen lovers in this lurid tale of fatal attraction. Garfield steals the show as the streetwise drifter who blows into town and lights a fire in Turner. As their affair steams up the two conspire to do away with her husband and circumstances begin to spin out of control. Tense and compelling. A classic. **113m/B VHS.** Lana Turner, John Garfield, Cecil Kellaway, Hume Cronyn, Leon Ames, Audrey Totter, Alan Reed; ***D:*** Tay Garnett; ***M:*** George Bassman.

The Postman Always Rings Twice 🦴🦴 **1981 (R)** It must be true because he's ringing again in Mamet's version of James M. Cain's depression-era novel. This time Nicholson plays the drifter and Lange the amoral wife with an aged husband. Truer to the original story than the 1946 movie in its use of brutal sex scenes, it nevertheless lacks the power of the original. Nicholson works well in this time era and Lange adds depth and realism to the character of Cora. But in the end it remains dreary and easily forgettable. **123m/C VHS, DVD.** Jack Nicholson, Jessica Lange, John Colicos, Anjelica Huston, Michael Lerner, John P. Ryan, Christopher Lloyd; ***D:*** Bob Rafelson; ***W:*** David Mamet; ***C:*** Sven Nykvist; ***M:*** Michael Small.

Postmark for Danger 🦴🦴½ *Portrait of Alison* **1956** Detectives do their best to smash a diamond smuggling ring that operates between Britain and the U.S. Along the way a number of people are killed. **84m/B VHS.** *GB* Terry Moore, Robert Beatty, William Sylvester, Josephine Griffin, Geoffrey Keen, Henry Oscar; ***D:*** Guy Green.

Postmortem 🦴🦴 **1998 (R)** Sheen is an FBI serial killer profiler who leaves the job to become a novelist and find peace in a small town. But his quiet life is shattered by a murderer who writes the obituaries of his victims before he kills. **105m/C VHS, DVD.** Charlie Sheen, Michael Halsey, Stephen McCole, Gary Lewis, Hazel Ann Crawford; ***D:*** Albert Pyun; ***W:*** John Lamb; ***C:*** George Mooradian; ***M:*** Tony Riparetti.

Pot o' Gold 🦴🦴 *The Golden Hour* **1941** Stewart plays a wealthy young man who signs on with a struggling band. He convinces his uncle, who has a radio program, to let the band perform during a radio giveaway show he has concocted. Slight comedy, Stewart notwithstanding. **87m/B VHS, DVD.** Paulette Goddard, James Stewart, Charles Winninger, Horace Heidt, Art Carney; ***D:*** George Marshall; ***W:*** Walter DeLeon; ***C:*** Hal Mohr.

Pot, Parents, and Police 🦴 *The Cat Ate the Parakeet* **1971** A 13-year-old boy goes crazy when his dog dies and soon gets in with a hippie crowd, drops acid, and gets in trouble with the cops. **86m/C VHS.** Phillip Pine, Robert Mantell, Madelyn Keen, Arthur Battanides, Martin Margulies; ***D:*** Phillip Pine; ***W:*** Phillip Pine.

Pound Puppies and the Legend of Big Paw **1988** The Pound Puppies, known for breaking dogs out of pounds and delivering them to safe and secure homes, are featured in their first full-length musical (and merchandising effort). Fifties music. **76m/C VHS.** ***D:*** Pierre de Celles; ***W:*** Jim Carlson; ***V:*** Nancy Cartwright, George Rose, B.J. Ward, Ruth Buzzi, Brennan Howard.

Pouvoir Intime 🦴🦴½ **1987 (PG-13)** What happens when robbers of an armored car lock the guard in the vehicle, and he decides to fight back? This film offers one possible scenario. Available in dubbed or subtitled versions. **86m/C VHS.** *FR* Marie Tifo, Pierre Curzi, Yvan Ponton, Jaques Lussier; ***D:*** Yves Simoneau.

P.O.W. Deathcamp 🦴🦴 **1989** A combat unit is captured and tortured by the Vietcong in this typical Vietnam story. **92m/C VHS.** Charles Black, Bill Balbridge, Rey Malonzo; ***D:*** Jett C. Espirtu.

The P.O.W. Escape 🦴½ *Behind Enemy Lines* **1986 (R)** The adventures of a surly American commander captured as a POW during the final days of the Vietnam War. **90m/C VHS.** David Carradine, Mako, Charles R. Floyd, Steve James; ***D:*** Gideon Amir; ***W:*** Malcolm Barbour, James Bruner, Jeremy Lipp, John Langley.

Powaqqatsi: Life in Transformation 🦴🦴🦴½ **1988 (G)** Director Reggio's follow-up to "Koyaanisqatsi" doesn't pack the wallop of its predecessor. Still, the cinematography is magnificent and the music of Philip Glass is exquisitely hypnotic as we are taken on a spellbinding video collage of various third world countries and see the price they've paid in the name of progress. Part 2 of a planned trilogy. **95m/C VHS.** ***D:*** Godfrey Reggio; ***M:*** Philip Glass.

Powder 🦴🦴 **1995 (PG-13)** An electromagnetic albino with an I.Q. off the charts is discovered living in his grandparents' cellar and brought to live in a school for troubled teens. Despite harrassment from the crude locals, Powder (Flanery) manages to exude compassion and electricity all over the place with the help of sensitive school director Steenbergen and wacky science teacher Goldblum. Hyper-sentimentality, convoluted and contradictory writing, absurd messianic overtones, and a cop-out climax barely scratch the surface of film's problems. Revelations of Salva's criminal conviction for child molestation cast some scenes in a disturbing light and caused major headaches for Disney's publicity department. **111m/C VHS, DVD.** Sean Patrick Flanery, Mary Steenburgen, Lance Henriksen, Jeff Goldblum, Brandon Smith, Bradford Tatum, Susan Tyrrell, Missy (Melissa) Crider, Ray Wise, Esteban Louis Powell; ***D:*** Victor Salva; ***W:*** Victor Salva; ***C:*** Jerzy Zielinski; ***M:*** Jerry Goldsmith.

Powder Burn 🦴½ **1996** Detective Jack Becker seeks to protect a Beverly Hills client's young daughter when he uncovers unsavory goings-on at her home. And then discovers he's being set up to be the patsy for a murder. **92m/C VHS.** Jay Irwin, Elizabeth Barry.

Powder Keg 🦴🦴 **1970** Railroad company hires a rowdy team of investigators to retrieve a hijacked train. Action never quits. Inspired the TV pilot "The Bearcats." **93m/C VHS.** Rod Taylor, Dennis Cole, Michael Ansara, Fernando Lamas, Tisha Sterling; ***D:*** Douglas Heyes.

Powdersmoke Range 🦴½ **1935** Crooked frontier politician plots to steal valuable ranch property. The new owners, however, have other ideas. First in "The Three Mesquiteer" series. **71m/B VHS.** Harry Carey Sr., Hoot Gibson, Tom Tyler, Guinn "Big Boy" Williams, Bob Steele, Sam Hardy, Patricia "Boots" Mallory, Franklyn Farnum, William Desmond, William Farnum, Buzz Barton, Wally Wales, Art Mix, Buffalo Bill Jr., Buddy Roosevelt; ***D:*** Wallace Fox.

Power 🦴🦴½ **1928** Two dam-building construction workers vie with each other for the local girls. Silent. **60m/B VHS.** William Boyd, Alan Hale, Carole Lombard, Joan Bennett; ***D:*** Howard Higgin.

Power 🦴🦴½ *Jew Suss* **1934** A Jewish ghetto inhabitant in 18th-century Wurtemburg works his way out of the gutter and into some authority by pleasing the whims of an evil duke. Based on the novel by

Leon Fuechtwangler. **105m/B VHS.** *GB* Conrad Veidt, Benita Hume, Frank Vosper, Cedric Hardwicke, Gerald du Maurier, Pamela Ostrer, Joan Maude, Paul Graetz, Mary Clare, Percy Parsons, Dennis Hoey, Gibb McLaughlin, Francis L. Sullivan; ***D:*** Lothar Mendes.

The Power 🦴½ **1980 (R)** An ancient clay idol that was created by the Aztecs and possesses incredible destructive power is unleashed on modern man. **87m/C VHS.** Warren Lincoln, Susan Stokey, Lisa Erickson, Jeffrey Obrow, Chad Christian, Ben Gilbert, Chris Morrill, Rod Mays; ***D:*** Stephen Carpenter, Jeffrey Obrow; ***W:*** Stephen Carpenter, John Penney, Jeffrey Obrow; ***C:*** Stephen Carpenter; ***M:*** Christopher Young.

Power 🦴🦴½ **1986 (R)** A study of corporate manipulations. Gere plays a ruthless media consultant working for politicians. Fine cast can't find the energy needed to make this great, but it's still interesting. Lumet did better with same material in "Network." **111m/C VHS, DVD.** Richard Gere, Julie Christie, E.G. Marshall, Gene Hackman, Beatrice Straight, Kate Capshaw, Denzel Washington, Fritz Weaver, Michael Learned, E. Katherine Kerr, Polly Rowles, Matt Salinger, J.T. Walsh; ***D:*** Sidney Lumet; ***W:*** David Himmelstein; ***C:*** Andrzej Bartkowiak; ***M:*** Cy Coleman.

Power 98 🦴 **1996 (R)** L.A. shock-jock Karlin Pickett (Roberts) takes inexperienced Jon Price (Gedrick) as his protege, much to the dismay of girlfriend Sharon (Garth). Since Pickett will do anything to get higher ratings, she's right to worry, especially after a caller confesses to murder during Pickett's show. Roberts refrains from scenery-chewing but co-stars Gedrick and Garth give new meaning to bland. **89m/C VHS.** Eric Roberts, Jason Gedrick, Jennie Garth, Larry Drake, Stephen Tobolowsky; ***D:*** Jaime Hellman; ***W:*** Jaime Hellman; ***C:*** Kent Wakeford; ***M:*** Jeff Beal.

Power of Attorney 🦴🦴 **1994 (R)** Ambitious up-from-the-streets lawyer Paul Diehl (Koteas) decides to defend Mafia don Joseph Scassi (Aiello) against federal charges of murder and extortion, convincing himself that the mobster is telling the truth. But Scassi decides to make certain his lawyer will do his best by threatening Diehl's drug-dealing brother Frankie (Wilson). **97m/C VHS.** Danny Aiello, Elias Koteas, Nina Siemaszko, Rae Dawn Chong, Roger Wilson; ***D:*** Howard Himelstein; ***W:*** George Erschbamer, Jeff Barmash; ***M:*** Hal Beckett.

The Power of One 🦴🦴 **1992 (PG-13)** Good cast is generally wasted in liberal white look at apartheid. Set in South Africa during the 1940s, P.K. is a white orphan of British descent who is sent to a boarding school run by Afrikaaners (South Africans of German descent). Humiliated and bullied, particularly when England and Germany go to war, P.K. is befriended by a German pianist and a black boxing coach who teach him to box and stand up for his rights. Preachy and filled with stereotypes. Based on the novel by Bryce Courtenay. **126m/C VHS, DVD, Wide.** Stephen Dorff, Armin Mueller-Stahl, Morgan Freeman, John Gielgud, Fay Masterson, Marius Weyers, Tracy Brooks Swope, John Osborne, Daniel Craig, Dominic Walker, Alois Mayo, Ian Roberts, Maria Marais; ***D:*** John G. Avildsen; ***W:*** Robert Mark Kamen; ***C:*** Dean Semler; ***M:*** Hans Zimmer.

The Power of the Ninjitsu 🦴 **1988** A young man inherits the leadership of a martial arts crime gang, the Scorpions, but the elder members muscle him out of his place. He returns for revenge and has the old ones running scared. Power to the Ninjitsu! **90m/C VHS.** Britton Lee, Adam Frank, Peter Ujaer; ***D:*** Joseph Lai.

Power, Passion & Murder 🦴½ **1983** A young, glamorous movie star has an affair with a married man which begins the end of her career in 1930s Hollywood. **104m/C VHS.** Michelle Pfeiffer, Darren McGavin, Stella Stevens; ***D:*** Paul Bogart, Leon Ichaso.

Power Play 🦴½ *Operation Overthrow* **1981** Young army colonel from a small European country joins forces with rebels to overthrow the government. After the coup, the group discovers that in their midst is a traitor. So who is it? Suspense never builds adequately. **95m/C VHS.** *CA GB* Peter O'Toole, David Hemmings, Donald Pleasence, Barry Morse; ***D:*** Martyn Burke; ***W:*** Martyn Burke.

The Power Within 🦴½ **1979** An electrified stuntman finds he can send electrical shocks from his hands and becomes the victim of a kidnapping plot. **90m/C VHS.** Eric (Hans Gudegast) Braeden, David Hedison, Susan Howard, Art Hindle; ***D:*** John Llewellyn Moxey.

The Power Within 🦴🦴½ **1995 (PG-13)** Evil Raymond Vonn has stolen an ancient ring of power but to acquire its complete strength he needs to find a second, matching ring. This is in the possession of teenaged Stan Dryer (Roberts), who must discover the ring's power if he expects to defeat Vonn. **97m/C VHS.** Ted Jan Roberts, Karen Valentine, Keith Coogan, John O'Hurley, Gary Morgan, Sean Fitzgerald, William Zabka; ***D:*** Art Camacho; ***W:*** Jacobsen Hart, Susan Bowen; ***M:*** Jim Halfpenny.

Powwow Highway 🦴🦴🦴½ **1989 (R)** Remarkably fine performances in this unusual, thought-provoking, poorly titled foray into the plight of Native Americans. Farmer shines as the unassuming, amiable Cheyenne traveling to New Mexico in a beat-up Chevy with his Indian activist buddy, passionately portrayed by Martinez. On the journey they are constantly confronted with the tragedy of life on a reservation. A sobering look at government injustice and the lingering spirit of a people lost inside their homeland. **105m/C VHS.** Gary Farmer, A. Martinez, Amanda Wyss, Rene Handren-Seals, Graham Greene; ***D:*** Joanelle Romero, Jonathan Wacks; ***W:*** Janet Heaney, Jean Stawarz; ***C:*** Toyomichi Kurita; ***M:*** Barry Goldberg. Sundance '89: Filmmakers Trophy.

Practical Magic 🦴🦴½ **1998 (PG-13)** Gillian (Kidman) and Sally (Bullock) are modern-day witch sisters whose family suffers from an unfortunate 100-year-old curse. Any man they fall in love with is doomed to an early death. One more dead body, Gillian's abusive boyfriend Jimmy (Visnjic), brings out detective Gary Hallet (Quinn) and his charms prove mighty attractive to the frantic Sally. Good cast, weak story. Based on the 1995 novel by Alice Hoffman. **105m/C VHS, DVD, Wide.** Sandra Bullock, Nicole Kidman, Aidan Quinn, Stockard Channing, Dianne Wiest, Goran Visnjic; ***D:*** Griffin Dunne; ***W:*** Robin Swicord, Akiva Goldsman, Adam Brooks; ***C:*** Andrew Dunn; ***M:*** Alan Silvestri.

The Practice of Love 🦴🦴 **1984** A woman journalist's investigation of a murder casts suspicion on her two male lovers. The film raises the question of whether love is even possible in a world dominated by men's struggles for power. In German with English subtitles. **90m/C VHS.** *GE* ***D:*** Valie Export.

Prairie Badmen 🦴½ **1946** Outlaws are after a treasure map in the possession of the owner of a medicine show. It's up to our hero to stop them. One of the "Billy Carson" western series. **55m/B VHS.** Buster Crabbe.

The Prairie King 🦴½ **1927** Will grants three people the same gold mine but stipulates only one may own it. Silent quandary. **58m/B VHS.** Hoot Gibson, Barbara Worth, Charles Sellon, Albert Priscoe.

Prairie Moon 🦴½ **1938** Autry becomes the guardian of three tough kids from Chicago after they inherit a ranch. The kids help Autry round up a gang of rustlers. **58m/B VHS.** Gene Autry, Smiley Burnette.

Prairie Pals 🦴½ **1942** Deputies go undercover to rescue a kidnapped scientist. **60m/B VHS.** William Boyd, Lee Powell, Art Davis, Charles "Blackie" King, John Merton, Kermit Maynard, Al "Fuzzy" St. John; ***D:*** Sam Newfield.

The Prairie Pirate 🦴🦴½ **1925** Carey is the western hero tracking down the dirty dogs who murdered his sister. Fast-paced. **59m/B VHS.** Harry Carey Sr., Lloyd Whitlock, Jean Dumas, Trilby Clark; ***D:*** Edmund Mortimer.

Praise 🦴🦴🦴 **1998** First-time director Curran scores big with this downbeat sex-and-drugs saga. Gordan (Fenton) has quit his convenience store job to spend his time drinking with his mates in his grubby Brisbane apartment. Former co-worker Cynthia (Holder) invites Gordon to her parents' empty house where the duo spend their time with various chemical substances, alcohol, and sex. They wind up sticking together out of mutual need and never rise above their marginal existence. Still, both director and actors deliver a powerful production. Adapted from the novel by McGahan, who wrote the screenplay. **97m/C VHS.** *AU* Peter Fenton, Sacha Holder; ***D:*** John Curran; ***W:*** Andrew McGahan; ***C:*** Dion Beebe. Australian Film Inst. '99: Actress (Holder), Adapt. Screenplay.

Prancer 🦴🦴 **1989 (G)** An eight-year-old girl whose mother has recently died thinks an injured reindeer she has found belongs to Santa. She lovingly nurses him back to health. Harmless family entertainment. **102m/C VHS, DVD, Wide.** Sam Elliott, Rebecca Harrell, Cloris Leachman, Rutanya Alda, John Joseph Duda, Abe Vigoda, Michael Constantine, Ariana Richards, Mark Rolston; ***D:*** John Hancock; ***W:*** Greg Taylor; ***C:*** Misha (Mikhail) Suslov; ***M:*** Maurice Jarre.

Prancer Returns 🦴🦴½ **2001 (G)** When dad cuts out, 8-year-old Charlie, his mom and his brother move to a small Michigan town where Charlie hears about a local legend. Seems a young girl nursed a wounded deer back to health and set it free on Christmas Eve. The deer turned out to be Prancer and he rejoined Santa just in time to help pull the sleigh. So when Charlie finds a baby reindeer in the woods, he decides it must be a new Prancer and he has to make sure that the deer gets to Santa in time for Christmas. **90m/C VHS, DVD, Wide.** Jack Palance, John Corbett, Stacy Edwards, Gavin Fink, Michael O'Keefe; ***D:*** Joshua Butler; ***W:*** Greg Taylor. **CABLE**

Pray for Death 🦴🦴 **1985 (R)** When a mild-mannered Japanese family is victimized by a crime syndicate in L.A., a master ninja comes to the rescue. Higher quality production than most ninja adventures. **93m/C VHS.** James Booth, Robert Ito, Sho Kosugi, Shane Kosugi, Kane (Takeshi) Kosugi, Donna Kei Benz; ***D:*** Gordon Hessler; ***W:*** James Booth.

Pray for the Wildcats 🦴½ **1974** Three advertising executives' promotional trip from (or to?) Hell. Anything to please a client. **96m/C VHS.** Andy Griffith, William Shatner, Angie Dickinson, Janet Margolin, Marjoe Gortner, Lorraine Gary; ***D:*** Robert Lewis.

Pray TV 🦴🦴 *KGOD* **1980 (PG)** A sly con man turns a failing TV station into a profitable one when the station starts to broadcast around-the-clock religious programming. **92m/C VHS.** Dabney Coleman, Archie Hahn, Joyce Jameson, Nancy Morgan, Roger E. Mosley, Marcia Wallace; ***D:*** Rick Friedberg; ***W:*** Nick Castle. **TV**

Pray TV 🦴🦴 **1982** Expose of broadcast religion in which a young preacher chooses between orthodox religion and lots of money. Not as cutting an indictment as it could have been. **100m/C VHS.** John Ritter, Ned Beatty, Madolyn Smith, Richard Kiley, Louise Latham, Jonathan Prince, Michael Currie, Lois Areno; ***D:*** Robert Markowitz. **TV**

A Prayer for Katarina Horovitzova 🦴🦴🦴½ **1969** Stunning tale of a Polish singer who struggles to find the meaning and beauty of life while working to trade Nazi prisoners in U.S. jails for Jews hoping to emigrate. Based on the Arnost Lustig novel. Confiscated by the Czech Communist government and kept from the screen for 21 years. In Czechoslovakian with English subtitles. **60m/C VHS.** *CZ* Jiri Adamira, Lenka Fiserova, Cestmir Randa.

Prayer for the Dying 🦴🦴½ **1987 (R)** An IRA hitman longs to quit, but he has to complete one last assignment. The hit is witnessed by a priest who becomes an unwitting associate when the hitman hides out at the church. Fine performances from Bates and Rourke, though Hodges and Rourke were not satisfied with finished film. **104m/C VHS.** Mickey Rourke, Alan Bates, Bob Hoskins, Sammi Davis, Liam Neeson, Alison Doody, Christopher Fulford; ***D:*** Mike Hodges; ***W:*** Edmund Ward, Martin Lynch; ***M:*** Bill Conti.

A Prayer in the Dark 🦴🦴½ **1997 (PG-13)** Pious Quaker wife and mother, Emily Hayworth (Carter), is taken hostage in her own home by a former Quaker friend, Jimmy (Ferguson). He's escaped from prison with two armed cons, demanding that Emily steal $4 million from the bank where she works. Since they're also holding her family, she agrees. But when Emily's out of the house, she and others in the Quaker community try to find a peaceful solution to the volatile situation. **91m/C VHS.** Lynda Carter, Colin Ferguson, Teri Polo. **CABLE**

Prayer of the Rollerboys 🦴🦴½ **1991 (R)** Violent, futuristic, funky action as Haim infiltrates a criminal gang of syncopated roller-blading neo-nazi youth with plans for nationwide domination. Though routinely plotted and predictable, it's got great skating stunts and a wry vision of tomorrow's shattered USA—broke, drug-soaked, homeless, foreign-owned; even sharper when you realize this is a Japanese-American co-production. **94m/C VHS.** Corey Haim, Patricia Arquette, Christopher Collet, Julius W. Harris, J.C. Quinn, Jake Dengel, Devin Clark, Mark Pellegrino, Morgan Weisser; ***D:*** Rick King; ***W:*** W. Peter Iliff; ***C:*** Phedon Papamichael; ***M:*** Stacy Widelitz.

Praying Mantis 🦴🦴 **1983 (PG-13)** The professor's scheming nurse murdered his family and plans to marry him for his money. She enlists the aid of the professor's assistant in her evil plot. **119m/C VHS.** Jonathan Pryce, Cherie Lunghi, Ann Cropper, Carmen (De Sautoy) Du Sautoy, Pinkas Braun; ***D:*** Jack Gold; ***M:*** Carl Davis.

Praying Mantis 🦴🦴½ **1993 (PG-13)** Seymour stars as a femme fatale who likes to get married and then, in a rage against her own abusive childhood, kill her new husbands off. So far her total is five dead hubbies with number six (Bostwick) in her sights. Only this time, her almost-sister-in-law (Fisher) is very suspicious of the bride-to-be. **90m/C VHS.** Jane Seymour, Barry Bostwick, Frances Fisher, Chad Allen; ***D:*** James Keach; ***W:*** Duane Poole, William F. Delligan; ***M:*** John Debney. **CABLE**

Pre-Madonnas: Rebels Without a Clue 🦴🦴½ *Social Suicide* **1995 (PG-13)** Kim Sterling (Sturges) decides to rig the Beverly Hills Las Madonnas debutante ball to teach the snobs a lesson. **98m/C VHS.** Shannon Sturges, Bobbie Bresee, Peter Anthony Elliott, Kenn Cooper; ***D:*** Lawrence Foldes.

Preacherman 🦴½ **1983 (R)** Phony preacher travels through the South, fleecing gullible congregations (and providing for their sexual desires) wherever he goes. **90m/C VHS.** Amos Huxley, Marian Brown, Adam Hesse, Ilene Kristen, W. Henry Smith; ***D:*** Albert T. Viola; ***W:*** Albert T. Viola, Harvey Flaxman; ***M:*** W. Henry Smith, Roland Pope.

The Preacher's Wife 🦴🦴 **1996 (PG)** Remake of 1947's "The Bishop's Wife" finds troubled Newark minister Henry Biggs (Vance) praying for heavenly intervention. His prayers are answered with angel Dudley (Washington)—who isn't so holy that he can't appreciate the minister's choir-leading wife Julia (Houston). While trying to save his cash-strapped church from a greedy developer (Hines), Rev. Biggs is so mired in material problems that he is unable to believe that Dudley is actually an angel. Washington is the dictionary definition of debonair as the angel with a touch of the devil in his eye. All problems are, of course, wrapped up neatly with a bow on top in the end. The real stars of this Christmas tale, however, are Houston's vocal cords. Fans of her singing will love this movie, while others may want to rent the original. **124m/C VHS.** Shari Headley, Denzel Washington, Whitney Houston, Courtney B. Vance, Gregory Hines, Jenifer Lewis, Loretta Devine, Lionel Richie, Paul Bates, Justin Pierre Edmund, Darvel Davis Jr., William James Stiggers Jr.; ***D:*** Penny Marshall; ***W:*** Nat Mauldin, Allan Scott; ***C:*** Miroslav Ondricek; ***M:*** Hans Zimmer.

Precious Find 🦴🦴 **1996 (R)** In 2049 there's a new gold rush—this time into outer space. The moon's enclosed city is a staging area for mining operations throughout the solar system and draws the attention of three prospectors: Ben, who can "smell" gold, Crille (Hauer), who has a high-tech treasure map, and Sam (James), who owns a space hauler. They're all anxious to cash in when a newly discovered asteroid turns out to be a literal gold mine as is claim jumper Camilla (Chen). **90m/C VHS.** Rutger Hauer, Brion James, Harold P. Pruett, Joan Chen; ***D:*** Philippe Mora; ***W:*** Jane Ubell, John Remark; ***C:*** Walter Bal; ***M:*** Roy Hay.

Predator 🦴🦴½ **1987 (R)** Schwarzenegger leads a team of CIA-hired mercenaries into the Central American jungles to rescue hostages. They encounter an alien force that begins to attack them one by one. Soon it's just Arnold and the Beast in this attention-grabbing, but sometimes silly, suspense film. **107m/C VHS, DVD, Wide.** Arnold Schwarzenegger, Jesse Ventura, Sonny Landham, Bill Duke, Elpidia Carrillo, Carl Weathers, R.G. Armstrong, Richard Chaves, Shane Black, Kevin Peter Hall; ***D:*** John McTiernan; ***W:*** Jim Thomas, John Thomas; ***C:*** Donald McAlpine; ***M:*** Alan Silvestri.

Predator 2 🦴🦴 **1990 (R)** Tough cop takes time away from battling drug dealers to deal with malicious extraterrestrial who exterminated Arnold's band of commandos in "Predator." Miss-billed as sequel, its only resemblance to the original is that the predator has inexplicably returned (this time to the thick of L.A.). Gory action aplenty, little logic. Fine cast dominated by minority performers can't save this one. **105m/C VHS, Wide.** Kevin Peter Hall, Steve Kahan, Michael (Mike) Papajohn, Danny Glover, Gary Busey, Ruben Blades, Maria Conchita Alonso, Bill Paxton, Robert Davi, Adam Baldwin, Kent McCord, Morton Downey Jr., Calvin Lockhart, Teri Weigel; ***D:*** Stephen Hopkins; ***W:*** John Thomas, Jim Thomas; ***C:*** Peter Levy; ***M:*** Alan Silvestri.

Prefontaine 🦴🦴½ **1996 (PG-13)** Sports bio has appeal, thanks to lead actor Leto, in covering the brief career of early '70s runner Steve Prefontaine. Cocky and outspoken, the charismatic University of Oregon star soon owns every American record for distances between 2,000 and 10,000 meters. He's expected to gold at the 1972 Munich Olympics but falters, thanks in part to the tragedy surrounding the games. Returning home, the flamboyant Pre becomes a sports activist for athletes' rights before dying in a car crash in 1975 at the age of 24. Relatively straight narrative and little psychological insight make for few lasting impressions. **107m/C VHS.** Jared Leto, R. Lee Ermey, Ed O'Neill, Amy Locane, Lindsay Crouse, Laurel Holloman, Breckin Meyer, Kurtwood Smith, Brian McGovern, Peter Anthony Jacobs; ***D:*** Steve James; ***W:*** Steve James, Eugene Corr; ***C:*** Peter Gilbert; ***M:*** Mason Daring.

Prehistoric Bimbos in Armageddon City woof! **1993** Trianna and her tribe of Prehistoric Bimbos must prevent post-nuclear domination in Old Chicago City, the last remaining civilization after WWIII, by defeating the evil ruler Nemesis and his cyborgs. "Enough bimbos to fill two post-nuclear action comedies." So bad its gotta be good. **70m/C VHS.** Robert Vollrath, Tonia Monahan, Deric Bernier.

Prehistoric Women woof! **1950** A tribe of prehistoric women look for husbands the old-fashioned way—they drag them back to their caves from the jungle. So bad it's almost good. **74m/C VHS.** Laurette Luez, Allan Nixon, Mara Lynn, Joan Shawlee, Judy Landon; ***D:*** Greg Tallas.

Prehistoric Women 🦴 *Slave Girls* **1967** Essentially, an equally tacky remake of the 1950 woofer. Great white hunter David Marchant (Latimer) gets lost in a jungle where the local tribe worship the white rhino. He escapes from one group, only to recapture by some Amazons, who take the hunter to their queen, Kari (Beswick—the only reason to waste your time), who gives him two options—satisfy her or die. **90m/C VHS, DVD.** *GB* Michael Latimer, Martine Beswick, Edina Ronay, Carol White; ***D:*** Michael Carreras; ***W:*** Henry (Michael Carreras) Younger; ***C:*** Michael Reed; ***M:*** Carlo Martelli.

Prehysteria 🦴🦴½ **1993 (PG)** Fantasy/adventure about a widower, his 11-year-old son and teenage daughter, and what happens when some mysterious eggs from South America accidentally wind up at their farm. Imagine their surprise when the eggs hatch and out pop a brood of pygmy dinosaurs. The dinosaurs are cute (as is the family), the villain is dumb, and the violence minimal. **84m/C VHS.** Brett Cullen, Austin O'Brien, Samantha Mills, Colleen Morris, Tony Longo, Stuart Fratkin, Stephen Lee; ***D:*** Albert Band, Charles Band; ***W:*** Greg Suddeth, Mark Goldstein.

Prehysteria 2 🦴🦴½ **1994 (PG)** While their adoptive family is on vacation the pygmy dinosaurs get loose and aid a lonely rich boy whose governess is plotting to send him to military boarding school. **81m/C VHS.** Kevin R. Connors, Jennifer Harte, Dean Scofield, Bettye Ackerman, Larry Hankin, Greg Lewis, Alan Palo, Michael Hagiwara, Owen Bush; ***D:*** Albert Band; ***W:*** Brent Friedman, Michael Paul Davis; ***M:*** Richard Band.

Prehysteria 3 🦴🦴½ **1995 (PG)** The mini-dinos take up miniature golf. Seems Thomas MacGregor's (Willard) putt-putt business is about to sink when his daughter Ella (Anderson) finds the pygmy dinosaurs and a promotional bonanza is born. But Thomas' evil brother Hal (Weitz) hatches a plot to take over the now-successful enterprize. DeCoteau used the pseudonym Julian Breen. **85m/C VHS.** Fred Willard, Bruce Weitz, Whitney Anderson, Pam Matteson; ***D:*** David DeCoteau; ***W:*** Michael Paul Davis, Neil Ruttenberg.

Prelude to a Kiss 🦴🦴 **1992 (PG-13)** Disappointing screen adaptation of Craig Lucas' hit play features Baldwin and Ryan as young lovers in this romantic fantasy. Ryan is Rita, a free-spirited bartender and Baldwin is Peter, a conservative writer, who decide to marry after a whirlwind courtship. At their wedding reception, Rita obligingly kisses one of their guests, an old man (Walker). Then, on their honeymoon, Peter begins to notice a number of changes to Rita's character and comes to realize this is truly not the girl he married. The delicate fantasy which worked on stage struggles to survive the "opening up" of the screen adaptation though Baldwin (who reprises his stage role) and Ryan are appealing. **106m/C VHS, DVD, Wide.** Alec Baldwin, Meg Ryan, Sydney Walker, Ned Beatty, Patty Duke, Kathy Bates, Stanley Tucci; ***D:*** Norman Rene; ***W:*** Craig Lucas; ***C:*** Stefan Czapsky; ***M:*** Howard Shore.

Prelude to War **1942** A compact look at the events of 1931-39; includes a series of contrasts between free societies and totalitarian governments. From the "Why We Fight" series. **53m/B VHS.** ***D:*** Frank Capra. Oscars '42: Feature Doc.

Premature Burial 🦴🦴 **1962** A cataleptic Englishman's worst fears come true when he is buried alive. He escapes and seeks revenge on his doctor and his greedy wife. Based upon the story by Edgar Allan Poe. **81m/C VHS.** Ray Milland, Richard Ney, Hazel Court, Heather Angel, Alan Napier, John Dierkes, Dick Miller, Brendan Dillon Jr., Clive Halliday; ***D:*** Roger Corman; ***W:*** Charles Beaumont, Ray Russell; ***C:*** Floyd Crosby; ***M:*** Ronald Stein.

Premonition 🦴½ **1971 (PG)** Three drug-riddled '60s college students experience similar premonitions of death, and subsequently either die or become tormented. **83m/C VHS.** Carl Crow, Tim Ray, Winfrey Hester Hill, Victor Izay; ***D:*** Alan Rudolph; ***W:*** Alan Rudolph; ***C:*** John Bailey.

The Premonition 🦴🦴½ **1975 (PG)** Parapsychologist searching for a missing child is drawn into a frightening maze of dream therapy and communication with the dead. Well-done paranorm tale filmed in Mississippi. **94m/C VHS.** Richard Lynch, Sharon Farrell, Jeff Corey, Ellen Barber, Edward Bell, Danielle Brisebois; ***D:*** Robert Allen Schnitzer; ***W:*** Anthony Mahon.

Premonition 🦴🦴 **1998 (R)** Lloyd and Preston are tabloid reporters who investigate supernatural phenomena. Their latest find is a mental patient who predicts events that wind up leading back to a past they both share. Unfortunately, the film is more a series of horror cliches and makes little sense. **93m/C VHS, DVD.** Christopher Lloyd, Adrian Paul, Cynthia Preston, Blu Mankuma; ***D:*** Gavin Wilding; ***W:*** Gavin Wilding, Raul Inglis, John Fairley; ***C:*** Glen Winter. **VIDEO**

Prep School 🦴 **1981 (PG-13)** A very proper New England prep school is turned topsy-turvy by two rambunctious co-eds. They're determined to break every one of the school's cardinal rules. **97m/C VHS.** Leslie Hope, Andrew Sabiston; ***D:*** Paul Almond.

The Preppie Murder 🦴🦴½ **1989** Made for TV crime drama based on the killing of Jennifer Levin in New York City's Central Park in 1987, with Baldwin cast as prep school grad Robert Chambers. Amid sensational headlines, the story told of drugs, sexual games, and idle and disaffected youth. **100m/C VHS.** William Baldwin, Lara Flynn Boyle, Danny Aiello, Joanna (Joanna DeVarona) Kerns, Dorothy Fielding, James Handy, William Devane; ***D:*** John Herzfeld. **TV**

Preppies 🦴½ **1982 (R)** Yet another teen sex comedy, but this time Ivy Leaguer Drake must pass his exams to receive his $50 million inheritance. Lots of skirt chasing as his conniving cousin leads him astray. **83m/C VHS.** Dennis Drake, Peter Brady Reardon, Steven Holt, Nitchie Barrett, Cindy Manion, Katt Shea, Lynda Wiesmeier; ***D:*** Chuck Vincent.

Prescott Kid 🦴🦴 **1936** Legendary western star McCoy plays a law-abiding cowboy mistaken for the new Marshall in the outlaw town of San Lorenzo, which has been targeted by a gang of cattle rustling killers. **58m/B VHS.** Tim McCoy, Sheila (Manors) Mannors, Alden Chase, Hooper Atchley, Walter Brennan; ***D:*** David Selman; ***W:*** Ford Beebe.

Presenting Lily Mars 🦴🦴 **1943** A small-town girl comes to New York to make it on Broadway. Based on the Booth Tarkington novel. ♫When I Look at You; Three O'Clock in the Morning; Kulebiaka; Is It Love? (Or The Gypsy in Me); Broadway Rhythm; Sweethearts of America; Where There's Music; Every Little Movement Has a Meaning All Its Own; Tom, Tom the Piper's Son. **105m/B VHS.** Judy Garland, Van Heflin, Fay Bainter, Richard Carlson, Tommy Dorsey; ***D:*** Norman Taurog; ***C:*** Joseph Ruttenberg.

The President's Analyst 🦴🦴🦴½ **1967** A superbly written, brilliantly executed satire from the mind of Theodore J. Flicker, who wrote as well as directed. Coburn steals the show as a psychiatrist who has the dubious honor of being appointed "secret shrink" to the President of the U.S. Pressures of the job steadily increase his paranoia until he suspects he is being pursued by agents and counter agents alike. Is he losing his sanity or...? Vastly entertaining. **104m/C VHS.** James Coburn, Godfrey Cambridge, Severn Darden, Joan Delaney, Pat Harrington, Will Geer, William Daniels, Barry McGuire, Jill Banner, Arte Johnson; ***D:*** Theodore J. Flicker; ***W:*** Theodore J. Flicker; ***C:*** William A. Fraker; ***M:*** Lalo Schifrin.

President's Mistress 🦴½ **1978** A security agent searches for his sister's murderer, while trying to obscure the fact that she was having an affair with the President. **97m/C VHS.** Beau Bridges, Susan Blanchard, Larry Hagman, Joel Fabiani, Karen Grassle; ***D:*** John Llewellyn Moxey.

The President's Mystery 🦴½ *One For All* **1936** A lawyer decides to turn his back on society by giving up his practice and his marriage. Eventually he meets and falls in love with another woman. The most interesting aspect of the film is that it is based on a story by Franklin D. Roosevelt, which was published in "Liberty" magazine. The story was supposedly better than its screen adaptation. **80m/B VHS.** Henry Wilcoxon, Betty Furness, Sidney Blackmer, Evelyn Brent; ***D:*** Phil Rosen.

The President's Plane Is Missing 🦴🦴 **1971** When Air Force One disappears, the less than trustworthy Vice President takes control. Could there be a dire plot in the making? Based on a novel by Rod Serling's brother Robert J. Serling. **100m/C VHS.** Buddy Ebsen, Peter Graves, Arthur Kennedy, Rip Torn, Louise Sorel, Raymond Massey, James Wainwright, Mercedes McCambridge, Dabney Coleman, Joseph Campanella; ***D:*** Daryl Duke.

President's Target 🦴🦴 **1993** An anti-drug mission in South America is ambushed and CIA operative Peter Caine is the only survivor. Now he's out to see who planned the double-cross and how best to get his revenge. **82m/C VHS.** John Coleman, Martin Kove, Bo Hopkins, Brigitte Audrey; ***D:*** Yvan Chiffre.

The Presidio 🦴🦴 **1988 (R)** An easy going police detective must investigate a murder on a military base where he and the base commander have sparred before. The commander becomes downright nasty when his daughter shows an interest in the detective. Good action scenes in San Francisco almost covers up script weaknesses, but not quite. **97m/C VHS, DVD, 8mm.** Sean Connery, Mark Harmon, Meg Ryan, Jack Warden, Mark Blum, Jenette Goldstein; ***D:*** Peter Hyams; ***W:*** Larry Ferguson; ***M:*** Bruce Broughton.

Pressure Point 🦴🦴🦴 **1962** Poitier stars as a prison psychiatrist treating an inmate who is a racist and a member of the Nazi party. Darin gives an excellent performance as the Nazi patient in this intelligent drama based on a true case. **87m/B VHS.** Sidney Poitier, Bobby Darin, Peter Falk, Carl Benton Reid, Barry J. Gordon, Howard Caine, Mary Munday; ***D:*** Hubert Cornfield; ***M:*** Ernest Gold.

Presumed Guilty 🦴 **1991** An innocent man is released from prison only to find he is once again a wanted man! So he gets his gal, who happens to be the sheriff's daughter, is beaten up and in the end winds up living happily ever after. **91m/C VHS.** Jack Vogel, Holly Floria, Sean Holton, Wayne Zanelotti, Bradley Rockwell, Sharon Young, Al Schuerman; ***D:*** Lawrence L. Simeone; ***W:*** Lawrence L. Simeone.

Presumed Innocent 🦴🦴🦴 **1990 (R)** Assistant district attorney is the prime suspect when a former lover turns up brutally murdered. Cover-ups surround him, the political climate changes, and friends and enemies switch sides. Slow-paced courtroom drama with excellent performances from Ford, Julia, and Bedelia. Skillfully adapted from the best-seller by Chicago attorney Scott Turow. **127m/C VHS, DVD, 8mm, Wide.** Harrison Ford, Brian Dennehy, Bonnie Bedelia, Greta Scacchi, Raul Julia, Paul Winfield, John Spencer, Joe Grifasi, Anna Maria Horsford, Sab Shimono, Christine Estabrook, Michael (Lawrence) Tolan, Tom Mardirosian; ***D:*** Alan J. Pakula; ***W:*** Frank Pierson, Alan J. Pakula; ***C:*** Gordon Willis; ***M:*** John Williams.

Pretty Baby 🦴🦴🦴 **1978 (R)** Shield's launching pad and Malle's first American film is a masterpiece of cinematography and style, nearly upstaged by the plodding storyline. Carradine manages to be effective but never succeeds at looking comfortable as the New Orleans photographer besotted with, and subsequently married to, an 11-year-old prostitute (Shields). Low key, disturbingly intriguing story, beautifully photographed by Sven Nykvist. **109m/C VHS.** Brooke Shields, Keith Carradine, Susan Sarandon, Barbara Steele, Diana Scarwid, Antonio Fargas, Frances Faye, Gerrit Graham, Mae Mercer; ***D:*** Louis Malle; ***W:*** Polly Platt; ***C:*** Sven Nykvist; ***M:*** Jerry Wexler.

Pretty in Pink 🦴🦴½ **1986 (PG-13)** More teen angst from the pen of Hughes. Poor girl falls for a rich guy. Their families fret, their friends are distressed, and fate conspires against them. If you can suspend your disbelief that a teenager with her own car and answering machine is financially inferior, then you may very well be able to accept the entire premise. Slickly done and adequately, if not enthusiastically, acted. In 1987, Hughes essentially rewrote this film with "Some Kind of Wonderful," the same story with the rich/pauper characters reversed by gender. **96m/C VHS, 8mm.** Molly Ringwald, Andrew McCarthy, Jon Cryer, Harry Dean Stanton, James Spader, Annie Potts, Andrew (Dice Clay) Silverstein, Margaret Colin, Alexa Kenin, Gina Gershon, Dweezil Zappa, Kristy Swanson; ***D:*** Howard Deutch; ***W:*** John Hughes; ***C:*** Tak Fujimoto; ***M:*** Michael Gore.

Pretty Poison 🦴🦴🦴½ **1968** You won't need an antidote for this one. Original, absorbing screenplay, top-notch acting, and on target direction combine to raise this low-budget, black comedy above the crowd. Perkins at his eerie best as a burned-out arsonist who cooks up a crazy scheme and enlists the aid of a hot-to-trot high schooler, only to discover too late she has some burning desires of her own. Weld is riveting as the turbulent teen. **89m/C VHS.** Anthony Perkins, Tuesday Weld, Beverly Garland, John Randolph, Dick O'Neill; ***D:*** Noel Black. N.Y. Film Critics '68: Screenplay.

Pretty Smart woof! **1987 (R)** Two diametrically opposed sisters at a European finishing school team up against a drug-dealing, voyeuristic teacher. Pretty lame. **84m/C VHS.** Tricia Leigh Fisher, Patricia Arquette, Dennis Cole, Lisa Lorient; ***D:*** Dimitri Logothetis; ***M:*** Eddie Arkin.

Pretty Village, Pretty Flame 🦴🦴🦴 *Lepa Sela, Lepo Gore* **1996** Powerful story of the Bosnian conflict that is loosely based on a true incident. Story flashes from the days of Yugoslavian unity under Marshal Tito to 1992 when members of a Serbian patrol are trapped (along with an American journalist) by Muslim militiamen in a tunnel connecting Zagreb and Belgrade with no hope for escape. Serbo-Croatian with subtitles. **125m/C VHS, DVD, Wide.** Dragan Bjelogric, Nikola Kojo, Bata Zivojinovic, Dragan Maksimovic, Zoran Cvijanovic, Nikola Pejakovic, Lisa Moncure; ***D:*** Srdjan Dragojevic; ***W:*** Srdjan Dragojevic, Vanja Bulic, Nikola Pejakovic; ***C:*** Dusan Joksimovic; ***M:*** Lazar Ristovski.

Pretty Woman 🦴🦴🦴 **1990 (R)** An old story takes a fresh approach as a successful but stuffy business man hires a fun-loving, energetic young hooker to be his companion for a week. The film caused some controversy over its upbeat portrayal of prostitution, but its popularity at the boxoffice catapulted Roberts to stardom. **117m/C VHS, DVD.** Richard Gere, Julia Roberts, Ralph Bellamy, Jason Alexander, Laura San Giacomo, Hector Elizondo, Alex Hyde-White, Elinor Donahue, Larry Miller, Jane Morris; ***D:*** Garry Marshall; ***W:*** J.F. Lawton; ***C:*** Charles Minsky; ***M:*** James Newton Howard. Golden Globes '91: Actress—Mus./Comedy (Roberts).

Prettykill woof! **1987 (R)** A confusing storyline with numerous subplots involves detective with a paramour/prostitute (Hubley) attempting to stalk a mad killer while contending with her split personality. **95m/C VHS.** David Birney, Susannah York, Season Hubley, Yaphet Kotto, Suzanne Snyder, Germane Honde; ***D:*** George Kaczender; ***W:*** Sandra K. Bailey; ***C:*** Joao Fernandes.

The Prey 🦴 **1980 (R)** Poorly done horror show about a predator who is looking for a mate in the Colorado Rockies and kills five campers in the process. **80m/C VHS.** Debbie Thurseon, Steve Bond, Lori Lethin, Jackie Coogan; ***D:*** Edwin Scott Brown; ***W:*** Edwin Scott Brown, Summer Brown.

Prey for the Hunter 🦴 **1992 (R)** Four businessmen on a big-game hunt decide they're bored with their usual prey. They persuade a photojournalist to join them in a game with paint pellet guns except they decide to use real bullets and the journalist becomes their new target. An old and tired plot with nothing new to distinguish it. **90m/C VHS.** Todd Jensen, Andre Jacobs, Michelle Bestbier, Evan J. Klisser, David Butler, Allan Granville; ***D:*** John H. Parr.

Prey of the Chameleon 🦴 **1991 (R)** A female serial killer escapes from her asylum, ready to rip more men to shreds. However a tough lady cop has other ideas and goes all out to put an end to the madwoman's doings. Can she stop this fiend before the man she loves becomes the next victim? **91m/C VHS.** Daphne Zuniga, James Wilder, Alexandra Paul, Don Harvey; ***D:*** Fleming Fuller.

A Price above Rubies 🦴🦴½ **1997 (R)** Evils of patriarchal society are exposed in this tale of an Orthodox Jewish wife who seeks fulfillment outside the lonely and oppressive world in which she lives. Zellweger shines as Sonia, who defies her frigid Hasidic husband Mendel (Fitzgerald) to take a job as a jeweler, then falls in love with a Puerto Rican artist (Payne). Eccleston is Mendel's brother, who has a strange relationship with Sonia, and Margulies is his more traditional wife who tries to help Sonia fit in with their way of life. Interesting, though not earth-shatteringly deep, characterization beyond film's female lead is scanty, with one-dimensional male models on display here. Second feature from writer/director Yakin. **117m/C VHS, DVD.** Renee Zellweger, Christopher Eccleston, Glenn Fitzgerald, Allen Payne, Julianna Margulies, Kim Hunter, John Randolph, Kathleen Chalfant, Edie Falco, Tim Jerome, Phyllis Newman; ***D:*** Boaz Yakin; ***W:*** Boaz Yakin; ***C:*** Adam Holender; ***M:*** Lesley Barber.

Price of Glory 🦴🦴 **2000 (PG-13)** After seeing hs promising boxing career destroyed by an unscrupulous manager, Arturo Ortega (Smits) tries to live his dreams through his three sons. Sonny (Seda) is the best boxer but can't please his father, Jimmy (Collins) is the rebel, and Johnny (Hernandez) shares his dad's passion and has talent. Complicating matters are a powerful promoter (Perlman) and Arturo's self-destructive tendencies. You've seen this story before, even if the setting is changed to the Southwest, and except for excellent performances by Smits and Seda, there's nothing here to cover for the lack of originality and less-than-stellar execution. **118m/C VHS, DVD, Wide.** Jimmy Smits, Jon Seda, Clifton (Gonzalez) Collins Jr., Maria Del Mar, Sal Lopez, Louis Mandylor, Paul Rodriguez, Ron Perlman, Danielle Camastra, Ernesto Hernandez; ***D:*** Carlos Avila; ***W:*** Phil Berger; ***C:*** Alfonso Beato; ***M:*** Joseph Julian Gonzalez.

Priceless Beauty 🦴🦴½ **1990 (R)** Musician Lambert was only looking when he spotted the bottle which changed his life. Beautiful genie (Lane) lives inside, and is waiting just for him! Fun premise, good score, nice chemistry between the actors. **94m/C VHS.** Christopher Lambert, Diane Lane, Francesco Quinn, J.C. Quinn, Claudia Ohana, Monica Scattini, Joaquim de Almeida; ***D:*** Charles Finch.

Prick Up Your Ears 🦴🦴🦴 **1987 (R)** Film biography of popular subversive playwright Joe Orton depicts his rise to fame and his eventual murder at the hands of his homosexual lover in 1967. Acclaimed for its realistic and sometimes humorous portrayal of the relationship between two men in a society that regarded homosexuality as a crime, the film unfortunately pays scant attention to Orton's theatrical success. The occasional sluggishness of the script detracts a bit from the three leads' outstanding performances. **110m/C VHS.** *GB* Gary Oldman, Alfred Molina, Vanessa Redgrave, Julie Walters, Lindsay Duncan, Wallace Shawn, James Grant, Frances Barber, Janet Dale, Dave Atkins; ***D:*** Stephen Frears; ***W:*** Alan Bennett; ***C:*** Oliver Stapleton; ***M:*** Stanley Myers. N.Y. Film Critics '87: Support. Actress (Redgrave).

Pride and Prejudice 🦴🦴🦴½ **1940** Classic adaptation of Austen's classic novel of manners as a young marriageable woman spurns the suitor her parents choose for her. Excellent cast vividly recreates 19th century England, aided by the inspired set design that won the film an Oscar. **114m/B VHS.** Greer Garson, Laurence Olivier, Edmund Gwenn, Edna May Oliver, Mary Boland, Maureen O'Sullivan, Ann Rutherford, Frieda Inescort; ***D:*** Robert Z. Leonard; ***C:*** Karl Freund.

Pride and Prejudice 🦴🦴½ **1985** BBC miniseries adaptation of Jane Austen's novel about 19th-century British mores and the attempts of five sisters to get married. **226m/C VHS.** *GB* Elizabeth Garvie, David Rintoul; ***D:*** Cyril Coke. **TV**

Pride and Prejudice 🦴🦴🦴 **1995** Lavish TV adaptation of the Jane Austen novel finds bright Elizabeth Bennet (Ehle) unwillingly smitten by the wealthy, mysterious, and arrogant Mr. Darcy (Firth). Her family, filled with unmarried daughters, is rather silly and, of course, Elizabeth should be looking to get married (or at least not hinder her sisters' chances). Filmed on location in Derbyshire. On six cassettes. **300m/C VHS, DVD.** *GB* Jennifer Ehle, Colin Firth, Susannah Harker, Alison Steadman, Julia Sawalha, Benjamin Whitrow, Crispin Bonham Carter, Anna Chancellor, David Bamber, David Bark-Jones, Polly Maberly, Lucy Briers, Barbara Leigh-Hunt, Adrian Lukis; ***D:*** Simon Langton; ***W:*** Andrew Davies; ***C:*** John Kenway; ***M:*** Carl Davis.

The Pride and the Passion 🦴🦴 **1957** A small group of resistance fighters battling for Spanish independence in 1810 must smuggle a 6-ton cannon across the rugged terrain of Spain. Miscasting, especially of Sinatra as a Spanish peasant, hurts this film. **132m/C VHS, DVD, Wide.** Cary Grant, Frank Sinatra, Sophia Loren, Theodore Bikel, John Wengraf, Jay Novello, Philip Van Zandt; ***D:*** Stanley Kramer; ***W:*** Edward Anhalt; ***C:*** Franz Planer; ***M:*** George Antheil.

Pride of Jesse Hallum 🦴½ **1981** An illiterate man (played by country singer Cash) learns, after much trial and tribulation, to read. **105m/C VHS.** Johnny Cash, Brenda Vaccaro, Eli Wallach; ***D:*** Gary Nelson. **TV**

Pride of St. Louis 🦴🦴 **1952** A romanticized and humorous portrait of famed baseball player-turned-commentator Dizzy Dean. **93m/B VHS.** Dan Dailey, Joanne Dru, Richard Crenna, Richard Haydn, Hugh Sanders; ***D:*** Harmon Jones; ***W:*** Herman J. Mankiewicz.

Pride of the Bowery 🦴 *Here We Go Again* **1941** The Dead End Kids versus a boxing hopeful in training camp. **60m/B VHS.** Leo Gorcey, David Gorcey, Huntz Hall, Gabriel Dell, Billy Halop, Bobby Jordan; ***D:*** Joseph H. Lewis.

Pride of the Clan 🦴🦴½ **1918** Silent drama with Pickford and Moore as Scottish sweethearts battling a bit of adversity. When Pickford's father is lost at sea, she moves onto his fishing boat. She meets Moore, a fishing boy, and falls in love. But, he inherits a fortune and his parents forbid him to see Pickford. He goes off to live the good life but comes back to dramatically rescue Pickford. **80m/B VHS.** Mary Pickford, Matt Moore; ***D:*** Maurice Tourneur.

The Pride of the Yankees 🦴🦴🦴½ **1942** Excellent portrait of baseball great Lou Gehrig. Beginning as he joined the Yankees in 1923, the film follows this great American through to his moving farewell speech as his career was tragically cut short by the disease that bears his name. Cooper is inspiring in the title role. **128m/B VHS, DVD.** Gary Cooper, Teresa Wright, Babe Ruth, Walter Brennan, Dan Duryea; ***D:*** Sam Wood; ***W:*** Herman J. Mankiewicz, Jo Swerling; ***C:*** Rudolph Mate; ***M:*** Leigh Harline. Oscars '42: Film Editing.

Priest 🦴🦴 **1994 (R)** Father Greg (an intense performance by Roache) is a young, idealistic priest who gets a rude awakening when he's assigned to a tough inner-city Liverpool parish. His superior, Father Matthew (Wilkinson), is a middle-aged rabble rouser who's openly having an affair with their black housekeeper Maria (Tyson). But Father Greg has a secret of his own—despite struggles with his sexuality he gets involved with Graham (Carlyle), a man he meets in the local gay bar. Greg's inner turmoil is heightened when a young parishoner confesses that her father is sexually abusing her but, because of the seal of the confessional, the priest cannot report the problem. Director Bird walks a fine line between criticism and condemnation of Catholic doctrine. British TV feature provoked a storm of controversy in the U.S.; originally released at 105 minutes. **98m/C VHS, DVD.** *GB* Linus Roache, Tom Wilkinson, Cathy Tyson, Robert Carlyle, James Ellis, John Bennett, Rio Fanning, Jimmy Coleman, Lesley Sharp, Robert Pugh, Christine Tremarco; ***D:*** Antonia Bird; ***W:*** Jimmy McGovern; ***C:*** Fred Tammes; ***M:*** Andy Roberts.

Priest of Love 🦴🦴½ **1981 (R)** Arty account of the final years of the life of then-controversial author D.H. Lawrence, during which time he published "Lady Chatterly's Lover." A slow-moving but interesting portrayal of this complex man and his wife as they grapple with his imminent death from tuberculosis. **125m/C VHS.** *GB* Ian McKellen, Janet Suzman, John Gielgud, Helen Mirren, Jorge (George) Rivero; ***D:*** Christopher Miles; ***W:*** Alan Plater; ***C:*** Ted Moore.

Primal Fear 🦴🦴 **1996 (R)** Chicago defense attorney Martin Vail (Gere) is torn between the fight for justice and the lure of fame. He seems to have found the spotlight when a gentle altar boy (newcomer Norton is a standout) is accused of savagely murdering an archbishop. This leads to some courtroom fireworks due, in part, to the fact that the prosecutor (Linney) is Vail's former lover. Gere turns in a satisfying performance but, except when he's with his client, can't keep the script afloat. Lame plot revelations and an obvious "shocker" ending don't help matters. Feature directorial debut of Hoblit, Emmy winner for TV's "Hill Street Blues," "L.A. Law," and "NYPD Blue." Adapted from the book by William Diehl. **130m/C VHS, DVD.** Richard Gere, Laura Linney, Edward Norton, John Mahoney, Alfre Woodard, Frances McDormand, Terry O'Quinn, Andre Braugher, Steven Bauer, Joe Spano, Tony Plana, Stanley Anderson, Maura Tierney, Jon Seda; ***D:*** Gregory Hoblit; ***W:*** Steve Shagan, Ann Biderman; ***C:*** Michael Chapman; ***M:*** James Newton Howard. Golden Globes '97: Support. Actor (Norton); L.A. Film Critics '96: Support. Actor (Norton); Natl. Bd. of Review '96: Support. Actor (Norton).

Primal Impulse 🦴½ **1974** An astronaut, stranded on the moon because of a sinister experimental double-cross, unleashes a mental scream which possesses a young woman's mind back on earth. **90m/C VHS.** Klaus Kinski.

Primal Rage 🦴 **1990 (R)** A student is bitten by an experimental monkey, and begins to manifest his primal urges physically. Special effects by Carlo Rimbaldi. **92m/C VHS.** Bo Svenson, Patrick Lowe, Mitch Watson, Cheryl Arutt, Sarah Buxton; ***D:*** Vittoria Rambaldi.

Primal Scream 🦴½ *Hellfire* **1987 (R)** The Year is 1993. Earth's fuel sources are rapidly decaying and the top secret project to mine a revolutionary new energy source is underway—independently managed by a corrupt corporation. **95m/C VHS.** Kenneth John McGregor, Sharon Mason, Julie Miller, Jon Maurice, Mickey Shaughnessy; ***D:*** William Murray.

Primal Secrets 🦴🦴½ *Trick of the Eye* **1994** Artist Tilly, who specializes in illusionary trompe l'oeil paintings, is commissioned to paint a mural for reclusive socialite/widow Burstyn but there's a lot of mystery surrounding the job, especially when Burstyn begins to take an overly avid interest in Tilly's life. Based on the novel by Jane Stanton Hitchcock. Made for TV. **93m/C VHS.** Meg Tilly, Ellen Burstyn, Barnard Hughes; ***D:*** Ed Kaplan. **TV**

Primary Colors 🦴🦴½ **1998 (R)** Joe Klein's anonymously published political satire is adapted for the big screen, starting off humorously and shifting into somber. Southern good ole boy, Gov. Jack Stanton (Travolta), and his savvy wife (Thompson) are after the presidential nomination and surrounded by crazy associates, including skeptical first-time campaign manager Henry Burton (Lester). More about Henry's political baptism by fire than anything else, as he tries to accommodate his conscience to the continuous scandals and double-dealing. It really doesn't matter whether Travolta's channeling Clinton or if Thompson acts like Hilary, since the film has bigger problems. The change in tone is jarring, characters and situations disappear without warning. And given that the press act like salivating wolverines at the merest hint of scandal, the situation surrounding opponent Fred Picker (Hagman) seems far-fetched at best. Still the goings-on will hold your attention until they're over—and you realize it's all smoke-and-mirrors. **138m/C VHS, DVD.** John Travolta, Emma Thompson, Adrian Lester, Kathy Bates, Billy Bob Thornton, Larry Hagman, Maura Tierney, Stacy Edwards, Diane Ladd, Gia Carides, Paul Guilfoyle, Tommy Hollis, Robert Klein, J.C. Quinn, Rob Reiner, Caroline Aaron, Allison Janney, Mykelti Williamson, Tony Shalhoub, John Vargas, Ben Jones, Bonnie Bartlett; ***D:*** Mike Nichols; ***W:*** Elaine May; ***C:*** Michael Ballhaus; ***M:*** Ry Cooder. British Acad. '98: Adapt. Screenplay; Screen Actors Guild '98: Support. Actress (Bates); Broadcast Film Critics '98: Support. Actress (Bates).

Primary Motive 🦴🦴 **1992 (R)** Taut political thriller with Nelson as Andy Blumenthal, a press secretary who finds that an opposing candidate's campaign is covered by a web of lies. Blumenthal exposes the lies, but the candidate denies them and pulls further ahead in the polls. When the candidate's wife gives Blumenthal an extremely damaging piece of information, will the polls finally turn against him? **93m/C VHS.** Judd Nelson, Richard Jordan, Sally Kirkland, Justine Bateman, John Savage; ***D:*** Daniel Adams; ***W:*** William Snowden III, Daniel Adams; ***M:*** John Cale.

Primary Target 🦴 **1989 (R)** A mercenary reunites his 'Nam guerilla unit to rescue a diplomat's wife kidnapped by a Laotian jungle lord. **85m/C VHS.** John Calvin, Miki Kim, Joey Aresco, Chip Lucio, John Ericson, Colleen Casey; ***D:*** Clark Henderson.

Prime Cut 🦴🦴½ **1972 (R)** Veritable orgy of drug trafficking, prostitution, extortion, loan sharking, fisticuffs and gangsters getting ground into mincemeat. Sleazy but well-made crime melodrama has its followers, but is best known as Spacek's film debut. **86m/C VHS.** Lee Marvin, Gene Hackman, Sissy Spacek, Angel Tompkins, Gregory Walcott; ***D:*** Michael Ritchie; ***W:*** Robert Dillon; ***M:*** Lalo Schifrin.

Prime Evil 🦴🦴 **1988 (R)** A brave and determined nun infiltrates a sect of devil worshipping monks in an attempt to end their demonic sacrifices. The question is, will this sister slide beneath Satan's cleaver? **87m/C VHS, DVD.** William Beckwith, Christine Moore; ***D:*** Roberta Findlay.

The Prime Gig 🦴🦴 **2000** Wise (Vaughn) works a telephone scam for a run-down company manafed by Mick (Tobolowsky) that soon goes under. He's then recruited by Caitlin (Ormond) for a telemarketing scheme involving selling stocks in a gold mine for guru Kelly Grant (Harris), whose previous schemes cost him jail time. Wise is a success but despite the money (and the girl) you know there's trouble ahead. Predictable plot with Harris giving the strong performance. **96m/C VHS, DVD, Wide.** Vince Vaughn, Julia Ormond, Ed Harris, Rory Cochrane, Wallace Shawn, George Wendt, Stephen Tobolowsky; ***D:*** Gregory Mosher; ***W:*** William Wheeler; ***C:*** John A. Alonzo; ***M:*** David Robbins.

The Prime of Miss Jean Brodie 🦴🦴🦴 **1969 (PG)** Oscar-winning performance by Smith as a forward-thinking teacher in a Scottish girls' school during the 1920s. She captivates her impressionable young students with her fascist ideals and free-thinking attitudes in this adaptation of the play taken from Muriel Spark's novel. **116m/C VHS.** *GB* Maggie Smith, Pamela Franklin, Robert Stephens, Celia Johnson, Gordon Jackson, Jane Carr; ***D:*** Ronald Neame; ***W:*** Jay Presson Allen; ***C:*** Ted Moore. Oscars '69: Actress (Smith); British Acad. '69: Actress (Smith), Support. Actress (Johnson); Golden Globes '70: Song ("Jean"); Natl. Bd. of Review '69: Support. Actress (Franklin).

Prime Risk 🦴½ **1984 (PG-13)** A young engineer who discovers an electronic method to break into automated teller machines finds that it leads to more trouble when she discovers that foreign agents are hot on her trail. **98m/C VHS.** Toni Hudson, Lee Montgomery, Sam Bottoms; ***D:*** W. Farkas; ***C:*** Mac Ahlberg.

Prime Suspect 🦴🦴 **1982** An honest citizen becomes the prime suspect after the coverage of a murder by an overambitious television reporter. **100m/C VHS, DVD.** Mike Farrell, Teri Garr, Veronica Cartwright, Lane Smith, Barry Corbin, James Sloyan, Charles Aidman; ***D:*** Noel Black; ***C:*** Reynaldo Villalobos; ***M:*** Charles Gross. **TV**

Prime Suspect 🦴🦴 **1988** A young man escapes from a mental institution to clear his name after being wrongfully accused of murdering his girlfriend. **89m/C VHS.** Susan Strasberg, Frank Stallone, Billy Drago, Doug McClure; ***D:*** Mark Rutland.

Prime Suspect 🦴🦴🦴 **1992** Mirren stars as Detective Chief Inspector Jane Tennison in this British TV police procedural. When a male inspector dies of a heart attack while investigating a rape-murder, Tennison, the only women of senior police status, wants the case. But she runs into multiple obstructions, not the least being the smug male police system. Then the case really takes a turn when it appears Tennison is searching for a serial killer. But Jane is no quitter and she has both the brains and the guts to back up her orders. Adapted from the book by Lynda La Plante, who also wrote the teleplay. Several other TV movies followed. **240m/C VHS, DVD.** *GB* Helen Mirren, Tom Bell, Zoe Wanamaker, John Bowe, Tom Wilkinson, Ralph Fiennes; ***D:*** Christopher Menaul; ***W:*** Lynda La Plante. **TV**

Prime Target 🦴🦴 **1991 (R)** Small-town cop John Bloodstone (Heavener) is recruited by the FBI to transfer a mafia boss (Curtis) from a safehouse to the courthouse. He has to keep the former mobster alive long enough to testify against the "family." Their cross-country adventure is heightened by a murderous confrontation with evil forces that want them both dead. **87m/C VHS.** David Heavener, Tony Curtis, Isaac Hayes, Jenilee Harrison, Robert Reed, Andrew (Andy) Robinson, Don Stroud; ***D:*** David Heavener; ***W:*** David Heavener; ***M:*** Chris Boardman.

The Prime Time woof! **1960** Horrid film about a teen girl who leaves home and gets involved with a teen gang and a slimy detective. She's also kidnapped by a weird beatnik artist who forces her to pose nude. Black's film debut. Also known as "Hellkitten." **76m/B VHS.** JoAnn LeCompte, Frank Roche, James Brooks, Ray Gronwold, Maria Pavelle, Robert Major, Karen Black; ***D:*** Herschell Gordon Lewis.

Prime Time 🦴½ **1980 (R)** Forgotten satirical comedy about what would happen if the censors took a day off from American TV. **73m/C VHS.** Warren Oates, David Spielberg.

Prime Time Murder 🦴½ **1992 (R)** Freelance TV journalist hooks up with eccentric ex-cop to trail a psycho stalking street people. **95m/C VHS.** Tim Thomerson, Sally Kirkland, Anthony Finetti, Laura Reed; ***D:*** Gary Skeen Hall.

The Primitive Lover 🦴🦴 **1916** Early silent comedy about young wife who decides she deserves more than her marriage is giving her. **67m/B VHS.** Constance Talmadge, Kenneth Harlan, Harrison Ford; ***D:*** Sidney Franklin.

Primrose Path 🦴🦴½ **1940** Melodramatic soaper with comedic touches about a wrong-side-of-the-tracks girl falling for and then losing an ambitious young go-getter running a hamburger stand. **93m/B VHS.** Ginger Rogers, Joel McCrea, Marjorie Rambeau, Henry Travers, Miles Mander, Queenie Vasser, Joan Carroll, Vivienne Osborne; ***D:*** Gregory La Cava.

The Prince 🦴🦴 **1995** Young toy company executive Roy (Riley) is given cutthroat corporate advice by a sinister bartender (Williams) who uses the treatise on power by Machiavelli as his bible. Soon Roy is manipulating with the best of them and will do anything to get ahead. **89m/C VHS.** *CA* Billy Dee Williams, Michael Riley, Henry Silva, Lou Rawls, Timothy Bottoms, Liat Goodson, Edie McClurg; ***D:*** Pinchas Perry; ***W:*** Pinchas Perry; ***C:*** Hanania Baer; ***M:*** David Michael Frank.

Prince and the Great Race 🦴🦴 **1983** Three Australian children search the outback to find their kidnapped horse who is scheduled to run in the big New Year's Day Race. **91m/C VHS.** *AU* John Ewart, John Howard, Nicole Kidman.

The Prince and the Pauper 🦴🦴🦴 **1937** Satisfying adaptation of the classic Mark Twain story of a young street urchin who trades places with the young king of England. Wonderful musical score by noted composer Korngold who provided the music for many of Flynn's adventure films. Also available in a computer-colorized version. **118m/B VHS.** Errol Flynn, Claude Rains, Alan Hale, Billy Mauch, Montagu Love, Henry Stephenson, Barton MacLane; ***D:*** William Keighley; ***M:*** Erich Wolfgang Korngold.

The Prince and the Pauper 🦴🦴 **1962** A prince and a poor young boy swap their clothes and identities, thus causing a lot of confusion for their families. Based on the story by Mark Twain. **93m/C VHS.** Guy Williams, Laurence Naismith, Donald Houston, Jane Asher, Walter Hudd.

The Prince and the Pauper 🦴🦴½ *Crossed Swords* **1978 (PG)** Remake of the 1937 Errol Flynn film employing lavish sets and a tongue-in-cheek attitude among the all-star cast, who occasionally wander adrift when the director stops for tea. When an English prince and a pauper discover that they have identical appearances, they decide to trade places with each other. From Mark Twain's classic. **113m/C VHS, DVD, Wide.** *GB* Oliver Reed, Raquel Welch, Mark Lester, Ernest Borgnine, George C. Scott, Rex Harrison, Charlton Heston, Sybil Danning; ***D:*** Richard Fleischer; ***W:*** Berta Dominguez, George MacDonald Fraser, Pierre Spengler; ***C:*** Jack Cardiff; ***M:*** Maurice Jarre.

The Prince and the Pauper 🦴🦴½ **2001** Yet another version of the Mark Twain classic covers all the familiar bases but is briskly paced and has a good cast. Prince Edward (Jonathan Timmins) exchanges identities with peasant Tom Canty (Robert Timmins) and both learn that whether you're rich or poor life will always be a challenge. **90m/C VHS.** Jonathan Timmins, Robert Timmins, Aidan Quinn, Alan Bates, Jonathan Hyde; ***D:*** Giles Foster; ***W:*** Duke Fenady, Dominic Minghella. **CABLE**

The Prince and the Showgirl 🦴🦴½ **1957** An American showgirl in 1910 London is wooed by the Prince of Carpathia. Part of the "A Night at the Movies" series, this tape simulates a 1957 movie evening, with a Sylvester the Cat cartoon, "Greedy for Tweety," a newsreel and coming attractions for "Spirit of St. Louis." **127m/C VHS, DVD.** Laurence Olivier, Marilyn Monroe, Sybil Thorndike, Jeremy Spenser, Richard Wattis; ***D:*** Laurence Olivier; ***W:*** Terence Rattigan; ***C:*** Jack Cardiff.

The Prince and the Surfer 🦴🦴½ **1999 (PG)** A modern young prince, Edward, wants a chance to be a regular guy and changes places with his surfer teen double, Cash. Updated version of the Mark Twain story. **90m/C VHS, DVD.** Vincent Schiavelli, Arye Gross, Robert Englund, Timothy Bottoms, C. Thomas Howell, Linda Cardellini; ***D:*** Gregory Gieras. **VIDEO**

Prince Brat and the Whipping Boy 🦴🦴🦴 *The Whipping Boy* **1995 (G)** Orphaned Jemmy (Munro) is living on the streets of the 18th-century German town of Brattenburg with his younger sister Annyrose (Salt). Neglected, spoiled Prince Horace (Knight) has been causing mischief in the castle but instead of being punished himself, the king's men catch Jemmy and use him as a punishment stand-in. Jemmy escapes the castle to get back to his sister and the Prince decides to go along for the adventure. Filmed on location in North Rhine-Westphalia and Burgundy, Germany. Adventurous TV movie with spunky leads; adapted from Sid Fleischman's novella. **96m/C VHS.** Truan Munro, Nic Knight, Karen Salt, George C. Scott, Kevin Conway, Vincent Schiavelli, Andrew Bicknell, Jean Anderson, Mathilda May; ***D:*** Syd Macartney; ***W:*** Max Brindle; ***M:*** Lee Holdridge.

Prince Jack 🦴🦴 **1983** Profiles the turbulent political career of President John F. Kennedy. **100m/C VHS.** Lloyd Nolan, Dana Andrews, Robert Guillaume, Cameron Mitchell; ***D:*** Bert Lovitt; ***M:*** Elmer Bernstein.

Prince of Bel Air 🦴½ **1987 (R)** A pool-cleaning playboy who makes a habit of one night stands meets a woman and starts falling in love with her. **95m/C VHS.** Mark Harmon, Kirstie Alley, Robert Vaughn, Patrick Laborteaux, Deborah Harmon; ***D:*** Charles Braverman; ***M:*** Robert Folk. **TV**

The Prince of Central Park 🦴🦴🦴 **1977** Two young orphans are forced by circumstance to live in a tree in New York's Central Park until they are befriended by a lonely old woman. An above-average adaptation of the novel by Evan H. Rhodes, the story was later used for a Broadway play. **76m/C VHS.** Ruth Gordon, T(imothy) J(ohn) Hargrave, Lisa Richards, Brooke Shields, Marc Vahanian, Dan Hedaya; ***D:*** Harvey Hart. **TV**

Prince of Central Park 🦴½ **2000 (PG-13)** JJ Somerled (Nasso) is a 12-year-old stuck in the abusive foster home of Mrs. Ardis (Moriarty). Fed up, he takes off for the carousel at Central Park, where he had his last happy memory of his long-gone mother. In the park, JJ is befriended by all sorts of do-gooders and eccentrics. Bland non-musical reworking of a musical play. **105m/C VHS, DVD, Wide.** Frank Nasso, Kathleen Turner, Danny Aiello, Harvey Keitel, Cathy Moriarty, Lauren Velez, Jerry Orbach, Tina Holmes; ***D:*** John Leekley; ***W:*** John Leekley; ***C:*** Jonathan Herron; ***M:*** Theodore Shapiro.

Prince of Darkness 🦴½ **1987 (R)** University students release Satan, in the form of a mysterious chemical, unwittingly on the world. Written by Martin Quatermass (a pseudonym of Carpenter). Strong personnel does not save this dreary and slow-moving cliche plot. **102m/C VHS, DVD.** Alice Cooper, Donald Pleasence, Lisa Blount, Victor Wong, Jameson Parker, Dennis Dun, Susan Blanchard, Anne Howard, Ken Wright, Dirk Blocker; ***D:*** John Carpenter; ***W:*** John Carpenter; ***C:*** Gary B. Kibbe; ***M:*** John Carpenter.

Prince of Egypt 🦴🦴🦴 **1998 (PG)** First animated musical from Dreamworks manages to tell the story of the Exodus without turning it into Mickey Moses. Kilmer voices the young Moses, who is adopted by the royal family: imperious pharaoh Seti (Stewart), his stately Queen (Mirren) and jockish son Rameses (Fiennes). Happily wed to Tzipporah (Pfeiffer), he's living it up at the dawn of civilization until a chance meeting with his real sister Miriam (Bullock) twists his conscience and destiny. Steve Martin and Martin Short provide a short comic break, but overall the joking is kept to a minimum. Successful in combining epic feeling with stylized animation. **93m/C VHS, DVD.** ***D:*** Simon Wells, Brenda Chapman, Steve Hickner; ***M:*** Hans Zimmer; ***V:*** Val Kilmer, Michelle Pfeiffer, Helen Mirren, Steve Martin, Martin Short, Ralph Fiennes, Sandra Bullock, Jeff Goldblum, Danny Glover, Patrick Stewart, Ofra Haza, James Avery, Eden Riegel. Oscars '98: Song ("When You Believe"); Broadcast Film Critics '98: Song ("When You Believe").

Prince of Pennsylvania 🦴½ **1988 (R)** A mild comedy about a spaced-out youth who kidnaps his own father in hopes of nabbing a family inheritance. **113m/C VHS.** Keanu Reeves, Fred Ward, Amy Madigan, Bonnie Bedelia, Jeff Hayenga; ***D:*** Ron Nyswaner; ***W:*** Ron Nyswaner; ***M:*** Thomas Newman.

Prince of Poisoners: The Life and Crimes of William Palmer 🦴🦴½ **1998** A true crime story set in mid-19th century England. Dr. William Palmer (Allen) appears to be a successful surgeon with a devoted wife, Annie (Ashbourne), and happy family. But the doctor has a secret passion for racehorses and gambling and his good life is about to crumble because of his debts. So what's his solution? Why, murder of course, so Palmer can collect on various insurance policies and dispose of his gambling rivals. **180m/C VHS.** *GB* Keith Allen, Jayne Ashbourne, Judy Cornwell, Richard Coyle, Freddie Jones, Stephen Moore; ***D:*** Alan Dossor; ***W:*** Glenn Chandler; ***C:*** Allan Pyrah; ***M:*** Christopher Gunning. **TV**

Prince of the City 🦴🦴🦴 **1981 (R)** Docu-drama of a police officer who becomes an informant in an effort to end corruption within his narcotics unit, but finds he must pay a heavy price. Based on the true story told in Robert Daly's book, the powerful script carries the tension through what would otherwise be an overly long film. Excellent performances make this a riveting character study. **167m/C VHS.** Treat Williams, Jerry Orbach, Richard Foronjy, Don Billett, Ken Marino, Lindsay Crouse, Lance Henriksen; ***D:*** Sidney Lumet; ***W:*** Jay Presson Allen, Sidney Lumet; ***C:*** Andrzej Bartkowiak. N.Y. Film Critics '81: Director (Lumet).

The Prince of Thieves 🦴🦴 **1948** Robin Hood helps Lady Marian extricate herself from a forced marriage in this adventure made with younger audiences in mind. **72m/C VHS.** Jon Hall, Patricia Morison, Adele Jergens, Alan Mowbray, Michael Duane; ***D:*** Howard Bretherton.

The Prince of Tides 🦴🦴🦴½ **1991 (R)** Conroy's sprawling southern-fried saga is neatly pared down to essentials in this tale of the dysfunctional Wingo family, whose dark tragedies are gradually revealed as twins Tom and Savannah come to grips with personal demons under the ministering aid of psychiatrist Streisand. Bravura performance by Nolte in what may be his best role to date; Streisand is restrained in both her performance and direction although a subplot dealing with her bad marriage and rebellious son is a predictable distraction. The South Carolina low country, and even New York City, never looked better. Conroy adapted the screenplay from his novel of the same name with Johnston's help. **132m/C VHS, DVD, 8mm, Wide.** Nick Nolte, Barbra Streisand, Blythe Danner, Kate Nelligan, Jeroen Krabbe, Melinda Dillon, George Carlin, Jason Gould, Brad Sullivan; ***D:*** Barbra Streisand; ***W:*** Pat Conroy, Becky Johnston; ***C:*** Stephen Goldblatt; ***M:*** James Newton Howard. Golden Globes '92: Actor—Drama (Nolte); L.A. Film Critics '91: Actor (Nolte).

Prince Valiant 🦴🦴½ **1954 (PG-13)** When his royal dad is exiled by an evil tyrant, brave young Wagner brushes aside bangs and journeys to Camelot to seek the help of King Arthur. Based on Harold Foster's classic comic strip. **100m/C VHS.** James Mason, Janet Leigh, Robert Wagner, Debra Paget, Sterling Hayden, Victor McLaglen, Donald Crisp, Brian Aherne, Barry Jones, Mary (Phillips) Philips; ***D:*** Henry Hathaway; ***W:*** Dudley Nichols.

Prince Valiant 🦴🦴½ **1997 (PG-13)** We're back at Camelot with a lot of colorful pageantry and old-fashioned action. Young orphaned Valiant (Moyer) is the squire to Sir Gawain (Hickox), one of King Arthur's (Fox) knights. He is given the task of escorting Princess Ilene (Heigl) to her home in Wales and naturally the young twosome fall in love. Meanwhile, the sword Excalibur has been stolen by Viking leader Thagnar (Kretschmann) and somehow become embedded in his castle's stone floor. Then Ilene gets kidnapped and it's up to Valiant to rescue both Ilene and Excalibur. Based on the comic strip created by Harold R. Foster. **91m/C VHS.** *GB GE IR* Stephen Moyer, Katherine Heigl, Thomas Kretschmann, Edward Fox, Benjamin Pullen, Anthony Hickox, Udo Kier, Warwick Davis, Zach Galligan, Ron Perlman, Joanna Lumley, Gavan O'Herlihy, Walter Gotell; ***D:*** Anthony Hickox; ***W:*** Michael Frost Beckner, Anthony Hickox; ***C:*** Roger Lanser; ***M:*** David Bergeaud.

Princes in Exile 🦴🦴½ **1990 (PG-13)** Young people struggle with their life-threatening illnesses at a special summer camp. They find that love and friendship hold the key to dreams about the future. Excellent cast of newcomers. Based on a novel of the same name by Mark Schreiber. **103m/C VHS.** *CA* Zachary Ansley, Nicholas Shields, Stacy Mistysyn, Alexander Chapman, Chuck Shamata; ***D:*** Giles Walker.

Princess Academy 🦴 **1987 (R)** A self-respecting young debutante battles the ways of her elitist finishing school. **91m/C VHS.** *FR* Eva Gabor, Lu Leonard, Richard Paul, Lar Park Lincoln, Carole (Raphaelle) Davis; ***D:*** Bruce Block; ***M:*** Paul Antonelli, Roger Bellon.

The Princess & the Call Girl 🦴 **1984** Call girl Lucy Darling asks her look-alike college girlfriend Audrey Swallow (Levy in a dual role) to take her place in Monaco for a lavishly erotic weekend. Then when Audrey gets delayed, Lucy winds up taking her place in New York—at Audrey's engagement party. Weaker than Metzger's usual sexual romps. **90m/C VHS, DVD.** Carol Levy, Shannah Hall, Victor Bevine; ***D:*** Radley Metzger.

The Princess and the Goblin 🦴🦴½ **1994 (G)** Little kiddies may enjoy this animated adventure but it's a bland story with mediocre animation. Groups of ugly, underground-dwelling goblins like nothing better than to scare humans, especially castle-dwelling Princess Irene. Brave working-class Curdie helps to save the day. Based on a book by George MacDonald. **82m/C VHS.** *GB HU* ***V:*** Sally Ann Marsh, Peter Murray, Claire Bloom.

The Princess and the Pea **1983** From "Faerie Tale Theatre" comes the story of a princess who tries to prove that she's a blueblood by feeling the bump of a tiny pea under the thickness of 20 mattresses. **60m/C VHS.** Liza Minnelli, Tom Conti, Tim Kazurinsky, Pat McCormick, Beatrice Straight; ***D:*** Tony Bill. **CABLE**

The Princess and the Pirate 🦴🦴🦴 **1944** Hope at his craziest as a vaudvillian who falls for a beautiful princess while on the run from buccaneers on the Spanish Main. Look for Crosby in a closing cameo performance. Available in digitally remastered stereo with original movie trailer. **94m/C VHS, DVD.** Bob Hope, Walter Slezak, Walter Brennan, Virginia Mayo, Victor McLaglen, Bing Crosby; ***D:*** David Butler; ***W:*** Everett Freeman, Don Hartman, Melville Shavelson; ***C:*** Victor Milner; ***M:*** David Rose.

The Princess and the Warrior 🦴🦴🦴 *Der Krieger und die Kaiserin* **2000 (R)** Writer/director Twyker reunites with Potente, the star of his breakthrough feature "Run Lola Run." Potente plays Sissi, a mental institution nurse whose life is saved by small-time crook Bodo (Furmann). On the way to the bank (which he was about to rob), she is run over by a truck (in an accident that he helped cause). He crawls under the truck to avoid the police, but ends up saving her as she's about to choke to death on her own blood. After she recovers, she sets out to find Bodo, feeling that he is her one true love. Bodo, still grieving the loss of his wife, resists. Impossible to pigeonhole in one genre, as Twyker is clearly more concerned with his characters than with shoving them into a conveniently labeled plot. **130m/C VHS, DVD, Wide.** *GE* Franka Potente, Benno Furmann, Joachim Krol, Marita Breuer, Lars Rudolph, Jurgen Tarrach, Melchior Beslon, Ludger Pistor; ***D:*** Tom Tykwer; ***W:*** Tom Tykwer; ***C:*** Frank Griebe; ***M:*** Tom Tykwer, Johnny Klimek, Reinhold Heil.

The Princess Bride 🦴🦴🦴½ **1987 (PG)** A modern update of the basic fairy tale crammed with all the cliches, this adventurously irreverent love story centers around beautiful maiden Buttercup (Wright Penn) and her young swain Westley (Elwes) as they battle the evils of the mythical kingdom of Florin to be reunited with one another. Great dueling scenes and offbeat satire of the genre make this fun for adults as well as children. Based on William Goldman's cult novel. **98m/C VHS, DVD, Wide.** Cary Elwes, Mandy Patinkin, Robin Wright Penn, Wallace Shawn, Peter Falk, Andre the Giant, Chris Sarandon, Christopher Guest, Billy Crystal, Carol Kane, Fred Savage, Peter Cook, Mel Smith; ***D:*** Rob Reiner; ***W:*** William Goldman; ***C:*** Adrian Biddle; ***M:*** Mark Knopfler.

Princess Caraboo 🦴🦴½ **1994 (PG)** Fluffy quasi-fairy tale (but based on a true story) finds an exotic beauty (Cates) appearing in an English village in 1817. She speaks a language no one understands and is taken under the wing of the local gentry, the Worralls, who believe she is an Asian princess washed ashore during a shipwreck. Meanwhile, the local journalist (Rea) is suspicious but protective, an Oxford linguist (Lithgow) is determined to prove her a fraud, and she must put up with the Worrall family's pompous Greek butler (Cate's husband Kline at his showy best). **97m/C VHS, DVD.** Phoebe Cates, Stephen Rea, John Lithgow, Kevin Kline, Jim Broadbent, Wendy Hughes, Peter Eyre, Jacqueline Pearce, John Lynch, John Sessions, Arkie Whiteley, John Wells; ***D:*** Michael Austin; ***W:*** Michael Austin, John Wells; ***C:*** Freddie Francis; ***M:*** Richard Hartley.

Princess Cinderella 🦴🦴 **193?** A live-action dramatization of the famous fantasy. Dubbed in English. **75m/B VHS.** *SP* Silvana Jachino, Roberto Villa.

The Princess Comes Across 🦴🦴🦴 **1936** Deft comedy-mystery finds Brooklyn actress Lombard deciding to take an ocean voyage and pass herself off as a Swedish princess in the hopes of furthering her career. Bandleader MacMurray is smitten but an old beau recognizes the ruse and demands hush money. Then he turns up dead and the duo fall under the suspicious eye of a German passenger (Rumann) who happens to be a detective. From the novel by Louis Lucien Rogger. **77m/B VHS.** Carole Lombard, Fred MacMurray, Alison Skipworth, Sig Rumann, Douglass Dumbrille, William Frawley, Porter Hall, George Barbier, Lumsden Hare, Mischa Auer, Tetsu Komai; ***D:*** William K. Howard; ***W:*** Walter DeLeon, Francis Martin, Frank Butler, Don Hartman; ***C:*** Ted Tetzlaff.

Princess Daisy 🦴 **1983** A beautiful model claws her way to the top of her profession while trying to find true love and avoid the clutches of her rotten half-brother. Adapted from Judith Krantz's glitzy best-selling novel. **200m/C VHS.** Merete Van Kamp, Lindsay Wagner, Claudia Cardinale, Stacy Keach, Ringo Starr, Barbara Bach; ***D:*** Waris Hussein. **TV**

The Princess Diaries 🦴🦴½ **2001 (G)** Gently amusing comedy perfect for tweenies who worry about being misfits. Modern-day Cinderella story finds brainy-but-clumsy San Francisco teen Mia (newcomer Hathaway, who's a real find) learning that she's the heir to the European kingdom of Genovia after the death of her long-absent dad. And to teach her the ways of royalty is her very regal grandmama (Andrews). Think Henry Higgins and Eliza Doolittle. Of course, Mia has her doubts about being a princess, especially when the kids at school learn her secret. There's even a little first romance thrown in for good measure. Based on the novel by Meg Cabot. **114m/C VHS, DVD, Wide.** *US* Anne Hathaway, Julie Andrews, Hector Elizondo, Heather Matarazzo, Erik von Detten, Mandy Moore, Robert Schwartzman, Caroline Goodall, Larry Miller, Sandra Oh, Sean O'Bryan; ***D:*** Garry Marshall; ***W:*** Gina Wendkos; ***C:*** Karl Walter Lindenlaub; ***M:*** John Debney.

Princess Mononoke 🦴🦴🦴 **1998 (PG-13)** Stunning animated feature by Japanese master Hayao Miyazaki is a bit too long and graphic for small children, but is a must-see for fans of anime. Dubbed into English by an all-star cast, the tale follows the plight of Ashitaka (Crudup), who tries to find some way to lift a curse inflicted upon him after he accidentally kills a rampaging forest spirit. He discovers the cause is the encroaching civilization of Iron Town, led by the cold Lady Eboshi (Driver) and its conflict with the forest spirits and their champion San (Danes)—the princess of the title. Also lending their voices are Billy Bob Thornton as a mischievous monk and Gillian Anderson as San's wolf protector. Became the first feature of any kind to gross over $150 million at the box office in its native Japan. **133m/C VHS, DVD, Wide.** ***D:*** Hayao Miyazaki; ***W:*** Neil Gaiman; ***M:*** Joe Hisaishi; ***V:*** Claire Danes, Billy Crudup, Minnie Driver, Gillian Anderson, Jada Pinkett Smith, Billy Bob Thornton.

Princess of Thieves 🦴🦴½ **2001** An aging Robin Hood and Will Scarlett return to England with a mortally wounded King Richard. Robin knows that Prince John will stop at nothing to assume the throne, including killing Richard's son Phillip. Unfortunately, the duo are captured by the Sheriff of Nottingham and it's up to Robin's feisty daughter Gwyn, who disguises herself as a boy, to rescue her father and Will and stop the bad guys from taking over the kingdom. **88m/C VHS, DVD.** Malcolm McDowell, Keira Knightley, Roger Ashton-Griffiths, Jonathan Hyde, Del Synnott, Stephen Moyer, Stuart Wilson; ***D:*** Peter Hewitt; ***W:*** Sally Robinson, Robin Lerner. **TV**

Princess Tam Tam 🦴🦴🦴 **1935** Pleasing French adaptation of Shaw's "Pygmalion," as a beautiful native African woman is "westernized" by a handsome writer and then introduced to high society as an exotic princess. A musical notable for its spectacular choreography and on-location Tunisian scenery. Story by Pepito Abatino, who was then Baker's husband. In French with English subtitles. **77m/B VHS.** *FR* Josephine Baker, Albert Prejean, Germaine Aussey, Viviane Romance; ***D:*** Edmond T. Greville.

The Princess Who Never Laughed **1984** A stern king holds a laugh-off contest to make his morose daughter happy in this adaptation of the Brothers Grimm story from the "Faerie Tale Theatre" series. **60m/C VHS.** Ellen Barkin, Howard Hesseman, Howie Mandel, Mary Woronov.

Princess Yang Kwei Fei 🦴🦴🦴 *Yokihi; The Empress Yang Kwei Fei* **1955** Set in 8th-century China and based on the life of the last T'ang emperor and the beautiful servant girl he loves and makes his bride. She falls victim to court jealousies and he to his greedy family, though even death cannot end their love. Beautifully filmed and acted romantic tragedy. In Japanese with English subtitles. **91m/C VHS.** *JP* Machiko Kyo, Masayuki Mori, Eitaro (Sakae, Saka Ozawa) Ozawa, So Yamamura; ***D:*** Kenji Mizoguchi.

The Principal 🦴🦴½ **1987 (R)** A tough, down-on-his-luck high school teacher is hired as the principal of a relentlessly violent, uncontrollable high school. Naturally he whips it into shape. **109m/C VHS.** James Belushi, Louis Gossett Jr., Rae Dawn Chong, Michael Wright, Esai Morales, J.J. (Jeffrey Jay) Cohen, Troy Winbush; ***D:*** Christopher Cain; ***W:*** Frank Deese; ***C:*** Arthur Albert; ***M:*** Jay Gruska.

The Principal Takes a Holiday 🦴🦴½ **1998** John's (Bryan) parents threaten to deprieve him of his grandmother's inheritance if he doesn't keep out of trouble during his senior year. But his latest prank is already underway and when the principal is mistakenly hospitalized because of it, John decides to manipulate the situation and sets up anti-establishment drifter Franklin (Nealon) as the school's temporary replacement. **89m/C VHS.** Kevin Nealon, Zachery Ty Bryan, Jessica Steen; ***D:*** Robert King; ***W:*** Mark Amin. **VIDEO**

Prison 🦴½ **1988 (R)** The zombified body of an unjustly executed inmate haunts Creedmore Prison, stalking the guard that killed him. His search is aided by the terrified inmates. **102m/C VHS.** Lane Smith, Chelsea Field, Viggo Mortensen, Lincoln Kilpatrick, Tom Everett, Tommy (Tiny) Lister; ***D:*** Renny Harlin; ***W:*** C. Courtney Joyner; ***C:*** Mac Ahlberg; ***M:*** Richard Band.

Prison Break 🦴🦴 **1938** A convict plans a daring prison escape in order to clear his name for a murder he did not commit. **72m/B VHS.** Barton MacLane, Glenda Farrell, Ward Bond.

Prison for Children 🦴🦴½ **1993** Sixteen-year-old Chris is orphaned and put into a boys home where a supervisor sees his potential and helps him achieve it. **96m/C VHS.** Raphael Sbarge, Kenny Ransom, Jonathan Chapin, Josh Brolin, James Callahan, Betty Thomas, John Ritter; ***D:*** Larry Peerce.

Prison of Secrets 🦴🦴½ **1997** Mom Zimbalist gets convicted of racketeering and sent to the big house where she learns that some of the prison guards are pimping the inmates. After suffering degradation herself, Zimbalist finally decides to expose the abuse but she needs the other women to testify as well. **91m/C VHS, DVD.** Stephanie Zimbalist, Dan Lauria, Finola Hughes, Rusty Schwimmer, Gary Frank, Kimberly Russell; ***D:*** Fred Gerber; ***W:*** Layce Gardner; ***C:*** John Fleckenstein; ***M:*** Nan Miskin. **CABLE**

Prison on Fire 🦴🦴 **1987** A mobster sent to prison for murdering his wife becomes friends with an innocent prisoner who has been framed. Violent portrayal of prison life. In Cantonese with English subtitles. **98m/C VHS, DVD.** *HK* Chow Yun-Fat, Tony Leung Ka-Fai; ***D:*** Ringo Lam; ***W:*** Yin Nam; ***M:*** Lowell Lo.

Prison on Fire 2 🦴🦴 *Tao Fan; Jian Yu Feng Yun Xu Ji* **1991** Ching is a hard-timer in a Hong Kong prison troubled by an ongoing battle between local inmates and those from Mainland China. He manages to escape to see his young son but is soon returned to prison where evil security chief Zau sets him up against the Mainland gang, led by Dragon. There are more escapes, a riot, revenge, and lots of action. Subtitled. **107m/C DVD, Wide.** *HK* Chow Yun-Fat, Elvis Tsui, Kam-Kong Tsui, Yu Li; ***D:*** Ringo Lam; ***M:*** Lowell Lo.

Prison Planet 🦴½ **1992 (R)** In the year 2200 Earth is under the dictatorship of an evil king, with only a band of intrepid rebels to oppose him. Blaine, one of the rebels, gets himself arrested and sent to prison in search of the true ruler, the king's brother. But the prison is protected by a brutal warlord and his equally sadistic warriors, whom Blaine must battle if he ever hopes to find truth and justice. **90m/C VHS.** James Phillips, Jack Willcox, Michael Foley, Deborah Thompson-Carlin; *D:* Armand Gazarian; *W:* Armand Gazarian.

Prison Shadows 🦴 **1936** Contrived programmer about a fighter (Nugent) who attempts to make a comeback after having served three years of a five-year sentence for killing an opponent in the boxing ring. He makes his comeback, but deals yet another mortal blow. Turns out that a gambling ring is behind the bizarre murders of the fighters and Nugent is their next victim. **67m/B VHS.** Eddie Nugent, Lucille Lund, Joan Barclay, Forrest Taylor, Syd Saylor, Monte Blue; *D:* Robert F. "Bob" Hill; *W:* Al Martin.

Prison Stories: Women on the Inside 🦴🦴🦴 **1991** Three short dramatic stories depict the life of women inside prison walls. "New Chicks," directed by Spheeris, tells the story of two lifelong friends and partners in crime. "Esperanza," directed by Deitch, tells the story of a woman on the inside trying to prevent her family from following the same destructive path. Silver's "Parole Board" features Davidovich as a murderess up for parole but reluctant to leave the security of the prison. Blunt and gritty portrayal of prison gangs, the lifestyle of female inmates, and their fears of returning to life on the outside. **94m/C VHS.** Rae Dawn Chong, Annabella Sciorra, Lolita (David) Davidovich, Talisa Soto, Rachel Ticotin, Grace Zabriskie, Silvania Gallardo, Francesca Roberts; *D:* Donna Deitch, Penelope Spheeris, Joan Micklin Silver; *W:* Dick Beebe. **CABLE**

Prison Train 🦴🦴½ *People's Enemy* **1938** Travelogue of a convicted murderer's cross-country journey to begin his prison sentence at Alcatraz. **84m/B VHS.** Fred Keating, Dorothy Comingore, Clarence Muse, Faith Bacon, Alexander Leftwich, Nestor Paiva, Franklyn Farnum; *D:* Gordon Wiles.

The Prisoner 🦴🦴🦴 **1955** Gritty drama about a Cardinal imprisoned in a Soviet bloc country as his captors attempt to break his determination not to be used as a propaganda tool. Interactions between the prisoner and his interogator are riveting. Based on the real-life experiences of Cardinal Mindszenty, a Hungarian activist during and after WWII. **91m/B VHS.** *GB* Alec Guinness, Jack Hawkins, Raymond Huntley, Wilfred Lawson; *D:* Peter Glenville.

The Prisoner *Jackie Chan Is the Prisoner; Huo Shao Dao* **1990 (R)** Even though the cover of this bizarre import says "Jackie Chan Is The Prisoner," he doesn't even show up for the first 20 minutes or so. Actually, the film is something of an ensemble piece that cheerfully borrows from American prison movies (most blatantly "Cool Hand Luke") between action scenes. The free-wheeling plot has Jackie, Sammo Hung, and Tony Leung battling fellow prisoners and corrupt officials. **94m/C DVD, Wide.** *HK* Jackie Chan, Sammo Hung, Tony Leung Ka-Fai; *D:* Yen Ping Chu; *W:* Fu Lai, Yeh Yuen Chiao; *C:* Chan Wing Su; *M:* Eckart Seeber.

Prisoner in the Middle 🦴🦴 **1974 (PG)** Janssen is the only man who can stop a nuclear warhead from falling into the hands of rival Middle East factions. Originally released as "Warhead." **87m/C VHS, 8mm.** David Janssen, Karin Dor, Christopher Stone, Turia Tan, David Semadar, Art Metrano; *D:* John O'Conner.

Prisoner of Honor 🦴🦴🦴 **1991 (PG)** A cable retelling of notorious Dreyfus Affair, in which a Jewish officer in the 19th-century French military was accused of treason based on little evidence and lots of bigotry. George Piquart (Dreyfuss), the anti-semitic counterintelligence head, grows to realize Dreyfuss's innocence and fights zealously for the truth. Russell's flamboyant direction takes the heroic tale into the realm of the surreal; this may not be a thoroughly accurate account, but it's one of the more eye-filling. **90m/C VHS.** Richard Dreyfuss, Oliver Reed, Peter Firth, Jeremy Kemp, Brian Blessed, Peter Vaughan, Kenneth Colley, Lindsay Anderson; *D:* Ken Russell. **CABLE**

Prisoner of Love 🦴½ **1999 (R)** After bartender Tracy (Campbell) witnesses a shakedown gone wrong, low-level stooge Jonny (Thal) is told to get rid of her. But since he's fallen in lust with Tracy after flirting with her in a nightclub, Jonny kidnaps her and holds her prisoner in a warehouse until he can figure out how to keep them both alive. Not nearly as kinky as it sounds—in fact the sheer blandness makes this a miss. **100m/C VHS, DVD.** Eric Thal, Naomi Campbell, Beau Starr, Carl Marotte; *D:* Steve DiMarco; *M:* Norman Orenstein.

Prisoner of Rio 🦴🦴 **1989** Satire of scruple-less TV evangelists and their nefarious schemes at acquiring their audience's money. **90m/C VHS.** Steven Berkoff, Paul Freeman; *D:* Lech Majewski; *M:* Hans Zimmer. **CABLE**

Prisoner of Second Avenue 🦴🦴½ **1974 (PG)** A New Yorker in his late 40s faces the future, without a job or any confidence in his ability, with the help of his understanding wife. Based on the Broadway play by Neil Simon. **98m/C VHS, Wide.** Jack Lemmon, Anne Bancroft, Gene Saks, Elizabeth Wilson, Sylvester Stallone, F. Murray Abraham; *D:* Melvin Frank; *W:* Neil Simon; *M:* Marvin Hamlisch.

Prisoner of the Mountains 🦴🦴🦴 *Kavkazsky Plennik; Prisoner of the Caucasus* **1996 (R)** A modern-day, freely adapted version of Leo Tolstoy's novella "Prisoner of the Caucasus." Two Russian soldiers find themselves taken hostage in a remote Muslim village high in the Caucasus Mountains. Their captor, Abdul-Mourant (Sikharulidze), wishes to exchange them for his own captive son. Seasoned veteran Sacha (Menshikov) and young recruit Vanya (Bodrov Jr.) slowly form a bond, not only with each other but gradually with their captors. But there's a tragic inevitability to the entire untenable situation. Russian with subtitles. **98m/C VHS.** *RU* Sergei Bodrov Jr., Oleg Menshikov, Djemal Sikharulidze, Susanna Mekhralieva, Alexander Burejev, Alexei Zharkov, Valentina Fedotova; *D:* Sergei Bodrov; *W:* Sergei Bodrov, Arif Aliev, Boris Giller; *C:* Pavel Lebeshev; *M:* Leonid Desyatnikov.

Prisoner of Zenda 🦴🦴🦴½ **1937** An excellent cast and splendid photography make this the definitive film adaptation of Anthony Hope's swashbuckling novel. A British commoner is forced to pose as his cousin, the kidnapped king of a small European country, to save the throne. Complications of the romantic sort ensue when he falls in love with the queen. Excellent acting, robust sword play, and beautifully designed costumes make this an enjoyable spectacle. **101m/B VHS.** Ronald Colman, Douglas Fairbanks Jr., Madeleine Carroll, David Niven, Raymond Massey, Mary Astor, Sir C. Aubrey Smith, Montagu Love, Byron Foulger, Alexander D'Arcy, Charles Halton; *D:* John Cromwell; *W:* Donald Ogden Stewart, John Lloyd Balderston, Wells Root; *C:* James Wong Howe. Natl. Film Reg. '91.

Prisoner of Zenda 🦴🦴½ **1952** Less-inspired remake of the 1937 version of Anthony Hope's novel, of a man resembling the monarch of a small country who is forced to pose as King during the coronation ceremony, becomes enamored with the queen, and finds himself embroiled in a murder plot. Worth watching for the luxurious costumes and lavish sets. Cast as a Cardinal here, Stone starred in the 1922 version. **101m/C VHS.** Stewart Granger, Deborah Kerr, Louis Calhern, James Mason, Jane Greer, Lewis Stone; *D:* Richard Thorpe; *C:* Joseph Ruttenberg.

Prisoner of Zenda 🦴🦴 **1979 (PG)** Flat comedic interpretation of Anthony Hope's swashbuckling tale of two identical men who switch places, only to find things complicated by a murder. Sellers stars in the double role of Prince Rudolph of Ruritania and Syd, the cockney cab driver who doubles for Rudolph when the Prince is imprisoned by his jealous brother Michael. **108m/C VHS.** Peter Sellers, Jeremy Kemp, Lynne Frederick, Lionel Jeffries, Elke Sommer; *D:* Richard Quine; *W:* Dick Clement, Ian LaFrenais; *M:* Henry Mancini.

Prisoners of Inertia 🦴🦴½ **1989 (R)** Two newlyweds travel to New York city and find themselves caught up in a whirlwind adventure in this well-acted but lazily scripted comedy drama. **92m/C VHS.** Amanda Plummer, Christopher Rich, John C. McGinley; *D:* Jay Noyles Seles.

Prisoners of the Lost Universe 🦴½ **1984** Talk-show hostess and her buddy are transported to a hostile universe by a renegade scientist. The two terrified humans search desperately for the dimensional door that is their only hope of escape. **94m/C VHS.** Richard Hatch, Kay Lenz, John Saxon; *D:* Terry Marcel. **TV**

Prisoners of the Sun 🦴🦴🦴 *Blood Oath* **1991 (R)** Right after WWII an Australian captain fights to convict Japanese officers for atrocities against Allied POWs, but he's stonewalled by both the U.S. military and still-defiant enemy prisoners. This fiery drama from Down Under packs a punch as it questions whether wartime justice even exists; similar in that way to Brown's earlier "Breaker Morant." Takei (Sulu of the original "Star Trek") makes an imposing Japanese admiral. **109m/C VHS.** *AU* Bryan Brown, George Takei, Terry O'Quinn, John Back, Toshi Shioya, Deborah Kara Unger; *D:* Stephen Wallace.

Private Affairs 🦴 **1989 (R)** The mistress of a well-known surgeon becomes jealous when the doctor decides to have a fling with a gorgeous young swim instructor. Italian-made cheapie. **83m/C VHS.** *IT* Guiliana de Sio, Kate Capshaw, David Naughton, Luca Barbareschi, Michele Placido; *D:* Francesco Massaro.

The Private Affairs of Bel Ami 🦴🦴🦴 **1947** "This is the story of a scoundrel," proclaims the opening. Sanders is ideally cast as a suave cad who rises in 1880s Parisian society, largely through the strategic seduction of prominent women. Moralistically minded Old Hollywood toned down the talky adaptation of the Guy de Maupassant novel, but it's still drama of a high order. **112m/B VHS.** George Sanders, Angela Lansbury, Ann Dvorak, Frances Dee, John Carradine, Susan Douglas, Hugo Haas, Marie Wilson, Albert Bassermann, Warren William, Katherine Emery, Richard Fraser; *D:* Albert Lewin; *W:* Albert Lewin.

Private Benjamin 🦴🦴½ **1980 (R)** Lighthearted fare about a pampered New York Jewish princess who impulsively enlists in the U.S. Army after her husband dies on their wedding night. Hawn, who also produced, creates a character loveable even at her worst moments and brings a surprising amount of depth to this otherwise frivolous look at high society attitudes. Basis for a TV series. **110m/C VHS, DVD.** Goldie Hawn, Eileen Brennan, Albert Brooks, Robert Webber, Armand Assante, Barbara Barrie, Mary Kay Place, Sally Kirkland, Craig T. Nelson, Harry Dean Stanton, Sam Wanamaker; *D:* Howard Zieff; *W:* Nancy Meyers, Charles Shyer, Harvey Miller; *C:* David M. Walsh; *M:* Bill Conti. Writers Guild '80: Orig. Screenplay.

Private Buckaroo 🦴🦴 **1942** War time entertainment in which Harry James and his orchestra get drafted. They decide to put on a show for the soldiers and get help from the Andrews Sisters. ♫Don't Sit Under the Apple Tree with Anyone Else But Me; Three Little Sisters; Private Buckaroo; Johnny Get Your Gun Again; We've Got a Job to Do; You Made Me Love You; Six Jerks in a Jeep; That's the Moon My Son; I Love the South. **70m/B VHS.** The Andrews Sisters, Harry James, Joe E. Lewis, Dick Foran, Shemp Howard, Mary Wickes, Donald O'Connor; *D:* Edward F. (Eddie) Cline.

Private Confessions 🦴🦴 **1998** Continues Bergman's exploration of his parents' unhappy marriage (following "The Best Intentions"), set mostly in 1925. Restless Anna (August) is constantly at odds with her clergyman husband, Henrik (Froler), and she has an affair with divinity student Tomas (Hanzon). Anna confesses the affair to Pastor Jacob (von Sydow), who she regards as a surrogate uncle, and he advises her to tell Henrik. Anna's confrontation with Henrik will leave lasting scars—as Anna once again reveals to Jacob some ten years later. Swedish with subtitles. **127m/C VHS.** *SW* Pernilla August, Samuel Froler, Max von Sydow, Thomas Hanzon; *D:* Liv Ullmann; *W:* Ingmar Bergman; *C:* Sven Nykvist.

Private Contentment 🦴🦴 **1983** This is a drama about a young soldier's experiences before he goes off to war in 1945. **90m/C VHS.** Trini Alvarado, Peter Gallagher, John McMartin, Kathryn Walker; *D:* Vivian Matalon.

Private Duty Nurses 🦴½ *Young L.A. Nurses 1* **1971 (R)** Three nurses take on racism, war wounds, and a menage-a-trois (between one nurse, a doctor, and a drug addict). Second in Roger Corman's "nurse" quintet takes itself too seriously to be entertaining, but the gals make good use of those exciting new inventions, waterbeds. Preceded by "The Student Nurses" and followed by "Night Call Nurses," "The Young Nurses," and "Candy Stripe Nurses." **80m/C VHS.** Katherine (Kathy) Cannon, Joyce Williams, Pegi Boucher, Joseph Kaufmann, Dennis Redfield, Herbert Jefferson Jr., Paul Hampton, Paul Gleason; *D:* George Armitage; *W:* George Armitage; *C:* John McNichol; *M:* Sky.

The Private Eyes 🦴½ **1980 (PG)** Light and uneven comedic romp with Knotts and Conway as bungling sleuths engaged to investigate two deaths. They're led on a merry chase through secret passages to a meeting with a ghostly adversary. **91m/C VHS, DVD.** Don Knotts, Tim Conway, Trisha Noble, Bernard Fox; *D:* Lang Elliott; *W:* John Myhers, Tim Conway; *C:* Jacques Haitkin; *M:* Peter Matz.

The Private Files of J. Edgar Hoover 🦴🦴½ **1977 (PG)** Scandal-mongering "biography" of J. Edgar Hoover's private, sex-filled life. **112m/C VHS.** Broderick Crawford, Dan Dailey, Jose Ferrer, Rip Torn, Michael Parks, Raymond St. Jacques, Ronee Blakley; *D:* Larry Cohen; *W:* Larry Cohen.

A Private Function 🦴🦴½ **1984 (PG)** A ribald gag-fest dealing with Palin as a Yorkshireman who steals and fattens a wily contraband pig against the backdrop of post-WWII rationing. The satire ranges from biting to downright nasty, but Palin is always likeable in the center of it all. **96m/C VHS.** *GB* Michael Palin, Maggie Smith, Denholm Elliott, Bill Paterson, Liz Smith, Richard Griffiths, Tony Haygarth, John Normington, Alison Steadman, Pete Postlethwaite; *D:* Malcolm Mowbray; *W:* Alan Bennett; *C:* Tony Pierce-Roberts; *M:* John Du Prez. British Acad. '84: Actress (Smith), Support. Actor (Elliott), Support. Actress (Smith).

Private Hell 36 🦴🦴 **1954** Two detectives become guilt-ridden after keeping part of some stolen money recovered after a robbery. Co-produced by Lupino. **81m/B VHS.** Ida Lupino, Howard Duff, Steve Cochran, Dean Jagger, Dorothy Malone, Bridget Duff, Jerry Hausner, Dabbs Greer, Chris O'Brien, Kenneth Patterson, George Dockstader, Jimmy Hawkins, King Donovan; *D:* Donald Siegel; *W:* Ida Lupino; *C:* Burnett Guffey; *M:* Leith Stevens.

The Private History of a Campaign That Failed 🦴½ **1987** Adaptation of the Mark Twain story about a cowardly troop of Confederate soldiers. **89m/C VHS.** Pat Hingle, Edward Herrmann.

Private Investigations 🦴½ **1987 (R)** A made-for-video thriller about a nosey reporter who gets himself and his adult son in trouble while investigating drug-pushing cops. **91m/C VHS.** Ray Sharkey, Clayton Rohner, Talia Balsam, Anthony Zerbe, Paul LeMat; *D:* Nigel Dick; *W:* John Dahl, David Warfield.

Private Lessons 🦴🦴 **1981 (R)** Teenage boy is left alone for the summer in the care of an alluring maid and a scheming chauffeur. **83m/C VHS.** Eric Brown, Sylvia Kristel, Howard Hesseman; *D:* Alan Myerson; *C:* Jan De Bont.

Private Lessons **19??** A boy can't concentrate on his piano lessons when he gets a beautiful new teacher. You won't be able to concentrate on anything but comedy. **90m/C VHS.** Carroll Baker.

Private Lessons, Another Story 🦴½ **1994 (R)** A New York photographer (Morgan) is sick of her philandering husband and decides to experience some sexual excitement of her own by heading off to Miami. All that tropical heat inspires passion with her Cuban chauffeur (Garaza). **86m/C VHS.** Mariana Morgan, Ray Garaza, Theresa Morris; ***D:*** Dominique Othenin-Girard; ***W:*** William Mernit.

Private Life 🦴🦴½ *Chastnaya Zhizn* **1982** Suddenly with time on his hands, a Soviet official scrutinizes his relationships. After a number of revelations, he is forced to make new choices based on what he has learned. Oscar nominee in 1983. In Russian with English subtitles. **103m/C VHS.** *RU* Mikhail Ulyanov, Ita Sanvina, Irina Gubanova; ***D:*** Edgar Ryazanov; ***W:*** Andrew Davies.

Private Life of Don Juan 🦴🦴 *Don Juan* **1934** Appropriately slow-moving British costume drama set in 17th-century Spain finds an aging Don Juan struggling to maintain his usual antics in the pursuit of beautiful women. Furthermore, his reputation is being upstaged by a young imposter. Notable only as the last film appearance by Douglas Fairbanks Sr., and based on the play by Henri Bataille. **87m/B VHS.** *GB* Douglas Fairbanks Sr., Merle Oberon, Binnie Barnes, Melville Cooper, Joan Gardner, Benita Hume, Athene Seyler; ***D:*** Alexander Korda; ***C:*** Georges Perinal.

The Private Life of Henry VIII 🦴🦴🦴🦴 **1933** Lavish historical spectacle lustily portraying the life and lovers of notorious British Monarch, King Henry VIII. A tour de force for Laughton as the robust 16th-century king, with outstanding performances by the entire cast. **97m/B VHS.** *GB* Charles Laughton, Binnie Barnes, Elsa Lanchester, Robert Donat, Merle Oberon, Miles Mander, Wendy Barrie, John Loder, Lady Tree, Franklin Dyall, Claud Allister, William Austin, Gibb McLaughlin, Sam Livesey, Lawrence Hanray, Everley Gregg, Judy Kelly, John Turnbull, Frederick Culley, Hay Petrie, Wally Patch; ***D:*** Alexander Korda; ***W:*** Arthur Wimperis, Lajos Biro; ***C:*** Georges Perinal. Oscars '33: Actor (Laughton).

The Private Life of Sherlock Holmes 🦴🦴🦴½ **1970 (PG-13)** A unique perspective on the life of the famous detective reveals a complex character. Beautifully photographed, with fine performances by the supporting cast, the film boasts a haunting musical score but received suprisingly little recognition despite Wilder's high caliber direction. **125m/C VHS.** *GB* Robert Stephens, Colin Blakely, Genevieve Page, Irene Handl, Stanley Holloway, Christopher Lee, Clive Revill, Catherine Lacey, Tamara Toumanova, Mollie Maureen, Michael Balfour; ***D:*** Billy Wilder; ***W:*** Billy Wilder, I.A.L. Diamond; ***C:*** Christopher Challis; ***M:*** Miklos Rozsa.

Private Lives 🦴🦴🦴½ **1931** Stylish adaptation of Noel Coward play starring Shearer and Montgomery as a couple with a tempestuous relationship. Although once married, they have since divorced and married other mates. While honeymooning at the same french hotel (Quelle coincidence!), they have trouble showing affection to their new spouses and realize they still feel passionately about one another. Excellent acting combined with Coward's witty dialogue makes this film a treat. **92m/B VHS.** Norma Shearer, Robert Montgomery, Reginald Denny, Una Merkel, Jean Hersholt; ***D:*** Sidney Franklin.

The Private Lives of Elizabeth & Essex 🦴🦴🦴 **1939** Cast reads like a Who's Who in Hollywood in this lavishly costumed dramatization of the love affair between Queen Elizabeth I (Davis) and Robert Devereaux (Flynn), the second Earl of Essex. Forced to choose between her Kingdom and her lover, Davis' monarch is the epitome of a regal women. Fabray made her first film appearance as an adult in this adaptation of Maxwell Anderson's 1930 play "Elizabeth the Queen." **106m/C VHS.** Bette Davis, Errol Flynn, Vincent Price, Nanette Fabray, Olivia de Havilland, Alan Hale, Donald Crisp, Leo G. Carroll; ***D:*** Michael Curtiz.

Private Manoeuvres woof! **1983** A comely Swiss military adviser gives her all to uplift the morale of the men at Camp Samantha. **79m/C VHS.** Zachi Noy, Joseph Shiloah, Dvora Bekon.

A Private Matter 🦴🦴🦴 **1992 (PG-13)** Based on the true story of Sherri Finkbine (hostess of TV's "Romper Room") and the controversy surrounding her decision to terminate her pregnancy in 1962. Pregnant with her fifth child, she discovered her sleeping medication contained thalidomide, known to cause severe birth defects. Although technically illegal, her doctor agreed to quietly perform an abortion. Sherri warned a local newspaper reporter about the drug's dangers and her identity was mistakenly revealed. A storm of adverse publicity forced her to Sweden for the abortion. Great performances highlight this complex and traumatic issue. **89m/C VHS.** Sissy Spacek, Aidan Quinn, Estelle Parsons, Sheila McCarthy, Leon Russom, William H. Macy; ***D:*** Joan Micklin Silver; ***W:*** William Nicholson. **CABLE**

Private Navy of Sgt. O'Farrell 🦴🦴 **1968** Serviceable World War II service comedy casts Hope as the titular NCO who must salvage a cargo ship full of beer that was sunk by the Japanese. He also tries to get some nurses assigned to the remote Pacific island where he's stationed. But Phyllis Diller proves to be a poor morale booster. The film doesn't come close to the "Road" comedies, but it's still worth a mild recommendation to the star's fans. **92m/C DVD.** Bob Hope, Phyllis Diller, Jeffrey Hunter, Dick Sargent, Mako, Gina Lollobrigida; ***D:*** Frank Tashlin; ***W:*** Frank Tashlin; ***C:*** Alan Stenvold.

Private Obsession 🦴½ **1994 (R)** Model Emanuelle Griffith (Whirry) is missing—kidnapped by obsessed admirer Richard (Christian) who wants the beauty for himself alone. Emanuelle may be blonde but she's not dumb and she decides to turn the tables on her captor. **93m/C VHS, DVD.** Shannon Whirry, Michael Christian, Bo Svenson, Rip Taylor; ***D:*** Lee Frost; ***W:*** Lee Frost; ***C:*** William Boatman; ***M:*** Dean Andre.

Private Parts 🦴🦴 **1972 (R)** A bizarre first attempt at feature length for Bartel. Black comedy featuring a runaway, a voyeuristic photographer and a hotel full of strange people who participate in murder and a variety of freakish sexual acts. **87m/C VHS.** Ayn Ruymen, Lucille Benson, John Ventantonio, Laurie Main, Stanley Livingston, Charles Woolf, John Lupton, Dorothy Neumann, Gene Simms; ***D:*** Paul Bartel; ***W:*** Philip Kearney, Les Rendelstein; ***C:*** Andrew Davis; ***M:*** Hugo Friedhofer.

Private Parts 🦴🦴½ *Howard Stern's Private Parts* **1996 (R)** Stern makes his movie debut as...himself! Self-effacing yet self-aggrandizing bio traces Stern's rise from gawky kid to gawky college student to awkward small-market DJ to New York madman to inauguration as self-proclaimed King of All Media. Funny, and at times, touching flick features good performances by the rookie actors in Stern's inner circle, as well as by the pros. Giamatti is exceptional as the young WNBC exec assigned to tame Howard. Script manages to show Stern's outrageousness and still make him likeable. While this is clearly a whitewash job, and under other circumstances Stern himself might make fun of its sentimentality, pic should please everyone but the most rabid Stern-hater. **109m/C VHS, DVD.** Howard Stern, Robin Quivers, Mary McCormack, Paul Giamatti, Fred Norris, Gary Dell'Abate, Bobby Borriello, Michael Maccarone, Matthew Friedman, Jackie Martling, Carol Alt, Richard Portnow, Kelly Bishop, Henry Goodman, Jonathan Hadary, Paul Hecht, Allison Janney, Michael Murphy, James Murtaugh, Reni Santoni, Lee Wilkof, Theresa Lynn, Amber Smith; ***D:*** Betty Thomas; ***W:*** Len Blum, Michael Kalesniko; ***C:*** Walt Lloyd; ***M:*** Van Dyke Parks.

Private Passions 🦴 **1985** A sultry woman gives her teenaged cousin a lesson in love during his European vacation. **86m/C VHS.** Sybil Danning.

Private Resort 🦴🦴 **1984 (R)** Curious house detective and a bumbling thief interrupt the highjinks of two girl-crazy teens on a quest for fun at an expensive Miami hotel. Occasionally funny plodder. **82m/C VHS.** Johnny Depp, Rob Morrow, Karyn O'Bryan, Emily Longstreth, Tony Azito, Hector Elizondo, Dody Goodman, Leslie Easterbrook, Andrew (Dice Clay) Silverstein; ***D:*** George Bowers.

Private Road: No Trespassing **1987 (R)** A stock car racer and a top engineer compete over a military project, cars and a rich heiress. **90m/C VHS.** George Kennedy, Greg Evigan, Mitzi Kapture; ***D:*** Raphael Nussbaum.

Private School 🦴½ **1983 (R)** Two high school girls from the exclusive Cherryvale Academy for Women compete for the affections of a young man from nearby Freemount Academy for Men, while Cherryvale's headmistress is trying to raise funds to build a new wing. Banal teen sexploitation comedy with better-than-average cast. **89m/C VHS.** Phoebe Cates, Betsy Russell, Kathleen Wilhoite, Sylvia Kristel, Ray Walston, Matthew Modine, Michael Zorek, Fran Ryan, Jonathan Prince, Kari Lizer, Richard Stahl; ***D:*** Noel Black; ***C:*** Walter Lassally.

The Private Secretary 🦴½ **1935** Horton is a mild-mannered clergyman who finds out his identity has been usurped by a young man with a great many angry creditors. Horton has some amusing comic bits but the film, based on a popular Victorian farce "Der Bibliotheker" by Van Moser, did not translate well to the screen. **70m/B VHS.** *GB* Edward Everett Horton, Barry Mackay, Oscar Asche, Judy Gunn, Michael Shepley, Alastair Sim; ***D:*** Henry Edwards.

Private War 🦴½ **1990 (R)** Training for an elite force turns deadly when the commanding officer makes the rules. Now it's a private war between two brutal fighting machines. Adapted from a Jan Guillou story. **95m/C VHS.** Martin Hewitt, Joe Dallesandro, Kimberly Beck; ***D:*** Frank De Palma; ***W:*** Frank De Palma, Terry Borst.

The Private War of Major Benson 🦴🦴½ **1955** Tough Army officer Major Bernard Benson (Heston) has his work cut out for him when he's ordered to take over an ROTC program at a military academy. First he finds out the school's run by nuns and then he treats his young cadets as he would adult troops, which naturally makes him very unpopular. But he manages to unbend enough to try for a romance with the school's doctor (Adams). And of course the kids teach him how to become a human being. Remade in 1995 as "Major Payne." **104m/C VHS.** Charlton Heston, Julie Adams, Milburn Stone, Nana Bryant, William Demarest, Tim Considine, Sal Mineo; ***D:*** Jerry Hopper; ***W:*** William Roberts, Richard Alan Simmons; ***C:*** Harold Lipstein.

Private Wars 🦴🦴 **1993 (R)** A law-abiding community falls victim to gangland violence until the inhabitants hire a down-and-out private eye (Railsback) to show them how to fight back. He finds out that a greedy land developer (Whitman) has bribed the Chief of Police (Champion) to let his goons do anything to get the people out so he can redevelop the land. **94m/C VHS.** Steve Railsback, Michael Champion, Stuart Whitman, Holly Floria, Dan Tullis Jr., Michael Delano, James Lew, Brian Patrick Clark; ***D:*** John Weidner; ***W:*** Ken Lamplugh, John Weidner.

Privates on Parade 🦴🦴½ **1984 (R)** Film centering around the comic antics of an Army song-and-dance unit entertaining the troops in the Malayan jungle during the late '40s. Occasionally inspired horseplay based on Peter Nichols play. **107m/C VHS.** *GB* John Cleese, Denis Quilley, Simon Jones, Joe Melia, Nicola Pagett, Julian Sands; ***D:*** Michael Blakemore.

Prix de Beaute 🦴½ *Miss Europe* **1930** A woman's boyfriend does not know that she has won a beauty contest. Brooks' last starring role and the only film she did in France. In French with English subtitles. **93m/B VHS.** *FR* Louise Brooks, Jean Bradin, George Charlia, Gaston Jacquet; ***D:*** Augusto Genina.

The Prize 🦴🦴🦴 **1963** Gripping spy story laced with laughs based on a novel by Irving Wallace (adapted by Lehman). In Stockholm, writer accepts the Nobel prize for dubious reasons and then finds himself in the midst of political intrigue. Newman and Sommer turn in great performances in this action drama. **136m/C VHS.** Paul Newman, Edward G. Robinson, Elke Sommer, Leo G. Carroll, Diane Baker, Micheline Presle, Gerard Oury, Sergio Fantoni; ***D:*** Mark Robson; ***W:*** Ernest Lehman; ***C:*** William H. Daniels; ***M:*** Jerry Goldsmith.

Prize Fighter 🦴🦴 **1979 (PG)** Comedy team of Knotts and Conway take on Depression-era boxing. Fight manager Knotts and his pugilistic protege Conway unknowingly get involved with a powerful gangster, who convinces them to fight in a fixed championship match. Most enjoyable if intelligence is suspended at onset. **99m/C VHS.** Tim Conway, Don Knotts; ***D:*** Michael Preece; ***W:*** Tim Conway.

Prize of Peril 🦴🦴 **1984** A French TV game show rewards it winners with wealth and its losers with execution. Not always the best policy to learn what's behind Door #1. **95m/C VHS.** *FR* Michel Piccoli, Marie-France Pisier; ***D:*** Yves Boisset.

The Prize Pulitzer 🦴🦴 *Roxanne: The Prize Pulitzer* **1989** Watered-down account of the scandalous divorce between publishing heir Herbert "Pete" Pulitzer and his young wife Roxanne. Based on the book "The Prize Pulitzer" by Roxanne Pulitzer. **95m/C VHS.** Perry King, Chynna Phillips, Courteney Cox Arquette, Betsy Russell, Sondra Blake, Caitlin Brown; ***D:*** Richard A. Colla. **TV**

The Prizefighter and the Lady 🦴🦴🦴 *Every Woman's Man* **1933** In his first film role boxer Baer (who won the heavyweight boxing crown in 1934) is a natural as a fighter who falls for a beautiful nightclub singer (Loy). Baer and Loy get, but don't stay, together but she does turn out to be his lucky charm in the big fight finale. Fellow professional boxer Carnera, Baer's opponent in the climactic fight scene, refused to lose as the script indicated and the film ending was eventually rewritten. The likeable Baer later earned his living as an actor. **102m/B** Max Baer Sr., Myrna Loy, Otto Kruger, Primo Carnera, Walter Huston, Vince Barnett, Muriel Evans; ***D:*** Woodbridge S. Van Dyke.

Prizzi's Honor 🦴🦴🦴 **1985 (R)** Highly stylized, sometimes leaden black comedy about Vharley Partana (Nicholson), an aging and none-to-bright hit man from a New York mob family who breaks with family loyalties when he falls for Irene Walker (Turner), an upwardly mobile tax consultant who's also a hired killer. Skirting caricature in every frame, Nicholson is excellent in his portrayal of the thick-skulled mobster, as are Angelica Huston as the hot-to-trot Mafia daughter Maerose and Hickey as Don Prizzi. Adapted by Condon and Roach from Condon's novel. **130m/C VHS, DVD.** Jack Nicholson, Kathleen Turner, Robert Loggia, John Randolph, Anjelica Huston, Lawrence Tierney, William Hickey, Lee Richardson, Michael Lombard, Joseph Ruskin, CCH Pounder; ***D:*** John Huston; ***W:*** Richard Condon, Janet Roach; ***C:*** Andrzej Bartkowiak; ***M:*** Alex North. Oscars '85: Support. Actress (Huston); British Acad. '85: Adapt. Screenplay; Golden Globes '86: Actor—Mus./Comedy (Nicholson), Actress—Mus./Comedy (Turner), Director (Huston), Film—Mus./Comedy; L.A. Film Critics '85: Support. Actress (Huston); N.Y. Film Critics '85: Actor (Nicholson), Director (Huston), Film, Support. Actress (Huston); Natl. Soc. Film Critics '85: Actor (Nicholson), Director (Huston), Support. Actress (Huston); Writers Guild '85: Adapt. Screenplay.

Probable Cause 🦴🦴 **1995 (R)** A knife-wielding serial killer specializes in murdering cops and the clues seem to point to a troubled veteran cop (Ironside), newly paired with a beautiful detective (Vernon). Some unexpected twists and a surprise ending. **90m/C VHS.** Michael Ironside, Kate Vernon, Kirk Baltz, Craig T. Nelson, M. Emmet Walsh; ***D:*** Paul Ziller; ***W:*** Hal Salwen; ***C:*** Danny Nowak.

Probation 🦴🦴 *Second Chances* **1932** A dashing young man in trouble with the law receives an unusual sentence; he must become a chauffeur for a spoiled society girl. Grable's first film role is a small one. **60m/B VHS.** Sally Blane, J. Farrell MacDonald, Eddie (Edward) Phillips, Clara Kimball Young, Betty Grable; ***D:*** Richard Thorpe.

Probe ✌✌½ **1972** A detective uses computer-age technology to apprehend criminals. Pilot for the TV series "Search." **95m/C VHS.** Hugh O'Brian, Elke Sommer, John Gielgud, Burgess Meredith, Angel Tompkins, Lilia Skala, Kent Smith, Alfred Ryder, Jaclyn Smith; ***D:*** Russ Mayberry; ***W:*** Leslie Stevens. **TV**

Problem Child ✌½ **1990 (PG)** Ritter decides to adopt Oliver out of the goodness of his heart, but it seems young Oliver's already got a father figure named Beelzebub. Potential for laughs is unmet. **81m/C VHS, DVD.** John Ritter, Michael Oliver, Jack Warden, Amy Yasbeck, Gilbert Gottfried, Michael Richards, Peter Jurasik; ***D:*** Dennis Dugan; ***W:*** Scott M. Alexander, Larry Karaszewski; ***C:*** Peter Collister; ***M:*** Miles Goodman.

Problem Child 2 ✌ **1991 (PG-13)** Ritter and his nasty adopted son are back, but this time there's an equally malevolent little girl. They team up to prevent Ritter's upcoming marriage to a socialite. Low slapstick junk. **91m/C VHS.** John Ritter, Michael Oliver, Laraine Newman, Amy Yasbeck, Jack Warden, Ivyann Schwan, Gilbert Gottfried, James Tolkan, Charlene Tilton, Alan Blumenfeld, Paul Sutera; ***D:*** Brian Levant; ***W:*** Scott M. Alexander, Larry Karaszewski.

The Prodigal ✌✌½ **1955** Luke's New Testament Bible story of the son seduced by greed slickly transfered to the silver screen by MGM. A colorful cast is the main attraction. **113m/C** Lana Turner, Edmund Purdom, Louis Calhern, Audrey Dalton, Neville Brand, Walter Hampden, Taina Elg, Francis L. Sullivan, Joseph Wiseman, Sandy Descher, John Dehner, Cecil Kellaway, Henry Daniell, Paul Cavanagh, Tracey Roberts, Jay Novello, Dorothy Adams, Richard Devon; ***D:*** Richard Thorpe; ***C:*** Joseph Ruttenberg.

The Prodigal ✌✌ **1983 (PG)** A born-again family drama in which a sundered family is brought together by the return of a once-estranged son. **109m/C VHS.** John Hammond, Hope Lange, John Cullum, Morgan Brittany, Ian Bannen, Arliss Howard, Joey Travolta, Billy Graham; ***M:*** Bruce Broughton.

The Prodigal Planet ✌ **1988** Small group of believers continue their struggle against the world government UNTIE by disrupting their communication network. Sequel to "Thief in the Night," "A Distant Thunder," and "Image of the Beast." **67m/C VHS.** William Wellman Jr., Linda Beatie, Cathy Wellman, Thom Rachford; ***D:*** Donald W. Thompson.

The Prodigal Son ✌✌½ **1982** Small-town martial arts champ Biao learns all his fights were fixed by his wealthy father. Determined to prove himself fairly, Biao learns the true wisdom and skills of kung fu from traveling entertainer Ying. Typically over-the-top fight scenes. Chinese with subtitles or dubbed. **100m/C VHS, DVD, Wide.** *HK* Yuen Biao, Lam Ching Ying, Sammo Hung; ***D:*** Sammo Hung; ***W:*** Jing Wong.

The Prodigy ✌✌ **1998** Well-intentioned but far-fetched drama posits that Nathan Jones (Earl), an illiterate 12-year-old black boy, is "adopted" by a fraternity and enrolled as a student as a child prodigy. Sounds like an after-school special gone tragically awry. **104m/C DVD.** Robert Foreman, Jeremy Isiah Earl, Jennifer Rochester; ***D:*** Edward T. McDougal; ***W:*** Edward T. McDougal, Dale Chapman, Christopher Panneck; ***C:*** Ben Kufrin.

The Producers ✌✌✌½ **1968** A hilarious farce follows an attempted swindle by theater producer/con artist Max Bialystock (Mostel), who convinces his meek accountant Leo Bloom (Wilder) to go along with a scheme to deliberately stage a Broadway flop and abscond with the investors' money. They pick what they believe will be a surefire disaster, a musical entitled "Springtime for Hitler," only to see their plan backfire. Film achieved cult status and is considered one of Brooks' best. The phony play was later actually produced by Alan Johnson. **90m/C VHS, 8mm, Wide.** Zero Mostel, Gene Wilder, Dick Shawn, Kenneth Mars, Estelle Winwood, Lee Meredith, Frank Campanella, Mel Brooks; ***D:*** Mel Brooks; ***W:*** Mel Brooks; ***C:*** Joseph Coffey; ***M:*** John Morris. Oscars '68: Story & Screenplay, Natl. Film Reg. '96;; Writers Guild '68: Orig. Screenplay.

The Professional ✌✌ *Leon; The Cleaner* **1994 (R)** Leon (Reno) is an eccentric French hit man, working New York's mean streets, when his 12-year-old neighbor Mathilda (Portman) comes knocking. Seems her family has been murdered by minions of crooked drug enforcement agent Stansfield (Oldman) and she'd like Leon to teach her how to be a "cleaner" so she can get revenge. And Leon obliges. The lovely young Portman (in her film debut) is a little too Lolita-ish for comfort as she manipulates the stolid Reno, with Oldman suitably extravagant in the role of sadistic psycho. **109m/C VHS, DVD, Wide.** *FR* Jean Reno, Natalie Portman, Gary Oldman, Danny Aiello, Michael Badalucco, Ellen Greene; ***D:*** Luc Besson; ***W:*** Luc Besson; ***C:*** Thierry Arbogast; ***M:*** Eric Serra.

Professional Killers 1 ✌ **1973** Trio of hired assassins wanders about the countryside killing people during Japan's Feudal Era. **87m/C VHS.** Jiro Tamiya, Koji Takahashi.

The Professionals ✌✌✌½ **1966 (PG-13)** Action and adventure count for more than a storyline in this exciting western about four mercenaries hired by a wealthy cattle baron to rescue his young wife from Mexican kidnappers. Breathtaking photography recreates turn-of-the-century Mexico in this adaptation of the Frank O'Rourke novel. **117m/C VHS, DVD, Wide.** Burt Lancaster, Lee Marvin, Claudia Cardinale, Jack Palance, Robert Ryan, Woody Strode, Ralph Bellamy; ***D:*** Richard Brooks; ***W:*** Richard Brooks; ***C:*** Conrad L. Hall; ***M:*** Maurice Jarre.

The Professor ✌✌ **1958** Rare sci-fi thriller featuring a werewolf, an eccentric scientist and a communist plot. Also includes several 'werewolf' oriented movie trailers. **30m/C VHS.** Doug Hobart, John Copeland, Irene Barr.

Profile ✌✌½ **1954** A newsman gets an editorial job for a magazine called "Profile," and promptly falls in love with the boss's daughter. Complications arise when the boss's wife puts the moves on him. As if that isn't trouble enough, he finds himself accused of embezzlement. Average entertainment with some notable performances and an interesting chase scene. **65m/B VHS.** John Bentley, Kathleen Byron, Thea Gregory, Stuart Lindsell; ***D:*** Francis Searle.

Profile for Murder ✌✌ *The Fifth Season* **1996 (R)** Criminal profiler Hanna Carras (Severance) and Detective Andy Sachs (Michael) are assigned by DA Michael Weinberg (Wincott) to investigate investment banker Adrian Cross (Henriksen), the primary suspect in a series of grisly murders of young women. Cross likes to play mind games and soon Carras is very personally involved with the suspect but does that also make him the killer? **95m/C VHS.** Joan Severance, Lance Henriksen, Jeff Wincott, Ryan Michael; ***D:*** David Winning; ***W:*** Steve Fisher; ***C:*** Bruce Worrall; ***M:*** Barron Abramovitch.

Progeny ✌✌ **1998** Familiar horror ground with some scary creatures. Craig (Vosloo) and Sherry (McWhirter) are zapped by a bright light while in bed and don't remember what happened until a shrink (Crouse) and UFO investigator Clavell (Dourif) hypnotize them. Then Sherry remembers she was abducted and apparently impregnated by some slimy, tentacled aliens and it's all just kind of predictably gross from there on out. **100m/C VHS, DVD, Wide.** Arnold Vosloo, Jillian McWhirter, Brad Dourif, Lindsay Crouse, Wilford Brimley; ***D:*** Brian Yuzna; ***W:*** Aubrey Solomon; ***C:*** James Hawkinson; ***M:*** Steven Morrell. **VIDEO**

The Program ✌✌½ **1993 (R)** Sensitive tearjerker about college football players getting caught up in the drive for a championship. As the season takes its toll on both mind and body, players prepare for the Big Game. Caan is the team's gruff coach, who's willing to look the other way as long as his boys are winning. Film sparked controversy when the Disney studio pulled and recut it after release because one scene, where Sheffer's character lies down in traffic, sparked copy-cat actions and several deaths. The scene was not restored for the video version. **110m/C VHS.** James Caan, Craig Sheffer, Kristy Swanson, Halle Berry, Omar Epps, Duane Davis, Abraham Benrubi, Jon Maynard Pennell, Andrew Bryniarski, Joey Lauren Adams; ***D:*** David S. Ward; ***W:*** David S. Ward, Aaron Latham; ***M:*** Michel Colombier.

Programmed to Kill ✌✌ *Retaliator* **1986 (R)** A beautiful terrorist is captured by the CIA and transformed into a buxom bionic assassin. **91m/C VHS.** Robert Ginty, Sandahl Bergman, James Booth, Louise Caire Clark; ***D:*** Allan Holzman.

Project A ✌✌✌½ *Jackie Chan's Project A; A Gai Waak* **1983 (PG-13)** This period piece has several excellent physical routines. As Dragon Ma, a coast guard officer in 19th-century Hong Kong, Jackie Chan (who also directed) performs some of his most ingenious stunts, and pays overt homage to one of his greatest influences, Harold Lloyd. **105m/C VHS, DVD, Wide.** *HK* Jackie Chan, Sammo Hung, Yuen Biao; ***D:*** Jackie Chan; ***W:*** Edward Tang, Jackie Chan; ***M:*** Nicholas Rivera.

Project A: Part 2 **1987** Dragon Ma, the only honest cop in Hong Kong on the high seas at the turn of the century is back with a new set of adventures. In Cantonese with English subtitles. **101m/C VHS.** *HK* Jackie Chan, Maggie Cheung, Carina Lau, David Lam; ***D:*** Jackie Chan; ***W:*** Edward Tang, Jackie Chan.

Project: Alien ✌✌ **1989 (R)** Science fiction fans in search of a good extra-terrestrial flick should avoid this teaser, for it has nothing to do with aliens. As the film begins, Earth is allegedly being attacked by beings from space, and a vast array of scientists, militia and journalists track the aliens. What's actually happening revolves around the testing of deadly biological weapons. Shot in Yugoslavia. **92m/C VHS.** Michael Nouri, Darlanne Fluegel, Maxwell Caulfield, Charles Durning; ***D:*** Frank Shields; ***W:*** Anthony Able.

Project: Eliminator ✌½ **1991 (R)** A group of terrorists kidnap a designer of "smart" weapons, and it's up to a hard-hitting special forces unit to get him back. Filmed in New Mexico. **89m/C VHS, DVD.** David Carradine, Frank Zagarino, Drew Snyder, Hilary English, Vivian Schilling; ***D:*** H. Kaye Dyal; ***W:*** H. Kaye Dyal, Morris Asgar; ***C:*** Gerry Lively; ***M:*** John McCallum.

Project: Genesis ✌✌½ **1993** Pascal and a beautiful Alien Woman are shipwrecked on a desolate planet in the 23rd century. As they watch the worlds around them clash in war, they know it is up to them to create a new beginning at the end of the Universe. **79m/C VHS.** David Ferry, Olga Prokhorova; ***D:*** Philip Jackson; ***W:*** Philip Jackson; ***M:*** Andy McNeill.

Project: Kill! ✌ **1977** Head of a murder-for-hire squad suddenly disappears and his former assistant is hired to track him down dead or alive. **94m/C VHS.** Leslie Nielsen, Gary Lockwood, Nancy Kwan.

Project Metalbeast: DNA Overload ✌✌½ **1994 (R)** A CIA agent, cryogenically frozen for 10 years, becomes the guinea pig when a group of scientists decide to unthaw him for a DNA experiment involving living metallic skin. Too bad he turns into a metal beast by the light of the full moon. Sci-fi take on the werewolf saga. **92m/C VHS.** Kim Delaney, Barry Bostwick; ***D:*** Allessandro DeGaetano; ***W:*** Timothy E. Sabo; ***M:*** Conrad Pope.

Project Moon Base ✌½ **1953** Espionage runs rampant on a spaceship headed by a female officer. Eventually the ship is stranded on the moon. Actually filmed for the TV series "Ring Around the Moon." A cold-war sexist relic. **64m/B VHS, DVD.** Donna (Dona Martel) Martell, Hayden Rourke, Ross Ford, Larry Johns, Herb Jacobs; ***D:*** Richard Talmadge; ***W:*** Robert Heinlein, Jack Seaman; ***C:*** William C. Thompson; ***M:*** Herschel Burke Gilbert. **TV**

Project: Nightmare ✌½ **1985** Seems not all dreams are wish fulfillment, when these nightmares start coming true. **75m/C VHS.** Elly Koslo, Lance Dickson; ***D:*** Donald M. Jones.

Project: Shadowchaser ✌½ **1992 (R)** Action-packed would-be thriller about a billion dollar android who escapes from a top secret government laboratory. Programmed with superhuman strength and no human emotions the android and five terrorists take over a hospital (located in a skyscraper no less). Their hostages include the President's daughter and the terrorists demand a $150 million ransom. With a four-hour deadline the FBI calls in the hospital architect to advise them—only they've got the wrong man—and the android's creator, who wants his creation back—no matter what the cost. A low-budget Terminator clone. **97m/C VHS.** Martin Kove, Meg Foster, Frank Zagarino, Paul Koslo, Joss Ackland; ***D:*** John Eyres.

Project Shadowchaser 3000 ✌½ **1995 (R)** Deep space satellite station collides with a mining vessel carrying a killer android. The seven surviving crew are then hunted by the android as the ship's nuclear core is also threatening to explode. **99m/C VHS.** Frank Zagarino, Sam Bottoms, Christopher Atkins, Musetta Vander, Christopher Neame; ***D:*** John Eyres; ***W:*** Nick Davis; ***M:*** Steve Edwards.

Project Vampire ✌½ **1993** Vampire concocts a serum that will change humans into vampires within three days. His first guinea pig fights to stop the evil from succeeding. **90m/C VHS.** Brian Knudson, Mary-Louise Gemmill, Christopher Cho, Myron Natwick; ***D:*** Peter Flynn.

Project X ✌✌½ **1987 (PG)** A bemused Air Force pilot is assigned to a special project involving chimpanzees. He must decide where his duty lies when he realizes the semi-intelligent chimps are slated to die. **107m/C VHS.** Matthew Broderick, Helen Hunt, William Sadler, Johnny Rae McGhee, Jonathan Stark, Robin Gammell, Stephen Lang, Jean Smart, Dick Miller; ***D:*** Jonathan Kaplan; ***W:*** Stanley Weiser, Lawrence Lasker; ***C:*** Dean Cundey; ***M:*** James Horner.

The Projectionist ✌✌✌ **1971 (PG)** A must-see for movie buffs, Dangerfield made his screen debut in this story about a projectionist in a seedy movie house whose real-life existence begins to blur into the films he continuously watches. Made on a limited budget, this creative effort by Hurwitz was the first film to utilize the technique of superimposition. **84m/C VHS, DVD, Wide.** Rodney Dangerfield, Chuck McCann, Ina Balin, Jara Kohout, Harry Hurwitz, Stephen Phillips, Clara Rosenthal, Jacquelyn Glenn, Robert Staats; ***D:*** Harry Hurwitz; ***W:*** Harry Hurwitz; ***C:*** Victor Petrashevich; ***M:*** Igo Kantor, Erma E. Levin.

Prom Night ✌✌ **1980 (R)** A masked killer stalks four high school girls during their senior prom as revenge for a murder which occurred six years prior. Sequelled by "Hello Mary Lou: Prom Night 2," "Prom Night 3: The Last Kiss," and "Prom Night 4: Deliver Us from Evil." **91m/C VHS, DVD.** *CA* Jamie Lee Curtis, Leslie Nielsen, Casey Stevens, Eddie Benton, Antoinette Bower, Michael Tough, Pita Oliver, David Mucci, Joy Thompson, Mary Beth Rubens; ***D:*** Paul Lynch; ***W:*** William Gray; ***C:*** Robert New; ***M:*** Paul Zaza.

Prom Night 3: The Last Kiss ✌ **1989 (R)** The second sequel, in which the reappearing high school ghoul beguiles a lucky teenager. **97m/C VHS.** Tim Conlon, Cyndy Preston, Courtney Taylor, David Stratton, Dylan Neal, Jeremy Ratchford; ***D:*** Ron Oliver, Peter Simpson; ***W:*** Ron Oliver; ***C:*** Rhett Morita.

Prom Night 4: Deliver Us from Evil ✌ **1991 (R)** Yet another gory entry in the Prom series (one would hope it will be the last). Another group of naive teens decide that they can have more fun at a private party than at the prom. They host the party in a summer home that was once a monastery, but the festive affair soon turns into a night of terror when an uninvited guest crashes the party. For true fans of slasher flicks. **95m/C VHS.** *CA* Nikki DeBoer, Alden Kane, Joy Tanner, Alle Ghadban, James Carver; ***D:*** Clay Borris; ***W:*** Richard Beattie.

The Promise ☙½ *Face of a Stranger* **1979 (PG)** Weepie outdated story about star-crossed lovers Michael (Collins) and Nancy (Quinlan). A car accident leaves Michael comatose and Nancy badly disfigured. Michael's mother (Straight), who loathes Nancy, sees her chance to finally break them up. She offers to pay for Nancy's plastic surgery if she'll leave Michael forever, then Mom tells her son his girlfriend's dead. A year later Nancy, with her new face and new identity, and Michael meet. From the novel by Danielle Steele. **97m/C VHS.** Stephen Collins, Kathleen Quinlan, Beatrice Straight, Laurence Luckinbill, William Prince, Michael O'Hare; ***D:*** Gilbert Cates; ***W:*** Garry Michael White; ***M:*** David Shire.

The Promise ☙☙½ *Das Versprechen* **1994 (R)** Young lovers Konrad (Zoller and Zirner) and Sophie (Harfouch and Becker) find themselves separated by the Berlin Wall after a botched escape attempt in 1961. The estranged lovers meet only four times during the next three decades as they adjust to the systems under which they're forced to live. Somewhat contrived and cliched, this bittersweet romance uses Konrad and Sophie as symbols of the social and political turmoil and triumphs of the divided Germany. Received some criticism from East Germans who found the film's severe portrayal of Communist rule too harsh. Gets points for being the first post-fall film to explore the Wall's legacy. **115m/C VHS.** *GE* Corinna Harfouch, Meret Becker, August Zirner, Anian Zollner, Jean-Yves Gautier, Eva Mattes, Suzanne Uge, Hans Kremer, Pierre Besson, Tina Engel, Otto Sander, Hark Bohm; ***D:*** Margarethe von Trotta; ***W:*** Peter Schneider, Margarethe von Trotta; ***C:*** Franz Rath; ***M:*** Jurgen Knieper.

Promise Her Anything ☙☙ **1966** A widow (Caron) with a baby decides to make her boss (Cummings), a child psychologist who hates kids, her new husband. So she stashes the kid with her upstairs neighbor (Beatty), a would-be filmmaker who earns his living making blue movies. But the filmmaker has romantic designs on the widow and decides the baby may be his way to make a good impression. Beatty isn't very believable in this type of light-romantic comedy and the farcical situations are forced. **98m/C VHS.** *GB* Warren Beatty, Leslie Caron, Robert Cummings, Hermione Gingold, Lionel Stander, Keenan Wynn, Cathleen Nesbitt; ***D:*** Arthur Hiller; ***W:*** William Peter Blatty.

Promise to Murder ☙½ **1956** An early murder-drama episode from the "Climax" TV series. **60m/B VHS.** Peter Lorre, Louis Hayward, Ann Harding.

Promised a Miracle ☙☙½ **1988 (PG)** Based on the true story of a religious couple who sought help for their diabetic son through prayer rather than conventional medical means. Following the boy's death in 1974, the couple were charged with manslaughter. From the non-fiction account "We Let Our Son Die" by Larry Parker. **94m/C VHS.** Rosanna Arquette, Judge Reinhold, Tom Bower, Gary Bayer, Maria O'Brien, Giovanni Ribisi; ***D:*** Stephen Gyllenhaal; ***W:*** David Hill; ***C:*** Thomas Burstyn. **TV**

Promised Land ☙☙☙ *Young Hearts* **1988 (R)** Two high school friends from the rural northwestern U.S. come together several years after graduation under tragic circumstances. Writer Hoffman's semi-autobiographical, disillusioned look at the American Dream was re-discovered by movie goers due to its excellent dramatic performances, notable also as the first film produced by Robert Redford's Sundance Institute. **110m/C VHS.** Kiefer Sutherland, Meg Ryan, Tracy Pollan, Jason Gedrick, Googy Gress, Deborah Richter, Sandra Seacat, Jay Underwood, Oscar Rowland; ***D:*** Michael Hoffman; ***W:*** Michael Hoffman; ***M:*** James Newton Howard.

Promises in the Dark ☙☙½ **1979 (PG)** Drama focusing on the complex relationship between a woman doctor and her 17-year-old female patient who is terminally ill with cancer. Hellman's directorial debut. **118m/C VHS.** Marsha Mason, Ned Beatty, Kathleen Beller, Susan Clark, Paul Clemens, Donald Moffat, Michael Brandon; ***D:*** Jerome Hellman.

Promises! Promises! ☙½ *Promise Her Anything* **1963** Having difficulty getting pregnant, a woman goes on a cruise with her husband. While on board, they meet another couple, all get drunk, and change partners. Of course, both women find themselves pregnant, leaving the paternity in doubt. Famous primarily as the movie Mansfield told "Playboy" magazine she appeared "completely nude" in. **90m/B VHS.** Jayne Mansfield, Marie McDonald, Tommy Noonan, Fritz Feld, Claude Stroud.

The Promoter ☙☙☙ *The Card* **1952** Horatio Alger comedy stars Guinness as an impoverished student who gives himself a surreptitious leg up in life by altering his school entrance exam scores. Outstanding performances enliven this subtle British comedy of morals. **87m/B VHS.** *GB* Alec Guinness, Glynis Johns, Petula Clark, Valerie Hobson, Michael Hordern; ***D:*** Ronald Neame; ***W:*** Eric Ambler.

Pronto ☙☙½ **1997 (R)** Semi-retired bookie Harry Arno (Falk) is forced to head out of Miami when his mobster boss realizes Harry's been skimming. So he takes off for the Italian Riviera with ex-stripper girlfriend Joyce (Headly), while being trailed by doofus U.S. Marshal Raylan Givens (LeGros), who's trying to keep Harry alive so the feds can get his testimony against his gangster cohorts. Falk's gruff, Headly's smart, LeGros is a laugh, and the movie's vivid since it's taken from Elmore Leonard's 1993 novel. **100m/C VHS.** Peter Falk, Glenne Headly, James LeGros, Sergio Castellitto, Bradford Tatum, Walter Olkewicz, Glenn Plummer, Luis Guzman; ***D:*** Jim McBride; ***W:*** Michael Butler; ***C:*** Alfonso Beato; ***M:*** John Altman. **CABLE**

Proof ☙☙☙ **1991 (R)** Directorial debut of Moorhouse tells a tale of manipulation, friendship, and obsessive love between a blind photographer, Martin, his housekeeper, and the young man he befriends. Martin, mistrustful of the world around him, takes photographs as "proof" of the reality of his life. A chance meeting with Andy provides Martin with his "eyes" and the opportunity to expand his world and emotions—something his housekeeper, Celia, would be only too happy to help him with. Unhealthy triangle leads all three to a re-evaluation of their lives. Propelled by terrific performances and enough humor to balance its emotional content. **90m/C VHS.** *AU* Hugo Weaving, Genevieve Picot, Russell Crowe, Heather Mitchell, Jeffrey Walker, Frank Gallacher; ***D:*** Jocelyn Moorhouse; ***W:*** Jocelyn Moorhouse. Australian Film Inst. '91: Actor (Weaving), Director (Moorhouse), Film, Film Editing, Screenplay, Support. Actor (Crowe).

Proof of Life ☙☙½ **2000 (R)** When Alicia's (Ryan) engineer husband (Morse) is kidnapped by anti-government guerrillas in South America, she hires professional negotiator Terry Thorne (Crowe) to get him back. Complications arise when Terry falls for the wife. Complications also arose when Ryan fell for Crowe and her marriage to Dennis Quaid fell apart. Crowe and Ryan subsequently broke up just in time for the marketing push, leaving director Hackford without his two biggest stars to promote the film. Despite the offscreen heat, the movie's a lot better when dealing with the husband's predicament and the rescue operations than when exploring Ryan's angst and the budding romance. **135m/C VHS, DVD, Wide.** Russell Crowe, Meg Ryan, David Morse, David Caruso, Pamela Reed, Anthony Heald, Stanley Anderson, Gottfried John, Alun Armstrong, Michael Kitchen, Margo Martindale, Mario Ernesto Sanchez, Pietro Sibille, Vicky Hernandez, Norma Martinez, Diego Trujillo; ***D:*** Taylor Hackford; ***W:*** Tony Gilroy; ***C:*** Slawomir Idziak; ***M:*** Danny Elfman.

Proof of the Man ☙ **1984** A Japanese co-production about a murder in Tokyo that takes on international importance. **100m/C VHS.** *JP* George Kennedy, Broderick Crawford, Toshiro Mifune.

Prophecy ☙½ **1979 (PG)** A doctor and his wife travel to Maine to research the effects of pollution caused by the lumber industry. They encounter several terrifying freaks of nature and a series of bizarre human deaths. Laughable horror film. **102m/C VHS, DVD, Wide.** Talia Shire, Robert Foxworth, Armand Assante, Victoria Racimo, Richard Dysart, George Clutesi; ***D:*** John Frankenheimer; ***W:*** David Seltzer; ***C:*** Harry Stradling Jr.

The Prophecy ☙☙½ **1995 (R)** Modern variation of "Paradise Lost" carries a heavy load including possession, Native American mythology, and Walken as the archangel Gabriel. Not surprisingly, it stumbles under the weight. Gabriel is at odds with good angel Simon (Stolz) over the souls of humans, a battle that has its final showdown in a small Arizona community and crosses the paths of homicide detective Thomas Dagget (Koteas) and school teacher Katherine (Madsen). Successfully mixes humor and horror, but biblical jargon can lose horror fans just looking for a cheap thrill. Directorial debut of screenwriter Widen. **97m/C VHS, DVD.** Christopher Walken, Eric Stoltz, Elias Koteas, Virginia Madsen, Amanda Plummer, Viggo Mortensen; ***D:*** Gregory Widen; ***W:*** Gregory Widen; ***C:*** Bruce Douglas Johnson, Richard Clabaugh; ***M:*** David Williams.

The Prophecy 2: Ashtown ☙☙½ **1997 (R)** It's post-apocalyptic L.A. and power-hungry fallen angel Gabriel (Walken) returns from hell to stop the creation of a half-human/half-angelic child who's prophesized as the new savior of mankind. Angel Danyael (Wong) is intended as the dad while nurse Valerie (Beals) is the woman chosen as the mother. The good guys get some help from angel Michael (Roberts). Lots of action and good special effects, though viewers who haven't seen the first film may be confused. **83m/C VHS, DVD.** Christopher Walken, Russell Wong, Eric Roberts, Jennifer Beals, Bruce Abbott, Brittany Murphy, Steve Hytner, Glenn Danzig; ***D:*** Greg Spence; ***W:*** Greg Spence, Matt Greenberg; ***C:*** Richard Clabaugh; ***M:*** David Williams. **VIDEO**

The Prophecy 3: The Ascent ☙☙ **1999 (R)** Half-human/half-angel Danyael (Buzzotta) has grown up to be an anti-religious street preacher and is out to destroy new angel, Piriel (Cleverdon). This doesn't sit well with angel Zophael (Spano) who decides to stop him. Walken seems to be having the most fun as he once again appears as Gabriel, who's become content in his mortal guise and with human pleasure. **83m/C VHS, DVD, Wide.** Christopher Walken, Vincent Spano, Brad Dourif, Dave Buzzotta, Steve Hytner, Scott Cleverdon, Kayren Ann Butler; ***D:*** Patrick Lussier; ***W:*** Joel Soisson, Carl DuPre; ***C:*** Nathan Hope. **VIDEO**

The Prophet's Game ☙☙ **1999 (R)** Retired Seattle detective Vincent Swan (Hopper) gets a message from the Prophet, a serial killer that Swan supposedly killed years before. Then new victims turn up in L.A., killed in the Prophet's distinctive manner. So Swan heads south to help with the investigation and figure out is he dealing with a copycat—or did he just kill the wrong man? **107m/C VHS, DVD.** Dennis Hopper, Geoffrey Lewis, Stephanie Zimbalist, Joe Penny, Greg Lauren, Shannon Whirry, Michael Dorn, Don Swayze, Robert Ginty, Sondra Locke; ***D:*** David Worth; ***W:*** Carol Chrest; ***C:*** David Worth. **VIDEO**

The Proposal ☙☙½ **2000 (R)** Moran is an undercover cop who's forced to take on partner Esposito, who has no such experience, because he needs someone to pose as his wife in order to trap crime boss Lang. Only Esposito and Lang are starting to get a little too friendly, so Moran wonders how much she can be trusted. **90m/C VHS, DVD, Wide.** Nick Moran, Jennifer Esposito, Stephen Lang, William B. Davis; ***D:*** Richard Gale; ***W:*** Maurice Hurley; ***C:*** Curtis Petersen; ***M:*** Joseph Conlan.

The Proposition ☙☙½ **1996 (R)** Unless widow Catherine Morgan (Russell) can find the money to pay her late husband's gambling debts, she and her two daughters will be evicted from their Welsh farm. She refuses to take the easy way and marry local sheriff Huw (Lynch), instead making a bargain with his rakish, drunken bastard brother Rhys (Bergin) to drive her cattle to Gloucester market. Huw takes exception to this plan and tries every dirty trick he can to thwart them and naturally, Catherine and Rhys become more than antagonistic allies along the rough journey. **99m/C VHS.** Theresa Russell, Patrick Bergin, Richard Lynch, Richard Harrington, Jennifer Vaughan, Ifan Huw Dafydd, Nick McGaughey, Owen Garmon; ***D:*** Strathford Hamilton; ***W:*** Paul Matthews; ***C:*** David Lewis; ***M:*** Ben Heneghan, Ian Lawson.

The Proposition ☙☙ *Tempting Fate; Shakespeare's Sister* **1997 (R)** Convoluted and clunky story centering on wealthy-but-sterile Boston industrialist Hurt and his feminist writer wife Stowe, who decide to hire a surrogate (Harris) to get Stowe pregnant. But faltering priest Branagh, whom the couple consult, has some concerns. After the surrogate is murdered, the melodrama starts to fly and the movie plays out like a daytime soap opera, complete with dirty little secrets and earth-shaking revelations dropped with the sublety usually reserved for an anvil on Wile E. Coyote. Hurt and Stowe give their characters a little fire, but everybody else seems to be wandering around on their own little acting planet. **115m/C VHS.** Kenneth Branagh, William Hurt, Madeleine Stowe, Blythe Danner, Neil Patrick Harris, Robert Loggia, Josef Sommer, David Byrd; ***D:*** Leslie Linka Glatter; ***W:*** Rick Ramage; ***C:*** Peter Sova; ***M:*** Stephen Endelman.

The Proprietor ☙☙ **1996 (R)** Thinly disguised as a returning-to-your-roots and facing-your-ghosts drama, film is actually a celluloid shrine to its Gallic star, the legendary Moreau, who plays a legendary Gallic novelist, Adrienne Mark. Mark, after residing in New York for 30 years, reclaims her Jewish identity and returns to Paris to buy the home in which she grew up with her mother, who was killed in WWII. Famous for writing the novel "Call Me French," which became a highly acclaimed French film and a current American remake, Mark's primary struggle to come to grips with her mother's death is overshadowed by a bevy of subplots that compete with one another. Young as a sassy and somewhat stereotypical Hollywood producer; Carter as Milly the loyal housekeeper; Waterston, an antique dealer; and Billy, NYC video artist and adoring Mark fan, all add to the confusion. Moreau tries her best to give life to the saintly lead figure, but the coma-inducing sugar level of her character's goodness is overwhelming. Director Merchant's sophomore effort, though well-acted, is a good idea, poorly told. **105m/C VHS.** Jeanne Moreau, Sean Young, Sam Waterston, Nell Carter, Austin Pendleton, Pierre Vaneck, Christopher Cazenove, Jean-Pierre Aumont, Josh Hamilton, Marc Tissot; ***D:*** Ismail Merchant; ***W:*** Jean-Marie Besset, George Trow; ***C:*** Larry Pizer; ***M:*** Richard Robbins.

Prospero's Books ☙☙☙ **1991 (R)** Greenaway's free-ranging adaptation of Shakespeare's "The Tempest" has all his usual hallmarks of the bizarre. Gielgud is the aged Propsero, exiled to a magical island with his innocent daughter Miranda, and 24 beloved books containing the magician's recipe for life, each of which becomes a separate chapter in the film. Greenaway mixes film and high-definition video to create, with cinematographer Sacha Vierny, dazzling visuals that threaten to overwhelm but don't quite, thanks to both Greenaway's skill and the astonishing performance of the then 87-year-old Gielgud. **129m/C VHS.** John Gielgud, Michel Blanc, Erland Josephson, Isabelle Pasco, Tom Bell, Kenneth Cranham, Michael Clark, Mark Rylance; ***D:*** Peter Greenaway; ***W:*** Peter Greenaway; ***C:*** Sacha Vierny; ***M:*** Michael Nyman.

Protector ☙ **1985 (R)** A semi-martial arts cops 'n' robbers epic about the cracking of a Hong Kong-New York heroin route. **94m/C VHS, DVD.** Jackie Chan, Danny Aiello; ***D:*** James Glickenhaus.

Protector ☙☙ *Valentine's Day* **1997 (R)** Undercover cop Jack Valentine (Van Peebles) is supposed to be protecting a witness, who winds up being murdered. The cop is given 10 days to solve the crime or lose his badge. **97m/C VHS, DVD.** Mario Van Peebles, Randy Quaid, Rae Dawn Chong, Ben Gazzara; ***D:*** Duane Clark. **VIDEO**

Proteus 1995 (R) Survivors of a boat wreck wash up on an off-shore oil rig that's actually a secret lab financed by loony millionaire Brinkstone (Bradley), who's seeking immortality. His DNA experiments have led to the creation of a disgusting parasite that travels from body to body. Naturally, the boat survivors also seek to survive this latest health threat. Based on the novel "Slimer" by Harry Adam Knight. **97m/C VHS.** *GB* Doug Bradley, Craig Fairbrass, Toni Barry; *D:* Bob Keen.

Protocol 1984 (PG) A series of comic accidents lead a Washington cocktail waitress into the U.S. State Department's employ as a protocol official. Once there she is used as a pawn to make an arms deal with a Middle Eastern country. Typical Hawn comedy with an enjoyable ending. **100m/C VHS, DVD.** Goldie Hawn, Chris Sarandon, Andre Gregory, Cliff DeYoung, Ed Begley Jr., Gail Strickland, Richard Romanus, Keith Szarabajka, James Staley, Kenneth Mars, Kenneth McMillan, Archie Hahn, Amanda Bearse; *D:* Herbert Ross; *W:* Nancy Meyers, Harvey Miller, Charles Shyer, Buck Henry; *C:* William A. Fraker; *M:* Basil Poledouris.

Prototype 1983 TV revision of the Frankenstein legend has award-winning scientist Plummer as the creator of the first android. Fearful of the use the military branch of government has in mind for his creation, he attempts to steal back his discovery, in this suspenseful adventure. **100m/C VHS.** Christopher Plummer, David Morse, Frances Sternhagen, James Sutorius; *D:* David Greene; *M:* Billy Goldenberg. **TV**

Prototype X29A ½ 1992 (R) The year is 2057 in a desolate, lawless Los Angeles. A research scientist is conducting experiments on a crippled ex-soldier named Hawkins when they suddenly go awry, turning him into a half-man, half-machine robot. Known as Prototype, the creature goes on a hunting and killing spree. Lame "Terminator" & "Robocop" takeoff. **98m/C VHS.** Brenda Swanson, Robert Tossberg, Lane Lenhart; *D:* Phillip J. Roth; *W:* Phillip J. Roth.

The Proud and the Damned *Proud, Damned, and Dead* 1972 (PG) Five Civil-War-veteran mercenaries wander into a Latin American war and get manipulated by both sides. **95m/C VHS.** Chuck Connors, Aron Kincaid, Cesar Romero; *D:* Ferde Grofe Jr.

Proud Men 1987 A cattle rancher and his expatriate son are separated by bittnerness toward each other. Good acting from Heston and Strauss, and good action sequences, but ordinary script. **95m/C VHS.** Charlton Heston, Peter Strauss, Nan Martin, Alan Autry, Belinda Balaski, Red West; *D:* William A. Graham.

The Proud Ones ½ *Les Orgueilleux* 1953 An aristocratic French woman and her husband are traveling through Mexico when he suddenly dies of a mysterious illness. Left penniless in a decaying seaside town, she falls for the local doctor who is mourning the death of his wife. Adaptation of the Satre novel "L'Amour Redempteur." In French with English subtitles. **105m/B VHS.** *FR* Gerard Philipe, Michele Morgan, Victor Manuel Mendoza; *D:* Yves Allegret.

Proud Rebel 1958 A character study of a stubborn widower who searches for a doctor to aid him in dealing with the problems of his mute son, and of the woman who helps to tame the boy. Ladd's real-life son makes his acting debut. **99m/C VHS, DVD.** Alan Ladd, Olivia de Havilland, Dean Jagger, Harry Dean Stanton; *D:* Michael Curtiz; *W:* Lillie Hayward, Joseph Petracca; *C:* Ted D. McCord; *M:* Jerome Moross.

Providence 1977 (R) An interesting score highlights this British fantasy drama of a dying writer envisioning his final novel as a fusion of the people from his past with the circumstances he encounters on a daily basis. The first English-language effort by French director Resnais. **104m/C VHS.** *GB* John Gielgud, Dirk Bogarde, Ellen Burstyn, David Warner, Elaine Stritch; *D:* Alain Resnais; *W:* David Mercer; *C:* Ricardo Aronovich; *M:* Miklos Rozsa. Cesar '78: Art Dir./Set Dec., Director (Resnais), Film, Sound, Writing, Score; N.Y. Film Critics '77: Actor (Gielgud).

Provincial Actors 1979 Ambitious Christopher is the leading actor of a rural theatre troupe, who dreams of moving to the city and becoming a star. But his wife Anna is fed up with his dreams and leaves him and Christopher must make a choice between his career and his marriage. Polish with subtitles. **104m/C VHS.** *PL* Tadeysz Huk, Halina Labonarska, Ewa Dalkowska, Jerzy Stuhr; *D:* Agnieszka Holland.

Provocateur *Agent Provocateur* 1996 (R) Story revolves around the 1994 power struggle in North Korea. Spy Sook Hee (March), with close ties to dictator Kim Il Sung, takes a job as a nanny in South Korea in order to get access to sensitive info from her boss, a U.S. colonel. But her loyalties are torn when she befriends her young charge and then falls in love with the colonel's teenaged son Chris (Brancato). When her true identity is revealed, there's trouble for all. **104m/C VHS.** Jane March, Nick Mancuso, Lillo Brancato, Cary-Hiroyuki Tagawa; *D:* Jim Donovan.

Provoked ½ 1989 What would you do if your husband were being held hostage by a gang of ruthless, but stupid, escaped cons? Well, Maranne actually wants her husband back (maybe 'cause they're newleyweds) and no by-the-book police chief (Jones) is gonna stop her. This bride gets her hands on some automatic weaponry and look out! Shot in eight days with a $130,000 budget. **90m/C VHS.** Cindy Maranne, McKeiver Jones III, Harold W. Jones, Sharon Blair, Bob Fall, Joe Sprosty, Phyllis Durant, Tara Untiedt; *D:* Rick Pamplin; *W:* Tara Untiedt, Steve Pake.

Prowler ½ 1951 Heflin is a cop who responds to a prowler scare and finds the beautiful married Keyes worried about an intruder. He learns she will inherit a lot of money if anything happens to her husband so he seduces her and then "accidentally" kills her husband, supposedly mistaking him for a prowler. Keyes then marries Heflin but when she learns the truth her own life is in danger. Tidy thriller with Heflin doing a good job as the unpredictable villain. **92m/B VHS.** Van Heflin, Evelyn Keyes, Katherine Warren, John Maxwell, Emerson Treacy, Madge Blake, Wheaton Chambers, Sherry Hall, Robert Osterloh, Matt Dorff; *D:* Joseph Losey; *W:* Hugo Butler, Dalton Trumbo; *C:* Arthur C. Miller; *M:* Lyn Murray.

The Prowler *Rosemary's Killer* 1981 (R) A soldier returns from duty during WWII, only to find his girl in bed with another guy. He kills them, and for unclear reasons, returns to the same town 35 years later to kill more people. An effects-fest for Tom Savini. **87m/C VHS.** Vicky Dawson, Christopher Goutman, Cindy Weintraub, Farley Granger, John Seitz, Lawrence Tierney; *D:* Joseph Zito; *W:* Neal Barbera; *M:* Richard Einhorn.

Proximity ½ 2000 (R) William Conroy (Lowe) gets prison time for vehicular manslaughter and learns that the big house is hazardous to his health. Seems the inmates have a bad habit of getting killed and Conroy is next when he learns too much about what's going on. Conroy manages to escape and seeks help to expose the whole sleazy situation. Unfortunately, the movie is really dopey and dull. **86m/C VHS, DVD.** Rob Lowe, James Coburn, Kelly Rowan, Sonya A. Avakian; *D:* Scott Ziehl; *W:* Ben Queen, Seamus Ruane; *M:* Stephen Cullo.

PSI Factor ½ 1980 A civilian researcher working at the NASA space track station observes and records signals coming from planet Serius B. **91m/C VHS.** Peter Mark Richman, Gretchen Corbett, Tommy Martin; *D:* Bryan Trizers; *W:* Quentin Masters.

Psych-Out ½ 1968 A deaf girl searches Haight-Ashbury for her runaway brother. She meets hippies and flower children during the Summer of Love. Psychedelic score with Strawberry Alarm Clock and The Seeds. Somewhere in the picture, Nicholson whangs on lead guitar. **95m/C VHS.** Jack Nicholson, Bruce Dern, Susan Strasberg, Dean Stockwell, Henry Jaglom; *D:* Richard Rush; *W:* Richard Rush.

The Psychic woof! *Copenhagen's Psychic Loves* 1968 An ad executive gains psychic powers after he falls off a ladder and tries to conquer the world. A later effort by gore-king Lewis, notable only for sex scenes inserted by Lewis to make the movie salable. **90m/C VHS.** Dick Genola, Robin Guest, Bobbi Spencer, Carol Saenz, Sandra Wolsfeld; *D:* Herschell Gordon Lewis, James F. Hurley; *C:* Herschell Gordon Lewis; *M:* Vincent Oddo.

The Psychic 1978 (R) A psychic envisions her own death and attempts to alter the prediction. **90m/C VHS.** Jennifer O'Neill, Marc Porel, Evelyn Stewart, Gabriele Ferzetti, Gianni "John" Garko; *D:* Lucio Fulci.

Psychic ½ 1991 (R) A college student with psychic powers believes he knows who the next victim of a demented serial killer will be. The problem is: no one will believe him. And the victim is the woman he loves. **92m/C VHS.** Michael Nouri, Catherine Mary Stewart, Zach Galligan.

Psychic Killer ½ 1975 (PG) A wrongfully committed asylum inmate acquires psychic powers and decides to use them in a deadly revenge. Good cast in cheapie horror flick. **89m/C VHS, DVD, Wide.** Jim Hutton, Paul Burke, Julie Adams, Neville Brand, Aldo Ray, Rod Cameron, Della Reese; *D:* Ray Danton; *W:* Ray Danton, Mikel Angel, Greydon Clark; *C:* Herb Pearl; *M:* William Craft.

Psycho 1960 Hitchcock counted on his directorial stature and broke all the rules in this story of violent murder, transvestism, and insanity. Based on Robert Bloch's novelization of an actual murder, Leigh plays a fleeing thief who stops at the secluded Bates Motel where she meets her death in Hitchcock's classic "shower scene." Shot on a limited budget in little more than a month, "Psycho" changed the Hollywood horror film forever. Followed by "Psycho 2" (1983), "Psycho 3" (1986), "Psycho 4: The Beginning" (1990), and a TV movie. **109m/B VHS, DVD.** Anthony Perkins, Janet Leigh, Vera Miles, John Gavin, John McIntire, Martin Balsam, Simon Oakland, Ted (Edward) Knight, John Anderson, Frank Albertson, Patricia Hitchcock, Alfred Hitchcock; *D:* Alfred Hitchcock; *W:* Joseph Stefano; *C:* John L. "Jack" Russell; *M:* Bernard Herrmann; *V:* Virginia Gregg, Jeanette Nolan. AFI '98: Top 100; Golden Globes '61: Support. Actress (Leigh), Natl. Film Reg. '92.

Psycho ½ 1998 (R) Since Hitchcock's "Psycho" is one of the most famous movies of all time, it would seem redundant to summarize the plot here. Although, redundant is a fitting description of Gus Van Sant's shot-for-shot recreation. Wisely, Van Sant doesn't meddle with a good thing. On the other hand, ya pretty much have to ask, "what's the point?" Significant to the success of the original was that it pushed the envelope in 1960. (A shot of a toilet flushing! A woman taking a shower! Blasphemy!) But by today's standards, "Psycho" is utterly tame. Performances are excellent all around. As talented as Vaughn is, however, the inevitable comparison between him and Anthony Perkins reveals that Vaughn is just too cool for this role. Perkins' Norman Bates was geeky and frail, Vaughn just isn't. As the saying goes, "if it ain't broke, don't fix it." **106m/C VHS, DVD.** Vince Vaughn, Anne Heche, Julianne Moore, William H. Macy, Viggo Mortensen, Robert Forster, Philip Baker Hall, Anne Haney, Chad Everett, Rance Howard, Rita Wilson, James Remar, James LeGros; *D:* Gus Van Sant; *W:* Joseph Stefano; *C:* Christopher Doyle; *M:* Bernard Herrmann. Golden Raspberries '98: Worst Remake/Sequel, Worst Director (Van Sant).

Psycho 2 1983 (R) This sequel to the Hitchcock classic finds Norman Bates returning home after 22 years in an asylum to find himself haunted by "mother" and caught up in a series of murders. In a surprisingly good horror film, Perkins and Miles reprise their roles from the original "Psycho." Perkins went on to direct yet another sequel, "Psycho 3." **113m/C VHS, DVD.** Claudia Bryar, Osgood Perkins II, Anthony Perkins, Vera Miles, Meg Tilly, Robert Loggia, Dennis Franz; *D:* Richard Franklin; *W:* Tom Holland; *C:* Dean Cundey; *M:* Jerry Goldsmith.

Psycho 3 1986 (R) The second sequel to Hitchcock's "Psycho" finds Norman Bates drawn into his past by "mother" and the appearance of a woman who reminds him of this original victim. Perkins made his directorial debut in this film that stretches the plausibility of the storyline to its limits, but the element of parody throughout makes this an entertaining film for "Psycho" fans. **93m/C VHS, DVD.** Anthony Perkins, Diana Scarwid, Jeff Fahey, Roberta Maxwell, Robert Alan Browne, Hugh Gillin, Lee Garlington; *D:* Anthony Perkins; *W:* Charles Edward Pogue; *C:* Bruce Surtees; *M:* Carter Burwell.

Psycho 4: The Beginning 1990 (R) Prequels "Psycho" when, at the behest of a radio talk show host, Norman Bates recounts his childhood and reveals the circumstances that aided in the development of his peculiar neuroses. Stefano wrote the original screenplay and the original score is used, but this doesn't even come close to the original. **96m/C VHS.** Anthony Perkins, Henry Thomas, Olivia Hussey, CCH Pounder, Warren Frost, Donna Mitchell; *D:* Mick Garris; *W:* Joseph Stefano; *C:* Rodney Charters; *M:* Bernard Herrmann, Graeme Revell.

Psycho Beach Party ½ 2000 Busch adapted his own play—a spoof of 60s teen beach movies and psycho/thrillers. Perky teen tomboy Florence (Ambrose) desperately wants to fit into her SoCal ocean lifestyle by becoming the first female accepted into the local surfers who are led by hipster Kanaka (Gibson). The newly christened "Chicklet" has a dark side, however, a separate sultry personality named Anne that she fears is responsible for a series of murders that are thinning out the teen population. Busch plays the investigating officer, and former Kanaka girlfriend, Capt. Monica Stark. **95m/C VHS, DVD.** Lauren Ambrose, Thomas Gibson, Nicholas Brendon, Charles Busch, Kimberly Davies, Matt Keeslar, Nathan Bexton, Buddy Quaid, Beth Broderick, Amy Adams, Danni Wheeler, Kathleen Robertson; *D:* Robert Lee King; *W:* Charles Busch; *C:* Arturo Smith; *M:* Ben Vaughn.

Psycho Cop ½ 1988 Six college undergrads on a weekend retreat are menaced and picked off one at a time by a crazed local cop. **89m/C VHS.** Bobby Ray Shafer; *D:* Wallace Potts.

Psycho Cop 2 ½ 1994 (R) Four buddies plan a raunchy bachelor party, commandeering the company conference room for an after-hours orgy. Only Psycho Cop is on their case. Gore. Rifkin used the pseudonym Rif Coogan. **80m/C VHS.** Bobby Ray Shafer, Barbara Lee (Niven) Alexander, Julie Strain; *D:* Adam Rifkin.

Psycho from Texas *The Butcher* 1983 (R) Quiet Southern town is disrupted by the kidnapping of a wealthy oil man, followed by a string of meaningless murders. **85m/C VHS.** John King III, Candy Dee, Janel King.

Psycho Girls 1986 (R) Very low budget horror flick redeemed by spurts of weird black humor. Crazed woman is released from institution to seek out sister who should have been put away in the first place. She crashes anniversary celebration and, well, let's just say she's not the life of the party. Never released theatrically. **87m/C VHS.** *CA* John Haslett Cuff, Darlene Mignacco, Agi Gallus, Rose Graham, Silvio Oliviero, Michael Hoole, Pier Giorgia DiCicco, Fernne Kane; *D:* Gerard Ciccoritti; *W:* Gerard Ciccoritti, Michael Boekner.

Psycho Sisters ½ 1998 As children, Jackie (North) and Jane (Lynn) witness shocking events that traumatize them into the titular killers. Actually, after seeing so many young women pursued by homicidal maniacs, it's nice that a couple of them get to turn the tables. This low-budget horror has developed a strong cult following. **90m/C DVD, Wide.** J.J. North, Theresa Lynn; *D:* Pete Jacelone; *W:* Pete Jacelone, James L. Edwards; *C:* Timothy Healy.

Psychomania ½ *Violent Midnight* 1963 Semi-limpid mystery thriller about a former war hero and painter who is suspected of being the demented killer stalking girls on campus. To prove his innocence, he tracks the killer himself. **95m/C VHS.** Lee Philips, Shepperd Strudwick, Jean Hale,

Dick Van Patten, Sylvia Miles, James Farentino; *D:* Richard Hilliard.

Psychomania 🦴🦴 *The Death Wheelers* **1973 (R)** A drama of the supernatural, the occult, and the violence which lies just beyond the conventions of society for a group of dead motorcyclists, the Living Dead, who all came back to life after committing suicide with the help of the devil. **89m/C VHS, DVD, Wide.** *GB* George Sanders, Beryl Reid, Nicky Henson, Mary Laroche, Patrick Holt; *D:* Don Sharp; *W:* Arnaud d'Usseau; *C:* Ted Moore.

Psychopath 🦴½ **1968** A film about a modern-day, slightly unhinged, Robin Hood and his escapades, stealing from other thieves and giving to the victimized. **90m/C VHS.** *GB* Klaus Kinski, George Martin, Ingrid Schoeller; *D:* Guido Zurli.

Psychopath 🦴 *An Eye for an Eye* **1973 (PG)** A nutso children's TV personality begins to murder abusive parents. Fairly gory, and definitely not for family viewing. **85m/C VHS.** Tom Basham, Gene Carlson, Gretchen Kanne; *D:* Larry G. Brown; *M:* John Williams.

Psychopath 🦴🦴½ *Twist of Fate* **1997 (R)** D.A. Rachel Dwyer (Amick) needs the help of serial killer Lennox (Mulkey), who targets female law students, in solving another crime. Low on the histrionics and high on the courtroom drama as well as being well-acted. **95m/C VHS, DVD.** Madchen Amick, Chris Mulkey, Bruce Dinsmore, Don Jordan, Lynne Adams, Cas Anvar, Tara Slone, James Bradford; *D:* Max Fischer; *W:* Cameron Kent, William Lee; *C:* Guy Kinkead; *M:* Normand Corbeil. **CABLE**

Psychos in Love woof! **1987** A psychotic murderer who hates grapes of any kind finds the woman of his dreams—she's a psychotic murderer who hates grapes! Together they find bliss—until the plumber discovers their secret! **90m/C VHS.** Carmine Capobianco, Debi Thibeault, Frank Stewart; *D:* Gorman Bechard.

The Psychotronic Man 🦴½ **1991** An innocent man suddenly finds he possesses amazing and dangerous powers, enabling him to control outside events with a thought. **88m/C VHS.** Peter Spelson, Christopher Carbis, Curt Colbert, Robin Newton, Paul Marvel; *D:* Jack M. Sell.

PT 109 🦴🦴 **1963** The WWII exploits of Lieutenant (j.g.) John F. Kennedy in the South Pacific. Part of the "A Night at the Movies" series, this tape simulates a 1963 movie evening, with a Foghorn Leghorn cartoon ("Banty Raids"), a newsreel on the JFK assassination, and coming attractions for "Critic's Choice" and "Four for Texas." **159m/C VHS, Wide.** Cliff Robertson, Ty Hardin, Ty Hardin, Robert (Bobby) Blake, Robert Culp, James Gregory; *D:* Leslie Martinson.

P.T. Barnum 🦴🦴½ **1999** Bio of Phineas Taylor Barnum (Beau Bridges) and his development of "The Greatest Show on Earth." A shopkeeper from Connecticut, P.T. was determined to make his fortune in New York, eventually purchasing Scudder's American Museum and its exhibits, which he turned into a traveling big top event, thanks to his promotional skills. Barnum's zest for work, however, made for a less than happy home life. Beau's son Jordan plays the young Barnum. Filmed in Montreal and Vancouver, Canada. **138m/C VHS.** Beau Bridges, Cynthia Dale, Natalie Radford, Jordan Bridges, George Hamilton, Henry Czerny, Charles Martin Smith, Josh Ryan Evans, R.H. Thomson, Stephanie Morgenstern, Isabelle Cyr, Michelle-Barbara Pelletier, Victoria Sanchez; *D:* Simon Wincer; *W:* Lionel Chetwynd; *C:* Pierre Mignot. **CABLE**

Pterodactyl Woman from Beverly Hills 🦴 **1997 (R)** California housewife Pixie Chandler (D'Angelo) is the victim of an eccentric witch doctor (James) when her paleontologist husband Dick (Wilson) disturbs an ancient burial site and the doc curses Pixie by turning her into a dinosaur. This is the first so-called family release from those madcap Troma people who brought you the Toxic Avenger. **97m/C VHS.** Beverly D'Angelo, Brion James, Brad Wilson, Moon Zappa, Aron Eisenberg; *D:* Philippe Mora; *W:* Philippe Mora; *C:* Walter Bal; *M:* Roy Hay.

Puberty Blues 🦴🦴½ **1981 (R)** Two Australian girls become part of the local surfing scene in order to be accepted by the "in crowd" at their high school. **86m/C VHS.** *AU* Neil Schofield, Jad Capelja; *D:* Bruce Beresford.

Public Access 🦴🦴 **1993 (R)** Newcomer Whiley Pritcher (Marquette) manages to cause trouble in the small town of Brewster when he begins broadcasting a call-in program over a public-access cable station that encourages complaining about the town's problems. Skeletons start falling out of closets, leading to unexpected tragedy. Feature-film directorial debut of Singer. **90m/C VHS, DVD.** Ron Marquette, Dina Brooks, Burt Williams, Charles Kavanaugh, Larry Maxwell, Brandon Boyce; *D:* Bryan Singer; *W:* Bryan Singer, Christopher McQuarrie, Michael Feit Dougan; *C:* Bruce Douglas Johnson; *M:* John Ottman. Sundance '93: Grand Jury Prize.

A Public Affair 🦴½ **1962** Exposes the evils and abuses of collection agencies without even a shred of humor. Certainly gets its point across, but will bore any audience to tears or spontaneous naps. **71m/B VHS.** Myron McCormick, Edward Binns, Harry Carey Jr.

Public Cowboy No. 1 🦴½ **1937** Cattle thieves use a radio, airplanes, and refrigerator trucks in their updated rustling schemes. **54m/B VHS.** Gene Autry, William Farnum.

Public Enemies 🦴🦴 **1996 (R)** It's nefarious Ma Barker (Russell) and her boys on a '30s crime spree that gets even bigger when they hook up with criminal Alvin Karpis (Stallone). But when Ma's lover Arthur (Roberts) dreams up a kidnapping plot, it's a fast road to ruin. **95m/C VHS.** Theresa Russell, Eric Roberts, Frank Stallone, Alyssa Milano, Joseph Lindsey, Richard Eden, James Marsden, Dan Cortese; *D:* Mark L. Lester; *W:* C. Courtney Joyner; *M:* Christopher Franke.

Public Enemy 🦴🦴🦴½ *Enemies of the Public* **1931** Cagney's acting career was launched by this story of two Irish boys growing up in a Chicago shantytown to become hoodlums during the prohibition era. Tom (Cagney) and Matt (Woods) work their way up the criminal ladder, hooking up with molls Kitty (Clarke) and Mamie (Blondell) on their rise to the top. Harlow's a tough blonde who knows how to handle Cagney when he gets tired of Clarke. Considered the most realistic "gangster" film, Wellman's movie is also the most grimly brutal due to its release prior to Hollywood censorship. The scene where Cagney smashes a grapefruit in Clarke's face was credited with starting a trend in abusing film heroines. **85m/B VHS.** James Cagney, Edward (Eddie) Woods, Leslie Fenton, Joan Blondell, Mae Clarke, Jean Harlow, Donald Cook, Beryl Mercer; *D:* William A. Wellman; *W:* Harvey Thew, John Bright, Kubec Glasmon; *C:* Devereaux Jennings. Natl. Film Reg. '98.

The Public Eye 🦴🦴🦴½ **1992 (R)** Underappreciated film noir homage casts Pesci as a crime photographer with an unsuspected romantic streak. It's 1942 in NYC and cynical freelancer Leon "Bernzy" Bernstein's always looking for the perfect shot. Hershey's the recent widow whose nightclub-owner husband had mob ties and decides Pesci would be a likely patsy for helping her out. Hershey seems decorative and the romantic angle never quite develops, but Pesci delivers a rich, low-key performance as the visionary, hard-boiled artist. Climatic mob shootout is cinematic bullet ballet. Based loosely on the career of '40s photog Weegee, who defined New York and its times in his work. **98m/C VHS, Wide.** Joe Pesci, Barbara Hershey, Stanley Tucci, Richard Foronjy, Richard Riehle, Jared Harris, Jerry Adler, Dominic Chianese, Gerry Becker; *D:* Howard Franklin; *W:* Howard Franklin; *M:* John Barry.

Pucker Up and Bark Like a Dog 🦴 **1989 (R)** A young artist and his inspirationally lovely actress girl-friend find themselves in strange and crazy situations. Good cast gives this potential. **94m/C VHS.** Lisa Zane, Jonathan (Jon Francis) Gries, Paul Bartel, Robert Culp; *D:* Paul S. Parco.

Pudd'nhead Wilson 🦴½ **1987** An adaptation of a Mark Twain story about a small-town lawyer who discovers the illicit exchange of a white infant for a light-skinned negro infant by a slave woman. Made as an "American Playhouse" presentation on PBS. **87m/C VHS.** Ken Howard; *D:* Alan Bridges. **TV**

Pueblo Affair 🦴🦴🦴 **1973** A dramatization of the capture of the American spy ship "Pueblo" by the North Koreans, during which time the crew was tortured, imprisoned, and all intelligence documents were confiscated. **99m/C VHS.** Hal Holbrook, Andrew Duggan, Richard Mulligan, George Grizzard, Gary Merrill, Mary Fickett; *D:* Anthony Page. **TV**

Pufnstuf 🦴🦴½ **1970 (G)** Surreal theatrical feature based on the "H.R. Pufnstuff" children's series by Sid and Marty Kroft. Jimmy (Wild) takes his talking flute to Living Island, where objects, plants, and animals can speak and where he meets mayor Pufnstuf, a dragon. But Jack's magic flute is stolen by Witchiepoo (Hayes) who wants to be named "Witch of the Year" at the annual witches convention. **95m/C VHS.** Jack Wild, Billie Hayes, Martha Raye, "Mama" Cass Elliott, Billy Barty; *D:* Hollingsworth Morse; *W:* John Fenton Murray; *C:* Kenneth Peach Sr.; *M:* Charles Fox.

Pulp 🦴🦴½ **1972 (PG)** Caine, playing a mystery writer, becomes a target for murder when he ghostwrites the memoirs of a movie gangster from the 1930s, played deftly by Rooney. **95m/C VHS.** *GB* Michael Caine, Mickey Rooney, Lionel Stander, Lizabeth Scott, Nadia Cassini, Dennis Price, Al Lettieri; *D:* Mike Hodges; *W:* Mike Hodges.

Pulp Fiction 🦴🦴🦴🦴 **1994 (R)** Tarantino moves into the cinematic mainstream with his trademark violence and '70s pop culture mindset intact in this stylish crime trilogy. A day in the life of a criminal community unexpectedly shifts from outrageous, esoteric dialogue to violent mayhem with solid scripting that takes familiar stories to unexplored territory. Offbeat cast offers superb performances, led by Travolta in his best role to date as a hit man whose adventures with partner Jackson tie the seemingly unrelated stories together. Clever, almost gleeful look at everyday life on the fringes of mainstream society. Inspired by "Black Mask" magazine. A special collector's edition includes never-before-seen footage and commentary by Tarantino. **154m/C VHS, DVD, Wide.** Paul Calderon, Bronagh Gallagher, Stephen Hibbert, Angela Jones, Phil LaMarr, Duane Whitaker, Kathy Griffin, John Travolta, Samuel L. Jackson, Uma Thurman, Harvey Keitel, Tim Roth, Amanda Plummer, Maria De Medeiros, Ving Rhames, Eric Stoltz, Rosanna Arquette, Christopher Walken, Bruce Willis, Frank Whaley, Steve Buscemi, Peter Greene, Alexis Arquette, Julia Sweeney, Quentin Tarantino, Dick Miller; *D:* Quentin Tarantino; *W:* Roger Roberts Avary, Quentin Tarantino; *C:* Andrzej Sekula; *M:* Karyn Rachtman. Oscars '94: Orig. Screenplay; AFI '98: Top 100; British Acad. '94: Orig. Screenplay, Support. Actor (Jackson); Cannes '94: Film; Golden Globes '95: Screenplay; Ind. Spirit '95: Actor (Jackson), Director (Tarantino), Film, Screenplay; L.A. Film Critics '94: Actor (Travolta), Director (Tarantino), Film, Screenplay; MTV Movie Awards '95: Film, Dance Seq. (John Travolta/Uma Thurman); Natl. Bd. of Review '94: Director (Tarantino), Film; N.Y. Film Critics '94: Director (Tarantino), Screenplay; Natl. Soc. Film Critics '94: Director (Tarantino), Film, Screenplay.

Pulse 🦴🦴 **1988 (PG-13)** Electricity goes awry in this science-fiction thriller about appliances and other household devices that become super-charged and destroy property and their owners. **90m/C VHS.** Cliff DeYoung, Roxanne Hart, Joey Lawrence, Charles Tyner, Dennis Redfield, Robert Romanus, Myron Healey; *D:* Paul Golding; *C:* Peter Collister; *M:* Jay Ferguson.

Pulsebeat woof! **1985** Flick about warring health club owners. As boring as it sounds unless you're in the mood for lots of on-screen aerobics. If so, rent Jane Fonda instead. Dubbed. **92m/C VHS.** *SP* Daniel Greene, Lee Taylor Allen, Bob Small, Alice Moore, Helga Line, Alex Intriago, Peter Lupus; *D:* Marice Tobias.

The Puma Man woof! **1980** Puma Man is a super hero who must stop the evil Dr. Kobras from using an ancient mask in his attempt to become ruler of the world. Unreleased theatrically in the U.S., this low budget sci-fi/horror mix is so bad one wonders why an actor like Pleasence would sign on. Special effects these days are so extraordinary that the ones employed here are laughable. **80m/C VHS.** *IT* Donald Pleasence, Walter George Alton, Sydne Rome, Miguel Angel Fuentes; *D:* Alberto De Martino.

Pump Up the Volume 🦴🦴½ **1990 (R)** High school newcomer leads double life as Hard Harry, sarcastic host of an illegal radio broadcast and Jack Nicholson soundalike. Anonymously popular with his peers, he invites the wrath of the school principal due to his less than flattering comments about the school administration. Slater seems to enjoy himself as defiant deejay while youthful cast effectively supports. **105m/C VHS, DVD, 8mm.** Christian Slater, Scott Paulin, Ellen Greene, Samantha Mathis, Cheryl Pollak, Annie Ross, Andy Romano, Mimi Kennedy; *D:* Allan Moyle; *W:* Allan Moyle; *C:* Walt Lloyd; *M:* Cliff Martinez.

The Pumpkin Eater 🦴🦴🦴 **1964** British housewife Jo (Bancroft) has seemingly found contentment with her third husband, famous and wealthy writer Jake (Finch), and her eight children. But as Jo struggles to face middle age she discovers Jake is chronically unfaithful and goes into an emotional tailspin. Last film for Hardwicke. Slow-paced film with fine performances; based on the novel by Penelope Mortimer. **110m/C VHS.** *GB* Anne Bancroft, Peter Finch, James Mason, Richard Johnson, Cedric Hardwicke, Maggie Smith, Alan Webb, Eric Porter; *D:* Jack Clayton; *W:* Harold Pinter; *C:* Oswald Morris; *M:* Georges Delerue. British Acad. '64: Screenplay.

Pumpkinhead 🦴🦴½ *Vengeance: The Demon* **1988 (R)** A farmer evokes a demon from the earth to avenge his son's death. When it continues on its murdering rampage, the farmer finds he no longer has any control over the vicious killer. **89m/C VHS, DVD.** Lance Henriksen, John DiAquino, Kerry Remsen, Matthew Hurley, Jeff East, Kimberly Ross, Cynthia Bain, Joel Hoffman, Florence Schauffler, George "Buck" Flower, Tom Woodruff Jr.; *D:* Stan Winston; *W:* Mark Patrick Carducci, Gary Gerani; *C:* Bojan Bazelli; *M:* Richard Stone.

Pumpkinhead 2: Blood Wings 🦴½ **1994 (R)** Five typically stupid teenagers resurrect a demon and the creature goes on a bloodthirsty rampage. His leaves his signature, a calling card in the shape of wings, at each murder scene. **88m/C VHS.** Ami Dolenz, Andrew (Andy) Robinson, Kane Hodder, R.A. Mihailoff, Linnea Quigley, Steve Kanaly, Caren Kaye, Gloria Hendry, Soleil Moon Frye, Mark McCracken, Roger Clinton; *D:* Jeff Burr; *W:* Ivan Chachornia, Constantin Chachornia.

Punch the Clock 🦴🦴 **1990 (R)** Attractive female thief finds her bail bondsman very exciting; he's ready to help her any way he can. **88m/C VHS.** Michael Rogan, Chris Moore, James Lorinz; *D:* Eric L. Schlagman.

Punchline 🦴🦴 **1988 (R)** A look at the lives of stand-up comics, following the career ups-and-downs of an embittered professional funny-man and a frustrated housewife hitting the stage for the first time. Some very funny and touching moments and some not-so-funny and touching as the movie descends into melodrama without a cause. **100m/C VHS, DVD.** Tom Hanks, Sally Field, John Goodman, Mark Rydell, Kim Greist, Barry Sobel, Paul Mazursky, Pam Matteson, George Michael McGrath, Taylor Negron, Damon Wayans; *D:* David Seltzer; *W:* David Seltzer; *C:* Reynaldo Villalobos. L.A. Film Critics '88: Actor (Hanks).

The Punisher 🦴 **1990 (R)** Lundgren portrays Frank Castle, the Marvel Comics anti-hero known as the Punisher. When his family is killed by the mob Castle set his eyes on revenge. Filmed in Australia. **92m/C VHS, DVD.** Dolph Lundgren, Louis Gossett Jr., Jeroen Krabbe, Kim Miyori; *D:* Mark Goldblatt; *W:* Boaz Yakin; *C:* Ian Baker; *M:* Dennis Dreith.

Punk Rock Movie 1978 The musical explosion known as punk rock is documented here in its early days (circa 1977) at the Roxy in England. Includes a look at leading punk rock artists such as the Sex Pistols, the Clash, Slits, and others, and the entire counterculture that was punk. **80m/C VHS.**

Punk Vacation 🦴 1990 A gang of motorcycle mamas terrorize a small town. The usual biker stuff. **90m/C VHS.** Stephen Falchi, Roxanne Rogers, Don Martin, Sandra Bogan; ***D:*** Stanley Lewis.

P.U.N.K.S. 🦴🦴½ 1998 (PG) Preteen Drew (Redwine) and his friends are regularly beaten up by school bullies. Then they realize that evil industrialist Edward Crow (Winkler) has stolen an invention that turns weaklings into hulks and they decide to steal it back. **99m/C VHS.** Randy Quaid, Cathy Moriarty, Henry Winkler, Ted Redwine, Patrick Renna; ***D:*** Sean McNamara. **VIDEO**

Puppet Master 🦴🦴½ 1989 (R) Four psychics are sent to investigate a puppet maker who they think may have discovered the secret of life. Before they know it, they are stalked by evil puppets. Great special effects, not-so-great script. **90m/C VHS, DVD.** Paul LeMat, Jimmie F. Skaggs, Irene Miracle, Robyn Frates, Barbara Crampton, William Hickey, Matt Roe, Kathryn O'Reilly; ***D:*** David Schmoeller; ***W:*** Joseph G. Collodi; ***C:*** Sergio Salvati; ***M:*** Richard Band.

Puppet Master 2 🦴🦴 1990 (R) Puppets on a rampage turn hotel into den of special effects. Less effective string pulling than in original. Long live Pinocchio. **90m/C VHS, DVD.** Elizabeth MacLellan, Collin Bernsen, Greg Webb, Charlie Spradling, Nita Talbot, Steve Welles, Jeff Weston; ***D:*** David Allen; ***W:*** David Pabian; ***C:*** Thomas Denove; ***M:*** Richard Band.

Puppet Master 3: Toulon's Revenge 🦴🦴 1990 (R) Prequel about the origin of the whole gory Puppet Master shebang, set in Nazi Germany. The weapon-hungry Third Reich tries to wrest secrets of artificial life from sorceror Andre Toulon, who sics his deadly puppets on them. Toulon's a good guy here, one of many contradictions in the series. Fine cast, but strictly for the followers. **86m/C VHS, DVD.** Guy Rolfe, Ian Abercrombie, Sarah Douglas, Richard Lynch, Walter Gotell; ***D:*** David DeCoteau; ***W:*** C. Courtney Joyner; ***C:*** Adolfo Bartoli; ***M:*** Richard Band.

Puppet Master 4 🦴🦴 1993 (R) It's the puppets versus the totems, equally loathsome midget creatures who derive their power from the same eternal force as the puppets. No one wants to share and there's lots of gore while they battle for supremacy. **80m/C VHS, DVD.** Gordon Currie, Chandra West, Jason Adams, Teresa Hill, Guy Rolfe; ***D:*** Jeff Burr; ***W:*** Todd Henschell, Steven E. Carr, Jo Duffy, Douglas Aarniokoski, Keith Payson; ***M:*** Richard Band.

Puppet Master 5: The Final Chapter 🦴½ 1994 Greedy Dr. Jennings has come to Bodega Bay Inn to capture the puppets and discover the secret formula for their animation so he can sell it to the highest bidder. But he's not the only threat, it seems the demonic Eyad, a being from another dimension, also wants the secret and has sent his own evil puppet to kill the puppet master and steal their magic. **81m/C VHS, DVD.** Gordon Currie, Chandra West, Ian Ogilvy, Teresa Hill, Nicholas Guest, Willard Pugh, Diane McBain, Kaz Garas, Guy Rolfe; ***D:*** Jeff Burr; ***W:*** Douglas Aarniokoski, Jo Duffy, Todd Henschell, Keith Payson, Steven E. Karr; ***C:*** Adolfo Bartoli; ***M:*** Richard Band.

The Puppet Masters 🦴🦴 *Robert A. Heinlein's The Puppet Masters* 1994 (R) Government official (Sutherland) discovers aliens are taking over the bodies of humans and if he doesn't find a way to stop the parasites they'll soon rule the Earth. Yes, it does sound like "Invasion of the Body Snatchers" but the film is based on Robert A. Heinlein's 1951 novel, written five years before. The parasites are sufficiently yucky but, unfortunately, this adaptation is mediocre and generally wastes a talented cast. **109m/C VHS.** Donald Sutherland, Eric Thal, Julie Warner, Keith David, Will Patton, Richard Belzer, Yaphet Kotto, Dale Dye; ***D:*** Stuart Orme; ***W:*** Terry Rossio, David S. Goyer, Ted Elliott; ***M:*** Colin Towns.

Puppet on a Chain 🦴🦴 1972 (PG) American narcotics officer busts an Amsterdam drug ring and the leader's identity surprises him. Slow-moving thriller based on the Alistair MacLean novel. **97m/C VHS.** *GB* Sven-Bertil Taube, Barbara Parkins, Alexander Knox, Patrick Allen, Geoffrey Reeve; ***D:*** Geoffrey Reeve; ***C:*** Jack Hildyard.

The Puppetoon Movie 1987 (G) A compilation of George Pal's famous Puppetoon cartoons from the 1940s, marking his stature as an animation pioneer and innovator. Hosted by Gumby, Pokey, Speedy Alka Seltzer and Arnie the Dinosaur in newly directed scenes. **80m/C VHS, DVD.** ***D:*** Arnold Leibovit; ***M:*** Buddy (Norman Dale) Baker.

Pups 🦴🦴 1999 Surburban 13-year-old Stevie (Van Hoy) finds his mom's gun, which he shows to equally young girlfriend, Rocky (Barton). Instead of going to school, Stevie impulsively decides to rob a nearby bank, and nearly gets away with it until the cops and the FBI show up. Now the kids have hostages and no clue as to what they're doing, while hostage negotiator Daniel Bender (Reynolds) tries to get a volatile Stevie to listen to reason. **103m/C VHS.** Cameron Van Hoy, Mischa Barton, Burt Reynolds, Darling Narita; ***D:*** Ash; ***W:*** Ash; ***C:*** Carolos Arguello.

The Purchase Price 🦴🦴 1932 After a less than amorous beginning, farmer Brent and mail order bride Stanwyck fall into love and financial despair in this drama bordering on comedy. Good neighbor Landau is willing to help the poor agriculturalist out in exchange for Stanwyck. Tragedy strikes again when Stanwyck's bootlegger ex-boyfriend shows up and further disasters continue to test the couple's commitment. Based on the story "The Mud Lark" by Arthur Stringer. **70m/B VHS.** Barbara Stanwyck, George Brent, Lyle Talbot, Hardie Albright, David Landau; ***D:*** William A. Wellman; ***W:*** Robert Lord.

Pure Country 🦴🦴½ 1992 (PG) An easygoing movie about a familiar subject is held together by the charm of Strait (in his movie debut) and the rest of the cast. Strait plays a country music superstar, tired of the career glitz, who decides to get out and go back to his home in Texas. He falls in love with the spunky Glasser and decides to run his career his own way. Warren is effective as his tough manager and old-time cowboy Calhoun is finely weathered as Glasser's gruff dad. **113m/C VHS, DVD, Wide.** George Strait, Isabel Glasser, Lesley Ann Warren, Rory Calhoun, Kyle Chandler, John Doe, Molly McClure; ***D:*** Christopher Cain; ***W:*** Rex McGee; ***C:*** Rick Bota; ***M:*** Steve Dorff.

Pure Danger 🦴🦴½ 1996 (R) Short order cook Johnny (Howell) and his waitress girlfriend Becky (Linn) stumble upon a bag of diamonds and think all their troubles are over. Wrong—they're just beginning, since some very nasty men want the jewels and don't care who they kill to get them. Howell keeps his directorial debut fast-paced and surprisingly entertaining. **99m/C VHS.** C. Thomas Howell, Teri Ann Linn, Leon, Michael Russo; ***D:*** C. Thomas Howell; ***W:*** William Applegate Jr., John Barmettler; ***C:*** Ken Blakey; ***M:*** K. Alexander Wilkinson.

A Pure Formality 🦴🦴 *Una Pura Formalita; Une Pure Formalite* 1994 (PG-13) Murky psycho-drama finds a disheveled man (Depardieu) winding up at an isolated police station in a nameless country (in the middle of a rainstorm, no less). The Inspector (Polanski) suspects him of a local murder, especially after he claims to be a famous writer named Onoff, yet, can remember nothing. The Inspector wants a confession and spends the night trying to exact one from his guileful suspect. French with subtitles. Film is rated at a much younger level than will possibly understand or enjoy it. **111m/C VHS.** *FR IT* Gerard Depardieu, Roman Polanski, Sergio Rubini; ***D:*** Giuseppe Tornatore; ***W:*** Giuseppe Tornatore, Pascal Quignard; ***C:*** Basco Giurato; ***M:*** Ennio Morricone.

The Pure Hell of St. Trinian's 🦴🦴½ 1961 In this sequel to "Blue Murder at St. Trinian's," a sheik who desires to fill out his harem tries recruiting at a rowdy girls' school. Although it isn't as funny as the first, due to the lack of Alistair Sim, it is still humorous. Followed by "The Great St. Trinian's Train Robbery." Based on the cartoon by Ronald Searle. **94m/B VHS.** *GB* Cecil Parker, Joyce Grenfell, George Cole, Thorley Walters; ***D:*** Frank Launder; ***M:*** Malcolm Arnold.

Pure Luck 🦴½ 1991 (PG) A who-asked-for-it remake of a 1981 Franco-Italian film called "La Chevre." The premise is the same: an accident-prone heiress disappears in Mexico, and her father tries to locate her using an equally clumsy accountant. The nebbish and an attendant tough private eye stumble and bumble south of the border until the plot arbitrarily ends. Pure awful. **96m/C VHS.** Martin Short, Danny Glover, Sheila Kelley, Scott Wilson, Sam Wanamaker, Harry Shearer; ***D:*** Nadia Tass; ***W:*** Herschel Weingrod, Timothy Harris.

Purgatory 🦴 1989 While travelling abroad, two innocent women find themselves unjustly jailed. During their confinement they are tortured and raped. **90m/C VHS.** Tanya Roberts, Julie Pop; ***D:*** Ami Artzi; ***W:*** Paul Aratow.

Purgatory 🦴🦴½ 1999 A group of desperadoes head for what they think is the defenseless town of Refuge, where the sheriff (Shepard) doesn't carry a gun or allow cussing. But the town and its inhabitants are not what they seem and these cowpoke bad guys are in for quite a surprise. **94m/C VHS.** Sam Shepard, Eric Roberts, Randy Quaid, Peter Stormare, Donnie Wahlberg; ***D:*** Uli Edel; ***W:*** Gordon Dawson. **CABLE**

Purlie Victorious 🦴🦴 1963 Presentation of the award-winning Broadway hit, which takes a look at racial integration. **93m/C VHS.** Ossie Davis, Ruby Dee, Godfrey Cambridge, Alan Alda; ***D:*** Nicholas Webster.

The Purple Heart 🦴🦴½ 1944 An American Air Force crew is shot down over Tokyo and taken into brutal POW camps. Intense wartime melodramatics. **99m/B VHS.** Dana Andrews, Richard Conte, Farley Granger, Donald (Don "Red") Barry, Sam Levene, Kevin O'Shea, Tala Birell, Nestor Paiva, Benson Fong, Marshall Thompson, Richard Loo; ***D:*** Lewis Milestone; ***C:*** Arthur C. Miller.

Purple Hearts 🦴½ 1984 (R) Wahl stars as a Navy doctor who falls in love with nurse Ladd against the backdrop of the Vietnam war. Overlong and redundant. **115m/C VHS.** Cheryl Ladd, Ken Wahl, Stephen Lee, Annie McEnroe, Paul McCrane, Cyril O'Reilly; ***D:*** Sidney J. Furie; ***W:*** Sidney J. Furie, Ron Nyswaner; ***M:*** Robert Folk.

The Purple Monster Strikes 🦴🦴 1945 A martian plots to conquer Earth to save his dying planet. Serial in 15 episodes. **188m/B VHS.** Dennis Moore, Linda Stirling, Roy Barcroft; ***D:*** Spencer Gordon Bennet.

Purple Noon 🦴🦴🦴 *Plein Soleil; Lust for Evil* 1960 (PG-13) Don't let the ratings fool you, this isn't teen fodder. The gorgeous Delon stars as opportunistic Tom Ripley, who's hired by the father of his rich, arrogant playboy friend Philippe (Ronet) to persuade him to return home to San Francisco. Instead, Ripley covets the man's yacht, beautiful girlfriend Marge (Laforet), and money, so when Philippe pushes Tom too far he disposes of him and tries to divert police suspicions. Film noir set in the hedonistic Mediterranean sun. Based on the novel "The Talented Mr. Ripley" by Patricia Highsmith, although the ending of novel and film differ greatly. French with subtitles. **118m/C VHS, DVD, Wide.** *FR* Alain Delon, Maurice Ronet, Marie Laforet, Erno Crisa, Billy Kearns; ***D:*** Rene Clement; ***W:*** Rene Clement, Paul Gegauff; ***C:*** Henri Decae; ***M:*** Nino Rota.

Purple People Eater 🦴 1988 (PG) The alien of the title descends to earth to mix with young girls and rock 'n' roll. Based on the song of the same name whose performer, Sheb Wooley, appears in the film. Harmless, stupid fun for the whole family. **91m/C VHS.** Ned Beatty, Shelley Winters, Neil Patrick Harris, Kareem Abdul-Jabbar, Little Richard, Chubby Checker, Peggy Lipton; ***D:*** Linda Shayne.

Purple Rain 🦴🦴½ 1984 (R) A quasi-autobiographical video showcase for the pop-star Prince. Film tells the tale of his struggle for love, attention, acceptance, and popular artistic recognition in Minneapolis. Not a bad film, for such a monumentally egotistical movie. **113m/C VHS, DVD.** Prince, Apollonia, Morris Day, Olga Karlatos, Clarence Williams III; ***D:*** Albert Magnoli; ***W:*** William Blinn; ***C:*** Donald E. Thorin; ***M:*** Michel Colombier. Oscars '84: Orig. Song Score and/or Adapt.

The Purple Rose of Cairo 🦴🦴🦴 1985 (PG) A diner waitress, disillusioned by the Depression and a lackluster life, escapes into a film playing at the local movie house where a blond film hero, tiring of the monotony of his role, makes a break from the celluloid to join her in the real world. The ensuing love story allows director-writer Allen to show his knowledge of old movies and provide his fans with a change of pace. Farrow's film sister is also her real-life sister Stephanie, who went on to appear in Allen's "Zelig." **82m/C VHS, DVD, Wide.** Mia Farrow, Jeff Daniels, Danny Aiello, Dianne Wiest, Van Johnson, Zoe Caldwell, John Wood, Michael Tucker, Edward Herrmann, Milo O'Shea, Glenne Headly, Karen Akers, Deborah Rush; ***D:*** Woody Allen; ***W:*** Woody Allen; ***C:*** Gordon Willis; ***M:*** Dick Hyman. British Acad. '85: Film, Orig. Screenplay; Cesar '86: Foreign Film; Golden Globes '86: Screenplay; N.Y. Film Critics '85: Screenplay.

The Purple Taxi 🦴🦴½ 1977 (R) Romantic drama revolving around several wealthy foreigners who have taken refuge in beautiful southern Ireland. From Michel Deon's bestselling novel. **93m/C VHS.** *FR* Fred Astaire, Charlotte Rampling, Peter Ustinov, Philippe Noiret, Edward Albert; ***D:*** Yves Boisset.

Purple Vigilantes 🦴½ *The Purple Riders* 1938 The Three Mesquiteers uncover a gang of vigilantes. Part of the series. **54m/B VHS.** Robert "Bob" Livingston, Ray Corrigan, Max Terhune.

Pursued 🦴🦴🦴 1947 Excellent performances by Mitchum and Wright mark this suspenseful Western drama of a Spanish-American war veteran in search of his father's killer. **105m/B VHS.** Teresa Wright, Robert Mitchum, Judith Anderson, Dean Jagger, Alan Hale, Harry Carey Jr., John Rodney; ***D:*** Raoul Walsh; ***C:*** James Wong Howe; ***M:*** Max Steiner.

Pursuit 🦴🦴🦴 1972 A terrorist threatens to release a toxic nerve gas throughout a city hosting a political convention. Tension mounts as federal agents must beat the extremists' countdown to zero. Based on the novel by Crichton. **73m/C VHS.** Ben Gazzara, E.G. Marshall, Martin Sheen, Joseph Wiseman, William Windom; ***D:*** Michael Crichton; ***M:*** Jerry Goldsmith.

Pursuit 🦴🦴 1990 (R) A mercenary comes out of retirement to join a renegade team recovering stolen gold. But they turn on him, stealing the treasure and taking a hostage. Now he must track them down, or there's no movie. **94m/C VHS.** James Ryan, Andre Jacobs; ***D:*** John H. Parr.

The Pursuit of D.B. Cooper 🦴🦴 1981 (PG) Based on an actual hijacking that occurred on Thanksgiving Eve in 1971 in which J.R. Meade (alias D.B. Cooper) parachuted out of an airliner with $200,000 of stolen money. Although his fate and whereabouts have remained a mystery, this story speculates about what may have happened. **100m/C VHS.** Robert Duvall, Treat Williams, Kathryn Harrold, Ed Flanders; ***D:*** Roger Spottiswoode; ***C:*** Harry Stradling Jr.; ***M:*** James Horner.

The Pursuit of Happiness 🦴🦴½ 1970 (PG) An idealistic man is convicted of manslaughter after accidentally running down a woman. Once in prison, he's faced with the decision to try to escape. **85m/C VHS.** Michael Sarrazin, Arthur Hill, E.G. Marshall, Barbara Hershey, Robert Klein; ***D:*** Robert Mulligan.

Pursuit of the Graf Spee 🦴🦴½ *The Battle of the River Plate* 1957 Three small British ships destroy the mighty Graf Spee, a WWII German battleship. **106m/C VHS.** *GB* Anthony Quayle, Peter Finch, Ian Hunter; ***D:*** Michael Powell.

Pursuit to Algiers 🦴🦴½ **1945** The modernized Holmes and Watson guard over the King of fictional Rovenia during a sea voyage, during which assassins close in. **65m/B VHS.** Basil Rathbone, Nigel Bruce, Martin Kosleck, Marjorie (Reardon) Riordan, Rosalind Ivan, John Abbott; ***D:*** Roy William Neill.

Pushed to the Limit 🦴½ **1992 (R)** Harry Lee, the most feared gangster in Chinatown, is about to meet his match in martial-arts queen Lesseos. She's out for revenge when she learns that Lee is responsible for her brother's murder but first she must get by Lee's lethal bodyguard, the equally skilled Inga. **88m/C VHS.** Mimi Lesseos.

Pusher 🦴🦴 **1996** Violent thriller was the directorial debut of 24-year-old Refn. Frank (Bodnia) and his buddy Tonny (Mikkelsen) sell heroin in Copenhagen. Their drug supplier is a Serbian gangster named Milo (Buric), to whom Frank owes money. Things get worse when Frank dumps his latest supply before being arrested—Milo warns him if he doesn't pay his debts in the next couple of days, he's a dead man. The more Frank tries to get the money, the worse things get for him. Danish with subtitles. **105m/C VHS, DVD, Wide.** *DK* Kim Bodnia, Zlatko Buric, Mads Mikkelsen, Laura Drasbaek, Slavko Labovic, Lisbeth Rasmussen; ***D:*** Nicolas Winding Refn; ***W:*** Nicolas Winding Refn, Jens Dahl; ***C:*** Morten Soborg; ***M:*** Povl Kristian Mortensen.

Pushing Hands 🦴🦴½ **1992** Aging tai chi master Mr. Chu (Lung) leaves Beijing to live with his son Alex (Wang) and daughter-in-law Martha (Snyder) in suburban New York. High-strung Martha doesn't understand her tranquilly stubborn father-in-law, nor does Chu find disposable American society much to his liking. Naturally, and slowly, some accomodations are made. The title is a tai chi reference to keeping your opponent off-balance while maintaining your own equilibrium. Director Lee's debut feature is also the first in his trilogy of family films—followed by the more accomplished "The Wedding Banquet" and "Eat Drink Man Woman." English and Mandarin Chinese with subtitles. **100m/C VHS, DVD.** Sihung Lung, Deb Snyder, Bo Z. Wang, Lai Wang; ***D:*** Ang Lee; ***W:*** Ang Lee; ***C:*** Jong Lin; ***M:*** Xiao-Song Qu.

Pushing Tin 🦴🦴🦴 **1999 (R)** Nick (Cusack) and Russell (Thornton) are rival air traffic controllers at the Long Island tower that oversees New York's three main airports (JFK, La Guardia, and Newark). Nick is a cool professional and a family man, with stay-at-home wife Connie (Blanchett) and two kids. Russell is a cowboy whose wife Mary (Jolie)is young, wild, and usually drunk. The guys' rivalry at work is intensified when Nick sleeps with Mary and his paranoia and guilt get to him. The technical and journalistic aspects (it's based on a New York Times article) of the tower scenes get things started in surprisingly exciting fashion, and the four leads keep the intensity going with excellent performances despite some script lapses and questionable plot devices at the end. **124m/C VHS, DVD.** John Cusack, Billy Bob Thornton, Cate Blanchett, Angelina Jolie, Vicki Lewis, Jake Weber, Kurt Fuller, Matt Ross, Jerry Grayson, Michael Willis; ***D:*** Mike Newell; ***W:*** Glen Charles, Les Charles; ***C:*** Gale Tattersall; ***M:*** Anne Dudley.

Puss 'n Boots **1984** From "Faerie Tale Theatre" comes the story of a cat who makes his poor master a rich landowning nobleman. **60m/C VHS.** Ben Vereen, Gregory Hines; ***D:*** Robert Iscove. **CABLE**

Putney Swope 🦴🦴🦴 **1969 (R)** Comedy about a token black ad man mistakenly elected Chairman of the board of a Madison Avenue ad agency who turns the company upside-down. A series of riotous spoofs on commercials is the highpoint in this funny, though somewhat dated look at big business. **84m/B VHS, DVD.** Arnold Johnson, Laura Greene, Stanley Gottlieb, Mel Brooks; ***D:*** Robert Downey; ***W:*** Robert Downey; ***C:*** Gerald Cotts; ***M:*** Charles Cura.

Puzzle 🦴🦴½ **1978** Franciscus searches for the urn that contains the remains of Buddha but instead finds danger and intrigue. **90m/C VHS.** *AU* James Franciscus, Wendy Hughes, Robert Helpmann, Peter Gwynne, Gerald Kennedy, Kerry McGuire; ***D:*** Gordon Hessler. **TV**

Pygmalion 🦴🦴🦴½ **1938** Oscar-winning film adaptation of Shaw's play about a cockney flower-girl who is transformed into a "lady" under the guidance of a stuffy phonetics professor. Shaw himself aided in writing the script in this superbly acted comedy that would be adapted into the musical, "My Fair Lady," first on Broadway in 1956 and for the screen in 1964. **96m/B VHS, DVD.** *GB* Leslie Howard, Wendy Hiller, Wilfred Lawson, Marie Lohr, Scott Sunderland, David Tree, Everley Gregg, Leueen McGrath, Jean Cadell, Eileen Beldon, Frank Atkinson, O.B. Clarence, Esme Percy, Violet Vanbrugh, Iris Hoey, Viola Tree, Irene Browne, Kate Cutler, Cathleen Nesbitt, Cecil Trouncer, Stephen Murray, Wally Patch, H.F. Maltby; ***D:*** Anthony Asquith, Leslie Howard; ***W:*** W.P. Lipscomb, Anatole de Grunwald, Cecil Lewis, Ian Dalrymple, George Bernard Shaw; ***C:*** Harry Stradling Sr. Oscars '38: Screenplay; Venice Film Fest. '38: Actor (Howard).

Pyrates 🦴 **1991 (R)** Real life husband-wife team of Bacon and Sedgwick try to provide fireworks as hot, hot lovers in the forgettable one. For the price of this one you can buy a newspaper and chewing gum instead. Use both at the same time and you'll be ahead of everyone involved in this senseless hoot. **98m/C VHS.** Kevin Bacon, Kyra Sedgwick, Bruce Payne, Kristin Dattilo-Hayward; ***D:*** Noah Stern.

A Pyromaniac's Love Story 🦴🦴 **1995 (PG)** Offbeat tale of romance has a neigborhood bakery burning down and every major character confessing to the crime. Earnest working stiffs, snotty rich kids, and kindly old shop owners all have really confusing reasons for wanting to take the heat, most of which have to do with unrequited love. At times charming, but ultimately too whimsical for its own good. The quirky characters and goofy plot twists sabotage any attempt to ignite much interest. **99m/C VHS.** John Leguizamo, Sadie Frost, William Baldwin, Erika Eleniak, Michael Lerner, Joan Plowright, Armin Mueller-Stahl, Richard Crenna; ***D:*** Joshua Brand; ***W:*** Morgan Ward; ***C:*** John Schwartzman; ***M:*** Rachel Portman.

Python 🦴½ **2000 (R)** Intelligence organization develops a perfect weapon in a gigantic python. Of course, the government screws up, the snake gets loose, and there's hell to pay. **90m/C VHS, DVD, Wide.** Robert Englund, Casper Van Dien, Jenny McCarthy, Wil Wheaton, Frayne Rosenoff; ***D:*** Richard Clabaugh; ***W:*** Chris Neal, Gary Hershberger, Paul J.M. Bogh; ***C:*** Patrick Rousseau; ***M:*** David J. Nelsen. **VIDEO**

Python Wolf 🦴🦴 *C.A.T. Squad: Python Wolf* **1988 (R)** It's non-stop action in South Africa as a counter-terrorist group sets out to thwart a drug smuggler's plans to export plutonium. As usual, intense pacing from director Friedkin. Sequel to "C.A.T. Squad" (1986). **100m/C VHS.** Joe Cortese, Jack Youngblood, Steve James, Deborah Van Valkenburgh, Miguel Ferrer, Alan Scarfe; ***D:*** William Friedkin; ***M:*** Ennio Morricone. **TV**

The Pyx 🦴🦴🦴 *The Hooker Cult Murders* **1973 (R)** Canadian suspense thriller about the murder of a prostitute with satanic overtones. Poice sergeant investigates the crime and enters a world of devil worship and decadence. Based on the novel by John Buell. **111m/C VHS.** *CA* Karen Black, Christopher Plummer, Donald Pilon; ***D:*** Harvey Hart.

Q & A 🦴🦴 **1990 (R)** Semi-taut thriller with Nolte playing a totally corrupt, hair-trigger cop trying to make his murder of a drug dealer look like self-defense. Assigned to the case is an ex-cop turned assistant DA (Hutton) who's supposed to sweep the case under the rug. Then he finds out another dealer (Assante) is a witness and he happens to be romancing Hutton's former girlfriend (film debut of director Lumet's daughter). Lots of violence and raw language. **132m/C VHS, DVD.** Dominic Chianese, Nick Nolte, Timothy Hutton, Armand Assante, Patrick O'Neal, Lee Richardson, Luis Guzman, Charles S. Dutton, Jenny Lumet, Paul Calderon, Fyvush Finkel; ***D:*** Sidney Lumet; ***W:*** Sidney Lumet; ***C:*** Andrzej Bartkowiak; ***M:*** Ruben Blades.

Q Ships 🦴🦴½ **1928** Silent German drama about a submarine commander who has inner conflicts with his country's war effort. Uses actual WWI footage. **78m/B VHS.** *GE* J.P. Kennedy, Roy Travers, Johnny Butt, Philip Hewland; ***D:*** Geoffrey Barkas, Michael Barringer.

Q (The Winged Serpent) 🦴🦴🦴 *Q; The Winged Serpent* **1982 (R)** A cult of admirers surrounds this goony monster flick about dragonlike Aztec god Quetzlcoatl, summoned to modern Manhattan by gory human sacrifices, and hungry for rooftop sunbathers and construction teams. Direction and special effects are pretty ragged, but witty script helps the cast shine, especially Moriarty as a lowlife crook who's found the beast's hidden nest. **92m/C VHS, DVD, Wide.** Michael Moriarty, Candy Clark, David Carradine, Richard Roundtree, Malachy McCourt, James Dixon, Eddie Jones, Bruce Carradine, Tony Page, Fred J. Scollay, Mary Louise Weller; ***D:*** Larry Cohen; ***W:*** Larry Cohen; ***C:*** Fred Murphy; ***M:*** Robert O. Ragland.

QB VII 🦴🦴🦴½ **1974** A knighted physician brings a suit for libel against a novelist for implicating him in war crimes. Hopkins as the purportedly wronged doctor and Gazzara as the writer are both superb. Ending is stunning. Adapted from the novel by Leon Uris. **313m/C VHS, DVD.** Anthony Hopkins, Ben Gazzara, Lee Remick, Leslie Caron, Juliet Mills, John Gielgud, Anthony Quayle; ***D:*** Tom Gries; ***W:*** Edward Anhalt; ***M:*** Jerry Goldsmith. **TV**

Quackser Fortune Has a Cousin in the Bronx 🦴🦴🦴 *Fun Loving* **1970 (R)** An Irish fertilizer salesman meets an exchange student from the U.S., who finds herself attracted to this unlearned, but not unknowing, man. An original love story with drama and appeal. **88m/C VHS, DVD, Wide.** *IR* Gene Wilder, Margot Kidder, Eileen Colgan, May Ollis, Seamus Ford, Danny Cummins, Liz Davis; ***D:*** Waris Hussein; ***W:*** Gabriel Walsh; ***C:*** Gilbert Taylor; ***M:*** Michael Dress.

Quadrophenia 🦴🦴🦴 **1979 (R)** Pete Townshend's excellent rock opera about an alienated youth looking for life's meaning in Britain's music scene circa 1963. Jimmy (Daniels) and his pals are Mods who brawl with their rivals, the Rockers. Music by The Who is powerful and apt. Fine performance by Sting in his acting debut as The Ace Face. **115m/C VHS, DVD, Wide.** *GB* Phil Daniels, Mark Wingett, Philip Davis, Leslie Ash, Sting, Garry Cooper, Gary Shail, Toyah Willcox, Trevor Laird, Ray Winstone; ***D:*** Franc Roddam; ***W:*** Franc Roddam, Martin Stellman, Dave Humphries, Pete Townshend; ***C:*** Brian Tufano; ***M:*** John Entwhistle, Pete Townshend.

Quake 🦴½ **1992 (R)** Railsback stars as a stalker who takes advantage of the 1990 San Franscisco earthquake to finally obtain the woman of his dreams. A surveillance expert, he's after a beautiful lawyer (Anderson) and when the earthquake leaves her trapped he rushes to rescue her—only to hold her captive himself. **83m/C VHS.** Steve Railsback, Erika Anderson, Eb Lottimer, Dick Miller; ***D:*** Louis Morneau; ***W:*** Mark Evan Schwartz.

Quality Street 🦴🦴 **1937** English lovers Tone and Hepburn are separated when he leaves to fight in the Napoleonic Wars. When Tone returns years later, he's forgotten his erstwhile heartthrob. He also fails to recognize that the 16-year old coquette who's caught his eye is his old beloved in disguise. Cast works hard to overcome the absurd premise, based on the play by Sir James Barrie. **84m/B VHS.** Katharine Hepburn, Franchot Tone, Fay Bainter, Eric Blore, Cora Witherspoon, Estelle Winwood, Florence Lake, Bonita Granville; ***D:*** George Stevens; ***W:*** J.M. Barrie.

Quarantine 🦴🦴½ **1989 (R)** Quarantine camps for carriers of a fatal virus are the serious measures taken by the nation. The solution is clear to a rebel and an inventor; all must be liberated or exterminated. **92m/C VHS.** Beatrice Boepple, Garwin Sanford, Jerry Wasserman, Charles Wilkinson; ***D:*** Charles Wilkinson; ***W:*** Charles Wilkinson.

The Quarrel 🦴🦴½ **1993** Chaim Kovler is a New York poet visiting Montreal in 1948. In a park he notices a group of Orthodox Jews and discovers one is his childhood friend Hersh. Fifteen years earlier their friendship broke over Chaim's decision to give up the religious life for his writing. Having lost their families to the Holocaust in Poland, both men have immigrated to new lives in North America. They immediately pick up their quarrel over religious faith and its value, particularly in light of the Holocaust. The two characters serve too much as careful ideologues to be compelling and the story turns cloyingly sentimental. Based on a short story by Yiddish writer Chaim Grade. **88m/C VHS, DVD.** *CA* Saul Rubinek, R.H. Thomson, Arthur Grosser; ***D:*** Eli Cohen; ***W:*** David Brandes; ***M:*** William Goldstein.

The Quarry 🦴🦴 **1998** A nameless fugitive (Lynch) accepts a ride from a minister, whom he accidentally kills. He takes over the man's identity and possessions and journeys to the minister's new posting in a nearby isolated South African town. When his goods are in turn stolen by a poor young black man, Valentine, the town's racist white police chief not only arrests Valentine for the theft but links him to the murder when the minister's body is discovered. The original fugitive is consumed by guilt but will justice prevail? Based on the novel by Damon Galgut. English and Afrikaans with subtitles. **112m/C VHS, DVD, Wide.** *SA* John Lynch, Serge-Henri Valcke, Jonny Phillips, Oscar Petersen, Jody Abrahams, Sylvia Esau; ***D:*** Marion Hansel; ***W:*** Marion Hansel; ***C:*** Bernard Lutic; ***M:*** Takashi Kako.

Quarterback Princess 🦴🦴 **1985** Workaday telling of the real-life girl who goes out for football and becomes homecoming queen. Heartwarming, if you like that kinda stuff, but not exciting, except for the early appearances of such '90s stars as Helen Hunt (as said quarterback), Daphne Zuniga as her sister, and Tim Robbins as a teammate. **96m/C VHS.** Helen Hunt, Don Murray, John Stockwell, Barbara Babcock, Daphne Zuniga, Kathleen Wilhoite, Tim Robbins; ***D:*** Noel Black. **TV**

Quartet 🦴🦴🦴 **1981 (R)** A young French woman is taken in by an English couple after her husband goes to prison. The husband seduces her, and she becomes trapped emotionally and socially. Superbly acted, claustrophobic drama based on a Jean Rhys novel. **101m/C VHS.** *GB FR* Isabelle Adjani, Alan Bates, Maggie Smith, Anthony (Corlan) Higgins; ***D:*** James Ivory; ***W:*** Ruth Prawer Jhabvala. Cannes '81: Actress (Adjani).

Quartier Mozart 🦴🦴 **1992** Sexual farce presenting the assimilation of African American pop-culture into African traditions. A local sorceress uses witchcraft to give Queen of the 'Hood a first-hand look at sexual politics. The young girl enters the body of a boy struggling to find his place in the male hierarchy established by neighborhood Casanovas. In French with English subtitles. **80m/C VHS.** ***D:*** Jean-Pierre Bekolo.

Quatermass 2 🦴🦴🦴 *Enemy from Space* **1957** In the well made sequel to "Quatermass Experiment," (also known as "The Creeping Unknown") Professor Quatermass battles blobs and brainwashed zombies to rescue government officials whose bodies have been invaded by aliens. "Five Million Years to Earth" concluded the trilogy. **84m/B VHS, DVD, Wide.** *GB* Brian Donlevy, John Longden, Sidney James, Bryan Forbes, William Franklyn, Vera Day, John Van Eyssen, Michael Ripper, Michael Balfour; ***D:*** Val Guest; ***W:*** Val Guest, Nigel Kneale; ***C:*** Gerald Gibbs; ***M:*** James Bernard.

Quatermass and the Pit 🦴🦴½ **1958** From the original BBC production. Professor Quatermass is up to his ears in trouble as a Martian spacecraft is found by subway workers. Not long after a monster stalks the streets of London. Remade cinematically in 1968 as "Five Million Years to Earth." **180m/B VHS.** *GB* Andre Morell, Cec Linder.

Quatermass Conclusion ☙☙ **1979** An elderly British scientist comes out of retirement to stop an immobilizing death ray from outer space from destroying Earth. Edited version of a TV miniseries continues earlier adventures of Quatermass on film and television. **105m/C VHS.** *GB* John Mills, Simon MacCorkindale, Barbara Kellerman, Margaret Tyzack; ***D:*** Piers Haggard. **TV**

The Quatermass Experiment ☙☙☙ *The Creeping Unknown* **1956** Excellent British production about an astronaut who returns to Earth carrying an alien infestation that causes him to turn into a horrible monster. Competent acting and tense direction. Followed by "Enemy From Space." **78m/B VHS.** *GB* Brian Donlevy, Margia Dean, Jack Warner, Richard Wordsworth; ***D:*** Val Guest; ***M:*** James Bernard.

Quatorze Juliet ☙☙½ **1932** A taxi driver and a flower girl meet on Bastille Day and fall in love. When he becomes involved with gangsters, she steers him back to virtue in this minor French relic from director Clair. **85m/B VHS.** *FR* Anabella Rigaud, Jorge (George) Rigaud; ***D:*** Rene Clair.

Que Viva Mexico ☙☙☙ *Da Zdravstvuyet Meksika* **1932** Eisenstein's grand unfinished folly on the history of Mexico, reconstructed and released in 1979 by his protege, Grigori Alexandrov. Divided into four sections: "Sandunga" covers the Tehuantepec jungles and its inhabitants; "Manguei" is about a peasant and his bride; "Fiesta" devotes itself to bullfighting and romance; and "Soldadera" depicts the 1910 Mexican revolution through frescoes. Along with "Greed" and "Napoleon," it remains as one of cinema's greatest irrecoverable casualties. Russian narration with English subtitles. **85m/B VHS, DVD.** *RU* ***D:*** Sergei Eisenstein; ***W:*** Sergei Eisenstein, Grigori Alexandrov; ***C:*** Eduard Tisse.

Queen ☙☙☙ **1993** Epic miniseries from Pulitzer Prize-winner Alex Haley chronicles the life of his paternal great-grandmother, who bore a baby girl, Queen, to her white slave master. At the heart is Queen's quest for identity as she experiences unique problems due to her mixed race. She finally finds love with a ferry operator (Glover) whose role is powerful but unfortunately brief. It is this union that produces Alex's father, Simon. Although Haley died during production, he had spent considerable time sharing his vision with the staff, who also worked with him on the original "Roots." Good casting and a nice interpretation of Haley's tale is above average. Worth a watch. **360m/C VHS.** Halle Berry, Ann-Margret, Jasmine Guy, Timothy Daly, Danny Glover, Madge Sinclair, Martin Sheen, Paul Winfield, Ossie Davis, Raven-Symone, Victor Garber, Lonette McKee, Sada Thompson, Elizabeth Wilson; ***D:*** John Erman; ***W:*** David Stevens. **TV**

Queen Bee ☙☙½ **1955** Crawford is at her manipulative best as Southern belle Eva Phillips, married to wealthy Georgia mill owner Avery (Sullivan). The ruthless Eva is despised by her bitter, tippling husband who finds a chance at romance when cousin Jennifer (Marlow) comes to visit. Naturally, Eva can't stand any competition, though she doesn't care about Avery, and tries to break up the duo even as she seeks to renew her own affair with a former lover (Ireland). Based on the novel by Edna Lee. **94m/B VHS, DVD, Wide.** Joan Crawford, Barry Sullivan, John Ireland, Lucy Marlow, Betsy Palmer, Fay Wray; ***D:*** Ranald MacDougall; ***W:*** Ranald MacDougall; ***C:*** Charles B(ryant) Lang Jr.; ***M:*** George Duning.

Queen Christina ☙☙☙½ **1933** A stylish, resonant star vehicle for Garbo, portraying the 17th-century Swedish queen from ascension to the throne to her romance with a Spanish ambassador. Alternately hilarious and moving, it holds some of Garbo's greatest and most memorable moments. Gilbert's second to last film and his only successful outing after the coming of sound. **101m/B VHS.** Greta Garbo, John Gilbert, Lewis Stone, Sir C. Aubrey Smith, Ian Keith, Reginald Owen, Elizabeth Young; ***D:*** Rouben Mamoulian; ***C:*** William H. Daniels.

Queen for a Day ☙☙½ *Horsie* **1951** Three differing vignettes, based on a rather notorious radio and TV game show of the time, in which "deserving" (or sufficiently pathetic) working-class women were rewarded for their selflessness. Part one concerns a perfect suburban family whose son contracts polio. Part two has a teen spooking his immigrant parents by working as a carnival high diver to earn college cash. The finale is a Dorothy Parker farce about a homely but kindhearted nurse caring for the child of an unappreciative couple. So popular was this segment that the film was retitled after the main character. Overall, not bad considering the source. **107m/B VHS.** Phyllis Avery, Darren McGavin, Tristram Coffin, Adam Williams, Tracey Roberts, Jack Bailey, Jim Morgan, Fort Pearson; ***D:*** Arthur Lubin.

Queen Kelly ☙☙☙ **1929** The popularly known, slapdash version of von Stroheim's famous final film, in which an orphan goes from royal marriage to white slavery to astounding wealth. Never really finished, the film is the edited first half of the intended project, prepared for European release after von Stroheim had been fired. Even so, a campy, extravagant and lusty melodrama. Silent. **113m/B VHS, 8mm.** Gloria Swanson, Walter Byron, Seena Owen, Tully Marshall, Madame Sul Te Wan; ***D:*** Erich von Stroheim; ***W:*** Erich von Stroheim; ***C:*** Paul Ivano, Gordon Pollock.

Queen Margot ☙☙☙½ *La Reine Margot* **1994 (R)** Blood-soaked period of French history is duly rendered on screen in big-budget costume epic. Beautiful Catholic Princess Marguerite de Valois (Adjani), is the pawn of her devious mother, the widowed queen Catherine de Medici (Lisi). Mom skillfully manipulates unstable son Charles IX (Anglade), the nominal ruler of 1570s France, while she plots to marry Margot off to Protestant Henri de Navarre (Auteuil). Margot is contemptuous of her new husband, preferring to find her amatory amusements in the Paris streets, where she takes a handsome lover de la Mole (Perez). But both Margot and Henri are united against the Queen when Catherine's minions order the murder of the rival Huguenots—a notably violent affair known as the St. Bartholomew's Day Massacre. The history's confusing, the violence graphic, the acting flamboyant, and the visuals top-notch. Based on the novel by Alexandre Dumas. French with subtitles; originally released at 161 minutes. **135m/C VHS.** *FR* Isabelle Adjani, Daniel Auteuil, Virna Lisi, Jean-Hugues Anglade, Vincent Perez, Pascal Greggory, Miguel Bose, Dominique Blanc, Claudio Amendola, Asia Argento, Julien Rassam, Jean-Claude Brialy; ***D:*** Patrice Chereau; ***W:*** Patrice Chereau, Daniele Thompson; ***C:*** Philippe Rousselot; ***M:*** Goran Bregovic. Cannes '94: Special Jury Prize, Actress (Lisi); Cesar '95: Actress (Adjani), Cinematog., Costume Des., Support. Actor (Anglade), Support. Actress (Lisi).

Queen of Diamonds ☙☙ **198?** A woman pulls off the biggest diamond heist of all time. **90m/C VHS.** Claudia Cardinale, Stanley Baker, Henri Charriere.

Queen of Diamonds ☙☙ **1991** The "Queen of Diamonds" is an alienated blackjack dealer in Vegas who, in between dealing cards, casually searches for her missing husband and looks after an old man in a motel. **77m/C VHS.** Tinka Menkes; ***D:*** Nina Menkes; ***W:*** Nina Menkes.

Queen of Hearts ☙☙☙½ **1989 (PG)** Excellent, original romantic comedy is a directorial triumph for Amiel in his first feature. An Italian couple defy both their families and marry for love. Four children later, we find them running a diner in England. Humorous, dramatic, sad—everything a move can and should be. Fine performances. **112m/C VHS.** *GB* Anita Zagaria, Joseph Long, Eileen Way, Vittorio Duse, Vittorio Amandola, Ian Hawkes; ***D:*** Jon Amiel; ***M:*** Michael Convertino.

The Queen of Mean ☙½ *Leona Helmsley: The Queen of Mean* **1990** Tabloid TV-movie based on Ransdell Pierson's scandal-sheet bio of the hotel magnate and convicted tax cheat. See Leona connive. See Leona bitch. See Leona get hers. What's the point? If you ask that you're too bright to watch. **94m/C VHS.** Suzanne Pleshette, Lloyd Bridges, Bruce Weitz, Joe Regalbuto; ***D:*** Richard Michaels; ***C:*** Hanania Baer. **TV**

Queen of Outer Space woof! **1958** Notorious male-chauvinist sci-fi cheapie starts out slow, but then the laughs keep coming as the cast plays the hyperdumb material straight. Space cadets crash on Venus, find it ruled by women—and the dolls have wicked plans in store for mankind. Don't be surprised if you've seen the sets before since they were borrowed from "Forbidden Planet," "World Without End," and "Flight to Mars." **80m/C VHS.** Zsa Zsa Gabor, Eric Fleming, Laurie Mitchell, Paul Birch, Barbara Darrow, Dave Willcock, Lisa Davis, Patrick Waltz, Marilyn Buferd, Marjorie Durant, Lynn Cartwright, Gerry Gaylor; ***D:*** Edward L. Bernds; ***W:*** Charles Beaumont; ***C:*** William F. Whitley; ***M:*** Marlin Skiles.

The Queen of Spades ☙☙☙ **1949** Mystical drama about a Russian soldier who ruins his life searching for winning methods of card playing. Well-made version of the Pushkin story. **95m/B VHS.** *GB* Anton Walbrook, Edith Evans, Ronald Howard, Mary Jerrold, Yvonne Mitchell, Anthony Dawson; ***D:*** Thorold Dickinson.

Queen of the Amazons ☙½ **1947** A girl searches for her fiance and finds him reluctantly held captive by a tribe of women who rule the jungle. **60m/B VHS.** Robert Lowery, Patricia Morison, J. Edward Bromberg, John Miljan.

Queen of the Damned ☙☙ **2002 (R)** Based on the third book in Anne Rice's "Vampire Chronicles" resurrects vampire Lestat (Townsend) to rock the new millennium after a 200-year nap. He's awakened to become the singing sensation of a goth band (what's *more* goth than a vampire?). He soon meets up with Jesse (Moreau) a reckless vampire researcher and fellow vampires Marius (Perez), and Maharet (Olin). Lestat's new lady love, however, is Akasha (late pop star Aaliyah), the mother of all the vampires who has big plans for her and her bloodsucking beau, to, (what else?) rule the world. Her followers feel differently, however. Camp, but not camp enough to excuse it's lameness and host of lifeless performances. One dimensional characters and lackluster plot leave this drag of a *Queen* to Rice and vampire fans only. **101m/C VHS, DVD.** *US AU* Aaliyah, Stuart Townsend, Marguerite Moreau, Vincent Perez, Lena Olin, Paul McGann, Claudia Black, Bruce Spence, Christian Manon; ***D:*** Michael Rymer; ***W:*** Scott Abbott; ***C:*** Ian Baker; ***M:*** Richard Gibbs, Jonathan Davis.

Queen of the Jungle ☙ **1935** Re-edited adventure serial featuring a white woman cast off in a hot-air balloon and landing in Africa, where she is hailed as a Queen. High camp, starring ex-Our Ganger Kornman. **85m/B VHS, 8mm.** Mary Kornman, Reed Howes; ***D:*** Robert F. "Bob" Hill.

Queen of the Road ☙☙ **1984** A feisty Aussie schoolteacher starts a new life as a tractor-trailer driver. **96m/C VHS.** *AU* Joanne Samuel, Amanda Muggleton; ***D:*** Bruce Best.

Queen of the Stardust Ballroom ☙☙☙ **1975** Well-made drama about a lonely widow who goes to a local dance hall, where she meets a man and begins an unconventional late love. **98m/C DVD.** Maureen Stapleton, Charles Durning, Michael Strong, Charlotte Rae, Sam O'Steen; ***D:*** Michael Brandon; ***M:*** Billy Goldenberg. **TV**

Queenie ☙☙½ **1987** Miniseries loosely based on the life of actress Merle Oberon, exploring her rise to stardom. Based on the best-selling novel by Michael Korda, Oberon's nephew by marriage. Many long, dry passages fit for leaving the room for snacks. **233m/C VHS.** Mia Sara, Kirk Douglas, Martin Balsam, Claire Bloom, Chaim Topol, Joel Grey, Sarah Miles, Joss Ackland; ***D:*** Larry Peerce; ***M:*** Georges Delerue. **TV**

Queens Logic ☙☙½ **1991 (R)** Ensemble comedy in the tradition of "The Big Chill" featuring the trials and tribulations of the "old-neighborhood" gang, who gather again on hometurf and reminisce. Most of the film centers around Olin and girlfriend Webb and whether or not he will chicken out of their wedding. Not bad comedy, with Mantegna delivering most of the good lines. **116m/C VHS, DVD.** John Malkovich, Kevin Bacon, Jamie Lee Curtis, Linda Fiorentino, Joe Mantegna, Ken Olin, Tom Waits, Chloe Webb, Ed Marinaro, Kelly Bishop, Tony Spiridakis; ***D:*** Steve Rash; ***W:*** Tony Spiridakis; ***C:*** Amir M. Mokri; ***M:*** Joe Jackson.

Queens of Comedy ☙☙½ **2001 (R)** This "sort of" companion piece to Spike Lee's "Original Kings of Comedy" is a concert recorded at the Orpheum Theatre in Memphis starring four black stand-up comediennes—Miss Laura Hayes, Adel Givens, Sommore, and Mo'Nique. **79m/C DVD.** Adele Givens, Mo'Nique, Miss Laura Hayes, Sommore; ***D:*** Steve Purcell.

Querelle ☙☙½ **1983 (R)** Querelle, a handsome sailor, finds himself involved in a bewildering environment of murder, drug smuggling, and homosexuality in the port of Brest. Highly stylized and erotic sets, along with a dark look, give the film an interesting feel. Nice performances by Davis, Nero, and Moreau. Fassbinder's controversial last film, based on the story by Jean Genet. Strange, difficult narrative (such as it is), alternately boring and engrossing. **106m/C VHS, DVD, Wide.** *GE* Brad Davis, Jeanne Moreau, Franco Nero, Laurent Malet; ***D:*** Rainer Werner Fassbinder; ***W:*** Rainer Werner Fassbinder, Burkhard Driest; ***C:*** Xaver Schwarzenberger, Josef Vavra; ***M:*** Peer Raben.

The Quest ☙☙ **1986 (PG)** Australian film never released theatrically in the United States. A young boy (Thomas, of "E.T." fame) raised in the outback investigates a local Aboriginal superstition about a monster living in an ancient cemetery. Not bad, just dull. **94m/C VHS.** *AU* Henry Thomas, Tony Barry, John Ewart, Rachel Friend, Tamsin West, Dennis Miller, Katya Manning; ***D:*** Brian Trenchard-Smith.

The Quest ☙☙ **1996 (PG-13)** In his directorial debut, Van Damme plays pickpocket Christopher Dubois, who finds his adventures just beginning when he hops a freighter heading for the Far East in order to escape police trouble. He learns about a prestigious martial arts competition, where the prize could set him up for life, if he can manage to get into the invitation-only event. After many films set in the future, Van Damme chose to set this one in the '20s, with fairly good results. He piles on the beautiful location shots until the inevitable martial arts melee toward the end. Pacing is sketchy but Van Damme does display directorial talent. **95m/C VHS, DVD, Wide.** Jean-Claude Van Damme, Roger Moore, Aki Aleong, James Remar, Jack McGee, Janet Gunn, Abdel Qissi, Louis Mandylor; ***D:*** Jean-Claude Van Damme; ***W:*** Stuart Klein, Paul Mones; ***C:*** David Gribble; ***M:*** Randy Edelman.

Quest for Camelot ☙☙½ **1998 (G)** Camelot's future lies in the hands of heroine Kayley, who sees an opportunity to win a spot at King Arthur's roundtable when Excalibur is stolen by evil knight Ruber (Oldman). On her quest to recover the sword, she meets blind hermit Garrett and two-headed dragon Devon and Cornwall (Idle and Rickles). With an all-star cast, this first full-length animated feature from Warner Bros. wants to be a contender for the Disney animation crown, but can't quite overcome its familiar story, one-dimensional villain, and forgettable songs. However, Kayley and Garrett are strong, non-stereotypical characters that children and adults will welcome. Based on the children's novel "The King's Damosel" by Vera Chapman. **85m/C VHS, DVD.** ***D:*** Frederick Du Chan; ***W:*** Kirk De Micco, William Schifrin, David Seidler; ***M:*** Patrick Doyle; ***V:*** Jessalyn Gilsig, Cary Elwes, Gary Oldman, Eric Idle, Don Rickles, Jane Seymour, Pierce Brosnan, Gabriel Byrne, Bronson Pinchot, Jaleel White, John Gielgud. Golden Globes '99: Song ("The Prayer").

Quest for Fire ☙☙☙ **1982 (R)** An interesting story sans the usual dialogue thing. A group of men (McGill, Perlman, El-Kadi) during the Ice Age must wander the land searching for fire after they lose theirs fending off an attack. During their quest, they encounter and battle various animals and tribesmen in order to survive. The special language they speak was developed by Anthony Burgess, while the primitive movements were Desmond "The Naked Ape" Morris. Perlman went on to become the Beast in TV's "Beauty and the Beast"; Chong, as a primitive babe, is the daughter of Tommy Chong of the comic duo Cheech and Chong. **75m/C VHS, Wide.** *FR* Everett McGill, Ron Perlman, Nameer El-Kadi, Rae Dawn Chong; ***D:*** Jean-Jacques Annaud; ***W:*** Gerard Brach. Oscars '82: Makeup; Genie '83: Actress (Chong).

Quest for Love 🦴🦴½ **1971** Quirky sci-fi story of a man who passes through a time warp and finds himself able to maintain two parallel lives. Based on John Wyndham's short story. **90m/C VHS.** *GB* Joan Collins, Tom Bell, Denholm Elliott, Laurence Naismith; ***D:*** Ralph Thomas.

Quest for the Mighty Sword 🦴 **1990 (PG-13)** A warrior battles dragons, demons and evil wizards. D'Amato used the pseudonym David Hills. **94m/C VHS.** Eric Allen Kramer, Margaret Lenzey, Donald O'Brien, Dina Marrone, Chris Murphy; ***D:*** Joe D'Amato.

Quest of the Delta Knights 🦴🦴½ **1993 (PG)** Swashbuckling fantasy about a kingdom suffering under an evil ruler and his equally sinister queen. They are opposed by the heroic Delta Knights whose only chance to defeat the fiendish powers of darkness is by unearthing a legendary storehouse containing technology from the age of Atlantis and all the powers of the Ancients. **97m/C VHS.** David Warner, Olivia Hussey, Corbin Allred, Brigid Conley Walsh, David Kriegel; ***D:*** James Dodson; ***W:*** Redge Mahaffey.

A Question of Attribution 🦴🦴½ **1991** Sir Anthony Blunt (Fox) is an internationally respected art expert who also serves as an art adviser to Queen Elizabeth II. His life unravels when an on-going British Intelligence investigation reveals him to be the fourth man in the Burgess-Maclean-Philby scandal involving Englishmen who spied for, and eventually defected to, the USSR. The investigation of Blunt's covert past is paralleled with his own art investigation of a painting attributed to Titian. Three men are depicted in the art work—with a fourth male figure discovered to have been painted over. Alan Bennett adapted his play for this TV drama. **90m/C VHS.** *GB* James Fox, David Calder, Geoffrey Palmer, Prunella Scales, Mark Payton, Jason Flemyng, Edward De Souza, Ann Beach; ***D:*** John Schlesinger; ***W:*** Alan Bennett. **TV**

Question of Faith 🦴🦴½ **1993** A happily married woman is diagnosed with a rare form of cancer. Much to her family's dismay, she turns to some unconventional medical therapies in order to heal herself. Based on a true story. Basically noble, Archer and Neill lift this tearjerker out of most of its maudlin aspects. **90m/C VHS.** Anne Archer, Sam Neill, Frances Lee McCain, James Tolkan, James Hong, CCH Pounder, Louis Giambalvo, Norman Parker, Michael Constantine; ***D:*** Stephen Gyllenhaal; ***W:*** Bruce Hart.

A Question of Guilt 🦴🦴 **1978** When her child turns up dead, a free-wheeling divorcee is the prime suspect. **100m/C VHS.** Tuesday Weld, Ron Leibman, Peter Masterson, Alex Rocco, Viveca Lindfors, Lana Wood; ***D:*** Robert Butler. **TV**

Question of Honor 🦴🦴½ **1980** Under governmental pressures, an honest narcotics cop decides to inform on his department's corruption. Co-written and produced by ex-cop Sonny Grosso, on whom "The French Connection" was based. Based on the book "Point Blank," by Grosso and Philip Rosenberg. **134m/C VHS.** Ben Gazzara, Paul Sorvino, Robert Vaughn, Tony Roberts, Danny Aiello, Anthony Zerbe; ***D:*** Jud Taylor; ***W:*** Budd Schulberg. **TV**

A Question of Love 🦴🦴🦴 **1978** Fine performances in this well-done TV movie about two lesbians—one of whom is fighting her ex-husband for custody of their child. **100m/C VHS.** Gena Rowlands, Jane Alexander, Ned Beatty, Clu Gulager, Bonnie Bedelia, James Sutorius, Jocelyn Brando; ***D:*** Jerry Thorpe; ***M:*** Billy Goldenberg. **TV**

Question of Silence 🦴🦴🦴 *De Stilte Rond Christine M* **1983 (R)** Three women, strangers to each other, stand trial for a murdering a man. Intricately analyzed courtroom drama with much to say about male domination. In Dutch with English subtitles or dubbed. **92m/C VHS.** *NL* Cox Habrema, Nelly Frijda, Henriette Tol, Edda Barends; ***D:*** Marleen Gorris.

Qui Etes Vous, Mr. Sorge? 🦴🦴 **1961** The story of German journalist Richard Sorge, who was hanged by the Japanese in 1944 for being a Soviet spy. Uninteresting docudrama which focuses on the opinions of various witnesses as to the accuracy of the espionage charge. In French with English subtitles. **130m/B VHS.** *FR* Thomas Holtzman, Keiko Kishi; ***D:*** Andre Girard.

Quick 🦴🦴½ **1993 (R)** Polo stars as Quick, a professional assassin whose latest job is Herschel (Donovan), a mob accountant turned federal witness. When Quick is double-crossed, she takes off with Herschel as her insurance and a couple of bad guys (Fahey and Davi) on her trail. Not too much sex and lots of violence to go along with the fast pacing. **99m/C VHS.** Teri Polo, Martin Donovan, Jeff Fahey, Robert Davi, Tia Carrere; ***D:*** Rick King; ***W:*** Frederick Bailey; ***M:*** Robert Sprayberry.

The Quick and the Dead 🦴🦴 **1987** Based on a Louis L'Amour story, this cable western features a lone gunslinger who protects a defenseless settler's family from the lawless West, only to become a source of sexual tension for the wife. **91m/C VHS.** Sam Elliott, Tom Conti, Kate Capshaw, Kenny Morrison, Matt Clark; ***D:*** Robert Day; ***C:*** Dick Bush; ***M:*** Steve Dorff. **CABLE**

The Quick and the Dead 🦴🦴 **1994 (R)** Stone is a tough gal gunslinger out to avenge the murder of her father. Ellen arrives in the frontier town of Redemption where arch-villain Herod (Hackman) rules by means of violence and intimidation. Director Raimi packs in so many cliches that you're amazed that it's not a parody of the spaghetti westerns it tries to emulate. Maybe if Stone and Raimi didn't take this film so seriously, it would have been a better movie. One redeeming quality of the film is its wildly staged gunfights and interesting camera angles. Another is the excellent work by Hackman and Crowe. **105m/C VHS, DVD, Wide.** Sharon Stone, Gene Hackman, Leonardo DiCaprio, Russell Crowe, Kevin Conway, Lance Henriksen, Roberts Blossom, Pat Hingle, Keith David, Michael Stone, Stacey Linn Ramsower; ***Cameos:*** Gary Sinise; ***D:*** Sam Raimi; ***W:*** Simon Moore; ***C:*** Dante Spinotti; ***M:*** Alan Silvestri.

Quick Change 🦴🦴½ **1990 (R)** Murray, Davis, and Quaid form bumbling trio of New York bank robbers who can't seem to exit the Big Apple with loot. Based on Jay Cronley's book, it's Murray's directing debut (with help from screenwriter Franklin). Engaging minor caper comedy displaying plenty of NYC dirty boulevards. **89m/C VHS, 8mm.** Tony Shalhoub, Stanley Tucci, Jack Gilpin, Reg E. Cathey, Bill Murray, Geena Davis, Randy Quaid, Jason Robards Jr., Bob Elliott, Victor Argo, Kathryn Grody, Philip Bosco, Phil Hartman, Kurtwood Smith, Jamey Sheridan; ***D:*** Bill Murray, Howard Franklin; ***W:*** Howard Franklin; ***C:*** Michael Chapman; ***M:*** Randy Edelman, Howard Shore.

Quick, Let's Get Married **woof!** *Seven Different Ways; The Confession* **1971** Quick, let's not watch this movie. Even the people who made it must have hated it: they waited seven years to release it. Rogers runs a whorehouse; Eden is a gullible, pregnant prostitute; Gould in his big-screen debut(!) is a deaf-mute. A must-not see. **96m/C VHS.** Ginger Rogers, Ray Milland, Barbara Eden, Carl Schell, Michael Ansara, Walter Abel, Scott Meyer, Cecil Kellaway, Elliott Gould; ***D:*** William Dieterle.

Quicker Than the Eye 🦴🦴 **1988** When a magician gets mixed up in an assassination plot, he must use his wit, cunning, and magic to get out of it. **94m/C VHS.** Ben Gazzara, Mary Crosby, Catherine Jarrett, Ivan Desny, Eb Lottimer, Sophie Carle, Wolfram Berger, Dinah Hinz, Jean Yanne; ***D:*** Nicolas Gessner.

Quicksand 🦴🦴½ **1950** Mechanic Rooney borrows $20 from his boss's cash register, intending to return it. One thing leads to another, the plot thickens, and it's downhill (for Rooney) from there. Good, tense suspense drama. **79m/B VHS, DVD.** Mickey Rooney, Peter Lorre, Jeanne Cagney; ***D:*** Irving Pichel; ***W:*** Robert Smith; ***C:*** Lionel Linden; ***M:*** Louis Gruenberg.

Quicksand: No Escape 🦴🦴 **1991 (PG-13)** Scott Reinhardt (Matheson) is a successful architect whose partner decides to secure a building contract by bribing a city official. When his partner is murdered Reinhardt is approached by a former cop (Sutherland) asking a lot of money for some incriminating evidence. Reinhardt is then drawn ever deeper into the illicit dealings, endangering his life. **93m/C VHS.** Tim Matheson, Donald Sutherland, Jay Acovone, Timothy Carhart, John Finn, Marc Alaimo, Felicity Huffman, Al Pugliese; ***D:*** Michael Pressman; ***W:*** Peter Baloff, Dave Wollert.

Quicksilver 🦴½ **1986 (PG)** A young stockbroker loses all, then quits his job to become a city bicycle messenger. Pointless, self-indulgent yuppie fantasy. **106m/C VHS.** Kevin Bacon, Jami Gertz, Paul Rodriguez, Rudy Ramos, Andrew Smith, Gerald S. O'Loughlin, Laurence "Larry" Fishburne, Louie Anderson; ***D:*** Tom Donnelly; ***W:*** Tom Donnelly; ***M:*** Tony Banks.

Quicksilver Highway 🦴🦴½ **1998 (R)** Storyteller Aaron Quicksilver (Lloyd) entertains with two horror tales, based on the stories "The Body Politic" by Clive Barker and "Chattery Teeth" by Stephen King. The Barker story has been re-set in America and now features a plastic surgeon whose hands decide to become independent from the rest of his body, while the King story is about a traveling salesman who purchases a pair of steel teeth at a Arizona gas station, which turn out to be lifesavers when he makes the mistake of picking up a nightmarish hitchhiker. **90m/C VHS.** Christopher Lloyd, Matt Frewer, Raphael Sbarge, Missy (Melissa) Crider, Veronica Cartwright, Bill Nunn, Amelia Heinle; ***Cameos:*** Clive Barker; ***D:*** Mick Garris; ***W:*** Mick Garris; ***C:*** Shelly Johnson; ***M:*** Mark Mothersbaugh. **TV**

Quiet Cool 🦴 **1986 (R)** When his former girlfriend's family is killed, a New York cop travels to a sleepy California town run by a pot-growing tycoon. He subsequently kills the bad guys in a Rambo-like fit of vengeance. Dopey exercise in sleepy-eyed bloodshed. **80m/C VHS.** James Remar, Daphne Ashbrook, Adam Coleman Howard, Jared Martin, Fran Ryan; ***D:*** Clay Borris; ***W:*** Clay Borris; ***M:*** Jay Ferguson.

Quiet Day in Belfast 🦴🦴🦴 **1974** Tragedy occurs when northern Irish patriots and British soldiers clash in an Irish betting parlor. Kidder plays a duel role: an Irish woman in love with a British soldier (Foster) and the woman's twin sister, newly arrived from Canada, who becomes the victim of a case of mistaken identity. Convincingly adapted from a Canadian stage play by Andrew Dalrymple. **92m/C VHS.** *CA* Barry Foster, Margot Kidder, Leo Leyden, Emmet Bergin, Joyce Campion, Sean McCann; ***D:*** Milad Bessada; ***W:*** Jack Gray.

Quiet Days in Hollywood 🦴🦴 *The Way We Are* **1997 (R)** Sexual roundelay in Hollywood involves a prostitute, an actor, a crook, a waitress, a rape, a gay triangle, various affairs, and related sexual experimentation. Less titillating than it sounds; German director Rusnak was making his U.S. feature debut. Maybe something got lost in the translation. **95m/C VHS, DVD.** Peter Dobson, Chad Lowe, Steven Mailer, Darryl (Chill) Mitchell, Bill Cusack, Meta Golding, Hilary Swank, Natasha Gregson Wagner; ***D:*** Josef Rusnak; ***W:*** Josef Rusnak; ***C:*** Dietrich Lohmann; ***M:*** Harold Kloser.

A Quiet Duel 🦴🦴 *A Silent Duel; Shizuka Naru Ketto* **1949** Kyoji (Mifune), a young, idealistic doctor working as an army surgeon, contracts syphillis from the blood of a patient during an operation. Because the disease was virtually incurable at the time, the tormented Kyoji abandons his fiance and decides to dedicate himself to his work. Based on a play by Kazuo Kikuta. Japanese with subtitles. **95m/B VHS.** *JP* Toshiro Mifune, Takashi Shimura, Kenjiro Uemura; ***D:*** Akira Kurosawa; ***W:*** Senkichi Taniguchi, Akira Kurosawa; ***M:*** Akira Ifukube.

The Quiet Earth 🦴🦴🦴 **1985 (R)** Serious science fiction film about a scientist who awakens to find himself seemingly the only human left on earth as the result of a misfired time/space government experiment. He later finds two other people, a girl and a Maori tribesman, and must try to repair the damage in order to save what's left of mankind. **91m/C VHS.** *NZ* Bruno Lawrence, Alison Routledge, Peter Smith, Norman Fletcher, Tom Hyde; ***D:*** Geoff Murphy; ***W:*** Sam Pillsbury, Bill Baer, Bruno Lawrence; ***C:*** James Bartle; ***M:*** John Charles.

Quiet Fire 🦴½ **1991 (R)** A health-club owner tries to get the goods on the arms-dealing congressman who killed his best friend. Hilton-Jacobs looks properly pumped up since his sweathog days on TV's "Welcome Back Kotter." **100m/C VHS.** Lawrence-Hilton Jacobs, Robert Z'Dar, Nadia Marie, Karen Black, Lance Lindsay; ***D:*** Lawrence-Hilton Jacobs.

The Quiet Man 🦴🦴🦴🦴 **1952** The classic incarnation of Hollywood Irishness, and one of Ford's best, and funniest films. Wayne is Sean Thornton, a weary American ex-boxer who returns to the Irish hamlet of his childhood and tries to take spirited lass Mary Kate (O'Hara) as his wife, despite the strenuous objections of her brawling brother Red Will (McLaglen). Thornton's aided by the leprechaun-like Michaleen Flynn (Fitzgerald) and the local parish priest (Bond). A high-spirited and memorable film filled with Irish stew, wonderful banter, and shots of the lush countryside. Listen for the Scottish bagpipes at the start of the horse race, a slight geographic inaccuracy. **129m/C VHS, DVD.** John Wayne, Maureen O'Hara, Barry Fitzgerald, Victor McLaglen, Arthur Shields, Jack MacGowran, Ward Bond, Mildred Natwick, Ken Curtis, Mae Marsh, Sean McClory, Francis Ford; ***D:*** John Ford; ***W:*** Frank Nugent; ***C:*** Archie Stout; ***M:*** Victor Young. Oscars '52: Color Cinematog., Director (Ford); Directors Guild '52: Director (Ford); Venice Film Fest. '52: Director (Ford).

The Quiet Room 🦴🦴 **1996 (PG)** A nameless seven-year-old girl (Chloe Ferguson) refuses to speak when she learns her constantly quarreling parents are separating. Film is shown from only the child's perspective and her fantasies of a different life as she goes about her daily routine. Although the girl remains silent, she answers her parents in her thoughts (the voiceover lets the viewer into the girl's world) and she has flashbacks to her younger self (played by Ferguson's sister Phoebe) and when her parents loved each other. **91m/C VHS.** *AU* Chloe Ferguson, Celine O'Leary, Paul Blackwell, Phoebe Ferguson; ***D:*** Rolf de Heer; ***W:*** Rolf de Heer; ***C:*** Tony Clark; ***M:*** Graham Tardiff.

Quiet Thunder 🦴 **1987 (PG-13)** A hard-drinking bush pilot in Africa and a beautiful senator's wife are thrown together on the run after both witness an assassination. Mindless, thoroughly derivative "adventure." **94m/C VHS.** Wayne Crawford, June Chadwick, Victor Steinbach; ***D:*** David Rice.

Quigley Down Under 🦴🦴½ **1990 (PG-13)** A Western sharpshooter moves to Australia in search of employment. To his horror, he discovers that he has been hired to kill aborigines. Predictable action is somewhat redeemed by the terrific chemistry between Selleck and San Giacomo and the usual enjoyable theatrics from Rickman as the landowner heavy. **121m/C VHS, DVD, 8mm, Wide.** *AU* Tom Selleck, Laura San Giacomo, Alan Rickman, Chris Haywood, Ron Haddrick, Tony Bonner, Roger Ward, Ben Mendelsohn, Jerome Ehlers, Conor McDermottroe; ***D:*** Simon Wincer; ***W:*** John Hill; ***C:*** David Eggby; ***M:*** Basil Poledouris.

The Quiller Memorandum 🦴🦴🦴 **1966** An American secret agent travels to Berlin to uncover a deadly neo-Nazi gang. Refreshingly different from other spy tales of its era. Good screenplay adapted from Adam Hall's novel, "The Berlin Memorandum." **103m/C VHS.** George Segal, Senta Berger, Alec Guinness, Max von Sydow, George Sanders; ***D:***

Michael Anderson Sr.; *W:* Harold Pinter; *M:* John Barry.

Quills ✂✂½ **2000 (R)** Follows the last years of the life of the Marquis de Sade (played by Rush), which he spent in an insane asylum as punishment for his erotic writings. Sade continues to write while imprisoned, and with the help of his secret courier, Madeleine (played by Winslet), is able to distribute his stories to the public. Unfortunately, the movie uses Sade's imprisonment to put forth lessons about the importance of freedom of expression and perils of censorship, thereby sacrificing a closer investigation of the real story—the man's boiling imagination. Worth viewing for the performances and for the glimpse into the life of one of histories most fascinating authors. Based on the off-Broadway play by David Wright. **123m/C VHS, DVD, Wide.** Geoffrey Rush, Kate Winslet, Joaquin Rafael (Leaf) Phoenix, Michael Caine; *D:* Philip Kaufman; *W:* Doug Wright; *C:* Rogier Stoffers; *M:* Stephen Warbeck. Natl. Bd. of Review '00: Film, Support. Actor (Phoenix).

Quilombo ✂✂½ **1984** The title refers to a legendary settlement of runaway slaves in 17th-century Brazil; an epic chronicles its fortunes as leadership passes from a wise ruler to a more militant one who goes to war against the government. Stunning scenery, tribal images, and folk songs, but the numerous characters seldom come to life as personalities. One of Brazil's most expensive films, in Portuguese with English subtitles. **114m/C VHS.** *BR* Vera Fischer, Antonio Pompeo, Zeze Motta, Toni Tornado; *D:* Carlos Diegues; *W:* Carlos Diegues.

Quintet ✂✂ **1979** Atypical Altman sci-fi effort. The stakes in "Quintet," a form of backgammon, are high—you bet your life. Set during the planet's final ice age. Newman and wife Fossey wander into a dying city and are invited to play the game, with Fossey losing quickly. Bizarre and pretentious, with heavy symbolic going. **118m/C VHS.** Paul Newman, Bibi Andersson, Fernando Rey, Vittorio Gassman, David Langton, Nina Van Pallandt, Brigitte Fossey; *D:* Robert Altman; *W:* Lionel Chetwynd, Patricia Resnick, Robert Altman, Frank Barhydt.

Quiz Show ✂✂✂✂ **1994 (PG-13)** Redford's intelligent, entertaining, and morally complex film about the TV game show scandals of the late '50s is his most accomplished work to date. At the center of the film is Charles Van Doren (Fiennes), an intellectual, golden boy who dethrones Herbert Stempel (Turturro), the reigning champion of the rigged "Twenty-One." The program's sponsor felt Stempel, a nerdy Jewish grad's everyman qualities were wearing thin and wanted a more polished image, which they found in handsome, sophisticated Van Doren. Federal investigator Goodwin (Morrow) suspects Van Doren's reign is a sham and sets out to expose him as a fraud. Acting is of the highest caliber with Fiennes, Turturro, and Morrow all giving beautiful performances. Notable among supporting cast is Scofield as Van Doren's Pulitzer prize-winning father. With strong script and gorgeous lensing, this modern Faust story is a brilliant reflection on corporate greed, class rivalry, and the powers of television. Based on the book "Remembering America: A Voice From the Sixties" by Richard N. Goodwin. **133m/C VHS, DVD.** John Turturro, Rob Morrow, Ralph Fiennes, Paul Scofield, David Paymer, Hank Azaria, Christopher McDonald, Johann Carlo, Elizabeth Wilson, Mira Sorvino, Griffin Dunne, Martin Scorsese, Barry Levinson; *D:* Robert Redford; *W:* Paul Attanasio; *C:* Michael Ballhaus; *M:* Mark Isham. British Acad. '94: Adapt. Screenplay; N.Y. Film Critics '94: Film.

Quo Vadis ✂✂½ **1912** One of the first truly huge Italian silent epics. The initial adaptation of the Henryk Sienkiewicz novel about Nero and ancient Rome. Probably the cinema's first great financial success. **45m/B VHS.** *D:* Enrico Guazzoni.

Quo Vadis ✂✂✂ **1951** Larger-than-life production about Nero and the Christian persecution. Done on a giant scale: features exciting fighting scenes, romance, and fabulous costumes. Definitive version of the classic novel by Henryk Siekiewicz. Remade for Italian TV in 1985. **171m/C VHS.** Robert Taylor, Deborah Kerr, Peter Ustinov, Patricia Laffan, Finlay Currie, Abraham Sofaer, Marina Berti, Buddy Baer, Felix Aylmer, Nora Swinburne, Elspeth March; ***Cameos:*** Sophia Loren, Elizabeth Taylor; *D:* Mervyn LeRoy; *C:* Robert L. Surtees; *M:* Miklos Rozsa; ***Nar:*** Walter Pidgeon. Golden Globes '52: Support. Actor (Ustinov).

Quo Vadis ✂✂½ **1985 (R)** Third screen version of Henryk Sienkiewicz's book. See the other two first. This one is slow and perfunctory. Brandauer is memorable as Nero; Quinn (in the lead) is the son of Anthony. **122m/C VHS.** *IT* Klaus Maria Brandauer, Frederic Forrest, Christina Raines, Maria Therese Relin, Francesco Quinn, Barbara DeRossi, Phillippe LeRoy, Max von Sydow, Gabriele Ferzetti, Massimo Girotti, Leopoldo Trieste; *D:* Franco Rossi.

Rabbit Test ✂½ **1978 (PG)** In Rivers' first directorial effort, a clumsy virginal guy becomes the world's first pregnant man. So irreverent it's almost never in good taste, and so poorly written it's almost never funny. **86m/C VHS.** Billy Crystal, Roddy McDowall, Imogene Coca, Paul Lynde, Alex Rocco, George Gobel; *D:* Joan Rivers.

Rabid ✂✂½ *Rage* **1977 (R)** A young girl undergoes a radical plastic surgery technique and develops a strange and unexplained lesion in her armpit. She also finds she has an unusual craving for human blood. **90m/C VHS, DVD.** *CA* Marilyn Chambers, Frank Moore, Joe Silver, Howard Ryshpan, Patricia Gage, Susan (Suzan) Roman, Roger Periard, Victor Desy; *D:* David Cronenberg; *W:* David Cronenberg; *C:* Rene Verzier.

Rabid Grannies woof! **1989 (R)** Wicked satire about two aging sisters who receive a surprise birthday gift from their devilworshipping nephew. The gift turns their party into a gorefest as they rip into various family members—literally. Any humor will be lost on any but the most diehard Troma fans. Dubbed. **89m/C VHS, DVD.** *BE* Catherine Aymerie, Caroline Brackman, Danielle Daven, Raymond Lescot, Anne Marie Fox, Richard Cotica, Patricia Davie; *D:* Emmanuel Kervyn; *W:* Emmanuel Kervyn; *C:* Hugh Labye; *M:* Jean-Bruno Castelain, Pierre-Damien Castelain.

Race Against Time ✂✂ **2000** Another bleak futuristic thriller but with fast-paced and suspenseful action. When Gabriel's (Roberts) son is diagnosed with a deadly virus, Gabirel learns that the vaccine will cost him mucho dinero—and he has only 12 hours to come up with the cash. So he agrees to sell his organs to Lifecorps for harvesting in a year's time, then it's bye-bye for Gabe. But when his son dies anyway, Gabriel tries to get out of the agreement, especially when it seems his son's death wasn't so straightforward. **90m/C VHS, DVD.** Eric Roberts, Cary Elwes, Sarah Wynter, Chris Sarandon; *D:* Geoff Murphy. **CABLE**

Race for Glory ✂½ **1989 (R)** A young motorcyclist builds a super-bike he hopes will help him win a world championship race. Will he win? Can you stand the suspense? Let's just say there's a happy ending. **102m/C VHS.** Alex McArthur, Peter Berg, Pamela Ludwig; *D:* Rocky Lang; *M:* Jay Ferguson.

Race for Life ✂½ *Mask of Dust* **1955** A race car driver attempts to make a comeback despite objections from his wife. He races around Europe (great scenery); she leaves him; he tries to win her back and salvage his career. Standard, un-gripping story. Car scenes are great. **69m/B VHS.** *GB* Richard Conte, Mari Aldon, George Coulouris; *D:* Terence Fisher.

Race for Your Life, Charlie Brown ✂✂½ **1977 (G)** Another in the popular series of "Peanuts" character films. This one features Charlie Brown, Snoopy, and all the gang spending an exciting summer in the American wilderness. **76m/C VHS.** *D:* Bill Melendez, Phil Roman; *W:* Charles M. Schulz; *M:* Ed Bogas; *V:* Gail Davis, Melanie Kohn, Duncan Watson, Gregory Felton, Stuart Brotman, Liam Martin, Ed Bogas.

Race the Sun ✂✂ **1996 (PG)** There's nothin' new under this sun. Tired story of a group of young losers who band together to beat the odds and compete in an unusual contest is trotted out once again for populist amusement. This time it's a Hawaiian high school solar car team traveling to Australia to go for the prize against the big shots and snobs. Based on true events, it features some nice scenery from Berry and the main locations, but not much else. Uninspired but basically harmless, this one's fine for the kids. **100m/C VHS, DVD.** Halle Berry, James Belushi, Casey Affleck, Eliza Dushku, Kevin Tighe, Anthony Michael Ruivivar, J. Moki Cho, Dion Basco, Sara Tanaka, Nadja Pionilla, Steve Zahn, Bill Hunter; *D:* Charles Kanganis; *W:* Barry Morrow; *C:* David Burr; *M:* Graeme Revell.

Race to Freedom: The Story of the Underground Railroad ✂✂½ **1994** Story of four fugitive slaves, in 1850, who struggle to get from North Carolina to the safety of Canada through a network of safe-houses and people willing to risk smuggling them to asylum. **90m/C VHS, DVD.** *CA* Courtney B. Vance, Janet Bailey, Glynn Turman, Tim Reid, Michael Riley, Dawnn Lewis, Ron White, Alfre Woodard; *D:* Don McBrearty; *W:* Nancy Trite Botkin, Diana Braithwaite; *M:* Christopher Dedrick. **CABLE**

Race with the Devil ✂½ **1975 (PG)** Vacationers are terrorized by devil worshippers after they witness a sacrificial killing. Heavy on car chases; light on plot and redeeming qualities. Don't waste your time. **88m/C VHS.** Peter Fonda, Warren Oates, Loretta Swit, Lara Parker, R.G. Armstrong; *D:* Jack Starrett; *W:* Wes Bishop, Lee Frost; *C:* Robert C. Jessup.

The Racers ✂✂½ *Such Men are Dangerous* **1955** Douglas brings power to the role of a man determined to advance to the winners' circle. Exciting European location photography, but not much plot. **112m/C VHS.** Gilbert Roland, Kirk Douglas, Lee J. Cobb, Cesar Romero, Bella Darvi; *D:* Henry Hathaway; *M:* Alex North.

Rachel and the Stranger ✂✂✂ **1948** A God-fearing farmer declares his love for his wife when a handsome stranger (Mitchum) nearly woos her away. Well-cast, well-paced, charming Western comedy-drama. **93m/B VHS.** Loretta Young, Robert Mitchum, William Holden, Gary Gray; *D:* Norman Foster.

The Rachel Papers ✂✂✂ **1989 (R)** Based on the Martin Amis novel, this is the funny/sad tale of an Oxford youth who plots via his computer the seduction of a beautiful American girl. For anyone who has ever loved someone just out of their reach. **92m/C VHS.** Dexter Fletcher, Ione Skye, James Spader, Jonathan Pryce, Bill Paterson, Michael Gambon, Lesley Sharp; *D:* Damian Harris; *W:* Damian Harris; *M:* Chaz Jankel.

Rachel, Rachel ✂✂✂½ **1968 (R)** Rachel teaches by day, wearing simple, practical dresses and her hair up. By night she caters to her domineering mother by preparing refreshments for her parties. This sexually repressed, spinster schoolteacher, however, gets one last chance at romance in her small Connecticut town. Woodward mixes just the right amounts of loneliness and sweetness in the leading role. A surprising award-winner that was an independent production of Newman. Based on Margaret Laurence's "A Jest of God." **102m/C VHS.** Joanne Woodward, James Olson, Estelle Parsons, Geraldine Fitzgerald, Donald Moffat; *D:* Paul Newman; *W:* Stewart Stern. Golden Globes '69: Actress—Drama (Woodward), Director (Newman); N.Y. Film Critics '68: Actress (Woodward), Director (Newman).

Rachel River ✂✂½ **1987 (PG-13)** A divorced radio personality struggles to make something of her life in her small Minnesota town. **88m/C VHS.** Pamela Reed, Craig T. Nelson, Viveca Lindfors, James Olson, Zeljko Ivanek, Jo Henderson, Alan North, Jon (John) DeVries; *D:* Sandy Smolan; *W:* Judith Guest; *M:* Arvo Part.

Rachel's Man ✂ **1975** A big-screen version of the Biblical love story of Jacob and Rachel. **115m/C VHS, DVD.** Mickey Rooney, Rita Tushingham, Leonard Whiting, Michal Bat-Adam; *D:* Moshe Mizrahi.

Racing Luck ✂✂ *Red Hot Tires* **1935** While working at a race track, a man is framed and forced to work for another stable. **56m/B VHS.** William Boyd, Barbara Worth, George Ernest, Esther Muir, Dick Curtis; *D:* Sam Newfield.

Racing with the Moon ✂✂✂ **1984 (PG)** Sweet, nostalgic film about two buddies awaiting induction into the Marines in 1942. They have their last chance at summer romance. Benjamin makes the most of skillful young actors and conventional story. Great period detail. Keep your eyes peeled for glimpses of many rising young stars including Hannah and Carvey. **108m/C VHS.** Sean Penn, Elizabeth McGovern, Nicolas Cage, John Karlen, Rutanya Alda, Max (Casey Adams) Showalter, Crispin Glover, Suzanne Adkinson, Page Hannah, Michael Madsen, Dana Carvey, Carol Kane, Michael Talbott; *D:* Richard Benjamin; *W:* Steven Kloves; *C:* John Bailey; *M:* Dave Grusin.

The Racket ✂✂✂ **1951** Police captain Mitchum tries to break up mob racket of gangster Ryan. Internecine strife on both sides adds complexity. Mitchum and especially Ryan are super; fine, tense melodrama. **88m/B VHS.** Robert Ryan, Robert Mitchum, Lizabeth Scott, Ray Collins, William Conrad, Don Porter; *D:* John Cromwell.

The Racketeer ✂✂½ **1929** A racketeer falls in love with a pretty girl and attempts to win her over. As part of his plan, the gangster arranges to help the girl's boyfriend begin his musical career in exchange for the girl's promise to marry him. **68m/B VHS.** Carole Lombard, Robert Armstrong, Hedda Hopper; *D:* Howard Higgin.

Racketeers of the Range ✂½ **1939** Cattleman fights a crooked attorney who wants to sell his client's stock to a large meat packing company. **62m/B VHS.** George O'Brien, Marjorie Reynolds, Chill Wills, Ray Whitley; *D:* David Ross Lederman.

Racquet ✂ **1979** Tennis pro Convy searches for true love and a tennis court of to call his own in Beverly Hills. Lame, sophomoric, and unfunny. **87m/C VHS.** Bert Convy, Edie Adams, Lynda Day George, Phil Silvers, Bobby Riggs, Bjorn Borg, Tanya Roberts; *D:* David Winters.

Rad ✂½ **1986 (PG)** Teenage drama revolving around BMX racing and such dilemmas as: can the good guys beat the bad guys, who's got the fastest bike, must you cheat to win, and should our hero miss his SAT tests to compete in "the big race.." Directed by stunt-expert Needham. **94m/C VHS.** Bill Allen, Bart Conner, Talia Shire, Jack Weston, Lori Loughlin; *D:* Hal Needham; *W:* Sam Bernard.

Radar Men from the Moon *Retik, the Moon Menace* **1952** Commando Cody, with his jet-pack, fights to defend the earth from invaders from the moon. Twelve-episode serial on two tapes. Silly sci-fi. **152m/B VHS, DVD.** George D. Wallace, Aline Towne, Roy Barcroft, William "Billy" Bakewell, Clayton Moore; *D:* Fred Brannon.

Radar Patrol vs. Spy King **1949** Special agent Alyn and his buxom Vargas girl Jean Dean battle the deadly Baroda and his ring of saboteurs, hell-bent on destroying America. 12 episodes of the serial edited onto two cassettes. **167m/B VHS.** Kirk Alyn, Jeanne Dean.

Radar Secret Service ✂½ **1950** Two servicemen witness the hijacking of a truck loaded with nuclear material. **59m/B VHS.** John Howard, Adele Jergens, Tom Neal, Ralph Byrd.

Radiance ✂✂ **1998** Three half-sisters reunite in their rundown family home, located in the sugar cane country of Australia's tropical north, to bury their mother. Resentful Mae (Morton-Thomas) feels she was trapped into caring alone for their prematurely senile mother while sophisticated Cressy (Maza) became a successfull opera singer and youngest sister Nona (Mailman) indulged her party girl ways. Old grievances are aired and the trio set off more than one kind of fireworks together. Adapted by Nowra from his play. **83m/C VHS.** *AU* Trisha Morton-Thomas, Rachel Maza, Deborah Mailman; *D:* Rachel Perkins; *W:* Louis Nowra; *C:* Warwick Thornton; *M:* Alistair Jones. Australian Film Inst. '98: Actress (Mailman).

Radio Days ✂✂✂ **1987 (PG)** A lovely, unpretentious remembrance of the pre-TV radio culture. Allen tells his story in a series of vignettes centering around his youth in Brooklyn, his eccentric extended family, and the legends of radio they all followed. The ubiquitous Farrow is a young singer hoping to make it big. **89m/C VHS, DVD, Wide.** Mia Farrow, Dianne Wiest, Julie Kavner, Michael Tucker, Wallace Shawn, Josh Mostel, Tony Roberts, Jeff Daniels, Kenneth Mars, Seth Green, William Magerman, Diane Keaton, Renee Lippin, Danny Aiello, Gina DeAngelis, Kitty Carlisle Hart, Mercedes Ruehl, Tito Puente; ***D:*** Woody Allen; ***W:*** Woody Allen; ***C:*** Carlo Di Palma; ***Nar:*** Woody Allen.

Radio Flyer **1992 (PG-13)** It's 1969 and Mike and Bobby have just moved to northern California with their divorced mom. Everything would be idyllic if only their mother hadn't decided to marry a drunken child abuser who beats Bobby whenever the mood strikes him. Mike decides to help Bobby escape by turning their Radio Flyer wagon into a magic rocketship that will carry Bobby to safety, but ultimately proves tragic. Appealing version of childhood dreams sans the child abuse angle (toned down though it was), which is abruptly and unsatisfactorily handled. **114m/C VHS.** Elijah Wood, Joseph Mazzello, Lorraine Bracco, Adam Baldwin, John Heard, Ben Johnson; ***D:*** Richard Donner; ***Nar:*** Tom Hanks.

Radio Inside ½ **1994** Aimless Matthew (McNamara) comes to live with older brother Michael (Walsh) after their dad's death. Matthew needs someone to listen to him but, unfortunately, his picks his brother's neglected girlfriend Natalie (Shue). Aimless story, as well. **91m/C VHS.** William McNamara, Dylan Walsh, Elisabeth Shue, Gil Goldstein; ***D:*** Jeffrey Bell; ***W:*** Jeffrey Bell. **CABLE**

Radio Patrol **1937** Plenty of action and thrills abound in this 12-chapter serial. Pinky Adams, radio cop, is assisted by his trusty canine partner, Irish (Silverwolf). A cop's best friend is his dog. **235m/B VHS.** Mickey Rentschler, Adrian Morris, Monte Montague, Jack Mulhall, Grant Withers, Catherine Hughes; ***D:*** Ford Beebe, Cliff Smith.

Radioactive Dreams **1986 (R)** Surreal, practically senseless fantasy wherein two men, trapped in a bomb shelter for 15 years with nothing to read but mystery novels, emerge as detectives into a post-holocaust world looking for adventure. **94m/C VHS.** John Stockwell, Michael Dudikoff, Lisa Blount, George Kennedy, Don Murray, Michelle Little; ***D:*** Albert Pyun; ***W:*** Albert Pyun.

Radioland Murders ½ **1994 (PG)** Looks overwhelm weak plot in this mystery-comedy about 1939 Chicago radio station WBN. Lots of stock types (befuddled director, preening announcer, lusty vamp) with Masterson as Penny, the secretary holding everything together except for her marriage to head writer Roger (Benben). Then bodies start piling up during the live broadcast and everyone runs around frantically trying to solve the crimes and keep the broadcast going. Tiring and cliched. **112m/C VHS, DVD.** Brian Benben, Mary Stuart Masterson, Ned Beatty, George Burns, Brion James, Michael Lerner, Michael McKean, Jeffrey Tambor, Scott Michael Campbell, Anita Morris, Stephen Tobolowsky, Christopher Lloyd, Larry Miller, Corbin Bernsen; ***Cameos:*** Robert Klein, Harvey Korman, Peter MacNicol, Joey Lawrence, Bob(cat) Goldthwait; ***D:*** Mel Smith; ***W:*** Willard Huyck, Gloria Katz, Jeff Reno, Ron Osborn; ***C:*** David Tattersall; ***M:*** Joel McNeely.

Rafferty & the Gold Dust Twins ½ *Rafferty and the Highway Hustlers* **1975 (R)** Two women kidnap a motor vehicle inspector at gunpoint in Los Angeles and order him to drive to New Orleans. En route, they become pals. Wandering, pointless female buddy flick. **91m/C VHS.** Alan Arkin, Sally Kellerman, MacKenzie Phillips, Charles Martin Smith, Harry Dean Stanton; ***D:*** Dick Richards; ***M:*** Artie Butler.

The Raffle ½ **1994 (R)** Frank and David travel the globe to find the world's most beautiful woman, who'll be the prize date of the lucky guy with the winning raffle ticket. **100m/C VHS.** Nicholas Lea, Bobby Dawson, Jennifer Clement, Teri-Lynn Rutherford, Jay Underwood, Mark Hamill; ***D:*** Gavin Wilding; ***W:*** John Fairley; ***M:*** Robert O. Ragland.

Raffles **1930** Debonair and dashing gentleman thief A.J. Raffles (Coleman) is a famed cricket player by day and a cat burglar by night, who's always been successful at eluding Scotland Yard. Then he falls for beautiful socialite Lady Gwen Manders (Francis) and gets invited to a weekend house party where Lady Kitty Melrose (Skipworth) just happens to own a very valuable necklace and one of the other guests is suspicious Scotland Yard inspector McKenzie (Torrance). Naturally Raffles goes after the jewels. Based on the novel "The Amateur Cracksman" by Ernest William Hornung. Director D'Arrast was fired by producer Goldwyn and Fitzmaurice finished the film. **72m/B VHS.** Ronald Colman, Kay Francis, Alison Skipworth, David Torrence, Bramwell Fletcher, Frances Dade; ***D:*** Harry D'Abbadie D'Arrast, George Fitzmaurice; ***W:*** Sidney Howard; ***C:*** George Barnes, Gregg Toland.

Rage **1972 (PG)** Scott's directorial debut. A military helicopter sprays peace-loving rancher Scott and his son with nerve gas. The son's death is covered up; the rancher embarks on a vengeful rampage. Scott's sudden transformation to avenging killer is implausible and overwrought. **100m/C VHS.** George C. Scott, Richard Basehart, Martin Sheen, Barnard Hughes, Kenneth Tobey, Ed Lauter, Nicolas Beauvy, Dabbs Greer; ***D:*** George C. Scott; ***C:*** Fred W. Koenekamp.

Rage **1980** Well-acted, well-written, nerve-wracking drama about a convicted rapist who finds help through difficult therapy. Focuses on how the sex-offender discovers the "whys" behind his assaults. **100m/C VHS.** David Soul, James Whitmore, Yaphet Kotto, Caroline McWilliams, Vic Tayback, Sharon Farrell, Craig T. Nelson, Garry Walberg; ***D:*** William A. Graham; ***C:*** Allen Daviau. **TV**

Rage ½ **1995 (R)** When Alex Gainer (Daniels) is kidnapped he becomes the target of a high-tech lab experiment. Injected with chemicals that induce blind and killing rages, Alex escapes and unwillingly goes on a murderous rampage. Now he must find the antidote and clear his name before it happens again. **94m/C VHS.** Gary Daniels, Ken Tigar, Jillian McWhirter, Fiona Hutchinson, Peter Jason, Mark Metcalf; ***D:*** Joseph Merhi; ***W:*** Jacobsen Hart, Joseph John Barmettler Jr.; ***C:*** Ken Blakey; ***M:*** Louis Febre.

The Rage **1996 (R)** Nick Travis (Lamas) is a burned-out FBI agent with a brand new partner Kelly McCord (Cloke), who has no field experience, and a tough assignment. He's after a gang of anti-government killers led by psycho Dacy (Busey). Good action sequences substitute for the lack of plot sense. **95m/C VHS.** Lorenzo Lamas, Gary Busey, Kristen (Kristin) Cloke, Roy Scheider, David Carradine; ***D:*** Sidney J. Furie; ***W:*** Greg Mellott; ***C:*** Donald M. Morgan; ***M:*** Paul Zaza.

Rage and Honor **1992 (R)** Rothrock stars as Kris Fairfield, a high-school teacher who spends her spare time tutoring students in the martial-arts. Her present students are a group of cops, including Aussie visitor Preston Michaels. When Michaels witnesses a drug deal, he gets set-up by the dealers for a murder he didn't commit and only Kris can help him prove his innocence. **93m/C VHS, Wide.** Cynthia Rothrock, Richard Norton, Brian Thompson, Terri Treas, Catherine Bach, Alex Datcher; ***D:*** Terence H. Winkless; ***W:*** Terence H. Winkless.

Rage and Honor 2: Hostile Takeover ½ **1993 (R)** Rothrock returns as black-belt CIA operative Kris Fairfield, whose latest assignment takes her to Jakarta where a banker is involved in a large-scale drug money laundering operation. She teams up with Preston Michaels (Norton), a renegade Australian cop, and winds up following a trail that leads to a fortune in diamonds and lots of trouble. **98m/C VHS.** Cynthia Rothrock, Richard Norton, Patrick Muldoon, Frans Tumbuan, Ron Vreeken, Alex Tumundo; ***D:*** Guy Norris; ***W:*** Louis Sun, Steven Reich.

Rage at Dawn ½ *Seven Bad Men* **1955** An outlaw gang is tracked by a special agent who must "bend" the rules a little in order to get the bad guys. Not surprisingly, he gets his girl as well. A solid standard of the genre, with some clever plot twists. **87m/C VHS, DVD, Wide.** Randolph Scott, Forrest Tucker, Mala Powers, J. Carrol Naish, Edgar Buchanan; ***D:*** Tim Whelan; ***W:*** Horace McCoy; ***C:*** Ray Rennahan; ***M:*** Paul Sawtell.

The Rage: Carrie 2 *Carrie 2* **1999 (R)** You don't need psychic powers to know that things probably aren't going to end well for the tormenting teens in this slightly altered sequel. The heroine this time is Rachel (Bergl), a semi-Goth outcast who has a crush on good guy jock Jesse (London). She also has the ability to rattle and explode things when she's upset. Sue (Irving), the sole survivor from Carrie White's little tantrum years earlier, discovers that Rachel is related to the late telekinetic prom queen and tries to warn her. Too late. Jesse's bitchy girlfriend sets out to humiliate Rachel at a big party held at an all too flammable mansion. Lacks the character development and shock value of the first installment. **97m/C VHS, DVD, Wide.** Emily Bergl, Amy Irving, Jason London, J. Smith-Cameron, Zachery Ty Bryan, John Doe, Gordon Clapp, Rachel Blanchard, Mena Suvari, Eddie Kaye Thomas, Dylan Bruno, Charlotte Ayanna, Justin Urich, Elijah Craig; ***D:*** Katt Shea; ***W:*** Rafael Moreu; ***C:*** Donald M. Morgan; ***M:*** Danny P. Harvey.

A Rage in Harlem **1991 (R)** The crime novels of Chester A. Himes were translated into the best movies of the early '70s blaxploitation era. Now, a Himes story gets the big budget Hollywood treatment with juice and aplomb. A voluptuous lady crook enters Harlem circa 1950 with a trunkful of stolen gold sought by competing crooks, and the chase is on, with one virtuous soul (Whitaker) who only wants the girl. Great cast and characters, much humor, but unsparing in its violence. **108m/C VHS.** Forest Whitaker, Gregory Hines, Robin Givens, Zakes Mokae, Danny Glover, Tyler Collins, Ron Taylor, T.K. Carter, Willard Pugh, Samm-Art Williams, Screamin' Jay Hawkins, Badja (Medu) Djola, John Toles-Bey, Stack Pierce, George D. Wallace; ***D:*** Bill Duke; ***W:*** John Toles-Bey, Bobby Crawford; ***M:*** Elmer Bernstein.

Rage of Angels **1983** Lengthy miniseries adaptation of the Sidney Sheldon novel about an ambitious female attorney, her furs, and her men. Followed by "Rage of Angels: The Story Continues" (1986). **192m/C VHS.** Jaclyn Smith, Ken Howard, Armand Assante, Ronald Hunter, Kevin Conway, George Coe, Deborah May; ***D:*** Buzz Kulik; ***M:*** Billy Goldenberg. **TV**

Rage of Angels: The Story Continues ½ **1986** In this sequel to the Sidney Sheldon trash-with-flash miniseries, Smith reprises her role as the beautiful lady lawyer who always gets involved with the wrong men. This time she tries to hide the fact of her illegitimate son from his father, who's about to become Vice President of the United States. **200m/C VHS.** Jaclyn Smith, Ken Howard, Michael Nouri, Susan Sullivan, Brad Dourif, Angela Lansbury, Mason Adams; ***D:*** Paul Wendkos; ***C:*** Jack Priestley; ***M:*** Billy Goldenberg. **TV**

Rage of Honor **1987 (R)** A high-kicking undercover cop seeks vengeance on bad guys for his partner's murder. Standard of its type; why bother? **92m/C VHS.** Sho Kosugi, Lewis Van Bergen, Robin Evans, Gerry Gibson; ***D:*** Gordon Hessler; ***W:*** Wallace C. Bennett.

The Rage of Paris **1938** Scheming ex-actress and head waiter hope to gain by helping a beautiful French girl (Darrieux) snag a rich hubby. She comes to her senses, realizing that love, true love, matters more than wealth. Well-acted, quaint comedy. **78m/B VHS.** Danielle Darrieux, Douglas Fairbanks Jr., Mischa Auer, Helen Broderick; ***D:*** Henry Koster; ***C:*** Joseph Valentine.

Rage of the Werewolf ½ **1999** Okay, try to follow this. It's 2010 in New York City after an asteroid has collided with the moon, which somehow causes thousands of people to become werewolves. Now Jake was already a werewolf, so he has more flexibility than these newbies, including evil brother Lazlo who wants to unite all the wolves and destroy humanity. But Jake doesn't want anything to do with this evil plot and goes on the run. And then there's some mystery babe with special powers who can possibly help Jake out. **90m/C VHS.** Santo Marotta, Tom Non-Dorf, Hollis Granville, Debbie Rochon, Sasha Graham, Michael (Mick) McCleery, Jon Sanborne; ***D:*** Kevin J. Lindenmuth; ***W:*** Kevin J. Lindenmuth, Santo Marotta. **VIDEO**

Rage of Wind **1982** Master boxer seeks revenge on a Japanese commandant who kidnaps his wife during WWII. **97m/C VHS.** Chen Hsing, Yasuka Kurata, Irene Ryder.

Rage to Kill ½ **1988 (R)** Jingoistic retelling of the 1982 Grenada invasion, complete with helpless American med students. Good-guy race car driver whips them into shape to fight the Soviet-supplied general (he's the bad guy). Guess who wins. **94m/C VHS.** Oliver Reed, James Ryan, Henry Cele, Cameron Mitchell; ***D:*** David Winters.

Raggedy Man **1981 (PG)** Spacek in her signature role as a lonely small-town woman. Here she's raising two sons alone in a small Texas town during WWII. Spacek's strong acting carries a well-scripted story, unfortunately marred by an overwrought ending. **94m/C VHS.** Sissy Spacek, Eric Roberts, Sam Shepard, Tracey Walter, William Sanderson, Henry Thomas; ***D:*** Jack Fisk; ***W:*** William D. Wittliff; ***C:*** Ralf Bode; ***M:*** Jerry Goldsmith.

The Raggedy Rawney ½ **1990 (R)** A young Army deserter dresses in women's clothing and hides out as a mad woman with a band of gypsies. Good first directing effort by English actor Bob Hoskins. Unpretentious and engaging. **102m/C VHS.** Bob Hoskins, Dexter Fletcher, Zoe Nathenson, David Hill, Ian Dury, Zoe Wanamaker, J.G. Devlin, Perry Fenwick; ***D:*** Bob Hoskins; ***W:*** Bob Hoskins, Nicole De Wilde; ***M:*** Michael Kamen.

Ragin' Cajun **1990** Retired kick-boxer is forced into a death match to save his girlfriend. **91m/C VHS.** David Heavener, Charlene Tilton, Sam Bottoms, Samantha Eggar; ***D:*** William B. Hillman.

Raging Angels **1995 (R)** L.A. couple Chris (Flanery) and Lila (Mazur) are struggling rock 'n' rollers when Lila gets a job as a backup singer to star Colin (Pare), who's part of a cult called the Coalition for World Unity. Turns out they're a recruiting org for Satan and are looking for new souls. Our young duo are aided by flamboyant evangelist Sister Kate (Ladd) but it all comes down to a sky battle over downtown L.A. between a good angel and a satanic creature. Lots of unintentional laughs. The director wisely opted for the industry's Smithee pseudonym. **97m/C VHS.** Sean Patrick Flanery, Monet Mazur, Michael Pare, Diane Ladd, Shelley Winters, Arielle Dombasle; ***D:*** Alan Smithee; ***W:*** Kevin Rock, David Markov, Chris Bittler; ***C:*** Bryan England; ***M:*** Terry Plumeri.

Raging Bull **1980 (R)** Scorsese's depressing but magnificent vision of the dying American Dream and suicidal macho codes in the form of the rise and fall of middleweight boxing champ Jake LaMotta, a brutish, dull-witted animal who can express himself only in the ring and through violence. A photographically expressive, brilliant drama, with easily the most intense and brutal boxing scenes ever filmed. De Niro provides a vintage performance, going from the young LaMotta to the aging has-been, and is ably accompanied by Moriarty as his girl and Pesci as his loyal, much beat-upon bro. **128m/B VHS, DVD, 8mm, Wide.** Robert De Niro, Cathy Moriarty, Joe Pesci, Frank Vincent, Nicholas Colasanto, Theresa Saldana; ***D:*** Martin Scorsese; ***W:*** Paul Schrader, Mardik Martin; ***C:*** Michael Chapman; ***M:*** Robbie Robertson. Oscars '80: Actor (De Niro), Film Editing; AFI '98: Top 100; Golden Globes '81: Actor—Drama (De Niro); L.A. Film Critics '80: Actor (De Niro), Film; Natl. Bd. of Review '80: Actor (De Niro), Support. Actor (Pesci), Natl. Film Reg. '90;; N.Y. Film Critics '80: Actor (De Niro), Actor (De Niro), Support. Actor (Pesci, Pesci); Natl. Soc. Film Critics '80: Cinematog., Director (Scorsese), Support. Actor (Pesci).

Rags to Riches **1987** A wealthy Beverly Hills entrepreneur decides to improve his public image by adopting six orphan girls. TV pilot. **96m/C VHS.** Joseph Bologna, Tisha Campbell. **TV**

Ragtime 🦴🦴🦴 **1981 (PG)** The lives and passions of a middle class family weave into the scandals and events of 1906 America. A small, unthinking act represents all the racist attacks on one man, who refuses to back down this time. Wonderful period detail. From the E.L. Doctorow novel, but not nearly as complex. Features Cagney's last film performance. **156m/C VHS.** Howard E. Rollins Jr., Kenneth McMillan, Brad Dourif, Mary Steenburgen, James Olson, Elizabeth McGovern, Pat O'Brien, James Cagney, Debbie Allen, Jeff Daniels, Moses Gunn, Donald O'Connor, Mandy Patinkin, Norman Mailer; ***D:*** Milos Forman; ***W:*** Michael Weller; ***M:*** Randy Newman.

Raid on Entebbe 🦴🦴🦴 **1977 (R)** Dramatization of the Israeli rescue of passengers held hostage by terrorists at Uganda's Entebbe Airport in 1976. A gripping actioner all the more compelling because true. Finch received an Emmy nomination in this, his last film. **113m/C VHS.** Charles Bronson, Peter Finch, Horst Buchholz, John Saxon, Martin Balsam, Jack Warden, Yaphet Kotto, Sylvia Sidney; ***D:*** Irvin Kershner; ***C:*** Bill Butler; ***M:*** David Shire. **TV**

Raid on Rommel 🦴½ **1971 (PG)** A British soldier (Burton) poses as a Nazi and tries to infiltrate Rommel's team with his rag-tag brigade of misfits. Predictable drivel. Contains action footage from the 1967 film "Tobruk." **98m/C VHS, DVD.** Richard Burton, John Colicos, Clinton Greyn, Wolfgang Preiss; ***D:*** Henry Hathaway; ***W:*** Richard M. Bluel; ***C:*** Earl Rath; ***M:*** Hal Mooney.

Raiders of Atlantis 🦴 *The Atlantis Interceptors* **1983** Battles break out when the lost continent surfaces in the Caribbean. The warriors in these apocalyptic frays deploy atomic arsenals. **100m/C VHS.** Christopher Connelly; ***D:*** Roger Franklin.

Raiders of Ghost City 🦴½ **1944** Serial in 13 chapters involves a Union Secret Service Agent after a ring of gold robbers who are posing as Confederate soldiers during the end of the Civil War. **?m/C VHS.** Dennis Moore, Lionel Atwill, Regis Toomey, Wanda McKay.

Raiders of Leyte Gulf 🦴🦴 **1963** Long-unavailable Philippine film from the early 1960s is a throwback to the propaganda that Hollywood produced during WWII. This one features sadistic bucktoothed Japanese soldiers. The protagonists are American POWs and Philippine guerrillas who are setting the stage for MacArthur's return. Director Romero would go on to a busy career in horror and other genres. **80m/B VHS, DVD.** *PH* Leopold Salcedo, Michael Parsons, Jennings Sturgeon, Liza Moreno; ***D:*** Eddie Romero; ***W:*** Carl Kuntze, E.F. Romero; ***C:*** F. Sacdalan; ***M:*** Tito Arevalo.

Raiders of Red Gap 🦴½ **1943** A cattle company tries running homesteaders off their land to get control of it. The Lone Rider saves the day. **56m/B VHS.** Al "Fuzzy" St. John, Robert "Bob" Livingston.

Raiders of Sunset Pass 🦴🦴 **1943** Wartime western quickie makes an interesting novelty today. With most cowboys off fighting the Axis, the ladies form the Women's Army of the Plains to watch out for 4-F rustlers. **57m/B VHS.** Eddie Dew, Smiley Burnette, Jennifer Holt, Roy Barcroft, Mozelle Cravens, Beverly Aadland, Nancy Worth, Kenne Duncan, Jack Rockwell, Budd Buster, Jack Ingram; ***D:*** John English.

Raiders of the Border 🦴 **1944** A white-hatted cowboy must prevent the takeover of a trading post. **55m/B VHS.** Johnny Mack Brown, Raymond Hatton, Ellen Hall.

Raiders of the Lost Ark 🦴🦴🦴🦴 **1981 (PG)** Classic '30s-style adventure reminiscent of early serials spawned two sequels and numerous rip-offs and made Ford a household name as dashing hero and intrepid archeologist Indiana Jones. Set in 1936, Indy battles mean Nazis, decodes hieroglyphics, fights his fear of snakes, and even has time for a little romance in his quest for the biblical Ark of the Covenant. Allen is perfectly cast as his feisty ex-flame Marion, more than a little irritated with the smooth talker who dumped her years earlier. Asks viewers to suspend belief as every chase and stunt tops the last. Unrelated opening sequence does a great job of introducing the character. **115m/C VHS, 8mm.** Harrison Ford, Karen Allen, Wolf Kahler, Paul Freeman, John Rhys-Davies, Denholm Elliott, Ronald Lacey, Anthony (Corlan) Higgins, Alfred Molina; ***D:*** Steven Spielberg; ***W:*** George Lucas, Philip Kaufman; ***M:*** John Williams. Oscars '81: Art Dir./Set Dec., Film Editing, Sound, Visual FX; AFI '98: Top 100, Natl. Film Reg. '99.

Raiders of the Sun 🦴 **1992 (R)** After the Earth has been ruined in a biological disaster, a futuristic warrior arrives to help restore world peace and order. Cheap "Mad Max" ripoff. **80m/C VHS.** Richard Norton, Rick Dean, William (Bill) Steis, Blake Boyd, Brigitta Stenberg, Ned Hourani, Nick Nicholson, Nigel Hogge, Paul Holmes, Ernie Satana; ***D:*** Cirio H. Santiago; ***W:*** Frederick Bailey, Thomas McKelvey Cleaver; ***C:*** Joe Batac; ***M:*** Gary Earl, Odette Springer.

Railroaded 🦴🦴 **1947** The police seek a demented criminal who kills his victims with perfumed-soaked bullets. Tense, excellent noir Anothony Mann crime drama. **72m/B VHS, DVD.** John Ireland, Sheila Ryan, Hugh Beaumont, Ed Kelly, Jane Randolph; ***D:*** Anthony Mann; ***W:*** John C. Higgins; ***C:*** Guy Roe; ***M:*** Alvin Levin.

Railrodder 🦴🦴🦴 **1965** Buster Keaton as the railroader in this slapstick short fumbles his way across Canada. As in the days of the silents, he speaks not a word. **25m/C VHS.** Buster Keaton; ***D:*** Gerald Potterton.

The Railway Children 🦴🦴🦴½ **1970** At the turn of the century in England, the father of three children is framed and sent to prison during Christmas. The trio and their mother must survive on a poverty stricken farm near the railroad tracks. They eventually meet a new friend who helps them prove their father's innocence. Wonderfully directed by Jeffries. From the classic Edith Nesbitt children's novel. **104m/C VHS.** *GB* Jenny Agutter, William Mervyn, Bernard Cribbins, Dinah Sheridan, Iain Cuthbertson, Sally Thomsett, Peter Bromilow, Ann Lancaster, Gary Warren, Gordon Whiting, David Lodge; ***D:*** Lionel Jeffries; ***W:*** Lionel Jeffries; ***C:*** Arthur Ibbetson.

The Railway Children 🦴🦴🦴 **2000** Heart-tugger about the three Waterbury children, who must move to a small village and live in reduced circumstances with their mother (Agutter) when their father (Kitchen) is wrongfully imprisoned. The threesome spend much of their time by the railroad with its stationmaster (Russell) and a kindly railroad tycoon (Attenborough), who takes an interest in their situation. Based on the novel by Edith Nesbitt. Agutter played the role of the eldest daughter in the 1970 film version. **90m/C VHS.** *GB* Jenny Agutter, Michael Kitchen, Jemima Rooper, Jack Blumenau, Clare Thomas, Richard Attenborough, Clive Russell, David Bamber, Gregor Fisher; ***D:*** Catherine Morshead; ***W:*** Simon Nye; ***C:*** John Daly; ***M:*** Simon Lacey. **TV**

The Railway Station Man 🦴🦴🦴 **1992** Set in present-day Ireland. Christie plays a widowed artist struggling to put her life back together after her husband's death in a terrorist bombing. She meets a mysterious American (Sutherland) who's working on restoring the local railway station and finds herself falling in love. When she stumbles upon an IRA bombing plot she also finds out some unpleasant truths about her new lover. Wonderful performances, tragic story. Shot on location in County Donegal, Northern Ireland. Based on the novel by Jennifer Johnston. **93m/C VHS.** Julie Christie, Donald Sutherland, John Lynch, Mark Tandy, Frank McCusker, Niall Cusack; ***D:*** Michael Whyte; ***W:*** Shelagh Delaney. **CABLE**

Rain 🦴🦴½ **1932** W. Somerset Maugham's tale of a puritanical minister's attempt to reclaim a "lost woman" on the island of Pago Pago. Crawford and Huston work up some static. Remake of the 1928 silent film "Sadie Thompson." Remade again in 1953 as "Miss Sadie Thompson." **92m/B VHS, DVD.** Joan Crawford, Walter Huston, William Gargan, Guy Kibbee, Beulah Bondi, Walter Catlett; ***D:*** Lewis Milestone; ***W:*** Maxwell Anderson; ***C:*** Oliver Marsh; ***M:*** Alfred Newman.

The Rain Killer 🦴 **1990 (R)** Big city cop and fed don goloshes to track serial killer who slays rich ladies during heavy precipitation. Soggy story. **94m/C VHS.** Ray Sharkey, David Beecroft, Maria Ford, Woody Brown, Tania Coleridge; ***D:*** Ken Stein; ***W:*** Ray Cunneff.

Rain Man 🦴🦴🦴½ **1988 (R)** When his father dies, ambitious and self-centered Charlie Babbit finds he has an older autistic brother who's been institutionalized for years. Needing him to claim an inheritance, he liberates him from the institution and takes to the road, where both brothers undergo subtle changes. The Vegas montage is wonderful. Critically acclaimed drama and a labor of love for the entire cast. Cruise's best performance to date as he goes from cad to recognizing something wonderfully human in his brother and himself. Hoffman is exceptional. **128m/C VHS, DVD, 8mm.** Dustin Hoffman, Tom Cruise, Valeria Golino, Jerry Molen, Jack Murdock, Michael D. Roberts, Ralph Seymour, Lucinda Jenney, Bonnie Hunt, Kim Robillard, Beth Grant; ***D:*** Barry Levinson; ***W:*** Ronald Bass, Barry Morrow; ***C:*** John Seale; ***M:*** Hans Zimmer. Oscars '88: Actor (Hoffman), Director (Levinson), Orig. Screenplay, Picture; Berlin Intl. Film Fest. '88: Golden Berlin Bear; Directors Guild '88: Director (Levinson); Golden Globes '89: Actor—Drama (Hoffman), Film—Drama.

The Rain People 🦴🦴🦴 **1969 (R)** Pregnant housewife Knight takes to the road in desperation and boredom; along the way she meets retarded ex-football player Caan. Well directed by Coppola from his original script. Pensive drama. **102m/C VHS.** Shirley Knight, James Caan, Robert Duvall, Tom Aldredge, Marya Zimmet, Andrew Duncan, Sally Gracie, Alan Manson, Laura Hope Crews; ***D:*** Francis Ford Coppola; ***W:*** Francis Ford Coppola; ***C:*** Bill Butler; ***M:*** Ronald Stein.

Rain Without Thunder 🦴🦴½ **1993 (PG-13)** Imagine the year 2042, a time when abortion is illegal and a fertilized egg has full Constitutional rights. Now imagine sitting through an 87 minute fake documentary that follows the story of a mother and daughter team who have been jailed for trying to go to Sweden so that the daughter can get an abortion. A one-sided, militant pro-choice effort that is neither entertaining nor informational. **87m/C VHS.** Betty Buckley, Jeff Daniels, Ali Thomas, Frederic Forrest, Carolyn McCormick, Linda Hunt, Robert Earl Jones, Graham Greene, Iona Morris, Austin Pendleton; ***D:*** Gary Bennett; ***W:*** Gary Bennett; ***M:*** Randall Lynch, Allen Lynch.

Rainbow 🦴🦴 **1978** Broadway's "Annie" is badly miscast as Judy Garland from her early years in vaudeville to her starring years at MGM. Based on the book by Christopher Finch. Directed by sometime-Garland flame Jackie Cooper. **100m/C VHS.** Andrea McArdle, Jack Carter, Don Murray; ***D:*** Jackie Cooper; ***M:*** Charles Fox. **TV**

The Rainbow 🦴🦴🦴 **1989 (R)** Mature, literate rendering of the classic D.H. Lawrence novel about a young woman's sexual awakening. Beautiful cinematography. Companion/prequel to director Russell's earlier Lawrence adaptation, "Women in Love" (1969). **104m/C VHS.** *GB* Sammi Davis, Amanda Donohoe, Paul McGann, Christopher Gable, David Hemmings, Glenda Jackson, Kenneth Colley; ***D:*** Ken Russell; ***W:*** Vivian Russell, Ken Russell; ***C:*** Billy Williams; ***M:*** Carl Davis.

Rainbow Bridge 🦴 **1971 (R)** The adventures of a group of hippies searching for their consciousness in Hawaii. Features concert footage from Jimi Hendrix's final performance. **74m/C VHS, DVD.** Chuck Wein, Herbie Fletcher, Pat Hartley; ***D:*** Chuck Wein; ***C:*** Vilis Lapenieks.

Rainbow Drive 🦴🦴½ **1990 (R)** Cop thriller promises great things but fails to deliver. Weller is a good cop trapped in the political intrigues of Hollywood. He discovers five dead bodies; when the official count is four, he detects funny business. From the novel by Roderick Thorp. **93m/C VHS.** Peter Weller, Sela Ward, Bruce Weitz, David Caruso, James Laurenson, Chris Mulkey, Kathryn Harrold; ***D:*** Bobby Roth; ***W:*** Roderick Thorp, Bill Phillips, Bennett Cohen; ***M:*** Tangerine Dream. **CABLE**

The Rainbow Gang 🦴 **1973** A trio of unlikely prospectors heads into a legendary mine in search of riches and fame. **90m/C VHS.** Donald Pleasence, Don Calfa, Kate Reid.

Rainbow over Broadway **1933** A former Broadway star mother is set against having her son and daughter try their luck on Broadway. **52m/C VHS.** Joan Marsh, Frank Albertson, Lucien Littlefield, Grace Hayes, Dell Henderson, Harry C. (Henry) Myers, Gladys Blake, Glen Boles, Nat Carr; ***D:*** Richard Thorpe.

Rainbow over Texas 🦴🦴 **1946** Roy and the Sons of the Pioneers head to his hometown on a promotional tour. Roy enters the local Pony Express race but some disgruntled locals try to make certain that he doesn't win. **65m/B VHS.** Roy Rogers, Dale Evans, George "Gabby" Hayes, Sheldon Leonard; ***D:*** Frank McDonald; ***W:*** Gerald Geraghty; ***C:*** Reggie Lanning.

Rainbow Ranch 🦴½ **1933** A Navy boxer returns home to his ranch to find murder and corruption. Needless to say, he rides off to seek revenge. **54m/B VHS.** Rex Bell, Cecilia Parker, Robert F. (Bob) Kortman, Henry Hall, Gordon DeMain; ***D:*** Harry Fraser.

Rainbow Warrior 🦴🦴½ **1994 (PG)** True story of the bombing of the Greenpeace vessel and the two men who set out to solve the crime. **90m/C VHS.** Sam Neill, Jon Voight, Kerry Fox, Bruno Lawrence; ***D:*** Michael Tuchner.

Rainbow's End 🦴🦴 **1935** Gibson must defend Gale, the female rancher, from an evil adversary who is trying to run Gale and her invalid father off of their land. Things get complicated when Gibson discovers that Richmond works for his father! **54m/B VHS.** Hoot Gibson, June Gale, Oscar Apfel, Ada Ince, Charles Hill, Warner Richmond; ***D:*** Norman Spencer.

Raining Stones 🦴🦴 **1993** A hard-up plumber becomes obsessed with buying an expensive first communion dress for his daughter and gets involved in numerous misadventures trying to get the money. Another of Loach's comedy-dramas about the British working class and their struggle to survive with dignity. **90m/C VHS, DVD.** *GB* Bruce Jones, Julie Brown, Ricky Tomlinson, Tom Hickey, Gemma Phoenix, Jonathan James; ***D:*** Ken Loach; ***W:*** Jim Allen; ***C:*** Barry Ackroyd; ***M:*** Stewart Copeland. Cannes '93: Special Jury Prize.

The Rainmaker 🦴🦴🦴 **1956** Reminiscent of "Elmer Gantry" in his masterful performance, Lancaster makes it all believable as a con man who comes to a small midwestern town and works miracles not only on the weather but on spinster Hepburn, although both were a little long in the tooth for their roles. Written by Nash from his own play. **121m/C VHS, DVD.** Burt Lancaster, Katharine Hepburn, Wendell Corey, Lloyd Bridges, Earl Holliman, Cameron Prudhomme, Wallace Ford; ***D:*** Joseph Anthony; ***W:*** N. Richard Nash; ***C:*** Charles B(ryant) Lang Jr.; ***M:*** Alex North. Golden Globes '57: Support. Actor (Holliman).

The Rains Came 🦴🦴½ **1939** Living within a loveless marriage in the mythical Indian city of Ranchipur, English socialite Loy pursues extramarital love interests, including the compassionate doctor Power, potential heir to the maharajah's throne. When an earthquake hits and brings major destruction to the city, Loy aids the doctor in helping the injured. Hankies should be kept handy. Adapted from the Louis Bromfield novel. **104m/B VHS.** Myrna Loy, Tyrone Power, George Brent, Brenda Joyce, Nigel Bruce, Maria Ouspenskaya, Joseph Schildkraut, Laura Hope Crews, Marilyn Nash, Jane Darwell, Marjorie Rambeau, Henry Travers, H.B. Warner, William Royle, C. Montague Shaw, Harry Hayden, Abner Biberman, George Regas; ***D:*** Clarence Brown; ***W:*** Philip Dunne, Julien Josephson; ***C:*** Arthur C. Miller; ***M:*** Alfred Newman.

Raintree County 🦴🦴½ **1957** A lavish, somewhat overdone epic about two lovers caught up in the national turmoil of the Civil War. An Indiana teacher (Clift) marries a southern belle (Taylor) just after the outbreak of war. The new wife battles mental illness. Producers had hoped this would be another "Gone with the Wind." Adapted from the novel by Ross Lockridge Jr. Film was delayed in mid-production by Clift's near-fatal and disfiguring car crash. **175m/C VHS, Wide.** Elizabeth Taylor, Montgomery Clift, Eva Marie Saint, Lee Marvin, Nigel Patrick, Rod Taylor, Agnes Moorehead, Walter Abel; *D:* Edward Dmytryk; *C:* Robert L. Surtees.

Raise the Red Lantern 🦴🦴🦴½ **1991 (PG)** Set in 1920s China, Zhang explores its claustrophobic world of privilege and humiliation. Songlian, an educated 19-year-old beauty, is forced into marriage as the fourth wife of a wealthy and powerful old man. She discovers that the wives have their own separate quarters and servants, and spend most of their time battling to attract their husband's attention. Over the course of a year, Songlian's fury and resentment grow until self-defeating rebellion is all she has. Gong Li is exquisite as the young woman struggling for dignity in a portrayal which is both haunting and tragic. **125m/C VHS.** *CH* Gong Li, Ma Jingwu, He Caifei, Cao Cuifeng, Jin Shuyuan, Kong Lin, Ding Weimin; *D:* Zhang Yimou. British Acad. '92: Foreign Film; L.A. Film Critics '92: Cinematog.; N.Y. Film Critics '92: Foreign Film; Natl. Soc. Film Critics '92: Cinematog., Foreign Film.

Raise the Titanic woof! **1980 (PG)** A disaster about a disaster. Horrible script cannot be redeemed by purported thrill of the ship's emergence from the deep after 70 years. It's a shame, because the free world's security hangs in the balance. Based on Clive Cussler's best seller. **112m/C VHS.** Jason Robards Jr., Richard Jordan, Anne Archer, Alec Guinness, J.D. Cannon; *D:* Jerry Jameson; *M:* John Barry.

A Raisin in the Sun 🦴🦴🦴🦴 **1961** Outstanding story of a black family trying to make a better life for themselves in an all-white neighborhood in Chicago. The characters are played realistically and make for a moving story. Each person struggles with doing what he must while still maintaining his dignity and sense of self. Based on the 1959 Broadway play by Hansberry, who also wrote the screenplay. Remade for TV in 1989 with Danny Glover. **128m/B VHS, DVD, Wide.** Diana Sands, John Fiedler, Ivan Dixon, Louis Gossett Jr., Sidney Poitier, Claudia McNeil, Ruby Dee; *D:* Daniel Petrie; *W:* Lorraine Hansberry; *C:* Charles Lawton Jr.; *M:* Laurence Rosenthal. Natl. Bd. of Review '61: Support. Actress (Dee).

A Raisin in the Sun 🦴🦴🦴 **1989** An "American Playhouse" presentation of the Lorraine Hansberry play about a black family threatened with dissolution by the outside forces of racism and greed when they move into an all-white neighborhood in the 1950s. **171m/C VHS.** Danny Glover, Esther Rolle, Starletta DuPois; *D:* Bill Duke. **TV**

Raising Arizona 🦴🦴🦴½ **1987 (PG-13)** Hi's an ex-con and the world's worst hold-up man. Ed's a policewoman. They meet, fall in love, marry, and kidnap a baby (one of a family of quints). Why not? Ed's infertile and the family they took the baby from has "more than enough," so who will notice? But unfinished furniture tycoon Nathan Arizona wants his baby back, even if he has to hire an axe murderer on a motorcycle to do it. A brilliant, original comedy narrated in notorious loopy deadpan style by Cage. Innovative camera work by Barry Sonnenfeld. Wild, surreal, and hilarious. **94m/C VHS, DVD.** Nicolas Cage, Holly Hunter, John Goodman, William Forsythe, Randall "Tex" Cobb, Trey Wilson, M. Emmet Walsh, Frances McDormand, Sam McMurray, T.J. Kuhn, Peter Benedek; *D:* Joel Coen; *W:* Ethan Coen, Joel Coen; *C:* Barry Sonnenfeld; *M:* Carter Burwell.

Raising Cain 🦴🦴 **1992 (R)** Thriller evoking poor man's Hitchcock about a child psychiatrist who just happens to be nuts features Lithgow in five roles. Seems his supposedly dead Norwegian father has come to the United States and needs his son's help to steal babies for a child development experiment, so the son's alter ego, Cain, shows up to commit the nasty deed. Unfortunately Lithgow also catches his wife with another man, and that's when the bodies start piling up. **95m/C VHS, DVD, Wide.** John Lithgow, Lolita (David) Davidovich, Steven Bauer, Frances Sternhagen, Cindy Girard, Tom Bower, Mel Harris, Gabrielle Carteris, Barton Heyman; *D:* Brian DePalma; *W:* Brian DePalma; *C:* Stephen Burum; *M:* Pino Donaggio.

Raising Heroes 🦴🦴 **1997** Josh (Sistillio) and Paul (White) are about to finalize their adoption of a child when Josh witnesses a mob hit. Now he's a target, trying to stay alive and protect his family as well. **85m/C VHS.** Troy Sistillio, Henry White; *D:* Douglas Langway; *W:* Douglas Langway.

Raising the Heights 🦴½ **1997 (R)** Tensions escalate in the Brooklyn neighbor of Crown Heights when a drug deal, involving a high school teacher, results in the death of a young girl. So the victim's brother, Michael, decides to take revenge by taking a teacher hostage, with reporter Judy Burke leading a media barrage about the tense situation. Good intentions can't quite make up for the amateur filmmaking. **86m/C VHS.** Gilbert Brown Jr., John Knox, Fia Perera; *D:* Max Gottlieb; *W:* Max Gottlieb.

Rambling Rose 🦴🦴🦴 **1991 (R)** Dern is Rose, a free-spirited, sexually liberated before her time young woman taken in by a Southern family in 1935. Rose immediately has an impact on the male members of the clan, father Duvall and son Haas, thanks to her insuppressible sexuality. This causes consternation with the strait-laced patriarch, who attempts to control his desire for the girl. Eventually Rose decides she must try to stick to one man, but this only causes further problems. Dern gives her best performance yet in this excellent period piece, and solid support is offered from the rest of the cast, in particular Duvall and Dern's real-life mother Ladd. **115m/C VHS, DVD, Wide.** Laura Dern, Diane Ladd, Robert Duvall, Lukas Haas, John Heard, Kevin Conway, Robert John Burke, Lisa Jakub, Evan Lockwood; *D:* Martha Coolidge; *W:* Calder Willingham; *C:* Johnny E. Jensen; *M:* Elmer Bernstein. Ind. Spirit '92: Director (Coolidge), Film, Support. Actress (Ladd).

Rambo: First Blood, Part 2 🦴🦴 **1985 (R)** If anyone can save Our Boys still held prisoner in Asia it's John Rambo. Along the way he's tortured, flexes biceps, grunts, and then disposes of the bad guys by the dozen in one of filmdom's bigger dead body parades. Mindless action best enjoyed by testosterone-driven fans of the genre. Sequel to "First Blood" (1982); followed by "Rambo 3" (1988). **93m/C VHS, DVD.** Sylvester Stallone, Richard Crenna, Charles Napier, Steven Berkoff, Julia Nickson-Soul, Martin Kove; *D:* George P. Cosmatos; *W:* Sylvester Stallone, James Cameron; *C:* Jack Cardiff; *M:* Jerry Goldsmith. Golden Raspberries '85: Worst Picture, Worst Actor (Stallone), Worst Screenplay, Worst Song ("Peace In Our Life").

Rambo 3 🦴½ **1988 (R)** John Rambo, the famous Vietnam vet turned Buddhist monk, this time invades Afghanistan to rescue his mentor. Meets up with orphan and fights his way around the country. Typically exploitative, kill now, ask questions later Rambo attack, lacking the sheer volume of no-brainer action of the first two Rambos. At the time, the most expensive film ever made, costing $58 million. Filmed in Israel. **102m/C VHS, DVD.** Sylvester Stallone, Richard Crenna, Marc De Jonge, Kurtwood Smith, Spiros Focas; *D:* Peter McDonald; *W:* Sylvester Stallone; *C:* John Stanier; *M:* Jerry Goldsmith. Golden Raspberries '88: Worst Actor (Stallone).

Rampage 🦴🦴 **1987 (R)** Seemingly all-American guy Charles Reece (McArthur) goes on a murder spree, killing and then mutiliating his victims. Fraser (Biehn) is a liberal district attorney who questions his own views as he argues during the trial that Reece was sane when he committed the murders and deserves the death penalty. Director Friedkin makes no bones about his concerns that the criminal insanity defense often spares the perpetrator while denying justice to the victims. Adapted from the book by William P. Wood and loosely based on killer Richard Chase. Filmed in 1987, the movie wasn't released until 1992 due to the production company's financial difficulties. **92m/C VHS.** Michael Biehn, Alex McArthur, Nicholas (Nick) Campbell, Deborah Van Valkenburgh, John Harkins, Art LaFleur; *D:* William Friedkin; *W:* William Friedkin; *M:* Ennio Morricone.

Ramparts of Clay 🦴🦴🦴 **1971 (PG)** A young woman in Tunisia walks the line between her village's traditional way of life and the modern world just after her country's independence from France. Brilliantly shot on location; exquisitely poignant. In Arabic with English subtitles. **87m/C VHS.** *FR* *D:* Jean-Louis Bertucelli.

Ramrod 🦴🦴 **1947** Lake is a tough ranch owner at odds with her father, who is being manipulated by a big-time cattleman into trying to put them out of business. She fights back, and McCrea is caught in the middle as the only good guy. Nothing special. **94m/B VHS.** Veronica Lake, Joel McCrea, Arleen Whelan, Don DeFore, Preston Foster, Charlie Ruggles, Donald Crisp, Lloyd Bridges; *D:* Andre de Toth.

Ran 🦴🦴🦴🦴 **1985 (R)** The culmination of Kurosawa's career stands as his masterpiece. Loosely adapting Shakespeare's "King Lear," with plot elements from "Macbeth," he's fashioned an epic, heartbreaking statement about honor, ambition, and the futility of war. Aging medieval warlord Hidetora gives control of his empire to his oldest son, creating conflict with two other sons. Soon he's an outcast, as ambition and greed seize the two sons. Stunning battle scenes illuminate the full-blown tragedy of Kurosawa's vision. Superb acting with a scene-stealing Harada as the revenge-minded Lady Kaede; period costumes took three years to create. Japanese with English subtitles. **160m/C VHS, DVD, Wide.** *JP FR* Tatsuya Nakadai, Akira Terao, Jinpachi Nezu, Daisuke Ryu, Meiko Harada, Hisashi Igawa, Peter, Kazuo Kato, Takeshi Kato, Jun Tazaki, Toshiya Ito, Yoshiko Miyazaki, Masayuki Yui, Norio Matsui, Takashi Nomura; *D:* Akira Kurosawa; *W:* Akira Kurosawa, Hideo Oguni, Masato Ide; *C:* Asakazu Nakai, Takao Saito, Masaharu Ueda; *M:* Toru Takemitsu. Oscars '85: Costume Des.; British Acad. '86: Foreign Film; L.A. Film Critics '85: Foreign Film; Natl. Bd. of Review '85: Director (Kurosawa); N.Y. Film Critics '85: Foreign Film; Natl. Soc. Film Critics '85: Cinematog., Film.

Rana: The Legend of Shadow Lake 🦴 **1975** Gold at the bottom of a lake is guarded by a frog-monster, but treasure hunters try to retrieve it anyway. **96m/C VHS.** Alan Ross, Karen McDiarmid, Jerry Gregoris.

The Ranch 🦴🦴 **1988 (PG-13)** An executive who loses everything inherits a dilapidated ranch and renovates it into a health spa. **97m/C VHS.** Andrew Stevens, Gary Fjellgaard, Lou Ann Schmidt, Elizabeth Keefe; *D:* Stella Stevens.

Rancho Deluxe 🦴🦴🦴 **1975** Offbeat western spoof starring Bridges and Waterston as two carefree cowpokes. Cult favorite featuring music by Buffett, who also appears in the film. **93m/C VHS, DVD, Wide.** Jeff Bridges, Sam Waterston, Elizabeth Ashley, Charlene Dallas, Clifton James, Slim Pickens, Harry Dean Stanton, Richard Bright, Jimmy Buffett; *D:* Frank Perry; *W:* Thomas McGuane; *C:* William A. Fraker; *M:* Jimmy Buffett.

Rancho Notorious 🦴🦴🦴 **1952** Kennedy, on the trail of his girlfriend's murderer, falls for dance hall girl Dietrich. Fine acting. A "period" sample oF '50s westerns, but different. A must for Dietrich fans. **89m/C VHS.** Marlene Dietrich, Arthur Kennedy, Mel Ferrer, William Frawley, Jack Elam, George Reeves; *D:* Fritz Lang; *W:* Daniel Taradash; *C:* Hal Mohr.

Rancid Aluminium 🦴½ **2000** Druggie Pete Thompson (Ifans) inherits his family's failing publishing business, which ticks off his friend (and the company's accountant) Sean Deeny (Fiennes). So Sean decides to take over the business by borrowing money from Russian mobster, Mr. Kant (Berkoff). Pete thinks Sean is just getting an additonal source of capital. Pete sleeps around and eventually learns what Sean is really up to. The Russian wants a return on his investment. And the viewer will wonder why he's wasting his time since this movie is dumb. Based on the novel by Hawes, who did the screenplay. **91m/C VHS, DVD.** *GB* Rhys Ifans, Joseph Fiennes, Steven Berkoff, Tara Fitzgerald, Sadie Frost, Dani Behr, Keith Allen, Nick Moran; *D:* Edward Thomas; *W:* James Hawes; *C:* Tony Imi; *M:* John E.R. Hardy.

Random Encounter 🦴½ **1998** Executive Berkley becomes invovled in extortion and a murder cover-up all because she takes a shine to a mystery man. **100m/C VHS, DVD.** *CA* Elizabeth Berkley, Joel Wyner, Frank Schorpion, Barry Flatman, Mark Walker, Ellen David, Susan Glover, Frank Fontaine; *D:* Douglas Jackson; *W:* Matt Dorff; *C:* Georges Archambault; *M:* Daniel Scott. **VIDEO**

Random Harvest 🦴🦴🦴 **1942** A masterful, tearjerking film based on the James Hilton novel. A shell-shocked WWI amnesiac meets and is made happy by a beautiful music hall dancer. He regains his memory and forgets about the dancer and their child. This is Garson's finest hour, and a shamelessly potent sobfest. **126m/B VHS.** Greer Garson, Ronald Colman, Reginald Owen, Philip Dorn, Susan Peters, Henry Travers, Margaret Wycherly, Bramwell Fletcher; *D:* Mervyn LeRoy; *C:* Joseph Ruttenberg.

Random Hearts 🦴🦴 **1999 (R)** If this film had stuck to overcoming tragedy and finding new love, it could have been a classic romantic weepie. But the addition of some police corruption malarkey and a slow pace undermine the emotional payoff. Congresswoman Kay Chandler (Scott Thomas) and internal affairs cop Dutch Van Den Broeck (Ford) discover that their respective spouses, who were killed in the same airliner crash, had been having an affair. Dutch needs to know all the sordid details when Kay, who's up for re-election, wants the potentially scandalous situation to remain quiet. Based on the novel by Warren Adler. **133m/C VHS, DVD.** Harrison Ford, Kristin Scott Thomas, Sydney Pollack, Charles S. Dutton, Bonnie Hunt, Dennis Haysbert, Richard Jenkins, Paul Guilfoyle, Susanna Thompson, Peter Coyote, Dylan Baker, Lynne Thigpen, Bill Cobbs, Susan Floyd, Edie Falco, Kate Mara; *D:* Sydney Pollack; *W:* Kurt Luedtke; *C:* Philippe Rousselot; *M:* Dave Grusin.

Randy Rides Alone 🦴🦴 **1934** Very young Wayne is good in this slappable but pleasant B effort. Wayne single-handedly cleans up the territory and rids the land of a passel o'bad guys. **53m/B VHS, DVD.** John Wayne, Alberta Vaughn, George "Gabby" Hayes; *D:* Harry Fraser; *W:* Lindsley Parsons.

Range Busters 🦴 **1940** Range Busters are called in to find the identity of the phantom killer. **55m/B VHS.** Ray Corrigan, Max Terhune.

Range Feud 🦴½ **1931** Wayne is a ranch owner's son falsely accused of murder. Just as he's about to hang, Jones, as the heroic sheriff, saves the day and reveals the real killer's identity. **58m/B VHS.** Buck Jones, John Wayne, Susan Fleming, William Walling, Wallace MacDonald, Harry Woods, Ed LeSaint; *D:* David Ross Lederman.

Range Law 🦴 **1931** Another entry in the infamous Maynard series of horseplay, cliche, and repetitive plot elements. **60m/B VHS.** Ken Maynard, Charles "Blackie" King, Lafe (Lafayette) McKee.

Range Law 🦴½ **1944** Ranchers are being terrorized for their silver mine and its up to Brown and Hatton to catch the villains. **59m/B VHS.** Johnny Mack Brown, Raymond Hatton, Lloyd Ingraham, Sarah Padden, Ellen Hall, Steve Clark, Jack Ingram, Bud Osborne; *D:* Lambert Hillyer.

Range of Motion 🦴🦴½ **2000** After an accident, Lainie Berman's (De Mornay) husband slips into a coma but she's positive he can recover if she has enough faith. Based on the book by Elizabeth Berg. **120m/C VHS, DVD.** Rebecca DeMornay, Henry Czerny, Melanie Mayron, Barclay Hope, Kimberly Roberts; *D:* Donald Wyre; *W:* Grace McKeaney; *C:* Malcolm Cross; *M:* Gary Chang. **CABLE**

Range Renegades 🦴½ **1948** Sheriff Wakely and his pals have their hands full when his deputy gets involved with the leader of a gang of outlaw women. Predictable B oater reflects the then developing trend of using wicked female characters in westerns. Paved the way for films like "Johnny Guitar" and "Rancho

Notorious." **54m/B VHS.** Jimmy Wakely, Dub Taylor, Dennis Moore, Jennifer Holt, John James, Steve Clark, Frank LaRue; ***D:*** Lambert Hillyer; ***W:*** Ronald Davidson, William Lively.

Range Riders **1935** A gunman poses as a wimp and cleans out an outlaw gang. **46m/B VHS.** Buddy Roosevelt.

Rangeland Empire 🦴 **1950** Shamrock and Lucky are at it again, implicated as being members of an outlaw gang until that gang attacks them. **59m/B VHS.** James Ellison, Russell Hayden, Stanley Price, John Cason.

Rangeland Racket 🦴½ **1941** The Lone Rider (Houston) has been wrongly accused of a crime. **60m/B VHS.** George Houston, Hillary Brooke, Al "Fuzzy" St. John.

Ranger and the Lady 🦴½ **1940** Texas Ranger Rogers romances the woman who is the leader of a wagon train. **54m/B VHS.** Roy Rogers, George "Gabby" Hayes; ***D:*** Joseph Kane.

Rangers 🦴🦴 **2000 (R)** McCoy leads an Army Rangers team in capturing a terrorist bomber and while they accomplish their mission, the unit is forced to leave behind Plummer, which turns out to be part of a government setup. Not happy about this, Plummer joins the terrorists to get revenge and goes after his ex-buddies while McCoy realizes there's a conspiracy going on. **100m/C VHS, DVD, Wide.** Matt McCoy, Glenn Plummer, Corbin Bernsen, Dartanyan Edmonds, Rene Rivera; ***D:*** Jim Wynorski; ***W:*** Steve Latshaw; ***C:*** Ken Blakey; ***M:*** David Wurst, Eric Wurst. **VIDEO**

Ranger's Roundup 🦴 **1938** The Rangers prove their courage by rounding up an outlaw gang. **57m/B VHS.** Fred Scott, Al "Fuzzy" St. John.

The Rangers Step In 🦴½ **1937** Allen leaves the Texas Rangers when a feud between his family and that of the girl he loves heats up again. Turns out rustlers are stirring things up in order to get some of the disputed land. **56m/B VHS.** Robert "Tex" Allen, Eleanor Stewart, John Merton, Hal Taliaferro, Jack Ingram, Jack Rockwell, Lafe (Lafayette) McKee, Robert F. (Bob) Kortman; ***D:*** Spencer Gordon Bennet.

Rangers Take Over 🦴½ **1943** Gunlords are driven out by the Texas Rangers. **62m/B VHS.** Dave O'Brien, James Newill.

Ransom 🦴🦴🦴 **1996 (R)** Tight and crafty thriller proves millionaire airline magnate Tom Mullen (Gibson) is a force to be reckoned with when son Sean (Nolte, son of actor Nick) is kidnapped. A vigilante Donald Trump (only gorgeous and brave), Mullen treats this like a high-stakes business deal and decides to get his kid back by announcing on TV that the $2 million ransom demand will instead become a bounty on the kidnappers. Wife Kate (Russo), predictably flips out but Mullen, after a few encounters with the heinous abductors, has sized them up and is convinced he's done the right thing. Lindo is a by-the-book fed with bad dialogue and Sinise is a bad cop playing for the other team. Gibson's emergency appendectomy delayed filming but he was soon leaping over cars for director Howard's well-staged action scenes. Based on the 1956 flick starring Glenn Ford. **121m/C VHS, DVD.** Mel Gibson, Rene Russo, Gary Sinise, Delroy Lindo, Brawley Nolte, Lili Taylor, Liev Schreiber, Evan Handler, Dan Hedaya, Paul Guilfoyle, Jose Zuniga, Donnie Wahlberg, Michael Gaston, Nancy Ticotin; ***Cameos:*** Richard Price; ***D:*** Ron Howard; ***W:*** Richard Price, Alexander Ignon; ***C:*** Piotr Sobocinski; ***M:*** James Horner.

Ransom Money 🦴½ **1988** A kidnapping scheme involving millions of dollars, in and around the Grand Canyon, backfires. **87m/C VHS.** Broderick Crawford, Rachel Romen, Gordon Jump, Randy Whipple; ***D:*** DeWitt Lee.

Ranson's Folly 🦴🦴½ **1926** Barthelmess makes a wager that he can impersonate a famous outlaw well enough to rob a stage with only a pair of scissors. When the army paymaster is killed, guess who gets caught with his swash unbuckled? **80m/B VHS.** Richard Barthelmess, Dorothy Mackaill, Anders Randolf, Pat Hartigan, Brooks Benedict; ***D:*** Sidney Olcott.

Rapa Nui 🦴🦴½ **1993 (R)** The title refers to the Polynesian name for Easter Island, with the film set in the 17th century (before Dutch explorers discovered the island). It depicts the annual rituals of the mysterious people who built the Island's moai—the famous giant stone statues. Lee plays the heroic Noroinia, with Morales as his rival Make, and Holt as Ramana, the object of their desires. Faux primitive but with some great on-location filming. **107m/C VHS.** Jason Scott Lee, Esai Morales, Sandrine Holt; ***D:*** Kevin Reynolds; ***W:*** Kevin Reynolds, Tim Rose Price; ***M:*** Stewart Copeland.

Rape 🦴 **198?** Two guys investigate a third pal's mysterious death. They discover that his supernatural-power-imbued girlfriend is at the root of the matter. **90m/C VHS.** Rick Joss, Gil Vidal.

Rape and Marriage: The Rideout Case 🦴🦴½ **1980** The true story of an Oregon wife who accused her husband of rape. Thoughtfully explores the legal and moral questions raised by the case. Interpreted well enough, though not superbly, by a decent cast (although Rourke is a little too intense). **96m/C VHS.** Mickey Rourke, Linda Hamilton, Rip Torn, Eugene Roche, Conchata Ferrell, Gail Strickland, Bonnie Bartlett, Alley Mills; ***D:*** Peter Levin. **TV**

Rape of Love 🦴🦴½ **1979** The story begins with one of the most chilling rape scenes on film and then attempts to analyze the emotional impact of rape on its victim. Well-acted and directed. In French with English subtitles. **117m/C VHS.** *FR* Nathalie Nell, Alain Foures; ***D:*** Yannick Bellon.

The Rape of the Sabines woof! *El Rapto de las Sabinas; The Mating of the Sabine Women; Shame of the Sabine Women* **1961** The story of Romulus, king of Rome, and how he led the Romans to capture the women of Sabina. The battles rage, the women plot, and Romulus fights and lusts. Dubbed in English. **101m/C VHS.** *IT FR* Roger Moore, Mylene Demongeot, Jean Marais; ***D:*** Richard Pottier.

Rapid Assault 🦴🦴 **1999 (R)** Terrorist Lars Rynark (Scribner) is set to detonate a biochemical agent in the Atlantic Ocean that will decimate the population—unless he gets paid a lot of cash. Three government ops are sent to get to the terrorist first. Typical action fodder—the plot making any sense is besides the point. **90m/C VHS, DVD.** Tim Abell, Don Scribner, Jeff Rector, Lisa Mazzetti; ***D:*** Sherman Scott. **VIDEO**

Rapid Fire 🦴 **1989** Cheap, made-for-video quickie about a good guy U.S. agent who battles terrorists. Easy to skip. **90m/C VHS.** Joe Spinell, Michael Wayne, Ron Waldron; ***D:*** David A. Prior.

Rapid Fire 🦴🦴½ **1992 (R)** Lee (son of martial arts cult film star Bruce Lee) is a Chinese-American art student who also happens to be a martial arts expert. He's tapped by the police to help stem the violence between the Asian and Italian gangs fighting for control over Chicago's drug trade. Typical martial arts movie is made better by uniquely choreographed action sequences and Lee's attractive presence. **96m/C VHS.** Brandon Lee, Powers Boothe, Nick Mancuso, Raymond J. Barry, Kate Hodge, Tzi Ma, Tony Longo, Michael Paul Chan, Dustin Nguyen, John Vickery; ***D:*** Dwight Little; ***W:*** Alan B. McElroy, Cindy Cirile, Paul Attanasio; ***M:*** Christopher Young.

Rappin' 🦴 **1985 (PG)** Ex-con Van Peebles gets into it with the landlord and a street gang leader. Forgettable action/music drivel. ♫Rappin'; Two of a Kind; Call Me; Born to Love; Killer; Itching for a Scratch; Snack Attack; Dodge; Golly Gee. **92m/C VHS.** Mario Van Peebles, Tasia Valenza, Harry Goz, Charles Flohe; ***D:*** Joel Silberg.

The Rapture 🦴🦴 **1991 (R)** A beautiful telephone operator engages in indiscriminate sexual adventures to relieve the boredom of her job and life. She becomes curious by, and eventually converted to, evangelical Christianity, which leads her to a contented marriage and the birth of a daughter. When her husband is tragically killed she becomes convinced that she and her child will be taken by God into heaven if she only waits for the proper sign. **100m/C VHS.** Mimi Rogers, David Duchovny, Patrick Bauchau, Will Patton; ***D:*** Michael Tolkin; ***W:*** Michael Tolkin; ***C:*** Bojan Bazelli.

Rapunzel **1982** A beautiful young woman locked in a tall tower is saved by the handsome prince who climbs her golden tresses. Part of Shelly Duvall's "Faerie Tale Theatre" series. **60m/C VHS.** Shelley Duvall, Gena Rowlands, Jeff Bridges.

Rare Birds 🦴🦴½ **2001** Quirky Canadian comedy finds Dave Purcell (Hurt) depressed. His restaurant, located in the small town of Cape Spear, Newfoundland, is failing as is his long-distance marriage. But his eccentric neighbor Alphonse (Jones) comes up with a plan—he spreads the word among birders that a rare duck has been sighted and soon the area is flooded with amateur ornithologists, which is certainly good for Dave's business and his love life as he gets together with waitress Alice (Parker). Oh yeah, there's also Alphonse's plans for a cocaine shipment he's salvaged from a sunken boat, if he can keep away from the product himself. Based on the novel by Riche. **101m/C VHS, DVD.** *CA* William Hurt, Molly Parker, Andy Jones, Cathy Jones, Sheila McCarthy, Vicky Hynes, Greg Malone; ***D:*** Sturla Gunnarsson; ***W:*** Edward Riche; ***C:*** Jan Kiesser; ***M:*** Jonathan Goldsmith.

The Rare Breed 🦴🦴½ **1966** Plodding but pleasant Western. A no-strings ranch hand (Stewart) agrees to escort a Hereford Bull to Texas, where the widow of an English breeder plans to crossbreed the bull with longhorn cattle. The widow (O'Hara) insists that she and her daughter accompany Stewart on the trip, which features every kind of western calamity imaginable. When all others believe the attempt to crossbreed has failed, Stewart sets out to prove them wrong. **97m/C VHS.** James Stewart, Maureen O'Hara, Brian Keith, Juliet Mills, Jack Elam, Ben Johnson; ***D:*** Andrew V. McLaglen; ***C:*** William Clothier; ***M:*** John Williams.

A Rare Breed 🦴½ **1981 (PG)** Real-life story of a kidnapped horse in Italy and a young girl's quest to retrieve it. Directed by David Nelson of TV's "Ozzie and Harriet" fame, this movie is cute and old-fashioned. **94m/C VHS.** George Kennedy, Forrest Tucker, Tracy Vaccaro, Tom Hallick, Don DeFore; ***D:*** David Nelson.

Rascal Dazzle **1981** Montage-like tribute to that best-loved group of children, the Our Gang kids. Includes scenes with Spanky, Alfalfa, Darla, and the rest of the gang. **100m/B VHS.** ***Nar:*** Jerry Lewis.

The Rascals 🦴🦴½ **1981 (R)** An irrepressible youth at a rural Catholic boys' school comes of age. **93m/C VHS.** *FR* Thomas Chabrol; ***D:*** Bernard Revon.

Rashomon 🦴🦴🦴🦴 *In the Woods* **1951** In 12th century Japan, two travelers attempt to discover the truth about an ambush/rape/murder. They get four completely different versions of the incident from the three people involved in the crime and the single witness. An insightful masterpiece that established Kurosawa and Japanese cinema as major artistic forces. Fine performances, particularly Mifune as the bandit. Visually beautiful and rhythmic. Remade as a western, "The Outrage," in 1964. In Japanese with English subtitles. **83m/B VHS, DVD.** *JP* Machiko Kyo, Toshiro Mifune, Masayuki Mori, Takashi Shimura, Minoru Chiaki, Kichijiro Ueda, Daisuke Kato; ***D:*** Akira Kurosawa; ***W:*** Akira Kurosawa, Shinobu Hashimoto; ***C:*** Kazuo Miyagawa; ***M:*** Fumio Hayasaka. Oscars '51: Foreign Film; Natl. Bd. of Review '51: Director (Kurosawa); Venice Film Fest. '51: Film.

Rasputin 🦴🦴🦴 *Agoniya* **1985** The long-censored and banned film of the story of the mad monk and his domination of the royal family before the Russian Revolution. Petrenko is superb. First released in the United States in 1988. In Russian with English subtitles. **104m/C VHS.** *RU* Alexei Petrenko, Anatoly Romashin, Velta Linne, Alice Freindlikh; ***D:*** Elem Klimov; ***W:*** Semyon Lunghin, Ilya Nusinov; ***M:*** Alfred Shnitke.

Rasputin and the Empress 🦴🦴🦴 *Rasputin: The Mad Monk* **1933** Lavish historical epic teamed the three Barrymore sibs for the first and only time, as they vied for scene-stealing honors. Ethel is Empress Alexandra of Russia, tied to the weak-willed Nicholas II (Morgan) and under the spell of Rasputin, played by Lionel. John is a nobleman who seeks to warn the Russian rulers of their perilous perch on the throne, made only worse by Rasputin's spreading power and corruption. Ethel's first talkie and Wynyard's first film role. Uncredited director Charles Brabin was replaced by Boleslawski due to his incompatability with the imperious Ethel. **123m/B VHS, DVD.** Ethel Barrymore, John Barrymore, Lionel Barrymore, Ralph Morgan, Diana Wynyard, Tad Alexander, C. Henry Gordon, Edward Arnold, Gustav von Seyffertitz, Anne Shirley, Jean Parker, Henry Kolker; ***D:*** Richard Boleslawski; ***W:*** Charles MacArthur; ***C:*** William H. Daniels.

Rasputin: Dark Servant of Destiny 🦴🦴🦴 **1996 (R)** Charismatic Russian peasant/mystic Grigori Rasputin (a mesmerizing Rickman), having received a vision of the Virgin Mary, comes to St. Petersburg in order to relieve the suffering of young hemophiliac, Prince Alexei (Findlay). Tsarina Alexandra (Scacchi) approves of anyone who can help her stricken son while Tsar Nicholas II (McKellen) tentatively agrees to accept the self-proclaimed holy man into the Russian court. Fine performances and beautiful photography. Filmed in St. Petersburg. **120m/C VHS.** Alan Rickman, Ian McKellen, Greta Scacchi, Freddie Findlay, David Warner, John Wood, James Frain, Diana Quick, Ian Hogg, Peter Jeffrey, Ian McDiarmid, Julian Curry; ***D:*** Uli Edel; ***W:*** Peter Bruce; ***C:*** Elemer Ragalyi; ***M:*** Brad Fiedel. **CABLE**

Rasputin the Mad Monk 🦴🦴 **1966** Hammer's version of Russian history of course emphasizes the evil powers of the mad Russian monk (Lee) who gains entry into the court of the czar. Poor script but Lee's good. **90m/B VHS, DVD, Wide.** *GB* Christopher Lee, Barbara Shelley, Richard Pasco, Francis Matthews, Suzan Farmer, Nicholas Pennell, Renee Asherson, Derek Francis; ***D:*** Don Sharp; ***W:*** John (Anthony Hinds) Elder; ***C:*** Michael Reed; ***M:*** Don Banks.

The Rat Pack 🦴🦴½ **1998 (R)** Warts-and-all bio of ole blue eyes, Frank Sinatra (Liotta) and his pals, including Dean Martin (Mantegna), Sammy Davis Jr. (Don Cheadle), Joey Bishop (Slayton), and Peter Lawford (McFayden). Story focuses on the time when Sinatra decides to support John F. Kennedy's (Petersen) bid for the presidency but his mobster ties eventually end their would-be association. TV effort is unauthorized and scorned by the late Sinatra's family. **120m/C VHS, DVD.** Ray Liotta, Don Cheadle, Angus Macfadyen, Joe Mantegna, Bobby Slayton, William L. Petersen, Zeljko Ivanek, Robert Miranda, Dan O'Herlihy, Deborah Kara Unger, Phyllis Lyons, Megan Dodds; ***D:*** Rob Cohen; ***W:*** Kario Salem; ***C:*** Shane Hurlbut; ***M:*** Mark Adler. **CABLE**

Rat Pfink a Boo-Boo woof! *Rat Pfink and Boo Boo* **1966** Parody on "Batman" in which a bumbling superhero and his sidekick race around saving people. Notoriously inept. Title story is legendary—it was misspelled accidentally and Steckler didn't have the cash to fix it. **72m/B VHS.** Vin (Ron Haydock) Saxon, Carolyn Brandt, Titus Moede, Mike Kannon, James Bowie, George Caldwell, Keith Wester; ***D:*** Ray Dennis Steckler; ***W:*** Ron Haydock; ***C:*** Ray Dennis Steckler; ***M:*** Henry Price.

The Rat Race 🦴🦴🦴 **1960** A dancer and a musician venture to Manhattan to make it big, and end up sharing an apartment. Their relationship starts pleasantly and becomes romantic. Enjoyable farce. Well photographed and scripted, with the supporting characters stealing the show. **105m/C VHS.** Tony Curtis, Debbie Reynolds, Jack Oakie, Kay Medford, Don Rickles, Joe Bushkin; ***D:*** Robert Mulligan; ***C:*** Robert Burks; ***M:*** Elmer Bernstein.

Rat Race 🦴🦴½ **2001 (PG-13)** Eccentric Las Vegas casino tycoon Cleese sends six ordinary gamblers on a treasure hunt for two million bucks while rich gamblers wager on the outcome. It's all in the tradition of "It's a Mad, Mad, Mad, Mad World" and the "Cannonball Run" movies, which means it's also old-fashioned. But in that good, solidly funny, anything-for-a-laugh way. But it doesn't go for the cheap, bodily-function humor that so many recent comedies have done to death. The mostly B-list cast has a lot of fun with the material, which is well-paced and expertly carried out by writer Breckman and director Zucker, who thankfully returns to the zany wall-to-wall comedy that put him on the map. **92m/C VHS, DVD, Wide.** *US* John Cleese, Whoopi Goldberg, Cuba Gooding Jr., Jon Lovitz, Breckin Meyer, Amy Smart, Seth Green, Kathy Najimy, Rowan Atkinson, Wayne Knight, Dean Cain, Vince Vieluf, Lanei Chapman, Paul Rodriguez; ***D:*** Jerry Zucker; ***W:*** Andy Breckman; ***C:*** Thomas Ackerman; ***M:*** John Powell.

Ratas, Ratones, Rateros 🦴🦴 *Rodents* **1999** In poverty-stricken Ecuador, young Salvador (Bustos) tries to make his way as a petty thief. His life manages to take a turn for the worse with the arrival of Salvador's ex-con cousin Angel (Valencia) who stays with him and leads the boy down a self-destructive path. Spanish with subtitles. **107m/C VHS, DVD, Wide.** Marco Bustos, Carlos Valencia, Simon Brauer, Cristina Davila; ***D:*** Sebastian Cordero; ***W:*** Sebastian Cordero; ***C:*** Matthew Jensen; ***M:*** Sergio Sacoto-Arias.

Ratboy 🦴🦴½ **1986 (PG-13)** An unscrupulous woman attempts to transform a boy with a rat's face into a celebrity, with tragic results. First directorial effort by Locke that gradually loses steam. **105m/C VHS.** Sondra Locke, Sharon Baird, Robert Townsend; ***D:*** Sondra Locke; ***W:*** Rob Thompson; ***C:*** Bruce Surtees; ***M:*** Lennie Niehaus.

Ratcatcher 🦴🦴½ **1999** Twelve-year-old James (Eadie) gets into a fight with another boy on the banks of the canal that runs through their 1970s working-class Glasgow neighborhood. Ryan falls in and drowns and James keeps quiet while being endlessly drawn back to the scene. Meanwhile there's trouble at home and the family's hopes for a better life (by moving to new council housing) is also in jeopardy. **93m/C VHS.** *GB* William Eadie, Tommy Flanagan, Mandy Matthews, Leanne Mullen, John Miller; ***D:*** Lynne Ramsay; ***W:*** Lynne Ramsay; ***C:*** Alwin Kuchler; ***M:*** Rachel Portman.

Rated X 🦴🦴 **2000 (R)** True story of smut kings, the Mitchell Brothers, as portrayed by brothers Sheen and Estevez. Porno pioneer Jim (Estevez) sees dollar signs and joins with younger brother Artie (Sheen) to film skin flicks in San Francisco, including their hard-core classic "Behind the Green Door." They get busted a lot on obscenity charges and fall victim to booze and drugs but while Jim finally cleans up his act, Artie just sinks deeper, leading to a deadly confrontation between the two. The brothers do a surprisingly impressive job but it's grim going. Based on the book by David McCumber. **114m/C VHS, DVD.** Emilio Estevez, Charlie Sheen, Megan Ward, Danielle Brett, Rafer Weigel, Terry O'Quinn, Nikki DeBoer, Peter Bogdanovich, Tracy Hutson; ***D:*** Emilio Estevez; ***W:*** Norman Snider, Anne Meredith, David Hollander; ***C:*** Paul Sarossy; ***M:*** Tyler Bates. CABLE

A Rather English Marriage 🦴🦴½ **1998** Aging Reggie (Finney) and Roy (Courtenay) meet in a hospital waiting room after their wives have just died. The odd couple (Reggie is blustery ex-military while Roy was a milkman) are further thrown together when a social worker suggests that both should share Reggie's house to help with chores and expenses (and neither man is used to living alone). The rest of the subdued drama is their adjustment to each other and their new situations with flashbacks to their younger selves. Based on the novel by Angela Carter. Finney and Courtenay starred together in 1983's "The Dresser." **104m/C VHS.** *GB* Albert Finney, Tom Courtenay, Joanna Lumley, Sean Murray; ***D:*** Paul Seed; ***W:*** Andrew Davies; ***C:*** Gavin Finney; ***M:*** Jim Parker. TV

Ratings Game 🦴🦴 *The Mogul* **1984** A bitter, out-of-work actor and a woman who works at the ratings service manage to mess up the TV industry. Early directorial effort by DeVito is uneven but funny. **102m/C VHS.** Danny DeVito, Rhea Perlman, Gerrit Graham, Kevin McCarthy, Jayne Meadows, Steve Allen, Ronny Graham, George Wendt; ***D:*** Danny DeVito; ***W:*** Michael Barrie, Jim Mulholland. CABLE

Rats 🦴🦴 *Rats: Night of Terror* **1983** In 2225, the beleaguered survivors of a nuclear holocaust struggle with a mutant rodent problem. Mattei used the pseudonym Vincent Dawn. **97m/C VHS, DVD, Wide.** Richard Raymond, Richard Cross, Alex McBride; ***D:*** Bruno Mattei; ***W:*** Claudio Fragasso.

The Rats Are Coming! The Werewolves Are Here! woof! **1972 (R)** Low-budget schlock revolves around a family of werewolves and the daughter who decides to put an end to the curse. Imaginative title promises much more than movie delivers. The killer rats were thrown in as an afterthought to increase the run time. **92m/C VHS.** Hope Stansbury, Jackie Skarvellis, Noel Collins, Joan Ogden, Douglas Phair, Bernard Kaler; ***D:*** Andy Milligan; ***W:*** Andy Milligan; ***C:*** Andy Milligan.

A Rat's Tale 🦴🦴 **1998 (G)** "Romeo & Juliet" for rats. A regular Joe, Manhattanite Monty Mad-Rat meets Isabella Noble-Rat, the daughter of the rat President, and soon Monty is a goner for this out-of-reach rodent whose family disapproves of the common sewer creature. Adding to the intrigue, a land developer (Ostendorf) appears with a scheme to obliterate the rat population and build a parking garage. The rats band together to raise money to buy their land and prevent ratricide. Admirably lo-tech, kid pic nonetheless suffers from the cute but expressionless and very much wired marionettes playing the rats—they're no muppets—and the broadly characterized roles of the human actors (Hutton, Stiller and D'Angelo). Marionettes complements of Germany's Augsburger Puppet Theatre. Based on the book by Tor Seidler. **90m/C VHS.** *GE* Lauren Hutton, Jerry Stiller, Beverly D'Angelo, Josef Ostendorf; ***D:*** Michael F. Huse; ***W:*** Werner Morganrath, Peter Scheerbaum; ***C:*** Piotr Lenar; ***M:*** Frederic Talgorn; ***V:*** Dee Bradley Baker, Lynsey Bartilson, Donald Arthur, Ray Guth, Scott MacDonald.

Rattle of a Simple Man 🦴🦴½ **1964** A naive, chaste, middle-aged bachelor (Corbett) who lives in London must spend the night with a waitress (Cilento) to win a bet. She knows of the bet and kindly obliges. Enjoyable sex comedy. **91m/B VHS.** *GB* Harry H. Corbett, Diane Cilento, Michael Medwin, Thora Hird; ***D:*** Muriel Box.

Rattled 🦴🦴½ **1996 (PG-13)** Indiana Jones won't be the only snake-hater after seeing what hundreds of rattlesnakes can do. When their den is disturbed by construction on a new water project, hundreds of rattlers slither down the mountainside ready to attack anyone in their path. Based on the book "Rattlers" by Joseph Gilmore. **90m/C VHS.** William Katt, Shanna Reed, Michael Galeota, Monica Creel, Clint Howard, Ian Abercrombie, Ed Lauter, Bibi Besch, Zack Eginton; ***D:*** Tony Randel; ***W:*** Jim Wheat, Ken Wheat.

Rattler Kid 🦴 **197?** Cavalry sergeant wrongly accused of murdering his commanding officer escapes from prison and finds the real killer. **86m/C VHS.** Richard Wyler, Brad Harris.

Rattlers 🦴 **1976 (PG)** TV movie featuring poisonous rattlesnakes who attack at random. **82m/C VHS.** Sam Chew, Elizabeth Chauvet, Dan Priest; ***D:*** John McCauley. TV

Ratz 🦴½ **1999** Dumb teen film about best friends Marci and Summer who get involved with a magic ring, an eccentric shopkeeper, and two rats (yes, the rodent kind) who are transformed into a couple of datable young hunks so the girls will have escorts to the big spring dance. **95m/C VHS, DVD.** Caroline Elliott, Vanessa Lengies, Jake Seeley, Levi James, Kathy Baker, Ron Silver, Barbara Tyson; ***D:*** Thom Eberhardt; ***W:*** Thom Eberhardt; ***C:*** Ric Waite. CABLE

Ravager 🦴½ **1997 (R)** When a space transport ship crashlands in the desert, former lovers Cooper Wayne (Payne) and Avedon Hammond (Butler), along with their crew, search for help. They discover an underground storage facility and some leaking hazardous material labeled "Ravenger" that infects one of their technicians. When they return the infected crewman to the ship, they also bring back a contagion that threatens the survival of everyone aboard. **92m/C VHS.** Bruce Payne, Yancy Butler, Juliet Landau, Salvator Xuereb; ***D:*** James D. Deck; ***W:*** James D. Deck.

The Ravagers 🦴🦴 **1965** Capt. Kermit Dowling (Saxon) and ex-con Gaudiel (Poe) led Filipino guerrillas against remnants of the Japanese forces on the Philippines. The Japanese have taken over a convent in their search for a ship of gold bullion and Gaudiel manages to sneak inside where he encounters American Shelia (Fitzsimmons), who's been sheltered by the nuns. In between the action, they take a liking to each other. **80m/B VHS, DVD.** John Saxon, Fernando Poe Jr., Bronwyn Fitzsimons, Robert Arevalo, Mike Parsons; ***D:*** Eddie Romero; ***W:*** Eddie Romero, Cesar Amigo; ***M:*** Tito Arevalo.

Rave Review 🦴🦴 **1995** Desperate L.A. theatrical director wants to scare a powerful critic into giving his latest production a glowing review so that his small theatre company can remain in business. Too bad he scares the critic to death. **91m/C VHS.** Jeff Seymour, Ed Begley Jr., Leo Rossi, Joe Spano, Bruce Kirby, James Handy; ***D:*** Jeff Seymour; ***W:*** Jeff Seymour.

The Raven 🦴🦴 **1915** An early, eccentric pseudo-biography of author Edgar Allan Poe. The film opens with a look at Poe's ancestors and follows the author to maturity when he turns to alcohol for solace. His drunken stupor produces hallucinations that lead to his tale of "The Raven." Silent with added music track. **80m/B VHS.** Henry B. Walthall, Wanda Howard; ***D:*** Charles Brabin.

The Raven 🦴🦴🦴 **1935** A lunatic surgeon (Lugosi), who has a dungeon full of torture gadgets inspired by Edgar Allan Poe's stories, is begged by a man to save his daughter's life. The surgeon does, and then falls in love with the girl. But when she rejects his love (she's already engaged), he plans revenge in his chamber of horrors. Karloff plays the criminal who winds up ruining the mad doctor's plans. Lugosi is at his prime in this role, and any inconsistencies in the somewhat shaky script can be overlooked because of his chilling performance. **62m/B VHS.** Boris Karloff, Bela Lugosi, Irene Ware, Lester Matthews, Samuel S. Hinds; ***D:*** Lew (Louis Friedlander) Landers; ***W:*** David Boehm, Jim Tully; ***C:*** Charles Stumar.

The Raven 🦴🦴🦴 **1963** This could-have-been monumental teaming of horror greats Karloff, Lorre, and Price is more of a satire than a true horror film. One of the more enjoyable of the Corman/Poe adaptations, the movie takes only the title of the poem. As for the storyline: Price and Karloff play two rival sorcerers who battle for supremacy, with Lorre as the unfortunate associate turned into the bird of the title. **86m/C VHS.** Vincent Price, Boris Karloff, Peter Lorre, Jack Nicholson, Hazel Court, Olive Sturgess; ***D:*** Roger Corman; ***W:*** Richard Matheson; ***C:*** Floyd Crosby; ***M:*** Les Baxter.

Raven 🦴½ **1997 (R)** Covert mercenary team codenamed Raven is after a Soviet satellite decoder. They're double-crossed by renegade CIA agents and their leader Reynolds decides to get his own brand of justice. **93m/C VHS, DVD.** Burt Reynolds, Krista Allen, Matt Battaglia, David Ackroyd, Richard Gant; ***D:*** Russell Solberg; ***W:*** Jacobsen Hart; ***C:*** John Dirlam; ***M:*** Harry Manfredini.

Ravenhawk 🦴🦴 **1995 (R)** Native American Ravenhawk (McLish) is falsely accused of murdering her parents and sent to a maximum security asylum. Twelve years later she returns to her home and learns that corporate slimeball Philip Thorne (Atherton) framed her. Now, he's built a nuclear waste plant on Shoshone land over the objections of the tribe and Ravenhawk is determined to even the score. **88m/C VHS.** Rachel McLish, John Enos, William Atherton, Ed Lauter, Mitch Pileggi; ***D:*** Albert Pyun; ***W:*** Kevin Elders; ***C:*** George Mooradian; ***M:*** Johnny Harris.

Ravenous 🦴🦴½ **1999 (R)** Off-kilter tale of cannibalism in the American West in 1847 (loosely based on the Donner Party) loses its way when it begins to use man-eating as a metaphor for settlers carving up the land. When stringy, twitching Colqhoun (Carlyle) shows up starving and nearly frozen at an army fort in the Sierra Nevadas, he tells Captain John Boyd (Pearce) that he was with a party that resorted to eating their dead when stranded. When a team is sent to investigate, more than the facts are digested. Soon Colqhoun is extolling the virtues of pan-frying your pals to Boyd. The unusual subject and offbeat attempts at humor make this a recipe not for all tastes. **100m/C VHS, DVD, Wide.** John Spencer, Stephen Spinella, Neal McDonough, David Arquette, Guy Pearce, Robert Carlyle, Jeremy Davies, Jeffrey Jones; ***D:*** Antonia Bird; ***W:*** Ted Griffin; ***C:*** Anthony B. Richmond; ***M:*** Michael Nyman, Damon Albarn.

Raven's Ridge 🦴🦴½ **1997 (R)** Imagine an exceptionally low-budget combination of Stanley Kubrick's heist movie "The Killing" and "Deliverance." That's essentially what this story boils down to. A group of friends knock over an armored car at a racetrack then stash the loot out in the woods. When they go to retrieve it, they're attacked by a grizzled local. **77m/C DVD.** William Kendall, Dawn Howard, John Rizzi; ***D:*** Mike Upton.

Ravishing Idiot 🦴🦴 *Agent 38-24-36; Adorable Idiot; The Warm-Blooded Spy; Bewitching Scatterbrain* **1964** An unemployed bank clerk becomes mixed up with Soviet spies. **99m/B VHS.** *FR* Brigitte Bardot, Anthony Perkins; ***D:*** Edouard Molinaro.

Raw Courage 🦴 *Courage* **1984** Three long-distance runners relax in New Mexico, but are kidnapped by vigilantes. Loosely based on a James Dickey novel. **90m/C VHS.** Ronny Cox, Lois Chiles, Art Hindle, Tim Maier, M. Emmet Walsh; ***D:*** Robert L. Rosen.

Raw Deal 🦴🦴🦴 **1948** Sadistic Rick Coyle (Burr) framed one-time associate Joe Sullivan (O'Keefe), who wound up in prison. Joe's moll Pat (Trevor) helps him to escape and they take prison social worker Ann (Hunt), who's befriended Joe, as a hostage. They go after Coyle and Joe begins to fall for the demure dame, who finds the underworld life exciting and even saves Joe from one of Coyle's henchmen. No good guys here but it is fine film noir. **79m/B VHS, DVD.** Dennis O'Keefe, Claire Trevor, Raymond Burr, Marsha Hunt, John Ireland, Curt Conway, Whit Bissell; ***D:*** Anthony Mann; ***W:*** John C. Higgins, Leopold Atlas; ***C:*** John Alton; ***M:*** Paul Sawtell.

Raw Deal 🦴½ **1986 (R)** Don't ever give Schwarzenegger a raw deal! FBI agent Schwarzie infiltrates the mob and shoots lots of people. **106m/C VHS, DVD, Wide.** Arnold Schwarzenegger, Kathryn Harrold, Darren McGavin, Sam Wanamaker, Paul Shenar, Steven Hill; ***D:*** John Irvin; ***W:*** Patrick Edgeworth, Gary De Vore; ***C:*** Alex Thomson.

Raw Force 🦴 *Shogun Island* **1981 (R)** Three karate buffs visit an island inhabited by a sect of cannibalistic monks who have the power to raise the dead (it could happen). They fix the villains by kicking them all in the head. **90m/C VHS.** *PH* Cameron Mitchell, Geoffrey Binney, John Dresden, John Locke, Ralph Lombardi; ***D:*** Edward Murphy.

Raw Justice 🦴🦴 **1993 (R)** When the daughter of a powerful Southern mayor is murdered, tough ex-cop Mace (Keith) is hired to get the killer. Mace enlists the reluctant help of call girl Sarah (Anderson) to help him trap Mitch (Hayes), his prime suspect. Only things don't work out as Mace planned and the wary threesome must work together to save themselves from certain death. **92m/C VHS.** David Keith, Pamela Anderson, Robert Hayes, Leo Rossi, Charles Napier, Stacy Keach; ***D:*** David A. Prior; ***W:*** David A. Prior.

Raw Nerve 🦴 **1991 (R)** A cast with possibilities can't overcome this poorly reasoned suspenser. A young man has visions of the local serial killer, but when he reports them to police he becomes the suspect. There are a few twists beyond that, none too thrilling. **91m/C VHS.** Glenn Ford, Traci Lords, Sandahl Bergman, Randall

"Tex" Cobb, Ted Prior, Jan-Michael Vincent; **W:** David A. Prior.

Raw Nerve ½ **1999 (R)** Rogue cop Blair (Van Peebles) has crossed the line one too many times and is being investigated for money laundering. He's in trouble with IAD and the mob, which also puts girlfriend Izabel (Sheridan) in danger. Blair turns for help to ex-cop buddy Ethan (Galligan) but won't change his violent ways and keeps sinking down. **102m/C VHS, DVD.** Mario Van Peebles, Nicolette Sheridan, Zach Galligan; **D:** Avi Nesher. **VIDEO**

Raw Target ½ **1995 (R)** Ex-kickboxer Johnny Rider (Cook) finds himself a police decoy in a drug bust and then learns that the drug gang's leader Sparks (Hill) was also involved in his brother's death. **92m/C VHS.** Dale "Apollo" Cook, Ron Hall, Nick (Nicholas, Niko) Hill, Mychelle Charters; **D:** Tim Spring; **W:** Larry Maddox; **C:** Bruce Dorfman; **M:** Jun Lupito.

Rawhead Rex ½ **1987 (R)** An ancient demon is released from his underground prison in Ireland by a plowing farmer, and begins to decapitate and maim at will. Adapted by Clive Barker from his own short story. But Barker later disowned the film, so make your own judgment. **89m/C VHS, DVD.** David Dukes, Kelly Piper, Niall Toibin, Niall O'Brien, Donal McCann, Gladys Sheehan, Cora Lunny, Heinrich von Schellendorf; **D:** George Pavlou; **W:** Clive Barker; **C:** John Metcalfe; **M:** Colin Towns.

Rawhide **1938** Rancher's Protection Association forces landowners to knuckle under resulting in friction. Lou Gehrig plays a rancher in a western released the year before he died. Bandleader Ballew could be more gripping in the lead. **60m/B VHS.** Lou Gehrig, Smith Ballew, Evalyn Knapp; **D:** Ray Taylor.

Rawhide *Desperate Siege* **1950** Four escaped convicts hijack a stagecoach way station and hold hostages while waiting for a shipment of gold. A suspenseful B-grade western with a bang-up ending. Well paced and cast with an abundance of good talent. A remake of "Show Them No Mercy" (1938). **86m/B VHS.** Tyrone Power, Susan Hayward, Hugh Marlowe, Jack Elam, Dean Jagger, George Tobias, Edgar Buchanan, Jeff Corey; **D:** Henry Hathaway; **C:** Milton Krasner.

Rawhide Romance **1934** Bill finds justice and love in this chap-slappin' opus, which finds him neglecting the thieves operating on the ranch as he romances his girl. Naturally he comes to his senses and goes after the crooks. **47m/B VHS.** Buffalo Bill Jr., Genee Boutell, Lafe (Lafayette) McKee, Si Jenks; **D:** Victor Adamson.

Razor Blade Smile **1998 (R)** Kinky vampire tale with a really killer babe fond of leather fetish wear. She's Lilith Silver (Daley), a vampire hitwoman working in London. Lilith has been hired to murder members of the Illuminati—a secret society that has made inroads into the highest levels of business and government. Turns out the head of the Illuminati is Sethane Blake (Adamson), the vampire who originally made Lilith one of the undead. Low-budget, bloody camp with some watchable twists and turns. Also available in an unrated version. **101m/C VHS, DVD.** *GB* Eileen Daley, Chris(topher) Adamson, Kevin Howarth, Jonathan Coote, Heidi James, David Warbeck; **D:** Jake West; **W:** Jake West; **C:** James Solan; **M:** Richard Wells.

The Razor: Sword of Justice **1972** Reasonably honest cop Hanzo Itami knows he won't get a promotion under his corrupt boss Inspector Onishi unless he can blackmail him into it. And he finds a way when he discovers condemned prisoner Kanbei is actually living with his mistress Omino, who it turns out is busy with Onishi as well. A little knowledge could get Hanzo killed but he's willing to take the risk. Japanese with subtitles. **90m/C VHS, Wide.** *JP* Shintaro Katsu, Asaoka Yukiji, Atsumi Mari, Nishimura Akira; **D:** Kenji Misumi.

Razorback **1984 (R)** Young American travels to the Australian outback in search of his missing journalist wife. During his quest, he encounters a giant killer pig that has been terrorizing the area. Firmly establishes that pigs, with little sense of natural timing, make lousy movie villains. **95m/C VHS.** *AU* Gregory Harrison, Bill Kerr, Arkie Whiteley, Judy Morris, Chris Haywood, David Argue; **D:** Russell Mulcahy; **W:** Everett De Roche; **C:** Dean Semler.

The Razor's Edge **1946** Adaptation of the W. Somerset Maugham novel. A rich young man spends his time between WWI & WWII searching for essential truth, eventually landing in India. A satisfying cinematic version of a difficult novel, supported by an excellent cast. Remade in 1984 with Bill Murray in the lead role. **146m/B VHS.** Tyrone Power, Gene Tierney, Anne Baxter, Clifton Webb, Herbert Marshall, John Payne, Elsa Lanchester, Lucile Watson, Frank Latimore, Cecil Humphreys, Harry Pilcer, Cobina Wright Sr., Noel Cravat, John Wengraf; **D:** Edmund Goulding; **W:** Lamar Trotti; **C:** Arthur C. Miller; **M:** Alfred Newman. Oscars '46: Support. Actress (Baxter); Golden Globes '47: Support. Actor (Webb), Support. Actress (Baxter).

The Razor's Edge ½ **1984 (PG-13)** A beautifully filmed but idiosyncratic version of the W. Somerset Maugham novel. WWI-ravaged Larry Darrell combs the world in search of the meaning of life. Murray is a little too old and sardonic to seem really tortured. Russell is great as the loser he rescues. Subtly unique, with real shortcomings. **129m/C VHS.** Bill Murray, Catherine Hicks, Theresa Russell, Denholm Elliott, James Keach, Peter Vaughan, Saeed Jaffrey, Brian Doyle-Murray; **D:** John Byrum; **W:** John Byrum; **M:** Jack Nitzsche.

Re-Animator **1984** Black humor cult classic, based on the H.P. Lovecraft story "Herbert West, The Re-Animator." Med student Herbert West (Combs) is determined to make a medical breakthrough by bringing the dead back to life. His experimental green goo is finally successful on a corpse from the med school morgue but, as usual, any resurrected cadaver becomes difficult to control. Grisly if somewhat self-conscious but there's an unforgettable sex scene invovling a lustful severed head and heroine Megan (Crampton). Followed by "Bride of Re-Animator." **86m/C VHS, DVD, Wide.** Jeffrey Combs, Bruce Abbott, Barbara Crampton, David Gale, Robert Sampson, Gerry Black, Carolyn Purdy-Gordon; **D:** Stuart Gordon; **W:** Stuart Gordon, Dennis Paoli, William J. Norris; **C:** Mac Ahlberg; **M:** Richard Band.

Reach for the Sky ½ **1956** WW II flying ace loses both legs in an accident and learns to fly again. He becomes a hero during the Battle of Britain, then is shot down over France and held prisoner by the Germans. At war's end he returns to England to lead 3,000 planes over London in a victory flight. Inspirationaly told true story. **123m/B VHS.** *GB* Kenneth More, Alexander Knox, Nigel Green; **D:** Lewis Gilbert; **M:** John Addison. British Acad. '56: Film.

Reach the Rock **1998 (R)** Robin (Nivola) is a minor troublemaker who gets tossed into his small hometown jail one hot summer night by Sgt. Quinn (Sadler), who blames Robin for his nephew's accidental drowning. Robin keeps escaping from lockup to cause more minor vandalism but always returns to his cell, since he's hoping his ex-girlfriend Lise (Langton), who's taking off for New York, will come and bail him out so they can have one last heart-to-heart. When she does so, Robin finally seems to reach some mature understanding (but the character is so weakly developed, it's hard to tell). **100m/C VHS.** Alessandro Nivola, William Sadler, Brooke Langton, Bruce Norris, Karen Sillas, Norman Reedus, Richard Hamilton; **D:** William Ryan; **W:** John Hughes; **C:** John Campbell; **M:** John McEntire.

Reaching for the Moon ½ **1917** A day-dreaming department store employee finds himself in the unlikely position of ruling a kingdom. Vintage Fairbanks fun, based on a story by Anita Loos. Silent. **62m/B VHS.** Douglas Fairbanks Sr., Eileen (Elaine Persey) Percy, Millard Webb; **D:** John Emerson.

Reaching for the Moon ½ **1931** Fairbanks is a businessman who falls for liquor and Daniels on a transatlantic cruise. Dull and cruel; not as light-hearted as it intends. One Irving Berlin song sung by Crosby. **62m/B VHS, 8mm.** Douglas Fairbanks Sr., Bebe Daniels, Bing Crosby, Edward Everett Horton; **D:** Edmund Goulding.

Reactor **1985** A low-budget sci-fi film about kidnapped scientists, alien ships and an activated nuclear reactor. **90m/C VHS.** Yanti Somer, Melissa Long, James R. Stuart, Robert Barnes, Nick Jordan.

Ready to Rumble **2000 (PG-13)** Sanitation workers and best buds Gordie (Arquette) and Sean (Caan) decide to mastermind the comeback of their favorite wrestler, Jimmy "the King" King (Platt). The reason he needs a comeback is that promoter Titus Sinclair (Pantaliano) has decided that he's outlasted his usefulness. Sort of like this movie. Arquette and wrestling are annoying enough individually, but put 'em together and it's almost painful to watch. The two buddies make Bill and Ted look like Rhodes scholars, and it's not like there's any point to further parodying the "sport" of wrestling. Hopefully, this was a worth a few mortgage payments to supporting players Platt, Landau, and Pantaliano. **100m/C VHS, DVD, Wide.** David Arquette, Scott Caan, Oliver Platt, Rose McGowan, Joe Pantoliano, Martin Landau, Richard Lineback, Chris Owen, Kathleen Freeman, Lewis Arquette, Diamond Dallas Page; **D:** Brian Robbins; **W:** Steven Brill; **C:** Clark Mathis; **M:** George S. Clinton.

Ready to Wear *Pret-a-Porter* **1994 (R)** Altman travels to Paris to take on the fashion industry with his trademark satire, ensemble cast, and cameo players in tow. The untimely death of a major industry player begins a swirl of random subplots involving a head-spinning array of fashion industry stereotypes. Loren and Mastroianni recreate their "Yesterday, Today and Tomorrow" boudoir striptease scene. Coterie of one-dimensional characters is set adrift with no discernable plot, which might make for interesting people watching, but results in a tedious movie. Altman did it better with "The Player" and "Short Cuts." **132m/C VHS, DVD.** Sophia Loren, Marcello Mastroianni, Julia Roberts, Tim Robbins, Kim Basinger, Stephen Rea, Anouk Aimee, Lauren Bacall, Lili Taylor, Sally Kellerman, Tracey Ullman, Linda Hunt, Rupert Everett, Forest Whitaker, Richard E. Grant, Danny Aiello, Teri Garr, Lyle Lovett, Jean Rochefort, Michel Blanc, Anne Canovos, Jean-Pierre Cassel, Francois Cluzet, Rossy de Palma, Kasia (Katarzyna) Figura, Sam Robards, Cher, Harry Belafonte, Issey Miyake, Sonia Rykiel, Jean-Paul Gaultier, Thierry Mugler; **D:** Robert Altman; **W:** Barbara Shulgasser, Robert Altman; **C:** Jean Lepine, Pierre Mignot; **M:** Michel Legrand.

A Real American Hero ½ *Hard Stick* **1978** Story of Tennessee sheriff Buford Pusser, the subject of three "Walking Tall" films. Here, he battles moonshiners, with the usual violence. **94m/C VHS, DVD.** Brian Dennehy, Brian Kerwin, Forrest Tucker; **D:** Lou Antonio. **TV**

The Real Blonde ½ **1997 (R)** Entertaining ensemble pic that daringly exposes the business of show features a disillusioned actor, his beleaguered girlfriend, and a successful soap star (Caulfield) searching for a peroxide-free blonde in New York. On-the-outs couple Joe and Mary (Modine and Keener) is main focus but is undercut by the industry mania that surrounds them. Intelligent writing and caustic wit provide a few memorable scenes, such as the "Il Piano" debate in a crowded restaurant over a thinly veiled "acclaimed independent film" and Bob's resolution to his blonde quest. Modine also revs things up in an emotional improv. Thomas stands out from the crowd as a pretentious fashion photog. DiCillo's latest feature tackles the movie biz from the other side of the camera than his 1995 acclaimed satire, "Living in Oblivion." **105m/C VHS, DVD, Wide.** Matthew Modine, Catherine Keener, Daryl Hannah, Maxwell Caulfield, Elizabeth Berkley, Marlo Thomas, Buck Henry, Bridgette Wilson, Christopher Lloyd, Kathleen Turner, Denis Leary, Steve Buscemi; **D:** Tom DiCillo; **W:** Tom DiCillo; **C:** Frank Prinzi; **M:** Jim Farmer.

Real Bullets **1990** Stunt team performs the real thing when two members get imprisoned in a bad guy's desert castle. **86m/C VHS.** John Gazarian, Martin Landau; **D:** Lance Lindsay.

The Real Charlotte ½ **1991** When young, lovely, and flirtatious Francie Fitzpatrick (Roth) is romantically betrayed by a young English officer, she then sets her mind on the one man (Bergin) whom her plain and middle-aged cousin Charlotte (Crowley) has long loved. Set in Victorian-era Ireland; made for British TV. **240m/C VHS.** *GB* Joanna Roth, Jeananne Crowley, Patrick Bergin. **TV**

Real Genius **1985 (PG)** Brainy kids in California work with lasers on a class project that is actually intended for use as an offensive military weapon. When they learn of the scheme, they use their brilliant minds to mount an amusingly elaborate strategic defense initiative of their own. Eccentric characters and an intelligent script provide a bevy of laughs for the family. **108m/C VHS, DVD, Wide.** Val Kilmer, Gabe Jarret, Jonathan (Jon Francis) Gries, Michelle Meyrink, William Atherton, Patti D'Arbanville, Severn Darden, Robert Prescott; **D:** Martha Coolidge; **W:** Peter Torokvei, Neal Israel, Pat Proft; **M:** Thomas Newman.

The Real Glory **1939** After the U.S. capture of the Philippine islands during the Spanish-American war, an uprising of Moro tribesmen spreads terror. After most of the islands are evacuated only a small group of Army officers is left to lead the Filipino soldiers against the rebels. Cooper plays the heroic doctor, who is not afraid to fight, especially when he comes to the rescue of the beseiged Army fort. Great action sequences and particularly good performances by Cooper and Niven. **95m/B VHS.** Gary Cooper, David Niven, Andrea Leeds, Reginald Owen, Broderick Crawford, Kay Johnson, Russell Hicks, Vladimir Sokoloff, Rudy Robles, Tetsu Komai, Roy Gordon, Henry Kolker, Soledad Jiminez; **D:** Henry Hathaway; **W:** Robert Presnell, Jo Swerling; **C:** Rudolph Mate; **M:** Alfred Newman.

The Real Howard Spitz ½ **1998 (PG)** Cranky has-been detective turned writer Spitz (Grammer) finds unlikely success with a children's book about a crime-solving cow, despite the fact that Howard hates kids. But even he can't resist 8-year-old Samantha's (Tessier) pleas to help her find her missing father. Amusing and Grammer even dresses in a cow costume. **93m/C VHS.** Kelsey Grammer, Amanda Donohoe, Genevieve Tessier, Cathy Lee Crosby; **D:** Vadim Jean; **W:** Jurgen Wolff; **C:** Glen MacPherson; **M:** John Murphy. **VIDEO**

Real Life **1979 (R)** Writer/comedian Brooks's first feature sags in places, but holds its own as a vehicle for his peculiar talent. Brooks plays a pompous director whose ambition is to make a documentary of a "typical" American family. Good, intelligent comedy. **99m/C VHS, DVD, Wide.** Charles Grodin, Frances Lee McCain, Albert Brooks; **D:** Albert Brooks; **W:** Monica Johnson, Harry Shearer, Albert Brooks; **C:** Eric Saarinen; **M:** Mort Lindsey.

The Real Macaw **1998 (G)** Mac (voiced by Goodman) is a 150-year-old parrot who lives with Benjamin Girdis (Robards), who is forced into a retirement home because of serious debt. Mac just happens to know where a pirate treasure is hidden and he's willing to share the info with Ben's grandson, Sam (Croft) and the two set off for the South Pacific. **92m/C VHS.** *AU* Jason Robards Jr., Jamie Croft, Deborra-Lee Furness; **D:** Mario Andreacchio; **W:** Bruce Hancock; **C:** David Foreman; **M:** Bill Conti; **V:** John Goodman. **VIDEO**

The Real McCoy ½ **1993 (PG-13)** Generally awful crime-caper film about female bank robber Karen McCoy (Basinger). Just out of prison, all Karen wants to do is go straight and raise her young son but her plans are thwarted by former associates who kidnap the child to force her into one last heist. Kilmer is the small-time thief, with a crush on Karen, who tries to help her out. Dumb, slow-moving story with a vapid performance by Basinger. **104m/C VHS, DVD, Wide.** Kim Basinger, Val Kilmer, Terence Stamp, Zach English, Gailard Sartain; *D:* Russell Mulcahy; *W:* William Davies, William Osborne; *C:* Denis Crossan; *M:* Brad Fiedel.

Real Men ♂½ **1987 (PG-13)** The junior Belushi brother is a spy forced to recruit ordinary guy Ritter to help him negotiate with aliens to save the world. Bizarre premise shows promise, but spy spoof doesn't fire on all comedic pistons. Nice try. **86m/C VHS.** James Belushi, John Ritter, Barbara Barrie; *D:* Dennis Feldman; *C:* John A. Alonzo; *M:* Miles Goodman.

The Real Thing ♂♂ *Livers Ain't Cheap* **1997 (R)** Ex-con Rupert (Russo) is trying the straight and narrow while his kid brother James (Buzzotta) continues to be a bad guy. But when James is shot, Rupert gets together with some criminal buddies to pull off a New Year's Eve heist to raise the money needed for James' care. This one's kind of dull until the ending shoot-out. **89m/C VHS.** James Russo, Jeremy Piven, Rod Steiger, Esai Morales, Gary Busey, Emily Lloyd, Dave Buzzotta, Ashley Laurence, Fabrizio Bentivoglio, Robert LaSardo; *D:* James Merendino; *W:* James Merendino; *C:* Greg Littlewood; *M:* Peter Leinheiser. **VIDEO**

A Real Young Girl ♂ **1975** Breillat's explicit film was never commercially released—being too weird even for French cinema (at least at the time). It deals with the budding sexuality of the teenaged Alice (Alexandra) during her summer vacation as she becomes infatuated with Jim (Keller), a hunky laborer at her father's saw mill. Based on the director's novel "Le Soupirail" ("The Air Duct"). In French with subtitles. **93m/C VHS, DVD, Wide.** *FR* Charlotta Alexandra, Hiram Keller, Rita Meiden, Bruno Balp, Shirley Stoler; *D:* Catherine Breillat; *W:* Catherine Breillat; *C:* Pierre Fattori; *M:* Mort Shuman.

Reality Bites ♂♂½ **1994 (PG-13)** Humorous look at four recent college grads living, working, and slacking in Houston. Script by newcomer Childress is at its best when highlighting the trends: 7-Eleven Big Gulps, tacky '70s memorabilia, and games revolving around episodes of old TV shows like "Good Times," to name a few. Definite appeal for those in their early 20s, but anyone over 25 may encounter a "Generation X-er" gap, a noticeable problem since "Reality" claims to speak for the entire 20-something generation. Decent directorial debut for Stiller; good cast, particularly Garofalo, in her film debut. **99m/C VHS, DVD, Wide.** Winona Ryder, Ethan Hawke, Ben Stiller, Janeane Garofalo, Steve Zahn, Swoosie Kurtz, Joe Don Baker, John Mahoney; ***Cameos:*** David Pirner, Anne Meara, Jeanne Tripplehorn, Karen Duffy, Evan Dando; *D:* Ben Stiller; *W:* Helen Childress; *C:* Emmanuel Lubezki; *M:* Karl Wallinger.

Really Weird Tales ♂♂½ **1986** Several SCTV alumni highlight this three-story movie, which is science fiction with a satirical edge. **85m/C VHS.** John Candy, Martin Short, Joe Flaherty, Catherine O'Hara, Olivia D'Abo, Sheila McCarthy, David McIlwraith; *D:* John Blanchard, Paul Lynch, Don McBrearty.

Reap the Wild Wind ♂♂½ **1942** DeMille epic about salvagers off the Georgia coast in the 1840s featuring Wayne as the captain and Massey and a giant squid as the villains. Good cast, lesser story, fine underwater photography. **123m/C VHS, DVD.** Ray Milland, John Wayne, Paulette Goddard, Raymond Massey, Robert Preston, Lynne Overman, Susan Hayward, Charles Bickford, Walter Hampden, Louise Beavers, Martha O'Driscoll, Elisabeth Risdon, Hedda Hopper, Raymond Hatton, Barbara Britton; *D:* Cecil B. DeMille; *W:* Charles Bennett, Jesse Lasky Jr., Alan LeMay; *C:* Victor Milner; *M:* Victor Young.

The Reaper ♂♂ **1997 (R)** A crime writer's most famous novel seems to be the basis for a copycat serial killer. Since the author is nearby the scene of every crime as well, he becomes the prime suspect. The investigating detective asks for his help but if the killer stays true to the plot, she's likely to become the next victim. **97m/C VHS, DVD.** *CA* Chris Sarandon, Catherine Mary Stewart, Vlasta Vrana, Joanna Noyes; *D:* John Bradshaw; *W:* Matt Dorff; *C:* Bruce Chun. **TV**

Rear Window ♂♂♂♂ **1954** A newspaper photographer with a broken leg (Stewart) passes the time recuperating by observing his neighbors through the window. When he sees what he believes to be a murder, he decides to solve the crime himself. With help from his beautiful girlfriend and his nurse, he tries to catch the murderer without getting killed himself. Top-drawer Hitchcock blends exquisite suspense with occasional on-target laughs. Based on the story by Cornell Woolrich. **112m/C VHS, DVD, Wide.** James Stewart, Grace Kelly, Thelma Ritter, Wendell Corey, Raymond Burr, Judith Evelyn; *D:* Alfred Hitchcock; *W:* John Michael Hayes; *C:* Robert Burks; *M:* Franz Waxman. AFI '98: Top 100, Natl. Film Reg. '97.

Rear Window ♂♂½ **1998** Reeve stars as paralyzed architect Jason Kemp, whose wheelchair-bound existence has brought out the voyeur in the man. Kemp becomes convinced one of his neighbors is a murderer and has gotten rid of his drunken wife. Now all he needs to do is convince his friend and fellow architect, Claudia (Hannah), to help him prove his theory to skeptical police detective Moore (Forster). Oh, and keep the murderer from discovering just what Kemp knows. Reeve's first acting role since his own 1995 accident. **89m/C VHS.** Christopher Reeve, Daryl Hannah, Robert Forster, Ruben Santiago-Hudson, Anne Twomey, Allison Mackie, Ritchie Coster; *D:* Jeff Bleckner; *W:* Larry Gross, Eric Overmyer; *C:* Ken Kelsch; *M:* David Shire. **TV**

A Reason to Believe ♂♂ **1995 (R)** Campus date rape drama filmed at writer/director Tirola's alma mater, Miami University. Charlotte (Smith) goes to her boyfriend Wesley's (Quinn) big frat party, even though he's away and asked her not to. She drinks and flirts (a lot) with his best friend Jim (Underwood) and eventually leaves to collapse in a stupor on Wesley's bed. Jim follows and rapes her, though he'll tell his buddies Charlotte was a willing participant, which Wesley angrily believes. Meanwhile, the traumatized Charlotte is taken up by Linda (Emelin), the leader of the student feminist organization who wants the fraternities disbanded. Somewhat preachy and predicatable. **109m/C VHS.** Allison Smith, Jay Underwood, Daniel Quinn, Georgia Emelin, Obba Babatunde; *D:* Douglas Tirola; *W:* Douglas Tirola; *C:* Sarah Cawley.

Reason to Die ♂ **1990 (R)** Bounty hunter uses his own girlfriend as a decoy to trap a psychotic prostitute killer. **86m/C VHS.** Liam Cundill, Wings Hauser, Anneline Kriel, Arnold Vosloo; *D:* Tim Spring.

A Reason to Live, a Reason to Die ♂♂ *Massacre at Fort Holman; Una Ragione Per Vivere e Una Per Morire* **1973** A bland Italian-French-German-Spanish western in which a group of condemned men attempt to take a Confederate fort. **90m/C VHS.** James Coburn, Telly Savalas, Bud Spencer, Robert Burton; *D:* Tonino Valerii.

Rebecca ♂♂♂♂ **1940** Based on Daphne Du Maurier's best-selling novel about a young unsophisticated girl who marries a moody and prominent country gentleman haunted by the memory of his first wife. Fontaine and Olivier turn in fine performances as the unlikely couple. Suspenseful and surprising. Hitchcock's first American film and only Best Picture Oscar. **130m/B VHS, DVD.** Joan Fontaine, Laurence Olivier, Judith Anderson, George Sanders, Nigel Bruce, Florence Bates, Gladys Cooper, Reginald Denny, Leo G. Carroll, Sir C. Aubrey Smith, Melville Cooper; *D:* Alfred Hitchcock; *W:* Joan Harrison, Robert Sherwood; *C:* George Barnes; *M:* Franz Waxman. Oscars '40: B&W Cinematog., Picture.

Rebecca ♂♂♂ **1997** Daphne du Maurier's tale of marriage and jealousy makes its second TV incarnation. Worldly widower Maxim de Winter (Dance) takes his nameless, shy young bride (Fox) back to Manderley, the family estate. There she must compete with the ghost of the first Mrs. de Winter—the glamorous Rebecca—family secrets, and obsessive housekeeper, Mrs. Danvers (Rigg). The 1980 TV version (with Jeremy Brett as Maxim) starred Joanna David in the title role, coincidentally newcomer Fox's mother. **240m/C VHS.** *GB* Emilia Fox, Charles Dance, Diana Rigg, Faye Dunaway, Geraldine James, Jonathan Cake; *D:* Jim O'Brien; *W:* Arthur Hopcraft. **TV**

Rebecca of Sunnybrook Farm ♂♂ **1917** The original film version of the tale about an orphan who spreads sunshine and good cheer to all those around her. Silent with organ score. Based on the popular novel by Kate Douglas Wiggin; remade with Shirley Temple in 1938. **77m/B VHS.** Mary Pickford, Eugene O'Brien, Marjorie Daw, Helen Jerome Eddy; *D:* Marshall Neilan; *M:* Gaylord Carter.

Rebecca of Sunnybrook Farm ♂♂½ **1938** Temple becomes a radio star over her aunt's objections in this bouncy musical that has nothing to do with the famous Kate Douglas Wiggin novel. Temple sings a medley of her hits, and dances the finale with Bill "Bojangles" Robinson. ♫On the Good Ship Lollipop/ When I'm With You/Animal Crackers medley; Crackly Corn Flakes; Alone With You; Happy Ending; Au Revoir; An Old Straw Hat; Come and Get Your Happiness; Parade of the Wooden Soldiers. **80m/B VHS.** Shirley Temple, Randolph Scott, Jack Haley, Phyllis Brooks, Gloria Stuart, Slim Summerville, Bill Robinson, Helen Westley, William Demarest; *D:* Allan Dwan; *C:* Arthur C. Miller.

Rebel ♂½ **1973 (PG)** Mumbling student radical must decide between his love for a country girl and his loyalty to an underground terrorist organization. Notable (or not) for display of early Stallone. **80m/C VHS.** Sylvester Stallone, Anthony Page, Rebecca Grimes.

Rebel ♂½ **1985 (R)** A U.S. Marine falls in love with a Sydney nightclub singer and goes AWOL during WWII. Stylish but empty and badly cast. **93m/C VHS.** *AU* Matt Dillon, Debbie Byrne, Bryan Brown, Bill Hunter, Ray Barrett; *D:* Michael Jenkins.

Rebel High ♂½ **1988 (R)** Hijinks occur at a high school where youngsters study guerilla warfare and teachers wear bullet-proof vests. **92m/C VHS.** Harvey Berger, Stu Trivax, Larry Gimple, Shawn Goldwater; *D:* Harry Jacobs.

Rebel Love ♂ **1985** Love grows between a northern widow and a Confederate spy. In better hands it might have been a good story. Here, it's overwrought and embarrassing historical melodrama. **84m/C VHS.** Terence Knox, Jamie Rose, Fred Ryan; *D:* Milton Bagby Jr.; *W:* Milton Bagby Jr.

Rebel Rousers ♂♂ **1969** A motorcycle gang wreaks havoc in a small town where a drag-race is being held to see who will get the pregnant girlfriend of Dern's high-school buddy as the prize. Young Nicholson in striped pants steals the show. **81m/C VHS, DVD.** Jack Nicholson, Cameron Mitchell, Diane Ladd, Bruce Dern, Harry Dean Stanton; *D:* Martin B. Cohen; *W:* Martin B. Cohen, Abe Polsky, Michael Kars; *C:* Laszlo Kovacs, Glen R. Smith; *M:* William Loose.

The Rebel Set ♂♂½ *Beatsville* **1959** The owner of a beat generation coffeehouse plans an armed robbery with the help of some buddies. Genuinely suspenseful, competently directed. **72m/B VHS.** Gregg (Hunter) Palmer, Kathleen Crowley, Edward Platt, John Lupton, Ned Glass, Don Sullivan, Vicki Dougan, I. Stanford Jolley; *D:* Gene Fowler Jr.; *C:* Karl Struss.

Rebel Storm ♂ **1990 (R)** A group of freedom fighters team up to rescue America from the totalitarian rulers that are in charge in A.D. 2099. **99m/C VHS.** Zach Galligan, Wayne Crawford, June Chadwick, Rod McCary, John Rhys-Davies, Elizabeth Kiefer; *D:* Francis Schaeffer.

Rebel Vixens woof! **1985** Even though the war is over, ex-confederate soldiers continue looting and raping, until a brothel-full of prostitutes concoct a plan that has a lot to do with softcore sex. **94m/C VHS.** Maria Lease, Roda Spain.

Rebel without a Cause ♂♂♂♂ **1955** James Dean's most memorable screen appearance. In the second of his three films (following "East of Eden"), he plays troubled teen Jim Stark, who's alienated from both his parents and peers. He befriends outcasts Judy (Wood) and Plato (Mineo) in a police station and together they find a common ground. Many memorable scenes, including the "chickie run" between Jim and black leather-jacketed Buzz (Allen). Superb young stars carry this in-the-gut story of adolescence. All three leads met with real-life tragic ends. **111m/C VHS, DVD, Wide.** James Dean, Natalie Wood, Sal Mineo, Jim Backus, Nick Adams, Dennis Hopper, Ann Doran, William Hopper, Rochelle Hudson, Corey Allen, Edward Platt; *D:* Nicholas Ray; *W:* Irving Shulman, Stewart Stern; *C:* Ernest Haller; *M:* Leonard Rosenman. AFI '98: Top 100, Natl. Film Reg. '90.

The Rebels ♂♂ **1979** In the sequel to the TV miniseries "The Bastard," Philip Kent (Stevens) continues his Revolutionary War battle on the side of American independence. He is assisted by Southerner Judson Fletcher (Johnson) in thwarting an assassination attempt on George Washington. In addition to Bosley's Ben Franklin, "The Rebels" offers Backus as John Hancock. Followed by "The Seekers"; based on the novel by John Jakes. **190m/C VHS.** Andrew Stevens, Don Johnson, Doug McClure, Jim Backus, Richard Basehart, Joan Blondell, Tom Bosley, Rory Calhoun, MacDonald Carey, Kim Cattrall, William Daniels, Anne Francis, Peter Graves, Pamela Hensley, Wilfrid Hyde-White, Nehemiah Persoff, William Smith, Forrest Tucker, Tanya Tucker, Robert Vaughn, Deborah Richter; *D:* Russ Mayberry; ***Nar:*** William Conrad. **TV**

Reborn ♂♂ **1978** A faith healer and a talent scout hire actors to be cured of fake ailments. **91m/C VHS.** Dennis Hopper, Michael Moriarty, Francesco Rabal, Antonella Murgia.

Rebound: The Legend of Earl "The Goat" Manigault ♂♂½ **1996 (R)** Earl "The Goat" Manigault (Cheadle) was a '60s Harlem playground basketball phenom who was taken under the wing of parks director Holcomb Rucker (Whitaker), who tries to steer the young man towards college and a career in the NBA. Unfortunately, the easily influenced Manigault also attracts the attention of local drug dealer Legrand (Beach) and when Manigault's life starts to fall apart, he drops out of college and turns to heroin, eventually winding up in prison. Since this is an inspirational true story, Manigault does turn his life around to found his own basketball tournament in Harlem. **111m/C VHS.** Don Cheadle, Michael Beach, James Earl Jones, Loretta Devine, Glynn Turman, Clarence Williams III, Ronny Cox, Eriq La Salle, Monica Calhoun, Tamara Tunie, Forest Whitaker; ***Cameos:*** Kareem Abdul-Jabbar; *D:* Eriq La Salle; *W:* Larry Golin, Alan Swyer; *C:* Alar Kivilo; *M:* Kevin Eubanks. **CABLE**

Reckless ♂♂ **1935** Harlow, in a role originally intended for Joan Crawford, plays a showgirl coveted by a millionaire and secretly loved by her manager. Unfortunately, Harlow couldn't pull off the acting (much less the singing and dancing), although the plot strangely paralleled her own life. Songs include "Reckless," "Ev'rything's Been Done Before," "Trocadero," "Hear What My Heart Is Saying" and "Cyclone." **96m/B VHS.** Jean Harlow, William Powell, Franchot Tone, May Robson, Ted Healy, Nat Pendleton, Rosalind Russell; *D:* Victor Fleming; *C:* George J. Folsey.

Reckless ♂♂½ **1984 (R)** A sincere movie about a "good" girl who finds herself obsessed with a rebel from the wrong side of her small town. Differs from 1950s' wrong-side-of-the-track flicks only in updated sex and music. **93m/C VHS.** Aidan Quinn, Daryl Hannah, Kenneth McMillan, Cliff DeYoung, Lois Smith, Adam Baldwin, Dan Hedaya, Jennifer Grey, Pamela Springsteen; *D:* James Foley; *W:* Chris Columbus; *C:* Michael Ballhaus; *M:* Thomas Newman.

Reckless ♂♂ **1995 (PG-13)** Rachel (Farrow) thinks she has a happy marriage and family but her husband (Goldwyn) informs her that he's hired a hit man to kill her. This startling revelation sends her on a 15-year journey in which she meets many other people who are not what they seem. Rene and Lucas go for an ultra-stylized fable theme, exploring Rachel's (and America's) aversion to dealing with the world as it really is. Quirky characters and situations are at turns amusing and annoying. Adapted by Lucas from his own play. **91m/C VHS.** Mia Farrow, Scott Glenn, Mary-Louise Parker, Tony Goldwyn, Stephen Dorff, Eileen Brennan, Giancarlo Esposito, Deborah Rush; ***D:*** Norman Rene; ***W:*** Craig Lucas; ***C:*** Frederick Elmes; ***M:*** Stephen Endelman.

Reckless **1997** British TV production's a combo of farce, romance, and drama that finds young doctor Owen Springer (Green) returning to Manchester to look after his feisty-but-ailing father (Bradley). He has a chance meeting with a beautiful middle-aged woman on the train, and then Anna Fairley (Annis) turns out to be his job interviewer. Reckless Owen falls impulsively in love—before learning Anna is also the wife of his new boss, Dr. Richard Crane (Kitchen). This doesn't deter Owen, and when he learns Crane is having an affair, Owen arranges for Anna to discover her husband's infidelity. Naturally, this leads to Owen and Anna hitting the sheets and things get very complicated. **312m/C VHS.** *GB* Robson Green, Francesca Annis, Michael Kitchen, David Bradley, Julian Rhind-Tutt, Daniela Nardini, Margery Mason, Conor Mullen; ***D:*** David Richards, Sarah Harding; ***W:*** Paul Abbott. **TV**

Reckless Disregard **1984** A doctor whose career is ruined by a news report accusing him of involvement in a drug scam sues the newscaster. Based on Dan Rather's "60 Minutes" story and ensuing lawsuit. **92m/C VHS.** Leslie Nielsen, Tess Harper, Ronny Cox, Kate Lynch; ***D:*** Harvey Hart. **TV**

Reckless Kelly **1993 (PG)** Australian bank robber, pop culture hero, and local video store owner Kelly is upset when his gang's island retreat is about to be sold to a Japanese conglomerate, unless he can come up with a higher offer. So he prepares for a last-ditch defense of his home. Slapstick homage to legendary Australian outlaw Ned Kelly. **81m/C VHS.** *AU* Yahoo Serious, Hugo Weaving, Melora Hardin, Alexei Sayle, Bob Maza, Kathleen Freeman; ***D:*** Yahoo Serious; ***W:*** Yahoo Serious.

Reckless Moment **1949** A mother commits murder to save her daughter from an unsavory older man, and finds herself blackmailed. Gripping, intense thriller. **82m/B VHS.** James Mason, Joan Bennett, Geraldine Brooks; ***D:*** Max Ophuls; ***C:*** Burnett Guffey.

Reckless: The Sequel **1998** A year later, Anna (Annis) has divorced philandering Richard (Kitchen) and is living with Owen (Green). The duo decide, somewhat impulsively, to marry, which drives the chronically jealous Richard into a frenzy and he vows to use any dirty trick necessary to break them up. But family interference and Anna and Owen's own doubts may do the job for him. **120m/C VHS.** *GB* Robson Green, Francesca Annis, Michael Kitchen, David Bradley. **TV**

The Reckless Way **1936** A young woman struggles for her big break into the movies. **72m/B VHS.** Marion (Marian) Nixon, Kane Richmond, Inez Courtney, Malcolm McGregor, Harry Harvey, Arthur Howard; ***D:*** Raymond K. Johnson.

Recoil **1997 (R)** L.A. detective Ray Morgan (Daniels) gets in trouble with a crime family and they target his wife and family. So, for Ray it's a kill or be killed situation. **96m/C VHS.** Gary Daniels, Gregory McKinney. **VIDEO**

Record of a Tenement Gentleman **1947** An abandoned child picks a grumpy, middle-aged widow as a surrogate mother and she and her crazy neighbors come to love the little boy. Surprise ending. Japanese with subtitles. **72m/B VHS.** *JP* Choko Iida, Hohi Aoki, Chishu Ryu, Eitaro (Sakae, Saka Ozawa) Ozawa; ***D:*** Yasujiro Ozu.

Recruits **1986 (R)** Sophomoric gagfest about an inept Californian police force. Typical '80s-style mindless "comedy": dumb gags ensue from perfunctory premise. **81m/C VHS.** Alan Deveau, Annie McAuley, Lolita (David) Davidovich; ***D:*** Rafal Zielinski.

The Rector's Wife **1994** Anna Bouverie (Duncan) has spent 20 years as a clergyman's wife, scrimping and slaving to raise a family, serve God, and work for the parish on limited means. Tired of the financial strain she takes a job at a local supermarket causing additional disturbances in her already shaky marriage, disapproval of the parish, and the sudden interest of three different men. Based on the novel by Joanna Trollope; on four cassettes. **208m/C VHS.** *GB* Lindsay Duncan, Jonathan Coy, Simon Fenton, Lucy Dawson, Joyce Redman, Stephen (Dillon) Dillane, Ronald Pickup, Miles Anderson, Prunella Scales, Jonathan Cecil; ***D:*** Giles Foster; ***W:*** Hugh Whitemore; ***M:*** Richard Hartley.

Red Alert **1977** Good, suspenseful, topical made for televison thriller about nuclear meltdown. Will Minneapolis be saved? Usually Barbeau's name in the credits is a red alert, but this one is better than most. **95m/C VHS.** William Devane, Ralph Waite, Michael Brandon, Adrienne Barbeau; ***D:*** Billy Hale. **TV**

The Red and the Black *Le Rouge et le Noir* **1957** A big budgeted French adaptation of the classic Stendhal novel. A young man from the country seeks success, first in the Church and later in the employment and seduction of the gentry. In French with English subtitles. **134m/B VHS.** *FR* Danielle Darrieux, Gerard Philipe; ***D:*** Claude Autant-Lara.

The Red and the White *Csillagosok, Katonak* **1968** Epic war drama about the civil war between the Red Army and the non-communist Whites in Russia in 1918. Told from the perspective of Hungarians who fought alongside the Reds. Little dialogue. In Hungarian with English subtitles. **92m/B VHS, DVD, Wide.** *HU* Tibor Molnar, Andras Kozak, Josef Madaras; ***D:*** Miklos Jancso; ***W:*** Miklos Jancso, Gyula Hernadi, Giorgi Mdivani; ***C:*** Tamas Somlo.

The Red Badge of Courage **1951** John Huston's adaptation of the Stephen Crane Civil War novel is inspired, despite cutting room hatchet job by the studio. A classic study of courage and cowardice. Sweeping battle scenes and intense personal drama. **69m/B VHS.** Audie Murphy, Bill Mauldin, Douglas Dick, Royal Dano, Andy Devine, Arthur Hunnicutt, John Dierkes, Richard Easton, Tim Durant; ***D:*** John Huston; ***W:*** Albert Band; ***C:*** Harold Rosson; ***M:*** Bronislau Kaper.

Red Ball Express **1952** Fast-paced action highlights this WWII story about the transportation corp that must supply the gas, food, and ammunition necessary for General Patton's tank assault on Nazi-held Paris. Tough company leader Lt. Campbell (Chandler) must get the cooperation of both his first sergeant (Nicol), who holds a pre-war grudge, and a black corporal (Poitier), who believes he's the target of racism, in order to accomplish his mission. **84m/B VHS.** Jeff Chandler, Alex Nicol, Sidney Poitier, Charles Drake, Hugh O'Brian, Jack Kelly, Judith Braun, Jacqueline Duval; ***D:*** Budd Boetticher; ***W:*** John Michael Hayes; ***C:*** Maury Gertsman.

The Red Balloon **1956** The story of Pascal, a lonely French boy who befriends a wondrous red balloon which follows him everywhere. Lovely, finely done parable of childhood, imagination and friendship. **34m/C VHS, 8mm.** *FR* Pascal Lamorisse; ***D:*** Albert Lamorisse. Oscars '56: Orig. Screenplay.

Red Barry **1938** A comic strip detective tries to track down criminals who threaten the world. Thirteen episodes on one videotape. **?m/B VHS.** Buster Crabbe, Frances Robinson, Edna Sedgwick, Cyril Delevanti, Frank Lackteen; ***D:*** Ford Beebe, Alan James.

Red Beard *Akahige* **1965** An uncharacteristic drama by Kurosawa, about a young doctor in Japan awakening to life and love under the tutelage of a compassionate old physician. Highly acclaimed; in Japanese with English subtitles. **185m/B VHS, Wide.** *JP* Toshiro Mifune, Yuzo Kayama, Yoshio Tsuchiya, Reiko Dan; ***D:*** Akira Kurosawa.

Red Blooded American Girl **1990 (R)** A scientist develops a virus that turns people into vampires. Those infected hit the streets in search of blood. **89m/C VHS.** *CA* Christopher Plummer, Andrew Stevens, Heather Thomas, Kim Coates; ***D:*** David Blyth.

Red Cherry *Hong Ying Tao* **1995 (PG-13)** Based on a true story that focuses on the aftermath of the Chinese revolution in 1940 and the horrors of war. The orphaned Chuchu (Ke-Yu) and Luo (Xiaoli) are sent to a Russian school outside of Moscow and begin to settle into their new lives. But their precarious happiness is shattered when German troops invade Russia during WWII. Chinese and Russian with subtitles. **120m/C VHS, DVD.** *CH* Guo Ke-Yu, Xu Xiaoli; ***D:*** Ye Ying.

Red Corner **1997 (R)** Wrong-man scenario features Gere as an American entertainment lawyer on business in China who is framed for murdering a Chinese model he spent the night with. A colossal bummer, Jack's beautiful, court-appointed attorney (Ling) explains the Chinese legal process: "If you plead not guilty, you will be shot within a week and the cost of the bullet will be charged to your family." Gruesome jail scenes involving excrement and a hell-on-wheels female judge don't help his case much, either. Pic suffers from some of the usual cliches but is aided by an acclaimed performance by Ling and one of the better recent Gere turns. Beijing was recreated on the DreamWorks studio lot in California. **118m/C VHS, DVD.** Richard Gere, Bai Ling, Byron Mann, Bradley Whitford, Peter Donat, Robert Stanton, Tsai Chin, James Hong, Tzi Ma, Richard Venture; ***D:*** Jon Avnet; ***W:*** Robert King; ***C:*** Karl Walter Lindenlaub; ***M:*** Thomas Newman.

Red Dawn **1984 (PG-13)** During WWIII, Russian invaders overrun America's heartland and take over the country. Eight small-town teenagers, calling themselves the Wolverines, hide out in the rugged countryside and fight the Russians. Swayze and Grey met again in "Dirty Dancing." **114m/C VHS, DVD, Wide.** Patrick Swayze, C. Thomas Howell, Harry Dean Stanton, Powers Boothe, Lea Thompson, Charlie Sheen, Ben Johnson, Jennifer Grey, Ron O'Neal, William Smith; ***D:*** John Milius; ***W:*** John Milius, Kevin Reynolds; ***C:*** Ric Waite; ***M:*** Basil Poledouris.

Red Desert **1950** The Pecos Kid is sent to track down the theft of a shipment of gold. **60m/B VHS, DVD.** Jack Holt, Donald (Don "Red") Barry, Tom Neal, Joseph Crehan, Tom London; ***D:*** Charles Marquis Warren.

The Red Desert *Il Deserto Rosso* **1964** Antonioni's first color film, depicting an alienated Italian wife who searches for meaning in the industrial lunar landscape of northern Italy, to no avail. Highly acclaimed, and a masterpiece of visual form. In Italian with English subtitles. **120m/C VHS, DVD.** *IT* Monica Vitti, Richard Harris, Carlos Chionetti; ***D:*** Michelangelo Antonioni; ***W:*** Michelangelo Antonioni, Tonino Guerra; ***C:*** Carlo Di Palma; ***M:*** Giovanni Fusco. Venice Film Fest. '64: Film.

Red Desert Penitentiary **1983** A spoof of movie-making featuring caricatures of industry-types. **104m/C VHS.** James Michael Taylor, Cathryn Bissell, Will Rose; ***D:*** George Sluizer.

Red Dirt **1999** Teenaged cousins Griffith (Montgomery) and Emily (Palladino) spent their days lazying around their Mississippi town, sometimes in the company of their crazy Aunt Summer (Black). That is until the older Lee (Goggins) rents a cottage from the family and Griffith has some confused reactions to the newcomer, much to Emily's dismay. Unfortunately, this coming of age story is tritely told with laborious performances. **111m/C VHS, DVD, Wide.** Dan Montgomery Jr., Walton Goggins, Aleksa Palladino, Karen Black, Glenn Shadix, John Mese, Peg O'Keef; ***D:*** Tag Purvis; ***W:*** Tag Purvis; ***C:*** Ted Cohen; ***M:*** Nathan Barr.

Red Dust **1932** Dennis Carson (Gable) is the overseer of a rubber plantation in Indochina who causes all kinds of trouble when he falls in love with an engineer's (Raymond) new wife, Barbara (Astor). Harlow's the tart Vantine also interested in the big lug. Filled with free-spirited humor and skillfully directed; remarkably original. Remade in 1940 as "Congo Maisie" and Gable did his own remake with 1954's "Mogambo," co-starring Ava Gardner and Grace Kelly. **83m/B VHS.** Tully Marshall, Clark Gable, Jean Harlow, Mary Astor, Gene Raymond, Donald Crisp; ***D:*** Victor Fleming; ***W:*** John Lee Mahin.

The Red Dwarf **1999 (R)** Somewhat mawkish melodramatic fantasy about love-starved dwarf Lucien Lhotte (Thual) who works as a law clerk. He's summoned by aging opera singer Countess Paola Bendoni (Ekberg), who wants a divorce. The duo become improbable lovers, although he's humiliated (and vengeful) when the Countess returns to her husband. Lucien is also innocently loved by young circus acrobat, Isis (Gauzy), and her profession leads Lucien to an unexpected escape from his restricted world. French with subtitles. **101m/B VHS, DVD, Wide.** *FR* Anita Ekberg, Jean-Yves Thual, Dyna Gauzy, Arno Chevrier; ***D:*** Yvan Le Moine; ***W:*** Yvan Le Moine; ***C:*** Danny Elsen; ***M:*** Alexei Shelegin, Daniel Brandt.

Red Earth *Voros Fold* **1982** A satire about life under Hungarian socialism. Szanto is a bauxite mixer whose pigs have rooted out high quality bauxite from his backyard. Only the local bauxite prospectors don't want to believe in luck (and pigs) and credit, instead, careful planning. When Szanto's village is turned into a vast open mine, he's blamed. In Hungarian with English subtitles. **105m/C VHS.** *HU* Imre Nemeth, Sandor Kocsis, Kalman Toronyi, Ferenc Togh, Vilmos Gadori; ***D:*** Laszlo Vitezy; ***W:*** Istvan Darday.

Red Firecracker, Green Firecracker *Paoda Shuang Deng* **1993 (R)** Set in northern China before the 1911 revolution, this gorgeous saga focuses on the fortunes of the Cai family. The family, whose wealth depends on their fireworks business, has no male heirs and is headed by daughter Chun Zhi (Jing). To assume this lofty position, Chun Zhi must dress like a man and is forbidden to marry but that doesn't stop her from falling in love with bold young travelling artist Nie Bao (Gang). The household is thrown into a frenzy by their affair and it's decided that all Chun Zhi's potential suitors must undergo a firecracker ritual in order to win her hand. Mandarin Chinese with subtitles. **111m/C VHS, DVD.** *HK CH* Ning Jing, Wu Gang, Zhao Xiaorui, Gai Yang; ***D:*** He Ping; ***W:*** Da Ying; ***C:*** Yang Lun.

Red Flag: The Ultimate Game **1981** Pilots rival for success in battle simulation training with terrible consequences. Fine performances cover plot weaknesses. Well-written dialogue. **100m/C VHS.** Barry Bostwick, William Devane, Joan Van Ark, Fred McCarren, Debra Feuer, George Coe, Linden Chiles, Arlen Dean Snyder; ***D:*** Don Taylor. **TV**

The Red Fury **1984** Young Indian boy struggles to overcome prejudice and caring for his horse shows him the way. Good family viewing. **105m/C VHS.** William Jordan, Katherine (Kathy) Cannon.

Red Garters **1954** A musical parody of old-time westerns which doesn't quite come off. Mitchell palys the cowpoke who comes to town to avenge the death of his brother with Clooney as the saloon singer who uses him to make boyfriend Carson jealous. The adequate songs include "Red Garters," "Man and Woman," "A Dime and a Dollar," and "Vaquero." **91m/C VHS.** Guy Mitchell, Rosemary Clooney, Jack Carson, Gene Barry, Pat(ricia) Crowley, Joanne Gilbert, Frank Faylen, Reginald Owen, Buddy Ebsen; ***D:*** George Marshall; ***W:*** Michael Fessier; ***M:*** Jay Livingston, Ray Evans.

The Red Half-Breed **1970** A lonely half-breed Indian, wrongly accused of murder, discovers the real killer while running from the law. **103m/C VHS.** Daniel Pilon, Genevieve Deloir; ***D:*** Gilles Carle.

Red Headed Stranger **1987 (R)** Willie Nelson vehicle based on his 1975 album. Nelson is a gun-totin' preacher who kills his wife and is led to salvation by a good farm woman. But honestly: Morgan Fairchild as Willie Nelson's wife? Please. **108m/C VHS.** Willie Nelson, Katharine Ross, Morgan Fairchild; ***D:*** William D. Wittliff; ***W:*** William D. Wittliff.

Red Headed Woman 🦴🦴🦴 **1932** Unscrupulous Lil (sultry Harlow in a red wig) vamps her boss Bill Legendre (Morris) into divorcing his wife (Hyams) and marrying her. But then she gets bored and takes up with the wealthier Gaerste (Stephenson), while keeping his chauffeur Albert (Boyer) on the side. Bill finally divorces her and Lil heads for Europe (with Albert) to play among the nobility. Audiences loved the scandalous material, but the Hays Office objected to the fact that the immoral woman goes unpunished. Boyer took the small but notable role in his third American film because of studio MGM's prestige and it made his career. **79m/B VHS.** Jean Harlow, Chester Morris, Lewis Stone, Leila Hyams, Una Merkel, Henry Stephenson, May Robson, Charles Boyer, Harvey Clark; ***D:*** Jack Conway; ***W:*** Anita Loos; ***C:*** Harold Rosson.

Red Heat 🦴½ **1985** Blair is a tourist in East Germany mistakenly arrested and sent to a rough women's prison. Her fiance tries to free her. Meanwhile, she has to deal with tough-lady fellow jail bird Kristel. Familiar and marginal. **104m/C VHS.** Linda Blair, Sylvia Kristel, Sue Kiel, William Ostrander; ***D:*** Robert Collector.

Red Heat 🦴🦴 **1988 (R)** Two cops—one from the Soviet Union, one from Chicago—team up to catch the Eastern Bloc's biggest drug czar. Lots of action, but at times it seems too similar to Hill's earlier hit "48 Hours." Film claims to be the first major U.S. production shot in Red Square, Moscow. **106m/C VHS, DVD, Wide.** Arnold Schwarzenegger, James Belushi, Peter Boyle, Ed O'Ross, Laurence "Larry" Fishburne, Gina Gershon, Richard Bright; ***D:*** Walter Hill; ***W:*** Walter Hill; ***C:*** Matthew F. Leonetti; ***M:*** James Horner.

Red Hot 🦴🦴½ **1995 (PG)** Alexi (Getty), a young Russian classical musician, is secretly smuggled American rock 'n' roll music (it's 1959) by his uncle. He immediately decides to form a band and plots the first underground Soviet rock concert. Too bad girlfriend Valentina's (Gugino) dad is a disapproving highly ranked Communist Party official and the KGB are giving Alexi the evil eye. **95m/C VHS.** Balthazar Getty, Carla Gugino, Donald Sutherland, Armin Mueller-Stahl; ***D:*** Paul Haggis; ***W:*** Paul Haggis, Michael Maurer.

The Red House 🦴🦴🦴 **1947** Robinson plays a crippled farmer who, after his daughter brings home a suitor, attempts to keep everyone from a mysterious red house located on his property. Madness and murder prevail. Strange film noir about tangled relationships and unsuccessful attempts to bury the horrid past. Based on the novel by George Agnew Chamberlain. **100m/B VHS, DVD.** Edward G. Robinson, Lon (Bud) McCallister, Judith Anderson, Allene Roberts, Rory Calhoun, Ona Munson, Julie London, Harry Shannon, Arthur Space, Walter Sande, Pat Flaherty; ***D:*** Delmer Daves; ***W:*** Delmer Daves; ***C:*** Bert Glennon; ***M:*** Miklos Rozsa.

The Red Inn 🦴🦴 *L'Auberge Rouge* **1951** Yes, it is a comedy. An innkeeper and his wife have a second career involving the robbery and murder of stagecoach travellers staying at their isolated inn. And it's up to a monk (Fernandel) to stop the mayhem. French with subtitles. Yves Montand sings on the soundtrack. **95m/B VHS.** *FR* Fernandel, Francoise Rosay, Julien Carette, Gregoire Aslan, Marie-Claire Olivia, Lud Germain; ***D:*** Claude Autant-Lara; ***W:*** Jean Aurenche, Pierre Bost; ***C:*** Andre Bac; ***M:*** Rene Cloerec.

Red Kimono 🦴🦴 **1925** Exploitative silent melodrama about a young woman ditched by her husband. She becomes a prostitute, but is redeemed by true love. Interesting slice of its period. **95m/B VHS.** Tyrone Power Sr., Priscilla Boner, Nellie Bly Baker, Mary Carr; ***D:*** Walter Lang.

Red King, White Knight 🦴🦴½ **1989 (R)** An assassin tries to kill Mikhail Gorbachev during superpower peace talks. Ex-spook Skerritt returns to duty to thwart him. Better than most "topical" thrillers. **106m/C VHS.** Tom Skerritt, Max von Sydow, Helen Mirren; ***D:*** Geoff Murphy. **CABLE**

Red Kiss 🦴🦴🦴 *Rouge Baiser* **1985** In 1952 Paris, Nadia, a 15-year-old French-Jewish Stalinist of Polish descent falls in love with Stephane, an older, apolitical photographer. She's torn between love and politics; he's worried (rightly) about her being under-age; and to make matters more complicated, her Polish mother has been reunited with her first love and Nadia's family may be split apart. The sensual Valandrey is a real find in her difficult coming-of-age role. In French with English subtitles. **110m/C VHS.** *FR* Charlotte Valandrey, Lambert Wilson, Marthe Keller, Gunter Lamprecht, Laurent Terzieff; ***D:*** Vera Belmont; ***W:*** Vera Belmont, David Milhaud, Guy Konopnicki; ***C:*** Ramon Suarez; ***M:*** Jean-Marie Senia. Berlin Intl. Film Fest. '86: Actress (Valandrey).

Red Letters 🦴🦴 **2000 (R)** The plot veers wildly but the performances are worth a watch. Widowed college prof Dennis Burke (Coyote) has an eye for the ladies. He flirts with the dean's sexy young daughter, Gretchen (Balk), and is so taken with the imprisoned Lydia (Kinski) that he helps her escape so she can prove her innocence in a murder conviction. Not a good idea. **102m/C VHS, DVD, Wide.** Peter Coyote, Nastassia Kinski, Fairuza Balk, Jeremy Piven, Ernie Hudson, Udo Kier; ***D:*** Bradley Battersby; ***W:*** Bradley Battersby, Tom Hughes; ***C:*** Steven Fierberg. **VIDEO**

The Red Light Sting 🦴 **1984** A Justice Department rookie (Bridges) and a call girl (Fawcett) reluctantly team up to con the Mafia in order to convict a San Francisco rackets czar. Goes down easy, but also easily forgotten or skipped. **96m/C VHS.** Farrah Fawcett, Beau Bridges, Harold Gould, Paul Burke, Sunny Johnson; ***D:*** Rod Holcomb.

Red Lights Ahead **1936** Grandpa tries to save the day as he fights against spiritualism and crystal balls to help a friend prove that he is not running a scam. **63m/C VHS.** Andy Clyde, Paula Stone, Roger Imhof, Frank "Junior" Coghlan, Ben Alexander, Matty Kemp, Sam Flint, Addison "Jack" Randall, Lucile Gleason, Dann Doran; ***D:*** Roland D. Reed.

Red Line 🦴½ **1996 (R)** Stock-car racer Jim (McQueen) loses his sponsorship, turns to petty crime to settle his debts, and winds up in trouble with the mob when he hooks up with a couple of hoods to steal some diamonds. **102m/C VHS, DVD.** Chad McQueen, Michael Madsen, Corey Feldman, Jan-Michael Vincent, Roxana Zal, Dom DeLuise, Julie Strain, Robert Z'Dar; ***D:*** John Sjogren; ***W:*** John Sjogren, Scott Ziehl, Rolfe Kanefsky; ***C:*** Kevin McKay; ***M:*** Craig Carothers, Junior Walker.

Red Line 7000 🦴🦴 **1965** High stakes auto racers drive fast cars and date women. Excellent racing footage in otherwise routine four-wheel fest. **110m/C VHS.** James Caan, Laura Devon, Gail Hire, Charlene Holt, Marianna Hill, George Takei; ***D:*** Howard Hawks; ***C:*** Milton Krasner.

Red Lion 🦴🦴½ *Akage* **1969** A bumbling horse-tender in feudal Japan impersonates a military officer to impress his family, only to be swept into leading a liberating revolution. In Japanese with English subtitles. **115m/C VHS.** *JP* Toshiro Mifune, Shima Iwashita; ***D:*** Kihachi Okamoto.

The Red Menace woof! **1949** Anti-Communist propaganda, made with unknown actors in documentary style has little to offer today's viewers other than unintentional laughs. Picture the Commies offering naive Americans money and sex to join the party, and you'll have an idea of the intellectual talent that went into this one. **87m/B VHS.** Robert Rockwell, Hannelore Axman, Shepard Menken, Betty Lou Gerson, Barbara Fuller; ***D:*** R.G. Springsteen.

Red Nightmare 🦴½ **1962** Anti-communist propaganda produced for the Department of Defense by Warner Bros. features the cast of "Dragnet." The story dramatizes the Red Menace, with communists conspiring to take over America, and shows what would happen to life in a small American town if the Commies took over. **30m/B VHS.** Jack Webb, Jack Kelly, Jeanne Cooper, Peter Brown.

Red Nights 🦴 **1987** A country boy goes to Hollywood seeking success and finds instead corruption, decadence, and dishonesty. Excellent soundtrack by Tangerine Dream. **90m/C VHS.** Chris Parker, Jack Carter, Brian Matthews; ***D:*** Izhak Hanooka.

Red Planet 🦴🦴½ **2000 (PG-13)** It's 2050, Earth is dying, and the crew of the Mars-1 has been sent to the red planet to find out what went wrong with a previous colonization mission. Alas, something goes wrong with this mission, too (those pesky gamma rays), and some of the crew are forced to shuttle to the surface of Mars, where yet another mishap leaves them stranded without means of communication or escape. To make matters worse, the crew's AMEE (Autonomous Mapping Evaluation and Evasion) robot has turned nasty and intends to further endanger them and their mission. Heavy with visual effects, yet the film tries to keep the focus on the human elements. Follows the unexceptional "Mission to Mars" in exploring the big red one. **110m/C VHS, DVD, Wide.** Val Kilmer, Tom Sizemore, Carrie-Anne Moss, Benjamin Bratt, Simon Baker, Terence Stamp; ***D:*** Antony Hoffman; ***W:*** Jonathan Lemkin, Chuck Pfarrer.

Red Planet Mars 🦴🦴 **1952** Anti-communist, pro-Christianity story about scientists discovering that the Voice of Radio Free Mars belongs to God. Incoherent film overburdened with messages about politics, religion, and science was ahead of its time. Based on the play "Red Planet" by John L. Balderson and John Hoare. **87m/B VHS.** Peter Graves, Andrea King, Marvin Miller, Herbert Berghof, House Peters Jr., Vince Barnett; ***D:*** Harry Horner; ***W:*** Anthony Veiller, John Lloyd Balderston.

The Red Pony 🦴🦴🦴 **1949** A young boy escapes from his family's fighting through his love for a pet pony. Based on the novel by John Steinbeck. Timeless classic that the whole family can enjoy. **89m/C VHS.** Myrna Loy, Robert Mitchum, Peter Miles, Louis Calhern, Shepperd Strudwick, Margaret Hamilton, Beau Bridges; ***D:*** Lewis Milestone; ***C:*** Gaetano Antonio "Tony" Gaudio; ***M:*** Aaron Copland.

The Red Pony 🦴🦴🦴 **1976** Excellent TV remake of a classic 1949 adaptation of John Steinbeck. Fonda is superb as a troubled young boy's difficult father. **101m/C VHS.** Henry Fonda, Maureen O'Hara, Clint Howard, Jack Elam, Ben Johnson; ***D:*** Robert Totten. **TV**

The Red Raven Kiss-Off 🦴 **1990 (R)** A seedy Hollywood detective becomes the key suspect in a movie-making murder. Based on the 1930s' Dan Turner mystery stories. **93m/C VHS.** Marc Singer, Tracy Scoggins, Nicholas Worth, Arte Johnson; ***D:*** Christopher Lewis. **VIDEO**

Red Riding Hood 🦴🦴½ **1988** Musical version of story of wolf who has little girl fetish. **81m/C VHS.** Isabella Rossellini, Craig T. Nelson, Rocco Sisto.

Red River 🦴🦴🦴🦴 **1948** The classic Hawks epic about a gruelling cattle drive and the battle of wills between father and son. Tom Dunston (Wayne), who owns a sprawling cattle empire, decide to make a difficult trek north, refusing to listen to any advice from his adopted son, Matthew Garth (Clift, in his first film). Matt is eventually forced to take over the drive from the obsessed Dunston, who swears revenge. Generally regarded as one of the best westerns ever made, with a great supporting cast headed by Brennan and Ireland, although Dru is a very nominal love interest. Restored version has eight minutes of previously edited material. Remade for TV in 1988 with James Arness and Bruce Boxleitner. **133m/B VHS, DVD.** John Wayne, Montgomery Clift, Walter Brennan, Joanne Dru, John Ireland, Noah Beery Jr., Paul Fix, Coleen Gray, Harry Carey Jr., Harry Carey Sr., Chief Yowlachie, Hank Worden; ***D:*** Howard Hawks; ***W:*** Borden Chase, Charles Schnee; ***C:*** Russell Harlan; ***M:*** Dimitri Tiomkin. Natl. Film Reg. '90.

Red River Valley 🦴🦴 *Man of the Frontier* **1936** Autry and partner Burnette go undercover to find out who's plaguing a dam construction site with explosions. Not to be confused with a 1941 Roy Rogers pic bearing the same title. **60m/B VHS.** Gene Autry, Smiley Burnette, Frances Grant, Boothe Howard, Sam Flint, George Chesebro, Charles "Blackie" King, Eugene Jackson, Frank LaRue, Lloyd Ingraham; ***D:*** B. Reeves Eason.

Red River Valley 🦴🦴 **1941** Rogers helps the local ranchers get enough money together to build a much-needed water reservoir. Only gambler Bardette cons them out of the money, until Roy comes to the rescue. **62m/B VHS.** Roy Rogers, George "Gabby" Hayes, Trevor Bardette, Sally Payne; ***D:*** Joseph Kane; ***W:*** Malcolm Stuart Boylan; ***C:*** Jack Marta.

Red Rock Outlaw 🦴 **1947** A sleazy character tries to kill his twin brother and takes his place as an honest rancher. **56m/B VHS.** Lee White.

Red Rock West 🦴🦴🦴½ **1993 (R)** Nothing is what it seems in this stylish and entertaining film noir set in a desolate Wyoming town. Perennial loser and nice guy Michael (Cage) is headed to a job at an oil rig, but blows his chance by admitting he has a bad leg. Landing in the tiny burg of Red Rock, he's mistaken for the hit man hired by local barkeep Walsh to kill his pretty wife (Boyle). Then Boyle doubles Walsh's offer—what's a film noir boy to do? And Hopper, the real killer, strides into town. Full of twists, turns, and shades of "El Mariachi," this enjoyable, well-acted thriller is a real gem that escaped directly to cable before being rescued by a San Francisco exhibitor. **98m/C VHS, DVD, Wide.** Nicolas Cage, Dennis Hopper, Lara Flynn Boyle, J.T. Walsh, Timothy Carhart, Dan Shor, Dwight Yoakam, Bobby Joe McFadden, Craig Reay, Vance Johnson, Robert Apel, Dale Gibson, Ted Parks, Babs Bram, Robert Guajardo, Sarah Sullivan; ***D:*** John Dahl; ***W:*** John Dahl, Rick Dahl; ***C:*** Marc Reshovsky; ***M:*** William Olvis.

The Red Rope 🦴½ **1937** A Western hero cuts his honeymoon short to track down some villains. **56m/B VHS.** Bob Steele, Lois January, Forrest Taylor, Charles "Blackie" King, Karl Hackett, Bobby Nelson; ***D:*** S. Roy Luby.

Red Salute 🦴🦴 **1935** Screwball comedy in the "It Happened One Night" tradition (only not as good) with an anti-Communist message. General's daughter Drue (Stanwyck) falls in love with a young communist. Patriotic dad tries to divert her attention by sending her on a Mexican vacation, where she meets an AWOL soldier. When the pair tries to sneak back into the U.S., he's arrested and she heads back to her leftist lover, whereupon dad releases her AWOL beau and causes more confusion. Film caused much consternation among the left-leaning intelligensia at the time of its release. **88m/B VHS.** Barbara Stanwyck, Robert Young, Hardie Albright, Ruth Donnelly, Cliff Edwards, Gordon Jones, Lester Dorr; ***D:*** Sidney Lanfield; ***W:*** Manuel Seff, Elmer Harris, Humphrey Pearson; ***C:*** Robert Planck.

Red Scorpion 🦴 **1989 (R)** A Soviet soldier journeys to Africa where he is to assassinate the leader of a rebel group. Will he succeed or switch allegiances? Poor acting and directing abound. **102m/C VHS, DVD.** Dolph Lundgren, M. Emmet Walsh, Al White, T.P. McKenna, Carmen Argenziano, Brion James, Regopstann; ***D:*** Joseph Zito; ***W:*** Arne Olsen, Jack Abramoff, Robert Abramoff; ***C:*** Joao Fernandes; ***M:*** Jay Chattaway.

Red Scorpion 2 🦴½ **1994 (R)** Another "Dirty Dozen" rip-off finds your average ethnically mixed good guys brought together by a government agency to be heroic. In this case the enemy is a neo-fascist businessman who uses skinheads to cause mayhem in minority communities. **90m/C VHS.** Matt McColm, John Savage, Jennifer Rubin, Michael Ironside, Michael Covert, Real Andrews, George Touliatos; ***D:*** Michael Kennedy; ***W:*** Troy Bolotnick, Barry Victor; ***M:*** George Blondheim.

Red Shoe Diaries 🦴🦴 **1992 (R)** After a woman's suicide her grieving lover discovers her diaries and finds out she led a secret erotic life, revolving around her shoe-salesman lover and a pair of sexy red shoes. Also available in an unrated version. **105m/C VHS, DVD.** David Duchovny, Billy Wirth, Brigitte Bako; ***D:*** Zalman King. **CABLE**

Red Shoe Diaries 2: Double Dare 🦴🦴 **1992 (R)** The erotic sequel to "Red Shoe Diaries" follows the libidinous fancies of three women. Severance begins a sexual affair with a stranger only be torn between love and lust. Johnson gets naked to tease an office worker in the building next door. Crosby is a cop who is rejected by the man she desires—so she arrests and handcuffs him in order to play some kinky games. Also available in an unrated version. **92m/C VHS.** Joan Severance, Laura Johnson, Denise Crosby, Steven Bauer, Arnold Vosloo, David Duchovny; ***D:*** Zalman King, Tibor Takacs. **CABLE**

Red Shoe Diaries 3: Another Woman's Lipstick 🦴🦴 **1993 (R)** Another sexual anthology focusing on three stories of desire. In "Another Woman's Lipstick" Zoey finds out her husband is having an affair and follows him to his liaison—only to become intrigued with his lover herself. "Just Like That" finds the uptight Trudie falling for two very opposite men. "Talk to Me Baby" finds Ida and her lover Bud caught up in a very obsessional relationship. Also available in an unrated version. **90m/C VHS.** Nina Siemaszko, Matt LeBlanc, Tcheky Karyo, Maryam D'Abo, Richard Tyson, Lydie Denier, Christina (Kristina) Fulton, Kevin Haley, David Duchovny; ***D:*** Ted Kotcheff, Rafael Eisenman, Zalman King; ***W:*** Zalman King, Chloe King. **CABLE**

Red Shoe Diaries 4: Auto Erotica 🦴🦴 **1993 (R)** Yet another compilation of erotic tales courtesy of the Zalman King series. The first story finds a maid finding her employer's secret chamber and uncovering a very private fantasy. The second has an architect lured by a mystery woman into a game of seduction and the third finds a couple engaged in competitive obsessions. Also available in an unrated version. **83m/C VHS.** Ally Sheedy, Scott Plank, David Duchovny, Sheryl Lee, Nicholas Chinlund; ***D:*** Zalman King. **CABLE**

Red Shoe Diaries 5: Weekend Pass 🦴🦴 **1995 (R)** Yet another erotic saga from the cable series that features a model (Barbieri) hustling a pool hustler, a bounty hunter (Stansfield) becoming captivated by her prey, and an army recruit (Pouget) whose furlough involves a sexy drifter. **85m/C VHS.** Paula Barbieri, Claire Stansfield, Ely Pouget, Francesco Quinn, Ron Marquette, Anthony Addabbo; ***D:*** Ted Kotcheff. **CABLE**

Red Shoe Diaries 6: How I Met My Husband 🦴🦴 **1995 (R)** Three more erotic vignettes from the cable series. "How I Met My Husband" finds Alice enrolling in a course on becoming a domanitrix and falling for Giuseppe, who's one of the training objects. Camille has inherited her father's vast fortune in "Naked in the Moonlight" on the condition that she take special care of his '57 Cadillac convertible—and the one mechanic allowed to work on the car. In "Midnight Bells," Claire reminisces about the mystery lover she meets on only one night of the year—New Year's Eve. **85m/C VHS.** Luigi Amodeo, Neith Hunter, Raven Snow, Carsten Norgaard, John Enos, Charlotte Lewis, David Duchovny; ***D:*** Anne Goursaud, Philippe Angers, Bernard Auroux. **CABLE**

Red Shoe Diaries 7: Burning Up 🦴🦴 **1996 (R)** Yet another trilogy of TV eroticism. "Burning Up" finds Lynn becoming obsessed with a handsome fireman, "Kidnap" features the workaholic Sara taken hostage during a bank robbery and finding out that her captor has decided to marry her, Alia is a top model in "Runway," who falls in lust with a cabby. **90m/C VHS.** Udo Kier, Ron Marquette, Jennifer Ciesar, Amber Smith, Anthony Guidera, Daniel Blasco, Alexandra Tydings, David Duchovny; ***D:*** Rafael Eisenman. **CABLE**

Red Shoe Diaries 8: Night of Abandon 🦴🦴 **1997 (R)** Three more erotic adventures from the cable series. "Night of Abandon" finds Isabelle visiting her grandma in Rio de Janeiro and indulging in Carnival. "Liar's Table" has photjournalist Corey assigned to record L.A.'s sex scene and becoming intriged by a very expensive call girl. Married Kathryn's life changes "In the Blink of an Eye" when she meets a young boxer who's in training with her husband. **86m/C VHS.** Erika Anderson, Audie England, Daniel Leza, Ann Cockburn, Terrence Sheahan, Laurie Simpson, Julien Maurel, Brian Edwards, David Duchovny; ***D:*** Rafael Eisenman, Rene Manzor, James Gavin Bedford. **CABLE**

Red Shoe Diaries: Four on the Floor 🦴🦴 **1996** The late-night cable series continues with three more stories concerning a psychiatrist and her patient, two couples stranded on a rainy night, and the meeting of a rap star and a dancer. Contents:" The Psychiatrist," "Four on the Floor," "Emily's Dance." **85m/C DVD.** Denise Crosby, Georges Corraface, Christopher Atkins, Nick Corri, David Duchovny, Demetra Hampton, Rachel Palieri, Freedom Williams, Marry Morrow, Kent Masters-King; ***D:*** Rafael Eisenman, Zalman King, David Womark; ***W:*** Richard Baskin, Nellie Allard, Joelle Bentolila; ***C:*** Etienne Fauduet, Manuel Teran, Marco Mazzei; ***M:*** George S. Clinton. **CABLE**

Red Shoe Diaries: Luscious Lola 🦴🦴½ **2000** In these three stories, shy Mimi (Phillips) fantasizes about winning her dream guy; a sailor on shore leave winds up with more women than he can handle; and a young woman toys with men. **87m/C DVD.** Bobbie Phillips, Michael C. Bendetti, Christina (Kristina) Fulton, Perrey Reeves, Ernie Banks, John Enos, Joseph Whipp, David Duchovny, Andrew Bilgore, Heidi Mark, Michael Reilly Burke; ***D:*** Zalman King, Stephen Halbert; ***W:*** John Enos, Chloe King, Pascal Franchot, Elize D'Haene; ***C:*** Eagle Egilsson, David Stockton; ***M:*** George S. Clinton. **CABLE**

Red Shoe Diaries: Strip Poker 🦴🦴 **1996** Contains the episodes "Strip Poker," "Slow Train," "Hard Labor". **87m/C DVD.** Athena Massey, Jennifer Ciesar, Carolyn Seymour, David Duchovny, Anfisa Nezinskaya, Larisa Tipikina, Andrew Calder, Mark Suelke, Maximo Morrone; ***D:*** Zalman King, Rafael Eisenman; ***W:*** Zalman King, Patricia Louisianna Knop, Julie Marie Myatt, Elize D'Haene; ***C:*** Eagle Egilsson, Alexei Rodionov; ***M:*** George S. Clinton. **CABLE**

Red Shoe Diaries: Swimming Naked 🦴🦴½ **2000** The mother of all late-night cable series is still the artsiest. As such, these stories about a lifeguard, a skydiver, and a dancer are told with lots of smoke and gauzy focus. Contents: "Swimming Naked," "Jump," "Tears." **83m/C DVD.** Michael Woods, Cyia Batten, Carolyn Seymour, Arabella Holzbog, David Duchovny, Kristi Frank, Omry Reznik, Sonya Ryzy-Ryski, Todd Gordon, Daniel Ezralow; ***D:*** Zalman King, Rafael Eisenman; ***W:*** Zalman King, Melanie Finn, Chloe King, Katarina Wittich, Kathryn MacQuarrie; ***C:*** Eagle Egilsson, David Knaus; ***M:*** George S. Clinton. **CABLE**

The Red Shoes 🦴🦴🦴🦴 **1948** British classic about a young ballerina torn between love and success. Boris Lermontov (Walbrook) is the impresario of a ballet company who hires dancer Victoria Page (Shearer) and composer Julian Craster (Goring), giving them the chance at a new ballet inspired by the Hans Christian Andersen fairy tale. But when the endeavor becomes a major success, Boris become jealous over the closeness that develops between his proteges. Noted for the 20-minute ballet at the heart of the film and for the lavish use of Technicolor. **136m/C VHS, DVD.** *GB* Anton Walbrook, Moira Shearer, Marius Goring, Leonide Massine, Robert Helpmann, Albert Bassermann, Ludmila Tcherina, Esmond Knight; ***D:*** Emeric Pressburger, Michael Powell; ***W:*** Emeric Pressburger, Michael Powell; ***C:*** Jack Cardiff; ***M:*** Brian Easdale. Oscars '48: Art Dir./Set Dec., Color, Orig. Dramatic Score; Golden Globes '49: Score.

Red Signals 🦴🦴 **1927** Mystery criminal makes trains collide. **70m/B VHS.** Wallace MacDonald, Earl Williams, Eva Novak, J(ohn) P(aterson) McGowan, Frank Rice; ***D:*** J(ohn) P(aterson) McGowan.

Red Snow 🦴 **1991** High in the Cascade Mountains, Kyle Lewis is the new snowboard instructor for the Hurricane Ridge Ski Resort. The job is fine in the beginning, until Kyle learns of the tragic fate of the last instructor. Before he knows it, Kyle is the next target and is framed for two murders. He secures the help of his fellow snowboard buddies in hopes of solving the mystery and getting the girl, too. High speed ski scenes and dangerous stunts are the film's only redeeming qualities. **86m/C VHS.** Carlo Scandiuzzi, Scott Galloway, Darla Slavens, Mitchell Cox, Tamar Tibbs, Brian Mahoney; ***D:*** Phillip J. Roth.

Red Sonja 🦴½ **1985 (PG-13)** Two warriors join forces against an evil queen in this sword and sorcery saga. Big, beautiful bodies everywhere, with Bergman returning from her Conan adventures. Little humor, few special effects, and weak acting make this a poor outing. **89m/C VHS.** Arnold Schwarzenegger, Brigitte Nielsen, Sandahl Bergman, Paul Smith; ***D:*** Richard Fleischer; ***M:*** Ennio Morricone. Golden Raspberries '85: Worst New Star (Nielsen).

Red Sorghum 🦴🦴🦴½ **1987** A stunning visual achievement, this new wave Chinese film (and Yimou's directorial debut) succeeds on many levels—as an ode to the color red, as dark comedy, and as a sweeping epic with fairy tale overtones. Set in rural China in the 1920s, during the period of the Japanese invasion. The sorghum plot nearby is a symbolic playing field in the movie's most stunning scenes. Here, people make love, murder, betray, and commit acts of bravery, all under the watchful eye of nature. In Mandarin with English subtitles. **91m/C VHS.** *CH* Gong Li, Jiang Wen, Ji Cun Hua; ***D:*** Zhang Yimou; ***C:*** Gu Changwei.

The Red Squirrel 🦴🦴 *La Ardilla Roja* **1993** Former pop star Jota (Novo) is distraught over breaking up with his girlfriend and contemplating throwing himself off a bridge when he witnesses a motorcycle accident and rushes to help the young woman (Suarez) involved. After learning she's suffering from amnesia, Jota tells both the woman and the hospital that her name is Lisa and he's her lover. Then Jota invents a fictitious life for her, according to his own desires. Spanish with subtitles. **104m/C VHS.** *SP* Nancho Novo, Emma Suarez, Maria Barranco, Carmelo Gomez, Ana Garcia; ***D:*** Julio Medem; ***W:*** Julio Medem; ***C:*** Gonzalo F. Berridi; ***M:*** Alberto Iglesias.

The Red Stallion 🦴½ **1947** Good film for animal lovers, but it loses something when it comes to human relationships. A young boy raises his pony into an award-winning racehorse that saves the farm when it wins the big race. Good outdoor photography. **82m/B VHS.** Robert Paige, Noreen Nash, Ted Donaldson, Jane Darwell; ***D:*** Lesley Selander.

Red Sun 🦴🦴 **1971** A gunfighter, a samurai, and a French bandit fight each other in various combinations in the 1860s. Ludicrous and boring. **115m/C VHS, DVD.** *FR IT SP* Charles Bronson, Toshiro Mifune, Alain Delon, Ursula Andress; ***D:*** Terence Young; ***W:*** William Roberts; ***M:*** Maurice Jarre.

Red Sun Rising 🦴½ **1994 (R)** Kyoto cop Thomas Hoshino (Wilson) heads to L.A. in order to extradite a Japanese gangster, Yamata (Oh), and teams up with local detective Karen Ryder (Ferrell). Seems Yamata wants to start a turf war between two L.A. street gangs so he can sell guns to both sides. **95m/C VHS.** Don "The Dragon" Wilson, Terry Farrell, Soon-Teck Oh, Mako, James Lew, Edward Albert, Michael Ironside; ***D:*** Francis Megahy; ***C:*** John Newby.

Red Surf 🦴🦴 **1990 (R)** Action abounds in this surfer film. A couple of hard-nosed wave-riders get involved with big money drug gangs and face danger far greater than the tide. **104m/C VHS, DVD.** George Clooney, Doug Savant, Dedee Pfeiffer, Gene Simmons, Rick Najera, Philip McKeon; ***D:*** H. Gordon Boos; ***W:*** Vincent Robert; ***C:*** John Schwartzman; ***M:*** Sasha Matson.

Red Tent 🦴🦴🦴 *Krasnaya Palatka* **1969 (G)** A robust, sweeping man-versus-nature epic based on the true story of the Arctic stranding of Italian explorer Umberto Nobile's expedition in 1928. A Russian-Italian co-production. **121m/C** Sean Connery, Claudia Cardinale, Peter Finch, Hardy Kruger, Massimo Girotti, Luigi Vannucchi; ***D:*** Mikhail Kalatozov; ***M:*** Ennio Morricone.

The Red Violin 🦴🦴½ *Le Violon Rouge* **1998 (R)** Spans 300 years in the life of one famed musical instrument that winds up in present-day Montreal on the auction block. Crafted by the Italian master Bussotti (Cecchi) in 1681, the red violin derives its unusual color from the human blood mixed into the finish. With this legacy, the violin travels to Austria, England, China, and Canada, leaving both beauty and tragedy in its wake. Most of the vignettes are dull, with the Montreal-set framing story holding the most interest. **131m/C VHS, DVD, Wide.** *CA* Samuel L. Jackson, Don McKellar, Carlo Cecchi, Irene Grazioli, Jean-Luc Bideau, Jason Flemyng, Greta Scacchi, Christoph Koncz, Sylvia Chang, Colm Feore, Monique Mercure, Liu Zi Feng; ***D:*** Francois Girard; ***W:*** Don McKellar, Francois Girard; ***C:*** Alan Dostie; ***M:*** John Corigliano. Oscars '99: Orig. Score; Genie '98: Art Dir./Set Dec., Cinematog., Costume Des., Director (Girard), Film, Screenplay, Score.

Red, White & Busted 🦴 *Outside In* **1975** Amnesty or prison? That is the scorching, virtually unanswerable question asked by indictment of America. We follow three friends during the Vietnam War and see how they were affected by the events, whether or not they went. **85m/C VHS.** Darrell Larson, Heather Menzies, Dennia Oliveri, John Bill.

Red Wind 🦴🦴 **1991 (R)** Kris Morrow is a psychotherapist whose latest patient, Lila, has a number of disturbing sadomasochistic fantasies. When Kris feels she's getting too close to the situation, she refers Lila to another therapist. But Lila calls and tells Kris she's already acted out one of her fantasies by killing her husband. In order to stop Lila from killing again, Kris goes on a dangerous search for her deadly patient. **93m/C VHS.** Lisa Hartman Black, Deanna Lund, Philip Casnoff, Christopher McDonald; ***D:*** Alan Metzger.

The Redeemer 🦴 **1976** Group of adults at their high school reunion play the children's game of hide-and-seek, with deadly results. **80m/C VHS.** F.G. Finkbinder, Damien Knight, Jeanetta Arnette; ***D:*** Constantine S. Gochis.

Redemption: Kickboxer 5 🦴 *Kickboxer 5* **1995 (R)** Retired kickboxer Matt Reeves (Dacascos) goes after the scum who murdered a friend. No surprises here. **87m/C VHS.** Mark Dacascos, James Ryan; ***D:*** Kristine Peterson; ***M:*** John Massari.

The Redhead from Wyoming 🦴🦴½ **1953** Spirited sagebrush adventure with fiery-tempered O'Hara as a saloon proprietress with feelings for both a local cattle rustler and the town's sheriff. Based on a story by James. **81m/C VHS.** Maureen O'Hara, Alex Nicol, William Bishop, Robert Strauss, Alexander Scourby, Jack Kelly, Jeanne Cooper, Dennis Weaver, Stacy Harris; ***D:*** Lee Sholem; ***W:*** Polly James, Herb Meadow.

Redline 🦴🦴 *Deathline* **1997 (R)** John Wade (Hauer) is double-crossed and murdered by his partner Merrick (Dacascos), who's involved with a Russian crime syndicate. But Wade is resurrected as a bionically-enhanced creation and hunts for revenge in a seedily futuristic Moscow. **96m/C VHS, DVD.** Rutger Hauer, Mark Dacascos, Yvonne Scio, John Thompson; ***D:*** Tibor Takacs, Brian Irving; ***W:*** Tibor Takacs, Brian Irving; ***C:*** Zoltan David; ***M:*** Guy Zerafa. **VIDEO**

Redneck 🦴 **1973** Implausible, distasteful purported "thriller" about criminals on the run. **92m/C VHS.** *IT GB* Telly Savalas, Franco Nero, Mark Lester, Ely Galleani, Duilio Del Prete, Maria Michi; ***D:*** Silvio Narizzano.

Redneck Zombies 🦴 **1988 (R)** A bunch of backwoods rednecks become zombies after chug-a-lugging some radioactive beer. Eating local tourists becomes a hard habit to break. Betcha can't have just one! **83m/C VHS, DVD.** Lisa DeHaven, W.E. Benson, Floyd Piranha, William-Livingston Dekkar, Zoofeet, James Housely, Anthony Burlington-Smith, Martin J. Wolfman, Boo Teasdale, Darla Deans, Tyrone Taylor, Frank Lantz, Pericles Lewnes; ***D:*** Pericles Lewnes; ***W:*** Fester Smellman; ***C:*** Ken Davis; ***M:*** Adrian Bond.

Reds 🦴🦴🦴 **1981 (PG)** The recreation of the life of author John Reed ("Ten Days that Shook the World"), his romance with Louise Bryant, his efforts to start an American Communist party, and his reporting of the Russian Revolution. A sweeping, melancholy epic using dozens of "witnesses" who reminisce about what they saw. See director Sergei Eisenstein's silent masterpiece "Ten Days that Shook the World," based on Reed's book, for the Russian view of some of the events depicted in Beatty's film. **195m/C VHS.** Warren Beatty, Diane Keaton, Jack Nicholson, Edward Herrmann, Maureen Stapleton, Gene Hackman, Jerzy Kosinski, George Plimpton, Paul Sorvino, William Daniels, M. Emmet Walsh, Dolph Sweet, Josef Sommer; ***D:*** Warren Beatty; ***W:*** Warren Beatty; ***M:*** Dave Grusin, Stephen Sondheim. Oscars '81: Cinematog., Director (Beatty), Support. Actress (Stapleton); British Acad. '82: Support. Actor (Nicholson), Support. Actress (Stapleton); Directors Guild '81: Director (Beatty); Golden Globes '82: Director (Beatty); L.A. Film Critics '81: Cinematog., Director (Beatty), Support. Actress (Stapleton); Natl. Bd. of Review '81: Director (Beatty), Support. Actor (Nicholson); N.Y. Film Critics '81: Film; Natl. Soc. Film Critics '81: Support. Actress (Stapleton); Writers Guild '81: Orig. Screenplay.

Redwood Curtain 🦴🦴½ **1995 (PG)** Geri Riordan (Salonga) is an Amerasian teenager, with a brilliant future as a concert pianist before her, until she becomes obsessed with learning about her past. Her wealthy adoptive father, Laird Riordan (Lithgow), provides understanding but no answers so she turns to her sympathetic Aunt Geneva (Monk), who lives in the redwood forest area of northern California. There Geri encounters homeless Vietnam vet Lyman Fellers (Daniels) and becomes convinced the troubled man is her birth father. Adapted from the play by Lanford Wilson; made for TV. **99m/C VHS.** Lea Salonga, John Lithgow, Jeff Daniels, Debra Monk, Catherine Hicks; ***D:*** John Korty; ***W:*** Ed Namzug; ***M:*** Lawrence Shragge. **TV**

Redwood Forest Trail 🦴🦴 **1950** Environmental-themed oater about a camp for underprivileged city boys. The boys of the camp are blamed for the death of a landowner whose daughter then refuses to renew the camp's mortgage. Allen and Switzer set out to prove that the real culprits are sawmill workers out to control the area timber. Smokey the Bear also makes an appearance to lecture about careless forest fires and the need to preserve the woods. **67m/B VHS.** Rex Allen, Jeff Donnell, Carl "Alfalfa" Switzer, Jane Darwell, Marten Lamont, Pierre Watkin; ***D:*** Philip Ford; ***W:*** Bradford Ropes.

Reed: Insurgent Mexico 🦴🦴 *Reed, Mexico Insurgente* **1973** Dramatization of John Reed's newspaper reporting on the Mexican Revolution. Spanish with subtitles. **104m/B VHS.** *MX* Claudio Obregon, Eduardo Lopez Rojas, Eracio Zepeda; ***D:*** Paul Leduc.

Reefer Madness *Tell Your Children; Dope Addict; Doped Youth; Love Madness; The Burning Question* **1938 (PG)** Considered serious at the time of its release, this low-budget depiction of the horrors of marijuana has become an underground comedy favorite. Overwrought acting and lurid script contribute to the fun. **67m/B VHS, DVD.** Dave O'Brien, Dorothy Short, Warren McCollum, Lillian Miles, Thelma White, Carleton Young, Josef Forte, Harry Harvey Jr., Pat Royale; ***D:*** Louis Gasnier; ***W:*** Paul Franklin, Arthur Hoerl; ***C:*** Jack Greenhalgh; ***M:*** Abe Meyer.

Reet, Petite and Gone 🦴🦴🦴 **1947** All-Black musical featuring the music of neglected jive singer Louis Jordan, and his band, The Tympany Five. A girl's mother dies; sneaky lawyer tries to cheat her. Slick and enjoyable. **75m/B VHS.** Louis Jordan, June Richmond; ***D:*** William Forest Crouch.

The Ref 🦴🦴🦴 **1993 (R)** The couple from hell turn the tables on Gus (Leary), a hard-nosed fugitive who takes Caroline (Davis) and her husband Lloyd (Spacey) hostage. Gus then finds himself trapped in the traditional Christmas ordeal of a family suffering from industrial-strength dysfunction. He plots his getaway while masquerading as the couple's marriage counselor, hence the film's title. This sometimes brutal, frequently hysterical satire of male-female relationships, family ties, and compulsory holiday rituals uses consistently sharp dialogue and superb acting to tell an absurd but convincing tale. **97m/C VHS.** J.K. Simmons, Raymond J. Barry, Richard Bright, Adam LeFevre, Elie Raab, Bill Raymond, Jim Turner, Robert Ridgely, Vincent Pastore, B.D. Wong, Rutanya Alda, Denis Leary, Judy Davis, Kevin Spacey, Glynis Johns, Robert J. Steinmiller Jr., Christine Baranski; ***D:*** Ted (Edward) Demme; ***W:*** Richard LaGravenese, Marie Weiss; ***M:*** David A. Stewart.

The Reflecting Skin 🦴🦴 **1991** In a 1950s prairie town a small boy sees insanity, child-murder, and radiation sickness, leading him to fantasize that the tormented young widow next door is a vampire. The pretentious drama/freak show rationalizes its ghastly events as symbolizing the hero's loss of youthful innocence. But the Hound knows the score; this is "Faces of Death" for the arts crowd, a grotesque menagerie that dares you to watch. The exploding-frog opener is already notorious. Beautiful photography, with vistas inspired by the painting of Andrew Wyeth. **116m/C VHS.** *GB* Viggo Mortensen, Lindsay Duncan, Jeremy Cooper, Duncan Fraser, Shiela Moore, David Longworth, Robert Koons, David Bloom, Evan Hall; ***D:*** Philip Ridley; ***W:*** Philip Ridley; ***C:*** Dick Pope; ***M:*** Nick Bicat.

A Reflection of Fear 🦴🦴 *Labyrinth* **1972 (PG)** Lame psycho-thriller about a young girl's jealously of her father's girlfriend, with family members dying of supernatural causes. **90m/C VHS.** Robert Shaw, Sally Kellerman, Sondra Locke, Mary Ure; ***D:*** William A. Fraker; ***W:*** Lewis John Carlino.

Reflections in a Golden Eye 🦴🦴½ **1967** Huston's film adaptation of Carson McCullers novel about repressed homosexuality, madness, and murder at a Southern Army base in 1948. Star-studded cast cannot consistently pull off convoluted lives of warped characters; not for everyone, though it holds some interest. **109m/C VHS.** Elizabeth Taylor, Marlon Brando, Brian Keith, Julie Harris; ***D:*** John Huston; ***C:*** Oswald Morris.

Reflections in the Dark 🦴🦴 *Reflections on a Crime* **1994 (R)** Beautiful Regina (Rogers) is on death row for murdering her overbearing husband James (Terry). On execution-eve, she relates her tale to young guard Colin (Zane), dispatching hubby by a different method each time she varies her story. Takes itself too seriously though Rogers gives a star performance. **83m/C VHS.** Mimi Rogers, Billy Zane, John Terry, Kurt Fuller, Lee Garlington, Nancy Fish; ***D:*** Jon Purdy; ***W:*** Jon Purdy; ***C:*** Teresa Medina.

Reflections of Murder 🦴🦴½ **1974** Evil schoolteacher's wife and mistress decide to kill him off and then are plagued by his phantom. Well-done TV remake of the French film "Diabolique." Suspenseful, with a great ending. **97m/C VHS.** Tuesday Weld, Joan Hackett, Sam Waterston, Lucille Benson, R.G. Armstrong, Michael Lerner, Ed Bernard, Lance Kerwin; ***D:*** John Badham; ***M:*** Billy Goldenberg. **TV**

Reform School Girl 🦴 **1957** A young girl ends up behind bars when her boyfriend steals a car to go joy-riding and is involved in a hit-and-run murder. Extremely cheap production and incredulous story. Look for Kellerman in a bit part in her first screen appearance. **71m/B VHS.** Gloria Castillo, Ross Ford, Edward Byrnes, Ralph Reed, Jack Kruschen, Sally Kellerman, Luana Anders, Yvette Vickers, Diana Darrin, Edmund Burns, Ross Hunter; ***D:*** Edward L. Bernds; ***W:*** Edward L. Bernds; ***C:*** Floyd Crosby; ***M:*** Ronald Stein.

Reform School Girls 🦴 **1986 (R)** Satiric raucous women's prison film, complete with tough lesbian wardens, brutal lesbian guards, sadistic lesbian inmates, and a single, newly convicted heterosexual heroine. Wendy O. Williams as a teenager? Come on. Overdone, over-campy, exploitative. **94m/C VHS, DVD, Wide.** Linda Carol, Wendy O. Williams, Pat Ast, Sybil Danning, Charlotte McGinnis, Sherri Stoner; ***D:*** Tom De Simone; ***W:*** Tom De Simone; ***C:*** Howard Wexler.

The Refrigerator 🦴½ **1991** Filmed on a miniscule budget, this comic/horror flick tells the story of the innocent Batemans of Ohio who move into a grubby New York apartment where they discover their battered Norge refrigerator is actually a doorway to hell. The fridge has a taste for flesh and tends to eat the unwary visitor as well as defrosting blood (very messy). All the previous tenants disappeared without a trace—will the Batemans be next? Cartoon satire is too amateurish to be successful. **86m/C VHS.** David Simonds, Julia McNeal, Angel Caban, Nena Segal, Jaime Rojo, Michelle DeCosta, Phyllis Sanz; ***D:*** Nicholas A.E. Jacobs; ***W:*** Nicholas A.E. Jacobs; ***C:*** Paul Gibson.

Regarding Henry 🦴🦴🦴 **1991 (PG-13)** A cold-hearted lawyer gets shot in the head during a holdup and survives with memory and personality erased. During recovery the new Henry displays compassion and conscience the old one never had. Though too calculated in its yuppie-bashing ironies, the picture works thanks to splendid acting and low-key, on-target direction. **107m/C VHS, Wide.** Harrison Ford, Annette Bening, Bill Nunn, Mikki Allen, Elizabeth Wilson, Robin Bartlett, John Leguizamo, Donald Moffat, Nancy Marchand; ***D:*** Mike Nichols; ***W:*** Jeffrey Abrams; ***C:*** Giuseppe Rotunno; ***M:*** Hans Zimmer.

Regeneration 🦴🦴 **1915** Irish hoodlum Owen (Fellowes) is saved from his life of crime by social worker Mamie Rose (Nilsson). Walsh filmed on location in New York's Bowery district and used actual gangsters in roles. Also features the 10-minute 1910 short "The Police Force of New York City," produced by Thomas Edison. **72m/B VHS, DVD.** Rockliffe Fellowes, Anna Q. Nilsson; ***D:*** Raoul Walsh; ***W:*** Raoul Walsh, Carl Harbaugh; ***C:*** Georges Benoit. Natl. Film Reg. '00.

Reggie Mixes In 🦴🦴🦴 **1916** Wealthy man brawls in bar room and falls for barmaid. Taking a job to be near his beloved, he wipes out local thugs while tending to her welfare. Exhilarating fight scenes in which Fairbanks fists it out with real life boxers. **58m/B VHS.** Douglas Fairbanks Sr., Bessie Love, Joseph Singleton, William E. (W.E., William A., W.A.) Lowery, Wilbur Higby, Frank Bennett; ***D:*** Christy Cabanne.

Regina 🦴🦴½ *Regina Roma* **1983** A woman controls all the activities of her husband and son. At age 36, her son is ready to leave home and she refuses to let him. Fine performances in this strange and disturbing film. **86m/C VHS, DVD.** *IT* Anthony Quinn, Ava Gardner, Ray Sharkey, Anna Karina; ***D:*** Jean-Yves Prate.

Reg'lar Fellers 🦴🦴 **1941** A gang of kids save the town and soften the heart of their grandmother, too. Production is sloppy. Based on a comic strip by Gene Byrnes. **66m/B VHS.** Billy Lee, Carl "Alfalfa" Switzer, Buddy Boles, Janet Dempsey, Sarah Padden, Roscoe Ates; ***D:*** Arthur Dreifuss.

Rehearsal for Murder 🦴🦴½ **1982** Movie star Redgrave is murdered on the night of her Broadway debut. Seems it might have been someone in the cast. Brought to you by the creative team behind "Columbo." Challenging whodunit a twist. Good cast. **96m/C VHS, DVD.** Robert Preston, Lynn Redgrave, Patrick Macnee, Lawrence Pressman, Madolyn Smith, Jeff Goldblum, William Daniels; ***D:*** David Greene; ***W:*** Richard Levinson, William Link; ***C:*** Stevan Larner; ***M:*** Billy Goldenberg. **TV**

Reign of Fire **2002** Dragons—the film has dragons as the bad guys. And it's not set in medieval fantasy times, it's set in a post-apocalyptic future where the beasties incinerate humans. American Van Zan (McConaughey), a British fireman (Bale), and a cutie helicopter pilot (Scorupco) hook up to give the critters a taste of their own medicine. Not yet reviewed. **?m/C VHS, DVD.** Matthew McConaughey, Christian Bale, Izabela Scorupco, Gerard Butler, Scott James Moutter; ***D:*** Rob Bowman.

Reign of Terror 🦴🦴 *The Black Book* **1949** British-made adventure set during the French Revolution, with everyone after the black book that holds the names of those arch-fiend Robespierre plans to guillotine in his ruthless bid for power. Well-mounted, but historical personages and events are reduced to cartoon form. **89m/B VHS.** Robert Cummings, Arlene Dahl, Richard Hart, Arnold Moss, Richard Basehart; ***D:*** Anthony Mann; ***W:*** Philip Yordan; ***C:*** John Alton.

Reilly: Ace of Spies 🦴🦴🦴 **1987** Covers the exploits of the real-life superspy and womanizer Sydney Reilly who uncovers Russian secrets in 1901, allowing the Japanese to sink the Russian fleet and invade China. After a lively spying career for the British, Reilly eventually plots against the Bolsheviks and comes close to overthrowing Lenin and installing himself as the new leader of the Russian government. Eleven episodes on four cassettes. **572m/C VHS.** *GB* Sam Neill, Sebastian Shaw, Jeananne Crowley; ***D:*** Jim Goddard.

The Reincarnate 🦴 **1971 (PG)** Cult guarantees lawyer will live forever if he can find a new body. Enter gullible sculptor; lawyer uses skill at persuasion. **89m/C VHS.** *CA* Jack Creley, Jay Reynolds, Trudy Young, Terry Tweed; ***D:*** Don Haldane.

The Reincarnation of Golden Lotus 🦴🦴🦴🦴 *Pan Jin Lian Zhi Qian Shi Jin Sheng* **1989** In this highly erotic story of love and revenge, Wong escapes China for decadent Hong Kong by marrying a wealthy but foolish man. She has numerous sadomasochistic affairs and begins having flashbacks, revealing her to be the reincarnation of Golden Lotus, a courtesan of ancient China. In Mandarin Chinese with English subtitles. **99m/C VHS.** *HK* Joi Wong, Eric Tsang, Lam Chen Yen; ***D:*** Clara Law.

The Reincarnation of Peter Proud 🦴🦴 **1975 (R)** A college professor has nightmares which lead him to believe the spirit of a murdered man is now possessing him. Kinda scary, but predictable. Screenplay by Ehrlich from his novel. **105m/C VHS.** Michael Sarrazin, Jennifer O'Neill, Margot Kidder, Cornelia Sharpe, Paul Hecht; ***D:*** J. Lee Thompson; ***W:*** Max Ehrlich; ***C:*** Victor Kemper; ***M:*** Jerry Goldsmith.

Reindeer Games 🦴 **2000 (R)** Too much talking and not nearly enough gun-toting action bog down this already inane crime thriller that tries way too hard to impress with loopy plot twists that come at a dizzying pace. A miscast Affleck is Rudy Duncan, a just released convict who takes on the identity of his recently deceased cellmate in order to get cozy with Ashley (Theron), who had established a correspondence with the dead inmate. The couple spends blissful days together via aerobic sex until Ashley's sadistic "brother" Gabriel (Sinise) forces Rudy to help him and his skanky gang rob an Indian casino on Christmas Eve. Pic is surprisingly flat, deadening the impact of the surprise endings that come in rapid succession, which unintentionally transform the film into a parody of itself. **98m/C VHS, DVD, Wide.** Ben Affleck, Charlize Theron, Gary Sinise, Clarence Williams III, Dennis Farina, Donal Logue, James Frain, Isaac Hayes, Danny Trejo; ***D:*** John Frankenheimer; ***W:*** Ehren Kruger; ***C:*** Alan Caso; ***M:*** Alan Silvestri.

The Reivers 🦴🦴🦴½ **1969 (PG)** Young boy and two adult pals journey from small town Mississippi (circa 1905) to the big city of Memphis in a stolen car. Picaresque tale is delightful onscreen, as in William Faulkner's enjoyable last novel. **107m/C VHS.** Steve McQueen, Sharon Farrell, Will Geer, Michael Constantine, Rupert Crosse; ***D:*** Mark Rydell; ***W:*** Harriet Frank Jr., Irving Ravetch; ***M:*** John Williams.

The Rejuvenator 🦴🦴½ *Rejuvenatrix* **1988 (R)** An oft-told film story: an aging actress discovers a "youth" serum but finds out that the serum affects things other than her aging. Well-done. **90m/C VHS.** Marcus Powell, John MacKay, James Hogue, Vivian Lanko, Jessica Dublin; ***D:*** Brian Thomas Jones; ***W:*** Simon Nuchtern; ***M:*** Larry Juris.

Relative Fear 🦴½ **1995 (R)** Little Adam has bad luck with his friends and relatives—they keep getting murdered all around him. His mother begins to suspect something unnatural is going on, and discovers Adam is not her natural child, but the son of a homicidal madwoman. Has Adam inherited some deadly traits? **94m/C VHS.** Darlanne Fluegel, M. Emmet Walsh, James Brolin, Denise Crosby, Martin Neufeld, Linda Sorensen, Matthew Dupuis; ***D:*** George Mihalka; ***W:*** Kurt Wimmer.

Relative Values 🦴🦴½ **1999 (PG-13)** The upper crusty Countess of Marshwood (Andrews) is appalled when her son Nigel (Atterton) wants to marry American starlet Miranda (Tripplehorn). And she isn't the only one—Miranda has jilted her Hollywood star boyfriend Don (Baldwin), who shows up at the Marshwood's country house to change her mind, and she also has a long-lost sister, Moxie

(Thompson), who happens to be the Countess' maid. Slight but witty confection, based on a 1951 Noel Coward play. **92m/C VHS, DVD, Wide.** *GB* Julie Andrews, Edward Atterton, Jeanne Tripplehorn, William Baldwin, Sophie Thompson, Colin Firth, Stephen Fry; ***D:*** Eric Styles; ***W:*** Paul Rattigan, Michael Walker; ***C:*** Jimmy Dibling; ***M:*** John Debney.

Relax... It's Just Sex! ½ **1998 (R)** Love and sex in the '90s surround gay looking-for-love writer Vincey (Anderson). His self-made extended family include best gal pal Tara (Tilly) and her boyfriend Gus (Perez), whose HIV-positive brother Javi (Garcia) has just attracted the attention of Buzz (Carson), the man Vincey had his eye on. Then there's troubled lesbian couple Megan (Scott Thomas), who has a fling with a guy (Wirth), and girlfriend Sarina (Williams), who's drawn into the arms of Robin (Petty). But romantic complications take a back seat when Javi and Vincey are subjected to a fag bashing in which Vincey violently turns the tables on one of his attackers. **110m/C VHS, DVD.** Mitchell Anderson, Jennifer Tilly, Cynda Williams, Serena Scott Thomas, Lori Petty, Eddie Garcia, Terrence "T.C." Carson, Timothy Paul Perez, Billy Wirth, Susan Tyrrell, Chris Cleveland, Gibbs Toldsdorf, Seymour Cassel, Paul Winfield; ***D:*** P.J. Castellaneta; ***W:*** P.J. Castellaneta; ***C:*** Lon Magdich; ***M:*** Lori Eschler Frystak.

Relentless **1989 (R)** Twisted psycho Nelson, once rejected by the LAPD Academy on psychological grounds, takes his revenge by murdering people and using his police training to cover his tracks. Good acting keeps sporadically powerful but cliched thriller afloat. **92m/C VHS.** Edward (Eddie) Bunker, Judd Nelson, Robert Loggia, Meg Foster, Leo Rossi, Pat O'Bryan, Mindy Seeger, Angel Tompkins, Ken Lerner, George "Buck" Flower; ***D:*** William Lustig.

Relentless 2: Dead On **1991 (R)** Rossi, the detective from the first film, tracks yet another murderer whose occult-style mutilations mask an international political conspiracy. So-so slaughter with artsy camera work. Honestly, how many "Relentless" fans can you name who've been waiting with anticipation? **93m/C VHS.** Leo Rossi, Ray Sharkey, Meg Foster, Miles O'Keeffe, Dale Dye; ***D:*** Michael Schroeder.

Relentless 3 **1993 (R)** A serial killer (Forsythe) likes to carve up his women victims and send various body parts to taunt the police. Then this sicko decides to really drive the cops crazy by stalking the beautiful girlfriend of the detective (Rossi) investigating the crimes. **84m/C VHS.** William Forsythe, Leo Rossi, Tom Bower, Robert Costanzo, Signy Coleman; ***D:*** James (Momel) Lemmo; ***W:*** James (Momel) Lemmo.

Relentless 4 ½ **1994 (R)** A psychiatrist with a secret (Janssen) is the only clue Detective Sam Dietz (Rossi) has to a serial killer. Seems all the victims knew the shrink but what does she know? **91m/C VHS.** Leo Rossi, Famke Janssen, Ken Lerner, Colleen T. Coffey; ***D:*** Oley Sassone; ***W:*** Mark Sevi, Terry Plumeri.

The Relic **1996 (R)** Quiz time! Which is more implausible: a huge reptilian creature from South American mythology who is crazy for decapitations running amok in a Chicago museum, or Miller as an evolutionary biologist? That's right! Both are equally implausible. But we're forced to accept both after a ship from Brazil arrives with crates for the museum and a completely headless crew (extra credit if you said it's implausible for people with no heads to pilot a ship). Superstitious police detective Vincent D'Agosto (Sizemore) decides to close down the museum's exhibit of...Superstition. That does not sit well with museum director Ann Cuthbert (Hunt), who decides she needs grant money (and the movie needs victims). The monster proceeds to suck brains until the sassy scientist decides she's had enough and takes off her high heels, which everyone knows means the end is near for the creature. Sound interesting? Only if you like Lifestyles of the Rich and Headless. **110m/C VHS, DVD.** Penelope Ann Miller, Tom Sizemore, Linda Hunt, James Whitmore, Clayton Rohner, Thomas Ryan, Lewis Van Bergen, Chi Muoi Lo, Robert Lesser; ***D:*** Peter Hyams; ***W:*** Amy Holden Jones, John Raffo, Rick Jaffa, Amanda Silver; ***C:*** Peter Hyams; ***M:*** John Debney.

The Reluctant Agent **1995** Waitress Linda (Jackee) is persuaded to take the place of injured twin sister Charlene, an FBI agent hot on the trail of shady-but-attractive businessman C. Gabriel Dash (Lawson). So, she goes undercover with the questionable assistance of agent John Fraser (Hedaya) to bring their criminal to justice. **94m/C VHS.** Jackee, Richard Lawson, Dan Hedaya, Bill Fagerbakke, Harold Sylvester, Cynthia Stevenson, Sharon Barr, Eda Reiss Merin; ***D:*** Paul Lynch; ***W:*** Jeff Cohn, Kristi Kane; ***M:*** Tim Truman.

The Reluctant Astronaut ½ **1967** Roy Fleming (Knotts) is a carnvial worker who operates the spaceship ride. Dad's upset the kid has no ambition and sends an application for Roy to NASA. Everyone's surprised when Roy gets accepted and he heads off to Florida but it turns out the job is janitorial. Still Roy does make friends with astronaut Red (Nielsen), who persuades NASA that Roy would be the perfect civilian to send up in an experimental capsule. Too bad Roy's terrified to fly in anything. **103m/C VHS.** Don Knotts, Leslie Nielsen, Joan Freeman, Arthur O'Connell, Jesse White, Jeanette Nolan, Joan Shawlee; ***D:*** Edward Montagne; ***W:*** James Fritzell, Everett Greenbaum; ***C:*** Rexford Wimpy; ***M:*** Vic Mizzy.

The Reluctant Debutante **1958** Harrison and Kendall are the urbane parents of Dee who are trying to find a suitable British husband for their girl. It seems their choices just won't do however, and Dee falls for American bad boy musician Saxon. A very lightweight yet extremely enjoyable romantic comedy thanks to Harrison and in particular his real-life wife Kendall, who unfortunately died the following year. **96m/C VHS, Wide.** Rex Harrison, Kay Kendall, John Saxon, Sandra Dee, Angela Lansbury, Diane Clare; ***D:*** Vincente Minnelli; ***C:*** Joseph Ruttenberg.

The Remains of the Day **1993 (PG)** If repression is your cup of tea then this is the film for you. Others may want to shake British butler par excellence Stevens (Hopkins) and tell him to express an emotion. In the 1930s, Stevens is the rigidly traditional butler to Lord Darlington (Fox). When Miss Kenton (Thompson) the almost vivacious new housekeeper expresses a quietly personal interest in Stevens his loyalty to an unworthy master prevents him from a chance at happiness. A quiet movie, told in flashback. Hopkins' impressive performance gets by strictly on nuance with Thompson at least allowed a small amount of natural charm. Based on the novel by Kazuo Ishiguro. **135m/C VHS, DVD, 8mm, Wide.** *GB* Anthony Hopkins, Emma Thompson, James Fox, Christopher Reeve, Peter Vaughan, Hugh Grant, Michael (Michel) Lonsdale, Tim Pigott-Smith; ***D:*** James Ivory; ***W:*** Ruth Prawer Jhabvala; ***C:*** Tony Pierce-Roberts; ***M:*** Richard Robbins. British Acad. '93: Actor (Hopkins); L.A. Film Critics '93: Actor (Hopkins); Natl. Bd. of Review '93: Actor (Hopkins).

Rembrandt **1936** Necessarily very visual biography of the great Dutch painter, Rembrandt. Superb acting by Laughton. **86m/B VHS, DVD.** *GB* Charles Laughton, Elsa Lanchester, Gertrude Lawrence, Walter Hudd; ***D:*** Alexander Korda; ***C:*** Georges Perinal.

Rembrandt—1669 **1977** A recreation of the controversial artist's last year, with his egotism clashing with his artistic impulses. In Dutch with English subtitles. **114m/C VHS.** *NL* Frans Stelling, Tom de Koff, Aye Fil; ***D:*** Jos Stelling.

Remedy for Riches **1940** The fourth "Dr. Christian" comedy, has the small-town doctor trying to uncover a real estate fraud before it bankrupts his community. Mildly funny. **66m/B VHS, 8mm.** Jean Hersholt, Dorothy Lovett, Edgar Kennedy, Jed Prouty, Walter Catlett; ***D:*** Erle C. Kenton.

Remember Me **1985** Just as a woman is starting to gain control of her life, her husband returns home from the mental hospital. **95m/C VHS.** Robert Grubb, Wendy Hughes, Richard Moir; ***D:*** Lex Marinos.

Remember the Night **1940** Another Sturges-scripted winner in which assistant D.A. MacMurray falls for sophisticated shoplifter Stanwyck, who has stolen a diamond bracelet amidst the Christmas holiday bustle. On a promise that she will return for the trial MacMurray postpones the trial and offers her a ride home for the holidays. Stanwyck is turned away by her mother and MacMurray brings her home for a real family Christmas, where love blooms. A sentimental, funny romance that boisters holiday cheer any time of year. **94m/B VHS.** Barbara Stanwyck, Fred MacMurray, Beulah Bondi, Elizabeth Patterson, Willard Robertson, Sterling Holloway; ***D:*** Mitchell Leisen; ***W:*** Preston Sturges; ***C:*** Ted Tetzlaff; ***M:*** Frederick "Friedrich" Hollander.

Remember the Titans **2000 (PG)** Black coach Herman Boone (Washington) is hired to lead the football team at racially tense T. C. Williams High School in Alexandria, Virginia, a school that has been forced to integrate in 1971. This forces white coach Bill Yoast (Patton), who was close to reaching an important milestone, into the role of assistant. He and his former players almost sit out the season, but decide warily to show up for the first practices. The team works through initial stages of mistrust and ignorance, but finally learn to work together. As the school year begins, racial tensions are eased by the success of the team, and the unified team goes to the state championship. A bit predictable and cliche-ridden, but heartfelt. Based on a true story. **114m/C VHS, DVD, Wide.** Denzel Washington, Will Patton, Donald Adeosun Faison, Wood Harris, Ethan Suplee, Nicole Parker, Hayden Panettiere, Kate (Catherine) Bosworth, Ryan Hurst, Kip Pardue, Craig Kirkwood, Burgess Jenkins, Earl C. Poitier, Ryan Gosling; ***D:*** Boaz Yakin; ***W:*** Gregory Allen Howard; ***C:*** Philippe Rousselot; ***M:*** Trevor Rabin.

Remembering the Cosmos Flower **1999** Teenager Akiko and her mother return to their small town home in Japan after seven years in South America. Akiko has contracted AIDS—a fact the entire community is aware of. While Akiko tries to cope with her illness, her childhood playmate Natsumi confronts the ignorance and fear of the village. Japanese with subtitles. **103m/C VHS, DVD, Wide.** *JP* Mari Natsuki, Megumi Matsushita, Akane Oda, Kai Shishido; ***D:*** Junichi Suzuki; ***W:*** Junichi Suzuki, Tetsutomo Kosugi; ***C:*** Kaz Tanaka; ***M:*** Mamoru Samurakouchi.

Remo Williams: The Adventure Begins *Remo: Unarmed and Dangerous* **1985 (PG-13)** Adaptation of "The Destroyer" adventure novel series with a Bond-like hero who can walk on water and dodge bullets after being instructed by a Korean martial arts master. Funny and diverting, and Grey is excellent (if a bit over the top) as the wizened oriental. The title's assumption is that the adventure will continue. **121m/C VHS.** Fred Ward, Joel Grey, Wilford Brimley, Kate Mulgrew, J.A. Preston, George Coe, Charles Cioffi, Patrick Kilpatrick, Michael Pataki, Marv Albert, Reginald Vel Johnson, William Hickey; ***D:*** Guy Hamilton; ***W:*** Warren B. Murphy, Christopher Wood; ***C:*** Andrew Laszlo; ***M:*** Craig Safan.

Remolino de Pasiones **1968** A young woman is driven to suicide after succumbing to her mother's persistent lover. **89m/C VHS.** *MX* Amparo Rivelles, Carlos Pinar, Susana Dosamantes; ***D:*** Alejandro Galindo; ***W:*** Alejandro Galindo; ***C:*** Alex Phillips Jr.; ***M:*** Gustavo Cesar Carrion.

Remote ½ **1993 (PG)** Thirteen-year-old Randy is a whiz designing high-tech remote-control gadgets. When one of his toys wipes out a friend's science project, Randy's parents try to put a halt to his tinkering but the kid has other plans. Innocuous rip-off of "Honey, I Shrunk the Kids" with some "Home Alone" thrown in as well. **80m/C VHS.** Chris Carrara, Jessica Bowman, John Diehl, Derya Ruggles, Tony Longo, Stuart Fratkin; ***D:*** Ted Nicolaou; ***W:*** Mike Farrow; ***M:*** Richard Band.

Remote Control ½ **1988 (R)** A circulating videotape of a 1950s sci-fi flick is turning people into murderous zombies, thanks to some entrepreneurial aliens. Silly, but performed by young actors with gusto. **88m/C VHS.** Kevin Dillon, Deborah Goodrich, Christopher Wynne, Jennifer Tilly; ***D:*** Jeff Lieberman; ***M:*** Peter Bernstein.

Remote Control ½ **1994** Quiet Axel lives with his mom, whose life revolves around the TV set, and his sister Maeja, who spends most of her time partying in a seedy club called Sodoma. Sodoma is run by three amateur gangsters who are anxious to get rid of a rival, Moli. Meanwhile, Axel falls in love with Moli's sister Unnur (who also happens to be Maeja's best friend). Then the gangsters kidnap Unnur and Axel sets out to rescue her. Icelandic with English subtitles. **85m/C VHS.** *IC* Bjorn Fridbjornsson, Margret H. Gustavsdottir, Helgi Bjornsson, Soley Eliasdottir; ***D:*** Oskar Jonasson; ***W:*** Oskar Jonasson.

Renaissance Man ½ **1994 (PG-13)** Skeptical new teacher inspires a classroom of underachievers and finds his true calling. Based loosely on the experiences of screenwriter Burnstein at a base in Michigan. Civilian Bill Rago (DeVito) is an unemployed ad exec assigned to teach Shakespeare to a group of borderline Army recruits led by Hardison. Add half a bone for the recruits and their Hamlet rap, a breath of fresh air in an otherwise stale plot. Some funny moments, reminiscent of "Stripes," but not quite as wacky. On the other hand, Marshall does endearing well. Look for rapper Marky Mark with his shirt on (hard to recognize). Shot with the cooperation of the Army. **128m/C VHS.** Danny DeVito, Gregory Hines, James Remar, Stacey Dash, Ed Begley Jr., Mark Wahlberg, Lillo Brancato, Kadeem Hardison, Richard T. Jones, Khalil Kain, Peter Simmons, Jenifer Lewis; ***Cameos:*** Cliff Robertson; ***D:*** Penny Marshall; ***W:*** Jim Burnstein, Ned Mauldin; ***M:*** Hans Zimmer.

Rendez-Moi Ma Peau ½ *Give Me Back My Skin* **1981** A modern-day witch gets in a traffic accident with a married couple and, as revenge, she transposes their personalities into the other's body. In French with subtitles. **82m/C VHS.** *FR* Jean-Luc Bideau, Erik Colin, Bee Michelin, Chantal Neuwirth; ***D:*** Patrick Schulmann; ***C:*** Jacques Assuerus, Andre Zarra; ***M:*** Patrick Schulmann.

Rendez-vous **1985 (R)** A racy, dark film about the sensitive balance between sex and exploitation, the real world and the stage world. Some may be disturbed by chillingly explicit scenes. Impressive tour de force of imagination, direction, and cinematography. In French with English subtitles. **82m/C VHS.** *FR* Juliette Binoche, Lambert Wilson, Wadeck Stanczak, Jean-Louis Trintignant; ***D:*** Andre Techine; ***W:*** Olivier Assayas; ***C:*** Philippe Angers. Cannes '85: Director (Techine).

Rendez-vous de Juillet ½ **1949** In postwar Paris Lucien dreams of becoming a documentary filmmaker, with his friends accompanying him to Africa to serve as his production team. His parents want him to get a regular job and Lucien's buddies are more concerned with love affairs, jazz, theatre, and other pleasures to take him too seriously. Includes a performance by American trumpeter Rex Stewart. French with subtitles; follows Becker's "Antoine et Antoinette." **110m/B VHS.** *FR* Daniel Gelin, Brigitte Auber, Nicole Courcel, Maurice Ronet, Bernard Lajarrige; ***D:*** Jacques Becker; ***W:*** Jacques Becker, Maurice Griffe; ***C:*** Claude Renoir; ***M:*** Jean Wiener.

Rendezvous in Paris *Les Rendez-vous de Paris* **1995** Includes three stories by Rohmer about the complications and disappointments of love. "Le Rendez-vous de 7 heures" finds Esther (Bellar) upset when boyfriend Horace (Basler) is spotted with another girl at a cafe. She decides to make him jealous by showing up at the same cafe with another man. A woman (Rauscher) decides to leave her boring fiance in "Les Bancs de Paris" and tries to decide on a possible new romance with a provincial professor (Renko). In "Mere et Enfant 1907," a painter (Kraft) goes to an art gallery where he spots a woman (Loyen) admiring Picasso's painting "Mother and Child" and he decides to pursue her. French with subtitles. **100m/C**

VHS. *FR* Clara Bellar, Antoine Basler, Mathias Megard, Judith Chancel, Aurore Rauscher, Serge Renko, Michael Kraft, Benedicte Loyen, Veronika Johansson; *D:* Eric Rohmer; *W:* Eric Rohmer; *C:* Diane Baratier; *M:* Sebastien Erms.

Renegade Girl 🦴 **1946** A special agent is sent west to capture the female head of a band of outlaws. **65m/B VHS.** Alan Curtis, Ann Savage, Edward Brophy, Ray Corrigan, Jack Holt; *D:* William Berke.

Renegade Trail 🦴🦴 **1939** Hopalong Cassidy helps a marshall and a pretty widow round up ex-cons and rustlers. The King's Men, radio singers of the era, perform a fistful of songs. **61m/B VHS.** William Boyd, George "Gabby" Hayes, Russell Hayden, Charlotte Wynters, Russell Hopton, Sonny Bupp, Jack Rockwell, Roy Barcroft, Eddie Dean; *D:* Lesley Selander.

Renegades 🦴🦴 **1989 (R)** A young cop from Philadelphia and a Lakota Indian begrudgingly unite to track down a gang of ruthless crooks. Good action, and lots of it; not much story. **105m/C VHS, DVD.** Kiefer Sutherland, Lou Diamond Phillips, Rob Knepper, Jami Gertz, Bill Smitrovich; *D:* Jack Sholder; *C:* Phil Meheux; *M:* Michael Kamen.

Renfrew of the Royal Mounted 🦴🦴 **1937** A Canadian Mountie goes after counterfeiters and sings a few songs in this mild adaptation of a popular kids' radio serial. Newill was a popular tenor of the day, but the Hound thinks Renfrew's dog 'Lightning' should have been the star. **57m/B VHS.** Carol Hughes, James Newill, Kenneth Harlan; *D:* Al(bert) Herman.

Renfrew on the Great White Trail 🦴½ *On the Great White Trail; Renfrew of the Royal Mounted on the Great White Trail* **1938** A frustrated fur trader takes off after a pack of thieves. **58m/B VHS.** James Newill, Terry Walker, Robert Frazer, Richard Alexander; *D:* Al(bert) Herman.

Reno and the Doc 🦴🦴½ **1984** Enjoyable comedy about two endearingly cranky middle-aged men battling mid-life crises join together and test their mettle in the world of professional skiing. **88m/C VHS.** *CA* Ken Walsh, Henry Ramer, Linda Griffiths; *D:* Charles Dennis.

Renoir Shorts 🦴🦴🦴 **1927** Two early silent Renoir fantasies: "The Little Matchgirl," a lyrical adaptation of the Hans Christian Anderson fairy tale, and "Charleston," in which a space-traveling African and Parisian girl dance comically. **50m/B VHS.** Catherine Hessling; *D:* Jean Renoir.

Rent-A-Cop 🦴🦴 **1988 (R)** A cop (Reynolds) is bounced from the force after he survives a drug-bust massacre under suspicious circumstances. He becomes a security guard and continues to track down the still-at-large killer with help from call girl Minnelli. **95m/C VHS, DVD.** Burt Reynolds, Liza Minnelli, James Remar, Richard Masur, Bernie Casey, John Stanton, John P. Ryan, Dionne Warwick, Robby Benson; *D:* Jerry London; *W:* Michael Blodgett; *C:* Giuseppe Rotunno; *M:* Jerry Goldsmith. Golden Raspberries '88: Worst Actress (Minnelli).

Rent-A-Kid 🦴🦴½ **1995 (G)** Businessman Harry Haber (Nielsen) is asked by his son to keep an eye out on the Mid-Valley Orphanage for a week. Then Harry meets a young couple who are unsure about having a family so, since Harry's business is renting all sorts of things, he decides to rent the couple three orphans so they can get a taste of parenting. **89m/C VHS.** Leslie Nielsen, Christopher Lloyd, Matt McCoy, Sherry Miller, Amos Crawley, Cody Jones, Tabitha Lupien, Tony Rosato; *D:* Fred Gerber; *W:* Paul Bernbaum; *C:* Rene Ohashi; *M:* Ron Ramin.

Rentadick 🦴🦴 **1972** A precursor to the Monty Python masterpieces, written by future members Chapman and Cleese. Private eye spoof isn't as funny as later Python efforts; but it is an indication of what was yet to come and fans should enjoy it. **94m/C VHS.** *GB* James Booth, Julie Ege, Ronald Fraser, Donald Sinden, Michael Bentine, Richard Briers, Spike Milligan, Tsai Chin, Kenneth Cope, John Wells; *D:* Jim Clark; *W:* Graham Chapman, John Cleese; *C:* John Coquillon; *M:* Carl Davis.

Rented Lips 🦴 **1988 (R)** Two documentary filmmakers sell out, taking over the production of a porno film at the request of a public television producer who promises to help their careers. Mull and Shawn are well supported by an impressive cast, but everyone's effort is wasted in unfunny attempt at comedy. **82m/C VHS.** Martin Mull, Dick Shawn, Jennifer Tilly, Kenneth Mars, Edy Williams, Robert Downey Jr., June Lockhart, Shelley Berman, Mel Welles, Pat McCormick, Eileen Brennan; *D:* Robert Downey.

Repentance 🦴🦴🦴 *Pokayaniye; Confession* **1987 (PG)** A popular, surreal satire of Soviet and Communist societies. A woman is arrested for repeatedly digging up a dead local despot, and put on trial. Wickedly funny and controversial; released under the auspices of glasnost. In Russian with English subtitles. **151m/C VHS.** *RU* Avtandil Makharadze, Zeinab Botsvadze, Ia Ninidze, Edisher Giorgobiani, Ketevan Abuladze, Kakhi Kavsadze; *D:* Tengiz Abuladze. Cannes '87: Grand Jury Prize.

The Replacement Killers 🦴🦴½ **1998 (R)** Hong Kong action star Chow Yun-Fat makes his American debut in this somewhat disappointing first feature from director Antoine Fuqua. Chow stars as John Lee, an assassin working for crime boss Mr. Wei (Tsang). When Lee decides not to carry out a hit on a cop's (Rooker) son, he becomes the target of the men sent to replace him. Needing a passport to get back to China, Lee goes to forger Meg Coburn (Sorvino). Before she can finish the papers, Wei's men begin the first of many high body count gun battles. Fuqua, who was heavily influenced by John Woo (one of the film's exec producers), does a passable job of conveying the style of Chow and Woo's Hong Kong work, but doesn't leave much room for the substance. Chow's sublety and charisma are crammed into a mechanical action plot, and only his talent saves the whole thing from imploding. **86m/C VHS, DVD, Wide.** Chow Yun-Fat, Mira Sorvino, Michael Rooker, Kenneth Tsang, Juergen Prochnow, Danny Trejo, Til Schweiger, Clifton (Gonzalez) Collins Jr., Carlos Gomez, Frank Medrano; *D:* Antoine Fuqua; *W:* Ken Sanzel; *C:* Peter Collister; *M:* Harry Gregson-Williams.

The Replacements 🦴½ **2000 (PG-13)** An NFL players' strike finds coach Hackman stuck with a bunch of replacement players, including washed-up quarterback Shane Falco (Reeves) and never-was receiver Clifford Franklin (Jones). If you can get past the fact that the heroes are scabs, this silly cliche-fest still isn't very good. It's better than it oughta be, but only because of Hackman's presence and Jones's comic talents. The odd assortment of misfits and goofballs is occasionally amusing, but nothing you haven't seen in all the other "rag-tag-team-fights-the-odds" sports comedies. Based on the 1987 strike when players filling in for the Washington Redskins won three straight games. **105m/C VHS, DVD, Wide.** Keanu Reeves, Gene Hackman, Jon Favreau, Orlando Jones, Jack Warden, Brooke Langton, Rhys Ifans, Brett Cullen, Gailard Sartain, Art LaFleur, Faizon Love, Michael "Bear" Taliferro, Troy Winbush, Michael Jace, Ace Yonamine, David Denman, Keith David, Pat Summerall, John Madden, Evan Dexter Parke; *D:* Howard Deutch; *W:* Vince McKewin; *C:* Tak Fujimoto; *M:* Alan Silvestri.

Replicant 🦴🦴½ **2001 (R)** It takes a killer to catch a killer. In this case Van Damme is cloned by the government so he can go after himself (the original is a vicious serial killer). Cop Rooker, who's been unsuccessfully hunting the psycho for several years, teams up with the duplicate to get results. Lots of chases, fights, and high-tech thrills. **100m/C VHS, DVD, Wide.** Jean-Claude Van Damme, Michael Rooker, Ian Robinson, Catherine Dent; *D:* Ringo Lam; *W:* Lawrence Riggins, Les Weldon; *C:* Mike Southon; *M:* Guy Zerafa. **VIDEO**

Replikator: Cloned to Kill 🦴½ **1994 (R)** In the 21st century, a ruthless criminal gets hold of replication techology that can duplicate anything, including people. So it's up to a cop and two cyberpunks to stop the destruction. **96m/C VHS.** Michael St. Gerard, Brigitte Bako, Ned Beatty; *D:* G. Philip Jackson; *W:* Tony Johnston, Michelle Bellerose, John Dawson.

Repo Jake 🦴½ **1990** Jake Baxter learns the myth of the carefree life of a repossession man in this action thriller. His illusion is destroyed by angry clients, pornography, a deadly underworld racetrack, and a sinister crime boss. **90m/C VHS.** Dan Haggerty, Robert Axelrod.

Repo Man 🦴🦴🦴½ **1983 (R)** An inventive, perversely witty portrait of sick modern urbanity, following the adventures of punk stock boy Otto (Estevez), who takes a job as a car repossessor under the jaundiced eye of veteran Bud (Stanton). Then there's the lobotomized physicist Parnell (Harris), who carries around a strang glowing object in the trunk of his car that's wanted by the government. The L.A. landscape is filled with pointless violence, no-frills packaging, media hypnosis, and aliens. Executive producer: none other than ex-Monkee Michael Nesmith. **93m/C VHS, DVD, Wide.** Emilio Estevez, Harry Dean Stanton, Sy Richardson, Tracey Walter, Olivia Barash, Fox Harris, Jennifer Balgobin, Vonetta McGee, Angelique Pettyjohn, Biff Yeager; *D:* Alex Cox; *W:* Alex Cox; *C:* Robby Muller; *M:* Tito Larriva, Iggy Pop.

The Report on the Party and the Guests 🦴🦴🦴🦴 **1966** A controversial, widely banned political allegory, considered a masterpiece from the Czech new wave. A picnic/lawn party deteriorates into brutality, fascist intolerance and persecution. Many Czech film makers, some banned at the time, appear. Based on a story by Ester Krumbachova, who also co-wrote the screenplay. In Czech with English subtitles. **71m/B VHS.** *CZ* Jiri Nemec, Evald Schorm, Ivan Vyskocil, Jan Klusak, Zdena Skvorecka, Pavel Bosek; *D:* Jan Nemec; *W:* Jan Nemec.

Report to the Commissioner 🦴🦴🦴 *Operation Undercover* **1974 (R)** A rough, energetic crime-in-the-streets cop thriller. A young detective accidentally kills an attractive woman who turns out to have been an undercover cop, then is dragged into the bureaucratic cover-up. **112m/C VHS.** Michael Moriarty, Yaphet Kotto, Susan Blakely, Hector Elizondo, Richard Gere, Tony King, Michael McGuire, Stephen Elliott; *D:* Milton Katselas; *W:* Abby Mann; *M:* Elmer Bernstein.

Repossessed 🦴🦴 **1990 (PG-13)** A corny, occasionally funny takeoff on the human-possessed-by-the-devil films with Blair, as usual, as the afflicted victim. Nielsen, in another typecast role, plays the goofy man of the cloth who must save the day. Numerous actors appear in brief comedy sequences which lampoon current celebrities and constitute the film's highlights. For fans of "Airplane" and "The Naked Gun"; not necessarily for others. **89m/C VHS.** Linda Blair, Ned Beatty, Leslie Nielsen, Anthony Starke, Jesse Ventura; *D:* Bob Logan; *W:* Bob Logan; *M:* Charles Fox. Golden Raspberries '90: Worst Song ("He's Comin' Back (The Devil!)").

The Reptile 🦴🦴 **1966** The inhabitants of yet another Cornish village are turning up dead—mysteriously from snakebite. When Harry (Barrett) investigates his brother's death, he finds out Anna (Pearce) is the victim of a curse, which causes her to turn into a snake. Rather sympathetic characters for the horror genre. **90m/C VHS, DVD.** *GB* Jacqueline Pearce, Ray Barrett, Noel Willman, Jennifer Daniel, Michael Ripper, John Laurie, Marne Maitland, Charles Lloyd Pack, George Woodbridge, David Baron; *D:* John Gilling; *W:* John (Anthony Hinds) Elder; *C:* Arthur Grant; *M:* Don Banks.

Reptilian 🦴 **1999 (PG-13)** Archeologists Campbell (Livingston) and Hughes (Young) are searching for remains of a gigantic dinosaur. But guess who gets to them first? Evil aliens! Who want to take over the earth! So they ray-zap the dino remains back to life and the creature goes on a rampage until the military puts him down. But it doesn't end there—although you'll certainly wish it had. **99m/C VHS, DVD, Wide.** *KN* Harrison Young, Donna Philipson, Richard B. Livingston; *D:* Hyung Rae Shim; *W:* Marty Poole; *C:* Hong Kim An; *M:* Chris Desmong, Seung Woo Cho.

Reptilicus 🦴🦴 **1962** Oil drillers in Lapland bring up a sample of prehistoric flesh from a frozen bog deep below the earth, which is transported to Copenhagen. It proves to be alive and growing; eventually a lightning storm frees it from its holding tank. Soon thereafter the army has a real problem on its hands when it reappears as a completely regenerated monster, crawling across the landscape, crushing buildings and eating farmers. The authorities have no luck ridding themselves of the scaly, snake-like dragon, until they corner it in the main square in downtown Copenhagen. This alternative epic comes in dead last in the list of movies where giant monsters attack cities. The several hundred extras who run politely through the streets in "panic" look bored or amused. Most of Reptilicus's scenes are artlessly shot in broad daylight, making its general artificiality even more obvious. **90m/C DVD, Wide.** *DK* Carl Ottosen, Ann Smyrner, Mimi Heinrich, Asbjorn Andersen, Bodil Miller, Bent Mejding, Dirch Passer, Ole Wisborg; *D:* Sidney Pink; *W:* Sidney Pink, Ib Melchior; *C:* Aage Wiltrup; *M:* Sven Gyldmark.

Repulsion 🦴🦴🦴½ **1965** Character study of a young French girl who is repulsed and attracted by sex. Left alone when her sister goes on vacation, her facade of stability begins to crack, with violent and bizarre results. Polanski's first film in English and his first publicly accepted full-length feature. Suspenseful, disturbing and potent. **105m/B VHS.** *GB* Catherine Deneuve, Yvonne Furneaux, Ian Hendry, John Fraser, Patrick Wymark, James Villiers, Renee Houston, Helen Fraser, Mike Pratt, Valerie Taylor; *D:* Roman Polanski; *W:* Roman Polanski, Gerard Brach, David Stone; *C:* Gilbert Taylor.

Requiem for a Dream 🦴🦴🦴½ **2000** Amazing performances from the entire cast, particularly Burstyn, propel this harrowing story of drug addiction and crumbled dreams. Harry (Leto) and his friend Tyrone (Wayans) decide to become small-time drug dealers in order to raise the cash needed to help his designer girlfriend Marion (Connelly) open a clothing store. Unfortunately, they begin to sample the merchandise, and their plans slip away until all they can plan is how to get the next fix. In a parallel storyline, Harry's mother Sara (Burstyn) receives a call that she may be a contestant on her favorite game show. She begins gobbling diet pills to improve her appearance and soon can't live without them. Director Aronofsky has stated that addiction is the hero of this movie. Based on the novel by Hubert Selby, Jr. **102m/C VHS, DVD, Wide.** Jared Leto, Ellen Burstyn, Jennifer Connelly, Marlon Wayans, Christopher McDonald, Louise Lasser, Keith David, Sean Gullette; *D:* Darren Aronofsky; *W:* Darren Aronofsky, Hubert Selby Jr.; *C:* Matthew Libatique; *M:* Clint Mansell. Ind. Spirit '01: Actress (Burstyn), Cinematog.

Requiem for a Heavyweight 🦴🦴🦴 **1956** Original TV version of the story about an American Indian heavyweight boxer played by Palance who risks blindness in order to help his manager pay off bookies. Highly acclaimed teleplay written for "Playhouse 90." **90m/B VHS.** Jack Palance, Keenan Wynn, Ed Wynn, Kim Hunter, Ned Glass; *D:* Ralph Nelson; *W:* Rod Serling. **TV**

Requiem for a Heavyweight 🦴🦴🦴 *Blood Money* **1962** After 17 years, Mountain Rivera (Quinn) is a washed-up heavyweight risking his life if he continues boxing. He tries to find another job but his manager, Maish Rennick (Gleason), owes the mob big, and persuades the fighter to help him pay off his debts by joining the wrestling circuit, so Mountain humiliates himself to help out his old friend. The 1956 TV version is still more compelling but the film's performances are all first-rate. **100m/B VHS, DVD, Wide.** Anthony Quinn, Jackie Gleason, Mickey Rooney, Julie Harris, Stanley Adams, Spivy Levoe, Muhammad Ali, Jack Dempsey; *D:* Ralph Nelson; *W:* Rod Serling; *C:* Arthur Ornitz; *M:* Laurence Rosenthal.

Requiem for Dominic 🦴🦴🦴½ *Requiem fur Dominic* **1991 (R)** A Communist-bloc country in the midst of revolution accuses a man of terrorist activities. Can his friend, exiled for years, help him discover the truth? Interesting and timely premise, matched with outstanding ensemble acting make for a superior thriller. Amnesty International receives partial proceeds from all sales of this video. In German with English subtitles. **88m/C VHS.** *GE* Felix Mitterer, Viktoria Schubert, August Schmolzer, Angelica Schutz; ***D:*** Robert Dornhelm.

Requiem for Murder 🦴½ **1999 (PG-13)** Psychotic fan of a classical radio DJ decides to murder her competition. **95m/C VHS, DVD.** Molly Ringwald, Chris Heyerdahl, Lynne Adams, Chris Mulkey, Jayne Heitmeyer; ***D:*** Douglas Jackson; ***W:*** Matt Dorff; ***C:*** Barry Gravelle; ***M:*** Milan Kymlicka. **VIDEO**

The Rescue 🦴½ **1988 (PG)** An elite team of U.S. Navy Seals is captured after destroying a disabled submarine. When the U.S. government writes off the men, their children decide to mount a rescue. Puerile, empty-headed trash for teens. **97m/C VHS.** Marc Price, Charles Haid, Kevin Dillon, Christina Harnos, Edward Albert; ***D:*** Ferdinand Fairfax; ***W:*** Jim Thomas, John Thomas; ***C:*** Russell Boyd; ***M:*** Bruce Broughton.

Rescue from Gilligan's Island 🦴½ **1978** Fifteen years after the cancellation of "Gilligan's Island" came this TV movie that reunited the principal cast (minus Tina Louise's original Ginger) and finally depicted the rescue of the castaways. When a tsunami sweeps the group's huts into the sea, they're discovered by the Coast Guard and return to civilization. Somewhat changed by their experiences on the island, the castaways face difficulties assimilating with modern life, while at the same time Gilligan is pursued by Russian spies sent to retrieve an information disc that landed on the island. This awkward return to the lame jokes and Keaton-inspired slapstick of the TV series seemed out of date even during the original broadcast, but the cast's chemistry is still evident. **92m/C VHS, DVD.** Bob Denver, Alan Hale Jr., Russell Johnson, Jim Backus, Natalie Schafer, Dawn Wells, Judith Baldwin; ***D:*** Leslie Martinson; ***W:*** David Harmon, Sherwood Schwartz, Elroy Schwartz, Al Schwartz; ***C:*** Robert Primes; ***M:*** Gerald Fried. **TV**

Rescue Me 🦴🦴½ **1993 (PG-13)** Geek photographer Fraser carries a torch for high school honey Ginny and just happens to be on the scene (with camera) when she's kidnapped. So he persuades a scruffy Vietnam vet to help him rescue his damsel in distress. Likeable adventure with lots of chases. **99m/C VHS.** Michael Dudikoff, Stephen Dorff, Peter DeLuise, Ami Dolenz, William Lucking, Dee Wallace Stone; ***D:*** Arthur Seidelman; ***W:*** Michael Snyder; ***C:*** Hanania Baer; ***M:*** Al Kasha, Joel Hirschhorn, David Waters.

The Rescuers 🦴🦴🦴 **1977 (G)** Bernard and Miss Bianca, two mice who are members of the Rescue Aid Society, attempt to rescue an orphan named Penny from the evil Madame Medusa, who's after the world's biggest diamond. They are aided by comic sidekick, Orville the albatross, and a group of lovable swamp creatures. Very charming in the best Disney tradition. Based on the stories of Margery Sharp. Followed by "The Rescuers Down Under." **76m/C VHS.** ***D:*** Wolfgang Reitherman, John Lounsbery; ***M:*** Artie Butler; ***V:*** Bob Newhart, Eva Gabor, Geraldine Page, Jim Jordan, Joe Flynn, Jeanette Nolan, Pat Buttram.

The Rescuers Down Under 🦴🦴½ **1990 (G)** "Crocodile" Dundee goes Disney; the followup to "The Rescuers" places its characters in Australia with only mild results for a Magic Kingdom product. Heroic mice Bernard and Bianca protect a young boy and a rare golden eagle from a poacher. The great bird closely resembles the logo of Republic Pictures. **77m/C VHS, DVD, Wide.** ***D:*** Hendel Butoy, Mike Gabriel; ***W:*** Jim Cox, Karey Kirkpatrick, Joe Ranft, Byron Simpson; ***M:*** Bruce Broughton; ***V:*** Bob Newhart, Eva Gabor, John Candy, Tristan Rogers, George C. Scott, Frank Welker, Adam Ryen.

Rescuers: Stories of Courage—Two Couples 🦴🦴🦴 **1998 (PG)** In "Aart and Joht Je Vos," Delaney and Donovan are Dutch newlyweds who turn their home into a refuge for Jews hiding from the Nazis. The second story, "Marie Taquet," features Hamilton in the title role as a Belgian who, along with her husband (Molina), hides Jewish students at their Catholic boarding school. These true stories are based on the book "Rescuers: Portraits of Moral Courage in the Holocaust." **109m/C VHS.** Dana Delany, Martin Donovan, Linda Hamilton, Alfred Molina, Jan Rubes, Nigel Bennett, James Kidnie, Nicholas Kilbertus, Scott Speedman; ***D:*** Tim Hunter, Lynne Litman; ***W:*** Paul Monash, Francine Carroll, Cy Chermack; ***C:*** Miroslaw Baszak; ***M:*** Pino Donaggio, Hummie Mann. **CABLE**

Rescuers: Stories of Courage "Two Women" 🦴🦴🦴 **1997 (PG-13)** Fact-based drama about Gentiles who sheltered Jews from Nazi persecution during WWII. In "Mamusha" Perkins plays Gertruda, a Catholic nanny in Poland, who poses as the mother of her orphaned Jewish charge. "The Woman on the Bicycle" is Frenchwoman Marie-Rose (Ward), who works for the Resistance and hides a Jewish family in the attic of her home. **107m/C VHS.** Elizabeth Perkins, Sela Ward, Fritz Weaver, Anne Jackson, Al Waxman, Gerard Parkes, Michael Landes; ***D:*** Peter Bogdanovich; ***W:*** Ernest Kinoy, Terry Norris; ***C:*** Miroslaw Baszak; ***M:*** Hummie Mann. **CABLE**

Reservoir Dogs 🦴🦴🦴½ **1992 (R)** Ultraviolent tale of honor among thieves. Six professional criminals known by code names to protect their identities (Misters Pink, White, Orange, Blonde, Blue, and Brown) are assembled by Joe Cabot (Tierney) to pull off a diamond heist. But two of the gang are killed in a police ambush. The survivors regroup in an empty warehouse and try to discover the informer in their midst. In probably the most stomach-churning scene (there is some competition here), a policeman is tortured (by Madsen) just for the heck of it to the tune of the Stealers Wheel "Stuck in the Middle with You." Unrelenting; auspicious debut for Tarantino with strong ensemble cast anchored by Keitel as the very professional Mr. White. **100m/C VHS, DVD, Wide.** Harvey Keitel, Tim Roth, Michael Madsen, Steve Buscemi, Christopher Penn, Lawrence Tierney, Kirk Baltz, Quentin Tarantino, Edward (Eddie) Bunker, Randy Brooks; ***D:*** Quentin Tarantino; ***W:*** Quentin Tarantino; ***C:*** Andrzej Sekula; ***M:*** Karyn Rachtman; ***V:*** Steven Wright. Ind. Spirit '93: Support. Actor (Buscemi).

Resident Evil 🦴🦴 **2002 (R)** Yet another noisy movie adapted from a videogame, which never gets as creepy as a zombie movie should. Umbrella Corp. (AKA the Hive) is the front for a secret military tech and genetics operations. Its security operations are controlled by a A.I. computer known as the Red Queen, which instigates a series of defensive measures to contain a virus (that can reanimate the dead) that has been released. A group of containment specialists (including heroine babe Jovanovich) are sent in and have to battle workers who have been contaminated and turned into flesh-munching creatures. **100m/C VHS, DVD.** *GE GB* Milla Jovovich, Michelle Rodriguez, Colin Salmon, Eric Mabius, James Purefoy, Stephen Billington; ***D:*** Paul Anderson; ***W:*** Paul Anderson; ***C:*** David Johnson; ***M:*** Marco Beltrami.

Resistance 🦴🦴 **1992** Apocalytic tale of rebels and soldiers. The poor have been driven from abandoned cities into working as farm hands for a large corporation. When the workers rebel, anti-terrorist squads manage to make the situation worse and a full-scale rebellion begins. **112m/C VHS, DVD.** Jack Thompson, Stephen Leeder, Robyn Nevin, Harold Hopkins, Helen Jones, Kris McQuade, Hugh Keays-Byrne; ***D:*** Paul Elliot.

A Respectable Trade 🦴🦴½ **1998** Frances Scott (Fielding) has lost her position as a governess in 1788 Bristol, England. A job-search letter gathers Frances a marriage proposal from Josiah Cole (Clarke), an older, earnest, social climbing businessman whose trade happens to be slaves. Josiah wishes Frances to teach English to some of his property so they may be sold as house servants and Frances begins to feel something special for one of the group—Moses (Bakare)—who turns out to be much more of an educated gentleman than her own husband. Based on Gregory's 1995 novel. **240m/C VHS.** *GB* Emma Fielding, Warren Clarke, Ariyon Bakare, Anna Massey; ***D:*** Suri Krishnamma; ***W:*** Philippa Gregory. **TV**

The Respectful Prostitute 🦴🦴½ **1952** Sartre's tale of hooker who is cajoled into providing false testimony as a witness in the trial of a member of a prominent family. English language version of French drama. **75m/B VHS.** *FR* Ivan Desny, Barbara Laage, Walter Bryan; ***D:*** Marcel Pagliero, Charles Brabant; ***W:*** Jean-Paul Sartre.

Rest in Pieces 🦴 **1987 (R)** A young woman inherits a Spanish mansion, and weird things begin to happen. It seems a cult of Satan worshippers is already living on the estate. As one might infer from the title, quite a bit of hacking and slashing ensues. **90m/C VHS.** Scott Thompson Baker, Lorin Jean, Dorothy Malone; ***D:*** Joseph (Jose Ramon Larraz) Braunstein.

Restaurant 🦴🦴½ **1998 (R)** Would-be showbiz types all work at the same swanky New Jersey restaurant while exploring their relationships and ambitions. Recovering alcoholic and aspiring playwright Chris (Brody) is still carrying a torch for ex-girlfriend, Leslie (Hill) who slept with actor/co-worker Kenny (Baker), who's been cast in Chris' new play, much to his dismay. Meanwhile, Chris is trying a new romance with singer/waitress Jeanine (Neal). Although race doesn't seem to be a problem in personal relations (Chris is white, both his girlfriends are black), it starts to raise ugly problems at work (and change the tenor of the movie). **107m/C DVD, Wide.** Adrien Brody, Elise Neal, David Moscow, Simon Baker, Catherine Kellner, Malcolm Jamal Warner, Lauryn Hill, John Carroll Lynch, Sybil Temchen, Vonte Sweet, Michael Stoyanov; ***D:*** Eric Bross; ***W:*** Tom Cudworth; ***C:*** Horacio Marquinez; ***M:*** Theodore Shapiro.

Restless 🦴 *The Beloved* **1972** A restless homemaker begins an affair with a childhood friend. Director Cosmatos later oversaw "Rambo." **75m/C VHS.** *GR* Raquel Welch, Richard Johnson, Jack Hawkins, Flora Robson; ***D:*** George P. Cosmatos.

The Restless Breed 🦴 **1958** Son is restless after dad, a secret service agent, is slain by gunrunners. Routine oater-revenge epic done in by listless script. **81m/C VHS.** Scott Brady, Anne Bancroft, Jay C. Flippen, Rhys Williams, Jim Davis; ***D:*** Allan Dwan.

Restless Spirits 🦴🦴½ *Dead Aviators* **1999** Sullen Katie (Wimbles) and her young brother Simon (Swan) arrive to stay with their grandmother Lydia (Mason) in Porter's Point, Newfoundland. Both children are still grieving over the death of their aviator father in a crash four years before. While exploring a remote pond, Katie encounters the ghosts of French airmen Nungesser (Bluteau) and Coli (Monty). In 1927, they left Paris in a biplane on a nonstop trans-Atlantic flight to New York and disappeared. It seems their plane crashed into Porter's Pond and until the plane can be recovered they are doomed to wander its banks. Katie's determined to help, though no one believes her story. **95m/C VHS, DVD.** *CA* Juliana Wimbles, Lothaire Bluteau, Michel Monty, Marsha Mason, Leslie Hope, Ben Cook, Eugene Lipinski, Nickolas Swan; ***D:*** David Wellington; ***W:*** Semi Chellas; ***C:*** Andre Pienaar; ***M:*** Ron Sures. **CABLE**

Restoration 🦴🦴🦴 **1994 (R)** Set in the 17th century after Charles II is restored to the British throne, the title may instead refer to the restoration of one man's values. After curing one of the king's dogs, physician Downey is elevated to courtier and falls into drunken debauchery. He is soon forced to marry (but not touch) the king's favorite mistress. Unfortunately, he is caught trespassing on his majesty's main squeeze and banished from the court. Cast among the common rabble, he encounters the plague and the Great Fire of London while trying to redeem himself. Strong cast and sumptuous set design help to propel Downey's performance. Adapted from Rose Tremain's 1989 novel. Release was delayed a year because no one could seem to come up with a marketing strategy. **118m/C VHS, DVD.** Robert Downey Jr., Meg Ryan, Sam Neill, Hugh Grant, David Thewlis, Polly Walker, Ian McKellen; ***D:*** Michael Hoffman; ***W:*** Rupert Walters; ***C:*** Oliver Stapleton; ***M:*** James Newton Howard. Oscars '95: Art Dir./Set Dec., Costume Des.

Restraining Order 🦴🦴 **1999 (R)** Lawyer Robert Woodfield (Roberts) witnesses a murder that's committed by a former client. He contacts a friend in the D.A.'s office but when that friend is also murdered and Woodfield's efforts to bring the killer to justice are futile, he decides to personally avenge the crimes. **95m/C VHS, DVD.** Eric Roberts, Hannes Jaenicke, Tatjana Patitz, Dean Stockwell; ***D:*** Lee H. Katzin; ***W:*** John Jarrell; ***M:*** David Wurst, Eric Wurst. **VIDEO**

The Resurrected 🦴🦴½ **1991 (R)** One of the best recent H.P. Lovecraft horror adaptations, a fairly faithful try at "The Case of Charles Dexter Ward." Ward learns he has a satanic ancestor who possessed the secret of resurrection and eternal life—but, as the warlock says, it is very messy. Surprisingly tasteful even with occasional gore and truly ghastly monsters; in fact this pic could have used a bit more intensity. **108m/C VHS.** John Terry, Jane Sibbett, Chris Sarandon, Robert Romanus; ***D:*** Dan O'Bannon; ***M:*** Richard Band.

Resurrection 🦴🦴🦴½ **1980 (PG)** After a near-fatal car accident, a woman finds she has the power to heal others by touch. She denies that God is responsible, much to her Bible Belt community's dismay. Acclaimed and well-acted. **103m/C VHS.** Ellen Burstyn, Sam Shepard, Roberts Blossom, Eva LeGallienne, Clifford David, Richard Farnsworth, Pamela Payton-Wright; ***D:*** Daniel Petrie; ***W:*** Lewis John Carlino; ***M:*** Maurice Jarre. Natl. Bd. of Review '80: Support. Actress (LeGallienne).

Resurrection 🦴🦴 **1999 (R)** Chicago detectives John Prudhomme (Lambert) and Andrew Hollinsworth (Orser) are tracking a serial killer (Joy) who is killing men named after Christ's 12 apostles. He intends to use parts of his victims to reassemble the body of Christ in time for Easter Sunday resurrection. **108m/C VHS, DVD.** Christopher Lambert, Leland Orser, Robert Joy, Rick Fox, Barbara Tyson, James Kidnie, David Cronenberg; ***D:*** Russell Mulcahy; ***W:*** Brad Mirman; ***C:*** Jonathan Freeman; ***M:*** Jim McGrath.

Resurrection Man 🦴🦴 **1997 (R)** Sociopath Victor Kelly (Townsend) is in his element in 1975's Belfast when he's recruited to lead a group of Loyalist killers known as the "Resurrection Men." The gang's violence draws the attention of journalist Ryan (Nesbitt), who makes them media stars, and local cop Ferguson (Thompson), who wants to bring them down. Soon, though, Victor's capacity for bloodshed begins to worry older hood, McLure (McGinley), who thinks they'll all be better off without Victor. Very creepy atmosphere sustained by some appalling violence. Based on the novel by McNamee, who also wrote the screenplay. **100m/C VHS.** *GB* Stuart Townsend, James Nesbitt, Sean McGinley, Derek Thompson, John Hannah, Geraldine O'Rawe, Brenda Fricker, James Ellis, B.J. Hogg, Zara Turner; ***D:*** Marc Evans; ***W:*** Eoin McNamee; ***C:*** Pierre Aim; ***M:*** David Holmes, Gary Burns, Keith Tenniswood.

Resurrection of Zachary Wheeler 🦴🦴½ **1971 (G)** A presidential candidate, who narrowly escaped death in an auto crash, is brought to a mysterious clinic in New Mexico. A reporter sneaks into the clinic and discovers the horrors of cloning. **100m/C VHS.** Angie Dickinson, Bradford Dillman, Leslie Nielsen, Jack Carter, James Daly; ***D:*** Bob Wynn.

Retreat, Hell! 🦴🦴 **1952** Korean War drama about the retreat from the Changjin Reservoir. Standard gun-ho military orientation with dismal results. **95m/B VHS.** Frank Lovejoy, Richard Carlson, Russ Tamblyn, Anita Louise; ***D:*** Joseph H. Lewis.

Retribution 🦴½ 1988 (R) Struggling artist survives suicide attempt only to find himself possessed by the spirit of a criminal who was tortured to death. Seeing the hood's gruesome demise in his dreams, the survivor sets out to bring his murderers face-to-face with their maker. **106m/C VHS.** Dennis Lipscomb, Hoyt Axton, Leslie Wing, Suzanne Snyder; ***D:*** Guy Magar.

Retribution 🦴🦴 *Complicity* 1998 (R) Cameron Colley (Miller) is an investigative journalist who constantly runs into trouble with his editors. He's also addicted to cigarettes, cocaine, computer games, and sex with the married Yvonne (Hawes). Now he's looking into a series of grisly murders that possibly lead back to the youthful protests of a group of activists. Tends to be confusing more than compelling. Based on the novel by Iain Banks. **99m/C VHS, DVD.** *GB* Jonny Lee Miller, Brian Cox, Keeley Hawes, Paul Higgins, Bill Paterson, Samuel West, Rachael Stirling, Jason Hetherington; ***D:*** Gavin Millar; ***W:*** Bryan Elsley; ***C:*** David Odd; ***M:*** Colin Towns.

Retrievers 🦴 1982 Young man and a former CIA agent team up to expose the unsavory practices of the organization. **90m/C VHS, DVD.** Max Thayer, Roselyn Royce, Richard Anderson, Shawn Hoskins, Mary McCormick, Lenard Miller; ***D:*** Elliot Hong; ***W:*** Elliot Hong; ***C:*** Stephen Kim; ***M:*** Ted Ashford.

Retro Puppet Master 🦴🦴 1999 (PG-13) Most recent entry in the "Puppet Master" series is officially the first, finding a young Toulon in pre-World War I Paris where he falls in love with the daughter of the Swiss ambassador. Of course, the puppets and other mini-critters are involved too. **90m/C DVD.** Guy Rolfe, Greg Sestero, Brigitta Dau, Jack Donner, Stephen Blackehart; ***D:*** Joseph Tennent; ***W:*** Benjamin Carr; ***C:*** Viorel Sergovici Jr.; ***M:*** John Massari.

Retroactive 🦴🦴 1997 (R) Scientist Brian (Whaley) has been experimenting with reversing time and finally manages to make his project work. Meanwhile, police psychologist Karen (Travis) has has car trouble and been given a ride by Frank (Belushi) and his wife Rayanne (Whirry). Karen soon realizes Frank is a psycho and escapes, stumbling into Brian's lab. But Brian's just reversed time and Karen winds up back in Frank's car, trying to change the sequence of events. **91m/C VHS, DVD, Wide.** James Belushi, Kylie Travis, Shannon Whirry, Frank Whaley, Jesse Borrego, M. Emmet Walsh, Guy Boyd; ***D:*** Louis Morneau; ***W:*** Robert Strauss, Phillip Badger; ***C:*** George Mooradian; ***M:*** Tim Truman.

The Return woof! *The Alien's Return* 1980 (PG) Vincent and Shepherd meet as adults and discover that they had both, as children, been visited by aliens who had given technology to a cattle-mutilating prospector. A mess with no idea of what sort of film it wants to be. **91m/C VHS.** Cybill Shepherd, Raymond Burr, Jan-Michael Vincent, Martin Landau, Vincent Schiavelli, Zachary Vincent, Farah Bunch, Neville Brand, Susan Kiger; ***D:*** Greydon Clark.

Return 🦴🦴 1988 (R) A woman believes that the man she loves is the reincarnation of her dead grandfather. Interesting concept, but overall, a disappointing mystery. **78m/C VHS.** Frederic Forrest, Anne Francis, Karlene Crockett, John Walcutt, Lisa Richards; ***D:*** Andrew Silver.

Return Engagement 🦴½ 1978 A lonely middle-aged ancient history professor falls in love with one of her students. **76m/C VHS.** Elizabeth Taylor, Joseph Bottoms, Peter Donat, James Ray; ***D:*** Joseph Hardy.

Return Fire 🦴½ 1991 (R) A former employee of the government finds that he must now fight the system if he wants to save his son. Trivial action fare. **97m/C VHS.** Adam West, Ron Marchini.

Return from Witch Mountain 🦴½ 1978 (G) A pair of evil masterminds use a boy's supernatural powers to place Los Angeles in nuclear jeopardy. Sequel to Disney's ever-popular "Escape to Witch Mountain." **93m/C VHS.** Christopher Lee, Bette Davis, Ike Eisenmann, Kim Richards, Jack Soo; ***D:*** John Hough; ***W:*** Malcolm Marmorstein.

The Return of a Man Called Horse 🦴🦴 1976 (PG) Sequel to "A Man Called Horse" tells the story of an English aristocrat who was captured and raised by Sioux Indians, and then returned to his native homeland. Contains more of the torture scenes for which this series is famous, but not much of Harris. **125m/C VHS.** Richard Harris, Gale Sondergaard, Geoffrey Lewis; ***D:*** Irvin Kershner; ***W:*** Jack DeWitt; ***C:*** Owen Roizman.

The Return of Boston Blackie 🦴½ 1927 The oft-filmed crook/detective tries to retrieve an heiress's stolen jewels. Silent. **77m/B VHS.** Raymond Glenn, Corliss Palmer, Strongheart, Rosemary Cooper, Coit Albertson; ***D:*** Harry Hoyt.

Return of Captain Invincible 🦴🦴½ *Legend in Leotards* 1983 (PG) Arkin is a derelict superhero persuaded to fight crime again in this unique spoof. One liners fly faster than a speeding bullet. Lee gives one of his best performances as the mad scientist. Musical numbers by Rocky Horror's O'Brien and Hartley sporadically interrupt. Made on a shoe-string budget, offbeat film is entertaining but uneven. **102m/C VHS, DVD, Wide.** *AU* Alan Arkin, Christopher Lee, Kate Fitzpatrick, Bill Hunter, Graham Kennedy, Michael Pate, Hayes Gordon, Max Phipps, Noel Ferrier; ***D:*** Philippe Mora; ***W:*** Steven E. de Souza, Andrew Gaty; ***C:*** Louis Irving, Mike Molloy; ***M:*** William Motzig, Richard O'Brien.

The Return of Casey Jones 🦴🦴 *Train 2419* 1934 Early adventure film featuring lots of great railroad action. **64m/B VHS.** Charles Starrett, Ruth Hall, George "Gabby" Hayes, Robert Elliott, Margaret Seddon, Jackie Searl; ***D:*** John P. McCarthy.

Return of Chandu 🦴🦴 1934 This serial in 12 chapters features Bela Lugosi as Chandu, who exercises his magical powers to conquer a religious sect of cat worshippers inhabiting the island of Lemuria. In the process, he fights to save the Princess Nadji from being sacrificed by them. **156m/B VHS.** Bela Lugosi, Maria Alba, Clara Kimball Young; ***D:*** Ray Taylor.

The Return of Count Yorga 🦴🦴 1971 (R) The vampire Count returns, taking up residence in a decrepit mansion nearby an orphanage. There he spies the toothsome Cynthia and Yorga decides to make her a vampiric bride. But the Count reckons without Cynthia's noble boyfriend who wants to keep his honey on this side of the grave. Preceded by "Count Yorga, Vampire." **97m/C VHS.** Robert Quarry, Mariette Hartley, Roger Perry, Yvonne Wilder, Rudy DeLuca, George Macready, Walter Brooke, Tom Toner, Karen Huston, Paul Hansen, Craig T. Nelson; ***D:*** Bob Kelljan; ***W:*** Bob Kelljan, Yvonne Wilder; ***C:*** Bill Butler.

The Return of Dr. Mabuse 🦴🦴½ *Im Stahlnetz Des Dr. Mabuse; Phantom Fiend* 1961 The evil doctor is back, this time sending his entranced slaves to attack a nuclear power plant. Frobe, the inspector, and Barker, the FBI man, team up to thwart him. Fun for fans of serial detective stories. **88m/B VHS.** *GE FR IT* Gert Frobe, Lex Barker, Daliah Lavi, Wolfgang Preiss, Fausto Tozzi, Rudolph Forster; ***D:*** Harald Reinl.

Return of Dracula 🦴🦴 *The Curse of Dracula; The Fantastic Disappearing Man* 1958 Low-budget film about the Count killing a Czech artist and assuming his identity as he makes his way to the States. Once there, he moves in with the dead man's family and begins acting rather strangely. Retitled "The Curse of Dracula" for TV. **77m/C VHS.** Francis Lederer, Norma Eberhardt, Ray Stricklyn, Jimmy Baird, John Wengraf, Virginia Vincent, Greta Granstedt; ***D:*** Paul Landres; ***W:*** Pat Fielder; ***C:*** Jack MacKenzie.

Return of Draw Egan 🦴½ 1916 Vintage silent western wherein Hart is an outlaw-turned-greenhorn sheriff of a lawless town. Music score. **64m/B VHS, 8mm.** William S. Hart, Louise Glaum; ***D:*** William S. Hart.

The Return of Eliot Ness 🦴🦴½ 1991 (R) Ness comes out of retirement in 1947 Chicago to track down a friend's killer. And with Al Capone dead, Chicago mob bosses are fighting for their piece of illegal turf. Stack reprises his "The Untouchables" TV role from the early '60s in this made for TV movie. **94m/C VHS.** Robert Stack, Charles Durning, Philip Bosco, Jack Coleman, Lisa Hartman Black, Anthony De Sando; ***D:*** James A. Contner. **TV**

Return of Frank Cannon 🦴🦴 1980 Portly private eye Frank Cannon comes out of retirement to investigate the alleged suicide of an old friend. **96m/C VHS.** William Conrad, Diana Muldaur, Joanna Pettet, Allison Argo, Arthur Hill, Ed Nelson; ***D:*** Corey Allen; ***M:*** Bruce Broughton. **TV**

Return of Frank James 🦴🦴🦴 1940 One of Lang's lesser Hollywood works, this is nonetheless an entertaining sequel to 1939's "Jesse James." Brother Frank tries to go straight, but eventually has to hunt down the culprits who murdered his infamous outlaw sibling. Tierney's first film. **92m/C VHS.** Henry Fonda, Gene Tierney, Jackie Cooper, Henry Hull, John Carradine, Donald Meek, J. Edward Bromberg; ***D:*** Fritz Lang.

The Return of Grey Wolf 🦴🦴 1922 A wild dog must fight for survival in Northern Quebec and is befriended by a fur trapper. An intelligent hound, he repays the trapper's generosity by helping him put the moves on some fur thieves. Silent. **62m/B VHS, 8mm.** Helen Lynch, Henry Pierce.

The Return of Jafar 1994 (G) Clumsy thief Abis Mal inadvertently releases evil sorcerer Jafar from his lamp prison and now the powerful "genie Jafar" plots his revenge. So it's up to Aladdin and friends to save the Sultan's kingdom once again. Contains five new songs. ♫Just Forget About Love; Nothing In the World (Quite Like a Friend); I'm Looking Out for Me; You're Only Second Rate; Arabian Nights. **66m/C VHS.** ***W:*** Kevin Campbell, Mirith J.S. Colao; ***V:*** Scott Weinger, Linda Larkin, Gilbert Gottfried, Val Bettin, Dan Castellaneta.

Return of Jesse James 🦴🦴 1950 Look-alike of dead outlaw Jesse James joins in with some former members of the James Gang, leading townsfolk to believe the notorious bank robber never died. It's up to brother Frank James, now an upstanding citizen, to set the record straight. A little slow moving at times, but still worth viewing. **77m/B VHS.** John Ireland, Ann Dvorak, Reed Hadley, Henry Hull, Hugh O'Brian, Tommy Noonan, Peter Marshall; ***D:*** Arthur Hilton.

The Return of Josey Wales 🦴 1986 (R) No match for the original featuring Clint Eastwood, the title character is played woodenly by Parks. This installment finds Wales pitted against a bumbling lawman. Sequel to 1976's "The Outlaw Josey Wales." **90m/C VHS.** Michael Parks, Rafael Campos, Bob Magruder, Paco Vela, Everett Sifuentes, Charlie McCoy; ***D:*** Michael Parks.

The Return of Martin Guerre 🦴🦴🦴½ *Le Retour de Martin Guerre* 1983 In this medieval tale, a dissolute village husband disappears soon after his marriage. Years later, someone who appears to be Martin Guerre returns, allegedly from war, and appears much kinder and more educated. Starring in a love story of second chances, Depardieu does not disappoint, nor does the rest of the cast. In French with English subtitles. Based on an actual court case. Remade in 1993 as "Sommersby." **111m/C VHS, DVD, Wide.** *FR* Gerard Depardieu, Roger Planchon, Maurice Jacquemont, Barnard Pierre Donnadieu, Nathalie Baye; ***D:*** Daniel Vigne; ***W:*** Daniel Vigne, Jean-Claude Carriere; ***C:*** Andre Neau; ***M:*** Michel Portal. Cesar '83: Writing, Score; Natl. Soc. Film Critics '83: Actor (Depardieu).

The Return of Peter Grimm 🦴🦴½ 1935 Man returns from death to try to tidy up the mess he left behind. Enjoyable if trite fantasy based on a play by David Belasco. **82m/B VHS.** Lionel Barrymore, Helen Mack, Edward Ellis, Donald Meek, George Breakston, James Bush; ***D:*** George Nicholls Jr.

The Return of Spinal Tap 🦴🦴½ 1992 Cult-fave mock rock group Spinal Tap is back with a feature-length video of performance and backstage footage from its recent reunion concert tour promoting their album "Break Like the Wind." Sequel to "This Is Spinal Tap" features lots of heavy metal songs including the title track, "Majesty of Rock," "Bitch School," "Diva Fever," "Clam Caravan," and "Stinkin' Up the Great Outdoors." Not as great as the original satire, but will appeal to Spinal Tap fans. **110m/C VHS.** Christopher Guest, Michael McKean, Harry Shearer, Rick Parnell, C.J. Vanston, June Chadwick; ***Cameos:*** Paul Anka, Jeff Beck, Jamie Lee Curtis, Richard Lewis, Martha Quinn, Kenny Rogers, Martin Short, Mel Torme, Rob Reiner, Paul Shaffer, Fred Willard, Bob Geldof; ***W:*** Christopher Guest, Michael McKean, Harry Shearer.

Return of Superfly 🦴 1990 (R) Man with insect moniker pesters drug dealers and cops in Harlem. Long-awaited sequel to urban epic "Superfly," scored again by Mayfield. **94m/C VHS.** Margaret Avery, Nathan Purdee, Sam Jackson; ***M:*** Ice-T, Curtis Mayfield.

The Return of Swamp Thing 🦴½ 1989 (PG-13) The DC Comics creature rises again out of the muck to fight mutants and evil scientists. Tongue-in-cheek, and nothing at all like the literate, ecologically oriented comic from which it was derived. **95m/C VHS.** Louis Jourdan, Heather Locklear, Sarah Douglas, Dick Durock; ***D:*** Jim Wynorski.

Return of the Aliens: The Deadly Spawn 🦴 *The Deadly Spawn* 1983 (R) Aliens infect the earth and violently destroy humans. Extremely violent and gory. Watch out for those officious offspring. **90m/C VHS.** Charles George Hildebrandt; ***D:*** Douglas McKeown.

Return of the Ape Man 🦴🦴 1944 Campy fun with Carradine and Lugosi. A mad scientist transplants Carradine's brain into the body of the "missing link." Hams galore. **51m/B VHS.** Bela Lugosi, John Carradine, George Zucco, Judith Gibson, Michael Ames, Frank Moran, Mary Currier; ***D:*** Phil Rosen.

Return of the Bad Men 🦴🦴 1948 Scott is a retired marshall who must fight against a gang of outlaws lead by the Sundance Kid. Sequel to "Badman's Territory." **90m/C VHS.** Randolph Scott, Robert Ryan, Anne Jeffreys, George "Gabby" Hayes, Jason Robards Sr., Jacqueline White; ***D:*** Ray Enright; ***W:*** Charles "Blackie" O'Neal.

The Return of the Borrowers 🦴🦴🦴 1996 Sweet sequel to 1993's "The Borrowers" finds the six-inch Clock family—father Pod (Holm), mother Homily (Wilton), and teenaged daughter Arrietty (Callard)—having to find a new home. Lots of misadventures ensue as they must avoid nasty humans, a giant bee, a storm, and other dangers on their way to safety. Based on the novels by Mary Norton. **165m/C VHS.** *GB* Ian Holm, Penelope Wilton, Rebecca Callard, Sian Phillips, Tony Haygarth, Judy Parfitt, Ben Chaplin, Paul Cross, Pamela Cundell, Ross McCall, Richard Vernon, Danny Newman; ***D:*** John Henderson; ***W:*** Richard Carpenter; ***C:*** Clive Tucker; ***M:*** Howard Goodall.

Return of the Dragon 🦴🦴½ 1973 (R) In Lee's last picture, a Chinese restaurant in Rome is menaced by gangsters who want to buy the property. On behalf of the owners, Lee duels an American karate champ in the Roman forum. The battle scenes between Lee and Norris are great and make this a must-see for martial arts fans. **91m/C VHS, DVD, Wide.** *CH* Bruce Lee, Nora Miao, Chuck Norris; ***D:*** Bruce Lee; ***W:*** Bruce Lee; ***C:*** Ho Lang Shang; ***M:*** Joseph Koo.

Return of the Evil Dead 🦴 *Return of the Blind Dead; El Ataque de los Muertos Sin Ojos* 1975 The sightless dead priests return to attack still more 1970s' Europeans in this second installment of the "blind dead" trilogy. Preceded by "Tombs of the Blind Dead" and followed by "Horror of the Zombies." Not to be confused with Raimi's "Evil Dead" slasher flicks. **85m/C VHS, DVD.** *SP PT* Tony Kendall, Esther Roy, Frank Blake, Fernando (Fernand) Sancho, Lone Fleming, Loreta Tovar, Jose Canalejas; ***D:*** Armando de Ossorio; ***W:*** Armando de Ossorio; ***C:*** Miguel Mila; ***M:*** Anton Abril.

Return of the Family Man 🦴 **1989** A mass murderer seems unstoppable as he continues to slash whole families at a time...the family man is redefined in this bloody gore-fest. **90m/C VHS.** Ron Smerczak, Liam Cundill, Terence Reis, Michelle Constant; ***D:*** John Murlowski.

Return of the Fly 🦴🦴 **1959** The son of the scientist who discovered how to move matter through space decides to continue his father's work, but does so against his uncle's wishes. He soon duplicates his dad's experiments with similar results. This sequel to "The Fly" doesn't buzz like the original. Followed by "Curse of the Fly." **80m/B VHS, DVD.** Vincent Price, Brett Halsey, John Sutton, Dan Seymour, David Frankham, Danielle De Metz, Ed Wolff; ***D:*** Edward L. Bernds; ***W:*** Edward L. Bernds, Brydon Baker.

Return of the Jedi 🦴🦴🦴½ *Star Wars: Episode 6—Return of the Jedi* **1983 (PG)** Third film in George Lucas' popular space saga. Against seemingly fearsome odds, Luke Skywalker battles such worthies as Jabba the Hut and heavy-breathing Darth Vader to save his comrades and triumph over the evil Galactic Empire. Han and Leia reaffirm their love and team with C3PO, R2-D2, Chewbacca, Calrissian, and a bunch of furry Ewoks to aid in the annihilation of the Dark Side. The special effects are still spectacular, even the third time around. Sequel to "Star Wars" (1977) and "The Empire Strikes Back" (1980). **132m/C VHS, Wide.** Mark Hamill, Carrie Fisher, Harrison Ford, Billy Dee Williams, David Prowse, James Earl Jones, Kenny Baker, Denis Lawson, Anthony Daniels, Peter Mayhew, Sebastian Shaw, Jeremy Bulloch, Toby Philpot; ***D:*** Richard Marquand; ***W:*** George Lucas, Lawrence Kasdan; ***C:*** Alan Hume; ***M:*** John Williams; ***V:*** Alec Guinness, Frank Oz. Oscars '83: Visual FX.

Return of the Killer Tomatoes! 🦴 **1988 (PG)** The man-eating plant-life from 1977's "Attack of the Killer Tomatoes" is back, able to turn into people due to the slightly larger budget. Astin is mad as the scientist. Not as bad as "Attack," representing a small hurdle in the history of filmdom. Followed by "Killer Tomatoes Strike Back." **98m/C VHS, DVD.** Anthony Starke, George Clooney, Karen Mistal, Steve Lundquist, John Astin, Charlie Jones, Rock Peace, Frank Davis, C.J. Dillon, Teri Weigel; ***D:*** John DeBello; ***W:*** John DeBello, Constantine Dillon, Steve Peace; ***C:*** Stephen Kent Welch; ***M:*** Neal Fox, Rick Patterson.

The Return of the King **1980** The third and final animated episode of J.R.R Tolkien's Middle Earth Trilogy. This saga features Frodo, relative to Hobbit Bilbo Baggins, and his faithful servant, making middle Earth safe from Orcs, Gollums and other ooky creatures. **120m/C VHS, DVD, Wide.** ***D:*** Arthur Rankin Jr., Jules Bass; ***M:*** Maury Laws; ***V:*** Orson Bean, Roddy McDowall, John Huston, Theodore Bikel, William Conrad, Glen Yarborough, Paul Frees, Casey Kasem, Sonny Melendrez.

Return of the Lash 🦴 **1947** Lash LaRue once again defends settlers' rights from ruthless outlaws. **53m/B VHS.** Lash LaRue, Al "Fuzzy" St. John, Mary Maynard, George Chesebro; ***D:*** Ray Taylor.

Return of the Living Dead 🦴🦴½ **1985 (R)** Poisonous gas revives a cemetery and a morgue rendering an outrageous spoof on the living-dead sub-genre with fast-moving zombies, punk humor, and exaggerated gore. Its humor does not diminish the fear factor, however. Sequel follows. Directed by "Alien" writer O'Bannon. **90m/C VHS.** Clu Gulager, James Karen, Linnea Quigley, Don Calfa, Jewel Shepard, Beverly Randolph, Miguel Nunez, Brian Peck; ***D:*** Dan O'Bannon; ***W:*** Dan O'Bannon, John A. Russo, Russell Streiner; ***C:*** Jules Brenner.

Return of the Living Dead 2 🦴½ **1988 (R)** An inevitable sequel to the original Dan O'Bannon satire about George Romero-esque brain-eating zombies attacking suburbia with zest and vigor. **89m/C VHS.** Dana Ashbrook, Marsha Dietlein, Philip Bruns, James Karen, Thom Mathews, Suzanne Snyder, Michael Kenworthy, Thor Van Lingen; ***D:*** Ken Wiederhorn; ***W:*** Ken Wiederhorn; ***C:*** Robert Elswit.

Return of the Living Dead 3 🦴½ **1993 (R)** When Curt's girlfriend Julie dies in a motorcycle accident you'd think that would be the end of romance. But not when your dad heads a secret project that involves reviving corpses. Only problem is now Julie's a zombie with long metal claws and glass spikes sticking out of various body parts. Hey, if it's true love Curt will get over it. Macabre special effects. Also available unrated. **97m/C VHS, DVD, Wide.** Melinda (Mindy) Clarke, J. Trevor Edmond, Kent McCord, Basil Wallace, Fabio Urena; ***D:*** Brian Yuzna; ***W:*** John Penney; ***C:*** Gerry Lively; ***M:*** Barry Goldberg.

Return of the Magnificent Seven 🦴🦴 *Return of the Seven* **1966** The first sequel to "The Magnificent Seven" features the group liberating a compatriot who is held hostage. Yawn. **97m/C VHS, DVD, Wide.** Yul Brynner, Warren Oates, Robert Fuller, Claude Akins, Julian Mateos, Elisa Montes, Emilio Fernandez; ***D:*** Burt Kennedy; ***W:*** Larry Cohen; ***C:*** Paul Vogel; ***M:*** Elmer Bernstein.

Return of the Man from U.N.C.L.E. 🦴🦴 **1983** Those dashing super agents Napoleon Solo and Illya Kuryakin come out of retirement to settle an old score with their nemesis THRUSH. **96m/C VHS.** Robert Vaughn, David McCallum, Patrick Macnee, Gayle Hunnicutt, Geoffrey Lewis; ***D:*** Ray Austin. **TV**

The Return of the Musketeers 🦴🦴½ **1989 (PG)** Lester's third Musketeers film (after his successful double-act in the '70s) is a good-natured but average costume/comedy/buddy film. Twenty years after D'Artagnan, Athos, Porthos, and Aramis saved the French queen from scandal it's time to do it all over again. Milady DeWinter, who hatched the first plot, is dead but her equally devious daughter Justine is more than able to take mama's scheming place. Just to add a little more excitement Athos' adopted son Raoul meets Justine and passions fly amidst the swordplay. Based on the Alexandre Dumas novel "Twenty Years After." **103m/C VHS.** *GB FR SP* Michael York, Oliver Reed, Frank Finlay, Richard Chamberlain, Kim Cattrall, C. Thomas Howell, Geraldine Chaplin, Roy Kinnear, Christopher Lee, Philippe Noiret, Jean-Pierre Cassel, Billy Connolly, Eusebio Lazaro; ***D:*** Richard Lester; ***W:*** George MacDonald Fraser.

The Return of the Native 🦴🦴½ **1994 (PG)** Wind-swept moors, a tempestuous heroine, two loves, and requisite tragedy all courtesy of Thomas Hardy's 1878 novel. Beautiful Eustacia Vye (Jones) longs to leave the boredom of Egdon Heath—even though she's involved with the roguish Damon Wildeve (Owen). Then businessman Clym Yeobright (Stevenson) returns from Paris and captures Eustacia's fancy. She marries him in the hope they'll return to the continent but she's bitterly disappointed when Clym wants to remain in Egdon. Meanwhile, Damon has married Clym's gentle cousin Thomasin (Skinner) but he and Eustacia can't seem to stay away from each other, leading to storms for all. **99m/C VHS.** Catherine Zeta-Jones, Clive Owen, Ray Stevenson, Claire Skinner, Joan Plowright, Steven Mackintosh, Celia Imrie, Paul Rogers; ***D:*** Jack Gold; ***W:*** Robert W. Lenski; ***M:*** Carl Davis. **TV**

Return of the Pink Panther 🦴🦴½ **1974 (G)** Bumbling Inspector Clouseau is called upon to rescue the Pink Panther diamond stolen from a museum. Sellers manages to produce mayhem with a vacuum cleaner and other devices that, in his hands, become instruments of terror. Clever opening credits. Fourth installment in the Pink Panther series but the first with Sellers since 1964's "A Shot in the Dark." **113m/C VHS, DVD.** Peter Sellers, Christopher Plummer, Catherine Schell, Herbert Lom, Victor Spinetti; ***D:*** Blake Edwards; ***W:*** Frank Waldman, Blake Edwards; ***C:*** Geoffrey Unsworth; ***M:*** Henry Mancini.

Return of the Rebels 🦴🦴 **1981** TV fluff with Eden as a motorcycle matron whose campground is rid of riff-raff by the crow-lined participants in a 25-year reunion of a biker gang. **100m/C VHS.** Barbara Eden, Robert Mandan, Jamie Farr, Patrick Swayze, Don Murray, Christopher Connelly; ***D:*** Noel Nosseck. **TV**

Return of the Secaucus 7 🦴🦴🦴½ **1980** Centers around a weekend reunion of seven friends who were activists during the Vietnam War in the turbulent '60s. Now turning 30, they evaluate their present lives and progress. Writer and director Sayles plays Howie in this excellent example of what a low-budget film can and should be. A less trendy predecessor of "The Big Chill" (1983) which, perhaps, was a few years ahead of its time. **110m/C VHS.** Mark Arnott, Gordon Clapp, Maggie Cousineau-Arndt, David Strathairn, Adam LeFevre, Bruce MacDonald, Maggie Renzi, Jean Passanante, Karen Trott, John Sayles; ***D:*** John Sayles; ***W:*** John Sayles; ***C:*** Austin De Besche; ***M:*** Mason Daring. L.A. Film Critics '80: Screenplay, Natl. Film Reg. '97.

Return of the Soldier 🦴🦴🦴 **1982** A shell-shocked WWI veteran has no memory of his marriage, leaving his wife, his childhood flame, and an unrequited love to vie for his affections. Adapted from the novel by Rebecca West. **101m/C VHS.** *GB* Glenda Jackson, Julie Christie, Ann-Margret, Alan Bates, Ian Holm, Frank Finlay; ***D:*** Alan Bridges; ***M:*** Richard Rodney Bennett.

Return of the Street Fighter 🦴½ *Satsujin-ken 2* **1974** Sequel to "The Street Fighter," finds Terry Tsuguri (Chiba) hired by a gang to silence a jailed informer. So, Terry gets arrested, practices his karate and does the guy in, and finds out the gang now wants to silence him. Big mistake! Notice a pattern yet? Followed by "The Street Fighter's Last Revenge" and "Sister Street Fighter." **88m/C VHS, DVD, Wide.** *JP* Sonny Chiba, Claude Gannyon; ***D:*** Shigehiro (Sakae) Ozawa; ***W:*** Steve Autrey, Koji Takada; ***C:*** Teiji Yoshida.

Return of the Tall Blond Man with One Black Shoe 🦴🦴½ *Le Retour du Grand Blond* **1974** Sequel to 1972's "The Tall Blond Man With One Black Shoe." Again a "klutz" is mistaken for a master spy and becomes unknowingly involved in the world of international intrigue. In French with English subtitles. Not quite as good as the original. **84m/C VHS.** *FR* Pierre Richard, Mireille Darc, Michael Duchaussoy, Jean Rochefort, Jean Carmet; ***D:*** Yves Robert; ***W:*** Francis Veber; ***M:*** Vladimir Cosma.

Return of the Tiger 🦴½ **1978** The Hovver Night Club in Bangkok fronts the operations of an international narcotics group headed by an American. When a rival Chinese gang tries to dominate the drug market, conflict and lots of kicking ensue. **95m/C VHS.** Bruce Li, Paul Smith, Chaing I, Angela (Mao Ying) Mao; ***D:*** Jimmy Shaw.

Return of the Vampire 🦴🦴 **1943** A Hungarian vampire and his werewolf servant seek revenge on the family who drove a spike through his heart two decades earlier. **69m/B VHS.** Bela Lugosi, Nina Foch, Miles Mander, Matt Willis, Frieda Inescort, Roland Varno, Gilbert Emery, Ottola Nesmith; ***D:*** Lew (Louis Friedlander) Landers; ***W:*** Griffin Jay; ***C:*** L.W. O'Connell, John Stumar.

Return of Wildfire 🦴½ **1948** Two sisters are left to run the family horse ranch when their brother is killed. A drifter aids the sisters in bringing the murderer to justice. **83m/B VHS.** Richard Arlen, Patricia Morison, Mary Beth Hughes.

Return to Africa 🦴🦴 **1989** Rebels threaten the familial paradise of the tightknit Mallory clan. **95m/C VHS.** Stan Brock, Anne Collings, David Tors, Ivan Tors, Peter Tors, Steven Tors; ***D:*** Leslie Martinson.

Return to Boggy Creek 🦴🦴 **1977 (PG)** Townspeople in a small fishing village learn from a photographer that a "killer" beast, whom they thought had disappeared, has returned and is living in Boggy Creek. Some curious children follow the shutterbug into the marsh, despite hurricane warnings, and the swamp monster reacts with unusual compassion. OK for the kiddies. Fictitious story unlike other "Boggy Creek" films, which are billed as semi-documentaries. Sequel to "Legend of Boggy Creek" and features Mary Ann from "Gilligan's Island." **87m/C VHS.** Dawn Wells, Dana Plato, Louise Belaire, John Hofeus; ***D:*** Tom (Thomas R.) Moore.

Return to Cabin by the Lake 🦴½ **2001** Psychos never die—they always return to do the sequel. Presumed dead writer/serial killer Stanley Caldwell (Nelson) isn't dead at all. In fact, he infiltrates a movie crew making a film adaptation of the circumstances of his killing spree. But Stanley doesn't like the way events are being portrayed, so he bumps off the director (Krause) and takes control. Campy rather than scary. **89m/C VHS, DVD.** Judd Nelson, Brian Krause, Dahlia Salem, Michael P. Northey, Emmanuelle Vaugier; ***D:*** Po Chich Leong; ***W:*** Jeffrey Reddick; ***C:*** Stephen M. Katz; ***M:*** Frankie Blue. **CABLE**

Return to Earth 🦴🦴 **1976** Drama deals with the self-doubts faced by Apollo 11 astronaut Buzz Aldrin after his triumphant return to Earth. Based on Aldrin's own novel. **74m/C VHS.** Cliff Robertson, Shirley Knight, Ralph Bellamy, Stefanie Powers, Charles Cioffi; ***D:*** Jud Taylor. **TV**

Return to Eden 🦴🦴 **1989** A young woman falls in love with her philosophy tutor, but he can't return her affections. An interesting comparison between the passion of the primitive and the tangle of modern-day romance. **90m/C VHS.** Sam Bottoms, Edward Binns, Renee Coleman; ***D:*** William Olsen.

Return to Fantasy Island 🦴½ **1977** Boss, boss, it's da plane! The second full-length TV treatment of the once-popular series wherein three couples get their most cherished fantasy fulfilled by Mr. Roarke and company. **100m/C VHS.** Ricardo Montalban, Herve Villechaize, Adrienne Barbeau, Pat(ricia) Crowley, Joseph Campanella, Karen Valentine, Laraine Day, George Maharis, Horst Buchholz, France Nuyen, Joseph Cotten, Cameron Mitchell, George Chakiris; ***D:*** George McCowan. **TV**

Return to Frogtown woof! **1992 (PG-13)** Sequel to "Hell Comes to Frogtown" finds Texas Rocket Ranger Ferrigno captured by mutant frogs. As unbelievably bad as it sounds. **90m/C VHS.** Lou Ferrigno, Charles Napier, Robert Z'Dar, Denice Duff, Don Stroud; ***D:*** Donald G. Jackson.

Return to Horror High 🦴 **1987 (R)** A horror movie producer makes a film in an abandoned and haunted high school, where a series of murders occurred years earlier. As in most "return" flicks, history repeats itself. **95m/C VHS, DVD, Wide.** Alex Rocco, Vince Edwards, Philip McKeon, Brendan Hughes, Lori Lethin, Scott Jacoby, George Clooney, Maureen McCormick; ***D:*** Bill Froelich; ***W:*** Bill Froelich, Mark Lisson, Dana Escalante, Greg H. Sims, Nancy Forner; ***C:*** Roy Wagner; ***M:*** Stacy Widelitz.

Return to Lonesome Dove 🦴🦴½ **1993** Routine sequel to successful western saga "Lonesome Dove" picks up after the burial of Gus McCrae in Texas by his friend, ex-Texas Ranger Woodrow F. Call (now played by Voight). The original dealt with a cattle drive, this one with horses. Along the way you'll run into the usual sidewinders as well as McCrae's lost love Clara (now Hershey) and Schroder, returning as Call's unacknowledged son Newt. Filmed on location in Montana. TV production was already underway when author Larry McMurtry gave the producers his then unpublished sequel "Streets of Laredo" which differed from the script. Some changes were made but the book and miniseries don't match. **330m/C VHS.** Jon Voight, William L. Petersen, Rick Schroder, Barbara Hershey, Louis Gossett Jr., Oliver Reed, Reese Witherspoon, Nia Peeples, Dennis Haysbert, Timothy Scott, Barry Tubb, Chris Cooper, CCH Pounder, William Sanderson; ***D:*** Mike Robe; ***W:*** John Wilder. **TV**

Return to Macon County 🦴🦴 **1975** Tale of three young, reckless youths who become involved with drag racing and a sadistic law enforcement officer. Nolte turns in a good performance in his first film, as does Johnson, despite a mediocre script and dialogue. Sequel to 1974's "Macon County Line." **90m/C VHS.** Nick Nolte, Don Johnson, Robin Mattson; ***D:*** Richard Compton; ***W:*** Richard Compton.

Return to Mayberry 🦴🦴 **1985** Andy Taylor returns to Mayberry after 20 years to obtain his old job as sheriff. Sixteen of the original actors reappeared for this nostalgia-fest. **95m/C VHS.** Andy Griffith, Ron Howard, Don Knotts, Jim Nabors, Aneta Corsaut, Jack Dodson, George Lindsey, Betty Lynn; *D:* Bob Sweeney. **TV**

Return to Me 🦴🦴½ **2000 (PG)** Widowed building contractor Bob (Duchovny) is uneasy about getting involved in a new romance (particularly after some pathetic blind dates) but meets waitress Grace (Driver) and suddenly love is in the air. However, Grace is reluctant to reveal that she's had a heart transplant. But what's she going to do when she discovers that the donor heart came from Bob's beloved late wife. The best romance, however, might be between the testily loving marrieds, the Daytons (Hunt, Belushi), who are Grace's best friends. Directorial debut of Hunt is soapy without being sappy. **113m/C VHS, DVD, Wide.** David Duchovny, Minnie Driver, James Belushi, Bonnie Hunt, Carroll O'Connor, Robert Loggia, David Alan Grier, Joely Richardson, Eddie Jones, Marianne Muellerleile, William Bronder; *D:* Bonnie Hunt; *W:* Bonnie Hunt, Don Lake; *C:* Laszlo Kovacs; *M:* Nicholas Pike.

Return to Never Land 🦴🦴½ **2002 (G)** Losing much of the charm and magic of the 1953 Disney animated classic "Peter Pan," this sequel picks up years after the other left off and finds Peter (Weaver), Tinker Bell, and the rest of the gang in Never Land. Wendy (Soucie), however, is now grown and married with a daughter of her own, the spunky Jane (Owen), whose skepticism about her mother's wild tales fades after she is kidnaped by Captain Hook (Burton), still on a quest for the treasure he believes Pan stole. She then finds her way to Peter and more adventure with her mom's old pals. Innocuous and generic but refined Disney entry works for the youngest viewers but older children and parents won't find anything deeper for them. Nice blend of digital and traditional animation. **72m/C VHS, DVD.** *D:* Robin Budd; *W:* Temple Mathews; *M:* Joel McNeely; *V:* Blayne Weaver, Harriet Owen, Corey Burton, Jeff Bennett, Kath Soucie, Roger Rees, Spencer Breslin, Andrew McDonough.

Return to Oz 🦴🦴½ **1985 (PG)** Picking up where "The Wizard of Oz" left off, Auntie Em and Uncle Ed place Dorothy in the care of a therapist to cure her "delusions" of Oz. A natural disaster again lands her in the land of the yellow brick road, where the evil Nome King and Princess Mombi are spreading terror and squalor. Based on a later L. Frank Baum book. Enjoyable for the whole family although some scenes may frighten very small children. **109m/C VHS, DVD.** Fairuza Balk, Piper Laurie, Matt Clark, Nicol Williamson, Jean Marsh; *D:* Walter Murch; *W:* Walter Murch, Gill Dennis; *C:* David Watkin; *M:* David Shire.

Return to Paradise 🦴🦴 **1953** Cooper is a soldier of fortune wandering through the Polynesian islands in the late 1920s. On a remote atoll he comes across a crazy missionary intent upon subduing the native population. Cooper falls in love with a native beauty (Haynes in her screen debut) and leads the natives in a revolt against authority. Cliched but with nice scenery from the location shoot in Samoa. Loose adaptation of the short story "Mr. Morgan" by James Michener. **100m/C VHS.** Gary Cooper, Roberta Haynes, Barry Jones, John Hudson, Moira MacDonald; *D:* Mark Robson; *W:* Charles Kaufman.

Return to Paradise 🦴🦴🦴 *All for One* **1998 (R)** Sheriff (Vaughn) and Tony (Conrad), along with their new friend Lewis (Phoenix), take a vice-filled vacation in Malaysia. Done with the partying, the two New Yorkers return home while Lewis stays in Asia to work with orangutans. Two years later, Lewis is in a Malaysian prison, facing execution for a brick of hashish, which Sheriff haphazardly tossed into the garbage. Enter Heche as lawyer Beth, who finds Sheriff and tells him that in order to save Lewis, he and Tony must return and take their share of the responsibility (and serve time in a squalid third-world prison). Despite contributing an important twist to the extremely powerful climax, Pinkett Smith's role feels too contrived and is the biggest flaw in the film. Loose retelling of the 1989 French film "Force Majeure." **112m/C VHS, DVD.** Vince Vaughn, Joaquin Rafael (Leaf) Phoenix, Anne Heche, David Conrad, Jada Pinkett Smith, Vera Farmiga, Nick Sandow; *D:* Joseph Ruben; *W:* Wesley Strick, Bruce Robinson; *C:* Reynaldo Villalobos; *M:* Mark Mancina.

Return to Peyton Place 🦴🦴½ **1961** A young writer publishes novel exposing town as virtual Peyton Place, and the townsfolk turn against her and her family. Sequel to the scandalously popular '50s original and inspiration for the just-as-popular soap opera. Astor is excellent as the evil matriarch. **122m/C VHS.** Carol Lynley, Jeff Chandler, Eleanor Parker, Mary Astor, Robert Sterling, Luciana Paluzzi, Tuesday Weld, Brett Halsey, Bob Crane; *D:* Jose Ferrer.

Return to Salem's Lot 🦴🦴 **1987 (R)** Enjoyable camp sequel to the Stephen King tale, this time involving a cynical scientist and his son returning to the town only to find it completely run by vampires. **101m/C VHS.** Michael Moriarty, Ricky Addison Reed, Samuel Fuller, Andrew Duggan, Evelyn Keyes, Jill Gatsby, June Havoc, Ronee Blakley, James Dixon, David Holbrook; *D:* Larry Cohen; *W:* Larry Cohen, James Dixon; *C:* Daniel Pearl.

Return to Savage Beach 🦴½ **1997 (R)** Top secret government agency L.E.T.H.A.L. is sent to retrieve a computer disk containing the location of a hidden treasure. Lots of action, babes, and hardbodies (you're not expecting acting talent, are you?). **98m/C VHS.** Julie Strain, Julie K. Smith, Shae Marks, Cristian Letelier; *D:* Andy Sidaris; *W:* Andy Sidaris; *C:* Howard Wexler. **VIDEO**

Return to Snowy River 🦴🦴🦴 **1988 (PG)** Continues the love story of the former ranch hand and the rancher's daughter in Australia's Victoria Alps that began in "The Man From Snowy River." Dennehy takes over from Kirk Douglas as the father who aims to keep the lovers apart. The photography of horses and the scenery is spectacular, making the whole film worthwhile. **99m/C VHS.** *AU* Tom Burlinson, Sigrid Thornton, Brian Dennehy, Nicholas Eadie, Mark Hembrow, Bryan Marshall; *D:* Geoff Burrowes; *W:* Geoff Burrowes.

Return to the Blue Lagoon 🦴 **1991 (PG-13)** Neither the acting nor the premise has improved with age. Another photogenic adolescent couple experiences puberty on that island; for continuity, the young man is the son of the lovers in the first "Blue Lagoon." Breathtaking scenery—just turn down the sound. **102m/C VHS.** Milla Jovovich, Brian Krause, Lisa Pelikan; *D:* William A. Graham; *C:* Robert Steadman.

Return to the Lost World 🦴🦴½ **1993 (PG)** Rival scientists Challenger and Summerlee set out for the Lost World and find it threatened by oil prospectors. With a volcano about to explode the scientists set out to save their prehistoric paradise and its dinosaur inhabitants. Based on a story by Sir Arthur Conan Doyle. Sequel to "The Lost World." **99m/C VHS.** John Rhys-Davies, David Warner, Darren Peter Mercer, Geza Kovacs; *D:* Timothy Bond.

Return to Two Moon Junction 🦴½ **1993 (R)** New York supermodel Savannah (Clarke) returns to her family's riverfront home in Georgia and promptly sheds her clothing for local sculptor Jake (Schafer). Must be something about the southern heat. This sequel should have the same video success as its predecessor since it keeps to the minimal plot/maximum teasing sex scenes outline. **96m/C VHS.** Melinda (Mindy) Clarke, John Clayton Schafer, Louise Fletcher; *D:* Farhad Mann.

Reuben, Reuben 🦴🦴🦴 **1983 (R)** Brilliant, but drunken poet Conti turns himself around when he falls in love with earthy college girl McGillis in her film debut. The student's dog Reuben unwittingly alters Conti's progress, however, in the film's startling conclusion. Based on the writings of Peter DeVries. **100m/C VHS.** Tom Conti, Kelly McGillis, Roberts Blossom, E. Katherine Kerr, Cynthia Harris, Joel Fabiani, Kara Wilson, Lois Smith; *D:* Robert Ellis Miller; *W:* Julius J. Epstein; *M:* Billy Goldenberg. Natl. Bd. of Review '83: Actor (Conti); Writers Guild '83: Adapt. Screenplay.

Reunion 🦴🦴🦴 **1988 (PG-13)** Robards stars as a Jewish businessman, living in the U.S., who returns to his boyhood home of Stuttgart, Germany some 50 years after his leaving in 1933. He hopes to find out what happened to a boyhood school chum—the son of an artistocractic (and Aryan) German family. Film uses extensive flashbacks to show the the rise of anti-Semitism and how it affects the friendship of both youths. Thoughtfull and well-acted though occasionally plodding drama based on Fred Uhlman's novel. **120m/C VHS.** *FR GE GB* Jason Robards Jr., Christien Anholt, Samuel West, Francoise Fabian, Maureen Kerwin, Barbara Jefford, Alexander Trauner; *D:* Jerry Schatzberg; *W:* Harold Pinter; *C:* Bruno de Keyzer.

Reunion in France 🦴🦴 *Mademoiselle France; Reunion* **1942** Parisian dress designer sacrifices her lifestyle to help an American flier flee France after the Nazis invade. Dated patriotic flag-waver. **104m/B VHS.** Joan Crawford, John Wayne, Philip Dorn, Reginald Owen, Albert Bassermann, John Carradine, Ann Ayars, J. Edward Bromberg, Henry Daniell, Moroni Olsen, Howard da Silva, Ava Gardner, John Considine; *D:* Jules Dassin.

Revelation 🦴 **2000** In the continuing adventures based on the "Left Behind" novels (a conservative Christian interpretation of the Book of Revelation), a counter-terrorism expert (Fahey) goes up against a Messiah (Mancuso) out to rule the world, etc., etc. **97m/C DVD.** Jeff Fahey, Nick Mancuso, Carol Alt, Leigh Lewis; *D:* Andre Van Heerden; *W:* Peter LaLonde, Paul LaLonde; *C:* George Tirl.

Revenge 🦴½ *Terror under the House; After Jenny Died; Inn of the Frightened People* **1971** The parents of a girl who was brutally killed take the law into their own hands in this bloody, vengeful thriller. **89m/C VHS, Wide.** *GB* Joan Collins, James Booth, Ray Barrett, Sinead Cusack, Kenneth Griffith; *D:* Sidney Hayers.

Revenge woof! **1986 (R)** Sequel to "Blood Cult" about a cult led by horror king Carradine. Seems these dog worshippers want McGowan's land and Senator Carradine will stop at nothing to get it. Woofer filled with gratuitous violence. **104m/C VHS, DVD.** Patrick Wayne, John Carradine, Bennie Lee McGowan, Josef Hanet, Stephanie Kropke; *D:* Christopher Lewis; *W:* Christopher Lewis; *C:* Steve McWilliams; *M:* Rod Slane.

Revenge 🦴🦴 **1990 (R)** Retired pilot Costner makes the mistake of falling in love with another man's wife. Quinn gives a first-rate performance as the Mexican crime lord who punishes his spouse and her lover, beginning a cycle of vengeance. Sometimes contrived, but artfully photographed with tantalizing love scenes. Based on the Jim Harrison novel. **123m/C VHS, DVD.** Kevin Costner, Anthony Quinn, Madeleine Stowe, Sally Kirkland, Joe Santos, Miguel Ferrer, James Gammon, Tomas Milian; *D:* Tony Scott; *W:* Jim Harrison; *M:* Jack Nitzsche.

Revenge in the House of Usher 🦴🦴 *Neurosis; Zombie 5* **1982** Mad Eric Usher, the last of his equally insane family, lives in a creepy cliffside house with vampire-ghost Helen. Then he invites Alan Harker for a visit, and Alan's accepting is a big mistake on his part. **90m/C VHS, DVD, Wide.** *FR* Howard Vernon, Anthony (Jose, J. Antonio, J.A.) Mayans, Dan Villers, Lina Romay; *D:* Jess (Jesus) Franco; *C:* Alain Hardy; *M:* Daniel White.

Revenge of Doctor X woof! **198?** A man/beast lies waiting for the pretty reporter who seeks her shipwrecked father in the jungles of an uncharted island. **90m/C VHS.** John Ashley, Ronald Remy, Angelique Pettyjohn.

The Revenge of Frankenstein 🦴🦴½ **1958** Frankenstein (Cushing) is rescued from the guillotine by his dwarf servant and decides to relocate to Carlsbruck where he becomes the popular society physician, Dr. Stein. But the misunderstood doc just can't stop his ghoulish experiments and plans to transfer his servant's brain into another sewn together creature. Nicely macabre sequel to "The Curse of Frankenstein"; followed by "The Evil of Frankenstein." **89m/C VHS.** *GB* Peter Cushing, Michael Gwynn, Francis Matthews, Oscar Quitak, Lionel Jeffries, Eunice Gayson, John Welsh; *D:* Terence Fisher; *W:* Jimmy Sangster.

Revenge of the Barbarians 🦴 **1964** As the barbarians descend on Rome, Olympus must decide whether to save the empire or the beautiful Gallo, the woman he loves. Decisions, decisions. **99m/C** Robert Alda, Anthony Steel.

Revenge of the Barbarians 🦴 *Hrafninn Flygur; When the Raven Flies* **1985** A Scandinavian adventure about a young Celt seeking revenge against the Viking hordes that killed his family. **95m/C VHS.** *IC* Helgi Skulason, Jakob Thor Einarsson, Edda Bjorgvinsdottir, Egill Olafsson, Flosi Olafsson; *D:* Hrafn Gunnlaugsson; *W:* Hrafn Gunnlaugsson; *C:* Tony Forsberg.

Revenge of the Cheerleaders 🦴 **1976 (R)** The cheerleaders pull out all the stops to save their school from a ruthless land developer. What spirit. **86m/C VHS.** Jerii Woods, Cheryl "Rainbeaux" Smith, Helen Lang, Patrice Rohmer, Susie Elene, Eddra Gale, William Bramley, Carl Ballantine, David Hasselhoff; *D:* Richard Lerner.

Revenge of the Creature 🦴🦴 **1955** In this follow up to "The Creature from the Black Lagoon," the Gill-man is captured in the Amazon and taken to a Florida marine park. There he is put on display for visitors and subjected to heartless experiments. Growing restless in his captive surroundings, the creature breaks free and makes for the ocean. Includes screen debut of Clint Eastwood as a lab technician. Originally shot in 3-D. Based on a story by William Alland. **82m/B VHS.** John Agar, Lori Nelson, John Bromfield, Nestor Paiva, Clint Eastwood, Robert B. Williams, Grandon Rhodes, Charles Cane; *D:* Jack Arnold; *W:* Martin Berkeley; *C:* Charles S. Welbourne; *M:* Joseph Gershenson.

Revenge of the Dead 🦴 **1984 (R)** European archeological team discovers the existence of a powerful force that allows the dead to return to life. **100m/C VHS.** *IT* Gabriele Lavia, Anne Canoras; *D:* Pupi Avati.

Revenge of the Living Zombies 🦴 **1988 (R)** Teens on a Halloween hayride run headlong into flesh-craving zombies. Available in a slightly edited version. **85m/C VHS.** Bill (William Heinzman) Hinzman, John Mowod, Leslie Ann Wick, Kevin Kindlin; *D:* Bill (William Heinzman) Hinzman.

Revenge of the Musketeers 🦴🦴½ *D'Artagnan's Daughter; La Fille de D'Artagnan* **1994 (R)** Exciting swashbuckler that finds the beautiful Eloise (Marceau) uncovering a dastardly plot by the Duc of Crassac (Rich) to kill King Louis XIV (Legros). She goes to her father, aging Musketeer D'Artagnan (Noiret), and he seeks the aid of old compatriots Athos (Bideau), Porthos (Billerey), and Aramis (Frey). Since Eloise can handle a sword as well as any of the Musketeers, she gets her own share of dering-do. French with subtitles. **130m/C VHS.** *FR* Sophie Marceau, Philippe Noiret, Jean-Luc Bideau, Raoul Billerey, Sami Frey, Claude Rich, Nils (Niels) Tavernier, Charlotte Kady, Stephane Legros, Luigi Proietti; *D:* Bertrand Tavernier; *W:* Michel Leviant; *C:* Patrick Blossier; *M:* Philippe Sarde.

Revenge of the Nerds 🦴🦴½ **1984 (R)** When nerdy college freshmen are victimized by jocks, frat boys and the school's beauties, they start their own fraternity and seek revenge. Carradine and Edwards team well as the geeks in this better than average teenage sex comedy. Guess who gets the girls? Sequel was much worse. **89m/C VHS, DVD, Wide.** Robert Carradine, Anthony Edwards, Timothy Busfield, Andrew Cassese, Curtis Armstrong, Larry B. Scott, Brian Tochi, Julia Montgomery, Michelle Meyrink, Ted McGinley, John Goodman, Bernie Casey; *D:*

Jeff Kanew; *W:* Tim Metcalfe, Jeff Buhai; *C:* King Baggot; *M:* Thomas Newman.

Revenge of the Nerds 2: Nerds in Paradise ♪ **1987 (PG-13)** The nerd clan from the first film (minus Edwards who only makes a brief appearance) travels to Fort Lauderdale for a fraternity conference. They fend off loads of bullies and jocks with raunchy humor. Boy can Booger belch. Not as good as the first Nerds movie; a few laughs nonetheless. **89m/C VHS, DVD.** Robert Carradine, Curtis Armstrong, Timothy Busfield, Andrew Cassese, Ed Lauter, Larry B. Scott, Courtney Thorne-Smith, Anthony Edwards, James Hong; *D:* Joe Roth; *W:* Dan Guntzelman, Steve Marshall; *C:* Charles Correll; *M:* Mark Mothersbaugh.

Revenge of the Nerds 3: The Next Generation ♪½ **1992** Adams College has nerd-loathing trustee Downey Jr. mobilizing those frat boys against the bespectacled geeks, who turn to founding nerd Carradine to save them. Cookie-cutter characters and the gags won't hold your attention. Let's hope this is the last in the series. **100m/C VHS.** Robert Carradine, Curtis Armstrong, Ted McGinley, Morton Downey Jr., Julia Montgomery.

Revenge of the Nerds 4: Nerds in Love ♪♪½ **1994** Yes, even nerds deserve a little love. This time the gang get together for Booger's (Armstrong) wedding—complete with nerd bachelor party and wedding shower. Too bad Booger's future father-in-law is so reluctant to have a nerd in the family that he hires a sleazy detective to dig up some dirt. Made for TV. **90m/C VHS.** Curtis Armstrong, Robert Carradine, Ted McGinley, Larry B. Scott, Donald Gibb, Joseph Bologna, Julia Montgomery, Corinne Bohrer, Christina Pickles, Jessica Tuck, Robert Picardo; *D:* Steve Zacharias; *W:* Steve Zacharias, Steve Buhai. **TV**

Revenge of the Ninja ♪♪½ **1983 (R)** Ninja Kosugi hopes to escape his past in Los Angeles. A drug trafficker, also ninja-trained, prevents him. The two polish off a slew of mobsters before their own inevitable showdown. Better-than the standard chop-socky fest from Cannon with amusing surreal touches like a battling grandma ninja. Sequel to "Enter the Ninja," followed by "Ninja III." **90m/C VHS.** Sho Kosugi, Arthur Roberts, Keith Vitali, Virgil Frye, Ashley Ferrare, Kane (Takeshi) Kosugi, John Lamotta, Grace Oshita, Melvin C. Hampton, Mario Gallo; *D:* Sam Firstenberg; *W:* James R. Silke; *M:* Rob Walsh, Michael W. Lewis.

Revenge of the Pink Panther ♪♪½ **1978 (PG)** Inspector Clouseau survives his own assassination attempt, but allows the world to think he is dead in order to pursue an investigation of the culprits in his own unique, bumbling way. The last "Pink Panther" film before Sellers died, and perhaps the least funny. **99m/C VHS, DVD, Wide.** Peter Sellers, Herbert Lom, Dyan Cannon, Robert Webber, Burt Kwouk, Robert Loggia; *D:* Blake Edwards; *W:* Frank Waldman, Blake Edwards, Ron Clark; *C:* Ernest Day; *M:* Henry Mancini.

Revenge of the Radioactive Reporter ♪♪ **1991** Nuclear plant honchos don't like journalist who's about to hang their dirty laundry, so they toss him into vat of nuclear waste. He returns as a reporter with a cosmetic peel. **90m/C VHS.** David Scammell, Kathryn Boese, Randy Pearlstein, Derrick Strange; *D:* Craig Pryce.

Revenge of the Red Baron ♪♪½ **1993 (PG-13)** Jim Spencer (Rooney) is the WWI pilot who shot down Germany's fearsome Red Baron. Now aged and infirm he's tormented by what he thinks is his enemy's ghost. A vengeful ghost who takes after Spencer's family. **90m/C VHS.** Mickey Rooney, Tobey Maguire, Laraine Newman, Cliff DeYoung; *D:* Robert Gordon; *W:* Michael James McDonald; *C:* Christian Sebaldt.

Revenge of the Stepford Wives ♪½ **1980** TV sequel to the Ira Levin fantasy about suburban husbands who create obedient robot replicas of their wives. In this installment, the wives are not robots, but are simply made docile by drugs. Strange casting pairs Johnson and Kavner as husband and stepford wife. Begat "The Stepford Children." **95m/C VHS.** Sharon Gless, Julie Kavner, Don Johnson, Audra Lindley, Mason Adams, Arthur Hill; *D:* Robert Fuest. **TV**

Revenge of the Teenage Vixens from Outer Space ♪♪ **1986** A low-budget film about three sex starved females from another planet who come to earth to find men. When the ones they meet do not live up to their expectations, the frustrated females turn the disappointing dudes are turned into vegetables. **84m/C VHS.** Lisa Schwedop, Howard Scott; *D:* Jeff Ferrell.

Revenge of the Virgins ♪ **1962** A tribe of topless 'Indian' women protect their sacred land from the white men. Exhumed exploitation for bad-film junkies, narrated by Kenne Duncan, an Ed Wood cohort. **53m/B VHS.** Jewell Morgan, Charles Veltman, Jodean Russo, Stanton Pritchard; *D:* Paul Perri; *Nar:* Kenne Duncan.

Revenge of the Zombies ♪½ **1943** In this sequel of sorts to "King of the Zombies," Carradine is creating an army of the undead for use by an evil foreign entity. **61m/B VHS.** John Carradine, Robert Lowery, Gale Storm, Veda Ann Borg, Mantan Moreland; *D:* Steve Sekely.

Revenge Quest ♪ **1996** In the year 2031, Trent McCormic, L.A.'s most violent serial killer, escapes from a maximum security prison on Mars. He's determined to kill Julie Myers, the woman who testified against him. LAPD detective Rick Castle is equally determined to protect her. **90m/C VHS, DVD.** Brian Gluhak, Christopher Michael Egger, Jennifer Agular; *D:* Alan De Herrera; *W:* Alan De Herrera; *C:* Alan De Herrera; *M:* Joseph Andalino. **VIDEO**

The Revenge Rider ♪♪ **1935** Orphan McCoy goes after the villains who killed his parents. Good performance from McCoy in an otherwise average film. **60m/B VHS.** Tim McCoy, Robert "Tex" Allen, Billie Seward, Edward Earle, Jack Clifford, Lafe (Lafayette) McKee; *D:* David Selman.

The Revenger ♪ **1990** A framed man returns from prison and finds that a mobster has kidnapped his wife and wants $50,000 to give her back. **91m/C VHS.** Oliver Reed, Frank Zagarino; *D:* Cedric Sundstrom.

Reversal of Fortune ♪♪♪½ **1990 (R)** True tale of wealthy socialite Claus von Bulow (Irons) accused of deliberately giving his wife Sunny (Close) a near-lethal overdose of insulin. Comatose Close narrates history of the couple's courtship and married life, a saga of unhappiness and substance abuse, while Silver (as lawyer Dershowitz) et al prepare von Bulow's defense. An unflattering picture of the idle rich that never spells out what really happened. Irons is excellent as the eccentric and creepy defendant and richly deserved his Best Actor Oscar. From the novel by Dershowitz. **112m/C VHS, DVD, 8mm, Wide.** Jeremy Irons, Glenn Close, Ron Silver, Annabella Sciorra, Uta Hagen, Fisher Stevens, Julie Hagerty, Jack Gilpin, Christine Baranski, John David (J.D.) Cullum; *D:* Barbet Schroeder; *W:* Nicholas Kazan; *C:* Luciano Tovoli; *M:* Mark Isham. Oscars '90: Actor (Irons); Golden Globes '91: Actor—Drama (Irons); L.A. Film Critics '90: Actor (Irons), Screenplay; Natl. Soc. Film Critics '90: Actor (Irons).

The Revolt of Job ♪♪♪ *Job Lazadasa* **1984** An elderly Jewish couple adopts an eight-year-old Gentile boy although it is illegal in WWII-torn Hungary and against the beliefs of the orthodox community. Moving story with fine performances. **98m/C VHS.** *GE HU* Fereno Zenthe, Hedi Tenessy; *D:* Imre Gyongyossy, Barna Kabay.

Revolt of the Barbarians ♪ **1964** Ancient Rome is plagued by barbarian invasion and piracy. A consul travels to Gaul to try to put an end to their misdeeds. **?m/C VHS.** *IT* Roland Carey, Grazia Maria Spina, Mario Feliciani.

Revolt of the Zombies ♪ **1936** A mad scientist learns the secret of bringing the dead to life and musters the zombies into an unique, gruesome military unit during WWI. Strange early zombie flick looks silly by today's standards. **65m/B VHS, DVD.** Dorothy Stone, Dean Jagger, Roy D'Arcy, Robert Noland, George Cleveland; *D:* Victor Halperin; *W:* Howard Higgin; *C:* Jockey A. Feindel, Arthur Martinelli.

Revolution ♪ **1985 (R)** The American Revolution is the setting for this failed epic centering on an illiterate trapper and his son who find themselves caught up in the fighting. Long and dull, which is unfortunate, because the story had some potential. The cast is barely believable in their individual roles. Where did you get that accent, Al? **125m/C VHS.** *GB* Al Pacino, Donald Sutherland, Nastassia Kinski, Annie Lennox, Joan Plowright, Steven Berkoff, Dave King; *D:* Hugh Hudson; *W:* Robert Dillon.

Revolution! A Red Comedy ♪♪♪ **1991** A group of students are lured away from their revolutionary tendencies by materialistic indulgences. This satirical comedy is in color and black and white. **84m/B VHS.** Kimberly Flynn, Christopher Renstrom, Georg Osterman; *D:* Jeff Kahn; *W:* Jeff Kahn.

Revolver ♪♪ **1992 (R)** FBI agent Nick Sastro is paralyzed by an assassin's bullet when he tries to stop Aldo Testi, an arms and drug smuggler. But Nick decides to come out of retirement when a chance to nail Testi comes his way. **96m/C VHS.** Robert Urich, Dakin Matthews, Steven Williams, Assumpta Serna, Craig Hill; *D:* Gary Nelson.

Rhapsody ♪♪½ **1954** Taylor plays a wealthy woman torn between a famous young violinist and an equally talented pianist in this long and overdrawn soap opera. Although Taylor gives a superb performance, it's not enough to save this sugarcoated musical romance. Includes lush European scenery and sequences of classical music dubbed in by Claudio Arrau and Michael Rabin. Based on the adaptation of the Henry Handel Richardson novel "Maurice Guest." **115m/C VHS.** Elizabeth Taylor, Vittorio Gassman, John Ericson, Louis Calhern, Michael Chekhov, Barbara Bates, Celia Lovsky; *D:* Charles Vidor; *W:* Michael Kanin, Fay Kanin.

Rhapsody in August ♪♪½ *Hachigatsu no Kyoshikyoku* **1991 (PG)** Talky family drama has four children spending the summer with their grandmother Kane in Nagasaki. They become obsessed with the memorials and bomb sites commemorating the dropping of the atomic bomb in 1945 and their grandmother's experiences. Then Kane's Eurasian nephew (Gere) comes for a visit, inciting more family discussions. Adapted from the novel "Nabe-no-Naka" by Kiyoko Murata. Minor Kurosawa; in Japanese with English subtitles. **98m/C VHS.** *JP* Sachiko Murase, Narumi Kayashima, Hisashi Igawa, Richard Gere; *D:* Akira Kurosawa; *W:* Akira Kurosawa; *C:* Takao Saito, Masaharu Ueda; *M:* Shinichiro Ikebe.

Rhapsody in Blue ♪♪♪ **1945** Standard Hollywood biography of the great composer features whitewashed and non-existent characters to deal with the spottier aspects of George Gershwin's life. Still, the music is the main attraction and it doesn't disappoint. ♫Rhapsody in Blue; Concerto in F; The Cuban Overture; Fascinatin' Rhythm; The Man I Love; Yankee Doodle Blues; Somebody Loves Me; Swanee; Mine. **139m/B VHS.** Robert Alda, Joan Leslie, Alexis Smith, Charles Coburn, Julie (Jacqueline Wells) Bishop, Albert Bassermann, Morris Carnovsky, Rosemary DeCamp, Herbert Rudley, Charles Halton, Robert Shayne, Johnny Downs, Al Jolson; *D:* Irving Rapper; *W:* Howard Koch; *M:* George Gershwin, Max Steiner, Ira Gershwin.

Rhinestone ♪ **1984 (PG)** A country singer claims she can turn anyone, even a cabbie, into a singing sensation. Stuck with Stallone, Parton prepares her protege to sing at New York City's roughest country-western club, The Rhinestone. Only die-hard Dolly and Rocky fans need bother with this bunk. Some may enjoy watching the thick, New York accented Stallone learn how to properly pronounce dog ("dawg") in country lingo. Yee-haw. **111m/C VHS.** Sylvester Stallone, Dolly Parton, Ron Leibman, Richard Farnsworth, Tim Thomerson; *D:* Bob (Benjamin) Clark; *W:* Sylvester Stallone, Phil Alden Robinson. Golden Raspberries '84: Worst Actor (Stallone), Worst Song ("Drinkenstein").

Rhodes ♪♪½ *Rhodes of Africa* **1936** The story of Cecil Rhodes, a man who was instrumental in the Boer War in Africa and established the Rhodes Scholarships with $10 million, is told in this biography. Fine performance by Huston and Homolka. **91m/B VHS.** *GB* Walter Huston, Oscar Homolka, Basil Sydney, Frank Cellier, Peggy Ashcroft, Renne De Vaux, Percy Parsons, Bernard Lee, Ndanisa Kumalo; *D:* Berthold Viertel.

Rhodes ♪♪½ **1997** British miniseries details the life of 19th-century colonialist, British-born Cecil Rhodes (Shaw), who makes his money in the South African diamond trade and decides to place as much African territory under Britain's flag as possible. Rhodes succeeded in begetting the nation of Rhodesia (now Zimbabwe), became involved in the bloody Boer War, and established the prestigious Rhodes scholarship at Oxford University. On three cassettes. **336m/C VHS.** *GB* Martin Shaw, Frances Barber, Tim Dutton, David Butler, Ken Stott, Raymond Coulthard, Neil Pearson; *D:* David Drury; *W:* Antony Thomas; *C:* Alec Curtis; *M:* Alan Parker. **TV**

Rhythm on the Range ♪♪½ **1936** Crosby stars as a singing cowboy who befriends freight car stowaway Farmer while transporting his prize steer back to his ranch in California. He invites her to his domicile and she falls in love with life on the range and with the rancher himself. Filled with lots of musical numbers, including an appearance from the Sons of the Pioneers featuring Roy Rogers. Comedy from Burns and Raye, who makes her feature film debut here, is as entertaining as always. Remade by Dean Martin and Jerry Lewis in 1956 as "Pardners." ♫I'm an Old Cowhand; Empty Saddles; I Can't Escape From You; The House That Jack Built for Jill; If You Can't Sing It You'll Have to Swing It; Roundup Lullaby; Drink It Down; Memories; Hang Up My Saddle. **88m/B VHS.** Bing Crosby, Frances Farmer, Bob Burns, Martha Raye, Samuel S. Hinds, Warren Hymer, Lucile Watson; *D:* Norman Taurog; *W:* John Moffitt, Sidney Salkow, Walter DeLeon, Francis Martin; *C:* Karl Struss.

Rhythm on the River ♪♪½ **1940** Famous Broadway songwriter Rathbone has lost his magic touch so he hires melody maker Crosby to ghost for him while also hiring Martin to be the wordsmith. When the two fall in love they decide to strike off on their own but can't get their music heard since everyone assumes they've been copying Rathbone. Lots of backstage jokes with Rathbone terrific as an insecure egomaniac. ♫Rhythm on the River; When the Moon Comes Over Madison Square; Ain't It a Shame About Mame?; What Would Shakespeare Have Said?; Only Forever; That's for Me; I Don't Want to Cry Anymore. **94m/B VHS.** Bing Crosby, Mary Martin, Basil Rathbone, Oscar Levant, Oscar Shaw, Charley Grapewin, William Frawley, Charles Lane; *D:* Victor Schertzinger; *W:* Dwight Taylor; *M:* Victor Young.

Rhythm Parade ♪♪ **1943** A woman takes off for Hawaii, leaving her infant in the care of an L.A. nightclub singer. A jealous rival of the singer takes the opportunity to cause problems. The thin plot serves as a vehicle for lots of singing. ♫Tootin' My Own Horn; Petticoat Army; Mimi From Tahiti; You're Drafted; Wait Till the Sun Shines Nellie; Sweet Sue; 'Neath the Yellow Moon In Old Tahiti. **68m/B VHS.** Nils T. Granlund, Gale Storm, Robert Lowery, Margaret Dumont, Chick Chandler, Cliff Nazarro, Jan Wiley, Candy Candido, Yvonne De Carlo; *D:* Howard Bretherton.

Rhythm Romance ♪♪½ *Some Like It Hot* **1939** Gene Krupa and his Orchestra are the reason to see this lesser Hope comedy. Nicky Nelson (Hope) is a Coney Island carnival barker, who's latest scheme is to make a buck off the swing craze with Krupa. Meanwhile, Nelson's girl, Lily Racquel (Ross), is miffed at him and decides to take a job as Krupa's girl singer. Based on the play "The Great Magoo" by Ben Hecht and Gene Fowler. ♫The Lady's in Love with You; Some Like it Hot; Heat and Soul. **65m/B VHS.** Bob Hope,

Shirley Ross, Gene Krupa, Una Merkel; *D:* George Archainbaud; *W:* Lewis R. Foster; *C:* Karl Struss.

Rhythm Thief 1994 No-budget independent film finds alienated New York hustler Simon (Andrews) eking out a living selling tapes of local underground bands he has illegally recorded. He wants to be left alone but circumstances won't allow it. He's got one of the enraged bands after him, he's pestered by local "admirers," and his eccentric former girlfriend Marty (Daniels) suddenly turns up—severely shaking Simon's emotionally barren existence. Quirky character study gets lots of impact from tiny bucks. **88m/B VHS.** Jason Andrews, Eddie Daniels, Kimberly Flynn, Kevin Corrigan, Sean Haggerty, Mark Alfred, Christopher Cooke; *D:* Matthew Harrison; *W:* Matthew Harrison, Christopher Grimm; *C:* Howard Krupa; *M:* Danny Brenner. Sundance '95: Special Jury Prize.

Ricco *Summertime Killer* **1974 (PG)** A young man swears vengeance against the mobsters who killed his father. He kidnaps the daughter of a mafia kingpin and the battle begins. **90m/C VHS.** *FR IT SP* Chris Mitchum, Karl Malden, Olivia Hussey, Raf Vallone, Claudine Auger, Gerard Tichy; *D:* Antonio (Isasi-Isasmendi) Isasi.

Rich and Famous 1981 (R) The story of the 25-year friendship of two women, through college, marriage, and success. George Cukor's last film. **117m/C VHS, DVD.** Jacqueline Bisset, Candice Bergen, David Selby, Hart Bochner, Meg Ryan, Steven Hill, Michael Brandon, Matt Lattanzi; *D:* George Cukor; *W:* Gerald Ayres; *M:* Georges Delerue. Writers Guild '81: Adapt. Screenplay.

Rich and Strange ½ *East of Shanghai* **1932** Early Hitchcock movie is not in the same class as his later thrillers. A couple inherits a fortune and journeys around the world. Eventually the pair gets shipwrecked. **92m/B VHS, DVD.** *GB* Henry Kendall, Joan Barry, Betty Amann, Percy Marmont, Elsie Randolph; *D:* Alfred Hitchcock; *W:* Alfred Hitchcock, Alma Reville; *C:* Jack Cox, Charles Martin.

Rich Girl 1991 (R) A winsome, wealthy wench hides her millions by going to work in a rock 'n' roll bar and falls in love with the local Bruce Springsteen wanna-be. Despite the thick coating of music, sex, drugs, and profanity, this consists of cliches that were old before talkies. Too earnestly acted to be campy fun. Poor movie. **96m/C VHS.** Jill Schoelen, Don Michael Paul, Ron Karabatsos, Sean Kanan, Willie Dixon, Paul Gleason; *D:* Joel Bender.

Rich in Love ½ 1993 (PG-13) Light-hearted look at the changes in a Southern family after matriarch Helen Odom leaves to pursue her own life, shattering the peaceful existence of those around her. Seen through the eyes of 17-year-old daughter Lucille who assumes the role of "mother" for her sister and father while trying to come to terms with her own confused feelings. Nice performances by newcomer Erbe and Finney can't overcome a mediocre script. Based on the novel by Josephine Humphreys. **105m/C VHS, Wide.** Albert Finney, Jill Clayburgh, Kathryn Erbe, Kyle MacLachlan, Piper Laurie, Ethan Hawke, Suzy Amis, Alfre Woodard; *D:* Bruce Beresford; *W:* Alfred Uhry; *M:* Georges Delerue.

Rich Kids ½ 1979 (PG) A young girl trying to cope with the divorce of her parents is aided by a boyfriend whose parents have already split. **97m/C VHS.** John Lithgow, Kathryn Walker, Trini Alvarado, Paul Dooley, David Selby, Jill Eikenberry, Olympia Dukakis; *D:* Robert M. Young; *C:* Ralf Bode.

Rich Man, Poor Man 1976 Classic TV miniseries covers 20 (sometimes bitter) years in the lives of the two Jordache brothers. It's 1945 in quiet Port Phillip, New York with embittered German baker Axel (Asner), his unfulfilled wife Mary (McGuire), and sons Tom (Nolte) and Rudy (Strauss). Tom is wild and irresponsible, Rudy is ambitious and college-bound, and Julie Prescott (Blakely), Rudy's girl, overshadows both their lives. Based on the novel by Irwin Shaw. The first series contained 12 episodes. A second series of 21 episodes primarily followed the tribulations of the next generation, although Strauss returned as Rudy. **720m/C VHS.** Peter Strauss, Nick Nolte, Susan Blakely, Ed Asner, Dorothy McGuire, Bill Bixby, Robert Reed, Ray Milland, Kim Darby, Talia Shire, Lawrence Pressman, Kay Lenz; *M:* Alex North. **TV**

The Rich Man's Wife ½ 1996 (R) Modern noir strands unhappy wife Josie (Berry) on Martha's Vineyard without her loathsome spouse (McDonald), where she makes the mistake of confiding her marital woes to sympathetic, yet obviously deranged stranger Cole (Greene). She tells Cole sometimes she wishes her husband was dead. Poof! Before you can say "foreshadowing," hubby's murdered and she's the prime suspect. Increasingly nutso Cole stalks our heroine, seemingly innocent, but possibly not as blameless as it appears. Failed mystery/thriller delivers little of either and the attempt at a "Strangers on a Train" premise and a "Usual Suspects" type ending fail miserably. **95m/C VHS, DVD, Wide.** Halle Berry, Christopher McDonald, Clive Owen, Peter Greene, Charles Hallahan, Frankie Faison, Clea Lewis; *D:* Amy Holden Jones; *W:* Amy Holden Jones; *C:* Haskell Wexler; *M:* John (Gianni) Frizzell.

Rich, Young and Pretty ½ 1951 Light-hearted, innocuous musical starring Powell as a Texas gal visiting Paris with her rancher father (Corey). Powell finds romance with Damone (in his screen debut) and a secret—the mother she has never known (Darrieux). Lamas (in his American screen debut) plays Darrieux's new heartthrob. ♫Dark is the Night; L'Amour Toujours, Tonight For Sure; Wonder Why; I Can See You; Paris; We Never Talk Much; How Do You Like Your Eggs in the Morning?; There's Danger in Your Eyes, Cherie; The Old Piano Roll Blues. **95m/C VHS.** Jane Powell, Danielle Darrieux, Wendell Corey, Vic Damone, Fernando Lamas, Marcel Dalio, Una Merkel, Richard Anderson, Jean Murat, Hans Conried; *D:* Norman Taurog; *W:* Sidney Sheldon, Dorothy Cooper; *M:* Sammy Cahn, Nicholas Brodszky.

Richard III *The Life and Death of King Richard III* **1912** According to the American Film Institute, this is the oldest surviving American feature film and, in 1912, the most ambitious adaptation of Shakespeare ever attempted. Despite changes in conventions, it's still a lively work that's brightened considerably by a new Ennio Morricone score. **58m/B DVD.** Frederick Warde, Robert Gomp, Albert Gardner, Violet Stuart; *D:* James Keane.

Richard III ½ 1955 This landmark film version of the Shakespearean play features an acclaimed performance by Laurence Olivier, who also directs. The plot follows the life of the mentally and physically twisted Richard of Gloucester and his schemes for the throne of England. **138m/C VHS, Wide.** *GB* Laurence Olivier, Cedric Hardwicke, Ralph Richardson, John Gielgud, Stanley Baker, Michael Gough, Claire Bloom; *D:* Laurence Olivier. British Acad. '55: Actor (Olivier), Director (Olivier), Film; Golden Globes '57: Foreign Film.

Richard III ½ 1995 (R) The Brits once again bring the Bard's most notorious monarch to the screen, this time in a new setting. McKellen stars in the title role of the deformed and ruthless English king, now in an imagined 1930s London of swanky Art Deco, Black Shirt thugs and modern media. Purists may resent major dialogue cuts, but famous speeches (such as the "winter of our discontent" opener) are amusingly staged in this modern take. Gorgeously polished visuals are perfect foil for the slimy, evil goings-on. Based on both Shakespeare's play and Richard Eyre's stage adaptation (in which McKellen also starred). **105m/C VHS.** *GB* Ian McKellen, Annette Bening, Jim Broadbent, Robert Downey Jr., Nigel Hawthorne, Kristin Scott Thomas, Maggie Smith, John Wood; *D:* Richard Loncraine; *W:* Ian McKellen, Richard Loncraine; *C:* Peter Biziou; *M:* Trevor Jones.

Richard Petty Story 1972 (G) The biography of race car driver Petty, played by himself, and his various achievements on the track. **83m/C VHS.** Richard Petty, Darren McGavin, Kathie Browne, Lynn(e) Marta, Noah Beery Jr., L.Q. (Justus E. McQueen) Jones.

Richard's Things 1980 (R) A man's wife and his girlfriend find love and comfort in each other after his death. Screenplay by Frederic Raphael, from his novel. Very slow and dreary, with a weak performance from Ullman. **104m/C VHS.** *GB* Liv Ullmann, Amanda Redman; *D:* Anthony Harvey; *W:* Frederic Raphael; *C:* Frederick A. (Freddie) Young; *M:* Georges Delerue.

Richie Rich ½ 1994 (PG) Yet another adaptation from the comics. Richie (Culkin), the world's richest boy, takes over the family business when his madcap parents Richard (Herrmann) and Regina (Ebersole) disappear thanks to the devious Laurence Van Dough (Larroquette). But there's kindly valet Cadbury (Hyde) and eccentric live-in inventor Keenbean (McShane) to help Richie save the day. Some silliness but Culkin has clearly outgrown this type of kid role. Biltmore, the 8,000 acre Vanderbilt estate in Asheville, North Carolina, serves as the Rich family home. **94m/C VHS.** Macaulay Culkin, John Larroquette, Edward Herrmann, Christine Ebersole, Jonathan Hyde, Michael McShane, Stephi Lineburg; *Cameos:* Reggie Jackson, Claudia Schiffer; *D:* Donald Petrie; *W:* Tom S. Parker, Jim Jennewein; *C:* Don Burgess; *M:* Alan Silvestri.

Ricky 1 ½ 1988 Mumbling pugilist spoof. Da Mob wants to make Ricky da fall guy, but uh, he's not as dumb as he looks. **90m/C VHS.** Michael Michaud, Maggie Hughes, James Herbert, Lane Montano; *D:* Bill Naud; *M:* Joel Goldsmith.

Ricochet 1991 (R) Rookie cop Washington causes a sensation when he singlehandedly captures notorious psychopath Lithgow. But this particular criminal is a twisted genius, and from his prison cell he comes up with a plan to destroy the young cop. Teaming up with old friend Ice-T, the rookie tries to outwit his evil archnemesis. Genuinely scary, tense and violent thriller. **104m/C VHS, DVD, Wide.** Denzel Washington, John Lithgow, Ice-T, Jesse Ventura, Kevin Pollak, Lindsay Wagner, Mary Ellen Trainor, Josh Evans, Victoria Dillard, John Amos, John Cothran Jr.; *D:* Russell Mulcahy; *W:* Steven E. de Souza; *C:* Peter Levy; *M:* Alan Silvestri.

The Riddle of the Sands ½ 1979 Two English yachtsmen in 1903 inadvertently stumble upon a German plot to invade England by sea. British film based on the Erskine Childers spy novel. **99m/C VHS.** *GB* Michael York, Jenny Agutter, Simon MacCorkindale, Alan Badel; *D:* Tony Maylam; *M:* Howard Blake.

Ride 1998 (R) This sometimes-amusing but mostly rude road comedy seems to be merely an excuse for getting MTV veejays and rap stars together without actually showing any videos. Freddy B (Campbell) is a superstar looking for street cred, so his director Bleau (Brown) sends Leta (DeSousa) to Harlem to bring a group of young street talents to Miami for a video shoot. There are too many storylines in the busload of passengers to develop fully, so they are skimmed over and defused with a mixture of generic road movie brawls and narrow escapes combined with sexual and scatalogical humor. Yoba does a good job as Poppa, who's trying to watch over reckless little brother Geronimo (Starr) while keeping the rest of the crew in line. **83m/C VHS.** Malik Yoba, Melissa De Sousa, Fredro Starr, John Witherspoon, Cedric the Entertainer, Sticky Fingaz, Kellie Williams, Idalis de Leon, Julia Garrison, Guy Torry, Reuben Asher, The Lady of Rage, Dartanyan Edmonds, Downtown Julie Brown; *Cameos:* Snoop Dogg; *D:* Millicent Shelton; *W:* Millicent Shelton; *C:* Frank Byers; *M:* Dunn Pearson Jr.

Ride a Wild Pony 1975 (G) A poor Australian farmer's son is allowed to pick a horse of his own from a neighboring rancher's herd. After he trains and grows to love the pony, the rancher's daughter, a handicapped rich girl, decides to claim it for herself. Enjoyable Disney story is based on the tale "Sporting Proposition," by James Aldridge. **86m/C VHS.** *AU* John Meillon, Michael Craig, Robert Bettles, Eva Griffith, Graham Rouse; *D:* Don Chaffey; *C:* Jack Cardiff; *M:* John Addison.

The Ride Back ½ 1957 Well-done western about lawman Hamish (Conrad) who decides to take outlaw Kallen (Quinn) across the Mexican border back to Texas—a four days' journey through hostile territory. At the site of a massacre they discover a lone survivor, a little girl whom they take with them. Then they are attacked by Apaches and when Hamish is wounded, Kallen sees his chance for escape. Good performances by the leads; feature debut for director Miner. **80m/B VHS.** William Conrad, Anthony Quinn, Lita Milan, Ellen Hope Monroe; *D:* Allen Miner; *W:* Antony Ellis; *C:* Joseph Biroc; *M:* Frank DeVol.

Ride Clear of Diablo ½ 1954 Crooked Sheriff Kenyon (Birch) and equally crooked lawyer Meredith (Pullen) murder Clay O'Mara's (Murphy) father and brother. He vows to get revenge, aided by gunslinger Whitey Kincade (Duryea). Then Laurie (Cabot), Kenyon's niece and Meredith's fiance, comes to Clay's attention. Macho Technicolor western with a likeable cast. **80m/C VHS.** Audie Murphy, Dan Duryea, Susan Cabot, Paul Birch, William Pullen, Abbe Lane, Russell Johnson, Jack Elam, Lane Bradford, Holly (Mike Ragan) Bane, Denver Pyle; *D:* Jesse Hibbs; *W:* George Zuckerman, D.D. Beauchamp; *C:* Irving Glassberg.

Ride 'Em Cowboy ½ 1942 Two peanut and hotdog vendors travel west to try their hand as cowpokes. Usual Abbott and Costello fare with a twist—there are lots of great musical numbers. ♫A Tisket, A Tasket; I'll Remember April; Wake Up Jacob; Beside the Rio Tonto; Rock 'n' Reelin'; Give Me My Saddle; Cow Boogie. **86m/B VHS.** Bud Abbott, Lou Costello, Anne Gwynne, Samuel S. Hinds, Dick Foran, Richard Lane, Johnny Mack Brown, Ella Fitzgerald, Douglass Dumbrille; *D:* Arthur Lubin.

Ride 'Em Cowgirl 1941 Singing cowgirl, Page, enters a horse race to expose the crook who cheated her father. **51m/B VHS.** Dorothy Page, Vince Barnett, Milton Frome; *D:* Samuel Diege.

Ride Him, Cowboy 1932 Entertaining oater has Wayne saving horse Duke from being sentenced to death. This was the first of six series films Wayne made for Warner's, all of which costarred his white wonder horse, Duke. Remake of the 1926 Ken Maynard silent "The Unknown Cavalier." Based on the story by Kenneth Perkins. **55m/B VHS.** John Wayne, Ruth Hall, Henry B. Walthall, Harry Gribbon, Otis Harlan, Charles Sellon; *D:* Fred Allen; *W:* Scott Mason.

Ride in a Pink Car 1974 (R) When a Vietnam vet returns home, he discovers that his welcoming committee is really a lynch mob. **83m/C VHS.** Glenn Corbett, Morgan Woodward, Ivy Jones; *D:* Robert Emery.

Ride in the Whirlwind 1966 Three cowboys are mistaken for members of a gang by a posse. Screenplay for the offbeat western by Nicholson. **83m/C DVD, Wide.** Jack Nicholson, Cameron Mitchell, Millie Perkins, Katherine Squire, Harry Dean Stanton, Rupert Crosse; *D:* Monte Hellman; *W:* Jack Nicholson; *C:* Gregory Sandor; *M:* Robert Jackson Drasnin.

Ride Lonesome ½ 1959 The heroic Scott is a bounty hunter looking for a killer (Best). It's not just the money, Scott hopes Best will lead him to the man who murdered Scott's wife. Along the trail he meets a pretty widow and two outlaws who hope if they capture Best, they'll get a pardon. A well-done example of a "B" western with good performances; Coburn's film debut. **73m/C VHS.** Randolph Scott, James Best, Karen Steele, Pernell Roberts, Lee Van Cleef, James Coburn; *D:* Budd Boetticher; *W:* Burt Kennedy.

Ride, Ranger, Ride ½ 1936 Texas Ranger Autry is out to stop a group of Comanches from raiding a wagon train. **56m/B VHS.** Gene Autry, Smiley Burnette, Kay Hughes, Max Terhune, Monte Blue, Chief Thundercloud; *D:* Joseph Kane.

Ride the High Country *Guns in the Afternoon* **1962** The cult classic western about two old friends who have had careers on both sides of the law. One, Joel McCrea, is entrusted with a shipment of gold, and the other, Randolph Scott, rides along with him to steal the precious cargo. Although barely promoted by MGM, the film became a critics' favorite. Grimacing and long in the tooth, McCrea and Scott enact a fitting tribute and farewell to the myth of the grand ol' West. **93m/C VHS, Wide.** Randolph Scott, Joel McCrea, Mariette Hartley, Edgar Buchanan, R.G. Armstrong, Ronald Starr, John Anderson, James Drury, L.Q. (Justus E. McQueen) Jones, Warren Oates, Jennie Jackson, John Chandler; ***D:*** Sam Peckinpah; ***W:*** N.B. Stone Jr.; ***C:*** Lucien Ballard; ***M:*** George Bassman. Natl. Film Reg. '92.

Ride the Man Down 🦴½ **1953** Story of a murderous land war between neighboring landowners tells the same old story: Greed knows no boundaries. **90m/C VHS.** Brian Donlevy, Chill Wills, Jack LaRue, Rod Cameron, Ella Raines, Barbara Britton; ***D:*** Joseph Kane.

Ride the Wild Fields 🦴🦴½ **2000** Tender adaptation of Vacarro's play "And the Home of the Brave" finds 11-year-old Opal Miller (Vega) and her mother Ruby (Whalley) struggling to manage their small North Carolina farm while Opal's dad serves overseas during WWII. Ruby is grateful for the help of drifter Tom (Flanery), though others are suspicious of the young man, but complications arise when the adults develop stronger feelings for one another. **101m/C VHS.** Joanne Whalley, Sean Patrick Flanery, Alexa Vega, Cotter Smith; ***D:*** Paul A. Kaufman; ***W:*** Rodney Vaccaro; ***C:*** Thom Best; ***M:*** Laura Kaufman. **CABLE**

Ride the Wild Surf 🦴🦴½ **1964** It's fun in the sun when surfers Fabian, Hunter, and Brown head to Hawaii in search of the ultimate waves. Throw in a little romance and a cool title song by Jan and Dean and you've got your better than average beach movie. The surfing footage is excellent. Cowabunga! **101m/C VHS.** Fabian, Tab Hunter, Barbara Eden, Peter Brown, Susan Hart, Shelley Fabares, Jim Mitchum; ***D:*** Don Taylor.

Ride the Wind 🦴🦴 **1966** "Bonanza" gang goes to the aid of the Pony Express. **120m/C VHS.** Michael Landon, Lorne Greene, Dan Blocker.

Ride to Glory 🦴🦴 *The Deserter; La Spina Dorsale del Diavolo* **1971** In 1886, a cavalry officer deserts his troops to seek revenge on the Apaches that brutally killed his family. Hearing this, a general offers to pardon him if he will lead a dangerous group of men on a mission against the Apaches. Fast-paced and very bloody. **90m/C VHS.** Bekim Fehmiu, Richard Crenna, Chuck Connors, Ricardo Montalban, Ian Bannen, Slim Pickens, Woody Strode, Patrick Wayne, John Huston; ***D:*** Burt Kennedy.

Ride with the Devil 🦴🦴½ **1999 (R)** Clunky Civil War saga adapted from Daniel Woodrell's novel "Woe to Live On." Lee concentrates on the 1862 Border Wars between the Southern-sympathizers known as the Bushwhackers and the pro-Union Jayhawkers. Best pals Jack Bull Chiles (Ulrich) and Jake Roedel (Maguire) join a group of Bushwhackers and both become involved with a young farm widow, Sue Lee (singer Jewel in her acting debut). After some loses, Jake and the remaining band join in Quantrill's (Ales) infamous raid on the abolitionist stronghold of Lawrence, Kansas. Film serves as a coming-of-age story for the teenaged Jake and Maguire, at least, is up to the challenge. **139m/C VHS, DVD, Wide.** Tobey Maguire, Skeet Ulrich, Jeffrey Wright, Jewel, Simon Baker, Jonathan Rhys Meyers, James Caviezel, Tom Guiry, Tom Wilkinson, Jonathan Brandis, John Ales, Matthew Faber, Steven Mailer, Zach Grenier, Margo Martindale, Mark Ruffalo, Celia Weston; ***D:*** Ang Lee; ***W:*** James Schamus; ***C:*** Frederick Elmes; ***M:*** Mychael Danna.

Rider from Tucson 🦴🦴 **1950** Two rodeo riders head out to Colorado for a friend's wedding. They find out the bride has been kidnapped by a bunch of claim jumpers after control of a gold mine. **60m/B VHS.** Tim Holt, Richard Martin, Elaine Riley, Douglas Fowley, Veda Ann Borg; ***D:*** Lesley Selander.

Rider of the Law 🦴 **1935** A government agent poses as a greenhorn easterner to nab a gang of outlaws. **56m/B VHS.** Bob Steele.

Rider on the Rain 🦴🦴🦴 *Lepassager de la Pluie* **1970** A young housewife is viciously raped by an escaped sex maniac. She kills him and disposes of his body, not knowing that he is being relentlessly pursued by mysterious American Bronson. Suspenseful, French-made thriller featuring one of Bronson's best performances. **115m/C VHS.** *FR* Marlene Jobert, Charles Bronson, Jill Ireland; ***D:*** Rene Clement. Golden Globes '71: Foreign Film.

Riders 🦴🦴½ *Jilly Cooper's Riders* **1988** Enemies since childhood, aristocratic Rupert Campbell-Black (Gilbert) and half-gypsy Jake Lovell (Praed) have carried their rivalry into the competitive equestrian field. Of course, there's the added complication of Rupert's wife, whom Jake is also interested in. Based on Jilly Cooper's steamy novel. **210m/C VHS.** *GB* Marcus Gilbert, Michael Praed, Stephanie Beacham, Gabrielle Beaumont, Serena Gordon, John Standing, Anthony Valentine, Cecile Paoli; ***D:*** Gabrielle Beaumont; ***W:*** Charlotte Bingham; ***C:*** Michael J. Davis; ***M:*** Roger Webb.

Riders of Death Valley 🦴🦴½ **1941** Splendid western action serial in 15 episodes. Foran, Jones, and Carillo head a passel o'men watching for thieves and claim jumpers in a mining area. **320m/B VHS.** Dick Foran, Buck Jones, Leo Carrillo, Lon Chaney Jr.; ***D:*** Ford Beebe, Ray Taylor.

Riders of Destiny 🦴🦴½ **1933** Wayne plays a government agent sent to find out who is stealing water from the local farmers. Very early Wayne has the Duke looking awfully young as an agent securing water rights for ranchers. **59m/B VHS, DVD.** John Wayne, George "Gabby" Hayes, Cecilia Parker, Forrest Taylor, Al "Fuzzy" St. John; ***D:*** Robert North Bradbury; ***W:*** Robert North Bradbury; ***C:*** Archie Stout.

Riders of Pasco Basin 🦴½ **1940** Outlaws are tricking ranchers out of their money by falsely promising to build a dam. So Brown and his cohorts come to set things right. **56m/B VHS.** Johnny Mack Brown, Fuzzy Knight, Bob Baker, Frances Robinson, Arthur Loft, Frank LaRue, Lafe (Lafayette) McKee, Kermit Maynard; ***D:*** Ray Taylor; ***W:*** Ford Beebe.

Riders of the Desert 🦴½ **1932** Steele tracks down the loot from a stagecoach robbery. **57m/B VHS.** Bob Steele.

Riders of the Purple Sage 🦴🦴½ **1925** When Texas Ranger Jim Lassiter's (Mix) sister and niece are kidnapped by the evil Walters (Oland), he devotes his life to finding them. While working on a ranch (and falling in love with the beautiful ranch owner), he learns Walters has changed his name and is passing himself off as a judge. Promptly shooting the skunk dead, Lassiter and his sweetie must run from a posse. Based on the Zane Grey novel. **63m/B VHS.** Tom Mix, Warner Oland, Mabel Ballin, Beatrice Burnham, Arthur Morrison, Fred Kohler Sr.; ***D:*** Lynn F. Reynolds; ***W:*** Edfrid Bingham.

Riders of the Purple Sage 🦴🦴½ **1996** Legendary gunman (are there any other kind?) Lassiter (Harris) helps save Bern (Thomas) from a beating in a town run by a conservative religious sect, led by Deacon Tull (Weisser). Seems Bern's befriended ranch owner (and nonmember) Jane (Madigan) and the Deacon is not only after Jane but her considerable land and cattle holdings. Lassiter rides to the rescue. Properly brooding TV adaptation of the 1912 Zane Grey novel (the Grey novel specifies that the sect are Mormons but this caused considerable fuss). Filmed in Utah. **90m/C VHS.** Ed Harris, Amy Madigan, Henry Thomas, Norbert Weisser, Robin Tunney, G.D. Spradlin; ***D:*** Charles Haid; ***W:*** Gill Dennis; ***C:*** William Wages; ***M:*** Arthur Kempel. **TV**

Riders of the Range 🦴🦴 **1924** Sheep invade the cattle range and a range war flares up between those who would herd and the ranchers. Silent flick of interest because of the stars. **62m/B VHS.** Edmund Cobb, Dolly Dale; ***D:*** Otis Thayer.

Riders of the Range 🦴 **1949** Cowboy rides into town just in time to save a girl's brother from gamblers. **60m/B VHS.** Tim Holt, Richard Martin.

Riders of the Rockies 🦴🦴½ **1937** An honest cowboy turns rustler in order to trap a border gang. One of Ritter's very best cowboy outings; good fun, and a very long fistfight with King. **60m/B VHS.** Tex Ritter, Yakima Canutt, Louise Stanley, Charles "Blackie" King, Snub Pollard; ***D:*** Robert North Bradbury.

Riders of the Storm 🦴½ *The American Way* **1988 (R)** A motley crew of Vietnam vets runs a covert TV broadcasting station from an in-flight B-29, jamming America's legitimate airwaves. Interesting premise with boring result. **92m/C VHS.** Dennis Hopper, Michael J. Pollard, Eugene Lipinski, James Aubrey, Nigel Pegram; ***D:*** Maurice Phillips; ***W:*** Scott Roberts.

Riders of the Timberline 🦴🦴 **1941** Unusual for a Hopalong Cassidy programmer in that it puts him in timber country. Yes, he's a lumberjack and he's okay, as he fights against land-grabbing crooks all day. **59m/B VHS.** William Boyd, Brad King, Andy Clyde, J. Farrell MacDonald, Elaine Stewart, Anna Q. Nilsson, Hal Taliaferro, Tom Tyler, Victor Jory; ***D:*** Lesley Selander.

Riders of the West 🦴 **1942** An honest cowpoke fights off a band of rustlers. **58m/B VHS.** Buck Jones, Tim McCoy, Raymond Hatton, Sarah Padden, Harry Woods; ***D:*** Howard Bretherton.

Riders of the Whistling Pines 🦴🦴 **1949** Our ever-so-bland hero solves a murder perpetrated by a passel of lumber thieves and saves the day for yet another damsel in distress. **70m/B VHS.** Gene Autry, Patricia Barry, Jimmy Lloyd; ***D:*** John English.

Riders of the Whistling Skull 🦴🦴½ *The Golden Trail* **1937** The Three Mesquiteers are guiding an expedition to an ancient Indian city. A gang of rustlers looting the city are holding an archeology professor hostage, and the Mesquiteers must rescue him. Swell cast; nifty, creepy plot; solid-as-usual leads. **58m/B VHS.** Robert "Bob" Livingston, Ray Corrigan, Max Terhune, Yakima Canutt, Roland Winters; ***D:*** Mack V. Wright.

Riders to the Sea 🦴½ **1988** A mother envisions the death of her last son in the same manner her other sons died—by drowning. Based on the play by Irish dramatist John Millington Synge. **90m/C VHS.** Geraldine Page, Amanda Plummer, Sachi (MacLaine) Parker, Barry McGovern; ***D:*** Ronan O'Leary.

Ridicule 🦴🦴🦴½ **1996 (R)** Fish-out-of-water drama has minor country aristocrat Ponceludon (Berling) enter the depraved world of the 18th-century court at Versailles. There, he hopes, the king will aid him in his quest to drain the disease-ridden swamps at his estate. The naive provincial finds he must master the weapons of choice for success within the court—wit, deadly ridicule, and impeccable lineage. After initial missteps due to lack of finesse, he quickly adapts, and finds some influential allies: the beautiful Madame de Blayac (Ardant) and sympathetic Marquis de Bellegarde (Rochefort). When the Marquis's spirited and attractive daughter, Mathilde (Godreche), shows up, the smitten Ponceludon must stop her loveless marriage of convenience. Perfectly cast, director Leconte's highly lauded period piece has all the emotional and technical elements of an engaging film. In French with subtitles. **102m/C VHS.** *FR* Charles Berling, Jean Rochefort, Fanny Ardant, Bernard Giraudeau, Judith Godreche, Bernard Dheran, Carlo Brandt, Jacques Mathou; ***D:*** Patrice Leconte; ***W:*** Remi Waterhouse, Michel Fessler, Eric Vicaut; ***C:*** Thierry Arbogast; ***M:*** Antoine Duhamel. Oscars '96: Foreign Film; Cesar '97: Director (Leconte), Film; Broadcast Film Critics '96: Foreign Film.

Ridin' Down the Canyon 🦴🦴½ **1942** Standard but entertaining entry in Rogers' popular series. It's Rogers to the rescue when a gang of outlaws are rustling cattle and selling to the government for wartime profits. Roy, along with the Sons of the Pioneers, also manages to croon a few tunes. Based on a story by Robert Williams and Norman Houston. **54m/B VHS.** Roy Rogers, George "Gabby" Hayes, Linda Hayes, Addison Richards, Adrian (Lorna Gray) Booth, James Seay; ***D:*** Joseph Kane; ***W:*** Albert De Mond.

Ridin' on a Rainbow 🦴½ **1941** Has-been performer on a steamboat decides to rob a bank in the hopes of starting a new life for himself and his daughter. The money he robs had just been deposited by some cattlemen, one of whom joins the steamboat's crew, wins the daughter's heart, and gets to the father. Slow and dull, with too much singing, and too little plot and scenery. **79m/B VHS.** Gene Autry, Smiley Burnette, Mary Lee; ***D:*** Lew (Louis Friedlander) Landers.

Ridin' the California Trail 🦴½ **1947** The Cisco Kid is wanted dead or alive in several states. **40m/B VHS.** Gilbert Roland.

Ridin' the Lone Trail woof! **1937** Steele attempts to stop some criminals who've been harassing a stagecoach line. Republic was better than this weak western would lead us to believe. Steele, who went on to better things, is a bright spot in a film that sounds and looks bad. Keep your ears open for the sound of airplanes—apparently Newfield forgot they hadn't been invented in the time of the wild west. From a story by E.B. Mann. **56m/B VHS.** Bob Steele, Claire Rochelle, Charles "Blackie" King, Ernie Adams, Lew Meehan, Julian Rivero; ***D:*** Sam Newfield; ***W:*** Charles Francis Royal.

Ridin' the Trail 🦴 **1940** Scott stars as a cowboy out to rid the countryside of bad guys in this western. **60m/B VHS.** Fred Scott, Iris Lancaster, Harry Harvey, Jack Ingram, John Ward; ***D:*** Raymond K. Johnson.

Ridin' Thru 🦴🦴 **1935** Another Tom Tyler western, in which the hero does battle with unscrupulous villains. **60m/B VHS.** Tom Tyler, Ruth Hiatt, Lafe (Lafayette) McKee, Philo (Philip, P.H., P.M.) McCullough, Lew Meehan, Bud Osborne; ***D:*** Harry S. Webb.

The Riding Avenger 🦴½ **1936** To gain the love of a beautiful lady, a cowboy vows never to fight again, but is forced to break his promise when the town is terrorized. Aw, shucks. **56m/B VHS.** Hoot Gibson, Ruth Mix, Buzz Barton; ***D:*** Harry Fraser.

Riding High 🦴🦴½ **1950** Capra remade his 1934 film "Broadway Bill" as this light-hearted musical. Horse trainer Crosby falls for the wealthy Gray who demands he choose between her and his horse. Bing chooses the horse who proves his loyalty by winning the big race and making Crosby a rich man. ♫Someplace on Anywhere Road; Sunshine Cake; We've Got a Sure Thing; The Horse Told Me; The Whiffenpoof Song; De Camptown Races. **112m/B VHS.** Bing Crosby, Coleen Gray, Charles Bickford, William Demarest, Frances Gifford, Raymond Walburn, James Gleason, Ward Bond, Percy Kilbride, Harry Davenport, Margaret Hamilton, Douglass Dumbrille, Gene Lockhart, Charles Lane, Frankie Darro, Paul Harvey, Marjorie Lord, Dub Taylor, Max Baer Sr., Oliver Hardy; ***D:*** Frank Capra; ***W:*** Robert Riskin, Melville Shavelson, Jack Rose; ***C:*** George Barnes.

Riding High 🦴 **1978** It's a battle for supremacy between the kings of the motorcycle stunt world. TV movie's soundtrack includes songs from The Police, Dire Straits, Jerry Lee Lewis, and more. **92m/C VHS.** Murray Salem, Marella Oppenheim, Eddie Kidd, Irene Handl; ***D:*** Ross Cramer. **TV**

Riding in Cars with Boys 🦴🦴 **2001 (PG-13)** Based on the memoir of Beverly Donofrio, the plot follows Beverly (Barrymore) from 1965, when she becomes pregnant at age 15, to 1986, when her son has grown up and she has completed her book. The story is more concerned with the way parents treat their children, however, and Beverly doesn't emerge as the spunky super-mom who prevailed despite the odds. Instead she comes off as a whiner who blames her loser husband Ray (Zahn) for getting her pregnant, her own parents (Woods and Bracco) for not talking to her, and even her son Jason (Garcia) for merely being around. Barrymore gives a good performance, but Zahn outdoes her by breaking his "goofy guy" typecast and adding texture to the woeful Ray. **132m/C VHS, DVD.** *US* Drew Barrymore, Steve Zahn, Brittany Murphy, Adam Garcia, Lorraine Bracco, James Woods, Sara Gilbert, Desmond Harrington, David Moscow, Maggie Gyllenhaal, Peter Facinelli, Marisa Ryan, Mika Boorem, Skye McCole Bartusiak, Logan Lerman; ***D:*** Penny Marshall; ***W:*** Morgan Ward; ***C:*** Miroslav Ondricek; ***M:*** Hans Zimmer.

Riding On && **1937** Hayseed falls for the daughter of his father's arch rival. While his father battles it out over cattle, he pines for his enemy's daughter. Lots of action which is typical fare in mediocre western production. **59m/B VHS.** Tom Tyler, Germaine Greer, Rex Lease, John Elliott, Earl Dwire; ***D:*** Harry S. Webb.

Riding on Air && **1937** Small-town newspaper editor Brown discovers that his bumbling methods get him the right results. Smugglers and crazy inventions in a ho-hum Brown entry. **58m/B VHS.** Joe E. Brown; ***D:*** Edward Sedgwick.

Riding Speed & **1935** Our hero breaks up a gang of smugglers along the Mexican border. **50m/B VHS.** Buffalo Bill Jr.

Riding the Sunset Trail &&& **1941** Top-notch tale of Keene trying to stop a con from cashing in on his dead half-brother's fortune. Solid production values and an enthusiastic performance by Keene make this one of his best films after a string of flops. **56m/B VHS.** Tom (George Duryea) Keene, Betty Miles, Frank Yaconelli, Sugar Dawn, Slim Andrews, Kenne Duncan; ***D:*** Robert Emmett Tansey; ***W:*** Robert Emmett, Frances Kavanaugh.

The Riding Tornado &&½ **1932** Bronc rider McCoy takes a job on Grey's ranch, promptly falling for her. Ranch foreman Oakman, who's really the leader of a gang of rustlers, kidnaps Grey and McCoy goes after them. **63m/B VHS.** Tim McCoy, Shirley Grey, Wheeler Oakman, Wallace MacDonald, Russell Simpson, Montagu Love, Lafe (Lafayette) McKee, Bud Osborne; ***D:*** David Ross Lederman.

Riding with Death **1976** A man who can become invisible, thanks to a military experiment, uses his power to uncover a dastardly plot by a mad scientist. So-so TV pilot. **97m/C VHS.** Ben Murphy, Andrew Prine, Katherine Crawford, Richard Dysart; ***D:*** Alan J. Levi. **TV**

Riel && **1979** The story of Louis Riel, a half-French, half-Indian visionary who challenged the Canadian army in his fight for equality and self-rule. **150m/C VHS.** Raymond Cloutier, Arthur Hill, William Shatner, Christopher Plummer, Leslie Nielsen; ***D:*** George Bloomfield.

Riff Raff && *Riffraff* **1935** Melodramatic story about the relationship of two waterfront workers in the tuna fishing business. Confusing script saddled with too many characters, but there is some good sharp dialogue between the leads. Also features the scenic California waterfront. **80m/B VHS.** Jean Harlow, Spencer Tracy, Joseph Calleia, Una Merkel, Mickey Rooney, Victor Kilian, J. Farrell MacDonald, Roger Imhof; ***D:*** J. Walter Ruben.

Riff-Raff &&½ **1947** Various dramatic and comic complications arise when a dying man gives Panama City con man O'Brien a map to oil deposits. Interesting and quick-moving melodrama. **80m/B VHS.** Pat O'Brien, Walter Slezak, Anne Jeffreys, Jason Robards Sr., Percy Kilbride, Jerome Cowan; ***D:*** Ted Tetzlaff.

Riff Raff &&& **1992** Unsparing black comedy about the British working-class by director Loach. Ex-con Stevie comes to London from Scotland to look for work and escape his thieving past. He finds a nonunion job on a construction site, takes up squatter's rights in an abandoned apartment, and finds a girlfriend in equally struggling singer Susie, who turns out to be a junkie. Loach's characters deal with their unenviable lot in life through rough humor and honest sentiment. Regional accents are so thick that the film is subtitled. **96m/C VHS.** *GB* Robert Carlyle, Emer McCourt, Jimmy Coleman, George Moss, Ricky Tomlinson, David Finch, Bill Jesse; ***D:*** Ken Loach; ***W:*** Bill Jesse; ***M:*** Stewart Copeland.

Rififi &&&½ *Du Rififi Chez les Hommes* **1954** Perhaps the greatest of all "heist" movies. Four jewel thieves pull off a daring caper, only to fall prey to mutual distrust. The long scene of the actual theft, completely in silence, will have your heart in your throat. In French with English subtitles. **115m/B VHS, DVD.** *FR* Jean Servais, Carl Mohner, Robert Manuel, Jules Dassin; ***D:*** Jules Dassin; ***W:*** Jules Dassin; ***C:*** Philippe Agostini; ***M:*** Georges Auric. Cannes '55: Director (Dassin).

Rift &½ **1996** Bland romantic triangle set among Manhattan 20-somethings. Shy Tom (Sage) pines for Lisa (Bransford), the wife of his best friend, Bill (Cavanaugh). In fact, Tom begins having overwhelming nightmares, involving murder, about the situation. Not that you'll care since Tom is a mope, Lisa's a whiner, and Bill's a nasty-tempered bore. **87m/C VHS.** William Sage, Timothy Cavanaugh, Jennifer Bransford, Alan Davidson; ***D:*** Edward S. Barkin; ***W:*** Edward S. Barkin; ***C:*** Lee Daniel.

The Right Hand Man &½ **1987 (R)** A brother and sister must deal with their crusty patriarch's demise in the Victorian-era Australian outback. Disappointing and overwrought. **101m/C VHS.** *AU* Rupert Everett, Hugo Weaving, Arthur Dignam; ***D:*** Di Drew.

Right of Way &&½ **1984** Stewart plays an elderly man who makes a suicide pact with his wife (Davis) when he learns of her terminal illness. Davis and Stewart's first film together is disappointing and stodgy, with an abrupt ending that looks like bad editing by a frightened studio. Made for TV. **102m/C VHS.** James Stewart, Bette Davis, Priscilla Morrill, Melinda Dillon; ***D:*** George Schaefer; ***M:*** Brad Fiedel. **TV**

The Right Stuff &&& **1983 (PG)** A rambunctious adaptation of Tom Wolfe's nonfiction book about the beginnings of the U.S. space program, from Chuck Yeager's breaking of the sound barrier to the last of the Mercury missions. Featuring an all-star cast and an ambitious script. Rowdy, imaginative, and thrilling, though broadly painted and oddly uninvolving. Former astronaut John Glenn was running for president when this was out. **193m/C VHS, DVD, Wide.** Ed Harris, Dennis Quaid, Sam Shepard, Scott Glenn, Fred Ward, Charles Frank, William Russ, Kathy Baker, Barbara Hershey, Levon Helm, David Clennon, Kim Stanley, Mary Jo Deschanel, Veronica Cartwright, Pamela Reed, Jeff Goldblum, Harry Shearer, Donald Moffat, Scott Paulin, Lance Henriksen, Scott Wilson, John P. Ryan, Royal Dano; ***D:*** Philip Kaufman; ***W:*** Philip Kaufman; ***C:*** Caleb Deschanel; ***M:*** Bill Conti. Oscars '83: Film Editing, Sound, Orig. Score.

The Right Temptation &&½ **2000 (R)** Female PI Derian (De Mornay) is hired by a jealous wife (Delaney) to get the dirt on her adulterous rich husband (Sutherland). Too bad the PI then falls for her target, who may also be in bed with the mob. **93m/C VHS, DVD, Wide.** Kiefer Sutherland, Rebecca DeMornay, Dana Delany, Adam Baldwin; ***D:*** Lyndon Chubbuck.

The Right to Remain Silent && **1995 (R)** Rookie cop Christine Paley (Thompson) learns all about human foibles in her job processing incoming suspects. Based on a play by Brent Briscoe and Mark Fauser. **96m/C VHS.** Lea Thompson, Amanda Plummer, Christopher Lloyd, Laura San Giacomo, Judge Reinhold, Carl Reiner, L.L. Cool J., Patrick Dempsey, Fisher Stevens, Robert Loggia; ***D:*** Hubert de la Bouillerie.

Rikisha-Man &&&½ *Rickshaw Man; Muhomatsu no Issho* **1958** A tragic melodrama about a rickshaw puller who helps raise a young boy after his father has died, and loves the boy's mother from afar. Inagaki's remake of his original 1943 version. In Japanese with English subtitles. **105m/B VHS.** *JP* Toshiro Mifune; ***D:*** Hiroshi Inagaki.

Rikky and Pete &&½ **1988 (R)** An engaging Australian comedy about a bizarre, precociously eccentric brother and sister. He's a Rube Goldberg-style mentor; she's a scientist-cum-country singer. They move together to the outback and meet a score of weird characters. A worthy follow-up to director Tass's "Malcolm." **103m/C VHS.** *AU* Nina Landis, Stephen Kearney, Tetchie Agbayani, Bruce Spence, Bruno Lawrence, Bill Hunter, Dorothy Allison, Don Reid, Lewis Fitz-Gerald; ***D:*** Nadia Tass; ***W:*** David Parker; ***M:*** Phil Judd.

Rikyu &&& **1990** Set in 16th century Japan, Rikyu is a Buddhist priest who elevated the tea ceremony to an art form. To him it is a spiritual experience, to his master, Lord Hideyoshi Toilyotomi, the ruler of Japan, mastery of the ceremony is a matter of prestige. Conflict arises between Rikyu's ideal of profound simplicity, symbolized by the ceremony, and Toilyotomi's planned conquest of China, which Rikyu opposes. In Japanese with English subtitles. **116m/C VHS, DVD.** *JP* Rentaro Mikuni, Tsutomu Yamazaki; ***D:*** Hiroshi Teshigahara; ***W:*** Hiroshi Teshigahara, Genpei Akasegawa; ***C:*** Fujio Morita; ***M:*** Toru Takemitsu.

Rim of the Canyon &½ **1949** Autry has a dual role as a lawman tracking villains who were jailed by his father years before. **70m/B VHS.** Gene Autry, Nan Leslie, Thurston Hall, Clem Bevans, Walter Sande, Jock Mahoney, Alan Hale Jr., Denver Pyle; ***D:*** John English.

Rimfire &&½ **1949** An undercover agent tracks down some stolen U.S. Army gold, aided by the ghost of a wrongly hanged gambler. Fun B western. **65m/B VHS.** Mary Beth Hughes, Henry Hull, Fuzzy Knight, James Millican, Victor Kilian, Margia Dean, Jason Robards Sr., Reed Hadley; ***D:*** B. Reeves Eason.

Rin Tin Tin, Hero of the West && **1955** In one of his last adventures, the famous German Shepherd proves his courage and hyper-canine intelligence. Colorized. **75m/C VHS.** James Brown, Lee Aaker.

The Ring &&½ **1927** Very early Hitchcock about boxer who marries carnival girl, loses carnival girl, and wins carnival girl back again. Standard romantic punch and roses yarn interesting as measure of young director's developing authority. **82m/B VHS, DVD.** *GB* Carl Brisson, Lillian Hall-Davis, Ian Hunter, Gordon Harker; ***D:*** Alfred Hitchcock; ***W:*** Alfred Hitchcock; ***C:*** Jack Cox.

The Ring &&½ **1952** Poignant early fight movie that gives a lesson in prejudice against Chicanos. The main character feels that the only way to get respect from the world is to fight for it. Well-directed and perceptive. **79m/B VHS.** Gerald Mohr, Rita Moreno, Kiri Te Kanawa, Robert Arthur, Art Aragon, Jack Elam; ***D:*** Kurt Neumann.

Ring of Bright Water &&& **1969 (G)** Well done story of a pet otter from Gavin Maxwell's autobiography. The film stars the couple that made the delightful "Born Free." Beautiful Scottish Highlands photography adds to this captivating and endearing tale of a civil servant who purchases an otter from a pet store and moves to the country. **107m/C VHS, DVD, Wide.** *GB* Bill Travers, Virginia McKenna, Peter Jeffrey, Archie Duncan; ***D:*** Jack Couffer; ***W:*** Jack Couffer, Bill Travers; ***C:*** Wolfgang Suschitzky; ***M:*** Frank Cordell.

Ring of Death &½ **1972** A tough cop investigating a routine case becomes a hunted man after someone kills the man he is following. **93m/C VHS.** Franco Nero, Florinda Bolkan, Adolfo Celi.

Ring of Fire &½ **1991 (R)** Wilson is one of very few modern American kung-fu heroes of Asian descent, and he works messages against prejudice into this interracial Romeo-and-Juliet chopsocky tale. What foot through yonder window breaks? **100m/C VHS, DVD.** Don "The Dragon" Wilson, Maria Ford, Vince Murdocco, Dale Jacoby, Michael Delano, Eric Lee; ***D:*** Richard W. Munchkin.

Ring of Fire 2: Blood and Steel &½ **1992 (R)** Wilson returns as Dr. Johnny Wu in this martial-arts actioner which finds the good doctor the witness to a robbery. When one of the robbers is killed, the gang's leader kidnaps Johnny's fiance and holds her for ransom. He decides to bypass the police and use his own expertise to rescue her. **94m/C VHS.** Don "The Dragon" Wilson, Maria Ford, Sy Richardson, Michael Delano, Dale Jacoby, Vince Murdocco, Evan Lorie, Gary Robbins, Charlie Ganis, Ron Yuan; ***D:*** Richard W. Munchkin.

Ring of Fire 3: Lion Strike &½ **1994 (R)** Johnny Wu is supposed to be on vacation with his son and a beautiful forest ranger when they find themselves in the way of a violent group known as the Global Mafia. Seems Johnny has a computer disk that the gangsters want. **90m/C VHS.** Don "The Dragon" Wilson, Bobbie Phillips, Robert Costanzo; ***D:*** Rick Jacobson.

Ring of Steel && **1994 (R)** Alex, a one-time Olympic hopeful in fencing, is enticed into combat by the mysterious owner of a decadent nightclub where gladiator-type matches are staged for the thrill of the bored and jaded super-rich. Unaware of the high stakes, Alex wins a duel and is showered with money and the attention of a beautiful, yet dangerous woman. When Alex discovers the club's dark secret, he no longer wants to fight, but blackmail draws him in even deeper. **94m/C VHS.** Joe Don Baker, Carol Alt, Robert Chapin, Gary Kasper, Darlene Vogel; ***D:*** David Frost; ***W:*** Robert Chapin; ***M:*** Jeff Beal.

Ring of Terror & **1962** College boy who wants to join a fraternity must survive the initiation rights, which include stealing a ring from a corpse. Unfortunately, this seemingly invincible guy has a deadly terror of the dead. Cheaply made flop alledgedly based on a composite of actual hazing incidents. **72m/B VHS.** George Mather, Esther Furst, Austin Green, Joseph Conway; ***D:*** Clark Paylow.

Ring of the Musketeers &&½ **1993 (PG-13)** Contemporary spoof of the Musketeers saga finds three descendants of the swashbuckling heroes carrying on the family tradition of protecting the weak and innocent. They even get stuck with a Musketeer-wanna-be when they come to the rescue of a young boy who is kidnapped to prevent his dad from testifying against mobsters. **86m/C VHS.** David Hasselhoff, Alison Doody, Thomas Gottschalk, Richard "Cheech" Marin, Corbin Bernsen, John Rhys-Davies; ***D:*** John Paragon; ***W:*** Joel Surnow.

Ringmaster woof! *Jerry Springer's Ringmaster* **1998 (R)** Okay, this is it. Hug the kids, empty the bank accounts. It's the apocalypse. Jerry Springer's made a movie. And the first question would be: why? To cash in, of course, and to try to justify the show's existence. The second question is: Why should you bother? The answer is a resounding "You shouldn't." In case you couldn't guess the plot, Jerry welcomes a stepdad (Dudikoff) who's doing it with his 15-year-old stepdaughter (Pressly), and a woman (Robinson) who caught her man (White) with her best friend. Sexual escapades and the thrill of being on "the TEE-vee" ensue. **89m/C VHS, DVD.** Jerry Springer, John Capodice, Jaime Pressly, Molly Hagan, Michael Dudikoff, Michael Jai White, William McNamara, Dawn Maxey, Wendy Raquel Robinson, Tangie Ambrose, Nicki Micheaux, Ashley Holbrook; ***D:*** Neil Abramson; ***W:*** Jon Bernstein; ***C:*** Russell Lyster; ***M:*** Kennard Ramsey. Golden Raspberries '98: Worst New Star (Springer).

Ringside &½ **1949** A concert pianist turns boxer to avenge his brother who was blinded in a fight. **64m/B VHS.** Donald (Don "Red") Barry, Sheila Ryan, Tom Brown.

The Rink &&& **1916** Chaplin plays a waiter who spends his lunch hour on roller skates. Silent with musical soundtrack added. **20m/B VHS.** Charlie Chaplin; ***D:*** Charlie Chaplin.

Rio Bravo &&&½ **1959** John T. Chance (Wayne) is the sheriff of a Texas border town who takes murderer Joe (Akins) into custody. Since Joe is the brother of powerful local cattle baron Nathan Burdette (Russell), the sheriff faces a blockade of gunmen hired to keep his prisoner from being brought to justice. Long, but continually entertaining. Chance has to make do with the help of a cripple (Brennan), a drunk (Martin), and a hot-headed kid (Nelson). Lond, but continually entertaining film that didn't impress critics at the time but its reputation has improved over the years. Sequel: "El Dorado." Semi-remake was called "Assault on Precinct 13." **140m/C VHS, DVD, Wide.** John

Wayne, Dean Martin, Angie Dickinson, Ricky Nelson, Walter Brennan, Ward Bond, Claude Akins, Bob Steele, John Russell, Harry Carey Jr., Pedro Gonzalez-Gonzalez; *D:* Howard Hawks; *W:* Leigh Brackett, Jules Furthman; *C:* Russell Harlan; *M:* Dimitri Tiomkin.

Rio Conchos 🦴🦴🦴 **1964** Nifty nonstop action in this western set in Texas after the Civil War. Three Army buddies search for 2,000 stolen rifles. Boone is understated, O'Brien is good, and Brown memorable in his debut. **107m/C VHS.** Richard Boone, Stuart Whitman, Edmond O'Brien, Anthony (Tony) Franciosa, Jim Brown; *D:* Gordon Douglas; *M:* Jerry Goldsmith.

Rio Diablo 🦴🦴½ **1993** Country Western singers abound in—what else—a made-for-TV Western movie. A bounty hunter (Rogers) and newlywed groom (Tritt) set off after a gang of thieving kidnappers who have snatched the young bride (Harring). Judd shows up as the owner of a desert hostelry, who happens to cross paths with the hunters. Watch out—this could be more fun than a Partridge Family reunion. **120m/C VHS.** Kenny Rogers, Travis Tritt, Naomi Judd, Stacy Keach, Brion James, Bruce Greenwood, Laura Harring; *M:* Larry Brown.

Rio Grande 🦴🦴🦴 **1950** The last entry in Ford's cavalry trilogy following "Fort Apache" and "She Wore a Yellow Ribbon." A U.S. cavalry unit on the Mexican border conducts an unsuccessful campaign against marauding Indians. The commander of the lonely outpost, Lt. Col. Kirby Yorke (Wayne), plays no favorites when his only son, Jeff (Jarman Jr.), arrives as a new recruit and is soon followed by Yorke's estranged wife, Kathleen (O'Hara). Featuring an excellent Victor Young score and several songs by the Sons of the Pioneers. **105m/B VHS, DVD.** John Wayne, Maureen O'Hara, Ben Johnson, Claude Jarman Jr., Harry Carey Jr., Victor McLaglen, Chill Wills, J. Carrol Naish; *D:* John Ford; *W:* James Kevin McGuinness; *C:* Bert Glennon; *M:* Victor Young.

Rio Grande Raiders 🦴 **1946** A Stagecoach driver discovers that his kid brother is working for a crooked rival stage company. **54m/B VHS.** Sunset Carson, Linda Stirling, Bob Steele.

Rio Lobo 🦴🦴½ **1970 (G)** Hawks's final film takes place after the Civil War, when Union Colonel Wayne goes to Rio Lobo to take revenge on two traitors. Disappointing. The Duke has to carry weak supporting performances on his brawny shoulders—and nearly does. **114m/C VHS.** John Wayne, Jorge (George) Rivero, Jennifer O'Neill, Jack Elam, Chris Mitchum, David Huddleston, George Plimpton; *D:* Howard Hawks; *C:* William Clothier; *M:* Jerry Goldsmith.

Rio Rattler 🦴½ **1935** Tyler takes the place of a murdered lawman in order to find his killer. **60m/B VHS.** Tom Tyler, Marion Shilling, Eddie Gribbon, William (Bill) Gould, Tom London; *D:* Franklin Shamray.

Rio Rita 🦴🦴½ **1942** Abbott & Costello are working on a ranch and somehow become involved with Nazi spies. Provides a few original comic bits for the duo but is otherwise mediocre. An updated remake of the 1929 Wheeler & Woolsey comedy. **91m/B VHS.** Bud Abbott, Lou Costello, Kathryn Grayson, John Carroll, Patricia Dane, Tom Conway, Peter Whitney; *D:* Sylvan Simon; *C:* George J. Folsey.

Riot 🦴🦴½ **1969 (R)** Men in cages throw tantrums until warden returns from vacation. Filmed in Arizona State Prison with real convicts as extras. Strong performances by fullback Brown and durable Hackman. Based on story by ex-con Frank Elli. Too oft-played theme song sung by Bill Medley of the Righteous Brothers. **97m/C VHS.** Gene Hackman, Jim Brown, Mike Kellin, Ben Carruthers, Frank Eyman; *D:* Buzz Kulik; *W:* James Poe.

Riot 🦴 **1996 (R)** Dumb actioner set on Christmas Eve, 1999, amidst some L.A. riots. British Special Air Service officer Shane Alcott (Daniels) must rescue his kidnapped ex-girlfriend Anna-Lisa (Rowland), who just happens to be the British ambassador's daughter. She's being held by ghetto gangster Leon (Sanders), whose gang turn out to be pawns for IRA leader O'Flaherty (Kilpatrick), who has a score to settle. Predictable fights, lots of explosions. **95m/C VHS.** Gary Daniels, Ray "Sugar Ray" Leonard, Patrick Kilpatrick, Paige Rowland, Dex Elliot Sanders, Charles Napier; *D:* Joseph Merhi; *W:* John Barmettler, William Applegate Jr.; *C:* Ken Blakey; *M:* Jim Halfpenny.

Riot in Cell Block 11 🦴🦴🦴 **1954** A convict leads four thousand prisoners in an uprising to improve prison conditions. Based on producer/ex-con Walter Wanger's own experience. Powerful and still timely. Filmed at Folsom Prison. **80m/B VHS.** Neville Brand, Leo Gordon, Emile Meyer, Frank Faylen; *D:* Donald Siegel.

Riot in the Streets 🦴🦴 *Riot* **1996 (R)** Four intertwined stories revolving around the 1992 Los Angeles riots, on the day the Rodney King verdict was announced. Concerned are an African-American family, a white police officer, a Latino family, and Asian-American shopowners. Documentary footage of the actual riots is also included. **95m/C VHS.** Mario Van Peebles, Melvin Van Peebles, Cicely Tyson, Luke Perry, Peter Dobson, Dante Basco, Mako, Kieu Chinh, Alexis Cruz, Douglas Spain, Yelba Osorio, John Ortiz; *D:* C. David Johnson, Richard Dilello, Galen Yuen, Alex Munoz; *W:* C. David Johnson, Richard Dilello, Galen Yuen, Joe Vasquez; *C:* Paul Elliott. **CABLE**

Riot Squad 🦴🦴 **1941** An intern poses as a doctor in order to find out who was responsible for putting a mob hit on a police captain. **55m/B VHS.** Richard Cromwell, Rita Quigley, John Miljan, Mary Ruth, Herbert Rawlinson, Mary Gordon, Arthur Space; *D:* Edward Finney.

Rip-Off 🦴 **1977** Two Greek wanderers enter the American way of life via sex, drugs, syndicated crime, and terrorism. **78m/C VHS.** Michael Benet, Michelle Simone, James Masters, Johnny Dark; *D:* Manolis Tsafos.

The Rip Off 🦴 **1978 (R)** A colorful gang of hoodlums goes for the biggest heist of their lives—six million bucks in diamonds! **99m/C VHS.** Lee Van Cleef, Karen Black, Robert Alda, Edward Albert; *D:* Anthony (Antonio Margheriti) Dawson.

Rip Roarin' Buckaroo 🦴 **1936** A fighter sets out to avenge himself when he is framed in a dishonest fight. **51m/B VHS.** Tom Tyler, B.J. Quinn Jr., Beth Marion, Charles "Blackie" King; *D:* Robert F. "Bob" Hill.

Rip van Winkle **1985** Sleepy Coppola adaptation of the Washington Irving story about a man who falls asleep for 20 years after a group of ghosts get him drunk. From the "Faerie Tale Theatre" series. **60m/C VHS.** Harry Dean Stanton, Talia Shire; *D:* Francis Ford Coppola.

Ripe 🦴🦴 **1997 (R)** Fourteen-year-old fraternal twins Violet (Keena) and Rosie (Eagan) decide to make it on their own after their abusive parents are killed in a car crash. They wind up on a derelict southern army base where they're befriended by caretaker Pete (Currie) and M.P. Ken (Brice), who may not have the most innocent of intentions. **93m/C VHS.** Monica Keena, Daisy Eagan, Gordon Currie, Ron Brice, Karen (Lynn) Gorney, Vincent Laresca; *D:* Mo Ogrodnik; *W:* Mo Ogrodnik; *C:* Wolfgang Held; *M:* Anton Sanko.

The Ripper woof! **1986** The spirit of Jack the Ripper possesses a university professor's body. Ultra-violent. Shot on videotape for the video market. **90m/C VHS.** Wade Tower, Tom Schreir, Mona Van Pernis, Andrea Adams; *D:* Christopher Lewis.

The Ripper 🦴🦴 **1997 (R)** Yet another version of the Jack the Ripper saga. In 1888 London, ambitious Scotland Yard inspector Jim Hansen (Bergin) is investigating the murders of several East End prostitutes. Clues direct him to a member of the nobility, in fact, Queen Victoria's grandson, Prince Edward (West), but pursuing his inquiries could lead to the end of Hansen's career. **100m/C VHS.** Patrick Bergin, Gabrielle Anwar, Michael York, Samuel West, Essie Davis, Olivia Hamnett; *D:* Janet Meyers; *W:* Robert Rodat; *C:* Martin McGrath; *M:* Mason Daring. **CABLE**

Ripper: Letter from Hell 🦴🦴 **2001 (R)** Thankfully, there's more terror than gore in this slasher, which could be a bummer if you prefer the bloodier the better. Molly Keller (Cook) enrolls in a forensic science program taught by criminologist Marshall Kane (Payne). There's a spate of recent campus murders that Molly and her study group are investigating and the modus operandi resembles that of Jack the Ripper. Then they start becoming the killer's next victims. **113m/C VHS, DVD, Wide.** A.J. Cook, Bruce Payne, Ryan Northcott, Juergen Prochnow, Claire Keim, Derek Hamilton, Emmanuelle Vaugier; *D:* John Eyres; *W:* Patrick Bermel; *C:* Thomas M. Harting; *M:* Peter Allen. **VIDEO**

Ripper Man 🦴½ **1996 (R)** Ex-cop is accused of murder when he finds a body at a nightclub and then becomes the killer's next target. **93m/C VHS.** Mike Norris. **VIDEO**

Riptide 🦴🦴🦴 **1934** Shearer is a carefree American married to stuffy English lord Marshall. He goes off to America on a business trip, she's bored and goes to a costume party (everyone dresses as insects!) where she meets old flame Montgomery. He gets drunk, follows her home in an effort to rekindle their passion, and winds up in the hospital after a drunken fall. The returning Marshall is appalled by the scandalous press and instigates divorce proceedings. Eventually, they come to their senses and decide they do love each other. Quality production with an entertaining cast. **90m/B VHS.** Norma Shearer, Herbert Marshall, Robert Montgomery, Richard "Skeets" Gallagher, Ralph Forbes, Lilyan Tashman; *D:* Edmund Goulding; *W:* Edmund Goulding.

The Rise and Fall of Legs Diamond 🦴🦴½ **1960** Not quite historically accurate but fast-paced and entertaining gangster bio of legendary booze trafficker Legs Diamond. Danton's debut. **101m/B VHS.** Ray Danton, Karen Steele, Jesse White, Simon Oakland, Robert Lowery, Elaine Stewart; *D:* Budd Boetticher.

The Rise & Rise of Daniel Rocket 🦴🦴 **1986** A exceptional young boy believes he can fly without the aid of a flying machine. From the "American Playhouse" series. **90m/C VHS.** Tom Hulce, Timothy Daly, Valerie Mahaffey; *D:* Emile Ardolino.

The Rise of Louis XIV 🦴🦴🦴 *La Prise de Pouvoir Par Louis XIV* **1966** A masterful docudrama detailing the life and court intrigues of Louis XIV of France. Successfully captures the attitudes and mores of the royalty at the time. One of a series of historical films directed by Rossellini. Made for French TV; subtitled. **100m/C VHS.** *FR* Jean-Marie Patte, Raymond Jourdan, Dominique Vincent, Silvagni, Pierre Barrat; *D:* Roberto Rossellini. **TV**

Rising Son 🦴🦴🦴 **1990** A family man who loves his job faces trauma when his factory closes at the same time his son informs him he's quitting medical school. Solid family drama and parable of economic hard times of the early '80s, sustained by top-drawer performances by Dennehy, Damon, and Laurie. Well directed by Coles. **92m/C VHS.** Brian Dennehy, Matt Damon, Piper Laurie, Graham Beckel, Ving Rhames, Jane Adams, Richard Jenkins, Emily Longstreth; *D:* John David Coles; *W:* Bill Phillips. **CABLE**

Rising Sun 🦴🦴🦴 **1993 (R)** When a prostitute is found murdered in the boardroom of a powerful Japanese-owned corporation, seasoned cop (and Japanese expert) Connery and new partner Snipes are sent to investigate. Complicated yarn about business, prejudice, cops, and the differences between east and west. Filmed with stylized camera techniques, quick action, and good rapport between the two leads. Based on the book by Crichton, which offered ominous theories about international politics and business. These aspects had the film labeled as Japan-bashing, one of the reasons the script was rewritten to focus more on the murder mystery. **129m/C VHS, DVD, Wide.** Sean Connery, Wesley Snipes, Tia Carrere, Harvey Keitel, Kevin Anderson, Stan(ford) Egi, Mako, Cary-Hiroyuki Tagawa, Ray Wise, Tatjana Patitz; *D:* Philip Kaufman; *W:* Michael Backes, Michael Crichton, Philip Kaufman; *C:* Michael Chapman; *M:* Toru Takemitsu.

Risk 🦴🦴🦴 **1994** Maya (Sillas) is a struggling, emotionally distant, New York artist when she meets overly friendly Joe (Ilku) on a bus. He follows her home and manages to entice Maya into letting him spend the night but Joe has some psychological problems, including criminal behavior, which manifests itself when he steals a car. Maya, nevertheless, agrees to drive with him to his older sister's home in rural Connecticut and finds bad blood and more mental anguish that she knows how to deal with. Terrifically honest performance by Sillas and an equally touching one by Ilku are highlights of this adult attempt at romance. **85m/C VHS.** Karen Sillas, David Ilku, Molly Price, Jack Gwaltney; *D:* Deirdre Fishel; *W:* Deirdre Fishel; *C:* Peter Pearce; *M:* John Paul Jones.

Risk 🦴🦴½ **2000 (R)** Shady insurance guy John Kriesky (Brown) is tutoring young Ben (Long) in money, sex, and shifty deals, including involving him in insurance fraud. Then Kriesky's lawyer/girlfriend Louise (Karvan) decides to give Ben a few personal lessons as well. Fast-paced thriller with a cast that's well worth watching. **89m/C VHS, DVD, Wide.** *AU* Bryan Brown, Tom Long, Claudia Karvan, Jason Clarke; *D:* Alan White; *W:* John Armstrong; *C:* Simon Duggan; *M:* Don Miller-Robinson. **CABLE**

Risky Business 🦴🦴 **1928** Fortune-seeking mother disapproves of daughter's doctor fiance, and educates girl in marital woes. Video includes early Pollard short "Sold at Auction." **104m/B VHS.** Vera Reynolds, ZaSu Pitts, Ethey Clayton; *D:* Alan Hale.

Risky Business 🦴🦴🦴 **1983 (R)** With his parents out of town and awaiting word from the college boards, a teenager becomes involved in unexpected ways with a quick-thinking prostitute, her pimp, and assorted others. Cruise is likeable, especially when dancing in his underwear. Funny, well-paced, stylish prototypical '80s teen flick reintroduced Ray-Bans as the sunglasses for the wanna-be hip. What a party! **99m/C VHS, DVD, 8mm, Wide.** Tom Cruise, Rebecca DeMornay, Curtis Armstrong, Bronson Pinchot, Joe Pantoliano, Kevin Anderson, Richard Masur, Raphael Sbarge, Nicholas Pryor, Janet Carroll; *D:* Paul Brickman; *W:* Paul Brickman; *C:* Reynaldo Villalobos, Bruce Surtees; *M:* Tangerine Dream.

Rita Hayworth: The Love Goddess 🦴½ **1983** Drama details the tragic life of the beautiful film star. Carter, lovely though she is, plays Rita weakly and without depth. **100m/C VHS.** Lynda Carter, Michael Lerner, Alejandro Rey, John Considine; *D:* James Goldstone. **TV**

Rita, Sue & Bob Too 🦴🦴🦴 **1987 (R)** A middle-aged Englishman gets involved in a menage a trois with two promiscuous teenagers, until the whole town gets wind of it. A raunchy, amoral British comedy. **94m/C VHS.** *GB* Michelle Holmes, George Costigan, Siobhan Finneran, Lesley Sharp, Willie Ross, Patti Nicholls, Kulvinder Ghir; *D:* Alan Clarke; *W:* Andrea Dunbar; *C:* Ivan Strasburg; *M:* Michael Kamen.

The Rite 🦴🦴 *The Ritual; Riten* **1969** Members of a famous theatrical troupe are called before a judge to answer charges that a production is obscene. The judge's interrogation exposes their private and painful neuroses until the performers decide to turn on their accuser. Pessimistic even by Bergman standards and the first film the director made specifically for TV. Swedish with subtitles. **75m/B VHS.** *SW* Ingrid Thulin, Gunnar Bjornstrand, Erik Hell, Anders Ek; *D:* Ingmar Bergman; *W:* Ingmar Bergman; *C:* Sven Nykvist.

Rites of Passage 🦴🦴 **1999 (R)** Suspenser about fathers, sons, and masculinity has both awkwardness and intensity. Del Farraday (Stockwell) and his son D.J. (Keith) travel to their secluded mountain cabin for a heart-to-heart chat, only to discover the place is being used by Farley's estranged gay son, Campbell (Behr). As if there weren't enough family angst, the trio are joined by violent escaped cons Frank (Remar) and Red (Woolvett). Tempers flare between Del and Frank and the entire situation is worsened by a secret that Campbell is keeping. Good performances. **94m/C VHS, DVD.** Dean Stockwell, James Remar, Jaimz Woolvett, Jason Behr, Robert Keith; ***D:*** Victor Salva; ***W:*** Victor Salva; ***C:*** Don E. Fauntleroy; ***M:*** Bennett Salvay.

Rituals 🦴½ *The Creeper* **1979** Group of five calm, rational men suddenly turn desperate after a chain of nightmarish events on a camping trip. Yet another low-budget "Deliverance" rip off. **100m/C VHS.** *CA* Hal Holbrook, Lawrence Dane; ***D:*** Peter Carter.

The Ritz 🦴🦴🦴 **1976 (R)** Weston tries to get away from his gangster brother-in-law by hiding out in a gay bathhouse in New York. Moreno plays a talentless singer Googie Gomez, who performs in the bathhouse while waiting for her big break. Moreno is great reprising her Tony-winning stage role, and Lester's direction is spiffy. Written by Terence McNally from his play. **91m/C VHS.** Rita Moreno, Jack Weston, Jerry Stiller, Kaye Ballard, Treat Williams, F. Murray Abraham; ***D:*** Richard Lester.

Rivals 🦴½ *Deadly Rivals* **1972 (R)** Shallow, unconvincing drama about a stepfather challenged by his stepson, who wants to kill this new contender for his mother's love. Nice handling of cast credits, but other details—like acting, directing and photography—leave much to be desired. **103m/C VHS.** Robert Klein, Joan Hackett, Scott Jacoby; ***D:*** Krishna Shah.

The River 🦴🦴🦴🦴 **1951** A massively lauded late film by Renoir about three British girls growing up in Bengal, India, all developing crushes on a one-legged American vet. Lyrical and heartwarming, with hailed cinematography by Claude Renoir. Rumer Godden wrote the novel, and co-scripted the screenplay with director Renoir. Satyajit Ray, one of India's greatest filmmakers, assisted Renoir. **99m/C VHS.** *FR* Patricia Walters, Adrienne Corri, Nora Swinburne, Radha, Arthur Shields, Thomas E. Breen, Esmond Knight; ***D:*** Jean Renoir; ***W:*** Jean Renoir; ***C:*** Claude Renoir; ***Nar:*** June Hillman.

The River 🦴🦴 **1984 (PG)** Farmers battle a river whose flood threatens their farm. Spacek, as always, is strong and believable as the wife and mother, but Gibson falters. Beautiful photography. The third in an onslaught of films in the early '80s that dramatized the plight of the small American farmer. "The River" isn't as strong as "Country" and "Places in the Heart" which managed to convey important messages less cloyingly. **124m/C VHS, DVD, Wide.** Mel Gibson, Sissy Spacek, Scott Glenn, Billy Green Bush; ***D:*** Mark Rydell; ***W:*** Julian Barry, Robert Dillon; ***C:*** Vilmos Zsigmond; ***M:*** John Williams.

River Beat 🦴🦴 **1954** A woman aboard an American freighter is unwittingly used as diamond smuggler, and is arrested when the ship docks in London. An inspector does his best to clear the hapless woman. **70m/B VHS.** Phyllis Kirk, John Bentley, Robert Ayres, Lenny White, Glyn Houston, Charles Lloyd Pack; ***D:*** Guy Green.

The River Niger 🦴🦴½ **1976 (R)** Jones is riveting, and Tyson is good in an otherwise muddling adaptation of the Tony-award winning play about black ghetto life. Realistic emotions and believable characters. **105m/C VHS.** James Earl Jones, Cicely Tyson, Glynn Turman, Louis Gossett Jr., Roger E. Mosley, Jonelle Allen; ***D:*** Krishna Shah.

River of Death 🦴½ **1990 (R)** Absurd adventure, based on an Alistair McLean novel, about a white man entering the Amazon jungle world of a forgotten tribe in search of wealth, tripping over Neo-Nazi scientists and war criminals. Too complex to be harmlessly enjoyable; too mindless for the complexity to be worth unraveling. **103m/C VHS.** Michael Dudikoff, Robert Vaughn, Donald Pleasence, Herbert Lom, L.Q. (Justus E. McQueen) Jones, Cynthia Erland, Sarah Maur-Thorp; ***D:*** Steve Carver.

River of Diamonds 🦴 **1990** A daring adventurer, with the standard beautiful woman at his side, battles evil curses and Nazis buried alive to find a fortune in diamonds. Yeah, sure. Another miserable "Indiana Jones" rip off. **88m/C VHS.** Dack Rambo, Angela O'Neill, Ferdinand "Ferdy" Mayne, Graham Clark, David Sherwood, Tony Caprari, Dominique Tyawa; ***D:*** Robert J. Smawley.

River of Evil 🦴½ **1964** Action/adventure in which a young girl travels through the Amazon jungle searching for clues to her father's death. **?m/C VHS.** Barbara Rutting, Harald Leipnitz.

River of Grass 🦴½ **1994** No-budget noirish crime/romance set in the swampy, low-rent Florida area between Miami and the Everglades. Uncaring and frankly dumb housewife/mom Cozy (Bowman) hooks up with the boozing Lee Ray (Fessenden) and the dim duo take an illegal dip in a private pool. Cozy manages to fire off Lee's gun and thinks she hit a man who suddenly appeared. Not bothering to find out if this is true, they decide to hold up in a motel until they can figure out what to do. You won't really care but director Reichardt does have a way with visuals so things aren't a total loss. **80m/C VHS.** Lisa Bowman, Larry Fessenden, Dick Russell; ***D:*** Kelly Reichardt; ***W:*** Jesse Hartman, Kelly Reichardt; ***C:*** Jim Denault.

River of No Return 🦴🦴½ **1954** During the gold rush, an itinerant farmer and his young son help a heart-of-gold saloon singer search for her estranged husband. Rather crummy script is helped by the mere presence of Mitchum and Monroe. Marilyn sings the title song, "Down in the Meadow," and "I'm Going to File My Claim." **91m/C VHS, DVD, Wide.** Robert Mitchum, Marilyn Monroe, Tommy Rettig, Rory Calhoun, Murvyn Vye, Douglas Spencer; ***D:*** Otto Preminger; ***W:*** Frank Fenton; ***C:*** Joseph LaShelle; ***M:*** Cyril Mockridge.

River of Unrest 🦴🦴½ *Ourselves Alone* **1937** Remarkable visual expressiveness and emotional power mark this depiction of terrorism and open warfare during the Irish Rebellion. Based on a play, hence slow; but good acting pulls it up half a bone. **69m/B VHS.** John Lodge, John Loder, Antoinette Cellier.

The River Pirates 🦴🦴½ **1994 (PG)** Mississippi boy discovers a lot about life over the summer of his 12th birthday in 1942. He finds the secret hiding place of a band of river thieves, endures a tornado, has some adventures with his friends, and finds out that his crush on the prettiest girl in town is reciprocated. Based on a novel by Willie Morris. **108m/C VHS.** Ryan Francis, Richard Farnsworth, Gennie James, Doug Emerson, Anne Ramsey, Maureen O'Sullivan; ***D:*** Tom G. Robertson.

The River Rat 🦴🦴½ **1984 (PG)** Ex-con Jones is reunited with his daughter after spending 13 years in prison. There's something in there about stashed loot that should have been jettisonned in favor of more getting-to-know-you father-daughter drama, which is good. **93m/C VHS.** Tommy Lee Jones, Brian Dennehy, Martha Plimpton, Shawn Smith, Melissa Davis; ***D:*** Tom Rickman.

River Red 🦴🦴 **1998 (R)** Trying to save his younger brother Tom (Moscow) from the beatings Dad regularly gives him, Dave Holden (Scott), stabs their father to death. As a minor (and therefore subject to a lighter sentence), Tom takes the rap and is sent to a juvenile home until he is 21. Dave's guilt (and the debts his father has left him) cause him to become physically violent, leading him into a life of crime. When the brothers reunite, emotions come to a head. Based on Drilling's one-act stage play, film boasts fine performances but nevertheless fails to take advantage of its controversial plot and deep psychological themes. A more thorough examination of the motivations would have made for a heightened outcome and a more interesting film overall. **104m/C VHS.** Tom Everett Scott, David Moscow, Cara Buono, Denis O'Hare, Leo Burmester, Tibor Feldman, James Murtaugh, David Lowery, Michael Kelly; ***D:*** Eric Drilling; ***W:*** Eric Drilling; ***C:*** Steven Schlueter; ***M:*** Johnny Hickman.

A River Runs Through It 🦴🦴🦴½ **1992 (PG)** Contemplative exploration of family ties and coming of age with impact falling just short of the novel's is another well-crafted American tale directed by Redford. Set in Montana during the early part of the century, a Presbyterian minister teaches his two sons, one troubled and one on his way to success, about life and religion via fly-fishing. Based on the novel by Norman Maclean. **123m/C VHS, DVD, 8mm, Wide.** Craig Sheffer, Brad Pitt, Tom Skerritt, Brenda Blethyn, Emily Lloyd, Edie McClurg, Stephen Shellen, Susan Taylor; ***D:*** Robert Redford; ***W:*** Richard Friedenberg; ***C:*** Philippe Rousselot; ***M:*** Mark Isham. Oscars '92: Cinematog.

River Street 🦴🦴 **1995** Ambitious real estate agent Ben Egan (Young) is engaged to marry Sharon (MacIntosh), his shady boss Vincent Pierce's (Hunter) daughter. But when he blows a big deal and winds up striking a cop, Ben's sentenced to community service at a dilapidated center for street kids. He takes an interest in good-hearted center director Wendy (Davis) but can't change his ways so easily. The center stands on valuable river front property and if Ben can get the land, he'll get back both his job and Sharon. The relationships don't convince and Ben's change of heart seems forced. **88m/C VHS.** *AU* Aden Young, Bill Hunter, Essie Davis, Tammy MacIntosh, Sullivan Stapleton, Lois Ramsey; ***D:*** Tony Mahood; ***W:*** Philip Ryall; ***C:*** Martin McGrath; ***M:*** David Bridie, John Phillips.

The River Wild 🦴🦴½ **1994 (PG-13)** Dissatisfied wife Gail (Streep) plans a family white-water rafting vacation with 10-year-old son Roarke (Mazzello) and workaholic husband Tom (Strathairn). A former guide (and white-water expert) Gail comes to the aid of river novices Wade (boyishly menacing Bacon) and Terry (Reilly), who quickly turn out to be violent criminals needing Gail's help with their escape. Slow start leads to nonstop thrills with Streep an adept action heroine, though undercut by the flic's need to do something with Strathairn's thankless role. Beautiful Montana and Oregon settings. **111m/C VHS, DVD.** Meryl Streep, David Strathairn, Joseph Mazzello, Kevin Bacon, John C. Reilly, Benjamin Bratt; ***D:*** Curtis Hanson; ***W:*** Raynold Gideon; ***C:*** Robert Elswit; ***M:*** Jerry Goldsmith.

Riverbend 🦴🦴 **1989 (R)** A renegade black Army major escapes a rigged court martial only to be persecuted by racist whites in a small Southern town. **106m/C VHS.** Steve James, Tony Frank, Julius Tennon, Margaret Avery; ***D:*** Sam Firstenberg. **TV**

River's Edge 🦴🦴🦴 **1987 (R)** Drug-addled high school student strangles his girlfriend and casually displays the corpse to his apathetic group of friends, who leave the murder unreported for days. Harrowing and gripping; based on a true story. Aging biker Hopper is splendid. **99m/C VHS, DVD, 8mm, Wide.** Keanu Reeves, Crispin Glover, Daniel Roebuck, Joshua John Miller, Dennis Hopper, Ione Skye, Roxana Zal, Tom Bower, Constance Forslund, Leo Rossi, Jim Metzler; ***D:*** Tim Hunter; ***W:*** Neal Jimenez; ***C:*** Frederick Elmes; ***M:*** Jurgen Knieper. Ind. Spirit '88: Film, Screenplay; Sundance '87: Special Jury Prize.

RKO 281 🦴🦴🦴 **1999 (R)** This retelling of Orson Welles' (Schrieber) battles to make 1941's "Citizen Kane" is all about egos. Welles had the arrogance of youth and Hearst the arrogance of power. The film, written with Herman J. Mankiewicz (Malkovich), was a thinly disguised look at newspaper magnate William Randolph Hearst (Cromwell) and his life with longtime mistress, blond actress Marion Davies (Griffith). Hearst was so outraged by Welles' movie that he tried to use his considerable influence with the Hollywood studios to have the film destroyed. Naturally, the story is both streamlined and altered but the leading roles are dramatically well served. **87m/C VHS, DVD.** Liev Schreiber, John Malkovich, James Cromwell, Melanie Griffith, Brenda Blethyn, Roy Scheider, David Suchet, Fiona Shaw, Liam Cunningham, Tim Woodward; ***D:*** Ridley Scott; ***W:*** John Logan; ***C:*** Mike Southon; ***M:*** John Altman. **CABLE**

The Road 🦴🦴 *El Camino* **2000** Manuel is on his way to a family funeral (by motorcycle) when he meets photographer Caroline on the road. Their romance is tested when Manuel is suddenly arrested and thrown in jail—only to escape after seeing a cop beat an inmate to death. The lovers are on the run but the end of the road is not the end of the journey. Spanish with subtitles. **107m/C VHS, DVD.** *AR* Ezequiel Rodriquez, Antonella Costa, Daniel Valenzuela, Hector Anglada, Alejandro Awada, Ruben Patagonia; ***D:*** Javier Olivera; ***W:*** Hector Olivera, Javier Olivera; ***C:*** Cristian Cottet; ***M:*** Axel Krygier.

Road Agent 🦴½ *Texas Road Agent* **1926** Hoxie is the Kansas Kid, a fugitive hired by a crooked lawyer to pose as the long-lost heir to a ranching fortune. Only the Kid develops a soft spot for his "family" and may not be able to go through with the evil plot. **70m/B VHS.** Al Hoxie; ***D:*** J(ohn) P(aterson) McGowan.

Road Ends 🦴🦴½ **1998 (R)** Small town sheriff Hopper and local innkeeper Hemingway unwittingly offer refuge to runaway FBI informant, Maceda (Sarandon), who's supposed to testify against his drug trafficking boss. FBI agent Gere (Coyote) is after Maceda as well as his ex-employers—and it's just a matter of who catches up to him first. **98m/C VHS, DVD.** Chris Sarandon, Peter Coyote, Dennis Hopper, Mariel Hemingway, Joanna Gleason; ***D:*** Rick King; ***W:*** Bill Mesce Jr.; ***C:*** Bruce Douglas Johnson; ***M:*** David Mansfield.

The Road from Coorain 🦴🦴½ **2002** Based on the 1989 memoir by historian Jill Ker Conway who was born and raised on a vast and isolated Australian sheep ranch called Coorain. The story, which opens in the early 1940s, deals with Jill's difficult relationship with her stoical mother Eve (Stevenson), who keeps Coorain even after being widowed and moving her family to Sydney. Jill proves to be an exceptional student and excels at university but family tragedies continue to haunt the Kers. **120m/C VHS.** *AU* Juliet Stevenson, Richard Roxburgh, Katherine Slattery, Alex Tomasetti, Tim Guinee, John Howard, Bernard Curry, Sean Hall; ***D:*** Brendan Maher; ***W:*** Sue Smith; ***C:*** Tristan Milani; ***M:*** Stephen Rae. **TV**

Road Games 🦴🦴 **1981 (PG)** Trucker Keach is drawn into a web of intrigue surrounding a series of highway "Jack the Ripper"-style murders. Curtis is a hitchhiker. Nothing special. Director Franklin later helmed "Psycho II." **100m/C VHS.** *AU* Stacy Keach, Jamie Lee Curtis, Marion Edwards, Grant Page, Bill Stacey, Thaddeus Smith, Alan Hopgood; ***D:*** Richard Franklin; ***W:*** Everett De Roche; ***C:*** Vincent Monton; ***M:*** Brian May.

The Road Home 🦴🦴½ **1995 (PG)** Depression-era heart-tugger features two orphaned brothers who ride the rails from New York to Nebraska in search of a new home at Father Flanagan's Boys Town. **90m/C VHS.** Keegan Macintosh, Will Estes, Kris Kristofferson, Charles Martin Smith, Danny Aiello, Dee Wallace Stone, Mickey Rooney; ***D:*** Dean Hamilton.

The Road Home 🦴🦴🦴 *Wo De Fu Qin Mu Qin* **2001 (G)** Sweet story about enduring love. Luo Yuseng (Honglei) returns to his Chinese village to bury his father. He learns his mother wants to have a funeral ritual performed as a mark of respect, which involves carrying the coffin to the cemetery. Flashbacks show how young illiterate beauty Zhao Di (Ziyi) caught the eye of Luo Changyu (Hao), the new schoolteacher, who comes from the city and is of a higher class. But Changyu falls victim to the political climate of the '50s and must leave her behind, promising to return. And she promises to wait. The flashbacks are filmed in color while the present is filmed in B&W. Chinese with subtitles. **89m/C VHS, DVD, Wide.** *CH* Zhang Ziyi, Sun Honglei, Zheng Hao, Zhao Yuelin, Li Bin; ***D:*** Zhang Yimou; ***W:*** Bao Shi; ***C:*** Hou Yong; ***M:*** San Bao.

Road House 🦴🦴½ **1948** Nightclub singer Lupino inspires noir feelings between jealous road house owner Widmark and his partner Wilde. Widmark sets up Wilde to take the fall for a faked robbery, convinces the law to release him into his custody, then dares him to escape. **95m/B VHS.** Richard Widmark, Ida Lupino, Cornel Wilde, Celeste Holm, O.Z. Whitehead; *D:* Jean Negulesco.

Road House ♪½ **1989 (R)** Bouncer Swayze is hired to do the impossible: clean up the toughest bar in Kansas City. When he lays down his rules he makes a lot of enemies, including ex-bar employees and local organized crime. Ample violence; an example of formula filmmaking at its most brain-numbing, with a rock soundtrack. **115m/C VHS, 8mm, Wide.** Patrick Swayze, Sam Elliott, Kelly Lynch, Ben Gazzara, Kevin Tighe, Marshall Teague, Julie Michaels, Jeff Healey; *D:* Rowdy Herrington; *C:* Dean Cundey; *M:* Michael Kamen.

Road Kill USA ♪♪½ **1993** Two sleazy drifters on a cross-country murder spree pick up a hitchhiking college student and expect him to join in the fun. When he refuses, he has two choices: kill or be killed. **98m/C VHS.** Andrew Porter, Sean Bridges, Deanna Perry; *D:* Tony Elwood.

The Road Killers ♪♪ **1995 (R)** Sickening psycho Cliff (well-played by Sheffer) is head of a brutal quartet that terrorizes a family driving along a remote desert highway. Cliff kidnaps the family daughter and her mild-mannered dad (Lambert) must rescue her. **89m/C VHS.** Christopher Lambert, Craig Sheffer, Adrienne Shelly; *D:* Deran Sarafian; *W:* Tedi Sarafian.

Road Movie ♪♪½ **1972** Cult favorite about a pair of brutish truck drivers (Bostwick and Drivas) who pick up a prostitute (Baff) on a trip across America. Baff delivers an emotional performance as the beaten and furious hooker who, after being abused and rejected, seeks her revenge. **82m/C DVD, Wide.** Barry Bostwick, Robert Drivas, Regina Baff; *D:* Joseph Strick; *W:* Judith Rascoe; *C:* Don Lenzer.

Road Racers ♪♪ **1959** The roar of the engine, fast cars, and family ties combine in this movie about the thrill of speed. **73m/B VHS.** Joel Lawrence, Marian Collier, Skip Ward; *D:* Arthur Swerdloff; *W:* Stanley Kallis, Ed Lasko.

Road Show ♪♪½ **1941** Menjou stars as a young man wrongfully committed to an insane asylum. He escapes and joins a bankrupt carnival owned by Landis. Some really zany stuff keeps this from being just standard fare. Co-written by silent film comic Langdon. **87m/B VHS.** Adolphe Menjou, Carole Landis, John Hubbard, Charles Butterworth, Patsy Kelly, George E. Stone, Polly Ann Young, Edward Norris, Marjorie Woodworth, Florence Bates; *D:* Hal Roach; *W:* Harry Langdon.

The Road to Bali ♪♪♪ **1953** Sixth Bob-n-Bing road show, the only one in color, is a keeper. The boys are competing for the love of—that's right—Lamour. She must be some gal, cuz they chase her all the way to Bali, where they meet cannibals and other perils, including the actual Humphrey Bogart. Jones's debut, in a bit role. ♫Moonflowers; Chicago Style; Hoots Mon; To See You; The Merry-Go-Runaround; Chorale for Brass, Piano, and Bongo (instrumental). **90m/C VHS, DVD.** Bob Hope, Bing Crosby, Dorothy Lamour, Murvyn Vye, Ralph Moody, Jane Russell, Jerry Lewis, Dean Martin, Carolyn Jones; *D:* Hal Walker; *W:* Frank Butler, Hal Kanter, William Morrow; *C:* George Barnes.

The Road to El Dorado ♪♪½ **2000 (PG)** Spanish con men Tulio (Kline) and Miguel (Branagh) search for the legendary Lost City of Gold in this animated mix of the Crosby-Hope "Road" pictures and Kipling's "Man Who Would Be King." The duo hitch a ride with Cortes's expedition to South America, land among the natives, and are mistaken for gods. They also run into a beautiful local (Perez) who's onto their game and agrees to help them, and run afoul of the local priest, who's fond of human sacrifice and wants to overthrow the kindly chief (Olmos). As usual, the animation is superb, and there are enjoyable moments throughout, but a weak plot and nondescript characters add up to a somewhat disappointing outing. **90m/C VHS, DVD, Wide.** *D:* Eric Bergeron, Don Paul; *W:* Ted Elliott, Terry Rossio; *M:* Elton John, Hans Zimmer, John Powell, Tim Rice; *V:* Kevin Kline, Kenneth Branagh, Rosie Perez, Armand Assante, Edward James Olmos; *Nar:* Elton John.

The Road to Galveston ♪♪♪ **1996 (PG-13)** Texas widow Jordan Roosevelt (Tyson) needs to pay her mortgage so she turns her home into a residence for three Alzheimer patients. When her financial problems only worsen, Jordan decides to fulfill her lifetime goal and takes everyone on a trip to Galveston to see the ocean. Sentimental, fact-based TV movie cuts the saccharine through compelling performances. **93m/C VHS.** Cicely Tyson, Piper Laurie, Tess Harper, Salle Ellis, Starletta DuPois, James McDaniel, Penny Johnson, Clarence Williams III, Stephen (Steve) Root; *D:* Michael Toshiyuki Uno; *W:* Tony Lee; *M:* Stanley Clarke.

The Road to Hong Kong ♪♪½ **1962** Last of the Crosby/Hope team-ups shows some wear, but still manages charm and humor. Lamour appears only briefly in this twisted comedy of hustlers caught in international espionage and cosmic goings-on. ♫Teamwork; Let's Not Be Sensible; It's The Only Way to Travel; We're On the Road to Hong Kong; Warmer Than a Whisper. **91m/B VHS.** Bob Hope, Bing Crosby, Joan Collins, Dorothy Lamour, Peter Sellers; *D:* Norman Panama; *W:* Norman Panama; *C:* Jack Hildyard.

The Road to Lebanon ♪♪ **1960** An original musical comedy featuring many stars, spoofing the famous Hope-Crosby "Road" films. **50m/B VHS.** Danny Thomas, Bing Crosby, Bob Hope, Hugh Downs, Claudine Auger, Sheldon Leonard.

The Road to Life ♪♪ *Putyovka V Zhizn* **1931** In the turmoil caused by Russia's Revolutionary and Civil wars, thousands of orphans roam the countryside resorting to petty crime to survive. One group is sent to a collective as part of an experimental program where they can be reformed and learn a trade but their criminal pasts seem inescapable. Russian with subtitles. **100m/B VHS.** *RU* Nikolai Batalov, Maria Gonfa, Tsifan Kyria; *D:* Nicolai Ekk; *W:* Nicolai Ekk; *M:* Yakov Stollyar.

The Road to Morocco ♪♪♪½ **1942** The third in the road movie series finds Hope and Crosby in Morocco, stranded and broke. To get some money, Crosby sells Hope into slavery to be the princess's (Lamour) personal plaything. Feeling guilty, Crosby returns to the palace to rescue Hope, only to find that he and the princess are getting married because the royal astrologer said it was in the stars. Crosby then tries to woo Lamour and, when the astrologer discovers the stars were mistaken, those two decide to marry. Quinn, however, also wants her and hilarious scenes ensue when the boys rescue Lamour from him. One of the funniest in the series. Watch for the camel at the end. ♫Constantly; Moonlight Becomes You; Ain't Got a Dime to My Name; Road to Morocco. **83m/C VHS, DVD.** Bing Crosby, Bob Hope, Dorothy Lamour, Anthony Quinn, Dona Drake, Vladimir Sokoloff, Yvonne De Carlo; *D:* David Butler; *W:* Frank Butler, Don Hartman; *C:* William Mellor. Natl. Film Reg. '96.

Road to Nashville ♪♪ **1967 (G)** An agent travels to Nashville to enlist talent for a new musical. Why do so many of these semi-musicals insist on having a plot? Good music. **110m/C VHS, DVD.** Marty Robbins, Johnny Cash, Doodles Weaver, Connie Smith, Richard Arlen; *D:* Robert Patrick.

Road to Nhill ♪♪ **1997** Very Aussie comedy filled with eccentric characters. An isolated, rural community is thrown into a tizzy when four female members of the local bowling team are in an accident that traps them in their overturned car. Volunteer emergency services rush into action but head off in the wrong direction and the women finally manage to free themselves, with various local yokels inept aid at the scene. Ensemble cast is fine. **95m/C VHS.** *AU* Lynette Curran, Patricia Kennedy, Lois Ramsey, Monica Maughan, Paul Chubb, Bill Hunter, Kerry Walker, Matthew Dyktynski, Terry Norris, Bill Young, Tony Barry, Alwyn Kurts; *D:* Sue Brooks; *W:* Alison Tilson; *C:* Nicolette Freeman; *M:* Elizabeth Drake.

Road to Perdition **2002 (R)** Michael Sullivan (Hanks) is a Depression-era hitman, known as "the Angel of Death," who wants revenge on those who killed his wife and younger son, while taking his teenaged son (Hoechlin) along for the ride. Based on the 1998 graphic novel by Max Allan Collins and Richard Piers Rayner. Not yet reviewed. **?m/C VHS, DVD.** Tom Hanks, Paul Newman, Jude Law, Tyler Hoechlin, Jennifer Jason Leigh, Stanley Tucci; *D:* Sam Mendes; *W:* David Self.

The Road to Rio ♪♪♪½ **1947** The wisecracking duo travel to Rio De Janeiro to prevent Spanish beauty Lamour (there she is again) from going through with an arranged marriage. Top-notch entry; fifth in the "Road" series. ♫But Beautiful; You Don't Have To Know the Language; For What?; Experience; Apalachicola, Florida; Cavaquinho; Brazil. **100m/B VHS, DVD.** Bing Crosby, Bob Hope, Dorothy Lamour, Gale Sondergaard, Frank Faylen, The Andrews Sisters; *D:* Norman Z. McLeod; *W:* Jack Rose; *C:* Ernest Laszlo.

The Road to Ruin ♪♪ **1928** The evils of smoking and drinking plummet a girl into a life of prostitution in this melodramatic, moralistic tale. An unintentional laugh-riot right up there with "Reefer Madness." Silent. **45m/B VHS, DVD.** Helen Foster, Grant Withers, Virginia Roye; *D:* Norton S. Parker; *W:* Erik Anjou; *C:* James Diamond.

Road to Ruin ♪♪ **1991 (R)** A rich playboy pretends to lose all his money to see if his girlfriend loves him for himself or for his wealth. But when his business partner embezzles his fortune, he must regain both his money and his girlfriend's trust. **94m/C VHS.** Peter Weller, Carey Lowell, Michael Duchaussoy; *D:* Charlotte Brandstrom.

Road to Salina ♪♪♪ **1968 (R)** A drifter is mistaken for (and might actually be) a desert-restaurant owner's long-lost son. He plays along, eventually seducing the family's daughter, who might be his sister. **97m/C VHS.** *FR* Robert Walker Jr., Rita Hayworth, Mimsy Farmer, Ed Begley Sr.; *D:* Georges Lautner.

The Road to Singapore ♪♪½ **1940** This is the movie that started it all. Crosby and Hope decide to swear off women and escape to Singapore to enjoy the free life. There they meet Lamour, a showgirl who is abused by Quinn. The boys rescue Lamour, but soon find they are both falling for her. She's in love with one of them, but won't reveal her feelings. Who will get the girl? Not as funny as some of the other road movies, but it's great for a first try. ♫Captain Custard; The Moon and the Willow Tree; Sweet Potato Piper; Too Romantic; Kaigoon. **84m/C VHS, DVD.** Bing Crosby, Bob Hope, Dorothy Lamour, Charles Coburn, Judith Barrett, Anthony Quinn, Jerry Colonna, Johnny Arthur, Pierre Watkin; *D:* Victor Schertzinger; *W:* Frank Butler, Don Hartman; *C:* William Mellor.

The Road to Utopia ♪♪♪ **1946** Fourth of the "Road" films, wherein the boys wind up in Alaska posing as two famous escaped killers in order to locate a secret gold mine. One of the series' funniest and most spontaneous entries, abetted by Benchley's dry, upper-crust comments. ♫Put It There, Pal; Welcome to My Dreams; Would You?; Personality; Sunday, Monday, or Always?; Goodtime Charlie; It's Anybody's Spring. **90m/B VHS, DVD.** Bing Crosby, Bob Hope, Dorothy Lamour, Jack LaRue, Robert Benchley, Douglass Dumbrille, Hillary Brooke, Robert Barrat, Nestor Paiva; *D:* Hal Walker; *W:* Norman Panama, Melvin Frank; *C:* Lionel Lindon; *M:* Johnny Burke, Leigh Harline, James Van Heusen.

The Road to Wellville ♪♪ **1994 (R)** Corn flake magnate John Harvey Kellogg takes good health to an intestine-invading extreme in this spa satire featuring Hopkins as the buck-toothed Kellogg. Broderick and Fonda portray a wealthy couple who visit the turn-of-the-century sanitarium in search of Kellogg's cure, but receive only sexual frustration and anal humiliations. Bowel jokes and an essentially plotless scenario overshadow a gifted, but helpless cast. Adapted from T. Coraghessan Boyle's not-so-easily-adaptable novel. **120m/C VHS.** Anthony Hopkins, Bridget Fonda, Matthew Broderick, John Cusack, Dana Carvey, Michael Lerner, Colm Meaney, John Neville, Lara Flynn Boyle, Traci Lind, Roy Brocksmith, Norbert Weisser; *D:* Alan Parker; *W:* Alan Parker; *C:* Peter Biziou; *M:* Rachel Portman.

The Road to Yesterday ♪♪♪½ **1925** Two couples together on a crashing train are somehow thrown into the 18th century in roles parallel to their own lives. DeMille's first independent film; intriguing action/melodrama. Silent with musical soundtrack. **136m/B VHS.** Joseph Schildkraut, William Boyd, Jetta Goudal, Vera Reynolds, Iron Eyes Cody; *D:* Cecil B. DeMille.

The Road to Zanzibar ♪♪♪ **1941** After selling a fake diamond mine to a criminal, Crosby and Hope flee to Zanzibar, where they meet up with Lamour and Merkel. The guys put up the money for a safari, supposedly to look for Lamour's brother, but they soon discover that they too have been tricked. Deciding to head back to Zanzibar, Crosby and Hope find themselves surrounded by hungry cannibals. Will they survive, or will they be someone's dinner? Not as funny as the other road movies, but amusing nonetheless. ♫It's Always You; You're Dangerous; On the Road to Zanzibar; You Lucky People You; Birds of a Feather; African Etude. **92m/C VHS, DVD.** Bing Crosby, Bob Hope, Dorothy Lamour, Una Merkel, Eric Blore, Iris Adrian, Lionel Royce; *D:* Victor Schertzinger; *W:* Frank Butler, Don Hartman; *C:* Ted Tetzlaff.

Road Trip ♪♪½ **2000 (R)** Extremely low-brow comedy about four college buddies who set out on an 1,800-mile road trip (from New York to Texas) in order to intercept an incriminating videotape Josh (Meyer) has mistakenly mailed to his long-distance girlfriend. Green does disgusting things to a defenseless white mouse, and there's the usual frat-house sexual humor, but like most teen comedies these days, it's quotable, laugh-even-though-you-know-better funny, and basically harmless. **91m/C VHS, DVD, Wide.** Breckin Meyer, Seann William Scott, Rachel Blanchard, DJ Qualls, Fred Ward, Andy Dick, Paulo Costanzo, Tom Green, Amy Smart, Anthony Rapp, Ethan Suplee; *D:* Todd Phillips; *W:* Todd Phillips, Scot Armstrong; *C:* Mark Irwin; *M:* Mike Simpson.

The Road Warrior ♪♪♪½ *Mad Max 2* **1982 (R)** The first sequel to "Mad Max" takes place after nuclear war has destroyed Australia. Max helps a colony of oil-drilling survivors defend themselves from the roving murderous outback gangs and escape to the coast. The climactic chase scene is among the most exciting ever filmed; this film virtually created the "action-adventure" picture of the 1980s. **95m/C VHS, DVD, Wide.** *AU* Mel Gibson, Bruce Spence, Emil Minty, Vernon Wells, Virginia Hey, Max Phipps, Mike (Michael) Preston, William Zappa; *D:* George Miller; *W:* George Miller, Terry Hayes; *C:* Dean Semler; *M:* Brian May. L.A. Film Critics '82: Foreign Film.

Roadhouse Girl ♪ *Marilyn* **1953** A sexy woman kindles a romance with one of her husband's employees and the result is murder. Reminiscent of "The Postman Always Rings Twice," but with poor production values and performances. **70m/B VHS.** *GB* Maxwell Reed, Sandra Dorne, Leslie Dwyer, Vida Hope, Ferdinand "Ferdy" Mayne; *D:* Wolf Rilla; *W:* Wolf Rilla.

Roadhouse 66 ♪½ **1984 (R)** Utterly unoriginal broke-down-in-a-hick-town nonsense. Snooty Reinhold and scruffy Dafoe go through the motions, and of course find a pair of female companions. Soundtrack features Los Lobos, the Pretenders, and Dave Edmunds. **90m/C VHS.** Willem Dafoe, Judge Reinhold, Karen Lee, Kate Vernon, Stephen Elliott; *D:* John Mark Robinson; *C:* Thomas Ackerman.

Roadie ♪½ **1980 (PG)** Supposedly a look at the back-stage world of rock 'n' roll, but the performance and direction leave a lot to be desired. Meatloaf is a roadie who desperately wants to meet Alice Cooper, and spends the movie trying to do so. Features Art Carney, and musical names like Blondie, Roy Orbison, Hank Williams Jr., and Don Cornelius (of "Soul Train" fame). **105m/C VHS.** Meat Loaf Aday, Kaki Hunter, Art Carney, Gailard Sartain, Alice Cooper, Roy Orbison, Hank Williams Jr., Ramblin' Jack Elliot; **D:** Alan Rudolph; **W:** Alan Rudolph, Michael Ventura.

Roadkill 🦴 **1989** Cheap thriller about Ramona (Buhagiar), a concert promoter who tries to find a lost band, "The Children of Paradise," in the Canadian north woods. Along the way, she meets a would-be serial killer and other assorted weirdos. **85m/B VHS.** *CA* Valerie Buhagiar, Don McKellar, Bruce McDonald; **D:** Bruce McDonald; **W:** Don McKellar. Toronto-City '89: Canadian Feature Film.

Roadracers 🦴🦴 **1994 (R)** Made as part of Showtime's "Rebel Highway" series, Rodriguez basically takes the title from the 1959 AIP low-budgeter and goes his own way. Leather-clad rebel Dude Delaney (Arquette) has a voluptuous Latino dreamgirl named Donna (Hayek) and a gang which faces off against the clique led by rival Teddy Leather (Wiles) in drag races and roller rinks all around town. Great rockabilly soundtrack. **95m/C VHS.** David Arquette, Jason Wiles, Salma Hayek, John Hawkes, William Sadler, O'Neal Compton, Lance LeGault, Karen Landry, Tommy Nix; **D:** Robert Rodriguez; **W:** Robert Rodriguez, Tommy Nix; **C:** Roberto Schaefer; **M:** Paul Boll, Johnny Reno. CABLE

Roads to the South 🦴🦴½ *Les Routes du Sud* **1978** One-time Spanish revolutionary turned screenwriter returns to his homeland to fight fascism, but finds himself attracted to his son's beautiful girlfriend. Much soul searching. In French with English subtitles. **100m/C VHS.** *FR* Yves Montand, Miou-Miou, Laurent Malet, Mario Gonzalez, Jose Luis Gomez, Jeannine Mestre, Roger Planchon, Didier Sauvegrain; **D:** Joseph Losey; **W:** Jorge Semprun; **C:** Gerry Fisher; **M:** Michel Legrand.

Roadside Prophets 🦴🦴 **1992 (R)** Counter-culture road trip, striving to be the '90s version of "Easy Rider," follows factory worker/biker Joe (Doe) on his mission to transport the ashes of a fellow biker to Nevada. He is accompanied by the pesky younger Sam (Horovitz), and together they meet up with lots of eccentrics and stay at lots of cheap motels. Interesting cast meanders through sentimental and slow-moving buddy flick from debut director Wool, who wrote "Sid and Nancy." Cusack completes the cameo hat trick, with appearances here and in 1992's "The Player" and "Shadows and Fog." **96m/C VHS.** John Doe, Adam Horovitz, David Carradine, Timothy Leary, Arlo Guthrie, Barton Heyman, Jennifer Balgobin, John David (J.D.) Cullum; ***Cameos:*** John Cusack; **D:** Abbe Wool; **W:** Abbe Wool.

The Roamin' Cowboy 🦴🦴 **1937** In a town where the local ranchers are being threatened, a drifter comes to their rescue and wins both a girl and a job. **56m/B VHS.** Fred Scott, Al "Fuzzy" St. John, Lois January, Forrest Taylor, Roger Williams; **D:** Robert F. "Bob" Hill.

Roamin' Wild 🦴🦴½ **1936** Exciting, action-packed early western with marshal Tyler saving a lady's stagecoach line from unsavory varmints. **60m/B VHS.** Tom Tyler, Carol Wyndham, Al Ferguson, George Chesebro, Max Davidson, Fred Parker; **D:** Bernard B. Ray.

Roanoak 🦴🦴½ **1986** A dramatization in three parts of the mysterious fate of the early English settlement of Roanoak in North Carolina, which disappeared without a trace. Long, but intriguing. Made for PBS: "American Playhouse." **180m/C** Will Sampson, Victoria Racimo, Porky White, Adrian Sparks, Patrick Kilpatrick; **D:** Jan Egleson. TV

Roarin' Lead 🦴½ **1937** Three Mesquiteers fight with a gang of rustlers while helping the orphans' and cattlemen's associations. **54m/B VHS.** Robert "Bob" Livingston, Ray Corrigan, Max Terhune.

Roaring City 🦴½ **1951** A hard-boiled detective searches for the person behind the murders of gangsters and prize fighters. **58m/B VHS.** Hugh Beaumont, Edward Brophy, Richard Travis; **D:** William Berke.

Roaring Guns 🦴🦴½ **1936** An unflappable McCoy rides in to thwart a despicable landowner trying to drive all the small ranchers out of business. Low-budget fun. **66m/B VHS.** Tim McCoy, Rex Lease, Wheeler Oakman; **D:** Sam Newfield.

Roaring Ranch 🦴½ **1930** Gibson is trying to protect his ranch from the evil Oakman while attempting to care for a baby as well. **65m/B VHS.** Hoot Gibson, Wheeler Oakman, Sally Eilers, Bobby Nelson, Frank Clark; **D:** B. Reeves Eason; **W:** B. Reeves Eason.

The Roaring Road 🦴🦴½ **1919** Romantic comedy about a car salesman named Toodles, who drives for his company in a big race. Vintage racing footage; silent with original organ music. **57m/B VHS, 8mm.** Wallace Reid, Ann Little, Theodore Roberts; **D:** James Cruze.

Roaring Roads 🦴 **1935** An heir to a fortune acquires a lust for race car driving, and his family thinks, a reckless death wish. **60m/B VHS.** Gertrude Messinger, David Sharpe.

Roaring Six Guns 🦴½ **1937** Maynard protects his property against his crooked partner and his fiancee's father. **60m/B VHS.** Kermit Maynard, Mary Hayes, John Merton, Edward Cassidy.

Roaring Speedboats 🦴 *Mile a Minute Love* **1937** Bakewell is a speedboat racer up against crooks who want to con him out of his money by tinkering with his invention. **62m/B VHS, 8mm.** William "Billy" Bakewell, Arletta Duncan, Duncan Renaldo, Vivien Oakland, Wilfrid Lucas; **D:** Elmer Clifton.

The Roaring Twenties 🦴🦴🦴½ **1939** Eddie (Cagney), George (Bogart), and Lloyd (Lynn) are three WWI buddies who find their lives intersecting unexpectedly in Prohibition-era New York. Eddie becomes a bootlegger and vies with George for status as crime boss. Lloyd is the attorney working to prosecute them. Great gangster flick was the last time Bogart and Cagney worked together after "Angels with Dirty Faces" (1938) and "The Oklahoma Kid" (1939). Cheesy script delivered with zest by top pros. **106m/B VHS.** James Cagney, Humphrey Bogart, Jeffrey Lynn, Priscilla Lane, Gladys George, Frank McHugh, Paul Kelly, Joseph (Joe) Sawyer; **D:** Raoul Walsh; **W:** Robert Rossen, Richard Macaulay; **C:** Ernest Haller; **M:** Heinz Roemheld, Ray Heindorf.

Rob Roy 🦴🦴🦴 **1995 (R)** Kilt-raising though overlong tale of legendary Scot Robert Roy MacGregor mixes love and honor with bloodlust and revenge. Neeson's rugged clan leader fends off a band of dastardly nobles led by Cunningham (Roth), a foppish twit with an evil bent. Misty highland scenery and intense romantic interplay between Neeson and Lange as the spirited Mary MacGregor lend a passionate twist to an otherwise earthy, robust adventure of lore capped by one of the best sword fights in years. Both Neeson and Lange provide a gutsy substance to their characters: Neeson's Celtic hero is sexy and steadfast (and generally sports an Irish accent), while Lange inhabits a soulful and tenacious Mary. Roth's delightfully hammy performance as MacGregor's loathsome, bewigged nemesis delivers zip amid the high-minded speeches, plot lulls, and separated body parts. Visually stunning, with on-location shooting in the Scottish Highlands. More ambience is provided by Buswell's evocative score. **144m/C VHS, DVD.** Liam Neeson, Jessica Lange, Tim Roth, John Hurt, Eric Stoltz, Andrew Keir, Brian Cox, Brian McCardie, Gilbert Martin, Vicki Masson, David Hayman, Jason Flemyng, Shirley Henderson, Gilly Gilchrist, John Murtagh, Ewan Stewart; **D:** Michael Caton-Jones; **W:** Alan Sharp; **C:** Karl Walter Lindenlaub, Roger Deakins; **M:** Carter Burwell. British Acad. '95: Support. Actor (Roth).

Rob Roy—The Highland Rogue 🦴½ *Rob Roy* **1953** In the early 18th century, Scottish Highlander Rob Roy must battle against the King of England's secretary, who would undermine the MacGregor clan to enact his evil deeds. Dull Disney drama. **84m/C VHS.** Richard Todd, Glynis Johns, James Robertson Justice, Michael Gough; **D:** Harold French.

Robbers of the Sacred Mountain 🦴🦴 *Falcon's Gold* **1983** TV rip-off of "Raiders of the Lost Ark," loosely based on Arthur Conan Doyle's story "Challenger's Gold." Adventurers seek meteorites in the Mexican jungle. Billed as the first made-for-cable movie. **95m/C VHS.** John Marley, Simon MacCorkindale, Louise Vallance, George Touliatos; **D:** Bob Schulz. CABLE

Robbery 🦴🦴½ **1967** Unoriginal but competent rendition of the hackneyed British Royal Mail robbery. Thieves plan and execute a heist of a late-night mail train carrying $10 million. **113m/C VHS.** *GB* Stanley Baker, James Booth, Joanna Pettet, Frank Finlay, Barry Foster; **D:** Peter Yates.

Robbery 🦴 **1985** A six-man platoon of Vietnam war veterans endeavors to assault and rob a mob of shiftless bookies. **91m/C VHS.** John Sheerin, Tony Rickards, Tim Hughes; **D:** Michael Thornhill.

Robbery under Arms 🦴🦴½ **1957** From Australia in the 1800s, similar to the American wild west, comes a tale of love and robbery. Finch is the leader of a band of outlaws. Rather dull story redeemed by excellent photography of beautiful landscape. **83m/C VHS.** *GB* Peter Finch, Ronald Lewis, Laurence Naismith, Maureen Swanson, David McCallum, Jill Ireland; **D:** Jack Lee.

Robby 🦴🦴 **1968** A young white boy and a young black boy shipwrecked on an island form a strong friendship that sees them through a series of adventures. **60m/C VHS.** Warren Raum, Ryp Siani, John Garces; **D:** Ralph Blumke.

The Robe 🦴🦴½ **1953** This moving, religious portrait follows the career and religious awakening of drunken and dissolute Roman tribune Marcellus (Burton), after he wins the robe of the just-crucified Christ in a dice game. Mature plays Burton's slave surprisingly well, and reprised the role in the sequel, "Demetrius and the Gladiators"; Burton is wooden. "The Robe" was the first movie to be filmed in CinemaScope. Based on the novel by Lloyd C. Douglas. **133m/C VHS, DVD, Wide.** Richard Burton, Jean Simmons, Victor Mature, Michael Rennie, Richard Boone, Dean Jagger, Jeff Morrow, Jay Robinson, Dawn Addams, Ernest Thesiger, Torin Thatcher; **D:** Henry Koster; **W:** Albert (John B. Sherry) Maltz, Philip Dunne; **C:** Leon Shamroy. Oscars '53: Art Dir./Set Dec., Color, Costume Des. (C); Golden Globes '54: Film—Drama; Natl. Bd. of Review '53: Actress (Simmons).

Robert et Robert 🦴🦴🦴 **1978** Two 'ineligible' bachelors resort to using a computerized matrimonial agency to find the girls of their dreams. They become friends while they wait for their dates. Sensitive tale of loneliness and friendship. Warm and witty with fine performances throughout. French with English subtitles. **105m/C VHS.** *FR* Charles Denner, Jacques Villeret, Jean-Claude Brialy, Macha Meril, Germaine Montero, Regine; **D:** Claude Lelouch; **W:** Claude Lelouch; **C:** Jacques Lefrancois. Cesar '79: Support. Actor (Villeret).

Robert Kennedy and His Times 🦴🦴½ **1990** Another look at the Kennedy clan, this time from the Bobby angle. Good acting. Based on the book by Arthur Schlesinger. **309m/C VHS.** Brad Davis, Veronica Cartwright, Cliff DeYoung, Ned Beatty, Beatrice Straight, Jack Warden; **D:** Marvin J. Chomsky.

Robert Louis Stevenson's St. Ives 🦴🦴½ *St. Ives; All for Love* **1998 (R)** During the Napoleonic Wars, dashing French officer, Captain Jacques St. Ives (Barr), is captured during battle and sent to a POW camp in the Scottish Highlands that is run by Major Chevening (Grant). St. Ives and the Major become friends but that doesn't mean that he won't try to escape, especially since Jacques has the aid of plucky lassie Flora (Friel). A leisurely paced costume romp. **90m/C VHS, DVD, Wide.** *GB* Jean-Marc Barr, Anna Friel, Richard E. Grant, Miranda Richardson, Michael Gough, Jason Isaacs, Tim Dutton, Cecile Pallas; **D:** Harry Hook; **W:** Allan Cubitt; **C:** Robert Alazraki.

Robert Louis Stevenson's The Game of Death 🦴🦴½ *The Suicide Club; The Game of Death; Robert Louis Stevenson's The Suicide Club* **1999 (R)** This version sticks to the spirit of Stevenson's story (which was filmed in 1936 as "Trouble for Two") but adds plotlines and characters. It's 1899 and Henry Joyce (Morrissey) has decided to kill himself because of his lover's betrayal. He and pal, Captain May (Shuke), meet the equally suicidal Shaw (Bettany), who takes them along to the Suicide Club. Run by the mysterious Bourne (Pryce), its members willingly want to die—and both the next victim and their murderer are selected by a drawing of the cards. And you aren't allowed to change your mind. **89m/C VHS, DVD, Wide.** David Morrissey, Jonathan Pryce, Paul Bettany, Neil Stuke, Catherine Siggins; **D:** Rachel Samuels; **W:** Lev L. Spiro; **C:** Chris Manley; **M:** Adrian Johnston.

Roberta 🦴🦴🦴 **1935** A football player inherits his aunt's Parisian dress shop and finds himself at odds with an incognito Russian princess. Dumb plot aside, this is one of the best Astaire-Rogers efforts. A later remake was titled "Lovely to Look At." ♫Let's Begin; Yesterdays; Smoke Gets in Your Eyes; I'll Be Hard to Handle; I Won't Dance; Lovely to Look At; Back Home Again in Indiana; The Touch of Your Hand; You're Devasting. **85m/B VHS.** Fred Astaire, Ginger Rogers, Irene Dunne, Lucille Ball, Randolph Scott; **D:** William A. Seiter; **M:** Max Steiner.

Robin and Marian 🦴🦴 **1976 (PG)** After a separation of 20 years, Robin Hood is reunited with Maid Marian, who is now a nun. Their dormant feelings for each other are reawakened as Robin spirits her to Sherwood Forest. In case you wanted to see Robin Hood robbed of all magic, spontaneity, and fun. Connery is dull, dull, dull, working with an uninspired script. **106m/C VHS.** *GB* Sean Connery, Audrey Hepburn, Robert Shaw, Richard Harris, Denholm Elliott, Ian Holm, Nicol Williamson, Ronnie Barker; **D:** Richard Lester; **C:** David Watkin; **M:** John Barry.

Robin and the 7 Hoods 🦴🦴½ **1964** Runyon-esque Rat Pack version of 1920s Chicago, with Frank and the boys as do-good gangsters in their last goround. Fun if not unforgettable. ♫Bang! Bang!; Style; Mister Booze; Don't Be a Do-Badder; My Kind of Town. **124m/C VHS, DVD, Wide.** Frank Sinatra, Bing Crosby, Dean Martin, Sammy Davis Jr., Peter Falk, Barbara Rush, Victor Buono, Hank Henry, Robert Foulk, Allen Jenkins, Jack LaRue, Edward G. Robinson, Hans Conried, Tony Randall; **D:** Gordon Douglas; **W:** John Fenton Murray; **C:** William H. Daniels; **M:** Nelson Riddle, James Van Heusen.

Robin Hood 🦴🦴🦴½ **1922** Extravagant production casts Fairbanks as eponymous gymnastic swashbuckler who departs for Crusades as Earl of Huntington and returns as the hooded one to save King Richard's throne from the sinister Sheriff of Nottingham. Best ever silent swashbuckling. **110m/B VHS, DVD.** Douglas Fairbanks Sr., Wallace Beery, Sam DeGrasse, Enid Bennett, Paul Dickey, William E. (W.E., William A., W.A.) Lowery, Roy Coulson, Bill Bennett, Merrill McCormick, Wilson Benge, Willard Louis, Alan Hale, Maine Geary, Lloyd Talman; **D:** Allan Dwan; **W:** Douglas Fairbanks Sr.; **C:** Arthur Edeson.

Robin Hood 🦴🦴🦴 **1973** This time the Sherwood Forest crew are portrayed by appropiate cartoon animals, hence, Robin is a fox, Little John a bear, etc. Good family fare, but not as memorable as other Disney features. **83m/C VHS, DVD.** **D:** Wolfgang Reitherman; **M:** George Bruns; **V:** Roger Miller, Brian Bedford, Monica Evans, Phil Harris, Andy Devine, Carol(e) Shelley, Peter Ustinov, Terry-Thomas, Pat Buttram, George Lindsey, Ken Curtis.

Robin Hood 🦴🦴🦴 **1991** Dark version of the medieval tale. Bergin's Prince of Thieves is well developed and Thurman is a graceful Marion. Three studios announced plans to remake "Robin Hood" in 1990 and two were completed, including this one which was scaled down for cable TV. **116m/C VHS.** Patrick Bergin, Uma Thurman, Juergen Prochnow, Edward Fox, Jeroen Krabbe, Jeff Nuttal, David Morrisey, Owen Teale; **D:** John Irvin; **M:** Geoffrey Burgon. CABLE

Robin Hood: Men in Tights 🦴🦴½ *Men in Tights* **1993 (PG-13)** Brooksian rendition of the classic legend inspires guffaws, but doesn't hit the bullseye on all it promises. Hood afficionados will appreciate the painstaking effort taken to spoof the 1938 Errol Flynn classic while leaving plenty of room to poke fun at the more recent Costner non-classic "Robin

Hood: Prince of Thieves." Elwes, last seen swinging swords in "The Princess Bride," is well cast as the Flynn look-alike. Expect the usual off-color humor that's so prevalent in all Brooks outings. **105m/C VHS.** Cary Elwes, Richard Lewis, Roger Rees, Amy Yasbeck, Dave Chappelle, Isaac Hayes, Tracey Ullman, Mark Blankfield, Megan Cavanagh, Eric Allen Kramer, Tony Griffin, Dick Van Patten, Mel Brooks; ***D:*** Mel Brooks; ***W:*** Mel Brooks, J. David Shapiro, Evan Chandler; ***M:*** Hummie Mann.

Robin Hood of Texas 🦴🦴½ **1947** Autry finds his calm life disturbed when he is falsely accused of robbing a bank. Pretty good plot for once, in Autry's last Republic western, and plenty of action. **71m/B VHS.** Gene Autry, Lynne Roberts, Sterling Holloway, Adele Mara; ***D:*** Lesley Selander.

Robin Hood of the Pecos 🦴🦴½ **1941** Ex-Confederate soldier takes on northern post-war politicians and carpetbaggers. Decent Rogers/Hayes outing. **56m/B VHS.** Roy Rogers, George "Gabby" Hayes, Marjorie Reynolds, Jay Novello, Roscoe Ates; ***D:*** Joseph Kane.

Robin Hood: Prince of Thieves 🦴🦴½ **1991 (PG-13)** Costner is the politically correct Rebel with a Cause, but a thinker, not a doer—and therein lies the problem. His quiet thoughtfulness doesn't add up to leadership and Rickman easily overpowers him as the wicked, crazed Sheriff of Nottingham. Freeman is excellent as a civilized Moor who finds England, and its people, inhospitable, dangerous, and not a little stupid. Mastrantonio, a last minute choice, excels as the lovely Lady Marian. Great action sequences, a gritty and morbid picture of the Middle Ages, and some fun scenes with the Merry Men. Revisionist in its ideas about the times and people, critics generally disapproved of the changes in the story and Costner's performance, though their comments about his lack of an English accent seem nitpicky in light of some basic plot problems. Still has lots of fun for lovers of action, romance and fairy tales. **144m/C VHS, DVD, Wide.** Kevin Costner, Morgan Freeman, Mary Elizabeth Mastrantonio, Christian Slater, Alan Rickman, Geraldine McEwan, Michael McShane, Brian Blessed, Michael Wincott, Nick Brimble, Harold Innocent, Jack Wild; ***Cameos:*** Sean Connery; ***D:*** Kevin Reynolds; ***W:*** Pen Densham, John Watson; ***C:*** Billy Milton; ***M:*** Michael Kamen. British Acad. '91: Support. Actor (Rickman); MTV Movie Awards '92: Song ("(Everything I Do) I Do for You"); Golden Raspberries '91: Worst Actor (Costner).

Robin Hood: The Movie 1955 A colorized and re-mixed version of several episodes of the British TV series adds up to a fine version of the classic tale. Excellent cast, clever editing, and stunning colorization. **90m/C VHS.** *GB* Richard Greene, Bernadette O'Farrell, Alan Wheatley; ***D:*** Ralph Smart, Daniel Birt, Terence Fisher. **TV**

Robin Hood...The Legend: Herne's Son 🦴🦴½ **1985** When Robin Hood is killed by the Sheriff of Nottingham, he begs Robert of Huntington (Connery) to continue his work. Connery refuses, the band dissolves, Maid Marion is kidnapped, and they reunite to save her. Good entry in the BBC series. **101m/C VHS.** *GB* Jason Connery, Oliver Cotton, Michael Craig, Nickolas Grace, George Baker; ***D:*** Robert M. Young. **TV**

Robin Hood...The Legend: Robin Hood and the Sorcerer 🦴🦴½ **1983** Robin Hood is chosen by the mystical Herne the Hunter to thwart the evil Sheriff of Nottingham and protect the English peasantry. He must defeat the supernatural powers of a sorcerer and gather together his men in this pilot for British TV. **115m/C VHS.** *GB* Michael Praed, Anthony Valentine, Nickolas Grace, Clive Mantle, Peter Williams; ***D:*** Ian Sharp. **TV**

Robin Hood...The Legend: The Swords of Wayland 🦴🦴½ **1983** A wicked sorceress provides a supernatural threat to Robin and his merry men. Second entry in the BBC series. Convoluted, breathless plot makes for swashbuckling fun and much derring-do. **115m/C VHS.** *GB* Michael Praed, Rula Lenska, Nickolas Grace; ***D:*** Robert M. Young. **TV**

Robin Hood...The Legend: The Time of the Wolf 🦴🦴½ **1985** Robin Hood finds out that an old enemy is about to release his evil doings on the world and only he can stop him, while Maid Marian comes to a momentous decision. **105m/C VHS.** *GB* Jason Connery, Nickolas Grace, Richard O'Brien; ***D:*** Syd Roberson. **TV**

Robin of Locksley 🦴🦴½ **1995 (PG)** A modern-day, teenaged Robin Hood (Sawa) battles the bullies at his private boys school (thanks to his archery prowess), meets a girl named Marian, and takes on sinister FBI agent Nottingham. **97m/C VHS.** Devon Sawa, Sarah Chalke, Joshua Jackson; ***D:*** Michael Kennedy.

Robinson Crusoe 🦴🦴 **1936** A real oddity: a British silent film originally made in 1927, re-edited ten years later. Music and sound effects were added, along with a narration by children's radio personality Carney. Follows the plot of the famous adventure story by Daniel Defoe. **34m/B VHS.** ***Nar:*** Uncle Don Carney.

Robinson Crusoe & the Tiger 🦴½ **1972 (G)** A tiger tells the famous story of how Robinson Crusoe became stranded on a desert island. **109m/C VHS.** Hugo Stiglitz, Ahui; ***D:*** Rene Cardona Jr.

Robinson Crusoe of Clipper Island 🦴🦴 **1936** Fourteen-episode serial featuring the investigative expertise of Mala, a Polynesian in the employ of the U.S. Intelligence Service. Each episode runs 16 minutes. Shortened version titled "Robinson Crusoe of Mystery Island." **256m/B VHS.** Mala, Rex, Buck, Kate Greenfield, John Ward, Tracy Lane, Robert F. (Bob) Kortman, Herbert Rawlinson; ***D:*** Mack V. Wright.

Robinson Crusoe of Mystery Island 🦴🦴 **1936** A Polynesian employed by the U.S. Intelligence Service investigates saboteurs on a mysterious island. Would-be cliffhanger is a yawner; where are the chills and thrills? Edited from the serial "Robinson Crusoe of Clipper Island." **100m/B VHS.** Mala, Rex, Buck, Herbert Rawlinson, Ray Taylor; ***D:*** Mack V. Wright.

Robinson Crusoe on Mars 🦴 **1964** Sci-fi interpretation of Defoe classic. West is one of two daring scientists who take a monkey with them on a mission to outer space. When a meteor strikes their ship, it hurtles out of control towards the red planet and only Mantee and Mona survive the wreckage. They meet Lundin, an escaped slave and teach him English until evil slave traders spoil the fun. **109m/C** Adam West, Vic Lundin, Paul Mantee; ***D:*** Byron Haskin; ***W:*** Ib Melchior, John C. Higgins; ***C:*** Winton C. Hoch; ***M:*** Nathan Van Cleave.

Robo-Chic *Cyber-Chic* **1989** A woman who is part cop, part machine, becomes a defender of justice. **90m/C VHS.** Kathy Shower, Jack Carter, Burt Ward, Lyle Waggoner; ***D:*** Ed Hansen, Jeffrey Mandel.

Robo Warriors 🦴🦴 **1996 (PG-13)** In the year 2036, Earth has been conquered by the Terridaxx, a half-human, half-reptile race. But 12-year-old Zac finds the last high-tech fighting machine, the Robo Warrior (Remar), and convinces him to help destroy the invaders. **94m/C VHS.** James Remar, James Lew.

RoboCop 🦴🦴🦴 **1987 (R)** A nearly dead Detroit cop, Alex Murphy (Weller), is used as the brain for a crime-fighting robot in this bleak vision of the future. Humor, satire, action, and violence keep this moving in spite of its underlying sadness. Slick animation techniques from Phil Tippet. Verhoeven's first American film. **103m/C VHS, DVD, Wide.** Peter Weller, Nancy Allen, Ronny Cox, Kurtwood Smith, Ray Wise, Miguel Ferrer, Dan O'Herlihy, Robert DoQui, Felton Perry, Paul McCrane, Del Zamora; ***D:*** Paul Verhoeven; ***W:*** Michael Miner, Edward Neumeier; ***C:*** Jan De Bont; ***M:*** Basil Poledouris.

RoboCop 2 🦴🦴 **1990 (R)** Grimer, more violent sequel to the initial fascinating look at the future, where police departments are run by corporations hungry for profit at any cost. A new and highly addictive drug has made Detroit more dangerous than ever. Robocop is replaced by a stronger cyborg with the brain of a brutal criminal. When the cyborg goes berserk, Robocop battles it and the drug lords for control of the city. Dark humor and graphic savagery, with little of the tenderness and emotion of the original. **117m/C VHS, DVD, Wide.** Peter Weller, Nancy Allen, Belinda Bauer, Dan O'Herlihy, Tom Noonan, Gabriel Damon, Galyn Gorg, Felton Perry, Patricia Charbonneau; ***D:*** Irvin Kershner; ***W:*** Walon Green; ***C:*** Mark Irwin; ***M:*** Leonard Rosenman.

RoboCop 3 🦴½ **1991 (PG-13)** Robocop's new Japanese owners plan to build a huge, new, ultra-modern city (in place of the decrepit 21st-century Detroit) but first must evict thousands of people in this third installment of the "Robocop" films (which sat on the studio shelf before finally being released in 1993). There's an android Ninja warrior to do battle with Robo who's gone over to the rebel underground but the plot and action sequences are rehashed from better films. Watch the original. **104m/C VHS, DVD, Wide.** Stephen (Steve) Root, Robert John Burke, Nancy Allen, John Castle, CCH Pounder, Bruce Locke, Rip Torn, Remi Ryan, Felton Perry; ***D:*** Fred Dekker; ***W:*** Frank Miller, Fred Dekker; ***C:*** Gary B. Kibbe; ***M:*** Basil Poledouris.

Roboman 🦴🦴½ *Who?* **1975 (PG)** American scientist gets in car crash in Soviet Union. When he returns to the States as a cyborg, his friends seem to notice a change. **91m/C VHS.** *GB GE* Elliott Gould, Trevor Howard, Joe Bova, Ed Grover, James Noble, John Lehne; ***D:*** Jack Gold.

Robot Holocaust 🦴🦴 **1987** Somewhere in the doomed future, after the Earth is laid waste by robots with superior intelligence, a human survivor dares to challenge them. If you're doomed to watch this, you just might survive; it's so-so, unsurprisingly sci-fi. **79m/C VHS.** Norris Culf, Nadine Hart, Joel von Ornsteiner, Jennifer Delora, Andrew Howarth, Angelika Jager, Rick Gianasi; ***D:*** Tim Kincaid; ***W:*** Tim Kincaid.

Robot in the Family 🦴🦴 **1994** Slapstick comedy about Alex and his wacky but endearing robot who embark on a race against time through the streets of New York to track down a priceless antique that could save Alex's family from financial ruin. **92m/C VHS.** Joe Pantoliano, John Rhys-Davies, Danny Gerard, Amy Wright, Tom Signorelli, Peter Maloney, John Wylie, David Shuman, Matthew Locricchio; ***D:*** Mark Richardson, Jack Shaoul; ***W:*** Jack Shaoul; ***M:*** Papo Gely, Ted Mason; ***V:*** Don Peoples.

Robot Jox 🦴½ **1990 (PG)** Two futuristic warriors battle to the finish in giant mechanical robots. Preteen fare. **84m/C VHS.** Gary (Rand) Graham, Anne-Marie Johnson, Paul Koslo, Robert Sampson, Danny Kamekona, Hilary Mason, Michael Alldredge; ***D:*** Stuart Gordon; ***W:*** Joe Haldeman; ***C:*** Mac Ahlberg.

Robot Monster 🦴🦴½ *Monster from Mars; Monsters from the Moon* **1953** Ludicrous cheapie is widely considered one of the worst films of all time, as a single alien dressed in a moth-eaten gorilla suit and diving helmet conspires to take over the Earth from his station in a small, bubble-filled California cave. Available in original 3-D format. **84m/B VHS, DVD.** George Nader, Claudia Barrett, Gregory Moffett, Selena Royle, John (Jack) Mylong, George Barrows; ***D:*** Phil Tucker; ***W:*** Wyott Ordung; ***C:*** Jack Greenhalgh; ***M:*** Elmer Bernstein; ***V:*** John Brown.

Robot Pilot 🦴 *Emergency Landing* **1941** Tucker stars as a WWII test pilot trying to promote a friend's invention. Along the way, he's involved in a subplot with enemy agents who steal a bomber. He also finds time to become romantically entangled with the boss' spoiled daughter. **68m/B VHS, 8mm.** Forrest Tucker, Carol Hughes, Evelyn Brent, Emmett Vogan, William (Bill) Halligan; ***D:*** William Beaudine.

The Robot vs. the Aztec Mummy **woof!** *El Robot Humano; La Momia Azteca Contra el Robot Humano* **1959** Grade-Z Mexican horror film pits a jealous mummy who guards a tomb against tomb robbers and the robot they invent. Special effects are laughable today—the robot's ears are lightbulbs—but true mummy movie fans might want to watch this one. Everyone else will probably be better off skipping it. **65m/B VHS.** *MX* Ramon Gay, Rosita (Rosa) Arenas, Crox Alvarado, Luis Aceves Castaneda, Emma Rolden; ***D:*** Rafael Portillo; ***W:*** Alfredo Salazar; ***C:*** Enrique Wallace; ***M:*** Antonio Diaz Conde.

Robot Wars 🦴🦴 **1993 (PG)** When what seems to be the last mega-robot on earth falls into enemy hands, a renegade pilot unearths another with the help of an engineer and archeologist to fight for the future of mankind. **106m/C VHS.** Don Michael Paul, Barbara Crampton, James Staley, Lisa Rinna, Danny Kamekona, Yuji Okumoto, J. Downing, Peter Haskell; ***D:*** Albert Band.

Rocco and His Brothers 🦴🦴🦴½ *Rocco et Ses Freres; Rocco E I Suoi Fratelli* **1960** A modern classic from top director Visconti, about four brothers who move with their mother from the Italian countryside to Milan. Very long, sometimes ponderous, but engrossing, complex drama. Available shortened to 90 minutes, but the unedited version is much more rewarding. In Italian with English subtitles. **168m/B VHS, DVD, Wide.** *IT* Alain Delon, Renato Salvatori, Annie Girardot, Katina Paxinou, Claudia Cardinale, Roger Hanin, Alessandra Panaro, Spiros Focas, Max Cartier; ***D:*** Luchino Visconti; ***W:*** Luchino Visconti, Suso Cecchi D'Amico, Pasquale Festa Campanile, Enrico Medioli, Massimo Franciosa; ***C:*** Giuseppe Rotunno; ***M:*** Nino Rota.

The Rock 🦴🦴🦴 **1996 (R)** Cage follows up his Oscar win with a big-budget action hero turn, with great results. In an attempt to get benefits for the families of soldiers killed in various covert operations, a decorated general (Harris) and his commando squad occupy Alcatraz island, taking hostages and threatening to unleash a deadly gas bomb on San Francisco. Biochemical weapons expert Stanley Goodspeed (Cage) is called in to disarm the rockets, aided by John Patrick Mason (Connery), only man to successfully escape from the island prison. Like most Simpson/Bruckheimer productions, credibility is stretched to the limit, but the action scenes and crisp pacing don't leave much time for pondering details, anyway. Connery, cool as ever, hasn't lost a step. Cage effectively plays up his character's inexperience at being the hero. Co-producer Don Simpson died of drug overdose during production. **136m/C VHS, DVD, Wide.** Nicolas Cage, Sean Connery, Ed Harris, Michael Biehn, William Forsythe, David Morse, John Spencer, John C. McGinley, Tony Todd, Bokeem Woodbine, Danny Nucci, Vanessa Marcil, Claire Forlani, Gregory Sporleder; ***D:*** Michael Bay; ***W:*** Jonathan Hensleigh; ***C:*** John Schwartzman; ***M:*** Nick Glennie-Smith. MTV Movie Awards '97: On-Screen Duo (Sean Connery/Nicolas Cage).

Rock-A-Bye Baby 🦴🦴½ **1957** Clayton Poole (Lewis) is a big fan of glamorous movie star Carla Naples (Maxwell), a recent widow who gives birth to triplets—a fact she wants kept hush-hush since she's starring as a virgin in a religious epic. So Clayton comes to the rescue by agreeing to be the little bundles' babysitter. And as a job bonus he gets to fall in love with Carla's sweet sister, Sandy (Stevens). A very loose adaptation of the Preston Sturges comedy "The Miracle of Morgan's Creek." **103m/C VHS.** Jerry Lewis, Marilyn Maxwell, Connie Stevens, Salvatore Baccaloni, Reginald Gardiner, Hans Conried, Ida Moore, George Sanders, James Gleason; ***D:*** Frank Tashlin; ***W:*** Frank Tashlin; ***C:*** Haskell Boggs; ***M:*** Walter Scharf.

Rock-a-Doodle 🦴🦴½ **1992 (G)** Little Edmond is knocked out during a storm and has an Elvis-influenced vision. He sees Chanticleer, the sun-raising rooster, tricked into neglecting his duties by an evil barnyard owl. Humiliated and scorned, the earnest young fowl leaves the farm and winds up in a Las Vegas-like city as an Elvis-impersonating singer (complete with pompadour) where he meets with success and all its trappings. Mildly amusing, but bland by today's standards of animation, with music which is certainly nothing to crow about. **77m/C VHS, DVD.** ***D:*** Don Bluth; ***W:*** David N. Weiss; ***M:*** Robert Folk; ***V:*** Glen Campbell, Christopher Plummer, Phil Harris, Sandy Duncan, Ellen Greene, Charles Nelson Reilly, Eddie Deezen, Toby Scott Granger, Sorrell Booke.

Rock All Night ✓✓ **1957** Typically trashy Corman quickie (filmed in five days on one set) about some wild '50s teens and, in this case, a couple of murderers. Seems Cloud Nine, the local teen hangout, is invaded by a couple of murderers who hold the kids hostage. It's up to the hipster bartender, known as Shorty because he's five-foot-one, to save the day. Unrelated concert footage of the Platters and the Blockbusters opens the film. **62m/B VHS.** Dick Miller, Abby Dalton, Russell Johnson, Jonathan Haze, Robin Morse, Chris Alcaide, Beach Dickerson, Bruno VeSota, Mel Welles; *D:* Roger Corman; *W:* Charles B. Griffith; *C:* Floyd Crosby.

Rock & Roll Cowboys ✓ **1992** Set in the near-future. Mickey LaGrange is a roadie who has dreams of playing his own songs and becoming a rock and roll star himself. When he meets the mysterious Damien Shard he just may get the opportunity and a lot more besides. Shard is the inventor of an instrument that taps directly into the brain to transform thought into music. When Mickey uses the instrument he becomes an instant success—until he notices some horrifying side effects. **83m/C VHS.** Peter Phelps, David Franklin, John (Roy Slaven) Doyle; *D:* Robert Stewart.

Rock & Rule ✓✓ **1983** Animated sword & sorcery epic with a rock soundtrack. Voices are provided by Deborah Harry, Cheap Trick, Lou Reed, and Iggy Pop. **85m/C VHS.** *D:* Clive A. Smith; *M:* Deborah Harry, Lou Reed, Iggy Pop; *V:* Paul LeMat, Susan (Suzan) Roman, Don Francks, Dan Hennessey, Chris Wiggins, Catherine Gallant, Catherine O'Hara.

Rock & the Money-Hungry Party Girls ✓ **1989** A struggling musician battles against Gabor-sister-worshipping bimbos in an effort to find unpublished songs by a '50s music legend. **90m/C VHS.** Paul Sercu, Adam Small, Judi Durand, Mary Baldwin, Debra Lamb; *D:* Kurt MacCarley.

Rock, Baby, Rock It ✓ **1957** Weak and silly rock-and-roll crime drama about teens trying to fight the Mafia in Dallas in 1957. Features performances by many regional bands including Kay Wheeler, the Cell Block Seven, Johnny Carroll, Preacher Smith and the Deacons, and the Five Stars. If you grew up in Dallas in the '50s, the musical groups may bring back some fond memories; otherwise, this obscure film probably isn't worth your time. **84m/B VHS.** Kay Wheeler, John Carroll; *D:* Murray Douglas Sporup.

Rock House ✓✓ **1992 (R)** When an L.A. narcotics officer's wife is murdered by drug runners he goes on an obsessive revenge mission to destroy the city's cocaine operations. **98m/C VHS.** Joseph Jennings, Michael Robbin, Alan Shearer; *D:* Jack Vacek; *W:* Jack Vacek.

Rock Hudson's Home Movies **1992** Farr re-creates the character of the late actor over numerous film clips used to suggest homoerotic themes in Hudson's movies. Low-budget and high camp. **63m/C VHS.** Eric Farr; *D:* Mark Rappaport; *W:* Mark Rappaport.

Rock 'n' Roll High School ✓✓✓ **1979 (PG)** The music of the Ramones highlights this non-stop high-energy cult classic about a high school out to thwart the principal at every turn. If it had been made in 1957, it would have been the ultimate rock 'n' roll teen movie. As it is, its 1970s' milieu works against it, but the performances are perfect for the material and the Ramones are great. Songs include "Teenage Lobotomy," "Blitzkrieg Bop," "I Wanna Be Sedated," and the title track, among others. Followed less successfully by "Rock 'n' Roll High School Forever." ♫Teenage Lobotomy; Blitzkrieg Bop; I Wanna Be Sedated; Rock and Roll High School. **94m/C VHS, DVD, Wide.** P.J. Soles, Vincent Van Patten, Clint Howard, Dey Young, Mary Woronov, Alix Elias, Dick Miller, Paul Bartel, Don Steele, Dee Dee Ramone, Joey Ramone, Johnny Ramone, Marky Ramone; *D:* Allan Arkush; *W:* Joe Dante, Russ Dvonch, Joseph McBride, Richard Whitley; *C:* Dean Cundey; *M:* The Ramones.

Rock 'n' Roll High School Forever ✓ **1991 (PG-13)** Jesse Davis and his band just want to rock 'n' roll, but the new principal doesn't share their enthusiasm. Way late, way lame sequel to "Rock 'n' Roll High School" doesn't come close to the originality that made it a cult classic. Soundtrack includes music from The Divinyls, Dee Dee Ramone, Mojo Nixon, Will and the Bushmen, The Pursuit of Happiness, and more. **94m/C VHS.** Corey Feldman, Mary Woronov, Mojo Nixon, Evan Richards, Michael Ceveris, Patrick Malone, Larry Linville, Sarah Buxton, Liane (Alexandra) Curtis, Lewis Arquette, Jason Lively; *D:* Deborah Brock; *W:* Deborah Brock; *C:* James Mathers.

Rock 'n' Roll Nightmare ✓½ *The Edge of Hell* **1985 (R)** A rock band is pursued by demons from another dimension. The usual lame garbage. **89m/C VHS.** *CA* Jon Mikl Thor, Paula Francescatto, Rusty Hamilton, Jillian Peri, Frank Dietz, David Lane, Teresa Simpson, Liane Abel, Nancy Bush; *D:* John Fasano; *W:* Jon Mikl Thor; *C:* Mark MacKay.

Rock, Pretty Baby ✓ **1956** Early rock-'n'-roll movie about a teenage band and high school riots. **89m/B VHS.** Sal Mineo, John Saxon, Rod McKuen, Luana Patten, Fay Wray, Edward Platt, Alan Reed Jr.; *D:* Richard Bartlett; *M:* Henry Mancini.

Rock River Renegades ✓ **1942** The Range Busters capture a band of renegades and restore peace to the territory once more. **59m/B VHS.** Ray Corrigan, John "Dusty" King.

Rock, Rock, Rock ✓✓½ **1956** A young girl tries to earn enough money for a prom gown after her father closes her charge account. Screen debut of Tuesday Weld. Ultra-low-budget, but a classic after a fashion. Includes classic musical numbers performed by Chuck Berry and other rock 'n' roll pioneers. **78m/B VHS.** Alan Freed, Chuck Berry, Fats Domino, Tuesday Weld; *D:* Will Price.

Rock Star ✓✓ **2001 (R)** Not a number one hit, but thanks to Mark Wahlberg, at least you won't choke on your own vomit. Working class Chris (Wahlberg) spends his off hours as the lead singer in Blood Pollution, a "tribute band" (don't call them a cover band!) to heavy metal demigods Steel Dragon. He gets a little too obsessive in the worship of his heroes, alienates the rest of the band, and is finally replaced for telling guitarist Rob (Olyphant) how to play. In a fantastical twist (and a none-too-subtle reference to real-life rockers Judas Priest), the musicians in Steel Dragon fire their secretly gay lead singer Bobby Beers (Flemyng) and recruit the amazed Chris to replace him. Real rock musicians and former rock star wives are scattered throughout the cast, but they don't add any glam to a rather bland depiction of a raunchy time period. **106m/C VHS, DVD, Wide.** *US* Mark Wahlberg, Jennifer Aniston, Timothy Olyphant, Timothy Spall, Jason Flemyng, Dominic West, Matthew Glave, Beth Grant, Stephan Jenkins, Jason Bonham, Heidi Mark, Michael Shamus Wiles, Dagmara Dominczyk, Rachel Hunter; *D:* Stephen Herek; *W:* John Stockwell; *C:* Ueli Steiger; *M:* Trevor Rabin.

Rockabye ✓✓½ **1986** Single mother Bertinelli is visiting New York with her two-year-old son when she's attacked and her child stolen. In her search for the boy, she discovers a black market in baby selling. **?m/C VHS.** Valerie Bertinelli, Rachel Ticotin, Jason Alexander, Ray Baker, Dick Latessa, James Rebhorn, Lynne Thigpen; *D:* Richard Michaels. **TV**

Rocket Attack U.S.A. woof! **1958** Antiquated and ridiculous tale of nuclear warfare about the time of Sputnik, with Russia's first strike blowing up New York City and environs. Mercifully short, with time for a little romance. Everything about this movie is so bad it's good for a laugh. **70m/B VHS.** Monica Davis, John McKay, Dan Kern, Edward Czerniuk, Art Metrano; *D:* Barry Mahon.

Rocket Gibraltar ✓✓✓ **1988 (PG)** On the occasion of a crusty patriarch's birthday, a large family unites on his remote estate to carry out his special birthday wish. Fine performance by Lancaster. Supported by a solid cast, overcomes a slim story, Culkin, later of "Home Alone," is loveable as the precocious five-year-old. Picturesque Long Island scenery. **92m/C VHS.** Burt Lancaster, Bill Pullman, John Glover, Suzy Amis, Macaulay Culkin, Patricia Clarkson, Frances Conroy, Sinead Cusack, Bill Martin, Kevin Spacey; *D:* Daniel Petrie; *W:* Amos Poe; *M:* Andrew Powell.

Rocket to the Moon ✓✓ **1986** An adaptation of the Clifford Odets story about the mundane life of a 30-year-old Manhattan dentist and how he comes to terms with his life. From the PBS "American Playhouse" series. **118m/C VHS.** Judy Davis, John Malkovich, Eli Wallach; *D:* John Jacobs.

The Rocketeer ✓✓✓ **1991 (PG)** Lightheaded fun. A stunt flyer in the 1930s finds a prototype jet backpack sought by Nazi spies. Donning a mask, he becomes a flying superhero. Breezy family entertainment with stupendous effects; even better if you know movie trivia, as it brims with Hollywood references, like a great villain (Dalton) clearly based on Errol Flynn. **109m/C VHS, DVD, Wide.** Billy Campbell, Jennifer Connelly, Alan Arkin, Timothy Dalton, Paul Sorvino, Melora Hardin, Tiny Ron, Terry O'Quinn, Ed Lauter, James Handy; *D:* Joe Johnston; *W:* Paul DeMeo, Danny Bilson; *C:* Hiro Narita; *M:* James Horner.

RocketMan ✓½ *Rocket Man* **1997 (PG)** Houston, we have a gastrointestinal problem. Well, dumb astronaut Fred Z. Randall (Williams) does, anyway. The bumbling computer geek is picked to go on the first manned mission to Mars, much to the dismay of crew commander "Wild Bill" Overbeck (Sadler) and specialist Julie Ford (Lundy). Beau Bridges plays Bud Nesbitt, the veteran astronaut back at NASA headquarters who is Randall's only supporter. While too much of the humor revolves around flatulence, Williams shows some talent while raiding the Disney archive for impressions. Remember, in space no one can hear you...pull my finger. **93m/C VHS.** Harland Williams, Jessica Lundy, Beau Bridges, William Sadler, Jeffrey DeMunn, James Pickens Jr., Peter Onorati; *D:* Stuart Gillard; *W:* Craig Mazin, Greg Erb; *C:* Steven Poster; *M:* Michael Tavera.

Rocketship ✓✓ **1936** Flash Gordon battles sea monsters, ray guns, and robots in this sci-fi adventure, which is an edited version of a Flash serial. **97m/B VHS.** Buster Crabbe, Jean Rogers, Charles Middleton.

Rocketship X-M ✓✓½ *Expedition Moon* **1950** A lunar mission goes awry and the crew lands on Mars, where they discover ancient ruins. Well acted and nicely photographed. Contains footage, a tinted sequence and previews of coming attractions from classis science fiction files. **77m/B VHS, DVD.** Lloyd Bridges, Osa Massen, John Emery, Hugh O'Brian, Noah Beery Jr.; *D:* Kurt Neumann; *W:* Kurt Neumann, Dalton Trumbo; *C:* Karl Struss; *M:* Ferde Grofe Jr.

Rockin' Road Trip ✓ **1985 (PG-13)** A guy meets a girl in a Boston bar, and finds himself on a drunken, slapstick road trip down the Eastern seaboard with a rock band. **101m/C VHS.** Garth McLean, Katherine Harrison, Margeret Currie, Steve Boles.

The Rocking Horse Winner ✓✓½ **1949** Poignant tale of a young boy who discovers he can predict racehorse winners by riding his rocking horse. His spendthrift mother's greed leads to tragedy. Based on the short story by D.H. Lawrence. **91m/B VHS.** *GB* John (Howard) Davies, Valerie Hobson, Hugh Sinclair; *D:* Anthony Pelissier.

Rocktober Blood ✓½ **1985 (R)** A convicted and executed rock star comes back from the grave and starts killing people all over again. Yet another gorefest. **88m/C VHS.** Donna Scoggins, Tray Loren, Nigel Benjamin, Beverly Sebastian; *D:* Ferd Sebastian.

Rockula ✓½ **1990 (PG-13)** Teen rock comedy about a young-yet-300-year-old vampire looking to lose his virginity. Recommended only for hard-core Diddley fans. **90m/C VHS.** Dean Cameron, Bo Diddley, Tawny (Ellis) Fere, Susan Tyrrell, Thomas Dolby, Toni Basil; *D:* Luca Bercovici; *W:* Luca Bercovici.

Rockwell: A Legend of the Wild West ✓✓½ **1993** Black heroics in the wild west. U.S. Marshall Porter Rockwell and his posse of sharp shooters are after a vicious gang murdering supposed claim jumpers who just happen to be Rockwell's friends. **?m/C VHS.** Randy Gleave, Karl Malone, Michael Rudd, George Sullivan.

Rocky ✓✓✓½ **1976 (PG)** Boxoffice smash about a young man from the slums of Philadelphia who dreams of becoming a boxing champion. Stallone plays Rocky, the underdog hoping to win fame and self-respect. Rags-to-riches story seems to parallel Stallone's life; he had been previously virtually unknown before this movie. Intense portrayal of the American Dream; loses strength in the subsequent (and numerous) sequels. **125m/C VHS, DVD, 8mm, Wide.** Sylvester Stallone, Talia Shire, Burgess Meredith, Burt Young, Carl Weathers; *D:* John G. Avildsen; *W:* Sylvester Stallone; *C:* James A. Crabe; *M:* Bill Conti. Oscars '76: Director (Avildsen), Film Editing, Picture; AFI '98: Top 100; Directors Guild '76: Director (Avildsen); Golden Globes '77: Film—Drama; L.A. Film Critics '76: Film; Natl. Bd. of Review '76: Support. Actress (Shire); N.Y. Film Critics '76: Support. Actress (Shire).

Rocky 2 ✓✓ **1979 (PG)** Time-marking sequel to the boxoffice smash finds Rocky frustrated by the commercialism that followed his match to Apollo, but considering a return bout. Meanwhile, his wife fights for her life. The overall effect is to prepare you for the next sequel. **119m/C VHS, DVD.** Sylvester Stallone, Talia Shire, Burt Young, Burgess Meredith, Carl Weathers; *D:* Sylvester Stallone; *W:* Sylvester Stallone; *C:* Bill Butler; *M:* Bill Conti.

Rocky 3 ✓✓½ **1982 (PG)** Rocky is beaten by big, mean Clubber Lang (played to a tee by Mr. T). He realizes success has made him soft, and has to dig deep to find the motivation to stay on top. Amazingly, Stallone regains his underdog persona here, looking puny next to Mr. T, who is the best thing about the second-best "Rocky" flick. **103m/C VHS.** Sylvester Stallone, Talia Shire, Burgess Meredith, Carl Weathers, Mr. T, Leif Erickson, Burt Young; *D:* Sylvester Stallone; *W:* Sylvester Stallone; *C:* Bill Butler; *M:* Bill Conti.

Rocky 4 ✓½ **1985 (PG)** Rocky travels to Russia to fight the Soviet champ who killed his friend during a bout. Will Rocky knock the Russkie out? Will Rocky get hammered on the head a great many times and sag around the ring? Will Rocky ever learn? Lundgren isn't nearly as much fun as some of Rocky's former opponents and Stallone overdoes the hyper-patriotism and relies too heavily on uplifting footage from earlier "Rocky" movies. **91m/C VHS, DVD.** Sylvester Stallone, Talia Shire, Dolph Lundgren, Brigitte Nielsen, Michael Pataki, Burt Young, Carl Weathers; *D:* Sylvester Stallone; *W:* Sylvester Stallone; *C:* Bill Butler; *M:* Bill Conti, Vince DiCola. Golden Raspberries '85: Worst Actor (Stallone), Worst Support. Actress (Nielsen), Worst Director (Stallone), Worst Screenplay, Worst New Star (Nielsen).

Rocky 5 ✓✓ **1990 (PG)** Brain damaged and broke, Rocky finds himself back where he started on the streets of Philadelphia. Boxing still very much in his blood, Rocky takes in a protege, training him in the style that made him a champ (take a lickin' and keep on tickin'). However an unscrupulous promoter has designs on the young fighter and seeks to wrest the lad from under the former champ's wing. This eventually leads to a showdown between Rocky and the young boxer in a brutal streetfight. Supposedly the last "Rocky" film, it's clear the formula has run dry. **105m/C VHS, 8mm.** Sylvester Stallone, Talia Shire, Burt Young, Sage Stallone, Tom Morrison, Burgess Meredith; *D:* John G. Avildsen; *W:* Sylvester Stallone; *C:* Steven Poster; *M:* Bill Conti.

The Rocky Horror Picture Show ✓✓✓ **1975 (R)** When a young couple take refuge in a haunted castle, they find themselves the unwilling pawns in a warped scientist's experiment. Cult camp classic has been a midnight movie favorite for years and has developed an entire subculture built around audience participation. The tape includes a seven-minute short detailing the story behind the movie's popularity. May not be as much fun watching it on the little screen unless you bring the rice and squirt guns. ♫The Time Warp; Science Fiction Double Feature; Wedding Song; Sweet Transvestite; The Sword of Damocles; Charles Atlas Song; Whatever Happened to Saturday Night; Touch-a Touch-a Touch-a Touch Me; Eddie's Teddy. **105m/C VHS, DVD, Wide.** *GB* Tim Curry, Susan Sarandon, Barry Bostwick, Little Nell, Richard O'Brien, Patricia Quinn, Jonathan Adams, Peter Hinwood, Meat Loaf Aday, Charles Gray, Koo Stark; ***D:*** Jim Sharman; ***W:*** Jim Sharman, Richard O'Brien; ***C:*** Peter Suschitzsky; ***M:*** Richard Hartley, Richard O'Brien.

Rocky Jones, Space Ranger: Renegade Satellite 🦴½ **1954** Nostalgia freaks may embrace this revived edition of the infamous early live-TV space cadet show. Rocky squares off against enemies of the United Solar System like Dr. Reno and Rudy DeMarco. Really cheap. **69m/B VHS.** Richard Crane, Sally Mansfield, Maurice Cass.

Rocky Marciano 🦴🦴½ **1999 (R)** Boxing biopic about the up-from-poverty Rocky (Favreau) who, as heavyweight champ, had 43 knock-outs and who retired in 1956 undefeated. (He was killed in a 1969 plane crash.) Marciano has the usual tribulations—greedy managers and overly-interested mobsters—and a climatic bout with his childhood hero, an aging Joe Louis (Davis). LoBiano, who plays a mobster, starred as Marciano in the 1979 TV movie, "Marciano." **90m/C VHS.** Jon Favreau, Judd Hirsch, Penelope Ann Miller, George C. Scott, Tony LoBianco, Duane Davis, Rhoda Gemignani, Rino Romano; ***D:*** Charles Winkler; ***W:*** Charles Winkler, Larry Golin; ***C:*** Paul Sarossy; ***M:*** Stanley Clarke. **CABLE**

Rocky Mountain Rangers 🦴🦴 **1940** The Three Mesquiteers do what they do best: save a town from bad guys. **58m/B VHS.** Robert "Bob" Livingston, Raymond Hatton, Duncan Renaldo, Leroy Mason, Dennis Moore, John St. Polis; ***D:*** George Sherman.

Rodan 🦴🦴 *Radon; Radon the Flying Monster* **1956** A gigantic prehistoric bird is disturbed from his slumber by H-bomb tests. He awakens to wreak havoc on civilization. Big bugs also run amok. From the director of "Godzilla" and a host of other nuclear monster movies. **74m/C VHS.** *JP* Kenji Sahara, Yumi Shirakawa; ***D:*** Inoshiro Honda.

Rodeo Girl 🦴🦴½ **1980** Ross is a restless housewife who joins the rodeo in this drama based on the life of cowgirl Sue Pirtle. Particularly strong supporting cast of Hopkins, Clark, and Brimley. **100m/C VHS.** Katharine Ross, Bo Hopkins, Candy Clark, Jacqueline Brookes, Wilford Brimley, Parley Baer; ***D:*** Jackie Cooper. **TV**

Rodeo King and the Senorita 🦴🦴 **1951** Rex and his horse Koko are hired on to a Wild West show, which DiSimone is struggling to run after the death of her dad. Her situation is more difficult because of a series of accidents that Rex doesn't think are so accidental. Remake of the 1946 Roy Rogers/Trigger movie "My Pal Trigger." **67m/B VHS.** Rex Allen, Buddy Ebsen, Roy Barcroft, Bonnie DeSimone, Mary Ellen Kay, Tristram Coffin; ***D:*** Philip Ford; ***W:*** John K. Butler; ***C:*** Walter Strenge.

Rodgers & Hammerstein's South Pacific 🦴🦴½ *South Pacific* **2001** Close may be a little mature to be cockeyed optimist and smalltown nurse Nellie Forbush but she gives it her all (and served as one of the exective producers) in this TV remake of the Rodgers and Hammerstein musical. Filmed in Australia and Tahiti, the scenery, music, and capable cast (who can sing just fine), all contribute. Of course, Connick Jr. (as romantic Lt. Cable) has an advantage in the vocal area but Serbedzija's plantation owner Emile de Becque has charisma to spare. **135m/C VHS, DVD.** Glenn Close, Rade Serbedzija, Harry Connick Jr., Robert Pastorelli, Jack Thompson, Ilene Graff, Lori Tan Chinn, Natalie Mendoza, Simon Burke, Steve Le Marquand, Steve Bastoni, Damon Herriman; ***D:*** Richard Pearce; ***W:*** Lawrence D. Cohen; ***C:*** Stephen Windon; ***M:*** Richard Rodgers. **TV**

Rodrigo D.: No Future 🦴🦴 **1991** Gritty, realistic portrayal of the youth-killing culture of Medellin, Columbia. Minimal plot involves a young drummer and his drug-running friends. The actors used are actual untrained street kids, several of whom died after the film's completion. In Spanish with English subtitles. **92m/C VHS.** Ramiro Meneses, Carlos Mario Resrepo; ***D:*** Victor Gaviria.

Roe vs. Wade 🦴🦴🦴 **1989** Hunter is excellent as the single woman from Texas who successfully challenged the nation's prohibitive abortion laws in a landmark Supreme Court case. Based on the actual 1973 case of Norma McCorvey. **92m/C VHS.** Holly Hunter, Amy Madigan, Terry O'Quinn, Stephen Tobolowsky, Dion Anderson, Kathy Bates, James Gammon, Chris Mulkey; ***D:*** Gregory Hoblit. **TV**

Roger & Me 🦴🦴🦴½ **1989 (R)** Hilarious, controversial and atypical semi-documentary details Moore's protracted efforts to meet General Motors president Roger Smith and confront him with the poverty and despair afflicting Flint, Michigan, after GM closed its plants there. Includes some emotionally grabbing scenes: a Flint family is evicted just before Christmas; a woman makes a living by selling rabbits for food or pets; and a then soon-to-be Miss America addresses the socioeconomic impact of GM's decision. One of the highest-grossing non-fiction films ever released, and Moore's first. **91m/C VHS.** Michael Moore, Anita Bryant, Bob Eubanks, Pat Boone; ***D:*** Michael Moore; ***W:*** Michael Moore; ***C:*** Kevin Rafferty, Chris Beaver, John Prusak, Bruce Schermer.

RoGoPaG 🦴🦴 **1962** Four episodic films by four European masters (the title refers to their last names), satirizing the human condition. Rossellini's "Virginity" finds an airline stewardess (Schiaffino) fending off an amorous passenger (Balabin). Godard's "The New World" features a post-nuclear Paris and its effect on romance. "La Ricotta" is Pasolini's controversial take on religion with Welles as the director of a religious epic. Gregoretti's "The Range Grown Chicken" finds Tognazzi the frazzled head of a family beset by consumerism. A mixed bag with Pasolini and Godard offering the most disturbing essays. **122m/B VHS.** *IT* Orson Welles, Ugo Tognazzi, Rosanna Schiaffino, Alexandra Stewart, Jean-Mark Bory, Renato Salvatori, Lisa Gastoni, Bruce Balabin; ***D:*** Roberto Rossellini, Jean-Luc Godard, Pier Paolo Pasolini, Ugo Gregoretti; ***W:*** Roberto Rossellini, Jean-Luc Godard, Pier Paolo Pasolini, Ugo Gregoretti; ***M:*** Carlo Ristichelli.

Rogue 🦴 **1976 (R)** The Rogue is a ruthless man who can make beautiful women do anything that he desires; so, of course, he does. **87m/C VHS.** Milan Galvonic, Barbara Bouchet, Margaret Lee; ***D:*** Gregory Simpson.

Rogue Force 🦴½ **1999 (R)** A renegade SWAT commander (Patrick) leads a vigilante group of ex-police officers in assassinating a number of mobsters. The murders are being investigating by federal agent Rooker and homicide detective DiLascio, who have no idea where their assignment is leading them. Predictable but delivers the action required of the genre. **90m/C VHS, DVD.** Robert Patrick, Michael Rooker, Louis Mandylor, Diane DiLascio; ***D:*** Martin Klinert. **VIDEO**

Rogue Male 🦴🦴½ **1976** TV movie finds '30s British aristocrat O'Toole plotting to assassinate Hitler. When his plan fails, he's on the run from both the Gestapo and the British police. Based on the novel by Geoffrey Household. **100m/C VHS.** *GB* Peter O'Toole, Alastair Sim, John Standing, Cyd Hayman; ***D:*** Clive Donner; ***W:*** Frederic Raphael.

Rogue of the Range 🦴 **1936** A lawman pretends that he is a bandit in order to track down an outlaw gang. **60m/B VHS.** Johnny Mack Brown.

Rogue of the Rio Grande 🦴½ **1930** Musical western in which the renowned bandit El Malo arrives in the peace-loving town of Sierra Blanca. One of Loy's earlier films. ♫Argentine Moon; Carmita; Song of the Bandoleros. **60m/B VHS.** Myrna Loy, Jose Bohr, Raymond Hatton, Carmelita Geraghty.

Rogue Trader 🦴🦴 **1998 (R)** Unremarkable recreation of the true story of futures trader Nick Leeson (McGregor), who singlehandedly brought down the Barings Merchant Bank in 1995. Working the floor of the Singapore International Money Exchange, Leeson quickly realizes he's completely out of his depth but can't admit it, so he hides his losses and continues to gamble until the deficit adds up to a $1 billion. Based on the book by Nicholas Leeson and Edward Whitley. The real Leeson was paroled from a Singapore jail in 1999. **101m/C VHS, DVD.** *GB* Ewan McGregor, John Standing, Anna Friel, Yves Beneyton, Tim (McInnerny) McInnerny, Betsy Brantley, Caroline Langrishe; ***D:*** James Dearden; ***W:*** James Dearden; ***C:*** Jean-Francois Robin; ***M:*** Richard Hartley.

Rogue's Gallery 🦴🦴 **1944** A reporter and photographer covering the story of an inventor and his latest device are caught up in intrigue when he is found murdered. **60m/B VHS.** Frank Jenks, Robin Raymond, H.B. Warner, Ray Walker, Davison Clark, Robert E. Homans, Frank McGlynn, Pat Gleason, Edward (Ed Kean, Keene) Keane; ***D:*** Al(bert) Herman.

Rogue's Tavern 🦴🦴 **1936** In this grade B curio, a blood-thirsty killer stalks the occupants of a country inn, bodies are found with their throats crushed, and a psycho psychic is on the loose. Surprise ending. **70m/B VHS.** Wallace Ford, Joan Woodbury, Clara Kimball Young, Barbara Pepper, Jack Mulhall, John Elliott; ***D:*** Robert F. "Bob" Hill.

Rogue's Yarn 🦴🦴 **1956** An investigator probes the death of a woman, ostensibly the result of a boating accident. Gradually he uncovers a plot involving the woman's husband and his mistress in this semi-entertaining British mystery. **80m/B VHS.** *GB* Nicole Maurey, Derek Bond, Elwyn Brook-Jones, Hugh Latimer; ***D:*** Vernon Sewell.

Roland the Mighty 🦴½ **1958** Muscular, Herculeanesque hero takes on all comers in this sword and sandal epic set in the Asian steppes. **98m/C VHS.** *IT* Rick Battaglia, Rosanna Schiaffino.

Roll Along Cowboy 🦴½ **1937** A vintage sagebrush saga about a cowboy caught by love. Based on Zane Grey's "The Dude Ranger." **55m/B VHS.** Smith Ballew, Cecilia Parker; ***D:*** Gus Meins.

Roll of Thunder, Hear My Cry 🦴🦴½ **1978** A black family struggles to survive in Depression-era Mississippi in this inspiring, if somewhat predictable, production. Look for the always impressive Freeman in a supporting role. Based on the novels of Mildred Taylor. **110m/C VHS.** Claudia McNeil, Janet MacLachlan, Morgan Freeman; ***D:*** Jack Smight. **TV**

Roll on Texas Moon 🦴 **1946** A cowpoke is hired to prevent a feud between the sheep men and the cattle ranchers. **68m/B VHS.** Roy Rogers, George "Gabby" Hayes, Dale Evans, Dennis Hoey; ***D:*** William Witney.

Roll, Wagons, Roll 🦴½ **1939** Tex Ritter leads a wagon train to Oregon. **52m/B VHS.** Tex Ritter; ***D:*** Al(bert) Herman.

Roller Blade 🦴 **1985** In a post-holocaust world a gang of Amazon-style nuns, who worship a "have a nice day" happy face, battle the forces of evil with martial arts and mysticism. Has to be seen to be believed. Extremely low-budget outing. **88m/C VHS.** Suzanne Solari, Jeff Hutchinson, Shaun Mitchelle, Michelle (McClellan) Bauer, Lisa Marie, Barbara Peckinpaugh; ***D:*** Donald G. Jackson; ***M:*** Robert Garrett.

Roller Blade Warriors: Taken By Force 🦴🦴 **1990** Roller babes battle evil mutant while balancing on big boots with small wheels. **90m/C VHS.** Kathleen Kinmont, Rory Calhoun, Abby Dalton, Elizabeth Kaitan.

Roller Boogie woof! **1979 (PG)** A truly awful film made at the time of the mercifully brief roller-disco craze. Blair runs away from home and winds up helping some friends thwart a businessman looking to close the local roller rink. Everything about this one reeks amateur. **103m/C VHS.** Linda Blair, Jim Bray, Beverly Garland, Roger Perry, James Van Patten, Kimberly Beck, Mark Goddard, Stoney Jackson, Sean McClory; ***D:*** Mark L. Lester; ***W:*** Barry Schneider; ***C:*** Dean Cundey.

Rollerball 🦴🦴½ **1975 (R)** Caan is utterly convincing in this futuristic tale in which a brutal sport assumes alarming importance to a sterile society. Flashy, violent, sometimes exhilirating. **123m/C VHS, DVD, Wide.** James Caan, John Houseman, Maud Adams, Moses Gunn, John Beck; ***D:*** Norman Jewison; ***W:*** William Harrison; ***C:*** Douglas Slocombe; ***M:*** Andre Previn.

Rollerball 🦴 **2002 (PG-13)** Re-imagination of the 1975 cult classic. The sport of the near-future attracts extreme sports enthusiast Jonathan Cross (Klein), drawn by the big bucks and buddy (LL Cool J), who convinces him to try out. The sport itself, is sort of like pro wrestling on skates and motorcycles. Fleeing the law in the U.S., Jonathan heads to a former Soviet republic where the league is run by ex-KGB agent Petrovich (Reno) who wants to increase the sport's blood and gore factor to gain a stateside cable TV deal. Jonathan finds love with fellow baller Aurora (Romijn-Stamos) whose nearly unnoticeable "deformity" doesn't dissuade her suicidal suitor. Laughable scenarios, seriously ailing editing, corny script, lackluster performances and grave miscasting (the sensitive Klein as a macho macho man) make this one a prime candidate for contraction. **98m/C VHS, DVD, Wide.** *US* Chris Klein, L.L. Cool J., Rebecca Romijn-Stamos, Jean Reno, Naveen Andrews, Oleg Taktarov, David Hemblen; ***D:*** John McTiernan; ***W:*** Larry Ferguson, John Pogue; ***C:*** Steve Mason; ***M:*** Eric Serra.

Rollercoaster 🦴🦴 **1977 (PG)** A deranged extortionist threatens to sabotage an amusement park ride. Plucky Segal must stop him. Video renters will be spared the nauseating effects of film's original "Sensurround." **119m/C VHS, DVD, Wide.** George Segal, Richard Widmark, Timothy Bottoms, Henry Fonda, Susan Strasberg, Harry Guardino; ***D:*** James Goldstone; ***W:*** William Link; ***C:*** David M. Walsh; ***M:*** Lalo Schifrin.

Rollin' Plains 🦴 **1938** A Texas Ranger tries to settle a feud between cattlemen and sheepmen over water rights. **60m/B VHS.** Tex Ritter; ***D:*** Al(bert) Herman.

Rolling Home 🦴🦴 **1948** Tame tale about aging cowpoke, his grandson, and a really swell horse. Saddle up and snooze. **71m/B VHS.** Jean Parker, Russell Hayden, Pamela Blake, Buss Henry, Raymond Hatton.

Rolling Thunder 🦴🦴½ **1977 (R)** Vietnam vet turns vigilante when he arrives home from POW camp and sees his family slaughtered. Graphically violent, potentially cathartic. Typical of screenwriter Paul Schrader. **99m/C VHS.** William Devane, Tommy Lee Jones, Linda Haynes; ***D:*** John Flynn; ***W:*** Paul Schrader, Heywood Gould; ***C:*** Jordan Cronenweth.

Rolling Vengeance 🦴½ **1987 (R)** Enterprising fellow constructs powerful truck to better facilitate the extermination of gang members who earlier slaughtered his family. Keep on truckin'. **90m/C VHS.** Don Michael Paul, Ned Beatty, Lawrence Dane, Lisa Howard; ***D:*** Steven Hilliard Stern.

Rollover 🦴½ **1981 (R)** Turgid big-budget drama about Arab undermining of American economy. Kristofferson is lifeless, Fonda is humorless. Supporting players Sommer and Cronyn fare better. **117m/C VHS.** Jane Fonda, Kris Kristofferson, Hume Cronyn, Bob Gunton, Josef Sommer, Martha Plimpton; ***D:*** Alan J. Pakula.

Roman Holiday 🦴🦴🦴½ **1953** Hepburn's first starring role is a charmer as a princess bored with her official visit to Rome who slips away and plays at being an "average Jane." A reporter discovers her little charade and decides to cash in with an exclusive story. Before they know it, love calls. Blacklisted screenwriter Trumbo was "fronted" by Ian McLellan Hunter, who accepted screen credit and the Best Story Oscar in Trumbo's stead. The Academy voted to posthumously award Trumbo his own Oscar in 1993. **118m/B VHS, 8mm.** Audrey Hepburn, Gregory Peck, Eddie Albert, Tullio Carminati; ***D:*** William

Wyler; *W:* Dalton Trumbo. Oscars '53: Actress (Hepburn), Costume Des. (B&W), Story; British Acad. '53: Actress (Hepburn); Golden Globes '54: Actress—Drama (Hepburn), Natl. Film Reg. '99;; N.Y. Film Critics '53: Actress (Hepburn).

Roman Scandals ℰℰ½ **1933** A penniless young man daydreams himself back to ancient Rome with uproarious results. Lucille Ball appears as one of the Goldwyn Girls. Dance sequences were choreographed by Busby Berkeley. ♫No More Love; Build A Little Home; Keep Young and Beautiful; Rome Wasn't Built in a Day; Put a Tax on Love. **91m/B VHS.** Eddie Cantor, Ruth Etting, Gloria Stuart, Edward Arnold, Lucille Ball, Busby Berkeley; *D:* Frank Tuttle; *C:* Gregg Toland.

Roman Spring of Mrs. Stone ℰℰℰ *The Widow and the Gigolo* **1961** An aging actress determines to revive her career in Rome but finds romance with a gigolo instead in this adaptation of Tennessee Williams's novella. Leigh and Beatty are compelling, but Lenya nearly steals the show as Leigh's distinctly unappealing confidant. **104m/C VHS.** Warren Beatty, Vivien Leigh, Lotte Lenya, Bessie Love, Jill St. John, Elspeth March; *D:* Jose Quintero; *W:* Gavin Lambert.

Romance ℰℰ **1930** In only her second talkie, Garbo stars as an Italian opera star who seduces a young priest. Poor story and weak acting from everyone with the exception of Garbo. Even she can't save this one. Adapted from the play "Signora Caclini." **77m/B VHS.** Greta Garbo, Lewis Stone, Gavin Gordon, Elliott Nugent, Florence Lake, Clara Blandick; *D:* Clarence Brown; *C:* William H. Daniels.

Romance ℰℰ **1999** This journey of erotic self-discovery caused raised eyebrows even among the blase French. Schoolteacher Marie (Ducey) is sexually rejected by her bored male model boyfriend Paul (Stevenin). This so distresses her that Marie flings herself into sexual escapades, including bar-pickup Paolo (Italian porn star Siffredi) and bondage sessions with school principal Robert (Berleand). Very talky, very self-serious, and very explicit. French with subtitles. **93m/C VHS, DVD, Wide.** *FR* Caroline Ducey, Sagamore Stevenin, Francois Berleand, Rocco Siffredi; *D:* Catherine Breillat; *W:* Catherine Breillat; *C:* Yorgos Arvanitis; *M:* D.J. Valentin, Raphael Tidas.

Romance in Manhattan ℰℰ **1934** Recent immigrant to New York struggles to build new life, in spite of unemployment, language barriers, and loneliness. He meets Broadway chorine Rogers and song and dance ensues. America, ain't it a great place? **78m/B VHS.** Ginger Rogers, Francis Lederer, J. Farrell MacDonald; *D:* Stephen Roberts; *M:* Max Steiner.

Romance of a Horsethief ℰℰ½ **1971 (PG)** Brynner leads this entertaining but slow-paced "Fiddler on the Roof" comedic romp without the music. In 1904 Poland, a Cossack captain takes horses for the Russo-Japanese war. The residents of the town rise up, goaded on by Birkin. **100m/C VHS.** *YU* Yul Brynner, Eli Wallach, Jane Birkin, Oliver Tobias, Lainie Kazan, David Opatoshu; *D:* Abraham Polonsky.

Romance on the High Seas ℰℰℰ **1948** A woman is scheduled to take a cruise vacation but skips the boat when she believes her husband is cheating on her. Her husband believes she is taking the cruise to cheat on him and hires a private detective to follow her. Pleasant comedy features the film debut of Doris Day. ♫It's Magic; It's You or No One; The Tourist Trade; Put 'Em in a Box, Tie 'Em with a Ribbon, and Throw 'Em in the Deep Blue Sea; Two Lovers Met in the Night; Run, Run, Run; I'm in Love; Cuban Rhapsody. **99m/C VHS.** Jack Carson, Janis Paige, Don DeFore, Doris Day, Oscar Levant, S.Z. Sakall, Eric Blore, Franklin Pangborn, Leslie Brooks, William "Billy" Bakewell; *D:* Michael Curtiz; *W:* Julius J. Epstein.

Romance on the Orient Express ℰ½ **1989** Sparks fly when former lovers meet again on the Orient Express. Don't expect any flesh, though, as this was made for TV. **96m/C VHS.** Cheryl Ladd, Stuart Wilson, John Gielgud; *D:* Lawrence Gordon Clark. **TV**

Romance on the Range ℰ½ **1942** Rogers sets out to trap a gang of fur thieves and finds romance. **60m/B VHS.** Roy Rogers, George "Gabby" Hayes, Sally Payne.

Romance with a Double Bass ℰℰℰ **1974** When a musician and a princess take a skinny dip in the royal lake and get their clothes stolen, comic complications arise. Reminiscent of Cleese's sojourn as a Monty Python member, with surreal, frequently raunchy humor. **40m/C VHS.** *GB* John Cleese, Connie Booth, Graham Crowden, Desmond Jones, Freddie Jones, Andrew Sachs; *D:* Robert M. Young.

Romancing the Stone ℰℰℰ **1984 (PG)** Uptight romance novelist Joan (Turner) lives out her fantasies after she receives a mysterious map from her murdered brother-in-law and her sister is kidnapped in South America—the ransom being the map. Out to rescue her sister, she's helped and hindered by American soldier of fortune Jack (Douglas) whose main concern is himself and the hidden treasure described in the map. Great chemistry between the stars and loads of clever dialogue in this appealing adventure comedy. First outing with Turner, Douglas, and DeVito. Followed by "The Jewel of the Nile." **106m/C VHS, DVD, Wide.** Mary Ellen Trainor, Michael Douglas, Kathleen Turner, Danny DeVito, Zack Norman, Alfonso Arau, Ron Silver; *D:* Robert Zemeckis; *W:* Diane Thomas; *C:* Dean Cundey; *M:* Alan Silvestri. Golden Globes '85: Actress—Mus./Comedy (Turner), Film—Mus./Comedy; L.A. Film Critics '84: Actress (Turner).

Romantic Comedy ℰℰ **1983 (PG)** Writing duo never seem to synchronize their desires for each other in this dull comedy. Engaging stars don't inspire each other much, and supporting cast can't make up the difference. Adapted from the Bernard Slade play. **102m/C VHS, DVD, Wide.** Dudley Moore, Mary Steenburgen, Frances Sternhagen, Ron Leibman; *D:* Arthur Hiller; *W:* Bernard Slade; *C:* David M. Walsh; *M:* Marvin Hamlisch.

Romantic Englishwoman ℰℰℰ **1975 (R)** Literate comedy-drama about the intertwined lives of several sophisticated and restrained Brits. Caine is a successful novelist with writer's block whose wife falls for another man while on a trip alone. He then invites his wife's lover to stay with them in order to generate ideas for his writing until his jealousy begins to surface. **117m/C VHS.** *GB* Glenda Jackson, Michael Caine, Helmut Berger, Kate Nelligan; *D:* Joseph Losey; *W:* Tom Stoppard, Thomas Wiseman.

Rome Adventure ℰℰ *Lovers Must Learn* **1962** Spinster librarian Pleshette takes Roman vacation hoping to meet handsome prince. Donahue takes shine to her while girlfriend Dickinson is away, as does suave Roman Brazzi. Soapy, ill-paced romance. **119m/C VHS.** Troy Donahue, Angie Dickinson, Suzanne Pleshette, Rossano Brazzi, Constance Ford, Al Hirt, Chad Everett; *D:* Delmer Daves; *W:* Delmer Daves; *M:* Max Steiner.

Rome '78 ℰℰ½ **1978** Acclaimed underground film centered around Caligula and the Queen of Sheba in ancient Rome. **60m/C VHS.** Eric Mitchell; *D:* James Nares.

Romeo and Juliet ℰℰℰ½ **1936** One of MGM producer Irving Thalberg's pet projects (and starring Thalberg's wife, Norma Shearer), this Shakespeare classic was given the spare-no-expense MGM treatment. Physically too old to portray teenage lovers, both Howard and Shearer let their acting ability supply all necessary illusions. Also notable is Barrymore's over-the-top portrayal of Mercutio. **126m/B VHS.** Leslie Howard, Norma Shearer, John Barrymore, Basil Rathbone, Edna May Oliver; *D:* George Cukor; *C:* William H. Daniels.

Romeo and Juliet ℰℰ **1954** Unfulfilling adaptation of Shakespeare's timeless drama of young love cast against family antagonisms. Peculiar supporting cast features both Cabot and ubiquitous master Gielgud. **138m/C VHS.** *IT* Laurence Harvey, Susan Shantall, Aldo Zollo, Sebastian Cabot, Flora Robson, Mervyn Johns, Bill Travers, John Gielgud; *D:* Renato Castellani; *C:* Robert Krasker. Natl. Bd. of Review '54: Director (Castellani).

Romeo and Juliet ℰℰℰ½ **1968 (PG)** Young couple share love despite prohibitive conflict between their families in this adaptation of Shakespeare's classic play. Director Zeffirelli succeeds in casting relative novices Whiting and Hussey in the leads, but is somewhat less proficient in lending air of free-wheeling '60s appeal to entire enterprise. Kudos, however, to cinematographer Pasquale De Santis and composer Nina Rota. Also available in a 45-minute edited version. **138m/C VHS, DVD, Wide.** *GB IT* Olivia Hussey, Leonard Whiting, Michael York, Milo O'Shea; *D:* Franco Zeffirelli; *W:* Franco Zeffirelli, Franco Brusati, Maestro D'Amico; *C:* Pasqualino De Santis; *M:* Nino Rota; *Nar:* Laurence Olivier. Oscars '68: Cinematog., Costume Des.; Golden Globes '69: Foreign Film; Natl. Bd. of Review '68: Director (Zeffirelli).

Romeo Is Bleeding ℰℰ½ **1993 (R)** Jack (Oldman) is a police detective accepting mobster payoffs from boss Falcone (Scheider) for fingering federally protected witnesses. But the next target proves Jack's undoing—hitwoman Mona (Olin), who's more than a match for any man. Oldman's character is played for a patsy by everyone while Olin's is a kinky psycho-villainess with an enjoyment of violence, red lipstick, and a constant, maniacal laugh. Sciorra is generally wasted as Jack's unhappy wife while Lewis is annoying as his young and vacuous mistress. Part homage, part satire of film noir is overly stylized with intrusive narration but some effective shocks. **110m/C VHS, DVD, Wide.** Gary Oldman, Lena Olin, Annabella Sciorra, Juliette Lewis, Roy Scheider, Michael Wincott, David Proval, Paul Butler, Will Patton, Larry Joshua, James Cromwell, Ron Perlman; *D:* Peter Medak; *W:* Hilary Henkin; *C:* Darius Wolski; *M:* Mark Isham.

Romeo Must Die ℰℰ½ **2000 (R)** Romance is decidedly secondary to action in this kung fu/hip hop hybrid. After an over-extended (but flashy) credits sequence, the story kicks in. Black crime lord Isaak O'Day (a magnetic Lindo) and Asian crime boss Ch'u Sing (O) are maintaining an uneasy truce in order to do a mega-business deal. Then Sing's useless younger son is killed and soon O'Day's son bites the dust as well. Into the mix springs good guy/ex-cop Han Sing (Li), who's out to avenge his brother's death, and lovely Trish O'Day (Aaliyah), who wants the same for her brother. (This is the chastest romantic pairing in modern movies.) The action sequences are frequent and frequently amazing and Li has minimal English dialogue to worry about. The supporting players, including Wong and Washington, are also solidly watchable. There's also humor, including Li's introduction to touch football. **115m/C VHS, DVD, Wide.** Jet Li, Aaliyah, Delroy Lindo, Henry O, Isaiah Washington IV, Russell Wong, DMX, DB Woodside, Edoardo Ballerini, Anthony Anderson, Jon Kit Lee, Francoise Yip; *D:* Andrzej Bartkowiak; *W:* Eric Bernt, John Jarrell; *C:* Glen MacPherson; *M:* Stanley Clarke, Timbaland.

Romero ℰℰ½ **1989** Julia is riveting as the Salvadoran archbishop who championed his destitute congregation despite considerable political opposition. A stirring biography financed by the United States Roman Catholic Church. **102m/C VHS, DVD.** Raul Julia, Richard Jordan, Ana Alicia, Eddie Velez, Alejandro Bracho, Tony Plana, Lucy Reina, Harold Gould, Al Ruscio, Robert Viharo; *D:* John Duigan; *W:* John Sacret Young; *C:* Geoff Burton; *M:* Gabriel Yared.

Romola ℰℰ½ **1925** Silent adventure. After Powell and his father are attacked by pirates, Powell escapes. But instead of rescuing his father, he opts for a life of corruption. Dad eventually escapes and returns to exact vengeance. A rather expensive film in its day, troubled by modern-day sights in what was supposed to be old Florence. Gish's drowning scene had to be re-shot because she wouldn't sink. Colman arranged for his then-wife Raye to have a bit part, but they were divorced soon after the film was finished. **120m/B VHS.** Lillian Gish, Dorothy Gish, William Powell, Ronald Colman, Charles Lane, Herbert Grimwood, Bonaventure Ibanez, Frank Puglia, Thelma Raye; *D:* Henry King.

Romper Stomper ℰℰ **1992 (R)** Violent confrontations between Australian skinheads and the Vietnamese community mixed in with a disturbed love story. Suburban rich girl Gabe (McKenzie) is drawn to the charasmatic Hando (Crowe), the certifiably loony leader of a group of Melbourne's skinheads. Any romance takes a backseat to the carnage brought by the skinheads' attacks on the local Asian community, who fight back with equal force. Disquieting look at a brutal world which can't be ignored. Film caused a furor upon its Australian release with debates about whether the extreme violence was intended to titilate or explicate the plot. An unrated version at 89 minutes is also available. **85m/C VHS, DVD, Wide.** *AU* Alex Scott, Leigh Russell, Daniel Wylie, James McKenna, Samantha Bladon, Russell Crowe, Jacqueline McKenzie, Daniel Pollock; *D:* Geoffrey Wright; *W:* Geoffrey Wright; *C:* Ron Hagen; *M:* John Clifford White. Australian Film Inst. '92: Actor (Crowe), Sound, Score.

Romy and Michele's High School Reunion ℰ½ **1997 (R)** Two vacuous ditz queens, Romy (Sorvino) and Michele (Kudrow), best friends and roommates since high school, decide they must impress at their 10-year Tucson high school reunion by passing themselves off as wealthy and successful. Since they're barely bright enough to walk and chew gum at the same time, this proves to be a challenge, especially when the arrival of cynical Heather (Garofalo), who knows the truth, threatens their deception. Music's good, and there are a (very) few funny moments, but you'll concentrate most on trying to ignore those annoying accents. You don't laugh with these would-be babes, you laugh at them. And even then, not all that much. Based on Schiff's play "The Ladies' Room." **91m/C VHS, DVD.** Mira Sorvino, Lisa Kudrow, Janeane Garofalo, Alan Cumming, Julia Campbell, Elaine Hendrix, Jacob Vargas, Camryn Manheim; *D:* David Mirkin; *W:* Robin Schiff; *C:* Reynaldo Villalobos; *M:* Steve Bartek.

Ronin ℰℰ½ **1998 (R)** What a cast! What a director! What a disappointment! Okay, so it's not that bad—the scenery's spectacular (the action takes place between Paris and Nice) and there are some amazing car chases. But, they go on much too long and the story's less than involving. Sam (De Niro) is a world-weary, possibly ex-spy who gets involved with several international players (including Reno, Skarsgard, and Bean) to do a job for tough Irish lass Deirdre (McElhone). She's fronting (for the violent Pryce) a project to retrieve a mysterious suitcase from some Russian bad guys. One of the best things the film's got going for it is the wary buddy relationship that builds between De Niro and Reno. Title refers to a Japanese legend concerning 47 masterless samurai. Richard Weisz is the pseudonym for a rewriting David Mamet. **118m/C VHS, DVD, Wide.** Robert De Niro, Jean Reno, Stellan Skarsgard, Natascha McElhone, Jonathan Pryce, Skipp (Robert L.) Sudduth, Michael (Michel) Lonsdale, Sean Bean, Jan Triska, Feodor Atkine, Bernard Bloch, Katarina Witt; *D:* John Frankenheimer; *W:* David Mamet, J.D. Zeik; *C:* Robert Fraisse; *M:* Elia Cmiral.

Ronnie and Julie ℰℰ½ **1997 (PG)** Yet another contemporary variation of "Romeo & Juliet" with high-school sweethearts Ronnie (Jackson) and Julie's (Finley) relationship threatened by their respective parents political rivalry in a mayoral campaign. At least this one has a happy ending. **99m/C VHS.** Teri Garr, Joshua Jackson, Margot Finlay, Alexandra Purvis, Tom Butler, Garwin Sanford; *D:* Philip Spink; *C:* Bruce Worrall.

The Roof ℰℰ **1956** Uninteresting outing about a young couple who married against their families' wishes and find that setting up a home of their own is more difficult than they thought. In Italian with English subtitles. **98m/B VHS.** *IT* Gabriella Pallotta, Giorgio Listuzzi; *D:* Vittorio De Sica.

Rooftops 🦴½ **1989 (R)** Peculiar but predictable, centering on love between Hispanic girl and white youth who has mastered martial arts dancing. Director Wise is a long way from his earlier "West Side Story." See this one and be the only person you know who has. **108m/C VHS.** Jason Gedrick, Troy Beyer, Eddie Velez, Tisha Campbell; *D:* Robert Wise; *W:* Allan Goldstein, Terrence (Terry) Brennan; *M:* Michael Kamen.

The Rookie 🦴🦴 **1990 (R)** Routine cop drama has worldly veteran and wide-eyed newcomer team to crack stolen-car ring managed by Germans. Eastwood and Sheen are reliable, but Hispanics Julia and Braga, though miscast, nonetheless steal this one as the German villains. **121m/C VHS, 8mm, Wide.** Clint Eastwood, Charlie Sheen, Raul Julia, Sonia Braga, Lara Flynn Boyle, Pepe Serna, Marco Rodriguez, Tom Skerritt, Roberta Vasquez; *D:* Clint Eastwood.

The Rookie 🦴🦴🦴½ **2002 (G)** Texas high school teacher and baseball coach Jim Morris (Quaid) challenges his also-ran team by promising to go on a major league tryout if they win the regional championship. The team wins, and the former minor-leaguer keeps his promise and attends a Devil Rays tryout and finds his now-rejuvenated arm can throw a baseball 98 mph. During his journey to the majors, he deals with his relationship with his old man, and life on the other side of 30. If this were't a true story, it'd be one of the hokiest movies ever, but because you know it's real, it's, well...inspiring. It helps that Quaid nails the role, and Jones, as son Hunter, walks off with every scene he's in. One of the producers, Mark Ciardi, is a former teammate of Morris, from his original go-round in the minors. Based on Morris's book "The Oldest Rookie." **127m/C VHS, DVD.** Dennis Quaid, Rachel Griffiths, Angus T. Jones, Brian Cox, Beth Grant, Chad Lindberg, Royce D. Applegate, Jay Hernandez, Russell Richardson, Raynor Scheine, David Blackwell, Edward "Blue" Deckert, Dan Kamin, Trevor Morgan, Rick Gonzalez, Angelo Spizzirri; *D:* John Lee Hancock; *W:* Mike Rich; *C:* John Schwartzman; *M:* Carter Burwell.

Rookie of the Year 🦴🦴½ **1993 (PG)** Kid's fluff fantasy come true. Twelve-year-old baseball fanatic Henry has dreams of making it to the big league. He falls, breaks his arm, and when it heals strangely is blessed with a pitching arm so spectacular he finds himself not only playing for the Chicago Cubs, but leading them to the World Series. Enjoyable family outing for first-time director Stern (who also plays a seasoned and very incredulous ballplayer). Keep your eyes peeled for appearances by real-live sluggers Pedro Guerrero, Barry Bonds, and others. **103m/C VHS, DVD, Wide.** Thomas Ian Nicholas, Daniel Stern, Gary Busey, Dan Hedaya; *D:* Daniel Stern; *W:* Sam Harper; *C:* Jack N. Green; *M:* Bill Conti. Blockbuster '95: Family Movie, V.

The Room 🦴🦴 **1987** Altman takes on Pinter in this brooding mini-play about two young strangers who try to rent the room already occupied by a disconnected woman and her semi-catatonic husband. **48m/C VHS.** Julian Sands, Linda Hunt, Annie Lennox, David Hemblen, Donald Pleasence; *D:* Robert Altman; *W:* Harold Pinter. **TV**

Room at the Top 🦴🦴🦴½ **1959** Ambitious factory man forsakes true love and marries boss's daughter instead in this grim drama set in industrial northern England. Cast excels, with Harvey and Sears as the worker and his wife. Signoret is also quite compelling as the abandoned woman. Adapted from John Braine's novel and followed by "Life at the Top" and "Man at the Top." **118m/B VHS, DVD.** *GB* Laurence Harvey, Simone Signoret, Heather Sears, Hermione Baddeley, Avril Ungar, Donald Wolfit, Wendy Craig, Allan Cuthbertson, Ian Hendry, Donald Houston, Raymond Huntley, Miriam Karlin, Wilfred Lawson, Richard Pasco, Mary Peach, Prunella Scales, Beatrice Varley, John Westbrook, Delena Kidd; *D:* Jack Clayton; *W:* Neil Paterson; *C:* Freddie Francis; *M:* Mario Nascimbene. Oscars '59: Actress (Signoret), Adapt. Screenplay; British Acad. '58: Actress (Signoret), Film; Cannes '59: Actress (Signoret).

Room 43 🦴½ *Passport to Shame* **1958** Campy fable about a British cab driver who falls in love with a French girl, and stumbles onto a white-slavery ring when she falls victim to it. Features a young Caine and future novelist Collins in bit parts. **93m/B VHS.** Diana Dors, Herbert Lom, Eddie Constantine, Michael Caine, Jackie Collins; *D:* Alvin Rakoff.

Room Service 🦴🦴½ **1938** The Marx Brothers provide less than the usual mayhem here with Groucho as a penniless theatrical producer determined to remain in his hotel room until he can secure funds for his next play. Ball doesn't help matters much either. Not bad, but certainly not up to the zany Marx clan's usual stuff. **78m/B VHS.** Groucho Marx, Harpo Marx, Chico Marx, Lucille Ball, Ann Miller, Frank Albertson, Donald MacBride, Charles Halton; *D:* William A. Seiter; *W:* Morrie Ryskind; *C:* J. Roy Hunt; *M:* Roy Webb.

Room to Let 🦴🦴 **1949** An elderly woman and her daughter take in boarders in Victorian England. They rent a room to a man who claims to be a doctor, but the two women eventually become prisoners of fear, believing the man is actually Jack the Ripper. Will there be a vacancy soon? Somewhat disturbing and suspenseful. **68m/B VHS.** *GB* Jimmy Hanley, Valentine Dyall, Christine Silver, Merle Tottenham, Charles Hawtrey, Connie Smith, Laurence Naismith; *D:* Godfrey Grayson.

A Room with a View 🦴🦴🦴🦴 **1986** Engaging adaptation of E.M. Forster's novel of requited love. Lucy Honeychurch (Bonham Carter) is the feisty British idealist who rejects dashing George (Sands) for supercilious Cecil (Day-Lewis), then repents and finds (presumably) eternal passion. A multi-Oscar nominee, with great music (courtesy of Puccini), great scenery (courtesy of Florence), and great performances (courtesy of practically everybody, but supporters Smith, Dench, Callow, and Elliott must be particularly distinguished). Truly romantic, and there's much humor too. **117m/C VHS, DVD, Wide.** *GB* Helena Bonham Carter, Julian Sands, Denholm Elliott, Maggie Smith, Judi Dench, Simon Callow, Daniel Day-Lewis, Rupert Graves, Rosemary Leach; *D:* James Ivory; *W:* Ruth Prawer Jhabvala; *C:* Tony Pierce-Roberts; *M:* Richard Robbins. Oscars '86: Adapt. Screenplay, Art Dir./Set Dec., Costume Des.; British Acad. '86: Actress (Smith), Film, Support. Actress (Dench); Golden Globes '87: Support. Actress (Smith); Ind. Spirit '87: Foreign Film; Natl. Bd. of Review '86: Support. Actor (Day-Lewis); N.Y. Film Critics '86: Cinematog., Support. Actor (Day-Lewis); Writers Guild '86: Adapt. Screenplay.

Roommate **1984** A valedictorian church-goer and a rebellious iconoclast room together at Northwestern University in 1952, with the expected humorous results. Public TV presentation based on a John Updike story. **96m/C VHS.** Lance Guest, Barry Miller, Elaine Wilkes, Melissa Ford, David Bachman; *D:* Neil Cox. **TV**

Roommates 🦴🦴½ **1995 (PG)** Rocky Holeczek (Falk) is a cantankerous coot who, at age 75, decides to care for orphaned seven-year-old grandson Michael. Over the 30 years they are together, they fight over Rocky's old school ways and a grown-up Michael's (Sweeney) attempt to have a family of his own. But despite their bickering, Michael soon realizes that his 107-years-old grandfather's words are truly pearls of wisdom when faced with tragedy. Film hits the right sentimental buttons without going overboard with the tissues and Falk's performance, underneath the layers of latex make-up, is charmingly irascible. Based on co-writer Apple's own grandfather. **108m/C VHS.** Peter Falk, D.B. Sweeney, Julianne Moore, Ellen Burstyn; *D:* Peter Yates; *W:* Max Apple, Stephen Metcalfe; *C:* Mike Southon; *M:* Elmer Bernstein.

Rooster Cogburn 🦴🦴½ **1975 (PG)** A Bible-thumping schoolmarm joins up with a hard-drinking, hard-fighting marshal in order to capture a gang of outlaws who killed her father. Tired sequel to "True Grit" but the chemistry between Wayne and Hepburn is right on target. **107m/C VHS, DVD, Wide.** John Wayne, Katharine Hepburn, Richard Jordan, Anthony Zerbe, John McIntire, Strother Martin, Paul Koslo; *D:* Stuart Millar; *W:* Martin Julien; *C:* Harry Stradling Jr.; *M:* Laurence Rosenthal.

Rooster: Spurs of Death! woof! **1983 (PG)** An expose on cock fighting, in which a young idealist tries to stop the thriving sport in a small southern town. Dog of a movie that (not surprisingly) went straight to video. **90m/C VHS.** Vincent Van Patten, Ty Hardin, Kristine DeBell, Ruta Lee. **VIDEO**

Roosters 🦴🦴½ **1995 (R)** Gallo Morales (Olmos) is returning home, after serving seven years in prison for manslaughter, anxiously awaited by wife Juana (Braga), 20-year-old rebellious son Hector (Nucci), neglected adolescent daughter Angela (Lassez), and sexy sister Chata (Alonso). Gallo is a noted breeder of fighting cocks, which for him represent machismo and power but, to his resentment, it's Hector who owns a potential prize-winning bird, precipitating some explosive family conflicts. Adapted by Sanchez-Scott from her 1987 play. **93m/C VHS.** Edward James Olmos, Sonia Braga, Maria Conchita Alonso, Danny Nucci, Sarah Lassez; *D:* Robert M. Young; *W:* Milcha Sanchez-Scott; *C:* Reynaldo Villalobos; *M:* David Kitay.

Rootin' Tootin' Rhythm 🦴 *Rhythm on the Ranch* **1938** All's not quiet on the range, but Autry comes along to sing things back to normal. Goofy, clumsy, ubiquitous sidekick Burnette is a symbol for this whole effort. **55m/B VHS.** Gene Autry, Smiley Burnette, Monte Blue; *D:* Mack V. Wright.

Roots 🦴🦴🦴🦴 **1977** The complete version of Alex Haley's saga following a black man's search for his heritage, revealing an epic panorama of America's past. Dramatizing the shared heritage of millions of African Americans in an ennobling fashion, this milestone miniseries brought together dozens of black actors to create an accurate, if simplified, picture of several generations in one black family. The story begins with Kunta Kinte (Burton) going through his manhood trials in his Gambian village in Africa, only to be captured by slavers and shipped away to America. **573m/C VHS, DVD.** John Amos, Maya Angelou, Ed Asner, Lloyd Bridges, LeVar Burton, Chuck Connors, Cicely Tyson, Ben Vereen, Sandy Duncan, Tanya Boyd, Lynda Day George, Lorne Greene, Burl Ives, O.J. Simpson, Todd Bridges, Georg Stanford Brown, MacDonald Carey, Olivia Cole, Leslie Uggams, Ossie Davis; *D:* David Greene, Marvin J. Chomsky, John Erman, Gilbert Moses; *W:* William Blinn, Ernest Kinoy, M. Charles Cohen, James Lee; *C:* Stevan Larner, Joseph M. Wilcots; *M:* Quincy Jones, Gerald Fried. **TV**

Roots of Evil 🦴½ **1991 (R)** This erotic thriller follows a cop on the trail of a murderer who specializes in killing Hollywood's most beautiful prostitutes. Also available in unrated and Spanish-language versions. **?m/C VHS.** Alex Cord, Delia Sheppard, Charles Dierkop, Jillian Kesner; *D:* Gary Graver.

Roots: The Gift 🦴🦴 **1988** It's Christmas 1770, and Kunte Kinte (Burton) and Fiddler (Gossett) try to escape slavery via the Underground Railroad. In their attempt, they wind up giving the gift of freedom to several of their fellow slaves. **94m/C VHS.** Louis Gossett Jr., LeVar Burton, Michael Learned, Avery Brooks, Kate Mulgrew, Shaun Cassidy, John McMartin; *D:* Kevin Hooks; *C:* John A. Alonzo. **TV**

Roots: The Next Generation 🦴🦴🦴 **1979** Sequel to the landmark TV miniseries continuing the story of author Alex Haley's ancestors from the Reconstruction era of the 1880s to 1967, culminating with Haley's visit to West Africa where he is told the story of Kunta Kinte. **685m/C VHS.** Georg Stanford Brown, Lynne Moody, Henry Fonda, Richard Thomas, Marc Singer, Olivia de Havilland, Paul Koslo, Beah Richards, Stan Shaw, Harry (Henry) Morgan, Irene Cara, Dorian Harewood, Ruby Dee, Paul Winfield, James Earl Jones, Debbie Allen; *Cameos:* Al Freeman Jr., Marlon Brando. **TV**

Rope 🦴🦴🦴½ **1948 (PG)** In New York City, two gay college students murder a friend for kicks and store the body in a living room trunk. They further insult the dead by using the trunk as the buffet table and inviting his parents to the dinner party in his honor. Very dark humor is the theme in Hitchcock's first color film, which he innovatively shot in uncut ten-minute takes, with the illusion of a continuous scene maintained with tricky camera work. Based on the Patrick Hamilton play and on the Leopold-Laeb murder case. **81m/C VHS, DVD.** James Stewart, John Dall, Farley Granger, Cedric Hardwicke, Constance Collier; *D:* Alfred Hitchcock; *W:* Arthur Laurents; *C:* William V. Skall, Joseph Valentine; *M:* David Buttolph.

Rorret 🦴🦴🦴 **1987** "Rorret" is "terror" spelled backwards—a good indication of the psychological and physical terror Mr. Rorret, the owner of the Peeping Tom Cinema, inflicts upon his female patrons. The Cinema is devoted to the horror film and Rorret himself dresses like Peter Lorre in "M"; lives behind the movie screen, watching the films in mirror image; and enjoys the frightened reactions of his female patrons. He enjoys their reactions so much that he later stalks the women for real. Highlighted by recreated sequences from such psycho-terror classics as "Psycho," "Dial M for Murder," "Strangers on a Train," and "Peeping Tom." In Italian with English subtitles. **105m/C VHS.** *IT* Lou Castel, Anna Galiena, Massimo Venturiello; *D:* Fulvio Wetzl; *W:* Fulvio Wetzl.

Rosa Luxemburg 🦴🦴 **1986** Based on the life of the Jewish political radical, murdered in 1919. Involving herself with the German Social Democratic Party, Luxemburg undergoes numerous imprisonments and maintains a tempestuous personal life. Based primarily on Luxemburg's letters and speeches; charismatic performance by Sukowa. In German with English subtitles. **122m/C VHS.** *GE* Barbara Sukowa, Daniel Olbrychski, Otto Sander, Adelheid Arndt; *D:* Margarethe von Trotta; *W:* Margarethe von Trotta. Cannes '86: Actress (Sukowa).

Rosalie 🦴🦴½ **1938** A gridiron great from West Point falls for a mysterious beauty from Vassar. He soon learns that her father reigns over a tiny Balkan nation. Expensive, massive, imperfect musical; exotic romantic pairing fails to conceal plot's blah-ness. Oh well, at least Porter's music is good. ♫I've a Strange New Rhythm in My Heart; Why Should I Care?; Spring Love Is in the Air; Rosalie; It's All Over But the Shouting; Who Knows?; In the Still of the Night; To Love or Not to Love; Close (instrumental). **118m/B VHS.** Nelson Eddy, Eleanor Powell, Frank Morgan, Ray Bolger, Ilona Massey, Reginald Owen, Edna May Oliver, Jerry Colonna; *D:* Woodbridge S. Van Dyke; *M:* Cole Porter.

Rosalie Goes Shopping 🦴🦴🦴 **1989 (PG-13)** Satire about American consumerism hiding behind slapstick comedy, and it works, most of the time. Misplaced Bavarian (Sagebrecht) moves to Arkansas and begins spending wildly and acquiring "things." Twisty plot carried confidently by confident wackiness from Sagebrecht and supporters. **94m/C VHS.** *GE* Marianne Sagebrecht, Brad Davis, Judge Reinhold, Willie Harlander, Alex Winter, Erika Blumberger, Patricia Zehentmayr; *D:* Percy Adlon; *W:* Eleonore Adlon, Percy Adlon; *M:* Bob Telson.

The Rosary Murders 🦴🦴 **1987 (R)** Based on the William X. Kienzle mystery about a serial killer preying on nuns and priests. Father Koesler (Sutherland) must betray the confessional to stop him. Interesting, though sometimes muddled and too rarely tense. Filmed on location in Detroit. **105m/C VHS.** Donald Sutherland, Charles Durning, Belinda Bauer, Josef Sommer, James Murtaugh, John Danelle, Addison Powell, Kathleen Tolan, Janet Smith; *D:* Fred Walton; *W:* Fred Walton, Elmore Leonard; *C:* David Golia.

The Rose 🦴🦴🦴 **1979 (R)** Modeled after the life of Janis Joplin, Midler plays a young, talented and self-destructive blues/rock singer. Professional triumphs don't stop her lonely restlessness and confused love affairs. The best exhibition of the rock and roll world outside of documentaries. Electrifying film debut for Midler features an incredible collection of songs. ♫Fire Down Below; I've Written A Letter to Daddy; Let Me Call You Sweetheart; The Rose; Stay With Me; Camellia; Sold My

Soul To Rock 'n' Roll; Keep On Rockin'; When A Man Loves a Woman. **134m/C VHS.** Bette Midler, Alan Bates, Frederic Forrest, Harry Dean Stanton, David Keith; ***D:*** Mark Rydell; ***C:*** Vilmos Zsigmond. Golden Globes '80: Actress—Mus./Comedy (Midler), Song ("The Rose"); Natl. Soc. Film Critics '79: Support. Actor (Forrest).

The Rose and the Jackal ♂♂ **1990** Fun, intriguing fictionalization about the founder of the Pinkerton detective agency. During the Civil War, bearded, Scottish Reeve tries to persuade a wealthy Southern lady to help save the Union. **94m/C VHS.** Christopher Reeve, Madolyn Smith, Granville Van Dusen, Carrie Snodgress, Kevin McCarthy; ***D:*** Jack Gold. **CABLE**

The Rose Garden ♂♂½ **1989 (PG-13)** In modern Germany, a Holocaust survivor is put on trial for assaulting an elderly man. The victim, it turns out, was a Nazi guilty of heinous war crimes. Ullmann and Schell lend substance, though treatment of a powerful theme is inadequate. **112m/C VHS.** Liv Ullmann, Maximilian Schell, Peter Fonda, Jan Niklas, Kurt Hubner; ***D:*** Fons Rademakers; ***W:*** Paul Hengge; ***M:*** Egisto Macchi.

Rose Marie ♂♂♂ *Indian Love Call* **1936** An opera star falls in love with the mountie who captured her escaped convict brother. Hollywood legend has it that when a British singer was presented with the first line in "Indian Love Song," which is "When I'm calling you-oo-oo-oo-oo-oo-oo," the confused performer sang, "When I'm calling you, double oh, double oh, double oh..." Maybe true, maybe not, but funny anyway. Classic MacDonald-Eddy operetta. Remade in 1954. ♫Indian Love Call; Pardon Me, Madame; The Mounties; Rose Marie; Totem Tom Tom; Just for You; Tex Yeux; St. Louis Blues; Dinah. **112m/B VHS.** Jeanette MacDonald, Nelson Eddy, James Stewart, Allan Jones, David Niven, Reginald Owen; ***D:*** Woodbridge S. Van Dyke; ***C:*** William H. Daniels; ***M:*** Rudolf Friml.

Rose Marie ♂♂♂ **1954 (G)** Blyth is a lonely Canadian woman wooed by a mean spirited fur trapper and a gallant mountie. Unremarkable remake of the Eddy/MacDonald musical is saved by spectacular technicolor and CinemaScope photography. Choreography by Busby Berkeley. ♫Rose Marie; Indian Love Call; Totem Tom Tom; The Mounties; I Have the Love; The Right Place For A Girl; Free to be Free; The Mountie Who Never Got His Man. **115m/C VHS, Wide.** Ann Blyth, Howard Keel, Fernando Lamas, Bert Lahr, Marjorie Main, Joan Taylor, Chief Yowlachie, Abel Fernandez, Al Ferguson, Dabbs Greer, Lumsden Hare; ***D:*** Mervyn LeRoy; ***C:*** Paul Vogel.

Rose of Rio Grande ♂ **1938** A western musical about a Mexican gang that avenges the deaths of members of the upper strata. **60m/B VHS.** John Carroll, Movita, Antonio Moreno, Lena Basquette, Duncan Renaldo; ***D:*** William Nigh.

Rose of Washington Square ♂♂½ **1939** Singer Faye gets involved with the no-account Power, much to the dismay of her friend Jolson. They marry, and she becomes a singing sensation in the Ziegfeld Follies while he becomes an embarassment, eventually winding up on the wrong side of the law. Jolson stole the movie, singing some of his best numbers. This thinly disguised portrait of Fanny Brice caused the performer to sue for defamation of character; she eventually settled out of court. ♫California, Here I Come; My Mammy; Pretty Baby; Toot Toot Tootsie Goodbye; Rock-A-Bye Your Baby with a Dixie Melody; My Man; I'm Just Wild About Harry; I Never Knew Heaven Could Speak; Rose of Washington Square. **86m/B VHS.** Alice Faye, Tyrone Power, Al Jolson, William Frawley, Joyce Compton, Hobart Cavanaugh, Moroni Olsen; ***D:*** Gregory Ratoff; ***W:*** Nunnally Johnson; ***C:*** Karl Freund.

The Rose Tattoo ♂♂♂½ **1955** Magnani, in her U.S. screen debut, is just right as a Southern widow who cherishes her husband's memory, but falls for virile trucker Lancaster. Williams wrote this play and screenplay specifically for Magnani, who was never as successful again. Interesting character studies, although Lancaster doesn't seem right as an Italian longshoreman. **117m/B VHS.** Anna Magnani, Burt Lancaster, Marisa Pavan, Ben Cooper, Virginia Grey, Jo Van Fleet; ***D:*** Daniel Mann; ***W:*** Tennessee Williams, Hal Kanter; ***C:*** James Wong Howe; ***M:*** Alex North. Oscars '55: Actress (Magnani), Art Dir./Set Dec., B&W, B&W Cinematog.; British Acad. '56: Actress (Magnani); Golden Globes '56: Actress—Drama (Magnani), Support. Actress (Pavan); N.Y. Film Critics '55: Actress (Magnani).

Roseanne: An Unauthorized Biography ♂ **1994** Boring TV movie about the boorish (ex-)duo of Tom Arnold and Roseanne Barr Pentland Arnold. Recounts her troubled upbringing in Salt Lake City, her stormy marriage, and her long slog toward fame as a "domestic goddess" stand-up comedienne and TV series star. Miscasting of both leads hurts any chance this poor substitute had. **90m/C VHS.** Denny Dillon, David Graf, John Walcutt, John Karlen, Judith Scarpone, Danielle Harris.

Rosebud ♂ **1975 (PG)** Embarassingly dull film finds a group of PLO terrorists kidnapping five young women who were vacationing aboard O'Toole's yacht. He's supposedly a journalist but actually works for the CIA. Action ping-pongs between the plight of the victims and what's being done to rescue them but it's so boring you won't care. "Rosebud" is the name of the yacht. Based on a novel by Joan Hemingway and Paul Bonnecarrere. **126m/C VHS.** Peter O'Toole, Richard Attenborough, Kim Cattrall, Brigitte Ariel, Isabelle Huppert, Lalla Ward, Deborah Berger, Cliff Gorman, Claude Dauphin, Peter Lawford, Raf Vallone, Adrienne Corri; ***D:*** Otto Preminger; ***W:*** Eric Lee Preminger, Marjorie Kellogg.

Rosebud Beach Hotel ♂ *The Big Lobby; The No-Tell Hotel* **1985 (R)** Wimpy loser tries his hand at managing a rundown hotel in order to please his demanding girlfriend. Camp is okay, but this softporn excuse is horrible in every other way. **82m/C VHS.** Colleen Camp, Peter Scolari, Christopher Lee, Fran Drescher, Eddie Deezen, Chuck McCann, Hank Garrett, Hamilton Camp, Cherie Currie; ***D:*** Harry Hurwitz; ***C:*** Joao Fernandes.

Roseland ♂♂♂ **1977 (PG)** Three interlocking stories, set at New York's famous old Roseland Ballroom, about lonely people who live to dance. Not fully successful, but strong characters, especially in the second and third stories, make it worth watching, although it lacks energy. **103m/C VHS.** Christopher Walken, Geraldine Chaplin, Joan Copeland, Teresa Wright, Lou Jacobi; ***D:*** James Ivory; ***W:*** Ruth Prawer Jhabvala.

Rosemary's Baby ♂♂♂♂ **1968 (R)** A young woman, innocent and religious, and her husband, ambitious and agnostic, move into a new apartment. Soon the woman is pregnant, but she begins to realize that she has fallen into a coven of witches and warlocks, and that they claim the child as the antichrist. Gripping and powerful, subtle yet utterly horrifying, with luminous performances by all. Polanski's first American film; from Levin's best-seller. **134m/C VHS, DVD, Wide.** Mia Farrow, John Cassavetes, Ruth Gordon, Sidney Blackmer, Maurice Evans, Patsy Kelly, Elisha Cook Jr., Ralph Bellamy, Charles Grodin, Hanna Landy, Emmaline Henry, William Castle; ***D:*** Roman Polanski; ***W:*** Roman Polanski; ***C:*** William A. Fraker; ***M:*** Krzysztof Komeda; ***V:*** Tony Curtis. Oscars '68: Support. Actress (Gordon); Golden Globes '69: Support. Actress (Gordon).

Rosencrantz & Guildenstern Are Dead ♂♂♂ **1990 (PG)** Playwright Stoppard adapted his own absurdist 1967 play to film—which at first look makes as much sense as a "Swan Lake" ballet on radio. Patience is rewarded for those who stick with it. Two tragicomic minor characters in "Hamlet" squabble rhetorically and misperceive Shakespeare's plot tightening fatally around them. Uprooted from the stage environment, it's arcane but hilarious if you're paying attention. Roth and Oldman are superb as the doomed duo. **118m/C VHS.** *GB* Gary Oldman, Tim Roth, Richard Dreyfuss, Iain Glen, Joanna Roth, Donald (Don) Sumpter, Sven Medvesck, Joanna Miles, Ian Richardson, John Burgess, Vili Matula, Ljubo Zecevic; ***D:*** Tom Stoppard; ***W:*** Tom Stoppard; ***C:*** Peter Biziou; ***M:*** Stanley Myers. Venice Film Fest. '91: Picture.

Roses Bloom Twice ♂½ **1977** When a middle-aged widow decides to make up for some of the wild living that she missed during her marriage, she shocks her children. **87m/C VHS.** Glynis McNicoll, Michael Craig, Diane Craig, John Allen, Jennifer West; ***D:*** David Stevens.

Rosetta ♂♂ **1999 (R)** Rosetta (Dequenne) is a desperate 17-year-old Belgian who lives in a trailer with her alcoholic mother. Her joyless routine includes caring for her passed-out mom and frantically searching for some kind of employment, even if it means betraying her one friend, Riquet (Rongione), who works at a waffle stand and whose job Rosetta comes to covet. Claustrophobic and depressing. French with subtitles. **95m/C VHS, DVD.** *FR BE* Emilie Dequenne, Fabrizio Rongione, Anne Yernaux, Olivier Gourmet; ***D:*** Jean-Pierre Dardenne, Luc Dardenne; ***W:*** Jean-Pierre Dardenne, Luc Dardenne; ***C:*** Alain Marcoen. Cannes '99: Actress (Dequenne), Film.

Rosewood ♂♂♂ **1996 (R)** Based on the true story of the well-off African American community of Rosewood, Florida, which was destroyed by a white mob in 1923. Rhames is Mr. Mann, a war vet and Voight a white shopkeeper who, together, try to save innocent people from the tragic massacre that begins when a woman falsely accuses a black man of rape. Accurately shows the tensions present between blacks and whites of the time. Voight's character is not overly romanticized as the great white hope. The real hero is the reticent Rhames, a fictitious blend of real-life characters and Hollywood machismo. Both performances are strong and film succeeds as a detailed visual reminder of country's tragic history. Real-life survivors of the bloodshed finally won reparation from the Florida legislature in 1993. Singleton's location shoots in the Florida swamps caused problems for the crew, one of whom was sent to the hospital after a snake bite. **142m/C VHS, DVD.** Ving Rhames, Jon Voight, Don Cheadle, Michael Rooker, Bruce McGill, Loren Dean, Esther Rolle, Elise Neal, Catherine Kellner, Akosua Busia, Paul Benjamin, Mark Boone Jr., Muse Watson, Badja (Medu) Djola, Kathryn Meisle, Jaimz Woolvett; ***D:*** John Singleton; ***W:*** Gregory Poirier; ***C:*** Johnny E. Jensen; ***M:*** John Williams.

Rosie ♂♂ **1999** Rosie (Coppens) is 13 and is first seen living in an institution for delinquents. Her desperate story is told in flashbacks as the girl grows up in industrial Antwerp in a cramped apartment with her mother, Irene (de Roo), who insists Rosie say they are sisters when men come to visit, which they do frequently. When her moocher Uncle Michel (Vercruyssen) arrives, Rosie is even kicked out of her bedroom. It's no wonder she escapes into a romantic dreamworld she shares with a would-be boyfriend, Jimi (Wijnant), and the dangerous turn her real life takes. Flemish with subtitles. **97m/C VHS.** *BE* Aranka Coppens, Sara de Roo, Joost Wijnant, Frank Vercruyssen; ***D:*** Patrice Toye; ***W:*** Patrice Toye; ***C:*** Richard Van Oosterhout; ***M:*** John Parish.

Rosie: The Rosemary Clooney Story ♂♂½ **1982** Above average biography of Clooney's up-and-down career. Locke lip-synches Clooney's voice in songs. Orlando doesn't help matters portraying Jose Ferrer. **100m/C VHS.** Sondra Locke, Tony Orlando, Penelope Milford, Katherine Helmond, Kevin McCarthy, John Karlen, Cheryl Anderson, Robert Ridgely, Joey Travolta; ***D:*** Jackie Cooper. **TV**

Roswell: The U.F.O. Cover-Up ♂♂½ **1994 (PG-13)** Fact-based drama finds intelligence officer Major Jesse Marcel (McLachlan) investigating the wreckage of a craft near his Roswell, New Mexico air base in the summer of 1947. Marcel believes the craft is extraterrestrial—as are the strange bodies recovered from the wreckage. An Air Force press release announces a UFO but is quickly retracted and Marcel's suspicions ridiculed. A 30-year reunion still finds him obsessed and seeking to clear his name but this time Marcel's investigations may finally lead to the truth. Made for TV; based on the book "UFO Crash at Roswell" by Kevin D. Randle and Donald R. Schmitt. **91m/C VHS.** Kyle MacLachlan, Dwight Yoakam, Kim Greist, Martin Sheen, Xander Berkeley, J.D. Daniels, Doug Wert, John M. Jackson, Peter MacNicol, Bob Gunton, Charles Martin Smith; ***D:*** Jeremy Paul Kagan; ***W:*** Jeremy Paul Kagan, Arthur Kopit, Paul Davids; ***C:*** Steven Poster; ***M:*** Elliot Goldenthal. **TV**

R.O.T.O.R. ♂ **1988** R.O.T.O.R. (Robotic Officer of Tactical Operations Research) is a law enforcement robot that is supposed to stop criminals. But watch out! It might go beserk and wreck your town. **90m/C VHS.** Richard Gesswein, Margaret Trigg, Jayne Smith; ***D:*** Cullen Blaine.

Rough Cut ♂♂ **1980 (PG)** American diamond thief Reynolds lives in London, pursued by an aging Scotland Yard detective who wants to end his career in a blaze of glory. A beautiful lady is the decoy. Good chemistry; lousy script. **112m/C VHS.** Burt Reynolds, Lesley-Anne Down, David Niven, Timothy West, Joss Ackland, Patrick Magee; ***D:*** Donald Siegel; ***W:*** Larry Gelbart; ***C:*** Frederick A. (Freddie) Young.

Rough Justice ♂½ **1987** Spaghetti western about a lone gunfighter tracking down three killers. Kinski is a sexually aroused bad guy in this miserable excuse. What could he have been thinking? **95m/C VHS.** *IT* Klaus Kinski, Steven Tedd; ***D:*** Mario Costa.

Rough Magic ♂♂ *Miss Shumway; Jette un Sort* **1995 (PG-13)** Fantasy-noir-romance-comedy-on-the-road-movie-nostalgia-fest can't decide what it wants to be when it grows up. Fonda is a magician's assistant, with latent powers of her own, who flees to Mexico after witnessing a murder. Her fiance (Moffett) turns out to be the culprit and he hires drifter Crowe to track her down. Along the way, they meet a quack doctor (Broadbent) trying to find a magic Mayan potion, a garage owner who becomes a sausage, and a shaman. Sure, it's confusing, but the performances are good, and you could always play "Name That Genre" afterwards. Adapted from the novel "Miss Shumway Waves a Wand" by James Hadley Chase. **104m/C VHS.** *GB FR* Bridget Fonda, Russell Crowe, Jim Broadbent, D.W. Moffett, Paul Rodriguez, Euva Anderson; ***D:*** Clare Peploe; ***W:*** Clare Peploe, Robert Mundy, William Brookfield; ***C:*** John Campbell; ***M:*** Richard Hartley.

Rough Night in Jericho ♂½ **1967** Martin plays unredeemable scum in this cliched western. He's an ex-lawman trying to take over the town of Jericho and all that's left to own is the stagecoach line run by Simmons and McIntire. Coming to Simmons aid is Peppard, a former deputy marshall turned gambler. Predicatably violent. **104m/C VHS, DVD, Wide.** Dean Martin, Jean Simmons, George Peppard, John McIntire, Slim Pickens, Don Galloway; ***D:*** Arnold Laven; ***W:*** Sydney Boehm, Marvin H. Albert; ***C:*** Russell Metty; ***M:*** Don Costa.

Rough Riders ♂♂½ **1997** Miniseries covering the adventures of the Volunteer Cavalry, led by a pre-presidential Teddy Roosevelt (Berneger), and their travails during the Spanish-American War in 1898. Fighting in Cuba, the Calvary were a mixture of western outlaws and cowboys and eastern bluebloods—all of whom would have to learn to fight together. Filmed on locations in Texas. **240m/C VHS.** Tom Berenger, Sam Elliott, Gary Busey, Brad Johnson, Christopher Noth, Brian Keith, George Hamilton, R. Lee Ermey, Nicholas Chinlund, Dale Dye, Holt McCallany, Illeana Douglas, Geoffrey Lewis, William Katt, Adam Storke, Dakin Matthews, Francesco Quinn, Titus Welliver, Mark Moses; ***D:*** John Milius; ***W:*** John Milius, Hugh Wilson; ***C:*** Anthony B. Richmond; ***M:*** Peter Bernstein. **CABLE**

Rough Riders of Cheyenne ♂½ **1945** Sunset Carson ends the feud between the Carsons and the Sterlings. **54m/B VHS.** Sunset Carson, Peggy Stewart.

Rough Riders' Roundup ♂♂ **1939** Roy and the boys rid a mining town of its crooked manager. Less yodeling than later Roger's outings; also better all around. **54m/B VHS.** Roy Rogers, Raymond Hatton, Lynne Roberts, Dorothy Sebastian, Duncan Renaldo, George Montgomery; *D:* Joseph Kane.

Rough Ridin' Rhythm ♂½ **1937** Wallace is kidnapped to care for the orphaned child of a bandit's sister with Maynard being accused of having murdered the woman. But he's innocent and fights the gang to clear his name. Based on the story "Getting a Start in Life" by James Oliver Curwood. **58m/B VHS.** Kermit Maynard, Beryl Wallace, Ralph Peters, Betty Mack, Curly Dresden; *D:* J(ohn) P(aterson) McGowan.

Rough Riding Rangers ♂½ *The Secret Stranger* **1935** Threatening letters plague a western ranch family. **57m/B VHS.** Rex Lease, Janet Chandler.

Roughnecks ♂½ **1980** A team of Texas oil drillers attempt to dig the deepest oil well in history and chase women on the side. Too long, and not particularly action-packed or gripping. **240m/C VHS.** Sam Melville, Cathy Lee Crosby, Vera Miles, Harry (Henry) Morgan, Steve Forrest, Stephen McHattie, Wilford Brimley; *D:* Bernard McEveety. **TV**

Round Midnight ♂♂♂ **1986 (R)** An aging, alcoholic black American jazz saxophonist comes to Paris in the late 1950s seeking an escape from his self-destructive existence. A devoted young French fan spurs him to one last burst of creative brilliance. A moody, heartfelt homage to such expatriate bebop musicians as Bud Powell and Lester Young. In English and French with English subtitles. Available in a Spanish-subtitled version. **132m/C VHS, DVD, Wide.** *FR* Dexter Gordon, Lonette McKee, Francois Cluzet, Martin Scorsese, Herbie Hancock, Sandra Reaves-Phillips; *D:* Bertrand Tavernier; *W:* Bertrand Tavernier, David Rayfiel; *C:* Bruno de Keyzer. Oscars '86: Orig. Score.

Round Numbers ♂½ **1991 (R)** Judith Schweitzer believes her husband "Big Al the Muffler King" is having an affair with the gorgeous Muffler Mate of the Month, Mitzi (Playboy Playmate Hope Marie Carlton). Determined to get revenge, Judith books herself into the same health spa that Mitzi attends and the result is pure comedy. **98m/C VHS.** Kate Mulgrew, Samantha Eggar, Marty Ingels, Hope Marie Carlton, Shani Wallis, Natalie Barish, Debra Christofferson; *D:* Nancy Zala; *W:* Nancy Zala.

Round Trip to Heaven ♂♂ **1992 (R)** Party guy Larry (Feldman) and his innocent cousin (Galligan) take off in a borrowed Rolls Royce to go meet Larry's dream centerfold in a super model contest. Unfortunately, the Rolls' trunk is loaded with stolen money and Stoneface (Sharkey), the felon who stashed the cash, wants the money back. With Stoneface in pursuit these guys are in for the ride of their lives. For the teen set only. Also available with Spanish subtitles. **97m/C VHS.** Corey Feldman, Zach Galligan, Julie McCullough, Rowanne Brewer, Ray Sharkey; *D:* Alan Roberts.

The Round Up ♂♂½ *Szegenylegenyek Nehezeletuck; The Hopeless Ones; The Poor Outlaws* **1966** Brutal tale spins a realistic political web of fear. Set in 1868 in a prison camp, suspected Hungarian subversives, largely peasants and herdsmen, are thrown into jail and tortured. A direct and shocking exploration of life under dehumanizing, totalitarian rule. In Hungarian with English subtitles. **90m/B VHS.** *HU* Janos Gorbe, Tibor Molnar, Andras Kozak; *D:* Miklos Jancso; *W:* Gyula Hernadi.

Round-Up Time in Texas ♂♂ **1937** Autry delivers a herd of horses to his diamond-prospector brother in South Africa and has to deal with bandits after the jewels. Typical early Autry entry, with singin' on the side. **54m/B VHS.** Gene Autry, Smiley Burnette; *D:* Joseph Kane.

The Rounders ♂♂½ **1965** Two aging, no-account cowboys (Ford and Fonda) dream of giving up their broncobusting ways to open a bar in Tahiti where they can watch the world go by. But they have a habit of blowing all their money on women, whiskey, and bad bets. An ornery unbreakable horse may be the key to changing their luck. Mild-mannered comedy with beautiful Arizona scenery. **85m/C VHS.** Glenn Ford, Henry Fonda, Sue Ane Langdon, Hope Holiday, Chill Wills, Edgar Buchanan, Kathleen Freeman, Joan Freeman, Denver Pyle; *D:* Burt Kennedy; *W:* Burt Kennedy; *C:* Paul Vogel.

Rounders ♂♂½ **1998 (R)** Damon plays Mike, a law student who used to be a poker hustler, but is now ready to leave the game and settle down with girlfriend Jo (Mol). His good intentions are undermined by his "friend" Worm (Norton), whose gambling debts are mounting. Mike's return to the table doesn't reduce the debt; instead, he loses money and his reputation. Knowing he must get the money himself, Mike sets up a final showdown with Teddy KGB (Malkovich)—a tense game of Texas Hold 'Em in which Malkovich's drawn-out accent provides the most fun of the movie. Damon holds his own, using some elaborate monologues reminiscent of "Good Will Hunting," while Norton and Malkovich add a lot of spark. It's all style over substance, but that's what makes it (mostly) work. **120m/C VHS, DVD.** Matt Damon, Edward Norton, John Turturro, Gretchen Mol, Famke Janssen, John Malkovich, Martin Landau, Michael Rispoli, Melina Kanakaredes, Josh Mostel, Lenny Clarke, Tom Aldredge; *D:* John Dahl; *W:* David Levien, Brian Koppelman; *C:* Jean-Yves Escoffier; *M:* Christopher Young.

Rounding Up the Law ♂♂½ **1922** Good guy dupes bad guy while organ plays. **62m/B VHS, 8mm.** Russell Gordon, Chet Ryan, Patricia Palmer, William (Bill, Billy) McCall, Guinn "Big Boy" Williams; *D:* Charles Seeling.

Roustabout ♂♂½ **1964 (PG)** A roving, reckless drifter joins a carnival and romances the owner's daughter. Elvis rides on good support from Stanwyck et al. Welch has a bit part in her film debut; look for Terri Garr as a dancer. ♫Roustabout; Poison Ivy League; One Track Heart; Little Egypt; Wheels on My Heels; It's a Wonderful World; It's Carnival Time; Hard Knocks; There's a Brand New Day on the Horizon. **101m/C VHS, DVD.** Elvis Presley, Barbara Stanwyck, Joan Freeman, Leif Erickson, Sue Ane Langdon, Pat Buttram, Joan Staley, Dabbs Greer, Steve Brodie, Jack Albertson, Marianna Hill, Beverly Adams, Billy Barty, Richard Kiel, Raquel Welch; *D:* John Rich.

The Rousters ♂♂½ **1990 (PG)** Descendants of Wyatt Earp run a carnival in a small Western town. Comic misadventures arise when a modern varmint named Clayton comes looking for action. Cannell (of "The A-Team" and "Riptide" fame) cowrote and produced—with his usual extraordinary mix of the absurd and the dangerous. Unusual vehicle for Rogers, but she keeps her style and humor. Made for TV. **72m/C VHS.** Jim Varney, Mimi Rogers, Chad Everett, Maxine Stuart, Hoyt Axton; *D:* E.W. Swackhamer; *W:* E.W. Swackhamer, Stephen J. Cannell. **TV**

Route 9 ♂♂ **1998 (R)** Cliched story has some decent performances. Two smalltown sheriff's deputies (MacLachlan and Williams) discover a couple of dead bodies, drugs, and a stash of cash, which they decide to keep. But their boss (Coyote) gets suspicious and then the feds come investigating. **102m/C VHS, DVD.** Kyle MacLachlan, Wade Andrew Williams, Peter Coyote, Roma Maffia, Amy Locane, Miguel (Michael) Sandoval, Scott Coffey; *D:* David Mackay; *W:* Brendan Broderick, Rob Kerchner; *C:* Brian Sullivan; *M:* Don Davis. **CABLE**

Route 666 ♂♂½ **2001 (R)** Some very slick stylistic touches are brought to this action/horror that aspires to be another "From Dusk Til Dawn." Marshals Jack (Phillips) and Stephanie (Petty) are escorting a witness to a grand jury in Los Angeles when they become lost on a remote highway. Years ago, a chain gang was murdered there, and they return as inmates of the living dead for revenge. The ultra-violence is silly but some of the visual tricks are pretty cool. **90m/C DVD, Wide.** Lou Diamond Phillips, Lori Petty, Steven Williams, Dale Midkiff, Alex McArthur, Mercedes Colon, L.Q. (Justus E. McQueen) Jones; *D:* William Wesley; *W:* William Wesley, Thomas N. Weber, Scott Fivelson; *C:* Philip Lee; *M:* Terry Plumeri.

The Rover ♂½ *The Adventurer* **1967** Peyrol (Quinn) is involved in counterrevolutionary forces during the Napoleonic War and takes refuge in the home of Caterina (Hayworth), where he falls in love with her shy and mentally slow niece, Arlette (Schiaffino). Very dull adaptation of the Joseph Conrad novel. **103m/C VHS.** *IT* Anthony Quinn, Rosanna Schiaffino, Rita Hayworth, Richard Johnson; *D:* Terence Young; *W:* Luciano Vincenzoni, Jo Eisinger; *C:* Leonida Barboni; *M:* Ennio Morricone.

Rover Dangerfield ♂♂ **1991 (G)** Lovable Las Vegas hound Rover Dangerfield searches for respect but finds none. The results are hilarious. Quality animation from a project developed by Rodney Dangerfield and Harold Ramis. **78m/C VHS, 8mm.** *D:* Jim George; *W:* Harold Ramis; *M:* David Newman; *V:* Rodney Dangerfield.

Row Your Boat ♂♂ **1998** Ex-con Jamey (Bon Jovi), who took a burglary rap for his brother (Forsythe), is determined to go straight after his release from prison. He gets a job as a census taker, which is how he meets Asian immigrant single mom Chun Hua (Ling) who will become a part of a scheme by Jamey's no-good brother. **106m/C VHS, DVD.** Jon Bon Jovi, William Forsythe, Bai Ling, Jill(ian) Hennessey, John Ventimiglia; *D:* Sollace Mitchell; *W:* Sollace Mitchell; *C:* Michael Barrow, Zoltan David; *M:* Phil Ramone.

The Rowdy Girls ♂♂ **2000** Sharp-shooting Tweed disguises herself as a nun and meets up with bullwhip-wielding wild woman Strain and runaway bride Brooks in order to cross the western frontier. And no amount of scurvy outlaws are going to stop them. Ogle to your heart's content. **88m/C VHS, DVD.** Shannon Tweed, Julie Strain, Deanna Brooks, Laszlo Vargo; *D:* Steve Nevius; *W:* India Allen. **VIDEO**

Rowing Through ♂♂ **1996** Tiff Wood (Ferguson) is a top sculler at Harvard who is sacrificing everything in his obsession to win gold at the 1980 Moscow Olympics. And he has the best chance—until the U.S. decides to boycott the games. But Tiff refuses to give up his dream and struggles four more years towards the '84 Olympics—even though it means proving himself against a younger group of competitors. **115m/C VHS, DVD.** *CA JP* Colin Ferguson, Leslie Hope, Peter Murnik, Kenneth Welsh, Michiko Hada, Helen Shaver, James Hyndman, Christopher Jacobs; *D:* Masato Harada; *W:* Masato Harada, Will Aitken; *C:* Sylvain Brault; *M:* Masahiro Kawasaki.

Rowing with the Wind ♂♂ *Remando al Viento* **1988 (R)** The story behind Mary Shelley's (McInnerny) writing of "Frankenstein," amidst the decadence of Mary and Percy B.'s (Pelka) 1816 Swiss sojourn with Lord Byron (Grant). Hurley has the relatively small role of Claire, Mary's half-sister and Byron's former lover. **95m/C VHS.** *SP* Lizzy McInnerny, Hugh Grant, Valentine Pelka, Elizabeth Hurley, Jose Luis Gomez, Aitana Sanchez-Gijon; *D:* Gonzalo Suarez; *W:* Gonzalo Suarez; *C:* Carlos Suarez.

Roxanne ♂♂♂ **1987 (PG)** A modern comic retelling of "Cyrano de Bergerac." The romantic triangle between a big nosed, small town fire chief, a shy fireman and the lovely astronomer they both love. Martin gives his most sensitive and believable performance. Don't miss the bar scene where he gets back at a heckler. A wonderful adaptation for the modern age. **107m/C VHS, DVD, 8mm, Wide.** Steve Martin, Daryl Hannah, Rick Rossovich, Shelley Duvall, Michael J. Pollard, Fred Willard, John Kapelos, Max Alexander, Damon Wayans, Matt Lattanzi, Kevin Nealon; *D:* Fred Schepisi; *W:* Steve Martin; *C:* Ian Baker; *M:* Bruce Smeaton. L.A. Film Critics '87: Actor (Martin); Natl. Soc. Film Critics '87: Actor (Martin); Writers Guild '87: Adapt. Screenplay.

Roxie Hart ♂♂½ **1942** Sassy '20s Chicago dance hall girl Roxie (Rogers) decides to take the fall when hubby (Chandler) murders a man. (She sees it as a publicity boost to her career). Slick lawyer Billy Flynn (Menjou) knows he can get the tootsie off if she justs flashes the jury her considerable sex appeal. Montgomery's a smitten reporter who catches Roxie's eye. Based on the play "Chicago" by Maurine Watkins and previously filmed in 1927. Bob Fosse later adapted the play for a Broadway musical. **75m/B VHS.** Ginger Rogers, Adolphe Menjou, George Montgomery, Lynne Overman, Nigel Bruce, Phil Silvers, Sara Allgood, William Frawley, Spring Byington, George Chandler; *D:* William A. Wellman; *W:* Nunnally Johnson; *C:* Leon Shamroy; *M:* Alfred Newman.

The Royal Bed ♂♂½ *The Queen's Husband* **1931** King Eric's queen really wears the pants in the family, and when she leaves on a trip, he's left helpless and hapless. A revolution erupts, and his daughter announces she plans to marry a commoner. What's a king to do? **74m/B VHS.** Lowell Sherman, Nance O'Neil, Mary Astor, Anthony Bushell, Gilbert Emery, Robert Warwick, J. Carrol Naish; *D:* Lowell Sherman.

Royal Deceit ♂½ *Prince of Jutland* **1994 (R)** Young Amled (Bale) is heir to the 6th century kingdom of Jutland. But when his father is murdered by Amled's jealous uncle Fenge (Byrne), the youth feigns insanity to save himself and then begins to plot his revenge. Very familiar story doesn't arouse more than mild interest despite the cast. **85m/C VHS.** Gabriel Byrne, Helen Mirren, Christian Bale, Brian Cox, Kate Beckinsale, Steven Waddington, Tom Wilkinson, Tony Haygarth, Saskia Wickham, Brian Glover; *D:* Gabriel Axel; *C:* Henning Kristiansen; *M:* Per Norgard.

Royal Flash ♂♂♂ **1975 (PG)** Satirical adventure picture, witty and fast paced, with a few real life period characters thrown in for good measure. Cowardly swashbuckler Flashman, wanting to enter high society, is used to advance a political cause when he is forced to impersonate a Prussian nobleman and marry a duchess. Script by Fraser and based on his series of novels featuring the Flashman character. **98m/C VHS.** *GB* Malcolm McDowell, Alan Bates, Florinda Bolkan, Oliver Reed, Britt Ekland, Lionel Jeffries, Tom Bell, Alastair Sim, Michael Hordern, Joss Ackland, Christopher Cazenove, Bob Hoskins; *D:* Richard Lester; *W:* George MacDonald Fraser; *C:* Geoffrey Unsworth.

A Royal Scandal ♂♂½ **1996** And you thought Chuck and Di made a hash of their marriage. The British should be used to marital scandal as this saga on the disasters befalling Princess Caroline of Brunswick (Lynch) and Prince George (Grant), aptly demonstrates. The extravagant George is forced to marry through political and financial pressure but loathes the unrefined Caroline practically on sight. As soon as a royal heir is on the way, they cease to live together and George goes back to his mistresses. But although Caroline will agree to a settlement, she refuses a divorce and when George becomes King George IV, Caroline fully intends to be Queen. **60m/C VHS.** *GB* Richard E. Grant, Susan Lynch, Frances Barber, Michael Kitchen, Denis Lawson, Oliver Ford Davies, Irene Richards; *D:* Sheree Folkson; *W:* Stanley Price; *C:* John Daly; *M:* John Altman; *Nar:* Ian Richardson.

The Royal Tenenbaums ♂♂♂½ **2001 (R)** Anderson and Wilson's third and most ambitious film concerns a wildly eccentric family of kid geniuses who converge upon their childhood home as unhappy adults, just as their long-estranged father shows up looking for handouts and understanding, and mother is considering remarriage to the family accountant. Book lovers will appreciate the literary allusions—the Tenenbaum house seems lifted from the pages of J.D. Salinger or John Irving—and storybook styling, down to the chapter headings and gruff narration. Inventive script and quirky dialogue carry a story that sometimes becomes cartoonish, as most of the characters are one-dimensional. Some may find the film's overt weirdness a bit much, but there's a heart underneath it all. Hackman's performance as the dastardly, tactless, and yet wholly lovable Royal is a supreme comic feat. Depression has never been so fun. **108m/C VHS, DVD.** *US* Gene Hackman, Anjelica Huston, Gwyneth Paltrow, Ben Stiller, Luke Wilson, Owen C. Wilson, Bill Murray, Danny Glover, Seymour Cassel, Kumar Pallana, Grant Rosenmeyer, Jonah Meyerson, Stephen Lea Sheppard; *D:* Wes Anderson; *W:* Owen C. Wilson, Wes Anderson; *C:* Robert Yeoman; *M:* Mark Mothersbaugh; *Nar:* Alec Baldwin. Golden Globes '02: Actor—Mus./Comedy (Hackman); Natl. Soc. Film Critics '01: Actor (Hackman).

Royal Warriors *In the Line of Duty; Police Assassins; Ultra Force; Huang Jia Zhan Shi* **1986** Watch Michelle kick major butt! Policewoman Yeoh teams up with a retired Japanese cop and an airport security officer to prevent a terrorist highjacking. When the terrorist's associates decide to get even, the three must continue to fight together to save themselves. Chinese with subtitles or dubbed. **85m/C VHS, DVD.** *HK* Michelle Yeoh, Henry Sanada, Michael Wong; ***D:*** David Chung.

Royal Wedding *Wedding Bells* **1951** Astaire and Powell play a brother-and-sister dance team who go to London during the royal wedding of Princess Elizabeth, and find their own romances. Notable for the inspired songs and Astaire's incredible dancing on the ceiling and walls; Lerner's first screenplay. The idea came from Adele Astaire's recent marriage to a British Lord. ♫Too Late Now; Sunday Jumps; How Can You Believe Me When I Said I Love You When You Know I've Been A Liar All My Life?; You're All the World to Me; The Happiest Day of My Life; Open Your Eyes; Ev'ry Night at Seven; I Left My Hat in Haiti; What A Lovely Day For A Wedding. **93m/C VHS, DVD.** Fred Astaire, Jane Powell, Peter Lawford, Keenan Wynn, Sarah Churchill; ***D:*** Stanley Donen; ***W:*** Alan Jay Lerner; ***C:*** Robert Planck; ***M:*** Johnny Green, Burton Lane, Albert Sendry.

Royce **1993 (R)** After a successful mission, Royce's CIA team is disbanded. But some former agents aren't happy with early retirement and decide to go into business for themselves. **98m/C VHS.** James Belushi, Chelsea Field, Miguel Ferrer, Peter Boyle; ***D:*** Rod Holcomb; ***W:*** Paul Bernbaum.

R.P.M. **1997 (R)** Professional car thief Luke (Arquette) takes up an offer to steal a prototype fuel-less supercar for a very large sum of money. However, he's not the only one after the goods. **91m/C VHS, DVD.** David Arquette, Famke Janssen, Emmanuelle Seigner, Jerry Hall; ***D:*** Ian Sharp; ***C:*** Harvey Harrison; ***M:*** Alan Lisk. **VIDEO**

R.P.M.* (*Revolutions Per Minute) ½ **1970 (R)** Another chance to relive the '60s. Student activists force the university hierarchy to appoint their favorite radical professor president. Hip prof-turned-prez Quinn is between a rock and a hard place, and allows police to crack down. Could have been intriguing, but loses steam; in any case, the script and direction both stink. **90m/C VHS.** Anthony Quinn, Paul Winfield, Gary Lockwood, Ann-Margret, Rigg Kennedy; ***D:*** Stanley Kramer; ***W:*** Erich Segal; ***M:*** Perry Botkin.

R.S.V.P. ½ **1984 (R)** Hollywood party honoring a writer turns tragic when a body is found in the guest of honor's pool. Most interesting part is watching the porn stars who make up most of the cast fail at acting while dressed. **87m/C VHS.** Harry (Herbert Streicher) Reems, Lynda Wiesmeier; ***D:*** Lem Amero.

Rubberface **1981 (PG)** Tony Maroni (Carrey) is a very bad but very determined comedian. And he may just catch a break when he teams up with joke writer Janet (Glassbourg). Made for Canadian TV. **48m/C VHS.** *CA* Jim Carrey, Adah Glassbourg; ***D:*** Glen Salzman, Rebecca Yates. **TV**

Rubdown **1993** An ex-baseball player, turned Beverly Hills masseur, finds himself the victim of a frame-up when one of his clients is murdered. **88m/C VHS.** Jack Coleman, Michelle Phillips, Kent Williams, Alan Thicke, Catherine Oxenberg, William Devane; ***D:*** Stuart Cooper; ***W:*** Clyde Allen Hayes; ***M:*** Gerald Gouriet.

Rubin & Ed **1992 (PG-13)** Ed is a real estate groupie who bribes the eccentric Rubin to attend a get-rich-quick seminar. Rubin decides to cash in on the favor by taking Ed on the road in search of the perfect gravesite for Rubin's long-dead feline. If that sounds wacky, just wait—the fun really begins when the duo is stranded in Death Valley and begins to suffer from sunstroke and hallucinations. Those who dream of weirdos bonding in the desert may be enthused but other viewers may thirst for something more. **82m/C VHS.** Crispin Glover, Howard Hesseman, Karen Black, Michael Greene, Brittney Lewis; ***D:*** Trent Harris; ***W:*** Trent Harris; ***C:*** Bryan Duggan.

Ruby **1977 (R)** A young woman, christened in blood and raised in sin, has a love affair with the supernatural and murders up a storm at a drive-in. Confused, uneven horror a step up from most similar flicks. **85m/C VHS, DVD, Wide.** Roger Davis, Janit Baldwin, Piper Laurie, Stuart Whitman; ***D:*** Curtis Harrington; ***W:*** Barry Schneider; ***C:*** William Mendenhall; ***M:*** Don Ellis.

Ruby ½ **1992 (R)** Another in the increasing number of Kennedy assassination and conspiracy dramas—this one told from the viewpoint of Jack Ruby, Lee Harvey Oswald's killer. Confusing plot, somewhat redeemed by the performances of Aiello and Fenn. Combines actual footage of Ruby shooting Oswald with black-and-white filmed scenes. Based on the play "Love Field" by Stephen Davis. **111m/C VHS.** Joe (Johnny) Viterelli, Danny Aiello, Sherilyn Fenn, Arliss Howard, Tobin Bell, David Duchovny, Richard Sarafian, Joe Cortese, Marc Lawrence; ***D:*** John MacKenzie; ***W:*** Stephen Davis; ***C:*** Phil Meheux; ***M:*** John Scott.

Ruby Bridges ½ **1998** On November 14, 1960, six-year-old Ruby Bridges (Monet) became the first black student to integrate the New Orleans public school system. She started her first day of first grade classes at William Frantz Elementary School escorted by four federal marshalls, enduring hostile crowds and death threats because of her mother Lucielle's (Rochon) desire for her daughter to get an equal education despite what the Bridge's family would endure. **90m/C VHS.** Michael Beach, Penelope Ann Miller, Lela Rochon, Chaz Monet, Kevin Pollak, Diana Scarwid; ***D:*** Euzhan Palcy; ***W:*** Toni Johnson. **TV**

Ruby Gentry ½ **1952** White-trash girl Jones, cast aside by man-she-loves Heston, marries wealthy Malden to spite him, then seeks revenge. Classic Southern theme of comeuppance, good direction and acting lift it a notch. **82m/B VHS.** Charlton Heston, Jennifer Jones, Karl Malden; ***D:*** King Vidor.

Ruby in Paradise **1993 (R)** Leaving her dead-end life in Tennessee, Gissing (Judd) moves to Panama City, Florida and lands a job selling souvenirs for no-nonsense Mildred Chambers (Lyman). Although pursued by two very different men, Ruby concentrates more on self-exploration, recording her thoughts in a journal. A seemingly effortless portrayal of Ruby Lee by Judd (daughter of Naomi and sister of Wynonna Judd) makes for a pleasurable character study of a young woman on her own. **115m/C VHS.** Ashley Judd, Todd Field, Bentley Mitchum, Allison Dean, Dorothy Lyman, Betsy Dowds; ***D:*** Victor Nunez; ***W:*** Victor Nunez; ***C:*** Alex Vlacos; ***M:*** Charles Engstrom. Ind. Spirit '94: Actress (Judd); Sundance '93: Grand Jury Prize.

Ruby Jean and Joe **1996 (PG-13)** Aging rodeo star Joe Wade (Selleck) doesn't want to leave the circuit even though it's obvious that his body can't take the punishment anymore. Joe gets more depressed until he picks up hitchhiker Ruby Jean (Johnson), a sarcastic teenager in search of a future. The unlikely duo form a friendship that may offer salvation to them both. **100m/C VHS.** Tom Selleck, JoBeth Williams, Rebekah Johnson, Ben Johnson; ***D:*** Geoffrey Sax; ***W:*** James Lee Barrett; ***C:*** James L. Carter; ***M:*** Stephen Graziano. **CABLE**

Ruby's Dream *Dear Mr. Wonderful* **1982** A bowling alley and nightclub owner dreams of making it big in Las Vegas. After his dreams crash to the ground, however, he realizes what is truly important in life. **100m/C VHS.** Joe Pesci, Ed O'Ross, Evan Handler, Ivy Ray Browning; ***D:*** Peter Lilienthal; ***W:*** Sam Koperwas; ***C:*** Michael Ballhaus; ***M:*** Claus Bantzer.

Ruckus *The Loner* **1981 (PG)** A Vietnam vet uses his training to defend himself when he runs into trouble in a small Alabama town. Less obnoxious than "First Blood," (which came later), but basically the same movie. **91m/C VHS, DVD, Wide.** Dirk Benedict, Linda Blair, Ben Johnson, Richard Farnsworth, Matt Clark; ***D:*** Max Kleven; ***W:*** Max Kleven; ***C:*** Don Burgess; ***M:*** Willie Nelson.

Ruddigore **197?** The Lords of Ruddigore have been bound for centuries by a terribly inconvenient curse; they must commit a crime every day or die a horribly painful death. When the Lord of Ruddigore passes his mantle on to the new heir, the young heir loses both his good reputation and his very proper fiancee. A new version of Gilbert and Sullivan's opera. **112m/C VHS.** Vincent Price, Keith Michell, Sandra Dugdale.

Rude **1996 (R)** Rude's (Lewis) a Jamaican-Canadian pirate-radio DJ in Toronto, who narrates three stories about urban life: window dresser Maxine (Crawford) struggles to recover from an abortion after her lover leaves her; frightened boxer Jordan (Chevolleau) tries to deal with his own homosexuality after participating with friends in a gay bashing; and ex-con Luke (Wint) returns to his wife (now a police officer) and young son. He tries to resist returning to his drug dealing past and cope with a jealous younger brother (Johnson). Debut for director Virgo. **90m/C VHS, DVD.** *CA* Sharon M. Lewis, Richard Chevolleau, Rachael Crawford, Maurice Dean Wint, Stephen Ellen, Clark Johnson, Melanie Nicholls-King, Stephen Shellen; ***D:*** Clement Virgo; ***W:*** Clement Virgo; ***C:*** Barry Stone; ***M:*** Aaron David.

Rude Awakening ½ **1981** A real estate agent is tortured by bizarre nightmares which lead to an unusual series of events. Part of the "Thriller Video" series. **60m/C VHS.** Denholm Elliott, James Laurenson, Pat Heywood; ***D:*** Peter Sasdy.

Rude Awakening **1989 (R)** Hippies Cheech and Roberts (where's Chong?) settled in a South American commune 20 years ago. Now they're back, and don't know what to make of old pals Carradine and Hagerty who have become—that's right—yuppies. Rip Van Winkle-ian farce draws a few yuks, but could have been much funnier. Points for trying. **100m/C VHS.** Eric Roberts, Richard "Cheech" Marin, Julie Hagerty, Robert Carradine, Buck Henry, Louise Lasser, Cindy Williams, Andrea Martin, Cliff DeYoung; ***D:*** Aaron Russo, David Greenwalt; ***W:*** Richard LaGravenese; ***M:*** Jonathan Elias.

Rudy ½ **1993 (PG)** Likeable, true story about a little guy who triumphs over big odds. Daniel "Rudy" Ruettiger (Astin) dreams of playing football for Notre Dame, no matter how farfetched the dream. He's a mediocre student, physically unsuitable for big time college ball, but sheer determination helps him attain his dream. Astin delivers an engaging performance and is backed up by a good supporting cast. Sentimental story stretches the truth with typical shameless Hollywood manipulation, but is still entertaining. From the director and writer of another David beats Goliath sports film, "Hoosiers." **112m/C VHS, DVD, 8mm, Wide.** Robert J. Steinmiller Jr., Vince Vaughn, Sean Astin, Ned Beatty, Charles S. Dutton, Lili Taylor, Robert Prosky, Jason Miller, Ron Dean, Chelcie Ross, Jon Favreau, Greta Lind, Scott Benjaminson, Christopher Reed; ***D:*** David Anspaugh; ***W:*** Angelo Pizzo; ***C:*** Oliver Wood; ***M:*** Jerry Goldsmith.

Rudyard Kipling's The Jungle Book ½ *The Jungle Book* **1994 (PG)** Respectable live-action version from Disney of the Rudyard Kipling tale of Mowgli (Lee), the boy who's raised by a wolf pack after getting lost in an Indian jungle. This time around Mowgli gets to grow up—enough to have a romantic interest in the lovely Kitty (Headey), the daughter of British officer, Major Brydon (Neill). His rival is the supercilious Captain Boone (Elwes), who learns Mowgli knows the location of a hidden jungle treasure. Now Mowgli must count on his friends, Grey Brother the wolf, Baloo the bear, and Bagheera the black panther, to defeat the greedy Boone and win Kitty. Filmed in India. **111m/C VHS.** Jason Scott Lee, Cary Elwes, Sam Neill, Lena Headey, John Cleese; ***D:*** Stephen Sommers; ***W:*** Stephen Sommers.

Rudyard Kipling's the Second Jungle Book: Mowgli and Baloo *Jungle Book 2; Mowgli and Baloo: Jungle Book 2; The Second Jungle Book: Mowgli and Baloo* **1997 (PG)** Actually a prequel to "Rudyard Kipling's The Jungle Book," the story centers on the ten-year-old Mowgli (Williams) and his efforts to stay among his animal friends in the jungle. After he is spotted by a scout for P.T. Barnum's circus (Campbell), he must elude the hastily organized group that's out to capture and exploit him. He must also dodge the Bandars, a group of funky monkeys who want to make Mowgli their unwilling leader. The special effects are nowhere near as good as its predecessor, with matte shots that make some of the animals look like they were added with magic markers. The story is a classic, however, and the performances (especially Williams') are good. **88m/C VHS.** Jamie Williams, Billy Campbell, Roddy McDowall, Cornelia Hayes O'Herlihy, David Paul Francis, Gulsham Grover, Dyrk Ashton, B.J. Hogg, Amy Robbins, Hal Fowler; ***D:*** Duncan McLachlan; ***W:*** Bayard Johnson, Matthew Horton; ***C:*** Adolfo Bartoli; ***M:*** John Scott.

The Rue Morgue Massacres ½ **1973 (R)** A modern reprise of the Poe story with touches of Frankensteinia thrown in; plenty of gore. **90m/C VHS.** *SP* Paul (Jacinto Molina) Naschy, Rossana Yanni, Maria Perschy, Vic Winner, Mary Ellen Arpon, Jacinto (Jack) Molina; ***D:*** Javier Aguirre.

Ruggles of Red Gap **1935** Classic comedy about an uptight British butler who is "won" by a barbarous American rancher in a poker game. Laughton as the nonplussed manservant is hilarious; supporting cast excellent. Third and far superior filming of Harry Leon Wilson story. One of the all-time great comedies, the film was remade musically with Bob Hope and Lucille Ball as "Fancy Pants" (1950). **90m/B VHS.** Charles Laughton, Mary Boland, Charlie Ruggles, ZaSu Pitts, Roland Young, Leila Hyams, James Burke, Maude Eburne; ***D:*** Leo McCarey; ***W:*** Walter DeLeon; ***M:*** Ralph Rainger. N.Y. Film Critics '35: Actor (Laughton).

Rugrats in Paris: The Movie **2000 (G)** There are enough pop culture references and sly humor for the parents and enough diaper, booger and barf jokes for the kids to make this entertaining viewing for the entire family. Tommy, Chuckie and the rest of the gang from the animated Nickelodeon series return for their second full-length feature, this time trekking off to France as Tommy's inventor dad tries to fix a mechanical dinosaur at a very EuroDisney-style theme park. Also, Chuckie's dad Chas is wooed by the kid-hating park operator Coco La Bouche (voice of Susan Sarandon), who only wants to marry him because she thinks that there's a promotion in it for her. This all leads to a bizarre chase through Paris involving the giant dinosaur and a huge escargot. **80m/C VHS, DVD, Wide.** ***D:*** Stig Bergqvist, Paul Demeyer; ***W:*** David N. Weiss, Jill Gorey, Barbara Herndon, Kate Boutilier; ***M:*** Mark Mothersbaugh; ***V:*** Elizabeth (E.G. Dailey) Daily, Christine Cavanaugh, Susan Sarandon, Jack Riley, Michael Bell, Melanie Chartoff, Tara Charendoff, Kath Soucie, John Lithgow, Debbie Reynolds, Mako, James D. Stern, Cheryl Chase, Julia Kato, Lisa McClowry.

The Rugrats Movie **1998 (G)** Precocious one-year-old Tommy is afraid he'll be forgotten by his parents with the arrival of baby brother Dil, so he and his pals decide to return the infant to the hospital. Boarding a talking wagon named Reptar (invented by Tommy's father), they embark on an adventure that takes them to a scary forest where they run into wolves, a "wizard," and a band of escaped circus monkeys that kidnap Dil in the film's most frightening sequence. While dishing out lessons about responsibility, bravery, friendship, and jealousy, film also contains parodies of and homages to several films, including "Raiders of the Lost Ark." The humor works on many levels, so this one is enjoyable for all ages. **79m/C VHS, DVD, Wide.** ***D:*** Norton Virgien, Igor Kovalyov; ***W:*** David N. Weiss, J. David Stem; ***M:*** Mark Mothersbaugh; ***V:*** Elizabeth (E.G. Dailey) Daily, Christine Cavanaugh, Tara Charendoff, Melanie Chartoff, Jack Riley, Joe Alaskey, Phil(ip) Proctor, Whoopi Goldberg, David

Spade, Kath Soucie, Cheryl Case, Cree Summer, Michael Bell, Tress MacNeille, Busta Rhymes.

Rule #3 🦴🦴 **1993** "Never believe everything you see." That's the rule con artist Travis West lives by. This time he's got two scams planned—a Las Vegas real estate swindle and a cash ripoff of a former nemesis. Double- and triple-crosses abound. Based on the true story of West, who swindled more than $9 million in 15 years. **93m/C VHS.** Mitchell Cox, Marcia Swayze; ***D:*** Mitchell Cox.

Rulers of the City 🦴 **1971** Young gangster avenges his father's death. **91m/C VHS.** Jack Palance, Edmund Purdom, Al Cliver, Harry Baer.

Rules of Engagement 🦴🦴½ **2000 (R)** Marine Childers (Jackson) is assigned the task of rescuing an ambassador and his family from a hostile area in Yemen. The mission goes terribly wrong and an order is given by Childers, resulting in the death of 83 Yemeni women and children. To keep the US from suffering any terrorist backlash, Childers is charged with mass murder. Effective courtroom drama (which spares us the cliched surprise witness), although it merely grazes the complex issues of military decision-making due to its skeletal script. Intensity and momentum is sustained by the towering performances of leads Jackson and Jones as Childers's buddy and lawyer. After two weeks as box-office leader, film received some protest over its negative portrayal of Arab-Americans. Based on a story by ex-Secretary of the Navy James Webb. **128m/C VHS, DVD, Wide.** Elayne J. Taylor, Samuel L. Jackson, Tommy Lee Jones, Guy Pearce, Bruce Greenwood, Blair Underwood, Philip Baker Hall, Anne Archer, Ben Kingsley, Mark Feuerstein, Dale Dye; ***D:*** William Friedkin; ***W:*** Stephen Gaghan; ***C:*** Nicola Pecorini, William A. Fraker; ***M:*** Mark Isham.

The Rules of the Game 🦴🦴🦴🦴 *Le Regle du Jeu* **1939** Renoir's masterpiece, in which a group of French aristocrats, gathering for a weekend of decadence and self-indulgence just before WWII, becomes a metaphor for human folly under siege. The film was banned by the French government, pulled from distribution by the Nazis, and not restored to its original form until 1959, when it premiered at the Venice Film Festival. A great, subtle, ominous film landmark. In French with English subtitles. Heavily copied and poorly remade in 1989 as "Scenes from the Class Struggle in Beverly Hills." **110m/B VHS, 8mm.** Marcel Dalio, Nora Gregor, Jean Renoir, Mila Parely, Julien Carette, Gaston Modot, Roland Toutain, Paulette Dubost, Odette Talazac; ***D:*** Jean Renoir; ***W:*** Jean Renoir.

The Ruling Class 🦴🦴🦴½ **1972 (PG)** The classic cult satire features O'Toole as the unbalanced 14th Earl of Gurney, who believes that he is either Jesus Christ or Jack the Ripper. Tongue-in-cheek look, complete with dance and music, at eccentric upper-class Brits and their institutions. Uneven, chaotic, surreal and noteworthy. **154m/C VHS, DVD, Wide.** *GB* Peter O'Toole, Alastair Sim, Arthur Lowe, Harry Andrews, Coral Browne, Nigel Green, Michael Bryant, William Mervyn, Carolyn Seymour, James Villiers; ***D:*** Peter Medak; ***W:*** Peter Barnes; ***C:*** Ken Hodges; ***M:*** John Cameron. Natl. Bd. of Review '72: Actor (O'Toole).

Rumble Fish 🦴🦴🦴 **1983 (R)** A young street punk worships his gang-leading older brother, the only role model he's known. Crafted by Coppola into an important story of growing up on the wrong side of town, from the novel by S.E. Hinton. Ambitious and experimental, with an atmospheric music score; in black and white. **94m/B VHS, DVD.** Matt Dillon, Mickey Rourke, Dennis Hopper, Diane Lane, Vincent Spano, Nicolas Cage, Diana Scarwid, Christopher Penn, Tom Waits; ***D:*** Francis Ford Coppola; ***W:*** Francis Ford Coppola; ***C:*** Stephen Burum; ***M:*** Stewart Copeland.

Rumble in the Bronx 🦴🦴½ **1996 (R)** Singapore action star Chan plays a Hong Kong cop who comes to the South Bronx to attend his uncle's wedding and winds up caught in a crime war between the mob and a vicious motorcycle gang. Living special effect Chan choreographed and performed all of his own stunts, and they are remarkable (pay special attention to the hovercraft scene). Over-the-top cheesy dubbing and streets that are obviously not New York (filmed in Vancouver) add to the cartoonish fun. After several attempts to break into the American market, this is Chan's first release in the United States. **91m/C VHS, DVD, Wide.** *HK* Jackie Chan, Anita (Yim-Fong) Mui, Francoise Yip, Bill Tung, Morgan Lam, Marc Akerstream; ***D:*** Stanley Tong; ***W:*** Edward Tang, Fibe Ma; ***C:*** Jingle Ma; ***M:*** J. Peter Robinson.

Rumble in the Streets 🦴½ **1996 (R)** Street-smart young Rowe discovers that a psycho cop has decided to clean up the streets of Dallas by hunting down and killing kids like her and she must use her own toughness to survive. **74m/C VHS.** Kimberly Rowe, David Courtemarche, Patrick DeFazio; ***D:*** Bret McCormick.

The Rumor Mill 🦴🦴½ *Malice in Wonderland* **1986** The careers and titanic rivalry of influential Hollywood gossip writer Hedda Hopper and Louella Parsons, played with verve by Taylor and Alexander. Fictionalized script based on the book "Hedda and Louella" by George Eels. **94m/C VHS.** Elizabeth Taylor, Jane Alexander, Richard Dysart, Joyce Van Patten; ***D:*** Gus Trikonis; ***W:*** Jacqueline Feather, David Seidler; ***M:*** Charles Bernstein. **TV**

A Rumor of Angels 🦴🦴 **2000 (PG-13)** Cloying coming-of-age tale somewhat redeemed by Redgrave's performance as eccentric recluse Maddy Bennett. 12-year-old James (Morgan) is spending the summer on the Maine coast. His mother died in a car accident, he resents his new stepmom Mary (McCormack), doesn't get along with his neglectful father Nathan (Liotta), and also has his misfit Uncle Charlie (Livingston) to deal with. After James vandalizes Maddy's property, the two become unlikely confidantes and Maddy helps him to deal with his problems. **94m/C VHS, DVD.** Vanessa Redgrave, Trevor Morgan, Ray Liotta, Catherine McCormack, Ron Livingston; ***D:*** Peter O'Fallon; ***W:*** Peter O'Fallon, James Eric, Jamie Horton; ***C:*** Roy Wagner; ***M:*** Tim Simonec.

A Rumor of War 🦴🦴🦴½ **1980** The first big Vietnam drama for TV is a triumph, portraying the real-life experience of author Philip Caputo (based on his bestseller), from naive youth to seasoned soldier to bitter murder suspect at court martial. Succeeds where Stone's later, much-ballyhooed "Born on the Fourth of July" fails. Adapted by John Sacret Young. **195m/C VHS.** Brad Davis, Keith Carradine, Michael O'Keefe, Stacy Keach, Steve Forrest, Richard Bradford, Brian Dennehy, John Friedrich, Perry Lang, Chris Mitchum, Dan Shor, Jeff Daniels, Laurence "Larry" Fishburne, Lane Smith, Gail Youngs, Bobby Ellerbee; ***D:*** Richard T. Heffron; ***W:*** John Sacret Young; ***C:*** Stevan Larner, Jorge Stahl Jr.; ***M:*** Charles Gross.

Rumpelstiltskin **1982** From "Faerie Tale Theatre" comes the story of a woman who can spin straw into gold (Duvall) and the strange man who saves her life (Villechaize). Enjoyable for the whole family. **60m/C VHS.** Bud Cort, Ned Beatty, Shelley Duvall, Herve Villechaize, Paul Dooley. **CABLE**

Rumpelstiltskin 🦴🦴 **1986 (G)** Musical retelling of the classic Brother Grimm fairy tale. Irving plays a young girl who says she can spin straw into gold. Barty is a dwarf who helps her. The catch: she must give up her first born to pay him. Lackluster direction and uninspired acting make this version a yawner. Irving's real-life mother (Pointer) and brother have roles too. **84m/C VHS.** Amy Irving, Billy Barty, Robert Symonds, Priscilla Pointer, Clive Revill, John Moulder-Brown; ***D:*** David Irving.

Rumpelstiltskin woof! **1996 (R)** First director Jones inflicts "Leprechaun" upon us and now there's another warped dwarf on the loose. Single L.A. mom Shelly (Johnston-Ulrich) finds a wishing stone in a thrift shop and unwittingly summons up the little demon, who immediately tries to steal her young son. **91m/C VHS.** Kim Johnston-Ulrich, Tommy Blaze, Max Grodenchik, Allyce Beasley; ***D:*** Mark Jones; ***W:*** Mark Jones; ***C:*** Doug Milsome; ***M:*** Charles Bernstein.

Run 🦴½ **1991 (R)** A high energy action cartoon, with little plot but lots of stunts. Dempsey is a super-smart law student hired to drive a car to Atlantic City. A stop on the way starts trouble. Instant romance with a local girl balances mayhem from crime boss. Expect no more than physical feats and you'll be happy with this lightweight fare. **91m/C VHS.** Patrick Dempsey, Kelly Preston, Ken Pogue, Alan C. Peterson, Sean McCann; ***D:*** Geoff Burrowes; ***W:*** Michael Blodgett; ***C:*** Bruce Surtees.

Run, Angel, Run! 🦴½ **1969 (R)** Ex-biker Angel is on the run from his former gang after he helps expose them in a magazine article. He settles on a sheep ranch with his girl and then the gang shows up with revenge in mind. Prime drive-in fare with title song sung by none other than Ms. Tammy Wynette. **90m/C VHS.** William Smith, Margaret Markov, Valerie Starrett; ***D:*** Jack Starrett.

Run for the Dream: The Gail Devers Story 🦴🦴½ **1996 (PG-13)** Inspirational biopic on U.S. track star Devers (Woodard) who won a gold medal in the 100m sprint in the 1992 Olympics. But 17 months before, Devers suffers complications from a debilitating thyroid condition, Graves's Disease, which could not only cost her her career but her life. **99m/C VHS.** Alfre Woodard, Louis Gossett Jr., Robert Guillaume. **CABLE**

Run for the Roses 🦴½ *Thoroughbred* **1978 (PG)** "National Velvet" clone about a young Puerto Rican boy and a champion race horse in Kentucky. Cheery family fare. **93m/C VHS.** Lisa Eilbacher, Vera Miles, Stuart Whitman, Sam Groom; ***D:*** Henry Levin.

Run If You Can 🦴 **1987 (R)** A woman sees a brutal murderer killing his victims on her TV. Will she be next? **92m/C** Martin Landau, Yvette Nipar, Jerry Van Dyke; ***D:*** Virginia Lively Stone.

Run Lola Run 🦴🦴🦴½ *Lola Rennt* **1998 (R)** Berlin punkette Lola (Potente) receives a frantic phone call from her small-time criminal boyfriend Manni (Bleibtreu). He's lost a bag of money he was delivering to his boss and has only 20 minutes to make good or he's history. Lola then sprints off in a manic attempt to find the money needed to save her man. The plot comes roaring to a halt, and is then repeated with different outcomes based on small changes in Lola's path, with different styles to match. Writer/director Tom Tykwer's energetic style helps push this creative and technically brilliant thriller across the winner's line. German with subtitles. **81m/C VHS, DVD.** *GE* Franka Potente, Moritz Bleibtreu, Joachim Krol, Herbert Knaup, Armin Rohde; ***D:*** Tom Tykwer; ***W:*** Tom Tykwer; ***C:*** Frank Griebe; ***M:*** Tom Tykwer. Ind. Spirit '00: Foreign Film.

Run of the Arrow 🦴🦴 *Hot Lead* **1956** Rather than surrender to the North at the end of the Civil War, an ex-Confederate soldier (Steiger) joins the Sioux nation, engaged in war against the white man. Steiger's Irish brogue is weird and distracting, and the intriguing premise fails to satisfy, but the cast is competent and interesting. **85m/C VHS.** Rod Steiger, Brian Keith, Charles Bronson, Ralph Meeker, Tim McCoy; ***D:*** Samuel Fuller; ***W:*** Samuel Fuller.

The Run of the Country 🦴🦴🦴 **1995 (R)** Amid the scenic splendor of a small town south of the North Irish border in County Cavan, Danny (Keeslar) comes of age, sometimes the hard way. His relationship with his bullying dad (Finney), the local Garda officer, begins to crumble after the tragic death of his mum. So he runs away to live with the town malcontent Prunty (Brophy) and falls in love with the beautiful Annagh (Smurfit), who lives north of the border. Life gets even more complicated when Annagh learns she's pregnant. Director Yates, reunited with Finney for the first time since they won Oscars for "The Dresser," sometimes digs too deep into a big crock of standard Irish stew, occasionally delivering Celtic melodrama instead of poignant slice of life. The usual themes of family dysfunction, religious rebellion and moral dilemma are augmented by the occasional appearance of the IRA. As the frustrated, violent father, Finney shines. In their debut, Keeslar and Smurfit are fine, but Brophy's Prunty is the one you'll remember. Adapted by Connaughton (who used similar geography for "The Playboys") from his novel. **109m/C VHS.** Albert Finney, Matt Keeslar, Victoria Smurfit, Anthony Brophy, David Kelly; ***D:*** Peter Yates; ***W:*** Shane Connaughton; ***C:*** Mike Southon; ***M:*** Cynthia Millar.

Run, Rebecca, Run 🦴🦴½ **1981** Interesting family adventure yarn for the family about a South American refugee who tries to stop a young girl from leaving from an Australian island where they are both stranded. She eventually befriends him, and attempts to get permission for him to enter the country. **90m/C VHS.** *AU* Simone Buchanan, Henri Szeps; ***D:*** Peter Maxwell.

Run Silent, Run Deep 🦴🦴🦴 **1958** Submarine commander Gable battles his officers, especially the bitter Lancaster who vied for the same command, while stalking the Japanese destroyer that sunk his former command. Top-notch WWII sub action, scripted from Commander Edward L. Beach's novel. **93m/B VHS, DVD, Wide.** Burt Lancaster, Clark Gable, Jack Warden, Don Rickles, Brad Dexter, Nick Cravat, Joe Maross, Mary Laroche, Eddie Foy III, Rudy Bond, H.M. Wynant, Joel Fluellen, Ken Lynch, John Bryant; ***D:*** Robert Wise; ***W:*** John Gay; ***C:*** Russell Harlan; ***M:*** Franz Waxman.

Run, Stranger, Run 🦴🦴 *Happy Mother's Day, Love, George* **1973 (PG)** The inhabitants of a seaside house in Nova Scotia are paralyzed with fear when a number of brutal murders occur. A couple of sicko slasher scenes, but hard to swallow. **110m/C VHS.** Ron Howard, Patricia Neal, Cloris Leachman, Bobby Darin; ***D:*** Darren McGavin; ***C:*** Walter Lassally.

Runaway 🦴½ **1984 (PG-13)** A cop and his sidekick track down a group of killer robots wreaking havoc. Self-serious, sorry sci-fi. Features Simmons of the rock group KISS. **100m/C VHS, DVD, Wide.** Tom Selleck, Cynthia Rhodes, Gene Simmons, Stan Shaw, Kirstie Alley; ***D:*** Michael Crichton; ***W:*** Michael Crichton; ***C:*** John A. Alonzo; ***M:*** Jerry Goldsmith.

The Runaway 🦴🦴½ **2000** Luke Winter (Newton) and Joshua Monroe (McLaughlin) are best friends growing up in 1940s rural Georgia despite the fact that one is black and one white. While on an adventure, they make a discovery that leads new sheriff Frank Richards (Cain) into reopening the investigation into the unsolved murders of three local black men. The town wants to hush up the whole incident but the sheriff wants justice to prevail. **98m/C VHS, DVD.** Dean Cain, Maya Angelou, Debbi (Deborah) Morgan, Pat Hingle, Kathryn Erbe, Cliff DeYoung, Cody Newton, Duane McLaughlin, Roxanne Hart, Sonny Shroyer; ***D:*** Arthur Allan Seidelman; ***W:*** Ron Raley; ***C:*** Ron Garcia; ***M:*** Ernest Troost. **TV**

The Runaway Barge 🦴🦴 **1975** Tiresomely ordinary TV yarn about three adventurers earning their living on a riverboat. The usual cliches are present, including a gang of bad guys. **78m/C VHS.** Bo Hopkins, Tim Matheson, Jim Davis, Nick Nolte, Devon Ericson, Christina Hart, James Best; ***D:*** Boris Sagal.

Runaway Bride 🦴🦴🦴 **1999 (PG)** If you don't mind being manipulated by masters (and you really won't), the predictability of this romantic comedy won't bother you either. Hey, if you weren't looking for a happy ending, you wouldn't be watching a romantic comedy. New York columnist Ike Graham (Gere) gets into hot water (as in fired) when his story on Maggie Carpenter (Roberts), the bolting bride (three trips down the aisle and no vows), is filled with errors. So Ike decides to go to Maggie's hometown, where she's on her fourth engagement, and get the real scoop. Of course, he falls for the would-be bride and she for him but things aren't all hearts and flowers. Appealing performances and boy, does Roberts know how to wear a wedding dress. **116m/C VHS, DVD, Wide.** Julia

Roberts, Richard Gere, Joan Cusack, Hector Elizondo, Christopher Meloni, Rita Wilson, Paul Dooley, Laurie Metcalf, Jean Schertler, Donal Logue, Reg Rogers, Yul Vazquez, Lisa Roberts Gillan, Sela Ward, Tom Mason; *D:* Garry Marshall; *W:* Josann McGibbon, Sara Parriott; *C:* Stuart Dryburgh; *M:* James Newton Howard.

The Runaway Bus 🦴🦴 1954 Filled with the requisite motley crew of passengers, including a gold-carrying thief and the ever-befuddled Margaret Rutherford, a bus gets lost between airports and ends up in a deserted village. Would-be wacky comedy. **78m/B VHS.** *GB* Frankie Howerd, Margaret Rutherford, Petula Clark, George Coulouris, Belinda Lee, Reginald Beckwith, Terence Alexander, Toke Townley, John Horsley, Anthony Oliver, Stringer Davis, Lisa Gastoni, Frank Phillips; *D:* Val Guest; *W:* Val Guest; *C:* Stanley Pavey; *M:* Ronald Binge.

Runaway Father 🦴🦴½ 1991 Pat Bennett's husband fakes his own death in an attempt to abandon his family. When Bennett discovers he's alive she works to set a legal precedent—17 years worth of back child support. Based on a true story. **94m/C VHS.** Donna Mills, Jack Scalia, Chris Mulkey, Jenny Lewis; *D:* John Nicolella. **TV**

Runaway Nightmare 🦴 1984 Two western worm ranchers are kidnapped by a female gang whose members torture and initiate them, then talk about their plan to steal from organized criminals. Just another typical worm rancher flick. **104m/C VHS.** Michael Cartel, Al Valletta; *D:* Michael Cartel.

Runaway Train 🦴🦴🦴 1985 (R) A tough jailbird and his sidekick break out of the hoosegow and find themselves trapped aboard a brakeless freight train heading for certain derailment in northwestern Canada. Harrowing existential action drama based on a screenplay by Akira Kurosawa. Voigt is superb. **112m/C VHS, DVD, Wide.** Edward (Eddie) Bunker, Jon Voight, Eric Roberts, Rebecca DeMornay, John P. Ryan, T.K. Carter, Kenneth McMillan, John Bloom; *D:* Andrei Konchalovsky; *W:* Andrei Konchalovsky, Djordje Milicevic, Edward (Eddie) Bunker; *C:* Alan Hume; *M:* Trevor Jones. Golden Globes '86: Actor—Drama (Voight).

The Runaways 🦴🦴 1975 A boy runs away from an unhappy foster home situation and becomes friends with a leopard that has escaped from an animal park. Sentimental but well-done family fun. **76m/C VHS.** Dorothy McGuire, John Randolph, Neva Patterson, Josh Albee; *D:* Harry Harris.

Runaways 🦴 1984 A corrupt politician's wife falls in love with the man who saved her when she attempted suicide. The two try to escape her husband's wrathful vengeance. **95m/C VHS.** Steve Oliver, Sondra Currie, John Russell.

The Runestone 🦴🦴 1991 (R) After the eponymous viking relic is unearthed, an archaeologist's meddling frees a long-imprisoned wolf-beast that terrorizes New York. An adequate horror flick that taps the seldom-explored vein of Norse mythology. Based on a novel by Mark E. Rogers. **105m/C VHS.** Peter Riegert, Joan Severance, William Hickey, Tim Ryan, Chris Young, Alexander Godunov; *D:* Willard Carroll; *W:* Willard Carroll; *M:* David Newman.

The Runner 🦴🦴 1999 (R) Eldard stars as a compulsive Vegas gambler who's so deeply in debt he agrees to his shady uncle's (Mantegna) offer to get him a job with gangster Goodman. Eldard places bets with sports bookies (with mob money) and falls for cocktail waitress Cox, using some of Goodman's money to buy her a diamond ring. The vengeful Goodman doesn't take kindly to this. **95m/C VHS, DVD.** Ron Eldard, John Goodman, Courteney Cox Arquette, Joe Mantegna, Bokeem Woodbine; *D:* Ron Moler; *W:* Anthony E. Zuiker, Dustin Lee Abraham; *C:* James Glennon; *M:* Anthony Marinelli.

The Runner Stumbles 🦴½ 1979 (R) Dated melodrama about a priest who goes on trial for murdering the nun with whom he fell in love in a mining town in the 1920s. Based on a true incident, from the play by Milan Stiff. Van Dyke in an unwanted serious role is miserably grim and wooden. **109m/C VHS.** Dick Van Dyke, Kathleen Quinlan, Maureen Stapleton, Ray Bolger, Beau Bridges, Tammy Grimes; *D:* Stanley Kramer; *M:* Ernest Gold.

The Runnin' Kind 🦴🦴½ 1989 (R) A yuppie expecting to inherit his father's Ohio law firm goes on a wild spree with an all-girl rock band. Sexy drummer Howard shows him the sights of certain parts of L.A. Original, fun comedy. Independent. **89m/C VHS.** David Packer, Pleasant Gehman, Brie Howard, Susan Strasberg; *D:* Max Tash.

Running Against Time 🦴🦴½ 1990 (PG) A teacher tries to change history (and erase his brother's Vietnam War death) by time-warping back to 1963 and preventing JFK's murder. Cable TV movie takes an offhanded gee-whiz approach to a tantalizing premise, as temporal paradoxes multiply in "Back to the Future" style. No assassination-conspiracy theories, by the way, but Lyndon Johnson fans may not like his portrayal here. Based on the novel "A Time to Remember" by Stanley Shapiro. **93m/C VHS.** Robert Hays, Catherine Hicks, Sam Wanamaker, James DiStefano, Brian Smiar; *D:* Bruce Seth Green; *W:* Robert Glass. **CABLE**

Running Away 🦴🦴 1989 (PG-13) Bittersweet story of WWII romance, with a twist of adventure. Strong cast creates good chemistry, but somehow the story is not engaging. Loren and Penny are mother and daughter, leaving Rome for the hills and encountering dangers. **101m/C VHS.** Sophia Loren, Sydney Penny, Robert Loggia, Andrea Occhipinti; *D:* Dino Risi.

Running Blind 🦴🦴 1978 Espionage/adventure thriller has a double agent and a beautiful woman on the run in Iceland. **120m/C VHS.** *GB* Stuart Wilson, Heidi Steindorsottir.

Running Brave 🦴🦴 1983 (PG) The true story of Billy Mills, a South Dakota Sioux Indian who won the Gold Medal in the 10,000 meter run at the 1964 Tokyo Olympics. Not bad, but hokey in the way of many of these plodding true-story flicks. **90m/C VHS.** Robby Benson, Claudia Cron, Pat Hingle, Denis Lacroix; *D:* D.S. Everett; *W:* Henry Bean.

Running Cool 🦴🦴 1993 (R) Two easy-going bikers join up with an old friend to protect his wetlands property from a lowlife developer and his stooges. Chicks (there's a romance with a local biker babe), motorcyles, fighting, and saving the environment—what more could you want? **106m/C VHS.** Andrew Divoff, Tracy Sebastian, Dedee Pfeiffer, James Gammon, Paul Gleason, Arlen Dean Snyder, Bubba Baker; *D:* Beverly Sebastian, Ferd Sebastian; *W:* Beverly Sebastian, Ferd Sebastian.

Running Delilah 🦴🦴½ 1993 Delilah (Cattrall) is a secret agent who is apparently killed by a vicious arms dealer. Only her fellow agent (Zane) resurrects her and Delilah is transformed into a cybernetic super agent. And her assignment is to go after a terrorist who's building a nuclear weapon with plutonium supplied by Delilah's killer. **85m/C VHS.** Kim Cattrall, Billy Zane, Diana Rigg.

Running Free 🦴½ 1994 (PG) Sullen Garrett joins his naturalist mother in the Alaskan wilderness and establishes a friendship with a wolverine cub (who's smarter than the kid). **90m/C VHS, DVD.** Jesse Montgomery Sythe, Jayme Lee Misfeldt, Michael Pena; *D:* Steve Kroschel.

Running Hot 🦴🦴½ *Highway to Hell; Lucky 13* 1983 (R) Seventeen-year-old convicted murderer Stoltz gets love letter in prison from older woman Carrico. When he escapes, they flee the law together. Quick-paced and entertaining. **88m/C VHS.** Monica Carrico, Eric Stoltz, Stuart Margolin, Virgil Frye, Richard Bradford, Sorrels Pickard, Juliette Cummins; *D:* Mark Griffiths; *W:* Mark Griffiths.

The Running Man 🦴🦴½ 1987 (R) Special-effects-laden adaptation of the Stephen King novel (under his Richard Bachman pseud) about a futuristic TV game show. Convicts are given a chance for pardon—all they have to do is survive an on going battle with specially trained assassins in the bombed-out sections of Los Angeles. Sci-fi with an attitude. **101m/C VHS, DVD.** Edward (Eddie) Bunker, Arnold Schwarzenegger, Richard Dawson, Maria Conchita Alonso, Yaphet Kotto, Mick Fleetwood, Dweezil Zappa, Jesse Ventura, Jim Brown; *D:* Paul Michael Glaser; *W:* Steven E. de Souza; *C:* Thomas Del Ruth; *M:* Harold Faltermeyer.

Running Mates 🦴🦴🦴 1986 (PG-13) Occasionally intriguing drama of two teens who fall in love, but are kept apart by their fathers' local political rivalry. Could have been better, but cardboard characters abound. **90m/C VHS.** Greg Webb, Barbara Howard, J. Don Ferguson, Clara Dunn; *D:* Thomas L. Neff.

Running Mates 🦴🦴🦴 1992 (PG-13) Cynically amusing political satire about a bachelor politician and his too intelligent lady love. Harris is Hugh, a U.S. senator looking forward to the presidential primaries when he meets widowed children's novelist Aggie (Keaton). She hates politics and he's Mr. Slick, although decent enough behind the political expediency. Aggie, however, has a potentially damaging secret in her past which causes the scandal-scenting pack of press hounds to bay in salivating anticipation. Will Hugh stick by Aggie and will Aggie overcome her natural political distaste for everything to end happily? A well-played romp. **88m/C VHS.** Ed Harris, Diane Keaton, Ed Begley Jr., Ben Masters, Robert Harper, Brandon Maggart, Russ Tamblyn; *D:* Michael Lindsay-Hogg; *W:* A.L. Appling. **CABLE**

Running Mates 🦴🦴½ 2000 Liberal governor James Pryce (Selleck) is a shoo-in for the presidential nomination at the L.A. Democratic convention. But he still has to choose his veep running mate. And he's got four powerful women giving him opinions, including his wife Jenny (Travis), his campaign manager Lauren (Linney), Hollywood fundraiser Shawna (Hatcher), and boozy socialite Meg (Dunaway), who's the wife of Pryce's mentor (Culp). So will he go with the idealistic senator (Gunton) or the power broker (McGill)? **90m/C VHS, DVD, Wide.** Tom Selleck, Laura Linney, Nancy Travis, Teri Hatcher, Bruce McGill, Bob Gunton, Faye Dunaway, Robert Culp, Caroline Aaron, Matt Malloy; *D:* Ron Lagomarsino; *W:* Claudia Salter; *C:* Alan Caso; *M:* John Debney. **CABLE**

Running on Empty 🦴🦴🦴 1988 (PG-13) Two 1960s radicals are still on the run in 1988 for a politically motivated Vietnam War-era crime. Though they have managed to stay one step ahead of the law, their son wants a "normal" life, even if it means never seeing his family again. Well-performed, quiet, plausible drama. **116m/C VHS, DVD, 8mm.** Christine Lahti, River Phoenix, Judd Hirsch, Martha Plimpton, Jonas Arby, Ed Crowley, L.M. Kit Carson, Steven Hill, Augusta Dabney, David Margulies, Sidney Lumet; *D:* Sidney Lumet; *W:* Naomi Foner; *C:* Gerry Fisher; *M:* Tony Mottola. Golden Globes '89: Screenplay; L.A. Film Critics '88: Actress (Lahti); Natl. Bd. of Review '88: Support. Actor (Phoenix).

Running out of Luck 🦴½ 1986 (R) A light, song-packed story about a rock star very much like Jagger who is abandoned in South America and believed dead, until he returns to his world. Features songs from Jagger's solo album "She's the Boss." **88m/C VHS.** Mick Jagger, Dennis Hopper, Jerry Hall, Rae Dawn Chong; *D:* Julien Temple.

Running Out of Time 🦴🦴 *Dias Contados; Numbered Days* 1994 Antonio (Gomez) is a Basque who belongs to a terrorist organization. He's sent to Madrid to carry out an assignment, winds up getting involved with drug-addicted prostitute Charo (Gabriel), and finds that his mission overlaps with his relationship. Spanish with subtitles. **93m/C VHS, DVD, Wide.** *SP* Carmelo Gomez, Ruth Gabriel, Javier Bardem, Karra Elejalde, Candela Pena; *D:* Imanol Uribe; *W:* Imanol Uribe; *C:* Javier Aguirresarobe; *M:* Jose Nieto.

Running out of Time 🦴🦴🦴 1999 Jewel thief Andy (Lau) knows that he has only two weeks to live. He goes ahead and pulls a job that sets him against Sean (Wan), a canny police negotiator. Director Johnny To employs some flashy visuals in this overachieving crime movie and he got first-rate performances from his leads, particularly Lau Ching Wan, a tremendous character actor. **89m/C DVD, Wide.** *HK* Andy Lau, Lau Ching Wan, Waise Lee, Hui Siu Hung, Yoyo Mung; *D:* Johnny To; *W:* Yau Nai Hoi; *C:* Cheng Siu Keung; *M:* Wong Ying Wah.

Running Scared 🦴🦴 1979 (PG) Two young men, returning from military service as stowaways aboard an Army cargo plane, are caught by an intelligence agent and thought to be spies, because Reinhold has unknowingly photographed a secret U.S. base with his stolen Army-issue camera. Not-bad spy thriller with a twist—the "spies" are hapless nobodies, now on the lam. **92m/C VHS.** Ken Wahl, Judge Reinhold, John Saxon, Annie McEnroe, Bradford Dillman, Pat Hingle; *D:* Paul Glickler.

Running Scared 🦴🦴½ 1986 (R) Hip, unorthodox Chicago cops Hines and Crystal have to handle an important drug arrest before taking an extended vacation in Key West. Not as relentless as "48 Hrs," but more enjoyable in some ways. Ever wonder what it's like to ride in a car at high speed on the tracks? Find out here. **107m/C VHS, DVD, Wide.** Gregory Hines, Billy Crystal, Dan Hedaya, Jimmy Smits, Darlanne Fluegel, Joe Pantoliano, Steven Bauer; *D:* Peter Hyams; *W:* Gary De Vore; *C:* Peter Hyams.

Running Wild 🦴🦴 1927 Early silent comedy starring mustachioed Fields as an eternal coward who suddenly turns into a lion by hypnosis. Odd, often unfunny Fields entry sometimes hits the mark. He's awfully mean, though. **68m/B VHS.** W.C. Fields, Mary Brian, Claud Buchanan; *D:* Gregory La Cava; *M:* Gaylord Carter.

Running Wild 🦴🦴½ 1973 (G) A free-lance photographer becomes involved in a dispute to save a corral of wild mustang horses. The usual great Colorado scenery enhances a good, family-view story. **102m/C VHS.** Lloyd Bridges, Dina Merrill, Pat Hingle, Gilbert Roland, Morgan Woodward; *D:* Robert McCahon; *W:* Robert McCahon.

Running Wild 🦴 1994 (R) Beautiful woman abandons her much older fiance to go on a wild road trip with his son that includes sex and crime. **91m/C VHS.** Jennifer Barker, Daniel Dupont, Daniel Spector, Eliott Keener; *D:* Philippe Blot.

Running Wild 🦴🦴½ 1999 Harrison stars as Maj. Matt Robinson, a retired Air Force pilot who has taken a position with the U.N. to track elephant migrations in Africa. He takes his children Angela (Nevin) and Nicholas (Jones) with him. Once they arrive in Africa, Matt meets a pretty veternarian, Rachel (Hallier) and a guide, Isaac (Kanaventi). They enjoy a great adventure until Matt realizes that there are many elephant-hunting poachers in the area, and when they threaten Angela and Nicholas, Matt and Rachel spring into action to rescue the children. Fun film for the entire family, although a bit too preachy at times concerning the plight of endangered animals. Contains fine performances, as well as breathtaking nature photography. Horror-industry vet Harry Alan Towers executive produced this family film, which was directed by the writer of the slasher classic "Happy Birthday to Me"! **92m/C VHS, DVD.** Gregory Harrison, Lori Hallier, Cody Jones, Brooke Nevin, Munyaradzi Kanaventi; *D:* Timothy Bond. **CABLE**

Running Woman 🦴🦴 1998 (R) Emily Russo (Russell) is accused of the mysterious death of her young son and goes on the lam to prove her inncence. With the police on her trail, Emily's quest leads her to a gang that's terrorizing some seedier parts of L.A. **84m/C VHS.** Theresa Russell, Andrew (Andy) Robinson, Gary (Rand) Graham, Eddie Velez, Anthony Crivello, Robert LaSardo, Chris Pennock; *D:* Rachel Samuels; *W:* Rachel Samuels; *C:* Chris Manley; *M:* Christopher Lennertz. **VIDEO**

Rupert's Land 🦴🦴½ 1998 British lawyer Rupert is reunited for the first time since childhood with his hard-living half-brother Dale, a British Columbia fisherman, at the funeral of their father. The Canadian side of Rupert's family seems to be more than a little eccentric, including Dale's mother Trudy, the keeper of the family's sordid secrets. Rupert and Dale suffer through a series of misadventures as they try to reunite as brothers and deal with their father's flawed legacy. **95m/C**

VHS. *CA* Samuel West, Ian Tracey, George Wendt, Susan Hogan, Gabrielle Miller; ***D:*** Jonathan Tammuz; ***W:*** Graeme Manson; ***C:*** Gregory Middleton; ***M:*** Phil Marshall.

Rush **1984** A post-nuclear world war movie in which a rebel named Rush battles the rulers of a slave colony. **83m/C VHS.** *IT* Conrad Nichols, Gordon Mitchell, Laura Trotter, Rita Furlan; ***D:*** Tonino Ricci.

Rush **1991 (R)** Texas drug culture, circa 1975, is portrayed in this bleak cop drama. Rookie narcotics officer Kristen Cates (Leigh) goes undercover with the experienced Raynor (Patric) to catch a big-time dealer, menancingly played by Allman, and their bosses don't much care how they do it. Cates falls in love with Raynor and is drawn ever deeper into the drug-addicted world they are supposed to destroy. Fine performances and a great blues score by Clapton. The directorial debut of Zanuck. Based on ex-narcotics cop Kim Wozencraft's autobiographical novel. **120m/C VHS.** Jason Patric, Jennifer Jason Leigh, Gregg Allman, Max Perlich, Sam Elliott, Tony Frank, William Sadler, Special K. McCray; ***D:*** Lili Fini Zanuck; ***W:*** Pete Dexter; ***C:*** Kenneth Macmillan; ***M:*** Eric Clapton.

Rush Hour ½ **1998 (PG-13)** Cliched buddy film that's sauced up a bit with the unlikely pairing of loud-mouthed Tucker and swift-footed Chan. Motormouth L.A. detective James Carter (Tucker) is temporarily assigned to the FBI to babysit Hong Kong detective Lee (Chan) and keep him away from a kidnapping case that Lee is anxious to solve for personal reasons. Chan is more subdued stuntwise than in his own pictures but nonetheless a charmer against the abrasive Tucker. The culture clash scenes and some high gloss action moments make for a rousing action-comedy. Film was a surprise boxoffice smash. **98m/C VHS, DVD.** Jackie Chan, Chris Tucker, Tzi Ma, Julia Hsu, Philip Baker Hall, Rex Linn, Elizabeth Pena, Mark Rolston, Tom Wilkinson; ***D:*** Brett Ratner; ***W:*** Jim Kouf, Ross LaManna; ***C:*** Adam Greenberg; ***M:*** Lalo Schifrin. MTV Movie Awards '99: On-Screen Duo (Chris Tucker/Jackie Chan).

Rush Hour 2 **2001 (PG-13)** Director Ratner and stars Tucker and Chan all reteam for the sequel to their $250 million 1998 comedy. Det. Carter (Tucker) travels to Hong Kong with his new buddy, Det. Lee (Chan), where they get involved in a criminal conspiracy. The jokes aren't as funny or fresh as in the original, and that situation isn't helped by the fact that before the movie's half over you just want Tucker to shut up. Chan does a fine job with his duties, which are A) continue to amusingly mangle the English language, and B) do some more of those great martial-arts stunts. He gets some help in the acrobatic martial-arts department from Ziyi, Lone, and a nice cameo by Cheadle. They should stop now, but they won't. RH3 is almost guaranteed. **91m/C VHS, DVD, Wide.** *US* Chris Tucker, Jackie Chan, Harris Yulin, Zhang Ziyi, John Lone, Alan King, Roselyn Sanchez, Kenneth Tsang, Ernie Reyes Jr., Jeremy Piven, Saul Rubinek, Don Cheadle; ***D:*** Brett Ratner; ***W:*** Jeff Nathanson; ***C:*** Matthew F. Leonetti; ***M:*** Lalo Schifrin, Kathy Nelson.

Rush It ½ **1977** Scriptwriters ponder possible plots over capucino: "I've got it! 'Bike Messengers in Love'!" "Nah. The title's too obvious. Why don't we call it 'Rush It?'" Much hard work and many months later, the result is forgettable. **78m/C VHS.** Tom Berenger, Jill Eikenberry.

Rush Week **1988 (R)** Dead coeds populate campus during frat week. Greg Allman has bit part and the Dickies perform two songs. **93m/C VHS, DVD.** Dean Hamilton, Gregg Allman, Kathleen Kinmont, Roy Thinnes, Pamela Ludwig; ***D:*** Bob Bravler; ***W:*** Michael W. Leighton, Russell V. Manzatt; ***C:*** Jeff Mart.

Rushmore ½ **1998 (R)** Fresh and original comedy from Wes Anderson follows 15-year-old Max (Schwartzman), an underachieving yet overconfident student at Rushmore Academy. He has romantic designs on teacher Miss Cross (Williams), and enlists the help of wealthy alum Herman Blume (Murray) in his quest to impress her. Blume also falls for the woman, however, instigating a war of nasty tricks between the two quirky rivals. Murray drops his trademark smirk and gives his best performance to date. Also shining is newcomer Schwartzman, who is the son of Talia Shire. At this rate, the Coppola show biz clan may take over Hollywood by sheer population as well as talent. **93m/C VHS, DVD.** Bill Murray, Jason Schwartzman, Olivia Williams, Seymour Cassel, Brian Cox, Mason Gamble, Sara Tanaka, Connie Nielsen, Kim Terry, Stephen McCole, Ronnie McCawley, Keith McCawley; ***D:*** Wes Anderson; ***W:*** Wes Anderson, Owen C. Wilson; ***C:*** Robert Yeoman; ***M:*** Mark Mothersbaugh. Ind. Spirit '99: Director (54938), Support. Actor (Murray); L.A. Film Critics '98: Support. Actor (Murray); N.Y. Film Critics '98: Support. Actor (Murray); Natl. Soc. Film Critics '98: Support. Actor (Murray).

Russell Mulcahy's Tale of the Mummy *Tale of the Mummy; Talos the Mummy* **1999 (R)** Archeologists break open the sealed tomb of an Egyptian prince and are destroyed by the curse of Talos. Fifty years later, Samantha Turkel (Lombard) discovers her grandfather's logbook and decides to retrace the course of his deadly expedition. She recovers a sacred amulet and suddenly the power of Talos threatens again. The film was originally released at 119 minutes under the title "Talos the Mummy." **87m/C VHS, DVD.** Jason Scott Lee, Louise Lombard, Sean Pertwee, Lysette Anthony, Michael Lerner, Jack Davenport, Honor Blackman, Christopher Lee, Shelley Duvall, Jon Polito; ***D:*** Russell Mulcahy; ***W:*** Russell Mulcahy, John Esposito; ***C:*** Gabriel Beristain. **VIDEO**

The Russia House ½ **1990 (R)** Russian scientist Brandauer attempts to publish book debunking Soviet Union's claims of military superiority by passing it through ex-lover Pfeiffer to British editor Connery, apparently unaware of impending glasnost. Star-studded spy thriller aspires to heights it never quite reaches. Adapted from John Le Carre's novel, Stoppard's screenplay is very fine, actually making some aspects of the novel work better. **122m/C VHS, DVD, 8mm, Wide.** Sean Connery, Michelle Pfeiffer, Roy Scheider, James Fox, John Mahoney, Klaus Maria Brandauer, Ken Russell, J.T. Walsh, Michael Kitchen, David Threlfall, Ian McNeice, Christopher Lawford; ***D:*** Fred Schepisi; ***W:*** Tom Stoppard; ***C:*** Ian Baker; ***M:*** Jerry Goldsmith.

Russian Roulette **1975** The Russian premier is visiting Vancouver in 1970, and the Mounties must prevent a dissident KGB terrorist from assassinating him. Un-thrilling spy yarn fails to deliver on intriguing premise. **100m/C VHS.** George Segal, Christina Raines, Bo Brundin, Denholm Elliott, Louise Fletcher; ***D:*** Lou Lombardo.

Russian Roulette ½ **1993** Routine story about an American woman on vacation in Russia who finds herself in the middle of a plot to locate a hidden Czarist artifact and smuggle it out of the country. Everyone on her tour group is suspect, an American businessman becomes involved, and a killer starts eliminating the number of players. Great location scenery. **89m/C VHS.** Susan Blakely, Barry Bostwick, E.G. Marshall, Jeff Altman; ***D:*** Greydon Clark.

The Russian Terminator **1990 (R)** An FBI agent is up against a one-man "death squad." **90m/C VHS.** Helena Michaelson, Frederick Offrein, Harley Melin, Tina Tjung; ***D:*** Mats Helge; ***W:*** Mats Helge.

The Russians Are Coming, the Russians Are Coming **1966** Based on the comic novel "The Off-Islanders" by Nathaniel Benchley, this is the story of a Russian sub which accidentally runs aground off the New England coast. The residents falsely believe that the nine-man crew is the beginning of a Soviet invasion, though the men are only looking for help. A memorable set of silly events follows the landing, engineered by a gung-ho police chief and a town filled with overactive imaginations. **126m/C VHS.** Alan Arkin, Carl Reiner, Theodore Bikel, Eva Marie Saint, Brian Keith, Paul Ford, Jonathan Winters, Ben Blue, Tessie O'Shea, Doro Merande, John Phillip Law; ***D:*** Norman Jewison; ***C:*** Joseph Biroc. Golden Globes '67: Actor—Mus./Comedy (Arkin), Film—Mus./Comedy.

Russkies ½ **1987 (PG)** A jolly comedy about three adorable American kids who capture, and eventually grow to like, a stranded Russian sailor. Friendly and peace-loving, but dull. **98m/C VHS.** Joaquin Rafael (Leaf) Phoenix, Whip Hubley, Peter Billingsley, Stefan DeSalle, Susan Walters; ***D:*** Rick Rosenthal; ***M:*** James Newton Howard.

Rustler's Hideout *Rustler's Roundup* **1944** One of numerous westerns starring Crabbe as cowboy do-gooder Billy Carson, here plodding through standard histrionics against rustlers, a cardsharp, and a business fraud. **60m/C VHS.** Buster Crabbe, Al "Fuzzy" St. John, Charles "Blackie" King, John Merton, Lane Chandler, Hal Price, Edward Cassidy, Bud Osborne; ***D:*** Sam Newfield.

Rustlers of Red Dog ½ **1935** A 12-chapter western serial about Indian wars and cattle rustlers. **235m/B VHS.** Johnny Mack Brown, Raymond Hatton, Joyce Compton, Walter Miller, Harry Woods, William Desmond, Wally Wales, Chief Thundercloud, Art Mix, Bill(y) (William Patten) Patton, Bud Osborne, Lafe (Lafayette) McKee; ***D:*** Lew (Louis Friedlander) Landers.

Rustler's Paradise **1935** Carey seeks revenge on the man who stole his wife and daughter. **59m/B VHS.** Harry Carey Sr., Gertrude Messinger, Edmund Cobb; ***D:*** Harry Fraser.

Rustler's Rhapsody **1985 (PG)** A singing cowboy rides into a small western town and encounters all kinds of desperados in this earnest would-be satire of '40s B-movie westerns. **89m/C VHS.** Tom Berenger, Patrick Wayne, G.W. Bailey, Andy Griffith, Marilu Henner; ***D:*** Hugh Wilson; ***W:*** Hugh Wilson; ***C:*** Jose Luis Alcaine; ***M:*** Steve Dorff.

Rustler's Roundup ½ **1933** Mix rides to the rescue of Sinclair, whose daddy has been murdered by villains out to steal the ranch. **58m/B VHS.** Tom Mix, Diane Sinclair, Noah Beery Jr., Douglass Dumbrille, Roy Stewart, Nelson McDowell, William Desmond, Frank Lackteen, Pee Wee Holmes, Bud Osborne; ***D:*** Henry MacRae.

Rustler's Valley **1937** Hopalong Cassidy is a ranch foreman who tries to save his employer from the clutches of a crooked lawyer. Pretty fun ordinary range-ridin' saga. **59m/B VHS.** William Boyd, George "Gabby" Hayes, Lee J. Cobb; ***D:*** Nate Watt.

Rusty's Birthday ½ **1949** Danny searches for the lost Rusty who's been taken in by a family of transient workers. When Danny discovers his pal, he finds the young son of the family doesn't want to give Rusty up. **61m/B VHS.** Ted Donaldson, John Litel, Ann Doran, Jimmy Hunt, Ray Teal; ***D:*** Seymour Friedman; ***W:*** Brenda Weisberg.

The Rutanga Tapes ½ **1990 (R)** Soviet bloc country has representatives in Africa producing deadly chemicals used for war and a dissident has taped evidence of native deaths. Reporter babe Simpson wants an exclusive, Petersen wants the dissident, Libyan agents want the tapes, and you'll want to fast forward to the end. **88m/C VHS.** Henry Cele, Arnold Vosloo, Wilson Dunster, David Dukes, Susan Anspach; ***D:*** David Lister.

The Rutherford County Line **1987** A tough small-town sheriff searches for the killer of his deputies. **98m/C VHS.** Earl Owensby; ***D:*** Thom McIntyre.

The Ruthless Four *Every Man For Himself; Each One For Himself; Sam Cooper's Gold; Each Man For Himself* **1970** Quartet of unlikely mining partners match wills and wits and battle the elements. Not-so-hot spaghetti western, with good lead from Heflin. **97m/C VHS.** *IT* Van Heflin, Klaus Kinski, Gilbert Roland, George Hilton; ***D:*** Giorgio Capitani.

Ruthless People **1986 (R)** DeVito and his mistress spend a romantic evening plotting his obnoxious wife's untimely demise. Before he can put his plan into action, he's delighted to discover she's been kidnapped by some very desperate people—who don't stand a chance with Bette. High farcical entertainment is a variation on the story "The Ransom of Red Chief," by O. Henry. **93m/C VHS, DVD, Wide.** Bette Midler, Danny DeVito, Judge Reinhold, Helen Slater, Anita Morris, Bill Pullman; ***D:*** David Zucker, Jim Abrahams, Jerry Zucker; ***W:*** Dale Lanner; ***C:*** Jan De Bont; ***M:*** Michel Colombier.

Ruyblas **1948** Revenge and romance beset the court of Charles II in this tale of mistaken identity (with Marais in a dual role). Based on the novel by Victor Hugo. **90m/B VHS.** *FR* Jean Marais, Danielle Darrieux; ***D:*** Pierre Billon; ***W:*** Jean Cocteau.

Ryan's Daughter ½ **1970 (PG)** Irish woman (Miles) marries a man she does not love and then falls for a shell-shocked British major who arrives during the 1916 Irish uprising to keep the peace. Not surprisingly, she is accused of betraying the local IRA gunrunners to her British lover. Tasteful melodrama with lots of pretty scenery that goes on a bit too long. **194m/C VHS, Wide.** *GB* Sarah Miles, Robert Mitchum, John Mills, Trevor Howard, Christopher Jones, Leo McKern; ***D:*** David Lean; ***W:*** Robert Bolt; ***C:*** Frederick A. (Freddie) Young; ***M:*** Maurice Jarre. Oscars '70: Cinematog., Support. Actor (Mills); Golden Globes '71: Support. Actor (Mills).

Ryder P.I. **1986 (PG-13)** P.I Ryder and his sidekick fight crime and solve weird cases in the big city. **92m/C VHS.** Bob Nelson, Dave Hawthorne, John Mulrooney, Howard Stern; ***D:*** Karl Hosch, Chuck Walker; ***W:*** Bob Nelson, Dave Hawthorne, Karl Hosch, Chuck Walker; ***C:*** Phil Arfman; ***M:*** Kevin Kelly.

Sabaka *The Hindu* **1955** Adventure set in India about a scary religious cult. Karloff and the cast of stalwart "B" movie performers have fun with this one, and you should, too. **81m/C VHS.** Boris Karloff, Reginald Denny, Victor Jory, Lisa Howard, Jeanne Bates, Jay Novello, June Foray; ***D:*** Frank Ferrin.

Sabotage *A Woman Alone; Hidden Power* **1936** Early Hitchcock thriller based on Conrad's "The Secret Agent." A woman who works at a movie theatre (Sidney) suspects her quiet husband (Homolka) might be the terrorist planting bombs around London. Numerous sly touches of the Master's signature humor. **81m/B VHS, DVD, 8mm.** Oscar Homolka, Sylvia Sidney, John Loder, Desmond Tester, Joyce Barbour, Matthew Boulton, S.J. Warmington, William Dewhurst, Austin Trevor, Torin Thatcher, Aubrey Mather, Peter Bull, Charles Hawtrey, Martita Hunt, Hal Walters, Frederick Piper; ***D:*** Alfred Hitchcock; ***W:*** Charles Bennett, Ian Hay, Alma Reville, E.V.H. Emmett, Helen Simpson; ***C:*** Bernard Knowles.

Saboteur **1942** A man wrongly accused of sabotaging an American munitions plant during WWII sets out to find the traitor who framed him. Hitchcock uses his locations, including Boulder Dam, Radio City Music Hall, and the Statue of Liberty, to greatly intensify the action. Stunning resolution. **108m/B VHS, DVD.** Priscilla Lane, Robert Cummings, Otto Kruger, Alan Baxter, Norman Lloyd, Charles Halton; ***D:*** Alfred Hitchcock; ***W:*** Alfred Hitchcock, Peter Viertel; ***C:*** Joseph Valentine; ***M:*** Frank Skinner.

Sabre Jet **1953** Run-of-the-mill wartime drama of hubbies flying combat missions in Korea and long-suffering spouses on the home front. **90m/C VHS.** Robert Stack, Amanda Blake, Louis King; ***D:*** Louis King.

Sabrina *Sabrina Fair* **1954** Two wealthy brothers, one an aging businessman (Bogart) and the other a dissolute playboy (Holden), vie for the attention of their chauffeur's daughter (Hepburn), who has just returned from a French cooking school. Typically acerbic, in the Wilder manner, with Bogart and Holden cast interestingly against type (but it's Hepburn's picture anyway). Based on the play "Sabrina Fair" by Samuel Taylor. **113m/B VHS.** Audrey Hepburn, Humphrey Bogart, William Holden, Walter Hampden, Francis X. Bushman, John Williams, Martha Hyer, Marcel Dalio; ***D:*** Billy Wilder; ***W:*** Billy Wilder, Ernest Lehman; ***C:*** Charles B(ryant) Lang Jr. Oscars '54: Costume Des. (B&W); Directors Guild '54: Director (Wilder); Golden Globes '55: Screenplay; Natl. Bd. of Review '54: Support. Actor (Williams).

Sabrina ½ **1995 (PG)** Updated version of Billy Wilder's 1954 fairytale that starred a luminous Audrey Hepburn. This time around the pretty Ormond is the chauffeur's daughter who gets closely involved with the wealthy Larrabees. And this time the emphasis is more on workaholic business mogul Linus (Ford), who plays a dangerous game when he decides to transfer Sabrina's affections from his feckless engaged brother David (Kinnear) to himself in order to protect a business merger. Ford's a little too stodgy (you'll wonder why Sabrina bothers except she's probably just too nice to say no) but Kinnear's suitably charming (in his film debut) and Marchand properly matriarchal. **127m/C VHS, DVD, Wide.** Harrison Ford, Julia Ormond, Greg Kinnear, Nancy Marchand, John Wood, Richard Crenna, Angie Dickinson, Lauren Holly, Fanny Ardant, Dana Ivey, Patrick Bruel, Miriam Colon, Elizabeth Franz; ***D:*** Sydney Pollack; ***W:*** David Rayfiel, Barbara Benedek; ***C:*** Giuseppe Rotunno; ***M:*** John Williams.

Sabrina the Teenage Witch ♂♂½ **1996 (PG)** Based on the Archie Comics, this lighthearted movie finds 16-year-old Sabrina (Hart) being told by her two eccentric aunts, Hilda (Miller) and Zelda (Fernetz), that she is a witch, descended from a long line of good witches and warlocks. Sabrina's having enough trouble fitting in at Riverdale High without this kind of news but she does find that her magical powers have their advantages. Pilot for the TV series. **90m/C VHS.** Melissa Joan Hart, Charlene Fernetz, Sherry Miller, Michelle Beaudoin, Ryan Reynolds, Tobias Mehler, Lalainia Lindbjerg; ***D:*** Tibor Takacs; ***W:*** Barney Cohen, Kathryn Wallack, Nicholas Factor. **CABLE**

Sacco & Vanzetti ♂♂ *Sacco e Vanzetti* **1971 (PG)** Two Italian immigrants and acknowledged anarchists are caught amidst communist witch-hunts and judicial negligence when they are tried and executed for murder in 1920s America. Based on the true-life case, considered by some a flagrant miscarriage of justice and political martyrdom, by others, honest American judicial-system proceedings. Well-made and acted. Joan Baez sings the title song "The Ballad of Sacco and Vanzetti." **120m/C VHS, DVD.** Gian Marie Volonte, Riccardo Cucciolla, Milo O'Shea, Cyril Cusack, Geoffrey Keen; ***D:*** Guiliano Montaldo; ***M:*** Ennio Morricone. Cannes '71: Actor (Cucciolla).

The Sacketts ♂♂½ **1979** Follows the adventures of three Tennessee brothers who migrate to the West after the Civil War. Based on two Louis L'Amour novels. **198m/C VHS.** Jeffery Osterhage, Tom Selleck, Sam Elliott, Glenn Ford, Ben Johnson, Mercedes McCambridge, Ruth Roman, Jack Elam, Gilbert Roland; ***D:*** Robert Totten. **TV**

Sacred Ground ♂♂ **1983 (PG)** A trapper and his pregnant Apache wife unknowingly build shelter on the Paiute Indians' sacred burial ground. When the wife dies in childbirth, the pioneer is forced to kidnap a Paiute woman who has just buried her own deceased infant. Average western drama. **100m/C VHS.** Tim McIntire, Jack Elam, L.Q. (Justus E. McQueen) Jones, Mindi Miller; ***D:*** Charles B. Pierce; ***W:*** Charles B. Pierce.

The Sacrifice ♂♂♂ **1986 (PG)** Tarkovsky's enigmatic final film, released after his death. Deals with a retired intellectual's spiritually symbolic efforts at self-sacrifice in order to save his family on the eve of a nuclear holocaust. Stunning cinematography by Nykvist. Acclaimed, but sometimes slow going; not everyone will appreciate Tarkovsky's visionary spiritualism. In Swedish and Russian with English subtitles. **145m/C VHS, DVD, Wide.** *FR SW* Erland Josephson, Susan Fleetwood, Valerie Mairesse, Allan Edwall, Gudrun Gisladottir, Sven Wollter, Filippa Franzen; ***D:*** Andrei Tarkovsky; ***W:*** Andrei Tarkovsky; ***C:*** Sven Nykvist. British Acad. '87: Foreign Film.

Sacrifice ♂♂ **2000 (R)** Serial killer has murdered the daughter of felon Tyler Pearce, who escapes from prison to get revenge. He hooks up with an ex-prostitute (Luner) but he'll have to avoid an FBI agent who wants to put Tyler back behind bars. **91m/C VHS, DVD.** Michael Madsen, Bokeem Woodbine, Jamie Luner, Joshua Leonard; ***D:*** Mark L. Lester. **VIDEO**

Sacrilege ♂½ **1986** A nun and a nobleman engage in a hot love affair that fosters scandal, murder and, revenge. Cynical use of religious theme masks otherwise ordinary sex/romance flick. Controversial Italian-made erotic drama. **104m/C VHS.** *IT* Myriem Roussel, Alessandro Gassman; ***D:*** Luciano Odorisio.

The Sad Sack ♂♂ **1957** A bumbling hero with a photographic memory winds up in Morocco as a member of the French Foreign Legion. Although a success at the box office, Lewis's second movie (without partner Dean Martin) seems jerky and out of sorts today. Based on the comic strip character by George Baker, but not effectively. **98m/B VHS.** Jerry Lewis, Phyllis Kirk, David Wayne, Peter Lorre, Gene Evans, Mary Treen; ***D:*** George Marshall; ***C:*** Loyal Griggs; ***M:*** Burt Bacharach, Hal David.

Sadat ♂♂½ **1983 (PG)** Gossett Jr. well plays his title role of Egyptian leader and Nobel Peace Prize-winner Anwar el Sadat. But the controversial life and peace efforts of the president (assassinated in 1981) are given a quick overview in this average drama. **195m/C VHS.** Louis Gossett Jr., John Rhys-Davies, Jeremy Kemp, Nehemiah Persoff, Madolyn Smith, Anne Heywood, Jeffrey Tambor, Barry Morse; ***D:*** Richard Michaels; ***M:*** Charles Bernstein. **TV**

Saddle Buster ♂♂ **1932** A rodeo cowboy loses his nerve after being thrown by a tough horse, but gets it back again by the end of the hour. Actual rodeo footage is incorporated into this low-budget bronco saga. **59m/B VHS.** Tom (George Duryea) Keene, Helen Foster, Charles Quigley, Marie Quillen, Robert Frazer, Charles "Slim" Whitaker; ***D:*** Fred Allen.

Saddle Mountain Round-Up ♂ **1941** The Range Busters are on the trail again as they smoke out a murderer. **61m/B VHS.** Ray Corrigan, John "Dusty" King, Max Terhune.

Sadie McKee ♂♂♂ **1934** A melodrama with Crawford as a maid searching for love in the big city. She falls for a self-destructive ne'er-do-well, marries an alcoholic millionaire, and eventually finds true love with the wealthy Tone (who would become Crawford's third husband). Professional acting and directing elevate the story. **90m/B VHS.** Joan Crawford, Franchot Tone, Gene Raymond, Edward Arnold; ***D:*** Clarence Brown.

Sadie Thompson ♂♂♂ **1928** Swanson plays a harlot with a heart of gold, bawdy and good-natured, in the South Seas. A zealot missionary (Barrymore) arrives and falls in love with her. The last eight minutes of footage have been recreated by using stills and the original title cards, to replace the last reel which had decomposed. Remade as "Rain," "Dirty Gertie From Harlem," and "Miss Sadie Thompson." Based on W. Somerset Maugham's "Rain." **97m/B VHS, DVD.** Gloria Swanson, Lionel Barrymore, Raoul Walsh, Blanche Frederici, Charles Lane, James A. Marcus; ***D:*** Raoul Walsh; ***W:*** Raoul Walsh; ***C:*** George Barnes, Robert B. Kurrle, Oliver Marsh.

The Sadist ♂♂½ *The Profile of Terror* **1963** Three teachers on their way to Dodger Stadium find themselves stranded at a roadside garage and terrorized by a snivelling lunatic. Tense and plausible. **95m/B VHS, DVD.** Arch Hall Jr., Helen Hovey, Richard Alden, Marilyn Manning; ***D:*** James Landis; ***W:*** James Landis; ***C:*** Vilmos Zsigmond.

Safari 3000 ♂½ **1982 (PG)** "Playboy" writer is assigned to do a story on a three-day, 3,000 kilometer car race in Africa. Doesn't take itself too seriously, and neither should we. Dumb, dull, and disjointed. **91m/C VHS.** Stockard Channing, David Carradine, Christopher Lee; ***D:*** Harry Hurwitz; ***M:*** Ernest Gold.

Safe ♂♂♂ **1995 (R)** Surburban California housewife Carol (Moore) literally becomes allergic to her environment and winds up seeking relief in a holistic center in Albuquerque, where director Haynes takes a shot at the New Age and finds a link to the AIDS crisis. Serious, stylistically detached look at a near future riddled with environmental toxins is led by Moore's performance as the sunny suburbanite undone by the unseen. **119m/C VHS, DVD, Wide.** Julianne Moore, Peter Friedman, Xander Berkeley, Susan Norman, James LeGros, Mary Carver, Kate McGregor Stewart, Jessica Harper, Brandon Cruz; ***D:*** Todd Haynes; ***W:*** Todd Haynes; ***C:*** Alex Nepomniaschy; ***M:*** Ed Tomney.

Safe House ♂♂½ **1999** Comedy-thriller with a terrific lead performance by Stewart. A retiree succumbing to Alzheimer's, Mace Sowell's become increasingly paranoid and taken to carrying a gun and maintaining an elaborate security system around his L.A. home. Mace claims to be an ex-government agent, marked for death by his former boss who's now a presidential candidate. His fears are dismissed by his shrink (Elizondo) and his daughter forces him to get an in-home caregiver, Andi Travers (Williams). But soon Andi begins to think her charge may not be crazy after all. **125m/C VHS, DVD.** Patrick Stewart, Kimberly Williams, Hector Elizondo, Craig Shoemaker; ***D:*** Eric Steven Stahl; ***W:*** Eric Steven Stahl, Sean McLain; ***C:*** Vincent Donohue; ***M:*** Kevin Kiner. **CABLE**

Safe Men ♂½ **1998 (R)** Goofy, low-budget indie comedy whose pieces don't quite fit together. Set in Providence, R.I., talentless would-be singers Sam (Rockwell) and Eddie (Zahn) are mistaken by the local Jewish mafia for a couple of expert safecrackers. The inept duo are pressured by Big Fat Bernie Gayle (Lerner) and his henchman Veal Chop (Giamatti) to break into the home of Bernie's rival, Good Stuff Leo (Fierstein). Some dumb luck and a lot of coincidence work in the guys favor. But then the real safecracking team turns up. **89m/C VHS.** Sam Rockwell, Steve Zahn, Paul Giamatti, Michael Lerner, Harvey Fierstein, Mark Ruffalo; ***D:*** John Hamburg; ***W:*** John Hamburg; ***C:*** Michael Barrett; ***M:*** Theodore Shapiro.

Safe Passage ♂♂ **1994 (PG-13)** Grueling family drama with Sarandon and Shepherd portraying an unhappily married couple who are the parents of seven sons, one of whom is missing and presumed dead in the Sinai Desert war. One by one the grown boys arrive home to await any further news. They rehash memories, watch old videos, open old wounds, and generally affirm life. None of the performances, with the exception of Sarandon, are truly believable. She is the only one that brings any depth to her character as the tough matriarch that holds the family together. Feels like a TV movie, albeit one with classier names. Based on the novel by Ellyn Bache. **98m/C VHS.** Susan Sarandon, Sam Shepard, Robert Sean Leonard, Sean Astin, Marcia Gay Harden, Nick Stahl, Jason London, Philip Bosco, Matt Keeslar; ***D:*** Robert Ackerman; ***W:*** Deena Goldstone; ***C:*** Ralf Bode; ***M:*** Mark Isham.

Safety Last ♂♂♂ **1923** Lloyd silent comedy about an average guy who goes to the big city to become a success, and his misadventures. Hilarious and still awe-inspiring building climbing scene set new standards for movies in sight gags and comedy-thrill stunts, which became Lloyd's trademark. **78m/B VHS.** Harold Lloyd, Mildred Davis, Bill Strothers, Noah Young; ***D:*** Fred Newmeyer, Sam Taylor. Natl. Film Reg. '94.

Safety Patrol ♂♂½ **1998** Clumsy 11-year-old Scout (Hall) is determined to join his school's safety patrol team and instead winds up involved with a mother/son team of con artists. **92m/C VHS.** Bug Hall, Leslie Nielsen, Lainie Kazan, Wink Martindale, Ed McMahon, Curtis Armstrong, Charlene Tilton, Alex McKenna, Kurtwood Smith, Stephanie Faracy; ***D:*** Steve Holland. **VIDEO**

Saga of Death Valley ♂♂½ **1939** Rogers battles a band of outlaws and discovers that their leader is his own brother. Exciting and likeable early Rogers western. **56m/B VHS.** Roy Rogers, George "Gabby" Hayes, Donald (Don "Red") Barry, Doris Day; ***D:*** Joseph Kane.

The Saga of the Draculas ♂ *Dracula Saga; Dracula: The Bloodline Continues...; The Saga of Dracula* **1972 (R)** An aging vampire wishes to continue his bloodline and seeks to convert his niece's baby to his bloodsucking ways. **90m/C VHS.** *SP* Narciso Ibanez Menta, Tina Sainz, Tony Isbert, Maria Koski, Cristina Suriani, Helga Line; ***D:*** Leon Klimovsky.

Saga of the Vagabond ♂♂½ *Sengoku Gunto-Den* **1959** Arranged by master director Akira Kurosawa. A band of ruthless outlaws careen across a civil war-torn countryside. With English subtitles. **115m/C VHS.** *JP* Toshiro Mifune, Michiyo Aratama; ***D:*** Toshio Sugie.

Sagebrush Law ♂½ **1943** Western yarn has Holt playing a young man trying to clear the name of his bank president father. Barclay serves as the love interest and "Ukulele Ike" Edwards provides needed comic and music relief. **56m/B VHS.** Tim Holt, Cliff Edwards, Joan Barclay, Edward Cassidy, Karl Hackett, Roy Barcroft, Ernie Adams; ***D:*** Sam Nelson; ***W:*** Bennett Cohen.

Sagebrush Trail ♂♂♂ **1933** Wayne's second-ever western, complete with all sorts of tumbleweed and white-hat cliches. Our hero is wrongly accused of killin' a man, and busts out of the hoosegow to clear his name. Interesting plot twists makes for fun, compelling viewing. **53m/B VHS, DVD.** John Wayne, Yakima Canutt, Wally Wales; ***D:*** Armand Schaefer; ***W:*** Lindsley Parsons; ***C:*** Archie Stout.

Sahara ♂♂♂ **1943** A British-American unit must fight the Germans for their survival in the Libyan desert during WWII. Plenty of action and suspense combined with good performances makes this one a step above the usual war movie. **97m/B VHS, DVD.** Humphrey Bogart, Dan Duryea, Bruce (Herman Brix) Bennett, Lloyd Bridges, Rex Ingram, J. Carrol Naish, Richard Nugent, Pat O'Moore, Kurt Kreuger, John Wengraf, Carl Harbord, Louis Mercier, Guy Kingsford, Peter Lawford; ***D:*** Zoltan Korda; ***W:*** Zoltan Korda, John Howard Lawson, James O'Hanlon; ***C:*** Rudolph Mate; ***M:*** Miklos Rozsa.

Sahara woof! **1983 (PG)** Disappointing "Perils of Pauline" type adventure. Shields disguises herself as a man (sure) to complete a race across the desert in honor of her late father, and a sheik captures her. **111m/C VHS.** Brooke Shields, Lambert Wilson, Horst Buchholz, John Rhys-Davies, Ronald Lacey, John Mills, Steve Forrest, Perry Lang, Cliff (Potter) Potts; ***D:*** Andrew V. McLaglen; ***W:*** James R. Silke; ***M:*** Ennio Morricone.

Saigon Commandos ♂ **1988 (R)** Commandos, on the eve of the fall of Saigon in the 1970s, attempt to prevent heroin dealers from toppling the already-shaky government. So-so war/action flick. **84m/C VHS.** Richard Young, P.J. Soles, John Allen Nelson, Jimi B Jr.; ***D:*** Clark Henderson.

Saigon: Year of the Cat ♂ **1987** Drama about an American ambassador, a CIA operative, and a British bank clerk who try to leave Saigon in 1974 before the Vietcong enter the city. **106m/C VHS.** *GB* Frederic Forrest, E.G. Marshall, Judi Dench; ***D:*** Stephen Frears; ***W:*** David Hare; ***M:*** George Fenton. **TV**

Sailing Along ♂♂ **1938** British musical about a young starlet who sacrifices her career for true love. **80m/B VHS.** *GB* Jessie Matthews, Barry Mackay, Jack Whiting, Roland Young, Noel Madison, Athene Seyler, Patrick Barr; ***D:*** Sonnie Hale.

The Sailor Who Fell from Grace with the Sea ♂♂ **1976 (R)** Perverse tale of a disillusioned sailor who rejects the sea for the love of a lonely young widow and her troubled son. Graphic sexual scenes. Based on the novel by Yukio Mishima, the film suffers from the transition of Japanese culture to an English setting. **105m/C VHS.** *GB* Sarah Miles, Kris Kristofferson, Jonathan Kahn, Margo Cunningham; ***D:*** Lewis John Carlino; ***W:*** Lewis John Carlino.

The Saint ♂♂ **1968** Moore is Simon Templar, Leslie Charteris's mysterious British detective/hero in this adventure tale that takes him to Naples. Revival of and improvement on earlier movie series, and based on the very popular British TV show. **98m/C VHS, DVD.** *GB* Roger Moore, Ian Hendry.

The Saint ♂♂½ **1997 (PG-13)** The plot makes about as much sense as that of "Mission: Impossible," the villains are average ego-driven bad guys, and Shue's naive scientist/babe is totally unbelieveable (she's like a deer caught in a car's headlights). The only reason the movie works at all is due to the debonair, if angst-ridden, charms of Kilmer as super-thief and master of disguise Simon Templar. He's hired by Russian strongman Ivan Tretiak (Serbedzija) to steal the formula for cold fusion from scientist Emma Russell (Shue) so that Tretiak can save a freezing Moscow by delivering cheap energy and thus make Russia a formidable power once again (with himself as leader, natch). Only problem is Templar, who names all his alter egos after saints, falls for Emma and tries to get them out of harm's way by double-crossing Tretiak. At least the Moscow and Oxford settings are scenic. Templar's exploits are featured in a series of novels by Leslie Charteris, and previously appeared in earlier movies and on TV. **118m/C VHS, DVD.** Val Kilmer, Elisabeth Shue, Rade Serbedzija, Valery (Valeri Nikolayev) Nikolaev, Henry Goodman, Alun Armstrong, Michael Byrne, Eugene Lazarev, Charlotte Cornwell, Irina Apeximova, Emily Mortimer; ***D:*** Phillip Noyce; ***W:*** Jonathan Hensleigh, Wesley Strick; ***C:*** Phil Meheux; ***M:*** Graeme Revell.

St. Benny the Dip 🦴🦴½ *Escape If You Can* **1951** Three con-men evade police by posing as clergymen, and end up going straight after a series of adventures in a skid row mission. Funny in parts but extremely predictable. Still, good for a few laughs. **80m/B VHS.** Dick Haymes, Nina Foch, Roland Young, Lionel Stander, Freddie Bartholomew; ***D:*** Edgar G. Ulmer.

St. Elmo's Fire 🦴🦴½ **1985 (R)** Seven Georgetown graduates confront adult problems during their first post-graduate year. Reminiscent of "The Big Chill," but a weak story wastes lots of talent and time. **110m/C VHS.** Rob Lowe, Demi Moore, Andrew McCarthy, Judd Nelson, Ally Sheedy, Emilio Estevez, Mare Winningham, Martin Balsam, Jenny Wright, Joyce Van Patten, Andie MacDowell, Anna Maria Horsford; ***D:*** Joel Schumacher; ***W:*** Carl Kurlander, Joel Schumacher; ***C:*** Stephen Burum; ***M:*** David Foster. Golden Raspberries '85: Worst Support. Actor (Lowe).

Saint-Ex: The Story of the Storyteller 🦴🦴 **1995 (PG)** Ambitious bio based on famous French aviator, and author of the children's classic "The Little Prince," Antoine de Saint-Exupery (Ganz). Flashbacks show his childhood obsession with flying that eventually lead to Saint-Exuprey's perilous North African mail flights during WWII. Beyond his passion for flying is his marriage to Consuelo (Richardson), who comes to resent his frequent absences, and the later, more-supportive love of Genevieve (McTeer). Striking visuals but that's about all. **90m/C VHS.** *GB* Bruno Ganz, Miranda Richardson, Janet McTeer, Ken Stott, Katrin Cartlidge, Eleanor Bron, Brid Brennan, Karl Johnson; ***D:*** Anand Tucker; ***W:*** Frank Cottrell-Boyce; ***C:*** David Johnson; ***M:*** Barrington Pheloung.

The St. Francisville Experiment 🦴🦴 **2000 (PG-13)** Psychic, amateur ghost hunter, history student, and filmmaker fly to Louisiana to investigate a haunted house plagued by the spirit of slaves. **79m/C VHS, DVD.** Tim Baldini, Madison Charap, Ryan Larson, Paul Palmer, Paul James, Paul Salamoff, Troy Taylor; ***D:*** Tim Thompson.

St. Helen's, Killer Volcano 🦴🦴½ **1982** A young man and an old man develop a deep friendship amid the devastation, fear, greed, and panic surrounding the eruption of the Mt. St. Helen's volcano. Based on the true story of Harry Truman (!), who refused to leave his home. Pretty good. **95m/C VHS.** Art Carney, David Huffman, Cassie Yates, Bill McKinney, Ron O'Neal, Albert Salmi, Cesare Danova; ***D:*** Ernest Pintoff.

The Saint in London 🦴🦴 **1939** The Saint investigates a gang trying to pass counterfeit banknotes. The third in "The Saint" series. **72m/B VHS.** George Sanders, Sally Gray; ***D:*** John Paddy Carstairs.

The Saint in New York 🦴🦴 **1938** The Saint, Simon Templar, turns Robin Hood to help the Civic Committee clean up a gang of desperados. First of "The Saint" series. **71m/B VHS.** Louis Hayward, Kay Sutton, Jack Carson, Charles Halton; ***D:*** Ben Holmes.

St. Ives 🦴🦴 **1976 (PG)** Former police reporter Bronson agrees to recover some stolen ledgers and finds himself dealing with betrayal and murder. Bisset is sultry and the tale is slickly told, but dumb. Co-stars Travanti, later of TV's "Hill Street Blues." **94m/C VHS.** Charles Bronson, Jacqueline Bisset, John Houseman, Harry Guardino, Maximilian Schell, Harris Yulin, Elisha Cook Jr., Daniel J. Travanti; ***D:*** J. Lee Thompson; ***W:*** Barry Beckerman; ***M:*** Lalo Schifrin.

Saint Jack 🦴🦴🦴 **1979 (R)** The story of a small-time pimp with big dreams working the pleasure palaces of late-night Singapore. Engrossing and pleasant. Based on Paul Theroux's novel. **112m/C VHS, DVD, Wide.** Ben Gazzara, Denholm Elliott, Joss Ackland, George Lazenby, Peter Bogdanovich; ***D:*** Peter Bogdanovich; ***W:*** Peter Bogdanovich; ***C:*** Robby Muller.

Saint Joan 🦴🦴 **1957** Film of the George Bernard Shaw play, adapted by Graham Greene, about the French Maid of Orleans at her trial. Otto Preminger went on a nationwide talent hunt for his leading actress and chose the inexperienced Seberg (her screen debut). A good thing for her career, but not for this ill-begotten, overambitious opus. Seberg doesn't fit. Also available colorized. **131m/B VHS.** Jean Seberg, Anton Walbrook, Richard Widmark, John Gielgud, Harry Andrews, Felix Aylmer, Richard Todd; ***D:*** Otto Preminger; ***C:*** Georges Perinal.

Saint Maybe 🦴🦴🦴 **1998** Quietly affecting family saga adapted from the novel by Anne Tyler. Heedless Ian Bedloe (McCarthy) is disturbed when his older brother Danny (Nordling) impulsively marries scatty divorcee Lucy (Parker) who has two kids. When Lucy gets pregnant, Ian's interference results in a double tragedy. Seeking to atone for his mistake, Ian discovers the Church of the Second Chance and he decides to raise his brother's three children. **98m/C VHS.** Thomas McCarthy, Blythe Danner, Edward Herrmann, Mary-Louise Parker, Jeffrey Nordling, Melina Kanakaredes, Glynnis O'Connor, Amy Hargreaves, Kristoffer Ryan Winters, Denis O'Hare, Rene Augesen, Bethel Leslie; ***D:*** Michael Pressman; ***W:*** Robert W. Lenski; ***C:*** Shelly Johnson; ***M:*** Ernest Troost. **TV**

St. Michael Had a Rooster 🦴🦴 *San Michele Aveva un Gallo* **1972** In 19th-century Italy, idealist anarchist Giulio Manieri (Brogi) hopes to inspire the local peasantry through armed raids. Imprisoned for his trouble, Manieri learns upon his release after 10 years that his political struggles have been forgotten and he has to make a difficult adjustment to life on the outside. Based on the Leo Tolstoy story "The Divine and the Human." Italian with subtitles. **87m/C VHS.** *IT* Giulio Brogi, Danielle Dublino, Renato Scarpa; ***D:*** Paolo Taviani, Vittorio Taviani; ***W:*** Paolo Taviani, Vittorio Taviani; ***C:*** Mario Masini.

The Saint of Fort Washington 🦴🦴½ **1993 (R)** Sweetly naive and schizophrenic Matthew (Dillon) is homeless and through government screw-ups is sent to the Fort Washington Armory, which houses more than 700 homeless men. Harassed by others, Matthew is befriended by Jerry, a kindly Vietnam vet, who tries to care for him. Subject is taken seriously but slips into mawkishness; good performances by the leads. **104m/C VHS, Wide.** Danny Glover, Matt Dillon, Rick Aviles, Nina Siemaszko, Ving Rhames, Joe Seneca; ***D:*** Tim Hunter; ***W:*** Lyle Kessler; ***C:*** Frederick Elmes; ***M:*** James Newton Howard.

St. Patrick: The Irish Legend 🦴🦴½ **2000** Unfortunately neither the impressive cast, the beautiful scenery, or the special effects can transform this costumer from being bland and boring. Patrick (who allegedly drove all the snakes out of Ireland) was the privileged son of a nobleman in 5th century Britian, who suffered through six years as a slave before finding his religious calling. Over great opposition, he's eventually appointed as the first bishop of Ireland though he must still struggle with his enemies in the Church of England. **120m/C VHS, DVD.** Patrick Bergin, Malcolm McDowell, Alan Bates, Susannah York, Luke Griffin, Eamon Owens, Stephen Brennan, Chris McHallen, Michael Caven; ***D:*** Robert C. Hughes; ***W:*** Robert C. Hughes, Martin Duffy; ***C:*** James Mathers. **CABLE**

St. Patrick's Day 🦴🦴 **1999 (PG-13)** Widowed Mary McDonaugh (Laurie) is the matriarch of a dysfunctional Irish-American family. Four generations gather at her house for St. Patrick's Day where she announces she has taken the pledge and refuses to allows any whiskey in her home (which is ignored by certain members). As the day progresses, family secrets are revealed, including romantic feelings finally acknowledged, divorcing spouses, extramarital affairs, and other sexual shenanigans. **106m/C VHS, DVD.** Piper Laurie, Joanne Baron, Jim Metzler, Julie Strain, Herta Ware, Redmond M. Gleeson, David Ault, Colleen (Ann) (Vitamin C) Fitzpatrick, Chris Valenti, Stephen O'Mahoney; ***D:*** Hope Perello; ***W:*** Hope Perello; ***C:*** Denise Brassard; ***M:*** Michael Muhlfriedel.

The Saint Strikes Back 🦴🦴 **1939** Sanders debuts as the mysterious Simon Templar in this competent series. On a trip to San Francisco, the Saint aims to clear the name of a murdered man. The second in the series. **67m/B VHS.** George Sanders, Wendy Barrie, Jonathan Hale, Jerome Cowan, Neil Hamilton, Barry Fitzgerald, Edward (Ed) Gargan, Robert Strange; ***D:*** John Farrow.

The Saint Strikes Back: Criminal Court 🦴🦴 **1946** A suspense double feature: The Saint helps a daughter clear the name of her murdered father, a San Francisco police commissioner in "The Saint Strikes Back," and a young lawyer becomes involved in murder in "Criminal Court." **127m/B VHS.** George Sanders, Wendy Barrie, Barry Fitzgerald, Tom Conway, Steve Brodie; ***D:*** John Farrow.

The Saint Takes Over 🦴🦴 **1940** More adventures with the British mystery man; this time involving racetrack gambling. An original story that wasn't based on a Leslie Charteris novel as were the others. **69m/B VHS.** George Sanders, Jonathan Hale, Wendy Barrie, Paul Guilfoyle, Morgan Conway, Cy Kendall; ***D:*** Jack Hively.

The St. Tammany Miracle 🦴🦴½ **1994** Predictable, good-natured sports film about young coach Lootie Pfannder (Luner) who takes a job at a prep school and turns the losing girls basketball team into winners. Her broadcaster boyfriend Carl (Grosselaar) thinks she's crazy but aided by her assistant (Frye), Lootie is determined to prove everyone wrong. **90m/C VHS.** Jamie Luner, Mark Paul Gosselaar, Soleil Moon Frye, Jeffrey Meek, Julie McCullough; ***Cameos:*** Steve Allen; ***D:*** Joy Houck Jr.; ***W:*** Jim McCullough Jr.; ***M:*** Jay Weigel.

The St. Valentine's Day Massacre 🦴🦴½ **1967** Corman's big studio debut recreates the events leading to one of the most violent gangland shootouts in modern history: the bloodbath between Chicago's Capone and Moran gangs on February 14, 1929. Uninspired and unremittingly violent. Watch for Jack Nicholson's bit part. **100m/C VHS.** Jason Robards Jr., Ralph Meeker, Jean Hale, Joseph Campanella, Bruce Dern, Clint Ritchie, Richard Bakalyan, George Segal, Harold J. Stone, Jonathan Haze, Dick Miller, Barboura Morris, Jack Nicholson, Frank Silvera, Milton Frome, Alex Rocco, John Agar, Tom Signorelli; ***D:*** Roger Corman; ***W:*** Howard Browne; ***C:*** Milton Krasner; ***M:*** Lionel Newman.

A Saintly Switch 🦴🦴½ **1999** Aging quarterback Grier has just moved his pregnant wife Fox and their kids to a New Orleans. Mom's very unhappy and the kids are worried that their parents are going to split up—at least until they manage to mysteriously swap their parents' bodies. So now dad gets to be pregnant and mom has to learn to score touchdowns. **90m/C VHS.** David Alan Grier, Vivica A. Fox, Rue McClanahan, Al Waxman; ***D:*** Peter Bogdanovich. **TV**

Saints and Sinners 🦴½ **1995 (R)** Street-smart "Pooch" Puccia (Chapa) returns to his 'hood as an undercover cop to set up childhood buddy, drug dealer Big Boy Baynes (Plank), and winds up getting involved with seductive bad girl Eve (Rubin), who's also bedding Baynes. Then Pooch discovers his police contact is in the pay of the mob. Lots of macho posturing (attractive actors). **99m/C VHS.** Damian Chapa, Scott Plank, Jennifer Rubin, Damon Whitaker, Panchito Gomez, William Atherton; ***D:*** Paul Mones; ***W:*** Paul Mones; ***C:*** Michael Bonvillain.

The Saint's Double Trouble 🦴🦴 **1940** Leslie Charteris' suave detective becomes embroiled in another mystery, this one involving jewel thieves. Sanders plays a dual role as the hero and the crook. The fourth in the series. **68m/B VHS.** George Sanders, Helene Whitney, Jonathan Hale, Bela Lugosi, Donald MacBride, John Hamilton; ***D:*** Jack Hively.

Sakharov 🦴🦴🦴 **1984** The true story of the Russian physicist who designed the H-bomb and then rose to lead the Soviet dissident movement and win the Nobel Peace Prize. Robards is excellent. Topical and powerful. **120m/C VHS.** Glenda Jackson, Jason Robards Jr., Michael Bryant; ***D:*** Jack Gold; ***M:*** Carl Davis. **CABLE**

Salaam Bombay! 🦴🦴🦴 **1988** A gritty film about a child street beggar in the slums of Bombay trying to raise enough money to return to his mother's house in the country. The boy experiences every variety of gutter life imaginable, from humiliation to love. Moving and searing. Filmed on location, with actual homeless children; Nair's first feature. In Hindi with subtitles. **114m/C VHS.** *IN GB* Shafiq Syed, Hansa Vithal, Chanda Sharma, Nana Patekar, Aneeta Kanwar, Sarfuddin Quarassi, Raju Barnad, Raghubir Yadav; ***D:*** Mira Nair; ***W:*** Sooni Taraporevala; ***C:*** Sandi Sissel; ***M:*** L. Subramaniam.

The Salamander 🦴½ **1982 (R)** A French detective tries to find the assassin of the leaders of a neo-fascist underground movement in Italy and follows clues that lead back to WWII. Disappointing, overwrought adaptation of a Morris West novel. **101m/C VHS.** *GB* Franco Nero, Anthony Quinn, Martin Balsam, Sybil Danning, Christopher Lee, Cleavon Little, Paul Smith, Claudia Cardinale, Eli Wallach; ***D:*** Peter Zinner; ***M:*** Jerry Goldsmith.

Salammbo 🦴🦴½ **1914** An early silent epic in the grand Italian tradition. Loosely based on Flaubert's novel about ancient Carthage. **49m/B VHS.** *IT* Ernesto Pagani; ***D:*** Giovanni Pastrone.

Salem's Lot 🦴🦴½ *Blood Thirst* **1979 (PG)** Based on Stephen King's novel about a sleepy New England village which is infiltrated by evil. A mysterious antiques dealer takes up residence in a forbidding hilltop house—and it becomes apparent that a vampire is on the loose. Generally creepy; Mason is good, but Soul only takes up space in the lead as a novelist returning home. **112m/C VHS, DVD.** David Soul, James Mason, Lance Kerwin, Bonnie Bedelia, Lew Ayres, Ed Flanders, Elisha Cook Jr., Reggie Nalder, Fred Willard, Kenneth McMillan, Marie Windsor; ***D:*** Tobe Hooper; ***W:*** Paul Monash; ***C:*** Jules Brenner; ***M:*** Harry Sukman. **TV**

Sallah 🦴🦴🦴 **1963** A North African Jew takes his family to Israel in 1949 in hopes of making his fortune. He finds himself in a transit camp and runs up against the local bureaucracy in a quest for permanent housing as well as the European work ethic. Amusing and enjoyable satire. In Hebrew with English subtitles. **105m/B VHS.** *IS* Chaim Topol, Geula Noni, Gila Almagor, Arik Einstein, Shraga Friedman, Esther Greenberg; ***D:*** Ephraim Kishon; ***C:*** Floyd Crosby. Golden Globes '65: Foreign Film.

Sally Hemings: An American Scandal 🦴🦴½ **2000** Soap opera-ish romance based on the relationship between widowed ambassador (and third President) Thomas Jefferson (Neill) and his young mulatto house slave Sally Hemings (Ejogo)—an affair that lasted for 38 years. (DNA proved Jefferson to be the father of one and possible all six of Heming's children.) Sally remains dignified through the years as does Jefferson. The most excitement is Sally castigating her lover about his contradictory attitudes towards slavery. **173m/C VHS.** Carmen Ejogo, Sam Neill, Diahann Carroll, Mare Winningham, Rene Auberjonois, Mario Van Peebles; ***D:*** Charles Haid; ***W:*** Tina Andrews; ***C:*** Donald M. Morgan; ***M:*** Joel McNeely. **TV**

Sally of the Sawdust 🦴🦴½ **1925** Fields's first silent feature; he is carnival barker Professor Eustace McGargle who's the guardian of orphaned Sally (Dempster). Then Sally's wealthy grandfather (Alderson), a stern judge, becomes determined to claim her from showbiz lowlifes. Fields gets to demonstrate his talent for juggling, conning customers, and car chasing. Interesting movie caught director Griffith on the decline and Fields on the verge of stardom. Remade as a talkie in 1936 entitled "Poppy." Includes musical score. **113m/B VHS, DVD.** W.C. Fields, Carol Dempster, Erville Alderson; ***D:*** D.W. Griffith; ***W:*** Forrest Halsey; ***C:*** Harry Fischbeck, H. Sintzenich.

Salmonberries 🦴½ **1991 (R)** East German Roswitha (Zech) is devastated when her lover is killed trying to scale the Berlin Wall. She manages to escape and finds herself stuck in a remote Eskimo community in Alaska where she becomes involved with Kotzebue (lang in her film debut), who poses as a man to work on the Alaskan pipeline. The title has something to do with preserved berries—don't bother, it makes about as much sense as the entire movie. English and German with English subtitles. **94m/C VHS.** *GE CA* Rosel Zech, k.d. lang, Chuck Connors, Jane Lind, Oscar Kawagley, Wolfgang Steinberg, Wayne Waterman, Christel Merian; ***D:*** Percy Adlon; ***W:*** Percy Adlon, Felix Adlon; ***C:*** Newton Thomas (Tom) Sigel.

Salo, or the 120 Days of Sodom 🦴🦴 **1975** Extremely graphic film follows 16 children (eight boys and eight girls) who are kidnapped by a group of men in Fascist Italy. On reaching a secluded villa in the woods, the children are told to follow strict rules and then subjected to incredible acts of sadomasochism, rape, violence, and mutilation. This last film of Pasolini's was taken from a novel by the Marquis de Sade. Viewers are strongly recommended to use their utmost discretion when watching this controversial film. In Italian with English subtitles. **117m/C VHS, DVD, Wide.** *IT FR* Caterina Boratto, Giorgio Cataldi, Umberto P. Quintavalle, Paolo Bonacelli; ***D:*** Pier Paolo Pasolini; ***W:*** Pier Paolo Pasolini, Sergio Citti; ***C:*** Tonino Delli Colli; ***M:*** Ennio Morricone.

Salome 🦴🦴½ **1922** Garish silent rendition of Oscar Wilde's scandalous tale. **54m/B VHS.** Alla Nazimova, Madame Rose (Dion) Dione, Mitchell Lewis, Earl Schenck; ***D:*** Charles Bryant. Natl. Film Reg. '00.

Salome 🦴🦴 **1953** An over-costumed version of Oscar Wilde's Biblical story about King Herod's lascivious stepdaughter who danced her way to stardom and tried to save the life of John the Baptist. Talented cast can't overcome hokey script. **103m/C VHS.** Rita Hayworth, Stewart Granger, Charles Laughton, Judith Anderson, Cedric Hardwicke, Basil Sydney, Maurice Schwartz; ***D:*** William Dieterle; ***C:*** Charles B(ryant) Lang Jr.; ***M:*** George Duning.

Salome 🦴½ **1985 (R)** An updated and graphic version of the Oscar Wilde historical fantasy about the temptress Salome who helped topple Herod's Biblical kingdom with her dance of the Seven Veils. Not really a remake of the 1953 film since this is set during the 1940s. **100m/C VHS.** Jo Champa, Tomas Milian, Pamela Salem; ***D:*** Claude D'Anna; ***C:*** Pasqualino De Santis.

Salome, Where She Danced 🦴 **1945** Set during the Franco-Prussian war. A European dancer helps an American reporter in a spy scheme. She eventually relocates to America and becomes the toast of San Francisco. Somehow, De Carlo managed to spring from this ridiculous camp outing to stardom. **90m/C VHS.** Yvonne De Carlo, Rod Cameron, David Bruce, Walter Slezak; ***D:*** Charles Lamont; ***C:*** William Howard Greene, Hal Mohr.

Salome's Last Dance 🦴🦴 **1988 (R)** A theatrical, set-surreal adaptation of the Wilde story. Typically flamboyant Russell. **113m/C VHS, DVD.** Glenda Jackson, Stratford Johns, Nickolas Grace, Douglas Hodge, Imogen Millais Scott; ***D:*** Ken Russell; ***W:*** Ken Russell; ***C:*** Harvey Harrison.

Salsa 🦴🦴 **1988 (PG)** An auto repairman would rather dance in this "Dirty Dancing" clone. Rosa was formerly a member of the pop group Menudo. **97m/C VHS.** Robby Rosa, Rodney Harvey, Magali Alvarado, Miranda Garrison, Moon Orona; ***D:*** Boaz Davidson; ***W:*** Boaz Davidson, Tomas Benitez.

Salt of the Earth 🦴🦴🦴½ **1954** Finally available in this country after being suppressed for 30 years, this controversial film was made by a group of blacklisted filmmakers during the McCarthy era. It was deemed anti-American, communist propaganda. The story deals with the anti-Hispanic racial strife that occurs in a New Mexico zinc mine when union workers organize a strike. **94m/B VHS, DVD, CD-I.** Rosaura Revueltas, Will Geer, David Wolfe; ***D:*** Herbert Biberman; ***W:*** Michael Wilson; ***C:*** Stanley Meredith, Leonard Stark; ***M:*** Sol Kaplan. Natl. Film Reg. '92.

The Salton Sea 🦴🦴 **2002 (R)** Feature debut by helmer Caruso is very good at getting down into the sleaze and grime of the world of methedrine addicts, dealers, and victims. Maybe too good. The parade of degradation drowns out everything else; the performances of Kilmer as the nominal hero, and D'Onofrio as kingpin/sadist Pooh-Bear, the time-addled plot that begs for concentration, and any sense that anything good will come from viewing this film. What it does, it does well, the question is, does anyone have the stomach to see it done? **103m/C VHS, DVD.** *US* Val Kilmer, Vincent D'Onofrio, Adam Goldberg, Luis Guzman, Doug Hutchison, Anthony LaPaglia, Glenn Plummer, Peter Sarsgaard, Deborah Kara Unger, Chandra West, B.D. Wong, R. Lee Ermey, Shalom Harlow, Shirley Knight, Meat Loaf Aday, Azura Skye, Danny Trejo, Josh Todd; ***D:*** D.J. Caruso; ***W:*** Tony Gayton; ***C:*** Amir M. Mokri; ***M:*** Thomas Newman.

Salty 🦴🦴 **1973** A lovable but mischievous sea lion manages to complicate two brothers' lives when they volunteer to help a friend renovate a Florida marina, which is threatened by a mortgage foreclosure. Straightforward and inoffensive tale. **93m/C VHS.** Clint Howard, Mark Slade, Nina Foch; ***D:*** Ricou Browning.

Salut l'Artiste 🦴🦴🦴 **1974** Two bad actors try to make it in the industry. Delightfully funny with an excellent cast, especially Mastroianni. Snide and irreverant, yet loving and comic look at the world of acting. In French with English subtitles. **96m/C VHS.** *FR* Marcello Mastroianni, Jean Rochefort, Francoise Fabian, Carla Gravina; ***D:*** Yves Robert; ***M:*** Vladimir Cosma.

Salute John Citizen 🦴🦴🦴 **1942** The life of an average English family during the early days of WWII is depicted, focusing on the deprivation and horror of the Nazi blitzkrieg. **74m/B VHS.** Peggy Cummins, Stanley Holloway, Dinah Sheridan, Jimmy Hanley.

Salvador 🦴🦴🦴½ **1986 (R)** Photo journalist Richard Boyle's unflinching and sordid adventures in war-torn El Salvador. Boyle (Woods) must face the realities of social injustice. Belushi and Woods are hard to like, but excellent. Early critical success for director Stone. **123m/C VHS, DVD, Wide.** James Woods, James Belushi, John Savage, Michael Murphy, Elpidia Carrillo, Cynthia Gibb, Tony Plana, Colby Chester, Will MacMillan, Jose Carlos Ruiz, Jorge Luke, Juan Fernandez, Valerie Wildman; ***D:*** Oliver Stone; ***W:*** Oliver Stone, Richard Boyle; ***C:*** Robert Richardson; ***M:*** Georges Delerue. Ind. Spirit '87: Actor (Woods).

Salvation! 🦴🦴½ *Salvation! Have You Said Your Prayers Today?* **1987 (R)** A mean-tempered, timely satire about a money-hungry TV evangelist beset by a family of fervent, equally money-hungry followers, who proceed to cheat, seduce and blackmail him. Occasionally quite funny, but sloppy and predictable. Underground director Beth B's first above-ground film. **80m/C** Stephen McHattie, Exene Cervenka, Dominique Davalos, Viggo Mortensen, Rockets Redglare, Billy Bastiani; ***D:*** Beth B; ***W:*** Beth B.

The Salzburg Connection 🦴½ **1972 (PG)** A list of Nazi collaborators is discovered in Austria. A vacationing American lawyer is caught up in the battle for its possession. Filmed on location, it's still a poor, cheesy adaptation of the Helen MacInnes novel. **94m/C VHS.** Barry Newman, Anna Karina, Klaus Maria Brandauer, Karen Jensen; ***D:*** Lee H. Katzin.

Samantha 🦴🦴½ **1992 (PG)** Twenty-one year-old Samantha discovers she was left on her parents' doorstep in a basket and decides to find out where she came from. Good cast and high charm quotient help this film along. **101m/C VHS.** Martha Plimpton, Dermot Mulroney, Hector Elizondo, Mary Kay Place, Ione Skye; ***D:*** Steven La Rocque; ***W:*** John Golden, Steven La Rocque.

Samar 🦴🦴½ **1962 (PG)** A liberal penal colony commandant rebels against his superiors by leading his prisoners through the Philippine jungles to freedom. Original action drama with an interesting premise. **89m/C VHS.** George Montgomery, Gilbert Roland, Joan O'Brien, Ziva Rodann; ***D:*** George Montgomery.

Samaritan: The Mitch Snyder Story 🦴🦴🦴 **1986** Effective TV drama based upon the true story of Vietnam vet Mitch Snyder (Sheen) who battles various government agencies and ultimately fasts to call national attention to his crusade against homelessness. (Snyder eventually committed suicide.) Tyson appears as a bag lady. **90m/C VHS.** Martin Sheen, Roxanne Hart, Joe Seneca, Stan Shaw, Cicely Tyson; ***D:*** Richard T. Heffron. **TV**

Same Old Song 🦴🦴🦴 *On Connait la Chanson* **1997** Amusing melodrama that replaces some dialogue with lip-synched popular song lyrics ala Dennis Potter's "Pennies from Heaven" and "The Singing Detective." (Pic is dedicated to Potter). Camille (Jaoui) is helping her sister Odile (Azema) and brother-in-law Claude (Arditti) look for a new Paris apartment, while beginning an affair with real estate broker Marc (Wilson) and ignoring the overtures of love-sick Simon (Dussollier). Meanwhile, Nicolas (Bacri), Odile's now-married ex-flame is also apartment hunting and Odile's vulnerable since Claude doesn't love her anymore. Everybody lies to everybody else (and themselves) and misinterprets all the situations. French with subtitles. **122m/C VHS.** *FR* Agnes Jaoui, Jean-Pierre Bacri, Andre Dussollier, Sabine Azema, Lambert Wilson, Pierre Arditti, Jane Birkin, Jean-Paul Roussillon; ***D:*** Alain Resnais; ***W:*** Agnes Jaoui, Jean-Pierre Bacri; ***C:*** Renato Berta; ***M:*** Bruno Fontaine. Cesar '98: Actor (Dussollier), Film, Film Editing, Sound, Support. Actor (Bacri), Support. Actress (Jaoui), Writing.

Same River Twice 🦴🦴½ **1997** Four men who became friends while working as river rafting guides decide to have a reunion on the same river some 13 years after the death of a friend in a rafting accident. But each man realizes that the years have brought a certain amount of caution and that they are no longer young daredevils. Likewise, their personal quirks must be overcome if they are to successfully negogiate the white water rapids ahead of them. **103m/C VHS, DVD.** John Putch, Dwier Brown, Shea Farrell, Robert Curtis-Brown; ***D:*** Scott Featherstone; ***W:*** Scott Featherstone; ***C:*** Art Wilder; ***M:*** Bradley Smith. **VIDEO**

Same Time, Next Year 🦴🦴🦴 **1978** A chance meeting between an accountant and a housewife results in a sometimes tragic, always sentimental 25-year affair in which they meet only one weekend each year. Well-cast leads carry warm, touching story based on the Broadway play by Bernard Slade. **119m/C VHS.** Ellen Burstyn, Alan Alda; ***D:*** Robert Mulligan; ***C:*** Robert L. Surtees; ***M:*** Marvin Hamlisch. Golden Globes '79: Actress—Mus./Comedy (Burstyn).

Sammy & Rosie Get Laid 🦴🦴🦴 **1987** An unusual social satire about a sexually liberated couple living in London whose lives are thrown into turmoil by the arrival of the man's father—a controversial politician in India. Provides a confusing look at sexual and class collisions. From the makers of "My Beautiful Laundrette." **97m/C VHS.** *GB* Shashi Kapoor, Frances Barber, Claire Bloom, Ayub Khan-Din, Roland Gift, Wendy Gazelle, Meera Syal; ***D:*** Stephen Frears; ***W:*** Hanif Kureishi; ***C:*** Oliver Stapleton; ***M:*** Stanley Myers.

Sammy, the Way-Out Seal 🦴🦴 **1962** Two young boys bring a mischievous seal to live in their beach house and try to keep it a secret from their parents. Disney in its early '60s phase. **89m/C VHS.** Michael McGreevey, Billy Mumy, Patricia Barry, Robert Culp; ***D:*** Norman Tokar.

Sam's Son 🦴🦴 **1984 (PG)** Sentimental, autobiographical tale about how a young man's athletic prowess opens the door for an acting career in Hollywood. Good performance by Wallach as the boy's father. Self-indulgent, though entertaining. **107m/C VHS.** Eli Wallach, Anne Jackson, Timothy Patrick Murphy, Hallie Todd, James Karen, Allan Hayes, Joanna Lee, Michael Landon; ***D:*** Michael Landon; ***W:*** Michael Landon.

Samson 🦴 **1961** Samson attempts to keep wits and hair about him. **90m/C VHS.** *IT* Brad Harris, Brigitte Corey, Alan Steel, Serge Gainsbourg, Mara Berni; ***D:*** Gianfranco Parolini.

Samson Against the Sheik 🦴 *Maciste Contro lo Sceicco* **1962** Samson survives long enough to battle a sheik in the Middle Ages. **106m/C VHS.** *IT* Ed Fury, Carlo Latimer, Pierro Lulli, Adriano Micantoni; ***D:*** Domenico Paolella; ***W:*** Gian Paolo Callegari, Alessandro Ferrau; ***C:*** Carlo Bellero; ***M:*** Carlo Savina.

Samson and Delilah 🦴🦴🦴 **1950** The biblical story of the vindictive Delilah, who after being rejected by the mighty Samson, robbed him of his strength by shearing his curls. Delivered in signature DeMille style. Wonderfully fun and engrossing. Mature is excellent. **128m/C VHS.** Victor Mature, Hedy Lamarr, Angela Lansbury, George Sanders, Henry Wilcoxon, Olive Deering, Fay Holden; ***D:*** Cecil B. DeMille; ***C:*** George Barnes. Oscars '50: Art Dir./Set Dec., Color, Costume Des. (C).

Samson and Delilah 🦴🦴 **1984** TV version of the biblical romance, semi-based on DeMille's 1950 version. Original Samson (Mature) plays Samson's father. Too long but inoffensive; see the DeMille version instead. **95m/C VHS.** Antony Hamilton, Belinda Bauer, Max von Sydow, Jose Ferrer, Victor Mature, Maria Schell; ***D:*** Lee Philips; ***M:*** Maurice Jarre. **TV**

Samson and Delilah 🦴🦴 **1996** Another in TNT's biblical retellings, this time with Israelite shepherd Samson (Thal), who also the strongest man alive, falling for beautiful-but-treacherous Philistine Delilah (Hurley). Seems Samson is causing havoc with General Tariq's (Hopper) Philistine army and Delilah is to discover the secret of his strength. **180m/C VHS.** Eric Thal, Elizabeth Hurley, Dennis Hopper, Michael Gambon, Diana Rigg, Ben Becker, Paul Freeman, Daniel Massey, Pinkas Braun, Debora Caprioglio, Alessandro Gassman, Mark McGann, Jonathan Rhys Meyers; ***D:*** Nicolas Roeg; ***W:*** Allan Scott; ***C:*** Raffaele Mertes; ***M:*** Marco Frisina. **CABLE**

Samson and His Mighty Challenge 🦴½ **1964** In this rarely seen muscle epic, Hercules, Maciste, Samson and Ursus all take part in a battle royale. **?m/C VHS.** *IT* Alan Steel, Red Ross; ***D:*** Giorgio Capitani.

Samson and the 7 Miracles of the World 🦴🦴 *Maciste Alla Corte Del Gran Khan; Maciste at the Court of the Great Khan; Goliath and the Golden City* **1962** This time the hero known as Maciste (renamed Samson for Americans) is in the 13th century battling brutal Tartar warlords. The very Earth itself shakes when our hero goes into battle! **80m/C VHS.** *FR IT* Gordon Scott, Yoko Tani, Gabriele Antonini, Leonardo Severini, Valeri Inkizhinov, Helene Chanel; ***D:*** Riccardo (Robert Hampton) Freda; ***M:*** Les Baxter.

Samson in the Wax Museum 🦴½ *Santo en el Museo de Cera; Santo in the Wax Museum* **1963** Masked Mexican wrestling hero Santo (here called Samson) does battle with a scientist who has discovered a way to make wax monsters come to life. **92m/B VHS.** *MX* Santo, Claudio Brook, Ruben Rojo, Norma Mora, Roxana Bellini; ***D:*** Alfonso Corona Blake.

Samson vs. the Vampire Women 🦴½ **1961** Santo (here called Samson) the masked hero and athlete, battles the forces of darkness as a horde of female vampires attempt to make an unsuspecting girl their next queen. Not bad if you're into the Mexican wrestling genre. **89m/B VHS.** *MX* Santo, Lorena Lalazquez, Jaime Fernandez, Maria Duval; ***D:*** Alfonso Corona Blake.

Samurai 1: Musashi Miyamoto ½ **1955** The first installment in the film version of Musashi Miyamoto's life, as he leaves his 17th century village as a warrior in a local civil war only to return beaten and disillusioned. Justly award-winning. In Japanese with English subtitles. **92m/C VHS, DVD.** *JP* Toshiro Mifune, Kaoru Yachigusa, Rentaro Mikuni, Eiko Miyoshi; ***D:*** Hiroshi Inagaki; ***W:*** Hiroshi Inagaki, Tikuhei Wakao; ***C:*** Jun Yasumoto; ***M:*** Ikuma Dan. Oscars '55: Foreign Film.

Samurai 2: Duel at Ichijoji Temple ½ **1955** Inagaki's second film depicting the life of Musashi Miyamoto, the 17th century warrior, who wandered the disheveled landscape of feudal Japan looking for glory and love. In Japanese with English subtitles. **102m/C VHS, DVD.** *JP* Toshiro Mifune, Akihiko Hirata, Daisuke Kato, Mariko Okada, Sachio Sakai, Kaoru Yachigusa; ***D:*** Hiroshi Inagaki; ***W:*** Hiroshi Inagaki; ***C:*** Jun Yasumoto; ***M:*** Ikuma Dan.

Samurai 3: Duel at Ganryu Island ½ **1956** The final film of Inagaki's trilogy, in which Musashi Miyamoto confronts his lifelong enemy in a climactic battle. Depicts Miyamoto's spiritual awakening and realization that love and hatred exist in all of us. In Japanese with English subtitles. **102m/C VHS, DVD.** *JP* Toshiro Mifune, Koji Tsurata, Kaoru Yachigusa, Mariko Okada; ***D:*** Hiroshi Inagaki; ***W:*** Hiroshi Inagaki, Tikuhei Wakao; ***C:*** Kazuo Yamada; ***M:*** Ikuma Dan.

Samurai Cowboy **1993** Sato (Go) is a successful Japanese businessman who worships the American western ideal so he decides to give up the rat race by moving to Running Moose, Montana, and buying a cattle ranch. Talk about culture shock! Inoffensive fish-out-of-water comedy. Go is a popular singer in his native Japan. **101m/C VHS.** Hiromi Go, Catherine Mary Stewart, Robert Conrad, Conchata Ferrell, Matt McCoy; ***D:*** Michael Keusch; ***W:*** Michael Keusch; ***M:*** Osamu Kitajima.

Samurai Rebellion *Rebellion* **1967** Isaburo (Mifune) is a reknowned swordsman in 18th-century Japan who is the model of loyalty until his overlord demands the return of a former mistress, who is now Isaburo's daughter-in-law. This insult to his family forces Isaburo to take a deadly stand, which turns out to be against his best friend (Nakadai) who's trying to uphold the feudal code. Lots of swordplay. Last in Kobayashi's trilogy following "Harakiri" (1962) and "Kwaidan" (1964). Japanese with subtitles. **121m/B VHS.** *JP* Toshiro Mifune, Tatsuya Nakadai; ***D:*** Masaki Kobayashi; ***W:*** Shinobu Hashimoto.

Samurai Reincarnation **1981** After the Shogunate government kills 18,000 Christian rioters in the revolt of 1638, and publicly beheads the leader Shiro Amakusa, Shiro reincarnates during a monstrous thunderstorm. Consumed with hatred, he discards the teachings of Jesus Christ and seeks revenge. In Japanese with English subtitles. **122m/C VHS.** *JP* ***D:*** Kinji Fukasaku.

San Antonio **1945** A bad girl working in a dance hall turns over a new leaf on meeting the good guy. Trite plot, but good production. **105m/C VHS.** Errol Flynn, Alexis Smith, S.Z. Sakall, Victor Francen, Florence Bates, John Litel, Paul Kelly; ***D:*** David Butler; ***M:*** Max Steiner.

San Demetrio, London ½ **1947** Set in 1940, the crew of a crippled tanker endures harrowing situations to reach port. A decent anti-war movie in its time, it's now showing its age. Based on a true story, the plot sags with unbelievable scenes and holes on the plot side. **76m/B VHS.** Walter Fitzgerald, Mervyn Johns, Ralph Michael, Robert Beatty, Charles Victor, Frederick Piper; ***D:*** Charles Frend.

San Fernando Valley *San Fernando* **1944** Another lawman-in-evil-town epic. Rogers received his first on-screen kiss in 1944's biggest western. Fairly typical, pleasant cowboy tale. **54m/B VHS.** Roy Rogers, Dale Evans.

San Francisco ½ **1936** The San Francisco Earthquake of 1906 serves as the background for a romance between an opera singer and a Barbary Coast saloon owner. Somewhat overdone but gripping tale of passion and adventure in the West. Wonderful special effects. Finale consists of historic earthquake footage. Also available colorized. ♫San Francisco; A Heart That's Free; Would You?; Air des Bijoux; Sempre Libera. **116m/B VHS.** Jeanette MacDonald, Clark Gable, Spencer Tracy, Jack Holt, Jessie Ralph, Al Shean; ***D:*** Woodbridge S. Van Dyke; ***W:*** Anita Loos. Oscars '36: Sound.

Sanctuary **1998 (R)** A former government agent, Luke Connolly has completely changed his life by becoming a clergyman. However, when his old agency discovers his whereabouts, the deadly skills he's renounced may be all that can save him. **110m/C VHS, DVD.** Mark Dacascos, Kylie Travis, Jaimz Woolvett, Alan Scarfe; ***D:*** Tibor Takacs; ***W:*** Michael Stokes; ***M:*** Norman Orenstein. **VIDEO**

Sanctuary of Fear ½ *Girl in the Park* **1979** A priest in New York City helps an actress subjected to a series of terrorizing incidents. Uninspired would-be TV pilot based on Chesterton's "Father Brown" series. **98m/C VHS.** George Hearn, Barnard Hughes, Kay Lenz, Michael McGuire, Robert Schenkkan, David Rasche, Fred Gwynne, Elizabeth Wilson; ***D:*** John Llewellyn Moxey. **TV**

Sand **2000** Tyler Briggs (Vartan) wants to start over—away from his violent father (Quaid) and brothers. So after his mother's death, he heads to the quiet beach town where his mom grew up. There Tyler falls for Sandy (Wuhrer) and starts to make a peaceful new life but trouble and family follow. **90m/C VHS, DVD.** Michael Vartan, Denis Leary, Randy Quaid, Kari Wuhrer, Marshall Bell, Julie Delpy, Rodney Eastman, Bodhi (Pine) Elfman, Emilio Estevez, John Hawkes, Jon Lovitz, Norman Reedus, Peter Simmons, Harry Dean Stanton; ***D:*** Matt Palmieri; ***W:*** Matt Palmieri; ***C:*** John Skotchdopole.

Sand and Blood ½ *Blood and Sand; De Sable et de Sang* **1987** A young matador who wishes to escape poverty and a young, cultivated doctor, who despises bullfighting, meet and eventually become friends. A woman enters the picture and completes the love triangle. Widely praised by critics. Interesting and moving. In French with English subtitles. **101m/C VHS.** *FR* Sami Frey, Andre Dussollier, Clementine Celarie, Patrick Catalifo, Maria Casares, Catherine Rouvel; ***D:*** Jeanne Labrune; ***W:*** Jeanne Labrune.

The Sand Pebbles ½ **1966** An American expatriate engineer, transferred to a gunboat on the Yangtze River in 1926, falls in love with a missionary teacher. As he becomes aware of the political climate of American imperialism, he finds himself at odds with his command structure; the treatment of this issue can be seen as commentary on the situation in Vietnam at the time of the film's release. Considered one of McQueen's best performances, blending action and romance. **193m/C VHS, DVD, Wide.** Steve McQueen, Richard Crenna, Richard Attenborough, Candice Bergen, Marayat Andriane, Mako, Larry Gates, Gavin MacLeod, Simon Oakland, James Hong, Richard Loo, Barney (Bernard) Phillips, Tommy Lee, Ford Rainey, Walter Reed, Gus Trikonis, Joe Turkel, Glenn Wilder; ***D:*** Robert Wise; ***W:*** Robert Anderson; ***C:*** Joe MacDonald; ***M:*** Jerry Goldsmith. Golden Globes '67: Support. Actor (Attenborough).

Sand Trap ½ **1997 (R)** Wealthy businessman Nelson Yeager (Koepenick) gets pushed over a cliff by his best friend, Jack (James). But when Jack and Nelson's not-so-grieving widow Margo (Morehead) report the accident and the local sheriff (Thompson) goes to find the body, it's not there. Now a murder plot turns into a desire for revenge. Low-budget modern noir. **99m/C VHS.** Elizabeth Morehead, David John James, Brad Koepenick, Bob Thompson; ***D:*** Harris Done; ***W:*** Harris Done; ***C:*** Mark W. Gray. **VIDEO**

Sandakan No. 8 *Brothel 8; Sandakan House 8* **1974** A Japanese woman working as a journalist befriends an old woman who was sold into prostitution in Borneo in the early 1900s. Justly acclaimed feminist story dramatizes the role of women in Japanese society. Japanese with English subtitles. **121m/C VHS.** *JP* Kinuyo Tanaka, Yoko Takakashi, Komake Kurihara, Eitaro (Sakae, Saka Ozawa) Ozawa; ***D:*** Kei Kumai. Berlin Intl. Film Fest. '75: Actress.

Sanders of the River *Bosambo* **1935** A British officer in colonial Africa must work with the local chief to quell a rebellion. Tale of imperialism. Dated but still interesting and of value. Robeson is very good; superb location cinematography. **80m/B VHS.** *GB* Paul Robeson, Leslie Banks, Robert Cochran; ***D:*** Zoltan Korda; ***C:*** Georges Perinal.

Sandflow ½ **1937** Well-made Western with Jones playing a man whose father has cheated many ranchers. Jones is out to avenge all of his father's misdeeds and build a new life for himself in this above-average oater. **58m/B VHS.** Buck Jones, Lita Chevret, Robert F. (Bob) Kortman, Arthur Aylesworth, Robert Terry, Enrique DeRosas; ***D:*** Lesley Selander.

The Sandlot **1993 (PG)** Young Scotty (Guiry) moves to a new neighborhood in California in 1962 and tries to make friends despite not knowing anything about playing baseball. His scrappy teammates include the friendly Benny (Vitar), a chubby loud-mouthed catcher named Ham (Renna), and Squints (Leopardi), a would-be Lothario before his time. Action revolves around Scotty's attempt to get baseball autographed by Babe Ruth out of the clutches of giant killer junkyard dog owned by Jones before dad Leary discovers it's missing. Small wonder is nostalgic without being sentimental, and tells its tale with grace and humor, supported by a period soundtrack. **101m/C VHS, DVD, Wide.** Tom Guiry, Mike Vitar, Patrick Renna, Chauncey Leopardi, Marty York, Brandon Adams, Denis Leary, Karen Allen, James Earl Jones, Maury Wills, Art LaFleur, Marley Shelton, Brooke Adams; ***D:*** David Mickey Evans; ***W:*** David Mickey Evans, Robert Gunter; ***C:*** Anthony B. Richmond; ***M:*** David Newman; ***V:*** Arliss Howard.

The Sandpiper **1965** Free-spirited artist Taylor falls in love with Burton, the married headmaster of her son's boarding school. Muddled melodrama offers little besides starpower. Filmed at Big Sur, California. ♫The Shadow of Your Smile. **117m/C VHS.** Elizabeth Taylor, Richard Burton, Charles Bronson, Eva Marie Saint, Robert Webber, Morgan Mason; ***D:*** Vincente Minnelli; ***C:*** Milton Krasner. Oscars '65: Song ("The Shadow of Your Smile").

Sandra of a Thousand Delights *Sandra; Of a Thousand Delights; Vaghe Stelle Dell'Orsa* **1965** Haunting drama with strong women (and weak men). Sandra returns to Italy from her American home in order to attend a ceremony honoring her father—a Jewish scientist who died in a Nazi concentration camp. Back with her family, Sandra tries to deal with her past, including her mother's possible betrayal of her father and her brother's incestuous longings. Italian with subtitles. **100m/B VHS.** *IT* Claudia Cardinale, Jean Sorel, Marie Bell, Michael Craig, Renzo Ricci; ***D:*** Luchino Visconti; ***W:*** Luchino Visconti, Suso Cecchi D'Amico; ***M:*** Cesar Franck.

Sands of Iwo Jima ½ **1949** Wayne earned his first Oscar nomination as a tough Marine sergeant, in one of his best roles. He trains a squad of rebellious recruits in New Zealand in 1943. Later they are responsible for the capture of Iwo Jima from the Japanese—one of the most difficult campaigns of the Pacific Theater. Includes striking real war footage. **109m/B VHS, DVD.** John Wayne, Forrest Tucker, John Agar, Richard Jaeckel, Adele Mara, Wally Cassell, James Brown, Richard Webb, Arthur Franz, Julie (Jacqueline Wells) Bishop, William Murphy, George Tyne, Hal Baylor, John McGuire, Martin Milner, William (Bill) Self, Peter Coe, I. Stanford Jolley, Col. D.M. Shoup, Lt. Col. H.P. Crowe, Capt. Harold G. Shrier, Rene A. Gagnon, Ira H. Hayes, John H. Bradley; ***D:*** Allan Dwan; ***W:*** Harry Brown, James Edward Grant; ***C:*** Reggie Lanning; ***M:*** Victor Young.

Sands of Sacrifice ½ *Tangled Trails* **1921** Hart, a Northwest Mountie, seeks an unscrupulous promoter who's selling worthless mining stock. **56m/B VHS.** Neal Hart, Violet Palmer, Gladys Hampton, Jules Cowles, Jean Bary, Ed Roseman; ***D:*** Charles Bartlett.

The Sandy Bottom Orchestra ½ **2000** Sandy Bottom, Wisconsin is a quaint small town that is resistant to change. Big city Ingrid (Headly), a former classical pianist, discovered this when she married local dairy farmer Norman (Irwin). Norman is also having problems—he wants to include a classical concert in the town's annual summer festival rather than the usual marching band and is meeting with opposition. Their daughter Rachel (Zima) also longs to fit in but her musical talent has outgrown the limited resources of the community and decisions must be made. **100m/C VHS, DVD.** Glenne Headly, Tom Irwin, Madeline Zima, Jane Powell, Richard McMillan, Tamara Hope, Roger Dunn, Bradley Reid; ***D:*** Bradley Wigor; ***W:*** Joseph Maurer; ***C:*** Robert Primes; ***M:*** David Bell. **CABLE**

Sanjuro *Tsubaki Sanjuro* **1962** In this offbeat, satiric sequel to "Yojimbo," a talented but lazy samurai comes to the aid of a group of naive young warriors. The conventional ideas of good and evil are quickly tossed aside; much less earnest than other Kurosawa Samurai outings. In Japanese with English subtitles. **96m/B VHS, DVD.** *JP* Toshiro Mifune, Tatsuya Nakadai, Keiju Kobayashi, Yuzo Kayama; ***D:*** Akira Kurosawa; ***W:*** Akira Kurosawa, Ryuzo Kikushima, Hideo Oguni; ***C:*** Fukuzo Koizumi, Takao Saito; ***M:*** Masaru Sato.

Sans Soleil *Sunless* **1982** A female narrator reads and comments on the letters she receives from a friend, a freelance cameraman traveling through Japan, West Africa, and Iceland. The cameraman meditates on the cultural dislocation he feels and the meaning of his work and of life itself. Both narrator and cameraman remain unseen with the visuals being the cameraman's work in progress. **100m/C VHS.** *FR* ***D:*** Chris Marker; ***W:*** Chris Marker; ***Nar:*** Alexandra Stewart.

Sanshiro Sugata **1943** Kurosawa's first film. A young man learns discipline in martial arts from a patient master. Climactic fight scene is early signature Kurosawa. In Japanese with English subtitles. **82m/B VHS.** *JP* Denjiro Okochi, Yukiko Todoroki, Ranko Hanai, Ryonosuke Tsukigata, Sugisaku Aoyama, Kokuten Kodo, Susumo Fusuita, Takashi Shimura; ***D:*** Akira Kurosawa.

Sansho the Bailiff *The Bailiff; Sansho Dayu* **1954** A world masterpiece by Mizoguchi about feudal society in 11th century Japan. A woman and her children are sold into prostitution and slavery. As an adult, the son seeks to right the ills of his society. Powerful and tragic, and often more highly esteemed than "Ugetsu." In Japanese with English subtitles. **132m/B VHS.** *JP* Kinuyo Tanaka, Yoshiaki Hanayagi, Kyoko Kagawa, Eitaro Shindo, Ichiro Sugai; ***D:*** Kenji Mizoguchi; ***W:*** Yoshikata Yoda; ***M:*** Fumio Hayasaka.

Santa Claus woof! **1959** Santa Claus teams up with Merlin the Magician to fend off an evil spirit who would ruin everyone's Christmas. Mexican camp classic. **94m/C VHS.** *MX* Jose Elias Moreno, Cesareo Quezadas; ***D:*** Rene Cardona Sr.; ***Nar:*** Ken Smith.

Santa Claus Conquers the Martians *Santa Claus Defeats the Aliens* **1964** A Martian spaceship comes to Earth and kidnaps Santa Claus and two children. Martian kids, it seems, are jealous that Earth tykes have Christmas. Features then-child star Pia Zadora. **80m/C VHS.** John Call, Leonard Hicks, Vincent Beck, Victor Stiles, Donna Conforti, Bill McCutcheon, Christopher Month, Pia Zadora; ***D:*** Nicholas Webster; ***W:*** Glenville Mareth; ***C:*** David Quaid; ***M:*** Milton Delugg.

Santa Claus: The Movie **1985 (PG)** A big-budgeted spectacle about an elf who falls prey to an evil toy maker and almost ruins Christmas and Santa Claus. Boring, 'tis-the-season fantasy-drama meant to warm our cockles. **112m/C VHS, DVD, Wide.** Dudley Moore, John Lithgow, David Huddleston, Judy Cornwell, Burgess Meredith; ***D:*** Jeannot Szwarc; ***W:*** David Newman; ***C:*** Arthur Ibbetson; ***M:*** Henry Mancini.

The Santa Clause 🦴🦴½ **1994 (PG)** If you like Allen, you'll enjoy this lightweight holiday comedy about divorced workaholic dad Scott Calvin and eight-year-old son Charlie (Lloyd). Seems Santa injures himself falling off the Calvin roof and dad winds up putting on Santa's suit. But as it turns out when you put on Santa's suit, you become Santa, including a noticeable weight gain, a fluffy beard, and all those reindeer and elves to deal with (but where's Mrs. Claus?). **97m/C VHS, DVD.** Tim Allen, Eric Lloyd, Judge Reinhold, Wendy Crewson, David Krumholtz, Mary Gross; ***D:*** John Pasquin; ***W:*** Leonardo Benvenuti, Steve Rudnick; ***C:*** Walt Lloyd; ***M:*** Michael Convertino. Blockbuster '95: Male Newcomer, T. (Allen).

Santa Fe 🦴🦴 **1951** Action-packed western with Scott playing a Confederate soldier who heads West to take a job with the Santa Fe Railroad. However, his brothers, with their wounded rebel pride, have different ideas for forgetting the defeat. Refusing to take money from Northern businesses, they become outlaws. Based on a story by Louis Stevens and the novel by James Marshall. **89m/C VHS.** Randolph Scott, Janis Carter, Jerome Courtland, Peter Thompson, John Archer, Warner Anderson, Roy Roberts, Billy House; ***D:*** Irving Pichel; ***W:*** Kenneth Gamet.

Santa Fe 🦴🦴½ **1997 (R)** Muddled romantic drama with an appealing cast. It's taken cop Paul Thomas (Cole) eight months to recover from bullet wounds suffered in a shoot-out with a local cult. In the meantime, wife Leah's (Kelley) distanced herself from the marriage but still urges Paul into group counseling with charismatic Eleanor (Davidovich). Despite Paul's mistrust of her guru-like status, he's naturally drawn to Eleanor (and she to him). There's some tedious subplot stuff but the leads do fine. **97m/C VHS, DVD.** Gary Cole, Lolita (David) Davidovich, Sheila Kelley, Tina Majorino, Jere Burns, Pamela Reed, Phyllis Frelich, Mark Medoff, Tony Plana, Jeffrey Jones; ***D:*** Andrew Shea; ***W:*** Andrew Shea, Mark Medoff; ***C:*** Paul Elliott; ***M:*** Mark Governor.

Santa Fe Bound 🦴🦴 **1937** Tyler must work to clear his name when he is falsely accused of having murdered a man. **58m/B VHS.** Tom Tyler, Jeanne Martel, Richard Cramer, Charles "Slim" Whitaker, Edward Cassidy, Lafe (Lafayette) McKee, Dorothy Woods, Charles "Blackie" King; ***D:*** Harry S. Webb.

Santa Fe Marshal 🦴🦴 **1940** The 27th Hopalong Cassidy movie, if anyone's counting. In the title job the Hopster goes undercover with a medicine show to smash a criminal gang. A little different than usual, right up to the surprise identity of the crooked mastermind. **66m/B VHS.** William Boyd, Russell Hayden, Marjorie Rambeau, Bernadene Hayes, Earle Hodgins, Kenneth Harlan, Eddie Dean; ***D:*** Lesley Selander.

Santa Fe Stampede 🦴🦴½ **1938** The Three Mesquiteers join an old prospector in his claim but when he is killed, one of them (Wayne) is framed. The photography makes up for the weak storyline and direction. **58m/B VHS.** John Wayne, Ray Corrigan, Max Terhune, William Farnum, June Martel, Leroy Mason, Yakima Canutt, Curly Dresden; ***D:*** George Sherman.

Santa Fe Trail 🦴🦴½ **1940** Historically inaccurate but entertaining tale about the pre-Civil War fight for "bloody Kansas." The action-adventure depicts future Civil War Generals J.E.B. Stuart (Flynn) and George Armstrong Custer (Reagan!) as they begin their military career (although Custer was really just a youth at this time). Good action scenes. Also available colorized. **110m/B VHS, DVD.** Errol Flynn, Olivia de Havilland, Ronald Reagan, Van Heflin, Raymond Massey, Alan Hale; ***D:*** Michael Curtiz; ***W:*** Robert Buckner; ***C:*** Sol Polito; ***M:*** Max Steiner.

Santa Fe Uprising 🦴🦴½ **1946** Red Ryder has to save Little Beaver from kidnappers. Good first entry for Lane in the "Red Ryder" series. **54m/B VHS.** Allan "Rocky" Lane, Robert (Bobby) Blake.

Santa Sangre 🦴🦴🦴 **1990 (R)** A circus in Mexico City, a temple devoted to a saint without arms, and a son who faithfully dotes upon his armless mother are just a few of the bizarre things in this wildly fantastic film. Fenix acts as his mother's arms, plays the piano for her, and carries out any wish she desires—including murder. Visually intoxicating but strange outing may prove too graphic for some viewers. Not as rigorous as other Jodorowsky outings. Also available in an NC-17 version. **123m/C VHS.** *IT MX* Axel Jodorowsky, Sabrina Dennison, Guy Stockwell, Blanca Guerra, Thelma Tixou, Adan Jodorowsky, Faviola Tapia, Jesus Juarez; ***D:*** Alejandro Jodorowsky; ***W:*** Robert Leoni, Claudio Argento, Alejandro Jodorowsky; ***C:*** Danielle Nannuzzi; ***M:*** Simon Boswell.

Santa with Muscles 🦴½ **1996 (PG)** Cartoonish holiday-themed comedy finds the Hulkster as Scrooge-like millionaire Blake Thorne. Through a series of stupid circumstances, Thorne winds up in a Santa suit in a shopping mall hiding from the cops. But a blow to the head makes him believe he's the Jolly-Old-Elf himself and he comes to the aid of a local orphanage, whose tykes are about to be evicted. Silly's the kindest thing to say. **97m/C VHS.** Hulk Hogan, Don Stark, Ed Begley Jr., Clint Howard, Robin Curtis, Garrett Morris, Adam Wylie; ***D:*** John Murlowski; ***W:*** Jonathan Bond, Fred Mata, Dorrie Krum Raymond; ***C:*** Michael Gfelner; ***M:*** James Covell.

Santee 🦴🦴 **1973 (PG)** A father-son relationship develops between a bounty hunter and the son of a man he killed. Good, but not great, Western. **93m/C VHS.** Glenn Ford, Dana Wynter, Jay Silverheels, John Larch, Michael Burns; ***D:*** Gary Nelson.

Santitos 🦴🦴 **1999 (R)** Esperanza Diaz (Heredia) is a young Mexican widow whose 12-year-old daughter Blanca (Zapata) has supposedly died, although her mother never saw the child's body. When Esperanza's favorite saint, St. Jude the patron of lost causes, starts appearing to her, she begins a search for her lost child that takes her to the La Casa Rosa brothel in Tijuana. But faith and motherly love will help Esperanza survive anything. Disarmingly innocent film based on the novel by Escandon, who also wrote the screenplay. Spanish with subtitles. **99m/C VHS.** *MX* Dolores Heredia, Fernando Torre Lapham, Juan Duarte, Ana Bertha Espin, Maya Zapata, Roberto Cobo; ***D:*** Alejandro Springall; ***W:*** Maria Ampara Escandon; ***C:*** Xavier Perez Grobet; ***M:*** Carlo Nicolau, Rosino Serrano.

The Saphead 🦴🦴½ **1921** Keaton's first outing as the rich playboy has him playing the none-to-bright son of a Wall Street mogul. Some great moments provide a glimpse of cinematic greatness to come from the budding comedic genius. Based on the play "The New Henrietta" by Winchell Smith and Victor Mapes. Silent. **70m/B VHS, DVD.** William H. Crane, Buster Keaton, Carol Holloway, Edward Connelly, Irving Cummings; ***D:*** Herbert Blache; ***W:*** June Mathis; ***C:*** Harold Wenstrom.

Sapphire 🦴🦴🦴 **1959** Two Scotland Yard detectives seek the killer of a beautiful black woman who was passing for white. Good mystery and topical social comment; remains interesting and engrossing. Superbly acted all around. **92m/C VHS.** *GB* Nigel Patrick, Yvonne Mitchell, Michael Craig, Paul Massie, Bernard Miles; ***D:*** Basil Dearden. British Acad. '59: Film.

Saps at Sea 🦴🦴½ **1940** A doctor advises Ollie to take a rest away from his job at a horn factory. He and Stan rent a boat, which they plan to keep tied to the dock, until an escaped criminal happens by and uses the boys (and their boat) for his getaway. Cramer is a good bad guy; Stan and Ollie cause too much trouble, as always. **57m/B VHS.** Stan Laurel, Oliver Hardy, James Finlayson, Ben Turpin, Richard Cramer; ***D:*** Gordon Douglas.

Sara Dane 🦴🦴 **1981** A strong young woman in the 18th century rises in the world through marriage and business acumen. Interesting but imperfect and slow. **150m/C VHS.** *AU* Harold Hopkins, Brenton Whittle, Barry Quin, Sean Scully; ***D:*** Rod Hardy, Gary Conway.

Sarafina! 🦴🦴🦴 **1992 (PG-13)** Part coming-of-age saga, part political drama, part musical, and all emotionally powerful. Sarafina is a young girl in a township school in Soweto, South Africa in the mid-'70s, gradually coming into a political awakening amid the Soweto riots. Khumalo recreates her stage role as the glowing and defiant Sarafina with both Goldberg and Makeba good in their roles as Sarafina's outspoken and inspirational teacher and her long-suffering mother, respectively. Adapted from Ngema's stage musical. **98m/C VHS.** Leleti Khumalo, Whoopi Goldberg, Miriam Makeba, John Kani, Mbongeni Ngema; ***D:*** Darrell Roodt; ***W:*** Mbongeni Ngema, William Nicholson; ***M:*** Stanley Myers.

The Saragossa Manuscript 🦴🦴½ *Rekopis Znaleziony W Saragossie* **1965** Ambitious fantasy based on the 1813 novel "Sanatorium under the Hourglass" by Bruno Schultz. A romantic Belgian army officer, travelling to Spain, meets two beautiful princesses who send him on a fantastic journey to prove himself worthy of their affections. Polish with subtitles. **174m/B VHS.** *PL* Zbigniew Cybulski, Iga Cembrzynska, Joanna Jedryka, Slawomir Linder; ***D:*** Wojciech Has; ***W:*** Tadeusz Kwiatkowski; ***C:*** Mieczyslaw Jahoda; ***M:*** Krzysztof Penderecki.

Sarah, Plain and Tall 🦴🦴🦴 **1991 (G)** New England school teacher (Close) travels to Kansas circa 1910 to care for the family of a widowed farmer who has advertised for a wife. Superior entertainment for the whole family. Adapted from Patricia MacLachlan's novel of the same name by MacLachlan and Carol Sobieski. Nominated for nine Emmy Awards. A "Hallmark Hall of Fame" presentation. **98m/C VHS, DVD.** Glenn Close, Christopher Walken, Lexi (Faith) Randall, Margaret Sophie Stein, Jon (John) DeVries, Christopher Bell; ***D:*** Glenn Jordan; ***W:*** Carol Sobieski; ***C:*** Mike Fash; ***M:*** David Shire. **TV**

Sarah, Plain and Tall: Skylark 🦴🦴½ *Skylark* **1993 (G)** In a sequel to Hallmark Hall of Fame's hugely successful "Sarah, Plain and Tall," the whole Kansas crew shows up for more of their little-farm-on-the-prairie life. After two years in America's squarest state, mail-order bride Sarah (Close) loves Jacob (Walken), but not the scenery and still yearns for the lush greenery of Maine. When drought and fire threaten the farm, Jacob fears for the family's health and safety, and sends them back East for a visit. Close's "tough Yankee" expression grows a bit tiresome in a plot that is a tad predictable, yet the simplistic charm and nostalgia are unresistable and work to propel this quality Hallmark production. **98m/C VHS, DVD.** Glenn Close, Christopher Walken, Lexi (Faith) Randall, Christopher Bell, Tresa Hughes, Lois Smith, Lee Richardson, Elizabeth Wilson, Margaret Sophie Stein, Jon (John) DeVries, James Rebhorn, Woody Watson; ***D:*** Joseph Sargent; ***W:*** Patricia MacLachlan; ***C:*** Mike Fash; ***M:*** David Shire. **TV**

Sarah, Plain and Tall: Winter's End 🦴🦴🦴 *Winter's End* **1999 (G)** The third installation of the "Sarah" saga is set in 1918. A harsh winter is making life difficult for Sarah (Close), Jacob (Walken), and their three children. Then their lives take a strange turn when Jacob's father, John Witting (Palance), who abandoned his family when Jacob was a boy, suddenly shows up on their farm. A devastating storm proves just as paralyzing as the unresolved feelings between Jacob and John, but Sarah is determined to do what's best for her family. **99m/C VHS, DVD.** Glenn Close, Christopher Walken, Jack Palance, Lexi (Faith) Randall, Christopher Bell; ***D:*** Glenn Jordan; ***C:*** Ralf Bode; ***M:*** David Shire. **TV**

Sarah's Child 🦴🦴½ **1996** Sarah LaMere is devastated to learn that she can never have children. While husband Michael tries to accept, Sarah's upbringing has led her to believe that's her only purpose in life and she becomes increasingly unbalanced. Seemingly out of nowhere children's clothes and toys appear in their home and soon a strange young girl named Melissa appears, whom Sarah treats as her own child. When their landlady dies horribly after questioning Melissa, Michael is afraid the line between reality and fantasy has been breached but just how can he fight? **90m/C VHS.** Mary Parker Williams, Michael Berger, Ruth Hale, Bryce Chamberlain; ***D:*** Ron Beckstrom; ***W:*** Muffy Mead Thomas; ***C:*** Gregg Stouffer; ***M:*** Jim Ball, Glenn Workman.

Saratoga 🦴🦴½ **1937** Gable plays a bookie and Harlow the daughter of an impoverished horse breeder in this romantic comedy centered around the race tracks. This was the final film appearance for Harlow, who died before the film's completion. Mary Dees was chosen as her stand-in and had to finish many of the scenes. "Saratoga" was released just a month after Harlow's death and became one of the biggest moneymakers of the year. **94m/B VHS.** Jean Harlow, Clark Gable, Lionel Barrymore, Walter Pidgeon, Frank Morgan, Una Merkel, Cliff Edwards, George Zucco, Hattie McDaniel, Jonathan Hale; ***D:*** Jack Conway; ***W:*** Anita Loos, Robert Hopkins.

Saratoga Trunk 🦴🦴½ **1945** Lavish, if slow-moving, version of Edna Ferber's romance novel reteams Cooper and Bergman (who starred in "For Whom the Bell Tolls"). It's 1875 New Orleans and bitter Clio, the half-Creole illegitimate daughter of a local, is determined to marry rich. But first, she gets involved with Texas gambler Clint Maroon (Cooper). He's in a business deal with wealthy Van Steed (Warburton), about the Saratoga railroad line, and Clio decides to go after him. Of course, she really wants Clint and they go through lots of bother before ending up together. Filmed in 1943 but release was delayed because of WWII. **135m/B VHS.** Gary Cooper, Ingrid Bergman, John Warburton, Flora Robson, Florence Bates, Jerry Austin; ***D:*** Sam Wood; ***W:*** Casey Robinson; ***C:*** Ernest Haller; ***M:*** Max Steiner.

Sardinia Kidnapped 🦴🦴½ **1975** A beautiful girl is trapped in a clash between two powerful families while on vacation in Sardinia, where the peasants' custom is to kidnap a member of a rival family and then exchange the victim for land. Former documentary maker Mingozzi creates a realistic and uncompromising look at culture and change. In Italian; dubbed. **95m/C VHS.** *IT* Charlotte Rampling, Franco Nero; ***D:*** Gianfranco Mingozzi.

Sartana's Here...Trade Your Pistol for a Coffin 🦴 **1970** A soldier of fortune searches for a missing shipment of gold in the Old West. **92m/C VHS.** George Hilton, Charles Southwood, Erika Blanc, Linda Sini.

S.A.S. San Salvador 🦴 **1984** A CIA agent tries to prevent a psychotic from running amok in El Salvador. **95m/C VHS.** Miles O'Keeffe, Dagmar Lassander, Catherine Jarrett.

Sasquatch woof! **1976** Purported "documentary" about the mythical creature Bigfoot. Includes pictures of the "actual" monster. For those real stupid moods. **94m/C VHS.** George Lauris; ***D:*** Ed Ragozzini.

Satan in High Heels 🦴½ **1961** Sordid show-biz tale of a carnival dancer (Myles) who dreams of making it big on Broadway. First she finagles her way into a position as a nightclub singer and the mistress of a convenient millionaire. But she loses it all for love when she falls for the millionaire's misbehaving son. Flamboyant performance by Hall as the lesbian nightclub owner. **90m/B VHS, DVD.** Meg Myles, Grayson Hall, Del Tenney, Mike Keene, Robert Yuro, Sabrina, Earl Hammond, Paul Scott; ***D:*** Jerald Intrator; ***W:*** John T. Chapman; ***C:*** Bernard Herschensen; ***M:*** Mundell Lowe.

The Satan Killer 🦴½ **1993** A vicious serial killer is targeted by two tough police detectives. What makes it personal is Detective Stephen's fiance is one of the killer's victims and he's not going to let justice stand in the way of his revenge. **90m/C VHS.** Steve Sayre, Billy Franklin, James Westbrook, Belinda Creason, Cindy Healy; ***D:*** Stephen Calamari.

Satan Met a Lady 🦴🦴½ **1936** A weak adaptation of Dashiell Hammett's "Maltese Falcon." This version has Davis employing a private detective to track down a mysterious woman. The hunted woman is herself searching for a valuable collectible. **74m/B VHS.** Bette Davis, Warren William, Alison Skipworth, Arthur Treacher, Marie

Wilson, Porter Hall, Olin Howlin; *D:* William Dieterle.

The Satanic Rites of Dracula 🦴🦴 *Count Dracula and His Vampire Bride; Dracula Is Dead and Well and Living in London* **1973** Count Dracula is the leader of a satanic cult of prominent scientists and politicians who develop a gruesome plague virus capable of destroying the human race. Preceded by "Dracula A.D. 1972" and followed by "The 7 Brothers Meet Dracula." **88m/C VHS, DVD.** *GB* Christopher Lee, Peter Cushing, Michael Coles, William Franklyn, Freddie Jones, Joanna Lumley, Richard Vernon, Patrick Barr, Barbara Yo Ling; *D:* Alan Gibson; *W:* Don Houghton; *C:* Brian Probyn; *M:* John Cacavas.

Satanik 🦴 **1969 (R)** A hideous old hag is turned into a lovely young woman by a stolen potion, but it doesn't last long and she becomes a monster. **85m/C VHS.** *IT SP* Magda Konopka, Julio Pena, Luigi Montini, Armando Calvo, Umberto Raho; *D:* Piero Vivarelli.

Satan's Black Wedding 🦴 **1975 (R)** The ghouls arrive at a Monterey monastery in their Sunday best to celebrate devildom's most diabolical ritual, the "Black Wedding." **61m/C VHS.** Greg Braddock, Ray Miles, Lisa Milano.

Satan's Brew 🦴🦴 *Satansbraten* **1976** Aspiring poet (Raab) murders his mistress and assumes the identity of 19th-century symbolist poet Stefan George, including his idol's homosexual tastes. Fassbinder at his most excessive. German with subtitles. **100m/C VHS.** *GE* Kurt Raab, Margit Carstensen, Volker Spengler, Ingrid Caven, Helen Vita; *D:* Rainer Werner Fassbinder; *W:* Rainer Werner Fassbinder; *C:* Michael Ballhaus; *M:* Peer Raben.

Satan's Cheerleaders woof! **1977 (R)** A demonic high school janitor traps a bevy of buxom cheerleaders at his Satanic altar for sacrificial purposes. The gals use all of their endowments to escape the clutches of the evil sheriff and his fat wife. Is it ever campy! **92m/C VHS, DVD.** John Carradine, John Ireland, Yvonne De Carlo, Kerry Sherman, Jacqulin Cole, Hilary Horan, Alisa Powell, Sherry Marks, Jack Kruschen, Sydney Chaplin; *D:* Greydon Clark; *W:* Greydon Clark, Alvin L. Fast; *C:* Dean Cundey; *M:* Gerald Lee.

Satan's Harvest 🦴½ **1965** American detective inherits estate in Johannesburg, only to find the place is being used by drug smugglers. Sidesteps the political climate and shows the beauty of the land. And a good thing: the story is virtually nonexistent. **88m/C VHS.** George Montgomery, Tippi Hedren; *D:* Ferde Grofe Jr.

Satan's Princess 🦴 **1990** Satanic cult with a female leader runs amuck. Sloppy and forgettable. **90m/C VHS.** Robert Forster, Caren Kaye, Lydie Denier, Phillip Glasser, Michael (M.K.) Harris, Ellen Geer, Jack Carter; *D:* Bert I. Gordon; *W:* Stephen Katz.

Satan's Sadists 🦴 **1969 (R)** Tamblyn and his biker gang terrorize folks in the Southern California desert, including a retired cop, a Vietnam vet and a trio of vacationing coeds. Violent film will probably be best appreciated by Adamson completists. **88m/C VHS, DVD.** Russ Tamblyn, Regina Carrol, Gary Kent, Jackie Taylor, John Cardos, Kent Taylor, Robert Dix, Scott Brady, Evelyn Frank, Greydon Clark, Bill Bonner, Bobby Clark, Yvonne Stewart, Cheryl Anne, Randee Lynn, Bambi Allen, Breck Warwick; *D:* Al Adamson; *W:* Dennis Wayne; *C:* Gary Graver; *M:* Harley Hatcher.

Satan's School for Girls 🦴½ **1973** When a young woman investigates the circumstances that caused her sister's suicide, it leads her to a satanic girl's academy. Dumb and puerile made for TV "horror." **74m/C VHS.** Pamela Franklin, Roy Thinnes, Kate Jackson, Lloyd Bochner, Jamie Smith-Jackson, Jo Van Fleet, Cheryl Ladd, Gwynne Gilford, Bing Russell; *D:* David Lowell Rich; *W:* Arthur Ross; *M:* Laurence Rosenthal. **TV**

Satan's Touch woof! **1984 (R)** A simpleton worships the Devil and gets burned for his trouble. **86m/C VHS.** James Lawless, Shirley Venard.

Satanwar woof! **1979** A fictional look at various forms of Satan worship. **95m/C VHS.** Bart LaRue, Sally Schermerhorn, Jimmy Drankovitch.

Satisfaction 🦴 **1988 (PG-13)** An all-girl, high school rock band play out the summer before college. The Keatons should have sent Bateman to her room for this stunt. **93m/C VHS.** Justine Bateman, Trini Alvarado, Britta Phillips, Julia Roberts, Scott Coffey, Liam Neeson, Deborah Harry; *D:* Joan Freeman; *W:* Charles Purpura; *M:* Michel Colombier.

Saturday Night and Sunday Morning 🦴🦴🦴½ **1960** This "kitchen sink" drama finds the 23-year-old Finney in star form as working-class Arthur Seaton, who's devoted to good times, spending his weekends with boozing, brawling, and willing women. He's having an affair with the older, married Brenda (Roberts) and pursuing the strictly moral Doreen (Field), who refuses to sleep with him without a commitment. Arthur thinks he's falling in love and is (eventually) ready for marriage but not without complications and not before warning Doreen that he's unlikely to completely change his carefree ways. Reisz's first feature film; Sillitoe adapted from his novel. Finney was voted the most promising newcomer at the British Academy's (BAFTA) awards. **98m/B VHS, DVD, Wide.** *GB* Albert Finney, Rachel Roberts, Shirley Anne Field, Bryan Pringle, Norman Rossington, Hylda Baker, Robert Cowdra, Elsie Wagstaff, Frank Pettitt; *D:* Karel Reisz; *W:* Alan Sillitoe; *C:* Freddie Francis; *M:* John Dankworth. British Acad. '60: Actress (Roberts), Film; Natl. Bd. of Review '61: Actor (Finney).

Saturday Night Fever 🦴🦴½ **1977 (R)** Brooklyn teenager (Travolta), bored with his daytime job, becomes the nighttime king of the local disco. Based on a story published in "New York Magazine" by Nik Cohn. Acclaimed for its disco dance sequences, memorable soundtrack by the Bee Gees, and carefree yet bleak script; extremely dated, although it made its mark on society in its time. Followed by the sequel "Staying Alive." Also available in a 112-minute "PG" rated version. ♫Staying Alive; Night Fever; More Than a Woman; How Deep Is Your Love?. **118m/C VHS.** John Travolta, Karen (Lynn) Gorney, Barry Miller, Donna Pescow, Joseph Cali, Bruce Ornstein, Paul Pape, Fran Drescher; *D:* John Badham; *W:* Norman Wexler; *C:* Ralf Bode; *M:* David Shire. Natl. Bd. of Review '77: Actor (Travolta).

Saturday Night Special 🦴½ **1992 (R)** Country singer/songwriter Travis (played by Nashville stalwart Burnette) gets a job fronting the house band of Tennessee tavern owner T.J. (Dean). Travis also takes up with ambitious Darlene (Ford), who happens to be T.J.'s wife. But it's Darlene who has the brains in this unpleasant trio, she decides to get rid of hubby and sets Travis up to take the fall. It's all been done before (and better). **75m/C VHS.** Billy Burnette, Maria Ford, Rick Dean; *D:* Dan Golden; *W:* Jonathan Banks; *M:* Billy Burnette, Nicholas Rivera.

Saturday the 14th 🦴½ **1981 (PG)** A parody of the popular axe-wielding-maniac genre, about a family inheriting a haunted mansion. Poorly made; not funny or scary. Followed by even worse sequel: "Saturday the 14th Strikes Back." **91m/C VHS, DVD.** Richard Benjamin, Paula Prentiss, Severn Darden, Jeffrey Tambor, Kari Michaelsen, Kevin Brando, Rosemary DeCamp, Stacy Keach; *D:* Howard R. Cohen; *W:* Howard R. Cohen, Jeff Begun; *C:* Daniel Lacambre; *M:* Parmer Fuller.

Saturday the 14th Strikes Back 🦴 **1988** Continuing the name, but not the storyline, cast, or characters of the original, this one concerns the invasion of a birthday party by a vampire (Stonebrook) and her monstrous friends. The monsters decide that the birthday boy (Presson) should be their new leader. Pretty lame, even by the original's standards. **91m/C VHS, DVD.** Ray Walston, Avery Schreiber, Patty McCormack, Julianne McNamara, Rhonda Aldrich, Daniel Will-Harris, Joseph Ruskin, Pamela Stonebrook, Phil Leeds, Jason Presson, Michael Berryman, Victoria Morsell; *D:* Howard R. Cohen; *W:* Howard R. Cohen; *C:* Levie Isaacks; *M:* Parmer Fuller.

Saturn 3 🦴½ **1980 (R)** Two research scientists create a futuristic Garden of Eden in an isolated sector of our solar system, but love story turns to horror story when a killer robot arrives. Sporadically promising, but ultimately lame; dumb ending. For Farrah fans only. **88m/C VHS, DVD.** *GB* Farrah Fawcett, Kirk Douglas, Harvey Keitel, Ed Bishop; *D:* Stanley Donen; *W:* Martin Amis; *C:* Billy Williams; *M:* Elmer Bernstein.

Saul and David *Saul e David* **1968** Beautifully filmed story of David's life with King Saul, the battle with Goliath, and the tragic end of Saul. From the "Bible" series. **120m/C VHS.** Norman Wooland, Gianni "John" Garko.

Savage! woof! *Black Valor* **1973 (R)** A savage foreign mess with ex-baseball star Iglehart killing people with grenades and guns, abetted by an army full of murderous models. **81m/C VHS.** *MX* James Iglehart, Lada Edmund, Carol Speed, Rossana Ortiz, Sally Jordan, Aura Aurea, Vic Diaz; *D:* Cirio H. Santiago.

Savage 🦴🦴 **1996 (R)** Mad scientist discovers the gateway to a future world, which unleashes a powerful guardian known known as the Savage (Gruner). The Savage must prevent the doorway between the worlds from exploding and causing an apocalypse, even as he hunts his nemesis. **103m/C VHS.** Olivier Gruner, Kario Salem, Jennifer Grant, Sam McMurray, Kristin Minter; *D:* Avi Nesher; *W:* Patrick Highsmith, Peter Sagal; *C:* Peter Fernberger; *M:* Roger Neill.

Savage Abduction 🦴 **1973 (R)** Two girls visiting Los Angeles are kidnapped by a bizarre man. **84m/C VHS.** Tom Drake, Stephen Oliver, Sean Kenney; *D:* John Lawrence.

Savage Attraction 🦴½ *Hostage: The Christine Maresch Story; Hostage* **1983 (R)** True story of a 16-year-old girl forced to marry an ex-Nazi, and her hellish life thereafter. Frustrating because it could have been much better. **93m/C VHS.** *AU GE* Kerry Mack, Ralph Schicha; *D:* Frank Shields.

Savage Beach 🦴 **1989 (R)** A pair of well-endowed female federal agents battle assorted buccaneers on a remote Pacific isle over a rediscovered cache of gold from WWII. Exploitative, pornographic, and degrading to watch. Sequel to "Picasso Trigger." **90m/C VHS.** Dona Speir, Hope Marie Carlton, Bruce Penhall, Rodrigo Obregon, John Aprea, Teri Weigel, Lisa London; *D:* Andy Sidaris.

The Savage Bees 🦴🦴 **1976** A South American ship harbored at New Orleans during Mardi Gras unleashes killer bees into the celebratory crowds. Not bad, relatively exciting, TV thriller. **90m/C VHS.** Ben Johnson, Michael Parks, Paul Hecht, Horst Buchholz, Gretchen Corbett; *D:* Bruce Geller.

Savage Capitalism 🦴🦴 *Capitalismo Salvaje* **1993** Melodramatic romance between a reporter and a mining company exec crumbles when the exec's presumed dead wife returns. Meanwhile, the reporter uncovers the truth behind the company's plans to mine in the interior of Brazil, which could cause ecological ruin. Portuguese with subtitles. **86m/C VHS.** *BR* Fernanda Torres, Jose Mayer, Marisa Orth, Marcelo Tass; *D:* Andre Klotzel; *W:* Andre Klotzel, Djalma Batista.

Savage Dawn 🦴½ **1984 (R)** In yet another desert town, yet another pair of combat-hardened vets are confronted by yet another vicious motorcycle gang. Haven't we seen this one before? **102m/C VHS.** George Kennedy, Karen Black, Richard Lynch, Lance Henriksen, William Forsythe; *D:* Simon Nuchtern.

Savage Drums 🦴½ **1951** Sabu returns to his South Seas island to help end tribal warfare there. Dated and dumb, but fun-to-watch melodrama/action. **70m/B VHS.** Sabu, Lita Baron; *D:* William Berke.

Savage Fury 🦴 *Call of the Savage* **1933** Feature-length version of the popular movie serial. **80m/B VHS.** Noah Beery Jr., Dorothy Short.

The Savage Girl 🦴 **1932** A hunter journeys through the darkest jungle in search of prey. Instead, he stumbles across a beautiful white jungle girl, falls in love with her and attempts to take her back with him. **64m/B VHS.** Rochelle Hudson, Walter Byron, Harry C. (Henry) Myers, Ted Adams, Adolph Milar, Floyd Schackleford; *D:* Harry Fraser.

Savage Hearts 🦴½ **1995** Terminally ill mob hitwoman Beatrice Baxter (D'Abo) has six months left to live and she wants her last days to be spent in style. So she steals \$2 million from her mob employer Roger Focely (Harris)—who's determined to get the money back. **90m/C VHS.** Maryam D'Abo, Richard Harris, Myriam Cyr, Jerry Hall; *D:* Mark Ezra.

Savage Hunger 🦴 **1984** Ten plane crash survivors struggle to survive in the Baja desert. **90m/C VHS.** Chris Makepeace, Scott Hylands, Anne Lockhart; *D:* Sparky Green.

Savage Instinct 🦴🦴 **1991** A woman stumbles across a drug ring and becomes a target when they fear she could expose them. Only Mongo and his crew are even more surprised when she decides to fight back. **95m/C VHS.** Debra Sweaney, Brian Oldfield.

Savage Intruder 🦴 **1968 (R)** A wandering opportunist worms his way into the heart and home of a rich ex-movie star. She soon discovers that he's a sexual deviant who mutilates and murders for fun. Twisted doings with Hopkins in her final role. **90m/C VHS.** John David Garfield, Miriam Hopkins, Gale Sondergaard, Florence Lake, Joe Besser, Minta Durfee; *D:* Donald Wolfe.

Savage Is Loose woof! **1974 (R)** Drivel about a scientist, his wife, and their son stranded on a deserted island for 20 years. Not surprisingly, as junior matures he realizes there isn't a woman for him—or is there? Completely lacking in redeeming qualities. Absurd pseudo-Freudian claptrap produced by Scott. **114m/C VHS.** George C. Scott, Trish Van Devere, John David Carson, Lee Montgomery; *D:* George C. Scott.

Savage Island 🦴½ **1985 (R)** Women's prison in the tropics sets the scene for the usual exploitative goings-on. Blair is actually in the film only for a few minutes. Chopped-up, even worse version of "Escape From Hell." **74m/C VHS.** *SP IT* Nicholas Beardsley, Linda Blair, Anthony Steffen, Ajita Wilson, Christina Lai, Leon Askin; *D:* Edward (Edoardo Mulargia) Muller; *W:* Nicholas Beardsley. Golden Raspberries '85: Worst Actress (Blair).

Savage Journey 🦴½ **1983 (PG)** A wagon train of pioneers has difficulty on its westward journey. Simple story with no real appeal. **99m/C VHS.** Richard Moll, Maurice Grandmaison, Faith Clift; *D:* Tom McGowan.

Savage Justice 🦴 **1988** A young woman seeks revenge against leftist rebels (boo, hiss) in a Southeast Asian country who killed her parents and raped her. She hooks up with an ex-Green Beret, and they fight and love their way through the jungle. The usual nudity and violence; derivative and dumb. **90m/C** Julia Montgomery, Steven Memel.

Savage Land 🦴🦴½ **1994 (PG)** Family western finds a young brother and sister travelling by stage to meet up with their father. The stage is robbed by some bumbling bad guys, who then pursue the kids and two other passengers across the frontier. The kids, of course, are smarter than most of the adults, and manage to get the best of the bad hombres. **91m/C VHS.** Graham Greene, Corbin Bernsen, Vivian Schilling, Mercedes McNab, Corey Carrier, Brion James, Bo Svenson, Charlotte Ross.

Savage Messiah 🦴🦴🦴 **1972 (R)** Bio of young French sculptor Henri Gaudier and his intense, though platonic, affair with a refined Polish woman 20 years his senior. Stylized drama is spared most of director Russell's noted excesses but he manages to believably show their magnetic attraction. Gaudier was killed in WWI at the age of 24. Based on the biography by H.S. Ede. **96m/C VHS.** *GB* Scott Antony, Dorothy Tutin, Helen Mirren, Lindsay Kemp, Peter Vaughan, Michael Gough; *D:* Ken Russell; *W:* Christopher Logue; *C:* Dick Bush.

Savage Run 🦴🦴🦴 *Run, Simon, Run* **1970** Reynolds is a Papago Indian framed and imprisoned for his brother's murder. Sprung from the pen, he heads back to the reservation to find the real killers and to avenge his brother's death. Convincing drama. Stevens's last role before her suicide. **73m/C VHS.** Burt Reynolds, Inger Stevens, James Best, Rodolfo Acosta, Don Dubbins, Joyce

Jameson, Barney (Bernard) Phillips, Eddie Little Sky; *D:* George McCowan. **TV**

Savage Sam 1963 Intended as a sequel to "Old Yeller." Sam, the offspring of the heroic dog named Old Yeller, tracks down some children kidnapped by Indians. Fun, but not fully successful. **103m/C VHS.** Tommy Kirk, Kevin Corcoran, Brian Keith, Dewey Martin, Jeff York, Marta Kristen; *D:* Norman Tokar; *C:* Edward Colman.

The Savage Seven 1968 An underground classic where everyone loses. A motorcycle gang rides into an Indian town which is at the mercy of corrupt businessmen. The gang's leader becomes involved in the Indians' problems but the businessmen and the cops cause trouble for all concerned. Less than memorable. Produced by Dick Clark. **96m/C VHS.** Larry Bishop, Joanna Frank, Adam Roarke, Robert Walker Jr.; *D:* Richard Rush.

Savage Streets ½ 1983 (R) Blair seeks commando-style revenge on the street gang that raped her deaf sister. Extended rape scene betrays the exploitative intentions, though other bits are entertaining, in a trashy kind of way. **93m/C VHS.** Linda Blair, John Vernon, Sal Landi, Robert Dryer, Debra Blee, Linnea Quigley; *D:* Danny Steinmann; *M:* John D'Andrea. Golden Raspberries '85: Worst Actress (Blair).

Savage Weekend woof! *The Killer Behind the Mask; The Upstate Murders* 1980 (R) A killer behind a ghoulish mask stalks human prey in the boonies, of course. Astoundingly, there is one interesting role—William Sanderson's looney. Otherwise, throw this one no bones. **88m/C VHS.** Christopher Allport, James Doerr, Marilyn Hamlin, Caitlin (Kathleen Heaney) O'Heaney, David Gale, William Sanderson; *D:* David Paulsen, John Mason Kirby; *W:* David Paulsen.

Savage Wilderness ½ *The Last Frontier* 1955 When a trio of fur trappers lose a year's worth of skins to a band of marauding Indians, they decide to take scouting jobs at a cavalry outpost. But they find the new commander (Preston) hasn't gotten his nickname as the "Butcher of Shiloh" without reason. Adapted from the novel "The Gilded Rooster" by Richard Emery Roberts. **98m/C VHS.** Victor Mature, Robert Preston, Guy Madison, James Whitmore, Anne Bancroft, Russell Collins, Peter Whitney, Pat Hogan, Manuel Donde, Guy Williams; *D:* Anthony Mann; *W:* Philip Yordan, Russell S. Hughes; *M:* Leigh Harline.

The Savage Woman 1991 Marianna escapes from a desperate situation and is found unconscious in the woods by Elysee. He nurses her back to health, learns her terrible secret, and tries to help Marianna decide whether to turn herself into the police or keep running. In French with English subtitles. **100m/C VHS.** *CA* Patricia Tulasne, Matthias Habich; *D:* Lea Pool.

Savages 1972 A group of savages descend on a palatial mansion, and after living there for some time, become refined ladies and gentlemen. The moral savages and "civilized" men are really the same. **106m/C VHS.** Lewis J. Stadlen, Anne Francine, Thayer David, Salome Jens, Susan Blakely, Kathleen Widdoes, Sam Waterston; *D:* James Ivory; *C:* Walter Lassally.

Savages ½ 1975 Griffith as a demented nut-case stalking another man in the desert? That's right, Opie. "The Most Dangerous Game" remade-sort of-for TV. **74m/C VHS.** Andy Griffith, Sam Bottoms, Noah Beery Jr.; *D:* Lee H. Katzin.

Savages from Hell *Big Enough and Old Enough* 1968 (R) Greasy biker dude beats up a young black guy because he was flirting with the biker's woman. The biker also tries to rape a migrant farmworker's daughter because he lusts after her. Trashy exploitation film. **79m/C VHS.** Bobbie Byers, Cyril Poitier, Diwaldo Myers, Viola Lloyd, William P. Kelley; *D:* Joseph Prieto; *W:* Joseph Prieto.

Savannah Smiles ½ 1982 (PG) Poor little rich girl Anderson runs away from home, into the clutches of two ham-handed crooks. She melts their hearts, and they change their ways. Decent, sentimental family drama. **104m/C VHS, DVD.** Bridgette Andersen, Mark Miller, Donovan Scott, Peter Graves, Chris Robinson, Michael Parks; *D:* Pierre De Moro.

Save Me 1993 (R) Jim Stevens' (Hamlin) wife has left him and his boss is involved in some dirty deals that could cost Jim his job. So things couldn't get worse, could they? Well, of course they could—and do. Because Jim meets Ellie (Anthony), a sexual adventuress just destined to bring trouble to a lonely guy. Also available in an unrated version. **89m/C VHS.** Harry Hamlin, Lysette Anthony, Michael Ironside, Olivia Hussey, Bill Nunn, Steve Railsback; *D:* Alan Roberts; *W:* Neil Ronco; *M:* Rick Marvin.

Save the Lady 1982 Plucky kids fight city hall to save an old ferry, the Lady Hope, from the scrap heap. Nothing offensive here—just a pleasant family flick. **76m/C VHS.** Matthew Excell, Robert Clarkson, Miranda Cartledge, Kim Clifford; *D:* Leon Thau.

Save the Last Dance ½ 2001 (PG-13) "Fame" (or "Flashdance" or "Saturday Night Fever") meets "Romeo and Juliet" (or "West Side Story" or any trashy talk show) in this clearly not-so-original but solid teen drama. White, middle-class Sara (Stiles) adjusts to life and rediscovers her passion for dance in an all-black, inner-city Chicago high school when she must give up her dreams of attending Juilliard and move in with her down-on-his-luck father (Kinney) on the South Side. There, she befriends Chenille (Washington), who helps her get hip, and falls for her smart, ambitious brother Derek (Thomas), who helps her learn hip-hop. Stiles and Thomas turn in good performances despite somewhat stereotypical cast of characters. **112m/C VHS, DVD, Wide.** *US* Julia Stiles, Sean Patrick Thomas, Fredro Starr, Kerry Washington, Terry Kinney, Bianca Lawson, Garland Whitt, Vince Green; *D:* Thomas Carter; *W:* Duane Adler, Cheryl Edwards; *C:* Robbie Greenberg; *M:* Mark Isham.

Save the Tiger 1973 (R) A basically honest middle-aged man sees no way out of his failing business except arson. The insurance settlement will let him pay off his creditors, and save face. David, as the arsonist, and Gilford, as Lemmon's business partner, are superb. Lemmon is also excellent throughout his performance. **100m/C VHS.** Jack Lemmon, Jack Gilford, Laurie Heineman, Patricia Smith, Norman Burton, Thayer David; *D:* John G. Avildsen; *M:* Marvin Hamlisch. Oscars '73: Actor (Lemmon); Writers Guild '73: Orig. Screenplay.

Saved by the Light ½ 1995 On September 17, 1975, ruthless Dannion Brinkley's (Roberts) life was changed forever—he died. Struck by a bolt of lightning, Brinkley was declared dead, only to wake up 28 minutes later in the morgue. A changed man, which some of Brinkley's acquaintances find hard to believe, he becomes a public speaker, telling about his trip to heaven and his belief in love and salvation. TV movie based on Brinkley's book about his near-death experience. **95m/C VHS.** Eric Roberts, Lynette Walden, K. Callan; *D:* Lewis Teague. **TV**

Saving Grace 1986 (PG) A tale of the fictional youngest Pope of modern times, Pope Leo XIV (Conti). Beset by duty, he decides to shed his robes and get in touch with the world's peasantry. Improbable, but that's okay; the mortal sin is that it's improbable and slow and boring. **112m/C VHS, 8mm.** Tom Conti, Fernando Rey, Giancarlo Giannini, Erland Josephson, Donald Hewlett, Edward James Olmos; *D:* Robert M. Young; *W:* David S. Ward; *M:* William Goldstein.

Saving Grace ½ 2000 (R) Widowed Blethyn finds out her late hubby has left her deeply in debt and in order to maintain her comfortable lifestyle, her gardener (Ferguson) suggests that she grow pot and sell it. Quaint comedy has the trademark quirky characters and gently bawdy humor you'd expect. Blethyn and Ferguson are fine, and it's all veddy cheerful. Low-key approach lends itself well to the small screen. **93m/C VHS, DVD, Wide.** *GB* Brenda Blethyn, Craig Ferguson, Martin Clunes, Tcheky Karyo, Jamie Foreman, Valerie Edmond, Tristan Sturrock; *D:* Nigel Cole; *W:* Craig Ferguson, Mark Crowdy; *C:* John de Borman.

Saving Private Ryan 1998 (R) Big-budget WWII Spielberg epic finds eight soldiers, led by army captain Hanks, forced to go behind enemy lines in order to rescue downed paratrooper James Ryan (Damon). He's the sole surviving brother of four soldier siblings and the government wants some good PR—the men pulling the duty are less than enthusiastic, however. Pick your favorite reviewer-speak word—gripping, moving, intense, masterpiece—any or all of them will work. The opening 25-minute graphic depiction of Omaha Beach on D-Day is, on its own, Oscar-worthy. Hanks and the rest of the cast (which included a few surprise cameos) are excellent. Spielberg deglamorizes war, without belittling the sacrifices made by those who fought. The actors (except Damon) went through boot camp in England in order to get the proper attitude. **175m/C VHS, DVD.** Tom Hanks, Edward Burns, Tom Sizemore, Jeremy Davies, Giovanni Ribisi, Adam Goldberg, Barry Pepper, Vin Diesel, Matt Damon, Ted Danson, Dale Dye, Dennis Farina, Harve Presnell, Paul Giamatti, Bryan Cranston, David Wohl, Leland Orser, Joerg Stadler, Maximillian Martini, Amanda Boxer, Harrison Young; *D:* Steven Spielberg; *W:* Robert Rodat, Frank Darabont; *C:* Janusz Kaminski; *M:* John Williams. Oscars '98: Cinematog., Director (Spielberg), Film Editing, Sound, Sound FX Editing; British Acad. '98: Sound; Directors Guild '98: Director (Spielberg); Golden Globes '99: Director (Spielberg), Film—Drama; L.A. Film Critics '98: Cinematog., Director (Spielberg), Film; N.Y. Film Critics '98: Film; Broadcast Film Critics '98: Director (Spielberg), Film, Score.

Saving Silverman *Evil Woman* 2001 (PG-13) Testosterone-driven comedy has three buddies' bond threatened by ball-breaking fiancee of one of the boys. Peet is the whip-wielding control freak Judith Snodgrass-Fessbeggler, out to tame Neil Diamond-loving loser Darren (Biggs) and despised by best buds Wayne (Zahn) and J.D. (Black). The boys scheme to break up the duo by kidnaping Judith and re-acquainting Darren with his first love, now an aspiring nun. Black and Zahn provide much-needed comic relief, as do the scenes with their Diamond cover band. However, over-the-top characters and sophomoric humor mixed with increasingly gross gags ultimately not so much save but sink "Silverman." **90m/C VHS, DVD, Wide.** *US* Jason Biggs, Steve Zahn, Jack Black, Amanda Peet, R. Lee Ermey, Amanda Detmer, Neil Diamond; *D:* Dennis Dugan; *W:* Hank Nelken, Greg DePaul; *C:* Arthur Albert; *M:* Mike Simpson.

Savior 1998 (R) After his wife and son are killed in a terrorist bombing, an American officer (Quaid) turns mercenary and assumes a new identity. As Guy, he's a soulless killing machine, working for the Serbs in Bosnia. At a prisoner exchange, he is told to take a pregnant young Serbian woman, Vera (Ninkovic), back to her village. Guy winds up delivering the baby and protecting Vera on their hazardous (and ultimately tragic) journey as he slowly regains flickers of his own humanity. Excellent change-of-pace performance by Quaid in a gut-wrenching film inspired by a true story. **104m/C VHS, DVD.** Dennis Quaid, Natasa Ninkovic, Sergej Trifunovic, Stellan Skarsgard, Nastassia Kinski; *D:* Pedrag (Peter) Antonijevic; *W:* Robert Orr; *C:* Ian Wilson; *M:* David Robbins.

Sawbones 1995 (R) Medical school reject Willy Knapp (Harvey) takes out his frustrations by murdering people and then performing gruesome surgeries on the bodies. Cop But Miller (Baldwin) investigates. **78m/C VHS.** Don Harvey, Adam Baldwin, Barbara Carrera, Nina Siemaszko, Nicholas Sadler, Don Stroud; *D:* Catherine Cyran; *C:* Christopher Baffa. **CABLE**

Sawdust & Tinsel *The Naked Night; Sunset of a Clown; Gycklarnas Afton* 1953 Early Bergman film detailing the grisly, humiliating experiences of a traveling circus rolling across the barren Swedish countryside. Lonely parable of human relationships. In Swedish with English subtitles. **87m/B VHS.** *SW* Harriet Andersson, Ake Gronberg; *D:* Ingmar Bergman; *W:* Ingmar Bergman.

Say Anything 1989 (PG-13) A semi-mature, successful teen romance about an offbeat loner Lloyd Dobler (Cusack, in a winning performance), whose interested in the martial arts and going after the beautiful class brain, Diane Court (Skye), of his high school. Things are complicated when her father James (Mahoney) is suspected of embezzling by the IRS. Joan Cusack, John's real-life sister, also plays his sister in the film. Works well on the romantic level without getting too sticky. **100m/C VHS, DVD, Wide.** John Cusack, Ione Skye, John Mahoney, Joan Cusack, Lili Taylor, Richard Portnow, Pamela Segall, Jason Gould, Loren Dean, Bebe Neuwirth, Aimee Brooks, Eric Stoltz, Chynna Phillips, Joanna Frank, Jeremy Piven, Don "The Dragon" Wilson; *D:* Cameron Crowe; *W:* Cameron Crowe; *C:* Laszlo Kovács; *M:* Anne Dudley, Richard Gibbs, Nancy Wilson.

Say Goodbye, Maggie Cole ½ 1972 A widow goes to work as a doctor in a Chicago street clinic and becomes emotionally involved with a dying child. Hayward's final role in moving made-for-TV drama. **78m/C VHS.** Susan Hayward, Darren McGavin, Michael Constantine, Nichelle Nichols, Dane Clark; *D:* Jud Taylor.

Say Hello to Yesterday ½ 1971 (PG) A May-December romance that takes place entirely in one day. An unhappy housewife meets an exciting young traveler while both are in London. Cast and director try hard but fail to get the point across to the audience. **91m/C VHS.** *GB* Jean Simmons, Leonard Whiting, Evelyn Laye; *D:* Alvin Rakoff.

Say It Isn't So ½ 2001 (R) The Farrelly brothers produced this tale of boy-meets-girl, boy-gets-girl, boy-finds-out-girl-is-his-sister. They should've kept their money and done it themselves, it might've been a better movie. Klein stars as good-guy orphan Gilly, who meets cute with Jo (Graham), an inept hairdresser with the most screwed-up family this side of the Mansons. Her mom (Field) decides Gilly isn't upwardly mobile enough so she makes everyone think the couple are kin. Gilly sets out to set things right amid Farrelly-approved gross-out gags and humiliations galore. First-time helmer Rogers lacks the Farrelly sense of timing and sentiment, which results in most of the jokes falling flat or not developing at all. **95m/C VHS, DVD, Wide.** *US* Chris Klein, Heather Graham, Orlando Jones, Sally Field, Richard Jenkins, John Rothman, Jack Plotnick, Eddie Cibrian, Mark Pellegrino, Richard Riehle, Brent Briscoe, Henry Cho, Suzanne Somers, Brent Hinkley; *D:* James B. Rogers; *W:* Peter Gaulke, Gerry Swallow; *C:* Mark Irwin; *M:* Mason Daring.

Say Yes! ½ 1986 (PG-13) A nutty millionaire (Winters) bets $250 million that his inept nephew cannot get married within 24 hours. Three times the length of usual wacky sitcom, alas. **87m/C VHS.** Jonathan Winters, Art Hindle, Logan Ramsey, Lissa Layng; *D:* Larry Yust.

Sayonara 1957 An Army major is assigned to a Japanese airbase during the Korean conflict at the behest of his future father-in-law. Dissatisfied with his impending marriage, he finds himself drawn to a Japanese dancer and becomes involved in the affairs of his buddy who, against official policy, marries a Japanese woman. Tragedy surrounds the themes of bigotry and interracial marriage. Based on the novel by James Michener. **147m/C VHS, DVD, Wide.** Marlon Brando, James Garner, Ricardo Montalban, Patricia Owens, Red Buttons, Miyoshi Umeki, Martha Scott, Kent Smith, Miiko Taka; *D:* Joshua Logan; *W:* Paul Osborn; *C:* Ellsworth Fredericks; *M:* Franz Waxman. Oscars '57: Art Dir./Set Dec., Sound, Support. Actor (Buttons), Support. Actress (Umeki); Golden Globes '58: Support. Actor (Buttons).

The Scalawag Bunch 1975 Yet another retelling of Robin Hood and his Merry Men and their adventures in Sherwood Forest. **100m/C VHS.** *IT* Mark Damon, Luis Davila, Silvia Dionisio; *D:* George Ferron.

Scalp Merchant 1977 Private investigator Cliff Rowan hunts for a missing payroll. Someone would rather see him dead than successful. **108m/C VHS.** Cameron

Mitchell, John Waters, Elizabeth Alexander, Margaret Nelson; *D:* Howard Rubie.

Scalpel ♪♪ *False Face* **1976 (R)** After his daughter's death, a plastic surgeon creates her image on another woman to get an inheritance. Violent and graphic, with a surprise ending. Not too bad; interesting premise. **95m/C VHS.** Robert Lansing, Judith Chapman, Arlen Dean Snyder, Sandy Martin, David Scarroll; *D:* John Grissmer; *W:* John Grissmer.

The Scalphunters ♪♪½ **1968** Semi-successful, semi-funny western about an itinerant trapper (Lancaster) who is forced by Indians to trade his pelts for an educated black slave (Davis); many chases and brawls ensue. Good performances. **102m/C VHS.** Burt Lancaster, Ossie Davis, Telly Savalas, Shelley Winters, Nick Cravat, Dabney Coleman, Paul Picerni; *D:* Sydney Pollack; *W:* William W. Norton Sr.; *M:* Elmer Bernstein.

Scalps ♪♪ **1983 (R)** Hunted Indian princess and man whose family was killed by Indians form uneasy alliance in old West. **90m/C VHS.** Karen Wood, Alberto (Albert Farley) Farnese, Benny Cardosa, Charlie Bravo, Vassili Garis; *D:* Werner Knox.

Scam ♪♪½ **1993 (R)** Maggie and her partner Barry are con artists making their living scamming high rollers in Miami Beach. Then Maggie tries to pull a con on the wrong man. Jack Shanks is an ex-FBI agent with a score to settle and he blackmails Maggie into helping him. **102m/C VHS.** Christopher Walken, Lorraine Bracco, Miguel Ferrer; *D:* John Flynn.

Scandal ♪♪ *Shuban* **1950** Handsome artist (Mifune) and beautiful concert singer (Yamaguchi) become the victims of a libelous article in a gossip magazine. The artist decides to sue but, being softhearted, chooses a questionable lawyer because the man's young daughter is dying. Then the unethical lawyer accepts a bribe to prejudice the case. Japanese with subtitles. **105m/B VHS.** *JP* Toshiro Mifune, Takashi Shimura, Yoshiko Yamaguchi; *D:* Akira Kurosawa; *W:* Ryuzo Kikushima, Akira Kurosawa; *M:* Fumio Hayasaka.

Scandal ♪♪♪ **1989 (R)** A dramatization of Britain's Profumo government sex scandal of the 1960s. Hurt plays a society doctor who enjoys introducing pretty girls to his wealthy friends. One of the girls, Christine Keeler, takes as lovers both a Russian government official and a British Cabinet Minister. The resulting scandal eventually overturned an entire political party, and led to disgrace, prison, and death for some of those concerned. Also available in an unedited 115-minute version which contains more controversial language and nudity. Top-notch performances make either version well worth watching. **105m/C VHS, DVD.** *GB* John Hurt, Joanne Whalley, Ian McKellen, Bridget Fonda, Jeroen Krabbe, Britt Ekland, Roland Gift, Daniel Massey, Leslie Phillips, Richard Morant; *D:* Michael Caton-Jones; *W:* Michael Thomas; *C:* Mike Molloy; *M:* Carl Davis.

Scandal in a Small Town ♪♪ **1988** A cocktail waitress in a small town has to defend herself and her daughter from the town's critical eye and hateful actions. Self-righteous made for TV drama rehashes several earlier plots. **90m/C VHS.** Raquel Welch, Christa Denton, Peter Van Norden, Ronny Cox; *D:* Anthony Page. **TV**

A Scandal in Paris ♪♪½ *Thieves Holiday* **1946** Based on the real-life escapades of 19th-century criminal Francois Eugene Vidocq. Vidocq (Sanders) escapes from prison, briefly joins Napoleon's army, and catches the eye of Therese (Hasso), whose father is an important official. Under an assumed name, Vidocq joins the Paris police force in order to perpetrate his biggest crime. Instead, thanks to Therese's love, he goes straight. Sanders does an excellent job. **100m/B VHS.** George Sanders, Signe Hasso, Akim Tamiroff, Carole Landis, Gene Lockhart, Alan Napier, Vladimir Sokoloff, Alma Kruger; *D:* Douglas Sirk; *W:* Ellis St. Joseph; *C:* Guy Roe; *M:* Hanns Eisler, Heinz Roemheld.

Scandal Man ♪♪½ **1967** A French photographer gets in over his head when he snaps the daughter of an American KKK leader embracing a black man in a nightclub. In French with English subtitles. **86m/C VHS.** Maurice Ronet; *D:* Richard Balducci.

Scandalous ♪½ **1984 (PG)** A bumbling American TV reporter becomes involved with a gang of British con artists. Starts well but peters out. Look for the scene where Gielgud attends a Bow Wow Wow concert. **93m/C VHS.** Robert Hays, Pamela Stephenson, John Gielgud, Jim Dale, M. Emmet Walsh; *D:* Rob Cohen; *W:* Rob Cohen, Larry Cohen, John Byrum; *C:* Jack Cardiff; *M:* Dave Grusin.

Scandalous ♪ **1988** A duke and his uncle work together to find a secretary who disappeared after witnessing a murder. **90m/C VHS.** Albert Fortell, Lauren Hutton, Ursula Carven, Capucine; *D:* Robert W. Young.

Scandalous John ♪♪ **1971 (G)** Comedy western about a last cattle drive devised by an aging cowboy (Keith) in order to save his ranch. Keith's shrewd acting as the ornery cattle man who won't sell to developers carries this one. **113m/C VHS.** Brian Keith, Alfonso Arau, Michele Carey, Rick Lenz, John Ritter, Harry (Henry) Morgan; *D:* Robert Butler.

Scanner Cop ♪½ **1994 (R)** When deranged scientist Sigmund Glock escapes from prison, he's determined to take revenge on Peter Harrigan, the cop who put him behind bars. With the aid of an evil assistant and a mind-altering drug, Glock kidnaps and programs innocent citizens into cop-killing maniacs. Harrigan's only weapon is a rookie cop with the Scanner power to read minds—and then destroy them. **94m/C VHS.** Daniel Quinn, Darlanne Fluegel, Richard Lynch, Mark Rolston, Hilary Shepard, Gary Hudson, Cyndi Pass, Luca Bercovici, Brion James; *D:* Pierre David; *W:* John Bryant, George Saunders.

Scanner Cop 2: Volkin's Revenge ♪♪ **1994 (R)** Scanner cop Sam Staziak (Quinn) has become curious about his family, asking Carrie Goodart (Haje) to find out what she can. But Carrie's attacked by evil scanner Carl Volkin (Kilpatrick), whom Sam once sent to prison, and left in a coma. Then Sam discovers Volkin is draining the life force of other scanners in order to make himself invincible when he and Sam have their final showdown. **95m/C VHS.** Daniel Quinn, Patrick Kilpatrick, Khrystyne Haje, Robert Forster, Stephen Mendel; *D:* Steve Barnett; *W:* Mark Sevi; *C:* Thomas Jewett.

Scanners ♪♪½ **1981 (R)** "Scanners" are telepaths who can will people to explode. One scanner in particular harbors Hitlerian aspirations for his band of psychic gangsters. Gruesome but effective special effects. **102m/C VHS, DVD, Wide.** *CA* Stephen Lack, Jennifer O'Neill, Patrick McGoohan, Lawrence Dane, Michael Ironside, Robert A. Silverman; *D:* David Cronenberg; *W:* David Cronenberg; *C:* Mark Irwin; *M:* Howard Shore.

Scanners 2: The New Order ♪♪½ **1991 (R)** This not-bad sequel to the 1981 cult classic finds a powermad police official out to build a psychic militia of captured Scanners. More story than last time, plus more and better special effects. **104m/C VHS.** *CA* David Hewlett, Deborah Raffin, Yvan Ponton, Isabelle Mejias, Valentin Trujillo, Tom Butler, Vlasta Vrana, Dorothee Berryman, Raoul Trujillo; *D:* Christian Duguay; *W:* B.J. Nelson; *M:* Marty Simon.

Scanners 3: The Takeover ♪½ **1992 (R)** The third sequel in which Scanner siblings battle for control of the world. Lacks the creativity and storyline of the first two films. **101m/C VHS.** Steve Parrish, Liliana Komorowska, Valerie Valois; *D:* Christian Duguay.

Scanners: The Showdown ♪½ **1994 (R)** Carl Volkin (Kilpatrick), the "scanner" killer, has escaped jail and is stalking the streets of L.A. His ultimate target is Sam Staziak (Quinn), the scanner cop who sent him away. Since Volkin's powers grow with every kill, Staziak better get to Volkin in a hurry. **95m/C VHS.** Patrick Kilpatrick, Daniel Quinn, Khrystyne Haje, Stephen Mendel, Brenda Swanson, Jewel Shepard, Robert Forster; *D:* Steve Barnett; *W:* Mark Sevi.

The Scar ♪♪½ *Hollow Triumph* **1948** A cunning criminal robs the mob, then hides by "stealing" the identity of a lookalike psychologist. But he's overlooked one thing...or two. Farfetched film noir showcases a rare villainous role for Henreid (who also produced). Based on a novel by Murray Forbes. **83m/B VHS.** Paul Henreid, Joan Bennett, Eduard Franz, Leslie Brooks, John Qualeh, Mabel Paige, Herbert Rudley; *D:* Steve Sekely.

Scar of Shame ♪♪ **1927** Explores the ill-fated romance between a successful black concert pianist and the lower-class woman he marries. Gives a look at the color caste system and divisions within the black community of the era. **90m/B VHS.** Harry Henderson, Lucia Lynn Moses, Ann Kennedy, Norman Johnstone; *D:* Frank Peregini.

Scaramouche ♪♪♪½ **1952** Thrilling swashbuckler about a nobleman (Granger, very well cast) searching for his family during the French Revolution. To avenge the death of a friend, he joins a theatre troupe where he learns swordplay and becomes the character "Scaramouche." Features a rousing six-and-a-half-minute sword battle. **111m/C VHS.** Stewart Granger, Eleanor Parker, Janet Leigh, Mel Ferrer, Henry Wilcoxon, Nina Foch, Richard Anderson, Robert Coote, Lewis Stone, Elisabeth Risdon, Howard Freeman; *D:* George Sidney; *C:* Charles Rosher.

Scarecrow ♪♪½ **1973 (R)** Two homeless drifters (Hackman and Pacino) walk across America, heading toward a car wash business they never reach. An oft-neglected example of the early 70s extra-realistic subgenre initiated by "Midnight Cowboy." Engrossing until the end, when it falls flat. Filmed on location in Detroit. **112m/C VHS.** Gene Hackman, Al Pacino, Ann Wedgeworth, Eileen Brennan, Richard Lynch; *D:* Jerry Schatzberg; *C:* Vilmos Zsigmond. Cannes '73: Film.

Scared Stiff ♪♪♪ **1953** Fleeing a murder charge, Martin and Lewis find gangsters and ghosts on a Caribbean island. Funny and scary, a good remake of "The Ghost Breakers," with cameos by Hope and Crosby. ♫San Domingo; Song of the Enchilada Man; Mama Yo Quiero; You Hit the Spot; I Don't Care If the Sun Don't Shine; I'm Your Pal; When Somebody Thinks You're Wonderful. **108m/B VHS.** Dean Martin, Jerry Lewis, Lizabeth Scott, Carmen Miranda, Dorothy Malone; *Cameos:* Bob Hope, Bing Crosby; *D:* George Marshall.

Scared Stiff ♪ **1987 (R)** Three people move into a mansion once owned by a sadistic slave trader. Once there, they become unwilling victims of a voodoo curse. Bad special effects and script, not redeemed by decent but unoriginal story. **85m/C VHS.** Andrew Stevens, Mary Page Keller; *D:* Richard S. Friedman; *W:* Richard S. Friedman, Mark Frost, Daniel F. Bacaner.

Scared to Death ♪½ **1946** Begins with a woman dying of fright when shown the death mask of the man she framed. Dead woman then proceeds to narrate remainder of the story, which focuses on events leading up to her unfortunate, untimely, and fairly uninteresting demise. Memorable as Lugosi's only color film. DVD version is paired with 1941's "The Devil Bat." **60m/C VHS, DVD.** Bela Lugosi, George Zucco, Douglas Fowley, Nat Pendleton, Joyce Compton; *D:* Christy Cabanne.

Scared to Death ♪ **1980 (R)** A scientific experiment goes awry as a mutation begins killing off the residents of Los Angeles. **93m/C VHS.** John Stinson, Diana Davidson, David Moses, Kermit Eller; *D:* William Malone; *M:* Tom Chase.

Scarface ♪♪♪ *Scarface: The Shame of a Nation* **1931** The violent rise and fall of 1930s Chicago crime boss Tony Camonte—magnetically played by Muni—and based on the life of notorious gangster Al Capone. Release was held back by censors due to the amount of violence and its suggestion of incest between the title character and his sister (Dvorak). Morley is ice-cold ad Tony's moll Poppy. Producer Howard Hughes recut and filmed an alternate ending, without director Hawks' approval, to pacify the censors, and both versions of the film were released at the same time. Almost too violent and intense at the time. Remains brilliant and impressive. Remade in 1983. **93m/B VHS.** Paul Muni, Ann Dvorak, Karen Morley, Osgood Perkins, George Raft, Boris Karloff, W.R. Burnett, Ben Hecht, John Lee Mahin, Seton I. Miller; *D:* Howard Hawks; *W:* Fred Pasley; *C:* Lee Garmes; *M:* Gus Arnheim, Adolph Tandler. Natl. Film Reg. '94.

Scarface ♪♪♪ **1983 (R)** Al Pacino is a Cuban refugee who becomes powerful in the drug trade until the life gets the better of him. A remake of the 1932 classic gangster film of the same name, although the first film has more plot. Extremely violent, often unpleasant, but not easily forgotten. **170m/C VHS, DVD, Wide.** Al Pacino, Steven Bauer, Michelle Pfeiffer, Robert Loggia, F. Murray Abraham, Mary Elizabeth Mastrantonio, Harris Yulin, Paul Shenar, Oliver Stone; *D:* Brian DePalma; *W:* Oliver Stone; *C:* John A. Alonzo; *M:* Giorgio Moroder.

Scarface Mob ♪♪ *Tueur de Ch Icago* **1962** This is the original TV pilot film for the popular series "The Untouchables," about Eliot Ness's band of good guys battling Chicago's crime lord, Al Capone. Still strong stuff. Narrated by Walter Winchell. **120m/B VHS.** Robert Stack, Neville Brand, Barbara Nichols; *D:* Phil Karlson; *W:* Paul Monash; *Nar:* Walter Winchell. **TV**

The Scarlet & the Black ♪♪½ **1983** A priest clandestinely works within the shield of the Vatican's diplomatic immunity to shelter allied soldiers from the Nazis in occupied Rome. His efforts put him at odds with the Pope and target him for Gestapo assassination. Swashbuckling adventure at its second-best. Based on the nonfiction book "The Scarlet Pimpernel of the Vatican" by J.P. Gallagher. **145m/C VHS.** Gregory Peck, Christopher Plummer, John Gielgud, Raf Vallone; *D:* Jerry London; *M:* Ennio Morricone. **TV**

The Scarlet Car ♪♪ **1917** Chaney is a bank cashier who discovers his boss has been embezzling funds. A fight causes Chaney to believe he has killed his employer and he hides out in a remote cabin where guilt preys on his mind. **50m/B VHS.** Lon Chaney Sr., Franklyn Farnum, Edith Johnson, Sam DeGrasse; *D:* Joseph DeGrasse.

Scarlet Claw ♪♪♪ *Sherlock Holmes and the Scarlet Claw* **1944** Holmes and Watson solve the bloody murder of an old lady in the creepy Canadian village of Le Mort Rouge. The best and most authentic of the Sherlock Holmes series. **74m/B VHS.** Basil Rathbone, Nigel Bruce, Miles Mander, Gerald Hamer, Kay Harding; *D:* Roy William Neill.

The Scarlet Clue ♪♪ **1945** A better script and faster pacing improved this Monogram entry in the Chan series. Charlie investigates a series of mysterious deaths which lead to a plot to steal secret government radar plans. **65m/B VHS.** Sidney Toler, Benson Fong, Mantan Moreland, Robert E. Homans, Helen Devereaux; *D:* Phil Rosen.

Scarlet Dawn ♪♪½ **1932** Lavish sets and costumes abound in this romantic drama starring Fairbanks as a Russian aristocrat and Carroll as his maid servant. Together they flee Russia during the Revolution, marry, and settle into the life of the common working class. Restless under his new status, Fairbanks pursues Tashman and tries his hand at swindling. A slow but interesting love story. Adapted from the novel "Revolt" by Mary McCall. **58m/B VHS.** Douglas Fairbanks Jr., Nancy Carroll, Lilyan Tashman, Sheila Terry, Guy Kibbee, Richard Alexander, Frank Reicher; *D:* William Dieterle; *W:* Douglas Fairbanks Jr., Niven Busch, Erwin Gelsey.

Scarlet Empress ♪♪♪½ **1934** One of Von Sternberg's greatest films tells the story of Catherine the Great and her rise to power. Dietrich stars as the beautiful royal wife who outwits her foolish husband Peter (Jaffe) to become empress of Russia. Incredibly rich decor is a visual feast for the eye, as perfectionist von Sternberg fussed over every detail. Dietrich is excellent as Catherine, and von Sternberg's mastery of lighting and camera work makes for a highly extravagant film. Based on the diary of Catherine the Great. **110m/B VHS, DVD.** Marlene Dietrich, John Lodge, Sam Jaffe, Louise Dresser, Maria Sieber, Sir C. Aubrey Smith, Ruthelma Stevens, Olive Tell; ***D:*** Josef von Sternberg; ***W:*** Manuel Komroff; ***C:*** Bert Glennon.

The Scarlet Letter ♂♂ **1934** Unlikely comic relief provides only measure of redemption for this poorly rendered version of Hawthorne's classic novel about sin and Hester Prynne. **69m/B VHS.** Colleen Moore, Hardie Albright, Henry B. Walthall, Alan Hale, Cora Sue Collins, Betty Blythe; ***D:*** Robert G. Vignola.

The Scarlet Letter ♂♂♂ **1973** A studied, thoughtful, international production of the Nathaniel Hawthorne classic about a woman's adultery which incites puritanical violence and hysteria in colonial America. Fine modernization by Wenders. In German with English subtitles. **90m/C VHS.** *SP GE* Senta Berger, Lou Castel, Yella Rottlaender, William Layton, Yelena Samarina, Hans-Christian Blech; ***D:*** Wim Wenders.

The Scarlet Letter ♂♂♂ **1979** Faithful yet passionate TV adaptation of Hawthorne's classic novel of 17th-century New England. Hester Prynne (Foster) is condemned by her Puritan fellows for having a child out of wedlock and is forced to wear a scarlet letter A for adultery. Secretly sharing Hester's torment is the Rev. Arthur Dimmesdale (Heard), the baby's father, and Hester's vengeful back-from-the-dead husband, Roger Chillingsworth (Conway). **240m/C VHS.** Meg Foster, John Heard, Kevin Conway, Josef Sommer; ***D:*** Rick Hauser; ***W:*** Allan Knee, Alvin Sapinsley; ***M:*** John Morris.

The Scarlet Letter woof! **1995 (R)** Ewwwwww—ego-driven stinker of '95 ("Showgirls" not-withstanding). Feisty Hester Prynne (Moore) is condemned to wear the scarlet letter "A" of adultery by her 17th-century Puritan neighbors because she bore a child out of wedlock. Oldman is the lusty Reverend Arthur Dimmesdale (her partner in illicit passion) while Duvall chews scenery as Hester's wronged hubby. This "freely adapted" version of the 1850 American classic should have set author Nathaniel Hawthorne spinning in his grave as his moral saga of sin and redemption meets 20th-century moviemaking by having the passion made explicit and a happy ending tacked on. **135m/C VHS.** Demi Moore, Gary Oldman, Robert Duvall, Robert Prosky, Edward Hardwicke, Joan Plowright, Roy Dotrice, Dana Ivey, Sheldon Peters Wolfchild, Diane Salinger, Lisa Jolliff-Andoh, Amy Wright, Tim Woodward; ***D:*** Roland Joffe; ***W:*** Douglas Day Stewart; ***C:*** Alex Thomson; ***M:*** John Barry. Golden Raspberries '95: Worst Remake/Sequel.

The Scarlet Pimpernel ♂♂♂½ **1934** Sir Percy Blakeney (Howard) is a supposed dandy of the English court who assumes the identity of "The Scarlet Pimpernel" in order to outwit the French Republicans and aid innocent aristocrats during the French Revolution. The frustrated French send sinister ambassador Chauvelin (Massey) to discover the rogue's identity and involve Blakeney's French wife, Marguerite (Oberon) in their plot. Classic rendering of Baroness Orczy's novel, full of exploits, 18th century costumes, intrigue, damsels, etc. Produced by Alexander Korda, who fired the initial director, Rowland Brown. Remade twice for TV. **95m/B VHS, DVD.** *GB* Leslie Howard, Joan Gardner, Merle Oberon, Raymond Massey, Anthony Bushell, Nigel Bruce, Bramwell Fletcher, Walter Rilla, O.B. Clarence, Ernest Milton, Edmund Breon, Melville Cooper, Gibb McLaughlin, Morland Graham, Allan Jeayes; ***D:*** Harold Young; ***W:*** Robert Sherwood, Arthur Wimperis, Lajos Biro; ***C:*** Harold Rosson; ***M:*** Arthur Benjamin.

The Scarlet Pimpernel ♂♂♂ **1982** Remake of the classic about a British dandy who saved French aristocrats from the Reign of Terror guillotines during the French Revolution. Almost as good as the original 1935 film, with beautiful costumes and sets and good performances from Seymour and Andrews. **142m/C VHS.** *GB* Anthony Andrews, Jane Seymour, Ian McKellen, James Villiers, Eleanor David; ***D:*** Clive Donner; ***M:*** Nick Bicat. **TV**

The Scarlet Pimpernel ♂♂½ **1999** Wealthy, foppish English aristocrat, Sir Percy Blakeney (Grant), is not the fool he seems. Indeed, he masquerades as the daring Scarlet Pimpernel, the rescuer of those persecuted by the French Revolution, and the bane of French spy Chauvelin (Shaw). Why Percy has even managed to fool his lovely French wife, Marguerite (McGovern), who was once involved with Chauvelin, and who comes to see her husband in a more heroic light. Based on the novels by Baroness Emmuska Orczy. **120m/C VHS, DVD.** Richard E. Grant, Elizabeth McGovern, Martin Shaw, Anthony Green, Ronan Vibert, Christopher Fairbank, Jonathan Coy, Emilia Fox, Dominic Mafham; ***D:*** Patrick Lau; ***W:*** Richard Carpenter; ***C:*** Simon Kossoff; ***M:*** Michael Pavlicek. **CABLE**

The Scarlet Pimpernel 2: Mademoiselle Guillotine ♂♂½ **1999** The Scarlet Pimpernel and wife Marguerite head to France to save the daughter of a French nobleman from the clutches of Gabrielle Damiens (Black), AKA Mademoiselle Guillotine, and her band of revolutionaries. The disgraced Chauvelin is also involved and then Marguerite gets captured, so quite a lot of rescuing needs to be done. Based on the books by Baroness Emmuska Orczy. **90m/C VHS.** Richard E. Grant, Elizabeth McGovern, Martin Shaw, Anthony Green, Ronan Vibert, Christopher Fairbank, Jonathan Coy, Denise Black, James Callis, Peter Jeffrey, Julie Cox; ***D:*** Patrick Lau; ***W:*** Richard Carpenter; ***C:*** Simon Kossoff; ***M:*** Michael Pavlicek. **CABLE**

The Scarlet Pimpernel 3: The Kidnapped King ♂♂½ **1999** France's 10-year-old Dauphin is under the control of Robespierre when he is captured by a masked figure. As Sir Percy investigates, all clues point to legendary swordsman Chevalier D'Orly. Meanwhile, Marguerite has supposedly left Sir Percy and although Robespierre isn't convinced, Chauvelin is plotting to win back his former love. Based on the books by Baroness Emmuska Orczy. **90m/C VHS.** Richard E. Grant, Elizabeth McGovern, Martin Shaw, Anthony Green, Ronan Vibert, Christopher Fairbank, Jonathan Coy, Suzanne Bertish, Jerome Willis, Bryce Engstrom, Dalibor Sipek; ***D:*** Edward Bennett; ***W:*** Richard Carpenter; ***C:*** John Hooper; ***M:*** Michael Pavlicek. **CABLE**

Scarlet Spear woof! **1954** Filmed in Nairobi National Park in Kenya. A great white hunter convinces a young African chief that the ancient practices of his people are uncivilized. Pathetically stated and culturally offensive by today's standards. **78m/C VHS.** John Bentley, Martha Hyer, Morasi; ***D:*** George Breakston.

Scarlet Street ♂♂♂ **1945** A mild-mannered, middle-aged cashier becomes an embezzler when he gets involved with a predatory, manipulating woman. Lang remake of Jean Renoir's "La Chienne" (1931). Set apart from later attempts on the same theme by excellent direction by Lang and acting. Also available Colorized. **95m/B VHS.** Edward G. Robinson, Joan Bennett, Dan Duryea, Samuel S. Hinds; ***D:*** Fritz Lang; ***C:*** Milton Krasner.

The Scarlet Tunic ♂♂½ **1997** Based on the novella "The Melancholy Hussar of the German Legion" by Thomas Hardy. It's 1802 in Hardy's fictional Wessex countryside where a light cavalry regiment of bored Germans, fighting with the British against Napoleon, has an encampment on the land of retired doctor Edward Groves (Shepherd). Groves' pretty daughter Frances (Fielding) is engaged to local businessman Humphrey Gould (Sessions) but, of course, she falls for dashing German hussar Matthaus Singer (Barr). Since this is a Hardy story, don't expect any happy endings. **101m/C VHS.** *GB* Jean-Marc Barr, Emma Fielding, Simon Callow, John Sessions, Jack Shepherd, Andrew Tiernan, Thomas Lockyer; ***D:*** Stuart St. Paul; ***W:*** Stuart St. Paul, Mark Jenkins, Colin Clements; ***C:*** Malcolm McLean; ***M:*** John Scott. **TV**

Scarlett ♂♂½ **1994 (PG-13)** Well, fiddle-dee-dee. While purists may object to any tampering of "Gone With the Wind," this epic TV miniseries, from the Alexandra Ripley novel, manages to be good if overlong fun for those willing to sit back and relax. Scarlett tries to get back Tara and Rhett (they divorce but still battle continuously); explores her Irish family ties and even moves to Ireland; then gets involved with the wrong man and is accused of murder so Rhett can save her and everything can turn out okay (there's lots more). The big budget is up on-screen with lavish costumes and sets and a big cast—although why two Brits got the leads in this Southern melodrama is anyone's guess (Whalley and Dalton try hard). **360m/C VHS, DVD.** Joanne Whalley, Timothy Dalton, Ann-Margret, Barbara Barrie, Sean Bean, Brian Bedford, Stephen Collins, John Gielgud, Annabeth Gish, George Grizzard, Julie Harris, Tina Kellegher, Melissa Leo, Colm Meaney, Esther Rolle, Jean Smart, Elizabeth Wilson, Paul Winfield, Betsy Blair, Peter Eyre, Pippa Guard, Ronald Pickup, Gary Raymond, Dorothy Tutin; ***D:*** John Erman; ***W:*** William Hanley; ***M:*** John Morris. **TV**

Scarred ♂½ *Street Love; Red on Red* **1984 (R)** Unwed teenage mother becomes prostitute to support baby. Predictable plot and acting pull this one down. **85m/C VHS.** Jennifer Mayo, Jackie Berryman, David Dean; ***D:*** Rosemarie Turko; ***W:*** Rosemarie Turko.

Scarred City ♂♂ **1998 (R)** Cliched and predictable actioner with a decent cast. Trigger-happy cop John Trace (Baldwin) is forced to join an elite crime unit, headed by Laine Devon (Palminteri), which uses any means necessary to get the job done. But Trace soon decides that his fellow cops are basically just fulfilling their own violent impulses. Then Trace saves hooker Candy (Carrere) from a mob hit and his buddies decide they'd be better off without him. **95m/C VHS, DVD.** Chazz Palminteri, Stephen Baldwin, Tia Carrere, Gary Dourdan, Michael Rispoli, Steve Flynn; ***D:*** Ken Sanzel; ***W:*** Ken Sanzel; ***C:*** Michael Slovis; ***M:*** Anthony Marinelli.

The Scars of Dracula ♂♂½ **1970 (R)** A young couple tangles with Dracula in their search for the man's missing brother. Gory, creepy, violent, sexy tale from the dark side. Don't see it late at night. Preceded by "Taste the Blood of Dracula" and followed by "Dracula A.D. 1972." **96m/C VHS, DVD, Wide.** *GB* Christopher Lee, Jenny Hanley, Dennis Waterman, Wendy Hamilton, Patrick Troughton, Michael Gwynn, Anouska (Anoushka) Hempel, Michael Ripper, Christopher Matthews, Delta Lindsay; ***D:*** Roy Ward Baker; ***W:*** John (Anthony Hinds) Elder; ***M:*** James Bernard.

Scary Movie ♂½ **2000 (R)** If the last few Leslie Nielsen outings didn't convince you that the genre spoof was played out, this parody of "Scream" and all its progeny will. The Wayans brothers go for quantity of jokes and targets, and quality definitely suffers for it. Fart gags and gratuitous cussing (neither of which we often object to, but we have our limits) are substituted for focused satire. If you're looking for well-done genre spoofery, rent "Airplane" and "I'm Gonna Git You Sucka" and leave this one to the discount previously viewed bin. **85m/C VHS, DVD, Wide.** Keenen Ivory Wayans, Marlon Wayans, Shawn Wayans, Carmen Electra, Jon Abrahams, Shannon Elizabeth, Lochlyn Munro, Cheri Oteri, Anna Faris, Regina Hall, Kurt Fuller, David Lander, Dave Sheridan, Dan Joffre; ***D:*** Keenen Ivory Wayans; ***W:*** Marlon Wayans, Shawn Wayans; ***C:*** Francis Kenny; ***M:*** David Kitay.

Scary Movie 2 ♂ **2001 (R)** You knew they were lying when the tagline of the first film declared "No mercy, no shame, no sequel," especially since the spoof brought in more than $144 mil worldwide. The plot, such as it is, consists of a spooky doctor (Curry) convincing the cast from the original to spend the night in a haunted house to study insomnia. Familiar, no? But it's really just an excuse for the Wayans to parody a whole new batch of movies and do a lot (and we mean A LOT) of bodily fluid and sex jokes. Unfortunately, they don't do it any better than they did the first time, and whatever freshness the original had is long gone. **82m/C VHS, DVD, Wide.** *US* Anna Faris, Tim Curry, Shawn Wayans, Marlon Wayans, Chris Elliott, Tori Spelling, Christopher K. Masterson, Kathleen Robertson, Regina Hall, James Woods, David Cross, Andy Richter, Natasha Lyonne, Veronica Cartwright, Richard Moll; ***D:*** Keenen Ivory Wayans; ***W:*** Shawn Wayans, Marlon Wayans, Alyson Fouse, Greg Grabianski, Dave Polsky, Michael Anthony Snowden, Craig Wayans; ***C:*** Steven Bernstein.

Scavenger Hunt ♂ **1979 (PG)** Action begins when a deceased millionaire's will states that his 15 would-be heirs must compete in a scavenger hunt, and whoever collects all the items first wins the entire fortune. Big cast wanders about aimlessly. **117m/C VHS.** Richard Benjamin, James Coco, Ruth Buzzi, Cloris Leachman, Cleavon Little, Roddy McDowall, Scatman Crothers, Tony Randall, Robert Morley, Richard Mulligan, Dirk Benedict, Willie Aames, Vincent Price; ***D:*** Michael A. Schultz; ***M:*** Billy Goldenberg.

Scavengers ♂ **1987 (PG-13)** A man and a woman become involved in a spy plot and wind up in all sorts of danger. Pathetic excuse for a "thriller." **94m/C VHS.** Kenneth Gilman, Brenda Bakke, Ken Gampu, Norman Anstey, Crispin De Nys; ***D:*** Duncan McLachlan.

Scenario du Film Passion ♂♂♂ **1982** A classically self-analyzing video piece by Godard, in which he recreates on tape the scenario for his film "Passion," resulting in a reflexive, experimental essay on the process of image-making and conceptualizing films, especially Godard's. In French with English subtitles. **54m/C VHS.** ***D:*** Jean-Luc Godard, Anne-Marie Mieville, Barnard Menoud.

Scene of the Crime ♂♂½ **1985** Three short mysteries, which the audience is asked to solve: "The Newlywed Murder," "Medium Is the Murder," and "Vote for Murder." **74m/C VHS.** Markie Post, Alan Thicke, Ben Piazza; ***D:*** Walter Grauman; ***Nar:*** Orson Welles. **TV**

Scene of the Crime ♂♂♂ **1987** Beautiful widow, trapped in small French town, is sexually awakened by escaped convict hiding out near her home. Acclaimed, but sometimes distracting camera technique and slow pace undermine the film. In French with English subtitles. **90m/C VHS.** *FR* Catherine Deneuve, Danielle Darrieux, Wadeck Stanczak, Victor Lanoux, Nicolas Giraudi, Jean Bousquet, Claire Nebout; ***D:*** Andre Techine; ***W:*** Olivier Assayas.

Scenes from a Mall ♂♂ **1991 (R)** Conspicuous consumers spend 16th wedding anniversary waltzing in mall while marriage unravels with few laughs. Surprisingly superficial comedy given the depth of talent of Allen and Midler. **87m/C VHS.** Woody Allen, Bette Midler, Bill Irwin, Daren Firestone, Rebecca Nickels; ***Cameos:*** Fabio Lanzoni; ***D:*** Paul Mazursky; ***W:*** Paul Mazursky; ***C:*** Fred Murphy.

Scenes from a Marriage ♂♂♂♂ **1973 (PG)** Originally produced in six one-hour episodes for Swedish TV, this bold and sensitive film excruciatingly portrays the painful, unpleasant, disintegration of a marriage. Ullmann is superb. Realistic and disturbing. Dubbed. **168m/C VHS.** *SW* Liv Ullmann, Erland Josephson, Bibi Andersson, Jan Malmsjo, Anita Wall; ***D:*** Ingmar Bergman; ***W:*** Ingmar Bergman; ***C:*** Sven Nykvist. Golden Globes '75: Foreign Film; N.Y. Film Critics '74: Actress (Ullmann), Screenplay; Natl. Soc. Film Critics '74: Actress (Ullmann), Film, Screenplay, Support. Actress (Andersson).

Scenes from a Murder ♂½ **1972** A killer (Savalas) stalks a beautiful actress (Heywood). Dull excuse for a suspense flick. **91m/C VHS.** *IT* Telly Savalas, Anne Heywood, Giorgio Piazza; ***D:*** Alberto De Martino.

Scenes from the Class Struggle in Beverly Hills ♂♂½ **1989 (R)** Social satire about the wealthy, their servants, and their hangers-on in two Hollywood households. Two chauffeurs spend their spare time lusting after their lovely employers, and bet to see who can accomplish reality first. All kinds of erotic capers result. Usually funny and irreverent; occasionally misfires or takes itself too seriously. Reunites the trio from cult classic "Eating Raoul": Bartel, Woronov, and Beltran. Remake of Renoir's "The Rules of the Game." **103m/C VHS.** Jacqueline Bisset, Ray Sharkey, Mary Woronov, Robert Beltran, Ed Begley Jr., Wallace Shawn, Paul Bartel, Paul Mazursky, Arnetia Walker, Rebecca Schaeffer, Edith Diaz; ***Cameos:*** Little Richard, Michael Feinstein; ***D:*** Paul Bartel; ***W:*** Bruce Wagner; ***C:*** Steven Fierberg; ***M:*** Stanley Myers.

Scenes from the Goldmine 🦴½ **1987 (R)** A young woman joins a rock band and falls in love with its lead singer. Realistic but bland; music not memorable (performed mostly by the actors themselves). **99m/C VHS.** Catherine Mary Stewart, Cameron Dye, Joe Pantoliano, John Ford Coley, Steve Railsback, Timothy B. Schmit, Jewel Shepard, Alex Rocco, Lee Ving, Lesley-Anne Down; ***D:*** Marc Rocco.

The Scent of a Woman 🦴🦴½ *Sweet Smell of Woman; Profumo di Donna* **1975** An acclaimed dark comedy that may be an acquired taste for some. A blinded military officer and his valet take a sensual tour of Italy, the sightless man seducing beautiful women on the way. But at the end of the journey awaits a shock, and the real point of the tale, based on a novel by Giovanni Arpino. In Italian with English subtitles. Remade in 1992 as "Scent of a Woman." **103m/C VHS, DVD.** *IT* Vittorio Gassman; ***D:*** Dino Risi.

Scent of a Woman 🦴🦴🦴 **1992 (R)** Pacino is a powerhouse (verging on caricature) in a story that, with anyone else in the lead, would be your run-of-the-mill, overly sentimental coming of age/redemption flick. Blind, bitter, and semi-alcoholic Pacino is a retired army colonel under the care of his married niece. He's home alone over Thanksgiving, under the watchful eye of local prep school student Charlie (O'Donnell). Pacino's abrasive (though wonderfully intuitive and romantic) colonel makes an impact on viewers that lingers like a woman's scent long after the last tango. O'Donnell is competently understated in key supporting role, while the tango lesson between Pacino and Anwar dances to the tune of "classic." Boxoffice winner is a remake of 1975 Italian film "Profumo di Donna." **157m/C VHS, DVD, Wide.** Al Pacino, Chris O'Donnell, James Rebhorn, Gabrielle Anwar, Philip Seymour Hoffman, Richard Venture, Bradley Whitford, Rochelle Oliver, Margaret Eginton, Tom Riis Farrell, Frances Conroy, Ron Eldard; ***D:*** Martin Brest; ***W:*** Bo Goldman; ***C:*** Donald E. Thorin; ***M:*** Thomas Newman. Oscars '92: Actor (Pacino); Golden Globes '93: Actor—Drama (Pacino), Film—Drama, Screenplay.

The Scent of Green Papaya 🦴🦴🦴 *Mui du du Xanh* **1993** Tranquil film, set in 1951 Vietnam, follows 10-year-old peasant girl Mui as she spends the next 10 years as a servant in a troubled family, gracefully accommodating herself to the small changes in her life. At 20, she finds a fairy-tale romance with her next employer, a young pianist. Presents a romanticized view of the stoicism of Vietnamese women but is visually beautiful. Directorial debut of Hung is based on his childhood memories of Vietnam, which he re-created on a soundstage outside Paris. In Vietnamese with English subtitles. **104m/C VHS, DVD.** *VT* Tran Nu Yen-Khe, Lu Man San, Truong Thi Loc, Vuong Hoa Hoi; ***D:*** Tran Anh Hung; ***W:*** Tran Anh Hung, Patricia Petit; ***C:*** Benoit Delhomme; ***M:*** Ton That Tiet.

Schemes 🦴🦴 **1995 (R)** Grieving widower Paul Stewart (McCaffrey) becomes interested in Laura Pierce (Hope), a lovely young woman who said she knew his late wife. Then, Paul's business partner Evelyn (Draper) discovers Laura's not on the up and up and is really interested in Paul's substantial insurance payoff. Laura's part of a con job set up by volaile Victor (Glover), but since Evelyn's also in love with Paul, things aren't at all what they seem. **95m/C VHS.** John Glover, Polly Draper, Leslie Hope, James McCaffrey, John de Lancie, Allison Mackie; ***D:*** Derek Westervelt; ***W:*** Derek Westervelt; ***C:*** Claudio Obregon; ***M:*** Mark Chait.

Schindler's List 🦴🦴🦴🦴 **1993 (R)** Spielberg's staggering evocation of the Holocaust finds its voice in Oscar Schindler (Neeson), womanizing German businessman and aspiring war profiteer, who cajoled, bribed, and bullied the Nazis into allowing him to employ Jews in his Polish factories during WWII. By doing so he saved over 1,000 lives. The atrocities are depicted matter of factly as a by-product of sheer Nazi evil. Shot in black and white and powered by splendid performances. Neeson uses his powerful physique as a protective buffer; Kingsley is watchful as his industrious Jewish accountant; and Fiennes personifies evil as Nazi Amon Goeth. Based on the novel by Thomas Keneally, which itself was based on survivor's memories. Filmed on location in Cracow, Poland; due to the sensitive nature of the story, sets of the Auschwitz concentration camp were reconstructed directly outside the camp after protests about filming on the actual site. A tour de force and labor of love for Spielberg, who finally garnered the attention and respect as a filmmaker he deserves. **195m/B VHS, Wide.** Liam Neeson, Ben Kingsley, Ralph Fiennes, Embeth Davidtz, Caroline Goodall, Jonathan Sagalle, Mark Ivanir, Malgoscha Gebel, Shmulik Levy, Beatrice Macola, Andrzej Seweryn, Friedrich von Thun, Norbert Weisser, Michael Schneider, Anna Mucha; ***D:*** Steven Spielberg; ***W:*** Steven Zaillian; ***C:*** Janusz Kaminski; ***M:*** John Williams. Oscars '93: Adapt. Screenplay, Art Dir./Set Dec., Cinematog., Director (Spielberg), Film Editing, Picture, Orig. Score; AFI '98: Top 100; British Acad. '93: Adapt. Screenplay, Director (Spielberg), Film, Support. Actor (Fiennes); Directors Guild '93: Director (Spielberg); Golden Globes '94: Director (Spielberg), Film—Drama, Screenplay; L.A. Film Critics '93: Cinematog., Film; Natl. Bd. of Review '93: Film; N.Y. Film Critics '93: Cinematog., Film, Support. Actor (Fiennes); Natl. Soc. Film Critics '93: Cinematog., Director (Spielberg), Film, Support. Actor (Fiennes); Writers Guild '93: Adapt. Screenplay.

Schizo 🦴 *Amok; Blood of the Undead* **1977 (R)** Devious intentions abound as a middle-aged man is overcome by weird scenes and revelations, caused by the impending wedding of the figure skater he adores. Confusing tale of insanity, obsession, and skating. **109m/C VHS, DVD, Wide.** *GB* Lynne Frederick, John Leyton, Stephanie Beacham, John Fraser, Jack Watson, John McEnery; ***D:*** Pete Walker; ***W:*** John M. Watson Sr.; ***C:*** Peter Jessop.

Schizoid 🦴 *Murder by Mail* **1980 (R)** Advice-to-the-lovelorn columnist Hill receives a series of threatening letters causing her to wonder whether psychiatrist Kinski is bumping off his own patients. Boring blood dripper that's difficult to follow. **91m/C VHS.** Klaus Kinski, Marianna Hill, Craig Wasson; ***D:*** David Paulsen.

Schizopolis 🦴🦴 **1997** Experimental, empty satire on modern spirituality and communication combines a number of weird and wacky devices that are not particularly entertaining. In an interesting premise, Soderburgh takes the lead in a dual role as Fletcher Munson, a manically neurotic employee of a self-help guru and his own look-alike, a ho-hum dentist having an affair with Fletcher's wife. Soderburgh's real-life ex, actress Brantley, plays his wife, who also has a double that shows up at the dentist. Things grow more bizarre for no apparent reason, as secondary cast members speak in other languages or just complete nonsense while strange sound effects confuse, in a film which also lists no credits (the title is shown in film on a character's t-shirt). Soderburgh, who wrote, directed and lensed this surrealist homage, shot on a super-low $250,000 budget as a way of expressing ideas not allowed in bigger budget, conventional films. To most, this just looks like expensive therapy. **96m/C VHS.** Steven Soderbergh, Betsy Brantley, David Jensen; ***D:*** Steven Soderbergh; ***W:*** Steven Soderbergh; ***C:*** Steven Soderbergh.

Schlock 🦴🦴 *The Banana Monster* **1973 (PG)** Accurately titled horror parody is first directorial effort for Landis, who does double duty as a missing link who kills people and falls in love with blind girl. Look for cameo appearance by Forrest J. Ackerman; ape-makeup by Rick Baker. **78m/C VHS, DVD, Wide.** John Landis, Saul Kahan, Joseph Piantadosi, Eliza (Simons) Garrett, Emil Hamaty, Eric Allison; ***Cameos:*** Forrest J Ackerman; ***D:*** John Landis; ***W:*** John Landis; ***C:*** Robert E. Collins; ***M:*** David Gibson.

Schnelles Geld 🦴½ **1984** A mild-mannered guy gets involved with a prostitute, and is plunged into a world of crime and drugs. In German with English subtitles. **90m/C VHS.** *GE* Dieter Schidor, Anne Bennent, Hub Martin, Gila von Weitershausen; ***D:*** George Moorse; ***W:*** George Moorse; ***C:*** Wolfgang Dickmann.

School Daze 🦴🦴🦴 **1988 (R)** Director/writer/star Lee's second outing is a rambunctious comedy (with a message, of course) set at an African-American college in the South. Skimpy plot revolves around the college's homecoming weekend and conflict among frats and sororities and African-Americans who would lose their racial identity and others who assert it. Entertaining and thought provoking. A glimpse at Lee's "promise," fulfilled in "Do the Right Thing." **114m/C VHS, DVD, Wide.** Spike Lee, Laurence "Larry" Fishburne, Giancarlo Esposito, Tisha Campbell, Ossie Davis, Joe Seneca, Art Evans, Ellen Holly, Branford Marsalis, Bill Nunn, Kadeem Hardison, Darryl M. Bell, Joie Lee, Tyra Ferrell, Jasmine Guy, Gregg Burge, Kasi Lemmons, Samuel L. Jackson, Phyllis Hyman, James Bond III; ***D:*** Spike Lee; ***W:*** Spike Lee; ***C:*** Ernest R. Dickerson; ***M:*** Bill Lee.

School for Scandal 🦴🦴 **1965** British TV adaptation of Richard Sheridan's comedic play of the morals and manners of 18th-century England. **100m/B VHS.** *GB* Joan Plowright, Felix Aylmer. **TV**

School Spirit 🦴 **1985 (R)** A hormonally motivated college student is killed during a date. He comes back as a ghost to haunt the campus, disrupt the stuffy president's affair, and fall in love. Forgettable, lame, low-grade teen sex flick. **90m/C VHS.** Tom Nolan, Elizabeth Foxx, Larry Linville; ***D:*** Allan Holleb; ***W:*** Geoffrey Baere; ***M:*** Tom Bruner.

School Ties 🦴🦴🦴 **1992 (PG-13)** Encino man Fraser does a dramatic turn as a talented 1950s quarterback who gets a scholarship to the elite St. Matthew prep school. To conform with the closed-mindedness of the McCarthy era, both his father and coach suggest that he hide his Jewish religion. Fraser's compliance results in his big-man-on-campus status, until his rival in football and his love interest both find out that he is Jewish, creating an ugly rift in the school. What easily could have been just another teen hunk flick looks at much more than just Fraser's pretty face in successful, unflinching treatment of anti-Semitism. **110m/C VHS, DVD, Wide.** Brendan Fraser, Matt Damon, Chris O'Donnell, Randall Batinkoff, Andrew Lowery, Cole Hauser, Ben Affleck, Anthony Rapp, Amy Locane, Peter Donat, Zeljko Ivanek, Kevin Tighe, Michael Higgins, Ed Lauter; ***D:*** Robert Mandel; ***W:*** Darryl Ponicsan, Dick Wolf; ***C:*** Freddie Francis; ***M:*** Maurice Jarre.

Schtonk 🦴🦴 **1992** Hermann Willie is a down-and-out journalist who thinks he's come upon the find of the century when he's given what are supposedly Hitler's diaries. Based on the 1983 scandal when the German publication "Der Stern" paid $5 million and printed what turned out to be not-very-clever forgeries. Director Dietl mocks the greedy gullibility of the journal, the ingenuity of the forger, as well as the nostalgia of the ex- and neo-Nazis of the modern Germany. The title is a meaningless expletive uttered by Charlie Chaplin in "The Great Dictator." German with subtitles. **115m/C VHS.** *GE* Goetz George, Uwe Ochsenknecht, Rolf Hoppe; ***D:*** Helmut Dietl; ***W:*** Helmut Dietl. Berlin Intl. Film Fest. '92: Actor (George), Director (Dietl), Film.

Sci-Fighters 🦴🦴½ **1996 (R)** Renegade cop Cameron Grayson (Piper) is tracking rapist Adrian Dunn (Drago) in 2009 Boston and discovers that Dunn has been exposed to a deadly, mutating virus. It's actually changing the bad guy into an alien methane-breathing lifeform that, of course, wants to inhabit the earth. Appropriately gross alien makeup and some decent special effects. **94m/C VHS, DVD.** Roddy Piper, Billy Drago, Jayne Heitmeyer; ***D:*** Peter Svatek; ***W:*** Mark Sevi; ***C:*** Barry Gravelle; ***M:*** Milan Kymlicka.

Science Crazed 🦴½ **1990** A scientist creates a monster who could conceivably destroy the world. **90m/C VHS.** *CA* Cameron Klein; ***D:*** Ron Switzer.

Scissors 🦴½ **1991 (R)** Yes, this Hitchcock imitation needs trimming. An unstable young woman contends with a rapist, devious lookalikes, birds, and a prison-like apartment, not all of which are relevant to the plot. An unsharp stab at suspense from novelist/filmmaker DeFelitta. **105m/C VHS.** Sharon Stone, Steve Railsback, Michelle Phillips, Ronny Cox, Albert "Poppy" Popwell; ***D:*** Frank De Felitta; ***W:*** Frank De Felitta.

Scooby-Doo **2002 (PG)** Fred (Prinze) is out to debunk the apparent haunting of theme-park Spooky Island, accompanied by Daphne (Gellar), Velma (Cardellini), Shaggy (Lillard), and Scooby, of course (who's completely CGI, which made the film's budget very expensive). Based on the 1969 cartoon, "Scooby-Doo, Where Are You?" Not yet reviewed. **?m/C VHS, DVD.** Freddie Prinze Jr., Sarah Michelle Gellar, Matthew Lillard, Linda Cardellini, Rowan Atkinson; ***D:*** Raja Gosnell; ***W:*** James Gunn, Craig Titley.

Scorchers 🦴🦴 **1992 (R)** Back in the bayou, Splendid (Lloyd), a newlywed who won't sleep with her husband, and her cousin Talbot (Tilly), a preacher's daughter whose husband prefers the town whore Thais (Dunaway), find their lives intertwined because of their marital and sexual problems. A real "scorcher." **81m/C VHS.** Faye Dunaway, Denholm Elliott, James Earl Jones, Emily Lloyd, Jennifer Tilly, Leland Crooke, James Wilder, Anthony Geary; ***D:*** David Beaird; ***W:*** David Beaird.

Scorchy 🦴 **1976 (R)** Low-budget female cop action flick about a narcotics agent (Stevens) on the trail of a drug kingpin. Blood and guts, guns, and violence. Poor casting. **100m/C VHS.** Connie Stevens, William Smith, Cesare Danova, Marlene Schmidt; ***D:*** Howard (Hikmet) Avedis; ***W:*** Howard (Hikmet) Avedis.

Score 🦴🦴 **1972** Swinging marrieds Jack and Elvira turn their attention to a newlywed couple in order to indulge their sexual desires. Campy, culty erotica. **89m/C VHS, DVD.** Calvin Culver, Claire Wilbur, Lynn Lowry, Gerald Grant, Carl Parker; ***D:*** Radley Metzger; ***W:*** Jerry Douglas; ***C:*** Franco Vodopivec.

The Score 🦴🦴½ **2001 (R)** Slow-starting crime comedy with De Niro as a semi-retired thief, living a quiet life running a Montreal jazz club, until his fence (Brando) and a wannabe thief (Norton) talk him into pulling another job in Montreal's customs house. Bassett is DeNiro's squeeze (good taste there) who wants him out of the life. Excrutiatingly painstaking but realistic in its portrayal of the preparation and events leading to the heist, but when things finally get going, it crackles with tense "will-they-get-caught" moments and double-crosses aplenty. De Niro is solid, as always, but he seems like he may be getting to old for this stuff. Norton gets most of the screen time, and uses it well. Brando is surprisingly understated in an amusing way. **124m/C VHS, DVD, Wide.** *US* Robert De Niro, Edward Norton, Marlon Brando, Angela Bassett, Gary Farmer, Paul Soles, Jamie Harold; ***D:*** Frank Oz; ***W:*** Kario Salem, Scott Marshall Smith, Lem Dobbs; ***C:*** Rob Hahn; ***M:*** Howard Shore.

Scorned 🦴🦴 **1993 (R)** Seductive Patricia Langley loves her husband Truman so much that she'll do anything to help him get that promotion, including seducing another man. Too bad Alex Weston gets the promotion instead. Really too bad, since Patricia decides Alex has ruined her life and she's going to get revenge by ruining his. Also available in an unrated version. **100m/C VHS.** Shannon Tweed, Andrew Stevens, Michael D. Arenz, Kim Morgan Greene, Stephen Young, Daniel McVicar; ***D:*** Andrew Stevens; ***W:*** Barry Avrich.

Scorned 2 🦴½ **1996 (R)** Amanda (McClure) seems happily married to psych prof Mark—even if she is having those bad dreams. But when her hubby is tempted by a pretty coed and Amanda finds out—well this is one woman that should never be scorned. **105m/C VHS, DVD.** Tane McClure, Wendy Schumacher, Myles O'Brien,

John McCook, Andrew Stevens, Seth Jaffe; *D:* Rodney McDonald; *W:* Sean McGinley; *C:* Gary Graver; *M:* Patrick Seymour.

Scorpio ½ **1973 (PG)** Okay cat-and-mouse espionage tale about a wily, veteran CIA agent (Lancaster) who may have turned traitor. He's set-up to be killed by a CIA boss but the assassin, code-name Scorpio (Delon), has some trouble fulfilling his assignment. Cross- and double-cross abound. **114m/C VHS, DVD.** Burt Lancaster, Alain Delon, Paul Scofield, John Colicos, Gayle Hunnicutt, J.D. Cannon, Joanne Linville, Melvin Stewart, James B. Sikking, Vladek Sheybal, William (Bill) Smithers, Celeste Yarnall; *D:* Michael Winner.

The Scorpio Factor **1990** Murder and mayhem follow microchip heist. **87m/C VHS, DVD.** Attila Bertalan, David Nerman, Wendy Dawn Wilson; *D:* Michel Waehniuc; *W:* Carole Sauve, June Pinheiro; *C:* Bruno Philip; *M:* Richard Gresko.

Scorpion **1986 (R)** A karate-master and anti-terrorist expert defuses a skyjacking and infiltrates international assassination conspiracies. Ex-real life karate champ Tulleners is a ho-hum hero, and the story is warmed over. **98m/C VHS.** Tonny Tulleners, Allen Williams, Don Murray; *D:* William Reed.

The Scorpion King **2002 (PG-13)** Billed as a prequel to "The Mummy" series, this actioner is more in the "Sword 'n' Sandals" vein. The Rock is the title star, an assassin hired by a group of beleaguered tribes to defeat the evil warlord Memnon (Brand). The warlord is helped, somewhat unenthusiastically, by a sorceress (Hu) who can foresee the outcome of battles. Yes, it's cheesy, and downright silly at times, but it doesn't really strive for any more than that. The only motivation behind the whole endeavor seems to be to make The Rock a movie star, and if he sticks with action pics, he seems to be on his way. All the men do the requisite amount of killing, and discussing killing, and the women are all scantily clad. The target audience should be overjoyed. **94m/C VHS, DVD.** *US* Dwayne "The Rock" Johnson, Michael Clarke Duncan, Steven Brand, Kelly Hu, Bernard Hill, Grant Heslov, Peter Facinelli, Ralph (Ralf) Moeller, Branscombe Richmond, Roger Rees, Sherri Howard, Conrad Roberts; *D:* Chuck Russell; *W:* Stephen Sommers, William Osborne, David Hayter; *C:* John R. Leonetti; *M:* John Debney.

Scorpion Spring **1996 (R)** Drug runner Astor (Morales) is on the lam through the desert with a beautiful hostage (Aviles) when two unsuspecting travelers (Molina and McGaw) offer the stranded duo a ride. But drug lord El Rojo (McConaughey) wants Astor dead and doesn't care who gets in his way and there's also a border patrol officer (Blades) on their trail as well. **89m/C VHS.** Esai Morales, Alfred Molina, Patrick McGaw, Matthew McConaughey, Angel Aviles, Ruben Blades, Miguel (Michael) Sandoval, Richard Edson, John Doe; *D:* Brian Cox; *W:* Brian Cox; *C:* Nancy Schreiber; *M:* Lalo Schifrin.

Scorpion with Two Tails **1982** In an underworld of terror, people die grotesque deaths that a woman dreams of. **99m/C VHS.** John Saxon, Van Johnson.

The Scorpion Woman **1989** A female Viennese judge becomes entwined in an unusual case which partially parallels her own life. Her new young lover turns out to be bisexual. Not gripping. In German with English subtitles. **101m/C VHS.** *GE* Angelica Domrose, Fritz Hammel; *D:* Susanne Zanke.

The Scorpion's Tail **1971** Graphic murder scenes rev up this early thriller by Martino filmed with plot twists and visual games. Dubbed in English. **90m/C VHS.** *IT SP* Evelyn Stewart, Anita Strindberg, George Hilton, Luigi Pistilli, Janine Reynaud; *D:* Sergio Martino; *W:* Sauro Scavolini, Ernesto Gastaldi; *M:* Bruno Nicolai.

Scotland, PA ½ **2002 (R)** Shakespeare's "Macbeth" meets Mcjobs in director Morrissette's original black comedy set in 1970's rural Pennsylvania. Far from royalty, these McBeths, Slacker Mac (LeGros) and wife Pat (Tierney), are burger flippers at Duncan's, toiling away on minimum wage. At Pat's urging, they off nepotistic restaurant owner Norm Duncan (Rebhorn) after a promotion goes to his two sons. After a fryer "mishap" and a cover-up, the power-hungry couple are then free to have it their way, remodeling the restaurant and changing the name to McBeth's, complete with a (wink-wink) giant M. However, vegetarian cop McDuff (Walken) is assigned to find Duncan's killer. Falls just short of reaching full potential, but Tierney is especially great and the black humor should prove enjoyable for both Shakespeare and non-Shakespeare fans alike. **102m/C VHS, DVD.** *US* Maura Tierney, James LeGros, Christopher Walken, Kevin Corrigan, James Rebhorn, Tom Guiry, Amy Smart, Andy Dick, Josh Pais, Geoff Dunsworth; *D:* Billy Morrissette; *W:* Billy Morrissette; *C:* Wally Pfister; *M:* Anton Sanko.

Scotland Yard Inspector *Lady in the Fog* **1952** An American newspaperman (Romero) in London looks for a killer. Nothing special. **73m/B VHS.** *GB* Cesar Romero, Bernadette O'Farrell; *D:* Sam Newfield.

Scott of the Antarctic ½ **1948** Drama of doomed British expedition of 1911 struggling to be the first group to reach the South Pole. Much of the stunning location filming was shot in the Swiss Alps. Story is authentic, but oddly uninvolving, as though seen from afar. **111m/C VHS.** *GB* John Mills, Christopher Lee, Kenneth More, Derek Bond; *D:* Charles Frend; *C:* Geoffrey Unsworth.

Scott Turow's The Burden of Proof ½ *The Burden of Proof* **1992** Attorney Alejandro "Sandy" Stern (Elizondo) struggles to discover the reasons behind his wife's baffling suicide and deal with the problems caused by the federal investigation of his brother-in-law's commodities business. The character of Stern was also featured in the film "Presumed Innocent" (played by Raul Julia). TV movie; on two cassettes. **184m/C VHS.** Hector Elizondo, Brian Dennehy, Mel Harris, Stefanie Powers, Victoria Principal, Adrienne Barbeau, Anne Bobby, Gail Strickland, Concetta Tomei, Jeffrey Tambor; *D:* Mike Robe; *C:* Kees Van Oostrum.

Scoumoune ½ **1974** The local "fixer" and heavy gets into trouble and no one comes to help. A movie that searches for honesty. Dubbed in English. **87m/C VHS.** *FR* Jean-Paul Belmondo, Claudia Cardinale.

The Scout **1994 (PG-13)** Brooks is an about-to-be-canned scout for the New York Yankees who discovers a weird, though genuine, phenom pitcher (Fraser) on a trip to Mexico. He convinces the Yankees to take the phenom on, though he's not sure whether Fraser isn't a few innings shy of a complete game. But with a 100 mph fast ball and a bat that would have made Babe Ruth envious, who cares? Film straddles sports comedy and melodrama territories, satisfying in neither. Fraser plays variation on Encino Man. Brooks rewrote part of the script, adding much needed biting humor, but not enough. Bombastic real-life team owner Steinbrenner plays himself. **101m/C VHS, DVD, Wide.** Albert Brooks, Brendan Fraser, Dianne Wiest, Lane Smith, Michael Rapaport, Steve Garvey, Bob Costas, Roy Firestone, Anne Twomey, Tony Bennett; *D:* Michael Ritchie; *W:* Albert Brooks, Andrew Bergman, Monica Johnson; *C:* Laszlo Kovacs; *M:* Bill Conti.

Scout's Honor **1980** An orphan (Coleman) is determined to become the best Cub Scout ever when he joins a troop led by an executive who dislikes children. Harmless, enjoyable family tale includes several former child stars as Scout parents. **96m/C VHS.** Gary Coleman, Katherine Helmond, Wilfrid Hyde-White, Pat O'Brien, Joanna Moore, Meeno Peluce, Jay North, Harry (Henry) Morgan, Angela Cartwright; *D:* Henry Levin. **TV**

Scream **1983 (R)** Vacationers on a raft trip down the Rio Grande are terrorized by a mysterious murderer. Hopelessly dull. **86m/C VHS.** Pepper Martin, Hank Worden, Alvy Moore, Woody Strode, John Ethan Wayne; *D:* Byron Quisenberry.

Scream *Scary Movie* **1996 (R)** Director Craven playfully tweaks the cliches of teen slasher pics (which he helped create with "Nightmare on Elm Street") with this tongue-in-cheek thriller. Yep, where there's a mad slasher on the loose, there must be a group of teenagers "just out for a good time." The difference is both the killer and the victims have been raised on '80s splatter movies and, therefore, know all the rules. Sexual activity and/or substance abuse? Start picking out coffins. The stalker uses his cellular phone to terrorize his victims. He also uses it to ask his prey trivia questions or offer critiques of low-grade horror movies. Campbell plays the virginal heroine in the tight sweater, with Ulrich playing opposite as the sexually frustrated boyfriend. More fun than a bucket full of Karo syrup with red dye #3. **111m/C VHS, DVD.** Drew Barrymore, Neve Campbell, Courteney Cox Arquette, David Arquette, Skeet Ulrich, Rose McGowan, Henry Winkler, Liev Schreiber, W. Earl Brown, Jamie Kennedy, Lawrence Hecht; ***Cameos:*** Wes Craven, Linda Blair; *D:* Wes Craven; *W:* Kevin Williamson; *C:* Mark Irwin; *M:* Marco Beltrami. MTV Movie Awards '97: Film.

Scream 2 *Scream Again* **1997 (R)** Sidney (Campbell) trades psychotherapy for college, only to be harassed by a lunatic willing to duplicate her nightmares from the original. All the cast that survived the first pic are back (and some new faces, with O'Connell as Sidney's new boyfriend) including TV-tabloider Gale Weathers (Cox), who has turned a best-seller about the murders into a movie called "Stab"; lovable, huggable sheriff Dewey (Arquette); and horror film fanatic Randy (Kennedy). Director Craven and writer Williamson add more of the satirical spark that propelled its predecessor into boxoffice success. By following the rules of sequels, they increase the suspense (everyone is a suspect) and gore to tantalizing fun, making this entry to the popular franchise a hard one to top. **120m/C VHS, DVD.** Courteney Cox Arquette, Neve Campbell, Jerry O'Connell, David Arquette, Jada Pinkett Smith, Jamie Kennedy, Liev Schreiber, Sarah Michelle Gellar, Laurie Metcalf, Elise Neal, Lewis Arquette, Duane Martin, Omar Epps, David Warner, Timothy Olyphant, Rebecca Gayheart, Portia de Rossi; ***Cameos:*** Tori Spelling, Heather Graham; *D:* Wes Craven; *W:* Kevin Williamson; *C:* Peter Deming; *M:* Marco Beltrami. MTV Movie Awards '98: Female Perf. (Campbell).

Scream 3 ½ **2000 (R)** The filmmakers swear that this series is indeed only a trilogy. Good thing because, while entertaining enough, this third film is showing wear. Sidney is working as a crisis counselor and living in blessed anonymity in northern California. However, the actors involved in "Stab 3" are being offed and it ties in to her mother's mysterious past, so Sid is forced to resurface. Ambitious Gale (Cox Arquette) returns as does dopey Dewey (Arquette) and newcomer LAPD detective Kincaid (Dempsey) tries to figure out if there are any film rules that will help him catch a killer. **116m/C VHS, DVD, Wide.** Neve Campbell, David Arquette, Courteney Cox Arquette, Patrick Dempsey, Scott Foley, Lance Henriksen, Matt Keeslar, Jenny McCarthy, Emily Mortimer, Parker Posey, Deon Richmond, Patrick Warburton, Liev Schreiber, Heather Matarazzo, Jamie Kennedy, Carrie Fisher, Kevin Smith, Jason Mewes, Roger Corman; *D:* Wes Craven; *W:* Ehren Kruger; *C:* Peter Deming; *M:* Marco Beltrami.

Scream and Scream Again ½ *Screamer* **1970 (PG)** Price is a sinister doctor who tries to create a super race of people devoid of emotions. Cushing is the mastermind behind the plot. Lee is the agent investigating a series of murders. Three great horror stars, a psychadelic disco, great '60s fashions; it's all here. **95m/C VHS.** *GB* Vincent Price, Christopher Lee, Peter Cushing, Judy Huxtable, Alfred Marks, Anthony Newlands, Uta Levka, Judi Bloom, Yutte Stensgaard; *D:* Gordon Hessler; *W:* Christopher Wicking; *C:* John Coquillon.

Scream, Baby, Scream *Nightmare House* **1969** An unsuccessful artist switches from sculpting clay to carving young models' faces into hideous deformed creatures. **86m/C VHS.** Ross Harris, Eugenie Wingate, Chris Martell, Suzanne Stuart, Larry Swanson, Brad Grinter; *D:* Joseph Adler.

Scream Blacula Scream **1973 (R)** Blacula returns from his dusty undoing in the original movie to once again suck the blood out of greater Los Angeles. A voodoo priestess (Grier) is the only person with the power to stop him. A weak follow up to the great "Blacula," but worth a look for Marshall and Grier. **96m/C VHS.** William Marshall, Don Mitchell, Pam Grier, Michael Conrad, Richard Lawson, Lynne Moody, Janee Michelle, Barbara Rhoades, Bernie Hamilton; *D:* Bob Kelljan.

Scream Bloody Murder woof! **1972 (R)** A young boy grinds his father to death with a tractor but mangles his own hand trying to jump off. After receiving a steel claw and being released from a mental institution he continues his murderous ways in and around his home town. Inspiring. **90m/C VHS.** Fred Holbert, Leigh Mitchell, Robert Knox, Suzette Hamilton; *D:* Robert Emery.

Scream Dream **1989 (R)** A beautiful rock star uses her supernatural powers to control her fans, turning them into revenge-seeking monsters when she wants to. Heavy on the blood and skin; heavily exploitative. **80m/C VHS.** Melissa Moore, Carole Carr, Nikki Riggins, Jesse Ray; *D:* Donald Farmer; *W:* Donald Farmer.

Scream for Help **1986 (R)** A young girl discovers that her cheating stepfather is plotting to murder her mother, but no one will believe her. Is she paranoid? So bad it's funny; otherwise, it's just bad, and far from suspenseful. **95m/C VHS.** Rachael Kelly, David Brooks, Marie Masters; *D:* Michael Winner; *W:* Tom Holland.

Scream of Fear *Taste of Fear* **1961** A wheelchair-bound young woman goes to visit her father and new stepmother only to find her father is away on business. But she believes she sees her father's corpse. Is someone trying to drive her mad? Abounds in plot twists and mistaken identities. A truly spooky film, suspenseful, and well-made. **81m/B VHS.** *GB* Susan Strasberg, Ronald Lewis, Ann Todd, Christopher Lee; *D:* Seth Holt; *W:* Jimmy Sangster.

Scream of the Demon Lover woof! **1971 (R)** A young biochemist has a busy day as she works for a reclusive Baron. She fantasizes about him, tries to track down a murderer, and eventually discovers a mutant in the cellar. About as bad as they come, but short! **75m/C VHS.** Jennifer Hartley, Jeffrey Chase; *D:* Jose Luis Merino.

Scream of the Wolf **1974** Author and ex-hunter John (Graves) is called on to help the police in their investigation of a series of murders that seem to have been caused by a wolf that can walk on two legs. He turns to Byron (Walker), an old friend and obsessive hunter (think Zaroff in "The Most Dangerous Game") for help, but Byron refuses, arguing that the murders are making the people in the community feel more alive than ever. Byron involves John in a battle of brawn and hunting skill that will ultimately reveal the truth behind the killings. Passable TV movie by director Curtis feels like another attempt to create a "Kolchak: The Night Stalker"-type TV series, complete with Graves's flashy red Corvette, and a jazzy '70s "wokka-chikka" soundtrack. **74m/C VHS, DVD.** Peter Graves, Clint Walker, JoAnn Pflug, Phil Carey, James Storm; *D:* Dan Curtis; *W:* Richard Matheson, David Case; *C:* Paul Lohmann; *M:* Robert Cobert. **TV**

Screamer **1974** A woman wants revenge after she is viciously attacked and raped. Now every man she sees is her attacker as she becomes more and more unbalanced. **71m/C VHS.** Pamela Franklin, Donal McCann.

Screamers *L'Isola Degli Uomini Pesce; Island of the Fishmen; Something Waits in the Dark* **1980 (R)** A mad scientist on a desert island gleefully turns escaped convicts into grotesque monstrosities. Gory and gratuitous. **83m/C VHS.** Richard Johnson, Joseph Cotten, Barbara Bach; *D:* Dan T. Miller, Sergio Martino.

Screamers 🦴🦴 **1996 (R)** In the year 2078, Colonel Joe Hendricksson (Weller) and a small band of survivors fight a civil war on the radiation contaminated planet Sirius 6B. They run up against the screamers—mechanical creatures with razor-sharp claws, originally designed to protect humans. The screamers are bent on destroying all life in the universe while somehow mutating and breeding on their own. Unfortunately, director Duguay doesn't give any indication how this is taking place. Some fine stunt work and special effects redeem standard action adventure. Based on the novella "Second Variety" by Philip K. Dick ("Blade Runner"). **107m/C VHS, DVD.** Peter Weller, Jennifer Rubin, Andrew Lauer, Charles Powell, Ron White, Michael Caloz; ***D:*** Christian Duguay; ***W:*** Dan O'Bannon, Miguel Tejada-Flores; ***C:*** Rodney Gibbons; ***M:*** Normand Corbeil.

The Screaming Dead 🦴 *Dracula vs. Frankenstein* **1972** Monsters rise from the tomb to do battle with planet Earth and each other. Not to be confused with the Al Adamson epic "Dracula vs. Frankenstein." **84m/C VHS.** *SP* Dennis Price, Howard Vernon, Alberto Dalbes, Mary Francis, Genevieve Deloir, Josianne Gibert, Fernando Bilbao; ***D:*** Jess (Jesus) Franco.

The Screaming Skull 🦴½ **1958** Man redecorates house with skulls in attempt to drive already anxious wife insane. **68m/B VHS, DVD, Wide.** William (Bill) Hudson, Peggy Webber, Toni Johnson, Russ Conway, Alex Nicol; ***D:*** Alex Nicol; ***M:*** Ernest Gold.

Screams of a Winter Night 🦴 **1979 (PG)** Ghostly tale of an evil monster from the lake and the terror he causes. **92m/C VHS.** Matt Borel, Gil Glasco; ***D:*** Philippe Mora; ***W:*** Philippe Mora.

Screamtime 🦴 **1983 (R)** Two fiendish friends filch a trilogy of horror tapes for home viewing. After the show, real scary things happen. **89m/C VHS.** Jean Anderson, Robin Bailey, Dora Bryan, David Van Day; ***D:*** Al Beresford.

Screen Test woof! **1985 (R)** Oversexed silly teenagers arrange fake screen tests in order to meet girls. **84m/C VHS.** Michael Allan Bloom, Robert Bundy, Paul Lueken, David Simpatico, Cynthia Kahn, Mari Laskarin, Katherine Sullivan, Monique Gabrielle, Michelle (McClellan) Bauer, Tracey Adams; ***D:*** Sam Auster; ***W:*** Sam Auster; ***C:*** Jeffrey Jur.

Screw Loose 🦴🦴 *Svitati* **1999 (R)** Bernardo's (Greggio) dying father (Barra) has one last request—he wants a reunion with his American WWII buddy Jake (Brooks). So being a dutiful son, Bernardo comes to America and discovers Jake is in an L.A. mental institution. Nevertheless, he breaks him out and flies Jake back to Italy with him—followed by Jake's doctor, Barbara (Condra). And it turns out maybe Jake isn't the only one with a few loose screws. Slapsticky, with a weak script. **85m/C VHS, DVD, Wide.** *IT* Mel Brooks, Ezio Greggio, Gianfranco Barra, Julie Condra, Randi Ingerman; ***D:*** Ezio Greggio; ***W:*** Rudy DeLuca, Steve Haberman; ***C:*** Luca Robecchi.

Screwball Academy 🦴½ **1986 (R)** A beautiful female director makes a soft-core film on a secluded island, and gets trouble from thugs, evangelists, horny crew members and others. Former "SCTV" director John Blanchard understandably used a pseudonym to direct this lame effort. **90m/C VHS.** Colleen Camp, Kenneth Welsh, Christine Cattall; ***D:*** Reuben Rose.

Screwballs 🦴 **1983 (R)** Freewheeling group of high school boys stirs up trouble for their snooty and virginal homecoming queen. Another inept teen sex comedy with no subtlety whatsoever. Sequel: "Loose Screws." **80m/C VHS.** Peter Keleghan, Lynda Speciale; ***D:*** Rafal Zielinski; ***W:*** Jim Wynorski.

Screwed woof! **2000 (PG-13)** Chauffeur MacDonald tries kidnapping his mean boss's dog for ransom but things get screwed up so badly that the boss thinks it's the chauffeur that's been kidnapped. Lame physical and gross-out "comedy" ensues. Just who the title refers to is never made clear, but it seems like it's the producers, who had to pay the actors and writer/directors for this, ahem, dog. DeVito is the only one on screen who seems to know what he's doing, and Alexander and Karaszewski look to be cashing in on some far superior prior screenwriting work. **82m/C VHS, DVD, Wide.** Norm MacDonald, Elaine Stritch, Danny DeVito, Dave Chappelle, Daniel Benzali, Sherman Hemsley, Malcolm Stewart; ***D:*** Scott M. Alexander, Larry Karaszewski; ***W:*** Scott M. Alexander, Larry Karaszewski; ***C:*** Robert Brinkmann; ***M:*** Michel Colombier.

Scrooge 🦴🦴🦴 **1935** On Christmas Eve a miser changes his ways after receiving visits from the ghosts of Christmas past, present, and future. Co-scripter Hicks gives an interesting performance as Ebeneezer Scrooge. Based on the classic novel "A Christmas Carol" by Charles Dickens. **61m/B VHS, DVD.** *GB* Sir Seymour Hicks, Maurice Evans, Robert Cochran, Donald Calthrop, Mary Glynne, Oscar Asche; ***D:*** Henry Edwards; ***W:*** Sir Seymour Hicks; ***C:*** Sydney Blythe, William Luff.

Scrooge 🦴🦴½ **1970 (G)** Well done musical version of Charles Dickens' classic "A Christmas Carol," about a miserly old man who is faced with ghosts on Christmas Eve. Finney is memorable in the title role. ♫The Beautiful Day; Happiness; Thank You Very Much; A Christmas Carol; Christmas Children; I Hate People; Farver Chris'mas; See the Phantoms; December the 25th. **86m/C VHS.** *GB* Albert Finney, Alec Guinness, Edith Evans, Kenneth More; ***D:*** Ronald Neame; ***W:*** Leslie Bricusse; ***C:*** Oswald Morris; ***M:*** Leslie Bricusse. Golden Globes '71: Actor—Mus./Comedy (Finney).

Scrooged 🦴🦴 **1988 (PG-13)** Somewhat disjointed big-budgeted version of the hallowed classic. A callous TV executive staging "A Christmas Carol" is himself visited by the three ghosts and sees the light. Kane is terrific as one of the ghosts. Film is heavy-handed, Murray too sardonic to be believable. **101m/C VHS, DVD, 8mm, Wide.** Mary Ellen Trainor, Bill Murray, Carol Kane, John Forsythe, David Johansen, Bob(cat) Goldthwait, Karen Allen, Michael J. Pollard, Brian Doyle-Murray, Alfre Woodard, John Glover, Robert Mitchum, Buddy Hackett, Robert Goulet, Jamie Farr, Mary Lou Retton, Lee Majors; ***D:*** Richard Donner; ***W:*** Mitch Glazer, Michael O'Donoghue; ***C:*** Michael Chapman; ***M:*** Danny Elfman.

Scrubbers 🦴 **1982 (R)** Young girl is sent to reform school where she's forced to survive in a cruel and brutal environment. Low-budget "reform school" movie with no point, but lots of lesbianism. **93m/C VHS.** *GB* Amanda York, Chrissie Cotterill, Elizabeth Edmonds, Kate Ingram, Debbie Bishop, Dana Gillespie; ***D:*** Mai Zetterling.

Scruffy **1980** An orphan and his dog survive with the help of two crooks who are reformed through their love for the little boy. Animated. **72m/C VHS.** ***V:*** Alan Young, June Foray, Hans Conried, Nancy McKeon.

Scruples 🦴🦴½ **1980** Set in the glamorous, jet-setting world of Beverly Hills, this top-rated miniseries follows the career of Billy Ikehorn (Wagner) as she weds a wealthy industrialist and opens a clothing boutique named "Scruples." She caters to high society's haute couture, and encounters unscrupulous individuals who threaten to dethrone her from her position of power and privilege. Based on the best-selling novel by Judith Krantz. **279m/C VHS.** Lindsay Wagner, Barry Bostwick, Kim Cattrall, Gavin MacLeod, Connie Stevens, Efrem Zimbalist Jr., Gene Tierney; ***M:*** Charles Bernstein.

The Sculptress 🦴🦴 **1997** Troubled writer Rosalind Leigh (Goodall) prepares to interview convicted killer Olive Martin (Quirke), who five years before was found with the dead bodies of her mother and sister. Nicknamed "The Sculptress" for the gruesome nature of the murders, the equally troubled Olive is also a convincing liar. Although Olive says she's guilty, Roz is certain she's hiding something and becomes determined to discover the truth. Very creepy. Made for British TV; based on the novel by Minette Walters. **180m/C VHS.** *GB* Caroline Goodall, Pauline Quirke, Christopher Fulford, Dermot Crowley, David Horovitch, Jay Villiers, Lynda Rooke; ***D:*** Stuart Orme; ***W:*** Reg Gadney; ***C:*** Gavin Finney; ***M:*** Colin Towns. **TV**

Scum 🦴🦴🦴 **1979** Adapted from Roy Minton's acclaimed play, this British production looks at the struggle among three young men in a British Borstal (a prison for young convicts.) Portrays the physical, sexual, and psychological violence committed. Horrifying and powerful. **96m/C VHS.** *GB* Phil Daniels, Mick Ford, Ray Winstone; ***D:*** Alan Clarke.

Scum of the Earth 🦴½ **1963** Early '60s skin flick about innocent young Kim (Miles), who is cruelly tricked into posing topless for a photographer and is then blackmailed into a downward spiral of sleaze that ends in murder and suicide. The film features much of the cast and crew of director Lewis's "Blood Feast." **73m/B DVD.** Vicki (Allison Louise Downe) Miles, Lawrence Wood, Mal Arnold, Thomas Sweetwood, Sandy Sinclair; ***D:*** Herschell Gordon Lewis; ***W:*** Herschell Gordon Lewis.

Sea Chase 🦴🦴½ **1955** An odd post-war sea adventure, wherein a renegade German freighter captain is pursued by British and German navies as he leaves Australia at the outbreak of WWII. A Prussian Wayne rivaled only by his infamous Genghis Khan in "The Conqueror" for strange character selection. Turner is on board as Wayne's girlfriend. **117m/C VHS, Wide.** John Wayne, Lana Turner, Tab Hunter, James Arness, Lyle Bettger, David Farrar, Richard (Dick) Davalos, Claude Akins, John Qualen; ***D:*** John Farrow; ***C:*** William Clothier.

Sea Devils 🦴 **1931** Sentenced to prison for a crime he didn't commit, a man escapes and joins a boatload of treasure hunters, but mutiny is afoot. Don't get soaked by this cheapie. **77m/B VHS.** Walter Long, Edmund Burns, Henry Otto, James Donnelly; ***D:*** Joseph Levering.

Sea Devils 🦴🦴 **1937** The tale of a sea captain and his lovely daughter who have differing opinions on whom she should marry. While her father would like her to marry a tame gentlemen under his command, she has her heart set on another beau. Sound predictable? It is, but fun. **88m/B VHS.** Victor McLaglen, Preston Foster, Ida Lupino, Donald Woods, Gordon Jones; ***D:*** Ben Stoloff.

Sea Devils 🦴🦴 **1953** A smuggler and a beautiful spy come together during the Napoleonic Wars in this sea romance filled with intrigue and adventure. **86m/C VHS.** *GB* Rock Hudson, Yvonne De Carlo, Maxwell Reed; ***D:*** Raoul Walsh.

Sea Gypsies 🦴🦴 **1978 (G)** A sailing crew of five is shipwrecked off the Aleutian Islands. They must escape before winter or learn to survive. Passable family drama. **101m/C VHS.** Robert F. Logan, Mikki Jamison-Olsen, Heather Rattray, Cjon Damitri; ***D:*** Stewart Raffill; ***W:*** Stewart Raffill.

The Sea Hawk 🦴🦴🦴½ **1940** An English privateer learns the Spanish are going to invade England with their Armada. After numerous adventures, he is able to aid his queen and help save his country, finding romance along the way. One of Flynn's swashbuckling best. Available colorized. **128m/B VHS.** Errol Flynn, Claude Rains, Donald Crisp, Alan Hale, Flora Robson, Brenda Marshall, Henry Daniell, Gilbert Roland, James Stephenson, Una O'Connor; ***D:*** Michael Curtiz; ***W:*** Howard Koch.

Sea Hound **1947** A 15-part series set in the late 1940s that charts the voyage of a group of pirates searching for buried treasure. Everything goes well until Crabbe emerges to wreck their hopes. **?m/B VHS.** Buster Crabbe, Jimmy Lloyd, Pamela Blake, Ralph Hodges, Bob Barron; ***D:*** Walter B. Eason, Mack V. Wright.

Sea Lion 🦴🦴 **1921** A vicious sea captain, embittered by a past romance, becomes sadistic and intolerable, until the truth emerges. Lots of action, but plodding, rehashed plot. Silent. **50m/B VHS.** Hobart Bosworth.

Sea of Dreams 🦴 **1990** Don't expect much in the way of a script from this soft-core production. **80m/C VHS.** Jon Rodgers, Chad Scott, Jacky Peel, Renee O'Neil.

Sea of Love 🦴🦴🦴½ **1989 (R)** A tough, tightly wound thriller about an alcoholic cop with a mid-life crisis. While following the track of a serial killer, he begins a torrid relationship with one of his suspects. Pacino doesn't stand a chance when Barkin heats up the screen. **113m/C VHS, DVD, Wide.** Al Pacino, Ellen Barkin, John Goodman, Michael Rooker, William Hickey, Richard Jenkins; ***D:*** Harold Becker; ***W:*** Richard Price; ***C:*** Ronnie Taylor; ***M:*** Trevor Jones.

Sea of Sand 🦴🦴½ *Desert Patrol* **1958** Typical actioner set in WWII finds a British desert patrol's latest mission is to blow up Rommel's fuel supply before the battle of El Alamein. Lots of heroics against the Nazis and stiff upper lips. **97m/B VHS.** *GB* Richard Attenborough, John Gregson, Michael Craig, Vincent Ball, Ray McAnally; ***D:*** Guy Green; ***W:*** Robert Westerby; ***C:*** Wilkie Cooper; ***M:*** Clifton Parker.

Sea People 🦴🦴 **2000** Teen swimmer Amanda (Moss) rescues elderly John McRae (Cronyn) after he leaps from a bridge into the water. But she discovers that John wasn't trying to commit suicide and that he and his wife, Bridget (Gregson), have a very unique relationship with the sea. **92m/C VHS, DVD.** Hume Cronyn, Tegan Moss, Joan Gregson, Ron Lea, Don McKellar, Cedric Smith; ***D:*** Vic Sarin. **CABLE**

Sea Racketeers 🦴½ **1937** Soggy old tribute to the Coast Guard inadvertently makes them look like a bunch of bumblers, as they belatedly uncover a fur-smuggling racket working under their noses from a floating nightclub. **64m/B VHS.** Weldon Heyburn, Jeanne Madden, Warren Hymer, Dorothy McNulty, J. Carrol Naish, Joyce Compton, Charles Trowbridge, Syd Saylor, Lane Chandler, Benny Burt; ***D:*** Hamilton MacFadden.

The Sea Serpent 🦴½ **1985** A young sea captain and a crusty scientist unite to search out a giant sea monster awakened by atomic tests. Not one of Milland's better films. **92m/C VHS.** *SP* Timothy Bottoms, Ray Milland, Jared Martin; ***D:*** Gregory Greens.

The Sea Shall Not Have Them 🦴🦴½ **1955** A British bomber crashes into the North Sea during WWII. Film tells of the survivors' rescue by the Air-Sea Rescue Unit. Decent drama/adventure. **92m/B VHS.** Michael Redgrave, Dirk Bogarde; ***D:*** Lewis Gilbert; ***M:*** Malcolm Arnold.

The Sea Wolf 🦴🦴🦴½ **1941** Jack London's adventure novel about brutal, canny Captain Wolf Larsen (Robinson), his rebellious crew, and some unexpected passengers. Knox and Lupino are shipwreck survivors, picked up by Robinson and forced into working aboard his ship, the aptly named "Ghost." Crewman Garfield falls for Lupino and tries to rally his shipmates into resisting the meglomaniacal Robinson. Fine performances by all, especially Robinson as the personification of malevolent ego. Screen debut of Knox. Director Curtiz filmed entirely in studio tanks, sets, and pervasive fog machines. Previously filmed three times; later remade as "Barricade" and "Wolf Larsen." **90m/C VHS.** Edward G. Robinson, Alexander Knox, John Garfield, Ida Lupino, Gene Lockhart, Barry Fitzgerald, Stanley Ridges, Francis McDonald, David Bruce, Howard da Silva, Frank Lackteen, Ralf Harolde; ***D:*** Michael Curtiz; ***W:*** Robert Rossen.

The Sea Wolf 🦴🦴 **1993** Yet another adaptation of Jack London's classic battle of wills tale. Captain Wolf Larsen (Bronson) commands a surly ship of seal hunters through sheer ruthlessness and ego. He rescues snobbish theatre critic Van Weyden (Reeve) and pretty scam artist Flaxen (Stewart) from a capsized ferry. The self-educated captain wants to test out his theories about survival of the fittest by making the rich Van Weyden his cabin boy (Flaxen gets leered at). Lots of teeth-gnashing and bellowing in this turgid TV remake, although Revill has fun as the sniveling Cookie. See the Edward G. Robinson version instead. **120m/C VHS.** Charles Bronson, Christopher Reeve, Catherine Mary Stewart, Clive Revill; ***D:*** Michael Anderson Sr.; ***W:*** Andrew J. Fenady; ***M:*** Charles Bernstein.

Sea Wolves 🦴🦴½ **1981 (PG)** True WWII story about a commando-style operation undertaken by a group of middle-aged, retired British cavalrymen in India in 1943. Decent acting, though Peck's British accent fades in and out, with Moore as Bond. **120m/C VHS, DVD, Wide.** *GB* Gregory Peck, Roger Moore, David Niven, Trevor Howard, Patrick Macnee; ***D:*** Andrew V. McLaglen; ***W:*** Reginald Rose.

The Seagull **1971** A pensive, sensitive adaptation of the famed Chekhov play about the depressed denizens of an isolated country estate. In Russian with English subtitles. **99m/B VHS.** Alla Demidova, Lyudmila Savelyeva, Yuri Yakovlev; ***D:*** Yuri Karasik.

Seance on a Wet Afternoon ½ **1964** Dark, thoughtful film about a crazed pseudo-psychic who coerces her husband into a kidnapping so she can gain recognition by divining the child's whereabouts. Directed splendidly by Forbes, and superb acting from Stanley and Attenborough, who co-produced with Forbes. **111m/B VHS.** *GB* Kim Stanley, Richard Attenborough, Margaret Lacey, Maria Kazan, Mark Eden, Patrick Magee; ***D:*** Bryan Forbes; ***M:*** John Barry. British Acad. '64: Actor (Attenborough); Natl. Bd. of Review '64: Actress (Stanley); N.Y. Film Critics '64: Actress (Stanley).

The Search ½ **1948** Clift, an American solider stationed in post-WWII Berlin, befriends a homeless nine-year-old amnesiac boy (Jandl) and tries to find his family. Meanwhile, his mother has been searching the Displaced Persons camps for her son. Although Clift wants to adopt the boy, he steps aside, and mother and son are finally reunited. "The Search" was shot on location in the American Occupied Zone of Germany. Jandl won a special juvenile Oscar in his first (and only) film role. This was also Clift's first screen appearance, although this movie was actually filmed after his debut in "Red River," it was released first. **105m/B VHS.** Montgomery Clift, Aline MacMahon, Ivan Jandl, Jarmila Novotna, Wendell Corey; ***D:*** Fred Zinnemann; ***W:*** Paul Jarrico. Oscars '48: Story; Golden Globes '49: Screenplay.

Search and Destroy *Striking Back* **1981 (PG)** Deadly vendetta is begun by a Vietnamese official during the war. It is continued in the U.S. as he hunts down the American soldiers he feels betrayed him. Sub-par, forgettable war/action flick. **93m/C VHS.** Perry King, Don Stroud, Park Jong Soo, George Kennedy, Tisa Farrow; ***D:*** William Fruet.

Search and Destroy **1988 (R)** Sci-fi action flick about the capture of a secret biological warfare research station. Lotsa action, that's for sure—where's the plot? **87m/C VHS, DVD.** Stuart Garrison Day, Dan Kuchuck, Peggy Jacobsen; ***D:*** J. Christian Ingvordsen; ***W:*** J. Christian Ingvordsen; ***C:*** Steven Kaman; ***M:*** Chris Burke.

Search and Destroy **1994 (R)** Complex story finds bankrupt businessman Martin Mirkheim (Dunne) trying to overcome his financial woes by making a film based on a book by self-help guru, Dr. Luther Waxling (Hopper). Of course, since Martin's broke, he first has to find someone willing to invest in his venture, and the shady duo (Walken and Turturro) he does just leave him with more problems. Tediously stagy adaptation of Howard Korders' play. Directorial debut by artist Salle at least looks great and provides some quirky moments. **91m/C VHS, DVD.** Griffin Dunne, Dennis Hopper, Rosanna Arquette, Christopher Walken, John Turturro, Illeana Douglas, Ethan Hawke; ***Cameos:*** Martin Scorsese; ***D:*** David Salle; ***W:*** Michael Almereyda; ***C:*** Michael Spiller, Bobby Bukowski; ***M:*** Elmer Bernstein.

The Search for Bridey Murphy **1956** Long before channelers, Ramtha and New-Age profiteers, there was a Colorado housewife who under hypnosis described a previous life as an Irish girl. Her famous claim was never proven—but that didn't stop this well-acted but dull dramatization. Neither sensationalist, nor likely to persuade skeptics. Based on the book by Morey Bernstein, hypnotist in the case. **84m/B VHS.** Teresa Wright, Louis Hayward, Nancy Gates, Kenneth Tobey, Richard Anderson; ***D:*** Noel Langley; ***W:*** Noel Langley.

The Search for One-Eyed Jimmy **1996 (R)** Good-natured slice-of-life comedy about lowlife friends in the Brooklyn neighborhood of Red Hook. Film school grad Les (McCallany) returns to his old stomping grounds to make a documentary and decides missing local character Jimmy (Rockwell) will be his topic. Only no one except Jimmy's parents seem really concerned and Les' friends are such dimwits that they couldn't find a hole in the ground anyway. **86m/C VHS.** Holt McCallany, Nicholas Turturro, Steve Buscemi, Michael Badalucco, Ray "Boom Boom" Mancini, Anne Meara, John Turturro, Samuel L. Jackson, Sam Rockwell; ***D:*** Sam Henry Kass; ***W:*** Sam Henry Kass; ***C:*** Charles Levey; ***M:*** William Bloom.

Search for Signs of Intelligent Life in the Universe **1991 (PG-13)** Tomlin's brilliant one-woman show has been expanded into a wonderful film. As Tomlin's cast of 12 female and male characters meet and interact, they show every viewer his/her own humanity. **120m/C VHS.** Lily Tomlin; ***D:*** John Bailey; ***W:*** Jane Wagner; ***M:*** Jerry Goodman.

Search for the Gods ½ **1975** A dig in the Southwest turns interesting when one of the archeologists comes across an exquisite ancient medallion that could answer questions about alien visitors. Pilot for a TV series that didn't make it. **100m/C VHS.** Kurt Russell, Stephen McHattie, Ralph Bellamy, Victoria Racimo, Raymond St. Jacques; ***D:*** Jud Taylor. **TV**

The Searchers **1956** The classic Ford western, starring John Wayne as a hard-hearted frontiersman who spends years doggedly pursuing his niece, who was kidnapped by Indians. A simple western structure supports Ford's most moving, mysterious, complex film. Many feel this is the best western of all time. **119m/C VHS, DVD, Wide.** John Wayne, Jeffrey Hunter, Vera Miles, Natalie Wood, Ward Bond, John Qualen, Harry Carey Jr., Olive Carey, Antonio Moreno, Henry (Kleinbach) Brandon, Hank Worden, Lana Wood, Dorothy Jordan, Patrick Wayne; ***D:*** John Ford; ***W:*** Frank Nugent; ***C:*** Winton C. Hoch; ***M:*** Max Steiner. AFI '98: Top 100, Natl. Film Reg. '89.

Searching for Bobby Fischer ½ **1993 (PG)** Seven-year-old Josh Waitzkin (Pomeranc, in his debut) shows an amazing gift for chess, stunning his parents, who must then try to strike the delicate balance of developing his abilities while also allowing him a "normal" childhood. Excellent cast features Mantegna and Allen as his parents, Kingsley as demanding chess teacher Pandolfini, and Fishburne as an adept speed-chess hustler. Pomeranc is great, and his knowledge of chess (he's a ranked player) brings authenticity to his role. Title comes from Pandolfini's belief that Josh may equal the abilities of chess whiz Bobby Fischer. Underrated little gem based on a true story and adapted from the book by Waitzkin's father. **111m/C VHS, DVD, Wide.** Joe Mantegna, Max Pomeranc, Joan Allen, Ben Kingsley, Laurence "Larry" Fishburne, Robert Stephens, David Paymer, William H. Macy, Hal Scardino; ***D:*** Steven Zaillian; ***W:*** Steven Zaillian; ***C:*** Conrad L. Hall; ***M:*** James Horner. MTV Movie Awards '94: New Filmmaker (Zaillian).

Seaside Swingers ½ *Every Day's a Holiday* **1965** A group of teenagers at a seaside resort work to win a talent competition on TV. But where is the talent? Dumb teen romance comedy with accidental plot. ♫All I Want Is You; A Girls Needs a Boy; Second Time Around; Indubitably Me; Love Me, Please; Now, Ain't That Somethin'—Caw Blimey; Romeo Jones; What's Cookin. **94m/C VHS.** *GB* Michael Sarne, Grazina Frame, John Leyton; ***D:*** James Hill.

Season for Assassins ½ **1971** Police commissioner Castroni is the only man who can stop a wave of violence enveloping Rome. **102m/C VHS.** Joe Dallesandro, Martin Balsam.

A Season for Miracles ½ **1999** Because their drug-addict mother, Berry (Dern), is in jail, Alanna (Whitman) and younger brother J.T. (Sabara) are about to be placed in foster care. Instead, they go on the lam with their devoted Aunt Emilie (Gugino), whose car breaks down in the quaint community of Bethlehem (hey, it's a Christmas movie!). The family are taken under the eccentric wing of a diner waitress (Duke) and the trio warily settle in—with Emilie even drawing the romantic interest of handsome cop Nathan (Conrad). Of course, trouble comes calling when their secret is exposed. (It's Christmas—there's a happy ending.) Adapted from the book by Marilyn Papano. **90m/C VHS.** Carla Gugino, David Conrad, Kathy Baker, Laura Dern, Patty Duke, Lynn Redgrave, Mae Whitman, Evan Sabara, Faith Prince, Mary Louise Wilson; ***D:*** Michael Pressman; ***W:*** Maria Nation; ***C:*** Shelly Johnson; ***M:*** Craig Safan. **TV**

Season of Change ½ **1994** Tepid coming of age saga set in rural Montana, circa 1946. Thirteen-year-old Sally Mae (Tom) notices the tensions between her Bible-bound mother (Anderson) and war vet dad (Madsen), who's worried about finding a job to support his family. Sally Mae tries to understand all these adult notions even as she herself becomes attracted to teen mechanic Bobby (Randall). Cliched script and awkward performances don't help. **93m/C VHS.** Nicholle Tom, Michael Madsen, Jo Anderson, Hoyt Axton, Ethan (Randall) Embry; ***D:*** Robin Murray; ***W:*** Shirley Hillard.

Season of Fear ½ **1989 (R)** A young man visits his estranged father's home. Abandoned as a child, he's embroiled in a murder scheme engineered by his father's beautiful young wife. Intriguing premise, forgettable execution. **89m/C VHS.** Michael Bowen, Clancy Brown, Clare Wren, Ray Wise, Michael J. Pollard; ***D:*** Doug Campbell; ***W:*** Doug Campbell.

Season of the Witch ½ *Hungry Wives; Jack's Wife* **1973 (R)** A frustrated housewife becomes intrigued with a neighboring witch and begins to practice witchcraft herself, through murder and seduction. Meant to be suspenseful, thrilling, and topical, it is none of these. Poorly acted at best. Originally 130 minutes! **89m/C** Jan White, Ray Laine, Bill Thunhurst, Joedda McClain, Virginia Greenwald, Ann Muffly, Neil Fisher, Esther Lapidus, Dan Mallinger, Ken Peters; ***D:*** George A. Romero; ***W:*** George A. Romero; ***C:*** George A. Romero.

Sebastian ½ *Mr. Sebastian* **1968** Mathematics whiz is employed by the British to decipher codes. He falls in love with York, another code breaker, and becomes involved in international intrigue. A bit too fast-paced and busy, but enjoyable spy drama. Sutherland has a small role. **100m/C VHS.** *GB* Dirk Bogarde, Susannah York, Lilli Palmer, John Gielgud, Margaret Johnston, Nigel Davenport, Donald Sutherland; ***D:*** David Greene; ***M:*** Jerry Goldsmith.

Sebastiane **1979** An audacious film version of the legend of St. Sebastian, packed with homoerotic imagery and ravishing visuals. Honest, faithful rendering of the Saint's life and refusal to obey Roman authorities. Jarman's first film, in Latin with English subtitles. **90m/C VHS.** *GB* Leonardo Treviglio, Barney James, Richard James, Neil Kennedy, Richard Warwick, Lindsay Kemp; ***D:*** Derek Jarman, Paul Humfress; ***W:*** Derek Jarman, Paul Humfress; ***C:*** Peter Middleton; ***M:*** Brian Eno.

The Second Awakening of Christa Klages *Das Zweite Erwachen der Christa Klages* **1978** Young divorced mother Christa (Engel) decides to finance her money-troubled day-care center by robbing a bank with her lover Werner (Muller-Westernhagen). Werner's killed and Christa becomes a fugitive, taking refuge with her friend Ingrid (Reize). German with subtitles. **90m/C VHS.** *GE* Tina Engel, Sylvia Reize, Marius Muller-Westernhagen, Peter Schneider, Katharina Thalbach; ***D:*** Margarethe von Trotta; ***W:*** Margarethe von Trotta, Luisa Francia; ***C:*** Franz Rath; ***M:*** Klaus Doldinger.

Second Best **1994 (PG-13)** Quiet, intimate drama about a lonely Welsh postmaster (Hurt) who decides to adopt a son (Miles). James, the 11-year-old boy he considers adopting, comes from a troubled background and is prone to violent outbursts. Graham, the village postmaster, is dealing with emotional demons of his own, and his problems are interwoven with those of the deprived, temperamental James. Although Hurt seems miscast as a shy, middle-aged Welshman, he turns in one of the best performances of his career. Richly acted and flawlessly directed, Menges has created a convincing and effective father-son drama. Based on David Cook's novel. **105m/C VHS.** *GB* William Hurt, Chris Cleary Miles, Keith Allen, Prunella Scales, Jane Horrocks, Alan Cumming, John Hurt; ***D:*** Chris Menges; ***W:*** David Cook; ***M:*** Simon Boswell.

Second Best Secret Agent in the Whole Wide World ½ *Licensed to Kill* **1965** A klutzy agent attempts to prevent a Swedish anti-gravity formula from falling into Russian hands. Surprisingly good early spoof of the James Bond genre. **93m/C VHS.** *GB* Tom Adams, Veronica Hurst, Peter Bull, Karel Stepanek, John Arnatt; ***D:*** Lindsay Shonteff.

Second Chance ½ **1953** A former prizefighter (Mitchum) travels to Mexico where he protects a gangster's moll (Darnell) targeted for murder. But Palance is on their tail. Originally released theatrically on a wide screen in 3-D. Good melodrama. **82m/C VHS.** Robert Mitchum, Linda Darnell, Jack Palance, Reginald (Reggie, Reggy) Sheffield, Roy Roberts; ***D:*** Rudolph Mate.

Second Chance **1980** When a woman finds her husband is in love with another, her marital happiness is shattered. She leaves her betrayer and struggles to adapt to life as a single mother. **270m/C VHS.** *GB* Susannah York, Ralph Bates; ***D:*** Gerry Mill, Richard Handford. **TV**

Second Chances ½ **1998** Think a family version of "The Horse Whisperer." 10-year-old Sunny is left unable to walk without crutches after a car accident and becomes emotionally withdrawn. She and her mom move next door to former rodeo champ Ben Taylor and Sunny develops a rapport with both Ben and a crippled horse named Ginger. **107m/C VHS.** Tom Amandes, Kelsey Mulrooney, Isabel Glasser, Stuart Whitman, Theodore Bikel, Terry Moore, Madeline Zima; ***D:*** James Fargo. **VIDEO**

Second Chorus ½ **1940** Rivalry of two trumpet players for a girl and a job with Artie Shaw Orchestra. Music, dance, and romance. Nothing great, but pleasant. ♫Would You Like to Be the Love of My Life?; Poor Mr. Chisholm; (I Ain't Hep to That Step) But I'll Dig It; Swing Concerto; Sweet Sue; I'm Yours. **83m/B VHS.** Fred Astaire, Paulette Goddard, Burgess Meredith, Artie Shaw, Charles Butterworth; ***D:*** H.C. Potter.

The Second Civil War ½ **1997 (R)** Political satire falls apart at the end but until then manages to provide some dark comedy. In the near future, Idaho Governor Farley (Bridges) closes his state's borders to a planeload of refugee children from a Pakistan-India nuclear war. The President (Hartman), who wants to look tough, gives Farley 72 hours to change his mind and the media, led by executive producer Mel Burgess (Hedaya), goes into a typical frenzy. **105m/C VHS.** Beau Bridges, Phil Hartman, James Coburn, Dan Hedaya, Elizabeth Pena, Kevin Dunn, Denis Leary, James Earl Jones, Ron Perlman, Joanna Cassidy; ***D:*** Joe Dante; ***W:*** Martyn Burke; ***C:*** Mac Ahlberg; ***M:*** Hummie Mann. **CABLE**

Second Coming of Suzanne ½ **1980** Young actress encounters a hypnotic film director. Her role: to star in a crucifixion—which may be more real than she imagines. Winner of two international film festivals. **90m/C VHS.** Sondra Locke, Richard Dreyfuss, Gene Barry, Paul Sand, Jared Martin; ***D:*** Michael Barry; ***W:*** Michael Barry; ***C:*** Isidore Mankofsky.

Second Fiddle ½ *Irving Berlin's Second Fiddle* **1939** Power is a studio flack who's hired to mount a huge talent search for a girl to star in a new film epic (very clear parallels to the Scarlett O'Hara "Gone With the Wind" hunt). He's sent to smalltown Minnesota where he meets Henie, who lives with her forbidding aunt (Oliver), who doesn't want her niece to go to wicked Hollywood. Nevertheless, Henie gets the part, becomes a success, and falls for her co-star Vallee. But it's all a publicity stunt on his part and Power is the one who really loves the girl. Henie gets to do some skating. ♫Back to Back; I'm Sorry for Myself; I Poured My Heart Into Song; An Old-Fashioned Tune is Always New; When Winter Comes; Song of the Metronome. **86m/B VHS.** Sonja Henie, Tyrone Power, Rudy Vallee, Edna May Oliver, Mary Healy, Lyle Talbot, Alan Dinehart, Minna Gombell; ***D:*** Sidney Lanfield; ***W:*** Harry Tugend; ***M:*** Irving Berlin.

Second Sight ✌ **1989 (PG)** A detective (Larroquette) and a goofy psychic (Pinchot) set out to find a kidnapped priest. Flick is sidetracked along the way by such peculiarities as a pixieish nun for romantic, not religious, intrigue. Remember this one? No? That's because you blinked when it was released to theatres. Eminently missable. **84m/C VHS.** Dominic Chianese, John Larroquette, Bronson Pinchot, Bess Armstrong, James Tolkan, Christine Estabrook, Cornelia Guest, Stuart Pankin, William Prince, John Schuck; ***D:*** Joel Zwick; ***W:*** Patricia Resnick, Tom Schulman.

Second Sight ✌✌✌ **1999** Hard-charging Detective Chief Inspector Ross Tanner (Owen) is called to investigate the murder of a college student who was beaten to death within yards of his family's home. But beyond the murder, Tanner has a serious personal problem—a rare eye disease is causing him to go blind. Trying to keep his condition a secret, Tanner is forced to rely on new Detective Inspector Catherine Tully (Skinner), who has her own reasons for keeping quiet. **180m/C VHS.** *GB* Clive Owen, Claire Skinner, Stuart Wilson, Phoebe Nicholls, Tom Mullion, Louise Atkins, Eddie Marsan, Rebecca Egan, Benjamin Smith; ***D:*** Charles Beeson; ***W:*** Paula Milne; ***C:*** Richard Maidment. **TV**

Second Skin ✌✌½ **2000 (R)** Sam Kane (MacFayden) falls in love with Crystal (Henstridge), who's suffering from amnesia after a car crash. Sam tries to help her out and Crystal remembers that she and Sam have a previous and dangerous connection. **91m/C VHS, DVD, Wide.** Angus Macfadyen, Natasha Henstridge, Peter Fonda, Liam Waite; ***D:*** Darrell Roodt.

Second Thoughts ✌ **1983 (PG)** Frustrated woman attorney divorces her stuffy husband and takes up with an aging hippie. She comes to regret her decision when it becomes obvious that her new man has his head firmly stuck in the 60s. Comedy-drama lacking real laughs or drama. **109m/C VHS.** Lucie Arnaz, Craig Wasson, Ken Howard, Joe Mantegna; ***D:*** Lawrence Turman; ***W:*** Steve Brown; ***M:*** Henry Mancini.

Second Time Lucky ✌ **1984** The devil makes a bet with God that if the world began all over again Adam and Eve would repeat their mistake they made in the Garden of Eden. Bites off a lot, but has no teeth nor laughs. **98m/C VHS.** *AU NZ* Diane Franklin, Roger Wilson, Robert Morley, Jon Gadsby, Bill Ewens; ***D:*** Michael Anderson Sr.

Second Victory ✌✌½ **1987 (PG)** Major Mark Hanlon has been appointed an Occupation Officer in the winter of 1945. He expects this will be his chance to work for peace but when a good friend is brutally murdered all his thoughts turn to revenge. Based on the novel by Morris West. **95m/C VHS.** Anthony Andrews, Max von Sydow, Renee Soutendijk; ***D:*** Gerald Thomas.

Second Wind ✌✌ **1990 (PG)** Wagner and Naughton are trying to settle into their new life together, but find they must make a variety of difficult choices. **93m/C VHS.** Lindsay Wagner, James Naughton.

The Second Woman ✌✌½ *Here Lies Love; Twelve Miles Out* **1951** An architect, suffering from blackouts and depression, believes himself responsible for the death of his fiancee. Well-done psycho-drama. **91m/B VHS, DVD.** Robert Young, Betsy Drake, John Sutton; ***D:*** James V. Kern; ***W:*** Mort Briskin, Robert Smith; ***C:*** Hal Mohr.

Seconds ✌✌✌ **1966 (R)** Aging banker Arthur Hamilton (Randolph) is frantic to escape his dead-end existence and accepts an invitation from a mysterious organization to give him a second chance at life. Through surgery, Arthur's transformed into handsome artist Tony Wilson (Hudson). Uncomfortably living in Malibu, he soons finds out all his new neighbors are also "seconds," who are afraid he'll betray their secrets. Wilson decides he wants out of his new arrangement and back to his former life but it comes at a very high price. Eerie film manages to (mostly) overcome its plot problems, with a fine performance by Hudson. Based on the novel by Donald Ely. **107m/B VHS, DVD, Wide.** Rock Hudson, John Randolph, Salome Jens, Will Geer, Jeff Corey, Richard Anderson, Murray Hamilton, Karl Swenson, Khigh (Kaie Deei) Deigh, Frances Reid, Wesley Addy; ***D:*** John Frankenheimer; ***W:*** Lewis John Carlino; ***C:*** James Wong Howe; ***M:*** Jerry Goldsmith.

Secre of the Andes ✌✌½ **1998 (PG)** Rebellious Diana (Belle) travels to Argentina with her mother (Allen) to visit her estranged father (Keith). He's an archeologist searching for gold and Diana dabbles in the supernatural to help him out. **102m/C VHS, DVD.** David Keith, Nancy Allen, John Rhys-Davies, Camilla Belle, Jerry Stiller; ***D:*** Alejandro Azzano.

The Secret ✌✌½ **1993** Businessman and political candidate Mike Dunsmore (Douglas) comes to terms with his lifelong battle with dyslexia when his grandson begins to show signs of the same affliction. Set in picturesque New England fishing village. **92m/C VHS, DVD.** Kirk Douglas, Bruce Boxleitner, Brock Peters, Laura Harrington; ***D:*** Karen Arthur.

Secret Admirer ✌✌ **1985 (R)** A teenager's unsigned love letter keeps falling into the wrong hands. Intends to be funny, and sometimes is; too often, though, it surrenders to obviousness and predictability. **98m/C VHS.** C. Thomas Howell, Cliff DeYoung, Kelly Preston, Dee Wallace Stone, Lori Loughlin, Fred Ward, Casey Siemaszko, Corey Haim, Leigh Taylor-Young; ***D:*** David Greenwalt.

The Secret Agent ✌✌✌ **1936** Presumed dead, a British intelligence agent (Gielgud) reappears and receives a new assignment. Using his faked death to his advantage, he easily journeys to Switzerland where he is to eliminate an enemy agent. Strange Hitchcockian melange of comedy and intrigue; atypical, but worthy offering from the Master. **83m/B VHS, DVD.** *GB* Madeleine Carroll, Peter Lorre, Robert Young, John Gielgud, Lilli Palmer, Percy Marmont, Charles Carson, Florence Kahn; ***D:*** Alfred Hitchcock; ***W:*** Charles Bennett; ***C:*** Bernard Knowles; ***M:*** Louis Levy.

The Secret Agent ✌✌ *Joseph Conrad's The Secret Agent* **1996 (R)** Rain, rain go away. In this waterlogged adaptation of the Conrad novel, Hoskins plays Adolf Verloc, a cowardly agent provocateur who heads a group of anarchists in soggy Victorian England. His real mission, however, is to report the actions of the expatriates to the Russian government. After he is bullied into a terrorist attack on the Greenwich Observatory by his contact at the Russian embassy, the lives of Verloc, his wife Winnie (Arquette) and her mentally disabled brother Stevie (Bale) are blown to pieces (sometimes literally) by the consequences. The only spark in the otherwise dank and gloomy production is Williams (listed as George Spelvin) as the demented explosives expert known only as the Professor. Alfred Hitchcock also used a loose interpretation of Conrad's novel for "Sabotage." **95m/C VHS.** *GB* Bob Hoskins, Patricia Arquette, Gerard Depardieu, Robin Williams, Jim Broadbent, Christian Bale, Elizabeth Spriggs, Peter Vaughan, Julian Wadham; ***D:*** Christopher Hampton; ***W:*** Christopher Hampton; ***C:*** Denis Lenoir; ***M:*** Philip Glass.

Secret Agent 00 ✌ *Operation Kid Brother* **1967 (R)** A master criminal plans to blackmail the western world and only special Secret Agent 00 can stop him. Bad spy genre ripoff, interesting only as the screen debut of Sean Connery's brother. **97m/C VHS.** *IT* Neil Connery, Daniela Bianchi, Adolfo Celi; ***D:*** Alberto De Martino; ***M:*** Ennio Morricone.

The Secret Agent Club ✌½ **1996 (PG)** Secret agent Ray Chase (Hogan) steals a laser gun that evil Eve (Down) is determined to sell to the highest bidder. Ray returns home and, under the pretext of his job as a toy store owner, hides the gun in the store where his son Jeremy (McCurley) assumes it's a new toy. Eve's henchmen manage to capture Ray but not before Jeremy gets the gun and plans a rescue mission with his friends. **90m/C VHS.** Hulk Hogan, Richard Moll, Lesley-Anne Down, Mathew McCurley, Edward Albert, Lyman Ward, James Hong, Barry Bostwick, Jack Nance; ***D:*** John Murlowski; ***W:*** Rory Johnston; ***C:*** S. Douglas Smith.

Secret Agent 00-Soul ✌½ **1989** International spy decides to fulfill his dream of opening a detective agency in his old neighborhood. Release of this direct-to-video mishmash was delayed until '95. **71m/C VHS.** Billy Dee Williams, Amanda Le Flore, Marjean Holden, Tommy (Tiny) Lister; ***D:*** Julius Le Flore.

Secret Agent Super Dragon ✌ *Super Dragon* **1966** The CIA calls in the agent known as "Super Dragon" when it is discovered that a Venezuelan drug czar plans to spike U.S. gum and candy with an LSD-like drug. Less than competent production offers some unintended laughter. Ferroni used the pseudonym Calvin Jackson Padget. **95m/C VHS.** *FR IT GE* Ray Danton, Marisa Mell, Margaret Lee, Jess Hahn, Carlo D'Angelo, Andriana Ambesi; ***D:*** Giorgio Ferroni.

Secret Beyond the Door ✌✌ **1948** A wealthy heiress marries a widower and soon discovers that he murdered his first wife. Understandably, she wonders what plans he might have for her. Capably done chiller, but the plot is hackneyed pseudo-Hitchcock. **99m/B VHS.** Joan Bennett, Michael Redgrave, Barbara O'Neil, Anne Revere; ***D:*** Fritz Lang; ***M:*** Miklos Rozsa.

Secret Ceremony ✌✌½ **1969 (R)** An aging prostitute and a young, aimless waif resemble each other's dead mother and dead daughter, respectively, and the relationship goes on, strangely, from there. This original big-screen version is very good Freudian psycho-drama; 101-minute TV version is unfortunately greatly diluted. **109m/C VHS.** Elizabeth Taylor, Robert Mitchum, Mia Farrow, Pamela Brown, Peggy Ashcroft; ***D:*** Joseph Losey; ***M:*** Richard Rodney Bennett.

The Secret Code **1942** A 15-chapter serial with the Black Commando (Kelly) thwarting the Nazis' attempts at sabotage. After each chapter's cliffhanger ending a new form of secret code is explained and decoded. **315m/B VHS.** Paul Kelly, Anne Nagel, Clancy Cooper, Trevor Bardette, Gregory Gay, Ludwig Donath, Eddie (Ed, Eddy, Edwin) Parker; ***D:*** Spencer Gordon Bennet.

The Secret Diary of Sigmund Freud ✌✌ **1984** Spoofy look at the early years of Sigmund Freud, the father of modern psychoanalysis. Freud (Cort) has an affair with lisping nurse Kane while tending to patient Shawn and answering to mama Baker, who's carrying on with mad doctor Kinski. Talented cast falls asleep on couch. **129m/C VHS.** Bud Cort, Carol Kane, Carroll Baker, Klaus Kinski, Marisa Berenson, Dick Shawn, Ferdinand "Ferdy" Mayne; ***D:*** Danford B. Greene.

Secret File of Hollywood ✌½ *Secret File: Hollywood* **1962** A down-and-out private eye gets a job taking photos for a sleazy Hollywood scandal sheet and finds himself in the midst of a blackmail plot masterminded by his editor. An often childish potboiler, perhaps inspired by the once-feared Confidential Magazine. **85m/B VHS.** Robert Clarke, Francine York, Syd Mason, Maralou Gray, John Warburton; ***D:*** Ralph Cushman.

The Secret Four ✌✌ *The Four Just Men* **1940** Three young men seek to avenge the death of their friend at the hands of British traitors, and become involved in a plot to sabotage the Suez canal. Poorly adapted from the novel by Edgar Wallace. **79m/B VHS.** *GB* Hugh Sinclair, Griffith Jones, Francis L. Sullivan, Frank Lawton, Anna Lee, Alan Napier, Basil Sydney; ***D:*** Walter Forde.

Secret Games ✌½ **1992 (R)** An unhappily married woman (Brin) is searching for relief from her restrictive marriage. At the "Afternoon Demitasse," an exclusive brothel where women are paid for fulfilling their ultimate fantasies, she meets a man (Hewitt) who pushes her beyond her sexual limits and threatens to totally possess her. **90m/C VHS, DVD.** Martin Hewitt, Michele Brin, Delia Sheppard, Billy Drago; ***D:*** Alexander Gregory (Gregory Dark) Hippolyte; ***W:*** Georges des Esseintes; ***C:*** Wally Pfister, Thomas Denove; ***M:*** Joseph Smith.

Secret Games 2: The Escort ✌½ **1993 (R)** A performance artist (Hewitt) learns how to seduce women from a beautiful escort (Rochelle). However, he falls for his trainer despite being a star pupil who could have anyone he wanted. Plot conveniently lends itself to lots of steamy love scenes. Also available in an unrated version. **84m/C VHS.** Martin Hewitt, Amy Rochelle, Sara Suzanne Brown, Marie Leroux; ***D:*** Alexander Gregory (Gregory Dark) Hippolyte; ***W:*** Russell Lavalle; ***M:*** Ashley Irwin.

Secret Games 3 ✌½ **1994 (R)** A bored doctor's wife gets her kicks by visiting a club catering to women's fantasies. But then she meets a criminal who wants her all to himself. An unrated version is available at 91 minutes. **82m/C VHS, DVD.** Woody Brown, Brenda Swanson, Rochelle Swanson; ***D:*** Alexander Gregory (Gregory Dark) Hippolyte; ***C:*** Wally Pfister; ***M:*** Ashley Irwin.

The Secret Garden ✌✌✌ **1949** Orphaned Mary Lennox (O'Brien) is sent to live with her cold and uncaring Uncle Archibald Craven (Marshall), wh has never recovered from his wife's death. He keeps his crippled son, Colin (Stockwell), a virtual prisoner in the house until Mary discovers his presence and befriends him. She also discovers a neglected hidden garden, once the pride of Mrs. Craven, which Mary secretly begins to tend. Touching tearjerker based on the novel by Frances Hodgson Burnett. O'Brien leads an outstanding cast in one of her final juvenile roles. In black and white, with Technicolor for later garden scenes. **92m/B VHS.** Margaret O'Brien, Herbert Marshall, Dean Stockwell, Gladys Cooper, Elsa Lanchester, Brian Roper; ***D:*** Fred M. Wilcox; ***C:*** Ray June; ***M:*** Bronislau Kaper.

The Secret Garden ✌✌½ **1984** Orphaned Mary Lennox is sent to live with her mysterious uncle after her parents die. Mary is willful and spoiled and her uncle's house holds a number of secrets, including a crippled cousin. When Mary discovers a mysteriously abandoned locked garden she makes it her mission to restore the garden to life. Based on the children's classic by Frances Hodsgon Burnett. **107m/C VHS.** *GB* Sarah Hollis Andrews, David Patterson; ***D:*** Katrina Murray. **TV**

The Secret Garden ✌✌✌ **1987 (PG)** Lonely orphan Mary Lennox is sent to live with her uncle in England after her parent's deaths. Mary, who has grown up in India, is selfish and unhappy until she discovers two secrets on her uncle's estate. Class production of the children's classic by Frances Hodgson Burnett with wonderful performances; added prologue and afterword showing Mary as an adult are unnecessary, but don't detract either. Made for television as a "Hallmark Hall of Fame" special. **100m/C VHS.** Gennie James, Barret Oliver, Jadrien Steele, Michael Hordern, Derek Jacobi, Billie Whitelaw, Lucy Gutteridge, Julian Glover, Colin Firth, Alan Grint. **TV**

The Secret Garden ✌✌½ **1993 (G)** Rekindled interest in Frances Hodgon Burnett's classic tale has prompted a Broadway musical, two TV movies, and this latest big screen version. Mary Lennox is an orphan sent to live in her reclusive uncle's forbidding mansion filled with secrets, including a crippled cousin she didn't know she had. She discovers a secret neglected garden and becomes determined to bring it back to life. Befitting director Holland's reputation this version is beautiful but dark, with children prey to very adult anxieties. **102m/C VHS, DVD, Wide.** Kate Maberly, Maggie Smith, Haydon Prowse, Andrew Knott, John Lynch; ***D:*** Agnieszka

Holland; ***W:*** Caroline Thompson; ***C:*** Roger Deakins; ***M:*** Zbigniew Preisner. L.A. Film Critics '93: Score.

Secret Honor 🦴🦴🦴 *Lords of Treason; Secret Honor: The Last Testament of Richard M. Nixon; Secret Honor: A Political Myth* **1985** Idiosyncratic, single-set, one-man film version adapted by Donald Freed and Arnold Stone from their stage play about Richard Nixon coping with the death of his presidency on the night he's decided to blow his brains out. Made with students at the University of Michigan, and carried by the ranting and raving of Hall as a tragic Shakespearean Nixon with plenty of darkly humorous lines. **90m/C VHS.** Philip Baker Hall; ***D:*** Robert Altman; ***W:*** Donald Freed, Arnold Stone; ***C:*** Pierre Mignot; ***M:*** George Burt.

Secret Ingredient 🦴½ **1992** A legendary cognac recipe is the secret formula of the monks of St. Celare, whose monastery is located in the mountains of Yugoslavia. A wealthy American sends his flighty heiress daughter to pry the secret recipe from the monks but she runs into more than she bargains for when she falls for a handsome friar and gets caught up with a band of bumbling gypsies and the inept state police. **95m/C VHS.** Rick Rossovich, Catherine Hicks, Gary Kroeger, Jeff Corey, Brad Dexter, Sam Wanamaker; ***D:*** Slobodan Shijan.

Secret Life of an American Wife 🦴🦴 **1968** A bored housewife (Jackson) tries to seduce a client of her husband's, with less than hilarious results. Too much dialogue, not enough genuine humor. Disappointing inversion of director Axelrod's "The Seven Year Itch." **97m/C VHS.** Walter Matthau, Anne Jackson, Patrick O'Neal, Edy Williams; ***D:*** George Axelrod; ***W:*** George Axelrod.

The Secret Life of Girls 🦴🦴½ **1999** Fifteen-year-old Natalie (Delfino) is caught in the midst of family turmoil when her unhappy mother, Ruby (Hamilton), reveals that Natalie's college professor father, Hugh (Levy), has been fooling around with one of his students. Natalie hides out in the university library where she shyly flirts with a cute boy, but the family chaos continues when Hugh suffers the pangs of conscience. **90m/C VHS.** Majandra Delfino, Linda Hamilton, Eugene Levy, Kate Vernon, Meagan Good, Aeryk Egan, Andrew Ducote; ***D:*** Holly Goldberg Sloan.

The Secret Life of Walter Mitty 🦴🦴🦴 **1947** An entertaining adaptation of the James Thurber short story about a meek man (Kaye) who lives an unusual secret fantasy life. Henpecked by his fiancee and mother, oppressed at his job, he imagines himself in the midst of various heroic fantasies. While Thurber always professed to hate Kaye's characterization and the movie, it scored at the box-office and today stands as a comedic romp for Kaye. Available with digitally remastered stereo and original movie trailer. **110m/C VHS, DVD.** Danny Kaye, Virginia Mayo, Boris Karloff, Ann Rutherford, Fay Bainter, Florence Bates; ***D:*** Norman Z. McLeod; ***W:*** Everett Freeman, Ken Englund, Philip Rapp; ***C:*** Lee Garmes; ***M:*** Sylvia Fine, David Raksin.

Secret Mission 🦴🦴½ **1942** Four British intelligence agents are sent into occupied France to assess the strength of Nazi forces. But after discovering the information, their cover is blown and it's a race to get the intelligence into the right hands before the Nazis get to them first. **94m/B VHS.** *GB* James Mason, Hugh Williams, Roland Culver, Michael Wilding, Carla Lehmann, Nancy Price, Percy Walsh, Karel Stepanek, Herbert Lom, Stewart Granger; ***D:*** Harold French; ***W:*** Anatole de Grunwald, Basil Bartlett; ***C:*** Bernard Knowles, Cyril Knowles; ***M:*** Mischa Spoliansky.

Secret Obsession 🦴 **1988 (PG)** A love triangle among a father, his illegitimate son, and the woman they both love, set in North Africa in 1955. Sounds intriguing, but don't be fooled. Slow, dull, and poorly acted. **82m/C VHS.** Julie Christie, Ben Gazzara, Patrick Bruel, Jean Carmet; ***D:*** Henri Vart.

The Secret of El Zorro 🦴½ **1957** Don Diego's friend, Don Ricardo, threatens to unmask Zorro's secret identity when he challenges the legendary swordsman to a duel. **75m/B VHS.** Guy Williams.

The Secret of My Success 🦴🦴 **1987 (PG-13)** Country bumpkin Fox goes to the Big Apple to make his mark. He becomes the corporate mailboy who rises meteorically to the top of his company (by impersonating an executive) in order to win the love of an icy woman executive. He spends his days running frantically between his real job in the mailroom and his fantasy position, with various sexual shenanigans with the boss's wife thrown in to keep the viewer alert. Fox is charismatic while working with a cliche-ridden script that ties up everything very neatly at the end. **110m/C VHS, DVD, Wide.** Michael J. Fox, Helen Slater, Richard Jordan, Margaret Whitton, Fred Gwynne; ***D:*** Herbert Ross; ***W:*** Jim Cash, Jack Epps Jr., A.J. Carothers; ***C:*** Carlo Di Palma; ***M:*** David Foster.

The Secret of Navajo Cave 🦴🦴 *Legend of Cougar Canyon* **1976 (G)** Fair family adventure. Two young friends explore the mysterious Navajo cave, where one can be assured that a secret awaits. **84m/C VHS.** Holger Kasper, Steven Benally Jr., Johnny Guerro; ***D:*** James T. Flocker; ***Nar:*** Rex Allen.

The Secret of NIMH 🦴🦴🦴 **1982 (G)** Animated tale, produced by a staff of Disney-trained artists led by "American Tail's" Bluth; concerns a newly widowed mouse who discovers a secret agency of superintelligent rats (they've escaped from a science lab) who aid her in protecting her family. As is usually the case with Bluth films, the animation is superb while the socially aware plot struggles to keep pace. That aside, it's still an interesting treat for the youngsters. Adapted from Robert C. O'Brien's "Mrs. Frisby and the Rats of N.I.M.H." **84m/C VHS, DVD, 8mm.** ***D:*** Don Bluth; ***W:*** Don Bluth; ***M:*** Jerry Goldsmith; ***V:*** John Carradine, Derek Jacobi, Dom DeLuise, Elizabeth Hartman, Peter Strauss, Aldo Ray, Edie McClurg, Wil Wheaton.

The Secret of Roan Inish 🦴🦴🦴½ **1994 (PG)** Irish myth comes to life in this fantasy about the importance of family and place, seen through the eyes of 10-year-old Fiona Coneelly (newcomer Courtney) who's sent to live with her grandparents in post-WWII County Donegal. Fiona's drawn to her grandfather's stories about the family's ancestral home on the island of Roan Inish and the loss of her baby brother Jamie, who was carried out to sea. Another family tale is about a Selkie—a beautiful seal/woman captured by a Coneelly fisherman who eventually returned to her ocean home. When Fiona visits Roan Inish she becomes convinced that Jamie is alive and being cared for by the island's seals. Director Sayles keeps a firm grip on the cuteness factor while cinematographer Wexler works his usual magic on the sea, sky, and land of Ireland. Based on the 1957 novel "Secret of the Ron Mor Skerry" by Rosalie K. Fry. **102m/C VHS, DVD, Wide.** Jeni Courtney, Michael Lally, Eileen Colgan, John Lynch, Richard Sheridan, Susan Lynch, Cillian Byrne; ***D:*** John Sayles; ***W:*** John Sayles; ***C:*** Haskell Wexler; ***M:*** Mason Daring.

The Secret of Santa Vittoria 🦴🦴½ **1969 (PG)** Italo Bambolini (Quinn) is an amiable drunk who unexpectedly becomes the mayor of his wine-making village during WWII. Hearing the Nazis are headed toward Santa Vittoria to loot their supply of vintage wines, Italo and his savvy wife, Rosa (Magnani), enlist the villagers to hide most of the bottles in a cave outside of town, leaving a token amount to satisfy suspicious German Commander Von Prum (Kruger), who tries to learn the truth. Overly long but still amusing. Based on the novel by Robert Crichton. **139m/C VHS.** Anthony Quinn, Anna Magnani, Hardy Kruger, Virna Lisi, Renato Rascel, Giancarlo Giannini, Valentina Cortese, Sergio Franchi; ***D:*** Stanley Kramer; ***W:*** William Rose, Ben Maddow; ***C:*** Giuseppe Rotunno; ***M:*** Ernest Gold.

Secret of the Black Trunk 🦴🦴½ **1962** Chilling Edgar Wallace story about a series of murders at a famed English hotel. Filmed in Great Britain. **96m/C VHS.** *GE* Joachim Hansen, Senta Berger, Hans Reiser, Leonard Steckel, Peter Carsten; ***D:*** Werner Klinger.

The Secret of the Golden Eagle 🦴🦴 **1991** A boy and his new adventurer friend are on a quest to find the strange "Golden Statue" that causes people to grow old before their time. They must take it from criminals who are using it for evil purposes. A good adventure/fantasy for the entire family. **90m/C VHS.** Michael Berryman, Brandon McKay; ***D:*** Cole McKay.

Secret of the Ice Cave 🦴 **1989 (PG-13)** A motley band of explorers, hijackers and mercenaries go after a secret treasure in the remote mountains. **106m/C VHS.** Michael Moriarty, Sally Kellerman, David Mendenhall, Virgil Frye, Gerald Anthony, Norbert Weisser; ***D:*** Radu Gabrea.

The Secret of the Loch 🦴½ **1934** Scottish scientist claims to have seen Loch Ness Monster but everyone thinks his bagpipe's blown a reed. **80m/B VHS.** *GB* Sir Seymour Hicks, Nancy O'Neil, Gibson Gowland, Frederick Peisley; ***D:*** Milton Rosmer.

The Secret of the Telegian 🦴🦴½ *The Telegian* **1961** Rare Japanese sci-fi flick about a soldier who uses a teleportation device to kill fellow soldiers who tried to kill him. He could find his victims wherever they hid. **85m/C VHS.** *JP* Koji Tsurata, Yumi Shirakawa, Akihiko Hirata, Tadao Nakamura; ***D:*** Jun Fukuda.

Secret of Yolanda 🦴 **1982 (R)** Steamy romance about a young deaf-mute whose guardian and riding instructor both fall for her. **90m/C VHS.** Aviva Ger, Asher Zarfati, Shraga Harpaz.

The Secret Passion of Robert Clayton 🦴🦴 **1992 (R)** When Robert Clayton Jr. (Valentine) returns to his home town to take the position of D.A., he is forced to go head to head in a lurid murder trial with the defense attorney (Mahoney), who also happens to be his own father. **92m/C VHS.** John Mahoney, Scott Valentine, Eve Gordon, Kevin Conroy; ***D:*** E.W. Swackhamer; ***W:*** Brian Ross; ***C:*** Billy Dickson.

Secret Passions 🦴½ **1978** A young couple are haunted by a dark, romance-novel-type secret. **99m/C VHS.** John James, Susan Lucci; ***D:*** Michael Pressman. **TV**

Secret Places 🦴🦴½ **1985 (PG)** On the brink of WWII, a German girl in an English school finds friendship with a popular classmate. Touching and involving, but somehow unsatisfying. **98m/C VHS.** *GB* Maria Therese Relin, Tara MacGowran, Claudine Auger, Jenny Agutter; ***D:*** Zelda Barron; ***W:*** Zelda Barron.

The Secret Policeman's Other Ball 🦴🦴🦴 **1982 (R)** Engaging live performance by most of the Monty Python troupe and guest rock artists, staged for Amnesty International. Follows 1979's "The Secret Policeman's Ball," and followed by 1987's "The Secret Policeman's Third Ball." **101m/C VHS.** *GB* John Cleese, Graham Chapman, Michael Palin, Terry Jones, Pete Townshend, Sting, Billy Connolly, Bob Geldof; ***D:*** Julien Temple; ***W:*** Michael Palin.

Secret Policeman's Private Parts 🦴🦴½ **1981** Various sketches and performances from the various Secret Policeman occasions, featuring classic Python sketches including "I'm a Lumberjack and I'm OK." Also featured are performances by Phil Collins, Pete Townshend, Donovan, and Bob Geldof. Thank you very much. **77m/C VHS.** *GB* John Cleese, Michael Palin, Terry Jones, Eric Idle, Graham Chapman, Terry Gilliam, Pete Townshend, Julien Temple, Phil Collins, Peter Cook, Donovan, Bob Geldof; ***D:*** Roger Graef, Julien Temple.

The Secret Rapture 🦴🦴 **1994 (R)** Two sisters clash in this family drama, adapted by Hare from his 1988 play. The bohemian Isobel (Stevenson) and her estranged sister, the forbidding Marion (Wilton), are brought together by their father's death. While Isobel grieves, Marion seeks to gain advantage in the family business, and both must deal with their young, alcoholic, and volatile stepmother Katherine (Whalley-Kilmer). Emotional intensity with good performances but abrupt shifts in tone. **96m/C VHS.** *GB* Juliet Stevenson, Penelope Wilton, Joanne Whalley, Alan Howard, Neil Pearson, Robert Stephens, Hilton McRae; ***D:*** Howard Davies; ***W:*** David Hare; ***C:*** Ian Wilson; ***M:*** Richard Hartley.

A Secret Space 🦴🦴½ **1988** Story of a young man, born of secular parents, searching for the meaning of his Jewish roots as he nears his Bar Mitzvah. He is helped along by a group of Jews who are also searching for this meaning. **80m/C VHS.** Robert Klein, Phyllis Newman, John Matthews, Sam Schacht, Virginia Graham; ***D:*** Roberta Hodes.

The Secret War of Harry Frigg 🦴½ **1968 (R)** Non-conformist WWII Private Harry Frigg is promoted to general as part of a scheme to help five Allied generals escape from the custody of the Germans. Rare Newman bomb; dismal comedy. **123m/C VHS.** Paul Newman, Sylva Koscina, John Williams, Tom Bosley, Andrew Duggan; ***D:*** Jack Smight; ***C:*** Russell Metty.

Secret Weapon 🦴🦴 **1990** An Israeli technician flees his country with atomic secrets and a beautiful government agent is sent to induce him to return. Based on the true case of Mordecai Vanunu. Slow-paced and not very suspenseful. **95m/C VHS.** Griffin Dunne, Karen Allen, Stuart Wilson, Jeroen Krabbe, Brian Cox, John Rhys-Davies, Ian Mitchell; ***D:*** Ian Sharp. **CABLE**

Secret Weapons 🦴½ *Secrets of the Red Bedroom* **1985** Sexy Russian babes are KGB-trained to get any secret from any man. Strains credibility as well as patience. Made for TV. **100m/C VHS.** Linda Hamilton, Sally Kellerman, Hunt Block, Viveca Lindfors, Christopher Atkins, Geena Davis, James Franciscus; ***D:*** Don Taylor; ***M:*** Charles Bernstein. **TV**

The Secretary 🦴½ **1994 (R)** Another bland variation of "The Temp." Career woman Ellen Bradford (Harris) has a new fast-track job and a highly efficient secretary in Deidre (Kelley). But it turns out Deidre's also lethally efficient in disposing of co-workers through a series of inexplicable accidents and "suicides." So just what's Ellen going to do to show Deidre who's boss? **94m/C VHS.** Mel Harris, Sheila Kelley, Barry Bostwick, James Russo; ***D:*** Andrew Lane; ***C:*** Steven Bernstein; ***M:*** Louis Febre.

Secretary **2002 (R)** Kinky romantic comedy finds released mental patient Gyllenhaal getting a job as secretary to Spader's buttoned-down businessman who, it turns out, likes spanking and leather. His secretary is only too happy to comply. Not yet reviewed. **104m/C VHS, DVD.** James Spader, Maggie Gyllenhaal, Lesley Ann Warren, Jeremy Davies, Patrick Bauchau; ***D:*** Steven Shainberg; ***W:*** Erin Cressida Wilson.

Secrets 🦴½ **1971 (R)** A wife, her husband, and her daughter each have a sexual experience which they must keep secret. Bisset's nude love scene is an eye-opener. Fast forward through the rest of this dull, overwrought drama. **86m/C VHS.** Jacqueline Bisset, Per Oscarsson, Shirley Knight, Robert Powell, Tarka Kings, Martin C. Thurley; ***D:*** Philip Saville; ***M:*** Michael Gibbs.

Secrets 🦴 **1977** An unhappy young bride starts having numerous affairs when her mother dies. Hardly worth the effort. **100m/C VHS.** Susan Blakely, Roy Thinnes, Joanne Linville, John Randolph, Anthony Eisley, Andrew Stevens; ***D:*** Paul Wendkos. **TV**

Secrets 🦴🦴 **1982** British drama about the confused life of an innocent schoolgirl who's the victim of a mess of authoritative misunderstandings. One of David Puttnam's "First Love" series. **79m/C VHS.** *GB* Helen Lindsay, Anna Campbell-Jones, Daisy Cockburn; ***D:*** Gavin Millar.

Secrets 🦴🦴½ **1994 (PG-13)** Teenager Anna Berter, growing up in turn-of-the-century Iowa, is told by her snobbish mother Etta (Hamel) not to befriend the help, which include the woman who raised Anna alongside her granddaughter Edwina. When Edwina is seduced by a Berter family friend and left pregnant, Etta decides to adopt her baby daughter—whether Edwina wants to let the baby go or not.

All this obsessive behavior leads Anna to discover some very unhappy family secrets surrounding her own birth. Made for TV. **92m/C VHS.** Veronica Hamel, Julie Harris, Richard Kiley, Thomas Gibson, Shae D'Lyn, Jessica Bowman, Reed Edward Diamond; *D:* Jud Taylor. **TV**

Secrets and Lies 🦴🦴 **1995 (R)** Too-long film focusing on family and identity. The adoptive parents of black Yuppie Londoner Hortense (Jean-Baptiste) have just died and she decides it's time to seek out her birth parents. She's warned about the emotional consequences, especially upon discovering her biological mother is white—factory worker Cynthia (Blethyn), who has another daughter, Roxanne (Rushbrook), who doesn't get along with mum. Naturally, when Hortense is introduced to the rest of Cynthia's family, there's lots of dysfunction to explore. Good performances, although Hortense's character is bland, but pacing drags. **142m/C VHS.** *GB* Brenda Blethyn, Marianne Jean-Baptiste, Timothy Spall, Claire Rushbrook, Phyllis Logan, Lee Ross, Ron Cook, Leslie Manville, Irene Handl; *Cameos:* Alison Steadman; *D:* Mike Leigh; *W:* Mike Leigh; *C:* Dick Pope; *M:* Andrew Dickson. Australian Film Inst. '97: Foreign Film; British Acad. '96: Actress (Blethyn), Orig. Screenplay; Cannes '96: Actress (Blethyn), Film; Golden Globes '97: Actress—Drama (Blethyn); L.A. Film Critics '96: Actress (Blethyn), Director (Leigh), Film.

Secrets of a Married Man 🦴 **1984** A married man's philandering ways are his ruination when he falls hard for a beautiful prostitute. Shatner and Shepherd contain their laughter as they make their way through this hyper-earnest family drama. **96m/C VHS.** William Shatner, Cybill Shepherd, Michelle Phillips, Glynn Turman; *D:* William A. Graham.

Secrets of a Soul 🦴🦴½ **1925** A visually impressive presentation of Freudian psychoanalytic theory, in which a professor, wanting a child and jealous of his wife's childhood sweetheart, moves toward madness (we did say Freudian) and is cured through dream interpretation. Great dream sequences bring out the arm-chair psychoanalyst. Silent. **94m/B VHS.** *GE* Werner Krauss, Ruth Weyher, Jack Trevor; *D:* G.W. Pabst.

Secrets of Sweet Sixteen woof! **1974 (R)** Gag-fest about budding sexuality in high school. **84m/C VHS.** Suzie Atkins.

Secrets of Three Hungry Wives 🦴 **1978** When a multi-millionaire is killed, the women with whom he was having affairs are suspected. Tacky TV flick. **97m/C VHS.** Jessica Walter, Gretchen Corbett, Eve Plumb, Heather MacRae, James Franciscus, Craig Stevens; *D:* Gordon Hessler. **TV**

Secrets of Women 🦴🦴🦴 *Kvinnors Vantan; Waiting Women* **1952** A rare Bergman comedy about three sisters-in-law who tell about their affairs and marriages as they await their husbands at a lakeside resort. His first commercial success, though it waited nine years for release (1961). In Swedish with English subtitles. **114m/B VHS.** *SW* Anita Bjork, Karl Arne Homsten, Eva Dahlbeck, Maj-Britt Nilsson, Jarl Kulle; *D:* Ingmar Bergman; *W:* Ingmar Bergman.

The Secrets of Wu Sin 🦴🦴 **1932** A suicidal news writer in Chinatown is given a reason to live by a news editor who gives her a job. She starts investigating a ring smuggling Chinese workers, with the trail leading to, of course, Chinatown. Low-budget crime thriller. **65m/B VHS.** Lois Wilson, Grant Withers, Dorothy Revier, Robert Warwick, Toschia Mori; *D:* Richard Thorpe.

Seduce Me: Pamela Principle 2 🦴½ *Pamela Principle 2* **1994 (R)** Charles is a bored, married, architectural photographer who decides a change of pace is in order. So he starts shooting lingerie fashion spreads and gets seduced by model Pamela, who likes her men married. The only connection to the 1991 film is the married man/affair angle. **96m/C VHS.** Alina Thompson, Nick Rafter, India Allen; *D:* Edward Holzman.

Seduced 🦴🦴 **1985** When a rich businessman turns up dead, the ambitious politician who was involved with his wife must find the killer. Not memorable or exceptional, but not boring or offensive either. **100m/C VHS.** Gregory Harrison, Cybill Shepherd, Jose Ferrer, Adrienne Barbeau, Michael C. Gwynne, Karmin Murcelo, Paul Stewart; *D:* Jerrold Freedman. **TV**

Seduced and Abandoned 🦴🦴🦴 *Sedotta e Abbandonata* **1964** A lothario seduces his fiancee's young sister. When the girl becomes pregnant, he refuses to marry her. Family complications abound. A comic look at the Italian code of honor. In Italian with English subtitles. **118m/B VHS, Wide.** *IT* Saro Urzi, Stefania Sandrelli, Aldo Puglisi, Leopoldo Trieste; *D:* Pietro Germi; *W:* Pietro Germi. Cannes '64: Actor (Urzi).

Seduced by Evil 🦴🦴 **1994** A journalist (Somers) is investigating a story in a small Southwest town when she encounters a sorcerer (Vargas) who decides he wants her for himself alone. Even if it means destroying everyone she holds dear. Adapted from the novel "Brujo" by Jann Arrington Wolcott. **88m/C VHS.** Suzanne Somers, John Vargas, Julie Carmen, James B. Sikking, Mindy Spence, Nancy Moonves; *D:* Tony Wharmby; *W:* Bill Svanoe.

The Seducer 🦴🦴 **1982 (R)** Things get dangerous when a playboy's goals turn from love to death. **72m/C VHS.** Christopher Mathews; *D:* Donovan Winters.

The Seducers 🦴 **1970** An acid-dropping mother takes her shy, withdrawn son on a Mediterranean cruise and asks along some of her girlfriends in the hopes of stoking his libido. However, she finds it difficult to control her own impulses. The boy gets a chance when the ship runs aground on a remote island and he meets an innocent native girl. His mother, though, has designs of her own. Dubbed from Italian. **84m/C VHS.** *GE* Rosalba (Sara Bay) Neri, Edwige Fenech, Maud de Belleroche, Maurizio Bonuglia, Ruggero Miti, Ewa Thulin; *D:* Ottavio Alessi.

Seducers 🦴 *Death Game* **1977 (R)** Wealthy, middle-aged man unsuspectingly allows two young lesbians to use his telephone. A night of bizarre mayhem and brutal murder begins. They tease him, tear apart his house, and generally make him miserable. Why? Good question. **90m/C VHS.** Sondra Locke, Colleen Camp, Seymour Cassel, Beth Brickell; *D:* Peter S. Traynor.

Seducing Maarya 🦴🦴 **1999** Maarya is an East Indian/Canadian working in a Montreal restaurant. She agrees to an arranged marriage with the restaurant owner's son, even though he's gay, and then begins a romance with the 60something dad. No one seems too concerned by the situation until Maarya's violent brother turns up, exposing a family secret, and Maarya announces her pregnancy. Melodramatic. **107m/C VHS, DVD, Wide.** *CA* Nandana Sen, Mohan Agashe, Vijay Mehta, Ryan Holliman, Cas Anvar; *D:* Hunt Hoe; *W:* Hunt Hoe; *C:* Michael Wees; *M:* Dino Giancola, Janet Lumb.

The Seduction 🦴 **1982 (R)** Superstar TV anchorwoman is harassed by a psychotic male admirer. Usual run of the mill exploitive "B" thriller with no brains behind the camera. **104m/C VHS.** Morgan Fairchild, Michael Sarrazin, Vince Edwards, Andrew Stevens, Colleen Camp, Kevin Brophy; *D:* David Schmoeller; *W:* David Schmoeller; *C:* Mac Ahlberg; *M:* Lalo Schifrin.

The Seduction of Joe Tynan 🦴🦴½ **1979 (R)** Political drama about a young senator (Alda) torn between his family, his political career, and his mistress (Streep). Alda also wrote the thin screenplay, which reportedly is loosely based on the remarkable life of Ted Kennedy. Relatively shallow treatment of the meaty themes of power, hypocrisy, sex, and corruption in our nation's capital. **107m/C VHS.** Alan Alda, Meryl Streep, Melvyn Douglas, Barbara Harris, Rip Torn; *D:* Jerry Schatzberg; *W:* Alan Alda; *M:* Bill Conti. L.A. Film Critics '79: Support. Actor (Douglas), Support. Actress (Streep); Natl. Bd. of Review '79: Support. Actress (Streep); N.Y. Film Critics '79: Support. Actress (Streep); Natl. Soc. Film Critics '79: Support. Actress (Streep).

Seduction of Mimi 🦴🦴🦴 *Mimi Metallurgico Ferito Nell'Onore* **1972 (R)** Comic farce of politics and seduction about a Sicilian laborer's escapades with the Communists and the local Mafia. Giannini is wonderful as the stubborn immigrant to the big city who finds himself in trouble. One of the funniest love scenes on film. Basis for the later movie "Which Way is Up?" Italian with subtitles. **92m/C VHS, DVD, Wide.** *IT* Giancarlo Giannini, Mariangela Melato, Turi Ferro, Agostina Belli, Elena Fiore; *D:* Lina Wertmuller; *W:* Lina Wertmuller; *C:* Dario Di Palma; *M:* Piero Piccioni.

Seduction: The Cruel Woman 🦴🦴 **1989** A curiously uninvolving look at sexual games and fantasies. Wanda is a dominatrix, who also owns a sado-masochistic gallery where her various friends and current and formers lovers act out their basest desires. Stylized, with some graphic sex. Based on the novel "Venus in Furs" by Leopold Sacher-Masoch. In German with English subtitles. **84m/C VHS.** *GE* Mechthild Grossmann, Carola Regnier, Udo Kier, Sheila McLaughlin; *D:* Elfi Mikesch, Monika Treut; *W:* Elfi Mikesch, Monika Treut.

The Seductress 🦴½ **2000** Beautiful Alexis (O'Brien) is a black widow with a string of murdered wealthy husbands behind her. Kay Sanders (Hall) is a researcher obsessed with keeping tabs on each of Alexis's new identities, especially when the babe goes after Kay's boyfriend Paul (Smith). But it turns out that Kay and Alexis have a closer connection than that. The R-rated version is a mere 70 minutes. **82m/C VHS, DVD.** Shauna O'Brien, Gabriella Hall, Jonathan Smith; *D:* J Edie Martin. **VIDEO**

See How She Runs 🦴🦴🦴 **1978** Running becomes a central and redefining experience for a 40-year-old divorced schoolteacher (Woodward). Her training culminates with a run in the Boston marathon. Her loved ones, though concerned for her health and sanity, cheer her on. Excellent made for TV drama. Screen daughter Newman is also Woodward's real-life daughter. **92m/C VHS.** Joanne Woodward, John Considine, Lissy Newman, Barbara Manning; *D:* Richard T. Heffron. **TV**

See No Evil 🦴🦴🦴 *Blind Terror* **1971 (PG)** A blind girl gradually discovers the murdered bodies of her uncle's family. Trapped in the family mansion, she finds herself pursued by the killer. Chilling and well crafted. **90m/C VHS.** Mia Farrow, Dorothy Allison, Robin Bailey; *D:* Richard Fleischer; *W:* Brian Clemens; *M:* Elmer Bernstein.

See No Evil, Hear No Evil 🦴🦴 **1989 (R)** Another teaming for Pryor and Wilder, in which they portray a blind man and a deaf man both sought as murder suspects. Pryor and Wilder deserve better. **103m/C VHS, DVD, 8mm, Wide.** Gene Wilder, Richard Pryor, Joan Severance, Anthony Zerbe, Kevin Spacey; *D:* Arthur Hiller; *W:* Andrew Kurtzman, Eliot Wald, Earl Barret, Arne Sultan, Gene Wilder; *C:* Victor Kemper; *M:* Stewart Copeland.

See Spot Run woof! **2001 (G)** How can you not like a movie with dogs? Easy, put David Arquette in it. Spot, an FBI-trained dog, has a contract on his life after removing "one of the family jewels" of crime family boss Sonny Talia (Sorvino) and ends up in a doggie witness protection program. He lands in the possession of James (Jones), his mother (Bibb), and babysitter neighbor Gordon (Arquette). One may find the true essence of the movie in the middle of a large pile of Spot's morning business, where Gordon eventually finds himself. More scatological humor and other crass gags send "Spot" to the doghouse. Duncan is the sole high point as the dog's FBI handler. **97m/C VHS, DVD, Wide.** *US* David Arquette, Michael Clarke Duncan, Leslie Bibb, Angus T. Jones, Joe (Johnny) Viterelli, Paul Sorvino, Anthony Anderson; *D:* John Whitesell; *W:* George Gallo, Dan Baron, Chris Faber; *C:* John Bartley; *M:* John Debney.

See You in the Morning 🦴½ **1989 (PG-13)** Ill-conceived romantic comedy-drama about a divorced psychiatrist and a widow, both of whom had unhappy marriages, who meet and marry. They must cope with their respective children, family tragedies, and their own expectations, in order to make this second marriage work. **119m/C VHS.** Jeff Bridges, Alice Krige, Farrah Fawcett, Drew Barrymore, Lukas Haas, Macaulay Culkin, David Dukes, Frances Sternhagen, Theodore Bikel, George Hearn, Linda Lavin; *D:* Alan J. Pakula; *W:* Alan J. Pakula.

Seedpeople 🦴🦴½ **1992** Mindless horror flick has bloodthirsty plants inhabiting peaceful Comet Valley after their seeds fall from outer space and germinate. These "seedpeople" possess tremendous powers and soon have the rural residents transformed into zombies. Bears an uncanny resemblance to "Invasion of the Bodysnatchers," and is so bad it's almost good. Also available with Spanish subtitles. **87m/C VHS.** Sam Hennings, Andrea Roth, Dane Witherspoon, David Dunard, Holly Fields, Bernard Kates, Anne Betancourt, Sonny Carl Davis; *D:* Peter Manoogian; *W:* Jackson Barr; *M:* Bob Mithoff.

Seeds of Doubt 🦴🦴½ **1996 (R)** Formula thriller finds reporter Jennifer Kingsley (Watson) working to free convicted murderer Crawford (Lando) from prison because she thinks he's innocent (and she's fallen for him). Detective Dexter (Coyote) is unsucessful in convincing her otherwise but Jennifer begins to have her own doubts when a new series of killings begin after Crawford's release. **94m/C VHS.** Alberta Watson, Peter Coyote, Joe Lando; *D:* Peter Foldy.

Seeds of Evil 🦴🦴 *The Gardener* **1976 (R)** Warhol alumnus Dallesandro is a strange gardener who grows flowers that can kill. He can also turn himself into a tree and figures to seduce rich and bored housewife Houghton (niece of Katharine Hepburn) after he finishes tending her garden. Strange, quirky horror flick. **97m/C VHS.** Katharine Houghton, Joe Dallesandro, Rita Gam; *D:* James H. Kay.

Seeing Red 🦴🦴½ **1999** British soap opera star Coral Atkins (Lancashire) is doing a charity event in the 1970s at a children's home where she finds the conditions untenable. Having survived a terrible childhood herself, Coral improbably decides to switch careers and open her own home for abused children, though British social bureaucracy thwarts her every decision. Based on Atkins' 1990 memoir. **100m/C VHS.** *GB* Nicholas Gecks, Sarah Lancashire; *D:* Graham Theakston; *W:* Christopher Monger. **TV**

The Seekers 🦴🦴 **1979** The story of the Kent family continues, as Abraham Kent, his wife and young son are forced to leave the safety of Boston for the rugged, untamed Pacific Northwest. TV movie based on the novel by John Jakes; preceded by "The Bastard" and "The Rebels." **200m/C VHS.** Randolph Mantooth, Edie Adams, Neville Brand, Delta Burke, John Carradine, George DeLoy, Julie Gregg, Roosevelt "Rosie" Grier, George Hamilton, Alex Hyde-White, Brian Keith, Ross Martin, Gary Merrill, Martin Milner, Vic Morrow, Timothy Patrick Murphy, Hugh O'Brian, Robert Reed, Allan Rich, Barbara Rush, Sarah Rush, Stuart Whitman, Ed Harris, Jeremy Licht, Eric Stoltz; *D:* Sidney Hayers.

Seems Like Old Times 🦴🦴½ **1980 (PG)** A sweet lawyer (Hawn) finds herself helping her ex-husband (Chase) when two robbers force him to hold up a bank. Grodin is the new spouse threatened by Chase's appearance and by the heavies he's trying to escape. Better-than-average script, with funny and appealing characters. **102m/C VHS, DVD, Wide.** Goldie Hawn, Chevy Chase, Charles Grodin, Robert Guillaume, Harold Gould, George Grizzard, T.K. Carter; *D:* Jay Sandrich; *W:* Neil Simon; *C:* David M. Walsh; *M:* Marvin Hamlisch.

Seize the Day 🦴🦴🦴 **1986** A man approaching middle age (Williams) feels that he is a failure. Brilliant performances by all, plus a number of equally fine actors in small roles. Based on the short novel by Saul Bellow. **93m/C VHS.** Robin Williams, Joseph Wiseman, Jerry Stiller, Glenne Headly, Tony Roberts; *D:* Fielder Cook.

Seizure 🦴🦴 **1974 (PG)** Three demonic creatures from a writer's dreams come to life and terrorize him and his houseguests at a weekend party. Slick but disjointed; Stone's directorial debut. Interesting cast includes Tattoo from "Fantasy Island." **93m/C VHS.** *CA* Jonathan Frid, Herve Villechaize, Christina Pickles, Martine Beswick, Joseph Sirola, Troy Donahue, Mary Woronov, Anne Meacham; *D:* Oliver Stone; *W:* Oliver Stone, Edward Andrew (Santos Alcocer) Mann; *C:* Roger Racine.

Seizure: The Story of Kathy Morris 🦴🦴 **1982** The real-life anguish and struggle of a young music student who must have brain surgery and comes out of it unable to read or count. Workaday dramatization. **104m/C VHS.** Leonard Nimoy, Penelope Milford; *D:* Gerald I. Isenberg.

Selena 🦴🦴½ **1996 (PG)** Lopez is appealing in the title role of the 23-year-old Tejano superstar singer who was just breaking into international prominence when she was murdered by the president of her fan club in 1995. Flashbacks show dad Abraham's (Olmos) dashed musical aspirations and he serves as a stage father to his children, recognizing his daughter Selena's exceptional voice. Film covers her marriage to guitarist Chris Perez (Seda) and her building success until the final tragedy (which isn't shown). Film concludes with concert footage of the real Selena. **127m/C VHS, DVD, Wide.** Jennifer Lopez, Edward James Olmos, Jon Seda, Constance Marie, Jacob Vargas, Lupe Ontiveros, Jackie Guerra, Sal Lopez, Rebecca Lee Mezza; *D:* Gregory Nava; *W:* Gregory Nava; *C:* Edward Lachman; *M:* Dave Grusin.

Self-Defense 🦴½ **1988 (R)** When a city's police force goes on strike, the citizens band together into vigilante troops. **85m/C VHS.** Tom Nardini, Brenda Bazinet.

A Self-Made Hero 🦴🦴🦴 *Un Heros Tres Discret; A Very Discreet Hero* **1995** Albert Delhousse (Kassovitz) is a young Frenchman who manages to avoid military service in WWII. His one great talent is his confidence and his ability as a salesman. So, with some help from a true freedom fighter known as the Captain (Dupontel), he sells himself as a hero of the Resistance in 1945 Paris and manages to do so very effectively for the rest of his life. Kassovitz does an excellent job as the assured imposter. Based on the novel by Jean-Francoise Deniau; French with subtitles. **105m/C VHS, Wide.** *FR* Mathieu Kassovitz, Anouk Grinberg, Albert Dupontel, Sandrine Kimberlain, Jean-Louis Trintignant, Nadia Barentin; *D:* Jacques Audiard; *W:* Jacques Audiard, Alain Le Henry; *C:* Jean-Marc Fabre; *M:* Alexandre Desplat.

Sell Out 🦴🦴½ **1976 (PG)** A former spy living in Jerusalem is called out of retirement; his protege, who defected to the Soviets, now wants out. **102m/C VHS, DVD.** Richard Widmark, Oliver Reed, Gayle Hunnicutt, Sam Wanamaker; *D:* Peter Collinson; *W:* Judson Kinberg, Murray Smith; *C:* Arthur Ibbetson; *M:* Colin Frichter.

Selma, Lord, Selma 🦴🦴½ **1999** Civil rights drama focuses on the youngest two participants in a 1965 voting-rights march from Selma to Montgomery. Preteen Sheyann Webb (Smollett) is inspired by Dr. Martin Luther King Jr.'s (Powell) message of nonviolent demonstration and becomes dedicated to the cause, along with her best friend Rachel Nelson (Peyton). Things come to a climax with the March 7th march to the Edmund Pettus Bridge in Selma, a day that became known as "Bloody Sunday" when state troopers attacked the demonstrators. Adapted from the book "Selma, Lord, Selma" by Webb-Christburg, Nelson, and Frank Sikora. **88m/C VHS.** Jurnee Smollett, Stephanie Zandra Peyton, Clifton Powell, Yolanda King; *D:* Charles Burnett; *W:* Cynthia Whitcomb. **TV**

Semi-Tough 🦴🦴½ **1977 (R)** Likeable, still current social satire involving a couple of pro-football buddies and their mutual interest in their team owner's daughter. Romantic comedy, satire of the sports world, zany highjinks—it's all here, though not enough of any of these. Pleasant and enjoyable. Based on the novel by Dan Jenkins. **107m/C VHS, DVD, Wide.** Burt Reynolds, Kris Kristofferson, Jill Clayburgh, Lotte Lenya, Robert Preston, Bert Convy, Richard Masur, Carl Weathers, Brian Dennehy, John Matuszak, Ron Silver; *D:* Michael Ritchie; *W:* Walter Bernstein.

The Senator Was Indiscreet 🦴🦴🦴 *Mr. Ashton was Indiscreet* **1947** A farcical comedy concerning a slightly loony senator with presidential aspirations. He thinks he can win the nomination because he keeps a diary that would prove embarrassing to numerous colleagues. The diary then falls into the hands of a journalist. Powell is wonderful as the daffy politician. Playwright Kaufman's only directorial effort. **75m/B VHS.** William Powell, Ella Raines, Hans Conried; *D:* George S. Kaufman; *C:* William Mellor. N.Y. Film Critics '47: Actor (Powell).

Send Me No Flowers 🦴🦴🦴 **1964** Vintage Hudson-Day comedy. Hudson plays a hypochondriac who thinks his death is imminent. He decides to provide for his family's future by finding his wife a rich husband. She thinks he's feeling guilty for having an affair. **100m/C VHS.** Rock Hudson, Doris Day, Tony Randall, Paul Lynde; *D:* Norman Jewison; *W:* Julius J. Epstein; *C:* Daniel F. Fapp.

The Sender 🦴🦴 **1982 (R)** An amnesiac young man is studied by a psychiatrist. She discovers that her patient is a "sender," who can transmit his nightmares to other patients at a hospital. **92m/C VHS.** *GB* Kathryn Harrold, Zeljko Ivanek, Shirley Knight, Paul Freeman, Sean Hewitt, Harry Ditson, Marsha A. Hunt, Al Matthews, Angus MacInnes, Olivier Pierre; *D:* Roger Christian; *W:* Thomas Baum; *M:* Trevor Jones.

The Sender 🦴🦴½ **1998 (R)** Naval officer Dallas Grayson (Madsen) and his daughter Lisa are possessed of a mysterious power they may have inherited from Dallas' long-missing father, a Naval pilot shot down in the '60s. Whatever they have, the government wants, and they don't care how they get it. **98m/C VHS.** Michael Madsen, Dyan Cannon, Robert Vaughn, R. Lee Ermey, Steven Williams, Brian Bloom, Shelli Lether; *D:* Richard Pepin; *W:* Richard Preston Jr., Nathan Long; *C:* Michael Weaver.

Senior Trip 🦴 **1981** N.Y.C. will never be the same after a bunch of rowdy Midwestern high school seniors tear up the town on their graduation trip. **96m/C VHS.** James Carroll, Scott Baio, Mickey Rooney, Faye Grant, Vincent Spano, Jane Hoffman; *D:* Kenneth Johnson. **TV**

Senior Week woof! **1988** A batch of girl-hungry teens have a wacky time on their Florida vacation just before graduation. **97m/C VHS.** Michael St. Gerard, Devon Skye, Leesa Bryte; *D:* Stuart Goldman.

The Seniors 🦴🦴 **1978 (R)** A group of college students decide to open a phony sex clinic, but the joke is on them when the clinic becomes a success. Better than it sounds. Pretty good acting and much harmless goofiness. **87m/C VHS.** Dennis Quaid, Priscilla Barnes, Jeffrey Byron, Gary Imhoff; *D:* Rod Amateau.

Senora Tentacion 🦴🦴 **1949** Musical melodrama about a composer who fights to leave his mother, sister, and girlfriend in order to flee with Hortensia, a famous singer. In Spanish with English subtitles. **82m/B VHS.** David Silva, Susana Guizar, Ninon Sevilla.

Sensation 🦴🦴 **1994 (R)** A college co-ed agrees to participate in a professor's paranormal experiments in order to test her psychic abilities. Unfortunately what she senses is her prof involved in the unsolved sex-murder of a former student. **102m/C VHS.** Kari Wuhrer, Eric Roberts, Ron Perlman, Ed Begley Jr., Paul LeMat, Claire Stansfield, Kieran Mulroney, Tracey Needham; *D:* Brian Grant; *W:* Doug Wallace; *M:* Arthur Kempel.

Sensations 🦴🦴 **1987 (R)** A woman and a man who aren't exceptionally fond of one another share a lottery ticket and win. Vincent is best known as a former director of porno flicks, and he manages to work in sexual overtones. **91m/C VHS.** Rebecca Lynn, Blake Bahner, Jennifer Delora, Rick Savage, Loretta Palma, Frank Stewart; *D:* Chuck Vincent.

Sensations of 1945 🦴🦴½ *Sensations* **1944** A press agent turns his firm over to one of his clients, a dancer with some wild promotional ideas. Brings together numerous variety and musical acts. W. C. Fields has a cameo in his last film role. Mostly unremarkable, occasionally fun musical. **86m/B VHS.** Eleanor Powell, Dennis O'Keefe, Sir C. Aubrey Smith, Eugene Pallette, Cab Calloway, Sophie Tucker, Woody Herman, Lyle Talbot, Marie Blake; *Cameos:* W.C. Fields; *D:* Andrew L. Stone.

Sense & Sensibility 🦴🦴 **1985** BBC miniseries adaptation of Jane Austen's first novel concerning two sisters striving for happiness in their well-ordered lives. **174m/C VHS, DVD.** *GB* Irene Richard, Tracey Childs; *D:* Rodney Bennett. **TV**

Sense and Sensibility 🦴🦴🦴½ **1995 (PG)** Thanks to the machinations of greedy relatives, the impecunious Dashwood family is forced to move to a country cottage when father dies. Sensible Elinor (Thompson) looks after the household while overly romantic Marianne (Winslet) pines for passion—ignoring the noble attentions of middle-aged neighbor Brandon (Rickman) for the far more dashing Willoughby (Wise). Elinor has her own hopes for marriage with boyishly ineffectual Edward (Grant) but all three men have secrets that could crush romantic dreams (at least temporarily). Somewhat slow-paced but witty adaptation (by Thompson) of Jane Austen's first novel, well-acted and beautifully photographed (oh, to be in the English countryside). **135m/C VHS, DVD, 8mm.** *GB* Emma Thompson, Kate Winslet, Hugh Grant, Alan Rickman, Greg Wise, Robert Hardy, Elizabeth Spriggs, Emile Francois, Gemma Jones, James Fleet, Harriet Walter, Imogen Stubbs, Imelda Staunton, Hugh Laurie, Richard Lumsden; *D:* Ang Lee; *W:* Emma Thompson; *C:* Michael Coulter; *M:* Patrick Doyle. Oscars '95: Adapt. Screenplay; British Acad. '95: Actress (Thompson), Film, Support. Actress (Winslet); Golden Globes '96: Film—Drama, Screenplay; L.A. Film Critics '95: Screenplay; Natl. Bd. of Review '95: Actress (Thompson), Director (Lee), Film; N.Y. Film Critics '95: Director (Lee); Screen Actors Guild '95: Support. Actress (Winslet); Writers Guild '95: Adapt. Screenplay; Broadcast Film Critics '95: Film, Screenplay.

A Sense of Freedom 🦴🦴🦴 **1978 (R)** A hopeless racketeering criminal is thrust from institution to institution until the Scottish authorities decide on an innovative style of reform. Based on Jimmy Boyle's autobiographical book. Excellent and disturbing. **81m/C VHS.** *GB* David Hayman, Alex Norton, Jake D'Arcy, Sean Scanlan, Fulton Mackay; *D:* John MacKenzie.

Senseless 🦴🦴 **1998 (R)** Darryl (Wayans) is a poverty stricken college student trying to work his way through school while still supporting his family back home. He agrees to be a medical test subject for a procedure intended to heighten the senses. Unfortunately, as one sense is amplified, the others are drowned out, and Darryl becomes a flailing buffoon. Meanwhile he is in a competition against smarmy frat boy Scott (Spade, who looks about ten years late for his last Econ class) that would land him a job on Wall Street. After dealing with sounds that are too loud and smells that are too pungent, his body adjusts itself. The slapstick bits are hit and miss, but the likable Wayans and dislikable Spade prop up the movie fairly well. **93m/C VHS, DVD.** Marlon Wayans, David Spade, Matthew Lillard, Rip Torn, Tamara Taylor, Brad Dourif, Ken Lerner, Ernie Lively, Richard McGonagle, Esther Scott, Kenya Moore; *D:* Penelope Spheeris; *W:* Greg Erb, Craig Mazin; *C:* Daryn Okada; *M:* Yello.

Senso 🦴🦴🦴 *The Wanton Contessa* **1954** Tragic story of romance and rebellion as Italian patriots battle the Austro-Hungarian empire for independence in 1866. An Italian noblewoman betrays her marriage, and almost her country, to be with a cynical Austrian soldier in this visually stunning piece of cinematography. In Italian with English subtitles or dubbed. **125m/C VHS, DVD.** *IT* Alida Valli, Massimo Girotti, Heinz Moog, Farley Granger; *D:* Luchino Visconti; *C:* Robert Krasker.

The Sensual Man 🦴½ **1974 (R)** Hot-blooded Italian falls in love and gets married only to find out that his wife cannot consummate their marriage. Exploitative, misogynistic, and unfunny. **90m/C VHS.** Giancarlo Giannini, Rossana Podesta, Lionel Stander; *D:* Marco Vicario.

Sensual Partners woof! **1987** Young actresses are lured to Tangier by a fake movie producer and sold as sex slaves. Emphasis on soft-focus, soft-core flesh. **87m/C VHS.** Gina Jansen, Eric Falk.

The Sensuous Nurse 🦴🦴 **1976 (R)** Italian comedy about a beautiful nurse hired by the greedy, treacherous relatives of a weak-hearted count in hopes that her voluptuousness will give him a heart attack. It doesn't, and she falls in love. Mindless, but fun and sexy. Dubbed in English. **79m/C VHS.** *IT* Ursula Andress, Mario Pisu, Dulio Del Prete, Jack Palance; *D:* Nello Rosatti.

Sensuous Summer 🦴½ **1993 (R)** When Bobby returns home to the town of Elk Lake he finds the family business, run by his brother Nick, is in deep trouble. It seems Alex, an unscrupulous banker, wants to foreclose. But business comes second to pleasure when Bobby is reunited with old flame Jill and Nick takes up again with ex-girlfriend Cindy. **80m/C VHS.** Tom Case, Christina Campbell, Brittany McGrea, Gina Jorand.

The Sensuous Teenager woof! *Libido; Forbidden Passions* **1970 (R)** Overwhelmingly erotic and uncontrollably seductive, a teenage girl aims to please by releasing all the sensuality within her. **80m/C VHS.** Sandra Jullien, Janine Reynaud, Michel Lemoine; *D:* Max Pecas.

The Sentinel 🦴🦴 **1976 (R)** A model, who has moved into a New York City brownstone, encounters an aging priest and some unusual neighbors. When she investigates strange noises she finds out that the apartment building houses the doorway to hell—and that she's intended to be the next doorkeeper. Modest suspense film with a good cast and enough shock and special effects to keep the viewer interested. **92m/C VHS, DVD.** Chris Sarandon, Christina Raines, Ava Gardner, Jose Ferrer, Sylvia Miles, John Carradine, Burgess Meredith, Tom Berenger, Beverly D'Angelo, Jeff Goldblum, Arthur Kennedy, Deborah Raffin, Eli Wallach, Christopher Walken; *D:* Michael Winner; *W:* Michael Winner, Jeffrey Konvitz; *C:* Richard Kratina; *M:* Gil Melle.

Separate but Equal 🦴🦴🦴½ **1991 (PG)** One of TV's greatest history lessons, a powerful dramatization of the 1954 Brown vs. The Board of Education case that wrung a landmark civil rights decision from the Supreme Court. Great care is taken to humanize all the participants, from the humblest schoolchild to NAACP lawyer Thurgood Marshall (Poitier). On two cassettes. **194m/C VHS.** Sidney Poitier, Burt Lancaster, Richard Kiley, Cleavon Little, John McMartin, Graham Beckel, Lynne Thigpen, Albert Hall; *D:* George Stevens Jr.; *W:* George Stevens Jr.

Separate Lives 🦴½ **1994 (R)** Psych prof Lauren Porter (Hamilton) is in need of some counseling herself. Seems she has a sexy alter ego calling herself Lena and Lauren fears she may have killed someone in her Lena persona. So she turns to her student Tom (Belushi), who happens to be an ex-cop, for help. Sketchy characters and a tired formula make this one a yawner. **101m/C VHS.** Linda Hamilton, James Belushi, Vera Miles, Elissabeth (Elisabeth, Elizabeth, Liz) Moss, Drew Snyder, Mark Lindsay Chapman, Marc Poppel, Elizabeth Arlen; *D:* David Madden; *W:* Steven Pressfield; *M:* William Olvis.

A Separate Peace 🦴🦴 **1973 (PG)** Two young men in a New England prep school during WWII come to grips with the war, coming of age, and a tragic accident. Cheap rendition of a not-so-great novel by John Knowles. **104m/C VHS.** John Heyl, Parker Stevenson, William Roerick; *D:* Larry Peerce; *M:* Charles Fox.

Separate Tables 🦴🦴🦴½ **1958** Adaptation of the Terence Rattigan play about a varied cast of characters living out their personal dramas in a British seaside hotel. Guests include a matriarch and her shy daughter, a divorced couple, a spinster, and a presumed war hero. Their secrets and loves are examined in grand style. Fine acting all around. **98m/B VHS, DVD, Wide.** Burt Lancaster, David Niven, Rita Hayworth, Deborah Kerr, Wendy Hiller, Rod Taylor, Gladys Cooper, Felix Aylmer, Cathleen Nesbitt, Audrey Dalton, May Hallatt, Priscilla Morgan, Hilda Plowright; ***D:*** Delbert Mann; ***W:*** John Gay; ***C:*** Charles B(ryant) Lang Jr.; ***M:*** David Raksin. Oscars '58: Actor (Niven), Support. Actress (Hiller); Golden Globes '59: Actor—Drama (Niven); N.Y. Film Critics '58: Actor (Niven).

Separate Tables 🦴🦴½ **1983 (PG)** A remake of the 1958 film adapted from Terence Rattigan's play. Separated into two parts, "Table by the Window" and "Table Number Seven." The lives of the lonely inhabitants of a hotel are dramatized through wonderful acting by Christie and Bates. **50m/C VHS.** Julie Christie, Alan Bates, Claire Bloom, Irene Worth; ***D:*** John Schlesinger. **CABLE**

Separate Vacations 🦴½ **1986 (R)** A married man leaves his wife and kids to take a separate vacation, hoping he'll find exciting sex. Wife and kids end up at a ski resort, where romance comes her way. A lightweight, old story. **91m/C VHS.** David Naughton, Jennifer Dale, Mark Keyloun; ***D:*** Michael Anderson Sr.

Separate Ways 🦴½ **1982 (R)** Unhappily married couple involved in various affairs split up in order to deal with themselves and their marriage. Good cast; bad script wandering down Maudlin Lane. **92m/C VHS.** Karen Black, Tony LoBianco, David Naughton, Sybil Danning; ***D:*** Howard (Hikmet) Avedis; ***C:*** Dean Cundey.

The Separation 🦴🦴 **1994** Emotions (and fine performances) rather than action move along this domestic drama. Anne (Huppert) and Pierre (Auteuil) are living together in Paris with their toddler son when Anne suddenly announces that she's involved with another man. Anne doesn't see why this this should cause any rift in their domestic arrangements but Pierre slowly falls to pieces. Adapted from the novel by Dan Franck; French with subtitles. **85m/C VHS.** *FR* Isabelle Huppert, Daniel Auteuil, Karin Viard, Jerome Deschamps; ***D:*** Christian Vincent; ***W:*** Christian Vincent, Dan Franck; ***C:*** Denis Lenoir.

Sepia Cinderella 🦴🦴 **1947** A songwriter, who finds himself with a hit, abandons his current life and love to try high society. He finds out it's not what he wants after all. **67m/B VHS.** Sheila Guyse, Rubel Blakely, Freddie Bartholomew, Sid Catlett, Deke Wilson.

September 🦴🦴½ **1988 (PG-13)** Woody does Bergman again with a shuttered, claustrophobic drama about six unhappy people trying to verbalize their feelings in a dark summer house in Vermont. Well-acted throughout and interesting at first, but the whining and angst attacks eventually give way to boredom. Of course, the Woodman went on to "Crimes and Misdemeanors," blending his dark and comedic sides masterfully, so the best way to look at this is as a training film. **82m/C VHS, DVD, Wide.** Mia Farrow, Dianne Wiest, Denholm Elliott, Sam Waterston, Elaine Stritch, Jack Warden; ***D:*** Woody Allen; ***W:*** Woody Allen; ***C:*** Carlo Di Palma; ***M:*** Art Tatum.

September Affair 🦴🦴½ **1950** A married engineer and a classical pianist miss their plane from Naples. When the plane crashes, they're presumed dead, and they find themselves free to continue their illicit love affair. They find they cannot hide forever and must make peace with their pasts. Features the hit "September Song," recorded by Walter Huston. **104m/B VHS.** Joseph Cotten, Joan Fontaine, Francoise Rosay, Jessica Tandy, Robert Arthur; ***D:*** William Dieterle; ***C:*** Charles B(ryant) Lang Jr. Golden Globes '52: Score.

September Gun 🦴🦴½ **1983** A nun hires an aging gunfighter to escort her and a group of Apache children to a church school 200 miles away. Preston is excellent as the ornery varmint in this enjoyable, pleasant western comedy. **94m/C VHS.** Robert Preston, Patty Duke, Christopher Lloyd, Geoffrey Lewis, Sally Kellerman; ***D:*** Don Taylor. **TV**

September 30, 1955 🦴🦴½ *9/30/55* **1977 (PG)** A college undergrad (Thomas) in a small Arkansas town is devastated when he learns of the death of his idol, James Dean. (The title refers to the day Dean died.) Jimmy gathers a group of friends together for a vigil which turns into a drinking-binge, resulting in police chases and, finally, tragedy. Film debut of Quaid. **107m/C VHS.** Richard Thomas, Lisa Blount, Deborah Benson, Tom Hulce, Dennis Christopher, Dennis Quaid, Susan Tyrrell; ***D:*** James Bridges; ***W:*** James Bridges.

Serendipity 🦴🦴½ **2001 (PG-13)** Romance finds Jonathan (Cusack) and Sara (Beckinsale) falling in love one cold New York winter's night but then they part company because Sara believes if it's meant to be, fate will bring them back together. Sara's a twinkling twit. Ten years later both are engaged, but Jon and Sara also become separately convinced that they are destined to be together—if they can find each other again. Lots of near-misses and travel between New York and San Francisco until the inevitable happens. Swoony romanticism and more dippy than serendipitous but done in an expert manner. **87m/C VHS, DVD, Wide.** *US* John Cusack, Kate Beckinsale, Molly Shannon, John Corbett, Jeremy Piven, Bridget Moynahan, Eugene Levy; ***D:*** Peter Chelsom; ***W:*** Marc Klein; ***C:*** John de Borman; ***M:*** Alan Silvestri.

Sgt. Bilko 🦴½ **1995 (PG)** Popular '50s sitcom doesn't march so much as limp to the big screen with Martin leading the troops as the wise-cracking title character, crafted so brilliantly by Phil Silvers on the small screen. Martin flims and flams with frenetic energy as he tries to save his base from Washington cutbacks and the film from utter disaster. Enter Major Thorn (Hartman), Bilko's old adversary, who's plotting revenge on the con artist sergeant. Aykroyd's Bilko's naive boss, Col. Hall, but has little to do. Director Lynn finds his usual comic flair on leave this time around—too few laughs, spread too thin. Sentimental stroke has Catherine Silvers, Phil's daughter, playing Lt. Monday. **95m/C VHS, DVD, Wide.** Steve Martin, Dan Aykroyd, Phil Hartman, Glenne Headly, Darryl (Chill) Mitchell, Max Casella, Brian Leckner, Pamela Segall, Eric Edwards, Dan Ferro, John Marshall Jones, Brian Ortiz, Dale Dye; ***D:*** Jonathan Lynn; ***W:*** Andy Breckman; ***C:*** Peter Sova; ***M:*** Alan Silvestri.

Sgt. Kabukiman N.Y.P.D. woof! **1994** When New York cop Harry Griswold (Gianasi) investigates the death of a famous Japanese Kabuki actor, he suddenly finds himself in a kimono, having really bad hair-days, and vested with the powers of "Kabukiman." With the help of his beautiful teacher Lotus (Byun), he learns to channel his commmand of such amazing weapons as suffocating sushi rolls and lethal chopsticks into crime fighting. Stupid and insulting (deliberately so), all at the same time. A PG-13 version runs 95 minutes. **104m/C VHS, DVD.** Rick Gianasi, Susan Byun, Brick Bronsky, Bill Weeden, Thomas Crnkovich, Larry Robinson, Noble Lee Lester; ***D:*** Lloyd Kaufman, Michael Herz; ***W:*** Lloyd Kaufman, Andrew Osborn; ***C:*** Bob Williams; ***M:*** Bob Mithoff.

Sergeant Matlovich vs. the U.S. Air Force 🦴🦴½ **1978** A serviceman fights to remain in the Air Force after admitting his homosexuality. Compelling theme (from a true story) and good lead performance from Dourif are not enough to carry a rather flat made for TV script. **100m/C VHS.** Brad Dourif, Marc Singer, Frank Converse, William Daniels, Stephen Elliott, David Spielberg, Rue McClanahan, Mitchell Ryan, David Ogden Stiers; ***D:*** Paul Leaf. **TV**

Sgt. Pepper's Lonely Hearts Club Band woof! **1978 (PG)** "Rip-off" would be putting it kindly. A classic album by one of the greatest rock bands of all time deserves the respect of not having a star-studded extravaganza "filmization" made of it. Gratuitous, weird casting, bad acting give it a surreal feel. And the Bee Gees? Please. A nadir of '70s popular entertainment. ♫Sgt. Pepper's Lonely Hearts Club Band; With a Little Help From My Friends; Fixing a Hole; Getting Better; Here Comes the Sun; I Want You (She's So Heavy); Good Morning, Good Morning; Nowhere Man; Polythene Pam. **113m/C VHS.** Takaaki Yamashita, Maurice Gibb, Peter Frampton, Barry Gibb, Steve Martin, George Burns, Donald Pleasence; ***D:*** Michael A. Schultz.

Sergeant Rutledge 🦴🦴🦴 **1960** The story of a court-martial, told in flashback, about a black cavalry officer on trial for rape and murder. A detailed look at overt and covert racism handled by master director Ford. It is always apparent Strode (as Rutledge) is a heroic, yet human, figure who refuses to be beaten down by circumstances. The courtroom setting is deliberately oppressive but does make the film somewhat static. Based on the novel "Captain Buffalo" by James Warner Bellah. **112m/C VHS.** Woody Strode, Jeffrey Hunter, Constance Towers, Billie Burke, Juano Hernandez, Carleton Young, Charles Seel, Jan Styne, Mae Marsh; ***D:*** John Ford; ***W:*** Willis Goldbeck, James Warner Bellah; ***M:*** Howard Jackson.

Sergeant Ryker 🦴🦴½ **1968** Confident lead acting from Marvin as a U.S. serviceman accused of treason during the Korean War carries this otherwise blah army/courtroom drama. Remake of 1963 TV film "The Case Against Sergeant Ryker." Dillman is good as Marvin's energetic lawyer. **85m/C VHS.** Lee Marvin, Bradford Dillman, Vera Miles, Peter Graves, Lloyd Nolan, Murray Hamilton; ***D:*** Buzz Kulik; ***M:*** John Williams.

Sergeant York 🦴🦴🦴🦴 **1941** Timely and enduring war movie based on the true story of Alvin York, the country boy from Tennessee drafted during WWI. At first a pacifist, Sergeant York (Cooper, well cast in an Oscar-winning role) finds justification for fighting and becomes one of the war's greatest heros. Gentle scenes of rural life contrast with horrific battlegrounds. York served as a consultant. **134m/B VHS.** Gary Cooper, Joan Leslie, Walter Brennan, Dickie Moore, Ward Bond, George Tobias, Noah Beery Jr., June Lockhart, Stanley Ridges, Margaret Wycherly, James Anderson, David Bruce, Lane Chandler, Elisha Cook Jr., Erville Alderson, Howard da Silva, Donald Douglas, Frank Faylen, Pat Flaherty, Joseph Girard, Creighton Hale, Russell Hicks, George Irving, Selmer Jackson, Jack Pennick, Harvey Stephens, Kay Sutton, Clem Bevans, Charles Trowbridge, Guy Wilkerson, Gig Young; ***D:*** Howard Hawks; ***W:*** Abem Finkel, Harry Chandler, Howard Koch, John Huston; ***C:*** Sol Polito; ***M:*** Max Steiner. Oscars '41: Actor (Cooper), Film Editing; N.Y. Film Critics '41: Actor (Cooper).

Sergio Lapel's Drawing Blood 🦴 *Drawing Blood* **1999** Artist/vampire Diana (Spinella) fulfills her artistic visions with blood instead of oils or watercolors. Her human slave Edmond (Wilson) supplies a constant flow of "models" until he meets homeless prostitute Dee (Smith) and decides to take control of his life. Edmond also has his hands full keeping his ever-horny dad (Palatta) out of trouble. The Troma label says it all: non-existent production values, mediocre acting, plenty of flowing red stuff, and ample female exposure (although this time there's a genuine narrative logic to all the nudity). **90m/C DVD.** Kirk Wilson, Larry Palatta, Dawn Spinella, Leo Otero, Erin Smith; ***D:*** Sergio Lapel; ***W:*** Noel Anderson; ***C:*** Shawn Lewallen.

Serial 🦴🦴🦴 **1980 (R)** Fun spoof of hyper-trendiness—open marriage, health foods, fad religions, navel-gazing—in Marin County, the really cool place to live across the Golden Gate from San Francisco. Mull in his first lead is the oddly normal guy surrounded by fruits and nuts. Based on Cyra McFadden's novel. **90m/C VHS.** Martin Mull, Sally Kellerman, Tuesday Weld, Tom Smothers, Bill Macy, Peter Bonerz, Barbara Rhoades, Christopher Lee; ***D:*** Bill Persky; ***W:*** Rich Eustis, Michael Elias.

Serial Bomber 🦴🦴 **1996 (R)** A would-be bomber in Seattle targets his ex-girlfriend but his plan is foiled by an FBI agent. So the bomber shifts targets. Based on the novel "Christmas Apocalypse" by Toshiyuki Tajima. **89m/C VHS, DVD.** Jason London, Lori Petty, James LeGros, Yuki Amami; ***D:*** Keoni Waxman.

Serial Killer 🦴🦴 **1995 (R)** Selby Younger (Delaney) is able to think like a killer in order to catch them. That's how the beautiful cop captured serial killer William Lucian Morrano (Bell) who has now escaped—Selby's his ultimate target but first he wants revenge. So he uses her friends as bait and leaves the bodies for Selby to discover. **94m/C VHS, DVD.** Kim Delaney, Gary Hudson, Tobin Bell, Pam Grier, Marco Rodriguez, Lyman Ward, Cyndi Pass, Andrew Prine; ***D:*** Pierre David; ***W:*** Mark Sevi; ***C:*** Thomas Jewett; ***M:*** Louis Febre.

Serial Mom 🦴🦴🦴 **1994 (R)** June Cleaver-like housewife Turner is nearly perfect, except when someone disrupts her orderly life. Didn't rewind your videotape? Chose the white shoes after Labor Day? Uh oh. Stardom reigns after she's caught and the murderer-as-celebrity phenomenon is exploited to the fullest. Darkly funny Waters satire tends toward the mainstream and isn't as perverse as earlier efforts, but still maintains a shocking edge (vital organs are good for an appearance or two). Turner's chameleonic performance as the perfect mom/crazed killer is right on target, recalling "The War of the Roses." Waterston, Lake, and Lillard are terrific as her generic suburban family. **93m/C VHS, DVD, Wide.** Kathleen Turner, Sam Waterston, Ricki Lake, Matthew Lillard, Mink Stole, Traci Lords, Suzanne Somers, Joan Rivers, Patty (Patricia Campbell) Hearst, Mary Jo Catlett, Justin Whalin, Susan Lowe, Alan J. Wendl, Mary Vivian Pearce; ***D:*** John Waters; ***W:*** John Waters; ***C:*** Robert Stevens; ***M:*** Basil Poledouris; ***V:*** John Waters.

Series 7: The Contenders 🦴🦴½ **2001 (R)** Reality TV takes to the big screen in this morbid but insightful portrayal of a fictional show called "The Contenders" in which the participants hunt each other down to their ultimate, televised, demise. Pic is presented in the form of a marathon of the show, which stars eight-months pregnant Dawn (Smith), the champ who takes on five new challengers, including an 18-year-old girl (Wever), a cancer victim and artist who was also, coincidentally, Dawn's first boyfriend (Fitzgerald). Revealing portrayals make all the contestants sympathetic, but Dawn and Jeff's unique plight is the most interesting. A scene where Dawn casually guns people down in a convenience store while bystanders look on is a highlight in this interesting social satire. **86m/C VHS, DVD, Wide.** *US* Brooke Smith, Glenn Fitzgerald, Merritt Wever, Michael Kaycheck, Richard Venture, Donna Hanover, Marylouise Burke, Nada Despotovich, Danton Stone, Jennifer Van Dyck, Angelina Phillips, Tanny McDonald; ***D:*** Daniel Minahan; ***W:*** Daniel Minahan; ***C:*** Randy Drummond; ***M:*** Girls Against Boys; ***Nar:*** Will Arnett.

The Serpent and the Rainbow woof! **1987 (R)** A good, interesting book (by Harvard ethnobotanist Wade Davis) offering serious speculation on the possible existence and origin of zombies in Haiti was hacked and slashed into a cheap Wes Craven-ized screen semblance of itself. And a shame it is: the result is racist, disrespectful, exploitative, and superficial. **98m/C VHS, DVD.** Paul Guilfoyle, Bill Pullman, Cathy Tyson, Zakes Mokae, Paul Winfield, Conrad Roberts, Badja (Medu) Djola, Theresa Merritt, Brent Jennings, Michael Gough; ***D:*** Wes Craven; ***W:*** Richard Maxwell, A.R. Simoun; ***C:*** John Lindley; ***M:*** Brad Fiedel.

Serpent Island 🦴½ **1954** Two seamen fight over a Caribbean woman amid voodoo rituals, sea monsters and buried treasure. **63m/C VHS.** Sonny Tufts.

The Serpent's Egg 🦴½ *Das Schlangenei* **1978 (R)** Big disappointment from the great Bergman in his second film in English. Ullmann is not sultry and Carradine is horrible. Big budget matched by big Bergman ego, making a big, bad parody of himself. The plot concerns a pair of Jewish trapeze artists surviving in Berlin during Hitler's rise by working in a grisly and mysterious medical clinic. **119m/C VHS.** *GE* David Carradine, Liv Ullmann, Gert Frobe, James Whitmore; ***D:*** Ingmar Bergman; ***W:*** Ingmar Bergman; ***C:*** Sven Nykvist.

The Serpent's Kiss **1997 (R)** Great cast can't quite overcome the story's predictability. In 1699, young Dutch landscape artist Meneer Chrome (MacGregor) accepts a job at the remote English estate of Thomas Smithers (Postlethwaite) who wants a magnificent garden to present to his bored wife, Julianna (Scacchi). But Chrome is secretly employed by Juliana's scheming cousin, James Fitzmaurice (Grant), to bankrupt Smithers so that James can regain Juliana affections. Of course, Julianna casts her eyes on the handsome gardener instead, and then there's the matter of the Smithers' teenaged daughter, Thea (Chaplin). Rousselot is better known as a cinematographer (this is his first directorial effort) and the film at least looks gorgeous. **110m/C VHS, DVD, Wide.** *GB FR* Ewan McGregor, Greta Scacchi, Pete Postlethwaite, Richard E. Grant, Carmen Chaplin, Donal McCann, Charley Boorman; ***D:*** Philippe Rousselot; ***W:*** Tim Rose Price; ***C:*** Jean-Francois Robin; ***M:*** Goran Bregovic.

Serpent's Lair **1995 (R)** Tom (Fahey) and Alex (Medway) have just moved into what's supposed to be their dream apartment in L.A. Too bad there's lots of secrets and Tom's soon drawn into the web of sultry beauty Lillith (Lisa B.), who's not just your average femme fatale. **90m/C VHS.** Jeff Fahey, Heather Medway, Lisa B(arbuscia), Anthony Palermo, Kathleen Noone, Taylor Nichols, Patrick Bauchau; ***D:*** Jeff Reiner; ***W:*** Marc Rosenberg; ***C:*** Feliks Parnell; ***M:*** Vinnie Golia.

Serpico **1973 (R)** Based on Peter Maas's book about the true-life exploits of Frank Serpico, a New York undercover policeman who exposed corruption in the police department. Known as much for his nonconformism as for his honesty, the real Serpico eventually retired from the force and moved to Europe. South Bronx-raised Pacino gives the character reality and strength. Excellent New York location photography. **130m/C VHS.** Al Pacino, John Randolph, Jack Kehoe, Barbara Eda-Young, Cornelia Sharpe, F. Murray Abraham, Tony Roberts; ***D:*** Sidney Lumet. Golden Globes '74: Actor—Drama (Pacino); Natl. Bd. of Review '73: Actor (Pacino); Writers Guild '73: Adapt. Screenplay.

The Servant ½ **1963** A dark, intriguing examination of British class hypocrisy and the master-servant relationship. Wealthy, bored aristocratic playboy Tony (Fox) is ruined by his socially inferior but crafty and ambitious Cockney manservant Hugo (Bogarde). Playwright Harold Pinter wrote the adaptation of Robin Maugham's novel in his first collaboration with expatriate American director Losey. The best kind of British societal navel-gazing. **112m/B VHS, DVD.** *GB* Dirk Bogarde, James Fox, Sarah Miles, Wendy Craig, Catherine Lacey, Richard Vernon; ***D:*** Joseph Losey; ***W:*** Harold Pinter; ***C:*** Douglas Slocombe; ***M:*** John Dankworth. British Acad. '63: Actor (Bogarde); N.Y. Film Critics '64: Screenplay.

Servants of Twilight **1991 (R)** Religious zealots target a small boy for assassination because their cult leader says he's the anti-Christ. Adaptation of the Dean R. Koontz novel. Packed with action, its spell on the viewer hinges on a cruel shock ending that undercuts what came before. **95m/C VHS, DVD.** Bruce Greenwood, Belinda Bauer, Grace Zabriskie, Richard Bradford, Jarrett Lennon, Carel Struycken, Jack Kehoe, Kelli Maroney, Dale Dye; ***D:*** Jeffrey Obrow; ***W:*** Stephen Carpenter. CABLE

Serving in Silence: The Margarethe Cammermeyer Story **1995** Army nurse Margarethe Cammermeyer (Close) has had a distinguished career for 24 years, a bronze star earned in Vietnam, and obtained the rank of colonel. During a security clearance interview, she admits to the military that she is a lesbian and finds herself reluctantly in the eye of the media storm. The TV film won 3 EMMY awards: Best Actress for Close; Best Supporting Actress for Davis (as Margarethe's lover); and Best Screenplay. **92m/C VHS.** Glenn Close, Judy Davis, Jan Rubes, Wendy Makkena, William Converse-Roberts, Susan Barnes, Colleen Flynn, William Allen Young; ***D:*** Jeff Bleckner; ***W:*** Allison Cross. TV

Serving Sara **2002 (PG-13)** Perry plays the guy who's serving Hurley with divorce papers from her Texas hubby Campbell and ends up falling in love with her. Not yet reviewed. **?m/C VHS, DVD.** Matthew Perry, Elizabeth Hurley, Bruce Campbell, Vincent Pastore, Cedric the Entertainer; ***D:*** Reginald (Reggie) Hudlin; ***W:*** Jay Scherick, David Ronn.

Sesame Street Presents: Follow That Bird *Follow That Bird* **1985 (G)** Big Bird suffers an identity crisis, and leaves Sesame Street to join a family of real birds. He soon misses his home, and returns, in a danger-filled journey. **92m/C VHS, DVD.** Sandra Bernhard, John Candy, Chevy Chase, Joe Flaherty, Dave Thomas, Waylon Jennings; ***D:*** Ken Kwapis; ***W:*** Judy Freudberg, Tony Geiss; ***C:*** Curtis Clark; ***M:*** Lennie Niehaus; ***V:*** Carroll Spinney, Jim Henson, Frank Oz.

Session 9 **2001 (R)** Hazardous materials contractor Gordon (Mullan) bids on a job to remove asbestos from a rundown insane asylum. He secures the contract by promising to complete the work in a week, although under ideal circumstances it should take a month. Unfortunately, "ideal circumstances" are not afoot in the creepy booby hatch. The oppressive atmosphere soon gets to Gordon and his crew, who begin turning on each other after the discovery of nine audio tapes confirming rumors of satanic rituals and torture of patients. Somewhat marred by editing that gives away the plot too early, and also by the fact that for workers under a deadline, these guys stand around getting freaked out way too much. Shot using Sony's CineAlta HD digital video cameras instead of film. **100m/C VHS, DVD, Wide.** *US* Peter Mullan, David Caruso, Joshua Lucas, Brendan Sexton III, Paul Guilfoyle, Stephen Gevedon; ***D:*** Brad Anderson; ***W:*** Brad Anderson, Stephen Gevedon; ***C:*** Uta Briesewitz; ***M:*** Climax Gold Twins.

Sessions **1983** Mentally exhausted by her roles as sister, single parent, lover, exercise enthusiast, and high-priced prostitute, Leigh Churchill (Hamel) seeks professional counselling. Hamel's first role after "Hill Street Blues" is only average in this made for TV drama. **96m/C VHS.** Veronica Hamel, Jeffrey DeMunn, Jill Eikenberry, David Marshall Grant, George Coe, Henderson Forsythe, Deborah Hedwall; ***D:*** Richard Pearce. TV

Set It Off ½ **1996 (R)** Lethal "Waiting to Exhale," finds four female friends in Los Angeles pushed over the edge and taking up bank robbery to escape poverty and strike a blow against "the man." The felonious, funky divas of crime include Stony (Pinkett, who seems to be having fun with this role) and Latifah as Cleo, in a powerhouse performance. Butt-kicking action scenes are most entertaining combined with a soundtrack, including Seal, En Vogue, the Fugees and Brandy, to match. Melodramatic sequences, including Stony's romance with Keith (Underwood), drag. **121m/C VHS, DVD.** Jada Pinkett Smith, Queen Latifah, Vivica A. Fox, Kimberly Elise, Blair Underwood, John C. McGinley, Anna Maria Horsford, Ella Joyce, Charles Robinson, Chaz Lamas Shepard, Vincent Baum, Van Baum, Tom Byrd, Samantha MacLachlan; ***D:*** F. Gary Gray; ***W:*** Kate Lanier, Takashi Bufford; ***C:*** Marc Reshovsky; ***M:*** Christopher Young.

Set Me Free ½ *Emporte-Moi* **1999** Thirteen-year-old Hanna is trying to deal with her loneliness in 1963's Montreal. Her Polish immigrant father (Manojlovic) is a frustrated writer who takes his problems out on his family while his depressed wife (Pussieres) slaves in a garment factory to support them. Hanna tries to find solace at the cinema where she becomes enamored of actress Anna Karina, the sultry star of Jean-Luc Godard's "My Life to Live," in which she plays an independent prostitute (not a first-choice role model). Hanna's confusion and unhappiness go unresolved, but then she still has a lot of living to do. French with subtitles. **95m/C VHS, Wide.** *CA SI* Karine Vanasse, Miki (Predrag) Manojlovic, Pascale Bussieres, Alexandre Merineau, Charlotte Christeler, Nancy Huston, Monique Mercure; ***D:*** Lea Pool; ***W:*** Lea Pool, Monique H. Messier, Nancy Huston; ***C:*** Jeanne Lapoirie.

The Set-Up ½ **1949** Excellent, original if somewhat overwrought morality tale about integrity set in the world of boxing. Filmed as a continuous narrative covering only 72 minutes in the life of an aging fighter Stoker Thompson (Ryan). His manager (Tobias) takes a gangster's bribe for Thompson to throw the fight (without informing him), never believing the washed-up boxer has a chance to win. Powerful, with fine performances, especially from Ryan in the lead. Inspired by Joseph Moncure March's narrative poem. **72m/B VHS.** Robert Ryan, Audrey Totter, George Tobias, Alan Baxter, James Edwards, Wallace Ford; ***D:*** Robert Wise; ***W:*** Art Cohn; ***C:*** Milton Krasner.

The Set Up ½ **1995 (R)** Electronic engineer-turned-cat burglar Charlie Thorpe (Zane) is now apparently reformed after a prison stint and works designing and installing security systems. His latest job is for Chairman Jeremiah Cole (Coburn) at Charter Trust bank where he begins romancing the beautiful Gina (Sara). But she becomes the hostage of Charlie's ex-prison buddy Kliff (Russo), who wants Charlie's help in breaking into the bank. However, there's a doublecross (or maybe even a triplecross) that has Charlie scrambling to save his life. Based on the book "My Laugh Comes Last" by James Hadley Chase. **103m/C VHS.** Billy Zane, Mia Sara, James Coburn, James Russo; ***D:*** Strathford Hamilton; ***W:*** Michael Thoma; ***C:*** David Lewis; ***M:*** Conrad Pope.

The Settlement **1999** Con men Jerry and Pat try to make money by buying life insurance policies on the terminally ill. Unfortunately for them, their clients have been living a lot longer than anticipated. Then they meet the seriously ill Barbara and things begin to change. **92m/C VHS, DVD.** Kelly McGillis, John C. Reilly, William Fichtner, Dan Castellaneta, David Rasche; ***D:*** Mark Steilen; ***C:*** Judy Irola; ***M:*** Brian Tyler.

Seven ½ **1979 (R)** Freelance desperado Smith takes $7 million of your tax dollars at work from the feds to get rid of Hawaiian gangsters. Might be tongue in cheek, though sometimes it's hard to tell. Fun action pic unfortunately characterized by bad camera work and over-earnest direction. Features the original of a gag made famous in "Raiders of the Lost Ark." **100m/C VHS.** William Smith, Barbara Leigh, Guich Koock, Art Metrano, Martin Kove, Richard Le Pore, Susan Kiger; ***D:*** Andy Sidaris.

Seven *Se7en* **1995 (R)** If this grim thriller can't make you jump, you're dead, and you won't be the only one. Arrogant, ignorant detective David Mills (Pitt) is newly partnered with erudite old-timer William Somerset (Freeman) and they're stuck with the bizarre case of a morbidly obese man who was forced to eat himself to death. The weary Somerset is certain it's just the beginning and he's right—the non-buddy duo are on the trail of a serial killer who uses the seven deadly sins (gluttony, greed, sloth, pride, lust, envy, and wrath) as his modus operandi. Since most of the film is shot in dark, grimy, and unrelentingly rainy circumstances, much of the grotesqueness of the murders is left to the viewer's imagination—which will be in overdrive. **127m/C VHS, DVD, Wide.** Brad Pitt, Morgan Freeman, Gwyneth Paltrow, Kevin Spacey, R. Lee Ermey, Richard Roundtree, John C. McGinley, Julie Araskog, Reg E. Cathey, Peter Crombie; ***D:*** David Fincher; ***W:*** Andrew Kevin Walker; ***C:*** Darius Khondji; ***M:*** Howard Shore. MTV Movie Awards '96: Film, Most Desirable Male (Pitt), Villain (Spacey); Natl. Bd. of Review '95: Support. Actor (Spacey); N.Y. Film Critics '95: Support. Actor (Spacey); Broadcast Film Critics '95: Support. Actor (Spacey).

Seven Alone ½ *House Without Windows* **1975 (G)** Family adventure tale (based on Monroe Morrow's book "On to Oregon," based in turn on a true story) about seven siblings who undertake a treacherous 2000-mile journey from Missouri to Oregon, after their parents die along the way. Inspiring and all that; good family movie. **85m/C VHS.** Dewey Martin, Aldo Ray, Anne Collins, Dean Smith, Stewart Peterson; ***D:*** Earl Bellamy.

Seven Beauties *Pasqualino Settebellezze; Pasqualino: Seven Beauties* **1976** Very dark war comedy about a small-time Italian crook in Naples with seven ugly sisters to support. He survives a German prison camp and much else; unforgettably, he seduces the ugly commandant of his camp to save his own life. Good acting and tight direction. **116m/C VHS, DVD, Wide.** *IT* Giancarlo Giannini, Fernando Rey, Shirley Stoler, Elena Fiore, Enzo Vitale; ***D:*** Lina Wertmuller; ***W:*** Lina Wertmuller; ***C:*** Tonino Delli Colli.

Seven Brides for Seven Brothers ½ **1954** The eldest of seven fur-trapping brothers in the Oregon Territory brings home a wife. She begins to civilize the other six, who realize the merits of women and begin to look for romances of their own. Thrilling choreography by Michael Kidd—don't miss "The Barn Raising." Charming performances by Powell and Keel, both in lovely voice. Based on Stephen Vincent Benet's story. Thrills, chills, singin', dancin'—a classic Hollywood good time. ♫When You're In Love; Spring, Spring, Spring; Sobbin' Women; Bless Your Beautiful Hide; Goin' Co'tin; Wonderful, Wonderful Day; June Bride; Lonesome Polecat Lament. **103m/C VHS, DVD, 8mm, Wide.** Howard Keel, Jane Powell, Russ Tamblyn, Julie Newmar, Jeff Richards, Tommy (Thomas) Rall, Virginia Gibson; ***D:*** Stanley Donen; ***W:*** Albert Hackett, Frances Goodrich, Dorothy Kingsley; ***C:*** George J. Folsey. Oscars '54: Scoring/Musical.

Seven Chances ½ **1925** Silent classic that Keaton almost didn't make, believing instead that it should go to Harold Lloyd. Desperate lawyer Jimmie Shannon (Keaton) finds that he can inherit $7 million from his grandfather's estate if he marries by 7:00 p.m. on his 27th birthday, which is that day. After his girlfriend (Dwyer) turns down his botched proposal, chaos breaks loose when Jimmie advertises for someone—anyone—to marry him and make him rich. Suddenly he finds what seems to be hundreds of women willing to make the sacrifice, setting up one of the great film pursuits. Memorable boulder sequence was re-shot after preview audience indicated climax was lacking that certain something. Based on the play by David Belasco and remade with Chris O'Donnell as "The Bachelor" (1990). **60m/B VHS, DVD.** Buster Keaton, T. Roy Barnes, Snitz Edwards, Ruth Dwyer, Frankie Raymond; ***D:*** Buster Keaton; ***W:*** Clyde Bruckman, Jean C. Havez, Joseph A. Mitchell; ***C:*** Byron Houck, Elgin Lessley.

Seven Cities of Gold **1955** An expedition of Spanish conquistadors and missionaries descend on 18th-century California, looking for secret Indian caches of gold. Semi-lavish costume epic. **103m/C VHS.** Anthony Quinn, Michael Rennie, Richard Egan, Rita Moreno, Jeffrey Hunter, Eduardo Noriega, John Doucette; ***D:*** Robert D. Webb.

Seven Days in May ½ **1964** Topical but still gripping Cold War nuclear-peril thriller. After President Jordan Lyman (March) signs a nuclear disarmament treaty with the Soviets, General James M. Scott (Lancaster), the leader of the Joint Chiefs of Staff, plans a military takeover because he considers the president's pacifism traitorous. Lyman learns of the potential coup and works to expose the plot before it's too late. Highly suspenseful, with a breathtaking climax. Based on a novel by Fletcher Knebel and Charles Waldo Bailey II. **117m/B VHS, DVD, Wide.** Burt Lancaster, Kirk Douglas, Edmond O'Brien, Fredric March, Ava Gardner, Martin Balsam, George Macready, Whit Bissell, Hugh Marlowe, Richard Anderson, Andrew Duggan, John Houseman; ***D:*** John Frankenheimer; ***W:*** Rod Serling; ***C:*** Ellsworth Fredericks; ***M:*** Jerry Goldsmith. Golden Globes '65: Support. Actor (O'Brien).

Seven Days' Leave ✓✓ 1942 Radio star-crammed musical comedy about a soldier who must marry a certain already betrothed gal (Ball) within a week so he can inherit a fortune. Songs include "Can't Get Out of this Mood," "A Touch of Texas," and "Baby, You Speak My Language." Following the completion of the film, Mature joined the Coast Guard. Lively but not memorable. **87m/B VHS.** Victor Mature, Lucille Ball, Harold (Hal) Peary, Mary Cortes, Ginny Simms, Marcy McGuire, Peter Lind Hayes, Walter Reed, Wallace Ford, Arnold Stang, Buddy Clark, Charles Victor; ***D:*** Tim Whelan.

Seven Days to Live ✓✓½ 2001 (R) Ellen (Plummer) and her hubby Martin Shaw (Pertwee) move to a remote country house to recover from the death of their son. Of course, the house just happens to be built over a graveyard and Ellen is haunted by warnings that she has only, well, the title tells it all. Quite creepy. **96m/C VHS, DVD, Wide.** Amanda Plummer, Sean Pertwee, Nick Brimble, Gina Bellman; ***D:*** Sebastian Niemann.

Seven Deadly Sins ✓✓✓ 1953 A collection of tales concerning destructive emotions and the downfalls they cause. Contains shorts from some of Europe's finest directors (five French and two Italian). Stories and their directors are "Avarice and Anger" (de Filippo), "Sloth" (Dreville), "Lust" (Allegret), "Envy" (Rossellini), "Gluttony" (Rim), "Pride" (Autant-Lara) and "The Eighth Sin" (Lacombe). **127m/B VHS.** *FR IT* Eduardo de Filippo, Isa Miranda, Jacqueline Plessis, Louis de Funes, Paolo Stoppa, Frank Villard, Jean Richard, Francoise Rosay, Jean Debucourt, Louis Seigner; ***D:*** Eduardo de Filippo, Jean Dreville, Yves Allegret, Roberto Rossellini, Carlo Rim, Claude Autant-Lara, Georges Lacombe.

Seven Deaths in the Cat's Eye ✓✓ 1972 A ravenous beast slaughters people in a small Scottish village. This flick reveals a little-known fact about felines. **90m/C VHS.** *IT* Anton Diffring, Jane Birkin; ***D:*** Anthony (Antonio Margheriti) Dawson.

Seven Doors to Death ✓ 1944 Young architect tries to solve a crime to avoid being placed under suspicion. The suspects are six shop owners in this low-budget attempt at a murder mystery. **70m/B VHS.** Chick Chandler, June Clyde, George Meeker, Gregory Gay, Edgar Dearing; ***D:*** Elmer Clifton.

7 Faces of Dr. Lao ✓✓✓ 1963 Dr. Lao is the proprietor of a magical circus that changes the lives of the residents of a small western town. Marvelous special effects and makeup (Randall plays seven characters) highlight this charming family film in the Pal tradition. Charles Finney adapted from his novel. **101m/C VHS, DVD, Wide.** Tony Randall, Barbara Eden, Arthur O'Connell, Lee Patrick, Noah Beery Jr., John Qualen, John Ericson, Royal Dano; ***D:*** George Pal; ***W:*** Charles Beaumont; ***C:*** Robert J. Bronner; ***M:*** Leigh Harline.

Seven Girlfriends ✓✓ 2000 (R) Melancholy romantic comedy has thirty-something bachelor Jesse (Daly) so disheartened by his string of failed romances that he seeks out seven ex-girlfriends to find out what went wrong. Good cast. **100m/C VHS, DVD, Wide.** Timothy Daly, Laura Leighton, Mimi Rogers, Olivia D'Abo, Jami Gertz, Elizabeth Pena, Melora Hardin, Arye Gross, Katy Selverstone; ***D:*** Paul Lazarus; ***W:*** Paul Lazarus, Stephen Gregg; ***C:*** Don E. Fauntleroy; ***M:*** Christopher Tyng.

The Seven Hills of Rome ✓✓½ 1958 Quiet story of a TV star (Lanza) who follows his girlfriend (Castle) to Rome after a lovers' quarrel, and there falls in love with Allasio. Fantastic music makes up for a weak plot. Based on a story by Giueseppi Amato. ♫Arrivederci Roma; Seven Hills of Rome; Never Till Now; Earthbound; Come Dance With Me; Lolita; There's Gonna Be a Party Tonight; Italian Calypso; Questa o Quella. **107m/C VHS.** Mario Lanza, Peggy Castle, Renato Rascel, Marisa Allasio, Clelia Matania, Rosella Como; ***D:*** Roy Rowland; ***W:*** Giorgio Prosperi, Art Cohn; ***M:*** Georgie Stoll.

Seven Hours to Judgment ✓✓ 1988 (R) When the punks who murdered his wife go free, a psychotic man (Leibman) decides to take justice into his own hands. He kidnaps the wife of the judge in charge (Bridges, who also directed) and leads him on a wild goose chase. Leibman steals the film as the psycho. Ex-Springsteen spouse Phillips plays the judge's wife. Ambitious but credulity-stretching revenge/crime drama. Screenplay written by de Souza under the pseudonym Elliot Stephens. **90m/C VHS.** Beau Bridges, Ron Leibman, Julianne Phillips, Al Freeman Jr., Reggie Johnson; ***D:*** Beau Bridges; ***W:*** Steven E. de Souza, Walter Halsey Davis; ***C:*** Hanania Baer; ***M:*** John Debney.

Seven Keys to Baldpate 1917 Early version of the famous stage play by George M. Cohen in which George Washington Magee accepts a challenge that he can finish a novel in 24 hours while staying at the deserted Baldpate Inn. **66m/B VHS.** Hugh Ford, Anna Q. Nilsson, George M. Cohan, Hedda Hopper, Corene Uzzell, Joseph Smiley, Armand Cortes, C. Warren Cook; ***D:*** Mae Gaston.

Seven Keys to Baldpate 1929 Early talkie version of the film which was based on the famous stage play of the same name by George M. Cohan which follows an author into a deserted Baldpate Inn on a bet that he can't finish a novel in 24 hours while in the Inn. **70m/B VHS.** Richard Dix, Miriam Seegar, Crauford Kent, Margaret Livingston, Lucien Littlefield; ***D:*** Reginald Barker.

The Seven Little Foys ✓✓✓ 1955 Enjoyable musical biography of Eddie Foy (played ebulliantly by Hope) and his famed vaudevillian troupe. Cagney's appearance as George M. Cohan is brief, but long enough for a memorable dance duet with Hope. ♫Mary's a Grand Old Name; I'm a Yankee Doodle Dandy; I'm the Greatest Father of Them All; Nobody; Comedy Ballet; I'm Tired; Chinatown, My Chinatown. **95m/C VHS, DVD.** Bob Hope, Milly Vitale, George Tobias, Angela Clark, James Cagney; ***D:*** Melville Shavelson; ***W:*** Melville Shavelson, Jack Rose.

Seven Magnificent Gladiators ✓ 1984 (PG) Seven gladiators team up to save a peaceful Roman village from total annihilation. Dismal effort at a remake of "The Seven Samurai"—see the original instead, please. Ferrigno was "The Incredible Hulk" on TV. **86m/C VHS.** Lou Ferrigno, Sybil Danning, Brad Harris, Dan Vadis, Carla Ferrigno; ***D:*** Bruno Mattei.

Seven Minutes in Heaven ✓✓ 1986 (PG) Sensitive love story about a 15-year-old girl who invites her platonic male friend to live in her house, and finds it disturbs her boyfriend, as these things will. Ever so tasteful (unlike most other teen comedies), with gentle comedy—but forgettable. **90m/C VHS.** Jennifer Connelly, Byron Thames, Maddie Corman, Lauren Holly; ***D:*** Linda Feferman; ***W:*** Jane Bernstein; ***C:*** Steven Fierberg.

The Seven-Per-Cent Solution ✓✓✓ 1976 (PG) Dr. Watson (Duvall) persuades Sherlock Holmes (Nicholson) to meet with Sigmund Freud (Arkin) to cure his cocaine addiction. Holmes and Freud then find themselves teaming up to solve a supposed kidnapping. Adapted by Nicholas Meyer from his own novel. One of the most charming Holmes films; well-cast, intriguing blend of mystery, drama, and fun. Title refers to the solution of cocaine Holmes injects. **113m/C VHS, DVD.** Alan Arkin, Nicol Williamson, Laurence Olivier, Robert Duvall, Vanessa Redgrave, Joel Grey, Samantha Eggar, Jeremy Kemp, Charles Gray, Regine; ***D:*** Herbert Ross; ***W:*** Nicholas Meyer; ***C:*** Oswald Morris; ***M:*** John Addison.

Seven Samurai ✓✓✓✓ *Shichinin No Samurai; The Magnificent Seven* 1954 Kurosawa's masterpiece, set in 16th-century Japan. A small farming village, beset by marauding bandits, hires seven professional soldiers to rid itself of the scourge. Wanna watch a samurai movie? This is the one. Sweeping, complex human drama with all the ingredients: action, suspense, comedy. Available in several versions of varying length, all long—and all too short. Splendid acting. In Japanese with English subtitles. **204m/B VHS, DVD.** *JP* Toshiro Mifune, Takashi Shimura, Yoshio Inaba, Kuninori Kodo, Isao (Ko) Kimura, Seiji Miyaguchi, Minoru Chiaki, Daisuke Kato, Bokuzen Hidari, Kamatari (Keita) Fujiwara, Yoshio Kosugi, Yoshio Tsuchiya, Jun Tatara, Sojin, Kichijiro Ueda, Jun Tazaki, Keiji Sakakida, Keiko Tsushima, Gen Shimizu; ***D:*** Akira Kurosawa; ***W:*** Akira Kurosawa, Shinobu Hashimoto, Hideo Oguni; ***C:*** Asakazu Nakai; ***M:*** Fumio Hayasaka. Venice Film Fest. '54: Silver Prize.

Seven Sinners ✓✓✓ *Cafe of the Seven Sinners* 1940 A South Seas cabaret singer (Dietrich) attracts sailors like flies, resulting in bar brawls, romance, and intrigue. Manly sailor Wayne falls for her. A good-natured, standard Hollywood adventure. Well cast; performed and directed with gusto. **83m/B VHS.** Marlene Dietrich, John Wayne, Albert Dekker, Broderick Crawford, Mischa Auer, Billy Gilbert, Oscar Homolka; ***D:*** Tay Garnett.

Seven Thieves ✓✓✓ 1960 Charming performances and nice direction make this tale of the perfect crime especially watchable. Robinson, getting on in years, wants one last big heist. With the help of Collins and Steiger, he gets his chance. From the Max Catto novel "Lions at the Kill." Surprisingly witty and lighthearted for this subject matter, and good still comes out ahead of evil. **102m/C VHS.** Joan Collins, Edward G. Robinson, Eli Wallach, Rod Steiger; ***D:*** Henry Hathaway; ***C:*** Sam Leavitt.

The Seven-Ups ✓½ 1973 (PG) An elite group of New York City detectives seeks to avenge the killing of a colleague and to bust crooks whose felonies are punishable by jail terms of seven years or more. Unoriginal premise portends ill; plotless cop action flick full of car chases. Scheider tries hard. Directed by the producer of "The French Connection." **109m/C VHS.** Roy Scheider, Tony LoBianco, Larry Haines, Jerry Leon; ***D:*** Phil D'Antoni.

The Seven Year Itch ✓✓✓ 1955 Classic, sexy Monroe comedy. Stunning blonde model (who else?) moves upstairs just as happily married guy Ewell's wife leaves for a long vacation. Understandably, he gets itchy. Monroe's famous blown skirt scene is here, as well as funny situations and appealing performances. **105m/C VHS, DVD, Wide.** Marilyn Monroe, Tom Ewell, Evelyn Keyes, Sonny Tufts, Victor Moore, Doro Merande, Robert Strauss, Oscar Homolka, Carolyn Jones; ***D:*** Billy Wilder; ***W:*** Billy Wilder, George Axelrod; ***C:*** Milton Krasner; ***M:*** Alfred Newman. Golden Globes '56: Actor—Mus./Comedy (Ewell).

Seven Years Bad Luck ✓✓✓ 1920 French comic Linder has the proverbial seven years' bad luck all in one day (!) after he breaks a mirror. Original and quite funny; full of fetching sophisticated sight gags. Silent with music score. **67m/B VHS.** Max Linder.

Seven Years in Tibet ✓✓½ 1997 (PG-13) Big budget epic of a cold-hearted Austrian mountaineer Heinrich Harrer (Pitt) who becomes a WWII POW in a British internment camp in India. When he and fellow climber Peter Aufschnaiter (Thewlis) escape, they travel to Tibet where Harrer bonds with and becomes a tutor to the young Dalai Lama (Wangchuk). Sweeping vistas and snow-capped mountain scenery does little to aid the sluggish and unfocused narrative, which tries to cover too many subplots and doesn't really get going until halfway through. Pitt's screen presence is forceful and his performance capable but hampered by a somewhat labored Austrian accent. Based on Harrer's memoirs, film ran into numerous problems, including the revelation that Harrer had Nazi ties, China's sensitivity to the storyline, and India's refusal to allow filming. Director Annaud wound up substituting the Argentine Andes for the Himalayas. **131m/C VHS, DVD.** Brad Pitt, David Thewlis, B.D. Wong, Jamyang Jamtsho Wangchuk, Mako, Victor Wong, Ingeborga Dapkounaite; ***D:*** Jean-Jacques Annaud; ***W:*** Becky Johnston; ***C:*** Robert Fraisse; ***M:*** John Williams.

Seventeen Again ✓✓ 2000 Willie (Tahj Mowry) is doing a science project involving an anti-aging formula that accidentally gets mixed into some soap that his divorced grandparents, Cat (Clarke) and Gene (Hooks), wind up using. This turns them both in 17-year-olds (Tamara Mowry as Cat and Taylor as Gene). Cat winds up going to high school with look-alike granddaughter Sydney (Tia Mowry) and has a second chance with the teenaged Gene. Meanwhile, Willie is searching for an antidote since his formula has some potentially serious flaws. That the story is silly isn't the problem—it's also incoherent. **97m/C VHS, DVD.** Tia Mowry, Tamera Mowry, Tahj Mowry, Mark Taylor, Hope Clarke, Robert Hooks; ***D:*** Jeff Byrd; ***W:*** Stewart St. John; ***C:*** John Tarver; ***M:*** Christopher Franke, Shawm Stockman. CABLE

1776 ✓✓✓ 1972 (G) Musical comedy about America's first Continental Congress. The delegates battle the English and each other trying to establish a set of laws and the Declaration of Independence. Adapted from the Broadway hit with many members of the original cast. ♫The Lees of Old Virginia; He Plays the Violin; But, Mr. Adams; Sit Down John; Till Then; Piddle, Twiddle and Resolve; Yours, Yours, Yours; Mama, Look Sharp; The Egg. **141m/C VHS, Wide.** William Daniels, Howard da Silva, Ken Howard, Donald Madden, Blythe Danner, Ronald Holgate, Virginia Vestoff, Stephen Nathan, Ralston Hill; ***D:*** Peter H. Hunt; ***C:*** Harry Stradling Jr.

The Seventeenth Bride ✓✓ 1984 Set in a Czechoslovakian town; a strong-willed young woman is slowly destroyed by the insanity of war and racism. **92m/C VHS.** Lisa Hartman Black, Rosemary Leach; ***D:*** Israeli Nadav Levitan.

Seventh Cavalry ✓✓½ 1956 A somewhat different look at Custer's defeat at the Little Big Horn. A soldier who was branded a coward for not taking part in the festivities tries to assuage his guilt by heading up the burial detail. The muddled ending tries to tell us that the Indians were afraid of Custer's horse. **75m/C VHS.** Randolph Scott, Barbara Hale, Jay C. Flippen, Jeanette Nolan, Frank Faylen, Leo Gordon, Denver Pyle, Harry Carey Jr., Michael Pate, Donald Curtis, Frank Wilcox, Pat Hogan, Russell Hicks; ***D:*** Joseph H. Lewis; ***C:*** Ray Rennahan.

The Seventh Coin ✓✓½ 1992 (PG-13) The legendary King Herod minted seven coins bearing his image which have become coin collector Emil Saber's (O'Toole) obsession. (He's a homicidal lunatic who thinks he's the reincarnation of Herod anyway.) Saber has found six of the coins but the seventh has fallen into the unsuspecting hands of Salim (Chowdhry), a pickpocket who has actually snatched it from the equally unsuspecting Ronnie (Powers), an American teenager visiting Jerusalem (good local color). The two become allies when Saber comes after them. They're an appealing couple; O'Toole camps it up shamelessly; and the movie is easygoing escapism. **92m/C VHS.** Alexandra Powers, Navin Chowdhry, Peter O'Toole, John Rhys-Davies, Ally Walker; ***D:*** Dror Soref; ***W:*** Michael Lewis, Dror Soref; ***C:*** Avi (Avraham) Karpik.

The 7th Commandment ✓½ 1961 Unlikely melodrama about a man afflicted with amnesia following an auto accident. He becomes a successful evangelist only to be blackmailed by an old girlfriend. Don't you just hate when that happens? **82m/B VHS.** Jonathan Kidd, Lynn Statten; ***D:*** Irvin Berwick.

The Seventh Cross ✓✓✓ 1944 Tracy stars as one of seven men who escape from a German concentration camp. When it is discovered they're gone, the commandant nails seven crosses to seven trees, intending them for the seven escapees. Watch for Tandy ("Driving Miss Daisy") in her first screen appearance. Effective war-time drama. From the novel by Anna Seghers. **110m/B VHS.** Spencer Tracy, Signe Hasso, Hume Cronyn, Jessica Tandy, Agnes Moorehead, Herbert Rudley, Felix Bressart, Ray Collins, Alexander Granach, George Macready, Steven Geray, Karen Verne, George Zucco, Katherine Locke, Paul Guilfoyle, Kurt Katch,

Konstantin Shayne, John Wengraf, Eily Malyon; *D:* Fred Zinnemann; *W:* Helen Deutsch; *C:* Karl Freund; *M:* Roy Webb.

The Seventh Dawn 🦴🦴 **1964** Cliched adventure romance set in Malaysia in 1945. Guerrilla fighter Ferris (Holden) decides to become a landowner and stay on with mistress Dhana (Capucine) after the war. Ferris's old buddy Ng (Tamba) takes off for Moscow and returns indoctrinated and determined to convert the country to Communism. Ng and his fighters exclude Ferris from their attacks until British governor Trumphrey (Goodliffe) accuses Dhana of treason and threatens to execute her. So Ferris has to get Ng or risk Dhana. The young York plays Candace, the governor's daughter who has a crush on Ferris and helps him out. Based on the novel "The Durian Tree" by Michael Koen. **123m/C VHS.** *GB US* William Holden, Capucine, Susannah York, Tetsuro Tamba, Michael Goodliffe, Allan Cuthbertson, Maurice Denham, Beulah Quo; *D:* Lewis Gilbert; *W:* Karl Tunberg; *C:* Frederick A. (Freddie) Young; *M:* Riz Ortolani.

The Seventh Floor 🦴½ **1993 (R)** Kate's computer-controlled apartment becomes her prison when a psycho takes charge of the system. **99m/C VHS, DVD.** *AU* Brooke Shields, Masaya Kato, Craig Pearce, Linda Cropper; *D:* Ian Barry.

Seventh Heaven 🦴🦴 **1998** Married Mathilde (Kiberlain) is sunk in a serious depression that only begins to lessen when she meets a mysterious doctor (Berleand) who specializes in hynosis and alternative medicine. He tells her there are seven levels of heaven—the last a sort of self-fulfilled bliss. After a successful session with the doctor, Mathilde is suddenly sexually and emotionally rejuvenated—much to the consternation of her (til then) dominating spouse, Nico (Lindon). The more Mathilde takes control, the less Nico is able to cope with their role reversals. French with subtitles. **91m/C VHS.** *FR* Sandrine Kimberlain, Vincent Lindon, Francois Berleand; *D:* Benoit Jacquot; *W:* Benoit Jacquot, Jerome Beaujour; *C:* Romain Winding.

The Seventh Seal 🦴🦴🦴🦴 *Det Sjunde Inseglet* **1956** As the plague sweeps through Europe a weary knight convinces "death" to play one game of chess with him. If the knight wins, he and his wife will be spared. The game leads to a discussion of religion and the existence of God. Considered by some Bergman's masterpiece. Von Sydow is stunning as the knight. In Swedish with English subtitles. **96m/B VHS, DVD, 8mm.** *SW* Gunnar Bjornstrand, Max von Sydow, Bibi Andersson, Bengt Ekerot, Nils Poppe, Gunnel Lindblom; *D:* Ingmar Bergman; *W:* Ingmar Bergman; *C:* Gunnar Fischer; *M:* Erik Nordgren. Cannes '57: Grand Jury Prize.

The Seventh Sign 🦴🦴 **1988 (R)** A pregnant woman realizes that the mysterious stranger boarding in her house and the bizarre events that accompany him are connected to Biblical prophesy and her unborn child. Tries hard, but it's difficult to get involved in the supernatural goings-on. **105m/C VHS, DVD, Wide.** Demi Moore, Juergen Prochnow, Michael Biehn, John Heard, Peter Friedman, Manny Jacobs, John Taylor, Lee Garlington, Akosua Busia; *D:* Carl Schultz; *W:* W.W. Wicket; *C:* Juan Ruiz-Anchia; *M:* Jack Nitzsche.

The Seventh Stream 🦴🦴½ **2001** Filmed on location in the west of Ireland and based on the Celtic legend of the selkies. Owen Quinn (Glenn) is a fisherman whose life is empty since the death of his wife. Then he comes to the rescue of Mairead (Burrows), a beautiful and mysterious woman with strong ties to the sea. Owen opens his heart and home to her but will Mairead vanish as easily as she appeared? **98m/C VHS.** Scott Glenn, Saffron Burrows, John Lynch, Fiona Shaw, Eamon Morrissey; *D:* John Gray; *W:* John Gray; *C:* Seamus Deasy; *M:* Ernest Troost. **TV**

The Seventh Veil 🦴🦴🦴½ **1946** A concert pianist loses the use of her hands in a fire, and with it her desire to live. Through the help of her friends and a hypnotizing doctor, she regains her love for life. Superb, dark psycho-drama. Todd as the pianist and Mason as her guardian are both unforgettable. Wonderful music and staging. **91m/B VHS.** *GB* James Mason, Ann Todd, Herbert Lom, Hugh McDermott, Albert Lieven; *D:* Compton Bennett. Oscars '46: Orig. Screenplay.

The Seventh Victim 🦴🦴🦴 **1943** Another Val Lewton-produced low-budget exercise in shadowy suggestion, dealing with a woman searching for her lost sister, who'd gotten involved with Satanists. The Hays Office's squeamishness regarding subject matter makes the film's action a bit cloudy but it remains truly eerie. **71m/B VHS.** Kim Hunter, Tom Conway, Jean Brooks, Hugh Beaumont, Erford Gage, Isabel Jewell, Evelyn Brent; *D:* Mark Robson; *W:* Charles "Blackie" O'Neal.

The Seventh Voyage of Sinbad 🦴🦴🦴 **1958 (G)** Sinbad seeks to restore his fiancee from the midget size to which an evil magician (Thatcher) has reduced her. Ray Harryhausen works his animation magic around a well-developed plot and engaging performances by the real actors. Great score and fun, fast-moving plot. **94m/C VHS, DVD.** Kerwin Mathews, Kathryn Grant, Torin Thatcher, Richard Eyer, Alec Mango, Danny Green, Harold Kasket, Alfred Brown; *D:* Nathan (Hertz) Juran; *W:* Kenneth Kolb; *C:* Wilkie Cooper; *M:* Bernard Herrmann.

The '70s 🦴🦴½ **2000** Follows "The '60s" miniseries with the same superficial exploration of the decade seen through the eyes of four friends and lots of music. (Disco rules!) Dexter (Torry), Byron (Rowe), Eileen (Shaw), and Christine (Smart) are all at Kent State on that fateful day with the National Guard and their lives continue through numerous hot-button issues, including Watergate, feminism, drugs, sex, the Black Panthers, the environment, and religious cults. Cast is surprisingly strong. **170m/C VHS, DVD.** Brad Rowe, Guy Torry, Vinessa Shaw, Amy Smart, Kathryn Harrold, Graham Beckel, Tina Lifford, Chandra West, Robert Joy, Jeanetta Arnette, Michael Easton, Peggy Lipton; *D:* Peter Werner; *W:* Mitch Brian, Kevin Willmott; *C:* Neil Roach; *M:* Peter Manning Robinson. **TV**

Severance 🦴 **1988** An ex-pilot attempts to save his daughter from the world of drugs and violence. **93m/C VHS.** Lou Liotta, Lisa Nicole Wolpe, Linda Christian-Jones; *D:* David Max Steinberg.

The Severed Arm woof! **1973 (R)** Trapped in a cave, five men are compelled to cut off the arm of a companion in order to ward off starvation. Then as luck would have it, they're rescued. Years later, one by one they meet a bloody demise. Is it the one-armed man? **89m/C VHS.** Deborah Walley, Marvin Kaplan, Paul Carr, John Crawford, David Cannon; *D:* Thomas Alderman.

Severed Ties 🦴½ **1992 (R)** Brilliant genetic scientist experiments with human limb regeneration in order to re-grow his accidentally severed arm. His strange mixture of lizard and serial-killer genes results in a repulsive repitilian limb with a nasty habit of slithering out of his shoulder. His mother discovers his experiments and tries to sell his discovery to the Nazis but her son escapes into a bizarre subterranean society and vows revenge. So bad it's just bad. **95m/C VHS.** Billy Morrissette, Elke Sommer, Oliver Reed, Garrett Morris; *D:* Damon Santostefano.

Sex 🦴🦴½ **1920** Interesting dated relic. Morality play about a Broadway star who uses her charms to destroy a marriage only to dump her lover for richer prospects. The businessman she lands then shamelessly betrays her. What a title, especially for its time! **87m/B VHS.** Adrienne Renault, Louise Glaum, Irving Cummings, Peggy Pearce, Myrtle Stedman; *D:* Fred Niblo.

Sex Adventures of the Three Musketeers woof! **198?** Soft-core spoof of the Dumas classic. Dubbed. **79m/C VHS.** Inga Steeger, Achim Hammer, Peter Graf, Jurg Coray.

Sex and Buttered Popcorn **1991 (R)** Stylish and entertaining documentary of the Hollywood sexploitation moguls, and their films, from the 1920s through the 1950s. These films shamelessly catered to audience's prurient interests, but typically delivered saccharin-coated morality messages and stock footage of routine baby births or the horrible effects of sexually transmitted diseases. Hosted by Ned Beatty, and featuring clips from the actual films, plus an interview with the widow of Kroger Babb, the most notorious of the exploiteers. A real hoot. **70m/C VHS, DVD.** David Friedman; *D:* Sam Harrison.

Sex & Mrs. X 🦴🦴½ **2000** New York magazine journalist Joanna Scott (Hamilton) thought her marriage was as successful as her career—until husband Dale (Bick) leaves her for a younger woman. So Joanna is happy to go to Paris to interview the notorious Madame Simone (Bisset), but she winds up learning just as much about herself and how to face her new future. **91m/C VHS, DVD.** Linda Hamilton, Jacqueline Bisset, Paolo Seganti, Stewart Bick, Peter MacNeill, Tracy Bregman, Daniel Pilon; *D:* Arthur Allan Seidelman; *W:* Elisa Bell; *C:* Don E. Fauntleroy; *M:* Joseph Conlan. **CABLE**

Sex and the College Girl 🦴 **1964** Folks talk about their relationship problems while vacationing in Puerto Rico. Tame talkfest providing Grodin with his first role. Included as part of Joe Bob Brigg's "Sleaziest Movies in the History of the World" series, probably just for the title. **?m/C VHS.** Charles Grodin, Richard Arlen, Luana Anders; *D:* Joseph Adler.

Sex and the Other Man 🦴🦴 *Captive* **1995 (R)** Bill's (Eldard) having this little impotence problem, which girlfriend Jessica (Wuhrer) naturally finds frustrating. So much so that she succumbs to the charms of her married boss, Arthur (Tucci). But when Bill catches them together in bed, his reaction is something none of them expected. Based on the play "Captive" by Paul Weitz. **89m/C VHS, DVD.** Ron Eldard, Kari Wuhrer, Stanley Tucci; *D:* Karl Slovin; *W:* Karl Slovin; *C:* Frank Prinzi; *M:* Anton Sanko.

Sex and the Single Girl 🦴🦴½ **1964** Curtis is a reporter for a trashy magazine who intends to write an expose on "The International Institute of Advanced Marital and Pre-Marital Studies," an organization run by Wood. Curtis poses as a man having marital trouble, using his neighbor's name and marital problems, in order to get close to Wood. Things get sticky when Wood wants to meet Curtis' wife and three women show up claiming to be her. This confusing but amusing tale twists and turns until it reaches a happy ending. Loosely based on the book by Helen Gurley Brown. **114m/C VHS.** Tony Curtis, Natalie Wood, Henry Fonda, Lauren Bacall, Mel Ferrer, Fran Jeffries, Leslie Parrish, Edward Everett Horton, Larry Storch, Count Basie; *D:* Richard Quine; *C:* Charles B(ryant) Lang Jr.; *M:* Neal Hefti.

Sex and the Single Parent 🦴½ **1982** St. James and Farrell, both divorced, both with kids, have a relationship. Complications set in—just how does one be a single parent and have a fulfilling sex life in this day and age? **98m/C VHS.** Susan St. James, Mike Farrell, Dori Brenner, Warren Berlinger, Julie Sommars, Barbara Rhoades; *D:* Jackie Cooper. **TV**

Sex and Zen 🦴🦴 **1993** Softcore Hong Kong sex film based on the 17th century novel "Prayer Mat for the Flesh" by Li Yu. Mei Yang (Ng) gets married to beautiful Yuk Heung (Yip) but intends to commit adultery as often as possible. There's lots of bizarre sexual practices and Yuk ends up in a brothel while Mei finds his decadent lifestyle not quite as entertaining as he imagined. Cantonese with subtitles or dubbed. **99m/C VHS, DVD.** *HK* Lawrence Ng, Amy Yip, Kent Cheng, Isabella Chow, Lo Lieh, Carrie Ng; *D:* Michael Mak; *W:* Lee Ying Kit; *C:* Peter Ngor; *M:* Chan Wing Leung.

Sex Crimes 🦴🦴 **1992** A tough female judge is brutally raped and she keeps the attack a secret. However, she does ask a friendly police detective to teach her how to use a gun. He's suspicious of her reasons and decides to trail her as she sets out for revenge on her attacker. Predictable actioner. **90m/C VHS, DVD.** Jeffery Osterhage, Maria Richwine, Fernando Garzon, Craig Alan, Grace Morley; *D:* David Garcia.

Sex, Drugs, and Rock-n-Roll woof! **1984** Several girls frequent a rock club looking for all the action they can get their hands on. **90m/C VHS.** Jeanne Silver, Sharon Kane, Tish Ambrose, Josey Duval.

Sex, Drugs, Rock & Roll: Eric Bogosian **1991 (R)** Bogosian's 1990 concert performance, taped live at the Wilur Theate in Boston, exhibits the electricity and finely nuanced characters for which he is justly famous. The characters share a depressingly negative side, however, which keeps this film from being strictly belly-laugh territory. **96m/C VHS.** Eric Bogosian; *D:* John McNaughton; *W:* Eric Bogosian.

Sex Is Crazy 🦴 **1979** A melange from Italian horror director Franco containing some epic, some horror, some sex, some sitcom, and some documentary. Little green aliens touch down and impregnate earth women in one skit. In another, a gambler's girlfriend demands two thugs ravage her for the sheer sexual thrill. And in a third, a severed hand commands a heroine to martyr herself to the great god Cucufat. Spanish with English subtitles. **81m/C VHS.** *SP* Lina Romay, Anthony (Jose, J. Antonio, J.A.) Mayans, Tony Skios; *D:* Jess (Jesus) Franco.

sex, lies and videotape 🦴🦴🦴 **1989 (R)** Acclaimed, popular independent film by first-timer Soderbergh, detailing the complex relations among a childless married couple, the wife's adulterous sister, and a mysterious college friend of the husband's obsessed with videotaping women as they talk about their sex lives. Heavily awarded, including first prize at Cannes. Confidently uses much (too much?) dialogue and slow (too slow?) pace. **101m/C VHS, DVD, Wide.** James Spader, Andie MacDowell, Peter Gallagher, Laura San Giacomo, Ron Vawter, Steven Brill; *D:* Steven Soderbergh; *W:* Steven Soderbergh; *C:* Walt Lloyd; *M:* Cliff Martinez. Cannes '89: Actor (Spader), Film; Ind. Spirit '90: Actress (MacDowell), Director (Soderbergh), Film, Support. Actress (San Giacomo); L.A. Film Critics '89: Actress (MacDowell); Sundance '89: Aud. Award.

Sex, Love and Cold Hard Cash 🦴🦴½ **1993 (PG-13)** Sarah (Williams) is a high-priced hooker whose life savings ($20 million in stocks and bonds) have just been stolen. She hires an ex-con (Denison) to help recover the money and the two partners find themselves on the wrong side of some Mob trouble as well. Enough twists to keep a viewer interested as well as the prerequisite amount of shootings and chase scenes. **86m/C VHS.** JoBeth Williams, Anthony John (Tony) Denison; *D:* Harry S. Longstreet; *W:* Harry S. Longstreet.

The Sex Machine woof! **1976 (R)** In the year 2037, a scientist finds two of the world's greatest lovers and unites them so he can transform their reciprocating motion into electricity. It worked on paper. **80m/C VHS.** Agostina Belli.

Sex on the Run woof! *Cassanova and Co.; Some Like It Cool* **1978 (R)** Love-starved wife of an oil-rich sheik, stimulated by the idea of having Casanova for her lover, teases her master into delivering him, but Casanova finds peace in the arms of three convent lovelies. Disgusting, amateurish, and offensive. **88m/C VHS.** Tony Curtis, Marisa Berenson, Britt Ekland; *D:* Francosis Legrand.

Sex Through a Window 🦴 *Extreme Close-Up* **1972 (R)** TV reporter becomes an obsessive voyeur after filing a report on high tech surveillance equipment. Flimsy premise is a yucky, lame excuse to show skin. **81m/C VHS.** James McMullan, James A. Watson Jr., Kate Woodville, Bara Byrnes, Al Checco, Antony Carbone; *D:* Jeannot Szwarc; *W:* Michael Crichton.

Sex with a Smile 🦴 **1976 (R)** Five slapstick episodes by five different directors with lots of sexual satire pointed at religion and politics in Italy. Don't know much about Italy? Then you'll be left out of the joke here. And really, only one episode is funny anyway (the one with Feldman of "Young Frankenstein" fame). **100m/C VHS.** *IT* Marty Feldman, Edwige Fenech, Alex Marino, Enrico Monterrano, Giovanna Ralli; *D:* Sergio Martino.

Sexpot 🦴 **1988 (R)** A voluptuous woman's rich husbands mysteriously keep dying, but not before they leave their fortunes to her. **95m/C VHS.** Ruth (Coreen) Collins, Troy Donahue, Joyce Lyons, Gregory Patrick, Frank Stewart, Jack Carter; *D:* Chuck Vincent.

Sextette woof! **1978 (PG)** Lavish film about an elderly star who is constantly interrupted by former spouses and well-wishers while on a honeymoon with her sixth husband. West unwisely came out of retirement for this last film role, based on her own play. Exquisitely embarrassing to watch. Interesting cast. **91m/C VHS, DVD.** Mae West, Timothy Dalton, Ringo Starr, George Hamilton, Dom DeLuise, Tony Curtis, Alice Cooper, Keith Moon, George Raft, Rona Barrett, Walter Pidgeon, Regis Philbin; *D:* Ken Hughes; *W:* Herbert Baker; *C:* James A. Crabe; *M:* Artie Butler.

Sexton Blake and the Hooded Terror 🦴🦴 **1938** Sexton Blake a British private detective a la Holmes, is after "The Snake," a master criminal, and his gang The Hooded Terror. One of a series of melodramatic adventures interesting chiefly for Slaughter's performance as the gangleader. **70m/B VHS.** *GB* Tod Slaughter, Greta Gynt, George Curzon; *D:* George King.

Sexual Intent 🦴🦴 **1994 (R)** Based on the true story of pathological liar John Walsome, known as "the Sweetheart Scammer," who seduced and robbed more than 40 women. This con artist transformed himself into whatever kind of Mr. Right his victim needed—until he picked on the wrong woman. **88m/C VHS.** Gary Hudson, Michele Brin, Sarah Hill; *D:* Kurt MacCarley; *W:* Kurt MacCarley.

The Sexual Life of the Belgians 🦴½ *La Vie Sexuelle des Belges* **1994** Autobiographical comedy of sexual manners covering 1950 to 1978. Jan Bucquoy (Compere) grows up with a grim mother and immediately takes an interest in sex and beautiful women, which only heightens as he winds up in Brussels during the hedonistic '60s. He has a short, disastrous marriage, lots of affairs, not much sense, and a mocking disregard for Belgian provincialism. French with subtitles. **80m/C VHS.** *BE* Jean-Henri Compere, Isabella Legros, Sophie Schneider, Michele Shor; *D:* Jan Bucquoy; *W:* Jan Bucquoy; *C:* Michel Baudour.

Sexual Malice 🦴🦴 **1993 (R)** Another erotic thriller finds a bored wife involved in an obsessive affair with a mystery man who has murder on his mind. Also available in an unrated version. **96m/C VHS, DVD.** Diana Barton, John Laughlin, Chad McQueen, Edward Albert, Don Swayze, Kathy Shower, Samantha (Sam) Phillips; *D:* Jag Mundhra; *W:* Carl Austin; *C:* James Mathers.

Sexual Response 🦴🦴 **1992 (R)** Eve, a radio talk show "sexologist," is ironically unhappy in her marriage but scoffs at her producer's suggestion of an affair. That is until she meets a brash sculptor and they begin a torrid, and increasingly obsessive, romance. Her lover suggests that her husband have an "accident" with his hunting rifle, but Eve refuses and throws him out. The sculptor, however, breaks into the husband's loft to steal the rifle and finds some news clippings about the man's past that could ruin the lives of many. Little more than an excuse for torrid love scenes. Also available in an unrated version. **87m/C VHS.** Shannon Tweed, Catherine Oxenberg, Vernon Wells, Emile Levisetti; *D:* Yaky Yosha.

Sexual Roulette 🦴 **1996 (R)** A distaff and decidedly raunchier "Indecent Proposal." Jed and Sally wind up in money trouble and get in deeper by trying to recoup their loses (and losing bigtime) in a Vegas horse race. Then a rich blonde with some kinky preferences makes Jed an offer he can't afford to refuse. The unrated version is six minutes longer. **90m/C VHS, DVD.** Tane McClure, Tim Abell, Gabriella Hall, Richard Gabai, Myles O'Brien, G. Gordon Brer; *D:* Gary Graver; *W:* Sean McGinley; *C:* Gary Graver.

Sexus 🦴½ *Nuit la Plus Longue; Enfer Dans la Peau* **1964** Beautiful Virginia (de Solen) is kidnapped by Blackie (Tissier) and his cohorts and held in an abandoned farmhouse until her father pays her ransom. In the meantime, her looks provoke both jealousy and passion. French with subtitles. **88m/B VHS.** *FR* Willy Braque, Virginia De Soten, Yves Duffaut, Annie Jasse, Alain Tissier; *D:* Jose Benazeraf; *W:* Jose Benazeraf; *C:* Alain Derobe; *M:* Chet Baker.

Sexy Beast 🦴🦴🦴½ **2000 (R)** This British suspense/thriller is not only tense and caustically funny at times, it also has the guy who played Gandhi as a snarling, bad-ass gangster. Ben Kingsley plays Logan, who's sent to southern Spain to lure retired gangster "Gal" Dove (Winstone) back to England for the standard "one last job." When Gal refuses, Logan threatens non-non-violence on Gal's wife Deedee (Redman) and pals Aitch (Kendall, in his last role) and Jackie (White). Gal is forced into accepting after some unfortunate events, and the plot, masterminded by Logan's boss Teddy (McShane), is carried out. After the caper is done, however, Gal will have a harder time relaxing poolside with the reminders of the "sexy beast" of his criminal life all too close. Kingsley dominates the movie as the profanity-spewing Logan, but the rest of the cast also turn in outstanding performances. **88m/C VHS, DVD, Wide.** *GB* Ray Winstone, Ben Kingsley, Ian McShane, Amanda Redman, James Fox, Robert Atiko, Julianne White, Cavan Kendall, Alvaro Monje; *D:* Jonathan Glazer; *W:* Louis Mellis, David Scinto; *C:* Ivan Bird; *M:* Roque Banos. Broadcast Film Critics '02: Support. Actor (Kingsley).

S.F.W. 🦴🦴 **1994 (R)** Get out your cliche-o-meter for another look at Generation X. Suburban teen Cliff Spab (Dorff) unwillingly becomes a media sensation during a terrorist hostage crisis at a convenience store. The phrasemaking teen's apathetic words are adopted by his peers just as he realizes that there is something he actually cares about—fellow hostage Wendy Pfister (Witherspoon), a cheerleader who wouldn't have given him the time of day before. A somewhat heavy-handed commentary on fame in our tabloid-intensive society. Title acronym stands for "So F***ing What." Many reviewers had a similar reaction. Based on the novel by Andrew Wellman. **92m/C VHS.** Stephen Dorff, Reese Witherspoon, Jake Busey, Joey Lauren Adams, Pamela Gidley, David Barry Gray, Jack Noseworthy, Richard Portnow; *D:* Jefery Levy; *W:* Jefery Levy, James Foley.

Shack Out on 101 🦴🦴🦴 **1955** A waitress (Moore) in an isolated cafe on a busy highway notices suspicious doings among her customers. What could they be up to? Communist subversion, of course. Of-its-era anti-pinko propoganda, but with a twist: Moore uncovers commie plots, pleases her customers, and fends off unwelcome lecherous advances all in 80 minutes, on a single set! **80m/B VHS.** Lee Marvin, Terry Moore, Keenan Wynn, Frank Lovejoy, Whit Bissell, Jess Barker, Donald Murphy, Frank De Kova, Len Lesser, Fred Gabourie; *D:* Edward Dein; *W:* Edward Dein, Mildred Dein; *C:* Floyd Crosby; *M:* Paul Dunlap, Louis Prima.

Shackleton 🦴🦴🦴 **2002** Stirring adventure about the ill-fated expedition of Sir Ernest Shackleton (Branagh) to Antarctica in 1914. His ship, the Endurance, gets trapped in ice and eventually sinks, leaving Shackleton and his crew of 27 to set up camp on a nearby island. Shackleton and two of the crew set out for help to a whaling station on South Georgia Island—an unbelievably difficult journey of survival for those travelling and those left behind. **200m/C VHS, DVD, Wide.** Kenneth Branagh, Kevin McNally, Chris Larkin, Mark McGann, Lorcan Cranitch, Nicholas (Nick) Rowe, Pip Torrens, Shaun Dooley, Matt(hew) Day; *D:* Charles Sturridge; *W:* Charles Sturridge; *C:* Henry Braham; *M:* Adrian Johnston. **CABLE**

Shades of Black 🦴🦴 **1993** Young, small-town photographer/athlete Kate becomes the romantic obsession of charismatic, older artist Lilly. But Lilly's manipulations also hide the deeper secret of her mental instability, which soon proves dangerous to Kate. **115m/C VHS.** *D:* Mary Haverstick.

Shades of Fear 🦴🦴 *Great Moments in Aviation* **1993 (R)** Adventurous would-be aviatrix Gabriel Angel (Ayola), who's sailing from Grenada to England, is mistakenly assigned a room with Duncan (Pryce) and decides to pose as his wife to avoid a scandal. But a fellow passenger (Hurt) believes Duncan is also the art forger who ran off with his wife and caused her death. On their last night at sea, there's a final confrontation. **93m/C VHS.** *GB* Jonathan Pryce, Rakie Ayola, John Hurt, Vanessa Redgrave, Dorothy Tutin; *D:* Beeban Kidron. **TV**

Shadey 🦴🦴½ **1987 (PG-13)** The premise for this oddball comedy came to someone in the wee hours: I've got it! Mild-mannered mechanic can film people's thoughts; wants to use his gift only for good, but needs money for a sex-change operation. Assorted bad guys want to use him for evil purposes. Strange, but not bad; Helmond's character is memorable. **90m/C VHS.** *GB* Anthony Sher, Billie Whitelaw, Patrick Macnee, Katherine Helmond, Leslie Ash, Larry Lamb, Bernard Hepton; *D:* Philip Saville; *W:* Snoo Wilson; *C:* Roger Deakins; *M:* Colin Towns.

The Shadow 🦴½ **1936** Scotland Yard pulls out all the stops to track down a murderous extortionist, enlisting the aid of a novelist in their efforts. Long on talk and short on action. **63m/B VHS, DVD.** *GB* Henry Kendall, Elizabeth Allan, Jeanne Stuart, Felix Aylmer, Cyril Raymond; *D:* George Cooper.

The Shadow 🦴🦴½ **1994 (PG-13)** Who knows what evil lurks in the hearts of men? Why "The Shadow" of course, as is shown in this highly stylized big screen version of the '30s radio show that once starred Orson Welles. Billionaire playboy Lamont Cranston (Baldwin) is a master of illusion and defender of justice thanks to his alter ego. Aided by companion Margo Lane (Miller), da Shadow battles super-criminal Shiwan Khan (Lone), the deadliest descendant of Ghenghis Khan. Numerous and elaborate special effects provide icing on the cake for those in the mood for a journey back to the radio past or a quick superhero fix. **112m/C VHS, DVD.** Alec Baldwin, John Lone, Penelope Ann Miller, Peter Boyle, Ian McKellen, Tim Curry, Jonathan Winters; *D:* Russell Mulcahy; *W:* David Koepp; *C:* Stephen Burum; *M:* Jerry Goldsmith.

The Shadow Box 🦴🦴🦴 **1980** Three terminally ill people at a California hospice confront their destinies. Pulitzer Prize-winning play by Michael Cristofer is actually improved by director Newman and a superb, well-chosen cast. Powerful. **96m/C VHS.** Joanne Woodward, Christopher Plummer, Robert Urich, Valerie Harper, Sylvia Sidney, Melinda Dillon, Ben Masters, John Considine, James Broderick; *D:* Paul Newman; *M:* Henry Mancini.

The Shadow Conspiracy 🦴 **1996 (R)** Laughable innocent-on-the-run tale of presidential advisor Bobby Bishop (Sheen), who finds himself smack in the middle of an assassination conspiracy against the Prez (Waterston). Accused of murder, Bishop hooks up with ex-gal pal, reporter Amanda Givens (Hamilton) to get to the truth before the police and the bad guys get to them. Hunting the duo is a pro known as "The Agent" (Lang). Lang's lethal Agent comes off as one of the only believable characters here, perhaps because he has absolutely no dialogue to sabotage him. Sutherland fares better than most as Chief of Staff Conrad Jacob. Ludicrous plot twists and unconvincing performances by leads Sheen and Hamilton. **103m/C VHS.** Charlie Sheen, Linda Hamilton, Stephen Lang, Donald Sutherland, Sam Waterston, Ben Gazzara, Nicholas Turturro, Charles Cioffi, Theodore Bikel, Stanley Anderson, Dey Young, Gore Vidal, Paul Gleason, Terry O'Quinn; *D:* George P. Cosmatos; *W:* Rick Gibbs, Wayne Beach; *C:* Buzz Feitshans IV; *M:* Bruce Broughton.

Shadow Creature 🦴 **1996 (R)** Detective investigating a series of grisly murders finds a mad scientist and a mysterious formula that could unlock the secrets of immortality. The downside being the entire mutation of all life on earth into monsters. **?m/C VHS.** Shane Minor, Dennis Keefe, Scott Heim; *D:* James Gribbins.

Shadow Dancer 🦴🦴 **1996 (R)** Formulaic Corman exploitation finds L.A. stripper Narita (Hall) under investigation for the murder of two fellow dancers. **89m/C VHS.** Gabriella Hall, Robert Donovan, Kate McNeil, Ron Johnson; *D:* Stan Kane. **VIDEO**

Shadow Dancing 🦴🦴🦴 **1988 (PG)** The proprietor of the auspicious Beaumont Theater of Dance is haunted by one of his former dancers who died unexpectedly during a performance of "Medusa." Now, over 50 years later, Jessica, the pick for the lead in a new production, begins to take on her predecessor's mannerisms and spirit as she faces her impending doom. Surprisingly believable and suspenseful—and scary! **100m/C VHS.** Nadine Van Der Velde, James Kee, John Colicos, Shirley Douglas, Christopher Plummer; *D:* John Furey; *M:* Jay Gruska.

Shadow Force 🦴½ **1992** Homicide detective Rick Kelly is investigating the murders of a district attorney and a police sergeant. With the help of Mary, the usual beautiful female journalist, he uncovers a plot to assassinate key law enforcement officers. **?m/C VHS.** Dirk Benedict, Lance LeGault, Lise Cutter, Jack Elam, Glenn Corbett, Bob Hastings; *D:* Darrell Davenport.

Shadow Magic 🦴🦴½ **2000 (PG)** Englishman Raymond Wallace (Harris) turns up in Peking in 1902 with a hand-cranked, black and white, soundless camera and projector, thus bringing the first moving images to China. Local photographer Liu Jinglun (Yu), intrigued by the new technolgy, bridges the cultural barriers between Raymond and the community, causing problems of loyalty with his own family and friends and even jeopardizing his marriage chances. Mandarin with subtitles. **115m/C VHS, DVD, Wide.** *GE* Jared Harris, Xia Yu, Liu Peiqi, Lu Liping, Xing Yufei, Wang Jingming, Li Yusheng; *D:* Ann Hu; *W:* Ann Hu, Huang Dan, Tang Louyi, Kate Raisz, Bob McAndrew; *C:* Nancy Schreiber; *M:* Zhang Lida.

The Shadow Man 🦴🦴 *Street of Shadows* **1953** A casino operator in London (Romero) is accused of killing a former girlfriend and works to clear himself. Family conventional action mystery: nothing to write home about. **76m/B VHS.** *GB* Cesar Romero, Simone Silva, Kay Kendall, John Penrose, Edward Underdown; *D:* Richard Vernon.

Shadow Man 🦴🦴 **1975 (PG)** A mysterious thief, a master of disguise, sets out to steal the Treasure of the Knights Templar and nothing will stand in his way. **89m/C VHS.** Josephine Chaplin, Gert Frobe, Gayle Hunnicutt.

Shadow of a Doubt 🦴🦴🦴½ **1943** Uncle Charlie has come to visit his relatives in Santa Rosa. Although he is handsome and charming, his young niece slowly comes to realize he is a wanted mass murderer—and he comes to recognize her suspicions. Hitchcock's personal favorite movie; a quietly creepy venture into Middle American menace. Good performances, especially by Cronyn. From the story by Gordon McConnell. **108m/B VHS, DVD.** Teresa Wright, Joseph Cotten, Hume Cronyn, MacDonald Carey, Henry Travers, Wallace Ford; *D:* Alfred Hitchcock; *W:* Thornton Wilder, Sally Benson, Alma Reville; *C:* Joseph Valentine; *M:* Dimitri Tiomkin. Natl. Film Reg. '91.

Shadow of a Scream 🦴🦴 **1997 (R)** Detective Alice Redmond (Massey) goes undercover to investigate a suspected killer (Chokachi) and discovers his rough sexual fantasies appeal to the less staid side of her nature. So much so that she gets a little too up close and personal with this possible murderer. **84m/C VHS.** Athena Massey, David Chokachi, Cyril O'Reilly, Timothy Busfield; *D:* Howard McCain.

Shadow of Angels 🦴🦴 *Schatten der Engel* **1976** Beautiful prostitute Lily Brest's (Caven) latest client, a wealthy real estate investor (Lowitsch), just wants to talk and Lily's a good listener. So good, that more and more of her clients tell her all their darkest secrets and fears, leaving Lily herself falling into such a deep depression that she wonders if she can go on. Based on Fassbinder's play "The Garbage, the City and Death"; Fassbinder himself appears as a pimp. German with subtitles. **103m/C VHS.** *GE* Ingrid Caven, Klaus Lowitsch; ***Cameos:*** Rainer Werner Fassbinder; ***D:*** Daniel Schmid; ***W:*** Rainer Werner Fassbinder, Daniel Schmid.

Shadow of Chikara ♂ *Thunder Mountain; The Curse of Demon Mountain* **1977 (PG)** A Confederate Army Captain and an orphan girl encounter unexpected adventures as they search for a fortune in diamonds hidden in a river in northern Arkansas. **96m/C VHS.** Joe Don Baker, Sondra Locke, Ted Neeley, Slim Pickens.

Shadow of China ♂♂♂ **1991 (PG-13)** A young man struggles for power and love in Hong Kong, while an English beauty and an Asian activist hold the keys to his future and a past which could destroy him. Excellent acting, stunning location photography. Exotic and intense. Based on the Japanese best-seller "Snakehead." **100m/C VHS.** John Lone, Sammi Davis, Vivian Wu; ***D:*** Mitsuo Yanagimachi; ***W:*** Mitsuo Yanagimachi, Richard Maxwell.

Shadow of Chinatown ♂½ **1936** Mad scientist creates wave of murder and terror in Chinatown. Edited version of a 15-chapter serial. **70m/B VHS, DVD.** Bela Lugosi, Bruce (Herman Brix) Bennett, Joan Barclay, Luana Walters, Maurice Liu, William Buchanan; ***D:*** Robert F. "Bob" Hill.

Shadow of Doubt ♂♂½ **1998 (R)** L.A. defense attorney Kitt Devereux (Griffiths) likes high-profile cases. And her latest has the added tension of being prosecuted by ex-lover, Asst. D.A. Jack Campioni (Berenger). Kitt works with an investigaotr (Lewis) to prove a rapper (Dominguez) innocent of murder while being threatened by an accused rapist (Sheffer) and a prominent Senator, who's angling for a presidential nomination. How everything ties together is something Kitt will have to figure out if she wants to discover the truth. **103m/C VHS.** Melanie Griffith, Tom Berenger, Craig Sheffer, Huey Lewis, John Ritter, Wade Dominguez; ***D:*** Randal Kleiser; ***W:*** Raymond De Felitta, Myra Byanka.

Shadow of the Eagle **1932** Former wartime flying ace Wayne is accused of being a criminal known as "The Eagle." He's using his flying skills (which include skywriting) to threaten a corporation which has stolen plans for a new invention. But can Wayne really be our villain? 12-chapter serial. **226m/B VHS, DVD.** John Wayne, Dorothy Gulliver, Walter Miller; ***D:*** Ford Beebe.

Shadow of the Thin Man ♂♂♂ **1941** In the fourth "Thin Man" film, following "Another Thin Man," Nick and Nora stumble onto a murder at the racetrack. The rapport between Powell and Loy is still going strong, providing us with some wonderful entertainment. Followed by "The Thin Man Goes Home." **97m/B VHS.** William Powell, Myrna Loy, Barry Nelson, Donna Reed, Sam Levene, Alan Baxter, Dickie Hall, Loring Smith, Joseph Anthony, Henry O'Neill; ***D:*** Woodbridge S. Van Dyke.

Shadow of the Vampire ♂♂♂ **2000** Behind the scenes look at what possibly went on during the making of the silent vampire classic, 1922's "Nosferatu." Director F.W. Murnau (Malkovich) and his crew head for Czechoslovakia for location shooting on his version of "Dracula" and the first meeting of the dedicated actor who will play the title role—a very eccentric Max Schreck (Dafoe). Only Murnau has struck a devil's bargain with Schreck, who is an actual vampire—the leading man gets leading lady Greta (McCormack) as a reward—and a snack. But it seems Schreck can't wait, as the crew starts to fall mysteriously ill. A little slow going but strangely compelling and the two lead performances are outstanding. **93m/C VHS, DVD, Wide.** *GB* John Malkovich, Willem Dafoe, Catherine McCormack, Cary Elwes, Eddie Izzard, Udo Kier, Ronan Vibert, Aden (John) Gillett; ***D:*** Edmund Elias Merhige; ***W:*** Steven Katz; ***C:*** Lou Bogue; ***M:*** Dan Jones. L.A. Film Critics '00: Support. Actor (Dafoe).

Shadow of the Wolf ♂♂ *Agaguk: Shadow of the Wolf* **1992 (PG-13)** Phillips is Agaguk, the son of the village leader, in this epic saga of survival set against the wilderness of the Arctic. Agaguk decides he cannot accept the white man's intrusion, so he sets out on his own. His father believes his departure to be the ultimate betrayal and casts upon him the "curse of the white wolf." Now Agaguk and his companion (Tilly) must face the harsh tundra alone and struggle to stay alive in the Great White North. Based on the novel "Agaguk" by Yves Theriault. **108m/C VHS, Wide.** *CA* Lou Diamond Phillips, Donald Sutherland, Jennifer Tilly, Toshiro Mifune; ***D:*** Jacques Dorfman; ***W:*** Rudy Wurlitzer, Evan Jones. Genie '93: Art Dir./Set Dec., Costume Des.

Shadow on the Sun ♂½ **1988** The life of Beryl Markham, pioneer female aviator and adventurer of the 1930s. Way too long and boring TV answer to "Out of Africa." **192m/C VHS.** Stefanie Powers, Claire Bloom, Frederic Forrest, James Fox, John Rubinstein, Jack Thompson; ***D:*** Tony Richardson. **TV**

Shadow Play ♂½ **1986 (R)** A successful female playwright is haunted by visions of a past lover. Her life slowly falls apart, but not before this film does. **98m/C VHS.** Dee Wallace Stone, Cloris Leachman; ***D:*** Susan Shadburne; ***W:*** Susan Shadburne.

The Shadow Riders ♂♂ *Louis L'Amour's "The Shadow Riders"* **1982 (PG)** Two brothers who fought on opposite sides during the Civil War return home to find their brother's fiancee kidnapped by a renegade Confederate officer who plans to use her as ransom in a prisoner exchange. They set out to rescue the woman. Preceded by "The Sacketts" and based on the works of Louis L'Amour. **96m/C VHS, DVD.** Tom Selleck, Sam Elliott, Ben Johnson, Katharine Ross, Jeffery Osterhage, Gene Evans, R.G. Armstrong, Marshall Teague, Dominique Dunne, Jeanetta Arnette; ***D:*** Andrew V. McLaglen; ***W:*** Jim Byrnes; ***C:*** Jack Whitman; ***M:*** Jerrold Immel. **TV**

The Shadow Strikes ♂½ **1937** Adaptation of the radio serial. The sleuth pursues a killer and a gangster. Meanwhile, the police try to pin a robbery on the "Shadow." Who did it? The Shadow knows! **61m/B VHS.** Rod La Rocque, Lynn Anders.

Shadow Warriors ♂½ **1995 (R)** Greedy security expert Connors (O'Quinn) sells computerized bodyguards that are created from human corpses, aided by doctor Natalie (Graham). Only one of the latest creations has just gone on a killing spree, so they use another "technosapien" (Lurie) to prevent further mayhem. **80m/C VHS.** Evan Lurie, Terry O'Quinn, Russ Tertyask, Ashley Anne Graham, Timothy Patrick Cavanaugh; ***D:*** Lamar Card; ***C:*** M. David Mullen.

Shadow Warriors ♂♂ *Assault on Devil's Island* **1997** Navy SEALS, led by Mike McBride (Hogan), plan an assault on the island hideaway of drug lord Gallindo (Drago). Lending assistance is undercover DEA agent Hunter Wiley (being that the part is played by Tweed she's never really covered, appearing in a variety of lingerie and bikinis while kicking butt). However, when the SEALS get Gallindo, his crew retaliates. **94m/C VHS, DVD.** Hulk Hogan, Carl Weathers, Shannon Tweed, Martin Kove, Billy Drago, Trevor Goddard, Billy Blanks; ***D:*** Jon Cassar. **CABLE**

Shadow Warriors 2: Hunt for the Death Merchant ♂♂½ **1997 (R)** The elite commando unit of Hogan, Weathers, and Tweed return—and this time they must rescue a group of American gymnasts who are being held hostage. If you enjoyed the first movie, you'll enjoy this one since it's more of the action-filled same. **95m/C VHS.** Hulk Hogan, Carl Weathers, Shannon Tweed, Martin Kove; ***D:*** Jon Cassar. **CABLE**

A Shadow You Soon Will Be ♂♂ *Una Sombra Ya Pronto Seras* **1994** An allegory of the emptiness of contemporary Argentinian society, following the end of military rule, and based on a 1990 novel by Soriano, who co-wrote the screenplay. A man known merely as "The Engineer" (Sola) returns from Europe where he's lived in exile during the military dictatorship. Without family or friends, he wanders through the southern pampas, briefly communicating with other eccentric travelers, and non-commitally watching the world go by. Spanish with subtitles. **105m/C VHS, DVD.** *AR* Miguel Angel Sola, Eusebio Poncela, Pepe Soriano, Alicia Bruzzo, Luis Brandoni, Diego Torres, Gloria Carra; ***D:*** Hector Olivera; ***W:*** Hector Olivera, Osvaldo Soriano; ***C:*** Felix Monti; ***M:*** Osvaldo Montes.

Shadowhunter ♂♂ **1993 (R)** Glenn stars as a burned-out big city detective who is sent to a Navajo reservation in Arizona to bring a murder suspect back to Los Angeles. When the alleged killer escapes custody Glenn must track him across forbidding desert territory and face his suspect's unusual mystical powers. **98m/C VHS.** Scott Glenn; ***D:*** J.S. Cardone; ***W:*** J.S. Cardone; ***C:*** Dick Bush.

Shadowlands ♂♂♂ *C.S. Lewis Through the Shadowlands* **1985** A look at the later life of bachelor-scholar C.S. Lewis (also the author of the "Chronicles of Narnia"). A devout proponent of Christianity, the middle-aged Lewis fell in love and married Joy Gresham, a divorced American poet with two young sons. Joy was diagnosed with cancer and her illness provided Lewis with the clearest test of his faith. Wonderful performances by both Ackland and Bloom. **90m/C VHS.** *GB* Joss Ackland, Claire Bloom, Rupert Baderman; ***D:*** Norman Stone.

Shadowlands ♂♂♂ **1993 (PG)** Touching, tragic story of the late-in-life romance between celebrated author and Christian theologian C.S. Lewis (Hopkins) and brash New York divorcee Joy Gresham (Winger). Attenborough's direction is rather stately and sweeping and Winger is really too young for her role but Hopkins is excellent as (another) repressed man who finds more emotions than he can handle. Critically acclaimed adaptation of Nicholson's play will require lots of kleenex. **130m/C VHS, DVD.** *GB* Anthony Hopkins, Debra Winger, Edward Hardwicke, Joseph Mazzello, Michael Denison, John Wood, Peter Firth, Peter Howell; ***D:*** Richard Attenborough; ***W:*** William Nicholson; ***C:*** Roger Pratt; ***M:*** George Fenton. British Acad. '93: Film; L.A. Film Critics '93: Actor (Hopkins); Natl. Bd. of Review '93: Actor (Hopkins).

Shadows ♂♂ **1922** A Chinese laundryman (Chaney) lives with a group of his countrymen in a New England seacoast village. All is peaceful until the local minister decides to convert the "heathen" Chinese. Ludicrous but worth seeing for Chaney's fun performance. Silent with music score. **70m/B VHS, DVD.** Lon Chaney Sr., Harrison Ford; ***D:*** Tom Forman; ***W:*** Eve Unsell, Hope Loring; ***C:*** Harry Perry; ***M:*** Gaylord Carter.

Shadows ♂♂♂ **1960** Director Cassavettes' first indie feature finds jazz player Hugh (Hurd) forced to play dives to support his brother Ben (Carruthers) and sister Lelia (Goldoni). Light-skinned enough to pass for white, Lelia takes on the uptown New York art crowd and gets involved with the white Tony (Ray), who leaves when he finds out her true heritage. Meanwhile, Ben drifts along with his friends who abandon him when trouble finds them. Script was improvised by cast. **87m/B VHS.** Hugh Hurd, Lelia Goldoni, Ben Carruthers, Anthony Ray, Rupert Crosse, Tom Allen; ***D:*** John Cassavetes; ***C:*** Erich Kollmar; ***M:*** Charles Mingus, Shifi Hadi. Natl. Film Reg. '93.

Shadows and Fog ♂♂ **1992 (PG-13)** Offbeat, unpredictable Allen film that is little more than an exercise in expressionistic visual stylings. The action centers around a haunted, alienated clerk (Allen) who is awakened in the middle of the night to join a vigilante group searching the streets for a killer. Although reminiscent of a silent film, Carlo DiPalma's black-and-white cinematography is stunning. Several stars appear briefly throughout this extremely unfocused comedy. **85m/B VHS, DVD, Wide.** Woody Allen, Kathy Bates, John Cusack, Mia Farrow, Jodie Foster, Fred Gwynne, Julie Kavner, Madonna, John Malkovich, Kenneth Mars, Kate Nelligan, Donald Pleasence, Lily Tomlin, Philip Bosco, Robert Joy, Wallace Shawn, Kurtwood Smith, Josef Sommer, David Ogden Stiers, Michael Kirby, Anne Lange; ***D:*** Woody Allen; ***W:*** Woody Allen; ***C:*** Carlo Di Palma.

Shadows in the Storm ♂♂ **1988 (R)** A librarian/poet retreats to a secluded forest after losing his job. There he meets an exotically beautiful young woman who becomes his lover. With her love, she brings blackmail, murder, and mystery. **90m/C VHS.** Ned Beatty, Mia Sara, Michael Madsen; ***D:*** Terrell Tannen.

Shadows of Death ♂½ **1945** Crabbe is the hero who must track down a gang of outlaws who kill to grab the land along the path of a new railroad. One of the "Billy Carson" series. **60m/B VHS.** Buster Crabbe, Al "Fuzzy" St. John.

Shadows of Forgotten Ancestors ♂♂♂ *Tini Zabutykh Predkiv; Shadows of Our Ancestors; Shadows of Our Forgotten Ancestors; Wild Horses of Fire* **1964** Set in rural Russia in the early 20th century. Brings to expressive life the story of a man whose entire life has been overtaken by tragedy. Folk drama about a peasant who falls in with the daughter of his father's killer, then marries another woman. Strange, resonant and powerful with distinctive camera work. In Ukrainian with English subtitles. **99m/C VHS.** *RU* Ivan Micholaichuk, Larisa Kadochnikova; ***D:*** Sergei Paradjanov.

Shadows of the Orient **1937** Two detectives are out to smash a Chinese smuggling ring. **70m/B VHS.** Regis Toomey, Esther Ralston.

Shadows of Tombstone ♂½ **1953** There's corruption in the western town of Shadow Rock as the crooked sheriff and saloonkeeper make things miserable for the inhabitants. Rex and Slim try to right the wrongs but take their time about it. **54m/B VHS.** Rex Allen, Slim Pickens, Roy Barcroft, Emory Parnell, Jeanne Cooper; ***D:*** William Witney; ***W:*** Gerald Geraghty; ***C:*** Bud Thackery; ***M:*** R. Dale Butts.

Shadows on the Stairs ♂♂ **1941** A creepy boarding house is the scene of a number of mystery-drenched murders. A bizarre assortment of suspects make things even crazier. **63m/B VHS.** Frieda Inescort, Paul Cavanagh, Heather Angel, Bruce Lester, Miles Mander, Lumsden Hare, Turhan Bey; ***D:*** David Ross Lederman.

Shadows over Shanghai ♂½ **1938** This adventure relic was set during the Japanese invasion of China prior to WWII and uses much newsreel footage of that infamy. As for the plot, it's a groaner about good guys and bad skulking around the eponymous port in search of a treasure. **66m/B VHS.** James Dunn, Ralph Morgan, Robert Barrat, Paul Sutton, Edward (Eddie) Woods; ***D:*** Charles Lamont.

Shadows Run Black ♂½ **1984** A police detective must save a college coed from the clutches of a maniac wielding a meat cleaver. Ordinary slash-'em-up. Bet Costner's embarrassed now about this early role—like Stallone's porno role in "The Italian Stallion." **89m/C VHS.** William J. Kulzer, Elizabeth Trosper, Kevin Costner; ***D:*** Howard Heard.

Shadowzone ♂♂ **1989 (R)** As a result of NASA experiments in dream travel, an interdimensional monster invades our world in search of victims. Begins well, with slightly interesting premise, but degenerates into typical monster flick. Good special effects. **88m/C VHS, DVD.** Louise Fletcher, David Beecroft, James Hong, Shawn Weatherly, Lu Leonard; ***D:*** J.S. Cardone; ***W:*** J.S. Cardone.

ShadowZone: The Undead Express ♂♂½ **1996 (PG-13)** Teenaged Zach (Leopardi) winds up in New York's subway tunnels where he meets the vampire Valentine (Silver) and his fellow bloodsuckers. Based on the book by J.R. Black. **98m/C VHS.** Chauncey Leopardi, Ron Silver, Natanya Ross, Tony T. Johnson, Ron White; ***Cameos:*** Wes Craven; ***D:*** Stephen Williams; ***W:*** Roy Swallows; ***C:*** Curtis Petersen; ***M:*** Reg Powell. **CABLE**

Shadrach ♂♂½ **1998 (PG-13)** The Dabneys run-down Depression Era southern farm was once a rich tobacco plantation and, as they learn, the former home to aged black man Shadrach (Sawyer) who returns in order to die on the land where he grew up. Flawed family patriarch Vernon (Keitel) gives his word to the ex-slave that he can be buried on the land, but learns otherwise from the local sheriff. Still, Vernon tries to fulfill his promise. Director Susanna Styron's lethargic adaptation of her father William's 1978 short story proves that the story should have stayed shorter than ninety minutes. Although the relatively small budget shows, the cast provides good performances. **88m/C VHS, DVD.** Edward (Eddie) Bunker, Harvey Keitel, John Franklin Sawyer, Andie MacDowell, Scott Terra, Monica Bugajski, Darrell Larson, Deborah Hedwall, Daniel Treat; *D:* Susanna Styron; *W:* Susanna Styron, Bridget Terry; *C:* Hiro Narita; *M:* Van Dyke Parks.

Shaft 🦴🦴🦴 **1971 (R)** A black private eye (Roundtree) is hired to find a Harlem gangster's (Gunn) kidnapped daughter. Lotsa sex and violence; suspenseful and well directed by notable "Life" photographer Parks. Great ending. Academy Award-winning theme song by Isaac Hayes, the first music award from the Academy to an African American. Adapted from the novel by Ernest Tidyman. Followed by "Shaft's Big Score" and "Shaft in Africa." ♫Theme From Shaft. **98m/C VHS, DVD.** Richard Roundtree, Moses Gunn, Charles Cioffi, Christopher St. John, Gwen Mitchell, Lawrence Pressman, Victor Arnold, Antonio Fargas, Drew "Bundini" Brown; *D:* Gordon Parks; *W:* John D.F. Black, Ernest Tidyman; *C:* Urs Furrer; *M:* Isaac Hayes, J.J. Johnson. Oscars '71: Song ("Theme from Shaft"); Golden Globes '72: Score, Natl. Film Reg. '00.

Shaft 🦴🦴🦴 *Shaft Returns* **2000 (R)** Singleton's updated the 1971 blaxploitation flick with Jackson starring as the nephew of the coolest private dick ever (Roundtree has a cameo in his original role). But Jackson can more than hold his own in the cool department as he tracks down rich-kid murderer Walter Wade Jr. (Bale), who's after the only witness to his crime, a scared waitress (Collette). Wade hires a Latino drug dealer (Wright, in a standout performance almost equal to Jackson's) and a couple of bad cops to find the girl and kill Shaft, setting off much gunfire and snappy dialoque. Jackson has charisma to burn, but other characters, as well as potentially interesting plot points, get short shrift. This is most likely a result of Wright's part being (deservedly) beefed up from the original screenplay (about which Singleton and Jackson were said to be not entirely happy). **98m/C VHS, DVD.** Samuel L. Jackson, Christian Bale, Vanessa L(ynne) Williams, Jeffrey Wright, Philip Bosco, Toni Collette, Angela Pietropinto, Dan Hedaya, Josef Sommer, Richard Roundtree, Ruben Santiago-Hudson, Lynne Thigpen, Pat Hingle, Busta Rhymes, Mekhi Phifer, Zach Grenier, Catherine Kellner, Isaac Hayes, Lee Tergesen, Gloria Reuben, Gordon Parks, Daniel von Bargen; *D:* John Singleton; *W:* Richard Price; *C:* Stuart Dryburgh; *M:* Isaac Hayes, David Arnold.

Shaft in Africa 🦴🦴½ **1973 (R)** Violent actioner finds detective Shaft forced into helping an African nation stop some modern-day slave trading. Second sequel, following "Shaft's Big Score." **112m/C VHS, DVD, Wide.** Richard Roundtree, Frank Finlay, Vonetta McGee, Neda Arneric, Jacques Marin; *D:* John Guillermin; *W:* Stirling Silliphant.

Shaft's Big Score 🦴🦴½ **1972 (R)** This first sequel to the extremely sucessful "Shaft" has Roundtree's detective trying to mediate between several mobsters while investigating a friend's murder. Lots of action and an exciting Brooklyn chase scene involving cars, helicopters, and boats but still routine when compared to the original. Followed by "Shaft in Africa." **105m/C VHS, DVD, Wide.** Richard Roundtree, Moses Gunn, Joseph Macolo, Drew "Bundini" Brown, Wally Taylor, Kathy Imrie, Julius W. Harris, Rosalind Miles, Joe Santos; *D:* Gordon Parks; *W:* Ernest Tidyman; *M:* Gordon Parks.

Shag: The Movie 🦴🦴🦴 **1989 (PG)** The time is 1963, the setting Myrtle Beach, South Carolina, the latest craze shaggin' when four friends hit the beach for one last weekend together. Carson (Cates) is getting ready to marry staid Harley (Power); Melaina (Fonda) wants to be discovered in Hollywood; and Pudge (Gish) and Luanne (Hannah) are off to college. They encounter lots of music, boys, and dancing in this delightful film. Not to be confused with other "teen" movies, this one boasts a good script and an above average cast. **96m/C VHS, DVD, Wide.** Phoebe Cates, Annabeth Gish, Bridget Fonda, Page Hannah, Scott Coffey, Robert Rusler, Tyrone Power Jr., Jeff Yagher, Carrie Hamilton, Shirley Anne Field, Leilani Sarelle Ferrer; *D:* Zelda Barron; *W:* Robin Swicord, Lanier Laney, Terry Sweeney; *C:* Peter Macdonald.

The Shaggy D.A. 🦴🦴 **1976 (G)** Wilby Daniels is getting a little worried about his canine alter ego as he is about to run for District Attorney. Fun sequel to "The Shaggy Dog." **90m/C VHS.** Dean Jones, Tim Conway, Suzanne Pleshette, Keenan Wynn; *D:* Robert Stevenson; *M:* Buddy (Norman Dale) Baker.

The Shaggy Dog 🦴🦴½ **1959 (G)** When young Wilby Daniels utters some magical words from the inscription of an ancient ring he turns into a shaggy dog, causing havoc for family and neighbors. Disney slapstick is on target at times, though it drags in places. Followed by "The Shaggy D.A." and "Return of the Shaggy Dog." **101m/B VHS.** Fred MacMurray, Jean Hagen, Tommy Kirk, Annette Funicello, Tim Considine, Kevin Corcoran; *D:* Charles T. Barton; *C:* Edward Colman.

Shaka Zulu 🦴🦴🦴 **1983** British miniseries depicting the career of Shaka, king of the Zulus (Cele). Set in the early 19th century during British ascendency in Africa. Good, absorbing cross-cultural action drama would have been better with more inspired directing by Faure. **300m/C VHS, DVD.** *GB* Edward Fox, Robert Powell, Trevor Howard, Christopher Lee, Fiona Fullerton, Henry Cele; *D:* William C. Faure. **TV**

Shake Hands with Murder 🦴🦴 **1944** Three people spend their time bailing criminals out of jail for profit. One is murdered, and the other two become implicated in comedy. **63m/B VHS.** Iris Adrian, Frank Jenks, Douglas Fowley, Jack Raymond, Claire Rochelle, Herbert Rawlinson, Forrest Taylor; *D:* Al(bert) Herman.

Shake Hands with the Devil 🦴🦴🦴 **1959** It's the Irish Republican Army against the British Black and Tans as Ireland fights for independence in 1921. Cagney is a teaching surgeon who is secretly a militant, obsessed with the idea of gaining Irish freedom. He urges his students to join with him, which Irish-American Murray does. When Murray learns that Cagney is out to sabotage a peace treaty, he must decide whether to betray Cagney in order to stop further violence. Cagney is excellent as the hard-bitten revolutionary who can't see beyond his own ideals. Filmed on location in Dublin, which further heightens the film's tension. **110m/B VHS.** James Cagney, Don Murray, Dana Wynter, Glynis Johns, Michael Redgrave, Sybil Thorndike, Harry Brogan, Robert Brown; *D:* Michael Anderson Sr.; *W:* Ivan Goff.

Shake, Rattle and Rock 🦴🦴½ **1957** A deejay wants to open a teen music club playing rock 'n' roll, which has all the conservative parents up in arms. A court case follows (which the kids win). Incidental plot to the great music by Fats Domino, Joe Turner, Annita Ray, and Tommy Charles. Songs include "Ain't It a Shame," "Honey Chile," "I'm in Love Again," "Feelin' Happy," and "Sweet Love on My Mind." **76m/C VHS.** Mike Connors, Lisa Gaye, Sterling Holloway, Margaret Dumont, Raymond Hatton, Douglass Dumbrille; *D:* Edward L. Cahn; *W:* Lou Rusoff.

Shake, Rattle & Rock! 🦴🦴½ **1994 (PG-13)** Remake of the 1957 flick. Teenager Susan (Zellweger) scandalizes her uptight mom (Dunn) and the other conservative adults in town because of her love of that evil rock 'n' rock music—and bad boy Lucky (Doe). Made as part of Showtime's "Rebel Highway" series. **83m/C VHS, DVD.** Renee Zellweger, John Doe, Nora Dunn, Howie Mandel, Patricia Childress, Mary Woronov, Max Perlich, Dick Miller, William Schallert, Paul Anka; *D:* Allan Arkush; *W:* Trish Soodik; *C:* Jean De Segonzac; *M:* Joseph (Joey) Altruda. **CABLE**

Shakedown 🦴🦴½ *Blue Jean Cop* **1988 (R)** Power-packed action film. An overworked attorney and an undercover cop work together to stop corruption in the N.Y.P.D. Although lacking greatly in logic or plot, the sensational stunts make this an otherwise entertaining action flick. **96m/C VHS, DVD.** Sam Elliott, Peter Weller, Patricia Charbonneau, Antonio Fargas, Blanche Baker, Richard Brooks, Jude Ciccolella, George Loros, Tom Waits, Shirley Stoler, Rockets Redglare, Kathryn Rossetter; *D:* James Glickenhaus; *W:* James Glickenhaus; *C:* John Lindley; *M:* Jonathan Elias.

Shakedown 🦴🦴 **2002 (R)** Perlman is the leader of a doomsday cult that plans to steal a biological weapon and unleash it on the population. They take over the L.A. bank where the weapon is stored just at the same time that an earthquake hits, which traps the bad guys. When the military discovers the situation, a general (Dryer) decides to destroy the bank to prevent the virus from escaping. **92m/C VHS, DVD, Wide.** Ron Perlman, Erika Eleniak, Fred (John F.) Dryer, Wolf Larson, Matt Westmore; *D:* Brian Katkin; *W:* Brian Katkin; *C:* Yoram Astrakhan; *M:* Chris Farrell. **VIDEO**

Shaker Run 🦴½ **1985** A stunt car driver and his mechanic transport a mysterious package. They don't know what to do—they're carrying a deadly virus that every terrorist wants! Car chases galore, and not much else. However, if you like chase scenes... **91m/C VHS.** *NZ* Leif Garrett, Cliff Robertson, Lisa Harrow; *D:* Bruce Morrison.

Shakes the Clown 🦴 **1992 (R)** Chronicles the rise and fall of Shakes, an alcoholic clown wandering through the all-clown town of Palukaville. Framed for the murder of his boss by his archrival, Binky, Shakes takes it on the lam in order to prove his innocence, aided by his waitress girlfriend Judy, who dreams of becoming a professional bowler. Meant as a satire of substance-abuse recovery programs and the supposed tragedies of a performer's life, the film is sometimes zany, but more often merely unpleasant and unamusing. Williams has an uncredited role as a mime. **83m/C VHS, DVD, Wide.** Bob(cat) Goldthwait, Julie Brown, Blake Clark, Adam Sandler, Tom Kenny, Sydney Lassick, Paul Dooley, Tim Kazurinsky, Florence Henderson, LaWanda Page; *Cameos:* Robin Williams; *D:* Bob(cat) Goldthwait; *W:* Bob(cat) Goldthwait; *C:* Bobby Bukowski, Elliot Davis.

Shakespeare in Love 🦴🦴🦴🦴 **1998 (R)** Lively romantic comedy about a frustrated Elizabethan playwright suffering from writer's block—who just happens to be William Shakespeare (Fiennes). Will owes a comedy to bankrupt theater manager Henslowe (Rush) but just can't come up with a suitable story. His creative (and other) juices are sparked by wealthy beauty Viola De Lesseps (Paltrow), who so loves the theater that she disguises herself as a boy in order to act. (Women are forbidden to be seen on the stage.) But their affair is bittersweet since Viola is about to be married. Ah well, at least Will comes up with "Romeo and Juliet." Terrific script, fine performances, spectacular costumes and cinematography, and you don't have to be a Shakespeare scholar to enjoy yourself. **122m/C VHS, DVD, Wide.** Joseph Fiennes, Gwyneth Paltrow, Ben Affleck, Geoffrey Rush, Colin Firth, Judi Dench, Simon Callow, Tom Wilkinson, Imelda Staunton, Jim Carter, Rupert Everett, Martin Clunes, Anthony Sher, Joe Roberts; *D:* John Madden; *W:* Marc Norman, Tom Stoppard; *C:* Richard Greatrex; *M:* Stephen Warbeck. Oscars '98: Actress (Paltrow), Art Dir./Set Dec., Costume Des., Orig. Screenplay, Picture, Support. Actress (Dench), Orig. Mus./Comedy Score; British Acad. '98: Film, Film Editing, Support. Actor (Rush), Support. Actress (Dench); Golden Globes '99: Actress—Mus./Comedy (Paltrow), Film—Mus./Comedy, Screenplay; MTV Movie Awards '99: Kiss (Joseph Fiennes/Gwyneth Paltrow); N.Y. Film Critics '98: Screenplay; Natl. Soc. Film Critics '98: Support. Actress (Dench); Screen Actors Guild '98: Actress (Paltrow), Cast; Writers Guild '98: Orig. Screenplay; Broadcast Film Critics '98: Orig. Screenplay.

Shakespeare Wallah 🦴🦴🦴½ **1965** Tender, plausible drama of romance and postcolonial relations in India. A troupe of threadbare traveling Shakespeareans quixotically tours India trying to make enough money to return to England. Wonderfully acted and exquisitely and sensitively directed by Ivory. Based in part on the real-life experiences of the theatrical kendal family. **120m/B VHS.** Felicity Kendal, Shashi Kapoor, Madhur Jaffrey, Geoffrey Kendal, Laura Liddell; *D:* James Ivory; *W:* James Ivory, Ruth Prawer Jhabvala; *C:* Subrata Mitra; *M:* Satyajit Ray.

The Shakiest Gun in the West 🦴🦴½ **1968** Remake of Bob Hope's "Paleface" has Philadelphia dentist Jesse W. Heywood (Knotts) heading off for a new practice in the wild west of Big Springs. There he unwittingly takes on bad guys and sultry Penny (Rhoades), an undercover government agent who ropes the nervous dentist into marriage for the sake of her job. **101m/C VHS.** Don Knotts, Barbara Rhoades, Jackie Coogan, Donald (Don "Red") Barry, Ruth McDevitt, Dub Taylor, Noriyuki "Pat" Morita; *D:* Alan Rafkin; *W:* James Fritzell, Everett Greenbaum.

Shaking the Tree 🦴🦴½ **1992 (PG-13)** Group of four high school buddies are still in quest of self-fulfillment ten years after high school as they grapple with problems in the real world of adulthood, seeking distraction in adventure, romance, friendship, and sex. **97m/C VHS.** Arye Gross, Gale Hansen, Doug Savant, Steven Wilde, Courteney Cox Arquette, Christina Haag, Michael Arabian, Nathan Davis; *D:* Duane Clark; *W:* Duane Clark; *M:* David E. Russo.

Shakma 🦴½ **1989** A group of medical researchers involved with experiments on animal and human tendencies toward aggression take a night off to play a quiet game of "Dungeons and Dragons." The horror begins when their main experimental subject comes along and turns things nasty! **101m/C VHS.** Roddy McDowall, Christopher Atkins, Amanda Wyss, Ari Meyers; *D:* Hugh Parks.

Shalako 🦴🦴 **1968** Connery/Bardot pairing promises something special, but fails to deliver. European aristocrats on a hunting trip in New Mexico, circa 1880, are menaced by Apaches. U.S. Army scout tries to save captured countess Bardot. Strange British attempt at a Euro-western. Poorly directed and pointless. Based on a Louis L'Amour story. **113m/C VHS, DVD.** Brigitte Bardot, Sean Connery, Stephen Boyd, Honor Blackman, Woody Strode, Alexander Knox; *D:* Edward Dmytryk; *W:* Scot (Scott) Finch, J.J. Griffith, Hal Hopper, Clarke Reynolds; *C:* Ted Moore; *M:* Robert Farnon.

Shall We Dance 🦴🦴🦴 **1937** And shall we ever! Seventh Astaire-Rogers pairing has a famous ballet dancer and a musical-comedy star embark on a promotional romance and marriage, to boost their careers, only to find themselves truly falling in love. Score by the Gershwins includes memorable songs. Thin, lame plot—but that's okay. For fans of good singing and dancing, and especially of this immortal pair. ♫Slap That Bass; Beginner's Luck; Let's Call the Whole Thing Off; Walking the Dog; They All Laughed; They Can't Take That Away From Me; Shall We Dance. **116m/B VHS.** Fred Astaire, Ginger Rogers, Edward Everett Horton, Eric Blore; *D:* Mark Sandrich; *M:* George Gershwin, Ira Gershwin.

Shall We Dance? 🦴🦴🦴 *Shall We Dansu?* **1996** A timid Japanese businessman (Yakusyo) is lured to ballroom dancing when he glimpses a beautiful, sad-eyed teacher (Kusakari) through a window. As much commentary on controlled Japanese society as a spirited discovery of learning to live and dance. Well-drawn, quirky characters and good humor amid the observant social commentary should put this one at the top of the anyone's foreign film dance card. In Japanese with subtitles. **118m/C VHS.** *JP* Koji Yakusho, Tamiyo Kusakari, Naoto Takenaka, Akira (Tsukamoto) Emoto, Eriko Watanabe, Yu Tokui, Hiromasa Taguchi, Reiko Kusamura; *D:* Masayuki Suo; *W:* Masayuki Suo; *C:* Naoke Kayano; *M:* Yoshikazu Suo. Natl. Bd. of Review '97: Foreign Film; Broadcast Film Critics '97: Foreign Film.

Shallow Grave 🦴½ **1987 (R)** Four coeds en route to Florida witness a murder in rural Georgia and then are pursued relentlessly by the killer, a local sheriff. Decent premise and talented cast could have offered something better, given a meatier script. **90m/C VHS.** Tony March, Lisa Stahl, Tom Law, Carol Cadby; ***D:*** Richard Styles.

Shallow Grave 🦴🦴½ **1994 (R)** Juliet (Fox), David (Eccleston), and Alex (McGregor), three completely unlikable housemates, face a moral dilemma when their new roomie, Hugo (Allen), turns up dead of a drug overdose, leaving behind a suitcase stuffed with cash. Their decision to chop up the body, bury the bits, and keep the loot leads to a well-deserved descent into paranoia, betrayal, and dementia. Interesting character study in which the veneer of civility is totally destroyed at the first hint of temptation. Style wins out over substance as the characters are never humanized before they're demonized. **91m/C VHS, DVD.** *GB* Kerry Fox, Christopher Eccleston, Ewan McGregor, Keith Allen, Ken Stott, Colin McCredie, John Hodge; ***D:*** Danny Boyle; ***W:*** John Hodge; ***C:*** Brian Tufano; ***M:*** Simon Boswell.

Shallow Hal 🦴🦴 **2001 (PG-13)** Dumpy loser Hal (Black), along with buddy Mauricio (Alexander), will only go after supermodel-perfect women (with predictable results), until self-help guru Tony Robbins hypnotizes him into seeing the inner beauty of the women he encounters. This leads him to meet and pursue Rosemary (Paltrow), who he sees as the physical ideal, but the rest of the world knows to be 300 pounds. The Farrellys try to have it both ways, making fat jokes while projecting the message that appearance shouldn't matter. They're only moderately and intermittently successful. Paltrow does a good job of showing Rosemary's wariness and self-acceptance, while Black at times seems to be trying a little too hard. **114m/C VHS, DVD.** *US* Jack Black, Gwyneth Paltrow, Jason Alexander, Joe (Johnny) Viterelli, Bruce McGill, Susan Ward, Rene Kirby, Tony Robbins, Zen Gesner, Brooke Burns, Rob Moran, Nan Martin; ***D:*** Bobby Farrelly, Peter Farrelly; ***W:*** Bobby Farrelly, Peter Farrelly, Sean Moynihan; ***C:*** Russell Carpenter.

The Shaman 🦴½ **1987 (R)** Members of a family succumb to the hypnotic spell of the Shaman as he searches for the perfect one to inherit his powers. **88m/C VHS.** Michael Conforti, Elvind Harum, James Farkas, Lynn Weaver; ***D:*** Michael Yakub.

Shame 🦴🦴🦴½ *The Intruder; I Hate Your Guts; The Stranger* **1961** Strangely unsuccessful low-budget Corman effort, starring pre-"Star Trek" Shatner as a freelance bigot who travels around Missouri stirring up opposition to desegregation. Moralistic and topical but still powerful. Adapted from the equally excellent novel by Charles Beaumont. Uses location filming superbly to render a sense of everydayness and authenticity. **84m/B VHS, DVD.** William Shatner, Frank Maxwell, Jeanne Cooper, Robert Emhardt, Leo Gordon, Charles Beaumont, Beverly Lunsford, William F. Nolan, George Clayton Johnson; ***D:*** Roger Corman; ***W:*** Charles Beaumont; ***C:*** Taylor Byars; ***M:*** Herman Stein.

The Shame 🦴🦴🦴½ **1968 (R)** A Bergman masterpiece focusing on the struggle for dignity in the midst of war. Married concert musicians Ullmann and von Sydow flee a bloody civil war for a small island off their country's coast. Inevitably, the carnage reaches them and their lives become a struggle to endure and retain a small measure of civilized behavior as chaos overtakes them. Deeply despairing and brilliantly acted. In Swedish with English subtitles. **103m/C VHS.** *SW* Max von Sydow, Liv Ullmann, Gunnar Bjornstrand, Sigge Furst, Birgitta Valberg, Hans Alfredson, Ingvar Kjellson; ***D:*** Ingmar Bergman; ***W:*** Ingmar Bergman; ***C:*** Sven Nykvist. Natl. Soc. Film Critics '68: Actress (Ullmann), Director (Bergman), Film.

Shame 🦴🦴 **1987 (R)** Strange Australian revenge drama about a female lawyer/biker who rides into a small town and finds herself avenging the rape of a 16-year-old girl. Is it a genuinely feminist movie about justice and a strong woman taking charge? Or is it exploitative trash using a politically correct theme and "message" as a peg for much—very much—gratuitous violence? Hard to tell. Cultish for sure; made on a B budget. **95m/C VHS.** *AU* Deborra-Lee Furness, Tony Barry, Simone Buchanan, Gillian Jones; ***D:*** Steve Jodrell; ***W:*** Beverly Blakenship, Michael Brindley.

Shame 🦴🦴 **1992** In a small logging town a group of violent high school thugs get away with rape because the women are too terrified to go to the cops. Then lawyer Diana Cadell (Donohoe) gets stuck in town when her motorcycle breaks down. When she finds out what's been happening, she urges one victim (Balk) to speak out and suddenly they become the targets of both the vicious attackers and a town which would like to hush the entire mess up. Very strong performances by Donohoe and Balk. U.S. version of the same-titled 1987 Australian movie. **91m/C VHS.** Amanda Donohoe, Fairuza Balk, Dean Stockwell, Dan Gauthier; ***D:*** Dan Lerner; ***W:*** Rebecca Soladay. **CABLE**

Shame of the Jungle **1990 (R)** Animated spoof of Tarzan featuring the voices of John Belushi, Bill Murray, and Johnny Weissmuller Jr. **73m/C VHS.** ***D:*** Boris Szulzinger, Picha; ***V:*** Johnny Weissmuller Jr., John Belushi, Bill Murray, Brian Doyle-Murray, Christopher Guest, Andrew Duncan.

Shame, Shame on the Bixby Boys 🦴½ **1982** Somewhere in the Old West, outside a small town, lives a band of misfits who persist in rustling cattle. The Bixby Boys and their Pa have made a bad habit into a family tradition. **90m/C VHS.** Monte Markham, Sammy Jackson; ***D:*** Anthony Bowers.

Shame, Shame, Shame 🦴½ **1998 (R)** Pretty much lives up to its title. A Ph.D candidate working on her thesis asks her subjects to disrobe as part of her interviewing process and discovers as they shed their clothes they shed their secrets and inhibitions as well. **87m/C VHS.** Heidi Schanz, Costas Mandylor, Audie England, Valerie Perrine, Olivia Hussey; ***D:*** Zalman King. **VIDEO**

Shameless 🦴🦴 *Mad Dogs and Englishmen* **1994 (R)** Wealthy Antonia Dyer (Hurley) is the self-centered, drug addict daughter of aristocrat Sir Harry Dyer (Treves). Her dealer is upper-class Tony Vernon-Smith (Brett), who's involved with Sandy (Delamere), the daughter of corrupt narcotics cop Stringer (Ackland). Stringer discovers the two girls know each other and irrationally blames Antonia for his daughter's heroin habit. Meanwhile, American student Mike (Howell) has been trying to get girlfriend Antonia off the drugs. Hurley's properly snooty and manipulative while Howell seems out-of-place and uncomfortable. **99m/C VHS, DVD.** *GB* Elizabeth Hurley, C. Thomas Howell, Joss Ackland, Jeremy Brett, Frederick Treves, Claire Bloom, Louise Delamere, Chris(topher) Adamson; ***D:*** Henry Cole; ***W:*** Tim Sewell; ***C:*** John Peters; ***M:*** Barrie Guard.

The Shaming 🦴½ *The Sin; Good Luck, Miss Wyckoff* **1971 (R)** Puritanical schoolteacher is raped by a janitor, then develops a voracious sexual appetite. Horrible script, offensive premise can't be saved by good cast. Based on a novel by William Inge. **90m/C VHS.** Anne Heywood, Donald Pleasence, Robert Vaughn, Carolyn Jones; ***D:*** Marvin J. Chomsky.

Shampoo 🦴🦴½ **1975 (R)** A satire of morals (and lack thereof) set in Southern California, concerning a successful hairdresser (Beatty) and the many women in his life. A notable scene with Julie Christie is set at a 1968 presidential election-night gathering. Fisher's screen debut, only one year before "Star Wars" made her famous. Has a healthy glow in places and a perky bounce, but too many split ends. **112m/C VHS, Wide.** Warren Beatty, Julie Christie, Goldie Hawn, Jack Warden, Lee Grant, Tony Bill, Carrie Fisher, William Castle, Howard Hesseman; ***D:*** Hal Ashby; ***W:*** Warren Beatty, Robert Towne; ***M:*** John Barry. Oscars '75: Support. Actress (Grant); Natl. Soc. Film Critics '75: Screenplay; Writers Guild '75: Orig. Screenplay.

Shamus 🦴🦴 **1973 (PG)** Private dick Reynolds investigates a smuggling ring, beds a sultry woman, gets in lotsa fights. Classic Burt vehicle meant as a send-up. Unoriginal but fun. **91m/C VHS.** Burt Reynolds, Dyan Cannon, John P. Ryan; ***D:*** Buzz Kulik; ***W:*** Barry Beckerman; ***M:*** Jerry Goldsmith.

Shane 🦴🦴🦴🦴 **1953** A retired gunfighter, now a drifter, comes to the aid of a homestead family threatened by a land baron and his hired gun. Ladd is the mystery man who becomes the idol of the family's young son. Classic, flawless Western. Pulitzer prize-winning western novelist A.B. Guthrie Jr. adapted from the novel by Jack Schaefer. Long and stately; worth savoring. **117m/C VHS, DVD.** Alan Ladd, Jean Arthur, Van Heflin, Brandon de Wilde, Jack Palance, Ben Johnson, Elisha Cook Jr., Edgar Buchanan, Emile Meyer; ***D:*** George Stevens; ***W:*** Jack Sher; ***C:*** Loyal Griggs; ***M:*** Victor Young. Oscars '53: Color Cinematog.; AFI '98: Top 100; Natl. Bd. of Review '53: Director (Stevens), Natl. Film Reg. '93.

The Shanghai Cobra 🦴½ **1945** Below-average mystery has Chan hired by the government to investigate several supposed cobra bite murders. All motives lead to stealing a supply of radium. **64m/B VHS.** Sidney Toler, Benson Fong, Mantan Moreland, Walter Fenner, James B. Cardwell, Joan Barclay, James Flavin; ***D:*** Phil Karlson.

Shanghai Express 🦴🦴🦴½ **1932** Dietrich is at her most alluring in this mystical and exotic story that made legends out of both star and director. Dietrich plays Shanghai Lily, a woman of objectionable reputation, who has a reunion of sorts with ex-lover Brook aboard a slow-moving train through China. Remade as "Peking Express." Based on a story by Harry Hervey. **80m/B VHS.** Marlene Dietrich, Clive Brook, Anna May Wong, Warner Oland, Eugene Pallette, Lawrence Grant, Louise Closser Hale; ***D:*** Josef von Sternberg; ***W:*** Jules Furthman; ***C:*** Lee Garmes. Oscars '32: Cinematog.

The Shanghai Gesture 🦴🦴½ **1942** A wildly baroque, subversive melodrama. An English financier tries to close a gambling den, only to be blackmailed by the female proprietor—who tells him not only is the man's daughter heavily indebted to her, but that she is the wife he abandoned long ago. Based on a notorious Broadway play. Von Sternberg had to make numerous changes to the script in order to get it past the Hays censors; the director's final Hollywood work, and worthy of his oeuvre, but oddly unsatisfying. **97m/B VHS, DVD.** Walter Huston, Gene Tierney, Victor Mature, Ona Munson, Albert Bassermann, Eric Blore, Maria Ouspenskaya, Phyllis Brooks, Mike Mazurki; ***D:*** Josef von Sternberg; ***W:*** Josef von Sternberg, Jules Furthman, Geza Herczeg, Karl Vollmoller; ***C:*** Paul Ivano; ***M:*** Richard Hageman.

Shanghai Noon 🦴🦴½ **2000 (PG-13)** Goofy, good-natured, western action/comedy finds Chinese imperial guard Chon Wang (Chan) in trouble for not preventing Princess Pei Pei (Liu) from running off to America (circa 1880) with her American tutor (Connery). But it all turns out to be a kidnapping scheme and Wang winds up in Nevada, helping to deliver the ransom gold. Through some unlikely events, Wang hooks up with talkative, unsuccessful outlaw, Roy O'Bannon (Wilson), learns some of the west's wilder ways, and the buds set out to rescue the damsel, who's no shrinking flower herself. Chan and Wilson are both throughly ingratiating and you've got the Chan stunts to look forward to as well. **110m/C VHS, DVD, Wide.** Jackie Chan, Lucy Alexis Liu, Owen C. Wilson, Roger Yuan, Xander Berkeley, Jason Connery, Henry O, Walton Goggins, Russ Badger, Rafael Baez, Brandon Merrill; ***D:*** Tom Dey; ***W:*** Alfred Gough, Miles Millar; ***C:*** Dan Mindel; ***M:*** Randy Edelman.

Shanghai Surprise 🦴½ **1986 (PG-13)** Tie salesman Penn and missionary Madonna (yeah, right) are better than you'd think, and the story (of opium smuggling in China in the '30s) is intrepid and wildly fun, but indifferently directed and unsure of itself. Executive producer George Harrison wrote the songs and has a cameo. **90m/C VHS.** Sean Penn, Madonna, Paul Freeman, Richard Griffiths; ***Cameos:*** George Harrison; ***D:*** Jim Goddard; ***W:*** Robert Bentley; ***M:*** George Harrison, Michael Kamen. Golden Raspberries '86: Worst Actress (Madonna).

Shanghai Triad 🦴🦴🦴½ *Yao a Yao Yao Dao Waipo Qiao* **1995 (R)** Seventh collaboration of director Yimou and star Li takes place in violent crime dynasty of 1930s Shanghai. Here, eight days are seen through the eyes of a young boy (Cuihua) initiated into the Triad to be the lackey of the mob boss's arrogant mistress (Li). The trio and some trusty associates flee to the country after things heat up with a rival mob. Yimou subtly distinguishes the dichotomy between the jaded criminals and the naive youth with the move from the city to the country and his use of color and tone while avoiding cliche. Plot twists are fresh and technical aspects impeccable. Chinese with subtitles. **108m/C VHS, DVD, Wide.** *FR CH* Gong Li, Li Bao-Tian, Li Xuejian, Shun Chun Shusheng, Wang Xiaoxiao Cuihua, Jiang Baoying; ***D:*** Zhang Yimou; ***W:*** Bi Feiyu; ***C:*** Lu Yue; ***M:*** Zhang Guangtain.

Shanty Tramp 🦴 **1967** Small-town tramp puts the moves on an evangelist, a motorcycle gang, and a young black man, who risks his life trying to save her from her loose morals. Another cheesy flick made for the drive-in crowd. **72m/B VHS.** Lee Holland, Bill Rogers, Lawrence Tobin; ***D:*** Joseph Prieto. **TV**

Shark! 🦴½ *Man-Eater; Un Arma de Dos Filos* **1968 (PG)** American gun smuggler Reynolds, stranded in a tiny seaport in Africa, joins the crew of a marine biologist's boat. He soon discovers the boat's owner and his wife are trying to retrieve gold bullion that lies deep in shark-infested waters. Typical Reynoldsian action-infested dumbness. Like "Twilight Zone: The Movie," earned notoriety because of on-location tragedy: a stunt diver really was killed by a shark. Edited without the consent of Fuller, who disowned it. **92m/C VHS.** Burt Reynolds, Barry Sullivan, Arthur Kennedy; ***D:*** Samuel Fuller; ***W:*** Samuel Fuller.

Shark Attack 🦴½ **1999 (R)** A marine biologist investigates a rash of shark attacks terrorizing an African fishing village that have claimed the life of a friend. **95m/C VHS, DVD.** *SA* Casper Van Dien, Ernie Hudson, Bentley Mitchum, Jenny McShane; ***D:*** Bob Misiorowski; ***W:*** Scott Devine, William Hooke; ***C:*** Lawrence Sher. **VIDEO**

Shark Hunter 🦴 **1984 (PG)** Shark hunter gets ensnared in the mob's net off the Mexican coast as they race for a cache of sunken millions. The usual garden-variety B-grade adventure. **95m/C VHS.** Franco Nero, Jorge Luke, Mike Forrest.

Shark River 🦴½ **1953** A man attempts to get his brother, a Civil War veteran accused of murder, through the Everglades and send him to safety in Cuba. Good photography of the great swamp; disappointing story. **80m/C VHS.** Steve Cochran, Carole Mathews, Warren Stevens; ***D:*** John Rawlins; ***W:*** Lewis Meltzer, Louis Lantz.

Sharks' Treasure 🦴½ **1975 (PG)** A band of escaped convicts commandeer a boat filled with gold. Old fashioned sunken-treasure tale unexceptional except as a virtual one man show by writer/actor/director/producer/fitness nut Wilde. **96m/C VHS.** Cornel Wilde, Yaphet Kotto, John Nellson, Cliff Osmond, David Canary, David Gilliam; ***D:*** Cornel Wilde.

Sharky's Machine 🦴🦴½ **1981 (R)** A tough undercover cop (Reynolds) is hot on the trail of a crooked crime czar. Meanwhile he falls for a high-priced hooker. Well done but overdone action, with much violence. Based on the William Diehl novel. **119m/C VHS, DVD.** Burt Reynolds, Rachel Ward, Vittorio Gassman, Brian Keith, Charles Durning, Bernie Casey, Richard Libertini, Henry Silva, John Fiedler, Earl Holliman; ***D:*** Burt Reynolds; ***W:*** Gerald Di Pego; ***C:*** William A. Fraker.

Sharma & Beyond 🦴 **1984** A teenage would-be science fiction writer falls in love with the daughter of a famous sci-fi author. **85m/C VHS.** Suzanne Burden, Robert Urquhart, Michael Maloney; ***D:*** Brian Gilbert; ***M:*** Rachel Portman.

Sharon's Secret 🦴🦴½ **1995 (R)** When the mutilated bodies of wealthy Richard Harly and his wife are discovered, investigating detective Thomas McGregor (Henry) looks to place the blame on their traumatized 16-year-old daughter Sharon (Cameron), who'll inherit a fortune. Psychiatrist Laurel O'Connor (Harris) is assigned to help Sharon recover and she's defended by family attorney Frank Bowdin (McArthur) but it seems everyone has something to hide. **91m/C VHS.** Candace Cameron, Mel Harris, Gregg Henry, Alex McArthur, Paul Regina, Elaine Kagan, James Pickens Jr.; ***D:*** Michael Scott; ***W:*** Mark Homer. **CABLE**

Sharpe's Battle 🦴🦴½ **1994** Sharpe (Bean) must prepare the Royal Irish company, led by Lord Kiely (Durr) and used to only ceremonial duties, for their first battle. Meanwhile, Kiely's wife (Byrne) goes to Sharpe for help with a personal matter and there's more trouble with the French. Based on the novel by Bernard Cornwell; made for British TV. **100m/C VHS, DVD.** *GB* Sean Bean, Daragh O'Malley, Hugh Fraser, Jason Durr, Allie Byrne; ***D:*** Tom Clegg; ***W:*** Russell Lewis. **TV**

Sharpe's Company 🦴🦴½ **1994** Sharpe (Bean) sets out to rescue Spanish lover Teresa (Serna) and his infant daughter, trapped in the French-held city of Badajoz, which is about to be stormed by British troops. To make matters worse, Sharpe must also deal with the machinations of underhanded madman Sergeant Obadiah Hakeswill (Postlethwaite), an old enemy with a grudge to settle. Based on the novel by Bernard Cornwell; made for British TV. **100m/C VHS, DVD.** *GB* Sean Bean, Assumpta Serna, Daragh O'Malley, Pete Postlethwaite, Hugh Fraser, Clive Francis, Louise Germaine; ***D:*** Tom Clegg; ***W:*** Charles Wood. **TV**

Sharpe's Eagle 🦴🦴½ **1993** Sharpe (Bean) and his chosen band of sharpshooters are once again in the thick of battle against Napoleon's troops but this time they have the misfortune to be led by the imbecilic Sir Henry Simmerson (Cochrane). Thanks to Simmerson's cowardice, the regimental colors are captured and a heroic officer Sharpe admires is killed. Setting out for revenge, Sharpe is determined to capture the French mascot, a carved golden eagle carried into battle, and settle some personal scores. Based on the novel by Bernard Cornwell; made for British TV. **100m/C VHS, DVD.** *GB* Sean Bean, Assumpta Serna, Brian Cox, David Troughton, Daragh O'Malley, Michael Cochrane, Katia Caballero; ***D:*** Tom Clegg; ***W:*** Eoghan Harris; ***C:*** Ivan Strasburg; ***M:*** Dominic Muldowney. **TV**

Sharpe's Enemy 🦴🦴½ **1994** Sharpe (Bean) is sent to a mountain stronghold, held by a band of deserters, to ransom Isabella (Hurley), the bride of English colonel, Sir Augustus Farthingdale (Child). But the evil Hakeswill (Postlethwaite) is leading the criminals and he refuses to make things easy for our hero—nor will the French troops leave the English soldiers in peace. Based on the novel by Bernard Cornwell; made for British TV. **100m/C VHS, DVD.** *GB* Sean Bean, Assumpta Serna, Pete Postlethwaite, Daragh O'Malley, Hugh Fraser, Elizabeth Hurley, Michael Byrne, Jeremy Child, Nicholas (Nick) Rowe; ***D:*** Tom Clegg; ***W:*** Eoghan Harris. **TV**

Sharpe's Gold 🦴🦴½ **1994** Circa 1813 and Richard Sharpe (Bean) has now been promoted to Major—still leading his band of renegade sharpshooters. This time they're assigned to trade rifles for deserters held by the partisans and search for hidden Aztec gold, as Wellington (Fraser) prepares to push on into France. Sharpe must also protect Wellington's cousin Bess (Linehan) and her daughter Ellie (Ashbourne) as they search for Bess' missing husband. Based on the novel by Bernard Cornwell; made for British TV. **100m/C VHS, DVD.** *GB* Sean Bean, Daragh O'Malley, Hugh Fraser, Rosaleen Linehan, Jayne Ashbourne, Abel Folk, Peter Eyre; ***D:*** Tom Clegg; ***W:*** Nigel Kneale. **TV**

Sharpe's Honour 🦴🦴½ **1994** Sharpe (Bean) becomes a pawn of French spy Pierre Ducos when he's forced to cross enemy lines, disguised as a Spanish rebel, in order to defend himself against allegations of dishonor. Sharpe's also unable to resist the attractions of the Marquesa Dorada (Krige), who's also part of Ducos' plan. Based on the novel by Bernard Cornwell; made for British TV. **100m/C VHS, DVD.** *GB* Sean Bean, Daragh O'Malley, Alice Krige, Hugh Fraser, Michael Byrne, Ron Cook; ***D:*** Tom Clegg; ***W:*** Colin MacDonald. **TV**

Sharpe's Justice 🦴🦴½ **1997** Having cleared his name, Richard Sharpe (Bean) returns to England and is ordered north where he's to command the local militia. But Sharpe soon has to decide whether to support the local gentry or the working class in a time of social unrest. Based on the novel by Bernard Cornwell. **100m/C VHS, DVD.** *GB* Sean Bean, Daragh O'Malley, Abigail Cruttenden, Alexis Denisof, Douglas Henshall, Caroline Langrishe, Philip Glenister; ***D:*** Tom Clegg. **TV**

Sharpe's Legend 🦴🦴½ **1997** Highlights from the British TV series detailing the life, loves, and career of 19th-century British soldier/hero Richard Sharpe (Bean). Narrated by Rifleman Cooper (Mears). **90m/C VHS.** *GB* Sean Bean, Michael Mears; ***D:*** Paul Wilmshurst. **TV**

Sharpe's Mission 🦴🦴½ **1996** Sharpe (Bean) joins with Colonel Brand (Strong) and his men to blow up an ammunition depot as Wellington continues his invasion of France. But Brand arouses Sharpe's suspicions that the supposedly heroic Colonel is actually a French spy. Based on the novel by Bernard Cornwell. **100m/C VHS, DVD.** *GB* Sean Bean, Daragh O'Malley, Hugh Fraser, James Laurenson, Mark Strong, Abigail Cruttenden; ***D:*** Tom Clegg; ***W:*** Eoghan Harris. **TV**

Sharpe's Regiment 🦴🦴½ **1996** Wellington prepares for the invasion of France in June, 1813 but the South Essex batallion needs more men. So Sharpe (Bean) and Harper (O'Malley) are sent back to London for recruits and uncover corruption in high places. Based on the novel by Bernard Cornwell. **100m/C VHS, DVD.** *GB* Sean Bean, Daragh O'Malley, Nicholas Farrell, Michael Cochrane, Abigail Cruttenden, Caroline Langrishe, James Laurenson; ***D:*** Tom Clegg; ***W:*** Eoghan Harris. **TV**

Sharpe's Revenge 🦴🦴½ **1997** The Penisular War is over but Sharpe (Bean) is accused of stealing Napoleon's treasures by old enemy Ducos. Abandoned by his wife when he's convicted of the crime, Sharpe escapes from prison and crosses postwar France in search of the truth. Based on the novel by Bernard Cornwell. **100m/C VHS, DVD.** *GB* Sean Bean, Daragh O'Malley, Abigail Cruttenden, Feodor Atkine, Alexis Denisof, Cecile Paoli, Philip Whitchurch; ***D:*** Tom Clegg; ***W:*** Eoghan Harris. **TV**

Sharpe's Rifles 🦴🦴½ **1993** Swashbuckling heroics dominate as the Duke of Wellington's British soldiers battle Napoleon's French forces in the 1809 Penisular War (fought in Spain and Portugal). Common soldier Richard Sharpe (Bean) has just been promoted and given the unenviable task of leading a group of malcontent sharpshooters on a secret mission to aid Britain's Spanish allies. But it's not all hard times for Sharpe since the Spanish commander happens to be a very lovely woman. Adapted from the novel by Bernard Cornwall; made for British TV. **100m/C VHS, DVD.** *GB* Sean Bean, Assumpta Serna, Brian Cox, David Troughton, Daragh O'Malley, Julian Fellowes, Timothy Bentinck, Simon Andreu, Michael Mears, John Tams, Jason Salkey, Paul Trussell; ***D:*** Tom Clegg; ***W:*** Eoghan Harris; ***C:*** Ivan Strasburg; ***M:*** Dominic Muldowney. **TV**

Sharpe's Siege 🦴🦴½ **1996** In the winter of 1813, Napoleon Bonaparte sends his best spy, Major Ducos (Atkine), to find out where Wellington plans to invade France. The newly married Sharpe (Bean) is forced to leave his ill wife, Jane (Cruttenden), and capture a French fort while preventing Duclos' treachery. Based on the novel by Bernard Cornwell. **100m/C VHS, DVD.** *GB* Sean Bean, Daragh O'Malley, Hugh Fraser, Abigail Cruttenden, James Laurenson, Feodor Atkine; ***D:*** Tom Clegg; ***W:*** Eoghan Harris. **TV**

Sharpe's Sword 🦴🦴½ **1994** Sharpe's (Bean) sent to protect Wellington's top spy, El Mirador, and finds himself up against Napoleon's top swordsman Colonel Leroux (Fierry). When Sharpe's wounded, it's up to Lass (Mortimer), a young mute convent girl, to save our hero's life. Based on the novel by Bernard Cornwell; made for British TV. **100m/C VHS, DVD.** *GB* Sean Bean, Daragh O'Malley, Patrick Fierry, Emily Mortimer, John Kavanagh; ***D:*** Tom Clegg; ***W:*** Eoghan Harris. **TV**

Sharpe's Waterloo 🦴🦴½ **1997** Sharpe's (Bean) making a new life with new love Lucille (Paoli) at their French chateau. But when Napoleon returns from exile, Sharpe returns to the army and the Chosen Men to organize a defense before the battle of Waterloo. Based on the novel by Bernard Cornwell. **100m/C VHS, DVD.** *GB* Sean Bean, Daragh O'Malley, Hugh Fraser, Cecile Paoli, Alexis Denisof, Paul Bettany; ***D:*** Tom Clegg. **TV**

Shattered 🦴🦴🦴 *Scherben* **1921** Key film in Germany's kammerspiel (chamber play) movement, which emphasized naturalism with a minimum number of characters. A railway worker's daughter is seduced by her father's supervisor. When the man abandons her, the girl's father takes revenge. **62m/B VHS.** *GE* Werner Krauss, Edith Posca, Paul Otto; ***D:*** Lupu Pick; ***W:*** Carl Mayer.

Shattered 🦴½ *Something to Hide* **1972 (R)** Finch plays Harry, a man blamed for a failed marriage, held hostage in his home by his own paranoia, and driven to bouts of drinking. Slowly his tenuous grip on sanity slips and at any moment his fragile and crumbling life may be shattered. Tired, overwrought domestic drama. **100m/C VHS.** *GB* Peter Finch, Shelley Winters, Colin Blakely; ***D:*** Alastair Reid.

Shattered 🦴🦴 **1991 (R)** An architect recovering from a serious automobile accident tries to regain the memory that he has lost. As he begins to put together the pieces of his life, some parts of the puzzle don't quite fit. For example, he recalls his now loving wife's affair as well as his own. He remembers that he hired a private detective to follow his wife and shockingly, he remembers that he once believed his wife had planned to kill him. Are these memories the real thing, or are they all part of some mad, recuperative nightmare? Who knows. **98m/C VHS, 8mm, Wide.** Tom Berenger, Bob Hoskins, Greta Scacchi, Joanne Whalley, Corbin Bernsen, Theodore Bikel; ***D:*** Wolfgang Petersen; ***W:*** Wolfgang Petersen.

Shattered Dreams 🦴🦴½ **1994** TV movie about domestic violence finds Wagner as the battered wife of a prominent, high-profile government official. Based on a true story. **94m/C VHS.** Lindsay Wagner, Michael Nouri.

Shattered Image 🦴🦴½ **1993 (R)** Confusing thriller about the FBI's involvement in the kidnapping of the owner of a model agency, as well as plastic surgery, and a big money scam. **100m/C VHS.** Bo Derek, Jack Scalia, John Savage, Dorian Harewood, Ramon Franco, Carol Lawrence, Michael (M.K.) Harris, David McCallum; ***D:*** Fritz Kiersch. **CABLE**

Shattered Image 🦴🦴½ **1998** Jessie (Parillaud) is either a cold-blooded hit woman dreaming she's a honeymooner, or a newlywed dreaming she's a psycho assassin. Or both. After whacking a businessman in the men's room at a Seattle restaurant, our heroine goes home to bed, and wakes up a different woman. Literally. On her way to Jamaica with her new husband (Baldwin), Jessie again nods off and she's back in Seattle on her next hit. Each reality features characters from the alternate one, although (like Jessie) each has a different personality. Ruiz fills the screen with stunning homages (Wellesian mirror shots and Hitchcockian split personalities), a truly outrageous ending, and the surrealistic feel of a dream, making for psychotic, if not completely convincing, fun. **102m/C VHS, DVD.** Anne Parillaud, William Baldwin, Lisanne Falk, Graham Greene, Bulle Ogier, Billy Wilmott, O'Neil Peart, Leonie Forbes; ***D:*** Raul Ruiz; ***W:*** Duane Poole; ***C:*** Robby Muller; ***M:*** Jorge Arriagada.

Shattered Silence 🦴½ *When Michael Calls* **1971** A woman is tormented by phone calls that seem to be coming from her dead son as her life is torn apart by divorce. Leaves unanswered the question: Will there be any suspense? Made for TV. Worthless and dumb. **73m/C VHS.** Elizabeth Ashley, Ben Gazzara, Michael Douglas, Karen Pearson; ***D:*** Philip Leacock. **TV**

Shattered Spirits 🦴½ **1991 (PG-13)** Quiet family man cracks and goes on a rampage through his normally peaceful surburban neighborhood. Been done before and better. **93m/C VHS.** Martin Sheen, Melinda Dillon, Matthew Laborteaux, Roxana Zal, Lukas Haas.

Shattered Vows 🦴🦴 **1984** A young nun struggles with her love for a priest and her desire for a child. Bertinelli is convincing as the confused teen in otherwise ordinary TV drama. Adapted from the true story of Dr. Mary Gilligan Wong as told in her book, "Nun: A Memoir." **95m/C VHS.** Valerie Bertinelli, David Morse, Caroline McWilliams, Patricia Neal, Millie Perkins, Leslie Ackerman, Lisa Jane Persky; ***D:*** Jack Bender.

The Shawshank Redemption 🦴🦴🦴½ **1994 (R)** Bank veep Andy (Robbins) is convicted of the murder of his wife and her lover and sentenced to the "toughest prison in the Northeast." While there he forms a friendship with lifer Red (Freeman), experiences the brutality of prison life, adapts, offers financial advice to the guards, and helps the warden (Gunton) cook the prison books...all in a short 19 years. In his theatrical debut, director Darabont avoids belaboring most prison movie cliches while Robbins' talent for playing ambiguous characters is put to good use, and Freeman brings his usual grace to what could have been a thankless role. Adapted from the novella "Rita Hayworth and the Shawshank Redemption" by Stephen King. **142m/C VHS, DVD.** Tim Robbins, Morgan Freeman, Bob Gunton, William Sadler, Clancy Brown, Mark Rolston, Gil Bellows, James Whitmore; ***D:*** Frank Darabont; ***W:*** Frank Darabont; ***C:*** Roger Deakins; ***M:*** Thomas Newman.

She 🦴🦴½ **1921** H. Rider Haggard's famous story about the ageless Queen Ayesha, (Blythe), who renews her life force periodically by walking through a pillar of cold flame. Story and titles by Haggard. Blythe is a stirringly mean queen, and the story remains fresh and fun. Silent film with music score. **69m/B VHS.** Betty Blythe, Carlyle Blackwell, Mary Odette.

She 🦴🦴½ **1935** First sound version of H. Rider Haggard's popular 1887 adventure tale, although the film's location was changed from Africa to the frozen Arctic. Explorers Scott and Bruce are searching for a fire that preserves rather than destroys life. They are captured by a mysterious tribe and discover a living goddess—She-Who-Must-Be-Obeyed (Gahagan)—who bathed in the Flame of Life and is now eternal. She falls for Scott, who doesn't return her love, and there's trouble. Fantastic Art Deco sets and special effects. **95m/B VHS, DVD.** Helen Gahagan, Randolph Scott, Nigel Bruce, Helen Mack, Gustav von Seyffertitz; ***D:*** Irving Pichel, Lansing C. Holden; ***W:*** Dudley Nichols, Ruth Rose; ***C:*** J. Roy Hunt; ***M:*** Max Steiner.

S*H*E 🦴🦴 **1979** A flashy made for TV spy thriller. The female agent S*H*E (Securities Hazards Expert) must save the world's oil; good locations, nifty plot and looker Sharpe as the she-Bond add up to a reasonably fun time. Scripted by "Bond"-writer Maibaum. **100m/C VHS.** Cornelia Sharpe, Robert Lansing, William Taylor, Isabella Rye, Anita Ekberg; ***Cameos:*** Omar Sharif; ***D:*** Robert Lewis; ***W:*** Richard Maibaum; ***M:*** Michael Kamen. **TV**

She 🦴 **1983** A beautiful female warrior rules over the men in a post-holocaust world. She is kidnapped by a wealthy merchant who uses her to fight evil mutants. Utter rubbish vaguely based on the Haggard novel. **90m/C VHS.** Sandahl Bergman, Harrison Muller, Quin Kessler, David Goss; ***D:*** Avi Nesher.

She and He 🦴🦴½ **1963** Hani's look at the oppression of women, marital and spiritual discontent, and class divisions. Naoko is a bored housewife, living in a sterile high-rise apartment with her equally dissatisfied husband, and yearning for something to express her inner feelings. She accidentally meets an old classmate of her husband's who has become a poor ragpicker and tries to aid him. But all her efforts only lead to further tragedies. In Japanese with English subtitles. **110m/C VHS.** *JP* Sachiko Hidari, Eiji Okada, Kikuji Yamashita; ***D:*** Susumu Hani.

The She-Beast 🦴½ *Il Lago di Satana; The Revenge of the Blood Beast; La Sorella de Satan; The Sister of Satan* **1965** Burned at the stake in 18th-century Transylvania, a witch returns in the body of a beautiful young English woman on her honeymoon (in Transylvania?!), and once again wreaks death and destruction. Caution, Barbara Steele fans: she appears for all of 15 minutes. Sporadically funny. **74m/C VHS.** *IT YU* Barbara Steele, Ian Ogilvy, Mel Welles, Lucretia Love; ***D:*** Michael Reeves.

She Came on the Bus woof! **1969** Young thugs break into a well-kept suburban home and terrorize the housewife through rape and torture. Then they kidnap a bus and pose as the drivers until they can find more victims. Contains scenes of graphic violence which would be considered offensive even by today's standards. **58m/C VHS.** ***D:*** Harry Vincent.

She Came to the Valley 🦴 *Texas in Flames* **1977 (PG)** A tough pioneer woman becomes embroiled in political intrigue during the Spanish-American War. Based on Cleo Dawson's book. **90m/C VHS.** Ronee Blakley, Dean Stockwell, Scott Glenn, Freddy Fender.

She Couldn't Say No 🦴🦴 *Beautiful But Dangerous* **1952** A wealthy oil heiress (Simmons) with good intentions plans to give her money away to those friends who had helped her when she was struggling. Things don't go quite as planned; her philanthropy leads to unexpected mayhem in her Arkansas hometown. Passable, but not memorable comedy. Mitchum as a small-town doctor? **88m/B VHS.** Robert Mitchum, Jean Simmons, Arthur Hunnicutt, Edgar Buchanan, Wallace Ford; ***D:*** Lloyd Bacon.

She Creature 🦴🦴½ *Mermaid Chronicles Part 1: She Creature* **2001 (R)** In 1905, carnival barker Angus Shaw (Lily) is traveling in Ireland with his girlfriend Lily (Gugino) posing as a mermaid in a sideshow attraction. They meet drunken ex-sailor Woolrich (Morris) who takes them to his home where he has his own attraction—a real live mermaid (Kilhstedt). Angus steals the mermaid and sails for America but the mermaid begins attacking crewman and Lily develops a symbiotic relationship with the creature. Very loosely based on the AIP 1956 B-movie of the same title, this was one of a series of cable remakes under the umbrella title "Creature Features." **91m/C VHS, DVD, Wide.** Rufus Sewell, Carla Gugino, Rya Kihlstedt, Aubrey Morris, Jim Piddock, Gil Bellows, Reno Wilson; ***D:*** Sebastian Gutierrez; ***W:*** Sebastian Gutierrez; ***C:*** Thomas Callaway; ***M:*** David Reynolds. **CABLE**

She Demons woof! **1958** Pleasure craft loaded with babes crashes into a remote island controlled by a mad ex-Nazi scientist who transforms pretty girls into rubber-faced Frankensteins. Incomprehensible, to say the least. **68m/B VHS, DVD.** Irish McCalla, Tod Griffin, Victor Sen Yung, Rudolph Anders, Tod Andrews, Gene Roth, Bill Coontz, Billy Dix; ***D:*** Richard Cunha; ***W:*** Richard Cunha, H.E. Barrie; ***C:*** Meredith Nicholson; ***M:*** Nicholas Carras.

She-Devil 🦴🦴½ **1989 (PG-13)** A comic book version of the acidic Fay Weldon novel "The Life and Loves of a She-Devil"; a fat, dowdy suburban wife (Arnold) becomes a vengeful beast when a smarmy romance novelist steals her husband. Uneven comedic reworking of a distinctly unforgiving feminist fiction. Arnold is given too much to handle (her role requires an actual range of emotions); Streep's role is too slight, though she does great things with it. **100m/C VHS, DVD, Wide.** Meryl Streep, Roseanne, Ed Begley Jr., Linda Hunt, Elizabeth Peters, Bryan Larkin, A. Martinez, Sylvia Miles; ***D:*** Susan Seidelman; ***W:*** Mark Burns, Barry Strugatz; ***C:*** Oliver Stapleton; ***M:*** Howard Shore.

She Devils in Chains 🦴🦴 *American Beauty Hostages; Ebony, Ivory, and Jade; Foxforce* **1976 (PG)** A group of traveling female athletes are kidnapped by a groups of sadists who torture and beat them. In the end, however, the girls get their revenge, and it's bloody. **82m/C VHS, DVD.** Colleen Camp, Rosanne Katon, Sylvia Anderson, Ken Washington, Leo Martinez; ***D:*** Cirio H. Santiago; ***M:*** Eddie Nova.

She-Devils on Wheels woof! **1968** Havoc erupts as an outlaw female motorcycle gang, known as "Maneaters on Motorbikes," terrorizes a town—especially the men. Really, really bad biker flick finely honed by Lewis. **83m/C VHS.** Betty Connell, Christie Wagner, Pat Poston, Nancy Lee Noble, Ruby Tuesday, Roy Collodi, David Harris, Steve White; ***D:*** Herschell Gordon Lewis; ***W:*** Allison Louise Downe; ***C:*** Roy Collodi; ***M:*** Larry Wellington.

She Done Him Wrong 🦴🦴🦴 **1933** Singer Lady Lou (West) fronts an 1890s Bowery saloon for her shady boss, Gus Jordan (Beery Sr.) Gus gives her diamonds but when she gets an eyeful of young Salvation Army Capt. Cummings (Grant), Lou starts to think there's other things in life worth having. West imparts the screen version of her Broadway hit "Diamond Lil" with her usual share of double entendres and racy comments. ♫Silver Threads Among the Gold; Masie, My Pretty Daisy; Easy Rider; I Like a Guy What Takes His Time; Frankie and Johnny. **65m/B VHS.** Mae West, Cary Grant, Owen Moore, Noah Beery Sr., Gilbert Roland, Louise Beavers, Rafaela (Rafael, Raphaella) Ottiano; ***D:*** Lowell Sherman; ***W:*** Harvey Thew, John Bright; ***C:*** Charles B(ryant) Lang Jr.; ***M:*** Ralph Rainger, David Landau. Natl. Film Reg. '96.

She-Freak 🦴 *Alley of Nightmares* **1967** Remake of Tod Brownings' "Freaks." A cynical waitress burns everyone in a circus and gets mauled by the resident freaks. Pales beside its unacknowledged, classic original. **87m/C VHS, DVD.** Claire Brennan, Lynn Courtney, Bill McKinney, Lee Raymond, Madame Lee, Claude Smith, Ben Moore; ***D:*** Byron Mabe; ***W:*** David Friedman; ***C:*** William G. Troiano; ***M:*** Billy Allen.

She Gods of Shark Reef 🦴 *Shark Reef* **1956** Typical no-budget Corman exploitation tale of two brothers shipwrecked on an island inhabited by beautiful pearl-diving women. Filmed in Hawaii. **63m/C VHS.** Bill Cord, Don Durant, Lisa Montell, Carol Lindsay, Jeanne Gerson; ***D:*** Roger Corman.

She Goes to War 🦴🦴 **1929** King's first part-sound effort that takes place in the milieu of WWI. Boardman plays a spoiled rich girl who grows up fast when confronted with the horrors of the frontline while working in a canteen. **50m/B VHS, 8mm.** Eleanor Boardman, Alma Rubens, Al "Fuzzy" St. John; ***D:*** Henry King.

She Must Be Seeing Things 🦴🦴 **1987** Filmmaker Jo (Weaver) is making a picture about a 17th-century woman who lived her life as a man. Jo's lover Agatha (Dabney) becomes disturbed when she reads Jo's diary, learns she's been having affairs with men, and begins to fantasize about Jo's unfaithfulness with the men in her film crew. Agatha's insecurities finally lead her to disguising herself as a man in order to spy on Jo—mirroring what's happening in Jo's film. **95m/C VHS.** Sheila Dabney, Lois Weaver, Kyle DiCamp, John Erdman; ***D:*** Sheila McLaughlin; ***W:*** Sheila McLaughlin.

She Shall Have Music 🦴½ **1936** A magnate hires a dance band to broadcast from a cruise ship. Features music by Jack Hylton and his band, one of Britain's most popular orchestras of the 1930s. **76m/B VHS.** *GB* Jack Hylton, June Clyde, Claude Dampier, Bryan Lawrence, Gwen Farrar.

She Shoulda Said No 🦴 *The Devil's Weed; Wild Weed; Marijuana the Devil's Weed* **1949** Funny smelling cigarettes ruin the lives of all who inhale. Viewers' advice: just say no. Leed's actual drug bust with Robert Mitchum got her the lead. **70m/B VHS, DVD.** Lila Leeds, Alan Baxter, Lyle Talbot, Jack Elam, David Gorcey; ***D:*** Sam Newfield.

She Waits 🦴🦴 **1971** When a newlywed couple moves into an old house, the bride becomes possessed by the spirit of her husband's first wife. Unoriginal and mediocre horror. **74m/C VHS.** Dorothy McGuire, Patty Duke, David McCallum; ***D:*** Delbert Mann. **TV**

She Wolf of London 🦴½ **1946** In turn of the century London, Phyllis Allenby (Lockhart) learns that people are being murdered by a wolf in a nearby park. Since the Allenby family suffers from a werewolf curse, Phyllis decides that she must be the killer (though she doesn't remember doing anything). But her fiance Harry (Porter) is determined to prove her innocent. **62m/B VHS, DVD.** June Lockhart, Don Porter, Sara Haden, Jan Wiley, Lloyd Corrigan, Dennis Hoey, Martin Kosleck, Eily Malyon, Frederick Worlock; ***D:*** Jean Yarbrough; ***W:*** George Bricker, William Lava; ***C:*** Maury Gertsman.

She Wore a Yellow Ribbon 🦴🦴🦴½ **1949** An undermanned cavalry outpost makes a desperate attempt to repel invading Indians. Wayne shines as an officer who shuns retirement in order to help his comrades. Still fun and compelling. The second chapter in director Ford's noted cavalry trilogy, preceded by "Fort Apache" and followed by "Rio Grande." **93m/C VHS.** John Wayne, Joanne Dru, John Agar, Ben Johnson, Harry Carey Jr., Victor McLaglen, Mildred Natwick, George O'Brien, Arthur Shields, Noble Johnson, Harry Woods, Michael Dugan, Jack Pennick, Paul Fix, Francis Ford, Cliff Lyons, Tom Tyler, Chief John Big Tree; ***D:*** John Ford; ***W:*** Frank Nugent, Laurence Stallings; ***C:*** Winton C. Hoch, Charles P. Boyle; ***M:*** Richard Hageman. Oscars '49: Color Cinematog.

Sheba, Baby 🦴🦴 **1975 (PG)** A female dick (Grier) heads to Louisville where someone is trying to threaten her rich father and his loan company. Oddly non-violent for action-flick vet Grier; poorly written and directed. **90m/C VHS, DVD, Wide.** Pam Grier, Rudy Challenger, Austin Stoker, D'Urville Martin, Charles Kissinger; ***D:*** William Girdler; ***W:*** William Girdler; ***C:*** William Asman; ***M:*** Alex Brown.

Sheena woof! **1984 (PG)** TV sportscaster aids a jungle queen in defending her kingdom from being overthrown by an evil prince. Horrid bubble-gum "action" fantasy. **117m/C VHS.** Tanya Roberts, Ted Wass, Donovan Scott, Elizabeth Toro; ***D:*** John Guillermin; ***W:*** David Newman; ***C:*** Pasqualino De Santis.

The Sheep Has Five Legs 🦴🦴½ **1954** Quintuplet brothers return from around the world for a reunion in their small French village. Fernandel plays the father and all five sons; otherwise, comedy is only average-to-good. In French with English subtitles. **96m/B VHS, 8mm.** *FR* Fernandel, Edouard Delmont, Louis de Funes, Paulette Dubost; ***D:*** Henri Verneuil.

Sheer Madness 🦴🦴🦴 **1984** Focuses on the intense friendship between a college professor and a troubled artist, both women. Engrossing and subtle exposition of a relationship. Ambiguous ending underscores film's general excellence. Subtitled. **105m/C VHS.** *GE FR* Hanna Schygulla, Angela Winkler; ***D:*** Margarethe von Trotta; ***W:*** Margarethe von Trotta; ***C:*** Michael Ballhaus.

The Sheik 🦴🦴🦴 **1921** High camp Valentino has English woman fall hopelessly under the romantic spell of Arab sheik who flares his nostrils. Followed by "Son of the Sheik." **80m/B VHS.** Agnes Ayres, Rudolph Valentino, Adolphe Menjou, Walter Long, Lucien Littlefield, George Waggner, Patsy Ruth Miller; ***D:*** George Melford.

She'll Be Wearing Pink Pajamas 🦴🦴 **1984** Eight women volunteer for a rugged survival course to test their mettle. The intense shared experience gives them all food for thought. Well acted from a pretty thin story. **90m/C VHS.** Julie Walters, Anthony (Corlan) Higgins; ***D:*** John Goldschmidt; ***M:*** John Du Prez.

The Shell Seekers 🦴🦴½ **1989 (PG)** The widowed Penelope Keeling (Lansbury) is recovering from a heart attack and her three grown children want her to take things easy. But the scare has convinced Penelope to revisit her past and the happiness she once knew. So she returns to her childhood home in Cornwall to see what she can discover. Fine cast in a heart-tugger (with some lovely scenery from Cornwall, England and the island of Ibiza). Adapted from the novel by Rosamunde Pilcher. A Hallmark Hall of Fame presentation. **94m/C VHS.** *GB* Angela Lansbury, Sam Wanamaker, Anna Carteret, Michael Gough, Christopher Bowen, Patricia Hodge, Denis Quilley, Sophie Ward, Irene Worth; ***D:*** Waris Hussein; ***W:*** John Pielmeier. **TV**

Shell Shock 🦴½ *Betzilo Shel Helem Krav; China Ranch* **1963** Four GI's fight off the Germans and the longings for home during WWII. Hebrew with subtitles. **90m/C VHS.** *IS* Anat Atzmon, Gili Ben-Uzilo, Stanislav Chaplin, Dan Turgeman, Asher Tzarfati; ***D:*** Yoel Sharon; ***W:*** Yoel Sharon; ***C:*** Yoav Kosh; ***M:*** Edward Reyes, Arik Rudich.

Shelter 🦴🦴 **1998 (R)** ATF agent Martin Roberts (Allen) is set up by his commanding officer and has a bounty on his head. He takes refuge with a crime lord (Onorati), whom the bad guys feds are also after, and plans how to get even. **92m/C VHS, DVD.** John Allen Nelson, Peter Onorati, Brenda Bakke, Costas Mandylor, Charles Durning, Linden Ashby, Kurtwood Smith; ***D:*** Scott Paulin; ***W:*** Max Strom; ***C:*** Eric Goldstein; ***M:*** David Williams.

The Sheltering Sky 🦴🦴🦴 **1990 (R)** American couple Winger and Malkovich flee the plasticity of their native land for a trip to the Sahara desert where they hope to renew their spirits and rekindle love. Accompanied by socialite acquaintance Scott with whom Winger soon has an affair, their personalities and belief systems deteriorate as they move through the grave poverty of North Africa in breathtaking heat. Based on the existential novel by American expatriate Paul Bowles who narrates and appears briefly in a bar scene. Overlong but visually stunning, with cinematography by Vittorio Storaro. **139m/C VHS, Wide.** Debra Winger, John Malkovich, Campbell Scott, Jill Bennett, Timothy Spall, Eric Vu-An, Sotigui Koyate, Amina Annabi, Paul Bowles; ***D:*** Bernardo Bertolucci; ***W:*** Mark Peploe, Bernardo Bertolucci; ***C:*** Vittorio Storaro; ***M:*** Ryuichi Sakamoto, Richard Horowitz. Golden Globes '91: Score; N.Y. Film Critics '90: Cinematog.

Shenandoah 🦴🦴🦴 **1965** A Virginia farmer (Stewart, in a top-notch performance) who has raised six sons and a daughter, tries to remain neutral during the Civil War. War takes its toll as the daughter marries a Confederate soldier and his sons become involved in the fighting. Screen debut for Ross. **105m/C VHS.** James Stewart, Doug McClure, Glenn Corbett, Patrick Wayne, Rosemary Forsyth, Katharine Ross, George Kennedy, Phillip Alford, James Best, Charles Robinson, James McMullan, Tim McIntire, Eugene Jackson, Paul Fix, Denver Pyle, Harry Carey Jr., Dabbs Greer, Strother Martin, Warren Oates; ***D:*** Andrew V. McLaglen; ***W:*** James Lee Barrett; ***C:*** William Clothier; ***M:*** Frank Skinner.

Shep Comes Home 🦴 **1949** Shep the wonder canine accompanies an orphan through the Midwest where he nabs a band of bankrobbers. Sequel to "My Dog Shep." **62m/B VHS.** Robert Lowery, Sheldon Leonard.

Shepherd 🦴🦴 **1999 (R)** Offers plenty of cheap thrills as long as you don't expect the plot to make any sense. You've got your basic futuristic nightmare world—this time ruled by rival religious cults who use guns to extend their power. Howell is a sharpshooting mercenary who decides not to follow orders anymore—and there's hell to pay. **86m/C VHS.** C. Thomas Howell, Roddy Piper, Robert Carradine, Heidi von Palleske; ***D:*** Peter Hayman. **VIDEO**

The Shepherd of the Hills 🦴🦴🦴 **1941** Young Ozark mountain moonshiner Matt Matthews (Wayne) vows to one day find and kill the unknown father who deserted his family, leading to the early death of Matt's mother. His hatred is so strong that his girlfriend Sammy

(Field) refuses to marry him because of it. Then a stranger, Daniel Howitt (Carey Sr.), comes to town and his kind deeds have everyone calling him "The Shepherd." Even Matt warms to the man—until he discovers that Howitt is his father. Based on the novel by Harold Bell Wright. **89m/B VHS.** John Wayne, Harry Carey Sr., Betty Field, Beulah Bondi, James Barton, Marjorie Main, Ward Bond, Fuzzy Knight; ***D:*** Henry Hathaway; ***W:*** Grover Jones, Stuart Anthony; ***C:*** Charles B(ryant) Lang Jr., William Howard Greene; ***M:*** Gerard Carbonara.

Sheriff of Tombstone 🦴½ **1941** Trouble begins when a "judge" takes a sharpshooter in a poker game. **60m/B VHS.** Roy Rogers.

Sherlock Holmes and the Deadly Necklace 🦴🦴½ *Sherlock Holmes Und Das Halsband des Todes; Valley of Fear* **1962** Once again, Holmes and Watson are up against their old nemesis Moriarty. This time, Moriarty wants to get his hands on a necklace stolen from Cleopatra's tomb. Not only does Scotland Yard not consider him a suspect, they seek his advice. Enter Holmes and Watson, and the game's afoot. The offbeat casting and direction help make this one of the odder versions of Conan Doyle's work. **84m/B VHS.** *GE* Christopher Lee, Senta Berger, Hans Sohnker, Hans Nielsen, Ivan Desny, Leon Askin, Thorley Walters; ***D:*** Terence Fisher.

Sherlock Holmes and the Incident at Victoria Falls 🦴½ *Incident at Victoria Falls* **1991** A substandard Holmes excursion brings the Baker Street sleuth out of retirement to transport the world's largest diamond from Africa to London. The resulting mystery involves Teddy Roosevelt, the inventor of radio, and poor plotting. **120m/C VHS.** *GB* Christopher Lee, Patrick Macnee, Jenny Seagrove; ***D:*** Bill Corcoran.

Sherlock Holmes and the Secret Weapon 🦴🦴🦴 *Secret Weapon* **1942** Based on "The Dancing Men" by Sir Arthur Conan Doyle. Holmes battles the evil Moriarty in an effort to save the British war effort. Good Holmes mystery with gripping wartime setting. Hoey is fun as bumbling Inspector Lestrade. Available colorized. **68m/B VHS, DVD.** Basil Rathbone, Nigel Bruce, Karen Verne, William Post Jr., Dennis Hoey, Holmes Herbert, Mary Gordon, Henry Victor, Philip Van Zandt, George Eldredge, Leslie Denison, James Craven, Paul Fix, Hugh Herbert, Lionel Atwill; ***D:*** Roy William Neill; ***W:*** W. Scott Darling; ***C:*** Lester White; ***M:*** Frank Skinner.

Sherlock Holmes Faces Death 🦴🦴🦴 **1943** Dead bodies are accumulating in a mansion where the detecting duo are staying. Underground tunnels, life-size dress boards, and unanswered mysteries... Top-notch Holmes. Peter Lawford appears briefly as a sailor. Also available with "Hound of the Baskervilles" on Laser Disc. **68m/B VHS.** Basil Rathbone, Nigel Bruce, Hillary Brooke, Milburn Stone, Halliwell Hobbes, Arthur Margetson, Gavin Muir; ***D:*** Roy William Neill.

Sherlock Holmes in Washington 🦴🦴½ **1943** A top-secret agent is murdered; seems it's those blasted Nazis again! Holmes and Watson rush off to Washington, D.C. to solve the crime and to save some vitally important microfilm. Heavily flag-waving Rathbone-Bruce episode. Dr. Watson is dumbfounded by bubble gum. **71m/B VHS.** Basil Rathbone, Nigel Bruce, Henry Daniell, George Zucco, Marjorie Lord, John Archer; ***D:*** Roy William Neill.

Sherlock Holmes: The Voice of Terror 🦴🦴½ **1942** Holmes and Watson try to decode German radio messages during WWII. First Rathbone-as-Holmes effort for Universal, and first in which we are asked to believe the Victorian sleuth and his hairdo could have lived in this century. Patriotic and all that—and lots of fun. **65m/B VHS.** Basil Rathbone, Nigel Bruce, Hillary Brooke, Reginald Denny, Evelyn Ankers, Montagu Love; ***D:*** John Rawlins.

Sherlock: Undercover Dog 🦴🦴½ **1994 (PG)** Billy (Eroen) arrives on Catalina island to spend the summer with his father, an eccentric inventor. He makes a human friend in Emma (Cameron) and a canine companion in Sherlock, a police dog who's able to talk but naturally only to the two kids. Seems Sherlock's policeman master has been kidnapped by bumbling smugglers and its up to the trio to come to the rescue. **80m/C VHS.** Benjamin Eroen, Brynne Cameron, Anthony Simmons, Margy Moore, Barry Philips; ***D:*** Richard Harding Gardner; ***W:*** Richard Harding Gardner; ***M:*** Lou Forestieri.

Sherlock's Rivals & Where's My Wife 🦴½ **1927** Double feature includes a detective movie in which two used car dealers become amateur sleuths and a comedy in which a man has a hard time enjoying his weekend at a seashore resort. **53m/B VHS.** Milburn (Milt) Morante, Montague (Monty) Banks.

Sherman's March: An Improbable Search for Love **1986** McElwee's "epic" which was originally planned as a historical documentary about General Sherman's catastrophic march through the South, ends up being about the filmmaker himself, and his disastrous quest for love. When his girlfriend dumps him, he puts Sherman's story aside and films his own battle for romance, which includes help from his meddling family. The melodramatic women he meets and the neurotic energy of McElwee make this a very funny, uncensored film. **155m/C VHS.** ***D:*** Ross McElwee; ***W:*** Ross McElwee. Natl. Film Reg. '00.

She's All That 🦴🦴 **1999 (PG-13)** There are no surprises to be found in this formulaic Pygmalion-via-MTV teen comedy. Zack (Prinze Jr.) is the BMOC in yet another broadly drawn high school pecking order. After he's dumped by girlfriend Taylor (O'Keefe) for vain semi-celebrity Brock (Lillard, in an amusing send-up of MTV's "The Real World"), he accepts a bet from a pal that he can make artsy wallflower Laney (Cook) into a prom queen. The intelligent Laney suspects his motives, but proceeds with the makeover with caution. When Taylor decides she wants her man back, the stage is set for a predictable prom night showdown. **97m/C VHS, DVD.** Rachael Leigh Cook, Freddie Prinze Jr., Matthew Lillard, Paul Walker, Jodi Lyn O'Keefe, Kevin Pollak, Anna Paquin, Kieran Culkin, Elden (Ratliff) Henson, Usher Raymond, Gabrielle Union, Dule Hill, Kimberly (Lil' Kim) Jones; ***D:*** Robert Iscove; ***W:*** R. Lee Fleming Jr.; ***C:*** Francis Kenny; ***M:*** Stewart Copeland.

She's Back 🦴½ **1988 (R)** Murderee Fisher pesters hubby Joy from beyond the grave to avenge her death at the hands of a motorcycle gang. Uneven, but occasionally funny. **89m/C VHS.** Bobby DiCicco, Carrie Fisher, Robert Joy; ***D:*** Tim Kincaid.

She's Dressed to Kill 🦴🦴 *Someone's Killing the World's Greatest Models* **1979** Beautiful models are turning up dead during a famous designer's comeback attempt at a mountain retreat. Who could be behind these grisly deeds? Suspenseful in a made for TV kind of way, but not memorable. **100m/C VHS.** Eleanor Parker, Jessica Walter, John Rubinstein, Connie Sellecca; ***D:*** Gus Trikonis. **TV**

She's Gotta Have It 🦴🦴🦴 **1986 (R)** Lee wrote, directed, edited, produced and starred in this romantic comedy about an independent-minded black girl in Brooklyn and the three men and one woman who compete for her attention. Full of rough edges, but vigorous, confident, and hip. Filmed entirely in black and white except for one memorable scene. Put Lee on the film-making map. **84m/B VHS.** Tracy C. Johns, Spike Lee, Tommy Redmond Hicks, Raye Dowell, John Canada Terrell, Joie Lee, S. Epatha Merkerson, Bill Lee, Cheryl Burr, Aaron Dugger, Stephanie Covington, Renata Cobbs, Cheryl Singleton, Monty Ross, Lewis Jordan, Erik Todd Dellums, Reginald (Reggie) Hudlin, Eric Payne, Marcus Turner, Gerard Brown, Ernest R. Dickerson; ***D:*** Spike Lee; ***W:*** Spike Lee; ***C:*** Ernest R. Dickerson; ***M:*** Bill Lee. Ind. Spirit '87: First Feature.

She's Having a Baby 🦴🦴½ **1988 (PG-13)** Newlyweds Bacon and McGovern tread the marital waters with some difficulty, when news of an impending baby further complicates their lives. Told from Bacon's viewpoint as the tortured young writer/husband, who wonders if the yuppie life they lead is trapping him. Hughes's first venture into the adult world isn't as satisfying as his teen angst flicks, although the charming leads help. Major drawbacks are the arguably sexist premise and dull resolution. Great soundtrack; observant viewers will notice the beemer's license plate is the title's acronym: "SHAB." **106m/C VHS, DVD, Wide.** Kevin Bacon, Elizabeth McGovern, William Windom, Paul Gleason, Alec Baldwin, Cathryn Damon, Holland Taylor, James Ray, Isabel Lorca, Dennis Dugan, Edie McClurg, John Ashton; ***D:*** John Hughes; ***W:*** John Hughes; ***C:*** Don Peterman; ***M:*** Stewart Copeland.

She's in the Army Now 🦴 **1981** Farce about military life. Two bubble-headed females undergo basic training. "Private Benjamin" ripoff was meant as a TV pilot. **97m/C VHS.** Jamie Lee Curtis, Kathleen Quinlan, Melanie Griffith, Susan Blanchard, Julie Carmen, Janet MacLachlan; ***D:*** Hy Averback; ***M:*** Artie Butler. **TV**

She's Out of Control 🦴½ **1989** Dad Danza goes nuts when teen daughter Dolenz (real-life daughter of Monkee Mickey Dolenz) takes the advice of Dad's girlfriend on how to attract boys. Formulaic plot could almost be an episode of "Who's the Boss?" Danza is appealing, but not enough to keep this one afloat. **95m/C VHS, 8mm.** Tony Danza, Catherine Hicks, Wallace Shawn, Dick O'Neill; ***D:*** Stan Dragoti; ***M:*** Alan Silvestri.

She's So Lovely 🦴🦴½ *She's De Lovely; Call It Love* **1997 (R)** Troubled young alcoholic Eddie (Penn) disappears for three days on his pregnant wife Maureen (Wright), and returns to discover that she has been brutalized by a neighbor. Retaliation costs him 10 years in a mental institution. Upon his release, Eddie decides to find his now ex-wife and the daughter he's never known. Maureen's moved on—she's happily married to Joey (Travolta), has two daughters by him, and is justifiable worried that Eddie's love (which is as strong as ever) will upset the balance of her new life. Somewhat unevenly directed by Nick Cassavetes from a screenplay written by his late father John, who had already cast Penn and was set to direct when he became ill. Film revels in the style that made the elder Cassavetes famous (or infamous), and is best appreciated as a tribute. Travolta and Penn play well off each other. **97m/C VHS, DVD, Wide.** Sean Penn, Robin Wright Penn, John Travolta, Harry Dean Stanton, Debi Mazar, James Gandolfini, Gena Rowlands, Kelsey Mulrooney, David Thornton, Susan Traylor, Chloe Webb, Burt Young; ***D:*** Nick Cassavetes; ***W:*** John Cassavetes; ***C:*** Thierry Arbogast; ***M:*** Joseph Vitarelli. Cannes '97: Actor (Penn).

She's the One 🦴🦴½ **1996 (R)** Another Irish family saga from Burns covering lots of the same territory as "The Brothers McMullen." Semi-slacker taxi driver Mickey Fitzpatrick (Burns) impulsively marries passenger Hope (Bahns) and their romance is contrasted with the disintegrating marriage of Mickey's younger brother, buttoned-down stockbroker Francis (McGlone) and his frustrated wife Rene (Aniston). No wonder she's frustrated, Francis is having an affair with slutty Heather (Diaz), who turns out to be Mickey's former flame. Mahoney offers a typically fine performance, along with bad marital advice as the boys' father. Again the blustering men don't have a clue about the usually smarter women. **95m/C VHS, DVD, Wide.** Edward Burns, Mike McGlone, Jennifer Aniston, Cameron Diaz, Maxine Bahns, John Mahoney, Leslie Mann, George McCowan, Amanda Peet, Anita Gillette, Frank Vincent; ***D:*** Edward Burns; ***W:*** Edward Burns; ***C:*** Frank Prinzi; ***M:*** Tom Petty.

Shifting Sands **1918** Compelling film tells the tale of a young girl looking to be a successful artist. Her landlord makes constant overtures towards her. She refuses, so he has her thrown in jail for prostitution as an act of revenge. She fears her past may prevent her from obtaining true love. **52m/B VHS, 8mm.** Gloria Swanson, Joe King, Lillian Langdon.

Shiloh 🦴🦴½ **1997 (PG)** Schmaltzy but redeeming story about small town West Virginia 11-year-old Marty (Heron), who seeks to rescue and care for mistreated hunting dog Shiloh, who belongs to mean hermit Judd (Wilson). Goes beyond the typical "boy and his dog" theme with moral and ethical issues that Marty faces when he takes the dog from its owner. Frannie (who plays Shiloh) is a very cute and expressive beagle. Adapted from the Newberry award-winning novel by Phyllis Reynolds Naylor. **93m/C VHS, DVD, Wide.** Blake Heron, Michael Moriarty, Scott Wilson, Rod Steiger, Ann Dowd, Bonnie Bartlett; ***D:*** Dale Rosenbloom; ***W:*** Dale Rosenbloom; ***C:*** Frank Byers; ***M:*** Joel Goldsmith.

Shiloh 2: Shiloh Season 🦴🦴½ **1999** Low-key rural drama finds 12-year-old Marty Preston (Browne) claiming responsibility for lovable beagle Shiloh from his hard-drinking owner, Judd Travers (Wilson). But when Travers is injured in an accident, the kid has enough compassion to ask his parents to help him with the ornery cuss. Adapted from the novel by Phyllis Reynolds Naylor. **96m/C VHS, DVD, Wide.** Zachary Browne, Scott Wilson, Michael Moriarty, Ann Dowd, Rod Steiger, Bonnie Bartlett, Joe Pichler; ***D:*** Sandy Tung; ***W:*** Dale Rosenbloom; ***C:*** Troy Smith; ***M:*** Joel Goldsmith.

Shin Heike Monogatari 🦴🦴🦴🦴 *New Tales of the Taira Clan* **1955** Mizoguchi's second to last film, in which a deposed Japanese emperor in 1137 endeavors to win back the throne from the current despot, who cannot handle the feudal lawlessness. Acclaimed; his second film in color. In Japanese with English subtitles. **106m/C VHS.** *JP* Raizo Ichikawa, Ichijiro Oya, Michiyo Kogure, Eijiro Yanagi, Tatsuya Ishiguro, Yoshiko Kuga; ***D:*** Kenji Mizoguchi.

Shinbone Alley **1970 (G)** Animated musical about Archy, a free-verse poet reincarnated as a cockroach, and Mehitabel, the alley cat with a zest for life. Based on the short stories by Don Marquis. **83m/C VHS.** ***D:*** John D. Wilson; ***V:*** Carol Channing, Eddie Bracken, John Carradine, Alan Reed.

Shine 🦴🦴🦴½ **1995 (PG-13)** Astonishing true portrayal of musical genius and its cost. Teenaged pianist David Helfgott (Taylor) is a prodigy in his native Australia but is pushed to the limit by his authoritarian father Peter (Mueller-Stahl). Eventually defying his father's strictures, David accepts a scholarship to London's Royal College of Music where he triumphs under the tutelege of professor Cecil Parkes (Gielgud), but then collapses from strain. For 15 years, he is confined to psychiatric hospitals, unable to play the piano, until the now-adult David (Rush) has a chance meeting with the loving Gillian (Redgrave), whose support enables him to resume his career. Helfgott himself plays piano for his screen counterparts. **105m/C VHS, DVD, Wide.** *AU* Geoffrey Rush, Noah Taylor, Armin Mueller-Stahl, Lynn Redgrave, John Gielgud, Googie Withers, Chris Haywood, Sonia Todd, Alex Rafalowicz, Randall Berger; ***D:*** Scott Hicks; ***W:*** Jan Sardi; ***C:*** Geoffrey Simpson; ***M:*** David Hirschfelder. Oscars '96: Actor (Rush); Australian Film Inst. '96: Actor (Rush), Cinematog., Director (Hicks), Film, Film Editing, Orig. Screenplay, Sound, Support. Actor (Mueller-Stahl), Score; British Acad. '96: Actor (Rush); Golden Globes '97: Actor—Drama (Rush); L.A. Film Critics '96: Actor (Rush); Natl. Bd. of Review '96: Film; N.Y. Film Critics '96: Actor (Rush); Screen Actors Guild '96: Actor (Rush); Broadcast Film Critics '96: Actor (Rush).

Shine on, Harvest Moon 🦴🦴 **1938** Rogers brings a band of outlaws to justice and clears an old man suspected of being their accomplice. Title bears no relation to storyline. **60m/B VHS.** Roy Rogers, Lynne Roberts, Stanley Andrews; ***D:*** Joseph Kane.

The Shining 🦴🦴½ **1980 (R)** Very loose adaptation of the Stephen King horror novel about a writer and his family, snowbound in a huge hotel, who experience various hauntings caused by either the hotel itself or the writer's dementia. Technically stunning, and pretty dang scary, but too long, pretentious and implausible. Nicholson is excellent as the failed writer gone off the deep end. **143m/C**

VHS, DVD. Jack Nicholson, Shelley Duvall, Danny Lloyd, Scatman Crothers, Joe Turkel, Barry Nelson, Philip Stone, Lia Beldam, Billie Gibson, Barry Dennan, David Baxt, Lisa Burns, Alison Coleridge, Kate Phelps, Anne Jackson, Tony Burton; ***D:*** Stanley Kubrick; ***W:*** Stanley Kubrick, Diane Johnson; ***C:*** John Alcott; ***M:*** Walter (Wendy) Carlos, Rachel Elkind.

The Shining Hour ₰₰½ **1938** A compelling melodrama in which Crawford portrays a New York night club dancer who is pursued by the rather conservative Douglas. His brother tries to persuade him from marrying Crawford, but then he soon finds himself attracted to her. A devastating fire wipes out all problems of family dissension in this intelligent soap opera. **76m/B VHS.** Joan Crawford, Margaret Sullavan, Melvyn Douglas, Robert Young, Fay Bainter, Allyn Joslyn; ***D:*** Frank Borzage; ***W:*** Ogden Nash, Jane Murfin; ***C:*** George J. Folsey.

A Shining Season ₰₰₰ **1979** Tearjerker about a potential-packed long-distance runner, John Baker, stricken with cancer. He spends his last year training a girls' track team to a championship. Earnest, well-performed and involving. Based on a true story. Made for TV. **100m/C VHS.** Timothy Bottoms, Rip Torn, Allyn Ann McLerie, Ed Begley Jr., Benjamin Bottoms, Mason Adams, Constance Forslund, Ellen Geer; ***D:*** Stuart Margolin; ***M:*** Richard Bellis. **TV**

Shining Star ₰½ *That's the Way of the World* **1975 (PG)** A recording company is run by the mob. Potentially interesting film is hampered by quality of sound and photography and general lack of purpose or direction. **100m/C VHS.** Harvey Keitel, Ed Nelson, Cynthia Bostick, Bert Parks; ***D:*** Sig Shore.

Shining Through ₰₰½ **1992 (R)** Baby-voiced Griffith as a spy sent behind enemy lines without training? Douglas as a spy sent behind enemy lines without speaking German? Old-fashioned blend of romance, espionage, and derring-do where noble hero saves spunky heroine from nasty Nazis in WWII Germany works despite thin plot. Series of flash-forwards to an aged Griffith is annoying and tends to stop action cold, but everyone tries hard and period flavor is authentic. Adapted from best-selling Susan Isaacs novel, but bears little resemblance to book. **133m/C VHS.** Michael Douglas, Melanie Griffith, Liam Neeson, Joely Richardson, John Gielgud, Francis Guinan, Patrick Winczewski, Sylvia Syms; ***D:*** David Seltzer; ***W:*** David Seltzer; ***C:*** Jan De Bont; ***M:*** Michael Kamen. Golden Raspberries '92: Worst Picture, Worst Actress (Griffith), Worst Director (Seltzer).

Ship Ahoy ₰₰½ **1942** Songs, comedy, a spy spoof, and some patriotism thrown in for good measure. Powell plays a dancer who works with Tommy Dorsey and his orchestra. They're on their way to Puerto Rico, via ocean liner, along with her pulp fiction writer boyfriend (Skelton). Emery, posing as an FBI man, convinces Powell to smuggle a package for him but he's really a spy and the whole thing's a con which turns out to be based on one of Skelton's potboiler plots. An uncredited Frank Sinatra is the singer with the Dorsey band, along with drummer Buddy Rich and trumpeter Ziggy Elman who provide some great musical solos. ♫Last Call For Love; Poor You; On Moonlight Bay; Tampico; I'll Take Tallulah; Cape Dance; Ship Ahoy. **95m/B VHS.** Eleanor Powell, Red Skelton, Bert Lahr, Virginia O'Brien, John Emery, William Post Jr.; ***D:*** Edward Buzzell; ***W:*** Harry Kurnitz, Harry Clork, Irving Brecher.

Ship of Fools ₰₰₰ **1965** A group of passengers sailing to Germany in the '30s find mutual needs and concerns, struggle with early evidence of Nazi racism, and discover love on their voyage. Twisted story and fine acting maintain interest. Appropriate tunes written by Ernest Gold. Based on the Katherine Ann Porter novel. Leigh's last film role; she died two years later. Kramer grapples with civil rights issues in much of his work. **149m/B VHS.** Vivien Leigh, Simone Signoret, Jose Ferrer, Lee Marvin, Oskar Werner, Michael Dunn, Elizabeth Ashley, George Segal, Jose Greco, Charles Korvin, Heinz Ruehmann; ***D:*** Stanley Kramer; ***W:*** Abby Mann; ***C:*** Ernest Laszlo; ***M:*** Ernest Gold. Oscars '65: Art Dir./Set Dec., B&W, B&W Cinematog.; Natl. Bd. of Review '65: Actor (Marvin); N.Y. Film Critics '65: Actor (Werner).

The Shipping News ₰₰ **2001 (R)** Spacey is Quoyle, a middle-aged lifetime loser who returns to his childhood home of Newfoundland with his daughter and aunt (Dench) after his adulterous wife (Blanchett) dies. There, among the absurdly quirky citizenry, he meets Wavey (Moore) a widow who runs the day-care center and may hold the key to changing Quoyle's life around. Those who read the book (and there are many), will be deeply disappointed, and those who haven't may merely be deeply depressed. The desolate landscape is beautifully shot, but Spacey is badly miscast as the sad-sack loser, and subplots that could lead to some drama are dropped inexplicably. Blanchett and Moore distinguish themselves nicely. **120m/C VHS, DVD.** *US* Kevin Spacey, Judi Dench, Cate Blanchett, Julianne Moore, Pete Postlethwaite, Scott Glenn, Rhys Ifans, Gordon Pinsent, Jason Behr, Larry Pine, Jeanetta Arnette, Robert Joy, Alyssa Gainer, Kaitlyn Gainer, Lauren Gainer; ***D:*** Lasse Hallstrom; ***W:*** Robert Nelson Jacobs; ***C:*** Oliver Stapleton; ***M:*** Christopher Young. Natl. Bd. of Review '01: Support. Actress (Blanchett).

Ships in the Night ₰₰ **1928** Logan is the plucky heroine who is searching for her missing brother who has been captured by pirates. She is aided in her search by handsome hero Mower. **86m/B VHS.** Frank Moran, Jacqueline Logan, Jack Mower, Andy Clyde.

Shipwrecked ₰₰½ *Haakon Haakonsen* **1990 (PG)** Kiddie swashbuckler based on the 1873 popular novel "Haakon Haakonsen." A cabin boy is marooned on an island where he defends the hidden pirate treasure he finds by boobytrapping the island. **93m/C VHS, Wide.** *NO* Gabriel Byrne, Stian Smestad, Louisa Haigh, Trond Munch, Bjorn Sundquist, Eva Von Hanno, Kjell Stormoen; ***D:*** Nils Gaup; ***W:*** Nils Gaup, Nick Thiel; ***M:*** Patrick Doyle.

Shirley Valentine ₰₰₰ **1989** A lively middle-aged English housewife gets a new lease on life when she travels to Greece without her husband. Collins reprises her London and Broadway stage triumph. The character frequently addresses the audience directly to explain her thoughts and feelings; her energy and spunk carry the day. Good script by Russell from his play. From the people who brought us "Educating Rita." **108m/C VHS, 8mm.** *GB* Pauline Collins, Tom Conti, Alison Steadman, Julia McKenzie, Joanna Lumley, Bernard Hill, Sylvia Syms; ***D:*** Lewis Gilbert; ***W:*** George Hadjinassios, Willy Russell; ***C:*** Alan Hume; ***M:*** Willy Russell. British Acad. '89: Actress (Collins).

The Shock ₰₰½ **1923** Crippled low-life Chaney becomes restored spiritually by a small-town girl and rebels against his Chinese boss. This causes an unfortunate string of melodramatic tragedies, including the San Francisco earthquake of 1906. Silent. Odd, desultory tale with bad special effects is worth seeing for Chaney's good acting. **96m/B VHS.** Lon Chaney Sr., Virginia Valli; ***D:*** Lambert Hillyer.

Shock! ₰₰ **1946** A psychiatrist is called on to treat a woman on the edge of a nervous breakdown. He then discovers she saw him murder his wife, and tries to keep her from remembering it. Interesting premise handled in trite B style. Price's first starring role. **70m/B VHS.** Vincent Price, Lynn Bari, Frank Latimore, Anabel Shaw; ***D:*** Alfred Werker.

Shock ₰₰½ *Beyond the Door 2; Shock (Transfer Suspense Hypnos); Suspense; Al 33 di Via Orologio fa Sempre Freddo* **1979 (R)** Better treatment of the possession theme, but this time the door is to the home of a new family: Colin (from the original) plays a boy possessed by his dead father, who seeks revenge on his widow and her new husband. Director Bava's last feature. **90m/C VHS, DVD, Wide.** *IT* John Steiner, Daria Nicolodi, David Colin Jr., Ivan Rassimov, Nicola Salerno; ***D:*** Mario Bava; ***W:*** Lamberto Bava, Franco Barbieri, Dardano Sacchetti, Paolo Brigenti; ***C:*** Alberto Spagnoli.

Shock Corridor ₰₰₰ **1963** A reporter, dreaming of a Pulitzer Prize, fakes mental illness and gets admitted to an asylum, where he hopes to investigate a murder. He is subjected to disturbing experiences, including shock therapy, but does manage to solve the murder. However, he suffers a mental breakdown in the process and is admitted for real. Disturbing and lurid. **101m/B VHS, DVD, Wide.** Peter Breck, Constance Towers, Gene Evans, Hari Rhodes, James Best, Philip Ahn, Larry Tucker, Paul Dubov; ***D:*** Samuel Fuller; ***W:*** Samuel Fuller; ***C:*** Stanley Cortez; ***M:*** Paul Dunlap. Natl. Film Reg. '96.

Shock 'Em Dead ₰₰ **1990 (R)** A devil worshipper trades his life to Lucifer for a chance at rock and roll fame and beautiful Miss Lords. Sexy thriller, with a good share of violence and tension. Ironically, ex porn great Lords is one of the few starlets who doesn't disrobe in the film. **94m/C VHS.** Traci Lords, Aldo Ray, Troy Donahue, Stephen Quadros, Tim Moffett, Karen Russell, Gina Parks, Laurel Wiley, Tyger Sodipe; ***D:*** Mark Freed; ***W:*** Mark Freed, Andrew Cross, Dave Tedder; ***C:*** Ron Chapman.

Shock! Shock! Shock! ₰ **1987** Another low-budget slasher flick, with a homicidal lunatic wielding a butcher knife. Space alien jewel thieves add an element, for what it's worth. Makes one ponder the cosmic question: What's the diff between a bad slasher flick and a spoof of a bad slasher flick? Whichever this one is, it's really bad! **60m/B VHS.** Brad Issac, Cyndy McCrossen, Allen Rickman, Brian Fuorry; ***D:*** Todd Rutt, Arn McConnell.

A Shock to the System ₰₰₰ **1990 (R)** Business exec. Caine is passed over for a long-deserved promotion in favor of a younger man. When he accidentally pushes a panhandler in front of a subway in a fit of rage, he realizes how easy murder is and thinks it may be the answer to all his problems. Tries to be a satire take on corporate greed, etc., but somehow loses steam. Excellent cast makes the difference; Caine adds class. Based on the novel by Simon Brett. **88m/C VHS.** Michael Caine, Elizabeth McGovern, Peter Riegert, Swoosie Kurtz, Will Patton, Jenny Wright, John McMartin, Barbara Baxley; ***D:*** Jan Egleson; ***W:*** Andrew Klavan; ***C:*** Paul Goldsmith; ***M:*** Gary Chang.

Shock Treatment ₰½ *Traitement de Choc* **1981 (PG)** Seldom-seen mediocre semi-sequel to the cult classic, "The Rocky Horror Picture Show" (1975). Brad and Janet, now married and portrayed by different leads, find themselves trapped on a TV gameshow full of weirdos. Same writers, same director, and several original cast members do make an appearance. **94m/C VHS.** Richard O'Brien, Jessica Harper, Cliff DeYoung, Patricia Quinn, Charles Gray, Ruby Wax, Nell Campbell, Rik Mayall, Barry Humphries, Darlene Johnson, Manning Redwood; ***D:*** Jim Sharman; ***W:*** Jim Sharman, Richard O'Brien; ***C:*** Mike Molloy; ***M:*** Richard Hartley, Richard O'Brien.

Shock Waves ₰₰ *Death Corps; Almost Human* **1977 (PG)** Group of mutant-underwater-zombie-Nazi-soldiers terrorizes stranded tourists staying at a deserted motel on a small island. Cushing is the mad scientist intent on recreating the Nazi glory days with the seaweed-attired zombies. Odd B-grade, more or less standard horror flick somehow rises (slightly) above badness. Halpin's name was erroneously listed as Halprin—even on the original movie poster! **90m/C VHS.** Peter Cushing, Brooke Adams, John Carradine, Luke Halpin, Jack Davidson, Fred Buch; ***D:*** Ken Wiederhorn; ***W:*** Ken Wiederhorn, John Kent Harrison; ***C:*** Reuben Trane; ***M:*** Richard Einhorn.

Shocker ₰₰½ **1989 (R)** Another Craven gore-fest. A condemned serial killer is transformed into a menacing electrical force after being fried in the chair. Practically a remake of Craven's original "Nightmare on Elm Street." Great special effects, a few enjoyable weird and sick moments. What's Dr. Timothy Leary doing here? **111m/C VHS, DVD, Wide.** Michael Murphy, Peter Berg, Camille (Cami) Cooper, Mitch Pileggi, Richard Price, Timothy Leary, Heather Langenkamp, Theodore (Ted) Raimi, Richard Brooks, Sam Scarber; ***D:*** Wes Craven; ***W:*** Wes Craven; ***C:*** Jacques Haitkin; ***M:*** William Goldstein.

The Shoes of the Fisherman ₰½ **1968 (G)** Morris West's interesting, speculative best seller about Russian Pope brought to the big screen at much expense, but with little care or thought. Siberian prison-camp vet Quinn, elected Pope, tries to arrest nuclear war. Director Anderson wasted the prodigious talents of Olivier, Gielgud, et al. Sloppy use of good cast and promising plot. **160m/C VHS, Wide.** Anthony Quinn, Leo McKern, Laurence Olivier, John Gielgud, Vittorio De Sica, Oskar Werner, David Janssen; ***D:*** Michael Anderson Sr.; ***M:*** Alex North. Golden Globes '69: Score; Natl. Bd. of Review '68: Support. Actor (McKern).

Shoeshine ₰₰₰₰ **1947** Two shoeshine boys struggling to survive in post-war Italy become involved in the black market and are eventually caught and imprisoned. Prison scenes detail the sense of abandonment and tragedy that destroys their friendship. A rich, sad achievement in neo-realistic drama. In Italian with English subtitles. **90m/B VHS.** *IT* Franco Interlenghi, Rinaldo Smordoni, Annielo Mele, Bruno Ortensi, Pacifico Astrologo; ***D:*** Vittorio De Sica; ***W:*** Cesare Zavattini, Sergio Amidei, Adolfo Franci, C.G. Viola.

Shogun ₰₰₰½ *James Clavell's Shogun* **1980** Miniseries chronicling the saga of a shipwrecked English navigator who becomes the first Shogun, or Samurai warrior chief, from the Western world. Colorfully adapted from the James Clavell bestseller. Also released in a two-hour version, but this full-length version is infinitely better. **550m/C VHS.** Richard Chamberlain, Toshiro Mifune, Yoko Shimada, John Rhys-Davies, Damien Thomas; ***D:*** Jerry London; ***M:*** Maurice Jarre; ***Nar:*** Orson Welles. **TV**

Shogun Assassin ₰₰½ **1980 (R)** Story of a proud samurai named Lone Wolf who served his Shogun master well as the Official Decapitator, until the fateful day when the aging Shogun turned against him. Extremely violent, with record-breaking body counts. Edited from two other movies in a Japanese series called "Sword of Vengeance"; a tour de force of the cutting room. The samurai pushes his son's stroller through much of the film-sets it aside to hack and slash. **89m/C VHS.** *JP* Tomisaburo Wakayama, Kayo Matsuo, Shin Kishida, Masahiro Tomikawa; ***D:*** Kenji Misumi, Robert Houston; ***W:*** Robert Houston, David Weisman, Kazuo Koike; ***C:*** Chishi Makiura; ***M:*** Michael W. Lewis, Mark Lindsay.

Shogun's Ninja ₰½ **1983** In 16th-century Japan, an age-old rivalry between two ninja clans sparks a search for a dagger which will lead to one clan's hidden gold. Martial arts performed and directed by Sonny Chiba. In Japanese with usual poor English dubbing. **112m/C VHS, DVD, Wide.** *JP* Henry Sanada, Sue Shiomi, Sonny Chiba; ***D:*** Noribumi Suzuki.

Shoot ₰ **1985 (R)** Five hunting buddies fall prey to a group of crazed killers after one man is shot by accident. What's the message: Anti-gun? Anti-hunting? Silly, unbelievable, irresponsibly moralistic, and gratuitously violent. **98m/C VHS.** *CA* Ernest Borgnine, Cliff Robertson, Henry Silva, Helen Shaver; ***D:*** Harvey Hart.

Shoot ₰₰ **1992 (R)** Photographer Katie Tracy goes undercover to expose an illegal gambling ring fronted by an exotic nightclub. The latest gambling stakes involve the Emperor's pearls, offered in a private auction which could turn deadly, especially when Katie gets involved with the group's handsome ringleader. **90m/C VHS.** Dedee Pfeiffer, Miles O'Keeffe, Christopher Atkins; ***D:*** Hugh Parks.

Shoot It Black, Shoot It Blue ₰½ **1974** Rogue cop shoots a black purse snatcher and thinks he has gotten away with it. Unknown to him, a witness has filmed the incident and turns the evidence over to a lawyer. **93m/C VHS.** Michael Moriarty.

Shoot Loud, Louder, I Don't Understand! ₰½ *Spara Forte, Piu Forte...Non Capisco* **1966** A sculptor who has a hard time separating reality from dreams thinks he witnessed a murder. Shenanigans follow. Meant to be a black comedy, but when not dull, it is confusing. Welch looks good, as usual, but doesn't show acting talent here. In Italian with English subtitles. **101m/C VHS.** *IT* Marcello Mastroianni, Raquel Welch; ***D:*** Eduardo de Filippo; ***M:*** Nino Rota.

Shoot Out 🦴½ *Shootout* **1971** Hamfisted western based on Will James' novel "The Lone Cowboy" and previously filmed in 1934. Clay Lomax (Peck) gets out a prison and wants revenge on the partner, Sam Foley (Gregory), who doublecrossed him. So Foley hires a young gunslinger (Lyons) to take care of Lomax. In addition, Lomax gets stuck with an orphaned 8-year-old girl, who's the daughter of an ex-lover (and may be Lomax's flesh-and-blood). Peck's just too nice while Lyons chews all the scenery. **94m/C DVD.** Gregory Peck, Robert F. Lyons, Susan Tyrrell, Jeff Corey, James Gregory, Rita Gam, Pepe Serna, John Davis Chandler, Paul Fix, Arthur Hunnicutt, Nicolas Beauvy; ***D:*** Henry Hathaway; ***W:*** Marguerite Roberts; ***C:*** Earl Rath; ***M:*** Dave Grusin.

Shoot the Living, Pray for the Dead 🦴🦴 **1973** While travelling through Mexico, the leader of a band of killers promises his guide half of a share in stolen gold if he can lead them to it. **90m/C VHS.** Klaus Kinski.

Shoot the Moon 🦴🦴½ **1982 (R)** A successful writer, married and with four children, finds his life unrewarding and leaves his family to take up with a younger woman. The wife must learn to deal with her resentment, the fears of her children, and her own attempt at a new love. Fine acting but a worn-out story. **124m/C VHS.** Diane Keaton, Albert Finney, Karen Allen, Peter Weller, Dana Hill, Viveka Davis, Tracey Gold, Tina Yothers; ***D:*** Alan Parker; ***W:*** Bo Goldman.

Shoot the Piano Player 🦴🦴🦴🦴 *Tirez sur le Pianiste; Shoot the Pianist* **1962** Former concert pianist (Aznavour, spendidly cast) changes his name and plays piano at a low-class Paris cafe. A convoluted plot ensues; he becomes involved with gangsters, though his girlfriend wants him to try a comeback. Lots of atmosphere, character development, humor, and romance. A Truffaut masterpiece based on a pulp novel by David Goodis. In French with English subtitles. **92m/B VHS, DVD, Wide.** *FR* Charles Aznavour, Marie DuBois, Nicole Berger, Michele Mercier, Albert Remy; ***D:*** Francois Truffaut; ***W:*** Marcel Moussey, Francois Truffaut; ***C:*** Raoul Coutard; ***M:*** Georges Delerue.

Shoot the Sun Down 🦴½ **1981 (PG)** Four offbeat characters united in a search for gold turn against each other. "Gilligan's Island"-style assortment of characters (Indian; gunfighter; girl; sea captain) are cast away in a pointless plot from which they never escape. Too bad: talented cast could have done better. **102m/C VHS.** Christopher Walken, Margot Kidder, Geoffrey Lewis, Bo Brundin, Sacheen Little Feather; ***D:*** David Leeds.

Shoot to Kill 🦴🦴½ **1947** B-grade noir-esque mystery about a crooked D.A. and a gangster who bite the dust. Suspenseful, dark, street-level crime drama uncovered by ambitious journalist Ward. **64m/B VHS.** Russell Wade, Susan Walters, Nestor Paiva, Edmund MacDonald, Vince Barnett; ***D:*** William Berke.

Shoot to Kill 🦴🦴🦴 **1988 (R)** A city cop (Poitier, better than ever after 10 years off the screen) and a mountain guide (Berenger) reluctantly join forces to capture a killer who is part of a hunting party traversing the Pacific Northwest and which is being led by the guide's unsuspecting girlfriend (Alley). Poitier may be a bit old for the role, but he carries the implausible plot on the strength of his performance. Good action. **110m/C VHS.** Sidney Poitier, Tom Berenger, Kirstie Alley, Clancy Brown, Richard Masur, Andrew (Andy) Robinson, Frederick Coffin, Kevin Scannell; ***D:*** Roger Spottiswoode; ***W:*** Michael Burton, Harv Zimmel, Dan Petrie Jr.; ***C:*** Michael Chapman; ***M:*** John Scott.

Shoot to Kill 🦴🦴 *Disparen a Matar* **1990** An innocent young man is murdered during a police round-up while his mother watches helplessly. The police try a whitewash—proclaiming the victim a criminal—but she launches a long campaign for justice. Spanish with subtitles. **90m/C VHS.** *VZ* ***D:*** Carlos Azpurua.

The Shooter 🦴🦴½ **1997** The frontier town of Kingston is being terrorized by outlaw Krantz (Smith) and his gang until gunfighter Michael Atherton (Dudikoff) becomes their reluctant defender. Modest budget but lots of action. **93m/C VHS.** Michael Dudikoff, Randy Travis, Andrew Stevens, William Smith; ***D:*** Fred Olen Ray. **VIDEO**

Shooters 🦴½ **1989** A wacky platoon of misfits is paired off against a group of vicious killers in a "war game" training session. Not completely unfunny or worthless. **84m/C VHS.** Ben Schick, Robin Sims, Aldo Ray.

Shootfighter: Fight to the Death 🦴½ **1993 (R)** Two boys become experts in the martial arts and constant rivals. Now grown-up they take their rivalry to a deadly level in a "shootfight," a game which has no rules and is so brutal it's banned as a sport. Not that this stops them. An unrated version is also available. **94m/C VHS.** Bolo Yeung, Martin Kove, William Zabka, Michael Bernardo, Maryam D'Abo, Edward Albert, Kenn Scott; ***D:*** Patrick Allen; ***W:*** Judd B. Lynn, Larry Feliz Jr., Peter Shaner.

Shootfighter 2: Kill or Be Killed! 🦴½ **1996 (R)** The Miami underworld is placed on alert when a police chief, seeking to avenge the death of his son, joins with a martial arts master to recruit and train a group of fighters. Then they'll infiltrate the illegal spectator games of to-the-death-combat and see what mayhem they can cause. **90m/C VHS.** Bolo Yeung, Michael Bernardo, William Zabka; ***D:*** Paul Ziller; ***W:*** Peter Shaner, Greg Mellott.

The Shooting 🦴🦴🦴 **1966** A mysterious woman, bent on revenge, persuades a former bounty hunter and his partner to escort her across the desert, with tragic results. Offbeat, small film filled with strong performances by Nicholson and Oates. Filmed concurrently with "Ride in the Whirlwind," with the same cast and director. Bang-up surprise ending. **82m/C VHS, DVD, Wide.** Warren Oates, Millie Perkins, Jack Nicholson, Will Hutchins; ***D:*** Monte Hellman; ***W:*** Adrien (Carole Eastman) Joyce; ***C:*** Gregory Sandor; ***M:*** Richard Markowitz.

Shooting 🦴 **1982** Three boys run away when they think they have killed a man in a hunting accident. **60m/C VHS.** Lynn Redgrave, Lance Kerwin, Barry Primus.

Shooting Elizabeth 🦴½ **1992 (PG-13)** A fed-up husband decides to shut his loudmouthed wife up—permanently. Only before he can kill her, she disappears. The police don't buy it and want to charge him with murder. Can he find his wife before things really get serious? **96m/C VHS.** Jeff Goldblum, Mimi Rogers; ***D:*** Baz Taylor.

Shooting Fish 🦴🦴½ **1998 (PG)** London con-artists Dylan (Futterman) and Jez (Townsend) hire perky temp Georgie (Beckinsale) to lend an air of authenticity to one of their scams. She charms them both, while figuring out that they're not the legit businessmen they pretend to be. When one of their scams goes awry, landing them in prison, Georgie helps them out. All the whiile, she's trying to figure out a way to save her retarded brother's home from her greedy fiance. Breezy, fun comedy benefits from great chemistry between the likable leads, but suffers from plot overload near the end. **109m/C VHS, DVD, Wide.** *GB* Dan Futterman, Stuart Townsend, Kate Beckinsale, Dominic Mafham, Claire Cox, Nickolas Grace, Peter Capaldi, Annette Crosbie, Jane Lapotaire; ***D:*** Stefan Schwartz; ***W:*** Stefan Schwartz, Richard Holmes; ***C:*** Henry Braham; ***M:*** Stanislas Syrewicz.

The Shooting Party 🦴🦴½ **1977** Told in flashbacks, a story of a crime of passion, an innocent man, and guilty secrets. A magistrate cannot admit his love for a woodsman's daughter so she falls into a loveless marriage and a decadent affair. In a fit of passion, the magistrate kills her and then decides to prosecute her innocent husband for the crime. Based on a story by Chekhov. In Russian with English subtitles. **105m/C VHS.** *RU* Oleg (Yankovsky) Jankowsky, Galina Belyayeva; ***D:*** Emil Loteanu.

The Shooting Party 🦴🦴🦴½ **1985** A group of English aristocrats assemble at a nobleman's house for a bird shoot on the eve of WWI. Splendid cast crowned Mason, in his last role. Fascinating crucible class anxieties, rich with social scheming, personality conflicts, and things left unsaid. Adapted from Isabel Colegate's novel. **97m/C VHS.** *GB* James Mason, Dorothy Tutin, Edward Fox, John Gielgud, Robert Hardy, Cheryl Campbell, Judi Bowker; ***D:*** Alan Bridges; ***W:*** Julian Bond. L.A. Film Critics '85: Support. Actor (Gielgud); Natl. Soc. Film Critics '85: Support. Actor (Gielgud).

Shooting Stars 🦴 **1985** Two actors who play private eyes on TV are pushed out of their jobs by a jealous co-star. They take to the streets as "real" crime-fighting dicks. Interesting premise goes nowhere. **96m/C VHS.** Billy Dee Williams, Parker Stevenson, Efrem Zimbalist Jr., Edie Adams; ***D:*** Richard Lang. **TV**

Shooting the Past 🦴🦴½ **1999** Christopher Anderson (Cunningham) is a wealthy American developer who has just purchased an old London mansion, which he is intending to convert into a business school. The mansion presently houses the Fallon Photo Library, consisting of some 10 million historical pictures. The indifferent Anderson says the pictures must be sold or destroyed within a week. But Anderson reckons without the library's impervious employees, who will do whatever is necessary to save their library. **180m/C VHS.** *GB* Liam Cunningham, Lindsay Duncan, Timothy Spall, Emilia Fox; ***D:*** Stephen Poliakoff; ***W:*** Stephen Poliakoff. **TV**

The Shootist 🦴🦴🦴½ **1976 (PG)** Wayne, in a supporting last role, plays a legendary gunslinger afflicted with cancer who seeks peace and solace in his final days. Town bad guys Boone and O'Brian aren't about to let him rest and are determined to gun him down to avenge past deeds. One of Wayne's best and most dignified performances about living up to a personal code of honor. Stewart and Bacall head excellent supporting cast. Based on Glendon Swarthout's novel. **100m/C VHS, DVD, Wide.** John Wayne, Lauren Bacall, Ron Howard, James Stewart, Richard Boone, Hugh O'Brian, Bill McKinney, Harry (Henry) Morgan, John Carradine, Sheree North, Scatman Crothers; ***D:*** Donald Siegel; ***W:*** Scott Hale, Miles Hood Swarthout; ***C:*** Bruce Surtees; ***M:*** Elmer Bernstein.

Shop Angel 🦴🦴 **1932** A department store dress designer encounters romance and scandal in this low-budget drama of intrigue and romance. She falls in love with the fiance of her boss's daughter, and schemes to blackmail him (the boss). Competently rendered if unexceptional tale. **66m/B VHS, 8mm.** Marion Shilling, Holmes Herbert, Creighton Hale; ***D:*** E. Mason Hopper.

The Shop Around the Corner 🦴🦴🦴½ **1940** A low-key romantic classic in which Stewart and Sullavan are feuding clerks in a small Budapest shop, who unknowingly fall in love via a lonely hearts club. Charming portrayal of ordinary people in ordinary situations. Adapted from the Nikolaus Laszlo's play "Parfumerie." Later made into a musical called "In the Good Old Summertime" and, on Broadway, "She Loves Me." **99m/B VHS.** Margaret Sullavan, James Stewart, Frank Morgan, Joseph Schildkraut, Sara Haden, Felix Bressart, Charles Halton; ***D:*** Ernst Lubitsch; ***C:*** William H. Daniels. Natl. Film Reg. '99.

The Shop on Main Street 🦴🦴🦴🦴 *The Shop on High Street; Obch Od Na Korze* **1965** During WWII, a Slovak takes a job as an "Aryan comptroller" for a Jewish-owned button shop. The owner is an old deaf woman; they slowly build a friendship. Tragedy ensues when all of the town's Jews are to be deported. Sensitive and subtle. Surely among the most gutwrenching portrayals of human tragedy ever on screen. Exquisite plotting and direction. In Czechoslovakian with English subtitles. **111m/B VHS, DVD.** *CZ* Ida Kaminska, Josef Kroner, Hana Slivkoua, Frantisek Holly, Martin Gregor; ***D:*** Jan Kadar, Elmar Klos; ***W:*** Jan Kadar, Elmar Klos; ***C:*** Vladimir Novotny; ***M:*** Zdenek Liska. Oscars '65: Foreign Film; N.Y. Film Critics '66: Foreign Film.

Shopping 🦴🦴 **1993 (R)** A crumbling British industrial city (filmed at London's docklands) is the bleak setting for gangs of aimless youth who steal cars, crash into the windows of various shops, grab whatever comes to hand, and then lead the police on high-speed chases. Adrenaline junkie Billy (Law) is accompanied by thrill-seeking girlfriend Jo (Frost) on one such escapade while fending off rival Tommy (Pertwee), who doesn't like his burgeoning criminal empire disturbed. Tries too hard for that rebel youth feeling. **86m/C VHS, DVD.** *GB* Jude Law, Sadie Frost, Sean Pertwee, Fraser James, Sean Bean, Marianne Faithfull, Jonathan Pryce, Danny Newman; ***D:*** Paul Anderson; ***W:*** Paul Anderson; ***C:*** Tony Imi; ***M:*** Barrington Pheloung.

Shopworn Angel 🦴🦴🦴 **1938** Weepy melodrama about a sophisticated actress who leads on a naive Texas soldier who's in New York prior to being shipped out for WWI duty. Later, just before she goes on stage, she learns he's been killed at the front. She rallys to sing "Pack Up your Troubles in Your Old Kit Bag and Smile, Smile, Smile." Lots of tears. Adapted from the story "Private Pettigrew's Girl" by Dana Burnet. This remake of the same-titled 1929 film considerably softened the characters. Remade again in 1959 as "That Kind of Woman." **85m/B VHS.** Margaret Sullavan, James Stewart, Walter Pidgeon, Nat Pendleton, Alan Curtis, Sam Levene, Hattie McDaniel, Charley Grapewin, Charles D. Brown; ***D:*** H.C. Potter; ***W:*** Waldo Salt; ***C:*** Joseph Ruttenberg.

Shore Leave 🦴🦴🦴 **1925** Dressmaker Mackaill isn't getting any younger. Tough-guy sailor Bilge Smith (Barthelmess, in top form) meets her on shore leave; little does he realize her plans for him! She owns a dry-docked ship, you see, and it (and she) will be ready for him when he comes ashore next. Lovely, fun (if rather plodding) romantic comedy. Later made into musicals twice, as "Hit the Deck" and "Follow the Fleet." **74m/B VHS.** Richard Barthelmess, Dorothy Mackaill; ***D:*** John S. Robertson.

Short Circuit 🦴🦴 **1986 (PG)** A newly developed robot designed for the military is hit by lightning and begins to think it's alive. Sheedy and Guttenberg help it hide from the mean people at the weapons lab who want to take it home. Followed two years later, save Sheedy and Guttenberg, by the lame "Short Circuit 2." **98m/C VHS, DVD, Wide.** Steve Guttenberg, Ally Sheedy, Austin Pendleton, Fisher Stevens, Brian McNamara; ***D:*** John Badham; ***W:*** S.S. Wilson, Brent Maddock; ***C:*** Nick McLean; ***M:*** David Shire.

Short Circuit 2 🦴½ **1988 (PG)** A sequel to the first adorable-robot-outwits-bad-guys tale. The robot, Number Five, makes his way through numerous plot turns without much human assistance or much purpose. Harmless (unless you have to spend time watching it), but pointless and juvenile. Very occasional genuinely funny moments. **95m/C VHS, DVD, Wide.** Fisher Stevens, Cynthia Gibb, Michael McKean, Jack Weston, David Hemblen; ***D:*** Kenneth Johnson; ***W:*** Brent Maddock, S.S. Wilson; ***C:*** John McPherson; ***M:*** Charles Fox.

Short Cuts 🦴🦴🦴½ **1993 (R)** Multi-storied, fish-eyed look at American culture with some 22 characters intersecting—profoundly or fleetingly—through each other's lives. Running the emotional gamut from disturbing to humorous, Altman's portrait of the contemporary human condition is nevertheless fascinating. Based on nine stories and a prose poem by Raymond Carver. **189m/C VHS.** Annie Ross, Lori Singer, Jennifer Jason Leigh, Tim Robbins, Madeleine Stowe, Frances McDormand, Peter Gallagher, Lily Tomlin, Tom Waits, Bruce Davison, Andie MacDowell, Jack Lemmon, Lyle Lovett, Fred Ward, Buck Henry, Huey Lewis, Matthew Modine, Anne Archer, Julianne Moore, Lili Taylor, Christopher Penn, Robert Downey Jr., Jarrett Lennon, Zane Cassidy; ***D:*** Robert Altman; ***W:*** Frank Barhydt, Robert Altman; ***C:*** Walt Lloyd; ***M:*** Mark Isham. Ind. Spirit '94: Director (Altman), Film, Screenplay; Natl.

Soc. Film Critics '93: Support. Actress (Stowe); Venice Film Fest. '93: Film.

Short Eyes 🦴🦴🦴½ *The Slammer* **1979 (R)** When a child molester (Davison) enters prison, the inmates act out their own form of revenge against him. Filmed on location at New York City's Men's House of Detention, nicknamed "The Tombs." Script by Manuel Pinero from his excellent play; he also acts in the film. Top-notch performances and respectful direction from Young bring unsparingly realistic prison drama to the screen. Title is prison jargon for child molester. **100m/C VHS.** Bruce Davison, Miguel Pinero, Nathan George, Donald Blakely, Curtis Mayfield, Jose Perez, Shawn Elliott; ***D:*** Robert M. Young.

Short Fuse 🦴½ *Good to Go* **1988 (R)** A Washington, D.C. reporter uncovers the truth behind the rape and murder of a nurse. Interesting "go-go" music from the Washington D.C. ghetto aids an otherwise uninteresting film. **91m/C VHS.** Art Garfunkel, Robert DoQui, Harris Yulin, Richard Brooks, Reginald Daughtry; ***D:*** Blaine Novak.

Short Time 🦴🦴🦴 **1990 (PG-13)** Somewhere between "Tango & Cash" and "Airplane" is where you'll find "Short Time." Non-stop action/comedy stars Dabney Coleman and Teri Garr as partners in crime and humor. Coleman is a cop days from retirement; wrongly told he is dying, he tries hard to get killed so his family will be provided for. Coleman is wonderful. Garr, no longer the long-suffering wife of "Oh, God" and "Close Encounters," is appealing here as the indulgent sidekick. **100m/C VHS.** Dabney Coleman, Teri Garr, Matt Frewer, Barry Corbin, Joe Pantoliano, Xander Berkeley, Rob Roy, Kaj-Erik Eriksen; ***D:*** Gregg Champion; ***W:*** John Blumenthal, Michael Berry; ***M:*** Ira Newborn.

The Shot 🦴🦴½ **1996** Shot in 14 days for $40,000 (and sometimes showing it), this independent release follows out-of-work actors Dern Reel (Bell) and Patrick St. Patrick (Rivkin) as they try to break into the movie business. The foil for the two sensitive artist-types is the shallow but successful director David Egoman. Offended by his brainless action movies, the duo decide to "kidnap" the only print of his latest epic. Although production values are low and the sound is a bit dicey, indie fans will probably like this depiction of Hollywood's shady side. Gained some publicity when ten reels of Kevin Spacey's "Albino Alligator" were swiped from an airport baggage claim shortly after its release. **84m/C VHS.** Dan Bell, Michael Rivkin, Mo Gaffney, Michael DeLuise, Vincent Ward, Jack Kehler, Theodore (Ted) Raimi, Jude Horowitz; ***Cameos:*** Dana Carvey; ***D:*** Dan Bell; ***W:*** Dan Bell; ***C:*** Alan Caudillo; ***M:*** Dan Sonis.

A Shot in the Dark 🦴½ **1933** A minister suspects murder when a despised miser is thought to have committed suicide. He takes it on himself to investigate in this routine mystery. **53m/B VHS.** *GB* Dorothy Boyd, O.B. Clarence, Jack Hawkins, Russell Thorndike, Michael Shepley; ***D:*** George Pearson.

A Shot in the Dark 🦴🦴 **1935** When his son is murdered at a New England college, a distraught dad takes it on himself to investigate. Movie cowboy Starrett plays the sleuthing pop in this undistinguished mystery. **69m/B VHS.** Charles Starrett, Robert Warwick, Edward Van Sloan, Marion Shilling, Doris Lloyd, Helen Jerome Eddy, James Bush; ***D:*** Charles Lamont.

A Shot in the Dark 🦴🦴🦴½ **1964** Second and possibly the best in the classic "Inspector Clouseau-Pink Panther" series of comedies. The bumbling Inspector Clouseau (Sellers, of course) investigates the case of a parlor maid (Sommer) accused of murdering her lover. Clouseau's libido convinces him she's innocent,even though all the clues point to her. Classic gags, wonderful music. After this film, Sellers as Clouseau disappears until 1975's "Return of the Pink Panther" (Alan Arkin played him in "Inspector Clouseau," made in 1968 by different folks). **101m/C VHS, DVD, Wide.** Peter Sellers, Elke Sommer, Herbert Lom, George Sanders, Bryan Forbes; ***D:*** Blake Edwards; ***W:*** William Peter Blatty, Blake Edwards; ***C:*** Christopher Challis; ***M:*** Henry Mancini.

Shot in the Heart 🦴🦴🦴 **2001 (R)** In 1977, shortly after the Supreme Court reinstated capital punishment, convicted murderer Gary Gilmore (Koteas) requested execution by a Utah firing squad, becoming the first person executed in a decade. But Gilmore's brothers, Frank Jr. (Tergesen), and his younger brother, writer Mikal (Ribisi), come to Draper Prison to plead with him to change his mind. Alienated for years, the brothers' uneasy reunion brings up lots of twisted family memories. Haunting movie about internal demons and brotherly ties; based on Mikal's 1994 memoir of the same name. **98m/C VHS, DVD, Wide.** Giovanni Ribisi, Elias Koteas, Lee Tergesen, Sam Shepard, Amy Madigan, Eric Bogosian; ***D:*** Agnieszka Holland; ***W:*** Frank Pugliese; ***C:*** Jacek Petrycki. CABLE

Shot Through the Heart 🦴🦴🦴 **1998 (R)** Based on a true story of the ethnic conflict that tore apart the former Yugoslavia and started a civil war between 1992 and 1995. Serbian Slavko (Perez) and Croat Vlado (Roache), whose wife Maida (William) is a Muslim, are childhood friends and former teammates on the Yugoslavian target-shooting team. Slavko is drafted into the Serbian army and urges his friend to flee Sarajevo. Instead, Vlado and his family are trapped in the city and Vlado is forced to take up his rifle in defense against deadly Serbian snipers. Which leads him to a final confrontation with Slavko. Filmed in Sarajevo and Budapest. **115m/C VHS, DVD.** Linus Roache, Vincent Perez, Lothaire Bluteau, Adam Kotz, Lia Williams, Karianne Henderson; ***D:*** David Attwood; ***W:*** Guy Hibbert; ***M:*** Ed Shearmur. CABLE

Shotgun 🦴🦴½ **1955** A sheriff on the trail of a killer is accompanied by a girl he's saved from Indians. Average western cowritten by western actor Rory Calhoun, who had hoped to star in the film, but was turned down by the studio. **81m/C VHS.** Sterling Hayden, Zachary Scott, Yvonne De Carlo; ***D:*** Lesley Selander; ***C:*** Ellsworth Fredericks.

The Shout 🦴🦴🦴 **1978 (R)** From a strange Robert Graves story, an even stranger film. A lunatic befriends a young couple, moves in with them, and gradually takes over their lives. The movie's title refers to the man's ability to kill by shouting, a power he learned from his Australian aboriginal past. **88m/C VHS.** *GB* Alan Bates, Susannah York, John Hurt, Tim Curry; ***D:*** Jerzy Skolimowski; ***W:*** Michael Austin; ***M:*** Tony Banks. Cannes '78: Grand Jury Prize.

Shout 🦴🦴 **1991 (PG-13)** Romance and rebellion set in a sleepy Texas town during the 1950s. Jesse Tucker's (Walters) rebellious ways land him in the Benedict Home for Boys and he seems lost until Jack Cabe (Travolta) enters town. Jack introduces Jesse and the gang to the exciting new sounds of rock 'n' roll. Been done before and better. **93m/C VHS, DVD.** John Travolta, James Walters, Heather Graham, Richard Jordan, Linda Fiorentino, Scott Coffey; ***D:*** Jeffrey Hornaday; ***C:*** Robert Brinkmann; ***M:*** Randy Edelman.

Shout at the Devil 🦴½ **1976 (PG)** English officer Moore and Irish-American adventurer Marvin seek to blow up a German battleship out for repairs in East Africa before the outbreak of WWI. There's also some intrigue about ivory smuggling. From the novel by Wilbur Smith and based on an actual incident, but that doesn't make the comedy adventure any more palatable. Marvin's hamming is ludicrous, Moore is unusually wooden, and the big budget permits any number of fairly pointless action-oriented excursions and explosions. **128m/C VHS.** *GB* Lee Marvin, Roger Moore, Barbara Parkins, Ian Holm; ***D:*** Peter Hunt; ***M:*** Maurice Jarre.

The Show 🦴🦴 **1995 (R)** Choppy and incoherent behind-the-scenes look at the attitude and people who make up the explosive hip-hop and rap scene. Mixes black and white concert footage and interviews with Russell Simmons, LL Cool J and Snoop Doggy Dogg, who discuss their music and fans. Will be a disappointment for those looking for a more in-depth study of the music, as this exercise merely scratches the surface. Includes an abundance of cameos from today's top hip hop artists such as Notorious B.I.G., Naughty by Nature and Wu-Tang Clan. **90m/B VHS.** Craig Mack, Dr. Dre, Run DMC, Slick Rick, Warren G, Kurtis Blow; ***D:*** Brian Robbins; ***C:*** Larry Banks, Steven Consentino, Ericson Core, John L. Demps Jr., Todd A. Dos Reis.

Show Boat 🦴🦴🦴🦴 **1936** The second of three film versions of the Jerome Kern/Oscar Hammerstein musical (based on the Edna Ferber novel), filmed previously in 1929, about a Mississippi showboat and the life and loves of its denizens. Wonderful romance, unforgettable music. Director Whale also brought the world "Frankenstein." The laser edition includes a historical audio essay by Miles Kreuger, excerpts from the 1929 version, Ziegfeld's 1932 stage revival, "Life Aboard a Real Showboat" (a vintage short), radio broadcasts, and a 300-photo essay tracing the history of showboats. Remade 15 years later. ♫Ol' Man River; Ah Still Suits Me; Bill; Can't Help Lovin' Dat Man; Only Make Believe; I Have the Room Above Her; You Are Love; Gallivantin' Around; Cotton Blossom. **110m/B VHS.** Irene Dunne, Allan Jones, Paul Robeson, Helen Morgan, Hattie McDaniel, Charles Winninger, Donald Cook, Bobs Watson; ***D:*** James Whale; ***W:*** Oscar Hammerstein; ***M:*** Oscar Hammerstein, Jerome Kern. Natl. Film Reg. '96.

Show Boat 🦴🦴½ **1951** Third movie version of the 1927 musical about the life and loves of a Mississippi riverboat theatre troupe. Terrific musical numbers, with fun dance routines from Champion, who went on to great fame as a choreographer. Grayson is somewhat vapid, but lovely to look at and hear. Gardner didn't want to do the part of Julie, although she eventually received fabulous reviews—her singing was dubbed by Annette Warren. The 171-foot "Cotton Blossom" boat was built on the Tarzan lake on the MGM back lot at an astounding cost of $126,468. Warfield's film debut—his "Ole Man River"—was recorded in one take. excerpts from "Broadway," "Silent Film," and radio Version of "Show Boat," a documentary featuring life on a real show boat, and a commentary on the performers, the film, and the history of show boats. ♫Make Believe; Can't Help Lovin' Dat Man; I Might Fall Back On You; Ol' Man River; You Are Love; Why Do I Love You?; Bill; Life Upon the Wicked Stage; After the Ball. **115m/C VHS, DVD.** Kathryn Grayson, Howard Keel, Ava Gardner, William Warfield, Joe E. Brown, Agnes Moorehead, Gower Champion; ***D:*** George Sidney; ***W:*** George Wells, Jack McGowan; ***C:*** Charles Rosher; ***M:*** Jerome Kern, Oscar Hammerstein.

Show Business 🦴🦴🦴 **1944** Historically valuable film record of classic vaudeville acts, especially Cantor and Davis. A number of vaudevillians recreate their old acts for director Marin—unforgettable slapstick and songs. All this pegged on a plot that follows Cantor's rise to fame with the Ziegfeld Follies. ♫Alabamy Bound; I Want a Girl (Just Like the Girl Who Married Dear Old Dad); It Had to Be You; Makin' Whoopee; Why Am I Blue; They're Wearing 'Em Higher in Hawaii; The Curse of an Aching Heart; While Strolling in the Park One Day; You May Not Remember. **92m/B VHS.** Eddie Cantor, Joan Davis, George Murphy; ***D:*** Edwin L. Marin.

Show Me Love 🦴🦴 **1999** Sixteen-year-old Agnes (Liljeberg) is the new girl in the boring, small Swedish town of Amal. Agnes isn't cool enough to be with the popular crowd (she's a brainy vegetarian) and she's rumored to be a lesbian as well. Agnes does have a crush on bored beauty, Elin (Dahlstrom), who goes to extremes to get her kicks, even making a bet with her sister Jessica (Carlson) about kissing Agnes. Then, shocked by her own reactions, Elin makes out with convenient Johan (Rust). But Elin's betrayal of self leads to self-discovery—for both girls. Swedish with subtitles. **89m/C VHS, DVD.** *SW* Rebecca Liljeberg, Alexandra Dahlstrom, Mathias Rust, Erica Carlson, Stefan Horberg, Ralph Carlsson, Maria Hedborg; ***D:*** Lukas Moodysson; ***W:*** Lukas Moodysson; ***C:*** Ulf Brantas.

A Show of Force 🦴🦴 **1990 (R)** Reporter Irving investigates the coverup of a murder with political ramifications. Brazilian director Barreto cast (surprise!) his girlfriend in the lead; she doesn't exactly carry the day. Phillips is good, but you'll end up feeling cheated if you expect to see much of highly billed Duvall or Garcia. Based on a real incident of 1978, but hardly believable as political realism or even moralism. **93m/C VHS.** Erik Estrada, Amy Irving, Andy Garcia, Robert Duvall, Lou Diamond Phillips; ***D:*** Bruno Barreto; ***W:*** Evan Jones; ***M:*** Georges Delerue.

The Show Off 🦴🦴½ **1926** Irresponsible Aubrey Piper's (Sterling) incessant boasting wrecks havoc with his wife Amy (Wilson) and their life together. Brooks has a small role as the girl-next-door. **82m/B VHS, DVD.** Ford Sterling, Lois Wilson, Louise Brooks, Claire McDowell, C.W. Goodrich, Gregory Kelly; ***D:*** Malcolm St. Clair; ***W:*** Pierre Collins; ***C:*** Lee Garmes; ***M:*** Timothy Brock.

The Show-Off 🦴½ **1946** Aubrey Piper (Skelton) has big dreams which far out weigh his modest talents. He tells outlandish tales to impress girlfriend Amy (Maxwell) and schemes to make them come true. Dated material which even gifted comedian Skelton can't rescue. Adapted from a play by George Kelly and previously filmed in 1926, 1929, and 1934. **83m/B VHS.** Red Skelton, Marilyn Maxwell, Marjorie Main, Virginia O'Brien, Eddie Anderson, George Cleveland, Leon Ames, Marshall Thompson, Jacqueline White, Lila Leeds, Emory Parnell; ***D:*** Harry Beaumont; ***W:*** George Wells.

Show People 🦴🦴🦴 **1928** A pretty girl from the boonies tries to make it big in Tinseltown. But as a slapstick star?! She wanted to be a leading lady! Enjoyable, fun silent comedy shows Davies's true talents. Interesting star cameos, including director Vidor at the end. **82m/B VHS.** Marion Davies, William Haines, Dell Henderson, Paul Ralli, William S. Hart, Rod La Rocque; ***Cameos:*** King Vidor; ***D:*** King Vidor.

Show Them No Mercy 🦴🦴🦴 *Tainted Money* **1935** A couple and their baby out for a drive unwittingly stumble into a kidnapping that doesn't go as planned. Tense gangster drama reincarnated as the Western "Rawhide." **76m/B VHS.** Rochelle Hudson, Cesar Romero, Bruce Cabot, Edward Norris, Edward Brophy, Warren Hymer, Herbert Rawlinson; ***D:*** George Marshall.

The Showdown 🦴🦴 **1940** The title actually refers to a tricky poker game, the highlight of yet another Hopalong Cassidy versus hoss thieves quickie epic. Kermit Maynard is the brother of cowboy hero Ken Maynard. **65m/B VHS.** William Boyd, Russell Hayden, Britt Wood, Morris Ankrum, Jan Clayton, Roy Barcroft, Kermit Maynard; ***D:*** Howard Bretherton.

The Showdown 🦴🦴½ **1950** Elliott plays trail boss Shad Jones who knows one of his fellow cowhands has murdered his brother. Jones is determined to find out who it is and even the score. Brennan is cast against type as a greedy cattle baron. Elliott's last film for Republic. **86m/B VHS.** Wild Bill Elliott, Walter Brennan, Marie Windsor, Harry (Henry) Morgan, Rhys Williams, Jim Davis, Leif Erickson, Yakima Canutt; ***D:*** Stuart E. McGowan, Dorrell McGowan; ***W:*** Stuart E. McGowan, Dorrell McGowan.

Showdown 🦴🦴½ **1973 (PG)** Billy Massey (Martin) and Chuck Garvis (Hudson) had been friends since childhood, until they fell out over the attentions of the pretty Kate (Clark), whom Chuck married. Chuck became the honest town sheriff while Billy took to train robbing. Now it's up to Chuck to bring Billy to justice. Director Seaton's final film. **99m/C VHS.** Dean Martin, Rock Hudson, Susan Clark, Donald Moffat, John McLiam, Ed Begley Jr.; ***D:*** George Seaton; ***W:*** Theodore Taylor; ***C:*** Ernest Laszlo; ***M:*** David Shire.

Showdown 🦴½ **1993 (R)** A small southern town is taken over by a motorcycle gang whose leader, Kincade, decides to set up his fencing and drug operations there. But the local law enforcement has other ideas, calling in a martial arts expert who wants revenge against Kincade for the death of his partner. **92m/C VHS.** Leo

Fong, Werner Hoetzinger, Richard Lynch, Michelle McCormick, Frank Marth, Tom MacDowell, Troy Donahue; *D:* Leo Fong; *W:* Leo Fong.

Showdown ½ **1993 (R)** Ken, the new kid in a particularly nasty high school, gets picked on by the martial-arts expert school bully. After getting beaten up a lot Ken finds out the school janitor can help turn him into a high-kicking fighter. Lots of fast-paced fight scenes which is all the genre demands. An edited PG-13 version is also available. **90m/C VHS.** Kenn Scott, Billy Blanks, Patrick Kilpatrick, Kenneth McLeod; *D:* Robert Radler.

Showdown *Lookin' Italian* **1994 (R)** New Yorker Vinny (Acovone) has left the family crime business and moved to California for a quieter life. But when his fast-living nephew Anthony (LeBlanc) moves in, Vinny reluctantly finds himself drawn back into violence. **90m/C VHS, DVD.** Jay Acovone, Matt LeBlanc, Lou Rawls, John Lamotta, Stephanie Richards, Real Andrews; *D:* Guy Magar; *W:* Guy Magar; *C:* Gerry Lively; *M:* Jeff Beal.

Showdown at Boot Hill **1958** A U.S. Marshal (Bronson) kills a wanted murderer but cannot collect the reward because the townspeople will not identify the victim. **76m/B VHS.** Charles Bronson, Robert Hutton, John Carradine; *D:* Gene Fowler Jr.

Showdown at Williams Creek ½ *Kootenai Brown* **1991 (R)** A graphic Canadian Western set in the old Montana territory, where an outcast settler goes on trial for killing an old man. Testimony recounts a shocking history of greed and betrayal. The dark side of the Gold Rush, generally well-acted. Inspired by an actual incident. **97m/C VHS.** *CA* Tom Burlinson, Donnelly Rhodes, Raymond Burr, Michael Thrush, John Pyper-Ferguson, Alex Bruhanski; *D:* Allen Kroeker; *W:* John Gray; *M:* Michael Conway Baker.

Showdown in Little Tokyo **1991 (R)** Lundgren stars as a martial arts master/L.A. cop who was raised in Japan, and has all the respect in the world for his "ancestors" and heritage. Brandon Lee (son of Bruce) is Lundgren's partner, and he's a bona fide American-made, pop-culture, mall junkie. Together, they go after a crack-smuggling gang of "yakuza" (Japanese thugs). Lots of high-kicking action and the unique angle on stereotypes make this a fun martial arts film. **78m/C VHS, DVD, 8mm.** Dolph Lundgren, Brandon Lee, Tia Carrere, Cary-Hiroyuki Tagawa; *D:* Mark L. Lester; *W:* Caliope Brattlestreet; *C:* Mark Irwin; *M:* David Michael Frank.

Shower *Xizao* **2000 (PG-13)** Da Ming (Xin) is a successful modern businessman who returns to Beijing after receiving alarming news from his retarded younger brother Er Ming (Wu) about their father, Liu (Xu). But the worst thing Liu has to worry about is the closure of the old-fashioned bathhouse he runs, which provides a quiet haven for its denizens. Da Ming slowly begins to reconnect to his family and working class roots but what will happen if the bathhouse really does close? Sentimental comic saga. Chinese with subtitles. **94m/C VHS, DVD.** *CH* Zhu Xu, Jiang Wu, Pu Cun Xin; *D:* Yang Zhang; *W:* Yang Zhang; *C:* Jian Zhang; *M:* Ye Xiao Gang.

The Showgirl Murders ½ **1995 (R)** Stripper Jessica (Ford) goes into management when she turns a failing Las Vegas bar into a money-maker but this femme fatale wants owner Mitch (Preston) to stop sharing the wealth with his boozy wife Carolyn (Case). Meanwhile, blackmailing DEA agent Ridley (McFarland) and hitman Joey (Alber) cause problems. **84m/C VHS.** Maria Ford, Matt Preston, Jeff Douglas, D.S. Case, Kevin Alber, Bob McFarland; *D:* Gene Hertel; *W:* Christopher Wooden.

Showgirls woof! **1995 (NC-17)** Long on ridiculous dialogue and bad acting and short on costumes, coming-of-age tale follows one young woman as she nakedly climbs the ladder of success as a Vegas showgirl. Oh, the things she must do to be headliner. Berkley makes the jump from TV's "Saved by the Bell" to portray Nomi, the young lap dancer with the gift of pelvic thrust and the will to succeed. Whether cavorting clothed or nude, Berkley is uniformly wooden, a mass of lip gloss and mascara struggling to emote. Gershon, as her sly nemesis, brings some wit and splash to her role as the jaded headliner. Eszterhas script descends below its maker's usual standards, which are not particularly high. Titanic amount of female flesh on display fails to give film even a faint hint of sexuality, proof that there is a hell. Rent it, and be prepared to fast forward (to what, we're not sure, though there is a certain camp element that might have been amusing if not imprisoned here). Also available in "R" and unrated versions. **131m/C VHS, DVD, Wide.** Elizabeth Berkley, Gina Gershon, Kyle MacLachlan, Glenn Plummer, Alan Rachins, Robert Davi, Gina Ravera; *D:* Paul Verhoeven; *W:* Joe Eszterhas; *C:* Jost Vacano; *M:* David A. Stewart. Golden Raspberries '95: Worst Picture, Worst Actress (Berkley), Worst Director (Verhoeven), Worst Screenplay, Worst Song ("Walk into the Wind"), Worst New Star (Berkley).

Showtime **2002 (PG-13)** Murphy hams and De Niro grimaces as they both plod through this lame buddy cop comedy. The odd couple are the fiery LAPD detective Preston (De Niro), who's forced to star in a reality-based TV cop show with beat cop/frustrated actor Sellars (Murphy) after Preston impulsively shoots out a network camera and must avoid a law suit. Russo is the show's producer and has little to do here. The rest of the action involves tracking down some robbers who are also the owners of a really, really big gun. Shatner briefly injects some life into the lackluster action as he coaches the boys on how to play to the camera. Although the two leads are unarguably cast correctly and easy to watch doing what they do best, the premise lets them, and the audience, down. **95m/C VHS, DVD.** *US* Robert De Niro, Eddie Murphy, Rene Russo, Frankie Faison, Dante "Mos Def" Beze, William Shatner, Pedro Damian, Nestor Serrano, Drena De Niro, Kadeem Hardison, TJ Cross, Judah Friedlander; *D:* Tom Dey; *W:* Alfred Gough, Keith Sharon, Miles Millard; *C:* Thomas Kloss; *M:* Alan Silvestri.

Shredder Orpheus **1989** Rock star Orpheus skateboards through hell to stop deadly TV transmissions and rescue his wife. **93m/C VHS.** Jesse Bernstein, Robert McGinley, Vera McCaughan, Megan Murphy, Carlo Scandiuzzi; *D:* Robert McGinley.

Shrek **2001 (PG)** Animated tale from DreamWorks about a grumpy green ogre, Shrek (Myers), who's upset when some annoying fairy types overrun his swamp. So he makes a deal with the local hotshot, Lord Farquaad (Lithgow), to save his home by rescuing Princess Fiona (Diaz) from a tower that's guarded by your not-so-basic dragon type so Farquaad can marry her. Along as Shrek's unwelcome sidekick is a smart-mouthed donkey (Murphy), who insists on helping the ogre out. This one has some eye-popping visuals as well as inside jokes (and digs at Disney) to keep the adults amused. Based (loosely) on the children's book by William Steig. **89m/C VHS, DVD, Wide.** *US* *D:* Andrew Adamson, Victoria Jenson; *W:* Ted Elliott, Terry Rossio, Roger S.H. Schulman, Joe Stillman; *M:* Harry Gregson-Williams, John Powell; *V:* Mike Myers, Cameron Diaz, Eddie Murphy, John Lithgow, Vincent Cassel, Kathleen Freeman, Conrad Vernon. Oscars '01: Animated Film; British Acad. '01: Adapt. Screenplay; L.A. Film Critics '01: Animated Film; Broadcast Film Critics '01: Animated Film.

Shriek If You Know What I Did Last Friday the 13th ½ **2000 (R)** If you're a member of the no joke is too cheap to laugh at club, you'll like this parody of parodies. There's a killer on the loose and he's targeting a group of friends who go to Bulimia High. The humor may date quickly. **86m/C VHS, DVD, Wide.** Harley Cross, Tiffani-Amber Thiessen, Coolio, Tom Arnold, Julie Benz, Aimee Graham, Majandra Delfino, Shirley Jones, Rose Marie, Mink Stole, Simon Rex, Danny Strong; *D:* John Blanchard; *W:* Sue Bailey, Joe Nelms; *C:* David J. Miller; *M:* Tyler Bates. CABLE

Shriek in the Night ½ **1933** Two rival reporters (Rogers and Talbot, previously paired in "The Thirteenth Guest") turn detective to solve a string of apartment murders. Made on a proverbial shoestring, but not bad. **66m/B VHS.** Ginger Rogers, Lyle Talbot, Harvey Clark; *D:* Albert Ray.

Shriek of the Mutilated woof! **1974 (R)** An anthropological expedition on a deserted island turns into a night of horror as a savage beast kills the members of the group one by one. **85m/C VHS.** Alan Brock, Jennifer Stock, Michael (M.K.) Harris, Tawn Ellis, Darcy Brown; *D:* Michael Findlay; *W:* Ed Adlum, Ed Kelleher; *C:* Roberta Findlay.

Shrieker **1997 (R)** Six college students are squatting in an abandoned hospital that just happens to be the scene of a 50-year-old massacre. So, one gets the bright idea of conjuring up the creature that did the deed after learning that it will only kill five victims—and the sixth will become the creature's master. This one's really lame. **80m/C VHS.** Tanya Dempsey, Jamie Gannon, Parry Shen; *D:* Victoria Sloan; *W:* Benjamin Carr.

The Shrieking *Hex* **1973 (PG)** Black magic women hang out with biker types in Nebraska in 1919. **93m/C VHS.** Keith Carradine, Christina Raines, Gary Busey, Robert Walker Jr., Dan Haggerty, John Carradine, Scott Glenn; *D:* Leo Garen; *M:* Charles Bernstein.

The Shrimp on the Barbie ½ **1990 (R)** When daddy refuses to bless her marriage to dim bulb boyfriend, Australian Samms hires L.A. low life Marin to pose as new beau. Another pseudonymous Smithee effort. **86m/C VHS.** Richard "Cheech" Marin, Emma Samms, Vernon Wells, Bruce Spence, Carole (Raphaelle) Davis; *D:* Alan Smithee.

Shrunken Heads ½ **1994 (R)** Inspired by their comic book heroes three boys try to take on neighborhood thugs only to be gunned down. But along comes Mr. Sumatra, a retired voodoo specialist, who revives the three (in a somewhat smaller form) so they can fight the good fight once again. Title theme music by director Richard's brother, Danny Elfman. **86m/C VHS.** Aeryk Egan, Meg Foster, Julius W. Harris, Becky Herbst, A.J. Damato, Bo Sharon, Darris Love, Leigh-Allyn Baker, Troy Fromin; *D:* Richard Elfman; *W:* Matthew Bright; *M:* Richard Band.

Shy People **1987 (R)** An urbanized New York journalist and her spoiled daughter journey to the Louisiana bayou to visit long-lost relatives in order to produce an article for "Cosmopolitan." They find ignorance, madness, and ancestral secrets and are forced to examine their motives, their relationships and issues brought to light in the watery, murky, fantastic land of the bayous. Well-acted melodrama with an outstanding performance by Hershey as the cajun matriarch. **119m/C VHS.** Edward (Eddie) Bunker, Jill Clayburgh, Barbara Hershey, Martha Plimpton, Mare Winningham, Merritt Butrick, John Philbin, Don Swayze, Pruitt Taylor Vince; *D:* Andrei Konchalovsky; *W:* Gerard Brach, Marjorie David; *C:* Chris Menges; *M:* Tangerine Dream. Cannes '87: Actress (Hershey).

Siam Sunset ½ **1999** Mild fish-out-of-water comedy finds British chemist Perry (Roache), who works on devising new paint colors, caught up in every conceivable disaster while on an Australian holiday. The recent widower (his wife was crushed by a refrigerator) wins his vacation, which turns out to be a decidedly third-rate bus trip cross-country with a petty tyrant operator (Billing) and a number of Aussie eccentrics. Title refers to a particular shade of red that Perry is trying to develop. **91m/C VHS.** *AU* Linus Roache, Danielle Cormack, Roy Billing, Alan Brough, Ian Bliss, Victoria Hill, Rebecca Hobbs; *D:* John Polson; *W:* Max Dann, Andrew Knight; *C:* Brian J. Breheny; *M:* Paul Grabowsky.

Siberiade **1979** Depicts life in a Siberian village from 1909 to 1969 for a wealthy family and a peasant clan and how Soviet society affects them. Rambling narrative with strong characters. In Russian with subtitles. **190m/C VHS.** *RU* Vladimir Samoilov, Vitaly Solomin, Nikita Mikhalkov, Ludmila Gurchenko, Nathalia Andretchenko; *D:* Andrei Konchalovsky; *W:* Valentin Yezhov, Andrei Konchalovsky; *M:* Eduard Artemyev. Cannes '79: Grand Jury Prize.

Siberian Lady Macbeth ½ *Fury Is a Woman; Sibirska Ledi Magbet* **1961** A Polish version of Shakespeare's Macbeth which ranks with the greatest film translations of his work. In Czarist Russia the passionate wife of a plantation owner begins an affair with a farm hand, and poisons her father-in-law when he finds them out. As her madness grows, she plots the murder of the husband and other suspicious family members. In Serbian with English subtitles. **93m/B VHS, DVD, Wide.** *RU* Olivera Markovic, Ljuba Tadic, Kapitalina Eric; *D:* Andrzej Wajda; *W:* Sveta Lukic; *C:* Aleksandar Sekulovic.

The Sibling *Psycho Sisters; So Evil, My Sister* **1972 (PG)** Two sisters become involved in the accidental murder of a man who was a husband to one woman and lover to the other. Of course, one sister has just been released from the mental rehabilitation clinic. **85m/C VHS, DVD.** Susan Strasberg, Faith Domergue, Sydney Chaplin, Steve Mitchell; *D:* Reginald LeBorg.

Sibling Rivalry **1990 (PG-13)** Repressed doctor's wife (redundant) Alley rolls in hay with soon to be stiff stranger upon advice of footloose sister. Stranger expires from heart attack in hay and Alley discovers that the corpse is her long-lost brother-in-law. Slapstick cover-up ensues. **88m/C VHS, 8mm.** Kirstie Alley, Bill Pullman, Carrie Fisher, Sam Elliott, Jami Gertz, Ed O'Neill, Scott Bakula, Frances Sternhagen, Bill Macy; *D:* Carl Reiner.

The Sicilian ½ **1987** Adapted from the Mario Puzo novel and based on the life of Salvatore Giuliano. Chronicles the exploits of the men who took on the government, the Catholic Church, and the Mafia in an effort to make Sicily secede from Italy and become its own nation in the 1940s. Pretentious, overdone, and confused. This long, uncut version was unseen in America, but hailed by European critics; the 115-minute, R-rated American release is also available, but isn't as good. See "Salvatore Giuliano" (Francesco Rosi, 1962) instead of either version. **146m/C VHS, DVD.** Christopher Lambert, John Turturro, Terence Stamp, Joss Ackland, Barbara Sukowa; *D:* Michael Cimino; *W:* Steve Shagan; *C:* Alex Thomson; *M:* David Mansfield.

Sicilian Connection ½ **1974** A narcotics agent poses as a nightclub manager to bust a drug-smuggling organization. **100m/C VHS.** *IT* Ben Gazzara, Silvia Monti, Fausto Tozzi.

The Sicilian Connection *The Pizza Connection* **1985 (R)** Two brothers in the mob serve out vendettas and generally create havoc wherever they go. **117m/C VHS.** Michele Placido, Mark Switzer, Simona Cavallari.

Sid & Nancy ½ *Sid & Nancy: Love Kills* **1986 (R)** The tragic, brutal, true love story of The Sex Pistols' Sid Vicious and American groupie Nancy Spungen, from the director of "Repo Man." Remarkable lead performances in a very dark story that manages to be funny at times. Depressing but engrossing; no appreciation of punk music or sympathy for the self-destructive way of life is required. Oldman and Webb are superb. Music by Joe Strummer, the Pogues, and Pray for Rain. **111m/C VHS, DVD, Wide.** *GB* Gary Oldman, Chloe Webb, Debbie Bishop, David Hayman, Andrew Schofield, Tony London, Xander Berkeley, Biff Yeager, Courtney Love, Iggy Pop; *D:* Alex Cox; *W:* Alex Cox, Abbe Wool; *C:* Roger Deakins; *M:* The Pogues, Pray for Rain, Joe Strummer. Natl. Soc. Film Critics '86: Actress (Webb).

Side by Side **1988** In the same vein as "Cocoon," three senior citizens who aren't ready to retire decide to start their own business and launch a sportswear company designed for seniors. A witty portrayal of graceful aging that is uneven at times. **100m/C VHS.** Milton Berle, Sid Caesar, Danny Thomas; *D:* Jack Bender.

Side Out 🦴½ **1990 (PG-13)** The first major film about volleyball!? What a claim! What a bore. Midwestern college guy spends summer in Southern Cal. working for slumlord uncle; instead enters "the ultimate" beach volleyball touring. Bogus. Don't see it, dude. **100m/C VHS.** C. Thomas Howell, Peter Horton, Kathy Ireland, Sinjin Smith, Randy Stoklos, Courtney Thorne-Smith, Harley Jane Kozak, Christopher Rydell; ***D:*** Peter Israelson.

Side Show 🦴 **1984** A runaway teen joins the circus, witnesses a murder, and must use his wits to stay out of reach of the killer. Forced "suspense" and "drama" of the bad made for TV ilk. **98m/C VHS.** Lance Kerwin, Red Buttons, Anthony (Tony) Franciosa, Connie Stevens; ***D:*** William Conrad; ***M:*** Ralph Burns.

Sideburns 🦴🦴 **1991** The Pushkin Club, a group of reactionaries who try to remove the western influence from Russia, attack first a rock band, then innocent civilians as they act as a social cleaning service. Uses humor to try and warn people against the rising fascism in Russia because of the battle between conservative and reformist forces. In Russian with English subtitles. **110m/C VHS.** *RU* ***D:*** Yuri Mamin.

Sidekicks 🦴🦴 **1993 (PG)** Cutesy ego vehicle for executive producer Norris. (Brandis) is bullied by the kids at school and doesn't find much support at home from his well-meaning but ineffectual dad. He has a severe case of hero-worship for Norris, who appears as himself in a series of daydream karate sequences, saving the good guy and maiming the bad. Director Norris is actor Norris' brother. Predictable and sappy. **100m/C VHS, 8mm.** Chuck Norris, Jonathan Brandis, Beau Bridges, Mako, Julia Nickson-Soul, Danica McKellar, Richard Moll, Joe Piscopo; ***D:*** Aaron Norris; ***W:*** Donald W. Thompson, Lou Illar; ***C:*** Joao Fernandes; ***M:*** Alan Silvestri, David Shire.

Sidewalks of London 🦴🦴🦴 *St. Martin's Lane* **1938** Laughton's a sidewalk entertainer who takes in homeless waif Leigh and puts her in his act and in his heart. Harrison steals her away and before long she's a star in the music halls. Meanwhile, Laughton has fallen on hard times. Memorable performances. **86m/B VHS.** *GB* Charles Laughton, Vivien Leigh, Rex Harrison, Larry Adler, Tyrone Guthrie, Gus McNaughton, Bart Cormack, Edward Lexy, Maire O'Neill, Basil Gill, Claire Greet, David Burns, Cyril Smith, Ronald Ward, Romilly Lunge, Helen Haye, Jerry Verno; ***D:*** Tim Whelan; ***W:*** Clemence Dane; ***C:*** Jules Kruger; ***M:*** Arthur Johnson.

Sidewalks of New York 🦴🦴½ **1931** A hapless New York millionaire (Keaton) falls for tenement gal Page and tries to win her heart by saving her street urchin brother from joining the local gang of toughs. Keaton was a silent screen classic as a comedian but his talkie career was disappointing as he lost creative control and battled alcohol problems. **74m/B VHS.** Buster Keaton, Anita Page, Cliff Edwards, Frank LaRue, Frank Rowan, Norman Phillips Jr.; ***D:*** Jules White, Zion Myers.

Sidewalks of New York 🦴🦴 **2001 (R)** Burns's lightweight comedy about various New Yorkers looking for sex and/or romance suffered from post-Sept. 11 disdain for anything frivoluos. But it also suffers from weak writing, obvious "borrowing" from Woody Allen when he was still funny, and too few characters the audience can connect with. Burns is recently-dumped TV producer Tommy, who hooks up with recently-divorced teacher Maria (Rosario), whose ex, Ben (Crumholtz) thinks they can reunite, before he meets young waitress Ashley (Murphy), who's having an affair with a dentist (Tucci), who's married to Tommy's real-estate agent (Graham), in whom he naturally becomes interested. Oh, and they're all being interviewed for a documentary on love and sex in NYC. Even if it doesn't work on many levels, the performances are generally fine, with Tucci standing out in the meatiest role. **107m/C VHS, DVD, Wide.** *US* Edward Burns, Heather Graham, Rosario Dawson, Dennis Farina, David Krumholtz, Brittany Murphy, Stanley Tucci, Callie (Calliope) Thorne, Aida Turturro, Nadia Dajani, Michael Leydon Campbell; ***D:*** Edward Burns; ***W:*** Edward Burns; ***C:*** Frank Prinzi.

Sidewinder One 🦴 **1977 (PG)** Motocross racing is the setting for a romance between a racer and an heiress. Good racing footage, but where's the plot? If you like cars a whole lot... **97m/C VHS.** Michael Parks, Marjoe Gortner, Susan Howard, Alex Cord, Charlotte Rae; ***D:*** Earl Bellamy; ***W:*** Nancy Voyles Crawford.

Sidney Sheldon's Bloodline woof! *Bloodline* **1979 (R)** Wealthy businesswoman Hepburn finds she is marked for death by persons unknown. Exquisitely bad trash from another Sheldon bestseller. **116m/C VHS.** Audrey Hepburn, Ben Gazzara, James Mason, Michelle Phillips, Omar Sharif, Irene Papas, Romy Schneider, Gert Frobe, Maurice Ronet, Beatrice Straight; ***D:*** Terence Young; ***C:*** Frederick A. (Freddie) Young; ***M:*** Ennio Morricone.

The Siege 🦴🦴½ *Against All Enemies* **1998 (R)** Controversial political suspense/action movie caused quite a ruckus when first released. Although protested by Arab-American groups for alleged negative stereotyping, it actually points the finger at the U.S. military as the bad guys. First half centers on FBI honcho Hubbard (Washington) and his prominently Lebanese-American partner Haddad (Shaloub) as they try to stop terrorist bombings of New York. After the bombings escalate, martial law is declared in Brooklyn. Under semi-fascist Gen. Devereaux, all Constitutional rights are suspended and young Arab-Americans are rounded up and imprisoned. Hubbard forms a shaky alliance with shady CIA lady Elise Kraft to break the terrorist ring and restore freedom. Substitutes cardboard cutouts spouting political platitudes for characters. **116m/C VHS, DVD.** Denzel Washington, Tony Shalhoub, Annette Bening, Bruce Willis, Sami Bouajila, David Proval, Jack Gwaltney, Chip Zien, Victor Slezak, Will Lyman, Dakin Matthews, John Rothman, E. Katherine Kerr, Jimmie Ray Weeks, Lance Reddick, Mark Valley, Liana Pai, Amro Salama; ***D:*** Edward Zwick; ***W:*** Edward Zwick, Menno Meyjes, Lawrence Wright; ***C:*** Roger Deakins; ***M:*** Graeme Revell. Golden Raspberries '98: Worst Actor (Willis).

The Siege of Firebase Gloria 🦴½ **1989** Story of the Marines who risked their lives defending an outpost against overwhelming odds during the 1968 Tet offensive in Vietnam. Purportedly patriotic war drama made by an Australian director; lead Hauser is a disgusting sadist, and plot is hopelessly hackneyed. **95m/C VHS.** Wings Hauser, R. Lee Ermey, Mark Neely, Gary Hershberger, Clyde Jones, Margi Gerard, Richard Kuhlman, David Anderson, Robert Arevalo, John Calvin, Albert "Poppy" Popwell; ***D:*** Brian Trenchard-Smith; ***W:*** Tony Johnston, William Nagle; ***C:*** Joe Batac; ***M:*** Paul Schutze.

Siegfried 🦴🦴🦴🦴 *Siegfrieds Tod; Siegfried's Death* **1924** Half of Lang's epic masterpiece "Der Niebelungen," based on German mythology. Title hero bathes in the blood of a dragon he has slain. He marries a princess, but wicked Queen Brumhilde has him killed. Part two, in which Siegfried's widow marries Attila the Hun, is titled "Kriemheld's Revenge." These dark, brooding, archetypal tours de force were patriotic tributes, and were loved by Hitler. Silent with music score. **100m/B VHS.** *GE* Paul Richter, Margareta Schoen; ***D:*** Fritz Lang.

Siesta 🦴🦴½ **1987 (R)** Barkin is a professional stunt woman who leaves her current lover/manager, played by Sheen, and returns to visit her former lover and trainer, Byrne, on the eve of his marriage to another woman. Her trip, marked by flashbacks and flights of seemingly paranoid fantasy, leads to the discovery of murder, but she cannot remember who, when, why, or where. The film distorts time, reality, and perception in a sometimes fascinating, sometimes frustrating psychological mystery. Attractively filmed by video director Lambert. Barkin and Byrne were married in real life a year after the film's release. **97m/C VHS.** Ellen Barkin, Gabriel Byrne, Jodie Foster, Julian Sands, Isabella Rossellini, Martin Sheen, Grace Jones, Alexei Sayle; ***D:*** Mary Lambert; ***W:*** Patricia Louisianna Knop; ***M:*** Miles Davis, Marcus Miller.

The Sign of Four 🦴½ **1983** Sherlock Holmes and the ever-faithful Watson are hired by a young woman who has been anonymously sent an enormous diamond. An inept production which looks good but that's all. **97m/C VHS, DVD.** *GB* Ian Richardson, David Healy, Thorley Walters, Cherie Lunghi; ***D:*** Desmond Davis; ***W:*** Charles Edward Pogue; ***C:*** Denis Lewiston; ***M:*** Harry Rabinowitz.

The Sign of Four 🦴🦴½ **2001** Holmes (Frewer), Watson (Welsh), and the Baker Street Irregulars are invovled in murder, poison darts, a fortune in Indian jewels, and much suspicious behavior. **120m/C VHS.** *CA* Matt Frewer, Kenneth Welsh, Marcel Jeannin, Sophie Lorain, Edward Yankie, Michel Perron, Kevin Woodhouse; ***D:*** Rodney Gibbons; ***W:*** Joe Wiesenfeld; ***C:*** Eric Cayla; ***M:*** Marc Ouellette. CABLE

The Sign of the Cross 🦴🦴½ **1933** Depraved Emperor Nero (Laughton) decides he wants a new city so he burns down Rome—blaming the fire on the Christians he also wants to get rid of (preferably by the lions in the arena). Meanwhile, Marcus (March), the Roman Prefect, has fallen for the virginal Christian Mercia (Landi) and risks his life to save her. Besides Laughton's overwhelmingly hammy performance, Colbert slinks seductively as the emperor's vixenish wife, Poppaea. Again, lots of crowd scenes (DeMille's specialty). Based on the play by Wilson Barrett. **125m/B VHS.** Fredric March, Elissa Landi, Charles Laughton, Claudette Colbert, Ian Keith, Harry Beresford, Arthur Hohl, Nat Pendleton; ***D:*** Cecil B. DeMille; ***W:*** Waldemar Young, Sidney Buchman; ***M:*** Rudolph Kopp.

The Sign of Zorro 🦴🦴 **1960** Adventures of the masked swordsman as he champions the cause of the oppressed in early California. Full-length version of the popular late-50s Disney TV series. **89m/C VHS.** Guy Williams, Henry Calvin, Gene Sheldon, Romney Brent, Britt Lomond, George Lewis, Lisa Gaye; ***D:*** Norman Foster, Lewis R. Foster.

Signal 7 🦴🦴 **1983** An improvised, neo-verite document of a night in the lives of two San Francisco taxi drivers. Nilsson's first major release and a notable example of his unique scriptless, tape-to-film narrative technique. **89m/C VHS.** Bill Ackridge, Dan Leegant; ***D:*** Rob Nilsson; ***W:*** Rob Nilsson.

Signs **2002** Shyamalan takes on crop circles. Widowed father and lapsed minister Gibson is living on a farm with younger brother Phoenix when the mysterious circles appear in the cornfields. Film was shot in the director's native Pennsylvania. Not yet reviewed. **?m/C VHS, DVD.** Mel Gibson, Joaquin Rafael (Leaf) Phoenix, Rory Culkin, Abigail Breslin, Cherry Jones, Michael Showalter; ***D:*** M. Night Shyamalan; ***W:*** M. Night Shyamalan.

Signs & Wonders 🦴🦴 **2000** Commodities trader Alec (Skarsgard) has been living in Athens with wife Marjoire (Rampling) and their children. He begins an affair with sultry co-worker Katherine (Unger) and abandons his family to go to the States with her and then changes his mind. However, when he returns to Athens, Alec discovers Marjorie has moved on with her own lover, Andreas (Katalifos). But Alec isn't giving up and the consequences are unexpected. **108m/C VHS, DVD.** *FR* Stellan Skarsgard, Charlotte Rampling, Deborah Kara Unger, Dimitris Katalifos, Ashley Remy, Michael Cook; ***D:*** Jonathan Nossiter; ***W:*** Jonathan Nossiter, James Lasdun; ***C:*** Yorgos Arvanitis; ***M:*** Adrian Utley.

Signs of Life 🦴🦴 *Lebenszeichen* **1968** German soldier Stroszek (Brogle), injured during the occupation of Crete, is sent to recuperate on the remote island of Kos. With his Greek wife Nora, Stroszek has nothing to do but guard a deserted fortress and a store of abandoned ammunition. But soon the suspicious natives and the isolation begin to drive Stroszek to madness and he decides to blow up the ammunition dump (and the island along with it). German with subtitles. **90m/B VHS.** *GE* Peter Brogle, Wolfgang Reichmann, Athina Zacharopoulous, Wolfgang Stumpf; ***D:*** Werner Herzog; ***W:*** Werner Herzog; ***C:*** Thomas Mauch; ***M:*** Stavros Xarchakos.

Signs of Life 🦴🦴½ *One for Sorrow, Two for Joy* **1989 (PG-13)** A boat-building company in Maine closes its doors after centuries in business; the employees and families whose lives have been defined by it for generations learn to cope. Wonderful performances compensate only partly for a week script. An episode on PBS's "American Playhouse." **95m/C VHS.** Beau Bridges, Arthur Kennedy, Vincent D'Onofrio, Kevin J. O'Connor, Will Patton, Kate Reid, Michael Lewis, Kathy Bates, Mary-Louise Parker, Georgia Engel; ***D:*** John David Coles; ***W:*** Mark Malone; ***C:*** Elliot Davis; ***M:*** Howard Shore.

Silas Marner 🦴🦴🦴 **1985** Superb adaptation of the 1861 George Eliot classic about an itinerant weaver subjected to criminal accusation, poverty, and exile. Wonderful detail and splendid acting. Shot on location in the Cotswold district of England. **92m/C VHS.** *GB* Ben Kingsley, Jenny Agutter, Patrick Ryecart, Patsy Kensit; ***D:*** Giles Foster; ***M:*** Carl Davis. TV

The Silence 🦴🦴🦴 *Tystnaden* **1963** A brutal, enigmatic allegory about two sisters, one a nymphomaniac, the other a violently frustrated lesbian, traveling with the former's young son to an unnamed country beset by war. Fascinating and memorable but frustrating and unsatisfying: What is it about? What is it an allegory of? Where is the narrative? The third in Bergman's crisis-of-faith trilogy following "Through a Glass Darkly" and "Winter Light." In Swedish with English subtitles or dubbed. **95m/B VHS.** *SW* Ingrid Thulin, Gunnel Lindstrom, Birger Malmsten; ***D:*** Ingmar Bergman; ***W:*** Ingmar Bergman; ***C:*** Sven Nykvist.

Silence 🦴🦴 *Crazy Jack and the Boy* **1973 (G)** An autistic boy gets lost in the wilderness and faces an array of difficulties while his foster parents search for him. **82m/C VHS.** Will Geer, Ellen Geer, Richard Kelton, Ian Geer Flanders, Craig Kelly; ***D:*** John Korty.

Silence Like Glass 🦴🦴½ **1990 (R)** Diagnosed with life-threatening illness, two young women struggle to overcome their anger at their fate. They find friendship and together, search for reasons to live. Fine performances, with pacing that keeps the melodrama to a minimum. **102m/C VHS.** Jami Gertz, Martha Plimpton, George Peppard, Rip Torn, James Remar; ***D:*** Carl Schenkel; ***M:*** Anne Dudley.

The Silence of Neto 🦴🦴 *Silencio de Neto* **1994** A sheltered young boy comes of age in Guatemala during the early 1950s, a period marked by political upheaval and Cold War paranoia. His relationship with his socialist-leaning uncle causes family friction as it reflects on a repressive society and calls for reform. Spanish with subtitles. **106m/C VHS.** ***D:*** Luis Argueta; ***W:*** Luis Argueta; ***C:*** Ramon Suarez.

Silence of the Hams 🦴½ **1993 (R)** Very feeble parody of "The Silence of the Lambs" and others in the thriller/horror genre. Director/writer Greggio also stars as the murder victim, stabbed in the shower, who narrates the story in flashback. There's an eager FBI recruit, a femme fatale, assorted cameo turns, and DeLuise, chewing more scenery than even Anthony Hopkins could swallow, as nutcase Dr. Animal Cannibal Pizza. **85m/C VHS.** Ezio Greggio, Dom DeLuise, Billy Zane, Joanna Pacula, Charlene Tilton, Martin Balsam; ***Cameos:*** Stuart Pankin, John Astin, Phyllis Diller, Bubba Smith, Larry Storch, Rip Taylor, Shelley Winters, Mel Brooks, John Landis, John Carpenter, Joe Dante; ***D:*** Ezio Greggio; ***W:*** Ezio Greggio; ***C:*** Jacques Haitkin.

Silence of the Heart 🦴🦴🦴 **1984** Mother copes with aftermath of suicide of teenage son following her recent divorce. Hartley is captivating in this gripping drama. **100m/C VHS.** Mariette Hartley, Dana Hill, Howard Hesseman, Chad Lowe, Charlie Sheen; ***D:*** Richard Michaels; ***W:*** Phil Penningroth; ***M:*** Georges Delerue.

The Silence of the Lambs 🦴🦴🦴½ **1991 (R)** Foster is FBI cadet Clarice Starling, a woman with ambition, a cum laude degree in psychology, and a traumatic childhood. When a serial killer begins his ugly rounds, the FBI wants psychological profiles from other serial killers and she's sent to collect a profile from one who's exceptionally clever—psychiatrist Hannibal Lecter, a vicious killer prone to dining on his victims. Brilliant performances from Foster and Hopkins, finely detailed supporting characterizations, and elegant pacing from Demme. Some brutal visual effects. Excellent portrayals of women who refuse to be victims. Based on the Thomas Harris novel. **118m/C VHS, DVD, Wide.** Jodie Foster, Anthony Hopkins, Scott Glenn, Ted Levine, Brooke Smith, Charles Napier, Roger Corman, Anthony Heald, Diane Baker, Chris Isaak; ***D:*** Jonathan Demme; ***W:*** Ted Tally; ***C:*** Tak Fujimoto; ***M:*** Howard Shore. Oscars '91: Actor (Hopkins), Actress (Foster), Adapt. Screenplay, Director (Demme), Picture; AFI '98: Top 100; British Acad. '91: Actor (Hopkins), Actress (Foster); Directors Guild '91: Director (Demme); Golden Globes '92: Actress—Drama (Foster); Natl. Bd. of Review '91: Director (Demme), Film, Support. Actor (Hopkins); N.Y. Film Critics '91: Actor (Hopkins), Actress (Foster), Director (Demme), Film; Writers Guild '91: Adapt. Screenplay.

Silence of the North 🦴🦴½ **1981 (PG)** A widow (Burstyn) with three children struggles to survive under rugged pioneer conditions on the Canadian frontier. The scenery is, not surprisingly, stunning. Based on a true but generic story. **94m/C VHS.** *CA* Ellen Burstyn, Tom Skerritt; ***D:*** Allan Winton King; ***M:*** Michael Conway Baker.

The Silencer 🦴🦴 **1992 (R)** Walden stars as Harley-riding Angel who is out to stop a slavery and prostitution ring that abuses young runaways. Video-arcades hold the clues, and Angel must learn to kill without a conscience. Every time she kills, Angel seeks comfort in the arms of anonymous lovers. However, what she doesn't know is that her demented ex-boyfriend is watching. **85m/C VHS.** Lynette Walden, Chris Mulkey, Paul Ganus, Morton Downey Jr.; ***D:*** Amy Goldstein; ***W:*** Amy Goldstein, Scott Kraft.

The Silencer 🦴🦴 **1999 (R)** FBI agent Jason Wells (Elliott) fakes his own death in order to assume a new identity for a new assignment. Now known as Jason Black, he's an eager would-be assassin who wants to join the terrorist organization Division 5 where he can learn from master marksman Quinn Simmons (Dudikoff). But when Jason learns what's really behind his mission, things aren't so simple after all. **92m/C VHS.** *CA* Michael Dudikoff, Brennan Elliott, Gabrielle Miller, Terence Kelly, Peter Lacroix; ***D:*** Robert Lee; ***M:*** Peter Allen. **VIDEO**

The Silencers 🦴🦴½ **1966** Rompy spy spoof is the first of Martin's Matt Helm films, made to take advantage of the James Bond craze. Sexy secret agent man Helm must save the American atomic missile system from sabotage by Big O, the organization headed by Tung-Tze (Buono). That is if Matt can stay away from the babes and the booze. Based on the novels "The Silencers" and "Death of a Citizen" by Donald Hamilton. Followed by "Murderer's Row" (1966), "The Ambushers" (1967), and "The Wrecking Crew" (1968). **103m/C VHS.** Dean Martin, Victor Buono, Stella Stevens, Daliah Lavi, Arthur O'Connell, Robert Webber, James Gregory, Nancy Kovack, Roger C. Carmel, Cyd Charisse; ***D:*** Phil Karlson; ***W:*** Oscar Saul; ***C:*** Burnett Guffey; ***M:*** Elmer Bernstein.

The Silencers 🦴🦴½ **1995 (R)** Secret Service agent Chuck Rafferty (Scalia) discovers that his latest enemies, known as the Men In Black, are actually human-appearing aliens seeking to conquer Earth. Now Rafferty's only hope is to team up with inter-galactic peace officer Condor (Christopher) to defeat this evil. **103m/C VHS.** Jack Scalia, Dennis Christopher, Clarence Williams III, Carlos Lauchu, Lucinda Weist; ***D:*** Richard Pepin.

The Silences of the Palace 🦴🦴🦴 *Les Silences du Palais* **1994** Set in 1950s Tunisia at the end of the ruling monarchy. Twenty-five-year-old Alia (Lacroix) returns to the run-down palace where she was born and grew up as the daughter of a lifelong servant, Khedija (Hedhili), who was also the sexual favorite of her master, Prince Sidi Ali (Fazaa). She remembers the limited, repressed existence they endured and realizes that, ten years after leaving the palace, she has traded one form of subjugation for another and has yet to find her own independence. Arabic with subtitles. **116m/C VHS.** *FR* Ghalia Lacroix, Amel Hedhili, Kamel Fazaa, Hend Sabri, Najia Overghi; ***D:*** Moufida Tlatli; ***W:*** Moufida Tlatli, Nouri Bouzid; ***C:*** Youssef Ben Youssef.

Silent Assassins 🦴🦴 **1988** Fists and bullets fly when a scientist is kidnapped in order to gain secrets to biological warfare. Chong and Rhee, real-life owners of a martial arts studio, produced and choreographed the film. Blair is here, but doesn't figure much. A notch up from most similar martial arts pics. **92m/C VHS.** Sam Jones, Linda Blair, Jun Chong, Phillip Rhee; ***D:*** Scott Thomas, Lee Doo-yong.

Silent Code 🦴 **1935** A Mountie is framed for the murder of a young miner. **55m/B VHS.** Tom Tyler, Blanche Mehaffey, Kane Richmond.

The Silent Enemy 🦴🦴½ **1958** The true-life exploits of British frogmen battling Italian foes during WWII. Suspenseful and engrossing; good performances and good rendering of underwater action. Video release snips 20 minutes from the original and adds color. **91m/C VHS.** *GB* Laurence Harvey, John Clements, Michael Craig, Dawn Addams, Sidney James, Alec McCowen, Nigel Stock; ***D:*** William Fairchild.

Silent Fall 🦴½ **1994 (R)** Grisly double murder of his parents is witnessed by autistic nine-year-old, Tim Warden (Faulkner), and his traumatized over-protective teenaged sister Sylvie (Tyler). Retired psychiatrist Jake Rainier (Dreyfuss) is reluctant to get involved, ever since an autistic child in his care died, but when authoritarian rival Dr. Harlinger (Lithgow) is called instead, Jake changes his mind. Second half of film takes a lurid turn as Jake probes Tim's damaged psyche to discover the killer. Trite, clueless whodunnit that generally wastes the talent involved; Tyler and Faulkner make their film debuts. **101m/C VHS, DVD, Wide.** Richard Dreyfuss, Ben Faulkner, John Lithgow, Liv Tyler, Linda Hamilton, J.T. Walsh; ***D:*** Bruce Beresford; ***W:*** Akiva Goldsman; ***C:*** Peter James; ***M:*** Stewart Copeland.

Silent Hunter 🦴½ **1994 (R)** Undercover cop Jim Paradine (O'Keeffe) retreats to a remote mountains cabin when his family is killed by a gang of bank robbers. Naturally, the thugs just happen to crash land on Paradine's mountain top with their stolen loot and he goes off to hunt them down. **97m/C VHS.** Miles O'Keeffe, Fred Williamson, Lynne Adams, Peter Colvey, Jason Cavalier, Sabine Karsenti; ***D:*** Fred Williamson.

Silent Killers 🦴½ **19??** A scientist is responsible for the deaths of many people because of his research in germ warfare. He's haunted by the ghosts of his victims. Is he losing his mind or is it a sinister plot? **90m/C VHS.** Stephen Soul, Daniel Garfield.

Silent Madness 🦴 **1984 (R)** A psychiatrist must stop a deranged killer, escaped from an asylum, from slaughtering helpless college coeds in a sorority house. Meanwhile, hospital execs send orderlies to kill the patient, to conceal their mistake. Ludicrous. **93m/C VHS.** Belinda J. Montgomery, Viveca Lindfors, Sydney Lassick; ***D:*** Simon Nuchtern.

The Silent Mr. Sherlock Holmes 🦴🦴 **1912** These two silent shorts are a rare treat for Holmes fans. "The Copper Beeches" was produced with the "personal supervision of Arthur Conan Doyle." In "The Man with the Twisted Lip," Holmes is hired to find out whether a banker was murdered. **68m/B VHS.** *GB* Ellie Norwood.

Silent Motive 🦴🦴½ **1991** Laura is a Hollywood screenwriter who's shocked to discover that a killer is using her recent script as an outline for a series of film-industry murders. She's even more unnerved when a detective makes Laura his number one suspect. **90m/C VHS.** Patricia Wettig, Mike Farrell, Ed Asner, Rick Springfield, David Packer; ***D:*** Lee Philips; ***W:*** William Bekkala.

Silent Movie 🦴🦴½ **1976 (PG)** A has-been movie director (Brooks) is determined to make a comeback and save his studio from being taken over by a conglomerate. Hilarious at times but uneven. An original idea; not as successful as it could have been. Has music and sound effects, but only one word of spoken dialogue by famous mime Marceau. **88m/C VHS.** Mel Brooks, Marty Feldman, Dom DeLuise, Burt Reynolds, Anne Bancroft, James Caan, Liza Minnelli, Paul Newman, Sid Caesar, Bernadette Peters, Harry Ritz, Marcel Marceau; ***D:*** Mel Brooks; ***W:*** Mel Brooks, Ron Clark, Rudy DeLuca, Barry Levinson.

Silent Night, Bloody Night 🦴🦴 *Night of the Dark Full Moon; Death House* **1973 (R)** An escaped lunatic terrorizes a small New England town, particularly a mansion that was once an insane asylum. Not great, but well done by director Gershuny, with some nail-biting suspense and slick scene changes. **83m/C VHS.** Patrick O'Neal, John Carradine, Walter Abel, Mary Woronov, Astrid Heeren, Candy Darling; ***D:*** Theodore Gershuny.

Silent Night, Deadly Night 🦴 **1984 (R)** A psycho ax-murders people while dressed as jolly old St. Nick. Violent and disturbing, to say the least. Caused quite a controversy when it was released to theatres. Santa gimmick sold some tickets at the time, but resist the urge to rent it: it's completely devoid of worth, whatever the killer's outfit. As if one were not enough, we've been blessed with four sequels. **92m/C VHS.** Lilyan Chauvin, Gilmer McCormick, Toni Nero; ***D:*** Charles E. Sellier; ***M:*** Perry Botkin.

Silent Night, Deadly Night 2 🦴 **1987 (R)** The psychotic little brother of the psychotic, Santa Claus-dressed killer from the first film exacts revenge, covering the same bloody ground as before. Almost half this sequel consists of scenes lifted whole from the original. **88m/C VHS.** Eric Freeman, James Newman, Elizabeth (Kaitan) Cayton, Jean Miller; ***D:*** Lee Harry; ***M:*** Michael Armstrong.

Silent Night, Deadly Night 3: Better Watch Out! 🦴½ **1989 (R)** The now grown-up psycho goes up against a young blind woman. Santa is no longer the bad guy, thank goodness. The least bad of the lot, with black humor—though not enough to make it worth seeing. **90m/C VHS.** Richard Beymer, Bill Moseley, Samantha Scully, Eric (DaRe) Da Re, Laura Herring, Robert Culp; ***D:*** Monte Hellman.

Silent Night, Deadly Night 4: Initiation 🦴 **1990 (R)** A secret L.A. cult of she-demons use the slasher Ricky for their own ends—making for more mayhem and horror. Has virtually nothing to do with the other "sequels"—which is not to say it's very good. **90m/C VHS.** Maud Adams, Allyce Beasley, Clint Howard, Reggie Bannister; ***D:*** Brian Yuzna.

Silent Night, Deadly Night 5: The Toymaker 🦴🦴 **1991 (R)** A young boy's Christmas is overrun by murderous Santas and viscious stuffed animals. Definitely for fans of the genre only. **90m/C VHS.** Mickey Rooney, William Thorne, Jane Higginson.

Silent Night, Lonely Night 🦴🦴 **1969** Two lonely middle-aged people (Bridges and Jones) begin an affair at Christmas to stem the pain of their separately disintegrating marriages. Poignant but not successfully credible. Based on the play by Robert Anderson. **98m/C VHS.** Lloyd Bridges, Shirley Jones, Jeff Bridges, Cloris Leachman, Carrie Snodgress, Lynn Carlin; ***D:*** Daniel Petrie; ***M:*** Billy Goldenberg. **TV**

The Silent One 🦴½ **1986** Featuring underwater photography by Ron and Valerie Taylor, this is the odd story of a mysterious Polynesian boy who has a nautical relationship with a sea turtle. **96m/C VHS.** *NZ* Telo Malese, George Henare; ***D:*** Yvonne Mackay.

The Silent Partner 🦴🦴🦴 **1978** A bank teller (Gould) foils a robbery, but manages to take some money for himself. The unbalanced robber (Plummer) knows it and wants the money. Good script and well directed, with emphasis on suspense and detail. Unexpectedly violent at times. Early, non-comedic role for big guy Candy. **103m/C VHS.** *CA* Elliott Gould, Christopher Plummer, Susannah York, John Candy; ***D:*** Daryl Duke; ***W:*** Curtis Hanson; ***C:*** Billy Williams.

The Silent Passenger 🦴🦴½ **1935** Amateur sleuth Lord Peter Wimsey makes cinematic debut investigating murder and blackmail on the British railway. Dorothy Sayer's character later inspired BBC mystery series. **75m/B VHS.** *GB* John Loder, Peter Haddon, Mary Newland, Austin Trevor, Donald Wolfit, Leslie Perrins, Aubrey Mather, Ralph Truman; ***D:*** Reginald Denham.

Silent Predators 🦴🦴 **1999** SNAKE! Of course, not any any snake but mean hybrid rattlesnakes who slither over a small California desert town when an explosion at a construction site disturbs their home. And it's up to fire chief Hamlin to save the town! If the snakes are half as creepy as the video box art, this is one seriously scary snake movie. **91m/C VHS.** Harry Hamlin, Shannon Sturges, Patty McCormack, Jack Scalia, David Spielberg, Beau Billingslea; ***D:*** Noel Nosseck; ***W:*** John Carpenter, Matt Dorff; ***C:*** John Stokes; ***M:*** Michael Tavera. **CABLE**

Silent Rage 🦴 **1982 (R)** Sheriff Norris of a small Texas town must destroy killer Libby who has been made indestructible through genetic engineering. Chuck Norris meets Frankenstein, sort of. Nice try, but still thoroughly stupid and boring. **100m/C VHS, DVD, 8mm, Wide.** Chuck Norris, Ron Silver, Steven Keats, Toni Kalem, Brian Libby, Stephen Furst; ***D:*** Michael Miller; ***W:*** Joseph Fraley; ***C:*** Robert C. Jessup, Neil Roach; ***M:*** Peter Bernstein.

Silent Raiders 🦴 **1954** A commando unit is sent to France in 1943 to knock out a Nazi communications center. **72m/B VHS.** Richard Bartlett, Earle Lyon, Jeanette Bordeau; ***M:*** Elmer Bernstein.

Silent Rebellion 🦴½ **1982** A Greek immigrant (Savalas) and his son return to Greece, where they reunite with mother and brother and re-discover their heritage and each other. Cross-cultural misunderstandings abound; could have been interesting, but the story is just too generic and uninspired. **90m/C VHS.** Telly Savalas, Keith Gordon, Michael Constantine, Yula Gavala.

Silent Running 🦴🦴🦴 **1971 (G)** Members of a space station orbiting Saturn care for the last vegetation of a nuclear-devastated earth. When orders come to destroy the vegetation, Dern takes matters into his own hands. Speculative sci-fi at its best. Trumbull's directorial debut; he created special effects for "2001" and "Close Encounters." Strange music enhances the alien atmosphere. **90m/C VHS, DVD, Wide.** Bruce Dern, Cliff (Potter) Potts, Ron Rifkin; ***D:*** Douglas Trumbull; ***W:*** Michael Cimino, Deric Washburn, Steven Bochco; ***C:*** Charles F. Wheeler; ***M:*** Prof. Peter Schickele.

Silent Scream 🦴½ **1980 (R)** College kids take up residence with the owners of an eerie mansion complete with obligatory murders. Obvious to the point of being gratuitous—and just plain uninteresting. **87m/C VHS.** Rebecca Balding, Cameron Mitchell, Avery Schreiber, Barbara Steele, Steve Doubet, Brad Reardon, Yvonne De Carlo; ***D:*** Denny Harris; ***W:*** Wallace C. Bennett, Jim Wheat, Ken Wheat; ***C:*** Michael D. Murphy, David Shore.

Silent Scream 🦴 **1984** A former Nazi concentration camp commandant collects unusual animals and humans as a hobby. **60m/C VHS.** *GB* Peter Cushing, Brian Cox, Elaine Donnelly; ***D:*** Alan Gibson.

Silent Tongue 🦴🦴 **1992 (PG-13)** Weird western finds the crazed Talbot Roe (Phoenix) alone in the wilderness, guarding the tree that is the burial place of his half-breed wife Awbonnie (Tousey). Roe's father (Harris) bought his son's bride from her greedy and abusive father McCree (Bates). In an effort to return Talbot to some semblance of normality, Roe offers to buy McCree's other daughter (Ardondo) for his son. But Talbot is haunted by his wife's angry ghost, who wants her spirit set free by ritual burning, and McCree himself fears the vengeance of his one-time Indian wife Silent Tongue

(Cardinal). Messy, over-the-top plot with some poignant performances, especially Phoenix's. **101m/C VHS.** River Phoenix, Sheila Tousey, Richard Harris, Alan Bates, Jeri Arredondo, Dermot Mulroney, Tantoo Cardinal; ***Cameos:*** Bill Irwin, David Shiner; ***D:*** Sam Shepard; ***W:*** Sam Shepard; ***C:*** Jack Conroy; ***M:*** Patrick O'Hearn.

The Silent Touch 🦴🦴½ **1994 (PG-13)** Irascible, aged composer Henry Kesdi (Von Sydow), living in Denmark with his long-suffering wife Helena (Miles), hasn't written a note in 40 years. Music student Stefan (Blutheau) dreams of a composition he believes Henry started but never completed. So Stefan naturally sets out to help Henry finish his symphony by mystically healing his composer's block. Yes, it does sound hokey but the fluff is saved by Von Sydow's buoyantly funny performance. **92m/C VHS.** *PL DK GB* Max von Sydow, Lothaire Bluteau, Sarah Miles, Sofie Graboel, Aleksander Bardini, Peter Hesse Overgaard; ***D:*** Krzysztof Zanussi; ***W:*** Peter Morgan, Mark Wadlow; ***M:*** Wojciech Kilar.

Silent Trigger 🦴🦴 **1997 (R)** Special Forces commando Shooter (Lundgren) becomes a paid assassin for an undercover agency but an ill-fated mission causes him and partner Spotter (Bellman) to question the agency, who then decide the duo are expendable. Fast-paced with some eye-catching action sequences. **94m/C VHS.** Dolph Lundgren, Gina Bellman, George Jenesky; ***D:*** Russell Mulcahy; ***W:*** Sergio D. Altieri; ***C:*** David Franco; ***M:*** Stefano Mainetti.

Silent Valley 🦴 **1935** Adventure of the Old West with American cowboy star Tom Tyler. **60m/B VHS.** Tom Tyler.

Silent Victim 🦴🦴½ **1992 (R)** Greene stars as Bonnie Jackson, a Georgia housewife whose marriage has not only gone wrong but turned violent. She takes a drug overdose in a suicide attempt but it results only in a miscarriage. Her furious husband sues her for the murder of their unborn child while an ambitious district attorney petitions the state to charge Bonnie with committing an illegal abortion. Bonnie's torment soon becomes a media circus as she goes on trial. Based on a true story. **116m/C VHS.** Michele Greene, Kyle Secor, Ely Pouget, Alex Hyde-White, Dori Brenner, Leann Hunley; ***D:*** Menahem Golan; ***W:*** Nelly Adnil, Jonathan Platnick; ***M:*** William T. Stromberg.

Silent Victory: The Kitty O'Neil Story 🦴🦴🦴 **1979** Genuinely stirring real-life-overcoming-adversity story of the deaf woman who became a top stunt woman in Hollywood and holder of the land speed record for women. Channing is very good as O'Neil. Made for television. **96m/C** Stockard Channing, Brian Dennehy, Colleen Dewhurst, Edward Albert, James Farentino; ***D:*** Lou Antonio. **TV**

Silent Witness 🦴 **1985 (R)** A woman (Bertinelli) witnesses her brother-in-law and his friend rape a young woman. She must decide whether to testify against them or keep the family secret. Exploitative and weakly plotted. Rip-off of the much-discussed Massachusetts barroom rape case. **97m/C VHS.** Valerie Bertinelli, John Savage, Chris Nash, Melissa Leo, Pat Corley, Steven Williams, Jacqueline Brookes, Alex McArthur, Katie McCombs; ***D:*** Michael Miller. **TV**

Silent Witness 🦴🦴½ *Do Not Disturb* **1999 (R)** Walter Richmond (Hurt) and his wife Cathryn (Tilly) are in Amsterdam with their mute daughter Melissa so Walter can close a business deal. But Melissa witnesses a murder and then disappears, leaving her frantic parents to find her before the killers do. This one turns out to be more of a parody of the thriller genre than a serious example. **94m/C VHS, DVD.** William Hurt, Jennifer Tilly, Denis Leary, Francesca Brown, Michael Chiklis, Michael Goorjian; ***D:*** Dick Maas.

Silhouette 🦴🦴 **1991 (R)** Detained in a small Texas town, a woman witnesses the murder of a local girl—but in silhouette, so the killer's identity takes a feature-length running time to resolve. A fair but contrived thriller that the leading lady coproduced. **89m/C VHS.** Faye Dunaway, David Rasche, John Terry, Carlos Gomez, Ron Campbell, Margaret Blye, Talisa Soto, Ritch Brinkley; ***D:*** Carl Schenkel; ***W:*** Victor Buell. **CABLE**

Silicon Towers 🦴½ **1999 (PG-13)** Charlie Cook (Quint) is suddenly promoted to an executive position at Silicon Towers. But a mysterious e-mail warns him that the corporation is illegally accessing bank accounts worldwide and then Charlie gets accused of embezzling. **95m/C VHS, DVD.** Jonathan Quint, Brian Dennehy, Daniel Baldwin, Robert Guillaume, Brad Dourif; ***D:*** Serge Rodnunsky; ***W:*** Serge Rodnunsky. **VIDEO**

Silk 🦴 **1986 (R)** A beautiful and bloodthirsty detective cuts a swath through local heroin rings. **84m/C VHS.** Cec Verrell, Bill McLaughlin, Fred Bailey; ***D:*** Cirio H. Santiago.

Silk 2 🦴 **1989 (R)** A foreign-made sequel, in which a beautiful cop stops crime in Honolulu. Ludicrous plot, bad acting, lots of skin and violence—what more could you want? Dreadful. **85m/C VHS.** Monique Gabrielle, Peter Nelson, Jan Merlin, Maria Clair; ***D:*** Cirio H. Santiago.

Silk Degrees 🦴½ **1994 (R)** Actress witnesses a murder and is targeted for elimination by the killer. She's supposed to be protected by a couple of federal agents but it seems there's a traitor around. **81m/C VHS.** Deborah Shelton, Marc Singer, Mark Hamill, Michael Des Barres, Charles Napier, Gilbert Gottfried, Adrienne Barbeau; ***D:*** Armand Garabidian; ***W:*** Stuart Gibbs, Douglas J. Sloan, Robert Gottlieb; ***M:*** Larry Wolff.

Silk 'n' Sabotage 🦴½ *Wildchild 2* **1994** Serious-minded Jamie comes up with a program for a new computer game. When it's stolen by a con artist, Jamie and her frivolous roommates team up to retrieve it. Since the roomies operate a lingerie business there's lots of pulchritude on display. Also available unrated. **70m/C VHS, DVD.** Cherilyn Shea, Stephanie Champlin, Julie Skiru; ***D:*** Joe Cauley.

The Silk Road 🦴🦴½ **1992 (PG-13)** In 11th-century China the ancient trading route leads to Dun Huang, a desert city that is the last Chinese outpost on the road. Zhao, a young scholar, travels in a caravan which is attacked by Chinese mercenaries. His life is spared and when his new home is attacked by a neighboring nation, he hides the city's treasures in nearby caves. Adapted from the novel by Yashushi Inoue, which was based on the Thousand Buddha Caves, where a treasure of Buddhist icons and scrolls were discovered in 1900. Billed as an epic, there's lots of pageantry and some impressive battle scenes but is too stately and overdone to be more than merely interesting. In Japanese with English subtitles. **99m/C VHS.** *CH JP* Koichi Sato, Toshiyuki Nishida, Anna Nakagawa, Tsunehiko Watase, Daijiro Harada, Takahiro Tamura; ***D:*** Junya Sato; ***M:*** Masaru Sato.

Silk Stockings 🦴🦴🦴 **1957** Splendid musical comedy adaptation of "Ninotchka," with Astaire as a charming American movie man, and Charisse as the cold Soviet official whose commie heart he melts. Music and lyrics by Cole Porter highlight this film adapted from George S. Kaufman's hit Broadway play. Director Mamoulian's last film. ♫Too Bad; Paris Loves Lovers; Fated to Be Mated; The Ritz Roll 'n Rock; Silk Stockings; Red Blues; All of You; Stereophonic Sound; Josephine. **117m/C VHS, Wide.** Fred Astaire, Cyd Charisse, Janis Paige, Peter Lorre, George Tobias; ***D:*** Rouben Mamoulian; ***W:*** Mary St. Feint; ***M:*** Andre Previn.

Silkwood 🦴🦴🦴 **1983 (R)** The story of Karen Silkwood, who died in a 1974 car crash under suspicious circumstances. She was a nuclear plant worker and activist who was investigating shoddy practices at the plant. Streep acts up a storm, disappearing completely into her character. Cher surprises with her fine portrayal of a lesbian co-worker, and Russell is also good. Nichols has a tough time since we already know the ending, but he brings top-notch performances from his excellent cast. **131m/C VHS, DVD.** Meryl Streep, Kurt Russell, Cher, Diana Scarwid, Bruce McGill, Fred Ward, David Strathairn, Ron Silver, Josef Sommer, Craig T. Nelson; ***D:*** Mike Nichols; ***W:*** Nora Ephron, Alice Arlen; ***C:*** Miroslav Ondricek; ***M:*** Georges Delerue. Golden Globes '84: Support. Actress (Cher).

Silver Bandit 🦴 **1947** A bookkeeper is sent to investigate a mine theft. Along the way he sings country and western songs. **54m/B VHS.** Spade Cooley.

Silver Bears 🦴🦴 **1978 (PG)** Las Vegas mobster Balsam hires con man Caine and sends him to Switzerland to buy a bank for laundering purposes. Only a bankrupt prince (Jourdan) entices Caine into a scheme to control the world's silver market and he ends up being swindled himself. So-so entry adapted from the novel by Paul Erdman. **114m/C VHS.** Michael Caine, Cybill Shepherd, Louis Jourdan, Stephane Audran, David Warner, Tom Smothers, Martin Balsam, Jay Leno, Charles Gray, Joss Ackland; ***D:*** Ivan Passer; ***M:*** Claude Bolling.

The Silver Bullet **1934** Follows the adventures of Tom, the sheriff of a small gold mining town. **55m/C VHS.** Tom Tyler, Jayne Regan, Lafe (Lafayette) McKee, Charles King, George Chesebro, Charles "Slim" Whitaker, Lew Meehan, Franklyn Farnum, Walt Williams; ***D:*** Bernard B. Ray.

Silver Bullet 🦴🦴 *Stephen King's Silver Bullet* **1985 (R)** Adapted from Stephen King's "Cycle of the Werewolf," about a town whose inhabitants are being brutally murdered. It finally dawns on them the culprit is a werewolf. Action moves along at a good clip and the film has its share of suspense. **94m/C VHS, DVD, Wide.** Corey Haim, Gary Busey, Megan Follows, Everett McGill, Robin Groves, Leon Russom, Terry O'Quinn, Bill Smitrovich, Kent Broadhurst, Lawrence Tierney; ***D:*** Daniel Attias; ***W:*** Stephen King; ***C:*** Armando Nannuzzi.

The Silver Chalice 🦴 **1954** Newman's career somehow survived his movie debut in this bloated, turgid Biblical epic about the momentous events that befall a young Greek sculptor who fashions a holder for the cup that was used at the Last Supper. Newman later took out an ad in Variety to apologize for the film, in which Greene also made his debut. Based on the novel by Thomas Costain. **135m/C VHS.** Paul Newman, Virginia Mayo, Pier Angeli, Jack Palance, Natalie Wood, Joseph Wiseman, Lorne Greene, E.G. Marshall; ***D:*** Victor Saville; ***M:*** Franz Waxman.

Silver City 🦴🦴 **1984 (PG)** A saga depicting the plight of Polish refugees in Australia in 1949. A pair of lovers find each other in a crowded refugee camp. He's married to her friend. Too-complex, slow but earnest effort. **110m/C VHS.** *AU* Gosia Dobrowolska, Ivar Kants; ***D:*** Sophia Turkiewicz.

Silver City Bonanza 🦴🦴½ **1951** Lots of action in this outrageous oater that includes a haunted ranch and an undersea battle as plot devices. Singing cowboy Allen and sidekick Ebsen use a seeing-eye dog to track down the killer of a blind man. Since Roy Rogers and Republic parted company the year of this film's release, singing star Allen was groomed to become the new "King of the Cowboys." However, by this time, the singing-cowboy craze was almost old hat. **67m/B VHS.** Rex Allen, Buddy Ebsen, Mary Ellen Kay, Billy Kimbley, Alix Ebsen, Bill Kennedy, Gregg Barton, Clem Bevans; ***D:*** George Blair; ***W:*** Bob Williams; ***C:*** John MacBurnie; ***M:*** Stanley Wilson.

Silver City Kid 🦴 **1945** Two mine owners learn about a rich mineral vein under a rancher's land, kill him, and then try to steal the property from his sister. So it's up to ranch foreman Jack Adams (Lane) to expose the plot and bring the guilty to justice. **56m/B VHS.** Allan "Rocky" Lane.

Silver Dream Racer 🦴½ **1983 (PG)** An English grease monkey wants to win the World Motorcycle Championship title away from an American biker. He's also after someone else's girlfriend. Boring, stilted, unoriginal "Big Race" flick. **103m/C VHS.** Beau Bridges, David Essex, Christina Raines, Diane Keen, Harry H. Corbett; ***D:*** David Wickes; ***M:*** David Essex.

The Silver Horde 🦴🦴½ **1930** Alaskan salmon fishery owner McCrea battles villainous competitor Gordon for both his livelihood and his ladyfriend—dancehall dame Brent. Arthur's the society gal who briefly catches McCrea's eye. Silent screen star Sweet ended her career with a brief role. Based on a novel by Rex Beach. **80m/B VHS.** Joel McCrea, Evelyn Brent, Jean Arthur, Gavin Gordon, Louis Wolheim, Raymond Hatton, Blanche Sweet; ***D:*** George Archainbaud.

Silver Lode 🦴🦴½ **1954** A man accused of murder on his wedding day attempts to clear his name while the law launches an intensive manhunt for him. Ordinary story improved by good, energetic cast. **92m/C VHS.** John Payne, Dan Duryea, Lizabeth Scott, Stuart Whitman; ***D:*** Allan Dwan.

Silver Queen 🦴🦴 **1942** A woman finds out her father has gambled away a silver mine and left her with debts. She opens a saloon, only to have her fiance use the money to hunt for more silver. **81m/B VHS.** Priscilla Lane, George Brent, Bruce Cabot, Eugene Pallette; ***D:*** Lloyd Bacon.

Silver River 🦴½ **1948** Average western that marked the final collaboration between director Walsh and star Flynn. It never even comes close to their previous works. Flynn plays a no-good, power-hungry cad who will stop at nothing to get what he wants. He happens to want Sheridan, who is married to Bennett, so Flynn schemes to get rid of him. Overall, Flynn acts as though he really isn't interested in the material and had to make a pact with Walsh that he would stay sober until five in the afternoon while filming. Based on an unpublished novel by Stephen Longstreet. **108m/B VHS.** Errol Flynn, Ann Sheridan, Thomas Mitchell, Bruce (Herman Brix) Bennett, Tom D'Andrea, Barton MacLane, Monte Blue, Jonathan Hale; ***D:*** Raoul Walsh; ***W:*** Stephen Longstreet, Harriet Frank Jr.; ***M:*** Max Steiner.

Silver Spurs 🦴½ **1943** Villain tries to get some oil-rich property by murdering the ranch's owner. Ranch foreman Rogers saves the day. **60m/B VHS.** Roy Rogers, Jerome Cowan, John Carradine, Phyllis Brooks, Smiley Burnette, Joyce Compton; ***D:*** Joseph Kane.

Silver Stallion 🦴½ **1941** Thunder the Wonder Horse plays the title character, who fights rattlesnakes, wild dogs and hoss thieves. Too bad he doesn't give acting lessons to the humans in this frail family western with nice scenery and action scenes. **59m/C VHS.** David Sharpe, Carol Hughes, Leroy Mason, Walter Long; ***D:*** Edward Finney.

The Silver Stallion: King of the Wild Brumbies 🦴🦴½ *The Silver Brumby* **1993 (G)** The adolescent Indi is enthralled as her writer-mother relates each new chapter in the saga of Thara, the amazing silver stallion. And she images each adventure as the horse triumphs over evil men, other horses, and the elements to become leader of the herd. Based on the Australian children's novel "The Silver Brumby" by Elyne Mitchell. **93m/C VHS.** *AU* Caroline Goodall, Ami Daemion, Russell Crowe; ***D:*** John Tatoulis; ***W:*** John Tatoulis, Jon Stephens; ***M:*** Tassos Ioannides.

Silver Star 🦴🦴 **1955** Man elected sheriff of a western town turns down the job because he is a pacifist. He changes his mind when his defeated opponent hires a trio of killers to come after him. **73m/B VHS.** Jimmy Wakely, Edgar Buchanan, Marie Windsor.

Silver Strand 🦴🦴½ **1995 (R)** Hunky Brian Del Piso (Bellows), a naval cadet in the S.E.A.L. training school, makes the big mistake of falling for sexy Michelle (Sheridan), who just happens to be an officer's wife. As if he didn't have enough challenges, should their affair be exposed Brian might just as well kiss his career goodbye. **104m/C VHS.** Gil Bellows, Nicolette Sheridan; ***D:*** George Miller; ***W:*** Douglas Day Stewart; ***C:*** David Connell; ***M:*** Joseph Conlan.

The Silver Streak 🦴🦴 **1934** The sickly son of a diesel train designer needs an iron lung—pronto. A rival's super-fast locomotive is the only hope for the boy. Murders, runaway engines, and a crew that would rather walk enliven this race against time. **72m/B VHS.** Sally Blane, Charles Starrett, Arthur Lake, Edgar Kennedy, William Farnum; ***D:*** Thomas Atkins.

Silver Streak 🦴🦴🦴 1976 (PG) Pooped exec Wilder rides a train from L.A. to Chicago, planning to enjoy a leisurely, relaxing trip. Instead he becomes involved with murder, intrigue, and a beautiful woman. Energetic Hitchcock parody features successful first pairing of Wilder and Pryor. **113m/C VHS.** Gene Wilder, Richard Pryor, Jill Clayburgh, Patrick McGoohan, Ned Beatty, Ray Walston, Richard Kiel, Scatman Crothers; ***D:*** Arthur Hiller; ***W:*** Colin Higgins; ***M:*** Henry Mancini.

Silverado 🦴🦴🦴 1985 (PG-13) Affectionate pastiche of western cliches has everything a viewer could ask for—except Indians. Straightforward plot has four virtuous cowboys rise up against a crooked lawman in a blaze of six guns. No subtlety from the first big Western in quite a while, but plenty of fun and laughs. **132m/C VHS, DVD, Wide.** Kevin Kline, Scott Glenn, Kevin Costner, Danny Glover, Brian Dennehy, Linda Hunt, John Cleese, Jeff Goldblum, Rosanna Arquette, Jeff Fahey; ***D:*** Lawrence Kasdan; ***W:*** Lawrence Kasdan; ***C:*** John Bailey; ***M:*** Bruce Broughton.

Simba 🦴🦴🦴 1955 A young Englishman arrives at his brother's Kenyan farm to find him murdered in a local skirmish between the Mau Maus and white settlers. Well made, thoughtful look at colonialism, racial animosity, and violence. **98m/C VHS.** *GB* Dirk Bogarde, Donald Sinden, Virginia McKenna, Orlando Martins; ***D:*** Brian Desmond Hurst; ***C:*** Geoffrey Unsworth.

Simon 🦴🦴½ 1980 (PG) A group of bored demented scientists brainwash a college professor into believing he is an alien from a distant galaxy, whereupon he begins trying to correct the evil in America. Screwball comedy, or semi-serious satire of some kind? Hard to tell. Some terrific set pieces but the movie as a whole doesn't quite hold together. Directorial debut of Brickman, who previously worked as a scriptwriter with Woody Allen ("Sleeper," etc.). **97m/C VHS.** Alan Arkin, Madeline Kahn, Fred Gwynne, Adolph Green, Wallace Shawn, Austin Pendleton; ***D:*** Marshall Brickman; ***W:*** Marshall Brickman, Thomas Baum.

Simon Birch 🦴🦴 *A Small Miracle* 1998 (PG) Young Simon Birch (Smith) believes he's destined to become a hero, and that his disability—dwarfism resulting from Morquio's syndrome—is actually a gift from God to facilitate his destiny. After his best friend Joe's idolized mother dies, the two decide to track down Joe's father, who hasn't been seen for years. The quest leads to the climactic disaster that is the impetus for the heroics Simon has been waiting for. Smith's onscreen presence is the main attraction, as most of the emotion and inspiration in the source material, John Irving's novel "A Prayer for Owen Meany," is absent. Irving demanded both the character name change (Meany to Birch) and a screen credit change—from "based on" to "suggested by." **110m/C VHS, DVD.** Ian Michael Smith, Joseph Mazzello, Ashley Judd, Oliver Platt, David Strathairn, Dana Ivey, Jan Hooks, Beatrice Winde, Ceciley Carroll, Sumela-Rose Keramidopulos, Sam Morton; ***D:*** Mark Steven Johnson; ***W:*** Mark Steven Johnson; ***C:*** Aaron Schneider; ***M:*** Marc Shaiman; ***Nar:*** Jim Carrey.

Simon Bolivar 🦴🦴½ 1969 The title character leads the Venezuelan revolution in 1817. **110m/C VHS.** Maximilian Schell, Rosanna Schiaffino.

Simon, King of the Witches 🦴🦴½ 1971 (R) An L.A. warlock who lives in a sewer drain finds himself the center of attention when his spells actually work. This interesting hippie/witchcraft entry bogs down now and then but Prine's performance is droll and lively. **90m/C VHS.** Andrew Prine, Brenda Scott, George Paulsin, Norman Burton, Ultra Violet; ***D:*** Bruce Kessler; ***W:*** Robert Phippeny; ***C:*** David L. Butler.

Simon of the Desert 🦴🦴🦴½ *Simon del Desierto* 1966 Not Bunuel's very best, but worthy of the master satirist. An ascetic stands on a pillar in the desert for several decades—closer to God, farther from temptation. Pinal is a gorgeous devil that tempts Simon. Hilarious, irreverent, sophisticated. What's with the weird ending, though? In Spanish with English subtitles. **46m/B VHS.** Claudio Brook, Silvia Pinal, Enrique Alvarez Felix; ***D:*** Luis Bunuel; ***W:*** Luis Bunuel; ***C:*** Gabriel Figueroa; ***M:*** Raul Lavista.

Simon Sez 🦴½ 1999 (PG-13) Convoluted spy thriller stars basketball bad boy Dennis Rodman as Simon, an Interpol agent on the trail of effete illegal arms dealer Ashton (Pradon). He must be posing undercover as a gigantic space-age punk rock coloring book, because the nose rings, tattoos and shock treatment hair don't exactly say "inconspicuous." He is approached for help by his old friend and colleague Nick (Cook), a private eye who's in over his head on a kidnapping case. The two cases just happen to be connected, but the plot is just an excuse to show car chases and shoot 'em up action sequences. Rodman shows some decent acting skills, and he's still as bad as he wants to be. Unfortunately, the movie is a lot worse than he wants it to be. **85m/C VHS, DVD.** Dennis Rodman, Dane Cook, Natalia Cigliuti, Filip Nicolic, John Pinette, Jerome Pradon, Ricky Harris; ***D:*** Kevin Elders; ***W:*** Andrew Miller, Andrew Lowery; ***C:*** Avi (Avraham) Karpik; ***M:*** Brian Tyler. **VIDEO**

Simone 2002 (PG-13) Pacino plays a washed-up filmmaker who gets back to the big time when the star of his new movie becomes a media darling. Only problem is Simone is digitally created, which causes publicity problems. Not yet reviewed. **?m/C VHS, DVD.** Al Pacino, Catherine Keener, Jay Mohr, Jason Schwartzman, Pruitt Taylor Vince; ***D:*** Andrew Niccol; ***W:*** Andrew Niccol.

Simone Barbes 🦴🦴 *Simone Barbes ou la Vertu* 1980 Simone (Bourgoin) ushers at a porn theatre where she likes to embarass the clientele. One Parisian night she visits the seedy nightclub where her lesbian lover performs burlesque and decides to embark on some of her own erotic adventures, which prove dangerous. French with subtitles. **80m/C VHS.** *FR* Ingrid Bourgoin, Michel Delahaye, Martine Simonet, Pascal Bonitzer; ***D:*** Maire-Claude Treilhou; ***W:*** Maire-Claude Treilhou, Michel Delahaye; ***C:*** Jean-Yves Escoffier.

Simpatico 🦴🦴½ 1999 (R) Excellent performances and a disappointing script mark this adaptation of the Sam Shephard play. Nolte is Vinnie, who has evidence of horse breeder Carter's (Bridges) involvement in a past race fixing and blackmail scheme. Vinnie's been blackmailing Carter for years and summons him to California on the pretense of helping Vinnie out of a sexual misconduct rap. The supposed victim (Keener) of the misconduct is unaware that any took place and agrees to help Carter. Vinnie then steals Carter's I.D, car, and plane ticket and visits their old blackmail victim (Finney), and then Carter's wife Rosie (Stone), who was also in on the con. In a haze of confused motivations and implausible plot macinations, the three try to redeem their past deeds, with Vinnie and Carter seemingly switching places. **106m/C VHS, DVD, Wide.** Nick Nolte, Sharon Stone, Jeff Bridges, Catherine Keener, Albert Finney, Shawn Hatosy, Kimberly Williams, Liam Waite; ***D:*** Matthew Warchus; ***W:*** Matthew Warchus, David Nicholls; ***C:*** John Toll; ***M:*** Stewart Copeland.

Simple Justice 🦴½ 1989 (R) Mindless, justice-in-own-hands anti-liberal hogwash. Overwrought, smug, and violent story of a young couple beaten by robbers who remain at large. **91m/C VHS.** Cesar Romero, John Spencer, Doris Roberts, Candy McClain; ***D:*** Deborah Del Prete.

The Simple Life of Noah Dearborn 🦴🦴½ 1999 (PG) Simple morality tale with an affecting performance by Poitier. Noah Dearborn is a 91-year-old carpenter and farmer who refuses to sell his Georgia property to developers. So they try to declare the old man incompetent. **87m/C VHS.** Sidney Poitier, Mary-Louise Parker, Dianne Wiest, George Newbern; ***D:*** Gregg Champion. **TV**

Simple Men 🦴🦴🦴 1992 (R) Oddball brothers Bill (a petty criminal) and Dennis (a shy college student) decide to track down their missing father in this fractured comedy. Dad, a former big-league baseball player who bombed the Pentagon in the '60s, is a long-time fugitive hiding out somewhere in the wilds of Long Island. Their search leads them to two equally opposite women, the wary Kate, whom Bill immediately falls for, and the sexy Elina, who turns out to know dear old dad quite well. Deliberately deadpan and cliched, Hartley's quirky style can either irritate or illuminate via the weird turnings of his characters' lives. **105m/C VHS.** Robert John Burke, William Sage, Karen Sillas, Elina Lowensohn, Martin Donovan, Mark Bailey, John MacKay, Jeffrey Howard, Holly Marie Combs; ***D:*** Hal Hartley; ***W:*** Hal Hartley; ***C:*** Michael Spiller; ***M:*** Hal Hartley.

A Simple Plan 🦴🦴🦴 1998 (R) Hank (Paxton), his "slow" brother Jacob (Thornton), and Jacob's best bud, alcoholic Lou (Briscoe) find the wreckage of a small plane in the snowy Minnesota woods. The pilot is dead and there's a bag filled with $4 million in cash, which they decide is drug money. The trio decide to keep quiet about the find and keep the money hidden until the plane is discovered by someone else. But having all that loot brings out the greed in everyone and soon nasty things begin to happen to all those involved. Adapted from the 1993 novel by Scott Smith. **121m/C VHS, DVD.** Bill Paxton, Billy Bob Thornton, Brent Briscoe, Bridget Fonda, Gary Cole, Becky Ann Baker, Chelcie Ross, Jack Walsh; ***D:*** Sam Raimi; ***W:*** Scott B. Smith; ***C:*** Alar Kivilo; ***M:*** Danny Elfman. L.A. Film Critics '98: Support. Actor (Thornton); Broadcast Film Critics '98: Adapt. Screenplay, Support. Actor (Thornton).

A Simple Story 🦴🦴🦴 *Une Histoire Simple* 1979 A woman faces her 40th birthday with increasing uneasiness, though her life seems perfect from the outside. She evaluates her chances at love, childbearing, and friendship, after having an abortion and breaking up with her lover. Schneider's performance is brilliant in this gentle, quiet drama. In French with English subtitles. **110m/C VHS.** *FR* Romy Schneider, Bruno Cremer, Claude Brasseur; ***D:*** Claude Sautet.

A Simple Twist of Fate 🦴🦴½ 1994 (PG-13) Comedy drama gives Martin chance to flex serious muscles with this update of George Eliot's "Silas Marner." Adoptive father Michael McMann wants to keep his daughter Mathilda (played by the prerequisite adorable twins) in the face of demands from her biological father (Byrne), who happens to be a local politician. Then revelations brought out at the custody hearing threaten the politician's career. Cuddly dad is hardly Martin's image (in spite of "Parenthood"), though strong cast limits the sugar. **106m/C VHS.** Steve Martin, Gabriel Byrne, Catherine O'Hara, Stephen Baldwin, Alana Austin, Alyssa Austin, Laura Linney, Anne Heche, Michael Des Barres, Byron Jennings; ***D:*** Gilles Mackinnon; ***W:*** Steve Martin; ***M:*** Cliff Eidelman.

A Simple Wish 🦴🦴½ 1997 (PG) Equal employment opportunities now even extend to the fairy godmother realm. Anabel (Wilson) knows her dad (Pastorelli) wants to become a Broadway actor. So she wishes for a fairy godmother—and gets stuck with Murray (Short), the first affirmative-action male practitioner, who's really not very good at spellcasting. Both Anabel and Murray have bigger problems—evil fairy godmother Claudia (Turner) is after all the fairy godmothers' magic wands so she can rule the world's wishes. Short's brand of comic energy plays right into the kid audience, and Wilson lights up every scene she's in. **95m/C VHS, DVD, Wide.** Mara Wilson, Martin Short, Kathleen Turner, Robert Pastorelli, Amanda Plummer, Teri Garr, Francis Capra, Jonathan Hadary, Alan Campbell, Ruby Dee; ***D:*** Michael Ritchie; ***W:*** Jeff Rothberg; ***C:*** Ralf Bode; ***M:*** Bruce Broughton.

Simply Irresistible 🦴 1999 (PG-13) Romantic comedy in which failing restaurant owner/chef Amanda Shelton (Gellar) falls for exec Tom Barlett (Flanery). Thanks to the intervention of fairy-godfather O'Reilly (Durang) Amanda suddenly possesses a unique culinary ability—every emotion she's feeling goes into her food and winds up affecting her customers. Tries too hard (this kind of whimsical comedy should be lighter than a souffle) and the leads, appealing as they may be, don't generate any heat when together. The film also sounds like an Americanized version of "Like Water for Chocolate," even if no one's admitting to the notion. **95m/C VHS, DVD.** Sarah Michelle Gellar, Sean Patrick Flanery, Patricia Clarkson, Dylan Baker, Christopher Durang, Larry Gilliard Jr., Betty Buckley; ***D:*** Mark Tarlov; ***W:*** Judith Roberts; ***C:*** Robert Stevens; ***M:*** Gil Goldstein.

Sin and Redemption 🦴🦴 1994 (PG-13) Billie (Gibb) is raped by an unknown assailant and gives birth to a daughter from the attack. Several years later, she marries Jim (Grieco). But her daughter has an unusual medical condition that leads Billie to believe her new husband was also her rapist. **94m/C VHS.** Cynthia Gibb, Richard Grieco, Concetta Tomei, Cheryl Pollak, Chapelle Jaffe, Ralph Waite; ***D:*** M. Neema Barnette; ***W:*** Ellen Weston; ***C:*** Tobias Schliessler; ***M:*** David Bell. **TV**

Sin of Adam & Eve 🦴½ *El Pecado de Adan y Eva* 1967 (R) The story of Adam and Eve in the Garden of Eden and their fall from grace. Voice-over narrator is only sound in this strange dialogue-less story of the Adam and Eve, how they got kicked out of the Garden of Eden, and how they lose and then find each other outside. Ancient plot, to say the least. **72m/C VHS.** Candy Wilson, Jorge (George) Rivero; ***D:*** Michael Zachary.

The Sin of Harold Diddlebock 🦴🦴½ *Mad Wednesday* 1947 A man gets fired from his job, stumbles around drunk, and wins a fortune gambling. He then buys a circus and uses a lion to frighten investors into backing him. Inventive comedy, but missing the spark and timing of "The Freshman" (1925), of which it is a sequel. The final feature film for Lloyd (who did all his own stunts), made at the urging of director Sturges. **89m/B VHS.** Harold Lloyd, Margaret Hamilton, Frances Ramsden, Edgar Kennedy, Lionel Stander, Rudy Vallee, Franklin Pangborn; ***D:*** Preston Sturges.

The Sin of Madelon Claudet 🦴🦴🦴 *The Lullaby* 1931 Hayes plays common thief who works her way into upper crust of Parisian society only to tumble back into the street, all in the name of making a better life for her illegitimate son. Very sudsy stuff, with an outstanding performance by Hayes. **74m/B VHS.** Helen Hayes, Lewis Stone, Neil Hamilton, Robert Young, Cliff Edwards, Jean Hersholt, Marie Prevost, Karen Morley, Charles Winninger, Alan Hale; ***D:*** Edgar Selwyn. Oscars '32: Actress (Hayes).

Sin Takes a Holiday 🦴🦴½ 1930 A woman marries her boss to save him from his girl friend. On a trip to Paris, she is wooed by a refined European gentleman, but finds that she really does love her husband. By today's standards, it doesn't sound like much, but in the '30s, it was pretty sophisticated stuff. **81m/B VHS.** Constance Bennett, Kenneth MacKenna, Basil Rathbone, Rita La Roy, ZaSu Pitts, Fred Walton, Richard Carle, Helen Johnson; ***D:*** Paul Stein.

Sin You Sinners 🦴 1963 Aging stripper gets ahold of an amulet that allows her to look youthful and manipulate the lives of others. When she loses the amulet, however, bad things happen. Twisted ending. **73m/B VHS.** June Colbourne, Dian Lloyd, Derek Murcott, Beverly Nazarow, Charles Clements; ***D:*** Anthony Farrar.

Sinai Commandos 🦴🦴½ *Sinai Commandos: The Story of the Six Day War; Ha'Matarah Tiran* 1968 The story of a group of commandos in the Israeli Six-Day War in 1967 who are assigned to destroy important Arab radar installations. Includes actual combat footage. **99m/C VHS.** Robert Fuller; ***D:*** Raphael Nussbaum.

Sinatra 🦴🦴½ 1992 TV biopic chronicles the stormy life of crooner Frank Sinatra. Begins with his childhood in Hoboken, New Jersey and works its way through his big band tours, bobby soxer days, career skids, and triumphant comeback with his Oscar-winning performance in "From Here to Eternity," as well as his three marriages, "Rat Pack" friends, and mob connections. Executive Producer Tina Sinatra, Frank's daughter, doesn't gloss over her father's less savory character points and Casnoff does well with his leading role. Songs are lip-synched to classic Sinatra tunes with a few early recordings redone by actor Tom Burlinson and Frank Sinatra Jr. **245m/C VHS.** Philip Casnoff, Olympia Dukakis, Joe Santos, Gina Gershon, Nina Siemaszko, Marcia Gay Harden, Rod Steiger, Bob Gunton, David Raynr, James F. Kelly, Matthew Posey, Jay Robinson, Robin Gammell, Todd Waring, Joris Stuyck, Danny Gans, Jeff Corey; ***D:*** James Sadwith; ***W:*** William Mastrosimone; ***C:*** Reynaldo Villalobos. **TV**

Sinbad ⚘⚘ **1971** A sardonic portrait of an aging hedonist as he tries to hold onto the pleasures of drink, sex and gluttony. In Magyar (Hungarian), with English subtitles. **98m/C VHS.** *HU* ***D:*** Zoltan Huszarik.

Sinbad and the Eye of the Tiger ⚘⚘ **1977 (G)** The swashbuckling adventures of Sinbad the Sailor as he encounters the creations of Ray Harryhausen's special effects magic. Don't see this one for the plot, which almost doesn't exist. Otherwise, mildly fun. **113m/C VHS, DVD, Wide.** *GB* Patrick Wayne, Jane Seymour, Taryn Power, Margaret Whiting; ***D:*** Sam Wanamaker; ***W:*** Beverley Cross; ***C:*** Ted Moore; ***M:*** Roy Budd.

Sinbad of the Seven Seas ⚘½ **1989** Italian muscle epic based on the ancient legends. Ferrigno isn't green, but he's still a hulk, and he still can't act. It's poorly dubbed, which makes little difference; it would be stupid regardless. **90m/C VHS.** *IT* Lou Ferrigno, John Steiner, Leo Gullotta, Teagan Clive; ***D:*** Enzo G. Castellari.

Sinbad, the Sailor ⚘⚘⚘ **1947** Fairbanks fits well in his luminent father's swashbuckling shoes, as he searches for the treasure of Alexander the Great. Self-mocking but hamhanded, and confusing if you seek the hidden plot. Still, it's all in fun, and it is fun. **117m/C VHS.** Douglas Fairbanks Jr., Maureen O'Hara, Anthony Quinn, Walter Slezak, George Tobias, Jane Greer, Mike Mazurki, Sheldon Leonard; ***D:*** Richard Wallace; ***C:*** George Barnes.

Since You Went Away ⚘⚘⚘½ **1944** An American family copes with the tragedy, heartache and shortages of wartime in classic mega-tribute to the home front. Be warned: very long and bring your hankies. Colbert is superb, as is the photography. John Derek unobtrusively made his film debut, as an extra. **172m/B VHS.** Claudette Colbert, Jennifer Jones, Shirley Temple, Joseph Cotten, Agnes Moorehead, Monty Woolley, Guy Madison, Lionel Barrymore, Robert Walker, Hattie McDaniel, Keenan Wynn, Craig Stevens, Albert Bassermann, Alla Nazimova, Lloyd Corrigan, Terry Moore, Florence Bates, Ruth Roman, Andrew V. McLaglen, Dorothy Dandridge, Rhonda Fleming, Addison Richards, Jackie Moran; ***D:*** John Cromwell; ***W:*** David O. Selznick; ***C:*** Stanley Cortez, Lee Garmes; ***M:*** Max Steiner. Oscars '44: Orig. Dramatic Score.

Since You've Been Gone ⚘⚘ *Dogwater* **1997 (R)** The Clear View High School class of 1987 has their ten-year reunion and rivalries and romance are rediscovered. Grace (Boyle) has a penchant for nasty practical jokes she's never gotten over while Marie (Hatcher) is a self-important would-be exec who insults her one-time classmates and Rob (Schwimmer) is the still-loathed class president. **95m/C VHS.** David Schwimmer, Lara Flynn Boyle, Teri Hatcher, Joey Slotnick, Tom (Thomas E.) Hodges, Philip Rayburn Smith, Heidi Stillman, David Catlin, Laura Eason; ***Cameos:*** Marisa Tomei, Jon Stewart, Liev Schreiber, Molly Ringwald, Jennifer Grey; ***D:*** David Schwimmer.

Sincerely Charlotte ⚘⚘⚘ *Signe Charlotte* **1986** Huppert directs her sister in this film about a beautiful singer framed for her boyfriend's murder. She enlists an old lover to help her flee across the countryside. Love story/thriller is pleasingly odd and absorbing. In French with English subtitles. **92m/C VHS.** *FR* Isabelle Huppert, Niels Arestrup, Christine Pascal; ***D:*** Caroline Huppert; ***C:*** Bruno de Keyzer.

Sincerely Yours woof! **1956** Liberace wisely stayed away from acting after inauspiciously debuting in this horrible, maudlin remake of "The Man Who Played God." He plays a pianist who loses his hearing and decides to become a philanthropist to help those less fortunate than himself. Laughably cheesy. Thirty-one musical numbers, including Liberace's inimitable arrangement of "Chopsticks." **116m/C VHS.** Liberace, Joanne Dru, Dorothy Malone, William Demarest; ***D:*** Gordon Douglas; ***W:*** Irving Wallace.

A Sinful Life ⚘⚘ **1989 (R)** A strained, offbeat, B-grade comedy about an odd, infantile mother fighting to keep her unusual child from being taken away. Definitely not a must-see; can be irritating and obnoxious, depending on viewer and mood. Morris is at her oddball comedic best as the mother and former show dancer. Adult Tefkin plays her little girl. Based on the play "Just Like the Pom Pom Girls." **112m/C VHS.** Anita Morris, Rick Overton, Dennis Christopher, Blair Tefkin, Mark Rolston, Cynthia Szigeti; ***D:*** William Schreiner.

Sing ⚘½ **1989 (PG-13)** The students in the real-life Brooklyn public school "Sing" program endure the trials of adolescence while putting together a musical revue. Hurtles over the edge into cheesiness from the start, with way too much (cheesy) music. From the creator of "Fame" and "Footloose." **111m/C VHS.** Lorraine Bracco, Peter Dobson, Jessica Steen, Louise Lasser, George DiCenzo, Patti LaBelle; ***D:*** Richard Baskin; ***M:*** Jay Gruska.

Sing, Cowboy, Sing ⚘⚘ **1937** Decent adventure story about a wagon train heading west that runs into a band of outlaws doing outlaw stuff and must somehow get through. **60m/B VHS.** Tex Ritter.

Sing Sing Nights ⚘½ *Reprieved* **1935** A world-famous journalist is killed with three bullets. Three men have confessed, but only one could have actually done it. A professor sets out to solve the case. **60m/B VHS.** Conway Tearle, Mary Doran, Hardie Albright, Patricia "Boots" Mallory, Ferdinand Gottschalk, Berton Churchill, Jameson Thomas; ***D:*** Lewis D. Collins.

Sing Your Worries Away ⚘⚘ **1942** Songwriter Ebsen inherits $3 million and finds the money causes him nothing but trouble. Band of crooks cause the requisite wacky complications. Fun, harmless musical comedy. ♫It Just Happened to Happen; Sally, My Dear Sally; Sing Your Worries Away; Cindy Lou McWilliams; How Do You Fall in Love. **71m/B VHS.** Buddy Ebsen, Bert Lahr, June Havoc, Patsy Kelly, Margaret Dumont; ***D:*** Edward Sutherland.

Singapore ⚘⚘½ **1947** Rather boring romantic drama finds pearl smuggler Matt Gordon (MacMurray) returning to Singapore to resume his illegal trade at the end of WWII. He spots Linda (Gardner), the love of his life, but discovers she's suffering from amnesia and has married another man. Gangsters want Matt's hidden supply of pearls and kidnap Linda to get his cooperation. Remade with equal dullness in 1956 as "Istanbul." **80m/B VHS.** Fred MacMurray, Ava Gardner, Roland Culver, Richard Haydn, Thomas Gomez, Spring Byington, Porter Hall; ***D:*** John Brahm; ***W:*** Seton I. Miller, Robert Thoeren; ***C:*** Maury Gertsman; ***M:*** Daniele Amfitheatrof.

Singin' in the Rain ⚘⚘⚘⚘ **1952** One of the all-time great movie musicals—an affectionate spoof of the turmoil that afflicted the motion picture industry in the late 1920s during the changeover from silent films to sound. Don Lockwood (Kelly) and Lina Lamont (Hagen) are a popular romantic silent screen team when sound comes along. To continue, temperamental Lina must have her terrible voice dubbed by aspiring actress Kathy Selden (Reynolds), whom Don falls for. O'Connor's an acrobatic marvel as Don's best pal, Cosmo Brown, and of course there's Kelly's classic much-copied title dance. Later a Broadway musical. ♫All I Do is Dream of You; Should I?; Singin' in the Rain; Wedding of the Painted Doll; Broadway Melody; Would You; I've Got a Feelin' You're Foolin'; You Are My Lucky Star; Broadway Rhythm. **103m/C VHS, DVD.** Gene Kelly, Donald O'Connor, Jean Hagen, Debbie Reynolds, Rita Moreno, King Donovan, Millard Mitchell, Cyd Charisse, Douglas Fowley, Madge Blake, Joi Lansing; ***D:*** Gene Kelly, Stanley Donen; ***W:*** Adolph Green, Betty Comden; ***C:*** Harold Rosson; ***M:*** Nacio Herb Brown, Lennie Hayton. AFI '98: Top 100; Golden Globes '53: Actor—Mus./Comedy (O'Connor), Natl. Film Reg. '89.

The Singing Blacksmith ⚘⚘½ **1938** A relic of American Yiddish cinema, adapting popular 1909 play by David Pinski. A married blacksmith is wooed by another woman and falls victim to alcoholism. Overlong, but Oysher and his rich baritone voice still shine. In Yiddish with English subtitles. **95m/B VHS.** *PL* Miriam Riselle, Florence Weiss, Moishe Oysher; ***D:*** Edgar G. Ulmer.

Singing Buckaroo ⚘⚘ **1937** Dastardly bandits try to pilfer money from pretty blonde damsel and have to battle with yodelin' cowboy. B-level western good guy Scott belts out a few numbers and saves the day. Innocuously pleasant. **58m/B VHS.** Fred Scott, Victoria Vinton, Cliff Nazarro; ***D:*** Tom Gibson.

The Singing Cowgirl ⚘ **1939** Band of outlaws murder a ranch owner to get to a gold mine. Heroine Page rides in to save the day but gets shot down by western stereotypes. **60m/B VHS.** Dorothy Page, Dave O'Brien, Vince Barnett, Stanley Price; ***D:*** Samuel Diege; ***W:*** Arthur Hoerl.

The Singing Detective **1986** A musical/mystery/fantasy British miniseries, based on the work by Dennis Potter. Pulp fiction writer Phillip Marlowe (Gambon) is confined to his hospital bed, unable to move due to extreme psoriasis. In his lucid moments he tries to figure out the cause of his condition, but in his elaborate daydreams he's a detective (and big band singer) who's working to solve a series of murders. Six episodes: "Skin," "Heat," "Lovely Days," "Clues," "Pitter Patter," and "Who Done It." **420m/C VHS.** *GB* Michael Gambon, Patrick Malahide, Janet Suzman, Joanne Whalley; ***D:*** Jon Amiel. **TV**

The Singing Nun ⚘⚘ **1966** The true story of a Belgian nun who takes a liking to a motherless little boy. She writes a song for him, and a kind-hearted priest talks to a record producer to see about getting the song to go somewhere. The song soon becomes an international hit, and the nun ends up on the "Ed Sullivan Show." Sentimental and sugary sweet, but a big boxoffice hit. **98m/C VHS.** Debbie Reynolds, Ricardo Montalban, Greer Garson, Agnes Moorehead, Chad Everett, Katharine Ross, Juanita Moore, Ricky Cordell, Michael Pate, Tom Drake; ***D:*** Henry Koster; ***C:*** Milton Krasner.

Singing the Blues in Red ⚘⚘⚘ **1987** Dark, pessimistic character study of a protest singer/songwriter who leaves his native East Germany to escape repression and finds his loyalties divided. A moving personal story, as well as insightful, subtle social commentary. In English and German with subtitles. **110m/C VHS.** *GE* Gerulf Pannach, Fabienne Babe, Cristine Rose, Trevor Griffiths; ***D:*** Ken Loach; ***W:*** Trevor Griffiths; ***C:*** Chris Menges.

Single Bars, Single Women ⚘½ **1984** Utterly formulaic made for TV comedy-drama based on Dolly Parton's song is not entirely without merit. Lonely people gather in a local pick-up joint and share their miseries and hopes. **96m/C VHS.** Shelley Hack, Christine Lahti, Tony Danza, Mare Winningham, Keith Gordon, Paul Michael Glaser; ***D:*** Harry Winer; ***M:*** Basil Poledouris. **TV**

A Single Girl ⚘⚘½ *La Fille Seule* **1996** Follows, in real time, a young woman as she tells her boyfriend that she's pregnant, (Ledoyen) through her job handling room service at a Paris hotel, then again with her boyfriend after work. French with subtitles. Part sexual hotel fantasy, part observation of an ordinary couple going about daily life. **90m/C VHS, DVD, Wide.** *FR* Virginie Ledoyen, Benoit Magimel, Vera Briole, Dominique Valadie; ***D:*** Benoit Jacquot; ***W:*** Benoit Jacquot, Jerome Beaujour; ***C:*** Caroline Champetier; ***M:*** Kvarteto Mesta Prahi.

Single Room Furnished ⚘½ **1968** The fall of a buxom blonde from uncorrupted innocence through pregnancies to desperate prostitution. Fails to demonstrate any range of talent in Mansfield, who died before it was completed. Exploitative and pathetic. **93m/C VHS.** Jayne Mansfield, Dorothy Keller; ***D:*** Matt Cimber, Matteo Ottaviano.

The Single Standard ⚘⚘ **1929** San Francisco deb Garbo flings with artsy Asther and finds out the Hayes Code is just around the corner. **93m/B VHS.** Greta Garbo, Nils Asther, Johnny Mack Brown, Dorothy Sebastian, Lane Chandler, Zeffie Tilbury; ***D:*** John S. Robertson.

Single White Female ⚘⚘½ **1992 (R)** Psycho thriller casts Fonda as chic Manhattan computer consultant Allison Jones, who advertises for a roommate after a falling out with her boyfriend. Leigh is the frumpy, shy, bookstore clerk Hedra who answers the ad and moves into Allie's great Upper West Side apartment. They hit it off, that is until Allie notices Hedra's beginning to look and sound very familiar. Hmm... Derivative, though bonus points for creative murder implements and interesting performances throughout, including Friedman as Allie's gay upstairs neighbor. Based on the novel "SWF Seeks Same" by John Lutz. **107m/C VHS, DVD.** Bridget Fonda, Jennifer Jason Leigh, Steven Weber, Peter Friedman, Stephen Tobolowsky, Frances Bay, Renee Estevez, Kenneth Tobey; ***D:*** Barbet Schroeder; ***W:*** Don Roos; ***C:*** Luciano Tovoli; ***M:*** Howard Shore. MTV Movie Awards '93: Villain (Leigh).

Singles ⚘⚘⚘ **1992 (PG-13)** Seattle's music scene is the background for this lighthearted look at single 20-somethings in the '90s. Hits dead on thanks to Crowe's tight script and a talented cast, and speaks straight to its intended audience—the "Generation X" crowd. Real life band Pearl Jam plays alternative band Citizen Dick and sets the tone for a great soundtrack featuring the hot Seattle sounds of Alice in Chains, Soundgarden, and Mudhoney. The video contains six extra minutes of footage after the credits that was thankfully edited out of the final cut. Look for Horton, Stoltz (as a mime), Skerritt, and Burton in cameos. **100m/C VHS, DVD, Wide.** Matt Dillon, Bridget Fonda, Campbell Scott, Kyra Sedgwick, Sheila Kelley, Jim True, Bill Pullman, James LeGros, Ally Walker, Devon Raymond, Camillo Gallardo, Jeremy Piven; ***Cameos:*** Peter Horton, Eric Stoltz, Tim Burton, Tom Skerritt; ***D:*** Cameron Crowe; ***W:*** Cameron Crowe; ***C:*** Ueli Steiger; ***M:*** Paul Westerberg.

Singleton's Pluck ⚘⚘⚘ *Laughterhouse* **1984** Touching British comedy about a determined farmer who must walk his 500 geese 100 miles to market because of a strike. He becomes a celebrity when the TV stations start covering his odyssey. **89m/C VHS.** *GB* Ian Holm, Penelope Wilton, Bill Owen, Richard Hope; ***D:*** Richard Eyre.

The Sinister Invasion ⚘ *Alien Terror; The Incredible Invasion; Invasion Siniestra* **1968** A turn-of-the-century scientist (Karloff) discovers a death ray. Aliens, who would like a closer peek at what makes it work, use a sex-fiend's body to do so. One of Karloff's last four films, made simultaneously in Mexico. The great horror master's final offering. Excruciating. **95m/C VHS.** *MX* Boris Karloff, Enrique Guzman, Jack Hill, Yerye Beirut, Maura Monti, Tere Valdez; ***D:*** Juan Ibanez, Jack Hill; ***W:*** Luis Enrique Vergara, Karl Schanzer; ***C:*** Raul Dominguez, Austin McKinney.

The Sinister Urge woof! *The Young and the Immortal; Hellborn* **1960** Vice cops Duncan and Moore search for the murderer of three women. Seems the disturbed slayer is unbalanced because he's been looking at pictures of naked ladies. Was this meant to be taken seriously at the time? The last film by camp director Wood, maker of the infamous "Plan 9 from Outer Space." A must see for Wood fans. **82m/B VHS.** Kenne Duncan, Duke Moore, Jean Fontaine, Carl Anthony, Harvey B. Dunn, Dino Fantini, Reed Howes, Conrad Brooks; ***D:*** Edward D. Wood Jr.; ***W:*** Edward D. Wood Jr.; ***C:*** William C. Thompson.

Sink or Swim ⚘⚘½ *Hacks* **1997 (R)** TV writer/producer Brian (a suitably hang-dog Rea) is suffering from creative burnout and depression. His agent, Danny (Arnold), has just landed Brian a new job writing a TV series that he's dreading. His weekly poker buddies (and fellow writers) offer possible scenarios, amidst their backstabbing, but Brian may have reignited his creative spark after witnessing a romantic encounter between two silhouetted figures in a hotel window. He thinks the woman may be Georgia (Douglas), whom he meets in a bar, and Brian wants her story—at practically any price. **93m/C VHS, DVD.** Stephen Rea, Illeana Douglas, Tom Arnold, John Ritter, Dave Foley, Richard Kind, Ryan O'Neal, Ricky Jay, Jason Priestley, Olivia D'Abo, Bob Odenkirk; ***D:*** Gary Rosen; ***W:*** Gary Rosen; ***C:*** Ralf Bode; ***M:*** Anthony Marinelli.

Sink the Bismarck 🦴🦴🦴 **1960** British navy sets out to locate and sink infamous German battleship during WWII. Good special effects with battle sequences in this drama based on real incidents. One of the better of the plethora of WWII movies, with stirring naval battles and stylish documentary-style direction. **97m/B VHS.** *GB* Kenneth More, Dana Wynter, Karel Stepanek, Carl Mohner, Laurence Naismith, Geoffrey Keen, Michael Hordern, Maurice Denham, Esmond Knight, Michael Goodliffe, Jack Watling, Jack (Gwyllam) Gwillim, Mark Dignam, Ernest Clark, John Horsley, Sydney Tafler, John Stuart, Walter Hudd, Sean Barrett, Peter Burton, Edward R. Murrow; ***D:*** Lewis Gilbert; ***W:*** Edmund H. North; ***C:*** Christopher Challis; ***M:*** Clifton Parker.

Sinners 🦴 **1989** Outrageous portrait of an Italian family in the Big Apple trying to come to terms with the violence that surrounds their neighborhood. **90m/C VHS.** Joey Travolta, Robert Gallo, Joe Palese, Lou Calvelli, Angie Daglas, Sabrina Ferrand; ***D:*** Charles Kanganis.

Sinner's Blood woof! **1970 (R)** Bikers terrorize and torture a small town. **81m/C VHS.** Stephen Jacques, Crusty Beal, Nancy Sheldon, Parker Herriott, Julie Connors; ***D:*** Neil Douglas.

Sinners in Paradise 🦴🦴 **1938** An assortment of trouble-plagued characters alternately hide and face up to their mysterious pasts when their plane crashes on a deserted island. Interesting "crucible" premise runs out of steam, but plucky, resourceful cast and competent direction keep it going. **64m/B VHS.** Madge Evans, John Boles, Bruce Cabot, Marion Martin, Gene Lockhart, Dwight Frye, Charlotte Wynters, Nana Bryant, Milburn Stone, Donald (Don "Red") Barry, Morgan Conway; ***D:*** James Whale.

Sins **1985** On her way up the ladder of success in the fashion industry, Helene has stepped on a few toes. Those rivals and her ever-increasing acquisition of power and money make this film an exciting drama. **336m/C VHS.** Joan Collins, Timothy Dalton, Catherine Mary Stewart, Gene Kelly, James Farentino; ***D:*** Douglas Hickox.

Sins of Desire 🦴🦴 **1992** Highly erotic thriller with Roberts going undercover as a nurse in a sex therapy clinic. It seems her sister was a former patient at the clinic and has since died a mysterious death. Linking up with private eye Cassavetes, Roberts sets out to investigate the doctors who treated her sister, searching for clues to her untimely death. **90m/C VHS.** Tanya Roberts, Jay Richardson, Delia Sheppard, Nick Cassavetes, Jan-Michael Vincent; ***D:*** Jim Wynorski; ***W:*** Mark Thomas McGee, Peter Paul Liapis.

The Sins of Dorian Gray 🦴 **1982 (PG)** A modernized adaptation of "The Portrait of Dorian Grey" by Oscar Wilde, with Dorian as a beautiful woman who remains young for 30 years, while a video screen test ages, like the original character's mirror image. Might have been intriguing and stylish; instead, only disappointing and incompetent. **95m/C VHS.** Belinda Bauer, Joseph Bottoms, Anthony Perkins; ***D:*** Tony Maylam. **TV**

Sins of Jezebel 🦴 **1954** Biblical epic about Jezebel, who worships an evil god. She marries the king of Israel and brings the kingdom nothing but trouble. **74m/C VHS.** Paulette Goddard, George Nader, John Hoyt, Eduard Franz; ***D:*** Reginald LeBorg.

Sins of Rome 🦴🦴 **1954** Spartacus risks it all in a bold attempt to free his fellow slaves. Not nearly the equal of Kirk Douglas's "Spartacus," but much better than later Italian adventure epics. **75m/B VHS.** *IT* Ludmila Tcherina, Massimo Girotti, Gianna Maria Canale, Yves Vincent; ***D:*** Riccardo (Robert Hampton) Freda.

Sins of the Father 🦴🦴🦴 **2001** Thomas Frank Cherry (Sizemore) is a middle-aged Texan who comes to believe that his father, Bobby Frank Cherry (Jenkins), was one of four KKK members who bombed the Sixteenth Street Baptist Church in Birmingham, Alabama, in 1963. Four young black girls were killed in the explosion and the investigation dragged on and off for 38 years. When the investigation is revived once again, Tom decides to give testimony before a grand jury that casts down on his father's original alibi. Cherry was convicted of murder in 2002. **93m/C VHS, DVD.** Tom Sizemore, Ving Rhames, Richard Jenkins, Colm Feore; ***D:*** Robert Dornhelm; ***W:*** John Pielmeier; ***C:*** Derick Underschultz; ***M:*** Harold Kloser. **CABLE**

Sins of the Mind 🦴🦴 **1997 (R)** Michelle (Crider), the 25-year-old daughter of Eve (Clayburgh) and William (Farrell) Widener, awakens from a coma after a car accident and turns out to have psychological damage. Previously a conservative, hard-working artist, she's now a hedonist, given to erratic impulses and sexual compulsions. Michelle's actions threaten her family but her father is convinced he can still get his little girl back. **92m/C VHS.** Missy (Melissa) Crider, Mike Farrell, Jill Clayburgh, Louise Fletcher, Michael Mantell, Robert Pine, Cyia Batten, Grayson McCouch; ***D:*** James Frawley. **CABLE**

Sins of the Night 🦴 **1993 (R)** An ex-con insurance investigator is hired to find a sultry exotic dancer. Also available in an unrated version. **82m/C VHS.** Nick Cassavetes, Deborah Shelton.

Sinthia: The Devil's Doll 🦴🦴 **1970** A little girl is thought to be possessed by a demon after she has horrible dreams about killing her father. **?m/C VHS.** Shula Roan, Diane Webber; ***D:*** Ray Dennis Steckler.

Sioux City 🦴🦴½ **1994 (PG-13)** Jesse Rainfeather Goldman (Phillips) is a Lakota Sioux adopted away from the reservation of his birth and raised in Beverly Hills by a Jewish family. Jesse's curious when his birth mother suddenly contacts him, but when he arrives at the Sioux City reservation, he discovers she's suddenly died under mysterious circumstances. So Jesse sticks around to find out what's going on and discovers his heritage along the way. Well-meaning but dull. **102m/C VHS.** Lou Diamond Phillips, Salli Richardson, Melinda Dillon, Ralph Waite, Adam Roarke, Bill Allen, Gary Farmer; ***D:*** Lou Diamond Phillips; ***W:*** L. Virginia Browne; ***M:*** Christopher Lindsey.

Sioux City Sue 🦴🦴 **1946** Talent scouts looking to cast a western musical find Autry, then trick him into being the voice of a singing donkey in an animated production. But, the yodelin' cowboy belts out a number or two, and the poobahs give him the lead. Singin' and fancy ridin' abound in Autry's first post-WWII role. **69m/B VHS.** Gene Autry, Lynne Roberts, Sterling Holloway.

Sir Arthur Conan Doyle's The Lost World 🦴½ *The Lost World* **1998 (R)** In the '30s, zoologist George Challenger (Bergin) recruits a team of scientists to help him find a mythic land where dinosaurs and other prehistoric creatures exist. Lots of cliches although the special effects aren't bad. **96m/C VHS.** Patrick Bergin, David Nerman, Jayne Heitmeyer, Julian Casey; ***D:*** Bob Keen; ***W:*** Jean LaFleur; ***C:*** Barry Gravelle; ***M:*** Milan Kymlicka. **VIDEO**

Sirens 🦴🦴½ **1994 (R)** Staid minister Anthony Campion (Grant) takes Australian artist Norman Lindsay to task for submitting scandalous works to public exhibitions. Noted by one reviewer as "Enchanted April with nipples," comedy of manners is witty but lacks plot and looks remarkably like a centerfold layout. Ample displays of nudity as the models (including supermodel MacPherson in her acting debut) frolic in the buff. Grant is terrific as the seemingly enlightened but easily shocked minister, but Neill's Lindsay is thinly written and too often takes a back seat to the vamping models. Fictionalized account of a true incident from the 1930s; Lindsay's home and some of his artworks were used. Check out writer/director Duigan as a pompous village minister. **96m/C VHS, DVD, Wide.** *AU GB* Hugh Grant, Tara Fitzgerald, Sam Neill, Elle Macpherson, Kate Fischer, Portia de Rossi, Pamela Rabe, Ben Mendelsohn, John Polson, Mark Gerber, Julia Stone, Ellie MacCarthy, Vincent Ball; ***Cameos:*** John Duigan; ***D:*** John Duigan; ***W:*** John Duigan; ***C:*** Geoff Burton; ***M:*** Rachel Portman.

Sirens 🦴🦴 **1999 (R)** The sirens in this case are those attached to police cars. Sally Rawlings (Delany) gets a big promotion and decides to share the good news with her ex-hubby (Curtis Hall). They wind up parked under a bridge, steaming up the windows, when a cop car comes along. Trigger-happy cop (Carradine) winds up shooting the unarmed ex dead and the police try to cover up the bad shooting. Of course, Sally wants justice—no matter what it costs. **102m/C VHS.** Dana Delany, Keith Carradine, Vondie Curtis-Hall, Brian Dennehy, Justin Theroux; ***D:*** John Sacret Young; ***W:*** John Sacret Young; ***C:*** Eagle Egilsson; ***M:*** Brian Tyler. **CABLE**

Siringo 🦴🦴½ **1994** U.S. Deputy Marshal Charlie Siringo (Johnson) is out to capture escaped convict Wade Lewis (Macht). The two antagonists share a nasty history as Siringo, along with a young deputy, heads out to the ranch of former prostitute Kaitlin (Bernard) for a final showdown. **90m/C VHS.** Brad Johnson, Stephen Macht, Chad Lowe, Crystal Bernard; ***D:*** Kevin G. Cremin.

Sirocco 🦴🦴½ **1951** An American gun-runner (Bogart) stuck in Syria in 1925 matches wits with a French intelligence officer amid civil war and intrigue. About the underbelly of human affairs. **111m/B VHS.** Humphrey Bogart, Lee J. Cobb, Zero Mostel, Everett Sloane, Gerald Mohr; ***D:*** Curtis Bernhardt; ***C:*** Burnett Guffey.

Sister Act 🦴🦴½ **1992 (PG)** Surprising boxoffice hit casts Goldberg as a Reno lounge singer, Deloris, who's an inadvertent witness to a mob murder by her boyfriend Vince (Keitel). The cops hide her in a convent—where she's as comfortable in a habit as a fish is out of water. Much to the dismay of the poker-faced Mother Superior (Smith), Deloris takes over the ragtag choir and molds them into a swinging, religious version of a '60s girls group. Stock characters and situations are deflected by some genuinely funny moments and good performances, especially by Najimy and Makkena. Coached by the very clever Shaiman, Whoopi handles her singing bits with gusto, highlight of which is "My God," sung to the tune of "My Guy." **100m/C VHS, DVD, Wide.** Whoopi Goldberg, Maggie Smith, Harvey Keitel, Bill Nunn, Kathy Najimy, Wendy Makkena, Mary Wickes, Robert Miranda, Richard Portnow, Joseph Maher; ***D:*** Emile Ardolino; ***W:*** Joseph Howard; ***C:*** Adam Greenberg; ***M:*** Marc Shaiman.

Sister Act 2: Back in the Habit 🦴🦴 **1993 (PG)** Mediocre retread finds Goldberg once again donning her nun's habit and getting a choir rocking. Deloris has established her singing career in Vegas, but she's persuaded by her nun friends to whip the incorrigible music students at a troubled inner-city high school into shape for an all-state choral competition. The musical numbers and singing are catchy and well-done but Goldberg seems to have phoned her work in; given her reported $7,000,000 salary, a little more life is expected. She's still sharp with the one-liners but it's all familiar ground. Geared directly towards young viewers. **107m/C VHS, DVD.** Whoopi Goldberg, Kathy Najimy, James Coburn, Maggie Smith, Wendy Makkena, Barnard Hughes, Mary Wickes, Sheryl Lee Ralph, Michael Jeter, Robert Pastorelli, Thomas Gottschalk, Lauryn Hill, Brad Sullivan, Jennifer Love Hewitt; ***D:*** Bill Duke; ***W:*** James Orr, Jim Cruickshank, Judi Ann Mason; ***C:*** Oliver Wood; ***M:*** Miles Goodman. Blockbuster '95: Comedy Actress, V. (Goldberg).

Sister Dora 🦴🦴½ **1977** An idealistic young woman joins a nursing sisterhood in 19th century England but she questions her vocation when she falls in love. Adapted from a popular romance novel. **147m/C VHS.** *GB* Dorothy Tutin, James Grout, Peter Cellier; ***D:*** Mark Miller.

The Sister-in-Law 🦴🦴 **1974 (R)** Shady dealings, seduction, and adultery run rampant. Savage (who also wrote and sings the folk score) reluctantly agrees to deliver a package across the Canadian border for his brother. Intriguing. **80m/C VHS.** John Savage, Anne Saxon, W.G. McMillan, Meridith Baer; ***D:*** Joseph Rubin.

The Sister-in-Law 🦴🦴½ **1995 (PG-13)** Chilling cable suspenser finds the beautiful and evil Sarah Preston (Vernon) assuming the identity of the woman she's just killed—the widow of wealthy George Richards's (McCarthy) estranged son. George is dying and pathetically eager to accept Sarah at face value as is his vulnerable daughter Madlyn (Reed). But Sarah has not chosen the Richards family at random—she has a longtime grudge and plans to take her revenge slowly—so be prepared for a few more bodies to turn up. **95m/C VHS.** Kate Vernon, Kevin McCarthy, Shanna Reed, Craig Wasson; ***D:*** Noel Nosseck; ***W:*** David Callaway, Megan Marks. **CABLE**

Sister Kenny 🦴🦴🦴 **1946** Follows the story of a legendary Australian nurse crusading for the treatment of infantile paralysis. Stirring, well-made screen biography. Based on Elizabeth Kenny's memoir, "And They Shall Walk." **116m/B VHS.** Rosalind Russell, Dean Jagger, Alexander Knox, Philip Merivale, Beulah Bondi, Charles Halton; ***D:*** Dudley Nichols; ***C:*** George Barnes. Golden Globes '47: Actress—Drama (Russell).

Sister My Sister 🦴🦴 **1994 (R)** True crime story that served as the inspiration for Jean Genet's play "The Maids." In a French provincial town lives the authoritarian Madame Danzard (Walters), who stifles daughter Isabelle (Thursfield), and subjects her two maids, sisters Christine (Richardson) and Lea (May), to an equally harsh discipline. The tension between the four women reaches a high-strung crescendo, leading to violence. Claustrophobic character study. **89m/C VHS, DVD.** *GB* Julie Walters, Joely Richardson, Jodhi May, Sophie Thursfield; ***D:*** Nancy Meckler; ***W:*** Wendy Kellelman; ***C:*** Ashley Ropwe; ***M:*** Stephen Warbeck.

Sister, Sister 🦴🦴 **1987 (R)** A Congressional aide on vacation in Louisiana takes a room in an old mansion. He gradually discovers the secret of the house and its resident sisters. Dark Southern gothicism, full of plot surprises, with a twisted ending. **91m/C VHS, DVD, Wide.** Eric Stoltz, Judith Ivey, Jennifer Jason Leigh, Dennis Lipscomb, Anne Pitoniak, Natalija Nogulich; ***D:*** Bill Condon; ***W:*** Ginny Cerrella, Bill Condon, Joel Cohen; ***M:*** Richard Einhorn.

Sister Street Fighter 🦴 **1976** Action star Sonny Chiba takes a rest from his "Street Fighter" series in favor of protege Long, who's determined to deliver her own brand of deadly justice in this martial arts fest. **81m/C VHS, DVD, Wide.** Sue Shiomi, Sonny Chiba; ***D:*** Kazuhiko Yamaguchi.

The Sisterhood 🦴 **1988 (R)** A pair of amazons fight for women's rights in a post-nuclear future. Cheap feminist theme laid over warmed-over sci-fi plot. **75m/C VHS.** Rebecca Holden, Chuck Wagner, Lynn-Holly Johnson, Barbara Hooper; ***D:*** Cirio H. Santiago.

The Sisters 🦴🦴🦴 **1938** Lavish film of three sisters and their marital problems in turn of the century San Francisco. Davis gives a great performance as the oldest sister with the most trouble—notably in the form of unreliable sports reporter Flynn. Look for Susan Hayward in a bit role, as well as Bogart's wife, Mayo Methot. Based on the bestselling novel by Myron Brinig. **98m/B VHS.** Bette Davis, Errol Flynn, Anita Louise, Jane Bryan, Ian Hunter, Henry Travers, Beulah Bondi, Donald Crisp, Dick Foran, Patric Knowles; ***D:*** Anatole Litvak; ***M:*** Max Steiner.

Sisters 🦴🦴🦴 **1973 (R)** Siamese twins are separated surgically, but one doesn't survive the operation. The remaining sister is scarred physically and mentally with her personality split into bad and good. The bad side commits a murder, witnessed (or was it?) by an investigative reporter. And then things really get crazy. DePalma's first ode to Hitchcock, with great music by Hitchcock's favorite composer, Bernard Herrmann. Scary and suspenseful. **93m/C VHS, DVD, Wide.** Margot Kidder, Charles Durning, Barnard Hughes, Jennifer Salt, William Finley, Lisle Wilson, Mary Davenport, Dolph Sweet; ***D:*** Brian DePalma; ***W:*** Brian DePalma, Louisa Rose; ***C:*** Gregory Sandor; ***M:*** Bernard Herrmann.

Sisters of Death 🦴🦴 **1976 (PG)** Five members of a sorority gather together for a reunion in a remote California town. Little do they know, a psychopath is stalking them, one by one. Could it have something to do with the terrible secret they each keep? Good, cheap thrills and some Bicentennial fashions to boot. **87m/C VHS.** Arthur Franz, Claudia Jennings, Cheri Howell, Sherry Boucher, Paul Carr; ***D:*** Joseph Mazzuca.

Sisters of Satan 🦴🦴½ **1975 (R)** The nuns of the infamous convent St. Archangelo choose to survive by trading God for the devil. **91m/C VHS.** *MX* Claudio Brook, David Silva, Tina Romero, Susana Kamini; ***D:*** Juan Lopez Moctezuma.

Sisters of the Gion 🦴🦴 *Gion No Shimai* **1936** Story follows two geisha sisters, illuminating the plight of women in Japan. Elder sister Umekichi is traditional and dependent on her patrons while her modern younger sister Omocha exploits her customers as much as possible. But no matter the difference in their attitudes, both remain trapped by circumstances. Adapted from the novel "Yama" by Alexander Ivanovich Kuprin. Japanese with subtitles. **66m/B VHS.** *JP* Isuzu Yamada, Yoko Umemura, Eitaro Shindo, Benkei Shiganoya; ***D:*** Kenji Mizoguchi; ***W:*** Kenji Mizoguchi, Yoshikata Yoda; ***C:*** Minoru Miki.

Sisters, Or the Balance of Happiness 🦴🦴 *Schwestern Oder die Balance des Glucks* **1979** Orderly Maria (Lampe) runs the household for her resentful, dependent sister Anna (Gabriel). Opposites in temperment, the dysfunctional duo can neither live with or without each other. When Anna commits suicide, Maria tries to makeover young typist Miriam (Fruh) to take her sister's place. German with subtitles. **97m/C VHS.** *GE* Jutta Lampe, Gudrun Gabriel, Jessica Fruh; ***D:*** Margarethe von Trotta; ***W:*** Margarethe von Trotta; ***C:*** Franz Rath; ***M:*** Konstantin Wecker.

Sitcom 🦴🦴 **1997** Family dysfunction taken to the extreme. There's a pet rat, a new maid whose African husband seduces the son of the family, a daughter who becomes a paraplegic dominatrix, orgies, incest, and dad, who kills everyone when they throw him a surprise birthday party. Or does he? Or does it matter, anyway? French with subtitles. **80m/C VHS.** *FR* Evelyne Dandry, Francois Marthouret, Marina de Van, Adrien de Van, Stephane Rideau, Lucia Sanchez, Jules-Emmanuel Eyoum Deido; ***D:*** Francois Ozon; ***W:*** Francois Ozon; ***C:*** Yorick Le Saux; ***M:*** Eric Neveux.

Sitting Ducks 🦴🦴🦴 **1980 (R)** Mild-mannered accountant and lecherous pal rip off and then attempt to outrun the mob—all while swapping songs and confessions. Emil and Norman make it up as they go along; their hilarious repartee is largely improvised. They pick up a gorgeous lady (Townsend) and go about their way. **88m/C VHS.** Michael Emil, Zack Norman, Patrice Townsend, Richard Romanus, Irene Forrest, Henry Jaglom; ***D:*** Henry Jaglom; ***W:*** Henry Jaglom.

Six Days, Seven Nights 🦴🦴½ **1998 (PG-13)** Brash magazine editor Robin Monroe (Heche) is on a tropical vacation with fiance Frank (Schwimmer) when a deadline crisis forces her to ask gruff cargo pilot Quinn Harris (Ford) for a lift to Tahiti. A plane crash strands the incompatible duo on a remote island and naturally they need each other to survive. This started out as a routine romantic comedy but the action quotient was upped as filming progressed, thanks to a storyline involving modern-day pirates that's a waste of time. Also a waste are scenes involving Frank with Quinn's bodacious babe, Angelica (Obradors). Why does the only other woman with a significant part have to be a coochie-coo Charo impersonator? Thankfully, Ford and Heche do have considerable sass between them. Filmed on location in Kauai. **101m/C VHS, DVD.** Harrison Ford, Anne Heche, David Schwimmer, Temuera Morrison, Jacqueline Obradors, Allison Janney, Danny Trejo; ***D:*** Ivan Reitman; ***W:*** Michael Browning; ***C:*** Michael Chapman; ***M:*** Randy Edelman.

Six Degrees of Separation 🦴🦴½ **1993 (R)** Some believe that any two people, anywhere in the world, are connected by links to only six other people, hence the six degrees of separation. For the upper crust New Yorker Kittredges, Ouisa (Channing) and Flan (Sutherland), this becomes an issue when they encounter a charming young man (Smith) who claims to be Sidney Poitier's son and a friend of their children. The story unfolds as they realize they've been hustled—and don't understand why. Guare adapted his hit play, but what worked well there is almost too talky here. Channing, reprising her stage role, is very good as the stuffy Ouisa, with Sutherland delivering another interesting performance. Incredibly, the play was based on a true story. **112m/C VHS, DVD, Wide.** Stockard Channing, Will Smith, Donald Sutherland, Mary Beth Hurt, Bruce Davison, Ian McKellen, Richard Masur, Anthony Michael Hall, Heather Graham, Eric Thal, Anthony Rapp, Osgood Perkins II, Kitty Carlisle Hart, Catherine Kellner; ***D:*** Fred Schepisi; ***W:*** John Guare; ***C:*** Ian Baker; ***M:*** Jerry Goldsmith.

Six Gun Gospel 🦴🦴 **1943** Hatton masquerades as a preacher to investigate some shady dealings. Laughs come when the women of the congregation prevail upon him to sing, and he croons a ballad about Jesse James! **59m/B VHS.** Johnny Mack Brown, Raymond Hatton, Inna Gest, Eddie Dew, Roy Barcroft, Kenneth MacDonald, Bud Osborne; ***D:*** Lambert Hillyer.

Six Gun Rhythm 🦴½ **1939** Novelty western plot has football player traveling to Texas to avenge his father's murder. **59m/B VHS.** Tex Fletcher.

633 Squadron 🦴🦴½ **1964** A skilled R.A.F. pilot attempts to lead his squadron on a mission deep into the fjords of Norway in search of a Nazi fuel plant. Robertson tries hard, as always, but is really not British officer material. Well-made war flick, based on a true story. **102m/C VHS.** Cliff Robertson, George Chakiris, Maria Perschy, Harry Andrews; ***D:*** Walter Grauman; ***W:*** James Clavell.

Six in Paris 🦴🦴½ *Paris vu Par* **1968** Six short films by acclaimed French New Wave directors, each depicting a different Parisian neighborhood. "Saint-Germain-des-Pres" finds an American girl disillusioned by two French boys. "Gare du Nord" has a woman meeting a handsome stranger who announces he's going to kill himself. A shy dishwasher brings a prostitute to his room in the "Rue Saint-Denis." When a salesman is accosted by a derelict in the "Place de l'Etoile" he hits him with his umbrella and then thinks he's killed the man. "Montparnasse-Levallois" has a woman thinking she's mixed-up her meetings with her two lovers. "La Muette" finds a small boy buying earplugs to shut out the noise of his parents constant arguing. In French with English subtitles. **93m/C VHS.** *FR* Barbara Wilkin, Jean-Francois Chappey, Jean-Pierre Andreani, Nadine Ballot, Barbet Schroeder, Gilles Queant, Micheline Dax, Claude Melki, Jean-Michel Rouziere, Marcel Gallon, Joanna Shimkus, Philippe Hiquilly, Serge Davri, Stephane Audran, Gilles Chusseau, Dinah Saril, Claude Chabrol; ***D:*** Jean Douchet, Jean Rouch, Jean-Daniel Pollet, Eric Rohmer, Jean-Luc Godard, Claude Chabrol; ***W:*** Jean Douchet, George Keller, Jean Rouch, Jean-Daniel Pollet, Eric Rohmer, Jean-Luc Godard, Claude Chabrol; ***C:*** Nestor Almendros.

Six of a Kind 🦴🦴🦴 **1934** When Flora (Boland) and J. Pinkham Whinney (Ruggles) decide to drive to California for a second honeymoon, they advertise for another couple to share expenses. Unfortunately, it's Burns and Allen and their exceptionally large Great Dane that answer the ad. There's numerous complications, including bank clerk Whinney's being suspected of embezzlement, prompting Sheriff "Honest John" Hoxley (Fields) to go after the supposed criminals. Veteran comedy performers make this one a delight. **63m/B VHS.** Charlie Ruggles, Mary Boland, Gracie Allen, George Burns, W.C. Fields, Alison Skipworth; ***D:*** Leo McCarey; ***W:*** Walter DeLeon, Harry Ruskin; ***C:*** Henry Sharp; ***M:*** Ralph Rainger.

Six Pack 🦴½ **1982 (PG)** The Gambler goes auto racing. Rogers, in his theatrical debut, stars as Brewster Baker, a former stock car driver. He returns to the racing circuit with the help of six larcenous orphans (the six-pack, get it?) adept at stripping cars. Kinda cute if you're in the mood for sugar-powered race car story. **108m/C VHS.** Kenny Rogers, Diane Lane, Erin Gray, Barry Corbin, Anthony Michael Hall; ***D:*** Daniel Petrie; ***M:*** Charles Fox.

Six Shootin' Sheriff 🦴🦴 **1938** A cowboy framed for bank robbery is released and seeks to rid his town of all evil. And he gets the girl! **59m/B VHS.** Ken Maynard, Marjorie Reynolds, Walter Long; ***D:*** Harry Fraser.

Six-String Samurai 🦴🦴 **1998 (PG-13)** In 1957 the USSR bombs and assumes control of the U.S., and Las Vegas is the only safe haven of freedom. Forty years later, a rock musician/samurai is on an odyssey across the desert to replace the recently deceased Elvis as king of the neon city; challenging his quest is another guitar-slinger, Death (Gauger), and his cronies. Our hero Buddy (played by martial artist Falcon as a cross between Buddy Holly and Yojimbo) and his sidekick The Kid (McGuire) must face all the bad guys we've come to expect in a post-apocalyptic adventure. Filled with campy dialogue and well-staged Hong Kong-style action (directed by Falcon), basically all the makings of a good midnight movie, but it doesn't quite come together. **89m/C VHS, DVD.** Jeffrey Falcon, Justin McGuire, Stephane Gauger, John Sakisian; ***D:*** Lance Mungia; ***W:*** Lance Mungia, Jeffrey Falcon; ***C:*** Kristian Bernier; ***M:*** Brian Tyler.

Six Ways to Sunday 🦴🦴 **1999 (R)** Weird mob drama about a hitman and his Oedipal relationship with mom. Passive, repressed teenager, Harry Odum (Reedus), lives with his domineering mother, Kate (Harry), who controls his life. That is, until Harry assists his hoodlum buddy Arnie (Brody) with a job and manages to impress Arnie's boss, Mr. Varga (Adler). Since Harry turns out to have a latent talent for violence, he's soon elevated to hit man—although mom's still a problem. Based on the 1962 novel "Portrait of a Young Man Drowning" by Charles Perry. **97m/C VHS, DVD.** Norman Reedus, Deborah Harry, Adrien Brody, Jerry Adler, Peter Appel, Elina Lowensohn, Isaac Hayes, Anna Thompson; ***D:*** Adam Bernstein; ***W:*** Adam Bernstein, Marc Gerald; ***C:*** John Inwood; ***M:*** Theodore Shapiro.

Six Weeks 🦴🦴 **1982 (PG)** A young girl dying of leukemia brings together her work-driven mother and an aspiring married politician. Manipulative hanky-wringer has good acting from both Moores but oddly little substance. **107m/C VHS.** Dudley Moore, Mary Tyler Moore, Katherine Healy; ***D:*** Tony Bill; ***M:*** Dudley Moore.

Six Wives of Henry VIII 🦴🦴🦴 **1971** Michell has been called the definitive Henry VIII, and this BBC Classic (shown as part of "Masterpiece Theatre" on PBS) was perhaps the most praised series on British TV. Henry's wives were: Catherine of Aragon, Anne Boleyn, Jane Seymour, Anne of Cleves, Catherine Howard, and Catherine Parr. Each episode tells of their (sometimes tragic) fates as pawns in Henry's quest for an heir, and his changes from an eager young man to aged, bitter monarch. **540m/C VHS.** *GB* Keith Michell, Annette Crosbie, Dorothy Tutin, Anne Stallybrass, Elvi Hale, Angela Pleasence, Rosalie Crutchley. **TV**

Sixteen 🦴🦴 *Like a Crow on a June Bug* **1972 (R)** A naive country lass is attracted to the glitter and hum of the outside world. Her determination and optimism help her triumph. **84m/C VHS.** Mercedes McCambridge, Parley Baer, Ford Rainey, Beverly (Hills) Powers, John Lozier, Simone Griffeth, Maidie Norman; ***D:*** Lawrence (Larry) Dobkin.

Sixteen Candles 🦴🦴🦴 **1984 (PG)** Over a decade after hitting the theatres, "Sixteen Candles" is still popular—reaching near cult status among generation X-ers. Hilarious comedy of errors features the pouty Ringwald as an awkard teen who's been dreaming of her 16th birthday. But the rush of her sister's wedding causes everyone to forget, turning her birthday into her worst nightmare. Hughes may not be critically acclaimed, but his movies are so popular they nearly take on a life of their own. Ringwald and Hall are especially charming as the angst-ridden teens, encountering one trauma after another. Great soundtrack includes the title song by The Stray Cats. **93m/C VHS, DVD, Wide.** Molly Ringwald, Justin Henry, Michael Schoeffling, Haviland (Haylie) Morris, Gedde Watanabe, Anthony Michael Hall, Paul Dooley, Carlin Glynn, Blanche Baker, Edward Andrews, Carole Cook, Max (Casey Adams) Showalter, Liane (Alexandra) Curtis, John Cusack, Joan Cusack, Brian Doyle-Murray, Jami Gertz, Cinnamon Idles, Zelda Rubinstein, Billie Bird; ***D:*** John Hughes; ***W:*** John Hughes; ***C:*** Bobby Byrne; ***M:*** Ira Newborn.

Sixteen Fathoms Deep 🦴🦴 **1934** A sponge fisherman risks it all, including his love, when a mean businessman threatens his operation. Good underwater photography, but otherwise undistinguished. **57m/B VHS.** Lon Chaney Jr., Sally O'Neil, George Regas, Maurice Black, Russell Simpson; ***D:*** Armand Schaefer.

The 6th Day 🦴🦴½ **2000 (PG-13)** Arnold's a family guy in the near-future who finds out a clone has taken over his life. Not only that, but the evil corporation behind the clone doesn't want the original around to muck up their nefarious plans. Typical (although somewhat toned-down) Ah-nuld type mayhem ensues. Schwarzenegger has fun with his image, and the supporting players get some fine moments, too. Thought-provoking questions about human cloning add an interesting dimension, raising this one slightly above the genre-pic/star-vehicle level. **124m/C VHS, DVD, Wide.** Arnold Schwarzenegger, Tony Goldwyn, Sarah Wynter, Michael Rooker, Robert Duvall, Michael Rapaport, Wendy Crewson, Rodney Rowland, Ken Pogue, Wanda Cannon, Christopher Lawford, Terry Crews, Colin Cunningham, Taylor Anne Reid, Jennifer Gareis, Don McManus, Steve Bacic; ***D:*** Roger Spottiswoode; ***W:*** Cormac Wibberly, Marianne S. Wibberly; ***C:*** Pierre Mignot; ***M:*** Trevor Rabin.

The Sixth Man 🦴½ **1997 (PG-13)** College basketball star Antoine Tyler (Hardison) dies but returns as a ghost to help his brother (Wayans) lead their team to the NCAA finals. Basketball seems to be the sport of choice for Hollywood lately, so you'd think they'd be able to get one of these movies right. Once again, they blow the layup. The first half features the requisite flashback and tearjerker death scene, both of which are surprisingly effective. But then the focus turns to "hilarious" on-court hijinks and the all-time sports cliche champion: the second-half rally from an impossible deficit. Hardison and Wayans are the bright spots, displaying fine comic and dramatic chemistry. **107m/C VHS.** Kadeem Hardison, Marlon Wayans, David Paymer, Michael Michele, Kevin Dunn, Gary Jones, Vladimir Cuk, Chris Spencer, Kirk Baily, Saundra McClain, Lorenzo Orr, Travis Ford, Harold Sylvester; ***D:*** Randall Miller; ***W:*** Christopher Reed, Cynthia Carle; ***C:*** Michael Ozier; ***M:*** Marcus Miller.

The Sixth Sense 🦴🦴🦴 **1999 (PG-13)** Creepy psycho thriller about a traumatized young boy who can communicate with the dead (this is not the film's big surprise). Failed child shrink Malcolm Crowe (Willis in an excellent subdued performance) takes on the case of 9-year-old Cole (a touching Osment, carrying the picture on frail shoulders), who's divorced mom, Lynn (Collette), is worried about her terrified son's nightmares and episodes of acting out. Well, if you saw dead people all the time, you'd be scared too. When Crowe (who's dealing with traumas of his own) finally believes Cole, it leads to a breakthrough and an unexpected twist on what's happened before. **107m/C VHS, DVD.** Bruce Willis, Haley Joel Osment, Toni Collette, Olivia Williams, Donnie Wahlberg, Glenn Fitzgerald,

Trevor Morgan, Mischa Barton, Bruce Norris; *D:* M. Night Shyamalan; *W:* M. Night Shyamalan; *C:* Tak Fujimoto; *M:* James Newton Howard. MTV Movie Awards '00: Breakthrough Perf. (Osment); Broadcast Film Critics '99: Breakthrough Perf. (Osment).

The '60s 2½ 1999 (PG-13) A quick trip through the decade of peace, love, and Vietnam, told with all the usual cliches. Film uses the parallel stories of two families to hit the high points—the white, middleclass Herlihy family of Chicago and the black Taylor family of Mississippi. You've got hippies, Black Panthers, civil rights, the war, the anti-war movement, drugs, and rock 'n' roll. The soundtrack may be the best thing the miniseries has going for it. **171m/C VHS, DVD.** Jerry O'Connell, Josh Hamilton, Julia Stiles, Bill Smitrovich, Annie Corley, Leonard Roberts, Charles S. Dutton, Jordana Brewster, David Alan Grier, Jeremy Sisto, Cliff Gorman, Donovan Leitch, Carnie Wilson, Rosanna Arquette; *D:* Mark Piznarski; *W:* Jeffrey Alladin Fiskin; *C:* Michael D. O'Shea. **TV**

61* 3 2001 Crystal's nostalgic and meticulous telling of the 1961 home run race between Mickey Mantle (Jane) and Roger Maris (Pepper) clears the fence. Pepper and Jane are excellent as the "M & M Boys," and the rest of the solid cast is up to the task as well. The fine script mixes the baseball action with the behind the scenes material well. Crystal and writer Steinberg take great pains to show the tremendous pressure and outside distractions with which both players had to contend. With the exception of a few sportswriters (the obligatory villains), most of the characters are fleshed out nicely, instead of becoming a checklist of familiar names. Baseball geeks will find nits to pick, but for the most part, the baseball scenes and historical facts are right on the mark. Crystal's daughter plays Mrs. Maris. **128m/C VHS, DVD, Wide.** Thomas Jane, Barry Pepper, Chris Bauer, Christopher McDonald, Anthony Michael Hall, Bob Gunton, Bruce McGill, Richard Masur, Bobby Hosea, Donald Moffat, Renee Taylor, Joe Grifasi, Michael Nouri, Paul Borghese, Jennifer Crystal Foley, Seymour Cassel, Peter Jacobson, Robert Joy, Pat Crowley, Robert Costanzo; *D:* Billy Crystal; *W:* Hank Steinberg; *C:* Haskell Wexler; *M:* Marc Shaiman. **CABLE**

'68 1 1987 (R) A Hungarian family struggles with the generation gap in 1968 America. **99m/C VHS, DVD, Wide.** Eric Larson, Terra Vandergaw, Neil Young, Sandor Tecsi; *D:* Steven Kovacks; *C:* Daniel Lacambre; *M:* Shony Alex Braun, John Cipollinam.

Sizzle 2 1981 When her boyfriend is murdered by the mob, nightclub singer Anderson, newly arrived from Hicksville in Roaring '20s Chicago, stops at nothing to get revenge. Bad-guy gangster Forsythe falls for her charms. Fun but unsophisticated. Made for TV. **100m/C VHS.** Loni Anderson, John Forsythe, Leslie Uggams, Roy Thinnes, Richard Lynch, Michael Goodwin; *D:* Don Medford; *M:* Artie Butler. **TV**

Sizzle Beach U.S.A. 1 *Malibu Hot Summer* 1974 (R) Three aspiring young actresses want a shot at becoming famous and travel to Los Angeles where they spend their time at the beach with little budget and no particular purchase. Re-released and renamed in 1986 when Costner (in his film debut) became more well-known. **89m/C VHS, DVD.** Terry Congie, Leslie Brander, Roselyn Royce, Kevin Costner; *D:* Richard Brander.

Skag 3 1979 Disabled following a stroke, a Pittsburgh steel worker confronts a change in family roles and long-ignored family problems during his convalescence. Malden is exceptional and believable as a Joe Lunchbucket in this well-written, well-cast TV outing, pilot for the NBC series. **145m/C VHS.** Karl Malden, Piper Laurie, Craig Wasson, Leslie Ackerman, Peter Gallagher, Kathryn Holcomb, Powers Boothe; *D:* Frank Perry. **TV**

Skateboard 1 1977 (PG) A down-and-out Hollywood agent creates a pro skateboarding team and enters them in a race worth $20,000. Quickie premise executed lamely. **97m/C VHS.** Allen (Goorwitz) Garfield, Kathleen Lloyd, Chad McQueen, Leif Garrett, Richard Van Der Wyk, Tony Alva, Antony Carbone; *W:* Dick Wolf.

The Skateboard Kid 1½ 1993 (PG) When an outsider finds a magical talking skateboard, he suddenly becomes the envy of the in-group of skateboarding thrashers. **90m/C VHS.** Bess Armstrong, Timothy Busfield; *D:* Larry Swerdlove; *W:* Roger Corman; *V:* Dom DeLuise.

The Skateboard Kid 2 2 1994 (PG) Mystery creature helps Sammy build his dream skateboard, which turns out to have a mind of its own. **95m/C VHS.** Trenton Knight, Dee Wallace Stone, Bruce Davison, Andrew Stevens; *D:* Andrew Stevens.

Skeeter 1½ 1993 (R) Yes, it's the attack of the killer mosquito! Not just any mosquito of course, but a new gigantic species bred on toxic waste. They're invading the quiet desert town of Mesquite—and they're out for blood! **95m/C VHS.** Tracy Griffith, Jim Youngs, Charles Napier, Michael J. Pollard; *D:* Clark Brandon; *W:* Clark Brandon, Lanny Horn; *M:* David Lawrence.

Skeezer 2½ 1982 A dog becomes a key factor in a sympathetic doctor's efforts to communicate with emotionally unstable children. Based on reality, and a good cast makes it believable and moving. Quality family fare. **100m/C VHS.** Karen Valentine, Dee Wallace Stone, Tom Atkins, Mariclare Costello, Leighton Greer, Justine Lord; *D:* Peter H. Hunt.

Skeleton Coast 1 *Fair Trade* 1989 (R) Borgnine plays a retired U.S. Marine colonel who organizes a Magnificent Seven-like group of tough mercenaries to go into eastern Africa to save hostages held by Angolan terrorists. Cliches abound, including a token large-breasted woman, Mulford, getting her t-shirt ripped open. No plot and a bad script. **94m/C VHS.** Ernest Borgnine, Robert Vaughn, Oliver Reed, Herbert Lom, Daniel Greene, Nancy Mulford, Leon Isaac Kennedy; *D:* John Cardos.

Skeletons 2 1996 (R) Journalist Peter Crane (Silver) decides to leave New York after suffering a heart attack and moves his family to what he thinks will be the quiet of Saugatuck, Maine. They're settling in when Peter is approached by the mother of a young man, who's standing trial for murder, who claims her son is innocent. When Peter investigates, the townspeople suddenly turn hostile and the man is found hanged in his cell. Turns out this town's skeletons go back 100 years and the secrets are deadly. **91m/C VHS.** Ron Silver, James Coburn, Christopher Plummer, Dee Wallace Stone, Kyle Howard, Thomas Wilson Brown; *Cameos:* Paul Bartel; *D:* David DeCoteau.

Skeletons in the Closet 2½ 2000 (R) Seth Reed (Jackson) is more than just a rebellious teenager. A loner, he's given to violent outbursts that have his widowed father, Will (Williams), worried. Especially when a series of murders are committed in their New Hampshire town. But since Will is still suffering from the aftermath of his wife's death in a fire, maybe it's his sanity that's in question. Creepy, if sometimes cliched, thriller. **86m/C VHS, DVD.** Treat Williams, Jonathan Jackson, Linda Hamilton, Schuyler Fisk, Gordon Clapp; *D:* Wayne Powers; *W:* Wayne Powers, Donna Powers; *C:* Michael Barrett; *M:* Christopher Stone. **VIDEO**

Sketch Artist 2 1992 (R) Jack Whitfield (Fahey) is a police sketch artist whose latest rendering of a murder suspect looks suspiciously like his wife. Jack decides to keep this information to himself while he does some quiet investigating but he may not have any time. The police have a new murder suspect in mind—Jack! **89m/C VHS.** Jeff Fahey, Sean Young, Drew Barrymore, Frank McRae, Tcheky Karyo, James Tolkan, Charlotte Lewis; *D:* Phedon Papamichael; *W:* Michael Angeli. **CABLE**

Sketch Artist 2: Hands That See 2½ 1994 Fahey returns as police artist Jack Whitfield, who's asked to draw a sketch of a serial rapist/murderer. Near-victim Emmy (Cox) just happens to be blind but describes to Jack how the rapist looked as she felt his face. Emmy's hubby Glenn (Silverman) is concerned, especially when the creep warns Emmy about her trip to the cops. Solid characters build to good courtroom climax. **95m/C VHS.** Jeff Fahey, Courteney Cox Arquette, Jonathan Silverman, Michael Beach, Brion James, James Tolkan, Leilani Sarelle Ferrer, Michael Nicolosi, Scott Burkholder; *D:* Jack Sholder; *W:* Michael Angeli; *M:* Tim Truman.

Sketches of a Strangler 1½ 1978 A psychotic art student sketches, then murders prostitutes. Interesting lead character but hardly chilling—just horrible to watch. Made for TV. **91m/C VHS.** Allen (Goorwitz) Garfield, Meredith MacRae; *D:* Paul Leder. **TV**

Ski Bum 1 1975 (R) A ski bum discovers corruption and violence at a Colorado Rockies resort. Eminently forgettable trash. Scantily based on a novel by Romain Gary. **94m/C VHS.** Charlotte Rampling, Zalman King, Dimitra Arliss, Anna Karina; *D:* Bruce (B.D.) Clark.

Ski Patrol 2 1989 (PG) Wacky ski groupies try to stop an evil developer. Good ski action in a surprisingly plotful effort from the crazy crew that brought the world "Police Academy." **85m/C VHS.** Roger Rose, Yvette Nipar, T.K. Carter, Leslie Jordan, Ray Walston, Martin Mull; *D:* Richard Correll.

Ski School 1 1991 (R) Rival ski instructors compete for jobs and babes. Brow lowering. **89m/C VHS.** Ava Fabian, Dean Cameron, Tom Breznahan, Stuart Fratkin; *D:* Damian Lee.

Ski School 2 1½ 1994 (R) Former ski instructor Dave finds that both his job and his ex-gal have been acquired by a jerk. So Dave decides to get them both back. **92m/C VHS.** Dean Cameron, Wendy Hamilton, Heather Campbell, Brent Sheppard, Bill Dwyer; *D:* David Mitchell; *W:* Jay Naples.

Ski Troop Attack 2 1960 During WWII, an American ski patrol is sent behind Nazi lines to blow up a German railway bridge. Unexceptional low-budget Corman outing; not among the greatest of war movies. **61m/B VHS.** Michael Forest, Frank Wolff, Sheila Carol.

Skier's Dream 1988 This spectacular action-packed film focuses on a young executive in search of the ultimate run. Shot on the most exotic ski locations in the world; covers freestyle skiing, powder skiing, snowboarding, extreme skiing, cliff jumping, paragliding, and wave riding. **75m/C VHS.** John Eaves, Ian Boyd; *M:* Jimi Hendrix, Tom Cochrane.

Skin 1½ *Howard Beach: Making the Case for Murder* 1989 (PG-13) Prosecutor seeks the truth after a black man is chased into highway traffic by a gang of white teenaged thugs from Queens. Based on the true story of the death of a young black man in Howards Beach, Queens. Made for TV. **95m/C VHS.** Daniel J. Travanti, Joe Morton, Dan Lauria, William Daniels; *C:* Ron Fortunato. **TV**

Skin Art 1½ 1993 (R) Very offbeat character study focusing on Will, a tormented tattoo artist who specializes in decorating the backs of the young Asian prostitutes who work in a nearby brothel. Haunted by his memories as a Vietnam POW, Will decides to exorcise some demons on his latest female canvas. **90m/C VHS.** Kirk Baltz, Jake Weber, Nora Ariffin; *D:* W(illiam) Blake Herron; *W:* W(illiam) Blake Herron.

Skin Deep 1½ 1989 (R) A boyish Don Juan tries everything to win back his ex-wife. Ritter whines about his mid-life crisis and seduces women; this substitutes for plot. A few funny slapstick scenes still don't make this worth watching. **102m/C VHS.** John Ritter, Vincent Gardenia, Julianne Phillips, Alyson Reed, Nina Foch, Chelsea Field, Denise Crosby; *D:* Blake Edwards; *W:* Blake Edwards; *M:* Henry Mancini.

Skin Deep 2 1994 Lesbian filmmaker Alex is obsessed with making her first feature, which is about the pleasure and pain associated with body art. She places an ad in a tattoo magazine for an assistant and is intrigued by respondent, Chris, who's still dealing with her transgendered experience. As Alex gets deeper into her movie, she fails to notice Chris' growing infatuation with her until Chris decides to do something desperate to gain Alex's attention. **82m/C VHS.** *CA* Natsuko Ohama, Keram Malicki-Sanchez, Dana Brooks, Melanie Nicholls-King, David Crean; *D:* Midi Onodera; *W:* Midi Onodera, Barbara O'Kelly.

Skin Game 1½ 1931 Two British families feud over land rights. Not thrilling; not characteristic of working with Hitchcock. Way too much talking in excruciating, drawn-out scenes. Adapted from the play of the same name. **87m/B VHS, DVD.** *GB* Phyllis Konstam, Edmund Gwenn, Frank Lawton, C.V. France, Jill Esmond, Helen Haye; *D:* Alfred Hitchcock; *W:* Alfred Hitchcock; *C:* Jack Cox.

Skin Game 3 1971 (PG) A fast talking con-artist (Garner) and his black partner (Gossett) travel throughout the antebellum South setting up scams—Gossett is sold to a new owner by Garner, who helps him escape. Garner and Gossett make a splendid comedy team in this different kind of buddy flick. All is well until Asner turns the tables on them. Finely acted comedy-drama. **102m/C VHS.** James Garner, Louis Gossett Jr., Susan Clark, Ed Asner, Andrew Duggan; *D:* Paul Bogart; *M:* David Shire.

Skinheads: The Second Coming of Hate 1 1988 (R) Neo-fascists run rampant. Exploitative effort from schlock-doyen Clark. **93m/C VHS.** Chuck Connors, Barbara Bain, Brian Brophy, Jason Culp, Elizabeth Sagal; *D:* Greydon Clark; *W:* Greydon Clark.

Skinned Alive woof! 1989 A woman and her children travel cross-country to sell leather goods. When a detective discovers where the leather comes from he's hot on their trail. **90m/C VHS.** Mary Jackson, Scott Spiegel; *D:* Jon Killough; *W:* Jon Killough.

Skinner 1 1993 (R) Psychopath Dennis Skinner (Raimi) more than lives up to his grisly name with his penchant for stalking hookers with carving knives and cleavers. Now he's going after his innocent landlady (Lake) and it's up to Heidi (Lords), a victim who managed to get away, to find him before he can kill again. Lords in lingerie (and nasty scars) and some really disgusting skinning scenes. **89m/C VHS, DVD.** Theodore (Ted) Raimi, Traci Lords, Ricki Lake; *D:* Ivan Nagy; *W:* Paul Hart-Wilden; *C:* Greg Littlewood.

Skinner's Dress Suit 2½ 1926 Meek, hen-pecked office clerk tells domineering wife he got a raise so she'll get off his back. She quickly insinuates them into upper crusty social circle, where the fib pays off big. Remake of the 1917 version based on Henry Irving Dodge's novel. **79m/B VHS.** Reginald Denny, Laura La Plante, Arthur Lake, Hedda Hopper; *D:* William A. Seiter.

Skipped Parts 1½ 2000 (R) Fourteen-year-old Sam Callahan (Hall) and his bad-girl mom, Lydia (Leigh), have been exiled to Wyoming in 1963 by Lydia's southern big daddy, Caspar (Ermey). Lydia promptly takes up with the wrong guy (Greyeyes) and encourages Sam in sexual experimentation with schoolmate Maurey (Barton), with unfortunate results. Based on Sandlin's coming-of-age trilogy, the film is flat and predictable. **93m/C VHS, DVD, Wide.** *US* Jennifer Jason Leigh, Bug Hall, Michael Greyeyes, Mischa Barton, Peggy Lipton, Brad Renfro, R. Lee Ermey, Angela Featherstone, Alison Pill, Drew Barrymore, Gerald Lenton-Young; *D:* Tamra Davis; *W:* Tim Sandlin; *C:* Claudio Rocha; *M:* Stewart Copeland.

Skirts Ahoy! 2 1952 Williams, Evans, and Blaine are three WAVES who have their eyes set on three handsome men. To get them, of course, they must sing and dance a lot, and Williams must perform one of her famous water ballets. ♫Oh By Jingo; Hold Me Close to You; What Makes a WAVE?; What Good is a Gal Without a Guy?; Skirts Ahoy!; Glad to Have You Aboard; The Navy Waltz; I Get a Funny Feeling; We Will Fight. **109m/C VHS.** Esther Williams, Joan Evans, Vivian Blaine, Barry Sullivan, Keefe Brasselle, Billy Eckstine, Debbie Reynolds; *D:* Sidney Lanfield.

The Skull 2 1965 Horror abounds when Cushing gets his hands on the skull of the Marquis de Sade that has mysterious, murderous powers. Based on a story by Robert Bloch. **83m/C VHS.** Peter Cushing, Patrick Wymark, Christopher Lee, Nigel Green, Jill Bennett, Michael Gough, George Coulouris, Patrick Magee; *D:* Freddie Francis.

Skull: A Night of Terror 🦴🦴 **1988 (R)** A cop vows not to use guns after a tragic accident, then single-handed and unarmed, takes on terrorists who kidnap his family. **80m/C VHS.** Nadia Capone, Robert Bideman, Robbie Fox, Paul Sanders; ***D:*** Robert Bergman; ***W:*** Robert Bergman, Gerard Ciccoritti.

Skull & Crown 🦴🦴 **1935** Rin Tin Tin Jr. helps the hero break up a group of smugglers. A favorite of Tin fans everywhere. **58m/B VHS.** Regis Toomey, Jack Mulhall, James Murray.

Skullduggery 🦴½ **1970 (PG)** When a peaceful race of blond ape-people are discovered in New Guinea, a courtroom battle ensues to prevent their slaughter at the hands of developers. Interesting premise sadly flops. **105m/C VHS.** Burt Reynolds, Susan Clark, Roger C. Carmel, Chips Rafferty, Edward Fox, Wilfrid Hyde-White, Rhys Williams; ***D:*** Gordon Douglas.

Skullduggery woof! *Warlock* **1979 (PG)** Costume-store minion Haverstock carries a curse that makes him kill and mutilate. The usual unspeakable horror ensues for a group of medieval-game players. **95m/C VHS.** Thom Haverstock, Wendy Crewson, David Calderisi; ***D:*** Ota Richter.

The Skulls 🦴½ **2000 (PG-13)** Well, you just can't trust those darn secret societies. Teen star Jackson is Luke, an ambitious kid from the wrong side of the tracks at an "unnamed" Ivy League school that starts with "Y." Because he's the captain of the rowing team, he's asked to join the elite secret society the "Skulls." After the requisite hazing and initiation, Luke is showered with money and other perks. Membership has its privileges. But when his best friend Will (Harper) is found dead after snooping in Skull business, Luke suspects foul play and the movie goes from laughable to ludicrous. This secret society, led by evil judge Litten Mandrake (Nelson), does a lot of its business, including duels and car chases, out in the open. Another entry using the teen-paranoia-adults-are-bad theme, which should, mercifuly, help kill off the genre for a while. **106m/C VHS, DVD, Wide.** Joshua Jackson, Paul Walker, Hill Harper, Leslie Bibb, Christopher McDonald, Steve Harris, William L. Petersen, Craig T. Nelson; ***D:*** Rob Cohen; ***W:*** John Pogue; ***C:*** Shane Hurlbut; ***M:*** Randy Edelman.

The Skulls 2 🦴🦴 **2002 (R)** College student Ryan (Dunne) becomes a member of the secret fraternity the Skulls but when he sees a girl fall off the fraternity's roof, the situation turns ugly. **100m/C VHS, DVD, Wide.** *CA* Robin Dunne, Aaron Ashmore, Ashley Lyn Cafagna, Christopher Ralph, Nathan West, James Callanders, Lindy Booth; ***D:*** Joe Chappelle; ***W:*** Hans Rodionoff, Michele Colucci-Zieger; ***C:*** Steve Danyluk; ***M:*** Christophe Beck. **VIDEO**

The Sky Above, the Mud Below *Le Ciel et le Boue* **1961** An acclaimed documentary following a band of explorers transversing New Guinea in 1959, and their confrontations with native rituals, heretofore unknown cannibal tribes and physical calamities. In HiFi. **90m/C VHS.** ***D:*** Pierre-Dominique Gaisseau. Oscars '61: Feature Doc.

Sky Bandits 🦴½ **1940** Mounties uncover the mystery of a disappearing plane carrying gold from a Yukon mine. Last of the "Renfrew of the Mounties" pictures. **56m/B VHS, 8mm.** James Newill, Dave O'Brien, Louise Stanley; ***D:*** Ralph Staub; ***W:*** Edward Halperin; ***C:*** Mack Stengler.

Sky Hei$t 🦴🦴 **1975** Criminals plan robbery of police helicopter carrying fortune in gold bullion. **96m/C VHS.** Stefanie Powers, Joseph Campanella, Don Meredith, Larry Wilcox, Frank Gorshin, Shelley Fabares, Ken Swofford, Ray Vitte, Nancy Belle Fuller, Suzanne Somers; ***D:*** Lee H. Katzin. **TV**

Sky High 🦴🦴½ **1922** Mix is an immigration agent after a gang smuggling Chinese laborers across the Mexican border. Thrills involve an airplane and mountaintop battles as well as some terrific location footage from the Grand Canyon. **58m/B VHS.** Tom Mix, Eva Novak, J. Farrell MacDonald, Sid Jordan; ***D:*** Lynn F. Reynolds; ***W:*** Lynn F. Reynolds. Natl. Film Reg. '98.

Sky High 🦴 **1951** A spy at an Air Force base is trying to get hold of the plans to a secret plane. A GI is recruited to catch him. **60m/B VHS.** Sid Melton, Mara Lynn, Douglas Evans.

Sky High 🦴 **1984** Three college students become immersed in international intrigue when the C.I.A. and the K.G.B. pursue them through Greece looking for a secret Soviet tape. **103m/C VHS.** Daniel Hirsch, Clayton Norcross, Frank Schultz, Lauren Taylor; ***D:*** Nico Mastorakis.

Sky Liner 🦴 **1949** An FBI agent is trailing a spy who has taken secret documents aboard a west-bound flight. **62m/B VHS.** Richard Travis, Pamela Blake.

The Sky Pilot 🦴🦴½ **1921** Young clergyman sets up a parish on North Pacific coast and finds he must prove himself to the cowboys. He saves young woman from stampede, but her father blames him for her maimed legs and sets the preacher's church on fire, providing girl with excuse to overcome handicap. **63m/B VHS.** John Bowers, Colleen Moore, David Butler, Donald Ian Macdonald; ***D:*** King Vidor.

Sky Pirates woof! **1987** Space epic deals about pieces of ancient stone left by prehistoric extraterrestrials, now lost in a time warp. Bad stunts, bad script and notably bad acting make it a woofer in any era. **88m/C VHS.** *AU* John Hargreaves, Max Phipps, Meredith Phillips; ***D:*** Colin Eggleston.

Sky Riders 🦴🦴½ **1976 (PG)** Hang-gliders risk it all to take on a group of political kidnappers. Fine hang-gliding footage and glorious Greek locations make up for garden-variety plot. **93m/C VHS.** James Coburn, Susannah York, Robert Culp, Charles Aznavour, Harry Andrews, John Beck; ***D:*** Douglas Hickox; ***W:*** Jack DeWitt, Garry Michael White; ***M:*** Lalo Schifrin.

Skyline 🦴🦴🦴 *La Linea Del Cielo* **1984 (R)** A Spanish photographer comes to New York City to work for a magazine and tries to adjust to his cultural dislocation. Quietly funny, with a startling ending. Partly in Spanish with English subtitles. **84m/C VHS.** *SP* Antonio Resines, Beatriz Perez-Porro, Jaime Nos, Roy Hoffman; ***D:*** Fernando Colomo.

The Sky's the Limit 🦴🦴½ **1943** Astaire spends his leave in Manhattan and falls in love with fetching journalist Leslie. He's in civvies, so little does she know he's a war hero. Nothing-special semi-musical, with Fred-Ginger spark missing. ♫One For My Baby; My Shining Hour; I've Got a Lot in Common With You. **89m/B VHS.** Fred Astaire, Joan Leslie, Robert Benchley, Robert Ryan, Elizabeth Patterson; ***D:*** Edward H. Griffith.

Skyscraper 🦴 **1995 (R)** Gun-wielding helicopter pilot/heroine Carrie Wink (Smith) must battle villainous mercenaries holding hostages in an LA skyscraper. But she stills manages to find time for lots of steamy showers (to best display the only assets the film has). **96m/C VHS, DVD.** Anna Nicole Smith, Richard Steinmetz; ***D:*** Raymond Martino; ***W:*** William Applegate Jr.; ***C:*** Frank Harris; ***M:*** Jim Halfpenny.

Skyscraper Souls 🦴🦴🦴 **1932** William stars as David Dwight, a ruthless businessman who manipulates stock prices and double-crosses lovers in order to have complete control of a 100-story office building. He sacrifices everything and everyone in this story of big business. Based on the novel "Skyscraper" by Faith Baldwin. **98m/B VHS.** Warren William, Maureen O'Sullivan, Gregory Ratoff, Anita Page, Verree Teasdale, Norman Foster, Jean Hersholt, Wallace Ford; ***D:*** Edgar Selwyn.

Slacker 🦴🦴🦴 **1991 (R)** Defines a new generation: Overwhelmed by the world and it's demands, "Slackers" react by retreating into lives of minimal expectations. Filmed as a series of improvisational stories about people living on the fringes of the working world and their reactions (or lack thereof) to the life swirling around them. First feature for writer/director Linklater on a budget of $23,000; filmed on location in Austin, Texas with a cast of primarily non-professional actors. **97m/C VHS.** Richard Linklater, Rudy Basquez, Jean Caffeine, Jan Hockey, Stephan Hockey, Mark James, Samuel Dietert; ***D:*** Richard Linklater; ***W:*** Richard Linklater; ***C:*** Lee Daniel.

Slackers 🦴½ **2002 (R)** Schwartzman is wasted as Ethan, a social outcast college student with his stalker-like eye on the prize—an intelligent college girl with model good looks (former model King). Nicknaming himself "Cool Ethan," our semi-delusional hero blackmails three of the campus's best and brightest, who have gotten that rep entirely through cheating. Ethan demands the boys use their unique methods of chicanery to get him his dream girl, or he'll get them all expelled. Leader of the gang Dave (Sawa) leads the fix-up charade but ends up falling for the cutie himself. Uninteresting, annoying characters, awkward plotting, and the requisite ton of sophomoric, sexual, and gross-out humor, including a gratuitous septugenarian sponge bath. **86m/C VHS, DVD, Wide.** *US* Devon Sawa, Jason Schwartzman, James King, Jason Segel, Michael Maronna, Laura Prepon, Mamie Van Doren, Joe Flaherty, Leigh Taylor-Young, Sam Anderson, Cameron Diaz; ***D:*** Dewey Nicks; ***W:*** David H. Steinberg; ***C:*** James R. Bagdonas; ***M:*** Joseph (Joey) Altruda.

Slam 🦴🦴 **1998 (R)** Documentarian Levin makes his feature film debut with this part-prison, part-ghetto drama. Street-smart, low-level drug dealer Ray (Williams) is living in gang-ridden D.C. when he's busted for possession and suspicion of murdering his supplier. Jail's just as rough as the streets since two local inside gangs each want Ray's allegiance. Ray wants to keep to himself and work on his writing—the poetry he composes about what he sees in life. He manages to get bail and then has a lot of hard decisions to make. **100m/C VHS, DVD.** Saul Williams, Sonja Sohn, Bonz Malone; ***D:*** Marc Levin; ***W:*** Marc Levin, Saul Williams, Sonja Sohn, Bonz Malone, Richard Stratton; ***C:*** Mark Benjamin. Sundance '98: Grand Jury Prize.

Slam Dunk Ernest 🦴½ **1995 (PG-13)** Ernest (Varney) becomes a basketball star in a city league exhibition game when the Basketball Angel (Abdul-Jabbar) loans him his magic shoes. **93m/C VHS.** Jim Varney, Kareem Abdul-Jabbar, Jay Brazeau; ***D:*** John R. Cherry III; ***W:*** John R. Cherry III, Daniel Butler; ***M:*** Mark Adler.

Slamdance 🦴½ **1987 (R)** A struggling cartoonist is framed for the murder of a beautiful young woman while being victimized by the real killer. A complicated murder mystery with a punk beat and visual flash. But the tale is unoriginal—and where's the slamdancing? **99m/C VHS.** Tom Hulce, Virginia Madsen, Mary Elizabeth Mastrantonio, Harry Dean Stanton, Adam Ant, John Doe; ***D:*** Wayne Wang.

Slammer Girls 🦴 **1987 (R)** In this sex-drenched, unfunny spoof on women's prison films, the inmates of Loch Ness Penitentiary try to break out using their sexual wiles. The actresses are pseudonymous porn stars. **82m/C VHS.** Tally Brittany, Jane (Veronica Hart) Hamilton, Jeff Eagle, Devon Jenkin; ***D:*** Chuck Vincent.

The Slap *La Gifle* **1976 (PG)** French teens learn about love the French way. **103m/C VHS.** *FR* Isabelle Adjani, Lino Ventura; ***D:*** Claude Pinoteau; ***M:*** Georges Delerue.

Slap Shot 🦴🦴🦴 **1977 (R)** Profane satire of the world of professional hockey. Over-the-hill player-coach of the third-rate Charlestown Chiefs, Reggie Dunlop (Newman), gathers an odd-ball mixture of has-beens and young players and reluctantly initiates them, using violence on the ice to make his team win. The on-ice striptease by star player Ned Braden (Ontkean) needs to be seen to be believed. Charming in its own bone-crunching way. **123m/C VHS, DVD.** Allan Nicholls, Paul D'Amato, Brad Sullivan, Stephen Mendillo, Kathryn Walker, Paul Dooley, Yvon Barrette, Jeff Carlson, Steve Carlson, Dave Hanson, Ned Dowd, Paul Newman, Michael Ontkean, Jennifer Warren, Lindsay Crouse, Jerry Houser, Melinda Dillon, Strother Martin, Andrew Duncan, M. Emmet Walsh, Nancy Dowd, Swoosie Kurtz; ***D:*** George Roy Hill; ***W:*** Nancy Dowd; ***C:*** Victor Kemper; ***M:*** Elmer Bernstein.

Slap Shot 2: Breaking the Ice 🦴🦴 **2002 (R)** Okay, it took 25 years to make a sequel—is this a record? Rude and crude hockey comedy finds the Charlestown Chiefs being sold to media mogul Busey, who moves the team to Omaha, Nebraska. But the team is not supposed to play "real" hockey; they are only supposed to take the money and serve as comic foils to the game, which upsets the geeky Hanson brothers and team captain Baldwin. **104m/C VHS, DVD, Wide.** Stephen Baldwin, Jeff Carlson, Steve Carlson, Dave Hanson, Gary Busey, Callum Keith Rennie, Jessica Steen; ***D:*** Steve Boyum; ***W:*** Broderick Miller; ***C:*** Joel Ransom. **VIDEO**

Slappy and the Stinkers 🦴🦴½ **1997 (PG)** Five young misfits, known as "The Stinkers," are constantly in trouble with their stuffy school principal Morgan Brinway (Wong). On a class trip to the acquarium, the Stinkers meet Slappy the sea lion and decide to liberate him (they think he looks unhappy), stowing Slappy in Mr. Brinway's hot tub. Then the kids find out that evil animal thief Boccoli (McMurray) wants to steal the critter and sell him to a circus. Just as silly as it sounds but Slappy is really cute. **78m/C VHS.** B.D. Wong, Bronson Pinchot, Sam McMurray, Joseph Ashton, Travis Tedford, Gary LeRoi Gray, Carl Michael Lindner, Scarlett Pomers, Jennifer Coolidge; ***D:*** Barnet Kellman; ***W:*** Michael Scott, Bob Wolterstorff.

Slapstick of Another Kind 🦴½ **1984 (PG)** Lewis and Kahn play dual roles as an alien brother and sister and their adoptive Earth parents, who are being pursued by U.S. agents. Rather miserable rendition of a Kurt Vonnegut novel. **85m/C VHS.** Jerry Lewis, Madeline Kahn, Marty Feldman, Jim Backus, Noriyuki "Pat" Morita, Samuel Fuller, Orson Welles; ***D:*** Steven Paul.

Slash 🦴½ **1987** Each of four people caught in a political takeover harbors a secret that could harm one of the others. Extremely violent. **90m/C VHS.** Romano Kristoff, Michael Monty, Gwen Hung; ***D:*** John Gale.

Slashdance woof! **1989** A really pathetic thriller follows a lady cop undercover in a chorus line to find out who's been murdering the dancers. The acting is on the level of pro wrestling. Don't be fooled by the naked babes on the cassette box—there's no nudity. **83m/C VHS.** Cindy Maranne, James Carroll Jordan, Queen Kong, Joel von Ornsteiner, Jay Richardson; ***D:*** James Shyman; ***W:*** James Shyman.

Slashed Dreams 🦴🦴 *Sunburst* **1974 (R)** Hippie couple travels to California wilderness in search of a friend. A pair of woodsmen assault them and rape the woman, which really messes with their heads. Retitled and packaged as slasher movie. **74m/C VHS.** Peter Hooten, Kathrine Baumann, Ric Carrott, Anne Lockhart, Robert Englund, Rudy Vallee, James Keach, David Pritchard, Peter Brown; ***D:*** James Polakof; ***W:*** James Keach, David Pritchard.

The Slasher woof! **1974** A policeman must find the madman who has been killing off unfaithful married women. Miserably gory, pointless slasher (hence the title) interesting only as an early example of its kind. **88m/C VHS.** Farley Granger, Sylva Koscina, Susan Scott.

Slate, Wyn & Me 🦴 **1987 (R)** Two bank-robbing, kidnapping brothers flee cross-country from the law, and fall in love with the girl they've snatched. Pointless, and pointlessly violent and vulgar. **90m/C VHS.** Sigrid Thornton, Simon Burke, Martin Sacks; ***D:*** Don McLennan; ***C:*** David Connell.

Slaughter 🦴 **1972 (R)** After his parents are murdered, a former Green Beret goes after their killers. Plenty of brutality. Followed by "Slaughter's Big Ripoff." **92m/C VHS, DVD, Wide.** Jim Brown, Stella Stevens, Rip Torn, Cameron Mitchell, Don Gordon, Marlene Clark; ***D:*** Jack Starrett; ***W:*** Mark Hanna, Don Williams; ***C:*** R. Solano; ***M:*** Luchi De Jesus.

Slaughter High 🦴 **1986 (R)** A high school nerd is accidentally disfigured by a back-firing prank. Five years later, he returns to exact bloody revenge. Available in an unrated version. **90m/C VHS.** Caroline

Munro, Simon Scuddamore, Kelly Baker; ***D:*** George Dugdale.

Slaughter Hotel 🦴 *Asylum Erotica; La Bestia Uccide a Sangue Freddo* **1971 (R)** An asylum already inhabited by extremely bizarre characters is plagued by a series of gruesome murders. Lots of skin and lots of blood; Neri shines as a nymphomaniacal lesbian nurse. **72m/C VHS.** Klaus Kinski, Rosalba (Sara Bay) Neri, Margaret Lee, John Ely; ***D:*** Fernando Di Leo.

Slaughter in San Francisco 🦴 *Chuck Norris vs. the Karate Cop; Yellow Faced Tiger; Karate Cop* **1981 (R)** A Chinese-American cop leads a one-man fight against corruption in the department in Daly City, near San Francisco. Norris is the bad guy; made in 1973 but not released until he had an established following (and he still has only some 18 minutes of film footage). Plenty of kicking and karate chops. **92m/C VHS.** *CH* Chuck Norris, Don Wong; ***D:*** William Lowe.

Slaughter of the Innocents 🦴🦴 **1993 (R)** FBI agent Broderick (Glenn) is sent to Salt Lake City to investigate the murders of two children which are found to be connected to a series of bizarre killings that have occurred around Monument Valley. Unbeknownst to his associates, Broderick often uses his 11-year-old whiz-kid son Jesse's (Cameron-Glickenhaus) computer skills to aid his research. Only this time, his inquisitive son gets too close to a serial killer and unless Dad can figure things out on his own, Jesse will be the next victim. **104m/C VHS.** Scott Glenn, Jesse Cameron-Glickenhaus, Sheila Tousey, Darlanne Fluegel, Zitto Kazann; ***D:*** James Glickenhaus; ***W:*** James Glickenhaus.

The Slaughter of the Vampires woof! *Curse of the Blood-Ghouls; Curses of the Ghouls* **1962** Newlyweds meet a bloodthirsty vampire in a Viennese chalet. Real, real bad horror flick, poorly dubbed. **81m/C VHS.** *IT* Walter Brandi, Dieter Eppler, Graziella Granta; ***D:*** Robert (Roberto) Mauri; ***W:*** Robert (Roberto) Mauri.

Slaughter Trail 🦴🦴 **1951** Rancher-turned-stage robber Young shoots two Indians and cavalry colonel Donlevy has to deal with the fallout. Peace returns when Young dies. Ordinary western with balladeer device helping the plot along, or trying to. **78m/C VHS.** Brian Donlevy, Gig Young, Virginia Grey, Andy Devine, Robert Hutton; ***D:*** Irving Allen.

Slaughterday 🦴½ **1977 (R)** An innocent woman is caught in the middle of an ex-con's elaborate scheme to commit the largest heist of his life. **87m/C VHS.** Rita Tushingham, William Berger, Frederick Jaeger, Michael Hauserman, Gordon Mitchell; ***D:*** Peter Patzak.

Slaughterhouse woof! **1987 (R)** A rotund, pig-loving country boy kills, maims, and eats numerous victims. Features the requisite dumb teens and plenty of blood. **87m/C VHS, DVD.** Joe Barton, Sherry Bendorf, Don Barrett, Bill Brinsfield; ***D:*** Rick Roessler; ***W:*** Rick Roessler; ***C:*** Richard Benda.

Slaughterhouse Five 🦴🦴 **1972 (R)** A suburban optometrist becomes "unstuck" in time and flits randomly through the experiences of his life, from the Dresden bombing to an extraterrestrial zoo. Noticed at Cannes but not at theatres; ambitious failure to adapt Kurt Vonnegut's odd novel. **104m/C VHS, DVD.** Sharon Gans, Roberts Blossom, Michael Sacks, Valerie Perrine, Ron Leibman, Eugene Roche, Perry King; ***D:*** George Roy Hill; ***W:*** Stephen Geller; ***C:*** Miroslav Ondricek; ***M:*** Glenn Gould. Cannes '72: Special Jury Prize.

Slaughterhouse Rock woof! **1988 (R)** The ghost of a sexy rock star draws a young man into a confrontation with a sadistic spirit that rules a deserted prison. There's also some cannibalism involved. Music group Devo did the score for this flick. **90m/C VHS.** Nicholas Celozzi, Donna Denton, Toni Basil, Hope Marie Carlton; ***D:*** Dimitri Logothetis.

Slaughter's Big Ripoff 🦴½ **1973 (R)** Slaughter is back battling the Mob with guns, planes and martial arts. This undistinguished sequel features McMahon as a mob boss. **92m/C VHS, DVD, Wide.** Jim Brown, Brock Peters, Don Stroud, Ed McMahon, Art Metrano, Gloria Hendry; ***D:*** Gordon Douglas; ***W:*** Charles Johnson; ***C:*** Charles F. Wheeler; ***M:*** James Brown, Fred Wesley.

Slave Girls from Beyond Infinity 🦴🦴 **1987 (R)** In this B-movie spoof, two beautiful intergalactic slave girls escape their penal colony, land on a mysterious planet, and meet a cannibalistic despot. Fun spoof of '50s "B" sci-fi movies. **80m/C VHS, DVD.** Elizabeth (Kaitan) Cayton, Cindy Beal, Brinke Stevens, Don Scribner, Carl Horner, Kirk Graves, Randolph Roehbling, Bud Graves; ***D:*** Ken Dixon; ***W:*** Ken Dixon; ***C:*** Thomas Callaway, Kenneth Wiatrak; ***M:*** Carl Dante.

A Slave of Love 🦴🦴🦴 **1978** Poignant love story set in the Crimea as the Bolshevik Revolution rages around a film crew attempting to complete a project. Interesting as ideological cinema but also enjoyable romantic drama. In Russian with English subtitles. **94m/C VHS.** *RU* Elena Solovei, Rodion Nakhapetov, Alexander Kalyagin; ***D:*** Nikita Mikhalkov; ***M:*** Eduard Artemyev.

Slavers 🦴🦴 **1977 (R)** Detailed depiction of the 19th century African slave trade with a little romance thrown in. **102m/C VHS.** *GE* Trevor Howard, Britt Ekland, Ron Ely, Cameron Mitchell, Ray Milland; ***D:*** Jurgen Goslar.

Slaves in Bondage 🦴 **1937** Young country girls are lured into the big city and initiated into a life of ill repute in this exploitation classic. A must for camp fans of the '30s. **70m/C VHS.** Lona Andre, Wheeler Oakman, Donald Reed, Florence Dudley, John Merton, Richard Cramer; ***D:*** Elmer Clifton; ***W:*** Robert Dillon; ***C:*** Edward Linden.

Slaves of Hollywood 🦴🦴½ **1999** Paulette (Morgan) is filming a documentary about five aspiring Hollywood wannabe execs as they work their way up the Tinseltown ladder. Lots of stylish flourishes highlight a familiar tale of the backstabbing, schmoozing movie biz. **80m/C VHS.** Nicholas Worth, Katherin Morgan, Amy Lyndon, Tim Duquette, Hill Harper, Andre Barron, Rob Hyland, Elliot Markman; ***D:*** Terry Keefe, Michael J. Wechsler; ***W:*** Terry Keefe, Michael J. Wechsler; ***C:*** David Alan Parks; ***M:*** Joseph (Joey) Altruda, Bradford T. Ellis.

Slaves of New York 🦴½ **1989 (R)** Greenwich Village artists worry about life and love in the '80s and being artistic enough for New York. Adapted from the stories of Tama Janowitz, who also wrote the screenplay and appears as Abby. Disastrous adaptation of a popular novel. **115m/C VHS.** Bernadette Peters, Chris Sarandon, Mary Beth Hurt, Madeleine Potter, Adam Coleman Howard, Nick Corri, Mercedes Ruehl, Joe Leeway, Charles McCaughan, John Harkins, Anna (Katerina) Katarina, Tama Janowitz; ***D:*** James Ivory; ***W:*** Tama Janowitz.

Slaves to the Underground 🦴½ **1996 (R)** Love affair between Seattle bandmates Shelly (Gross) and Suzy (Ryan) runs into problems when Shelly's ex-boyfriend Jimmy (Bortz) re-enters the picture and some old feelings are also re-ignited. Mediocre yet abrasive, with that dated postgrunge, Seattle-is-so-over feeling. **90m/C VHS, DVD.** Jason Bortz, Molly Gross, Marisa Ryan; ***D:*** Kristine Peterson; ***W:*** Bill Cody; ***C:*** Zoran Hochstatter; ***M:*** Mike Martt.

The Slayer woof! *Nightmare Island* **1982 (R)** It's movies like this that give getting back to nature a bad name. That horrible monster is after those nice young people again! This time it's on an island off the coast of Georgia. **95m/C VHS.** ***D:*** J.S. Cardone; ***W:*** J.S. Cardone; ***M:*** Robert Folk.

Slayground 🦴½ **1984 (R)** Man, distraught at the accidental death of his daughter, hires a hitman to exact revenge. Excruciating adaptation of the novel by Richard Stark (Donald E. Westlake). **85m/C VHS.** *GB* Peter Coyote, Mel Smith, Billie Whitelaw, Philip Sayer, Kelli Maroney; ***D:*** Terry Bedford; ***M:*** Colin Towns.

SLC Punk! 🦴🦴 **1999 (R)** Lillard is Stevo, a punk rocker rebelling against "the establishment" in mid-'80s Salt Lake City, Utah before it's time to head off to Harvard Law. He and his friends wander aimlessly from fights with rednecks and hippies to trashy clubs to various girlfriends. Nothing really funny or particularly dramatic happens in the comedy-drama, which seems like an excuse for director/writer Merendino to relive his carefree college years. **97m/C VHS, DVD.** Matthew Lillard, Michael Goorjian, Annabeth Gish, Jennifer Lien, Christopher McDonald, Devon Sawa, James Duval, Til Schweiger, Kevin Breznahan, Jason Segel, Summer Phoenix, Adam Pascal, Chiara Barzini; ***D:*** James Merendino; ***W:*** James Merendino; ***C:*** Greg Littlewood; ***M:*** Melanie Miller.

The Sleazy Uncle 🦴🦴 *Lo Zio Indegno* **1989** A successful but bored businessman is energized by an encounter with his vice-ridden uncle, a mooching, womanizing beatnik poet who knows how to enjoy life. An energetic but rather formulaic comedy. In Italian with English subtitles. **104m/C VHS.** *IT* Giancarlo Giannini, Vittorio Gassman, Andrea Ferreol, Stefania Sandrelli; ***D:*** Franco Brusati; ***W:*** Franco Brusati, Leonardo Benvenuti, Piero De Bernardi; ***C:*** Romano Albani.

Sledgehammer woof! **1983** A madman is wreaking havoc on a small town, annihilating young women with a sledgehammer. **87m/C VHS.** Ted Prior, Doug Matley, Steven Wright.

Sleep of Death 🦴½ **1979** Young Englishman's pursuit of a blue-blooded woman seems to set off a series of bizarre and mysterious murders. A gothic thriller based on Sheridan Le Fanu's short story. **90m/C VHS.** Brendan Price, Marilu Tolo, Patrick Magee, Curt Jurgens, Per Oscarsson; ***D:*** Calvin Floyd.

Sleep with Me 🦴🦴½ **1994 (R)** What happens when love comes between friendship? Sarah (Tilly), Joseph (Stoltz), and Frank (Sheffer) are soon to find out. Sarah and Joseph are about to get married when their best friend Frank realizes he's in love with Sarah. So he sets out to seduce her and when Joseph realizes what's going on, he not only questions Frank's friendship but wonders just what signals Sarah's been giving off (although Joseph's hardly blameless). Six writers each wrote one of the social scenes detailing their triangular troubles, including a party where Tarantino does a hilarious riff on the homoerotic subtext in "Top Gun." Kelly's directorial debut. **117m/C VHS.** Craig Sheffer, Eric Stoltz, Meg Tilly, Todd Field, Adrienne Shelly, Lewis Arquette, Susan Traylor, Tegan West, Parker Posey, Dean Cameron, Thomas Gibson, June Lockhart, Quentin Tarantino, Joey Lauren Adams; ***D:*** Rory Kelly; ***W:*** Rory Kelly, Roger Hedden, Neal Jimenez, Michael Steinberg, Duane Dell'Amico, Joe Keenan; ***M:*** David Lawrence.

Sleepaway Camp 🦴 **1983 (R)** Crazed killer hacks away at the inhabitants of a peaceful summer camp in this run-of-the-mill slasher. **88m/C VHS, DVD, Wide.** Mike Kellin, Jonathan Tiersten, Felissa Rose, Christopher Collet; ***D:*** Robert Hiltzik; ***W:*** Robert Hiltzik; ***C:*** Benjamin Davis; ***M:*** Edward Bilous.

Sleepaway Camp 2: Unhappy Campers 🦴½ **1988 (R)** A beautiful camp counselor is actually a blood-thirsty, murdering madwoman. Sequel to the 1983 slasher, "Sleepaway Camp." **82m/C VHS.** Pamela Springsteen, Renee Estevez, Walter Gotell, Brian Patrick Clark; ***D:*** Michael A. Simpson.

Sleepaway Camp 3: Teenage Wasteland woof! **1989 (R)** This second sequel is as bad as the first two movies. Another disturbed camper hacks up another bevy of teenagers. Better luck at the Motel Six. **80m/C VHS.** Pamela Springsteen, Tracy Griffith, Michael J. Pollard; ***D:*** Michael A. Simpson.

Sleeper 🦴🦴🦴½ **1973 (PG)** Hapless nerd Allen is revived two hundred years after an operation gone bad. Keaton portrays Allen's love interest in a futuristic land of robots and giant vegetables. He learns of the hitherto unknown health benefits of hot fudge sundaes; discovers the truth about the nation's dictator, known as The Leader; and gets involved with revolutionaries seeking to overthrow the government. Hilarious, fast-moving comedy, full of slapstick and satire. Don't miss the "orgasmatron." **88m/C VHS, DVD, Wide.** Woody Allen, Diane Keaton, John Beck, Howard Cosell; ***D:*** Woody Allen; ***W:*** Marshall Brickman, Woody Allen; ***C:*** David M. Walsh; ***M:*** Woody Allen.

Sleepers 🦴🦴½ **1996 (R)** Tense, gritty drama based on Lorenzo Carcaterra's book about four teenaged friends from Hell's Kitchen who get into trouble and wind up being sent to a reform school, where they're brutalized by guards. John (Eldard) and Tommy (Crudup), who grow up to be hit men, recognize their chief abuser (Bacon) years later and kill him. Their trial is prosecuted by Michael (Pitt), another of the gang, who's now the assistant DA. It's supposed to be a true story (the book is published as non-fiction) but doubt has been cast on Carcaterra's veracity (his character is the fourth member, journalist Lorenzo, played by Patric). De Niro and Hoffman excel in relatively minor, but pivotal, roles. **150m/C VHS, DVD.** Brad Pitt, Jason Patric, Ron Eldard, Billy Crudup, Kevin Bacon, Robert De Niro, Dustin Hoffman, Vittorio Gassman, Minnie Driver, Terry Kinney, Brad Renfro, Jonathan Tucker, Joe Perrino, Geoff Wigdor, Bruno Kirby, Aida Turturro, Frank Medrano; ***D:*** Barry Levinson; ***W:*** Barry Levinson; ***C:*** Michael Ballhaus; ***M:*** John Williams.

Sleeping Beauty 🦴🦴🦴 **1959 (G)** Classic Walt Disney version of the famous fairy tale is set to the music of Tchaikovsky's ballet. Lavishly produced. With the voices of Mary Costa, Bill Shirley, and Vera Vague. **75m/C VHS.** ***D:*** Clyde Geronimi, Eric Larson, Wolfgang Reitherman, Les Clark; ***M:*** George Bruns; ***V:*** Mary Costa, Bill (William) Shirley, Barbara Luddy, Taylor Holmes, Verna Felton, Barbara Jo Allen, Pinto Colvig, Marvin Miller.

Sleeping Beauty **1983** Peters is the princess put to sleep by the evil queen. Handsome prince Reeve comes to the rescue in this classy retelling of the Sleeping Beauty legend. Combines live action and animation. From Shelley Duvall's "Faerie Tale Theatre." **60m/C VHS.** Christopher Reeve, Bernadette Peters, Beverly D'Angelo.

Sleeping Beauty 🦴½ **1989** Live action version of the beloved fairy tale, with Welch in the title role. **92m/C VHS.** Tahnee Welch, Morgan Fairchild, Nicholas Clay, Sylvia Miles, Kenny Baker.

The Sleeping Car 🦴🦴 **1990** A vindictive ghost haunts a group of people living in an old railway car. Fairly fun, fairly competent horror. **87m/C VHS.** David Naughton, Judie Aronson, Kevin McCarthy, Jeff Conaway, Dani Minnick, John Carl Buechler; ***D:*** Douglas Curtis.

Sleeping Car to Trieste 🦴🦴 **1945** Conspirators in the theft of a diplomat's diary ride the Orient Express, as a wily detective on board tries to piece together murder clues. Based on the story "Rome Express" by Clifford Grey. **95m/B VHS.** Jean Kent, Albert Lieven, David Tomlinson, Finlay Currie; ***D:*** John Paddy Carstairs.

Sleeping Dogs 🦴🦴½ **1977** A man in near-future New Zealand finds it hard to remain neutral when he is caught between a repressive government and a violent resistance movement. The first New Zealand film ever to open in the U.S., and a fine debut for director Donaldson. **107m/C VHS.** *NZ* Sam Neill, Ian Mune, Nevan Rowe, Dona Akersten, Warren Oates; ***D:*** Roger Donaldson.

The Sleeping Tiger 🦴🦴½ **1954** A thief breaks into the home of a psychiatrist, who captures him. In exchange for his freedom, the thief agrees to become a guinea pig for the doctor's rehabilitation theories with ultimately tragic results. Director Losey was originally compelled to release the film under a pseudonym, "Victor Hanbury," because he had been blacklisted by Hollywood during the 1950s red scare. First pairing of Losey and Bogarde, who collaborated on several later films, including "Modesty Blaise" (1966) and "Accident" (1967). **89m/B VHS.** Alexis Smith, Alexander Knox, Dirk Bogarde, Hugh Griffith; ***D:*** Joseph Losey; ***W:*** Harold Buchman, Carl Foreman; ***M:*** Malcolm Arnold.

Sleeping with Strangers 🦴🦴½ **1994 (R)** Two hoteliers in a small British Columbia town find their rivalry increasing as one hotel gets a boost when a drunken rock star and his Hollywood starlet arrive with their entourage in tow. Of course, the media follows and so does the comedic hysteria. **103m/C VHS.** Adrienne Shelly, Neil Duncan, Shawn Thompson, Kymberley Huffman, Scott McNeil; ***D:*** William T. Bolson; ***W:*** Joan Carr-Wiggin.

Sleeping with the Enemy 🦴🦴½ **1991 (R)** Roberts escapes from abusive husband by faking death, flees to Iowa, falls for drama professor, and, gasp, is found by psycho husband. Occasionally chilling but oft predictable thriller based on novel by Nancy Price. **99m/C VHS.** Julia Roberts, Kevin Anderson, Patrick Bergin, Elizabeth Lawrence, Kyle Secor, Claudette Nevins; ***D:*** Joseph Ruben; ***W:*** Ronald Bass; ***M:*** Jerry Goldsmith.

Sleepless 🦴🦴 **2001** Argento, the master of arty gore, returns in a familiar story. Retired inspector von Sydow is called back into service when a series of murders is identical to a prostitute murder spree (committed by a dwarf!) that the inspector solved 17 years earlier. Also back is the only witness (Dionisi) from the earlier crimes. **117m/C VHS, DVD.** *IT* Max von Sydow, Stefano Dionisi, Chiara Caselli; ***D:*** Dario Argento; ***W:*** Dario Argento, Franco Ferrini; ***C:*** Ronnie Taylor; ***M:*** The Goblins. **VIDEO**

Sleepless in Seattle 🦴🦴🦴½ **1993 (PG)** Witty, sweet romantic comedy explores the differences between men and women when it comes to love and romance. When widower Sam Bladwin (Hanks) talks about his wife on a national talk show, recently engaged Annie Reed (Ryan) responds. Writer/director Ephron's humorous screenplay is brought to life by a perfectly cast ensemble; it also breathed new life into the classic weepie "An Affair to Remember," comparing it to "The Dirty Dozen" in an unforgettable scene. A movie full of fine detail, from Sven Nykvist's camera work to the graphic layout of the opening credits to the great score. Captured millions at the boxoffice, coming in as the fourth highest grossing movie of 1993. **105m/C VHS, DVD, 8mm, Wide.** Tom Hanks, Meg Ryan, Bill Pullman, Ross Malinger, Rosie O'Donnell, Gaby Hoffman, Victor Garber, Rita Wilson, Barbara Garrick, Carey Lowell, Rob Reiner, Sarah Trigger; ***D:*** Nora Ephron; ***W:*** Jeffrey Arch, Larry Atlas, David S. Ward, Nora Ephron; ***C:*** Sven Nykvist; ***M:*** Marc Shaiman.

Sleepstalker: The Sandman's Last Rites 🦴🦴 **1994 (R)** A serial killer known as the Sandman (Harris) is executed but returns as a shape-shifting horror who can strip the flesh off his victims with whirling sand. He haunts the nightmares of a reporter (Underwood), the only survivor of one of the killer's massacres, who teams up with a photographer (Morris) to learn the creature's origins and defeat him. Good special effects. **101m/C VHS.** Jay Underwood, Michael (M.K.) Harris, Kathryn Morris; ***D:*** Turi Meyer.

Sleepwalk 🦴🦴 **1988 (R)** Odd independent effort about a bored New York desk worker who is given an ancient text of Chinese fairy tales to translate, and finds they're manifesting themselves in dangerous ways in real life. **78m/C VHS.** Suzanne Fletcher, Ann Magnuson; ***D:*** Sara Driver; ***C:*** Frank Prinzi, Jim Jarmusch.

Sleepwalkers 🦴½ *Stephen King's Sleepwalkers* **1992 (R)** When Mary and her son Charles arrive in the small town of Travis, Indiana, ugly things begin to happen. And no wonder, it seems the deadly duo are sleepwalkers—fiendish, cat-like vampire creatures who can only survive by sucking the life force out of unsuspecting virgins. Gory but not without some humor, particularly in Krige's portrayal of the sexy and too-loving mother. Not nearly as good as some of King's other horror classics. **91m/C VHS, DVD, Wide.** Brian Krause, Madchen Amick, Alice Krige, Jim Haynie, Cindy Pickett, Lyman Ward, Ron Perlman, Stephen King, Tobe Hooper, Mark Hamill, Glenn Shadix, Joe Dante, Clive Barker, John Landis, Dan Martin; ***D:*** Mick Garris; ***W:*** Stephen King; ***C:*** Rodney Charters; ***M:*** Nicholas Pike.

Sleepy Eyes of Death: The Chinese Jade 🦴🦴 **1963** Master swordsman Nemuri Kyoshireo slaughters six would-be ambushers and has the seductive Chisa trying to set him against her master's enemy, Chen Sun, all for the sake of discovering the secret of the Chinese Jade. Adapted from the novel by Shibata Renzaburo. Japanese with subtitles. **82m/C VHS, Wide.** *JP* Raizo Ichikawa, Tamao Nakamura, Jo Kenzaburo; ***D:*** Tokuzo Tanaka.

Sleepy Hollow 🦴🦴🦴 **1999 (R)** Gorgeous and grisly Burtonized version of Washington Irving's tale "The Legend of Sleepy Hollow." In this retelling, Ichabod Crane (Depp) is a New York constable who believes in reason and science, which won't do him much good when he's sent to the upstate hamlet of Sleepy Hollow to investigate a series of decapitation murders. Crane is housed by wealthy Balthus Van Tassel (Gambon), whose somewhat fey daughter Katrina (Ricci) falls for the quaking Crane, who refuses to believe that a ghost is committing mayhem. He's soon confronted by the graphic evidence of his own eyes. (Heads do certainly roll). Landau has a wordless cameo as the second victim. **105m/C VHS, DVD, Wide.** Johnny Depp, Christina Ricci, Miranda Richardson, Michael Gambon, Christopher Walken, Casper Van Dien, Jeffrey Jones, Richard Griffiths, Ian McDiarmid, Michael Gough, Christopher Lee, Marc Pickering, Lisa Marie, Steven Waddington, Claire Skinner, Alun Armstrong, Mark Spalding, Jessica Oyelowo; ***Cameos:*** Martin Landau; ***D:*** Tim Burton; ***W:*** Andrew Kevin Walker; ***C:*** Emmanuel Lubezki; ***M:*** Danny Elfman. Oscars '99: Art Dir./Set Dec.; British Acad. '99: Art Dir./Set Dec., Costume Des.

The Slender Thread 🦴🦴🦴 **1965** Based on a true story, Poitier plays a college student who volunteers at a crisis center and must keep would-be suicide Bancroft on the phone until the police can find her. Filmed on location in Seattle. First film for director Pollack. **98m/C VHS.** Sidney Poitier, Anne Bancroft, Telly Savalas, Steven Hill; ***D:*** Sydney Pollack; ***W:*** Stirling Silliphant; ***C:*** Loyal Griggs; ***M:*** Quincy Jones.

Sleuth 🦴🦴🦴½ **1972 (PG)** Milo (Caine), the owner of a chain of hair salons, is invited to the home of detective novelist Andrew Wyke (Olivier), who reveals that he Milo and Wyke's wife Marguerite are lovers. He persuades Milo to assist him with a fake robbery and an insurance scam that will help them both. Of course, Shaffer's complex plot (taken from his play) results in ever shifting, elaborate, and diabolical plots against each man, complete with red herrings, traps, and tricks. Playful, cerebral mystery thriller from top director Mankiewicz. **138m/C VHS, DVD, Wide.** Laurence Olivier, Michael Caine, John Matthews, Alec Cawthorne, Teddy Martin; ***D:*** Joseph L. Mankiewicz; ***W:*** Anthony Shaffer; ***C:*** Oswald Morris; ***M:*** John Addison. N.Y. Film Critics '72: Actor (Olivier).

Sliding Doors 🦴🦴½ **1997 (R)** The sliding doors are those of a London subway train. If Helen (Paltrow) makes it through before they close, her life (and loves) go one way. If she's left on the platform, they go another, and the audience is let in on both options. She'll either dump or stick with cheating boyfriend Gerry (Lynch), who has been sleeping with ultra-bitchy ex-girlfriend Lydia (Tripplehorn). And she will either strike up a relationship with a charming stranger (Hannah) on the train and become fabulously successful, or end up slinging hash in a diner while pregnant with her scumbag boyfriend's baby. The concept and story of the dual possibilities is pulled off well, although it is a bit too cute at times. Will you like it? Depends on if it's already been rented when you're at the video store. If it's out, be careful what you pick, because apparently the small stuff really does matter. **98m/C VHS, DVD.** Gwyneth Paltrow, John Lynch, John Hannah, Jeanne Tripplehorn, Virginia McKenna, Zara Turner, Douglas McFerran, Paul Brightwell, Nina Young; ***D:*** Peter Howitt; ***W:*** Peter Howitt; ***C:*** Remi Adefarasin; ***M:*** David Hirschfelder.

A Slight Case of Murder 🦴🦴½ **1999** Cable TV critic Terry Thorpe (Macy) is in a panic after accidentally killing one of his girlfriends. Instead of confessing, Terry tries to keep the truth from the cops (Arkin, Pickens Jr.) and his surviving gal pal (Huffman). Then along comes a suspicious PI (Cromwell) with a blackmail scheme. Goofy film noir that gets too complicated. Based on the novel "A Travesty" by Donald E. Westlake. **94m/C VHS.** William H. Macy, Adam Arkin, Felicity Huffman, James Cromwell, James Pickens Jr.; ***D:*** Steven Schachter; ***W:*** William H. Macy, Steven Schachter. **CABLE**

Slightly Honorable 🦴🦴½ **1940** A lawyer gets involved in political scandals and becomes a murder suspect. Snappy comedy-drama with good performances but too many subplots. Based on the novel "Send Another Coffin" by F. G. Presnell. **75m/B VHS.** Pat O'Brien, Broderick Crawford, Edward Arnold, Eve Arden, Evelyn Keyes, Phyllis Brooks; ***D:*** Tay Garnett.

A Slightly Pregnant Man 🦴🦴 **1979 (PG)** Comic complications abound as a construction worker becomes the world's first pregnant man. Surprise ending saves this simple and not very exciting film. **92m/C VHS.** Catherine Deneuve, Marcello Mastroianni; ***D:*** Jacques Demy.

Slightly Scarlet 🦴🦴½ **1956** Small-time hood Payne carries out an assignment from boss DeCorsia to smear a law-and-order politico running for mayor. He falls in love with the candidate's secretary, tries to go straight, and ends up running the mob when DeCorsia flees town. A spiffy, low-budget noir crime drama based on the James M. Cain novel "Love's Lovely Counterfeit." **99m/C VHS, DVD, Wide.** Rhonda Fleming, Arlene Dahl, John Payne, Kent Taylor, Ted de Corsia; ***D:*** Allan Dwan; ***W:*** Robert Blees; ***C:*** John Alton; ***M:*** Louis Forbes.

Slime City 🦴 **1989** The widow of an alchemist poisons her tenants so they will join her husband in the hereafter. Very low-budget; occasionally funny. **90m/C VHS.** Robert C. Sabin, Mary Huner, T.J. Merrick, Dick Biel; ***D:*** Gregory Lamberson.

The Slime People woof! **1963** Huge prehistoric monsters are awakened from long hibernation by atomic testing in Los Angeles. They take over the city, creating the fog they need to live. Thank goodness for scientist Burton, who saves the day. Filmed in a butcher shop in Los Angeles. **76m/B VHS, DVD.** Robert Hutton, Robert Burton, Susan Hart, William Boyce, Les Tremayne, John Close, Judee Morton; ***D:*** Robert Hutton; ***W:*** Vance Skarstedt; ***C:*** William G. Troiano.

Sling Blade 🦴🦴🦴½ **1996 (R)** Mildly retarded killer Karl Childers (Thornton, making his feature directorial debut) is released from a mental hospital, where he was placed after killing his mother and her lover, after 25 years. Returning to his hometown, he befriends a boy (Black) with problems of his own. His mother is living with a mean, bullying drunkard (Yoakam, in a brilliant performance) who has no use for anyone, least of all mom's openly gay co-worker (Ritter). Thornton's excellent script moves at the slow pace of its hero, providing the superb cast plenty of opportunity to explore the rich characterization and dialogue. Filmed in Thornton's home state of Arkansas. **134m/C VHS, DVD, Wide.** Billy Bob Thornton, Dwight Yoakam, John Ritter, Lucas Black, Natalie Canerday, James Hampton, Robert Duvall, J.T. Walsh, Rick Dial, Brent Briscoe, Christy Ward, Col. Bruce Hampton, Vic Chesnutt, Mickey Jones, Jim Jarmusch, Ian Moore; ***D:*** Billy Bob Thornton; ***W:*** Billy Bob Thornton; ***C:*** Barry Markowitz; ***M:*** Daniel Lanois. Oscars '96: Adapt. Screenplay; Ind. Spirit '97: First Feature; Writers Guild '96: Adapt. Screenplay.

The Slingshot 🦴🦴🦴 **1993 (R)** Quirky coming-of-age tale, set in 1920s Stockholm, finds 12-year-old Roland (Salen) trying to survive childhood dilemmas. His mother (Frydman) is a Russian Jew (who sells condoms illegally) and his father (Skarsgard) is a zealous socialist, so Roland is subjected to unceasing bullying and prejudice. But the resourceful Roland doesn't let society get him down—he uses the contraband condoms in an inventive slingshot design that brings him an unwarranted amount of attention. Based on the novel by Roland Schutt. Swedish with subtitles. **102m/C VHS.** *SW* Jesper Salen, Stellan Skarsgard, Basia Frydman, Niclas Olund, Ernst-Hugo Jaregard, Jacob Leygraf; ***D:*** Ake Sandgren; ***W:*** Bjorn Isfalt, Ake Sandgren.

The Slipper and the Rose 🦴🦴½ **1976 (G)** Lavish musical adaptation of the fairy tale "Cinderella." Chamberlain is a very princely prince and the lovely Craven makes a fine and spunky servant girl, whom he can't help falling in love with. Besides the lively musical numbers, viewers will also enjoy the beautiful Austrian scenery. **127m/C VHS, DVD, Wide.** *GB* Richard Chamberlain, Gemma Craven, Annette Crosbie, Edith Evans, Christopher Gable, Michael Hordern, Margaret Lockwood, Kenneth More, Julian Orchard, Lally Bowers, Sherrie Hewson, Rosalind Ayres, John Turner, Keith Skinner, Polly Williams, Norman Bird, Roy Barraclough, Peter Graves; ***Cameos:*** Bryan Forbes; ***D:*** Bryan Forbes; ***W:*** Bryan Forbes, Robert B. Sherman, Richard M. Sherman; ***C:*** Tony Imi; ***M:*** Robert B. Sherman, Richard M. Sherman.

Slipping into Darkness 🦴½ **1988 (R)** Three spoiled, rich college girls are held responsible for a retarded local boy's death. Honest and overwrought. **86m/C VHS.** Belle Mitchell, Laslo Papas, Beverly Ross, T.J. McFadden, Michelle Johnson, John DiAquino; ***D:*** Eleanor Gaver; ***W:*** Eleanor Gaver.

Slipstream 🦴🦴 **1972** "Turgid" and "gloomy" are the words for this romantic drama set in remote Alberta. The minor plot concerns a young woman who teaches a lonely disc jockey a lesson about life and love. This film feels like a long Canadian winter. **93m/C VHS.** *CA* Julie Askew, Patti Oatman, Eli Rill.

Slipstream 🦴🦴 **1989 (PG-13)** A sci-fi adventure set on a damaged Earthscape where people seek to escape a giant jetstream. While tracking down a bounty hunter gone bad, a futuristic cop follows his quarry into the dangerous river of wind. Ambitious "Blade Runner" clone with big names (Hamill is good) was never released theatrically in the US. **92m/C VHS, DVD.** *GB* Mark Hamill, Bill Paxton, Bob Peck, Eleanor David, Kitty Aldridge, Robbie Coltrane, Ben Kingsley, F. Murray Abraham; ***D:*** Steven Lisberger; ***W:*** Tony Kayden; ***C:*** Frank Tidy; ***M:*** Elmer Bernstein.

Slither 🦴🦴🦴 **1973 (PG)** Caan and Boyle become wrapped up in a scheme to recover $300,000 in cash, stolen seven years previously. Along the way they pick up speed freak Kellerman, who assists them in a variety of loony ways. Frantic chase scenes are the highlight. **97m/C VHS.** James Caan, Peter Boyle, Sally Kellerman, Louise Lasser, Allen (Goorwitz) Garfield, Richard B. Shull, Alex Rocco; ***D:*** Howard Zieff; ***W:*** W.D. Richter.

Slithis woof! *Spawn of the Slithis* **1978 (PG)** Slithis, the nuclear-waste creature, is the menace of Venice, California. Keep your pets (and yourself) indoors! **86m/C VHS.** Alan Blanchard, Judy Motulsky, Mello Alexandria, Dennis Lee Falt, Win Condict; ***D:*** Stephen Traxler; ***W:*** Stephen Traxler; ***C:*** Robert Caramico; ***M:*** Steve Zuckerman.

Sliver 🦴½ **1993 (R)** Another voyeuristic thriller starring Stone. She's Carly Norris, a lonely book editor who moves into one of Manhattan's toothpick thin buildings (the "sliver" of the title). She meets pulp novelist Jack (Berenger), whose libido is as overheated as his prose, but gets involved in a steamy affair with handsome neighbor Zeke (Baldwin), a computer whiz who also owns the building. Oh, by the way, he's installed video cameras in every unit that reveal many intimate secrets. Lots of sex and murders. Murky and underdeveloped and the ending, which was reshot, still leaves much to be desired. Lots of hype, little to recommend. **106m/C VHS, CD-I, Wide.** Sharon Stone, William Baldwin, Tom Berenger, Martin Landau, Polly Walker, Colleen Camp, CCH Pounder, Nina Foch, Keene Curtis; ***D:*** Phillip Noyce; ***W:*** Joe Eszterhas; ***C:*** Vilmos Zsigmond; ***M:*** Howard Shore. MTV Movie Awards '94: Most Desirable Male (Baldwin).

Sloane woof! **1984** Typical sleazy sex and violence flick. For the record: organized crime baddies kidnap good guy Resnick's girlfriend and he seeks revenge. **95m/C VHS.** Robert Resnick, Debra Blee, Paul Aragon; ***D:*** Dan Rosenthal.

Slow Burn 🦴🦴 **1986** An ex-reporter tries some detective work in the seamy side of Palm Springs, and becomes embroiled in the standard drug, kidnapping, murder routine. Based on the novel "Castles Burning" by Arthur Lyons. **92m/C VHS.** Eric Roberts, Beverly D'Angelo, Dan Hedaya, Dennis Lipscomb; *D:* Matthew Chapman; *W:* Matthew Chapman; *M:* Loek Dikker. **CABLE**

Slow Burn 🦴 **1990 (R)** The Mafia and Chinese Triads are having troubles and a tired cop attempts to reach a peaceful solution. **90m/C VHS.** William Smith, Anthony James, Ivan Rogers.

Slow Burn 🦴🦴½ **2000 (R)** Trina (Driver) is searching for a family heirloom—a box of missing diamonds—that were lost in the Mexican desert when her grandmother died. While she hunts around, the goods have already been discovered by a couple of escaped cons (Spader and Brolin) who take Trina hostage and steal her car. But when her car is disabled, things in the desert start to steam, with Trina trying to play both men against one another so she can make off with the treasure. **97m/C VHS, DVD.** Minnie Driver, James Spader, Josh Brolin, Stuart Wilson; *D:* Christian Ford; *W:* Christian Ford, Roger Soffer; *C:* Mark Vicente; *M:* Anthony Marinelli. **VIDEO**

Slow Moves 🦴½ **1984** Slow story of slow people who meet slowly, have sluggish affair, and find tragedy eventually. **93m/C VHS.** Roxanne Rogers; *D:* Jon Jost.

The Slugger's Wife 🦴½ *Neil Simon's The Slugger's Wife* **1985 (PG-13)** The marriage between an Atlanta Braves outfielder and a rock singer suddenly turns sour when their individual careers force them to make some tough choices. **105m/C VHS.** Michael O'Keefe, Rebecca DeMornay, Martin Ritt, Randy Quaid, Loudon Wainwright III, Cleavant Derricks, Lynn Whitfield; *D:* Hal Ashby; *W:* Neil Simon; *C:* Caleb Deschanel.

Slugs woof! **1987 (R)** A health inspector discovers that spilled toxic waste is being helpfully cleaned up by the slug population, saving Uncle Sam countless dollars. But wait! The slugs are mutating into blood-thirsty man-eaters. Is this the answer to military cut-backs? **90m/C VHS, DVD, Wide.** Michael Garfield, Kim Terry, Philip Machale, Alicia Moro, Santiago Alvarez, Emilio Linder, Concha Cuetos; *D:* J(uan) Piquer Simon; *W:* J(uan) Piquer Simon; *C:* Julio Bragado; *M:* Tim Souster.

Slumber Party '57 🦴½ **1976 (R)** At a slumber party, six girls get together and exchange stories of how they lost their virginity. Lots of great music by the Platters, Big Bopper, Jerry Lee Lewis, the Crewcuts, and Paul and Paula but complete schlock otherwise. **89m/C VHS.** Noelle North, Bridget Hollman, Debra Winger, Mary Ann Appleseth, Cheryl "Rainbeaux" Smith, Janet Wood, R.L. Armstrong, Rafael Campos, Larry Gelman, Will Hutchins, Joyce Jillson, Victor Rogers, Joe E. Ross, Bill (Billy) Thurman; *D:* William A. Levey; *M:* Miles Goodman.

Slumber Party Massacre 🦴½ **1982 (R)** A psychotic killer with a power drill terrorizes a high school girls' slumber party. Contrived and forced, but not always unfunny. **84m/C VHS, DVD, Wide.** Michele Michaels, Robin Stille, Andre Honore, Michael Villela, Debra Deliso, Gina Mari, Brinke Stevens, Jean Vargas, Ryan Kennedy; *D:* Amy Holden Jones; *W:* Rita Mae Brown; *C:* Stephen Posey; *M:* Ralph Jones.

Slumber Party Massacre 2 woof! **1987** Drowsy babes in lingerie are drilled to death by a perverse madman. Another disappointing sequel. **75m/C VHS, DVD.** Crystal Bernard, Kimberly McArthur, Juliette Cummins, Patrick Lowe; *D:* Deborah Brock; *W:* Deborah Brock; *C:* Thomas Callaway; *M:* Richard Ian Cox.

Slumber Party Massacre 3 woof! **1990 (R)** Parents: Don't let your daughters have any slumber parties! Yes, it's a drill—for the third time. **76m/C VHS, DVD.** Keely Christian, Brittain Frye, Michael (M.K.) Harris, David Greenle, Hope Marie Carlton, Maria Ford; *D:* Sally Mattison; *W:* Catherine Cyran; *C:* Jurgen Baum; *M:* Jaime Sheriff.

Slums of Beverly Hills 🦴🦴🦴½ **1998 (R)** Every few months, Murray Abromowitz (Arkin) packs up daughter Vivian (Lyonne) and sons Ricky (Marienthal) and Ben (Krumholtz) to sneak out of their current dumpy apartment (without paying the rent) and move on to the next one, always within Beverly Hills so the kids can stay in a good school. When cousin Rita (Tomei) escapes from a rehab center, Murray takes her in. While Murray's main concern is the kids' education, Vivian is more obsessed with the size of her breasts and exploring her adolescent sexuality. Semi-autobiographical first film for Jenkins, who scripted while at the Sundance Institute, has lots of character and charm, and just enough bite. Lyonne has no trouble being the center of attention and injects comedy into the many awkward social situations that a teenage girl must endure. **91m/C VHS, DVD, Wide.** Natasha Lyonne, Alan Arkin, Marisa Tomei, Kevin Corrigan, David Krumholtz, Carl Reiner, Eli Marienthal, Jessica Walter, Rita Moreno; *D:* Tamara Jenkins; *W:* Tamara Jenkins; *C:* Tom Richmond; *M:* Rolfe Kent.

The Small Back Room 🦴🦴🦴 *Hour of Glory* **1949** A crippled WWII munitions expert leads a tormented existence and laments government bureaucracy. Powerfully presented adult storyline. **106m/B VHS.** David Farrar, Jack Hawkins, Cyril Cusack, Kathleen Byron, Anthony Bushell, Michael Gough, Robert Morley; *D:* Michael Powell, Emeric Pressburger.

Small Change 🦴🦴🦴🦴 *L'Argent de Poche* **1976 (PG)** Pudgy, timid Desmouceaux and scruffy, neglected Goldman lead a whole pack of heartwarming tykes. A realistically and tenderly portrayed testament to the great director's belief in childhood as a "state of grace." Criticized for sentimentality, "Small Change" followed Truffaut's gloomy "The Story of Adele H." Steven Spielberg suggested the English translation of "L'Argent de Poche." In French with English subtitles. **104m/C VHS, DVD, Wide.** *FR* Geory Desmouceaux, Philippe Goldman, Jean-Francois Stevenin, Chantal Mercier, Claudio Deluca, Frank Deluca, Richard Golfier, Laurent Devlaeminck, Francis Devlaeminck, Sylvie Grezel, Pascale Bruchon, Nicole Felix, Francois Truffaut; *D:* Francois Truffaut; *W:* Suzanne Schiffman, Francois Truffaut; *C:* Pierre William Glenn; *M:* Maurice Jaubert.

A Small Circle of Friends 🦴½ **1980 (R)** Three Harvard students struggle through their shifting relationships during their college years in the 1960s. **112m/C VHS.** Brad Davis, Jameson Parker, Karen Allen, Shelley Long; *D:* Rob Cohen.

Small Faces 🦴🦴🦴 **1995 (R)** Semi-autobiographical account of three brothers growing up in a working class, gang-ridden section of Glasgow in 1968. Scottish lad Lex MacLean (Robertson) is at the crucial age of 13 and caught between two completely opposite brothers and two warring gangs. Sensitive brother Alan (McFadden) has the stigma of being an artist in a conscientiously macho society, while older brother Bobby (Duffy) has no such problem, being a gang member and all-around punk. When Lex unfortunately injures the eye of gang leader Malky (McKidd) with an air-gun, he unknowingly sets in motion a dangerous chain of events, forcing him to ally with both brothers. Writer/director MacKinnon makes sure even the most tense situations are offset with dark humor, and stages the violent scenes beautifully. Garnering comparisons with other Scottish youth fables like "Trainspotting," film follows somewhat the same storytelling formula, but is much more low-key. Character and film greatly benefits from an outstanding performance by Robertson. CNT Violence and language. **108m/C VHS.** *GB* Iain Robertson, Clare Higgins, Ian McElhinney, Kevin McKidd, Joseph McFadden, J.S. Duffy, Laura Fraser, Garry Sweeney, Mark McConnochie, Steven Singleton, David Walker; *D:* Gilles Mackinnon; *W:* Gilles Mackinnon, Billy Mackinnon; *C:* John de Borman; *M:* John Keane.

Small Hotel 🦴🦴 **1957** After discovering that he is to be replaced as headwaiter by a young woman, Harker plots to save his job through espionage, blackmail and cajolery. Average comedy, adapted from a popular British stage play as a star vehicle for Harker. **59m/B VHS.** Gordon Harker, Marie Lohr, John Loder, Irene Handl, Janet Munro, Billie Whitelaw, Francis Matthews, Dora Bryan; *D:* David MacDonald.

Small Kill 🦴½ **1993 (R)** Burghoff leaves his lovable MASH character far behind, testing his acting skills as a psycho who disguises himself as a female fortune teller to rob his victims of their life savings so he can become head druglord of his town (what a goal). Two cops try to stop him/her. **86m/C VHS.** Gary Burghoff, Rebecca Ferratti, Donnie Kehr, Jason Miller, Fred Carpenter; *D:* Robert M. Fresco; *W:* Fred Carpenter, James McTernan.

A Small Killing 🦴🦴 **1981** An undercover cop and a college professor pose as a wino and a bag lady, when trying to put the tabs on a druglord. Made for TV mystery/romance based on "The Rag Bag Clan" by Richard Barth. **100m/C VHS.** Ed Asner, Jean Simmons, Sylvia Sidney, Andrew Prine, J. Pat O'Malley, Anne Ramsey; *D:* Steven Hilliard Stern. **TV**

Small Sacrifices 🦴🦴½ **1989** The true story of Diane Downs, an Oregon woman who may have murdered her own three children in 1983. Fine performance from Fawcett, who seems to like made for TV tales of true-life domestic violence as an antidote to her earlier ditzy persona as a Charlie's Angel. Gripping, with a superb script. **159m/C VHS.** Farrah Fawcett, Ryan O'Neal, John Shea, Emily Perkins, Gordon Clapp; *D:* David Greene; *W:* Joyce Eliason. **TV**

Small Soldiers 🦴🦴½ **1998 (PG-13)** Why do kids today get all the really cool toys? G.I. Joe with the Kung Fu Grip never held any small Ohio towns under siege, and his fingers eventually fell off. But thanks to former defense supplier turned toy maker Globotech and its chairman Gil Mars (Leary), the residents of Winslow Corners receive a shipment of action figures called the Commando Elite. These toys are designed to interact with their owners. And do they ever—they take on a life of their own and wage war, thanks to being mistakenly implanted with military intelligence chips. Led by Chip Hazard (voice of Jones), these commandoes take on the previously quiet town in their quest to eradicate their toy rivals, the peaceful alien Gorgonites. Led by the gentle Archer (voice of Langella), the Gorgonites enlist the help of teens Alan (Smith) and Christy (Dunst) to battle this miniature menace. Combo of computer animation, Stan Winston's animatronic puppets, and live-action bring the toys to life. **110m/C VHS, DVD.** Gregory Edward Smith, Kirsten Dunst, Phil Hartman, Ann Magnuson, Jay Mohr, Denis Leary, Kevin Dunn, Wendy Schaal, Dick Miller, David Cross, Robert Picardo; *D:* Joe Dante; *W:* Gavin Scott, Adam Rifkin, Ted Elliott, Terry Rossio; *C:* Jamie Anderson; *M:* Jerry Goldsmith; *V:* Tommy Lee Jones, Frank Langella, Ernest Borgnine, Jim Brown, Bruce Dern, George Kennedy, Clint Walker, Christopher Guest, Michael McKean, Harry Shearer, Sarah Michelle Gellar, Christina Ricci.

Small Time 🦴🦴 **1991** Chronicles the downfall of a young, small-time Harlem thief. Vince knows nothing but the streets and peer pressure, indifference, and police abuse lead him inexorably to a fatal crime. Near documentary style only heightens the tensions. **88m/B VHS.** Richard Barboza, Carolyn Hinebrew, Keith Allen, Scott Ferguson, Jane Williams; *D:* Norman Loftis; *W:* Norman Loftis; *M:* Arnold Bieber.

Small Time Crooks 🦴🦴½ **2000 (PG)** Ex-con dishwasher Allen and his manicurist wife Ullman decide to become rich by robbing a New York City bank. Problem is, they team up with three bumblers (Lovitz, Rapaport, Darrow) to pull off the heist. As a result of the mishaps, the couple accidentally gains fame and fortune only to find it doesn't suit them at all. Grant is a well-bred snob trying to teach the lower classes some couth. Ullman, as usual, is endearing, while Allen is hard to fathom as a blue-collar guy turned crook. Hailed by some as Allen's triumphant return to his comedy stylings of old, the comedy in "Small Time Crooks" actually just seems old and tired. **94m/C VHS, DVD, Wide.** Woody Allen, Tracey Ullman, Hugh Grant, Jon Lovitz, Michael Rapaport, Elaine May, Tony Darrow, Elaine Stritch, George Grizzard; *D:* Woody Allen; *W:* Woody Allen; *C:* Fei Zhao. Natl. Soc. Film Critics '00: Support. Actress (May).

Small Town Boy 🦴🦴 **1937** The cast does what they can with the brief, hackneyed story of a guy whose personality changes for the worse when he finds a "fortune" (1000 pre-inflationary dollars). **61m/B VHS.** Stuart Erwin, Joyce Compton, Jed Prouty, Clara Blandick, James "Doc" Blakely; *D:* Glenn Tryon; *W:* Glenn Tryon.

Small Town Girl 🦴🦴½ *One Horse Town* **1953** Typical romantic musical of the era, as a city slicker picked up for speeding in a hick town is pursued by the sheriff's daughter. Several Busby Berkeley blockbuster musical numbers are shoehorned incongruously into the rural doings. ♫Take Me To Broadway; I've Got To Hear That Beat; My Flaming Heart; Fine, Fine, Fine; The Fellow I'd Follow; Lullaby of the Lord; Small Towns Are Smile Towns; My Gaucho. **93m/C VHS.** Jane Powell, Farley Granger, Bobby Van, Ann Miller, Billie Burke, Robert Keith, S.Z. Sakall, Fay Wray, Nat King Cole, Chill Wills; *D:* Leslie Kardos; *M:* Andre Previn.

A Small Town in Texas 🦴🦴 **1976 (PG)** An ex-con returns home looking for the sheriff who framed him on a drug charge, and who has stolen his woman. Not-too-violent, predictable revenge flick. **96m/C VHS.** Timothy Bottoms, Susan George, Bo Hopkins; *D:* Jack Starrett; *W:* William W. Norton Sr.; *M:* Charles Bernstein.

Small Vices: A Spenser Mystery 🦴🦴½ **1999** Robert B. Parker's erudite Boston sleuth, Spenser (Mantegna), makes a return appearance along with his associate, Hawk (Mahmud-Bey), and lover Susan Silverman (Harden). This time Spenser is asked to check out a possible miscarriage of justice—did a streetwise young black man actually rape and murder a white suburban college student, the crime for which he's been convicted. But as things turn increasingly dangerous, it's clear someone doesn't want Spenser snooping around. **100m/C VHS.** Joe Mantegna, Marcia Gay Harden, Shiek Mahmud-Bey, Eugene Lipinski, Wood Harris; *Cameos:* Robert B. Parker; *D:* Robert Markowitz; *W:* Robert B. Parker; *C:* Ron Garcia; *M:* David Shire. **CABLE**

The Smallest Show on Earth 🦴🦴🦴 *Big Time Operators* **1957** A couple inherit not only an old movie house, but the three people who work there as well. Very funny and charming, with a wonderful cast. Sellers is delightful as the soused projectionist. **80m/B VHS.** *GB* Bill Travers, Virginia McKenna, Margaret Rutherford, Peter Sellers, Bernard Miles, Leslie Phillips, Stringer Davis, Francis De Wolff, Sidney James, June Cunningham; *D:* Basil Dearden; *W:* William Rose, John Eldridge; *C:* Douglas Slocombe.

Smalltime 🦴🦴 **1999 (R)** Mobster, The Dutchman, needs to deliver a bag full of drugs to a desolate ranch and then wait for someone to pick up the goods and pay him. He decides to pass the job along to lower-level goon, Ben, who figures his two friends should be in on the caper. They get bored waiting and decide to call some girls to have a party, during which time the drugs get used up. Now, they've got nothing to switch for the money. This is going to make a lot of people unhappy. **96m/C VHS, DVD.** Jeff Fahey, Glenn Plummer, Rae Dawn Chong, Darren McGavin.

Smart Alecks 🦴½ **1942** The Bowery Boys get involved with gangsters when Jordan helps capture a crook. The usual wise-cracking from Hall and Gorcey helps keep things moving. **88m/B VHS.** Leo Gorcey, Huntz Hall, Gabriel Dell, Gale Storm, Roger Pryor Jr., Walter Woolf King, Herbert Rawlinson, Joe (Joseph) Kirk, Marie Windsor; *D:* Wallace Fox.

Smart House 🦴🦴 **2000** Ben lives with his widowed dad and his younger sister in a typical suburban house. But Ben likes to enter contests and he actually wins a "Smart House," a house designed to take care of all those pesky daily choices thanks to a computer, for his family and persuades his dad to move in. But Ben's dad falls for the house's creator and the house itself gets jealous and decides to keep the family trapped inside. Although the premise has been used for horror movies, this one is strictly a comedy. **82m/C VHS.** Ryan Merriman, Kevin Kilner, Jessica Steen, Susan Haskell; *D:* LeVar Burton; *V:* Katey Sagal. **CABLE**

Smart Money 🦴🦴½ **1988** A wrongly jailed man enlists the help of his oddball pals to get revenge on the real thief who committed the computer fraud that put him behind bars. They get even while padding their pockets. **88m/C VHS, DVD.** Spencer Leigh, Alexandra Pigg, Ken Campbell.

Smash Palace 🦴🦴½ **1982** A compelling drama of a marriage jeopardized by his obsession with building a race car and her need for love and affection. Melodramatic, but worth watching. Robson as their young daughter is wonderful. **100m/C VHS.** *NZ* Bruno Lawrence, Anna Jemison, Greer Robson, Keith Aberdein; *D:* Roger Donaldson; *W:* Bruno Lawrence.

Smash-Up: The Story of a Woman 🦴🦴🦴 *A Woman Destroyed* **1947** A famous nightclub singer gives up her career for marriage and a family, only to become depressed when her husband's career soars. She turns to alcohol and her life falls apart. When her husband sues for divorce and custody of their child, she fights to recover from alcoholism. Hayward's first major role. **103m/B VHS.** Susan Hayward, Lee Bowman, Marsha Hunt, Eddie Albert; *D:* Stuart Heisler; *W:* John Howard Lawson.

Smashing Time woof! **1967** Abysmal British comedy was never widely released on this side of the Atlantic and it's easy to see why. The film follows two small-town girls—Brenda (Tushingham), who's mousy and bony, and Yvonne (Redgrave), who's loud and pushy—who come to London at the swinging '60s. Unfortunately, they are two of the most unattractive comic heroines ever to hit the screen, and apparently that's a choice the filmmakers made deliberately. Moreover, their accents are difficult to understand and their voices could blister an elephant's hide. **96m/C VHS, DVD, Wide.** *GB* Rita Tushingham, Lynn Redgrave, Michael York, Anna Quayle, Irene Handl, Ian Carmichael; *D:* Desmond Davis; *W:* George Melly; *C:* Manny Wynn; *M:* John Addison.

Smile 🦴🦴🦴 **1975 (PG)** Barbed, merciless send-up of small-town America focusing on a group of naive California girls who compete for the "Young American Miss" crown amid rampant commercialism, exploitation and pure middle-class idiocy. Hilarious neglected '70s-style satire. Early role for Griffith. **113m/C VHS.** Bruce Dern, Barbara Feldon, Michael Kidd, Nicholas Pryor, Geoffrey Lewis, Colleen Camp, Joan Prather, Annette O'Toole, Melanie Griffith, Denise Nickerson, Titos Vandis; *D:* Michael Ritchie; *W:* Jerry Belson; *C:* Conrad L. Hall; *M:* Daniel Osborn, Leroy Holmes.

Smile, Jenny, You're Dead 🦴🦴 **1974** Janssen discovers that close friend's son-in-law has been murdered, and falls in love with the daughter, the main suspect. Pilot for Janssen's "Harry-O" detective series. **100m/C VHS.** David Janssen, John Anderson, Howard da Silva, Martin Gabel, Clu Gulager, Zalman King, Jodie Foster, Barbara Leigh; *D:* Jerry Thorpe. **TV**

A Smile Like Yours 🦴½ **1996 (R)** Too-cute yuppie couple Danny and Jennifer (Kinnear and Holly) decide to start a family, only to discover that Danny's "boys" can't swim. Many formulaic and predictable gags about masturbation and the possiblilty of infidelity ensue. Unfortunately, laughs do not. Kinnear comes off as amiable enough, while Holly turns in an aggravatingly over-the-top performance. Thomas and Cusack, as the couple's best friends, fare better than anyone, with the possible exception of scene-stealer Meullerleile as the cranky clinic nurse. Writer/director Samples is the former head of now-defuct Rysher Entertainment (flick's producing company). Coincidence? We think not. **99m/C VHS.** Greg Kinnear, Lauren Holly, Jill(ian) Hennessey, Christopher McDonald, Joan Cusack, Jay Thomas, Donald Moffat, France Nuyen, Marianne Muellerleile; ***Cameos:*** Shirley MacLaine; *D:* Keith Samples; *W:* Keith Samples, Kevin Meyer; *C:* Richard Bowen; *M:* William Ross.

Smiles of a Summer Night 🦴🦴🦴½ *Sommarnattens Leende* **1955** The best known of Bergman's rare comedies; sharp satire about eight Swedish aristocrats who become romantically and comically intertwined over a single weekend. Inspired Sondheim's successful Broadway musical "A Little Night Music," and Woody Allen's "A Midsummer Night's Sex Comedy." In Swedish with English subtitles. **110m/B VHS.** *SW* Gunnar Bjornstrand, Harriet Andersson, Ulla Jacobsson, Eva Dahlbeck, Jarl Kulle, Margit Carlquist; *D:* Ingmar Bergman; *W:* Ingmar Bergman.

Smilin' Through 🦴🦴🦴 **1933** First sound version of this melodrama/romance which Franklin had directed as a silent in 1922. Shearer is set to marry Howard when jealous rival March shows up armed at the wedding and accidentally kills the bride. March escapes and Howard spends his years as a recluse until his young niece, the image of his dead fiance (naturally, since she's also played by Shearer) arrives to live with him. She meets a young man who turns out to be March's son (played again by March) and they fall in love. Pure sentiment done with high gloss. Remade in 1941. **97m/B VHS.** Norma Shearer, Fredric March, Leslie Howard, O.P. Heggie, Ralph Forbes, Beryl Mercer, Margaret Seddon; *D:* Sidney Franklin; *C:* Lee Garmes.

Smilin' Through 🦴🦴½ **1941** Third filming, second with sound, first in color, of a popular melodrama. An embittered man whose wife was murdered on their wedding day raises an orphaned niece, only to have her fall in love with the son of her aunt's murderer. Made MacDonald into a singing star. Songs include title tune and "A Little Love, a Little Kiss." **101m/C VHS.** Jeanette MacDonald, Brian Aherne, Gene Raymond, Ian Hunter, Frances Robinson; *D:* Frank Borzage.

Smiling Fish & Goat on Fire 🦴🦴½ **1999 (R)** Title refers to the childhood nicknames that Chris Remi (Derick Martini) and his brother Tony (Steven Martini) were given by their Native American/Italian grandma. Accountant Chris and aspiring actor Tony share a house in L.A. and have trouble with women. Their current relationships are falling apart, but new ones are looming, and the confused bros get some sage advice from their elderly friend, Clive (Henderson). Low-budget, wry slice-of-life. **90m/C VHS, DVD, Wide.** Steven Martini, Derick Martini, Bill Henderson, Christa Miller, Amy Hathaway, Rosemarie Addeo, Heather Jae Marie, Nicole Rae, Wesley Thompson; *D:* Kevin Jordan; *W:* Kevin Jordan, Steven Martini, Derick Martini; *C:* Fred Iannone; *M:* Chris Horvath.

Smilla's Sense of Snow 🦴🦴 **1996 (R)** Thriller starts off well but fails to sustain the suspense of the Peter Hoeg mystery on which it is based. Solitary scientist Smilla Jasperson (Ormond) is a half-Inuit, half-American (Danish in the book) resident of Copenhagen who's an expert on snow and ice. Born and raised in Greenland, Smilla is drawn back to her home when the body of six-year-old Isaiah (Miano), whom she's grudgingly befriended, is discovered at their apartment building. Smilla believes the boy was murdered and when she begins investigating it leads to the Greenland mining company where Isaiah's late father worked and which is run by the suspicious Tork (Harris). Location cinematography is particularly impressive. **121m/C VHS, DVD, Wide.** *GE DK SW* Julia Ormond, Gabriel Byrne, Richard Harris, Vanessa Redgrave, Robert Loggia, Jim Broadbent, Mario Adorf, Bob Peck, Tom Wilkinson, Peter Capaldi, Emma Croft, Clipper Miano; *D:* Bille August; *W:* Ann Biderman; *C:* Jorgen Persson; *M:* Hans Zimmer, Harry Gregson-Williams.

Smith! 🦴🦴½ **1969 (G)** Naive but well intentioned look at present-day treatment of Native Americans. Rancher Ford becomes embroiled in the trial of murder suspect Ramirez. Based on Paul St. Pierre's novel "Breaking Smith's Quarter Horse." **101m/C VHS.** Glenn Ford, Frank Ramirez, Keenan Wynn; *D:* Michael O'Herlihy; *W:* Louis Pelletier; *M:* Robert F. Brunner.

Smithereens 🦴🦴½ **1982 (R)** Working-class girl leaves home for New York's music scene. Rugged, hip character study. Director Seidleman's first feature. **90m/C VHS.** Susan Berman, Brad Rinn, Richard Hell, Christopher Noth; *D:* Susan Seidelman; *W:* Ron Nyswaner, Peter Askin.

Smoke 🦴🦴½ **1970** A young boy nurses a lost German sheperd back to health with the help of his new stepfather, whom he learns to trust. Then he runs away with the dog when the original owners show up. Disney fare starring Opie/Richie (and later successful director) Howard. **89m/C VHS.** Earl Holliman, Ron Howard, Andy Devine; *D:* Vincent McEveety. **TV**

Smoke 🦴🦴 **1993** Three days in the life of Michael, as he travels between fantasy and reality, past and present, searching for love with the perfect older man. **90m/C VHS.** *D:* Mark D'Aruia; *M:* Arnold Bieber.

Smoke 🦴🦴 **1995 (R)** Brooklyn slice of life centers around the local cigar store run by Auggie Wren (Keitel). An ensemble piece, divided into five chapters, which includes such characters as down-on-his luck novelist Paul (Hurt), troubled black teenager Rashid (Perrineau Jr.), Augie's ex-wife Ruby (Channing) and supposed daughter (Judd), and many more (some of whom get lost in the shuffle). Wonderfully acted but the stories tend to disappear in a wisp of smoke. Based on a story by Auster. Wang and Auster also made an impromptu companion film "Blue in the Face." **112m/C VHS.** Harvey Keitel, William Hurt, Stockard Channing, Forest Whitaker, Harold Perrineau Jr., Ashley Judd, Mary Ward, Victor Argo, Jared Harris, Giancarlo Esposito, Mel Gorham; *D:* Wayne Wang; *W:* Paul Auster; *C:* Adam Holender; *M:* Rachel Portman.

Smoke in the Wind 🦴½ **1975 (PG)** Subpar western about men accused of complicity with the Union in postbellum Arkansas. Minor role for Brennan was his last; also director Kane's last film. **93m/C VHS.** John Ashley, Walter Brennan, John Russell, Myron Healey; *D:* Joseph Kane.

Smoke Signals 🦴🦴 **1998 (PG-13)** Serious themes are treated in a deceptively simple and humorous manner, based on stories from Alexie's book "The Lone Ranger and Tonto Fistfight in Heaven." Geeky, orphaned Thomas (Adams) lives on the Coeur d'Alene reservation in Idaho where he's reluctantly looked after by stoic Victor (Beach), whose long-gone father Arnold (Farmer) saved Thomas from the fire that killed his parents. When Victor learns of Arnold's death in Phoenix, Thomas says he'll pay the expenses of the trip if he can accompany Victor. The young men reach an understanding during their travels, while Victor struggles to deal with his complicated feelings about his father and the past. **88m/C VHS, DVD.** Adam Beach, Evan Adams, Irene Bedard, Gary Farmer, Tantoo Cardinal, Michelle St. John, Robert Miano, Molly Cheek, Elaine Miles, Michael Greyeyes, Chief Leonard George, John Trudell, Tom Skerritt, Cody Lightning, Cynthia Geary, Simon Baker; *D:* Chris Eyre; *W:* Sherman Alexie; *C:* Brian Capener; *M:* B.C. Smith. Ind. Spirit '99: Debut Perf. (Adams); Sundance '98: Aud. Award, Filmmakers Trophy.

The Smokers 🦴 **2000 (R)** Bleech—this would-be revenge comedy is guaranteed to leave a bad taste in your mouth with its unappealing characters and storyline. Boarding school friends Jefferson (Swain), Karen (Philipps), and Lisa (Pratt) are sick of boys treating them wrong. So with a stolen gun; they are determined to have the miscreants make amends. **97m/C VHS, DVD, Wide.** Dominique Swain, Keri Lynn Pratt, Busy Philipps, Oliver Hudson, Ryan Browning, Joel West, Thora Birch, Nicholas M. Loeb; *D:* Christina Peters; *W:* Christina Peters, Kenny Golde; *C:* J.B. Letchinger; *M:* Lawrence Gingold.

Smokescreen 🦴🦴½ **1990 (R)** A young ad exec meets the girl of his dreams, and finds himself working for her gangster boyfriend. Competently made and acted, but phoney ending wrecks it. **91m/C VHS.** Kim Cattrall, Dean Stockwell, Matt Craven, Kim Coates, Brian George, Michael Hogan; *D:* Martin Lavut.

Smokey and the Bandit 🦴🦴½ **1977 (PG)** The first and best of the series about bootlegger Reynolds is one long car chase. Reynolds makes a wager that he can deliver a truckload of Coors beer—once unavailable east of Texas—to Atlanta from Texas in 28 hours. Gleason is a riot as the "smokey" who tries to stop him. Field is the hitchhiker Reynolds picks up along the way. Great stunts; director Needham was a top stunt man. **96m/C VHS, DVD.** Susan McIver, John Schneider, Hank Worden, Sonny Shroyer, Burt Reynolds, Sally Field, Jackie Gleason, Jerry Reed, Mike Henry, Paul Williams, Pat McCormick; *D:* Hal Needham; *W:* Hal Needham, Charles Shyer; *C:* Bobby Byrne; *M:* Bill Justis, Jerry Reed.

Smokey and the Bandit 2 🦴 *Smokey and the Bandit Ride Again* **1980 (PG)** Pathetic sequel to "Smokey and the Bandit" proved a boxoffice winner, grossing $40 million. The Bandit is hired to transport a pregnant elephant from Miami to the Republican convention in Dallas. Sheriff Buford T. Justice and family are in hot pursuit. **101m/C VHS.** David Huddleston, John Anderson, Brenda Lee, Mel Tillis, Burt Reynolds, Sally Field, Jackie Gleason, Jerry Reed, Mike Henry, Dom DeLuise, Pat McCormick, Paul Williams; ***Cameos:*** Joe "Mean Joe" Greene, Don Williams, Terry Bradshaw; *D:* Hal Needham; *W:* Brock Yates, Jerry Belson, Michael Kane; *C:* Michael C. Butler.

Smokey and the Bandit, Part 3 🦴 **1983 (PG)** You thought the second one was bad? Another mega car chase, this time sans Reynolds and director Needham. **88m/C VHS.** Jackie Gleason, Jerry Reed, Paul Williams, Pat McCormick, Mike Henry, Colleen Camp; ***Cameos:*** Burt Reynolds; *D:* Dick Lowry; *W:* Stuart Birnbaum, David Dashev.

Smokey & the Hotwire Gang 🦴½ **1979** A convoy of truckers try to track down a beautiful woman driving a stolen car. **85m/C VHS.** James Keach, Stanley Livingston, Tony Lorea, Alvy Moore, George Barris.

Smokey & the Judge 🦴 **1980 (PG)** Police officer has his hands full with a trio of lovely ladies. **90m/C VHS.** Gene Price, Wayde Preston, Juanita Curiel.

Smokey Bites the Dust 🦴 **1981 (PG)** Car-smashing gag-fest about a sheriff's daughter kidnapped by her smitten beau. Near-plotless and literally unoriginal: lifted footage from several other Corman-produced flicks, a technique that can aptly be called garbage picking. **87m/C VHS.** Janet (Johnson) Julian, Jimmy (James Vincent) McNichol, Patrick Campbell, Kari Lizer, John Blythe Barrymore Jr., Kedrick Wolfe, Walter Barnes; *D:* Charles B. Griffith; *W:* Max Apple; *C:* Gary Graver; *M:* Bent Myggen.

Smokey Smith 🦴½ **1936** Ubiquitous Hayes and steely Steele hunt down the slayers of an elderly couple. Ordinary oater directed by Steele's father, Bradbury. **59m/B VHS.** Bob Steele, George "Gabby" Hayes; *D:* Robert North Bradbury.

Smoking/No Smoking 🦴🦴 **1994** Two linked films director Resnais adapted from writer Alan Ayckbourn's eight-play cycle "Intimate Exchanges" (although the screenwriters have only used six stories). Azema and Arditti plays nine characters in various tableaus on marriage and affairs set at a Yorkshire school. The opening sequence of each episode provides the title tie-in, as faculty wife Celia goes onto the terrace, finds a pack of cigarettes, and decides whether or not to light up. A studio set provides all the frankly fake backdrops. Very slight and very long. French with subtitles. **285m/C VHS.** *FR* Sabine Azema, Pierre Arditti; *D:* Alain Resnais; *W:* Jean-Pierre Bacri, Agnes Jaoui. Cesar '94: Actor (Arditti), Art Dir./Set Dec., Director (Resnais), Film, Writing.

A Smoky Mountain Christmas 🦴🦴 **1986** Dolly gets away from it all in a secluded cabin that has been appropriated by a gang of orphans, and sings a half dozen songs. Innocuous seasonal country fun. Winkler's TV directing debut. **94m/C VHS.** Dolly Parton, Bo Hopkins, Dan Hedaya, Gennie James, David Ackroyd, Rene Auberjonois, John Ritter, Anita Morris, Lee Majors; *D:* Henry Winkler; *W:* Dolly Parton. **TV**

Smooth Talk 1985 (PG-13) An innocent, flirtatious teenager catches the eye of a shady character, played by Williams. Disturbing and thought-provoking film that caused some controversy when it opened. Dern gives a brilliant performance as the shy, sheltered girl. Based on the Joyce Carol Oates story "Where Are You Going, Where Have You Been?" Made for PBS' "American Playhouse" series. **92m/C VHS.** Laura Dern, Treat Williams, Mary Kay Place, Levon Helm, William Ragsdale, Margaret Welsh, Sarah Inglis; ***D:*** Joyce Chopra; ***W:*** Tom Cole; ***C:*** James Glennon. Sundance '86: Grand Jury Prize. **TV**

Smooth Talker woof! 1990 (R) A serial killer stalks the women of a 976 party line. Bad acting, bad dialog, not a scare to be found. **89m/C VHS.** Joe Guzaldo, Peter Crombie, Stuart Whitman, Burt Ward, Sydney Lassick, Blair Weickgenant; ***D:*** Tom Milo.

Smouldering Fires ½ 1925 A tough businesswoman falls in love with an ambitious young employee, who is 15 years her junior. After they marry, problems arise in the form of the wife's attractive younger sister. Surprisingly subtle melodrama, if that's not an oxymoron. **100m/B VHS.** Pauline Frederick, Laura La Plante, Tully Marshall, Malcolm McGregor, Wanda (Petit) Hawley, Helen Lynch, George Cooper, Bert Roach; ***D:*** Clarence Brown.

Smugglers *Lover of the Great Bear* 1975 Opportunistic smugglers take advantage of the Russian Revolution to sack the land and make a bundle. **110m/C VHS.** *IT* Senta Berger, Giuliano Gemma; ***D:*** Valintino Orsini.

Smugglers' Cove 1948 Gorcey wrongly believes he has inherited a mansion. He and the Bowery Boys move in, only to stumble across a smuggling ring. Plenty of slapsticks; the boys at their best. **66m/B VHS.** Leo Gorcey, Huntz Hall, Gabriel Dell; ***D:*** William Beaudine.

Snake Eyes ½ 1998 (R) Stylish thriller with Nick Cage at his wild-eyed best. Cage is corrupt Atlantic City cop Rick Santoro, investigating the bold assassination of Secretary of Defense Kirkland (Fabiani) during a heavyweight boxing match. The first half of the film packs a visual punch, with De Palma's trademark jazzy camera work, but shortly after Santoro partners with his Navy officer pal Kevin Dunne (Sinise), and realizes nothing is what it seems, story is ko'd with a combination of implausibility and a lackluster climax. De Palma's first film since directing the b.o. smash "Mission Impossible." Shot exclusively in a Montreal skating arena. **99m/C VHS, DVD.** Nicolas Cage, Gary Sinise, Carla Gugino, John Heard, Stan Shaw, Kevin Dunn, Michael Rispoli, Joel Fabiani, Luis Guzman, Tamara Tunie; ***D:*** Brian DePalma; ***W:*** David Koepp; ***C:*** Stephen Burum; ***M:*** Ryuichi Sakamoto.

The Snake Hunter Strangler 1966 A young girl is rescued after 15 years from an evil cult of snake people. **65m/C VHS.** Guy Madison, Ivan Desny; ***D:*** Luigi Capuano.

The Snake People *Isle of the Snake People; Cult of the Dead; La Muerte Viviente; Isle of the Living Dead* 1968 A police captain investigates a small island littered with LSD-experimenting scientists, snake-worshippers, and voodoo. One of the infamous quartet of Karloff's final films, all made in Mexico. **90m/C VHS.** *MX* Boris Karloff, Julissa, Carlos East; ***D:*** Enrique Vergara.

The Snake Pit ½ 1948 One of the first films to compassionately explore mental illness and its treatment. Following an emotional collapse Virginia (de Havilland) is placed in a mental institution by her husband, Robert (Stevens). The severity of her depression causes her sympathetic doctor (Genn) to try such treatments as electric shock, hydrotherapy, and drugs, along with the psychoanalysis which gradually allows her to accept her fears and make her recovery. Tour-de-force performance by de Havilland. Based on the novel by Mary Jane Ward. **108m/B VHS.** Olivia de Havilland, Mark Stevens, Leo Genn, Celeste Holm, Glenn Langan, Helen Craig, Leif Erickson, Beulah Bondi; ***D:*** Anatole Litvak; ***W:*** Frank Partos, Millen Brand; ***C:*** Leo Tover; ***M:*** Alfred Newman. Oscars '48: Sound; N.Y. Film Critics '48: Actress (de Havilland).

The Snake Woman 1961 A herpetologist working in a small English village during the 1890s is conducting strange experiments to try to cure his wife's madness. He tries injecting his pregnant wife with snake venom and she gives birth to a cold-blooded daughter, who, when she grows up, has the ability to change herself into a deadly snake. She promptly begins killing the local male populace until Scotland Yard is called in to investigate. The curvy Travers is appropriately snakey but this movie is dull. **68m/C VHS.** *GB* John P. McCarthy, Susan Travers, Arnold Marle; ***D:*** Sidney J. Furie.

SnakeEater 1989 (R) Loner cop tracks down swine who killed his parents and kidnapped his sister. "Rambo" rip-off with little plot, but lots of action. Followed by two sequels. **89m/C VHS.** Lorenzo Lamas, Larry Csonka, Ron Palillo; ***D:*** George Erschbamer.

SnakeEater 2: The Drug Buster 1989 (R) A cop goes nuts and kills four drug dealers. As a result he is committed to an institution. Iron bars don't make a prison for this guy though, and he's soon back on the streets fighting crime with his pal "Speedboat." Silly sequel is quite bad; followed by yet another. **93m/C VHS.** Lorenzo Lamas, Larry B. Scott, Michelle Scarabelli, Harvey Atkin, Jack Blum, Kathleen Kinmont; ***D:*** George Erschbamer.

SnakeEater 3: His Law 1992 (R) Tough cop Jack Kelly (Lamas), aka SnakeEater, is out to avenge a woman's beating by a gang of thug bikers. Lots of action and violence, not much plot; based on W. Glenn Duncan's novel "Rafferty's Rules." **109m/C VHS.** Lorenzo Lamas, Minor Mustain, Tracy Cook, Holly Chester, Scott "Bam Bam" Bigelow; ***D:*** George Erschbamer; ***W:*** John Dunning.

Snap Decision ½ 2001 Widowed mom Jen (Winningham) allows her friend Carrie (Huffman), a professional photographer, to take candid pictures of her three children when Carrie visits. But the owner of a photo-developing shop gets flustered by what she sees and contacts the police about the "obscene" material. The kids are taken away from Jen and she faces prison time for child pornography in this true story that is every parent's nightmare. **92m/C VHS.** Mare Winningham, Felicity Huffman, Chelcie Ross, Chuck Shamata, Megan Fahlenbock, Ronn Sarosiak, Robert Bockstael, Don Allison; ***D:*** Alan Metzger; ***W:*** Ara Watson, Sam Blackwell; ***C:*** Rhett Morita; ***M:*** James McVay. **CABLE**

Snapdragon 1993 (R) Police psychologist is led astray by his libido while investigating a luscious amnesiac. His sensible vice cop girlfriend then discovers the sexpot is actually a psycho serial killer calling herself the Snapdragon but will her boyfriend even care? **96m/C VHS, DVD.** Steven Bauer, Pamela Anderson, Chelsea Field; ***D:*** Worth Keeter; ***W:*** Gene Church; ***C:*** James Mathers; ***M:*** Michael Linn.

The Snapper ½ 1993 (R) Originally made for BBC TV, Frears creates a small comic gem based on the second novel of Doyle's Barrytown trilogy. Set in Dublin, 20-year-old Sharon Curley (Kellegher) finds herself unexpectedly pregnant and refuses to name the father. Family and friends are understanding—until they discover the man's identity. Affecting performances, particularly from Meaney as Sharon's dad who takes a much greater interest in the birth of his grandchild than he ever did with his own children. Cheerful semi-sequel to "The Commitments" serves up domestic upheavals graced with humor and a strong sense of family loyalty. **95m/C VHS.** *IR* Tina Kellegher, Colm Meaney, Ruth McCabe, Colm O'Byrne, Pat Laffan, Eanna MacLiam, Ciara Duffy; ***D:*** Stephen Frears; ***W:*** Roddy Doyle. **TV**

Snapshot 1977 (R) Typical grade Z sex comedy; a free-lance photographer ogles lots of variously dishabilled young women through his lens. **84m/C VHS.** Jim Henshaw, Susan Petrie.

Snatch 2000 (R) A la "Lock, Stock and 2 Smoking Barrels," director Ritchie's second film is another well-populated and disorganized crime caper, this time with descriptively named lowlifes trying to heist a stolen 84-carat diamond. Leading the mayhem are Turkish (Statham) and Tommy (Graham), two boxing promoters who sign Mickey (Pitt), an Irish Gypsy, to take a dive. Meanwhile, Franky Four Fingers (Del Toro) transports the red-hot rock to London and his boss Avi (Farina), where it promptly gets lifted. Enter Bullet Tooth Tony (Jones) to find missing Franky and a host of others whose seemingly unrelated subplots eventually meet. Casting, lots of action, and Ritchie's dialogue are spot on. Ritchie's usual use of heavy Cockney accents are upstaged by Pitt's Gypsy pugilist and his much talked about thick-as-Guinness brogue which even the other characters can't decipher. The elaborate and sometimes confusing plotlines are aided by titles and narration and effective use of Ritchie's usual slo-mo, fast cutting, and split-screen. **104m/C VHS, DVD, Wide.** *GB* Benicio Del Toro, Dennis Farina, Brad Pitt, Vinnie Jones, Rade Serbedzija, Jason Statham, Lennie James, Ewen Bremner, Alan Ford, Mike Reid, Robbie Gee, Jason Flemyng, Sorcha Cusack, Stephen Graham; ***D:*** Guy Ritchie; ***W:*** Guy Ritchie; ***C:*** Tim Maurice-Jones; ***M:*** John Murphy.

Snatched 1972 The wives of three wealthy men are held for ransom, but one man doesn't want to pay, while one of the victims needs insulin. Standard TV fare. **73m/C VHS.** Howard Duff, Leslie Nielsen, Sheree North, Barbara Parkins, Robert Reed, John Saxon, Tisha Sterling; ***D:*** Sutton Roley; ***M:*** Randy Edelman. **TV**

Sneakers ½ 1992 (PG-13) Competent thriller about five computer hackers with questionable pasts and an equally questionable government job. Of course, nothing is as it seems. Rather slow-going considering the talents and suspense involved but includes enough turns to keep a viewer's interest. **125m/C VHS, DVD, Wide.** Robert Redford, Sidney Poitier, River Phoenix, Dan Aykroyd, Ben Kingsley, David Strathairn, Mary McDonnell, Timothy Busfield, George Hearn, Eddie Jones, James Earl Jones, Stephen Tobolowsky; ***D:*** Phil Alden Robinson; ***W:*** Lawrence Lasker, Walter F. Parkes, Phil Alden Robinson; ***C:*** John Lindley; ***M:*** James Horner, Branford Marsalis.

Sniper *The Deadly Tower* 1975 Suspenseful drama based on true story of Charles Whitman, who shot at University of Texas students from Texas Tower on a summer day in 1966. Disney alumunus Russell breaks type as mass killer, with fine support by Yniguez as a police officer on the scene and Beatty as the passerby who lends a hand. Finely crafted re-creation of disturbing, true event. **85m/C VHS, DVD.** Kurt Russell, Richard Yniguez, John Forsythe, Ned Beatty, Pernell Roberts, Clifton James, Paul Carr, Alan Vint, Pepe Serna; ***D:*** Jerry Jameson. **TV**

The Sniper ½ 1987 A law-abiding citizen becomes a vigilante killer after witnessing a violent crime. **90m/C VHS.** Claudia Cardinale.

Sniper ½ 1992 (R) Less than compelling shoot-'em-up set in Panama. Lead characters include Sgt. Beckett (Berenger), a seasoned assassin who gets a rush from killing. Also assigned to the case is Richard Miller (Zane), a newcomer who knows his guns but not his jungles. Together they go in search of their target, a politician planning a coup with the help of a druglord. Action is poorly choreographed and plot is cursory at best. **99m/C VHS, DVD, 8mm, Wide.** Tom Berenger, Billy Zane, J.T. Walsh, Aden Young, Ken Radley, Reinaldo Arenas, Carlos Alvarez, Roy Edmonds, Dale Dye; ***D:*** Luis Llosa; ***W:*** Michael Frost Beckner, Crash Leyland; ***C:*** Bill Butler; ***M:*** Gary Chang.

Sno-Line 1985 (R) A New York gangster moves to Texas and begins to wipe out the competition on his way to building his drug and gambling dynasty. Bo-ring excuse for entertainment. No hope, no redemption, no titillation: just ultra-"realistic" depiction of organized crime, poorly acted. **89m/C VHS.** Vince Edwards, Paul Smith, June Wilkinson; ***D:*** Douglas F. Oneans.

Snow Country ½ 1957 Romantic drama of an unsuccessful, married artist from Tokyo who travels to a mountain resort to find himself. He requests a Geisha for the evening and, when none are available, the beautiful adopted daughter of the local music teacher is sent to him instead. Based on the novel by Nobel Prize winner Yasunari Kawabata. In Japanese with English subtitles. Remade in 1965. **104m/B VHS.** *JP* Ryo Ikebe, Keiko Kishi, Akira Kubo, Kaoru Yachigusa, Hisaya Morishige, Mineko Yorozuyo, Etsuko Ichihara, Noriko Sengoku, Kumeko Urabe, Eiko Miyoshi, Akira Tan, Chieko Naniwa, Daisuke Kato, Haruo Tanaka; ***D:*** Shiro Toyoda.

The Snow Creature woof! 1954 Stupid troop of explorers bring back a snow creature from the Himalayas. Critter escapes in L.A. and terrorizes all in its path before blending in with club crowd. Very bad monster epic (the first about a snow monster) that strains credibility frame by frame. Occasionally, depending upon camera angle, light, and viewer mood, monster appears to be something other than guy in bad suit sweating. Directed by Billy Wilder's brother and another argument against genetic consistency. **72m/B VHS.** Paul Langton, Leslie Denison; ***D:*** W. Lee Wilder.

Snow Day ½ 2000 (PG) Goofy, innocuous family comedy may provide a distraction for the little monsters if you're stuck with a snow day of your own. Tom (Chase) is the hapless weatherman who's as surprised as anyone when the white stuff falls. Meanwhile, the nieghborhood kids seek to foil the efforts of the evil Snowplowman (Elliott) who is out to destroy their dream of having more than one day off from school. **89m/C VHS, DVD, Wide.** Chevy Chase, Chris Elliott, Mark Webber, Jean Smart, Schuyler Fisk, Iggy Pop, Pam Grier, John Schneider, Emmanuelle Chriqui; ***D:*** Chris Koch; ***W:*** Will McRobb, Chris Viscardi; ***C:*** Robbie Greenberg; ***M:*** Steve Bartek.

Snow Dogs 2002 (PG) Gooding leads this kid flick as Ted Brooks, a dentist who only finds out about his adoption after his biological mom's death in Alaska. Aside from a rather dilapidated house, mom's estate included a team of frisky Siberian husky sled dogs. Displaced city boy Ted, who's from Miami, hates the cold and the dogs but stays to take care of the estate, seek out his real father, and get better acquainted with friendly local bar owner Barb (Bacalso). Meanwhile, the grizzled Thunder Jack (Coburn) is on Ted's tail, trying to get him to sell the dogs. The expected Iditarod-type dog race ensues. Gooding mugs amiably and the good natured physical humor and action should amuse the young and undiscrimination. **99m/C VHS, DVD.** *US* Cuba Gooding Jr., James Coburn, Sisqo, Nichelle Nichols, M. Emmet Walsh, Graham Greene, Brian Doyle-Murray, Joanna Bacalso, Michael Bolton; ***D:*** Brian Levant; ***W:*** Jim Kouf, Tommy Swerdlow, Michael Goldberg, Mark Gibson, Philip Halprin; ***C:*** Thomas Ackerman; ***M:*** John Debney.

Snow Falling on Cedars 1999 (PG-13) Visually beautiful but remarkably dull adaptation of David Guterson's novel. In 1954, journalist and WWII vet, the portentiously-named Ishmael Chambers (Hawke), confronts his past when he's assigned to report on the trial of Japanese-American Kazuo Miyamoto (Yune), who's accused of murdering a fellow fisherman (Thal) in a small community north of Puget Sound. Kazuo just happens to be married to Ishmael's former flame, Hatsue (Kudoh)—their romance having been thwarted by the prejudicial times. Lots of impressionistic flashbacks complicate matters while the story meanders along, not helped by Hawke's blank-faced performance. **128m/C VHS, DVD.** Ethan Hawke, Youki Kudoh, Rick Yune, Sam Shepard, Max von Sydow, James Cromwell, James Rebhorn, Richard Jenkins, Eric Thal, Celia Weston, Max Wright; ***D:*** Scott Hicks; ***W:*** Scott Hicks, Ronald Bass; ***C:*** Robert Richardson; ***M:*** James Newton Howard.

Snow Kill 𝒮½ 1990 Five city-dwellers travel into the mountains for a fun survival training weekend, but the fun turns deadly when they accidentally come across a murderous drug gang. Pseudo-'30s suspense adventure fails to thrill or surprise. **90m/C VHS.** Terence Knox, Patti D'Arbanville, David Dukes; ***D:*** Thomas J. Wright; ***W:*** Harv Zimmel. **CABLE**

The Snow Queen 1983 From "Fairie Tale Theatre" comes this adaptation of the Hans Christian Andersen tale. A boy and girl who grow up together are separated by evil when the boy is held captive in the icy palace of the Snow Queen. The girl sets out to rescue him. **60m/C VHS.** Lauren Hutton, Linda Manz, David Hemmings, Melissa Gilbert, Lee Remick, Lance Kerwin; ***D:*** Peter Medak. **CABLE**

Snow: The Movie 𝒮 1983 Rates creative zero for title, though there is snow, as well as skiing, growing up, romance, and good times among the young people involved. Filmed in Australia. **83m/C VHS.** David Argue, Lance Curtis; ***D:*** Robert Gibson.

Snow Treasure 𝒮 1967 (G) With the help of an underground agent, Norwegian children smuggle gold out of the country right under the noses of the Nazis. Based on the novel by Marie McSwigan. **96m/C VHS.** James Franciscus, Paul Anstad; ***D:*** Irving Jacoby.

Snow White 𝒮𝒮 1989 The incomparable Rigg stars in this witty retelling of the beautiful girl and her seven little friends. **85m/C VHS.** Diana Rigg, Sarah Patterson, Billy Barty; ***D:*** Michael Berz.

Snow White: A Tale of Terror 𝒮𝒮½ *Snow White in the Black Forest; Grimm Brothers' Snow White* 1997 (R) This definitely puts the grim in the Grimm Brothers version of the fairy tale. In medieval Austria, beautiful Claudia (Weaver) marries widowed Frederick who, unfortunately, has an even-more beautiful daughter, Lilli (Keena), who's put out by this rival for her father's affections. The stepmom/stepdaughter battle increases when Claudia's own long-awaited baby is still-born and the wrathful and unbalanced Claudia orders Lilli's death. Only she's rescued by seven outcasts (only one of whom is a dwarf) living in the forest. The witchy Claudia does still like to talk to her mirror, however. Filmed in the Czech Republic. **101m/C VHS, DVD.** Sigourney Weaver, Sam Neill, Monica Keena, Gil Bellows, Taryn Davis; ***D:*** Michael Cohn; ***W:*** Thomas Szollosi, Deborah Serra; ***C:*** Mike Southon; ***M:*** John Ottman.

Snow White and the Seven Dwarfs 𝒮𝒮𝒮𝒮 1937 (G) Classic adaptation of the Grimm Brothers fairy tale about the fairest of them all. Beautiful animation, memorable characters, and wonderful songs mark this as the definitive "Snow White." Set the stage for other animated features after Walt Disney took an unprecedented gamble by attempting the first animated feature-length film, a project which took over two years to create and $1.5 million to make, and made believers out of those who laughed at the concept. Lifelike animation was based on real stars; Margery Belcher (later Champion) posed for Snow, Louis Hightower was the Prince, and Lucille LaVerne gave the Queen her nasty look. ♫Some Day My Prince Will Come; One Song; With a Smile and a Song; Whistle While You Work; Bluddle-Uddle-Um-Dum; The Dwarfs' Yodel Song; Heigh Ho; I'm Wishing; Isn't This a Silly Song?. **83m/C VHS, DVD.** ***D:*** David Hand; ***W:*** Ted Sears, Otto Englander, Earl Hurd, Dorothy Blank, Richard Creedon, Dick Richard, Merrill De Maris, Webb Smith; ***M:*** Frank Churchill, Paul J. Smith, Larry Morey, Leigh Harline; ***V:*** Adriana Caselotti, Harry Stockwell, Lucille LaVerne, Moroni Olsen, Billy Gilbert, Pinto Colvig, Otis Harlan, Scotty Matraw, Roy Atwell, Stuart Buchanan, Marion Darlington, Jim Macdonald. AFI '98: Top 100, Natl. Film Reg. '89.

Snow White and the Seven Dwarfs 1983 From "Faerie Tale Theatre" comes the story of a princess who befriends seven little men to protect her from the jealous evil queen. **60m/C VHS.** Elizabeth McGovern, Rex Smith, Vincent Price, Vanessa Redgrave; ***D:*** Peter Medak. **CABLE**

Snow White and the Three Stooges 𝒮 *Snow White and the Three Clowns* 1961 The Stooges fill in for the Seven Dwarfs when they go off prospecting in King Solomon's mines. Alas, see any Stooge movie but this one. **107m/C VHS.** Moe Howard, Larry Fine, Joe DeRita, Carol Heiss, Patricia Medina, Edson Stroll; ***D:*** Walter Lang; ***W:*** Noel Langley, Elwood Ullman; ***C:*** Leon Shamroy; ***M:*** Lyn Murray.

Snow White: The Fairest of Them All 𝒮𝒮 2002 Kreuk certainly looks the title part and Richardson makes a fine wicked stepmother and queen but this version of the fairy tale is lame. Snow's mother dies when she's a baby and her father (Irwin) unwittingly places his daughter under a curse when he marries the witchy Elspeth (Richardson). Oh, and the dwarves are rainbow-colored and named after the days of the week. But Snow still gets stuck in that glass coffin until the prince comes along. **90m/C VHS, DVD.** Kristen Kreuk, Miranda Richardson, Tom Irwin, Vera Farmiga, Vincent Schiavelli, Warwick Davis, Michael J. Anderson, Clancy Brown, Tyron Leitso; ***D:*** Caroline Thompson; ***W:*** Caroline Thompson, Julie Hickson; ***C:*** Jon Joffin; ***M:*** Michael Covertino. **TV**

Snowball Express 𝒮𝒮 1972 (G) When a New York City accountant inherits a hotel in the Rocky Mountains, he decides to move his family west to attempt to make a go of the defunct ski resort, only to find that the place is falling apart. Run-of-the-mill Disney comedy, based on the novel "Chateau Bon Vivant" by Frankie and John O'Rear. **120m/C VHS.** Dean Jones, Nancy Olson, Harry (Henry) Morgan, Keenan Wynn; ***D:*** Norman Tokar; ***M:*** Robert F. Brunner.

Snowballin' 𝒮 1985 A ski instructor gives private lessons to a bunch of snow bunnies. **90m/C VHS.** Seline Lomez, Daniel Pilon.

Snowballing 𝒮 1985 (PG) Part of the polluted wave of teen-sex flicks of the 1980s, this is very mild for the genre but still no prize. Lusty high schoolers at a skiing competition look for action on and off the slopes, end up exposing a resort fraud. **96m/C VHS.** Mary (Elizabeth) McDonough, Bob Hastings.

Snowbeast 𝒮½ 1977 The residents of a ski resort are being terrorized by a half-human, half-animal beast leaving a path of dead bodies in its wake. "Jaws" hits the slopes. Not scary or even funny. Made for TV. **96m/C VHS.** Bo Svenson, Yvette Mimieux, Sylvia Sidney, Clint Walker, Robert F. Logan; ***D:*** Herb Wallerstein. **TV**

Snowblind 𝒮𝒮 *Ski Lift to Death* 1978 Two ski gondolas derail, placing the passengers in jeopardy. Among the passengers is a mobster being pursued by an assassin. **98m/C VHS.** Deborah Raffin, Charles Frank, Howard Duff, Don Galloway, Gail Strickland, Don Johnson, Veronica Hamel, Clu Gulager, Lisa Reeves, Suzy Chaffee; ***D:*** William Wiard.

Snowboard Academy 𝒮½ 1996 (PG) Chris Barry (Haim), the younger son of a ski resort owner, gets into trouble when his crazy snowboarder pals take over the slopes. Chris' older brother challenges him to start a school that will turn the bumblers into racers in just two weeks. Filmed at Le Chantecler resort in the Laurentian Mountains near Montreal. **89m/C VHS.** Corey Haim, Jim Varney, Brigitte Nielsen, Joe Flaherty, Paul Hopkins; ***D:*** John Shepphird; ***W:*** Rudy Rupak, James Salisko; ***C:*** Bruno Philip; ***M:*** Ross Vannelli.

Snowbound: The Jim and Jennifer Stolpa Story 𝒮𝒮½ 1994 Based on a true story, this TV drama finds Jim (Harris) Stolpa, his wife Jennifer (Williams), and their 5-month-old baby fighting for survival when they're trapped in the open by a Nevada snowstorm for eight days. **120m/C VHS.** Neil Patrick Harris, Kelli Williams, Susan Clark, Michael Gross, Richard Cox; ***D:*** Christian Duguay; ***W:*** Jonathan Rintels; ***C:*** Peter Woeste; ***M:*** Lou Natale. **TV**

The Snows of Kilimanjaro 𝒮𝒮𝒮 1952 Called by Hemingway "The Snows of Zanuck," in reference to the great producer, this film is actually an artful pastiche of several Hemingway short stories and novels. The main story, "The Snows of Kilimanjaro," acts as a framing device, in which the life of a successful writer is seen through his fevered flashbacks as he and his rich wife, while on safari, await a doctor to save his gangrenous leg. **117m/C VHS, DVD.** Gregory Peck, Susan Hayward, Ava Gardner, Hildegarde Neff, Leo G. Carroll, Torin Thatcher, Ava Norring, Helene Stanley, Marcel Dalio, Vincente Gomez, Richard Allen, Leonard Carey; ***D:*** Henry King; ***W:*** Casey Robinson; ***C:*** Leon Shamroy; ***M:*** Bernard Herrmann.

Snuff-Bottle Connection 𝒮 1982 Russian envoy is spying for the government while delivering a gift to a Ching dynasty emperor. **96m/C VHS.** Hwang Jang Lee, John Liu, Roy Horan.

Snuffy Smith, Yard Bird 𝒮½ *Private Snuffy Smith; Snuffy Smith* 1942 The pint-sized moonshiner finds himself in the Army, clashing with his sergeant. Followed by "Hillbilly Blitzkrieg" later the same year. Duncan is perfect for the part, and Kennedy is right on as his foil. **67m/B VHS.** Bud Duncan, Edgar Kennedy, Sarah Padden, Doris Linden, J. Farrell MacDonald, Frank Austin, Jimmie Dodd; ***D:*** Edward F. (Eddie) Cline.

So Close to Paradise 𝒮𝒮 *Biandan, Guniang* 1998 Buddies Dong Zi and Gao Ping are farm workers who migrate to Shanghai for better lives. Dong gets a menial job on the docks while Gao turns to petty crime to survive. When a gang boss cheats Gao, he gets revenge by kidnapping the man's mistress, Vietnamese nighclub singer Ruan Hong. After some violence, Gao and Ruan fall in what passes for love but this story is not about to have a happy ending. A Chinese version of B-movie, Hollywood noir. Mandarin with subtitles. **90m/C VHS, DVD.** *CH* Guo Tao, Tong Wang, Yu Shi, Tao Wu; ***D:*** Xiaoshuai Wang; ***W:*** Xiaoshuai Wang, Pang Ming; ***C:*** Tao Yang; ***M:*** Lin Liu.

So Dear to My Heart 𝒮𝒮𝒮½ 1949 A farm boy and his misfit black sheep wreak havoc at the county fair. Several sequences combine live action with animation. Heartwarming and charming; straightforward and likeable but never sentimental. Wonderful, vintage Disney. ♫Sourwood Mountain; Billy Boy; So Dear To My Heart; County Fair; Stick-To-It-Ivity; Ol' Dan Patch; It's Whatcha Do With Watcha Got; Lavender Blue (Dilly Dilly). **82m/C VHS.** Bobby Driscoll, Burl Ives, Beulah Bondi, Harry Carey Sr., Luana Patten; ***D:*** Harold Schuster.

So Ends Our Night 𝒮𝒮𝒮 1941 German scorns Nazi ideology, flees Austria, and meets young Jewish couple seeking asylum. Fine adaptation of Erich Maria Remarque's novel "Flotsam," with splendid performances from Sullavan (on loan from Universal) and young Ford. **117m/B VHS.** Fredric March, Margaret Sullavan, Frances Dee, Glenn Ford, Anna Sten, Erich von Stroheim; ***D:*** John Cromwell; ***C:*** William H. Daniels.

So Fine 𝒮𝒮½ 1981 (R) Absent-minded English professor O'Neal tries to rescue his father's clothing business from going bottom-up. He accidentally invents peek-a-boo bottomed jeans, which become an immediate hit and make him rich. Comedy smorgasbord, setting outing from sometime novelist Bergman, hits and misses. O'Neal is memorable, as is the ubiquitous Warden and his sidekick. **91m/C VHS.** Ryan O'Neal, Jack Warden, Mariangela Melato, Richard Kiel; ***D:*** Andrew Bergman; ***W:*** Andrew Bergman; ***M:*** Ennio Morricone.

So I Married an Axe Murderer 𝒮𝒮½ 1993 (PG-13) Combination comedy/romance/thriller. Charlie is a hip bookstore owner with a commitment problem. When he finally falls in love with a butcher, he comes to suspect she's a serial killer and he's in line as her next victim. "Saturday Night Live" star Myers has a dual role: as Charlie and as Scottish dad Stuart, allowing him to be fanatically Scottish as Stuart and somewhat more restrained as the angst-ridden Charlie. One-gag movie counted on Myers' "Wayne's World" popularity, which didn't pan out at the boxoffice. Best appreciated by Myers' fans, this one is better on the small screen. **92m/C VHS, DVD, 8mm, Wide.** Mike Myers, Nancy Travis, Anthony LaPaglia, Amanda Plummer, Brenda Fricker, Matt Doherty; ***Cameos:*** Charles Grodin, Phil Hartman, Steven Wright, Alan Arkin, Michael Richards; ***D:*** Thomas Schlamme; ***W:*** Robbie Fox, Mike Myers; ***M:*** Bruce Broughton.

So Proudly We Hail 𝒮𝒮𝒮 1943 True story of the lives of three war-front nurses and their heroism under fire during WWII. Colbert is Lt. Davidson in charge of nine Red Cross Army nurses serving in the Pacific. Lake and Goddard play the other leads. With the popularity of its stars and the patriotic spirit of the film, the picture hit boxoffice gold. Critics praised its authenticity, as the film never fell victim to the usual standards of Hollywood glamour. Fans of Lake beware: she has short hair in this film because the government requested that she not appear as a servicewoman with her famous peek-a-boo hair style because female factory workers were getting their long Lake-inspired hair caught in the machinery. **126m/B VHS.** Claudette Colbert, Paulette Goddard, Veronica Lake, George Reeves, Barbara Britton, Walter Abel, Sonny Tufts, John Litel, Mary Servoss, Ted Hecht, Mary Treen, Helen Lynd, Lorna Gray, Dorothy Adams, Ann Doran, Jean Willes, Jan Wiley, Lynn Walker, Joan Tours, Kitty Kelly, James Bell, Dick Hogan, Bill Goodwin, James Flavin; ***D:*** Mark Sandrich; ***W:*** Allan Scott; ***C:*** Charles B(ryant) Lang Jr.; ***M:*** Miklos Rozsa.

So This Is Paris 𝒮𝒮𝒮 1926 Roguish pre-Hayes Code dancing duo seeks spice through alternative lovemates. Classic sophisticated Lubitsch, with outstanding camera work and a bit of jazz. **68m/B VHS.** Monte Blue, Patsy Ruth Miller, Lilyan Tashman, Andre de Beranger, Myrna Loy; ***D:*** Ernst Lubitsch.

So This Is Washington 𝒮𝒮½ 1943 The comedy team go to Washington with wacky inventions to help the war effort. Turns out there's too entirely too much nonsense going around, and the boys give 'em a piece of their mind. Fun, featherweight wartime comedy. **70m/B VHS.** Lum & Abner, Alan Mowbray.

Soapdish 𝒮𝒮𝒮 1991 (PG-13) The back stage lives of a daytime soap opera, "The Sun Also Sets," and its cast. When the soap's ratings fall, a character written out of series via decapitation is brought back to give things a lift. While the writer struggles to make the reincarnation believable, the cast juggles old and new romances, and professional jealousies abound. Some genuinely funny moments as film actors spoof the genre that gave many of them a start. **97m/C VHS, DVD, 8mm, Wide.** Sally Field, Kevin Kline, Robert Downey Jr., Cathy Moriarty, Whoopi Goldberg, Elisabeth Shue, Carrie Fisher, Garry Marshall, Teri Hatcher, Paul Johansson, Costas Mandylor, Stephen Nichols, Leeza Gibbons, John Tesh, Kathy Najimy, Sheila Kelley, Finola Hughes; ***D:*** Michael Hoffman; ***W:*** Andrew Bergman, Robert Harling; ***C:*** Ueli Steiger; ***M:*** Alan Silvestri.

S.O.B. 𝒮𝒮½ 1981 (R) Blake Edwards' bitter farce about Hollywood and the film industry wheelers and dealers who inhabit it. When a multi-million dollar picture bombs at the boxoffice, the director turns suicidal, until he envisions re-shooting it with a steamy, "X"-rated scene starring his wife, a star with a goody-two-shoes image. Edwards used his real-life wife, Julie ("Mary Poppins") Andrews, for the scene in which she bared her breasts. Oft-inspired, but oft-terrible. Zestfully uvengeful. William Holden's last film. **121m/C VHS, Wide.** William Holden, Robert Preston, Richard Mulligan, Julie Andrews, Robert Webber, Shelley Winters, Robert Vaughn, Larry Hagman, Stuart Margolin, Loretta Swit, Craig Stevens, Larry Storch, Jennifer Edwards, Robert Loggia, Rosanna Arquette, Marisa Berenson; ***D:*** Blake Edwards; ***W:*** Blake Edwards; ***C:*** Harry Stradling Jr.; ***M:*** Henry Mancini. Natl. Soc. Film Critics '81: Support. Actor (Preston).

Soccer Dog: The Movie 𝒮𝒮½ 1998 (PG) Clay Newlin (Foley) discovers the small town he's just moved to doesn't seem very friendly. His joins the local soccer team but isn't having much luck and Clay's only friend is stray dog Lincoln, who likes to watch the games. Then, when the team is short a player and in danger of forfeiting, the coach drafts Lincoln and the team actually wins. If you've watch the "Air Bud" movies, you've seen this before. **98m/C VHS.** Jeremy Foley, James Marshall, Olivia D'Abo; ***D:*** Tony Giglio; ***W:*** Daniel Forman. **VIDEO**

Social Error 🦴🦴 **1935** An heiress mistakes her guards for a group of kidnappers. **60m/B VHS.** Gertrude Messinger, David Sharpe.

Social Intercourse woof! **2001** Waste of celluloid concerning the social reclamation of cyber geek Todd (Taylor, who also edited, produced, directed, and co-scripted) at a friend's blow-out bash. If horny hijinks, tough-talking chicks, and a water-balloon sniper constituted good plot elements, then "Social Intercourse" would be the "Citizen Kane" of party films. **88m/C DVD.** Steve Taylor, Lee Abbott, Kim Little, Ashley Davis, Steve Grabowsky; ***D:*** Steve Taylor; ***W:*** Steve Taylor, Roger Kristian Jones; ***C:*** Armand Gazarian.

Social Misfits 🦴🦴 **2000** Twelve troubled teenagers, including our narrator Skylar (co-writer Tann), are sent to Camp Resurrection outside Fresno for a weekend of "re-education." The film claims to be based on events that took place on March 14, 1997, but this alternative boot-camp seems to consist mostly of unsupervised psycho-drama as each of the kids tells his or her story. The whole thing is produced with more enthusiasm than experience or talent. (Note the visible camera shadows.) Production values are minimal but adequate to the subject matter. **91m/C DVD.** Boris Cabrera, Le'Mark Cruise, Gabriel Damon, Isait de la Fuente, Ryan Francis, Bev Land, Eric Gray, Paul Gleason, Tyronne Tann; ***D:*** Rene Villar-Rios; ***W:*** Le'Mark Cruise, Tyronne Tann; ***C:*** Eric Leach; ***M:*** William Richter.

The Social Secretary 🦴🦴½ **1916** Driven from the rat race by lecherous men, Talmadge gets new job as rich woman's secretary, where she down-dresses to avoid further lewd encounters. She falls for her boss's son, but isn't considered marriage material until she proves herself. **56m/B VHS.** Norma Talmadge, Kate Lester, Helen Weir, Gladden James, Herbert Frank; ***D:*** John Emerson.

Society 🦴 **1992 (R)** A teenager wonders if his visions are real or hallucinations when he believes his family, and everyone else around him, are flesh-eating predators. The puzzle isn't much but wait for the special-effects ladened ending to get your fill of gore. **99m/C VHS.** Billy Warlock, Devin Devasquez, Evan Richards; ***D:*** Brian Yuzna.

Sodbusters 🦴🦴½ **1994 (PG-13)** Western spoof about homesteaders versus a greedy cattle baron and the railroad in 1875 Colorado. A lascivious farmer's wife and a mysterious gunslinger—as well as a couple of gay cowboys—are included for additional fun. **97m/C VHS.** Kris Kristofferson, John Vernon, Fred Willard, Wendel Meldrum, Max Gail, Steve Landesberg, Don Lake, James Pickens Jr., John Hemphill; ***D:*** Eugene Levy; ***W:*** John Hemphill, Eugene Levy. **TV**

Sodom and Gomorrah 🦴🦴 *Sodome et Gomorrhe; The Last Days of Sodom and Gomorrah* **1962** The Italian-made, internationally produced epic about Lot, the Hebrews and the destruction of the two sinful biblical cities. Moderately entertaining—but ponderous, to say the least, and very long. **154m/C VHS.** *IT* Stewart Granger, Stanley Baker, Pier Angeli, Anouk Aimee, Rossana Podesta; ***D:*** Robert Aldrich; ***M:*** Miklos Rozsa.

Sofie 🦴🦴½ **1992** Sweet family melodrama about a late 19th Jewish family in Denmark. Sofie (Mynster) is the unmarried 28-year-old daughter of loving, protective parents. She has fallen in love with a gentile artist (Christensen) but gives him up to marry within her faith. Unsuited, Sofie and Jonas (Zeller) lead melancholy lives, which Sofie redeems through her joy in her son. Self-effacing drama is Ullmann's directorial debut. Adapted from the novel "Mendel Philipsen & Son" by Henri Nathansen. In Swedish with English subtitles. **145m/C VHS, Wide.** *SW* Karen-Lise Mynster, Ghita Norby, Erland Josephson, Jesper Christensen, Henning Moritzen, Torben Zeller, Stig Hoffmeyer, Kirsten Rolffes, Lotte Herman; ***D:*** Liv Ullmann; ***W:*** Liv Ullmann, Peter Poulsen.

Soft and Hard 🦴🦴½ **1985** Video by Godard and Mieville intends to address the role of media and television in everyday life via a seemingly informal look at the couple's daily existence and the propensity for image production in it. In French; subtitled. **48m/C VHS.** *FR* ***D:*** Anne-Marie Mieville, Jean-Luc Godard. **TV**

Soft Deceit 🦴🦴½ **1994 (R)** Master criminal Trent (Bergin) gets caught in the heist of $l6 million in mob money. Then Anne (Vernon) shashays into prison offering Trent a deal—half the cash in exchange for breaking him out. She succeeds but maybe a doublecross is next on the agenda. **95m/C VHS.** Patrick Bergin, Kate Vernon, John Wesley Shipp, Gwynyth Walsh, Nigel Bennett, Damir Andrei; ***D:*** Jorge Montesi; ***W:*** Jorge Montesi.

Soft Fruit 🦴🦴½ **1999 (R)** Patsy (Drynan) is dying of cancer and, though her grumpy husband (Haft) isn't happy about it, her four children show up to care for her—the first time in 15 years that all the family has been together. The three sisters (Lemon, Horler, Talbot) have a long-standing case of sibling rivalry and son Bo (Dykstra) is only out on a prison parole because of his mother's condition. But Patsy has some definite ideas about how she wants to spend her last days, whatever her family thinks. **101m/C VHS.** *AU* Jeanie Drynan, Genevieve Lemon, Sacha Holder, Linal Haft, Alicia Talbot, Russell Dykstra; ***D:*** Christina Andreef; ***W:*** Christina Andreef; ***C:*** Laszlo Baranyai; ***M:*** Antony Partos. Australian Film Inst. '99: Actor (Dykstra), Support. Actress (Holder).

The Soft Kill 🦴🦴 **1994 (R)** LA private eye Jack Ramsey (Bernsen) becomes the prime murder suspect when his girlfriend is strangled. Can he prove his innocence before more bodies pile up and the cops catch him? **95m/C VHS.** Corbin Bernsen, Brion James, Matt McCoy, Michael (M.K.) Harris, Kim Morgan Greene, Carrie-Anne Moss; ***D:*** Eli Cohen.

The Soft Skin 🦴🦴🦴 *Le Peau Douce; Silken Skin* **1964** A classic portrayal of marital infidelity by the master director. A writer and lecturer has an affair with a stewardess. After the affair ends, his wife confronts him, with tragic results. Cliche plot is forgivable; acted and directed to perfection. Frequent Truffaut star Jean-Pierre Leaud served here as an apprentice director. In French with English subtitles. **120m/B VHS, DVD.** *FR* Jean Desailly, Nelly Benedetti, Francoise Dorleac, Daniel Ceccaldi; ***D:*** Francois Truffaut; ***W:*** Francois Truffaut, Jean-Louis Richard; ***C:*** Raoul Coutard; ***M:*** Georges Delerue.

Soggy Bottom U.S.A. 🦴🦴 **1984 (PG)** A sheriff has his hands full trying to keep the law enforced in a small Southern town. Quite-good cast keeps the plot from disappearing altogether. **90m/C VHS.** Don Johnson, Ben Johnson, Dub Taylor, Ann Wedgeworth, Lois Nettleton, Anthony Zerbe; ***D:*** Theodore J. Flicker.

Sois Belle et Tais-Toi 🦴🦴½ *Look Beautiful and Shut Up; Be Beautiful but Shut Up; Be Beautiful and Shut Up; Blonde for Danger* **1958** A police detective tracks jewel thieves and falls in love with a young waif. Several interesting and later famous actors have small parts. Light-hearted adventure. Subtitled in English. **110m/B VHS.** *FR* Henri Vidal, Mylene Demongeot, Jean-Paul Belmondo, Alain Delon, Hugh Brooks, Roger Hanin; ***D:*** Marc Allegret; ***W:*** Roger Vadim, Odette Joyeux, William Benjamin, Jean Marsan, Gabriel Arout; ***C:*** Armand Thirard.

Solar Crisis 🦴🦴½ **1992 (PG-13)** Eye-popping special effects highlight this Earth-on-the-edge-of-destruction sci-fier. In 2050 the sun has gone on self-destruct and begins throwing off giant solar flares which turn the Earth extra-crispy. A space team is sent to divert the flares but the mission may become a victim of sabotage. Director Sarafian actually forgoes credit for the standard Smithee pseudonym. **111m/C VHS, DVD, Wide.** Tim Matheson, Charlton Heston, Peter Boyle, Annabel Schofield, Jack Palance, Corin "Corky" Nemec; ***D:*** Richard Sarafian, Alan Smithee; ***W:*** Joe Gannon, Tedi Sarafian; ***C:*** Russell Carpenter; ***M:*** Maurice Jarre.

Solar Force 🦴🦴 **1994 (R)** Cop (Pare), stationed on the moon, is sent to earth to find a stolen chemical that is capable of restoring a destroyed environment. But there are secrets behind the assignment which could cost him his life. **91m/C VHS, DVD.** Michael Pare, Billy Drago, Walker Brandt; ***D:*** Boaz Davidson; ***W:*** Terrence Pare; ***C:*** Avi (Avraham) Karpik; ***M:*** Don Peake.

Solarbabies 🦴 **1986 (PG-13)** Rollerskating youths in a drought-stricken future vie for a mysterious power that will replenish the Earth's water. Shades of every sci-fi movie you've ever seen, from "Mad Max" to "Ice Pirates." Pathetic. **95m/C VHS.** Richard Jordan, Sarah Douglas, Charles Durning, Lukas Haas, Jami Gertz, Jason Patric; ***D:*** Alan Johnson; ***W:*** Walon Green; ***M:*** Maurice Jarre.

Solaris 🦴🦴 *Solyaris* **1972** With this the USSR tried to eclipse "2001: A Space Odyssey" in terms of cerebral science-fiction. Some critics thought they succeeded. You may disagree now that the lumbering effort is available on tape. Adapted from a Stanislaw Lem novel, it depicts a dilapidated space lab orbiting the planet Solaris, whose ocean, a vast fluid "brain," materializes the stir-crazy cosmonauts' obsessions—usually morose ex-girlfriends. Talk, talk, talk, minimal special effects. In Russian with English subtitles. In a two-cassette package, with a letterbox format preserving Tarkovsky's widescreen compositions. **167m/C VHS, DVD, Wide.** *RU* Donatas Banionis, Natalya Bondarchuk, Juri Jarvet, Vladislav Dvorzhetsky, Nikolai Grinko, Anatoli (Otto) Solonitzin, Sos Sarkisyan; ***D:*** Andrei Tarkovsky; ***W:*** Andrei Tarkovsky; ***C:*** Vadim Yusov; ***M:*** Eduard Artemyev. Cannes '72: Grand Jury Prize.

Soldat Duroc...Ca Va Etre Ta Fete! 🦴🦴 *Soldier Duroc* **1975** Days after the 1944 liberation of Paris, a French soldier crosses back over the French lines to see his lover, and is caught as a German sympathizer by American troops. **105m/C VHS.** *FR* Pierre Tornade, Robert Webber, Michel Galabru, Roger Carel; ***D:*** Michel Gerard.

The Soldier 🦴 *Codename: The Soldier* **1982 (R)** The Russians are holding the world at ransom with a pile of stolen plutonium, and a soldier finds himself in the position to carry out an unauthorized and dangerous plan to preserve the balance of world power. Wildly implausible, gratuitously violent spy trash. **90m/C VHS.** Ken Wahl, Klaus Kinski, William Prince, Alberta Watson; ***D:*** James Glickenhaus.

Soldier 🦴🦴 **1998 (R)** Steals trite scenes from other post-apolyptic sci-fi shoot-'em-ups just to prove that 47-year-old Kurt Russell had been working out. Genetically engineered soldier Russell is discarded as obsolete on a garbage dump planet inhabited by a freedom-loving survivalist (Pertwee) and his band of human flotsam. When a force led by next-generation soldier Jason Scott Lee invades the planet, Russell helps save the skanky-looking group of squatters. Robbed of his Snake Plissken smirk, Russell delivers a hollow character who is hard to like. The garbage planet set recycles props used in "Demolition Man," "Executive Decision," and "Event Horizon." The movie recycles ideas from every other sci-fi flick. **99m/C VHS, DVD, Wide.** Kurt Russell, Jason Scott Lee, Gary Busey, Michael Chiklis, Sean Pertwee, Jason Isaacs, Connie Nielsen, Brenda Wehle, Mark Bringleson, K.K. Dodds; ***D:*** Paul Anderson; ***W:*** David Peoples; ***C:*** David Tattersall; ***M:*** Joel McNeely.

Soldier Blue 🦴🦴 **1970 (R)** Two survivors of an Indian attack make their way back to an army outpost. The cavalry then seeks revenge on the Cheyenne tribe accused of the attack. Gratuitously violent Vietnam-era western hits hard on racial themes. Based on the novel "Arrow in the Sun" by Theodore V. Olsen on the Sand Creek Indian massacre. **109m/C VHS.** Candice Bergen, Peter Strauss, Donald Pleasence, Dana Elcar, Jorge (George) Rivero; ***D:*** Ralph Nelson; ***W:*** John Gay; ***C:*** Robert B. Hauser.

Soldier Boyz 🦴½ **1995 (R)** Ex-Marine Major Howard Tolliver (Dudikoff), who now runs a high-security prison for youthful offenders, is called on to rescue a United Nations worker who's being held hostage by a group of revolutionaries in Vietnam. For help, he takes along six of his toughest prisoners. A variation of "The Dirty Dozen." **91m/C VHS.** Michael Dudikoff, Cary-Hiroyuki Tagawa, Tyrin Turner, David Barry Gray, Channon Roe, Cedrick Terrell, Demetrius Navarro, Jacqueline Obradors; ***D:*** Louis Morneau; ***W:*** Darryl Quarles.

Soldier in Love 🦴🦴 **1967** Teleplay from "George Schaefer's Showcase Theatre" is based on the life of John Churchill, first Duke of Marlborough, and his wife Sarah. The ambitious young couple held the favor of Queen Anne for a time, until political intrigue brought about their downfall. **76m/C VHS.** Jean Simmons, Claire Bloom, Keith Michell; ***D:*** George Schaefer. **TV**

Soldier in the Rain 🦴🦴½ **1963** An unusual friendship develops between career sergeant Gleason and wheeler-dealer McQueen. Gleason is in good form, but McQueen is listless, and the story (set in a Southern army camp) is unsatisfying. Weld is the comely teen who makes for an intriguing love triangle. From the novel by William Goldman. **88m/B VHS.** Steve McQueen, Jackie Gleason, Tuesday Weld, Tony Bill, Tom Poston, Ed Nelson; ***D:*** Ralph Nelson; ***W:*** Blake Edwards; ***M:*** Henry Mancini.

Soldier of Fortune 🦴🦴½ **1955** A woman (Hayward) enlists mercenaries to help find her lost husband in Red China. Late Gable vehicle with the formula beginning to feel the post-war strain and the star looking a trifle long in the tooth. Still, a fun adventure from a top star. Hayward had been among the myriad starlets vying for the Scarlett O'Hara roles nearly two decades earlier. **96m/C VHS, DVD.** Clark Gable, Susan Hayward, Gene Barry, Alexander D'Arcy, Michael Rennie, Tom Tully, Anna Sten, Russell Collins, Leo Gordon, Jack Kruschen, Robert Quarry; ***D:*** Edward Dmytryk; ***W:*** Ernest K. Gann; ***C:*** Leo Tover; ***M:*** Hugo Friedhofer.

Soldier of Fortune Inc. 🦴🦴 **1997 (R)** Retired Major Matt Shepherd (Johnson) is recruited by Washington insider Xavier Trout (Selby), who works for a mystery organization that handles covert operations, to extract American POWs from Iraq. Matt puts together a specialized and secret unit in order to accomplish his mission. Action-packed TV pilot of the syndicated series. **98m/C VHS.** Brad Johnson, David Selby, Melinda (Mindy) Clarke, Tim Abell, Real Andrews, Mark Sheppard, Brian Cousins; ***D:*** Robert Radler. **TV**

Soldier of Orange 🦴🦴🦴 *Soldaat van Oranje* **1978** The lives of six Dutch students are forever changed by the WWII invasion of Holland by the Nazis. Based on the true-life exploits of Dutch resistance leader Erik Hazelhoff. Exciting and suspenseful; cerebral; carefully made and well acted. Made Rutger Hauer an international star. **144m/C VHS, DVD, Wide.** *NL* Derek De Lint, Rutger Hauer, Jeroen Krabbe, Edward Fox, Susan Penhaligon; ***D:*** Paul Verhoeven; ***W:*** Paul Verhoeven, Gerard Soeteman, Kees Holierhoek; ***C:*** Jan De Bont; ***M:*** Roger van Otterloo. L.A. Film Critics '79: Foreign Film.

Soldier of the Night 🦴½ **1984** Toy-store worker by day, vigilante killer by night. Israeli thriller set in Tel Aviv lacks vim and is badly dubbed. **89m/C VHS.** ***D:*** Dan Wolman.

A Soldier's Daughter Never Cries 🦴🦴½ **1998 (R)** American novelist and WWII vet Bill Willis (Kristofferson) lives in 1960s Paris with his sexy, free-thinking and -drinking wife Marcella (Hershey), their adopted French son Billy (Gruen), and teenage daughter Channe, the center of the story. Her relationships with her brother and a rude (yet likable) classmate (Costanzo) provide much of the film's emotional punch. Bill develops heart problems and takes the family home to the States. Against the backdrop of social and political turmoil, Bill's core values help the family through their own challenges. Ivory and Merchant make an admirable leap into the 20th century. Unfortunately, the film's episodic jumps are too confusing to make it a complete success. Based on the 1990 book by Kaylie Jones, daughter of novelist James Jones. **128m/C VHS.** Kris

Kristofferson, Barbara Hershey, Leelee Sobieski, Jesse Bradford, Anthony Roth Costanzo, Dominique Blanc, Jane Birkin, Virginie Ledoyen, Isaach de Bankole, Samuel Gruen, Luisa Conlon; ***D:*** James Ivory; ***W:*** James Ivory, Ruth Prawer Jhabvala; ***C:*** Jean-Marc Fabre; ***M:*** Richard Robbins.

Soldier's Fortune ½ **1991 (R)** A traveling gun for hire leaves the combat of Central America for the jungles of Los Angeles, only to find out that his daughter had been taken hostage. That's the last thing these kidnappers will ever do when they are found by this tough guy looking for his child. **96m/C VHS.** Gil Gerard, Charles Napier, Dan Haggerty, P.J. Soles, Barbara Bingham, Janus Blythe; ***D:*** Arthur N. Mele.

Soldier's Revenge **1984** A Vietnam vet has a hard time adjusting to life at home. **92m/C VHS.** John Savage.

A Soldier's Story **1984 (PG)** A black army attorney is sent to a Southern base to investigate the murder of an unpopular sergeant. Features WWII, Louisiana, jazz and blues, and racism in and outside the corps. From the Pulitzer-prize winning play by Charles Fuller, with most of the Broadway cast. Fine performances from Washington and Caesar. **101m/C VHS, DVD, Wide.** Howard E. Rollins Jr., Adolph Caesar, Denzel Washington, Patti LaBelle, Robert Townsend, Scott Paulin, Wings Hauser, Art Evans, Larry Riley, David Alan Grier; ***D:*** Norman Jewison; ***W:*** Charles Fuller; ***C:*** Russell Boyd; ***M:*** Herbie Hancock. L.A. Film Critics '84: Support. Actor (Caesar).

A Soldier's Sweetheart ½ **1998 (R)** Bored Vietnam soldier, Rat (Sutherland), narrates the unlikely story of Marianne (Gates). Her high school boyfriend, Fossie (Ulrich), is a lonely medic who manages to bring Marianne over to join him. All the guys in the squad fall for her, but Marianne falls in love with the excitement/uncertainty/terror of war. Adapted from the story "Sweetheart of the Song Tra Bong" by Tim O'Brien. **111m/C VHS.** Kiefer Sutherland, Skeet Ulrich, Georgina Cates, Daniel London, Larry Gilliard Jr., Christopher Birt, Louis Vanaria; ***D:*** Thomas Michael Donnelly; ***W:*** Thomas Michael Donnelly; ***C:*** Jacek Laskus; ***M:*** Gary Chang. **CABLE**

A Soldier's Tale **1991 (R)** During WWII, a menage-a-trois develops that can only lead to tragedy, yet the participants find themselves unable to resist. **96m/C VHS, DVD.** Gabriel Byrne, Marianne Basler, Judge Reinhold, Paul Wyett; ***D:*** Larry Parr; ***W:*** Larry Parr; ***C:*** Alun Bollinger; ***M:*** John Charles.

Sole Survivor ½ **1984 (R)** A group of zombies are searching for a beautiful advertising executive who was the sole survivor of a plane crash. **85m/C VHS.** Anita Skinner, Kurt Johnson, Caren Larkey, Brinke Stevens, Leon Robinson; ***D:*** Thom Eberhardt; ***C:*** Russell Carpenter.

Solid Gold Cadillac **1956** Holliday is a winning lead as Laura Patridge, an idealistic, small-time stockholder who discovers that the corporate board of directors are crooked. She makes waves at a stockholders meeting, gets noticed by the press, finds romance with former CEO Edward McKeever (Douglas), and works to oust the scalawags from power. The title comes from Laura's fervent desire to own a—you guessed it—solid gold cadillac. Based on the Broadway play by George S. Kaufman and Howard Teichmann. **99m/B VHS.** Judy Holliday, Paul Douglas, Fred Clark, Neva Patterson, Arthur O'Connell, Ray Collins; ***D:*** Richard Quine; ***W:*** Abe Burrows; ***C:*** Charles B(ryant) Lang Jr.; ***M:*** Cyril Mockridge; ***Nar:*** George Burns. Oscars '56: Costume Des. (B&W).

Solitaire for 2 ½ **1994 (R)** Sweet-natured romantic comedy about a rogue and a psychic. Handsome Daniel Becker (Frankel) is a behavioral psychologist who specializes in interpreting body language and using his expertise to bed as many beautiful women as happen his way. Uptight paleontologist Katie (Pays) has a problem with men—she can literally read their minds and gets angry at their lewd thoughts. So the path to true commitment is going to get a bit bumpy. **105m/C VHS.** *GB* Mark Frankel, Amanda Pays, Roshan Seth, Maryam D'Abo, Jason Isaacs, Annette Crosbie; ***D:*** Gary Sinyor; ***W:*** Gary Sinyor; ***C:*** Henry Braham; ***M:*** David A. Hughes, John Murphy.

The Solitary Man **1982** Glum look at a family breakup, from the husband's point of view. Holliman is good, but the exercise at large is regularly blues-inducing, and not especially inspiring or artful. **96m/C VHS.** Earl Holliman, Carrie Snodgress, Lara Parker, Lane Smith, Nicolas Coster, Michelle Pfeiffer; ***D:*** John Llewellyn Moxey. **TV**

Solo **1977 (PG)** Young hitchhiker Peers enters the lives of fire patrol pilot Gil and his teenage son. A plotless friendship develops, headed nowhere—like this movie. Great New Zealand scenery might be worth the price of rental. **90m/C VHS.** Vincent (Vince Gill) Gil, Perry Armstrong, Martyn Sanderson, Lisa Peers; ***D:*** Tony Williams.

Solo **1996 (PG-13)** Fast-paced actioner stars Van Peebles as Solo, an android assassin with a heart of gold. It seems the muscle-bound, computerized killer is programmed with not only amazing fighting skills but the ability to think and learn. Solo who, being naughty in the sight of one-dimensional government bigwigs, is scheduled for replacement by a fighting machine that won't be so fickle when it comes to pulling the trigger. The chase is on when Solo learns of their plot and takes to the jungles of Central America, where together with the local peasants, the rebellious robot fights to preserve his humanity and his life. Poor man's "Terminator" is sprinkled with the kind of glib one-liners usually reserved for Schwarzenegger, although Van Peebles' performance hikes this rehashed premise up a notch. Adapted from Robert Mason's novel "Weapon." **106m/C VHS, DVD.** Mario Van Peebles, William Sadler, Seidy Lopez, Barry Corbin, Adrien Brody, Abraham Verduzo, Jaime Gomez, Damian Bechir, Joaquin Garrido; ***D:*** Norberto Barba; ***W:*** David Corley; ***C:*** Chris Walling; ***M:*** Christopher Franke.

Solo Sunny **1980** Pop singer Sunny (Krossner) is constantly on the road with a mediocre band, trying to make a living. When she's kicked out of the group for consistently resisting the leader's sexual advances, she tries her hand at a solo career in Berlin. But things don't work out well, and Sunny is getting increasingly desperate. German with subtitles. **102m/C VHS.** *GE* Renate Krossner, Alexander Lang, Dieter Montag, Heide Kipp, Klaus Brasch; ***D:*** Konrad Wolf; ***W:*** Wolfgang Kohlhaase; ***C:*** Eberhard Geick; ***M:*** Gunther Fischer.

Solo Voyage: The Revenge **1990** A Russian "Rambo" goes on a murderous rampage, the likes of which humanity has not yet seen. **91m/C VHS.** *RU* Mikhail Nojkine, Alexandre Fatiouchine; ***D:*** Mikhail Toumanichulli.

Solomon ½ **1998** Solomon is crowned King of Israel and vows to build a temple to house the Ark of the Covenant. In return, he is granted the gift of widom, which he doesn't seem to make much use of. He falls deeply in love with the Queen of Sheba but when she is forced to return to her homeland, Solomon falls into such a depression that he neglects his kingdom and allows corruption to spread. **172m/C VHS, DVD.** Ben Cross, Vivica A. Fox, Anouk Aimee, Max von Sydow, Maria Grazia Cucinotta, Stefania Rocca, David Suchet, Richard Dillane; ***D:*** Roger Young. **CABLE**

Solomon and Gaenor **1998 (R)** Around 1911, a young Jewish peddler named Solomon (Gruffudd) meets Gaenor (Roberts), the daughter of Welsh mineworkers. Hiding his Orthodox Jewish origins, Solomon calls himself Sam and the young duo are soon in love. Gaenor winds up pregnant and her family wants to send her away and force her to give up the baby. She finally tracks down Solomon's family but they are equally upset that their son is involved with a gentile. Amidst all this family turmoil, is a violent dispute between the workers and the mine owners. Conventional tear-stained period piece. **103m/C VHS, DVD, Wide.** *GB* Ioan Gruffudd, Nia Roberts, Mark Lewis Jones, William Thomas, Maureen Lipman, David Horovitch; ***D:*** Paul Morrison; ***W:*** Paul Morrison; ***C:*** Nina Kellgren; ***M:*** Ilona Sekacz.

Solomon and Sheba **1959** King Solomon's brother and the Egyptian Pharaoh send the Queen of Sheba to Israel to seduce King Solomon so they may gain his throne. Tyrone Power had filmed most of the lead role in this silly, overwrought epic when he died of a heart attack. The role was reshot, with Brynner (with a full head of hair) replacing him. Director Vidor's unfortunate last film. Shot on location in Spain. **139m/C VHS, Wide.** Yul Brynner, Gina Lollobrigida, Marisa Pavan, George Sanders, Alejandro Rey; ***D:*** King Vidor; ***C:*** Frederick A. (Freddie) Young; ***M:*** Malcolm Arnold.

The Sombrero Kid **1942** The Kid unwittingly gets involved in a murder and is nearly hanged before his friends help him discover the real culprits. Plenty of action in this straight forward, fun western. **54m/B VHS.** Donald (Don "Red") Barry, Lynn Merrick, Rand Brooks; ***D:*** George Sherman.

Some Call It Loving **1973 (R)** Bad, pretentious modern version of Sleeping Beauty, set in L.A. King buys the sleeping girl (Farrow) from a carnival show, but she doesn't live up to his ideal. **103m/C VHS.** Zalman King, Carol White, Tisa Farrow, Richard Pryor, Pat Priest; ***D:*** James B. Harris.

Some Came Running **1958** James Jones's follow-up novel to "From Here to Eternity" does not translate nearly as well to the screen. Overlong and with little plot, the action centers around a would-be writer, his floozy girl friend, and the holier-than-thou characters which populate the town in which he grew up and to which he has now returned. Strong performances by all. **136m/C VHS, Wide.** Frank Sinatra, Dean Martin, Shirley MacLaine, Martha Hyer, Arthur Kennedy, Nancy Gates; ***D:*** Vincente Minnelli; ***C:*** William H. Daniels; ***M:*** Elmer Bernstein.

Some Folks Call It a Sling Blade **1994** The short film that became 1996's critically acclaimed "Sling Blade." This stark black-and-white short, penned by Billy Bob Thornton and directed by George Hickenlooper ("Hearts of Darkness: A Filmmaker's Apocalypse"), premiered at Sundance. The original version only involves a young reporter's (Ringwald) interview with Karl Childers (Thorton), in which he recalls the events that led him to be in the institution. Also includes "The Making of 'Some Folks Call It a Sling Blade'" (color, 13 minutes) which comprises interviews the stars, director, and producer. **29m/B VHS, DVD, Wide.** Billy Bob Thornton, Molly Ringwald, J.T. Walsh, Jefferson Mays, Suzanne Cryer; ***D:*** George Hickenlooper; ***W:*** Billy Bob Thornton; ***C:*** Kent Wakeford; ***M:*** Bill Boll.

Some Girls ½ *Sisters* **1988 (R)** A man goes to Quebec to see his college girlfriend who informs him that she is not in love with him anymore. But she has two sisters ready to comfort him! Strange black comedy; Gregory as the girl's father elevates so-so story. **104m/C VHS.** Patrick Dempsey, Andre Gregory, Lila Kedrova, Florinda Bolkan, Jennifer Connelly, Sheila Kelly; ***D:*** Michael Hoffman; ***M:*** James Newton Howard.

Some Kind of Hero **1982 (R)** A Vietnam prisoner of war returns home to a changed world. Pryor tries hard, but can't get above this poorly written, unevenly directed film. **97m/C VHS.** Richard Pryor, Margot Kidder, Ray Sharkey, Ronny Cox, Lynne Moody, Olivia Cole; ***D:*** Michael Pressman; ***W:*** Robert Boris.

Some Kind of Wonderful **1987 (PG-13)** A high-school tomboy has a crush on a guy who also happens to be her best friend. Her feelings go unrequited as he falls for a rich girl with snobbish friends. In the end, true love wins out. Deutch also directed (and John Hughes also produced) the teen flick "Pretty in Pink," which had much the same plot, with the rich/outcast characters reversed by gender. OK, but completely predictable. **93m/C VHS.** Eric Stoltz, Lea Thompson, Mary Stuart Masterson, Craig Sheffer, John Ashton, Elias Koteas, Molly Hagan; ***D:*** Howard Deutch; ***W:*** John Hughes.

Some Like It Hot **1959** Two unemployed musicians witness the St. Valentine's Day massacre in Chicago. They disguise themselves as women and join an all-girl band headed for Miami to escape the gangsters' retaliation. Flawless cast includes a fetching Monroe at her best; hilarious script. Curtis does his Cary Grant impression. Classic scenes between Lemmon in drag and Joe E. Brown as a smitten suitor. Brown also has the film's famous closing punchline. Monroe sings "I Wanna Be Loved By You," "Running Wild," and "I'm Through With Love." One of the very funniest movies of all time. **120m/B VHS, DVD, Wide.** Marilyn Monroe, Tony Curtis, Jack Lemmon, George Raft, Pat O'Brien, Nehemiah Persoff, Joe E. Brown, Joan Shawlee, Mike Mazurki; ***D:*** Billy Wilder; ***W:*** Billy Wilder, I.A.L. Diamond; ***C:*** Charles B(ryant) Lang Jr.; ***M:*** Adolph Deutsch. Oscars '59: Costume Des. (B&W); AFI '98: Top 100; British Acad. '59: Actor (Lemmon); Golden Globes '60: Actor—Mus./Comedy (Lemmon), Actress—Mus./Comedy (Monroe), Film—Mus./Comedy, Natl. Film Reg. '89.

Some Mother's Son *Sons and Warriors* **1996 (R)** Young IRA members Gerard Quigley (Gillen) and Frank Higgins (O'Hara) are sentenced to long prison terms after an attack on the British army. Tough, politically active Annie Higgins (Flanagan) has already lost one son to "The Troubles" and is willing to support Frank in whatever he does. But her son Gerard's involvement takes apolitical schoolteacher Kathleen (Mirren) completely by surprise. When their sons join in a prison hunger strike, the two mothers must face the choice of supporting their sons' possible deaths by starvation or allowing the prison's officials to force-feed them. The leads give tough, terrific performances in a heartwrenching story. **112m/C VHS.** *IR GB* Helen Mirren, Fionnula Flanagan, Aidan Gillen, David O'Hara, John Lynch, Tim Woodward, Ciaran Hinds, Gerard McSorley, Geraldine O'Rawe; ***D:*** Terry George; ***W:*** Jim Sheridan, Terry George; ***C:*** Geoffrey Simpson; ***M:*** Bill Whelan.

Somebody Has to Shoot the Picture **1990 (R)** Photographer Scheider is hired by a convicted man to take a picture of his execution. Hours before the event, Scheider uncovers evidence that leads him to believe the man is innocent. He then embarks in a race against time to save him. Adapted by Doug Magee from his book "Slow Coming Dark." Unpretentious, tough drama. **104m/C VHS, DVD.** Roy Scheider, Bonnie Bedelia, Robert Carradine, Andre Braugher, Arliss Howard; ***D:*** Frank Pierson; ***W:*** Doug Magee; ***C:*** Bojan Bazelli; ***M:*** James Newton Howard. **CABLE**

Somebody Is Waiting ½ **1996 (R)** Charlotte Ellis (Kinski) tries to be the best mom she can to her five kids after her abusive, drunken husband Roger (Byrne) finally abandons them. Eighteen-year-old Leon (Whitworth) seems to be headed down the same dark road after being arrested for drunk driving. Charlotte agrees to set up a bank account for Leon, if he'll move out, and is then killed in a robbery, where Leon is injured. Roger then shows up to look after his shattered family but it's only a matter of time before things get even worse. Pros Bryne and Kinski do what they can but the script is certainly no help. **90m/C VHS.** Gabriel Byrne, Nastassia Kinski, Johnny Whitworth, Rebecca Gayheart, Shirley Knight, Brian Donovan; ***D:*** Martin Donovan; ***W:*** Martin Donovan; ***C:*** Greg Gardiner; ***M:*** Elia Cmiral.

Somebody to Love ½ **1994 (R)** Spunky taxi dancer Mercedes (Perez) wants to be an actress despite the bad luck actor/boyfriend Harry (a subdued Keitel) has. One of her clients is the bumpious Ernesto (De Lorenzo), who quickly becomes infatuated by Mercedes and, to impress her, takes a job with local racketeer Emillio (Quinn). Ernesto even decides to take a contract hit to get the money Mercedes needs to help out Harry, leading to tragedy. Confusing look at the fringes of the L.A. showbiz scene, with lots of missed chances though Perez gets some flashy diva scenes. **103m/C VHS.** Edward (Eddie) Bunker, Rosie Perez, Harvey Keitel, Michael De Lorenzo, Anthony Quinn, Steve Buscemi, Stanley Tucci, Gerardo Mejia, Paul Herman; ***Cameos:***

Angel Aviles, Quentin Tarantino; *D:* Alexandre Rockwell; *W:* Alexandre Rockwell, Sergei Bodrov.

Somebody Up There Likes Me 1956 Story of Rocky Graziano's (Newman) gritty battle from his poor, street-wise childhood to his prison term (where he developed his boxing skills) and his eventual success as the middleweight boxing champion of the world. Adapted from Graziano's autobiography. Superior performance by Newman (in his third screen role, after the miserable "The Silver Chalice" and forgettable "The Rack"); screen debuts for McQueen and Loggia. **113m/B VHS.** Paul Newman, Pier Angeli, Everett Sloane, Eileen Heckart, Sal Mineo, Robert Loggia, Steve McQueen; *D:* Robert Wise; *W:* Ernest Lehman; *C:* Joseph Ruttenberg; *M:* Bronislau Kaper. Oscars '56: Art Dir./Set Dec., B&W, B&W Cinematog.

Someone at the Door 1950 Reporter Medwin arranges to be suspected of killing his sister, thus providing him with a good story and advancing his career. His plan almost backfires, when he is almost executed. Remake of a 1936 film of the same name. **65m/B VHS.** *GB* Michael Medwin, Garry Marsh, Yvonne Owen, Hugh Latimer; *D:* Francis Searle.

Someone Behind the Door ½ *Two Minds for Murder; Quelqu' Un Derriere la Porte* **1971 (PG)** Evil brain surgeon Perkins implants murderous suggestions into psychopathic amnesia victim Bronson's mind, then instructs him to kill his (the surgeon's) wife and her lover. **97m/C VHS.** Charles Bronson, Anthony Perkins, Jill Ireland, Henri Garcin; *D:* Nicolas Gessner.

Someone Else's America 1996 (R) Euro-"Grumpy Old Men" explores friendship and the modern immigrant experience in Brooklyn. Bayo (Manojlovic) is a comical, sad-sack Serb who works at the bar of Alonso (Conti), a Spaniard who immigrated with his blind mother (Casares). Story follows Bayo's family as they illegally immigrate to chase the American dream and adapt to life once they arrive. Touchingly funny highlight involves a scheme by the men which enables Alonso's homesick mother to revisit her village in Spain. Filmed in Germany with sets built to resemble Brooklyn, picture has an appealingly unreal quality. Cast and crew together formed its own melting pot, with over 20 nationalities contributing. English and Serbo-Croatian with subtitles. **116m/C VHS.** *FR GB GE* Tom Conti, Miki (Predrag) Manojlovic, Maria Casares, Zorka Manojlovic, Sergej Trifunovic, Chia-ching Niu, Andjela Stojkovic, Ananda Ellis; *D:* Goran Paskalyevic; *W:* Gordan Mihic; *C:* Yorgos Arvanitis; *M:* Andrew Dickson.

Someone I Touched ½ 1975 Way-overdone melodrama starring Leachman as a finally pregnant woman who learns her husband and a teenager he slept with have venereal disease. **74m/C VHS.** Cloris Leachman, James Olson, Glynnis O'Connor, Andrew (Andy) Robinson, Allyn Ann McLerie; *D:* Lou Antonio.

Someone Like You ½ 2001 (PG-13) New Yorker Jane (Judd) is a talk-show talent booker who falls for the program's new exec, Ray (Kinnear), who seems to be very serious about her too. In fact, Jane gives up her apartment expecting to move in with Ray, then is suddenly dumped. Homeless, Jane agrees to temporarily share the loft of co-worker Eddie (Jackman), a one-night only stud. Well, it does give Jane a chance to test her theory comparing men to bulls, who aren't interested in a cow (or girlfriend) they've had before. Gets by because the cast is so darn cute. Based on the novel "Animal Husbandry" by Laura Zigman. **97m/C VHS, DVD, Wide.** *US* Ashley Judd, Hugh Jackman, Greg Kinnear, Marisa Tomei, Ellen Barkin, Peter Friedman, Catherine Dent, Laura Regan; *D:* Tony Goldwyn; *W:* Elizabeth Chandler; *C:* Anthony B. Richmond; *M:* Rolfe Kent.

Someone to Die For 1995 (R) Accused murderer (and cop) Bernsen is out to prove his innocence but learns that the real killer may be very close to home. **98m/C VHS.** Corbin Bernsen, Ally Walker, Robert Stewart; *D:* Clay Borris.

Someone to Love 1987 (R) Rootless filmmaker gathers all his single friends together and interviews them about their failed love lives. Welles's last film as an actor. Wildly uneven, interesting experiment. **110m/C VHS.** Henry Jaglom, Orson Welles, Sally Kellerman, Andrea Marcovicci, Michael Emil, Oja Kodar, Stephen Bishop, Ronee Blakley, Kathryn Harrold, Monte Hellman; *D:* Henry Jaglom; *W:* Henry Jaglom; *C:* Hanania Baer.

Someone to Watch Over Me 1987 (R) After witnessing the murder of a close friend, beautiful and very wealthy Claire Gregory (Rogers) must be protected from the killer. Working-class New York detective Mike Keegan (Berenger), who's assigned the duty, is more than taken with her, despite the fact that he has both a wife (a knowing Bracco) and son at home. A highly watchable, stylish romantic crime thriller. **106m/C VHS, DVD.** Tom Berenger, Mimi Rogers, Lorraine Bracco, Jerry Orbach, Andreas Katsulas, Tony DiBenedetto, James Moriarty, John Rubinstein; *D:* Ridley Scott; *W:* Howard Franklin; *C:* Steven Poster; *M:* Michael Kamen.

Something About Sex *Denial* **1998 (R)** Acerbic bachelor Art (Alexander) broaches the subject of marital fidelity with three couples at a dinner party. All the couples publicly denounce flings while privately not practicing what they preach. **92m/C VHS, DVD.** Patrick Dempsey, Jonathan Silverman, Christine Taylor, Amy Yasbeck, Jason Alexander, Leah Lail, Ryan Alosio; ***Cameos:*** Adam Rifkin; *D:* Adam Rifkin; *W:* Adam Rifkin; *C:* Francis Kenny.

Something for Everyone ½ *The Rook; Black Flowers for the Bride* **1970 (R)** A corrupt footman uses sex and murder in an attempt to take over the estate of an aristocratic Bavarian family in post-WWII Germany. He nearly succeeds in marrying the countess (Lansbury), but someone has been keeping tabs on him. Funny, ambitious black comedy. From the novel "The Code" by Harry Kressing. **112m/C VHS.** Angela Lansbury, Michael York, Anthony (Corlan) Higgins, Heidelinde Weis; *D:* Harold Prince; *C:* Walter Lassally.

Something in Common ½ 1986 A woman discovers her 22-year-old son is having an affair with a woman her own age. Nicely done comedy; Burstyn and Weld both make good use of a solid script. Made for TV. **94m/C VHS.** Ellen Burstyn, Tuesday Weld, Don Murray, Patrick Cassidy, Eli Wallach; *D:* Glenn Jordan; *W:* Susan Rice; *M:* John Addison. **TV**

Something in the Wind ½ 1947 Mary Collins (Durbin) is a DJ having a sort of romance with Donald Read (Dall), who gets the mistaken idea that she was once his wealthy Uncle Chester's (Winninger) mistress and is still after the family money. O'Connor gets to steal the show as Durbin's ally, Charlie. ♫Something in the Wind; Turntable Song; It's Only Love; You Wanna Keep Your Baby Lookin' Right; Happy Go Lucky and Free. **89m/B VHS.** Deanna Durbin, Donald O'Connor, John Dall, Charles Winninger, Helena Carter, Margaret Wycherly; *D:* Irving Pichel; *W:* William Bowers, Harry Kurnitz; *C:* Milton Krasner; *M:* Johnny Green.

Something More 1999 (R) Sam (Gooojian), the romantic loser, and best bud Jim (Lovgren), the obnoxious womanizer, both fall for Kelly (West). The usual romantic complications abound as do all the usual romantic cliches. Cute cast. **97m/C VHS, DVD.** Michael Goorjian, Chandra West, David Lovgren, Jennifer Beals, Tom Cavanagh; *D:* Rob King; *W:* Peter Bryant; *C:* Jon Kranhouse; *M:* Rob Bryanton.

Something of Value 1957 Good ensemble performances in a serious colonial story about the Mau Mau rebellion in Kenya. Hudson and Poitier are torn between their friendship and their opposing loyalties. Drama solidly grounded in fact from the book by Robert Ruark. **113m/B VHS.** Rock Hudson, Sidney Poitier, Wendy Hiller, Dana Wynter, Juano Hernandez; *D:* Richard Brooks; *W:* Richard Brooks; *M:* Miklos Rozsa.

Something Short of Paradise ½ 1979 (PG) The owner of a Manhattan movie theatre has an on again/off again romance with a magazine writer. Would-be Allenesque romantic comedy is too talky and pretentious. **87m/C VHS.** David Steinberg, Susan Sarandon, Jean-Pierre Aumont, Marilyn Sokol; *D:* David Helpern; *W:* Fred Barron.

Something Special ½ *Willy Milly; I Was a Teenage Boy* **1986 (PG-13)** A 14-year-old girl has her wish come true when she is turned into a boy. Charming, original fantasy-comedy is fun for young and old. **93m/C VHS.** Pamela Segall, Patty Duke, Eric Gurry, John Glover, Seth Green; *D:* Paul Schneider; *W:* Walter Carbone.

Something to Sing About *Battling Hoofer* **1936** Musical melodrama about a New York bandleader's attempt to make it big in Hollywood. Allows Cagney the opportunity to demonstrate his dancing talents; he also sings. Rereleased in 1947. Also available colorized. Frawley was Fred on "I Love Lucy." ♫Any Old Love; Right or Wrong; Loving You; Out of the Blue; Something to Sing About. **84m/B VHS.** James Cagney, William Frawley, Evelyn Daw, Gene Lockhart; *D:* Victor Schertzinger.

Something to Talk About ½ *Grace Under Pressure* **1995 (R)** Romantic comedy/drama finds Grace (Roberts) running her overbearing father Wyly's (Duvall) horsebreeding operation and learning that her husband Eddie (the ever-charming Quaid) is tomcatting around. So Grace tosses him out and makes a temporary move with daughter Caroline (Aull) back home. Tart-tongued sister Emma Rae (Sedgwick) is sympathetic but long-suffering mama Georgia (Rowlands) thinks Grace should make the best of things (the way she's done). Naturally, Eddie wants his family back but the frazzled Grace is just coming to terms with what she wants out of life. Star appeal from both leads lends this familiar plot some spark. **106m/C VHS, DVD.** Julia Roberts, Dennis Quaid, Robert Duvall, Gena Rowlands, Kyra Sedgwick, Brett Cullen, Haley Aull, Muse Watson, Anne Shropshire; *D:* Lasse Hallstrom; *W:* Callie Khouri; *C:* Sven Nykvist; *M:* Hans Zimmer.

Something Weird woof! 1968 McCabe is disfigured horribly in an electrical accident. A seemingly beautiful witch fixes his face, on condition that he be her lover. The accident also gave him ESP—and it gets cheesier from there. **80m/C VHS, DVD, Wide.** Tony McCabe, Elizabeth Lee, William Brooker, Mudite Arums, Taed Heil, Lawrence Wood, Larry Wellington, Roy Colodi, Jeffrey Allen, Stan Dale, Richard Nilsson, Carolyn Smith, Norm Lenet, Louis Newman, Dick Gaffield, Janet Charlton, Lee Ahsmann, Roger Papsch, Daniel Carrington; *D:* Herschell Gordon Lewis; *W:* James F. Hurley; *C:* Herschell Gordon Lewis, Andy Romanoff.

Something Wicked This Way Comes 1983 (PG) Two young boys discover the evil secret of a mysterious traveling carnival that visits their town. Bradbury wrote the screenplay for this much-anticipated, expensive adaptation of his own novel. Good special effects, but disappointing. **94m/C VHS, DVD.** Jason Robards Jr., Jonathan Pryce, Diane Ladd, Pam Grier, Richard (Dick) Davalos, James Stacy, Royal Dano, Vidal Peterson, Shawn Carson; *D:* Jack Clayton; *W:* Ray Bradbury; *C:* Stephen Burum; *M:* James Horner.

Something Wild ½ 1986 (R) Mild-mannered business exec Daniels is picked up by an impossibly free-living vamp with a Louise Brooks hairdo, and taken for the ride of his up-till-then staid life, eventually leading to explosive violence. A sharp-edged comedy with numerous changes of pace. Too-happy ending wrecks it, but it's great until then. Look for cameos from filmmakers John Waters and John Sayles. **113m/C VHS, DVD.** Jeff Daniels, Melanie Griffith, Ray Liotta, Margaret Colin, Tracey Walter, Dana Peru, Jack Gilpin, Su Tissue, Kenneth Utt, Sister Carol East, John Sayles, John Waters, Charles Napier; *D:* Jonathan Demme; *W:* E. Max Frye; *C:* Tak Fujimoto; *M:* Rosemary Paul, John Cale, Laurie Anderson, David Byrne.

Sometimes a Great Notion *Never Give an Inch* **1971 (PG)** Trouble erupts in a small Oregon town when a family of loggers decide to honor a contract when the other loggers go on strike. Newman's second stint in the director's chair; Fonda's first role as an old man. Based on the novel by Ken Kesey. **115m/C VHS.** Paul Newman, Henry Fonda, Lee Remick, Richard Jaeckel, Michael Sarrazin; *D:* Paul Newman; *W:* John Gay; *M:* Henry Mancini.

Sometimes They Come Back 1991 (R) Another Stephen King tale of terror. Matheson plays a man haunted by the tragedy in his past. A witness to his brother's death, he also witnesses the fiery crash of his brother's killers. Only now the killers have returned from the dead, to take their revenge on him. **97m/C VHS, DVD.** Tim Matheson, Brooke Adams, Robert Rusler, William Sanderson; *D:* Tom McLoughlin; *W:* Mark Rosenthal, Larry Konner; *C:* Bryan England; *M:* Terry Plumeri. **TV**

Sometimes They Come Back... Again ½ 1996 (R) Psychologist John Porter (Gross) and his teenaged daughter (Swank) return to Porter's hometown after his mother's mysterious death. He should know you can never go home again since they're both soon threatened by a young man (Arquette) involved in the ritualistic murder of Porter's sister years before. Gruesome special effects are the highlight. **98m/C VHS, DVD.** Michael Gross, Hilary Swank, Alexis Arquette, Jennifer Elise Cox; *D:* Adam Grossman; *W:* Adam Grossman; *C:* Christopher Baffa; *M:* Peter Manning Robinson.

Sometimes They Come Back... For More 1999 (R) Two military officers investigate the disappearances of crew members at a government outpost in Antarctica. **89m/C VHS, DVD, Wide.** Clayton Rohner, Chase Masterson, Faith Ford, Max Perlich, Damian Chapa; *D:* Daniel Berk.

Somewhere I'll Find You 1942 Clark and Turner heat up the screen as correspondents running all over the war-torn world in their second film together. ("Honky Tonk" was their first.) Notable mainly because Gable's beloved wife, Carole Lombard, was killed in a plane crash only three days into production. Gable forced himself to finish the film and it became one of the studio's biggest hits. Although critics applauded his determination to complete the film, many felt his performance was subdued and strained. Film debut of Wynn. Based on a story by Charles Hoffman. **108m/B VHS.** Clark Gable, Lana Turner, Robert Sterling, Reginald Owen, Lee Patrick, Charles Dingle, Tamara Shayne, Leonid Kinskey, Diana Lewis, Molly Lamont, Patricia Dane, Sara Haden, Keenan Wynn; *D:* Wesley Ruggles; *W:* Walter Reisch, Marguerite Roberts.

Somewhere in Sonora 1933 Early Wayne Western set in Old Mexico. Wayne plays a rodeo performer who joins an outlaw gang to save a friend and a silver mine. Like most of the other films of the series, this was a remake of a Ken Maynard silent. Based on a story and the novel "Somewhere South in Sonora" by Will Levington Comfort. **59m/B VHS.** John Wayne, Henry B. Walthall, Shirley Palmer, J(ohn) P(aterson) McGowan, Frank Rice, Billy Franey, Paul Fix, Ralph Lewis; *D:* Mack V. Wright; *W:* Joe Roach.

Somewhere in the City ½ 1997 Covers the screwy lives of six tenants of a Lower East Side New York apartment building. Betty (a subdued Bernhard) is an unlucky-in-love therapist who's still neurotically trying. She agrees to help out Chinese exchange student Lu Lu (Ling) who's desperately seeking a green card marriage. Then there's unhappy wife Marta (Muti), whose upstairs lover, Frankie (Burke), is a completely incompetent crook. There's also gay actor Graham (Stormare), who's disappointed personally and professionally, and basement-dwelling Che (Stewart), a trust-fund baby who wants to be a radical revolutionary. Sporadically amusing with a talented cast. **93m/C VHS.** Sandra Bernhard, Bai Ling, Ornella

Muti, Robert John Burke, Peter Stormare, Paul Anthony Stewart, Bulle Ogier; ***Cameos:*** Edward I. Koch; ***D:*** Ramin Niami; ***W:*** Ramin Niami, Patrick Dillon; ***C:*** Igor Sunara; ***M:*** John Cale.

Somewhere in Time 🦴½ **1980 (PG)** Playwright Reeve (in his first post-Clark Kent role) falls in love with a beautiful woman in an old portrait. Through self-hypnosis he goes back in time to 1912 to discover what their relationship might have been. The film made a star of the Grand Hotel, located on Mackinac Island in Michigan, where it was shot. Drippy rip-off of the brilliant novel "Time and Again" by Jack Finney. Reeve is horrible; Seymour is underused. All in all, rather wretched. **103m/C VHS, DVD, Wide.** Christopher Reeve, Jane Seymour, Christopher Plummer, Teresa Wright; ***D:*** Jeannot Szwarc; ***W:*** Richard Matheson; ***C:*** Isidore Mankofsky; ***M:*** John Barry.

Somewhere Tomorrow 🦴🦴½ **1985 (PG)** A lonely, fatherless teenage girl is befriended by the ghost of a young man killed in a plane crash. Charming and moving, if not perfect. **91m/C VHS.** Sarah Jessica Parker, Nancy Addison, Tom Shea; ***D:*** Robert Wiemer.

Sommersby 🦴🦴½ **1993 (PG-13)** A too-good-to-be-true period romance based on the film "The Return of Martin Guerre." A Civil War veteran (Gere) returns to his wife's (Foster) less-than-open arms. She soon warms up to his kind, sensitive and caring manner, but can't quite believe the change that the war has wrought. Neither can the neighbors, especially the one (Pullman) who had his own eye on Laurel Sommersby. So is he really Jack Sommersby or an all too clever imposter? Lots of hankies needed for the tender-hearted. Strong performance by Foster. Filmed in Virginia (passing for the state of Tennessee.) **114m/C VHS, DVD, Wide.** Richard Gere, Jodie Foster, Bill Pullman, James Earl Jones, William Windom, Brett Kelley, Richard Hamilton, Maury Chaykin, Lanny Flaherty, Frankie Faison, Wendell Wellman, Clarice Taylor, R. Lee Ermey; ***D:*** Jon Amiel; ***W:*** Nicholas Meyer, Sarah Kernochan; ***C:*** Philippe Rousselot; ***M:*** Danny Elfman.

Son-in-Law 🦴½ **1993 (PG-13)** Surfer-dude comic Shore's a laconic fish out of water as a city-boy rock 'n' roller who falls in love with a country beauty, marries her, and visits the family farm to meet the new in-laws. Once there, he weirds out family and neighbors before showing everyone how to live, Pauly style. Silly entertainment best appreciated by Shore fans. **95m/C VHS, DVD.** Pauly Shore, Carla Gugino, Lane Smith, Cindy Pickett, Mason Adams, Patrick Renna, Dennis Burkley, Dan Gauthier, Tiffani-Amber Thiessen; ***D:*** Steve Rash; ***W:*** Adam Small, Shawn Schepps, Fax Bahr; ***C:*** Peter Deming; ***M:*** Richard Gibbs.

Son of a Gun 🦴½ **1919** A loveable but ornery cowboy gets banished from the county for disturbing the peace. However, he wins the favor of the townspeople when he stands up to a gang of gambling swindlers. Silent. **68m/B VHS.** "Broncho" Billy Anderson.

Son of Ali Baba 🦴🦴 **1952** Kashma Baba, son of Ali Baba, enters the military academy to learn to withstand adversity. He has other ideas however, until he must suddenly fill his father's shoes and fight the evil Caliph. He fights bravely with the help of his childhood friend, a beautiful princess, in this swashbuckler. **85m/C VHS.** Tony Curtis, Piper Laurie, Susan Cabot, Victor Jory, Hugh O'Brian, William Reynolds, Gerald Mohr; ***D:*** Ross Hunter.

Son of Captain Blood 🦴½ *Il Figlio del Capitano Blood* **1962 (G)** The son of the famous pirate meets up with his father's enemies on the high seas. The son of the famous actor Errol Flynn—Sean—plays the son of the character the elder Flynn played in "Captain Blood." Let's just say the gimmick didn't work. **90m/C VHS.** *IT SP* Sean Flynn, Ann Todd; ***D:*** Tulio Demicheli.

Son of Dracula 🦴🦴🦴 *Young Dracula* **1943** In this late-coming sequel to the Universal classic, a stranger named Alucard is invited to America by a Southern belle obsessed with eternal life. It is actually Dracula himself, not his son, who wreaks havoc in this spine-tingling chiller. **80m/B VHS.** Lon Chaney Jr., Evelyn Ankers, Frank Craven, Robert Paige, Louise Allbritton, J. Edward Bromberg, Samuel S. Hinds; ***D:*** Robert Siodmak; ***W:*** Eric Taylor; ***C:*** George Robinson.

Son of Flubber 🦴🦴½ **1963** Sequel to "The Absent Minded Professor" finds Fred MacMurray still toying with his prodigious invention, Flubber, now in the form of Flubbergas, which causes those who inhale it to float away. Disney's first-ever sequel is high family wackiness. **96m/C VHS.** Fred MacMurray, Nancy Olson, Tommy Kirk, Leon Ames, Joanna Moore, Keenan Wynn, Charlie Ruggles, Paul Lynde; ***D:*** Robert Stevenson; ***C:*** Edward Colman; ***M:*** George Bruns.

Son of Frankenstein 🦴🦴🦴 **1939** The second sequel (after "The Bride of Frankenstein") to the 1931 version of the horror classic. The good doctor's skeptical son returns to the family manse and becomes obsessed with his father's work and with reviving the creature. Full of memorable characters and brooding ambience. Karloff's last appearance as the monster. **99m/C VHS, DVD.** Basil Rathbone, Bela Lugosi, Boris Karloff, Lionel Atwill, Josephine Hutchinson, Donnie Dunagan, Emma Dunn, Edgar Norton, Lawrence Grant, Lionel Belmore; ***D:*** Rowland V. Lee; ***W:*** Willis Cooper; ***C:*** George Robinson.

Son of Fury 🦴🦴🦴 **1942** Dashing Ben Blake (Power) is left penniless when his sinister uncle (Sanders) wrongfully takes the family fortune. Ben escapes to sea and then to an island paradise—all the while plotting his revenge. But he still finds time to fall for the beautous Tierney. Fine 18th-century costumer done in grand style. Based on the novel "Benjamin Blake" by Edison Marshall. **98m/C VHS.** Tyrone Power, Gene Tierney, George Sanders, Frances Farmer, Roddy McDowall, John Carradine, Elsa Lanchester, Harry Davenport, Kay Johnson, Dudley Digges, Halliwell Hobbes, Marten Lamont, Arthur Hohl, Pedro de Cordoba, Dennis Hoey, Heather Thatcher; ***D:*** John Cromwell; ***W:*** Philip Dunne; ***M:*** Alfred Newman.

Son of Gascogne 🦴🦴½ *Les Fils de Gascogne* **1995** Offbeat comedy about identity, romance, and wish fullfillment. Gawky Harvey (Colin) is serving as a travel guide to a group of Georgian folksingers who are giving concerts in Paris. Harvey falls for their pretty teenaged interpreter, Dinara (Droukarova), who reciprocates. The duo meet Marco (Dreyfus), a chauffeur/con man, who insists that Harvey is the son of the late legendary director Gascogne (Harvey doesn't know who his father is) and insists on introducing him to his dad's cinematic colleagues (thus supplying cameos of numerous French cinema greats). French with subtitles. **106m/C VHS, DVD, Wide.** *FR* Gregoire Colin, Jean Claude Dreyfus, Dinara Droukarova, Bernadette LaFont, Alexandra Stewart, Stephane Audran, Jean-Claude Brialy, Bulle Ogier, Marie-France Pisier, Anemone, Patrice Leconte, Marina Vlady; ***D:*** Pascal Aubier; ***W:*** Pascal Aubier, Patrick Modiano; ***C:*** Jean-Jacques Flori; ***M:*** Angelo Zurzulo.

Son of God's Country 🦴½ **1948** Utterly hackneyed, near-comic attempt at a western. Good-guy U.S. Marshal poses as a crook to get the lowdown on the varmints. **60m/B VHS.** Monte Hale, Pamela Blake, Adrian (Lorna Gray) Booth.

Son of Godzilla 🦴🦴 *Gojira no Musuko; Monster Island's Decisive Battle: Godzilla's Son* **1966** Dad and junior protect beauty Maeda from giant spiders on a remote island ruled by a mad scientist. Fun monster flick with decent special effects. **86m/C VHS.** *JP* Akira Kubo, Beverly Maeda, Tadao Takashima, Akihiko Hirata, Kenji Sahara; ***D:*** Jun Fukuda; ***W:*** Shinichi Sekizawa, Kazue Shiba; ***C:*** Kazuo Yamada; ***M:*** Masaru Sato.

Son of Hercules in the Land of Darkness 🦴 **1963** Argolis (Vadis) must rescue prisoners trapped in an underground city. **74m/B VHS.** Dan Vadis, Carol Brown, Spela Rozin.

Son of Ingagi 🦴½ **1940** Lonely ape-man kidnaps woman in search of romance. Early all-black horror film stars Williams of "Amos 'n' Andy." **70m/B VHS.** Zack Williams, Laura Bowman, Alfred Grant, Spencer Williams Jr., Daisy Bufford, Arthur Ray; ***D:*** Richard C. Kahn; ***W:*** Spencer Williams Jr.; ***C:*** Roland Price, Herman Schopp.

Son of Kong 🦴🦴½ **1933** King Kong's descendant is discovered on an island amid prehistoric creatures in this often humorous sequel to RKO's immensely popular "King Kong." Hoping to capitalize on the enormous success of its predecessor, director Schoedsack quickly threw this together. As a result, its success at the boxoffice did not match the original's, and didn't deserve to, but it's fun. Nifty special effects from Willis O'Brien, the man who brought them to us the first time. **70m/B VHS.** Robert Armstrong, Helen Mack; ***D:*** Ernest B. Schoedsack; ***M:*** Max Steiner.

Son of Lassie 🦴🦴½ **1945 (G)** It seems that Lassie's son Laddie just isn't quite as smart as his mother. After the dog sneaks onto his master's plane during WWII, the plane gets shot down, and Lawford parachutes out with Laddie in his arms. The dog goes to get help because Lawford is hurt, but he brings back two Nazis! A sequel to "Lassie Come Home." **102m/C VHS.** Peter Lawford, Donald Crisp, June Lockhart, Nigel Bruce, William Severn, Leon Ames, Donald Curtis, Nils Asther, Robert Lewis; ***D:*** Sylvan Simon.

The Son of Monte Cristo 🦴🦴½ **1940** Illegitimate offspring of the great swashbuckler with Robert Donat proves they made pathetic, pointless sequels even back then. **102m/B VHS, DVD.** Louis Hayward, Joan Bennett, George Sanders, Florence Bates, Montagu Love, Ralph Byrd, Clayton Moore; ***D:*** Rowland V. Lee; ***W:*** George Bruce; ***C:*** George Robinson; ***M:*** Edward Ward.

Son of Paleface 🦴🦴🦴½ **1952** Hilarious sequel to the original Hope gagfest, with the Harvard-educated son of the original character (again played by Hope) heading west to claim an inheritance. Hope runs away with every cowboy cliche and even manages to wind up with the girl. Songs include "Buttons and Bows" (reprised from the original), "There's a Cloud in My Valley of Sunshine," and "Four-legged Friend." **95m/C VHS, DVD.** Bob Hope, Jane Russell, Roy Rogers, Douglass Dumbrille, Iron Eyes Cody, Bill Williams, Harry von Zell; ***D:*** Frank Tashlin; ***W:*** Frank Tashlin, Joseph Quillan, Robert L. Welch; ***C:*** Harry Wild.

Son of Rusty 🦴🦴½ **1947** Danny and his friends are warned to stay away from the farm of suspicious Jed Barlow. But Rusty keeps running away to see Jed's dog Barb and Danny gets to know Jed. Then Danny must stand by his new friend when word of Jed's past turns folks against him. (Rusty and Barb have puppies too.) **70m/B VHS.** Ted Donaldson.

Son of Samson 🦴½ *Le Geant de la Vallee Das Rois* **1962** Man with large pectoral muscles puts an end to the evil Queen of Egypt's reign of terror **89m/C VHS.** *FR IT YU* Mark Forest, Chelo Alonso, Angelo Zanolli, Vira (Vera) Silenti, Frederica Ranchi; ***D:*** Carlo Campogalliani.

Son of Sinbad 🦴🦴 *Nights in a Harem* **1955** Sinbad, captured by the Khalif of Baghdad, must bring him the secret of Greek fire to gain his freedom and free the city from the forces of mighty Tamerlane. About three dozen nubile young women wear very little and gambol with our hero herein; much-anticipated skinfest caused a scandal, nurtured by Howard Hughes for profit. **88m/C VHS.** Dale Robertson, Sally Forrest, Vincent Price, Lili St. Cyr, Mari Blanchard, Joi Lansing; ***D:*** Ted Tetzlaff.

Son of the Morning Star 🦴🦴🦴 **1991 (PG-13)** Lavish made for TV retelling of Custer's famed-butt kicking. Complex characterizations and unusual points of view, based on the book by Evan S. Connell. **186m/C VHS.** Gary Cole, Rosanna Arquette, Dean Stockwell, Rodney A. Grant, Terry O'Quinn, David Strathairn, Stanley Anderson, George American Horse; ***D:*** Mike Robe. **TV**

Son of the Pink Panther 🦴½ *Blake Edwards' Son of the Pink Panther* **1993 (PG)** Lame leftover from the formerly popular comedy series. Director Edwards has chosen not to resurrect Inspector Clouseau, instead opting for his son (Benigni), who turns out to be just as much of a bumbling idiot as his father. Commissioner Dreyfus (Lom), the twitching, mouth-foaming former supervisor of the original Clouseau is looking for a kidnapped princess (Farentino) along with Clouseau, Jr., who himself does not know he is the illegitimate son of his partner's dead nemesis. Many of the sketches have been recycled from previous series entrants. Rather than being funny, they seem used and shopworn like a threadbare rug. **115m/C VHS.** Roberto Benigni, Herbert Lom, Robert Davi, Debrah Farentino, Claudia Cardinale, Burt Kwouk, Shabana Azmi; ***D:*** Blake Edwards; ***W:*** Blake Edwards; ***C:*** Dick Bush; ***M:*** Henry Mancini.

The Son of the Shark 🦴🦴 *Le Fils du Requin* **1993** Simon (Da Silva) and Martin Vanderhoes (Vandendaele) have been abandoned by their mother and prefer to live as homeless delinquents rather than with their drunken father. The boys commit petty crimes and vandalism to survive (always escaping from foster homes and institutions) while Martin dreams of running away to his true home in the ocean—proclaiming himself to be "the son of a female shark." Depressing and casually cruel; based on a true story. French with subtitles. **88m/C VHS.** *FR* Ludovic Vandendaele, Erick Da Silva, Sandrine Blancke, Maxime LeRoux; ***D:*** Agnes Merlet; ***W:*** Agnes Merlet; ***C:*** Gerard Simon; ***M:*** Bruno Coulais.

Son of the Sheik 🦴🦴🦴 **1926** This sequel to Valentino's star-making "The Sheik" (1921) also turned out to be his last film. Ahmed (Valentino) falls in love with dancing girl Yasmin (Banky). He gets kidnapped by Ghabah (Love), the leader of a group of thieves, who tells the sheik's son that Yasmin has betrayed him. After his escape, Ahmed takes revenge by kidnapping Yasmin. Eventually, all the misunderstandings are resolved. Based on the novel by E.M. Hull. **62m/B VHS, DVD.** Rudolph Valentino, Vilma Banky, Montagu Love, George Fawcett, Karl (Daen) Dane, Agnes Ayres; ***D:*** George Fitzmaurice; ***W:*** Frances Marion; ***C:*** George Barnes.

Son of Zorro **1947** Zorro takes the law into his own hands to protect ranchers from bandits. A serial in 13 chapters. **164m/B VHS.** George Turner, Peggy Stewart, Roy Barcroft, Edward Cassidy.

Sonatine 🦴🦴🦴 **1996 (R)** Middle-age Yakuza mobster Murakama (director Kitano, using his screen name Beat Takeshi) wishes to retire but is instead sent to mediate a low-level gang war. Upon arrival, an attempt is made on his life, so he and his men hole up at a beach house. The young punks of the gang engage in horseplay and antics that indicate their violent natures and signal that all will not remain calm for long. Kitano's performance, writing, and direction are superb, understating the violence while not glamorizing it, and showing the effect it has on the man who carries it out. The relatively tranquil setting of the hideout allows some humor and character development, as well as preventing the cliches that usually pop up in this type of movie. Ever on the prowl for Far East gangster chic, Tarantino's Rolling Thunder brought this one to U.S. shores. Japanese with subtitles. **93m/C VHS.** *JP* Takeshi "Beat" Kitano, Aya Kokumai, Tetsu Watanabe, Masanobu Katsumura, Susumu Terashima, Ren Ohsugi, Tonbo Zushi, Eiji Minakata, Kenichi Yajima; ***D:*** Takeshi "Beat" Kitano; ***W:*** Takeshi "Beat" Kitano; ***C:*** Katsumi Yanagishima; ***M:*** Jo Hasaishi.

A Song Is Born 🦴🦴🦴 **1948** A group of music professors try to trace the history of music. Kaye is in charge of a U.S. music foundation whose research has led him up to ragtime. He is soon, however, thrust into the sometimes seedy world of jazz joints and night spots, all in the name of research. Enter love interest Mayo, a woman on the run from her gangster boyfriend who hides out at the foundation. Not one of Kaye's funniest or best, but if you enjoy big band music, you'll love this. Includes music by Louis Armstrong and his orchestra, Tommy Dorsey and his orchestra, and Charlie Barnet and his orchestra. This was Kaye's last film for

Goldwyn. ♫A Song is Born; Bach Boogie; Anitra's Dance; I'm Getting Sentimental Over You; Blind Barnabas; Mockin' Bird; Redskin Rhumba; The Goldwyn Stomp; Daddy-O. **113m/B VHS.** Danny Kaye, Virginia Mayo, Benny Goodman, Hugh Herbert, Steve Cochran, J. Edward Bromberg, Felix Bressart; ***D:*** Howard Hawks; ***C:*** Gregg Toland.

Song o' My Heart **1929** An early musical starring popular Irish tenor McCormack as a singer forced to abandon his career when he marries a woman he does not love. A tour de force for the lead in his movie debut. ♫Little Boy Blue; Paddy Me Lad; I Hear You Calling Me; A Fair Story by the Fireside; Just For a Day; Kitty My Love; The Rose of Tralee; A Pair of Blue Eyes; I Feel You Near Me. **91m/B VHS.** John McCormack, Maureen O'Sullivan, John Garrick, J.M. Kerrigan, Tommy Clifford, Alice Joyce; ***D:*** Frank Borzage.

Song of Arizona **1946** Rogers and the Sons of the Pioneers arrive to aid their pal Hayes against a gang of bank robbers in this modern-day oater. Eight songs perpetually punctuate the perfunctory plot, particularly "Will Ya Be My Darling," "Half-a-Chance Ranch," and the title tune. **54m/B VHS.** Roy Rogers, Dale Evans, George "Gabby" Hayes, Lyle Talbot, Bob Nolan; ***D:*** Frank McDonald.

The Song of Bernadette **1943** Depicts the true story of a peasant girl who sees a vision of the Virgin Mary in a grotto at Lourdes in 1858. The girl is directed to dig at the grotto for water that will heal those who believe in its powers, much to the astonishment and concern of the townspeople. Based on Franz Werfel's novel. Directed with tenderness and carefully cast, and appealing to religious and sentimental susceptibilities, it was a boxoffice smash. **156m/B VHS.** Charles Bickford, Lee J. Cobb, Jennifer Jones, Vincent Price, Anne Revere, Gladys Cooper; ***D:*** Henry King; ***C:*** Arthur C. Miller; ***M:*** Alfred Newman. Oscars '43: Actress (Jones), B&W Cinematog., Orig. Dramatic Score; Golden Globes '44: Actress—Drama (Jones), Director (King), Film—Drama.

Song of Freedom ½ **1936** John Zinga (Robeson) is a British-born black dockworker whose voal gifts are discovered by an opera impresario. After realizing a career as a concert performer, Zinga ventures to Africa to investigate his ancestry and finds he has royal roots, and that his tribe have fallen under the grip of corrupt spiritualists. Robeson turns in a fine performance in what is otherwise an average film. ♫Sleepy River; Lonely Road; Song of Freedom; The Black Emperor. **80m/B VHS, DVD.** *GB* Paul Robeson, Elisabeth Welch, George Mozart; ***D:*** J. Elder Wills; ***W:*** Ingram D'Abbes, Fenn Sherie; ***C:*** Eric Cross, Harry Rose.

Song of Nevada ½ **1944** Rogers woos the high-society daughter (Evans, of course) of a rancher (Hall). Quintenssential Roy-n-Dale. ♫It's Love, Love, Love; New Moon Over Nevada; Hi Ho Little Dogies; The Harum Scarum Baron of the Harmonium; What Are We Going to Do?; A Cowboy Has to Yodel in the Morning. **60m/B VHS.** Roy Rogers, Dale Evans, Thurston Hall; ***D:*** Joseph Kane.

Song of Norway **1970 (G)** A dramatization of the early life of the beloved Norwegian Romantic composer Edvard Grieg. Filmed against the beautiful mountains, waterfalls, and forests of Norway and based on the popular '40s stage production. The scenery is the best thing because Grieg's life was dull—even with cinematic liberties taken. ♫Strange Music; The Song of Norway; The Little House; Be a Boy Again; Three There Were; A Rhyme and a Reason; Wrong to Dream; I Love You; The Solitary Wanderer. **143m/C VHS.** Toralv Maurstad, Florence Henderson, Edward G. Robinson, Christina Schollin, Frank Porretta, Oscar Homolka, Robert Morley, Harry Secombe; ***D:*** Andrew L. Stone.

Song of Old Wyoming ½ **1945** Three of those songs are presented in the course of an ordinary western about a spunky widow driving badmen out of Wyoming territory. La Rue plays the villainous Cheyenne Kid; this was before he got his own series as the heroic "Lash" La Rue. **65m/C VHS.** Eddie Dean, Sarah Padden, Lash LaRue, Jennifer Holt, Emmett Lynn, John Carpenter, Ian Keith, Bob Barron; ***D:*** Robert Emmett Tansey.

Song of Scheherazade **1947** Superficial musical bio of Russian composer Rimsky-Korsakov (Aumont) and his romance with dancer Cara de Talavera (De Carlo), who inspires him to write the "Song of Scheherazade." **106m/C VHS.** Jean-Pierre Aumont, Yvonne De Carlo, Brian Donlevy, Eve Arden, Philip Reed, John Qualen; ***D:*** Walter Reisch; ***W:*** Walter Reisch; ***C:*** Hal Mohr, William V. Skall.

The Song of Songs ½ **1933** Orphaned Lily (Dietrich) is living with her elderly Aunt Rasmussen (Skipworth) in Berlin and falling for sculptor, Richard (Aherne). He wants her to pose for a nude statue, based on the Song of Solomon, after getting a gander at Lily's legs. However, wealthy Baron von Merzbach (Atwill), who's Richard's art patron, eventually persuades both Aunt and Richard that Lily needs a better life than either can offer. Their marriage has the Baron making Lily over, so she'll socially be a worthy Baroness, but these situations never work out as anticipated. Based on the novel by Hermann Sudermann and the play by Edward Sheldon. **89m/B VHS.** Marlene Dietrich, Brian Aherne, Lionel Atwill, Alison Skipworth, Hardie Albright, Helen Freeman; ***D:*** Rouben Mamoulian; ***W:*** Samuel Hoffenstein, Leo Birinski; ***C:*** Victor Milner; ***M:*** Karl Hajos, Milan Roder.

Song of Texas ½ **1943** When a young woman journeys west to visit her father at "his" ranch, Roy and his pals must keep the father's secret that he is just another hired hand. Whenever possible, everyone breaks into song. **54m/B VHS.** Roy Rogers, Harry Shannon, Pat Brady, Barton MacLane, Arline Judge; ***D:*** Joseph Kane.

Song of the Exile ½ **1990** A Chinese/Japanese student living in London in the early 1970s faces racial discrimination and decides to return to her native Hong Kong. But on the home front, she and her family clash emotionally until daughter and mother come to a gradual understanding of how the past affects the present. In Cantonese and Japanese with English subtitles. **100m/C VHS.** *CH* Maggie Cheung, Shwu-Fen Chang; ***D:*** Ann Hui.

Song of the Gringo *The Old Corral* **1936** Tex Ritter stars in his first singing western as a sheriff going after a gang of claim jumpers. **57m/B VHS.** Tex Ritter, Monte Blue, Joan Woodbury, Fuzzy Knight, Richard Adams, Warner Richmond; ***D:*** John P. McCarthy.

Song of the Islands ½ **1942** Landing families in Hawaii feud over a beach, while the son of one (Mature) and the daughter of the other (Grable) fall in love. Plenty of songs, and dancing to display Grable's legs. Of course happiness and concord reign at the end. Songs include "O'Brien Has Gone Hawaiian," "Sing Me a Song of the Islands," and "What's Buzzin', Cousin?" **75m/C VHS.** Betty Grable, Victor Mature, Jack Oakie, Thomas Mitchell, Billy Gilbert; ***D:*** Walter Lang.

The Song of the Lark ½ **2001** Thea Kronborg (Elliott) is a minister's daughter in 1890's Colorado who is encouraged by local doctor Howard Archie (Howard) to pursue her musical dreams. At first, Thea travels to Chicago to study piano but her teacher (Hules) realizes that Thea's true gift is her voice. Handsome brewery heir Fred Ottenburg (Goldwyn) offers to sponsor her career but their romance is rocky and Thea must eventually make her own way. Based on the novel by Willa Cather. **120m/C VHS.** Alison Elliott, Arliss Howard, Tony Goldwyn, Maximilian Schell, Norman Lloyd, Robert Floyd, Endre Hules, Nan Martin, Christian Meoli; ***D:*** Karen Arthur; ***W:*** Joseph Maurer; ***M:*** Charles Fox. **TV**

Song of the Thin Man ½ **1947** The sixth and final "Thin Man" mystery. This time Nick and Nora Charles (Powell and Loy) investigate the murder of a bandleader. Somewhat more sophisticated than its predecessor, due in part to its setting in the jazz music world. Sequel to "The Thin Man Goes Home." **86m/B VHS.** William Powell, Myrna Loy, Keenan Wynn, Dean Stockwell, Philip Reed, Patricia Morison, Gloria Grahame, Jayne Meadows, Don Taylor, Leon Ames, Ralph Morgan, Warner Anderson; ***D:*** Edward Buzzell; ***C:*** Charles Rosher.

Song of the Trail ½ **1936** Our hero saves an old man hornswoggled at cards. **65m/B VHS.** Kermit Maynard, George "Gabby" Hayes, Fuzzy Knight, Wheeler Oakman, Evelyn Brent, Andrea Leeds; ***D:*** Russell Hopton.

Song Spinner ½ **1995 (G)** In a mysterious land, a stranger gives a young girl the power of music, which she hopes to share with the king. But first she must get past the kingdom's noise police. **95m/C VHS.** Meredith Henderson, Patti LuPone, John Neville; ***D:*** Randy Bradshaw.

A Song to Remember **1945** With music performed by Jose Iturbi, this film depicts the last years of the great pianist and composer Frederic Chopin, including his affair with famous author George Sand, the most renowned French woman of her day. Typically mangled film biography. ♫Valse in D Flat (Minute Waltz); Mazurka In B Flat, Opus 7, No. 1; Fantasie Impromptu, Opus 66; Etude In A Flat, Opus 25, No. 1 (partial); Polonaise In A Flat, Opus 53 (partial); Scherzo In B Flat Minor; Etude In C Minor, Opus 10, No. 12; Nocturne In C Minor, Opus 48, No. 1; Nocturn In E Flat, Opus 9, No. 2. **112m/C VHS.** Cornel Wilde, Paul Muni, Merle Oberon, Nina Foch, George Coulouris; ***D:*** Charles Vidor; ***C:*** Gaetano Antonio "Tony" Gaudio; ***M:*** Miklos Rozsa.

Song Without End ½ **1960** This musical biography of 19th century Hungarian pianist/composer Franz Lizst is given the Hollywood treatment. The lavish production emphasizes Liszt's scandalous exploits with married women and his life among the royal courts of Europe rather than his musical talents. Features music from several composers including Handel, Beethoven, Bach and Schumann. This film marked the debut of Capucine. Director Vidor died during filming and Cukor stepped in, so there is a noticeable change in style. Although there is much to criticize in the story, the music is beautiful. ♫Mephisto Waltz; Spozalizio; Sonata In B Minor; Un Sospiro; Fantasy on Themes From "Rigoletto"; Consolation in D Flat; Liebestraum; Les Preludes; Piano Concerto No. 1. **130m/C VHS.** Dirk Bogarde, Capucine, Genevieve Page, Patricia Morison, Ivan Desny, Martita Hunt, Lou Jacobi; ***D:*** Charles Vidor, George Cukor; ***C:*** James Wong Howe; ***M:*** Morris Stoloff, Harry Sukman. Oscars '60: Scoring/Musical; Golden Globes '61: Film—Mus./Comedy.

Songcatcher **1999** Turn-of-the-century musicologist Dr. Lily Penleric (McTeer) heads for Appalachia in a huff after the all-male review board of the East Coast university where she teaches refuses to grant her tenure. She begins teaching at her sister Elna's (Adams) mountain school, harboring a superior attitude toward the rubes she's teaching. She discovers to her amazement that the songs the rustic people sing, dance and live to are barely altered from the time they were brought over from Europe. She rushes to record the native folk music, but meets resistance from local Tom (Quinn) who feels that if the hillbillies have something civilized folk want, they should be payed for it. Excellent performances and visuals throughout. **113m/C VHS, DVD.** Janet McTeer, Aidan Quinn, Pat Carroll, Jane Adams, Emmy Rossum, Mike Harding, Iris DeMent, Greg Cook, David Patrick Kelly, E. Katherine Kerr, Taj Mahal, Muse Watson, Stephanie Ross; ***D:*** Maggie Greenwald; ***W:*** Maggie Greenwald; ***C:*** Enrique Chediak; ***M:*** David Mansfield.

Songs and Bullets ½ **1938** Simple zen-like title sums it up. The songs total five in number, the bullets somewhat more as hero cowboys battle rustlers in routine fashion. One of a handful of films (westerns and comedies) produced by funnyman Stan Laurel. **57m/B VHS.** Fred Scott, Al "Fuzzy" St. John, Alice Ardell, Charles "Blackie" King, Karl Hackett, Frank LaRue, Budd Buster; ***D:*** Sam Newfield.

Songwriter ½ **1984 (R)** A high-falutin' look at the lives and music of two popular country singers with, aptly, plenty of country tunes written and performed by the stars. Singer-businessman Nelson needs Kristofferson's help keeping a greedy investor at bay. Never mind the plot; plenty of good music. ♫How Do You Feel About Foolin' Around?; Songwriter; Who'll Buy My Memories; Write Your Own Songs; Nobody Said It Was Going To Be Easy; Good Times; Eye of the Storm; Crossing the Border; Down to Her Socks. **94m/C VHS.** Willie Nelson, Kris Kristofferson, Rip Torn, Melinda Dillon, Lesley Ann Warren; ***D:*** Alan Rudolph.

Sonic Impact ½ **1999 (R)** Nutjob hijacks an airliner and threatens to crash it into the nearest large city. So a group of commandoes led by Nick Halton (Russo) makes plans to stop him. **94m/C VHS, DVD.** James Russo, Ice-T, Mel Harris; ***D:*** Rodney McDonald. **VIDEO**

Sonny and Jed *La Banda J.&S. Cronaca Criminale del Far West* **1973 (R)** An escaped convict and a free-spirited woman travel across Mexico pillaging freely, followed determinedly by shiny-headed lawman Savalas. Lame rip-off of the Bonnie and Clyde legend. **85m/C VHS.** *IT* Tomas Milian, Telly Savalas, Susan George, Rosanna Janni, Laura Betti; ***D:*** Sergio Corbucci; ***M:*** Ennio Morricone.

Sonny Boy woof! **1987 (R)** A transvestite and a psychopath adopt a young boy, training him to do their bidding, which includes murder. **96m/C VHS.** *IT* David Carradine, Paul Smith, Brad Dourif, Conrad Janis, Sydney Lassick, Savina Gersak, Alexandra Powers, Steve Carlisle, Michael Griffin; ***D:*** Robert Martin Carroll; ***W:*** Graeme Whifler; ***C:*** Roberto D'Ettorre Piazzoli; ***M:*** Carlo Maria Cordio.

Sonora Stagecoach **1944** Okay sagebrush saga with an interesting lineup; two cowboys, a heroic Indian, and a tough gal pilot escort a murder suspect in the title conveyance and manage to clear him when the real bad guys attack. **61m/B VHS.** Hoot Gibson, Bob Steele, Chief Thundercloud, Rocky Camron, Betty Miles, Glenn Strange, George Eldredge, Karl Hackett; ***D:*** Robert Emmett Tansey.

Sons **1991** A Vietnam veteran's son joins the military, causing strains within the family. **?m/C VHS.** ***D:*** Alexandre Rockwell; ***W:*** Alexandre Rockwell, Brandon Cole.

Sons of Katie Elder **1965** After their mother's death, four brothers are reunited. Wayne is a gunman; Anderson is a college graduate; silent Holliman is a killer; and Martin is a gambler. When they learn that her death might have been murder, they come together to devise a way to seek revenge on the killer. The town bullies complicate matters; the sheriff tells them to lay off. Especially strong screen presence by Wayne, in his first role following cancer surgery. One of the Duke's most popular movies of the '60s. **122m/C VHS, DVD, Wide.** John Wayne, Dean Martin, Earl Holliman, Michael Anderson Jr., Martha Hyer, George Kennedy, Dennis Hopper, Paul Fix, James Gregory; ***D:*** Henry Hathaway; ***W:*** Harry Essex, Allan Weiss, William Wright; ***C:*** Lucien Ballard; ***M:*** Elmer Bernstein.

Sons of Steel **1935** Two brothers, owners of a steel mill, lead vastly different lives. They raise their sons in their own images, causing problems. **65m/B VHS.** Charles Starrett, Polly Ann Young, William "Billy" Bakewell, Walter Walker, Aileen Pringle, Holmes Herbert, Florence Roberts, Adolf Millar, Lloyd Ingraham; ***D:*** Charles Lamont.

Sons of the Desert *Sons of the Legion; Convention City; Fraternally Yours* **1933** Laurel and Hardy in their best-written film. The boys try to fool their wives by pretending to go to Hawaii to cure Ollie of a bad cold when in fact, they are attending their lodge convention in Chicago. Also includes a 1935 Thelma Todd/Patsy Kelly short, "Top Flat." **73m/B VHS.** Stan Laurel, Oliver Hardy, Mae Busch, Charley Chase, Dorothy Christy; ***D:*** William A. Seiter.

Sons of the Pioneers 🦴🦴 **1942** Small town sheriff Hayes hires cowboy Roy to rid town of outlaws. **61m/B VHS.** Roy Rogers, George "Gabby" Hayes, Maris Wrixon, Forrest Taylor; ***D:*** Joseph Kane.

Sons of Trinity 🦴 **1995 (PG)** The two sons, Bambino (Neubert) and Trinity (Kizzier), of legendary cowpokes first meet when Bambino is about to be hung for horse thieving in the town of San Clementino. When Trinity gets his new friend off, they wind up as sheriff and deputy of the same town. Lots of physical comedy. **90m/C VHS.** Heath Kizzier, Keith Neubert, Ronald Nitschke, Siegfried Rauch; ***D:*** E.B. (Enzo Barboni) Clucher; ***C:*** Juan Amoros; ***M:*** Stefano Mainetti.

Sooner or Later 🦴½ **1978** 13-year-old girl passes herself off as 16 with a local rock idol and must decide whether to go all the way. **100m/C VHS.** Rex Smith, Judd Hirsch, Denise Miller, Morey Amsterdam, Lynn Redgrave; ***D:*** Bruce Hart. **TV**

Sophia Loren: Her Own Story 🦴🦴 **1980** Bio of Sophia Loren, watching her grow from a spindly child in working-class Naples to a world-renowned movie star, beauty queen, and mother. Loren plays herself and her mother in this tedious account. Based on the biography by A.E. Hotchner. **150m/C VHS.** Sophia Loren, Armand Assante, Ed Flanders, John Gavin; ***D:*** Mel Stuart; ***W:*** Joanna Crawford. **TV**

Sophie's Choice 🦴🦴🦴½ **1982 (R)** A haunting modern tragedy about Sophie Zawistowska, a beautiful Polish Auschwitz survivor settled in Brooklyn after WWII. She has intense relationships with a schizophrenic genius and an aspiring Southern writer. An artful, immaculately performed and resonant drama, with an astonishing, commanding performance by the versatile Streep; a chilling portrayal of the banality of evil. From the best-selling, autobiographical novel by William Styron. **157m/C VHS, DVD.** Meryl Streep, Kevin Kline, Peter MacNicol, Rita Karin, Stephen D. Newman, Josh Mostel; ***D:*** Alan J. Pakula; ***W:*** Alan J. Pakula; ***C:*** Nestor Almendros; ***M:*** Marvin Hamlisch. Oscars '82: Actress (Streep); Golden Globes '83: Actress—Drama (Streep); L.A. Film Critics '82: Actress (Streep); Natl. Bd. of Review '82: Actress (Streep); N.Y. Film Critics '82: Actress (Streep), Cinematog.; Natl. Soc. Film Critics '82: Actress (Streep).

Sophisticated Gents 🦴🦴🦴 **1981** Nine boyhood friends, members of a black athletic club, reunite after 25 years to honor their old coach and see how each of their lives has been affected by being black men in American society. Based on the novel "The Junior Bachelor Society" by John A. Williams. **200m/C VHS.** Paul Winfield, Roosevelt "Rosie" Grier, Bernie Casey, Raymond St. Jacques, Thalmus Rasulala, Dick Anthony Williams, Ron O'Neal, Rosalind Cash, Denise Nicholas, Alfre Woodard, Melvin Van Peebles; ***D:*** Harry Falk; ***W:*** Melvin Van Peebles. **TV**

Sorcerer 🦴🦴½ *Wages of Fear* **1977 (PG)** To put out an oil fire, four men on the run in South America agree to try to buy their freedom by driving trucks loaded with nitroglycerin over dangerous terrain—with many natural and man-made obstacles to get in their way. Remake of "The Wages of Fear" is nowhere as good as the classic original, but has exciting moments. Puzzlingly retitled, which may have contributed to the boxoffice failure, and the near demise of Friedkin's directing career. **121m/C VHS, DVD.** Roy Scheider, Bruno Cremer, Francesco Rabal, Soudad Amidou, Ramon Bieri; ***D:*** William Friedkin; ***W:*** Walon Green; ***C:*** Dick Bush, John Stephens; ***M:*** Tangerine Dream.

Sorceress woof! **1982 (R)** The Harris girls are sisters who use their powers of sorcery and fighting skills to battle demons, dragons, and evil. Yeah, sure. Really, they're just a pair of babes parading for the camera. **83m/C VHS.** Leigh Anne Harris, Lynette Harris, Bob Nelson, David Milbern, Bruno Rey, Anna De Sade; ***D:*** Brian Stuart; ***W:*** Jim Wynorski.

Sorceress 🦴🦴🦴 *Le Moine et la Sorcière* **1988** A friar in medieval Europe feels insecure in his religious beliefs after encountering a woman who heals through ancient practices. Historically authentic and interestingly moody. Written, produced, and directed by two women: an art history professor and a collaborator of Francois Truffaut's. In French with English subtitles or dubbed. **98m/C VHS.** *FR* Tcheky Karyo, Christine Boisson, Jean Carmet, Raoul Billerey, Catherine Frot, Feodor Atkine; ***D:*** Suzanne Schiffman; ***W:*** Pamela Berger, Suzanne Schiffman; ***C:*** Patrick Blossier.

Sorceress 🦴½ **1994 (R)** Larry Barnes (Poindexter) is on his way to a partnership at his law firm, especially since his wife Erica (Strain) eliminates his competition—permanently. But Erica goes after the wrong guy when she comes up against Howard Reynolds (Albert). Seems Howard's loving spouse Amelia (Blair) happens to be a witch and she has her own evil spells to cast. **93m/C VHS, DVD.** Julie Strain, Larry Poindexter, Linda Blair, Edward Albert; ***D:*** Jim Wynorski; ***W:*** Mark Thomas McGee; ***C:*** Gary Graver; ***M:*** Chuck Cirino, Darryl Way.

Sorority Babes in the Slimeball Bowl-A-Rama 🦴🦴 *The Imp* **1987 (R)** An ancient gremlin-type creature is released from a bowling alley, and the great-looking sorority babes have to battle it at the mall, with the help of a wacky crew of nerds. Horrible horror spoof shows plenty of skin. **80m/C DVD.** Linnea Quigley, Brinke Stevens, Andras Jones, John Wildman, Robin Rochelle, Michelle (McClellan) Bauer, George "Buck" Flower; ***D:*** David DeCoteau; ***W:*** Sergei Hasenecz; ***C:*** Scott Ressler, Stephen Blake; ***M:*** Guy Moon; ***V:*** Michael Sonye.

Sorority Boys 🦴 **2002 (R)** Three frat boys (Williams, Rosenbaum and Watson) become bosom buddies when they don don girlish garb to pass as sorority sisters in this contrived campus comedy. After being accused of a theft in their frat house, the badly disguised trio head to the notorious loser Delta Omega Gamma (DOG) house to stay in school. The boys teeter in their high heels, can't find dresses big enough for their ample "cabooses," and generally begin to understand the drag of being a gal while the film continues to serve up a kegful of gross-out and misogynist humor. Another in a string of misguided homages to "Animal House," with alums Daughton, Metcalf, Furst, and Vernon showing up for paychecks. Although Williams is considered to be the best of the three leads, all are terrible. Tepid romantic subplot with DOG house president doesn't help matters any. **93m/C VHS, DVD.** *US* Barry Watson, Michael Rosenbaum, Harland Williams, Melissa Sagemiller, Tony Denman, Brad Beyer, Heather Matarazzo, Kathryn Stockwood, Yvonne Scio; ***D:*** M. Wallace Wolodarsky; ***W:*** Joe Jarvis, Greg Coolidge; ***C:*** Michael D. O'Shea; ***M:*** Mark Mothersbaugh.

Sorority Girl 🦴½ **1957** Camp classic in which beautiful co-ed Cabot is presented as a malicious rich kid involved in everything from petty fights to blackmail. Cheap production from the Corman factory. **60m/B VHS.** Susan Cabot, Dick Miller, Barbara Crane, June Kenney, Fay Baker, Jeane Wood, Barboura Morris; ***D:*** Roger Corman; ***W:*** Leo Lieberman, Ed Waters; ***C:*** Monroe Askins; ***M:*** Ronald Stein.

Sorority House Massacre woof! **1986 (R)** A knife-wielding maniac stalks a sorority girl while her more elite sisters are away for the weekend. Yawn—haven't we seen this one before? Unfortunately for us we'll see it again because this one's followed by a sequel. **74m/C VHS, DVD.** Angela O'Neill, Wendy Martel, Pamela Ross, Nicole Rio; ***D:*** Carol Frank; ***W:*** Carol Frank; ***C:*** Marc Reshovsky; ***M:*** Michael Wetherwax.

Sorority House Massacre 2: Nighty Nightmare woof! **1992** Another no-brainer with a different cast and director. This time around three lingerie-clad lovelies are subjected to the terrors of a killer their first night in their new sorority house. College just keeps getting tougher all the time. **80m/C VHS, DVD.** Melissa Moore, Robin Harris, Stacia Zhivago, Dana Bentley, Shannon Wilsey; ***D:*** Jim Wynorski; ***W:*** James B. Rogers, Bob Sheridan; ***M:*** Chuck Cirino.

Sorority House Party 🦴 **1992 (R)** A famous rock guitarist is held against his will at the sexiest sorority house on campus. He definitely has mixed feelings about the experience considering the inhabitants saunter around in bikinis and "force" him to party with them. Anders and Attila are transplants from the modeling circuit. **95m/C VHS.** Attila, April Lerman, Kim Little, Avalon Anders, Joe Mundi, Rachel Latt, Mark Stulce, Michael Xavier; ***D:*** David Michael Latt; ***W:*** John Murdy, Steve Taylor.

Sorority House Vampires 🦴½ **1995** Sexy college coed Buffy fights to save her man and her sorority from Natalia, Queen of Darkness, and Count Vlad. **90m/C VHS.** Eugenie Bondurant, Robert Bucholz, Kathy Presgrave; ***D:*** Geoffrey de Valois. **VIDEO**

Sorrento Beach 🦴🦴 *Hotel Sorrento* **1995 (R)** A beachside community outside Melbourne, Australia, Sorrento is home to the Moynihans. The three Moynihan sisters—Meg (Goodall), Hillary (Gillmer), and Pippa (Morice)—are reunited after 10 years by their father's sudden death. Lots of tensions, rivalries, and jealousies come to the surface as well as old secrets regarding a family tragedy. Talky film hasn't quite cast off its stage origins (it's adapted from a play by Hannie Rayson) but the performances are noteworthy. **112m/C VHS.** *AU* Caroline Goodall, Caroline Gillmer, Tara Morice, Joan Plowright, John Hargreaves, Ray Barrett, Ben Thomas, Nicholas Bell; ***D:*** Richard Franklin; ***W:*** Richard Franklin, Peter Fitzpatrick, Hannie Rayson; ***C:*** Geoff Burton; ***M:*** Nerida Tyson-Chew. Australian Film Inst. '95: Adapt. Screenplay, Support. Actor (Barrett).

The Sorrow and the Pity 🦴🦴🦴½ **1971** A classic documentary depicting the life of a small French town and its resistance during the Nazi occupation. Lengthy, but totally compelling. A great documentary that brings home the atrocities of war. In French with English narration. **265m/B VHS, DVD, Wide.** *FR* Pierre Mendes-France, Sir Anthony Eden, Dr. Claude Levy, Denis Rake, Louis Grave, Maurice Chevalier; ***D:*** Marcel Ophuls; ***C:*** Mandre Gazut, Jurgen Thieme.

Sorrowful Jones 🦴🦴 **1949** A "Little Miss Marker" remake, in which bookie Hope inherits a little girl as collateral for an unpaid bet. Good for a few yuks, but the original is much better. **88m/B VHS.** Bob Hope, Lucille Ball, William Demarest, Bruce Cabot, Thomas Gomez, Mary Jane Saunders; ***D:*** Sidney Lanfield; ***W:*** Jack Rose, Melville Shavelson; ***C:*** Daniel F. Fapp.

Sorrows of Gin 🦴🦴½ **1979** Eight-year-old girl searches for a sense of family amid her parents' lives. Her efforts to deal with alienation and emotional isolation lead her to run away from home. From a short story by John Cheever. **60m/C VHS.** Edward Herrmann, Sigourney Weaver, Mara Hobel, Eileen Heckart, Rachel Roberts.

The Sorrows of Satan 🦴🦴🦴 **1926** Dempster and Cortez star as writers in love with each other, but Cortez can't take his poverty and the rejection of publishers. As he is about to end it all, the devil appears to him in disguise and makes an offer he can hardly refuse. He is introduced to London society and winds up marrying a fortune hunter. When he discovers this he goes back to Dempster, who still loves him, and vows to give up everything for her. Menjou then reveals himself to be the devil but Dempster's faith is so strong that the evil is vanquished. **111m/B VHS.** Adolphe Menjou, Carol Dempster, Ricardo Cortez, Lya de Putti; ***D:*** D.W. Griffith.

Sorry, Wrong Number 🦴🦴🦴½ **1948** A wealthy, bedridden wife overhears two men plotting a murder on a crossed telephone line, and begins to suspect that one of the voices is her husband's. A classic tale of paranoia and suspense. Based on a radio drama by Louise Fletcher, who also wrote the screenplay. Remade for TV in 1989. **89m/B VHS, DVD.** Barbara Stanwyck, Burt Lancaster, Ann Richards, Wendell Corey, Harold Vermilyea, Ed Begley Sr.; ***D:*** Anatole Litvak; ***W:*** Lucille Fletcher; ***C:*** Sol Polito; ***M:*** Franz Waxman.

Sorry, Wrong Number 🦴½ **1989** Cable remake of the 1948 Barbara Stanwyck thriller about a bed-ridden woman trying to get help after she realizes she's being stalked by a killer. Offers a new twist (drug dealing), but doesn't even approach the Stanwyck original. From the story by Lucille Fletcher. **90m/C VHS.** Loni Anderson, Hal Holbrook, Patrick Macnee, Miguel Fernandes, Carl Weintraub; ***D:*** Tony Wharmby; ***W:*** Ann Louise Bardach; ***M:*** Bruce Broughton. **CABLE**

S.O.S. Coast Guard 🦴🦴½ **1937** A fiendish scientist creates a disintegrating gas and the U.S. Coast Guard must stop him from turning it over to unfriendly foreigners. Loads of action in this 12-part serial. **224m/B VHS.** Ralph Byrd, Bela Lugosi, Maxine Doyle.

S.O.S. Pacific 🦴🦴 **1960** A seaplane crashes on a nuclear-test island and the survivors find that they have only five hours before they get nuked. Even though there is plenty of the usual action one would expect from such a film, the story really revolves around the characters. The British and U.S. versions have different endings. **91m/B VHS.** *GB* Eddie Constantine, Pier Angeli, Richard Attenborough, John Gregson, Eva Bartok; ***D:*** Guy Green.

S.O.S. Titanic 🦴🦴½ **1979** The story of the Titanic disaster, recounted in flashback, in docu-drama style. James Costigan's teleplay of the familiar story focuses on the courage that accompanied the horror and tragedy. Thoroughly professional, absorbing TV drama. **102m/C VHS, DVD, Wide.** *GB* Beverly Ross, David Janssen, Cloris Leachman, Susan St. James, David Warner, Ian Holm, Helen Mirren, Harry Andrews, David Battley, Ed Bishop, Peter Bourke, Shevaun Briars, Nick Brimble, Jacob Brooke, Catherine Byrne, Tony Caunter, Warren Clarke, Nicholas Davies, Deborah Fallender; ***D:*** Billy Hale; ***W:*** James Costigan; ***C:*** Christopher Challis; ***M:*** Howard Blake. **TV**

Sotto, Sotto 🦴🦴½ **1985 (R)** A minor Wertmuller comedy about an Italian businessman who is constantly suspicious of his wife's fidelity. As it happens, she's attracted to another woman (de Santis). Massimo Wertmuller is Lina's nephew. Entertaining. In Italian with English subtitles. **104m/C VHS.** *IT* Enrico Montesano, Veronica Lario, Massimo Wertmuller, Luisa de Santis; ***D:*** Lina Wertmuller; ***W:*** Lina Wertmuller.

Soul-Fire 🦴🦴 **1925** South Pacific high seas induce Cupid's arrow. Silent. **100m/B VHS.** Richard Barthelmess, Bessie Love, Walter Long, Arthur Metcalfe; ***D:*** John S. Robertson.

Soul Food 🦴🦴½ **1997 (R)** In between the mouth watering servings of fried-chicken, collard greens and catfish unfolds the lives of sisters Williams, Fox, and Long. They struggle to hold their family together by keeping up their mother's Sunday dinner tradition after she becomes ill. As mom's health deteriorates, so do the sisters' relationships with their significant others, turning things a bit soapy and predictable. Unfulfilling appetizer for those looking for a stark urban drama, but with an attractive ensemble cast which brings to life truthful characters, it's a hearty feast for those hungry for a heartwarming, contemporary tale. Warmth and humor won over audiences across color lines. Boasts many promising debuts, including director/writer Tillman and young narrator Hammond. Produced by music producer Kenneth (Babyface) Edmonds. **114m/C VHS, DVD, Wide.** Vanessa L(ynne) Williams, Vivica A. Fox, Nia Long, Michael Beach, Mekhi Phifer, Irma P. Hall, Jeffrey D. Sams, Gina Ravera, Brandon Hammond, Carl Wright, Mel Jackson, Morgan Michelle Smith, John M. Watson Sr.; ***D:*** George Tillman Jr.; ***W:*** George Tillman Jr.; ***C:*** Paul Elliott; ***M:*** Wendy Melvoin, Lisa Coleman.

Soul Hustler woof! **1976 (PG)** A con man becomes rich and famous as a tent-show evangelist. Pathetic drivel. **81m/C VHS.** Fabian, Casey Kasem, Larry Bishop, Nai Bonet; ***D:*** Burt Topper.

Soul Man 🦴🦴 **1986 (PG-13)** Denied the funds he expected for his Harvard tuition, a young white student (Howell) masquerades as a black in order to get a minority scholarship. As a black student at Harvard, Howell learns about racism and bigotry. Pleasant lightweight comedy with romance thrown in (Chong is the black girl he falls for), and with pretensions to social satire that it never achieves. **112m/C VHS, DVD, Wide.** C. Thomas Howell, Rae Dawn Chong, James Earl Jones, Leslie Nielsen, Arye Gross; ***D:*** Steve Miner; ***W:*** Carol Black; ***C:*** Jeffrey Jur; ***M:*** Tom Scott.

Soul of the Beast 🦴½ **1923** An elephant repeatedly saves Bellamy from the villainous Beery. Silent with original organ score. **77m/B VHS, 8mm.** Madge Bellamy, Cullen Landis, Noah Beery Sr.

Soul of the Game 🦴🦴🦴 **1996 (PG-13)** Cable movie follows the lives of three talented players in the Negro League during the 1945 season as they await the potential integration of baseball. Brooklyn Dodgers general manager Branch Rickey (Herrmann) has his scouts focusing on three men in particular: flashy, aging pitcher Satchel Paige (Lindo), mentally unstable catcher Josh Gibson (Williamson), and the young, college-educated Jackie Robinson (Underwood). Manages to resist melodrama through terrific performances. **105m/C VHS, DVD, Wide.** Delroy Lindo, Mykelti Williamson, Blair Underwood, Edward Herrmann, R. Lee Ermey, Gina Ravera, Salli Richardson, Obba Babatunde, Brent Jennings; ***D:*** Kevin Rodney Sullivan; ***W:*** David Himmelstein; ***C:*** Sandi Sissel; ***M:*** Lee Holdridge. **CABLE**

Soul Patrol 🦴 **1980 (R)** Black newspaper reporter clashes with the all-white police department in a racist city. **90m/C VHS.** Nigel Davenport, Ken Gampu, Peter Dyneley; ***D:*** Christopher Rowley.

Soul Survivor 🦴🦴½ **1995 (PG-13)** Set in Toronto's Jamaican community, this urban drama focuses on 20-something Tyrone (Williams) who's stuck in a custodial job and looking to make some easy money. He goes to work making collections for local gangster Winston (Harris), who tries to reassure his protege that money buys respect. But when Tyrone falls for straight-living social worker Annie (Scott), he begins to see the potholes in the path he's on. **89m/C VHS.** *CA* Peter Williams, George Harris, Judith Scott, Clark Johnson, David Smith; ***D:*** Stephen Williams; ***W:*** Stephen Williams; ***C:*** David Franco; ***M:*** John McCarthy.

Soul Survivors woof! **2001 (R)** Perhaps the worst slash and burn editing job in the history of film was used to chop this muddled horror flick from an R to a PG-13 rating. Cassie (Sagemiller) and her boyfriend Sean (Affleck) go to one last party with their friends Annabel (Dushku) and Matt (Bentley). The party is a nasty Goth rave held in a cathedral, seemingly run by juvenile delinquent vampires. Sean gets upset when he misinterprets an innocent kiss between Cassie and Matt, who is also her ex. On the way home, a distracted Cassie crashes the car while trying to iron things out with Sean, killing him. Or not, as the case may be, because Cassie keeps seeing her dead boyfriend wherever she goes. Also, she keeps being chased by creepy Goth skanks. So is Cassie crazy? Is Sean alive? Frankly, you won't care even if you make it to the end of this contorted mess. **85m/C VHS, DVD, Wide.** *US* Melissa Sagemiller, Wes Bentley, Casey Affleck, Eliza Dushku, Luke Wilson; ***D:*** Steve Carpenter; ***W:*** Steve Carpenter; ***C:*** Fred Murphy; ***M:*** Daniel Licht.

Soul Vengeance 🦴 *Welcome Home Brother Charles* **1975** Black man is jailed and brutalized for crime he didn't commit and wants revenge when he's released. Many afros and platform shoes. Vintage blaxploitation. **91m/C VHS.** Marlo Monte, Reatha Grey, Stan Kamber, Tiffany Peters, Ven Bigelow, Jake Carter; ***D:*** Jamaa Fanaka; ***W:*** Jamaa Fanaka.

The Souler Opposite 🦴🦴 **1997 (R)** Buddies Barry (Meloni) and Robert (Busfield) haven't grown up—especially where women are concerned. Most of struggling comic Barry's material is about his failed relationships while complacent, married Robert learns that his wife has decided she's a lesbian. Then sexist Barry meets feminist Thea (Moloney) and sparks fly—but can "souler" opposites really come together? First-time writer/director Kalmenson knows the territory since he's a stand-up comedian himself. **104m/C VHS, DVD, Wide.** Christopher Meloni, Timothy Busfield, Janel Moloney, Allison Mackie, John Putch, Rutanya Alda, Steve Landesberg; ***D:*** Bill Kalmenson; ***W:*** Bill Kalmenson; ***C:*** Amit Bhattacharya; ***M:*** Peter Himmelman.

Souls at Sea 🦴🦴½ **1937** Good buddy work by Cooper and Raft highlight this complicated seafaring yarn. In the 1840s sailor and abolitionist Nuggin Taylor (Cooper) is secretly sabotaging slave ships, working undercover for the British Navy. With loyal friend Powdah (Raft), Taylor tries to gather evidence against British officer Tarryton (Wilcoxon) even though he's fallen for Tarryton's sister Margaret (Dee). But after a sea disaster, Taylor's accused of murder and brought to trial. Will the truth come out in time to save him? **93m/B VHS.** Gary Cooper, George Raft, Henry Wilcoxon, Frances Dee, Olympe Bradna, George Zucco, Harry Carey Sr., Robert Cummings, Porter Hall, Joseph Schildkraut; ***D:*** Henry Hathaway; ***W:*** Grover Jones, Dale Van Every; ***C:*** Charles B(ryant) Lang Jr.

Soultaker 🦴½ **1990 (R)** The title spirit is after a young couple's souls, and they have just an hour to reunite with their bodies after a car crash. Meanwhile, they're in limbo (literally) between heaven and earth. The ending's OK, if you can make it that far. **94m/C VHS, DVD.** Joe Estevez, Vivian Schilling, Gregg Thomsen, David Shark, Jean Reiner, Chuck Williams, Robert Z'Dar; ***D:*** Michael Rissi; ***W:*** Vivian Schilling; ***C:*** James Rosenthal; ***M:*** John McCallum.

The Sound and the Silence 🦴🦴½ **1993** Bio of inventor Alexander Graham Bell (Bach). The Scottish Bell's father was a speech specialist and his beloved mother Eliza (Fricker) was severely hearing impaired. Bell himself trained to work with the deaf in Boston and experimented with transmitting speech electronically—a project which only grew when Bell married the deaf Mable Hubbard (Quinn). Bell's lifelong devotion lead to his development of the telephone as well as numerous other inventions (and his founding of "National Geographic" magazine). Bell was hardly a lively character but this TV drama is lavishly done. In two parts. **93m/C VHS.** John Bach, Elizabeth Quinn, Brenda Fricker, Ian Bannen; ***D:*** John Kent Harrison; ***W:*** Tony Foster, William Schmidt, John Kent Harrison; ***M:*** John Charles. **TV**

Sound of Horror 🦴½ *El Sonido de la Muerte; Sound From a Million Years Ago; The Prehistoric Sound* **1964** The Hound usually admires creative efforts to keep budgets down, but this is too much (or too little). A dinosaur egg hatches, and out lashes an invisible predator. Yes, you'll have to use your imagination as archaeologists are slashed to bits by the no-show terror. **85m/B VHS.** *SP* James Philbrook, Arturo Fernandez, Soledad Miranda, Ingrid Pitt; ***D:*** Jose Antonio Nieves-Conde.

Sound of Love 🦴 **1977** The mutual attraction between a deaf female hustler and a deaf race car driver leads to a deep relationship where they both learn about their own fears and desires. **74m/C VHS.** Celia de Burgh, John Jarratt.

Sound of Murder **1982** A successful children's book writer wants to exact revenge on his adulterous wife, but is himself murdered before he can "execute" his plan. **114m/C VHS.** Michael Moriarty, Joanna Miles.

The Sound of Music 🦴🦴🦴🦴 **1965** The classic film version of the Rodgers and Hammerstein musical based on the true story of the singing von Trapp family of Austria and their escape from the Nazis just before WWII. Beautiful Salzburg, Austria location photography and an excellent cast. Andrews, fresh from her Oscar for "Mary Poppins," is effervescent, in beautiful voice, but occasionally too good to be true. Not Rodgers & Hammerstein's most innovative score, but lovely to hear and see. Plummer's singing was dubbed by Bill Lee. Marni Nixon, behind-the-scenes songstress for "West Side Story" and "My Fair Lady," makes her on-screen debut as one of the nuns. ♫I Have Confidence In Me; Something Good; The Sound of Music; Preludium; Morning Hymn; Alleluia; How Do You Solve A Problem Like Maria?; Sixteen, Going on Seventeen; My Favorite Things. **174m/C VHS, DVD, Wide.** Julie Andrews, Christopher Plummer, Eleanor Parker, Peggy Wood, Charmian Carr, Heather Menzies, Marni Nixon, Richard Haydn, Anna Lee, Norma Varden, Nicholas Hammond, Angela Cartwright, Portia Nelson, Duane Chase, Debbie Turner, Kym Karath; ***D:*** Robert Wise; ***W:*** Ernest Lehman; ***C:*** Ted D. McCord; ***M:*** Richard Rodgers, Oscar Hammerstein. Oscars '65: Adapt. Score, Director (Wise), Film Editing, Picture, Sound; AFI '98: Top 100; Directors Guild '65: Director (Wise); Golden Globes '66: Actress—Mus./Comedy (Andrews), Film—Mus./Comedy, Natl. Film Reg. '01.

Sounder 🦴🦴🦴🦴 **1972 (G)** The struggles of a family of black sharecroppers in rural Louisiana during the Depression. When the father is sentenced to jail for stealing in order to feed his family, they must pull together even more, and one son finds education to be his way out of poverty. Tyson brings strength and style to her role, with fine help from Winfield. Moving and well made, with little sentimentality and superb acting from a great cast. Adapted from the novel by William Armstrong. **105m/C VHS.** Paul Winfield, Cicely Tyson, Kevin Hooks, Taj Mahal, Carmen Mathews, James Best, Janet MacLachlan; ***D:*** Martin Ritt; ***W:*** Lonnie Elder III; ***C:*** John A. Alonzo; ***M:*** Taj Mahal. Natl. Bd. of Review '72: Actress (Tyson); Natl. Soc. Film Critics '72: Actress (Tyson).

Sounds of Silence 🦴🦴 **1991** A young deaf boy fears that a killer arsonist may be at large—but can he prove it? One of a number of obscure oddities featuring former youth idol Donahue. **108m/C VHS.** Troy Donahue, Peter Nelson.

Soup for One 🦴🦴½ **1982 (R)** Writer-director Kaufer's first film is a solid entry in the Woody Allen-esque Manhattanite's angst genre. Young Jewish guy Rubinek pines for the woman of his dreams, finds her, is rejected, persists, gets her, wonders if she's what he wants after all. If you like Woody Allen, this is worth seeing. **84m/C VHS.** Saul Rubinek, Marcia Strassman, Gerrit Graham, Richard Libertini, Andrea Martin; ***D:*** Jonathan Kaufer.

Sour Grapes 🦴🦴 **1998 (R)** "Seinfeld" co-creator David's feature directorial debut has cousins Evan and Richie (Weber and Bierko) feuding over an Atlantic City slot machine jackpot. Evan, a successful neurosurgeon lends Richie, an extroverted loser, two quarters for one last pull on the slots. Of course, Richie wins $400,000. Escalating revenge schemes, petty greed, and quirky small talk scream sitcom episode, as do the TV quality production values, and lighting. The dialogue is biting and clever, but on the whole there's not enough here to justify 90 minutes of screen time. Robyn Peterman, the real-life daughter of J. Peterman, plays Richie's girlfriend. If you liked "Seinfeld," this flick's for you. **91m/C VHS, DVD.** Steven Weber, Craig Bierko, Karen Sillas, Matt Keeslar, Robyn Peterman, Jennifer Leigh Warren, Richard Gant, James MacDonald, Philip Baker Hall, Ann Guilbert; ***D:*** Larry David; ***W:*** Larry David; ***C:*** Victor Hammer.

Sourdough 🦴🦴 **1977** Fur trapper Perry escapes the hustle and bustle of modern life by fleeing to the Alaskan wilderness. Near-plotless travelog depends heavily on scenery—and there's plenty of that, for sure. **94m/C VHS.** Gil Perry, Charles Brock, Slim Carlson, Carl Clark; ***D:*** Martin J. Spinelli.

Sous Sol 🦴🦴 *Not Me* **1996** In 1967 Montreal, overly sensitive 11-year-old Rene (Moffatt) spies on his parents while they make love and the next morning learns his father has died. Rene becomes certain that sex leads to death, which puts a crimp in his budding sexuality. As a matter of fact he literally refuses to grow up, remaining in his pre-adolescent state for several years while Mom Reine (Portal) eventually hooks up with a new boyfriend Roch (Godin), who moves in. This causes a few more problems for Rene. French with subtitles. **90m/C VHS.** *CA* Louise Portal, Richard Moffatt, Isabelle Pasco, Patrice Godin; ***D:*** Pierre Gang; ***W:*** Pierre Gang; ***C:*** Pierre Mignot; ***M:*** Anne Bourne, Ken Myrh. Genie '96: Orig. Screenplay.

South Beach 🦴🦴 **1992 (R)** Two ex-football players turned private eyes are living the good life and partying it up in Miami Beach. However, their leisurely lifestyles are soon disrupted when they accept a mysterious challenge from the beautiful Vanity. **93m/C VHS.** Fred Williamson, Gary Busey, Vanity, Peter Fonda; ***D:*** Fred Williamson; ***W:*** Mark Montgomery; ***M:*** Joe Renzetti.

South Beach Academy 🦴 **1996 (R)** Eye candy focusing on a beach school that specializes in surfing, swimming, and volleyball rather than the usual academics. Maybe that's why the school's about to close—unless the lightly clad student body can come up with a plan to save their alma mater. **91m/C VHS.** Corey Feldman, Al Lewis, James Hong, Elizabeth Kaitan; ***D:*** Joe Esposito.

South Bronx Heroes 🦴½ *The Runaways; Revenge of the Innocents* **1985 (R)** A police officer helps two children when they discover their foster home is the headquarters for a pornography ring. **105m/C VHS, DVD.** Brendan Ward, Mario Van Peebles, Megan Van Peebles, Melissa Esposito, Martin Zurla, Jordan Abeles; ***D:*** William Szarka; ***W:*** William Szarka, Don Shiffrin; ***C:*** Eric Schmitz; ***M:*** Al Zima.

South Central 🦴🦴 **1992 (R)** A low-budget urban drama set in a gang-infested L.A. neighborhood. Bobby is a young black man, and former gang leader, who has spent ten years in prison for murder. His wife has become a drug addict and his young son Jimmie has begun running with his dad's old gang. Now paroled, Bobby hopes to re-establish the bond with his son—enough to protect him from following in his nowhere-to-go-but-down footsteps. Worthy effort with an emotional ending. Feature debut of director Anderson. Based on the novel "Crips" by Donald Bakeer. **99m/C VHS, DVD, Wide.** Glenn Plummer, Carl Lumbly, Christian Coleman, LaRita Shelby, Byron Keith Minns; ***D:*** Steve (Stephen M.) Anderson; ***W:*** Steve (Stephen M.) Anderson; ***C:*** Charlie Lieberman; ***M:*** Tim Truman.

South of Heaven, West of Hell 🦴½ **2000 (R)** A marshal (Yoakam), who once ran with an outlaw clan, must deal with his past when the bandits show up to terrorize the Arizona town he's sworn to protect. Yoakam's not much of a leading man and there's a lot of brutal violence to contend with. **133m/C VHS, DVD, Wide.** Dwight Yoakam, Bridget Fonda, Vince Vaughn, Billy Bob Thornton, Peter Fonda, Bud Cort, Michael Jeter, Paul (Pee-wee Herman) Reubens; ***D:*** Dwight Yoakam; ***W:*** Dwight Yoakam; ***C:*** James Glennon; ***M:*** Dwight Yoakam.

South of Hell Mountain 🦴½ **1970 (R)** On the run from a gold mine robbery where they left 20 dead, the McHenry brothers meet a mother-daughter team that slows them down. **87m/C VHS.** Ann Stewart, Sam Hall, Nicol Britton; ***D:*** William Sachs, Louis Leahman.

South of Monterey 🦴½ **1947** Western adventure with the Cisco kid. **63m/B VHS.** Gilbert Roland, Martin Garralaga, Frank Yaconelli, Marjorie (Reardon) Riordan; ***D:*** William Nigh.

South of Pago Pago 🦴🦴½ **1940** The unsuspecting natives of a tropical isle are exploited by a gang of pirates searching for a seabed of rare pearls. A notch up from most similar adventure outings, with great violent action and excellent cinematography. Leading lady Farmer was thought to be a rising star, but retired at 29 in 1942 because of alcoholism and spent some time in mental institutions. "Frances" (1982), with Jessica Lange, is based on her life. **98m/B VHS.** Victor McLaglen, Jon Hall, Frances Farmer, Gene Lockhart; ***D:*** Alfred E. Green.

South of Reno 🦴🦴½ **1987 (R)** A man living a secluded life in the desert dreams of moving to Reno and learns his wife is cheating on him. Odd, minimal plot. Impressive first feature for Polish diretor Rezyka, who cut his teeth on music videos. **98m/C VHS.** Jeffery Osterhage, Lisa Blount, Joe Phelan, Lewis Van Bergen, Julia Montgomery, Brandis Kemp, Danitza Kingsley, Mary Grace Canfield, Bert Remsen; *D:* Mark Rezyka; *M:* Nigel Holton.

South of St. Louis ♂♂½ **1948** A peaceful cattle rancher turns renegade gunrunner during the Civil War when his stock is destroyed by Union guerrillas. Overplotted but exciting and action-packed western, with Smith dazzling in a plethora of costumes. **88m/C VHS.** Joel McCrea, Zachary Scott, Victor Jory, Douglas Kennedy, Alexis Smith, Alan Hale, Dorothy Malone; *D:* Ray Enright; *C:* Karl Freund; *M:* Max Steiner.

South of Santa Fe ♂♂ **1932** Mexican rebels give the hero a hard time in this standard Western. **60m/B VHS.** Bob Steele, Janis Elliott, Chris-Pin (Ethier Crispin Martini) Martin, Jack Clifford, Eddie Dunn, Robert Burns, Hank Bell, Allan Garcia; *D:* Bert Glennon.

South of Santa Fe ♂♂ **1942** Rogers and friends take on the mob—yes, the mob, armed with machine guns and airplanes—after they are falsely implicated in a crime. In lulls between the rootin' tootin' gunfights, Rogers belts out "We're Headin' for the Home Corral," "Down the Trail," and "Open Range Ahead." **60m/B VHS.** Roy Rogers, George "Gabby" Hayes, Linda Hayes, Paul Fix, Judy Clark; *D:* Joseph Kane.

South of the Border ♂♂ **1939** Autry and Burnette are government agents sent to Mexico to investigate a possible revolution instigated by foreign agents. Propaganda-heavy singing western appeared just before the U.S. entered WWII; did well at the boxoffice and boosted Autry's career. **70m/B VHS.** Gene Autry, Smiley Burnette.

South of the Rio Grande ♂½ **1945** The Cisco Kid rides again as he comes to the aid of a rancher whose horses were stolen. Garden-variety law-and-order western. **60m/B VHS.** Duncan Renaldo; *D:* Lambert Hillyer.

South Pacific ♂♂♂½ **1958** A young American Navy nurse and a Frenchman fall in love during WWII. Expensive production included much location shooting in Hawaii. Based on Rodgers and Hammerstein's musical; not as good as the play, but pretty darn good still. The play in turn was based on James Michener's novel "Tales of the South Pacific." ♫My Girl Back Home; Dites-Moi; Bali Ha'i; Happy Talk; A Cockeyed Optimist; Soliloquies; Some Enchanted Evening; Bloody Mary; I'm Gonna Wash That Man Right Out of My Hair. **167m/C VHS, DVD, Wide.** Mitzi Gaynor, Rossano Brazzi, Ray Walston, France Nuyen, John Kerr, Juanita Hall, Tom Laughlin; *D:* Joshua Logan; *W:* Paul Osborn; *C:* Leon Shamroy; *M:* Richard Rodgers, Oscar Hammerstein; *V:* Giorgio Tozzi. Oscars '58: Sound.

South Park: Bigger, Longer and Uncut ♂♂½ **1999 (R)** The most unlikely critical darling of the summer of 1999 caught everyone's attention with it's MPAA-baiting language and sexual subject matter, and made audiences laugh—a lot—along the way. Stan, Kenny, Cartman, and Kyle sneak into an R-rated movie and shock their families with what they learn. So, concerned South Park parents form a censorship board to take on Canada (which results in a war, with enough bloody violence to make Sam Peckinpah sick, but didn't faze the MPAA), and the kids decide to fight back. Like most TV shows adapted for the big screen, this one flags at times, but has enough inspired comic moments to (mostly) justify the hype. The easily offended should definitely pass. **80m/C VHS, DVD, Wide.** *D:* Trey Parker; *W:* Trey Parker, Matt Stone, Pam Brady; *M:* Marc Shaiman, Trey Parker; *V:* Trey Parker, Matt Stone, Isaac Hayes, George Clooney, Minnie Driver, Mike Judge, Eric Idle, Mary Kay Bergman, Brent Spiner, Nick Rhodes, Stewart Copeland.

South Riding ♂♂½ **1937** Estate owner Robert Carne (Richardson) lives with teenaged daughter Midge (Johns) and has money woes from keeping ill wife Madge (Todd) in a mental hospital. A city councilman as well, Carne's drawn into a plan that will supposedly built decent housing for the lower classes but is actually a scam (which he discovers). Adapted from the novel by Winifred Holtby. **85m/B VHS.** *GB* Ralph Richardson, John Clements, Edna Best, Glynis Johns, Ann Todd, Edmund Gwenn, Marie Lohr, Milton Rosmer; *D:* Victor Saville; *W:* Ian Dalrymple; *C:* Harry Stradling Sr.; *M:* Richard Addinsell.

South Seas Massacre woof! **19??** A cop and a prisoner, shackled together, try to survive modern-day pirates, natives, and each other. They may make it through, but viewers may wish they didn't. **60m/C VHS.** Troy Donahue; *D:* Pablo Santiago.

Southern Comfort ♂♂♂ **1981 (R)** A group of National Guardsmen are on weekend maneuvers in the swamps of Louisiana. They run afoul of some of the local Cajuns, and are marked for death in this exciting and disturbing thriller. Boothe is excellent in a rare exploration of a little-understood way of life. Lots of blood. If you belong to the National Guard, this could make you queasy. **106m/C VHS, DVD, Wide.** Ned Dowd, Powers Boothe, Keith Carradine, Fred Ward, Franklyn Seales, Brion James, T.K. Carter, Peter Coyote; *D:* Walter Hill; *W:* David Giler, Michael Kane, Walter Hill; *M:* Ry Cooder.

A Southern Yankee ♂♂½ *My Hero* **1948** Skelton plays a bumbling bellboy who ends up as a Union spy during the Civil War. Enjoyable comedy, thanks largely to the off-screen input of Buster Keaton. **90m/B VHS.** Red Skelton, Brian Donlevy, Arlene Dahl, George Coulouris, Lloyd Gough, John Ireland, Minor Watson, Charles Dingle, Art Baker, Reed Hadley, Arthur Space, Addison Richards, Joyce Compton, Paul Harvey, Jeff Corey; *D:* Edward Sedgwick.

The Southerner ♂♂♂♂ **1945** A man used to working for others is given some land by an uncle and decides to pack up his family and try farming for himself. They find hardships as they struggle to support themselves. A superb, naturalistic celebration of a family's fight to survive amid all the elements. From the story "Hold Autumn in Your Hand," by George Sessions Perry. Novelist Faulkner had an uncredited hand in the script. He thought Renoir the best contemporary director, and later said "The Southerner" gave him more pleasure than any of his other Hollywood work (though this is faint praise; Faulkner is said to have hated Hollywood). **91m/B VHS, DVD, 8mm.** Zachary Scott, Betty Field, Beulah Bondi, Norman Lloyd, Bunny Sunshine, Jay Gilpin, Estelle Taylor, Blanche Yurka, Percy Kilbride, J. Carrol Naish; *D:* Jean Renoir; *W:* Jean Renoir, Hugo Butler, William Faulkner; *C:* Lucien N. Andriot; *M:* Werner Janssen. Natl. Bd. of Review '45: Director (Renoir); Venice Film Fest. '46: Film.

Southie ♂♂ **1998 (R)** Another return of the native son drama offers some decent performances but nothing much that is new. Danny Quinn (Wahlberg) is a South Boston bad boy returning to home turf after a sojourn in New York. Danny's pals are tied up with one Irish gangster crew while his own family is involved with oldtimer Colie (Tierney) and Danny himself has a score to settle with longtime rival, Joey (Cummings). **95m/C VHS, DVD.** Donnie Wahlberg, Rose McGowan, Lawrence Tierney, James (Jimmy) Cummings, Anne Meara, Amanda Peet, John Shea; *D:* John Shea; *W:* James (Jimmy) Cummings, John Shea, Dave McLaughlin; *C:* Allen Baker; *M:* Wayne Sharp.

Southward Ho! ♂♂ **1939** In the first western to team Rogers with sidekick Gabby Hayes, they portray ranchers investigating bloodshed in their valley, Roy meanwhile yodelin' four tunes. Fun outing. **56m/B VHS.** Roy Rogers, George "Gabby" Hayes.

Souvenir ♂♂ **1988 (R)** A German soldier returns to France after WWII to find the woman he left behind and the daughter he never saw. Might have been good, but too melodramatic and overwrought, with lukewarm acting. **93m/C VHS.** Christopher Plummer, Catherine Hicks, Christopher Cazenove, Michael (Michel) Lonsdale; *D:* Geoffrey Reeve.

Soylent Green ♂♂½ **1973 (PG)** In the 21st Century, hard-boiled police detective Heston investigates a murder and discovers what soylent green—the people's principal food—is made of. Robinson's final film is a disappointing end to a great career. Its view of the future and of human nature is relentlessly dark. Don't watch it with kids. **95m/C VHS.** Charlton Heston, Leigh Taylor-Young, Chuck Connors, Joseph Cotten, Brock Peters, Paula Kelly, Edward G. Robinson, Stephen Young, Whit Bissell, Dick Van Patten; *D:* Richard Fleischer; *W:* Stanley R. Greenberg; *C:* Richard H. Kline; *M:* Fredric Myrow.

Space Cowboys ♂♂♂ **2000 (PG-13)** Eastwood, starring and directing again, plays a retired Air Force pilot who was passed over for the astronaut training program in the late 1950s. However, now NASA needs his expertise when an ailing 1960's satellite poses a threat if it crashes to Earth. He agrees to go into space and repair it only if he can bring his equally codgerly buddies, Sutherland, Jones, and Garner, to assist. Hey, if John Glenn can go back into space at age 77, why not Eastwood? Fun ensemble piece that successfully weaves some action and thrills into the final act. **123m/C VHS, DVD, Wide.** Clint Eastwood, Tommy Lee Jones, James Garner, James Cromwell, Donald Sutherland, Marcia Gay Harden, Loren Dean, William Devane, Rade Serbedzija, Courtney B. Vance, Barbara Babcock, Blair Brown; *D:* Clint Eastwood; *W:* Ken Kaufman, Howard Klausner; *C:* Jack N. Green; *M:* Lennie Niehaus.

Space Jam ♂♂½ **1996 (PG)** Expensive live action-animation combo finds basketball great Jordan forced to play ball against evil intergalatic invaders who are out to capture Bugs Bunny and the rest of the Looney Tunes characters. It's all fairly silly but the kids will enjoy it. **87m/C VHS, DVD.** Michael Jordan, Bill Murray, Wayne Knight, Theresa Randle; *D:* Joe Pytka; *C:* Michael Chapman; *M:* James Newton Howard; *V:* Danny DeVito.

Space Marines ♂½ **1996 (R)** Cheesy cable thriller finds intergalactic marines battling 21st century space pirates who've stolen a nuclear cargo and taken hostages. **93m/C VHS.** Billy Wirth, John Pyper-Ferguson, Meg Foster, Edward Albert, James Shigeta, Cady Huffman; *D:* John Weidner; *C:* Garett Griffin. CABLE

Space Monster woof! *First Woman into Space; Voyage beyond the Sun* **1964** Really bad, low-budget flick with a rubber monster and a climactic crash into a "sea of monsters" which is really a fish tank full of crabs. Ultra cheap production with handed down cast and props. **80m/B VHS.** Russ Bender, Francine York, James Brown, Baynes Barron; *D:* Marlin Skiles; *W:* Marlin Skiles; *C:* Leonard Katzman; *M:* Robert Tobey.

Space Mutiny ♂ **1988 (PG)** Spaceship falls under the attack of the mutinous Kalgan. To keep everyone from being sold into slavery, a small band of loyal passengers strike back. Will they be successful in thwarting the attack? Who cares? **93m/C VHS.** Reb Brown, James Ryan, John Phillip Law, Cameron Mitchell; *D:* David Winters; *W:* Maria Dante.

Space Rage ♂ *Trackers* **1986 (R)** A criminal sentenced to life on a prison planet leads a revolt of the inmates. Lame, formula western set in outer space. **78m/C VHS.** Michael Pare, Richard Farnsworth, John Laughlin, Lee Purcell; *D:* Conrad Palmisano.

Space Raiders ♂♂ *Star Child* **1983 (PG)** A plucky 10-year-old blasts off into a futuristic world of intergalactic desperados, crafty alien mercenaries, starship battles and cliff-hanging dangers. Recycled special effects (from producer Corman's movie factory) and plot (lifted near-whole from "Star Wars"). **84m/C VHS.** Vince Edwards, David Mendenhall; *D:* Howard R. Cohen; *W:* Howard R. Cohen.

Space Riders woof! **1983 (PG)** Action-adventure about the world's championship motorcycle race, with a rock soundtrack featuring Duran Duran, Simple Minds and Melba Moore. **93m/C VHS.** Barry Sheene, Gavan O'Herlihy, Toshiya Ito, Stephanie McLean, Sayo Inaba; *D:* Joe Massot.

Space Soldiers Conquer the Universe ♂♂ **1940** Edited version of the Flash Gordon serial "Flash Gordon Conquers the Universe." The evil Emperor Ming introduces a horrible plague from outer space called "The Purple Death." Dr. Zarkov, Dale, and Flash Gordon travel from the frozen wastes of Frigia to the palaces of Mongo and must take risk after risk. Twelve chapters at 20 minutes each. **240m/B VHS.** Buster Crabbe, Charles Middleton, Carol Hughes.

Space Truckers ♂♂ **1997 (PG-13)** Sci-fi spoof about space haulage-truckers in the 21st century. Veteran hauler John Canyon (Hopper) accepts a dangerous assignment when he agrees to transport some sealed containers to Earth—no questions asked. Canyon, girlfriend Cindy (Mazar), and newbie driver Mike (Dorff) have their ship boarded by space pirates, led by Capt. Macaunudo (Dance), who's part-machine. The cargo turns out to be murderous androids, sent to conquer Earth. Canyon and his crew must perform various heroics to save the planet! Lots of campy bad taste. **97m/C VHS, DVD.** *IR* Dennis Hopper, Stephen Dorff, Charles Dance, Debi Mazar, George Wendt, Shane Rimmer, Vernon Wells, Barbara Crampton; *D:* Stuart Gordon; *W:* Ted Mann; *C:* Mac Ahlberg; *M:* Colin Towns.

Spaceballs ♂♂½ **1987 (PG)** A humorous Brooks parody of recent science fiction pictures, mostly notably "Star Wars," with references to "Alien," the "Star Trek series," and "The Planet of the Apes." Disappointingly tame and tentative, but chuckle-laden enough for Brooks fans. The great man himself appears in two roles, including puny wise man/wise guy Yogurt. **96m/C VHS, DVD, Wide.** Mel Brooks, Rick Moranis, John Candy, Bill Pullman, Daphne Zuniga, Dick Van Patten, John Hurt, George Wyner, Joan Rivers, Lorene Yarnell, Sal Viscuso, Stephen Tobolowsky, Dom DeLuise, Michael Winslow; *D:* Mel Brooks; *W:* Mel Brooks, Ronny Graham, Thomas Meehan; *M:* John Morris.

SpaceCamp ♂♂ **1986 (PG)** Gang o'teens and their instructor at the U.S. Space Camp are accidentally launched on a space shuttle, and then must find a way to return to Earth. Hokey plot, subpar special effects; why bother? Well, it is "inspirational." **115m/C VHS.** Kate Capshaw, Tate Donovan, Joaquin Rafael (Leaf) Phoenix, Kelly Preston, Larry B. Scott, Tom Skerritt, Lea Thompson, Terry O'Quinn; *D:* Harry Winer; *M:* John Williams.

Spaced Invaders ♂½ **1990 (PG)** Five ultra-cool aliens crash-land in a small midwestern town at Halloween. Local denizens mistake them for trick-or-treaters. Poorly made and a waste of time. **102m/C VHS.** Douglas Barr, Royal Dano, Ariana Richards, Kevin Thompson, Jimmy Briscoe, Tony Cox, Debbie Lee Carrington, Tommy Madden; *D:* Patrick Read Johnson; *W:* Scott Lawrence Alexander; *C:* James L. Carter.

Spaced Out woof! *Outer Reach* **1980 (R)** Naughty sci-fi sex comedy that parodies everything from "Star Wars" to "2001," though not very well. The sultry female aliens are visually pleasing, though. Watch this one with the sound turned off. **85m/C VHS.** Barry Stokes, Glory Annen; *D:* Norman J. Warren.

Spacehunter: Adventures in the Forbidden Zone ♂½ **1983 (PG)** Galactic bounty hunter agrees to rescue three damsels held captive by a cyborg. Strauss ain't no Harrison Ford. Filmed in 3-D, but who cares? **90m/C VHS, DVD, Wide.** *CA* Peter Strauss, Molly Ringwald, Michael Ironside, Ernie Hudson, Andrea Marcovicci; *D:* Lamont Johnson; *W:* Len Blum; *C:* Frank Tidy; *M:* Elmer Bernstein.

Spacejacked ♂½ **1998 (R)** In the future, the wealthy take pleasure trips to the Moon. Only greedy Barnes (Bernsen) sabotages the ship in order to extort money from the passengers—promising them a safe passage home in the escape pod. Of course, Barnes tries to double-cross everyone. Filled with low-budget cliches. **89m/C VHS.** Corbin Bernsen, Amanda Pays, Steve Bond; *D:* Jeremiah Cullinane; *W:* Brendan Broderick, Daniella Purcell; *C:* Laurence Manly; *M:* Siobhan Cleary.

Spaceship ♂½ *The Creature Wasn't Nice; Naked Space* **1981 (PG)** Misguided attempt to spoof creature-features. Mad scientist tries to protect kindly monster from crazed crew. Not very funny, with the exception of the song-and-dance routine by the monster. **88m/C VHS.** Cindy Williams, Bruce Kimmel, Leslie Nielsen, Gerrit Graham, Patrick Macnee, Ron Kurowski; *D:* Bruce Kimmel.

Spaceways 🦴½ **1953** Scientist Duff is beset by all sorts of troubles: his experimental rockets explode, his wife has an affair with an ambitious scientist, and when they disappear together, he's accused of killing them and placing their bodies in the exploded rocket. All in all, a pretty bad (and long) day for our hero. Why should we suffer through it with him? **76m/B VHS, DVD.** Howard Duff, Eva Bartok, Ceclie Cheyreau, Andrew Osborn; ***D:*** Terence Fisher; ***W:*** Richard H. Landau, Paul Tabori; ***C:*** Reg Wyer; ***M:*** Ivor Stanley.

Spaghetti House 🦴½ **1982** A handful of waiters are held hostage by ruthless killers in this innocuous but worthless Italian comedy. Dubbed. **103m/C VHS.** *IT* Nino Manfredi, Rita Tushingham; ***D:*** Giullo Paradisi.

Spaghetti Western 🦴½ **1969** A farmer and a publisher take on the vile oil baron who is taking over the town. A parody—or is it?—of Eastwoodian B-grade spaghetti westerns. No director credited. **90m/C VHS.** Franco Nero, Martin Balsam, Sterling Hayden.

Spalding Gray: Terrors of Pleasure **1988** The ultra-cool Gray tells the story of one man's dream to own land in his own inimitable way. HBO comedy special. **60m/C VHS.** Spalding Gray; ***D:*** Thomas Schlamme.

Spangles 🦴 **1926** Silent circus drama. **58m/B VHS.** Marion (Marian) Nixon, Hobart Bosworth, Pat O'Malley, Gladys Brockwell; ***D:*** Frank O'Connor.

The Spaniard's Curse 🦴🦴½ **1958** When a man is convicted for a murder he did not commit, he puts a curse on the judge and jury responsible. Mysteriously, the marked people begin dying. Is he responsible? Then he dies and the mystery thickens. Intriguing but sloppy murder mystery. **80m/B VHS.** *GB* Tony Wright, Lee Patterson, Michael Hordern, Ralph Truman, Henry Oscar; ***D:*** Ralph Kemplen.

The Spanish Gardener 🦴🦴🦴 **1957** A boy in a prominent family spends more time with the gentle gardner than with the domineering father, so dad arranges for his rival to be framed and sent to prison. An affecting British adaptation of the A.J. Cronin novel, turned into a showcase for Bogarde in the title role. **95m/C VHS.** Dirk Bogarde, Jon Whiteley, Michael Hordern, Cyril Cusack, Maureen Swanson, Lyndon Brook, Josephine Griffin, Bernard Lee; ***D:*** Philip Leacock.

Spanish Judges 🦴½ **1999 (R)** Boring crime drama set in L.A. finds three criminals—muscle Max (D'Onofrio), brains Jack (Lillard), and vamp Jamie (Golino)—looking to steal a couple of valuable Spanish pistols. Yes, it does sound roughly like the plot to "The Mexican" but this film is much worse. **98m/C VHS, DVD, Wide.** Vincent D'Onofrio, Matthew Lillard, Valeria Golino, Sam Hiona; ***D:*** Oz Scott; ***W:*** William Rehor; ***C:*** Stephen McNutt.

The Spanish Main 🦴🦴½ **1945** Typical, gusto-laden swashbuckler, RKO's first in Technicolor. Evil Spanish governor Slezak captures Dutch crew led by Henreid. They escape and kidnap his fiancee (O'Hara) off a ship coming from Mexico. Henreid forces her to marry him, but his crew uses the might of the armada and returns O'Hara to Slezak behind Henreid's back. Wow! **100m/C** Paul Henreid, Maureen O'Hara, Walter Slezak, Binnie Barnes, John Emery, Barton MacLane; ***D:*** Frank Borzage; ***C:*** George Barnes.

The Spanish Prisoner 🦴🦴🦴 **1997 (PG)** Playwright-filmmaker Mamet goes Hitchcockian in his latest thriller involving an elaborate con game. Naive inventor Joe Ross (Scott) develops a formula for something called "the Process" and soon finds himself a victim of industrial espionage. In a bit of stunt casting that works, Martin plays a sinister, wealthy businessman who befriends Joe and advises him about his corporate employers. No one is what they appear to be (if they were, it wouldn't be much of a thriller) in this unpredictable and seductive puzzle. Although the staccato dialogue is grating at times, and the emotional payoff is slight, there's enough twists throughout to keep you intrigued. Title comes from an old scam that feeds on the greed and lust of the mark. **112m/C VHS, DVD.** Campbell Scott, Steve Martin, Rebecca Pidgeon, Ben Gazzara, Ricky Jay, Felicity Huffman, Ed O'Neill; ***D:*** David Mamet; ***W:*** David Mamet; ***C:*** Gabriel Beristain; ***M:*** Carter Burwell.

Spanking the Monkey 🦴🦴🦴 **1994 (R)** "What'd ya do on your summer vacation?" Ray Aibelli (Davies) has an interesting answer in this dark comedy about family dysfunction, sexual politics, incest and masturbation, topics which guarantee it a special place on the video shelf. Returning from his freshman year at M.I.T., Ray learns he must give up a prestigious internship to care for his bedridden mother (Watson) while Dad goes on an extended "business" trip. Much sexual and emotional confusion follows. Mom, it seems, is rather attractive, controlling, and in need of hands-on assistance. Black comedy is understated and sensitive, focusing attention on the story and characters rather than the delicate subject matter, but you'll be aware of the delicate subject matter, nonetheless. Sharp directorial debut by Russell features fine performances by mostly unknown cast, elevating low-budget feel. See it with a relative. **99m/C VHS.** Jeremy Davies, Alberta Watson, Benjamin Hendrickson, Carla Gallo, Matthew Puckett; ***D:*** David O. Russell; ***W:*** David O. Russell; ***C:*** Mike Mayers. Ind. Spirit '95: First Feature, First Screenplay; Sundance '94: Aud. Award.

Spare Me 🦴🦴½ **1992** Family and personal dysfunction mark the long-awaited home video debut of Harrison's cult fave "bowling noir" debut film. Theo (Paseka) is put on suspension from the Pro Bowler's Tour for attacking an opponent with his bowling ball. He searches out his bowling-legend father, Buzz (Alfred), who might be able to help him out. Along the way he meets and falls for a pyromaniac waitress (MacFayden), whose father is evil bowling kingpin Miles Kastle, and her brother is escaped psycho patient Junior. When Theo finds Pop, he's in cahoots with Miles, helping him run an illegal midget bowling circuit. Harrison's excellent low-budget direction, and a hilarious, if completely twisted script, enables this one to pick up the difficult 7-10 split of cinematic success. **85m/C VHS.** Mark Alfred, Christopher Cook, Lawton Paseka, Christopher Grimm, Christie MacFadyen, Richard W. Sears Jr., Bill Christ, Sean Haggerty; ***D:*** Matthew Harrison; ***W:*** Christopher Grimm, Matthew Harrison; ***C:*** Mike Mayers; ***M:*** Danny Brenner.

Spare Parts woof! **1985** Guests at a remote hotel discover that it is run by black marketeers who kill guests and sell the body parts. Of course, they don't bother signing out. **108m/C VHS.** Judith Speidel, Wolf Roth.

Sparkle 🦴🦴½ **1976 (PG)** The saga of three singing sisters struggling to rise to the top of the charts in the 1950s. Sound familiar? Well done but cliched fictional version of the Supremes' career. McKee shines. Alcohol, drugs, and mobsters get in the way. Excellent musical score. **98m/C VHS.** Irene Cara, Lonette McKee, Dwan Smith, Philip Michael Thomas, Mary Alice, Dorian Harewood, Tony King; ***D:*** Sam O'Steen; ***W:*** Joel Schumacher; ***M:*** Curtis Mayfield.

Sparkler 🦴🦴½ **1999 (R)** Effervescemt Melba May (Overall) is a trailer-park wife, living just off the highway to Vegas. She leaves husband, Flint (Harvey), for cheating on her and eventually winds up in Vegas with three young men she just met and her old high-school buddy Dottie (Cartwright), who's now a stripper. And everybody gets an education of sorts. Doesn't have a consistent tone, with Overall and Cartwright providing the best performances. **96m/C VHS.** Park Overall, Veronica Cartwright, Jamie Kennedy, Steven Petrarca, Freddie Prinze Jr., Don Harvey, Grace Zabriskie, Sandy Martin; ***D:*** Darren Stein; ***W:*** Darren Stein, Catherine Eads; ***C:*** Rodney Taylor; ***M:*** David E. Russo.

Sparrows 🦴🦴🦴 **1926** Hidden in a southern swamp, the evil Grimes (von Seyffertz) runs a baby farm, where unwanted children are sent and used a slave labor. The eldest, nicknamed Mama Mollie (Pickford), tries to protect the others from Grimes's cruelty. They eventually plan their escape but must cross treacherous quicksand with Grimes in pursuit. Silent melodrama features a notable performance by Pickford. **109m/B VHS, DVD.** Mary Pickford, Gustav von Seyffertitz, Charlotte Mineau, Roy Stewart, Mary Louise Miller, "Spec" (Walter) O'Donnell, Mary Frances McLean, Camilla Johnson, Seesel Ann Johnson; ***D:*** William Beaudine; ***W:*** C. Gardner Sullivan, Winifred Dunn; ***C:*** Charles Rosher, Karl Struss, Hal Mohr; ***M:*** William Perry.

Spartacus 🦴🦴🦴🦴 **1960 (PG-13)** The true story of a gladiator who leads other slaves in a rebellion against the power of Rome in 73 B.C. The rebellion is put down and the rebels are crucified. Douglas, whose political leanings are amply on display herein, also served as executive producer, surrounding himself with the best talent available. Magnificent climactic battle scene features 8,000 real, live Spanish soldiers to stunning effect. A version featuring Kubrick's "director's cut" is also available, featuring a restored, controversial homoerotic bath scene with Olivier and Curtis. Anthony Mann is uncredited as co-director. A boxoffice triumph that gave Kubrick much-desired financial independence. **196m/C VHS, DVD, Wide.** Kirk Douglas, Laurence Olivier, Jean Simmons, Tony Curtis, Charles Laughton, Herbert Lom, Nina Foch, Woody Strode, Peter Ustinov, John Gavin, John Ireland, Charles McGraw, Joanna Barnes; ***D:*** Stanley Kubrick; ***W:*** Dalton Trumbo; ***C:*** Russell Metty; ***M:*** Alex North. Oscars '60: Art Dir./Set Dec., Color, Color Cinematog., Costume Des. (C), Support. Actor (Ustinov); Golden Globes '61: Film—Drama.

Spasms woof! *Death Bite* **1982 (R)** Reed is the unfortunate big game hunter who encounters The Demon Serpent, known as N'Gana Simbu, the deadliest snake in the world. Lame-brained horror fantasy; the producers should have released the nifty Tangerine Dream soundtrack and chucked the movie. Based on the novel "Death Bite" by Michael Maryk and Brent Monahan. **92m/C VHS.** *CA* Peter Fonda, Oliver Reed, Kerrie Keane, Al Waxman, Miguel Fernandes, Marilyn Lightstone, Laurie Brown, Gerard Parkes; ***D:*** William Fruet; ***W:*** Don Enright.

Spawn 🦴🦴🦴 **1997 (PG-13)** Government agent Al Simmons (White) returns to earth, six years after being murdered, in the form of Spawn, a hell-born creature with supernatural powers. He wants to avenge his death and also save his loved ones from the evil Violator (Leguizamo). With green eyes and a friendship with Satan, Spawn's more of a lethal weapon and way more sinister looking than the villain. An unrecognizable Leguizamo and sleazy Sheen team up as adequate adversaries. Extravagant special effects, and a complex, dark story put a unique spin on the over-exposed superhero premise. Adapted from the best-selling comic book. An R-rated director's cut, which includes a "making of" feature and an interview with Todd McFarlane, is also available. **97m/C VHS, DVD.** Michael (Mike) Papajohn, Michael Jai White, John Leguizamo, Martin Sheen, Theresa Randle, D.B. Sweeney, Nicol Williamson, Melinda (Mindy) Clarke, Miko Hughes; ***D:*** Mark Dippe; ***W:*** Alan B. McElroy; ***C:*** Guillermo Navarro; ***M:*** Graeme Revell.

Spawn of the North 🦴🦴½ **1938** Alaska's the final frontier in the early 1900s as fisherman Jim Kimmerlee (Fonda) tries to earn an honest buck. But former friend Tyler Dawson (Raft) has joined a group of Russian pirates who plunder the nets of others and the two men are forced into a deadly confrontation. Solid cast, weak script, and a special Oscar for photographic and sound effects (a glacier's involved). Based on the novel by Barrett Willoughby; remade in 1954 as "Alaska Seas." **110m/B VHS.** Henry Fonda, George Raft, Dorothy Lamour, John Barrymore, Akim Tamiroff, Louise Platt, Fuzzy Knight, Duncan Renaldo; ***D:*** Henry Hathaway; ***W:*** Jules Furthman, Talbot Jennings; ***C:*** Charles B(ryant) Lang Jr.; ***M:*** Dimitri Tiomkin.

The Spawning 🦴 **1982 (R)** The sequel to "Piranha." At Club Elysium the main course is the vacationers themselves. **88m/C VHS.** Steve Marachuk; ***D:*** James Cameron.

Speak Easily 🦴🦴½ **1932** Keaton is bored with his dull life as a college professor. Durante tries to spice things up with a phony inheritance letter, and Keaton decides to spend his supposed money backing a stage show. Keaton is the star, but Durante steals the show. Great supporting cast. **82m/B VHS.** Buster Keaton, Jimmy Durante, Ruth Selwyn, Thelma Todd, Hedda Hopper, Sidney Toler, Lawrence Grant, Henry Armetta, Edward Brophy; ***D:*** Edward Sedgwick.

Speak of the Devil 🦴 **1990** A New Orleans evangelist who seduces his followers moves to Los Angeles and strikes a bargain with Satan. Exploitative, unthinking spoof of Swaggart/Bakker scandals of recent years. **99m/C VHS.** Robert Elarton, Jean Miller, Bernice Tamara Goor, Louise Sherill, Walter Kay, Shawn Patrick Greenfield.

Speak Up! It's So Dark 🦴🦴 *Tala! Det ar sa Morkt* **1993** Soren (Norrthon) is a skinhead who gets beaten up at a neo-Nazi rally. He meets Jewish shrink Jacob (Glaser) on a train and Jacob offers to tend to Soren's wounds. Although Soren continually parrots hateful doctrine, Jacob (whose family died at Auschwitz) tries to help him and Soren slowly begins to see he's wrong. Swedish with subtitles. **83m/C VHS.** *SW* Etienne Glaser, Simon Norrthon; ***D:*** Suzanne Osten; ***W:*** Niklas Radstrom; ***C:*** Peter Mokrosinski.

Speaking Parts 🦴🦴🦴 **1989** VCR-obsessed laundry worker and another woman battle for the attention of bit-part actor McManus who works in ritzy hotel. A telling picture of the inextricable nature of modern technology. **92m/C VHS, DVD.** *CA* Michael McManus, Arsinee Khanjian, David Hemblen, Gabrielle Rose, Tony Nardi, Patricia Collins, Gerard Parkes; ***D:*** Atom Egoyan; ***W:*** Atom Egoyan; ***C:*** Paul Sarossy; ***M:*** Mychael Danna.

Special Bulletin 🦴🦴🦴 **1983** A pacifistic terrorist threatens to blow up Charleston, South Carolina, with a nuclear warhead. Done quite well in docu-drama style as a TV news bulletin. Interesting examination of the media's treatment of dramatic events. Top-notch made-for-TV fare. **105m/C VHS.** Ed Flanders, Christopher Allport, Kathryn Walker, Roxanne Hart; ***D:*** Edward Zwick; ***W:*** Marshall Herskovitz, Edward Zwick. **TV**

A Special Day 🦴🦴🦴 *Una Giornata Speciale; The Great Day* **1977** The day of a huge rally celebrating Hitler's visit to Rome in 1939 serves as the backdrop for an affair between weary housewife Loren and lonely, unhappy homosexual radio announcer Mastroianni. Good performances from two thorough pros make a depressing film well worth watching. In Italian with English subtitles or dubbed. **105m/C VHS, Wide.** *IT* Sophia Loren, Marcello Mastroianni, John Vernon, Francoise Berd; ***D:*** Ettore Scola; ***W:*** Ettore Scola, Ruggero Maccari, Maurizio Costanzo; ***C:*** Pasqualino De Santis; ***M:*** Armando Trovajoli. Golden Globes '78: Foreign Film.

Special Delivery 🦴🦴½ **1976 (PG)** Three unemployed Vietnam veterans decide to rob a bank but their getaway plans go awry. Svenson, the only robber who escapes, stashes the cash in a mailbox only to have it discovered by nutty artist, Shepherd, and crooked barkeep Gwynne. **99m/C VHS.** Bo Svenson, Cybill Shepherd, Vic Tayback, Michael C. Gwynne, Tom Atkins, Sorrell Booke, Deidre Hall, Gerrit Graham, Jeff Goldblum; ***D:*** Paul Wendkos; ***C:*** Harry Stradling Jr.; ***M:*** Lalo Schifrin.

Special Effects 🦴🦴 **1985 (R)** A desperate movie director murders a young actress, then makes a movie about her death. Solid, creepy premise sinks in the mire of flawed execution; a good film about Hollywood ego trips and obsession is lurking inside overdone script. **103m/C VHS.** *GB* Zoe Tamerlis, Eric Bogosian, Kevin J. O'Connor, Brad Rijn, Bill Oland, Richard Greene; ***D:*** Larry Cohen; ***W:*** Larry Cohen.

Special Forces *Hell in Normandy* **1968** Eight specially trained soldiers drop behind enemy lines to rescue prisoners of war in WWII. **90m/C VHS.** Peter Lee Lawrence, Guy Madison, Erika Blanc, Tony Norton.

Special Investigator ½ **1936** Dix is a criminal attorney who specializes in getting his mob clients freed. Then his FBI brother gets killed by the same criminals he's been defending. So Dix becomes a special agent and sets out to get the mob boss responsible for his brother's murder. Climax is the big shootout at the gang's hideaway. Based on the novel by Earle Stanley Gardner. **60m/B VHS.** Richard Dix, J. Carrol Naish, Margaret Callahan, Erik Rhodes, Owen Davis Jr., Ray Mayer, Joseph (Joe) Sawyer; ***D:*** Louis King.

Special Olympics **1978** A father attempts to care for his three sons, one of whom is mentally retarded, following the death of his wife. **104m/C VHS.** Charles Durning, Philip Brown, George Parry, Irene Tedrow, Mare Winningham, Herb Edelman, Debra Winger, Constance McCashin; ***D:*** Lee Philips. **TV**

Special Police ½ **1985** Police inspector protecting old friend's murder-witnessing sister learns that important politicians are involved with a seedy underground political movement. French thriller also available dubbed. **92m/C VHS.** *FR* Richard Berry, Carole Bouquet, Fanny Cottencon; ***D:*** Michael Vianey; ***W:*** Michael Vianey.

The Specialist ½ **1975 (R)** Lawyer West thinks he has seduced stunning Capri, but she has lured him into her clutches—she's been hired to kill him. Campy crud. It's old home week for '60s TV alums: West was Batman; bailiff Moore was Mr. Kimbell on Green Acres. **93m/C VHS, DVD, Wide.** Adam West, John Anderson, Ahna Capri, Alvy Moore; ***D:*** Howard (Hikmet) Avedis; ***W:*** Howard (Hikmet) Avedis, Marlene Schmidt, Ralph B. Potts; ***C:*** Massoud Joseph; ***M:*** Shorty Rogers.

The Specialist ½ **1994 (R)** Buffed bods do not a movie make—at least not in this mechanical actioner featuring Stone as the revenge-minded May Munro. Seems May's parents were killed by Cuban gangsters, led by father/son thugs Joe (Steiger) and Tomas Leon (Roberts), and she decides ex-CIA bomb specialist Ray Quick (Stallone) is just the man she needs to settle the score. But Quick has his own reasons for accepting—his expartner is nutball Ned Trent (Woods), who's now working for the Leons. Things blow up a lot, the two leads show off their toned flesh (but not much acting), and Woods gets to steal the movie with his amusing scenery chewing. **110m/C VHS, DVD, Wide.** Sylvester Stallone, Sharon Stone, James Woods, Eric Roberts, Rod Steiger; ***D:*** Luis Llosa; ***W:*** Alexandra Seros; ***C:*** Jeffrey L. Kimball; ***M:*** John Barry. Golden Raspberries '94: Worst Actress (Stone).

The Specials **2000** This is the movie that "Mystery Men" wanted to be. It's a smart comic book spoof that depends on good acting and well-written characters. The Specials are the sixth or seventh greatest team of superheroes in the business. Headquarters is a suburban house in Silver Lake. Their immediate goal—if they can quit bickering among themselves—it to get a line of action figures on the market. **89m/C DVD, Wide.** Rob Lowe, Jamie Kennedy, Thomas Haden Church, Paget Brewster, Judy Greer, James Gunn, Sean Gunn, Jordan Ladd, Kelly Coffield; ***D:*** Craig Mazin; ***W:*** James Gunn; ***C:*** Eliot Rockett; ***M:*** Brian Langsbard, Spring Aspers.

Species ½ **1995 (R)** A "friendly" galactic message containing a recipe on how to combine extraterrestrial DNA with human DNA is sent to scientists on Earth. The scientists, led by Fitch (Kingsley), whip up a batch of genetic material resulting in a sexy half alien, half human procreating/killing machine named Sil (model Henstridge's film debut). Naturally, Sil escapes from the lab, leaving the scientists with the unenviable task of catching her/it. All-star special effects team, including "Alien" designer H. R. Giger, create over-the-top, stomach-churning thrills. Dips liberally into the tricks of many sci-fi classics. For avid gore-meisters only. **108m/C VHS, DVD.** Ben Kingsley, Michael Madsen, Alfred Molina, Forest Whitaker, Marg Helgenberger, Natasha Henstridge, Michelle Williams; ***D:*** Roger Donaldson; ***W:*** Dennis Feldman; ***C:*** Andrzej Bartkowiak; ***M:*** Christopher Young. MTV Movie Awards '96: Kiss (Natasha Henstridge/Anthony Guidera).

Species 2 ½ **1998 (R)** Genetic scientists, in their quest to see an actual babe who will talk to genetic scientists, create a clone named Eve (Henstridge) from the monster in the original movie. Meanwhile, the U.S. has managed to successfully put an underwear model who can't act on Mars. Astronaut Patrick Ross (Lazard) has been infected with spores of alien DNA. Soon Ross' urge to procreate takes over and nasty alien babies are exploding out of screaming women all over town Government assassin Press Lennox (Madsen) and Dr. Laura Baker (Helgenberger) are once again called in to help track down the new species, with the help of Eve. Can they stop Ross and his brood before they mature? Can they stop Eve and Ross from making the beast with several scaly slimy multi-appendaged backs? Can they please stop making this movie again? **95m/C VHS, DVD.** Natasha Henstridge, Justin Lazard, Michael Madsen, Marg Helgenberger, Mykelti Williamson, George Dzundza, James Cromwell, Myriam Cyr, Baxter Harris; ***D:*** Peter Medak; ***W:*** Chris Brancato; ***C:*** Matthew F. Leonetti; ***M:*** Ed Shearmur.

Specimen ½ **1997 (R)** Twenty-four years ago, aliens impregnated Carol Hillary and she gave birth to a son, Mark. Now, the aliens have returned to claim him, only he doesn't want to go. **85m/C VHS, DVD.** *CA* Mark Paul Gosselaar, Doug O'Keefe, Michelle Johnson, Andrew Jackson; ***D:*** John Bradshaw; ***W:*** Damian Lee, Sheldon Inkol; ***C:*** Gerald R. Goozie; ***M:*** Terence Gowan.

The Speckled Band **1931** Set in 1930, this early talkie is a Sherlock Holmes adventure wherein the great detective must solve the mysterious death of a young woman. Massey makes his screen debut as Holmes, making the sleuth cynical, unhappy and pessimistic. Interesting prototypical Holmes case, faithful to the like-titled Conan Doyle story. **84m/B VHS, 8mm.** Raymond Massey, Lyn Harding, Athole Stewart, Angela Baddeley, Nancy Price; ***D:*** Jack Raymond; ***C:*** Frederick A. (Freddie) Young.

Specters *Spettri* **1987** Archaeologists excavating the Roman catacombs break open the gates of hell. Hellishly confused plot is unoriginal, to boot; decent production values hardly compensate. **95m/C VHS.** *IT* Donald Pleasence, John Pepper, Erna Schurer, Katrine Michelsen; ***D:*** Marcello Avallone; ***W:*** Marcello Avallone, Andrea Purgatori, Dardano Sacchetti, Maurizio Tedesco.

Spectre *House of the Damned; Roger Corman Presents: House of the Damned* **1996 (R)** Maura South (Paul) is the heiress to a old mansion in Ireland and when she, husband Will (Evigan), and their young daughter Aubrey (played by Evigan's daughter Briana) move in they discover it's haunted by the vengeful spirit of a young girl. When they discover the girl's body, the family hope a proper burial will set her spirit to rest but the ghost has other ideas. Filmed in Ireland. **82m/C VHS.** Greg Evigan, Alexandra Paul, Briana Evigan, Eamon Draper, Dick Donaghue; ***D:*** Scott Levy; ***W:*** Brendan Broderick; ***C:*** Christopher Baffa; ***M:*** Christopher Lennertz. **CABLE**

The Spectre of Edgar Allen Poe ½ **1973** The horridly fictionalized writer of horror fiction visits the asylum where his love Lenore is being held, and discovers murder and torture. Based very loosely on Poe's own torments. Dorky, rip-off horror. **87m/C VHS.** Cesar Romero, Robert Walker Jr., Tom Drake; ***D:*** Mohy Quandour.

Spectre of the Rose ½ **1946** Strange film set in the world of ballet. An impressario contends with an over-the-hill ballerina and a young male dancer with a deadly affinity for knives. **90m/B VHS.** Judith Anderson, Michael Chekhov, Ivan Kirov, Viola Essen, Lionel Stander; ***D:*** Ben Hecht; ***W:*** Ben Hecht.

Speechless ½ **1994 (PG-13)** Cute romantic comedy about sparring speechwriters who fall in love, and then briefly turn enemies when they discover they're working at professional odds. Davis is the idealistic liberal working for senatorial candidate Wannamaker, while Keaton is a TV sitcom writer doing a one-shot deal for a millionaire businessman, Republican Garvin. Both stars do a likable job; the supporting cast fares better with Reeve as an egotistical TV reporter, as well as Davis's fiance, and Bedelia as Keaton's ex-wife/campaign press secretary. Although the film parallels the real-life romance of rival Bush-Clinton spin doctors Mary Matalin and James Carville, it was written prior to the last presidential race. **99m/C VHS, DVD, Wide.** Michael Keaton, Geena Davis, Christopher Reeve, Bonnie Bedelia, Ernie Hudson, Charles Martin Smith, Gailard Sartain, Ray Baker, Mitchell Ryan; ***D:*** Ron Underwood; ***W:*** Robert King; ***C:*** Don Peterman; ***M:*** Marc Shaiman.

Speed ½ **1994 (R)** Excellent dude Reeves has grown up (and bulked up) as Los Angeles SWAT cop Jack Traven, up against bomb expert Howard Payne (Hopper, more maniacal than usual), who's after major ransom money. First it's a rigged elevator in a very tall building. Then it's a rigged bus—if it slows, it will blow, bad enough any day, but a nightmare in LA traffic. And that's still not the end. Terrific directorial debut for cinematographer De Bont, who certainly knows how to keep the adrenaline pumping. Fine support work by Daniels, Bullock, and Morton and enough wit in Yost's script to keep you chuckling. Great nonstop actioner from the "Die Hard" school. **115m/C VHS, DVD, Wide.** Keanu Reeves, Dennis Hopper, Sandra Bullock, Joe Morton, Jeff Daniels, Alan Ruck, Glenn Plummer, Richard Lineback, Beth Grant, Hawthorne James, David Kriegel, Carlos Carrasco, Natsuko Ohama, Daniel Villarreal; ***D:*** Jan De Bont; ***W:*** Graham Yost; ***C:*** Andrzej Bartkowiak; ***M:*** Mark Mancina. Oscars '94: Sound; MTV Movie Awards '95: Female Perf. (Bullock), Most Desirable Female (Bullock), On-Screen Duo (Keanu Reeves/Sandra Bullock), Villain (Hopper), Action Seq.; Blockbuster '95: Movie, V., Action Actress, V. (Bullock), Action Actress, T. (Bullock).

Speed 2: Cruise Control **1997 (PG-13)** Bigger's certainly not better in this lame sequel. Annie's (Bullock) got a new beau, hot-headed cop Alex (Patric), and the twosome decide to go on a Caribbean cruise for a little romance. Annie's luck with transportation holds as the ship is taken over by villainous computer geek-with-a-grudge John Giger (a particularly wild-eyed Dafoe), who sends the liner on a collision course with an oil tanker. Since Alex is off performing heroics, there's not much togetherness and Annie's left to get taken hostage (again). De Bont spent $25 mil on the ship's endless crash into a Caribbean island, which still manages to look fake and only elicits "you've got to be kidding me" disappointment. Bullock's feisty but powerless to save the flick. Patric's bland, and Dafoe is never menancing enough to create any thrills. This sea disaster crashes against the rocks of high expectations and poor execution. **123m/C VHS, DVD.** Richard Speight Jr., Joe Morton, Enrique Murciano, Sandra Bullock, Jason Patric, Willem Dafoe, Temuera Morrison, Brian McCardie, Glenn Plummer, Royale Watkins, Colleen Camp, Lois Chiles, Michael G. (Mike) Hagerty, Kimmy Robertson, Christine Firkins, Bo Svenson, Patrika Darbo; ***Cameos:*** Tim Conway; ***D:*** Jan De Bont; ***W:*** Jan De Bont, Jeff Nathanson, Randall McCormick; ***C:*** Jack N. Green; ***M:*** Mark Mancina. Golden Raspberries '97: Worst Remake/Sequel.

The Speed Lovers **1968** Stock car driver Lorenzen plays himself as an inspiration to a young man to join the auto racing circuit. More of a pat on the industry's back than a serious drama. Features footage from a number of race tracks around the country although shot principally in Atlanta. ♫Speed Lovers. **102m/C VHS.** Fred Lorenzen, William F. McGaha, Peggy O'Hara, David Marcus, Carol Street, Glenda Brunson; ***D:*** William F. McGaha; ***W:*** William F. McGaha, Elaine Wilkerson, Fred Tuch.

Speed Reporter **1936** Talmadge is the intrepid reporter investigating a phony reform movement that's really a front for a gang of criminals. Mediocre drama with Talmadge's thick German accent a hindrance. **56m/B VHS.** Richard Talmadge, Luana Walters, Richard Cramer; ***D:*** Bernard B. Ray.

The Speed Spook **1924** Silent ghost races car and steals documents. **85m/B VHS.** Johnny Hines, Warner Richmond; ***D:*** Charles Hines.

Speed Zone **1988 (PG)** Comic celebrities take over a high speed auto race when a redneck cop locks up the real drivers. Unfunny sequel to "Cannonball Run." **96m/C VHS.** Melody Anderson, Peter Boyle, Tim Matheson, Donna Dixon, John Candy, Eugene Levy, Joe Flaherty, Matt Frewer, Shari Belafonte, Tom Smothers, Dick Smothers, Brooke Shields, Lee Van Cleef, Jamie Farr, John Schneider, Michael Spinks; ***D:*** Jim Drake. Golden Raspberries '89: Worst Support. Actress (Shields).

Speeding Up Time **1971 (R)** An angry man wants to ice the dudes who torched his mother's tenement. **90m/C VHS.** Winston Thrash, Pamela Donegan.

Speedtrap **1978 (PG)** Typical chase scenes and cross-gender sparring characterize this tale of a private detective and a police officer pursuing car thieves. Good cast and fun chemistry between the leads; weak, typical script. **101m/C VHS.** Joe Don Baker, Tyne Daly, Richard Jaeckel, Robert Loggia, Morgan Woodward, Timothy Carey; ***D:*** Earl Bellamy.

Speedway **1968 (G)** Elvis the stock car driver finds himself being chased by Nancy the IRS agent during an important race. Will Sinatra keep to the business at hand? Or will the King melt her heart? Some cameos by real-life auto racers. Watch for a young Garr. Movie number 27 for Elvis. ♫Speedway; He's Your Uncle, Not Your Dad; There Ain't Nothing Like a Song. **90m/C VHS.** Elvis Presley, Nancy Sinatra, Bill Bixby, Gale Gordon, William Schallert, Carl Ballantine, Ross Hagen; ***Cameos:*** Richard Petty, Cale Yarborough, Teri Garr; ***D:*** Norman Taurog; ***C:*** Joseph Ruttenberg.

Speedway Junky ½ **1999** Army brat Johnny (Bradford) dreams of being an auto racing champion. So he runs away from his home in California determined to make it to North Carolina and get a job with driver Richard Petty's crew. At a stop in Vegas, naive Johnny gets robbed and comes to the attention of seasoned hustler Eric (Brower) who offers to teach Johnny the ropes. Johnny agrees but will only deal with women clients—while the gay Eric falls in love with the new kid in town. **105m/C VHS, DVD.** Jesse Bradford, Jordan Brower, Jonathan Taylor Thomas, Daryl Hannah, Patsy Kensit, Tiffani-Amber Thiessen; ***D:*** Nickolas Perry; ***W:*** Nickolas Perry; ***C:*** Steve Adcock; ***M:*** Stan Ridgway.

Speedy **1928** Lloyd comes to the rescue when the last horse car in NYC, operated by his fiance's grandfather, is stolen by a gang. Thoroughly phoney, fun pursuit/action comedy shot on location. Look for a brief appearance by Babe Ruth. **72m/B VHS.** Harold Lloyd, Bert Woodruff, Ann Christy; ***D:*** Ted Wilde.

Speedy Death *The Mrs. Bradley Mysteries: Speedy Death* **1999** Gladys Mitchell wrote some 66 mysteries starring the witty and clever Mrs. Adela Bradley (Rigg). A wealthy divorcee, Mrs. Bradley has a knack for investigations and a helpful chauffeur, George Moody (Dudgeon). In 1929, Adela is invited to the country estate of friends to celebrate Eleanor Bing's (Fielding) engagement. Only her fiance is murdered and then doesn't turn out to be what he seemed. But then, neither does anyone else. **90m/C VHS.** *GB* Diana Rigg, Neil Dudgeon, John Alderton, Emma Fielding, Tristan Gemmill, Tom Butcher, Sue Devaney, John Conroy, Michael Troughton; ***D:*** Audrey Cooke; ***W:*** Simon Booker. **TV**

The Spell **1977** An obese 15-year-old girl has the power to inflict illness and death on the people she hates. Necessarily mean-spirited, if we're being asked to sympathize with the main character. Therein lies the rub. Made for TV. **86m/C VHS.** Lee Grant, James Olson, Susan

Myers, Barbara Bostock, Lelia Goldoni, Helen Hunt; *D:* Lee Philips. TV

The Spellbinder ✓½ **1988 (R)** L.A. lawyer Daly falls in love with a woman he saves from an attacker, then discovers she's a fugitive from a satanic cult that wants her back. Unoriginal, but slickly made. **96m/C VHS.** Timothy Daly, Kelly Preston, Rick Rossovich, Audra Lindley; *D:* Janet Greek; *W:* Tracy Torme; *M:* Basil Poledouris.

Spellbound ✓✓ *The Spell of Amy Nugent* **1941** Broken-hearted over dead girlfriend, young college student attempts to contact her through spiritualism, succeeds, and suffers nervous breakdown. **75m/B VHS, DVD.** *GB* Derek Farr, Vera Lindsay, Frederick Leister, Hay Petrie, Felix Aylmer; *D:* John Harlow.

Spellbound ✓✓✓½ **1945** Peck plays an amnesia victim accused of murder. Bergman plays the psychiatrist who uncovers his past through Freudian analysis and ends up falling in love with him. One of Hitchcock's finest films of the 1940s, with a riveting dream sequence designed by Salvador Dali. Full of classic Hitchcock plot twists and Freudian imagery. Based on Francis Beeding's novel "The House of Dr. Edwardes." **111m/B VHS, DVD.** Ingrid Bergman, Gregory Peck, Leo G. Carroll, Michael Chekhov, Wallace Ford, Rhonda Fleming, Regis Toomey; *D:* Alfred Hitchcock; *W:* Ben Hecht; *C:* George Barnes; *M:* Miklos Rozsa. Oscars '45: Orig. Dramatic Score; N.Y. Film Critics '45: Actress (Bergman).

Spellbreaker: Secret of the Leprechauns ✓✓½ **1996 (G)** Youngster Mike Dennehy (Smith) is on summer vacation in Fairyhill, Ireland where he meets, what else, a band of leprechauns. He finds out the wee folk are battling sinister sorceress Nula, Queen of the Dead, who wants to seize the leprechauns power and destroy them. But not if Mike can stop her! **85m/C VHS.** Gregory Edward Smith, Madeleine Potter, Godfrey James, Tina Martin, Sylvester McCoy, James Ellis; *D:* Ted Nicolaou; *W:* Ted Nicolaou; *C:* Adolfo Bartoli; *M:* Richard Kosinski.

Spellcaster ✓ **1991 (R)** An evil wizard invites a DJ and a band of rock 'n' roll fanatics to his 1000-year-old Italian castle for an evil and bloodcurdling treasure hunt. **83m/C VHS.** Richard Blade, Gail O'Grady, Harold P. Pruett, Bunty Bailey, Rafal Zielinski, Adam Ant; *D:* Rafal Zielinski.

Spencer's Mountain ✓✓½ **1963** Fonda plays the larger-then-life patriarch of nine (with O'Hara as his wife), who's inherited the Wyoming mountain land claimed by his father. Fonda's dream is to build a new house large enough to contain his brood but something always gets in his way. This time it's eldest son MacArthur's dream of a college education. Sentimental family fare based on a novel by Earl Hamner Jr., which also became the basis for the TV series "The Waltons." **118m/C VHS.** Henry Fonda, Maureen O'Hara, James MacArthur, Donald Crisp, Wally Cox, Mimsy Farmer, Virginia Gregg, Lillian Bronson, Whit Bissell, Hayden Rorke, Dub Taylor, Victor French, Veronica Cartwright; *D:* Delmer Daves; *W:* Delmer Daves; *M:* Max Steiner.

Spenser: Ceremony ✓✓½ **1993** Urich resumes his role as Robert B. Parker's Boston PI, which he played in the TV series "Spenser: For Hire." This time around Spenser is searching for a troubled runaway who's gotten involved in prostitution. But her suburban dad, who has political aspirations, seems reluctant to have her found. Brooks returns as Spenser's menacing associate Hawk. Toronto stands in for Boston. Based on Parker's novel "Ceremony." **95m/C VHS.** Robert Urich, Avery Brooks, Barbara Williams, Tanya Allen, David Nichols, Lynne Cormack; *D:* Paul Lynch; *W:* Joan H. Parker, Robert B. Parker. CABLE

Spenser: Pale Kings & Princes ✓✓½ **1994** Spenser's (Urich) new case involves the murder of a reporter who was investigating a drug-ridden small New England town. But was the journalist killed for what he found out about a Colombian cocaine connection or did his womanizing have deadly consequences? Adapted from Robert B. Parker's novel. **95m/C VHS.** Robert Urich, Avery Brooks, Barbara Williams. CABLE

Spent ✓✓½ **2000** Gambling addict/occassional actor Max (London) has a girlfriend, Brigette (Spradling), who has a drinking problem, and a roommate, Grant (Park), who won't admit he's gay although his crush on Max seems pretty obvious. In fact, any communication is a big problem, since no one really wants to see their lives for what they are. Film coasts along without much happening. **90m/C VHS, DVD.** Jason London, Charlie Spradling, James Parks, Phill Lewis, Richmond Arquette, Barbara Barrie, Gilbert Cates, Rain Phoenix, Margaret Cho; *D:* Gil Cates Jr.; *W:* Gil Cates Jr.; *C:* Robert D. Tomer; *M:* Stan Ridgway.

Spetters ✓✓½ **1980 (R)** Four Dutch teenagers follow the motorcycle racing circuit and motocross champ Hauer. Misdirected youth film with a spicy performance from Soutendijk. Plenty of violence, sex, and gripping photography. Verhoeven went on to direct "Robocop" and "Total Recall." **108m/C VHS.** *NL* Rutger Hauer, Renee Soutendijk; *D:* Paul Verhoeven; *C:* Jan De Bont.

Sphere ✓½ **1997 (PG-13)** It must've looked good on paper, but bringing Michael Crichton's decade-old novel to the screen turned out to be a big mistake for all involved. Hoffman, Jackson, and Stone are a team of researchers sent underwater to investigate a mysterious 300-year-old space ship. After realizing the ship has American origins, they stumble across a huge liquid metal sphere that can make their deepest fears come true, in the form of huge squids and sea snakes. Never lives up to the promising premise or high-class looks. Despite three mega-stars and an A-list director, it's a hollow excursion low on thrills and originality, but there's plenty of existential ramblings about the power of the mind. **152m/C VHS, DVD, Wide.** Dustin Hoffman, Sharon Stone, Samuel L. Jackson, Peter Coyote, Queen Latifah, Liev Schreiber; *D:* Barry Levinson; *W:* Paul Attanasio, Stephen Hauser; *C:* Adam Greenberg; *M:* Elliot Goldenthal.

The Sphinx ✓✓½ **1933** A murderer causes havoc for his deaf-mute twin (Atwill, good in a dual role) when he frames him for his own crimes. Remade as "The Phantom Killer." **63m/B VHS.** Lionel Atwill, Theodore Newton, Sheila Terry, Paul Hurst, Luis Alberni, George "Gabby" Hayes; *D:* Phil Rosen.

Sphinx woof! **1981 (PG)** Woman archaeologist searches for hidden riches in the tomb of an Egyptian king. The scenery is impressive, but otherwise, don't bother. Based on the novel by Robin Cook. **117m/C VHS.** Lesley-Anne Down, Frank Langella, John Gielgud, Maurice Ronet, John Rhys-Davies; *D:* Franklin J. Schaffner; *W:* John Byrum.

Spice World: The Movie ✓½ **1997 (PG)** Clear some space on the video rack next to "Cool as Ice," the Spice Girls made a movie! Stretching their acting ability, the pop group plays a band of marginally talented singers who are inexplicably thrown to the top of the charts by a bitter twist of pop culture fate. What passes for the plot is stolen from "A Hard Day's Night," by the Beatles, depicting five days before a sellout concert at Albert Hall. The courageous champions of girl power do battle with the hassles of fame, bossy managers, and the media in their quest to get to the show. They find the time to visit a pregnant ex-Spice, change their clothes a kajillion times, and generally poke fun at themselves along the way. Unfortunately (at least for those over 13) they're not poked with anything really sharp. Loads of celebrity cameos (Elton John, Elvis Costello, Bob Hoskins), some of whom run off screen faster than if they were on fire. **92m/C VHS, DVD.** *GB* Emma (Baby Spice) Bunton, Geri (Ginger Spice) Halliwell, Victoria (Posh Spice) Adams, Melanie (Sporty Spice) Chisholm, Melanie (Scary Spice) Brown, Richard E. Grant, Alan Cumming, George Wendt, Claire Rushbrook, Mark McKinney, Richard O'Brien, Roger Moore, Barry Humphries, Jason Flemyng, Meat Loaf Aday, Bill Paterson, Stephen Fry, Richard Briers, Michael Barrymore, Naoki Mori, Hugh Laurie, Jennifer Saunders; *Cameos:* Elvis Costello, Bob Geldof, Bob Hoskins, Elton John; *D:* Bob Spiers; *W:* Kim Fuller, Jamie Curtis; *C:* Clive Tickner; *M:* Paul Newcastle. Golden Raspberries '98: Worst Actress (The Spice Girls).

Spices ✓✓✓ **1986** Poor woman Sonbai revolts against the sexist mores of rural colonial India in the 1940s. Features actress Patil in her final role. In Hindi with English subtitles. **98m/C VHS.** *IN* Smita Patil; *D:* Ketan Mehta.

The Spider and the Fly ✓✓½ **1994 (PG-13)** Mystery writer Dianna Taylor (Harris) and her friends like to play a murder mystery charade known as "The Game." Their latest unsuspecting patsy is crime writer Michael Moore (Shackelford)—who falls for Dianna bigtime. Then their publisher is killed—in the same sort of murder scenario one of them devised. **87m/C VHS.** Mel Harris, Ted Shackleford, Kim Coates, Colm Feore, Frankie Faison, Cynthia Belliveau, Kenneth Welsh, Peggy Lipton; *D:* Michael Katleman; *W:* Robert Pucci, Alanna Hamill; *M:* Richard Bellis. CABLE

Spider Baby ✓ *The Liver Eaters; Spider Baby, or the Maddest Story Ever Told; Cannibal Orgy, or the Maddest Story Ever Told* **1964** A tasteless horror-comedy about a chauffeur who takes care of a psychotic family. Theme song sung by Lon Chaney. **86m/B VHS, DVD.** Lon Chaney Jr., Mantan Moreland, Carol Ohmart, Sid Haig, Beverly Washburn, Jill Banner, Quinn (K.) Redeker, Mary Mitchell; *D:* Jack Hill; *W:* Jack Hill; *C:* Alfred Taylor; *M:* Ronald Stein.

Spider-Man ✓✓✓ **2002 (PG-13)** Raimi does a little 21st-century updating of the Marvel comic hero, who first made his appearance back in 1962, but remembers to keep the heart along with the action. Peter Parker (Maguire) is a nerdy teenager who gets tongue-tied every time he's around the babe of his dreams—Mary Jane Watson (Dunst). His life changes—not necessarily for the better—when he gets bitten by a genetically altered spider and takes on weird arachnid traits, such as strength, agility, wall crawling, web shooting, and swinging. After a family tragedy, the newly monickered Spider-Man becomes a crime fighter. His nemesis is, of course, the Green Goblin (Dafoe), who himself has a dual identity. **121m/C VHS, DVD.** *US* Tobey Maguire, Willem Dafoe, Kirsten Dunst, James Franco, Cliff Robertson, Rosemary Harris, J.K. Simmons, Gerry Becker, Bill Nunn, Jack Betts, Joe Manganiello, Stanley Anderson, Ron Perkins, Theodore (Ted) Raimi, Larry Joshua, Michael (Mike) Papajohn; *Cameos:* Bruce Campbell, Lucy Lawless; *D:* Sam Raimi; *W:* David Koepp; *C:* Don Burgess; *M:* Danny Elfman.

Spider Woman ✓✓✓ *Sherlock Holmes and the Spider Woman* **1944** A modernized Holmes and Watson adventure as the duo track down a woman responsible for a series of murders. His adversary uses poisonous spiders to do her work. Zestful, superior Holmes. **62m/B VHS.** Basil Rathbone, Nigel Bruce, Gale Sondergaard, Dennis Hoey; *D:* Roy William Neill.

Spiderman: The Deadly Dust **1978** A live-action episode of Spiderman, from the TV seies, as he attempts to prevent a city-destroying plutonium accident. **93m/C VHS.** Nicholas Hammond, Robert F. Simon, Chip Fields; *D:* Ron Satlof. TV

Spiders ✓✓✓ **1918** One of the earliest surviving films by director Lang, and predates Indiana Jones by almost 60 years. In these first two chapters ("The Golden Lake" and "The Diamond Ship") of an unfinished 4-part thriller, Carl deVogt battles with the evil Spider cult for a mystically powerful Incan diamond. Restored version has original color-tinted scenes. Silent with organ score. **137m/B VHS, DVD.** *GE* Lil Dagover; *D:* Fritz Lang; *M:* Gaylord Carter.

Spiders ✓✓½ **2000 (R)** Throwback to the "big bug" sci-fi horrors of the 1950s also borrows heavily from "The X-Files." College reporter Marci (Parrilla) and a couple of her pals sneak into a desert military base in time to witness the secret landing of a space shuttle. On board is a spider that has been injected with alien DNA and is doing absolutely disgusting things. It all ends with an arachnid attack on Phoenix! Can the city be saved? **93m/C VHS, DVD, Wide.** David Carpenter, Lana Parrilla; *D:* Gary Jones. VIDEO

The Spider's Stratagem ✓✓✓ **1970** Thirty years after his father's murder by the facists, a young man returns to a small Italian town to learn why his father was killed. The locals resist his efforts, and he is trapped in a mysterious web where history and lies exert a stranglehold on the truth. Intriguing, high literate thriller; outrageously lovely color photography. Based on a short story by Jorge Luis Borges. In Italian with English subtitles. **97m/C VHS.** *IT* Giulio Brogi, Alida Valli; *D:* Bernardo Bertolucci; *W:* Bernardo Bertolucci.

Spies ✓✓✓½ *Spione* **1928** A sly criminal poses as a famous banker to steal government information and create chaos in the world in this silent Lang masterpiece. Excellent entertainment, tight plotting and pacing, fine performances. Absolutely relentless intrigue and tension. **88m/B VHS, DVD.** *GE* Rudolf Klein-Rogge, Lupu Pick, Fritz Rasp, Gerda Maurus, Willy Fritsch; *D:* Fritz Lang.

Spies, Lies and Naked Thighs ✓½ **1991** A pair of crackpot CIA agents find themselves in a whirlpool of comedic madness when they are assigned to track down a deadly assassin. The problem? The assassin happens to be the ex-wife of one of the guys. Can he go another round with her and this time come out on top? Who cares? **90m/C VHS.** Harry Anderson, Ed Begley Jr., Rachel Ticotin, Linda Purl, Wendy Crewson; *D:* James Frawley.

Spies Like Us ✓✓½ **1985 (PG)** Chase and Aykroyd meet while taking the CIA entry exam. Caught cheating on the test, they seem the perfect pair for a special mission. Pursued by the Soviet government, they nearly start WWIII. Silly, fun homage to the Bing Crosby-Bob Hope "Road" movies that doesn't capture those classics' quota of guffaws, but comes moderately close. Look for several cameos by film directors. **103m/C VHS, DVD.** Chevy Chase, Dan Aykroyd, Steve Forrest, Bruce Davison, William Prince, Bernie Casey, Tom Hatton, Donna Dixon, Frank Oz, Michael Apted, Constantin Costa-Gavras, Terry Gilliam, Ray Harryhausen, Joel Coen, Martin Brest, Bob Swaim; *D:* John Landis; *W:* Lowell Ganz, Babaloo Mandel, Dan Aykroyd; *C:* Robert Paynter; *M:* Elmer Bernstein.

Spike of Bensonhurst ✓✓½ **1988 (R)** A Brooklyn street kid dreams of becoming a championship boxer. He tries to gain the mob's help by courting the local Don's daughter. Hip-but-stereotyped Morrissey effort is helped by great cast. **101m/C VHS.** Sasha Mitchell, Ernest Borgnine, Maria Pitillo, Talisa Soto, Sylvia Miles, Anne DeSalvo, Geraldine Smith, Rick Aviles, Antonia Rey; *D:* Paul Morrissey; *W:* Paul Morrissey, Alan Bowne; *C:* Steven Fierberg; *M:* Coati Mundi.

Spin the Bottle ✓✓ **1997** Jonah (Graham) invites four childhood friends, whom he hasn't seen in 10 years, for a weekend reunion at his Vermont lakefront summer house, which leads to sexual hijinks and sweet revenge. Yerkes's debut feature. **83m/C VHS, DVD, Wide.** Holter Graham, Jessica Faller, Mitchell Riggs, Kim Winter, Heather Goldenhersch; *D:* Jamie Yerkes; *W:* Amy Sohn; *C:* Harlan Bosmajian.

Spinout ✓✓ *California Holiday* **1966** A pouty traveling singer decides to drive an experimental race car in a rally. Usual Elvis fare with the King being pursued by an assortment of beauties. ♫Adam and Eve; Stop, Look, Listen; All That I Am; Am I Ready; Smorgasbord; Never Say Yes; Beach Shack; I'll Be Back; Spinout. **93m/C VHS.** Elvis Presley, Shelley Fabares, Carl Betz, Diane McBain, Cecil Kellaway, Jack Mullaney, Deborah Walley, Una Merkel, Warren Berlinger, Will Hutchins, Dodie Marshall; *D:* Norman Taurog.

The Spiral Staircase ✓✓✓ **1946** A mute servant, working in a creepy Gothic mansion, may be the next victim of a murderer preying on women afflicted with deformities, especially when the next murder occurs in the mansion itself. Great performance by McGuire as the terrified victim. Remade for TV in 1975. **83m/B VHS, DVD.** Dorothy McGuire, George Brent, Ethel Barrymore, Kent Smith, Rhonda Fleming, Gordon Oliver, Elsa Lanchester, Sara Allgood; *D:* Robert Siodmak; *W:* Mel Dinelli; *C:* Nicholas Musuraca; *M:* Roy Webb.

Spiral Staircase 🦴½ **1975** Mild TV remake of the 1946 classic about a mute servant who is menaced by a psychopathic killer. Why didn't they just show the original? **99m/C VHS.** *GB* Jacqueline Bisset, Christopher Plummer, John Phillip Law, Mildred Dunnock, Sam Wanamaker, Gayle Hunnicutt; ***D:*** Peter Collinson; ***W:*** Allan Scott, Chris Bryant.

Spirit Lost 🦴🦴 **1996 (R)** John (Leon) and wife Willy (Taylor) move to an old seaside home, where he hopes to find artistic inpiration. Instead, he finds an attractive ghost, Arabella (Williams), who has been hanging around for 200 years after her lover's betrayal. And the jealous Arabella wants to get her new lover's wife out of the way. Yes, ghosts CAN do it. Based on the book by Nancy Thayer. **90m/C VHS.** Leon, Regina Taylor, Cynda Williams, James Avery, Juanita Jennings; ***D:*** M. Neema Barnette; ***W:*** Joyce Renee Lewis; ***C:*** Yuri Neyman; ***M:*** Lionel Cole.

Spirit of St. Louis 🦴🦴🦴 **1957** A lavish Hollywood biography of famous aviator Charles Lindbergh and his historic transatlantic flight from New York to Paris in 1927, based on his autobiography. Intelligent; Stewart shines as the intrepid airman. Inexplicably, it flopped at the boxoffice. **137m/C VHS.** James Stewart, Patricia Smith, Murray Hamilton, Marc Connelly; ***D:*** Billy Wilder; ***W:*** Billy Wilder, Wendell Mayes; ***M:*** Franz Waxman.

Spirit of '76 🦴½ **1991 (PG-13)** In the 22nd century, the Earth faces certain disaster as a magnetic storm wipes out all of American culture. Now time travellers must return to 1776 to reacquire the Constitution to fix things up. But when their computer goes on the blink, the do-gooders land, not in 1776, but in 1976 at the beginning of disco fever! **82m/C VHS.** David Cassidy, Olivia D'Abo, Leif Garrett, Geoff Hoyle, Jeff McDonald, Steve McDonald, Liam O'Brien, Barbara Bain, Julie Brown, Thomas Chong, Iron Eyes Cody, Don Novello, Carl Reiner, Rob Reiner, Moon Zappa, Mark Mothersbaugh, Lucas Reiner; ***D:*** Lucas Reiner; ***W:*** Lucas Reiner; ***C:*** Stephen Lighthill; ***M:*** David Nichtern.

Spirit of the Beehive 🦴🦴🦴 *El Espiritu de la Colmena* **1973** An acclaimed and haunting film about a young Spanish girl enthralled by the 1931 "Frankenstein," embarking on a journey to find the creature in the Spanish countryside. One of the best films about children's inner life; in Spanish with subtitles. **95m/C VHS.** *SP* Fernando Gomez, Teresa Gimpera, Ana Torrent, Isabel Telleria, Laly Soldevilla; ***D:*** Victor Erice; ***W:*** Victor Erice; ***C:*** Luis Cuadrado; ***M:*** Luis De Pablo.

Spirit of the Eagle 🦴🦴 **1990 (PG)** Man and young son wander in mountains and make friends with feathered creature. Then boy is kidnapped, creating problems for dad. Somnolent family fare. **93m/C VHS, DVD.** Dan Haggerty, Bill Smith, Don Shanks, Jeri Arredondo, Trever Yarrish; ***D:*** Boon Collins; ***W:*** Boon Collins; ***C:*** Lew V. Adams; ***M:*** Parmer Fuller.

Spirit of the West 🦴½ **1932** Rodeo star Gibson and his ranch foreman brother work together to save a fair damsel's land from a gang of rustlers. Routine western of its era. **61m/B VHS.** Hoot Gibson, Hooper Atchley; ***D:*** Otto Brower.

The Spirit of West Point 🦴½ **1947** The true story of West Point's two All-American football greats, Doc Blanchard and Glenn Davis (who play themselves), while on leave after graduation from the title school. **77m/B VHS.** Felix "Doc" Blanchard, Glenn Davis, Tom Harmon, Alan Hale Jr., Anne Nagel, Robert Shayne; ***D:*** Ralph Murphy.

The Spirit of Youth 🦴🦴 **1937** Joe Louis supports his family with menial jobs until he shows his knack as a fighter. When he's knocked down, his gal appears at ringside to inspire him, and does. **70m/B VHS.** Joe Louis, Mantan Moreland.

Spirit Rider 🦴🦴🦴 **1993** Jesse Threebears is a sullen 16-year-old Ojibway who has been shuttled from foster homes since the age of six. Repatriated to his family's Canadian reservation, he's left in the care of his grandfather, Joe Moon. The entire community works to make Jesse's return successful but there are Jesse's resentments and some family tragedies to be overcome first. Based on the novel "Winners" by Mary-Ellen Lang Collura. **120m/C VHS.** *CA* Herbie Barnes, Adam Beach, Graham Greene, Tantoo Cardinal, Gordon Tootoosis, Tom Jackson, Michelle St. John.

Spirit: Stallion of the Cimarron 🦴🦴 **2002 (G)** Spirit is a wild stallion and leader of his herd, who is captured and treated badly by a Cavalry Colonel (Cromwell) until he escapes with the help of a young Lakota brave, Little Creek (Studi). Action sequences are impressive, even breathtaking, but the simplistic story and constant musical clues to the moods expressed on screen wear quickly. Combination of traditional 2-D and computer-generated 3-D elements doesn't always work, either. On the other hand, the animals don't speak (except for some of Spirit's thoughts in a voiceover provided by Damon), and there are no wacky sidekicks to clutter what is a pretty serious story for an animated feature. **85m/C VHS, DVD.** *US* ***D:*** Kelly Asbury, Lorna Cook; ***W:*** John Fusco; ***M:*** Hans Zimmer, Bryan Adams; ***V:*** Matt Damon, James Cromwell, Daniel Studi.

Spiritism 🦴🦴 *Espiritismo* **1961** Mother uses one of her three wishes to bring back her dead son. Adapted from the "Monkey's Paw." **85m/B VHS.** *MX* Nora Veyran, Jose Luis Jimenez, Jorge Mondragon, Rene Cardona Jr.; ***D:*** Benito Alazraki.

Spirits 🦴½ **1990 (R)** A priest tormented by his lust-filled dreams breaks his vows of chastity with a woman who turns out to be a murderer. Bad luck. **88m/C VHS.** Erik Estrada, Carol Lynley, Robert Quarry, Brinke Stevens, Oliver Darrow, Kathrin Lautner; ***D:*** Fred Olen Ray.

Spirits of the Dead 🦴🦴🦴 *Histoires Extraordinaires; Tre Passi nel Delirio; Tales of Mystery; Tales of Mystery and Imagination; Trois Histoires Extraordinaires d'Edgar Poe* **1968 (R)** Three Edgar Allan Poe stories adapted for the screen and directed by three of Europe's finest. "Metzengerstein," directed by Roger Vadim stars the Fonda siblings in a tale of incestuous lust. "William Wilson" finds Louis Malle directing Delon and Bardot in the story of a vicious Austrian army officer haunted by a murder victim. Finally, Fellini directs "Never Bet the Devil Your Head" or "Toby Dammit" in which Stamp plays a drunken British film star who has a gruesome date with destiny. Although Fellini's segment is generally considered the best (and was released on its own) all three provide an interesting, atmospheric vision of Poe. French and Italian with subtitles. **117m/C VHS, DVD, Wide.** *IT FR* Jane Fonda, Peter Fonda, Carla Marlier, Francoise Prevost, James Robertson Justice, Brigitte Bardot, Alain Delon, Katia Christine, Terence Stamp, Salvo Randone; ***D:*** Roger Vadim, Louis Malle, Federico Fellini; ***W:*** Roger Vadim, Louis Malle, Federico Fellini, Daniel Boulanger, Barnardino Zapponi; ***C:*** Tonino Delli Colli, Claude Renoir, Giuseppe Rotunno; ***M:*** Nino Rota, Diego Masson; ***Nar:*** Vincent Price, Clement Biddle Wood.

Spite Marriage 🦴🦴🦴 **1929** When Sebastian's lover dumps her like yesterday's garbage, she marries Keaton out of spite. Much postnuptual levity follows. Keaton's final silent. **82m/B VHS.** Buster Keaton, Dorothy Sebastian, Edward Earle, Leila Hyams, William Bechtel, Hank Mann; ***D:*** Edward Sedgwick.

Spitfire 🦴🦴🦴 **1934** Sentimental comedy-drama starring Hepburn as a hillbilly faith healer from the Ozarks who falls into a love triangle. One in a string of early boxoffice flops for Hepburn. She wanted to play a role other than patrician Eastern Seaboard, and did, but audiences didn't buy it. **90m/B VHS, 8mm.** Katharine Hepburn, Robert Young, Ralph Bellamy, Sidney Toler; ***D:*** John Cromwell; ***M:*** Max Steiner.

Spitfire 🦴🦴🦴 *The First of the Few* **1942** True story of Reginald J. Mitchell, who designed "The Spitfire" fighter plane, which greatly assisted the Allies during WWII. Howard's last film. Heavily propagandist but enjoyable and uncomplicated biography, with a splendid score. **88m/B VHS.** *GB* Leslie Howard, David Niven, Rosamund John, Roland Culver, David Horne, J.H. Roberts, Patricia Medina; ***D:*** Leslie Howard; ***C:*** Georges Perinal; ***M:*** William Walton.

Spitfire 🦴½ **1994 (R)** Feisty gymnast Charlie Case (Phillips) has some super secret info slipped to her by her secret agent father (Henrikson) that is desired by evil Carla Davis (Douglas). With the help of reporter Rex Beacham (Thomerson), Charlie's gonna save the day. **95m/C VHS.** Kristie Phillips, Sarah Douglas, Lance Henriksen, Tim Thomerson; ***D:*** Albert Pyun; ***W:*** Albert Pyun; ***C:*** George Mooradian; ***M:*** Tony Riparetti.

The Spitfire Grill 🦴🦴½ *Care of the Spitfire Grill* **1995 (PG-13)** Newly released from prison, Perry Talbott (Elliott) moves to smalltown Gilead, Maine, and gets a waitressing job at the Spitfire Grill, run by the cranky Hannah (Burstyn). Perry's upfront about her jail time, which doesn't endear her to the suspicious locals. Particularly censorious is businessman Nahum Goddard (Patton), who sends his downtrodden wife Shelby (Harden) to keep an eye on Perry. There are a number of personal dilemmas that take their toll in this familiar setting—redeemed by strong performances. **117m/C VHS, DVD.** Alison Elliott, Ellen Burstyn, Marcia Gay Harden, Will Patton, Kieran Mulroney, Gailard Sartain, Louise De Cormier, John M. Jackson; ***D:*** Lee David Zlotoff; ***W:*** Lee David Zlotoff; ***C:*** Rob Draper; ***M:*** James Horner. Sundance '96: Aud. Award.

Spittin' Image 🦴 **1983** After falling from her mean-spirited father's wagon, a young girl befriends a kind mountain man. She learns the ways of the wilderness and tobacco spitting. **92m/C VHS.** Lloyd "Sunshine" Parker, Trudi Cooper, Sharon Barr, Karen Barr; ***D:*** Russell Kern.

Splash 🦴🦴½ **1984 (PG)** A beautiful mermaid ventures into New York City in search of a man she's rescued twice when he's fallen overboard. Now it's her turn to fall—in love. Charming performances by Hanks and Hannah. Well-paced direction from Howard, with just enough slapstick. Don't miss the lobster scene. **109m/C VHS, DVD, 8mm, Wide.** Tom Hanks, Daryl Hannah, Eugene Levy, John Candy, Dody Goodman, Shecky Greene, Richard B. Shull, Bobby DiCicco, Howard Morris; ***D:*** Ron Howard; ***W:*** Babaloo Mandel, Lowell Ganz; ***C:*** Don Peterman; ***M:*** Lee Holdridge. Natl. Soc. Film Critics '84: Screenplay.

Splatter University woof! **1984** A deranged killer escapes from an asylum and begins to slaughter and mutilate comely coeds at a local college. Abysmally motiveless killing and gratuitous sex. Also available in a 78-minute "R" rated version. **79m/C VHS.** Francine Forbes, Dick Biel, Cathy Lacommaro, Ric Randing, Dan Eaton, Denise Texeira, Mary Ellen David, Joanna Mihalakis; ***D:*** Richard W. Haines; ***W:*** Richard W. Haines, John Michaels, Michael Cunningham; ***M:*** Chris Burke.

Splendor 🦴🦴½ **1935** Typical romantic weepie finds beautiful-but-poor Phyllis (Hopkins) marrying into the snobby clan of Brighton Lorrimore (McCrea). His family (whose fortunes are sliding) want to break the duo up and push Phyllis towards an affair with wealthy broker Martin (Cavanagh). There's a scandal and the Lorrimore's separate but true love conquers all, as you expect. **77m/B VHS.** Miriam Hopkins, Joel McCrea, Paul Cavanagh, Helen Westley, Billie Burke, Katherine Alexander, David Niven, Arthur Treacher; ***D:*** Elliott Nugent; ***W:*** Rachel Crothers; ***C:*** Gregg Toland.

Splendor 🦴🦴½ **1999 (R)** A '90s screwball comedy about an unconventional sexual arrangement. Veronica (Robertson) is an aspiring L.A. actress who enjoys her sexual exploits and who falls for two men on the opposite ends of the romantic spectrum. Abel (Schaech) is a freelance music critic who's intelligent and handsome while punk rock drummer Zed (Keeslar) is dumb but really sexy. Veronica refuses to choose between the two, so both move in with her (and prove to be more immature than the lady herself). Then Veronica meets successful and wealthy TV director, Ernest (Mabius), and wonders if it's time for a real adult relationsip. Surprisingly sweet and stylish fluff from Araki. **93m/C VHS, DVD, Wide.** Kathleen Robertson, Johnathon Schaech, Matt Keeslar, Eric Mabius, Kelly Macdonald; ***D:*** Gregg Araki; ***W:*** Gregg Araki; ***C:*** Jim Fealy; ***M:*** Daniel Licht.

Splendor in the Grass 🦴🦴🦴 **1961** A drama set in rural Kansas in 1925, concerning a teenage couple who try to keep their love on a strictly intellectual plane and the sexual and family pressures that tear them apart. After suffering a mental breakdown and being institutionalized, the girl returns years later in order to settle her life. Film debuts of Beatty, Dennis, and Diller. Inge wrote the screenplay specifically with Beatty in mind, after the actor appeared in one of Inge's stage plays. Filmed not in Kansas, but on Staten Island and in upstate New York. **124m/C VHS, DVD.** Natalie Wood, Warren Beatty, Audrey Christie, Barbara Loden, Zohra Lampert, Phyllis Diller, Sandy Dennis; ***D:*** Elia Kazan; ***W:*** William Inge; ***C:*** Charles Durnham; ***M:*** David Amram. Oscars '61: Story & Screenplay.

Split 🦴 **1990** Humanoids from another dimension manipulate earth activity. **85m/C VHS.** John Flynn, Timothy Dwight, Chris Shaw, Joan Bechtel; ***D:*** Chris Shaw.

Split Decisions 🦴🦴 **1988 (R)** An Irish family of boxers, dad and his two sons, slug it out emotionally and physically, as they come to terms with career choices and each other. Good scenes in the ring but the drama leans toward melodrama. Decent family drama, but somewhat of a "Rocky" rip-off. **95m/C VHS, 8mm.** Gene Hackman, Craig Sheffer, Jeff Fahey, Jennifer Beals, John McLiam, Eddie Velez, Carmine Caridi, James Tolkan; ***D:*** David Drury; ***W:*** David Fallon; ***M:*** Basil Poledouris.

Split Image 🦴🦴🦴 **1982 (R)** An all-American boy comes under the spell of a cult. His parents then hire a deprogrammer to bring the boy back to reality. Exceptional performances by Dennehy and Woods. This is a worthwhile film that spent far too little time in theatres. **113m/C VHS.** Michael O'Keefe, Karen Allen, Peter Fonda, Brian Dennehy, James Woods; ***D:*** Ted Kotcheff; ***W:*** Robert Mark Kamen; ***M:*** Bill Conti.

Split Second 🦴🦴½ **1953** An escaped prisoner holds hostages in a Nevada atomic bomb testing area. McNally's excellent performance as the kidnapper, in addition to strong supporting performances, enhance a solid plot. Powell's directorial debut. **85m/B VHS.** Paul Kelly, Richard Egan, Jan Sterling, Alexis Smith, Stephen McNally; ***D:*** Dick Powell; ***W:*** William Bowers, Irving Wallace.

Split Second 🦴½ **1992 (R)** Hauer is a futuristic cop tracking down a vicious alien serial killer in London in the year 2008. The monster rips out the hearts of his victims and then eats them in what appears to be a satanic ritual in this blood-soaked thriller wanna-be. Hauer gives a listless performance and overall, the action is quite dull. The music soundtrack also manages to annoy with the Moody Blues song "Nights in White Satin" playing at the most inappropriate times. A British/American co-production. **91m/C VHS, DVD.** *GB* Rutger Hauer, Kim Cattrall, Neil Duncan, Michael J. Pollard, Alun Armstrong, Pete Postlethwaite, Ian Dury, Roberta Eaton; ***D:*** Tony Maylam; ***W:*** Gary Scott Thompson; ***C:*** Clive Tickner; ***M:*** Francis Haines, Stephen Parsons.

Splitting Heirs 🦴🦴½ **1993 (PG-13)** Idle stars as the offspring of titled parents who is accidentally abandoned in a restaurant as an infant and raised by poor Pakistanis. (His mother winds up claiming the wrong abandoned baby.) When he discovers he's actually the 15th Duke of Bournemouth he plots, ineffectually, to kill off the present unknowing imposter, a nitwit American (Moranis). Cleese pops in as a shabby lawyer hired by Idle to help him claim the title with Hershey as Idle's real mother, the addle-brained and sex-starved Duchess. Convoluted plot, bland comedy. **87m/C VHS.** Eric Idle, Rick Moranis, Barbara Hershey, John Cleese, Catherine Zeta-Jones, Sadie Frost, Stratford Johns, Brenda Bruce, William Franklyn, Jeremy Clyde; ***D:*** Robert M. Young; ***W:*** Eric Idle; ***M:*** Michael Kamen.

Splitz woof! **1984 (PG-13)** An all-girl rock band agrees to help out a sorority house by participating in a series of sporting events. **89m/C VHS.** Robin Johnson, Patti

Lee, Shirley Stoler, Raymond Serra; *D:* Domonic Paris.

Spoiled Children 🦴🦴½ *Les Enfants Gates* **1977** A famous film director (Piccoli) tries to work on his new script at home but is too distracted by his family life. So he rents a high-rise apartment for peace and quiet but winds up involved in a tenant/landlord dispute and with a girl half his age. In French with English subtitles. **113m/B VHS.** *FR* Michel Piccoli, Christine Pascal, Michel Aumont, Gerard Jugnot, Arlette Bonnard; *D:* Bertrand Tavernier; *W:* Christine Pascal, Charlotte Dubreuil, Bertrand Tavernier; *M:* Philippe Sarde.

The Spoilers 🦴🦴½ **1914** Virtually unstaged account of gold hunting in the Alaskan wilderness enhanced by gritty film quality. Was a gold mine when released. **110m/B VHS.** William Farnum, Thomas Santschi, Kathlyn Williams, Bessie Eyton, Frank Clark, Wheeler Oakman; *D:* Colin Campbell.

The Spoilers 🦴🦴🦴 **1942** Two adventurers in the Yukon are swindled out of their gold mine and set out to even the score. A trademark scene of all versions of the movie (and there are many) is the climactic fistfight, in this case between hero Wayne and bad-guy Scott. One of the better films adapted from the novel by Rex Beach. William Farnum, who starred in both the 1914 and the 1930 versions, has a small part. **88m/B VHS.** John Wayne, Randolph Scott, Marlene Dietrich, Margaret Lindsay, Harry Carey Sr., Richard Barthelmess, Charles Halton; *D:* Ray Enright; *C:* Milton Krasner.

Spontaneous Combustion 🦴🦴 **1989 (R)** A grisly horror film detailing the travails of a hapless guy who has the power to inflict the title phenomenon on other people. **97m/C VHS.** Brad Dourif, Jon Cypher, Melinda Dillon, Cynthia Bain, William Prince, Dey Young, Dick Butkus, John Landis, Dale Dye; *D:* Tobe Hooper; *W:* Tobe Hooper, Howard Goldberg; *C:* Levie Isaacks; *M:* Graeme Revell.

Spook Busters 🦴🦴½ **1948** The Bowery Boys take jobs as exterminators, only to find themselves assigned the unenviable task of ridding a haunted house of ghosts. To make matters worse, the resident mad scientist wants to transplant Sach's brain into a gorilla. Essential viewing for anyone who thought "Ghostbusters" was an original story. **68m/B VHS.** Leo Gorcey, Huntz Hall, Douglass Dumbrille, Bobby Jordan, Gabriel Dell, William Benedict, David Gorcey, Bernard Gorcey, Tanis Chandler, Maurice Cass, Charles Middleton; *D:* William Beaudine.

The Spook Who Sat by the Door 🦴½ **1973 (PG)** A black CIA agent organizes an army of inner-city youths and launches a revolution. Based on the novel by Sam Greenlee. **95m/C VHS.** Lawrence Cook, Paula Kelly, J.A. Preston; *D:* Ivan Dixon; *M:* Herbie Hancock.

Spookies woof! **1985 (R)** An old master sorcerer who lives in a run-down haunted house sacrifices humans to give eternal life to his unconscious bride. He needs only a few more victims when a group of teenagers come along to explore the house. **85m/C VHS.** Felix Ward, Dan Scott, Maria Pechukas, Brendan Faulkner, Eugine Joseph; *D:* Thomas Doran.

Spooks Run Wild 🦴🦴½ **1941** The East Side Kids seek refuge in a spooky mansion owned by the eerie Lugosi. A fun horror-comedy with the Kids' antics playing off Lugosi's scariness quite well. Co-scripter Carl Foreman later cowrote "High-Noon," "The Bridge on the River Kwai," and "The Guns of Navarone." Not the same movie as "Ghosts on the Loose" which followed in '43 and also featured Lugosi and the Kids. **64m/B VHS.** Huntz Hall, Leo Gorcey, Bobby Jordan, Sammy (Earnest) Morrison, Dave O'Brien, Dennis Moore, Bela Lugosi; *D:* Phil Rosen; *W:* Carl Foreman.

Spooky Encounters 🦴🦴½ *Encounters of the Spooky Kind* **1980** Writer/director/star Samo Hung is Cheung, a simple-minded braggart who takes a bet to spend one night in a haunted temple. But it's a set-up. His unfaithful wife's lover hires an evil sorcerer to raise the dead. The film covers practically the entire palette of Chinese horror, including hopping vampires and flesh-eating zombies, along with flying undead and plenty of black magic. Samo pulls the film off easily, using his trademark humor to soften the horrific edge. **94m/C DVD, Wide.** *HK* Sammo Hung, Chung Fat; *D:* Sammo Hung; *W:* Sammo Hung.

The Sporting Club woof! **1972 (R)** A semi-gothic melodrama about a strict all men's club which, during a 100th anniversary party, reverts to savagery and primitive rites. **104m/C VHS.** Robert Fields, Margaret Blye, Nicolas Coster, Ralph Waite, Jack Warden, Linda Blair; *D:* Larry Peerce.

Spotlight Scandals 🦴🦴 **1943** A barber and a vaudevillian team up and endure the ups and downs of showbiz life in this low-budget musical from prolific B-movie director Beaudine. ♫The Restless Age; Goodnight Now; The Lilac Tree; Tempo of the Trail; Oh Johnny. **79m/B VHS.** Billy Gilbert, Frank Fay, Bonnie Baker; *D:* William Beaudine.

Spraggue 🦴🦴 **1984** A Boston professor and his eccentric aunt put the moves on a doctor who may have committed murder. Served as a TV pilot for a series that never materialized. **78m/C VHS.** Michael Nouri, Glynis Johns, James Cromwell, Mark Herrier, Patrick O'Neal, Andrea Marcovicci; *D:* Larry Elikann. **TV**

The Spree 🦴½ **1996** Cliched crime thriller with wooden dialogue has cat burglar Xinia (Beals) luring cop Hatcher (Boothe) into the nasty side of life. **98m/C VHS.** Jennifer Beals, Powers Boothe, Garry Chalk, John Cassini, Nathaniel DeVeaux, Rita Moreno; *D:* Tommy Lee Wallace; *W:* Livia Linden, Percy Angress; *C:* Richard Leiterman; *M:* Peter Manning Robinson. **CABLE**

The Spring 🦴½ **1989** Two archaeologists search Florida for the fountain of youth after they find new clues to its whereabouts. However, a greedy industrialist and an evil priest are both on their trail, fighting to keep the secret for themselves at any cost. **110m/C VHS.** Dack Rambo, Gedde Watanabe, Shari Shattuck, Steven Keats; *D:* John D. Patterson.

The Spring 🦴🦴½ **2000 (PG-13)** Widower Dennis Conway (MacLachlan) and his son Nick (Cross) stop in the small town of Springville when travelling and Nick has an accident. The kid has to spend some time in the hospital where Dennis becomes involved with his son's doctor, Sophie Weston (Eastwood). But the town hides a secret—the local spring is a modern-day fountain of youth, the residents are much older than they appear, and none can ever leave. Based on the novel by Clifford Irving. **90m/C VHS, DVD.** Kyle MacLachlan, Alison Eastwood, Joseph Cross, George Eads, Zachary Ansley, Aaron Pearl; *D:* David Jackson; *W:* J.B. White. **TV**

Spring Break 🦴 **1983 (R)** Four college students go to Fort Lauderdale on their spring vacation and have a wilder time that they bargained for, though viewer is deprived of excitement. **101m/C VHS.** Perry Lang, David Knell, Steve Bassett, Paul Land, Jayne Modean, Corinne Alphen; *D:* Sean S. Cunningham.

Spring Fever 🦴½ **1981** Heartaches of the junior tennis circuit are brought to the screen in this sports comedy. Previews promised a lot more than this film could ever hope to deliver. Even tennis fans will be disappointed. **93m/C VHS.** *CA* Susan Anton; *D:* Joseph L. Scanlan.

Spring Symphony 🦴🦴½ *Fruhlingssinfonie* **1986 (PG-13)** A moody, fairy-tale biography of composer Robert Schumann, concentrating on his rhapsodic love affair with pianist Clara Weick. Kinski is very good as the rebellious daughter, while the music is even better. Reasonably accurate in terms of history; dubbed. **102m/C VHS, DVD.** *GE* Nastassia Kinski, Rolf Hoppe, Herbert Gronemeyer; *D:* Peter Schamoni; *W:* Peter Schamoni; *C:* Gerard Vandenburg.

Springfield Rifle 🦴🦴½ **1952** Based on the real-life story of Major Les Kearney, who joined forces with outlaws to catch the thief stealing government weapons. Average. **93m/C VHS.** Gary Cooper, Phyllis Thaxter, David Brian, Lon Chaney Jr., Paul Kelly, Phil Carey, Guinn "Big Boy" Williams; *D:* Andre de Toth; *M:* Max Steiner.

Springtime in the Rockies 🦴🦴 **1937** Autry is a cattle-ranch foreman whose employer decides to try raising sheep. This doesn't set well with the other ranchers, but Autry manages to save the day and sing a little too. **60m/B VHS.** Gene Autry, Polly Rowles, Smiley Burnette; *D:* Joseph Kane.

Springtime in the Rockies 🦴🦴½ **1942** A Broadway duo Vicky (Grable) and Dan (Payne) just can't get along despite being in love with each other. So Vicky decides to partner up with Victor (Romero) while Dan tries to make Vicky jealous by dating his Brazilian secretary Rosita (Miranda). Top-notch musical, with a touch of romantic tension and comedy. Beautifully filmed in the Canadian Rockies. ♫I Had the Craziest Dream; Run Little Rainrop Run; A Poem Set to Music; Pan American Jubilee; I Like to Be Love by You; Chattanooga Choo Choo; Tic Tac Do Meu Coracao. **91m/C VHS.** Betty Grable, John Payne, Carmen Miranda, Cesar Romero, Charlotte Greenwood, Edward Everett Horton, Jackie Gleason; *D:* Irving Cummings; *W:* Ken Englund, Walter Bullock; *C:* Ernest Palmer.

Springtime in the Sierras 🦴🦴½ *Song of the Sierra* **1947** Rogers and Devine band together to fight a gang of poachers who prey on the wildlife of a game preserve. Features a number of songs by Rogers and The Sons of the Pioneers. **54m/B VHS.** Roy Rogers, Andy Devine, Jane Frazee, Stephanie Bachelor; *D:* William Witney.

The Sprinter 🦴🦴½ **1984** A young homosexual, while trying to submerge his confusion in professional track and field, gets to know a homely shot-putter and is seduced by her. In German with English subtitles. **90m/C VHS.** *GE* Dieter Eppler, Jurgen Mikol, Renate Muri; *D:* Christoph Boll; *W:* Christoph Boll; *C:* Peter Gauhe.

Sprung 🦴🦴 **1996 (R)** The dating scene among four young African Americans is examined in this well-intended, yet unfocused romantic comedy. Couple A are Brandy (Campbell) and Montel (Cundieff) who realize that they have a chance at true love. Couple B are their friends Adina (Parker) and Clyde (Torry) who try to sabatoge Brandy and Montel's happiness in order to save them from being "sprung" (in love) with each other. The camaraderie between the couples is funny, some of the time, but the humor often turns from vulgar to juvenile and scenes drag on a bit. Cundieff and Campbell are too bland to carry over the used plot but Torry is a comedic find who makes the film tolerable. **105m/C VHS, DVD.** Tisha Campbell, Paula Jai Parker, Rusty Cundieff, Joe Torry, John Witherspoon, Clarence Williams III; *D:* Rusty Cundieff; *W:* Darin Scott, Rusty Cundieff; *C:* Joao Fernandes; *M:* Stanley Clarke.

Spurs 🦴🦴 **1930** A rodeo star takes on a whole gang of rustlers and their imposing machine gun. This transitional western was made both with and without sound. **60m/B VHS.** Hoot Gibson, Robert E. Homans; *D:* B. Reeves Eason.

Sputnik 🦴🦴 *A Dog, a Mouse, and a Sputnik* **1961** A Frenchman, amnesiac after a car crash, comes up against Russian scientists, space-bound dogs, and weightlessness. Pleasant and charming family fun though clearly dated. Another fine performance from Auer. Dubbed. **80m/B VHS.** *FR* Noelia Noel, Mischa Auer, Denise Grey; *D:* Jean Dreville.

Spy 🦴🦴 **1989** A former spy who knows too much becomes the target of a renegade agency. **88m/C VHS.** Ned Beatty, Tim Choate, Bruce Greenwood, Catherine Hicks, Jameson Parker, Michael Tucker; *D:* Philip Frank Messina. **TV**

Spy Game 🦴🦴 **2001 (R)** It's 1991, and cagey veteran spy Nathan Muir (Redford) is on the verge of retirement, when he discovers that former protege Tom Bishop (Pitt) is to be executed in a Chinese prison for espionage. Muir has 24 hours to rescue Bishop, and to do it, he must first outwit his CIA superiors, who would rather lose the rogue agent than risk damaging an international trade agreement. Story's core is implausible but script is dense with information and drama, and the ultra-brisk editing leaves little time to consider the inadequacies. The use of geopolitical atrocities to add weight to a romantic subplot between Bishop and a British foreign-aid worker (McCormack) feels forced and, at times, insensitive. But Redford's cool and sarcastic performance, recalling his role in "Three Days of the Condor," makes up for some deficiencies and anchors the film nicely. **127m/C VHS, DVD, Wide.** *US* Robert Redford, Brad Pitt, Catherine McCormack, Stephen (Dillon) Dillane, Larry Bryggman, Michael Paul Chan, Marianne Jean-Baptiste, David Hemmings, Matthew Marsh, Todd Boyce, Charlotte Rampling; *D:* Tony Scott; *W:* Michael Frost Beckner, David Arata; *C:* Dan Mindel; *M:* Harry Gregson-Williams.

Spy Games 🦴½ *History is Made at Night* **1999** CIA agent Harry (Pullman) and Russian SVR agent Natasha (Jacob) dash around Helsinki chasing a videotape that contains U.S. satellite codes and spatting romantically. Old-fashioned and lame. **94m/C VHS, DVD.** *GB* Bill Pullman, Irene Jacob, Bruno Kirby, Glenn Plummer, Udo Kier, Andre Oumansky, Feodor Atkine; *D:* Ilkka Jarvilaturi; *W:* Patrick Amos; *C:* Michel Amathieu; *M:* Courtney Pine.

Spy Hard 🦴 **1996 (PG-13)** Nielsen does yet another genre spoof—this time a combo of "Die Hard" meets James Bond. Agent Dick Steele aka WD40 (Nielsen) is brought out of retirement to thwart the plans of crazed General Rancor (Griffith) for world domination. Not much else plotwise, which ropes Nielsen along in domino fashion through the myriad of unimaginative spoofs on such films as "Speed" and "Pulp Fiction." Minus the charm and pace of parody pioneers Zucker/Abrahams/Zucker, this latest entry should retire the whole genre. Directorial debut of Friedberg. **80m/C VHS, DVD.** Leslie Nielsen, Nicolette Sheridan, Andy Griffith, Charles Durning, Marcia Gay Harden, Barry Bostwick; *D:* Rick Friedberg; *W:* Rick Friedberg, Dick Chudnow, Jason Friedberg, Aaron Seltzer; *C:* John R. Leonetti; *M:* Bill Conti.

Spy in Black 🦴🦴🦴 *U-Boat 29* **1939** A German submarine captain returns from duty at sea during WWI and is assigned to infiltrate one of the Orkney Islands and obtain confidential British information. Known in the U.S. as "U-Boat 29," this film is based on a J. Storer Clouston novel. This was the first teaming of director Powell and writer Pressburger, who followed with "Contraband" in 1940. **82m/B VHS.** *GB* Conrad Veidt, Valerie Hobson, Sebastian Shaw, Marius Goring, June Duprez, Helen Haye, Cyril Raymond, Hay Petrie; *D:* Michael Powell; *M:* Miklos Rozsa.

Spy Kids 🦴🦴🦴 **2001 (PG)** Rare live-action kid's movie that doesn't talk down to its target audience has pre-teens Carmen (Vega)and Juni Cortez (Sabara) bemoaning their boring life and dealing with troublesome bullies until their parents disappear. It seems that Mom (Gugino) and Dad (Banderas) are retired superspies who get kidnapped while on one last mission. It's up to the kids, along with perennial sidekick Marin, to save their folks (and the world) from evil kid-show host Fegan Floop (Cumming, bidding for the title of world's busiest screen villian) and Minion (Shalhoub). Director/writer/editor/composer Rodriquez makes a concerted effort to provide family entertainment with zero objectionable material but plenty of gee-whiz gadgetry, fanciful set design, and exciting action. He said he wanted to make a movie that he'd be proud to show his children and his parents. He has succeeded. **88m/C VHS, DVD, Wide.** *US* Alexa Vega, Daryl Sabara, Antonio Banderas, Carla Gugino, Alan Cumming, Tony Shalhoub, Teri Hatcher, Richard "Cheech" Marin, Robert Patrick, Danny Trejo, George Clooney; *D:* Robert Rodriguez; *W:* Robert Rodriguez; *C:* Guillermo Navarro; *M:* Robert Rodriguez, Danny Elfman, John Debney.

Spy Kids 2: The Island of Lost Dreams **2002 (PG)** Carmen (Vega) and Juni (Sabara) have to fight rival spy kids when they take on a mystery man and his creatures on a distant island. Not yet reviewed. **?m/C VHS, DVD.** Antonio Banderas, Carla Gugino, Alexa Vega, Daryl Sabara, Mike Judge, Steve Buscemi; *D:* Robert Rodriguez; *W:* Robert Rodriguez.

Spy of Napoleon 🦴🦴 **1936** A French aristocrat agrees to marry the illegitimate daughter of Emperor Napoleon III and finds himself working to uncover traitors to the throne. Based on Baroness Orczy's novel. **77m/B VHS.** *GB* Richard Barthelmess, Dolly Haas, Francis L. Sullivan.

Spy Smasher **1942** A war reporter uses his supposed death (and a covenient twin brother) to go underground and fight Nazi counterfeiters trying to wreck the economy. 12-episode serial. "Spy Smasher Returns" is actually a condensed-version not a sequel. **185m/B VHS.** Kane Richmond, Marguerite Chapman, Sam Flint, Hans Schumm, Tristram Coffin; *D:* William Witney.

Spy Smasher Returns **1942** The exciting 12-part serial "Spy Smasher" was cut and edited into feature length and released under this title. The masked marvel and his twin brother battle enemy agents during WWII. This new version is just as exciting as the original cliffhanger. **185m/B VHS.** Kane Richmond, Marguerite Chapman, Sam Flint, Hans Schumm, Tristram Coffin; *D:* William Witney.

Spy Trap 🦴🦴½ **1992** Four junior-high school friends concoct bogus military plans using futuristic toys for blueprints. The "secret" plans get sold to the Russians and the kids find themselves chased by the unhappy KGB and the CIA. Family adventure. **96m/C VHS.** Elya Baskin, Danielle Du Clos, Jason Kristofer, Cameron Johann, Devin Ratray, Kimble Joyner; *D:* Arthur Sherman.

The Spy Who Came in from the Cold 🦴🦴🦴½ **1965** The acclaimed adaptation of the John Le Carre novel about an aging British spy who attempts to infiltrate the East German agency. Prototypical Cold War thriller, with emphasis on de-glamorizing espionage. Gritty and superbly realistic with a documentary style which hampered it at the boxoffice. **110m/B VHS.** Richard Burton, Oskar Werner, Claire Bloom, Sam Wanamaker, Peter Van Eyck, Cyril Cusack, Rupert Davies, Michael Hordern; *D:* Martin Ritt; *C:* Oswald Morris. British Acad. '66: Film; Golden Globes '66: Support. Actor (Werner).

The Spy Who Loved Me 🦴🦴 **1977 (PG)** James Bond teams up with female Russian Agent XXX to squash a villain's plan to use captured American and Russian atomic submarines in a plot to destroy the world. The villain's henchman, 7'2" Kiel, is the steel-toothed Jaws. Carly Simon sings the memorable, Marvin Hamlisch theme song, "Nobody Does It Better." **136m/C VHS, DVD, Wide.** *GB* Roger Moore, Barbara Bach, Curt Jurgens, Richard Kiel, Caroline Munro, Walter Gotell, Geoffrey Keen, Valerie Leon, Bernard Lee, Lois Maxwell, Desmond Llewelyn; *D:* Lewis Gilbert; *W:* Christopher Wood, Richard Maibaum; *C:* Claude Renoir, Lamar Boren; *M:* Marvin Hamlisch, Paul Buckmaster.

Spy with a Cold Nose 🦴🦴 **1966** A sporadically funny spy spoof about a bugged dog passed between British and Soviet intelligence. Hard-working cast keeps it from collapsing. **93m/C VHS.** *GB* Laurence Harvey, Daliah Lavi, Lionel Jeffries; *D:* Daniel Petrie.

The Spy Within 🦴🦴 *Flight of the Dove* **1994 (R)** Spy Alex (Russell) is working undercover as a call girl and Will (Glenn) is an explosives expert on the run from his past. The two share more than a mutual attraction since a covert organization wants them both dead. Confusing plot but fast-paced action. Railsback's directorial debut. **92m/C VHS.** Theresa Russell, Scott Glenn, Lane Smith, Terence Knox, Katherine Helmond, Alex Rocco, Joe Pantoliano, Rudy Ramos; *D:* Steve Railsback; *W:* Lewis Green.

Spymaker: The Secret Life of Ian Fleming 🦴🦴½ *Spymaker* **1990** Fictionalized account of the creator of the ultimate spy, James Bond, and his early days in the British Secret Service. Fans of the Bond movies will appreciate the numerous inside jokes. Connery is the son of Sean. **96m/C VHS.** *GB* Jason Connery, Kristin Scott Thomas, Joss Ackland, Patricia Hodge, David Warner, Fiona Fullerton, Richard Johnson; *D:* Ferdinand Fairfax. **TV**

S*P*Y*S 🦴 **1974 (PG)** An attempt to cash in on the success of "M*A*S*H," this unfunny spy spoof details the adventures of two bumbling CIA men who botch a Russian defection, and get both sides after them. Usually competent director Kershner had a bad day. **87m/C VHS.** Donald Sutherland, Elliott Gould, Joss Ackland, Zouzou, Shane Rimmer, Vladek Sheybal, Nigel Hawthorne; *D:* Irvin Kershner; *W:* Malcolm Marmorstein, Lawrence J. Cohen; *M:* Jerry Goldsmith.

Squanto: A Warrior's Tale 🦴🦴🦴 **1994 (PG)** Family adventure fare about 17th-century Massachusetts brave Squanto (Beach), who's captured by English traders and taken to Plymouth, England for display as a "savage." He manages to escape, eventually hiding aboard a trading vessel bound for America, and on returning home even brings about a peace between fearful Pilgrims and a neighboring tribe (which culminates in the first Thanksgiving feast). It may be history lite but it's also a thoughtful, adventurous saga with good performances, and fine location filming in Nova Scotia and Cape Breton, Canada. **101m/C VHS.** Adam Beach, Mandy Patinkin, Michael Gambon, Nathaniel Parker, Eric Schweig, Donal Donnelly, Stuart Pankin, Alex Norton, Irene Bedard; *D:* Xavier Koller; *W:* Darlene Craviotto; *M:* Joel McNeely.

Square Dance 🦴🦴½ *Home is Where the Heart Is* **1987 (PG-13)** A Texas teenager leaves the farm where she's been raised by her grandfather to live in the city with her promiscuous mother (Alexander, cast against type) where she befriends a retarded young man (yes, it's Lowe, also cast against type). Too slow, but helped by good acting. **118m/C VHS.** Jane Alexander, Jason Robards Jr., Rob Lowe, Winona Ryder, Deborah Richter, Guich Koock, Elbert Lewis; *D:* Daniel Petrie; *W:* Alan Hines; *M:* Bruce Broughton.

Square Dance Jubilee 🦴½ **1951** TV scouts hit Prairie City in search of cowboy stars, and stumble onto cattle rustlers; 21 C&W tunes support a near-invisible plot, suitable for fridge runs. **78m/B VHS.** Mary Beth Hughes, Donald (Don "Red") Barry, Wally Vernon, John Eldridge; *D:* Paul Landres.

Square Shoulders 🦴½ **1929** Adventures of young military school student with geometric anatomy (Coghlan). **58m/B VHS.** Frank "Junior" Coghlan, Louis Wolheim, Anita Louise, C. Montague Shaw; *D:* E. Mason Hopper.

The Squeaker 🦴🦴½ *Murder on Diamond Row* **1937** Good Edgar Wallace mystery about a disgraced inspector trying to clear his name. **77m/C VHS.** Edmund Lowe, Sebastian Shaw; *M:* Miklos Rozsa.

The Squeaker 🦴🦴½ **1965** Complicated but interesting thriller about the underworld goings-on after a big-time diamond heist. German remake of an early (1930) British talkie, also done in 1937, based on the Edgar Wallace novel. **95m/B VHS.** *GE* Heinz Drache, Eddi Arent, Klaus Kinski, Barbara Rutting; *D:* Alfred Vohrer.

The Squeeze 🦴🦴 **1977 (R)** Scotland Yard detective Keach, fired for drunkeness, gets a chance to reinstate himself when his ex-wife is caught up in a brutal kidnapping scheme. Slim script gives good cast uphill work. Ordinary thriller. Available with Spanish subtitles. **106m/C VHS.** Stacy Keach, Carol White, David Hemmings, Edward Fox, Stephen Boyd; *D:* Michael Apted.

The Squeeze 🦴🦴 *Diamond Thieves; The Heist; Rip-Off* **1978 (R)** An explosive crime thriller... **93m/C VHS, DVD.** Lee Van Cleef, Karen Black, Edward Albert, Lionel Stander, Robert Alda; *D:* Anthony (Antonio Margheriti) Dawson; *W:* Paul Costello; *C:* Sergio d'Offizi; *M:* Paolo Vasile.

The Squeeze 🦴½ **1980** An aging safecracker is hired for a final job, but learns that his cohorts plan to kill him when the heist is finished. Blah revenge thriller. **93m/C VHS.** *IT* Lee Van Cleef, Karen Black, Edward Albert, Lionel Stander, Robert Alda; *D:* Anthony (Antonio Margheriti) Dawson.

The Squeeze woof! **1987 (PG-13)** Keaton is wasted in this attempt at a comedy about a small-time con artist who discovers a Mafia plan to fix a lottery electromagnetically. **101m/C VHS, DVD.** Michael Keaton, Rae Dawn Chong, John Davidson, Ric Abernathy, Bobby Bass, Joe Pantoliano, Meat Loaf Aday, Paul Herman; *D:* Roger Young; *C:* Arthur Albert; *M:* Miles Goodman.

Squeeze 🦴🦴 **1997 (R)** Self-conscious but not unappealing first effort made on a shoestring budget, with a director who teaches acting at a Boston youth center and who wrote his script based on the lives of his three teeanged lead actors. Tyson (Burton), Hector (Cutanda) and Boa (Duong) lead aimless lives on Boston's meaner streets where trouble finds them despite their efforts to stay (more-or-less) clear. **96m/C VHS, DVD, Wide.** Tyrone Burton, Eddie Cutanda, Phuong Duong, Geoffrey Rhue, Russell Jones, Leigh Williams; *D:* Robert Patton-Spruill; *W:* Robert Patton-Spruill; *C:* Richard Moos; *M:* Bruce Flowers.

Squeeze Play woof! **1979** Group of young women start a softball team and challenge the boyfriends to a game. Standard battle of the sexes takes places, with a wet T-shirt contest thrown in for good measure. Cheap, plotless, offensive trash from Troma. **92m/C VHS, DVD.** Al Corley, Jennifer Hetrick, Jim Metzler, Jim Harris, Rick Gitlin, Helen Campitelli, Rick Kahn, Diana Valentien; *D:* Lloyd Kaufman; *W:* Charles Kaufman, Haim Pekelis; *C:* Lloyd Kaufman.

Squirm 🦴🦴 **1976 (R)** Storm disrupts a highly charged power cable, electrifying a host of garden-variety worms. The worms then turn themselves into giant monsters that terrorize a small town in Georgia. The opening credits claim it's based on an actual 1975 incident. Yeah, right. Okay entry in the giant worm genre. **92m/C VHS.** Don Scardino, Patricia Pearcy, Jean Sullivan; *D:* Jeff Lieberman; *W:* Jeff Lieberman.

Squizzy Taylor 🦴🦴 **1984** The rise and fall of real-life Australian mob boss Squizzy Taylor in the 1920s. Colorful period gangster drama loses steam about halfway through. **82m/C VHS.** *AU* Jacki Weaver, Alan Cassell, David Atkins; *D:* Kevin James Dobson; *C:* Dan Burstall.

SS Girls woof! **1978** After the assassination attempt of July 1944, Hitler does not trust the Wehrmacht and extends the power of the SS over Germany. General Berger entrusts Hans Schillemberg to recruit a specially chosen group of prostitutes who must test the fighting spirit and loyalty of the generals. Seedy exploitation. **82m/C VHS.** Gabriele Carrara, Marina Daunia, Vassilli Karis, Macha Magal, Thomas Rudy, Lucic Bogoljub Benny, Ivano Staccioli.

Ssssss 🦴🦴½ **1973 (PG-13)** Campy, creepy story of snake expert Carl Stoner (Strother Martin) who's developed a serum from cobra venom that just happens to turn human beings into snakes. His latest unwitting guinea pig is reasearch assistant David Blake (Benedict). Cool makeup effects. **99m/C VHS.** Strother Martin, Dirk Benedict, Heather Menzies, Richard B. Shull, Tim O'Connor, Jack Ging; *D:* Bernard L. Kowalski; *W:* Hal Dresner; *C:* Gerald Perry Finnerman; *M:* Patrick Williams.

Stacey 🦴½ *Stacey and Her Gangbusters* **1973 (R)** Ex-Playmate Randall stars as Stacey Hansen, a beautiful, implausibly talented private detective. Hyper-convoluted plot, too much sex and violence detract from a potentially not-wretched whodunit. **87m/C VHS.** Anne Randall, Marjorie Bennett, Anitra Ford, Alan Landers, James Westmoreland, Christina Raines; *D:* Andy Sidaris.

Stacking 🦴🦴 *Season of Dreams* **1987 (PG)** In the 1950s, a Montana family is threatened with losing their farm. Typical, boring '80s farmland tragedy with coming of age tale. **95m/C VHS.** Christine Lahti, Megan Follows, Frederic Forrest, Peter Coyote, Jason Gedrick; *D:* Martin Rosen; *W:* Victoria Jenkins; *C:* Richard Bowen, Paul Elliott; *M:* Patrick Gleeson.

Stacy's Knights 🦴🦴 *Double Down* **1983 (PG)** A seemingly shy girl happens to have an uncanny knack for blackjack. With the odds against her and an unlikely group of "knights" to aid her, she sets up an implausible "sting" operation. Blah TV fodder for the big screen. **95m/C VHS, DVD.** Kevin Costner, Andra Millian; *D:* Jim Wilson; *W:* Michael Blake.

Stag 🦴🦴 **1997 (R)** Bachelor party goes out of control and it's every guy for himself. Best man Michael (Van Peebles) surprises groom-to-be Victor (Stockwell) by inviting guys to his bachelor party that he hasn't seen in years—for good reason—such as drug dealer Pete (McCarthy). But when stripper Kelly (McShane) is accidentally killed, Pete's the only one to keep his cool and lay out their options. And this group is a lot more interested in self-preservation than in doing the right thing. **92m/C VHS.** Mario Van Peebles, Andrew McCarthy, John Stockwell, Kevin Dillon, Taylor Dane, William McNamara, Jerry Stiller, Ben Gazzara, John Henson, Jenny McShane; *D:* Gavin Wilding; *W:* Evan Tylor; *C:* Maryse Alberti; *M:* Paul Zaza.

Stage Door 🦴🦴🦴½ **1937** An energetic ensemble peek at the women of the theatre. A boarding house for potential actresses houses a wide variety of talents and dreams. Patrician Hepburn and wisecracking Rogers make a good team in a talent-packed ensemble. Realistic look at the sub-world of Broadway aspirations includes dialogue taken from idle chat among the actresses between takes. Based on the play by Edna Ferber and George S. Kaufman, who suggested in jest a title change to "Screen Door," since so much had been changed. Watch for young stars-to-be like Ball, Arden, and Miller. **92m/B VHS.** Katharine Hepburn, Ginger Rogers, Lucille Ball, Eve Arden, Andrea Leeds, Jack Carson, Adolphe Menjou, Gail Patrick; *D:* Gregory La Cava. N.Y. Film Critics '37: Director (La Cava).

Stage Door Canteen 🦴🦴½ **1943** The Stage Door Canteens were operated by the American Theatre Wing during WWII for servicemen on leave. They were staffed by some of the biggest stars of the day, 65 of whom are featured here. The slight, hokey plot concerns three soldiers who fall for canteen workers while on furlough in NYC. Many musical numbers, cameos, and walk-ons by a plethora of stars. ♫We Mustn't Say Goodbye; Bombshell From Brooklyn; The Machine Gun Song; Sleep, Baby, Sleep in Your Jeep; Quick Sands; You're Pretty Terrific Yourself; Don't Worry Island; We Meet in the Funniest Places; A Rookie and His Rhythm. **135m/B VHS, DVD.** Cheryl Walker, William Terry, Marjorie (Reardon) Riordan, Lon (Bud) McCallister, Sunset Carson, Tallulah Bankhead, Merle Oberon, Katharine Hepburn, Paul Muni, Ethel Waters, Judith Anderson, Ray Bolger, Helen Hayes, Harpo Marx, Gertrude Lawrence, Ethel Merman, Edgar Bergen, George Raft, Benny Goodman, Peggy Lee, Count Basie, Kay Kyser, Guy Lombardo, Xavier Cugat, Johnny Weissmuller; *D:* Frank Borzage; *W:* Delmer Daves; *C:* Harry Wild; *M:* Al Dubin, Freddie Rich.

Stage Fright 🦴🦴🦴 **1950** Wyman will stop at nothing to clear her old boyfriend, who has been accused of murdering the husband of his mistress, an actress (Dietrich). Disguised as a maid, she falls in love with the investigating detective, and discovers her friend's guilt. Dietrich sings "The Laziest Gal in Town." The Master's last film made in England until "Frenzy" (1971). **110m/B VHS.** *GB* Jane Wyman, Marlene Dietrich, Alastair Sim, Sybil Thorndike, Michael Wilding, Kay Walsh; *D:* Alfred Hitchcock.

Stage Fright 🦴 **1983** Bashful actress is transformed into a homicidal killer after a latent psychosis in her becomes active. **82m/C VHS.** Jenny Neumann, Gary Sweet; *M:* Brian May.

Stage Struck 🦴🦴½ **1957** Strasberg reprises the role made famous by Katharine Hepburn as a determined, would-be actress in this mediocre remake of "Morning Glory" (1933). Christopher Plummer's screen debut shows little of his later talent. **95m/B VHS.** Henry Fonda, Susan Strasberg, Christopher Plummer, Herbert Marshall, Joan Greenwood; *D:* Sidney Lumet; *M:* Alex North.

Stage to Mesa City 🦴🦴 **1948** Marshal LaRue must find out who is behind the pesky attacks on the stage line to Mesa City. Chesebro, as usual, is a good bad guy. A few chuckles between fist fights and shoot-em-ups. **52m/B VHS.** Lash LaRue, Al "Fuzzy" St. John, George Chesebro, Jennifer Holt, Russell Arms; *D:* Ray Taylor.

Stagecoach 🦴🦴🦴🦴 **1939** Varied group of characters with nothing in common are stuck together inside a coach besieged by bandits and Indians. Considered structurally perfect, with excellent direction by Ford, it's the film that made Wayne a star as the Ringo Kid, an outlaw looking to avenge the murder of his brother and father. The first pairing of Ford and Wayne changed the course of the modern western. Stunning photography by Bert Glennon and Ray Binger captured the mythical air of Monument Valley, a site that Ford was often to revisit. Based on the story "Stage to Lordsburg" by Ernest Haycox. Remade miserably with in 1966 and again—why?—as a TV movie in 1986. **100m/B VHS, DVD.** John Wayne, Claire Trevor, Thomas Mitchell, George Bancroft, John Carradine, Andy Devine, Donald Meek, Louise Platt, Berton Churchill, Tim Holt, Tom Tyler, Chris-Pin (Ethier Crispin Martini) Martin, Francis Ford, Jack Pennick; ***D:*** John Ford; ***W:*** Dudley Nichols; ***C:*** Bert Glennon, Ray Binger. Oscars '39: Support. Actor (Mitchell), Score; AFI '98: Top 100, Natl. Film Reg. '95;; N.Y. Film Critics '39: Director (Ford).

Stagecoach 🦴 **1986** A forgettable remake of the classic 1939 western about a motley crew of characters in a cross-country coach beset by thieves and Indians. **95m/C VHS.** Willie Nelson, Waylon Jennings, Johnny Cash, Kris Kristofferson, John Schneider, Elizabeth Ashley, Mary Crosby, Anthony Newley, Anthony (Tony) Franciosa; ***D:*** Ted Post; ***M:*** Willie Nelson. **TV**

Stagecoach to Denver 🦴🦴 **1946** Lane as Red Ryder investigates a stagecoach wreck and uncovers a land-grabbing plot led by-who else?—the pillar of the community (Barcroft). Well-directed "Red Ryder" episode. **53m/B VHS.** Allan "Rocky" Lane, Roy Barcroft, Robert (Bobby) Blake, Peggy Stewart, Martha Wentworth; ***D:*** R.G. Springsteen.

Stagefright 🦴 **1987** A maniacal serial killer tries to cover his trail by joining the cast of a play about mass murder. The other actors soon have more to worry about than remembering their lines. Typical low-grade horror. **95m/C VHS, DVD, Wide.** David Brandon, Barbara Cupisti, Robert Gligorov; ***D:*** Michele (Michael) Soavi; ***W:*** Luigi Montefiore.

Stairway to Heaven 🦴🦴🦴½ *A Matter of Life and Death* **1946 (PG)** Wonderful romantic fantasy features Niven as RAF pilot Peter D. Carter, who falls in love with American WAC June (Hunter). Forced to bail out during a mission, Peter is rescued and must undergo a risky operation. What's riskier is an angel (Goring) has made a mistake and realizes that Peter should have died. While on the operating table, Peter's spirit travels to Heaven and pleads his case for life against a harsh prosecutor (Massey) and a group of judges. Terrific work by cinematographer Cardiff. **104m/C VHS.** *GB* David Niven, Kim Hunter, Marius Goring, Raymond Massey, Roger Livesey, Robert Coote, Kathleen Byron, Richard Attenborough; ***D:*** Michael Powell, Emeric Pressburger; ***W:*** Michael Powell, Emeric Pressburger; ***C:*** Jack Cardiff; ***M:*** Allan Gray.

Stakeout 🦴🦴 **1962** An ex-con tries to start life anew, but every time he finds a good job, his past catches up with him. A return to the life of crime looks tempting. Predictable and familiar plot, but performances are sincere. **81m/B VHS.** Bing Russell, Billy Hughes, Bill Hale, Jack Harris; ***D:*** James Landis; ***W:*** James Landis.

Stakeout 🦴🦴½ **1987 (R)** A sometimes violent comedy-thriller about a pair of detectives who stake out a beautiful woman's apartment, hoping for a clue to the whereabouts of her psycho boyfriend who has broken out of prison. One of them (Dreyfuss) then begins to fall in love with her. Natural charm among Estevez, Dreyfuss, and Stowe that adds to the proceedings, which are palpably implausible and silly. Slapstick sequel "Another Stakeout" followed in 1993. **117m/C VHS, 8mm.** Richard Dreyfuss, Emilio Estevez, Madeleine Stowe, Aidan Quinn, Forest Whitaker, Dan Lauria, Earl Billings; ***D:*** John Badham; ***W:*** Jim Kouf; ***M:*** Arthur B. Rubinstein.

Stalag 17 🦴🦴🦴🦴 **1953** A group of American G.I.s in a German POW camp during WWII suspects the opportunistic Sefton (Holden) of being the spy in their midst. One of the very best American movies of the 1950s, adapted from the play by Donald Bevan and Edmund Trzcinski. Wilder, so good at comedy, proved himself equally adept at drama, and brought a top-drawer performance out of Holden. Features superb photography from Ernest Laszlo, and a wonderful score. **120m/B VHS, DVD.** William Holden, Don Taylor, Peter Graves, Otto Preminger, Harvey Lembeck, Robert Strauss, Sig Rumann, Richard Erdman, Neville Brand, Gil Stratton, Robinson Stone, Robert Shawley, Jay Lawrence; ***D:*** Billy Wilder; ***W:*** Billy Wilder, Edwin Blum; ***C:*** Ernest Laszlo; ***M:*** Franz Waxman. Oscars '53: Actor (Holden).

Stalag Luft **19??** Senior British officer James Forrester (Fry) is regarded by fellow POWs as a first-class idiot, since he has a record 23 escapes and re-captures. But he's determined to break all 327 prisioners out of their Nazi camp while the nervous German Kommandant keeps one eye on the advancing Allied army and the other on his prisoners. **103m/C VHS.** *GB* Stephen Fry, Geoffrey Palmer, Nicholas Lyndhurst.

Stalin 🦴🦴½ **1992** The story of the leader of the Soviet Union who ruled with an iron fist from 1924-53. One of the most feared men of the 20th century, he wrenched the largest country in the world singlehandedly from a backward, pastoral farmland to an industrial landscape. He was also responsible for the feared purges of the late 1930s where more than a million people were executed. Also explored is the dictator's relationships with his family, including how marriage to a cunning, sadistic, paranoid tyrant affected his wife. Filmed at actual historical locations in Russia. **173m/C VHS.** Robert Duvall, Julia Ormond, Jeroen Krabbé, Joan Plowright, Maximilian Schell, Frank Finlay, Roshan Seth, Daniel Massey, Miriam Margolyes, Jim Carter, Joanna Roth, Andras Balint; ***D:*** Ivan Passer; ***W:*** Paul Monash; ***C:*** Vilmos Zsigmond. **CABLE**

Stalingrad 🦴🦴 **1994** Group of German stormtroopers fall victim to the brutal war of attrition over Stalingrad in 1942 and 1943. Realistic depiction of war is not for the fainthearted. Originally a TV miniseries; German with subtitles. **150m/C VHS, DVD.** *GE* Dominique Horwitz, Thomas Kretschmann, Jochen Nickel; ***D:*** Joseph Vilsmaier; ***W:*** Joseph Vilsmaier; ***C:*** Joseph Vilsmaier; ***M:*** Norbert J. Schneider.

Stalk the Wild Child 🦴½ **1976** Well-intentioned but unconvincing American remake of Truffaut's "The Wild Child," about a child psychologist's efforts to rehabilitate a boy raised by wolves. TV pilot inspired "Lucan," a short-lived series. **78m/C VHS.** David Janssen, Trish Van Devere, Benjamin Bottoms, Joseph Bottoms; ***D:*** William Hale. **TV**

Stalked 🦴½ **1994 (R)** Daryl Gleeson (Underwood) saves the life of the widowed Brooke's (D'Abo) young son (Fennell). Naturally, she's grateful—only Daryl takes her gratitude for something more intimate and becomes fixated on her every move. **95m/C VHS.** Maryam D'Abo, Jay Underwood, Tod Fennell, Lisa Blount, Alex Karzis, Karen Robinson, Vivian Reis; ***D:*** Douglas Jackson.

Stalked woof! **1999** Macedonian transplant Aleksandr (Ognenovski) wakes up to an American nightmare, finding himself the target of a small town's wrath when framed for murder. Mayhem ensues, but not without those forced moments of pathos, romance, and testosterone-infused male bonding. Writer/director/star Ognenovski retreads the formula from early Stallone, Schwarzenegger, and Van Damme films: an outsider trapped in a hostile environment with only his wits and a few hundred rounds to protect him. Here, the cliches pile up faster than the body count. Add abysmal dialog, casting misfires (like the actor with a thick Russian accent playing the mayor of a small American town), and fight scenes rife with punches that don't connect, and we are in the presence of a potential Ed Wood for the action crowd. Sublime schlock, any way you slice it. **93m/C DVD, Wide.** Jorgo Ognenovski, Meto Jovanovski, Lisa Marie Wilson; ***D:*** Jorgo Ognenovski; ***W:*** Jorgo Ognenovski, Mary Quijano; ***C:*** Ricardo Jacques Gale.

Stalker 🦴🦴🦴 **1979** A meteorite, crashing to Earth, has caused a wasteland area known as the Zone. The Zone is forbidden to anyone except special guides called Stalkers. Three Stalkers enter the region searching for its center, which contains a room that supposedly reveals fantasies. From the Soviet team that made "Solaris." Filmed with both color and black-and-white sequences. Suspenseful atmosphere due to the director's use of long takes, movement, and color. In Russian with English subtitles. **160m/C VHS.** *RU* Alexander Kaidanovsky, Nikolai Grinko, Anatoli (Otto) Solonitzin, Alice Freindlikh; ***D:*** Andrei Tarkovsky; ***M:*** Eduard Artemyev.

Stalker 🦴½ *Fatal Affair* **1998 (R)** And what a very dumb, psychopathic stalker he is too. Family man Mack Maddox (Howell) is selected for jury duty and realizes that the murder victim is a woman with whom he had an affair. What's worse is the accused killer (Underwood) finds out that Maddox was involved with his wife and begins, well, stalking him and his family, even though Maddox has confessed his involvement to his wife and the cops. The plot never does make any sense and the flat performances don't help either. **93m/C VHS, DVD.** *CA* C. Thomas Howell, Jay Underwood, Mark Camacho, Maxim Roy, Bryn McAuley; ***D:*** Marc S. Grenier; ***W:*** Michael Rauch; ***C:*** Georges Archambault; ***M:*** Normand Corbeil. **VIDEO**

Stalking Danger 🦴½ *C.A.T. Squad* **1986 (PG)** A secret government group must terminate an assassination plot by a terrorist organization. **97m/C VHS.** Joe Cortese, Steve James, Patricia Charbonneau, Jack Youngblood; ***D:*** William Friedkin; ***M:*** Ennio Morricone.

Stalking Laura 🦴½ *I Can Make You Love Me: The Stalking of Laura Black* **1993** Laura Black (Shields) has just landed her first job at a California engineering firm where she meets co-worker Richard Farley (Thomas). He asks her out—she turns him down—he starts harassing her. Laura reports it to the company, who eventually fire Farley, and obtains a restraining order. He goes on a murderous rampage. Fact-based TV movie with Thomas effective as the dangerous obsessive. **90m/C VHS.** Brooke Shields, Richard Thomas, Viveka Davis, William Allen Young, Richard Yniguez, Scott Bryce.

The Stalking Moon 🦴½ **1969 (G)** Indian scout Peck, ready to retire, meets a woman and her half-breed son who have been captives of the Apaches for 10 years. He agrees to help them escape but learns that the woman's Indian husband is hunting them down. Skeletal plot with little meat on it; great scenery but you wouldn't know it. **109m/C VHS.** Gregory Peck, Eva Marie Saint, Robert Forster, Noland Clay; ***D:*** Robert Mulligan; ***W:*** Alvin Sargent.

Stamp of a Killer 🦴 **1987 (PG)** A tough cop tries to decipher the pattern of a rampaging serial killer. **95m/C VHS.** Jimmy Smits, Judith Light, Audra Lindley, Michael Parks, Rhea Perlman; ***D:*** Larry Elikann. **TV**

Stand Alone 🦴🦴 **1985 (R)** WWII vet Durning battles local dope dealers in his New York neighborhood. Self-serious anti-drug flick miscasts Durning (overweight and looking silly in fight scenes) and Grier. **94m/C VHS.** Charles Durning, Pam Grier, James Keach; ***D:*** Alan Beattie; ***W:*** Roy Carlson.

Stand and Deliver 🦴🦴 **1928** War vet joins Greek ranks for the smell of gunpowder in the morning and meets woman of his dreams. Kidnapped by infamous outlaws, he pledges allegiance to them before turning them over to the authorities, and he's free to live happily ever after with heartthrob. **57m/B VHS.** Rod La Rocque, Lupe Velez, Warner Oland, James Dime, Frank Lanning, Donald Crisp; ***D:*** Donald Crisp.

Stand and Deliver 🦴🦴🦴 **1988 (PG)** A tough teacher inspires students in an East L.A. barrio to take the Advanced Placement Test in calculus. A superb, inspirational true story, with a wonderful performance from Olmos. **105m/C VHS, DVD, 8mm.** Edward James Olmos, Lou Diamond Phillips, Rosana De Soto, Andy Garcia, Will Gotay, Ingrid Oliu, Virginia Paris, Mark Eliot, Eugene Glazer; ***D:*** Ramon Menendez; ***W:*** Ramon Menendez, Tom Musca; ***C:*** Tom Richmond; ***M:*** Craig Safan. Ind. Spirit '89: Actor (Olmos), Director (Menendez), Film, Screenplay, Support. Actor (Phillips), Support. Actress (De Soto).

Stand by Me 🦴🦴🦴 **1986 (R)** A sentimental, observant adaptation of the Stephen King novella "The Body." Four 12-year-olds trek into the Oregon wilderness to find the body of a missing boy, learning about death and personal courage. Told as a reminiscence by narrator "author" Dreyfuss with solid performances from all four child actors. Too much gratuitous obscenity, but a very good, gratifying film from can't-miss director Reiner. **87m/C VHS, DVD, 8mm, Wide.** River Phoenix, Wil Wheaton, Jerry O'Connell, Corey Feldman, Kiefer Sutherland, Richard Dreyfuss, Casey Siemaszko, John Cusack; ***D:*** Rob Reiner; ***W:*** Raynold Gideon; ***C:*** Thomas Del Ruth; ***M:*** Jack Nitzsche.

Stand-In 🦴🦴🦴 **1937** When a Hollywood studio is threatened with bankruptcy, the bank sends in timid efficiency expert Howard to save it. Satire of studio executives and big-budget movie making. Bogart is interestingly cast and effective in his first comedy role, playing a drunken producer in love with star Shelton. **91m/B VHS.** Humphrey Bogart, Joan Blondell, Leslie Howard, Alan Mowbray, Marla Shelton, Jack Carson; ***D:*** Tay Garnett.

Stand-In 🦴 **1985** A strange comedy-action film that takes a behind-the-scenes look at sleaze films and organized crime. **87m/C VHS.** Danny Glover; ***D:*** Robert Zagone.

Stand-Ins 🦴🦴½ **1997** Would-be actresses in pre-WWII Hollywood find themselves looking for fame and unwillingly settling for stand-in status. The girls all hang out at Jack's (Mandylor) bar, where Greta Garbo-double, druggie Shirley (Zuniga), battles with cynical Bette Davis stand-in, Monica (Ladd), as they celebrate the birthday of Jean Harlowish Martha Anne (Davis), along with Mae West clone Peggy (Chatton) and Marlene Dietrich stand-in Rhonda (Crider). This desperate gang are bitchy and frustrated and, of course, theatrical. Based on Kelleher's one-act play. **89m/C VHS, DVD.** Daphne Zuniga, Jordan Ladd, Sammi Davis, Missy (Melissa) Crider, Charlotte Chatton, Costas Mandylor, Katherine Heigl; ***D:*** Harvey Keith; ***W:*** Harvey Keith, Ed Kelleher; ***C:*** Andrzej Sekula; ***M:*** Bill Elliott.

Stand Off 🦴½ **1989** Two young hoodlums with guns take 18 girls hostage in a dormitory. In Hungarian with English subtitles. **97m/C VHS.** *HU* Ary Beri, Gabor Svidrony, Zbigniew Zapasiewicz, Istvan Szabo; ***D:*** Gyula Gazdag.

Stand Off 🦴🦴½ *April One* **1993 (PG-13)** Dramatization of a 14-hour hostage incident that took place at the Bahamanian High Commission in Ottawa on April Fools Day in 1986. Ex-con David Maltby (Shellen) politely demands that an empty firehall become a shelter for women by taking the High Commissioner for the Bahamas, Jane Briscoe (Sears), as a hostage. Somewhat flawed but psychologically interesting. **90m/C VHS.** *CA* Stephen Shellen, Djanet Sears, David Strathairn, Gordon Clapp, Pierre Curzi, Wayne Robson; ***D:*** Murray Battle; ***W:*** Murray Battle; ***M:*** Jonathan Goldsmith.

Stand Up and Cheer 🦴🦴½ **1934 (PG)** The new federal Secretary of Entertainment organizes a huge show to raise the country's depressed spirits. Near-invisible plot, fantastic premise are an excuse for lots of imagery, dancing, and comedy, including four-year-old Temple singing "Baby Take a Bow." Also available colorized. ♫I'm Laughing; We're Out of the Red; Broadway's Gone Hillbilly; Baby Take a Bow; This Is Our Last Night Together; She's Way Up Thar; Stand Up and Cheer. **80m/B VHS.** Shirley Temple, Warner Baxter, Madge Evans, Nigel Bruce, Stepin Fetchit, Frank Melton, Lila Lee, James Dunn, John Boles, Scotty Beckett; ***D:*** Hamilton MacFadden; ***W:*** Will Rogers, Ralph Spence; ***C:*** Ernest Palmer.

Standing Tall 🦴🦴 **1978** A small-time cattle rancher takes on a high-class land baron in this average, made-for-TV western set during the Depression. Playing a "half-breed," Forster carries an otherwise mediocre effort. **100m/C VHS.** Robert Forster, Linda Evans, Will Sampson, L.Q. (Justus E. McQueen) Jones; ***D:*** Harvey Hart.

Standoff 🦴🦴½ **1997 (R)** A botched FBI raid on a Texas cult stronghold lead the four fed survivors to seek shelter in an abandoned farmhouse. Surrounded by gunfire, they're soon not any safer inside, especially when they capture two of the cult's female recruits. **91m/C VHS.** Robert Sean Leonard, Natasha Henstridge, Dennis Haysbert, Keith Carradine, Tricia Vessey; ***D:*** Andrew Chapman; ***W:*** Andrew Chapman.

Stanley 🦴½ **1972 (PG)** Seminole Vietnam veteran Robinson uses rattlesnakes as his personal weapon of revenge against most of mankind. Thoroughly wretched effort in the gross-pets vein of "Willard" and "Ben." **108m/C VHS.** Chris Robinson, Alex Rocco, Susan Carroll; ***D:*** William Grefe.

Stanley and Iris 🦴🦴½ **1990 (PG-13)** Blue collar recent widow Fonda meets co-worker De Niro, whose illiteracy she helps remedy. Romance follows, inevitably but excruciatingly. Leads' strong presence helps along a very slow, underdeveloped plot. **107m/C VHS, Wide.** Jane Fonda, Robert De Niro, Swoosie Kurtz, Martha Plimpton, Harley Cross, Jamey Sheridan, Feodor Chaliapin Jr., Zohra Lampert, Loretta Devine, Julie Garfield; ***D:*** Martin Ritt; ***W:*** Harriet Frank Jr., Irving Ravetch; ***M:*** John Williams.

Stanley and Livingstone 🦴🦴🦴 **1939** The classic Hollywood kitsch version of the Victorian legend-based-on-fact. American journalist Tracy sets out into darkest Africa to locate a long lost Brisith explorer. Lavish, dramatically solid fictionalized history. (The real Stanley did not become a missionary—but hey, this is the movies). Tracy is excellent, as usual, and low-key. **101m/B VHS.** Spencer Tracy, Cedric Hardwicke, Nancy Kelly, Walter Brennan, Richard Greene, Charles Coburn, Henry Hull, Henry Travers, Miles Mander, Holmes Herbert, Paul Stanton, Brandon Hurst, Joseph Crehan, Russell Hicks; ***D:*** Henry King; ***C:*** George Barnes; ***M:*** Alfred Newman.

Star! 🦴🦴 *Those Were the Happy Times* **1968** Campy showbiz extravaganza based on the life of famed musical comedy performer Gertrude Lawrence (Andrews), star of the London and Broadway stage. Film follows Lawrence's adventures from the British music halls to her fateful meeting with Noel Coward (Massey), who would not only become her dearest friend but perform with and write for her as well. A tumultuous private life is also on display. 17 lavishly staged musical numbers helped boost the cost of the film to $14 million—big bucks in '68. Movie was a colossal flop on opening and was recut, deleting 50 minutes, but still didn't recoup its losses. Has gained a cult following. ♫Down at the Old Bull and Bush; Piccadilly; Star!; Oh, It's a Lovely War; In My Garden of Joy; Forbidden Fruit; Parisian Pierrot; Someday I'll Find You; Has Anybody Seen Our Ship?. **172m/C VHS, Wide.** Julie Andrews, Daniel Massey, Richard Crenna, Michael Craig, Robert Reed, Bruce Forsyth, Beryl Reid, John Collin, Alan Oppenheimer, Anthony Eisley, Jenny Agutter, J. Pat O'Malley, Richard Karlan, Lynley Laurence, Harvey Jason, Elizabeth St. Clair; ***D:*** Robert Wise; ***W:*** William Fairchild; ***C:*** Ernest Laszlo.

The Star Chamber 🦴🦴 **1983 (R)** A conscientious judge (Douglas) sees criminals freed on legal technicalities and wonders if he should take justice into his own hands. He finds a secret society that administers justice extra-legally. Implausible yet predictable. **109m/C VHS.** Michael Douglas, Hal Holbrook, Yaphet Kotto, Sharon Gless, James B. Sikking; ***D:*** Peter Hyams; ***W:*** Peter Hyams, Roderick Taylor.

Star Crash 🦴🦴½ *Stella Star* **1978 (PG)** Trio of adventurers (woman, man, and robot) sent by emperor Plummer square off against interstellar evil (Spinell) by using their wits and technological wizardry. Semi-funny and cheesy sci-fi, done with style beyond its limited budget. **92m/C VHS.** *IT* Caroline Munro, Marjoe Gortner, Christopher Plummer, David Hasselhoff, Robert Tessier, Joe Spinell, Nadia Cassini, Judd Hamilton; ***D:*** Lewis (Luigi Cozzi) Coates; ***W:*** Lewis (Luigi Cozzi) Coates; ***M:*** John Barry.

Star Crystal 🦴 **1985 (R)** Aboard a spaceship, an indestructible alien hunts down the human crew. Cheap imitation of "Alien." **93m/C VHS.** C. Jutson Campbell, Faye Bolt, John W. Smith; ***D:*** Lance Lindsay.

Star 80 🦴🦴½ **1983 (R)** Based on the true-life tragedy of Playmate of the Year Dorothy Stratten and her manager-husband Paul Snider as they battle for control of her body, her mind, and her money, with gruesome results. Roberts is overpowering as the vile Snider, but the movie is generally unpleasant. Fosse's last film. **104m/C VHS, DVD.** Mariel Hemingway, Eric Roberts, Cliff Robertson, David Clennon, Josh Mostel, Roger Rees, Carroll Baker; ***D:*** Bob Fosse; ***W:*** Bob Fosse; ***C:*** Sven Nykvist; ***M:*** Ralph Burns.

Star Hunter 🦴½ **1995 (R)** When a bus filled with football players and cheerleaders takes a wrong turn, it winds up in an intergalatic hunting ground where the humans become the prey. Lots of lame chase and would-be action scenes. **80m/C VHS.** Roddy McDowall, Stella Stevens, Ken Stott, Zack (Zach) Ward, Wendy Schumacher; ***D:*** Cole McKay.

A Star Is Born 🦴🦴🦴½ **1937** A movie star declining in popularity marries a shy girl and helps her become a star. Her fame eclipses his and tragic consequences follow. Shows Hollywood-behind-the-scenes machinations. Stunning ending is based on the real-life tragedy of silent film star Wallace Reid, who died of a morphine overdose in 1923 at age 31. Remade twice, in 1954 and 1976. **111m/C VHS, DVD.** Janet Gaynor, Fredric March, Adolphe Menjou, May Robson, Andy Devine, Lionel Stander, Franklin Pangborn; ***D:*** William A. Wellman; ***W:*** William A. Wellman, David O. Selznick, Dorothy Parker; ***C:*** William Howard Greene; ***M:*** Max Steiner. Oscars '37: Story.

A Star Is Born 🦴🦴🦴½ **1954 (PG)** Aging actor helps a young actress to fame. She becomes his wife, but alcoholism and failure are too much for him. She honors his memory. Remake of the 1937 classic was Garland's triumph, a superb and varied performance. Newly restored version reinstates over 20 minutes of long-missing footage, including three Garland musical numbers. ♫I'll Get By; You Took Advantage of Me; Black Bottom; Peanut Vendor; My Melancholy Baby; Swanee; It's a New World; Gotta Have Me Go with You; Somewhere There's Someone. **175m/C VHS, DVD, Wide.** Judy Garland, James Mason, Jack Carson, Tommy Noonan, Charles Bickford, Emerson Treacy, Charles Halton; ***D:*** George Cukor; ***W:*** Moss Hart; ***C:*** Sam Leavitt; ***M:*** Harold Arlen, Ira Gershwin. Golden Globes '55: Actor—Mus./Comedy (Mason), Actress—Mus./Comedy (Garland), Natl. Film Reg. '00.

A Star Is Born 🦴🦴 **1976 (R)** Miserable update of the 1937 and 1954 classics modified to permit Ms. Streisand to showcase her hit song "Evergreen." The tragic story of one rock star (the relentlessly un-hip Streisand) on her way to the top and another (good old boy Kristofferson) whose career is in decline. Kristofferson is miscast, Streisand eventually numbing, but film may interest those looking into big-budget, big-star misfires. ♫Watch Closely Now; Spanish Lies; Hellacious Acres; With One More Look At You; Woman in the Moon; Queen Bee; Everything; Crippled Cow; I Believe in Love. **140m/C VHS.** Barbra Streisand, Kris Kristofferson, Paul Mazursky, Gary Busey, Sally Kirkland, Oliver Clark, Marta Heflin, Robert Englund; ***D:*** Frank Pierson; ***W:*** Frank Pierson, Joan Didion, John Gregory Dunne; ***C:*** Robert L. Surtees; ***M:*** Paul Williams. Oscars '76: Song ("Evergreen"); Golden Globes '77: Actor—Mus./Comedy (Kristofferson), Actress—Mus./Comedy (Streisand), Film—Mus./Comedy, Song ("Evergreen"), Score.

Star Kid 🦴🦴🦴 *The Warrior of Waverly Street* **1997 (PG)** Twelve-year-old Spencer Griffith (Mazzello) is the new wimp in town, with a face that immediately attracts the fists of the biggest bully around, Turbo Bradley (Simmrin). On the run from Turbo, Spencer encounters Cy, an experimental cyber-battlesuit built by cutesy good aliens to save themselves from reptilian bad aliens. After inserting himself into Cy, and solving a few problems common to boy-inside-alien relationships, Spencer takes his first awkward steps, gets some humorous revenge on Turbo, and learns some lessons about confronting one's fears and accepting responsibility. Film delivers enough action and effects to keep everyone happy. **101m/C VHS, DVD.** Joseph Mazzello, Alex Daniels, Richard Gilliland, Joey Simmrin, Brian Simpson, Danny Masterson, Corinne Bohrer, Arthur Burghardt, Ashlee Levitch, Heidi Lotito; ***D:*** Manny Coto; ***W:*** Manny Coto; ***C:*** Ronn Schmidt; ***M:*** Nicholas Pike.

Star Knight 🦴 *Starknight* **1985 (PG-13)** Weird combo of sci fi and medieval romance. A spaceship lands near a European castle and the local princess falls for one of the visitors—much to her daddy's dismay. Very silly. **92m/C VHS.** *SP* Harvey Keitel, Klaus Kinski, Fernando Rey; ***D:*** Fernando Colomo.

The Star Maker 🦴🦴 *The Star Man; L'Uomo delle Stelle* **1995 (R)** Con man Joe Morelli (Castellitto) travels through the villages of 1950s Sicily claiming to be a movie talent scout. For a fee, he offers the locals a chance to shoot a screen test, which reveals various bits and pieces of their lives. There's a brief romance and Joe's scam eventually comes to light but the story's more nostalgia than narrative. Italian with subtitles. **107m/C VHS.** *IT* Sergio Castellitto, Tiziana Lodato; ***D:*** Giuseppe Tornatore; ***W:*** Giuseppe Tornatore, Fabio Rinaudo; ***C:*** Dante Spinotti; ***M:*** Ennio Morricone.

Star Maps 🦴🦴 **1997 (R)** Ambitious and ambiguous effort from first-time director Arteta has boyish Carlos (Spain) chase his dreams of movie stardom on the streets of Hollywood. Pimped by his manipulative and brutal father Pepe (Figueroa), Carlos sells "maps of the stars' homes" as a cover for his real job, male prostitute. Dad's hooker mistress (Murphy) mentors him in the family business. Add in a mother (Velez) "recovering" from a nervous breakdown by talking to long-dead Mexican comedy star Cantinflas, and a brother (Chandler) who acts out scenes from Mexican wrestling movies, and it's a wonder he doesn't make his screen debut on Jerry Springer. Despite fine performances and a solid debut effort from Arteta, the tragic elements don't fit well with the attempted comic tone of the rest of the movie. **80m/C VHS.** Douglas Spain, Efrain Figueroa, Lysa Flores, Kandeyce Jensen, Martha Velez, Annette Murphy, Vincent Chandler, Al Vincente, Herbert Siguenza, Robin Thomas, Jeff Michalski; ***D:*** Miguel Arteta; ***W:*** Miguel Arteta; ***C:*** Chuy Chavez; ***M:*** Lysa Flores.

Star of Midnight 🦴🦴 **1935** A lawyer/detective becomes involved in the disappearance of the leading lady in a Broadway show and the murder of a columnist. Powell and Rogers take on characters similar to Nick and Nora Charles, but the pizazz of the "Thin Man" series is missing. **90m/B VHS.** Ginger Rogers, William Powell, Paul Kelly; ***D:*** Stephen Roberts.

The Star Packer 🦴🦴 **1934** Wayne puts on a marshal's badge, straightens out a gang of crooks, and still finds time for romance. Implausible and kind of dull early Wayne vehicle. **53m/B VHS, DVD.** John Wayne, George "Gabby" Hayes, Earl Dwire, Yakima Canutt; ***D:*** Robert North Bradbury; ***W:*** Robert North Bradbury; ***C:*** Archie Stout.

Star Portal 🦴🦴 **1997 (R)** Alien Rena (Massey) comes to Earth seeking blood to help her dying race. Assuming the form of a babe, she falls in love with a hematologist (Bauer), and must battle a law-enforcer from her own planet. **83m/C VHS.** Athena Massey, Steven Bauer, Stephen Davies, Anthony Crivello; ***D:*** Jon Purdy. **VIDEO**

Star Quest 🦴 *Beyond the Rising Moon; Space 2074* **1989** A genetically engineered woman fights for freedom from her corporate creators. Mediocre effects and some pointless action; done much better by Ridley Scott in "Blade Runner." **90m/C VHS.** Tracy Davis, Hans Bachman, Michael Mack; ***D:*** Phillip Cook.

Star Quest 🦴🦴½ **1994 (R)** Eight astronauts, suspended in a cryogenic sleep for nearly 100 years, awaken to find the human race has been destroyed by a nuclear holocaust. **95m/C VHS.** Steven Bauer, Emma Samms, Alan Rachins, Brenda Bakke, Ming Na, Gregory McKinney, Cliff DeYoung; ***D:*** Rick Jacobson.

Star Reporter 🦴½ **1939** A son takes over his father's newspaper when dad is killed by gangsters. The son uses the paper in an attempt to destroy the underworld, but stumbles on some startling personal information that could drastically backfire on him. Generally interesting plot, but has some implausibility and too-broad characterization. **62m/B VHS.** Warren Hull, Marsha Hunt, Morgan Wallace, Clay Clement, Wallis (Clarke) Clark, Virginia Howell, Paul Fix, Joseph Crehan; ***D:*** Howard Bretherton.

Star Slammer 🦴½ **1987 (R)** A beautiful woman is unjustly sentenced to a brutal intergalactic prison ship. She leads the convicts to escape amid zany situations. Unevenly funny sci-fi comedy. **85m/C VHS, DVD, Wide.** Ross Hagen, John Carradine, Sandy Brooke, Aldo Ray; ***D:*** Fred Olen Ray; ***W:*** Michael Sonye; ***C:*** Paul Elliot; ***M:*** Anthony Harris.

Star Spangled Girl 🦴½ **1971 (G)** One of Neil Simon's lesser plays, one of his least movies. A pert, patriotic young lady captures the hearts of two left-wing alternative-newspaperguys next door; their political conflicts never rise above bland sitcom level. **94m/C VHS.** Sandy Duncan, Tony Roberts, Todd Susman, Elizabeth Allen; ***D:*** Jerry Paris; ***W:*** Neil Simon; ***C:*** Sam Leavitt; ***M:*** Charles Fox.

Star Spangled Rhythm 🦴🦴🦴 **1942** Movie studio guard (Moore) has told his son (Bracken), a sailor, that he's actually the head of the studio in this WW2 musical/comedy. When he learns his son and his pals are coming for a visit, he enlists the aid of a friendly studio switchboard operator (Hutton) to pull a fast one. (Luckily, the real studio boss is out of town). Plot doesn't matter anyway since its just an excuse for a lot of studio stars to show up and perform. ♫A Sweater, a Sarong and a Peek-a-Boo Bang; That Old Black Magic; Hit the Road to Dreamland; Old Glory; On the Swing Shift; Doing It for Defense; Sharp as a Tack; He Loved Me Till the All-Clear Came. **99m/B VHS, DVD.** Betty Hutton, Eddie Bracken, Victor Moore, Bing Crosby, Ray Milland, Bob Hope, Veronica Lake, Dorothy Lamour, Susan Hayward, Dick Powell, Mary Martin, Alan Ladd, Paulette Goddard, Cecil B. DeMille, Arthur Treacher, Preston Sturges, Eddie Anderson, William Bendix; ***D:*** George Marshall; ***W:*** Melvin Frank, George S. Kaufman, Norman Panama, Arthur Ross, Harry Tugend; ***C:*** Theodor Sparkuhl, Leo Tover.

Star Time 🦴½ **1992** Henry is a mentally ill loser who wants to be as happy and famous as his favorite TV stars. Deciding to kill himself, Henry is stopped by the mysterious Sam Bones, who offers him TV stardom—at a steep price. Henry achieves his 15 minutes of fame as a serial killer and his only link to reality is a female social worker. **85m/C VHS.** Michael St. Gerard, John P. Ryan, Maureen Teefy; ***D:*** Alexander Cassini; ***W:*** Alexander Cassini; ***C:*** Fernando Arguelles.

Star Trek: The Motion Picture 🦴🦴½ **1980 (G)** The Enterprise fights a strange alien force that threatens Earth in this first film adaptation of the famous TV series. Shatner's Kirk has been promoted to admiral and is called to take command of the vessel. He gets his old crew to tag along as well. Very slow moving; followed by numerous sequels. Twelve additional minutes of previously unseen footage have been added to this home video version of the theatrical feature. **143m/C VHS, DVD, Wide.** William Shatner, Leonard Nimoy, DeForest Kelley, James Doohan, Stephen Collins, Persis Khambatta, Nichelle Nichols, Walter Koenig, George Takei, Majel Barrett, Mark Lenard; ***D:*** Robert Wise; ***W:*** Harold Livingston; ***C:*** Richard H. Kline; ***M:*** Jerry Goldsmith.

Star Trek 2: The Wrath of Khan 🦴🦴🦴 **1982 (PG)** Picking up from the 1967 Star Trek episode "Space Seed," Admiral James T. Kirk and the crew of the Enterprise must battle Khan, an old foe out for revenge. Warm and comradly in the nostalgic mode of its successors. Introduced Kirk's former lover and unknown son to the series plot, as well as Mr. Spock's "death," which led to the next sequel (1984's "The Search for Spock"). **113m/C VHS, DVD, Wide.** William Shatner, Leonard Nimoy, Ricardo Montalban, DeForest Kelley, Nichelle Nichols, James Doohan, George Takei, Walter Koenig, Kirstie Alley, Merritt Butrick, Paul Winfield, Bibi Besch; ***D:*** Nicholas Meyer; ***W:*** Jack Sowards; ***C:*** Gayne Rescher; ***M:*** James Horner.

Star Trek 3: The Search for Spock 🦴🦴½ **1984 (PG)** Captain Kirk hijacks the USS Enterprise and commands the aging crew to go on a mission to the Genesis Planet to discover whether Mr. Spock still lives (supposedly he died in the last movie). Klingons threaten, as usual. Somewhat slow and humorless, but intriguing. Third in the series. **105m/C VHS, DVD, 8mm, Wide.** William Shatner, Leonard Nimoy, DeForest Kelley, James Doohan, George Takei, Walter Koenig, Mark Lenard, Robin Curtis, Merritt Butrick, Christopher Lloyd, Judith Anderson, John Larroquette, James B. Sikking, Nichelle Nichols, Cathie Shirriff, Miguel Ferrer, Grace Lee Whitney; ***D:*** Leonard Nimoy; ***W:*** Harve Bennett; ***C:*** Charles Correll; ***M:*** James Horner.

Star Trek 4: The Voyage Home 🦴🦴🦴 **1986 (PG)** Kirk and the gang go back in time (to the 1980s, conveniently) to save the Earth of the future from destruction. Filled with hilarious moments and exhilarating action; great special effects enhance the timely conservation theme. Watch for the stunning going-back-in-time sequence. Spock is particularly funny as he tries to fit in and learn the '80s lingo! Also available as part of Paramount's "director's series," in which Nimoy discusses various special effects aspects in the making of the film. The best in the six-part (so far) series. **119m/C VHS, DVD, 8mm, Wide.** William Shatner, DeForest Kelley, Catherine Hicks, James Doohan, Nichelle Nichols, George Takei, Walter Koenig, Mark Lenard, Leonard Nimoy, Michael Berryman, Majel Barrett, Brock Peters, John Schuck, Jane Wyatt; ***D:*** Leonard Nimoy; ***W:*** Nicholas Meyer, Harve Bennett, Peter Krikes, Steve Meerson; ***C:*** Don Peterman; ***M:*** Leonard Rosenman.

Star Trek 5: The Final Frontier 🦴½ **1989 (PG)** A renegade Vulcan kidnaps the Enterprise and takes it on a journey to the mythic center of the universe. Shatner's big-action directorial debut (he also co-wrote the script) is a poor follow-up to the Nimoy-directed fourth entry in the series. Heavy-handed and pretentiously pseudo-theological. **107m/C VHS, DVD, 8mm, Wide.** William Shatner, Leonard Nimoy, DeForest Kelley, James Doohan, Laurence Luckinbill, Walter Koenig, George Takei, Nichelle Nichols, David Warner, Melanie Shatner, Harve Bennett; ***D:*** William Shatner; ***W:*** David Loughery, William Shatner; ***C:*** Andrew Laszlo; ***M:*** Jerry Goldsmith. Golden Raspberries '89: Worst Picture, Worst Actor (Shatner), Worst Director (Shatner).

Star Trek 6: The Undiscovered Country 🦴🦴½ **1991 (PG)** The final chapter in the long running Star Trek series is finally here. The Federation and the Klingon Empire are preparing a much-needed peace summit but Captain Kirk has his doubts about the true intentions of the Federation's longtime enemies. When a Klingon ship is attacked, Kirk and the crew of the Enterprise, who are accused of the misdeed, must try to find the real perpetrator. Has an exciting, climactic ending. As is typical of the series, the film highlights current events—glasnost—in its plotlines. Meyer also directed Star Trek movie 2 ("The Wrath of Khan") and wrote the screenplay for 4 ("The Voyage Home"). **110m/C VHS, DVD, CD-I.** William Shatner, Leonard Nimoy, DeForest Kelley, James Doohan, George Takei, Walter Koenig, Nichelle Nichols, Christopher Plummer, Kim Cattrall, Iman, David Warner, Mark Lenard, Grace Lee Whitney, Brock Peters, Kurtwood Smith, Rosana De Soto, John Schuck, Michael Dorn, Christian Slater; ***D:*** Nicholas Meyer; ***W:*** Nicholas Meyer, Denny Martin Flinn; ***C:*** Hiro Narita; ***M:*** Cliff Eidelman.

Star Trek: First Contact 🦴🦴🦴 **1996 (PG-13)** The eighth big-screen Trek saga is firmly in the hands of the "Next Generation" cast as Picard and the Enterprise cross paths with the Borg and their sinister Queen. It's hard to tell whether the cry "Resistance is Futile" is coming from the Borg, or the Trek franchise itself, as this installment may well bring in new "Trekkers" with its "less techno-babble, more action" approach and the fact that this crew can act. The Borg attempt to change history by travelling back in time (to 2063) to prevent scientist Cromwell from inventing warp drive. While the less-interesting members of the crew stay on Earth to help out with the launch, the battle for the Enterprise rages on up in space. Trademark effects, humor, and idealism are in abundant supply and should please the long-time fan as well as the neophyte. **111m/C VHS, DVD.** Patrick Stewart, Jonathon Frakes, Brent Spiner, LeVar Burton, Michael Dorn, Marina Sirtis, Gates (Cheryl) McFadden, Alfre Woodard, James Cromwell, Alice Krige, Neal McDonough, Robert Picardo, Dwight Schultz; ***D:*** Jonathon Frakes; ***W:*** Brannon Braga, Ronald D. Moore; ***C:*** Matthew F. Leonetti; ***M:*** Jerry Goldsmith.

Star Trek: Generations 🦴🦴🦴 **1994 (PG)** The sci-fi phenomena continues with the first film spun off from the recently departed "Star Trek: The Next Generation" TV series and the seventh following the adventures of the Enterprise crew. Captain Kirk is propelled into the future thanks to an explosion and manages to hook up with current starship captain, Picard. Of course, just in time to save the galaxy from the latest space loon, the villainous Dr. Soren (McDowell), renegade Klingons, and your basic mysterious space entity. For comic relief, android Data gets an emotion chip. Terrific special effects (courtesy of Industrial Light and Magic) and yes, the heroic Kirk receives his mandatory grandiose death scene. Other original characters making a brief appearance are Scotty and Chekov. An entertaining romp through time and space. **117m/C VHS, DVD.** William Shatner, Patrick Stewart, Malcolm McDowell, Whoopi Goldberg, Jonathon Frakes, Brent Spiner, LeVar Burton, Michael Dorn, Gates (Cheryl) McFadden, Marina Sirtis, James Doohan, Walter Koenig, Alan Ruck; ***D:*** David Carson; ***W:*** Ronald D. Moore, Brannon Braga; ***C:*** John A. Alonzo; ***M:*** Dennis McCarthy; ***V:*** Majel Barrett.

Star Trek: Insurrection 🦴🦴½ **1998 (PG)** In the ninth film, Captain Picard (Stewart) goes to Data's (Spiner) rescue when the android seemingly goes berserk while on a scientific mission to investigate the non-techno culture of the peaceful Ba'ku. What Picard discovers is a planet that's virtually a fountain of youth and a dastardly plan by the Federation and the evil Son'a, led by bitter Ru'afro (Abraham), to gain the secret even though it means destroying the planet to do so. More humor and romance than usual done in the typical professional manner of the franchise. **100m/C VHS, DVD.** Patrick Stewart, Brent Spiner, Donna Murphy, F. Murray Abraham, Jonathon Frakes, LeVar Burton, Michael Dorn, Anthony Zerbe, Gates (Cheryl) McFadden, Marina Sirtis, Gregg Henry, Daniel Hugh-Kelly; ***D:*** Jonathon Frakes; ***W:*** Michael Piller; ***C:*** Matthew F. Leonetti; ***M:*** Jerry Goldsmith.

Star Wars 🦴🦴🦴🦴 *Star Wars: Episode 4—A New Hope* **1977 (PG)** First entry Lucas's "Star Wars" trilogy proved to be one of the biggest boxoffice hits of all time. A young hero, a captured princess, a hotshot pilot, cute robots, a vile villain, and a heroic and mysterious Jedi knight blend together with marvelous special effects in a fantasy tale about rebel forces engaged in a life or death struggle with the tyrant leaders of the Galactic Empire. Set a new cinematic standard for realistic special effects, making many pre-"Star Wars" effects seem almost laughable in retrospect. Followed by "The Empire Strikes Back" (1980) and "Return of the Jedi" (1983). **121m/C VHS, Wide.** Mark Hamill, Carrie Fisher, Harrison Ford, Alec Guinness, Peter Cushing, Kenny Baker, James Earl Jones, David Prowse, Anthony Daniels, Peter Mayhew; ***D:*** George Lucas; ***W:*** George Lucas; ***C:*** Gilbert Taylor; ***M:*** John Williams. Oscars '77: Art Dir./Set Dec., Costume Des., Film Editing, Sound, Visual FX, Orig. Score; AFI '98: Top 100; Golden Globes '78: Score; L.A. Film Critics '77: Film, Natl. Film Reg. '89.

Star Wars: Episode 1—The Phantom Menace 🦴🦴🦴 **1999 (PG)** Lucas' first "Star Wars" film in 16 years is also the beginning of his prequel trilogy. Jedi Master Qui-Gon Jinn (Neeson) and rebellious apprentice Obi-Wan Kenobi (McGregor) are sent to the peaceful planet Naboo to aid young Queen Amidala (Portman), who is being forced to sign a Trade Federation treaty. When the Jedis escape to Tatooine with Amidala, they encounter a slave boy, Anakin (Lloyd), whom Jinn realizes is enpowered by the Force, and are pursued by the Federation and evil Dark Lord, Darth Maul (Park). The special effects are all they're cracked up to be (practically the whole thing is computer generated, but doesn't look it), and the action scenes have the zip and excitement you'd expect. The characters and story may aim a little more at kids than some would like, but those kids will be the teenagers that flock to see the next two. Some plot holes, but that's to be expected in the first installment of a trilogy. **130m/C VHS, DVD, Wide.** Liam Neeson, Ewan McGregor, Natalie Portman, Jake Lloyd, Ian McDiarmid, Samuel L. Jackson, Ray Park, Pernilla August, Terence Stamp, Brian Blessed, Oliver Ford Davies, Hugh Quarshie, Ralph Brown, Sofia Coppola; ***D:*** George Lucas; ***W:*** George Lucas; ***C:*** David Tattersall; ***M:*** John Williams; ***V:*** Ahmed Best, Frank Oz. MTV Movie Awards '00: Action Seq.

Star Wars: Episode 2—Attack of the Clones 🦴🦴🦴½ **2002 (PG)** Ambitious Jedi knight Anakin (Christensen) goes further on his journey to the dark side while Obi-Wan (McGregor) tries to reign him in. He and Amidala (Portman), who's now a senator, have a forbidden romance, and the Republic continues to be plaqued by enemies from within and without. The romance angle, so touted in the pre-release hype, seems forced due to a lack of chemistry between the two leads, but everything else is spectacular. The exposition is handled much better that in Episode 1, (and really whets the appetite for Episode 3) and the action set pieces are (as expected) well done, and superbly choreographed. Christensen does a fine job of showing flashes of the personality changes to come in Anakin, while Jackson finally gets to show what he's got as the baddest Jedi this side of Yoda. **124m/C VHS, DVD.** *US* Ewan McGregor, Hayden Christensen, Natalie Portman, Ian McDiarmid, Temuera Morrison, Samuel L. Jackson, Christopher Lee, Pernilla August, Jimmy Smits, Jack Thompson, Rose Byrne, Oliver Ford Davies, Leanna (Leeanna) Walsman, Anthony Daniels, Kenny Baker, Ronald Falk; ***D:*** George Lucas; ***W:*** George Lucas, Jonathan Hales; ***C:*** David Tattersall; ***M:*** John Williams; ***V:*** Frank Oz, Ahmed Best, Andrew Secombe.

Starbird and Sweet William 🦴🦴 **1973 (G)** On a solo plane flight, a young Native American crashes in the wilderness. He must fight for survival in the harsh woods with his only friend, a bear cub. Good family fare. **95m/C VHS.** A. Martinez, Louise Fitch, Dan Haggerty, Skip Homeier; ***D:*** Jack B. Hively.

Starchaser: The Legend of Orin 🦴🦴½ **1985 (PG)** Animated fantasy about a boy who must save the world of the future from malevolent hordes. **107m/C VHS.** ***D:*** Steven Hahn; ***M:*** Andrew Belling.

Stardom 🦴🦴½ **2000 (R)** Price of fame, media-obsessed drama set in the world of modeling. Sultry teen Tina (Pare) is playing on a women's hockey team in smalltown Ontario when she's discovered. French photo Philippe (Berling) puts her on the road to stardom, American manager Renny (Gibson) moves her career forward, but her success causes trouble for the older man she becomes invovled with—celebrity restauranteur Barry Levine (Aykroyd) until Tina moves on. All the while she's part of the disposable, instant celeb culture by you're never too sure who's doing the manipulating and how much Tina is complicit in her own exploitation. **102m/C VHS, DVD, Wide.** *FR CA* Jessica Pare, Dan Aykroyd, Thomas Gibson, Charles Berling, Frank Langella, Robert Lepage; ***D:*** Denys Arcand; ***W:*** Denys Arcand, Jacob Potashnik; ***C:*** Guy Dufaux; ***M:*** Francois Dompierre.

Stardust Memories 🦴🦴½ **1980 (PG)** Allen's "8 1/2." A comic filmmaker is plagued with creative blocks, relationships, modern fears and fanatical fans. The last film in Allen's varying self-analysis, with explicit references to Fellini and Antonioni. **88m/B VHS, DVD.** Woody Allen, Charlotte Rampling, Jessica Harper, Marie-Christine Barrault, Tony Roberts, Helen Hanft, Cynthia Gibb, Amy Wright, Daniel Stern; ***D:*** Woody Allen; ***W:*** Woody Allen; ***C:*** Gordon Willis.

The Starfighters 🦴½ **1963** Air Force Lieutenant Dornan must prove his courage to his disapproving war hero Congressman father. Dornan flies his F-104 through a dangerous storm, thereby earning his father's respect, which leads them to form a bond. **84m/C VHS.** Robert Dornan, Richard Jordahl, Shirley Olmstead.

Starflight One 🦴🦴 *Starflight: the Plane that Couldn't Land* **1983** A space shuttle is called on to save the world's first hypersonic airliner trapped in an orbit above earth. The film features good special effects, but also a predictable "rescue-mission" plot. **155m/C VHS.** Ray Milland, Lee Majors, Hal Linden, Lauren Hutton, Robert Webber, Terry Kiser; ***D:*** Jerry Jameson.

Stargate 🦴🦴 **1994 (PG-13)** U.S. military probe of a ring-shaped ancient Egyptian artifact (your tax dollars at work) sends he-man colonel Russell and geeky Egyptologist Spader into a parallel universe. There they meet the builders of the pyramids who are enslaved by an evil despot (Davidson) posing as a sun god. Ambitious premise zapped from prepubescent imaginations gets an A for effort, but a silly plot that jumbles biblical epic panoramas and space odyssey special effects with otherworldly mysticism and needless emotional hang-ups trade shlock for style. Spader's shaggy scholar is neurotically fun, Russell's jarhead a bore, and Davidson's vampy villain an unintended hoot. **119m/C VHS, DVD.** Kurt Russell, James Spader, Jaye Davidson, Viveca Lindfors, Alexis Cruz, Leon Rippy, John Diehl, Erik Avari, Mili Avital; ***D:*** Roland Emmerich; ***W:*** Dean Devlin, Roland Emmerich; ***C:*** Jeff Okun; ***M:*** David Arnold.

Starhops 🦴½ **1978 (R)** A trio of buxom young women attract business to their drive-in restaurant by wearing skimpy outfits. Surprisingly inoffensive for an "R" rating. **92m/C VHS.** Dorothy Buhrman, Sterling Frazier, Jillian Kesner, Peter Paul Liapis, Paul Ryan, Anthony Mannino, Dick Miller; ***D:*** Barbara Peeters; ***W:*** Stephanie Rothman.

Stark 🦴½ **1985** Wichita detective journeys to Las Vegas in an effort to locate his missing sister. During his search, he finds himself taking on the mob. Pilot for a TV series that never happened, and Tidyman's last screenplay. A sequel, "Stark: Mirror Image," was made in 1986. **94m/C VHS.** Nicolas Surovy, Dennis Hopper, Marilu Henner, Seth Jaffe; ***D:*** Rod Holcomb; ***W:*** Ernest Tidyman. **TV**

Starlight 🦴½ **1997** Alien envoy searches for a genetic component (found in a half-alien/half-human hybrid) that will allow her people to live in a post-apocalytic Earth's polluted atmosphere. **100m/C VHS.** Rae Dawn Chong, Willie Nelson, Billy Wirth, Jim Byrnes, Deborah Wakeham; ***D:*** Jonathan Kay.

Starlight Hotel 🦴🦴½ **1990 (PG)** An unhappy teenage girl sets off to find her father, with the help of a shellshocked veteran wrongly accused of a crime. Set in New Zealand during the Depression. Lovely scenery and good acting highlight nice story of odd friendship. **90m/C VHS.** *NZ* Greer Robson, Peter Phelps, Marshall Napier, Pat Smythe, Alice Fraser; ***D:*** Sam Pillsbury.

Starman 🦴🦴🦴 **1984 (PG)** An alien from an advanced civilization lands in Wisconsin. He hides beneath the guise of a grieving young widow's recently deceased husband. He then makes her drive him across country to rendezvous with his spacecraft so he can return home. Well-acted, interesting twist on the "Stranger in a Strange Land" theme. Bridges is fun as the likeable starman; Allen is lovely and earthy in her worthy follow-up to "Raiders of the Lost Ark." **115m/C VHS, DVD, Wide.** Jeff Bridges, Karen Allen, Charles Martin Smith, Richard Jaeckel; ***D:*** John Carpenter; ***W:*** Bruce A. Evans, Raynold Gideon; ***C:*** Donald M. Morgan; ***M:*** Jack Nitzsche.

Starry Night 🦴🦴½ **1999 (PG-13)** So what would artist Vincent Van Gogh do if he suddenly found himself alive (a century after his death) in modern-day Los Angeles and discovered that his paintings, which were considered ugly and worthless in his lifetime, were collected by the wealthy and worth a fortune? Well, he might decide to steal them back, sell them himself, and give the money to other struggling artists. And he might also find himself falling in love with a pretty art student who inspires him to paint new masterpieces. **98m/C VHS, DVD.** Abbott Alexander, Lisa Waltz, Sally Kirkland, Lou Wagner; ***D:*** Paul Davids; ***W:*** Paul Davids; ***C:*** David W. Smith; ***M:*** Brad Warnaar.

Stars and Bars 🦴🦴 **1988 (R)** O'Connor misfire strands Day-Lewis in the midst of hillbillies. A stuffy English art expert travels from New York to Georgia to price a Renoir, and happens on a bizarre backwoods family marginally run by Stanton. Stereotypical pursuit of humor teeters precariously on the edge of black comedy without actually being funny. Stinky script dooms fine cast to just acting weird in a "Deliverance" sort of way. Based on the novel by William Boyd. **95m/C VHS.** Daniel Day-Lewis, Harry Dean Stanton, John Cusack, Joan Cusack, Spalding Gray, Will Patton, Martha Plimpton, Glenne Headly, Laurie Metcalf, Maury Chaykin; ***D:*** Pat O'Connor; ***W:*** William Boyd.

Stars and Stripes Forever 🦴🦴🦴 *Marching Along* **1952** Sumptious, Hollywoodized bio of composer John Phillip Sousa, based on his memoir "Marching Along," but more concerned with the romantic endeavors of young protege Wagner. Accuracy aside, it's solid entertainment even if you're not mad about march music. ♫Stars and Stripes Forever; El Capitan; Washington Post; King Cotton; The Battle Hymn of the Republic; Dixie; Light Cavalry; Turkey in the Straw; Hail to the Chief. **89m/C VHS.** Clifton Webb, Debra Paget, Robert Wagner, Ruth Hussey, Finlay Currie; ***D:*** Henry Koster.

The Stars Fell on Henrietta 🦴🦴½ **1994 (PG)** Down-on-his-luck wildcatter Mr. Cox (Duvall) searches for oil and redemption. He's looking for it on the failing farm of couple Don and Cora Day (Quinn and Fisher) in the middle of the 1930s Texas dustbowl with the reluctant backing of more successful oil man (Dennehy). Quiet character study of an obsessed wheeler-dealer playing with his last poker chip verges on the romantic in its quest for black gold, true to its message about never giving up hope. Directorial debut for Keach is led by typically excellent portrayals by Duvall and Dennehy, but Quinn and Fisher are given little to work with. Marks the first movie Clint Eastwood's Malpaso company has produced in which he didn't star or direct since "Ratboy." **110m/C VHS.** Robert Duvall, Aidan Quinn, Frances Fisher, Brian Dennehy, Lexi (Faith) Randall, Kaytlyn Knowles, Francesca Ruth Eastwood; ***D:*** James Keach; ***W:*** Philip Railsback; ***C:*** Bruce Surtees; ***M:*** David Benoit.

Stars in My Crown 🦴🦴🦴 **1950** McCrea provides a moving performance as the pistol-wielding preacher who helps the residents of a 19th-century small town battle a typhoid epidemic and KKK terrorism. Adapted from the novel by Joe David Brown. **89m/B VHS.** Joel McCrea, Ellen Drew, Dean Stockwell, Alan Hale, Lewis Stone, Amanda Blake, Juano Hernandez, Charles Kemper, Connie Gilchrist, Ed Begley Sr., James Arness, Jack Lambert, Arthur Hunnicutt; ***D:*** Jacques Tourneur; ***W:*** Margaret Fitts; ***M:*** Adolph Deutsch; ***Nar:*** Marshall Thompson.

The Stars Look Down 🦴🦴🦴 **1939** A mine owner forces miners to work in unsafe conditions in a Welsh town and disaster strikes. Redgrave is a miner's son running for office, hoping to improve conditions, and to escape the hard life. Forceful, well-directed effort suffered at the box-office, in competition with John Ford's similar classic "How Green Was My Valley." From the novel by A.J. Cronin. The original British version was released at 110 minutes. **96m/B VHS.** *GB* Michael Redgrave, Margaret Lockwood, Emlyn Williams, Cecil Parker; ***D:*** Carol Reed.

Starship 🦴 *Lorca and the Outlaws* **1987 (PG)** British sci-fi seems to be an oxymoron. To wit, this lame "Star Wars" ripoff is about human slaves on a planet run by evil robots. **91m/C VHS.** *GB* John Tarrant, Cassandra Webb, Donough Rees, Deep Roy, Ralph Cotterill; ***D:*** Roger Christian.

Starship Invasions 🦴 **1977 (PG)** Lee leads a group of bad aliens seeking to take over the Earth. He's thwarted by UFO expert Vaughn, who is aided by a group of good aliens. Cheesy special effects have this one looking like a bad sci-fi serial from the '40s. **89m/C VHS.** *CA* Christopher Lee, Robert Vaughn, Daniel Pilon, Helen Shaver, Henry Ramer, Victoria (Vicki) Johnson; ***D:*** Ed(ward) Hunt; ***W:*** Ed(ward) Hunt.

Starship Troopers 🦴🦴🦴 **1997 (R)** As Bugs Bunny would say, "Of course you know, this means war!" Giant arachnids prove to be an invincible opponent with zero tolerance for things with less than four legs in Verhoeven's comic-book styled, epic slaughter fest. The futuristic, fascist, co-ed Moblie Infantry, led by renegade Commander Rasczak (Ironside), does battle with the sinister arthropods, usually resulting in much human bloodshed. The high body count includes many young actors, but unlike Verhoeven's "Showgirls," their careers should remain relatively unscathed. The acting is straight out of a Mattel toy factory, but the action and confrontations with the enemy insects are a thrill thanks to computer animated special effects. Cheesy, bloody good fun, if you can ignore the fact that fascists are portrayed as the good guys. Based on the 1959 novel by Robert A. Heinlein. **129m/C VHS, DVD.** Casper Van Dien, Michael Ironside, Neil Patrick Harris, Clancy Brown, Denise Richards, Dina Meyer, Jake Busey, Patrick Muldoon, Seth Gilliam, Rue McClanahan, Marshall Bell, Eric Bruskotter, Blake Lindsley, Anthony Michael Ruivivar, Dean Norris, Dale Dye; ***D:*** Paul Verhoeven; ***W:*** Edward Neumeier; ***C:*** Jost Vacano; ***M:*** Basil Poledouris.

Starstruck 🦴🦴½ **1982 (PG)** Fun-loving folly about a teen who tries to help his talented cousin make it as a singer. Playfully tweeks Hollywood musicals. Enjoyable and fun. **95m/C VHS.** *AU* Jo Kennedy, Ross O'Donovan, Pat Evison; ***D:*** Gillian Armstrong; ***C:*** Russell Boyd.

Start the Revolution without Me 🦴🦴🦴 **1970 (PG)** Hilarious, Moliere-esque farce about two sets of identical twins (Wilder and Sutherland) separated at birth, who meet 30 years later, just before the French Revolution. About as hammy as they come; Wilder is unforgettable. Neglected when released, but now deservedly a cult favorite. **91m/C VHS.** Gene Wilder, Donald Sutherland, Orson Welles, Hugh Griffith, Jack MacGowran, Billie Whitelaw, Victor Spinetti, Ewa Aulin, Denise Coffey, Helen Fraser, Murray Melvin; ***D:*** Bud Yorkin; ***W:*** Lawrence J. Cohen, Fred Freeman; ***C:*** Jean Tournier; ***M:*** John Addison.

Starting Over 🦴🦴🦴 **1979 (R)** His life racked by divorce, Phil Potter learns what it's like to be single, self-sufficient, and lonely once again. When a blind date grows into a serious affair, the romance is temporarily halted by his hang-up for his ex-wife. Enjoyable love-triangle comedy loses direction after a while, but Reynolds is subtle and charming, and Bergen good as his ex, a very bad songwriter. Based on a novel by Dan Wakefield. **106m/C VHS.** Burt Reynolds, Jill Clayburgh, Candice Bergen, Frances Sternhagen, Austin Pendleton, Mary Kay Place, Kevin Bacon, Daniel Stern; ***D:*** Alan J. Pakula; ***W:*** James L. Brooks; ***C:*** Sven Nykvist; ***M:*** Marvin Hamlisch.

Starved 🦴🦴 **1997** Monica (Beaman) thinks she's found a terrific guy in Scott Dawson (Adams). He gives her flowers, writes her romantic notes, and offers her candle lit dinners. So naturally, Monica falls in love. Too bad, Scott's a sociopath. He takes her prisoner, keeps her in his basement, and uses mind games and starvation to try and break Monica's will. Monica's best friend Jane (Zobel) continues to search for her, even after the police have let the case go. But can she find her in time? Based on a true story. **90m/C VHS.** Lee Ann Beaman, Hal Adams, Toni Zobel; ***D:*** Guy Crawford, Yvette Hoffman.

State and Main 🦴🦴🦴 **2000 (R)** Hollywood filmmakers descend on a small New England town, which promptly becomes dazzled by all the showbiz glitter. Much of the story rotates around Hoffman, who plays the down-to-earth writer forced to rewrite his script entitled "The Old Mill" after the crew discovers the town's mill burned down years ago. Meanwhile, he becomes concerned when he realizes the film's star (Baldwin) has become involved with a local teenaged girl. Macy and LuPone, Mamet regulars, also enliven the cast. Entertaining, satirical look at Hollywood egos bumping up against middle America. Not too many guffaws, but nice to see Mamet lighten things up with a comedy. **90m/C VHS, DVD, Wide.** Alec Baldwin, Philip Seymour Hoffman, William H. Macy, Julia Stiles, David Paymer, Rebecca Pidgeon, Sarah Jessica Parker, Charles Durning, Patti LuPone; ***D:*** David Mamet; ***W:*** David Mamet; ***C:*** Oliver Stapleton; ***M:*** Theodore Shapiro.

State Department File 649 🦴½ **1949** Insipid spy drama set in northern China. Mongolian rebels hold U.S. agent Lundigan captive; he hopes to capture a Chinese warlord. **87m/C VHS.** Virginia Bruce, William Lundigan; ***D:*** Sam Newfield.

State Fair 🦴🦴🦴 *It Happened One Summer* **1945** The second version of the glossy slice of Americana about a family at the Iowa State Fair, featuring plenty of great songs by Rodgers and Hammerstein. Adapted from the 1933 screen version of Phil Stong's novel. Remade again in 1962. ♫It Might as Well Be Spring; It's a Grand Night for Singing; That's For Me; Isn't It Kinda Fun?; All I Owe Iowa; Our State Fair. **100m/C VHS, DVD.** Charles Winninger, Jeanne Crain, Dana Andrews, Vivian Blaine, Dick Haymes, Fay Bainter, Frank McHugh, Percy Kilbride, Donald Meek, William Marshall, Harry (Henry) Morgan; ***D:*** Walter Lang; ***W:*** Oscar Hammerstein; ***C:*** Leon Shamroy; ***M:*** Richard Rodgers, Oscar Hammerstein. Oscars '45: Song ("It Might as Well Be Spring").

State Fair 🦴🦴 **1962** The third film version of the story of a farm family who travel to their yearly state fair and experience life. The original songs are still there, but otherwise this is a letdown. Texas setting required dropping the song "All I Owe Iowa." ♫Our State Fair; It's a Grand Night for Singing; That's for Me; It Might as Well Be Spring; Isn't It Kinda Fun?; More Than Just a Friend; It's the Little Things in Texas; Willing and Eager; This Isn't Heaven. **118m/C VHS.** Pat Boone, Ann-Margret, Bobby Darin, Tom Ewell, Alice Faye, Pamela Tiffin, Wally Cox; ***D:*** Jose Ferrer; ***C:*** William Mellor.

State of Emergency 🦴🦴🦴½ **1994 (R)** John Novelli (Mantegna) is a cynical, overworked emergency-room doctor for an over-crowded, underequipped big-city hospital. His latest casualty is a head trauma case the hospital is ill-prepared to handle and as the patient's condition worsens both doctor and hospital are put at risk. **97m/C VHS.** Joe Mantegna, Lynn Whitfield, Paul Dooley; ***D:*** Leslie Linka Glatter; ***W:*** Susan Black, Lance Gentile. **TV**

State of Grace 🦴🦴🦴 **1990 (R)** Irish hood Penn returns to old NYC neighborhood as undercover cop and becomes involved with an Irish Westies mob in a fight for survival as urban renewal encroaches on their Hell's Kitchen turf. Shrinking client base for shakedown schemes and protection rackets forces them to become contract killers for the Italian mafia. Fine performances, with Penn tense but restrained, gang honcho Harris intense, and Oldman chewing up gritty urban scenery as psycho brother of Harris, but the story is long and meandering. Well-choreographed violence. **134m/C VHS.** Joe (Johnny) Viterelli, Sean Penn, Ed Harris, Gary Oldman, Robin Wright Penn, John Turturro, Burgess Meredith, John C. Reilly; ***D:*** Phil Joanou; ***W:*** Dennis McIntyre; ***C:*** Jordan Cronenweth; ***M:*** Ennio Morricone.

State of Siege 🦴🦴🦴 *Etat de Siege* **1973** Third pairing of Montand and Costa-Gavras, about the real-life death of USAID employee Daniel Mitrione, suspected to be involved in torture and murder in Uruguay in the '60s. Quietly suspenseful, with snazzy editing; conspiracy-theory premise is similar to Stone's "JFK," and similarly disturbing, whether you believe it or not. Dubbed. **119m/C VHS.** *FR* Yves Montand, Renato Salvatori, O.E. Hasse, Jacques Perrin; ***D:*** Constantin Costa-Gavras.

State of the Union 🦴🦴🦴½ *The World and His Wife* **1948** Liberal multimillionaire Tracy is seeking the Republican presidential nomination. His estranged wife (Hepburn) is asked to return so they can masquerade as a loving couple for the sake of his political career. Hepburn tries to help Tracy, as the backstage political machinations erode his personal convictions. Adapted from a highly successful, topical Broadway play; the writers changed dialogue constantly to reflect the news. Capra and his partners at Liberty Pictures originally hoped to cast Gary Cooper and Claudette Colbert. Hepburn and Menjou were at odds politically (over communist witch hunts in Hollywood) but are fine together onscreen. **124m/B VHS.** Spencer Tracy, Katharine Hepburn, Angela Lansbury, Van Johnson, Adolphe Menjou, Lewis Stone, Howard Smith; ***D:*** Frank Capra; ***C:*** George J. Folsey.

State of Things 🦴🦴🦴 **1982** Ostensibly a mystery involving a film crew trying to remake a B-movie, "The Most Dangerous Man On Earth," but also an in-depth look at the process of filmmaking, a scathing look at nuclear warfare and an homage to Roger Corman and Hollywood at large. An enigmatic, complex film from Wenders prior to his American years. In German with English subtitles; some dialogue in English. **120m/B VHS.** *GE* Patrick Bauchau, Allen (Goorwitz) Garfield, Isabelle Weingarten, Viva, Samuel Fuller, Paul Getty III, Roger Corman; ***D:*** Wim Wenders. Venice Film Fest. '82: Film.

Stateline Motel 🦴½ *Last Chance For a Born Loser* **1975 (R)** Cheap Italian ripoff of "The Postman Always Rings Twice," with a surprise ending but little of great interest. **86m/C VHS.** *IT* Eli Wallach, Ursula Andress, Fabio Testi, Barbara Bach; ***D:*** Maurizio Lucidi.

State's Attorney 🦴🦴½ *Cardigan's Last Case* **1931** A burned-out attorney finds himself falling in love with the least likely person, a prostitute he is defending. Contrived, improbable story succumbs to star-quality lead acting from Barrymore. Remade in 1937 with Lee Tracy as "Criminal Lawyer." **79m/B VHS.** John Barrymore, Jill Esmond, William "Stage" Boyd, Helen Twelvetrees; ***D:*** George Archainbaud; ***M:*** Max Steiner.

Static 🦴🦴½ **1987 (PG-13)** A strange, disquieting independent film about an eccentric youth who claims to have built a machine through which one can see heaven. Uneven, with some dull stretches. **89m/C VHS.** Keith Gordon, Amanda Plummer, Bob Gunton, Jane Hoffman, Barton Heyman, Lily Knight; ***D:*** Mark Romanek; ***W:*** Keith Gordon, Mark Romanek.

Station 🦴🦴½ **1981** A Japanese detective's love affair is corrupted by his ruthless search for a bloodthirsty cop killer. With English subtitles. **130m/C VHS.** *JP* Ken Takakura, Chieko Baisho; ***D:*** Yasuo Furuhata.

The Station 🦴🦴 **1992** A sophisticated woman, who has just abandoned her fiancee, waits in a tiny station for an early train. The only person around is the young and ordinary stationmaster. Gradually the two are drawn together in a number of charming and comic romantic fantasies. In Italian with English subtitles. **92m/C VHS.** *IT* Margherita Buy, Ennio Fantastichini; ***D:*** Sergio Rubini; ***W:*** Sergio Rubini.

Station West 🦴🦴🦴 **1948** A disguised Army officer is sent to uncover a mystery of hijackers and murderers. Along the way, he meets up with and falls for a beautiful woman who may be involved in the treachery. Good, solid western with a fine cast and plenty of fun action shot against the requisite beautiful western landscapes. Based on the Luke Short story. Also available colorized. **92m/B VHS.** Dick Powell, Jane Greer, Agnes Moorehead, Burl Ives, Tom Powers, Raymond Burr; *D:* Sidney Lanfield.

The Stationmaster's Wife ½ **1977** In Germay's Weimar Republic a provincial stationmaster's wife expresses her boredom with her pleasant ineffectual husband by having numerous meaningless affairs. Meant to invoke postwar German dread and the fake bourgeois morality which covered political and social resentments. Originally shown as a 200-minute miniseries for German TV; subtitled. **111m/C VHS.** *GE* Elisabeth Trissenaar, Kurt Raab, Gustal Bayrhammer, Bernard Helfrich, Udo Kier, Volker Spengler; *D:* Rainer Werner Fassbinder; *W:* Rainer Werner Fassbinder; *C:* Michael Ballhaus; *M:* Peer Raben. **TV**

The Statue **1971 (R)** Famed sculptress unveils a nude rendering of her Nobel Prize-winning husband. Much hilarity in the British vein is meant to ensue, but doesn't. Niven is OK, but this empty, plotless farce should have been much shorter. **84m/C VHS.** *GB* David Niven, Virna Lisi, Robert Vaughn, Ann Bell, John Cleese; *D:* Rod Amateau.

Stavisky **1974** Sumptuously lensed story of Serge Stavisky, a con-artist and bon-vivant whose machinations almost brought down the French government when his corruption was exposed in 1934. Belmondo makes as charismatic an antihero as you could find. Excellent score complements the visuals. In French with English subtitles. **117m/C VHS, DVD, Wide.** Jean-Paul Belmondo, Anny (Annie Legras) Duperey, Charles Boyer, Francois Perier, Gerard Depardieu; *D:* Alain Resnais; *W:* Jorge Semprun; *C:* Sacha Vierny; *M:* Stephen Sondheim. N.Y. Film Critics '74: Support. Actor (Boyer).

Stay As You Are ½ **1978** Aging French architect Mastroianni has designs on a teenager who may be his illegitimate daughter from an earlier affair. **95m/C VHS.** *FR* Marcello Mastroianni, Nastassia Kinski, Francesco Rabal; *D:* Alberto Lattuada.

Stay Awake **1987 (R)** A demon stalks, haunts and tortures eight young girls sleeping together at a secluded Catholic school. Title might be addressed to the viewer, who will be tempted to snooze. **90m/C VHS, DVD.** *SA* Shirley Jane Harris, Tanya Gordon, Jayne Hutton, Heath Porter; *D:* John Bernard.

Stay Away, Joe **1968 (PG)** The King is a singing half-breed rodeo star who returns to his reservation where he finds love and trouble. Utterly cliche, embarrassing, and stupid even by Elvis-movie standards. **98m/C VHS.** Elvis Presley, Burgess Meredith, Joan Blondell, Thomas Gomez, L.Q. (Justus E. McQueen) Jones, Katy Jurado, Henry Jones; *D:* Peter Tewkesbury.

Stay Hungry **1976 (R)** A wealthy southerner (Bridges) is involved in a real estate deal which depends on the sale of a gym where a number of body builders hang out. He becomes immersed in their world and finds himself in love with the working-class Field. Big Arnold's first speaking role in his own inimitable accent (his first role in "Hercules in New York" was dubbed.) Offbeat and occasionally uneven comedy-drama based on a novel by Charles Gaines is a sleeper. **102m/C VHS.** Jeff Bridges, Sally Field, Arnold Schwarzenegger, Robert Englund, Scatman Crothers; *D:* Bob Rafelson; *W:* Bob Rafelson.

Stay Tuned **1992 (PG-13)** Suburban yuppie couple buys a large-screen TV and satellite dish from Hellvision salesman, are sucked into their dish, and wind up starring in hellish TV shows such as "Wayne's Underworld," "Northern Overexposure," "Sadistic Home Videos," and "My Three Sons of Bitches." If they can survive for 24 hours, they'll be able to return to their normal lives. Clever idea for a film is wasted as this one never really gets off the ground; viewers may not want to stay tuned to the low comedy and frantic yucks. **90m/C VHS, DVD, Wide.** John Ritter, Pam Dawber, Jeffrey Jones, Eugene Levy, David Tom, Heather McComb; *D:* Peter Hyams; *W:* Tom S. Parker; *C:* Peter Hyams; *M:* Bruce Broughton.

Stay Tuned for Murder ½ **1988** A sexy news reporter gets caught in a web of financial wrongdoings and corruption. The financiers, lawyers, and other sinister types she's investigating decide to give her a story she will never forget—if she ever gets the chance to tell it! **92m/C VHS.** Terry Reeves Wolf, Christopher Ginnaven; *D:* Gary Jones.

Staying Alive ½ **1983 (PG)** "Saturday Night Fever" was the ultimate cheesy '70s musical, hence likeable in a dorky way. This pathetic sequel (directed by Stallone from a Rocky-esque script about beating the odds, etc.) is utterly predictable and forgettable. Music mostly by Frank Stallone, the great heir to Rodgers and Hammerstein. ♫The Woman In You; I Love You Too Much; Breakout; Someone Belonging to Someone; Life Goes On; Far From Over; Devils and Seducers; (We Dance) So Close to the Fire; Hope We Never Change. **96m/C VHS.** John Travolta, Cynthia Rhodes, Finola Hughes, Norma Donaldson; *D:* Sylvester Stallone; *W:* Sylvester Stallone; *M:* Frank Stallone.

Staying On ½ **1980** Based on the Paul Scott novel, this English drama follows the life of a post-colonial British colonel and his wife who chose to remain in India. **87m/C VHS.** *GB* Trevor Howard, Celia Johnson; *D:* Irene Shubik.

Staying Together ½ **1989 (R)** Three midwestern brothers go into a panic when their father decides to sell the restaurant they've worked at all their adult lives. Somehow they manage the transition and learn about life. Sloppy comedy-drama with way too many unresolved subplots. **91m/C VHS.** Dermot Mulroney, Tim Quill, Sean Astin, Stockard Channing, Melinda Dillon, Daphne Zuniga; *D:* Lee Grant; *W:* Monte Merrick; *C:* Dick Bush; *M:* Miles Goodman.

The Steagle **1971 (R)** The threat of the Cuban missile crisis lets a fantasizing professor loose to enact his wildest dreams. Odd Mitty-esque fantasy comedy might have worked, but ends up confusing and frustrating. **101m/C VHS.** Richard Benjamin, Cloris Leachman; *D:* Paul Sylbert.

Steal Big, Steal Little **1995 (PG-13)** Twins Robby and Reuben Martinez (Garcia) battle over the California ranch land left to Reuben by their mother. Evil, manipulative Robby, all fancy suits and slicked-back hair, wants to build condos while gentle, less-fashionable Reuben must fight to fulfill his dream of building a home for the migrant workers he employs. Yawn. Writer/director Davis' flashy action movie technique doesn't fit into the dramatic social commentary—it's too fast and forced to work. Garcia's radical character changes are impressive though. Arkin provides comic relief as the good-hearted used-car dealer who tries to save the day, if not the film. **130m/C VHS.** Andy Garcia, Alan Arkin, Rachel Ticotin, Joe Pantoliano, David Ogden Stiers, Charles Rocket, Holland Taylor; *D:* Andrew Davis; *W:* Lee Blessing, Jeanne Blake, Terry Kahn, Andrew Davis; *C:* Frank Tidy; *M:* William Olvis.

Steal the Sky **1988** Israeli agent Hemingway seduces Iraqi pilot Cross and persuades him to steal a Soviet MIG jet and defect to Israel. Unlikely plot but swell flying scenes. Hemingway is poorly cast, as she often is. **110m/C VHS.** Mariel Hemingway, Ben Cross, Etta Ankri; *D:* John Hancock. **CABLE**

Steal This Movie! *Abbie* **2000 (R)** Bio of anti-war activist and Yippie founder Abbie Hoffman tries to explore the counterculture of the 60s but bites off more than it can chew. Film's fragmented by its structure of using the flashback recollections of Abbie's (D'Onofrio) first wife Anita (Garofalo) and lawyer Gerry Lefcourt (Pollak) to explain the manic and charismatic Hoffman, who wound up spending most of the 70s an underground fugitive and who died a suicide. Garity, who's the son of Tom Hayden and Jane Fonda, plays his activist dad. **111m/C VHS, DVD, Wide.** Vincent D'Onofrio, Janeane Garofalo, Jeanne Tripplehorn, Donal Logue, Kevin Pollak, Kevin Corrigan, Troy Garity, Alan Van Sprang; *D:* Robert Greenwald; *W:* Bruce Graham; *C:* Denis Lenoir; *M:* Mader.

Stealing Beauty ½ **1996 (R)** The film's main asset, besides the beautiful Tuscan scenery, is the coltish charm of Tyler, who stars as virginal teenager Lucy Harmon. An innocent abroad, she's spending the summer with family friends after her mother's suicide. Ostensibly artist Ian Grayson (McCann) is doing her portrait but Lucy's more interested in finding romance with neighbor lad Niccolo (Zibetti), who bestowed her first kiss on a previous visit. Lucy's sunny appeal doesn't go unnoticed by the villa's other inhabitants, including dying playwright Alex (Irons), but it seems Lucy's growing up won't be easy on anyone (not even herself). **118m/C VHS, DVD, Wide.** *IT GB FR* Liv Tyler, Jeremy Irons, Donal McCann, Sinead Cusack, Jean Marais, D.W. Moffett, Stefania Sandrelli, Carlo Cecchi, Roberto Zibetti, Joseph Fiennes, Jason Flemyng, Leonardo Treviglio; *D:* Bernardo Bertolucci; *W:* Susan Minot, Bernardo Bertolucci; *C:* Darius Khondji; *M:* Richard Hartley.

Stealing Heaven ½ **1988 (R)** Based on the lives of Abelard and Heloise. In 12th-century Paris, a theologian and teacher falls in love with a beautiful young woman, and the two must defend their bond from all comers, including her righteous uncle. Steamy; trimmed to 108 minutes after threatened X rating. Attractive and cerebral. Available in a 115 minute-uncut, unrated version. **108m/C VHS.** *GB YU* Derek De Lint, Kim Thomson, Denholm Elliott, Mark Jax, Bernard Hepton, Kenneth Cranham, Angela Pleasence, Rachel Kempson; *D:* Clive Donner; *W:* Chris Bryant; *M:* Nick Bicat.

Stealing Home ½ **1988 (PG-13)** A washed-up baseball player learns his former babysitter (who was also his first love and inspiration), has committed suicide. Their bittersweet relationship is told through flashbacks. Foster's superb performance steals the show in this quiet sleeper. **98m/C VHS, DVD.** Mark Harmon, Jodie Foster, William McNamara, Blair Brown, Harold Ramis, Jonathan Silverman, John Shea, Helen Hunt, Richard Jenkins, Ted Ross, Thatcher Goodwin, Yvette Croskey; *D:* Steven Kampmann, Will Aldis; *W:* Steven Kampmann, Will Aldis; *C:* Bobby Byrne; *M:* David Foster.

Stealth Fighter ½ **1999 (R)** Naval pilot Owen Turner (Ice-T) fakes his own death and goes to work for the bad guys in South America. Then he steals a stealth fighter from a U.S. military base and starts bombing foreign military installations. So naval officer Ryan Mitchell (Mandylor) is sent to stop him. Wynorski directed under the pseudonym "Jay Andrews." **87m/C VHS, DVD, Wide.** Ice-T, Costas Mandylor, Ernie Hudson, Erika Eleniak, Andrew Divoff, John Enos, Steve Eastin; *D:* Jim Wynorski; *W:* Lenny Juliano; *C:* J.E. Bash; *M:* Alex Wilkinson. **VIDEO**

Steam: A Turkish Bath *Hamam: Il Bagno Turco* **1996** Francesco (Gassman) is a young Italian businessman married to the equally busy Marta (d'Aloja) and living a fashionable life in Rome. When he learns an aunt has left him a building in Istanbul, he leaves to check out his inheritance. What Francesco discovers is that he now possesses a traditional Turkish bath and that the family his aunt lived with and employed is eager for him to stay. Mysterious Istanbul begins to work its magic as does Francesco's unexpected (and mutual) growing attraction to the family's son, Mehmet (Gunsur). Of course, Marta does eventually show up. Italian and Turkish with subtitles. **96m/C VHS, DVD.** *TU IT SP* Alessandro Gassman, Francesca D'Aloja, Carlo Cecchi, Mehmet Gunsur, Serif Sezer, Basak Koklukaya, Halil Ergun, Alberto Molinari; *D:* Ferzan Ozpetek; *W:* Ferzan Ozpetek, Stefano Tummolini; *C:* Pasquale Mari; *M:* Aldo De Scalzi.

Steamboat Bill, Jr. ½ **1928** City-educated student returns to his small home-town and his father's Mississippi river boat, where he's an embarrassment to dad. But bond they do, to ward off the owner of a rival riverboat, whose daughter Keaton falls for. Engaging look at small-town life and the usual wonderful Keaton antics, including braving the big tornado. **75m/B VHS, DVD.** Buster Keaton, Ernest Torrence, Marion Byron, Tom Lewis; *D:* Charles Reisner; *W:* Carl Harbaugh; *C:* Bert Haines, Devereaux Jennings.

Steaming **1986 (R)** Six women get together in a London bathhouse and review their various troubles with men. Unfortunate adaptation of the good play by Nell Dunn. Where are the laughs—and what happened to the dramatic tension? The last film of Dors and director Losey. **102m/C VHS.** *GB* Vanessa Redgrave, Sarah Miles, Diana Dors; *D:* Joseph Losey.

Steel *Look Down and Die; Men of Steel* **1980 (R)** Construction workers on a mammoth skyscraper face insurmountable odds and strong opposition. Will they finish their building? Worth watching, if you don't have anything else to do. **100m/C VHS.** Lee Majors, Jennifer O'Neill, Art Carney, George Kennedy, Harris Yulin, Terry Kiser, Richard Lynch, Roger E. Mosley, Albert Salmi, R.G. Armstrong; *D:* Steve Carver; *W:* Leigh Chapman; *M:* Michel Colombier.

Steel ½ **1997 (PG-13)** Metal specialist John Henry Irons (O'Neal) has designed a top-secret military weapon that falls into the hands of a street gang. Donning a suit of armor he designed, he become super hero Steel and sets out to end the reign of terror of former colleague turned super villian Burke (Nelson). Adaptation of popular DC comic keeps target audience in mind with lots of action and plenty of humor. Shaq proves once again that as an actor he's a pretty good basketball player. **97m/C VHS.** Shaquille O'Neal, Judd Nelson, Annabeth Gish, Richard Roundtree, Irma P. Hall, Charles Napier, Kerrie Keane, Hill Harper, Thom Barry; *D:* Kenneth Johnson; *W:* Kenneth Johnson; *C:* Mark Irwin; *M:* Mervyn Warren.

Steel and Lace ½ **1990 (R)** Davison is the scientist brother of a classical pianist who commits suicide after being raped. He revives her as a cyborg, which promptly sets out to enact its revenge. Depressing, morbid sci-fi. **92m/C VHS.** Bruce Davison, Clare Wren, Stacy Haiduk, David Naughton, David Lander; *D:* Ernest Farino; *W:* Joseph Dougherty, Dave Edison; *C:* Thomas Callaway.

Steel Arena **1972 (PG)** Several real life stunt-car drivers appear in this action-packed film, crammed with spins, jumps, explosions and world-record-breaking, life risking stunts. **99m/C VHS.** Dusty Russell, Gene Drew, Buddy Love; *D:* Mark L. Lester.

The Steel Claw **1961** One-handed ex-Marine Montgomery organizes guerilla forces against the Japanese in the Philippines in WWII. Good location shooting and plenty of action. **95m/C VHS.** George Montgomery, Charito Luna, Mario Barri; *D:* George Montgomery.

Steel Cowboy **1978** With his marriage, sanity, and livelihood on the line, an independent trucker agrees to haul a hot herd of stolen steers. Passable made-for-TV macho adventure. **100m/C VHS.** James Brolin, Rip Torn, Jennifer Warren, Strother Martin, Melanie Griffith, Lou Frizzell; *D:* Harvey Laidman; *M:* Charles Bernstein.

Steel Dawn ½ **1987 (R)** Another "Mad Max" clone: A leather-clad warrior wields his sword over lots of presumably post-apocalyptic desert terrain. Swayze stars with his real-life wife Niemi in unfortunate follow-up to "Dirty Dancing." **90m/C VHS, DVD.** Arnold Vosloo, Patrick Swayze, Lisa Niemi, Christopher Neame, Brett Hool, Brion James, Anthony Zerbe; *D:* Lance Hool; *W:* Doug Lefler; *C:* George Tirl; *M:* Brian May.

Steel Frontier ½ **1994 (R)** Post-apocalypse actioner finds a group of survivors trying to make a new life in a town they call New Hope. But then a group of bandit soldiers take over—until a lone hero comes along to save the day. **94m/C VHS.** Joe Lara, Brion James, Bo Svenson, Stacie Foster; *D:* Paul G. Volk, Jacobsen Hart; *W:* Jacobsen Hart.

The Steel Helmet ½ **1951** Hurriedly made Korean War drama stands as a top-notch war film. Brooding and dark, GIs don't save the world for democracy or rescue POWs; they simply do their best to survive a horrifying situation. Pointless death, confused loyalties and cynicism abound in writer-director Fuller's scathing comment on the madness of war. **84m/B VHS.** Gene Evans, Robert Hutton, Steve Brodie, William Chun, James Edwards, Richard Loo, Harold Fong, Neyle Morrow, Sid Melton, Richard Monahan, Lynn Stalmaster; ***D:*** Samuel Fuller; ***W:*** Samuel Fuller; ***C:*** Ernest Miller; ***M:*** Paul Dunlap.

Steel Magnolias **1989 (PG)** Shelby Eatenton (Roberts) is a young woman stricken with severe diabetes who chooses to live her life to the fullest despite her bad health. Much of the action centers around a Louisiana beauty shop (run by Parton) where the women get together to discuss the goings-on of their lives. Screenplay by R. Harling, based on his partially autobiographical play. Sweet, poignant, and often hilarious, yet just as often overwrought. MacLaine is funny as a bitter divorcee; Parton is sexy and fun as the hairdresser; but Field and Roberts (as mother and daughter) go off the deep end and make it all entirely too weepy. **118m/C VHS, DVD, 8mm, Wide.** Sally Field, Dolly Parton, Shirley MacLaine, Daryl Hannah, Olympia Dukakis, Julia Roberts, Tom Skerritt, Sam Shepard, Dylan McDermott, Kevin J. O'Connor, Bill McCutcheon, Ann Wedgeworth, Janine Turner; ***D:*** Herbert Ross; ***W:*** Robert Harling; ***C:*** John A. Alonzo; ***M:*** Georges Delerue. Golden Globes '90: Support. Actress (Roberts).

Steel Sharks **1997 (R)** A military coup in Iran finds chemical weapons expert Dr. Van Tasset (Livingston) kidnapped by revolutionaries. Members of an elite squad of Navy SEALs are sent to rescue him, aided by a U.S. sub. But the good guys wind up prisoners on an Iranian sub and a deadly game of underwater hide-and-seek follows. **94m/C VHS.** Billy Dee Williams, Gary Busey, Tim Lounibos, Barry Livingston, Billy Warlock, Larry Poindexter, Tim Abell, Robert Miranda, David Roberson, Matthew St. Patrick; ***D:*** Rodney McDonald; ***W:*** Rodney McDonald, William Martell; ***C:*** Bryan Greenberg; ***M:*** David Lawrence. **VIDEO**

Steele Justice **1987 (R)** A tough 'Nam vet takes on the whole Vietnamese Mafia in Southern California after his friend is murdered. One of those head-scratchers: Should I laugh, or be offended? **96m/C VHS.** Martin Kove, Sela Ward, Ronny Cox, Bernie Casey, Joseph Campanella, Sarah Douglas; ***D:*** Robert Boris; ***W:*** Robert Boris.

Steele's Law **1991 (R)** A loner cop is forced to take the law into his own hands in order to track down an insane international assassin. **90m/C VHS, DVD.** Fred Williamson, Bo Svenson, Doran Inghram, Phyllis Cicero; ***D:*** Fred Williamson; ***W:*** Charles Eric Johnson; ***C:*** David Blood; ***M:*** Mike Logan.

Steelyard Blues *The Final Crash* **1973 (PG)** A motley-crew comedy about a wacky gang that tries to steal an abandoned WW II airplane. Zany pranks abound. Technically flawed direction from Myerson mars a potentially hilarious story. **93m/C VHS.** Jane Fonda, Donald Sutherland, Peter Boyle, Howard Hesseman, John Savage, Garry Goodrow; ***D:*** Alan Myerson; ***W:*** David S. Ward; ***M:*** David Shire.

Stella **1955** Mercouri's film debut has her as a free-spirited bar singer who gets involved in a tragic romantic triangle with a middle-class writer and a local football hero. Melodramatic but Mercouri's earthy joie de vivre is already apparent. In Greek with English subtitles. **94m/B VHS, DVD.** *GR* Melina Mercouri, Yiorgo Fountas, Aiekos Alexandrikis, Sophia Vembo; ***D:*** Michael Cacoyannis; ***W:*** Michael Cacoyannis; ***C:*** Costa Theodorides; ***M:*** Manos Hadjidakis.

Stella **1989 (PG-13)** Anachronistic remake update of "Stella Dallas" casts Midler as a single mother who sacrifices everything to give her daughter a better life. Barbara Stanwyck did it much better in 1937. Based on Olive Higgins Prouty's novel. **109m/C VHS.** Bette Midler, John Goodman, Stephen Collins, Eileen Brennan, Ben Stiller, Trini Alvarado, Marsha Mason; ***D:*** John Erman; ***W:*** Robert Getchell; ***C:*** Billy Williams.

Stella Dallas **1937** Uneducated Stella (Stanwyck) lets go of the daughter (Shirley) she loves when she realizes her ex-husband (Boles) can give the girl more advantages. What could be sentimental turns out believable and worthwhile under Vidor's steady hand. Stanwyck never makes a wrong step. From a 1923 novel by Olive Higgins Prouty. Remade in 1989 as "Stella," starring Bette Midler. **106m/B VHS, DVD.** Barbara O'Neil, Tim Holt, Barbara Stanwyck, Anne Shirley, John Boles, Alan Hale, Marjorie Main; ***D:*** King Vidor; ***W:*** Sarah Y. Mason, Victor Heerman; ***C:*** Rudolph Mate; ***M:*** Alfred Newman.

Stella Does Tricks **1996** Stella (Macdonald) is a teen runaway, working as a prostitute in London for pimp Mr. Peters (Bolam). She was abused by her dad (Stewart) and has revenge fantasies—some of which she takes out on clients, which leads to punishment by her boss. She briefly gets free of Peters and gets a legit job, but Stella has also become involved with junkie Eddie (Matheson) and his drug needs have him betraying Stella. No Cinderella stories here—Stella's life is bleak and violent, with Macdonald giving a powerhouse performance. **97m/C VHS, DVD.** *GB* Kelly Macdonald, James Bolam, Ewan Stewart, Hans Mathieson, Andy Serkis, Paul Chahidi; ***D:*** Coky Giedroye; ***W:*** A.L. Kennedy; ***C:*** Barry Ackroyd; ***M:*** Nick Bicat.

Stella Maris **1918** Pickford inspiringly plays two difficult roles. As Stella Maris, she's a wealthy orphaned cripple who's in love with the married John Risca (Tearle), whose wife, Louise (Ankewich), is an abusive alcoholic. John eventually leaves her and Louise takes out her anger on homely servant Unity Blake (Pickford's second role). When Unity is eventually rescued by John, she also falls in love with him. Brimming with the tragic consequences of love. **100m/B VHS, DVD.** Mary Pickford, Conway Tearle, Camille Ankewich, Ida Waterman, Herbert Standing; ***D:*** Marshall Neilan; ***W:*** Frances Marion; ***C:*** Walter Stradling.

The Stendahl Syndrome *La Sindrome di Stendhal* **1995** Psycho serial-killer thriller about a Rome police detective, Anna (Argento), who has an extreme hallucinatory reaction to artwork (the title syndrome). While visiting an art gallery, she collapses and is assisted by Alfredo (Kretschmann), who turns out to be the very rapist-killer whom she's hunting. Anna escapes from him once (after being tortured) but is captured again. However, she manages to fight back in ways squeamish viewers may want to avoid watching. Inspired by Graziella Magherini's novel "La Sindrome di Stendhal." **118m/C VHS, DVD.** *IT* Asia Argento, Thomas Kretschmann, Marco Leonardi, Luigi Diberti, Paolo Bonacelli, John Quentin; ***D:*** Dario Argento; ***W:*** Dario Argento; ***C:*** Giuseppe Rotunno; ***M:*** Ennio Morricone.

Step Lively **1944** A young playwright tries to recover the money he lent to a fast-talking Broadway producer and is forced to take the leading role in his play. Lively musical remake of "Room Service" (1938) was Sinatra's first starring role. Look for Dorothy Malone as a brunette switchboard operator. ♫Some Other Time; As Long As There's Music; Where Does Love Begin?; Come Out, Come Out, Wherever You Are; Why Must There Be an Opening Song?; And Then You Kissed Me; Ask the Madame. **88m/B VHS.** Frank Sinatra, Gloria De Haven, George Murphy, Walter Slezak, Adolphe Menjou, Anne Jeffreys; ***D:*** Tim Whelan.

The Stepdaughter **2000 (R)** After years of abuse in foster homes, Susan (Roth) wants to strike back at the birth mother who abandoned her. She tracks down the now happily married woman (Pickett), gets a job on the ranch where she lives, and plans her next deadly move. **92m/C VHS, DVD, Wide.** Andrea Roth, Lisa Dean Ryan, Jaimz Woolvett, Cindy Pickett, Gary Hudson, Gil Gerard, Matt Farnsworth, Lee Dawson; ***D:*** Peter Paul Liapis; ***W:*** Richard Dana; ***C:*** Maximo Munzi. **VIDEO**

The Stepfather **1987 (R)** Creepy thriller about a seemingly ordinary stepfather who is actually a homicidal maniac searching for the "perfect family." An independently produced sleeper tightly directed and well written. Followed by two inferior sequels. **89m/C VHS.** Terry O'Quinn, Shelley Hack, Jill Schoelen, Stephen Shellen, Charles Lanyer, Stephen E. Miller; ***D:*** Joseph Ruben; ***W:*** Donald E. Westlake; ***C:*** John Lindley; ***M:*** Patrick Moraz.

Stepfather 2: Make Room for Daddy **1989 (R)** A poor sequel to the suspenseful sleeper, wherein the psychotic family man escapes from an asylum and woos another suburban family, murdering anyone who may suspect his true identity. Followed by yet another sequel. **93m/C VHS.** Terry O'Quinn, Meg Foster, Caroline Williams, Jonathan Brandis, Henry Brown, Mitchell Laurance; ***D:*** Jeff Burr; ***W:*** John P. Auerbach; ***C:*** Jacek Laskus.

Stepfather 3: Father's Day **1992 (R)** The father from Hell is back! Escaping from the loony bin with a surgically altered face, the stepfather settles in a small town and gets a job at a nursery (the plant kind, not the children kind). His favorite gardening tool fast becomes the mulch machine, and soon locals are fertilizing the garden. Well below the original, but it may please fans of this genre. **110m/C VHS.** Robert Wightman, Priscilla Barnes, Season Hubley; ***D:*** Guy Magar; ***C:*** Alan Caso.

The Stepford Wives **1975** Joanna (Ross) and husband Walter (Masterson) move from bustling Manhattan to the supposedly idyllic Connecticut town of Stepford. Joanna gets suspicious when she notices all the wives are strangely content and subservient and when she meets fellow newcomer, Bobby (Prentiss), they decide to investigate. Creepy adaptation of the Ira Levin novel. **115m/C VHS, DVD, Wide.** Katharine Ross, Paula Prentiss, Peter Masterson, Nanette Newman, Patrick O'Neal, Tina Louise, Dee Wallace Stone, William Prince, Mary Stuart Masterson, Carol Rossen; ***D:*** Bryan Forbes; ***W:*** William Goldman; ***C:*** Owen Roizman; ***M:*** Michael Small.

Stephano Quantestorie **1993** Walter Mitty-ish story about day-dreaming cop Stephano (Nichetti) who falls for the prime suspect in a robbery he's investigating. He escapes his conflicting feelings by imagining himself living other lives—as a math professor, airline pilot, saxophone player, and thief, but soon all these alter ego are intruding into his work. Italian with subtitles. **90m/C VHS.** *IT* Maurizio Nichetti; ***D:*** Maurizio Nichetti; ***W:*** Maurizio Nichetti.

Stephen King's Golden Years *Golden Years* **1991** Stephen King creates a chilling vision of scientific progress gone awry in this shocking techno-thriller. After being accidentally exposed to exotic chemicals in a lab explosion, an aging janitor undergoes an extraordinary transformation and the government will sacrifice anything to learn more about it. **232m/C VHS, DVD.** Keith Szarabajka, Frances Sternhagen, Ed Lauter, R.D. Call, Stephen King, Felicity Huffman, Stephen (Steve) Root; ***D:*** Kenneth Fink, Stephen Tolkin, Allen Coulter, Michael G. Gerrick; ***W:*** Stephen King, Josef Anderson. **TV**

Stephen King's It **1990** A group of small town children, who were terrorized by an evil force in their youth, are traumatized again some 30 years later, when they learn a new series of child murders occurred in their Eastern home town. The adults, who now all have successful and diverse careers, must come to terms with the terrible secret they share, as "IT" has returned to wreak havoc in their New England home town. Based on horror master King's bestselling novel of the same name. **193m/C VHS.** Tim Reid, Richard Thomas, John Ritter, Annette O'Toole, Richard Masur, Dennis Christopher, Harry Anderson, Olivia Hussey, Tim Curry, Jonathan Brandis, Michael Cole; ***D:*** Tommy Lee Wallace; ***W:*** Stephen King; ***M:*** Richard Bellis. **TV**

Stephen King's Rose Red *Rose Red* **2002 (PG-13)** King released the ficitonal memoir "The Diary of Ellen Rimbauer" shortly before the miniseries aired, rather than the movie being based on an already successful novel. The "Diary's" editor, Dr. Joyce Reardon (Travis), is a college professor looking for the supernatural inside Rose Red, a decaying mansion known for its strange history. She gathers together various paranormals, including autistic teenager Annie (Brown) who has strong telekinetic powers. The house begins to feed off Annie's energy and all hell breaks loose. Last role for Dukes (as Joyce's nemesis Professor Miller) who died during filming. **254m/C VHS, DVD.** Nancy Travis, Kimberly J. Brown, Matt Keeslar, David Dukes, Julian Sands, Judith Ivey, Melanie Lynskey, Matt Ross, Kevin Tighe, Julia Campbell, Jimmi Simpson; ***D:*** Craig R. Baxley; ***W:*** Stephen King; ***C:*** David Connell; ***M:*** Gary Chang. **TV**

Stephen King's The Langoliers *The Langoliers* **1995 (PG-13)** Bloated variation of "Ten Little Indians" where 10 airline passengers dozing off on their L.A.-to-Boston flight and awakening to find their fellow passengers and the crew have vanished. Of course, one passenger (Morse) is a pilot and he gets them to Bangor, Maine (where the miniseries was filmed), only to discover the airport is deserted and very weird things are going on. Oh yeah, the "langoliers" look like flying cannonballs with piranha teeth and have something to do with neurotic Pinchot's character. Not that you'll care much. **180m/C VHS, DVD.** David Morse, Bronson Pinchot, Patricia Wettig, Dean Stockwell, Kate Maberly, Christopher Collet, Kimber Riddle, Mark Lindsay Chapman, Frankie Faison, Baxter Harris, Stephen King, Tom Holland; ***D:*** Tom Holland; ***W:*** Tom Holland; ***C:*** Paul Maibaum; ***M:*** Vladimir Horunzhy. **TV**

Stephen King's The Night Flier *The Night Flier* **1996 (R)** Portrays blood-sucking beings that prey upon the weakness of mortal men in order to survive. And besides tabloid journalists, there's vampires in it, too! Richard Dees (Ferrer) is a reporter/photographer for a National Enquirer-like paper who is not above staging lurid photos to grab Page One. His editor pits him in a contest with rookie papparazzo Katherine (Entwistle) for a story about a murderer who wears a black cape and tricorn hat, flies into small airports in a sinister black plane and drains his victims' blood. Dees follows the killer's trail in his own plane, stopping to ruthlessly grill survivors and doctor up a few pictures. Genuinely spooky showdown will leave only one monster standing. Who is it? Inquiring minds want to know. **97m/C VHS, DVD.** Michael H. Moss, Miguel Ferrer, Julie Entwisle, Dan Monahan, John Bennes, Beverly Skinner, Rob Wilds, Richard Olsen, Elizabeth McCormick; ***D:*** Mark Pavia; ***W:*** Mark Pavia, Jack O'Donnell; ***C:*** David Connell; ***M:*** Brian Keane. **CABLE**

Stephen King's The Stand *The Stand* **1994** Ghoulish made for TV adaptation of the King novel about a superflu/plague that decimates the U.S. population. The few survivors are soon divided into two camps—those dreaming of a godly old black woman known as Mother Abigail and others of the satanic Randall Flagg, the Walkin' Dude. Boulder, Colorado (where King was living when he wrote the novel) serves as headquarters for Abigail's brood while Las Vegas (where else) is Flagg territory. It all comes down to a battle of good vs. evil, with the future of mankind at stake. Religious allegory can get tedious but it's a varied cast with some scenes not for those with queasy stomachs. On four cassettes. **360m/C VHS, DVD.** Jamey Sheridan, Ruby Dee, Gary Sinise, Molly Ringwald, Miguel Ferrer, Laura San Giacomo, Rob Lowe, Adam Storke, Matt Frewer, Corin "Corky" Nemec, Ray Walston, Bill Fagerbakke, Ossie Davis, Shawnee Smith, Rick Aviles, John (Joe Bob Briggs) Bloom, Michael (Mike) Lookinland, Ed Harris, Kathy Bates, Kareem Abdul-Jabbar, Stephen King, Sam Raimi; ***D:*** Mick Garris; ***W:*** Stephen King; ***C:*** Edward Pei; ***M:*** W.G. Snuffy Walden. **TV**

Stephen King's The Storm of the Century *Storm of the Century* **1999 (PG-13)** Little Tall Island, Maine, is under siege—and not just from the most ferocious storm the island has seen in years. No, there's madness and murder afoot in the form of demonic stranger Andre Linoge (Feore). He seems to know everyone's secrets but what he wants is anybody's guess. Now it's up to amiable constable Michael Anderson (Daly) to control the rising hysteria and come up with a solution. **247m/C VHS, DVD.** Colm Feore, Timothy Daly, Debrah Farentino, Casey Siemaszko, Jeffrey DeMunn, Richard Blackburn; ***D:*** Craig R. Baxley; ***W:*** Stephen King; ***C:*** David Connell; ***M:*** Gary Chang. **TV**

Stephen King's The Tommyknockers 🦴🦴½ *The Tommyknockers* **1993 (R)** Another of King's creepy tales, adapted for TV. Bobbi (Helgenberger) and Gard (Smits) live in the small town of Haven, Maine (actually filmed on New Zealand's North Island). She's an aspiring writer; he's a fading poet with a drinking problem and a metal plate in his head (this is important). Walking in the woods, Bobbi stumbles over a long-buried spaceship which begins to take possession of the townspeople—their eyes shine green, their teeth fall out, and they act out their (often violent) fantasies—all but Gard. The whole thing's more silly than scary. The title comes from an old children's rhyme. **120m/C VHS, DVD.** Jimmy Smits, Marg Helgenberger, Joanna Cassidy, E.G. Marshall, Traci Lords, John Ashton, Allyce Beasley, Cliff DeYoung, Robert Carradine, Leon Woods, Paul McIver; ***D:*** John Power; ***W:*** Lawrence D. Cohen; ***M:*** Christopher Franke. **TV**

Stephen King's Thinner 🦴🦴 *Thinner* **1996 (R)** Holland takes all the meat out of this supernatural horror by turning it into a formulaic pursuit-of-justice bore. Porcine lawyer Billy Halleck (Burke) accidentally hits a gypsy with his car and is cursed with a case of perpetual weight loss. Conveniently for Billy, the client he has just gotten an acquittal for is local mobster Richie "The Hammer" Ginelli (Mantegna) who is now determined to save him. Ponderous plot and lackluster-looking latex is redeemed by decent acting. King makes his requisite cameo as Dr. Bangor (get it, Maine?) Originally published in 1984 under King's pseudonym Richard Bachman. **92m/C VHS, DVD.** Robert John Burke, Joe Mantegna, Lucinda Jenney, Michael Constantine, Kari Wuhrer, John Horton, Sam Freed, Daniel von Bargen, Elizabeth Franz, Joy Lentz, Jeff Ware; ***Cameos:*** Stephen King; ***D:*** Tom Holland; ***W:*** Michael McDowell, Tom Holland; ***C:*** Kees Van Oostrum; ***M:*** Daniel Licht.

Stepmom 🦴🦴🦴 **1998 (PG-13)** The opening scenes make it look like a comedic catfight-filled ride. Harris is a divorced dad with two kids, a supermom ex-wife (Sarandon), and a glamorous new girlfriend (Roberts), whose career seems more important than the kids. Jibes and glares are traded by the two women until mom is stricken with some form of untreatable terminal cancer. This changes the story from broad comedy to emotional drama as Sarandon must train the younger woman to be the new mom. Columbus seems comfortable with the shift, and manages to keep everything upbeat. The script, penned by five writers, becomes more cliched as the film goes on, but stays just this side of chick-flick. **124m/C VHS, DVD.** Julia Roberts, Susan Sarandon, Ed Harris, Jena Malone, Liam Aiken, Lynn Whitfield, Darrell Larson, Mary Louise Wilson; ***D:*** Chris Columbus; ***W:*** Jessie Nelson, Steven Rogers, Ronald Bass, Gigi Levangie, Karen Leigh Hopkins; ***C:*** Donald McAlpine; ***M:*** John Williams. Natl. Bd. of Review '98: Support. Actor (Harris).

Stepmonster 🦴½ **1992 (PG-13)** A boy tries to convince his father that his new stepmother is a monster—literally. Doesn't work any better than "My Stepmother Is an Alien." **?m/C VHS.** Alan Thicke, Robin Riker, Corey Feldman, John Astin, Ami Dolenz, George Gaynes.

The Stepmother 🦴½ **1971** Yet another Hitchcock ripoff story involving an evil stepmother. Rey is passable, but there's not much else to recommend this dredge. **100m/C VHS.** Alejandro Rey, John Anderson, Katherine Justice, John David Garfield, Marlene Schmidt, Claudia Jennings, Larry Linville; ***D:*** Howard (Hikmet) Avedis.

Steppenwolf 🦴🦴½ **1974 (PG)** Static, enigmatic film version of the famous Herman Hesse novel about a brooding writer searching for meaning and self-worth. Interesting to watch, but the offbeat novel doesn't translate to the screen; leaves you flat. **105m/C VHS.** *SI* Max von Sydow, Dominique Sanda, Pierre Clementi, Carla Rominelli, Roy Bosier; ***D:*** Fred Haines; ***W:*** Fred Haines; ***C:*** Tomislav Pinter; ***M:*** George Gruntz.

Stepping Out 🦴🦴🦴 **1991 (PG)** Minnelli stars as a would-be Broadway dancer who gives tap dancing lessons in an old church to an assortment of offbeat and interesting characters. When the troupe is asked to perform for a local charity, they make the most of their opportunity. A warm and touching ensemble piece that avoids over-sentimentalizing and utilizes its cast to best advantage. **113m/C VHS.** Liza Minnelli, Shelley Winters, Bill Irwin, Ellen Greene, Julie Walters, Robyn Stevan, Jane Krakowski, Sheila McCarthy, Andrea Martin, Carol Woods, Nora Dunn, Eugene Glazer; ***D:*** Lewis Gilbert; ***W:*** Richard Harris; ***M:*** Peter Matz.

Steps from Hell 🦴 **1992** Vald Tempest is an evil immortal in control of a cult of zombie women. He's stolen a sacred map that will lead to a gateway which, when opened, will unleash a supreme evil on the world. Unless the heroic John Clark can find a way to prevent it, of course. **90m/C VHS.** Bernardo Rosa, Rocky Tucker, Ron Odell, Philip Cable, Liz Stoeckel, Steve Quimby, Lisa Lund; ***D:*** James Tucker; ***W:*** James Tucker.

The Stepsister 🦴🦴 **1997 (PG-13)** Pediatrician Donna Canfield is lured to her death by one of her young patients. When daughter Darcy (Sofer) comes home to console her dad, Dr. Derek (Rachins), she finds her place usurped by the widowed Joan (Evans) and her sexpot daughter, Melinda (Wilson). Married in unseemly haste, the wealthy Derek dies equally quickly, leaving Darcy suspicious of her new stepfamily. **91m/C VHS.** Rena Sofer, Bridgette Wilson, Linda Evans, Alan Rachins; ***D:*** Matt Dorff; ***W:*** Matt Dorff; ***C:*** Laszlo George; ***M:*** Peter Manning Robinson. **CABLE**

Stepsisters woof! **1985** Murderous double-crosses occur among a pilot, his wife, and her sister. **75m/C VHS.** Hal Fletcher, Sharyn Talbert, Bond Gideon.

The Sterile Cuckoo 🦴🦴🦴 *Pookie* **1969 (PG)** An aggressive co-ed pursues a shy freshman who seems to embody her romantic ideal. Minnelli's performance is outstanding; Burton as the naive young man is also fine. Pakula's splendid first directing job. **108m/C VHS.** Liza Minnelli, Wendell Burton, Tim McIntire; ***D:*** Alan J. Pakula; ***W:*** Alvin Sargent; ***C:*** Milton Krasner.

Stevie 🦴🦴 **1978** Jackson brings her flawless skill to the role of British poet Stevie Smith. Excellent performance from Washbourne as Stevie's spinster aunt. Wooden, lifeless screen rendition for the Hugh Whitemore stage play is helped greatly by good performances, but is too talky and, frankly, rather dull and self-absorbed. **102m/C VHS.** *GB* Glenda Jackson, Mona Washbourne, Alec McCowen, Trevor Howard; ***D:*** Robert Enders; ***C:*** Frederick A. (Freddie) Young. L.A. Film Critics '78: Support. Actress (Washbourne); Montreal World Film Fest. '78: Actress (Jackson); N.Y. Film Critics '78: Support. Actress (Washbourne).

Stewardess School woof! **1986 (R)** Airline spoof aims at wackiness, but misses the runway. Generic title betrays probable badness which turns out to be all too real. An utter woofer. **84m/C VHS.** Sandahl Bergman, Wendie Jo Sperber, Judy Landers, Julia Montgomery, Corinne Bohrer; ***D:*** Ken Blancato; ***W:*** Ken Blancato; ***M:*** Robert Folk.

Stick 🦴½ **1985 (R)** Ex-con Stick (Reynolds, directing himself) wants to start a new life for himself in Miami. Lots of drug dealers and guns don't help the interest level in this dull underworld tale. Based upon the Elmore Leonard novel. **109m/C VHS.** Burt Reynolds, Candice Bergen, George Segal, Charles Durning, Dar Robinson; ***D:*** Burt Reynolds; ***W:*** Elmore Leonard; ***M:*** Steve Dorff.

The Stick-Up 🦴 *Mud* **1977** In 1935, a young American traveling in Great Britain is introduced to some rather illegal fun. Rather sorry attempt at romance/comedy/adventure. **101m/C VHS.** David Soul, Pamela McMyler; ***D:*** Jeffrey Bloom; ***W:*** Jeffrey Bloom.

Stickfighter 🦴 **1989 (PG)** The oppressive reign of an evil Spanish ruler of the Philippines is challenged by the world's best stickfighter. **102m/C VHS.** *PH* Dean Stockwell, Nancy Kwan, Alejandro Rey, Roland Dantes; ***D:*** Luis Nepomuceno.

Sticks 🦴🦴 **1998 (R)** Who knew cigars could cause so much trouble? Lenny (Brancato) discovers that an illicit shipment of Cuban cigars, the special private label of Castro himself, have been stolen. Maria (Machado) wants to swap the cigars for weapons to help liberate Cuba while her boyfriend Mark (Brunsmann) just wants some cold hard cash by selling the merchandise to a private Hollywood club frequented by high rollers. And Lenny sees a chance to make his own score. Too bad the mob and the feds have their own ideas. **94m/C VHS, DVD.** Lillo Brancato, Leo Rossi, Justina Machado, Keith Brunsmann; ***D:*** Brett Mayer; ***W:*** Brett Mayer; ***C:*** Nils Erickson; ***M:*** Bill Elliott. **VIDEO**

Sticks and Stones 🦴🦴 **1996 (PG-13)** Three high school friends are harassed by the local bully and the situation gets tragically out of control. **96m/C VHS.** Kirstie Alley, Gary Busey, Justin Isfeld, Max Goldblatt, Chauncey Leopardi; ***D:*** Neil Tolkin; ***W:*** Neil Tolkin; ***C:*** Avi (Avraham) Karpik; ***M:*** Hummie Mann. **VIDEO**

Sticky Fingers 🦴 **1988 (PG-13)** Two female musicians, asked to watch nearly a million bucks in drug money, go on a mega shopping spree. Completely incredible, unlikeable and mean-spirited attempt at zany comedy. **89m/C VHS.** Melanie Mayron, Helen Slater, Eileen Brennan, Carol Kane, Christopher Guest, Danitra Vance, Gwen Welles, Stephen McHattie, Shirley Stoler; ***D:*** Catlin Adams; ***W:*** Catlin Adams, Melanie Mayron; ***C:*** Gary Thieltges; ***M:*** Gary Chang.

The Sticky Fingers of Time 🦴🦴 **1997** New York writer Tucker (Matthews) is not having your average day. She goes out for coffee in 1953 and winds up in 1997 (thanks to some kind of atom-bomb mutation in her DNA). Turns out she's not the only time traveller, according to fellow freak, Isaac (Urbaniak). In fact, Isaac was responsible for bringing Tucker into the future so she wouldn't be murdered. Tucker (who's a pulp novelist) takes everything that happens with chain-smoking aplomb. **81m/B VHS, DVD.** Terumi Matthews, James Urbaniak, Belinda Becker, Nicole Zaray, Samantha Buck; ***D:*** Hilary Brougher; ***W:*** Hilary Brougher; ***C:*** Ethan Mass; ***M:*** Miki Navazio.

Stiff Upper Lips 🦴🦴½ **1996** Spoof of all the upper-crusty British costume dramas replete with sexual innuendoes and enlightening travel to hot climes. Twitish Edward (West) tries to pair off best chum Cedric (Portal) with his virgin sister, Emily (Cates). Only Emily prefers hearty servant, George (Pertwee). Snooty Aunt Agnes (Scales) decides everyone should take a restorative trip to Italy and later to India, where Aunt Agnes herself is subjected to a leering tea-planter, Horace (Ustinov). Meanwhile, Edward and Cedric are exploring their own "strange feelings" for one another. As with any film in this genre some gags work better than others. **85m/C VHS, DVD, Wide.** *GB* Samuel West, Robert Portal, Georgina Cates, Sean Pertwee, Prunella Scales, Peter Ustinov, Brian Glover, Frank Finlay; ***D:*** Gary Sinyor; ***W:*** Gary Sinyor, Paul Simpkin; ***C:*** Simon Archer; ***M:*** David A. Hughes, John Murphy.

Stigma 🦴½ **1973** "Miami Vice" star Thomas (then 23; later to restore his middle name, Michael) is a young doctor who treats a syphilis epidemic in a small town. He's indistinguishable, but better than anything else here. Ever seen close-ups of advanced syphilis? Here's your chance—but it's not pretty. **93m/C** Philip Michael Thomas, Harlan Cary Poe; ***D:*** David E. Durston.

Stigmata 🦴½ **1999 (R)** Disappointing horror flick that's campy instead of creepy. Airhead Pittsburgh beautician Frankie (Arquette) doesn't even believe in God, so why is she suddenly afflicted with visions and seizures that leave her with Christ-like wounds? Could it have anything to do with the rosary her vacationing mom sent her from Brazil? When the media picks up the story, the Vatican decides to send Father Kiernan (Byrne, who makes a very sexy priest) to check things out. Lots of hokey mumbo-jumbo ensues. **103m/C VHS, DVD.** Patricia Arquette, Gabriel Byrne, Jonathan Pryce, Portia de Rossi, Patrick Muldoon, Nia Long, Thomas Kopache, Rade Serbedzija, Enrico Colantoni, Dick Latessa, Ann Cusack; ***D:*** Rupert Wainwright; ***W:*** Rick Ramage, Tom Lazarus; ***C:*** Jeffrey L. Kimball; ***M:*** Elia Cmiral.

Stiletto 🦴½ **1969 (R)** Good cast is wasted in this mediocre depiction of the trouble encountered by a contract Mafia assassin when he decides to change careers. Based on the usual pulp cheese by Harold Robbins. **101m/C VHS.** Alex Cord, Britt Ekland, Patrick O'Neal, Joseph Wiseman, Barbara McNair, Roy Scheider, M. Emmet Walsh, Raul Julia; ***D:*** Bernard L. Kowalski; ***C:*** Jack Priestley.

Stiletto Dance 🦴🦴½ **2001 (R)** Anton (Doyle) is the head of the Russian mob in Buffalo, NY, who plans to sell a nuclear device to the Albanians. Undercover cop Kit Adrian (Roberts) has other ideas—before he makes the mistake of falling for a mob enforcer's wife (Laurier). **97m/C VHS, DVD.** Eric Roberts, Shawn Doyle, Brett Porter, Romano Orzari, Lucie Laurier, Yaphet Kotto, Mark Camacho, Justin Louis; ***D:*** Mario Azzopardi; ***W:*** Alfonse Ruggiero; ***C:*** Pierre Jodoin. **CABLE**

Still Breathing 🦴🦴½ **1997 (PG-13)** Romance with elements of the fantastical. Fletcher (Fraser) is an eccentric street performer in San Antonio, who dreams of a woman he knows will become his wife (it's a family thing). This turns out to be tough L.A. con woman Rosalyn (Going), whose next sting just happens to involve a Texan. When Fletcher flies to L.A. to find his would-be lady love, they meet cute and have a lot of mistaken assumptions before things come out right. Fraser's character may be wide-eyed but he's no fool and Going displays a needed touch of vulnerability for her manipulative bad girl. **109m/C VHS, DVD.** Brendan Fraser, Joanna Going, Ann Magnuson, Celeste Holm, Lou Rawls, Angus Macfadyen, Paolo Seganti; ***D:*** James F. Robinson; ***W:*** James F. Robinson; ***C:*** John Thomas; ***M:*** Paul Mills.

Still Crazy 🦴🦴🦴½ **1998 (R)** Twenty years after the breakup of his band Strange Fruit, Tony (Rea) is ready to give it a go again. With the Wisbech rock festival beckoning, he rounds up the others: lead singer Ray (Nighy), still a musician living in a mansion; drummer Beano (Spall), a gardener on the run from the tax collector; and singer-bassist Les (Nail), who runs a roofing business. One glitch: lead guitarist Brian (Robinson), the most popular band member, is supposedly dead. Luckily, love of the music (and money) forces the band to get it together. Inspired by a reunion tour of the Animals, but has more "Full Monty" fun and heart than "Spinal Tap" parody to it. The cast is superb and the actual concert makes you want to stand up and cheer, when you're done laughing. **96m/C VHS, DVD.** *GB* Stephen Rea, Billy Connolly, Jimmy Nail, Timothy Spall, Bill Nighy, Juliet Aubrey, Helena Bergstrom, Bruce Robinson, Hans Matheson, Rachael Stirling, Phil Daniels, Frances Barber, Philip Davis; ***D:*** Brian Gibson; ***W:*** Dick Clement, Ian LaFrenais; ***C:*** Ashley Rowe; ***M:*** Clive Langer.

Still Life 🦴🦴 **1992 (PG-13)** The press has dubbed him "the Art Killer," a serial murderer who makes scupltures out of his victims. He's a sensation—and not ready to stop. This sicko's next "Still Life" may just be a struggling young musician. **83m/C VHS.** Jason Gedrick, Jessica Steen, Stephen Shellen; ***D:*** Graeme Campbell; ***M:*** Mychael Danna.

Still Not Quite Human 🦴🦴 **1992** Teenage android Chip must do battle with unscrupulous industrialists and their robot weapon Spartacus to rescue his inventor father from their deadly clutches. **84m/C VHS.** Alan Thicke, Christopher Neame, Betsy Palmer, Adam Philipson, Rosa Nevin, Ken Pogue, Jay Underwood; ***D:*** Eric Luke; ***W:*** Eric Luke.

Still of the Night 🦴🦴 **1982 (PG)** A Hitchcock-style thriller about a psychiatrist infatuated with a mysterious woman who may or may not be a killer. **91m/C VHS.** Meryl Streep, Roy Scheider, Jessica Tandy, Joe Grifasi, Sara Botsford, Josef Sommer; ***D:*** Robert Benton; ***W:*** Robert Benton, David Newman; ***C:*** Nestor Almendros.

The Stilts 🦴🦴🦴 **1984** From modern Spanish cinema's preeminent director, this is a study of sexual dynamics revolving around a doomed love triangle. Aging professor Gomez wants young Del Sol to commit to him, but she won't; she has another, younger lover. Overwrought at times, but well acted. In Spanish with English subtitles. **95m/C VHS.** *SP* Laura Del Sol, Francesco Rabal, Fernando Gomez; ***D:*** Carlos Saura.

The Sting 🦴🦴🦴½ **1973 (PG)** Newman and Redford together again in this sparkling story of a pair of con artists in 1930s Chicago. They set out to fleece a big-time racketeer, pitting brain against brawn and pistol. Very inventive, excellent acting, Scott Joplin's wonderful ragtime music adapted by Marvin Hamlisch. The same directorial and acting team from "Butch Cassidy and the Sundance Kid" triumphs again. **129m/C VHS, DVD.** Paul Newman, Robert Redford, Robert Shaw, Charles Durning, Eileen Brennan, Harold Gould, Ray Walston; ***D:*** George Roy Hill; ***W:*** David S. Ward; ***C:*** Robert L. Surtees; ***M:*** Marvin Hamlisch. Oscars '73: Art Dir./Set Dec., Costume Des., Director (Hill), Film Editing, Picture, Story & Screenplay, Orig. Song Score and/or Adapt.; Directors Guild '73: Director (Hill).

The Sting 2 🦴½ **1983 (PG)** Complicated comic plot concludes with the final con game, involving a fixed boxing match where the stakes top $1 million and the payoff could be murder. Lame sequel to "The Sting" (1973). **102m/C VHS.** Jackie Gleason, Mac Davis, Teri Garr, Karl Malden, Oliver Reed; ***D:*** Jeremy Paul Kagan; ***W:*** David S. Ward; ***C:*** Bill Butler; ***M:*** Lalo Schifrin.

Sting of the West 🦴 **1976 (PG)** Journeyman con artist swindles his way across the Wild West. **90m/C VHS.** Jack Palance, Giancarlo (Timothy Brent) Prete, Lionel Stander.

Stingray 🦴½ **1978 (PG)** Two guys buy a Corvette, not knowing it's loaded with stolen heroin. Gangsters with an interest in the dope come after them, and the chase is on. Very violent and not all that funny. **105m/C VHS.** Chris Mitchum, Sherry Jackson, Les Lannom; ***D:*** Richard Taylor.

Stir 🦴 **1998** Scientist about to reveal a medical discovery is murdered in his hotel room. Months later, his wife and young son return to the hotel and the son, while sleeping, sees the night of the murder through his father's eyes. **100m/C VHS.** Tony Todd, Traci Lords, Daniel Roebuck, Seth Adkins, Karen Black, Michael J. Pollard, Andrew Heckler; ***D:*** Rodion Nakhapetov; ***W:*** Rodion Nakhapetov; ***C:*** Darko Suvak; ***M:*** Keith Bilderbeck. VIDEO

Stir Crazy 🦴🦴½ **1980 (R)** Two down-on-their luck losers find themselves convicted of a robbery they didn't commit and sentenced to 120 years behind bars with a mean assortment of inmates. Wilder and Pryor's second teaming isn't quite as successful as the first go-round, but still provides plenty of laughs. **111m/C VHS, DVD.** Richard Pryor, Gene Wilder, Nicolas Coster, Lee Purcell, Craig T. Nelson, JoBeth Williams; ***D:*** Sidney Poitier; ***W:*** Bruce Jay Friedman; ***C:*** Fred Schuler; ***M:*** Tom Scott, Michael Masser.

Stir of Echoes 🦴🦴½ **1999 (R)** The kid in "The Sixth Sense" isn't the only one seeing dead people, although blue-collar Tom Witzky (Bacon) really doesn't have a clue as to what's happening to him. After being hypnotized at a party by his witchy sister-in-law, Lisa (Douglas), Tom winds up with some very scary clairvoyant abilities, which link him to a neighborhood teenaged girl who's presumed missing but has, in fact, been murdered. Naturally, Tom's visions and obsessions lead to some problems with his family and friends. Based on the novel by Richard Matheson. **110m/C VHS, DVD, Wide.** Kevin Bacon, Illeana Douglas, Kathryn Erbe, Liza Weil, Kevin Dunn, Conor O'Farrell, Zachary David Cope, Jenny Morrison, Eddie Bo Smith Jr.; ***D:*** David Koepp; ***W:*** David Koepp; ***C:*** Fred Murphy; ***M:*** James Newton Howard.

Stitches 🦴 **1985 (R)** Adolescent comedy about med students playing practical jokes on the dean using laboratory specimens. So bad the director (actually Rod Holcomb) allegedly did not want his name associated with it. **92m/C VHS.** Eddie Albert, Parker Stevenson, Geoffrey Lewis, Brian Tochi; ***D:*** Alan Smithee; ***W:*** Michael Choquette.

The Stolen Children 🦴🦴🦴½ *Il Ladro di Bambini* **1992** Highly acclaimed Italian neo-realist film that tells the story of a shy carabiniere and two children who have been placed in his care. They are an emotionally battered 11-year-old girl who was forced into prostitution by her mother and her sullen 9-year-old brother. As they journey from Milan to Sicily and gradually get to know each other, all three of the characters undergo a slight transformation. Gracefully executed, this haunting masterpiece explores the overriding themes of guilt and innocence and keeps you thinking about them long after the movie's over. Italian with subtitles. **108m/C VHS.** *IT* Enrico Lo Verso, Valentina Scalici, Giuseppe Ieracitano, Florence Darel, Marina Golovine, Fabio Alessandrini; ***D:*** Gianni Amelio; ***W:*** Gianni Amelio, Sandro Petraglia, Stefano Rulli; ***M:*** Franco Piersanti. Cannes '92: Grand Jury Prize.

A Stolen Face 🦴🦴 **1952** Creepy, implausible drama of a plastic surgeon, spurned by a beautiful concert pianist, who transforms a female convict to look just like her. The convict runs away, but perhaps there's hope in the future with the pianist. **71m/B VHS.** *GB* Paul Henreid, Lizabeth Scott, Andre Morell, Susan Stephen; ***D:*** Terence Fisher; ***M:*** Malcolm Arnold.

Stolen Hearts 🦴 **1995 (R)** Instead of reporting con man Brandon Keyes (Finiani) to the cops after he takes her money, bar owner Dana Andrews (Aletonis) hires PI Justin Gibbons (Dale) to get back her savings. Justin happens to work with a psychic, Tess (Hall), and the twosome have a mutual attraction. They find the sleaze and get back the dough. Very boring. **82m/C VHS.** Landon Hall, Vincent Dale, Jim Finiani, Paula Aletonis; ***D:*** Ralph Portillo.

Stolen Hours 🦴½ **1963** Inferior remake of Bette Davis's "Dark Victory" casts Hayward as an oil-rich heiress who learns she has a fatal illness. Bring the tissues for this tearjerker. Based on the play "Dark Victory" by George Emerson Brewer Jr. and Bertram Block. **100m/C VHS.** Susan Hayward, Michael Craig, Diane Baker, Edward Judd, Paul Rogers; ***D:*** Daniel Petrie; ***W:*** Jessamyn West, Joseph Hayes.

Stolen Identity 🦴½ **1953** A Viennese cabbie sees his American dream dashed for lack of the proper papers. When an American businessman is murdered in his cab he is quick to seize the moment...and the dead man's identity. In no time at all he finds himself involved with the widow, entangled with the murderer and under suspicion for the killing. Predictable and sluggish, the story inches its way to the foregone conclusion. **81m/B VHS.** Francis Lederer, Donald Buka, Joan Camden, Adrienne Gessner; ***D:*** Gunther Fritsch.

Stolen Kisses 🦴🦴🦴½ *Baisers Voles* **1968** Sequel to "The 400 Blows," the story of Antoine Doinel: his unsuccessful career prospects as a detective in Paris, and his initially awkward but finally successful adventures with women. Made during Truffaut's involvement in a political crisis involving the sack of Cinematique Francais director Henri Langlois. Truffaut dedicated the film to Langlois and the Cinematique, but it is a thoroughly apolitical, small-scale, charming (some say too charming) romantic comedy, Truffaut-style. Followed by "Bed and Board." **90m/C VHS, DVD.** *FR* Jean-Pierre Leaud, Delphine Seyrig, Michael (Michel) Lonsdale, Claude Jade; ***D:*** Francois Truffaut; ***W:*** Francois Truffaut, Claude de Givray; ***C:*** Denys Clerval; ***M:*** Antoine Duhamel. Natl. Soc. Film Critics '69: Director (Truffaut).

A Stolen Life 🦴🦴 **1946** Remake of 1939 film of the same title starring Elisabeth Bergner. Oddly, Davis chose this as her first and last producing effort. Implausible tale of an evil twin (Davis) who takes her sister's (Davis) place so she can have the man they both love. Davis pulls it off as both twins; Ford is good as the hapless hubby. **107m/B VHS.** Bette Davis, Glenn Ford, Dane Clark, Walter Brennan, Charlie Ruggles, Bruce (Herman Brix) Bennett, Esther Dale, Peggy Knudsen; ***D:*** Curtis Bernhardt; ***M:*** Max Steiner.

The Stone Boy 🦴🦴🦴½ **1984 (PG)** A boy accidentally kills his older brother on their family's Montana farm. The family is torn apart by sadness and guilt. Sensitive look at variety of reactions during a crisis, with an excellent cast led by Duvall's crystal-clear performance. **93m/C VHS.** Mary Ellen Trainor, Glenn Close, Robert Duvall, Jason Presson, Frederic Forrest, Wilford Brimley, Linda Hamilton; ***D:*** Christopher Cain; ***W:*** Gina Berriault; ***C:*** Juan Ruiz-Anchia; ***M:*** James Horner, John Beal.

Stone Cold woof! **1991 (R)** Flamboyant footballer Bosworth made his acting debut in this sensitive human document, playing the usual musclebound, one-punk-army terminator cop, out to infiltrate a sadistic band of fascist biker barbarians engaged in drug running and priest shooting. Profane, lewd, gory, self-deifying; a crash course (accent on crashes) in everything despicable about modern action pics. **91m/C VHS, 8mm.** Brian Bosworth, Lance Henriksen, William Forsythe, Arabella Holzbog, Sam McMurray; ***D:*** Craig R. Baxley; ***W:*** Walter Doniger; ***C:*** Alexander Grusynski; ***M:*** Sylvester Levay.

Stone Cold Dead 🦴½ **1980 (R)** Rugged cop Crenna battles crime lord Williams (Paul Williams? Yeah, sure) over a prostitution ring. Meanwhile, a sniper starts killing hookers. Unoriginal and thoroughly dull would-be thriller. **100m/C VHS.** Richard Crenna, Paul Williams, Linda Sorensen, Belinda J. Montgomery; ***D:*** George Mendeluk; ***W:*** George Mendeluk.

Stone Fox 🦴🦴 **1987** Heartwarming family drama in which a young man must win a dogsled race to save the family farm. Based on John Reynolds Gardiner's popular children's book. **96m/C VHS.** Buddy Ebsen, Joey Cramer, Belinda J. Montgomery, Gordon Tootoosis; ***D:*** Harvey Hart.

The Stone Killer 🦴🦴½ **1973 (R)** Bronson stars as a tough plainclothes cop in this action-packed drama about a Mafia plot to use Vietnam vets in a mass killing. Violent but tense and action-packed revenge adventure set in the underworlds of New York and Los Angeles. **95m/C VHS.** Charles Bronson, Martin Balsam, Norman Fell, Ralph Waite, John Ritter; ***D:*** Michael Winner.

Stone of Silver Creek **1935** The owner of the Bonanza saloon, T. William Stone (Jones), discovers some of his unsavory patrons are planning to rob him. After a friend is shot trying to help him, Stone decides to even the score. Chapter 3 of "Gordon of Ghost City" finds Mary and Gordon entering a mine owned by Mary's grandfather, which turns out to be rich in gold. A figure sets an explosion and Mary and Gordon get trapped in the mine! **87m/B VHS.** Buck Jones, Noel Francis, Niles Welch, Marion Shilling, Peggy Campbell, Harry Semels, Madge Bellamy, Walter Miller; ***D:*** Nick Grinde, Ray Taylor.

Stonebrook 🦴🦴 **1998 (PG-13)** Two college roommates at a private university gamble to make their tuition money and wind up drawing the attention of a detective who wants to use their illegal activities to incriminate the mob. **90m/C VHS, DVD, Wide.** Seth Green, Brad Rowe, Zoe McLellan, William Mesnik, Stanley Kamel; ***D:*** Byron W. Thompson; ***W:*** Steven Robert Morris; ***C:*** John Tarver; ***M:*** Dean Grinsfelder.

The Stoned Age 🦴 **1994 (R)** Buddies look to get wasted and find some chicks. Set in the '70s. **90m/C VHS, DVD.** Michael Kopelow, China Kantner, Renee Griffen; ***D:*** James Melkonian.

Stones of Death 🦴 **1988 (R)** An aboriginal curse is invoked when a subdivision is built too close to an ancient burial site. Teenagers begin having all-too-real nightmares about death. **90m/C VHS.** Tom Jennings, Natalie McCurry, Zoe Carides, Eric Oldfield; ***D:*** James Bagle.

Stonewall 🦴🦴🦴 **1995 (R)** Fictional account of the June, 1969 police raid on Greenwich Village gay bar the Stonewall Inn, which is considered to have launched the modern gay rights movement. White-bread, midwestern activist Matty Dean (Weller) arrives in New York and gets thrown in jail for defending streetwise drag queen LaMiranda (Diaz) from harassing cops. They become lovers but Matty is also involved with conservative prepster Ethan (Corbalis), who thinks the flamboyant queens give the gay movement a bad name. Meanwhile, the drag queens at the mob-backed Stonewall are getting fed up with police raids and brutal treatment. Adapted from Martin Duberman's social history "Stonewall." Director Finch died during the final editing stages of the film. **93m/C VHS, DVD.** Frederick Weller, Guillermo Diaz, Brendan Corbalis, Bruce MacVittie, Duane Boutte, Peter Ratray, Luis Guzman; ***D:*** Nigel Finch; ***W:*** Rikki Beadle Blair; ***C:*** Chris Seager; ***M:*** Michael Kamen.

The Stooge 🦴🦴½ **1951** Singer Bill Miller (Martin) asks the antic Ted Rogers (Lewis) to join him in his vaudeville act, where Rogers' clowning has them on the road to success. But then Miller decides he wants to go solo. Sounds more than a little autobiographical. ♫A Girl Named Mary and a Boy Named Bill; Who's Your Little Whozis?; Just One More Chance; With My Eyes Wide Open I'm Dreaming; Louise; I'm Yours. **100m/B VHS.** Dean Martin, Jerry Lewis, Polly Bergen, Marion Marshall, Eddie Mayehoff, Richard Erdman, Frances Bavier; ***D:*** Norman Taurog; ***W:*** Martin Rackin, Fred Finklehoffe, Elwood Ullman; ***C:*** Daniel F. Fapp.

Stoogemania 🦴 **1985** A nerd becomes so obsessed with the Three Stooges that they begin to take over his life and ruin it. Harmless except as a waste of time. Includes actual Stooge footage including some colorized—but see an old Stooges movie instead. **95m/C VHS.** Josh Mostel, Melanie Chartoff, Sid Caesar, Mark Holton, Patrick DeSantis, Armin Shimerman, Thom Sharp, Joshua John Miller, Victoria Jackson, Ron House, Alan Shearman, Diz White; ***D:*** Chuck Workman; ***W:*** Chuck Workman, Jim Geoghan; ***C:*** Christopher Tufty; ***M:*** Hummie Mann, Gary Tigerman.

Stop Making Sense 🦴🦴🦴½ **1984** The Talking Heads perform 18 of their best songs in this concert filmed in Los Angeles. Considered by many to be the best concert movie ever made. The band plays with incredible energy and imagination, and Demme's direction and camera work is appropriately frenzied and original. Features such Talking Heads songs as "Burning Down the House," "Psycho Killer," and "Once in a Lifetime." Band member Tina Weymouth's Tom Tom Club also performs for the audience. **99m/C VHS, DVD, Wide.** ***D:*** Jonathan Demme; ***C:*** Jordan Cronenweth.

Stop! or My Mom Will Shoot 🦴 **1992 (PG-13)** Getty is an overbearing mother paying a visit to her cop son (Stallone) in Los Angeles. When mom witnesses a crime she has to stay in town longer than intended, which gives her time to meddle in her son's work and romantic lives. If Stallone wants to change his image this so-called comedy isn't the way to do it—because the joke is only on him. Viewers who rent this may find the joke is on them. **87m/C VHS.** Sylvester Stallone, Estelle Getty, JoBeth Williams, Roger Rees, Martin Ferrero, Gailard Sartain, Dennis Burkley; ***D:*** Roger Spottiswoode; ***W:*** William Osborne, William Davies, Blake Snyder; ***M:*** Alan Silvestri. Golden Raspberries '92: Worst Actor (Stallone), Worst Support. Actress (Getty), Worst Screenplay.

Stop That Cab 🦴½ **1951** Sloppy crooks accidentally leave precious jewels in the back seat of a taxi, and pursue and torture the cabby who found and hid them. Rather mean-spirited, uninteresting comedy. **56m/B VHS.** Sid Melton, Iris Adrian, Tom Neal.

Stopover Tokyo 🦴🦴 **1957** An American intelligence agent uncovers a plot to assassinate the American ambassador while on leave in Japan. Nice location shooting and scenery; limp story and characters. Based on a novel by John P. Marquand. **100m/C VHS.** Robert Wagner, Joan Collins, Edmond O'Brien, Ken Scott; ***D:*** Richard L. Breen.

The Stork Club 🦴🦴 **1945** A little song, a little dance, will Betty Hutton find romance? The actors manage to rise above the script in this silly, overdone fable. Hutton stars as the poor but spunky hatcheck girl who unwittingly saves the life of a cynical billionaire. His expressions of gratitude are less than appreciated by her G.I. beau. Done mainly as a vehicle for Hutton's promotion, so Betty's die-hard fans may find it to their liking. ♫Doctor, Lawyer, Indian Chief; Baltimore Oriole; I'm a Square in the Social Circle; If I Had a Dozen Hearts; Love Me; China Boy; In the Shade of the Old Apple Tree. **98m/B VHS.** Betty Hutton, Barry Fitzgerald, Don DeFore, Robert Benchley, Bill Goodwin, Iris Adrian, Noel Neill, Andy Russell; ***D:*** Hal Walker.

Storm 🦴½ **1987 (PG-13)** Uneven thriller finds college students on a camping trip who must fight for their lives when they are confronted by killer thieves. Somewhat contrived, but interesting ending to this low-budget outing. **99m/C VHS.** *CA* David Palfy, Stan Kane, Harry Freedman, Lawrence Elion, Tom Schioler; ***D:*** David Winning; ***M:*** Amin Bhatia.

Storm and Sorrow 🦴🦴 **1990** Molly Higgins is known as the "Spider-woman of the Rockies" for her legendary mountain climbing abilities. Then she joins a team looking to scale the 24,000-foot peaks of Russia's Pamir Mountains. The group meets deadly hazards—both natural and those caused by the ego-driven rivalries of the group's members. A fact-based drama based on the novel by Richard Craig. **96m/C VHS.** Lori Singer, Todd Allen, Steve (Stephen M.) Anderson, Jay Baker; ***W:*** Leigh Chapman.

Storm Catcher 🦴🦴 **1999 (R)** Air Force pilot Jack Holloway (Lundgren) is falsely convicted of stealing a prototype military aircraft. He manages to escape in order to find the real culprits, which also puts Hollway's family in danger. **95m/C VHS, DVD.** Dolph Lundgren, Mystro Clark, Yvonne Zime, Kylie Bax; ***D:*** Anthony Hickox; ***W:*** Bill Gucwa, Ed Masterson. **VIDEO**

Storm Chasers: Revenge of the Twister 🦴½ **1998** Having lost her husband in a plane crash, "storm chaser" Jaime (McGillis) throws herself into her work. Sent to Colorado to investigate a tornado, she hooks up with hunky FEMA coordinator, Will (Larson). There are some severe disturbances in the atmosphere causing problems—and disturbances on a more personal level as well. Dull and dumb. **96m/C VHS, DVD.** Kelly McGillis, Wolf Larson, Liz Torres, Adrian Zmed, James MacArthur; ***D:*** Mark Sobel. **VIDEO**

Storm in a Teacup 🦴🦴½ **1937** A reporter starts a campaign to save a sheepdog that the town magistrate has ordered killed because the owner, an old woman, is unable to pay the license tax. As the dog's fate hangs in the balance, this often humorous film provides an interesting look at British society of the 1930s. **80m/B VHS.** *GB* Vivien Leigh, Rex Harrison, Cecil Parker, Sara Allgood; ***D:*** Victor Saville.

Storm over Asia 🦴🦴🦴🦴 *The Heir to Genghis Khan* **1928** A Mongolian trapper is discovered to be descended from Genghis Khan and is made puppet emperor of a Soviet province. Beautiful and evocative. Silent masterpiece. **70m/B VHS, DVD.** *RU* I. Inkizhinov, Valeri Inkizhinov, A. Chistiakov, A. Dedinstev, V. Tzoppi, Paulina Belinskaya; ***D:*** Vsevolod Pudovkin; ***C:*** Anatoli Golovnya.

Storm over Wyoming 🦴🦴 **1950** The old sheep-and-cattle battle again; Holt and Martin find themselves haplessly embroiled in a Wyoming range war. Action-packed but thin, ordinary western. **60m/B VHS.** Tim Holt, Richard Martin.

Storm Rider 🦴🦴 **1957** A gunman hired to protect a group of ranchers from a powerful rancher falls in love with a local widow. After his job is done, however, he leaves her behind. Typical western fare. **70m/B VHS.** Scott Brady, Mala Powers, Bill Williams, Olin Howlin, William "Bill" Fawcett, John Goddard; ***D:*** Edward L. Bernds; ***W:*** Edward L. Bernds; ***M:*** Les Baxter.

Storm Tracker 🦴🦴½ *Storm* **1999 (PG-13)** Meteorologist Ron Young (Perry) develops a method of manipulating the path of deadly storms and is recruited by General Roberts (Sheen) to perfect his storm-tracking system for government use. Naturally, this isn't altruistic, the General wants to turn the violent storms on his enemies. **90m/C VHS, DVD.** Luke Perry, Martin Sheen, Alexandra Powers, David Moses, Renee Estevez; ***D:*** Harris Done. **CABLE**

Storm Trooper 🦴½ **1998** Abused wife Grace Tolson (Alt) is just cleaning up after killing her husband when the mysterious Stark (Laughlin) shows up at her back door. Closely following are a group of armed men who manage to wound the stranger, exposing wires and circuitry. Stark the cyborg gets Grace into a lot of danger but she's got a gun and she's not gonna take it anymore. **89m/C VHS.** Carol Alt, John Laughlin, Zach Galligan, Corey Feldman, Richard (Rick) Hill, Kool Moe Dee; ***D:*** Jim Wynorski; ***W:*** T.L. Lankford; ***C:*** J.E. Bash; ***M:*** Terry Plumeri. **VIDEO**

The Storm Within 🦴🦴🦴½ *Les Parents Terribles* **1948** Based on Cocteau's play, many consider this domestic drama of a troubled family's tortured existence to be his finest work. De Bray plays the domineering mother, Marais plays the son, and Day is the woman he (and his father) love in this complex story of sexuality, parental rivalry and jealousy. With the film set in only two locations, Cocteau creates a claustrophobic intimacy within the walls of de Bray's family apartment and Day's apartment. An inferior remake, "Intimate Relations" was released in Britain in 1953. In French with English subtitles. **98m/B VHS.** *FR* Jean Marais, Yvonne de Bray, Gabrielle Dorziat, Marcel Andre, Josette Day; ***D:*** Jean Cocteau; ***W:*** Jean Cocteau; ***Nar:*** Jean Cocteau.

Stormquest woof! **1987** Deep in the jungle, a band of women warriors live without men. When it is discovered that one of the group has a male lover, she is sentenced to death. Her man tries to rescue her, and it turns into a war of the sexes—literally. In Spanish with subtitles. **90m/C VHS.** *SP* Kai Baker, Brent Huff; ***D:*** Alex Sessa.

Stormswept 🦴½ **1995** Actress Brianna (Hughes) rents a haunted Louisiana mansion housing the spirit of a slave master. When a storm strands Brianna and friends, the spirit causes everyone to get up to all sorts of sexual escapades. **94m/C VHS, DVD, Wide.** Julie Hughes, Melissa Moore, Kathleen Kinmont, Justin Carroll, Lorissa McComas, Ed Wasser, Kim Kopf, Hunt Scarritt; ***D:*** David Marsh; ***W:*** David Marsh.

Stormy Monday 🦴🦴½ **1988 (R)** An American developer conspires to strike it rich in Newcastle, England real estate by resorting to violence and political manipulations. Sting plays the jazz club owner who opposes him. Slow plot, but acted and directed well; interesting photography. **108m/C VHS, 8mm.** *GB* Melanie Griffith, Tommy Lee Jones, Sting, Sean Bean, James Cosmo, Mark Long, Brian Lewis; ***D:*** Mike Figgis; ***W:*** Mike Figgis; ***C:*** Roger Deakins; ***M:*** Mike Figgis.

Stormy Nights 🦴½ **1997 (R)** Femme fatale Nicole (Spaulding) worms her way into the lives of Jennifer McCormick (Tweed) and her weak-willed hubby (Clark), leading to seduction and betrayal. **90m/C VHS.** Shannon Tweed, Tracy Spaulding, Brett (Baxter) Clark; ***D:*** Alberto Vidaurri; ***W:*** Michael Meyer; ***C:*** S. Douglas Smith; ***M:*** Jay Bolton.

Stormy Trails 🦴🦴 **1936** Bell battles bellicose bad guys who are after his property. At least all the gunfights should keep a viewer awake! **59m/B VHS.** Rex Bell.

Stormy Waters 🦴🦴½ *Remorques* **1941** A romantic French drama about a sea captain falling in love with a woman he rescues from a storm. He goes back to his wife, however, when she becomes critically ill. Director Gremillon insisted on realistic footage of storms at sea; production was delayed because of the difficulties of the German occupation. Dubbed. **75m/B VHS.** *FR* Jean Gabin, Michele Morgan, Madeleine Renaud; ***D:*** Jean Gremillon.

Stormy Weather 🦴🦴½ **1943** In this cavalcade of black entertainment, the plot takes a back seat to the nearly non-stop array of musical numbers, showcasing this stellar cast at their performing peak. ♫There's No Two Ways About Love; Stormy Weather; Ain't Misbehavin'; Rhythm Cocktail; Rang Tang Tang; Dat, Dot, Dah; That Ain't Right; I Can't Give You Anything But Love, Baby; Digga Digga Doo. **77m/B VHS.** Lena Horne, Bill Robinson, Fats Waller, Dooley Wilson, Cab Calloway; ***D:*** Andrew L. Stone; ***C:*** Leon Shamroy. Natl. Film Reg. '01.

The Story Lady 🦴🦴½ **1993** A retiree uses her story-telling abilities as a hostess on a public-access children's program. She becomes so popular that two network execs want to exploit her as a spokesperson for a toy company. Only a young girl can help her find a way to resist going commercial. **120m/C VHS, DVD.** Jessica Tandy, Lisa Jakub, Ed Begley Jr., Charles Durning, Stephanie Zimbalist; ***D:*** Larry Elikann; ***M:*** Lee Holdridge. **TV**

The Story of a Cheat 🦴🦴🦴 **1936** The hero of the film discovers at an early age that dishonesty is probably the best policy and he sets out to put his theory into use. Director/writer Guitry also turns in a great performance as the central character. Guitry was a major influence on such different directors as Welles, Resnais and Truffaut. Based on Guitry's novel "Memoires d'Un Tricheur." In French with English subtitles. **83m/B VHS.** *FR* Sacha Guitry; ***D:*** Sacha Guitry; ***W:*** Sacha Guitry.

Story of a Cowboy Angel 🦴 **1981** On the Christmas Mountain Ranch, a cowboy angel descends to Earth to bestow various beneficences. **90m/C VHS.** Slim Pickens.

The Story of a Love Story 🦴🦴½ *Impossible Object* **1973** Bates plays a writer whose imagination gets the better of him when he attempts an extra-marital affair. Was he with her or not? Unusual concept doesn't stand up in the long run. Fine cast is under-utilized. **110m/C VHS.** *FR* Alan Bates, Dominique Sanda, Evans Evans, Lea Massari, Michel Auclair, Laurence De Monaghan; ***D:*** John Frankenheimer; ***W:*** Alan Bates.

Story of a Prostitute 🦴🦴 *Joy Girls; Shunpuden* **1965** Lurid film adapted from a novel by Taijiro Tamura. A betrayed woman volunteers to become a prostitute for a garrison of soldiers stationed on the Manchurian front in WWII. Soon, the commander takes the woman as his sole property, though she has fallen for one of his junior officers. Japanese with subtitles. **86m/B VHS, Wide.** *JP* Yumiko Nogawa, Tamio Kawachi, Isao Tamagawa; ***D:*** Seijun Suzuki.

The Story of a Three Day Pass 🦴🦴½ *La Permission* **1968** A black American GI falls in love with a white French girl he meets in peacetime Paris. Based on Van Peebles book "La Permission." With English subtitles. Made on a low budget and flawed, but poignant and impressive. **87m/B VHS.** Harry Baird, Nicole Berger, Pierre Doris; ***D:*** Melvin Van Peebles; ***W:*** Melvin Van Peebles.

The Story of Adele H. 🦴🦴🦴 *L'Histoire d'Adele H* **1975 (PG)** The story of Adele Hugo, daughter of Victor Hugo, whose love for an English soldier leads to obsession and finally to madness after he rejects her. Sensitive and gentle unfolding of characters and story. Beautiful photography. In French with English subtitles. **97m/C VHS, DVD, Wide.** *FR* Isabelle Adjani, Bruce Robinson, Sylvia Marriott; ***D:*** Francois Truffaut; ***W:*** Suzanne Schiffman, Jean Gruault; ***C:*** Nestor Almendros; ***M:*** Maurice Jaubert. Natl. Bd. of Review '75: Actress (Adjani); N.Y. Film Critics '75: Actress (Adjani), Screenplay; Natl. Soc. Film Critics '75: Actress (Adjani).

The Story of Alexander Graham Bell 🦴🦴🦴 **1939** Lavish Fox biography on the inventor of the telephone provided Ameche with his most popular role. He's a serious Scot who comes to Boston to teach speech to the deaf and falls in love with the rich, beautiful and hearing impaired Young (whose three sisters, Georgianna, Polly Ann, and Sally are also in the film). Thanks to Young's rich daddy (Coburn), Bell gets the money to work on his invention, aided by enthusiastic assistant Watson (Fonda). No, it's not an entirely accurate retelling but it's well-done. **97m/B VHS.** Don Ameche, Loretta Young, Henry Fonda, Charles Coburn, Spring Byington, Gene Lockhart, Sally Blane, Polly Ann Young, Georgianna Young, Bobs Watson, Jonathan Hale, Harry Davenport; ***D:*** Irving Cummings; ***W:*** Lamar Trotti; ***C:*** Leon Shamroy.

The Story of Boys & Girls 🦴🦴🦴 *Storia de Ragazzi e di Ragazze* **1991** Two very different families come together for the wedding feast of their children, during which family secrets are revealed and we come to know and care for everyone present. A 20-course meal rivals the food scenes in "Babette's Feast" and is guaranteed to make your mouth water. Fine ensemble of actors, well directed, with a vivid evocation of 1930s Italy. In Italian with English subtitles. **92m/C VHS.** *IT* Lucrezia Lante della Rovere, Massimo Bonetti, Davide Bechini, Enrica Maria Modugno, Valeria Bruni Tadeschi, Lina Bernardi, Anna Bonaiuto, Alessandro Haber; ***D:*** Pupi Avati; ***W:*** Pupi Avati; ***M:*** Riz Ortolani.

The Story of David 🦴🦴🦴 **1976 (PG)** Well-done Old Testament Bible drama about the shepherd boy who slew Goliath, overcame the Philistines, and united Israel. Then, as King David, he winds up involved in an illicit love affair with Bathsheba that threatens to destroy his kingdom. Fine acting and a literate script highlight this TV production. **192m/C VHS.** Timothy Bottoms, Anthony Quayle, Jane Seymour, Keith Michell, Susan Hampshire; ***D:*** Alex Segal; ***W:*** Ernest Kinoy. **TV**

The Story of Dr. Wassell 🦴🦴½ **1944** Courageous true story of Corydon M. Wassell (Cooper), who won the Navy Cross for humanitarianism in WWII. Stationed in Java when the Japanese overrun the island, Wassell's placed in charge of evacuating the wounded. When he learns that stretcher cases must be left behind, he disobeys orders to rescue some badly wounded soldiers and get them to safety. (Naturally, there has to be some romance, so Cooper's paired with Day as a Red Cross nurse). Based on the book by James Hilton. **137m/C VHS.** Gary Cooper, Laraine Day, Signe Hasso, Dennis O'Keefe, Carol Thurston, Carl Esmond, Stanley Ridges, Paul Kelly, Elliott Reid, Philip Ahn, Barbara Britton; ***D:*** Cecil B. DeMille; ***W:*** Charles Bennett, Alan LeMay; ***C:*** Victor Milner; ***M:*** Victor Young.

The Story of Esther Costello 🦴🦴½ *Golden Virgin* **1957** Rich American Margaret Landi (Crawford) is visiting her Irish homeland when she meets Esther (Sears), a young girl rendered deaf, mute, and blind by a childhood trauma. The childless Margaret is persuaded to take Esther in as a surrogate daughter and the waif gradually begins to respond to her care, sparking a media frenzy over the inspirational saga. This brings Carlo (Brazzi), Margaret's estranged and money-grubbing husband, out of the woodwork, with some get-rich-quick schemes. Well-done melodrama adapted from the book by Nicholas Monsarrat. **102m/B VHS.** *GB* Joan Crawford, Heather Sears, Rossano Brazzi, Lee Patterson, Ron Randell, Fay Compton, John Loder, Denis O'Dea; ***D:*** David Miller; ***W:*** Charles Kaufman; ***C:*** Robert Krasker; ***M:*** Georges Auric.

The Story of Fausta 🦴🦴½ *Romance da Empregada* **1988 (R)** An unhappily married cleaning woman in the slums of Rio entices all the money and gifts she can out of an elderly widower. Decidely grim comedy-drama, well-done but unsparing in its depiction of overwhelming greed. In Portuguese with English subtitles. **90m/C VHS.** *BR* Betty Faria, Daniel Filho, Brandao Filho; ***D:*** Bruno Barreto; ***M:*** Ruben Blades.

The Story of G.I. Joe 🦴🦴🦴½ **1945** Grunt's-eye-view of the European theatre in WWII, based on the columns of war correspondent Ernie Pyle. Follows an infantry unit through Italy and concentrates on the everyday experiences of the soldiers, registering genuine emotion and realism. Mitchum's breakthrough role. Most of the actual unit played themselves. Pyle was killed by a sniper shortly before the film's release. **109m/B VHS, DVD.** Burgess Meredith, Robert Mitchum, Wally Cassell, William Benedict, William Murphy, Jimmy Lloyd, Fred Steele, William (Bill) Self, Jack Reilly, Tito Renaldo, Hal Boyle, Chris Cunningham, Jack Foisie, George Lah, Bob Landry, Clete Roberts, Robert Rueben, Don Whitehead; ***D:*** William A. Wellman; ***W:*** Leopold Atlas, Guy Endore, Philip Stevenson, Ernie Pyle; ***C:*** Russell Metty; ***M:*** Louis Applebaum, Ann Ronell.

The Story of Jacob & Joseph ♪♪♪ **1974 (R)** Fine biblical drama finds brothers Jacob and Esau fighting over their birthright, tearing apart their family for 20 years. When the brothers finally reconcile, it's only to cast an envious eye on youngest brother Joseph, whom they sell into slavery. Taken to Egypt Joseph uses his talents to become the Pharoah's chief advisor but he can never forget his family or what was done to him. All-around good acting, directing, and writing. **96m/C VHS, DVD.** Keith Michell, Tony LoBianco, Julian Glover, Colleen Dewhurst, Herschel Bernardi, Harry Andrews; ***D:*** Michael Cacoyannis; ***W:*** Ernest Kinoy; ***M:*** Mikis Theodorakis; ***Nar:*** Alan Bates. **TV**

The Story of Louis Pasteur ♪♪♪ **1936** Formulaic Hollywood biopic raised a notch or two by Muni's superb portrayal of the famous scientist and his career leading up to his most famous discoveries. Acclaimed in its time; excellent despite low budget. **85m/B VHS.** Paul Muni, Josephine Hutchinson, Anita Louise, Fritz Leiber, Donald Woods, Porter Hall, Akim Tamiroff, Walter Kingsford; ***D:*** William Dieterle; ***C:*** Gaetano Antonio "Tony" Gaudio. Oscars '36: Actor (Muni), Story.

The Story of O ♪♪ **1975 (NC-17)** A young woman's love for one man moves her to surrender herself to many men, in order to please him. Soft-core porn with bondage and S&M beautified by camera work. Based on the classic Freudian-erotic novel by Pauline Reage. **105m/C VHS, DVD.** Corinne Clery, Anthony Steel, Udo Kier, Jean Gaven, Christiane Minazolli, Martine Kelly, Nadine Perles; ***D:*** Just Jaeckin; ***W:*** Sebastien Japrisot; ***C:*** Robert Fraisse, Yves Rodallec; ***M:*** Pierre Bachelet.

The Story of O, Part 2 ♪ **1987** A sort-of sequel to the erotic classic, in which the somewhat soiled vixen takes over an American conglomerate by seducing everyone in it. **107m/C DVD.** Sandra Wey, Carole James.

The Story of Qiu Ju ♪♪♪ *Qiu Ju Da Guansi* **1991 (PG)** A simple story, beautifully directed and acted, about a peasant woman's search for justice. The pregnant Qiu Ju's husband is assaulted and injured by the head of their village. Outraged, Qui Ju slowly climbs the Chinese administrative ladder from official to higher official as she insistently seeks redress. Presents a close observance of daily life and customs with a strong female lead. Adapted from the novel "The Wan Family's Lawsuit" by Chen Yuan Bin. In Mandarin Chinese with English subtitles. **100m/C VHS.** *CH* Gong Li, Lei Lao Sheng, Liu Pei Qu, Ge Zhi Jun, Ye Jun, Yang Liu Xia, Zhu Qanging, Cui Luowen, Yank Huiquin, Wang Jianfa, Lin Zi; ***D:*** Zhang Yimou; ***W:*** Liu Heng; ***C:*** Chi Xiaonin, Yu Xaioqun; ***M:*** Zhao Jiping. Natl. Soc. Film Critics '93: Foreign Film; Venice Film Fest. '92: Actress (Li), Film.

The Story of Robin Hood & His Merrie Men ♪♪♪ *The Story of Robin Hood* **1952** Well-made swashbuckler based on the English legend was Disney's second live action feature. Almost, but not quite, as memorable as the 1938 Michael Curtiz "Adventures of Robin Hood." Curtiz's version had Errol Flynn, after all. **83m/C VHS.** Richard Todd, Joan Rice, Peter Finch, Martita Hunt; ***D:*** Ken Annakin.

The Story of Ruth ♪♪ **1960** Biblical saga of adventures of Ruth as she denounces her pagan gods and flees to Israel. Typically "epic" with overwrought performances. Alternately not too bad to downright boring. **132m/C VHS.** Elana Eden, Viveca Lindfors, Peggy Wood, Tom Tryon, Stuart Whitman, Jeff Morrow, Thayer David, Eduard Franz; ***D:*** Henry Koster.

The Story of Seabiscuit ♪♪½ *Pride of Kentucky* **1949** The famous racing winner Seabiscuit is featured in a fluffy story of a racetrack romance. Temple is in love with a jockey (McCallister) but wants him to give up racing. Her uncle (Fitzgerald), who is Seabiscuit's trainer, has other things in mind. **93m/C VHS.** Shirley Temple, Barry Fitzgerald, Lon (Bud) McCallister, Rosemary DeCamp; ***D:*** David Butler.

The Story of the Late Chrysanthemum ♪♪♪½ **1939** Classic drama about the son of a Kabuki actor who falls in love with a servant girl against his father's wishes. Their doomed affair is the center of the plot. Acclaimed and sensitive drama, in Japanese with English subtitles. **115m/B VHS.** *JP* Shotaro Hanayagi, Kakuo Mori, Kokichi Takada, Gonjuro Kawarazaki, Yoko Umemura; ***D:*** Kenji Mizoguchi.

The Story of Us ♪♪½ **1999 (R)** Hey attraction is easy but sustaining a relationship is hard—particularly after 15 years in a marriage of opposites. Crossword puzzle editor Katie (Pfeiffer) is a planner and organizer while hubby Ben (Willis), a TV comedy writer, is a spontaneous free-spirit. The kids are away at summer camp when the constantly bickering duo decide on a trial separation as they wonder what went wrong. Appealing leads but story is repetitive and sentimental. **98m/C VHS, DVD.** Bruce Willis, Michelle Pfeiffer, Rita Wilson, Paul Reiser, Rob Reiner, Tim Matheson, Julie Hagerty, Jayne Meadows, Tom Poston, Betty White, Red Buttons; ***D:*** Rob Reiner; ***W:*** Alan Zweibel, Jessie Nelson; ***C:*** Michael Chapman; ***M:*** Eric Clapton, Marc Shaiman.

The Story of Vernon and Irene Castle ♪♪♪ **1939** In this, their last film together for RKO, Astaire and Rogers portray the internationally successful ballroom dancers who achieved popularity in the early 1900s. Irene Castle served as technical advisor for the film and exasperated everyone on the set by insisting that Rogers be a brunette. Still fun, vintage Fred and Ginger. ♫Only When You're In My Arms; Missouri Waltz; Oh, You Beautiful Doll; Nights of Gladness; By the Beautiful Sea; Glow, Little Glow Worm; Destiny Waltz; Row, Row, Row; The Yama Yama Man. **93m/B VHS.** Fred Astaire, Ginger Rogers, Edna May Oliver, Lew Fields, Jack Perrin, Walter Brennan; ***D:*** H.C. Potter.

The Story of Women ♪♪♪ *Une Affaire de Femmes* **1988** Riveting factual account of a woman (Huppert) who was guillotined for performing abortions in Nazi-occupied France. In French with English subtitles. **110m/C VHS.** *FR* Isabelle Huppert, Francois Cluzet, Marie Trintignant, Nils (Niels) Tavernier, Louis Ducreux; ***D:*** Claude Chabrol; ***W:*** Claude Chabrol, Colo Tavernier O'Hagan; ***C:*** Jean Rabier; ***M:*** Matthieu Chabrol. L.A. Film Critics '89: Foreign Film; N.Y. Film Critics '89: Foreign Film; Venice Film Fest. '88: Actress (Huppert).

The Story of Xinghua ♪♪ **1993** Obedient wife Xinghua (Wenli) endures the cruelty of her greedy husband (Guoli) in a northern Chinese village, built within the shadow of the Great Wall. Working in the fields alongside handsome farmer Tulin (Shaojun), Xinghua is drawn to his gentleness and the two become lovers. When her husband hears that gold may be buried beneath one of the wall's watchtowers, he persuades his fellow villagers to help him dig beneath the stones—a decision that leads to tragedy. Mandarin with subtitles. **89m/C VHS.** *CH* Jiang Wehli, Zhang Guoli, Tian Shaoujun; ***D:*** Yin Li.

Storybook ♪♪½ **1995 (G)** Eight-year-old Brandon finds a magic storybook and enters into a realm of fantasy. He discovers the only way to return home from Storyland is to save the kingdom from the rule of Queen Evilia and along with Woody the Woodsman, Pouch the Boxing Kangaroo, and Hoot the Wise Owl, Brandon just may succeed. **88m/C VHS.** Sean Fitzgerald, William McNamara, Swoosie Kurtz, Robert Costanzo, James Doohan, Brenda Epperson, Gary Morgan, Richard Moll, Jack Scalia, Milton Berle; ***D:*** Lorenzo Doumani; ***W:*** Lorenzo Doumani, Susan Bowen.

Storytelling ♪♪♪ **2001 (R)** Anthology explores the roles that sex and dysfunction play in creativity. First story, "Fiction" explores the complex relationship of writing student Vi (Blair) and her boyfriend Marcus (Fitzpatrick), who has cerebral palsy. The two are using each other for different ends, most notably to read each other's writing. Vi moves on to an intense one-night stand with her formidable black writing professor (Wisdom). Shaken, Vi weaves the graphic, brutal, but fascinating encounter into a story of her own. In "Nonfiction," feature documentarian Toby (Giamatti) goes to the burbs to document the life of a teen, his extremely dysfunctional family, and their Salvadoran maid. Solondz's characteristic black humor and social satire offers a range of hot topics, including homosexuality, political correctness, social stereotypes, the Holocaust, race, poverty, and the disabled. **87m/C VHS, DVD.** *US* Selma Blair, Leo Fitzpatrick, Aleksa Palladino, Robert Wisdom, Noah Fleiss, Paul Giamatti, John Goodman, Julie Hagerty, Lupe Ontiveros, Franka Potente, Mike Schank, Mark Webber, Jonathan Osser; ***D:*** Todd Solondz; ***W:*** Todd Solondz; ***M:*** Belle & Sebastian, Nathan Larson.

Storyville ♪½ **1974 (PG)** Love and music overcome prostitution and poverty in this turn-of-the-century New Orleans jazz drama, but tragedy prevails. **96m/C VHS.** Tim Rooney, Jeannie Wilson, Butch Benit, Wayne Mack, Bond Gideon, Oley Sassone; ***D:*** Jack Weis.

Storyville ♪♪ **1992 (R)** Southern Gothic tale set in New Orleans about a feckless young lawyer running for a local congressional seat. Neither Cray nor his family are strong candidates for the family values vote. Cray is separated from his wife and willingly indulges in an affair with a beautiful and mysterious young woman. This leads to a blackmail plot when he finds out his lover has been videotaping their antics. There's also a murder investigation and a host of family skeletons rattling around. Robards is fine as the crafty uncle but Spader's low-key attitude works against the story. Directorial debut of Frost. **112m/C VHS.** James Spader, Joanne Whalley, Jason Robards Jr., Charlotte Lewis, Michael Warren, Piper Laurie, Michael Parks, Chuck McCann, Woody Strode, Charles Haid; ***D:*** Mark Frost; ***W:*** Mark Frost, Lee Reynolds; ***M:*** Carter Burwell.

Stowaway ♪♪♪ **1936 (G)** After her missionary parents are killed in a Chinese revolution, Shirley stows away on a San Francisco-bound liner and plays cupid to a bickering couple who adopt her. ♫Good Night, My Love; One Never Knows, Does One; You Gotta S-M-I-L-E to Be H-A-P-P-Y; I Wanna Go To the Zoo; That's What I Want For Christmas. **86m/B VHS.** Shirley Temple, Robert Young, Alice Faye, Eugene Pallette, Helen Westley, Arthur Treacher, Astrid Allwyn; ***D:*** William A. Seiter; ***C:*** Arthur C. Miller.

Straight for the Heart ♪♪ *A Corps Perdu* **1988** Photojournalist Pierre returns to Montreal after a harrowing assignment in Nicaragua. His homecoming is less than happy when he discovers both his lovers, David and Sarah, have deserted him. Pierre takes to wandering the Montreal streets, taking pictures, hoping they will help him make some sense of his life and help him re-establish a connection with beauty and humanity. In French with English subtitles. **92m/C VHS.** *CA* Matthias Habich, Johanne-Marie Tremblay; ***D:*** Lea Pool.

Straight Line ♪♪ **1988** T.S. Turner is a private investigator who goes after street gangs in order to prevent further violence in this action-packed story. **95m/C VHS.** Mr. T, Sean Roberge, Ron Ryan.

Straight out of Brooklyn ♪♪ **1991 (R)** A bleak, nearly hopeless look at a struggling black family in a Brooklyn housing project. The son seeks escape through crime, his father in booze. An up-close and raw look at part of society seldom shown in mainstream film, its undeniable power is sapped by ragged production values and a loose narrative prone to melodrama. Rich (seen in a supporting role) was only 19 years old when he completed this, funded partly by PBS-TV's "American Playhouse." **91m/C VHS.** George T. Odom, Ann D. Sanders, Lawrence Gilliard, Mark Malone, Reana E. Drummond, Barbara Sanon, Matty Rich; ***D:*** Matty Rich; ***W:*** Matty Rich; ***C:*** John Rosnell; ***M:*** Harold Wheeler. Ind. Spirit '92: First Feature; Sundance '91: Special Jury Prize.

Straight out of Compton ♪♪½ **2000** Stereotype-riddled saga of a tough Compton local, Henry "Hen" Alabaster, and his plan to score some big time cash and start his own record company. He targets a racist politician named Drake Norelli who's made a fortune laundering mob money. The whole thing seems to want to deliver the meaningful message that "you can't escape your past," but it's lost amidst a mess of cliches and offensive stereotypes. **?m/C DVD.** Ryan Combs, Johnny DeaRenzo, Jules Dupree, Sean Epps; ***D:*** Ryan Combs; ***W:*** Ryan Combs; ***C:*** Eric Green.

Straight Shooter ♪♪ **1999 (R)** Former Foreign Legionnaire Volker Bretz (Ferch) seeks revenge for his daughter's death by killing the politicians he thinks are responsible. Frank Hector (Hopper), his former trainer, may be the only one who can stop him but will he? Hopper's the only English-speaking actor in this German thriller—the other actors are dubbed. **98m/C VHS, DVD.** *GE* Dennis Hopper, Heino Ferch, Ulrich Muhe; ***D:*** Thomas Bohn.

Straight Shootin' ♪♪½ **1917** Ford's first major effort launched both Carey and Gibson to national fame. Prototypical western; great action, great scenery. Silent. **53m/B VHS.** Harry Carey Sr., Hoot Gibson, Mollie Malone; ***D:*** John Ford.

The Straight Story ♪♪♪½ **1999 (G)** Surprisingly sweet true story from the generally eccentric Lynch. Septuagenarian Alvin Straight (Farnsworth), who lives in Iowa, is determined to visit his ailing, estranged brother Lyle (Stanton) even though he can no longer drive a car. So, he hitches a small trailer to his riding mower and heads off at a stately 6 miles per hour—to Wisconsin (a 300 mile trip). Alvin realizes this is his last chance at both freedom and family and he's determined to make the most of it. Farnsworth plays Straight as a gruff, straight-talking old geezer and there's little or no sentimentality involved. **111m/C VHS, DVD, Wide.** Richard Farnsworth, Harry Dean Stanton, Sissy Spacek; ***D:*** David Lynch; ***W:*** John Roach; ***C:*** Freddie Francis; ***M:*** Angelo Badalamenti. Ind. Spirit '00: Actor (Farnsworth); N.Y. Film Critics '99: Actor (Farnsworth), Cinematog.

Straight Talk ♪♪½ **1992 (PG)** Shirlee (Parton), a down-home gal from Arkansas, heads for Chicago to start life anew. She finds a job as a receptionist at WNDY radio, but is mistaken for the new radio psychologist. Her homespun advice ("Get off the cross. Somebody needs the wood.") becomes hugely popular and soon "Dr." Shirlee is the toast of the town. Parton's advice is the funniest part of this flimsy movie, but she is helped immensely by Dunne and Orbach. Woods, however, is not in his element in a romantic comedy, and holds the movie down. **91m/C VHS.** Dolly Parton, James Woods, Griffin Dunne, Michael Madsen, Deirdre O'Connell, John Sayles, Teri Hatcher, Spalding Gray, Jerry Orbach, Philip Bosco, Charles Fleischer, Jay Thomas; ***D:*** Barnet Kellman; ***W:*** Craig Bolotin, Patricia Resnick; ***M:*** Brad Fiedel.

Straight Time ♪♪♪ **1978 (R)** Ex-con Hoffman hits the streets for the first time in six years and finds himself again falling into a life of crime. Well-told, sobering story flopped at the boxoffice and has never received the recognition it deserved. Convincing, realistic portrayal of a criminal. Hoffman was the original director, but gave the reins to Grosbard. Based on the novel "No Beast So Fierce" by Edward Bunker. **114m/C VHS.** Dustin Hoffman, Harry Dean Stanton, Gary Busey, Theresa Russell, M. Emmet Walsh, Kathy Bates, Edward (Eddie) Bunker; ***D:*** Ulu Grosbard; ***W:*** Jeffrey Boam, Alvin Sargent, Edward (Eddie) Bunker; ***C:*** Owen Roizman; ***M:*** David Shire.

Straight to Hell ½ **1987 (R)** A wildly senseless, anachronistic western spoof about a motley, inept gang of frontier thieves. An overplayed, indiscriminating punk spaghetti oat-opera. **86m/C VHS, DVD, Wide.** Dennis Hopper, Joe Strummer, Elvis Costello, Grace Jones, Jim Jarmusch, Dick Rude, Courtney Love, Sy Richardson, Biff Yeager, Xander Berkeley, Shane McGowan; ***D:*** Alex Cox; ***W:*** Alex Cox, Dick Rude; ***C:*** Tom Richmond; ***M:*** The Pogues, Pray for Rain.

Straight Up ½ **1990** A musical f/x-ridden attempts to warn MTV-era children about drugs, but visual gimmicks often overwhelm the message. Gossett sings nicely as a cosmic sage of abstinence, who cautions a boy against substance abuse. The smartest segment lambasts cigarette and alcohol ads. **75m/C VHS.** Chad Allen, Louis Gossett Jr.

Strait-Jacket ½ **1964** After Crawford is released from an insane asylum where she was sent 20 years for axing her husband and his mistress, mysterious axe murders begin to occur in the neighborhood. Coincidence? Aging axist Crawford is the prime suspect, and even she cannot say for sure who's doing it. Daughter Baker is there to help her adjust. Moderately creepy grade B+ slasher is lifted somewhat by Crawford. Written by Robert Bloch ("Psycho"). Never one to miss a gimmick, director Castle arranged for the distribution of cardboard "bloody axes" to all theatre patrons attending the movie. **89m/B VHS, DVD, Wide.** Joan Crawford, Leif Erickson, Diane Baker, George Kennedy, Howard St. John, Rochelle Hudson, Edith Atwater, Lee Majors, John Anthony Hayes, Mitchell Cox, Lee Yeary, Patricia Krest; ***D:*** William Castle; ***W:*** Robert Bloch; ***C:*** Arthur E. Arling; ***M:*** Van Alexander.

Stranded **1987 (PG-13)** A group of aliens escaping interplanetary persecution land on Earth and enlist the aid of an Earth family. Solid characters make it more than sci-fi; sort of a parable of intolerance, human (and alien) goodness, etc. **80m/C VHS.** Maureen O'Sullivan, Ione Skye, Cameron Dye; ***D:*** Tex Fuller; ***W:*** Alan Castle.

The Strange Affair of Uncle Harry ½ *Uncle Harry* **1945** Small-town gothic with fine acting by Sanders, an aging bachelor who plots murder when his romance is threatened by a jealous sister. A title card asks you not to reveal the 'surprise' ending—a hackneyed twist that appeased the censors but made producer Joan Harrison resign in protest. Based on a play by Robert Job. Tape suffers from poor film-video transfer. **80m/B VHS.** George Sanders, Geraldine Fitzgerald, Ella Raines, Sara Allgood, Moyna MacGill, Samuel S. Hinds, Harry von Zell; ***D:*** Robert Siodmak.

A Strange and Deadly Occurrence ½ **1974** Strange things start to happen to a family when they move to a house in a remote area. **74m/C VHS.** Robert Stack, Vera Miles, L.Q. (Justus E. McQueen) Jones, Herb Edelman; ***D:*** John Llewellyn Moxey. **TV**

Strange Awakening **1958** Traveling in France while recuperating from amnesia, Barker is trapped in a plot of fraud and theft. Confused and contrived. **75m/B VHS.** *GB* Lex Barker, Carole Mathews, Nora Swinburne, Richard Molinos, Peter Dyneley; ***D:*** Montgomery Tully.

Strange Bedfellows ½ **1965** Within 24 hours of Carter Hudson (Hudson) arriving to work in London, he's met and married eccentric Italian Toni Vincenti (Lollobrigida). Complete opposites, the marriage is soon over and Carter returns to the States. Seven years later, he's back in London, ready to officially divorce Toni but learns from company PR whiz Dick Bramwell (Young) that his big promotion is contingent on his happy marriage. Carter courts Toni again, and tries to support her liberal causes and friends, but it turns out her latest stunt is aimed at his firm. Supposedly a check of the closing credits shows the film was shot on a Universal back lot and not on location. **104m/C VHS.** Rock Hudson, Gina Lollobrigida, Gig Young, Edward Judd, Howard St. John, Nancy Kulp, Bernard Fox, Terry-Thomas; ***D:*** Melvin Frank; ***W:*** Melvin Frank, Michael Pertwee; ***C:*** Leo Tover; ***M:*** Leigh Harline.

Strange Behavior *Dead Kids; Small Town Massacre* **1981 (R)** In a small Midwestern town, the police chief follows the clues from a series of murders to the experimental lab of the local college. Seems there's a mad scientist involved... Grisly and creepy, but unduly ballyhooed when it appeared. Shot on location in New Zealand. **105m/C VHS.** Michael Murphy, Louise Fletcher, Dan Shor, Fiona Lewis, Arthur Dignam, Marc McClure, Scott Brady, Dey Young, Charles Lane; ***D:*** Michael Laughlin; ***W:*** Michael Laughlin, Bill Condon; ***C:*** Louis Horvath.

Strange Brew ½ **1983 (PG)** The screen debut of the SCTV alumni's characters Doug & Bob MacKenzie, the Great White North duo. They do battle with a powerful, megalomaniacal brew master over—what else?—a case of beer. Dumb, but what did you expect? Watch it, or be a hoser. **91m/C VHS.** *CA* Rick Moranis, Dave Thomas, Max von Sydow, Paul Dooley, Lynne Griffin, Angus MacInnes; ***D:*** Rick Moranis, Dave Thomas; ***W:*** Steve DeJarnatt, Rick Moranis, Dave Thomas; ***C:*** Steven Poster; ***M:*** Charles Fox; ***V:*** Mel Blanc.

Strange Cargo ½ **1940** Convicts escaping from Devil's Island are mystically entranced by a Christ-like fugitive en route to freedom. An odd, pretentious Hollywood fable waiting for a cult following. Gable and Crawford's eighth and final pairing. Adapted by Anita Loos from the book "Not Too Narrow...Not Too Deep" by Richard Sale. **105m/B VHS.** Clark Gable, Joan Crawford, Ian Hunter, Peter Lorre, Paul Lukas, Albert Dekker, J. Edward Bromberg, Eduardo Ciannelli, Frederick Worlock; ***D:*** Frank Borzage; ***W:*** Lesser Samuels; ***C:*** Robert Planck; ***M:*** Franz Waxman.

Strange Case of Dr. Jekyll & Mr. Hyde **1968** An adaptation of the classic Robert Louis Stevenson book about a scientist who conducts experiments on himself to separate good from evil. Palance is oddly but appealingly cast; Jarrott's bad direction wrecks it. Made for TV. **128m/C VHS, DVD.** Jack Palance, Leo Genn, Oscar Homolka, Billie Whitelaw, Denholm Elliott; ***D:*** Charles Jarrott; ***M:*** Robert Cobert. **TV**

Strange Case of Dr. Jekyll & Mr. Hyde ½ **1989** The Robert Louis Stevenson classic, with Hyde portrayed as an icy, well-dressed sociopath. An entry in Shelley Duvall's "Nightmare Classics" series. More psychological than special effect-y. **60m/C VHS.** Anthony Andrews, Laura Dern, George Murdock, Nicholas Guest; ***D:*** Michael Lindsay-Hogg. **CABLE**

The Strange Case of the End of Civilization As We Know It ½ **1993** Cleese stars as the detective grandson of Sherlock Holmes, who also has a reputation for making a mockery of police investigations. Nevertheless, the police commissioner summons him to capture that diabolical criminal Professor Moriarty. **55m/C VHS.** *GB* John Cleese, Stratford Johns, Connie Booth, Arthur Lowe.

Strange Confession **1945** Contains one of the truly rare Inner Sanctum Mysteries from Universal. **62m/C VHS.** Lon Chaney Jr., Brenda Joyce, J. Carrol Naish, Milburn Stone, Lloyd Bridges; ***D:*** John Hoffman; ***W:*** M. Coates Webster.

The Strange Countess **1961** A girl is almost murdered and no apparent motive can be found until a 20-year-old murder is uncovered in this Edgar Wallace story. **96m/C VHS.** *GE* Joachim Fuchsberger, Lil Dagover, Marianne Hoppe, Brigitte Grothum; ***D:*** Josef von Baky.

Strange Days **1995 (R)** It's 1999 in volatile L.A. and vice cop-turned-street-hustler Lenny Nero (Fiennes) is plying his SQUID trade—discs that offer the wearer the chance to experience any vice. The seedily likeable Lenny draws the line at peddling snuff clips until one capturing the murder of his friend, hooker Iris (Bako), shows up. Lenny's in way over his head and turns to self-sufficient security agent Mace (Bassett) to save him. The phenomenal Bassett heats up the screen (and kicks major butt) while the generally cerebral Fiennes shows why someone could care about his desperate lowlife. Bigelow's an action expert and struts on the film's dark visuals while offering some emotional impact with her society-on-the-eve-of-destruction saga. **145m/C VHS, DVD.** Kelly Hu, Michael Jace, Ralph Fiennes, Angela Bassett, Juliette Lewis, Tom Sizemore, Michael Wincott, Brigitte Bako, Vincent D'Onofrio, William Fichtner, Richard Edson, Glenn Plummer, Josef Sommer; ***D:*** Kathryn Bigelow; ***W:*** James Cameron, Jay Cocks; ***C:*** Matthew F. Leonetti; ***M:*** Graeme Revell.

The Strange Door ½ **1951** Laughton hams it up as the evil Alan de Maletroit (Laughton), who's imprisoned his brother Edmond (Cavanagh) for the crime of marrying Alan's one love. Now Maletroit wants to destroy his niece Blanche (Forrest) as well. But Edmond's faithful retainer Voltan (Karloff) is determined to stop the evil. Low-budget hokum adapted from the Robert Louis Stevenson story "The Sire de Maletroits's Door." **81m/B VHS.** Charles Laughton, Boris Karloff, Paul Cavanagh, Sally Forrest, Richard Stapley, Michael Pate, Alan Napier; ***D:*** Joseph Pevney; ***W:*** Jerry Sackheim; ***C:*** Irving Glassberg.

Strange Fits of Passion ½ **1999** Low-budget comedy/drama is McCredie's directorial debut. A nameless overly-romantic young woman (Noonan) is convinced that she has just let the perfect man (Finsterer) slip away and she becomes obsessive about finding him again. Her search does not stop her, however, from having some alternative romantic prospects in mind. **83m/C VHS.** *AU* Michela Noonan, Mitchell Butel, Samuel Johnson, Steve Adams, Anni Finsterer, Jack Finsterer; ***D:*** Elise McCredie; ***W:*** Elise McCredie; ***C:*** Jaems Grant; ***M:*** Cezary Skubiszewski.

Strange Fruit **1979** Based on Lillian Smith's novel, this program tells the story of a black painter in Georgia, 1948, who faces racism. At first avoiding voter registration, he becomes involved and is killed. His death serves as an inspiration to his community. **33m/C VHS.**

Strange Illusion ½ *Out of the Night* **1945** Unbalanced teen Lydon believes his mother, about to remarry, was responsible for his father's death. He feigns insanity in a plan to catch her, but is sent to an asylum, where he nearly goes insane for real. Slow and implausible, but creepy enough to hold your interest. **87m/B VHS, DVD.** Jimmy Lydon, Warren William, Sally Eilers, Regis Toomey, Charles Arnt, George Reed, Jayne Hazard; ***D:*** Edgar G. Ulmer; ***W:*** Adele Comandini; ***C:*** Philip Tannura; ***M:*** Leo Erdody.

Strange Impersonation ½ **1946** Dreamy noir has chemist Nora Goodrich (Marshall) injecting herself in order to test a new anesthetic she's developing. (This is never a good idea.) Then her life goes nuts when she can't separate reality from her dreams. **68m/B VHS, DVD.** Brenda Marshall, William Gargan, Hillary Brooke, George Chandler, Ruth Ford, H.B. Warner, Lyle Talbot, Mary Treen; ***D:*** Anthony Mann; ***W:*** Mindret Lord; ***C:*** Robert Pittack.

Strange Interlude *Strange Interval* **1932** Shearer is at her best in screen adaptation of talky Eugene O'Neill play in which she portrays a young wife who wants a child, but discovers that insanity runs in her husband's family. Doing the only sensible thing, she decides to have a child by another man (Gable). Interesting because the characters' thoughts are revealed to the audience through voice-overs. **110m/B VHS.** Norma Shearer, Clark Gable, May Robson, Ralph Morgan, Robert Young, Mary Alden, Maureen O'Sullivan, Henry B. Walthall; ***D:*** Robert Z. Leonard; ***C:*** Lee Garmes.

Strange Interlude ½ **1990** Slow PBS production of Eugene O'Neill's famous drama covering two decades of the lives and loves of an upper-class family. Excellent performances help to make up for talkiness. On two cassettes. **190m/C VHS.** Glenda Jackson, Jose Ferrer, David Dukes, Ken Howard, Edward Petherbridge; ***D:*** Herbert Wise.

Strange Invaders **1983 (PG)** Body-snatchers-from-space sci-fi with an attitude—fun spoof of '50s alien flicks. Space folks had taken over a mid-western town in the '50s, assuming the locals' appearance and attire before returning to their ship. Seems one of them married an earthling—but divorced and moved with her half-breed daughter to New York City. So the hicksters from space arrive in Gotham wearing overalls... **94m/C VHS, DVD, Wide.** Paul LeMat, Nancy Allen, Diana Scarwid, Michael Lerner, Louise Fletcher, Wallace Shawn, Fiona Lewis, Kenneth Tobey, June Lockhart, Charles Lane, Dey Young, Mark Goddard; ***D:*** Michael Laughlin; ***W:*** Bill Condon; ***C:*** Louis Horvath; ***M:*** John Addison.

Strange Justice: The Clarence Thomas and Anita Hill Story ½ **1999 (R)** Someone must have lied at the 1991 comfirmation hearings for Supreme Court Justice Clarence Thomas (Lindo) and this cable drama takes a look at playing hardball politics. Lobbyist Kenneth Duberstein (Patinkin) is assigned by the Bush White House to get Thomas appointed. But he doesn't anticipate the testimony of Anita Hill (Taylor) and her claims that her former boss sexually harassed her. Based on the non-fiction account by Jane Mayer and Jill Abramson. **111m/C VHS.** Delroy Lindo, Regina Taylor, Mandy Patinkin, Paul Winfield, Louis Gossett Jr.; ***D:*** Ernest R. Dickerson; ***W:*** Jacob Epstein. **CABLE**

The Strange Love of Martha Ivers **1946** Douglas is good in his screen debut as the wimpy spouse of unscrupulous Stanwyck. Stanwyck shines as the woman who must stay with Douglas because of a crime she committed long ago... Tough, dark melodrama; classic film noir. **117m/B VHS, DVD.** Barbara Stanwyck, Van Heflin, Kirk Douglas, Lizabeth Scott, Judith Anderson; ***D:*** Lewis Milestone; ***W:*** Robert Rossen; ***C:*** Victor Milner; ***M:*** Miklos Rozsa.

The Strange Love of Molly Louvain ½ *Molly Louvain* **1932** Unwed mother Dvorak finds herself in hiding after her criminal beau fatally shoots a police officer. She falls in love with the unsuspecting newsman (Tracy) hot on her trail. Good performance from Dvorak but the film in general lacks sparkle. Adapted from the play "Tinsel Girl" by Maurine Watkins. **70m/B VHS.** Ann Dvorak, Lee Tracy, Richard Cromwell, Guy Kibbee, Leslie Fenton, Frank McHugh, Evalyn Knapp, Charles Middleton, Mary Doran, C. Henry Gordon; ***D:*** Michael Curtiz; ***W:*** Erwin Gelsey, Brown Holmes.

Strange New World ½ **1975** Three astronauts awake from 188 years in the fridge to find cloning has arrived. Made for TV as a pilot for a hoped-for series that might have been even worse. **100m/C VHS.** John Saxon, Kathleen Miller, Keene Curtis, Martine Beswick, James Olson, Catherine Bach, Richard Farnsworth, Ford Rainey; ***D:*** Robert Butler. **TV**

The Strange One ½ **1957** Appropriate title for this dank drama based on Willingham's novel and play "End As a Man." Jacko De Paris (Gazzara) is the student leader at a Southern military school, who uses his power to intimidate and brutalize fellow cadets, aided by minions Knoble (Hingle) and Gatt (Olson). Finally a group of younger students, led by Marquales (Peppard, in his film debut) go after the tyrant. Also filmed as 1957's "Sorority Girl." **100m/B VHS.** Ben Gazzara, Pat Hingle, James Olson, George Peppard, Peter Mark Richman, Larry Gates, Clifton James, Arthur Storch; ***D:*** Jack Garfein; ***W:*** Calder Willingham; ***C:*** Burnett Guffey; ***M:*** Kenyon Hopkins.

Strange Shadows in an Empty Room *Blazing Magnums; Shadows in an Empty Room* **1976 (R)** Sleuth Whitman wants answers about the murder of his kid sis. He beats lots of people up, and the viewer leaves the empty living room to look at the inside of the fridge, which is more interesting. De Martino used the pseudonym Martin Herbert. **97m/C VHS.** Stuart Whitman, John Saxon, Martin Landau, Tisa Farrow, Carole Laure, Gayle Hunnicutt; ***D:*** Alberto De Martino.

The Strange Woman 🦴🦴 **1946** Uneventful Hollywood costume drama. Lamarr stalks man after man, but never creates much excitement in spite of Ulmer's fancy camera work and intense pace. **100m/B VHS, DVD.** Hedy Lamarr, George Sanders, Louis Hayward, Gene Lockhart, Hillary Brooke, June Storey; ***D:*** Edgar G. Ulmer; ***W:*** Herb Meadow; ***C:*** Lucien N. Andriot; ***M:*** Carmen Dragon.

Strange World of Coffin Joe 🦴 *O Estranho Mundo de Ze do Caixao* **1968** A collection of three shocking horror episodes about a truly disgusting dollmaker who becomes tempted by his human-like creations, a balloon seller's repulsive necrophiliac impulses, and a doctor (the disguised Coffin Joe) with a sadistic gift for excruciating torture. In Portugese with English subtitles. **?m/C VHS.** *BR* Jose Mojica Marins; ***D:*** Jose Mojica Marins.

The Strangeness woof! **1985** Miners in search of gold release a "strange" creature from far beneath the earth—eek! Made on a negative budget. **90m/C VHS.** Dan Lunham, Terri Berland; ***D:*** David Michael Hillman.

The Stranger 🦴🦴🦴½ **1946** Notably conventional for Welles, but swell entertainment nonetheless. War crimes tribunal sets Nazi thug Shayne free hoping he'll lead them to his superior, Welles. Robinson trails Shayne through Europe and South America to a small town in Connecticut. Tight suspense made on a tight budget saved Welles's directorial career. **95m/B VHS, DVD.** Edward G. Robinson, Loretta Young, Martha Wentworth, Konstantin Shayne, Richard Long, Orson Welles; ***D:*** Orson Welles; ***W:*** Victor Trivas; ***C:*** Russell Metty; ***M:*** Bronislau Kaper.

The Stranger 🦴½ **1973** Corbett crash-lands on a planet an awful lot like Earth—and must stay on the run. Uneven fugitive thriller in sci-fi drag. Made for TV. **100m/C VHS.** Cameron Mitchell, Glenn Corbett, Sharon Acker, Lew Ayres, George Coulouris, Dean Jagger; ***D:*** Lee H. Katzin. **TV**

The Stranger 🦴🦴🦴 **1987 (R)** Amnesiac car-wreck victim Bedelia begins regaining her memory, and realizes she witnessed several grisly murders. Is her shrink (Riegert) helping her remember, or keeping something from her? Good, neglected thriller. **93m/C VHS, 8mm.** *AR* Bonnie Bedelia, Peter Riegert, Barry Primus, David Spielberg, Julio de Grazia, Cecilia (Celia) Roth, Marcus Woinski; ***D:*** Adolfo Aristarain; ***W:*** Dan Gurskis; ***M:*** Craig Safan.

The Stranger 🦴🦴½ **1992** Quiet comedy about family loyalties and devalued traditions. The upper-middle-class life of Sudhindra Bose is disturbed by the arrival of his wife Anila's long-lost uncle Manomohan. Although their young son is excited by the visit of this mysterious relative, Anila is bewildered and her husband suspicious—he thinks the man may be an imposter after their money. The independent Manomohan realizes the family's discomfort and slowly turns the tables on all their questions. Ray's last film. In Bengali with English subtitles. **100m/C VHS.** *IN* Deepankar De, Mamata Shankar, Bikram Bhattacharya, Utpal Dutt, Dhritiman Chatterji, Rabi Ghosh, Subrata Chatterji; ***D:*** Satyajit Ray; ***W:*** Satyajit Ray.

The Stranger 🦴🦴 **1995 (R)** Mystery woman (Long) rides into small town and rids it of a vicious motorcycle gang. Femme version of the lone hero saga. **98m/C VHS.** Kathy Long, Andrew Divoff, Eric Pierpont, Robin Lynn Heath; ***D:*** Fritz Kiersch; ***W:*** Gregory Poirier.

A Stranger Among Us 🦴🦴 **1992 (PG-13)** A missing jeweler turns up dead and more than $1 million in diamonds has disappeared. NYPD Detective Emily Eden (Griffith) is called in to solve the case, and she decides she must go undercover in a community of Hasidic Jews to find the perpetrator. She not only finds the criminal, but she also falls in love with one of the group's most devout residents. Griffith is out of her element as a tough cop with her baby voice and cutesy style, but other actors, including Thal (in his movie debut) and Sara, perform splendidly, even though they're held back by a cumbersome script with many similarities to "Witness." **109m/C VHS, Wide.** James Gandolfini, Melanie Griffith, Eric Thal, John Pankow, Tracy Pollan, Lee Richardson, Mia Sara, Jamey Sheridan; ***D:*** Sidney Lumet; ***W:*** Robert J. Avrech; ***C:*** Andrzej Bartkowiak; ***M:*** Jerry Bock. Golden Raspberries '92: Worst Actress (Griffith).

The Stranger and the Gunfighter 🦴🦴 **1976** The baddest spaghetti western of all time—or is it a kung fu movie? Alcoholic cowpoke Van Cleef and kung fu master Lieh pair up to find hidden treasure. There is a map, but parts are printed on the assorted fannies of various women. **106m/C VHS.** *IT* Patty (Patti) Shepard, Lee Van Cleef, Lo Lieh; ***D:*** Anthony (Antonio Margheriti) Dawson.

Stranger by Night 🦴🦴 **1994 (R)** Detective Bobby Corcoran and his partner are hunting a mutilating serial killer. Since Corcoran suffers from black-outs and fits of rage the evidence begins pointing very close to home. **96m/C VHS, DVD.** Steven Bauer, William Katt, Jennifer Rubin, Michael Parks, Michele Greene, J.J. Johnston; ***D:*** Gregory (Gregory Dark) Brown; ***W:*** Daryl Haney; ***C:*** Wally Pfister; ***M:*** Ashley Irwin.

The Stranger from Pecos 🦴🦴 **1945** Brown fights a cheater who swindles people at poker and then uses the money to buy their mortgages. Meanwhile, his pal Hatton finds a novel way to help a robbery victim buy back his property. **55m/B VHS.** Johnny Mack Brown, Raymond Hatton, Kirby Grant, Christine McIntyre, Steve Clark, Kermit Maynard; ***D:*** Lambert Hillyer.

The Stranger from Venus woof! *Immediate Disaster; The Venusian* **1954** "The Day the Earth Stood Still" warmed over. Venusian Dantine tells earth lady Neal he's worried about the future of her planet. Real low budget. Includes previews of coming attractions from classic sci-fi. **78m/B VHS, DVD.** Patricia Neal, Helmut Dantine, Derek Bond; ***D:*** Bob Balaban; ***W:*** Hans Jacoby; ***C:*** Ken Talbot; ***M:*** Eric Spear.

Stranger in Paso Bravo 🦴 **1973** A distraught drifter returns to a strange Italian town to avenge the murders of his wife and daughter years before. Dubbed. **92m/C VHS.** *IT* Anthony Steffen, Giulia Rubini, Eduardo Fajardo, Andriana Ambesi.

Stranger in the House 🦴🦴 **1997 (R)** Jack (Railsback) hid a diamond necklace in an old house after his heist went bad. When he gets out of prison and goes to retrieve his loot, he discovers the house is now occupied by Joanna (Greene) and Dan (Dinsmore). Turns out Dan wants to kill Joanna for her money, and Jack's being pursued by an insurance adjuster (Vrana) after the necklace. **94m/C VHS.** Michele Greene, Steve Railsback, Bruce Dinsmore, Vlasta Vrana; ***D:*** Rodney Gibbons; ***W:*** Peter Paul Liapis, Steve Pesce; ***M:*** Marty Simon. **VIDEO**

A Stranger in the Kingdom 🦴🦴 **1998 (R)** Walt Andrews (Hudson) has been hired sight unseen to be the new minister in a small Vermont community in the fifties. The unseen part is a problem since the townspeople are shocked when Walt turns out to be black. Then Walt gets arrested for the murder of a young housekeeper, Claire (Bayne), whom he was sheltering from her abusive employer and the town seems determined to make him the scapegoat. Based on a Howard Frank Mosher novel. **111m/C VHS, DVD.** Ernie Hudson, David Lansbury, Jean (Louisa) Kelly, Martin Sheen, Sean Nelson, Jordan Bayne, Bill Raymond, Henry Gibson, Larry Pine, Tom Aldredge, Carrie Snodgress; ***D:*** Jay Craven; ***W:*** Jay Craven, Don Bredos; ***C:*** Philip Holahan.

Stranger in Town 🦴🦴 **1957** A young journalist looks into the murder of an American composer in a sleepy English village. He discovers blackmail and intrigue. So-so thriller. Based on the novel "The Uninvited" by Frank Chittenden. **73m/B VHS.** *GB* Alex Nicol, Ann Page, Mary Laura Wood, Mona Washbourne, Charles Lloyd Pack; ***D:*** George Pollock.

A Stranger in Town 🦴🦴½ **1995** Single mom Kay Tarses (Smart) has relocated to a small, quiet town with her infant son. But her peace is disturbed by menacing Barnes (Hines), a stranger who seems to know Kay has been lying about her past—and her child. When he seems determined to take her child, Kay has to decide whether to run, accept her fate, or fight. **93m/C VHS.** Jean Smart, Gregory Hines, Jeffrey Nordling, Lucinda Jenney, Richard Riehle; ***D:*** Peter Levin; ***M:*** Mark Snow. **TV**

A Stranger Is Watching 🦴½ **1982 (R)** Rapist-murderer Torn holds his victim's 10-year-old daughter hostage, along with a New York TV anchorwoman. Complicated and distasteful. **92m/C VHS.** Rip Torn, Kate Mulgrew, James Naughton; ***D:*** Sean S. Cunningham. **TV**

The Stranger: Kabloonak 🦴🦴½ **1998** Pioneering filmmaker Robert Flaherty (Dance) premieres his documentary "Nanook of the North" in 1922 and recalls (in flashback) his difficulties in making the film. History has been tweaked but the cinematography is gorgeous and Dance's lead performance is strong. **105m/C VHS.** Charles Dance; ***D:*** Claude Massot.

Stranger on the Third Floor 🦴🦴🦴 **1940** Reporter McGuire's testimony helped convict cabbie Cook of murder, but he begins to have doubts. Odd, shadowy psycho-thriller considered by some the first film noir. The reporter comes to be suspected of the crime...and his fiancee pounds the pavement to prove him innocent. Average acting, but great camera work gives the whole a deliciously menacing feel. **64m/B VHS.** Peter Lorre, John McGuire, Elisha Cook Jr., Margaret Tallichet, Charles Halton; ***D:*** Boris Ingster.

Stranger than Fiction 🦴½ **1999 (R)** Would-be horror thriller wastes its talented cast. Jared (Astin) arrives, hysterical and bloody, at the home of his best friend, Austin (Field), with some confusing tale about a murder in his apartment. Austin, Jared and their friends Emma (Meyer) and Violet (Wagner) return to the scene of the crime, only to discover that Jared has been less than honest with them. **100m/C VHS, DVD.** MacKenzie Astin, Todd Field, Dina Meyer, Natasha Gregson Wagner; ***D:*** Eric Bross; ***W:*** Tim Garrick, Scott Russell; ***C:*** Horacio Marquinez; ***M:*** Larry Seymour.

Stranger than Paradise 🦴🦴🦴 **1984 (R)** Would-be New York hipster Willie (Lurie) is a Hungarian emigre who is asked to look after his newly arrived teenaged cousin Eva (Balint). They develop a weird affectionate relationship before Eva heads to Cleveland to live with an aunt (Stark). When Willie realizes he misses her, he and buddy Eddie (Edson) drive to visit her and the threesome then decide to head to Florida for some fun in the sun. The thinking person's mindless flick. Inventive, independent comedy made on quite a low budget was acclaimed at Cannes. **90m/B VHS, DVD, Wide.** *GE* John Lurie, Eszter Balint, Richard Edson, Sara Driver, Cecillia Stark, Danny Rosen; ***D:*** Jim Jarmusch; ***W:*** Jim Jarmusch; ***C:*** Tom DiCillo; ***M:*** John Lurie. Natl. Soc. Film Critics '84: Film.

The Stranger Who Looks Like Me 🦴🦴 **1974** Adoptees Baxter and Bridges set out to find their real parents. Not-bad TV fare. Blake is Baxter's real-life mom. Look for a young Patrick Duffy. **74m/C VHS.** Meredith Baxter, Beau Bridges, Whitney Blake; ***D:*** Larry Peerce.

The Stranger Within 🦴½ **1974** Made-for-TV "Rosemary's Baby" rip-off. Eden is in a family way, though hubby Grizzard is impotent. The stranger within begins commanding her to do its bidding, just as if she were a genie. **74m/C VHS.** Barbara Eden, George Grizzard, Joyce Van Patten, Nehemiah Persoff; ***D:*** Lee Philips; ***M:*** Charles Fox. **TV**

The Stranger Wore a Gun 🦴🦴 **1953** Hoping to remove a black mark against his name, Jeff Travis (Scott) goes to Arizona and ends up foiling a stagecoach robbery. Features a great action sequence in a burning saloon. Originally shot in 3-D, this is based on the novel "Yankee Gold" by John M. Cunningham. **83m/C VHS.** Randolph Scott, Claire Trevor, Joan Weldon, George Macready, Alfonso Bedoya, Lee Marvin, Ernest Borgnine, Pierre Watkin, Joseph (Joe) Vitale; ***D:*** Andre de Toth.

Strangers 🦴🦴 **1990** Australian horror film revolves around a man in a troubled marriage who fools around with another woman, only to realize she is dead set on mating for life. When he hesitates, she vows to murder his wife. Very similar to the smash hit "Fatal Attraction." **83m/C VHS.** *AU* James Healey, Anne Looby; ***D:*** Craig Lahiff.

Strangers 🦴🦴 **1991 (R)** Features three provocative vignettes that take place far from home. Fiorentino, Chen, and Hutton each star in an erotic story played out in a foreign land. **85m/C VHS.** Linda Fiorentino, Joan Chen, Timothy Hutton; ***D:*** Joan Tewkesbury.

The Strangers 🦴 **1998** Seems Trent doesn't know as much about his lover Jade as he thinks—until she turns him into a werewolf. He gets away and hides out in the small town of Pine Fork, even beginning to fall in love. Then Jade shows up with her new boyfriend—looking for revenge and fresh meat. **90m/C VHS.** Richard Bent, Shanna Betz, Victoria Hunter, Jennifer Marks, Matt Martin, Jimmy Lord, J.J. Denton, Joe Durrenberger; ***D:*** Charles Solomon Jr., Peter Cohl; ***W:*** Charles Solomon Jr., Peter Cohl, Steven Weller; ***C:*** Anthony Moncado. **VIDEO**

Stranger's Gold 🦴 **1971** A mysterious gunslinger eliminates corruption in a western mining town. **90m/C VHS.** Gianni "John" Garko, Antonio Vilar, Daniela Giordano.

Strangers in Good Company 🦴🦴🦴 *The Company of Strangers* **1991 (PG)** A loving metaphor to growing older. Director Scott uses non-actors for every role in this quiet little film about a bus-load of elderly women lost in the Canadian wilderness. They wait for rescue without hystrionics, using the opportunity instead to get to know each other and nature. Beautifully made, intelligent, uncommon and worthwhile. **101m/C VHS, DVD.** *CA* Alice Diabo, Mary Meigs, Cissy Meddings, Beth Webber, Winifred Holden, Constance Garneau, Catherine Roche, Michelle Sweeney; ***D:*** Cynthia Scott; ***W:*** Cynthia Scott, David Wilson, Gloria Demers, Sally Bochner; ***M:*** Marie Bernard.

Strangers in Paradise 🦴½ **1984** A scientist who had cryogenically frozen himself to escape the Nazis is thawed out in the present, and his powers are used by a delinquent-obsessed sociopath. **81m/C VHS.** Ulli Lommel, Ken Letner, Geoffrey Barker, Thom Jones; ***D:*** Ulli Lommel; ***W:*** Ulli Lommel; ***M:*** William Pettyjohn.

Strangers in the City 🦴🦴 **1962** Puerto Ricans newly arrived in New York try to make their way. Serious but slightly overwrought immigrant-family melodrama. **80m/B VHS.** Robert Gentile, Camilo Delgado, Rosita De Triana; ***D:*** Rick Carrier.

Strangers Kiss 🦴🦴½ **1983 (R)** Circa 1955: Hollywood director encourages his two leads to have an off-screen romance to bring reality to his film. Conflict arises when the leading lady's boyfriend, the film's financier, gets wind of the scheme. Intriguing, fun, slightly off-center. Based on Stanley Kubrick's film "Killer Kiss." **93m/C VHS.** Peter Coyote, Victoria Tennant, Blaine Novak, Dan Shor, Richard Romanus, Linda Kerridge, Carlos Palomino; ***D:*** Matthew Chapman; ***W:*** Blaine Novak, Matthew Chapman; ***M:*** Gato Barbieri.

Strangers of the Evening 🦴🦴 **1932** In its day this dark comedy/mystery caught flak for its gruesomeness. There's been a mixup at the undertaker's, and the wrong body was buried— possibly alive. Good photography and acting make the humor work, intentionally or not. Based on the novel "The Illustrious Corpse," by Tiffany Thayer. **70m/B VHS.** ZaSu Pitts, Eugene Pallette, Lucien Littlefield, Tully Marshall, Miriam Seegar, Theodore von Eltz; ***D:*** H. Bruce Humberstone.

Strangers on a Train 🦴🦴🦴🦴 **1951** Long before there was "Throw Momma from the Train," there was this Hitchcock super-thriller about two passengers who accidentally meet and plan to "trade" murders. Amoral Walker wants the exchange and the money he'll inherit by his father's death; Granger would love to end his stifling marriage and wed Roman, a senator's daughter, but finds the idea ultimately sickening. What happens is pure Hitchcock. Screenplay co-written by murder-mystery great Chandler. Patricia Hitchcock, the director's only child, plays Roman's sister. The concluding "carousel" scene is a masterpiece. From the novel by Patricia Highsmith. **101m/B VHS, DVD.** Farley Granger, Robert Walker, Ruth Roman, Leo G. Carroll, Patricia Hitchcock, Marion Lorne; ***D:*** Alfred Hitchcock; ***W:*** Raymond Chandler; ***C:*** Robert Burks; ***M:*** Dimitri Tiomkin.

Strangers: The Story of a Mother and Daughter 🦴🦴🦴 **1979** Rowlands is the long-estranged daughter of Davis, who won an Emmy for her portrayal of the embittered widow. The great actress truly is at her recent best in this made-for-TV tearjerker, and Rowlands keeps pace. **88m/C VHS.** Bette Davis, Gena Rowlands, Ford Rainey, Donald Moffat; ***D:*** Milton Katselas.

Strangers When We Meet 🦴🦴½ **1960** A married architect and his equally married neighbor begin an affair. Their lives become a series of deceptions. Lavish but uninvolving soaper. Written by Evan Hunter and based on his novel. **117m/B VHS.** Kirk Douglas, Kim Novak, Ernie Kovacs, Walter Matthau, Barbara Rush, Virginia Bruce, Kent Smith; ***D:*** Richard Quine; ***C:*** Charles B(ryant) Lang Jr.

Stranglehold 🦴½ **1994 (R)** Cooper (Trimble) is the executive assistant of Congresswoman Fillmore (McWhirter), who becomes the hostage of a nerve gas holding nutcase (Wells). Cooper manages to evade the nutcase's thugs while using his martial arts prowess to rescue his boss. **73m/C VHS.** *AU* Jerry Trimble, Jillian McWhirter, Vernon Wells; ***D:*** Cirio H. Santiago.

The Strangler 🦴½ **1964** A confused, mother-fixated psychopath strangles young women. Made at the time the Boston Strangler was terrorizing Beantown. The film slayer strangles ten lasses before his love of dolls gives him away. **89m/B VHS.** Victor Buono, David McLean, Diane Sayer, Ellen Corby, Jeanne Bates, James B. Sikking; ***D:*** Burt Topper.

Strangler of Blackmoor Castle 🦴🦴 **1963** Someone is murdering people at an old English castle and Scotland Yard sends an investigator to track down the killer. **?m/C VHS.** *GE* Karin Dor, Ingmar Zeisberg.

Strangler of the Swamp 🦴½ **1946** The ghost of an innocent man wrongly hanged for murder returns to terrorize the village where he was lynched. Decidedly B-grade horror features an out-of-focus ghost and Edwards—on the other side of the camera—as one of his would-be victims. **60m/B VHS, DVD.** Rosemary La Planche, Blake Edwards, Charles Middleton, Robert Barrat; ***D:*** Frank Wisbar; ***W:*** Frank Wisbar; ***C:*** James S. Brown Jr.

Strapless 🦴🦴½ **1990 (R)** Just-turned-40 American doctor Brown lives and works in London. She has just ended a long-term romance, and takes up with suave foreigner Ganz. Her young sister Fonda, arrives for a visit. Good, interesting if sometimes plodding story of adult relationships. **99m/C VHS, DVD.** *GB* Blair Brown, Bridget Fonda, Bruno Ganz, Alan Howard, Michael Gough, Hugh Laurie, Suzanne Burden, Camille Coduri, Alexandra Pigg, Billy Roch, Gary O'Brien; ***D:*** David Hare; ***W:*** David Hare; ***C:*** Andrew Dunn; ***M:*** Nick Bicat.

Strapped 🦴🦴½ **1993** Earnest urban drama about a young man who needs quick cash and turns to selling guns to get it. ("Strapped" in street lingo means both carrying a gun and needing money.) Diquan's (Woodbine) pregnant girlfriend is in jail for selling crack and he doesn't have the bail money. So he and a partner begin selling guns but it turns out Diquan has also cut a deal with the cops and the deal doesn't stay a secret for long. Whitaker's directorial debut. **102m/C VHS.** Bokeem Woodbine, Kia Joy Goodwin, Fred "Fredro" Scruggs, Michael Biehn, Craig Wasson; ***D:*** Forest Whitaker; ***W:*** Dena Kleiman. **CABLE**

Strategic Air Command 🦴🦴½ **1955** A classic post-WWII chunk of Air Force patriotism. Veteran third baseman Stewart is recalled to flight duty at the hint of a nuclear war. He's already put in his time in the Big One and thinks he's being singled out now, but he answers his Uncle Sam's call. Allyson plays Stewart's wife for the third time. **114m/C VHS.** James Stewart, June Allyson, Frank Lovejoy, Barry Sullivan; ***D:*** Anthony Mann; ***C:*** William H. Daniels.

The Stratton Story 🦴🦴🦴 **1949** Stewart and Allyson teamed up for the first of the three pictures they'd make together in this true story of Monty Stratton, the Chicago White Sox pitcher. A baseball phenom, Stratton suffers a devastating hunting accident which leads to the amputation of one leg. Learning to walk with an artificial limb, Stratton also struggles to resume his baseball career. Stewart's fine as always, with Allyson lending noble support as the loving wife. Chisox manager Jimmy Dykes played himself as did pitcher Gene Bearden, lending further authenticity to an excellent production. **106m/B VHS.** James Stewart, June Allyson, Frank Morgan, Agnes Moorehead, Bill Williams, Bruce Cowling; ***D:*** Sam Wood; ***W:*** Guy Trosper, Douglas S. Morrow. Oscars '49: Story.

The Strauss Family 🦴🦴½ **1973** British miniseries covers the drama and scandal surrounding 85 years in the lives of the musical Strauss family of 19th-century Vienna. Woolfe is patriarch Johann Strauss, whose son Schanni (Wilson) will exclipse his egotistical father's talents. Music performed by the London Symphony Orchestra. On 4 cassettes. **390m/C VHS.** *GB* Eric Woolfe, Stuart Wilson, Anne Stallybrass, Derek Jacobi, Jane Seymour. **TV**

Straw Dogs 🦴🦴🦴 **1972 (R)** An American mathematician, disturbed by the predominance of violence in American society, moves with his wife to an isolated Cornish village. He finds that primitive savagery exists beneath the most peaceful surface. After his wife is raped, Hoffman's character seeks revenge. Hoffman is good, a little too wimpy at times. A violent, frightening film reaction to the violence of the 1960s. **118m/C VHS, DVD.** *GB* Sally Thomsett, Colin Welland, Peter Arne, Dustin Hoffman, Susan George, Peter Vaughan, T.P. McKenna, David Warner; ***D:*** Sam Peckinpah; ***W:*** Sam Peckinpah, David Zelag Goodman; ***C:*** John Coquillon; ***M:*** Jerry Fielding.

Strawberry and Chocolate 🦴🦴🦴 *Fresa y Chocolate* **1993 (R)** Sex, politics, and friendship set in 1979 Havana. University student David (Cruz) is sitting morosely in a cafe eating chocolate ice cream when he's spotted by older, educated, gay, strawberry-eating Diego (Perugorria), who manages to persuade David to visit him at his apartment. Resolutely hetero (and communist), David is appalled not only by Diego's sexuality but by his subversive politics. But gradually David's seduced by Diego's ideas and friendship into questioning the regime's harsh policies (and homophobia). Satiric and sympathetic—not only to the characters but to Cuba itself. Ill with cancer, Gutierrez Alea finished the film with the aid of Tabio. From the short story "The Wolf, the Forest and the New Man" by sceenwriter Paz. Spanish with subtitles. **110m/C VHS.** *CU* Jorge Perugorria, Vladimir Cruz, Mirta Ibarra, Francisco Gattorno, Jorge Angelino, Marilyn Solaya; ***D:*** Tomas Gutierrez Alea, Juan Carlos Tabio; ***W:*** Tomas Gutierrez Alea, Senel Paz; ***C:*** Mario Garcia Joya; ***M:*** Jose Maria Vitier.

Strawberry Blonde 🦴🦴🦴 **1941** A romantic comedy set in the 1890s, with Cagney as a would-be dentist infatuated with money-grubbing Hayworth (the strawberry blonde of the title), who wonders years later whether he married the right woman (chestnut brunette de Havilland). Attractive period piece remade from 1933's "One Sunday Afternoon," and revived yet again in 1948 by Raoul Walsh. **100m/B VHS.** James Cagney, Olivia de Havilland, Rita Hayworth, Alan Hale, George Tobias, Jack Carson, Una O'Connor, George Reeves; ***D:*** Raoul Walsh; ***W:*** Julius J. Epstein, Philip G. Epstein; ***C:*** James Wong Howe.

Strawberry Fields 🦴🦴 **1997** Rebellious teenaged Japanese-American Irene (Nakamura) takes off on a road trip of self-discovery with her boyfriend, whom she soon dumps to spend quality time alone in the Arizona desert figuring out life. **86m/C VHS, DVD, Wide.** Suzy Nakamura, James Sie, Chris Tashima, Marilyn Tokuda, Reiko Mathieu, Peter Yoshida, Heather Yoshimura, Takayo Fischer; ***D:*** Rea Tajiri; ***W:*** Rea Tajiri, Kerri Sakamoto; ***C:*** Zack Winestine; ***M:*** Bundy Brown.

Strawberry Roan 🦴🦴 **1933** Maynard plays a stubborn rodeo cowboy, out to prove he ain't whipped yet. One of Maynard's most popular films. Gene Autry bought the story to help him out in later years; the 1948 Autry "remake" uses only the title. **59m/B VHS.** Ken Maynard, Ruth Hall; ***D:*** Ken Maynard.

The Strawberry Statement 🦴🦴 **1970 (R)** Dated message film about a campus radical who persuades a college student to take part in the student strikes on campus during the '60s. Ambitious anti-violence message is lost in too many subplots. Soundtrack features songs by Crosby, Stills, Nash and Young and John Lennon. **109m/C VHS.** Kim Darby, Bruce Davison, Bud Cort, James Coco, Kristina Holland, Bob Balaban, David Dukes, Jeannie Berlin; ***D:*** Stuart Hagmann; ***W:*** Israel Horovitz. Cannes '70: Special Jury Prize.

The Stray 🦴🦴 **2000 (R)** When Vonna Grayson (Everhart) accidentally hits a homeless man (Lysenko) when she's driving home, she insists on having him recover at her ranch. Soon the relationship becomes romantic, but her "stray" has a hidden agenda and Vonna winds up in danger. **98m/C VHS, DVD.** Angie Everhart, Stefan Lysenko, Michael Madsen, Frank Zagarino, Seidy Lopez; ***D:*** Kevin Mock; ***W:*** Terry Cunningham; ***C:*** Ken Blakey; ***M:*** John Sponsler. **VIDEO**

Stray Bullet 🦴 **1998 (R)** Attorney John Burnside (Carradine) mistakenly picks up the luggage of fellow traveler Stella Crosby (Staab), who invites him to her home for a party. But John gets kidnapped from the party by some thugs who are owed money by Stella's husband, who they have mistaken John for. Instead of setting things straight, Stella persuades John to pose as her husband until she can works things out. John agrees because he has the hots for Stella. John's very dumb. **86m/C VHS.** Robert Carradine, Rebecca Staab, Fred (John F.) Dryer, Ian Beattie; ***D:*** Robert Spera; ***W:*** Christopher Wood; ***C:*** Jules Labarthe; ***M:*** Arthur Kempel. **VIDEO**

Stray Dog 🦴🦴🦴 **1949** A tense, early genre piece by Kurosawa, about a police detective who has his revolver picked from his pocket on a bus, and realizes soon after it's being used in a series of murders. Technically somewhat flawed, but tense and intense. Mifune's pursuit of the criminal with his gun becomes metaphorically compelling. In Japanese with English subtitles. **122m/B VHS.** *JP* Toshiro Mifune, Takashi Shimura, Isao Kimura; ***D:*** Akira Kurosawa.

Strays 🦴🦴 **1991 (R)** Here kitty kitty! A young couple move into their dream home, convinced it is the perfect place to raise their daughter. What they don't know is that the area is populated by a pack of wild cats. Before they can get rid of the kitties, one has marked their bedroom as his territory and they find themselves battling a swarm of mean kitties during a bad storm. **83m/C VHS.** Kathleen Quinlan, Timothy Busfield, Claudia Christian; ***D:*** John McPherson; ***W:*** Shaun Cassidy.

Streamers 🦴🦴 **1983 (R)** Six young soldiers in a claustrophobic army barracks tensely await the orders that will send them to Vietnam. Written by Rabe from his play. Well acted but downbeat and drawn out. **118m/C VHS.** Bill Allen, Matthew Modine, Michael Wright, Mitchell Lichtenstein, George Dzundza; ***D:*** Robert Altman; ***W:*** David Rabe.

The Street 🦴🦴½ **1923** A dark classic of German Kammerspiel film, notable for its expressionist treatment of Paris street life. A middle-aged man decides to abandon his wife and job to see what excitement he can find. He is duped by a prostitute, accused of murder, imprisoned, and nearly commits suicide before being rescued. Silent. **87m/B VHS.** *GE* ***D:*** Karl Grune; ***W:*** Karl Grune.

Street Asylum 🦴 **1990 (R)** Real-life Watergate spook Liddy is pathetically bad as an evil genius who cooks up a scheme to rid the streets of deadbeats and scumbags by implanting cops with a gizmo that makes them kill. Also available in a 94-minute unrated version. **94m/C VHS.** Wings Hauser, Alex Cord, Roberta Vasquez, G. Gordon Liddy, Marie Chambers, Sy Richardson, Jesse Doran, Jesse Aragon, Brion James; ***D:*** Gregory (Gregory Dark) Brown.

Street Corner Justice 🦴🦴 **1996** Typical vigilante action movie features excop Mike Justus (Singer), who's possessed of a short fuse and a strong sense of justice. He inherits a house in a crime-ridden L.A. neighborhood and finds himself coming to the aid of merchants who are being terrorized by the local drug-dealing gangs. **102m/C VHS.** Marc Singer, Steve Railsback, Kim Lankford, Willie Gee; ***D:*** Charles "Chuck" Bail; ***W:*** Charles "Chuck" Bail, Gary Kent, Stan Berkowitz; ***C:*** Doug O'Neons, David Golia; ***M:*** K. Alexander Wilkinson.

Street Crimes 🦴🦴 **1992 (R)** A street-wise cop convinces gang members to put down their weapons and settle their grudges in the boxing ring. But when a gang leader starts shooting down the police and civilians, the cop and his young partner must work together to keep the neighborhood safe. **?m/C VHS.** Dennis Farina, Max Gail, Mike Worth; ***D:*** Stephen Smoke; ***W:*** Stephen Smoke; ***M:*** John Gonzalez.

The Street Fighter 🦴½ *Satsujimken* **1974** Fast-paced martial arts action finds freelance fighter Terry Tsuguri (Chiba) hired to spring a convicted killer from prison. But after he succeeds, his employers renege on their payment. Big mistake. Dubbed from Japanese. Three sequels: "Return of the Street Fighter," "The Street Fighter's Last Revenge," and "Sister Street Fighter." **91m/C VHS, DVD, Wide.** *JP* Sonny Chiba, Gerald (Waichi) Yamada, Tony Cetera, Doris (Yutaka) Nakajima; ***D:*** Shigehiro (Sakae) Ozawa; ***W:*** Steve Autrey, Koji Takada; ***C:*** Ken Tsukakoshi; ***M:*** Toshiaki Tsushima.

Street Fighter 🦴½ **1994 (PG-13)** Yes, it's a movie based on a popular video game (guess no one worried about the colossal flop of "Super Mario Bros"). Van Damme is action-minded Colonel Guile who is assigned to defeat crazed dictator General Bison (Julia in one of his last roles) in order to rescue kidnapped relief workers. Yes, there's lots of cartoon action but the game's more exciting (and even makes more sense). Shot on location in Australia and Bangkok. **101m/C VHS, DVD, Wide.** Jean-Claude Van Damme, Raul Julia, Wes Studi, Ming Na, Damian Chapa, Simon Callow, Roshan Seth, Kylie Minogue, Byron Mann; ***D:*** Steven E. de Souza; ***W:*** Steven E. de Souza; ***C:*** William A. Fraker; ***M:*** Graeme Revell.

The Street Fighter's Last Revenge 🦴 *Revenge! The Killing Fist; Street Fighter Counterattacks* **1974** Third in the martial arts series finds Terry Tsuguri (Chiba) hired by a mob boss to do some dirty work and then getting double-crossed—resulting in the death of Terry's girl. So, Terry hunts the miscreants down one by one. Lots of action, not much acting. Followed by "Sister Street Fighter." **79m/C VHS, DVD, Wide.** *JP* Sonny Chiba, Sue Shiomi; ***D:*** Teru Ishii.

Street Girls 🦴 **1975 (R)** A father enters the world of urban drugs and prostitution to find his runaway daughter. **77m/C VHS.** Carol Case, Christine Souder, Paul Pompian; ***D:*** Michael Miller.

Street Gun 🦴 **1996** Small-time hood Joe Webster (Pagel) pines for some sense of accomplishment in his life. A tip from his hustler-friend lands Joe in the good graces of the local crime boss. As he ingratiates himself into his new malevolent world, the shadows yield betrayal, murder, and no place to hide. Potentially interesting premise is botched, with cowriter/director Milloy aping John Woo gun pyrotechnics and "Reservoir Dogs" attitude (a Woo rip-off once removed). There is also the thorny dilemma of rooting for a hero who aspires to be an exceptional thug. **92m/C DVD.** Justin Pagel, Scott Cooke, Michael Egan; ***D:*** Travis Milloy; ***W:*** Travis Milloy, Timothy Lee; ***C:*** Joel King.

Street Hawk 🦴 **1984** A government agent operates an experimental, crime-fighting motorcycle in battling against a high-powered drug smuggling ring. **60m/C VHS.** Rex Smith, Jayne Modean, Richard Venture, Christopher Lloyd.

Street Heart 🦴🦴 *Le Coeur au Poing* **1998** Louise has structured a very sheltered, controlled (if lonely) world for herself that gradually comes undone as both her sister and her lover abandon her. Feeling the need to reconnect with life, Louise goes about making contact in a dangerous manner. She begins to stop strangers on the street and offers to do whatever they would like for one hour. French with subtitles. **100m/C VHS.** *CA* Pascale Montpetit, Anne-Marie Cadieux, Guy Nadon, Guylaine Tremblay; ***D:*** Charles Biname; ***W:*** Monique Proulx, Charles Biname; ***C:*** Pierre Gill; ***M:*** Richard Gregoire, Yves Desrosiers.

Street Hero woof! **1984** A young thug is torn between familial common sense and Mafia connections. **102m/C VHS.** Vince Colosimo, Sigrid Thornton, Sandy Gore.

Street Hitz 🦴½ **1992** Two brothers in the South Bronx find their family loyalties tested. Joey wants to finish college and get away from the violence in the streets while his brother Junior turns to the gangs to survive. **92m/C VHS.** Angelo Lopez, Melvin Muza, Lyota Ramirez; ***D:*** Joseph B. Vasquez.

Street Hunter woof! **1990 (R)** Former cop turned freelance fighter quit the force when his integrity was questioned, but he still helps out now and then. Scumbag drug dealers line up a thug to waste him; epic kung fu battle ensues. **120m/C VHS.** Steve James, Reb Brown, John Leguizamo, Valarie Pettiford, Frank Vincent, Richie Havens; ***D:*** John A. Gallagher; ***C:*** Phil Parmet.

Street Justice 🦴½ **1989 (R)** Overcomplex tale of a CIA agent on the lam. Returning from years of Russian imprisonment, Ontkean finds his wife remarried, his daughter grown and both battling the corrupt town government. Good performances can't help the confusion of too many characters too flatly developed. **94m/C VHS.** Michael Ontkean, Joanna (Joanna DeVarona) Kerns, Catherine Bach, J.D. Cannon, Jeanette Nolan, Richard Cox, William Windom; ***D:*** Richard Sarafian.

The Street King 🦴½ *King Rikki* **2002 (R)** Rikki Ortega (Seda) wants to be top dog on the gang-ravaged streets of East L.A. And the one man to oppose him is his childhood buddy turned cop, Juan Vallejo (Lopez). It's alleged to be a modern reworking of Shakespeare's "Richard III." **90m/C VHS, DVD.** Jon Seda, Mario Lopez, Timothy Paul Perrez, Jill-Michele Melean; ***D:*** James Gavin Bedford; ***W:*** Jesse Graham; ***C:*** Rob Sweeney.

Street Knight 🦴🦴 **1993 (R)** Gang warfare in L.A. in a routine actioner. Jake is an ex-cop who gets drawn into a battle between two rival gangs when their truce is broken by mysterious murders on both sides. Seems there's an unsuspected third party involved—a para-military band of professional killers that want the gang violence to divert police interest from their own nefarious operations. **88m/C VHS.** Jeff Speakman, Christopher Neame, Lewis Van Bergen, Bernie Casey, Jennifer Gatti, Richard Coca; ***D:*** Albert Magnoli.

Street Law 🦴 **1979 (R)** Vivid and violent study of one man's frustrated war on crime. **77m/C VHS, DVD.** Franco Nero, Barbara Bach, Reno Palmer.

Street Law 🦴🦴 **1995 (R)** John Ryan (Wincott) is a down-on-his-luck trial lawyer whose childhood buddy Luis Calderone (Prieto) is willing to lend a helping hand. Too bad Luis is an ex-con who hasn't left his dangerous street ways behind him and now John is caught up in some unsavory action. **98m/C VHS, DVD.** Jeff Wincott, Paco Christian Prieto, Christina Cox; ***D:*** Damian Lee; ***W:*** Damian Lee; ***C:*** Gerald R. Goozie; ***M:*** Ronald J. Weiss.

Street Music 🦴🦴½ **1981** The elderly people living in an old hotel join forces with a young couple to organize a protest that may save their building. Well-directed urban comedy-drama; good location shooting in San Francisco's Tenderloin. **88m/C VHS.** Larry Breeding, Elizabeth (E.G. Dailey) Daily, Ned Glass, Marjorie Eaton, D'Alan Moss, David Parr; ***D:*** Jenny (H. Anne Riley) Bowen; ***W:*** Jenny (H. Anne Riley) Bowen; ***C:*** Richard Bowen. Sundance '82: Grand Jury Prize.

Street of Forgotten Women 🦴 **1925** Hollywood, in one of its periodic morality binges, came up with this purported expose on prostitution. An innocent girl is seduced and brutalized by a theatrical agent and eventually finds herself walking the pavement for less than moral purposes. Lots of shots of scantily clad showgirls and our heroine in her undies. **55m/B VHS.**

Street of Shame 🦴🦴🦴½ *Red-Light District; Akasen Chitai* **1956** A portrayal of the abused lives of six Tokyo prostitutes. Typically sensitive to the roles and needs of women and critical of the society that exploits them, Mizoguchi creates a quiet, inclusive coda to his life's work in world cinema. Kyo is splendid as a hardened hooker and has a memorable scene with her father. Kogure is also good. The great director's last finished work was instrumental in the outlawing of prostitution in Japan. In Japanese with English subtitles. **88m/B VHS.** *JP* Machiko Kyo, Aiko Mimasu, Michiyo Kogure; ***D:*** Kenji Mizoguchi.

Street People woof! **1976 (R)** Gratuitous car chases and violence do not a movie make, as in this case in point. Utter woofer has Brit Moore cast as a mafiosa. Yeah, right. **92m/C VHS.** Roger Moore, Stacy Keach, Ivo Garrani, Ettore Manni; ***D:*** Maurizio Lucidi.

Street Scene 🦴🦴🦴 **1931** Life in a grimy New York tenement district, circa 1930. Audiences nationwide ate it up when Elmer Rice adapted his own Pulitzer Prize-winning play and top helmsman Vidor gave it direction. **80m/B VHS, DVD, 8mm.** Sylvia Sidney, William "Buster" Collier Jr., Estelle Taylor, Beulah Bondi, David Landau; ***D:*** King Vidor; ***W:*** Elmer Rice; ***C:*** George Barnes; ***M:*** Alfred Newman.

Street Smart 🦴🦴½ **1987 (R)** Reeve was blah as Superman (let's be frank), and he's blah here as a desperate New York freelance writer who fakes a dramatic story about prostitution. When his deception returns to haunt him, he's in trouble with pimps and murderers, as well as the D.A. Freeman and Baker are both superb. Based on screenwriter David Freeman's own experience with "New York" magazine. **97m/C VHS.** Christopher Reeve, Morgan Freeman, Kathy Baker, Mimi Rogers, Andre Gregory, Jay Patterson, Anna Maria Horsford; ***D:*** Jerry Schatzberg; ***W:*** David Freeman; ***C:*** Adam Holender; ***M:*** Miles Davis. Ind. Spirit '88: Support. Actor (Freeman); L.A. Film Critics '87: Support. Actor (Freeman); N.Y. Film Critics '87: Support. Actor (Freeman); Natl. Soc. Film Critics '87: Support. Actor (Freeman), Support. Actress (Baker).

Street Soldiers 🦴½ **1991 (R)** Martial artists are out to take back the streets from the punks and scum who now rule them. **98m/C VHS.** Jun Chong, Jeff Rector, David Homb, Jonathan Gorman, Joon Kim, Katherine Armstrong, Joel Weiss; ***D:*** Lee Harry.

Street Trash woof! **1987** In Brooklyn, a strange poisonous liquor is being sold cheap to bums, making them melt and explode. A gross, cheap, tongue-in-cheek shocker from the makers of "The Toxic Avenger." **91m/C VHS.** Vic Noto, Mike Lackey, Bill Chepil, R.L. Ryan, James Lorinz, Miriam Zucker; ***D:*** Jim Muro; ***W:*** Roy Frumkes; ***C:*** David Sperling.

Street War 🦴 **197?** A cop pursues the Mob in the name of revenge as well as duty. **90m/C VHS.** James Mason, Cyril Cusack, Raymond Pellegrin.

Street Warriors woof! **1987** Ostensibly "serious" look at juvenile crime. Actually miserable, exploitative, offensive junk. **105m/C VHS.** Christa Leem, Nadia Windell, Victor Petit, Francisco (Frank) Brana; ***D:*** Jose Antonio De La Loma.

Street Warriors, Part 2 woof! **1987** Even worse than its predecessor, and that's saying something. Horrible dubbing from Spanish would be laughable, if the rapes weren't so graphic. **105m/C VHS.** Angel Luis Fernandez, Paul Ramirez, Teresa Giminez, Veronica Miriel, Conrad Tortosa; ***D:*** Jose Antonio De La Loma.

Street Wars 🦴½ **1991 (R)** Violent low-budgeter about 17-year-old Sugarpop, who takes over older brother Frank's Los Angeles drug operation, after Frank is murdered, and finds himself battling a rival gang. **90m/C VHS, DVD.** Alan Joseph, Bryan O'Dell, Clifford Shegog, Jean Pace, Vaughn Cromwell, Cardella Demilo; ***D:*** Jamaa Fanaka; ***W:*** Jamaa Fanaka; ***C:*** John L. Demps Jr.; ***M:*** Michael Dunlap, Yves Chicha.

The Street with No Name 🦴🦴🦴 **1948** In follow-up to "Kiss of Death," Widmark confirms rep as one disturbed guy playing psychotic career criminal whose life is grisly trail of murder and brutality. **93m/B VHS.** Mark Stevens, Richard Widmark, Lloyd Nolan, Barbara Lawrence, Ed Begley Sr., Donald Buka, Joseph Pevney; ***D:*** William Keighley.

A Streetcar Named Desire 🦴🦴🦴🦴 **1951 (PG)** Powerful film version of Tennessee Williams' play about a neurotic southern belle with a hidden past who comes to visit her sister and is abused and driven mad by her brutal brother-in-law. Grim New Orleans setting for terrific performances by all, with Malden, Leigh, and Hunter winning Oscars, and Brando making highest impact on audiences. Brando disliked the role, despite the great impact it had on his career. **122m/B VHS, DVD.** Vivien Leigh, Marlon Brando, Kim Hunter, Karl Malden; ***D:*** Elia Kazan; ***W:*** Tennessee Williams; ***C:*** Harry Stradling Sr.; ***M:*** Alex North. Oscars '51: Actress (Leigh), Art Dir./Set Dec., B&W, Support. Actor (Malden), Support. Actress (Hunter); AFI '98: Top 100; British Acad. '52: Actress (Leigh); Golden Globes '52: Support. Actress (Hunter), Natl. Film Reg. '99;; N.Y. Film Critics '51: Actress (Leigh), Director (Kazan), Film.

A Streetcar Named Desire 🦴🦴🦴 **1984** Excellent TV adaptation of the Tennessee Williams drama about fading southern belle Blanche du Bois (Ann-Margret in a terrific performance). D'Angelo is her plain sister Stella who lives with brutish husband Stanley (Williams) in the seamy French Quarter of New Orleans. Can't surpass the original but this version does have the advantage of not having to soft-pedal the drama for the '50s censors. **94m/C VHS.** Ann-Margret, Beverly D'Angelo, Treat Williams, Randy Quaid, Rafael Campos, Erica Yohn; ***D:*** John Erman; ***C:*** Bill Butler; ***M:*** Marvin Hamlisch. **TV**

A Streetcar Named Desire 🦴🦴½ **1995** Baldwin and Lange recreate their 1992 stage roles of brutal Stanley Kowalski and fragile Southern belle Blanche DuBois from the Broadway revival of Tennessee Williams 1947 Pulitzer Prize-winning play. This TV version is truer to the dialogue and situations of the original production than the censored '51 film. **156m/C VHS.** Jessica Lange, Alec Baldwin, Diane Lane, John Goodman, Frederick Coffin; ***D:*** Glenn Jordan; ***C:*** Ralf Bode; ***M:*** David Mansfield.

Streetfight 🦴½ *Coonskin* **1975 (R)** Semi-animated racist exploitation from the creator of "Fritz the Cat." Features some superb animation. **89m/C VHS.** Philip Michael Thomas, Scatman Crothers, Barry White, Charles Gordone; ***D:*** Ralph Bakshi; ***W:*** Ralph Bakshi; ***C:*** William A. Fraker; ***M:*** Chico Hamilton.

Streets 🦴🦴 **1990 (R)** Applegate (of Fox TV's "Married...With Children") is believable as an illiterate runaway teen. Good drama set in Venice, California about life on the streets is flawed by near-gratuitous pairing with story of a crazy prostitute-killing cop. **90m/C VHS.** Christina Applegate, David Mendenhall, Eb Lottimer; ***D:*** Katt Shea, Andy Ruben; ***W:*** Andy Ruben.

Streets of Fire 🦴🦴½ **1984** A soldier of fortune rescues his ex-girlfriend, now a famous rock singer, after she's been kidnapped by a malicious motorcycle gang. Violently energetic in its insistent barrage of imagery. Director Hill's never-never land establishes a retro-futuristic feel and is beautifully photographed, however vacuous the ending may be. **93m/C VHS, DVD.** Michael Pare, Diane Lane, Rick Moranis, Amy Madigan, Willem Dafoe, Deborah Van Valkenburgh, Richard Lawson, Rick Rossovich, Bill Paxton, Lee Ving, Stoney Jackson, Robert Townsend, Grand Bush, Mykelti Williamson, Elizabeth (E.G. Dailey) Daily, Lynne Thigpen, Marine Jahan, Ed Begley Jr., John Dennis Johnston, Olivia Brown; ***D:*** Walter Hill; ***W:*** Walter Hill, Larry Gross; ***C:*** Andrew Laszlo; ***M:*** Ry Cooder.

Streets of Gold 🦴🦴½ **1986 (R)** Brandauer is good as a Soviet boxer who defected and now washes dishes in Brooklyn. He trains a pair of street youngsters in the hope of beating his old coach in the Olympics. "Rocky"-like in the boxing, and in the rags-to-riches optimism. **94m/C VHS.** Klaus Maria Brandauer, Adrian Pasdar, Wesley Snipes; ***D:*** Joe Roth; ***W:*** Richard Price, Heywood Gould, Tom Cole; ***C:*** Arthur Albert; ***M:*** Jack Nitzsche.

The Streets of L.A. 🦴🦴½ **1979** A frustrated middle-aged woman teaches some punks from an L.A. barrio a thing or two about pride and motivation when she demands reimbursement for the tires they slashed. Without thoroughly professional Woodward to carry it, there would not be much of a movie. Woodward's character is resourceful, and so is the actress. Made for TV. **94m/C VHS.** Joanne Woodward, Robert Webber, Michael C. Gwynne; ***D:*** Jerrold Freedman; ***C:*** Allen Daviau. **TV**

The Streets of San Francisco 🦴🦴🦴 **1972** The pilot that spawned the popular TV series. A street-wise old cop and his young college-boy partner (who else but Malden and Douglas as Stone and Keller) investigate the murder of a young woman. Adapted from "Poor, Poor Ophelia" by Carolyn Weston. **120m/C VHS.** Karl Malden, Robert Wagner, Michael Douglas, Andrew Duggan, Tom Bosley, Kim Darby, Mako; ***D:*** Walter Grauman. **TV**

Streets of Sin 🦴🦴½ *Not Wanted* **1949** Written and produced by movie star Lupino (who also took over directing when credited director Clifton became ill), this morality play tells the story of a naive girl's tribulations when she becomes infatuated with a musician and then becomes pregnant by him. Shunned by the musician, she enters a home for unwed mothers to sort out her life and feelings for a crippled veteran who wants to marry her. **91m/B VHS.** Sally Forrest, Keefe Brasselle, Leonard Penn, Dorothy Adams, Rita Lupino; ***D:*** Elmer Clifton; ***W:*** Ida Lupino.

Streetwalkin' 🦴 **1985 (R)** Life in the Big Apple isn't always rosy for a brother and sister who must contend with prostitutes, drug dealers, and tough cops. She turns to prostitution to get by. Miserable, exploitative trash. **86m/C VHS.** Melissa Leo, Dale Midkiff, Leon Robinson, Julie Newmar, Randall Batinkoff, Annie Golden, Antonio Fargas; ***D:*** Joan Freeman; ***W:*** Joan Freeman, Robert Alden; ***C:*** Steven Fierberg.

Streetwise 🦴🦴🦴½ **1984** Eye-opening and candid documentary inspired by a "Life" magazine article. Frank and honest look at homeless children making a living on the streets. Seattle provides the backdrop to the story as the filmmakers hang around with the kids, earning their trust, and receive the truth from them. Cruel, funny, enraging, but always sobering look into a population of homeless in America. A deservedly acclaimed, terrifying vision of urban America. **92m/C VHS.** ***D:*** Martin Bell; ***W:*** Cheryl McCall; ***M:*** Tom Waits.

Strictly Ballroom 🦴🦴🦴½ **1992 (PG)** Offbeat, cheerfully tacky dance/romance amusingly turns every movie cliche slightly askew. Scott (Mercurio) has been in training for the Pan-Pacific ballroom championships since the age of six. While talented, he also refuses to follow convention and scandalizes the stuffy dance establishment with his new steps. When his longtime partner leaves him, Scott takes up with a love-struck beginner (Morice), with some surprises of her own. Ballet dancer Mercurio (in his film debut) is appropriately arrogant yet vulnerable, with Morice as the plain Jane turned steel butterfly. Wonderful supporting cast; great debut for director Luhrmann. **94m/C VHS, DVD, Wide.** *AU* Paul Mercurio, Tara Morice, Bill Hunter, Pat Thomsen, Barry Otto, Gia Carides, Peter Whitford, John Hannan, Sonia Kruger-Tayler, Kris McQuade, Pip Mushin, Leonie Page, Antonio Vargas, Armonia Benedito; ***D:*** Baz Luhrmann; ***W:*** Baz Luhrmann, Craig Pearce; ***C:*** Steve Mason; ***M:*** David Hirshfelder. Australian Film Inst. '92: Costume Des., Director (Luhrmann), Film, Film Editing, Screenplay, Support. Actor (Otto), Support. Actress (Thomsen).

Strictly Business ½ **1991 (PG-13)** An upwardly mobile black broker has his career aspirations in order until he meets a beautiful club promoter who finds him square and boring. Wanting to impress her he asks the advice of a young man who works in the mail room for the proper way to dress and talk. A low-rent Pygmalion story. **83m/C VHS.** Halle Berry, Tommy Davidson, Joseph C. Phillips; ***D:*** Kevin Hooks; ***M:*** Michel Colombier.

Strictly G.I. **1944** A collection of wartime patriotic shorts, including "All Star Bond Rally." The support and perception of WWII is historically intriguing. **45m/B VHS.** Bing Crosby, Frank Sinatra, Betty Grable, Judy Garland, Harpo Marx, Harry James, Bob Hope, Jerry Colonna.

Strike ½ **1924** Eisenstein's debut, and a silent classic. Stirring look at a 1912 clash between striking factory workers and Czarist troops. **94m/B VHS, DVD.** *RU* ***D:*** Sergei Eisenstein.

Strike a Pose ½ **1993 (R)** Erotic thriller finds international model-turned-fashion photographer Miranda Cross, her boyfriend LAPD detective Nick Carter, and Miranda's model friends stalked by a revenge-minded killer. Also available in an unrated version. **75m/C VHS, DVD.** Margie Peterson, Robert Eastwick, Michelle LaMothe; ***D:*** Dean Hamilton.

Strike Back **1980** A convict escapes from prison to find the girl he loves, and is hounded by the police and the mob. **89m/C VHS.** Dave Balko, Brigette Wollner; ***D:*** Carl Schenkel.

Strike Commando woof! **1987 (R)** Cheap, exploitative ripoff of the expensive, exploitative mega-action thriller "Rambo." Sleepwalking actors; horrible, overwrought script. Mattei used the pseudonym Vincent Dawn. **92m/C VHS.** Reb Brown, Christopher Connelly, Locs Kamme; ***D:*** Bruno Mattei.

Strike Force *Crack* **1975** A New York City cop, a Federal agent and a state trooper work together to battle a large drug ring. Failed made-for-TV pilot. Early Gere appearance; not related to later Robert Stack film with the same title. **74m/C VHS.** Cliff Gorman, Richard Gere, Donald Blakely; ***D:*** Barry Shear. **TV**

Strike Force **1981** The jurors on an embezzlement case turn up bloody and headless around town, so a special criminal strike force is brought in to solve the murders. Why do the murders happen only on Tuesdays? Made for TV. **90m/C VHS.** Robert Stack, Dorian Harewood, Herb Edelman; ***D:*** Richard Lang. **TV**

Strike It Rich ½ *Loser Take All* **1990 (PG)** A honeymooning couple find themselves resorting to the Monte Carlo gambling tables in order to raise money for the ride home. Lightweight fluff unfortunately adapted from Graham Greene's short novel "Loser Takes All." Only for hard-core Gielgudites. **86m/C VHS.** Molly Ringwald, Robert Lindsay, John Gielgud, Max Wall, Simon de la Brosse; ***D:*** James Scott; ***M:*** Cliff Eidelman.

Strike Me Pink **1936** Shy Eddie Pink (Cantor) decides to change his ways after reading a self-help book and takes on the management of the local amusement park. Then some crooks want to muscle in on the action and Eddie must prove his mettle. Merman as girlfriend Joyce gets to belt out a few songs. ♫The Lady Dances; Shake It Off with Rhythm; You Have Me High, You Have Me Low; Calabash Pipe. **100m/B VHS.** Eddie Cantor, Ethel Merman, Sally Eilers, William Frawley, Parkyakarkus (Harry Einstein), Brian Donlevy, Jack LaRue; ***D:*** Norman Taurog; ***W:*** Frank Butler, Walter DeLeon, Francis Martin; ***C:*** Gregg Toland, Merritt B. Gerstad; ***M:*** Harold Arlen.

Strike Up the Band ½ **1940** A high school band turns to hot swing music and enters a national radio contest. Rooney and Garland display their usual charm in this high-energy stroll down memory lane. ♫Over the Waves; The Light Cavalry Overture; Walkin Down Broadway; Five Foot Two, Eyes of Blue; After the Ball; Nobody; Strike Up the Band. **120m/B VHS.** Judy Garland, Mickey Rooney, Paul Whiteman, William Tracy, June Preisser; ***D:*** Busby Berkeley. Oscars '40: Sound.

Striker **1988 (R)** Mercenary John "Striker" Slade is sent to Nicaragua to free a captured American journalist, not knowing his superiors have betrayed him to the Contras and the Sandinistas. He battles it out with both groups while seeking revenge on the businessmen who set him up. **90m/C VHS.** Frank Zagarino, Melanie Rogers, Paul Werner; ***D:*** Stephen M. Andrews.

Striker's Mountain ½ **1987** Story of a sports enthusiast who creates heli-skiing and builds it into a business. Great ski scenes, but skip the rest. **99m/C VHS.** Bruce Greenwood, Mimi Kuzyk, Leslie Nielsen, August Schellenberg, Jessica Steen; ***D:*** Allen Simmonds.

Striking Distance ½ **1993 (R)** Tom Hardy (Willis) is a hard-nosed fifth-generation Pittsburgh homicide cop whose police detective father (Mahoney) is killed, apparently by a serial killer. Hardy insists the perp was really a fellow cop and winds up on the River Rescue squad (at least his partner is the fetching Parker). When the serial killer starts striking at women with some connection to Hardy, he finds scant support from his fellow cops. High action quotient backed by a fine cast, but the killer's identity won't be any surprise. **101m/C VHS, DVD.** Bruce Willis, Sarah Jessica Parker, Dennis Farina, Tom Sizemore, Brion James, Robert Pastorelli, Timothy Busfield, John Mahoney, Andre Braugher; ***D:*** Rowdy Herrington; ***W:*** Marty Kaplan, Rowdy Herrington; ***C:*** Mac Ahlberg; ***M:*** Brad Fiedel.

Striking Point ½ **1994 (R)** Police detectives are determined to stop ex-KGB commandoes from smuggling high-tech weapons into the country. **96m/C VHS.** Chris Mitchum, Tracy Spaulding.

Strip Search ½ **1997 (R)** Police detective Robby (Pare) gets seduced by easy money and sex when he gets involved with sex clubs and underworld gangs. **90m/C VHS, DVD.** *CA* Michael Pare, Pam Grier, Caroline Neron, Lucie Laurier, Maury Chaykin, Heidi von Palleske, MacKenzie Gray; ***D:*** Rod Hewitt.

Stripes ½ **1981 (R)** Feeling like losers and looking to straighten out their lives, two friends enlist in the Army under the mistaken impression that military life is something like a summer camp for grownups. A boxoffice success (despite a weak script) due in large part to Murray's charm and his verbal and sometimes physical sparring with Oates, who is good as the gruff-tempered platoon sergeant. Features humorous stints from various "Second City" players, including Candy, whom Murray turns into a "lean, mean fighting machine." **105m/C VHS, DVD, Wide.** Lance LeGault, Bill Murray, Harold Ramis, P.J. Soles, Warren Oates, John Candy, John Larroquette, Judge Reinhold, Sean Young, Dave Thomas, Joe Flaherty; ***D:*** Ivan Reitman; ***W:*** Len Blum, Harold Ramis; ***C:*** Bill Butler; ***M:*** Elmer Bernstein.

Stripped to Kill **1987 (R)** A female cop goes undercover to lure a psycho killing strippers. Not-bad entry from Corman and cohorts. Followed by—you guessed it—"Stripped to Kill II." **88m/C VHS.** Kay Lenz, Greg Evigan, Norman Fell, Pia Kamakahi, Tracy Crowder, Deborah Ann Nassar, Lucia Nagy Lexington, Carlye Byron, Athena Worthy, Michelle Foreman, Diana Bellamy; ***D:*** Katt Shea; ***W:*** Katt Shea, Andy Ruben; ***C:*** John LeBlanc; ***M:*** John O'Kennedy.

Stripped to Kill II: Live Girls **1989** A young woman with extra-sensory powers dreams of murders which she discovers are all too real. A weak sequel, despite the interesting premise. **83m/C VHS.** Maria Ford, Eb Lottimer, Karen Mayo Chandler, Marjean Holden, Birke Tan, Debra Lamb; ***D:*** Katt Shea; ***W:*** Katt Shea.

The Stripper ½ *Woman of Summer* **1963** A middle-aged stripper in a traveling show returns to the small Kansas town of her youth. Left stranded, she moves in with an old friend whose teenage son promptly falls in love with her. Based on the play "A Loss of Roses" by William Inge. **95m/B VHS.** Joanne Woodward, Richard Beymer, Claire Trevor, Carol Lynley, Robert Webber, Gypsy Rose Lee; ***D:*** Franklin J. Schaffner; ***M:*** Jerry Goldsmith.

Stripper ½ **1986 (R)** A good under-the-covers glimpse of the life and work of several real-life strippers, culminating in the First Annual Stripper's Convention in 1984. **90m/C VHS.** Janette Boyd, Sara Costa, Kimberly Holcomb; ***D:*** Jerome Gary; ***M:*** Jack Nitzsche.

Stripshow **1995 (R)** Veteran Vegas stripper shows the ropes to newcomer and then must vie with the upstart for her boyfriend's interest. **96m/C VHS, DVD.** Monique Parent, Tane McClure, Steven Tietsort; ***D:*** Gary Orona; ***W:*** Gary Orona.

Striptease ½ **1996 (R)** Single mom Erin Grant (Moore) loses custody of her daughter Angela (Moore's real-life offspring, Rumer) to her lowlife ex, Darrell (Patrick). In order to raise the money for an appeal, she dances at a Miami strip club, where she runs across politician David Dilbeck (Reynolds), who has a thing for both vaseline and Erin. Unlike "Showgirls," this one's intentionally funny and features some fine script work and performances, which got overlooked amidst all the hype, including Moore's record-setting (for an actress) $12 million paycheck, 4 mil of which reportedly was for agreeing to dance nude. Based on the novel by Carl Hiaasen. **115m/C VHS, DVD, Wide.** Paul Guilfoyle, Demi Moore, Burt Reynolds, Ving Rhames, Armand Assante, Robert Patrick, Rumer Willis; ***D:*** Andrew Bergman; ***W:*** Andrew Bergman; ***C:*** Stephen Goldblatt; ***M:*** Howard Shore. Golden Raspberries '96: Worst Picture, Worst Actress (Moore), Worst Director (Bergman), Worst Screenplay, Worst Song ("Pussy, Pussy, Pussy (Whose Kitty Cat Are You?)").

Stripteaser ½ **1995 (R)** Sicko psycho Dean holds dancers and patrons hostage in an L.A. strip joint where he provides various humiliations for his captives. Ford's the beautiful ecdysiast whose been the object of the fellow's secret obsessions. Also available unrated. **82m/C VHS.** Rick Dean, Maria Ford, Lance August; ***D:*** Dan Golden.

Stroke of Midnight ½ **1990 (PG)** Souped-up Cinderella with Lowe as egotistic high fashion designer, Grey as struggling shoe designer and a pumpkin-colored VW Bug. **102m/C VHS.** Rob Lowe, Jennifer Grey, Andrea Ferreol; ***D:*** Tom Clegg.

Stroker Ace woof! **1983 (PG)** Flamboyant stock car driver tries to break an iron-clad promotional contract signed with a greedy fried-chicken magnate. Off duty, he ogles blondes as dopey as he is. One of the worst from Reynolds—and that's saying something. **96m/C VHS, DVD.** Burt Reynolds, Ned Beatty, Jim Nabors, Parker Stevenson, Loni Anderson, Bubba Smith; ***D:*** Hal Needham; ***W:*** Hal Needham, Hugh Wilson; ***C:*** Nick McLean; ***M:*** Al Capps. Golden Raspberries '83: Worst Support. Actor (Nabors).

Stromboli ½ **1950** Bergman is a Czech refugee who marries an Italian fisherman in order to escape from her displaced persons camp. He brings her to his home island of Stromboli where she finds the life bleak and isolated and her marriage a trial. In Italian with English subtitles. The melodrama was even greater off-screen than on; this is the movie which introduced Bergman and Rossellini and began their (then) scandalous affair. **107m/B VHS.** *IT* Ingrid Bergman, Mario Vitale, Renzo Cesana; ***D:*** Roberto Rossellini.

Strong Man **1926** A WWI veteran, passing himself off as an unlikely circus strongman, searches an American city for the girl whose letters gave him hope during the war. Perhaps Langdon's best full-length film. **78m/B VHS.** Harry Langdon, Gertrude Astor, Tay Garnett; ***D:*** Frank Capra.

Strong Medicine ½ **1984** Strange, avant-garde film about a strange, off-written young woman. Cleverly directed experiment that's not for everyone. **84m/C VHS.** Carol Kane, Raul Julia, Wallace Shawn, Kate Manheim, David Warrilow; ***D:*** Guy Green.

Stroszek **1977** Three German misfits—a singer, a prostitute and an old man—tour the U.S. in search of their dreams. Touching, hilarious comedy-drama with a difference and an attitude. One of Herzog's easiest and also best films. In English and German with English subtitles. **108m/C VHS, DVD, Wide.** *GE* Eva Mattes, Bruno S, Clemens Scheitz; ***D:*** Werner Herzog; ***W:*** Werner Herzog; ***C:*** Thomas Mauch; ***M:*** Chet Atkins, Tom Paxton.

The Structure of Crystals ½ *Struktura Krysztalu* **1969** A member of the scientific elite meets with an old friend who has moved to a remote meteorological station and tries to persuade him to return to the city and resume his work. Zanussi's cerebral first feature was also the first of a series of films to explore the scientific community. In Polish with English subtitles. **76m/B VHS.** *PL* Andrzej Zarnecki, Jan Myslowicz, Barbara Wrzesinska, Wladyslaw Jarema, Daniel Olbrychski; ***D:*** Krzysztof Zanussi; ***W:*** Edward Zebrowski, Krzysztof Zanussi.

Struggle **1931** Unfortunately, Griffith's final directorial effort is a ludicrous melodrama about the evils of alcohol. Because of Prohibition, working man Jimmie Wilson (Skelly) takes to illegal hootch, which turns out to be tainted, causing Jimmie to abuse his wife and daughter and destroy their formerly happy home. **87m/B VHS.** Hal Skelly, Zita Johann, Evelyn Baldwin, Charlotte Wynters, Helen Mack, Kate Bruce, Jackson Halliday, Edna Hagan, Claude Cooper, Arthur Lipson, Charles Richman, Scott Moore, Dave Manley; ***D:*** D.W. Griffith; ***W:*** D.W. Griffith, Anita Loos, John Emerson; ***C:*** Joseph Ruttenberg; ***M:*** D.W. Griffith, Philip A. Scheib.

Stryker woof! **1983 (R)** The ever-lovin' nuclear holocaust has occurred, and good guys and bad guys battle it out for scarce water. If you liked "Mad Max," go see it again; don't watch this miserable effort. **86m/C VHS.** *PH* Steve Sandor, Andria Fabio; ***D:*** Cirio H. Santiago; ***W:*** Howard R. Cohen.

Stuart Bliss **1998** Curious little comedy mixes elements of "The X-Files" and "The Truman Show." Stuart Bliss (Zelnicker) is an ordinary guy who slowly succumbs to paranoia and apocalyptic religious visions. Of course, the question is: Is he crazy or well-informed? **88m/C VHS, DVD.** Michael Zelniker, Dea Lawrence, Derek McGrath, Ania Suli, Mark Fite; ***D:*** Neil Grieve; ***W:*** Michael Zelniker, Neil Grieve; ***C:*** Jens Sturup.

Stuart Little ½ **1999 (PG)** This bigscreen adaptation of E.B. White's 1945 children's classic is hardly faithful but has its own charms. Mr. (Laurie) and Mrs. (Davis) Little decide to expand their family through adoption and wind up with a tiny, talking, clothes-wearing white mouse named Stuart (Fox). Their son George (Lipnicki) has a hard time thinking of a mouse as his little brother and family cat Snowbell (Lane) thinks the rodent is snack food. When his attempt to eat Stuart fails, Snowbell turns to kidnapping. The array of digital effects is amazing. **92m/C VHS, DVD.** Geena Davis, Hugh Laurie, Jonathan Lipnicki, Brian Doyle-Murray, Estelle Getty, Julia Sweeney, Dabney Coleman; ***D:*** Rob Minkoff; ***W:*** M. Night Shyamalan, Greg Booker; ***C:*** Guillermo Navarro; ***M:*** Alan Silvestri; ***V:*** Michael J. Fox, Nathan Lane, Chazz Palminteri, Steve Zahn, Bruno Kirby, Jennifer Tilly, David Alan Grier, Jim Doughan.

Stuart Little 2 **2002 (PG)** Stuart (Fox) and a reluctant Snowbell (Lane) venture through NYC to rescue new friend, a pidgeon named Margalo (Griffith). Not yet reviewed. **?m/C VHS, DVD.** Geena Davis, Hugh Laurie, Jonathan Lipnicki; ***D:*** Rob Minkoff; ***W:*** Bruce Joel Rubin; ***V:*** Michael J. Fox, Nathan Lane, Melanie Griffith, James Woods, Steve Zahn.

Stuart Saves His Family **1994 (PG-13)** Fired from his self-help TV show on a Chicago public-access station, New-Age advice guru Smalley (Franken) returns home to help his pathetically dysfunctional family sort out their problems and an inheritance, a nonplot that gives Smalley a chance to do his 12-step shtick. And that's...O.K. A tolerable installment in the endless parade of mediocre "Saturday Night Live" sketches stretched for the big screen that takes a few surprisingly maudlin turns. Based on Franken's book of Smalley's "daily affirmations," "I'm Good Enough, I'm Smart Enough, and Doggone It, People Like Me!" **97m/C VHS, DVD, Wide.** Al Franken, Laura San Giacomo, Vincent D'Onofrio, Shirley Knight, Harris Yulin, Julia Sweeney, Aaron Lustig, Darrell Larson, Camille Saviola, Gerrit Graham, Theodore (Ted) Raimi, Joe Flaherty; ***D:*** Harold Ramis; ***W:*** Al Franken; ***C:*** Lauro Escorel; ***M:*** Marc Shaiman.

Stuck on You & **1984 (R)** Couple engaged in a palimony suit takes their case to a judge to work out their differences. Wing-clipped angel Gabriel (Corey) comes to earth to help them patch it up. Never mind. **90m/C VHS, DVD.** Prof. Irwin Corey, Virginia Penta, Mark Mikulski; ***D:*** Lloyd Kaufman, Michael Herz; ***W:*** Lloyd Kaufman, Michael Herz; ***C:*** Lloyd Kaufman.

Stuckey's Last Stand & **1978 (PG)** A group of camp counselors prepare to take 22 children on a nature hike they will never forget. Mindless teen fodder. **95m/C VHS.** Whit Reichert, Tom Murray, Rich Casentino.

The Stud woof! **1978 (R)** Owner of a fashionable "after hours" dance spot hires a young, handsome stud to manage the club and attend to her personal needs. Low-budget look and seemingly scriptless. Faithfully adapted by sister Jackie Collins from her novel. **90m/C VHS.** *GB* Joan Collins, Oliver Tobias; ***D:*** Quentin Masters; ***W:*** Jackie Collins.

The Student Affair & *The Lay of the Land* **1997 (R)** Lame would-be comedy based on Shapiro's stage play, which also starred Kellerman. She's college prof M.J. Dankworth, who suspects hubby Harvey (Begley Jr.) is tossing their tired marriage aside to shtupp his well-endowed grad student Muriel (Taylor). So she hires a P.I. (Margolin) to snoop but he's more interested in his client. Then the marrieds seek out (different) psychiatrists for help and M.J. indulges her rage in silly fantasy scenes. Don't waste your time. **94m/C VHS.** *CA* Sally Kellerman, Ed Begley Jr., Sandra Taylor, Stuart Margolin, Tyne Daly, Rance Howard, Avery Schreiber; ***D:*** Larry Arrick; ***W:*** Mel Shapiro; ***C:*** Frederic Goodich; ***M:*** Jeff Lass.

Student Affairs woof! **1988 (R)** A bunch of highschool misfits vie for roles in a movie about a bunch of high school misfits. **92m/C VHS.** Louie Bonanno, Jim Abele, Alan Fisler, Deborah (Tracey Adams) Blaisdell; ***D:*** Chuck Vincent.

Student Bodies woof! **1981 (R)** A "Halloween"-style spoof of high-school horror films, except it's not funny. And what's so funny about bloody murder anyway? When the on-the-set problems and strife arose (which they did), why didn't everyone just cut their losses and go home? **86m/C VHS.** Kristen Riter, Matthew Goldsby, Richard Brando, Joe Flood, Joe Talarowski, Mimi Weddell; ***D:*** Mickey Rose; ***W:*** Mickey Rose.

Student Confidential & **1987 (R)** A Troma-produced spoof of seedy high school youth movies, new and old, involving four students who are led into the world of adult vices by a mysterious millionaire. Badly made and dull. Douglas and Jackson both have brothers named Michael. **99m/C VHS.** Eric Douglas, Marlon Jackson, Susan Scott, Ronee Blakley, Elizabeth Singer; ***D:*** Richard Horian.

The Student Nurses && **1970 (R)** The adventures, amourous and otherwise, of four last-year nursing students. Followed by four sequels: "Private Duty Nurses," "Night Call Nurses," "The Young Nurses," and "Candy Stripe Nurses." Better than average exploitation fare. First release from Roger Corman's New World studios; it goes down hill from there. **89m/C VHS.** Elaine Giftos, Karen Carlson, Brioni Farrell, Barbara Leigh, Reni Santoni, Richard Rust, Lawrence Casey, Darrell Larson, Paul Camen, Richard Stahl, Scottie MacGregor, Pepe Serna; ***D:*** Stephanie Rothman; ***W:*** Don Spencer; ***C:*** Stevan Larner.

Student of Prague &&& **1913** Early silent classic based on the German Faust legend: a student makes a pact with the devil to win a beautiful woman. Poor fellow. With either German or English title cards. Music track. **60m/B VHS.** *GE* Lothar Koemer, Grete Berger, Paul Wegener; ***D:*** Paul Wegener, Stellan Rye.

The Student Prince && **1954** Delightful rendition of Sigmund Romberg's famous operetta in which Purdom stars as the Prince of Heidelberg who falls for barmaid Blyth. Lanza recorded the soundtrack, but could not star in this film because of his weight problem. Previously filmed in 1919 and 1927 without music. ♫Golden Days; Serenade; Deep in My Heart; To the Inn We're Marching; Drink, Drink, Drink; Come Boys, Let's All Be Gay, Boys; Summertime in Heidelberg; Beloved; I Walk With God. **107m/C VHS.** Ann Blyth, Edmund Purdom, John Ericson, Louis Calhern, Edmund Gwenn, S.Z. Sakall, Betta St. John; ***D:*** Richard Thorpe; ***C:*** Paul Vogel.

The Student Prince in Old Heidelberg &&½ *Old Heidelberg* **1927** Prince Karl Heinrich silently falls in love with lowly barmaid. **102m/B VHS.** Ramon Novarro, Norma Shearer; ***D:*** Ernst Lubitsch.

The Student Teachers &½ **1973** Yet another soft-core Corman product. Three student teachers sleep around, on screen. **79m/C VHS.** Susan Damante Shaw, Brooke Mills, Bob Harris, John Cramer, Chuck Norris; ***D:*** Jonathan Kaplan.

Studs Lonigan && **1960** Drifting, too artsy rendering a James T. Farrell's trilogy about an Irish drifter growing up in Chicago in the '20s. Good period detail, but oddly off-kilter and implausible as history. **96m/B VHS.** Christopher Knight, Frank Gorshin, Jack Nicholson; ***D:*** Irving Lerner; ***W:*** Philip Yordan; ***M:*** Jerry Goldsmith.

A Study in Scarlet && **1933** Owen played Watson the previous year in "Sherlock Holmes"; here he's miscast as Holmes, and the plot differs from the Doyle story of the same title. **77m/B VHS.** Reginald Owen, Alan Mowbray, Anna May Wong, June Clyde, Alan Dinehart; ***D:*** Edwin L. Marin; ***W:*** Reginald Owen.

A Study in Terror &&& *Sherlock Holmes Grosster Fall; Fog* **1966** A well-appointed Sherlock Holmes thriller, and the second one in color. Premise has a young, athletic Holmes in pursuit of an educated Jack the Ripper in 1880s London. **94m/C VHS.** *GE GB* John Neville, Donald Houston, Judi Dench, Anthony Quayle, Robert Morley, Frank Finlay, Cecil Parker; ***D:*** James Hill.

The Stuff &½ **1985 (R)** Surreal horror semi-spoof about an ice cream mogul and a hamburger king who discover that the new, fast-selling confection in town zombifies its partakers. Forced, lame satire from producer/director/writer Cohen. **93m/C VHS, DVD, Wide.** Michael Moriarty, Andrea Marcovicci, Garrett Morris, Paul Sorvino, Danny Aiello, Brooke Adams, Patrick O'Neal, Alexander Scourby, Scott Bloom, James Dixon, Tammy Grimes, Clara Peller, Abe Vigoda; ***D:*** Larry Cohen; ***W:*** Larry Cohen; ***C:*** Paul Glickman; ***M:*** Anthony Guefen.

Stuff Stephanie in the Incinerator & **1989 (PG-13)** A Troma gagfest about wealthy cretins who torture and kill young women. "Funny" title betrays utter, exploitive mindlessness. **97m/C VHS.** Catherine Dee, William Dame, M.R. Murphy, Dennis Cunningham; ***D:*** Don Nardo.

The Stunt Man &&&& **1980 (R)** A marvelous and unique exercise in metacinematic manipulation. O'Toole, in one of his very best roles, is a power-crazed movie director; Railsback is a fugitive sheltered by him from sherrif Rocco. When a stunt man is killed in an accident, O'Toole prevails on Railsback to replace him, leading Railsback to wonder if O'Toole wants him dead. A labor of love for director-producer Rush, who spent nine years working on it, and waited two years to see it released, by Fox. Based on the novel by Paul Brodeur. **129m/C VHS, DVD, Wide.** Peter O'Toole, Steve Railsback, Barbara Hershey, Charles "Chuck" Bail, Alex Rocco, Allen (Goorwitz) Garfield, Adam Roarke, Sharon Farrell, Philip Bruns; ***D:*** Richard Rush; ***W:*** Richard Rush, Lawrence B. Marcus; ***C:*** Mario Tosi; ***M:*** Dominic Frontiere. Golden Globes '81: Score; Montreal World Film Fest. '80: Film; Natl. Soc. Film Critics '80: Actor (O'Toole).

Stunt Pilot && **1939** A young man takes a job at a film studio as a stunt pilot and finds mayhem and romance on and off the ground. One in the "Tailspin Tommy" series. Well-paced and fun to watch. **61m/C VHS.** John Trent, Marjorie Reynolds, Milburn Stone, Jason Robards Sr., Pat O'Malley; ***D:*** George Waggner.

Stunts && *Who Is Killing the Stuntman* **1977 (PG)** See "The Stunt Man" instead. OK script hides near-invisible plot; stunt man engages in derring-do. **90m/C VHS.** Robert Forster, Fiona Lewis, Joanna Cassidy, Darrell Fetty, Bruce Glover, James Luisi; ***D:*** Mark L. Lester; ***M:*** Michael Kamen.

Stuntwoman &½ **1981** Welch plays a stuntwoman whose death-defying job interferes with her love life. What ever shall she do? **95m/C VHS.** Raquel Welch, Jean-Paul Belmondo; ***D:*** Claude Zidi.

The Stupids &½ **1995 (PG)** In the tradition of "Dumb and Dumber," the aptly named Stupids—dad Stanley (Arnold), mom Joan (Lundy), brother Buster (Hall), and sis Petunia (McKenna)—blunder unwittingly into and out of dangerous adventures involving their garbage. Landing Arnold for the lead seems like the casting coup of the decade but the movie itself is shaky and uninspired. Based on the children's best-selling books. Keep a lookout for Captain Kangaroo (Keeshan) and numerous other cameos. **93m/C VHS.** Tom Arnold, Jessica Lundy, Bug Hall, Alex McKenna, Mark Metcalf, Matt Keeslar, Frankie Faison, Christopher Lee, Bob Keeshan; ***Cameos:*** Robert Wise, Norman Jewison, Constantin Costa-Gavras, David Cronenberg, Atom Egoyan, Gillo Pontecorvo; ***D:*** John Landis; ***W:*** Brent Forrester; ***C:*** Manfred Guthe; ***M:*** Christopher Stone. Golden Raspberries '96: Worst Actor (Arnold).

Styx &&½ **2000 (R)** Nelson (Weller) decides to get out of the safecracking trade after his brother Mike (MacFadyen) rescues him from a botched bank heist that leaves several accomplices unaccounted for. Nelson tries to go straight but Mike is a losing gambler with a big debt to some loan sharks. Nelson agrees to do a diamond heist only to learn that his not-so-missing partner Art (Brown) is the mastermind and Art just may be holding a grudge. Pro cast and fast-paced action take this above the usual heist flicks. **94m/C VHS, DVD.** Peter Weller, Bryan Brown, Angus Macfadyen, Adrienne Pierce, Anthony Bishop, Nan Hamilton, Shane Howarth, Gerard Rudolf; ***D:*** Alexander Wright; ***W:*** George Ferris; ***C:*** Russell Lyster; ***M:*** Roy Hay.

Sub Down & **1997 (PG-13)** Silly underwater saga about a submarine trapped under the polar ice cap in the Bering Strait. Scientists Baldwin, Conti, and Anwar are aboard the USS Portland when it manages to collide with a Russian sub and sink. So they're running out of air and have to figure out a way to survive. Director Gregg Champion took his name off, so be warned. **91m/C VHS.** Stephen Baldwin, Gabrielle Anwar, Tom Conti, Chris Mulkey, Tony Plana, Joel Thomas Traywick, Doug McKeon; ***D:*** Alan Smithee; ***W:*** Howard Chesley; ***C:*** Hiro Narita; ***M:*** Stefano Mainetti. **CABLE**

The Subject Was Roses &&&½ **1968** Outstanding story of family dysfunction and love based on Gilroy's Pulitzer Prize-winning play. Timmy Cleary (Sheen) returns from WWII to find that his parents' marriage has disintegrated into open hostility. Formerly mom Nettie's (Neal) fave, Timmy finally starts to learn about blustery dad John (Albertson) and attempts to moderate between the rancorous duo. But he quickly discovers that each of his parents will use him against the other and Timmy decides the best thing for everyone would be if he strikes out on his own. First film for Neal after her recovery from a series of strokes. **107m/C VHS.** Martin Sheen, Patricia Neal, Jack Albertson; ***D:*** Ulu Grosbard; ***W:*** Frank D. Gilroy; ***C:*** Jack Priestley; ***M:*** Lee Pockriss. Oscars '68: Support. Actor (Albertson).

Submarine Attack && *Torpedo Zone; The Great Hope; La Grande Speranza* **1954** Unconventional war story posits an Italian submarine captain (Baldini) who decides to rescue the survivors of a Danish freighter that he has sunk. **92m/B VHS, DVD.** *IT* Renato Baldini, Lois Maxwell, Folco Lulli, Carlo Bellini, Earl Cameron; ***D:*** Duilio Coletti; ***C:*** Leonida Barboni; ***M:*** Nino Rota.

Submarine Seahawk && **1959** When a group of Japanese warships mysteriously disappear, allied intelligence suspect a big battle is brewing. An inexperienced commander who has been tracking the movement of the Japanese ships is put in charge of the submarine Seahawk, even though the crew lacks faith in his command abilities. His own men may prove a bigger obstacle than any of the Japanese. Lots of action and stock WWII footage. **83m/B VHS.** John Bentley, Brett Halsey, Wayne Heffley, Steve Mitchell, Henry McCann, Frank Gerstle; ***D:*** Spencer Gordon Bennet.

Submerged && **2000 (R)** Terrorists hijack a commerical airliner carrying a computer decoder that controls a national defense satellite capable of launching nuclear weapons. The hijackers deliberately plunge the plane into the Pacific Ocean and while the passengers struggle to survive, a team of Nacy SEALS attempt a rescue mission and a strike against the bad guys. **95m/C VHS, DVD, Wide.** Coolio, Nicole Eggert, Fred Williamson, Dennis Weaver, Maxwell Caulfield, Brent Huff, Tim Thomerson; ***D:*** Ed Raymond; ***W:*** Steve Latshaw; ***C:*** Thomas Callaway. **VIDEO**

Submission &½ **1977 (R)** A pharmacist's sensuality is reawakened when she has a provocative affair with a clerk in her shop. **107m/C VHS.** *IT* Franco Nero, Lisa Gastoni; ***D:*** Salvatore Samperi.

Subspecies &½ **1990 (R)** New improved vampire demons descend on earth. The first full-length feature film shot on location in Transylvania. For horror buffs only. **90m/C VHS, 8mm.** Laura Tate, Michael Watson, Anders (Tofting) Hove, Michelle McBride, Irina Movila, Angus Scrimm; ***D:*** Ted Nicolaou.

The Substance of Fire && **1996 (R)** Publisher Isaac Geldhart (Rifkin) is an autocrat in both his business and his personal life, which may be why he's having so much trouble with both. A Holocaust survivor, Geldhart's obsessive about publishing a lavish four-volume history of Nazi medical experiments that will bankrupt the family firm. So his children wind up ousting him from the company and Isaac slowly slips over the edge into madness. Very King Lear, with an astonishing performance by Rifkin who also played the character in Baitz's 1991 Off-Broadway play. **100m/C VHS.** Ron Rifkin, Tony Goldwyn, Timothy Hutton, Sarah Jessica Parker, Ronny Graham, Elizabeth Franz, Gil Bellows; ***D:*** Daniel Sullivan; ***W:*** Jon Robin Baitz; ***C:*** Robert Yeoman; ***M:*** Joseph Vitarelli.

The Substitute && **1993 (R)** Donohue plays a sexy high-school substitute teacher who turns out to have homicidal tendencies, which she decides to take out on her students. Film debut for rapper/underwear model Mark. **86m/C VHS.** Amanda Donohoe, Dalton James, Natasha Gregson Wagner, Eugene Glazer, Mark Wahlberg; ***D:*** Martin Donovan; ***W:*** Cynthia Verlaine; ***M:*** Gerald Gouriet.

The Substitute & **1996 (R)** Berenger plays a Vietnam vet mercenary who poses as a substitute teacher to uncover a drug ring after his girlfriend (Venora) is roughed up by the gang. At one point, he displays his unique teaching style by throwing some unruly students out of the second floor window. Hmm...wonder if that was on the test. Being a concerned teacher, he decides to uncover the kingpin of the unruly drug gang. Being an unruly drug gang, they decide to shoot at him...a lot. Unless you're a fan of heavy weaponry, banal one liners or yelling at the screen in frustration, substitute another movie for this one. **114m/C VHS, DVD.** Tom Berenger, Ernie Hudson, Diane Venora, Marc Anthony, Glenn Plummer, Cliff DeYoung, William Forsythe, Raymond Cruz, Sharron Corley, Richard Brooks, Rodney A. Grant, Luis Guzman; ***D:*** Robert Mandel; ***W:***

Alan Ormsby, Roy Frumkes, Rocco Simonelli; *C:* Bruce Surtees; *M:* Gary Chang.

The Substitute 2: School's Out 🦴🦴 **1997 (R)** Mercenary Carl Thomasson (Williams) poses as a high school substitute teacher to hunt down the New York gang bangers who murdered his brother during a carjacking. But his plans for revenge put innocent schoolchildren at risk as well. **90m/C VHS, DVD.** Treat Williams, B.D. Wong, Angel David, Michael Michele, Larry Gilliard Jr.; *D:* Steven Pearl; *W:* Roy Frumkes, Rocco Simonelli; *C:* Larry Banks; *M:* Joe Delia. **VIDEO**

The Substitute 3: Winner Takes All 🦴🦴½ **1999 (R)** Mercenary Karl Thomasson (Williams) visits Nicole, the daughter of a dead friend who's a teacher at an eastern college. After Nicole is badly beaten, Karl takes over as a substitute and has his fellow mercenaries investigate. They discover members of the football team are on steroids, thanks to an in with the son of the local crime boss, so Karl and his buddies decide to clean things up. **90m/C VHS, DVD.** Treat Williams, Rebecca Staab, Claudia Christian, James Black, Richard Portnow; *D:* Robert Radler; *W:* Roy Frumkes, Rocco Simonelli; *C:* Barry M. Wilson; *M:* Tor Hyams. **VIDEO**

The Substitute 4: Failure is Not an Option 🦴½ **2000 (R)** Undercover cop Karl Thomaason (Williams) poses as a teacher at a military academy and discovers a group of neo-Nazi cadets whose aims are supported by members of the staff. The more sequels, the less steam this series has—this one is definitely running on low. **91m/C VHS, DVD, Wide.** Treat Williams, Angie Everhart, Bill Nunn, Tim Abell, Simon Rhee, Patrick Kilpatrick, Michael Weatherly, Grayson Fricke; *D:* Robert Radler; *W:* Dan Gurskis; *C:* Richard Rawlings; *M:* Steve Edwards. **VIDEO**

The Substitute Wife 🦴🦴½ **1994 (PG-13)** Dying Nebraska frontier woman Amy Hightower (Thompson) decides to find her husband Martin (Weller) a new wife to help on the farm and look after their four children. But women are so scarce (and the farm is so isolated) that the only one willing to give it a try is prostitute Pearl (Fawcett), who's fed up with her profession but isn't exactly the motherly type (at least not at first). Amusing relationships develop between the two women and the bewildered husband. Made for TV. **92m/C VHS.** Farrah Fawcett, Lea Thompson, Peter Weller; *D:* Peter Werner; *W:* Stan Daniels; *C:* Neil Roach; *M:* Mark Snow. **TV**

Subterfuge 🦴🦴 **1968** When a special American security agent goes to England for a "vacation," his presence causes speculation and poses several serious questions for both British Intelligence and the underworld. Nothing special, with the occasional suspenseful moment. **89m/C VHS.** *GB* Tom Adams, Joan Collins, Gene Barry, Richard Todd; *D:* Peter Graham Scott.

Suburban Commando 🦴🦴 **1991 (PG)** A goofy, muscular alien mistakenly lands on Earth while on vacation. He does his best to remain inconspicuous, resulting in numerous hilarious situations. Eventually he is forced to confront his arch, interstellar nemesis in order to defend the family who befriended him. A harmless, sometimes cute vehicle for wrestler Hogan, which will certainly entertain his younger fans. **88m/C VHS.** Hulk Hogan, Christopher Lloyd, Shelley Duvall, Larry Miller, William Ball, JoAnn Dearing, Jack Elam, Roy Dotrice, Christopher Neame, Tony Longo; *D:* Burt Kennedy; *W:* Frank Cappello.

Suburban Roulette 🦴 **1967** "Adults only" feature from splattermaster Lewis caters to the prurient. Groovy themes like wife swapping and other very daring subjects. Totally '60s. Presented as part of Joe Bob Brigg's "Sleaziest Movies in the History of the World" series. **91m/C VHS.** Elizabeth Wilkinson, Ben Moore, Tony McCabe, Deborah Grant; *D:* Herschell Gordon Lewis; *W:* Herschell Gordon Lewis; *C:* Roy Collodi.

The Suburbans 🦴½ **1999 (R)** Bland and not very funny ensemble comedy. The Suburbans were an '80s one-hit wonder band who reunite 18 years later at member Gil's (Ferrell) wedding. Their impromptu reunion draws the attention of unlikely record company talent scout Kate (Hewitt), who decides she wants to resurrect their would-be music careers. The music satire is funny but the domestic angst is boring. **81m/C VHS, DVD, Wide.** Jennifer Love Hewitt, Will Ferrell, Donal Lardner Ward, Craig Bierko, Amy Brenneman, Bridgette Wilson, Tony Guma, Robert Loggia, Antonio Fargas, Ben Stiller, Jerry Stiller; *D:* Donal Lardner Ward; *W:* Donal Lardner Ward, Tony Guma; *C:* Michael Barrett; *M:* Robbie Kondor.

Suburbia 🦴 *The Wild Side* **1983 (R)** When a group of punk rockers move into a condemned suburban development, they become the targets of a vigilante group. Low budget, needless violent remake of anyone of many '50s rebellion flicks that tries to have a "message." **99m/C VHS, DVD.** Chris Pederson, Bill Coyne, Jennifer Clay, Timothy Eric O'Brien, Andrew Pece, Don Allen; *D:* Penelope Spheeris; *W:* Penelope Spheeris; *C:* Tim Suhrstedt; *M:* Alex Gibson.

subUrbia 🦴🦴 **1996 (R)** Ensemble piece featuring three aimless post-high school friends, Jeff (Ribisi), Buff (Zahn), and Tim (Katt) who spend their time hanging out in the parking lot of a convenience store. What's different about this night is that they're joined by Jeff's girlfriend Sooze (Carey) and her friend Bee-Bee (Spybey), and they actually have a purpose for waiting around. The guys are expecting a visit from their old buddy Pony (Bartok), a rock musician just finding success. But when Pony does appear, the fact that he has done something to get out and succeed turns the meeting hostile. Based on the play by Eric Bogosian. **118m/C VHS.** Giovanni Ribisi, Steve Zahn, Nicky Katt, Jayce Bartok, Amie Carey, Dina Spybey, Parker Posey, Ajay Naidu, Samia Shoaib; *D:* Richard Linklater; *W:* Eric Bogosian; *C:* Lee Daniel.

Subway 🦴½ **1985 (R)** Surreal, MTV-esque vision of French fringe life from the director of "Le Dernier Combat." A spike-haired renegade escapes the law by plunging into the Parisian subway system. Once there, he encounters a bizarre subculture living under the city. Plenty of angry-youth attitude, but where's the point? And frankly, too much bad New Wave music. **103m/C VHS, DVD.** *FR* Christopher Lambert, Isabelle Adjani, Jean-Hugues Anglade, Jean Reno, Richard Bohringer, Michel Galabru, Eric Serra, Arthur Simms; *D:* Luc Besson; *W:* Luc Besson, Pierre Jolivet, Alain Le Henry, Marc Perrier, Sophie Schmit; *C:* Carlo Varini; *M:* Rickie Lee Jones, Eric Serra. Cesar '86: Actor (Lambert), Art Dir./Set Dec., Sound.

Subway Stories 🦴🦴 **1997 (R)** Ten short films based on actual experiences on the New York subway system featuring such topics as harassment, flirtation, sex, food, and money. **82m/C VHS.** Bill Irwin, Kris Parker, Denis Leary, Christine Lahti, Steve Zahn, Jerry Stiller, Bonnie Hunt, Lili Taylor, Michael Rapaport, Mercedes Ruehl, Sarita Choudhury, Taral Hicks, Danny Hoch, Mike McGlone, Rosie Perez, Gregory Hines, Anne Heche; *D:* Ted (Edward) Demme, Abel Ferrara, Jonathan Demme, Julie Dash, Seth Zvi Rosenfeld, Bob Balaban, Alison Maclean, Lucas Platt, Patricia Benoit, Craig McKay; *W:* Danny Hoch, John Guare, Adam Brooks, Julie Dash, Lynn Grossman, Marla Hanson, Seth Zvi Rosenfeld, Joe Viola, Albert Innaurato, Angela Todd; *C:* Ken Kelsch, Adam Kimmel, Tom Hurwitz, Anthony C. "Tony" Jannelli.

Subway to the Stars 🦴🦴½ *Un Trem Para as Estrelas* **1987** Young saxophonist Fontes searches the back streets of Rio for his missing girlfriend. Realistic and sometimes depressing, if aimless at times. Overall, an intriguing "underworld" flick from Brazil. Portuguese with subtitles. **103m/C VHS.** *BR* Guilherme Fontes, Milton Gonçalves, Taumaturgo Ferreira, Ze Trindade, Ana Beatriz Wiltgen; *D:* Carlos Diegues.

Success Is the Best Revenge 🦴🦴½ **1984** A Polish film director living in London struggles with his rebellious teenage son. Both struggle with questions of exile and identity. Uneven but worthwhile and based on Skolimowski's own experiences. His better earlier film is "Moonlighting." **95m/C VHS.** *GB* Michael York, Michel Piccoli, Anouk Aimee, John Hurt, Jane Asher, Joanna Szerbic, Michael Lyndon, George Skolimowski; *D:* Jerzy Skolimowski; *M:* Hans Zimmer.

Such a Long Journey 🦴🦴🦴 **1998** Bank clerk Gustad Noble has a modest life that is beginning to fall apart. First his young daughter becomes very ill and then his son defies Gustad's ambitions for him. Finally, he receives a letter from an old friend asking for his help and Gustad finds himself caught up in unexpected danger and deception. Set in Bombay in 1971, as India prepares for war, and based on the novel by Rohinton Mistry. **110m/C VHS.** *CA GB* Roshan Seth, Om Puri, Kurush Deboo, Naseeruddin Shah, Ranjit Chowdhari; *D:* Sturla Gunnarsson; *W:* Sooni Taraporevala; *C:* Jan Kiesser. Genie '98: Actor (Seth), Film Editing.

The Sucker 🦴🦴 *Le Corniauds* **1965** Antoine Marecchal (Bouvril) is on his way to an Italian vacation when his car is wrecked in an accident. The businessman who smashed his car offers Antoine a Cadillac to drive but this turns him into a smuggler. However, Antoine isn't as dumb as he may appear and he makes the most of his unusual situation. French with subtitles. **90m/C VHS.** *FR* Bourvil, Louis de Funes; *D:* Gerard Oury.

Sucker Money 🦴½ *Victims of the Beyond* **1934** Newspaper reporter works to expose phony spiritualist. Good title; little else. Boring. **59m/B VHS.** Mischa Auer, Phyllis Barrington, Earl McCarthy, Ralph Lewis, Mae Busch; *D:* Dorothy Davenport Reid.

Sudden Death 🦴 **1950** Shamrock and Lucky are back as cowboys posing as hired gunmen in order to foil a wealthy, homesteader-hating land baron. **55m/B VHS.** James Ellison, Russell Hayden, Stanley Price, Raymond Hatton, Julie Adams.

Sudden Death 🦴 **1977 (R)** Two professional violence merchants put themselves up for hire. **84m/C VHS.** Robert Conrad, Felton Perry, Don Stroud, Bill Raymond, Ron Vawter, Harry Roskolenko; *D:* Richard Foreman.

Sudden Death 🦴 **1985 (R)** A beautiful businesswoman decides to kill every rapist she can find after she herself has been attacked. Exploitative in its own fashion; fueled and felled by rage. **95m/C VHS.** Denise Coward, Frank Runyeon, Jamie Tirelli; *D:* Sig Shore.

Sudden Death 🦴🦴 **1995 (R)** Terrorists invade a hockey arena where the Vice President and 17,000 fans, including Fire Marshal Jean-Claude and his kids, are watching the seventh game of the Stanley Cup Finals. The latest in the "Die Hard in a..." genre covers the territory with the now-standard lack of characterization, family member in peril, and ever-increasing body count. Boothe (playing Alan Rickman playing a bad guy) does most of the talking while Van Damme kicks people in the head and plays goalie. Producer Howard Baldwin owns the Pittsburgh Penguins, coincidentally one of the teams on the ice for the second pairing of "Timecop" vets Hyams and Van Damme. **110m/C VHS, DVD.** Jean-Claude Van Damme, Powers Boothe, Ross Malinger, Whittni Wright, Raymond J. Barry, Dorian Harewood, Kate McNeil, Audra Lindley; *D:* Peter Hyams; *W:* Gene Quintano; *C:* Peter Hyams; *M:* John Debney.

Sudden Fear 🦴🦴🦴 **1952** Successful playwright/heiress Myra Hudson (Crawford) has a whirlwind romance, leading to marriage, with oh-so-charming actor Lester Blaine (Palance). But Les is more interested in Myra's money and gets together with former flame Irene (always the bad girl Grahame) to get rid of his new bride and inherit her fortune. But Myra finds out about the plot and puts her writing talent to work in coming up with a new scenario. Good suspenser with fine performances. Adapted from the book by Edna Sherry. **111m/B VHS, DVD.** Joan Crawford, Jack Palance, Gloria Grahame, Bruce (Herman Brix) Bennett, Virginia Huston, Mike Connors; *D:* David Miller; *W:* Lenore Coffee, Robert Smith; *C:* Charles B(ryant) Lang Jr.; *M:* Elmer Bernstein.

Sudden Impact 🦴🦴½ **1983 (R)** Eastwood directs himself in this formula thriller, the fourth "Dirty Harry" entry. This time "Dirty Harry" Callahan tracks down a revenge-obsessed murderess and finds he has more in common with her than he expected. Meanwhile, local mobsters come gunning for him. This is the one where he says, "Go ahead. Make my day." Followed by "The Dead Pool." **117m/C VHS, 8mm, Wide.** Clint Eastwood, Sondra Locke, Pat Hingle, Bradford Dillman, Albert "Poppy" Popwell; *D:* Clint Eastwood; *W:* Joseph C. Stinson; *C:* Bruce Surtees; *M:* Lalo Schifrin.

Sudden Manhattan 🦴🦴 **1996** Unemployed single Donna (Shelly) thinks she witnesses a murder—over and over again. Of course, no one believes her and she tries to figure out the truth. Shelly's directorial debut. **80m/C VHS, DVD.** Adrienne Shelly, Tim Guinee, Roger Rees, Louise Lasser, Hynden Walch; *D:* Adrienne Shelly; *W:* Adrienne Shelly; *C:* Jim Denault; *M:* Pat Irwin.

Suddenly 🦴🦴🦴½ **1954** Crazed gunman John Baron (Sinatra) holds a family hostage in the hick town of Suddenly, California, as part of a plot to kill the president, who's stopping at the local train station. As things begin to go wrong, Baron begins to unravel. Tense thriller is a good display for Sinatra's acting talent. Unfortunately hard to find because Sinatra forced United Artists to take it out of distribution after hearing that Kennedy assassin Lee Harvey Oswald had watched "Suddenly" only days before November 22, 1963. Really, Ol' Blue Eyes should have stuck with making top-notch thrillers like this one, instead of degenerating into the world's greatest lounge singer. **75m/B VHS, DVD.** Frank Sinatra, Sterling Hayden, James Gleason, Nancy Gates, Paul Frees, Willis Bouchey, Kim Charney, Christopher Dark; *D:* Lewis Allen; *W:* Richard Sale; *C:* Charles Clarke; *M:* David Raksin.

Suddenly, Last Summer 🦴🦴🦴½ **1959** Brain surgeon is summoned to the mansion of a rich New Orleans matron who wishes him to perform a lobotomy on her niece, supposedly suffering from a mental breakdown. Based on the play by Tennessee Williams. Softened for the censors, though the themes of homosexuality, insanity, and murder, characterizations of evil, and unusual settings presage many movies of the next two decades. Extremely fine performances from Hepburn and Taylor. Clift never completely recovered from his auto accident two years before and does not come across with the strength of purpose really necessary in his character. Still, fine viewing. **114m/B VHS, DVD, Wide.** Elizabeth Taylor, Katharine Hepburn, Montgomery Clift, Mercedes McCambridge, Albert Dekker; *D:* Joseph L. Mankiewicz; *W:* Gore Vidal; *C:* Jack Hildyard; *M:* Malcolm Arnold. Golden Globes '60: Actress—Drama (Taylor).

Sudie & Simpson 🦴🦴🦴 **1990** Heart-tugging tale of friendship set in rural 1940s Georgia. Twelve-year-old white Sudie's forbidden friendship with the adult black Simpson provides a lot of talk in their small town. Racial barriers finally cause Simpson to be accused of child molestation and the odds of his survival, despite his innocence, don't seem great. Based on Sara Flanigan Carter's autobiographical novel. **95m/C VHS, DVD.** Sara Gilbert, Louis Gossett Jr., Frances Fisher, John M. Jackson, Paige Danahy, Ken Strong; *D:* Joan Tewkesbury; *W:* Sara Flanigan Carter, Ken Koser; *C:* Mario DiLeo; *M:* Michel Colombier. **CABLE**

Suds 🦴🦴½ **1920** Pickford is tragic laundress with major crush on a guy who left his shirt at the laundry. **75m/B VHS.** Mary Pickford, William Austin, Harold Goodwin, Madame Rose (Dion) Dione, Theodore Roberts; *D:* John Francis Dillon.

Suffering Bastards 🦴🦴½ **1990** Buddy and Al have never worked a day in their lives—Mom's nightclub always gave them something to do and a regular paycheck. But when Mom's swindled out of the family business, they decide it's time to take charge. Soon they're caught between bullets, babes, and belly laughs in this action-filled comedy. **95m/C VHS.** Eric Bogosian, John C. McGinley, David Warshofsky.

Sugar & Spice 🦴🦴🦴 **2001 (PG-13)** If there is such a thing as a smart cheerleader teen pic, this is it. Satire of offbeat pep squadders who cheer by day and rob banks by night include Suvari's rebellious Kansas and Shelton's permanently upbeat Diane. Diane meets Jack (Marsden), and two American kids do the best they can when they learn Diane is pregnant. They decide to marry, move more into a seedy apartment, and take up work at a local fast food joint. After losing said employment, the motivation becomes clear for the girls' ensuing illegal capers. Littered with pop culture references: the girls rent "Reservoir Dogs" to prepare for the heist, rob the banks in "Betty" masks, and deal with one of the girls' hots for Conan O'Brien. **81m/C VHS, DVD, Wide.** *US* Marley Shelton, James Marsden, Mena Suvari, Marla Sokoloff, Rachel Blanchard, Melissa George, Alexandra Holden, Sara Marsh, Sean Young; ***D:*** Francine McDougall; ***W:*** Mandy Nelson; ***C:*** Robert Brinkmann; ***M:*** Mark Mothersbaugh.

Sugar Cane Alley ♂♂♂ *Rue Cases Negres* **1983 (PG)** After the loss of his parents, an 11-year-old orphan boy goes to work with his grandmother on a sugar plantation. She realizes that her young ward's only hope is an education. Set in Martinique in the 1930s among black workers. Poignant and memorable. French with subtitles. **106m/C VHS.** *FR* Garry Cadenat, Darling Legitimus, Douta Seck; ***D:*** Euzhan Palcy; ***W:*** Euzhan Palcy; ***C:*** Dominique Chapuis.

Sugar Cookies woof! **1977 (R)** Erotic horror story in which young women are the pawns as a satanic satyr and an impassioned lesbian play out a bizarre game of vengeance, love, and death. **89m/C VHS.** Mary Woronov, Lynn Lowry, Monique Van Vooren; ***D:*** Michael Herz.

Sugar Hill ♂♂ **1994 (R)** Two brothers (Wright & Snipes) are heroin dealers who have built their own crime empire in the Sugar Hill section of Harlem. Snipes is moved to reconsider his career options when he falls for an aspiring actress (Randle). Jarring editing sequence recaps the seminal event in the brothers' upbringing and serves to explain how the wide-eyed boys became cold-blooded pushers. Good performances by all, but formulaic plot will leave viewers asking themselves if they haven't seen it before and why it was they saw it then. Junkie dad Williams was Linc on "The Mod Squad" on TV in the late '60s and director of "Tales from the Hood." **123m/C VHS.** Wesley Snipes, Michael Wright, Theresa Randle, Clarence Williams III, Abe Vigoda, Ernie Hudson, Larry Joshua, Leslie Uggams, Khandi Alexander, Raymond Serra, Joe Dallesandro, Vondie Curtis-Hall; ***D:*** Leon Ichaso; ***W:*** Barry Michael Cooper; ***C:*** Bojan Bazelli; ***M:*** Terence Blanchard.

Sugar Town ♂♂ **1999 (R)** Ambitions collide in this saga of the L.A. music scene. Savvy and unscrupulous young singer Gwen (Gordon) is determined to land a recording contract while a group of middle age rock stars (Taylor, Des Barres, and Kemp) want to recapture their fame—with music producer Burt (Klein) as their catalyst. There's also struggling studio musician Carl (Doe) and his woes with Latina singer, Rosio (Cavazos) and various other subplots—none of which hang together terribly well. **92m/C VHS.** Michael Des Barres, Jade Gordon, John Taylor, Martin Kemp, Larry Klein, John Doe, Lumi Cavazos, Lucinda Jenney, Rosanna Arquette, Ally Sheedy, Beverly D'Angelo, Richmond Arquette, Jeff McDonald, Vincent Berry, Polly Platt, Chris Mulkey; ***D:*** Allison Anders, Kurt Voss; ***W:*** Allison Anders, Kurt Voss; ***C:*** Kristian Bernier; ***M:*** Larry Klein.

Sugarbaby ♂♂♂ *Zuckerbaby* **1985 (R)** An acclaimed German film about a fat mortuary attendant living in Munich who transforms herself (but doesn't lose weight) in order to seduce a young, handsome subway conductor. Touching and warm film that introduced Sagebrecht to American audiences. A bit too cutting-edge cinematographically. In German with English subtitles. Remade as "Babycakes." Sagebrecht and director Adlon team up again for "Bagdad Cafe" and "Rosalie Goes Shopping." **103m/C VHS.** *GE* Marianne Saegebrecht, Eisi Gulp, Toni Berger, Will Spendler, Manuela Denz; ***D:*** Percy Adlon; ***W:*** Percy Adlon.

The Sugarland Express ♂♂♂ **1974 (PG)** To save her son from adoption, a young woman helps her husband break out of prison. In their flight to freedom, they hijack a police car, holding the policeman hostage. Speilberg's first feature film is a moving portrait of a couple's desperation. Based on a true story, adapted by Hal Barwood and Matthew Robbins. **109m/C VHS, Wide.** Goldie Hawn, Ben Johnson, Michael Sacks, William Atherton; ***D:*** Steven Spielberg; ***W:*** Steven Spielberg, Matthew Robbins, Hal Barwood; ***C:*** Vilmos Zsigmond; ***M:*** John Williams.

Sugartime ♂♂½ **1995 (R)** Based on the true-life romance of '60s Chicago mobster Sam Giacana (Turturro) and song bird Phyllis Maguire (Parker), one of the wholesome Maguire Sisters. Naturally, getting involved with a crime boss did little for her image and Maguire's career hit the skids while Giacana's volatile jealousy brought unwanted attention from both fellow gangsters and the feds. (He was murdered in 1975 and had broken off with Phyllis before that). The real Maguire denounced the inaccuracy of the TV production. Suggested by William F. Roemer, Jr.'s book "Roemer: Man Against the Mob." **108m/C VHS.** John Turturro, Mary-Louise Parker, Elias Koteas, Maury Chaykin, Louis Del Grande, Christopher Barry, Richard Blackburn; ***D:*** John N. Smith; ***W:*** Martyn Burke; ***C:*** Pierre Letarte.

Suicide Kings ♂♂ **1997 (R)** When the sister of one of four prep school friends is kidnapped, the guys decide to take retired mobster Charlie Barrett (Walken) hostage so he'll help them. The wanna-be "Reservoir Pups" lose control almost as soon as the caper begins, and the savvy Barrett takes advantage to turn his captors against each other with news that the girl's abduction may have been an inside job. Maze of a plot, which wanders into "Usual Suspects" is-this-all-real? territory, does nothing to help any of the young actors, who are clearly overmatched by Walken. Not much here for anyone except fans of Walken's patented Gangster Cool. **106m/C VHS, DVD.** Louis Lombardi, Christopher Walken, Jay Mohr, Henry Thomas, Sean Patrick Flanery, Denis Leary, Jeremy Sisto, Johnny Galecki, Cliff DeYoung, Laura San Giacomo, Laura Harris; ***D:*** Peter O'Fallon; ***W:*** Josh McKinney, Gina Goldman, Wayne Rice; ***C:*** Christopher Baffa; ***M:*** Graeme Revell, Tim Simonec.

Suicide Patrol ♂ **197?** A small band of saboteurs patrols a German-controlled Mediterranean island during WWII. **90m/C VHS.** Gordon Mitchell, Pierre Richard, Max Dean.

Suicide Ride ♂♂ **1997** Action-movie junkie Barney's (Quill) life is going nowhere, so looking for some real adventure he decides to hire a hitman (Hues) to off him. Only the hitman wants to retire and instead offers Barney his job, which he takes. This causes him lots of trouble. Quirky low-budgeter. **86m/C VHS.** Tim Quill, Matthias Hues, Frank Adonis; ***D:*** Samer Daboul, Trevor Sands.

Suite 16 ♂ **1994 (R)** A penthouse suite in a French Riviera hotel is occupied by rich, manipulative, wheelchair-bound Glover (Postlethwaite). Young gigolo/thief Chris (Kamerling), who believes he's killed his latest trick, is given refuge by Glover in exchange for allowing the aging voyeur to watch Chris (via camera) perform with a succession of prostitutes. Finally, Chris wants to leave but Glover offers him a huge amount of money for one final vicarious—and deadly—thrill. Eurotrash, with corny dialogue, but Postlethwaite's chillingly creepy. Also available in an R-rated version. **93m/C VHS, DVD.** *BE GB* Pete Postlethwaite, Antoine Kamerling, Geraldine Pailhas, Thom Jansen; ***D:*** Dominique Deruddere; ***W:*** Charles Higson, Lise Mayer; ***C:*** Jean-Francois Robin; ***M:*** Walter Hus.

The Suitors ♂ **1988** When a group of Iranians decide to sacrifice a lamb in their apartment, the New York police send in SWAT team assuming they're terrorists. First time effort by Ebrahimian, in Farsi with English subtitles. **106m/C VHS.** ***D:*** Ghasem Ebrahimian.

Sullivan's Travels ♂♂♂♂ **1941** Sturges' masterpiece is a sardonic, whip-quick romp about a Hollywood director tired of making comedies who decides to make a serious, socially responsible film and hits the road masquerading as a hobo in order to know hardship and poverty. Beautifully sustained, inspired satire that mercilessly mocked the ambitions of Depression-era social cinema. Gets a little over-dark near the end before the happy ending; Sturges insisted on 20-year-old Lake as The Girl; her pregnancy forced him to rewrite scenes and design new costumes for her. As ever, she is stunning. **90m/B VHS, DVD.** Joel McCrea, Veronica Lake, William Demarest, Robert Warwick, Franklin Pangborn, Porter Hall, Eric Blore, Byron Foulger, Robert Greig, Torben Meyer, Jimmy Conlin, Margaret Hayes, Chester Conklin, Alan Bridge; ***D:*** Preston Sturges; ***W:*** Preston Sturges; ***C:*** John Seitz; ***M:*** Leo Shuken. Natl. Film Reg. '90.

The Sum of All Fears ♂♂½ **2002 (PG-13)** Affleck takes over as Jack Ryan, who is now just an analyst, and has a girlfriend (Moynihan) who's a young doctor (hmmm...), but the film is still set in the present-day. That's just the first confusing element of this complicated spy thriller. The first half is spent on set pieces that seem to have no connection, until a climactic event (which takes place an hour in). Ryan is trying to prevent a nuclear war between the U.S. and Russia. Neo-Nazis are the baddies who put the world on the brink, and give the audience a safe, cartoony villian to make up for the now all-too-possible nuclear scenario. Affleck shows signs of growing into the role if the franchise continues, but he's not there yet. Pic is at its best when in the conference rooms of the White House and Kremlin, with each leader's advisors pressing their agendas. **118m/C VHS, DVD.** *US* Ben Affleck, Morgan Freeman, James Cromwell, Bridget Moynahan, Liev Schreiber, Ron Rifkin, Alan Bates, Ciaran Hinds, Philip Baker Hall, Bruce McGill, Colm Feore, Josef Sommer, Ken Jenkins, Michael Byrne, John Beasley, Jamie Harrold; ***D:*** Phil Alden Robinson; ***W:*** Paul Attanasio, Daniel Pyne; ***C:*** John Lindley; ***M:*** Jerry Goldsmith.

The Sum of Us ♂♂♂ **1994 (R)** Sweet and faithful adaptation of David Stevens' stage play about a father and his gay son. Widowed Harry Mitchell (Thompson) shares his house with son Jeff (Crowe), who's never made a secret of his sexual orientation. Affable Harry only wants what's best for his boy, including his over-enthusiastic welcome to Jeff's potential new boyfriend (Polson). Too bad Harry's not so lucky in love—his new woman friend Joyce (Kennedy) has problems with Jeff's sexuality. Well, she just has to adjust. Pervasive feel-good message may leave less well-adjusted viewer addled. Sensitive performances, though the film's antecedents as a play are highlighted by having the main characters talk directly to the camera. Aussie slang provides a challenge. **99m/C VHS.** *AU* Jack Thompson, Russell Crowe, John Polson, Deborah Kennedy, Mitch Mathews, Julie Herbert, Joss Moroney, Rebekah Elmaloglou; ***D:*** Kevin Dowling, Geoff Burton; ***W:*** David Stevens; ***C:*** Geoff Burton; ***M:*** Dave Faulkner. Australian Film Inst. '94: Adapt. Screenplay; Montreal World Film Fest. '94: Screenplay.

Summer ♂♂♂½ *Le Rayon Vert; The Green Ray* **1986 (R)** The fifth and among the best of Rohmer's "Comedies and Proverbs" series. A romantic but glum young French girl finds herself stuck in Paris during the tourist season searching for true romantic love. Takes time and patience to seize the viewer; moving ending makes it all worthwile. In French with English subtitles. **98m/C VHS, DVD.** *FR* Marie Riviere, Lisa Heredia, Beatrice Romand, Eric Hamm, Rosette, Isabelle Riviere; ***D:*** Eric Rohmer; ***W:*** Eric Rohmer; ***C:*** Sophie Maintigneux; ***M:*** Jean-Louis Valero.

Summer Affair ♂½ **1979** Two young lovers run away from their bickering parents and get shipwrecked on a desert island. **90m/C VHS.** *IT* Ornella Muti, Les Rannow; ***D:*** George S. Casorati.

Summer and Smoke ♂♂½ **1961** Repressed, unhappy Page falls for handsome doctor Harvey. A tour de force for Page, but that's all; adapted clumsily from the overwrought Tennessee Williams play. **118m/C VHS, Wide.** Laurence Harvey, Geraldine Page, Rita Moreno, Una Merkel, John McIntire, Thomas Gomez, Pamela Tiffin, Lee Patrick, Max (Casey Adams) Showalter, Earl Holliman, Harry Shannon, Pattee Chapman; ***D:*** Peter Glenville; ***C:*** Charles B(ryant) Lang Jr.; ***M:*** Elmer Bernstein. Golden Globes '62: Actress—Drama (Page); Natl. Bd. of Review '61: Actress (Page).

Summer Camp Nightmare ♂½ *The Butterfly Revolution* **1986 (PG-13)** See "Lord of the Flies" instead. A young fascist incites children at two summer camps to overthrow and imprison the adults. Barbarism rears its ugly head. Self-serious and anticlimatic. Based on the novel "The Butterfly Revolution" by William Butler. **89m/C VHS.** Chuck Connors, Charles Stratton, Harold P. Pruett, Tom Fridley, Adam Carl; ***D:*** Bert L. Dragin; ***C:*** Don Burgess.

Summer Catch ♂½ **2001 (PG-13)** Freddie Prinze, Jr. is really gonna have to learn to shake off some of the signs his agent is giving him. In this rip-off of every baseball movie of the last decade, Prinze plays underdog pitcher Ryan, on his last chance in his hometown Cape Cod league. Complicating matters are his flamboyant rival Eric (Pearson) and upperclass babe Tenley (Biel), who he falls for while cutting lawns for his irascible father (Ward). Can Ryan make it to the big leagues with help from grizzled manager Schiffner (Dennehy)? Will he win the bodacious babe despite protests from her blueblood father (Davison)? Will Lillard make another appearance in a Freddie Prinze, Jr. movie? If you don't know the answers to those questions, you deserve to watch this bush-league flick. **108m/C VHS, DVD, Wide.** *US* Freddie Prinze Jr., Jessica Biel, Matthew Lillard, Brian Dennehy, Fred Ward, Jason Gedrick, Brittany Murphy, Marc Blucas, Bruce Davison, Wilmer Valderrama, Christian Kane, Gabriel Mann, Cedric Pendleton, Zena Grey, Corey Pearson; ***D:*** Mike Tollin; ***W:*** Kevin Falls, John Gatins; ***C:*** Tim Suhrstedt; ***M:*** George Fenton.

Summer City ♂½ *Coast of Terror* **1977** Fun-and-sun surfing movie complete with romance, hot rods, murder and great shots of the sea features Gibson in his debut. Ever wonder what Australian surf bums do on weekends? The same as their California counterparts—except they talk funny. **83m/C VHS.** *AU* Mel Gibson, Phillip Avalon, John Jarratt, Christopher Fraser.

Summer Fantasy ♂ **1984** Mindless TV surf saga about a curvy teen who would rather watch the beach hunks then go to medical school. **96m/C VHS.** Julianne Phillips, Ted Shackleford, Michael Gross, Dorothy Lyman; ***D:*** Noel Nosseck; ***M:*** Peter Bernstein.

Summer Heat ♂½ **1987 (R)** In rural, mid-Depression North Carolina, a young, lonely wife and mother is seduced by a drifter and together they plot murder. Her husband neglects her, and you should neglect to see this utter yawner. Based on a Louise Shivers novel. **80m/C VHS.** Lori Singer, Anthony Edwards, Bruce Abbott, Kathy Bates; ***D:*** Michie Gleason; ***C:*** Elliot Davis.

Summer Holiday ♂♂½ **1948** Rooney comes of age with a vengeance during summer vacation in musical rendition of "Ah, Wilderness." Undistinguished musical numbers, inferior to the original, but jazzy Technicolor cinematography. Ended up in the red by over $1.5 million, lotsa money back then. ♫It's Our Home Town; Afraid to Fall in Love; All Hail, Danville High; The Stanley Steamer; It's Independence Day; I Think You're the Sweetest Kid I've Ever Known; Weary Blues. **92m/C VHS.** Mickey Rooney, Gloria De Haven, Walter Huston, Frank Morgan, Jackie "Butch" Jenkins, Marilyn Maxwell, Agnes Moorehead, Selena Royle, Anne Francis; ***D:*** Rouben Mamoulian.

The Summer House ♂♂½ **1994** Comedy of manners set in 1959 England about the manipulations of three middle-aged women (Moreau, Plowright, Walters) over the impending marriage of one's dreamy young daughter (Headey) to a dolt (Threlfall). Moreau stirs things up as the spirited and skeptical friend of Walters, the deluded bride's mother whom she must interrupt from her busy nuptial preparations and somehow communicate the obvious. Plowright is perfectly cast as the gimlet-eyed groom's mother, well aware of her son's flaws, who achieves an odd alliance with polar opposite Moreau. Strong performances from all the veterans carry the day. Based on the novel by Alice Thomas Ellis. **85m/C VHS.** *GB* Jeanne Moreau, Joan Plowright, Julie Walters, Lena Headey, David Threlfall, Padraig Casey, Britta Smith, John Wood; ***D:*** Waris Hussein; ***W:*** Martin Sherman; ***M:*** Stanley Myers.

Summer Interlude ½ *Illicit Interlude; Summerplay; Sommarlek* **1950** A ballerina recalls a romantic summer spent with an innocent boy, who was later tragically killed. Contains many earmarks and visual ideas of later Bergman masterpieces. In Swedish with English subtitles. **95m/B VHS.** *SW* Maj-Britt Nilsson, Birger Malmsten, Alf Kjellin; ***D:*** Ingmar Bergman; ***W:*** Ingmar Bergman.

Summer Lovers **1982 (R)** Summer vacation finds young couple traveling to the exotic Greek island of Santorini. They meet up with a fun-loving woman and discover three-way sexual tension, but little in the way of plot, dialogue, or acting. From the director of "Grease" and "Blue Lagoon" and best watched late at night while half conscious. **98m/C VHS.** Peter Gallagher, Daryl Hannah, Valerie Quennessen; ***D:*** Randal Kleiser; ***M:*** Basil Poledouris.

Summer Magic **1963** An impecunious recent widow is forced to leave Boston and settle her family in a small town in Maine. Typical, forgettable Disney drama; early Mills vehicle. A remake of "Mother Carey's Chickens." **116m/C VHS.** Hayley Mills, Burl Ives, Dorothy McGuire, Deborah Walley, Una Merkel, Eddie Hodges; ***D:*** James Neilson; ***M:*** Buddy (Norman Dale) Baker.

Summer Night with Greek Profile, Almond Eyes & Scent of Basil **1987 (R)** A wealthy woman tycoon hires an ex-CIA man to kidnap a high-priced, professional terrorist and hold him for ransom. An ironic battle of the sexes follows. In Italian with English subtitles. **94m/C VHS.** *IT* Mariangela Melato, Michele Placido, Roberto Herlitzka, Massimo Wertmuller; ***D:*** Lina Wertmuller; ***W:*** Lina Wertmuller.

The Summer of Aviya *Kayitz Shel Aviya* **1988** Ten-year-old Aviya has spent most of her life in orphanages as her partisan Jewish mother fought the Nazis. Now, Aviya faces the prospect of returning to a home and woman she doesn't really know, one who is also balanced on the edge of madness. Based on the memoirs of Almagor. Hebrew with subtitles. Followed by "Under the Domim Tree." **?m/C VHS.** *IS* Kaipo Cohen, Gila Almagor; ***D:*** Eli Cohen; ***W:*** Eli Cohen, Gila Almagor.

The Summer of Ben Tyler ½ **1996 (PG)** Temple Rayburn (Woods) is an up-and-coming lawyer in a small southern town in 1942 and the protege of influential Spencer Maitland (Cariou). Before his family's black housekeeper dies, Rayburn agrees to take in her mentally handicapped teenaged son, Ben (Mattocks), to the dismay of the white community. Then Maitland insists Rayburn defend his son Junius (Isola) against a drunk driving charge where a woman was killed. TV movie. **134m/C VHS.** James Woods, Len Cariou, Elizabeth McGovern, Charles Mattocks, Kevin Isola, Julia McIlvaine, Clifton James; ***D:*** Arthur Allan Seidelman; ***W:*** Robert Inman; ***C:*** Neil Roach; ***M:*** Van Dyke Parks; ***Nar:*** Judith Ivey. **TV**

Summer of Fear *Stranger in Our House* **1978** A happy young woman (Blair) must overcome evil forces when her cousin (a teenage witch not akin to Sabrina) comes to live with—and control—her family. Based on a novel by Lois Duncan, who also wrote the source novel for 1997's "I Know What You Did Last Summer." Pretty scary if ordinary, made-for-TV horror from later-famous Craven. **94m/C VHS.** Linda Blair, Lee Purcell, Jeremy Slate, Carol Lawrence, MacDonald Carey, Jeff McCracken, Jeff East, Fran Drescher; ***D:*** Wes Craven; ***M:*** Tom D'Andrea. **TV**

Summer of '42 **1971 (R)** Touching if sentimental story about 15-year-old Hermie's (Grimes) sexual coming of age during his summer vacation on an island off New England. While his friends are fumbling with girls their own age, he falls in love with a beautiful 22-year-old woman (O'Neill) whose husband is off fighting in the war. **102m/C VHS, DVD, Wide.** Jennifer O'Neill, Gary Grimes, Jerry Houser, Oliver Conant; ***D:*** Robert Mulligan; ***W:*** Herman Raucher; ***C:*** Robert L. Surtees; ***M:*** Michel Legrand; ***Nar:*** Robert Mulligan. Oscars '71: Orig. Dramatic Score.

The Summer of Miss Forbes *El Verano de la Senora Forbes* **1988** A governess rules over two young boys with an iron hand by day and cavorts nude and drunk by night. The boys fantasize about her murder, but fate has different plans. In Spanish with English subtitles. **85m/C VHS.** *SP* Hanna Schygulla, Alexis Castanares, Victor Cesar Villalobos, Guadalupe Sandoval, Fernando Balzaretti, Yuriria Munguia; ***D:*** Jaime Humberto Hermosillo.

The Summer of My German Soldier **1978** A young Jewish girl befriends an escaped German prisoner of war in a small town in Georgia during WWII. Occasionally sentimental but more often genuinely moving TV drama. Rolle won a deserved Emmy as the housekeeper. Adapted from Bette Green's novel. **98m/C VHS.** Kristy McNichol, Esther Rolle, Bruce Davison; ***D:*** Michael Tuchner. **TV**

Summer of Sam ½ **1999 (R)** Spike Lee's take on the summer of 1977, when serial killer Son of Sam traumatized New York City. The plot does not center on the actual crimes of David Berkowitz, but on the repercussions they had in the neighborhoods of New York. Leguizamo and Sorvino play a married Bronx couple who grow to question pal Ritchie (Brody), a newly converted punk rocker who leads a double life as a gay dancer. As the killer's attacks continue, fear begins to rise along with the temperature, and the neighborhood begins to tear itself apart. Lee's film drew highly publicized protests from the families of Berkowitz's victims. **142m/C VHS, DVD.** Adrien Brody, John Leguizamo, Spike Lee, Mira Sorvino, Jennifer Esposito, Michael Badalucco, Anthony LaPaglia, Patti LuPone, Ben Gazzara, Bebe Neuwirth, John Savage, Roger Guenveur Smith, Michael Rispoli; ***D:*** Spike Lee; ***W:*** Spike Lee; ***C:*** Ellen Kuras; ***M:*** Terence Blanchard.

Summer of the Monkeys ½ **1998 (G)** Fairly sappy family pic set in rural America. John Lee (Ontkean) is a hard-working farmer with a caring wife, Sara (Hope), precocious son Jay Berry (Sevier), and a crippled daughter, Daisy (Stuart). Gramps (Brimley) runs the local general store and Jay works there, hoping to save money to buy Daisy a pony. When a nearby train wreck leads to the escape of a foursome of circus monkeys, Jay aims to find them first and get the reward for their return. **101m/C VHS.** *CA* Michael Ontkean, Leslie Hope, Corey Sevier, Katie Stuart, Wilford Brimley, Don Francks, B.J. McLellan; ***D:*** Michael Anderson Sr.; ***W:*** Greg Taylor, Jim Strain; ***C:*** Michael Storey; ***M:*** George Blondheim.

A Summer Place **1959** Melodrama about summer liaisons amid the young and middle-aged rich on an island off the coast of Maine. Too slick; romantic drama is little more than skin-deep, and dialogue is excruciating. Donahue's first starring role. Based on the novel by Sloan Wilson. Featuring "Theme from a Summer Place," which was a number-one hit in 1959. **130m/C VHS.** Troy Donahue, Richard Egan, Sandra Dee, Dorothy McGuire, Arthur Kennedy, Constance Ford, Beulah Bondi; ***D:*** Delmer Daves; ***C:*** Harry Stradling Sr.; ***M:*** Max Steiner.

Summer Rental **1985 (PG)** That John Candy just can't win, can he? Here, as a hopeless, harried air traffic controller, he tries to have a few days to relax in sunny Florida. Enter mean rich guy Crenna. Candy can add something hefty to the limpest of plots, and does so here. Watch the first hour for yuks, then rewind. **87m/C VHS, DVD, 8mm, Wide.** John Candy, Rip Torn, Richard Crenna, Karen Austin, Kerri Green, John Larroquette, Pierrino Mascarino; ***D:*** Carl Reiner; ***W:*** Mark Reisman, Jeremy Stevens; ***C:*** Ric Waite; ***M:*** Alan Silvestri.

Summer School **1977 (R)** A teenaged boy's girlfriend will stop at nothing to prevent him from going out with the pretty new girl in town. **80m/C VHS.** John McLaughlin, Steve Rose, Phoebe Schmidt.

Summer School ½ **1987 (PG-13)** A high-school teacher's vacation plans are ruined when he gets stuck teaching remedial English in summer school. It seems all these students are interested in is re-enacting scenes from "The Texas Chainsaw Massacre." Actually, one of the better films of this genre. **98m/C VHS.** Mark Harmon, Kirstie Alley, Nels Van Patten, Courtney Thorne-Smith, Lucy Lee Flippin, Shawnee Smith, Robin Thomas, Dean Cameron; ***D:*** Carl Reiner; ***W:*** Jeff Franklin; ***M:*** Danny Elfman.

Summer School Teachers woof! **1975 (R)** Three sultry femmes bounce about Los Angeles high school and make the collective student body happy. Typical Corman doings; sequel to "The Students Teachers." **87m/C VHS.** Candice Rialson, Pat Anderson, Rhonda Leigh Hopkins, Christopher Wales; ***D:*** Barbara Peeters.

Summer Snow *Nuiyan, Seisap; Woman, Forty* **1994** Broad comedy mixed (not always successfully) with family drama. May (Siao) is forced to take in her father-in-law Sun (Chiao) after his wife dies. The old man immediately causes chaos with his habit of wandering off and bizarre behavior, which is finally diagnosed as being Alzheimer's disease. Working mother May tries to find a practical way to deal with her dilemmas but the strains are beginning to crack the family apart. Cantonese with subtitles. **106m/C VHS.** *HK* Josephine Siao, Roy Chiao, Law Karying, Allen Ting; ***D:*** Ann Hui; ***W:*** Chan Man-keung; ***C:*** Mark Lee Ping-Bin; ***M:*** Yoshihide Otomo. Berlin Intl. Film Fest. '94: Actress (Siao).

Summer Solstice ½ **1981** Fonda and Loy are splendid as a couple married half a century who revisit the beach where they first met. Fonda especially shines, as a crusty old artist. Yes, it is an awful lot like "On Golden Pond." **75m/C VHS.** Henry Fonda, Myrna Loy, Lindsay Crouse, Stephen Collins; ***D:*** Ralph Rosenblum. **TV**

Summer Stock *If You Feel Like Singing* **1950** Garland plays farm owner Jane Falbury whose sister, Abigail (DeHaven) arrives with a summer stock troupe, led by Joe Ross (Kelly), to rehearse a show in the family barn. Jane agrees, if the troupe will help her with the farm's harvest. When Abigail decamps for New York, leaving the leading lady role open, guess who steps into the breach. Slim plot papered over with many fun song-and-dance numbers. Also features Garland's first MGM short, "Every Sunday," made in 1936 with Deanna Durbin. ♫Friendly Star; Mem'ry Island; Dig-Dig-Dig For Your Dinner; If You Feel Like Singing, Sing; Howdy Neighbor; Blue Jean Polka; Portland Fancy; You, Wonderful You; Get Happy. **109m/C VHS.** Judy Garland, Gene Kelly, Gloria De Haven, Carleton Carpenter, Eddie Bracken, Phil Silvers, Hans Conried, Marjorie Main, Ray Collins; ***D:*** Charles Walters; ***W:*** George Wells, Sy Gomberg.

A Summer Story **1988 (PG-13)** Superbly acted, typically British period drama about beautiful farm girl Stubbs and city lawyer Wilby, who fall in love. But can they overcome difference of social class? From the story "The Apple Tree" by John Galsworthy. **97m/C VHS.** *GB* James Wilby, Imogen Stubbs, Susannah York, Sophie Ward, Kenneth Colley, Jerome Flynn; ***D:*** Piers Haggard; ***W:*** Penelope Mortimer; ***M:*** Georges Delerue.

A Summer to Remember *Seryozha* **1961** A five-year-old boy spends a summer with his stepfather on a Soviet collective farm. The two become deeply attached. Scenes of collective life will be of more interest to Westerners than the near-sentimental story. Star Bondarchuk later directed the epic, award-winning "War and Peace." **80m/B VHS, DVD.** *RU* Borya Barkhazov, Sergei Bondarchuk, Irana Skobtseva.

A Summer to Remember ½ **1984 (PG)** A deaf boy (played by Gerlis, himself deaf since birth) develops a friendship with an orangutan through sign language. Bad guys abduct the friendly ape—but all is right in the end. Nice, innocuous family viewing. Based on a story by Scott Swanton and Robert Lloyd Lewis. **93m/C VHS, DVD.** Tess Harper, James Farentino, Burt Young, Louise Fletcher, Sean Gerlis, Bridgette Andersen; ***D:*** Robert Lewis; ***C:*** Stephen W. Gray; ***M:*** Charles Fox. **TV**

Summer Vacation: 1999 *1999—Nen No Natsu Yasumi* **1988** Four boys are left behind at boarding school during their summer vacation. They experience all the early pangs of adolescence from love to jealousy. Their summer is then disturbed by the arrival of another boy who appears to be the reincarnation of a dead friend. Romantic look at youth caught between innocence and awareness. In Japanese with English subtitles. **90m/C VHS.** *JP* Eri Miyagima, Miyuki Nakano, Tomoko Otakra, Rie Mizuhara; ***D:*** Shusuke (Shu) Kaneko.

Summer Wishes, Winter Dreams **1973 (PG)** Woodward and Balsam are a materially prosperous middle-aged couple with little but tedium in their lives—a tedium accurately replicated, in what feels like real life, in this slow, dull film. The two leads and Sidney—in her first screen role in 17 years—are all excellent, but the story of regret and present unhappiness wears the viewer down. **95m/C VHS.** Joanne Woodward, Martin Balsam, Sylvia Sidney, Dori Brenner, Ron Richards; ***D:*** Gilbert Cates; ***W:*** Stewart Stern. British Acad. '74: Actress (Woodward); Natl. Bd. of Review '73: Support. Actress (Sidney); N.Y. Film Critics '73: Actress (Woodward).

Summerdog **1978 (G)** Harmless family tale about vacationers who rescue a cheerful, lovable mutt named Hobo. And a good thing they found him: He saves them from many perils. Thanks, Hobo! **90m/C VHS.** James Congdon, Elizabeth Eisenman, Oliver Zabriskie, Tavia Zabriskie; ***D:*** John Clayton.

Summer's Children **1984** Man who suffers from amnesia as a result of a car crash becomes the target of a mysterious killer. Forget about it. **90m/C VHS.** Tom Haoff, Paully Jardine, Kate Lynch.

Summer's End ½ **1999** In 1983, physician William Blakely (Jones) decides to retire to the small Georgia town where he grew up. But the lakeside community is lilywhite and hostile (Blakely's family was originally driven out by racial violence). However, fatherless 12-year-old Jamie (LeDoux) and the doc become friends, despite pressures on the boy to toe the racist line. **101m/C VHS, DVD.** James Earl Jones, Wendy Crewson, Brendan Fletcher, Jake LeDoux; ***D:*** Helen Shaver. **CABLE**

A Summer's Tale ½ *Conte d'Ete* **1996** Talky and slow-moving vacation comedy is the third in Rohmer's "Tales of the Four Seasons" series. Young Gaspard (Poupaud) is spending a month in a borrowed flat in the seaside resort of Dinard. He becomes friendly with waitress Margot (Langlet) while he waits for his girlfriend Lena (Nolin) to join him, but is also introduced to Margot's friend Solene (Simon), who's interested in a quick fling with Gaspard. When all three women agree to accompany him on a sightseeing trip, he's got more a than a little maneuvering to do. French with subtitles. **133m/C VHS, DVD.** *FR* Melvil Poupaud, Amanda Langlet, Aurelia Nolin, Gwenaelle Simon; ***D:*** Eric Rohmer; ***W:*** Eric Rohmer; ***C:*** Diane Baratier; ***M:*** Sebastien Erms, Philippe Eidel.

Summertime ½ *Summer Madness* **1955** Spinster Hepburn vacations in Venice and falls in love with Brazzi. She is hurt when inadvertently she learns he is married, but her life has been so bleak she is not about to end her one great romance. Moving, funny, richly photographed in a beautiful Old World city. From Arthur Laurents' play "The Time of the Cuckoo." **98m/C VHS, DVD.** Katharine Hepburn, Rossano Brazzi, Isa Miranda, Darren McGavin, Mari Aldon, MacDonald Parke, Jeremy Spenser; ***D:*** David Lean; ***W:*** David Lean, H.E. Bates; ***C:*** Jack Hildyard; ***M:*** Alessandro Cicognini. N.Y. Film Critics '55: Director (Lean).

Summertree **1971 (PG)** Douglas stars as a young musician in the 1960s trying to avoid the draft and the wrath of his parents. Contrived and heavy-handed. Produced by Douglas pere, Kirk. Adapted from the play by Ron Cower. **88m/C VHS.** Michael Douglas, Jack Warden, Brenda Vaccaro, Barbara Bel Geddes, Kirk Calloway, Bill Vint; ***D:*** Anthony Newley; ***M:*** David Shire.

The Sun Comes Up 🦴🦴 **1949** MacDonald, in her last screen appearance, plays a bitter widow whose life is changed by an orphan's love for a collie. Songbird MacDonald manages to sing a number of songs, some of them backed by a chorus of "orphans." Based on short stories by Marjorie Kinnan Rawlings. **93m/C VHS.** Jeanette MacDonald, Lloyd Nolan, Claude Jarman Jr., Lewis Stone, Dwayne Hickman; ***D:*** Richard Thorpe; ***W:*** William Ludwig; ***M:*** Andre Previn.

Sun Ra & His Intergalactic Solar Arkestra: Space Is the Place 🦴🦴 **1974** Space age flick starring most appropriately Sun Ra, space-age prophet/jazz musician. Sun Ra returns from a space odyssey and embarks on saving black youth from the world's oppressive control by bringing them back into space with him. The shaman's philosophy on film. ♫Watusi; Outer Spaceways Inc.; The Satellites are Spinning. **63m/C VHS.** ***D:*** John Coney; ***W:*** Joshua Smith.

The Sun Shines Bright 🦴🦴 **1953** Heavily stereotyped, contrived tale of a Southern judge with a heart of gold who does so many good deeds (defending a black man accused of rape; helping a desperate prostitute) that he jeopardizes his re-election. Set during Reconstruction. An unfortunate remake of Ford's own 1934 "Judge Priest," starring Will Rogers. **92m/B VHS.** Charles Winninger, Arleen Whelan, John Russell, Stepin Fetchit, Milburn Stone, Russell Simpson; ***D:*** John Ford; ***C:*** Archie Stout.

Sun Valley Serenade 🦴🦴½ **1941** Wartime musical fluff about a band that adopts a Norwegian refugee waif as a publicity stunt. She turns out to be a full-grown man-chaser who stirs up things at a ski resort. Fun, but it ends abruptly—because, they say, Henie fell during the huge skating finale, and Darryl Zanuck wouldn't greenlight a reshoot. One of only two feature appearances by Glenn Miller and his Orchestra (the other was "Orchestra Wives"), on video with a soundtrack restored from original dual-track recordings. ♫Chattanooga Choo Choo; I Know Why and So Do You; It Happened In Sun Valley; The Kiss Polka; In the Mood. **86m/C VHS.** Sonja Henie, John Payne, Glenn Miller, Milton Berle, Lynn Bari, Joan Davis, Dorothy Dandridge; ***D:*** H. Bruce Humberstone.

Sunburn 🦴½ **1979 (PG)** Insurance investigator Grodin hires model Fawcett to pretend to be his wife to get the scoop on a suicide/murder case of a rich guy in Acapulco. Made-for-TV drivel. **110m/C VHS.** Farrah Fawcett, Charles Grodin, Joan Collins, Art Carney, William Daniels; ***D:*** Richard Sarafian; ***W:*** James Booth. **TV**

Sunchaser 🦴½ **1996 (R)** Mishmash of medicine and mysticism focuses on yuppie UCLA oncologist Dr. Michael Reynolds (Harrelson) who's kidnapped by 16-year-old patient, Brandon "Blue" Monroe (Seda). Blue is a half-Navajo gang-banger whose cancer is inoperable and he needs the doc to drive him to a reservation in Arizona where he feels a medicine man and the waters of a supposedly magical lake can cure him. Reynolds naturally discovers some humanity on the trip and decides to help his truculent patient. Leads give sincere performances but film is half-baked at best. **123m/C VHS.** Woody Harrelson, Jon Seda, Anne Bancroft, Alexandra Tydings, Matt Mulhern, Talisa Soto, Lawrence Pressman, Michael O'Neill, Harry Carey Jr.; ***D:*** Michael Cimino; ***W:*** Charles Leavitt; ***C:*** Doug Milsome; ***M:*** Maurice Jarre.

Sundance and the Kid 🦴🦴 **1976 (PG)** Two brothers try to collect an inheritance against all odds. Originally known as "Sundance Cassidy and Butch the Kid." **84m/C VHS.** John Wade, Karen Blake; ***D:*** Arthur Pitt.

Sunday 🦴🦴 **1996** Basically a two-character study of mistaken identity among lonely, middleaged people. On a winter's Sunday morning in Queens, depressed Oliver (Suchet) is greeted by failing British actress Madeleine (Harrow), who mistakes him for a director she once met. She invites him to lunch and Oliver, who's actually a homeless former accountant, struggles to maintain the charade. The unstable Madeleine's bitter when she discovers his deception but is also unwillingly to let the connection between them die. **93m/C VHS.** David Suchet, Lisa Harrow, Larry Pine, Jared Harris, Joe Grifasi; ***D:*** Jonathan Nossiter; ***W:*** Jonathan Nossiter, James Lasdun; ***C:*** Michael Barrow, John Foster; ***M:*** Jonathan Nossiter. Sundance '97: Screenplay, Grand Jury Prize.

Sunday, Bloody Sunday 🦴🦴🦴 **1971 (R)** Adult drama centers around the intertwined love affairs of the homosexual Finch, the heterosexual Jackson, and self-centered bisexual artist Head, desired by both. Fully drawn characters brought to life by excellent acting make this difficult story well worth watching—though Head's central character is sadly rather dull. Day-Lewis makes his first (brief) screen appearance as a car vandalizing teenager. Powerful, sincere, and sensitive. **110m/C VHS, Wide.** *GB GB* Glenda Jackson, Peter Finch, Murray Head, Daniel Day-Lewis; ***D:*** John Schlesinger. British Acad. '71: Actor (Finch), Actress (Jackson), Director (Schlesinger), Film; Golden Globes '72: Foreign Film; N.Y. Film Critics '71: Screenplay; Natl. Soc. Film Critics '71: Actor (Finch), Screenplay; Writers Guild '71: Orig. Screenplay.

Sunday Daughters 🦴🦴🦴 **1980** A teenage girl kept in a detention home constantly tries to escape and find some kind of familial love. Stronge performances mix with keen direction. In Hungarian with English subtitles. **100m/C VHS.** *HU* Julianna Nyako; ***D:*** Janosz Rozsa.

A Sunday in the Country 🦴🦴🦴½ *Un Dimanche a la Campagne* **1984 (G)** A lush, distinctively French affirmation of nature and family life. This character study with a minimal plot takes place during a single summer day in 1910 France. An elderly impressionist painter-patriarch is visited at his country home by his family. Highly acclaimed, though the pace may be too slow for some. Beautiful location photography. In French with English subtitles. **94m/C VHS, DVD.** *FR* Louis Ducreux, Sabine Azema, Michel Aumont; ***D:*** Bertrand Tavernier; ***W:*** Bertrand Tavernier, Colo Tavernier O'Hagan; ***C:*** Bruno de Keyzer. Cannes '84: Director (Tavernier); Cesar '85: Actress (Azema), Cinematog., Writing; Natl. Bd. of Review '84: Support. Actress (Azema); N.Y. Film Critics '84: Foreign Film.

Sunday in the Park with George 🦴🦴🦴 **1986** Taped theatrical performance of the Tony, Grammy, and Pulitzer Prize-winning musical play, which is based upon impressionist Georges Seurat's painting "A Sunday Afternoon on the Island of Grande Jatte." Features a celebrated music score by Sondheim. **120m/C VHS, DVD.** Mandy Patinkin, Bernadette Peters, Barbara Byrne, Charles Kimbrough; ***D:*** James Lapine; ***M:*** Stephen Sondheim.

Sunday Too Far Away 🦴🦴🦴 **1974** The rivalries between Australian sheep shearers and graziers leads to an ugly strike at a remote outback area in 1955. An uncomplicated story and a joy to watch. **100m/C VHS.** *AU* Jack Thompson; ***D:*** Ken Hannam. Australian Film Inst. '74: Actor (Thompson), Film.

Sundays & Cybele 🦴🦴🦴½ *Les Dimanches de Ville d'Arvay; Cybele* **1962** A ragged war veteran and an orphaned girl develop a strong emotional relationship, which is frowned upon by the townspeople. Warm and touching. In French with English subtitles. Also available in a letterboxed edition. **110m/B VHS.** *FR* Hardy Kruger, Nicole Courcel; ***D:*** Serge Bourguignon; ***M:*** Maurice Jarre. Oscars '62: Foreign Film.

Sunday's Children 🦴🦴🦴½ **1994** Lyrical exploration of childhood continues trilogy that includes "Fanny and Alexander" and "Best Intentions." Wistful childhood memoir takes up the story of Ingmar Bergman's family eight years after the director was born. Many of the same familial issues surface, but story soon narrows its focus to the relationship between little Ingmar, whom everyone calls Pu, and his stern father Henrik. Deeply emotional and intense, film represents the steps toward forgiveness that the elder Bergman is finally able to take regarding the painful relationship he had with his own father. Father-son theme made more poignant with Ingmar's son Daniel making his feature debut as director. **118m/C VHS.** *SW* Thommy Berggren, Lena Endre, Henrik Linnros, Jacob Leygraf, Maria Bolme, Borje Ahlstedt, Per Myrberg; ***D:*** Daniel Bergman; ***W:*** Ingmar Bergman.

Sundown 🦴🦴½ **1941** In Africa at the beginning of WWII, a local girl aids the British against a German plot to run guns to the natives and start a rebellion. Engaging performances and efficient direction keep it above the usual cliches. Also available in a colorized version. **91m/B VHS, DVD.** Gene Tierney, Bruce Cabot, George Sanders, Harry Carey Sr., Cedric Hardwicke, Joseph Calleia, Dorothy Dandridge, Reginald Gardiner; ***D:*** Henry Hathaway; ***C:*** Charles B(ryant) Lang Jr.; ***M:*** Miklos Rozsa.

Sundown 🦴½ **1991 (R)** An ambitious shot at a vampire western fails because it drains almost all vampire lore and winds up resembling a standard oater. Carradine plays a reformed vampire king (guess who) running a desert clinic that weans bloodsuckers away from preying on humans. But undead renegades attack using sixguns and wooden bullets. The climax may outrage horror purists. **104m/C VHS.** David Carradine, Bruce Campbell, Deborah Foreman, Maxwell Caulfield, Morgan Brittany; ***D:*** Anthony Hickox.

Sundown Fury 🦴 **1942** Young cowboy fights against a group of bandits to hold a telegraph office. **56m/B VHS.** Donald (Don "Red") Barry.

Sundown Kid 🦴½ **1943** A Pinkerton agent goes undercover to break up a counterfeiting operation. Routine western. **55m/B VHS.** Donald (Don "Red") Barry.

Sundown Riders 🦴 **1948** Cowhands are victimized by noose-happy outlaws. Filmed in just over a week on a $30,000 budget and originally shot on 16mm to make it accessible to hospitals and schools with basic viewing equipment. The lesson here: it takes time and money to make a good western. **56m/B VHS.** Russell Wade, Andy Clyde, Jay Kirby; ***D:*** Lambert Hillyer.

Sundown Saunders 🦴 **1936** A standard oater about a cowboy whose prize for winning a horse race is a ranch. Trouble is, an outlaw wants the homestead as well. **64m/B VHS.** Bob Steele; ***D:*** Robert North Bradbury.

The Sundowners 🦴🦴🦴½ **1960** Slow, beautiful, and often moving epic drama about a family of Irish sheepherders in Australia during the 1920s who must continually uproot themselves and migrate. They struggle to save enough money to buy their own farm and wind up training a horse they hope will be a money-winner in racing. Well-acted by all, with Johns and Ustinov providing some humorous moments. Adapted from the novel by Jon Cleary. Filmed in Australia and London studios. **133m/C VHS.** Deborah Kerr, Robert Mitchum, Peter Ustinov, Glynis Johns, Dina Merrill, Chips Rafferty, Michael Anderson Jr., Lola Brooks, Wylie Watson; ***D:*** Fred Zinnemann; ***C:*** Jack Hildyard; ***M:*** Dimitri Tiomkin. Natl. Bd. of Review '60: Actor (Mitchum); N.Y. Film Critics '60: Actress (Kerr).

Sunny 🦴🦴 **1941** Another glossed-over, love-conquers-all musical with Neagle as a circus star who falls for a wealthy car maker's son. Dad and crew disapprove, putting a damper on the romance. In spite of the weak storyline and flat direction, Kerns' music and Bolger's dancing make it enjoyable. ♫Who?; D'ya Love Me?; Sunny; Two Little Bluebirds. **98m/B VHS.** Anna Neagle, Ray Bolger, John Carroll, Edward Everett Horton, Frieda Inescort, Helen Westley, Benny Rubin, Richard Lane, Martha Tilton; ***D:*** Herbert Wilcox.

Sunny Side Up 🦴🦴½ **1928** As stress of pickle factory work takes toll on woman's friend, she makes heroic effort to help her to the country to recover. **66m/B VHS.** Vera Reynolds, ZaSu Pitts, Edmund Burns, Sally Rand; ***D:*** Donald Crisp.

Sunny Skies 🦴 **1930** Bargain-basement retread has Lease donating a pint of blood. ♫Sunny Days; I Must Have You; Wanna Find a Boy; Must Be Love. **75m/B VHS.** Benny Rubin, Marceline Day, Rex Lease, Marjorie "Babe" Kane, Wesley Barry; ***D:*** Norman Taurog.

Sunnyside woof! **1979 (R)** Travolta plays a street kid trying to bring an end to the local gang warfare so he can move to Manhattan. Features a host of pop tunes in an attempt to ride the coattails of brother John's successful "Saturday Night Fever." Laughably bad. **100m/C VHS.** Joey Travolta, John Lansing, Stacey Pickren, Andrew Rubin, Michael Tucci, Talia Balsam, Joan Darling; ***D:*** Timothy Galfas.

Sunrise 🦴🦴🦴🦴 *Sunrise—A Song of Two Humans* **1927** Magnificent silent story of a simple country boy who, prodded by an alluring city woman, tries to murder his wife. Production values wear their age well. Gaynor won an Oscar for her stunning performance. Remade in Germany as "The Journey to Tilsit." Based on a story by Hermann Suderman. **110m/B VHS.** George O'Brien, Janet Gaynor, Bodil Rosing, Margaret Livingston, J. Farrell MacDonald, Carl Mayer; ***D:*** F.W. Murnau; ***C:*** Charles Rosher, Karl Struss. Oscars '28: Actress (Gaynor), Cinematog., Natl. Film Reg. '89.

Sunrise at Campobello 🦴🦴🦴 **1960** A successful adaptation of the Tony award-winning play by Schary, who wrote the screenplay and also produced the film. In 1921, the Roosevelt family is vacationing at Campbello when Franklin (Bellamy, re-creating his stage role) becomes ill with what turns out to be polio. His formidable mother Sara (Shoemaker) wants her paralyzed so to give up his political aspirations but politico pal Louis Howe (Cronyn) insists Franklin get on with living, aided by the strength of wife Eleanor (an excellent performance by Garson). **143m/C VHS.** Ralph Bellamy, Greer Garson, Hume Cronyn, Jean Hagen, Jack Perrin, Lyle Talbot, Ann Shoemaker, Tim Considine, Zena Bethune, Pat Close; ***D:*** Vincent J. Donehue; ***W:*** Dore Schary; ***C:*** Russell Harlan; ***M:*** Franz Waxman. Golden Globes '61: Actress—Drama (Garson); Natl. Bd. of Review '60: Actress (Garson).

Sunrise Trail 🦴🦴½ **1931** Lots of action with Steele working undercover for the sheriff, trying to stop a rustler. He also finds the time to fall for barmaid Mehaffey. **65m/B VHS.** Bob Steele, Blanche Mehaffey, Jack Clifford, Eddie Dunn; ***D:*** John P. McCarthy.

The Sun's Burial 🦴🦴🦴 **1960** Oshima's stylized and violent drama depicts life in Osaka's worst slum—a teeming underworld populated by teen gangs, prostitutes, and criminals. All want control of the area's most profitable business, an illegal blood-selling operation. In Japanese with English subtitles. **87m/C VHS.** *JP* Kayoko Honoo, Koji Nakahara, Masahiko Tsugawa, Fumio Watanabe; ***D:*** Nagisa Oshima.

Sunset 🦴🦴 **1988 (R)** Edwards wanders the range in this soft-centered farce about a couple of Western legends out to solve a mystery. On the backlots of Hollywood, silent screen star Tom Mix (Willis) meets aging marshal Wyatt Earp (Garner) and participates in a time-warp western circa 1927. They encounter a series of misadventures while trying to finger a murderer. Garner ambles enjoyably, lifting him a level above the rest of the cast. **101m/C VHS, DVD.** Bruce Willis, James Garner, Mariel Hemingway, Darren McGavin, Jennifer Edwards, Malcolm McDowell, Kathleen Quinlan, M. Emmet Walsh, Patricia Hodge, Richard Bradford, Joe Dallesandro, Dermot Mulroney; ***D:*** Blake Edwards; ***W:*** Blake Edwards, Rod Amateau; ***C:*** Anthony B. Richmond; ***M:*** Henry Mancini. Golden Raspberries '88: Worst Director (Edwards).

Sunset Boulevard 🦴🦴🦴½ **1950** Famed tale of Norma Desmond (Swanson), aging silent film queen, who refuses to accept that stardom has ended for her and hires young down-on-his-luck screenwriter Joe Gillis (Holden) to help engineer her movie comeback. The screenwriter, who becomes the actress' kept man, assumes he can manipulate her, but finds out otherwise. Reality was almost too close for comfort, as Swanson, von Stroheim (as her major domo Max), and others very nearly play themselves. A darkly humorous look at the legacy and loss of fame with witty dialog, stellar performances, and some now-classic scenes. Based on the story "A Can of Beans" by Brackett and Wilder. **100m/B VHS.** Gloria Swanson, William Holden, Erich von Stroheim, Nancy Olson, Buster Keaton, Jack Webb, Cecil B. DeMille, Fred Clark; ***D:*** Billy Wilder; ***W:*** Billy Wilder, Charles Brackett, D.M. Marshman Jr.; ***C:*** John Seitz; ***M:*** Franz Waxman. Oscars '50: Art Dir./Set Dec., B&W, Story & Screenplay, Orig. Dramatic Score; AFI '98: Top 100; Golden Globes '51: Actress—Drama (Swanson), Director (Wilder), Film—Drama, Score, Natl. Film Reg. '89.

Sunset Grill 🦴🦴 **1992 (R)** While investigating his wife's murder, detective Ryder Hart (Weller) discovers a pattern of grisly killings. Sexy singer Loren Duquesne (Singer) leads him south of the border to her boss and his bloody money-making scheme. Unrated version also available. **103m/C VHS.** Peter Weller, Lori Singer, Alexandra Paul, John Rhys-Davies, Michael Anderson Jr., Stacy Keach; ***D:*** Kevin Connor.

Sunset Heat 🦴🦴 *Midnight Heat* **1992 (R)** Former drug dealer (Pare) returns to his home in Los Angeles with a legit job as a photojournalist. He stays with an old friend who turns out to be involved with the obsessed drug czar that Pare used to work for. Trouble comes along when the drug lord is robbed and blames Pare for the crime. Action-packed, with some good plot twists. An unrated version contains two additional minutes of footage. **94m/C VHS.** Michael Pare, Dennis Hopper, Adam Ant, Daphne Ashbrook, Charlie Schlatter; ***D:*** John Nicolella.

Sunset in El Dorado 🦴½ **1945** Roy and Dale thwart a villainous scheme to defraud farmers of their land. **56m/B VHS.** Roy Rogers, Dale Evans, George "Gabby" Hayes, Hardie Albright, Roy Barcroft, Tom London, Edmund Cobb; ***D:*** Frank McDonald.

Sunset in the West 🦴🦴 **1950** Deputy sheriff Rogers figures out that local gunrunners are using the railroad to help them move their merchandise and he sets out to stop them. **67m/C VHS.** Roy Rogers, Gordon Jones, Penny Edwards, Estelita Rodriguez; ***D:*** William Witney; ***W:*** Gerald Geraghty; ***C:*** Jack Marta.

Sunset Limousine 🦴🦴½ **1983** An out-of-work stand-up comic gets thrown out by his girlfriend, then takes a job as a chauffeur. Standard vehicle with occasional bursts of speed. **92m/C VHS.** Charles Lane, John Ritter, Martin Short, Susan Dey, Paul Reiser, Audrie Neehan, Lainie Kazan; ***D:*** Terry Hughes.

Sunset on the Desert 🦴½ **1942** Rogers gets to wear a white hat and a black hat as both the leader of a gang of outlaws and the hero who brings them to justice. A poor man's Western omelette. **53m/B VHS.** Roy Rogers, George "Gabby" Hayes, Lynne Carver, Frank M. Thomas Sr., Bob Nolan, Beryl Wallace, Glenn Strange, Douglas Fowley, Roy Barcroft, Pat Brady; ***D:*** Joseph Kane.

Sunset Park 🦴🦴 **1996 (R)** Brooklyn phys ed teacher Phyllis Saroka (Perlman) becomes the coach of a high school basketball team that, despite her total lack of knowledge about the game, makes it to the city championships. The cast's excellent performances hold interest, even though the predictable storyline gives away all of its moves before it gets near the hoop. Starr (of the rap group Onyx) is outstanding as the most talented (and most troubled) member of the team. **100m/C VHS.** Rhea Perlman, Carol Kane, Terrence DaShon Howard, Camille Saviola, Fredro Starr, James Harris, Antwon Tanner, Shawn Michael Howard, De'Aundre Bonds; ***D:*** Steve Gomer; ***W:*** Seth Zvi Rosenfeld, Kathleen McGhee-Anderson; ***C:*** Robbie Greenberg; ***M:*** Kay Gee, Miles Goodman.

Sunset Range 🦴½ **1935** The "World's All-Around Champion Cowboy" of 1912 stars in this chaps-slappin', bitchompin', dust-raisin' saga of the plains. **59m/B VHS.** Hoot Gibson.

Sunset Serenade 🦴🦴 **1942** Roy and Gabby outwit murderous duo who plan to eliminate the new heir to a ranch. **60m/B VHS.** Roy Rogers, George "Gabby" Hayes, Helen Parrish; ***D:*** Joseph Kane.

Sunset Strip 🦴 **1985** A photographer investigates a friend's murder, and enters the seamy world of drugs and rock and roll in L.A. **83m/C VHS.** Tom Elpin, Cheri Cameron Newell, John Mayall.

Sunset Strip woof! **1991 (R)** A young dancer finds a job in a strip club and competes against the other women there to find the man of her dreams. The women take their jobs very seriously—even attending ballet classes to improve their performances. However, the viewer probably won't take this movie very seriously since it is just another excuse to show women in as little clothing as possible. **95m/C VHS.** Jeff Conaway, Michelle Foreman, Shelley Michelle; ***D:*** Paul G. Volk; ***M:*** John Gonzalez.

Sunset Trail 🦴 **1932** Routine Maynard sagebrush saga with the hero protecting a woman rancher from outlaws. **60m/B VHS.** Ken Maynard.

Sunshine 🦴🦴 **1999 (R)** Sprawling look at four generations of an assimilated Hungarian-Jewish family covers a lot of time at the expense of cohesiveness and character. Title refers to the health tonic that makes the family fortune and is a pun on the family's original name, Sonnenschein. Fiennes turns up in three roles as the family prospers in Budapest by changing their name to avoid the anti-Semitic society—eventually converting to Catholicism. It will not protect them, however, from the Nazi holocaust and the turbulent postwar period that leads to the Hungarian Revolution of 1956. **180m/C VHS, DVD, Wide.** *CA HU* Ralph Fiennes, Rosemary Harris, Rachel Weisz, Jennifer Ehle, Molly Parker, Deborah Kara Unger, James Frain, William Hurt, John Neville, Miriam Margolyes, Mark Strong; ***D:*** Istvan Szabo; ***W:*** Istvan Szabo, Israel Horovitz; ***C:*** Lajos Koltai; ***M:*** Maurice Jarre. Genie '99: Film.

The Sunshine Boys 🦴🦴🦴 **1975 (PG)** Two veteran vaudeville partners, who have shared a love-hate relationship for decades, reunite for a TV special. Adapted by Neil Simon from his play. Matthau was a replacement for Jack Benny, who died before the start of filming. Burns, for his first starring role since "Honolulu" in 1939, won an Oscar. **111m/C VHS.** George Burns, Walter Matthau, Richard Benjamin, Lee Meredith, F. Murray Abraham, Carol Arthur, Howard Hesseman; ***D:*** Herbert Ross; ***W:*** Neil Simon. Oscars '75: Support. Actor (Burns); Golden Globes '76: Actor—Mus./Comedy (Matthau), Film—Mus./Comedy, Support. Actor (Benjamin); Writers Guild '75: Adapt. Screenplay.

Sunshine Run 🦴½ *Black Rage* **1979 (PG)** Two escaped slaves and a young widow search for Spanish treasure in the Everglades. **102m/C VHS.** Chris Robinson, Ted Cassidy, David Legge, Phyllis Robinson; ***D:*** Chris Robinson.

Sunshine State **2002 (PG-13)** Sayles returns with a tale of developers invading a small Florida island as Falco and Bassett attempt to reconcile with their families. Not yet reviewed. **?m/C VHS, DVD.** Edie Falco, Angela Bassett, Timothy Hutton, James McDaniel, Mary Steenburgen, Marc Blucas; ***D:*** John Sayles; ***W:*** John Sayles.

Sunstroke 🦴🦴 **1992 (R)** Seymour plays a desperate mother searching for her kidnapped child through the Arizona desert. Framed for murder, she cannot contact the police but must track the kidnappers herself, until she meets a drifter with secrets of his own. **91m/C VHS.** Jane Seymour, Stephen Meadows, Steve Railsback, Ray Wise, Don Ameche; ***D:*** James Keach; ***W:*** Duane Poole.

The Super 🦴½ **1991 (R)** Pesci stars as a slumlord who faces a prison sentence thanks to his terminal neglect. The option given to him is to live in his own rat hole until he provides reasonable living conditions. This he does, and predictably learns a thing or two about his own greed and the people who suffer as a result of it. Pesci as always gives an animated performance but poor scripting laden with stereotypes and cliches successfully restricts effort. **86m/C VHS.** Joe Pesci, Vincent Gardenia, Madolyn Smith, Ruben Blades; ***D:*** Rod Daniel; ***C:*** Bruce Surtees.

Super Bitch 🦴½ *Mafia Junction* **1989** Nasty, cold, and uncaring woman uses men to keep up her expensive habits, then ruthlessly tosses them aside when she is done. She purposely entangles them in her drug trade and thinks nothing of their deaths. Proving once again that you get what you pay for. **90m/C VHS.** Stephanie Beacham, Patricia Hayes, Gareth Thomas; ***D:*** Massimo Dallamano.

Super Brother 🦴 **1990 (R)** The feared and respected leader of an oppressed people is imprisoned, much to everyone's regret. **90m/C VHS.** Woody Strode.

Super Force 🦴🦴 **1990** When astronaut Zach Stone (Olandt) returns from an assignment on Mars he finds his policeman brother has been murdered. He quits NASA and joins the force to get revenge, battling evil crime boss Tao Satori (Liddy). Stone also moonlights as a vigilante, complete with motorcycle and high-tech armoured suit. It's dumb but there's lots of action. **92m/C VHS.** Ken Olandt, G. Gordon Liddy, Larry B. Scott, Lisa Niemi, Marshall Teague; ***Cameos:*** Patrick Macnee; ***D:*** Richard Compton.

Super Fuzz 🦴½ *Supersnooper* **1981 (PG)** Rookie policeman develops super powers after being accidentally exposed to radiation. Somewhat ineptly, he uses his abilities to combat crime. Somewhat ineptly acted, written, and directed as well. **97m/C VHS.** Terence Hill, Joanne Dru, Ernest Borgnine; ***D:*** Sergio Corbucci; ***W:*** Sergio Corbucci.

Super Mario Bros. 🦴🦴½ **1993 (PG)** $42 million adventure fantasy based on the popular Nintendo video game. The brothers are in hot pursuit of the Princess Daisy who's been kidnapped by evil slime-bucket Hopper and taken to Dinohattan, a fungi-infested, garbage-strewn, rat-hole version of Manhattan. Hopper will amuse the adults, doing a gleeful reptilian version of Frank Booth from "Blue Velvet." Hoskins and Leguizamo act gamely in broad Nintendo style, enthusiastically partaking in high-tech wizardry and the many gags. Hits bullseye of target audience—elementary and junior high kids—with frenetic pace, gaudy special effects, oversized sets, and animatronic monsters. **104m/C VHS, Wide.** Bob Hoskins, John Leguizamo, Samantha Mathis, Fisher Stevens, Richard Edson, Dana Kaminsky, Dennis Hopper, Fiona Shaw, Mojo Nixon, Lance Henriksen; ***D:*** Rocky Morton, Annabel Jankel; ***W:*** Edward Solomon, Parker Bennett, Terry Runte; ***M:*** Alan Silvestri.

Super Seal 🦴 **1977 (G)** An injured seal pup disrupts a family's normal existence after the young daughter adopts him. **95m/C VHS.** Foster Brooks, Sterling Holloway, Sarah Brown; ***D:*** Michael Dugan.

Superargo 🦴🦴 *Il Re Dei Criminali; Superargo the Giant; The King of Criminals* **1967** A wrestler becomes a superhero with psychic powers and a bulletproof leotard, fighting a madman who is turning athletes into robots. Successful Italian hero who wouldn't last two minutes in the ring with Batman. **95m/C VHS.** *IT SP* Guy Madison, Ken Wood, Liz Barrett, Diana Loris; ***D:*** Paul Maxwell.

Superbug Super Agent 🦴½ **1976** Dodo, the wonder car puts the brakes on crime in this silly action-adventure tale. A lemon in a lot full of Herbies. **90m/C VHS.** Robert Mark, Heidi Hansen, George Goodman.

Superchick woof! **1971 (R)** Mild-mannered stewardess by day, sexy blonde with karate blackbelt by night. In addition to stopping a skyjacking she regularly makes love to men around the world. A superbomb that never gets off the ground. **94m/C VHS, DVD.** Joyce Jillson, Louis Quinn, Thomas Reardon, Uschi Digart; ***D:*** Ed Forsyth; ***W:*** Gary Crutcher; ***C:*** Paul Hipp; ***M:*** Allan Alper.

Supercop 🦴🦴½ *Police Story 3: Supercop* **1992 (R)** Super Hong Kong cop Kevin Chan (Chan) heads to China to assist the authorities in cracking an international drug ring. He's partnered with disciplined-but-beautiful Director Yang (Yeoh), who's also a terrific fighter, and the duo go undercover (as a married couple) to infiltrate the operation, which takes them to a Malaysian resort. Then Chan's girlfriend shows up, blowing their cover. Lots of action-packed fighting and wild chases. The 1996 American release loses about a half-hour of run time from the original. Dubbed from Cantonese. **93m/C VHS, DVD, Wide.** *HK* Jackie Chan, Michelle Yeoh, Maggie Cheung, Kenneth Tsang, Yuen Wah; ***D:*** Stanley Tong; ***W:*** Edward Tang, Fibe Ma, Lee Wai Yee; ***C:*** Ardy Lam; ***M:*** Joel McNeely.

Supercop 2 🦴🦴 *Police Story 3, Part 2* **1993 (R)** Rising star Inspector Jessica Yang (Yeoh) has her life disrupted when her boyfriend David is dishonorably discharged from the police force and leaves town. Several months later, Jessica is assigned to stop a crime ring that turns out to be headed by David. Chan has a brief cameo (in drag). **94m/C VHS, DVD.** *HK* Michelle Yeoh, Yukari Oshima, Eric Tsang, Rongguang Yu, Athene Chu, Siu-wong Fan, Jackie Chan, Emile Chau, Chu Yan; ***D:*** Stanley Tong; ***W:*** Stanley Tong, Mok Tang Han, Sui Lai Kang.

Superdad 🦴 **1973 (G)** A middle-aged parent is determined to bridge the generation gap by trying his hand at various teenage activities. Disney family fare that's about as complicated as a TV commercial. The adolescents are two-dimensional throwbacks to the fun-loving '50s. **94m/C VHS.** Bob Crane, Kurt Russell, Joe Flynn, Barbara Rush, Kathleen (Kathy) Cody, Dick Van Patten; ***D:*** Vincent McEveety; ***M:*** Buddy (Norman Dale) Baker.

Superfly 🦴🦴½ **1972 (R)** Controversial upon release, pioneering blaxploitation has Harlem dope dealer finding trouble with gangs and police as he attempts to establish retirement fund from one last deal. Excellent period tunes by Curtis Mayfield. Two lesser sequels. **98m/C VHS.** Ron O'Neal, Carl Lee, Sheila Frazier, Julius W. Harris, Charles McGregor; ***D:*** Gordon Parks Jr.; ***W:*** Phillip Fenty; ***C:*** James Signorelli; ***M:*** Curtis Mayfield.

Superfly T.N.T. woof! *Super Fly T.N.T* **1973 (R)** This confusing sequel to "Superfly" finds O'Neal returning as Youngblood Priest. The now ex-drug dealer has retired with his girlfriend to Rome where he is approached by an African gun-runner (Browne) for help in a revolution against an oppressive government. Cheap exploitation. **87m/C VHS.** Ron O'Neal, Roscoe Lee Browne, Sheila Frazier, Robert Guillaume, Jacques Sernas, William Berger; ***D:*** Ron O'Neal; ***W:*** Alex Haley.

Supergirl 🦴½ **1984 (PG)** Big-budget bomb in which Slater made her debut and nearly killed her career, with the help of Kryptonite. Unexciting and unsophisticated story of a young woman, cousin to Superman, with super powers, based on the comic book series. She's in pursuit of a magic paperweight, but an evil sorceress wants it too. Dunaway is a terrifically vile villainess with awesome black magic powers. Slater is great to look at, but is much better in almost any other film. **114m/C VHS, DVD, Wide.** *GB* Faye Dunaway, Helen Slater, Peter O'Toole, Mia Farrow, Brenda Vaccaro, Marc McClure, Simon Ward, Hart Bochner, Maureen Teefy, David Healy, Matt Frewer; ***D:*** Jeannot Szwarc; ***W:*** David Odell; ***C:*** Alan Hume; ***M:*** Jerry Goldsmith.

Supergrass 🦴🦴 **1987 (R)** A low-brow British farce about a nebbish who poses as a drug smuggler to impress his girlfriend, and is then mistaken for a real one by the authorities. **105m/C VHS.** *GB* Adrian Edmondson, Peter Richardson, Nigel Planer, Jennifer Saunders, Ronald Allen, Dawn French; ***D:*** Peter Richardson.

Superman: The Movie 🦴🦴🦴½ **1978 (PG)** The DC Comics legend comes alive in this wonderfully entertaining saga of Superman's life from a baby on the doomed planet Krypton (with Brando as Supe's dad) to Earth's own Man of Steel (a chiseled Reeve). Hackman and Beatty pair marvelously as super criminal Lex Luthor and his bumbling sidekick Otis, while Kidder is an intelligent Lois Lane. Award-winning special effects and a script that doesn't take itself too seriously make this great fun. Followed by three sequels. **152m/C VHS, DVD, Wide.** Christopher Reeve, Margot Kidder, Marlon Brando, Gene Hackman, Glenn Ford, Susannah York, Ned Beatty, Valerie Perrine, Jackie Cooper, Marc McClure, Trevor Howard, Sarah Douglas, Terence Stamp, Jack O'Halloran, Phyllis Thaxter; ***D:*** Richard Donner; ***W:*** Mario Puzo, Robert Benton, David Newman; ***C:*** Geoffrey Unsworth; ***M:*** John Williams. Oscars '78: Visual FX.

Superman 2 🦴🦴🦴 **1980 (PG)** The sequel to "the movie" about the Man of Steel. This time, he has his hands full with three super-powered villains from his home planet of Krypton. The romance between reporter Lois Lane and our superhero is made believable and the storyline has more pace to it than the original. A sequel that often equals the first film—leave it to Superman to pull off the impossible. **128m/C VHS, DVD, Wide.** Christopher Reeve, Margot Kidder, Gene Hackman, Ned Beatty, Jackie Cooper, Sarah Douglas, Jack O'Halloran, Susannah York, Marc McClure, Terence Stamp, Valerie Perrine, E.G. Marshall; ***D:*** Richard Lester; ***W:*** Mario Puzo, David Newman; ***C:*** Geoffrey Unsworth, Robert Paynter; ***M:*** John Williams.

Superman 3 🦴🦴 **1983 (PG)** Villainous businessman Ross Webster (Vaughn) tries to conquer Superman (Reeve) via the expertise of bumbling computer expert Gus Gorman (Pryor) and the judicious use of an artificial form of Kryptonite. Superman explores his darker side after undergoing transformation into sleaze ball. Promising satiric start ultimately defeated by uneven story and direction and boring physical comedy. Notable is the absence of Lois Lane as a main character, instead the big guy takes up with former flame Lana Lang (O'Toole). Followed by "Superman 4." **123m/C VHS, DVD, Wide.** Christopher Reeve, Richard Pryor, Annette O'Toole, Jackie Cooper, Margot Kidder, Marc McClure, Annie Ross, Robert Vaughn; ***D:*** Richard Lester; ***W:*** David Newman; ***C:*** Robert Paynter; ***M:*** John Williams.

Superman 4: The Quest for Peace 🦴🦴 **1987 (PG)** The third sequel, in which the Man of Steel endeavors to rid the world of nuclear weapons, thereby pitting himself against nuclear-entrepreneur Lex Luthor and his superpowered creation, Nuclear Man. Special effects are dime-store quality and it appears that someone may have walked off with parts of the plot. Reeve deserves credit for remaining true to character through four films. **90m/C VHS, DVD, Wide.** Christopher Reeve, Gene Hackman, Jon Cryer, Marc McClure, Margot Kidder, Mariel Hemingway, Sam Wanamaker; ***D:*** Sidney J. Furie; ***W:*** Mark Rosenthal; ***M:*** John Williams; ***V:*** Susannah York.

Superman & the Mole Men 🦴🦴½ *Superman and the Strange People* **1951** The cast of the popular 1950s' TV show made this rarely seen feature as a pilot for the series. Superman faces the danger threatened by the invasion of radioactive mole-men who make their way to the surface world from the bowels of the earth through an oil-well shaft. Simple fun. **58m/C VHS.** George Reeves, Phyllis Coates, Jeff Corey; ***D:*** Lee Sholem. **TV**

Supernatural 🦴🦴½ **1933** Roma (Lombard) falls prey to a phony medium (Dinehart) who promises to call up the spirit of her recently murdered twin brother. At the same moment of the seance a murderess dies in the electric chair and her body is used in Dr. Houston's (Warner) life-after-death experiment. Too bad Roma becomes possessed by the woman's evil spirit. Now the doctor and Roma's fiance (Scott) must undo the curse. A hokey B-grade movie disliked by Lombard. **78m/B VHS.** Carole Lombard, Randolph Scott, H.B. Warner, Alan Dinehart, Vivienne Osborne, Beryl Mercer, William Farnum, Willard Robertson; ***D:*** Victor Halperin; ***W:*** Harvey Thew, Brian Marlow; ***C:*** Arthur Martinelli.

The Supernaturals 🦴½ **1986 (R)** Confederate Civil War-era ghosts, bent on avenging their deaths, haunt a wooded area in which modern Yankee army maneuvers are practiced. Antebellum boredom. **85m/C VHS.** Bobby DiCicco, Maxwell Caulfield, LeVar Burton, Nichelle Nichols; ***D:*** Armand Mastroianni; ***C:*** Peter Collister.

Supernova 🦴½ **1999 (PG-13)** This one got stuck on the studio shelf for awhile and didn't improve with age. In fact, director Walter Hill was so incensed over studio re-editing that he removed his name, leaving the pseud. "Thomas Lee" to grace this space mishmash. Nick Vanzant (Spader) is stuck piloting a 22nd-century medical vessel after the captain (Forster) is killed. The craft receives a distress call and makes the mistake of rescuing Karl (Facinelli), an odd duck who proves to be very dangerous. You'll wonder what got left on the cutting-room floor. **91m/C VHS, DVD, Wide.** James Spader, Angela Bassett, Robin Tunney, Peter Facinelli, Lou Diamond Phillips, Wilson Cruz, Robert Forster; ***D:*** Walter Hill; ***W:*** David Campbell Wilson; ***C:*** Lloyd Ahern II; ***M:*** David Williams.

Supersonic Man woof! **1978 (PG)** Incoherent shoestring-budget Superman spoof with a masked hero fighting to save the world from the evil intentions of a mad scientist. **85m/C VHS.** *SP* Michael Coby, Cameron Mitchell, Diana Polakov; ***D:*** J(uan) Piquer Simon.

Superstar 🦴🦴 **1999 (PG-13)** Yet another SNL skit tries to stretch to feature film length and remain funny. Don't these people ever give up?! What's next? "Weekend Update: The Movie?" This time producer Lorne Michaels showcases klutzy Catholic schoolgirl Mary Katherine Gallagher (Shannon) as she tries to win a school talent contest and a kiss from the campus hunk (Ferrell). Of course, it's really about her strange armpit sniffing technique and panty-flashing behavior. The material doesn't translate well to movie length (shocking!), and the "teenagers" look like they're about twenty years late for homeroom. There are some funny bits, however, and if you like the character on the show you'll probably like the movie. Warning: There are scenes where Ms. Gallagher french kisses a tree, which sounds a lot funnier than it actually is. **82m/C VHS, DVD.** Molly Shannon, Will Ferrell, Elaine Hendrix, Glynis Johns, Mark McKinney, Harland Williams, Emmy Laybourne; ***D:*** Bruce McCulloch; ***W:*** Steve Koren; ***C:*** Walt Lloyd; ***M:*** Michael Gore.

Superstar: The Life and Times of Andy Warhol 🦴🦴🦴 **1990** Even if you didn't grok Andy's 'pop' artwork and self-created celebrity persona, this ironic, kinetic, oft-rollicking documentary paints a vivid picture of the wild era he inspired and exploited. Interviewees range from Warhol cohorts like Dennis Hopper to proud executives at the Campbell Soup plant. One highlight: a Warhol guest shot on "The Love Boat." **87m/C VHS, DVD.** Tom Wolfe, Sylvia Miles, David Hockney, Taylor Mead, Dennis Hopper, Viva, Allen Ginsberg, Ultra Violet, Paul Morrissey, Sally Kirkland, Fran Lebowitz, Lou Reed, Shelley Winters, Holly Woodlawn; ***D:*** Chuck Workman; ***W:*** Chuck Workman; ***C:*** Burleigh Wartes.

Superstition 🦴½ *The Witch* **1982** A reverend and his family move into a vacant house despite warnings about a curse from the townsfolk. Some people never learn. **85m/C VHS.** James Houghton, Albert Salmi, Lynn Carlin; ***D:*** James Robertson.

Supervixens 🦴🦴 *Russ Meyer's SuperVixens; SuperVixens Eruption; Vixens* **1975** True to Meyer's low-rent exploitation film canon, this wild tale is filled with characteristic Amazons, sex and violence. A gas station attendant is framed for the grisly murder of his girlfriend and hustles out of town, meeting a succession of well-endowed women during his travels. As if it needed further problems, it's hampered by a tasteless storyline and incoherent writing. **105m/C VHS.** Shari Eubank, Charles Napier, Uschi Digart, Charles Pitts, Henry Rowland, Sharon Kelly, Haji; ***D:*** Russ Meyer; ***W:*** Russ Meyer; ***C:*** Russ Meyer; ***M:*** William Loose.

Support Your Local Gunfighter 🦴🦴🦴 **1971 (G)** Garner plays a western con man with his tongue firmly in his cheek. He comes to the small town of Purgatory and is thought to be a notorious gunfighter. He decides to go with the mistaken identity and use it to his profitable advantage. Elam is his bumbling sidekick and Pleshette the love interest. A delightful, deliberately cliche-filled western. A follow-up, not a sequel, to "Support Your Local Sheriff" (1969). **92m/C VHS, DVD, Wide.** James Garner, Jack Elam, Suzanne Pleshette, Harry (Henry) Morgan, Dub Taylor, John Dehner, Joan Blondell, Ellen Corby, Henry Jones; ***D:*** Burt Kennedy; ***W:*** James Edward Grant; ***C:*** Harry Stradling Jr.; ***M:*** Jack Elliott, Allyn Ferguson.

Support Your Local Sheriff 🦴🦴🦴½ **1969 (G)** Amiable, irreverent western spoof with more than its fair share of laughs. When a stranger stumbles into a gold rush town, he winds up becoming sheriff. Garner is perfect as the deadpan sheriff, particularly in the scene where he convinces Dern to remain in jail, in spite of the lack of bars. Neatly subverts every western cliche it encounters, yet keeps respect for formula western. Followed by "Support Your Local Gunfighter." **92m/C VHS, DVD, Wide.** James Garner, Joan Hackett, Walter Brennan, Bruce Dern, Jack Elam, Harry (Henry) Morgan; ***D:*** Burt Kennedy; ***W:*** William Bowers; ***C:*** Harry Stradling Jr.

Suppose They Gave a War and Nobody Came? 🦴🦴½ *War Games* **1970 (G)** A small Southern town battles with a local army base in this entertaining but wandering satire. The different acting styles used as the producers wavered on making this a comedy or drama were more at war with one another than the characters involved. **113m/C VHS.** Tony Curtis, Brian Keith, Ernest Borgnine, Suzanne Pleshette, Ivan Dixon, Bradford Dillman, Don Ameche; ***D:*** Hy Averback; ***W:*** Don McGuire.

Supreme Sanction 🦴🦴 **1999 (R)** An assassin (Swanson) working for a covert government agency decides not to kill the journalist who's threatening to expose the corrupt organization that trained her. This doesn't please her bosses and they mark her for death. **95m/C VHS, DVD.** Michael Madsen, Kristy Swanson, David Dukes, Donald Adeosun Faison, Tommy (Tiny) Lister, Ron Perlman; ***D:*** John Terlesky; ***W:*** John Terlesky. **VIDEO**

Surabaya Conspiracy 🦴½ **1975** Mystery and intrigue surround a quest for gold in Africa. **90m/C VHS.** Michael Rennie, Richard Jaeckel, Barbara Bouchet, Mike (Michael) Preston; ***D:*** Roy Davis.

Sure Fire 🦴🦴 **1990** Wes (Blair) is a mercurial entrepreneur who thinks he has found the financial ticket to paradise with his vacation home scheme. Much to the chagrin of his wife Ellen (Dezina), he refuses to let anything stand in the way of his sure-fire fortune, even his family. Wes develops a little self-control as he realizes he's beginning to flake out, but it may be too late. Director Jost has put together a surprisingly unpretentious film with a virtually no-name cast, its plot speaking volumes on the American condition while unfolding in the bleak Utah desert. **86m/C VHS.** Tom Blair, Kristi Hager, Robert Ernst, Kate Dezina, Phillip R. Brown; ***D:*** Jon Jost; ***W:*** Jon Jost.

The Sure Thing 🦴🦴🦴 **1985 (PG-13)** College students who don't like each other end up travelling to California together, and of course, falling in love. Charming performances make up for predictability. Can't-miss director (and ex-Meathead) Reiner's second direct hit at the boxoffice. **94m/C VHS, 8mm.** John Cusack, Daphne Zuniga, Anthony Edwards, Boyd Gaines, Lisa Jane Persky, Viveca Lindfors, Nicolette Sheridan, Tim Robbins; ***D:*** Rob Reiner; ***W:*** Jonathan Roberts, Steven L. Bloom; ***C:*** Robert Elswit; ***M:*** Tom Scott.

Surf Nazis Must Die 🦴 **1987** A piece of deliberate camp in the Troma mold, about a group of psychotic neo-Nazi surfers taking over the beaches of California in the wake of a devastating earthquake. Tongue-in-cheek, tasteless and cheap, but intentionally so. **83m/C VHS, DVD.** Barry Brenner, Gail Neely, Michael Sonye, Dawn Wildsmith, Tom Shell, Bobbie Bresee; ***D:*** Peter George; ***W:*** John Ayre; ***C:*** Rolf Kestermann; ***M:*** John McCallum.

Surf Ninjas 🦴🦴½ *Surf Warriors* **1993 (PG)** Action comedy for the kiddies finds two young surfer dudes who are actually the long-lost crown princes of the obscure nation of Patu San. The country's incompetent (what a surprise, it's Nielsen) warlord wants the boys to stay lost. Lame jokes and tame martial arts sequences. **87m/C VHS.** Kelly Hu, Ernie Reyes Jr., Nick Cowen, Leslie Nielsen, Tone Loc, Rob Schneider, John Karlen, Ernie Reyes Sr.; ***D:*** Neal Israel; ***W:*** Dan Gordon; ***C:*** Arthur Albert; ***M:*** David Kitay.

Surf Party 🦴½ **1964** Romance among the sands of Malibu with Vinton as the owner of a surf shop. Risque in 1964; utterly campy today. ♫If I Were an Artist; That's What Love Is; Pearly Shells. **68m/C VHS.** Bobby Vinton, Jackie De Shannon, Patricia Morrow, Kenny Miller; ***D:*** Maury Dexter.

Surf 2 woof! *Surf 2: The End of the Trilogy* **1984 (R)** A most excellent group of surfers get sick from drinking tainted Buzz Cola concocted by demented chemist Deezen in most heinous effort to obliterate surfer population from Southern California. Bogus, dude. No, you didn't miss "Surf 1" (there's not one), the title is the sort of in-joke this exercise in mental meltdown perpetuates as comedy. Ha. **91m/C VHS.** Morgan Paull, Cleavon Little, Lyle Waggoner, Ruth Buzzi, Linda Kerridge, Carol Wayne, Eddie Deezen, Eric Stoltz, Brandis Kemp, Terry Kiser; ***D:*** Randall Badat; ***W:*** Randall Badat; ***M:*** Peter Bernstein.

Surface to Air 🦴🦴 **1998 (R)** Naval pilot Steven Madison (McQueen) is estranged from half-brother Zach (Madsen), who's in the Marines. But both wind up in Persian Gulf. Steve and fellow pilot Lori (Shatner) are captured by Iraqi terrorists and face certain death—unless Zach can come to the rescue. **93m/C VHS.** Michael Madsen, Chad McQueen, Melanie Shatner, Larry Thomas; ***D:*** Rodney McDonald. **VIDEO**

Surfacing woof! **1984** A girl braves the hostile northern wilderness to search for her missing father. This pseudo-psychological, sex-driven suspense flick makes little sense. **90m/C VHS.** Joseph Bottoms, Kathleen Beller, R.H. Thomson, Margaret Dragu; ***D:*** Claude Jutra.

The Surgeon 🦴 *Exquisite Tenderness* **1994 (R)** Routine hospital horror finds Dr. Theresa McCann (Glasser) caught up in murder when patients and doctors become poison victims. Aided by toxicologist Benjamin Hendricks (Remar), McCann finds a lollipop left behind and realizes the killer is ex-boyfriend/doctor Julian Matar (Haberle), whose unlawful experiments in tissue regeneration got him suspended. Now he's hiding out in the hospital and killing to get the pituitary glands necessary for his miracle serum. Film's original title "Exquisite Tenderness" is a term for the point when pain becomes so extreme it turns to pleasure—the film merely turns grisly. **100m/C VHS, DVD.** *GE* Isabel Glasser, James Remar, Sean Haberle, Charles Dance, Peter Boyle, Malcolm McDowell, Charles Bailey-Gates, Gregory West, Mother Love; ***D:*** Carl Schenkel; ***W:*** Patrick Cirillo; ***C:*** Thomas Burstyn; ***M:*** Christopher Franke.

Surprise Attack 🦴 **197?** The Spanish Civil War forms the backdrop for this action opus. **124m/C VHS.** Simon Andrew, Danny Martin, Patty (Patti) Shepard; ***D:*** J. Anthony (Jose Antonio de la Loma) Loma.

Surrender 🦴½ **1987 (PG)** A struggling woman artist and a divorced author fall in love but won't admit it for fear of being hurt again. Jumbled plot, unfortunate casting. Available in a Spanish-subtitled version. **95m/C VHS.** Michael Caine, Sally Field, Steve Guttenberg, Peter Boyle, Jackie Cooper, Julie Kavner, Louise Lasser, Iman; ***D:*** Jerry Belson; ***W:*** Jerry Belson; ***C:*** Juan Ruiz-Anchia; ***M:*** Michel Colombier.

Surrender Dorothy 🦴½ **1998** Weird psychosexual drama focuses on 26-year-old sexually confused Trevor (Pryor), who's afraid of women. He offers drugs and a place to crash to heroin addict Lahn (Di Novis) but their arrangement soons turn bizarre when Trevor desires Lahn to cross-dress as Dorothy, his concept of the ideal girlfriend, and then wants to take his obsession even farther. **97m/B**

VHS, DVD. Kevin Di Novis, Peter Pryor, Jason Centeno, Elizabeth Casey; ***D:*** Kevin Di Novis; ***W:*** Kevin Di Novis; ***C:*** Jonathan Koval; ***M:*** Christopher Matarazzo.

Surrogate **1988** A young couple fights to keep their marriage afloat by turning to a sex surrogate. Strong cast helps carry odd, confusing script, with plenty of (you guessed it) sex, and a mystery to solve. **100m/C VHS.** *CA* Art Hindle, Shannon Tweed, Carole Laure, Michael Ironside, Marilyn Lightstone; ***D:*** Don Carmody.

Survival Game **1987** A young combat expert (Chuck Norris's son) gets involved with some ex-hippies in search of a $2 million cache. High-kickin' action. **91m/C VHS.** Mike Norris, Deborah Goodrich, Seymour Cassel; ***D:*** Herb Freed.

Survival of Spaceship Earth **1990** Man, his world and the protection of its ecology are discussed in this beautiful and fascinating film. Winner of numerous international awards due to the strength of its production values and writing. Nominated for ten Emmy awards; winner of two. **63m/C VHS.** Rue McClanahan; ***D:*** Dirk Summers; ***W:*** Dirk Summers; ***Nar:*** Raymond Burr.

Survival Quest ½ **1989 (R)** Students in a Rocky Mountain survival course cross paths with a band of bloodthirsty mercenaries-in-training. A battle to the death ensues; you'll wish they'd all put each other out of their misery a lot sooner. **90m/C VHS.** Lance Henriksen, Dermot Mulroney, Mark Rolston, Steve Antin, Paul Provenza, Ben Hammer, Traci Lind, Catherine Keener, Reggie Bannister; ***D:*** Don A. Coscarelli; ***W:*** Don A. Coscarelli.

Survival Run **1980 (R)** Six California teenagers become stranded in the Mexican desert, where they witness Graves and Milland making a shady deal. The chase is on, the story is lame, the gory parts aren't gory—so why bother? **90m/C VHS.** Peter Graves, Ray Milland, Vincent Van Patten; ***D:*** Larry Spiegel; ***W:*** Gerard M. Cahill.

Survival Zone **woof! 1984 (R)** Nuclear holocaust survivors battle a violent band of marauding motorcyclists on the barren ranches of the 21st century. Advice to director Rubens and cohorts: Next time, find a plot that's not growing mold. **90m/C VHS.** Gary Lockwood, Morgan Stevens, Camilla Sparv; ***D:*** Percival Rubens.

The Survivalist **1987 (R)** An arms-ready survivalist nut defends his family and supplies against a panicked society awaiting nuclear war. Poorly acted, little tension, and ineffective plotting make boredom seem a more critical issue than survival. **96m/C VHS.** Steve Railsback, Susan Blakely, Marjoe Gortner, David Wayne, Cliff DeYoung; ***D:*** Sig Shore; ***W:*** Robert Dillon.

Surviving Desire **1991** Donovan plays Jude, a neurotic, romantic English professor who falls madly in love with an independently minded student, Sophie. Unfortunately, Sophie is more interested in how the seduction will advance her writing than how it will affect her life. The lovers explore their brief affair by analyzing every emotion and motive in a series of quirky conversations. Intelligent, amusing, and stylized film from director Hartley. The tape also includes two Hartley shorts: "Theory of Achievement" and "Ambition." **86m/C VHS, DVD.** Martin Donovan, Mary B. Ward, Matt Malloy, Rebecca Nelson; ***D:*** Hal Hartley; ***C:*** Michael Spiller.

Surviving Picasso ½ **1996 (R)** Merchant-Ivory team takes time off from bodice-rippers to tear into the personal life of the Cubist legend, Pablo Picasso. Takes an unglamourous look at the mythically famous artist, focusing on the rocky ten-year affair with Francoise Gilot (newcomer McElhone), who met the artist in Nazi-occupied Paris when she was 22 and he was 62. Hopkins is well-cast as the insufferable senior and adds a strong dose of charm to soften his portrayal. Scores high tech credits, especially picture's sumptuous look, compliments of production designer and frequent collaborator Luciana Arrighi. Unfortunately adapted from the decidedly one-sided biography "Picasso: Creator and Destroyer" by controversial author Arianna Huffington. Denied use of the artist's works by his estate, the filmmakers settled for some "work in progress" replicas. **126m/C VHS.** Anthony Hopkins, Natascha (Natasha) McElhone, Julianne Moore, Joss Ackland, Joan Plowright, Diane Venora, Peter Eyre, Jane Lapotaire, Joseph Maher, Bob Peck; ***D:*** James Ivory; ***W:*** Ruth Prawer Jhabvala; ***C:*** Tony Pierce-Roberts; ***M:*** Richard Robbins.

Surviving the Game **1994 (R)** Poorly made hunt-the-human story. Homeless Ice-T is hired by a group of men to assist them on their annual hunt. But wait, he's the prey. Unbelievable premise pits the streetwise, down and out Ice-T against the savvy and weapons rich group—and he beats them at their own game. Few high-impact action sequences. The violence, although there isn't as much as might be expected, is graphic. **94m/C VHS, DVD.** Rutger Hauer, Ice-T, F. Murray Abraham, Gary Busey, Charles S. Dutton, John C. McGinley, William McNamara, Jeff Corey; ***D:*** Ernest R. Dickerson; ***W:*** Eric Bernt; ***C:*** Bojan Bazelli; ***M:*** Stewart Copeland.

Survivor **1980** A jetliner crashes, leaving but one survivor, the pilot, who is then plagued by visions, tragedies, and ghosts of dead passengers. Viewers also suffer. **91m/C VHS.** *AU* Robert Powell, Jenny Agutter, Joseph Cotten, Angela Punch McGregor; ***D:*** David Hemmings; ***W:*** David Ambrose; ***M:*** Brian May.

Survivor **1987** A lone warrior on a post-nuclear holocaust wasteland battles a megalomaniac ruler. Moll as the evil villian is watchable, but overall the film is a wasteland, too. **92m/C VHS.** Chip Mayer, Richard Moll, Sue Kiel; ***D:*** Michael Shackleton.

The Survivor **1998 (R)** Yet another sci-fier where Earth is a mess—this time it's a rainforest-covered penal colony run by the violent Kyla (Moll) and his vicious minions. When the president's (Herd) spaceship crashes, convicted murderer Tarkin (Declie) tries to save him from Kyla. Not bad special effects and lots of action. **95m/C VHS.** Richard Moll, Xavier DeClie, Richard Herd; ***D:*** Nick Davis. **VIDEO**

Survivors **1983 (R)** Two unemployed men find themselves the target of a hit man, whom they have identified in a robbery attempt. One of the men goes gun-crazy protecting himself. Uneven comedy with wild Williams and laid-back Matthau. **102m/C VHS, DVD, Wide.** Robin Williams, Walter Matthau, Jerry Reed, John Goodman, James Wainwright, Kristen Vigard; ***D:*** Michael Ritchie; ***W:*** Michael Leeson; ***C:*** Billy Williams; ***M:*** Paul Chihara.

Susan and God *The Gay Mrs. Trexel* **1940** A selfish socialite returns from Europe and starts practicing a new religion, much to the dismay of her friends and family. Despite her preaching, her own domestic life is falling apart and she realizes that her preoccupation and selfish ways have caused a strain on her marriage and her relationship with her daughter. An excellent script and a fine performance from Crawford make this a highly satisfying film. **115m/B VHS.** Joan Crawford, Fredric March, Ruth Hussey, John Carroll, Rita Hayworth, Nigel Bruce, Bruce Cabot, Rose Hobart, Rita Quigley, Marjorie Main, Gloria De Haven; ***D:*** George Cukor; ***W:*** Anita Loos.

Susan Lenox: Her Fall and Rise ½ *The Rise of Helga; Rising to Fame* **1931** Garbo, the daughter of an abusive farmer, falls into the arms of the handsome Gable to escape an arranged marriage. Both stars are miscast, but the well-paced direction keeps the melodrama moving. **84m/B VHS.** Greta Garbo, Clark Gable, Jean Hersholt, John Miljan, Alan Hale, Hale Hamilton; ***D:*** Robert Z. Leonard; ***C:*** William H. Daniels.

Susan Slept Here ½ **1954** While researching a movie on juvenile delinquents, a Hollywood script writer (Powell) is given custody of a spunky 18-year-old delinquent girl (Reynolds) during the Christmas holidays. Cute sex comedy. Based on the play "Susan," by Alex Gottlieb and Steve Fisher. **98m/C VHS.** Dick Powell, Debbie Reynolds, Anne Francis; ***D:*** Frank Tashlin.

Susana **1951** Minor though still interesting Bunuel, in which a sexy delinquent young girl is rescued from vagrancy by a Spanish family, and how she subsequently undermines the family's structure through sexual allurement and intimidation. In Spanish with English subtitles. **87m/B VHS.** *MX* Rosita Quintana, Fernando Soler, Victor Manuel Mendoza, Matilde Palou; ***D:*** Luis Bunuel.

Susanna Pass **1949** Oil deposits underneath a fish hatchery lake attract bad guys. They set off explosions to destroy the fishery, but game warden Rogers investigates. Minor outing for Roy. **67m/C VHS.** Roy Rogers, Dale Evans, Estelita Rodriguez, Martin Garralaga, Robert Emmett Keane, Lucien Littlefield, Douglas Fowley; ***D:*** William Witney.

Susannah of the Mounties ½ **1939 (PG)** An adorable young girl is left orphaned after a wagon train massacre and is adopted by a Mountie. An Indian squabble gives Shirley a chance to play little peacemaker and teach Scott how to tap dance, too. Could she be any cuter? Available colorized. **78m/B VHS.** Shirley Temple, Randolph Scott, Margaret Lockwood, J. Farrell MacDonald, Moroni Olsen, Victor Jory; ***D:*** William A. Seiter; ***C:*** Arthur C. Miller.

Suspect ½ **1987 (R)** An overworked Washington, DC, public defender (Cher) is assigned to a controversial murder case in which her client is a deaf-mute, skid-row bum. A cynical lobbyist on the jury illegally researches the case himself. They work together to uncover a far-reaching conspiracy. Unrealistic plot, helped along by good performances and tight direction. **101m/C VHS, DVD, Wide.** Dennis Quaid, Cher, Liam Neeson, E. Katherine Kerr, Joe Mantegna, John Mahoney, Philip Bosco; ***D:*** Peter Yates; ***W:*** Eric Roth; ***C:*** Billy Williams; ***M:*** Michael Kamen.

Suspect Device ½ *Roger Corman Presents: Suspect Device* **1995 (R)** Nonsensical cable thriller finds government computer researcher Dan (Howell) mistakenly accessing a secret file and becoming an immediate assassination target. Then Dan discovers he isn't even human—he's really a genetically engineered cross between a robot and a nuclear bomb! Part "Terminator," part "Three Days of the Condor," and all silliness. **90m/C VHS.** C. Thomas Howell, Stacy Travis, Jed Allan, John Beck, Marcus Aurelius, Jonathan Fuller; ***D:*** Rick Jacobson; ***W:*** Alex Simon; ***C:*** John Aronson; ***M:*** Christopher Lennertz. **CABLE**

Suspended Alibi ½ *Suspected Alibi* **1956** British crime-drama about an adulterous man unjustly accused when his alibi is murdered. Overlook the convenient coincidence. **64m/B VHS.** *GB* Patrick Holt, Honor Blackman, Andrew Keir, Valentine Dyall; ***D:*** Alfred Shaughnessy.

Suspicion ½ **1941** Alfred Hitchcock's suspense thriller about a woman who gradually realizes she is married to a killer and may be next on his list. An excellent production unravels at the end due to RKO's insistence that Grant retain his "attractive" image. This forced the writers to leave his guilt or innocence undetermined. Available colorized. **99m/B VHS.** Cary Grant, Joan Fontaine, Cedric Hardwicke, Nigel Bruce, May Whitty, Leo G. Carroll, Heather Angel; ***D:*** Alfred Hitchcock; ***C:*** Harry Stradling Sr.; ***M:*** Franz Waxman. Oscars '41: Actress (Fontaine); N.Y. Film Critics '41: Actress (Fontaine).

Suspicion **1987** Remake of the chilling Hitchcock tale. Newlywed bride is consumed with fears about her wealthy new husband. The suspense builds as she comes to suspect that she is married to a cold-blooded killer. Curtin in way over her head. **97m/C VHS.** Jane Curtin, Anthony Andrews, Jeremy Northam, Ron Pember, Betsy Blair, Michael Hordern, Vivian Pickles, Jo Anderson; ***D:*** Andrew Grieve.

Suspicious Agenda ½ **1994 (R)** Cop with a past is assigned to a task force that's hunting down a sadistic vigilante. **97m/C VHS.** Richard Grieco, Nick Mancuso, Jim Byrnes; ***D:*** Clay Borris; ***W:*** Kevin Rock.

Suspicious Minds ½ **1996 (R)** PI Jack Ramsey (Bergin) is hired to get the goods on Isabelle's (Heitmeyer) alleged infidelities. But Jack winds up in an affair with the femme, whose other lover has just been murdered. **97m/C VHS.** Patrick Bergin, Jayne Heitmeyer, Gary Busey, Daniel Pilon; ***D:*** Alain Zaloum.

Suspiria **1977 (R)** An American dancer enters a weird European ballet academy and finds they teach more than movement as bodies begin piling up. Sometimes weak plot is aided by great-but-gory special effects, fine photography, good music, and a chilling opening sequence. Also available in unrated version. **99m/C VHS, DVD, Wide.** *IT* Jessica Harper, Joan Bennett, Alida Valli, Udo Kier, Stefania Casini, Flavio Bucci, Barbara Magnolfi, Rudolf Schuendler; ***D:*** Dario Argento; ***W:*** Dario Argento, Daria Nicolodi; ***C:*** Luciano Tovoli; ***M:*** Dario Argento, The Goblins.

Suture **1993** Quirky thriller is a homage to late '50s melodramas with its strange tale of mistaken identity. Vincent wants to hide his unsavory past by assuming the identity of his estranged half-brother, Clay, which should be difficult since Vincent is white and Clay is black but the movie's premise is that everyone confuses the two. Vincent tries to kill Clay in an explosion but he survives—with amnesia and with everyone in the hospital assuming he's Vincent. Shifting points of view as he struggles to piece together his memory offer disorientation not just for Clay but the viewer as well. Feature film debut for the directors. **96m/B VHS, DVD, Wide.** Dennis Haysbert, Sab Shimono, Mel Harris, Michael (M.K.) Harris, Dina Merrill, David Graf, Fran Ryan; ***D:*** Scott McGehee, David Siegel; ***W:*** Scott McGehee, David Siegel; ***C:*** Greg Gardiner; ***M:*** Cary Berger. Sundance '94: Cinematog.

Suzanne ½ **1980 (R)** Set in 1950s Quebec, the story of a good woman whose criminal boyfriend leaves her pregnant when he is sent to prison. Ten years later, he returns, threatening her happy marriage. Confused script can't be saved by valiant cast. **90m/C VHS.** Sondra Locke, Richard Dreyfuss, Gene Barry.

Suzy ½ **1936** Harlow's fourth film and her only one with Grant is a mixture of romance, action, and comedy set during WWI. Grant plays a French flier who falls in love with Harlow, although she is married to Tone. Excellent air footage and some good funny scenes keep this film moving right along. Even has Grant singing hit song, "Did I Remember?" **99m/B VHS.** Jean Harlow, Franchot Tone, Cary Grant, Benita Hume, Lewis Stone, Inez Courtney; ***D:*** George Fitzmaurice.

Svengali **1931** A music teacher uses his hypnotic abilities to manipulate one of his singing students and make her a star. Soon the young woman is singing for sell-out crowds, but only if her teacher is present. Barrymore in a hypnotic performance. Adapted from "Trilby" by George Du Maurier. Remade in 1955 and 1983. **76m/B VHS, DVD.** John Barrymore, Marian Marsh, Donald Crisp; ***D:*** Archie Mayo; ***W:*** J. Grubb Alexander; ***C:*** Barney McGill.

Svengali ½ **1955** Limp remake of the 1931 film about Trilby, an artist's model, falling under the mesmerizing spell of the title character, who is determined to make her into a famous singer. Chiefly notable for its visuals which were based on the illustrations from the original novel "Trilby" by George du Maurier. **82m/C VHS.** *GB* Hildegarde Neff, Donald Wolfit, Terence Morgan, Derek Bond, Paul Rogers, David Kossoff; ***D:*** Noel Langley; ***W:*** Noel Langley.

Svengali ½ **1983** Flamboyant but faded music star O'Toole mentors Foster, a young pop singer looking for stardom. Boring remake of the Barrymore classic. **96m/C VHS.** Peter O'Toole, Jodie Foster, Elizabeth Ashley, Larry Joshua, Pamela Blair, Barbara Byrne, Holly Hunter; ***D:*** Anthony Harvey; ***M:*** John Barry. **TV**

Swamp Fire ½ **1946** Mississippi river-boat captain Weissmuller, wrestles alligators and battles with Crabbe for the woman he loves in this turgid drama. Look for Janssen in an early screen performance. **69m/B VHS.** Johnny Weissmuller, Virginia Grey, Buster Crabbe, Carol Thurston, Edwin Maxwell, Pedro de Cordoba, Pierre Watkin, David Janssen; ***D:*** William H. Pine.

Swamp of the Lost Monster 🦴 **1965** An incredible Mexican horror/western/musical that features a mouse-like monster that'll scare the cheese out of you. **88m/B VHS.** *MX* Gaston Santos, Sarah Cabrera, Manuel Donde; ***D:*** Rafael Baledon Sr.

Swamp Thing 🦴🦴½ **1982 (PG)** Overlooked camp drama about scientist accidentally turned into tragic half-vegetable, half-man swamp creature, with government agent Barbeau caught in the middle, occasionally while topless. A vegetarian nightmare or ecology propaganda? You be the judge. Adapted from the comic book by Craven. **91m/C VHS, DVD, Wide.** Adrienne Barbeau, Louis Jourdan, Ray Wise, Dick Durock; ***D:*** Wes Craven; ***W:*** Wes Craven; ***C:*** Robbie Greenberg; ***M:*** Harry Manfredini.

Swamp Women 🦴 *Swamp Diamonds; Cruel Swamp* **1955** Four escaped women convicts, known as the "Nardo Gang," chase after a stash of diamonds in this super cheap, super bad action adventure from cult director Corman. **73m/C VHS.** Mike Connors, Marie Windsor, Beverly Garland, Carole Mathews, Susan Cummings, Jonathan Haze, Jill Jarmyn, Ed Nelson, Lou Place; ***D:*** Roger Corman; ***W:*** David Stern; ***M:*** Bill Holman.

The Swan 🦴🦴½ **1925** Princess' arranged marriage with a prince is complicated by a poor man also in love with her. Classic romantic comedy of the silent era. Remade in 1956. Based on a play by Ferenc Molnar. **50m/B VHS.** Adolphe Menjou, Ricardo Cortez, Frances Howard; ***D:*** Dimitri Buchowetzki.

The Swan 🦴🦴🦴 **1956** A twist on the Cinderella story with Kelly (in her last film before her marriage) as the charming beauty waiting for her prince. Both Guinness, as the crown prince, and Jourdan, as her poor tutor, want her hand (and the rest of her). Attractive cast, but story gets slow from time to time. Remake of a 1925 silent film. **112m/C VHS.** Grace Kelly, Louis Jourdan, Alec Guinness, Jessie Royce Landis, Brian Aherne, Estelle Winwood; ***D:*** Charles Vidor; ***C:*** Joseph Ruttenberg, Robert L. Surtees.

The Swan Princess 🦴🦴½ **1994 (G)** Formulaic prince-and-princess love story based loosely on "Swan Lake" takes a modern twist: Princess Odette, offended by the emphasis her intended, Prince Derek, places on her beauty, flees the kingdom. She's kidnapped by the evil Rothbart, an enchanter who turns her into a swan able to take human form only when touched by moonlight. A snappy trio of animal characters eventually helps Odette reunite with her newly P.C. love, with lots of zesty musical numbers and various Disney-inspired plot points along the way. Adults may yawn, but kiddies will be charmed just the same. **90m/C VHS.** ***D:*** Richard Rich; ***W:*** Richard Rich, Brian Nissen; ***M:*** Lex de Azevedo; ***V:*** Jack Palance, Michelle Nicastro, Howard McGillin, Liz Callaway, John Cleese, Steven Wright, Steve Vinovich, Dakin Matthews, Sandy Duncan, Mark Harelik, James Arrington, Davis Gaines, Joel McKinnon Miller.

The Swan Princess 2: Escape from Castle Mountain 🦴🦴½ **1997 (G)** Heroine Odette changes back into a swan to help husband Derek defeat evil magician Clavius. Some humor, some action, some nice tunes, and decent animation should keep the kids happy. ♫That's What You Do for a Friend; The Magic of Love; You Gotta Love It. **75m/C VHS.** ***D:*** Richard Rich; ***W:*** Brian Nissen; ***M:*** Lex de Azevedo; ***V:*** Michelle Nicastro, Douglas Sills, Jake Williamson, Christy Landers.

Swann 🦴½ **1996** Too many loose ends and weak direction from Benson Gyles (in her feature film debut) waste the efforts of a talented cast. Chicago-based writer Sarah Maloney (Richardson) is doing a biography of Mary Swann, wife/murder victim of a backwater Ontario farmer, who secretly wrote poetry (and gets compared to Emily Dickinson). Sarah heads to Nadeau to meet with Mary's friend Rose (Fricker) and discovers she may have altered some of the published poetry but there's not much there to really care about. Based on a novel by Carol Shields. **98m/C VHS.** *GB CA* Miranda Richardson, Brenda Fricker, Michael Ontkean, Sean McCann, John Neville, Sean Hewitt, Kyra Harper, David Cubitt, Geny Walter; ***D:*** Anna Benson Gyles; ***W:*** David Young; ***C:*** Gerald Packer; ***M:*** Richard Rodney Bennett.

Swann in Love 🦴🦴½ *Un Amour De Swann* **1984 (R)** A handsome, wealthy French aristocrat makes a fool of himself over a beautiful courtesan who cares nothing for him. Elegant production lacks spark. Based upon a section of Marcel Proust's "Remembrance of Things Past." In French with English subtitles or an English language version. **110m/C VHS.** *FR GE* Jeremy Irons, Ornella Muti, Alain Delon, Fanny Ardant, Marie-Christine Barrault; ***D:*** Volker Schlondorff; ***W:*** Peter Brook, Jean-Claude Carriere; ***C:*** Sven Nykvist. Cesar '85: Art Dir./Set Dec., Costume Des.

The Swap 🦴½ *Sam's Song* **1971 (R)** Ex-con searches for his brother's killer. Muddled story uses clips from early De Niro film "Sam's Song." **120m/C VHS, DVD.** Robert De Niro, Jered Mickey, Jennifer Warren, Terrayne Crawford, Martin Kelley; ***D:*** Jordan Leondopoulos; ***C:*** Alex Phillips Jr.; ***M:*** Gershon Kingsley.

Swap Meet 🦴 **1979 (R)** Wacky teen sex comedy about shenanigans at a small town swap meet. Strictly bargain basement. **86m/C VHS.** Ruth Cox, Deborah Richter, Danny Goldman, Cheryl Rixon, Jonathan (Jon Francis) Gries; ***D:*** Brice Mack.

The Swarm 🦴 **1978 (PG)** Low-brow insect contest as scientist Caine fends off a swarm of killer bees when they attack metro Houston. The bees are really just black spots painted on the film. And the acting is terrible. "B" movie on bees, but it's still better than "The Bees." **116m/C VHS.** Michael Caine, Katharine Ross, Richard Widmark, Lee Grant, Richard Chamberlain, Olivia de Havilland, Henry Fonda, Fred MacMurray, Patty Duke, Ben Johnson, Jose Ferrer, Slim Pickens, Bradford Dillman, Cameron Mitchell; ***D:*** Irwin Allen; ***W:*** Stirling Silliphant; ***C:*** Fred W. Koenekamp; ***M:*** Jerry Goldsmith, John Williams.

Swashbuckler 🦴 *Scarlet Buccaneer* **1976 (PG)** Jaunty pirate returns from sea to find his friends held captive by dastardly dictator for their political views. He rescues them, and helps them overthrow the erstwhile despot. **101m/C VHS, DVD, Wide.** Robert Shaw, James Earl Jones, Peter Boyle, Genevieve Bujold, Beau Bridges, Geoffrey Holder; ***D:*** James Goldstone; ***W:*** Jeffrey Bloom; ***C:*** Philip Lathrop; ***M:*** John Addison.

Swashbuckler 🦴½ *The Scarlet Buccaneer* **1984** Eighteenth-century pirate fracas that can't compete with Errol Flynn. **100m/C VHS.** *FR* Jean-Paul Belmondo, Marlene Jobert, Laura Antonelli, Michel Auclair, Julien Guiomar; ***D:*** Jean-Paul Rappeneau.

Sweater Girls woof! **1978 (R)** Sex comedy about two girls starting their own club called the "Sweater Girls." Terrible teen exploitaiton film. **90m/C VHS.** Charlene Tilton, Harry Moses, Meegan King, Noelle North, Kate Sarchet, Carol Seflinger, Tamara Barkley, Julie Parsons; ***D:*** Donald M. Jones.

Swedenhielms 🦴🦴½ **1935** A poor Swedish scientist struggles to support his family while hoping to win a Nobel prize, while his two sons get involved in a moneylending scandal. Bergman is the rich fiance of one son, to whom poverty is a puzzlement. Fine performances by Ekman and the 20-year-old Bergman (in her third film). In Swedish with English subtitles. **92m/B VHS.** *SW* Gosta Ekman, Karin Swanstrom, Bjorn Berglund, Hakan Westergren, Tutta Rolf, Ingrid Bergman, Sigurd Wallen; ***D:*** Gustaf Molander.

Sweeney Todd: The Demon Barber of Fleet Street **1984** A filmed performance of Sondheim's Tony-winning Broadway musical. Creepy thriller about a demon barber, his razor, and his wife's meatpies. **139m/C VHS.** *GB* Angela Lansbury, George Hearn; ***D:*** Harold Prince; ***M:*** Stephen Sondheim.

The Sweeper 🦴🦴½ **1995 (R)** LA cop Mark Goddard (Howell) has a problem—his suspects have a bad habit of dying in his custody. Then he's recruited by a secret police organization whose aim is to dispense their own brand of deadly justice and Mark discovers a key to his troubled past and the murder of his cop father (Fahey). **101m/C VHS.** C. Thomas Howell, Ed Lauter, Cynda Williams, Jeff Fahey; ***D:*** Joseph Merhi; ***W:*** William Applegate Jr.; ***C:*** Ken Blakey; ***M:*** K. Alexander Wilkinson.

Sweepers 🦴🦴 **1999 (R)** Former land mine sweeper Christian Erickson (Lundgren) is called out of retirement to help bomb expert Michelle Flynn (Stansfield) uncover a terrorist plan to plant landmines in the U.S. **96m/C VHS, DVD.** Dolph Lundgren, Claire Stansfield, Bruce Payne; ***D:*** Darby Black; ***W:*** Darby Black, Kevin Bernhardt; ***C:*** Yossi Wein. **VIDEO**

Sweet Adeline 🦴🦴 **1926** Small-time hayseed makes it big in the music business while brother steals his girl back home. Not easily put off, young songster perseveres. **60m/B VHS.** Charles Ray, Gertrude (Olmstead) Olmsted, Jack Clifford, Ida Lewis; ***D:*** Jerome Storm.

Sweet Adeline 🦴🦴½ **1935** Dunne attracts all the men in her father's Hoboken beer garden but Woods plays the songwriter with whom she finds real love. Wonderful score. ♫Play Us a Polka, Dot; Here Am I; We Were So Young; Why Was I Born?; Mollie O'Donahue; Lonely Feet; 'Twas Not So Long Ago; Don't Ever Leave Me. **87m/B VHS.** Irene Dunne, Donald Woods, Hugh Herbert, Ned Sparks, Joseph Cawthorn, Louis Calhern; ***D:*** Mervyn LeRoy; ***M:*** Jerome Kern, Oscar Hammerstein.

Sweet and Lowdown 🦴🦴½ **1999 (PG-13)** Slight jazzy comedy, set in the thirties, traces the up-and-down career of fictional musician Emmet Ray (Penn), who's haunted by the fact that he's the second-best jazz guitarist in the world (Django Reinhardt is the first). However talented Emmet is musically, he's scum as a human being, abandoning Hattie (Morton), the mute laundress who turns out to be the love of his life in favor of wealthy writer Blanche (Thurman). Fine cast, good look, great music. **95m/C VHS, DVD, Wide.** Sean Penn, Samantha Morton, Uma Thurman, Brian Markinson, Anthony LaPaglia, Gretchen Mol, Vincent Guastaferro, John Waters, James Urbaniak, Constance Schulman, Kellie Overbey, Michael Sprague, Woody Allen; ***D:*** Woody Allen; ***W:*** Woody Allen; ***C:*** Zhao Fei; ***M:*** Dick Hyman.

Sweet Beat 🦴 *The Amorous Sex* **1962** A young woman gets a chance to become a singer when she reaches the finals of a British beauty contest. Pedestrian story enlivened by music from popular British bands of the time. **66m/B VHS.** Julie Amber, Sheldon Lawrence, Irv Bauer, Billy Myles.

Sweet Bird of Youth 🦴🦴🦴 **1962** An acclaimed adaptation of the Tennessee Williams play about Chance Wayne, a handsome drifter who travels with an aging movie queen to his small Florida hometown, hoping she'll get him started in a movie career. However, coming home turns into a big mistake, as the town boss wants revenge on Chance for seducing his daughter, Heavenly. Williams's original stage ending was cleaned up, providing a conventional "happy" movie ending for the censors. Remade for TV in 1989 with Elizabeth Taylor and Mark Harmon in the lead roles. **120m/C VHS, Wide.** Paul Newman, Geraldine Page, Ed Begley Sr., Mildred Dunnock, Rip Torn, Shirley Knight, Madeline Sherwood; ***D:*** Richard Brooks; ***W:*** Richard Brooks; ***C:*** Milton Krasner. Oscars '62: Support. Actor (Begley); Golden Globes '63: Actress—Drama (Page).

Sweet Bird of Youth 🦴🦴 **1989 (R)** TV remake of the Tennessee Williams's play, which was filmed for the big screen in 1962, with Harmon and Taylor having the unenviable task of following in the roles played by Paul Newman and Geraldine Page. She is an egotistical, has-been movie star and he is her ambitious gigolo who wants a movie career of his own. Unfortunately, the trouble that drove him from his Florida hometown is still there when he reappears, actress in tow. Things don't bode well. The TV production uses Williams's original ending, which was cleaned up for a "happier" version in the '62 film. **95m/C VHS.** Elizabeth Taylor, Mark Harmon, Rip Torn, Valerie Perrine, Ruta Lee, Seymour Cassel, Kevin Geer, Michael Wilding Jr.; ***D:*** Nicolas Roeg; ***W:*** Gavin Lambert; ***M:*** Ralph Burns. **TV**

Sweet Charity 🦴🦴🦴 **1969** An ever-optimistic dime-a-dance girl has a hard time finding a classy guy to marry. MacLaine is appealing in this big-budget version of the popular Broadway musical by Neil Simon (derived from Fellini's "Notti di Cabiria"). Fosse's debut as film director. Watch for Cort as a flower child. ♫My Personal Property; It's a Nice Face; Hey, Big Spender; Rich Man's Frug; If My Friends Could See Me Now; There's Gotta Be Something Better Than This; Rhythm of Life; Sweet Charity; I'm a Brass Band. **148m/C VHS.** Shirley MacLaine, Chita Rivera, John McMartin, Paula Kelly, Sammy Davis Jr., Ricardo Montalban, Bud Cort; ***D:*** Bob Fosse; ***C:*** Robert L. Surtees; ***M:*** Cy Coleman.

Sweet Country 🦴½ **1987 (R)** During the overthrow of the Allende government in Chile, the lives of a Chilean family and an American couple intertwine. Heavy-going propaganda is a cross between tragedy and unintentional comedy. Made by the director of "Zorba the Greek." **147m/C VHS.** Jane Alexander, John Cullum, Carole Laure, Franco Nero, Joanna Pettet, Randy Quaid, Irene Papas, Jean-Pierre Aumont, Pierre Vaneck, Katia Dandoulaki; ***D:*** Michael Cacoyannis.

Sweet Country Road 🦴½ **1981** A rock singer journeys to Nashville to try to cross over into country music. **95m/C VHS.** Buddy Knox, Kary Lynn, Gordy Trapp, Johnny Paycheck, Jeanne Pruett.

Sweet Creek County War 🦴 **1982** Retired sheriff must leave his quiet ranch to battle a greedy businessman. **90m/C VHS.** Richard Egan, Albert Salmi, Nita Talbot, Slim Pickens.

Sweet Dreams 🦴🦴½ **1985 (PG-13)** Biography of country singer Patsy Cline (Lange), who is struggling until her recording of "Walking After Midnight" becomes a hit. Her second marriage to fan Charlie Dick (Harris) begin to unravel as his drinking and her success both increase and Charlie turns abusive. Patsy's rise to stardom ended in an early death. Fine performances thoughout, with Lange lip-synching to Cline's original recordings. ♫Walking After Midnight; Crazy; Sweet Dreams; San Antonio Rose; Blue Moon of Kentucky; Lovesick Blues; Seven Lonely Days; Foolin' Around; Your Cheatin' Heart. **115m/C VHS, DVD.** Jessica Lange, Ed Harris, Ann Wedgeworth, David Clennon, John Goodman, James Staley, Gary Basaraba, P.J. Soles; ***D:*** Karel Reisz; ***W:*** Robert Getchell; ***C:*** Robbie Greenberg; ***M:*** Charles Gross.

Sweet Ecstasy 🦴½ *Douce Violence; Sweet Violence* **1962** Wealthy shenanigans on the French Riviera. Olivier (Pezy) is the upright young man who can't sleep with anyone unless he's in love, much to sex bomb Elke's (Sommer) dismay. **75m/B VHS.** *FR* Elke Sommer, Pierre Brice, Christian Pezy, Claire Maurier; ***D:*** Max Pecas; ***M:*** Charles Aznavour.

Sweet Evil 🦴½ **1995 (R)** Naomi and Mike seek the help of a surrogate after a number of failed fertility treatments. Jenny seems to be perfect but after she moves into their home, they learn Jenny's got a nasty secret. **92m/C VHS, DVD.** Bridgette Wilson, Peter Boyle, Scott Cohen, Eiko Matsuda; ***D:*** Rene Eram. **VIDEO**

Sweet Evil 🦴 **1998** Anthony Thurman is the owner of a club that specializes in exotic dancers and sometimes the married Anthony gets a little too involved with the entertainment. His wife knows about his habits and doesn't mind until one of Anthony's affairs uncovers an old secret that was better left hidden. **87m/C VHS.** Al Sapienza, Andrea Riave, Douglas De Marco; ***D:*** Michael Paul Girard; ***W:*** Michael Paul Girard; ***C:*** Luis Escobar; ***M:*** Michael Paul Girard. **VIDEO**

Sweet 15 **1990** A young Hispanic girl learns that there is more to growing up than parties when she learns her father is an illegal alien. Originally aired on PBS as part of the "Wonderworks" family movie series. **120m/C VHS.** Karla Montana, Panchito

Gomez, Tony Plana, Jenny Gago, Susan Ruttan; *D:* Victoria Hochberg.

Sweet Georgia 🦴 **1972** Soft-core star Jordan is a lusty wife whose husband is an alcoholic, so she has a roll in the hay with almost every other cast member. Lots of action, too, including a pitchfork fight. Ride 'em cowboy. **80m/C VHS.** Marsha Jordan.

Sweet Hearts Dance 🦴🦴 **1988 (R)** Parallel love stories follow two longtime friends, one just falling in love, the other struggling to keep his marriage together. Charming performances from all, but a slow pace undermines the film. **95m/C VHS, DVD, Wide.** Don Johnson, Jeff Daniels, Susan Sarandon, Elizabeth Perkins, Justin Henry, Holly Marie Combs; *D:* Robert Greenwald; *W:* Ernest Thompson; *C:* Tak Fujimoto; *M:* Richard Gibbs.

The Sweet Hereafter 🦴🦴🦴½ **1996 (R)** A schoolbus crash kills 14 children in the small town of Sam Dent, British Columbia. Big city lawyer Mitchell Stephens (Holm) arrives to persuade the townspeople to begin a class-action suit targeting city authorities and the bus manufacturer, while struggling to deal with his drug-addicted daughter Zoe (Banks). Paralyzed teenaged survivor Nicole Burnell (Polley) tries to cope with the aftermath of the tragedy as does widower Billy Ansell (Greenwood), whose two children died in the crash. But the case soon begins to tear the reeling town apart as everyone struggles with loss and fate. Egoyan's intimate, lyrical adaptation of the novel by Russell Banks, is filled with wonderful performances, particularly by Polley. **110m/C VHS, DVD, Wide.** *CA* Ian Holm, Sarah Polley, Bruce Greenwood, Tom McCamus, Arsinee Khanjian, Alberta Watson, Gabrielle Rose, Maury Chaykin, David Hemblen, Earl Pastko, Peter Donaldson, Caerthan Banks, Brook Johnson, Stephanie Morgenstern; *D:* Atom Egoyan; *W:* Atom Egoyan; *C:* Paul Sarossy; *M:* Mychael Danna. Cannes '97: Grand Jury Prize; Genie '97: Actor (Holm), Cinematog., Director (Egoyan), Film, Film Editing, Sound, Score; Ind. Spirit '98: Foreign Film; Toronto-City '97: Canadian Feature Film.

Sweet Hostage 🦴🦴½ **1975** Escaped mental patient kidnaps uneducated farm girl and holds her captive in a remote cabin. Blair and Sheen turn in good performances. Adaptation of Nathaniel Benchley's "Welcome to Xanadu." **93m/C VHS.** Linda Blair, Martin Sheen, Jeanne Cooper, Lee DeBroux, Dehl Berti, Bert Remsen; *D:* Lee Philips. **TV**

Sweet Jane 🦴🦴½ **1998** Teenaged Tony (Gordon-Levitt) has AIDS and no family. He becomes infatuated with HIV-positive heroin addict Jane (Mathis), whom he sees in the hospital, and follows her into a dangerous street life. Although Jane treats him badly, Tony sticks around to "protect" her and they slowly establish a mutally dependent relastionship that offers surrogate family ties and solace for them both. **83m/C VHS, DVD.** Samantha Mathis, Joseph Gordon-Levitt, Bud Cort, William McNamara, Mary Woronov; *D:* Joe Gayton; *W:* Joe Gayton; *C:* Greg Littlewood; *M:* Walter Werzowa.

Sweet Justice 🦴½ **1992 (R)** This time its the women who get to be commandos, have all the adventures, and get revenge on various scum. The nominal plotline has Sunny Justice (Carter) and her group of gal-warriors avenging the sadistic murder of a friend. Martial arts, weapons, and action galore. **92m/C VHS, DVD.** Finn Carter, Kathleen Kinmont, Marc Singer, Frank Gorshin, Mickey Rooney; *D:* Allen Plone; *W:* Allen Plone, Jim Tabilio.

Sweet Killing 🦴🦴 **1993 (R)** A banker murders his shrewish wife to be with another woman. He thinks he has the perfect alibi, but then his fictitious excuse comes to life when a mysterious stranger begins stalking him. Based on the novel "Qualthrough" by Agnes Hall. **87m/C VHS.** Anthony (Corlan) Higgins, F. Murray Abraham, Leslie Hope, Michael Ironside, Andrea Ferreol; *D:* Eddy Matalon; *W:* Eddy Matalon.

Sweet Liberty 🦴🦴 **1986 (PG)** Alda's hometown is overwhelmed by Hollywood chaos during the filming of a movie version of his novel about the American Revolution. Pleasant but predictable. **107m/C VHS.** Alan Alda, Michael Caine, Michelle Pfeiffer, Bob Hoskins, Lillian Gish; *D:* Alan Alda; *W:* Alan Alda; *M:* Bruce Broughton.

Sweet Lies 🦴½ **1988 (R)** An insurance investigator tracking a scam artist in Paris is preyed upon by a group of single women betting one another that any man can be seduced. Slow comedy. **86m/C VHS.** Treat Williams, Joanna Pacula, Julianne Phillips, Laura Manszky, Norbert Weisser, Marilyn Dodd-Frank; *D:* Nathalie Delon; *M:* Trevor Jones.

Sweet Light in a Dark Room 🦴🦴🦴 *Romeo, Julia a Tma; Romeo, Juliet and Darkness* **1960** A student in Prague during the Nazi Occupation hides a Jewish girl. He falls in love with her but becomes the suspect in the murder of a Nazi officer. Directed by the great Czech filmmaker Weiss who was himself forced to leave his country during Nazi occupation. In Czech with English subtitles. **93m/B VHS.** *CZ* Ivan Mistrik, Dana Smutna; *D:* Jiri Weiss.

Sweet Lorraine 🦴🦴🦴 **1987 (PG-13)** A bittersweet, nostalgic comedy about the staff and clientele of a deteriorating Catskills hotel on the eve of its closing. **91m/C VHS.** Maureen Stapleton, Lee Richardson, Trini Alvarado, Freddie Roman, John Bedford Lloyd, Giancarlo Esposito, Edie Falco, Todd Graff, Evan Handler; *D:* Steve Gomer; *W:* Michael Zettler, Shelly Altman; *M:* Richard Robbins.

Sweet Love, Bitter 🦴🦴½ *It Won't Rub Off, Baby; Black Love, White Love* **1967** The downfall of a black jazz saxophonist in the 1950s. The character is loosely based on the life of legendary musician Charlie "Bird" Parker. Alto sax man Charles McPherson dubs Gregory's solos. Adapted from the novel "Night Song" by John A. Williams. **92m/C VHS.** Dick Gregory, Don Murray, Diane Varsi, Robert Hooks; *D:* Herbert Danska; *W:* Lewis Jacobs, Herbert Danska; *M:* Mal Waldron.

Sweet Movie 🦴🦴 **1975** A provocative cult classic concerning a South African tycoon who purchases a virgin bride and then exploits her sexually. In English and French with subtitles. **120m/C VHS.** *CA FR GE* Carole Laure, Pierre Clementi, Sami Frey, Anna Prucnall, Jane Mallet, John Vernon; *D:* Dusan Makavejev; *W:* Dusan Makavejev; *C:* Pierre Lhomme; *M:* Manos Hadjidakis.

Sweet Murder woof! **1993 (R)** "Single White Female" rip-off features Udy allowing Davidtz to share her apartment—with nasty consequences. **101m/C VHS.** Helene Udy, Embeth Davidtz, Russell Todd; *D:* Percival Rubens.

Sweet Nothing 🦴🦴🦴 **1996 (R)** Wall Street up-and-comer Angel (Imperioli) is given some crack by a buddy (Calderon) to celebrate the birth of his child. This starts a downward spiral into addiction and dealing. At first, his wife Monika (Sorvino) goes along, but as Angel deteriorates, she learns not to trust him. Excellent performances by Imperioli and Sorvino avoid over-the-top theatrics. Script provides a realistic look at how addiction affects real people, and steers clear of obvious cliches. Based on diaries found in a Bronx apartment building. Film's producers tracked down the author and paid for his rehab. **89m/C VHS.** Michael Imperioli, Mira Sorvino, Paul Calderon, Billie Neal; *D:* Gary Winick; *W:* Lee Drysdale.

Sweet November 🦴🦴 **1968** Tearjerker stars Dennis as Sara Deever, a terminally ill woman who shares her apartment with a different lover each month. She helps the guy with his particular hangup and he helps her, well, live. That is until Mr. November (Newley) refuses to leave when his month is up because he's fallen in love. Remade in 2001. **113m/C VHS.** Sandy Dennis, Anthony Newley, Theodore Bikel, Burr de Benning, Sandy Baron, Marj Dusay, Martin West, Virginia Vincent, King Moody; *D:* Robert Ellis Miller; *W:* Herman Raucher; *C:* Daniel F. Fapp; *M:* Michel Legrand.

Sweet November 🦴½ **2001 (PG-13)** Stale and contrived remake of the 1968 film stars Theron as a kooky, carefree boho looking to rehabilitate uptight businessmen one month at a time, until her inevitable demise from a mysterious illness. Nelson Moss (Reeves) is Mr. November, who is invited to live with Sara in exchange for losing his cell phone, monkeysuit, and too-tense attitude for a day at the beach (literally). As the November holiday looms and Sara's secret is sappily revealed, we can give thanks that the movie is almost over. Improbable story with decent performance by Theron, while Reeves's is less so, shocking no one. **114m/C VHS, DVD, Wide.** *US* Keanu Reeves, Charlize Theron, Jason Isaacs, Greg Germann, Liam Aiken, Lauren Graham, Michael Rosenbaum, Robert Joy, Jason Kravits, Frank Langella; *D:* Pat O'Connor; *W:* Kurt Voelker; *C:* Edward Lachman; *M:* Christopher Young.

Sweet Perfection 🦴🦴 **1990 (R)** Jackson plans a big promotion for her beauty contest. Who will be voted the "Perfect Woman?" Tired premise, but it has its moments. **90m/C VHS.** Stoney Jackson, Anthony Norman McKay, Catero Colbert, Liza Crusat, Reggie Theus, Tatiana Tumbtzen.

Sweet Poison 🦴🦴 **1991 (R)** Bobby Stiles is a ruthless criminal who has just broken out of prison. He wants to get home and settle the score with his brother, who actually committed the crime Bobby was imprisoned for. Henry and Charlene Odell are traveling cross-country when Bobby crosses their path and forces them to drive him home. Bobby's not too busy eluding the police to notice that his captives' marriage is a little shaky—and that Charlene is attractive and sexy. As Bobby and Charlene get closer husband Henry just becomes another problem. **101m/C VHS.** Steven Bauer, Patricia Healy, Edward Herrmann; *D:* Brian Grant.

Sweet Revenge 🦴🦴 **1987 (R)** TV journalist kidnapped by a white slavery ring in the Asian jungles. After escaping, she returns for vegeance. Meek drama. **79m/C VHS.** Ted Shackleford, Nancy Allen, Martin Landau; *D:* Mark Sobel.

Sweet Revenge 🦴🦴 **1990** When a judge tells a divorced couple that the woman must pay the man alimony, she hires an actress to marry her ex. The tables are turned in this way-out marriage flick, reminiscent of the screwball comedies of the 1940s. **89m/C VHS.** Rosanna Arquette, Carrie Fisher, John Sessions; *D:* Charlotte Brandstrom; *W:* Janet Brownell; *M:* Hubert Bougis.

Sweet Revenge 🦴½ *The Revengers' Comedies* **1998** Even this professional cast can't rescue this predictable black comedy that is condensed from two 1991 Alan Ayckbourn plays, "The Revengers' Comedies." After saving each other from committing suicide, depressed businessman Henry Bell (Neill) and orphaned aristocrat Karen Knightly (Bonham Carter) agree on reciprocal revenge plots. Karen will punish the guy (Coogan) who stole Henry's job while Henry will destroy the neurotic wife (Scott Thomas) whose husband was once Karen's lover. Then Henry discovers Karen hasn't been telling him the truth. Too much seems to be lost from the original source. **82m/C VHS, DVD, Wide.** *GB FR* Sam Neill, Helena Bonham Carter, Kristin Scott Thomas, Martin Clunes, Rupert Graves, Steve Coogan, John Wood, Liz Smith, Charlotte Coleman; *D:* Malcolm Mowbray; *W:* Malcolm Mowbray; *C:* Romain Winding; *M:* Alexandre Desplat. **CABLE**

Sweet Rosie O'Grady 🦴🦴½ **1943** Musical-comedy star Grable has returned to New York after success in England, where she caught the eye of nobleman Gardiner. Ex-boyfriend Young is a tabloid reporter who's expected by editor Menjou to get the scoop on her past. Seems she used to perform in Bowery saloons although that's not what Grable's been telling everyone. Slight story, charming performers, and lots of songs. Remade in 1948 as "That Wonderful Urge." ♫My Heart Tells Me; My Sam; Oh Where is the Groom?; The Wishing Waltz; Going to the Country Fair; Get Your Police Gazette; Battle Cry; Sweet Rosie O'Grady; Two Little Girls in Blue. **74m/C VHS.** Betty Grable, Robert Young, Adolphe Menjou, Reginald Gardiner, Virginia Grey, Phil Regan, Sig Rumann, Alan Dinehart; *D:* Irving Cummings; *C:* Ernest Palmer.

Sweet 16 🦴🦴 **1981 (R)** Serial killings in Texas town begin to set off muffled alarms in big head of sheriff Hopkins. Sixteen-year-old Melissa has recently moved into town. She's beautiful, mysterious, and promiscuous, and she has a big problem—all her boyfriends end up dead. No real puzzle. **90m/C VHS.** Susan Strasberg, Bo Hopkins, Don Stroud, Dana Kimmell, Patrick Macnee, Larry Storch; *D:* Jim Sotos.

Sweet Smell of Success 🦴🦴🦴½ **1957** Powerful and ruthless New York City gossip columnist J.J. Hunsecker (Lancaster) writes a syndicated newspaper column that pandering press agent Sidney Falco (Curtis) is desperate to have his clients be a part of. Hunsecker only cares about the welfare of his younger sister, Susan (Harrison), and is outraged over her budding romance with jazz musician Steve Dalls (Milner). So he strong arms Falco into breaking up the relationship, with unexpected consequences. Engrossing performances, great dialogue. **96m/C VHS, DVD, Wide.** Burt Lancaster, Tony Curtis, Martin Milner, Barbara Nichols, Sam Levene, Susan Harrison; *D:* Alexander MacKendrick; *W:* Ernest Lehman, Clifford Odets; *C:* James Wong Howe; *M:* Elmer Bernstein. Natl. Film Reg. '93.

Sweet Spirits woof! **198?** Soft-sell European fluff about a modern mannequin having a raucous affair with an artist. **87m/C VHS.** Erika Blanc, Farley Granger.

Sweet Sugar 🦴½ *Chaingang Girls; Captive Women 3: Sweet Sugar* **1972 (R)** Slave girls try to escape from a Costa Rican sugar cane plantation and its cruel owner. Needless to say, vulgar exploitation runs hither and yon in this film. **90m/C VHS.** Phyllis E. Davis, Ella Edwards, Pamela Collins, Cliff Osmond, Timothy Brown; *D:* Michel Levesque.

Sweet Sweetback's Baadasssss Song 🦴🦴🦴 **1971** A black pimp kills two policemen who beat up a black militant. He uses his street-wise survival skills to elude his pursuers and escape to Mexico. A thriller, but racist, sexist, and violent. **97m/C VHS.** Melvin Van Peebles, Simon Chuckster, Hubert Scales, John Dullaghan, Rhetta Hughes, John Amos, West Gale, Niva Rochelle, Nick Ferrari, Mario Van Peebles, Megan Van Peebles; *D:* Melvin Van Peebles; *W:* Melvin Van Peebles; *C:* Robert Maxwell; *M:* Melvin Van Peebles.

Sweet Talker 🦴🦴½ **1991 (PG)** Following his release from prison, a charming con man shows up in a small coastal village, thinking the townsfolk will be ripe for the picking. What he doesn't know is they can do some sweet talking of their own, and he soon finds himself caring for a pretty widow and her son. Enjoyable light comedy works thanks to likable leads. **91m/C VHS, DVD.** *AU* Bryan Brown, Karen Allen, Chris Haywood, Bill Kerr, Bruce Spence, Bruce Myles, Paul Chubb, Peter Hehir, Justin Rosniak; *D:* Michael Jenkins; *W:* Tony Morphett; *C:* Russell Boyd; *M:* Richard Thompson, Peter Filleul.

Sweet Thing 🦴🦴🦴 **2000 (R)** Well-constructed tale concerning a troubled young artist, Sean Fields (Fox), who begins a potentially meteoric rise with a series of controversial paintings. His abusive stepfather, Ray Fields (Lunning), a district judge, has announced his intention to run for U.S. Congress and his campaign success is mirrored by the growing popularity of Sean's work, although the graphic nature of the paintings sparks a warped media frenzy. **115m/C DVD, Wide.** Jeremy Fox, Amalia Stifter, Ev Lunning Jr.; *D:* Mark David; *W:* Mark David, Mark Spacek; *C:* Mark David, Levy Castleberry, Marc Wiskemann.

Sweet Trash woof! **1970 (R)** A vice cop, having an affair with a 17-year-old prostitute, is blackmailed by an underworld figure. Lives up to its name. **80m/C VHS.** Sebastian Gregory, Sharon Matt, Luke Perry, Bonnie Clark, Gene Blackey; *D:* John Hayes.

Sweet William 🦴🦴🦴 **1979 (R)** A philandering and seemingly irresistible young man finds that one sensitive woman hasn't the patience or time for his escapades. Adult comedy concerned with sex without displaying any on the screen. **88m/C VHS.** *GB* Sam Waterston, Jenny Agutter, Anna

Massey, Arthur Lowe; *D:* Claude Whatham; *W:* Beryl Bainbridge.

Sweet Young Thing 19?? Young students at a French girls' school receive all sorts of attention from the male staff. **83m/C VHS.** Jean Tolzac, Bernard Musson.

The Sweetest Gift ₰₰½ 1998 Two Florida neighbors (Carroll and Shaver) turn out to have many of the same problems—they're both single parents trying to raise their kids as best they can while dealing with poverty and prejudice. And despite the racial differences, their kids become friends. **90m/C VHS.** Helen Shaver, Diahann Carroll, Tisha Campbell; *D:* Stuart Margolin; *W:* Rosa Jordan; *C:* Ron Stannett; *M:* Lawrence Shragge. **CABLE**

The Sweetest Thing ₰₰ 2002 (R) Girls can be just as sex-obsessed and disgusting as boys as this raunchy comedy sets out to prove. San Francisco party girl Christina Walters (Diaz) isn't looking for Mr. Right—just Mr. Right Now. And she thinks she's met him when Christina and gal pal Courtney (Applegate) take the third of their Musketeer trio—the just-dumped Jane (Blair)—out to a dance club to drink and flirt. Christina meets cute with Peter (Jane) but doesn't follow through. After getting ragged on by Courtney, the babe duo decide to track him down at the oh-so-genteel wedding he's attending. Havoc ensues. Film's both giddy and sleazy but if you like Diaz at her daffiest, you'll sit through the tacky situations. **84m/C VHS, DVD.** *US* Cameron Diaz, Christina Applegate, Thomas Jane, Selma Blair, Jason Bateman, Parker Posey; *D:* Roger Kumble; *W:* Nancy M. Pimental; *C:* Anthony B. Richmond; *M:* Ed Shearmur.

Sweetheart of the Navy ₰½ 1937 Sailors help a cafe singer out of a jam, with one of them almost giving up his career for her. Standard fare, but Parker is well worth listening to. **63m/B VHS.** Eric Linden, Cecilia Parker, Roger Imhof, Bernadene Hayes, Jason Robards Sr., Don Barclay; *D:* Duncan Mansfield.

Sweethearts ₰₰₰ 1938 MacDonald and Eddy star as married stage actors trying to get some time off from their hectic schedule in this show-within-a-show. Trouble ensues when their conniving producer begs, pleads and tricks them into staying. Lots of well-staged musical numbers. ♫Wooden Shoes; Every Lover Must Meet His Fate; Sweethearts; Pretty as a Picture; Summer Serenade; On Parade. **114m/C VHS.** Jeanette MacDonald, Nelson Eddy, Frank Morgan, Florence Rice, Ray Bolger, Mischa Auer; *D:* Woodbridge S. Van Dyke.

Sweethearts ₰₰½ 1997 (R) Manic-depressive Jasmine (Garofalo) responds to a personal ad placed by Arliss (Rouse), so she'll have a date for her 31st birthday. When the experience goes badly, Jasmine prevents Arliss from leaving by pulling a gun on him. Offbeat and downbeat. **85m/C VHS.** Janeane Garofalo, Mitch Rouse, Margaret Cho, Bob(cat) Goldthwait; *D:* Aleks Horvat; *W:* Aleks Horvat; *C:* John Peters; *M:* Carl Schurtz.

Sweetie ₰₰₰ 1989 (R) Bizarre, expressive Australian tragicomedy about a pair of sisters—one a withdrawn, paranoid Plain Jane, the other a dangerously extroverted, overweight sociopath who re-enters her family's life and turns it upside down. Campion's first feature. **97m/C VHS.** *AU* Genevieve Lemon, Karen Colston, Tom Lycos, Jon Darling, Dorothy Barry, Michael Lake, Andre Pataczek; *D:* Jane Campion; *W:* Gerard Lee, Jane Campion; *M:* Martin Armiger.

Sweetwater: A True Rock Story ₰₰½ 1999 (PG-13) TV music journalist Cami Carlson (Williams) gets out of drug rehab and learns her new assignment is a "where are they now" story about '60s band Sweetwater, the opening act at Woodstock. Teenaged singer Nansi Nevins (Johnson) disappeared after the festival and the band soon broke up. Cami tracks down ex-band members and flashbacks show how the band started and what caused Nansi to take off. **95m/C VHS.** Kelli Williams, Amy Jo Johnson, Kurt Max Runte, Robert Moloney, Frederic Forrest, Michelle Phillips, Terry David Mulligan, Nancy Warren; *D:* Lorraine Senna; *W:* Victoria Wozniak; *C:* Bernard Couture. **CABLE**

Swept Away... ₰₰₰ *Swept Away...By an Unusual Destiny in the Blue Sea of August* 1975 (R) A rich and beautiful Milanese woman is shipwrecked on a desolate island with a swarthy Sicilian deck hand, who also happens to be a dedicated communist. Isolated, the two switch roles, with the wealthy woman dominated by the crude proletarian. Sexy and provocative. Italian with subtitles. **116m/C VHS, DVD, Wide.** *IT* Giancarlo Giannini, Mariangela Melato; *D:* Lina Wertmuller; *W:* Lina Wertmuller; *C:* Julio Battiferri; *M:* Piero Piccioni.

Swept from the Sea ₰₰½ *Amy Foster* 1997 (PG-13) Shipwrecked foreigner (Perez) and ostracized servant girl (Weisz) are star-crossed lovers in 19th century Cornwall. Told in flashback by Dr. Kennedy (McKellen) to Kathy Bates' invalid Miss Swaffer, he recalls how the native Ukrainian Yanko, who could speak no English, was thought to be an idiot by all in town, except the kind and gentle Amy, who found him washed up on the shore. Kennedy and Yanko bond through a game of chess, and the kindly doctor teaches him English. Armed with the native words of love, Yanko goes a'courtin' Miss Amy. Definitely for die-hard romantics, the films throws in all the melodrama it can muster and then some, but performances are worthy (especially McKellen's). Based on a short story by Joseph Conrad. **115m/C VHS, DVD.** *GB* Vincent Perez, Rachel Weisz, Kathy Bates, Ian McKellen, Joss Ackland, Tom Bell, Zoe Wanamaker, Tony Haygarth, Fiona Victory; *D:* Beeban Kidron; *W:* Tim Willocks; *C:* Dick Pope; *M:* John Barry.

Swift Justice ₰₰ 1988 Mayor of a small town thinks he's gotten away with murder after leaving a young girl for dead in a junk yard. However, the mayor and his violent pals are soon hunted by an ex-Green Beret with a penchant for justice. **90m/C VHS.** Jon Greene, Cindy Rome, Cameron Mitchell, Aldo Ray, Chuck "Porky" Mitchell, Wilson Dunster, Ted Leplat; *D:* Harry Hope.

Swifty ₰½ 1936 A cowpoke is accused of murder but escapes to track down the real culprit and win the hand of the girl he loves. **60m/B VHS.** Hoot Gibson.

Swim Team ₰ 1979 New coach for a terminally inept school swimming team whips them into shape. Doesn't hold much water. **81m/C VHS.** Stephen Furst, James Daughton, Jenny Neumann, Kim Day, Buster Crabbe; *D:* James Polakof.

The Swimmer ₰₰₰½ 1968 (PG) A lonely suburbanite swims an existential swath through the pools of his neighborhood landscape in an effort at self-discovery. A surreal, strangely compelling work based on a story by John Cheever. **94m/C VHS.** Burt Lancaster, Janice Rule, Janet Landgard, Marge Champion, Kim Hunter, Rose Gregorio, John David Garfield; *D:* Frank Perry; *M:* Marvin Hamlisch.

Swimming Pool ₰₰½ 1970 (PG) Two men and two women spend a weekend in a villa on the French Riviera, manipulating each other, playing sexual games, and changing partners. Their escapades end in murder. Romantic melodrama is sensuous if slow-moving. French film dubbed in English. **85m/C VHS.** *FR* Romy Schneider, Alain Delon, Maurice Ronet, Jane Birkin; *D:* Jacques Deray.

Swimming to Cambodia ₰₰₰ 1987 Gray tells the story of his bit part in "The Killing Fields," filmed in Cambodia, and makes ironic observations about modern life. It works. **87m/C VHS.** Spalding Gray; *D:* Jonathan Demme; *C:* John Bailey; *M:* Laurie Anderson.

Swimming with Sharks ₰₰₰ *The Buddy Factor* 1994 (R) Budding screenwriter Guy (Whaley) goes to work for notoriously insulting movie producer Buddy (Spacey). Soon, Guy grows tired of his boss's demeaning treatment and cruel means of communication and devises a scheme which would even the score. Hollywood satire has more bite than "The Player," and a devious cilmax, but it's mostly an opportunity for Spacey to hang his hams, which he does with glee. Debut for director Huang, who based his script on his experience as a production assistant. See it with your boss. **93m/C VHS, DVD.** Kevin Spacey, Frank Whaley, Michelle Forbes, Benicio Del Toro; *D:* George Huang; *W:* George Huang; *C:* Steven Firestone; *M:* Tom Heil. N.Y. Film Critics '95: Support. Actor (Spacey).

Swimsuit ₰½ 1989 A young ad executive decides to revitalize a swimsuit company's failing business by sponsoring a contest for the perfect swimsuit model in this TV fluff. **100m/C VHS, DVD.** William Katt, Catherine Oxenberg, Cyd Charisse, Nia Peeples, Tom Villard, Cheryl Pollak, Billy Warlock, Jack Wagner; *D:* Chris Thomson; *W:* Robert Schiff; *C:* Laszlo George; *M:* John D'Andrea. **TV**

Swindle ₰ 1992 Two life-long friends set up scam after scam in their quest for sex and money. Their latest con involves a phony marriage broker business, which provides the opportunity to meet a lot of lovely ladies. Only it turns out the hustlers may be the ones getting hustled. **85m/C VHS.** Robby West, Britt Houston, Elaina Dunn, Samantha Fong, Bobby Tess, Donna Thomas; *D:* Jason Holt.

The Swindle ₰₰ *Rien ne va plus* 1997 Chabrol's 50th film deals with femme fatale con woman Betty (Huppert) and her older partner, Victor (Serrault). Their modus operandi is for Betty to pick up a businessman, go to his hotel room, and after he passes out from the mickey she's put in his drink, Betty and Victor steal just enough to make it worth their time without raising immediate suspicions. But Betty wants to go for higher stakes and works her own scam with shady Maurice (Cluzet), which has unexpected consequences for the trio. French with subtitles. **105m/C VHS, Wide.** *FR* Isabelle Huppert, Michel Serrault, Francois Cluzet, Jean-Francois Balmer; *D:* Claude Chabrol; *W:* Claude Chabrol; *C:* Eduardo Serra; *M:* Matthieu Chabrol.

Swing ₰₰½ 1998 (R) Martin Luxford (Speer) is out on parole, having learned to play the sax in the slammer from his cellmate Jack (Clemons, who does the sax solos). So he decides to put together a neo-forties swing band in Liverpool with his sultry ex-girlfriend, singer Joan (Stansfield), who's now married to jealous cop, Andy (McCall). Martin has to recruit musicians, get them gigs, and manage to avoid getting into trouble that could land him back in jail (and win back Joan). It's an amusing "let's put on a show" Brit style. **98m/C VHS.** *GB* Hugo Speer, Lisa Stansfield, Tom Bell, Rita Tushingham, Paul Usher, Alexei Sayle, Danny McCall, Clarence Clemons, James Hicks, Scot Williams, Tom Georgeson; *D:* Nick Mead; *W:* Nick Mead; *C:* Ian Wilson.

Swing High, Swing Low ₰₰½ 1937 A trumpet player fights the bottle and the dice to become a hit in the jazz world and marry the woman he loves. Solid drama. From the stage play "Burlesque." Made first as "The Dance of Life," then as "When My Baby Smiles At Me." **95m/B VHS.** Carole Lombard, Fred MacMurray, Charles Butterworth, Dorothy Lamour; *D:* Mitchell Leisen.

Swing It, Professor ₰₰½ *Swing it Buddy* 1937 A stodgy music professor refuses to recognize jazz as a valid musical form and subsequently loses his job. During his unemployment, he wanders into a nightclub and discovers jazz isn't so bad after all. Nice camera work. ♫I'm Sorta Kinda Glad I Met You; An Old-Fashioned Melody; Richer Than A Millionaire. **62m/B VHS.** Pinky Tomlin, Paula Stone, Mary Kornman, Milburn Stone, Pat Gleason; *D:* Marshall Neilan.

Swing It, Sailor! ₰₰ 1937 Two footloose sailors go after the same woman while on shore leave. Decent screwball comedy. **61m/B VHS.** Wallace Ford, Ray Mayer, Isabel Jewell, Mary Treen; *D:* Raymond Cannon.

Swing Kids ₰₰ 1993 (PG-13) In 1939 in Germany, big band or "swing" music is the instrument used by a group of young people to rebel against the conformity demanded by Hitler. Highlights the politics of the era, but concentrates mainly on three teenagers and the strains that Nazi power put on their friendship. Although the premise is based in historic fact, there is still something disturbingly silly about the entire production. Dance sequences are lively and well-choreographed. Branagh (in an uncredited role) plays a smooth-talking Gestapo chief. Filmed on location in Prague, Czechoslovakia (as a substitute for Hamburg, Germany). **114m/C VHS.** Robert Sean Leonard, Christian Bale, Frank Whaley, Barbara Hershey, Tushka Bergen, David Tom, Kenneth Branagh, Noah Wyle; *D:* Thomas Carter; *W:* Jonathan Marc Feldman; *C:* Jerzy Zielinski; *M:* James Horner.

Swing Parade of 1946 ₰½ 1946 One of the multitude of 1940s musicals. Young songwriter falls in love with club owner. Highlights include an appearance by the Three Stooges. ♫Stormy Weather; Just a Little Fond Affection; Don't Worry About the Mule; A Tender Word Will Mend It All; On the Sunny Side of the Street; Oh, Brother; After All This Time; Caledonia. **74m/B VHS.** Gale Storm, Phil Regan, Moe Howard, Edward Brophy, Connee Boswell; *D:* Phil Karlson.

Swing Shift ₰₰½ 1984 (PG) When Hawn takes a job at an aircraft plant after her husband goes off to war, she learns more than riveting. Lahti steals the film as her friend and co-worker. A detailed reminiscence of the American home front during WWII that never seems to gel. Produced by Hawn. **100m/C VHS.** Goldie Hawn, Kurt Russell, Ed Harris, Christine Lahti, Holly Hunter, Chris Lemmon, Belinda Carlisle, Fred Ward, Roger Corman, Lisa Pelikan; *D:* Jonathan Demme; *W:* Ron Nyswaner, Bo Goldman; *C:* Tak Fujimoto. N.Y. Film Critics '84: Support. Actress (Lahti).

Swing Time ₰₰₰ 1936 Astaire, a dancer who can't resist gambling, is engaged to marry another woman, until he meets Ginger. One of the team's best efforts. ♫The Way You Look Tonight; Waltz in Swing Time; Never Gonna Dance; Pick Yourself Up; A Fine Romance; Bojangles of Harlem. **103m/B VHS.** Fred Astaire, Ginger Rogers, Helen Broderick, Betty Furness, Eric Blore, Victor Moore; *D:* George Stevens; *M:* Jerome Kern, Dorothy Fields. Oscars '36: Song ("The Way You Look Tonight").

Swingers ₰₰₰ 1996 (R) Hip, hilarious, and highly entertaining low-budget comedy features five young showbiz wanna-bes on the prowl for career breaks and beautiful "babies" in the Hollywood retro club scene. Mike (screenwriter Favreau) is a struggling actor/comedian from New York who's having trouble getting over his ex. His slick, handsome friend Trent (Vaughn, in a star-making turn) and the rest of his neo-Rat Pack buddies try to get him back in the game with nightly parties and lounge-hopping. Witty script and clever camera work make this one "money, baby, money!" **96m/C VHS, DVD.** Jon Favreau, Vince Vaughn, Ron Livingston, Patrick Van Horn, Alex Desert, Brooke Langton, Heather Graham, Deena Martin, Katherine Kendall, Blake Lindsley; *D:* Doug Liman; *W:* Jon Favreau; *C:* Doug Liman; *M:* Justin Reinhardt. MTV Movie Awards '97: New Filmmaker (Liman).

A Swingin' Summer ₰½ 1965 A bunch of groovy guys and gals go-go to the beach for a vacation of fun and sun and end up starting a rock 'n' roll concert series. Everybody gets part of the action...even the bespectacled Welch, who gets a chance to sing. Performances from the Righteous Brothers and rock semi-legends Donnie Brooks, Gary Lewis and the Playboys, and the Rip Chords. ♫Red Hot Roadster; Justine; Penny the Fool; Out to Lunch; Nitro; Ready to Groove. **81m/C VHS.** James Stacy, William Wellman Jr., Quinn O'Hara, Martin West, Mary Mitchell, Allan Jones, Raquel Welch; *D:* Robert Sparr; *W:* Leigh Chapman.

The Swinging Cheerleaders ₰₰½ 1974 (PG) A group of amorous cheerleaders turn on the entire campus in this typical sexploiter. **90m/C VHS, DVD.** Cheryl "Rainbeaux" Smith, Colleen Camp, Rosanne Katon, Jo Johnston, Mae Mercer, Bob Minor, George D. Wallace; *D:* Jack Hill; *W:* Betty Conklin; *C:* Alfred Taylor; *M:* William Allen Castleman, William Loose.

Swiss Conspiracy ₰₰ 1977 (PG) Against the opulent background of the world's richest financial capital and playground of the wealthy, one man battles to stop a daring and sophisticated blackmailer preying on the secret bank account set. Fast-paced, if sometimes confusing. **92m/C VHS, DVD.** *GE* David Janssen, Senta Berger, John Saxon, Ray Milland, Elke Sommer; *D:* Jack

Arnold; ***W:*** Norman Klenman, Philip Saltzman, Michael Stanley; ***M:*** Klaus Doldinger.

The Swiss Family Robinson 🦴🦴🦴 **1960** A family, seeking to escape Napoleon's war in Europe, sets sail for New Guinea, but shipwrecks on a deserted tropical island. There they build an idyllic life, only to be confronted by a band of pirates. Lots of adventure for family viewing. Filmed on location on the island of Tobago. Based on the novel by Johann Wyss. **126m/C VHS, DVD, Wide.** John Mills, Dorothy McGuire, James MacArthur, Tommy Kirk, Janet Munro, Sessue Hayakawa; ***D:*** Ken Annakin; ***W:*** Lowell S. Hawley; ***C:*** Harry Waxman; ***M:*** William Alwyn.

Swiss Miss 🦴🦴½ **1938** Stan and Ollie are mousetrap salesmen on the job in Switzerland. Highlights include Stan's tuba serenade and the gorilla-on-the-bridge episode. Also included on this tape is a 1935 Thelma Todd/Patsy Kelly short, "Hot Money." **97m/B VHS.** Stan Laurel, Oliver Hardy, Della Lind, Walter Woolf King, Eric Blore, Thelma Todd, Patsy Kelly; ***D:*** John Blystone.

The Switch 🦴🦴 **1989 (R)** An escaped convict takes the place of a talented conman and chaos ensues. **?m/C VHS.** Anthony Quinn, Adriano Celentano, Capucine, Corinne Clery.

Switch 🦴🦴🦴 **1991 (R)** A chauvinist louse, slain by the girlfriends he misused, is sent back to Earth as an alluring female to learn the other side's point of view. The plot may lack urgency, but this is a sparkling adult comedy that scores as it pursues the gimmicky concept to a logical, outrageous and touching conclusion. Barkin's act as swaggering male stuck in a woman's body is a masterwork of physical humor. **104m/C VHS, DVD, Wide.** Ellen Barkin, Jimmy Smits, JoBeth Williams, Lorraine Bracco, Perry King, Bruce Payne, Tony Roberts; ***D:*** Blake Edwards; ***W:*** Blake Edwards; ***C:*** Dick Bush; ***M:*** Henry Mancini.

Switchback 🦴🦴 *Going West in America* **1997 (R)** FBI agent Frank Lacrosse (Quaid) pursues the serial killer who kidnapped his son. Against the backdrop of a Texas sheriff's election and a Colorado snowstorm, the killer, who may or may not be a former rail worker (Glover) or the hitchhiking ex-doctor (Leto) he picked up, leads Lacrosse on a convoluted cat-and-mouse game with no apparent logic or motive. First-time director Stuart, who wrote "Die Hard" and "The Fugitive," wrote this one in film school, and it shows. Connect-the-dots set pieces and plot twists only provide Quaid more time to perfect his Harrison Ford impression and Glover more scenery and dialogue to chew. Ermey is impressive as the put-upon small-town sheriff. Stunt work is well done and the Colorado countryside looks great. **120m/C VHS, DVD.** Dennis Quaid, Danny Glover, Jared Leto, R. Lee Ermey, William Fichtner, Ted Levine, Leo Burmester, Merle Kennedy, Julio Mechoso; ***D:*** Jeb Stuart; ***W:*** Jeb Stuart; ***C:*** Oliver Wood; ***M:*** Basil Poledouris.

Switchblade Sisters woof! *The Jezebels; Playgirl Gang* **1975** Crime gang of female ex-cons wreaks pseudo-feminist havoc. Bruce is Lenny Bruce's daughter. **91m/C VHS, DVD, Wide.** Robbie Lee, Joanne Nail, Monica Gayle, Kitty Bruce, Asher Brauner, Chase Newhart, Marlene Clark, Janice Karman, Don Stark, Kate Murtagh, Bill Adler; ***D:*** Jack Hill; ***W:*** F.X. Maier; ***C:*** Stephen M. Katz; ***M:*** Les Baxter, Medusa, Chuck Day, Richard Person.

Switched at Birth 🦴🦴½ **1991 (PG)** A fact-based drama about two girls, switched in a hospital nursery at birth. Only when one girl dies, a decade later, do her parents discover that she could not have been their biological child. Their search for their daughter leads to an emotional conflict between the girl, the man that raised her, and the biological parents who seek to claim her. Beware of the sappy Hollywood ending; five years later the story of Kimberly Mays was still going through the U.S. judicial system. **200m/C VHS.** Bonnie Bedelia, Brian Kerwin, Ed Asner, Caroline McWilliams, John M. Jackson, Lois Smith, Eve Gordon, Judith Hoag, Ariana Richards; ***D:*** Waris Hussein. **TV**

Switching Channels 🦴🦴½ **1988 (PG)** A modernized remake of "His Girl Friday," and therefore the fourth version of "The Front Page." Beautiful TV anchorwoman (Turner) wants to marry handsome tycoon (Reeve), but her scheming ex-husband (Reynolds) gets in the way. Weak performances from everyone but Beatty and lackluster direction render this off-told story less funny than usual. **108m/C VHS.** Burt Reynolds, Kathleen Turner, Christopher Reeve, Ned Beatty, Henry Gibson, George Newbern, Al Waxman, Ken James, Joe Silver, Charles Kimbrough, Tony Rosato; ***D:*** Ted Kotcheff; ***W:*** Jonathan Reynolds; ***M:*** Michel Legrand.

Swoon 🦴🦴🦴 **1991** Kalin's directorial debut is a stylish rendering of the sensational 1924 kidnapping and murder of Bobby Franks by Richard Loeb and Nathan Leopold Jr. and their subsequent trial and imprisonment. Core elements of the case remain but Kalin imposes contemporary styles and morals on the past, particularly his protest against the homophobic attitudes influencing the trial while acknowledging the jaded and dispassionate behavior of the two young men. Previous cinematic versions of the murder case include "Rope" and "Compulsion" but Kalin graphically portrays the characters homosexuality, which was only hinted at in the earlier films. **95m/B VHS.** Daniel Schlachet, Craig Chester, Ron Vawter, Michael Kirby, Michael Stumm, Valda Z. Drabla, Natalie Stanford; ***D:*** Tom Kalin; ***W:*** Tom Kalin; ***C:*** Ellen Kuras; ***M:*** James Bennett. Sundance '92: Cinematog.

The Sword and the Cross 🦴½ **1958** A grade-B adventure about the life of Mary Magdelene. **93m/B VHS.** Yvonne De Carlo, Jorge Mistral; ***D:*** Carlo L. Bragaglia.

Sword & the Dragon 🦴🦴 *Ilya Mourometz* **1956** A young warrior must battle any number of giant mythical creatures. **81m/C VHS.** *RU* Boris Andreyer, Andrei Abrikosov; ***D:*** Alexander Ptushko.

The Sword & the Rose 🦴🦴½ *When Knighthood Was in Flower* **1953** Mary Tudor, sister of King Henry VIII, shuns the advances of a nobleman for the love of a commoner. Johns is an obstinate princess; Justice, a fine king. Based on the book "When Knighthood Was in Flower." **91m/C VHS.** Richard Todd, Glynis Johns, Michael Gough, Jane Barrett, James Robertson Justice; ***D:*** Ken Annakin; ***C:*** Geoffrey Unsworth.

Sword & the Sorcerer 🦴½ **1982 (R)** Young prince strives to regain control of his kingdom, now ruled by an evil knight and a powerful magician. Mediocre script and acting is enhanced by decent special effects. **100m/C VHS, DVD, Wide.** Lee Horsley, Kathleen Beller, George Maharis, Simon MacCorkindale, Richard Lynch, Richard Moll, Robert Tessier, Nina Van Pallandt, Anna Bjorn, Jeff Corey; ***D:*** Albert Pyun; ***W:*** Albert Pyun; ***C:*** Joseph Mangine; ***M:*** David Whitaker.

The Sword in the Stone 🦴🦴🦴 **1963 (G)** The Disney version of the first volume of T.H. White's "The Once and Future King" wherein King Arthur, as a boy, is instructed in the ways of the world by Merlin and Archimedes the owl. Although not in the Disney masterpiece fold, boasts the usual superior animation and a gripping mythological tale. **79m/C VHS, DVD.** ***D:*** Wolfgang Reitherman; ***W:*** Bill Peet; ***M:*** George Bruns; ***V:*** Ricky Sorenson, Sebastian Cabot, Karl Swenson, Junius Matthews, Alan Napier, Norman Alden, Martha Wentworth, Barbara Jo Allen.

Sword of Doom 🦴🦴🦴 *Daibosatsu Toge* **1967** A rousing samurai epic detailing the training of an impulsive, bloodlusting warrior by an elder expert. In Japanese with English subtitles. **120m/B VHS.** *JP* Tatsuya Nakadai, Toshiro Mifune; ***D:*** Kihachi Okamoto.

The Sword of El Cid 🦴½ *La Spada del Cid* **1962** Not much dash and very little daring-do in this poorly plotted, overly dramatic saga of good vs. evil, Spanish style. Rightful heir to the crown threatens, challenges and enevitably crosses swords with the pretender to his throne. Costume mavens may find something to hold their interest. **86m/C VHS.** *SP IT* Roland Carey, Sandro Moretti, Chantal Deberg, Iliana Grimaldi, Jose Luis Pellicena, Daniela Bianchi; ***D:*** Miguel Iglesias.

Sword of Gideon 🦴🦴½ **1986** An action-packed and suspenseful TV film about an elite commando group who set out to avenge the Munich Olympic killings of 1972. Adapted from "Vengeance" by George Jonas. **148m/C VHS.** Steven Bauer, Michael York, Rod Steiger, Colleen Dewhurst, Robert Joy, Laurent Malet, Lino Ventura, Leslie Hope; ***D:*** Michael Anderson Sr.; ***W:*** Chris Bryant; ***M:*** Georges Delerue. **TV**

Sword of Honor 🦴½ **1994 (R)** Undercover cop and martial arts expert Johnny Lee (Leigh) investigates his partner's mysterious death amidst the tawdry glamor of Vegas. **?m/C VHS.** Steven Leigh, Sophia Crawford, Angelo Tiffe, Jerry Tiffe, Jeff Pruitt, Debbie Scofield; ***D:*** Robert Tiffe; ***W:*** Robert Tiffe, Clay Ayers; ***M:*** David Rubinstein.

Sword of Lancelot 🦴🦴½ *Lancelot and Guinevere* **1963** A costume version of the Arthur-Lancelot-Guinevere triangle, with plenty of swordplay and a sincere respect for the old legend. **115m/C VHS.** *GB* Cornel Wilde, Jean Wallace, Brian Aherne, George Baker; ***D:*** Cornel Wilde.

Sword of Monte Cristo 🦴½ **1951** Masked female avenger, seeking the liberty of the French people, discovers a valuable sword that holds the key to a vast fortune. But the sword is also desired by an evil government minister. **80m/C VHS.** George Montgomery, Rita (Paula) Corday; ***D:*** Maurice Geraghty.

Sword of Sherwood Forest 🦴🦴½ **1960** The Earl of Newark plots the murder of the Archbishop of Canterbury in yet another rendition of the Robin Hood legend. Cushing is truly evil as the villain. **80m/C VHS.** *GB* Richard Greene, Peter Cushing, Niall MacGinnis, Richard Pasco, Jack (Gwyllam) Gwillim, Sarah Branch, Nigel Green, Oliver Reed; ***D:*** Terence Fisher.

Sword of the Valiant 🦴🦴 **1983 (PG)** The Green Knight arrives in Camelot to challenge Gawain. Remake of "Gawain And The Green Knight." Connery adds zest to a minor epic. **102m/C VHS.** *GB* Sean Connery, Miles O'Keeffe, Cyrielle Claire, Leigh Lawson, Trevor Howard, Peter Cushing, Wilfrid Brambell, Lila Kedrova, John Rhys-Davies; ***D:*** Stephen Weeks; ***W:*** Philip M. Breen; ***C:*** Frederick A. (Freddie) Young.

Sword of Venus 🦴 *Island of Monte Cristo* **1953** Uninspired production finds the son of the Count of Monte Cristo the victim in a scheme to deprive him of his wealth. **73m/B VHS.** Robert Clarke, Catherine McLeod, Dan O'Herlihy, William Schallert; ***D:*** Harold Daniels.

Swordfish 🦴🦴 **2001 (R)** CIA operative Gabriel Shear (Travolta) uses associate Ginger (Berry) to coerce a computer hacker (Jackman), who's just been released from prison, to steal nine billion dollars from a DEA slush fund. In return, the hacker gets a fresh start with his wife and daughter. The plot goes on from there, but it's too convoluted and pointless to bother with. As is usually the case with anything directed by Sena or produced by Joel Silver, the emphasis is on flash, high-energy action set pieces, and collateral damage, all of which is well done, if eventually repetitive, here. Travolta is an expert at playing the smirking supervillain, but it does wear. Jackman and Cheadle give better performances than the flick deserves, and Berry has fun with her obligatory femme fatale role. **99m/C VHS, DVD, Wide.** *US* John Travolta, Hugh Jackman, Halle Berry, Don Cheadle, Vinnie Jones, Sam Shepard, Zach Grenier, Camryn Grimes, Rudolf Martin, Drea De Matteo; ***D:*** Dominic Sena; ***W:*** Skip Woods; ***C:*** Paul Cameron; ***M:*** Christopher Young.

Swords of Death 🦴🦴 **1971** Final film by Uchida, released posthumously, deals with the adventurous period exploits of the irrepressible Miyamoto Musashi. With English subtitles. **76m/C VHS.** *JP* Kinnosuke Nakamura, Rentaro Mikuni; ***D:*** Tomu Uchida.

The Swordsman 🦴🦴½ **1992 (R)** The quest to return the stolen sword of the legendary Alexander the Great to a museum is muscular detective Lamas' assignment. Turns out the detective and his evil millionaire antagonist have been chasing each other through time in their endless quest for revenge and power. **98m/C VHS, DVD.** Lorenzo Lamas, Claire Stansfield, Michael Champion; ***D:*** Michael Kennedy; ***W:*** Michael Kennedy.

Sworn Enemies 🦴🦴½ **1996 (R)** Clifton Santier (Greene) goes on a killing spree in a small town where the local sheriff turns out to be his ex-partner, Pershing Quinn (Pare). Now the two enemies decide that only death will settle their old (and new) scores. **101m/C VHS, DVD.** *CA* Peter Greene, Michael Pare, Macha Grenon; ***D:*** Shimon Dotan; ***W:*** Rod Hewitt; ***C:*** Sylvain Brault; ***M:*** Walter Christian Rothe, Richard Anthony Boast.

Sworn to Justice 🦴½ **1997 (R)** Psychologist Jana Dane (Rothrock) wakes up with psychic powers after sustaining a serious head injury from the burglars who killed her sister and nephew. Jana then decides to put her new abilities to work for her by becoming a night time avenger. **90m/C VHS, DVD.** Cynthia Rothrock, Kurt McKinney, Tony LoBianco, Brad Dourif, Mako, Kenn Scott; ***D:*** Paul Maslak; ***W:*** Robert Easter; ***C:*** Richard Benda; ***M:*** John Coda.

Sybil 🦴🦴🦴 **1976** Fact-based story of a woman who developed 16 distinct personalities, and the supportive psychiatrist who helped her put the pieces of her ego together. Excellent production featuring Field's Emmy-winning performance. **122m/C VHS.** Sally Field, Joanne Woodward, Brad Davis, Martine Bartlett, Jane Hoffman; ***D:*** Daniel Petrie. **TV**

Sylvester 🦴🦴 **1985 (PG)** A 16-year-old girl and a cranky stockyard boss team up to train a battered horse named Sylvester for the National Equestrian trials. Nice riding sequences and good performances can't overcome familiar plot, but the kids will enjoy this one. **104m/C VHS.** Melissa Gilbert, Richard Farnsworth, Michael Schoeffling, Constance Towers; ***D:*** Tim Hunter.

Sylvia 🦴🦴½ **1986 (PG)** Biography of author/educator Sylvia Ashton-Warner, and her efforts to teach Maori children in New Zealand to read via unorthodox methods. David is a marvel. Based on Ashton-Warner's books "Teacher" and "I Passed This Way." **99m/C VHS.** *NZ* Eleanor David, Tom Wilkinson, Nigel Terry, Mary Regan; ***D:*** Michael Firth.

Sylvia and the Phantom 🦴🦴🦴 *Sylvia and the Ghost* **1945** A charming French comedy about a lonely young girl who is befriended by the ghost of a man killed decades earlier in a duel over the girl's grandmother. Based on the play by Alfred Adam. In French with English subtitles. **88m/B VHS.** *FR* Odette Joyeux, Jacques Tati, Francois Perier; ***D:*** Claude Autant-Lara.

Sylvia Scarlett 🦴🦴½ **1935** An odd British comedy about a woman who masquerades as a boy while on the run with her father, who causes all kinds of instinctive confusion in the men she meets. **94m/B VHS.** Katharine Hepburn, Cary Grant, Brian Aherne, Edmund Gwenn, Natalie Paley, Dennie Moore, Lennox Pawle, Daisy Belmore, Nola Luxford; ***D:*** George Cukor; ***C:*** Russell Metty.

Sympathy for the Devil 🦴🦴 *One Plus One* **1970** Rolling Stones provide music for confused, revolutionary documentary. Episodic jumble is odd, sometimes fascinating. **110m/C VHS.** *FR* Mick Jagger, Rolling Stones; ***D:*** Jean-Luc Godard.

Symphony in the Mountains 🦴🦴½ **1935** An early German sound romance, where an Austrian singing teacher falls in love with the sister of one of his student's. Featuring choral work by the Vienna Boys' Choir. In German with English subtitles. **75m/B VHS.** *GE*

Synapse 🦴🦴 **1995 (R)** Black-marketeer Andre (Makepeace) is doublecrossed by a partner and arrested by Life Corp., which runs this futuristic civilization. As an experimental punishment, his mind is implanted into the body of Celeste (Duffy), who manages to escape and join up with a band of revolutionaries determined to destroy the evil corporation. Fast-paced story and good special effects. **89m/C VHS.** Karen Duffy, Saul Rubinek, Matt McCoy, Chris Makepeace; ***D:*** Allan Goldstein.

Syngenor 🦴½ **1990 (R)** Syngenor stands for Synthesized Genetic Organism, to differentiate it from all other organisms. Created by science, it escapes, and a crack team of scientists and gung-ho military types are mobilized to track it down. **98m/C VHS.** Starr Andreeff, Mitchell Laurance, David Gale, Charles Lucia, Riva Spier, Jeff Doucette, Bill Gratton, Lewis Arquette, Jon Korkes, Melanie Shatner; ***D:*** George Elanjian Jr.; ***M:*** Tom Chase, Steve Rucker.

T-Bird Gang 🦴½ **1959** A high school student goes undercover to infiltrate a teen gang. When his cover is blown, things get hairy. Laughable sleazebag production. **75m/B VHS.** Ed Nelson, John Brinkley, Pat George, Beach Dickerson, Tony Miller; ***D:*** Richard Harbinger; ***M:*** Shelley Manne.

T Bone N Weasel 🦴🦴 **1992 (PG-13)** Hines and Lloyd play not-so-excons who steal a car and try to lead a life of ease. Crime doesn't pay. **94m/C VHS.** Gregory Hines, Christopher Lloyd. **CABLE**

T-Force 🦴🦴½ **1994 (R)** T-Force is a successful cybernetic law enforcement team set up in the year 2007. But when innocent people get caught in the T-Force crossfire, a team shutdown is ordered, causing the members to turn renegade and fight for their survival instead. The plot rarely gets in the way of the hard-hitting action. **101m/C VHS.** Jack Scalia, Erin Gray, Evan Lurie, Daron McBee; ***D:*** Richard Pepin.

T-Men 🦴🦴🦴 **1947** Treasury Department agents Dennis O'Brien (O'Keefe) and Tony Genaro (Ryder) infiltrate a mob counterfeiting gang. Filmed in semi-documentary style, exciting tale serves also as an effective commentary on the similarities between the agents and those they pursue. Mann and cinematographer Alton do especially fine work here. **96m/B VHS, DVD.** Alfred Ryder, Dennis O'Keefe, June Lockhart, Mary Meade, Wallace Ford, Charles McGraw; ***D:*** Anthony Mann; ***W:*** John C. Higgins; ***C:*** John Alton; ***M:*** Paul Sawtell.

Table for Five 🦴🦴½ **1983 (PG)** A divorced father takes his children on a Mediterranean cruise and while sailing, he learns that his ex-wife has died. The father and his ex-wife's husband struggle over who should raise the children. Sentimental and well-acted. **120m/C VHS.** Jon Voight, Millie Perkins, Richard Crenna, Robbie Kiger, Roxana Zal, Son Hoang Bui, Marie-Christine Barrault, Kevin Costner; ***D:*** Robert Lieberman; ***W:*** David Seltzer; ***M:*** Miles Goodman.

Table Settings 🦴🦴 **1984** A taped performance of James Lapines' comedy about the lives of three generations of a Jewish family. **90m/C VHS.** Robert Klein, Stockard Channing, Dinah Manoff, Eileen Heckart.

Tabloid! 🦴½ **1988** Unorthodox woman prints and sells racy trash for enquiring minds. **99m/C VHS.** Scott Davis, Glen Coburn; ***D:*** Bret McCormick, Matt Shaffen.

Tabu: A Story of the South Seas 🦴🦴🦴½ **1931** Fascinating docudrama about a young pearl diver's ill-fated romance. The gods have declared the young woman he desires "taboo" to all men. Filmed on location in Tahiti. Authored and produced by Murnau and Flaherty. Flaherty left in mid-production due to artistic differences with Murnau, who was later killed in an auto accident one week before the premiere of film. **81m/B VHS.** ***D:*** Robert Flaherty, F.W. Murnau; ***C:*** Floyd Crosby. Oscars '31: Cinematog., Natl. Film Reg. '94.

Tactical Assault 🦴🦴½ **1999 (R)** During the Gulf War, Air Force pilot John Holiday (Hauer) loses it under pressure and nearly shoots down an unarmed passenger jet. Pilot Lee Banning (Patrick) is forced to shoot down Holiday's plane instead to save the situation. But Holiday doesn't see things that way and decides to get revenge on Lee. Good action in what's really a revenge thriller. **89m/C VHS, DVD.** Rutger Hauer, Robert Patrick, Isabel Glasser, Ken Howard; ***D:*** Mark Griffiths. **VIDEO**

Tadpole **2002** Prep-schooler Oscar Grubman (Stanford) comes home to Manhattan to spend the holidays with his remarried dad (Ritter) and his new stepmom (Weaver) whom he promptly gets a crush on. Soon his unrequited love is soothed instead by her best friend (Neuwirth). Not yet reviewed. **?m/C VHS, DVD.** Aaron Stanford, Sigourney Weaver, John Ritter, Bebe Neuwirth, Robert Iler, Peter Appel, Adam LeFevre; ***D:*** Gary Winick; ***W:*** Heather McGowan, Niels Mueller.

Taffin 🦴½ **1988 (R)** An Irish bill collector battles a group of corrupt businessmen who want to replace the local soccer field with a hazardous chemical plant. Pretty dull fare, overall, with Brosnan much less charismatic than usual. **96m/C VHS, DVD.** *GB* Pierce Brosnan, Ray McAnally, Alison Doody, Patrick Bergin; ***D:*** Francis Megahy; ***W:*** David Ambrose.

Tag: The Assassination Game 🦴½ **1982 (PG)** An exciting new game has been discovered by a group of university students. Players act as spies and assassins, "killing" each other to make points. But a school newspaper sportswriter finds the game has become more real than make-believe. Timely topic in the early '80s when Dungeons and Dragons and other "war" games were popular on college campuses across the nation. **92m/C VHS.** Robert Carradine, Linda Hamilton, Michael Winslow, Kristine DeBell, Perry Lang; ***D:*** Nick Castle; ***W:*** Nick Castle.

Tagget 🦴 **1990 (PG-13)** A former CIA operative who has erased his nightmarish stint in Vietnam gradually begins to recall his past. When pieces of the puzzle begin to come together, he remembers a few things that the government would prefer he forget. Soon, CIA men are on his trail and their mission is to see that he forgets his past—permanently. **89m/C VHS.** Daniel J. Travanti, William Sadler, Roxanne Hart, Stephen Tobolowsky, Peter Michael Goetz, Sarah Douglas, Noel Harrison; ***D:*** Richard T. Heffron. **CABLE**

Tai-Pan 🦴½ **1986 (R)** A 19th century Scottish trader and his beautiful Chinese mistress are the main characters in this confusing attempt to dramatize the story of Hong Kong's development into a thriving trading port. Too many subplots and characters are introduced in a short time to do justice to James Clavell's novel of the same name, the basis for the movie. The first American production completely filmed in China. **130m/C VHS.** Bryan Brown, Joan Chen, John Stanton, Kyra Sedgwick, Tim Guinee, Russell Wong, Bert Remsen; ***D:*** Daryl Duke; ***W:*** John Briley; ***C:*** Jack Cardiff; ***M:*** Maurice Jarre.

Tail Lights Fade 🦴🦴 **1999 (R)** Angie (Allen) is living in Toronto when she learns her marijuana-dealing brother has been busted. So she convinces boyfriend Cole (Meyer) that they should drive to Vancouver in order to destroy his greenhouse crop before the cops discover it. And for some reason, Cole decides this would be a perfect opportunity to convince their friends Bruce (Busey) and Wendy (Richards) that they should indulge in a cross-country relay race. Dumb. Title comes from a Buffalo Tom song. **87m/C VHS, DVD.** *CA* Tanya Allen, Breckin Meyer, Jake Busey, Denise Richards, Lisa Marie, Elizabeth Berkley, Jaimz Woolvett; ***D:*** Malcolm Ingram; ***W:*** Matthew Gissing; ***C:*** Brian Pearson.

The Tailor of Panama 🦴🦴🦴½ **2000 (R)** British spy Andrew Osnard (Brosnan) threatens to expose the shady past of society tailor Harry Pendel (Rush) unless Harry passes on information about the political situation in Panama. But since Harry doesn't really know anything, he just makes up plausible lies. Le Carre and Boorman create a smart, cynical film from Le Carre's 1996 novel, utilizing Brosnan to treak his famous alter-ego and expose the corruption of post-Cold War espionage and Western foreign affairs. Well-written, with believable characterizations and subtle, consistent plotting, and as an added bonus, the performances match the high standards of the writing. **109m/C VHS, DVD, Wide.** *US IR* Pierce Brosnan, Geoffrey Rush, Jamie Lee Curtis, Brendan Gleeson, Catherine McCormack, Leonor Varela, Harold Pinter, Daniel Radcliffe, David Hayman, Mark Margolis, Martin Ferrero, John Fortune; ***D:*** John Boorman; ***W:*** John Boorman, Andrew Davies, John Le Carre; ***C:*** Philippe Rousselot; ***M:*** Shaun Davey.

Tails You Live, Heads You're Dead 🦴🦴 **1995 (R)** Cable thriller features Bernsen as psycho Neil Jones, who kills at random—and tells a stranger, Jeff Quint (McGinley), whom he met at a bar that the man is his next victim. After several unsuccessful attempts on his life, Quint turns to private detective McKinley (Matheson) for help. Based on the short story "Liar's Dice" by Bill Pronzini. **91m/C VHS.** Corbin Bernsen, Ted McGinley, Tim Matheson, Maria Del Mar; ***D:*** Tim Matheson; ***W:*** Miguel Tejada-Flores; ***C:*** Francois Protat; ***M:*** David Michael Frank. **CABLE**

Tailspin: Behind the Korean Airline Tragedy 🦴🦴 **1989** Made-for-TV docudrama on the 1983 downing of Korean Aire flight 007 in Soviet airspace. Purports to show the U.S. government's reaction to what became a major international incident. **82m/C VHS.** Michael Moriarty, Michael Murphy, Chris Sarandon, Harris Yulin, Gavan O'Herlihy, Ed O'Ross; ***D:*** David Darlow; ***M:*** David Ferguson.

Tailspin Tommy **1934** Features 12 chapters of the great action serial. **?m/B VHS.** Maurice Murphy, Noah Beery Jr., Walter Miller, Patricia Farr, Grant Withers, John Davidson, William Desmond, Charles A. Browne; ***D:*** Lew (Louis Friedlander) Landers.

Tainted 🦴½ **1988** Small-town woman tries to endure after being raped. Both her husband and the attacker are killed, and she is forced to conceal their deaths. Poorly scripted. **90m/C VHS.** Shari Shattuck, Park Overall, Gene Tootle, Magilla Schaus, Blaque Fowler; ***D:*** Orestes Matacena.

Tainted 🦴🦴½ **1998** Ever wonder what would happen if the guys from "Clerks" fell in with a bunch of vampires? Well, lucky you. Now you can find out. Video clerks Ryan and J.T. hitch a ride to the midnight movie with their new co-worker Alex, who just happens to be a vampire whose ex is shacking up with the new vamp in town, who wants to taint the city's blood supply with undead blood. Script has many laughs, lots of attitude, and plenty of pop-culture knowledge, but gets a bit windy at times. Sometimes the actors seem to to trying a little too hard, but it doesn't detract from the story. Filmed in Detroit with lots of excellent local product placement. **106m/C VHS.** Dusan "Dean" Cechvala, Greg James, Sean Farley, Jason Brouwer, Tina Kapousis, Edward Zeimis, Robert St. Mary, Brian Evans; ***D:*** Brian Evans; ***W:*** Sean Farley; ***C:*** Brian Evans; ***M:*** Jessie McClear. **VIDEO**

Tainted Blood 🦴🦴 **1993 (R)** Welch stars as an investigative reporter whose latest story has her attempting to find the teenage twin of a psychotic killer. **86m/C VHS.** Raquel Welch, Alley Mills, Kerri Green, Natasha Gregson Wagner, Joan Van Ark; ***D:*** Matthew Patrick; ***W:*** Kathleen Rowell, Ginny Cerrella; ***C:*** Billy Dickson.

Tainted Image 🦴🦴 **1991** Artist woman starts to lose sanity with help of boyfriend, psycho neighbor and rash of bizarre deaths. She turns to canvas for solace and decides she needs secret ingredient that can't be found in art supply store to complete masterpiece. **95m/C VHS.** Tom Saunders, Sandra Frances, Annetta Arpin, Ken La Mothe, Heidi Emerich, Steve Kornacki.

The Take 🦴🦴 **1990 (R)** Recovering alcoholic cop faces wrath of drug lord and marriage on the rocks. **91m/C VHS.** Ray Sharkey, R. Lee Ermey, Lisa Hartman Black, Larry Manetti, Joe Lala; ***D:*** Leon Ichaso; ***W:*** Edward Anhalt, Handel Glassberg; ***M:*** David Beal.

Take a Hard Ride 🦴½ **1975 (R)** Dull spaghetti western about a cowboy transporting money to Mexico, evading bandits and bounty hunters. **103m/C VHS.** *IT* Jim Brown, Lee Van Cleef, Fred Williamson, Jim Kelly, Barry Sullivan; ***D:*** Anthony (Antonio Margheriti) Dawson; ***M:*** Jerry Goldsmith.

Take Down 🦴🦴 **1979 (PG)** Hermann is charming as a high school English teacher turned reluctant wrestling coach. **96m/C VHS.** Lorenzo Lamas, Kathleen Lloyd, Maureen McCormick, Edward Herrmann, Nicolas Beauvy, Stephen Furst, Kevin Hooks; ***D:*** Keith Merrill.

Take Down 🦴🦴½ *Deliver Them from Evil: The Taking of Alta View* **1992 (PG-13)** Rick Worthington (Hamlin) takes hostages in a Utah hospital maternity ward, seeking revenge on the doctors who sterilized his wife. He threatens to detonate a bomb even as a hostage negogiator (O'Quinn) tries to defuse the situation. **96m/C VHS.** Harry Hamlin, Teri Garr, Terry O'Quinn, Gary Frank, Keith Coulouris; ***D:*** Peter Levin; ***W:*** John Miglis; ***C:*** Ronald Orieux; ***M:*** Mark Snow. **TV**

Take It Big 🦴½ **1944** Uninspired B-musical starring the Tin Man from the "Wizard of Oz." Haley is an impoverished actor who inherits a ranch and saves it by—surprise—putting on a show. ♫Sunday, Monday, and Always; Love and Learn; Life Can Be Beautiful; Take It Big; I'm a Big Success with You. **75m/B VHS.** Jack Haley, Harriet Hilliard Nelson, Mary Beth Hughes, Arline Judge, Nils T. Granlund, Fuzzy Knight, Ozzie Nelson; ***D:*** Frank McDonald.

Take It to the Limit 🦴🦴½ **2000** Troubled teen Rick (Fitzpatrick) is sent to stay with his uncle (Marlo) in hopes that it'll straighten him out. But that happens when Jill (Roenfeldt), a cute girl, introduces him to rock climbing. This is a pretty good movie for kids. It's a bit obvious, but it treats the characters seriously. **87m/C DVD.** Leo Fitzpatrick, John Marlo, Gretel Roenfeldt, Jason Bortz, Christin Couto; ***D:*** Sam Kieth; ***W:*** Arthur Jeon; ***C:*** Michael Anderson; ***M:*** Louis Gabriel Cowan.

Take Me Back to Oklahoma 🦴 **1940** Musical western with comedy. **64m/B VHS.** Tex Ritter, Terry Walker, Karl Hackett, George Eldredge; ***D:*** Al(bert) Herman.

Take Me Out to the Ball Game 🦴🦴½ *Everybody's Cheering* **1949** Williams manages a baseball team, locks horns with players Sinatra and Kelly, and wins them over with song. Naturally, there's a water ballet scene. Contrived and forced, but enjoyable. ♫Take Me Out to the Ball Game; The Hat My Father Wore on St. Patrick's Day; O'Brien to Ryan to Goldberg; The Right Girl for Me; It's Fate, Baby, It's Fate; Yes, Indeedy; Strictly U.S.A. **93m/C VHS, DVD.** Frank Sinatra, Gene Kelly, Esther Williams, Jules Munshin, Betty Garrett, Edward Arnold, Tom Dugan, Richard Lane; ***D:*** Busby Berkeley; ***W:*** Harry Tugend, George Wells; ***C:*** George J. Folsey; ***M:*** Roger Edens.

Take the Money and Run 🦴🦴🦴 **1969 (PG)** Allen's directing debut; he also co-wrote and starred. "Documentary" follows a timid, would-be bank robber who can't get his career off the ground and keeps landing in jail. Little plot, but who cares? Nonstop one-liners and slapstick. **85m/C VHS, DVD.** Woody Allen, Janet Margolin, Marcel Hillaire, Louise Lasser, Jacquelyn Hyde, Lonny (Loni) Chapman, Jan Merlin, James Anderson, Jackson Beck, Howard Storm; ***D:*** Woody Allen; ***W:*** Mickey Rose, Woody Allen; ***C:*** Lester Shorr; ***M:*** Marvin Hamlisch.

Take This Job & Shove It 🦴🦴 **1981 (PG)** The Johnny Paycheck song inspired this story of a hot-shot efficiency expert who returns to his hometown to streamline the local brewery. Encounters with old pals inspire self-questioning. Alternately inspired and hackneyed. Cameos by Paycheck and other country stars. **100m/C VHS.** Robert Hays, Art Carney, Barbara Hershey, David Keith, Martin Mull, Eddie Albert, Penelope Milford; ***Cameos:*** Johnny Paycheck, David Allen Coe, Charlie Rich, Lacy J. Dalton; ***D:*** Gus Trikonis; ***W:*** Barry Schneider.

Take Two 🦴 **1987 (R)** A woman has an affair with her husband's twin brother. Interesting metaphysically: Are you my husband or my lover? But is an adultery/murder drama with Frank Stallone worth 101 minutes of your time? **101m/C VHS.** Grant Goodeve, Robin Mattson, Frank Stallone, Warren Berlinger, Darwyn Swalve, Nita Talbot; ***D:*** Peter Rowe.

Take Your Best Shot 🦴½ **1982** Standard TV comedy about an out-of-work actor struggling with his low self-esteem and his failing marriage. **96m/C VHS.** Robert Urich, Meredith Baxter, Jeffrey Tambor,

Jack Bannon, Claudette Nevins; *D:* David Greene. **TV**

Taken 🦴🦴½ **1999 (R)** Businessman Coleman gets kidnapped only both his wife and business partners see a financial opportunity and decide not to pay the ransom. When he realizes this, Coleman thinks it prudent to befriend kidnapper Boutsikaris and hope that something can be worked out. **96m/C VHS.** *CA* Dabney Coleman, Dennis Boutsikaris, Linda Smith, Dorothee Berryman, Carl Alacchi; *D:* Max Fischer; *W:* Pierre Lapointe.

Taken Away 🦴🦴½ **1989** Struggling young divorcee Stephanie Monroe waits tables during the day and studies to be a computer tech at night in order to provide her eight-year-old daughter Abby with a better life. Unable to afford child care, Stephanie leaves Abby alone in the afternoon until she can get home from work. But when the welfare system finds out Stephanie is accused of child neglect and must fight a bureaucratic nightmare in order to get her child back. **94m/C VHS.** Valerie Bertinelli, Kevin Dunn, Joshua Maurer, Anna Maria Horsford, Juliet Sorcey, Nada Despotovich, Mathew Faison, James Arone; *D:* John D. Patterson; *W:* Robert Freedman, Selma Thomson. **TV**

The Takeover 🦴½ **1994 (R)** East coast crime boss Danny Stein (Drago) decides to take over the L.A. operations of rival Tony Valachi (Mancuso). Lots of mayhem ensues. **91m/C VHS.** Billy Drago, Nick Mancuso, John Savage, Eric (DaRe) Da Re, Cali Timmins, David Amos, Gene Mitchell; *D:* Troy Cook; *W:* Gene Mitchell; *M:* Jimmy Lifton.

Taking Care of Business 🦴½ *Filofax* **1990 (R)** Too familiar tale of switched identity has crazed Cubs fan Belushi find Grodin's Filofax, allowing him to pose as businessman. Old jokes and a story full of holes. **108m/C VHS, DVD.** James Belushi, Charles Grodin, Anne DeSalvo, Loryn Locklin, Veronica Hamel, Hector Elizondo, Mako, Gates (Cheryl) McFadden, Stephen Elliott; *D:* Arthur Hiller; *W:* Jeffrey Abrams; *C:* David M. Walsh; *M:* Stewart Copeland.

The Taking of Beverly Hills 🦴½ **1991 (R)** Deranged billionaire Bat Masterson designs a bogus toxic spill that leaves the wealth of Beverly Hills his for the taking. Football hero Boomer Hayes teams up with renegade cop Ed Kelvin to try and stop Masterson and save the city of Beverly Hills. **96m/C VHS, Wide.** Ken Wahl, Matt Frewer, Robert Davi, Harley Jane Kozak, Lee James, Branscombe Richmond, Lyman Ward, Michael Bowen, William Prince, Ken Swofford, George Wyner; *D:* Sidney J. Furie; *W:* Sidney J. Furie, David Burke.

The Taking of Flight 847: The Uli Derickson Story 🦴🦴🦴 *The Flight* **1988** Wagner plays the stewardess who acted as a go-between for the passengers during a 1985 terrorist hijacking, saving all but one life. True-story drama is suspenseful and entertaining, nominated for several Emmys. **100m/C VHS.** Laurie Walters, Sandy McPeak, Ray Wise, Leslie Easterbrook, Lindsay Wagner, Eli Danker, Joseph Naser; *D:* Paul Wendkos; *W:* Norman Merrill. **TV**

The Taking of Pelham One Two Three 🦴🦴🦴 **1974 (R)** A hijack team, lead by the ruthless Shaw, seizes a NYC subway car and holds the 17 passengers for $1 million ransom. Fine pacing keeps things on the edge. New cinematic techniques used by cameraman Owen Roizman defines shadowy areas like never before. **105m/C VHS, DVD, Wide.** Robert Shaw, Walter Matthau, Martin Balsam, Hector Elizondo, James Broderick, Earl Hindman, Dick O'Neill, Jerry Stiller, Tony Roberts, Doris Roberts, Kenneth McMillan, Julius W. Harris, Sal Viscuso; *D:* Joseph Sargent; *W:* Peter Stone; *C:* Owen Roizman; *M:* David Shire.

Taking the Heat 🦴🦴½ **1993 (R)** When mobster Arkin kills a sporting-goods dealer with a golf club the murder is witnessed by yuppie Goldwyn. Whitfield is the ambitious cop who wants Goldwyn to testify against the gangster—if she can keep him alive long enough to get him to court. One long chase scene. **91m/C VHS.** Lynn Whitfield, Tony Goldwyn, Alan Arkin, George Segal, Peter Boyle; *D:* Tom Mankiewicz; *W:* Dan Gordon. **CABLE**

Tale of a Vampire 🦴🦴½ **1992 (R)** In present day London, ageless vampire Alex (Sands) still mourns his long-lost vampiric love, Virginia, when he meets Anne (Hamilton) (who resembles Virginia). Alex doesn't know he's being stalked by Virginia's husband, Edgar (Cranham), also a vampire. Edgar decides to use Anne (with whom Alex has fallen in love) as bait, in a revenge plot. A tiny budget and slow pacing mar the film's fine visual style and good work by the two male leads. Film debut for director Sato. **93m/C VHS.** *GB* Julian Sands, Kenneth Cranham, Suzanna Hamilton; *D:* Shimako Sato; *W:* Jane Corbett, Shimako Sato; *M:* Julian Joseph.

The Tale of Ruby Rose 🦴🦴🦴 **1987 (PG)** Living in the mountains of Tasmania, Ruby Rose, her husband Henry, and their adopted son Gem, struggle to survive the '30s depression by hunting and trapping. Having spent all her life in the mountains, Ruby Rose has a very superstitious view of life and a terror of nightfall. But after an argument with her husband, Ruby Rose sets out on a cross-country journey to find her grandmother and discover the secrets of her past. **101m/C VHS.** *AU* Melita Jurisic, Chris Haywood; *D:* Roger Sholes; *W:* Roger Sholes; *M:* Paul Schutze.

A Tale of Springtime 🦴🦴½ **1989 (PG)** Comedy-romance is the first film in Rohmer's planned new series, the "Tales of the Four Seasons," not to be confused with his "Six Moral Tales" or his "Comedies and Proverbs." Centers around Jeanne, a high school philosophy teacher; Natacha, a young student; and Igor, Natacha's father. As characteristic of Rohmer films, texture and character largely overshadow linear plots and social messages. However, the efficiency and directness of his camera work make it a pleasure to watch. **107m/C VHS, DVD, Wide.** *FR* Anne Teyssedre, Hugues Quester, Florence Darel, Eloise Bennett, Sophie Robin; *D:* Eric Rohmer; *W:* Eric Rohmer; *C:* Luc Pages; *M:* Robert Schumann.

The Tale of the Frog Prince 🦴🦴🦴½ **1983** Superb edition of Shelley Duvall's "Faerie Tale Theatre" finds Williams the victim of an angry fairy godmother's spell. Garr to the rescue as the self-centered princess who saves him with a kiss. Directed and written by Idle of Monty Python fame. **60m/C VHS.** Robin Williams, Teri Garr; *D:* Eric Idle; *W:* Eric Idle.

A Tale of Two Cities 🦴🦴🦴🦴 **1936** Lavish production of the Dickens' classic set during the French Revolution, about two men who bear a remarkable resemblance to each other, both in love with the same girl. Carefree lawyer Sydney Carton (Colman) roused to responsibility, makes the ultimate sacrifice. A memorable Madame DeFarge from stage star Yurka in her film debut, with assistance from other Dickens' film stars Rathbone, Oliver, and Walthall. **128m/B VHS.** Ronald Colman, Elizabeth Allan, Edna May Oliver, Reginald Owen, Isabel Jewell, Walter Catlett, H.B. Warner, Donald Woods, Basil Rathbone, Blanche Yurka, Henry B. Walthall; *D:* Jack Conway; *W:* W.P. Lipscomb, S.N. Behrman; *M:* Herbert Stothart.

A Tale of Two Cities 🦴🦴🦴 **1958** A well-done British version of the Dickens' classic about a lawyer who sacrifices himself to save another man from the guillotine during the French Reign of Terror. The sixth remake of the tale. **117m/B VHS.** *GB* Dirk Bogarde, Dorothy Tutin, Christopher Lee, Donald Pleasence, Ian Bannen, Cecil Parker; *D:* Ralph Thomas.

A Tale of Two Cities 🦴🦴½ **1980** Impressive looking but bloodless adaptation of the Dickens novel set in the French Revolution. Saradon takes on the dual role of sacrificing English lawyer Carton and French nobleman Darnay, with Krige as the lovely woman caught between the two. **156m/C VHS.** Chris Sarandon, Alice Krige, Peter Cushing, Kenneth More, Barry Morse, Flora Robson, Billie Whitelaw; *D:* Jim Goddard; *W:* John Gay. **TV**

A Tale of Two Cities 🦴🦴🦴 **1991** Masterpiece Theatre production of the classic Dickens tale. The French revolution was a time of revenge and brutality, but also provided the proving ground for a love greater than life. Terrific cast and perfectly detailed production. **240m/C VHS, Wide.** James Wilby, Serena Gordon, John Mills, Jean-Pierre Aumont, Anna Massey.

Tale of Two Sisters 🦴🦴½ **1989** Sheen narrates sensual drama about two beautiful, ambitious sisters. **90m/C VHS, DVD.** Valerie Breiman, Claudia Christian, Sydney Lassick, Jeff Conaway, Peter Berg; *D:* Adam Rifkin; *W:* Charlie Sheen; *Nar:* Charlie Sheen.

A Tale of Winter 🦴🦴½ *Conte D'Hiver* **1992** Portrays the romantic trials of a young French woman who cannot choose between her two smitten lovers and her one true love, the long disappeared father of her child. Felicie (Very) hopelessly loves Charles (Van Den Driessche), whom she met five years before, but mistakenly gave the wrong address. Rohmer's trademark conversation-filled scenes find her brooding over her predicament, running from one lover and back again, until a revelation during a viewing of Shakespeare's "The Winter's Tale." A charming cast carries the story to a surprise twist of an ending. Second in the series "Tales of the Four Seasons." In French with English subtitles. **114m/C VHS.** *FR* Charlotte Very, Frederic Van Dren Driessche, Michel Voletti, Herve Furic, Ava Loraschi, Jean-Luc Revol, Haydee Caillot, Jean-Claude Biette, Rosette, Marie Riviere; *D:* Eric Rohmer; *W:* Eric Rohmer; *C:* Luc Pages; *M:* Sebastien Erms.

Talent for the Game 🦴🦴½ **1991 (PG)** A slight but handsomely produced baseball pleasantry about a talent scout who recruits a phenomenonal young pitcher, then sees the kid exploited by the team owner. More like an anecdote than a story, with an ending that aims a little too hard to please. Good for sports fans and family audiences. **91m/C VHS.** Edward James Olmos, Lorraine Bracco, Jeff Corbett, Jamey Sheridan, Terry Kinney; *D:* Robert M. Young; *W:* David Himmelstein, Tom Donnelly, Larry Ferguson; *M:* David Newman.

The Talented Mr. Ripley 🦴🦴½ **1999 (R)** Beautiful but ultimately hollow adaptation of Patricia Highsmith's chiller, which was previously filmed as 1960's "Purple Noon." This time around Damon takes on the title role as a poor nobody who is sent to Italy in 1958 to persuade rich playboy, Dickie Greenleaf (Law), to return to the bosom of his family in New York. Only the more the emotionally needy Ripley sees of Dickie's sybaritic lifestyle—the more he wants it for himself, even if it means killing Dickie and literally assuming his identity. Law is the draw and the movie suffers a letdown after his death. **139m/C VHS, DVD, Wide.** Matt Damon, Jude Law, Gwyneth Paltrow, Cate Blanchett, Philip Seymour Hoffman, Jack Davenport, James Rebhorn, Sergio Rubini, Philip Baker Hall, Lisa Eichhorn, Stefania Rocca; *D:* Anthony Minghella; *W:* Anthony Minghella; *C:* John Seale; *M:* Gabriel Yared. British Acad. '99: Support. Actor (Law); Natl. Bd. of Review '99: Director (Minghella), Support. Actor (Hoffman).

Tales from a Parallel Universe: Eating Pattern 🦴🦴 *Eating Pattern* **1997 (R)** The Lexx space cruiser is part machine and part organic matter, so it needs nourishment, as does its crew. But Zev and Stanley make a big mistake stopping for food at the planet Klaagya. Seems the inhabitants are controlled by parasitic worms that feed on their brains and they're always interested in a fresh meal. Now it's up to Kai to come to the rescue. Third episode in the series. **93m/C VHS.** Brian Downey, Eva Habermann, Michael McManus, Rutger Hauer; *D:* Rainer Matsutani; *W:* Paul Donovan; *C:* Les Krizsan; *M:* Marty Simon. **CABLE**

Tales from a Parallel Universe: Giga Shadow 🦴🦴 *Giga Shadow* **1997 (R)** The Lexx crew must make a dangerous attempt to replenish Kai's supply of proto-blood, which brings them perilously near their arch-enemy, His Shadow. The fourth (and last) film of the series. **93m/C VHS.** Brian Downey, Eva Habermann, Michael McManus, Malcolm McDowell; *D:* Robert Sigl; *W:* Paul Donovan; *C:* Les Krizsan; *M:* Marty Simon. **CABLE**

Tales from a Parallel Universe: I Worship His Shadow 🦴🦴 *I Worship His Shadow* **1997 (R)** Space rebels try to unseat a tyrannical ruler known as His Shadow, in this first of a four-part series. A prophecy states that the ruler will be defeated by a dying race and aiding that prediction are rebel leader Thodin (Bostwick), cowardly Stanley Tweedle (Downey), warrior Kai (McManus), and Zev (Habermann), His Shadow's unwilling love slave. Followed by the "Super Nova" episode. **95m/C VHS.** Brian Downey, Eva Habermann, Michael McManus, Barry Bostwick, Ellen Dubin; *D:* Paul Donovan; *W:* Paul Donovan; *C:* Les Krizsan; *M:* Marty Simon. **CABLE**

Tales from a Parallel Universe: Super Nova 🦴🦴 *Super Nova* **1997 (R)** A continuation of the "I Worship His Shadow" episode, which finds the rebels in possession of the mile-long spacecraft known as The Lexx, which also happens to be the most destructive weapon in the universe. But they don't want to destroy the craft, instead they use the Lexx to visit the lost planet of Brunnis in hopes of restoring their lost leader to life. Only the rebels get captured by the Poet Man (Curry), and their deaths could lead to the total annihilation of the universe. **93m/C VHS.** Brian Downey, Eva Habermann, Michael McManus, Ellen Dubin, Tim Curry; *D:* Ron Oliver; *W:* Paul Donovan; *C:* Les Krizsan; *M:* Marty Simon. **CABLE**

Tales from the Crypt 🦴🦴🦴 **1972 (PG)** A collection of five scary stories from the classic EC comics that bear the movie's title. Richardson tells the future to each of five people gathered in a cave, each tale involving misfortune and, of course, gore. **92m/C VHS.** *GB* Ralph Richardson, Joan Collins, Peter Cushing, Richard Greene, Ian Hendry; *D:* Freddie Francis.

Tales from the Crypt **1989** Three contemporary tales of the macabre, "The Man Who Was Death," "'Twas the Night Before," and "Dig That Cat...He's Real Gone," linked together by a special-effects host. Ry Cooder provides the musical score for the second episode. Based on stories published by William M. Gaines in EC Comics. **81m/C VHS.** William Sadler, Mary Ellen Trainor, Larry Drake, Joe Pantoliano, Robert Wuhl, Gustav Vintas; *D:* Richard Donner, Walter Hill, Robert Zemeckis; *M:* Ry Cooder, Alan Silvestri. **CABLE**

Tales from the Crypt Presents Bordello of Blood 🦴🦴 *Bordello of Blood* **1996 (R)** Detective Rafe Guttman (Miller) is on the case of a Bible thumper's (Eleniak) missing brother (Feldman). The trail leads him to a unique establishment, a brothel presided over by vampire queen Lilith (Everhart), whose clients all wind up dead (but probably with smiles on their faces), and the strange Reverend Current (Sarandon, who made a fine vampire himself in "Fright Night"). Crypt Keeper's second big screen outing showcases Miller's slant on the leading man gig and serves up campy fun with the blood. **87m/C VHS, DVD.** Dennis Miller, Angie Everhart, Chris Sarandon, Corey Feldman, Erika Eleniak; *D:* Gilbert Adler; *W:* Gilbert Adler, A.L. Katz; *C:* Tom Priestley; *M:* Chris Boardman.

Tales from the Crypt Presents Demon Knight 🦴🦴 *Demon Knight; Demon Keeper* **1994 (R)** Gruesomely garish big-screen version of the TV series that was inspired by the lurid 1950s E.C. comics. Horrormeister Crypt Keeper offers his usual pun-filled introduction to a tale set in a seedy boardinghouse. Brayker (Sadler) is the guardian of an ancient key that keeps the forces of darkness from overwhelming mankind, a key desired by the charismatic Collector (Zane), who unleashes a disgusting mix of demons against the house's inhabitants. Curious hybrid of spoof/splatter pic that doesn't quite work in either genre. **93m/C VHS, DVD.** Billy Zane, William Sadler, Jada Pinkett Smith, Brenda Bakke, CCH Pounder, Dick Miller, Thomas Haden Church, John Schuck, Gary Farmer, Charles Fleischer; *D:* Ernest R. Dickerson; *W:*

Ethan Reiff, Cyrus Voris, Mark Bishop; *C:* Rick Bota; *M:* Ed Shearmur; *V:* John Kassir.

Tales from the Darkside: The Movie ☙☙ **1990 (R)** Three short stories in the tradition of the ghoulish TV show are brought to the big screen, with mixed results. The plot centers around a boy who is being held captive by a cannibal. In order to prolong his life, he tells her horror stories. The tales were written by Sir Arthur Conan Doyle, Stephen King, and Michael McDowell. **93m/C VHS, DVD, Wide.** Deborah Harry, Christian Slater, David Johansen, William Hickey, James Remar, Rae Dawn Chong, Julianne Moore, Robert Klein, Steve Buscemi, Matthew Lawrence; *D:* John Harrison; *W:* George A. Romero, Michael McDowell; *C:* Rob Draper.

Tales from the Gimli Hospital ☙☙ **1988** A smallpox outbreak at the turn of the century finds Einar and Gunnar sharing a hospital room. They begin telling each other increasingly bizarre personal secrets and develop a serious rivalry. Sharp dialogue with some equally grotesque imagery. Director Maddin's first feature film. **68m/B VHS, DVD.** *CA* Kyle McCulloch, Michael Gottli, Angela Heck, Margaret Anne McLeod; *D:* Guy Maddin; *W:* Guy Maddin; *C:* Guy Maddin.

Tales from the Hood ☙☙ **1995 (R)** Horror anthology with that urban twist. Three young thugs search for lost drugs inside a funeral parlor run by creepy Mr. Simms (Williams III) and instead walk into a world of four chilling and funny stories of fright dealing with racism and black on black crime. Tales aren't very original and are often too preachy for true enjoyment, but its nice to see someone attempt to breath life into an old and familiar genre. Williams III, with his pop-eyed stares and Don King coif, is fitting as the eerie storyteller. **97m/C VHS, DVD.** Lamont Bentley, De'Aundre Bonds, Tom Wright, Michael Massee, Duane Whitaker, Brandon Hammond, Paula Jai Parker, Roger Guenveur Smith, Art Evans, Clarence Williams III, Corbin Bernsen, David Alan Grier, Wings Hauser, Rosalind Cash, Rusty Cundieff, Joe Torry, Anthony Griffith, Darin Scott; *D:* Rusty Cundieff; *W:* Rusty Cundieff, Darin Scott; *C:* Anthony B. Richmond; *M:* Christopher Young.

Tales from the Snow Zone **1991** "Tales from the Snow Zone" is the latest feature length ski film from RAP producers Jon Long and James Angrove. Filmed entirely in the 1991 ski season, this film captures the essence of the sport and lifestyle. "Tales" covers true extreme skiing, radical free skiing, moguls, downhill ski racing, telemarking, snowboarding, and monoskiing. Filmed in Europe and North America, "Tales" features skiers from the United States, Canada, France, Sweden, and Australia. **70m/C VHS.**

Tales of Beatrix Potter ☙☙☙½ *Peter Rabbit and Tales of Beatrix Potter* **1971 (G)** The Royal Ballet Company of England performs in this adaptation of the adventures of Beatrix Potter's colorful and memorable creatures. Beautifully done. **90m/C VHS.** *GB* *D:* Reginald Mills.

Tales of Erotica ☙☙ *Die Erotische Geschichten* **1993 (R)** Four stories made for German TV. "The Dutch Master" finds New Yorker Teresa (Sorvino) becoming obsessed with a Vermeer-style painting at a museum. She begins to dress like the lively characters and eventually disappears into the picture itself. "The Insatiable Mrs. Kirsch" finds a vacationing writer (Shepherd) becoming fascinated by a fellow guest (Baynes), who seems to be hiding something. In "Vroom Vroom Vroom" luckless Leroy (Barboza) asks a voodoo doctor for help with the girls and winds up with a motorcycle that transforms itself into a beautiful woman when ridden. "Wet" has bathroom-fixture salesman Bruce (Howard) enticed by persistent customer Davida (Williams), who insists they both try out the showroom hot tub before she'll consider buying. **104m/C VHS, DVD.** *GE* Mira Sorvino, Aida Turturro, Simon Shepherd, Hetty Baynes, Ken Russell, Richard Barboza, Arliss Howard, Cynda Williams; *D:* Ken Russell, Susan Seidelman, Melvin Van Peebles, Bob Rafelson; *W:* Susan Seidelman, Melvin Van Peebles, Bob Rafelson, Jonathan Brett; *C:* Maryse Alberti, Hong Manley, Igor Sunara; *M:* Melvin Van Peebles, Wendy Blackstone, David McHugh. **TV**

The Tales of Hoffmann ☙☙½ **1951** A ballet-opera consisting of three stories by Jacques Offenbach covering romance, magic and mystery arising out of a poet's misadventures in love. Lavishly designed and highly stylized. **138m/C VHS.** Robert Rounseville, Robert Helpmann, Moira Shearer; *D:* Michael Powell, Emeric Pressburger.

Tales of Manhattan ☙☙☙ **1942** Star-studded anthology about a tailor who curses a tailcoat that then travels, with varying degrees of good and bad fortune, from owner to owner. There's a love triangle, a love match, a concert appearance, a down-on-his-luck lawyer, a swanky party, a crook, and a windfall for some sharecroppers. Fields' party episode (he wears the coat to give a lecture and winds up wreaking havoc) was cut out of the original theatrical release. **118m/C VHS.** Charles Boyer, Rita Hayworth, Thomas Mitchell, Ginger Rogers, Henry Fonda, Cesar Romero, Elsa Lanchester, Charles Laughton, Edward G. Robinson, George Sanders, James Gleason, J. Carrol Naish, Paul Robeson, Ethel Waters, Eddie Anderson, W.C. Fields, Margaret Dumont; *D:* Julien Duvivier; *W:* Ben Hecht, Donald Ogden Stewart, Samuel Hoffenstein, Ferenc Molnar, Alan Campbell; *C:* Joseph Walker; *M:* Sol Kaplan.

Tales of Ordinary Madness ☙ **1983** Gazzara as a poet who drinks and sleeps with assorted women. Based on the stories of Charles Bukowski. Pretentious and dull. **107m/C VHS, DVD.** Ben Gazzara, Ornella Muti, Susan Tyrrell, Tanya Lopert, Roy Brocksmith, Katya Berger; *D:* Marco Ferreri; *W:* Marco Ferreri, Sergio Amidei, Anthony Foutz; *C:* Tonino Delli Colli; *M:* Philippe Sarde.

Tales of Robin Hood ☙½ **1952** A low-budget depiction of the Robin Hood legend. **59m/B VHS.** Robert Clarke, Mary Hatcher; *D:* James Tinling.

Tales of Terror ☙☙ *Poe's Tales of Terror* **1962** Three tales of terror based on stories by Edgar Allan Poe: "Morella," "The Black Cat," and the "The Case of M. Valdemar." Price stars in all three segments and is excellent as the bitter and resentful husband in "Morella." **90m/C VHS, DVD, Wide.** Vincent Price, Peter Lorre, Basil Rathbone, Debra Paget, Joyce Jameson, Maggie Pierce, Leona Gage, Edmund Cobb; *D:* Roger Corman; *W:* Richard Matheson; *C:* Floyd Crosby; *M:* Les Baxter.

Tales of the Kama Sutra 2: Monsoon ☙ **1998** Naval officer Kenneth Blake (Tyson) and his fiancee Sally (McShane) travel to the island of Goa, off the coast of India, to enjoy a resort vacation. But Blake is drawn into an affair with Leela (Brodie), who tells him that they are the reincarnation of legendary lovers who leaped to their death from the island's lighthouse 500 years before. It's one way to get a man interested. **96m/C VHS, DVD.** Richard Tyson, Helen Brodie, Jenny McShane, Matt McCoy, Doug Jeffery, Gulsham Grover; *D:* Jag Mundhra. **VIDEO**

Tales of the Kama Sutra: The Perfumed Garden ☙ *The Perfumed Garden* **1998 (R)** Not particularly erotic story centers on Americans Michael and Lisa, who have a rocky romantic relationship. Lisa follows Michael to India where he is helping to restore the erotic sculptures of Khajuraho. However, Michael's lust is aroused by a mysterious Indian woman (Kumar), who happens to resemble the statue he's repairing, which leads to a retelling of one Kama Sutra story about a royal courtesan set 1000 years earlier. **104m/C VHS, DVD.** Pravesh Kumar, Ivan Baccarat, Amy Lindsey, Rajeshwari Sachdev, Bhupinder Singh, Nasser; *D:* Jag Mundhra.

Tales of the Klondike: In a Far Country ☙☙ **1987** An adaptation of Jack London's story exploring the fears, dangers, and joys experienced by prospectors in the harsh wilderness of northwest Canadian gold country. **60m/C VHS.** Robert Carradine, Scott Hylands; *D:* Janine Manatis; *Nar:* Orson Welles. **TV**

Tales of the Klondike: Race for Number One ☙☙ **1987** Two men compete in a highly contested dog-sled race—the goal of which is to be the first to reach a tract of gold-laden land. Adapted from a story by Jack London. **60m/C VHS.** David Ferry, John Ireland; *D:* David Cobham; *Nar:* Orson Welles. **TV**

Tales of the Klondike: The Scorn of Women ☙☙ **1987** An available man is enthusiastically courted by every single woman in Dawson City, Alaska. From a story by Jack London. **60m/C VHS.** Tom Butler, Eva Gabor; *D:* Claude Fournier; *Nar:* Orson Welles. **TV**

Tales of the Klondike: The Unexpected ☙☙ **1987** Five gold prospectors grow rich, but lose all that is most valuable through overwhelming greed. Adapted from a story by Jack London. **60m/C VHS.** John Candy, Cherie Lunghi; *D:* Peter Pearson; *Nar:* Orson Welles. **TV**

Tales of the Unexpected ☙☙½ **1991** Four tales designed to startle the senses and provoke the imagination. Episodes include "People Don't Do Such Things," about a marriage gone awry, "Youth from Vienna," about a weird fountain of youth, "Skeleton in the Cupboard," which tells of a man desperately trying to hide some strange secret and finally, "Bird of Prey," in which a pet parrot leaves its owners an enormous egg before dying. **101m/C VHS.** Arthur Hill, Samantha Eggar, Don Johnson, Dick Smothers, Sharon Gless, James Carroll Jordan, Charles Dance, Zoe Wanamaker, Sondra Locke, Frank Converse; *D:* Gordon Hessler, Norman Lloyd, Paul Annett, Ray Danton.

Tales That Witness Madness ☙☙½ **1973 (R)** An asylum is the setting for four tales of horror, as a doctor tells a visitor how four patients ended up in his clinic. Stories are "Mr. Tiger," "Penny Farthing," "Mel" and "Luau." At the time this was Novak's first film appearance in four years. **90m/C VHS.** *GB* Jack Hawkins, Donald Pleasence, Suzy Kendall, Joan Collins, Kim Novak, Mary Tamm, Georgia Brown, Donald Houston, David Wood, Peter McEnery; *D:* Freddie Francis.

Talion ☙☙ *An Eye for an Eye* **1966 (PG)** A western revenge movie that features two disabled men, a rancher and a bounty hunter, who team up to find the gang that slaughtered the rancher's family. **92m/C VHS.** Robert Lansing, Slim Pickens, Patrick Wayne; *D:* Michael Moore.

Talisman ☙½ **1998 (R)** Theriel, the Black Angel, has been fused to an ancient Talisman for centuries. Summoned from his rest, he must offer seven human sacrifices to complete an evil ritual that will open the gates of hell and usher in the end of the world. Two teenagers are chosen to help Theriel but they've got other things in mind. Director DeCoteau used the pseud "Victoria Sloan" for this venture. **90m/C VHS.** Walter Jones, Jason Adelman, Billy Parish, Ilinca Goia; *D:* David DeCoteau; *W:* Benjamin Carr. **VIDEO**

Talk ☙☙ **1994** Sharp conversation between two 30-something women as they wander around the streets of Sydney. Stephanie (Milliken) and Julia (Longley) are collaborators on graphic novels—Stephanie's single and adventurous while Julia is seemingly settled in the country with her lover and child. As they talk, the women learn that both their lives have conflicts. Fantasy sequences, which slow the story down, find the women stepping into their own comic-book adventures. **86m/C VHS.** *AU* Victoria Longley, Angie Milliken, Richard Roxburgh, Jacqueline McKenzie, John Jarratt; *D:* Susan Lambert; *W:* Jan Cornall; *C:* Ron Hagen; *M:* John Clifford White.

Talk of Angels ☙☙ **1996 (PG-13)** Young Irish aristocrat Mary (Walker) leaves her homeland for Spain to serve as governess for a wealthy family, just as the country is about to erupt into civil war. She ignites passion in everyone she encounters, especially her married employer and his married son. This forbidden relationship serves as the crux of the story. Unfortunately, good looks alone (which both stars have) don't create chemistry, and Walker and Perez simply fizzle on screen. The film and its leads are certainly nice to look at, but there's something missing: an interesting story. With several obvious thefts from the ultimate wartime love story, "Gone With the Wind" (including a blatant rip-off of the famous scene where Scarlett walks among the sea of dead soldiers), the story is hardly original. **97m/C VHS.** Polly Walker, Vincent Perez, Frances McDormand, Franco Nero, Marisa Paredes, Penelope Cruz, Ruth McCabe, Francesco Rabal, Ariadna Gil, Rossy de Palma; *D:* Nick Hamm; *W:* Ann Guedes, Frank McGuinness; *C:* Alexei Rodionov; *M:* Trevor Jones.

Talk of the Town ☙☙☙ **1942** A brilliantly cast, strange mixture of screwball comedy and lynch-mob melodramatics. An accused arsonist, a Supreme Court judge and the girl they both love try to clear the former's name and evade the cops. **118m/B VHS.** Ronald Colman, Cary Grant, Jean Arthur, Edgar Buchanan, Glenda Farrell, Rex Ingram, Emma Dunn; *D:* George Stevens.

Talk Radio ☙☙☙ **1988 (R)** Riveting Stone adaptation of Bogosian's one-man play. An acidic talk radio host confronts America's evil side and his own past over the airwaves. The main character is loosely based on the life of Alan Berg, a Denver talk show host who was murdered by white supremacists. **110m/C VHS, DVD, Wide.** Eric Bogosian, Alec Baldwin, Ellen Greene, John Pankow, John C. McGinley, Michael Wincott, Leslie Hope; *D:* Oliver Stone; *W:* Eric Bogosian, Oliver Stone; *C:* Robert Richardson; *M:* Stewart Copeland.

Talk to Me ☙½ **1982** A successful New York accountant checks into the Hollins Communication Institute to cure his stuttering. While there, he meets and falls in love with a squirrel-hunting stuttering woman from Arkansas. **90m/C VHS.** Austin Pendleton, Michael Murphy, Louise Fletcher, Brian Backer, Clifton James.

Talkin' Dirty after Dark ☙☙ **1991 (R)** Sexy comedy starring Lawrence as a suave comedian who will do anything to get a late-night spot at Dukie's comedy club. **89m/C VHS.** Martin Lawrence, Jedda Jones, Phyllis Stickney, Darryl Sivad; *D:* Topper Carew; *W:* Topper Carew.

Talking about Sex ☙☙½ **1994** Publishing party for a shrink's self-help manual sparks many conversations about sex and romance among a group of fashionable Los Angelenos. The breezy party chatter is broken up by B&W pseudo-documentary interludes of women exchanging confidences. **83m/C VHS.** Kim Wayans, Marcy Walker, Daniel Beer, Randy Powell, Kerry Ruff, Joe Richards, Daria Lynn; *D:* Aaron Speiser; *W:* Aaron Speiser, Carl Nelson; *M:* Tim Landers.

Talking Walls ☙½ *Motel Vacancy* **1985** A college sociology student uses high-tech surveillance equipment to spy on the clients of a seedy motel, in order to complete his thesis on human sexuality. **85m/C VHS.** Stephen Shellen, Marie Laurin, Barry Primus, Sally Kirkland; *D:* Stephen Verona.

The Tall Blond Man with One Black Shoe ☙☙☙ *Le Grand Blond avec une Chassure Noire* **1972 (PG)** A violinist is completely unaware that rival spies mistakenly think he is also a spy, and that he is the center of a plot to booby-trap an overly ambitious agent at the French Secret Service. A sequel followed called "Return of the Tall Blond Man with One Black Shoe" which was followed by a disappointing American remake, "The Man with One Red Shoe." In French with English subtitles or dubbed. **90m/C VHS, 8mm.** *FR* Pierre Richard, Bernard Blier, Jean Rochefort, Mireille Darc, Jean Carmet; *D:* Yves Robert; *W:* Francis Veber; *M:* Vladimir Cosma.

Tall, Dark and Deadly ☙☙½ **1995 (R)** Roy (Scalia) romances Maggie (Delaney), a young woman he's met in a bar. The viewer's already clued in that Roy's a bad 'un (seein' as how he's killed one woman) and when he chains Maggie to a sink, she picks up on the idea that he's a wacko. Basic damsel-in-distress with a cast that manages to keep straight faces in the most preposterous of circumstances. **88m/C VHS.** Jack Scalia, Kim Delaney, Todd Allen, Gina Mastrogiacomo, Ely Pouget; *D:*

Kenneth Fink; *W:* MaryAnne Kasica, Michael Scheff; *M:* Joseph Vitarelli. CABLE

The Tall Guy 🦴🦴🦴 **1989 (R)** Goldblum is a too-tall actor who tries the scene in London and lands the lead in a musical version of 'The Elephant Man,' becoming an overnight success. Not consistently funny, but good British comedy, including an interesting sex scene. **92m/C VHS, DVD, Wide.** Jeff Goldblum, Emma Thompson, Rowan Atkinson, Geraldine James, Kim Thomson, Anna Massey; *D:* Mel Smith; *W:* Richard Curtis; *C:* Adrian Biddle; *M:* Peter Brewis.

Tall in the Saddle 🦴🦴½ **1944** A misogynist foreman (Wayne) finds himself accused of murder. Meanwhile, he falls in love with his female boss's niece. An inoffensive and memorable western. **79m/B VHS.** John Wayne, Ella Raines, George "Gabby" Hayes, Ward Bond; *D:* Edwin L. Marin.

Tall Lie 🦴🦴 *For Men Only* **1953** A student quits a fraternity hazing exercise. He's pursued by a psychotic bunch of his fraternity brothers and is killed in a smashup. A local doctor goes onto an anti-hazing campaign in the aftermath. **93m/B VHS.** Paul Henreid, Robert Sherman; *D:* Paul Henreid.

The Tall Men 🦴🦴 **1955** Standard western features frontier hands on a rough cattle drive confronting Indians, outlaws, and the wilderness while vying with each other for the love of Russell. **122m/C VHS.** Clark Gable, Jane Russell, Robert Ryan, Cameron Mitchell, Mae Marsh; *D:* Raoul Walsh.

Tall Story 🦴🦴 **1960** Perkins is a star basketball player who must pass a crucial test in order to continue to play the game. In addition to the pressure of the exam, he is being pressured by gamblers to throw a game against the Russians. Fonda makes her screen debut as a cheerleader who is so awe-struck by Perkins that she takes the same classes just to be close to him. Based on the play by Howard Lindsay and Russel Crouse, and the novel "The Homecoming Game" by Howard Nemerov. **91m/C VHS.** Anthony Perkins, Jane Fonda, Ray Walston, Marc Connelly, Anne Jackson, Tom Laughlin; *D:* Joshua Logan; *W:* Julius J. Epstein; *C:* Ellsworth Fredericks.

The Tall T 🦴🦴½ **1957** A veteran rancher (Pat) stumbles onto big trouble when by chance he catches a stage coach that is eventually overrun by an evil band of cut-throats. After killing everyone on the coach except Pat and the daughter of a wealthy copper mine owner (Doretta), the renegades decide to leave the scene with the unfortunate two as hostages. Pat and Doretta, although in dire straits, find time to fall in love and devise an intricate plan for their escape. Regarded in certain western-lover circles as a cult classic. **77m/B VHS.** Randolph Scott, Richard Boone, Maureen O'Sullivan, Arthur Hunnicutt, Skip Homeier, Henry Silva, Robert Burton, Robert Anderson; *D:* Budd Boetticher; *W:* Burt Kennedy. Natl. Film Reg. '00.

Tall Tale: The Unbelievable Adventures of Pecos Bill 🦴 **1995 (PG)** Having trouble with greedy land ownners out for his pa's land, Daniel Hackett (Stahl) summons the help of three Old West legends: Pecos Bill (Swayze), John Henry (Brown), and Paul Bunyan (Platt) to face off with the evil industrialist J.P. Stiles (Glenn). Disney's variation on the "Wizard of Oz" is riddled with cartoonish characters and sleep-inducing dialogue. It would truly be a tall tale if it were said that this movie was any good. **98m/C VHS.** Patrick Swayze, Oliver Platt, Roger Aaron Brown, Nick Stahl, Scott Glenn, Stephen Lang, Jared Harris, Catherine O'Hara; *D:* Jeremiah S. Chechik; *W:* Steven L. Bloom, Robert Rodat; *C:* Janusz Kaminski.

Tall, Tan and Terrific **1946** Things really go crazy when the owner of a nightclub in Harlem is accused of murder. **40m/C VHS.** Mantan Moreland, Monte Hawley, Francine Everett, Dots Johnson; *D:* Bud Pollard.

Tall Texan 🦴🦴½ **1953** A motley crew seeks gold in an Indian burial ground in the desert. Flawed but interesting and suspenseful. Greed, lust, Indians and desert heat. **82m/B VHS.** Lloyd Bridges, Lee J. Cobb, Marie Windsor, George Steele; *D:* Elmo Williams; *C:* Joseph Biroc.

Talons of the Eagle 🦴🦴 **1992 (R)** Martial arts adventure centers around three undercover agents who go up against crimelord Mr. Li (Hong). To impress Li, martial arts champion Tyler Wilson (Blanks) and vice detective Michael Reeds (Merhi) enter a deadly martial arts tournament. They later hook up with beautiful agent Cassandra Hubbard (Barnes), who has already investigated Li's drug, gambling, and prostitution rings. Features the most advanced fighting techniques ever filmed. **96m/C VHS.** Billy Blanks, Jalal Merhi, James Hong, Priscilla Barnes, Matthias Hues; *D:* Michael Kennedy; *W:* J. Stephen Maunder.

Tamango 🦴🦴 **1959** A confusing drama set on a slave ship travelling from Africa to Cuba in 1830. Jurgens is the ship's captain who takes the black Dandridge as his mistress. Meanwhile, the slaves are plotting a revolt, with Dandridge as a conspirator. The interracial romance does takes a secondary role to the racial conflicts. The title refers to the leader of the slave revolt, played by Cressan. Filmed in both English- and French-language versions. **98m/C VHS.** *FR* Curt Jurgens, Dorothy Dandridge, Jean Servais, Alex Cressan; *D:* John Berry.

The Tamarind Seed 🦴½ **1974** Andrews and Sharif are star-crossed lovers kept apart by Cold War espionage. Dated, dull and desultory. **123m/C VHS.** Julie Andrews, Omar Sharif, Anthony Quayle, Dan O'Herlihy, Sylvia Syms; *D:* Blake Edwards; *W:* Blake Edwards; *C:* Frederick A. (Freddie) Young; *M:* John Barry.

The Taming of the Shrew 🦴🦴½ **1929** Historically interesting early talkie featuring sole (if perhaps unfortunate) pairing of Pickford and Fairbanks. Features the legendary credit line "By William Shakespeare, with additional dialogue by Sam Taylor." Re-edited in 1966; 1967 Zeffirelli remake featured Taylor and Burton. **66m/B VHS.** Mary Pickford, Douglas Fairbanks Sr., Edwin Maxwell, Joseph Cawthorn; *D:* Sam Taylor; *C:* Karl Struss.

The Taming of the Shrew 🦴🦴🦴½ **1967** A lavish screen version of the classic Shakespearean comedy. Burton and Taylor are violently physical and perfectly cast as the battling Katherine and Petruchio. At the time the film was made, Burton and Taylor were having their own marital problems, which not only added an inner fire to their performances, but sent the interested moviegoers to the theatres in droves. **122m/C VHS, DVD, Wide.** *IT* Elizabeth Taylor, Richard Burton, Michael York, Michael Hordern, Cyril Cusack; *D:* Franco Zeffirelli; *W:* Franco Zeffirelli; *C:* Oswald Morris; *M:* Nino Rota.

Tammy and the Bachelor 🦴🦴½ **1957** A backwoods Southern girl becomes involved with a romantic pilot and his snobbish family. They don't quite know what to make of her but she wins them over with her down-home philosophy. Features the hit tune, "Tammy." Charming performance by Reynolds. **89m/C VHS.** Debbie Reynolds, Leslie Nielsen, Walter Brennan, Fay Wray, Sidney Blackmer, Mildred Natwick, Louise Beavers; *D:* Joseph Pevney; *W:* Oscar Brodney.

Tammy and the Doctor 🦴🦴 **1963** Sandra Dee reprises Debbie Reynolds's backwoods gal ("Tammy and the Bachelor"). Dee becomes a nurse's aide and is wooed by doctor Fonda, in his film debut. **88m/C VHS.** Sandra Dee, Peter Fonda, MacDonald Carey; *D:* Harry Keller; *W:* Oscar Brodney.

Tammy and the T-Rex 🦴🦴½ **1994 (PG-13)** All Michael (Walker) wanted was a date with the lovely Denise (Richards)—he didn't expect to almost die for her. Nor did he expect a mad scientist to transplant his brain into a mechanical three-ton dinosaur. Part teen angst—part camp horror—all good-natured hooey. **82m/C VHS.** Paul Walker, Denise Richards, Terry Kiser, John Franklin; *D:* Stewart Raffill.

Tampopo 🦴🦴🦴 *Dandelion* **1986** A hilarious, episodic Japanese comedy. Young restaurant hostess Tampopo (Miyamoto) is coached by 10 gallon-hatted stranger Goro (Yamazaki) in how to make the perfect noodle so she can open her own successful shop. There's also a food-loving gangster (Yakusho) who serves as an occasional narrator and gourmet. Popular, free-form hit that established Itami in the West. Japanese with subtitles. **114m/C VHS, DVD, Wide.** *JP* Ken(saku) Watanabe, Tsutomu Yamazaki, Nobuko Miyamoto, Koji Yakusho, Rikiya Yasuoka, Kinzo Sakura, Shoji Otake; *D:* Juzo Itami; *W:* Juzo Itami; *C:* Masaki Tamura; *M:* Kunihiko Murai.

Tangiers 🦴 **1983** The disappearance of a British intelligence agent in Gibraltar sets off a chain-reaction of violent incidents. **82m/C VHS.** Ronny Cox.

Tangled Destinies 🦴🦴½ **1932** Old dark house thriller involving a deserted mansion, murder, and faux diamonds. Good acting and a decent storyline make it one of the few successful independently made films of its time. **64m/B VHS.** Lloyd Whitlock, Glenn Tryon, Vera Reynolds, Doris Hill, Sidney Bracy; *D:* Frank Strayer; *W:* Edward T. Lowe.

Tango 🦴½ **1936** An early melodrama follows the ups and down of a chorus girl and the guy who sticks with her through thick and thin and poorly filmed dance routines. Based on a novel by Vida Hurst. **66m/B VHS.** Marion (Marian) Nixon, Chick Chandler, Matty Kemp, Marie Prevost, Warren Hymer, Herman Bing, Franklin Pangborn, George Meeker; *D:* Phil Rosen.

Tango 🦴🦴 **1998 (PG-13)** There's not much plot and it's not really needed when cinematographer Storaro so stunningly lenses Saura's semi-documentary look at Argentina's national dance. Middleaged Buenos Aires director Mario Suarez (Sola) is depressed after being abandoned by his wife, Laura (Narova), and decides to throw himself into making a movie about the tango. The film's shady investor, Angelo Larroca (Galiardo), insists Mario hire his young dancer mistress, Elena (Maestro), with whom Mario unwisely starts to fall in love. Spanish with subtitles. **115m/C VHS, DVD.** *SP* Miguel Angel Sola, Juan Luis Galiardo, Mia Maestro, Cecilia Narova; *D:* Carlos Saura; *W:* Carlos Saura; *C:* Vittorio Storaro; *M:* Lalo Schifrin.

Tango and Cash 🦴🦴 **1989 (R)** Stallone and Russell are L.A. cops with something in common: they both think they are the best in the city. Forced to work together to beat drug lord Palance, they flex their muscles a lot. Directing completed by Albert Magnoli, after Andrei Konchalovsky left in a huff. **104m/C VHS, DVD, 8mm, Wide.** Edward (Eddie) Bunker, Sylvester Stallone, Kurt Russell, Jack Palance, Brion James, Teri Hatcher, Michael J. Pollard, James Hong, Marc Alaimo, Robert Z'Dar; *D:* Andrei Konchalovsky; *W:* Randy Feldman; *C:* Donald E. Thorin; *M:* Harold Faltermeyer.

Tango Bar 🦴🦴½ **1988** A romantic triangle between a tango dancer who leaves Argentina during a time of political unrest, his former partner, and his wife, who both stay behind. They are reunited after years of separation. Gives the viewer a detailed vision of the historical and cultural significance of the tango. Charming, interesting and very watchable. In Spanish with English subtitles. **90m/C VHS.** *AR* Raul Julia, Valeria Lynch, Ruben Juarez; *D:* Marcos Zurinaga.

The Tango Lesson 🦴🦴½ **1997 (PG)** Semiautobiographical tale of director/star/writer and former dancer Potter ("Orlando" director), as Sally, who finds love and the meaning of life in the tango while living in Paris. While penning a noncommercial script called "Rage" about a paraplegic designer who stalks leggy models, Sally meets a tango instructor (Pablo) without a partner, and soon the two are doing more than just the tango. Sally grooms Pablo to star in her upcoming pic as long as he allows the headstrong director to take the lead while they dance. Occasionally departs from the story to the "Rage" script, played out in color. While light on their toes, performances by the real-life director and real-life tango instructor are as heavy and stilted as some of the dialogue. Using dance as the metaphor for control and power in relationships, Potter falls flat in a pretentious "Lesson." **101m/B VHS.** *GB* Sally Potter, Pablo Veron, Gustavo Naveira, Fabian Salas, David Toole, Carolina Iotti, Carlos Copello, Peter Eyre, Heathcote Williams; *D:* Sally Potter; *W:* Sally Potter; *C:* Robby Muller; *M:* Fred Frith, Sally Potter.

Tank 🦴½ **1983 (PG)** Retired Army officer Garner's son is thrown into jail on a trumped-up charge by a small town sheriff. Dad comes to the rescue with his restored Sherman tank. Trite and unrealistic portrayal of good versus bad made palatable by Garner's performance. **113m/C VHS, DVD.** James Garner, Shirley Jones, C. Thomas Howell, Mark Herrier, Sandy Ward, Jenilee Harrison, Dorian Harewood, G.D. Spradlin; *D:* Marvin J. Chomsky; *W:* Dan Gordon; *C:* Donald Birnkrant; *M:* Lalo Schifrin.

Tank Commando 🦴½ **1959** Mediocre WWII actioner, set in Italy, about a demolition squad of battle-hardened Americans trying to locate a secret German crossing point. It turns out to be an underwater bridge and an Italian orphan is the only one, besides the Germans, to know its location. Can the Americans persuade the kid to talk? **79m/B VHS.** Bob Barron, Wally Campo, Maggie Lawrence, Donato Farretta, Leo V. Metranga, Jack Sowards, Anthony Rich, Larry Hudson; *D:* Burt Topper; *W:* Burt Topper.

Tank Girl 🦴½ **1994 (R)** Big-budget adaption of the underground British comic book about a brash punker chick (Petty), her mutant friends, and the evil establishment in the post-apocalyptic future. The heavily armed pixie battles the tyrannical Department of Water and Power, run by evil Dr. Kesslee (McDowell), for control of the world's water supply in the year 2033. Straying a bit too far from the source comic, the plot (such as it is) is crammed into a rigid action-movie structure that lacks excitement. Plays like a cheap Gen-X marketing ploy with its bizarre mixture of pop culture references and a hipper-than-thou soundtrack coordinated by Courtney Love. **104m/C VHS, DVD, Wide.** Lori Petty, Malcolm McDowell, Ice-T, Naomi Watts, Jeff Kober, Reg E. Cathey, Scott Coffey, Ann Cusack, Don Harvey, Brian Wimmer, Stacey Linn Ramsower, Iggy Pop, Ann Magnuson; *D:* Rachel Talalay; *W:* Tedi Sarafian; *C:* Gale Tattersall; *M:* Graeme Revell.

Tanks a Million 🦴🦴 **1941** Despite the title, tanks aren't even mentioned in this. Tracy stars as a wacky genius who gets drafted. His excellent memory keeps getting him into one predicament after another. Though he gets promoted quickly, he shows himself no leader. Lots of time-worn gags, but they still work. **50m/B VHS.** William Tracy, James Gleason, Noah Beery Jr., Joseph (Joe) Sawyer, Elyse Knox, Douglas Fowley, Frank Faylen, Dick Wessel, Frank Melton, Harold Goodwin, William (Bill) Gould, Norman Kerry; *D:* Fred Guiol.

Tanner '88 *Tanner: A Political Fable* **1988** Murphy is excellent as a longshot politician on the trail of the Democratic presidential nomination. Precise political satire from a story by Gary "Doonesbury" Trudeau. **120m/C VHS.** Michael Murphy, Pamela Reed, Cynthia Nixon; *D:* Robert Altman. CABLE

Tanya's Island 🦴🦴½ **1981 (R)** Abused girlfriend fantasizes about life on deserted island and romance with an ape. Vanity billed as D.D. Winters. **100m/C VHS.** Vanity, Dick Sargent, Mariette Levesque, Don McCleod; *D:* Alfred Sole.

The Tao of Steve 🦴🦴🦴 **2000 (R)** Overweight, intelligent kindergarten teacher Dex (Logue) is a hit with the ladies, but feels a vague sense of wanting something more. The title of the film comes from Dex's personal philosophy of cool, which he takes from the images of such icons as Steve McQueen, Steve McGarrett, and Steve Austin—but is also tossed with equal parts Kierkegaard and Aquinas. He's ripe for some growing up, and only needs to find the perfect mate, who comes along in the form of Syd (played by Greer Goodman, sister of the director and one of the film's three screenwriters), one of Dex's one-night stands. A sweet romantic comedy that can thank Logue for much of its charm. **87m/C VHS, DVD, Wide.** Donal Logue, Greer Goodman, Kimo Wills, Ayelet Kaznelson, David Aaron Baker, Nina Jaroslaw; *D:* Jenniphr Goodman; ***W:*** Greer Goodman, Jenniphr Goodman, Duncan North; ***C:*** Teodoro Maniaci; ***M:*** Joe Delia.

Tap 𝒮𝒮½ **1989 (PG-13)** The son of a famous tap dancer, a dancer himself, decides to try to get away from his former life of crime by helping an aging hoofer revitalize the art of tap dancing. Fun to watch for the wonderful dancing scenes. Davis' last big screen appearance. Hines is sincere in this old-fashioned story, and dances up a storm. Captures some never-before filmed old hoofers. **106m/C VHS.** Gregory Hines, Sammy Davis Jr., Suzzanne Douglass, Joe Morton, Terrance McNally, Steve Condos, Jimmy Slyde, Harold Nicholas, Etta James, Savion Glover, Dick Anthony Williams, Sandman Sims, Bunny Briggs, Pat Rico, Arthur Duncan; ***D:*** Nick Castle; ***W:*** Nick Castle; ***M:*** James Newton Howard.

Tape 𝒮𝒮𝒮 **2001 (R)** Director Linklater makes digital technology an asset in this intriguing, claustrophobic character study based on a play by Stephen Belber. Johnny (Leonard) pays a visit to high school chum Vince (Hawke), who's working as a low-level drug dealer. Their casual conversation becomes increasingly hostile as Vince begins making accusations involving Johnny and his first love, Amy (Thurman), who soon pays a visit herself. Despite a tiny cast and only one location, story stays stimulating throughout, as the script deftly shifts viewer allegiance between characters and explores interesting themes of memory, subjectivity and ownership of one's past. Linklater's use of high-definition video gives the film a vitality and spontaneous feel that suits the material. **86m/C VHS, DVD.** *US* Ethan Hawke, Robert Sean Leonard, Uma Thurman; ***D:*** Richard Linklater; ***W:*** Stephen Belber; ***C:*** Maryse Alberti.

Tapeheads 𝒮𝒮½ **1989 (R)** Silly, sophomoric, sexy comedy starring Cusack and Robbins as young wanna-be rock-video producers who get mixed up with perverted politicos, conniving music-industry types, and asinine bands looking for MTV stardom before they eventually strike it big helping their childhood idols, The Swanky Modes. Many big-name music industry cameos and a great soundtrack help keep things lively when the plot goes out of control. Sam Moore and Junior Walker are the Sam & Dave-esque Modes. **93m/C VHS, DVD, Wide.** Courtney Love, Ebbe Roe Smith, Lee Arenberg, Rocky Giordani, John Marshall Jones, John Durbin, Milton Selzer, Zander Schloss, Jo Harvey Allen, Sy Richardson, Coati Mundi, John Fleck, John Cusack, Tim Robbins, Mary Crosby, Connie Stevens, Susan Tyrrell, Lyle Alzado, Don Cornelius, Katy Boyer, Doug McClure, Clu Gulager, Jessica Walter, Stiv Bators, Sam Moore, Junior Walker, Martha Quinn, Ted Nugent, Weird Al Yankovic, Bob(cat) Goldthwait, Michael Nesmith, Xander Berkeley, Bojan Bazelli; ***D:*** Bill Fishman; ***W:*** Bill Fishman, Peter McCarthy; ***C:*** Bojan Bazelli.

Taps 𝒮𝒮½ **1981 (PG)** Military academy students led by Hutton are so true to their school they lay siege to it to keep it from being closed. An antiwar morality play about excesses of zeal and patriotism. Predictable but impressive. **126m/C VHS, DVD, Wide.** Timothy Hutton, George C. Scott, Ronny Cox, Sean Penn, Tom Cruise; ***D:*** Harold Becker; ***W:*** Robert Mark Kamen, Darryl Ponicsan; ***C:*** Owen Roizman; ***M:*** Maurice Jarre.

Tar 𝒮𝒮 **1997** Female cop Prescott and crook Thigpen were high school sweethearts who went their separate ways. But they're reunited when Thigpen hijacks a squad car that just happens to be driven by guess who. There's also a story involving a group of black nationalists who kidnap white businessman and cover them in—you guessed it—tar. Likeable leads, improbable characters. **?m/C VHS.** Kevin Thigpen, Nicole Prescott, Seth Gilliam, Ron Brice, Frank Minucci; ***D:*** Goetz Grossmann; ***W:*** Goetz Grossmann; ***C:*** Lloyd Handwerker; ***M:*** John Hill.

Tarantella 𝒮𝒮½ **1995** Aspiring New York photographer Diane DiSorella (Sorvino) gets a shock when her mother dies suddenly. After returning to the New Jersey home and Italian-American community she rejected, Diane is given a journal her mother secretly kept by old family friend Pina (Gregorio). Small-scale story with Diane's big change being learning to accept where she came from. **84m/C VHS, DVD.** Mira Sorvino, Rose Gregorio, Stephen Spinella, Matthew Lillard, Antonia Rey, Frank Pellegrino; ***D:*** Helen DeMichiel; ***W:*** Helen DeMichiel, Richard Hoblock; ***C:*** Teodoro Maniaci; ***M:*** Norman Moll.

Tarantula 𝒮𝒮𝒮 **1955** If you're into gigantic killer insect movies this is one of the best with nifty special effects and some good action. Carroll plays a scientist working on a growth formula which he's testing on a spider when it accidentally gets loose. This eight-legged horror grows to 100 feet high and causes havoc in the Arizona desert until the Air Force napalms the sucker. Look for Eastwood in the final sequence as an Air Force pilot. **81m/B VHS.** Leo G. Carroll, John Agar, Mara Corday, Nestor Paiva, Ross Elliott, Clint Eastwood; ***D:*** Jack Arnold; ***W:*** Robert M. Fresco, Martin Berkeley.

Tarantulas: The Deadly Cargo 𝒮 **1977** Eek! Hairy spiders terrizing our sleepy town and destroying our orange crop! Made-for-TV cheapie not creepy; will make you sleepy. **100m/C VHS.** Claude Akins, Charles Frank, Deborah Winters, Pat Hingle, Sandy McPeak, Bert Remsen, Howard Hesseman, Tom Atkins, Charles Siebert; ***D:*** Stuart Hagmann.

Taras Bulba 𝒮𝒮½ **1962** Well-photographed costume epic on the 16th century Polish revolution. Brynner as the fabled Cossack; Curtis plays his vengeful son. Good score. Shot on location in Argentina. Based on the novel by Nikolai Gogol. **122m/C VHS, Wide.** Tony Curtis, Yul Brynner, Christine Kaufmann, Sam Wanamaker, George Macready, Vladimir Sokoloff, Perry Lopez; ***D:*** J. Lee Thompson.

Target 𝒮𝒮 **1985 (R)** Normal dad/hubby Hackman slips into a figurative phone booth and emerges as former CIA when his better half is kidnapped in Paris. Good action scenes, but poorly scripted and too long. **117m/C VHS.** Gene Hackman, Matt Dillon, Gayle Hunnicutt, Josef Sommer; ***D:*** Arthur Penn; ***W:*** Howard Berk.

Target Eagle 𝒮𝒮 **1984** Spanish police chief von Sydow hires mercenary Rivero to infiltrate drug ring. Good performances; ho-hum story. **99m/C VHS.** *SP MX* Max von Sydow, George Peppard, Maud Adams, Chuck Connors, Jorge (George) Rivero, Susana Dosamantes; ***D:*** J. Anthony (Jose Antonio de la Loma) Loma.

Target: Favorite Son 𝒮𝒮 **1987 (R)** An attractive, ammunition-laden woman sharp-shoots her way to power in this made-for-TV movie. **115m/C VHS.** Linda Kozlowski, Harry Hamlin, Robert Loggia, Ronny Cox, James Whitmore.

Target for Killing 𝒮𝒮 **1966** Mediocre thriller about a secret agent who must protect a young heiress from a Lebanese syndicate that's out to kill her. **93m/C VHS.** Stewart Granger, Curt Jurgens, Molly Peters, Adolfo Celi, Klaus Kinski, Rupert Davies; ***D:*** Manfred Kohler.

Targets 𝒮𝒮𝒮 **1968 (PG)** Bogdanovich's suspenseful directorial debut. An aging horror film star plans his retirement, convinced that real life is too scary for his films to have an audience. A mad sniper at a drive-in movie seems to prove he's right. Some prints still have anti-gun prologue, which was added after Robert Kennedy's assassination. **90m/C VHS.** Boris Karloff, James Brown, Tim O'Kelly, Peter Bogdanovich, Mary Jackson, Sandy Baron, Monte Landis, Mike Farrell, Nancy Hsueh, Arthur Peterson, Tanya Morgan, Randy Quaid; ***D:*** Peter Bogdanovich; ***W:*** Peter Bogdanovich; ***C:*** Laszlo Kovacs.

Tarnished Angels 𝒮𝒮𝒮 **1957** Reporter Burke Devlin (Hudson) is writing a story for the local New Orleans paper about a tormented trio of air circus barmstormers. A former WWI ace, Roger Shumann (Stack) cares more about flying than he does his sizzling wife Laverne (Malone), who's loved-from-afar by loyal mechanic Jiggs (Carson). When Roger's plane cracks up, he uses his wife to obtain use of an experimental aircraft in order to win a race—and brings disaster crashing around them all. Good action, fine cast. Based on William Faulkner's 1930 novel "Pylon." **91m/B VHS.** Rock Hudson, Robert Stack, Dorothy Malone, Jack Carson, Robert Middleton, Troy Donahue, Alan Reed, Robert J. Wilke, William Schallert; ***D:*** Douglas Sirk; ***W:*** George Zuckerman; ***C:*** Irving Glassberg; ***M:*** Frank Skinner.

Tart 𝒮𝒮 **2001 (R)** Cat Storm (Swain) is desperate to belong to the in-crowd at her New York prep school even if it means dumping her best friend, Delilah (Phillips). But privilege has its price. **94m/C VHS, DVD, Wide.** Dominique Swain, Brad Renfro, Bijou Phillips, Mischa Barton, Lacey Chabert, Alberta Watson, Myles Jeffrey, Scott Thompson, Melanie Griffith; ***D:*** Christina Wayne; ***W:*** Christina Wayne; ***C:*** Stephen Kazmierski; ***M:*** Jeehun Hwang.

Tartuffe 𝒮𝒮½ **1984** Popular French leading man Depardieu makes directorial debut with Moliere classic about religious hypocrisy and an imposter taking advantage of a wealthy merchant and his family. In French with English subtitles. **140m/C VHS.** *FR* Gerard Depardieu, Francois Perier, Elisabeth Depardieu; ***D:*** Gerard Depardieu.

Tartuffe 𝒮𝒮½ **1990** Moliere's famous comedy has Tartuffe posing as a holy man who has attracted the incredulous merchant Orgon. Orgon is willing to give Tartuffe anything—money, social position, even his daughter—and Tartuffe is more than happy to accept. **110m/C VHS.** Anthony Sher, Nigel Hawthorne, Alison Steadman; ***D:*** Bill Alexander.

Tarzan 𝒮𝒮𝒮 **1999 (G)** Disney animated film finds baby Tarzan lost in the jungle and raised by a gorilla family—patriarch Kerchak (Henriksen), nurturing mom Kala (Close), and bossy big sister Terk (O'Donnell). But, years later, a now grownup Tarzan's (Goldwyn) life is thrown into chaos when he first encounters humans—and realizes he is one. Eccentric gorilla scientist Professor Porter (Hawthorne) and his lovely daughter Jane (Driver) are willing to help, but jungle guide Clayton (Blessed) is the villain on the scene. Disney's animation is even more amazing than usual thanks to some new computer software that gives the jungle background unbelievable depth and Tarzan glides, surfs, and jumps in a wow! look! manner. **88m/C VHS, DVD.** ***D:*** Kevin Lima, Chris Buck; ***W:*** Tab Murphy, Bob Tzudiker, Noni White; ***M:*** Phil Collins; ***V:*** Tony Goldwyn, Minnie Driver, Rosie O'Donnell, Glenn Close, Lance Henriksen, Wayne Knight, Brian Blessed, Nigel Hawthorne, Alex D. Linz. Oscars '99: Song ("You'll Be In My Heart"); Golden Globes '00: Song ("You'll Be In My Heart").

Tarzan and His Mate 𝒮𝒮𝒮 **1934** Second entry in the lavishly produced MGM Tarzan series. Weissmuller and O'Sullivan cohabit in unmarried bliss before the Hays Code moved them to a tree house with twin beds. Many angry elephants, nasty white hunters, and hungry lions. **93m/B VHS.** Johnny Weissmuller, Maureen O'Sullivan, Neil Hamilton, Paul Cavanagh; ***D:*** Jack Conway; ***W:*** Leon Gordon, James Kevin McGuinness, Howard Emmett Rogers; ***C:*** Clyde De Vinna, Charles Clarke; ***M:*** William Axt.

Tarzan and the Green Goddess 𝒮½ *New Adventures of Tarzan* **1938** Tarzan searches for a statue that could prove dangerous if in the wrong hands. **72m/B VHS.** Bruce (Herman Brix) Bennett, Ula Holt, Frank Baker; ***D:*** Edward Kull.

Tarzan and the Lost City 𝒮𝒮½ *Tarzan and Jane; Greystoke 2: Tarzan and Jane* **1998 (PG)** Gorgeous locations in South Africa are a decided plus in this routine hero/adventure story. Lord Greystoke, AKA Tarzan (Van Dien), returns to Africa from England in order to save his home from mercenaries hunting the lost city of Opar. Spunky fiance Jane (March) heads to the jungle after her Ape Man and gets into (and out of) trouble with bad guy Nigel Ravens (Waddington). Not very convincing special effects but Van Dien looks good in his loincloth and has the action moves down cold. **84m/C VHS, DVD, Wide.** Casper Van Dien, Jane March, Steven Waddington, Winston Ntshona, Rapulana Seiphemo, Ian Roberts; ***D:*** Carl Schenkel; ***W:*** Bayard Johnson, J. Anderson Black; ***C:*** Paul Gilpin; ***M:*** Christopher Franke.

Tarzan and the Trappers 𝒮½ **1958** Bad-guy trappers and would-be treasure-seekers wish they hadn't messed with the ape man. **70m/B VHS, DVD, Wide.** Gordon Scott, Eve Brent, Ricky Sorenson, Maurice Marsac; ***D:*** Charles Haas, H. Bruce Humberstone, Sandy Howard.

Tarzan Escapes 𝒮𝒮𝒮 **1936** Jane is tricked by evil hunters into abandoning her fairy tale life with Tarzan, so the Ape Man sets out to reunite with his one true love. The third entry in MGM's Weissmuller/O'Sullivan series is still among the better Tarzan movies thanks to the leads, but the Hays Office made sure Jane was wearing a lot more clothes this time around. **95m/B VHS.** Johnny Weissmuller, Maureen O'Sullivan, John Buckler, Benita Hume, William Henry; ***D:*** Richard Thorpe.

Tarzan Finds a Son 𝒮𝒮𝒮 **1939** Weissmuller and O'Sullivan returned to their roles after three years with the addition of the five-year-old Sheffield as Boy. He's an orphan whose awful relatives hope he stays lost so they can collect an inheritance. Jane and Tarzan fight to adopt the tyke and when the new family are captured by a wicked tribe only an elephant stampede can save them! **90m/B VHS.** Johnny Weissmuller, Maureen O'Sullivan, John(ny) Sheffield, Ian Hunter, Henry Stephenson, Frieda Inescort, Henry Wilcoxon; ***D:*** Richard Thorpe.

Tarzan of the Apes 𝒮𝒮 **1917** Brawny Lincoln is the original screen Tarzan. Silent film well done and more faithful to the book than later versions. **63m/B VHS.** Elmo Lincoln, Enid Markey; ***D:*** Scott Sidney.

Tarzan, the Ape Man 𝒮𝒮𝒮 **1932** The definitive Tarzan movie; the first Tarzan talkie; the original of the long series starring Weissmuller. Dubiously faithful to the Edgar Rice Burroughs story, but recent attempts to remake, update or improve it (notably the pretentious 1984 Greystoke) have failed to near the original's entertainment value or even its technical quality. O'Sullivan as Jane and Weissmuller bring style and wit to their classic roles. **99m/B VHS.** Johnny Weissmuller, Maureen O'Sullivan, Neil Hamilton; ***D:*** Woodbridge S. Van Dyke; ***C:*** Clyde De Vinna.

Tarzan, the Ape Man woof! **1981 (R)** Plodding, perverted excuse to see Derek cavort nude in jungle. So bad not even hard-core Tarzan fans should bother. **112m/C VHS.** Bo Derek, Richard Harris, John Phillip Law, Miles O'Keeffe, Wilfrid Hyde-White, Akushula Selayah, Steven Strong, Laurie Main, Harold Ayer; ***D:*** John Derek; ***W:*** Gary Goddard; ***C:*** John Derek; ***M:*** Perry Botkin. Golden Raspberries '81: Worst Actress (Derek).

Tarzan the Fearless 𝒮½ **1933** Tarzan (Crabbe) helps a young girl find her missing father. **84m/B VHS, DVD, Wide.** Buster Crabbe, Julie (Jacqueline Wells) Bishop, E. Alyn Warren, Edward (Eddie) Woods, Philo (Philip, P.H., P.M.) McCullough, Matthew Betz; ***D:*** Robert F. "Bob" Hill; ***W:*** Walter Anthony; ***C:*** Joseph Brotherton, Harry Neuman.

Tarzan the Tiger **1929** Series of 15 chapters is loosely based on the Edgar Rice Burroughs novel entitled "Tarzan and the Jewels of Opar." These chapters were filmed as silent pieces, and were later released with a musical score and synchronized sound effects. Here Merrill is the first to sound the cry of the bull ape, Tarzan's trademark. **?m/B VHS.** Frank Merrill, Natalie Kingston, Lilian Worth, Al Ferguson; ***D:*** Henry MacRae.

Tarzana, the Wild Girl 𝒮 **1972** Jungle cheapie about an expedition that finds a beautiful, scantily clad girl living wildly in the jungle. **87m/C VHS.** Kenneth (Ken) Clark, Franca Polesello, Frank Ressel, Andrew Ray, James Reed; ***W:*** Philip Shaw.

Tarzan's New York Adventure 𝒮𝒮½ **1942** O'Sullivan's final appearance as Jane is a so-so adventure with some humorous moments when Tarzan meets the big city. When Boy is kidnapped by an evil circus owner, Tarzan, Jane, and Cheta head out to rescue him. Tarzan shows off his jungle prowess by climbing skyscrapers and diving off the Brooklyn Bridge into the East River. Lincoln, the screen's first Tarzan, has a cameo. **70m/B VHS.** Johnny Weissmuller, Maureen O'Sullivan, John(ny) Sheffield, Virginia Grey, Charles Bickford, Paul Kelly, Chill Wills, Russell Hicks, Cy Kendall; ***Cameos:*** Elmo Lincoln; ***D:*** Richard Thorpe.

Tarzan's Revenge 🦴 **1938** Morris is a better Olympic runner than actor; Holm is horrible. Only for serious Tarzan fans. **70m/B VHS.** Glenn Morris, Eleanor Holm, Hedda Hopper; ***D:*** David Ross Lederman.

Tarzan's Secret Treasure 🦴🦴½ **1941** Tarzan saves an expedition from a savage tribe only to be repaid by having the greedy hunters hold Jane and Boy hostage. They want Tarzan's help in finding a secret cache of gold. But Tarzan doesn't take kindly to threats to his family and teaches those evil-doers a lesson! **81m/B VHS.** Johnny Weissmuller, Maureen O'Sullivan, John(ny) Sheffield, Reginald Owen, Barry Fitzgerald, Tom Conway, Philip Dorn; ***D:*** Richard Thorpe.

Task Force 🦴🦴½ **1949** History of naval aviation and the development of the aircraft carrier highlighted by actual WWII combat footage (in color). Cooper and his naval buddies try to convince the brass that planes can be landed on the decks of ships. Slowly the Navy goes ahead and when Pearl Harbor is attacked, Cooper is given command of his own aircraft carrier. The use of the carriers proved very effective in Pacific battles and Cooper is finally vindicated. **116m/B VHS.** Gary Cooper, Jane Wyatt, Wayne Morris, Walter Brennan, Julie London, Bruce (Herman Brix) Bennett, Jack Holt, Stanley Ridges, John Ridgely, Richard Rober, Art Baker, Moroni Olsen; ***D:*** Delmer Daves; ***W:*** Delmer Daves.

A Taste for Flesh and Blood **1990 (R)** A monster from outer space comes to earth and is delighted with the easy pickings for his insatiable appetite. A brave boy and girl, and a NASA commander must join forces to take the alien out. This one is billed as a campy salute to '50s B movies. **84m/C VHS.** Rubin Santiago, Lori Karz, Tim Ferrante.

A Taste for Killing 🦴🦴 **1992 (R)** Two boys, both from well-to-do families, decide to take summer jobs on an offshore Texas oil rig. The best friends think a summer of adventure awaits them; however, their lives are made miserable by their blue-collar boss, who is resentful of their high society background. Then they meet Bo Landry, who befriends them and helps them survive. Unfortunately, Bo turns out to be anything but a friend as he reveals himself as a deadly con-artist in this intense psychological thriller. **87m/C VHS.** Jason Bateman, Henry Thomas, Michael Biehn, Edward "Blue" Deckert, Helen Cates; ***D:*** Lou Antonio; ***W:*** Dan Bronson.

A Taste of Blood 🦴½ **1967** Gore-meister Lewis's vampire film is actually fairly restrained when compared to "2000 Maniacs" and "Blood Feast." When John Stone (Rogers) drinks brandy containing the blood of Count Dracula, he turns into a green-faced killer bent on revenge against the ancestors of...oh, never mind. **118m/C DVD.** Bill Rogers, Elizabeth Wilkinson, Thomas Wood, Lawrence Tobin; ***D:*** Herschell Gordon Lewis; ***W:*** Donald Stanford; ***C:*** Andy Romanoff.

The Taste of Cherry 🦴🦴 *Ta'm e Guilass; Taste of Cherries* **1996** Despairing, middle-aged Mr. Badii (Ershadi) is contemplating suicide and looking for someone who will bury his corpse discreetly. (He's already dug his own shallow grave in the countryside.) He drives through the streets and picks up several different men—all of whom remind him that suicide goes against the teachings of Islam. Finally, one old Turkish man relates his own story of attempted suicide and seemingly persuades Badii to rethink his actions. **95m/C VHS, DVD, Wide.** *IA* Homayon Ershadi, Abdolrahma Bagheri, Afshin Bakhtiari; ***D:*** Abbas Kiarostami; ***W:*** Abbas Kiarostami; ***C:*** Homayun Payvar. Cannes '97: Film; Natl. Soc. Film Critics '98: Foreign Film.

Taste of Death 🦴 **1977** A youth discovers his courage within when he stands up to the bandits invading his village. **90m/C VHS.** John Ireland.

A Taste of Hell 🦴 **1973 (PG)** Two American soldiers fight a guerilla outfit in the Pacific during WWII. A low-budget film with few redeeming characteristics. **90m/C VHS.** William Smith, John Garwood.

A Taste of Honey 🦴🦴🦴 **1961** A plain working-class girl falls in love with a black sailor. When she becomes pregnant, a homosexual friend helps her out. A moving film with strong, powerful performances. Based on the London and Broadway hit play by Shelagh Delaney. **100m/B VHS.** *GB* Rita Tushingham, Robert Stephens, Dora Bryan, Murray Melvin, Paul Danquah; ***D:*** Tony Richardson; ***W:*** Tony Richardson, Shelagh Delaney; ***C:*** Walter Lassally; ***M:*** John Addison. British Acad. '61: Film, Support. Actress (Bryan); British Acad. '62: Screenplay; Cannes '62: Actor (Melvin), Actress (Tushingham).

Taste the Blood of Dracula 🦴🦴½ **1970 (PG)** Lee's Dracula only makes a brief appearance in this Hammer horror film which has three children taking over from the bloodsucker. Three Victorian dandies have killed the wizard who revived Dracula and he seeks their deaths by using their own children as the means of his revenge. Not enough Lee but still creepy. Preceded by "Dracula Has Risen from the Grave" and followed by "Scars of Dracula." **91m/C VHS.** *GB* Christopher Lee, Ralph Bates, Geoffrey Keen, Gwen Watford, Linda Hayden, John Carson, Peter Sallis, Isla Blair, Martin Jarvis, Roy Kinnear, Anthony (Corlan) Higgins, Michael Ripper; ***D:*** Peter Sasdy; ***W:*** John (Anthony Hinds) Elder; ***C:*** Arthur Grant; ***M:*** James Bernard.

Tatie Danielle 🦴🦴🦴 **1991** Pitch-black comedy from the director of "Life Is a Long Quiet River" sees a bitter, elderly widow moving in with her young nephew and making his life a hell. In French with yellow English subtitles. **114m/C VHS.** *FR* Tsilla Chelton, Catherine Jacob, Isabelle Nanty, Neige Dolsky, Eric Prat, Laurence Fevrier; ***D:*** Etienne Chatiliez; ***W:*** Etienne Chatiliez.

The Tattered Web 🦴🦴 **1971** A police sergeant confronts and accidently kills the woman with whom his son-in-law has been cheating. He's then assigned the case. When he tries to frame a wino for the murder, things get more and more messy. Fine performances. **74m/C VHS, DVD.** Lloyd Bridges, Frank Converse, Broderick Crawford, Murray Hamilton, Sallie Shockley; ***D:*** Paul Wendkos; ***M:*** Robert Jackson Drasnin. **TV**

Tattle Tale 🦴½ **1992 (PG)** Vindictive ex-wife writes book accusing her actor ex of abusing her and he loses out on his career-breaking role. So he decides to disguise himself and seduce her into telling the truth. Even dumber than it sounds. **96m/C VHS.** C. Thomas Howell, Ally Sheedy; ***D:*** Baz Taylor.

Tattoo 🦴🦴 **1981 (R)** A model becomes the object of obsession for a crazy tattoo artist. He relentlessly pursues her, leaving behind all his other more illustrated clients. Starts out fine, but deteriorates rapidly. Controversial love scene between Dern and Adams. **103m/C VHS.** Bruce Dern, Maud Adams, Leonard Frey, Rikke Borge, John Getz; ***D:*** Bob Brooks; ***W:*** Joyce Bunuel.

The Tavern 🦴🦴 **2000** Ronnie (Dye) is a bartender who wants to buy a Manhattan watering hole from its alleged Florida-bound owner, Kevin (Zittel). He borrows the money from a number of people, including his best friend Dave (Geer), who becomes his partner. But they're underfinanced and beset by competition and numerous other problems soon surface threatening their business survival. Unsentimental and downbeat. **88m/C VHS, DVD, Wide.** Cameron Dye, Kevin Geer, Margaret Cho, Greg Zittel, Nancy Ticotin, Steven Marcus, Carlo Alban, Kym Austin, Gary Perez; ***D:*** Walter Foote; ***W:*** Walter Foote; ***C:*** Kurt Lennig; ***M:*** Bill Lacey, Loren Toolajian.

Tax Season 🦴🦴 **1990 (PG-13)** A small-time businessman buys a Hollywood tax service sight-unseen, and finds it employing a hooker, a bookie and a variety of other unconventional types. **93m/C VHS.** Fritz Bronner, James Hong, Jana Grant, Toru Tanaka, Dorie Krum, Kathryn Knotts, Arte Johnson, Rob Slyker; ***D:*** Tom Law.

Taxi Blues 🦴🦴🦴½ **1990** A political allegory with the two protagonists representing the new and old Soviet Union. A hard-working, narrow-minded cabdriver keeps the saxophone of a westernized, Jewish, jazz-loving musician who doesn't have his fare. The two strike up a wary friendship as each tries to explain his view of life to the other. Good look at the street life of Moscow populated by drunks, punks, and black marketeers. Directorial debut of Lounguine. In Russian with English subtitles. **110m/C VHS.** *RU* Piotr Mamonov, Piotr Zaitchenko, Natalia Koliakanova, Vladimir Kachpour; ***D:*** Pavel (Lungin) Lounguine; ***W:*** Pavel (Lungin) Lounguine. Cannes '90: Director (Lounguine).

Taxi Dancers 🦴½ **1993** Smalltown Billie arrives in Hollywood with dreams of becoming an actress. Naturally, her dreams turn to despair and she resorts to "dancing" at the Shark Club where she becomes involved with a gambler who owes money to the wrong people. **97m/C VHS.** Sonny Landham, Robert Miano, Brittany McCrena, Tina Fite, Mirage Micheaux, Michele Hess, Randall Irwin; ***D:*** Norman Thaddeus Vane; ***W:*** Norman Thaddeus Vane; ***M:*** Larry Blank.

Taxi Driver 🦴🦴🦴 **1976 (R)** A psychotic NYC taxi driver tries to save a child prostitute and becomes infatuated with an educated political campaigner. He goes on a violent rampage when his dreams don't work out. Repellant, frightening vision of alienation and urban catharsis. On-target performances from Foster and De Niro. **112m/C VHS, DVD, 8mm, Wide.** Robert De Niro, Jodie Foster, Harvey Keitel, Cybill Shepherd, Peter Boyle, Albert Brooks, Leonard Harris, Joe Spinell, Martin Scorsese; ***D:*** Martin Scorsese; ***W:*** Paul Schrader; ***C:*** Michael Chapman; ***M:*** Bernard Herrmann. AFI '98: Top 100; British Acad. '76: Support. Actress (Foster); Cannes '76: Film; L.A. Film Critics '76: Actor (De Niro), Natl. Film Reg. '94;; N.Y. Film Critics '76: Actor (De Niro); Natl. Soc. Film Critics '76: Actor (De Niro), Director (Scorsese), Support. Actress (Foster).

The Taxi Mystery 🦴 **1926** Guy saves Broadway starlet from band of ne'er-do-wells thanks to deserted taxi, then tries to figure out who she is, unaware that her sinister understudy plans to do her in. **50m/B VHS.** Edith Roberts, Robert Agnew, Virginia Pearson, Phillips Smalley; ***D:*** Fred Windermere.

Taxi zum Klo 🦴🦴🦴 **1981** An autobiographical semi-documentary about the filmmaker's aimless existence and attempts at homosexual affairs after being fired from his job as a teacher. Explicit. In German with English subtitles. Sordid sexual situations. **98m/C VHS.** *GE* Bernd Broaderup, Frank Ripploh; ***D:*** Frank Ripploh.

A Taxing Woman 🦴🦴🦴½ *Marusa No Onna* **1987** Satiric Japanese comedy about a woman tax collector in pursuit of a crafty millionaire tax cheater. Followed by the equally hilarious "A Taxing Woman's Return." In Japanese with English subtitles. **127m/C VHS, DVD.** *JP* Nobuko Miyamoto, Tsutomu Yamazaki, Hideo Murota, Shuji Otaki; ***D:*** Juzo Itami; ***W:*** Juzo Itami; ***C:*** Yonezo Maeda; ***M:*** Toshiyuki Honda.

A Taxing Woman's Return 🦴🦴🦴 *Marusa No Onna II* **1988** Funny, sophisticated, action-packed. Miyamoto returns as the dedicated tax investigator to fight industrialists, politicians, and other big swindlers, who have contrived to inflate Tokyo's real estate values. Sequel to "A Taxing Woman." In Japanese with English subtitles. **127m/C VHS.** *JP* Nobuko Miyamoto, Rentaro Mikuni, Masahiko Tsugawa, Tetsuro Tamba, Toru Masuoka, Takeya Nakamura, Hosei Komatsu, Mihoko Shibata; ***D:*** Juzo Itami; ***W:*** Juzo Itami.

The Taxman 🦴🦴 **1998 (R)** Al Benjamin (Pantoliano) is an obsessive New York State tax investigator who stumbles across six dead bodies in a Brighton Beach gasoline company while on the job. He teams up with a pain-in-the-butt cop, Joseph Romero (Dominguez), who's proficient in Russian—a necessity in the immigrant community. Their sleuthing leads them to the Russian mob, a scam involving gasoline taxes, and a lot of violence. **95m/C VHS, DVD.** Joe Pantoliano, Wade Dominguez, Elizabeth Berkley, Michael Chiklis, Robert Townsend; ***D:*** Avi Nesher; ***W:*** Avi Nesher, Roger Berger; ***C:*** Jim Denault; ***M:*** Roger Neill.

TC 2000 🦴½ **1993 (R)** Jason Storm and Zoey Kinsella are cops working for The Controller, who has the unenviable task of protecting the community from roving gangs of vicious punks. When Zoey is killed, The Controller converts her into a super-cybernetic killing machine unleashed on the gangs. Meanwhile Jason is considered a liability and must battle the gangs, The Controller, and cyber-Zoey to save himself. Oh, there's also something about saving the Earth's atmosphere from nuclear destruction. Lots of action. **92m/C VHS.** Billy Blanks, Bobbie Phillips, Jalal Merhi, Bolo Yeung, Matthias Hues; ***D:*** T.J. Scott; ***W:*** T.J. Scott.

Tchaikovsky 🦴🦴½ **1971** The glorious music is all that saves this pedestrian biography of the 19th century Russian composer, which ignores his homosexuality and glosses over the dissolution of his marriage. Lead performance by Smoktunovsky does manage to rise above the moribund script. Originally released at 191 minutes. In Russian with English subtitles. **153m/C VHS, DVD, Wide.** *RU* Innokenti Smoktunovsky, Antonina Shuranova, Yevgeny Leonov, Maya Plisetskaya, Vladislav Strzeltchik, Alla Demidova, Kirill Lavrov; ***D:*** Igor Talankin; ***W:*** Igor Talankin, Yuri Nagibin, Budimir Metalnikov; ***C:*** Margarita Pilikhina.

Tchao Pantin 🦴🦴🦴 **1984** An acclaimed French film noir about an ex-cop being drawn into drug smuggling underground via a young Arab. English subtitles. Finely drawn characters skillfully portrayed make this a winner. **100m/C VHS.** *FR* Coluche, Richard Anconina, Agnes Soral; ***D:*** Claude Berri. Cesar '84: Actor (Coluche), Cinematog., Sound, Support. Actor (Anconina).

Tea and Sympathy 🦴🦴🦴 **1956** A young prep school student, confused about his sexuality, has an affair with an older woman, his teacher's wife. The three leads recreate their Broadway roles in this tame adaption of the Robert Anderson play which dealt more openly with the story's homosexual elements. **122m/C VHS, Wide.** Deborah Kerr, John Kerr, Leif Erickson, Edward Andrews, Darryl Hickman, Norma Crane, Dean Jones; ***D:*** Vincente Minnelli; ***W:*** Robert Anderson; ***C:*** John Alton.

Tea for Three 🦴🦴 **1984 (R)** Sexual trio develops and seeks therapy after a fledgling doctor has been having sexual relationships with two women, and the females finally meet. **89m/C VHS.** Iris Berben, Mascha Gonska, Heinz Marecek; ***D:*** Gerhard Janda.

Tea for Two 🦴🦴🦴 **1950** This takeoff on the Broadway play "No, No, Nanette" features Day as an actress who takes a bet that she can answer "no" to every question for 24 hours (life was less complex back then). If she can, she gets to finance and star in her own Broadway musical. ♫I Know That You Know; Crazy Rhythm; Charleston; I Only Have Eyes For You; Tea For Two; I Want to be Happy; Oh Me, Oh My; The Call of the Sea; Do Do Do. **98m/C VHS.** Doris Day, Gordon MacRae, Gene Nelson, Patrice Wymore, Eve Arden, Billy DeWolfe, S.Z. Sakall, Bill Goodwin, Virginia Gibson, Crauford Kent, Harry Harvey; ***D:*** David Butler.

Tea with Mussolini 🦴🦴 **1999 (PG)** Semiautobiographical account of director Zeffirelli's own childhood in fascist Italy. In 1935, young Luca (Lucas) is abandoned by his mother and his neglectful father is happy when the boy is taken in by a group of middleaged, eccentric Englishwomen, including Mary (Plowright), Lady Hester (Smith), and Arabella (Dench). Soon, their group is joined by flamboyantly wealthy (and Jewish) American Elsa (Cher). But as Mussolini consolidates his power and WWII begins, Luca is sent away to school, and the women find themselves unwelcome foreigners. **116m/C VHS, DVD.** *IT GB* Joan Plowright, Maggie Smith, Judi Dench, Cher, Baird Wallace, Charlie Lucas, Lily Tomlin, Paolo Seganti, Massimo Ghini, Claudio Spadaro; ***D:*** Franco Zeffirelli; ***W:*** Franco Zeffirelli, John Mortimer; ***C:*** David Watkin; ***M:*** Alessio Vlad, Stefano Arnaldi. British Acad. '99: Support. Actress (Smith).

Teach Me 🦴 **1997 (R)** Erotic romance novelist Sara Kane gets a story idea from observing a troubled couple at a restaurant. Janine's got some sexual fears that are causing problems in her marriage but Sara's willing to intercede and help ease her tensions. **90m/C VHS.** Shannon Leahy, Raasa Leela Shields, Greg Provance; ***D:*** Gary Delfiner. **VIDEO**

The Teacher 🦴🦴 *The Seductress* **1974 (R)** TV's "Dennis the Menace" (North) has an affair with his high school teacher; the pair is menaced by a deranged killer. Cheap but enjoyable. **97m/C VHS.** Angel Tompkins, Jay North, Anthony James; ***D:*** Howard (Hikmet) Avedis.

Teachers 🦴🦴 **1984 (R)** A lawsuit is brought against a high school for awarding a diploma to an illiterate student. Comedy-drama starts slowly and seems to condemn the school system, never picking up strength or resolving any issues, though Nolte is fairly intense. Shot in Columbus, Ohio. **106m/C VHS.** Nick Nolte, JoBeth Williams, Lee Grant, Judd Hirsch, Ralph Macchio, Richard Mulligan, Royal Dano, Morgan Freeman, Laura Dern, Crispin Glover, Madeline Sherwood, Zohra Lampert; ***D:*** Arthur Hiller.

Teacher's Pet 🦴🦴🦴 **1958** Cynical newspaper editor Jim Gannon (Gable) enrolls in a night college journalism course, believing that it won't teach anything of substance. But that's before he gets an eyeful of teacher Erica Stone (Day). Gannon decides to continue to pose as a student but watch the sparks fly when Erica finds out about his deception. Charming comedy with a well-written script and a superb comic performance by Young as Day's lovelorn suitor. **120m/B VHS.** Clark Gable, Doris Day, Mamie Van Doren, Gig Young, Nick Adams, Marion Ross, Jack Albertson, Charles Lane; ***D:*** George Seaton; ***W:*** Fay Kanin, Michael Kanin; ***C:*** Haskell Boggs; ***M:*** Roy Webb.

Teaching Mrs. Tingle 🦴🦴 *Killing Mrs. Tingle* **1999 (PG-13)** Williamson delivers a disappointing directorial debut in this teen horror/comedy adapted from one of his first scripts. Wrong-side-of-the-tracks Leigh Ann (Holmes) is anticipating being high school valedictorian until her sadistic English teacher Mrs. Tingle (Mirren) mistakenly accuses her of cheating. Leigh Ann and friends Jo Lynn (Coughlan) and Luke (Watson) go to Mrs. Tingle's house to plead their case and beg for mercy, but the heartless old hag refuses to listen to them. During an argument, Mrs. Tingle is knocked unconscious and the teens decide to tie her up and exact their revenge. **96m/C VHS, DVD.** Katie Holmes, Helen Mirren, Liz Stauber, Barry Watson, Jeffrey Tambor, Vivica A. Fox, Marisa Coughlan, Molly Ringwald, Michael McKean; ***D:*** Kevin Williamson; ***W:*** Kevin Williamson; ***C:*** Jerzy Zielinski; ***M:*** John (Gianni) Frizzell.

The Teahouse of the August Moon 🦴🦴½ **1956** An adaptation of the John Patrick play. Post-war American troops are assigned to bring civilization to a small village in Okinawa and instead fall for Okinawan culture and romance. Lively cast keeps it generally working, but assessments of Brando's comedic performance vary widely. **123m/C VHS, Wide.** Glenn Ford, Marlon Brando, Eddie Albert, Paul Ford, Machiko Kyo, Harry (Henry) Morgan; ***D:*** Daniel Mann; ***C:*** John Alton.

Teamster Boss: The Jackie Presser Story 🦴🦴🦴 **1992 (R)** Well-done cable movie powered by a riveting performance by Dennehy. Presser followed Jimmy Hoffa as president of the Teamsters and was equally caught between the mob and the government as he tried to do what he considered best for the union. **111m/C VHS.** Brian Dennehy, Jeff Daniels, Maria Conchita Alonso, Eli Wallach, Robert Prosky, Donald Moffat, Tony LoBianco, Kate Reid, Henderson Forsythe, Al Waxman; ***D:*** Alastair Reid. **CABLE**

Tearaway 🦴½ **1987 (R)** Australian story of a street punk with an alcoholic father. Story has potential, but ends up going nowhere. **100m/C VHS.** *NZ AU* Matthew Hunter, Mark Pilisi, Peter Bland, Kim Willoughby, Rebecca Saunders; ***D:*** Bruce Morrison.

Tears in the Rain 🦴🦴 **1988** Casey Cantrell (Stone) travels to London to deliver a deathbed letter from her mother to Lord Richard Bredon. While in England, she is pursued by two men, an heir to the Bredon fortune, and his wealthy friend. After she finds a love which is forbidden, she makes a bizarre discovery that changes her life forever. **100m/C VHS.** *GB* Sharon Stone, Christopher Cazenove, Leigh Lawson, Paul Daneman; ***D:*** Don Sharp. **TV**

Tecumseh: The Last Warrior 🦴🦴½ **1995** Oh-so-noble TV biography of the Shawnee leader (1768-1813) and his refusal to give up the battle against white settlement of the Indiana Territory. North Carolina substitutes for Ohio and Indiana. Based on the book "Panther in the Sky" by James Alexander Thom. **90m/C VHS.** Jesse Borrego, David Clennon, Tantoo Cardinal, David Morse, Holt McCallany, August Schellenberg, Jimmie F. Skaggs, Jeri Arredondo; ***D:*** Larry Elikann; ***W:*** Paul F. Edwards; ***M:*** David Shire.

Ted & Venus 🦴🦴½ **1993 (R)** Cort plays Ted, an oddball cult poet in love with Linda, a beach beauty who finds him repulsive. The more she rejects him, the more obsessed about her Ted gets, especially when his equally oddball friends offer him romantic advice. **100m/C VHS.** Bud Cort, Kim Adams, Rhea Perlman, James Brolin, Carol Kane; ***Cameos:*** Gena Rowlands, Martin Mull, Woody Harrelson, Andrea Martin, Timothy Leary, Cassandra Peterson; ***D:*** Bud Cort; ***W:*** Bud Cort, Paul Ciotti.

Teddy at the Throttle 🦴🦴 **1916** Teddy, the Great Dane, must rescue Gloria Swanson from a villain who has tied up her boyfriend. Silent. **20m/B VHS.** Bobby Vernon, Gloria Swanson, Wallace Beery; ***D:*** Clarence Badger.

Teen Alien 🦴 *The Varrow Mission* **1988 (PG)** On Halloween, a young boy and his friends run into a hostile alien. It could happen. **88m/C VHS.** Vern Adix; ***D:*** Peter Senelka.

Teen Vamp 🦴 **1988** Dorky high schooler is bitten by a prostitute; becomes a cool vampire. Mindless "comedy." **87m/C VHS.** Clu Gulager, Karen Carlson, Angela Brown; ***D:*** Samuel Bradford.

Teen Witch 🦴🦴 **1989 (PG-13)** A demure high schooler uses black magic to woo the most popular guy in school. **94m/C VHS.** Robin (Robyn) Lively, Zelda Rubinstein, Dan Gauthier, Joshua John Miller, Dick Sargent; ***D:*** Dorian Walker; ***W:*** Robin Menken.

Teen Wolf 🦴🦴½ **1985 (PG)** A nice, average teenage basketball player begins to show werewolf tendencies which suddenly make him popular at school when he leads the team to victory. The underlying message is to be yourself, regardless of how much hair you have on your body. Lighthearted comedy carried by the Fox charm; followed by subpar "Teen Wolf Too." **92m/C VHS, 8mm.** Michael J. Fox, James Hampton, Scott Paulin, Susan Ursitti; ***D:*** Rod Daniel; ***M:*** Miles Goodman.

Teen Wolf Too 🦴🦴 **1987 (PG)** The sequel to "Teen Wolf" in which the Teen Wolf's cousin goes to college on a boxing scholarship. More evidence that the sequel is rarely as good as the original. **95m/C VHS.** Jason Bateman, Kim Darby, John Astin, Paul Sand; ***D:*** Christopher Leitch; ***W:*** Timothy King.

Teenage 🦴 **1944** Low budget juvenile schlock film that tries to figure out what's wrong with modern youth. Pure camp. **?m/C VHS.** Herbert (Hayes) Heyes, Wheeler Oakman.

Teenage Bad Girl 🦴🦴½ *Bad Girl; My Teenage Daughter* **1959** A woman who edits a magazine for teenagers can't control her own daughter. The kid does time in the pen after staying out all night and generally running around with the wrong crowd. Syms first lead performance is memorable in an otherwise routine teensploitation flick. **100m/B VHS.** Anna Neagle, Sylvia Syms, Norman Wooland, Wilfrid Hyde-White, Kenneth Haigh, Julia Lockwood; ***D:*** Herbert Wilcox.

Teenage Bonnie & Klepto Clyde 🦴½ **1993 (R)** Like their '30s namesakes, Clyde Barrow and Bonnie Parker are just two high-spirited kids who let their need for excitement get in the way of their better judgment (ha!). Bonnie and Clyde meet in a fast-food joint, become shoplifting buddies, fall in love, graduate to armed robbery, try to run for the border, and die. **90m/C VHS.** Maureen Flannigan, Scott Wolf; ***Cameos:*** Don Novello.

Teenage Catgirls in Heat 🦴🦴 **2000** On their lighthearted commentary track, the filmmakers admit that they had originally titled this Texas-produced horror simply "Catgirls." It was the good folks at Troma who came up with the modifiers that turns it into an inspired piece of exploitation. If the film doesn't quite live up (or down) to it, that's not too surprising. It is a nice, silly little horror and nobody involved takes it very seriously. **90m/C DVD.** Gary Graves, Carrie Vanston, Dave Cox; ***D:*** Scott Perry; ***W:*** Scott Perry, Grace Smith; ***C:*** Thad Halci; ***M:*** Randy Buck, Nenad Vugrinec.

Teenage Caveman 🦴🦴 *Out of the Darkness; Prehistoric World* **1958** A teenage boy living in a post-apocalypse yet prehistoric world journeys across the river, even though he was warned against it, and finds an old man who owns a book about past civilizations in the 20th Century. Schlocky, and one of the better bad films around. The dinosaur shots were picked up from the film "One Million B.C." **66m/B VHS.** Robert Vaughn, Darrah Marshall, Leslie Bradley, Frank De Kova, Jonathan Haze, Beach Dickerson, Marshall Bradford, Robert Shayne, Joseph H. Hamilton, June Jocelyn, Charles P. Thompson; ***D:*** Roger Corman; ***W:*** Robert W(right) Campbell; ***C:*** Floyd Crosby; ***M:*** Albert Glasser.

Teenage Caveman 🦴🦴 **2001 (R)** Post-apocalyptic nightmare world has a small group of cave dwellers, led by elders who ban sex to keep the population down. But teenage hormones will out and David leads girlfriend Sarah and a group of friends into the wilderness where they meet Neil and Judith, who are the result of genetic experimentation that has some unpleasant side effects for our little band of survivors (think sex). A "Creature Features" remake of the 1958 movie. **100m/C VHS, DVD.** Andrew Keegan, Tara Subkoff, Richard Hillman, Shawn Elliot, Tiffany Limos, Stephen Jasso, Crystal Grant, Hayley Keenan, Paul Hipp; ***D:*** Larry Clark; ***W:*** Christos N. Gage; ***C:*** Steve Gainer; ***M:*** Zoe Poledouris. **CABLE**

Teenage Crime Wave 🦴 **1955** Route 66 provides thrills for a couple of teen punks, but things get out of hand when they blow a sheriff's head off. They scoop up a couple of babes and hightail it with the police close behind, ultimately confronting their destiny at a mountain top observatory. **77m/B VHS.** Tommy Cook, Mollie McCart, Sue England, Frank Griffin, James Bell, Kay Riehl; ***D:*** Fred F. Sears.

Teenage Devil Dolls 🦴 **1953** A cheap exploitation teenage flick wherein an innocent girl is turned on to reefer and goofballs, and eventually ends up on the street. **70m/C VHS.** Barbara Marks, Bramlef L. Price Jr.; ***D:*** B. Lawrence Price.

Teenage Doll 🦴🦴 **1957** Good old Corman teen exploitation pic features a good girl who's tired of being good and gets mixed up with some street punks. She even manages to set off a gang war by accidentally kiling a beat girl from a rival group. **71m/B VHS, DVD.** Fay Spain, John Brinkley, June Kenney, Collette Jackson, Barbara Wilson, Ed Nelson, Richard Devon, Ziva Rodann, Barboura Morris, Bruno VeSota; ***D:*** Roger Corman; ***W:*** Charles B. Griffith; ***C:*** Floyd Crosby; ***M:*** Walter Greene.

Teenage Exorcist 🦴½ **1993** Tired horror spoof finds the prim Diane (Stevens) renting a creepy house from an equally creepy real estate agent (Berryman). After she moves in, Diane begins having horrible nightmares and calls her family for help. When they arrive Diane has turned into a chainsaw-wielding seductress. The family is so distressed that they misdial the phone and wind up with a pizza delivery geek (Deezen) instead of the exorcist they need. **90m/C VHS.** Brinke Stevens, Eddie Deezen, Michael Berryman, Robert Quarry, Jay Richardson, Tom Shell, Elena Sahagun; ***D:*** Grant Austin Waldman; ***W:*** Brinke Stevens.

Teenage Frankenstein 🦴½ **1958** A descendent of Dr. Frankenstein makes his own scramble-faced monster out of a teenage boy. Lurid '50s drive-in fare (companion to "I Was a Teenage Werewolf") is campy fun in small doses only. **72m/B VHS.** Whit Bissell, Phyllis Coates, Robert Burton, Gary Conway, George Lynn, John Cliff; ***D:*** Herbert L. Strock.

Teenage Gang Debs 🦴 **1966** These chicks throw a sleazy coming out party the likes of which defy description. Simply the most important social function of 1966. **77m/B VHS, DVD.** Diana Conti, Linda Gale, Eileen Scott, Sandra Kane, Robin Nolan, Linda Cambi, Sue McManus, Geri Tyler, Joey Naudic, John Batis, Tom Yourk, Thomas Andrisano, George Winship, Doug Mitchell, Tom Eldred, Frank Spinella, Alec Primrose, Gene Marrin, Lyn Kennedy, Janet Banzet; ***D:*** Sande N. Johnsen; ***W:*** Hy Cahl; ***C:*** Harry Petricek; ***M:*** Steve Karmen.

Teenage Monster woof! *Meteor Monster* **1957** A young boy is hit by a meteor and is somehow transformed into a raving, slime-covered maniac. **65m/B VHS, DVD.** Gilbert Perkins, Stephen Parker, Anne Gwynne, Stuart Wade, Gloria Castillo, Chuck Courtney; ***D:*** Jacques "Jack" Marquette; ***W:*** Ray Buffum; ***C:*** Taylor Byars.

Teenage Mother woof! **1967** A Swedish sex education teacher comes to town and poisons the minds of the local high school kids. Naturally one becomes pregnant and has to try to trick the father into marrying her. More awful stuff from the director of "Girl On a Chain Gang." **78m/C VHS.** Arlene Sue Farber, Frederick Riccio, Julie Ange, Howard Le May, George Peters; ***D:*** Jerry Gross; ***W:*** Jerry Gross; ***C:*** Richard Brooks; ***M:*** Steve Karmen.

Teenage Mutant Ninja Turtles: The Movie 🦴🦴½ **1990 (PG)** Four sewer-dwelling turtles that have turned into warrior ninja mutants due to radiation exposure take it upon themselves to rid the city of crime and pizza. Aided by a television reporter and their ninja master, Splinter the Rat, the turtles encounter several obstacles, including the evil warlord Shredder. A most excellent live-action version of the popular comic book characters which will hold the kids' interest. Much head-kicking and rib-crunching action as Leonardo, Donatello, Raphael, and Michelangelo fight for the rights of pre-adolescents everywhere. Combines real actors with Jim Henson creatures. **95m/C VHS, DVD.** Judith Hoag, Elias Koteas; ***D:*** Steven Barron; ***W:*** Todd W. Langen; ***C:*** John Fenner; ***M:*** John Du Prez; ***V:*** Robbie (Reist) Rist, Corey Feldman, Brian Tochi, Kevin Clash, David McCharen.

Teenage Mutant Ninja Turtles 2: The Secret of the Ooze 🦴🦴 **1991 (PG)** Amphibious pizza-devouring mutants search for the toxic waste that turned them into marketable martial artist ecologically correct kid idols. Same formula as the first go-round with some new characters tossed in. Animatronic characters from the laboratory of Jim Henson, first screen appearance by rapper Vanilla Ice. Marked end of pre-teen turtle craze. **88m/C VHS.** Francois Chau, David Warner, Paige Turco, Ernie Reyes Jr., Vanilla Ice; ***D:*** Michael Pressman.

Teenage Mutant Ninja Turtles 3 🦴🦴 **1993 (PG)** Check it out dudes; the Teenage Mutant Ninja Turtles hit 17th century Japan to rescue loyal friend, reporter April O'Neil. Plenty of smoothly executed, blood-free martial arts moves keep the pace rolling, while the turtles battle an evil lord and English pirates. Seeing the TMNT's use a little more of their reptilian grey matter, and snarf a little less pizza should contribute to a relatively high adult tolerance level (considering the genre), and loads of good clean fun for the kiddies. **95m/C VHS, Wide.** Elias Koteas, Paige Turco, Stuart Wilson, Sab Shimono, Vivian Wu; ***D:*** Stuart Gillard; ***W:*** Stuart Gillard; ***M:*** John Du Prez; ***V:*** Randi Mayem Singer, Matt Hill, Jim Raposa, David Fraser.

Teenage Strangler woof! **1964** A homicidal teen terrorizes his school. Cheap film features drag races, rumbles, dances, babes, rock 'n' roll and more. One for the "bad enough to be fun" category. **61m/C VHS, DVD.** Bill A. Bloom, Jo Canterbury, John Ensign, Jim Asp, Johnny Haymer, Bill Mills, Ron Ormond; ***D:*** Bill Posner; ***W:*** Clark Davis; ***C:*** Fred Singer; ***M:*** Danny Dean.

Teenage Wolfpack 🦴½ 1957 Boring film about German juvenile delinquents, robbery, violence, and murder. **90m/C VHS.** *GE* Horst Buchholz, Karin Baal, Christian Doermer; ***D:*** Georg Tressler.

Teenage Zombies woof! 1958 Mad scientist on remote island kidnaps teenagers and uses her secret chemical formula to turn them into zombies as part of her plan to enslave the world. Not as good as it sounds. **71m/B VHS, DVD.** Don Sullivan, Katherine Victor, Chuck Niles; ***D:*** Jerry Warren; ***W:*** Jerry Warren; ***C:*** Allen Chandler.

Teenager 🦴 1974 (R) Three desperate, reckless individuals, all caught up in making a low budget movie, interact and eventually self-destruct. **91m/C VHS.** Andrea Cagan, Reid Smith, Susan Bernard; ***D:*** Gerald Seth Sindell.

Teenagers from Outer Space woof! *The Gargon Terror* 1959 Low-budget sci-fi effort finds extraterrestrial youngsters visiting earth to conquer it and find food for their "monstrous pets" (they're really lobster shadows.) So cheaply made and melodramatic that it just may be good for a laugh. **86m/B VHS, DVD.** Tom Graeff, Dawn Anderson, Harvey B. Dunn, Bryant Grant, Thomas Lockyer, King Moody, Bob Williams; ***D:*** Tom Graeff; ***W:*** Tom Graeff; ***C:*** Tom Graeff; ***M:*** Tom Graeff.

TekWar 🦴🦴½ 1994 It's 2044 and society is plagued by "Tek," an illegal, addictive drug-like computer disk that creates powerful but destructive virtual-reality fantasies. Jake Cardigan (Evigan) is an cop framed on drug and murder charges, fresh out of prison, who's trying to both clear his name and find out what happened to his now ex-wife and son. Shatner, who wrote the Tek novels, guests as Walter Bascom, the head of a detective agency who promises to help Cardigan if Jake helps find a missing scientist. Made for TV. **92m/C VHS.** Greg Evigan, Eugene C. Clark, Torri Higginson, William Shatner; ***D:*** William Shatner. **TV**

Telefon 🦴🦴 1977 (PG) Suspenseful, slick spy tale. Soviet agents battle a lunatic comrade who tries to use hypnotized Americans to commit sabotage. Daly, later of TV's "Cagney and Lacey," is memorable. **102m/C VHS.** Charles Bronson, Lee Remick, Donald Pleasence, Tyne Daly, Patrick Magee, Sheree North; ***D:*** Donald Siegel; ***W:*** Stirling Silliphant, Peter Hyams; ***M:*** Lalo Schifrin.

Telegraph Trail 🦴½ 1933 Weak Wayne entry about an Army scout who helps some workers complete the first transcontinental wire line. Of course, Wayne ends up getting tough with some Indians. Cheaply made, with most of the action footage lifted from the 1926 silent, "The Red Raiders." **60m/B VHS.** John Wayne, Marceline Day, Frank McHugh, Otis Harlan, Yakima Canutt, Lafe (Lafayette) McKee; ***D:*** Tenny Wright; ***W:*** Kurt Kempler.

The Telephone woof! 1987 (R) A neurotic out-of-work actress begins a comedic chain of events via a few prank phone calls. Goldberg has managed to salvage some bad material with the strength of her comedic performances, but not so here. In fact, she sued to prevent this version from ever seeing the light of day. Too bad she didn't have a better lawyer. Torn's directorial debut. **96m/C VHS.** Whoopi Goldberg, Elliott Gould, John Heard, Amy Wright; ***D:*** Rip Torn; ***W:*** Terry Southern.

Tell It to the Judge 🦴🦴½ 1949 Russell plays the exuberant ex-wife of lawyer Cummings. They repeatedly try reconciling but ditzy blonde McDonald always manages to catch Cummings' eye. Fed up Russell takes off for a holiday in the mountains where she meets Young. When her ex-hubby follows her, she decides to try and make him jealous using Young as the bait. **87m/B VHS.** Rosalind Russell, Robert Cummings, Gig Young, Marie McDonald, Harry Davenport, Louise Beavers; ***D:*** Norman Foster.

Tell Me a Riddle 🦴🦴½ 1980 (PG) A dying woman attempts to reconcile with her family in this poignant drama about an elderly couple rediscovering their mutual love after 47 years of marriage. Fine acting; Grant's directorial debut. **94m/C VHS.** Melvyn Douglas, Lila Kedrova, Brooke Adams, Peter Coyote; ***D:*** Lee Grant; ***W:*** Joyce Eliason.

Tell Me That You Love Me 🦴½ 1984 (R) A tear-jerking portrait of a disintegrating modern marriage. **88m/C VHS.** Nick Mancuso, Barbara Williams, Belinda J. Montgomery; ***D:*** Tzipi Trope.

Tell Me Where It Hurts 🦴🦴 1974 A middle-aged housewife changes her life when she forms a women's consciousness-raising group with her friends. The script won an Emmy. Stapleton's performance is redeeming in this otherwise slow movie. **78m/C VHS.** Maureen Stapleton, Paul Sorvino; ***D:*** Paul Bogart; ***M:*** David Shire. **TV**

The Tell-Tale Heart 🦴🦴½ *The Hidden Room of 1,000 Horrors* 1962 Daydreaming author fantasizes about falling for major babe and killing his best friend for her. Adapted Poe tale. **78m/B VHS.** *GB* Laurence Payne, Adrienne Corri, Dermot Walsh, Selma Vaz Dias, John Scott, John Martin, Annette Carell, David Lander; ***D:*** Ernest Morris; ***W:*** Brian Clemens.

Tell Them Willie Boy Is Here 🦴🦴🦴 1969 (PG) Western drama set in 1909 California about a Paiute Indian named Willie Boy and his white bride. They become the objects of a manhunt (led by the reluctant local sheriff, Redford) after Willie kills his wife's father in self-defense. This was once-blacklisted Polonsky's first film in 21 years. **98m/C VHS, Wide.** Robert Redford, Katharine Ross, Robert (Bobby) Blake, Susan Clark, Barry Sullivan, John Vernon, Charles McGraw; ***D:*** Abraham Polonsky; ***W:*** Abraham Polonsky; ***C:*** Conrad L. Hall; ***M:*** Dave Grusin.

Telling Lies in America 🦴🦴 1996 (PG-13) Semiautobiographical Eszterhaus-penned coming-of-ager allies a starstruck and naive Hungarian immigrant teen with dirty deejay on the take in early 60s Cleveland. Karchy Jones (Renfro) worships the slick polyester prince of the airwaves Billy Magic (Bacon), and through a contest at school, wins a chance to become his eager-beaver lackey. The twisted rock-n-roll mentor shows Karchy his own, highly cynical version of attaining the American Dream which, naturally, leads to trouble. Universally acclaimed performance by Bacon, who takes a one-dimensional persona and runs with it. Flockhart plays the "it" girl of Karchy's dreams. Smoothly told story suffers from a few of the usual cliches, but makes up for in heart. **101m/C VHS, DVD.** Kevin Bacon, Brad Renfro, Maximilian Schell, Calista Flockhart, Paul Dooley, Jonathan Rhys Meyers, Luke Wilson; ***D:*** Guy Ferland; ***W:*** Joe Eszterhas; ***C:*** Reynaldo Villalobos; ***M:*** Nicholas Pike.

Telling You 🦴🦴½ 1998 (R) Buddies Phil (Facinelli) and Dennis (Mihok) work at the local pizzeria and try to score but don't have much success since they're, basically, amiable losers. Fluff and Hewitt's role is small as Phil's ex-girlfriend. **94m/C VHS, DVD, Wide.** Peter Facinelli, Dash Mihok, Matthew Lillard, Jennifer Love Hewitt, Richard Libertini, Robert DeFranco, Frank Medrano, Jennifer Jostyn, Rick Rossovich, Jennie Garth; ***D:*** Robert DeFranco; ***W:*** Robert DeFranco, Marc Palmieri; ***C:*** Mark Doering-Powell; ***M:*** Russ Landau.

The Temp woof! 1993 (R) Unbelievably bad attempt at office horror. Beautiful, mysterious Kris temps for Hutton, a junior exec at the Mrs. Appleby baked goods company. She's almost too good to be true with unbelievable organizational skills and her dead serious ambition to climb the corporate ladder. Pyscho-drama has pyscho, but lacks drama, direction, plot development, intelligent dialogue, and anything resembling motive. While Hutton is tolerable, we nominate ex-Twin Peaker Boyle for the bad acting hall of shame as the conniving psycho. **99m/C VHS, DVD, Wide.** Timothy Hutton, Lara Flynn Boyle, Faye Dunaway, Dwight Schultz, Oliver Platt, Steven Weber, Scott Coffey, Colleen Flynn, Dakin Matthews, Maura Tierney; ***D:*** Tom Holland; ***W:*** Kevin Falls; ***C:*** Steve Yaconelli; ***M:*** Frederic Talgorn. Golden Raspberries '93: Worst Support. Actress (Dunaway).

The Tempest 🦴🦴🦴 1928 A Russian peasant soldier rises through the ranks to become an officer, only to be undone by his love for the daughter of his commanding officer. Silent with musical score. **105m/B VHS.** John Barrymore, Louis Wolheim; ***D:*** Sam Taylor; ***C:*** Charles Rosher.

The Tempest 🦴🦴½ 1963 Shakespeare's classic tale of the fantasy world of spirits, sorcerers, maidens, monsters, and scheming noblemen is brought to life in George Schaefer's ethereal production. **76m/C VHS.** Maurice Evans, Richard Burton, Roddy McDowall, Lee Remick, Tom Poston; ***D:*** George Schaefer. **TV**

The Tempest 🦴🦴🦴 1982 (PG) New York architect Phillip (Cassavettes), fed up with city living, chucks it all and brings his daughter Miranda (Ringwald in her screen debut), and singer Aretha (Sarandon) to live with him on a barren Greek island where then encounter a hermit named Kalibanos (Julia). Then, thanks to a shipwreck, all the other people in Phillip's life, including his unfaithful wife Antonia (Rowland), show up to complicate his midlife crisis. Loosley based on the Shakespeare play of the same name. Well-written, thoughtfully acted, and beautifully filmed. **140m/C VHS.** John Cassavetes, Gena Rowlands, Susan Sarandon, Vittorio Gassman, Molly Ringwald, Paul Stewart, Sam Robards, Raul Julia; ***D:*** Paul Mazursky; ***W:*** Paul Mazursky, Leon Capetanos; ***C:*** Donald McAlpine; ***M:*** Stomu Yamashta.

The Tempest 🦴🦴½ 1999 (PG-13) This time around the Shakespeare fantasy is transported to a Civil War-era Mississippi bayou, which is where magic-studying Gideon Prosper (Fonda) is living with his daughter, Miranda (Heigl), and a runaway slave, Ariel (Perrineau). Into this secluded world stumbles young Union soldier, Frederick Allen (Mills), with whom the lonely Miranda immediately falls in love, while Gideon is finally forced to reckon with the world in the form of his unscrupulous brother, Anthony (Glover). **90m/C VHS.** Peter Fonda, John Glover, Harold Perrineau Jr., Katherine Heigl, Eddie Mills, John Pyper-Ferguson, Dennis Redfield; ***D:*** Jack Bender; ***W:*** James Henerson; ***C:*** Steve Shaw. **TV**

Temptation 🦴🦴 1994 (R) Ex-con Eddie (Fahey) gets hired to work on a luxury yacht, which helps him keep track of his double-crossing former partner. Too bad for Eddie that the guy's wife is such a distraction. **91m/C VHS.** Jeff Fahey, Alison Doody, Philip Casnoff, David Keith, Patricia Durham, W. Paul Bodie; ***D:*** Strathford Hamilton.

Temptation of a Monk 🦴🦴 1994 Costume drama about China's 7th-century Tang Dynasty finds General Shi (Hsin-kuo) duped into an assassination plot against the crown prince. After a massacre, the General flees and finds sanctuary with a group of Buddhist monks at a remote temple. There's also the General's sometime lover and a mystery woman (both played by Chen). Sometimes slow-moving and confusing but with exotic visuals. Based on a novel by Lilian Lee; Mandarin with subtitles. **118m/C VHS, DVD.** *CH* Wu Hsin-kuo, Joan Chen, Zhang Fengyi, Michael Lee; ***D:*** Clara Law; ***W:*** Eddie L.C. Fong; ***C:*** Andrew Lesnie; ***M:*** Tats Lau.

The Temptations 🦴🦴½ 1998 Miniseries bio of the Motown group from its high school beginnings in 1958 (under various names) through a meeting with Motown founder Berry Gordy (Babatunde) and major success in the sixties. Told from the viewpoint of the last original Temp, Otis Williams (Whitfield), as he and buddies Melvin Franklin (Woodside) and Paul Williams (Payton) hook up with first lead singer Eddie Kendricks (Brooks). When Kendricks goes solo it's the turn of David Ruffin (Leon) but the group suffers various ego traumas and tragedies. Naturally, the music's the real highlight. **150m/C VHS, DVD.** Charles Malik Whitfield, DB Woodside, Terron Brooks, Christian Payton, Leon, Alan Rosenberg, Obba Babatunde, Charles Ley, Tina Lifford, Gina Ravera, Vanessa Bell Calloway, Chaz Lamar Shepherd; ***D:*** Allan Arkush; ***W:*** Kevin Arkadie, Robert P. Johnson; ***C:*** Jamie Anderson. **TV**

The Tempter 🦴 *L'Anticristo; The Antichrist* 1974 (R) Mirrors the gruesomeness of "The Exorcist," with story following an invalid's adventures with witchcraft, bestiality, and Satanism. **96m/C VHS.** *IT* Mel Ferrer, Carla Gravina, Arthur Kennedy, Alida Valli, Anita Strindberg, George Coulouris; ***D:*** Alberto De Martino; ***M:*** Ennio Morricone.

The Temptress 🦴🦴½ 1949 A doctor attempting to find a cure for polio is coerced by an irresistible woman into murder and blackmail. Well-told story, if somewhat grim. **85m/B VHS.** *GB* Joan Maude, Arnold Bell, Don Stannard, Shirley Quentin, John Stuart, Ferdinand "Ferdy" Mayne; ***D:*** Oswald Mitchell.

Temptress 🦴🦴 1995 (R) Photographer Karin Swann (Delaney) returns from a spiritual retreat in India obsessed with the deadly goddess Kali. Karin's new overtly sexual personality startles lover Matthew (Sarandon) while her work has also undergone some changes. When a friend is murdered, Matthew begins to wonder if Kali's evil powers have overtaken Karin. **93m/C VHS.** Kim Delaney, Chris Sarandon, Corbin Bernsen, Dee Wallace Stone, Jessica Walter, Ben Cross; ***D:*** Lawrence Lanoff; ***W:*** Melissa Mitchell; ***M:*** Michael Stearns.

Temptress Moon 🦴🦴 *Feng Yue* 1996 (R) 1920s Shanghai is displayed in all its decadence with opium-addicted Ruyi (Li) forced to officially head the Pang family after the death of her father. Power actually lies with distant male cousin Duanwen (Lin), who manages the household and is drawn to his cold relative. Ruyi's childhood playmate and fellow addict, Zhongliang (Cheung), is now a professional gigolo and blackmailer, working for a gangster (Tian) who wants him to seduce Ruyi and steal the Pang fortune. What happens is an obsessive affair between two beautiful manipulators. Chilly high-style soap opera. Mandarin with subtitles. **113m/C VHS.** *HK* Gong Li, Leslie Cheung, Kevin Lin, Xie Tian, Zhou Jie, He Saifei; ***D:*** Chen Kaige; ***W:*** Shu Kei; ***C:*** Christopher Doyle; ***M:*** Zhao Jiping.

10 🦴🦴½ 1979 (R) A successful songwriter who has everything finds his life is incomplete without the woman of his dreams, the 10 on his girl-watching scale. His pursuit brings surprising results. Also popularizes Ravel's "Bolero." **121m/C VHS, DVD.** Dudley Moore, Julie Andrews, Bo Derek, Dee Wallace Stone, Brian Dennehy, Robert Webber; ***D:*** Blake Edwards; ***W:*** Blake Edwards; ***C:*** Frank Stanley; ***M:*** Henry Mancini.

Ten Benny 🦴🦴 *Nothing to Lose* 1998 (R) Frustrated New Jersey shoe salesman Ray (Brody) borrows $10,000 from a local wiseguy in order to win enough money at the track to set himself up in business. Bad idea. As his luck continues a downward spiral, he abuses his wife (Temchen) into the arms of his buddy (Gallagher) and becomes more desparate to climb out of the hole he's dug for himself. First-time director Bross has obviously studied the Scorsese school of filmmaking, but must've skipped the classes on originality, subtlety, and characterization. Not much going on here that hasn't been done (better) somewhere else, but Brody turns in a fine performance. **98m/C VHS, DVD, Wide.** Adrien Brody, Sybil Temchen, Michael Gallagher, Tony Gillan, James Moriarty, Frank Vincent; ***D:*** Eric Bross; ***W:*** Eric Bross, Tom Cudworth; ***C:*** Horacio Marquinez; ***M:*** Chris Hajian.

The Ten Commandments 🦴🦴½ 1923 The silent epic that established DeMille as a popular directorial force and which he remade 35 years later as an even bigger epic with sound. Follows Moses' adventures in Egypt, plus a modern story of brotherly love and corruption. Features a new musical score by Gaylord Carter. Remade in 1956. **146m/B VHS.** Theodore Roberts, Richard Dix, Rod La Rocque, Edythe Chapman, Nita Naldi; ***D:*** Cecil B. DeMille; ***C:*** Archie Stout; ***M:*** Gaylord Carter.

The Ten Commandments 🦴🦴🦴 1956 (G) DeMille's remake of his 1923 silent classic (and his last film) is a lavish Biblical epic that tells the life story of Moses, who turned his back on a privileged life to lead his people to freedom outside of Egypt. Exceptional cast, with Fraser Heston (son of Charlton) as the baby Moses. Parting of Red Sea rivals any modern special effects. A 35th Anniversary Collector's Edition is available uncut at 245 minutes, in widescreen format and Dolby Surround stereo, and 1,000 copies of an Autographed Limited Edition that includes an engraved bronze plaque and an imprinted card written and personally signed by Charlton Heston are also available. **219m/C VHS, DVD, Wide.** Charlton Heston, Yul Brynner, Anne Baxter, Yvonne De Carlo, Nina Foch, John Derek, H.B. Warner, Henry Wilcoxon, Judith Anderson, John Carradine, Douglass Dumbrille, Cedric Hardwicke, Martha Scott, Vincent Price, Debra Paget; ***D:*** Cecil B. DeMille; ***W:*** Aeneas MacKenzie, Jesse Lasky Jr., Frederic M. Frank, Jack Gariss; ***C:*** Loyal Griggs; ***M:*** Elmer Bernstein. Natl. Film Reg. '99.

Ten Days That Shook the World 🦴🦴🦴½ *October; Oktyabr* **1927** Silent masterpiece based on American author John Reed's book of the same name. Eisenstein, commissioned by the Soviet government, spared no expense to chronicle the Bolshevik Revolution of 1917 (in a flattering Communist light, of course). He was later forced to cut his portrayal of Leon Trotsky, who was then an enemy of the state. Includes rare footage of the Czar's Winter Palace in Leningrad. Haunting score, combined with some of Eisenstein's most striking work. See Warren Beatty's "Reds" for a fictional look at Reed and the Russian Revolution. **104m/B VHS, DVD.** *RU* Nikandrov, N. Popov, Boris Livanov; ***D:*** Sergei Eisenstein, Grigori Alexandrov; ***W:*** Sergei Eisenstein, Grigori Alexandrov; ***C:*** Vladimir Popov, Eduard Tisse; ***M:*** Dimitri Shostakovich, Edmund Meisel.

Ten Days Wonder 🦴🦴½ *La Decade Prodigieuse* **1972 (PG)** Mystery/drama focuses on the patriarch of a wealthy family (Welles), his young wife, and his adopted son (Perkins), who is having an affair with his stepmother. It also turns out that Perkins is certifiable and is trying to break all of the Ten Commandments, which he succeeds in doing before killing himself (gruesomely). Based on the mystery novel by Ellery Queen. **101m/C VHS.** *FR* Orson Welles, Anthony Perkins, Marlene Jobert, Michel Piccoli, Guido Alberti; ***D:*** Claude Chabrol.

Ten Little Indians 🦴🦴½ *And Then There Were None* **1975 (PG)** Ten people are gathered in an isolated inn under mysterious circumstances. One by one they are murdered, each according to a verse from a children's nursery rhyme. British adaptation of the novel and stage play by Agatha Christie. **98m/C VHS, DVD.** *GB* Herbert Lom, Richard Attenborough, Oliver Reed, Elke Sommer, Charles Aznavour, Stephane Audran, Gert Frobe, Adolfo Celi, Orson Welles; ***D:*** Peter Collinson.

Ten Little Indians 🦴🦴 *Agatha Christie's Ten Little Indians* **1989 (PG)** A group of prize-winning vacationers find themselves embarking on an African adventure. They all wind up at the same camp, and realize that they are being murdered one by one. Based on the work of Agatha Christie. **100m/C VHS.** Donald Pleasence, Brenda Vaccaro, Frank Stallone, Herbert Lom, Sarah Maur-Thorp; ***D:*** Alan Birkinshaw.

The Ten Million Dollar Getaway 🦴🦴 **1991 (PG-13)** True story of the 1978 Lufthansa robbery at Kennedy Airport in which the criminals were forced to leave 10 of their $20 million heist behind when a pick-up van didn't show. Standard cable fare produced to cash in on the same scenario played out in "Goodfellas." **93m/C VHS.** John Mahoney, Karen Young, Tony LoBianco, Gerry Bamman, Joseph Carberry, Terrence Mann, Kenneth John McGregor, Christopher Murney; ***D:*** James A. Contner; ***W:*** Christopher Canaan. **CABLE**

Ten Nights in a Bar Room 🦴🦴 **1913** The evils of alcohol are dramatized when they ruin a man's life. One of many propaganda films about alcohol and the problems that it caused that were made during the prohibition era. Silent, with a musical score. Remade in 1931. **68m/B VHS.** Robert Lawrence, Marie Trado.

Ten Nights in a Bar-Room 🦴🦴 **1931** A turn-of-the-century mill owner succumbs to alcoholism and ruins his life and family. Later, he sees the error of his ways and gives up drinking. This was one of many films made during this era that chronicled the evils of alcohol and fanned the flames of the prohibition debate. Remake of the 1913 silent film. **60m/B VHS.** William Farnum, Thomas Santschi, John Darrow, Robert Frazer; ***D:*** William O'Connor.

Ten North Frederick 🦴🦴½ **1958** A shrewish wife (Fitzgerald) forces her gentle lawyer husband (Cooper) into cutthroat politics. He consoles himself in the arms of a much younger woman. Good performances, hokey script, based on the John O'Hara novel. **102m/B VHS.** Gary Cooper, Diane Varsi, Suzy Parker, Geraldine Fitzgerald, Tom Tully, Stuart Whitman; ***D:*** Philip Dunne; ***W:*** Philip Dunne.

10 Rillington Place 🦴🦴🦴 **1971 (PG)** A grimy, upsetting British film about the famed serial killer John Christie and the man wrongly hanged for his crimes, the incident that led to the end of capital punishment in England. Impeccably acted. One of Hurt's earliest films. **111m/C VHS.** *GB* Richard Attenborough, John Hurt, Judy Geeson, Gabrielle Daye, Andre Morell, Bernard Lee, Isobel Black, Pat Heywood; ***D:*** Richard Fleischer; ***W:*** Clive Exton; ***C:*** Denys Coop; ***M:*** John Dankworth.

Ten Speed 🦴🦴 **1976** Two advertising executives compete in a 400-mile bicycle race from San Francisco to Malibu. **89m/C VHS.** William Woodbridge, Patricia Hume, David Clover.

Ten Things I Hate about You 🦴🦴🦴 **1999 (PG-13)** This Bill Shakespeare guy must be raking in the royalties, dude! The Bard is once again adapted for teens in this update of his very un-PC comedy "The Taming of the Shrew." Obstetrician and single dad Walter (Miller) has seen enough teen pregnancies to fear all adolescent boys who show up with flowers. He decrees that his ultra-popular daughter Bianca (Oleynik) cannot date before her man-hating sister Kat (Stiles) does. Two lovesick suitors, vain Joey (Keegan) and sensitive guy Cameron (Gordon-Levitt), bribe new-kid-in-town Patrick (Ledger) to make advances on Kat in order to play "jumpeth the maiden" with Bianca. Kat and Patrick then engage in a duel of verbal thrusts and parries, gradually falling for each other. Incorporates some of Shakespeare's dialogue, but glosses over the more chauvinistic elements of his play. **97m/C VHS, DVD, Wide.** Julia Stiles, Heath Ledger, Larisa Oleynik, Joseph Gordon-Levitt, Andrew Keegan, David Krumholtz, Larry Miller, Susan May Pratt, Darryl (Chill) Mitchell, Allison Janney, David Leisure, Gabrielle Union; ***D:*** Gil Junger; ***W:*** Karen McCullah Lutz, Kirsten Smith; ***C:*** Mark Irwin; ***M:*** Richard Gibbs. MTV Movie Awards '00: Breakthrough Perf. (Stiles).

Ten to Midnight 🦴🦴 **1983 (R)** Vigilante Bronson is on the prowl again, this time as a police officer after a kinky serial murderer. The psychotic killer stalks his daughter and Dad's gonna stop him at any cost. **101m/C VHS.** Charles Bronson, Wilford Brimley, Lisa Eilbacher, Andrew Stevens; ***D:*** J. Lee Thompson; ***W:*** William Roberts.

10 Violent Women woof! **1979 (R)** Ten women who take part in a million dollar jewelry heist are tossed into a women's prison where brutal lesbian guards subject them to degradation and brutality. **97m/C VHS, DVD.** Sherri Vernon, Dixie Lauren, Sally Gamble; ***D:*** Ted V. Mikels; ***W:*** Ted V. Mikels; ***C:*** Yuval Shousterman; ***M:*** Nicholas Carras.

Ten Wanted Men 🦴 **1954** A successful cattle baron is confronted by a pistol-wielding landowner determined to ruin him. Standard fare, with better than average performances from Scott and Boone. **80m/C VHS.** Randolph Scott, Jocelyn Brando, Richard Boone, Skip Homeier, Leo Gordon, Jack Perrin, Donna (Dona Martel) Martell; ***D:*** H. Bruce Humberstone; ***W:*** Harriet Frank Jr., Irving Ravetch.

Ten Who Dared 🦴🦴 **1960** Ten Civil War heroes brave the Colorado River in an effort to chart its course. Although it's based on an actual historic event, the film is poorly paced and lacks suspense. **92m/C VHS.** Brian Keith, John Beal, James Drury; ***D:*** William Beaudine.

The Tenant 🦴🦴🦴½ *Le Locataire* **1976 (R)** Disturbing story of a hapless office worker who moves into a spooky Paris apartment house. Once lodged inside its walls, he becomes obsessed with the previous occupant, who committed suicide, and the belief that his neighbors are trying to kill him. Based on a novel by Roland Topor. **126m/C VHS.** *FR* Lila Kedrova, Claude Dauphin, Michel Blanc, Roman Polanski, Isabelle Adjani, Melvyn Douglas, Jo Van Fleet, Bernard Fresson, Shelley Winters; ***D:*** Roman Polanski; ***W:*** Gerard Brach, Roman Polanski; ***C:*** Sven Nykvist; ***M:*** Philippe Sarde.

The Tenant of Wildfell Hall 🦴🦴½ **1996** Anne Bronte gets her turn in the spotlight with this TV adaptation of her 1848 novel. When the mysterious Helen Graham (Fitzgerald) and her young son become the new tenants of decaying Wildfell Hall, they naturally elicit lots of gossip in their rural community. Then young farmer Gilbert Markham (Stephens) becomes romantically interested in Helen and she's eventually forced to reveal her secret—she's run away from her alcoholic and abusive husband Arthur Huntingdon (Graves), who has now kidnapped their son to force Helen to return. **180m/C VHS.** *GB CA* Tara Fitzgerald, Toby Stephens, Rupert Graves, Beatie Edney, James Purefoy, Jonathan Cake, Kenneth Cranham, Janet Dale; ***D:*** Mike Barker; ***W:*** Janet Barron, David Nokes; ***C:*** Daf Hobson; ***M:*** Richard G. Mitchell. **TV**

The Tender Age 🦴🦴 *The Little Sister* **1984** Troubled 18-year-old girl gets out of a detention home and is put on probation. She captivates her idealistic probation officer, whose interest may extend beyond professional concern. Fine idea, but under-played. **103m/C VHS.** John Savage, Tracy Pollan, Roxanne Hart, Richard Jenkins; ***D:*** Jan Egleson; ***W:*** Jan Egleson.

Tender Comrade 🦴🦴 **1943** Flag-waving violin-accompanied tearjerker about five women who live together to make ends meet while their men do manly things during WWII. Intended to puff your heart up with patriotic gusto. Ironically, thanks to the girls' communal living arrangement, director Dmytryk was later accused of un-American activities. **101m/B VHS.** Ginger Rogers, Robert Ryan, Ruth Hussey, Patricia Collinge, Mady Christians, Kim Hunter, Jane Darwell, Mary Forbes, Richard Martin; ***D:*** Edward Dmytryk.

Tender Flesh woof! **1997** Unashamed exercise in sleaze from the prolific Jess Franco is worth noting for only one scene wherein a woman urinates on camera. Beyond that dubious distinction, it's yet another unfocused variation on "The Most Dangerous Game." **90m/C DVD.** *SP* Lina Romay, Amber Newman, Monique Parent; ***D:*** Jess (Jesus) Franco; ***W:*** Jess (Jesus) Franco; ***M:*** Jess (Jesus) Franco.

Tender Is the Night 🦴🦴½ **1955** A TV adaptation of the F. Scott Fitzgerald classic, set in the roaring '20s, in which a psychiatrist marries one of his patients and then heads down the road to ruin, driven by his marriage and the times in which he lives. An entry from the "Front Row Center" series. **60m/B VHS.** Mercedes McCambridge, James Daly. **TV**

Tender Loving Care 🦴 **1973** Three nurses dispense hefty doses of T.L.C. in their hospital, and the patients aren't the only ones on the receiving end. **72m/C VHS, DVD.** Donna Desmond, Leah Simon, Anita King; ***D:*** Don Edmonds.

Tender Mercies 🦴🦴🦴 **1983 (PG)** Down-and-out country singer Mac Sledge (Duvall) gets roaring drunk after breaking up with his wife Dixie (Buckley) andfinds himself waking up at a motel/gas station run by religious widow, Rosa Lee (Harper). mac sticks arounds and finds his life redeemed by the love of a good woman and he also decides to attempt a comeback. Aided by Horton Foote's script, Duvall, Harper, and Barkin (as Mac's daughter Sue Anne) keep this from being simplistic and sentimental. Duvall wrote as well as performed the songs in his Oscar-winning performance. Wonderful, life-affirming flick. **88m/C VHS, DVD, Wide.** Robert Duvall, Tess Harper, Betty Buckley, Ellen Barkin, Wilford Brimley, Lenny Von Dohlen, Allan Hubbard; ***D:*** Bruce Beresford; ***W:*** Horton Foote; ***C:*** Russell Boyd; ***M:*** George Dreyfus. Oscars '83: Actor (Duvall), Orig. Screenplay; Golden Globes '83: Actor—Drama (Duvall); L.A. Film Critics '83: Actor (Duvall); N.Y. Film Critics '83: Actor (Duvall); Writers Guild '83: Orig. Screenplay.

The Tender Trap 🦴🦴½ **1955** Charlie Reader (Sinatra) is a bachelor not content with the many women in his life. He meets the innocent Julie Gillis (Reynolds) and falls head over heels for her. He then torments himself over a marriage proposal, unwilling to let go of his freedom. **111m/C VHS, Wide.** Frank Sinatra, Debbie Reynolds, Celeste Holm, David Wayne, Carolyn Jones, Lola Albright, Tom Helmore, Howard St. John, Willard Sage, James Drury, Benny Rubin, Frank Sully, David White; ***D:*** Charles Walters; ***W:*** Julius J. Epstein; ***C:*** Paul Vogel.

The Tender Warrior 🦴🦴 **1971 (G)** A beautifully photographed animal adventure with Haggerty as the woodsman. **85m/C VHS.** Dan Haggerty, Charles Lee, Liston Elkins; ***D:*** Stewart Raffill.

The Tender Years 🦴🦴 **1947** Sentimental drama of a minister trying to outlaw dog fighting, spurred on by his son's fondness for a particular dog. **81m/B VHS.** Joe E. Brown, Richard Lyon, Noreen Nash, Charles Drake, Josephine Hutchinson; ***D:*** Harold Schuster.

Tenderness of the Wolves 🦴🦴 *Die Zartlichkeit der Wolfe* **1973** Inspired by Fritz Lang's film "M" but sticking closer to its source material, the case of real-life mass murderer Peter Kurten, known as the Dusseldorf Vampire. Lommel's film is also given the "Fassbinder" spin (he's in the cast as well as the producer and editor). In 1925, black marketeer Fritz Haarmann (Raab) lures young runaway boys with the promise of a job, only to seduce and murder them—and sell their remains as meat. Raab rather resembles the Peter Lorre character but his Hartmann is all surface quiet and seething madness underneath. Very chilling. German with subtitles. **86m/C VHS, DVD, Wide.** *GE* Kurt Raab, Jeff Roden, Margit Carstensen, Rainer Werner Fassbinder, Wolfgang Schenck, Brigitte Mira, Ingrid Caven, Juergen Prochnow; ***D:*** Ulli Lommel; ***W:*** Kurt Raab; ***C:*** Jurgen Jurges; ***M:*** Peer Raben.

Tennessee Stallion 🦴 **1978** A low-class horse-trainer breaks into the world of aristocratic thoroughbred racing. **87m/C VHS.** Audrey Landers, Judy Landers, James Van Patten.

Tennessee's Partner 🦴🦴 **1955** Enjoyable, unexceptional buddy Western. Reagan intervenes in an argument and becomes Payne's pal. Adapted from a story by Bret Harte. **87m/C VHS, DVD.** Ronald Reagan, Rhonda Fleming, John Payne; ***D:*** Allan Dwan; ***W:*** D.D. Beauchamp, Milton Krims, Teddi Sherman, G. Graham Baker; ***C:*** John Alton; ***M:*** Louis Forbes.

Tension at Table Rock 🦴🦴 **1956** Accused of cowardice, a lone gunman must prove he killed in self-defense. Well-cast serious Western. **93m/C VHS.** Richard Egan, Dorothy Malone, Cameron Mitchell; ***D:*** Charles Marquis Warren.

Tentacles woof! *Tentacoli* **1977 (PG)** Cheesy Italian version of "Jaws" lacking only the suspense and cogent storytelling. Huston slums as the investigator charged with finding the octopus gone mad, while Fonda collects check and makes a quick exit. Hopkins is in charge of the killer whales that save the day. You'll cheer when Winters is devoured by sea pest. From the director of an "Exorcist" rip-off, "Beyond the Door" (that's not a recommendation). **90m/C VHS.** *IT* John Huston, Shelley Winters, Bo Hopkins, Henry Fonda, Cesare Danova, Delia Boccardo, Alan Boyd, Claude Akins; ***D:*** Oliver (Ovidio Assonitis) Hellman, Ovidio G. Assonitis; ***W:*** Steven W. Carabatsos, Tito Carpi, Sonia Molteni; ***C:*** Roberto D'Ettorre Piazzoli; ***M:*** Stelvio Cipriano.

Tentacles of the North 🦴🦴½ **1926** Two ships are trapped in the ice of the Arctic with the only survivor of one ship being a fearful young girl. Tinted print. **54m/B VHS.** Gaston Glass, Alice Calhoun, Al Ferguson, Joseph Girard; ***D:*** Louis Chaudet.

The 10th Kingdom 🦴🦴½ **2000** Overly long but visually impressive fairy-tale extravganza. New Yorkers Virginia (Williams) and her father Tony (Larroquette) find themselves magically transported into an alternate universe that consists of nine kingdoms filled with trolls, evil queens, human/beast hybrids, and all sorts of adventures. Their quest to return home (to what they learn is their own tenth kingdom) is consistently thwarted until they clear up a little good vs. evil battle that's raging. **350m/C VHS, DVD.** Kimberly Williams, John Larroquette, Scott Cohen, Ann-Margret, Rutger Hauer, Camryn Manheim, Ed O'Neill, Dianne Wiest, Daniel Lapaine, Dawnn Lewis, Jimmy Nail, Warwick Davis, Timothy Bateson, Robert Hardy, Aden (John) Gillett, Moira Lister; ***D:*** David Carson, Herbert Wise; ***C:*** Lawrence Jones, Chris Howard; ***M:*** Anne Dudley. **TV**

The Tenth Man 🦴🦴½ **1988** Hopkins stars as a wealthy French lawyer, captured by the Nazis and sentenced to death. He discovers a fellow prisoner who is willing to take his place in exchange for Hopkins's wealth going to support the man's family. After his release, Hopkins returns to his old home, now occupied by the dead man's family, but doesn't reveal his true identity. When an imposter appears, claiming to be Hopkins, another twist is added. Slow-going but the usual excellent performances by Hopkins and Jacobi. Based on a novella by Graham Greene. **99m/C VHS.** Anthony Hopkins, Kristin Scott Thomas, Derek Jacobi, Cyril Cusack, Brenda Bruce, Paul Rogers; ***D:*** Jack Gold. **TV**

Tenth Month 🦴🦴 **1979** Carol Burnett plays a divorced, middle-aged woman who becomes pregnant by a married man. She refuses help, choosing instead to live alone and keep an ever-hopeful vigil for the birth of her child. Sappy but touching TV drama. **123m/C VHS.** Carol Burnett, Keith Michell, Dina Merrill; ***D:*** Joan Tewkesbury.

10th Victim 🦴🦴🦴 *La Decima Vittima; La Dixieme Victime* **1965** Sci-fi cult film set in the 21st century has Mastroianni and Andress pursuing one another in a futuristic society where legalized murder is used as the means of population control. Intriguing movie where Andress kills with a double-barreled bra, the characters hang out at the Club Masoch, and comic books are considered literature. Based on "The Seventh Victim" by Robert Sheckley. **92m/C VHS, DVD, Wide.** *IT* Ursula Andress, Marcello Mastroianni, Elsa Martinelli, Salvo Randone, Massimo Serato; ***D:*** Elio Petri; ***W:*** Elio Petri, Tonino Guerra, Ennio Flaiano, Giorgio Salvioni; ***C:*** Gianni Di Venanzo; ***M:*** Piero Piccioni.

Teorema 🦴🦴 **1968** Scathing condemnation of bourgeois complacency. Stamp, either a devil or a god, mysteriously appears and enters into the life of a well-to-do Milanese family and raises each member's spirituality by sleeping with them. Ultimately, the experience leads to tragedy. In Italian with English subtitles. **98m/C VHS.** *IT* Terence Stamp, Silvana Mangano, Massimo Girotti, Anna Wiazemsky, Laura Betti, Andres Jose Cruz; ***D:*** Pier Paolo Pasolini; ***M:*** Ennio Morricone.

Tequila Body Shots 🦴 **1999 (R)** Low-budget nightmare is suffered not just by the portentously named main character, Johnny Orpheus (Lawrence). Johnny is convinced by some buddies to attend a Day of the Dead party held on a Mexican beach where he imbibes some whacked Tequila that enables him to read women's thoughts and experience some afterlife horrors, courtesy of evil spirit Hector (Moreno). Turns out Hector is after his reincarnated wife who just happens to be the girl (Mouser) that Johnny is interested in. Oh yeah, and its all played for laughs (but you won't be). **94m/C VHS, DVD, Wide.** Joey Lawrence, Dru Mouser, Rene L. Moreno, Nathan Anderson, Josh Marchette, Jennifer Lyons, Henry Darrow; ***D:*** Tony Shyu; ***W:*** Tony Shyu; ***C:*** Lawrence Schweich; ***M:*** Shayne Fair, Larry Herbstritt.

Tequila Sunrise 🦴🦴½ **1988 (R)** Towne's twisting film about two lifelong friends and a beautiful woman. Gibson is a (supposedly) retired drug dealer afraid of losing custody of his son to his nagging ex-wife. Russell is the cop and old friend who's trying to get the lowdown on a drug shipment coming in from Mexico. Pfeiffer runs the poshest restaurant on the coast and is actively pursued by both men. Questions cloud the plot and confuse the viewer; loaded with double-crosses, intrigue and surprises around every corner, still the photogenic leads are pleasant to watch. Steamy love scene between Pfeiffer and Gibson. **116m/C VHS, DVD, 8mm.** Mel Gibson, Kurt Russell, Michelle Pfeiffer, Raul Julia, Arliss Howard, Arye Gross, J.T. Walsh, Ann Magnuson; ***D:*** Robert Towne; ***W:*** Robert Towne; ***C:*** Conrad L. Hall; ***M:*** Dave Grusin.

Teresa Venerdi 🦴🦴🦴 *Doctor Beware* **1941** An unusual Italian comedy about a man and his financial difficulties. His mistress, his fiance and a young girl make his troubles more confusing. Unusually sweet and humorous DeSica. **90m/B VHS.** *IT* Vittorio De Sica, Irasema Dilian, Anna Magnani, Adriana Benetti, Arturo Bragaglia, Olga Vittoria Gentilli; ***D:*** Vittorio De Sica; ***W:*** Vittorio De Sica; ***C:*** Vincenzo Seratrice; ***M:*** Renzo Rossellini.

Teresa's Tattoo 🦴 **1994** A bimbo (Shelly) with a Chinese dragon tattoo somehow obtains a pair of earrings containing details of the U.S. space program. She's kidnapped by inept thugs and dies in a freak accident. Now the kidnappers need a look-alike for their extortion scheme so they kidnap another girl (Shelly again) and drug and tattoo her. Naturally, when she wakes up she manages to escape. Thin farce striving too hard to be madcap and whimsical. **88m/C VHS.** Adrienne Shelly, C. Thomas Howell, Nancy McKeon, Lou Diamond Phillips, Casey Siemaszko, Jonathan Silverman, Diedrich Bader; ***Cameos:*** Majel Barrett, Anthony Clark, Nanette Fabray, Tippi Hedren, k.d. lang, Joe Pantoliano, Mary Kay Place, Mare Winningham, Kiefer Sutherland, Melissa Etheridge; ***D:*** Julie Cypher; ***W:*** Georgie Huntington; ***C:*** Sven Kirsten; ***M:*** Melissa Etheridge.

Tereza 🦴🦴🦴 **1961** In politically chaotic Czechoslovakia, a female police detective tries to solve an intricate murder mystery. In Czech with English subtitles. **91m/B VHS.** *CZ* Jirina Svorcova; ***D:*** Pavel Blumenfeld.

Terminal Bliss 🦴½ **1991 (R)** Teen heartthrob Perry stars as a spoiled rich druggie in this "Less Than Zero" knock-off. Perry and childhood pal Owen grow up sharing everything—lacrosse, girlfriends, and drugs. However, their friendship is really put to the test when a beautiful new girl (Chandler) moves to town just before graduation. Release was delayed, but obviously wants to capitalize on Perry's popularity. **94m/C VHS.** Luke Perry, Timothy Owen, Estee Chandler, Sonia Curtis, Micah Grant, Alexis Arquette; ***D:*** Jordan Alan; ***W:*** Jordan Alan; ***C:*** Greg Smith; ***M:*** Frank Becker.

Terminal Choice 🦴½ **1985 (R)** Staff at a hospital conduct a betting pool on patients' life expectancies. Someone decides he should win more often and uses a computer to help hedge his bets. Wasted cast on this unsuspenseful and bloody film. **98m/C VHS.** Joe Spano, Diane Venora, David McCallum, Ellen Barkin; ***D:*** Sheldon Larry; ***W:*** Neal Bell.

Terminal Entry 🦴½ **1987 (R)** Teen computer geeks accidentally find a terrorist online network, and inadvertently begin transmitting instructions to destroy U.S. targets. The premise is intriguing but poorly done. **95m/C VHS.** Edward Albert, Yaphet Kotto, Kabir Bedi; ***D:*** John Kincade; ***C:*** James L. Carter.

Terminal Exposure 🦴🦴 **1989 (R)** Predictable but likeable comedy-mystery. A pair of Venice, CA, beach denizens capture a murder on film and try to solve it. **105m/C VHS.** Steve Donmyer, John Vernon, Ted Lange, Joe Phelan, Hope Marie Carlton, Mark Hennessy, Scott King; ***D:*** Nico Mastorakis.

Terminal Force 🦴 *Rescue Force* **1988 (R)** Stupid, poorly executed story of kidnapping and the mob. So bad it never saw the inside of a theatre; went straight to video. **83m/C VHS.** Troy Donahue, Richard Harrison, Dawn Wildsmith; ***D:*** Fred Olen Ray. **VIDEO**

Terminal Impact 🦴🦴 **1995 (R)** Bounty hunters Saint (Zagarino) and Max (Genesse) agree to a high-paying assignment at Delta Tech Labs without asking any questions. They discover that the lab's chairman Sheen (Roberts) is messing around with DNA and has been implanting insect DNA into unwilling human subjects, which turns them into killer cyborgs as well. **94m/C VHS.** Bryan Genesse, Frank Zagarino, Jennifer Miller, Ian Roberts; ***D:*** Yossi Wein; ***W:*** Jeff Albert, Dennis Dimster Denk; ***C:*** Rod Stewart.

Terminal Island 🦴½ **1973 (R)** Tough southern California penal colony is crowded with inmates from death row. When prison becomes coed, violence breaks out. Exploitative and unappealing. **88m/C VHS.** Phyllis E. Davis, Tom Selleck, Don Marshall, Ena Hartman, Marta Kristen; ***D:*** Stephanie Rothman.

Terminal Justice: Cybertech P.D. 🦴½ **1995 (R)** Cop Bobby Chase (Lamas) is assigned to protect VR sex babe, Pamela Travis (Wuhrer). Turns out wealthy VR game manufacturer, Reginald Matthews (Sarandon) has teamed up with sicko doctor, Deacon (Vivyan), to clone beautiful women so they can be used in snuff films. And Matthews wants Pam's DNA to begin the process. **95m/C VHS.** Lorenzo Lamas, Chris Sarandon, Kari Wuhrer, Peter Coyote; ***D:*** Rick King; ***W:*** Frederick Bailey; ***C:*** Chris Holmes Jr.; ***M:*** Michael Hoenig. **VIDEO**

The Terminal Man 🦴🦴½ **1974 (R)** A slick, visually compelling adaptation of the Michael Crichton novel. A scientist plagued by violent mental disorders has a computer-controlled regulator implanted in his brain. The computer malfunctions and he starts a murdering spree. Futuristic vision of man-machine symbiosis gone awry. Well acted, but still falls short of the novel. **107m/C VHS.** George Segal, Joan Hackett, Jill Clayburgh, Richard Dysart, James B. Sikking, Norman Burton; ***D:*** Mike Hodges; ***W:*** Mike Hodges.

Terminal Rush 🦴🦴 **1996 (R)** Army Ranger Johnny Price (Wilson) is thrown out of the service after being framed for a crime. But when terrorists (led by Piper) take over Hoover Dam, Price is the one person with the necessary skills to thwart this vindictive madman. **94m/C VHS, DVD.** Don "The Dragon" Wilson, Roddy Piper; ***D:*** Damian Lee. **VIDEO**

Terminal Velocity 🦴🦴 **1994 (PG-13)** Skydiving instructor Ditch Brodie (Sheen) thinks he sees student Chris Morrow (Kinski) plummet to her death, only it turns out she's not dead and certainly not a beginner. Upon further investigation, he finds the usual web of international intrigue descending upon him, and that the KGB definitely wants him to mind his own business. Still, he pushes on. Another no-brainer actioner with few surprises satisfies the guilty pleasures of action addicts only. **132m/C VHS, DVD.** Charlie Sheen, Nastassia Kinski, James Gandolfini, Christopher McDonald, Melvin Van Peebles; ***D:*** Deran Sarafian; ***W:*** David N. Twohy; ***C:*** Oliver Wood; ***M:*** Joel McNeely.

Terminal Virus 🦴🦴 **1996 (R)** A deadly sexually trasmitted disease has made reproduction impossible, so humanity is on the verge of extinction. It's up to an outlaw and a scientist to convince a suspicious population that a new serum is the cure everyone's been waiting for. **74m/C VHS.** James Brolin, Richard Lynch, Bryan Genesse; ***D:*** Dan Golden.

Termination Man 🦴🦴 **1997 (R)** Serbian terrorist blackmails NATO and the United Nations with a nerve gas threat and genetically enhanced agent Dylan Pope (Railsback), who may be immune to the gas, must lead a covert squad to save the day. Action by the numbers. **92m/C VHS, DVD.** Steve Railsback, Athena Massey, James Farentino, Eb Lottimer; ***D:*** Fred Gallo; ***W:*** Fred Gallo, Charles Philip Moore; ***C:*** Eugeny Guslinsky; ***M:*** Deddy Tzur. **VIDEO**

The Terminator 🦴🦴🦴 **1984 (R)** Futuristic cyborg (Schwarzenegger, suitably robotic and menacing) is sent to present-day Earth. His job: kill the woman, Sarah Connor (Hamilton), who will conceive the child destined to become the great liberator and arch-enemy of the Earth's future rulers. The cyborg is also pursued by another futuristic visitor, Kyle Reese (Biehn), who falls in love with the intended victim. Cameron's pacing is just right in this exhilarating, explosive thriller which displays Arnie as one cold-blooded villain who utters a now famous line: "I'll be back." Followed by "Terminator 2: Judgment Day." **108m/C VHS, DVD, Wide.** Arnold Schwarzenegger, Michael Biehn, Linda Hamilton, Paul Winfield, Lance Henriksen, Bill Paxton, Rick Rossovich, Dick Miller, Earl Boen; ***D:*** James Cameron; ***W:*** James Cameron; ***M:*** Brad Fiedel.

Terminator 2: Judgment Day 🦴🦴🦴½ **1991 (R)** He said he'd be back and he is, programmed to protect the boy who will be mankind's post-nuke resistance leader. But the T-1000, a shape-changing, ultimate killing machine, is also on the boy's trail. Twice the mayhem, five times the special effects, ten times the budget of the first, but without Arnold it'd be half the movie. The word hasn't been invented to describe the special effects, particularly THE scariest nuclear holocaust scene yet. Worldwide megahit, but the $100 million budget nearly ruined the studio; Arnold accepted his $12 million in the form of a jet. **139m/C VHS, DVD, 8mm, Wide.** Arnold Schwarzenegger, Linda Hamilton, Edward Furlong, Robert Patrick, Earl Boen, Joe Morton; ***D:*** James Cameron; ***W:*** James Cameron; ***C:*** Adam Greenberg; ***M:*** Brad Fiedel. Oscars '91: Makeup, Sound, Sound FX Editing, Visual FX; MTV Movie Awards '92: Film, Male Perf. (Schwarzenegger), Female Perf. (Hamilton), Breakthrough Perf. (Furlong), Most Desirable Female (Hamilton), Action Seq.

Termini Station 🦴🦴½ **1989** Dewhurst gives an excellent performance as the alcoholic matriarch of a small-town Canadian family. She drinks all day and dreams of traveling to Italy, while her children work and believe there is something more to life than their mundane existence. When they finally do leave, they discover an intriguing new world. Dewhurst and Follows also appear together in "Anne of Green Gables" and "Anne of Avonlea." **105m/C VHS.** *CA* Colleen Dewhurst, Megan Follows, Gordon Clapp, Hannah Lee, Leon Pownall, Debra McGrath, Elliott Smith, Norma Dell'Agnese; ***D:*** Allen King; ***M:*** Mychael Danna.

Terms of Endearment 🦴🦴🦴 **1983 (PG)** A weeper following the changing relationship between a young woman and her mother, over a 30-year period. Beginning as a comedy, turning serious as the years go by, this was Brooks' debut as screenwriter and director. Superb supporting cast headed by Nicholson's slyly charming neighbor/astronaut, with stunning performances by Winger and MacLaine as the two women who often know and love each other too well. Adapted from Larry McMurtry's novel. **132m/C VHS, DVD, Wide.** Shirley MacLaine, Jack Nicholson, Debra Winger, John Lithgow, Jeff Daniels, Danny DeVito; ***D:*** James L. Brooks; ***W:*** James L. Brooks; ***C:*** Andrzej Bartkowiak; ***M:*** Michael Gore. Oscars '83: Actress (MacLaine), Adapt. Screenplay, Director (Brooks), Picture, Support. Actor (Nicholson); Directors Guild '83: Director (Brooks); Golden Globes '84: Actress—Drama (MacLaine), Film—Drama, Screenplay, Support. Actor (Nicholson); L.A. Film Critics '83: Actress (MacLaine), Director (Brooks), Film, Screenplay, Support. Actor (Nicholson); Natl. Bd. of Review '83: Actress (MacLaine), Director (Brooks), Support. Actor (Nicholson); N.Y. Film Critics '83: Actress (MacLaine), Film, Support. Actor (Nicholson); Natl. Soc. Film Critics '83: Actress (Winger), Support. Actor (Nicholson); Writers Guild '83: Adapt. Screenplay.

Terraces 🦴🦴½ **1977** TV series pilot about high-rise tenants whose balconies are their only common ground. Good performances. **90m/C VHS.** Lloyd Bochner, Eliza (Simons) Garrett, Julie Newmar, Tim Thomerson; ***D:*** Lila Garrett. **TV**

Terranova 🦴🦴 **1991** Six characters in search of themselves, with the profound changes in their lives coming through an unlikely friendship. Rosetta is the poor matriarch of an Italian immigrant family while wealthy Noemi is an artistocratic landowner. But they share simiilar frustrations and the desire to change their lives. Set in a rural Venezuelan town in the 1950s; Spanish with subtitles. **96m/C VHS.**

IT Marisa Laurito, Mimi Lazo, Antonio Banderas, Patrick Bauchau, Massimo Bonetti, Nathalia Martinez; ***D:*** Calogero Salvo.

Terrified 🦴🦴½ **1994 (R)** Erotic thriller about a nympho being stalked by a mystery assailant. Genuinely creepy. **90m/C VHS, DVD.** Heather Graham, Lisa Zane, Rustam Branaman, Tom Breznahan, Max Perlich, Balthazar Getty, Richard Lynch, Don Calfa; ***D:*** James Merendino; ***W:*** James Merendino, Megan Heath.

The Terror 🦴🦴 **1938** A hostelry is the scene of a number of brutal murders. Remake of a 1928 film and based on a play by Edgar Wallace. Good story, but weak version of it. **63m/B VHS.** *GB* Wilfred Lawson, Bernard Lee, Arthur Wontner, Linden Travers, Henry Oscar, Alastair Sim; ***D:*** Richard Bird.

The Terror 🦴🦴 *Lady of the Shadows* **1963** A lieutenant in Napoleon's army chases a lovely maiden and finds himself trapped in a creepy castle by a mad baron. Movie legend has it Corman directed the movie in three days as the sets (from his previous movie "The Raven") were being torn down around them. **81m/C VHS, DVD.** Boris Karloff, Jack Nicholson, Sandra Knight, Dick Miller, Dorothy Neumann, Jonathan Haze; ***D:*** Roger Corman, Jack Hill, Francis Ford Coppola, Monte Hellman, Dennis Jacob, Jack Nicholson; ***W:*** Roger Corman, Leo Gordon, Jack Hill; ***C:*** John M. Nickolaus Jr.; ***M:*** Ronald Stein.

The Terror woof! **1979 (R)** After 100 years, a man reveals in a film that his family killed a witch. Friends who see the film are attacked by supernatural forces. Originally double-billed with "Dracula's Dog." **86m/C VHS.** John Nolan, Carolyn Courage, James Aubrey, Glynis Barber, Sarah Keller, Tricia Walsh; ***D:*** Norman J. Warren.

Terror at London Bridge 🦴🦴 *Bridge Across Time; Arizona Ripper* **1985** London Bridge is transported brick by brick to Arizona. It carries its history with it, including the havoc-wreaking spirit of Jack the Ripper. Campy made-for-TV effort. **96m/C VHS.** David Hasselhoff, Stephanie Kramer, Adrienne Barbeau, Randolph Mantooth; ***D:*** E.W. Swackhamer; ***C:*** Gil Hubbs.

Terror at Red Wolf Inn 🦴🦴 *Club Dead; Terror House; The Folks at Red Wolf Inn* **1972 (R)** Young woman wins a vacation; finds she's been invited for dinner, so to speak. Not campy enough to overcome stupidity. **90m/C VHS.** Linda Gillin, Arthur Space, John Neilson, Mary Jackson, Janet Wood, Margaret Avery; ***D:*** Bud Townsend; ***W:*** Allen Actor.

Terror at Tenkiller 🦴 **1986** Two girls vacationing in the mountains are seemingly surrounded by a rash of mysterious murders. **87m/C VHS.** Mike Wiles, Stacey Logan. **VIDEO**

Terror Beach 🦴 **198?** A doctor and his bride move to a coastal village, only to find it enmeshed in witchcraft and devil worship. **90m/C VHS.** Victor Petit, Julie James, Mary Costi, Sandra Mozar.

Terror Beneath the Sea 🦴🦴½ *Kaitei Daisenso; Water Cyborgs* **1966** A mad scientist wants to rule the world with his cyborgs. American and Japanese scientists unite to fight him. Fine special effects, especially the transformation from human to monster. **85m/C VHS.** *JP* Sonny Chiba, Peggy Neal, Franz Gruber, Gunther Braun, Andrew Hughes, Mike Daneen; ***D:*** Hajime Sato.

Terror by Night 🦴🦴½ **1946** Holmes and Watson attempt to solve the murder of the owner of a gigantic, beautiful jewel. Their investigation must be completed before their train arrives at its destination, where the murderer can escape. **60m/B VHS, DVD.** Basil Rathbone, Nigel Bruce, Alan Mowbray, Dennis Hoey, Renee Godfrey; ***D:*** Roy William Neill; ***W:*** Frank Gruber; ***C:*** Maury Gertsman.

Terror Creatures from the Grave 🦴 **1966** Husband summons medieval plague victims to rise from the grave to drop in on his unfaithful wife. Should've been better. **85m/C VHS.** *IT* Barbara Steele, Riccardo Garrone, Walter Brandi; ***D:*** Ralph Zucker.

Terror Eyes 🦴½ **1987 (PG-13)** Spoof-thriller revolves around an "agent from Hell," sent to Earth to recruit writers for a horror film. **90m/C VHS.** Daniel Roebuck, Vivian Schilling, Dan Bell, Lance August.

Terror in a Texas Town 🦴🦴½ **1958** George Hansen (Hayden) is a Swedish seaman who returns home to discover his farmer father has been gunned down by the greedy Johnny Crale (Young), who's after the land so he can drill for oil. So Hansen's out for revenge. There's a final showdown that not only includes six-shooters but a harpoon. **120m/B VHS.** Sterling Hayden, Nedrick Young, Sebastian Cabot, Victor Millan; ***D:*** Joseph H. Lewis; ***W:*** Dalton Trumbo; ***C:*** Ray Rennahan; ***M:*** Gerald Fried.

Terror in Beverly Hills woof! **1990** When the President's daughter is kidnapped, it's up to an ex-marine to save her. The trouble is, the head terrorist hates the marine's guts as he blames him for the deaths of his wife and children. So incredibly bad it's campy and fun. **88m/C VHS.** Frank Stallone, Cameron Mitchell, William Smith; ***D:*** John Myhers; ***W:*** John Myhers.

Terror in Paradise 🦴½ **1990 (R)** Jason and Vickie think they're going to have a romantic holiday on a beautiful island paradise. But they've picked the wrong spot to vacation. It seems the island harbors a terrorist group and when they see more than they should the lovers become the next targets. **93m/C VHS.** Joanna Pettet, Gary Lockwood, David Anthony Smith, Leslie Ryan; ***D:*** Peer J. Oppenheimer.

Terror in the Haunted House 🦴🦴½ *My World Dies Screaming* **1958** Newlyweds move into an old house. The bride remembers it from her nightmares. First release featured the first use of Psychorama, a technique in which scary words or advertising messages were flashed on the screen for a fraction of a second—just long enough to cause subliminal response. The technique was banned later in the year. **90m/C VHS, DVD.** Gerald Mohr, Cathy O'Donnell, William Ching, John Qualen, Barry Bernard; ***D:*** Harold Daniels; ***W:*** Robert C. Dennis; ***C:*** Frederick E. West; ***M:*** Darrell Calker.

Terror in the Jungle 🦴 **1968 (PG)** Plane crashes in Peruvian wilds and young boy survivor meets Jivaro Indians who think he's a god. Much struggling to survive and battling with horrible script. **95m/C VHS.** Jimmy Angle, Robert Burns, Fawn Silver; ***D:*** Tom De Simone; ***M:*** Les Baxter.

Terror in the Swamp 🦴 **1985 (PG)** When not hanging out in the local murky waters, a swamp creature terrorizes the residents of a small town. **89m/C VHS.** Billy Holliday; ***D:*** Joe Catalanotto.

Terror in the Wax Museum woof! **1973 (PG)** The owner of a wax museum is killed while mulling over the sale of the museum. The new owner has little better luck as the bodies continue to pile up. Production uses every out-of-work horror film actor of the time. The most suspenseful part of this low-budget flick is waiting to see how long the "wax dummies" can hold their breath. **94m/C VHS.** Ray Milland, Broderick Crawford, Elsa Lanchester, Louis Hayward, Maurice Evans, John Carradine; ***D:*** Georg Fenady; ***W:*** Jameson Brewer; ***M:*** George Duning.

Terror Is a Man 🦴🦴 *Blood Creature* **1959** A mad scientist attempts to turn a panther into a man on a secluded island. Early Filipino horror attempt inspired by H.G. Wells' "The Island of Doctor Moreau." **89m/B VHS, DVD.** *PH* Francis Lederer, Greta Thyssen, Richard Derr, Oscar Keesee; ***D:*** Gerardo (Gerry) De Leon; ***W:*** Harry Paul Harber; ***C:*** Emmanuel I. Rojas; ***M:*** Ariston Auelino.

Terror of Mechagodzilla 🦴½ *Monsters from the Unknown Planet; The Escape of Megagodzilla; Mekagojira No Gyakushu* **1978 (G)** It's monster vs. machine in the heavyweight battle of the universe as a huge mechanical Godzilla built by aliens is pitted against the real thing. The last Godzilla movie made until "Godzilla 1985." **79m/C VHS, DVD.** *JP* Katsuhiko Sasakai, Tomoko Al; ***D:*** Inoshiro Honda; ***W:*** Yukiko Takayama; ***C:*** Mototaka Tomioka; ***M:*** Akira Ifukube.

Terror of Rome Against the Son of Hercules 🦴 **1964** Musclebound gladiators battle it out in this low-budget Italian action flick. Dubbed. **100m/C VHS.** *FR IT* Mark Forest, Marilu Tolo; ***D:*** Mario Caiano.

Terror of the Bloodhunters 🦴 **1962** A French author is sentenced to Devil's Island for a crime he didn't commit. The warden's daughter takes a liking to him and arranges for him and a friend to escape, but numerous perils await them in the jungle. **60m/B VHS.** Robert Clarke, Steve Conte, Dorothy Haney; ***D:*** Jerry Warren; ***W:*** Jerry Warren.

Terror of the Steppes 🦴 **1964** Yet another sword and sandal extravaganza in which a musclebound hero conquers all. **?m/C VHS.** *IT* Kirk Morris; ***D:*** Tanio Boccia.

Terror of Tiny Town 🦴🦴 **1938** Main characteristic of this musical/western is its entire midget cast, all members of Jed Buell's Midgets. Otherwise the plot is fairly average and features a bad guy and the good guy who finally teaches him a lesson. Newfield plays up the cast's short stature—they walk under saloon doors and ride Shetland ponies. **63m/B VHS.** Billy Curtis, Yvonne Moray, "Little Billy" Rhodes, Billy Platt, John Bambury, Charles Becker; ***D:*** Sam Newfield; ***W:*** Fred Myton, Clarence Marks; ***C:*** Mack Stengler.

Terror on Alcatraz 🦴 **1986** The only prisoner to successfully escape from Alcatraz Island returns to retrieve the safety deposit box key he needs to get his stolen loot. And anyone who gets in his way is in for trouble. **96m/C VHS.** Veronica Porsche Ali, Sandy Brooke, Aldo Ray, Scott Ryder; ***D:*** Philip Marcus.

Terror on the 40th Floor 🦴 **1974** Seven people make an attempt to escape from the 40th floor of an inflamed skyscraper. Poorly done re-hash of "Towering Inferno." Uninspired. **98m/C VHS.** John Forsythe, Anjanette Comer, Don Meredith, Joseph Campanella; ***D:*** Jerry Jameson.

Terror on Tour woof! **1983** The Clowns, a rock group on their way up, center their stage performance around sadistic, mutilating theatrics. When real murders begin, they become prime suspects. Exploitive, bloody, disgusting. **90m/C VHS.** Dave Galluzzo, Richard Styles, Rick Pemberton; ***D:*** Don Edmonds.

Terror out of the Sky 🦴½ **1978** A scientist must disguise himself as one of the insects to divert the attention of a horde of killing bees from a busload of elementary children. Sub-par sequel to "The Savage Bees." **95m/C VHS.** Efrem Zimbalist Jr., Dan Haggerty; ***D:*** Lee H. Katzin; ***M:*** William Goldstein.

Terror Ship 🦴🦴 **1954** Three people find an abandoned yacht which they believe was used for smuggling. While searching it, they find that it was used to transport stolen uranium. Before the police can arrive, the thieves show up. Not a very good handling of what was actually an interesting idea. Released as "Dangerous Voyage" in Great Britain. **72m/B VHS.** *GB* William Lundigan, Naomi Chance, Vincent Ball, Jean Lodge, Richard Stewart; ***D:*** Vernon Sewell.

Terror Squad 🦴🦴 **1987** An unsuspecting high school population is put under siege by Libyan terrorists. The students get a hands-on lesson in revolution and guerrilla war tactics. **95m/C VHS.** Kerry Brennan, Bill Calvert, Chuck Connors, Greer Brodie; ***D:*** Peter Maris.

Terror Stalks the Class Reunion 🦴🦴½ **1993 (PG-13)** Kay (Nelligan) is a teacher who disappears at a class reunion. Police dismiss the case as a runaway wife, except for Virginia, a young detective (Beals) who doesn't accept that theory. And she's right—Kay is held hostage in a remote cabin by an obsessed former student (Davies). Kay needs all her wits to fend off her deranged and possibly deadly suitor while Virginia races to find her. Based on the novel by Mary Higgins Clark. **95m/C VHS.** Kate Nelligan, Jennifer Beals, Geraint Wyn Davies.

Terror Street 🦴 **1954** An Air Force pilot's wife is murdered. He has 36 hours to clear his name and find the killer. **84m/B VHS.** Dan Duryea, Elsy Albiin, Ann Gudrun, Eric Pohlmann.

Terror Tract 🦴🦴 **2000 (R)** Real estate agent Bob (Ritter) takes newlyweds Allen (DeLuise) and Mary Ann (Smith) to each of three homes he has for sale. But each home was the site of some horrible evil: in one a wife kills her abusive husband, only to fear he's not really dead; in the second, a father tries to stop the mischief caused by his daughter's evil pet monkey; and in the third house, a teenager finds himself psychically linked to a killer who blames the teen for his crimes. Comfortably scary fun. **97m/C VHS, DVD, Wide.** John Ritter, Marcus Bagwell, Bryan Cranston, Will Estes, Brenda Strong, Rachel York, Allison Smith, Carmine D. Giovinazzo, David DeLuise, Wade Andrew Williams, Frederic Lane; ***D:*** Geoffrey Wright, Lance Dreesen, Clint Hutchison; ***W:*** Clint Hutchison; ***C:*** Ken Blakey; ***M:*** Brian Tyler. **VIDEO**

Terror Trail 🦴½ **1933** As usual, Mix uses guns and fists to bring bad guys to justice, and gets the girl in the bargain. **62m/B VHS.** Tom Mix, Naomi Judge, Arthur (L.) Rankin, Raymond Hatton, Francis McDonald, Robert F. (Bob) Kortman, John St. Polis, Lafe (Lafayette) McKee, Buffalo Bill Jr.; ***D:*** Armand Schaefer.

Terror Train 🦴🦴 *Train of Terror* **1980 (R)** A masquerade party is held on a chartered train. But someone has more than mask-wearing in mind as a series of dead bodies begin to appear. Copperfield provides magic, Curtis provides screams in this semi-scary slasher movie. **97m/C VHS.** Jamie Lee Curtis, Ben Johnson, Hart Bochner, David Copperfield, Vanity, Howard Busgang, Michael Shanks, Amanda Tapping, Troy Kennedy Martin, Anthony Sherwood, Timothy Webber; ***D:*** Roger Spottiswoode; ***W:*** Alec Curtis; ***C:*** John Alcott.

Terror 2000 🦴½ *Intensivstation Deutschland* **1992** Satire/exploitation/slapstick and gross-out humor converge in a story about a husband and wife detective team sent to a German refugee camp to investigate the disappearance of a Polish family seeking asylum. The detectives discover the family has been kidnapped by a group of neo-Nazis. German with subtitles. **79m/C VHS.** *GE* Margit Carstensen, Alfred Edel, Udo Kier, Peter Kern, Gary Indiana; ***D:*** Christoph Schlingensief; ***W:*** Christoph Schlingensief.

The Terror Within 🦴 **1988 (R)** Reptilian mutants hit the streets searching for human women to breed with. Have the Teenage Mutant Ninja Turtles grown up? **90m/C VHS, DVD.** George Kennedy, Andrew Stevens, Starr Andreeff, Terri Treas; ***D:*** Thierry Notz; ***W:*** Thomas McKelvey Cleaver; ***C:*** Ronn Schmidt; ***M:*** Rick Conrad.

The Terror Within 2 🦴½ **1991 (R)** In a world destroyed by biological warfare, a warrior and the woman he rescued traverse the badlands occupied by hideous mutants. What they don't know is that the real terror comes from within. How can they possibly survive? Not without decent dialogue, that's for sure. **90m/C VHS.** Andrew Stevens, Stella Stevens, Chick Vennera, R. Lee Ermey; ***D:*** Andrew Stevens.

Terrorgram 🦴 **1990 (R)** Not a very special delivery. An offscreen James Earl Jones introduces three lesser tales of terror. Best seg: a sleazy filmmaker gets trapped in the world of his own exploitation scripts. The other two are bloody but negligible revenge-from-the-grave yarns. All start off with the receipt of a sinister package, hence a postal motif. **88m/C VHS.** Michael Hartson, J.T. Wallace; ***Nar:*** James Earl Jones.

The Terrorist 🦴🦴 *Malli* **1998** Malli (Dharkar) is a 19-year-old terrorist trained to kill from an early age and to die if necessary. She lives with her fellow militants in a camp and is chosen to kill a politician by detonating a bomb that will be strapped to her waist. But when Malli is forced to wait in the city for her victim, she begins to question her mission and her cause. Inspired by the 1991 assassination of Indian prime minister Rajiv Gandhi although the film itself never mentions country, group, or politics specifically. **95m/C VHS, DVD, Wide.** *IN* Ayesha Dharker; ***D:*** Santosh Sivan; ***W:*** Santosh Sivan; ***C:*** Santosh Sivan; ***M:*** Sonu Sisupal.

The Terrorists 🦴½ **1974 (PG)** Just as later he was a Scottish Lithuanian subcommander in "The Hunt for Red October" (1990), here Connery is a Scottish Norwegian security chief. Good cinematography and premise are wasted; generic title betrays sloppy execution. **89m/C VHS.** Sean Connery, Ian McShane, John Quentin; ***D:*** Casper Wrede; ***M:*** Jerry Goldsmith.

Terrorists 🦴 **1983** An Army investigator discovers a plot to assassinate the President. It's up to him to move quickly enough to stop it. Brutal action. **61m/C VHS.** Marland Proctor, Irmgard Millard.

The Terrornauts woof! **1967** When man begins space exploration, Earth is attacked by aliens. The defenders are taken to an out-dated fortress where they learn that their forebears were similarly attacked. Juvenile, lackluster, contrived, and really dumb. **77m/C VHS.** *GB* Simon Oates, Zena Marshall, Charles Hawtrey, Stanley Meadows; ***D:*** Montgomery Tully.

Terrorvision woof! **1986 (R)** OUR TV GAVE BIRTH TO SPACE ALIENS! It's amazing what modern technology can do: Suburban family buys a fancy satellite dish; bad black comedy and gory special effects result. **84m/C VHS.** Gerrit Graham, Mary Woronov, Diane Franklin, Bert Remsen, Alejandro Rey; ***D:*** Ted Nicolaou; ***W:*** Ted Nicolaou; ***M:*** Richard Band.

The Terry Fox Story 🦴🦴🦴 **1983** In the spring of 1980, a young man who had lost his right leg to cancer dipped his artificial limb into the Atlantic Ocean and set off on a fund-raising "Marathon of Hope" across Canada, drawing national attention. Inspiring true story is well-scripted and avoids corniness. Good acting from real-life amputee Fryer and, as usual, from Duvall. **96m/C VHS.** Eric Fryer, Robert Duvall, Chris Makepeace, Michael Zelniker, Rosalind Chao; ***D:*** Ralph L. (R.L.) Thomas; ***M:*** Bill Conti. Genie '84: Actor (Fryer), Film, Support. Actor (Zelniker). **TV**

Tess 🦴🦴🦴 **1980 (PG)** Sumptuous adaptation of the Thomas Hardy novel "Tess of the D'Ubervilles." Kinski is wonderful as an innocent farm girl who is seduced by the young aristocrat she works for and then finds marriage to a man of her own class only brings more grief. Polanski's direction is faithful and artful. Nearly three hours long, but worth every minute. **170m/C VHS.** *GB FR* Nastassia Kinski, Peter Firth, Leigh Lawson, John Collin; ***D:*** Roman Polanski; ***W:*** Roman Polanski, Gerard Brach; ***C:*** Ghislan Cloquet, Geoffrey Unsworth. Oscars '80: Art Dir./Set Dec., Cinematog., Costume Des.; Cesar '80: Cinematog., Director (Polanski), Film; Golden Globes '81: Foreign Film; L.A. Film Critics '80: Cinematog., Director (Polanski); N.Y. Film Critics '80: Cinematog.

Tess of the D'Urbervilles 🦴🦴½ **1998** Thomas Hardy's rural Victorian England is the setting for romantic tragedy. Tess Durbeyfield (Waddell) is a poor, naive 16-year-old who's unwillingly sent to work for the wealthy D'Urbervilles, whom her family believes are distant relatives. There, Tess becomes the target of wastrel Alec's (Flemyng) desires and he takes advantage of her. Several years later, Tess is now working as a dairymaid and falls in true love with Angel Clare (Milburn), but he can't accept her soiled past even though they've married. Heartbroken Tess falls deeper into hardship until Alec suddenly reappears in her life—and so does Angel. **180m/C VHS.** *GB* Justine Waddell, Jason Flemyng, Oliver Milburn, John McEnery, Lesley Dunlop, Gerald James, Debbie Chazen; ***D:*** Ian Sharp; ***W:*** Ted Whitehead; ***C:*** Richard Greatrex; ***M:*** Alan Lisk. **TV**

Tess of the Storm Country 🦴🦴½ **1922** Pickford remade her own 1914 film for the better, starring as poor Tessibel Skinner, who takes in her lover Frederick Graves' (Hughes) pregnant sister, Teola (Hope), and then says the child is hers to protect the unwed mom from her ruthless father (Torrence). Tessibel temporarily loses Frederick until the truth comes out. **120m/B VHS, DVD.** Mary Pickford, Lloyd Hughes, David Torrence, Gloria Hope, Jean Hersholt; ***D:*** John S. Robertson; ***W:*** Elmer Harris; ***C:*** Charles Rosher, Paul Eagler; ***M:*** Jeffrey Mark Silverman.

Test of Donald Norton 🦴🦴½ **1926** Good early Western. A young man raised by Indians finds work with the Hudson's Bay Company and does well, but is haunted by suspicions that he is a half-breed. **68m/B VHS, 8mm.** George Walsh, Tyrone Power Sr., Eugenia Gilbert, Robert Graves, Virginia True Boardman; ***D:*** B. Reeves Eason.

A Test of Love 🦴🦴 *Annie's Coming Out* **1984 (PG)** Incorrectly diagnosed as retarded, a young woman with cerebral palsy struggles to adjust to life outside an institution. Predictable but touching and well-acted. **93m/C VHS.** *AU* Angela Punch McGregor, Drew Forsythe, Tina Arhondis; ***D:*** Gil Brealey; ***W:*** Chris Borthwick. Australian Film Inst. '84: Film.

Test Pilot 🦴🦴🦴½ **1938** Gable and Spencer star as daring test pilot and devoted mechanic respectively. When Gable has to land his experimental craft in a Kansas cornfield, he meets and falls in love with farm girl Loy. The two marry and raise a family, all the while she worries over his dangerous profession. When the Air Force asks him to test their new B-17 bomber, she refuses to watch, thinking the test will end in tragedy. Superb aviation drama featuring excellent cast. **118m/B VHS.** Clark Gable, Myrna Loy, Spencer Tracy, Lionel Barrymore, Samuel S. Hinds; ***D:*** Victor Fleming.

Test Tube Babies woof! *Sins of Love; The Pill* **1948** A married couple's morals begin to deteriorate as they mourn the fact they can't have a child. The day is saved, however, when they learn about the new artificial insemination process. Amusing, campy propaganda in the vein of "Reefer Madness." Rereleased in 1967 as "The Pill" with extra scenes featuring Monica Davis and John Maitland. **83m/B VHS.** Dorothy Dube, Timothy Farrell, William Thomason; ***D:*** W. Merle Connell; ***W:*** Richard McMahan.

Test Tube Teens from the Year 2000 🦴 *Virgin Hunters* **1993 (R)** When sex is banned in the year 2000, horny teenagers are left with no choice but to travel through time for some action. **74m/C VHS.** Morgan Fairchild, Ian Abercrombie, Brian Bremer, Christopher Wolf, Michelle Matheson, Sara Suzanne Brown, Don Dowe, Chuck Borden, Robin Joi Brown, Conrad Brooks; ***D:*** David DeCoteau; ***W:*** Kenneth J. Hall; ***M:*** Reg Powell.

Testament 🦴🦴🦴 **1983 (PG)** Well-made and thought-provoking story of the residents of a small California town struggling to survive after a nuclear bombing. Focuses on one family who tries to accept the reality of post-holocaust life. We see the devastation but it never sinks into sensationalism. An exceptional performance from Alexander. **90m/C VHS.** Jane Alexander, William Devane, Ross Harris, Roxana Zal, Kevin Costner, Rebecca DeMornay; ***D:*** Lynne Littman; ***W:*** John Sacret Young; ***M:*** James Horner.

The Testament of Dr. Cordelier 🦴🦴🦴 *Testament in Evil; Le Testament du Docteur Cordelier* **1959** A strange, experimental fantasy about a Jekyll and Hyde-type lunatic stalking the streets and alleys of Paris. Originally conceived as a TV play, Renoir attempted to create a new mise-en-scene, using multiple cameras covering the sequences as they were performed whole. French with English subtitles. **95m/C VHS.** *FR* Jean-Louis Barrault, Michel Vitold, Teddy Billis, Jean Topart, Micheline Gary; ***D:*** Jean Renoir; ***W:*** Jean Renoir; ***C:*** Georges Leclerc; ***M:*** Joseph Kosma.

Testament of Dr. Mabuse 🦴🦴½ *The Crimes of Dr. Mabuse; The Last Will of Dr. Mabuse* **1962** The director of an asylum is controlled by the evil genius, Dr. Mabuse, who hypnotizes him in this well-done remake of Lang's 1933 classic. **?m/C VHS, DVD.** Gert Frobe, Wolfgang Preiss, Senta Berger.

The Testament of Orpheus 🦴🦴🦴½ *Le Testament D'Orphee* **1959** Superb, personal surrealism; writer-director Cocteau's last film. Hallucinogenic, autobiographical dream-journey through time. Difficult to follow, but rewarding final installment in a trilogy including "The Blood of the Poet" and "Orpheus." In French with English subtitles. **80m/B VHS, DVD.** *FR* Jean Cocteau, Edouard Dermithe, Maria Casares, Francois Perier, Yul Brynner, Jean-Pierre Leaud, Daniel Gelin, Jean Marais, Pablo Picasso, Charles Aznavour; ***D:*** Jean Cocteau; ***W:*** Jean Cocteau; ***C:*** Roland Pointoizeau; ***M:*** Georges Auric.

Testament of Youth 🦴🦴½ **1979** Based on the autobiography of British feminist, author, and pacifist Vera Brittain (Campbell). Vera is enjoying herself at Oxford University in 1913 until war is declared. Vera then becomes a nurse on the frontlines in France and her experiences eventually shatter her, leading her to painfully change her life. **200m/C VHS.** *GB* Cheryl Campbell, Rupert Frazer, Emrys James, Rosalie Crutchley, Joanna McCallum, Michael Troughton, Peter Woodward; ***D:*** Moira Armstrong; ***W:*** Elaine Morgan. **TV**

Tetsuo: The Iron Man 🦴🦴 *The Ironman* **1992** A weird live-action science-fiction cartoon about a white-collar Japanese worker who finds himself being gradually transformed into a walking metal collection of cables, drills, wires, and gears. The newly formed metal creature then faces off with an equally bizarre metals fetishist (played by the director). In Japanese with English subtitles. **67m/B VHS, DVD.** *JP* Tomoroh Taguchi, Kei Fujiwara, Shinya Tsukamoto; ***D:*** Shinya Tsukamoto; ***W:*** Shinya Tsukamoto; ***C:*** Shinya Tsukamoto; ***M:*** Chu Ishikawa.

Tetsuo 2: Body Hammer 🦴🦴 **1997** Taniguchi (Yaguchi) strikes back at the cyborgs who kidnapped and killed his young son by transforming himself into a killer robotic machine man. Japanese with subtitles. **83m/C VHS, DVD.** *JP* Tomoroh Taguchi; ***D:*** Shinya Tsukamoto; ***W:*** Shinya Tsukamoto; ***C:*** Shinya Tsukamoto.

Tevye 🦴🦴½ *Tevye der Milkhiker* **1939** Sholom Aleichem's story of Jewish family life, intermarriage, and turmoil in Poland. When Khave, the daughter of Tevye the dairyman, seeks to marry a Ukrainian peasant, Tevye must come to terms with his love for his daughter and his faith and loyalty to tradition. Also the basis for the musical "Fiddler on the Roof." In Yiddish with English subtitles. **96m/B VHS.** Maurice Schwartz, Miriam Riselle; ***D:*** Maurice Schwartz. Natl. Film Reg. '91.

Tex 🦴🦴½ **1982 (PG)** Fatherless brothers in Oklahoma come of age. Dillon is excellent. Based on the novel by S.E. Hinton. **103m/C VHS, DVD.** Matt Dillon, Jim Metzler, Meg Tilly, Bill McKinney, Frances Lee McCain, Ben Johnson, Emilio Estevez; ***D:*** Tim Hunter; ***W:*** Tim Hunter, Charles Haas; ***C:*** Ric Waite; ***M:*** Pino Donaggio.

Tex Rides with the Boy Scouts 🦴½ **1937** Scouts aid Ritter in capturing gold bandits with a little bit of singing thrown in for good measure. **60m/B VHS.** Tex Ritter.

The Texans 🦴🦴½ **1938** Ex-Confederate soldier Kirk Jordan (Scott) struggles to make a new life for himself as a trail boss, aiming to get 10,000 head of cattle to the railroad in Abilene. But there's temptation in the form of Ivy Preston (Bennett) and a scheme to reignite the war. Remake of 1924 silent "North of '36." **93m/B VHS.** Randolph Scott, Joan Bennett, Walter Brennan, May Robson, Robert Cummings, Raymond Hatton, Robert Barrat, Harvey Stephens, Chris-Pin (Ethier Crispin Martini) Martin, Francis Ford; ***D:*** James Hogan; ***W:*** Bertram Millhauser, Paul Sloane, William Wister Haines.

Texas 🦴🦴🦴 **1941** Two friends wander through the West after the Civil War getting into scrapes with the law and eventually drifting apart. Ford takes a job on a cattle ranch run by Trevor and discovers Holden has joined a gang of rustlers aiming to steal her herd. The two men vie for Trevor's affections. Although friends, a professional rivalry also existed between the two leading actors and they competed against each other, doing their own stunts during filming. Well-acted, funny, and enthusiastic Western. **94m/B VHS.** William Holden, Glenn Ford, Claire Trevor, Edgar Buchanan, George Bancroft; ***D:*** George Marshall.

Texas 🦴🦴½ *James A. Michener's Texas* **1994** Stephen Austin (Duffy) sets up a colony in 1821 Texas, with Mexican law requiring the settlers to become Mexican citizens. Eventually, calls for statehood begin and Austin's initial resistance is overturned by rebellion and prodding from Sam Houston (Keach) and Jim Bowie (Keith). Lots of action amidst the history, including the battle for the Alamo, but it's a routine extravaganza. Made for TV miniseries adapted from Michener's novel. Filmed on location in Del Rio, Texas. **180m/C VHS, DVD.** Patrick Duffy, Stacy Keach, David Keith, Maria Conchita Alonso, Anthony Michael Hall, Rick Schroder, Benjamin Bratt, Chelsea Field, John Schneider, Grant Show, Randy Travis, Woody Watson; ***D:*** Richard Lang; ***W:*** Sean Meredith; ***M:*** Lee Holdridge. **TV**

Texas across the River 🦴🦴½ **1966** Sam Hollis (Martin) is a wise-cracking gun runner who, along with Indian sidekick Kronk (Bishop), is recruiting men to help him ship guns through hostile Comanche territory. Don Andrea, a Spanish nobleman (played by Frenchman Delon) wrongly accused of murder, joins up and much comic misadventure ensues. **101m/C VHS, Wide.** Dean Martin, Alain Delon, Joey Bishop, Rosemary Forsyth, Tina Aumont, Peter Graves, Michael Ansara, Linden Chiles, Andrew Prine, Richard Farnsworth; ***D:*** Michael Gordon; ***W:*** Ben Starr, Wells Root, Harold Greene; ***C:*** Russell Metty.

Texas Bad Man 🦴½ **1932** Sheriff Mix goes undercover to get in with Kohler's gang of outlaws and bring them to justice. **60m/B VHS.** Tom Mix, Fred Kohler Sr., Lucille Powers, Ed LeSaint, Richard Alexander; ***D:*** Edward Laemmle.

Texas Buddies 🦴½ **1932** Steele plays a former military pilot who uses his trusty monoplane to round up outlaws. Interesting twist on standard oater, but suffers from poor execution. **57m/B VHS.** Bob Steele, Nancy Drexel, George "Gabby" Hayes, Francis McDonald, Harry Semels; ***D:*** Robert North Bradbury; ***W:*** Robert North Bradbury.

Texas Carnival 🦴🦴 **1951** Williams and Skelton star as carnival performers who operate the dunk tank. When Skelton is mistaken for an oil tycoon, he lives high on the hog until the mistake is discovered. Believe it or not, this musical has only one water ballet sequence. Songs include "It's Dynamite," "Whoa! Emma," and "Young Folks Should Get Married." **77m/C VHS.** Esther Williams, Red Skelton, Howard Keel, Ann Miller, Paula Raymond, Keenan Wynn, Tom Tully; ***D:*** Charles Walters.

The Texas Chainsaw Massacre 🦴🦴½ **1974 (R)** The movie that put the "power" in power tools. An idyllic summer afternoon drive becomes a nightmare for a group of young people pursued by a chainsaw-wielding maniac. Made with tongue firmly in cheek, this is nevertheless a mesmerizing saga of gore, flesh, mayhem, and violence. **86m/C VHS, DVD, Wide.** Marilyn Burns, Allen Danzinger, Paul A. Partain, William Vail, Teri McMinn, Edwin Neal, Jim Siedow, Gunnar Hansen, John Dugan, Jerry Lorenz; ***D:*** Tobe Hooper; ***W:*** Tobe Hooper, Kim Henkel; ***C:*** Daniel Pearl; ***M:*** Tobe Hooper, Wayne Bell; ***Nar:*** John Larroquette.

The Texas Chainsaw Massacre 2 woof! **1986 (R)** A tasteless, magnified sequel to the notorious blood-bucket extravaganza, about a certain family in southern Texas who kill and eat passing travelers. Followed by "Leatherface: The Texas Chainsaw Massacre 3." **90m/C VHS, DVD, Wide.** Dennis Hopper, Caroline Williams, Bill Johnson, Jim Siedow, Bill Moseley, Lou Perry, John (Joe Bob Briggs) Bloom; ***D:*** Tobe Hooper; ***W:*** L.M. Kit Carson; ***C:*** Richard Kooris; ***M:*** Tobe Hooper.

The Texas Chainsaw Massacre 4: The Next Generation 🦴🦴 *Return of the Texas Chainsaw Massacre* **1995 (R)** Heroine Jenny (Zellweger) and her three friends take a wrong turn down a dark country road and wind up in the nightmare clutches of homicidal tow-truck driver Vilmer (McConaughey), his accomplice Darla (Perenski), and the infamous Leatherface (Jacks). No restraint here—as the borderline sadism and tension builds to, unfortunately, something of a letdown. Feature debut for Henkel, who co-wrote Tobe Hooper's 1977 horror classic. Film finally got a release in 1997 after both McConaughey and Zellweger became stars in more mainstream films. Pay attention to "Love Theme from Texas Chainsaw Massacre," sung by Debbie Harry and Leatherface himself. **94m/C VHS, DVD.** Renee Zellweger, Matthew McConaughey, Robert Jacks, Tony Perenski, Lisa Marie Newmyer, John Dugan, Marilyn Burns; ***D:*** Kim Henkel; ***W:*** Kim Henkel; ***C:*** Levie Isaacks; ***M:*** Wayne Bell.

Texas Cyclone 🦴🦴 **1932** A stranger rides into a town that turns out to be incredibly friendly. Later he realizes the entire town thinks he is a prominent citizen who disappeared years ago. **58m/B VHS.** Tim McCoy, Wheeler Oakman, Shirley Grey, Walter Brennan, John Wayne, Wallace MacDonald, Vernon Dent, Mary Gordon; ***D:*** David Ross Lederman.

Texas Detour 🦴 **1977** On a trip across country, a trio of young Californians have their van stolen. They decide to take the law into their own hands when the redneck sheriff gives them no help. Dull, undistinguished "action" flick. **90m/C VHS.** Cameron Mitchell, Priscilla Barnes, Patrick Wayne, Mitch Vogel, Lindsay Bloom, R.G. Armstrong; ***D:*** Howard (Hikmet) Avedis.

A Texas Funeral 🦴🦴 **1999 (R)** Sheen is a Texas patriarch, seen only in flashbacks since it's his funeral that's being attended by his crazy family, which has a long tradition of dysfunction. Set in the late-'60s. **98m/C VHS.** Martin Sheen, Robert Patrick, Jane Adams, Christopher Noth, Isaiah Washington IV, Joanne Whalley, Grace Zabriskie, Olivia D'Abo, Quinton Jones; ***D:*** W(illiam) Blake Herron; ***W:*** W(illiam) Blake Herron; ***C:*** Michael Bonvillain; ***M:*** James Legg.

Texas Gunfighter 🦴🦴 **1932** Your basic western from the Maynard series, with everything a western could have. **60m/B VHS.** Ken Maynard.

Texas Guns 🦴🦴 *Once Upon a Texas Train* **1990 (PG)** A gritty western about an old-time gunman (Nelson) and his quest for one last robbery, killing those who stand in his way and some just for fun. Also watch for Cassidy's comeback. **96m/C VHS.** Willie Nelson, Richard Widmark, Shaun Cassidy, Angie Dickinson, Kevin McCarthy, Royal Dano, Chuck Connors, Ken Curtis, Dub Taylor.

Texas Jack 🦴½ **1935** The head of a medicine show tries to trace the disappearance of his sister. **55m/B VHS.** Jack Perrin, Jayne Regan, Nelson McDowell, Budd Buster, Lew Meehan; ***D:*** Bernard B. Ray.

Texas John Slaughter: Geronimo's Revenge 🦴🦴 **1960** An Indian-loving rancher frets and fights when Geronimo attacks innocent settlers. Compiled from Disney TV episodes. **77m/C VHS.** Tom Tryon, Darryl Hickman, Betty Lynn; ***D:*** Harry Keller. **TV**

Texas John Slaughter: Stampede at Bitter Creek 🦴🦴 **1962** Good guy Texas John Slaughter meets a variety of threatening obstacles when he tries to move his cattle herd into New Mexico. Originally from the "Walt Disney Presents" TV series. **90m/C VHS.** Tom Tryon; ***D:*** Harry Keller. **TV**

Texas Justice 🦴½ **1942** The "Lone Rider" cavorts around in the desert, dispensing justice in the guise of a monk. **60m/B VHS.** George Houston, Al "Fuzzy" St. John, Dennis Moore, Wanda McKay, Claire Rochelle; ***D:*** Sam Newfield.

Texas Kid 🦴½ **1943** A typical western. Hero helps a vengeance-minded kid catch the robber-gang who robbed and killed his father. Yee-Haw. **53m/B VHS.** Johnny Mack Brown, Kermit Maynard, Raymond Hatton, Shirley Patterson, Edmund Cobb, Charles "Blackie" King; ***D:*** Lambert Hillyer.

Texas Lady 🦴🦴 **1956** When a woman wins $50,000 gambling, she buys a Texas newspaper on the stipulation that she can edit it in this standard fare western. Good vehicle for Colbert to look beautiful, but the plot and script are average and uninspired. **86m/C VHS.** Claudette Colbert, Barry Sullivan, Gregory Walcott; ***D:*** Tim Whelan.

Texas Layover woof! **1975** Impossible-to-describe western/exploitation entry from trashmeister Adamson involving multiple stewardesses and the remnants of the Ritz Brothers. **88m/C VHS.** Yvonne De Carlo, Robert "Bob" Livingston, Donald (Don "Red") Barry, Connie Hoffman, Regina Carrol, Jimmy Ritz, Harry Ritz; ***D:*** Al Adamson.

Texas Legionnaires 🦴🦴 *Man from Music Mountain* **1943** Roy comes back to his home town and gets caught between feuding cattle and sheep herders. **71m/B VHS.** Roy Rogers, Ruth Terry, Paul Kelly, Ann Gillis, George Cleveland, Pat Brady; ***D:*** Joseph Kane.

Texas Lightning 🦴½ **1981 (R)** Innocuous B-grade touching movie about a father and son and their family woes. **93m/C VHS.** Cameron Mitchell, Channing Mitchell, Maureen McCormick, Peter Jason.

Texas Masquerade 🦴🦴 **1944** Standard good cowboys versus land-grabbers action filler. William Boyd plays Hopalong Cassidy. Andy Clyde plays California Carson. Jimmy Rogers plays...Jimmy Rogers. **59m/B VHS.** William Boyd, Andy Clyde, Jimmy Rogers, Mady Correll, Don Costello, Russell Simpson, Nelson Leigh, Francis McDonald, J. Farrell MacDonald; ***D:*** George Archainbaud.

Texas Payback 🦴🦴 **1995 (R)** Convicted killer Cody Giles (Hudson) busts out of prison in order to get revenge on the now-retired-and-working-in-Vegas Texas Ranger Louis Gentry (Jones) who put him away. **96m/C VHS.** Sam Jones, Gary Hudson, Kathleen Kinmont, Bo Hopkins; ***D:*** Richard W. Munchkin; ***W:*** Brian Page; ***C:*** Mark Morris; ***M:*** Jim Halfpenny.

Texas Pioneers 🦴½ *The Blood Brother* **1932** A frontier scout is sent to an outpost town besieged by crooks. **54m/B VHS.** Bill Cody.

The Texas Rangers 🦴🦴½ **1936** Banditos Jim Hawkins (MacMurray) and Wahoo Jones (Oakie) roam the Texas frontier until the Rangers come in, establishing order. So, they switch over to the good guys but are then told to bring in their old partner-in-crime Sam McGee (Nolan). Lots of confronting villains and battling varmints. Based on the book by Walter Prescott Webb. Followed by "The Texas Rangers Ride Again" and remade as "The Streets of Laredo" (1949). **99m/B VHS.** Fred MacMurray, Jack Oakie, Lloyd Nolan, Jean Parker, Edward Ellis, Fred Kohler Sr., George "Gabby" Hayes; ***D:*** King Vidor; ***W:*** Louis Stevens.

The Texas Rangers 🦴🦴 **1951** A prisoner is given the opportunity to capture the notorious Sam Bass gang in exchange for freedom. Good B Western; lotsa shootin'. **68m/C VHS.** George Montgomery, Gale Storm, Jerome Courtland, Noah Beery Jr.; ***D:*** Phil Karlson.

Texas Rangers 🦴🦴 **2001 (PG-13)** Western featuring Van Der Beek and Kucher (they're dreamy!) as greenhorns who volunteer to fight bandits along the Rio Grande in 1875 Texas. McDermott's Ranger McNelly of the famous Texas Rangers is their demanding mentor who teaches them a'ropin' and a'shootin'. All are robbed of their families by the bad guys, and there's a passel o' gunfights, but taming the West takes a backseat to the real drama centered mostly around the ailing McNelly's fate in this revenge actioner. Cast is good but hindered by a weak script and direction. After sitting on the shelf for two years, yella-bellied studio execs denied the stale oater an advance screening, well aware of its weak appeal. **90m/C VHS, DVD, Wide.** *US* James Van Der Beek, Dylan McDermott, Ashton Kutcher, Usher Raymond, Robert Patrick, Rachael Leigh Cook, Leonor Varela, Randy Travis, Jon Abrahams, Matt Keeslar, Vincent Spano, Marco Leonardi, Oded Fehr, Joe Spano, Tom Skerritt, Alfred Molina; ***D:*** Steve Miner; ***W:*** Scott Busby, Martin Copeland; ***C:*** Daryn Okada; ***M:*** Trevor Rabin.

The Texas Rangers Ride Again 🦴🦴½ **1940** When cattle keep disappearing from the Dangerfield ranch, owner Robson secretly calls in the Texas Rangers to find out what's going on. Howard and Crawford work undercover to root out the criminals while Howard also finds the time to make goo-goo eyes at Robson's granddaughter Drew. **68m/B VHS.** John Howard, Broderick Crawford, May Robson, Ellen Drew, Anthony Quinn, Akim Tamiroff, Charley Grapewin, Harvey Stephens; ***D:*** James Hogan; ***W:*** William R. Lipman, Horace McCoy.

Texas Terror 🦴🦴 **1935** Young Wayne resigns his badge when he mistakenly believes he has shot and killed his friend. He later rescues his friend's sister, learns the truth, and (naturally) finds true love. **50m/B VHS.** John Wayne, George "Gabby" Hayes, Lucille Browne.

Texas to Bataan 🦴½ **1942** The Range Busters ship horses to the Philippines and encounter enemy spies. Part of the "Range Busters" series. **56m/B VHS.** John "Dusty" King, David Sharpe, Max Terhune; ***D:*** Robert Emmett Tansey.

Texas Trouble 🦴½ *Billy the Kid's Range War* **1941** Hackett is out to stop Barclay's road building by using a Billy the Kid imposter to halt construction. But the real Billy is ticked off and comes to the rescue. **?m/B VHS.** Bob Steele, Al "Fuzzy" St. John, Carleton Young, Joan Barclay, Karl Hackett, Rex Lease; ***D:*** Sam Newfield; ***W:*** William Lively; ***C:*** Jack Greenhalgh; ***M:*** Lew Porter.

Texas Wildcats 🦴½ **1939** A cowboy helps make sure that sinister adversaries are brought to justice on the American Frontier. **60m/B VHS.** Tim McCoy.

Texasville 🦴🦴½ **1990 (R)** Sequel to "The Last Picture Show" finds the characters still struggling after 30 years, with financial woes from the energy crisis, mental illness inspired by the Korean War, and various personal tragedies. Lacks the melancholy sensitivity of its predecessor, but has some of the wit and wisdom that comes with age. Based again on a Larry McMurtry novel. Not well received during its theatrical release. **120m/C VHS.** Timothy Bottoms, Jeff Bridges, Annie Potts, Cloris Leachman, Eileen Brennan, Randy Quaid, Cybill Shepherd, William McNamara; ***D:*** Peter Bogdanovich; ***W:*** Peter Bogdanovich.

The Texican 🦴½ **1966** Former sheriff Jess Carlin (Murphy) is living in Mexico but must return to the Texas town of Rim Rock when his newspaperman brother is murdered. Town boss Luke Starr (Crawford) is behind the crime but the townspeople are too scared to help Carlin out—except for saloon gal Kit (Lorys). **86m/C VHS.** Audie Murphy, Broderick Crawford, Diana Lorys, Aldo Sambrel, Antonio Casas; ***D:*** Lesley Selander; ***W:*** John C. Champion; ***C:*** Francis Marin.

Thank God It's Friday 🦴½ **1978 (PG)** Episodic and desultory disco-dancing vehicle which won the Best Song Oscar for Donna Summer's rendition. Life is irony. Co-produced by Motown. ♫Last Dance; After Dark; Find My Way; It's Serious; Let's Make A Deal; Romeo and Juliet; You're the Reason I Feel Like Dancing; From Here to Eternity; Dance All Night. **100m/C VHS.** Valerie Landsburg, Teri Nunn, Chick Vennera, Jeff Goldblum, Debra Winger; ***D:*** Robert Klane; ***W:*** Armyan Bernstein. Oscars '78: Song ("Last Dance").

Thank You & Good Night **1991** Director Oxenberg gathers members of her own family around a purple armchair of grandma's to talk about life, love, and family memories, including grandma's illness and recent death. **81m/C VHS.** ***D:*** Jan Oxenberg; ***W:*** Jan Oxenberg; ***C:*** Claudia Raschke.

Thank Your Lucky Stars 🦴🦴🦴 **1943** A lavish, slap-dash wartime musical that emptied out the Warner's lot for an array of uncharacteristic celebrity turns. Features Shore in her movie debut. ♫They're Either Too Young or Too Old; Blues in the Night; Hotcha Cornia; Ridin' For A Fall; We're Staying Home Tonight; Goin' North; Love Isn't Born, It's Made; No You, No Me; Ice Cold Katie. **127m/B VHS.** Eddie Cantor, Dinah Shore, Joan Leslie, Errol Flynn, Bette Davis, Edward Everett Horton, Humphrey Bogart, John Garfield, Alan Hale, Ann Sheridan, Ida Lupino, Jack Carson, Dennis Morgan, Olivia de Havilland; ***D:*** David Butler; ***W:*** Norman Panama.

Thanks for the Memory 🦴🦴 **1938** After Hope and Ross sang "Thanks for the Memory" in "The Big Boradcast of 1938," Paramount decided to capitalize on its popularity in this lame comedy. Steve Merrick (Hope) tends to the house while trying to write a novel. Meanwhile, wife Anne (Ross) is working as a model to support the couple. Steve rebels against being a "kept man" and their marriage enters shaky ground until they come to their senses. **79m/B VHS.** Bob Hope, Shirley Ross, Charles Butterworth, Otto Kruger, Hedda Hopper, Laura Hope Crews, Eddie Anderson; ***D:*** George Archainbaud; ***W:*** Lynn Starling; ***C:*** Karl Struss.

Tharus Son of Attila 🦴 **1987** A couple of sword-wielding barbarians battle each other and an evil emperor. **89m/C VHS.** Jerome Courtland, Rik von Nutter, Lisa Gastoni; ***D:*** Robert Montero.

That Brennan Girl 🦴½ **1946** A maudlin soap opera about how a girl's upbringing by an inconsiderate mother makes her a devious little wench. Fortunately her second husband had a better mom, and redemption is at hand. **95m/B VHS.** James Dunn, Mona Freeman, William Marshall, June Duprez, Frank Jenks, Charles Arnt; ***D:*** Alfred Santell.

That Certain Age 🦴🦴½ **1938** Alice (Durbin) is charmed by her newspaper-owning father's houseguest, older and sophisticated journalist Vincent Bullitt (Douglas). She gets a big crush and dumps boyfriend Ken (Cooper), causing much consternation to all. ♫That Certain Age; You're as Pretty as a Picture; Be a Good Scout; Has Anybody Ever Told You Before?; My Own. **101m/B VHS.** Deanna Durbin, Melvyn Douglas, Jackie Cooper, John Halliday, Irene Rich, Nancy Carroll, Jackie Searl, Charles Coleman; ***D:*** Edward Ludwig; ***W:*** Bruce Manning; ***C:*** Joseph Valentine.

That Certain Thing 🦴🦴½ **1928** Very early silent Capra comedy about a bachelor with a silver spoon in his mouth who loses his inheritance when he marries for love. It's got that certain Capra screwball feeling. **65m/B VHS.** Viola Dana, Ralph Graves, Burr McIntosh, Aggie Herring, Syd Crossley; ***D:*** Frank Capra.

That Certain Woman 🦴🦴½ **1937** Sentimental drama with Davis portraying a gangster's widow who wants to make a new life for herself. Fonda plays the rich playboy with whom she falls in love. Because of Davis' star power, she demanded that Fonda play opposite her. It seems Davis had a real life crush on him when they were both players in a stock company several years earlier. Remake of Goulding's "The Trespasser" which starred Gloria Swanson. **91m/B VHS.** Bette Davis, Henry Fonda, Ian Hunter, Anita Louise, Donald Crisp, Katherine Alexander, Minor Watson; ***D:*** Edmund Goulding; ***W:*** Edmund Goulding; ***M:*** Max Steiner.

That Championship Season 🦴🦴 **1982 (R)** Long-dormant animosities surface at the reunion of a championship basketball team. Unfortunate remake of Miller's Pulitzer-prize winning play, with none of the fire which made it a Broadway hit. **110m/C VHS.** Martin Sheen, Bruce Dern, Stacy Keach, Robert Mitchum, Paul Sorvino, Jason Miller; ***D:*** Jason Miller; ***C:*** John Bailey; ***M:*** Bill Conti.

That Championship Season 🦴🦴 **1999 (R)** Tom Daley (Sinise) returns to his hometown for the 20th anniversary of his high-school basketball team's championship victory. A night of nostalgia with Daley, his brother (Kinney), some friends (Shalhoub, D'Onofrio), and their coach (Sorvino, who directed this remake), turns into a drunken rehash of old grievances and the airing of some dirty laundry. Miller adapted his 1973 Pulitzer Prize-winning play, which he also directed for the big screen in 1982. **126m/C VHS.** Gary Sinise, Terry Kinney, Vincent D'Onofrio, Tony Shalhoub, Paul Sorvino; ***D:*** Paul Sorvino; ***W:*** Jason Miller; ***C:*** Bruce Surtees; ***M:*** Larry Blank. **CABLE**

That Cold Day in the Park 🦴🦴½ **1969 (R)** Early Altman. An unhappy woman takes in a homeless young man from the park near her home. The woman (Dennis) is obsessive and odd; so is the film. Dennis is excellent. Reminiscent of "The Collector." **91m/C VHS.** Sandy Dennis, Michael Burns, Susanne Benton, Michael Murphy, John David Garfield; *D:* Robert Altman.

That Darn Cat 🦴🦴½ **1965 (G)** Vintage Disney comedy about a Siamese cat that helps FBI Agent Jones thwart kidnappers. Could be shorter, but suspenseful and funny with characteristic Disney slapstick. Based on the book "Undercover Cat" by The Gordons. **115m/C VHS.** Hayley Mills, Dean Jones, Dorothy Provine, Neville Brand, Elsa Lanchester, Frank Gorshin, Roddy McDowall; *D:* Robert Stevenson; *C:* Edward Colman; *M:* Robert F. Brunner.

That Darn Cat 🦴🦴½ **1996 (PG)** Innocuous Disney remake of the 1965 Disney comedy falls into the "why bother" category. Bored 16-year-old Patti (Ricci) finds some unexpected excitement when her alley-wandering cat D.C. (for Darned Cat) returns home from a prowl with a wristwatch around his neck. Turns out it's a clue in a bungled kidnapping and Patti manages to convince rookie FBI agent Zeke (Doug) to investigate. Jones, who played the FBI agent in the original, is the wealthy husband of would-be kidnap victim Cannon. Ricci's appealing as the sarcastic teen and Elvis the cat has a certain scrappy charm as well. Based on the novel "Undercover Cat" by Mildred and Gordon Gordon. **89m/C VHS.** Christina Ricci, Doug E. Doug, Dean Jones, George Dzundza, Peter Boyle, Michael McKean, Bess Armstrong, Dyan Cannon, John Ratzenberger, Estelle Parsons, Rebecca Schull, Thomas F. Wilson, Brian Haley, Mark Christopher Lawrence; *D:* Bob Spiers; *W:* Scott M. Alexander, Larry Karaszewski; *C:* Jerzy Zielinski; *M:* Richard Gibbs.

That Darn Sorceress 🦴 **1988** A child witch has grown up, and so has her power. To keep her disciples, she must perform increasingly horrible feats. **89m/C VHS.** Pauline Adams, Bettie (Betty) Page; *D:* Whitney Bain.

That Eye, the Sky 🦴🦴 **1994** Alice (Harrow) and Sam (Fairall) Flack live on a small farm with their two children and senile grandmother. Sam's in a serious car crash and is eventually returned home still in a deep coma. Alice, who's having trouble coping, is grateful when wandering evangelist Harry Warburton (Coyote) shows up on her doorstep offering his help. But is this mystery man offering a miracle or more heartache? Based on the book by Tim Winton. **105m/C VHS.** *AU* Lisa Harrow, Peter Coyote, Mark Fairall, Jamie Croft, Amanda Douge, Alethea McGrath; *D:* John Ruane; *W:* John Ruane, Jim Barton; *C:* Ellery Ryan; *M:* David Bridie. Australian Film Inst. '95: Support. Actress (Douge).

That Forsyte Woman 🦴🦴 *The Forsyte Saga* **1950** Based on the novel "A Man of Property" by John Galsworthy, a married Victorian woman falls for an architect engaged to be wed. Remade later (and better) for BBC-TV as "The Forsythe Saga." **112m/C VHS.** Errol Flynn, Greer Garson, Walter Pidgeon, Robert Young, Janet Leigh, Harry Davenport, Stanley Logan, Lumsden Hare, Aubrey Mather, Matt Moore; *D:* Compton Bennett; *C:* Joseph Ruttenberg.

That Gang of Mine 🦴🦴 **1940** "East Side Kids" episode about gang member Mugg's ambition to be a jockey. Good racing scenes. **62m/B VHS.** Bobby Jordan, Leo Gorcey, Clarence Muse, Dave O'Brien; *D:* Joseph H. Lewis.

That Girl from Paris 🦴🦴½ **1936** An opera singer from Paris stows away on an ocean liner to be near the swing bandleader she has fallen in love with. An entertaining film with many songs; remade as "Four Jacks and a Jill." ♫Una Voce Poco Fa; The Blue Danube; Love and Learn; The Call to Arms; Seal It With A Kiss; My Nephew From Nice; Moon Face; Tarantella. **105m/B VHS.** Lily Pons, Gene Raymond, Jack Oakie, Herman Bing, Lucille Ball, Mischa Auer, Frank Jenks; *D:* Leigh Jason.

That Hamilton Woman 🦴🦴🦴 *Lady Hamilton* **1941** Screen biography of the tragic 18th-century love affair between British naval hero Lord Nelson and Lady Hamilton. Korda exaggerated the film's historical distortions in order to pass the censor's production code about adultery. Winston Churchill's favorite film which paralleled Britain's heroic struggles in WWII. **125m/B VHS.** Laurence Olivier, Vivien Leigh, Gladys Cooper, Alan Mowbray, Sara Allgood, Henry Wilcoxon; *D:* Alexander Korda; *M:* Miklos Rozsa. Oscars '41: Sound.

That Long Night in '43 🦴🦴½ *The Long Night of '43; La Lunga Notte del '43* **1960** Young married woman has an affair with an Army deserter during WWII while the local fascist leader makes a power grab by executing his opposition, including the deserter's father. Italian with subtitles. **110m/B VHS.** *IT* Belinda Lee, Gabriele Ferzetti, Enrico Maria Salerno; *D:* Florestano Vancini; *W:* Florestano Vancini, Ennio de Concini, Pier Paolo Pasolini; *C:* Carlo Di Palma; *M:* Carlo Rustichelli.

That Lucky Touch 🦴🦴 **1975** York is a reporter covering NATO games; Moore is Bond warmed over as an arms dealer. Sexual and professional tension becomes unlikely romance. Slight and dull. Cobb's last film. **92m/C VHS.** Roger Moore, Susannah York, Shelley Winters, Lee J. Cobb, Jean-Pierre Cassel, Raf Vallone, Sydne Rome; *D:* Christopher Miles; *W:* John Briley.

That Man Bolt 🦴🦴 **1973** Jefferson Bolt (Williamson) is a kung fu expert who agrees to carry $1 million from Hong Kong to Mexico City while being pursued by a government agent. Typical blaxpoitation feature. **102m/C VHS.** Fred Williamson, Teresa Graves, Byron Webster, Miko Mayama, Satoshi Nakamura, Jack Ging, Vassili Lambrinos, John Orchard; *D:* Henry Levin, David Lowell Rich; *W:* Quentin Werty; *C:* Gerald Perry Finnerman; *M:* Charles Bernstein.

That Man from Rio 🦴🦴½ *L'Homme de Rio; L'Uomo di Rio* **1964** Engaging adventure spoof with Belmondo as a pilot whose girlfriend (Dorleac) has just been kidnapped. Her father led an expedition to South America in search of an Amazon treasure and the kidnappers think she knows how to find it. So of course Belmondo does some international adventuring in order to rescue her. In French with English subtitles. **114m/C VHS.** *FR IT* Jean-Paul Belmondo, Francoise Dorleac, Jean Servais, Simone Renant; *D:* Philippe de Broca; *W:* Philippe de Broca, Jean-Paul Rappeneau; *M:* Georges Delerue. N.Y. Film Critics '64: Foreign Film.

That Midnight Kiss 🦴🦴½ **1949** Glossy production of a musical romance featuring Lanza in his film debut. Thin plot has Lanza starring as a singing truck driver who is discovered by opera diva Grayson. ♫They Didn't Believe Me; I Know, I Know, I Know; Three O'Clock in the Morning; Santa Lucia; Down Among the Sheltering Palms; Revolutionary Etude; Cara Nome; Celeste Aida; Una Furtiva Lacrima. **96m/C VHS.** Kathryn Grayson, Jose Iturbi, Ethel Barrymore, Mario Lanza, Keenan Wynn, J. Carrol Naish, Jules Munshin; *D:* Norman Taurog; *C:* Robert L. Surtees.

That Naughty Girl 🦴🦴 **1958** The bored daughter of a nightclub owner decides to experience all life has to offer. **77m/C VHS.** *FR* Brigitte Bardot, Jean Bretonniere, Francoise Fabian; *D:* Michel Boisrond.

That Night 🦴🦴½ **1993 (PG-13)** A view of romance through the eyes of a young girl, circa 1961. Ten-year-old Alice (Dushku) is the confidant of rebellious 17-year-old neighbor Cheryl (Lewis), who enlists the young girl's aid as a go-between with her wrong-side-of-the tracks boyfriend Rick (Howell). 21 soundtrack oldies are featured. Directorial debut for screenwriter Bolotin. Based on a novel by Alice McDermott. **89m/C VHS.** C. Thomas Howell, Juliette Lewis, Eliza Dushku, Helen Shaver, John Dossett; *D:* Craig Bolotin; *W:* Craig Bolotin.

That Obscure Object of Desire 🦴🦴🦴½ *Cet Obscur Objet du Desir* **1977 (R)** Bunuel's last film, a comic nightmare of sexual frustration. A rich Spaniard obtains a beautiful girlfriend who, while changing physical identities, refuses to sleep with him. Based on a novel by Pierre Louys, which has been used as the premise for several other films, including "The Devil is a Woman," "La Femme et le Pantin," and "The Female." Available with subtitles or dubbed. **100m/C VHS, DVD, Wide.** *SP* Fernando Rey, Carole Bouquet, Angela Molina, Julien Bertheau; *D:* Luis Bunuel; *W:* Luis Bunuel, Jean-Claude Carriere; *C:* Edmond Richard. L.A. Film Critics '77: Foreign Film; Natl. Bd. of Review '77: Director (Bunuel); Natl. Soc. Film Critics '77: Director (Bunuel).

That Old Feeling 🦴🦴 **1996 (PG-13)** Bitter ex-spouses Lilly (Midler) and Dan (Farina) are reunited at the wedding of their daughter and things turn ugly. They cause a scene and are sent out of the reception to cool down. Instead, their old passion flares up and they're found reeling in that old feeling in the back seat of a Porshe. After leaving to see where their whirlwind of romance takes them, they are trailed by their daughter (Marshall), her weenie husband (Denton), and their respective current spousal units Rowena (O'Grady) and Alan (Rasche). Fluffy romantic comedy carried mostly by the performances of Midler and Farina. **105m/C VHS, DVD.** Bette Midler, Dennis Farina, Danny Nucci, Paula Marshall, Gail O'Grady, David Rasche, Jayne (Jane) Eastwood; *D:* Carl Reiner; *W:* Leslie Dixon; *C:* Steve Mason; *M:* Patrick Williams.

That Sinking Feeling 🦴🦴🦴 **1979 (PG)** A group of bored Scot teenagers decide to steal 90 sinks from a plumber's warehouse. Well received early film from Forsyth is genuinely funny as the boys try to get rid of the sinks and turn a profit. **82m/C VHS.** *GB* Robert Buchanan, John Hughes, Billy Greenlees, Alan Love; *D:* Bill Forsyth; *W:* Bill Forsyth; *C:* Michael Coulter.

That Summer of White Roses 🦴🦴½ **1990 (R)** Compelling action drama about a lifeguard working at a resort in Nazi-occupied Yugoslavia and his love for a woman resistance fighter and her child. **98m/C VHS.** Tom Conti, Susan George, Rod Steiger; *D:* Rajko Grlic.

That Thing You Do! 🦴🦴🦴 **1996 (PG)** The Wonders, a small-town foursome, hit the big time in 1964 after a substitute drummer (like that could ever happen) adds some kick to the band's new song and sets the local kids a-fruggin'. Developed by freshman director/screenwriter Hanks (who also plays the band's Svengali-like record exec) as a diversion from Oscar hype, it's nostalgic and uncomplicated to a fault, but engaging nonetheless. Hanks clone Scott puts the beat into the charmingly wholesome quartet, while the underused Tyler is disarming as the put-upon girlfriend. Look quick or you'll miss bosom buddy Scolari as a TV host. Can't-get-it-out-of-your-head title track (played 11 times in the film) was selected from over 300 submissions after Hanks put out the call to music publishers. **110m/C VHS, DVD, Wide.** Giovanni Ribisi, Bryan Cranston, Holmes Osborne, Dawn Maxey, Sean M. Whalen, Clint Howard, Kathleen Kinmont, Barry Sobel, Gedde Watanabe, Jonathan Demme, Marc McClure, Colin Hanks, Tom Everett Scott, Johnathon Schaech, Liv Tyler, Steve Zahn, Ethan (Randall) Embry, Tom Hanks, Charlize Theron, Obba Babatunde, Peter Scolari, Alex Rocco, Bill Cobbs, Rita Wilson, Chris Isaak, Kevin Pollak; *D:* Tom Hanks; *W:* Tom Hanks; *C:* Tak Fujimoto; *M:* Howard Shore.

That Touch of Mink 🦴🦴½ **1962** In New York City, an unemployed secretary finds herself involved with a business tycoon. On a trip to Bermuda, both parties get an education as they play their game of "cat and mouse." Enjoyable romantic comedy. **99m/C VHS, DVD, Wide.** Cary Grant, Doris Day, Gig Young, Audrey Meadows, John Astin, Dick Sargent; *D:* Delbert Mann; *W:* Stanley Shapiro, Nate Monaster; *C:* Russell Metty; *M:* George Duning. Golden Globes '63: Film—Mus./Comedy.

That Uncertain Feeling 🦴🦴½ **1941** Light comedy about a couple's marital problems increasing when she develops the hiccups and a friendship with a flaky piano player. A remake of the earlier Lubitsch silent film, "Kiss Me Again." Available colorized. **86m/B VHS, DVD.** Merle Oberon, Melvyn Douglas, Burgess Meredith, Alan Mowbray, Eve Arden, Sig Rumann, Harry Davenport; *D:* Ernst Lubitsch; *W:* Donald Ogden Stewart, Walter Reisch; *C:* George Barnes; *M:* Werner R. Heymann.

That Was Then...This Is Now 🦴🦴 **1985 (R)** Lame adaptation of S.E. Hinton teen novel about a surly kid who is attached to his adoptive brother and becomes jealous when the brother gets a girlfriend. **102m/C VHS.** Emilio Estevez, Craig Sheffer, Kim Delaney, Jill Schoelen, Barbara Babcock, Frank Howard, Larry B. Scott, Morgan Freeman; *D:* Christopher Cain; *W:* Emilio Estevez.

That'll Be the Day 🦴🦴½ **1973 (PG)** The early rock 'n' roll of the 1950s is the only outlet for a frustrated young working-class Brit. Prequel to "Stardust." Good, meticulous realism; engrossing story. **91m/C VHS, DVD, Wide.** Ringo Starr, Keith Moon, David Essex, Rosemary Leach, James Booth, Billy Fury, Rosalind Ayres, Robert Lindsay, Brenda Bruce, Verna Harvey, James Ottoway, Deborah Watling, Beth Morris, Daphne Oxenford, Kim Braden, Ron Hackett, Johnny Shannon, Susan Holderness, The Debonairs; *D:* Claude Whatham; *W:* Ray Connolly; *C:* Peter Suschitzsky.

That's Adequate 🦴🦴 **1990 (R)** Mock documentary about a fictional film studio. Lampoons just about every movie made in the last 60 years. Premise might have been adequate for a sketch, but hardly for a feature-length film. Zaniness gets old quickly. **82m/C VHS.** Tony Randall, Robert Downey, Rocky Aoki, Bruce Willis, Robert Townsend, James Coco, Jerry Stiller, Peter Riegert, Susan Dey, Richard Lewis, Robert Vaughn, Renee Taylor, Stuart Pankin, Brother Theodore, Anne Bloom, Chuck McCann, Anne Meara; *D:* Harry Hurwitz; *W:* Harry Hurwitz.

That's Dancing! **1985 (G)** This anthology features some of film's finest moments in dance from classical ballet to break-dancing. **104m/C VHS.** Fred Astaire, Ginger Rogers, Ruby Keeler, Cyd Charisse, Gene Kelly, Shirley MacLaine, Liza Minnelli, Sammy Davis Jr., Mikhail Baryshnikov, Ray Bolger, Jennifer Beals, Dean Martin; *D:* Jack Haley Jr.; *M:* Henry Mancini.

That's Entertainment **1974 (G)** A compilation of scenes from the classic MGM musicals beginning with "The Broadway Melody" (1929) and ending with "Gigi" (1958). Great fun, especially for movie buffs. **132m/C VHS, Wide.** Judy Garland, Fred Astaire, Frank Sinatra, Gene Kelly, Esther Williams, Bing Crosby; *D:* Jack Haley Jr.; *M:* Henry Mancini.

That's Entertainment, Part 2 **1976 (G)** A cavalcade of great musical and comedy sequences from MGM movies of the past. Also stars Jeanette MacDonald, Nelson Eddy, the Marx Brothers, Laurel and Hardy, Jack Buchanan, Ann Miller, Mickey Rooney, Louis Armstrong, Oscar Levant, Cyd Charisse, Elizabeth Taylor, Maurice Chavalier, Bing Crosby, Jimmy Durante, Clark Gable, and the Barrymores. Not as unified as its predecessor, but priceless nonetheless. **129m/C VHS.** Fred Astaire, Gene Kelly.

That's Entertainment, Part 3 **1993 (G)** Third volume contains 62 MGM musical numbers from over 100 films, hosted by nine of the original stars, and is based on outtakes and unfinished numbers from studio archives. One new technique used here is a split-screen showing both the actual film with a behind-the-scenes shot that includes cameramen, set designers, and dancers scurrying around. Although it has its moments, TE3 doesn't generate the same reverence for Hollywood's Golden Age that its predecessors managed to do. That 18-year gap between sequels may say something about what the studio execs thought of their film vault's remainders. **113m/C VHS.** *D:* Bud Friedgen, Michael J. Sheridan; *W:* Bud Friedgen, Michael J. Sheridan; *M:* Marc Shaiman.

That's Life! 🦴🦴 **1986 (PG-13)** A lackluster semi-home movie starring Edwards' family and friends. A single weekend in the lives of a writer who's turning 60, his singer wife who has been diagnosed with cancer, and their family. **102m/C VHS, DVD.** Jack Lemmon, Julie Andrews, Sally Kellerman, Chris Lemmon, Emma Walton, Rob Knepper, Robert Loggia, Jennifer Edwards; *D:* Blake Edwards; *W:* Blake Edwards; *M:* Henry Mancini.

That's My Baby! 🦴 **1988 (PG-13)** A man wants his girlfriend to have their baby, but the only thing she wants is a career. War between the sexes poorly done. **97m/C VHS.** Sonja Smits, Timothy Webber; *D:* Edie Yolles, John Bradshaw.

That's the Way I Like It ½ **1999 (PG-13)** Homage to disco but set in the East rather than the West. It's 1977 and Sinapore clerk Hock (Pang) wants to win a disco tournament so he can buy a motorcycle. He drops his usual partner (Tang) for the flashier Julie (Francis) and the rivalry between the dance teams gets intense. But Hock just happens to have the spirit of the legendary "Saturday Night Fever" studster himself, Tony Manero (Pace), to give him that extra dance fever. **92m/C VHS, DVD, Wide.** Adrian Pang, Anna Belle Francis, Dominic Pace, Madeline Tang, Caleb Goh; ***D:*** Glen Goei; ***W:*** Glen Goei; ***C:*** Brian J. Breheny; ***M:*** Guy Gross.

Theatre of Blood *Much Ado about Murder* **1973 (R)** Shakespearean ham actor Edward Lionheart (Price) committed suicide after losing an award and being ridiculed by the critics. Now those same critics are being murdered in bizarre ways—in fact, their deaths parallel those in the plays of the Bard. Well, it's no big surprise to discover that Lionheart is indeed alive and committing the inventive crimes with the assistance of his lovely daughter, Edwina (Rigg). Top drawer comedy noir with a great supporting cast of Britain's best (and quite a bit of gore). **104m/C VHS, DVD, Wide.** *GB* Vincent Price, Diana Rigg, Ian Hendry, Robert Morley, Dennis Price, Diana Dors, Milo O'Shea, Harry Andrews, Coral Browne, Robert Coote, Jack Hawkins, Michael Hordern, Arthur Lowe; ***D:*** Douglas Hickox; ***W:*** Anthony Greville-Bell; ***C:*** Wolfgang Suschitzky; ***M:*** Michael Lewis.

Theatre of Death ½ *Blood Fiend; Female Fiend* **1967** Horror master Lee is back, this time as a theatre director in Paris. Meanwhile, police are baffled by a series of mysterious murders, each bearing a trace of vampirism. Well-plotted suspense. A racy voodoo dance sequence, often cut, is available on some video versions. **90m/C VHS, DVD, Wide.** Christopher Lee, Lelia Goldoni, Julian Glover, Evelyn Laye, Jenny Till, Ivor Dean; ***D:*** Samuel Gallu; ***W:*** Ellis Kadison, Roger Marshall; ***C:*** Gilbert Taylor.

Thelma & Louise **1991 (R)** Hailed as the first "feminist-buddy" movie, Sarandon and Davis bust out as best friends who head directly into one of the better movies of the year. Davis is the ditzy Thelma, a housewife rebelling against her dominating, unfaithful, abusive husband (who, rather than being disturbing, provides some of the best comic relief in the film). Sarandon is Louise, a hardened and world-weary waitress in the midst of an unsatisfactory relationship. They hit the road for a respite from their mundane lives, only to find violence and a part of themselves they never knew existed. Outstanding performances from Davis and especially Sarandon, with Pitt notable as the stud who gets Davis' motor revved. Director Scott has a fine eye for set details. **130m/C VHS, DVD, 8mm, Wide.** Susan Sarandon, Geena Davis, Harvey Keitel, Christopher McDonald, Michael Madsen, Brad Pitt, Timothy Carhart, Stephen Tobolowsky, Lucinda Jenney; ***D:*** Ridley Scott; ***W:*** Callie Khouri; ***C:*** Adrian Biddle; ***M:*** Hans Zimmer. Oscars '91: Orig. Screenplay; Natl. Bd. of Review '91: Actress (Sarandon), Actress (Davis); Natl. Soc. Film Critics '91: Support. Actor (Keitel); Writers Guild '91: Orig. Screenplay.

Them! **1954** A group of mutated giant ants wreak havoc on a southwestern town. The first of the big-bug movies, and far surpassing the rest, this is a classic fun flick. See how many names you can spot among the supporting cast. **93m/B VHS.** James Whitmore, Edmund Gwenn, Fess Parker, James Arness, Onslow Stevens, Jack Perrin, Joan Weldon, Sean McClory, Sandy Descher, Dub Taylor, William Schallert, Leonard Nimoy, Richard Deacon; ***D:*** Gordon Douglas; ***W:*** Ted Sherdeman; ***C:*** Sid Hickox; ***M:*** Bronislau Kaper.

The Theme *Tema* **1979** Esenin is a mediocre middle-aged playwright who knows his success comes from kowtowing to the party line. Trying to find inspiration he visits his native village where he meets the young Sasa, an artist who has refused to compromise. Although Esenin falls for her, Sasa has only contempt for his lack of principles and stays with her poet/lover, who is reduced to digging graves and has decided to emigrate to Israel. The film went unreleased for eight years because of its themes of artistic freedom and emigration. In Russian with English subtitles. **100m/C VHS.** *RU* Mikhail Ulyanov, Inna Churikova, Stanislav Lyubshin, Evgeny Vesnik, Sergei Nikonenko, Natalya Selezneva; ***D:*** Gleb Panfilov. Berlin Intl. Film Fest. '79: Golden Berlin Bear.

Theodora Goes Wild **1936** Tiny, priggish Lynnfield, Connecticut is shocked to discover that a scandalous best seller about smalltown life has been written pseudonymously by their very own Theodora Lynn (Dunne). When Theodora gets a chance to meet sophisticated New Yorker Michael Grant (Douglas), who did the illustrations for her book, she falls for him. But both must throw aside their own (and everyone else's) expectations and limitations for them to be happy. Dunne's first comedic lead role. **94m/B VHS.** Irene Dunne, Melvyn Douglas, Thomas Mitchell, Thurston Hall, Rosalind Keith, Spring Byington, Elisabeth Risdon, Margaret McWade; ***D:*** Richard Boleslawski; ***W:*** Sidney Buchman; ***C:*** Joseph Walker; ***M:*** Morris Stoloff.

Theodore Rex ½ **1995 (PG)** Futuristic comedy finds cynical, seasoned cop Katie Coltrane (Goldberg) furious at being teamed with Teddy, who just happens to be an eight-foot-tall, three-ton, returned-from-extinction Tyrannosaurus Rex (who has a taste for cookies). And Teddy's not exactly the brightest dinosaur on the block, which makes Katie's job all the harder when they stumble across a major crime caper. **92m/C VHS.** Whoopi Goldberg, Armin Mueller-Stahl, Richard Roundtree, Juliet Landau; ***D:*** Jonathan Betuel; ***W:*** Jonathan Betuel; ***C:*** David Tattersall; ***M:*** Robert Folk.

The Theory of Flight **1998 (R)** Awkward film reflects the relationship between Jane Hatchard (Bonham Carter), a wheelchair-bound woman suffering from a motor-neurological disease, and her eccentric, reluctant caregiver, Richard (Branagh). Richard is an artist who dreams of human flight, and one of his attempts gets him assigned to community service and to the independent, dying Jane. Her one wish is to lose her virginity but Richard won't oblige, although he's willing to set her up with a gigolo (Stevenson). Flirts with bad taste and is generally worth watching because of Bonham Carter's fierce performance. **98m/C VHS.** *GB* Helena Bonham Carter, Kenneth Branagh, Gemma Jones, Holly Aird, Ray Stevenson; ***D:*** Paul Greengrass; ***W:*** Richard Hawkins; ***C:*** Ivan Strasburg; ***M:*** Rolfe Kent.

There Goes Barder *Ca Va Barder* **1954** Constantine plays a con-man who's hired by a crooked ship owner to be a security agent. **90m/B VHS.** *FR* Eddie Constantine, May Britt, Jean Carmet, Jean Danet, Monique Van Vooren; ***D:*** John Berry; ***W:*** John Berry; ***C:*** Jacques Lemare.

There Goes Kelly ½ **1945** Moran and Miller are page boys at a radio station who try to get the station receptionist a singing job. When the vocalist on a popular show is murdered, the duo not only get their protege a break but get themselves a mystery to solve as well. **62m/B VHS.** Jackie Moran, Sidney Miller, Wanda McKay, Ralph Sanford, Jan Wiley, Anthony Warde; ***D:*** Phil Karlson.

There Goes My Baby ½ **1992 (R)** Eight California high school grads confront their futures on two nights in '65 (as the Watts riots ignite). There are Vietnam protests, flower children, would-be rock stars, friendships, and romantic complications. Yes, it sounds a lot like "American Graffiti" but the cast are winning and there's a good deal of affection without sinking to mawkishness. **99m/C VHS.** Dermot Mulroney, Rick Schroder, Kelli Williams, Jill Schoelen, Noah Wyle, Kristin Minter, Lucy Deakins, Kenny Ransom, Seymour Cassel, Paul Gleason, Frederick Coffin, Andrew (Andy) Robinson, Shon Greenblatt, J.E. Freeman; ***D:*** Floyd Mutrux; ***W:*** Floyd Mutrux.

There Goes the Neighborhood ½ **1992 (PG-13)** A dying convict tells prison psychiatrist Daniels where he has buried $8.5 million—under the home of neighbor O'Hara. Daniels and O'Hara try to discreetly dig up the fortune but when the neighborhood finds out everyone wants a chance at the cash. **88m/C VHS.** Jeff Daniels, Catherine O'Hara, Dabney Coleman, Hector Elizondo, Judith Ivey, Rhea Perlman, Harris Yulin, Jonathan Banks, Chazz Palminteri, Mary Gross; ***D:*** Bill Phillips; ***M:*** David Bell.

There Was a Crooked Man ½ **1970 (R)** An Arizona town gets some new ideas about law and order when an incorruptible and innovative warden takes over the town's prison. The warden finds he's got his hands full with one inmate determined to escape. Offbeat western black comedy supported by an excellent and entertaining production, with fine acting all around. **123m/C VHS.** Kirk Douglas, Henry Fonda, Warren Oates, Hume Cronyn, Burgess Meredith, John Randolph, Arthur O'Connell, Alan Hale Jr., Lee Grant; ***D:*** Joseph L. Mankiewicz; ***W:*** Robert Benton, David Newman; ***C:*** Harry Stradling Jr.

Theremin: An Electronic Odyssey **1995 (PG)** Profiles the life of Russian scientist Leon Theremin (who died in 1993), founder of electronic music, and his revolutionary musical invention, the Theremin. Martin located the 95-year-old Theremin in Moscow in 1991, interviewed him on camera, then brought him back to the U.S. to film reunions with friends and colleages he hadn't seen in 50 years. Martin's focus is on the impact of the Theremin on Hollywood movie scores heard in '50s sci-fi and thriller classics ("The Day the Earth Stood Still") and in popular music (The Beach Boys' "Good Vibrations" is commented on by Brian Wilson). Theremin's life proves as curious as his instrument, with his controversial interracial marriage to a ballet star, abduction by Russian agents, and imprisonment in a Soviet mental hospital. "Theremin" provides a fascinating and heartfelt tribute to the man's work and life. **84m/C VHS.** ***D:*** Steven M. Martin; ***W:*** Steven M. Martin; ***C:*** Robert Stone, Edward Lachman, Chris Lombardi; ***M:*** Hal Willner.

There's a Girl in My Soup **1970 (R)** Sellers is a gourmet who moonlights as a self-styled Casanova. Early post "Laugh-In" Hawn is the young girl who takes refuge at his London love nest when her boyfriend dumps her. Lust ensues. Has its funny parts, but not a highlight of anyone's career. Based on the hit play. **95m/C VHS.** *GB* Peter Sellers, Goldie Hawn, Diana Dors; ***D:*** Roy Boulting.

There's No Business Like Show Business **1954** A top husband and wife vaudevillian act make it a family affair. Filmed in CinemaScope, allowing for full and lavish musical numbers. Good performances and Berlin's music make this an enjoyable film. ♫When the Midnight Choo-Choo Leaves for Alabam; Let's Have Another Cup of Coffee; Play a Simple Melody; After You Get What You Want You Don't Want It; You'd Be Surprised; A Sailor's Not a Sailor; A Pretty Girl is Like a Melody; If You Believe Me; A Man Chases a Girl Until She Catches Him. **117m/C VHS, DVD, Wide.** Ethel Merman, Donald O'Connor, Marilyn Monroe, Dan Dailey, Johnny Ray, Mitzi Gaynor, Frank McHugh, Hugh O'Brian; ***D:*** Walter Lang; ***W:*** Phoebe Ephron, Henry Ephron; ***C:*** Leon Shamroy; ***M:*** Irving Berlin, Lionel Newman, Alfred Newman.

There's Nothing out There **1990** A group of seven teenagers spends Spring Break at a secluded mountain cabin. It sounds wonderful, but one of the boys (who claims to have seen every horror movie on video) knows the signs of a horror movie just waiting to happen. **91m/C VHS, DVD, Wide.** Craig Peck, Wendy Bednarz, Mark Collver, Bonnie Bowers, John Carhart III, Claudia Flores, Jeff Dachis, Lisa Grant; ***D:*** Rolfe Kanefsky; ***W:*** Rolfe Kanefsky; ***C:*** Ed Hershberger; ***M:*** Christopher Thomas.

There's Something about Mary **1998 (R)** Outrageously funny comedy that only veers from the gutter when it feels like taking a dip in the sewer. Set in 1985, the prologue introduces us to geeky Ted (Stiller), who gets a prom date with class knockout Mary (Diaz) after sticking up for her retarded brother Warren (Brown). The big date is not to be, however, for a vicious tuxedo zipper to the privates incapacitate Ted. Thirteen years later, Ted is still depressed over the incident, and still carries a torch for Mary. He hires Pat (Dillon), an oily detective with enormous choppers, to find her. Unfortunately for Ted, Pat is instantly smitten with Mary and lies. Ted learns the truth and heads to Miami to find her himself. Merely looking at the plot does not do justice to this lowbrow masterpiece. **118m/C VHS, DVD.** Ben Stiller, Matt Dillon, Cameron Diaz, Chris Elliott, Lee Evans, Lin Shaye, Jeffrey Tambor, Markie Post, Keith David, Jonathan Richman, W. Earl Brown, Khandi Alexander, Richard Tyson, Rob Moran, Lenny Clarke, Zen Gesner, Harland Williams, Richard Jenkins; ***Cameos:*** Brett Favre; ***D:*** Bobby Farrelly, Peter Farrelly; ***W:*** Bobby Farrelly, Peter Farrelly, Edward Decter, John J. Strauss; ***C:*** Mark Irwin; ***M:*** Jonathan Richman. MTV Movie Awards '99: Film, Female Perf. (Diaz), Villain (Dillon), Fight; N.Y. Film Critics '98: Actress (Diaz).

Therese **1986** Stylish biography of a young French nun and her devotion to Christ bordering on romantic love. Explores convent life. Real-life Therese died of TB and was made a saint. A directorial tour de force for Cavalier. In French with English subtitles. **90m/C VHS.** *FR* Catherine Mouchet, Aurore Prieto, Sylvie Habault, Ghislaine Mona; ***D:*** Alain Cavalier; ***W:*** Alain Cavalier; ***C:*** Isabelle Dedieu. Cannes '86: Special Jury Prize; Cesar '87: Cinematog., Director (Cavalier), Film, Writing.

Therese & Isabelle ½ **1967** Story of growing love and physical attraction between two French schoolgirls. On holiday together, they confront their mutual desires. Richly photographed soft porn based on the novel by Violet Leduc. Not vulgar, but certainly for adults. French with subtitles. **118m/B VHS, DVD.** Essy Persson, Anna Gael, Barbara Laage, Anne Vernon; ***D:*** Radley Metzger; ***W:*** Jesse Vogel; ***C:*** Hans Jura; ***M:*** Georges Auric.

These Girls Won't Talk **192?** Three female stars of early silent pictures are featured separately in: "Her Bridal Nightmare," "Campus Carmen," and "As Luck Would Have It." **50m/B VHS.** Colleen Moore, Carole Lombard, Betty Compson.

These Old Broads ½ **2001** Three actresses—Addie Holden (Collins), Kate Westbourne (MacLaine), and Piper Grayson (Reynolds)—starred in a '60s musical that over the years has become a cult hit. A TV exec (Carbonell) wants to engineer a TV reunion special but the trio hate each other. Maybe the agent (Taylor) they all share can persuade them. **95m/C VHS.** Debbie Reynolds, Joan Collins, Shirley MacLaine, Elizabeth Taylor, Jonathan Silverman, Peter Graves, Gene Barry, Pat Harrington; ***D:*** Matthew Diamond; ***W:*** Carrie Fisher, Elaine Pope; ***C:*** Eric Van Haren Noman; ***M:*** Guy Moon, Steve Tyrell. **TV**

These Three ½ **1936** A teenaged girl ruins the lives of two teachers by telling a malicious lie. Excellent cast. Script by Lillian Hellman, based on her play "The Children's Hour." Remade by the same director as "The Children's Hour" in 1961. **92m/B VHS.** Miriam Hopkins, Merle Oberon, Joel McCrea, Bonita Granville, Marcia Mae Jones, Walter Brennan, Margaret Hamilton, Catherine Doucet, Alma Kruger, Carmencita Johnson, Mary Ann Durkin, Frank McGlynn; ***D:*** William Wyler; ***W:*** Lillian Hellman; ***C:*** Gregg Toland; ***M:*** Alfred Newman.

Thesis *Tesis; Snuff* **1996 (R)** Angela (Torrent) is a university student writing her thesis on violence in the media. She comes across a snuff film that shows a girl being tortured to death. While trying to discover if the film is real, Angela finds out that the girl was a university student and that the film was actually shot on campus. Now it's Angela's life in danger. Suspenseful with a shocker ending. Spanish with subtitles. **121m/C VHS, DVD.** *SP* Ana Torrent, Fele Martinez, Eduardo Noriega; *D:* Alejandro Amenabar; *W:* Alejandro Amenabar, Mateo Gil; *C:* Hans Burman; *M:* Alejandro Amenabar, Mariano Marin.

They *Invasion from Inner Earth; Hell Fire* **1977** Beings from beneath the earth's crust take their first trip to the surface. **88m/C VHS.** Paul Dentzer, Debbie Pick, Nick Holt; *D:* Ito Rebane.

They All Kissed the Bride **1942** Tough cookie Margaret Drew (Crawford) must take over the family's trucking business when dad dies and support her ditzy mother (Burke) and younger sister Vivian (Parrish). Crusading newspaperman Michael Holmes (Douglas) blasts Margaret's business practices in print but when they finally meet, the sparks fly. Crawford manages the physical comedy well and Douglas is suitably charming. **87m/B VHS.** Joan Crawford, Melvyn Douglas, Billie Burke, Helen Parrish, Roland Young, Allen Jenkins, Emory Parnell; *D:* Alexander Hall; *W:* Andrew Solt, P.J. Wolfson; *C:* Joseph Walker; *M:* Werner R. Heymann.

They All Laughed **1981 (PG)** Three detectives become romantically involved with the women they were hired to investigate. Essentially light-hearted fluff with little or no script. Further undermined by the real-life murder of Stratten before the film's release. **115m/C VHS.** Ben Gazzara, John Ritter, Audrey Hepburn, Colleen Camp, Patti Hansen, Dorothy Stratten, Elizabeth Pena; *D:* Peter Bogdanovich; *W:* Peter Bogdanovich.

They Bite woof! **1995 (R)** A pornographic filmmaker's latest epic about lustful gill-men is filming at the same Florida beach where a zoologist is investigating reports of man-like fish monsters killing swimmers. Just a coincidence? Ultra- (and deliberately) cheesy; an unrated version is also available. **96m/C VHS.** Donna Frotscher, Nick Baldasare, Charlie Barnett, Ron Jeremy; *D:* Bret Piper; *W:* Bret Piper.

They Call It Sin *The Way of Life* **1932** Often told story of a young country girl heading to the Big Apple in search of her big break and "Mr. Right." Young is a chorus line girl romantically involved with her married producer (Calhern) while faithful admirer Brent waits nearby. Predictable plot adapted from the novel by Alberta Stedman Eagan. **68m/B VHS.** Loretta Young, George Brent, David Manners, Louis Calhern, Una Merkel, Joseph Cawthorn, Helen Vinson; *D:* Thornton Freeland; *W:* Lillie Hayward, Howard J. Green.

They Call Me Bruce? *A Fist Full of Chopsticks* **1982 (PG)** A bumbling Bruce Lee look-alike meets a karate-chopping Mafia moll in this farce. Silly premise creates lots of laughs. Followed by a sequel, "They Still Call Me Bruce." **88m/C VHS.** Johnny Yune, Margaux Hemingway; *D:* Elliot Hong; *W:* Tim Clawson.

They Call Me Mr. Tibbs! **1970 (R)** Lieutenant Virgil Tibbs (Poitier) investigates the murder of a prostitute. The prime suspect is his friend, the Reverend Logan Sharpe (Landau). He is torn between his duty as a policeman, his concern for the reverend, and the turmoil of his domestic life. Less tense, less compelling sequel to "In the Heat of the Night." **108m/C VHS, DVD, Wide.** Sidney Poitier, Barbara McNair, Martin Landau, Juano Hernandez, Anthony Zerbe, Ed Asner, Norma Crane, Jeff Corey; *D:* Gordon Douglas; *W:* Alan R. Trustman; *C:* Gerald Perry Finnerman; *M:* Quincy Jones.

They Call Me Sirr **2000** Based on the true story of Sirr Parker (Scott), a talented but poverty-stricken high school football player in South Central L.A. After Sirr and his younger brother are abandoned by their mother, Sirr struggles to look after his family (including an ailing grandmother) while keeping his place on the team. But the teen is finally forced to turn to his coach (Duncan) for help. **97m/C VHS, DVD.** Kente Scott, Michael Clarke Duncan; *D:* Robert Munic; *W:* Robert Munic; *C:* David Perrault; *M:* Sharon Farber. CABLE

They Call Me Trinity *Lo Chiamavano Trinita* **1972 (G)** Lazy drifter-gunslinger and his outlaw brother join forces with Mormon farmers to rout bullying outlaws. Spoofs every western cliche with relentless comedy, parodying "The Magnificent Seven" and gibing the spaghetti western. Followed by "Trinity is Still My Name." Dubbed. **110m/C VHS.** *IT* Terence Hill, Bud Spencer, Farley Granger, Steffen Zacharias; *D:* E.B. (Enzo Barboni) Clucher.

They Came from Beyond Space **1967** Aliens invade the earth and possess the brains of humans. They only want a few slaves to help them repair their ship which crashed on the moon. The only person able to stop them is a scientist with a steel plate in his head. Silly and forgettable. **86m/C VHS.** *GB* Robert Hutton, Michael Gough; *D:* Freddie Francis.

They Came from Within *Shivers; The Parasite Murders; Frissons* **1975 (R)** The occupants of a high-rise building go on a sex and violence spree when stricken by an aphrodisiac parasite. Queasy, sleazy, and weird. First major film by Cronenberg. **87m/C VHS, DVD.** *CA* Paul Hampton, Joe Silver, Lynn Lowry, Barbara Steele, Susan Petrie, Allan Migicovsky, Ronald Mlodzik; *D:* David Cronenberg; *W:* David Cronenberg; *C:* Robert Saad; *M:* Ivan Reitman.

They Came to Cordura **1959** Mexico, 1916: a woman and six American soldiers—five heroes and one who has been branded a coward—begin a journey to the military headquarters in Cordura. Slow journey brings out personalities. Look for "Bewitched" hubby Dick York. Based on Glendon Swarthout's best-seller. **123m/C VHS.** Gary Cooper, Rita Hayworth, Van Heflin, Tab Hunter, Dick York, Richard Conte; *D:* Robert Rossen.

They Died with Their Boots On **1941** The Battle of Little Big Horn is recreated Hollywood style. Takes liberties with historical fact, but still an exciting portrayal of General Custer's last stand. The movie also marks the last time de Havilland worked with Flynn. Also available colorized. **141m/B VHS.** Errol Flynn, Sydney Greenstreet, Anthony Quinn, Hattie McDaniel, Arthur Kennedy, Gene Lockhart, Regis Toomey, Olivia de Havilland, Charley Grapewin, G.P. (Tim) Huntley Jr., Frank Wilcox, Joseph (Joe) Sawyer, Eddie Acuff, Minor Watson, Tod Andrews, Stanley Ridges, John Litel, Walter Hampden, Joseph Crehan, Selmer Jackson, Gig Young, Dick Wessel; *D:* Raoul Walsh; *W:* Aeneas MacKenzie; *C:* Bert Glennon; *M:* Max Steiner.

They Drive by Night *The Road to Frisco* **1940** Two truck-driving brothers break away from a large company and begin independent operations. After an accident to Bogart, Raft is forced to go back to the company where Lupino, the boss's wife, becomes obsessed with him and kills her husband to gain the company and win Raft. When he rejects her, she accuses him of the murder. Well-plotted film with great dialogue. Excellent cast gives it their all. **97m/B VHS.** Humphrey Bogart, Ann Sheridan, George Raft, Ida Lupino, Alan Hale, Gale Page, Roscoe Karns, Charles Halton; *D:* Raoul Walsh.

They Got Me Covered **1943** Two WWII-era journalists get involved in a comic web of murder, kidnapping and romance. Hope is very funny and carries the rest of the cast. Look for Doris Day in a bit part and listen for Bing Crosby singing whenever Hope opens his cigarette case. **95m/B VHS, DVD.** Doris Day, Bob Hope, Dorothy Lamour, Otto Preminger, Eduardo Ciannelli, Donald Meek, Walter Catlett; *D:* David Butler; *W:* Harry Kurnitz; *C:* Rudolph Mate; *M:* Leigh Harline; *V:* Bing Crosby.

They Knew What They Wanted **1940** A lonely San Francisco waitress begins a correspondence romance with a grape grower and agrees to marry him after he sends her a photo which shows him as being young and handsome. She arrives to discover Laughton had sent her a picture of another man. An accident, an affair, and a pregnancy provide further complications before a satisfactory ending is suggested. Flawed adaptation of Sidney Howard's play still has strong performances from Lombard and Laughton. **96m/B VHS.** Charles Laughton, Carole Lombard, Harry Carey Sr., Karl Malden, William Gargan; *D:* Garson Kanin; *C:* Harry Stradling Sr.

They Live *Creepers* **1988 (R)** A semi-serious science-fiction spoof about a drifter who discovers an alien conspiracy. They're taking over the country under the guise of Reaganism, capitalism and yuppiedom. Screenplay written by Carpenter under a pseudonym. Starts out fun, deteriorates into cliches and bad special effects makeup. **88m/C VHS, DVD, Wide.** Roddy Piper, Keith David, Meg Foster, George "Buck" Flower, Peter Jason, Raymond St. Jacques, John Lawrence, Sy Richardson, Jason Robards III, Larry Franco, Wendy Brainard, Dana Bratton; *D:* John Carpenter; *W:* John Carpenter, Frank Armitage; *C:* Gary B. Kibbe; *M:* John Carpenter, Alan Howarth.

They Live by Night *The Twisted Road; Your Red Wagon* **1949** Bowie (Granger) is a naive young criminal who joins a prison break with hardened cons Chickamaw (da Silva) and T-Dub (Flippen) who then use him as an extra pair of hands in a bank heist. Bowie tries to go straight by marrying young Keechie (O'Donnell) but gets sucked back in by his criminal compatriots and winds up a fugitive with no hope. Classic film noir was Ray's first attempt at directing. Based on Edward Anderson's novel "Thieves Like Us," under which title it was remade in 1974. Compelling and suspenseful. **95m/B VHS.** Cathy O'Donnell, Farley Granger, Howard da Silva, Jay C. Flippen, Helen Craig, William Wright; *D:* Nicholas Ray; *W:* Nicholas Ray, Charles Schnee; *C:* George E. Diskant; *M:* Leigh Harline.

They Made Me a Criminal *I Became a Criminal; They Made Me a Fugitive* **1939** A champion prizefighter, believing he murdered a man in a drunken brawl, runs away. He finds refuge in the West with the Dead End Kids. Remake of "The Life of Jimmy Dolan." Berkeley was best-known for directing and choreographing musicals and surprisingly did very well with this movie. **92m/B VHS, DVD.** John Garfield, Ann Sheridan, Claude Rains, Leo Gorcey, Huntz Hall, Gabriel Dell, Bobby Jordan, Billy Halop; *D:* Busby Berkeley; *W:* Sig Herzig; *C:* James Wong Howe; *M:* Max Steiner.

They Made Me a Fugitive *I Became a Criminal; They Made Me a Criminal* **1947** Former RAF officer Clem Morgan (Howard) gets drawn into the excitement of the black market after the war but then is framed by his gang boss Narcey (Jones) when Morgan won't deal drugs. After he gets out of jail, Morgan heads back to Soho to get his revenge. Based on the novel "A Convict Has Escaped" by Jackson Budd. **96m/B VHS.** *GB* Trevor Howard, Griffith Jones, Sally Gray, Rene Ray, Mary Merrall, Vida Hope, Charles Farrell, Ballard Berkeley; *D:* Alberto Cavalcanti; *W:* Noel Langley; *C:* Otto Heller; *M:* Marius Francois Gaillard.

They Meet Again **1941** The final segment of the Dr. Christian series. The country doctor sets out to prove the innocence of a man who has been wrongly accused of stealing money. Slow moving and not particularly exciting. **68m/B VHS, 8mm.** Jean Hersholt, Dorothy Lovett; *D:* Erle C. Kenton.

They Met in Bombay **1941** Two jewel thieves team up in this romantic action-comedy, complete with exotic locations and two big boxoffice stars. A Japanese invasion makes Russell reconsider her life of crime and gives Gable a chance to play hero. Look for Alan Ladd in a bit part in his pre-"This Gun for Hire" days. Based on a story by John Kafka. **86m/B VHS.** Clark Gable, Rosalind Russell, Peter Lorre, Jessie Ralph, Reginald Owen, Eduardo Ciannelli, Alan Ladd; *D:* Clarence Brown; *W:* Anita Loos, Edwin Justus Mayer, Leon Gordon.

They Might Be Giants **1971 (G)** Woodward is a woman shrink named Watson who treats retired judge Scott for delusions that he is Sherlock Holmes. Scott's brother wants him committed so the family loot will come to him. Very funny in places; Woodward and Scott highlight a solid cast. **98m/C VHS, DVD.** George C. Scott, Joanne Woodward, Jack Gilford, Eugene Roche, Kitty Winn, F. Murray Abraham, M. Emmet Walsh; *D:* Anthony Harvey; *W:* James Goldman; *C:* Victor Kemper; *M:* John Barry.

They Never Come Back **1932** A boxer is thrown in jail and then stages a comeback. **62m/B VHS.** Regis Toomey, Dorothy Sebastian.

They Only Kill Their Masters **1972 (PG)** Garner plays a California police chief investigating the death of a wild beach town resident, supposedly killed by her doberman pinscher. He discovers the woman was actually drowned and there are any number of secrets to uncover. Mild whodunit. **98m/C VHS.** James Garner, Katharine Ross, June Allyson, Hal Holbrook, Harry Guardino, Christopher Connelly, Tom Ewell, Peter Lawford, Edmond O'Brien, Arthur O'Connell, Ann Rutherford, Art Metrano; *D:* James Goldstone; *M:* Perry Botkin.

They Paid with Bullets: Chicago 1929 *Tempo di Charleston - Chicago 1929* **1969** The story of one man's rise to power, and eventual downfall as a Mafia consigliatore. **88m/C VHS.** *SP* Peter Lee Lawrence, Ingrid Schoeller, William Bogart; *D:* Julio Diamante; *W:* Odoardo Fiory; *C:* Emilio Foriscot; *M:* Enrico Simonetti.

They Saved Hitler's Brain woof! *Madmen of Mandoras; The Return of Mr. H* **1964** Fanatical survivors of the Nazi holocaust gave eternal life to the brain of their leader in the last hours of the war. Now it's on a Caribbean island giving orders again. One of the truly great "bad" movies. Shot in pieces in the U.S., the Philippines, and elsewhere, with chunks of other films stuck in to hold the "story" together. **91m/B VHS, 8mm.** Walter Stocker, Audrey Caire, Nestor Paiva, Carlos Rivas, Dani Lynn, Bill Freed, John Holland, Scott Peters, Marshall Reed; *D:* David Bradley; *W:* Richard Miles, Steve Bennett; *C:* Stanley Cortez; *M:* Don Hulette.

They Shall Have Music *Melody of Youth; Ragged Angels* **1939** A poverty-stricken child hears a concert by violinist Heifetz and decides to become a musician. He joins Brennan's nearly bankrupt music school and persuades Heifetz to play at a benefit concert. Hokey but enjoyable Goldwyn effort to bring classical music to the big screen. ♫Rondo Capriccioso; Hora Staccato; Estrellita; Melody; Concerto in E Minor for Violin and Orchestra; Waltz in D Flat, Opus 64, No. 1; Cara Nome; Casta Diva. **101m/B VHS.** Walter Brennan, Joel McCrea, Gene Reynolds, Jascha Heifetz, Marjorie Main, Porter Hall, Andrea Leeds, Terence (Terry) Kilburn; *D:* Archie Mayo.

They Shoot Horses, Don't They? **1969 (R)** Powerful period piece depicting the desperation of the Depression Era. Contestants enter a dance marathon in the hopes of winning a cash prize, not realizing that they will be driven to exhaustion. Fascinating and tragic. **121m/C VHS, DVD.** Jane Fonda, Michael Sarrazin, Susannah York, Gig Young, Red Buttons, Bonnie Bedelia, Bruce Dern, Allyn Ann McLerie, Chaing I, Al Lewis, Michael Conrad; *D:* Sydney Pollack; *W:* James Poe; *C:* Philip Lathrop; *M:* Johnny Green. Oscars '69: Support. Actor (Young); British Acad. '70: Support. Actress (York); Golden Globes '70: Support. Actor (Young); N.Y. Film Critics '69: Actress (Fonda).

They Still Call Me Bruce **1986 (PG)** A Korean searches for the American who saved his life when he was young and instead becomes big brother to an orphan. Supposedly a sequel to "They Call Me Bruce," but has little in common with it. Poorly done and not particularly entertaining. **91m/C VHS.** Johnny Yune, Robert Guillaume, Pat Paulsen; *D:* Johnny Yune.

They Watch *They* **1993 (PG-13)** Workaholic Bergin neglects his family and suffers the consequences when his young daughter dies in an auto accident. In fact, he's so distressed that he relies on blind psychic Redgrave to get in touch with his little girl's spirit. Based on the story "They" by Rudyard Kipling. **100m/C VHS.** Patrick Bergin, Vanessa Redgrave, Valerie Mahaffey; *D:* John Korty; *W:* Edithe Swensen; *M:* Gerald Gouriet. TV

They Went That-a-Way & That-a-Way woof! **1978 (PG)** Two bumbling deputies pose as convicts in this madcap prison caper. Terrible re-hash of

Laurel-and-Hardy has nothing going for it. **96m/C VHS.** Sonny Shroyer, Tim Conway, Richard Kiel, Chuck McCann; ***D:*** Edward Montagne; ***W:*** Tim Conway.

They Were Expendable ♂♂♂½ **1945** Two American captains pit their PT boats against the Japanese fleet. Based on the true story of a PT boat squadron based in the Philippines during the early days of WWII. One of the best (and most underrated) WWII films. Also available in a colorized version. **135m/B VHS, DVD.** Robert Montgomery, John Wayne, Donna Reed, Jack Holt, Ward Bond, Cameron Mitchell, Leon Ames, Marshall Thompson, Paul Langton, Donald Curtis, Jeff York, Murray Alper, Jack Pennick, Alex Havier, Charles Trowbridge, Robert Barrat, Bruce Kellogg, Louis Jean Heydt, Russell Simpson, Philip Ahn, Betty Blythe, William B. Davidson, Pedro de Cordoba, Arthur Walsh, Harry Tenbrook, Tim Murdock, Vernon Steele; ***D:*** John Ford; ***W:*** Frank Wead; ***C:*** Joseph August; ***M:*** Herbert Stothart, Eric Zeisl.

They Were So Young ♂♂½ **1955** European models become the pawns of wealthy Brazilian magnates when they are sent to South America. They are threatened with death if they do not cooperate. The scenes were shot in Italy and Berlin. Well acted and believable, although rather grim story. **78m/B VHS.** *GE* Scott Brady, Johanna (Hannerl) Matz, Raymond Burr; ***D:*** Kurt Neumann.

They Were Ten ♂♂½ **1961** Ten Soviet Jews make Palestine their home in the 1800s despite Arab and Turkish persecution and pressures among themselves. In Hebrew with English subtitles. **105m/B VHS.** *IS* Ninette, Oded Teomi, Leo Filer, Yosef Safra; ***D:*** Baruch Dienar.

They Won't Believe Me ♂♂♂ **1947** A man plots to kill his wife, but before he does, she commits suicide. He ends up on trial for her "murder." Interesting acting by Young and Hayward against type. Surprising, ironic ending. **95m/B VHS.** Robert Young, Susan Hayward, Rita Johnson, Jane Greer; ***D:*** Irving Pichel.

They Won't Forget ♂♂♂½ **1937** When a young girl is murdered in a southern town, personal interests take precedence over justice. Turner is excellent in her first billed role, as are the other actors. Superb script, and expert direction by LeRoy pulls it all together. Based on Ward Greene's "Death in the Deep South." **95m/B VHS.** Claude Rains, Otto Kruger, Lana Turner, Allyn Joslyn, Elisha Cook Jr., Edward Norris; ***D:*** Mervyn LeRoy; ***W:*** Robert Rossen, Aben Kandel.

They're Playing with Fire woof! **1984 (R)** An English teacher seduces a student and gets him involved in a murder plot to gain an inheritance. Turns out someone else is beating them to the punch. Sleazy semi-pornographic slasher. **96m/C VHS.** Sybil Danning, Eric Brown, Andrew Prine, Paul Clemens, K.T. Stevens, Alvy Moore; ***D:*** Howard (Hikmet) Avedis; ***W:*** Howard (Hikmet) Avedis.

Thick as Thieves ♂♂½ **1999 (R)** Master thief Mackin (Baldwin) likes to get the job done and then return to his quietly sophisticated private life. Pointy (White) is the arrogant up-and-comer, with mob ties, who wants to eliminate the competition by setting Mackin up for a crime. The dual between the duo upsets mob boss Sal Capetti (Byrd) and has police officer Petrone (DeMornay) also very interested. **93m/C VHS, DVD, Wide.** Alec Baldwin, Michael Jai White, Rebecca DeMornay, Andre Braugher, Bruce Greenwood, David Byrd, Richard Edson, Khandi Alexander, Robert Miano, Janeane Garofalo, Julia Sweeney, Ricky Harris, Michael Jace; ***D:*** Scott Sanders; ***W:*** Scott Sanders, Arthur Krystal; ***C:*** Chris Walling; ***M:*** Christophe Beck. CABLE

Thicker Than Water ♂♂ **1993** Eerie psychological thriller exploring the relationship between identical twins. Sam Crawford (Pryce) is a successful doctor, happily married to Jo (Russell), whose sister Debbie (Russell again) is completely different in temperament. The two share a strong psychic bond, however, and when Jo dies in a suspicious hit-and-run accident Debbie feels compelled to make Sam her own. Based on the novel by Dylan Jones. **150m/C VHS, DVD.** *GB* Theresa Russell, Jonathan Pryce, Robert Pugh; ***D:*** Marc Evans; ***W:*** Trevor Preston.

The Thief ♂♂ **1952** An American commits treason and is overcome by guilt. Novel because there is not one word of dialogue, though the gimmmick can't sustain the ordinary story. A product of the Communist scare of the 1950s, it tends to be pretentious and melodramatic. **84m/B VHS, DVD.** Ray Milland, Rita Gam, Martin Gabel, Harry Bronson, John McKutcheon; ***D:*** Russell Rouse; ***W:*** Russell Rouse, Clarence Greene; ***C:*** Sam Leavitt; ***M:*** Herschel Burke Gilbert.

Thief **1971** A successful businessman (Crenna) attempts to put his criminal past behind him. He's trapped when looking for a quick way to get some money to pay off a gambling debt. Well-written and -directed drama with tepid acting. **74m/C VHS.** Richard Crenna, Angie Dickinson, Cameron Mitchell, Hurd Hatfield, Robert Webber; ***D:*** William A. Graham. TV

Thief ♂♂♂ *Violent Streets* **1981 (R)** A big-time professional thief likes working solo, but decides to sign up with the mob in order to make one more big score and retire. He finds out it's not that easy. Taut and atmospheric thriller is director Mann's feature film debut. **126m/C VHS, DVD.** James Caan, Tuesday Weld, Willie Nelson, James Belushi, Elizabeth Pena, Robert Prosky, Dennis Farina; ***D:*** Michael Mann; ***W:*** Michael Mann; ***C:*** Donald E. Thorin; ***M:*** Tangerine Dream.

The Thief ♂♂ *Vor* **1997 (R)** Postwar Russian drama set in 1952. Katya (Rednikova) is a young widow with a six year-old-son, Sanya (Philipchuk). She's traveling by train when a soldier named Tolyan (Mashkov) enters their compartment. But the end of the trip, Katya's decided to go off with Tolyan and the threesome become a family. But Tolyan harbors a violent streak and Katya also discovers that Tolyan is an imposter—he's not a soldier but a thief. Still, she loves him and soon becomes his accomplice. Russian with subtitles. **92m/C VHS, DVD, Wide.** *RU* Vladimir Mashkov, Ekaterina Rednikova, Misha Philipchuk; ***D:*** Pavel Chukhrai; ***W:*** Pavel Chukhrai; ***C:*** Vladimir Klimov; ***M:*** Vladimir Dashkevich.

The Thief and the Cobbler ♂♂♂½ **1996 (G)** Musically animated fairy tale about Tack, a humble cobbler (Broderick) who aids the clever and beautiful Princess Yum Yum (Beals) when their town's golden treasures are stolen. Legendary villain Price lends his voice as the evil Zig Zag. Three time Oscar winning director Williams (of "Who Framed Roger Rabbit?" fame), and a team of animators led by Harris (part of the team that created Bugs Bunny) created sophisticated optical illusions that the team dubbed "two and a half dimensional." Incorporating intricate lighting, shadows and smooth motion, the project took almost three decades to complete. Soundtrack performed by the London Symphony Orchestra. **72m/C VHS.** ***D:*** Richard Williams; ***W:*** Richard Williams; ***C:*** John Leatherbarrow; ***M:*** Robert Folk; ***V:*** Vincent Price, Matthew Broderick, Jennifer Beals, Eric Bogosian, Toni Collette, Jonathan Winters, Clive Revill, Kenneth Williams, Clinton Sundberg, Thick Wilson.

The Thief of Bagdad ♂♂♂½ **1940** A wily young thief enlists the aid of a powerful genie to outwit the Grand Vizier of Baghdad. An Arabian Nights spectacular with lush photography, fine special effects, and striking score. Outstanding performance by Ingram as the genie. **106m/C VHS.** *GB* Sabu, Conrad Veidt, June Duprez, Rex Ingram, John Justin, Miles Malleson, Morton Selten, Mary Morris; ***D:*** Tim Whelan, Michael Powell, Ludwig Berger, Alexander Korda, Zoltan Korda, William Cameron Menzies; ***W:*** Lajos Biro, Miles Malleson; ***C:*** Georges Perinal; ***M:*** Miklos Rozsa. Oscars '40: Color Cinematog.

The Thief of Baghdad ♂♂♂ **1924** The classic silent crowd-pleaser, about a roguish thief who uses a genie's magic to outwit Baghdad's evil Caliph. With famous special effects in a newly struck print, and a new score by Davis based on Rimsky-Korsakov's "Scheherezade." Remade many times. **153m/B VHS, DVD.** Douglas Fairbanks Sr., Snitz Edwards, Charles Belcher, Anna May Wong, Etta Lee, Brandon Hurst, Sojin, Julanne Johnston; ***D:*** Raoul Walsh; ***M:*** Carl Davis. Natl. Film Reg. '96.

Thief of Baghdad ♂♂ *Il Ladro Di Bagdad; Le Voleur De Bagdad* **1961** An Arabian Nights fantasy about a thief in love with a Sultan's daughter who has been poisoned. He seeks out the magical blue rose which is the antidote. Not as lavish as the previous two productions by this title, nor as much fun. **89m/C VHS.** *IT* Georgia Moll, Steve Reeves; ***D:*** Arthur Lubin.

The Thief of Baghdad ♂♂½ **1978 (G)** A fantasy-adventure about a genie, a prince, beautiful maidens, a happy-go-lucky thief, and magic. Easy to take, but not an extraordinary version of this oft-told tale. Ustinov is fun as he tries to marry off his daughter. **101m/C VHS.** Peter Ustinov, Roddy McDowall, Terence Stamp, Frank Finlay, Ian Holm; ***D:*** Clive Donner. TV

Thief of Hearts ♂♂ **1984 (R)** A thief steals a woman's diary when he's ransacking her house. He then pursues the woman, using his secret knowledge. Slick, but too creepy. Re-edited with soft porn scenes in some video versions. Stewart's first film. **101m/C VHS, DVD, Wide.** Steven Bauer, Barbara Williams, John Getz, Christine Ebersole, George Wendt; ***D:*** Douglas Day Stewart; ***W:*** Douglas Day Stewart; ***C:*** Andrew Laszlo; ***M:*** Harold Faltermeyer.

The Thief Who Came to Dinner ♂♂ **1973 (PG)** A computer analyst and a wealthy socialite team up to become jewel thieves and turn the tables on Houston's high society set. Comedy plot gets complex, though O'Neal and Bisset are likeable. Early Clayburgh role as O'Neal's ex. Based on a novel by Terence Lore Smith. **103m/C VHS.** Ryan O'Neal, Jacqueline Bisset, Warren Oates, Jill Clayburgh, Ned Beatty, Gregory Sierra, Michael Murphy, Austin Pendleton, John Hillerman, Charles Cioffi; ***D:*** Bud Yorkin; ***W:*** Walter Hill; ***M:*** Henry Mancini.

Thieves Like Us ♂♂♂½ **1974 (R)** Story of doomed lovers during the Depression is thoughtfully told by Altman. Older criminals Remsen and Schuck escape from jail with young killer Carradine. They only know one way to make a living—robbing banks—and it isn't long before they're once more working at their trade. They get a lot of press but they have a distinct problem. They're not really very good at what they do. Cops on their trail, the gang tries, unsuccessfully, to survive. Fletcher's film debut as Remsen's sister-in-law. Good period atmosphere and strong characters. Based on the novel by Edward Anderson and previously filmed as "They Live by Night." **123m/C VHS.** Keith Carradine, Shelley Duvall, Bert Remsen, John Schuck, Louise Fletcher, Anne Latham, Tom Skerritt; ***D:*** Robert Altman; ***W:*** Joan Tewkesbury, Calder Willingham, Robert Altman.

Thieves of Fortune woof! **1989 (R)** Former Miss Universe stars as a contestant in a high stakes fortune hunt that spans half the globe. She meets with more than her share of action-packed encounters among the ruffians who compete for the $28 million purse. Implausible; horrible script; cliched. **100m/C VHS.** Michael Nouri, Lee Van Cleef, Shawn Weatherly.

The Thin Blue Line ♂♂♂½ **1988** The acclaimed docudrama about the 1977 shooting of a cop in Dallas County, and the incorrect conviction of Randall Adams for the crime. A riveting, spellbinding experience. Due to the film's impact and continued lobbying by Morris, Adams is now free. **101m/C VHS.** ***D:*** Errol Morris; ***W:*** Errol Morris; ***C:*** Robert Chappell, Stefan Czapsky; ***M:*** Philip Glass. Natl. Film Reg. '01.

Thin Ice ♂♂♂ **1937** Successful musical romance featuring European prince Power falling for commoner Henie. A fine score, solid script, and Henie's excellent ice skating routines make this her best film. Based on the play "Der Komet" by Attila Obok. ♫I'm Olga from the Volga; My Swiss Hillbilly; My Secret Love Affair; Over Night. **78m/B VHS.** Sonja Henie, Tyrone Power, Arthur Treacher, Raymond Walburn, Joan Davis, Alan Hale, Sig Rumann, Melville Cooper, Maurice Cass, George Givot, Torben Meyer; ***D:*** Sidney Lanfield; ***W:*** Boris Ingster, Milton Sperling.

A Thin Line Between Love and Hate ♂ **1996 (R)** Writer/director/star Lawrence shows that there's no line between a crude, foulmouthed ego trip and an unfunny, unsuspenseful film. Darnell Wright is a smooth talker constantly on the lookout for women to conquer and discard. Eventually, he meets the wrong lady (Whitfield), a classic movie psycho who turns his life upside down. Drawing heavily from "Fatal Attraction," this halfhearted effort offers bad pacing, a weak script, and totally unsympathetic characters, which could almost be overlooked if it was at all funny. Whitfield holds the flick's only redeeming value as the femme fatale. **106m/C VHS, DVD.** Tracy Morgan, Martin Lawrence, Lynn Whitfield, Regina King, Bobby Brown, Della Reese, Roger E. Mosley, Malinda Williams, Darryl (Chill) Mitchell, Simbi Khali; ***D:*** Martin Lawrence; ***W:*** Martin Lawrence, Bentley Kyle Evans, Kenny Buford, Kim Bass; ***C:*** Francis Kenny; ***M:*** Roger Troutman.

The Thin Man ♂♂♂½ **1934** Married sleuths Nick (Powell) and Nora (Loy) Charles investigate the mysterious disappearance of a wealthy inventor. Charming and sophisticated, this was the model for all husband-and-wife detective teams that followed. Don't miss Asta, their wire-hair terrier. Based on the novel by Dashiell Hammett. Its enormous popularity triggered five sequels, starting with "After the Thin Man." **90m/B VHS.** William Powell, Myrna Loy, Maureen O'Sullivan, Cesar Romero, Porter Hall, Nat Pendleton, Minna Gombell, Natalie Moorhead, Edward Ellis; ***D:*** Woodbridge S. Van Dyke; ***W:*** Albert Hackett, Frances Goodrich; ***C:*** James Wong Howe. Natl. Film Reg. '97.

The Thin Man Goes Home ♂♂½ **1944** Married sleuths Nick and Nora Charles solve a mystery with Nick's disapproving parents looking on in the fifth film from the "Thin Man" series. Despite a three-year gap and slightly less chemistry between Powell and Loy, audiences welcomed the skinny guy. Sequel to "Shadow of the Thin Man"; followed by "Song of the Thin Man." **100m/B VHS.** William Powell, Myrna Loy, Lucile Watson, Gloria De Haven, Anne Revere, Harry Davenport, Helen Vinson, Lloyd Corrigan, Donald Meek, Edward Brophy, Charles Halton; ***D:*** Richard Thorpe.

The Thin Red Line ♂♂½ **1964** First adaptation of the James Jones novel about the fight for Guadalcanal focuses on the relationship between Sgt. Welsh (Warden) and Pvt. Doll (Dullea). As battle experience hardens Doll, the mutual hatred the two have changes to a grudging respect. Effectively portrays the dehumanizing psychological effects of war. **99m/B VHS, DVD.** Keir Dullea, Jack Warden, James Philbrook, Kieron Moore, Ray Daley, Merlyn Yordan, Bob Kanter, Stephen Levy; ***D:*** Andrew Marton; ***W:*** Bernard Gordon; ***C:*** Manuel Berenguer; ***M:*** Malcolm Arnold.

The Thin Red Line ♂♂♂ **1998 (R)** After a long hiatus, director Malick returns in this epic WWII saga about a rifle company fighting at Guadalcanal. Visually stunning and focused on the inner thoughts, feelings, and philosophical leanings of the soldiers, the film sacrifices plot and continuity to study the questions of Man vs. Nature and the Origin of Evil. Plot difficulties are highlighted by the physical similarities of relative newcomers Chaplin and Caviezel. Combat scenes are, naturally, beautifully shot and effective, while the relationship between Penn and Caviezel makes the biggest impression among the many subplots (some of which go nowhere) and the star-laden, large cast. Based on the 1962 novel by James Jones. **170m/C VHS, DVD.** Kirk Acevedo, Miranda Otto, Nick Stahl, James Caviezel, Adrien Brody, Sean Penn, Nick Nolte, John Cusack, George Clooney, Woody Harrelson, Ben Chaplin, Elias Koteas, Jared Leto, John Travolta, Tim Blake Nelson, John C. Reilly, John Savage, Arie Verveen, David Harrod, Thomas Jane, Paul Gleason, Penelope Allen, Don Harvey, Shawn Hatosy, Donal Logue, Dash Mihok, Larry Romano; ***D:*** Terrence Malick; ***W:*** Terrence Malick; ***C:*** John Toll; ***M:*** Hans Zimmer. N.Y. Film Critics '98: Director (Malick); Natl. Soc. Film Critics '98: Cinematog.

The Thing 🦴🦴🦴½ *The Thing from Another World* **1951** One of the best of the Cold War allegories and a potent lesson to those who won't eat their vegetables. Sci fi classic about an alien craft and creature (Arness in monster drag), discovered by an Arctic research team. The critter is accidentally thawed and then wreaks havoc, sucking the blood from sled dog and scientist alike. It's a giant seed-dispersing vegetable run amuck, unaffected by missing body parts, bullets, or cold. In other words, Big Trouble. Excellent direction, assisted substantially by producer Hawks, and supported by strong performances. Available colorized; remade in 1982. Loosely based on "Who Goes There?" by John Campbell. **87m/B VHS, Wide.** James Arness, Kenneth Tobey, Margaret Sheridan, Dewey Martin, Robert Cornthwaite, Douglas Spencer, James Young, Robert Nichols, William (Bill) Self, Eduard Franz, Sally Creighton, John Dierkes, George Fenneman; ***D:*** Christian Nyby, Howard Hawks; ***W:*** Charles Lederer, Ben Hecht; ***C:*** Russell Harlan; ***M:*** Dimitri Tiomkin. Natl. Film Reg. '01.

The Thing 🦴🦴½ **1982 (R)** A team of scientists at a remote Antarctic outpost discover a buried spaceship with an unwelcome alien survivor still alive. Bombastic special effects overwhelm the suspense and the solid cast. Less a remake of the 1951 science fiction classic than a more faithful version of John Campbell's short story "Who Goes There?," since the seeds/spores take on human shapes. **109m/C VHS, DVD.** Kurt Russell, Wilford Brimley, T.K. Carter, Richard Masur, Keith David, Richard Dysart, David Clennon, Donald Moffat, Thomas G. Waites, Charles Hallahan; ***D:*** John Carpenter; ***W:*** Bill Lancaster; ***C:*** Dean Cundey; ***M:*** Ennio Morricone.

The Thing Called Love 🦴🦴½ **1993 (PG-13)** Take last year's surprise hit "Singles" and replace grunge rock and Seattle with Country/Western and Nashville for this unsentimental tale of four 20-something singles trying to make their mark in the world of country music. The idea for the plot comes from the real-life Bluebird Cafe—the place where all aspiring singers and songwriters want to perform. Phoenix, Mathis, Mulroney, and Bullock did their own singing; look for Oslin as the Cafe owner. Phoenix's last completed film role. **116m/C VHS.** River Phoenix, Samantha Mathis, Sandra Bullock, Dermot Mulroney, K.T. Oslin, Anthony Clark, Webb Wilder; ***Cameos:*** Trisha Yearwood; ***D:*** Peter Bogdanovich; ***W:*** Allan Moyle, Carol Heikkinen; ***C:*** Peter James.

The Thing with Two Heads 🦴🦴½ **1972 (PG)** The inspired box copy says it all: "They share the same body...but hate each other's guts!" Max Kirshner (Milland), a white racist surgeon, plans to cheat death by having his head attached to another body. Imagine his surprise when he finds his noggin stitched onto black Jack Moss (Grier), right next to the original head. Nobody involved is taking the material too seriously. **93m/C DVD, Wide.** Ray Milland, Roosevelt "Rosie" Grier, Don Marshall, Roger Perry, Kathrine Baumann, Lee Frost, Wes Bishop, Rick Baker; ***D:*** Lee Frost; ***W:*** James Gordon White; ***C:*** Jack Steely; ***M:*** Robert O. Ragland.

Things 🦴 **198?** A man creates a monster during his freakish experiments with artificial insemination. The monster returns to his house seeking revenge, and the man's visiting brother and a friend disappear, probably a clever move given their lackluster circumstances. **90m/C VHS.** Barry Gillis, Amber Lynn, Doug Bunston, Bruce Roach; ***D:*** Andrew Jordan.

Things 🦴🦴½ **1993** Two horror tales told by a jilted wife who's holding her husband's mistress hostage. "The Box" finds evil Mayor Black (Delama) incensed about a newly opened brothel in his hick Nevada town. So he decides to teach the hookers a lesson with the help of a bizarre, boxed creature that's with him at all times. "Thing in a Jar" finds an abusive husband and his mistress plotting to kill his mousy wife. Only the murder victim comes back to haunt the deadly duo—at least parts of her do. Nicely grotesque special effects courtesy of Mike Tristano. **85m/C VHS.** Neil Delama, Trey Howard, Debra Stevens, Courtney Lercara, Kinder Hunt; ***Cameos:*** Jeff Burr; ***D:*** Dennis Devine, Jay Woelfel; ***W:*** Dennis Devine, Steve Jarvis, Mike Bowler.

Things 2 🦴🦴½ **1997** Sequel to 1993's "Things." When a pizza delivery girl gets stranded at the creepy home of a strange horror novelist he entertains her with two tales of terror. Oh yes, if the girl can solve the mysteries within the stories, she gets to live. If not, well... The first has a cheating wife plotting to rid herself of hubby by using the ferocious small creature (with big teeth) she's trained to kill on her command. But the creature has other ideas. The second story finds a fashion photographer suspecting that a serial killer stalking her neighborhood may not be human. **85m/C VHS.** Angela Eads, David Hussey, Rich Ward, Margie Rey; ***D:*** Steve Jarvis, Dennis Devine, Mike Bowler; ***W:*** Steve Jarvis, Dennis Devine, Mike Bowler; ***C:*** Craig Incardone; ***M:*** Adam Karpel.

Things Change 🦴🦴🦴 **1988 (PG)** An old Italian shoeshine guy agrees, for a fee, to be a fall guy for the Mafia. A lower-echelon mob hood, assigned to watch over him, decides to give the old guy a weekend of fun in Vegas before going to jail. Director Mamet co-wrote the screenplay with Silverstein, best-known for his children's books ("Where the Sidewalk Ends," "The Giving Tree"). Combines charm and menace with terrific performances, especially from Ameche and Mantegna. **114m/C VHS, DVD.** Joe Mantegna, Don Ameche, Robert Prosky, J.J. Johnston, Ricky Jay, Mike Nussbaum, Jack Wallace, Dan Conway, J.T. Walsh, William H. Macy; ***D:*** David Mamet; ***W:*** David Mamet, Shel Silverstein; ***M:*** Alaric Jans. Venice Film Fest. '80: Actor (Ameche); Venice Film Fest. '88: Actor (Mantegna).

Things Happen at Night 🦴 **1948** Scientist and insurance investigator determine that friendly ghost has possessed a family's youngest daughter. Not much happens. **79m/B VHS.** *GB* Gordon Harker, Alfred Drayton, Robertson Hare, Olga Lindo, Wylie Watson; ***D:*** Francis Searle.

Things in Their Season 🦴🦴½ **1974** Melodrama about the imminent death of the mother of a Wisconsin farm family who makes those around her realize the value of happiness. Neal is excellent, rest of cast better than average in a well-told and sincere film. **79m/C VHS.** Patricia Neal, Ed Flanders, Marc Singer, Meg Foster; ***D:*** James Goldstone. **TV**

The Things of Life 🦴🦴🦴 *Les Choses De La Vie* **1970** A car crash makes a man re-evaluate his life, goals, and loves. In the end he must choose the course of his future and decide between his wife and mistress. In French with English subtitles. **90m/C VHS, Wide.** *FR* Romy Schneider, Michel Piccoli, Lea Massari; ***D:*** Claude Sautet.

Things to Come 🦴🦴🦴½ **1936** Using technology, scientists aim to rebuild the world after a lengthy war, followed by a plague and other unfortunate events. Massey and Scott each play two roles, in different generations. Startling picture of the world to come, with fine sets and good acting. Based on an H.G. Wells story, "The Shape of Things to Come." **92m/B VHS, DVD.** *GB* Raymond Massey, Margaretta Scott, Ralph Richardson, Cedric Hardwicke, Derrick DeMarney, Maurice Braddell; ***D:*** William Cameron Menzies; ***W:*** H.G. Wells; ***C:*** Georges Perinal; ***M:*** Arthur Bliss.

Things to Do in Denver When You're Dead 🦴🦴🦴 **1995 (R)** Jimmy the Saint (Garcia) is an ex-mobster gone straight who is called upon by his former boss, the Man With the Plan (Walken), to do one last easy-money job. Jimmy agrees and rounds up his old gang, a colorfully off-color group which includes Pieces (Lloyd), a porn movie projectionist and Critical Bill (Williams), a hair-trigger psycho who works in a funeral parlor. The job goes awry and the group becomes a target of hitman Mr. Shhh (Buscemi). Hipster dialogue, crime-gone-wrong formula, and the presence of Buscemi instantly scream Tarantino rip-off, but the performances make it a worthwhile genre entry. **115m/C VHS, DVD.** Andy Garcia, Christopher Lloyd, William Forsythe, Bill Nunn, Treat Williams, Jack Warden, Steve Buscemi, Fairuza Balk, Gabrielle Anwar, Christopher Walken, Glenn Plummer, Don Cheadle, Bill Cobbs, Josh Charles, Michael Nicolosi, Marshall Bell, Sarah Trigger, Jenny McCarthy, Tommy (Tiny) Lister; ***D:*** Gary Fleder; ***W:*** Scott Rosenberg; ***C:*** Elliot Davis; ***M:*** Michael Convertino.

Things You Can Tell Just by Looking at Her 🦴🦴½ **2000 (PG-13)** Ensemble female cast tells five stories that intersect in odd ways. Dr. Keener (Close) gets unhappy romantic news from tarot card reader Christine (Flockhart), whose own lover, Lilly (Golino), is terminally ill. Meanwhile, Rebecca (Hunter) has an abortion (performed by Dr. Keener) and then has an emotional breakdown. Then there's single mother Rose (Baker), who becomes intrigued by her new neighbor—a dwarf (Woodburn), and finally staid Kathy (Brenneman) and her exhuberantly sexy blind sister Carol (Diaz). **106m/C VHS, DVD, Wide.** Cameron Diaz, Glenn Close, Calista Flockhart, Holly Hunter, Amy Brenneman, Kathy Baker, Valeria Golino, Matt Craven, Gregory Hines, Noah Fleiss, Miguel (Michael) Sandoval, Danny Woodburn, Roma Maffia; ***D:*** Rodrigo Garcia; ***W:*** Rodrigo Garcia; ***C:*** Emmanuel Lubezki; ***M:*** Ed Shearmur.

Think Big 🦴🦴½ **1990 (PG-13)** Former professional wrestlers, the Pauls are truck drivers in this silly, enjoyable comedy. They pick up a brilliant teenager running from bad guys. Mayhem ensues. **86m/C VHS.** Peter Paul, David Paul, Martin Mull, Ari Meyers, Richard Kiel, David Carradine, Richard Moll, Peter Lupus; ***W:*** Jim Wynorski, R.J. Robertson.

Think Dirty 🦴🦴 *Every Home Should Have One* **1970 (R)** Lascivious comedy about ad exec Feldman's attempt to develop a series of sexy commercials to sell cereal. At the same time his wife forms a "clean up TV" group. Not very interesting or funny. **93m/C VHS.** *GB* Marty Feldman, Judy Cornwell, Shelley Berman; ***D:*** Jim Clark.

Thinkin' Big 🦴 **1987 (R)** Guys and gals cavort on the Texas coast, except for one lonely fat guy who tries to increase his sexual prowess. The usual teen sex frenzy. **96m/C VHS.** Bruce Anderson, Kenny Sargent, Randy Jandt, Nancy Buechler, Darla Ralston; ***D:*** S.F. Brownrigg.

The Third 🦴🦴 *Der Dritte* **1972** Margit (Hoffmann) has two children and two divorces after marrying men who wanted her more than she wanted them. So when Margit decides to take a third chance on love, she resolves to do the choosing. She picks unsuspecting colleague Hrdlistchka (Ludwig) and is determined to get him to say yes. German with subtitles. **107m/C VHS.** *GE* Jutta Hoffmann, Rolf Ludwig, Armin Mueller-Stahl, Peter Kohnke, Barbara Dittus; ***D:*** Egon Gunther; ***W:*** Gunther Rucker; ***C:*** Erick Gusko; ***M:*** Karl-Ernst Sasse.

Third Degree Burn 🦴🦴 **1989** Mystery about a small-time detective hired by a businessman to follow a woman, only to become a suspect when the woman's real husband is killed. **97m/C VHS.** Treat Williams, Virginia Madsen, Richard Masur; ***D:*** Roger Spottiswoode. **CABLE**

The Third Key 🦴🦴½ *The Long Arm* **1957** A solid British crime drama follows a dogged detective as he probes serial safecrackings, with a climax set at London's Festival Hall. Based on the book by Robert Barr, who co-scripted. **96m/B VHS.** Jack Hawkins, Dorothy Allison, Geoffrey Keen, Richard Leech, Ian Bannen; ***D:*** Charles Frend.

The Third Man 🦴🦴🦴🦴 **1949** An American writer of pulp westerns (Cotten) arrives in post-war Vienna to take a job with an old friend, but discovers he has been murdered. Or has he? Based on Graham Greene's mystery, this classic film noir thriller plays on national loyalties during the Cold War. Welles is top-notch as the manipulative Harry Lime, black-market drugdealer extraordinare. The underground sewer sequence is not to be missed. With a haunting (sometimes irritating) theme by Anton Karas on unaccompanied zither. Special edition features trailer. **104m/B VHS, DVD, 8mm.** *GB* Joseph Cotten, Orson Welles, Alida Valli, Trevor Howard, Bernard Lee, Wilfrid Hyde-White, Ernst Deutsch, Erich Ponto, Siegfried Breuer, Hedwig Bleibtreu, Paul Hoerbiger, Herbert Halbik, Frederick Schreicker, Jenny Werner, Nelly Arno, Alexis Chesnakov, Leo Bieber, Paul Hardtmuth, Geoffrey Keen, Annie Rosar; ***D:*** Carol Reed; ***W:*** Graham Greene; ***C:*** Robert Krasker; ***M:*** Anton Karas. Oscars '50: B&W Cinematog.; AFI '98: Top 100; British Acad. '49: Film; Cannes '49: Film; Directors Guild '49: Director (Reed).

Third Man on the Mountain 🦴🦴½ *Banner in the Sky* **1959 (G)** A family epic about mountain climbing, shot in Switzerland and based on James Ramsey Ullman's "Banner in the Sky." A young man is determined to climb the "Citadel" as his ancestors have. He finds there's more to climbing than he imagined. Look for Helen Hayes (MacArthur's mother) in a cameo. Standard Disney adventure drama. **106m/C VHS.** James MacArthur, Michael Rennie, Janet Munro, James Donald, Herbert Lom, Laurence Naismith; ***Cameos:*** Helen Hayes; ***D:*** Ken Annakin.

The Third Miracle 🦴🦴½ **1999 (R)** Harris makes for one sexy and dynamic priest. He's Father Frank Shore who is struggling with his faith and is in a kind of voluntary retirement. However, he's summoned by power player, Bishop Cahill (Haid), to investigate the purported miracles of the late Helen O'Regan (Sukowa). A cult is growing up around her memory and the mention of sainthood (which requires three proven miracles) has the church wary. Film is set in Chicago in 1979 and based on the book by Richard Vetere. **119m/C VHS, DVD.** Ed Harris, Anne Heche, Charles Haid, Armin Mueller-Stahl, Michael Rispoli, Jean-Louis Roux, Ken James, James Gallanders, Barbara Sukowa; ***D:*** Agnieszka Holland; ***W:*** John Romano, Richard Vetere; ***C:*** Jerzy Zielinski; ***M:*** Jan A.P. Kaczmarek.

The Third Sex 🦴🦴 *Anders Als du und Ich* **1957** One of the first films to deal with homosexuality in which parents try to "straighten out" their gay son. German with subtitles. **90m/C VHS.** *GE* Paul Dahlke, Paula Wesley, Hans Nielsen, Christian Wolff, Friedrich Joloff, Hilde Korber, Gunther Theil; ***D:*** Veit Harlan; ***W:*** Felix Lutzkendorff; ***C:*** Kurt Grigoleit; ***M:*** Erwin Halletz.

Third Solution 🦴🦴 *Russicum* **1989 (R)** An Italian-made film about the discovery of a secret pact made between the Kremlin and the Vatican that may start WWIII. Well-cast, but poorly conceived spook drama, with music by Vangelis. **93m/C VHS, Wide.** *IT* Treat Williams, F. Murray Abraham, Danny Aiello, Nigel Court, Rita Rusic, Rossano Brazzi; ***D:*** Pasquale Squitieri; ***M:*** Vangelis.

Third Walker 🦴🦴🦴 **1979** A desperate woman sacrifices her marriage to immerse herself in efforts to reunite her twin sons, who were inadvertently separated at birth. An original and intriguing directorial debut by McLuhan. **85m/C VHS.** William Shatner, Colleen Dewhurst, Marshall McLuhan, Monique Mercure, Andree Pelletier; ***D:*** Teri McLuhan; ***W:*** Teri McLuhan, Robert Thom.

Third World Cop 🦴🦴 **1999 (R)** Detective Capone (Campbell) returns to his childhood home in Kingston and discovers that his best bud Ratty (Danvers) is the right-hand man for local crime boss One Hand (Bradshaw). Their friendship leaves the gangsters suspicious that Ratty is a police informer but even when he finally agrees to help Capone, things go wrong. Straight-ahead crime story does have the advantage of the Jamaican settings to take it out of the norm. **98m/C VHS, DVD.** *JM* Paul Campbell, Carl Bradshaw, Mark Danvers, Audrey Reid; ***D:*** Christopher Browne; ***W:*** Christopher Browne, Suzanne Fenn, Chris Salewicz; ***C:*** Richard Lannaman; ***M:*** Sly Dunbar, Robbie Shakespeare.

Thirst 🦴🦴 **1987 (R)** A girl is abducted by a secret society that wants her to become their new leader. There is just one catch: she has to learn to like the taste of human blood. Chilling but weakly plotted. **96m/C VHS.** David Hemmings, Henry Silva, Chantal Contouri; ***D:*** Rod Hardy.

The Thirsty Dead woof! *The Blood Cult of Shangri-La; Blood Hunt* **1974 (PG)** Maybe they could learn to like Gatorade. An eternally young jungle king is looking for a wife. She can be young forever too, if she's not above vampirism and sacrificing virgins. In spite of the jungle vampire slant, this Filipino-made movie is a woofer. **90m/C VHS.** *PH* John Considine, Jennifer Billingsley, Judith McConnell, Fredricka Meyers, Tani Phelps Guthrie; ***D:*** Terry Becker.

Thirteen Days &&&½ **2000** **(PG-13)** The Cuban Missile Crisis seen through the eyes of President JFK, Attorney General Robert Kennedy, and presidential aide Kenny O'Donnell (Costner). Director Donaldson wisely opts not to over-dramatize what was clearly a suspenseful story to begin with (and realizes, as well, that we know the outcome). The few sacrifices of historical accuracy made in the name of dramatic license are basically harmless. Greenwood and Culp ably handle the often difficult task of portraying the brothers Kennedy, and Costner is solid as the brothers' trusted confidante. Donaldson and Costner notably worked together on 1987's "No Way Out." **145m/C VHS, DVD, Wide.** Kevin Costner, Bruce Greenwood, Steven Culp, Dylan Baker, Michael Fairman, Kevin Conway, Tim Kelleher, Len Cariou, Bill Smitrovich, Dakin Matthews, Madison Mason, Christopher Lawford, Ed Lauter, Elya Baskin, Boris Krutonog, Peter White, James Karen, Tim Jerome, Olek Krupa, Lucinda Jenney, Henry Strozier, Frank Wood, Stephanie Romanov; ***D:*** Roger Donaldson; ***W:*** David Self; ***C:*** Andrzej Bartkowiak; ***M:*** Trevor Jones.

13 Ghosts &&½ **1960** A dozen ghosts need another member to round out their ranks. They have four likely candidates to choose from when a family moves into the house inhabited by the ghoulish group. Originally viewed with "Illusion-O," a technology much like 3-D, which allowed the viewing of the ghosts only through a special pair of glasses. **88m/C VHS, DVD, Wide.** Charles Herbert, Jo Morrow, Martin Milner, Rosemary DeCamp, Donald Woods, Margaret Hamilton, John van Dreelen; ***D:*** William Castle; ***W:*** Robb White; ***C:*** Joseph Biroc; ***M:*** Von Dexter.

13 Ghosts && **2001 (R)** Another attempt to meld humor and horror in a William Castle remake ala "House on Haunted Hill" misfires in this flashy screamfest. Arthur (Shalhoub) inherits a weird glass mansion from his shadowy Uncle Cyrus (Abraham). He moves into the house with his kids Kathy (Elizabeth) and Bobby (Roberts) and their nanny Maggie (Digga). Along for kicks is spastic psychic Rafkin (Lillard), which is good, because the mansion ends up being a gigantic infernal contraption powered by ghosts complete with whirling gears and sliding glass panels that attack the inhabitants. It seems that crazy Uncle Cyrus built the house to open the Eye of Hell and it's up to Arthur to stop it. The special effects are above average, but the plot is clearly not. **91m/C VHS, DVD, Wide.** Tony Shalhoub, Embeth Davidtz, Matthew Lillard, Shannon Elizabeth, Alec Roberts, Rah Digga, JR Bourne, F. Murray Abraham; ***D:*** Steve Beck; ***W:*** Richard D'Ovidio, Neal Marshall Stevens; ***C:*** Gale Tattersall; ***M:*** John (Gianni) Frizzell.

13 Rue Madeleine &&& **1946** Cagney plays a WWII spy who infiltrates Gestapo headquarters in Paris in order to find the location of a German missile site. Actual OSS footage is used in this fast-paced early postwar espionage propaganda piece. Rex Harrison rejected the part taken by Cagney. **95m/B VHS.** James Cagney, Annabella, Richard Conte, Frank Latimore, Walter Abel, Sam Jaffe, Melville Cooper, E.G. Marshall, Karl Malden, Red Buttons, Blanche Yurka, Peter Von Zerneck, Marcel Rousseau, Dick Gordon, Alfred Linder; ***D:*** Henry Hathaway; ***W:*** Sy Bartlett, John Monks Jr.; ***C:*** Norbert Brodine; ***M:*** David Buttolph.

Thirteenth Day of Christmas **1985** A psychotic boy is left alone by his parents on Christmas night. **60m/C VHS.** *GB* Patrick Allen, Elizabeth Spiggs. **TV**

The 13th Floor &½ **1988 (R)** A young girl fuses with the spirit of a young boy her father ruthlessly killed years before, and together they wreak havoc. **86m/C VHS, DVD.** Lisa Hensley, Tim McKenzie, Miranda Otto; ***D:*** Chris Roach.

The Thirteenth Floor &½ **1999** **(R)** Silly sci-fier with a confusing virtual-reality plot and a lot of visual effects. An investigation into the mysterious death of tycoon Hannon Fuller (Mueller-Stahl) leads to the realization that he lived in parallel worlds—one in the present and one in 1937. Exec Douglas Hall (Bierko) stands to inherit, which raises the suspicious of cop McBain (Haysbert), while mysterious femme Jane (Mol) shows up, claiming to be Fuller's daughter. And then there's Hall's colleague Whitney (D'Onofrio), who also exists in the 1937 as a barkeep with a very important letter. Not that any of this turns out to be particularly interesting. **100m/C VHS, DVD.** Craig Bierko, Vincent D'Onofrio, Armin Mueller-Stahl, Gretchen Mol, Dennis Haysbert, Steven Schub, Jeremy Roberts; ***D:*** Josef Rusnak; ***W:*** Josef Rusnak; ***C:*** Wedigo von Schultzendorff; ***M:*** Harold Kloser.

13th Guest && *Lady Beware* **1932** Two people try to solve a murder that occurred at a dinner party. An incredibly creaky early talkie melodrama that created some of the cliches of the genre. **70m/B VHS.** Ginger Rogers, Lyle Talbot, J. Farrell MacDonald, Paul Hurst; ***D:*** Albert Ray.

The Thirteenth Man &&½ **1937** When a journalist investigating the murder of a district attorney is also killed, the paper's gossip columnist takes the case. Entertaining, fast-paced mystery. **70m/B VHS.** Weldon Heyburn, Inez Courtney, Selmer Jackson, Milburn Stone, Matty Fain; ***D:*** William Nigh.

The 13th Mission &½ **1991** A low-budget overseas combat adventure, no better than the first 12. **95m/C VHS.** Robert Marius, Jeff Griffith, Michael Monty, David Morisson, Paul Home, John Falch, Albert Bronski, Chantal Manz; ***D:*** Antonio Perez.

Thirteenth Reunion & **1981** A newspaperwoman uncovers a bizarre secret society when she does a routine story on a health spa. **60m/C VHS.** Julia Foster, Dinah Sheridan, Richard Pearson; ***D:*** Peter Sasdy.

The 13th Warrior && *Eaters of the Dead* **1999 (R)** Banderas stars as Ahmed Ibn Fahdlan, a sophisticated Arabian poet and lover-turned-reluctant-warrior, who gets exiled from his homeland and caught up in a quest with a bunch of uncouth, slaughter-loving Vikings. Based on the 1976 book by Michael Crichton, this one has been sitting on the shelf a while after a rocky filming history. However, if you like bloody, action-packed epics it will satisfy your cravings. **103m/C VHS, DVD.** Antonio Banderas, Vladimir Kulich, Clive Russell, Omar Sharif, Diane Venora, Sven Wollter, Dennis Storhoi, Anders T. Anderson, Richard Bremmer, Neil Maffin, Tony Curran, Mischa Hausserman, Asbjorn Riis, Daniel Southern, Oliver Sveinall, Albie Woodington; ***D:*** Michael Crichton, John McTiernan; ***W:*** Michael Crichton; ***C:*** Peter Menzies Jr.; ***M:*** Jerry Goldsmith.

The 30-Foot Bride of Candy Rock & **1959** A junk dealer invents a robot, catapults into space and causes his girlfriend to grow to 30 feet in height. Lightweight, whimsical fantasy was Costello's only solo starring film, and his last before his untimely death. **73m/B VHS.** Lou Costello, Dorothy Provine, Gale Gordon; ***D:*** Sidney Miller.

30 Is a Dangerous Age, Cynthia &&½ **1968** Dudley Moore stars as a nightclub pianist who spends a lot of his time daydreaming about being rich, famous, and married to a beautiful woman. Moore determines to attain all these dreams before his 30th birthday, which is only six weeks away. **85m/C VHS.** *GB* Dudley Moore, Suzy Kendall, Eddie Foy Jr.; ***D:*** Joseph McGrath; ***W:*** Dudley Moore; ***M:*** Dudley Moore.

Thirty Seconds Over Tokyo &&& **1944** Dated but still interesting classic wartime flagwaver details the conception and execution of the first bombing raids on Tokyo by Lt. Col. James Doolittle and his men. Look for Blake Edwards, as well as Steve Brodie in his first screen appearance. Based on a true story. **138m/B VHS.** Spencer Tracy, Van Johnson, Robert Walker, Robert Mitchum, Phyllis Thaxter, Scott McKay, Stephen McNally, Louis Jean Heydt, Leon Ames, Paul Langton, Don DeFore, Tim Murdock, Alan Napier, Dorothy Morris, Jacqueline White, Selena Royle, Bill Phillips, Donald Curtis, Gordon McDonald, John R. Reilly, Douglas Cowan, Ann Shoemaker, Steve Brodie; ***D:*** Mervyn LeRoy; ***W:*** Dalton Trumbo; ***C:*** Robert L. Surtees, Harold Rosson; ***M:*** Herbert Stothart.

32 Short Films about Glenn Gould &&& **1993** Perceptive docudrama about the iconoclastic Canadian classical pianist who secluded himself in the studio, forsaking live performances for much of his career. A combination of dramatic recreation, archival material, and interviews depict the biographical details of the driven artist who died at the age of 50. Feore is memorable in the title role, especially since he's never actually shown playing the piano. Title and film structure refer to Bach's "Goldberg" Variations, a recording which made Gould's reputation. **94m/C VHS, DVD, Wide.** *CA* Colm Feore, Gale Garnett, David Hughes, Katya Ladan, Gerry Quigley, Carlo Rota, Peter Millard, Yehudi Menuhin, Bruno Monsaingeon; ***D:*** Francois Girard; ***W:*** Don McKellar, Francois Girard; ***C:*** Alan Dostie. Genie '93: Cinematog., Director (Girard), Film, Film Editing.

36 Fillete &&& **1988** Lili, an intellectually precocious 14-year-old French girl who's literally bursting out of her children's dress size 36 fillete, discovers her sexuality. So while on vacation with her family she becomes determined to see if she can seduce a middle-aged playboy. In French with English subtitles. **88m/C VHS, DVD.** *FR* Delphine Zentout, Etienne Chicot, Oliver Parniere, Jean-Pierre Leaud; ***D:*** Catherine Breillat; ***W:*** Catherine Breillat, Roger Salloch; ***C:*** Laurent Dailland.

36 Hours &&& **1964** Maj. Pike (Garner) is a high-ranking WWII Army officer with knowledge of top secret invasion plans who wakes up in an Army hospital with amnesia, a wife (Saint) he didn't know he had, and a shrink telling him that the war's been over for some time. But Pike's not sure what's real and what isn't, especially when the doc asks him to explain, in great detail, what happened just before he lost his memory. Are they telling the truth, or is this an elaborate hoax? Tight, suspenseful plot, and fine performances all around make this an enjoyable thriller even after that question is answered. Remade for TV in 1989 with Corbin Bernsen in the Garner role. **115m/B VHS.** James Garner, Eva Marie Saint, Rod Taylor, Werner Peters, John Banner, Russ Thorson, Alan Napier, Oscar Beregi, Edmund Gilbert, Sig Rumann, Celia Lovsky, Karl Held, Marjorie Bennett, Martin Kosleck, Henry Rowland, Hilda Plowright, Joseph Mell, Rudolph Anders, James Doohan; ***D:*** George Seaton; ***W:*** George Seaton, Roald Dahl, Carl K. Hittleman; ***C:*** Philip Lathrop; ***M:*** Dimitri Tiomkin.

Thirty-Six Hours of Hell &½ **1977** A troop of Marines battle Japanese forces in the South Pacific during WWII. Dubbed. **95m/C VHS.** Richard Harrison, Pamela Tudor; ***D:*** Roberto Marrtero.

36 Hours to Die &&½ **1999** Noah Stone (Williams) is a brewery owner recovering from heart bypass surgery. As if he doesn't have enough to worry about, a crime syndicate wants to use his business as a front in an extortion scam and he's got a day-and-a-half to make up his mind (hence the title). Stone's wife (Cattrall), her ex-cop uncle (O'Connor), and even Stone's bowling team unite to take on the bad guys. **96m/C VHS.** Treat Williams, Saul Rubinek, Kim Cattrall, Carroll O'Connor, George Touliatos, Scott Hylands; ***D:*** Yves Simoneau; ***W:*** Robert Rodat. **CABLE**

'38: Vienna before the Fall &&½ **1988** Wartime Vienna explodes with love and politics. Academy Award nominee for Best Foreign Language Film. In German with English subtitles. **97m/C VHS.** *GE* Tobias Engel, Sunnyi Melles; ***D:*** Wolfgang Gluck.

The 39 Steps &&&& **1935** The classic Hitchcock mistaken-man-caught-in-intrigue thriller, featuring some of his most often copied set-pieces and the surest visual flair of his pre-war British period. Remade twice, in 1959 and 1979. **81m/B VHS, DVD, 8mm.** *GB* Robert Donat, Madeleine Carroll, Godfrey Tearle, Lucie Mannheim, Peggy Ashcroft, John Laurie, Wylie Watson, Helen Haye, Frank Cellier, Gus McNaughton, Jerry Verno, Peggy Simpson, Hilda Trevelyan, John Turnbull, Elizabeth Inglis, Wilfrid Brambell; ***D:*** Alfred Hitchcock; ***W:*** Charles Bennett, Alma Reville, Ian Hay; ***C:*** Bernard Knowles; ***M:*** Louis Levy.

The Thirty-Nine Steps &&½ **1979** Hitchcock remake is a visually interesting, but mostly uninvolving, mystery. Powell is the man suspected of stealing plans to begin WWI. Above average, but not by much. **98m/C VHS, DVD.** *GB* Robert Powell, David Warner, Eric Porter, Karen Dotrice, John Mills, Andrew Keir; ***D:*** Don Sharp.

This Boy's Life &&& **1993 (R)** In 1957, Carolyn (Barkin) and her teenage son Toby (DiCaprio) are in search of a new life, far from her abusive ex-boyfriend. In the town of Concrete, just outside Seattle, she meets ex-military man Dwight (De Niro), a slick but none too suave mechanic who might be the answer to her dreams, but then again, he might not. Nicely crafted performances from all, but keep your eye on DiCaprio (great in his first major role) as the confused and abused teen divided between dreams of prep school and the allure of the going-nowhere crowd. Based on the memoirs of Tobias Wolff; director Caton-Jones sensitively illustrates the skewed understanding of masculinity in the 1950s. Vintage soundtrack takes you back. **115m/C VHS, Wide.** Robert De Niro, Ellen Barkin, Leonardo DiCaprio, Jonah Blechman, Eliza Dushku, Chris Cooper, Carla Gugino, Zachary Ansley, Tracey Ellis, Kathy Kinney, Gerrit Graham; ***D:*** Michael Caton-Jones; ***W:*** Robert Getchell; ***C:*** David Watkin; ***M:*** Carter Burwell.

This Could Be the Night &&½ **1957** Rocco and Tony are two small-fry gangsters who run a nightclub. Anne is a prim schoolteacher who takes a part-time job as their secretary. She falls for the handsome Tony much to the dismay of Rocco who knows his partner's less-than-sterling character. Sweet but minor comedy. Franciosa's first film. ♫This Could Be The Night; Hustlin' News Gal; I Got It Bad; I'm Gonna Live Till I Die; Taking a Chance on Love; Trumpet Boogie; Mamba Combo; Blue Moon; Dream Dancing. **105m/B VHS, Wide.** Jean Simmons, Paul Douglas, Anthony (Tony) Franciosa, Joan Blondell, Julie Wilson, Neile Adams, J. Carrol Naish, Rafael Campos, ZaSu Pitts, Tom Helmore; ***D:*** Robert Wise.

This England &½ **1942** Patriotic morale booster is a rather dull jog through Britain's fight for freedom as an American journalist, visiting England, learns a village's history from a country squire, including surviving the Norman conquest, Spanish Armada, Napoleonic Wars, WWI, and the 1940 air attacks. **84m/B VHS.** *GB* Emlyn Williams, John Clements, Constance Cummings; ***D:*** David MacDonald.

This Gun for Hire &&&½ **1942** In his first major film role, Ladd plays a hired gun seeking retribution from a client who betrays him. Preston is the cop pursuing him and hostage Lake. Ladd's performance as the cold-blooded killer with a soft spot for cats is stunning; his train-yard scene is an emotional powerhouse. Based on Graham Greene's novel "A Gun for Sale." Remade as "Short Cut to Hell." The first of several films using the Ladd-Lake team, but the only one in which Ladd played a villain. **81m/B VHS.** Alan Ladd, Veronica Lake, Robert Preston, Laird Cregar; ***D:*** Frank Tuttle; ***W:*** Albert (John B. Sherry) Maltz, W.R. Burnett.

This Gun for Hire && **1990 (R)** A professional assassin finds that he has been duped into killing a powerful political figure, whom he was told was a New Orleans mobster. Now on the run, he takes a nightclub performer hostage, unaware that she is the fiance of the FBI agent who is after him. All odds are against him, but the special relationship he forms with the woman may just be his ticket out. Adapted from novel by Graham Greene. **89m/C VHS.** Robert Wagner, Nancy Everhard, Frederic Lehne, John Harkins; ***D:*** Lou Antonio.

This Happy Breed 🦴🦴🦴½ **1947** A celebrated film version of Noel Coward's classic play depicts the changing fortunes of a large family in England between the world wars. Happiness, hardships, triumph and tragedy mix a series of memorable episodes, including some of the most cherished moments in popular British cinema, though its appeal is universal. **114m/C VHS.** *GB* Robert Newton, Celia Johnson, John Mills, Kay Walsh, Stanley Holloway, Amy Veness, Alison Leggatt, Eileen Erskine, John Blythe, Guy Verney, Betty Fleetwood, Merle Tottenham; ***D:*** David Lean; ***W:*** David Lean, Noel Coward, Ronald Neame; ***C:*** Ronald Neame; ***M:*** Noel Coward, Muir Mathieson; ***Nar:*** Laurence Olivier.

This Happy Feeling 🦴🦴½ **1958** Reynolds is a young woman who is romantically attracted to both Jurgens, a sophisticated retired actor, and Saxon, a younger suitor who is Jurgens' neighbor. Good acting all around. Charming telling of old tale. **83m/C VHS.** Curt Jurgens, Debbie Reynolds, John Saxon, Alexis Smith, Mary Astor, Estelle Winwood; ***D:*** Blake Edwards; ***W:*** Blake Edwards.

This Is a Hijack 🦴 **1975 (PG)** Gambler hijacks the plane carrying his wealthy boss to help pay his debts. What it lacks in suspense, it lacks in performance and direction as well. **90m/C VHS.** Adam Roarke, Neville Brand, Jay Robinson, Lynn Borden, Dub Taylor.

This Is Elvis 🦴🦴 **1981 (PG)** The life of Elvis, combining documentary footage with dramatizations of events in his life. Includes more than three dozen songs. Generally seen as an attempt to cash in on the myth, but was well-received by his fans. **144m/C VHS.** Elvis Presley; ***D:*** Malcolm Leo, Andrew Solt; ***W:*** Malcolm Leo, Andrew Solt; ***C:*** Gil Hubbs.

This Is My Father 🦴🦴½ **1999 (R)** Teacher Kieran Johnson (Caan) decides to research his Irish roots after discovering a photo of his mother with a mystery man who may have been his father. Told in flashback, it portraits the class differences in rural Ireland in the thirties and the doomed romance between wealthy, teenaged Fiona Flynn (Farrelly) and Kieran O'Dea (Quinn), a poor tenant farmer who works for the Flynn family. Affecting role for Aidan Quinn, who worked with brothers Paul and Declan. Script is based on a story Theresa Quinn told her children. **120m/C VHS, DVD, Wide.** Aidan Quinn, James Caan, Stephen Rea, Moya Farrelly, John Cusack, Jacob Tierney, Colm Meaney, Donal Donnelly, Brendan Gleeson; ***D:*** Paul Quinn; ***W:*** Paul Quinn; ***C:*** Declan Quinn; ***M:*** Donal Lunny.

This Is My Life 🦴🦴 **1992 (PG-13)** The story of a working mother torn between her skyrocketing career as a standup comic and her two daughters. Kavner plays the divorced mom who is determined to chuck her cosmetic sales job for comic success. Her career starts to really take off; she hires an agent and makes appearances on talk shows. As offers pour in, she eventually realizes that her girls are suffering as a result of her success. Good performances highlight an otherwise average drama. **105m/C VHS.** Julie Kavner, Samantha Mathis, Carrie Fisher, Dan Aykroyd, Gaby Hoffman; ***D:*** Nora Ephron; ***W:*** Nora Ephron, Delia Ephron.

This Is Not a Test 🦴🦴 **1962** When news comes of an impending nuclear attack, a state trooper at a roadblock offers sanctuary to passing travellers. The effectiveness of the film's social commentary is hindered by its small budget. **72m/B VHS, DVD.** Seamon Glass, Mary Morlass, Thayer Roberts, Aubrey Martin; ***D:*** Frederic Gadette; ***W:*** Frederic Gadette, Peter Abenheim, Betty Laskey; ***C:*** Brick Marquard; ***M:*** Greig McRitchie.

This Is Spinal Tap 🦴🦴🦴½ *Spinal Tap* **1984 (R)** Pseudo-rockumentary about heavy-metal band Spinal Tap, profiling their career from "England's loudest band" to an entry in the "where are they now file." Hilarious satire, featuring music performed by Guest, McKean, Shearer, and others. Included are Spinal Tap's music video "Hell Hole," and an ad for their greatest hits album, "Heavy Metal Memories." Features great cameos, particularly David Letterman's Paul Shaffer as a record promoter and Billy Crystal as a surly mime. First feature for Reiner (Meathead on "All in the Family"). Followed by "The Return of Spinal Tap." **82m/C VHS, DVD, 8mm, Wide.** Michael McKean, Christopher Guest, Harry Shearer, Tony Hendra, Bruno Kirby, Rob Reiner, June Chadwick, Howard Hesseman, Billy Crystal, Dana Carvey, Ed Begley Jr., Patrick Macnee, Fran Drescher, Paul Shaffer, Anjelica Huston, Fred Willard, Paul Benedict, Archie Hahn; ***D:*** Rob Reiner; ***W:*** Michael McKean, Christopher Guest, Harry Shearer, Rob Reiner; ***C:*** Peter Smokler; ***M:*** Michael McKean, Christopher Guest, Harry Shearer, Rob Reiner.

This Is the Army 🦴🦴½ **1943** A robust tribute to the American soldier of WWII based on the hit play by Irving Berlin. Murphy, who later was a senator from California, played Reagan's father. ♫Your Country and My Country; My Sweetie; Poor Little Me, I'm on K.P.; We're On Our Way to France; What Does He Look Like?; This is the Army, Mr. Jones; I'm Gettin' Tired So I Can Sleep; Mandy; Ladies of the Chorus. **105m/C VHS.** George Murphy, Joan Leslie, Ronald Reagan, Alan Hale, Kate Smith, George Tobias, Irving Berlin, Joe Louis; ***D:*** Michael Curtiz; ***M:*** Max Steiner. Oscars '43: Scoring/Musical.

This Is the Sea 🦴🦴½ **1996 (R)** Belfast Protestant teenager Hazel Stokes (Morton) falls in love with Catholic boy, Malachy McAliskey (McDade), with trouble sure to follow. Interesting cast but the film winds up being simplistic and cliched. Director McGuckian also appears as Cathy, Padhar McAliskey's girlfriend, who is played by McGuckian's husband, Lynch. Title comes from a 1985 Waterboys song. **104m/C VHS.** *IR* Mary McGuckian, Samantha Morton, Ross McDade, Richard Harris, John Lynch, Gabriel Byrne, Marc O'Shea, Des McAleer; ***D:*** Mary McGuckian; ***W:*** Mary McGuckian; ***C:*** Des Whelan.

This Island Earth 🦴🦴½ **1955** The planet Metaluna is in desperate need of uranium to power its defense against enemy invaders. A nuclear scientist and a nuclear fission expert from Earth are kidnapped to help out. The first serious movie about interplanetary escapades. Bud Westmore created pulsating cranium special effects make-up. **86m/C VHS, DVD.** Jeff Morrow, Faith Domergue, Rex Reason, Russell Johnson; ***D:*** Joseph M. Newman; ***M:*** Herman Stein.

This Land Is Mine 🦴🦴🦴 **1943** A timid French schoolteacher gathers enough courage to defy the Nazis when they attempt to occupy his town. Laughton's characterization is effective as the meek fellow who discovers the hero within himself in this patriotic wartime flick. **103m/B VHS.** Charles Laughton, Maureen O'Hara, George Sanders, Walter Slezak, George Coulouris, Una O'Connor; ***D:*** Jean Renoir. Oscars '43: Sound.

This Lightning Always Strikes Twice **1985** An elegant murder mystery made for British television. **60m/C VHS.** *GB* Claire Bloom, Trevor Howard, Charles Dance. **TV**

This Man Must Die 🦴🦴🦴½ *Que La Bete Meure; Uccidero Un Uomo; Killer!* **1970 (PG)** A man searches relentlessly for the driver who killed his young son in a hit-and-run. When found, the driver engages him in a complex cat-and-mouse chase. Another stunning crime and punishment tale from Chabrol. **112m/C VHS.** *FR* Michael Duchaussoy, Caroline Cellier, Jean Yanne, Anouk Ferjac, Maurice Pialat; ***D:*** Claude Chabrol; ***W:*** Paul Gegauff; ***C:*** Jean Rabier.

This Property Is Condemned 🦴🦴 **1966** It's a hot time down south once again in this adaptation of the Tennessee Williams play. Wood is the overly flirtatious southern charmer who takes a shine to the latest tenant of her loathsome mama's boardinghouse. And since it's Redford, who can blame her. Things steam up when he returns her interest but there's trouble a'brewin'. Both leads are lovely but the film itself is overly southern-fried. Williams was reportedly unhappy with the script and wanted his name removed from the film. **109m/C VHS.** Robert Redford, Natalie Wood, Charles Bronson, Kate Reid, Mary Badham, Jon(athan) Provost, Robert (Bobby) Blake, John Harding; ***D:*** Sydney Pollack; ***W:*** Francis Ford Coppola, Edith Sommer, Fred Coe.

This Special Friendship 🦴🦴½ *Les Amities Particulieres* **1967** Powerful, if overdone French drama about an emotionally sensitive young man at a Catholic boarding school. His sexual relationship with another boy leads to tragedy. Based on the novel by Roger Peyrefitte. **99m/B VHS.** *FR* Francis Lacombrade, Didier Haudepin, Lucien Nat, Louis Seigner, Michel Bouquet, Francois Leccia; ***D:*** Jean Delannoy.

This Sporting Life 🦴🦴🦴 **1963** A gritty, depressing portrait of former coal miner Frank Machin (Harris), who breaks into the violent world of professional rugby, and whose inability to handle social differences causes problems. He begins an affair with widow Mrs. Hammond (Roberts), from whom he rents a room, but finds they are capable of only a physical attachment. One of the best of the British early '60s working-class angry young man melodramas. **134m/B VHS, DVD.** *GB* Richard Harris, Rachel Roberts, Alan Badel, William Hartnell, Colin Blakely, Vanda Godsell, Arthur Lowe; ***D:*** Lindsay Anderson; ***W:*** David Storey; ***C:*** Denys Coop; ***M:*** Roberto Gerhard. British Acad. '63: Actress (Roberts); Cannes '63: Actor (Harris).

This Stuff'll Kill Ya! woof! **1971 (PG)** A backwoods preacher who believes in free love and moonshining runs into trouble with the locals when a series of gruesome religious murders are committed. Southern drive-in material from one of the genre's masters. Holt's last film. **100m/C VHS.** Jeffrey Allen, Tim Holt, Gloria King, Ray Sager, Eric Bradly, Terence McCarthy, Larry Drake; ***D:*** Herschell Gordon Lewis; ***W:*** Herschell Gordon Lewis; ***C:*** Alex Ameri; ***M:*** Herschell Gordon Lewis.

This Sweet Sickness 🦴🦴½ *Dites-Lui Que Je L'Aime* **1977** Destructive passion and sexual delusion is explored in this adaptation of the Patricia Highsmith novel. David seems to be a hardworking loner who is loved by the sweet Juliette. Rejected by him, Juliette then discovers that David has built a remote mountain chalet for the woman he does love, Lise, who's married and unaware of David's obsessional devotions. Extravagant emotions lead to tragedy. In French with English subtitles. **107m/C VHS.** *FR* Gerard Depardieu, Miou-Miou, Dominique Laffin, Claude Pieplu, Christian Clavier, Jacques Denis, Josiane Balasko, Veronique Silver, Jacqueline Jeanne, Michel Such; ***D:*** Claude Miller; ***W:*** Claude Miller, Luc Beraud; ***C:*** Pierre Lhomme.

This Time I'll Make You Rich 🦴 **1975 (PG)** Two American hoodlums work out a drug-ring heist in the Far East. Parolini used the pseudonym Frank Kramer. **97m/C VHS.** Antonio (Tony) Sabato, Robin McDavid; ***D:*** Gianfranco Parolini.

This World, Then the Fireworks 🦴🦴½ **1997 (R)** Long on style but short on substance, overwrought neo-noir tells the tragic tale of traumatized twins living a totally debauched life. After seeing their father murdered in a romantic triangle, which left their mother (McClanahan) with physical and emotional scars, brother Marty (Zane) and sister Carol (Gershon) cling to each other as they grow up and engage in an implied incestuous relationship. The duo winds up grifters, murdering and pillaging their way through a small coastal town in the 1950s. Lee plays a messed-up cop who, tragically, becomes an easy mark for Marty. Based on a 1955 short story by Jim Thompson, director Oblowitz's debut gets too caught up in the excesses of pulp and focuses on slick visuals and dramatic score over a coherent story. Well-cast performances are universally solid and engaging. **100m/C VHS.** Billy Zane, Gina Gershon, Sheryl Lee, Rue McClanahan, Seymour Cassel, Will Patton, Richard Edson, William Hootkins; ***D:*** Michael Oblowitz; ***W:*** Larry Gross; ***C:*** Tom Priestley; ***M:*** Pete Rugolo.

Thomas and the Magic Railroad **2000 (G)** Thomas, a spunky blue steam engine, is bullied by big bad engine, Diesel, and aided by Mr. Conductor (Baldwin), as well as young Lily (Wilson) and her train-loving grandad (Fonda) who also come to Thomas' rescue. Part live-action, part animation adaptation of the British children's series will be fine for the kidlets but parents will overdose on the whimsey factor. **84m/C VHS, DVD.** Mara Wilson, Alec Baldwin, Peter Fonda, Didi Conn; ***D:*** Britt Allcroft; ***W:*** Britt Allcroft; ***C:*** Paul Ryan; ***M:*** Hummie Mann.

The Thomas Crown Affair 🦴🦴🦴 *Thomas Crown and Company; The Crown Caper* **1968 (R)** A multi-millionaire (McQueen) decides to plot and execute the perfect theft, a daring daylight robbery of a bank. Dunaway is the gorgeous and efficient insurance investigator determined to nab him. One of the best visual scenes is the chess match between the two as they begin to fall in love. Strong production with Oscar-winning theme "The Windmills of Your Mind." ♫The Windmills of Your Mind. **102m/C VHS, DVD.** Steve McQueen, Faye Dunaway, Jack Weston, Yaphet Kotto, Gordon Pinsent; ***D:*** Norman Jewison; ***W:*** Alan R. Trustman; ***C:*** Haskell Wexler. Oscars '68: Song ("The Windmills of Your Mind"); Golden Globes '69: Song ("The Windmills of Your Mind").

The Thomas Crown Affair 🦴🦴🦴 **1999 (R)** Slick, lavish, updated, and loose adaptation of the 1968 Steve McQueen/Faye Dunaway caper. Thomas Crown (Brosnan) is a self-made New York billionaire, who just can't resist pulling off the perfect crime by stealing a Monet from the Metropolitan Museum of Art. Catherine Banning (Russo) is the gorgeous insurance investigator on his trail, who can't help falling for the very charming criminal. The fortysomething duo sizzle (how fantastic to see two age-appropriate lovers for a change) and if the ending has a tacked-on feel, it doesn't really matter. Dunaway makes a cameo appearance as Crown's therapist. **111m/C VHS, DVD.** Pierce Brosnan, Rene Russo, Denis Leary, Frankie Faison, Ben Gazzara, Fritz Weaver, Charles Keating, Mark Margolis, Faye Dunaway, Esther Canadas; ***D:*** John McTiernan; ***W:*** Leslie Dixon, Kurt Wimmer; ***C:*** Tom Priestley; ***M:*** Bill Conti.

Thomas Graal's Best Film 🦴🦴🦴 **1917** The famous comical adventures of a film scriptwriter wooing his secretary, followed by "Thomas Graal's First Child." Silent. **70m/B VHS.** *SW* Victor Sjostrom, Karin Molander; ***D:*** Mauritz Stiller.

Thomas Graal's First Child 🦴🦴🦴 **1918** The sequel to "Thomas Graal's Best Film." The comical screenwriter and actress couple attempt to raise a baby. Silent. **70m/B VHS.** Victor Sjostrom, Karin Molander; ***D:*** Mauritz Stiller.

Thompson's Last Run 🦴½ **1990** Boyhood friends grow up on either side of the law. They come face-to-face, though, when one is assigned to transport the other to prison. **95m/C VHS.** Robert Mitchum, Wilford Brimley, Kathleen York, Susan Tyrrell; ***D:*** Jerrold Freedman; ***M:*** Miles Goodman. **TV**

Thor and the Amazon Women 🦴 **1960** The mighty Thor leads his enslaved men on an attack against the evil Queen Nera and her female-dominated Amazon society. **85m/C VHS.** Joe Robinson, Susy Andersen.

The Thorn 🦴½ **1973 (R)** The Virgin Mary and Joseph try to raise Jesus Christ in the modern world. **90m/C VHS.** Bette Midler, John Bassberger.

The Thorn Birds 🦴🦴🦴 **1983** Pioneers find danger and romance in the Australian outback as they struggle to begin a dynasty. Charismatic priest sometimes hurts, sometimes helps them. One of Stanwyck's last performances; Ward's American TV debut. Originally a ten-hour TV miniseries based on Colleen McCullough novel. Emmy nominations for actor Chamberlain, supporting actors Brown and Plummer, supporting actress Laurie, direction, photography, music, costume design, and editing. **486m/C VHS.** Rachel Ward, Richard Chamberlain, Jean Simmons, Ken Howard, Mare Winningham, Richard Kiley, Piper Laurie, Bryan Brown, Christopher Plummer, Barbara Stanwyck; ***D:*** Daryl Duke; ***C:*** Bill Butler; ***M:*** Henry Mancini. **TV**

Thoroughbreds Don't Cry && ½ 1937 Rooney plays a jockey who throws a race so his no-good father can win enough money to pay for his supposed medical problems. The owner of the horse then drops dead from a heart attack. Rooney feels guilty, so he asks his father to loan the owner's grandson $1,000 to run in another race. His father says no, so Rooney steals the money from him, and when the father finds out he tells the track officials that Rooney threw the race. Garland is Rooney's best friend and moral support, and she sings a few songs too! A fairly good horse racing story. **80m/B VHS.** Judy Garland, Mickey Rooney, Sophie Tucker, Sir C. Aubrey Smith, Ronald Sinclair, Forrester Harvey; ***D:*** Alfred E. Green.

Thoroughly Modern Millie && ½ 1967 (G) Andrews is a young woman who comes to New York in the early 1920s where she meets another newcomer, the innocent Moore. Andrews decides to upgrade her image to that of a "modern" woman, a flapper, and sets out to realize her ambition, to become a stenographer and marry the boss. Meanwhile, Moore has become an object of interest to Lillie, who just happens to run a white-slavery ring. Lots of frantic moments and big production numbers in this campy film. Channing and Lillie are exceptional fun. ♫Thoroughly Modern Millie; The Tapioca; Jimmy; The Jewish Wedding Song; Baby Face; Do It Again; Poor Butterfly; Rose of Washington Square; I Can't Believe That You're In Love With Me. **138m/C VHS.** Julie Andrews, Carol Channing, Mary Tyler Moore, John Gavin, Beatrice Lillie, James Fox, Noriyuki "Pat" Morita; ***D:*** George Roy Hill; ***W:*** Richard Morris; ***C:*** Russell Metty; ***M:*** Elmer Bernstein. Oscars '67: Orig. Score; Golden Globes '68: Support. Actress (Channing).

Those Calloways && ½ 1965 (PG) A small town family attempts to establish a sanctuary for the flocks of wild geese who fly over the woods of Swiftwater, Maine. Fine Disney family fare, with good cast. Based on Paul Annixter's novel "Swiftwater." **131m/C VHS.** Brian Keith, Vera Miles, Brandon de Wilde, Walter Brennan, Ed Wynn, John Qualen, Linda Evans; ***D:*** Norman Tokar; ***W:*** Louis Pelletier; ***C:*** Edward Colman; ***M:*** Max Steiner.

Those Daring Young Men in Their Jaunty Jalopies && *Monte Carlo or Bust; Quei Temerari Sulle Loro Pazze, Scatenate, Scalcinate Carriole* 1969 (G) Daring young men in noisy slow cars trek 1500 miles across country in the 1920s and call it a race. **125m/C VHS.** *GB* Tony Curtis, Susan Hampshire, Terry-Thomas, Eric Sykes, Gert Frobe, Peter Cook, Dudley Moore, Jack Hawkins; ***D:*** Ken Annakin; ***W:*** Ken Annakin, Jack Davies.

Those Endearing Young Charms && 1945 Romance develops between a young Air Corps mechanic and a salesgirl. Complications arise when another man enters the scene. Light romantic comedy. Based on the play by Edward Chodorov. **82m/B VHS.** Robert Young, Laraine Day, Anne Jeffreys, Lawrence Tierney; ***D:*** Lewis Allen.

Those Fantastic Flying Fools && ½ *Blast-Off; Jules Verne's Rocket to the Moon* 1967 A mad race to be the first on the moon brings hilarious results. Loosely based on a Jules Verne story. **95m/C VHS.** *GB* Burl Ives, Troy Donahue, Gert Frobe, Terry-Thomas, Hermione Gingold, Daliah Lavi, Lionel Jeffries; ***D:*** Don Sharp.

Those Glory, Glory Days & ½ 1983 An English woman, secure in her position as an outstanding sports journalist, reminisces about the days when she and her friends idolized the boys on the soccer team. Nothing extraordinary, but nicely made. **92m/C VHS.** *GB* Zoe Nathenson, Liz Campion, Cathy Murphy; ***D:*** Philip Saville; ***M:*** Trevor Jones.

Those Lips, Those Eyes && ½ 1980 (R) A pre-med student takes a job as a prop boy in a summer stock company and winds up falling in love with the company's lead dancer. Subplot about aging actor is more interesting, better played by Langella. O'Connor is appropriately lovely. Nicely made, charming sleeper of a film. **106m/C VHS.** Frank Langella, Tom Hulce, Glynnis O'Connor, Jerry Stiller, Kevin McCarthy; ***D:*** Michael Pressman.

Those Magnificent Men in Their Flying Machines &&& 1965 In 1910, a wealthy British newspaper publisher is persuaded to sponsor an air race from London to Paris. Contestants come from all over the world and shenanigans, hijinks, double-crosses, and romance are found along the route. Skelton has fun in prologue, while Terry-Thomas is great as the villain. Fun from start to finish. **138m/C VHS, Wide.** *GB* Stuart Whitman, Sarah Miles, Robert Morley, Alberto Sordi, James Fox, Gert Frobe, Jean-Pierre Cassel, Flora Robson, Sam Wanamaker, Terry-Thomas, Irina Demick, Benny Hill, Gordon Jackson, Millicent Martin, Red Skelton; ***D:*** Ken Annakin; ***W:*** Ken Annakin, Jack Davies.

Those Who Love Me Can Take the Train && *Ceux Qui M'Aiment Predront le Train* 1998 Bisexual artist Jean-Baptiste Emmerich (Trintignant) has died in Paris but wished to be buried in his hometown of Limoges—a four-hour train trip for his motley group of mourners, which include friends, relatives, and former lovers of both sexes. Things don't calm down at the cemetery where yet more relatives await, including the artist's estranged twin brother. Rather than bonding in grief, the trip and funeral succeed in bringing out old hurts and rivalries and causing the shakeup of more than one relationship. French with subtitles. **122m/C VHS, DVD, Wide.** *FR* Jean-Louis Trintignant, Pascal Greggory, Charles Berling, Bruno Todeschini, Valeria Bruni-Tedeschi, Vincent Perez, Dominique Blanc, Sylvain Jacques, Marie Daems; ***D:*** Patrice Chereau; ***W:*** Patrice Chereau, Daniele Thompson, Pierre Trividic; ***C:*** Eric Gautier. Cesar '99: Cinematog., Director (Chereau), Support. Actress (Blanc).

Thou Shalt Not Kill...Except & *Stryker's War* 1987 A Vietnam vet seeks revenge on the violent cult who kidnapped his girlfriend. **84m/C VHS, DVD, Wide.** Brian Schulz, Robert Rickman, John Manfredi, Tim Quill, Cheryl Hansen, Sam Raimi, Perry Mallette, Theodore (Ted) Raimi, Glenn Barr, Scott Spiegel, Bruce Campbell, Paul Grabke; ***D:*** Josh Becker; ***W:*** Josh Becker, Scott Spiegel; ***C:*** Josh Becker; ***M:*** Joseph LoDuca.

Thoughts Are Free &&& ½ 1984 (PG) A young soldier, wounded in WWII, escapes from the train that is transporting him and his comrades to a Soviet labor camp and rejoins his family. Under the repressive communist regime, he plots his family's escape to the West but his plans are thwarted when the Berlin Wall is erected, leaving him in the West and his wife and daughter in the East. As the years go by, they can get together only by outwitting the bureaucrats. The film's title is taken from an old German folk song "Die Gedanken sind frei." **93m/C VHS.** Herbert Ludwig, Kathrin Kratzer; ***D:*** Josef Sommer.

A Thousand Acres && 1997 (R) Based on Jane Smiley's Pulitzer Prize-winning novel, it's "King Lear" set on an Iowa farm. Sisters (Pfeiffer, Lange, and Leigh) discover that their father has decided to divide the family's thousand-acre farm amongst the three of them. Then stranger Firth comes to town and divides Pfeiffer and Lange even further by showing an interest in both of them. Melodramatic and contrived, with every hot-button women's issue imaginable thrown into the mix. Director Moorhouse purportedly considered removing her name from the picture. **105m/C VHS, DVD.** Jessica Lange, Michelle Pfeiffer, Jennifer Jason Leigh, Colin Firth, Jason Robards Jr., Keith Carradine, Pat Hingle, Kevin Anderson, John Carroll Lynch, Anne Pitoniak, Vyto Ruginis, Michelle Williams, Elissabeth (Elisabeth, Elizabeth, Liz) Moss; ***D:*** Jocelyn Moorhouse; ***W:*** Laura Jones; ***C:*** Tak Fujimoto; ***M:*** Richard Hartley.

A Thousand and One Nights && ½ 1945 Handsome Aladdin (Wilde) falls in love with beautiful Princess Armina (Jergens) but fate steps in and Aladdin and sidekick Abdullah (Silvers) are off in search of a magic lamp. This time around the genie is a beautiful woman (Keyes), who falls for Aladdin herself and tries to thwart his would-be romance. Clever fun. **92m/C VHS.** Cornel Wilde, Evelyn Keyes, Adele Jergens, Phil Silvers, Rex Ingram, Dennis Hoey, Philip Van Zandt, Gus Schilling; ***D:*** Alfred E. Green; ***W:*** Jack Henley, Richard English; ***C:*** Ray Rennahan; ***M:*** Marlin Skiles.

A Thousand Clowns &&& 1965 A nonconformist has resigned from his job as chief writer for an obnoxious kiddie show in order to enjoy life. But his independence comes under fire when he becomes guardian for his young nephew and social workers take a dim view of his lifestyle. Balsam won an Oscar for his role as Robard's agent brother. Adapted from Herb Gardner's Broadway comedy. **118m/B VHS.** Jason Robards Jr., Barry J. Gordon, William Daniels, Barbara Harris, Gene Saks, Martin Balsam; ***D:*** Fred Coe; ***W:*** Herb Gardner; ***C:*** Arthur Ornitz. Oscars '65: Support. Actor (Balsam).

The Thousand Eyes of Dr. Mabuse && ½ *The Secret of Dr. Mabuse; The Diabolical Dr. Mabuse; The Shadow Versus the Thousand Eyes of Dr. Mabuse; Die Tausend Augen des Dr. Mabuse* 1960 Lang's last film is a return to his pre-war German character, the evil Dr. Mabuse. A series of strange murders occur in a Berlin hotel and police believe the killer thinks he's a reincarnation of the doctor. Disorienting chiller. German with subtitles. **103m/B VHS, DVD.** *GE* Dawn Addams, Peter Van Eyck, Gert Frobe, Wolfgang Preiss; ***D:*** Fritz Lang; ***W:*** Fritz Lang, Jan Fethke, Heinz Oskar Wuttig; ***C:*** Karl Lob; ***M:*** Gerhard Becker, Bert Grund.

A Thousand Heroes && ½ 1994 (PG) Based on the true story of United Airlines Flight 232 which took off on a flight from Denver to Chicago and then suffered engine explosions over Iowa. The jumbo jet crashed in a fiery explosion but some 200 people survived. **95m/C VHS.** Richard Thomas, Charlton Heston, James Coburn.

Thousand Pieces of Gold &&& 1991 (PG-13) A young Chinese woman is sold by her father to a marriage broker, but instead of a respectable marriage she is shipped to America and expected to work as a prostitute in an Idaho mining town. Instead she works taking in laundry as she tries to make her way in a man's world, finding a sweet romance of opposites along the way. Based on a true story. Excellent performances by Chao and Cooper. **105m/C VHS.** Rosalind Chao, Dennis Dun, Michael Paul Chan, Chris Cooper, Jimmie F. Skaggs, William Oldham, David Hayward, Beth Broderick; ***D:*** Nancy Kelly; ***W:*** Anne Makepeace; ***C:*** Bobby Bukowski; ***M:*** Gary Remal Malkin.

Thousands Cheer && ½ 1943 A flag-waving wartime musical about a tap-dancing Army private who falls in love with the colonel's daughter, culminating with an all-star (MGM) USO show. Songs include "Honeysuckle Rose," sung by Horne, and "The Joint Is Really Jumping Down at Carnegie Hall," sung by Garland. **126m/C VHS.** Gene Kelly, Kathryn Grayson, Judy Garland, Mickey Rooney, Mary Astor, John Boles, Lucille Ball, Eleanor Powell, Virginia O'Brien, Margaret O'Brien, Red Skelton, Lionel Barrymore, June Allyson, Frank Morgan, Kay Kyser, Bob Crosby, Lena Horne, Donna Reed; ***D:*** George Sidney; ***W:*** Paul Jarrico; ***C:*** George J. Folsey.

Thrashin' & 1986 (PG-13) A new-to-L.A. teen must prove himself to a tough gang on skateboards by skateboarding a certain treacherous race. For skateboarding fans only. **93m/C VHS.** Josh Brolin, Pamela Gidley, Robert Rusler, Chuck McCann; ***D:*** David Winters; ***W:*** Paul Brown; ***M:*** Barry Goldberg.

Threads &&& 1985 The famed dramatic re-creation of the effects of nuclear war on a British city and two of its families. A disturbing, uncompromising, and somewhat plausible drama. **110m/C VHS.** *GB* Karen Meagher, Rita May, David Brierly, Reece Dinsdale, Harry Beety; ***D:*** Mick Jackson. **TV**

Threat && ½ 1949 A killer escapes from jail and returns to settle the score with those who convicted him. Tense, fast-moving thriller. **66m/B VHS.** Michael O'Shea, Virginia Grey, Charles McGraw; ***D:*** Felix Feist.

Three Ages &&& 1923 A parody of D.W. Griffith's 1916 film "Intolerance." Keaton's first feature film casts him in prehistoric days, ancient Rome, and in modern times. Silent with musical score. **59m/B VHS, DVD.** Wallace Beery, Oliver Hardy, Buster Keaton; ***D:*** Buster Keaton, Edward F. (Eddie) Cline.

3 A.M. &&& 2001 Slice-of-life ensemble drama traces the doings of NYC cabbies over 36 hours. The struggling cab company, run by the owner's daughter Box (Choudhury), is on the verge of bankruptcy and her drivers are spooked by a serial killer targeting cabbies. Meawhile, Hershey (Glover) is stretching the patience of girlfriend George (Grier); Latina Salgado (Rodriguez) is tired of being sexually harassed; Bosian refugee Rasha (Tifunovic) is on the brink of being fired; and ambitious Jose (Cannavale) finds a briefcase of stolen money. **92m/C VHS, DVD.** Danny Glover, Pam Grier, Michelle Rodriguez, Sarita Choudhury, Sergej Trifunovic, Bobby Cannavale, Isaach de Bankole, Mike Starr, Paul Calderon; ***D:*** Lee Davis; ***W:*** Lee Davis; ***C:*** Enrique Chediak; ***M:*** Branford Marsalis. **CABLE**

Three Amigos && 1986 (PG) Three out-of-work silent screen stars are asked to defend a Mexican town from bandits; they think it's a public appearance stint. Spoof of Three Stooges and Mexican bandito movies that at times falls short, given the enormous amount of comedic talent involved. Generally enjoyable with some very funny scenes. Co-written by former "Saturday Night Live" producer Michaels. Short's first major film appearance. **105m/C VHS, DVD, Wide.** Chevy Chase, Steve Martin, Martin Short, Joe Mantegna, Patrice Martinez, Jon Lovitz, Phil Hartman, Randy Newman, Alfonso Arau; ***D:*** John Landis; ***W:*** Lorne Michaels, Steve Martin, Randy Newman; ***C:*** Ronald W. Browne; ***M:*** Elmer Bernstein.

The Three Avengers && ½ 1980 (R) Hung Tack (Lee) is the master of a kung fu school in a town plagued by two evil businessmen, who force Hung to take on the local gangs. During a fight, he's spotted by a talent scout and starts a career in the movies but is around to rescue a friend who's gotten into trouble. Hey, the fighting's the important part anyway. **93m/C VHS.** Bruce Lee.

Three Broadway Girls &&& *The Greeks Had a Word for Them* 1932 Three gold-diggers go husband-hunting. Well-paced, very funny telling of this old story. Remade many times, including "How to Marry a Millionaire," "Three Blind Mice," "Moon Over Miami," and "Three Little Girls in Blue." **78m/B VHS.** Joan Blondell, Ina Claire, Madge Evans, David Manners, Lowell Sherman; ***D:*** Lowell Sherman.

Three Brothers &&& *Tre Fratelli* 1980 (PG) An acclaimed Italian film by veteran Rosi about three brothers summoned to their small Italian village by a telegram saying their mother is dead. Sensitive and compassionate. In Italian with English subtitles. Adapted from Platonov's story "The Third Son." **113m/C VHS.** *IT* Philippe Noiret, Charles Vanel, Michele Placido, Vittorio Mezzogiorno, Andrea Ferreol; ***D:*** Francesco Rosi; ***W:*** Francesco Rosi; ***C:*** Pasqualino De Santis; ***M:*** Piero Piccioni.

Three Bullets for a Long Gun & ½ 1973 (PG) Two prairie renegades battle bandits as they search for an inherited gold mine. **89m/C VHS.** Keith Van Der Wat, Beau Brummel, Patrick Munhardt; ***D:*** Peter Henkel; ***W:*** Keith Van Der Wat.

Three by Hitchcock && 1928 Condensed versions of three of Hitchcock's early films (1927-28). Consists of "The Ring," "Champagne," and "The Manxman," his last silent film. **90m/B VHS.** ***D:*** Alfred Hitchcock.

The Three Caballeros && ½ 1945 (G) Donald Duck stars in this journey through Latin America. Full of music, variety, and live-action/animation segments. Stories include "Pablo the Penguin," "Little Gauchito," and adventures with Joe Carioca, who was first introduced in Disney's "Saludos Amigos." Today this film stands as one of the very best pieces of animation ever created. Great family fare. ♫The Three Caballeros; Baia. **71m/C VHS, DVD.** ***D:*** Norman Ferguson; ***V:*** Sterling Holloway, Aurora Miranda.

Three Came Home 1950 Colbert is an American married to a British administrator in the Far East during WWII. Conquering Japanese throw the whole family into a brutal POW concentration camp, and their confinement is recounted in harrowing and unsparing detail. Superior drama, also laudable for a fairly even-handed portrayal of the enemy captors. Based on an autobiographical book by Agnes Newton-Keith. **106m/B VHS, DVD.** Claudette Colbert, Patric Knowles, Sessue Hayakawa, Florence Desmond, Sylvia Andrew, Mark Keuning, Phyllis Morris, Howard Chuman; ***D:*** Jean Negulesco; ***W:*** Nunnally Johnson; ***C:*** William H. Daniels, Milton Krasner; ***M:*** Hugo Friedhofer.

Three Cases of Murder 1955 Three fast-paced tales of mayhem. "In the Picture" features a deranged taxidermist, a creepy house, and a hapless museum guide. From a story by Roderick Wilkinson. Two friends are in love with the same girl in "You Killed Elizabeth" and when she turns up dead it's clear one of them is guilty. From a story by Brett Halliday. The best features Welles as "Lord Mountdrago," who destroys the career of a fellow Parliament Member and is haunted by fears of retaliation. Based on a story by W. Somerset Maugham. **99m/B VHS.** *GB* Alan Badel, John Gregson, Orson Welles, Elizabeth Sellars, Hugh Pryse, Jack Lambert; ***D:*** Wendy Toye, David Eady, George More O'Ferrell; ***W:*** Donald Wilson, Sidney Carroll, Ian Dalrymple; ***C:*** Georges Perinal; ***M:*** Doreen Carwithen.

Three Charlies and One Phoney! 1918 Three of Charlie Chaplin's best comedy shorts, plus one featuring his best-known imitator—Billy West. Included are "Recreation" ("Fun is Fun") ("Spring Fever"), "His Musical Career" ("The Piano Movers") ("Musical Tramps"), "The Bond" (featuring Charlie in a Liberty Bond appeal) and "His Day Out" with Billy West imitating Chaplin. All but "His Day Out" were written and directed by Chaplin. **69m/B VHS, 8mm.** Charlie Chaplin, Mack Swain, Charley Chase, Edna Purviance, Sydney Chaplin, Albert Austin; ***D:*** Charlie Chaplin; ***W:*** Charlie Chaplin.

Three Coins in the Fountain 1954 Three women throw money into fountain and get romantically involved with Italian men. Outstanding CinemaScope photography captures beauty of Italian setting. Sammy Cahn theme song sung by Frank Sinatra. ♫Three Coins in the Fountain. **102m/C VHS.** Clifton Webb, Dorothy McGuire, Jean Peters, Louis Jourdan, Maggie McNamara, Rossano Brazzi; ***D:*** Jean Negulesco; ***C:*** Milton Krasner. Oscars '54: Color Cinematog., Song ("Three Coins in the Fountain").

Three Comrades 1938 Taylor, Tone, and Young are three friends, reunited in bleak, post-WWI Germany, who meet and befriend Sullavan, a tubercular beauty. Reluctant to marry because of her health, she's finally persuaded to wed Taylor, amidst the country's increasing unrest. Tragedy strikes Sullavan and the politicized Young and the two remaining comrades face an uncertain future. Bleak but forceful and passionate drama. Sullavan's performance is superb. Based on the novel by Erich Maria Remarque. Fitzgerald's script was heavily re-written because both Sullavan and producer Mankiewicz found his approach too literary with unspeakable dialogue. **99m/B VHS.** Robert Taylor, Margaret Sullavan, Robert Young, Franchot Tone, Lionel Atwill, Guy Kibbee, Henry Hull, George Zucco, Monty Woolley, Charley Grapewin, Spencer Charters, Sarah Padden; ***D:*** Frank Borzage; ***W:*** F. Scott Fitzgerald, Edward Paramore; ***C:*** Joseph Ruttenberg; ***M:*** Franz Waxman. N.Y. Film Critics '38: Actress (Sullavan).

Three Daring Daughters 1948 When her husband leaves her and she almost misses her daughter's graduation due to a fainting spell, MacDonald takes hiatus on a cruise ship where she meets and marries pianist Iturbi. Unknowing, the three daughters at home conspire to get Dad back in the family. Enraged when Mom returns with newfound hubby, the threesome do all in their power to make the newlyweds as miserable as possible. Happily ended musical-comedy is chock full of memorable tunes. Based on the play "The Bees and the Flowers" by Kohner and Albert Manning. ♫Route 66; The Dickey Bird Song; Alma Mater; Fleurette; Passepied; Where There's Love; Ritual Fire Dance; You Made Me Love You; Happy Birthday. **115m/C VHS.** Jeanette MacDonald, Jose Iturbi, Jane Powell, Edward Arnold, Harry Davenport, Moyna MacGill, Elinor Donahue, Ann E. Todd; ***D:*** Fred M. Wilcox; ***W:*** Sonya Levien, John Meehan, Albert Mannheimer, Frederick Kohner.

Three Days in Beirut 1983 **(PG)** A soldier of fortune and a beautiful interpreter join forces against a backdrop of Middle Eastern politics, espionage, and violence. **94m/C VHS.** Diana Sands, Calvin Lockhart; ***D:*** Michael A. Schultz.

Three Days of the Condor 1975 **(R)** CIA researcher Joe Turner (Redford) leaves the office to get sme lunch and returns to find all his colleagues murdered. He calls for help but learns his own organization is responsible for the slaughter. So Joe goes on the run until he can expose the conspiracy. Good performance by Dunaway as photographer Kathy Hale, who is forced by Joe to help him but then becomes a willing accomplice. A post-Watergate tale of paranoia and suspense. Based on "Six Days of the Condor" by James Grady. **118m/C VHS, DVD, Wide.** Robert Redford, Faye Dunaway, Cliff Robertson, Max von Sydow, John Houseman; ***D:*** Sydney Pollack; ***W:*** David Rayfiel; ***C:*** Owen Roizman; ***M:*** Dave Grusin.

Three Days to a Kill 1991 **(R)** Calvin Sims is a mercenary hired to rescue a kidnapped ambassador—by any means necessary. **90m/C VHS.** Fred Williamson, Bo Svenson, Henry Silva, Chuck Connors, Van Johnson, Sonny Landham; ***D:*** Fred Williamson.

Three Desperate Men 1950 Three brothers accused of murder become outlaws. Not innovative, but satisfactory tale of the Old West. **71m/B VHS.** Preston Foster, Virginia Grey, Jim Davis; ***D:*** Sam Newfield.

The Three Faces of Eve 1957 Emotionally disturbed Eve (Woodward) seeks the help of psychiatrist Dr. Luther (Cobb), who eventually discovers she has three distinct personalities: a downtrodden housewife, a party girl, and a well-educated, well-balanced woman. So Luther decides to integrate all three into one Eve. Although Woodward gives a powerful performance, the film has dated badly, particularly the narration by Cooke, which gives the film a now-stilted air. Although the film is fact-based, the story was deemed too implausible for the public to believe at the time without the assurances of the narrator. **91m/B VHS.** Joanne Woodward, David Wayne, Lee J. Cobb, Nancy Kulp, Edwin Jerome, Vince Edwards; ***D:*** Nunnally Johnson; ***W:*** Nunnally Johnson; ***C:*** Stanley Cortez; ***M:*** Robert Emmett Dolan; ***Nar:*** Alistair Cooke. Oscars '57: Actress (Woodward); Golden Globes '58: Actress—Drama (Woodward).

Three Faces West *The Refugee* 1940 A dust bowl community is helped by a Viennese doctor who left Europe to avoid Nazi capture. He's aided by the Duke in this odd combination of Western frontier saga and anti-Nazi propaganda. Works only part of the time. **79m/B VHS.** John Wayne, Charles Coburn, Sigrid Gurie, Sonny Bupp, Russell Simpson; ***D:*** Bernard Vorhaus.

3:15—The Moment of Truth 1986 **(R)** A vicious high school gang is confronted by an angry exmember in this so-so teen delinquent film. **86m/C VHS.** Adam Baldwin, Deborah Foreman, Rene Auberjonois, Danny De La Paz; ***D:*** Larry Gross; ***W:*** Sam Bernard; ***M:*** Gary Chang.

357 Magnum 1977 Jonathan Hightower, the CIA's special investigator in the Far East, speaks softly and carries a very big gun. **71m/C VHS.** Marland T. Stewart, James Whitworth, Kathryn Hayes.

Three for Bedroom C 1952 A movie star and a scientist make romance on a train bound for Los Angeles. Swanson's follow-up to "Sunset Boulevard." **74m/C VHS.** Gloria Swanson, Fred Clark, Steve Brodie, Hans Conried, Margaret Dumont; ***D:*** Milton Bren.

Three for the Road 1987 **(PG)** A young aspiring political aide and his roommate must escort a Senator's ill-mannered and spoiled daughter to a reform institution. On the road, they run into more than a few obstacles. Good performances elevate a bland script. Sheen made this movie before his riveting performance as a young GI in "Platoon." **98m/C** Charlie Sheen, Kerri Green, Alan Ruck, Sally Kellerman; ***D:*** Bill W.L. Norton; ***W:*** Tim Metcalfe; ***M:*** Barry Goldberg.

Three for the Show 1955 Julie (Grable) is a song-and-dance queen whose husband, Marty (Lemmon), was presumed dead in WWII. After she marries his songwriting partner, Vernon (Champion), Marty naturally shows up. Because she loves both men, Julie decides to set-up a household threesome until she can make up her mind. Champion's real-life spouse and dance partner, Marge, plays Grable's best friend. Some good dance numbers don't make up for the weak script. Based on the W. Somerset Maugham play "Too Many Husbands" and filmed under that title in 1940. ♫Someone to Watch Over Me; WHich One?; Down Boy!; I've Been Kissed Before; I've Got a Crush on You; How Come You Like Me Like You Do?; Three for the Show. **93m/C VHS.** Betty Grable, Jack Lemmon, Gower Champion, Marge Champion, Myron McCormick, Paul Harvey; ***D:*** H.C. Potter; ***W:*** Leonard Stern, Edward Hope; ***C:*** Arthur E. Arling; ***M:*** George Duning.

Three Fugitives 1989 **(PG-13)** An ex-con holdup man determined to go straight is taken hostage by a bungling first-time bank robber, who is only attempting the holdup in order to support his withdrawn young daughter. Ex-con Nolte winds up on the lam with the would-be robber and his daughter. The comedy is fun, the sentimental moments too sweet and slow. Remake of French "Les Fugitifs." **96m/C VHS, DVD, Wide.** Nick Nolte, Martin Short, James Earl Jones, Kenneth McMillan, Sarah Rowland Doroff, Alan Ruck; ***D:*** Francis Veber; ***W:*** Francis Veber; ***C:*** Haskell Wexler; ***M:*** David McHugh.

Three Godfathers 1948 A sweet and sentimental western has three half-hearted outlaws on the run, taking with them an infant they find in the desert. Dedicated to western star and Ford alumni Harry Carey Sr. (whose son is one of the outlaws in the film), who died of cancer the year before. Ford had first filmed the tale with Carey Sr. as "Marked Men" in 1919. **82m/C VHS.** John Wayne, Pedro Armendariz Sr., Harry Carey Jr., Ward Bond, Mae Marsh, Jane Darwell, Ben Johnson, Mildred Natwick, Guy Kibbee; ***D:*** John Ford; ***C:*** Winton C. Hoch.

Three Guys Named Mike 1951 Wyman plays an overly enthusiastic airline stewardess who finds herself the object of affection from three guys named Mike, including an airline pilot, an advertising man, and a scientist. A cute comedy. **89m/B VHS.** Jane Wyman, Van Johnson, Barry Sullivan, Howard Keel, Phyllis Kirk, Jeff Donnell; ***D:*** Charles Walters; ***W:*** Sidney Sheldon.

The 300 Year Weekend 1971 Ten people gather for a weekend-long group therapy session, led by Dr. Marshall (Tolan), that reveals what troubles them. You won't be interested. **123m/C VHS.** Michael (Lawrence) Tolan, William Devane, Gabriel Dell, Dorothy Lyman, James Congdon, Sharon Laughlin, Roy Cooper, M'el Dowd, Bernard Ward, Carole Demas; ***D:*** Victor Stoloff; ***W:*** William Devane, Victor Stoloff; ***C:*** Joseph Brun; ***M:*** Gilber Fuller.

The 317th Platoon 1965 An emotionally gripping war drama of the French-Vietnamese War in which the 317th Platoon of the French Army, consisting of four French commanders and 41 Laotians, is ordered to leave Luong Ba, Cambodia and retreat to Tao Tsai. The men begin their march and slowly succumb to the elements and ambushes. Days later, when what is left of the platoon finally reaches Tao Tsai, the camp is in enemy hands and the remnants of the 317th Platoon are killed in cold blood. Director Shoendoerffer portrays this struggle, conflict, and the quiet haunting tension of war with great skill. In French with English subtitles. **100m/B VHS.** *FR* Jacques Perrin, Bruno Cremer, Pierre Fabre, Manuel Zarzo; ***D:*** Pierre Schoendoerffer; ***W:*** Pierre Schoendoerffer; ***C:*** Raoul Coutard; ***M:*** Gregorio Garcia Segura, Pierre Jansen.

Three Husbands 1950 A deceased playboy leaves letters for the title characters incriminating their wives in extramarital affairs. The men's reactions are pure farce—even though this same concept was played straight with a sex change in the earlier "A Letter to Three Wives." **79m/B VHS.** Eve Arden, Ruth Warrick, Vanessa Brown, Howard da Silva, Shepperd Strudwick, Jane Darwell; ***D:*** Irving Reis.

Three in the Attic 1968 **(R)** A college student juggles three girlfriends at the same time. When the girls find out they are being two-timed, they lock their boyfriend in an attic and exhaust him with forced sexual escapades. Then they talk. Limited trashy and foolish appeal. **92m/C VHS.** Christopher Jones, Yvette Mimieux, John Beck; ***D:*** Richard Wilson.

Three in the Cellar *Up in the Cellar* 1970 **(R)** A disgruntled college student seeks revenge on the school president by seducing his wife, daughter and mistress. Good screenplay helps carry it off. **92m/C VHS.** Wes Stern, Joan Collins, Larry Hagman, Judy Pace; ***D:*** Theodore J. Flicker.

Three in the Saddle 1945 Ritter and the Texas Rangers fight for law and order. **61m/B VHS.** Tex Ritter, Dave O'Brien, Charles "Blackie" King; ***D:*** Harry Fraser.

Three Kinds of Heat 1987 **(R)** Three Interpol agents track down a warring Asian crime lord. Alternately tongue-in-cheek and silly. Never released in theatres—it found it's home on video. Stevens created "The Outer Limits" for TV. **88m/C VHS.** Robert Ginty, Victoria Barrett, Shakti; ***D:*** Leslie Stevens. **VIDEO**

Three Kings 1999 **(R)** Director Russell turns the war movie genre on its ear with his subversive, chaotic, and ultimately satisfying studio film debut. At the end of the Gulf War, Special Forces Major Gates (Clooney) recruits three Army reservists to join him on an illegal mission to steal gold bullion which Hussein's troops had stolen from Kuwait. They wind up learning too much about U.S. policies and broken promises in the Middle East. Clooney is perfect as the pragmatic Gates, and Russell supplies the right mix of cynicism, dark humor, and action-movie heroism. **115m/C VHS, DVD, Wide.** George Clooney, Mark Wahlberg, Ice Cube, Spike Jonze, Nora Dunn, Jamie Kennedy, Mykelti Williamson, Clifford Curtis, Said Taghmaoui, Judy Greer, Liz Stauber, Holt McCallany; ***D:*** David O. Russell; ***W:*** David O. Russell; ***C:*** Newton Thomas (Tom) Sigel; ***M:*** Carter Burwell. Broadcast Film Critics '99: Breakthrough Perf. (Jonze).

Three Legionnaires *Three Crazy Legionnaires* 1937 Three soldiers cavort in a post-WWI Siberian tank town. **67m/B VHS.** Robert Armstrong, Lyle Talbot, Fifi d'Orsay, Anne Nagel, Donald Meek.

The Three Little Pigs 1984 From "Faerie Tale Theatre" comes the story of three little pigs, the houses they lived in and the wolf that tried to do them in. **60m/C VHS.** Billy Crystal, Jeff Goldblum, Valerie Perrine; ***D:*** Howard Storm. **CABLE**

Three Little Words 1950 A musical biography of songwriting team Harry Ruby and Bert Kalmar, filled with Kalmar-Ruby numbers. Helen Kane (famous for her boop-boop-de-boops) dubbed "I Wanna Be Loved By You" for Reynolds. A musical in the best MGM tradition. ♫I Wanna Be Loved By You; Who's Sorry Now?; Three Little Words; I Love You So Much; She's Mine, All Mine; So-Long, Oo-Long; Hooray for Captain Spaulding; Up In the Clouds; All Alone Monday. **102m/C VHS.** Fred Astaire, Red Skelton, Vera-Ellen, Arlene Dahl, Keenan Wynn, Gloria De Haven, Debbie Reynolds, Gale Robbins; ***D:*** Richard Thorpe; ***M:*** Andre Previn. Golden Globes '51: Actor—Mus./Comedy (Astaire).

Three Lives and Only One Death 🦴🦴½ *Trois Vies et Une Seule Mort* **1996** Surrealist film features Mastroianni in four roles. Salesman Mateo Strano walks out on his wife Maria (Paredes) and doesn't see her for 20 years. When he finally returns, Mateo wants her back, although Maria's got a new husband, Andre (Atkine). Then there's Georges Vickers, negative anthropology professor-turned street tramp who takes up with hooker Tania (Galiena), who also has another identity. Then he's a butler who's trying to murder a young couple and steal their child and finally, Mastroianni's a rich industrialist who seems to be suffering from multiple personalities. And yes, somehow all the stories do tie together. French with subtitles. **124m/C VHS.** *FR* Marcello Mastroianni, Anna Galiena, Marisa Paredes, Melvil Poupaud, Chiara Mastroianni, Arielle Dombasle, Feodor Atkine, Jean-Yves Gautier, Pierre Bellemare, Lou Castel, Jacques Pieller; ***D:*** Raul Ruiz; ***W:*** Raul Ruiz, Pascal Bonitzer; ***C:*** Laurent Machuel; ***M:*** Jorge Arriagada.

The Three Lives of Karen 🦴🦴½ **1997 (PG-13)** Thriller finds Karen Winthrop (O'Grady) engaged to state trooper Matt (Guinee) and seemingly happy until Paul Riggs (Boutsikaris) shows up. He has proof that Karen is actually his wife Emily who disappeared four years before, abandoning him and their daughter Jessica (Bugajski). So the confused Karen returns with Paul to try and remember what happened to her. She learns that she's actually disappeared twice before and the flashbacks Karen has of her past are terrifying. **89m/C VHS.** Gail O'Grady, Dennis Boutsikaris, Tim Guinee, Monica Bugajski; ***D:*** David Burton Morris; ***W:*** David Chisholm; ***C:*** John L. Demps Jr. **CABLE**

The Three Lives of Thomasina 🦴🦴🦴 **1963 (PG)** In turn-of-the-century Scotland, a veterinarian orders his daughter's beloved cat destroyed when the pet is diagnosed with tetanus. After the cat's death (with scenes of kitty heaven), a beautiful and mysterious healer from the woods is able to bring the animal back to life and restore the animal to the little girl. Lovely Disney fairy tale with good performances by all. **95m/C VHS.** Patrick McGoohan, Susan Hampshire, Karen Dotrice, Matthew Garber; ***D:*** Don Chaffey; ***V:*** Elspeth March.

Three Men and a Baby 🦴🦴🦴 **1987 (PG)** The arrival of a young baby forever changes the lives of three sworn bachelors living in New York. Well-paced, charming and fun, with good acting from all. A remake of the French movie "Three Men and a Cradle." **102m/C VHS, DVD, 8mm, Wide.** Tom Selleck, Steve Guttenberg, Ted Danson, Margaret Colin, Nancy Travis, Philip Bosco, Celeste Holm, Derek De Lint, Cynthia Harris, Lisa Blair, Michelle Blair, Paul Guilfoyle; ***D:*** Leonard Nimoy; ***W:*** James Orr, Jim Cruickshank; ***C:*** Adam Greenberg; ***M:*** Marvin Hamlisch.

Three Men and a Cradle 🦴🦴🦴½ *Trois Hommes et un Couffin* **1985 (PG-13)** Three carefree bachelors, Jacques (Dussollier), Pierre (Giraud), and Michel (Boujenah), find a baby girl in a basket outside the door of the home they share. One is the father—although none of the men are sure which one it is. After the initial shock of learning how to take care of a child, they fall in love with her and won't let her go. There's a strange subplot about Jacques hiding heroin in the baby's diapers that gets them all involved with drug dealers. Still, everything is played for laughs and the film has heaps of charm. French with subtitles. Remade in 1987 as "Three Men and a Baby." **100m/C VHS.** *FR* Roland Giraud, Michel Boujenah, Andre Dussollier, Phillippe LeRoy, Marthe Villalonga, Dominque Lavanant; ***D:*** Coline Serreau; ***W:*** Coline Serreau; ***C:*** Jean-Yves Escoffier. Cesar '86: Film, Support. Actor (Boujenah), Writing.

Three Men and a Little Lady 🦴🦴½ **1990 (PG)** In this sequel to "Three Men and a Baby," the mother of the once abandoned infant decides that her child needs a father. Although she wants Selleck, he doesn't get the message and so she chooses a snooty British director. The rest of the movie features various semi-comic attempts to rectify the situation. **100m/C VHS, DVD.** Tom Selleck, Steve Guttenberg, Ted Danson, Nancy Travis, Robin Weisman, Christopher Cazenove, Fiona Shaw, Sheila Hancock, John Boswall, Jonathan Lynn, Sydney Walsh; ***D:*** Emile Ardolino; ***W:*** Charlie Peters, Sara Parriott, Josann McGibbon; ***C:*** Adam Greenberg; ***M:*** James Newton Howard.

Three Men on a Horse 🦴🦴🦴 **1936** Comedy classic about mild-mannered McHugh's ability to predict horse races and the bettors that try to take advantage of him. Blondell is great as the Brooklynese girlfriend of one of the bettors. Lots of laughs, but don't watch for the horse-racing scenes, because there aren't many. **88m/B VHS.** Frank McHugh, Joan Blondell, Carol Hughes, Allen Jenkins, Guy Kibbee, Sam Levene; ***D:*** Mervyn LeRoy.

The Three Musketeers 🦴🦴 *D'Artagnan* **1916** One of the many movie adaptation of Alexandre Dumas' adventure, but this one comes from the hand of famed movie pioneer Ince. D'Artagnan joins the title characters in saving France's Queen Anne from a nefarious plot. Silent with the original organ score. **74m/B VHS, 8mm.** Orin Johnson, Dorothy Dalton, Louise Glaum, Walt Whitman; ***D:*** Charles Swickard.

The Three Musketeers 🦴🦴🦴½ **1921** D'Artagnan swashbuckles silently amid stylish sets, scores of extras and exquisite costumes. Relatively faithful adaptation of Alexandre Dumas novel, slightly altered in favor of D'Artagnan's lover. Classic Fairbanks, who also produced. **120m/B VHS, DVD.** Douglas Fairbanks Sr., Leon Bary, George Siegmann, Eugene Pallette, Boyd Irwin, Thomas Holding, Sidney Franklin, Charles Stevens, Nigel de Brulier, Willis Robards, Mary MacLaren; ***D:*** Fred Niblo; ***W:*** Lotta Woods, Douglas Fairbanks Sr.; ***C:*** Arthur Edeson; ***M:*** Louis F. Gottschalk.

The Three Musketeers **1933** Modern adaptation of the classic tale by Alexander Dumas depicts the three friends as members of the Foreign Legion. Weakest of Wayne serials, in 12 parts. **215m/B VHS, DVD.** John Wayne, Raymond Hatton, Lon Chaney Jr.

The Three Musketeers 🦴🦴 **1935** Three swordsmen, loyal to each other, must battle the corrupt Cardinal Richelieu. Generally regarded as the least exciting adaptation of Alexander Dumas' classic tale. The first talking version. **95m/B VHS.** Walter Abel, Paul Lukas, Moroni Olsen, Ian Keith, Margot Grahame, Heather Angel, Onslow Stevens, Miles Mander; ***D:*** Rowland V. Lee; ***M:*** Max Steiner.

The Three Musketeers 🦴🦴½ *The Singing Musketeer* **1939** Musical-comedy version of the famed Alexandre Dumas swashbuckling saga. Ameche is a singing D'Artagnan and the three Ritz brothers are the inept and cowardly Musketeers (who turn out to be phonies, after all). Silly fun. ♫My Lady; Song of the Musketeers; Voila; Chicken Soup. **73m/B VHS.** Don Ameche, Al Ritz, Harry Ritz, Jimmy Ritz, Binnie Barnes, Lionel Atwill, Miles Mander, Gloria Stuart, Pauline Moore, Joseph Schildkraut, John Carradine, Douglass Dumbrille; ***D:*** Allan Dwan; ***W:*** M.M. Musselman, William A. Drake, Sam Hellman.

The Three Musketeers 🦴🦴½ **1948** The three musketeers who are "all for one and one for all" join forces with D'Artagnan to battle the evil Cardinal Richelieu in this rambunctious adaptation of the classic tale by Alexander Dumas. Good performances by the cast, who combined drama and comedy well. Turner's first color film. **126m/C VHS.** Lana Turner, Gene Kelly, June Allyson, Gig Young, Angela Lansbury, Van Heflin, Keenan Wynn, Robert Coote, Reginald Owen, Frank Morgan, Vincent Price, Patricia Medina; ***D:*** George Sidney.

The Three Musketeers 🦴🦴🦴½ **1974 (PG)** Extravagant and funny version of the Dumas classic. Three swashbucklers (Reed, Chamberlain, Finlay) and their country cohort (York), who wishes to join the Musketeers, set out to save the honor of the French Queen (Chaplin). To do so they must oppose the evil cardinal (Heston) who has his eyes on the power behind the throne and who is aided by cohort Milady (Dunaway). Welch is amusing as clumsy lady-in-waiting Constance. A strong cast leads this winning combination of slapstick and high adventure. Followed by "The Four Musketeers" and "The Return of the Musketeers." **105m/C VHS, DVD.** Richard Chamberlain, Oliver Reed, Michael York, Raquel Welch, Frank Finlay, Christopher Lee, Faye Dunaway, Charlton Heston, Geraldine Chaplin, Simon Ward, Jean-Pierre Cassel, William Hobbs; ***D:*** Richard Lester; ***W:*** George MacDonald Fraser; ***C:*** David Watkin; ***M:*** Michel Legrand. Golden Globes '75: Actress—Mus./Comedy (Welch).

The Three Musketeers 🦴🦴½ **1993 (PG)** Yet another version of the classic swashbuckler with Porthos, Athos, Aramis, and the innocent D'Artanan banding together against the evil Cardinal Richelieu and the tempting Milady DeWinter to save France. Cute stars, a little swordplay, a few jokes, and cartoon bad guys. Okay for the younger crowd. **105m/C VHS, DVD.** Kiefer Sutherland, Charlie Sheen, Chris O'Donnell, Oliver Platt, Rebecca DeMornay, Tim Curry, Gabrielle Anwar, Julie Delpy, Michael Wincott; ***D:*** Stephen Herek; ***W:*** David Loughery; ***C:*** Dean Semler; ***M:*** Michael Kamen.

3 Ninjas 🦴🦴½ **1992 (PG)** Lively kid's actioner about three brothers who are trained as ninjas by their grandpa. When a group of bad guys tries to kidnap the boys, they're in for trouble. Sort of a cross between "The Karate Kid" and "Home Alone" that is suitable for family viewing. Followed by "3 Ninjas Kick Back." **84m/C VHS.** Victor Wong, Michael Treanor, Max Elliott Slade, Chad Power, Rand Kingsley, Alan McRae, Margarita Franco, Toru Tanaka, Patrick Laborteaux; ***D:*** Jon Turteltaub; ***W:*** Edward Emanuel; ***M:*** Rick Marvin.

3 Ninjas: High Noon at Mega Mountain 🦴🦴 *Three Ninjas: Showdown at Mega Mountain* **1997 (PG)** Fourth installment of the kid-fantasy franchise finds brothers Rocky (Botuchis), Colt (O'Laskey), and Tum-Tum (Roeske) in the middle of a takeover at an amusement park. The ninja trained brothers, along with a computer-whiz neighbor (Earlywine) and retiring action hero Dave Dragon (Hogan) must save the day when Medusa (Anderson) and her henchmen ransom the park and its guests. Typically, the adults are incompetent when they're not busy being nasty. Pre-pubescent kids are the only ones likely to find this entertaining—if they're not too discriminating. The "action" is somewhere between cartoon and pro wrestling. Varney stands out as Medusa's lead henchman. **93m/C VHS.** Hulk Hogan, Loni Anderson, Jim Varney, Victor Wong, Mathew Botuchis, Michael J. O'Laskey II, J.P. Roeske II, Chelsey Earlywine, Alan McRae, Margarita Franco, Kirk Baily; ***D:*** Sean McNamara; ***W:*** Sean McNamara, Jeff Phillips; ***C:*** Blake T. Evans; ***M:*** John Coda.

3 Ninjas Kick Back 🦴🦴½ **1994 (PG)** Sequel to the popular "3 Ninjas." Three brothers help their grandfather protect a ceremonial knife won in a ninja tournament in Japan 50 years earlier. Gramps' ancient adversary in that tournament, now an evil tycoon, wants the sword back and he's willing to enlist the aid of his three American grandchildren, members of garage band Teenage Vomit, to get it. The showdown eventually heads to Japan, where "Kick Back," unlike predecessors, dispenses with the Japan-bashing. High-spirited action fare that kids will enjoy. **95m/C VHS, DVD, Wide.** Victor Wong, Max Elliott Slade, Sean Fox, Evan Bonifant, Sab Shimono, Dustin Nguyen, Jason Schombing, Caroline Junko King, Angelo Tiffe; ***D:*** Charles Kanganis; ***W:*** Mark Saltzman; ***C:*** Christopher Faloona; ***M:*** Rick Marvin.

3 Ninjas Knuckle Up 🦴🦴½ **1995 (PG-13)** Brothers Rocky (Treanor), Tum Tum (Power), and Colt (Slade) spend their summer vacation with ever-wise Grandpa Mori (Wong) and get to practice their martial arts skills on a variety of villains. Seems a waste management company has been illegally dumping toxins onto the nearby Indian reservation where the boys' friend Jo (Lightning) lives and have even kidnapped her dad (Shanks) to keep him silent. So it's our pint-sized heroes to the rescue. Filmed in '92 but released after "3 Ninjas Kick Back," which explains why Treanor and Power are missing from the second film. **94m/C VHS.** Victor Wong, Michael Treanor, Chad Power, Max Elliott Slade, Crystle Lightning, Patrick Kilpatrick, Don Shanks, Charles Napier, Nick Ramus, Vincent Schiavelli; ***D:*** Simon S. Sheen; ***W:*** Alex S. Kim; ***C:*** Eugene Shlugleit; ***M:*** Gary Stevan Scott.

Three Nuts in Search of a Bolt 🦴½ **1964 (R)** Three neurotics send a surrogate to a comely psychiatrist for help, but the shrink thinks the surrogate's a three-way multiple personality. Raunchy monkey-shines ensue. Includes Van Doren's infamous beer bath scene. **78m/C VHS.** Mamie Van Doren, Tommy Noonan, Paul Gilbert, Alvy Moore; ***D:*** Tommy Noonan.

301, 302 🦴 **1994** Confusing horror story told in flashbacks focuses on two women in neighboring high-rise apartments. A young policeman is investigating the disappearance of the woman from apartment 302 (Hwang). He questions the tenant across the hall in 301 (Pang), an obsessive cook who tries to share her culinary results with Hwang, who happens to be an anorexic writer. Both have dark secrets in their pasts, which they share, leading to a grotesque resolution of their friendship. **99m/C VHS.** *KN* Eun-Jin Bang, Sin-Hye Hwang, Chu-Ryun Kim; ***D:*** Chul-Soo Park; ***W:*** Suh-Goon Lee.

Three o'Clock High 🦴🦴½ **1987 (PG)** A nerdy high school journalist is assigned a profile of the new kid in school, who turns out to be the biggest bully, too. He approaches his task with great unease. Silly teenage farce is given souped-up direction by Spielberg protege Joanou. Features decent work by the young cast. **97m/C VHS.** Casey Siemaszko, Anne Ryan, Stacey Glick, Jonathan Wise, Richard Tyson, Jeffrey Tambor, Philip Baker Hall, John P. Ryan; ***D:*** Phil Joanou; ***W:*** Richard Christian Matheson, Thomas Szollosi; ***M:*** Tangerine Dream.

Three of Hearts 🦴½ **1993 (R)** Slick look at love in contemporary downtown New York. The triangle consists of Connie (Lynch), just dumped by bisexual girlfriend Ellen (Fenn), who is in turn seduced by hired escort Joe (Baldwin), who will break her heart, causing her to turn back to the sympathetic Connie. But guess what happens. Hiply superficial plot is transparent although the three leads are likeable, especially Lynch as the lanky lovelorn Connie. Don't read further if you don't want to know what happens since the film was shot with two endings. The U.S. release pairs Joe and Ellen for a typically American happy ending; the European release doesn't. **102m/C VHS.** Kelly Lynch, William Baldwin, Sherilyn Fenn, Joe Pantoliano, Gail Strickland, Cec Verrell, Claire Callaway, Tony Amendola; ***D:*** Yurek Bogayevicz; ***W:*** Adam Greenman; ***M:*** Richard Gibbs.

Three on a Match 🦴🦴🦴 **1932** An actress, a stenographer and a society woman get together for a tenth year reunion. They become embroiled in a world of crime when Blondell's gangster boyfriend takes a liking to Dvorak. She leaves her husband and takes up with the crook. The results are tragic. Bogart's first gangster role. **64m/B VHS.** Joan Blondell, Warren William, Ann Dvorak, Bette Davis, Lyle Talbot, Humphrey Bogart, Patricia Ellis, Grant Mitchell; ***D:*** Mervyn LeRoy.

Three on a Meathook woof! **1972** When a young man and his father living on an isolated farm receive female visitors, bloodshed is quick to follow. Essentially a remake of "Psycho," and very loosely based on the crimes of Ed Gein. Filmed in Louisville, Kentucky. **85m/C VHS.** Charles Kissinger, James Pickett, Sherry Steiner, Carolyn Thompson; ***D:*** William Girdler; ***W:*** William Girdler; ***C:*** William Asman; ***M:*** William Girdler.

The Three Penny Opera 🦴🦴🦴 *Die Dreigroschenoper* **1962** Mack the Knife presides over an exciting world of thieves, murderers, beggars, prostitutes and corrupt officials in a seedy section of London. Based on the opera by Kurt Weill and Bertold Brecht, which was based on "The Beggar's Opera" by John Gay. Remake of "The Threepenny Opera" (1931). **124m/C VHS.** *GE* Curt Jurgens, Hildegarde Neff, Gert

Frobe, June Ritchie, Lino Ventura, Sammy Davis Jr.

Three Seasons 🦴🦴 **1998 (PG-13)** First American indie production to be shot in Vietnam with native-speaking actors since the war (by Vietnam-born, U.S.-raised director Bui in his feature debut) has a number of beautiful shots but not much story to back it up. Bustling Saigon sets the stage for the intertwining fortunes of five characters: young flower seller Kien An (Hiep), street kid Woody (Duoc), cyclo driver Hai (Duong), prostitute Lan (Bui), and ex-Marine Hager (Keitel), who's searching for his Amer-Asian daughter. **110m/C VHS.** Harvey Keitel, Don Duong, Nguyen Ngoc Hiep, Zoe Bui, Nguyen Huu Duoc, Tran Manh Cuong; ***D:*** Tony Bui; ***W:*** Tony Bui; ***C:*** Lisa Rinzler; ***M:*** Richard Horowitz. Ind. Spirit '00: Cinematog.; Sundance '99: Cinematog., Aud. Award, Grand Jury Prize.

Three Secrets 🦴🦴½ **1950** A plane crashes and the only survivor is a five-year-old boy. Three women, each with a secret, seek to claim him as the child each gave up for adoption five years before. Tearjerker with good cast. **98m/B VHS.** Eleanor Parker, Patricia Neal, Ruth Roman, Frank Lovejoy, Leif Erickson; ***D:*** Robert Wise.

The Three Sisters 🦴🦴½ **1965** A stage production from the Actor's Studio of Chekhov's play about unhappy siblings in turn-of-the-century Russia. The three sisters believe all their problems are caused by liviing in the provinces and would be solved if they could return to their childhood home in Moscow. **167m/B VHS.** Shelley Winters, Sandy Dennis, Geraldine Page, Kevin McCarthy, Kim Stanley, Luther Adler, Robert Loggia, James Olson, Gerald Hiken; ***D:*** Paul Bogart.

Three Smart Girls 🦴🦴🦴½ **1936** Fast-moving musical features three high-spirited sisters who attempt to bring their divorced parents back together. Their plan is thwarted when they learn of their father's plan to marry a gold digger. 15-year-old singing sensation Durbin made her debut in this film. Based on a story by Commandini. Followed by "Three Smart Girls Grow Up." ♫My Heart is Singing; Someone to Care for Me. **84m/B VHS.** Deanna Durbin, Binnie Barnes, Alice Brady, Ray Milland, Charles Winninger, Mischa Auer, Nan Grey, Barbara Read; ***D:*** Henry Koster; ***W:*** Adele Comandini, Austin Parker; ***C:*** Joseph Valentine.

Three Smart Girls Grow Up 🦴🦴🦴 **1939** Durbin once again plays matchmaker, this time for her two older sisters and their fellas. A delightful mix of comedy and song, this lighthearted sequel turned out to be one of the top-grossing films of the year. Durbin sings "Because," which became one of her biggest hits. **88m/B VHS.** Deanna Durbin, Charles Winninger, Nan Grey, Helen Parrish, Robert Cummings, William Lundigan, Ernest Cossart; ***D:*** Henry Koster; ***W:*** Felix Jackson, Bruce Manning.

Three Sovereigns for Sarah 🦴🦴½ **1985** Witch-hunters tortured and toasted Sarah's two sisters for practicing witchcraft in the past. Now, accused of witchery herself, she struggles to prove the family's innocence. Excellent, made-for-PBS. Fine performances from all, especially Redgrave. **152m/C VHS.** Vanessa Redgrave, Phyllis Thaxter, Patrick McGoohan; ***D:*** Philip Leacock.

Three Stooges in Orbit 🦴🦴½ **1962** Three TV performers (you know who) looking for a shtick and a place to live, encounter a crazy scientist with a rocket-like invention. In a shocking plot twist, the boys accidently launch the rocket and must battle Martians to save the world and their TV career. **87m/B VHS.** Moe Howard, Larry Fine, Joe DeRita, Emil Sitka, Carol Christensen, Edson Stroll; ***D:*** Edward L. Bernds.

The Three Stooges Meet Hercules 🦴🦴½ **1961** The Three Stooges are transported back to ancient Ithaca by a time machine with a young scientist and his girlfriend. When the girl is captured, they enlist the help of Hercules to rescue her. **80m/B VHS.** Moe Howard, Larry Fine, Joe DeRita, Vicki Trickett, Quinn (K.) Redeker, Samson Burke, Lewis Charles, Marlin McKeever, Michael McKeever, John Cliff, George Neise; ***D:*** Edward L. Bernds; ***W:*** Elwood Ullman; ***C:*** Charles S. Welbourne; ***M:*** Paul Dunlap.

Three Stops to Murder 🦴 **1953** An FBI agent investigates the murder of a beautiful model in this early, unspectacular Hammer production. **76m/B VHS.** *GB* Tom Conway, Mila Parely, Naomi Chance, Eric Pohlmann, Andrew Osborn, Richard Wattis, Eileen Way, Delphi Lawrence; ***D:*** Terence Fisher.

Three Strange Loves 🦴🦴🦴 *Thirst* **1949** Men and women struggle with loneliness, old age, and sterility. Sometimes disjointed, but for the most part, well-made. Finely acted. In Swedish with English subtitles. **88m/B VHS.** *SW* Eva Henning, Brigit Tengroth, Birger Malmsten; ***D:*** Ingmar Bergman.

Three Strikes woof! **2000 (R)** Two-time loser Rob is released from jail determined to stay straight and thus avoid the harsh sentencing of California's "Three Strikes" law. But as luck, and a lame script filled with fart jokes and little esle would have it, his buddy picks him up from jail in a stolen car and promptly gets in a gunfight with the cops. On the run from the police and gang members, Rob tries to find a way to clear himself and get home. There's not much to redeem this disaster of a flick, unless you find embarrassingly stereotypical characters and "In Living Color" refect jokes amusing. **83m/C VHS, DVD, Wide.** Brian Hooks, N'Bushe Wright, Faizon Love, Starletta DuPois, David Alan Grier, Dean Norris, Meagan Good, De'Aundre Bonds, Antonio Fargas, Vincent Schiavelli, David Leisure, Gerald S. O'Loughlin, George Wallace, E40, Barima McNight, Mo'Nique, Shawn Fonteno; ***D:*** DJ Pooh; ***W:*** DJ Pooh; ***C:*** Johnny (John W.) Simmons; ***M:*** Aaron Anderson, Andrew Slack.

3:10 to Yuma 🦴🦴🦴½ **1957** In order to collect $200 he desperately needs, a poor farmer has to hold a dangerous killer at bay while waiting to turn the outlaw over to the authorities arriving on the 3:10 train to Yuma. Stuck in a hotel room with the outlaw's gang gathering outside, the question arises as to who is the prisoner. Farmer Heflin is continually worked on by the outlaw Ford, in a movie with more than its share of great dialogue. Suspenseful, well-made action western adapted from an Elmore Leonard story. **92m/B VHS, DVD, Wide.** Glenn Ford, Van Heflin, Felicia Farr, Richard Jaeckel; ***D:*** Delmer Daves; ***W:*** Halsted Welles; ***C:*** Charles Lawton Jr.; ***M:*** George Duning.

Three Texas Steers 🦴½ *Danger Rides the Range* **1939** A circus owner inherits some land that the government wants for a water project and her manager tries to get it for himself. Enter the terrific trio to set things right. Last of the series for Terhune. The scenes of the circus fire were taken from "Circus Girl" (1937). **59m/B VHS.** John Wayne, Ray Corrigan, Max Terhune, Carole Landis, Ralph Graves, Roscoe Ates; ***D:*** George Sherman.

Three the Hard Way 🦴🦴½ **1974 (R)** An insane white supremacist has a plan to eliminate blacks by contaminating water supplies. A big blaxploitation money maker and the first to team Brown, Williamson, and Kelly, who would go on to make several more pictures together. **93m/C VHS.** Jim Brown, Fred Williamson, Jim Kelly, Sheila Frazier, Jay Robinson, Alex Rocco; ***D:*** Gordon Parks.

3000 Miles to Graceland 🦴½ **2001 (R)** Shockingly original pic sets Elvis impersonators in Vegas, only these Presleys wanna rob, not rock. Ex-cellmates Russell and Costner are the lead Kings, Michael and Murphy, who team up with Arquette, Slater, and Woodbine, and head to the quaint desert burg to relieve its wagering establishments of some extra cash. After a strong opening segment, only moments of comic relief are scattered throughout the comedy, highlighted by the Elvii strutting through town in a "Reservoir Dogs" homage. Cox is adept at playing the lovelorn, single mom Cybil, pining for Michael. Gratuitous violence and cliched action doesn't help movie's one-note appeal but the look is slick and the boys drive cool cars. **125m/C VHS, DVD, Wide.** *US* Kevin Costner, Kurt Russell, Christian Slater, Bokeem Woodbine, David Arquette, Courteney Cox Arquette, Kevin Pollak, Jon Lovitz, Howie Long, Thomas Haden Church, Ice-T, David Kaye, Louis Lombardi; ***D:*** Demian Lichtenstein; ***W:*** Demian Lichtenstein, Richard Recco; ***C:*** David Franco; ***M:*** George S. Clinton.

Three to Tango 🦴½ **1999 (PG-13)** Dopey would-be romantic comedy only demonstrates that actors who make it big in TV series should think about sticking to the small screen. (Or being more careful about their big screen choices.) Married tycoon Charles Newman (McDermott) has it in his power to award a lucrative contract to struggling architect Oscar Novak (Perry) and his partner, Peter Steinberg (Peter). Somehow, Newman gets the impression that Oscar is gay and would be the perfect guy to spy on Newman's young mistress, Amy (Campbell), whom he fears is about to wander. Naturally, Oscar falls for the girl and then must work around all the mistaken assumptions. Yawn. **98m/C VHS, DVD.** Dylan McDermott, Neve Campbell, Matthew Perry, Oliver Platt, Cylk Cozart, John C. McGinley, Bob Balaban, Kelly Rowan, Deborah Rush, Patrick Van Horn; ***D:*** Damon Santostefano; ***W:*** Rodney Vaccaro, Aline Brosh McKenna; ***C:*** Walt Lloyd; ***M:*** Graeme Revell.

Three Violent People 🦴🦴 **1957** Family feud set in post-Civil War Old West features Heston and Baxter impulsively marrying and returning to run the family ranch. Heston's brother (Tryon) wants to sell the ranch in order to get his share of the inheritance and then Heston finds out Baxter was once a prostitute. In this case family squabbles don't make for an exciting film. **100m/C VHS.** Charlton Heston, Anne Baxter, Gilbert Roland, Tom Tryon, Forrest Tucker, Elaine Stritch, Bruce (Herman Brix) Bennett, Barton MacLane; ***D:*** Rudolph Mate; ***W:*** James Edward Grant; ***C:*** Loyal Griggs; ***M:*** Walter Scharf.

Three Warriors 🦴½ **1977** Young Native American boy is forced to leave the city and return to the reservation, where his contempt for the traditions of his ancestors slowly turns to appreciation and love. **100m/C VHS.** Charles White Eagle, Lois Red Elk, McKee "Kiko" Red Wing, Christopher Lloyd, Randy Quaid.

Three Way Weekend 🦴 **1981 (R)** Two young girls set off on a back-packing trip through the mountains of Southern California to enjoy camping and romance. **78m/C VHS.** Dan Diego, Jody Lee Olhava, Richard Blye, Blake Parrish; ***D:*** Emmett Alston.

The Three Weird Sisters 🦴🦴 **1948** The three weird sisters from "Macbeth" strive to maintain their life of luxury by plotting to kill their half-brother for the inheritance. Not a bad effort for Birt's first time out as director; script co-written by his wife, Louise and poet Thomas. **82m/B VHS.** *GB* Nancy Price, Mary Clare; ***D:*** Daniel Birt; ***W:*** Dylan Thomas, Louise Birt.

Three Wishes 🦴🦴 **1995 (PG)** Mysterious—and perhaps mystical—stranger Jack (Swayze) moves into the lives of a 1950s suburban widow (Mastrantonio) and her kids (Mazzello and Mumy) after she hits him with her car. Jack proceeds to use Zen philosophy, stories of a genie disguised as a dog, and nude sunbathing to help the kids' Little League team, make a boy fly, and scandalize the neighborhood. Adults will recognize the beatnik, Kerouac-influenced philosophy of nonconformity. They'll also recognize the sellout of that ideal with the sickeningly sappy ending. Mumy is the son of former "Lost in Space" child star Billy Mumy. **115m/C VHS, DVD, Wide.** Patrick Swayze, Mary Elizabeth Mastrantonio, Joseph Mazzello, David Marshall Grant, Michael O'Keefe, John Diehl, Jay O. Sanders, Diane Venora, Seth Mumy; ***D:*** Martha Coolidge; ***W:*** Elizabeth Anderson; ***C:*** Johnny E. Jensen; ***M:*** Cynthia Millar.

Three Word Brand 🦴🦴 **1921** Hart plays three roles in this film, a homesteader who is killed by Indians and his twin sons, who are separated after their father's death and reunited many years later. Silent with musical score. **75m/B VHS.** William S. Hart, Jane Novak, S.J. Bingham; ***D:*** Lambert Hillyer.

The Three Worlds of Gulliver 🦴🦴½ *The Worlds of Gulliver* **1959** A colorful family version of the Jonathan Swift classic about an Englishman who discovers a fantasy land of small and giant people. Visual effects by Ray Harryhausen. **100m/C VHS, DVD.** Kerwin Mathews, Jo Morrow, Basil Sydney, Mary Ellis; ***D:*** Jack Sher; ***W:*** Jack Sher, Arthur Ross; ***C:*** Wilkie Cooper; ***M:*** Bernard Herrmann.

The Threepenny Opera 🦴🦴 *Die Dreigroschenoper; L'Opera De Quat'Sous; Beggars' Opera* **1931** A musical about the exploits of gangster Mack the Knife. Adapted from Bertolt Brecht's play and John Gay's "The Beggar's Opera." In German with English subtitles. **107m/B VHS.** Rudolph Forster, Lotte Lenya, Carola Neher, Reinhold Schunzel, Fritz Rasp, Valeska Gert, Ernst Busch; ***D:*** G.W. Pabst; ***W:*** Ladislao Vajda, Bela Balazs, Leo Lania; ***C:*** Fritz Arno Wagner; ***M:*** Kurt Weill.

Three's Trouble 🦴🦴 **1985** A middle-class family erupts when a young male babysitter enters to care for its three mischievous sons. **93m/C VHS.** *AU* John Waters, Jacki Weaver, Steven Vidler; ***D:*** Chris Thomson.

Threesome woof! **1994 (R)** Another Generation X movie that tries hard to be hip, but fails miserably. Due to a college administrative error, Alex (Boyle) winds up sharing a suite with two male roommates, Eddy (Charles) and Stuart (Baldwin). Despite having completely different personalities, they soon become best friends and form one cozy little group, with cozy being the key word. Sexual tension abounds—Alex wants Eddy who wants Stuart who wants Alex. Filled with pathetic dialogue (most of it relating to bodily functions and body parts) and shallow, obnoxious characters, this menage a trois film is a flop. **93m/C VHS, DVD, 8mm, Wide.** Lara Flynn Boyle, Stephen Baldwin, Josh Charles, Alexis Arquette, Mark Arnold, Martha Gehman, Michelle Matheson; ***D:*** Andrew Fleming; ***W:*** Andrew Fleming; ***C:*** Alexander Grusynski; ***M:*** Thomas Newman.

Threshold 🦴🦴½ **1983 (PG)** An internationally acclaimed research biologist is frustrated by his inability to save a dying 20-year-old woman born with a defective heart. She becomes the recipient of the first artificial heart. Solid performances. **97m/C VHS.** *CA* Donald Sutherland, Jeff Goldblum, John Marley, Mare Winningham; ***D:*** Richard Pearce. Genie '83: Actor (Sutherland).

The Thrill Killers woof! *The Monsters Are Loose; The Maniacs Are Loose* **1965** Young murderous thugs rampage through Los Angeles suburbs, killing indiscriminately. Pretentious and exploitative. Sometimes shown with Hallucinogenic Hypo-Vision—a prologue announcing the special effect would be shown before the film, and on cue, hooded ushers would run through the theatre with cardboard axes. Weird. **82m/C VHS.** Cash (Ray Dennis Steckler) Flagg, Ray Dennis Steckler, Liz Renay, Brick (Ron Haydock) Bardo, Ron Haydock, Atlas King, Gary Kent, Carolyn Brandt, Herb Robins, Ron Burr, George Morgan, Arch (Archie) Hall Sr.; ***D:*** Ray Dennis Steckler; ***W:*** Gene Pollock, Ray Dennis Steckler; ***C:*** Joseph Mascelli; ***M:*** Henry Price.

Thrill of a Romance 🦴🦴 **1945** Johnson, an Army hero, meets Williams, a swimming instructor of all things, at a resort in the Sierra Nevadas. The only problem is that she's married. Typical swim-romance vehicle. ♫Please Don't Say No, Say Maybe; I Should Care; Lonely Night; Vive L'Amour; Schubert's Serenade; The Thrill of a Romance. **105m/C VHS.** Esther Williams, Van Johnson, Frances Gifford, Henry Travers, Spring Byington, Lauritz Melchior; ***D:*** Richard Thorpe.

The Thrill of It All! 🦴🦴½ **1963** An average housewife becomes a star of TV commercials, to the dismay of her chauvinist husband, a gynecologist. Fast and funny, with numerous acidic jokes about television sponsors and programs. **108m/C VHS.** James Garner, Doris Day, Arlene Francis, Edward Andrews, Carl Reiner, Elliott Reid, Reginald Owen, ZaSu Pitts; ***D:*** Norman Jewison; ***W:*** Carl Reiner; ***C:*** Russell Metty.

Thrill Seekers 🦴🦴½ *The Timeshifters* **1999 (PG-13)** Fast-pace helps overcome the plot holes in this sci-fi thriller. Merrick (Van Dien) is a tabloid reporter who is researching great past catastrophes. He discovers that aliens are traveling back in time (to earth's present) to take part in disasters of their own contrivance. Trying to prevent an arena fire, Merrick teams up with another reporter, Elizabeth (Bell), and they run into a couple of alien assassins (Saldana, Outerbridge). **92m/C VHS, DVD.** Casper Van Dien, Catherine Bell, Peter Outerbridge, Theresa Saldana, Martin Sheen, Mimi Kuzyk, Lawrence Dane, Catherine Van Dien; ***D:*** Mario Azzopardi; ***W:*** Kurt Inderbitzin, Gay Walch; ***C:*** Derick Underschultz; ***M:*** Fred Mollin. **CABLE**

Thrilled to Death 🦴½ **1988 (R)** An utterly naive husband and wife get caught in the middle of a lethal game when they befriend a scheming couple. **90m/C VHS.** Blake Bahner, Rebecca Lynn, Richard Maris, Christine Moore; ***D:*** Chuck Vincent.

Thrillkill 🦴 **1984** A young girl is enmeshed in a multi-million-dollar burglary scheme after her computer-whiz/embezzler sister disappears. **88m/C VHS.** Robin Ward, Gina Massey, Anthony Kramroither; ***D:*** Anthony D'Andrea.

Throne of Blood 🦴🦴🦴🦴 *Kumonosujo, Kumonosu-djo; Cobweb Castle; The Castle of the Spider's Web* **1957** Kurosawa's masterful adaptation of "Macbeth" transports the story to medieval Japan and the world of the samurai. Mifune and Chiaki are warriors who have put down a rebellion and are to be rewarded by their overlord. On their way to his castle they meet a mysterious old woman who prophesizes that Mifune will soon rule—but his reign will be short. She is dismissed as crazy but her prophesies come to pass. So steeped in Japanese style that it bears little resemblance to the Shakespearean original, this film is an incredibly detailed vision in its own right. In Japanese with English subtitles. **105m/B VHS.** *JP* Toshiro Mifune, Isuzu Yamada, Takashi Shimura, Minoru Chiaki, Akira Kubo; ***D:*** Akira Kurosawa; ***W:*** Hideo Oguni, Shinobu Hashimoto, Ryuzo Kikushima, Akira Kurosawa; ***C:*** Asakazu Nakai; ***M:*** Masaru Sato.

Throne of Fire woof! **1982** A mighty hero battles the forces of evil to gain control of the powerful Throne of Fire. Dubbed. **91m/C VHS.** *IT* Peter McCoy, Sabrina Siani; ***D:*** Franco Prosperi.

Through a Glass Darkly 🦴🦴🦴 *Sasom I En Spegel* **1961** Oppressive interactions within a family sharing a holiday on a secluded island: a woman recovering from schizophrenia, her husband, younger brother, and her psychologist father. One of Bergman's most mysterious, upsetting and powerful films. In Swedish with English subtitles. Part of Bergman's Silence-of-God trilogy followed by "Winter Light" and "The Silence." **91m/B VHS.** *SW* Harriet Andersson, Max von Sydow, Gunnar Bjornstrand, Lars Passgard; ***D:*** Ingmar Bergman; ***W:*** Ingmar Bergman; ***C:*** Sven Nykvist. Oscars '61: Foreign Film.

Through Naked Eyes 🦴🦴½ **1987** Thriller about two people who spy on each other. They witness a murder and realize that someone else is watching them. What a coincidence. **91m/C VHS.** David Soul, Pam Dawber; ***D:*** John Llewellyn Moxey. **TV**

Through the Breakers 🦴½ **1928** Heartbroken woman suffers silently on South Pacific isle. **55m/B VHS.** Margaret Livingston, Holmes Herbert, Clyde Cook, Natalie Joyce.

Through the Eyes of a Killer 🦴🦴½ **1992 (R)** Laurie Fisher (Helgenberger) has dumped cheating boyfriend Jerry (Pantoliano) and has declared her independence by finding a spacious but crummy New York apartment in desperate need of renovation. Enter handsome handyman Ray Bellano (Anderson), who's happy to work on the apartment—and Laurie as well. But where Laurie sees a fling, Ray sees true love, and since brooding Ray's got the prerequisite mystery past, you know Laurie's in for the shock of her life. Long-time nice guy Anderson does a credible turn as an obsessive psycho. Based on the short story "The Master Builder" by Christopher Fowler; made for TV. **94m/C VHS.** Richard Dean Anderson, Marg Helgenberger, Joe Pantoliano, David Marshall Grant, Melinda Culea, Tippi Hedren; ***D:*** Peter Markle; ***W:*** John Pielmeier; ***M:*** George S. Clinton. **TV**

Through the Olive Trees 🦴🦴🦴 *Under the Olive Trees; Zire Darakhtan Zeyton* **1994 (G)** Film-within-a-film is the last of a trilogy concerned with Persian village life, following "Where Is My Friend's House?" and "And Life Goes On." Director, filming in an earthquake-ravaged village, discovers that the young bricklayer playing the bridegroom in his film is actually in love with the local girl who's playing the bride. However, she's turned down his real-life marriage proposal, feeling that the uneducated man is beneath her. Farsi with subtitles. It may be rated G but considering the subject matter and the fact that the film is subtitled, don't consider this one for the kiddies. **104m/C VHS.** *IA* Hossein Rezai, Mohamad Ali Keshavarz, Taherek Ladania, Zarifeh Shivah; ***D:*** Abbas Kiarostami; ***W:*** Abbas Kiarostami; ***C:*** Hossein Jafarian, Farhad Saba.

Throw Down 🦴 **2000** Ex-Marine martial artist Max Finister (Wingster) comes home to find that drug pushers have taken over the neighborhood. The rest of the story follows the familiar formula. This is an unusually inept action picture. The fights (directed by Wingster) tend to be slow and director Cyrus Beyzavi tends to cut people's heads off. **90m/C DVD, Wide.** La'Mard J. Wingster, Mark G. Young, Maribel Velez, Wendy Fajardo, John "Kato" Hollis, Patrick "Gun" Ryan; ***D:*** Cyrus Beyzavi; ***C:*** Mike Dolgetta.

Throw Momma from the Train 🦴🦴🦴 **1987 (PG-13)** DeVito plays a man, henpecked by his horrific mother, who tries to persuade his writing professor (Crystal) to exchange murders. DeVito will kill Crystal's ex-wife and Crystal will kill DeVito's mother. Only mama isn't going to be that easy to get rid of. Fast-paced and entertaining black comedy. Ramsey steals the film. Inspired by Hitchcock's "Strangers on a Train." **88m/C VHS, DVD, Wide.** Danny DeVito, Billy Crystal, Anne Ramsey, Kate Mulgrew, Kim Greist, Branford Marsalis, Rob Reiner, Bruce Kirby; ***D:*** Danny DeVito; ***W:*** Stu Silver; ***C:*** Barry Sonnenfeld; ***M:*** David Newman.

The Throwback 🦴½ **1935** When Jones was a lad the townspeople accused his father of cattle rustling. When he returns as an adult he sets out to clear his father's name. **61m/B VHS.** Buck Jones, Muriel Evans, Eddie (Edward) Phillips, George "Gabby" Hayes, Bryant Washburn, Paul Fix, Frank LaRue; ***D:*** Ray Taylor.

Thumb Tripping 🦴🦴 **1972 (R)** A dated '60s/hippie film. Two flower children hitchhike and encounter all kinds of other strange people in their travels on the far-out roads. **94m/C VHS.** Meg Foster, Michael Burns, Bruce Dern, Marianna Hill, Michael Conrad, Joyce Van Patten; ***D:*** Quentin Masters.

Thumbelina **1982** From "Faerie Tale Theatre" comes the story of a tiny girl who gets kidnapped by a toad and a mole, but meets the man of her dreams in the nick of time. Adapted from the classic tale by Hans Christian Andersen. **60m/C VHS.** Carrie Fisher, William Katt, Burgess Meredith; ***D:*** Michael Lindsay-Hogg. **CABLE**

Thumbelina 🦴🦴½ *Hans Christian Andersen's Thumbelina* **1994 (G)** Ornery little girl named Mia gets magically sucked into the pages of the "Thumbelina" storybook she's reading and finds all sorts of adventures. Loose adaptation of Hans Christian Andersen fairy tale from Bluth is lackluster, with acceptable songs. Not up to the level of recent Disney animated features, but pleasant enough for the kids. **86m/C VHS, DVD, Wide.** ***D:*** Don Bluth, Gary Goldman; ***W:*** Don Bluth; ***M:*** William Ross, Barry Manilow, Barry Manilow, Jack Feldman, Bruce Sussman; ***V:*** Jodi Benson, Gary Imhoff, Charo, Gilbert Gottfried, Carol Channing, John Hurt, Will Ryan, June Foray, Kenneth Mars. Golden Raspberries '94: Worst Song ("Marry the Mole").

Thunder Alley 🦴½ **1985** In middle America, two friends and their rock group struggle for success. One of the friends dies after an accidental overdose and the other's grief propels him to stardom. ♫Can't Look Back; Just Another Pretty Boy; Sometimes in the Night; Heart to Heart; Can You Feel My Heart Beat; Do You Feel Alright?; Danger, Danger; Surrender; Gimme Back My Heart. **102m/C VHS.** Roger Wilson, Leif Garrett, Jill Schoelen; ***D:*** J.S. Cardone; ***W:*** J.S. Cardone.

Thunder and Lightning 🦴🦴 **1977 (PG)** A mismatched young couple chase a truckload of poisoned moonshine. Action-packed chases ensue. Nice chemistry between Carradine and Jackson. **94m/C VHS.** David Carradine, Kate Jackson, Roger C. Carmel, Sterling Holloway, Eddie Barth; ***D:*** Corey Allen.

Thunder & Mud **1989** Female mud wrestlers battle over their favorite rock band. Hahn's attempt to cash in on her notoriety after the Bakker scandal. **90m/C VHS.** Jessica Hahn; ***D:*** Penelope Spheeris.

Thunder Bay 🦴🦴🦴 **1953** Stewart and Duryea are a pair of Louisiana wildcat oil drillers who believe there is oil at the bottom of the Gulf of Mexico off the coast of the town of Port Felicity. They decide to construct an oil platform which the shrimp fisherman of the town believe will interfere with their livelihoods. Tensions rise between the two groups and violence seems likely. Action packed, with timely storyline as modern oil drillers fight to drill in waters that have historically been off-limits. **82m/C VHS.** James Stewart, Joanne Dru, Dan Duryea, Gilbert Roland, Marcia Henderson; ***D:*** Anthony Mann; ***W:*** John Michael Hayes; ***C:*** William H. Daniels.

Thunder County 🦴½ **1974** Federal agents and drug runners are after a group of four convicts who have just escaped from prison. **78m/C VHS.** Mickey Rooney, Ted Cassidy, Chris Robinson.

Thunder in God's Country 🦴 **1951** A dishonest gambler eyes a peaceful western town as the next Vegas-like gambling capital. Before this occurs he is exposed as a cheat. **67m/B VHS.** Rex Allen, Mary Ellen Kay.

Thunder in Paradise 🦴🦴½ **1993 (PG-13)** R.J. Hurricane Spencer (Hogan) is a soldier of fortune who heads into Cuba to help a woman and child escape political imprisonment, using his high-tech, weapon-filled speedboat. He has to fight off a small army and manages to find a buried treasure as well. Simple-minded TV pilot. **104m/C VHS.** Hulk Hogan, Robin Weisman, Chris Lemmon, Carol Alt, Patrick Macnee, Sam Jones, Charlotte Rae; ***D:*** Douglas Schwartz. **TV**

Thunder in Paradise 2 🦴½ **1994 (PG)** Damsel sends up a distress signal and it's the Hulkster and his pal to the rescue. Unfortunately, their commando raid fails and now they need an escape plan. From the syndicated TV series. **90m/C VHS.** Hulk Hogan, Chris Lemmon, Carol Alt, Patrick Macnee; ***D:*** Douglas Schwartz.

Thunder in Paradise 3 🦴½ **1994 (PG-13)** Hogan is on a top secret mission to capture a drug lord who's holding his daughter hostage. **88m/C VHS.** Hulk Hogan.

Thunder in the City 🦴🦴🦴 **1937** Robinson is an intense American promoter in the sales game who is sent to London by his employers to learn a more subdued way of doing business. Instead, he meets a pair of down-on-their-luck artistocrats whose only asset is an apparently worthless Rhodesian mine. Robinson, however, comes up with a way to promote the mine and get enough capital together to make it profitable. Good satire with Robinson well cast. Robinson wasn't taken with the script in its original form and persuaded his friend, playwright Robert Sherwood, to re-write it. **85m/B VHS.** *GB* Edward G. Robinson, Nigel Bruce, Ralph Richardson, Constance Collier; ***D:*** Marion Gering; ***M:*** Miklos Rozsa.

Thunder in the Desert 🦴 **1938** A cowhand joins an outlaw gang in order to catch his uncle's killer. **56m/C VHS.** Bob Steele, Louise Stanley, Don Barclay, Charles "Blackie" King, Lew Meehan, Budd Buster; ***D:*** Sam Newfield.

Thunder in the Pines 🦴 **1949** Two lumberjack buddies send for the same French girl to marry, unbeknownst to each other. When she arrives, the dismayed men agree to a contest to see who will marry her. Meanwhile the French girl falls for the local saloon owner and his jilted girlfriend vows to get even. She does, with the help of the lumberjacks. **61m/B VHS.** Denise Darcel, George Reeves, Ralph Byrd, Lyle Talbot, Michael Whalen, Roscoe Ates, Vince Barnett; ***D:*** Robert Edwards.

Thunder Mountain 🦴½ **1935** Zane Grey's novel about two prospectors who are bushwhacked on their way to file a claim comes to life on the screen. **56m/B VHS.** George O'Brien.

Thunder Over Texas 🦴 **1934** The cowboy hero gets embroiled in a railroad scandal that involves a kidnapping. Directed by Edgar G. Ulmer, who used the alias John Warner because he was moonlighting. His first western; previously he was best known for "The Black Cat." **52m/B VHS.** Marion Shilling, Helen Westcott, Victor Potel, Tiny Skelton; ***D:*** Edgar G. Ulmer.

Thunder Pass 🦴🦴 **1937** Gold and greed are the motives for murder as two young brothers become separated when their wagon train is attacked and their family is slaughtered. One brother searches for the other and finds him several years later. Based on the novel "Arizona Ames" by Zane Grey. Also released as "Thunder Trail." **58m/B VHS.** Charles Bickford, Marsha Hunt, Gilbert Roland, Monte Blue; ***D:*** Charles T. Barton.

Thunder Pass 🦴🦴 **1954** Routine story about a wagon train threatened by hostile Indians and the Army officer who leads them to safety. Based on a story by George Van Marter. **76m/B VHS.** Dane Clark, Dorothy Patrick, Andy Devine, Raymond Burr, John Carradine, Mary Ellen Kay; ***D:*** Frank McDonald; ***W:*** Tom Hubbard, Fred Eggers.

Thunder River Feud 🦴🦴 **1942** The Rangebusters help two ranchers avoid a range war. Part of "The Rangebusters" series. **58m/B VHS.** Ray Corrigan, John "Dusty" King, Max Terhune.

Thunder Road 🦴🦴🦴 **1958 (PG)** Luke Doolin (Mitchum) comes home to Tennessee from Korea and takes over the family moonshine business, fighting both mobsters and federal agents. An exciting chase between Luke and the feds ends the movie with the appropriate bang. Robert Mitchum not only produced, wrote and starred in this best of the moonshine-running films, but also wrote the theme song "Whippoorwill" (which later became a radio hit). Mitchum's teenaged son, James, made his film debut as brother Robin Doolin and later starred in a similar movie "Moonrunners." A cult favorite. **92m/B VHS, DVD.** Robert Mitchum, Jacques Aubuchon, Gene Barry, Keely Smith, Trevor Bardette, Sandra Knight, Jim Mitchum, Betsy Holt, Frances Koon, Mitchell Ryan, Peter Breck; ***D:*** Arthur Ripley; ***W:*** Walter Wise, Robert Mitchum; ***C:*** Alan Stenvold; ***M:*** Jack Marshall.

Thunder Run 🦴 **1986 (PG-13)** When a load of uranium needs to be transferred across Nevada, a retired trucker takes on the job. The trip is made more difficult since terrorists are trying to hijack the shipment to use for a bomb. **84m/C VHS.** Forrest Tucker, John Ireland, John Shepherd, Jill Whitlow, Wallace (Wally) Langham, Cheryl Lynn; ***D:*** Gary Hudson; ***W:*** Charles Davis.

Thunder Trail **1937** Set of twins, separated by a wagon trail massacre, meet up years later on opposite sides of the law. **58m/C VHS.** Gilbert Roland, Charles Bickford, Marsha Hunt, J. Carrol Naish, James Craig, Monte Blue; ***D:*** Charles T. Barton.

Thunder Warrior 🦴 *Thunder* **1985 (R)** A young Indian turns into a one-man army determined to punish the local authorities who are abusing his fellow tribe members. De Angelis used the pseudonym Larry Ludman. **84m/C VHS.** Raymond Harmstorf, Bo Svenson, Mark Gregory; ***D:*** Fabrizio de Angelis.

Thunder Warrior 2 🦴 **1985 (PG-13)** A tough Native American is provoked to violence by small-town prejudice. De Angelis used the pseudonym Larry Ludman. **114m/C VHS.** *IT* Mark Gregory, Karen Reel, Bo Svenson; ***D:*** Fabrizio de Angelis.

Thunder Warrior 3 🦴 **1988** The Indian Thunder has vowed to live in peace, but forswears the oath when his wife is kidnapped and family is terrorized. Revenge is the top priority as he torments the bad guys. De Angelis used the pseudonym Larry Ludman. **90m/C VHS.** Mark Gregory, John Phillip Law, Ingrid Lawrence, Werner Pochath, Horts Schon; ***D:*** Fabrizio de Angelis.

Thunderball 🦴🦴½ **1965 (PG)** The fourth installment in Ian Fleming's James Bond series finds 007 on a mission to thwart SPECTRE, which has threatened to blow up Miami by atomic bomb if 100 million pounds in ransom is not paid. One of the more tedious Bond entries but a big boxoffice success. Tom Jones sang the title song. Remade as "Never Say Never Again" in 1983 with Connery reprising his role as Bond after a 12-year absence. **125m/C VHS, DVD, Wide.** *GB* Sean Connery, Claudine Auger, Adolfo Celi, Luciana Paluzzi, Rik von Nutter, Martine Beswick, Molly Peters, Guy Doleman, Bernard Lee, Lois Maxwell, Desmond Llewelyn; ***D:*** Terence Young; ***W:*** John Hopkins, Richard Maibaum; ***C:*** Ted Moore; ***M:*** John Barry. Oscars '65: Visual FX.

Thunderbolt & Lightfoot 🦴🦴🦴 **1974 (R)** Eastwood is an ex-thief on the run from his former partners (Kennedy and Lewis) who believe he's made off with the loot from their last job, the robbery of a government vault. He joins up with drifter Bridges, who helps him to escape. Later, Eastwood manages to convince Kennedy he doesn't know where the money is. Bridges then persuades the men that they should plan the same heist and rob the same government vault all over again, which they do. But their getaway doesn't go exactly as planned. All-around fine acting; notable is Bridges' scene dressed in drag. First film for director Cimino. **115m/C VHS, DVD, Wide.** Clint Eastwood, Jeff Bridges, George Kennedy, Geoffrey Lewis, Gary Busey; ***D:*** Michael Cimino; ***W:*** Michael Cimino; ***C:*** Frank Stanley; ***M:*** Dee Barton.

Thunderground 🦴 **1989 (R)** A beautiful con artist teams with a fighter and together they travel to New Orleans to arrange a bout with the king of bare-knuckled fighting. **92m/C VHS.** Paul Coufos, Margaret Langrick, Jesse Ventura, M. Emmet Walsh; ***D:*** David Mitchell.

Thunderheart 🦴🦴🦴 **1992 (R)** Young FBI agent Kilmer is sent to an Oglala Sioux reservation to investigate a murder. He is himself part Sioux, but resents being chosen for the assignment because of it. Aided by a veteran partner (Shepard), Ray learns, professionally and personally, from a shrewd tribal police officer (well played by Greene). Set in the late '70s, the film is loosely based on actual events plaguing the violence-torn Native American community at that time. Great cinematography by Roger Deakins. Filmed on the Pine Ridge Reservation in South Dakota. Director Apted deals with the actual incidents this film is based on in his documentary about Leonard Peltier, "Incident at Oglala." **118m/C VHS, DVD, Wide.** Val Kilmer, Sam Shepard, Graham Greene, Fred Ward, Fred Dalton Thompson, Sheila Tousey, Chief Ted Thin Elk, John Trudell, Dennis Banks, David Crosby; ***D:*** Michael Apted; ***W:*** John Fusco; ***C:*** Roger Deakins; ***M:*** James Horner.

Thundering Forest 🦴🦴 **1941** Australian actioneer pitting loggers against saboteurs. **?m/C VHS.** *AU* Frank Leighton.

Thundering Gunslingers 🦴 **1940** A group of gunmen terrorizing townspeople finally meet their match in this Western. **61m/B VHS.** Buster Crabbe.

Thundering Trail 🦴 *Thunder on the Trail* **1951** Two cowboys encounter plenty of trouble before they take the President's newly appointed territorial governor to his office. **55m/B VHS.** Lash LaRue, Al "Fuzzy" St. John, Sally Anglim, Archie Twitchell, Ray Bennett.

Thundersquad 🦴 **1985** Mercenaries help a South American rebel leader rescue his kidnapped son. **90m/C VHS.** Sal Borgese, Julia Fursich, Antonio (Tony) Sabato.

Thursday 🦴🦴½ **1998 (R)** Familiarity does breed something close to contempt in this comic crime thriller. Ex-drug dealer Casey Wells (Jane) has left L.A. for the straight and narrow life of a married Houston architect. That is until his lowlife expartner Nick (Eckhart) turns up one Thursday with a briefcase full of dope and some gangster problems. A succession of other nasty characters then proceeds to darken Casey's doorway and his efforts to get his life back just cause things to spin further out of control. The leads do a good job but it's nothing you haven't seen before. Also available in an unrated version. **82m/C VHS.** Thomas Jane, Aaron Eckhart, Paulina Porizkova, James LeGros, Paula Marshall, Michael Jeter, Glenn Plummer, Mickey Rourke; ***D:*** Skip Woods; ***W:*** Skip Woods; ***C:*** Denis Lenoir.

Thursday's Child 🦴🦴 **1943** A child's success in films causes trouble for her family. Melodramatic and sappy, but Howes, as the kid, is excellent. One of Granger's early supporting roles. **95m/B VHS.** *GB* Stewart Granger, Sally Ann Howes, Wilfred Lawson, Kathleen O'Regan, Eileen Bennett, Marianne Davis, Gerhard Kempinski, Felix Aylmer, Margaret Yarde, Vera Bogetti, Percy Walsh, Ronald Shiner; ***D:*** Rodney Ackland; ***W:*** Rodney Ackland, Donald Macardle; ***C:*** Desmond Dickinson.

Thursday's Game 🦴🦴🦴 **1974 (PG)** Two crisis-besieged businessmen meet every Thursday, using poker as a ruse to work on their business and marital problems. Wonderful cast; intelligently written. **99m/C VHS.** Gene Wilder, Ellen Burstyn, Bob Newhart, Cloris Leachman, Nancy Walker, Valerie Harper, Rob Reiner; ***D:*** James L. Brooks; ***W:*** James L. Brooks. **TV**

THX 1138 🦴🦴🦴 **1971 (PG)** In the dehumanized world of the future, people live in underground cities run by computer, are force-fed drugs to keep them passive, and no longer have names—just letter/number combinations (Duvall is THX 1138). Emotion is also outlawed and when the computer-matched couple THX 1138 and LUH 3417 discover love, they must battle the computer system to escape. George Lucas' first film, which was inspired by a student film he did at USC. **88m/C VHS, Wide.** Robert Duvall, Donald Pleasence, Maggie McOmie; ***D:*** George Lucas; ***W:*** George Lucas; ***M:*** Lalo Schifrin.

Tiara Tahiti 🦴🦴 **1962** Intrigue, double-cross, romance, and violence ensue when two old army acquaintances clash in Tahiti. Very fine performances from the two leading men. **100m/C VHS.** James Mason, John Mills, Claude Dauphin, Rosenda Monteros, Herbert Lom; ***D:*** Ted Kotcheff.

The Tic Code 🦴🦴½ **1999 (R)** Twelve-year-old Miles (Marquette) aspires to be a jazz pianist but must practice at the local bar because his single mom Laura (Draper) can't afford a piano. But Miles has a bigger problem—he suffers from the misunderstood Tourette's syndrome, which brings him close to his idol, sax player Tyrone (Hines), who is similarly afflicted. Soon Tyrone is also playing some sweet music with Laura but the trio are on shaky ground since Tyrone can't deal with his illness. **91m/C VHS, DVD.** Gregory Hines, Polly Draper, James McCaffrey, Christopher Marquette, Carol Kane, Bill Nunn, Tony Shalhoub, Desmond Robertson, Fisher Stevens, Camryn Manheim, David Johansen; ***D:*** Gary Winick; ***W:*** Polly Draper; ***C:*** Wolfgang Held; ***M:*** Michael Wolff.

Ticker 🦴½ **2001 (R)** San Francisco detective Sizemore is tracking mad bomber Hopper (reprising his "Speed" role to little effect) aided by bomb squad leader Seagal. Nothing that hasn't been done a zillion times before (and much better). **92m/C VHS, DVD, Wide.** Tom Sizemore, Steven Seagal, Nas, Jaime Pressly, Dennis Hopper, Chilli, Peter Greene; ***Cameos:*** Ice-T; ***D:*** Albert Pyun; ***W:*** Paul B. Margolis. **VIDEO**

The Ticket 🦴🦴 **1997 (PG-13)** Keith Reicker (Marshall) works as a pilot for a financially ailing charter company. His marriage to CeCe (Doherty) is rocky but when Keith wins a lottery worth $l23 million, he's certain his life has finally turned around. He persuades CeCe and their 13-year-old son to fly with him and collect the money but the plane is sabotaged. Now they must not only survive the wilderness but whoever is out to steal the ticket and make certain the Reickers don't get out alive. **88m/C VHS.** John Tench, James Marshall, Shannen Doherty, Heidi Swedberg, Al Mancini; ***D:*** Stuart Cooper; ***W:*** David Alexander; ***C:*** Curtis Petersen; ***M:*** Charles Bernstein. **CABLE**

Ticket of Leave Man 🦴🦴 **1937** London's most dangerous killer fronts a charitable organization designed to help reform criminals. It actually steers them into a crime syndicate that cheats philanthropists out of their fortunes. **71m/B VHS.** *GB* Tod Slaughter, John Warwick, Marjorie Taylor.

Ticket to Heaven 🦴🦴🦴 **1981 (PG)** A young man, trying to deal with the painful breakup of a love affair, falls under the spell of a quasi-religious order. His friends and family, worried about the cult's influence, have him kidnapped in order for him to be de-programmed. Mancuso is excellent, as are his supporting players Rubinek and Thomson. **109m/C VHS, DVD.** *CA* Nick Mancuso, Meg Foster, Kim Cattrall, Saul Rubinek, R.H. Thomson, Jennifer Dale, Guy Boyd, Paul Soles; ***D:*** Ralph L. (R.L.) Thomas; ***W:*** Anne Cameron; ***C:*** Richard Leiterman; ***M:*** Micky Erbe. Genie '82: Actor (Mancuso), Film, Support. Actor (Rubinek).

Ticket to Tomahawk 🦴🦴½ **1950** A gunslinger is hired by a stagecoach company to sabotage a railroad. Look for Marilyn Monroe as a chorus girl in a musical number. **90m/C VHS.** Anne Baxter, Rory Calhoun, Walter Brennan, Charles Kemper, Connie Gilchrist, Arthur Hunnicutt, Victor Sen Yung; ***D:*** Richard Sale.

Tickle Me 🦴½ **1965** An unemployed rodeo star finds work at an all-girl health spa and dude ranch. He falls in love with a young lady who has a treasure map and keeps her safe from the evil men who want her fortune. For die-hard Elvis fans only. ♫(It's a) Long, Lonely Highway; Night Rider; It Feels So Right; Dirty, Dirty Feeling; (Such an) Easy Question; Put the Blame on Me; I'm Yours; I Feel That I've Known You Forever; Slowly but Surely. **90m/C VHS.** Elvis Presley, Julie Adams, Jack Mullaney; ***D:*** Norman Taurog.

Ticks 🦴½ *Infested* **1993 (R)** Mammoth mutant killer insects terrorize a Northern California campground! The predatory woodticks are the victims of steroids dumped in the water supply and a group of unwary teen campers fall prey to their deadly venom! And if that's not bad enough, a forest fire breaks out, trapping the teens! **85m/C VHS.** Ami Dolenz, Rosalind Allen, Alfonso Ribeiro, Peter Scolari; ***D:*** Tony Randel.

Tidal Wave 🦴½ *Nippon Chiubotsu; The Submersion of Japan; Japan Sinks* **1975 (PG)** Scientists discover that Japan is slowly sinking and order the island to be evacuated. Originally a popular Japanese production, the American version is a poorly dubbed, re-edited mess. **82m/C VHS.** *JP* Lorne Greene, Keiju Kobayashi, Rhonda Leigh Hopkins, Hiroshi Fujioka, Shiro Moriana; ***D:*** Andrew Meyer.

Tides of War 🦴🦴 **1990** In the twilight of WWII, a German officer begins to question his role in a proposed missile attack on Washington in light of the S.S. brutality he witnesses. **90m/C VHS.** Yvette Heyden, Rodrigo Obregon, David Soul, Bo Svenson; ***D:*** Neil Rossati.

Tidy Endings 🦴½ **1988** A man who died from AIDS leaves behind his male lover and his ex-wife. The two form a friendship as they both try to cope with the man's death. Based on the play by Fierstein. **54m/C VHS.** Harvey Fierstein, Stockard Channing; ***D:*** Gavin Millar; ***W:*** Harvey Fierstein.

Tie Me Up! Tie Me Down! 🦴🦴½ *Atame!* **1990 (NC-17)** A young psychiatric patient kidnaps a former porno actress he has always had a crush on, and holds her captive, certain that he can convince her to love him. Black comedy features a fine cast and is well directed. At least one fairly explicit sex scene and the bondage theme caused the film to be X-rated, although it was originally released unrated by the distributor. In Spanish with English subtitles. **105m/C VHS, DVD, Wide.** *SP* Victoria Abril, Antonio Banderas, Loles Leon, Francesco Rabal, Julieta Serrano, Maria Barranco, Rossy de Palma; ***D:*** Pedro Almodovar; ***W:*** Pedro Almodovar; ***C:*** Jose Luis Alcaine; ***M:*** Ennio Morricone.

The Tie That Binds 🦴 **1995 (R)** Insipid thriller is a cheap imitation of its cousin, "The Hand that Rocks the Cradle" (made by the same producers), but what the former movie did to the nanny business, this flick does to a whole genre. Leanne and John Netherwood (Hannah and Carradine) are psycho parents out to reclaim their daughter from the lame-brain yuppie couple (Spano and Kelly) who adopted her. Out of all the children there, they choose the one who likes to sleep with a butcher knife under her pillow. Duh! Every "family in danger from psychotic" cliche is employed in a vain attempt to build suspense for the silly conclusion. Dismal directorial debut of screenwriter Strick. **98m/C VHS, DVD, Wide.** Daryl Hannah, Keith Carradine, Moira Kelly, Vincent Spano, Julia Devin, Ray Reinhardt, Cynda Williams; ***D:*** Wesley Strick; ***W:*** Michael Auerbach; ***C:*** Bobby Bukowski; ***M:*** Graeme Revell.

Tiefland 🦴🦴½ **1944** Melodrama based on the libretto for D'Abert's opera about a gypsy dancer and her loves. Unreleased until 1954, this film is the last of Riefenstahl's career; she subsequently turned to still photography. In German with English subtitles. **98m/B VHS.** *GE* Leni Riefenstahl, Franz Eichberger, Bernard Minetti, Maria Koppenhofer, Luise Rainer; ***D:*** Leni Riefenstahl.

Tierra 🦴🦴 *Earth* **1995** Metaphysical messiness. Mystery exterminator Angel (Gomez) comes to Aragon, a land of red soil and lightning strikes, to fumigate the woodlice infesting the vineyards. He recruits some locals and gypsies to help him out while becoming involved with a couple of women—shy Angela (Suarez) and hot Mari (Klein). But Angel is also literally haunted by an alter ego—a situation that no doubt has some deep meaning that is never very clear. But neither is the rest of the movie. Spanish with subtitles. **122m/C VHS, DVD, Wide.** *SP* Carmelo Gomez, Emma Suarez, Silke Klein, Karra Elejalde, Nancho Novo, Txema Blasco; ***D:*** Julio Medem; ***W:*** Julio Medem; ***C:*** Javier Aguirresarobe; ***M:*** Alberto Iglesias.

Tieta of Agreste 🦴🦴 **1996** After many years, wealthy Tieta (Braga) returns to her village with her stepdaughter and immediately causes havoc for her greedy family. Based on a novel by Jorge Amado. Portuguese with subtitles. **140m/C VHS, DVD, Wide.** *BR* Sonia Braga, Marilia Pera, Zeze Motta, Jorge Amado; ***D:*** Carlos Diegues; ***W:*** Carlos Diegues; ***C:*** Edgar Moura; ***M:*** Caetano Veloso.

Tiffany Jones 🦴 **1975 (R)** Tiffany Jones is a secret agent who has information that presidents and revolutionaries are willing to kill for. **90m/C VHS.** Anouska (Anoushka) Hempel, Ray Brooks, Eric Pohlmann, Martin Benson, Susan Sneers; ***D:*** Pete Walker.

Tiger and the Pussycat 🦴🦴½ *Il Tigre* **1967 (R)** A successful Italian businessman's infatuation with an attractive American art student leads him to marital and financial woes. **110m/C VHS.** Ann-Margret, Vittorio Gassman, Eleanor Parker; ***D:*** Dino Risi.

Tiger Bay 🦴🦴🦴 **1959** A young Polish sailor, on leave in Cardiff, murders his unfaithful girlfriend. Lonely ten-year-old Gillie sees the crime and takes the murder weapon, thinking it will make her more popular with her peers. Confronted by a police detective, she convincingly lies but eventually the sailor finds Gillie and kidnaps her, hoping to keep her quiet until he can get aboard his ship. A delicate relationship evolves between the child and the killer as she tries to help him escape and the police close in. Marks Hayley Mills' first major role and one of her finest performances. **107m/B VHS, DVD.** *GB* John Mills, Horst Buchholz, Hayley Mills, Yvonne Mitchell, Megs Jenkins, Anthony Dawson, Kenneth Griffith, Michael Anderson Jr.; ***D:*** J. Lee Thompson; ***W:*** John Hawkesworth; ***C:*** John Hawkesworth; ***M:*** Laurie Johnson.

Tiger Claws 🦴½ **1991 (R)** The pretty, petite Rothrock has been called the female Bruce Lee. Perhaps, but at least he got a good script every once in a while. This time Rothrock's a kung-fu cop investigating the strange ritual-murders of martial-arts champions. **93m/C VHS, DVD.** Cynthia Rothrock, Bolo Yeung, Jalal Merhi; ***D:*** Kelly Markin; ***W:*** J. Stephen Maunder; ***C:*** Curtis Petersen, Mark Willis.

Tiger Fangs 🦴½ **1943** When Nazis threaten the Far East rubber production with man-eating tigers, real-life big game hunter Frank Buck comes to the rescue. **57m/B VHS.** Frank Buck, June Duprez, Duncan Renaldo; ***D:*** Sam Newfield.

Tiger Heart 🦴🦴½ **1996 (PG-13)** Teenaged karate champ Eric Chase (Roberts) is looking forward to a lazy summer with girlfriend Stephanie (Lyons) before heading off to college. But when his neighborhood comes under attack from an unscrupulous developer and Stephanie runs afoul of his goons, Eric decides to take action. **90m/C VHS.** Ted Jan Roberts, Jennifer Lyons, Robert LaSardo, Carol Potter, Timothy Williams; ***D:*** Georges Chamchoum; ***W:*** William Applegate Jr.; ***M:*** John Gonzalez.

Tiger Joe 🦴 **1985** There's trouble in Southeast Asia, and the U.S. military confuses things even more. **96m/C VHS.** Alan Collins, David Warbeck; ***D:*** Anthony (Antonio Margheriti) Dawson.

Tiger of the Seven Seas 🦴🦴 **1962** A female pirate takes over her father's command and embarks on adventures on the high seas. Generous portions of action, intrigue, and romance. Sequel to "Queen of the Pirates." **90m/C VHS.** *IT FR* Gianna Maria Canale, Anthony Steel, Grazia Maria Spina, Ernesto Calindri; ***D:*** Luigi Capuano.

Tiger Town 🦴🦴½ **1983 (G)** A baseball player, ending an illustrious career with the Detroit Tigers, sees his chance of winning a pennant slipping away. A young fan, however, proves helpful in chasing that elusive championship. **76m/C VHS.** Roy Scheider, Justin Henry, Ron McLarty, Bethany Carpenter, Noah Moazezi; ***D:*** Alan Shapiro; ***C:*** Robert Elswit. **CABLE**

A Tiger Walks 🦴🦴½ **1964** A savage tiger escapes from a circus and local children start a nationwide campaign to save its life. Notable for its unflattering portrayal of America's heartland and small town dynamics. Radical departure from most Disney films of the period. **88m/C VHS.** Sabu, Pamela Franklin, Brian Keith, Vera Miles, Kevin Corcoran, Peter Brown, Una Merkel, Frank McHugh, Edward Andrews; ***D:*** Norman Tokar; ***M:*** Buddy (Norman Dale) Baker.

Tiger Warsaw 🦴½ *The Tiger* **1987 (R)** A young man returns to the town where he once lived, before he shot his father. He hopes to sort out his life and repair family problems. Muddled and sappy. **92m/C VHS.** Patrick Swayze, Barbara Williams, Piper Laurie, Bobby DiCicco, Kaye Ballard, Lee Richardson, Mary McDonnell; ***D:*** Amin Q. Chaudhri.

The Tiger Woods Story 🦴🦴½ **1998 (PG-13)** Kain stars as the young man who, at 21, became the youngest player ever to win the Masters Golf Tournament. Based on the book "Tiger" by John Strege. **103m/C VHS.** Khalil Kain, Keith David, Freda Foh Shen; ***D:*** LeVar Burton; ***W:*** Takashi Bufford. **CABLE**

Tigerland 🦴🦴🦴 **2000 (R)** Irish newcomer Farrell made a big (and deserved) splash as Army draftee Roland Bozz, one of a group of grunts at the final stage of infantry training at Fort Polk, Louisiana in 1971. The title refers to the wilderness area designed for jungle combat simulation before the newbies are shipped out to Nam. But the rebellious, cynical Bozz gets away with defying every rule thrown at him to the disbelief of the others in the platoon. Familiar story but the ensemble cast is right on the mark and director Schumacher keeps tight control in this old-fashioned low-budget drama. **101m/C VHS, DVD, Wide.** *US* Colin Farrell, Matthew Davis, Clifton (Gonzalez) Collins Jr., Tom Guiry, Russell Richardson, Cole Hauser, Shea Whigham; ***D:*** Joel Schumacher; ***W:*** Ross Klaven, Michael McGruther; ***C:*** Matthew Libatique; ***M:*** Nathan Larsen.

Tigers in Lipstick 🦴½ *Wild Beds* **1980 (R)** Seven short vignettes featuring the beautiful actresses as aggressive women and the men that they influence. **88m/C VHS.** *IT* Laura Antonelli, Monica Vitti, Ursula Andress, Sylvia Kristel; ***D:*** Luigi Zampa.

A Tiger's Tale 🦴½ **1987 (R)** A middle-aged divorced nurse begins an affair with her daughters's ex-boyfriend. **97m/C VHS.** Ann-Margret, C. Thomas Howell, Charles Durning, Kelly Preston, Ann Wedgeworth, Tim Thomerson, Steven Kampmann, Traci Lind, Angel Tompkins, William Zabka; ***D:*** Peter Douglas; ***C:*** Tony Pierce-Roberts.

Tigershark 🦴 **1987 (R)** A martial arts expert goes to Southeast Asia to rescue his girlfriend, who has been kidnapped by communist forces and held captive for arms and ammunition. Strictly for fans of the martial arts. **97m/C VHS.** Mike Stone, John Quade, Pamela Bryant; ***D:*** Emmett Alston; ***W:*** Ivan Rogers.

Tight Spot 🦴🦴🦴 **1955** Been-around-the-block model Sherry Conley (Rogers) is serving time for a crime she didn't commit when she's offered a deal by U.S. attorney Lloyd Hallett (Robinson) if she'll testify against mob boss Benjamin Costain (Greene). But since no other potential witness lived to the trial date, Sherry's against cooperating. However, Hallett puts her up in a hotel with bodyguard Vince Striker (Keith) in hopes she'll change her mind. But Costain has a lot of clout and is determined to get to Sherry. Rogers gives an excellent performance in a dramatic role with fine support from the rest of the cast. **97m/B VHS.** Ginger Rogers, Edward G. Robinson, Brian Keith, Lorne Greene, Katherine Anderson; ***D:*** Phil Karlson; ***W:*** William Bowers; ***C:*** Burnett Guffey; ***M:*** George Duning.

Tightrope 🦴🦴🦴 **1984 (R)** Police inspector Wes Block pursues a killer of prostitutes in New Orleans' French Quarter. The film is notable both as a thriller and as a fascinating vehicle for Eastwood, who experiments with a disturbing portrait of a cop with some peculiarities of his own. **115m/C VHS.** Clint Eastwood, Genevieve Bujold, Dan Hedaya, Jennifer Beck, Alison Eastwood, Randi Brooks, Regina Richardson, Jamie Rose; ***D:*** Richard Tuggle; ***C:*** Bruce Surtees; ***M:*** Lennie Niehaus.

The Tigress 🦴½ **1993 (R)** In 1920s Berlin two con artists set out to scam a rich American using sex as a lure. Things don't go as planned. Also available in an unrated version. **89m/C VHS.** Valentina Vargas, James Remar, George Peppard.

Til There Was You 🦴½ **1996 (PG-13)** You know what most great romance movies have in common? The couples actually meet each other before the end of the movie. Not here. That's one of the reasons this one isn't even good. Ghostwriter Gwen (Tripplehorn) and architect Nick (McDermott), although seemingly destined for one another, have more near-misses than a drunken, near-sighted airline pilot. They're shown in the same room, in adjoining rooms, leaving a room as soon as the other enters, etc., etc. Meanwhile, minor characters appear, speak some ham-fisted dialogue and then disappear. This happens for 20 years. Then they meet and the movie is (thankfully) over. Parker, however, does an excellent job as a rehab-addicted former child star who has ties to both characters. Feature directorial debut for Winant. **113m/C VHS, DVD, Wide.** Dylan McDermott, Sarah Jessica Parker, Jeanne Tripplehorn, Jennifer Aniston, Ken Olin, Craig Bierko, Nina Foch, Alice Drummond, Christine Ebersole, Michael Tucker, Patrick Malahide, Kasi Lemmons, Karen Allen; ***D:*** Scott Winant; ***W:*** Winnie Holzman; ***C:*** Bobby Bukowski; ***M:*** Miles Goodman, Terence Blanchard.

Tilai 🦴🦴 *The Law* **1990** When Saga returns to his African village after a long absence, it's to discover that his young fiancee, Nogma, has been forced into marriage with his own father. According to his tribe's code of honor Saga can do nothing but love won't be denied and they begin an affair, which is deemed incestuous by the village. So Saga and Nogma flee, hoping to live out of the reach of tribal law. **81m/C VHS.** Rasmane Ouedraogo, Ina Cisse, Roukietou Barry; ***D:*** Idrissa Ouedraogo; ***W:*** Idrissa Ouedraogo; ***C:*** Pierre-Laurent Chenieux, Jean Monsigny; ***M:*** Abdullah Ibrahim. Cannes '90: Grand Jury Prize.

Till Death Do Us Part 🦴½ **1972 (PG)** Three married couples spend a weekend at a counseling retreat, unaware that the proprietor is a murderous maniac. **77m/C VHS.** James Keach, Claude Jutra, Matt Craven; ***D:*** Timothy Brand.

Till Death Do Us Part 🦴🦴 **1992 (R)** An ex-cop turns into an evil killer who seduces unsuspecting women and murders them for their insurance money. Contains footage not seen in the TV movie. Based on a true story and the book by Vincent Bugliosi. **93m/C VHS.** Treat Williams, Arliss Howard, Rebecca Jenkins; ***D:*** Yves Simoneau.

Till Marriage Do Us Part 🦴🦴½ *Dio Mio, Come Sono Caduta in Basso; How Long Can You Fall?* **1974 (R)** An innocent couple discovers on their wedding night that they are really brother and sister. Since they can't in good conscience get a divorce or consummate their marriage, they must seek sexual gratification elsewhere. Antonelli is deliciously tantalizing in this silly satire. In Italian with English subtitles. **97m/C VHS.** *IT* Laura Antonelli, Alberto Lionello, Jean Rochefort, Michele Placido, Karin Schubert; ***D:*** Luigi Comencini.

Till Murder Do Us Part 🦴🦴½ *A Woman Scorned: The Betty Broderick Story* **1992 (PG-13)** Based on the true story of Betty Broderick, an obsessively devoted wife and mother whose husband leaves her for another woman. Even after a bitter divorce, Betty refuses to let go. Until she commits murder. **95m/C VHS.** Meredith Baxter, Stephen Collins, Michelle Johnson, Kelli Williams, Stephen (Steve) Root; ***D:*** Dick Lowry. **TV**

Till the Clouds Roll By 🦴🦴½ **1946** An all-star, high-gloss musical biography of songwriter Jerome Kern, that, in typical Hollywood fashion, bears little resemblance to the composer's life. Filled with wonderful songs from his Broadway hit. ♫Showboat Medley; Till the Clouds Roll By; Howja Like to Spoon with Me?; The Last Time I Saw Paris; They Didn't Believe Me; I Won't Dance; Why Was I Born?; Who?; Sunny. **137m/C VHS, DVD.** Robert Walker, Van Heflin, Judy Garland, Frank Sinatra, Lucille Bremer, Kathryn Grayson, June Allyson, Dinah Shore, Lena Horne, Virginia O'Brien, Tony Martin; ***D:*** Richard Whorf; ***W:*** Myles Connolly, Jean Holloway; ***C:*** Harry Stradling Sr.; ***M:*** Conrad Salinger, Roger Edens, Lennie Hayton.

Till the End of the Night 🦴½ **1994 (R)** D'arcy (Enos) is an ex-con who will do anything to get back his ex-wife Diana Davenport (Lang) and it doesn't matter that she has a new husband, John (Valentine) and two kids. D'arcy manages to kidnap Diana and it's up to John to save his wife. **90m/C VHS.** John Enos, Katherine Kelly Lang, Scott Valentine, David Keith; ***D:*** Larry Brand; ***W:*** Larry Brand.

Till the End of Time 🦴🦴½ **1946** Three GIs have trouble adjusting to civilian life in their home town after WWII. Fine performances and excellent pacing. Popular title song. Adapted from "They Dream of Home" by Niven Busch. **105m/C VHS.** Robert Mitchum, Guy Madison, Bill Williams, Dorothy McGuire, William Gargan, Tom Tully; ***D:*** Edward Dmytryk.

Till There Was You 🦴 **1991 (PG-13)** A struggling musician travels to a faraway tropical isle to solve the mystery of his brother's death. **94m/C VHS.** Mark Harmon, Deborah Kara Unger, Jeroen Krabbe, Shane Briant; ***D:*** John Seale; ***M:*** Graeme Revell.

Tillie Wakes Up 🦴🦴½ **1917** Third in the Tillie series, following "Tillie's Punctured Romance" and "Tillie's Tomato Surprise." Tillie (Dressler) decides she needs a little fun in her life so she asks her henpecked nieghbor Mr. Pipkin (Hines) to spend the day with her on Coney Island. **48m/B VHS.** Marie Dressler, Johnny Hines, Frank Beamish, Ruby de Remer; ***D:*** Harry Davenport; ***W:*** Frances Marion.

Tillie's Punctured Romance 🦴🦴 **1914** The silent comedy which established Chaplin and Dressler as comedians. Chaplin, out of his Tramp character, is the city slicker trying to put one over on farm girl Dressler who pursues revenge. First feature length comedy film. Followed by "Tillie's Tomato Surprise" and "Tillie Wakes Up," which starred Dressler but not Chaplin. **73m/B VHS, DVD.** Charlie Chaplin, Marie Dressler, Mabel Normand, Mack Swain, Chester Conklin; ***D:*** Mack Sennett; ***W:*** Hampton Del Ruth; ***C:*** Frank D. Williams.

Tilt 🦴 **1978 (PG)** Flimsy storyline concerns a young runaway's adventures with an aspiring rock star. Shields' pinball expertise eventually leads her to a match against pinball champ Durning. **111m/C VHS.** Charles Durning, Ken Marshall, Brooke Shields, Geoffrey Lewis; ***D:*** Rudy Durand; ***W:*** Rudy Durand, Donald Cammell.

Tim 🦴🦴½ **1979** Follows the relationship between a handsome, mentally retarded young man and an attractive older businesswoman. Sappy storyline is redeemed by Gibson's fine performance in one of his first roles. Based on Colleen McCullough's first novel. **94m/C VHS, DVD.** *AU* Mel Gibson, Piper Laurie, Peter Gwynne, Alwyn Kurts, Pat Evison; ***D:*** Michael Pate; ***W:*** Michael Pate; ***C:*** Paul Onorato; ***M:*** Eric Jupp. Australian Film Inst. '79: Actor (Gibson).

Tim Tyler's Luck **1937** Lost but not forgotten serial in its 12-chapter entirety. The fearless Tim Tyler uses whatever he can to do battle with the sinister Spider Web gang. **235m/B VHS.** Frankie Thomas Jr., Frances Robinson, Al Shean, Norman Willis, Earl Douglas, Jack Mulhall, Frank Mayo, Pat O'Brien; ***D:*** Ford Beebe, Wyndham Gittens.

Timber Queen 🦴🦴 **1944** A WWII flier comes home and aids his best friend's widow, who must make a quota of timber or lose her sawmill to gangsters. Old-fashioned. **66m/B VHS.** Richard Arlen, Mary Beth Hughes, June Havoc, Sheldon Leonard, George E. Stone, Dick Purcell; ***D:*** Frank McDonald.

Time After Time 🦴🦴🦴 **1979 (PG)** In Victorian London, circa 1893, H.G. Wells is experimenting with his time machine. He discovers the machine has been used by an associate, who turns out to be Jack the Ripper, to travel to San Francisco in 1979. Wells follows to stop any further murders and the ensuing battle of wits is both entertaining and imaginative. McDowell is charming as Wells and Steenburgen is equally fine as Well's modern American love interest. **112m/C VHS.** Malcolm McDowell, David Warner, Mary Steenburgen, Patti D'Arbanville, Charles Cioffi; ***D:*** Nicholas Meyer; ***W:*** Nicholas Meyer; ***M:*** Miklos Rozsa.

Time and Tide 🦴🦴 *Seunlau Ngaklau* **2000 (R)** Non-stop action from Hark with the usual convoluted plot. Tyler (Tse) is working as a bodyguard for a client who turns out to be a Triad boss. Tyler's friend Jack (Bai) is an ex-mercenary whose pregnant wife, Hui (Lo), is the criminal's estranged daughter. And then Jack's former South American colleagues show up in Hong Kong with a plan to assassinate the Triad boss, among other gun battles. Oh, and Tyler is also about to become a father, courtesy of a one-night stand who doesn't want anything to do with him. Chinese with subtitles. **113m/C VHS, DVD, Wide.** *HK* Nicholas Tse, Wu Bai, Anthony Wong, Candy Lo, Cathy Chui, Joventino Couto Remotigue; ***D:*** Tsui Hark; ***W:*** Tsui Hark, Koan Hui; ***C:*** Herman Yau, Ko Chiu-lam; ***M:*** Tommy Wai.

Time at the Top 🦴🦴½ **1999** Fourteen-year-old Susan Shawson travels back in time (via her apartment's elevator) from the Philadelphia of the present to the same city in 1881. There Susan befriends Victoria Walker and her younger brother Robert, who need help with their family troubles. The trio manage to time travel back and forth and the change both the past and the present. Based on the book by Edward Ormondroyd. **96m/C VHS.** Timothy Busfield, Elisha Cuthbert, Gabrielle Boni, Mathew Harbour, Lynne Adams, Denys Chapdelaine; ***D:*** Jim Kaufman; ***W:*** Linda Brookover; ***C:*** Francois Protat; ***M:*** Simon Carpentier. **CABLE**

Time Bandits 🦴🦴½ **1981 (PG)** A group of dwarves help a young boy to travel through time and space with the likes of Robin Hood, Napoleon, Agamemnon, and other time-warp playmates. Epic fantasy from Monty Python alumni. **110m/C VHS, DVD, Wide.** *GB* John Cleese, Sean Connery, Shelley Duvall, Katherine Helmond, Ian Holm, Michael Palin, Ralph Richardson, Kenny Baker, Peter Vaughan, David Warner, Craig Warnock; ***D:*** Terry Gilliam; ***W:*** Terry Gilliam, Michael Palin; ***C:*** Peter Biziou; ***M:*** Mike Moran, George Harrison.

Time Chasers 🦴🦴 **1995** Nick Miller (Burch) invents a device that permits his airplane to travel through time. But, after selling his invention, he soon discovers that it has turned the future into a desolate wasteland. Now Nick must try to regain control and put things back to normal. **90m/C VHS.** Matthew Burch, Bonnie Pritchard, Peter Harrington; ***D:*** David Giancola.

Time Code 🦴🦴 *Timecode* **2000 (R)** Figgis shot his film in one day, using four digital video cameras and 28 actors to tell four separate (though inter-connected) stories that were shown simultaneously onscreen in four rectangular quadrants. The stories center around a film production company headed by producer Alex Green (Skarsgard), whose wife Emma (Burrows) plans to leave him because he is having an affair with actress Rose (Hayek), whose own relationship with Lauren (Tripplehorn) is falling apart. Then there's various producers, directors, and actors pitching ideas or auditioning for parts. It's not as confusing as might be imagined although how it will play on video is a challenge. **97m/C VHS, DVD.** Stellan Skarsgard, Saffron Burrows, Salma Hayek, Jeanne Tripplehorn, Richard Edson, Julian Sands, Xander Berkeley, Glenne Headly, Holly Hunter, Danny Huston, Kyle MacLachlan, Alessandro Nivola, Steven Weber, Viveka Davis, Aimee Graham, Andrew Heckler, Daphna Kastner, Leslie Mann, Mia Maestro; ***D:*** Mike Figgis; ***W:*** Mike Figgis; ***C:*** Patrick Alexander Stewart; ***M:*** Mike Figgis, Anthony Marinelli.

A Time for Miracles 🦴½ **1980** Dramatic biography of the first native-born American saint, Elizabeth Bayley Seton, who was canonized in 1975. **97m/C VHS.** Kate Mulgrew, Lorne Greene, Rossano Brazzi, John Forsythe, Jean-Pierre Aumont, Milo O'Shea; ***D:*** Michael O'Herlihy. **TV**

Time for Revenge 🦴🦴½ **1982** A demolitions worker attempts to blackmail his corrupt employer by claiming a workplace explosion made him speechless. He finds himself in a contest of silence and wits. In Spanish with English subtitles. **112m/C VHS.** *AR* Federico Luppi, Haydee Padilla, Julio de Grazia, Ulises Dumont; ***D:*** Adolfo Aristarain. Montreal World Film Fest. '82: Film.

The Time Guardian 🦴½ **1987 (PG)** Time-travelers of the future arrive in the Australian desert in 1988, intent on warning the local populace of the impending arrival of killer cyborgs from the 40th century. Muddled and confusing. **89m/C VHS, 8mm.** Tom Burlinson, Carrie Fisher, Dean Stockwell, Nikki Coghill; ***D:*** Brian Hannant; ***W:*** Brian Hannant, John Baxter; ***C:*** Geoff Burton.

Time Indefinite 🦴🦴 **1993** Cinema verite effort once again follows filmmaker McElwee who returns to his Southern roots to confront personal tragedy by recording every moment on film. It is an emotional journey in which he discovers that his camera may not be enough to protect him from his own feelings. Moving, with occasional lapses into self-absorption. Companion film to McElwee's "Sherman's March." **117m/C VHS.** ***D:*** Ross McElwee; ***W:*** Ross McElwee.

Time Lapse 🦴🦴 **2001 (PG-13)** Agent Clay Pierce (McNamara) is a member of a U.S. antiterrorist unit who unknowingly prevents an attempt to sell a nuclear device to the Iraquis. Too bad Clay is the only one who makes it back alive (more or less). He's got a lot of questions for his boss LaNova (Scheider), who turns out to be a double-dealer. And he deals with Clay by giving him an experimental drug that causes amnesia—so Clay is really confused about why people keep trying to kill him. **88m/C VHS, DVD.** Roy Scheider, William McNamara, Dina Meyer, Henry Rollins; ***D:*** David Worth. **VIDEO**

Time Lock 🦴🦴 **1957** An expert safecracker races against time to save a child who is trapped inside a bank's preset time-locked vault. Canada is the setting, although the film was actually made in England. Based on a play by Arthur Hailey. **73m/B VHS.** *GB* Robert Beatty, Betty McDowall, Vincent Winter, Lee Patterson, Sandra Francis, Alan Gifford, Robert Ayres, Victor Wood, Jack Cunningham, Peter Mannering, Gordon Tanner, Larry Cross, Sean Connery; ***D:*** Gerald Thomas; ***W:*** Peter Rogers; ***C:*** Peter Hennessy; ***M:*** Stanley Black.

The Time Machine 🦴🦴🦴 **1960** English scientist living near the end of the 19th century invents time travel machine and uses it to travel into various periods of the future. Rollicking version of H.G. Wells' classic cautionary tale boasts Oscar-winning special effects. Remade in 1978. **103m/C VHS, DVD, Wide.** Rod Taylor, Yvette Mimieux, Whit Bissell, Sebastian Cabot, Alan Young, Paul Frees, Bob Barran, Doris Lloyd; ***D:*** George Pal; ***W:*** David Duncan; ***C:*** Paul Vogel; ***M:*** Russell Garcia.

Time Machine 🦴½ **1978 (G)** Yet another adaptation of H.G. Wells' classic novel about a scientist who invents a machine that enables him to travel through time. Inferior remake of the 1960 version. **99m/C VHS.** John Beck, Priscilla Barnes, Andrew Duggan; ***D:*** Henning Schellerup.

The Time Machine 🦴🦴 **2002 (PG-13)** Well, the special effects are pretty cool but this sci-fi adventure has little to do with H.G. Wells' 1894 novel. Eccentric scientist Alexander Hartdegen (an anorexic-looking Pearce) lives in New York, circa 1900. He's devastated when his fiance Emma (Guillory) is killed and is determined to change fate by building a time machine. But going back in time changes nothing so Hartdegen goes forward to discover why he can't change things. He accidentally winds up in 800,000 when the Earth is once again pastoral and its inhabitants are divided into the gentle surface-dwelling Elois and the monstrous, cannibalistic subterranean Morlocks. Irish singer Mumba debuts as Mara, whom Hartdegen falls for, and a heavily made-up Irons is the Uber-Morlock. Unfortunately, the story is dull rather than what it should be—rousing in a who-cares-about-logic, B-movie way. **96m/C VHS, DVD.** *US* Guy Pearce, Samantha Mumba, Mark Addy, Sienna Guillory, Omera Mumba, Jeremy Irons, Orlando Jones, Phyllida Law, Yancey Arias; ***Cameos:*** Alan Young; ***D:*** Simon Wells; ***W:*** John Logan; ***C:*** Donald McAlpine; ***M:*** Klaus Badelt.

A Time of Destiny 🦴🦴 **1988 (PG-13)** During WWII, an American soldier vows to kill his brother-in-law, who he believes caused his father's death. Meanwhile, the two men have become good friends in the army, never realizing their connection. A strange, overblown family saga from the director of "El Norte." Beautiful photography, terrific editing. **118m/C VHS, 8mm.** William Hurt, Timothy Hutton, Melissa Leo, Stockard Channing, Megan Follows, Francesco Rabal; ***D:*** Gregory Nava; ***W:*** Gregory Nava, Anna Thomas; ***M:*** Ennio Morricone.

Time of Indifference 🦴🦴 *Gli Indifferenti; Les Deux Rivales* **1964** Based on the novel by Alberto Moravia. Tale of the disintegration of values in 1920s Italy is unable to take full advantage of its fine cast or potentially thought-provoking themes. **84m/B VHS.** *IT* Rod Steiger, Shelley Winters, Claudia Cardinale, Paulette Goddard, Tomas Milian; ***D:*** Francesco Maselli.

Time of the Gypsies 🦴🦴🦴 *Dom Za Vesanje* **1990 (R)** Acclaimed Yugoslavian saga about a homely, unlucky Gypsy boy who sets out to steal his way to a dowry large enough to marry the girl of his dreams. Beautifully filmed, magical, and very long. In the Gypsy language, Romany, it's the first feature film made in the Gypsy tongue. **136m/C VHS.** *YU* Davor Dujmovic, Sinolicka Trpkova, Ljubica Adzovic, Hunsija Hasimovic, Bora Todorovic; ***D:*** Emir Kusturica. Cannes '89: Director (Kusturica).

The Time of Their Lives 🦴🦴½ *The Ghost Steps Out* **1946** A pair of Revolutionary War-era ghosts haunt a modern country estate. One of the best A & C comedies. **82m/B VHS.** Bud Abbott, Lou Costello, Marjorie Reynolds, Binnie Barnes, Gale Sondergaard, John Shelton; ***D:*** Charles T. Barton.

The Time of Your Life 🦴🦴🦴½ **1948** The only Cagney film that ever lost money. A simple but engaging story of people trying to live their dreams. Cagney is delightful as a barroom philosopher who controls the world around him from his seat in the tavern. Although it was not very popular with audiences at the time, the critics hailed it as an artistic achievement. Based on William Saroyan's play. **109m/B VHS.** James Cagney, William Bendix, Jeanne Cagney, Broderick Crawford, Ward Bond, James Barton, Paul Draper, Natalie Schafer; ***D:*** H.C. Potter.

Time Out for Love 🦴🦴½ *Les Grandes Personnes; The Five Day Lover* **1961** An American girl travels to Paris in search of romance, but discovers more than she bargained for. In French with English subtitles. **91m/B VHS.** *IT FR* Jean Seberg, Micheline Presle, Maurice Ronet, Francoise Prevost, Annibale Ninchi, Nando (Fernando) Bruno; ***D:*** Jean Valere; ***M:*** Georges Delerue.

Time Runner 🦴🦴 **1992 (R)** It's 2022 and the Earth is being used as target practice by alien invaders. Space captain Hamill manages to find a hole in time and slip back to 1992 where he can battle the first of the alien infiltrators and maybe change Earth's destiny. The time-travel theme (including Hamill watching his own birth) is fun and the special effects are well done. **90m/C VHS.** Mark Hamill, Brion James, Rae Dawn Chong; ***D:*** Michael Mazo.

Time Served 🦴½ **1999 (R)** Typically sleazy women-in-prison movie. Sarah McKinney (Oxenberg) is wrongly convicted by a psycho judge and sent to the slammer where she faces a crooked warden and lecherous guards. Sarah also discovers that the prison's work release program means stripping at an underground sex club frequented by the judge and his cronies. Sarah wants to expose more than just herself and tries to get the truth out. **94m/C VHS.** Catherine Oxenberg, Louise Fletcher, Jeff Fahey, Bo Hopkins, James Handy; ***D:*** Glen Pitre. **CABLE**

Time Stands Still 🦴🦴🦴 *Megall Az Ido* **1982** Two brothers experience troubled youth in Budapest. Artful, somberly executed, with American pop soundtrack. Subtitled in English. **99m/C VHS.** *HU* Istvan Znamenak, Henrik Pauer, Aniko Ivan, Sander Soth, Peter Galfy; ***D:*** Peter Gothar; ***W:*** Peter Gothar; ***C:*** Lajos Koltai; ***M:*** Gyorgy Selmeczi. N.Y. Film Critics '82: Foreign Film.

Time to Die 🦴½ *Seven Graves for Rogan* **1983 (R)** WWII victim of heinous war crimes, obsessed with revenge, stalks his prey for a final confrontation, while eluding U.S. intelligence. Disappointing despite good cast working with Mario Puzo story. **89m/C VHS.** Edward Albert, Rex Harrison, Rod Taylor, Raf Vallone; ***D:*** Matt Cimber; ***M:*** Ennio Morricone.

A Time to Die 🦴½ **1991 (R)** Lords plays a police photographer who, well, photographs the police. But her camera catches one in the act of murder. Routine crime thriller. **93m/C VHS.** Traci Lords, Jeff Conaway, Richard Roundtree, Bradford Bancroft, Nitchie Barrett; ***D:*** Charles Kanganis; ***W:*** Charles Kanganis; ***M:*** Ennio Morricone.

Time to Kill *Tempo di Uccidere* **1989 (R)** A young soldier in Africa wanders away from his camp and meets a woman whom he rapes and kills. But when he returns to his outfit he finds he can't escape his tormenting conscience. **110m/C VHS.** Nicolas Cage, Giancarlo Giannini, Robert Liensol; ***D:*** Guiliano Montaldo; ***W:*** Furio Scarpelli; ***M:*** Ennio Morricone.

A Time to Kill 🦴🦴🦴½ **1996 (R)** Powerful story of revenge, racism, and the question of justice in the "new south." John Grisham had a lot of clout when he finally sold his first and favorite novel to the movies, including veto power over the leading man—director Schumacher was for Woody Harrelson, Grisham was opposed but both finally agreed on newcomer McConaughey. He's outstanding as idealistic smalltown Mississippi lawyer Jake Brigance, called to defend anguished father Carl Lee Hailey (Jackson), who's accused of killing the rednecks who raped his young daughter. Jake's assisted by former mentor Lucien Wilbanks (Sutherland) and ambitious northern law student Ellen Roark (Bullock) against ruthless prosecutor Rufus Buckley (Spacey). Is it emotionally manipulative? You betcha. But Grisham's done well on screen and Schumacher (who also did "The Client") knows how to get the most from his cast and script. **150m/C VHS, DVD, Wide.** Matthew McConaughey, Samuel L. Jackson, Sandra Bullock, Kevin Spacey, Donald Sutherland, Brenda Fricker, Oliver Platt, Charles S. Dutton, Kiefer Sutherland, Chris Cooper, Ashley Judd, Patrick McGoohan, Rae'ven (Alyia Larrymore) Kelly, John Diehl, Tonea Stewart, M. Emmet Walsh, Anthony Heald, Kurtwood Smith; ***D:*** Joel Schumacher; ***W:*** Akiva Goldsman; ***C:*** Peter Menzies Jr.; ***M:*** Elliot Goldenthal. MTV Movie Awards '97: Breakthrough Perf. (McConaughey).

A Time to Live 🦴½ **1985** Adaptation of Mary Lou Weisman's "Intensive Care" about a family's adjustment to a young boy's fight with Muscular Dystrophy. Minnelli's first appearance in a TV movie. **97m/C** Liza Minnelli, Jeffrey DeMunn, Swoosie Kurtz, Corey Haim, Scott Schwartz; ***D:*** Rick Wallace; ***M:*** Georges Delerue. **TV**

A Time to Live and a Time to Die 🦴🦴 *Tong Nien Wang Shi* **1985** Family from southern mainland China emigrate to Taiwan in the '40s to escape from hardship and are unable to return after the communist takeover. They find themselves cut off from their cultural heritage, and though the years pass, everyone still thinks of the mainland as home. Taiwanese with subtitles. **137m/C VHS.** *CH* ***D:*** Hou Hsaio-hsien.

A Time to Love & a Time to Die 🦴🦴½ **1958** Lush adaptation of Erich Maria Remarque novel about WWII German soldier who falls in love with a young girl during furlough. The two are married, only to be separated when he is forced to return to the Russian front. Sympathetic treatment of Germans opposed to Hitler's policies. Hutton's first film, credited to his real name, Dana J. Hutton. **133m/C VHS.** John Gavin, Lilo (Liselotte) Pulver, Jock Mahoney, Keenan Wynn, Klaus Kinski, Don DeFore, Thayer David, Dieter Borsche, Erich Maria Remarque, Barbara Rutting, Charles Regnier, Dorothea Wieck, Kurt Meisel, Clancy Cooper, John van Dreelen, Dana J. Hutton; ***D:*** Douglas Sirk; ***W:*** Orin Jannings; ***C:*** Russell Metty; ***M:*** Miklos Rozsa.

A Time to Remember 🦴½ **1990** Sticky with sentiment, this family film tells of a boy with a gift for singing, encouraged by a priest, discouraged by his father. At one point the kid loses his voice—he probably choked on the pathos. **90m/C VHS.** Donald O'Connor, Morgana King.

Time Tracers 🦴½ **1997** A group of scientists, detectives, and a reporter time travel back to the Civil War and the Jurassic period to correct a glitch that could alter earth's future. El tacky production reminiscent of Saturday matinee filler that uses stock footage for its monsters. **93m/C VHS.** Jeffrey Combs, Rocky Patterson, T.J. Myers, Tyler Mason; ***D:*** Bret McCormick.

Time Trackers 🦴🦴 **1988 (PG)** A Roger Corman cheapie about a race through time, from present-day New York to medieval England, to recover a time machine before it alters the course of history. **87m/C VHS.** Kathleen Beller, Ned Beatty, Will Shriner, Parley Baer, Robert Cornthwaite, Bridget Hoffman, Alex Hyde-White; ***D:*** Howard R. Cohen; ***W:*** Howard R. Cohen; ***C:*** Ronn Schmidt; ***M:*** Parmer Fuller.

The Time Travelers 🦴🦴 *Time Trap* **1964** Scientists discover and pass through a porthole leading to earth's post-armageddon future where they encounter unfriendly mutants. Frightened, they make a serious effort to return to the past. Remade as "Journey to the Center of Time." **82m/C VHS.** Preston Foster, Phil Carey, Merry Anders, John Hoyt, Joan Woodbury, Dolores Wells, Dennis Patrick; ***D:*** Ib Melchior.

Time Troopers *Morgen Grauen; Morning Terror* **1989 (R)** In another post-nuke society, special police must execute anyone who has misused their allotted "energy clips" for illicit behavior. Dime-store budget sci-fi. **90m/C VHS.** *AT* Albert Fortell, Hannelore Elsner; ***D:*** L.E. Neiman.

Time Walker **1982 (PG)** An archaeologist unearths King Tut's coffin in California. An alien living inside is unleashed and terrorizes the public. **86m/C VHS.** Ben Murphy, Nina Axelrod, Kevin Brophy, James Karen, Austin Stoker; ***D:*** Tom Kennedy; ***W:*** Tom Friedman, Karen Levitt; ***M:*** Richard Band.

Time Without Pity ½ **1957** Anti-capital punishment plea finds desperate alcoholic David Graham (Redgrave) discovering that his son Alec (McCowen) is about to be executed for murder. But David doesn't believe in the boy's guilt and has 24 hours to find the real killer. The audience knows Alec is innocent from the get-go, making for a certain suspense. Based on the play "Someone Waiting" by Emlyn Williams. **88m/B VHS.** *GB* Michael Redgrave, Alec McCowen, Ann Todd, Leo McKern, Peter Cushing, Renee Houston, Paul Daneman, Lois Maxwell, Richard Wordsworth, George Devine, Joan Plowright; ***D:*** Joseph Losey; ***W:*** Ben Barzman; ***C:*** Freddie Francis; ***M:*** Tristram Cary.

Timebomb ½ **1991 (R)** When someone attempts to kill Biehn, he turns to a beautiful psychiatrist for help. She triggers flashbacks that send her hunted patient on a dangerous, perhaps deadly, journey into his past. **96m/C VHS.** Michael Biehn, Patsy Kensit, Tracy Scoggins, Robert Culp, Richard Jordan, Raymond St. Jacques, Jim Maniaci, Billy Blanks, Ray "Boom Boom" Mancini, Steven J. Oliver; ***D:*** Avi Nesher; ***W:*** Avi Nesher; ***M:*** Patrick Leonard.

Timecop ½ **1994 (R)** "Terminator" rip-off is fodder for Van Damme followers with lots of action and special effects (you weren't expecting acting too). 2004 policeman Max Walker (Van Damme) must travel back in time to prevent corrupt politician Aaron McComb (Silver) from altering history for personal gain. It's also Walker's chance to alter his personal history since his wife Melissa (Sara) was killed in an explosion he can now prevent. Futuristic thriller based on a Dark Horse comic. **98m/C VHS, DVD.** Jean-Claude Van Damme, Ron Silver, Mia Sara, Bruce McGill, Scott Lawrence, Kenneth Welsh, Gabrielle Rose, Duncan Fraser, Ian Tracey, Gloria Reuben, Scott Bellis, Jason Schombing, Kevin McNulty, Sean O'Byrne, Malcolm Stewart, Alfonso Quijada, Glen Roald, Theodore Thomas; ***D:*** Peter Hyams; ***W:*** Mark Verheiden, Gary De Vore; ***C:*** Peter Hyams; ***M:*** Mark Isham.

Timeless ½ **1996** Hart's experimental feature debut uses Super-8, 16mm and 35mm formats to tell a familiar story. Eighteen-year-old Terry (Bryne) hangs out on the streets of Queens doing various odd jobs for a variety of small-time gamblers, dealers, and mobsters. He falls for Lyrica (Duge) and gets her away from her abusive lover and the teen twosome head out of town, hoping for a better life. **90m/C VHS, DVD, Wide.** Peter Byrne, Michael Griffiths, Melissa Duge; ***D:*** Chris Hart; ***W:*** Chris Hart.

Timelock **1999** In the 23rd century, asteroid Alpha 4 serves as a maximum security prison for the most dangerous criminals. However, the inmates have now gained controlled and its up to the reluctant heroics of a petty thief and a shuttle pilot to get the bad guys back in their cages. **100m/C VHS, DVD.** Maryam D'Abo, Arye Gross, Jeff Speakman, Jeffrey Meek, Martin Kove; ***D:*** Robert Munic; ***W:*** Joseph John Barmettler Jr.; ***C:*** Steve Adcock. **VIDEO**

Timemaster ½ **1995 (PG-13)** The orphaned 12-year-old Jesse (Cameron-Glickenhaus) dreams his parents are alive in another time, so he asks inventor Isaiah (Morita) for help. The duo discover Jesse's parents are being held hostage by a galactic dictator (Dorn), who's using them in sinister virtual-reality games and Jesse must time-travel to rescue them. **100m/C VHS.** Jesse Cameron-Glickenhaus, Noriyuki "Pat" Morita, Joanna Pacula, Michael Dorn, Duncan Regehr, Michelle Williams; ***D:*** James Glickenhaus; ***W:*** James Glickenhaus.

Timerider ½ *The Adventure of Lyle Swan* **1983 (PG)** Motorcyclist riding through the California desert is accidentally thrown back in time to 1877, the result of a scientific experiment that went awry. There he finds no gas stations and lots of cowboys. Co-written and co-produced by Michael Nesmith, best known for his days with the rock group "The Monkees." **93m/C VHS, DVD, Wide.** Fred Ward, Belinda Bauer, Peter Coyote, Richard Masur, Ed Lauter, L.Q. (Justus E. McQueen) Jones, Tracey Walter; ***D:*** William Dear; ***W:*** Michael Nesmith, William Dear; ***C:*** Larry Pizer; ***M:*** Michael Nesmith.

Times of Harvey Milk **1983** A powerful and moving documentary about the life and career of San Francisco supervisor and gay activist Harvey Milk. The film documents the assassination of Milk and Mayor George Moscone by Milk's fellow supervisor, Dan White. Highly acclaimed by both critics and audiences, the film gives an honest and direct look at the murder and people's reactions. News footage of the murders and White's trial is included. **90m/C VHS.** ***D:*** Robert Epstein. Oscars '83: Feature Doc.

Times Square ½ **1980 (R)** A 13-year-old girl learns about life on her own when she teams up with a defiant, anti-social child of the streets. Unappealing and unrealistic, the film features a New Wave music score. **111m/C VHS, DVD, Wide.** Tim Curry, Trini Alvarado, Robin Johnson, Peter Coffield, Elizabeth Pena, Anna Maria Horsford; ***D:*** Allan Moyle; ***W:*** Jacob Brackman; ***C:*** James A. Contner.

Times to Come *Lo Que Vendra* **1981** Taut thriller reminiscent of bleak futuristic movies like "Clockwork Orange." Three people try to survive in a desolate, aggressive, and unstable future. In Spanish with English subtitles. **98m/C VHS.** *AR* Hugo Soto, Juan Leyrado, Charly Garcia; ***D:*** Gustavo Mosquera.

Timestalkers ½ **1987** A college professor's infatuation with a young woman is complicated by their pursuit of a criminal from the 26th century into the past. Mildly entertaining adventure. Tucker's last film. **100m/C VHS.** William Devane, Lauren Hutton, Klaus Kinski, John Ratzenberger, Forrest Tucker, Gail Youngs; ***D:*** Michael A. Schultz. **TV**

Tin Cup **1996 (R)** You've got your romantic triangle, you've got your sports, you've got Costner reteamed with Shelton—"Bull Durham" on a golf course? Can lightening strike twice? Ron "Tin Cup" McAvoy (Costner) is a West Texas golf hustler who has the ability but not the steadiness to be on the pro tour. When McAvoy decides on a last-ditch effort to qualify for the U.S. Open, he turns to psychologist Dr. Molly Griswold (Russo) to get his game together. And the fact that Molly is the girlfriend of McAvoy's longtime rival—and successful PGA player—Don Simms (Johnson), well Tin Cup isn't adverse to playing for the lady's affections either. The U.S. Open scenes were filmed at Houston's Kingwood Country Club and the actors do hit their own shots. **133m/C VHS, DVD.** Kevin Costner, Don Johnson, Rene Russo, Richard "Cheech" Marin, Linda Hart, Dennis Burkley, Rex Linn, Lou Myers, Richard Lineback, Mickey Jones; ***D:*** Ron Shelton; ***W:*** Ron Shelton, John Norville; ***C:*** Russell Boyd; ***M:*** William Ross.

The Tin Drum *Die Blechtrommel* **1979 (R)** German child in the 1920s wills himself to stop growing in response to the increasing Nazi presence in Germany. He communicates his anger and fear by pounding on a tin drum. Memorable scenes, excellent cast. In German with English subtitles. Adapted from the novel by Gunter Grass. **141m/C VHS, DVD, Wide.** *GE* David Bennent, Mario Adorf, Angela Winkler, Daniel Olbrychski, Katharina Thalbach, Heinz Bennent, Andrea Ferreol, Charles Aznavour; ***D:*** Volker Schlondorff; ***W:*** Jean-Claude Carriere, Volker Schlondorff; ***C:*** Igor Luther; ***M:*** Maurice Jarre. Oscars '79: Foreign Film; Cannes '79: Film; L.A. Film Critics '80: Foreign Film.

Tin Man ½ **1983** Garage mechanic born totally deaf designs and builds a computer that can both hear and speak for him. His world is complicated, however, when a young speech therapist introduces him to new and wonderful sounds and unscrupulous and exploitative computer salesmen. Interesting premise and nice performances. **95m/C VHS.** Timothy Bottoms, Deana Jurgens, Troy Donahue; ***D:*** John G. Thomas.

Tin Men ½ **1987 (R)** Set in Baltimore in the 1960s, this bitter comedy begins with two aluminum-siding salesmen colliding in a minor car accident. They play increasingly savage pranks on each other until one seduces the wife of the other, ruining his marriage. Like "Diner," the movie is full of Levinson's idiosyncratic local Baltimore color. **112m/C VHS, DVD, Wide.** Richard Dreyfuss, Danny DeVito, Barbara Hershey, John Mahoney, Jackie Gayle, Stan Brock, Seymour Cassel, Bruno Kirby, J.T. Walsh, Michael Tucker; ***D:*** Barry Levinson; ***W:*** Barry Levinson; ***C:*** Peter Sova; ***M:*** David Steele.

Tin Pan Alley ½ **1940** Tin Pan Alley songwriters Oakie and Payne meet singing sisters Faye and Grable, who agree to plug their material. At first their music business thrives but when the women head off to sing in a hit London show, the business goes downhill. Since WWI has been declared, the boys enlist and wind up in England, where they get a second chance to see their gals. The first teaming of Faye and Payne, who would star together in three more films. Remade as "I'll Get By." ♫The Sheik of Araby; You Say the Sweetest Things, Baby; America I Love You; Goodbye Broadway, Hello France; K-K-K-Katy; Moonlight Bay; Honeysuckle Rose; Moonlight and Roses. **92m/B VHS.** Alice Faye, John Payne, Betty Grable, Jack Oakie, Allen Jenkins, Esther Ralston, John Loder, Elisha Cook Jr., Fred Keating, Billy Gilbert; ***D:*** Walter Lang; ***W:*** Robert Ellis, Helen Logan; ***C:*** Leon Shamroy; ***M:*** Alfred Newman. Oscars '40: Score.

The Tin Soldier ½ **1995 (PG)** Updated version of the Hans Christian Andersen story finds 12-year-old Billy (Knight) moving with his widowed mom (Sheedy) to a tough L.A. neighborhood. He's intimidated by the school bully to join a gang and smitten by a pretty girl who doesn't like his new friends. What's a guy to do? Why meet a mysterious toy shop owner (DeLuise), who gives Billy a tin soldier that magically transforms into a very real medieval knight named Yarik (Voight). Good intentions—no subtlety. Voight's directorial debut. **99m/C VHS.** Trenton Knight, Ally Sheedy, Dom DeLuise, Jon Voight; ***D:*** Jon Voight. **CABLE**

The Tin Star **1957** Perkins is the young sheriff who persuades veteran bounty hunter Fonda to help him rid the town of outlaws. Excellent Mann western balances humor and suspense. **93m/B VHS.** Henry Fonda, Anthony Perkins, Betsy Palmer, Neville Brand, Lee Van Cleef, John McIntire, Michel Ray; ***D:*** Anthony Mann; ***C:*** Loyal Griggs; ***M:*** Elmer Bernstein.

The Tingler **1959** Coroner Price discovers that a creepy creature is capable of growing on the human spine and increasing in size through fear. The only way to get rid of it is through constant screaming. Price takes what is probably the screen's first LSD trip and a partial color sequence fights nice red blood pouring from a faucet. One of Castle's cheesy best that originally wowed movie audiences in "Percepto" format, which consisted of installing electric buzzers under the seats for that true tingling sensation. **82m/B VHS, DVD.** Vincent Price, Darryl Hickman, Judith Evelyn, Philip Coolidge, Patricia Cutts, Pamela Lincoln; ***D:*** William Castle; ***W:*** Robb White; ***C:*** Wilfred M. Kline; ***M:*** Von Dexter.

Tinseltown **1997 (R)** Two broke screenwriters, who are living in a self-storage facility, suspect that the man who rents the space next to them is an infamous L.A. serial killer. Naturally, the desperate duo are inspired by his deeds to write a screenplay, which could make them his next victims. Based on the play "Self-storage" by Tony Spiridakis and Shem Bitterman. **84m/C VHS.** Arye Gross, Joe Pantoliano, Ron Perlman, Tom Wood, Kristy Swanson, Rebecca Gray, John Considine, David Dukes; ***D:*** Tony Spiridakis; ***W:*** Tony Spiridakis.

Tintorera...Tiger Shark woof! *Tintorera; Tintorera...Bloody Waters* **1978 (R)** Three shark hunters attempt to discover why buxom swimmers are disappearing. Phony takeoff of "Jaws." **91m/C VHS.** *GB MX* Susan George, Fiona Lewis, Jennifer Ashley; ***D:*** Rene Cardona Jr.

Tiny Toon Adventures: How I Spent My Vacation **1991** How the tiny toons of Acme Acres spend their summer vacation in this animated adventure that spoofs several popular films and amusements. Plucky Duck and Hampton Pig journey to "Happy World Land" (a takeoff on Walt Disney World), Babs and Buster Bunny's water adventure parodies "Deliverance," there's a spoof of "The Little Mermaid," and the Road Runner even makes a cameo appearance. Parents will be equally entertained by the level of humor and the fast-paced action. Based on the Steven Spielberg TV cartoon series, this is the first made-for-home-video animated feature ever released in the United States. **80m/C VHS, 8mm.**

The Tioga Kid ½ **1948** Dean takes on two roles here, that of a Texas Ranger and an outlaw who goes by the name of "The Tioga Kid." Andy Parker and the Plainsmen provide the cowboy tunes. **54m/B VHS.** Eddie Dean, Roscoe Ates, Jennifer Holt, Dennis Moore, William "Bill" Fawcett; ***D:*** Ray Taylor; ***W:*** Ed Earl Repp.

The Tip-Off ½ **1931** Lovable boxer (Armstrong) and vivacious girlfriend (Rogers) save less-than-bright friend from getting involved with mean mobster's girlfriend. Major chemistry between Rogers and Armstrong. **75m/B VHS.** Eddie Quillan, Robert Armstrong, Ginger Rogers, Joan Peers, Ernie Adams; ***D:*** Albert Rogell.

'Tis a Pity She's a Whore ½ *Addio, Fratello, Crudele* **1973 (R)** A brother and sister engage in an incestuous affair. She becomes pregnant and is married off. Her husband, however, becomes infuriated when he learns of his wife's pregnancy. Photography is by Vittorio Storaro in this highly stylized drama set in Renaissance Italy. **102m/C VHS.** *IT* Charlotte Rampling, Oliver Tobias, Fabio Testi, Antonio Falsi, Rick Battaglia, Angela Luce, Rino Imperio; ***D:*** Giuseppe Patroni-Griffi; ***M:*** Ennio Morricone.

Titan A.E. ½ **2000 (PG)** Animated adventure set after Earth is destroyed by aliens. Young Cale begins a journey through space to find a legendary lost ship—The Titan—that holds the secret to mankind's salvation. Visuals—both computer-generated and traditionally drawn—are breathtaking, but the script is earthbound. Dialogue too often falls flat, and the story, aimed at teen boys, never lives up to the epic visual dazzle. **95m/C VHS, DVD, Wide.** ***D:*** Don Bluth, Gary Goldman; ***W:*** Ben Edlund, John August, Joss Whedon; ***M:*** Graeme Revell; ***V:*** Matt Damon, Drew Barrymore, Bill Pullman, Nathan Lane, Janeane Garofalo, John Leguizamo, Tone Loc, Ron Perlman, Alex D. Linz, Jim Breuer.

Titanic **1953** Hollywoodized version of the 1912 sinking of the famous luxury liner sets the scene for the personal drama of a mother (Stanwyck) who wants to flee her husband (Webb) for a new life in America. Story gets a little too melodramatic, but it's not a bad retelling of the sea tragedy. Film is quite effective in conveying the panic and the calm of the actual sinking. A 20-foot-long model of the ship was built for the re-creation of that fateful moment when the "Titanic" hit the inevitable iceberg. **98m/B VHS.** Clifton Webb, Barbara Stanwyck, Robert Wagner, Richard Basehart, Audrey Dalton, Thelma Ritter, Brian Aherne; ***D:*** Jean Negulesco; ***W:*** Charles Brackett, Walter Reisch, Richard L. Breen. Oscars '53: Story & Screenplay.

Titanic ½ **1996 (PG-13)** Dull and draggy TV version of the 1912 tragedy between the luxury liner and an iceberg that resulted in the deaths of more than 1000 passengers. There are the usual romantic subplots, villains, and heroes, and Scott is properly noble as the veteran captain making his last voyage before retirement. Otherwise you've seen this many times before. **165m/C VHS, DVD.** George C. Scott, Peter Gallagher, Catherine Zeta-Jones, Eva Marie Saint, Tim Curry, Roger Rees, Harley Jane Kozak, Marilu Henner, Felicity Waterman, Scott Hylands, Kevin McNulty, Malcolm Stewart; ***D:*** Robert Lieberman; ***W:*** Ross LaManna, Joyce Eliason; ***C:*** David Hennings; ***M:*** Lennie Niehaus.

Titanic 🦴🦴🦴 **1997 (PG-13)** Skipper Cameron's mega-budget three-hour tour has had its own brushes with disaster with a mammoth budget (it's the most expensive movie ever made at $285 million) and a theatrical release that seemed unattainable. But instead of reaping hordes of criticism for what many thought was a joke, Cameron has accumulated praise and a boatload of Oscar hardware for his labor of love. A love story that happens to have the sinking of the historic ship as a backdrop, real characters and fictional characters are blended for a detailed re-enactment of the luxury liner's first and last voyage. The two lovebirds, Jack Dawson (DiCaprio) and debutante Rose Bukater (Winslet) are from different ends of the economic and social ladder. DiCaprio and Winslet are dynamic as the star-crossed lovers and make the running time less a chore to sit through. The special effects are impressive with a life-size version of the ship built just for this film. Cameron's prowess as a storyteller keeps the outcome of the ship suspenseful and tense even though the ending is no secret. Film has gone on to break boxoffice records set by "Star Wars" and "ET." **197m/C VHS, DVD.** Kate Winslet, Leonardo DiCaprio, Billy Zane, Kathy Bates, Frances Fisher, Gloria Stuart, Jonathan Hyde, Danny Nucci, David Warner, Bill Paxton, Bernard Hill, Victor Garber, Suzy Amis, Bernard Fox; ***D:*** James Cameron; ***W:*** James Cameron; ***C:*** Russell Carpenter; ***M:*** James Horner. Oscars '97: Art Dir./Set Dec., Cinematog., Costume Des., Director (Cameron), Film Editing, Picture, Song ("My Heart Will Go On"), Sound, Sound FX Editing, Visual FX, Orig. Score; Directors Guild '97: Director (Cameron); Golden Globes '98: Director (Cameron), Film—Drama, Song ("My Heart Will Go On"), Score; MTV Movie Awards '98: Film, Male Perf. (DiCaprio); Screen Actors Guild '97: Support. Actress (Stuart); Broadcast Film Critics '97: Director (Cameron).

Title Shot 🦴 **1981 (R)** A crafty manager convinces a millionaire to bet heavily on the guaranteed loss of his heavyweight contender in an upcoming fight. He doesn't realize the boxer is too stupid to throw the fight. **88m/C VHS.** Tony Curtis, Richard Gabourie, Susan Hogan, Robert Delbert; ***D:*** Les Rose.

Tito and Me 🦴🦴🦴 *Tito i Ja; Tito and I* **1992** Ten-year-old Zoran lives in 1954 Belgrade and is fascinated by Yugoslavian leader Marshall Tito. Crowded into a flat with his extended family, Zoran learns about volatility firsthand. Then there's romance—he has a crush on a classmate who breaks up with him when she is chosen as one of Tito's Young Pioneers, which means a two-week trip to the country. Political indoctrination means nothing but love—ahh. Debut role for the young Vojnov, who carries the weight of the movie with perfect aplomb. In Serbo-Croation with English subtitles. **104m/C VHS, DVD.** *YU* Dimitrie Vojnov, Lazar Ristovski, Anica Dobra, Predrag Manojlovic, Olivera Markovic; ***D:*** Goran Markovic; ***W:*** Goran Markovic; ***C:*** Radoslav Vladic; ***M:*** Zoran Simjanovic.

Titus 🦴🦴 **1999 (R)** Flashy version of a lesser-known early Shakespeare play, the gory "Titus Andronicus." Theatrical director Taymor makes her film debut with verve and a wild mixture of styles. Victorius Roman general Titus (Hopkins) has just defeated the Goths and has captured Tamora (Lange), the Goth Queen and her sons, one of whom Titus promptly sacrifices to appease the gods. Decadent Emperor Saturninus (Cumming) claims Tamora for his queen; her daughter Lavinia (Fraser) suffers a fate worse than death; Tamora wants revenge; Titus wants revenge; there's a villainous Moor, Aaron (Lennix); and a lot of campy fantasy and blood. **162m/C VHS, DVD, Wide.** Anthony Hopkins, Jessica Lange, Alan Cumming, Harry J. Lennix, Colm Feore, Laura Fraser, James Frain, Angus Macfadyen, Jonathan Rhys Meyers, Geraldine McEwan, Matthew Rhys; ***D:*** Julie Taymor; ***W:*** Julie Taymor; ***C:*** Luciano Tovoli; ***M:*** Elliot Goldenthal.

T.N.T. 🦴🦴 **1998 (R)** Gruner's managed to extricate himself from a covert fighting force but now they're threatening his family unless he does what he's told. **87m/C VHS, DVD.** Olivier Gruner, Eric Roberts, Randy Travis, Sam Jones, Rebecca Staab; ***D:*** Robert Radler; ***C:*** Bryan Duggan; ***M:*** Steve Edwards. **VIDEO**

TNT Jackson woof! **1975 (R)** A kung fu mama searches for her brother while everyone in Hong Kong tries to kick her out of town. **73m/C VHS.** Jeannie Bell; ***D:*** Cirio H. Santiago.

To All a Goodnight woof! **1980 (R)** Five young girls and their boyfriends are planning an exciting Christmas holiday until a mad Santa Claus puts a damper on things. Total gorefest, with few, if any, redeeming virtues. **90m/C VHS.** Jennifer Runyon, Forrest Swanson, Linda Gentile, William Lover; ***D:*** David A(lexander) Hess.

To All My Friends on Shore 🦴🦴🦴 **1971** Drama about a father dealing with his young son's sickle cell anemia. Fine performances, realistic script make this an excellent outing. **74m/C VHS.** Bill Cosby, Gloria Foster, Dennis Hines; ***D:*** Gilbert Cates. **TV**

To Be or Not to Be 🦴🦴🦴½ **1942** Sophisticated black comedy set in wartime Poland. Lombard and Benny are Maria and Josef Tura, the Barrymores of the Polish stage, who use the talents of their acting troupe to protect the Warsaw Resistance against the invading Nazis. The opening sequence is regarded as a cinema classic. One of Benny's finest film performances, the movie marks Lombard's final screen appearance—she was killed in a plane crash druing a war bond drive shortly after completing the film. Classic Lubitsch. Remade in 1983 with Mel Brooks and Anne Bancroft. **102m/B VHS.** Carole Lombard, Jack Benny, Robert Stack, Sig Rumann, Lionel Atwill, Felix Bressart, Helmut Dantine, Tom Dugan, Charles Halton, Stanley Ridges, George Lynn, Halliwell Hobbes, Miles Mander, Henry Victor, Leslie Denison, Frank Reicher, John Kellogg, James Finlayson, Roland Varno; ***D:*** Ernst Lubitsch; ***W:*** Ernst Lubitsch, Edwin Justus Mayer, Melchior Lengyel; ***C:*** Rudolph Mate; ***M:*** Werner R. Heymann, Miklos Rozsa. Natl. Film Reg. '96.

To Be or Not to Be 🦴🦴½ **1983 (PG)** In this remake of the 1942 film, Bancroft and Brooks are actors in Poland during WWII. They accidently become involved with the Polish Resistance and work to thwart the Nazis. Lots of laughs, although at times there's a little too much slapstick. **108m/C VHS.** Mel Brooks, Anne Bancroft, Charles Durning, Jose Ferrer, Tim Matheson, Christopher Lloyd; ***D:*** Alan Johnson; ***W:*** Ronny Graham.

To Be the Best 🦴½ **1993 (R)** Eric, a member of the U.S. Kickboxing Team, lets his love for the beautiful Cheryl and his hot temper get the best of him. When a ruthless gambler threatens to kill Cheryl if Eric doesn't throw his big match, he joins with his family, fellow teammates, and most feared opponent, to set things right. **99m/C VHS.** Mike Worth, Martin Kove, Phillip Troy, Brittney Powell, Alex Cord, Steven Leigh; ***D:*** Joseph Merhi; ***W:*** Michael January.

To Catch a Killer 🦴🦴🦴 **1992** A chilling performance by Dennehy highlights this true-crime tale of a detective's relentless pursuit of serial killer John Wayne Gacy, who preyed on young men and hid the bodies in his home. Made for television. **95m/C VHS, DVD.** Brian Dennehy, Michael Riley, Margot Kidder, Meg Foster; ***D:*** Eric Till; ***W:*** Judson Kinberg; ***C:*** Rene Ohashi; ***M:*** Paul Zaza. **TV**

To Catch a King 🦴🦴 **1984** Garr is a singer working in Wagner's nightclub in 1940s' Lisbon. The pair becomes involved in trying to foil the Nazi plot to kidnap the vacationing Duke and Duchess of Windsor. Average cable fare. **120m/C VHS.** Robert Wagner, Teri Garr, Horst Janson, Barbara Parkins, John Standing; ***D:*** Clive Donner; ***M:*** Nick Bicat. **CABLE**

To Catch a Thief 🦴🦴🦴 **1955** On the French Riviera, a reformed jewel thief falls for a wealthy American woman, who suspects he's up to his old tricks when a rash of jewel thefts occur. Oscar-winning photography by Robert Burks, a notable fireworks scene, and snappy dialogue. A change of pace for Hitchcock, this charming comedy-thriller proved to be as popular as his other efforts. Based on the novel by David Dodge. Kelly met future husband Prince Rainier during a photo shoot while she was attending the Cannes Film Festival. **103m/C VHS.** Cary Grant, Grace Kelly, Jessie Royce Landis, John Williams, Charles Vanel, Brigitte Auber; ***D:*** Alfred Hitchcock; ***W:*** John Michael Hayes; ***C:*** Robert Burks. Oscars '55: Color Cinematog.

To Catch a Yeti 🦴½ **1995 (PG)** Big game hunter Meat Loaf is all set for a trip to the Himalayas when the Yeti winds up being spotted in the canyons of Manhattan (and it turns out to be very tiny). **88m/C VHS.** Meat Loaf Aday; ***D:*** Bob Keen.

To Cross the Rubicon 🦴🦴½ **1991** Romantic comedy finds Kendall (Royce) getting dumped by David (Souther), her boyfriend of eight years, who then reconciles with former flame, Claire (Devon). Meanwhile, Kendall involves herself with James (Burke), a young musician, and becomes new best friends with—you guessed it—Claire. But will David and Kendall's previous relationship cause friction? **120m/C VHS, DVD.** Patricia Royce, J.D. Souther, Lorraine Devon, Billy Burke; ***D:*** Barry Caillier; ***W:*** Patricia Royce, Lorraine Devon; ***C:*** Christopher Tufty; ***M:*** Paul Speer, David Lanz.

To Dance with the White Dog 🦴🦴🦴 **1993 (PG)** Robert Samuel Peek (Cronyn) is a pecan-tree grower from rural Georgia who has been married to Cora (Tandy) for 57 years. Then she dies and their fussing daughters (Baranski and Wright) wonder how their father will survive. But Sam's increasing loneliness is checked when he befriends a stray white dog that it seems no one else can see. Based on the novel by Terry Kay. **98m/C VHS.** Hume Cronyn, Jessica Tandy, Christine Baranski, Amy Wright, Esther Rolle, Harley Cross, Frank Whaley, Terry Beaver, Dan Albright, David Dwyer; ***D:*** Glenn Jordan; ***W:*** Susan Cooper; ***C:*** Neil Roach. **TV**

To Die For 🦴½ *Dracula: The Love Story* **1989 (R)** A vampire stalks, woos, and snacks on a young real estate woman. **99m/C VHS, DVD.** Brendan Hughes, Scott Jacoby, Duane Jones, Steve Bond, Sydney Walsh, Amanda Wyss, Ava Fabian; ***D:*** Deran Sarafian; ***W:*** Leslie King; ***C:*** Jacques Haitkin; ***M:*** Cliff Eidelman.

To Die For 🦴🦴🦴 **1995 (R)** Beauteous, manipulative Suzanne Stone (Kidman) wants to be somebody—preferably a big TV personality—and nothing will stop her. She recruits a scruffy threesome to help her ice sweet-but-dim hubby, Larry (Dillon), even if it does means seducing aimless teenager Jimmy (Phoenix). Black comedy, loosely based on the Pamela Smart murder case and adapted from the novel by Joyce Maynard, takes on the media-obsessed culture with a wicked grin. Van Sant retains his fresh and hip storytelling in his first film for a major studio. Backed by Henry's zesty script, all the actors shine—with standout performances from Kidman as the monstrous Suzanne and Phoenix (River's younger brother) as the lost/horny Jimmy. Shot entirely in Canada. **103m/C VHS, DVD, 8mm.** Nicole Kidman, Matt Dillon, Joaquin Rafael (Leaf) Phoenix, Casey Affleck, Alison Folland, Illeana Douglas, Dan Hedaya, Wayne Knight, Kurtwood Smith, Holland Taylor, Maria Tucci, Susan Traylor; ***Cameos:*** George Segal, Buck Henry; ***D:*** Gus Van Sant; ***W:*** Buck Henry, Johnny Burne; ***C:*** Eric Alan Edwards; ***M:*** Danny Elfman. Golden Globes '96: Actress—Mus./Comedy (Kidman); Broadcast Film Critics '95: Actress (Kidman).

To Die For 2: Son of Darkness 🦴½ *Son of Darkness: To Die For 2* **1991 (R)** This far outclasses part one in terms of acting and production values, but the plot still isn't back from the grave. Strange, because all the vampires are; despite their fiery deaths last time they flock around the adoptive mother of a baby secretly sired by a bloodsucker. **95m/C VHS.** Rosalind Allen, Steve Bond, Scott Jacoby, Michael Praed, Jay Underwood, Amanda Wyss, Remy O'Neill, Vince Edwards; ***D:*** David F. Price.

To Die Standing 🦴½ **1991 (R)** Two mavericks team up to do what the D.E.A. and cops simply cannot... capture a dangerous international drug lord. High action. **87m/C VHS.** Cliff DeYoung, Robert Beltran, Jamie Rose, Gerald Anthony, Orlando Sacha, Michael Ford; ***D:*** Louis Morneau; ***W:*** Ross Bell, Daryl Haney.

To Each His Own 🦴🦴🦴 **1946** Top-notch melodrama finds middle-aged businesswoman Josephine Norris (de Havilland) recalling her past as she carries on through London's blitz. As a young woman, Josephine fell in love with a dashing WWI pilot (Lund), became pregnant, and had her lover killed in action. To avoid scandal, she gives the baby up for adoption, although she stays in touch with his adoptive mother (Anderson) and befriends the boy. When Gregory (Lund again) grows up, he too becomes a pilot and visits Josephine—who's still longing to tell him the truth. Lund's film debut. **100m/B VHS.** Olivia de Havilland, John Lund, Mary Anderson, Roland Culver, Virginia Welles, Bill Goodwin, Phillip Terry; ***D:*** Mitchell Leisen; ***W:*** Charles Brackett, Jacques Thery; ***C:*** Daniel F. Fapp; ***M:*** Victor Young. Oscars '46: Actress (de Havilland).

To Forget Venice 🦴🦴½ **1979** Portrays the sensitive relationships among four homosexuals, and their shared fears of growing older. Dubbed in English. **90m/C VHS.** *IT* Erland Josephson, Mariangela Melato, David Pontremoli, Elenora Giorgi; ***D:*** Franco Brusati.

To Gillian on Her 37th Birthday 🦴🦴 **1996 (PG-13)** Overly sentimental weeper explores the effects of a mother's death on the ones she's left behind. Gillian's been dead for two years but widower David Lewis (Gallagher) hasn't been able to let her spirit go and daughter Rachel (Danes) is having trouble growing up with a father who spends more time on the beach with his dead wife's ghost than with her. Enter nosy sister-in-law Esther (Baker) and annoying husband (Altman) who try to set him up on the anniversary of Gillian's death and you've got a mental family breakdown coming. Pfeiffer appears as Gillian in this script by husband Kelley, based on the play by Michael Brady. **92m/C VHS, DVD.** Peter Gallagher, Claire Danes, Kathy Baker, Wendy Crewson, Bruce Altman, Michelle Pfeiffer, Freddie Prinze Jr.; ***D:*** Michael Pressman; ***W:*** David E. Kelley; ***C:*** Tim Suhrstedt; ***M:*** James Horner.

To Grandmother's House We Go 🦴🦴½ **1994** The Olsen twins want to give mom a restful Christmas vacation so they decide to visit Grandma (on their own) and wind up in the hands of a pair of bumbling kidnappers. Made for TV movie. **89m/C VHS.** Ashley (Fuller) Olsen, Mary-Kate Olsen, Cynthia Geary, Rhea Perlman, J. Eddie Peck, Stuart Margolin; ***Cameos:*** Bob Saget, Lori Loughlin; ***D:*** Jeff Franklin; ***W:*** Jeff Franklin. **TV**

To Have & Have Not 🦴🦴🦴½ **1944** Martinique charter boat operator gets mixed up with beautiful woman and French resistance fighters during WWII. Top-notch production in every respect. Classic dialogue and fiery romantic bouts between Bogart and Bacall. Bacall's first film. Based on a story by Ernest Hemingway. Remade in 1950 as "The Breaking Point" and in 1958 as "The Gun Runners." **100m/B VHS.** Humphrey Bogart, Lauren Bacall, Walter Brennan, Hoagy Carmichael, Marcel Dalio, Dolores Moran, Sheldon Leonard, Dan Seymour; ***D:*** Howard Hawks; ***W:*** Jules Furthman, William Faulkner.

To Heal a Nation 🦴🦴½ **1988** The story of veteran Jan Scruggs, who spearheaded the movement to build the Vietnam Veterans memorial. The then little-known Ross Perot provided major financial support for Scruggs' dream. **100m/C VHS.** Eric Roberts, Conrad Bachmann, Glynnis O'Connor, Marshall Colt, Scott Paulin, Lee Purcell, Laurence Luckinbill, Linden Chiles, Brock Peters; ***D:*** Michael Pressman; ***W:*** Lionel Chetwynd. **TV**

To Hell and Back 1955 Adaptation of Audie Murphy's autobiography. Murphy plays himself, from his upbringing as the son of Texas sharecroppers to his Army career in WWII, where he was the most-decorated American soldier. Murphy won more than 20 medals, including the Congressional Medal of Honor. Features realistic battle sequences punctuated with grand heroics. **106m/C VHS, DVD.** Audie Murphy, Marshall Thompson, Jack Kelly, Charles Drake, Gregg (Hunter) Palmer, Paul Picerni, David Janssen, Bruce Cowling, Paul Langton, Art Aragon, Felix Noriego, Denver Pyle, Brett Halsey, Susan Kohner, Anabel Shaw, Mary Field, Gordon Gebert, Rand Brooks, Richard Castle, Gen. Walter Bedell Smith; ***D:*** Jesse Hibbs; ***W:*** Gil Doud; ***C:*** Maury Gertsman; ***M:*** Henry Mancini.

To Joy *Till Gladje* 1950 The rocky marriage of a violinist and his wife illuminate the problems of the young in Swedish society. Early Bergman. In Swedish with English subtitles or dubbed. **90m/B VHS.** *SW* Maj-Britt Nilsson, Birger Malmsten, Margit Carlquist, Stig Olin, John Ekman, Victor Sjostrom; ***D:*** Ingmar Bergman; ***W:*** Ingmar Bergman; ***C:*** Gunnar Fischer.

To Kill a Clown 1972 (R) Painter and his wife working to save their marriage are trapped on an isolated island and terrorized by a crazed Vietnam veteran. This helps pull them together. Some holes in the plot, but generally effective. **82m/C VHS.** Alan Alda, Blythe Danner, Heath Lamberts; ***D:*** George Bloomfield.

To Kill a Mockingbird 1962 Faithful adaptation of powerful Harper Lee novel, both an evocative portrayal of childhood innocence and a denunciation of bigotry. Peck's performance as southern lawyer Atticus Finch defending black Tom Robinson (Peters), who's accused of raping a white woman, is flawless. Duvall debuted as the dim-witted Boo Radley. Lee based her characterization of "Dill," the Finch children's "goin' on seven" friend, on Truman Capote, her own childhood friend. **129m/B VHS, DVD.** Gregory Peck, Brock Peters, Phillip Alford, Mary Badham, Robert Duvall, Rosemary Murphy, William Windom, Alice Ghostley, John Megna, Frank Overton, Paul Fix, Collin Wilcox-Paxton; ***D:*** Robert Mulligan; ***W:*** Horton Foote; ***C:*** Russell Harlan; ***M:*** Elmer Bernstein; ***Nar:*** Kim Stanley. Oscars '62: Actor (Peck), Adapt. Screenplay, Art Dir./Set Dec., B&W; AFI '98: Top 100; Golden Globes '63: Actor—Drama (Peck), Score, Natl. Film Reg. '95.

To Kill a Priest 1989 (R) Based on the true story of Father Jerzy Popieluszko, a young priest in 1984 Poland who defies his church and speaks out publicly on Solidarity. He is killed by the government as a result. Harris is good as the menacing police official. **110m/C VHS.** Christopher Lambert, Ed Harris, David Suchet, Tim Roth, Joanne Whalley, Pete Postlethwaite, Cherie Lunghi, Joss Ackland; ***D:*** Agnieszka Holland; ***W:*** Agnieszka Holland; ***C:*** Adam Holender; ***M:*** Georges Delerue.

To Kill a Stranger 1984 A beautiful pop singer is stranded in a storm, and then victimized by a mad rapist/murderer. **100m/C VHS.** Donald Pleasence, Dean Stockwell, Angelica Maria, Aldo Ray, Sergio Aragones.

To Live *Huozhe* 1994 Superb drama follows the lives of one family—weak but adaptable Fugui (You), his strong-willed wife Jiazhen (Li), and their young daughter and son—from prerevolutionary China in the 1940s through the '60s Cultural Revolution. Fugui loses the family fortune in the gambling houses, actually a blessing when the Communists come to power, and the family must struggle to survive financial and increasingly difficult political changes, where fate can change on a whim. Subtle saga about ordinary human lives reacting to terrifying conditions boasts extraordinary performances and evocative imagery. Adapted from the novel "Lifetimes" by Yu Hua. Chinese with subtitles. **130m/C VHS.** *CH* Ge You, Gong Li, Niu Ben, Guo Tao, Jiang Wu; ***D:*** Zhang Yimou; ***W:*** Lu Wei, Yu Hua; ***C:*** Lu Yue; ***M:*** Zhao Jiping. British Acad. '94: Foreign Film; Cannes '94: Actor (You), Grand Jury Prize.

To Live and Die in Hong Kong 1989 Two sailors arrive in Hong Kong for a little R & R, until they are mistaken for spies by both the Hong Kong police and the Chinese mob. Action-packed tale. **98m/C VHS.** Rowena Cortes, Lawrence Jan, Mike Kelly, Laurens C. Postma; ***D:*** Lau Shing Hon.

To Live & Die in L.A. 1985 (R) Fast-paced, morally ambivalent tale of cops and counterfeiters in L.A. After his partner is killed shortly before his retirement, a secret service agent sets out to track down his ruthless killer. Lots of violence; some nudity. Notable both for a riveting car chase and its dearth of sympathetic characters. **114m/C VHS.** William L. Petersen, Willem Dafoe, John Pankow, Dean Stockwell, Debra Feuer, John Turturro, Darlanne Fluegel, Robert Downey; ***D:*** William Friedkin; ***W:*** William Friedkin.

To Love Again 1980 A middle-aged love story about a reclusive college professor and the campus handyman. **96m/C VHS.** Lynn Redgrave, Brian Dennehy, Conchata Ferrell; ***D:*** Joseph Hardy.

To Paris with Love 1955 A British man and his son fall in love with a shop girl and her boss while on vacation in Paris. Charming and humorous, with a witty performance from Guinness. **75m/C VHS.** Alec Guinness, Odile Versois, Vernon Gray; ***D:*** Robert Hamer; ***M:*** Edwin Astley.

To Play or to Die 1991 The introverted Kees attends an all-boy school where powerful bullies and sadomasochistic games are the rule. Kees is fascinated by the handsome Charel, the bullies leader. He invites Charel to his home, intending to turn the tables on his tormentor, but nothing goes as planned. Intense and controversial look at gay teens. Directorial debut of Krom. In Dutch with English subtitles. **150m/C VHS, DVD, Wide.** *NL* Geert Hunaerts, Tjebbo Gerritsma; ***D:*** Frank Krom; ***W:*** Anne Van De Putte, Frank Krom; ***C:*** Nils Post; ***M:*** Kim Hayworth, Ferdinand Bakker.

To Play the King 1993 Sequel to "The House of Cards" finds Francis Urquhart (Richardson), having murdered his way to the Prime Ministery, now bored with his political situation. But things may be changing—the Queen has been succeeded by her liberal son (Kitchen) and Francis, goaded by his equally vicious wife (Fletcher), plots treachery to bring down the monarchy. Followed by "The Final Cut"; adapted from the novel by Michael Dobbs. **212m/C VHS.** *GB* Ian Richardson, Michael Kitchen, Diane Fletcher, Kitty Aldridge, Bernice Stegers, Colin Jeavons, Rowena King, Erika Hoffman, Nicholas Farrell; ***D:*** Paul Seed; ***W:*** Andrew Davies.

To Please a Lady *Red Hot Wheels* 1950 Romantic comedy-drama about race car driver Gable and reporter Stanwyck. Although leads do their best with the script, they're unable to generate any sparks. However, race track scenes are excellent. Filmed at the Indianapolis Speedway, the spectacular racing footage makes up for overall average film. **91m/B VHS.** Clark Gable, Barbara Stanwyck, Adolphe Menjou, Will Geer, Roland Winters; ***D:*** Clarence Brown; ***W:*** Barre Lyndon, Marge Decker.

To Protect and Serve 1992 (R) When crooked cops start getting killed, two young cops are assigned to investigate. Suspicion points to a rookie (Howell), who just may have decided to clean things up his own way. **93m/C VHS.** C. Thomas Howell, Lezlie (Dean) Deane, Richard Romanus, Joe Cortese; ***D:*** Eric Weston.

To Race the Wind 1980 Blind man wants to be treated like a normal person as he struggles through Harvard Law School. Based upon Harold Krents's autobiography "Butterflies Are Free." **97m/C VHS.** Steve Guttenberg, Lisa Eilbacher, Randy Quaid, Barbara Barrie; ***D:*** Walter Grauman. **TV**

To See Paris and Die *Uvidet Parizh i Umeret* 1993 Elena Orekhova (Vasilyeva) is a Russian stage mother who will do absolutely anything to ensure pianist son Yuri gets chosen for a prestigious competition in Paris—even though she knows secrets from her past could place a blight on his career. Russian with subtitles. **110m/C VHS.** *RU* Tatyana Vasilyeva, Dimitry Malikov, Stanislav Lyubshin, Vladimir Steklov, Nina Usatova; ***D:*** Alexander Proshkin; ***W:*** Georgi Branev; ***C:*** Boris Brozhovsky.

To Sir, with Love 1967 Teacher in London's tough East End tosses books in the wastebasket and proceeds to teach his class about life. Skillful and warm performance by Poitier as idealistic teacher; supporting cast also performs nicely. Based on the novel by E.R. Braithwaite. LuLu's title song was a big hit in 1967-68. **105m/C VHS, DVD, Wide.** *GB* Sidney Poitier, Lulu, Judy Geeson, Christian Roberts, Suzy Kendall, Faith Brook; ***D:*** James Clavell; ***W:*** James Clavell; ***C:*** Paul Beeson; ***M:*** Ron Grainer.

To Sleep with a Vampire 1992 (R) A Los Angeles bloodsucker is tired of his violent existence and craves the one thing he can't have—daylight. As he stalks his latest victim, a stripper, he decides to take her home and have her tell him about living in daytime. When she realizes what's going on, the intended victim decides to fight for her life. Action and eroticism raises this one above the norm. Remake of "Dance of the Damned." **90m/C VHS.** Scott Valentine, Charlie Spradling, Richard Zobel, Ingrid Vold, Stephanie Hardy; ***D:*** Adam Friedman; ***W:*** Patricia Harrington.

To Sleep with Anger 1990 (PG) At first a comic, introspective look at a black middle-class family going about their business in the heart of Los Angeles. Sly charmer Glover shows up and enthralls the entire family with his slightly sinister storytelling and a gnawing doom gradually permeates the household. Insightful look into the conflicting values of Black America. Glover's best performance. **105m/C VHS.** Danny Glover, Mary Alice, Paul Butler, Richard Brooks, Carl Lumbly, Vonetta McGee, Sheryl Lee Ralph; ***D:*** Charles Burnett; ***W:*** Charles Burnett; ***C:*** Walt Lloyd. Ind. Spirit '91: Actor (Glover), Director (Burnett), Screenplay, Support. Actress (Ralph); Natl. Soc. Film Critics '90: Screenplay; Sundance '90: Special Jury Prize.

To the Death 1993 (R) A kickboxer wants to retire from the boxing tournaments but the corrupt promoters refuse to let him go unless he manages to kill his rivals in the ring. **90m/C VHS.** John Barrett, Michael Quissi; ***D:*** Darrell Roodt.

To the Devil, a Daughter *Child of Satan* 1976 (R) A nun is put under a spell by a priest who has been possessed by Satan. She is to bear his child. A writer on the occult intervenes. Based on the novel by Dennis Wheatley. One of Kinski's early films. **93m/C VHS.** Richard Widmark, Christopher Lee, Nastassia Kinski, Honor Blackman, Denholm Elliott, Michael Goodliffe; ***D:*** Peter Sykes; ***W:*** Christopher Wicking; ***C:*** David Watkin.

To the Last Man 1933 An early Scott sagebrush epic, about two feuding families. Temple is seen in a small role. Based on Zane Grey's novel of the same name. **70m/B VHS.** Randolph Scott, Esther Ralston, Jack LaRue, Noah Beery Sr., Buster Crabbe, Gail Patrick, Barton MacLane, Fuzzy Knight, John Carradine, Jay Ward, Shirley Temple; ***D:*** Henry Hathaway.

To the Lighthouse 1983 The Ramsay family's annual proper British holiday at their Cornwall home turns into a summer of disillusionment in this adaptation of the Virginia Woolf novel. Made for British TV. **115m/C VHS.** Rosemary Harris, Michael Gough, Suzanne Bertish, Lynsey Baxter, T.P. McKenna, Kenneth Branagh; ***D:*** Colin Gregg. **TV**

To the Limit 1995 (R) Actioner finds the pulchritudinous Colette (Smith) revealing to mobster Frank (Travolta) that she's a CIA agent (and if you believe that I have a bridge in Brooklyn to sell you) and that they are the targets of a rogue agent (Richmond). No, Smith can't act but since she takes lots of showers and is supported by some professionals who can, this gets by on trash value alone. **96m/C VHS, DVD.** Anna Nicole Smith, Joey Travolta, Michael Nouri, Branscombe Richmond, John Aprea, Kathy Shower, Rebecca Ferratti, David Proval; ***D:*** Raymond Martino; ***W:*** Raymond Martino, Joey Travolta; ***C:*** Henryk Cymerman; ***M:*** Jim Halfpenny.

To the Shores of Hell 1965 Leaving his sweetheart behind, Major Greg Donahue attacks Da Nang and plots to rescue his brother from the Viet Cong. **82m/C VHS.** Marshall Thompson, Kiva Lawrence, Richard Jordahl.

To the Shores of Tripoli 1942 Wartime propaganda in the guise of drama, in which a smarmy playboy is transformed into a Marine in boot camp. **82m/C VHS.** John Payne, Maureen O'Hara, Randolph Scott, Nancy Kelly, Harry (Henry) Morgan, Maxie "Slapsie" Rosenbloom, William Tracy, Minor Watson, Alan Hale Jr., Hugh Beaumont, Hillary Brooke; ***D:*** H. Bruce Humberstone.

To Walk with Lions 1999 (PG) Continues the story of lion expert George Adamson, told previously in "Born Free" and "Living Free." Tony Fitzjohn (Michie) takes what he thinks will be a temporary job with Adamson (Harris) and his brother Terence (Bannen) in Kenya in the 1980s. The brothers are running a private wildlife preserve that rehabilitates zoo lions for life in the wild. Tony is naturally wary of his new employment and his curmudgeonly new employers but comes to value them all, even falling in love with anthropologist Lucy (Fox) who's working with the local tribes. Has some disturbing violence (both animal and human). **108m/C VHS, DVD.** *CA GB* Richard Harris, Ian Bannen, Kerry Fox, John Michie, Hugh Quarshie, Honor Blackman, Geraldine Chaplin; ***D:*** Carl Schultz; ***W:*** Keith Ross Leckie; ***C:*** Jean Lepine; ***M:*** Alan Reeves.

To Wong Foo, Thanks for Everything, Julie Newmar 1995 (PG-13) Hot on the high heels of "The Adventures of Priscilla, Queen of the Desert," comes the sanitized for your protection Yankee version. And its all about hanging on to your dreams and how we're all the same inside, with politically correct gay drag queens doing the sermonizing. Yes, this is the feel-good drag road movie for the 90s. Den mother Vida (Swayze), tough beauty queen Noxeema (Snipes), and hot-blooded Chi Chi (Leguizamo doing his best Rosie Perez) head to Hollywood in a 1967 Cadillac convertible that inconveniently breaks down in a tiny Nebraska town. The "girls" work their magic, and presumably the people of this uncultured, anachronistic backwater will never be the same. One-dimensional characters, flat direction, and inconsistent script undercut exceptional efforts by Swayze and Leguizamo. **108m/C VHS.** Wesley Snipes, Patrick Swayze, John Leguizamo, Stockard Channing, Blythe Danner, Melinda Dillon, Arliss Howard, Jason London, Christopher Penn; ***Cameos:*** Julie Newmar, Robin Williams; ***D:*** Beeban Kidron; ***W:*** Douglas Carter Beane; ***M:*** Rachel Portman.

The Toast of New Orleans 1950 A poor fisherman rises to stardom as an opera singer. Likable, though fluffy production features a plethora of musical numbers. ♫Be My Love; Tina Lina; I'll Never Love You; The Toast of New Orleans; Song of the Bayou; Boom Biddy Boom Boom. **97m/C VHS.** Kathryn Grayson, Mario Lanza, David Niven, Rita Moreno, J. Carrol Naish; ***D:*** Norman Taurog.

Toast of New York 1937 Arnold plays Jim Fisk, a New England peddler who rises to become one of the first Wall Street giants of industry. Atypical Grant performance. **109m/B VHS.** Edward Arnold, Cary Grant, Frances Farmer, Jack Oakie, Donald Meek, Billy Gilbert; ***D:*** Rowland V. Lee.

Tobor the Great 1954 Sentimental and poorly executed, this film tells the tale of a boy, his grandfather, and Tobor the robot. Villainous communists attempt to make evil use of Tobor, only to be thwarted in the end. **77m/B VHS.** Charles Drake, Billy Chapin, Karin Booth, Taylor Holmes, Joan Gerber, Steven Geray; ***D:*** Lee Sholem.

Tobruk 1966 American GI's endeavor to knock out the guns of Tobruk, to clear the way for a bombing attack on German fuel supply depots of North Africa in this WWII actioner. **110m/C VHS.** Rock Hudson, George Peppard, Guy Stockwell, Nigel Green; ***D:*** Arthur Hiller.

Toby McTeague ☙☙ 1987 (PG) A story about an Alaskan family that breeds Siberian Huskies. When his father is injured, the youngest son tries to replace him in the regional dog-sled race. **94m/C VHS.** Winston Rekert, Wannick Bisson, Timothy Webber; ***D:*** Jean-Claude Lord; ***W:*** Djordje Milicevic, Jamie Brown.

Toby Tyler ☙☙☙ 1959 (G) A boy runs off to join the circus, and teams up with a chimpanzee. A timeless and enjoyable Disney film that still appeals to youngsters. Good family-fare. **93m/C VHS.** Kevin Corcoran, Henry Calvin, Gene Sheldon, Bob Sweeney; ***D:*** Charles T. Barton.

Today I Hang ☙☙ 1942 A man is framed for murder and sentenced to hang. His buddies on the outside do their best to prove his innocence. Meanwhile, in prison, the accused encounters any number of interesting characters. **67m/B VHS.** Walter Woolf King, Mona Barrie, William Farnum, Harry Woods, James Craven; ***D:*** Oliver Drake.

Today We Kill, Tomorrow We Die ☙ 1971 (PG) A rancher is unjustly sent to prison; when his sentence is over he hires a gang to relentlessly track down the culprit who framed him. **95m/C VHS.** Montgomery Ford, Bud Spencer, William Berger, Tatsuya Nakadai, Wayde Preston; ***D:*** Tonino Cervi.

Today We Live ☙☙½ 1933 Triangle love story set in WWI. Crawford is a hedonistic Brit having a fling with her naval brother's (Tone) friend (Young). When American flyer Cooper appears she sets her sights on him but soon he's off to combat in France where he's reported killed. Crawford returns to Young but, naturally, reports of Cooper's death have been greatly exaggerated and the two eventually reunite. Faulkner co-scripted from his story "Turn About" which had no female character and concerned the rivalry between naval officers and fly boys. **113m/B VHS.** Gary Cooper, Joan Crawford, Franchot Tone, Robert Young, Roscoe Karns, Louise Closser Hale; ***D:*** Howard Hawks; ***W:*** Dwight Taylor, William Faulkner, Edith Fitzgerald.

The Todd Killings ☙½ *A Dangerous Friend; Skipper* 1971 (R) A psychotic young man commits a series of murders involving young women. Sleazy, forgettable picture wastes a talented cast. **93m/C VHS.** Robert F. Lyons, Richard Thomas, Barbara Bel Geddes, Ed Asner, Sherry Miles, Gloria Grahame, Belinda J. Montgomery; ***D:*** Barry Shear; ***W:*** Joel Oliansky.

Todd McFarlane's Spawn *Spawn* 1997 McFarlane's comic book creation makes his cable TV animated debut. Hellspawn was once human CIA assassin Al Simmons, murdered in the line of duty, who sold his soul to see his wife one last time. When he comes back from the grave with superhuman powers it's again as a killer with attitude, who leaves a high body count. A PG-13 version clocks in at 90 minutes. **147m/C VHS, DVD.** ***D:*** Eric Rademski; ***W:*** Alan B. McElroy, Gary Hardwick; ***V:*** Keith David, Richard Dysart, Ronny Cox. **CABLE**

Toga Party ☙ 1979 (R) Fraternity house throws a wild toga party in this raunchy low-rent depiction of college life. **82m/C VHS.** Bobby H. Charles, Mary Mitchell.

Together? ☙½ 1979 (R) Divorced woman and a male chauvinist test the limits of their sexual liberation as well as viewer patience. **91m/C VHS.** *IT* Maximilian Schell, Jacqueline Bisset, Terence Stamp, Monica Guerritore; ***D:*** Armenia Balducci; ***M:*** Burt Bacharach.

Togetherness ☙½ 1970 Two wealthy, good-for-nothing playboys chase after the same blonde, a Communist, in Greece. **101m/C VHS.** George Hamilton, Peter Lawford, Olinka (Schoberova) Berova, John Banner, Jesse White; ***D:*** Arthur Marks.

The Toilers and the Wayfarers ☙☙ 1997 New Ulm, Minnesota is an ultraconservative German-American community where the teenaged Dieter (Klemp) is the object of affection for best friend Phillip (Woodhouse). Although Dieter thinks he might be gay, he rejects Phillip, who soon takes off for Minneapolis. This leaves Dieter open to the attentions of slightly older, free-spirited Udo (Schirg). Dieter's father strongly disapproves and the young man leaves to join Phillip in the big bad city, with Udo in tow. But since none of the boys have any money, they're soon working the streets to survive. English and German with subtitles. **85m/C VHS, DVD.** Matt Klemp, Ralf Schirg, Andrew Woodhouse; ***D:*** Keith Froelich; ***W:*** Keith Froelich; ***C:*** Jim Tittle; ***M:*** Chan Poling.

Tokyo Cowboy ☙☙ 1994 Tokyo burger flipper No Ogawa (Ida) dreams of the wild west and becoming a cowboy, inspired by the letters of his childhood pen pal, Kate (Hirt). So he decides to head for Kate's small Canadian hometown and realize his fantasies. Kate's meddling mom makes him welcome but Kate herself, only recently returned home, is hiding the fact that her friend Shelly (Mortil) is also her lover. Both have some unrealistic expectations to overcome in their quest for happiness. **94m/C VHS, DVD.** Hiromoto Ida, Christianne Hirt, Janne Mortil, Anna Ferguson, Michael Ironside; ***D:*** Kathy Garneau; ***W:*** Caroline Adderson; ***C:*** Kenneth Hewlett; ***M:*** Ari Wise.

Tokyo Decadence ☙½ 1991 (NC-17) Ai is a high-paid prostitute working in Tokyo for an agency that specializes in sado-masochism. Film follows her various sexual escapades in humiliating detail as well as her drug-addled search for a client Ai thinks she's in love with. Since Ai remains a cipher, the film also remains unfocused except for its creepy and explicit sex scenes. Adaptation of director Murakami's novel "Topaz." In Japanese with English subtitles or dubbed. **92m/C VHS, DVD.** *JP* Miho Nikaido, Tenmei Kano, Yayoi Kusama, Sayoko Amano; ***D:*** Ryu Murakami; ***W:*** Ryu Murakami; ***C:*** Tadashi Aoki; ***M:*** Ryuichi Sakamoto.

Tokyo Drifter ☙☙ *Tokyo Nagaremono* 1966 Surreal yakuza film follows an honorable gangster hunted by both his own bosses and a rival mob, who chase him across Japan. Lots of camera trickery. Japanese with subtitles. **83m/C VHS, DVD, Wide.** *JP* Eiji Go, Chieko Matsubara, Tetsuya Watari, Tamio Kawachi, Hideaki Nitani, Ryuji Kita; ***D:*** Seijun Suzuki; ***W:*** Yasunori Kawauchi; ***C:*** Shigeyoshi Mine; ***M:*** So Kaburagi.

Tokyo-Ga ☙☙☙½ 1985 Impelled by his love for the films of Yasujiro Ozu, Wenders traveled to Tokyo and fashioned a caring document of both the city and of Ozu's career, using images that recall and comment on Ozu's visual motifs. **92m/C VHS.** ***D:*** Wim Wenders; ***W:*** Wim Wenders.

Tokyo Joe ☙½ 1949 A war hero/nightclub owner returns to Tokyo and becomes ensnared in blackmail and smuggling while searching for his missing wife and child. Slow-moving tale has never been considered one of Bogart's better movies. **88m/B VHS.** Humphrey Bogart, Florence Marly, Alexander Knox, Sessue Hayakawa, Jerome Courtland, Lore Lee Michel; ***D:*** Stuart Heisler.

Tokyo Olympiad 1966 A monumental sports documentary about the 1964 Olympic Games in its entirety. Never before available for home viewing. Letterboxed with digital sound. In Japanese with English subtitles. **170m/C VHS, Wide.** *JP* ***D:*** Kon Ichikawa; ***W:*** Kon Ichikawa; ***C:*** Kazuo Miyagawa.

Tokyo Pop ☙☙½ 1988 (R) A punk rocker travels to Japan to find stardom and experiences a series of misadventures. Enjoyable in its own lightweight way. Hamilton is the daughter of Carol Burnett. **99m/C VHS.** Carrie Hamilton, Yutaka Tadokoro, Tetsuro Tamba, Taiji Tonoyama, Masumi Harukawa; ***D:*** Fran Rubel Kuzui; ***W:*** Lynn Grossman, Fran Rubel Kuzui; ***M:*** Alan Brewer.

Tokyo Raiders ☙☙☙ 2000 (PG-13) Remarkably stylish Hong Kong action flick. Director Jingle Ma brings a music video sensibility to the proceedings. The plot concerns a detective (Tony Leung) and his hunt for a gangster, but that's a negligible excuse for a series of cleverly choreographed action scenes. The physical violence is carefully modulated for a young audience, and many gadgets are employed. **100m/C DVD, Wide.** *HK* Tony Leung Chiu-Wai, Ekin Cheng, Toru Nakamura, Hiroshi Abe, Kelly Chen, Kumiko Endo, Minami Shirakawa, Majyu Ozawa, Cecilia Cheung; ***D:*** Jingle Ma; ***W:*** Susan Chan, Felix Chong; ***C:*** Jingle Ma, Chan Chi Ying; ***M:*** Peter Kam.

Tokyo Story ☙☙☙☙ *Tokyo Monogatari* 1953 Poignant story of elderly couple's journey to Tokyo where they receive little time and less respect from their grown children. Masterful cinematography, and sensitive treatment of universally appealing story. In Japanese with English subtitles. **134m/B VHS.** *JP* Chishu Ryu, Chieko Higashiyama, So Yamamura, Haruko Sugimura, Setsuko Hara; ***D:*** Yasujiro Ozu; ***W:*** Yasujiro Ozu; ***C:*** Yushun Atsuta; ***M:*** Kojun Saito.

Tol'able David ☙☙ 1921 A simple tale of mountain folk, done in the tradition of Mark Twain stories. A family of hillbillies is embroiled in a feud with a clan of outlaws. When the community's mail is stolen by the troublesome ruffians, the family's youngest member, who harbors dreams of becoming a mail driver, comes to the rescue. Silent film. **91m/B VHS, DVD.** Richard Barthelmess, Gladys Hulette, Ernest Torrence; ***D:*** Henry King; ***W:*** Henry King, Edmund Goulding; ***C:*** Henry Cronjager.

The Toll Gate ☙☙½ 1920 Quick on the draw outlaw Black Deering (Hart) is betrayed by one of his own men but manages to escape the authorities. He heads into the wilderness and finds shelter with an abandoned young mother (Nilsson). But the law is on his trail. **73m/B VHS, DVD.** William S. Hart, Anna Q. Nilsson, Jack (H.) Richardson, Joseph Singleton; ***D:*** Lambert Hillyer; ***W:*** Lambert Hillyer; ***C:*** Joseph August.

Toll of the Desert ☙ 1935 A lawman learns that his father is a ruthless, back-stabbing renegade. Now he must try and catch him. **58m/B VHS.** Roger Williams, Ted Adams, Edward Cassidy, Tom London, John Elliott, Earl Dwire, Betty Mack, Fred Kohler Jr.; ***D:*** William Berke.

Tollbooth ☙☙ 1994 (R) Romantic dreamer Jack (Von Dohlen) mans a tollbooth on a stretch of Florida Keys highway while his equally longing honey Doris (Balk) works at a nearby gas station and has a thing going on the side with bait salesman Dash (Patton). The return of Doris' long-gone daddy Leon (Cassel) causes some family problems while Jack's new associate Vic (Wilder) has a scam that's drawing interest from the state police. Thin plot but lots of charm from the two leads helps hold interest in Breziner's first film. **108m/C VHS.** Fairuza Balk, Lenny Von Dohlen, Will Patton, Seymour Cassel, James Wilder, Louise Fletcher, William Katt; ***D:*** Salome Breziner; ***W:*** Salome Breziner; ***C:*** Henry Vargas; ***M:*** Adam Gorgoni.

Tom and Huck ☙☙☙ 1995 (PG) Tom Sawyer and pal Huck Finn are the only witnesses to a murder. Tom's friend Muff is framed for the crime and the boys are being tracked by the real killer, Injun Joe. They must decide to come forward, expose the true fiend, and risk their own hides or run away and let an innocent man hang. True to the Twain story, Thomas plays a mischievous Tom to Renfro's troublemaking Huck. Film was shot in Mooresville, Alabama, population 69, just down the road a piece from the Hannibal, Missouri of Twain fame. **91m/C VHS.** Jonathan Taylor Thomas, Brad Renfro, Eric Schweig, Charles Rocket, Amy Wright, Michael McShane, Marian Seldes, Rachael Leigh Cook, Lanny Flaherty, Courtland Mead, Peter M. MacKenzie, Heath Lamberts; ***D:*** Peter Hewitt; ***W:*** Stephen Sommers, David Loughery; ***C:*** Bobby Bukowski; ***M:*** Stephen Endelman.

Tom and Jerry: The Movie ☙☙ 1993 (G) Everybody's favorite animated cat/mouse duo (who began life in a 1940 MGM short "Puss Gets the Boot") hit the big screen, this time talking (unlike their animated shorts). Rather than cartoon mayhem our two protagonists are goody-two-shoes (with songs yet!) but still retain their charm. Kids will like it, but true "Tom and Jerry" fans should probably stick to the original cartoons. **84m/C VHS.** ***D:*** Phil Roman; ***W:*** Dennis Marks; ***M:*** Henry Mancini, Leslie Bricusse; ***V:*** Richard Kind, Dana Hill, Charlotte Rae, Henry Gibson, Rip Taylor, Howard Morris, Edmund Gilbert, David Lander.

Tom & Viv ☙☙☙ 1994 (PG-13) American T.S. Eliot (Dafoe) is an Oxford student in 1914 when he meets the moody, monied Vivien Haigh-Wood (Richardson). After a whirlwind courtship, they marry—disastrously. Eliot begins to establish himself as a poet, while Vivien serves as muse/typist and unsuccessfully battles her misdiagnosed illnesses with too much drinking and drugs, as well as embarrassing public scenes. As Eliot gains success, he increasingly distances himself from the unhappy Viv, until finally committing her to an asylum. Dafoe is fine as the chilly, withdrawn poet but Richardson steals the film as his flamboyant, lost wife. Based on the play by Michael Hastings, who co-wrote the screenplay. **115m/C VHS.** *GB* Willem Dafoe, Miranda Richardson, Rosemary Harris, Tim Dutton, Nickolas Grace, Philip Locke, Clare Holman, Joanna McCallum; ***D:*** Brian Gilbert; ***W:*** Michael Hastings, Adrian Hodges; ***M:*** Debbie Wiseman. Natl. Bd. of Review '94: Actress (Richardson), Support. Actress (Harris).

Tom Brown's School Days ☙☙½ *Adventures at Rugby* 1940 Depicts life among the boys in an English school during the Victorian era. Based on the classic novel by Thomas Hughes. Remade in 1951. **86m/B VHS.** *GB* Cedric Hardwicke, Jimmy Lydon, Freddie Bartholomew; ***D:*** Robert Stevenson.

Tom Brown's School Days ☙☙☙ 1951 Tom enrolls at Rugby and is beset by bullies in classic tale of English school life. British remake of the 1940 version. Based on the novel by Thomas Hughes. **93m/B VHS.** *GB* Robert Newton, John (Howard) Davies, James Hayter; ***D:*** Gordon Parry.

Tom Clancy's Netforce ☙☙ *Netforce* 1998 (R) In 2005, technology has become so advanced that a special unit of the FBI, known as Netforce, has been established to police the Internet. Alex Michaels (Bakula) heads the unit after the murder of predecessor Steve Day (Kristofferson), leading Michaels to believe that criminals are trying to cause a global computer crash. Michael's two prime suspects are computer mogul Will Stiles (Reinhold) and crime boss Leong Cheng (Tagawa). Based on a story co-written by Clancy. **90m/C VHS, DVD.** Scott Bakula, Joanna Going, Brian Dennehy, Kris Kristofferson, Judge Reinhold, Cary-Hiroyuki Tagawa, CCH Pounder, Paul Hewitt, Chelsea Field, Frank Vincent; ***D:*** Robert Lieberman; ***W:*** Lionel Chetwynd; ***C:*** David Hennings; ***M:*** Jeff Rona. **TV**

Tom, Dick, and Harry ☙☙½ 1941 Dreamy girl is engaged to three men and unable to decide which to marry. It all depends on a kiss. Remade as "The Girl Most Likely." **86m/B VHS.** Ginger Rogers, George Murphy, Burgess Meredith, Alan Marshal, Phil Silvers; ***D:*** Garson Kanin; ***W:*** Paul Jarrico.

Tom Horn ☙☙ 1980 (R) The final days of one of the Old West's legends. Gunman Tom Horn, hired by Wyoming ranchers to stop cattle rustlers, goes about his job with a zeal that soon proves embarrassing to his employers. Beautifully photographed and authentic in its attention to details of the period, the film nonetheless takes liberties with the facts of Horn's life and is lacking in other aspects of production. **98m/C VHS.** Steve McQueen, Linda Evans, Richard Farnsworth, Billy Green Bush, Slim Pickens; ***D:*** William Wiard; ***W:*** Thomas McGuane; ***C:*** John A. Alonzo; ***M:*** Ernest Gold.

Tom Jones ☙☙☙☙ 1963 Bawdy comedy based on Henry Fielding's novel about a rustic playboy's wild life in 18th century England. Hilarious and clever with a grand performance by Finney. One of the sexiest eating scenes ever. Redgrave's debut. Theatrically released at 129 minutes, the film was recut by the director, who decided it needed tightening before its 1992 re-release on video. **121m/C VHS, DVD, Wide.** *GB* Albert Finney, Susannah York, Hugh Griffith, Edith Evans, Joan Greenwood, Diane Cilento, George Devine, David Tomlinson, Joyce Redman, Lynn Redgrave, Julian Glover, Peter Bull, David Warner; ***D:*** Tony Richardson; ***W:*** John Osborne; ***C:*** Walter Lassally; ***M:*** John Addison. Oscars '63: Adapt. Screenplay, Director (Richardson), Picture, Orig. Score; British Acad. '63: Film, Screenplay; Directors Guild '63: Director

(Richardson); Golden Globes '64: Film—Mus./Comedy, Foreign Film; Natl. Bd. of Review '63: Director (Richardson); N.Y. Film Critics '63: Actor (Finney), Director (Richardson), Film.

Tom Jones 𝓑𝓑𝓑 **1998** Miniseries based on the Henry Fielding novel goes further than the hit 1963 movie by including Fielding (Sessions) as the narrator of Tom's bawdy adventures. Tom (Beesley) is an 18th-century orphan with a heart of gold, an affinity for trouble, and an eye for the ladies. His true love is Sophie (Morton), the daughter of the boisterous Squire Western (Blessed). But of course, the path of true love never runs smooth. Lavish adaptation and lots of fun. **300m/C VHS, DVD.** *GB* Max Beesley, Samantha Morton, Brian Blessed, John Sessions, Benjamin Whitrow, Frances De La Tour; *D:* Metin Huseyin; *W:* Simon Burke. CABLE

Tom Sawyer 𝓑𝓑𝓑 **1930** Winning adaptation of Mark Twain's oft told tale of boyhood in Hannibal, Missouri. Cast reprised their roles the following year in "Huckleberry Finn." **86m/B VHS.** Jackie Coogan, Mitzie Green, Lucien Littlefield, Tully Marshall; *D:* John Cromwell; *C:* Charles B(ryant) Lang Jr.

Tom Sawyer 𝓑𝓑½ **1973 (G)** Musical version of the Mark Twain tale of the boisterous Tom, his friend Becky Thatcher, and various adventures, including the fence whitewashing. Amusing kid fare shot on location in Missouri. ♫River Song; Gratification; Tom Sawyer; Freebootin'; Aunt Polly's Soliloquy; If'n I Was God; A Man's Gotta Be What He's Born To Be; How Come?; Hannibal, Mo. **104m/C VHS, Wide.** Johnny Whitaker, Jodie Foster, Celeste Holm, Warren Oates, Jeff East; *D:* Don Taylor; *M:* John Williams.

Tom Thumb 𝓑𝓑𝓑 **1958** Diminutive boy saves village treasury from bad guys. Adapted from classic Grimm fairy tale. Special effects combine live actors, animation, and puppets. **92m/C VHS, DVD, Wide.** *GB* Russ Tamblyn, Peter Sellers, Terry-Thomas; *D:* George Pal; *W:* Ladislas Fodor; *C:* Georges Perinal; *M:* Douglas Gamley.

Tomahawk 𝓑𝓑½ **1951** Indian sympathizer Jim Bridger (Heflin) is a local scout who anticipates trouble when the government decides to build a wagon route straight through Sioux hunting grounds in order to reach Montana's gold mines. The touchy situation is made worse by cavalry officer Dancy (Nicol) who thinks the only good Indian is a dead one. **82m/C VHS.** Van Heflin, Preston Foster, Yvonne De Carlo, Alex Nicol, Jack Oakie, Tom Tully, Rock Hudson, Ann Doran; *D:* George Sherman; *W:* Maurice Geraghty, Silvia Richards; *C:* Charles P. Boyle; *M:* Hans J. Salter.

Tomb 𝓑𝓑 **1986** Fortune seekers disturb the slumber of a magical, sadistic princess much to their everlasting regret. Adapted from a Bram Stoker novel. **106m/C VHS.** Cameron Mitchell, John Carradine, Sybil Danning, Richard Hench, Michelle (McClellan) Bauer, Susan Stokey, David Pearson, Francesca "Kitten" Natividad; *D:* Fred Olen Ray; *C:* Paul Elliott.

Tomb of Ligeia 𝓑𝓑𝓑 *Tomb of the Cat* **1964** The ghost of a man's first wife expresses her displeasure when groom and new little missus return to manor. One of the better Corman adaptations of Poe. Also available with "The Conqueror Worm" on Laser Disc. **82m/C VHS.** *GB* Vincent Price, Elizabeth Shepherd, John Westbrook, Oliver Johnston, Richard Johnson, Derek Francis, Richard Vernon, Ronald Adam, Frank Thornton, Penelope Lee, Denis Gilmore; *D:* Roger Corman; *W:* Robert Towne; *C:* Arthur Grant; *M:* Kenneth V. Jones.

Tomb of the Undead 𝓑½ **1972** The sadistic guards of a prison camp are rudely awakened by the prisoners they tortured to death when they return as flesh-eating zombies looking to settle the score. **60m/C VHS.** *GB* Duncan McLeod, Lee Frost, John Dennis; *D:* John Hayes.

Tomb of Torture woof! *Metempsycose* **1965** Murdered countess is reincarnated in the body of a newspaperman's mistress. Together they investigate monster reports in a murder-ridden castle. The butler may have something to do with it. Filmed in Sepiatone and dubbed. **88m/B VHS.** Annie Albert, Thony Maky, Mark Marian; *D:* William Grace.

The Tomboy 𝓑½ **1924** A young woman behaves boyishly in Colonial America. **64m/B VHS.** Dorothy Devore, Lotta Williams, Herbert Rawlinson, Harry Gribbon, Lee Moran; *D:* David Kirkland.

Tomboy 𝓑 **1940** Shy country boy and a not-so-shy city girl meet, fall in love, and overcome obstacles that stand in their path. **70m/B VHS.** Jackie Moran, Marcia Mae Jones.

Tomboy woof! **1985 (R)** A pretty auto mechanic is determined to win not only the race but the love and respect of a superstar auto racer. **91m/C VHS.** Betsy Russell, Eric Douglas, Jerry Dinome, Kristi Somers, Richard Erdman, Toby Iland; *D:* Herb Freed.

Tomboy & the Champ 𝓑𝓑 **1958** Despite many obstacles, a music-loving calf becomes a prize winner with the help of its loving owner. Kids will love it, but adults will find this one a little sugary. **82m/C VHS.** Candy Moore, Ben Johnson, Jesse White; *D:* Francis D. Lyon.

Tombs of the Blind Dead 𝓑𝓑½ *The Blind Dead; La Noche dell Terror Ciego; La Noche de la Muerta Ciega; Crypt of the Blind Dead; Night of the Blind Dead* **1972 (PG)** Blinded by crows for using human sacrifice in the 13th century, zombies rise from the grave to wreak havoc upon 20th-century Spaniards. Atmospheric chiller was extremely popular in Europe and spawned three sequels. The sequels, also on video, are "Return of the Evil Dead" and "Horror of the Zombies." **102m/C VHS, DVD.** *SP PT* Caesar Burner, Lone Fleming, Helen Harp, Joseph Thelman, Rufino Ingles, Maria Silva; *D:* Armando de Ossorio; *W:* Armando de Ossorio; *C:* Pablo Ripoll; *M:* Anton Abril.

Tombstone 𝓑𝓑𝓑 **1993 (R)** Saga of Wyatt Earp and his band of law-abiding large moustaches beat the Kasdan/Costner vehicle to the big screen by several months. Legendary lawman Wyatt (Russell) moves to Tombstone, Arizona, aiming to start a new life with his brothers, but alas, that's not to be. The infamous gunfight at the OK Corral is here, and so is best buddy Doc Holliday, gunslinger and philosopher, a role designed for scenery chewing (Kilmer excels). Romance is supplied by actress Josephine, though Delany lacks the necessary romantic spark. Russell spends a lot of time looking troubled by the violence while adding to the body count. Too self-conscious, suffers from '90s western revisionism, but blessed with a high energy level thanks to despicable villains Lang, Biehn, and Boothe. **130m/C VHS, DVD, Wide.** Kurt Russell, Val Kilmer, Michael Biehn, Sam Elliott, Dana Delany, Bill Paxton, Powers Boothe, Stephen Lang, Jason Priestley, Dana Wheeler-Nicholson, Billy Zane, Thomas Haden Church, Joanna Pacula, Michael Rooker, Harry Carey Jr., Billy Bob Thornton, Charlton Heston, Robert John Burke, John Corbett, Buck Taylor, Terry O'Quinn, Pedro Armendariz Jr., Chris Mitchum, Jon Tenney; *D:* George P. Cosmatos; *W:* Kevin Jarre; *C:* William A. Fraker; *M:* Bruce Broughton; *Nar:* Robert Mitchum.

Tombstone Canyon 𝓑½ **1935** Death rides the range until Maynard and his horse Tarzan put a halt to it. **60m/B VHS.** Ken Maynard, Sheldon Lewis, Cecilia Parker.

Tombstone Terror 𝓑 **1934** A cowboy is beleaguered by a case of mistaken identity. **55m/B VHS.** Bob Steele.

Tomcat: Dangerous Desires 𝓑𝓑 **1993 (R)** Tom (Grieco) suffers from a rare degenerative condition and agrees to become a guinea pig in a secret, genetic imprinting experiment that has him injected with feline RNA. Tom's health is restored but the side effects give him the predatory instincts of a cat and the need to kill to stay alive. **96m/C VHS.** Richard Grieco, Maryam D'Abo, Natalie Radford.

Tomcats woof! **2001 (R)** Writer/director Pourier takes a half-step down from his previous occupation of porn screenwriter with this steaming pile of misogyny. Michael (O'Connell) is a basically decent guy up to his ethics in gambling debt. The only way out is to marry off his last single friend, Kyle (Busey), in order to win a bet made with their other buddies. He tracks down Natalie (Elizabeth), the only one of Kyle's conquests that he regrets dumping, who agrees, for half the dough and a measure of revenge, but soon the plotters fall in love. Every woman here is depicted as some form of evil, and humiliated accordingly. This isn't new, but it wouuld help if something was at least chuckle-worthy. There's no such relief here, unless you find renegade cancerous sex organs amusing. **92m/C VHS, DVD.** *US* Jerry O'Connell, Shannon Elizabeth, Jake Busey, Jaime Pressly, Bernie Casey, David Ogden Stiers, Travis Fine, Heather Stephens, Horatio Sanz, Julia Schultz; *D:* Gregory Poirier; *W:* Gregory Poirier; *C:* Charles Minsky; *M:* David Kitay.

Tommy 𝓑𝓑 *The Who's Tommy* **1975 (PG)** Peter Townsend's rock opera as visualized in the usual hyper-Russell style about the deaf, dumb, and blind boy who becomes a celebrity due to his amazing skill at the pinball machines. A parade of rock musicians perform throughout the affair, with varying degrees of success. Despite some good moments, the film ultimately falls prey to ill-conceived production concepts and miscasting. ♫Underture; Captain Walker Didn't Come Home; It's a Boy; '51 Is Going to Be a Good Year; What About the Boy?; The Amazing Journey; Christmas; See Me, Feel Me; Eyesight to the Blind. **108m/C VHS, DVD, Wide.** *GB* Ann-Margret, Elton John, Oliver Reed, Tina Turner, Roger Daltrey, Eric Clapton, Keith Moon, Pete Townshend, Jack Nicholson, Robert Powell, Paul Nicholas, Barry Winch, Victoria Russell, Ben Aris, Mary Holland, Jennifer Baker, Susan Baker, Arthur Brown, John Entwhistle; *D:* Ken Russell; *W:* Ken Russell, Keith Moon, John Entwhistle; *C:* Ronnie Taylor, Dick Bush; *M:* Pete Townshend, John Entwhistle. Golden Globes '76: Actress—Mus./Comedy (Ann-Margret).

Tommy Boy 𝓑𝓑 **1995 (PG-13)** Not-too-bright rich kid Tommy (Farley) teams up with snide, officious accountant Richard (Spade) to save the family auto parts business after dad (Dennehy) buys the farm. Tommy and Richard must deal with a conniving stepmom and stepbrother (Derek and Lowe), a ruthless rival (Aykroyd), and a road trip from hell to drum up some new business. Not as bad as it sounds, but inconsistent direction and too-familiar characters offset the amusing chemistry between Farley and Spade. **98m/C VHS, DVD, Wide.** Chris Farley, David Spade, Brian Dennehy, Bo Derek, Dan Aykroyd, Julie Warner, Rob Lowe; *D:* Peter Segal; *W:* Bonnie Turner, Terry Turner; *C:* Victor Kemper; *M:* David Newman. MTV Movie Awards '96: On-Screen Duo (Chris Farley/David Spade).

Tomorrow 𝓑𝓑𝓑 **1972 (PG)** Powerful tale of the love of two lonely people. Outstanding performance by Duvall as lumber mill worker who falls for a pregnant woman. Based on the neglected Faulkner story. **102m/B VHS.** Robert Duvall, Olga Bellin, Sudie Bond; *D:* Joseph Anthony; *W:* Horton Foote.

Tomorrow at Seven 𝓑𝓑½ **1933** A mystery writer is determined to discover the identity of the Ace of Spades, a killer who always warns his intended victim, then leaves an ace of spades on the corpse as his calling card. **62m/B VHS.** Chester Morris, Vivienne Osborne, Frank McHugh, Allen Jenkins, Henry Stephenson; *D:* Ray Enright.

Tomorrow Is Forever 𝓑𝓑½ **1946** Welles and Colbert marry shortly before he goes off to fight in WWI. Badly wounded and disfigured, he decides to stay in Europe while Colbert, believing Welles dead, eventually marries Brent. Fast forward to WWII when Brent, a chemical manufacturer, hires a new scientist to work for him in the war effort (guess who). This slow-moving melodrama wastes a good cast. Six-year-old Wood debuts as Welles' adopted daughter. **105m/B VHS.** Claudette Colbert, Orson Welles, George Brent, Lucile Watson, Richard Long, Natalie Wood; *D:* Irving Pichel; *C:* Joseph Valentine; *M:* Max Steiner.

The Tomorrow Man 𝓑𝓑 **2001 (R)** Just go with the flow, cause this time travel adventure yarn doesn't make a whole lot of sense. Larry Mackey (Bernsen) is your average joe, living an average life in the 1970s with his son Bryon. Then Mackey's son is kidnapped by notorious criminal Mac (Rusler) who happens to have time-traveled from 30 years in the future. Larry gets together with a time cop (Kennedy) to get the kid back and discovers that Byron actually grows up to be Mac—and dad needs to figure out why. **95m/C VHS, DVD.** Corbin Bernsen, Zach Galligan, Beth Kennedy, Morgan Rusler, Adam Sutton; *D:* Doug Campbell. VIDEO

Tomorrow Never Comes 𝓑½ **1977** When he discovers his girlfriend has been unfaithful, a guy goes berserk and eventually finds himself in a stand-off with the police. Violent. **109m/C VHS.** Oliver Reed, Susan George, Raymond Burr, John Ireland, Stephen McHattie, Donald Pleasence; *D:* Peter Collinson.

Tomorrow Never Dies 𝓑𝓑 **1997 (PG-13)** 18th installment of the James Bond series is all style and little else packaged in a tedious action adventure. Our villain is a media mogul (Pryce) who plans to start WWIII in order to increase his newspaper revenues. (Rupert Murdoch, start your lawyers!) In between the blantant product placements (from Heineken to Visa), our secret agent Bond (Brosnan, who seems bored with the role in his second appearance) sets out to foil the nutty plans. Bond gets help from Hong Kong action queen Yeoh as a Chinese agent, and a bevy of toys from the antiquated Q, including a BMW controlled by remote. Direction and flow is on autopilot after the opening scene and despite Yeoh's energetic high-kicks and the sleek techno toys, it can't revitalize what has become a third-class imitator of its predecessors. **119m/C VHS, DVD.** Pierce Brosnan, Jonathan Pryce, Michelle Yeoh, Teri Hatcher, Judi Dench, Colin Salmon, Samantha Bond, Desmond Llewelyn, Joe Don Baker, Ricky Jay, Vincent Schiavelli, Geoffrey Palmer; *D:* Roger Spottiswoode; *W:* Bruce Feirstein; *C:* Robert Elswit; *M:* David Arnold.

Tomorrow the World 𝓑𝓑 **1944** This bizarre little wartime drama is dated in almost every respect. Emil Bruckner (Homeier) is a Hitler Youth who's sent to live with his uncle (March) in America. The conflict between a fascist mindset and liberal tolerance is painted with very broad strokes. Both acting and writing have an extravagant quality that contemporary audiences will have trouble accepting. **86m/B DVD.** Fredric March, Betty Field, Agnes Moorehead, Skip Homeier, Joan Carroll, Boots Brown, Edit Angold, Rudy Wiesler, Marvin Davis, Patsy Ann Thompson, Mary Newton, Tom Fadden; *D:* Leslie Fenton; *W:* Ring Lardner Jr., Leopold Atlas; *C:* Henry Sharp.

Tomorrow's Child 𝓑𝓑 **1982** TV drama about in vitro fertilization (test-tube babies) and surrogate motherhood. **100m/C VHS.** Stephanie Zimbalist, William Atherton, Bruce Davison, Ed Flanders, Salome Jens, James Shigeta, Susan Oliver, Arthur Hill; *D:* Joseph Sargent. TV

Tomorrow's Children 𝓑 **1934** An alarmist melodrama warning against the threat of government-induced female sterilization asks the question: if a woman's family is weird, should her tubes be tied? **55m/B VHS, DVD.** Sterling Holloway, Diana Sinclair, Sarah Padden, Don Douglas; *D:* Crane Wilbur.

The Tong Man 𝓑𝓑½ **1919** Robbins owes the tong money and Hayakawa, as the tong's executioner, is sent to kill him when he won't pay up. Only it turns out Hayakawa is in love with Eddy, Robbins daughter, and refuses. Then the tong decide to kill him for disobeying their orders. **58m/B VHS.** Sessue Hayakawa, Helen Jerome Eddy, Marc Robbins, Toyo Fujita; *D:* William Worthington.

Tongs: An American Nightmare 𝓑 **1988 (R)** Chinese-American street gangs in Chinatown battle over turf and drug shipments. **80m/C VHS.** Ian Anthony Leung, Christopher O'Conner, Simon Yam; *D:* Philip Chan.

Toni 𝓑𝓑𝓑½ **1934** An Italian worker falls for his landlady and they make plans to marry. A grim turn of events, however, brings tragic consequences. Based on the lives of several townsfolk in the village of Les Martiques, the film was shot in the town and members of the local populace were used as characters. In French with English subtitles. **90m/B VHS.** *FR* Charles Blavette, Jenny Helia, Edouard Delmont, Celia Montalvan; ***D:*** Jean Renoir; ***W:*** Jean Renoir; ***C:*** Claude Renoir; ***M:*** Paul Bozzi.

Tonight and Every Night 🦴🦴½ **1945** Cabaret singer and RAF pilot fall in love during WWII. Her music hall post puts her in the midst of Nazi bombing, and her dedication to her song and dance career puts a strain on the romance. Imaginative production numbers outweigh pedestrian storyline. ♫Cry and You Cry Alone; What Does an English Girl Think of a Yank; Anywhere; The Boy I Left Behind; You Excite Me; Tonight and Every Night. **92m/C VHS.** Rita Hayworth, Lee Bowman, Janet Blair, Marc Platt, Leslie Brooks; ***D:*** Victor Saville.

Tonight for Sure 🦴½ **1961** Coppola made this nudie, his first film, as a student at UCLA. Two men, one who spies on women and the other who imagines nude women everywhere, plan an escapade. **66m/B VHS.** ***D:*** Francis Ford Coppola; ***W:*** Francis Ford Coppola; ***M:*** Carmine Coppola.

Tonight or Never 🦴🦴 **1931** Nella (Swanson) is a young opera singer whose Venice debut is criticized for her lack of passion. So she spends the night with a nameless handsome admirer (Douglas), which does the trick. Nella is suddenly offered a contract with the Metropolitan Opera and learns that her new lover is a talent scout who arranged the whole thing and everything works out just peachy. Film is adapted from a play by Lili Hatvany, in which Douglas also starred. **80m/B VHS, DVD.** Gloria Swanson, Melvyn Douglas, Ferdinand Gottschalk, Alison Skipworth, Boris Karloff, Robert Greig; ***D:*** Mervyn LeRoy; ***W:*** Ernest Vajda, Frederic Hatton, Fanny Hatton; ***C:*** Gregg Toland; ***M:*** Alfred Newman.

Tonio Kroger 🦴🦴 **1965** A young writer travels through Europe in search of intellectual and sensual relationships and a home that will suit him. He must balance freedom and responsibility. Works best if one is familiar with the Thomas Mann novel on which film is based. In German with English subtitles. **92m/B VHS.** *GE* Jean-Claude Brialy, Nadja Tiller, Gert Frobe; ***D:*** Rolf Thiele.

Tonka 🦴🦴½ *A Horse Named Comanche* **1958** A children's story about a wild horse tamed by a young Indian, only to have it recruited for the Battle of Little Bighorn. Mineo is fine as the Indian brave determined to be reunited with his steed. The film also makes a laudable effort to portray the Indians as a dignified race. The movie, however, stumbles at its conclusion and is contrived throughout. **97m/C VHS.** Sal Mineo, Phil Carey, Jerome Courtland; ***D:*** Lewis R. Foster.

Tonto Basin Outlaws 🦴🦴 **1941** The Range Busters team up with Teddy Roosevelt's Rough Riders in order to stop a gang of cattle rustlers. Standard oater material. Based on the story by Earle Snell. **60m/B VHS.** Ray Corrigan, John "Dusty" King, Max Terhune, Jan Wiley, Tristram Coffin, Edmund Cobb; ***D:*** S. Roy Luby; ***W:*** John Vlahos.

The Tonto Kid 🦴 **1935** Action-packed western featuring Rex Bell. **56m/B VHS.** Rex Bell, Ruth Mix, Buzz Barton, Joseph Girard, Jack Rockwell, Murdock McQuarrie; ***D:*** Harry Fraser.

Tony Draws a Horse 🦴🦴½ **1951** An eight-year-old draws an anatomically correct horse on the door of his father's office, leading to a rift between the parents as they argue how to handle the heartbreak of precociousness. Somewhat uneven but engaging comedy, based on a play by Lesley Storm. **90m/B VHS.** Cecil Parker, Anne Crawford, Derek Bond, Barbara Murray, Mervyn Johns, Barbara Everest, David Hurst; ***D:*** John Paddy Carstairs.

Tony Rome 🦴🦴½ **1967** Tony Rome (Sinatra) is a P.I. living the good life on his boat in Miami. He's hired by wealthy builder Rudolph Kosterman (Oakland) to keep an eye on his erratic daughter, Diana (Lyons). Turns out there's organized crime and blackmail involved as well—oh, and a babe named Ann (St. John). An entertaining diversion based on the novel "Miami Mayhem" by Marvin H. Albert. Followed by "The Lady in Cement" (1968). **110m/C VHS.** Frank Sinatra, Jill St. John, Simon Oakland, Gena Rowlands, Richard Conte, Lloyd Bochner, Jeffrey Lynn, Sue Lyon; ***D:*** Gordon Douglas; ***W:*** Richard L. Breen; ***C:*** Joseph Biroc; ***M:*** Billy May.

Too Beautiful for You 🦴🦴 *Trop Belle pour Toi* **1988 (R)** A successful car salesman, married for years to an extraordinarily beautiful woman, finds himself head over heels for his frumpy secretary. Depardieu plays the regular guy who finds he's never believed in the love and fidelity of a woman he thinks is too beautiful for him. In French with English subtitles. **91m/C VHS.** *FR* Gerard Depardieu, Josiane Balasko, Carole Bouquet, Roland Blanche, Francois Cluzet; ***D:*** Bertrand Blier; ***W:*** Bertrand Blier; ***C:*** Philippe Rousselot. Cannes '89: Grand Jury Prize; Cesar '90: Actress (Bouquet), Director (Blier), Film, Writing.

Too Far to Go 🦴🦴🦴 **1979** Terrific TV adaptation of a series of John Updike stories focusing on the rocky longtime marriage of not-so-proper New Englanders Danner and Moriarty. **98m/C VHS.** Blythe Danner, Michael Moriarty, Glenn Close, Ken Kercheval; ***W:*** William Hanley.

Too Fast, Too Young 🦴 **1996 (R)** L.A. police captain Floyd Anderson (Ironside) finds himself shouldering the blame when violent offender Dalton (Tiller) escapes from prison and goes on a cop-killing spree. **90m/C VHS.** Michael Ironside, Patrick Tiller, James Wellington, Kasia (Katarzyna) Figura, Marshall Bell; ***D:*** Tim Everitt; ***W:*** Tim Everitt.

Too Good to Be True 🦴½ **1998** Jamie, Tina, and Silvia head to the beach at spring break for the usual ritual of sun, surf, and guys. First they attract nerds, then hoods, then hot guy Rick hits it off with Jamie and things seem to be going just swell. But the film isn't called "Too Good to Be True" for nuthin'. **91m/C VHS.** John O'Brien, Carole Bardwell, Spence Decker, Lisa Reissman, Angie Janu, Isaac Allan; ***D:*** Eric Swelstad; ***W:*** Cliff Hollingsworth; ***C:*** Scott Spears. **VIDEO**

Too Hot to Handle 🦴🦴🦴 **1938** Two rival photographers searching for a beautiful lady-pilot's missing brother wind up in Brazil, where they encounter a dangerous tribe of voodoo types. Amusing, if exaggerated, picture of the lengths to which reporters will go to for a story. Classic Gable. **105m/B VHS.** Clark Gable, Myrna Loy, Walter Pidgeon, Walter Connolly, Leo Carrillo, Virginia Weidler; ***D:*** Jack Conway.

Too Hot to Handle 🦴 **1976** Voluptuous lady contract killer fights against the mob with all the weapons at her disposal. Filmed on location in Manila. **88m/C VHS.** Cheri Caffaro, Aharon Ipale, Corinne Calvet, John van Dreelen, Vic Diaz, Jordan Rosengarten, Butz Aquino, Subas Herrero; ***D:*** Don Schain; ***W:*** J. Michael Sherman, Albert (Don) Buday; ***C:*** Fred Conde; ***M:*** Hugo Montenegro.

Too Late for Tears 🦴🦴🦴 *Killer Bait* **1949** An honest husband and his not so honest wife stumble on a load of mob-stolen cash and become entangled in a web of deceit and murder as the wife resorts to increasingly desperate measures to keep her newfound fortune. Atmospheric and entertaining film noir albeit sometimes confusing. **99m/B VHS.** Lizabeth Scott, Don DeFore, Dan Duryea, Arthur Kennedy, Kristine Miller, Barry Kelley, Denver Pyle, Jimmy Ames, Billy Halop, Jimmie Dodd; ***D:*** Byron Haskin; ***W:*** Roy Huggins; ***C:*** William Mellor; ***M:*** R. Dale Butts.

Too Late the Hero 🦴🦴🦴 *Suicide Run* **1970 (PG)** Unlikely band of allied soldiers battle Japanese force entrenched in the Pacific during WWII. Rousing adventure, fine cast. **133m/C VHS, DVD, Wide.** Michael Caine, Cliff Robertson, Henry Fonda, Ian Bannen, Harry Andrews, Denholm Elliott, William Beckley, Ronald Fraser, Percy Herbert, Patrick Jordan, Harvey Jason, Sam Kydd, Ken Takakura; ***D:*** Robert Aldrich; ***W:*** Robert Aldrich, Lois Heller; ***C:*** Joseph Biroc; ***M:*** Gerald Fried.

Too Many Crooks 🦴🦴 **1959** A British spoof of crime syndicate films. Crooks try to extort, but bungle the job. Terry-Thomas is fun, as always. **85m/B VHS.** *GB* Terry-Thomas, Brenda de Banzie, George Cole; ***D:*** Mario Zampi.

Too Many Girls 🦴🦴½ **1940** Beautiful heiress goes to a small New Mexico college to escape from a cadre of gold-digging suitors. Passable adaptation of the successful Rodgers and Hart Broadway show, with many original cast members and the original stage director. Lucy and Desi met while making this film, and married shortly after. ♫Spic and Spanish; Heroes in the Fall; Pottawatomie; 'Cause We All Got Cake; Love Never Went to College; Look Out; I Didn't Know What Time It Was; The Conga; You're Nearer. **85m/B VHS.** Lucille Ball, Richard Carlson, Eddie Bracken, Ann Miller, Desi Arnaz Sr., Hal LeRoy, Libby Bennett, Frances Langford, Van Johnson; ***D:*** George Abbott; ***M:*** George Bassman, Richard Rodgers, Lorenz Hart.

Too Much Sun 🦴½ **1990 (R)** A dying man can prevent his fortune from falling into the hands of a corrupt priest simply by having one of his two children produce an heir. The problem is, they're both gay! **97m/C VHS.** Robert Downey Jr., Ralph Macchio, Eric Idle, Andrea Martin, Laura Ernst, Jim Haynie; ***D:*** Robert Downey.

Too Pretty to Be Honest 🦴🦴 *Trop Jolie pour Etre Honette* **1972** Four women sharing an apartment witness a robbery and begin to suspect that their neighbor is the culprit. So they decide to steal the money from him. In French with subtitles. **95m/C VHS.** *FR* Jane Birkin, Bernadette LaFont, Serge Gainsbourg; ***D:*** Richard Balducci; ***M:*** Serge Gainsbourg.

Too Scared to Scream 🦴½ **1985 (R)** Policeman and an undercover agent team up to solve a bizarre series of murders at a Manhattan apartment house. **104m/C VHS.** Mike Connors, Anne Archer, Leon Isaac Kennedy, John Heard, Ian McShane, Maureen O'Sullivan, Murray Hamilton; ***D:*** Tony LoBianco; ***W:*** Neal Barbera.

Too Shy to Try 🦴🦴 **1982 (PG)** A incredibly shy man meets his dream girl, and enrolls in a psychology course to overcome his ineptitude. A ribald, slapstick French comedy. **89m/C VHS.** *FR* Pierre Richard, Aldo Maccione; ***D:*** Pierre Richard.

Too Smooth 🦴🦴 *Hairshirt* **1998 (R)** Danny (Paras) is a smooth-talking actor wannabe who lies to every woman he knows—until he meets naive Corey (Wright), whom he thinks is the girl of his dreams. But when his vindictive starlet ex (Campbell) learns about Corey's new romance, she becomes determined to expose him for the lying dog she's sure he remains. **91m/C VHS, DVD.** Dean Paras, Neve Campbell, Katie Wright, Rebecca Gayheart, Christian Campbell, David DeLuise, Stefan Brogren, Adam Carolla, Marley Shelton; ***D:*** Dean Paras; ***W:*** Dean Paras; ***M:*** Nathan Barr.

Too Wise Wives 🦴🦴 **1921** A story of would-be marital infidelity and misunderstandings. Silent. **90m/C VHS.** Louis Calhern, Claire Windsor; ***D:*** Lois Weber.

Too Young to Die 🦴🦴 **1990 (R)** Teenager Amanda (Lewis) hooks up with the wrong guy in sleazy Billy (Pitt), who hooks her on drugs and turns her into a prostitute. She meets nice guy Mike (O'Keefe), who briefly takes her away from the life but when their relationship falls apart, Amanda goes back to Billy. Billy eggs her on to get revenge for being dumped and Amanda winds up on trial for murder. Fact-based TV movie. **92m/C VHS.** Juliette Lewis, Brad Pitt, Michael Tucker, Michael O'Keefe, Emily Longstreth, Alan Fudge; ***D:*** Robert Markowitz; ***W:*** David Hill; ***C:*** Eric Van Haren Noman; ***M:*** Charles Bernstein.

The Toolbox Murders 🦴 **1978 (R)** Unknown psychotic murderer brutally claims victims one at a time, leaving police mystified and townsfolk terrified. Sick and exploitative, with predictably poor production values. **93m/C VHS.** Cameron Mitchell, Pamelyn Ferdin, Wesley Eure, Nicolas Beauvy, Aneta Corsaut, Tim Donnelly, Evelyn Guerrero; ***D:*** Dennis Donnelly; ***W:*** Robert Easter, Ann Kindberg; ***C:*** Gary Graver.

Toothless 🦴🦴½ **1997** Katherine Lewis (Alley) is a work-obsessed dentist who is struck by a car and wakes up in Limbo Land (yes, she's dead). The supervisor, Ms. Rogers (Redgrave), informs Katherine that because she had no emotional connections in life her entry into heaven will have to wait—and she's going to do her time as the Tooth Fairy. Katherine is not supposed to intervene with her charges but this sarcastic lady, who doesn't much care for her princess-like Tooth Fairy attire, does get involved with 12-year-old Bobby (Mallinger) and his widowed dad (Midkiff). **85m/C VHS.** Kirstie Alley, Ross Malinger, Dale Midkiff, Lynn Redgrave, Daryl (Chill) Mitchell, Melanie Mayron, Kimberly Scott, Helen Slater; ***W:*** Mark S. Kaufman. **TV**

Tootsie 🦴🦴🦴🦴 **1982 (PG)** Stubborn, unemployed actor Michael Dorsey (Hoffman) disguises himself as a woman named Dorothy Michaels to secure a part on a soap opera. As his popularity on TV mounts, his love life becomes increasingly soap operatic. Hoffman is delightful, as is the rest of the stellar cast, especially lange as the cast member he falls in love with. Debut of Davis; Murray's performance unbilled. Director Pollack plays Michael's put-upon agent, George Fields. **110m/C VHS, DVD, Wide.** Dustin Hoffman, Jessica Lange, Teri Garr, Dabney Coleman, Bill Murray, Charles Durning, Geena Davis, George Gaynes, Estelle Getty, Christine Ebersole, Sydney Pollack; ***D:*** Sydney Pollack; ***W:*** Larry Gelbart, Murray Schisgal, Don McGuire; ***C:*** Owen Roizman; ***M:*** Dave Grusin. Oscars '82: Support. Actress (Lange); AFI '98: Top 100; British Acad. '83: Actor (Hoffman); Golden Globes '83: Actor—Mus./Comedy (Hoffman), Film—Mus./Comedy, Support. Actress (Lange); L.A. Film Critics '82: Screenplay, Natl. Film Reg. '98;; N.Y. Film Critics '82: Director (Pollack), Screenplay, Support. Actress (Lange); Natl. Soc. Film Critics '82: Actor (Hoffman), Film, Screenplay, Support. Actress (Lange); Writers Guild '82: Orig. Screenplay.

Top Dog 🦴½ **1995 (PG-13)** Another cop-and-dog-team-up-to-get-the-bad-guys flick. This one, however, is meant to appeal to the kids who liked "Sidekicks." That raises a problem with the unfortunately topical right-wing-hate group-bombing plot. Jake Wilder (Norris), a beer-swillin' karate-choppin' loner cop, teams up with canine Reno, whose ex-partner was killed by the neo-Nazi terrorists. Weak script and erratic storyline can't find a comfortable balance between the too-cute pooch scenes and the (admittedly toned-down) violence. Reno steals every scene he's in, and provides the flick's few redeeming moments. **93m/C VHS, DVD, Wide.** Chuck Norris, Clyde Kusatsu, Michele Lamar Richards, Carmine Caridi, Peter Savard Moore, Erik von Detten, Herta Ware, Kai Wulff, Francesco Quinn, Timothy Bottoms; ***D:*** Aaron Norris; ***W:*** Ron Swanson; ***C:*** Joao Fernandes.

Top Gun 🦴🦴½ **1986 (PG)** Young Navy pilots compete against one another on the ground and in the air at the elite Fighter Weapons School. Cruise isn't bad as a maverick who comes of age in Ray Bans, but Edwards shines as his buddy. Awesome aerial photography and high-cal beefcake divert from the contrived plot and stock characters. The Navy subsequently noticed an increased interest in fighter pilots. Features Berlin's Oscar-winning song "Take My Breath Away." ♫Take My Breath Away; Danger Zone; Destination Unknown; Heaven in Your Eyes; Hot Summer Nights; Mighty Wings; Playing with the Boys; Through the Fire; Top Gun Anthem. **109m/C VHS, DVD, 8mm.** Tom Cruise, Kelly McGillis, Val Kilmer, Tom Skerritt, Anthony Edwards, Meg Ryan, Rick Rossovich, Michael Ironside, Barry Tubb, Whip Hubley, John Stockwell, Tim Robbins, Adrian Pasdar; ***D:*** Tony Scott; ***W:*** Jim Cash, Jack Epps Jr.; ***C:*** Jeffrey L. Kimball; ***M:*** Harold Faltermeyer. Oscars '86: Song ("Take My Breath Away"); Golden Globes '87: Song ("Take My Breath Away").

Top Hat 🦴🦴🦴🦴 **1935** Ginger isn't impressed by Fred's amorous attentions since she's mistaken him for a friend's other half. Many believe it to be the duo's best film together. Choreography by Astaire and score by Berlin makes this one a classic Hollywood musical. Look for a young Lucille Ball as a clerk in a flower shop. ♫Cheek to Cheek; Top Hat, White Tie and Tails; Isn't This A Lovely Day; The Piccolino; No Strings. **97m/B VHS, 8mm.** Fred Astaire, Ginger Rogers, Erik Rhodes, Helen Broderick, Edward Everett Horton, Eric Blore, Lucille Ball; ***D:*** Mark Sandrich; ***W:*** Dwight Taylor, Allan

Scott; *M:* Irving Berlin, Max Steiner. Natl. Film Reg. '90.

Top of the Heap 1972 (R) A cop is denied a promotion and gets angry. Deciding to chuck the laws of due process, he goes on a criminal-killing rampage. **91m/C VHS.** Christopher St. John, Paula Kelly, Patrick McVey; *D:* Christopher St. John.

Top of the World ½ 1997 (R) Newly released con Ray Mercer (Weller) travels to Vegas with his estranged wife, Rebecca (Carrere), who wants a quickie divorce. She's got a new boyfriend, casino manager Steve Atlas (Hopper). But Ray just happens to get caught in the middle of a heist planned by Atlas to cover up his embezzling at the casino. Sounds like it should be entertaining but it's not. **98m/C VHS, DVD.** Peter Weller, Tia Carrere, Dennis Hopper, Joe Pantoliano, Martin Kove, Peter Coyote, David Alan Grier, Cary-Hiroyuki Tagawa; *D:* Sidney J. Furie; *W:* Bart Madison; *C:* Alan Caso; *M:* Robert O. Ragland.

Top Secret! 1984 (PG) Unlikely musical farce parodies spy movies and Elvis Presley films. Young American rock star Nick Rivers goes to Europe on goodwill tour and becomes involved with Nazis, the French Resistance, an American refugee, and more. Sophisticated it isn't. From the creators of "Airplane!" **90m/C VHS.** Val Kilmer, Lucy Gutteridge, Christopher Villiers, Omar Sharif, Peter Cushing, Jeremy Kemp, Michael Gough, Billy Mitchell; *D:* Jim Abrahams, Jerry Zucker, David Zucker; *W:* Jim Abrahams, Jerry Zucker, David Zucker, Martyn Burke; *C:* Christopher Challis; *M:* Maurice Jarre.

Topaz 1969 (PG) American CIA agent and French intelligence agent combine forces to find information about Russian espionage in Cuba. Cerebral and intriguing, but not classic Hitchcock. Based on the novel by Leon Uris. **126m/C VHS, DVD, Wide.** John Forsythe, Frederick Stafford, Philippe Noiret, Karin Dor, Michel Piccoli; *D:* Alfred Hitchcock; *W:* Samuel A. Taylor; *C:* Jack Hildyard; *M:* Maurice Jarre. Natl. Bd. of Review '69: Director (Hitchcock), Support. Actor (Noiret).

Topaze 1933 A shy, depressed teacher is fired from his job at a private school and takes a new job, unaware that his boss is using him in a business scam. From the French play by Marcel Pagnol. An American version was also filmed in 1933; Pagnol produced his own version in '51. In French with English subtitles. **92m/B VHS.** *FR* Louis Jouvet, Edwige Feuillere, Marcel Vallee; *D:* Louis Gasnier; *W:* Marcel Pagnol; *M:* Max Steiner.

Topaze 1933 American adaptation of the Marcel Pagnol play, about an innocent, doltish schoolmaster who becomes the unknowing front for a baron's illegal business scam. Remade in two French versions, in 1933, and in 1951 by Pagnol. **127m/B VHS.** John Barrymore, Myrna Loy, Jobyna Howland, Jackie Searl; *D:* Harry D'Abbadie D'Arrast.

Topaze ½ 1951 After losing his job, a pathetic school teacher gets involved with the mob and winds up a powerful businessman. Remake of two earlier versions, one French and one American. Based on the play by director Pagnol. In French with English subtitles. **95m/B VHS.** *FR* Fernandel, Helen Perdriere, Pierre Larquey; *D:* Marcel Pagnol.

The Topeka Terror 1945 Lane stars as a federal agent who joins forces with a frontier lawyer to stop greedy land-grabber Barcroft from ripping off a group of homesteaders. Based on a story by Patricia Harper. **55m/B VHS.** Allan "Rocky" Lane, Linda Stirling, Roy Barcroft, Earle Hodgins, Bud Geary; *D:* Howard Bretherton; *W:* Patricia Harper, Norman S. Hall.

Topkapi 1964 An international bevy of thieves can't resist the treasures of the famed Topkapi Palace Museum, an impregnable fortress filled with wealth and splendor. Comic thriller based on Erie Ambler's "The Light of Day." **122m/C VHS, DVD, Wide.** Melina Mercouri, Maximilian Schell, Peter Ustinov, Robert Morley, Akim Tamiroff, Jess Hahn, Gilles Segal; *D:* Jules Dassin; *W:* Monja Danischewsky; *C:* Henri Alekan; *M:* Manos Hadjidakis. Oscars '64: Support. Actor (Ustinov).

Topper ½ 1937 Wealthy, madcap George (Grant) and Marion (Bennett) Kerby return as ghosts after a fatal car accident, determined to assist their morose banker pal Cosmo Topper (Young) to enjoy life. Of course, since Cosmo is the only one who can see the ghostly Kerbys his life becomes very complicated. Immensely popular at the boxoffice; followed by "Topper Takes a Trip" (1939) and "Topper Returns" (1941). The series uses trick photography and special effects to complement the comedic scripts. Based on Thorne Smith's novel, "The Jovial Ghosts." Inspired a TV series and remade in 1979 as TV movie. **97m/B VHS.** Cary Grant, Roland Young, Constance Bennett, Billie Burke, Eugene Pallette, Hoagy Carmichael; *D:* Norman Z. McLeod.

Topper Returns 1941 Cosmo Topper helps ghost find the man who mistakenly murdered her and warns her friend, the intended victim. Humorous conclusion to the trilogy preceded by "Topper" and "Topper Takes a Trip." Followed by a TV series. **87m/B VHS, DVD.** Roland Young, Joan Blondell, Dennis O'Keefe, Carole Landis, Eddie Anderson, H.B. Warner, Billie Burke; *D:* Roy Del Ruth; *W:* Gordon Douglas, Jonathan Latimer; *C:* Norbert Brodine.

Topper Takes a Trip 1939 Cosmo Topper and his wife have falling out and ghosts Kerby help them get back together. The special effects sequences are especially funny. Followed by "Topper Returns." Also available colorized. **85m/B VHS.** Constance Bennett, Roland Young, Billie Burke, Franklin Pangborn, Alan Mowbray; *D:* Norman Z. McLeod.

Topsy Turvy ½ 1984 (R) A comedy about reckless romance and not much else. **90m/C VHS.** Lisbet Dahl, Ebbe Rode; *D:* Edward Fleming.

Topsy Turvy ½ 1999 (R) The very contemporary Leigh takes a pass at Victorian England for his very long and chatty look at life in the theatre. His focus is on the comic-opera partnership of irascible lyricist W.S. Gilbert (Broadbent) and pleasure-loving composer, Sir Arthur Sullivan (Corduner). Their latest creation (after 10 hits) is a flop, causing a serious rift but Gilbert, after a visit to a Japanese art exhibit, is inspired to write "The Mikado" and pulls Sullivan back in. The film then follows the production of the opera from rehearsal to the 1885 premiere with all its difficulties and triumphs. **160m/C VHS, DVD, Wide.** *GB* Jim Broadbent, Allan Corduner, Leslie Manville, Eleanor David, Ron Cook, Timothy Spall, Kevin McKidd, Mark Benton, Shirley Henderson, Martin Savage, Jessie Bond; *D:* Mike Leigh; *W:* Mike Leigh; *C:* Dick Pope; *M:* Carl Davis. Oscars '99: Costume Des., Makeup; British Acad. '99: Makeup; N.Y. Film Critics '99: Director (Leigh), Film; Natl. Soc. Film Critics '99: Director (Leigh), Film.

Tor ½ 1964 Medieval barbarian endeavors to free an enslaved village from a band of murderous hoodlums. **94m/C VHS.** Joe Robinson, Bella Cortez, Harry Baird; *D:* Antonio Leonviola.

Tora! Tora! Tora! 1970 (G) The story of events leading up to December 7, 1941, is retold by three directors from both Japanese and American viewpoints in this tense, large-scale production. Well-documented and realistic treatment of the Japanese attack on Pearl Harbor that brought the U.S. into WWII; notable for its good photography but lacks a storyline equal to its epic intentions. **144m/C VHS, DVD, Wide.** Martin Balsam; So Yamamura, Joseph Cotten, E.G. Marshall, Tatsuya Mihashi, Wesley Addy, Jason Robards Jr., James Whitmore, Leon Ames, George Macready, Takahiro Tamura, Eijiro Tono, Shogo Shimada, Koreya Senda, Jun Usami, Richard Anderson, Kazuo Kitamura, Keith Andes, Edward Andrews, Neville Brand, Leora Dana, Walter Brooke, Norman Alden, Ron Masak, Edmon Ryan, Asao Uchida, Frank Aletter, Jerry Fogel; *D:* Richard Fleischer, Toshio Masuda, Kinji Fukasaku; *W:* Ryuzo Kikushima, Hideo Oguni, Larry Forrester; *C:* Sinsaku Himeda, Charles F. Wheeler, Osamu Furuya; *M:* Jerry Goldsmith. Oscars '70: Visual FX.

The Torch ½ 1950 Mexican revolutionary restores law and order when he captures a small town but then finds himself in turmoil as he falls for an aristocratic young woman. **90m/C VHS.** *MX* Gilbert Roland, Paulette Goddard, Pedro Armendariz Sr., Walter Reed; *D:* Emilio Fernandez.

Torch Song 1953 In this muddled melodrama, a tough, demanding Broadway actress meets her match when she is offered true love by a blind pianist. Contains a couple of notoriously inept musical numbers. Made to show off Crawford's figure at age 50. Crawford's singing in the movie is dubbed. **90m/C VHS.** Joan Crawford, Michael Wilding, Marjorie Rambeau, Gig Young, Harry (Henry) Morgan, Dorothy Patrick, Benny Rubin, Nancy Gates; *D:* Charles Walters.

Torch Song Trilogy ½ 1988 (R) Adapted from Fierstein's hit Broadway play about a gay man who "just wants to be loved." Still effective, but the rewritten material loses something in the translation to the screen. Bancroft heads a strong cast with a finely shaded performance as Fierstein's mother. **126m/C VHS.** Anne Bancroft, Matthew Broderick, Harvey Fierstein, Brian Kerwin, Karen Young, Charles Pierce; *D:* Paul Bogart; *W:* Harvey Fierstein; *C:* Mikael Salomon; *M:* Peter Matz.

Torchlight 1985 (R) A young couple's life begins to crumble when a wealthy art dealer teaches them how to free base cocaine. Heavy-handed treatment of a subject that's been tackled with more skill elsewhere. **90m/C VHS.** Pamela Sue Martin, Steve Railsback, Ian McShane, Al Corley, Rita Taggart; *D:* Thomas J. Wright.

Torero *Bullfighter* 1956 A young man becomes a bullfighter to overcome his fear of bulls. **89m/B VHS.** *MX* Luis Procuna, Manolete, Dolores Del Rio, Carlos Arruza; *D:* Carlos Velo; *W:* Carlos Velo, Hugo Butler.

Torment *Hets; Frenzy* 1944 Tragic triangle has young woman in love with fellow student and murdered by sadistic teacher. Atmospheric tale hailed by many as Sjoberg's finest film. Ingmar Bergman's first filmed script. In Swedish with English subtitles. **90m/B VHS.** *SW* Alf Kjellin, Mai Zetterling, Stig Jarrel, Olof Winnerstrand, Gunnar Bjornstrand; *D:* Alf Sjoberg; *W:* Ingmar Bergman; *C:* Martin Bodin; *M:* Hilding Rosenberg.

Torment 1985 (R) A mild-mannered fellow is secretly a mass murderer specializing in young lovers. He struggles to hide his secret as his daughter approaches dating age and a relentless detective gets closer to the truth. A low-budget slasher. **85m/C VHS.** Taylor Gilbert, William Witt, Eve Brenner; *D:* Samson Aslanian, John Hopkins; *W:* Samson Aslanian, John Hopkins.

Tormented ½ 1960 Man pushes his mistress out of a lighthouse, killing her. Her ethereal body parts return to haunt him. **75m/B VHS, DVD.** Richard Carlson, Susan Gordon, Juli Reding; *D:* Bert I. Gordon; *W:* Bert I. Gordon, George Worthing Yates; *C:* Ernest Laszlo; *M:* Albert Glasser, Calvin Jackson.

The Tormentors WOOF! 1971 (R) Vaguely neo-Nazi gangs rape and murder a man's family, and he kills them all in revenge. **78m/C VHS, DVD.** James Craig, Anthony Eisley, Chris Nole, William Dooley, Bruce Kemp, Inga Wede, James Gordon White; *D:* Boris Eagle; *W:* James Gordon White.

Torn Apart 1989 (R) Traditional Middle East hatreds undermine the love affair between two young people. Excellent performances from the principals highlight this drama. Adapted from the Chayin Zeldis novel "A Forbidden Love." **95m/C VHS.** Adrian Pasdar, Cecilia Peck, Machram Huri, Arnon Zadok, Barry Primus; *D:* Jack Fisher; *M:* Peter Arnow.

Torn Between Two Lovers 1979 A beautiful married woman has an affair with an architect while on a trip. Remick is enjoyable to watch, but it's a fairly predictable yarn. **100m/C VHS.** Lee Remick, Joseph Bologna, George Peppard, Giorgio Tozzi; *D:* Delbert Mann. **TV**

Torn Curtain ½ 1966 American scientist poses as a defector to East Germany in order to uncover details of the Soviet missile program. He and his fiancee, who follows him behind the Iron Curtain, attempt to escape to freedom. Derivative and uninvolving. **125m/C VHS, DVD, Wide.** Paul Newman, Julie Andrews, Lila Kedrova, David Opatoshu; *D:* Alfred Hitchcock; *W:* Brian Moore; *C:* John F. Warren; *M:* John Addison.

Tornado 1983 An army sergeant revolts against his superiors and the enemy when his captain leaves him stranded in Vietnam. **90m/C VHS.** Giancarlo (Timothy Brent) Prete, Tony Marsina, Alan Collins; *D:* Anthony (Antonio Margheriti) Dawson.

Tornado! ½ 1996 (PG) TV movie with cheesy special effects chronicles a week with tornado chaser Campbell, meteorologist Hudson, and government accountant Sturges who wants to stop funding for Hudson's new storm-warning device. Lame attempt to capture some of the "Twister" audience fails miserably. **90m/C VHS, DVD.** Bruce Campbell, Ernie Hudson, Shannon Sturges, L.Q. (Justus E. McQueen) Jones, Bo Eason; *D:* Noel Nosseck; *W:* John Logan; *C:* Paul Maibaum; *M:* Garry Schyman.

Torpedo Alley 1953 A guilt-ridden WWII Navy pilot feels responsible for the deaths of his crew. After the war, he joins a submarine crew and gradually learns to deal with his guilt. Average drama with plenty of submarine footage. **84m/B VHS.** Dorothy Malone, Mark Stevens, Charles Winninger, Bill Williams; *D:* Lew (Louis Friedlander) Landers.

Torpedo Attack 1972 Greek sailors, in an outdated submarine, bravely but hopelessly attack Mussolini's Italy during WWII. **88m/C VHS.** *GR* John Ferris, Sidney Kazan; *D:* George Law.

Torpedo Run 1958 Standard submarine melodramatics, about a U.S. sub that must torpedo a Japanese aircraft carrier which holds some of the crew's family members. Sometimes slow, generally worthwhile. **98m/C VHS.** Glenn Ford, Ernest Borgnine, Dean Jones, Diane Brewster, L.Q. (Justus E. McQueen) Jones; *D:* Joseph Pevney; *C:* George J. Folsey.

Torrents of Spring 1990 (PG-13) Based on an Ivan Turgenev story, this lavishly filmed and costumed drama concerns a young Russian aristocrat circa 1840 who is torn between two women. Predictably, one is a good-hearted innocent, the other a scheming seductress. **102m/C VHS.** Timothy Hutton, Nastassia Kinski, Valeria Golino, William Forsythe, Urbano Barberini, Francesca De Sapio, Jacques Herlin; *D:* Jerzy Skolimowski.

Torso WOOF! *I Corpi Presentano Tracce Di Violenza Carnale; Bodres Bear Traces of Carnal Violence* 1973 (R) Crazed psychosexual killer stalks beautiful women and dismembers them. Fairly bloodless and uninteresting, in spite of lovely Kendall. Italian title translates: The Bodies Showed Signs of Carnal Violence—quite an understatement for people missing arms and legs. **91m/C VHS, DVD.** *IT* Suzy Kendall, Tina Aumont, John Richardson; *D:* Sergio Martino; *W:* Sergio Martino, Ernesto Gastaldi; *C:* Giancarlo Ferrando; *M:* Maurizio de Angelis, Guido de Angelis.

Torso ½ 2001 (R) In the small Canadian town of Hamilton, Ontario, a butchered torso is discovered in 1946. Soon, femme fatale Evelyn Dick (Robertson) is accused of the brutal murder of her streetcar conductor husband. Evelyn admits to numerous affairs with wealthy and powerful men and a desire to lead the good life but did she really commit murder? **90m/C VHS, DVD.** Kathleen Robertson, Victor Garber, Callum Keith Rennie, Brenda Fricker, Jonathan Potts, John Henry Canavan; *D:* Alex Chapelle; *W:* Dennis Foon; *C:* Nikos Evdemon; *M:* Christopher Dedrick.

Tortilla Flat 1942 Based on the John Steinbeck novel of the same name, two buddies, Tracy and Garfield, struggle to make their way on the wrong side of the tracks in California. Garfield gets a break by inheriting a couple of houses, Tracy schemes to rip-off a rich, but eccentric, dog owner. In the meantime, both fall for the same girl, Lamarr, in perhaps the finest role of her career. Great performances from all, especially Morgan. **105m/B VHS.** Spencer Tracy, Hedy Lamarr, John Garfield, Frank Morgan, Akim Tamiroff,

Sheldon Leonard, John Qualen, Donald Meek, Connie Gilchrist; *D:* Victor Fleming; *C:* Karl Freund.

Tortilla Soup 🦴🦴½ **2001 (PG-13)** Widower Martin Naranjo (Elizondo) is a Mexican-American patriarch trying to control the lives of his three grown daughters. Schoolteacher Leticia (Pena) fears love has passed her by; successful Carmen (Obradors) questions her career choice; and Maribel (Mello) has graduated from high school and is just eager to leave home. Meanwhile, Martin is a chef who's lost his sense of taste and smell and is being pursued by divorced Hortensia (Welch). Food and family dinners bring the various crises out in the open. And yes, the film is the American version of the 1994 Taiwanese film "Eat, Drink, Man, Woman" with an equally engaging cast. **102m/C VHS, DVD, Wide.** *US* Hector Elizondo, Jacqueline Obradors, Elizabeth Pena, Tamara Mello, Nikolai Kinski, Raquel Welch, Paul Rodriguez, Joel Joan, Constance Marie; *D:* Maria Ripoli; *W:* Tom Musca, Ramon Menendez, Vera Blasi; *C:* Xavier Perez Grobet; *M:* Bill Conti.

Torture Chamber of Baron Blood 🦴🦴½ *Baron Blood; Gli Orrori del Castello di Norimberga; The Blood Baron; Chamber of Tortures; The Thirst of Baron Blood* **1972 (PG)** Baron with gorgeous thirst for the red stuff is reanimated and lots of innocent bystanders meet a grisly fate in this spaghetti gorefest. Familiar story has that certain Bava feel. **90m/C VHS, DVD.** *IT* Joseph Cotten, Elke Sommer, Massimo Girotti, Rada Rassimov, Antonio Cantafora; *D:* Mario Bava; *W:* Vincent Fotre, William Bairn; *M:* Les Baxter.

The Torture Chamber of Dr. Sadism 🦴🦴½ *Blood Demon; Castle of the Walking Dead; Die Schlangengrube und das Pendel* **1969** Decapitated and drawn and quartered for sacrificing 12 virgins, the evil Count Regula is pieced together 40 years later to continue his wicked ways. Great fun, terrific art direction. Very loosely based on Poe's "The Pit and the Pendulum." Beware of the heavily edited video version. **120m/C VHS.** *GE* Christopher Lee, Karin Dor, Lex Barker, Carl Lange, Vladimir Medar, Christiane Rucker, Dieter Eppler; *D:* Harald Reinl.

Torture Dungeon 🦴 **1970 (R)** Director Milligan tortures audience with more mindless medieval pain infliction from Staten Island. **80m/C VHS.** Jeremy Brooks, Susan Cassidy; *D:* Andy Milligan.

Torture Garden 🦴🦴 **1967** A sinister man presides over an unusual sideshow where people can see what is in store if they allow the evil side of their personalities to take over. Written by Bloch ("Psycho") and based on four of his short stories. **93m/C VHS.** *GB* Jack Palance, Burgess Meredith, Peter Cushing, Beverly Adams; *D:* Freddie Francis; *W:* Robert Bloch; *M:* Don Banks, James Bernard.

The Torture of Silence 🦴🦴½ *Mater Dolorosa* **1917** A simple little drama about a doctor's neglected wife seeking out the doctor's best friend for love, remade by Gance in 1932. **55m/B VHS.** *FR* Emmy Lynn, Firmin Gemier, Armand Tallier, Anthony Gildes, Paul Vermoyal; *D:* Abel Gance; *W:* Abel Gance; *C:* Leonce-Henri Burel.

Torture Ship 🦴½ **1939** Director Halperin, who earlier made the minor horror classic "White Zombie," was all at sea in this becalmed thriller about a mad doctor who uses convicts for glandular experiment in his shipboard laboratory. Based on the short story "A Thousand Deaths" by Jack London. **57m/B VHS.** Lyle Talbot, Irving Pichel, Julie (Jacqueline Wells) Bishop, Sheila (Manors) Mannors; *D:* Victor Halperin.

Torture Train 🦴½ **1983 (R)** Mayhem, murder, and knife-wielding psychosis occurs on board a train. **78m/C VHS.** Patty Edwards, Kay Beal.

Total Eclipse 🦴 **1995 (R)** Unfortunate look at the mutually destructive relationship between 19th-century French poets Arthur Rimbaud (DiCaprio) and Paul Verlaine (Thewlis). Rimbaud was a 16-year-old Parisian sensation for his iconoclastic work but what's presented is an obnoxious showoff, while the older, married Verlaine is a drunken lout who abuses his teenaged wife Mathilde (Bohringer). There's lots of dissolute, violent behavior and absolutely no insight into their work (which is the only reason to care). Ugly film wastes a lot of talent. **111m/C VHS, DVD.** Leonardo DiCaprio, David Thewlis, Romane Bohringer, Dominique Blanc; *D:* Agnieszka Holland; *W:* Christopher Hampton; *C:* Yorgos Arvanitis; *M:* Jan A.P. Kaczmarek.

Total Exposure 🦴 **1991 (R)** Total idiocy involving unclad babes and hormonally imbalanced men in blackmail and murder. 1990 Playboy Playmate Deborah Driggs proves there is life of sorts after playmatedom. **96m/C VHS.** Michael Nouri, Season Hubley, Christian Bocher, Robert Prentiss, Deborah Driggs, Jeff Conaway; *D:* John Quinn.

Total Reality 🦴½ **1997 (R)** In order to escape execution, disgraced soldier Anthony Rand (Bradley) undertakes to follow renegade general Tunis (Kretschmann) back through time and prevent the destruction of the universe. **97m/C VHS, DVD.** David Bradley, Thomas Kretschmann, Ely Pouget, Bill Shaw, Misa Koprova; *D:* Phillip J. Roth; *W:* Phillip J. Roth, Robert Tossberg; *C:* Andres Garreton. **VIDEO**

Total Recall 🦴🦴🦴 **1990 (R)** Mind-bending sci-fi movie set in the 21st century. Construction worker Quaid (Schwarzenegger) dreams every night about the colonization of Mars, so he decides to visit a travel service that specializes in implanting vacation memories into its clients' brains and buy a memory trip to the planet. Only during the implant, Quaid discovers his memories have been artificially altered and he must find out just what's real and what's not. Intriguing plot and spectacular special effects. Laced with graphic violence. Based on Phillip K. Dick's "We Can Remember It for You Wholesale." **113m/C VHS, DVD, 8mm, Wide.** Arnold Schwarzenegger, Rachel Ticotin, Sharon Stone, Michael Ironside, Ronny Cox, Roy Brocksmith, Marshall Bell, Mel Johnson Jr.; *D:* Paul Verhoeven; *W:* Gary Goldman, Dan O'Bannon; *C:* Jan De Bont; *M:* Jerry Goldsmith. Oscars '90: Visual FX.

Total Recall 2070: Machine Dreams 🦴🦴 **1999 (R)** Pilot movie for the brief series that had only a tentative connection to the Ah-nuld movie and the short stories of Philip K. Dick. David Hume (Easton) is a 21st century cop who is supposed to keep an eye on the Consortium, the group of private companies that unofficially now run the world. They create mayhem and he tries to clean it up. Hume must battle rogue androids and solve the murders that occurred at the virtual reality vacation agency, Total Rekall. **83m/C VHS, DVD.** Michael Easton, Karl Pruner, Cyndy Preston, Judith Krant, Nick Mancuso; *D:* Mario Azzopardi; *C:* Peter Wunstorf. **CABLE**

Totally F*ed Up** 🦴🦴 **1994** The first of director Araki's teen trilogy, followed by "The Doom Generation" and "Nowhere," concerns itself with the teen angst experienced by a loose group of friends—four gays and a lesbian couple. In short chapters, they meet, talk, and wander through a soulless L.A. as one of their group, film school student Steven (Luna), makes a video documentary about their situation (footage of which in intercut throughout the film). **80m/C VHS.** James Duval, Gilbert Luna, Lance May, Roko Belic, Susan Behshid, Jenee Gill, Alan Boyce; *D:* Gregg Araki; *W:* Gregg Araki; *C:* Gregg Araki.

Toto le Heros 🦴🦴🦴 *Toto the Hero* **1991 (PG-13)** Bitter old man, who as a child fantasized that he was a secret agent named Toto, harbors deep resentment over not living the life he's convinced he should have had. He maintains a childhood fantasy that he and his rich neighbor were switched at birth in the confusion of a fire at the hospital. Series of flashbacks and fast forwards show glimpses of his life, not necessarily as it was, but how he perceived it. Sounds complex, but it's actually very clear and fluid. Mix of comedy and tragedy, with lots of ironic twists, and precise visuals. In French with English subtitles. **90m/C VHS.** *FR* Michel Bouquet, Jo De Backer, Thomas Godet, Mireille Perrier, Sandrine Blancke, Didier Ferney, Hugo Harold Harrisson, Gisela Uhlen, Peter Bohlke; *D:* Jaco Van Dormael; *W:* Jaco Van Dormael; *C:* Walther Vanden Ende; *M:* Pierre Van Dormael. Cesar '91: Foreign Film.

The Touch 🦴½ *Be Roringen* **1971 (R)** Straightforward story of a woman who is satisfied with her husband until the arrival of a stranger. The stranger soon has her yearning for a life she has never known. Bergman's first English film lacks the sophistication of his earlier work. **112m/C VHS.** *SW* Bibi Andersson, Elliott Gould, Max von Sydow; *D:* Ingmar Bergman; *W:* Ingmar Bergman; *C:* Sven Nykvist.

Touch 🦴🦴½ **1996 (R)** Sleazebags, fundamentalists, and a maybe saint would seem to make for a surefire success in this easygoing adaptation of the offbeat Elmore Leonard novel. And while individual scenes and performances shine, the film doesn't completely hang together. Young Juvenal (Ulrich) is a former monk, now working at an L.A. alcohol rehab center, who possesses the stigmata and seems to have an authentic gift for healing. Naturally, this brings the crazies and the scammers out of the woodwork, including former preacher Bill Hill (Walken), whose partner (Fonda) falls for the lad, and paramilitary religious fanatic August Murray (Arnold). **96m/C VHS.** Skeet Ulrich, Bridget Fonda, Christopher Walken, Tom Arnold, Gina Gershon, Lolita (David) Davidovich, Paul Mazursky, Janeane Garofalo, John Doe, Conchata Ferrell, Mason Adams, Breckin Meyer, Anthony Zerbe; *D:* Paul Schrader; *W:* Paul Schrader; *C:* Edward Lachman; *M:* David Grohl.

Touch & Go 🦴🦴 **1980 (PG)** Three beautiful women commit grand larceny in order to raise funds for underprivileged children. **92m/C VHS.** *AU* Wendy Hughes; *D:* Peter Maxwell; *W:* Alan Ormsby.

Touch and Go 🦴½ **1986 (R)** Sentimental drama about a self-interested hockey pro who learns about love and giving through a young delinquent and his attractive mother. **101m/C VHS.** Michael Keaton, Maria Conchita Alonso, Ajay Naidu, Maria Tucci, Max Wright, John C. Reilly; *D:* Robert Mandel; *W:* Harry Colomby.

Touch Me Not 🦴🦴 *The Hunted* **1974 (PG)** A neurotic secretary is used by an industrial spy to gain information on her boss. Weak thriller. **84m/C VHS, DVD.** *GB* Lee Remick, Michael Hinz, Ivan Desny, Ingrid Garbo; *D:* Douglas Fifthian.

A Touch of Class 🦴🦴🦴 **1973 (PG)** Married American insurance adjustor working in London plans quick and uncommitted affair but finds his heart doesn't obey the rules. Jackson and Segal create sparkling record of a growing relationship. **105m/C VHS, DVD, Wide.** George Segal, Glenda Jackson, Paul Sorvino, Hildegard(e) Neil, K. Callan, Mary Barclay, Cec Linder; *D:* Melvin Frank; *W:* Jack Rose; *C:* Austin Dempster; *M:* John Cameron. Oscars '73: Actress (Jackson); Golden Globes '74: Actor—Mus./Comedy (Segal), Actress—Mus./Comedy (Jackson); Writers Guild '73: Orig. Screenplay.

Touch of Evil 🦴🦴🦴🦴 **1958 (PG-13)** Stark, perverse story of murder, kidnapping, and police corruption in Mexican border town. Welles portrays a police chief who invents evidence to convict the guilty. Filled with innovative photography reminiscent of "Citizen Kane," as filmed by Russell Metty. In 1998, Walter Murch restored the film working from Welles's notes, re-editing the work to what Welles had originally envisioned before studio intervention; this version is 101 minutes and is unrated. **108m/B VHS, DVD, Wide.** Charlton Heston, Orson Welles, Janet Leigh, Joseph Calleia, Akim Tamiroff, Marlene Dietrich, Valentin de Vargas, Dennis Weaver, Joanna Moore, Mort Mills, Victor Millan, Ray Collins; *Cameos:* Joi Lansing, Zsa Zsa Gabor, Mercedes McCambridge, Joseph Cotten; *D:* Orson Welles; *W:* Orson Welles; *C:* Russell Metty; *M:* Henry Mancini. Natl. Film Reg. '93.

The Touch of Satan 🦴 *The Touch of Melissa; Night of the Demon; Curse of Melissa* **1970 (PG)** Lost on the road, a young man meets a lovely young woman and is persuaded to stay at her nearby farmhouse. Things there are not as they seem, including the young woman—who turns out to be a very old witch. **90m/C VHS.** Michael Berry, Emby Mallay, Lee Amber, Yvonne Wilson, Jeanne Gerson; *D:* Don Henderson.

Touched 🦴🦴 **1982 (R)** Two young people struggle with the outside world after their escape from a mental institution. Although melodramatic and poorly scripted, the film is saved by fine performances by Hays and Beller. **89m/C VHS.** Robert Hays, Kathleen Beller, Ned Beatty, Gilbert Lewis; *D:* John Flynn.

Touched by Love 🦴🦴½ *To Elvis, With Love* **1980 (PG)** The true story of a handicapped child who begins to communicate when her teacher suggests she write to Elvis Presley. Sincere and well performed. **95m/C VHS.** Deborah Raffin, Diane Lane, Christina Raines, Clu Gulager, John Amos; *D:* Gus Trikonis; *W:* Hesper Anderson; *M:* John Barry.

Touching Evil 🦴🦴🦴 **1997** London police detective Dave Creegan (Green) and his fellow cops at the (fictional) Organized and Serial Crime Unit investigate three creepy cases in this three-tape series. The first concerns the kidnapping of three small boys; the second involves patients being drugged and killed while in hospital; and the third involves corpses, university students, and the Internet. The detectives are a fine, flawed unit and make for some interesting company. Followed by two sequels. **360m/C VHS.** *GB* Robson Green, Ian McDiarmid, Nicola Walker, Michael Feast, Adam Kotz, Kenneth MacDonald, Antony Byrne, Shaun Dingwall; *D:* Julian Jarrold, Marc Munden; *W:* Paul Abbott, Russell T. Davies; *C:* David Odd; *M:* Adrian Johnston. **TV**

Tough and Deadly 🦴½ **1994 (R)** CIA agent teams up with bounty hunter to stop a drug ring. **92m/C VHS.** Billy Blanks, Roddy Piper.

Tough Assignment 🦴 **1949** A reporter in the West discovers and infiltrates a gang of organized rustlers who are forcing butchers to buy inferior meat. **64m/B VHS.** Donald (Don "Red") Barry, Marjorie Steele, Steve Brodie.

Tough Enough 🦴🦴 **1983 (PG)** A country-western singer and songwriter decides to finance his fledgling singing career by entering amateur boxing matches. Insipid and predictable, with fine cast wasted. **107m/C VHS.** Dennis Quaid, Charlene Watkins, Warren Oates, Pam Grier, Stan Shaw, Bruce McGill, Wilford Brimley, Bob Watson; *D:* Richard Fleischer.

Tough Guy 🦴 **1953** Based on the play by Bruce Walker, a London hood carouses, mugs, breaks hearts and personifies his generation's anxiety. **73m/B VHS.** *GB* James Kenney, Hermione Gingold, Joan Collins; *D:* Lewis Gilbert.

Tough Guy 🦴 *Kung Fu: The Head Crusher* **1970** Two undercover policemen battle local gangsters in a bid to smash their crime ring. **90m/C VHS.** Chen Ying, Charlie Chiang; *D:* Chieng Hung.

Tough Guys 🦴🦴½ **1986 (PG)** Two aging ex-cons, who staged America's last train robbery in 1961, try to come to terms with modern life after many years in prison. Amazed and hurt by the treatment of the elderly in the 1980s, frustrated with their inability to find something worthwhile to do, they begin to plan one last heist. Tailor-made for Lancaster and Douglas, who are wonderful. Script becomes cliched at end. **103m/C VHS.** Burt Lancaster, Kirk Douglas, Charles Durning, Eli Wallach, Jake Steinfeld, Dana Carvey, Alexis Smith, Darlanne Fluegel, Billy Barty, Monty Ash; *D:* Jeff Kanew; *W:* James Orr, Jim Cruickshank; *M:* James Newton Howard.

Tough Guys Don't Dance 🦴🦴½ **1987 (R)** Mailer directed this self-satiric mystery thriller from his own novel. A writer may have committed murder—but he can't remember. So he searches for the truth among various friends, enemies, lovers, and cohorts. **110m/C VHS.** Ryan O'Neal, Isabella Rossellini, Wings Hauser, Debra Sandlund, John Bedford Lloyd, Lawrence Tierney, Clarence Williams III, Penn Jillette, Frances Fisher; *D:* Norman Mailer; *W:* Norman Mailer; *C:* John Bailey; *M:* Angelo Badalamenti. Golden Raspberries '87: Worst Director (Mailer).

Tough Kid & 1939 A bad kid with gang connections attempts to shield his boxer brother from corruption at the hands of the same gang. Poor production all around. **61m/B VHS.** Frankie Darro, Dick Purcell, Judith Allen, Lillian Elliot; ***D:*** Howard Bretherton.

Tough to Handle &½ 1937 ...And no picnic to watch, either. A reporter cracks a criminal racket that rips off lottery sweepstakes winners. A laughably inept production. **58m/B VHS.** Frankie Darro, Kane Richmond, Phyllis Fraser, Harry Worth; ***D:*** S. Roy Luby.

Tougher Than Leather & 1988 (R) The rap triumvirate battles criminals, vigilante-style, in their home neighborhood. Poorly executed and exploitative fare. **92m/C VHS.** Run DMC, The Beastie Boys, Slick Rick, Richard Edson, Jenny Lumet; ***D:*** Rick Rubin.

Toughlove && 1985 The parents of a juvenile delinquent organize a tough parental philosophy and a support group for other parents having a difficult time with their teens. **100m/C VHS.** Lee Remick, Bruce Dern, Piper Laurie, Louise Latham, Dana Elcar, Jason Patric, Eric Schiff, Dedee Pfeiffer; ***D:*** Glenn Jordan. **TV**

Touki Bouki && *Journey of the Hyena* 1973 Feeling alienated from their African society, Mory and Anta see freedom in the flashy consumerism of European culture and embark on a quest to meet happiness in Paris. A Bonnie & Clyde-like story symbolizing Africa's advancement toward a technological civilization. In Wolof with English subtitles. **85m/C VHS.** ***D:*** Djibril Diop Mambety.

Tour of Duty &&½ 1987 Follows the trials that the members of an American platoon face daily during the Vietnam war. Pilot for the TV series. **93m/C VHS.** Terence Knox, Stephen Caffrey, Joshua Maurer, Ramon Franco; ***D:*** Bill W.L. Norton. **TV**

Tourist Trap & 1979 (PG) While traveling through the desert, a couple's car has a flat. A woman's voice lures the man into an abandoned gas station, where he discovers that the voice belongs to a mannequin. Or is it? Not very interesting or suspenseful. **90m/C VHS, DVD, Wide.** Tanya Roberts, Chuck Connors, Robin Sherwood, Jocelyn Jones, Jon Van Ness, Dawn Jeffory, Keith McDermott; ***D:*** David Schmoeller; ***W:*** David Schmoeller; ***C:*** Nicholas Josef von Sternberg; ***M:*** Pino Donaggio.

Tourist Trap &&½ 1998 Frustrated banker George Piper (Stern) decides his family needs "together" time. So he buys an RV and shanghais his workaholic wife (Hagerty) and rebellious kids into a vacation. George decides to retrace the footsteps of his famous ancestor Jeremiah Piper and leads his brood into all kinds of comic misadventures. **89m/C VHS.** Daniel Stern, Julie Hagerty, Margot Finley, Blair Slater, Paul Giamatti, David Rasche, Ken Tremblett; ***D:*** Richard Benjamin. **VIDEO**

Tournament &&½ *Le Tournoi dans la Cite* 1929 Renoir's second-to-last silent film, in which Protestants and Catholics joust out their differences in era of Catherine de Medici. **90m/B VHS.** *FR* Aldo Nadi; ***D:*** Jean Renoir.

Tous les Matins du Monde &&& *All the Mornings of the World* 1992 Haunting tale of two 17th century French baroque composers and their relationship with each other and their music. Gerard Depardieu plays Marin Marais who eventually becomes a court composer at Versailles. As a young man, he studies under Sainte Colombe, a private and soulful musician, about whom little is known even today. Depardieu's son Guillaume (in his film debut) plays the young Marais, who startles the quiet Sainte Colombe home and has an affair with one of his daughters (Brochet). Filmmaker Corneau lends a quiet austere tone which parallels the life and music of Sainte Colombe. In French with English subtitles. **114m/C VHS.** *FR* Gerard Depardieu, Guillaume Depardieu, Jean-Pierre Marielle, Anne Brochet, Caroline Sihol, Carole Richert, Violaine Lacroix, Nadege Teron, Miriam Boyer, Michel Bouquet; ***D:*** Alain Corneau; ***W:*** Pascal Quignard, Alain Corneau; ***C:*** Yves Angelo; ***M:*** Jordi Savall. Cesar '92: Cinematog., Director (Corneau), Film, Support. Actress (Brochet), Score.

Toute Une Nuit &&& *All Night Long* 1982 Assorted people stumble melodramatically in and out of one another's lives on steamy summer night in Brussels. Fine combination of avant-garde technique and narrative. In French with English subtitles. **90m/C VHS.** *BE FR* Aurore Clement, Tcheky Karyo, Veronique Silver, Angelo Abazoglou, Natalia Ackerman; ***D:*** Chantal Akerman; ***W:*** Andra Akers.

Toward the Terra && 1980 In the distant future mankind is forced to evacuate Earth and settles on the planet Atarakusha. Society ruthlessly suppresses anything which could destabalize it in an effort to prevent the mistakes which destroyed the Earth. The most destablizing presence is the MU, a new race with incredible mental powers, who are ruthlessly hunted and eliminated. But the leader of the MU reaches out to a human with his own inexplicable powers to aid in establishing a new world. In Japanese with subtitles. **112m/C VHS.** *JP*

Tower of Evil woof! *Horror on Snape Island; Beyond the Fog* 1972 (R) Anthropologists and treasure hunters unite in search of Phoenician hoard on Snape Island. Suddenly, inanimate bodies materialize. Seems the island's single inhabitant liked it quiet. Cult favorite despite uneven performances. So bad it's not bad. **86m/C VHS, DVD, Wide.** *GB* Bryant Halliday, Jill Haworth, Jack Watson, Mark Edwards, George Coulouris; ***D:*** James O'Connolly; ***W:*** James O'Connolly; ***C:*** Desmond Dickinson; ***M:*** Kenneth V. Jones.

The Tower of London &&½ 1939 Tells the story of Richard III (Rathbone), the English monarch who brutally executed the people who tried to get in his way to the throne. This melodrama was considered extremely graphic for its time, and some of the torture scenes had to be cut before it was released. **93m/B VHS.** Basil Rathbone, Boris Karloff, Barbara O'Neil, Ian Hunter, Vincent Price, Nan Grey, John Sutton, Leo G. Carroll, Miles Mander; ***D:*** Rowland V. Lee; ***W:*** Robert N. Lee; ***C:*** George Robinson; ***M:*** Hans J. Salter, Frank Skinner.

Tower of London && 1962 A deranged lord (Price) murdering his way to the throne of England is eventually crowned Richard III. Sophisticated and well-made Poe-like thriller. More interesting as historic melodrama than as horror film. A remake of the 1939 version starring Basil Rathbone, in which Price played a supporting role. **79m/B VHS.** Vincent Price, Michael Pate, Joan Freeman, Robert Brown, Sandra Knight, Justice Watson; ***D:*** Roger Corman; ***W:*** Leo Gordon, F. Amos Powell, James B. Gordon; ***C:*** Arch R. Dalzell; ***M:*** Michael Anderson.

Tower of Screaming Virgins & 1968 The Queen of France maintains a tower in which she has her lovers killed—after she makes love to them. An extremely loose adaptation of a Dumas novel; with English subtitles. **89m/C VHS, 8mm.** *GE* Terry Torday, Jean Piat.

Tower of Terror &½ 1942 (NC-17) Woman escapes from a German concentration camp and takes refuge in a lighthouse. The proprietor sees in her an uncanny resemblance to his late wife, whom he killed, and soon plots to do away with her. Story hampered by poor acting. **62m/B VHS.** *GB* Wilfred Lawson, Movita, Michael Rennie, Morland Graham, John Longden, George Woodbridge; ***D:*** Lawrence Huntington.

Tower of Terror &&½ 1997 This Disney TV movie really isn't very scary and is related to the thrill ride located at Disney World. Disgraced reporter Buzzy (Guttenberg) and his niece (Dunst) investigate the 60-year-old murder of the family of a popular 1930s child star in a supposedly haunted hotel. **89m/C VHS.** Steve Guttenberg, Kirsten Dunst, Nia Peeples; ***D:*** D.J. MacHale. **TV**

The Towering Inferno && 1974 (PG) Raging blaze engulfs the world's tallest skyscraper on the night of its glamorous dedication ceremonies. Allen had invented the disaster du jour genre two years earlier with "The Poseidon Adventure." Features a new but equally noteworthy cast. ♫We May Never Love Like This Again. **165m/C VHS, DVD, Wide.** Steve McQueen, Paul Newman, William Holden, Faye Dunaway, Fred Astaire, Jennifer Jones, Richard Chamberlain, Susan Blakely, O.J. Simpson, Robert Vaughn, Robert Wagner; ***D:*** John Guillermin, Irwin Allen; ***W:*** Stirling Silliphant; ***C:*** Joseph Biroc, Fred W. Koenekamp; ***M:*** John Williams. Oscars '74: Cinematog., Film Editing, Song ("We May Never Love Like This Again"); British Acad. '75: Support. Actor (Astaire); Golden Globes '75: Support. Actor (Astaire).

Town and Country & 2001 (R) Yep, it's as bad as you've heard. The oft-delayed and much-discussed romantic-comedy features characters you don't care about (rich Manhattanites with more money than they need) in situations that've been done to death (bed-hopping amidst middle age angst and closet-hiding). Shandling and Beatty are the cad husbands who decide to risk 25-year marriages in the name of fighting boredom. Keaton and Hawn are the revenge-fueled wives. All are upstaged by Heston and Seldes as the gun-toting, foul-mouthed parents of one of Beatty's dalliances (McDowell). **104m/C VHS, DVD, Wide.** *US* Warren Beatty, Diane Keaton, Goldie Hawn, Andie MacDowell, Jenna Elfman, Garry Shandling, Charlton Heston, Marian Seldes, Tricia Vessey, Josh Hartnett, Nastassia Kinski, Katharine Towne, Buck Henry; ***D:*** Peter Chelsom; ***W:*** Buck Henry, Michael Laughlin; ***C:*** William A. Fraker; ***M:*** Rolfe Kent.

A Town Called Hell & *A Town Called Bastard* 1972 (R) Two men hold an entire town hostage while looking for "Aguila," the Mexican revolutionary. Greed, evil, and violence take over. Shot in Spain. Whatever you call it, just stay out of it. **95m/C VHS.** *GB SP* Robert Shaw, Stella Stevens, Martin Landau, Telly Savalas, Fernando Rey; ***D:*** Robert Parrish.

A Town Has Turned to Dust &½ 1998 Lame remake of a 1958 Rod Serling script for "Playhouse 90." Serling's story was set in the old west; this version goes for sci-fi and a futuristic desert town called Carbon run by mob boss Perlman who controls the water supply and the main industry, which is mining. But when Perlman hangs an innocent man, he finally provoking drunken sheriff Lang to take action. **91m/C VHS, DVD.** Ron Perlman, Stephen Lang, Gabriel Olds, Judy Collins; ***W:*** Rod Serling. **CABLE**

A Town Like Alice &&½ 1985 An Australian miniseries based on a novel by Nevil Shute. The story follows women prisoners of war during WWII. Jean Paget is a British prisoner in the camps of Malaya when she meets and falls in love with a fellow prisoner, the rugged Australian, Joe. Separated by their captors, they reunite years later and try to see if their love has survived. Remake of a 1951 film of the same name that is also known as "Rape of Malaya." **301m/C VHS.** *AU* Bryan Brown, Helen Morse, Gordon Jackson; ***D:*** David Stevens. **TV**

Town That Dreaded Sundown &&½ 1976 (R) A mad killer is on the loose in a small Arkansas town. Based on a true story, this famous 1946 murder spree remains an unsolved mystery. **90m/C VHS.** Ben Johnson, Andrew Prine, Dawn Wells, Jimmy Clem, Charles B. Pierce; ***D:*** Charles B. Pierce; ***W:*** Earl E. Smith; ***C:*** Jim Roberson.

Town without Pity &&½ *Stadt ohne Mitleid* 1961 Though the subject of this courtroom drama remains far too timely, its treatment is dated in some key scenes. Of course, being 40 years old will do that to a movie. In 1960, four American GIs (Blake, Jaeckel, Sutton, Sondock) stationed in Germany are accused of raping a local girl, Karin (Kaufmann). Lawyer Steve Garrett (Douglas) is brought in to defend them and elects to put the young woman on trial and on the stand. Gripping courtroom tale never fails to deliver dramatic punch. Based on the Manfred Gregor novel "The Verdict." Gene Pitney had his biggest hit with the Academy Award-nominated title song. **103m/B VHS, DVD.** *GE* Kirk Douglas, E.G. Marshall, Robert (Bobby) Blake, Richard Jaeckel, Frank Sutton, Alan Gifford, Barbara Rutting, Christine Kaufmann, Mal Sondock; ***D:*** Gottfried Reinhardt; ***W:*** Silvia Reinhardt, Georg Hurdalek; ***C:*** Kurt Hasse; ***M:*** Dimitri Tiomkin. Golden Globes '61: Song ("Town without Pity").

The Toxic Avenger &½ 1986 (R) Tongue-in-cheek, cult fave has 98-pound weakling Melvin (Torgl) fall into barrel of toxic waste to emerge as Toxie (Cohen), a lumbering, bloodthirsty hulk of sludge and mire. He falls for blind babe Sara (Maranda) and sets out to do good (and get revenge). Set in the legendary city of TromaVille. Billed as "The first Super-Hero from New Jersey." Followed by: "The Toxic Avenger, Part 2;" "The Toxic Avenger, Part 3: The Last Temptation of Toxie;" and "Citizen Toxie: The Toxic Avenger, Part 4." **90m/C VHS, DVD.** Mitchell Cohen, Andree Maranda, Jennifer Baptist, Robert Prichard, Cindy Manion, Mark Torgl, David Weiss; ***D:*** Michael Herz, Lloyd Kaufman; ***W:*** Joe Ritter; ***C:*** James London.

The Toxic Avenger, Part 2 &½ 1989 (R) Sequel to "Toxic Avenger." Hulky slimer targets Japanese corporations that built toxic chemical dump in Tromaville. Followed by "The Toxic Avenger, Part 3: The Last Temptation of Toxie." **90m/C VHS, DVD.** Ron Fazio, Phoebe Legere, Rick Collins, John Altamura, Rikiya Yasuoka, Lisa Gaye, Mayako Katsuragi; ***D:*** Michael Herz, Lloyd Kaufman; ***W:*** Lloyd Kaufman, Gay Partington Terry; ***C:*** James London; ***M:*** Barrie Guard.

The Toxic Avenger, Part 3: The Last Temptation of Toxie &½ 1989 (R) Unemployed superhero is tempted to sell out to greedy capitalists when his cutie Claire needs an eye operation. Also available in an unrated version. **102m/C VHS, DVD.** Ron Fazio, Phoebe Legere, John Altamura, Rick Collins, Lisa Gaye, Jessica Dublin; ***D:*** Michael Herz, Lloyd Kaufman; ***W:*** Gay Partington Terry, Lloyd Kaufman; ***C:*** James London; ***M:*** Christopher De Marco.

The Toy &½ 1982 (PG) Penniless reporter finds himself the new "toy" of the spoiled son of a multimillionaire oil man. Unfortunate casting of Pryor as the toy owned by Gleason, with heavy-handed lecturing about earning friends. Slow and terrible remake of the Pierre Richard comedy "Le Jouet." **102m/C VHS, DVD, Wide.** Richard Pryor, Jackie Gleason, Ned Beatty, Wilfrid Hyde-White, Scott Schwartz; ***D:*** Richard Donner; ***W:*** Carol Sobieski; ***C:*** Laszlo Kovacs; ***M:*** Patrick Williams.

Toy Soldiers &½ 1984 (R) A group of college students are held for ransom in a war-torn Central American country. When they escape, they join forces with a seasoned mercenary who leads them as a vigilante force. **85m/C VHS.** Cleavon Little, Jason Miller, Tim Robbins, Tracy Scoggins; ***D:*** David Fisher.

Toy Soldiers && 1991 (R) This unlikely action tale stops short of being laughable but still has a fair share of silliness. South American narco-terrorists seize an exclusive boys' school. The mischievous students turn their talent for practical jokes to resistance-fighting. Orbach has an uncredited cameo. Based on a novel by William P. Kennedy. **104m/C VHS, 8mm.** Sean Astin, Wil Wheaton, Keith Coogan, Andrew Divoff, Denholm Elliott, Louis Gossett Jr., Shawn (Michael) Phelan; ***Cameos:*** Jerry Orbach; ***D:*** Dan Petrie Jr.; ***W:*** Dan Petrie Jr.; ***C:*** Thomas Burstyn; ***M:*** Robert Folk.

Toy Story &&&& 1995 (G) First feature length, wholly computer animated film confirms what we suspected all along—toys do have lives of their own when we're not around. Pull-string cowboy Woody (Hanks), as favorite toy, presides over his fellow playthings in Andy's room. Enter new toy on the block, Buzz Lightyear (Allen), a space ranger action figure who thinks he's real. Jealous Woody and his delusional, high-tech companion soon find themselves in the outside world, where they must join forces to survive. Funny, intelligent script and voice characterizations that rival many live-action movies in depth and emotion. All this, and Don Rickles berating an actual hockey puck. **84m/C VHS, DVD, Wide.** ***D:*** John Lasseter; ***W:*** Joss Whedon, Joel Cohen, Alec Sokolow; ***M:*** Randy Newman; ***V:*** Tom Hanks, Tim Allen, Annie

Potts, John Ratzenberger, Wallace Shawn, Jim Varney, Don Rickles, John Morris, R. Lee Ermey, Laurie Metcalf, Erik von Detten.

Toy Story 2 🦴🦴🦴🦴 **1999 (G)** Woody is kidnapped by a greedy toy collector and finds out that he was the star of a popular '50s children's show (think Howdy Doody) with a posse of his own. Buzz and the other denizens of Andy's room set out to save him, and in the process meet up with Buzz's arch-nemesis Emperor Zurg. All of the original cast members return to their now-classic characters, and the plentiful new characters, in-jokes, and tributes to other movies keep this installment just as entertaining for kids and adults as the original was. This one actually has more depth than the first, dealing with issues such as mortality and the meaning of (a toy's) life. Watch for the outtakes reel while the final credits roll. **92m/C VHS, DVD, Wide.** ***D:*** John Lasseter, Lee Unkrich, Ash Bannon; ***W:*** Ash Bannon, Rita Hsiao, Doug Chamberlin, Chris Webb, Andrew Stanton; ***M:*** Randy Newman; ***V:*** Tom Hanks, Tim Allen, Joan Cusack, Don Rickles, John Ratzenberger, Annie Potts, Wayne Knight, Laurie Metcalf, Jim Varney, Estelle Harris, Kelsey Grammer, Wallace Shawn, John Morris, R. Lee Ermey, Jodi Benson, Jonathan Harris, Joe Ranft, Andrew Stanton, Robert Goulet. Golden Globes '00: Film—Mus./Comedy.

Toys 🦴½ **1992 (PG-13)** Diappointingly earnest comedy about Leslie (Williams), the whimsical son of a toy manufacturer who must fight to keep the playful spirit of the factory alive after it passes into the hands of his deranged uncle (Gambon). This uncle is a general who attempts to transform the factory into an armaments plant. Leslie receives assistance in this battle from his sister Alsatia (Cusack) and his cousin Patrick (L.L. Cool J). Flat characters; generally falls short by trying too hard to send a message to viewers about the folly of war. Does have extremely vivid and intriguing visuals and special effects. **121m/C VHS, DVD, Wide.** Robin Williams, Joan Cusack, Michael Gambon, L.L. Cool J., Robin Wright Penn, Donald O'Connor; ***D:*** Barry Levinson; ***W:*** Valerie Curtin, Barry Levinson; ***C:*** Adam Greenberg.

Toys in the Attic 🦴🦴½ **1963** A man returns to his home in New Orleans with his child bride, where they will live with his two impoverished, spinster sisters. Toned-down version of the Lillian Hellman play. **88m/B VHS.** Dean Martin, Geraldine Page, Yvette Mimieux, Wendy Hiller, Gene Tierney, Nan Martin, Larry Gates, Frank Silvera; ***D:*** George Roy Hill; ***W:*** James Poe; ***C:*** Joseph Biroc.

Trace of Stones 🦴🦴 *Spur der Steine* **1966** Building construction foreman Hannes Balla benevolently rules over a mammoth building site where he's supported by his workers because things run smoothly. Until, that is, a young female engineer, Kati Klee, and the new Party Secretary Werner Horrath show up. Balla soon isn't the top man anymore and, what's worse, he finds himself in a romantic triangle with Kati and Horrath. Based on the novel by Erik Neutsch. German with subtitles. **138m/B VHS.** *GE* Manfred Krug, Krystyna Stypulkowska, Eberhard Esche; ***D:*** Frank Beyer; ***W:*** Karl-Georg Egel; ***C:*** Gunter Marczinkowski.

Traces of Red 🦴🦴 **1992 (R)** Set in affluent Palm Beach, and filled with dead bodies, colorful suspects, and red herrings. The complex plot, often so serious it's funny, leads viewers through a convoluted series of events. Cop Jack Dobson (Belushi) is found dead in the opening scene; in homage to "Sunset Boulevard," his corpse acts as the narrator, a vehicle which unfortunately doesn't work as well here. He promises to recount the events leading up to his death which circle around a series of murders, and the people in his life who are possible suspects. Although Belushi's performance is average, Goldwyn, as Dobson's partner, shows off the talent he displayed in "Ghost." **105m/C VHS.** James Belushi, Lorraine Bracco, Tony Goldwyn, William Russ, Michelle Joyner, Joe Lisi, Jim Piddock; ***D:*** Andy Wolk; ***W:*** Jim Piddock; ***C:*** Tim Suhrstedt; ***M:*** Graeme Revell.

Track of the Moonbeast 🦴🦴 **1976** An American Indian uses mythology to capture the Moonbeast, a lizard-like creature that is roaming the deserts of New Mexico. **90m/C VHS.** Chase Cordell, Donna Leigh Drake; ***D:*** Richard Ashe.

Track of the Vampire 🦴½ *Blood Bath* **1966** Half an hour of leftover footage from a Yugoslavian vampire movie stuck into the story of a California painter who kills his models. Gripping and atmospheric, but disjointed. **80m/B VHS.** *YU* William Campbell, Jonathan Haze, Sid Haig, Marissa Mathes, Lori Saunders, Sandra Knight; ***D:*** Stephanie Rothman, Jack Hill.

Track 29 🦴½ **1988 (R)** A confusing black comedy about a lonely woman, her husband who has a model train fetish, and a stranger who claims to be her son. Filmed in North Carolina. **90m/C VHS.** Theresa Russell, Gary Oldman, Christopher Lloyd, Colleen Camp, Sandra Bernhard, Seymour Cassel, Leon Rippy, Vance Colvig; ***D:*** Nicolas Roeg; ***W:*** Dennis Potter.

Tracked 🦴🦴 *Dogboys* **1998** Prisoner Julian Taylor (Cain) is sent to the patrol-dog training detail and discovers that the twisted department head (Brown) "rents" out his dogs and prisoners to hunters who want human prey. Carrere is the beautiful D.A. who investigates the rash of inmate deaths and discovers Julian is the next quarry. **92m/C VHS.** Bryan Brown, Dean Cain, Tia Carrere, Ken James, Von Flores, Richard Chevolleau, Sean McCann; ***D:*** Ken Russell; ***W:*** David Taylor; ***C:*** Jamie Thompson; ***M:*** John Altman. **CABLE**

The Tracker 🦴🦴½ *Dead or Alive* **1988** HBO western about a retired gunman/tracker who must again take up arms. His college-educated son joins him as he searches for a murdering religious fanatic. Fairly decent for the genre. **102m/C VHS, DVD, Wide.** Kris Kristofferson, Scott Wilson, Mark Moses, David Huddleston, John Quade, Don Swayze, Brynn Thayer; ***D:*** John Guillermin; ***M:*** Sylvester Levay. **CABLE**

The Trackers 🦴½ **1971** A frontier man searches for the people who kidnapped his daughter and killed his son. He is joined by a cocky black tracker. Borgnine brings strength to his character as the rancher seeking revenge. **73m/C VHS.** Sammy Davis Jr., Ernest Borgnine, Julie Adams, Connie Kreski, Jim Davis; ***D:*** Earl Bellamy. **TV**

Tracks 🦴½ **1976 (R)** Vietnam veteran accompanies the body of a buddy on a long train ride home. He starts suffering flashbacks from the war and begins to think some of the passengers are out to get him. **90m/C VHS.** Dennis Hopper, Dean Stockwell, Taryn Power, Zack Norman, Michael Emil, Barbara Flood; ***D:*** Henry Jaglom; ***W:*** Henry Jaglom; ***C:*** Paul Glickman.

Tracks of a Killer 🦴🦴 **1995 (R)** David (Brolin) and Clair (LeBrock) Hawker are vacationing at their isolated winter retreat with corporate climber Patrick (Larsen) and his wife Bella (Taylor). When Bella is killed on David's snowmobile in an accident-that's-no-accident, it turns out Patrick is after David's company in the worst possible way. **100m/C VHS.** Kelly Le Brock, James Brolin, Wolf Larson, Courtney Taylor, George Touliatos; ***D:*** Harvey Frost; ***W:*** Michael Cooney; ***C:*** Bruce Worrall; ***M:*** Barron Abramovitch.

Trade Off 🦴🦴 **1995 (R)** Beautiful, unhappily married Jackie (Russell) seduces equally miserable married businessman Thomas (Baldwin) and jokes about getting rid of their respective spouses. Then Thomas' wife is killed in a car crash and Thomas learns Jackie caused the "accident." He should have watched "Strangers on a Train" to see where trading murders can get you. **92m/C VHS.** Theresa Russell, Adam Baldwin, Megan Gallagher, Barry Primus, Pat Skipper; ***D:*** Andrew Lane.

Trade Secrets 🦴🦴 **199?** Special investigator Jerry Morrison is assigned to probe the mysterious death of an heiress to a wine fortune. His investigation leads to the secrets and private fantasies of the woman's family and friends. **91m/C VHS.** Sam Waterston, Marisa Berenson, Lauren Hutton, Arielle Dombasle; ***D:*** Claude Feraldo; ***W:*** Claude Feraldo.

Trader Horn 🦴🦴½ **1931** Early talkie was the first Hollywood picture to be filmed in Africa. Carey and Renaldo are traders who tangle with a native tribe while searching for the long-lost daughter of a missionary, who turns out to be a tribal goddess. Based on a novel by Alfred Aloysius Horn and Ethelreda Lewis. Boring remake in 1973. **105m/B VHS.** Harry Carey Sr., Duncan Renaldo, Edwina Booth, Sir C. Aubrey Smith, Mutia Omoolu, Olive Carey; ***D:*** Woodbridge S. Van Dyke; ***W:*** Cyril Hume, Richard Schayer, Dale Van Every, John Thomas Neville; ***C:*** Clyde De Vinna.

Trader Tom of the China Seas **1954** A young island trader and a shipwrecked beauty get involved in espionage while helping the UN to safeguard the Asian corridor. A 12-part serial on two cassettes. **167m/B VHS.** Harry Lauter, Aline Towne, Lyle Talbot, Fred Graham.

Trading Favors 🦴🦴 **1997 (R)** Seductress Alex (Arquette) talks eager high-school student Lincoln (Gummersall) into giving her a ride, not knowing she's trying to escape from her violent boyfriend (Greene). But that's only the beginning of the trouble. **103m/C VHS.** Rosanna Arquette, Devon Gummersall, George Dzundza, Peter Greene, Julie Ariola, Alanna Ubach, Jason Hervey, Craig Nigh, Mary Jo Catlett, Lin Shaye, Richard Riehle, William Frankfather, Frances Fisher, Chad Lowe; ***D:*** Sondra Locke; ***W:*** Timothy Albaugh, Tag Mendillo; ***C:*** Jerry Sidell; ***M:*** Jeff Rona.

Trading Hearts 🦴🦴 **1987 (PG)** Over-the-hill baseball player falls for an unsuccessful singer and single mom at a Florida training camp set in the 1950s. **88m/C VHS.** Beverly D'Angelo, Raul Julia, Jenny Lewis, Parris Buckner, Robert Gwaltney; ***D:*** Neil Leifer; ***W:*** Frank Deford.

Trading Mom 🦴🦴½ **1994 (PG)** Harried single parent Spacek is erased from the lives of her three kids, who decide they want a parent who's more fun. So, thanks to some magic, they head off to the Mommy Mart to try out a trio of bizarre choices. This gives Spacek a chance at three more roles before the kids come to their senses. Based on "The Mommy Market" by Nancy Brelis; directorial debut for daughter Tia. **82m/C VHS.** Sissy Spacek, Anna Chlumsky, Aaron Michael Metchik, Asher Metchik, Maureen Stapleton; ***D:*** Tia Brelis; ***W:*** Tia Brelis; ***M:*** David Kitay.

Trading Places 🦴🦴½ **1983 (R)** Two elderly businessmen wager that environment is more important than heredity in creating a successful life, using a rich nephew and an unemployed street hustler as guinea pigs. Curtis is winning as a hooker-with-a-heart-of-gold who helps the hapless Aykroyd. Oft-told tale succeeds thanks to strong cast. Murphy's second screen appearance. **118m/C VHS, 8mm, Wide.** Eddie Murphy, Dan Aykroyd, Jamie Lee Curtis, Ralph Bellamy, Don Ameche, Denholm Elliott, Paul Gleason, James Belushi, Al Franken, Tom Davis, Giancarlo Esposito, Bill Cobbs, Stephen Stucker; ***D:*** John Landis; ***W:*** Herschel Weingrod, Timothy Harris; ***M:*** Elmer Bernstein. British Acad. '83: Support. Actor (Elliott), Support. Actress (Curtis).

Traffic 🦴🦴½ **1971** Eccentric auto designer Monsieur Hulot tries to transport his latest contraption from Paris to Amsterdam for an international auto show. As usual, everything goes wrong. Tati's last feature film and his fifth to feature Hulot. French with subtitles. **89m/C VHS.** *FR* Jacques Tati, Maria Kimberly, Marcel Fraval; ***D:*** Jacques Tati; ***W:*** Jacques Lagrange, Jacques Tati; ***C:*** Eddy van der Enden, Marcel Weiss; ***M:*** Charles Dumont.

Traffic 🦴🦴🦴½ **2000 (R)** Based on the 1990 British miniseries "Traffik," Soderbergh's film has three loosely intertwined stories about the drug trade: Supreme Court Justice Douglas is appointed as head of the National Drug Task Force but learns his own daughter is a heroin addict; San Diego socialite wife Zeta-Jones learns the drug trade when her drug lord hubby gets busted; and Mexican border cop Del Toro works on his power base. Soderbergh takes on a large, complex subject with a large, complex film populated by a large, uniformly excellent cast. The outcomes of the various storylines may not end happily or neatly (just like in real life), but the characters and ideas explored along the way are compelling. **147m/C VHS, DVD, Wide.** Michael Douglas, Catherine Zeta-Jones, Benicio Del Toro, Dennis Quaid, Benjamin Bratt, Albert Finney, Amy Irving, Don Cheadle, Luis Guzman, Steven Bauer, James Brolin, Erika Christensen, Clifton (Gonzalez) Collins Jr., Miguel Ferrer, Tomas Milian, D.W. Moffett, Marisol Padilla Sanchez, Peter Riegert, Jacob Vargas, Rena Sofer, Stacy Travis, Salma Hayek, Topher Grace, Beau Holden, Enrique Murciano; ***D:*** Steven Soderbergh; ***W:*** Stephen Gaghan; ***C:*** Steven Soderbergh; ***M:*** Cliff Martinez. Oscars '00: Adapt. Screenplay, Director (Soderbergh), Film Editing, Support. Actor (Del Toro); British Acad. '00: Adapt. Screenplay, Support. Actor (Del Toro); Golden Globes '01: Screenplay, Support. Actor (Del Toro); L.A. Film Critics '00: Director (Soderbergh); Natl. Bd. of Review '00: Director (Soderbergh); N.Y. Film Critics '00: Director (Soderbergh), Film, Support. Actor (Del Toro); Natl. Soc. Film Critics '00: Director (Soderbergh), Support. Actor (Del Toro); Screen Actors Guild '00: Actor (Del Toro), Cast; Writers Guild '00: Adapt. Screenplay; Broadcast Film Critics '00: Adapt. Screenplay, Director (Soderbergh).

Traffic in Souls 🦴🦴🦴 **1913** A silent melodrama dealing with white slavery. Immigrants and gullible country girls are lured into brothels where they are trapped with no hope of escape until, in a hail of bullets, the police raid the dens of vice and rescue them. **74m/B VHS.** Matt Moore, Jane Gail, William Welsh; ***D:*** George Tucker.

Traffic Jam 🦴🦴½ *Jutai* **1991** A light comedy about a Japanese family's attempt to travel on a holiday weekend. Tokyo couple and their two young children decide to visit the husband's family who happen to live on a distant island. Naturally, traffic's horrendous, they have very little time, and things continuously go wrong. Japanese with subtitles. **108m/C VHS.** *JP* Kenichi Hagiwara, Hitomi Kuroki, Ayako Takarada, Shingo Yazawa, Eiji Okada; ***D:*** Mitsuo Kurotsuchi.

Traffik 🦴🦴🦴 **1990** A tense, unnerving look at the international world of heroin smuggling. The British drama follows the lives of three men involved in the drug trade: a farmer in the poppy fields of Pakistan, a drug smuggler in Hamburg, and a Tory cabinet minister who heads his government's anti-drug cabinet and then comes to realize his own daughter is an addict. The basis for Steven Soderbergh's much-lauded 2000 film "Traffic." **360m/C VHS, DVD.** *GB* Lindsay Duncan, Bill Paterson, Jamal Shah, Talat Hussain, Fritz Muller-Scherz, Julia Ormond, Knut Hinz, Feryal Gauhar Shah, Peter Lakenmacher, Vincenzo Benestante; ***D:*** Alastair Reid; ***W:*** Simon Moore; ***C:*** Clive Tickner; ***M:*** Tim Souster. **TV**

The Tragedy of a Ridiculous Man 🦴🦴 *La Tragedia di un Uomo Ridicolo* **1981 (PG)** The missing son of an Italian cheese manufacturer may or may not have been kidnapped by terrorists. Lesser Bertolucci effort may or may not have a point. In Italian with English subtitles. **116m/C VHS.** *IT* Ugo Tognazzi, Anouk Aimee, Victor Cavallo, Ricky Tognazzi, Laura Morante; ***D:*** Bernardo Bertolucci; ***W:*** Bernardo Bertolucci; ***C:*** Carlo Di Palma; ***M:*** Ennio Morricone. Cannes '81: Actor (Tognazzi).

Tragedy of Flight 103: The Inside Story 🦴🦴🦴 **1991 (PG)** Dramatization of the events surrounding the destruction of Pan Am flight 103 over Lockerbie, Scotland, due to a terrorist-planted bomb. **89m/C VHS.** Ned Beatty, Peter Boyle, Vincent Gardenia, Timothy West, Michael Wincott, Harry Ditson, Aharon Ipale, John Shrapnel; ***D:*** Leslie Woodhead.

Trahir 🦴🦴🦴 *Betrayal* **1993** In 1948 Romania journalist George Vlaicu (Leysen) writes a controversial article on the death of democracy in his country and is imprisoned for 11 years. In 1959 he's offered a deal, go free as long as he talks weekly to a police inspector (Repan). He begins a new career as a poet and marries his former typist, Laura (Perrier), but after a tragedy learns that his meetings with the inspector aren't as innocuous as they've seemed. Excellent performances and a cold look at how a police state is able to control its artists and writers. Filmed primarily in Romania. Director Mihaileanu's first feature film. French with subtitles. **104m/C VHS.** *FR SI SP RO* Johan Leysen, Mireille Perrier, Alexandru Repan, Razvan Vasilescu, Maia Morgenstern, Radu Beligan; ***D:*** Radu Mihaileanu; ***W:*** Laurent Moussard, Radu Mihaileanu; ***M:*** Temistocle Popa. Montreal World Film Fest. '93: Actor (Leysen), Film.

Trail Beyond 🦴½ **1934** A cowboy and his sidekick go on the trek to the northwest to find a girl and a gold mine. **57m/B VHS, DVD.** John Wayne, Noah Beery Sr., Verna Hillie, Noah Beery Jr.; ***D:*** Robert North Bradbury; ***W:*** Lindsley Parsons; ***C:*** Archie Stout.

Trail Drive 🦴 **1935** Adventures of a cowboy during a big cattle drive. **63m/B VHS.** Ken Maynard.

Trail of a Serial Killer 🦴🦴 **1998 (R)** FBI agent Jason Enola (Penn) and detective Brad Abraham (Madsen) team up to find a serial killer leaving a trail of dismembered corpses. **95m/C VHS, DVD.** Christopher Penn, Michael Madsen, Jennifer Dale, Chad McQueen; ***D:*** Damian Lee. **VIDEO**

Trail of Robin Hood 🦴🦴½ **1950** Rogers sees to it that poor families get Christmas trees, in spite of the fact that a big business wants to raise the prices. Features a number of western stars, including Holt playing himself. **67m/C VHS.** Roy Rogers, Penny Edwards, Gordon Jones, Jack Holt, Emory Parnell, Rex Allen, Allan "Rocky" Lane, Clifton Young, Monte Hale, Kermit Maynard, Tom (George Duryea) Keene, Ray Corrigan, William Farnum; ***D:*** William Witney.

Trail of Terror 🦴 **1935** G-Man poses as an escaped convict to get the goods on a gang. **60m/B VHS.** Bob Steele, Beth Marion, Forrest Taylor, Charles "Blackie" King, Lloyd Ingraham, Charles French; ***D:*** Robert North Bradbury.

Trail of the Hawk 🦴 **1937** Saga of frontier justice and love on the plains. **50m/B VHS.** Yancey Lane, Betty Jordan, Dick(ie) Jones; ***D:*** Edward Dmytryk.

The Trail of the Lonesome Pine 🦴🦴🦴 **1936** The first outdoor film to be shot in three-color Technicolor. Two backwoods Kentucky clans, the Tolliver and the Falins, have been feuding so long no one remembers what started the fuss. But young engineer Jack Hale (MacMurray) gets stuck in the middle when he comes to build a railroad through the Blue Ridge Mountains. Hale saves the life of Dave Tolliver (Fonda) but Dave's not happy when the city slicker starts mooning over Dave's sister, June (Sidney). And the Falins aren't happy about the railroad, which leads to even more fighting. Based on the novel by John Fox Jr. and previously filmed in 1916 and 1923. **102m/C VHS.** Henry Fonda, Fred MacMurray, Sylvia Sidney, Robert Barrat, Fred Stone, Nigel Bruce, Beulah Bondi, George "Spanky" McFarland, Fuzzy Knight; ***D:*** Henry Hathaway; ***W:*** Grover Jones, Horace McCoy, Harvey Thew; ***C:*** William Howard Greene, Robert C. Bruce.

Trail of the Mounties 🦴 **1947** A Mountie gallops smack into a murdering slew of fur thieves. **41m/B VHS.** Donald (Don "Red") Barry, Robert Lowery, Tom Neal, Russell Hayden.

Trail of the Pink Panther 🦴🦴 **1982 (PG)** The sixth in Sellers' "Pink Panther" series. Inspector Clouseau disappears while he is searching for the diamond known as the Pink Panther. Notable because it was released after Sellers' death, using clips from previous movies to fill in gaps. Followed by "Curse of the Pink Panther." **97m/C VHS.** Peter Sellers, David Niven, Herbert Lom, Capucine, Burt Kwouk, Robert Wagner, Robert Loggia; ***D:*** Blake Edwards; ***W:*** Blake Edwards, Frank Waldman; ***C:*** Dick Bush; ***M:*** Henry Mancini.

Trail of the Silver Spurs 🦴½ **1941** A lone man remaining in a ghost town discovers gold and becomes rich. Part of the "Range Busters" series. **57m/B VHS.** Ray Corrigan, John "Dusty" King, Max Terhune, I. Stanford Jolley, Dorothy Short; ***D:*** S. Roy Luby.

Trail Riders 🦴½ **1942** The Range Busters set a trap to capture a gang of outlaws who killed the son of the town marshal during a bank robbery. Part of the "Range Busters" series. **55m/B VHS.** John "Dusty" King, David Sharpe, Max Terhune, Evelyn Finley, Forrest Taylor, Charles "Blackie" King.

Trail Street 🦴½ **1947** Scott is Bat Masterson, the western hero. He aids the struggle of Kansans as they conquer the land and local ranchers. **84m/B VHS.** Randolph Scott, Robert Ryan, Anne Jeffreys, George "Gabby" Hayes, Madge Meredith, Jason Robards Sr.; ***D:*** Ray Enright.

Trail to San Antone 🦴½ **1947** Gene trades the prairie for the racetrack when he helps out an injured jockey, whom Autry wants to ride for him in the big race. **67m/B VHS.** Gene Autry, Peggy Stewart, Sterling Holloway, William Henry; ***D:*** John English; ***W:*** Jack Natteford; ***C:*** William Bradford.

Trailer, the Movie 🦴🦴 **1999** Goofy experimental comedy combines elements of "Last Action Hero" and "Purple Rose of Cairo." In a black-and-white introduction, two lonely guys (McCrudden and Pope) sneak into a theatre one night and fall in love with two actresses (Hicks and Crigler) they see in a trailer. After the guys are tossed out, they wish their way into a color world where the rules of movies apply. Unfortunately, this well-meaning independent production lacks the wit to make full use of the engaging premise. **101m/C DVD.** Ian McCrudden, Will Pope, Miranda Hicks, Marjorie Crigler; ***D:*** Ian McCrudden; ***C:*** Matthew Uhry.

Trailin' 🦴🦴½ **1921** Mix stars as a cowboy in search of his parentage. Based on the Max Brand story. **58m/B VHS.** Tom Mix, Eva Novak, James Gordon; ***D:*** Lynn F. Reynolds.

Trailing Double Trouble 🦴½ **1940** A corrupt attorney murders a rancher to pursue a business scheme. Three ranch hands kidnap the rancher's orphaned baby to keep her safe from the attorney. The second entry in the "Range Busters" series. **56m/B VHS.** Ray Corrigan, John "Dusty" King, Max Terhune.

Trailing Trouble 🦴½ **1930** Gibson is a cowpoke who gets robbed of the money he received for a cattle sale. When he rescues a Chinese girl from danger she helps him recover the money. He also has to battle a rival for his girlfriend's affections. He should have battled for a better script. **58m/B VHS.** Hoot Gibson, Margaret Quimby, Peter Morrison, Olive Young, William (Bill, Billy) McCall; ***D:*** Arthur Rosson.

The Train 🦴🦴🦴🦴 *Le Train; Il Treno* **1965** During the German occupation of Paris in 1944, a German colonel (Scofield) is ordered to ransack the city of its art treasures and put them on a train bound for Germany. Word gets to the French Resistance who then persuade the train inspector (Lancaster) to sabotage the train. A battle of wills ensues between Scofield and Lancaster as each becomes increasingly obsessed in outwitting the other—though the cost to all turns out to be as irreplaceable as the art itself. Filmed on location in France. Frankenheimer used real locomotives, rather than models, throughout the film, even in the spectacular crash sequences. **133m/C VHS, DVD, Wide.** *FR IT* Burt Lancaster, Paul Scofield, Jeanne Moreau, Michel Simon, Suzanne Flon, Wolfgang Preiss, Albert Remy, Charles Millot, Jacques Marin, Donald O'Brien, Jean-Pierre Zola, Arthur Brauss, Howard Vernon, Richard Munch, Paul Bonifas, Jean-Claude Bercq; ***D:*** John Frankenheimer; ***W:*** Frank Davis, Walter Bernstein, Franklin Coen; ***C:*** Jean Tournier, Walter Wottitz; ***M:*** Maurice Jarre.

The Train Killer 🦴 **1983** A mad Hungarian is bent on destroying the Orient Express. **90m/C VHS.** Michael Sarrazin; ***D:*** Sandor Simo.

Train of Events 🦴🦴½ **1949** An interesting look at lives affected by a train wreck just outside London, taking the form of four short episodes. Three are frankly somber, depressing tales of the ill-fated train driver, a murderer and an escaped prisoner-of-war. The fourth segment is a refreshingly lighthearted piece about romantic jealousies in a traveling orchestra. A precursor to the later swarm of crass disaster movies, except here emphasis is on character over special effects. **89m/B VHS.** Jack Warner, Gladys Henson, Susan Shaw, Patric Doonan, Miles Malleson, Leslie Phillips, Joan Dowling, Laurence Payne, Valerie Hobson, John Clements, Peter Finch, Mary Morris, Laurence Naismith, Michael Hordern; ***D:*** Sidney Cole, Basil Dearden, Charles Crichton.

Train of Life 🦴🦴 *Train de Vie* **1998 (R)** Theatrical fable set in 1941 in a mountainous village shtetl near the Russian border. Schlomo the fool (Abelanski) tells the village elders that the Nazis are on their way. So the Rabbi (Harari) and the villagers decide to construct their own mock deportation train and make their way to Palestine. Mordechai (Rufus) plays the role of the Nazi commandant (a little too well), while the others delegate various roles and the train begins to roll out, with any number of problems along the way. French with subtitles. **103m/C VHS.** *FR* Rufus, Clement Harari, Agathe de la Fontaine, Lionel Abelanski, Michel Muller; ***D:*** Radu Mihaileanu; ***W:*** Radu Mihaileanu; ***C:*** Yorgos Arvanitis, Laurent Dailland; ***M:*** Goran Bregovic.

Train Robbers 🦴🦴 **1973 (PG)** A widow employs the services of three cowboys to help her recover some stolen gold in order to clear her late husband's name. At least that's what she says. **92m/C VHS, Wide.** John Wayne, Ann-Margret, Rod Taylor, Ben Johnson, Christopher George, Ricardo Montalban, Bobby Vinton, Jerry Gatlin; ***D:*** Burt Kennedy; ***W:*** Burt Kennedy; ***C:*** William Clothier.

Train Station Pickups 🦴 **197?** Trashy film about young girls who hook at a local train depot, until something goes wrong. **96m/C VHS.** Marco Knoger, Katja Carrol, Ingeborg Steinbach, Benjamin Carwath; ***D:*** Walter Boos.

Train to Hollywood 🦴🦴🦴 **1986** Marilyn Monroe-obsessed young Polish girl daydreams incessantly as she works on dining car. Funny and surreal. Polish dialogue with English subtitles. **96m/C VHS.** *PL* ***D:*** Radoslaw Piwowarski.

Train to Tombstone 🦴 **1950** A train running from Albuquerque to Tombstone carries a motley mob of the usual characters. **60m/B VHS.** Donald (Don "Red") Barry, Judith Allen, Robert Lowery, Tom Neal; ***D:*** Charles Reisner.

Trained to Kill 🦴½ **1988** Two brothers seek revenge on the mean streets of L.A. **94m/C VHS.** Frank Zagarino, Glen Eaton, Lisa Aliff, Marshall Teague, Robert Z'Dar, Henry Silva, Arlene Golonka, Ron O'Neal, Harold Diamond, Chuck Connors; ***D:*** H. Kaye Dyal; ***W:*** H. Kaye Dyal, Arthur Webb.

Trained to Kill, U.S.A. 🦴½ **1983 (R)** Vietnam veteran relives his war experiences when a gang of terrorists threaten his hometown. **88m/C VHS.** Stephen Sander, Heidi Vaughn, Rockne Tarkington.

Training Day 🦴🦴 **2001 (R)** Until the script finally goes completely off the rails, this cop corruption tale is worth watching for the ferocious performance of Washington alone. He's veteran undercover narc Alonzo Harris, who's been the big dog on the L.A. streets for so long, he's become morally bankrupt and works on the might makes right theory of justice. Opposing him is rookie Jake Hoyt (Hawke), who first wants to be a part of Harris's team and then learns just what it will cost him. Fuqua shot on location so you can definitely feel the grit. **120m/C VHS, DVD, Wide.** *US* Denzel Washington, Ethan Hawke, Scott Glenn, Clifford Curtis, Dr. Dre, Snoop Dogg, Tom Berenger, Harris Yulin, Raymond J. Barry, Charlotte Ayanna, Macy Gray, Eva Mendez, Nicholas Chinlund, Jaime Gomez, Raymond Cruz; ***D:*** Antoine Fuqua; ***W:*** David Ayer; ***C:*** Mauro Fiore; ***M:*** Mark Mancina. Oscars '01: Actor (Washington); L.A. Film Critics '01: Actor (Washington).

Trainspotting 🦴🦴🦴 **1995 (R)** From the same team who offered the violently comedic "Shallow Grave," comes an equally destructive look at a group of Edinburgh junkies and losers. Heroin-user Mark Renton (McGregor) once again decides to get off junk but to do so he has to get away from his friends: knife-wielding psycho Begbie (Carlyle), Sick Boy (Miller), Spud (Bremner), and Tommy (McKidd). He heads for a semi-respectable life in London but Begbie and Spud wind up involving him in a serious money drug deal that spells trouble. Strong fantasy visuals depict drug highs and lows while heavy Scottish accents (and humor) may prove difficult. Based on the 1993 cult novel by Irvine Welsh. Film drew much controversy for supposingly being pro-heroin but the junkie's life is hardly portrayed as being attractive in any way. **94m/C VHS, DVD, Wide.** *GB* Ewan McGregor, Ewen Bremner, Jonny Lee Miller, Robert Carlyle, Kevin McKidd, Kelly Macdonald, Shirley Henderson, Pauline Lynch; ***D:*** Danny Boyle; ***W:*** John Hodge; ***C:*** Brian Tufano. British Acad. '95: Adapt. Screenplay.

The Traitor 🦴½ **1936** Undercover man joins a gang of bandits. **57m/B VHS.** Tim McCoy; ***D:*** Sam Newfield.

Tramp & a Woman 🦴🦴 **1915** Two shorts made for the Essanay Company in 1915 which offer the Little Tramp wooing Purviance in typical Chaplin fashion. Silent with musical score. **45m/B VHS.** Charlie Chaplin, Edna Purviance.

Tramp at the Door 🦴🦴½ **1987** Delightful drama about a wandering, magical man who enters the lives of an embittered family. He helps them sort the skeletons in their closets, and works wonders on their relationships. **81m/C VHS.** Ed McNamara, August Schellenberg, Monique Mercure, Eric Peterson; ***D:*** Allen Kroeker.

Tramplers 🦴 **1966** A rebel father and son split over the hanging of a Yankee during the Civil War. Italian made spaghetti western without much plot and lots of gratuitous gunplay. **103m/C VHS.** *IT* Joseph Cotten, Gordon Scott; ***D:*** Albert Band, Mario Sequi.

Trancers 🦴🦴 *Future Cop* **1984 (PG-13)** A time-traveling cult from the future goes back in time to 1985 to meddle with fate. Only Jack Deth, defender of justice, can save mankind. Low-budget "Blade Runner." Followed by two sequels. **76m/C VHS, DVD.** Tim Thomerson, Michael Stefoni, Helen Hunt, Art LaFleur, Telma Hopkins; ***D:*** Charles Band; ***W:*** Danny Bilson.

Trancers 2: The Return of Jack Deth 🦴 **1990 (R)** Retro cop is back from the future again, but seems to have lost his wit and nerve in between sequels. Ward is miscast and the pacing undermines whatever suspense that might have been. **85m/C VHS.** Tim Thomerson, Helen Hunt, Megan Ward, Biff Manard, Martine Beswick, Jeffrey Combs, Barbara Crampton, Richard Lynch; ***D:*** Charles Band.

Trancers 3: Deth Lives 🦴½ **1992 (R)** In the third film of the "Trancers" series, time-traveling cop Jack Deth fights the deadliest form of government-sponsored Trancer yet—it has a brain. **83m/C VHS.** Tim Thomerson, Melanie Smith, Andrew (Andy) Robinson, Tony Pierce, Dawn Ann Billings, Helen Hunt, Megan Ward, Stephen Macht, Telma Hopkins; ***D:*** C. Courtney Joyner; ***W:*** C. Courtney Joyner; ***M:*** Richard Band.

Trancers 4: Jack of Swords 🦴🦴½ **1993 (R)** Time-traveling cop Jack Deth finds himself in a mystical new dimension where the blooksucking Trancers have enslaved the local population as feeders. If Jack expects to conquer he'll first need to survive an ancient wizard's prophecy of death. Filmed on location in Romania. **74m/C VHS.** Tim Thomerson, Stacie Randall, Ty Miller, Terri Ivens, Mark Arnold, Clare Hartley, Alan Oppenheimer, Stephen Macht, David Nutter; ***W:*** Peter David; ***M:*** Gary Fry.

Trancers 5: Sudden Deth 🦴🦴½ **1994 (R)** Irreverant time-travelling cop Jack Deth (Thomerson) returns to help the Tunnel Rats occupy the castle of Caliban. But the evil Lord Caliban is resurrected and his only desire is to destroy Jack. This is supposedly the final chapter of Deth's saga. **73m/C VHS.** Tim Thomerson, Stacie Randall, Ty Miller, Terri Ivens, Mark Arnold, Clare Hartley, Alan Oppenheimer, Jeff Moldovan, Lochlyn Munro, Stephen Macht; ***D:*** David Nutter; ***W:*** Peter David; ***M:*** Gary Fry.

Transatlantic Merry-Go-Round 🦴🦴 **1934** An early semi-musical mystery about an eclectic assortment of passengers aboard a luxury liner. ♫It Was Sweet of You; Rock and Roll; Moon Over Monte Carlo; Oh Leo, It's Love; If I Had a Million Dollars. **90m/B VHS.** Jack Benny, Gene Raymond, Nancy Carroll, Boswell Sisters, Ralph Morgan, Sidney Blackmer; *D:* Ben Stoloff.

Transatlantic Tunnel 🦴🦴½ *The Tunnel* **1935** An undersea tunnel from England to America is attempted, despite financial trickery and undersea disasters. Made with futuristic sets which were advanced for their time. **94m/B VHS.** *GB* Richard Dix, Leslie Banks, Madge Evans, Helen Vinson, Sir C. Aubrey Smith, George Arliss, Walter Huston; *D:* Maurice Elvey.

Transformations 🦴½ **1988 (R)** An interplanetary pilot battles a deadly virus that threatens life throughout the universe. Obscure space jetsam. **84m/C VHS.** Rex Smith, Patrick Macnee, Lisa Langlois, Christopher Neame; *D:* Jay Kamen; *W:* Mitch Brian.

Transformers: The Movie 🦴 **1986 (G)** A full-length animated film featuring the universe-defending robots fighting the powers of evil. These robots began life as real toys, so there's some marketing going on. **85m/C VHS, DVD.** *D:* Nelson Shin; *M:* Vince DiCola; *V:* Orson Welles, Eric Idle, Judd Nelson, Leonard Nimoy, Robert Stack.

Transmutations 🦴 *Underworld* **1985 (R)** Mad scientist Elliott develops a mind-altering drug which is tested by a group of young people. They find out too late that the drug causes horrible facial disfigurement, as well as leaving them hopelessly addicted, and they hide out underground, plotting their revenge. Cowper, a young hooker in the group, turns out to be immune to the side effects and works with her ex-mobster boss to get help. Confusing. Barker co-scripted from one of his stories but later disowned the film. **103m/C VHS.** *GB* Denholm Elliott, Steven Berkoff, Miranda Richardson, Nicola Cowper, Larry Lamb, Art Malik, Ingrid Pitt, Irina Brook, Paul Brown; *D:* George Pavlou; *W:* Clive Barker, James Caplin; *C:* Syd Macartney.

Transport from Paradise 🦴🦴½ *Transport Z Raje* **1965** Follows the story of Jewish life in the Terezin ghetto before the inhabitants are imprisoned and shipped off to Auschwitz as part of Hitler's final solution. Based on a novel by Arnold Lustig. In Czech with English subtitles. **93m/B VHS.** *CZ D:* Zbynek Brynych.

Transylvania 6-5000 🦴 **1985 (PG)** Agreeably stupid horror spoof about two klutzy reporters who stumble into modern-day Transylvania and encounter an array of comedic creatures. Shot in Yugoslavia. **93m/C VHS, DVD, Wide.** Jeff Goldblum, Joseph Bologna, Ed Begley Jr., Carol Kane, John Byner, Geena Davis, Jeffrey Jones, Norman Fell, Michael Richards; *D:* Rudy DeLuca; *W:* Rudy DeLuca; *C:* Tomislav Pinter; *M:* Lee Holdridge.

Transylvania Twist 🦴½ **1989 (PG-13)** Moronic comedy about vampires, teenage vampire hunters and half-naked babes. **90m/C VHS.** Robert Vaughn, Teri Copley, Steve Altman, Ace Mask, Angus Scrimm, Jay Robinson, Brinke Stevens; *D:* Jim Wynorski; *W:* R.J. Robertson.

The Trap 🦴🦴 **1922** Chaney kidnaps the son of a man he's sent to prison on false charges. Rather than give up the kid when the man is released, he plans a trap. **?m/B VHS.** Lon Chaney Sr., Alan Hale, Irene Rich; *D:* Robert Thornby; *W:* George C. Hall; *C:* Virgil Miller.

The Trap 🦴🦴½ *The Baited Trap* **1959** In trying to escape justice, a ruthless crime syndicate boss holds a small desert town in a grip of fear. **84m/C VHS.** Richard Widmark, Tina Louise, Lee J. Cobb, Earl Holliman, Lorne Greene, Carl Benton Reid; *D:* Norman Panama; *W:* Norman Panama.

Trap 🦴🦴 *L'Aventure Sauvage* **1966** A trapper buys a mute girl as his wife. Together they try to make a life for themselves in the Canadian wilderness. Fine telling of interesting western tale. Unusual and realistic. **106m/C VHS.** *GB CA* Rita Tushingham, Oliver Reed, Rex Sevenoaks; *D:* Sidney Hayers; *C:* Robert Krasker.

Trap on Cougar Mountain 🦴 **1972 (G)** A young boy begins a crusade to save his animal friends from the traps and bullets of hunters. **97m/C VHS.** Erik Larsen, Keith Larsen, Karen Steele; *D:* Keith Larsen.

Trap Them & Kill Them 🦴 **1984** American group traveling through the Amazon jungle encounter a terrifying aborigine tribe. Point of trip undergoes considerable reexamination. **90m/C VHS.** Gabriele Tinti, Susan Scott, Donald O'Brien.

Trapeze 🦴🦴🦴 **1956** Lancaster is a former trapeze artist, now lame from a triple somersault accident. Curtis, the son of an old friend, wants Lancaster to teach him the routine. Lollobrigida, an aerial acrobat, is interested in both men. Exquisite European locations, fine camera work. The actors perform their own stunts. **105m/C VHS, Wide.** Burt Lancaster, Tony Curtis, Gina Lollobrigida, Katy Jurado, Thomas Gomez; *D:* Carol Reed; *C:* Robert Krasker; *M:* Malcolm Arnold.

Trapped 🦴🦴½ **1949** Semi-documentary crime drama shows in semi-documentary style how the feds hunt down a gang of counterfeiters by springing one of their comrades from prison. Well-paced, suspenseful and believable. **78m/B VHS.** Lloyd Bridges, Barbara Payton, John Hoyt, James Todd; *D:* Richard Fleischer.

Trapped 🦴½ **1989 (R)** A woman working late in her high-rise office is stalked by a killer and must rely on her ingenuity to outwit him. **93m/C VHS.** Kathleen Quinlan, Bruce Abbott, Katy Boyer, Ben Loggins; *D:* Fred Walton; *W:* Fred Walton. **CABLE**

Trapped Alive 🦴½ **1993** Robin and Monica are abducted by three escaped convicts who want their car as a getaway vehicle. Trying to avoid a police roadblock the car crashes through the cover of a long-abandoned mine. When the group try to find their way out of the maze of tunnels they realize they're not down there alone. **92m/C VHS.** Alex Kubik, Elizabeth Kent, Michael Nash, Randolph Powell, Mark Witsken, Sullivan Hester, Laura Kallison, Cameron Mitchell; *D:* Leszek Burzynski; *W:* Leszek Burzynski.

Trapped by the Mormons 🦴🦴 *The Mormon Peril* **1922** Mormons seduce innocent young girls to add to their harems. An interesting piece of paranoid propaganda. Silent with original organ music. **97m/B VHS, 8mm.** Evelyn Brent, Lewis Willoughby.

Trapped in Paradise 🦴½ **1994 (PG-13)** Three bungling brothers make off with a bundle of cash from the Paradise—the town, not the afterlife—bank on Christmas Eve. The locals, naive refugees from a Rockwell painting, don't recognize the buffoons as criminals, and reward their crime with hospitality that would make Frank Capra proud. Chase scenes and subplots abound as the boys spend what seems an eternity trying to make their getaway. Routine, humdrum comedy is hampered by an obvious plot. Watchable only because of Carvey, Lovitz, and Cage. **111m/C VHS.** Nicolas Cage, Jon Lovitz, Dana Carvey, John Ashton, Madchen Amick, Donald Moffat, Richard Jenkins, Florence Stanley, Angela Paton, Vic Manni, Frank Pesce, Sean McCann, Paul Lazar, Richard B. Shull; *D:* George Gallo; *W:* George Gallo; *M:* Robert Folk.

Trapped in Silence 🦴🦴 **1986** Young Sutherland, abused since childhood, stops speaking to protect himself mentally and physically. Psychologist Mason is determined to break down the walls to help him confront his pain. Interesting cameo by Silver as a gay counselor forced out of his job when his sexual preference is discovered. Mildly melodramatic made-for-TV message drama. **94m/C VHS.** Marsha Mason, Kiefer Sutherland, John Mahoney, Amy Wright; *Cameos:* Ron Silver; *D:* Michael Tuchner.

Trapped in Space 🦴🦴½ **1994 (PG-13)** On a mission to Venus a space shuttle is damaged by a meteor strike, leaving only enough oxygen for one person. So, what's everyone else suppose to do? Based on a short story by Arthur C. Clarke. **87m/C VHS.** Jack Wagner, Jack Coleman, Craig Wasson, Sigrid Thornton, Kay Lenz; *D:* Arthur Seidelman; *W:* John Vincent Curtis, Melinda M. Snodgrass; *M:* Jay Gruska.

Trapper County War 🦴 **1989 (R)** A city boy and a Vietnam vet band together to rescue a young woman held captive by a backwoods clan. **98m/C VHS, DVD.** Robert Estes, Bo Hopkins, Ernie Hudson, Betsy Russell, Don Swayze, Noah Blake; *D:* Worth Keeter; *W:* Russell V. Manzatt; *C:* Irl Dixon; *M:* Shuki Levy.

Traps 🦴🦴½ **1993 (R)** Australian journalist Michael Duffield (Reynolds) and his English photographer wife Louise (Reeves) arrive for an assignment in 1950 French Indochina. Michael is to write about life on a French-owned rubber plantation, managed by Daniel (Frey), who lives with his rather peculiar daughter Viola (McKenzie). The plantation is troubled by the increasingly militant Viet-Minh rebels and it becomes clear that the four characters all have their own emotional difficulties to deal with, as well. Loosely adapted from the novel "Dreamhouse" by Kate Grenville. Feature film directing debut for Chan. **95m/C VHS.** *AU* Saskia Reeves, Robert Reynolds, Sami Frey, Jacqueline McKenzie; *D:* Pauline Chan; *W:* Pauline Chan, Robert Carter; *C:* Kevin Hayward; *M:* Douglas Stephen Rae.

Trash 🦴🦴 **1970** Andy Warhol's profile of a depraved couple (Warhol-veteran Dallesandro and female impersonater Woodlawn) living in a lower east side basement and scouting the streets for food and drugs. Not for those easily offended by nymphomaniacs, junkies, lice, and the like; a must for fans of underground film and the cinema verite style. **110m/C VHS, DVD.** Joe Dallesandro, Holly Woodlawn, Jane Forth, Michael Sklar, Geri Miller, Bruce Pecheur, Andrea Feldman; *D:* Paul Morrissey; *W:* Paul Morrissey; *C:* Paul Morrissey.

Trauma 🦴½ **1962** A girl suffers amnesia after the trauma of witnessing her aunt's murder. She returns to the mansion years later to piece together what happened. A sometimes tedious psychological thriller. **93m/C VHS.** John Conte, Lynn Bari, Lorrie Richards, David Garner, Warren Kemmerling, William Bissell, Bond Blackman, William Justine; *D:* Robert M. Young.

Traveling Man 🦴🦴 **1989** Drama about a veteran traveling salesman who's assigned an eager young apprentice when his sales go down. Lithgow gives a great performance as the burnt-out traveling salesman. **105m/C VHS.** John Lithgow, Jonathan Silverman, Margaret Colin, John Glover; *D:* Irvin Kershner; *M:* Miles Goodman. **CABLE**

Traveller 🦴🦴🦴 **1996 (R)** Deriving its name from the real-life group of wily Irish-American con men who prowl the Southeast, this view into the lives and clannish ways of its members may have you checking that brand-spankin' new driveway sealant. Their basic philosophy is: if you're not one of us, we're allowed to take all of your money. Bokky (Paxton) is the jack-of-all-tricks who takes the younger Pat (Wahlberg) under his wing after the boy is shunned by the rest of the group. Pat's father married outside the clan, and that's not allowed. Bokky falls into the same trap, however, when a beautiful bartender (Margulies), who he has just fleeced, steals his heart. Rather violent ending dims the good feeling that builds and may leave you feeling...well, cheated. Directorial debut of long-time Clint Eastwood cinematographer Jack Green, who also shot "Twister" with Paxton. **100m/C VHS, DVD.** Bill Paxton, Mark Wahlberg, Julianna Margulies, James Gammon, Luke Askew, Michael Shaner, Nikki Deloach, Danielle Wiener; *D:* Jack N. Green; *W:* Jim McGlynn; *C:* Jack N. Green; *M:* Andy Paley.

Travelling North 🦴🦴 **1987 (PG-13)** A belligerent retiree falls in love with a divorcee and they move together to a rustic retreat. They have an idyllic existence until the man discovers he has a serious heart condition. Adaptation of David Williamson's play has fine performances. **97m/C VHS.** *AU* Leo McKern, Julia Blake; *D:* Carl Schultz; *W:* David Williamson. Australian Film Inst. '87: Actor (McKern); Montreal World Film Fest. '87: Actor (McKern).

The Travelling Players 🦴🦴 *O Thiassos* **1975** Slow-going for those unfamiliar with Greek myths and modern Greek history as the country is continually oppressed and betrayed. A travelling company of provicial actors ply their trade over some 16 years (1936-1952) while their country experiences the upheavals of a fascist dictatorship, WWII, occupation, civil war, and repression by the right-wing regime. The focus is on ordinary people in ordinary surroundings (with Angelopoulous leaning towards the communist sensibility). Greek with subtitles. **230m/C VHS.** *GR* Eva Kotamanidou, Maria Vassilou, Petros Zarkadis, Alika Georgouli, Stratos Pahis; *D:* Theo Angelopoulos; *W:* Theo Angelopoulos; *C:* Yorgos Arvanitis; *M:* Loukianos Kilaidonis.

Travels with My Aunt 🦴🦴½ **1972 (PG)** A banker leading a mundane life is taken on a wild, whirlwind tour of Europe by an eccentric woman claiming to be his aunt. Based on Graham Greene's best-selling novel. **109m/C Wide.** Maggie Smith, Alec McCowen, Louis Gossett Jr., Robert Stephens, Cindy Williams; *D:* George Cukor; *W:* Jay Presson Allen. Oscars '72: Costume Des.

Traxx 🦴 **1987 (R)** Satire about an ex-cop soldier of fortune. Not surprisingly, Stevens doesn't do much with this lame script. **84m/C VHS.** Shadoe Stevens, Priscilla Barnes, William E. Pugh, John Hancock, Robert Davi, Rick Overton; *D:* Jerome Gary; *W:* Gary De Vore; *M:* Jay Gruska.

Treacherous Crossing 🦴🦴 **1992 (PG)** When her husband disappears on their honeymoon cruise heiress Wagner tries to get the ship's crew to help her. They think she's crazy, but aided by new friend Dickinson, Wagner intends to find out just what's going on. Based on the radio play "Cabin B-13" by John Dickson Carr. **88m/C VHS.** Lindsay Wagner, Angie Dickinson, Grant Show, Joseph Bottoms, Karen Medak, Charles Napier, Jeffrey DeMunn; *D:* Tony Wharmby; *W:* Elisa Bell.

Treasure Island 🦴🦴🦴½ **1934** Fleming's adaptation of Robert Louis Stevenson's 18th-century English pirate tale of Long John Silver is a classic. Beery is great as the pirate; Cooper has trouble playing the boy. Also available colorized. Multitudinous remakes. **102m/B VHS.** Wallace Beery, Jackie Cooper, Lionel Barrymore, Lewis Stone, Otto Kruger, Douglass Dumbrille, Charles "Chic" Sale, Nigel Bruce; *D:* Victor Fleming; *C:* Clyde De Vinna.

Treasure Island 🦴🦴🦴½ **1950 (PG)** Spine-tingling Robert Louis Stevenson tale of pirates and buried treasure, in which young cabin boy Jim Hawkins matches wits with Long John Silver. Some editions excise extra violence. Stevenson's ending is revised. Full Disney treatment, excellent casting. **96m/C VHS.** Bobby Driscoll, Robert Newton, Basil Sydney, Walter Fitzgerald, Denis O'Dea, Ralph Truman, Finlay Currie; *D:* Byron Haskin; *C:* Frederick A. (Freddie) Young.

Treasure Island 🦴🦴 *La Isla Del Tesoro* **1972 (G)** Unexceptional British reheat of familiar pirate tale. Welles' interpretation of Long John Silver may be truer to Stevenson, but it's one heckuva blustering binge. **94m/C VHS.** *GB* Orson Welles, Kim Burfield, Walter Slezak, Lionel Stander; *D:* John Hough; *W:* Orson Welles.

Treasure Island 🦴🦴½ **1989** Excellent cable version of the classic Robert Louis Stevenson pirate tale with Heston as Long John Silver. Written, produced, and directed by Fraser Heston, son of Charlton. **131m/C VHS.** Charlton Heston, Christian Bale, Julian Glover, Richard Johnson, Oliver Reed, Christopher Lee, Clive Wood, Nicholas Amer, Michael Halsey; *D:* Fraser Heston; *W:* Fraser Heston. **CABLE**

Treasure Island 🦴🦴½ **1999 (PG)** Appropriately adventurous version of Robert L. Stevenson's often-filmed tale of young Jim Hawkins, who has a treasure map and a boatload of pirates eager for the riches hidden on Treasure Island! Palance is notably snarly as peg-legged Long John Silver. **95m/C VHS, DVD.** *CA* Jack Palance, Kevin Zegers, Patrick Bergin; *D:* Peter Rowe; *W:* Peter Rowe; *C:* Marc Charlesbois.

Treasure Island 🦴🦴½ **1999** Near the end of WWII, two officers the fictional intelligence compound called "Treasure Island" are given a dead body and a covert assignment: construct a fake "backstory," including made-up letters to girlfriends, family members, etc., and fill the body's pockets with information. When dumped in the ocean, it is hoped that the false information will send the Japanese in the wrong direction. The two officers find themselves consumed by visions of the body, which seems to show up everywhere, including invading their (quite unusual) sex lives. Challenging and ambitious puzzle of a film which is filled from sprocket hole to sprocket hole with coded messages, encrypted dialogue, and implied meanings. Certainly not for all audiences, but a funny and fascinating exercise in style and cinematic invention. The basics of the story are simple and easy to follow, but the female characters (and their relationship to our protagonists) are a bit muddled. In a '40s period style, the film begins with a brief serial and newsreel that are absolutely perfect. **83m/B DVD.** Lance Baker, Nick Offerman, Jonah Blechman; ***D:*** Scott King; ***W:*** Scott King; ***C:*** Scott King, Phillip Glau; ***M:*** Chris Anderson.

Treasure of Arne ½ **1919** A 16th century Scottish mercenary kills and loots the estate of rich, well-to-do property owner Sir Arne. Famous early Swedish silent that established Stiller as a director. **78m/B VHS.** *SW* ***D:*** Mauritz Stiller.

The Treasure of Bengal ½ **1953** Sabu attempts to stop his chief from trading the village's precious gem (the largest ruby in the world) for firearms. **72m/C VHS.** Sabu.

Treasure of Fear ½ *Scared Stiff* **1945** A bungling newspaper reporter gets involved with four jade chessmen once owned by Kubla Khan. A few laughs in this contrived haunted house story. **66m/B VHS.** Jack Haley, Barton MacLane, Ann Savage, Veda Ann Borg; ***D:*** Frank McDonald.

The Treasure of Jamaica Reef ½ **1974 (PG)** Adventurers battle sharks and other nasty fish as they seek a sunken Spanish galleon and its cache of golden treasure. **96m/C VHS.** Cheryl Ladd, Stephen Boyd, Roosevelt "Rosie" Grier, David Ladd, Darby Hinton; ***D:*** Virginia Lively Stone.

The Treasure of Matecumbe **1976 (G)** A motley crew of adventurers led by a young boy search for buried treasure as they are pursued by Indians and other foes. Filmed in the Florida Key Islands. **107m/C VHS.** Billy Attmore, Robert Foxworth, Joan Hackett, Peter Ustinov, Vic Morrow; ***D:*** Vincent McEveety; ***M:*** Buddy (Norman Dale) Baker.

Treasure of Monte Cristo **1950** A woman marries a seaman said to be an ancestor of the Count for his inheritance. Instead, she finds love and mystery. **78m/B VHS.** *GB* Adele Jergens, Steve Brodie, Glenn Langan; ***D:*** William Berke.

Treasure of Pancho Villa ½ **1955** An American adventurer plots a gold heist to help Villa's revolution. He encounters every obstacle in the West while on his way to help the Mexican rebel. **96m/C VHS.** Rory Calhoun, Shelley Winters, Gilbert Roland; ***D:*** George Sherman.

The Treasure of the Amazon ½ *El Tesoro del Amazones* **1984** Three fortune hunters embark on a perilous search for wealth in the South American jungles. Silly and unnecessarily violent. **105m/C VHS.** *MX* Stuart Whitman, Donald Pleasence, Ann Sydney, Bradford Dillman, John Ireland; ***D:*** Rene Cardona Jr.

Treasure of the Four Crowns **1982 (PG)** Aging history professor hires a team of tough commandos to recover four legendary crowns containing the source of mystical powers. The crowns are being held under heavy guard by a crazed cult leader. **97m/C VHS.** *SP* Tony Anthony, Anna (Ana Garcia) Obregon, Gene Quintano; ***D:*** Ferdinando Baldi; ***W:*** Lloyd Battista, James Bryce; ***M:*** Ennio Morricone.

Treasure of the Golden Condor ½ **1953** A swashbuckler heads to the jungles of 18th-century Guatemala in search of ancient treasure. Contains interesting footage of Mayan ruins, but otherwise ordinary. A remake of "Son of Fury." **93m/C VHS.** Cornel Wilde, Connie Smith, Fay Wray, Anne Bancroft, Leo G. Carroll, Robert (Bobby) Blake; ***D:*** Delmer Daves.

Treasure of the Lost Desert ½ **1983** A Green Beret crushes a terrorist operation in the Middle East. **93m/C VHS.** Bruce Miller, Susan West, Larry Finch; ***D:*** Tony Zarindast.

Treasure of the Moon Goddess woof! **1988 (R)** A dizzy nightclub singer is mistaken by Central American pirates and natives for the earthly manifestation of their Moon Goddess. **90m/C VHS.** Don Calfa, Joann Ayres, Asher Brauner; ***D:*** Joseph Louis Agraz.

Treasure of the Sierra Madre **1948** Three prospectors in search of gold in Mexico find suspicion, treachery and greed. Bogart is superbly believable as the paranoid, and ultimately homicidal, Fred C. Dobbs. Huston directed his father and wrote the screenplay, based on a B. Traven story. **126m/B VHS.** Humphrey Bogart, Walter Huston, Tim Holt, Bruce (Herman Brix) Bennett, Barton MacLane, Robert (Bobby) Blake, Alfonso Bedoya; ***D:*** John Huston; ***W:*** John Huston; ***M:*** Max Steiner. Oscars '48: Director (Huston), Screenplay, Support. Actor (Huston); AFI '98: Top 100; Golden Globes '49: Director (Huston), Film—Drama, Support. Actor (Huston); Natl. Bd. of Review '48: Actor (Huston), Natl. Film Reg. '90;; N.Y. Film Critics '48: Director (Huston), Film.

Treasure of the Yankee Zephyr *Race for the Yankee Zephyr* **1983 (PG)** Trio joins in the quest for a plane that has been missing for 40 years...with a cargo of $50 million. They have competition in the form of Peppard and cronies. Decent cast muddles through the predictable plotting. **108m/C VHS.** *AU NZ* Ken Wahl, George Peppard, Donald Pleasence, Lesley Ann Warren, Bruno Lawrence, Grant Tilly; ***D:*** David Hemmings; ***M:*** Brian May.

The Treasure Seekers **1979** Four rival divers set off on a perilous Caribbean expedition in search of the legendary treasure of Morgan the Pirate. **88m/C VHS.** Rod Taylor, Stuart Whitman, Elke Sommer, Keenan Wynn, Jeremy Kemp.

A Tree Grows in Brooklyn ½ **1945 (PG)** Sensitive young Irish lass growing up in turn-of-the-century Brooklyn tries to rise above her tenement existence. Based on the novel by Betty Smith. Kazan's directorial debut. **128m/B VHS.** Peggy Ann Garner, James Dunn, Dorothy McGuire, Joan Blondell, Lloyd Nolan, Ted Donaldson, James Gleason, John Alexander, Charles Halton; ***D:*** Elia Kazan; ***C:*** Leon Shamroy; ***M:*** Alfred Newman. Oscars '45: Support. Actor (Dunn).

The Tree of Wooden Clogs ½ *L'Albero Degli Zoccoli* **1978** Epic view of the lives of four peasant families working on an estate in turn of the century Northern Italy. The title comes from the shoes the peasants wear. When a young boy breaks a shoe, his father risks punishment by cutting down one of his landlord's trees to make a new pair of clogs. Slow moving and beautiful, from former industrial filmmaker Olmi. In Italian with English subtitles. **185m/C VHS.** *IT* Luigi Ornaghi, Francesca Moriggi, Omar Brignoll, Antonio Ferrari; ***D:*** Ermanno Olmi; ***W:*** Ermanno Olmi; ***C:*** Ermanno Olmi. Cannes '78: Film; N.Y. Film Critics '79: Foreign Film.

Treehouse Hostage ½ **1999 (PG)** Timmy needs a reat current-events project if he doesn't want to get stuck in summer school. Fortunately, he and some friends manage to capture a escaped counterfeiter, Banks (Varney), and turn him in for a grade. Only it turns out that the school principal is actually the head of the counterfeiting ring. **90m/C VHS, DVD.** Jim Varney, Joey Zimmerman, Richard Kline; ***D:*** Sean McNamara.

Tree's Lounge ½ **1996 (R)** First time director/writer Buscemi takes a look at the downward spiraling life of Tommy Basilio (Buscemi), a working-class misfit who loses his job and then spends most of his time hanging out at the dreary local bar. He finally winds up driving an ice cream truck, only leading to more trouble when his teenaged helper, Debbie (Sevigny), develops a crush on him—a situation her hot-headed father Jerry (Baldwin) takes exception to. And the irresponsible Tommy is finally forced to realize that his ill-concerned actions have consequences. **94m/C VHS, DVD.** Steve Buscemi, Chloe Sevigny, Daniel Baldwin, Elizabeth Bracco, Anthony LaPaglia, Debi Mazar, Carol Kane, Seymour Cassel, Mark Boone Jr., Eszter Balint, Mimi Rogers, Kevin Corrigan, Samuel L. Jackson; ***D:*** Steve Buscemi; ***W:*** Steve Buscemi; ***C:*** Lisa Rinzler; ***M:*** Evan Lurie.

Tremors ½ **1989 (PG-13)** A tiny desert town is attacked by giant man-eating worm-creatures. Bacon and Ward are the handymen trying to save the town. Amusing, with good special effects. **96m/C VHS, DVD.** Kevin Bacon, Fred Ward, Finn Carter, Michael Gross, Reba McEntire, Bibi Besch, Bobby Jacoby, Charlotte Stewart, Victor Wong, Tony Genaros, Ariana Richards; ***D:*** Ron Underwood; ***W:*** S.S. Wilson, Brent Maddock; ***C:*** Alexander Grusynski; ***M:*** Ernest Troost.

Tremors 2: Aftershocks ½ **1996 (PG-13)** They're baaaaack! The Graboids have resurfaced to eat their way through Mexican oil fields and it's up to tough guys Earl Bassett (Ward) and Burt Gummer (Gross) to get rid of the toothy worms once and for all. Same mix of tongue-in-cheek humor and special effects as the first film. **100m/C VHS, DVD.** Fred Ward, Michael Gross, Helen Shaver, Christopher Gartin, Marcelo Tubert; ***D:*** S.S. Wilson; ***W:*** S.S. Wilson, Brent Maddock; ***C:*** Virgil Harper; ***M:*** Jay Ferguson.

Tremors 3: Back to Perfection **2001 (PG-13)** Gross returns to his hometown of Perfection, Nevada, and sees a cheesy theme park based on the Graboids has opened. Then real Graboids return to wreck havoc again. **104m/C VHS, DVD, Wide.** Michael Gross, Charlotte Stewart, Shawn Christian, Ariana Richards, Susan Chung, Helen Shaver, Christopher Gartin; ***D:*** Brent Maddock; ***W:*** John Whelpley; ***C:*** Virgil Harper; ***M:*** Kevin Kiner. VIDEO

Trenchcoat ½ **1983** Aspiring mystery writer travels to Malta to research her new novel and is drawn into a real-life conspiracy. Silly and contrived spoof of the detective genre. **95m/C VHS.** Margot Kidder, Robert Hays; ***D:*** Michael Tuchner; ***W:*** Jeffrey Price, Peter S. Seaman; ***M:*** Charles Fox.

Trespass *Looters* **1992 (R)** Violent crime tale set in East St. Louis, Illinois. Two redneck firemen learn about stolen gold artifacts supposedly hidden in an abandoned building and go on a treasure hunt. When they witness a murder they also get involved in a battle between two crime lords—who want these interlopers dead. What follows is a deadly game of cat-and-mouse. Lots of action but it's all fairly routine. Original release date of summer 1992 was delayed until the winter because of unfortunate similarities to the L.A. riots. **104m/C VHS, DVD, Wide.** Ice Cube, Ice-T, William Sadler, Bill Paxton, Art Evans; ***D:*** Walter Hill; ***W:*** Robert Zemeckis, Bob Gale; ***C:*** Lloyd Ahern; ***M:*** Ry Cooder.

Trespasser **1985** A painter has an affair with a young woman. He comes to regret destroying his family and their life together. Based on a D.H. Lawrence novel. **90m/C VHS.** Alan Bates, Dinah Stabb, Pauline Morgan, Margaret Whiting.

Trespasses **1986 (R)** Couple of drifters wander into a Texas town where they rape a local woman and kill a local rancher's son. So the fathers of the victims decide to get revenge. Brutal and tedious. **90m/C VHS.** Lou Diamond Phillips, Robert Kuhn, Ben Johnson, Adam Roarke, Mary Pillot, Van Brooks; ***D:*** Adam Roarke, Lauren Bivens; ***W:*** Lou Diamond Phillips.

The Trial *Le Proces; Der Prozess; Il Processo* **1963** Expressionistic Welles adaptation of classic Kafka novella about an innocent man accused, tried, and convicted of an unknown crime in an unnamed exaggeratedly bureaucratic country. Another Welles project that met with constant disaster in production, with many lapses in continuity. **118m/B VHS, DVD, Wide.** *FR* Anthony Perkins, Jeanne Moreau, Orson Welles, Romy Schneider, Akim Tamiroff, Elsa Martinelli; ***D:*** Orson Welles; ***W:*** Orson Welles; ***C:*** Edmond Richard; ***M:*** Jean Ledrut.

The Trial **1993** Spare adaptation of Franz Kafka's novel finds Prague bank clerk Joseph K (MacLachlan) arrested on unknown charges. His increasing guilt and paranoia fit well into a world where the most illogical things happen in the most matter of fact way. Good visuals. **120m/C VHS, DVD.** Kyle MacLachlan, Anthony Hopkins, Jason Robards Jr., Polly Walker, Juliet Stevenson, Alfred Molina; ***D:*** David Hugh Jones; ***W:*** Harold Pinter; ***C:*** Phil Meheux; ***M:*** Carl Davis.

Trial & Error ½ *The Dock Brief* **1962** Comedic satire, based on the play by John Mortimer, finds hapless lawyer Morgenhall (Sellers) thinking he's finally got his big chance when he defends wife murderer Fowle (Attenborough). Fowle wants to plead guilty but Morgenhall dreams of being a court star and insists on pleading his client innocent. It's a disaster just waiting to happen. **78m/B VHS, DVD.** *GB* Peter Sellers, Richard Attenborough, Beryl Reid, David Lodge, Frank Pettingell, Eric Woodburn; ***D:*** James Hill; ***W:*** Pierre Rouve; ***C:*** Edward Scaife; ***M:*** Ron Grainer.

Trial and Error ½ **1992** Peter Hudson (Matheson) is an overly zealous prosecutor who successfully convicts a small time criminal of murder, sending him to death row. This launches Hudson's political career and five years later he's about to be nominated for Lieutenant Governor, just as the felon's execution draws near. Suddenly, new evidence points to the man's innocence, but if Hudson investigates it could ruin his political future. But he's got a bigger problem—the real killer decides to make Hudson's wife his next victim. **91m/C VHS, Wide.** Tim Matheson, Helen Shaver, Sean McCann, Eugene C. Clark; ***D:*** Mark Sobel.

Trial and Error ½ **1996 (PG-13)** Courtroom comedy may remind you of another law oriented movie. No, not "Kramer vs. Kramer." It's "My Cousin Vinny," also directed by Lynn. Both feature fake lawyers defending hopeless clients in small towns. In this case, lawyer Charles Tuttle (Daniels) is too messed up from his bachelor party to make it to court for a case in which the defendent Benny (Torn), a relative of Chuck's big-wig future father-in-law, is accused of selling mail-order "commemorative copper Lincoln engravings" which are actually pennies. His best bud Richard (Richards), an actor, decides to stand in for him, and the legal slip-and-pratfalls ensue. Richards as the physical comedian and Daniels as the white bread straight man have great comic chemistry, but the plot won't surprise you much. **98m/C VHS, DVD.** Michael Richards, Jeff Daniels, Rip Torn, Charlize Theron, Jessica Steen, Austin Pendleton, Alexandra Wentworth, Lawrence Pressman, Dale Dye, Max Casella, Jennifer Coolidge; ***D:*** Jonathan Lynn; ***W:*** Sarah Bernstein, Gregory Bernstein; ***C:*** Gabriel Beristain; ***M:*** Phil Marshall.

Trial by Jury ½ **1994 (R)** Strong cast, lame script. Idealistic single mother Valerie Alston (Whalley-Kilmer) winds up on the jury trying notorious mobster Rusty Pirone (Assante). Rusty's henchman, Tommy Vesey (Hurt), lets Valerie know that her son is in mortal danger if she doesn't find his boss innocent. Of course DA Daniel Graham (Byrne) is equally adamant about a conviction and is willing to use Valerie any way he has to. **107m/C VHS, DVD, Wide.** Beau Starr, Mike Starr, John Capodice, Joanne Whalley, William Hurt, Gabriel Byrne, Armand Assante, Kathleen Quinlan, Stuart Whitman, Margaret Whitton, Ed Lauter, Joe Santos, Richard Portnow; ***D:*** Heywood Gould; ***W:*** Jordan Katz, Heywood Gould; ***C:*** Frederick Elmes; ***M:*** Terence Blanchard.

Trial by Media ½ *An American Daughter* **2000** Lyssa Dent Hughes (Lahti) is a prominent D.C. doctor (and senator's daughter) who has been nominated to become surgeon general. But thanks to media scrutiny, and some careless remarks, she becomes a target and her nomination is in jeopardy. Wasserstein scripted from her 1997 play "American Daughter." **92m/C VHS, DVD.** Christine Lahti, Tom Skerritt, Jay Thomas, Mark Feuerstein, Lynne Thigpen, Stanley Anderson, Blake Lindsley; ***D:*** Sheldon Larry; ***W:*** Wendy Wasserstein; ***C:*** Albert J. Dunk; ***M:*** Phil Marshall. CABLE

The Trial of Billy Jack woof! **1974 (PG)** Billy Jack takes on the feds and beats the hell out of a lot of people to prove that the world can live in peace. Awful, pretentious film. **175m/C VHS, DVD.** Tom Laughlin, Delores Taylor, Victor Izay, Teresa Laughlin, William Wellman Jr., Russell Lane, Michelle Wilson, Geo Ann Sosa, George Aguilar, Sacheen Little Feather; *D:* Frank Laughlin, Tom Laughlin; *W:* Tom Laughlin, Delores Taylor; *C:* Jack Marta; *M:* Elmer Bernstein.

The Trial of Lee Harvey Oswald **1977** What would've happened if Jack Ruby had not shot Oswald. Oswald's trial and its likely results are painstakingly created. **192m/C VHS.** Ben Gazzara, Lorne Greene, John Pleshette, Lawrence Pressman; *D:* Gordon Davidson. **TV**

Trial of the Catonsville Nine ½ **1972 (PG)** Riveting political drama that focuses on the trial of nine anti-war activists, including Father Daniel Berrigan, during the Vietnam War days of the late 1960s. Imperfect, but involving. **85m/C VHS.** Ed Flanders, Douglas Watson, William Schallert, Peter Strauss, Richard Jordan; *D:* Gordon Davidson.

The Trial of the Incredible Hulk **1989** The Hulk returns to battle organized crime and is aided by his blind superhero/lawyer friend Daredevil. Followed by "The Death of the Incredible Hulk." **96m/C VHS.** Bill Bixby, Lou Ferrigno, Rex Smith, John Rhys-Davies, Marta DuBois, Nancy Everhard, Nicholas Hormann; *D:* Bill Bixby. **TV**

The Trials of Oscar Wilde *The Man with the Green Carnation; The Green Carnation* **1960** Finch is the highlight as playwright/wit Wilde, who ill-advisedly sues the Marquis of Queensbury (Jeffries) for libel when the peer accuses him of being a sodomite. Wilde is, in fact, having an affair with the Marquis' son, Lord Alfred Douglas (Fraser), which eventually leads to Wilde's imprisonment and the destruction of his life. Based on the play "The Stringed Lute" by John Furnell and the book "The Trials of Oscar Wilde" by Montgomery Hyde. **123m/C VHS.** *GB* Peter Finch, John Fraser, Lionel Jeffries, Nigel Patrick, James Mason, Yvonne Mitchell, Maxine Audley, James Booth, Paul Rogers, Ian Fleming, Laurence Naismith; *D:* Ken Hughes; *W:* Ken Hughes; *C:* Ted Moore; *M:* Ronald Goodwin.

The Triangle **2001** This triangle is the Bermuda kind as friends charter a boat for their annual Caribbean fishing trip and instead discover the Queen of Scots, a ghostly luxury liner that has been missing for 60 years. Boarding the ship turns out to be a big mistake since the tragedy that overtook the lives of the passengers and crew lingers and begins to affect the present. **92m/C VHS, DVD.** Luke Perry, Dan Cortese, Olivia D'Abo, Dorian Harewood, Polly Shannon, David Hewlett; *D:* Lewis Teague; *W:* Ted Humphrey; *C:* Ric Waite; *M:* Lawrence Shragge. **CABLE**

The Triangle Factory Fire Scandal **1979** Based on the true-life Triangle factory fire at the turn of the century. The fire killed 145 garment workers and drastically changed industrial fire and safety codes. **100m/C VHS.** Tom Bosley, David Dukes, Tovah Feldshuh, Janet Margolin, Stephanie Zimbalist, Lauren Front, Stacey Nelkin, Ted Wass, Charlotte Rae, Milton Selzer, Valerie Landsburg; *D:* Mel Stuart. **TV**

Tribes ½ *The Soldier Who Declared Peace* **1970** When a hippie is drafted into the Marines, despite the furious efforts of his drill sergeant, he refuses to conform to military life. Soon his boot-camp mates are trying his methods of defiance and survival. Well-made mix of comedy and social commentary. **90m/C VHS.** Jan-Michael Vincent, Darren McGavin, Earl Holliman; *D:* Joseph Sargent. **TV**

Tribulation **2000** Police detective Tom Canboro (Busey) goes up against the evil Messiah (Mancuso) in another entry in the "Left Behind" series of adventures based on the Book of Revelation. **97m/C DVD.** Gary Busey, Howie Mandel, Margot Kidder, Nick Mancuso, Sherry Miller, Leigh Lewis; *D:* Andre Van Heerden; *W:* Peter LaLonde, Paul LaLonde; *C:* George Tirl.

Tribute **1980 (PG)** A dying man is determined to achieve a reconciliation with his estranged son. Adapted by Bernard Slade from his play. **125m/C VHS.** *CA* Jack Lemmon, Robby Benson, Lee Remick, Kim Cattrall; *D:* Bob (Benjamin) Clark.

Tribute to a Bad Man **1956** Hard-nosed rancher Cagney will stop at nothing to retain his worldly possessions in this 1870s Colorado territory western. His ruthless behavior drives girlfriend Papas into the arms of hired hand Dubbins. Spencer Tracy and Grace Kelly were originally cast for the roles of Jeremy Rodock and Jocasta Constantine, but Kelly backed out and Tracy was fired due to differences with director Wise. Based on the short story by Jack Schaefer. **95m/C VHS.** James Cagney, Don Dubbins, Stephen McNally, Irene Papas, Vic Morrow, Royal Dano, Lee Van Cleef, James Griffith, Onslow Stevens, James Bell, Jeanette Nolan, Bud Osborne, Tom London, Dennis Moore, Buddy Roosevelt, Carl Pitti; *D:* Robert Wise; *W:* Michael Blankfort; *M:* Miklos Rozsa.

Tricheurs *Cheaters* **1984** Scam artists hit largest casino in the world and look forward to golden years of retirement. From the director of "Reversal of Fortune." In French with English subtitles. **95m/C VHS.** *FR* Jacques Dutronc, Bulle Ogier, Kurt Raab, Virgilio Teixeira, Steve Baes; *D:* Barbet Schroeder.

Trick **1999 (R)** Cheery gay romantic comedy. Quiet Gabriel (Campbell) is a struggling Broadway composer with a horndog straight roommate (Beyer) who is constantly taking over their apartment for his one-nighters (and locking Gabe out). Which leaves Gabriel in a dilemma when he meets hunky go-go boy, Mark (Pitok), and the duo can't find a place to be alone. But as the night wears on, they discover that lust may be taking a backseat to some deeper feelings. **90m/C VHS, DVD.** Missi Pyle, Christian Campbell, John Paul (J.P.) Pitoc, Tori Spelling, Brad Beyer, Clinton Leupp, Lorri Bagley, Steve Hayes; *D:* Jim Fall; *W:* Jason Schafer; *C:* Terry Stacey; *M:* David Friedman.

Trick or Treat ½ **1986 (R)** A high school student is helped to exact violent revenge against his bullying contemporaries. His helper is the spirit of a violent heavy metal rock star who he raises from the dead. Sometimes clever, not terribly scary. **97m/C VHS.** Tony Fields, Marc Price, Ozzy Osbourne, Gene Simmons, Elaine Joyce, Glenn Morgan, Lisa Orgolini, Doug Savant; *D:* Charles Martin Smith; *W:* Joel Soisson, Michael S. Murphy, Rhet Topham; *C:* Robert Elswit.

Trick or Treats woof! **1982 (R)** Young boy's pranks on his terrified babysitter backfire on Halloween night. His deranged father, escaped from an asylum, shows up to help him "scare" her. Giroux doesn't look very frightened in this extremely tedious film from Welles' best camera man. **90m/C VHS.** Carrie Snodgress, David Carradine, Jackie Giroux, Steve Railsback, Chris Graver, Peter Jason, Jillian Kesner, Paul Bartel; *D:* Gary Graver.

Tricks **1997 (R)** Once a Las Vegas showgirl, Jackie (Rogers) is now a gift shop clerk in Reno, making some extra dough by turning tricks at night. After being beaten by a john, Jackie loses her job and has trouble finding work. Her roommate Sarah (Daly) introduces her to old-time gangster Big Sam (Walston), who offers to help her get even with the guy who beat her but it's not that easy. **96m/C VHS.** Mimi Rogers, Tyne Daly, Ray Walston, Callum Keith Rennie, Kevin McNulty; *D:* Kenneth Fink; *W:* Deborah Amelon; *C:* John Bartley; *M:* Patrick Seymour. **CABLE**

Tricks of the Trade **1988 (R)** Goody-two-shoe housewife and hooker accomplice search for husband's murderer. Racy TV fodder. **100m/C VHS.** Cindy Williams, Markie Post, Chris Mulkey, James Whitmore Jr., Scott Paulin, John Ritter, Apollonia; *D:* Jack Bender. **TV**

Trident Force **1988** International counter-terrorism team is ordered to destroy the Palestinian Revolutionary Legion by any means possible. **90m/C VHS.** Anthony Alonzo, Mark Gil, Nanna Anderson, Steve Rogers, Eddie M. Gaerlan; *D:* Richard Smith.

The Trigger Effect ½ **1996 (R)** Nightmare in yuppiedom when a suspicious electromagnetic pulse knocks out all electrical power, telephone, and broadcast signals for hundreds of miles around a tranquil southern California community, which becomes increasingly unsettled. Matt (MacLachlan), wife Annie (Shue), and friend Joe (Mulroney) hang out together during the mystery power outage with lots of mounting tension both within and without. Film, however dread-producing, doesn't really make that much sense. **103m/C VHS, DVD, Wide.** Kyle MacLachlan, Elisabeth Shue, Dermot Mulroney, Michael Rooker, Richard T. Jones, Bill Smitrovich, William Lucking, Molly Morgan, Richard Schiff; *D:* David Koepp; *W:* David Koepp; *C:* Newton Thomas (Tom) Sigel; *M:* James Newton Howard.

Trigger Happy ½ *Mad Dog Time* **1996 (R)** Director Bishop (son of Rat-Packer Joey, who's in the film) tells a tale of crime lord Vic (Dreyfuss) and various gangsters in what should be a knowingly cool story but isn't. Vic's about to get out of the loony bin and has informed his enforcer, Ben London (Byrne), to get rid of his rivals and disloyal fellow mobsters in time for his return. Meanwhile, his chief of staff, Mickey (Goldblum), has been romancing both Vic's gal Grace (Lane) and her jealous older sister, Rita (Barkin). This situation does not make Vic happy. The movie won't make you happy either. **93m/C VHS.** Richard Dreyfuss, Gabriel Byrne, Jeff Goldblum, Diane Lane, Ellen Barkin, Gregory Hines, Kyle MacLachlan, Larry Bishop, Burt Reynolds, Henry Silva; ***Cameos:*** Joey Bishop, Angie Everhart, Michael J. Pollard, Richard Pryor, Rob Reiner, Billy Idol; *D:* Larry Bishop; *W:* Larry Bishop; *C:* Frank Byers; *M:* Earl Rose.

Trigger, Jr. ½ **1950** Rogers and his Western Show find themselves in the middle of a dispute between intimidated ranchers and an evil local range patrol office. When Trigger is injured by a killer stallion, Roy turns to two unlikely allies—a 10-year-old boy who's scared of horses and frisky Trigger Jr. **67m/B VHS.** Roy Rogers, Dale Evans, Grant Withers, Pat Brady, Gordon Jones, Peter Miles, George Cleveland; *D:* William Witney; *W:* Gerald Geraghty.

Trigger Men ½ *Billy the Kid's Fighting Pals* **1941** Steele, Young, and St. John find a dying U.S. marshal who has been ambushed by the villainous Peil. Seems Peil and his gang have taken over a small border town in order to set up a smuggling operation with Mexico. So the trio avenge the marshal by putting a stop to the nefarious doings. Newfield directed under the pseudonym Sherman Scott. **59m/B VHS.** Bob Steele, Al "Fuzzy" St. John, Carleton Young, Edward Peil Sr., Phyllis Adair, Charles "Blackie" King, Curly Dresden, Hal Price, George Chesebro, Forrest Taylor, Budd Buster; *D:* Sam Newfield.

Trigger Pals ½ **1939** Jarrett stars in this basic oater about bringing a gang of rustlers to justice. Besides the usual gunplay, he also attempts to sing a few songs. **58m/B VHS.** Art Jarrett, Lee Powell, Al "Fuzzy" St. John, Dorothy Fay, Charles "Blackie" King, Frank LaRue; *D:* Sam Newfield.

Trigger Tricks ½ **1930** Gibson's brother becomes the victim of a vicious cattleman and Hoot is out for revenge. **60m/B VHS.** Hoot Gibson, Sally Eilers, Neal Hart, Monte Montague, Peter Morrison, Robert E. Homans, Jack (H.) Richardson; *D:* B. Reeves Eason.

The Trigger Trio ½ **1937** Rancher with diseased cattle kills a ranch inspector. The Three Mesquiteers are called in to crack the case. **54m/B VHS.** Ray Corrigan, Max Terhune, Ralph Byrd, Robert Warwick, Cornelius Keefe, Wally Wales; *D:* William Witney.

Trilby **1917** Original screen production of Du Maurier's classic tale of Svengali. **59m/B VHS.** Clara Kimball Young, Wilton Lackaye, Chester Barnett; *D:* Maurice Tourneur.

Trilogy of Terror ½ **1975** Black shows her versatility as she plays a tempting seductress, a mousy schoolteacher, and the terrified victim of an African Zuni fetish doll in three horror shorts. **78m/C VHS, DVD.** Karen Black, Robert Burton, John Karlen, Gregory Harrison, George Gaynes, James Storm, Kathryn Reynolds, Tracy Curtis; *D:* Dan Curtis; *W:* Richard Matheson; *C:* Paul Lohmann; *M:* Robert Cobert. **TV**

Trilogy of Terror 2 **1996 (R)** Curtis follows up his 1975 TV movie with an okay sequel headed by Anthony. "Graveyard Rats" features flesh-eating, cemetery-dwelling rodents and a greedy wife who bumped off her wealthy husband, a mother strikes a fiendish bargain to bring her drowned son back to life in "Bobby," and the deadly African Zuni fetish doll returns in "He Who Kills." **90m/C VHS, DVD.** Lysette Anthony, Richard Fitzpatrick, Geraint Wyn Davies, Matt Clark, Geoffrey Lewis, Blake Heron; *D:* Dan Curtis; *W:* Dan Curtis, William F. Nolan, Richard Matheson; *C:* Elemer Ragalyi; *M:* Robert Cobert. **CABLE**

Trinity Is Still My Name ½ *Continuavamo A Chiamarlo Trinita* **1975 (G)** Sequel to "They Call Me Trinity." Insouciant bumbling brothers Trinity and Bambino, oblivious to danger and hopeless odds, endure mishaps and adventures as they try to right wrongs. A funny parody of Western cliches that never becomes stale. **117m/C VHS, DVD.** *IT* Bud Spencer, Terence Hill, Harry Carey Jr.; *D:* E.B. (Enzo Barboni) Clucher.

Trio **1950** Sequel to "Quartet," featuring the W. Somerset Maugham stories "The Verger," "Mr. Knowall," and "Sanatorium Acclaimed." **88m/B VHS.** Jean Simmons, Michael Rennie, Bill Travers, James Hayter, Kathleen Harrison, Felix Aylmer, Nigel Patrick, Finlay Currie, John Laurie; *D:* Ken Annakin, Harold French; *C:* Geoffrey Unsworth, Reg Wyer.

The Trio **1997** Unconvincing German sex comedy finds gay middle-aged Zobel (George) and his daughter Lizzie (Hain) constantly on the move as they exercise their pickpocketing profession, along with Zobel's lover Karl (Redl). After Karl dies in an auto accident, Lizzie recruits hunky drifter Rudolf (Eitner) to take his place. Which Rudolf does in more ways than one, since he soon becomes the lover of both father and daughter. German with subtitles. **97m/C VHS, DVD, Wide.** *GE* Goetz George, Jeanette Hain, Felix Eitner, Christian Redl; *D:* Hermine Huntgeburth; *W:* Hermine Huntgeburth, Horst Sczerba, Volker Einrauch; *C:* Martin Kukula; *M:* Niki Reiser.

The Trip **1967** A psychedelic journey to the world of inner consciousness, via drugs. A TV director, unsure where his life is going, decides to try a "trip" to expand his understanding. Hopper is the drug salesman, Dern, the tour guide for Fonda's trip through sex, witches, torture chambers, and more. Great period music. **85m/C VHS.** Peter Fonda, Susan Strasberg, Bruce Dern, Dennis Hopper, Salli Sachse, Barboura Morris, Judith Lang, Luana Anders, Beach Dickerson, Dick Miller, Michael Nader, Michael Blodgett, Caren Bernsen, Katherine Walsh, Peter Bogdanovich, Tom Signorelli; *D:* Roger Corman; *W:* Jack Nicholson; *C:* Arch R. Dalzell; *M:* Barry Goldberg.

The Trip to Bountiful **1985 (PG)** An elderly widow, unhappy living in her son's fancy modern home, makes a pilgrimage back to her childhood home in Bountiful, Texas. Based on the Horton Foote play. Fine acting with Oscar-winning performance from Page. **102m/C VHS, 8mm.** Geraldine Page, Rebecca DeMornay, John Heard, Carlin Glynn, Richard Bradford; *D:* Peter Masterson; *W:* Horton Foote; *C:* Fred Murphy. Oscars '85: Actress (Page); Ind. Spirit '86: Actress (Page), Screenplay.

TripFall ½ **2000 (R)** Tom Williams (Ritter) decides he, wife Gina (Hunter), and their kids need some family time, so they head off on vacation. And run into the nightmare of Eddie (Roberts) and his gang of kidnappers. With his wife and kids in Eddie's slimy hands, Tom has one day to get more than a million bucks together if he wants them back alive. **95m/C VHS, DVD.** John Ritter, Eric Roberts, Rachel Hunter; *D:* Serge Rodnunsky; *W:* Serge Rodnunsky; *C:* Greg Patterson; *M:* Evan Evans. **VIDEO**

Triple Cross **1967** Plummer is a British safecracker imprisoned on the channel islands at the outbreak of WWII. When the Germans move in, he offers to work for them if they set him free. The Germans buy his story and send him to England, but once there he offers his services to the British as a double agent.

Based on the exploits of Eddie Chapman, adapted from his book, "The Eddie Chapman Story." **91m/C VHS.** *FR GB* Christopher Plummer, Romy Schneider, Trevor Howard, Gert Frobe, Yul Brynner, Claudine Auger, Georges Lycan, Jess Hahn, Howard Vernon; ***D:*** Terence Young.

Triple Echo *Soldier in Skirts* **1977 (R)** A young woman falls for an army deserter who is hiding from the military police by dressing as a woman. Mistrust and deception get the best of some of the involved parties. **90m/C VHS.** *GB* Glenda Jackson, Oliver Reed, Brian Deacon; ***D:*** Michael Apted; ***W:*** Robin Chapman.

Triple Impact **1992** Hall, Cook, and Riley are three martial-arts experts who join forces against illegal gambling syndicates who are staging full-contact bloodmatches. Their alliance leads them to Asia where the prize is death—or a fortune in gold. **97m/C VHS.** Dale "Apollo" Cook, Ron Hall, Bridgett "Baby Doll" Riley, Robert Marius, Steve Rogers, Nick Nicholson, Ned Hourani, Mike "Cobra" Cole; ***D:*** David Hunt; ***W:*** Steve Rogers.

TripleCross **1985** Three former cops strike it rich and although they love the money, they miss the game, so they get involved in a murder case. These wealthy detectives encounter high-level gangsters, a baseball scandal, and a hit man in their race to solve the perfect crime. **97m/C VHS.** Ted Wass, Markie Post, Gary Swanson; ***D:*** David Greene.

Triplecross **1995 (R)** Jewel thief Jimmy Ray (Bergin) is after a fortune in diamonds and obsessive FBI agent Oscar (Williams) is looking to bring him down. Oscar decides to use Jimmy Ray's ex-cell mate Teddy (Pare) but Teddy gets involved with J.R.'s girlfriend Julia (Laurence) instead of tending to business. Wooden crime caper. **95m/C VHS.** Patrick Bergin, Billy Dee Williams, Michael Pare, Ashley Laurence; ***D:*** Jeno Hodi. CABLE

Tripods: The White Mountains **1984** Sci-fi thriller about the takeover of earth by alien tripods. The conquerors start controlling human minds, but not until after they are 16 years old. Two boys seek to end the terror. **150m/C VHS.** John Shackley, Jim Baker, Cari Seel; ***D:*** Graham Theakston.

Trippin' **1999 (R)** Gregory (Richmond) is a daydreamer who can't keep his mind on his studies until he finds out that the prom queen, Cinny (Campbell), goes for the brainy type. Between fantasies of fame, fortune, and exotic locales, Gregory, with the help of his ne'er-do-well buddies Fish (Torry) and June (Faison), tries to improve his grades and get her to the prom. Likeable cast and a nice message about the importance of getting an education balance out a gratuitous subplot about a local crime boss recruiting June. Lightweight but amusing. **92m/C VHS, DVD.** Deon Richmond, Maia Campbell, Donald Adeosun Faison, Guy Torry, Harold Sylvester, Stoney Jackson, Michael Warren, Aloma Wright, Bill Henderson; ***D:*** David Raynr; ***W:*** Gary Hardwick; ***C:*** John Aronson.

Tripwire **1989 (R)** A vengeance-crazed government agent tracks down the terrorist who murdered his wife. **120m/C VHS.** Terence Knox, David Warner, Charlotte Lewis, Isabella Hofmann, Yaphet Kotto, Thomas Chong, Meg Foster; ***D:*** James (Momel) Lemmo.

Tristana **1970 (PG)** Allegorical tale of a beautiful girl (Deneuve) who moves in with a hypocritical benefactor following the death of her mother. She is quickly exploited and seduced by the one who would protect her, but runs away with an artist in pursuit of love. Searing in its commentary on Catholicism, death, lust, and the woebegone place of humanity in the world, the movie is also widely seen as a depiction of fascist Spain's attempt to find its place in the 20th century. Based on the novel by Benito Perez Galdos. In Spanish with English subtitles. **98m/C VHS.** *SP IT FR* Catherine Deneuve, Fernando Rey, Franco Nero, Lola Gaos, Antonio Casas, Jesus Fernandez, Vincent Solder; ***D:*** Luis Bunuel; ***W:*** Julio Alejandro, Luis Bunuel; ***C:*** Jose F. Aguayo.

The Triumph of Hercules *Trionfo di Ercole; Hercules and the Ten Avengers; Hercules vs. the Giant Warriors* **1966** Hercules gets stripped of his powers by a peeved Zeus and must try to battle a sorcercess and 10 giant bronze warriors without them, until Zeus reconsiders. **94m/C VHS.** *IT FR* Dan Vadis, Moira Orfei, Pierre (Peter Cross) Cressoy, Marilu Tolo, Pierro Lulli; ***D:*** Alberto De Martino; ***W:*** Robert Gianviti; ***C:*** Pier Ludovico Pavoni; ***M:*** Francesco De Masi.

The Triumph of Love **2001 (PG-13)** Not much of a triumph but not a complete waste of time either. Adapted from Pierre Marivaux's 18th-century play, Sorvino plays Princess Leonide, who knows that her family usurped their throne and she is determined to see its rightful owner, Prince Agis (Rodan), returned to power. Of course, he's a handsome prince and the princess has fallen in love but there are complications that involve her disguising herself as a male philosophy student and insinuating herself into his guardians' (Kingsley, Shaw) austere lives. Deceptions abound. **107m/C VHS, DVD.** *IT GB* Mira Sorvino, Ben Kingsley, Fiona Shaw, Jay Rodan, Rachael Stirling, Ignazio Oliva; ***D:*** Clare Peploe; ***W:*** Clare Peploe, Bernardo Bertolucci, Marilyn Goldin; ***C:*** Fabio Cianchetti; ***M:*** Jason Osborn, Jason Osborn.

The Triumph of Sherlock Holmes **1935** Wontner and Fleming teamed for an early series of Holmesian romps. In one of their best outings, Sherlock Holmes comes out of retirement as a series of bizarre murders of Pennsylvania coal miners lure him back into action. From "The Valley of Fear" by Sir Arthur Conan Doyle. **84m/B VHS.** *GB* Arthur Wontner, Ian Fleming; ***D:*** Leslie Hiscott.

Triumph of the Spirit **1989 (R)** Gritty account of boxer Salamo Arouch's experiences in Auschwitz. The boxer became champion in matches between prisoners conducted for the amusement of Nazi officers. Filmed on location in Auschwitz. **115m/C VHS, DVD, Wide.** Willem Dafoe, Robert Loggia, Edward James Olmos, Wendy Gazelle, Kelly Wolf, Costas Mandylor, Kario Salem; ***D:*** Robert M. Young; ***W:*** Robert M. Young, Shimon Arama, Andrzej Krakowski, Laurence Heath, Arthur Coburn, Millard Lampell; ***M:*** Cliff Eidelman.

Triumph of the Will *Triumph des Willens* **1934** Director Riefenstahl's formidable, stunning film, documenting Hitler and the Sixth Nazi Party Congress in 1934 in Nuernberg, Germany. The greatest and most artful propaganda piece ever produced. German dialogue. Includes English translation of the speeches. **115m/B VHS, DVD, Wide.** *GE* ***D:*** Leni Riefenstahl; ***W:*** Leni Riefenstahl; ***C:*** Sepp Allgeier; ***M:*** Herbert Windt.

Triumphs of a Man Called Horse **1983 (R)** An Indian must save his people from prospectors in order to keep his title as Peace, Chief of the Yellow Hand Sioux. Inadequate sequel to two previous films: "A Man Called Horse" and "The Return of a Man Called Horse." **91m/C VHS.** *MX* Richard Harris; ***D:*** John Hough; ***W:*** Carlos Aured, Jack DeWitt, Kenneth G. Blackwell.

Trixie **2000 (R)** Performances by a fine ensemble cast are mangled almost as badly as the English language in this wandering comedy-mystery. Trixie (Watson) is a malaprop-spouting security guard at a resort casino who wants to be a detective. She stumbles onto a murder mystery involving bombastic Senator Avery (Nolte) and decides that if she solves the crime, a career as a detective will surely follow. Many false leads are chased, and the theme that not everyone is as they appear is hammered home time and time again. Among the list of usual suspects are a golddigging barfly (Murphy), a washed-up lounge singer (Warren), a two-bit ladies man (Mulroney) and an impressionist/singer with a shady past (Lane). **117m/C VHS, DVD, Wide.** Emily Watson, Nick Nolte, Dermot Mulroney, Nathan Lane, Brittany Murphy, Lesley Ann Warren, Will Patton, Stephen Lang; ***D:*** Alan Rudolph; ***W:*** Alan Rudolph; ***C:*** Jan Kiesser; ***M:*** Mark Isham, Roger Neill.

Trois Couleurs: Blanc *White; Three Colors: White* **1994 (R)** Bittersweet comedic rags-to-riches tale spiced with revenge and lasting love. "White" focuses on equality and begins when a bewildered Polish hairdresser is divorced by his disdainful French wife, who takes him for everything he has. Returning to his family in Poland, Karol doggedly works his way into wealth. Then he decides to fake his death and leave his fortune to the ex he still loves—or does he? In Polish and French with English subtitles. Part 2 of Kieslowski's trilogy, following "Trois Couleurs: Bleu" and followed by "Trois Couleurs: Rouge." **92m/C VHS.** *FR SI PL* Zbigniew Zamachowski, Julie Delpy, Janusz Gajos, Jerzy Stuhr, Aleksander Bardini, Grzegorz Warchol, Cezary Harasimowicz, Jerzy Nowak, Jerzy Trela, Cezary Pazura, Michel Lisowski, Philippe Morier-Genoud; ***Cameos:*** Juliette Binoche, Florence Pernel; ***D:*** Krzysztof Kieslowski; ***W:*** Krzysztof Kieslowski, Krzysztof Piesiewicz; ***C:*** Edward Klosinski; ***M:*** Zbigniew Preisner. Berlin Intl. Film Fest. '94: Director (Kieslowski).

Trois Couleurs: Bleu *Three Colors: Blue; Blue* **1993 (R)** First installment of director Kieslowski's trilogy inspired by the French tricolor flag. "Blue" stands for liberty—here freedom is based on tragedy as Julie (Binoche) reshapes her life after surviving an accident which killed her famous composer husband and their young daughter. Excellent performance by Binoche, which relies on the internalized grief and brief emotion which flits across her face rather than overwhelming displays for expression. In French with English subtitles. **98m/C VHS, Wide.** *FR* Juliette Binoche, Benoit Regent, Florence Pernel, Charlotte Very, Helene Vincent, Philipe Volter, Claude Duneton, Hugues Quester, Florence Vignon, Isabelle Sadoyan, Yahn Tregouet, Jacek Ostaszewski; ***Cameos:*** Emmanuelle Riva; ***D:*** Krzysztof Kieslowski; ***W:*** Krzysztof Kieslowski, Krzysztof Piesiewicz, Slawomir Idziak, Agnieszka Holland, Edward Zebrowski; ***C:*** Slawomir Idziak; ***M:*** Zbigniew Preisner. Cesar '94: Actress (Binoche), Film Editing, Sound; L.A. Film Critics '93: Score; Venice Film Fest. '93: Actress (Binoche), Film.

Trois Couleurs: Rouge *Three Colors: Red; Red* **1994 (R)** "Red" is for fraternity in the French tricolor flag, and, in director Kieslowski's last film in his trilogy, emotional connections are made between unlikely couples. There's law student Auguste and his girlfriend Karin, young fashion model Valentine, and a nameless retired judge, brought together by circumstance and destined to change each other's lives. Subtle details make for careful viewing but it's a rewarding watch and a visual treat (keep an eye on cinematographer Sobocinski's use of the color red). Binoche and Delpy, who starred in the earlier films, also make an appearance, as Kieslowski uses the finale to tie up loose ends. In French with English subtitles. **99m/C VHS.** *FR PL SI* Irene Jacob, Jean-Louis Trintignant, Frederique Feder, Jean-Pierre Lorit, Samuel Le Bihan, Marion Stalens, Teco Celio, Bernard Escalon, Jean Schlegel, Elzbieta Jasinska; ***Cameos:*** Juliette Binoche, Julie Delpy, Benoit Regent, Zbigniew Zamachowski; ***D:*** Krzysztof Kieslowski; ***W:*** Krzysztof Kieslowski, Krzysztof Piesiewicz; ***C:*** Piotr Sobocinski; ***M:*** Zbigniew Preisner. Cesar '94: Score; Ind. Spirit '95: Foreign Film; L.A. Film Critics '94: Foreign Film; N.Y. Film Critics '94: Foreign Film; Natl. Soc. Film Critics '94: Foreign Film.

Trojan Eddie **1996** Stephen Rea puts his perpetual hangdog mug to good use as the hapless Trojan Eddie, so named for the make of the van in which he transports and sells stolen goods. He is married to the shrewish town tramp, who helps little in raising their two girls and makes fun of his dream of opening his own business. His boss is John Power (Harris), leader of a group of clannish con men. He is teamed with Power's nephew Dermot (Townsend), who's secretly romancing his uncle's much younger wife-to-be. The young lovers take off with the cache of wedding loot on the night of the nuptials, and Power involves Eddie in an all-out search for the couple. After they're caught and pardoned by Power, however, the spiral of betrayal and violence spins faster than ever, with Eddie always eyeing the chance to escape. Excellent rapport between Rea and Harris as their fortunes shift and reverse. **103m/C VHS.** Stephen Rea, Richard Harris, Brendan Gleeson, Sean McGinley, Angeline Ball, Brid Brennan, Stuart Townsend, Aislin McGuckin; ***D:*** Gilles Mackinnon; ***W:*** Billy Roche; ***C:*** John de Borman; ***M:*** John Keane.

The Trojan Horse *The Trojan War; The Mighty Warrior* **1962** Greek warrior Aeneas (Reeves), under the command of Ulysses (Barrymore), gets to hide out in the Trojan horse with his fellow fighters and then get those Trojans when they take the wooden beast into their city. When they're successful, Aeneas takes his guys and decides to go off and found the city of Rome. You were maybe expecting historical or mythological accuracy? **105m/C VHS.** *IT FR* Steve Reeves, John Blythe Barrymore Jr., Juliette Mayniel, Edy Vessel, Lidia Alfonsi, Luciana Angelillo, Arturo Dominici, Mimmo Palmara, Carlo Tamberlani, Nando Tamberlani; ***D:*** Giorgio Ferroni; ***W:*** Ugo Liberatore; ***C:*** Rino Filippini; ***M:*** Giovanni Fusco.

Trojan War **1997 (PG-13)** Yes, the title does refer to the condom brand. High schooler Brad Kimble (Friedle) has finally convinced dream girl Brooke (Shelton) to get romantic—if he has the proper protection, of course. But as his search is continually thwarted, this gives his best gal pal Lea (Hewitt)—who would like to be something more—the chance to show who really loves him. Harmless, although sexually overt, teen fluff. **90m/C VHS.** Lee Majors, Wendie Malick, David Patrick Kelly, Anthony Michael Hall, Jennifer Love Hewitt, Will Friedle, Marley Shelton; ***D:*** George Huang; ***W:*** Andy Burg, Scott Myers; ***C:*** Dean Semler; ***M:*** George S. Clinton.

Trojan Women **1971 (G)** Euripides' tragedy on the fate of the women of Troy after the Greeks storm the famous city. The play does not translate well to the screen, in spite of tour-de-force acting. **105m/C VHS.** Katharine Hepburn, Vanessa Redgrave, Irene Papas, Genevieve Bujold, Brian Blessed, Patrick Magee; ***D:*** Michael Cacoyannis. Natl. Bd. of Review '71: Actress (Papas).

Troll **1986 (PG-13)** A malevolent troll haunts an apartment building and possesses a young girl in hopes of turning all humans into trolls. Sometimes imaginative, sometimes embarrassing. Followed by a sequel. **86m/C VHS.** Noah Hathaway, Gary Sandy, Anne Lockhart, Sonny Bono, Shelley Hack, June Lockhart, Michael Moriarty, Jennifer Beck, Phil Fondacaro, Brad Hall, Julia Louis-Dreyfus, Albert Band, Charles Band; ***D:*** John Carl Buechler; ***W:*** Ed Naha; ***C:*** Romano Albani; ***M:*** Richard Band.

Troll 2 **1992 (PG-13)** A young boy can only rely on his faith in himself when no one believes his warnings about an evil coming to destroy his family. Entering into a nightmare world, Joshua must battle witches' spells and the evil trolls who carry out their bidding. **95m/C VHS.** Michael Stephenson, Connie McFarland; ***D:*** Drago Floyd; ***W:*** Clyde (Claudio Fragasso) Anderson.

A Troll in Central Park **1994 (G)** Animated fantasy about Stanley the troll, who is cast out of his kingdom (because he's a good guy) and winds up in New York's Central Park. There, Stanley brings happiness to a little girl and her skeptical brother, all the while battling the evil troll queen. Strictly average family fare. **76m/C VHS, DVD, Wide.** ***D:*** Don Bluth, Gary Goldman; ***W:*** Stu Krieger; ***M:*** Robert Folk; ***V:*** Dom DeLuise, Cloris Leachman, Jonathan Pryce, Hayley Mills, Charles Nelson Reilly, Phillip Glasser, Robert Morley, Sy Goraleb, Tawney Sunshine Glover, Jordan Metzner.

Troma's War woof! **1988 (R)** The survivors of an air crash find themselves amid a tropical terrorist-run civil war. Also available in a 105-minute, unrated version. Devotees of trash films shouldn't miss this one. **90m/C VHS, DVD.** Carolyn Beauchamp, Sean Bowen, Michael Ryder, Jessica Dublin, Steven Crossley, Lorayn Lane DeLuca, Charles Kay Hune, Ara Romanoff, Alex Cserhart, Aleida Harris; ***D:*** Michael Herz, Lloyd Kaufman; ***W:*** Lloyd Kaufman, Mitchell Dana, Eric Hattler, Thomas Martinek; ***C:*** James London; ***M:*** Christopher De Marco.

Tromba, the Tiger Man 🦴½ *Tromba* **1952** A circus tiger tamer uses a special drug that hypnotizes the critters into obeying his every whim. When he tries the same drug on women, things get out of hand. **62m/B VHS.** *GE* Rene Deltgen, Angelika Hauff, Gustav Knuth, Hilde Weissner, Grethe Weiser, Gardy Granass, Adrian Hoven; ***D:*** Helmut Weiss.

Tromeo & Juliet 🦴🦴 **1995 (R)** There've been many versions of Shakespeare, but the Bard may never recover from being "Tromatized." On the outskirts of New York City, teenaged Tromeo Que (Keenan) falls in lust with babe Juliet Capulet (Jensen), but the family feud is still around to cause major disharmony. There's lots of profanity, perversity, and gore to keep your interest. As the movie's tagline says, "Body Piercing. Kinky Sex. Dismemberment. The things that made Shakespeare great." The unrated version is 105 minutes. **95m/C VHS, DVD.** Will Keenan, Jane Jensen, Debbie Rochon, Lemmy, Valentine Miele, Sean Gunn; ***D:*** Lloyd Kaufman; ***W:*** James Gunn; ***C:*** Brendan Flynt; ***M:*** Willie Wisely.

Tron 🦴🦴 **1982 (PG)** A video game designer enters into his computer, where he battles the computer games he created and seeks revenge on other designers who have stolen his creations. Sounds better than it plays. Terrific special effects, with lots of computer-created graphics. **96m/C VHS, DVD, Wide.** Jeff Bridges, Bruce Boxleitner, David Warner, Cindy Morgan, Barnard Hughes, Dan Shor, Peter Jurasik, Tony Stephano; ***D:*** Steven Lisberger; ***W:*** Steven Lisberger; ***C:*** Bruce Logan; ***M:*** Walter (Wendy) Carlos.

Troop Beverly Hills 🦴 **1989 (PG)** Spoiled housewife Long isn't really spoiled, just misunderstood. She takes over leadership of her daughter's Wilderness Girls troop and finds the opportunity to redeem herself by offering her own unique survival tips to the uncooperative little brats who make up the troop. Everyone learns meaningful life lessons, Long is finally understood, and everyone lives happily ever after in posh Beverly Hills. Sheer silliness makes this one almost painful to watch, a shame since it boasts a good cast whose talent is totally wasted. **105m/C VHS, 8mm.** Shelley Long, Craig T. Nelson, Betty Thomas, Mary Gross, Stephanie Beacham, Audra Lindley, Edd Byrnes, Ami Foster, Jenny Lewis, Kellie Martin; ***D:*** Jeff Kanew; ***W:*** Pamela Norris, Margaret Grieco Oberman; ***M:*** Randy Edelman.

Tropic of Cancer 🦴🦴🦴 **1970 (NC-17)** Based on Henry Miller's once-banned, now classic novel, this film portrays the sexual escapades of the expatriate author living in 1920s Paris. Torn stars as the carefree, loose-living writer and Burstyn plays his disgusted wife. **87m/C VHS.** Rip Torn, James Callahan, Ellen Burstyn, David Bauer, Phil Brown; ***D:*** Joseph Strick.

Tropical Heat 🦴🦴 **1993 (R)** When the Maharajah is killed on safari, his grieving widow (D'Abo) files a $5 million insurance claim before returning to India. She's followed by an investigator (Rossovich) who becomes infatuated with the lovely D'Abo. Through palaces, primitive villages, and ancient jungle temples, they are drawn into a mystery involving blackmail and murder. Based on a story by Jag Mundhra, Michael W. Potts, and Simon Levy. **86m/C VHS.** Rick Rossovich, Maryam D'Abo, Lee Ann Beaman, Asha Siewkumar; ***D:*** Jag Mundhra; ***W:*** Michael W. Potts; ***M:*** Del Casher.

Tropical Snow 🦴 **1988 (R)** A pair of lovers living poorly in Colombia decide to enter the drug trade in exchange for passage to the U.S. offered to them by drug kingpin Carradine. Unfortunately, they get more than they bargained for. Shot on location. **87m/C VHS.** David Carradine, Madeleine Stowe, Nick Corri, Argermiro Catiblanco; ***D:*** Ciro Duran.

Trouble along the Way 🦴🦴½ **1953** Wayne is a once big-time college football coach who takes a coaching job at a small, financially strapped Catholic college in an effort to retain custody of his young daughter. His underhanded recruiting methods result in his firing—and the probable loss of his daughter. Unusual and sentimental role for Wayne proves he can handle comedy as well as action. **110m/B VHS.** John Wayne, Donna Reed, Charles Coburn, Tom Tully, Sherry Jackson, Marie Windsor, Tom Helmore, Dabbs Greer, Leif Erickson, Douglas Spencer; ***D:*** Michael Curtiz; ***W:*** Jack Rose, Melville Shavelson; ***M:*** Max Steiner.

Trouble Bound 🦴🦴 **1992 (R)** Madsen is Harry, a guy just out of prison, on his way to Nevada with trouble dogging him every step. He's got a dead body in the car trunk, drug dealers after him, and when he offers a lift to a pretty cocktail waitress (Arquette) his luck only gets worse. She plans to kill a Mob boss and it's no secret. Chases and violence. **90m/C VHS.** Michael Madsen, Patricia Arquette, Florence Stanley, Seymour Cassel, Sal Jenco; ***D:*** Jeff Reiner; ***W:*** Darrell Fetty, Francis Delia; ***M:*** Vinnie Golia.

Trouble Busters 🦴 **1933** Troubled locals worry about who to call when oil is discovered in their town, bringing evil profiteers with it. The Trouble Busters come into town to set things straight. **51m/B VHS.** Jack Hoxie, Lane Chandler; ***D:*** Lewis D. Collins.

Trouble in Mind 🦴🦴🦴 **1986 (R)** Stylized romance is set in the near future in a rundown diner. Kristofferson is an ex-cop who gets involved in the lives of a young couple looking for a better life. Look for Divine in one of her/his rare appearances outside of John Waters' works. **111m/C VHS, 8mm.** Kris Kristofferson, Keith Carradine, Genevieve Bujold, Lori Singer, Divine, Joe Morton, George Kirby, John Considine, Dirk Blocker, Gailard Sartain, Tracy Kristofferson; ***D:*** Alan Rudolph; ***W:*** Alan Rudolph; ***C:*** Toyomichi Kurita; ***M:*** Mark Isham. Ind. Spirit '86: Cinematog.

Trouble in Paradise 🦴🦴 **1988** Welch stars as a widow stranded in a tropical island paradise with an Australian sailor. The two must struggle as they are stalked by a gang of drug smugglers, hence the title. **92m/C VHS.** Raquel Welch, Jack Thompson, Nicholas Hammond, John Gregg; ***D:*** Di Drew. **TV**

Trouble in Store 🦴🦴½ **1953** A bumbling department store employee stumbles on a gangster's plot. Fun gags and a good cast. **85m/B VHS.** *GB* Margaret Rutherford, Norman Wisdom, Moira Lister, Megs Jenkins; ***D:*** John Paddy Carstairs.

Trouble in Texas 🦴🦴 **1937** Outlaws go to a rodeo and try to steal the prize money. Tex wants to find out who killed his brother and in his spare time, sings and tries to stop the crooks. Notable because it is the last film Hayworth made under her original stage name (Rita Cansino). **65m/B VHS.** Tex Ritter, Rita Hayworth, Earl Dwire, Yakima Canutt; ***D:*** Robert North Bradbury.

Trouble in the Glen 🦴🦴½ **1954** A Scottish-American soldier returns to his ancestral home and becomes involved in a dispute between the town residents and a lord over a closed road. Uneven script undermines comic idea. **91m/C VHS.** *GB* Orson Welles, Victor McLaglen, Forrest Tucker, Margaret Lockwood; ***D:*** Herbert Wilcox.

The Trouble with Angels 🦴🦴½ **1966 (PG)** Two young girls turn a convent upside down with their endless practical jokes. Russell is everything a Mother Superior should be: understanding, wise, and beautiful. **112m/C VHS.** Hayley Mills, June Harding, Rosalind Russell, Gypsy Rose Lee, Binnie Barnes; ***D:*** Ida Lupino; ***C:*** Lionel Lindon; ***M:*** Jerry Goldsmith.

The Trouble with Dick 🦴 **1988 (R)** An ambitious young science fiction writer's personal troubles begin to appear in his writing. Although the box cover displays a "Festival Winner" announcement, don't be fooled! Story becomes tedious after first five minutes. **86m/C VHS.** Tom Villard, Susan Dey, Elizabeth Gorcey, David Clennon, Marianne Muellerleile; ***D:*** Gary Walkow; ***W:*** Gary Walkow; ***C:*** Elaine Giftos, Daryl Studebaker; ***M:*** Roger Bourland. Sundance '87: Grand Jury Prize.

The Trouble with Girls (and How to Get into It) 🦴🦴🦴 *The Chautauqua* **1969 (G)** A 1920s traveling show manager tries to solve a local murder. Not as much singing as his earlier films, but good attention is paid to details. This is definitely one of the better Elvis vehicles. ♫Almost; Clean Up Your Own Back Yard. **99m/C VHS.** Elvis Presley, Marlyn Mason, Nicole Jaffe, Sheree North, Edward Andrews, John Carradine, Vincent Price, Joyce Van Patten, Dabney Coleman, John Rubinstein, Anthony Teague; ***D:*** Peter Tewkesbury.

The Trouble with Harry 🦴🦴🦴 **1955 (PG)** When a little boy finds a dead body in a Vermont town, it causes all kinds of problems for the community. No one is sure who killed Harry and what to do with the body. MacLaine's film debut and Herrmann's first musical score for Hitchcock. **90m/C VHS, DVD, Wide.** John Forsythe, Shirley MacLaine, Edmund Gwenn, Jerry Mathers, Mildred Dunnock, Mildred Natwick, Royal Dano; ***D:*** Alfred Hitchcock; ***W:*** John Michael Hayes; ***C:*** Robert Burks; ***M:*** Bernard Herrmann.

The Trouble with Spies 🦴 **1987 (PG-13)** A bumbling British spy goes to Ibizia to locate a Russian agent, makes a million mistakes and wins anyway. A loser of a film, wasted a fine cast. Made in 1984; no one bothered to release it for three years. **91m/C VHS.** Donald Sutherland, Malcolm Morley, Lucy Gutteridge, Ruth Gordon, Ned Beatty, Michael Hordern, Robert Morley; ***D:*** Burt Kennedy; ***W:*** Burt Kennedy.

Troublemakers 🦴½ **1994 (PG)** Travis (Hill) is the fastest gun in the west—but his brother Moses (Spencer) is the country's meanest bounty hunter. But their mother loves them, and wants both her boys home for Christmas. So she leaves it up to Travis to lure Moses back to the homestead. **98m/C VHS, DVD.** Terence Hill, Bud Spencer, Anne Kasprik, Ruth Buzzi, Ron Carey; ***D:*** Terence Hill; ***W:*** Jess Hill; ***C:*** Carlo Tafani; ***M:*** Pino Donaggio.

Troubles 🦴🦴½ **1988** In 1919, Major Brendan Archer arrives on the coast of Wicklow, Ireland to be reunited with his fiancee, Angela Spencer, at the family hotel, the decaying Majestic. Brendan is puzzled by the changes in both the hotel and Angela and begins to turn his interests to her friend, Sarah Devlin, who is a passionate Irish nationalist. But volatile Irish politics puts the romance in danger. Based on the 1970 novel by J.G. Farrell. **208m/C VHS, DVD.** *GB* Ian Charleson, Ian Richardson, Sean Bean, Emer Gillespie, Susannah Harker; ***D:*** Christopher Morahan; ***W:*** Charles Sturridge. **TV**

The Truce 🦴🦴🦴 *La Tregua* **1996** Adaptation of the novel by Primo Levi, based on his true account of traveling home across Europe after the liberation of Auschwitz at the end of WWII. Tells the story of Levi's arduous journey home to Turin through Eastern Europe, as well as his slow rediscovery of life and hope. Has the trappings of a grand historical epic, but works best as a quiet introspective look at a man trying to reclaim his humanity after experiencing unimaginable horror. Flashback scenes in the camp are appropriately harrowing, but the film loses focus when joining Levi and his ragtag compadres on the road home, sometimes slipping into banal sentimentality or outright melodrama, two things a story this powerful doesn't need. Turturro, who committed to the project several years ago, gives the performance of his career, understated and convincing. Levi committed suicide in 1987, shortly after giving Rosi's adaptation his blessing. **117m/C VHS.** *IT FR GE SI* John Turturro, Rade Serbedzija, Massimo Ghini, Stefano Dionisi, Teco Celio, Claudio Bisio, Roberto Citran, Andy Luotto, Agnieszka Wagner; ***D:*** Francesco Rosi; ***W:*** Stefano Rulli, Sandro Petraglia, Tonino Guerra, Francesco Rosi; ***C:*** Pasqualino De Santis, Marco Pontecorvo; ***M:*** Luis Bacalov.

Truck Stop 🦴 **19??** This truck stop has all a trucker needs—including the owner, voluptuous Pamela. **80m/C VHS.** Nikki Gentile, Elizabeth Turner; ***D:*** Jean Marie Pallardy.

Truck Stop Women 🦴🦴 **1974 (R)** Female truckers become involved in smuggling and prostitution at a truck stop. The mob wants a cut of the business and will do anything to get their way. Better than it sounds. **88m/C VHS.** Claudia Jennings, Lieux Dressler, John Martino, Dennis Fimple, Dolores Dorn, Gene Drew, Paul Carr, Jennifer Burton; ***D:*** Mark L. Lester.

Truck Turner 🦴½ **1974 (R)** He's a bounty hunter, he's black and he's up against a threadbare plot. Hayes methodically eliminates everyone involved with his partner's murder while providing groovy soundtrack. Quintessential blaxploitation. **91m/C VHS, DVD, Wide.** Isaac Hayes, Yaphet Kotto, Annazette Chase, Nichelle Nichols, Scatman Crothers, Dick Miller; ***D:*** Jonathan Kaplan; ***W:*** Leigh Chapman; ***C:*** Charles F. Wheeler; ***M:*** Isaac Hayes.

Trucker's Woman 🦴 **1983 (R)** Man takes a job driving an 18-wheel truck in order to find the murderers of his father. **90m/C VHS.** Michael Hawkins, Mary Cannon; ***D:*** Will Zens.

Trucks 🦴🦴 **1997 (R)** A group of residents are terrorized by driverless trucks going on a rampage through their small town, which happens to be located in Area 51. Based on the short story by Stephen King and previously filmed as 1986's "Maximum Overdrive." **99m/C VHS, DVD.** Timothy Busfield, Brenda Bakke, Brendan Fletcher, Jay Brazeau, Amy Stewart; ***D:*** Chris Thomson; ***W:*** Brian Taggert; ***C:*** Rob Draper, Keith Holland; ***M:*** Michael Richard Plowman. **CABLE**

True Believer 🦴🦴½ **1989 (R)** Cynical lawyer, once a '60s radical, now defends rich drug dealers. Spurred on by a young protege, he takes on the hopeless case of imprisoned Asian-American accused of gang-slaying. Tense thriller with good cast. **103m/C VHS, DVD, Wide.** James Woods, Robert Downey Jr., Yuji Okumoto, Margaret Colin, Kurtwood Smith, Tom Bower, Miguel Fernandes, Charles Hallahan; ***D:*** Joseph Ruben; ***W:*** Wesley Strick; ***C:*** John Lindley; ***M:*** Brad Fiedel.

True Blood 🦴🦴 **1989 (R)** A man returns to his home turf to save his brother from the same ruthless gang who set him up for a cop's murder. **100m/C VHS.** Chad Lowe, Jeff Fahey, Sherilyn Fenn; ***D:*** Peter Maris.

True Blue 🦴🦴 **2001 (R)** Rem Macy (Berenger) is supposed to be a seasoned NYPD detective. So why does he behave like a hormonally-challenged rookie? He's investigating a severed hand found floating in a Central Park pond that turns out to belong to the roommate of Nikki (Heuring). Nikki begs protection from Macy and he lets her stay in his apartment—which the Hound is sure is standard police procedure. Naturally, this is a really dumb move. **101m/C VHS, DVD, Wide.** Tom Berenger, Lori Heuring, Barry Newman, Pamela Gridley, Soon-Teck Oh, Richard Chevolleau, Leo Lee; ***D:*** J.S. Cardone; ***W:*** J.S. Cardone; ***C:*** Darko Suvak; ***M:*** Timothy S. Jones. **VIDEO**

True Colors 🦴🦴½ **1987 (PG-13)** A woman fights for her homeland of France in order to save the country from being taken over by Hitler. **160m/C VHS.** Noni Hazlehurst, John Waters, Patrick Ryecart, Shane Briant, Alan Andrews; ***D:*** Pino Amenta.

True Colors 🦴🦴 **1991 (R)** Law school buddies take divergent paths in post grad real world. Straight and narrow Spader works for Justice Department while dropout Cusack manipulates friends and acquaintances to further his position as Senator's aid. Typecast, predictable and, moralizing. **111m/C VHS.** Paul Guilfoyle, Dina Merrill, Philip Bosco, Brad Sullivan, Don McManus, John Cusack, James Spader, Imogen Stubbs, Mandy Patinkin, Richard Widmark; ***D:*** Herbert Ross.

True Confessions 🦴🦴🦴 **1981 (R)** Tale of corruption pits two brothers, one a priest and the other a detective, against each other. Nice 1940s period look, with excellent performances from De Niro and Duvall. Based on a true case from the Gregory Dunne novel. **110m/C VHS.** Robert De Niro, Robert Duvall, Kenneth McMillan, Charles Durning, Cyril Cusack, Ed Flanders, Burgess Meredith, Louisa Moritz; ***D:*** Ulu Grosbard; ***W:*** John Gregory Dunne, Joan Didion; ***C:*** Owen Roizman; ***M:*** Georges Delerue.

True Crime 🦴🦴½ *Dangerous Kiss* **1995 (R)** High school student turns detective when a classmate is killed, hooks up with a police cadet, and finds herself on the trail of a serial killer. **94m/C VHS, DVD.** Alicia Silverstone, Kevin Dillon, Bill Nunn, Michael Bowen; ***D:*** Pat Verducci; ***W:*** Pat Verducci; ***C:*** Chris Squires; ***M:*** Blake Leyh.

True Crime 🦴🦴½ **1999 (R)** Eastwood, who directs and stars, does a good job developing his character Steve Everett, a flawed reporter who has boozed and womanized his way out of the top of his profession. He is given the assignment to interview death row inmate Frank Beachum (Washington), who is scheduled to die in twenty-four hours. Everett becomes convinced that Beachum is innocent, and the plot erodes into a trite race against time to save the innocent man. Clint shows his acting chops before the story deflates, however, and his fans will certainly enjoy this one. **127m/C VHS, DVD, Wide.** Clint Eastwood, James Woods, Isaiah Washington IV, Denis Leary, Frances Fisher, Diane Venora, Mary McCormack, Lisa Gay Hamilton, Bernard Hill, Michael McKean, Michael Jeter, Hattie Winston, Laila Robins, Christine Ebersole, Anthony Zerbe, John Finn, Marissa Ribisi, Erik King, Graham Beckel, Sydney Tamiia Poitier, Penny Rae Bridges; ***D:*** Clint Eastwood; ***W:*** Larry Gross, Paul Brickman, Stephen Schiff; ***C:*** Jack N. Green; ***M:*** Lennie Niehaus.

True Friends 🦴🦴 **1998 (R)** Amateurish but earnest effort by the three lead actors (who also wrote, directed, and produced in various combinations). In 1980, three 12-year-old Bronx buddies witness local mob boss, Big Tony, kill a man. They've stayed friends and kept the secret for 15 years but now the crime comes back to haunt them. **98m/C VHS, DVD.** James Quattrochi, Loreto Mauro, Rodrigo Botero, Dan Lauria, MacKenzie Phillips, John Capodice, Peter Onorati, Bertilla Damas, Leo Rossi; ***D:*** James Quattrochi; ***W:*** James Quattrochi, Rodrigo Botero; ***C:*** Jeff Baustert; ***M:*** Charles Dayton.

True Grit 🦴🦴🦴 **1969 (G)** Hard-drinking U.S. Marshal Rooster Cogburn (Wayne) is hired by a young girl (Darby) to find her father's killer. Won Wayne his only Oscar. Based on the Charles Portis novel. Prompted sequel, "Rooster Cogburn." **128m/C VHS, DVD.** Jeremy Slate, Dennis Hopper, Alfred Ryder, Strother Martin, Jeff Corey, Ron Soble, John Fiedler, James Westerfield, John Doucette, Donald Woods, Edith Atwater, Carlos Rivas, Wilford Brimley, Jay Silverheels, Hank Worden, John Wayne, Glen Campbell, Kim Darby, Robert Duvall; ***D:*** Henry Hathaway; ***W:*** Marguerite Roberts; ***C:*** Lucien Ballard; ***M:*** Elmer Bernstein. Oscars '69: Actor (Wayne); Golden Globes '70: Actor—Drama (Wayne).

True Heart 🦴🦴½ **1997 (PG)** Bonnie (Dunst) and brother Sam (Bryan) are lost in the British Columbian wilderness after surviving a plane crash. They are befriended by a Native American elder (Schellenberg), who guides them through the dangers and back to civilization. Corny dialogue and beautiful scenery. **92m/C VHS.** Kirsten Dunst, Zachery Ty Bryan, August Schellenberg, Dey Young, Michael Gross; ***D:*** Catherine Cyran; ***W:*** Catherine Cyran; ***C:*** Christopher Baffa; ***M:*** Eric Allaman.

True Heart Susie 🦴🦴½ **1919** A simple, moving story about a girl who is in love with a man who marries another girl from the city. Silent. **87m/B VHS.** Lillian Gish, Robert "Bobbie" Harron; ***D:*** D.W. Griffith.

True Identity 🦴🦴 **1991 (R)** Henry, a comic superstar in England, stars as an innocent black man marked for death by the Mafia. He hides by disguising himself as white and gets a taste of life on the other side of the color line. The interesting premise was based on a classic Eddie Murphy sketch on "Saturday Night Live," but isn't treated with sufficient imagination or humor here. **94m/C VHS.** Lenny Henry, Frank Langella, Anne-Marie Johnson, Charles Lane; ***D:*** Charles Lane; ***W:*** Andy Breckman.

True Lies 🦴🦴½ **1994 (R)** Brain candy with a bang offers eye popping special effects and a large dose of unbelievability. Sort of like a big screen "Scarecrow and Mrs. King" as supposed computer salesman Harry Trasker (Ah-nuld) keeps his spy work secret from mousy, neglected and bored wife Helen (Curtis), who has a few secrets of her own and inadvertantly ends up right in the thick of things. Raunchy and extremely sexist, but not without charm; the stupidity is part of the fun. Perfectly cast sidekick Arnold holds his own as a pig, but Heston is wasted as the head honcho. Tons of special effects culiminate in a smashing finish. Very loosely adapted from the 1991 French comedy "La Total." **114m/C VHS, DVD, Wide.** Arnold Schwarzenegger, Jamie Lee Curtis, Tom Arnold, Bill Paxton, Tia Carrere, Art Malik, Eliza Dushku, Charlton Heston, Grant Heslov; ***D:*** James Cameron; ***W:*** James Cameron; ***C:*** Russell Carpenter; ***M:*** Brad Fiedel. Golden Globes '95: Actress—Mus./Comedy (Curtis); Blockbuster '96: Action Actress, V. (Curtis).

True Love 🦴🦴🦴 **1989 (R)** Low-budget, savagely observed comedy follows the family and community events leading up to a Bronx Italian wedding. Authentic slice-of-life about two young people with very different ideas about what marriage and commitment mean. Acclaimed script and performances. **104m/C VHS.** Annabella Sciorra, Ron Eldard, Aida Turturro, Roger Rignack, Michael J. Wolfe, Star Jasper, Kelly Cinnante, Rick Shapiro, Suzanne Costallos, Vincent Pastore; ***D:*** Nancy Savoca; ***W:*** Nancy Savoca, Richard Guay; ***C:*** Lisa Rinzler. Sundance '89: Grand Jury Prize.

True Romance 🦴🦴½ **1993 (R)** Geeky Clarence (Slater) and wide-eyed call girl Alabama (Arquette) meet and fall instantly in love (and marriage). The inept duo inadvertantly steals her pimp's coke and they head to L.A. with the mob in pursuit. Gem performances in small roles include Walken's icily debonair mafioso; Clarence's dad (Hopper), an ex-cop who runs afoul of Walken; Pitt's space-case druggie; Oldman's crazed pimp; and the ghost of Elvis (Kilmer), whom Clarence talks to in times of stress. Horrific violence mixed with very black humor clicks most of the time. Tarantino helped finance "Reservior Dogs" when he sold this script, his first. Unrated version also available. **116m/C VHS, DVD.** Maria Pitillo, Gregory Sporleder, Kevin Corrigan, Michael Beach, Frank Adonis, Victor Argo, Paul Ben-Victor, Paul Bates, Christian Slater, Patricia Arquette, Gary Oldman, Brad Pitt, Val Kilmer, Dennis Hopper, Christopher Walken, Samuel L. Jackson, Christopher Penn, Bronson Pinchot, Michael Rapaport, Saul Rubinek, Conchata Ferrell, James Gandolfini, Tom Sizemore, Ed Lauter; ***D:*** Tony Scott; ***W:*** Quentin Tarantino; ***C:*** Jeffrey L. Kimball; ***M:*** Hans Zimmer, Mark Mancina.

True Stories 🦴🦴🦴½ **1986 (PG)** Quirky, amusing look at the eccentric denizens of a fictional, off-center Texas town celebrating its 150th anniversary. Notable are Kurtz as the Laziest Woman in America and Goodman as a blushing suitor. Directorial debut of Byrne. Worth a look. **89m/C VHS, DVD.** David Byrne, John Goodman, Swoosie Kurtz, Spalding Gray, Annie McEnroe, Pops Staples, Tito Larriva, Alix Elias, Scott Valentine, Jo Harvey Allen; ***D:*** David Byrne; ***W:*** Beth Henley, Stephen Tobolowsky, David Byrne; ***C:*** Edward Lachman; ***M:*** David Byrne.

True Vengeance 🦴🦴 **1997 (R)** Navy operative finds himself on the run from a group of bounty hunters. **90m/C VHS.** Daniel Bernhardt, Miles O'Keeffe, Beverly Johnson; ***D:*** David Worth; ***W:*** Kurt Johnstad; ***C:*** David Worth. **VIDEO**

True West 🦴🦴🦴 **1986** Filmed performance of the acclaimed Sam Shepard play about two mismatched brothers. **110m/C VHS.** John Malkovich, Gary Sinise; ***D:*** Allan Goldstein. **TV**

True Women 🦴🦴½ **1997 (PG-13)** Sarah McClure (Delany) leaves Georgia with husband Bartlett (Boothe), settles in Texas, and raises her orphaned sister Euphemia (Majorino and Gish), as well as her own family, while Bartlett's off being a Texas Ranger. Euphemia's eventually reunited with her best friend, southern plantation beauty Georgia (Jolie), who's trying to hide the fact that she's part-Cherokee. The ladies suffer through Comanche attacks, the Alamo and the Mexican Army, the Civil War, Reconstruction, and various romantic trials and tribulations, all while being gosh-darn heroic. TV miniseries based on the historical novel by Janice Woods Windle. **170m/C VHS.** Dana Delany, Annabeth Gish, Angelina Jolie, Powers Boothe, Tina Majorino, Rachael Leigh Cook, Jeffrey Nordling, Michael Greyeyes, Tony Todd, Terrence Mann, Michael York, Salli Richardson, Irene Bedard, Charles S. Dutton, Julie Carmen, Matthew Glave, John Schneider; ***D:*** Karen Arthur; ***W:*** Christopher Lofton; ***C:*** Thomas Neuwirth; ***M:*** Bruce Broughton. **TV**

Truly, Madly, Deeply 🦴🦴🦴 **1991 (PG)** The recent death of her lover Jamie (Rickman) drives Nina (Stevenson) into despair and anger, until he turns up at her apartment one day. And decides to bring some of his ghostly buddies and hang out. Tender and well written tale of love and the supernatural, with believable characters and plot-line. Playwright Minghella's directorial debut. **107m/C VHS, DVD.** *GB* Juliet Stevenson, Alan Rickman, Bill Paterson, Michael Maloney, Christopher Rozycki, Keith Bartlett, David Ryall, Stella Maris; ***D:*** Anthony Minghella; ***W:*** Anthony Minghella; ***C:*** Remi Adefarasin; ***M:*** Barrington Pheloung. Australian Film Inst. '92: Foreign Film; British Acad. '91: Orig. Screenplay.

Truman 🦴🦴½ **1995 (PG)** Cable bio follows "Give 'em Hell" Harry (Sinise) from 1917 to 1968. The 33rd U.S. President, derided as a political hack, was determined to prove himself against the odds and by making the tough decisions, including authorizing use of the A-bomb on Japan. Sinise gives the appropriate nononsense performance, matched by Scarwid as ever-loyal wife Bess. Based on David McCullough's Pulitzer Prize-winning book. **?m/C VHS, DVD.** Gary Sinise, Diana Scarwid, Colm Feore, Richard Dysart, James Gammon, Tony Goldwyn, Pat Hingle, Harris Yulin, Leo Burmester, Zeljko Ivanek, David Lansbury, Marian Seldes, Lois Smith, Richard Venture, Daniel von Bargen; ***D:*** Frank Pierson; ***W:*** Tom Rickman; ***C:*** Paul Elliott; ***M:*** David Mansfield. **CABLE**

The Truman Show 🦴🦴🦴🦴 **1998 (PG)** Flawless execution of an eerie, yet fantastical premise, marked by outstanding performances, make this surreal fable a joy to watch from start to finish. Unbeknownst to insurance salesman Truman Burbank, (Carrey) his entire life has been broadcast live on TV in a 24-hour soap opera. When evidence of Truman's fabricated life begins to surface, he plans his escape, upsetting the grand scheme of producer, director and charismatic artist Christof (Harris in a stand-out performance). Carrey's sympathetic, low-key portrayal will make people forget the disappointment of "Cable Guy." Weir handles his satirical theme with craftmen-like precision, never letting his commentary on the power of the tube become too heavy-handed. Carrey reportedly took a pay cut from his $20 million fee in order to star. **102m/C VHS, DVD, Wide.** Jim Carrey, Ed Harris, Laura Linney, Noah Emmerich, Natascha (Natasha) McElhone, Holland Taylor, Paul Giamatti, Philip Baker Hall, Brian Delate, Una Damon; ***D:*** Peter Weir; ***W:*** Andrew Niccol; ***C:*** Peter Biziou; ***M:*** Philip Glass, Burkhard Dallwitz. British Acad. '98: Director (Weir), Orig. Screenplay; Golden Globes '99: Actor—Drama (Carrey), Support. Actor (Harris), Score; MTV Movie Awards '99: Male Perf. (Carrey); Natl. Bd. of Review '98: Support. Actor (Harris).

The Trumpet of the Swan 🦴½ **2001 (G)** Disappointing animated adaptation of E.B. White's 1970 children's book has Louis, a mute trumpeter swan, trying to overcome his disability. Louis befriends a human boy who persuades him to learn to read and write, which doesn't help him much in the animal world, but brings him fame in the human one. His father, distraught over his son's "defect," steals a trumpet for him, and Louis learns to play, becoming famous enough to assuage his father's guilt over the theft by paying for the instrument. The animation, story, and (surprisingly) the score, all seem flat, while the script provides nothing in the way of magic. Only the youngest (under 5) of viewers will be distracted, but probably not for very long. **75m/C VHS, DVD, Wide.** *US* ***D:*** Richard Rich, Terry L. Noss; ***W:*** Judy Rothman Rofe; ***M:*** Marcus Miller; ***V:*** Dee Baker, Jason Alexander, Mary Steenburgen, Reese Witherspoon, Seth Green, Carol Burnett, Joe Mantegna, Sam Gifaldi.

Trumps 🦴🦴 *Enormous Changes at the Last Minute* **1983 (R)** Three dramas about women and contemporary relationships in New York City. Based on three stories—"Faith's Story," "Virginia's Story," and "Alexandra's Story"—by Grace Paley. **90m/C VHS.** Ellen Barkin, Kevin Bacon, Maria Tucci, Ron McLarty, Zvee Scooler, David Strathairn, Jeffrey DeMunn, Sudie Bond; ***D:*** Mirra Bank, Ellen Hovde; ***W:*** John Sayles, Susan Rice.

Trust 🦴🦴 **1991 (R)** An obnoxious girl, tossed out by her family after becoming pregnant, forms a loving bond with a strange, possibly deranged guy from an abusive household. Similar in style and theme to Hartley's "The Unbelievable Truth"—a peculiar sardonic comedy/drama not for every taste. **107m/C VHS.** Adrienne Shelly, Martin Donovan, Merritt Nelson, Edie Falco, John MacKay, Marko Hunt; ***D:*** Hal Hartley; ***W:*** Hal Hartley; ***C:*** Michael Spiller; ***M:*** Phil Reed. Sundance '91: Screenplay.

Trust Me 🦴🦴 **1989 (R)** A cynical L.A. art dealer decides to promote a young artist's work and then kill him off to increase the value of his paintings. Satirical view of the Los Angeles art crowd. **94m/C VHS.** Adam Ant, Talia Balsam, David Packer, Barbara Bain, Joyce Van Patten, William DeAcutis; ***D:*** Bobby Houston.

Trusting Beatrice 🦴½ **1992 (PG)** Lame comedy finds feckless landscaper Claude (Jacobs) the bewildered caretaker of Beatrice (Jacob), a Frenchwoman stranded in America without a green card and with a young Cambodian refugee girl. So Claude decides to take Beatrice home to his determinedly eccentric family. Tries for quirky but fails miserably. **86m/C VHS.** Irene Jacob, Mark Evan Jacobs, Leonardo Cimino, Charlotte Moore, Steve Buscemi, Pat McNamara; ***D:*** Cindy Lou Johnson; ***W:*** Cindy Lou Johnson.

The Truth about Cats and Dogs 🦴🦴🦴 **1996 (PG-13)** Funny, intelligent Abby (Garofalo) hosts a popular radio call-in show for pet lovers. When a handsome Brit photographer (Chaplin) phones in with a Great Dane problem, he becomes intrigued by her voice, and asks for a date. Insecure about her looks, Abby asks her beautiful-but-dim girlfriend Noelle (Thurman) to fill in. Naturally, both women fall for the shy Englishman. Charming, updated version of "Cyrano de Bergerac" theme works because of strong lead performances, especially Garofalo, who steals the show with her dry, self-effacing wit. Entertaining romantic comedy features some nice scenes of Santa Monica, too. **97m/C VHS, DVD.** Bob Odenkirk, Janeane Garofalo, Uma Thurman, Ben Chaplin, Jamie Foxx, Richard Coca, Stanley DeSantis; ***D:*** Michael Lehmann; ***W:*** Audrey Wells; ***C:*** Robert Brinkmann; ***M:*** Howard Shore.

The Truth About Jane 🦴🦴½ **2000** Fifteen-year-old Jane (muth) is experiencing her first love. Unfortunately for her family and friends, it's with another girl and they just can't cope. Her mom, Janice (Channing), is especially upset and may lose Jane if she can't find a way to accept her. **91m/C VHS, DVD.** Stockard Channing, Ellen Muth, James Naughton, RuPaul Charles, Noah Fleiss, Kelly Rowan, Jenny O'Hara, Alicia Lagano; ***D:*** Lee Rose; ***W:*** Lee Rose; ***C:*** Eric Van Haren Noman; ***M:*** Terence Blanchard. **CABLE**

Truth about Women 🦴🦴 **1958** An old aristocrat recounts his youthful adventures to his son-in-law. A pale British comedy of manners. **107m/C VHS.** *GB* Laurence Harvey, Julie Harris, Mai Zetterling, Eva Gabor, Wilfrid Hyde-White, Derek Farr; ***D:*** Muriel Box.

Truth or Consequences, N.M. 🦴 **1997 (R)** Yes, the name of the town is real. No, Bob Barker is not the mayor. Dim parolee Raymond (Gallo) and his even dimmer girlfriend Addy (Dickens) are reunited and just want to settle down, to tell the truth. Instead, they fall immediately back into a life of crime. Along with their accomplices Marcus (Williamson) and Curtis (Sutherland), they plan to rip off a drug dealer for big bucks (no whammies!). The heist, of course, goes bad; they steal an RV and kidnap its owners Gordon (Pollack) and Donna (Phillips). An attempt to unload the drugs on a powerful Mafia boss (Steiger) also goes awry, and that starts a real family feud. As the mob hit man (Sheen), the cops, and the crooks all converge on the eponymous New Mexico town, everyone is in jeopardy. Not logical, not original and not good. Directorial debut for Sutherland, who should really quit playing coked-up psychopathic murderers. **106m/C VHS, DVD, Wide.** Vincent Gallo,

Kim Dickens, Kiefer Sutherland, Mykelti Williamson, Grace Phillips, Kevin Pollak, Martin Sheen, Rod Steiger, Rick Rossovich, John C. McGinley, Max Perlich; ***D:*** Kiefer Sutherland; ***W:*** Brad Mirman; ***C:*** Ric Waite; ***M:*** Jude Cole.

Truth or Dare? 🦴 **1986** The childhood game of truth or dare turns deadly in this violent thriller. **87m/C VHS.** John Brace, Mary Fanaro, Geoffrey Lewis Miller; ***D:*** Yale Wilson.

Truth or Dare 🦴🦴½ *In Bed with Madonna; Madonna Truth or Dare* **1991 (R)** A quasi-concert-documentary—here is music superstar Madonna tarted up in fact, fiction, and fantasy—exhibitionism to the nth power. Tacky, self-conscious,and ultimately, if you are a Madonna fan, moving. On camera Madonna stings ex-boyfriend Warren Beatty, disses admirer Kevin Costner, quarrels with her father, reminisces, and does sexy things with a bottle. Oh yes, she occasionally sings and dances. Both those who worship and dislike the Material Girl will find much to pick apart here. **118m/C VHS, DVD, Wide.** Madonna; ***D:*** Alek Keshishian.

Truth or Die 🦴🦴 *Doing Life* **1986 (PG-13)** This trite, cliched TV movie chronicles the life of convict Jerry Rosenberg, the first prisoner to earn a law degree from his cell. Still, an uncharacteristic role for sitcom guy Danza. Based on Rosenberg's book "Doing Life." **96m/C VHS.** Tony Danza, Jon (John) DeVries, Lisa Langlois, Rocco Sisto; ***D:*** Gene Reynolds.

Try and Get Me 🦴🦴 *Sound of Fury* **1950** A small town is incited into a manhunt for kidnappers who murdered their victim. Suspenseful melodrama analyzes mob rule and the criminal mind. **91m/B VHS.** Lloyd Bridges, Kathleen Ryan, Richard Carlson, Frank Lovejoy, Katherine Locke; ***D:*** Cy Endfield; ***W:*** Cy Endfield, Jo Pagano; ***C:*** Guy Roe.

Tryst 🦴½ **1994 (R)** Julia plots to kill her husband with the help of a detective, but when her housekeeper's son arrives, Julia decides another pawn is just what her deceitful plan needs. **101m/C VHS.** Barbara Carrera, Louise Fletcher, David Warner, Steve Bond, Andy Romano, Johnny LaSpada; ***D:*** Peter Foldy; ***W:*** Peter Foldy; ***M:*** Tom Howard.

The Tsar's Bride 🦴🦴🦴 *Tsarskaya Nevesta* **1966** A lovely young woman is chosen to be the bride of the horrible Tsar Glebov but when the Tsar's bodyguard falls for her, romantic difficulties ensue. A hybrid of the 1899 Rimsky-Korsakov opera and an 1849 play. **95m/B VHS.** *RU* Raisa Nedashkovskaya, Natalya Rudnaya, Otar Koberidze; ***D:*** Vladimir Gorikker.

Tucker: The Man and His Dream 🦴🦴🦴 **1988 (PG)** Portrait of Preston Tucker, entrepreneur and industrial idealist, who in 1946 tried to build the car of the future and was effectively run out of business by the powers-that-were. Ravishing, ultra-nostalgic lullaby to the American Dream. Watch for Jeff's dad, Lloyd, in a bit role. **111m/C VHS, DVD, 8mm, Wide.** Jeff Bridges, Martin Landau, Dean Stockwell, Frederic Forrest, Mako, Joan Allen, Christian Slater, Lloyd Bridges, Elias Koteas, Nina Siemaszko, Corin "Corky" Nemec, Marshall Bell, Don Novello, Peter Donat, Dean Goodman, Patti Austin; ***D:*** Francis Ford Coppola; ***W:*** Arnold Schulman, David Seidler; ***M:*** Joe Jackson, Carmine Coppola. Golden Globes '89: Support. Actor (Landau); N.Y. Film Critics '88: Support. Actor (Stockwell).

Tuesdays with Morrie 🦴🦴½ **1999** Detroit sportswriter Mitch Albom (Azaria) spots his old college prof, 78-year-old Morrie Schwartz (Lemmon), on ABC's "Nightline" discussing his battle with ALS and his thoughts on death. The workaholic Albom, who has not seen Morrie in 16 years, decides to pay his one-time mentor a visit in Boston. The relationship rekindles and they begin to meet every Tuesday, with Albom coming to question the path his life is taking. Based on Albom's best-selling book. **89m/C VHS.** Jack Lemmon, Hank Azaria, John Carroll Lynch, Wendy Moniz, Bonnie Bartlett, Caroline Aaron, Aaron Lustig, Bruce Nozick; ***D:*** Mick Jackson; ***W:*** Tom Rickman; ***C:*** Theo van de Sande; ***M:*** Marco Beltrami. **TV**

Tuff Turf 🦴🦴 **1985 (R)** The new kid in town must adjust to a different social lifestyle and a new set of rules when his family is forced to move to a low-class section of Los Angeles. He makes enemies immediately when he courts the girlfriend of one of the local toughs. Fast-paced with a bright young cast. Music by Jim Carroll, Lene Lovich, and Southside Johnny. **113m/C VHS, DVD, Wide.** James Spader, Kim Richards, Paul Mones, Matt Clark, Olivia Barash, Robert Downey Jr., Catya (Cat) Sassoon; ***D:*** Fritz Kiersch; ***W:*** Jette Rinck; ***C:*** Willy Kurant; ***M:*** Jonathan Elias.

Tulips 🦴½ **1981 (PG)** Would-be suicide takes a contract out on himself, and then meets a woman who makes life worth living again. Together they attempt to evade the gangland hit man. Limp comedy. **91m/C VHS.** *CA* Gabe Kaplan, Bernadette Peters, Henry Gibson; ***D:*** Stan Ferris.

Tulsa 🦴🦴🦴 **1949** High-spirited rancher's daughter begins crusade to save her father's oil empire when he's killed. Having become ruthless and determined to succeed at any cost, she eventually sees the error of her ways. Classic Hayward. **96m/C VHS.** Susan Hayward, Robert Preston, Chill Wills, Ed Begley Sr., Pedro Armendariz Sr.; ***D:*** Stuart Heisler; ***C:*** Winton C. Hoch.

Tumbledown Ranch in Arizona 🦴 **1941** After a rodeo accident, an unconscious college student dreams of adventure out west. Part of the "Range Busters" series. **60m/B VHS.** Ray Corrigan, John "Dusty" King, Max Terhune, Sheila (Rebecca Wassem) Darcy, Marian Kerby; ***D:*** S. Roy Luby.

Tumbleweed Trail 🦴½ **1942** Action-packed thundering western. **57m/B VHS.** William Boyd, Art Davis, Lee Powell, Jack Rockwell; ***D:*** Sam Newfield.

Tumbleweeds 🦴🦴🦴 **1925** William S. Hart's last western. Portrays the last great land rush in America, the opening of the Cherokee Strip in the Oklahoma Territory to homesteaders. Preceded by a sound prologue, made in 1939, in which Hart speaks for the only time on screen, to introduce the story. Silent, with musical score. **114m/B VHS.** William S. Hart, Lucien Littlefield, Barbara Bedford; ***D:*** King Baggot.

Tumbleweeds 🦴🦴½ **1998 (PG-13)** Mary Jo Walker (McTeer) has been married numerous times and been in even more relationships. 12-year-old daughter Ava (Brown) knows that when things go wrong with mom's romantic prospects they pack up and hit the road, which is why they're on their way to San Diego. Of course, Mary Jo meets trucker Jack (O'Connor) along the way and decides to shack up with him when they reach their destination, while the remarkably resilient Ava settles into another new life. But since Mary Jo has such lousy judgment (except about her love for Ava) this mother-daughter duo is headed for rocky times ahead. **104m/C VHS, DVD, Wide.** Janet McTeer, Kimberly J. Brown, Gavin O'Connor, Jay O. Sanders, Lois Smith, Laurel Holloman, Michael J. Pollard, Noah Emmerich; ***D:*** Gavin O'Connor; ***W:*** Angela Shelton, Gavin O'Connor; ***C:*** Dan Stoloff; ***M:*** David Mansfield. Golden Globes '00: Actress—Mus./Comedy (McTeer); Ind. Spirit '00: Debut Perf. (Brown); Natl. Bd. of Review '99: Actress (McTeer); Sundance '99: Filmmakers Trophy.

Tundra 🦴🦴½ *The Mighty Thunder* **1936** Quasi adventure-drama/documentary set in the Alaskan tundra. A young man, known only as the "Flying Doctor," tends to the sick in small villages throughout the wilderness. But his own survival is at stake when his small plane crashes. Filmed on location. **72m/B VHS.** Del Cambre; ***D:*** Norman Dawn.

The Tune 🦴🦴 **1992** 30,000 ink and watercolor drawings make up this animated gem which tells the story of Del (Neiden), a failed songwriter who gets a fresh start when he makes a wrong turn on the freeway and winds up in Flooby Nooby. The strange inhabitants of this town teach Del to throw out his rhyming dictionary and write about his experiences. Plympton's first full-length animated feature. Also includes "The Making of The Tune" and the animated short "Draw." **80m/C VHS, DVD.** ***D:*** Bill Plympton; ***W:*** Maureen McElheron, Bill Plympton, P.C. Vey; ***C:*** John Donnelly; ***M:*** Maureen McElheron; ***V:*** Daniel Neiden, Maureen McElheron, Marty Nelson, Emily Bindiger, Chris Hoffman.

Tune in Tomorrow 🦴🦴 **1990 (PG-13)** Lovesick young Martin (Reeves) wants to woo divorced older babe aunt-by-marriage Julia (Hershey) and is romantically counseled by wacky soap opera writer Pedro (Falk). Seems even soap operas draw on real life, and Martin's story is immortalized on the airwaves, circa 1951 New Orleans. The story-within-a-story also features Pedro's radio characters coming to hammy life. Sometimes funny, sometimes not (the Albanian jokes are tiresome). Adapted from the novel "Aunt Julia and the Scriptwriter" by Mario Vargas Llosa. **90m/C VHS.** Barbara Hershey, Keanu Reeves, Peter Falk, Bill McCutcheon, Patricia Clarkson, Peter Gallagher, Dan Hedaya, Buck Henry, Hope Lange, John Larroquette, Elizabeth McGovern, Robert Sedgwick, Henry Gibson; ***D:*** Jon Amiel; ***W:*** William Boyd; ***C:*** Robert Stevens; ***M:*** Wynton Marsalis.

Tunes of Glory 🦴🦴🦴½ **1960** Guinness and Mills are wonderful in this well made film about a brutal, sometimes lazy colonel and a disciplined and educated man moving up through the ranks of the British military. York's film debut. From the novel by James Kennaway, who adapted it for the screen. **107m/C VHS.** *GB* Alec Guinness, John Mills, Dennis Price, Kay Walsh, Susannah York; ***D:*** Ronald Neame; ***M:*** Malcolm Arnold.

The Tunnel 🦴🦴½ **1989 (R)** Obsessive romance film with a trace of suspense. Artist sees the woman of his dreams at a showing of his work. Her marriage, and her trepidation, don't keep his obsession from consuming him. **99m/C VHS.** Jane Seymour, Peter Weller, Fernando Rey; ***D:*** Antonio Drove.

The Tunnel of Love 🦴🦴½ **1958** Day and Widmark are a married couple who find themselves over their heads in red tape when they try to adopt a baby. A beautiful, disapproving adoption investigator also causes more problems for the couple when she believes Widmark is less than ideal father material. Widmark is not in his element at comedy but Day and Young (as their next-door neighbor) are fine in this lightweight adaptation of the Joseph Fields-Peter DeVries play. **98m/B VHS, Wide.** Doris Day, Richard Widmark, Gig Young, Gia Scala, Elisabeth Fraser, Elizabeth Wilson; ***D:*** Gene Kelly; ***W:*** Jerome Chodorov.

Tunnel Vision 🦴½ **1995 (R)** Detective Kelly Wheatstone (Kensit) and her partner Frank Yanovitch (Reynolds) are after a serial killer whose victims are all beautiful women killed in a ritualistic fashion. But all the clues begin to point to Yanovitch as the one committing the crimes. This one is routine all the way. **100m/C VHS.** *AU* Patsy Kensit, Robert Reynolds, Rebecca Rigg, Shane Briant; ***D:*** Clive Fleury; ***W:*** Clive Fleury; ***C:*** Paul Murphy; ***M:*** David Hirschfelder.

Tunnelvision 🦴🦴½ **1976 (R)** A spoof of TV comprised of irreverent sketches. Fun to watch because of the appearances of several now-popular stars. **70m/C VHS.** Chevy Chase, John Candy, Laraine Newman, Joe Flaherty, Howard Hesseman, Gerrit Graham, Al Franken, Tom Davis, Ron Silver; ***D:*** Neal Israel.

Turbo: A Power Rangers Movie 🦴 **1996 (PG)** The Power Rangers must battle the evil Divatox (Turner), who's kidnapped the wizard Lerigot so she can use his power to free her even more evil boyfriend Maligore. It's all around cheesy but if you're a five-year-old you may still enjoy the action. **99m/C VHS, DVD, Wide.** Jason David Frank, Stephen Antonio Cardenas, John Yong Bosch, Catherine Sutherland, Nakia Burrise, Blake Foster, Paul Schrier, Jason Narvy, Amy Jo Johnson, Austin St. John, Hilary Shepard Turner, Jon Simanton; ***D:*** David Winning, Shuki Levy; ***W:*** Shuki Levy, Shell Danielson; ***C:*** Ilan Rosenberg; ***M:*** Shuki Levy.

Turbulence 🦴½ **1996 (R)** When you fly, it's usually the turbulence that makes you throw up. Well, this movie isn't that bad, but you may experience a touch of nausea. Flight attendant Teri (Holly) is pushing the drink cart on a strangely vacant New York to L.A. Christmas Eve run. Among the passengers are convicted felons Ryan (Liotta) and Stubbs (Gleeson), who are either on their way to a more secure prison or fulfilling the "consumption of airline food" portion of their sentence. The prisoners seize a gun from the marshals and accidentally rub out the cockpit crew. With all the passengers locked away, Teri must battle the serial rapist/killer Ryan as well as learn to fly the plane through a horrible storm. Passengers on the left of the screen may look out and see "Passenger 57," while those on the right can see the ancient monument of "Airport 75." **103m/C VHS, DVD, Wide.** Ray Liotta, Lauren Holly, Hector Elizondo, Brendan Gleeson, Ben Cross, Rachel Ticotin, Jeffrey DeMunn, John Finn, Catherine Hicks; ***D:*** Robert Butler; ***W:*** Jonathan Brett; ***C:*** Lloyd Ahern; ***M:*** Shirley Walker.

Turbulence 2: Fear of Flying 🦴🦴 **1999** Group of scared to fly passengers try to overcome their fears aboard a jumbo 747. They will never set foot off the ground again after severe turbulance damages the plane and a nerve gas-carrying terrorist commandeers it. **100m/C VHS, DVD, Wide.** Tom Berenger, Craig Sheffer, Jennifer Beals, Jeffrey Nordling; ***D:*** David Mackay; ***W:*** Kevin Bernhardt, Brendan Broderick, Rob Kerchner. **VIDEO**

Turf Boy 🦴🦴 *Mr. Celebrity* **1942** Desperate for cash, a boy and his uncle try to get an old horse into prime condition for racing. A minor equine melodrama, just the right length for an old-time matinee double-feature. **68m/B VHS.** Robert "Buzzy" Henry, James Seay, Doris Day, William (Bill) Halligan, Gavin Gordon; ***D:*** William Beaudine.

Turk 182! 🦴½ **1985 (PG-13)** The angry brother of a disabled fireman takes on City Hall in order to win back the pension that he deserves. He attacks through his graffiti art. Hutton is too heavy for the over-all comic feel of this mostly silly film. **96m/C VHS.** Timothy Hutton, Robert Culp, Robert Urich, Kim Cattrall, Peter Boyle, Darren McGavin, Paul Sorvino; ***D:*** Bob (Benjamin) Clark.

Turkish Delight 🦴🦴½ **1973** Free spirit sculptor falls in love with free spirit gal from bourgeois family and artsy soft porn ensues. That is until a brain tumor puts an end to their fun, and he's left to wallow in flashbacks and more artsy soft porn. Dubbed. Verhoeven later became big boxoffice in the U.S. with "Total Recall." **100m/C VHS, DVD, Wide.** *NL* Monique Van De Ven, Rutger Hauer, Tonny Huurdeman, Wim Van Den Brink; ***D:*** Paul Verhoeven; ***W:*** Gerard Soeteman; ***C:*** Jan De Bont.

Turn It Up 🦴🦴 **2000 (R)** Diamond (Pras) is a talented musician who's involved in the drug trade with childhood friend Gage (Ja Rule). He wants to go legit so he can pursue his music dreams but Gage is a hothead who gets them into more trouble. Then Diamond's girlfriend announces she's pregnant, his mother unexpectedly dies, and his estranged father (Curtis-Hall) turns up. **87m/C VHS, DVD, Wide.** Pras, Vondie Curtis-Hall, Ja Rule, Tamala Jones, Jason Statham, Eugene C. Clark; ***D:*** Robert Adetuyi; ***W:*** Robert Adetuyi; ***C:*** Hubert Taczanowski; ***M:*** Gary Jones, Happy Walter.

Turn of the Blade 🦴 **1997** Predictable thriller finds photographer Sam Peyton (Christensen) upset that his wife Kelly (Owens) is more interested in her acting career than in having a baby. It may be safer to have the kid, since Kelly's the lust object for a seedy film director and then a dangerous stalker. Meanwhile, Sam has his own problems with his associate Wendy, who wants their relationship to get personal and wants Kelly out of the way. **91m/C VHS.** David Christensen, Crystal Owens, David Keith Miller, Julie Horvath; ***D:*** Bryan Michael Stoller; ***W:*** Mark Bark; ***C:*** Richard A. Jones; ***M:*** Greg Edmonson. **VIDEO**

The Turn of the Screw 🦴🦴 **1974** Supernatural powers vie with a young governess for control of the souls of the two children in her charge. Redgrave does well in this chilling film adapted from the Henry James story. **120m/C VHS.** Lynn Redgrave, Jasper Jacobs, Eva Griffith; ***D:*** Dan Curtis.

The Turn of the Screw 🦴🦴
1989 (R) The young charges of an English nanny are sought for their souls by a dark, unimaginable evil in the mansion. Another version of the Henry James classic. **60m/C VHS.** Amy Irving, David Hemmings; ***D:*** Graeme Clifford.

The Turn of the Screw 🦴🦴
1992 (R) Yet another version of the Henry James classic as a young governess struggles with sexual obsession and the two children in her care who are possessed by evil. **95m/C VHS.** Julian Sands, Patsy Kensit, Stephane Audran, Marianne Faithfull; ***D:*** Rusty Lemorande; ***M:*** Simon Boswell.

The Turn of the Screw 🦴🦴½
1999 Solid TV adaptation of the Henry James novel boasts some fine performances in a now familiar story. Miss (May) is the young, too-impressionable governess at Bly manor, whose charges are the overly well-behaved Miles (Sowerbutts) and his younger sister, Flora (Robinson). Soon Miss is seeing ghosts—those of the former governess and another servant, Peter Quint (Salkey), whom she believes are corrupting her innocent children. But maybe the emotional young woman is simply crazy. **80m/C VHS.** *GB* Jodhi May, Pam Ferris, Colin Firth, Joe Sowerbutts, Grace Robinson, Jason Salkey, Caroline Pegg, Jenny Howe; ***D:*** Ben Bolt; ***W:*** Nick Dear; ***C:*** David Odd; ***M:*** Adrian Johnston. **TV**

Turnaround **1987 (R)** Unusual action/suspense film set in a small town. Relentless gang rampages the citizens. Finally, a man decides he's had enough, and turns on the heathens with his knowledge of magic. **97m/C VHS.** Doug McKeon, Tim Maier, Eddie Albert, Gayle Hunnicutt; ***D:*** Ola Solum.

Turner and Hooch 🦴🦴 **1989 (PG)**
A dog witnesses a murder, and a fussy cop is partnered with the drooling mutt and a weak script in his search for the culprit. Drool as a joke will only go so far, but Hanks is his usual entertaining self. **99m/C VHS, DVD, Wide.** Tom Hanks, Mare Winningham, Craig T. Nelson, Scott Paulin, J.C. Quinn; ***D:*** Roger Spottiswoode; ***W:*** Michael Blodgett, Jim Cash, Jack Epps Jr.; ***C:*** Adam Greenberg; ***M:*** Charles Gross.

The Turning 🦴½ *Home Fires Burning*
1992 Twenty-two-year-old Cliff Harnish (Dolan) returns home after a four-year absence to shock his family with his strident Neo-Nazi beliefs. May be of curiosity value to Anderson's "X-Files" fans, since she appears (relatively briefly and partially nude) as the guy's girlfriend in a kitchen sex scene. Based on the play by Ceraso. **92m/C VHS, DVD.** Michael Dolan, Raymond J. Barry, Karen Allen, Tess Harper, Gillian Anderson; ***D:*** L.A. Puopolo; ***W:*** L.A. Puopolo, Chris Ceraso; ***C:*** J. Michael McClary.

The Turning Point 🦴🦴½ **1977**
(PG) A woman who gave up ballet for motherhood must come to terms as her daughter launches a ballet career and falls for the lead male dancer. The mother finds herself threatened by her daughter's affection toward an old friend who sacrificed a family life for the life of a ballerina. Baryshnikov's film debut. Melodramatic ending and problems due to ballet sequences. **119m/C VHS.** Shirley MacLaine, Anne Bancroft, Tom Skerritt, Leslie Browne, Martha Scott, Marshall Thompson, Mikhail Baryshnikov; ***D:*** Herbert Ross; ***W:*** Arthur Laurents; ***C:*** Robert L. Surtees. Golden Globes '78: Director (Ross), Film—Drama; L.A. Film Critics '77: Director (Ross); Natl. Bd. of Review '77: Actress (Bancroft), Support. Actor (Skerritt); Writers Guild '77: Orig. Screenplay.

Turtle Diary 🦴🦴🦴 **1986 (PG)** Two lonely Londoners collaborate to free giant turtles from the city aquarium with the aid of a zoo-keeper, and the turtles' freedom somehow frees them as well. Jackson and Kingsley are stunning. Adapted by Harold Pinter from the Russell Hoban book. **90m/C VHS.** *GB* Ben Kingsley, Glenda Jackson, Richard Johnson, Michael Gambon, Rosemary Leach, Jeroen Krabbe, Eleanor Bron; ***D:*** John Irvin; ***W:*** Harold Pinter; ***M:*** Geoffrey Burgon.

Turumba 🦴🦴🦴 **1984** A quiet satire about a family of papier-mache animal makers in a Philippine village who get a gargantuan order in time for the Turumba holiday, and desperately try to fill it. In Tagalog with English subtitles. **94m/C VHS.** *PH* ***D:*** Kidlat Tahimik.

The Tuskegee Airmen 🦴🦴🦴
1995 (PG-13) Cable drama based on the formation and WWII achievements of the U.S. Army Air Corps' first squadron of black combat fighter pilots, the "Fighting 99th" of the 332nd Fighter Group. They were nicknamed after the segregated military outpost where they trained in Tuskegee, Alabama and distinguished themselves in combat, never losing a single bomber, and receiving more than 800 medals. Cast all do a fine job in what turns out to essentially be a standard action/war movie. Based on a story by former Tuskegee airman, Robert W. Williams. **107m/C VHS, DVD, Wide.** Laurence "Larry" Fishburne, Cuba Gooding Jr., Allen Payne, Malcolm Jamal Warner, Courtney B. Vance, Andre Braugher, John Lithgow, Rosemary Murphy, Christopher McDonald, Vivica A. Fox, Daniel Hugh-Kelly, David Harrod, Eddie Braun, Bennet Guillory; ***D:*** Robert Markowitz; ***W:*** Paris Qualles, Ron Hutchinson, Trey Ellis; ***C:*** Ronald Orieux; ***M:*** Lee Holdridge. **CABLE**

Tusks 🦴½ *Fire in Eden* **1989 (R)** A ruthless hunter tries to kill elephants. **99m/C VHS.** Andrew Stevens, John Rhys-Davies, Lucy Gutteridge, Julian Glover; ***D:*** Tara Hawkins Moore.

Tut & Tuttle 🦴½ **1982** Young dabbler in magic is transported to ancient Egypt where he is able to demonstrate courage and wits against the evil Horemheb, who has kidnapped Prince Tut. **97m/C VHS.** Christopher Barnes, Eric Greene, Hans Conried, Vic Tayback.

The Tuttles of Tahiti 🦴🦴🦴
1942 The Tuttles lead a life of leisure in the South Seas. Laughton's child becomes enamoured of his rival's offspring, causing problems between the two families. More interesting than it sounds. **91m/C VHS.** Charles Laughton, Jon Hall, Peggy Drake, Victor Francen, Gene Reynolds, Florence Bates, Mala, Alma Ross, Curt Bois; ***D:*** Charles Vidor.

Tuxedo Warrior 🦴½ **1982** Set in South Africa, this film involves the adventures of a well-dressed mercenary who is caught between the police, diamond thieves, and an old girlfriend's bank robbing. **93m/C VHS.** John Wyman, Carol Royle, Holly Palance; ***D:*** Andrew Sinclair.

Twelfth Night 🦴🦴½ **1996 (PG)** Director Nunn's take on Shakespeare's gender-bending, romantic-comedy, which is now set in the 1890s. Shipwrecked on an unfriendly Illyrian shore, Viola (Stubbs), believing twin brother Sebastian (Mackintosh) to be dead, disguises herself in male attire and joins the retinue of the lovesick Duke Orsino (Stephens). He's pining for the Countess Olivia (Bonham Carter) and decides to use Viola-turned-Cesario as a surrogate wooer. Too bad Olivia's becoming more interested in her effeminate pseudo-suitor and that Orsino's having a few sexual quandries of his own. **133m/C VHS.** *GB* Imogen Stubbs, Helena Bonham Carter, Toby Stephens, Steven Mackintosh, Richard E. Grant, Nigel Hawthorne, Ben Kingsley, Imelda Staunton, Mel Smith, Nicholas Farrell; ***D:*** Trevor Nunn; ***W:*** Trevor Nunn; ***C:*** Clive Tickner; ***M:*** Shaun Davey.

Twelve Angry Men 🦴🦴🦴🦴
1957 Fonda sounds the voice of reason as a jury inclines toward a quick-and-dirty verdict against a boy on trial. Excellent ensemble work. Lumet's feature film debut, based on a TV play by Reginald Rose. **95m/B VHS, DVD, Wide.** Henry Fonda, Martin Balsam, Lee J. Cobb, E.G. Marshall, Jack Klugman, Robert Webber, Ed Begley Sr., John Fiedler, Jack Warden, George Voskovec, Edward Binns, Joseph Sweeney; ***D:*** Sidney Lumet; ***W:*** Reginald Rose; ***C:*** Boris Kaufman; ***M:*** Kenyon Hopkins. Berlin Intl. Film Fest. '57: Golden Berlin Bear; British Acad. '57: Actor (Fonda).

Twelve Angry Men 🦴🦴½ **1997**
(PG-13) Cable TV update of the 1954 "Studio One" teleplay/1957 movie (both written by Rose) that brings together an all-male jury (now with four black jurors) to decide the fate of a Latino murder suspect. Lemmon has the Henry Fonda role of the juror with reasonable doubts, determined to provide a fair hearing. **117m/C VHS.** George C. Scott, Jack Lemmon, Hume Cronyn, Tony Danza, Mykelti Williamson, Edward James Olmos, Courtney B. Vance, Ossie Davis, Armin Mueller-Stahl, Dorian Harewood, James Gandolfini, William L. Petersen, Mary McDonnell, Douglas Spain; ***D:*** William Friedkin; ***W:*** Reginald Rose. **CABLE**

The Twelve Chairs 🦴🦴🦴 **1970**
(PG) Take-off on Russian folktale first filmed in Yugoslavia in 1927. A rich matron admits on her deathbed that she has hidden her jewels in the upholstery of one of 12 chairs that are no longer in her home. A Brooksian treasure hunt ensues. **94m/C VHS, DVD.** Mel Brooks, Dom DeLuise, Frank Langella, Ron Moody, Bridget Brice; ***D:*** Mel Brooks; ***W:*** Mel Brooks; ***C:*** Djordje Nikolic; ***M:*** Mel Brooks, John Morris.

12 Monkeys 🦴🦴🦴 **1995 (R)** Forty years after a plague wipes out 99 percent of the human population and sends the survivors underground, scientists send prisoner James Cole (Willis) to the 1990s to investigate the connection between the virus and seriously deranged fanatic Jeffrey Goines (Pitt), whose father happens to be a renowned virologist. Director Gilliam's demented vision is a bit tougher and less capricious than usual, and the convoluted plot and accumulated detail require a keen attention span, but as each piece of the puzzle falls into place the story becomes a fascinating sci-fi spectacle. Pitt drops the pretty-boy image with a nutzoid performance that'll make revelers stop swooning in a heartbeat. Inspired by the 1962 French short "La Jetee." **131m/C VHS, DVD.** Bruce Willis, Madeleine Stowe, Brad Pitt, Christopher Plummer, David Morse, Frank Gorshin, Jon Seda; ***D:*** Terry Gilliam; ***W:*** David Peoples, Janet Peoples; ***C:*** Roger Pratt; ***M:*** Paul Buckmaster. Golden Globes '96: Support. Actor (Pitt).

Twelve o'Clock High 🦴🦴🦴½
1949 Epic drama about the heroic 8th Air Force, with Peck as bomber-group commander sent to shape up a hard-luck group, forced to drive himself and his men to the breaking point. Compelling dramatization of the strain of military command. Includes impressive footage of actual WWII battles. Best-ever flying fortress movie. **132m/B VHS, DVD.** Gregory Peck, Hugh Marlowe, Gary Merrill, Millard Mitchell, Dean Jagger, Paul Stewart, Robert Arthur, John Kellogg, Sam Edwards, Russ Conway, Lawrence (Larry) Dobkin; ***D:*** Henry King; ***W:*** Sy Bartlett, Beirne Lay Jr.; ***C:*** Leon Shamroy; ***M:*** Alfred Newman. Oscars '49: Sound, Support. Actor (Jagger), Natl. Film Reg. '98.

12:01 🦴🦴½ **1993 (PG-13)** It's the "Groundhog Day" premise played for thrills. Barry Thompson (Silverman) is an employee at a scientific research firm who finds himself reliving the same 24-hour period over and over again. And what a day it is—he discovers a secret project is causing the mysterious time warp, falls in love with beauteous scientist Lisa (Slater) and watches as she gets murdered. Can Barry figure out how to stop what's going on and change things enough to save her? Adaptation of the short story "12:01" by Richard Lupoff, which was previously made into a short film. **92m/C VHS.** Jonathan Silverman, Helen Slater, Martin Landau, Nicolas Surovy, Jeremy Piven; ***D:*** Jack Sholder. **TV**

12 Plus 1 🦴🦴🦴 *The Thirteen Chairs*
1970 (R) A man sells 13 chairs left to him by his aunt, only to find that one of them contained a hidden fortune. He chases across Europe in search of each of them. Some good cameos help move this re-make of a Russian folk-tale along, but it remains lightweight. Tate's last movie, before her death at the hands of Manson and his "family." **94m/C VHS.** *FR IT* Sharon Tate, Orson Welles, Vittorio Gassman, Mylene Demongeot, Terry-Thomas, Tim Brooke; ***Cameos:*** Vittorio De Sica; ***D:*** Nicolas Gessner.

Twentieth Century 🦴🦴🦴🦴 **1934**
Maniacal Broadway director Barrymore transforms shop girl Lombard into a smashing success adored by public and press. Tired of Barrymore's manic-excessive ways, she heads for the Hollywood hills, pursued by the Profile in fine form. **91m/B** Carole Lombard, John Barrymore, Walter Connolly, Roscoe Karns, Edgar Kennedy, Ralph Forbes, Charles Lane, Etienne Girardot, Snow Flake; ***D:*** Howard Hawks; ***W:*** Charles MacArthur, Ben Hecht.

Twenty Bucks 🦴🦴🦴 **1993 (R)**
Whimsical film follows a $20 bill from its "birth" at a cash machine to its "death" as it is returned to the bank, tattered and torn, for shredding. The bill is passed from owner to owner, sometimes simply and briefly, sometimes altering fate. The original screenplay is nearly 60 years old: Endre Bohem originally drafted it in 1935, and his son revised and updated it. Clever transitions allow the various stories and characters to blend almost seamlessly. The strongest character is Shue's, a young waitress and aspiring writer. Rosenfeld's directorial debut is worth a look. Filmed in Minneapolis. **91m/C VHS.** Linda Hunt, David Rasche, George Morfogen, Brendan Fraser, Gladys Knight, Elisabeth Shue, Steve Buscemi, Christopher Lloyd, Sam Jenkins, Kamal Holloway, Melora Walters, William H. Macy, Diane Baker, Spalding Gray, Matt Frewer, Concetta Tomei, Nina Siemaszko; ***D:*** Keva Rosenfeld; ***W:*** Leslie Bohem, Endre Bohem; ***C:*** Emmanuel Lubezki; ***M:*** David Robbins. Ind. Spirit '94: Support. Actor (Lloyd).

20 Dates 🦴🦴½ **1999 (R)** Writer/director Myles Berkowitz, recently divorced and having career problems, decided to combine these two problems into one. He filmed himself going on 20 dates, sometimes without the dates' knowledge (until he sprung the release form on 'em at the end of the night). Some of it's real, some staged, but all of it focuses on Berkowitz. He talks about himself, and the project, incessantly, which gets annoying after awhile, but the film has its moments. When one of the dates actually works out, and turns into a budding romance, he has to tell the girl that he's still obligated to play out the string. Some of the funnier moments are his conversations with his financial backer, who thought he was getting a sex romp flick. **88m/C VHS.** ***D:*** Myles Berkowitz; ***W:*** Myles Berkowitz; ***C:*** Adam Biggs; ***M:*** Bob Mann, Steve Tyrell.

Twenty Dollar Star 🦴½ **1991 (R)**
Steamy thriller about an prominent actress who leads a double life as a cheap hooker, and consequent occupational hazards. The title may as well refer to the budget. **92m/C VHS.** Rebecca Holden, Bernie White, Eddie Barth, Marilyn Hassett, Dick Sargent; ***D:*** Paul Leder.

20 Million Miles to Earth 🦴🦴½ **1957** A spaceship returning from an expedition to Venus crashes on Earth, releasing a fast-growing reptilian beast that rampages throughout Athens. Another entertaining example of stop-motion animation master Ray Harryhausen's work, offering a classic battle between the monster and an elephant. **82m/B** William Hopper, Joan Taylor, Frank Puglia, John Zaremba, Thomas B(rowne). Henry, Jan Arvan; ***D:*** Nathan (Hertz) Juran; ***W:*** Christopher Knopf, Bob Williams; ***C:*** Irving Lippman; ***M:*** Mischa Bakaleinikoff.

20,000 Leagues under the Sea 🦴🦴🦴 **1916** Outstanding silent adaptation of Jules Verne's "20,000 Leagues Under the Sea" and "The Mysterious Island" filmed with a then revolutionary underwater camera. Much octopus fighting. Look for newly mastered edition. **105m/B VHS, DVD.** Matt Moore, Allen Holubar, June Gail, William Welsh, Chris Benton, Dan Hamlon; ***D:*** Stuart Paton; ***W:*** Stuart Paton; ***C:*** Eugene Gaudio.

20,000 Leagues under the Sea 🦴🦴🦴½ **1954** From a futuristic submarine, Captain Nemo wages war on the surface world. A shipwrecked scientist and sailor do their best to thwart Nemo's dastardly schemes. Buoyant Disney version of the Jules Verne fantasy. **127m/C VHS, Wide.** James Mason, Kirk Douglas, Peter Lorre, Paul Lukas, Robert J. Wilke, Carleton Young; ***D:*** Richard Fleischer; ***W:*** Earl Felton; ***C:*** Franz Planer; ***M:*** Paul J. Smith. Oscars '54: Art Dir./Set Dec., Color.

20,000 Leagues Under the Sea 🦴½ **1997** Silly TV version of the oft-told Verne tale finds marine biologist Aronnax (Crenna) and his assistant/daughter Sophie (Cox) prisoners on Captain Nemo's (Cross) submarine. In the original Verne version, Sophie was a young man—the sex change now means there's lots of boring eye-batting between Sophie, harpoonist Ned Land (Gross), and the jealous Nemo. The underwater photography is nifty but the fish also provide more excitement than the cast. **91m/C VHS, DVD.** Ben Cross, Richard Crenna, Paul Gross, Julie Cox, Michael Jayston; ***D:*** Michael Anderson Sr.; ***W:*** Joe Wiesenfeld; ***C:*** Alan Hume; ***M:*** John Scott. **TV**

Twenty-One 🦴🦴½ **1991 (R)** Modern morality tale of a young English woman who moves to the U.S. to make a new start, but falls into the same old habits. Kensit is frank and charming, in spite of difficulties with her drug addict boyfriend and the illegal alien she marries. Director Boyd leaves it to the viewer to decide between right and wrong and where Kensit fits. **92m/C VHS.** *GB* Patsy Kensit, Jack Shepherd, Patrick Ryecart, Maynard Eziashi, Rufus Sewell, Sophie Thompson, Susan Wooldridge, Julia Goodman; ***D:*** Don Boyd; ***W:*** Don Boyd; ***C:*** Keith Goddard; ***M:*** Michael Berkeley.

21 Days 🦴🦴½ *Twenty-One Days Together; The First and the Last* **1937** Dull film somewhat redeemed by its stars. Leigh is a married woman carrying on with Olivier. When her husband confronts them, Olivier accidentally kills him in a fight. They keep quiet but then a mentally deranged man is taken into custody for the crime. Since he will be held 21 days before coming to trial, the lovers decide to spend the time together before Olivier confesses. Based on the play "The First and the Last" by John Galsworthy. **75m/C VHS.** *GB* Vivien Leigh, Laurence Olivier, Leslie Banks, Francis L. Sullivan, Hay Petrie, Esme Percy, Robert Newton; ***D:*** Basil Dean; ***W:*** Graham Greene, Basil Dean.

21 Hours at Munich 🦴🦴🦴 **1976** Made-for-TV treatment of the massacre of Israeli athletes by Arab terrorists at the 1972 Olympics. Well-done. The film was produced using the actual Munich locations. **100m/C VHS.** William Holden, Shirley Knight, Franco Nero, Anthony Quayle, Noel Willman; ***D:*** William A. Graham.

23 1/2 Hours Leave 🦴🦴 **1937** Amusing WWI service comedy as a barracks wiseacre bets that by the following morning he'll be breakfasting with a general. It's a song-filled remake of a 1919 film, whose star Douglas MacLean later produced this. **73m/B VHS.** James Ellison, Terry Walker, Morgan Hill, Arthur Lake, Paul Harvey; ***D:*** John Blystone.

Twenty-Four Eyes 🦴🦴🦴 *Nijushi No Hitomi* **1954** Miss Oishi (Takamine), a teacher on a remote Japanese island in the 1920s, attempts to transmit peaceful values to her 12 pupils amidst the clamor of a nation gearing up for war. As she watches them grow up, many of them doomed to an early death, she remains a pillar of quiet strength. In Japanese with English subtitles. **158m/B VHS.** *JP* Hideko Takamine, Chishu Ryu, Toshiko Kobayashi; ***D:*** Keisuke Kinoshita.

The 24 Hour Woman 🦴🦴½ **1999 (R)** Perez is Grace, a morning TV talk show producer who has her pregnancy announced on the air, to the surprise of the baby's father (and the show's co-host) Serrano. Heartless executive producer LuPone milks the pregnancy for every ratings point, then callously turns her back on her employee's problems once the baby is delivered. Pressured by the demands of her job and motherhood, Grace has a major mental meltdown in which she confronts her harpy boss on air. Perez shows a more mature side while still retaining her Latina buzzsaw comic gifts. **93m/C VHS.** Rosie Perez, Marianne Jean-Baptiste, Patti LuPone, Karen Duffy, Wendell Pierce, Melissa Leo, Aida Turturro, Diego Serrano, Rosana Desoto, Alicia Renee Washington; ***D:*** Nancy Savoca; ***W:*** Nancy Savoca, Richard Guay; ***C:*** Teresa Medina; ***M:*** Louis Vega, Kenny Gonzalez.

24 Hours in a Woman's Life 🦴🦴 **1961** A girl in love with an irresponsible guy hears a cautionary tale from grandma Bergman, who once had a whirlwind romance with a young gambler and naively thought she could reform him. A static TV adaptation of an oft-filmed Stefan Zweig novel, unusually lavish for its time but on the dull side. **90m/C VHS.** Ingrid Bergman, Rip Torn, John Williams, Lili Darvas, Jerry Orbach; ***D:*** Silvio Narizzano; ***W:*** John Mortimer.

24 Hours to Midnight 🦴½ **1992** A widow uses her ninja skills to wipe out the crime bosses and henchmen who killed her husband. **91m/C VHS.** Cynthia Rothrock, Stack Pierce; ***D:*** Leo Fong.

24 Nights 🦴🦴½ **1999** Twenty-four year old Jonathan Parker has never stopped believing in Santa Claus after a magical encounter at the age of four. Now a pot-smoking loser at life and love, he writes a letter to Santa asking for true romance. When Jonathan meets new co-worker Toby, he decides his letter has been answered even though Toby has a longtime boyfriend. But Jonathan will do anything to get what he believes is his Christmas wish. **97m/C VHS, DVD.** Kevin Isola, Aida Turturro, Steven Mailer, David Burtka, Mary Louise Wilson; ***D:*** Kieran Turner; ***W:*** Kieran Turner; ***C:*** Scott Barnard.

24-7 🦴🦴 **1997 (R)** Title is local Midlands English slang for 24 hours a day, seven days a week. And in this case it refers to the boredom suffered by the aimless, unemployed youth who live in the local housing estates in Thatcher's depressed '80s England. Middle-aged ex-boxer Alan Darcy (Hoskins in a sincere and sweet performance) decides to help the lads by reviving the amateur boxing club which saved him in his youth. Although it seems to work for a time, things slide downward as, eventually, does the distraught Darcy himself. Meadows' feature directorial debut. **96m/B VHS.** *GB* Bob Hoskins, Danny Nussbaum, James Hooton, Darren O. Campbell, Mat Hand, Jimmy Hynd, Justin Brady, Karl Collins, Johann Myers, Anthony Clarke, Bruce Jones, Frank Harper, Pamela Cundell; ***D:*** Shane Meadows; ***W:*** Shane Meadows, Paul Fraser; ***C:*** Ashley Rowe; ***M:*** Neil MacColl, Boo Hewerdine.

25 Fireman's Street 🦴🦴🦴 *Almok a hazrol; Tuzolto utca 25* **1973** An evocative drama about the residents of an old house in Hungary which is about to be torn down, and their evening of remembrances of life before, during and after WWII. In Hungarian with English subtitles. **97m/C VHS.** *HU* Rita Bekes, Peter Muller, Lucyna Winnicka, Andras Balint; ***D:*** Istvan Szabo; ***W:*** Istvan Szabo, Luca Karall; ***C:*** Sandor Sara.

The 27th Day 🦴🦴½ **1957** Temperate cold war allegory has aliens deliver five mysterious capsules to five Earthlings from different countries. Each capsule, if opened, is capable of decimating the population of the entire planet, but is rendered ineffective after 27 days or upon the death of the holder. Wild ending. Based on John Mantley novel. **75m/B VHS.** Gene Barry, Valerie French, George Voskovec, Arnold Moss, Stefan Schnabel, Ralph Clanton, Friedrich Ledebur, Mari Tsien.

28 Days 🦴🦴½ **2000 (PG-13)** Hard-partying New York journalist Gwen (Bullock) manages to destroy her sister's wedding reception when she gets drunk and manages to get arrested for DUI. The film's title refers to the amount of time Gwen must spend at a rehab clinic. Naturally, Gwen doesn't really believe she has a problem and that's the first attitude adjustment she has to make. Cliches galore although Bullock is welcomingly spiky rather than sweet. **103m/C VHS, DVD, Wide.** Sandra Bullock, Viggo Mortensen, Dominic West, Diane Ladd, Elizabeth Perkins, Steve Buscemi, Alan Tudyk, Reni Santoni, Marianne Jean-Baptiste, Michael O'Malley, Azura Skye, Margo Martindale; ***D:*** Betty Thomas; ***W:*** Susannah Grant; ***C:*** Declan Quinn; ***M:*** Richard Gibbs.

29th Street 🦴🦴½ **1991 (R)** Compelling comedy-drama based on the true story of Frank Pesce, a New York actor who won $6 million in that state's first lottery. Great performance from Aiello, as usual, but the direction falters in the dramatic sequences. Based on the book by Frank Pesce and James Franciscus. **101m/C VHS.** Danny Aiello, Anthony LaPaglia, Lainie Kazan, Frank Pesce, Donna Magnani, Rick Aiello, Vic Manni, Ron Karabatsos, Robert Forster, Joe Franklin, Pete Antico; ***D:*** George Gallo; ***W:*** George Gallo; ***C:*** Steven Fierberg; ***M:*** William Olvis.

Twice a Judas 🦴 *Dos Veces Judas; Due Volte Guida* **1969** An amnesiac is swindled and has his family killed by a ruthless renegade. He wants to get even, even though he can't remember who anyone is. **90m/C VHS.** *IT SP* Klaus Kinski, Antonio (Tony) Sabato, Emma Baron, Franco Beltramme, Jose Calvo; ***D:*** Nando Cicero; ***W:*** Jaime Jesus Balcazar; ***C:*** Francis Marin; ***M:*** Carol Pes.

Twice a Woman 🦴 **1979** Man and woman divorce, and then both fall in love with the same provocative young woman. It's complicated. **90m/C VHS.** Bibi Andersson, Anthony Perkins, Sandra Dumas.

Twice Dead woof! **1988** A family moves into a ramshackle mansion haunted by a stage actor's angry ghost. The ghost helps them battle some attacking delinquent boys. Uninteresting story, poorly done. Never released in theatres. **94m/C VHS.** Tom Breznahan, Jill Whitlow, Sam Melville, Brooke Bundy, Todd Bridges, Jonathan Chapin, Christopher Burgard; ***D:*** Bert L. Dragin; ***M:*** David Bergeaud.

Twice in a Lifetime 🦴🦴🦴 **1985 (R)** Middle-aged man takes stock of his life when he's attracted to Ann-Margret. Realizing he's married in name only, he moves in with his new love while his former wife and children struggle with shock, disbelief, and anger. Well-acted, realistic, and unsentimental. **117m/C VHS.** Gene Hackman, Ellen Burstyn, Amy Madigan, Ann-Margret, Brian Dennehy, Ally Sheedy; ***D:*** Bud Yorkin; ***W:*** Colin Welland.

Twice-Told Tales 🦴🦴🦴 *Nathaniel Hawthorne's "Twice Told Tales"* **1963** Horror trilogy based loosely on three Nathaniel Hawthorne tales, "Dr. Heidegger's Experiment," "Rappaccini's Daughter," and "The House of Seven Gables." Price is great in all three of these well-told tales. **120m/C VHS, DVD, Wide.** Beverly Garland, Richard Denning, Vincent Price, Sebastian Cabot, Brett Halsey; ***D:*** Sidney Salkow; ***W:*** Robert E. Kent; ***C:*** Ellis W. Carter; ***M:*** Richard LaSalle.

Twice upon a Yesterday 🦴🦴 **1998 (R)** Struggling London actor Victor (Henshall) is a romantic swine. He two-timed girlfriend Sylvia (Headey) and she wisely dumped him and found another guy, Dave (Strong), and they're going to get married. Through some time-travelling magic, Victor is able to relive his fateful moment and prevent Sylvia's going. But she winds up meeting Dave anyway while a confused Victor finds a sympathetic bartender, Louise (Cruz), to listen to his romantic trials. Things are just a little too sappy and meandering but the cast (especially Cruz) are worth watching. **94m/C VHS, DVD.** *GB* Douglas Henshall, Lena Headey, Mark Strong, Penelope Cruz, Elizabeth McGovern, Eusebio Lazaro, Charlotte Coleman, Gustavo Salmeron, Neil Stuke; ***D:*** Maria Ripoli; ***W:*** Rafa Russo; ***C:*** Javier Salmones.

Twilight 🦴🦴🦴 *The Magic Hour* **1998 (R)** It's a pleasure to see pros at work, even if the story is a familiar one. In the noir world of L.A., ex-cop, ex-drunk, ex-P.I. Harry Ross (Newman) is living above the garage at the estate of movie star marrieds Jack (Hackman) and Catherine (Sarandon) Ames, for whom Harry has done several jobs. The cancer-stricken Jack asks Harry to handle a blackmail payoff, which seems to resurrect the circumstances of femme fatale Catherine's first husband's alleged suicide. Also involved is Harry's colleague Raymond Hope (Garner)and Harry's ex-flame, Verna (Channing), a cop investigating a murder with ties to the entire ugly situation. **94m/C VHS, DVD.** Paul Newman, Susan Sarandon, Gene Hackman, James Garner, Stockard Channing, Reese Witherspoon, Giancarlo Esposito, Liev Schreiber, Margo Martindale, John Spencer, M. Emmet Walsh; ***D:*** Robert Benton; ***W:*** Robert Benton, Richard Russo; ***C:*** Piotr Sobocinski; ***M:*** Elmer Bernstein.

The Twilight Girls 🦴🦴 *Les Collegiennes* **1957** Young woman enters an exclusive girls boarding school and is immediately introduced to a clique of wealthy girls—one of whom develops a amorous attraction to the newcomer. Film was originally banned in New York because of the frankness of its lesbian scenes. **83m/B VHS.** *FR* Agnes Laurent, Elga Andersen, Estella Blain, Henri Guisol; ***D:*** Andrew Hunebelle; ***W:*** Jean Lambertie, Jacques Lancien.

Twilight in the Sierras 🦴🦴½ **1950** Lots of heroics and music in this action-packed western. An ex-outlaw gone straight is kidnapped for his notorious criminal finesse. Rogers must come to rescue. **67m/C VHS.** Roy Rogers, Dale Evans, Estelita Rodriguez, Pat Brady, Russ Vincent, George Meeker; ***D:*** William Witney.

Twilight Man 🦴🦴½ **1996 (R)** University professor and novelist Jordan Cooper (Matheson) finds his great life turned upside down when a brief altercation with a stranger turns into a nightmare. Turns out the stranger is very strange indeed—computer hacker Hollis Dietz (Stockwell) has made Cooper his own deadly obsession. Suddenly his medical records say he's schizophrenic and even a killer and Cooper must elude police to clear his name. **99m/C VHS.** Tim Matheson, Dean Stockwell, L. Scott Caldwell, Yvette Nipar, Georgann Johnson; ***D:*** Craig R. Baxley; ***W:*** Pablo F. Fenjves, Jim Korris; ***C:*** David Connell; ***M:*** Gary Chang.

Twilight of the Cockroaches 🦴½ *Gokiburi* **1990** Mr. Saito is a slovenly bachelor who winds up leaving the remains of his meals for the anthropomorphic cockroaches that infest his apartment. The cockroaches have had it so good for so long that they don't know about insecticides and fearing humans. That is, until Mr. Saito's fastidious new girlfriend makes her appearance and declares war on the vermin. A lifelessly animated tale too dumb for both children and adults and with decidedly unpleasant subject matter, despite the singing, dancing insects. In Japanese with English subtitles. **105m/C VHS.** *JP* ***D:*** Hiroaki Yoshida; ***V:*** Kaoru Kobayashi, Setsuko Karamsumarau.

The Twilight of the Golds 🦴🦴½ **1997 (PG-13)** The upper-middle class Jewish Gold family seem conventional if fretful: there's doctor dad Walter (Marshall), concerned mom Phyllis (Dunaway), married daughter Suzanne (Beals), and aspiring theatrical producer son David (Fraser), who's gay. It seems everyone's dealt with David's homosexuality until Suzanne's geneticist husband, Rob Stein (Tenney), informs his pregnant wife that tests on their unborn son show genes statistically link to him being gay. (The theory is unproven.) Suzanne considers abortion and David is understandably upset when no one tries to talk her out of it, beginning a family estrangement. Based on the play by Tolins. **90m/C VHS, DVD.** Garry Marshall, Faye Dunaway, Jennifer Beals, Brendan Fraser, Jon Tenney, Jack Klugman, Sean O'Bryan, Rosie O'Donnell; ***D:*** Ross Kagen Marks; ***W:*** Jonathan Tolins, Seth Bass; ***C:*** Tom Richmond; ***M:*** Lee Holdridge. **CABLE**

The Twilight of the Ice Nymphs 🦴🦴 **1997** Welcome once again to filmmaker Maddin's weird world. Peter Glahn (Whitney) is released from prison and travels back to his mythical home in Mandragora, where the sun never sets. At the family ostrich farm, his sister Amelia (Duvall) is smitten with Dr. Solti (Thompson) who has unearthed a mysterious statue of Venus that apparently has strange powers. And Peter gets involved with two women, Zephyr (Krige) and Julianna (Bussieres), who also have ties to the doctor. Deliberately artificial and hallucinatory. **91m/C VHS, DVD.** *CA* Pascale Bussieres, R.H. Thomson, Alice Krige, Nigel Whitney, Shelley Duvall, Frank Gorshin, Ross McMillan; ***D:*** Guy Maddin; ***W:*** George Toles; ***C:*** Michael Marshall; ***M:*** John McCulloch.

Twilight on the Rio Grande 🦴 **1941** Autry runs into a female knife thrower and some jewel smugglers in this far-fetched western. **54m/B VHS.** Gene Autry, Sterling Holloway, Adele Mara, Bob Steele; ***D:*** Frank McDonald.

Twilight on the Trail 🦴🦴 **1941** Cattle rustlers disappear and Hopalong Cassidy and his sidekicks become "dude" detectives to solve the crime. **54m/B VHS.** William Boyd, Brad King, Andy Clyde, Jack Rockwell, Wanda McKay, Howard Bretherton.

Twilight People woof! *Beasts* **1972 (PG)** When a mad scientist's creations turn on him for revenge, he runs for his life. Boring, gory, with bad make-up and even poorer acting. This one should fade away into the night. **84m/C VHS, DVD.** *PH* John Ashley, Pat(ricia) Woodell, Jan Merlin, Pam Grier, Eddie Garcia; ***D:*** Eddie Romero.

Twilight Zone: The Movie 🦴🦴½ **1983 (PG)** Four short horrific tales are anthologized in this film as a tribute to Rod Sterling and his popular TV series. Three of the episodes, "Kick the Can," "It's a Good Life" and "Nightmare at 20,000 Feet," are based on original "Twilight Zone" scripts. Morrow was killed in a helicopter crash during filming. **101m/C VHS.** Steven Williams, Dan Aykroyd, Albert Brooks, Vic Morrow, Kathleen Quinlan, John Lithgow, Billy Mumy, Scatman Crothers, Kevin McCarthy, Bill Quinn, Selma Diamond, Abbe Lane, John Larroquette, Jeremy Licht, Patricia Barry, William Schallert, Burgess Meredith, Cherie Currie, Nancy Cartwright, Dick Miller, Stephen Bishop; ***D:*** John Landis, Steven Spielberg, George Miller, Joe Dante; ***W:*** John Landis, George Clayton Johnson, Richard Matheson; ***C:*** Allen Daviau, John Hora, Stevan Larner; ***M:*** Jerry Goldsmith.

Twilight's Last Gleaming 🦴🦴½ **1977 (R)** A maverick general takes a SAC missile base hostage, threatening to start WWIII if the U.S. government doesn't confess to its Vietnam policies and crimes. Gripping film, with good performances. Based on a novel by Walter Wager, "Viper Three." **144m/C VHS.** Burt Lancaster, Charles Durning, Richard Widmark, Melvyn Douglas, Joseph Cotten, Paul Winfield, Burt Young, Roscoe Lee Browne, Richard Jaeckel, William Marshall, Vera Miles, Leif Erickson, Charles McGraw, William Smith, John Ratzenberger; ***D:*** Robert Aldrich; ***W:*** Ronald M. Cohen; ***C:*** Robert B. Hauser; ***M:*** Jerry Goldsmith.

Twin Beds 🦴🦴½ **1942** Screwball comedy has newlyweds Mike and Julie Abbott (Brent and Bennett) trying to get a little alone time away from their overly friendly neighbors. The interruptions include Julie's ex-boyfriend Larky (Truex) who's on the lookout for imaginary burglars, and an inebriated Russian (Auer) who can't find his own room. Both of their wives just add to the fun. Provides plenty of laughs, especially when Auer's on screen. Adapted from the Margaret Mayo/Salisbury Field play. **85m/B VHS.** Joan Bennett, George Brent, Mischa Auer, Glenda Farrell, Ernest Truex, Una Merkel, Margaret Hamilton, Charles Arnt, Charles Coleman, Cecil Cunningham, Thurston Hall; ***D:*** Tim Whelan; ***W:*** Eddie Moran, Kenneth Earl, Curtis Kenyon; ***C:*** Hal Mohr; ***M:*** Dimitri Tiomkin.

Twin Dragons 🦴🦴 *Shuang Long Hui* **1992 (PG-13)** Re-edited and redubbed English version of the Asian all-star film "Seung Lung Wui," a benefit for the Director's Guild of Hong Kong. Stealing the plot from Jean-Claude Van Damme of all people, Chan plays a dual role as twins separated at birth (as if there were any other kinds of twins in movie scripts) who grow up and cross paths. Chan's likable personality saves the trite, allegedly funny comedy jokelets from bouncing too hard, and the action is chop-sockety good. Cameos from Hong Kong big shots like Tsui Hark, Ringo Lam and John Woo. **89m/C VHS, DVD.** *HK* Jackie Chan, Maggie Cheung, Anthony Chan, Philip Chan, Nina Li Chi, Sylvia Chang, James Wong, Kirk Wong, Ringo Lam, John Woo, Tsui Hark, Teddy Robin; ***D:*** Ringo Lam, Tsui Hark; ***W:*** Barry Wong, Tsui Hark; ***C:*** Wing-hang Wong, Wong Ngor Tai; ***M:*** Michael Wandmacher, Phe Loung.

Twin Falls Idaho 🦴🦴🦴 **1999 (R)** Eerie romantic drama about a lonely pair of conjoined twins, Francis (Michael Polish) and Blake (Mark Polish) Falls. The handsome 25-year-olds are celebrating their birthday in a shabby hotel room on Idaho Street, which is where hooker Penny (Hicks) shows up. Blake (the strong twin) intends Penny as a present for his fragile brother Francis, whose weakened heart is seemingly kept beating by Blake's sheer will. Initially repulsed, Penny becomes fascinated by their situation and begins to fall for Blake. But just what will happen if Francis does indeed die? The talented Polish brothers are identical but not "Siamese" twins. **110m/C VHS, DVD, Wide.** Michael Polish, Mark Polish, Michele Hicks, Jonathan (Jon Francis) Gries, Patrick Bauchau, Garrett Morris, William Katt, Lesley Ann Warren, Teresa Hill, Holly Woodlawn; ***D:*** Michael Polish; ***W:*** Michael Polish, Mark Polish; ***C:*** M. David Mullen; ***M:*** Stuart Matthewman.

Twin Peaks: Fire Walk with Me 🦴🦴 **1992 (R)** Prequel to the cult TV series is weird and frustrating, chronicling the week before Laura Palmer's death. Suspense is lacking since we know the outcome, but Lynch manages to intrigue with dream-like sequences and interestingly offbeat characters. On the other hand, it's exploitative and violent enough to alienate series fans. Includes extremely brief and baffling cameos by Bowie as an FBI agent and Stanton as the manager of a trailer park. Several of the show's regulars are missing, and others appear and disappear very quickly. On the plus side are the strains of Badalamenti's famous theme music and Isaak as an FBI agent with amazingly acute powers of observation. **135m/C VHS, DVD, Wide.** *FR* Kyle MacLachlan, Sheryl Lee, Moira Kelly, David Bowie, Chris Isaak, Harry Dean Stanton, Ray Wise, Kiefer Sutherland, Peggy Lipton, Dana Ashbrook, James Marshall, David Lynch, Catherine Coulson, Julee Cruise, Eric (DaRe) Da Re, Miguel Ferrer, Heather Graham, Madchen Amick, Juergen Prochnow, Grace Zabriskie; ***D:*** David Lynch; ***W:*** David Lynch; ***C:*** Ron Garcia; ***M:*** Angelo Badalamenti.

Twin Sisters 🦴½ **1991** Woman discovers her missing twin sister was a high-priced prostitute and a detective tries to protect her from the lowlifes sis was involved with. **92m/C VHS.** Stephanie Kramer, Susan Almgren, Frederic Forrest, James Brolin; ***D:*** Tom Berry; ***M:*** Lou Forestieri.

Twin Town 🦴🦴½ **1997** Dark comedy about class warfare, escalating revenge, and drug abuse in a small seaside Welsh town features sharp, profane, and very funny dialogue, well-developed and played characters, and uneven direction. Brothers Julian (Evans) and Jeremy (Ifans) like to steal expensive cars and get high on any substance they can find and control. They live with their handyman dad Fatty (Ceredig) and massage parlor receptionist sister (Scorgie) on the wrong side of the tracks. Dad falls off a roof while working for the local contractor/drug kingpin (Thomas) and is not fairly compensated. This starts a cycle of revenge that begins with public urination and gets nasty from there. Sort of a Welsh "Trainspotting," which featured a cameo by "Twin" writer/director Allen. Some scenes may be too much for some viewers (especially animal lovers). **101m/C VHS.** *GB* Llyr Evans, Rhys Ifans, Huw Ceredig, William Thomas, Dorien Thomas, Dougray Scott; ***D:*** Kevin Allen; ***W:*** Kevin Allen, Paul Durden; ***C:*** John Mathieson; ***M:*** Mark Thomas.

Twin Warriors 🦴½ *The Tai-Chi Master; Tai ji Zhang San Feng* **1993 (R)** Junbao (Li) and Tianbao (Siu-hou) grow up together in a Shaolin temple where they secretly learn kung fu by observing the monks in training. Eventually, they're kicked out and Junbao joins a group of rebels while Tianbao enlists in the imperial army. He betrays the rebels and Junbao works to become a Tai Chi master in order to defeat his old friend. Dubbed from Cantonese. **91m/C VHS, DVD, Wide.** *HK* Jet Li, Chin Siu Ho, Michelle Yeoh; ***D:*** Woo-ping Yuen; ***W:*** Kwong Kim Yip; ***C:*** Tom Lau; ***M:*** Wai Lap Wu.

Twins 🦴🦴½ **1988 (PG)** A genetics experiment gone awry produces twins rather than a single child. One is a genetically engineered superman, the other a short, lecherous petty criminal. Schwarzenegger learns he has a brother, and becomes determined to find him, despite their having been raised separately. The two meet and are immediately involved in a contraband scandal. Amusing pairing of Schwarzenegger and DeVito. **107m/C VHS, DVD.** Arnold Schwarzenegger, Danny DeVito, Kelly Preston, Hugh O'Brian, Chloe Webb, Bonnie Bartlett, Marshall Bell, Trey Wilson, Nehemiah Persoff; ***D:*** Ivan Reitman; ***W:*** William Davies, William Osborne, Timothy Harris, Herschel Weingrod; ***C:*** Andrzej Bartkowiak; ***M:*** Georges Delerue, Randy Edelman.

Twins of Evil 🦴🦴 *The Gemini Twins; Twins of Dracula; The Virgin Vampires* **1971** Beautiful female twins fall victim to the local vampire, and their God-fearing uncle is out to save/destroy them. Hammer sex and blood-sucking epic starring the Collinsons, who were featured in the October 1970 issue of "Playboy" as the first twin Playmates. **86m/C VHS.** *GB* Madeleine Collinson, Mary Collinson, Peter Cushing, Kathleen Byron, Dennis Price, Damien Thomas, David Warbeck, Katya Wyeth, Maggie Wright, Luan Peters, Kristen Lindholm, Judy Matheson; ***D:*** John Hough; ***W:*** Tudor Gates; ***C:*** Dick Bush.

Twinsanity 🦴 *Goodbye Gemini* **1970 (R)** Evil twins are charged with the murder of a man who attempted to blackmail them. **91m/C VHS.** *GB* Judy Geeson, Martin Potter, Alexis Kanner, Michael Redgrave, Freddie Jones, Peter Jeffrey; ***D:*** Alan Gibson; ***W:*** Edmund Ward; ***M:*** Christopher Gunning.

Twinsitters 🦴🦴½ **1995 (PG-13)** Twins Peter and David Falcone (Peter and David Paul) find themselves unexpectedly saving the life of corrupt businessman Frank Hillhurst (Martin). Hillhurst is turning state's evidence on his crooked operations and his disturbed partners have threatened both his life and the lives of his twin 10-year-old nephews. So Hillhurst hires the Falcones to protect his hellacious pint-sized relatives—who manage to get themselves kidnapped. **93m/C VHS.** Peter Paul, David Paul, Christian Cousins, Joseph Cousins, Jared Martin, George Lazenby, Rena Sofer, Mother Love; ***D:*** John Paragon; ***W:*** John Paragon.

Twirl 🦴🦴 **1981** Satirical look at the cutthroat world of baton twirling. Parents apply relentless pressure on their daughters to win a contest. Decent made-for-TV movie. **100m/C VHS.** Stella Stevens, Charles Haid, Lisa Whelchel, Erin Moran, Edd Byrnes, Sharon Spelman, Matthew Tobin, Donna McKechnie, Rosalind Chao, Heather Locklear, Deborah Richter, Jamie Rose, Tracy Scoggins; ***D:*** Gus Trikonis.

Twist 🦴½ *Folies Bourgeoises* **1976** A tepid French drama chronicling the infidelities of various wealthy aristocrats. The aristocrats are boring, as is the film. In French with English subtitles or dubbed. **105m/C VHS.** *FR* Bruce Dern, Stephane Audran, Ann-Margret, Sydne Rome, Jean-Pierre Cassel, Curt Jurgens, Maria Schell, Charles Aznavour; ***D:*** Claude Chabrol; ***M:*** Manuel De Sica.

Twist & Shout 🦴🦴🦴 *Hab Og Karlighed* **1984 (R)** Sequel to the popular Danish import "Zappa," in which two teenage lovers discover sex and rock and roll. Transcends the teens discovering sex genre. Danish with English subtitles. Profanity, nudity, and sex. **107m/C VHS.** *DK* Lars Simonsen, Adam Tonsberg, Ulrikke Juul Bondo, Camilla Soeberg; ***D:*** Bille August; ***W:*** Bille August; ***C:*** Jan Weincke, Aldo (G.R. Aldo) Graziatti.

Twisted 🦴🦴 **1986 (R)** This curio from Slater's early career came out on tape to take advantage of his rising stardom. He's properly creepy as a brilliant but evil teen using electronics, psychology, and swordplay to terrorize victims. The suspense isn't too bad when direction doesn't go overboard, which unfortunately is half the time. Based on the play "Children! Children!" by Jack Horrigan. **87m/C VHS.** Lois Smith, Christian Slater, Tandy Cronyn, Brooke Tracy, Dina Merrill, Dan Ziskie, Karl Taylor, Noelle Parker, John Cunningham, J.C. Quinn; ***D:*** Adam Holender.

Twisted 🦴🦴 **1996** Apt title for a contemporary gay version of "Oliver Twist" set in New York. Homeless 10-year-old orphan Lee (Graves) is brought into the seedy world of brothel owner Andre (Hickey). The youngster is befriended by Angel (Norona) a drug-addicted hustler who's under the sway of abusive pimp Eddie (Crivello). Along with big-hearted drag queen Shiniqua (Porter), Angel tries to rescue Lee from a sordid life. A stylized, operatic melodrama. **100m/C VHS.** Keivyn McNeil Graves, William Hickey, David Norona, Anthony Crivello, Billy Porter; ***D:*** Seth Michael Donsky; ***W:*** Seth Michael Donsky; ***C:*** Hernan Toto.

Twisted 🦴🦴 **1996 (PG-13)** Four people become trapped in a fantasy world where nothing is as it seems. An airline passenger loses his identity, a houswife finds romance, a con man find a new mark, and a hired killer decides to retire—or at least that's what they believe. From the Australian TV series "Twisted Tales." **86m/C VHS, DVD.** *AU* Geoffrey Rush, Rachel Ward, Bryan Brown, Kimberly Davies, Shane Briant; ***D:*** Samantha Lang, Christopher Robbin Collins, Gregor Jordan, Catherine Millar; ***C:*** James Bartle; ***M:*** Nerida Tyson-Chew; ***Nar:*** Bryan Brown. **TV**

Twisted Brain 🦴 *Horror High* **1974 (R)** An honor student develops a serum that makes him half man and half beast. Now he can exact revenge on all the jocks and cheerleaders who have humiliated him in the past. Cardi is okay, the rest of the cast is awful. Silly, horrific teen monster epic. **89m/C VHS.** Pat Cardi, Austin Stoker, Rosie Holotik, John Niland, Joyce Hash, Jeff Alexander, Joe "Mean Joe" Greene; ***D:*** Larry N. Stouffer.

Twisted Justice 🦴½ **1989** Set in 2020, Heavener is a cop determined to stop a ruthless killer. Matters become complicated, however, when his gun is taken away. Now he's forced to rely on his cunning to outwit his sadistic opponent. **90m/C VHS, DVD.** David Heavener, Erik Estrada, Jim Brown, Shannon Tweed, James Van Patten, Don Stroud, Karen Black, Lori Warren; ***D:*** David Heavener; ***W:*** David Heavener; ***C:*** David Hue.

Twisted Love 🦴½ **1995 (R)** Wallflower becomes obsessed with the most popular guy in school. He has a motorcycle accident-that-was-no-accident and winds up in her tender care. Sounds like "Misery" to me. **80m/C VHS.** Lisa Dean Ryan, Mark Paul Gosselaar, Soleil Moon Frye; ***D:*** Eb Lottimer.

Twisted Nightmare 🦴 **1987 (R)** The people responsible for a young retarded boy's death are hunted by a strange figure lurking in the shadows. **95m/C** Rhonda Gray, Cleve Hall, Brad Bartrum, Robert Padilla; ***D:*** Paul Hunt.

Twisted Obsession 🦴🦴 **1990 (R)** A man becomes passionately obsessed with a woman, and it leads to murder. **109m/C VHS.** Jeff Goldblum, Miranda Richardson, Anemone, Dexter Fletcher, Daniel Ceccaldi, Liza Walker, Jerome Natali, Arielle Dombasle; ***D:*** Fernando Trueba; ***C:*** Jose Luis Alcaine; ***M:*** Antoine Duhamel.

Twister 🦴🦴 **1989 (PG-13)** An intriguing independent feature about a bizarre midwestern family, its feverish eccentricities and eventual collapse. Awaiting a cult following. **93m/C VHS.** Dylan McDermott, Crispin Glover, Harry Dean Stanton, Suzy Amis, Jenny Wright, Lindsay Christman, Lois Chiles, William S. Burroughs, Tim Robbins; ***D:*** Michael Almereyda; ***W:*** Michael Almereyda; ***C:*** Renato Berta; ***M:*** Hans Zimmer.

Twister 🦴🦴½ **1996 (PG-13)** Director De Bont's sophomore directorial effort is another non-stop adrenaline drive, but instead of a mad bomber, nature is the bad guy. Hunt leads a collegiate team of storm chasing scientists through Oklahoma in hopes of placing a robotic mechanism inside a tornado which, in turn, will help them predict and prepare for future funnel forces. There's also the matter of Hunt's soon-to-be ex-husband Paxton, and a competitor (Elwes) who's in charge of a slick group of rival scientists. There's a lot of things flying around, including trucks, houses, cows and the plausibility of the plot. But a contrived plot didn't keep from making $100 million in its first two weeks of release. Some nice chemistry between Hunt and Paxton, apparently the only people who can still look attractive in high winds and blowing debris. **105m/C VHS, DVD, Wide.** Bill Paxton, Helen Hunt, Cary Elwes, Jami Gertz, Alan Ruck, Lois Smith, Sean M. Whalen, Gregory Sporleder, Abraham Benrubi, Jake Busey, Joey Slotnick, Philip Seymour Hoffman, Jeremy Davies, Zach Grenier; ***D:*** Jan De Bont; ***W:*** Michael Crichton, Anne-Marie Martin; ***C:*** Jack N. Green; ***M:*** Mark Mancina. MTV Movie Awards '97: Action Seq.

Twists of Terror 🦴🦴½ **1998** Three horror stories narrated by an agoraphobic Los Angelenos. In "The People You Meet," a couple are terrorized while in the country; "The Clinic" has Mancuso confined to a hospital after a vicious dog attack, but the patient learns he can't check out; while "Stolen Moments" finds one young woman and two playboys with murder on their minds. **90m/C VHS.** Jennifer Rubin, Nick Mancuso, Carl Marotte, Francoise Robertson, Andrew Jackson; ***D:*** Douglas Jackson.

Twitch of the Death Nerve 🦴🦴 *Bay of Blood; Last House on the Left, Part 2; Carnage* **1971 (R)** Four vacationers are relentlessly pursued by a homicidal maniac armed with a sickle, bent on decapitation. Supposedly the inspiration for the "Friday the 13th" series. **87m/C VHS, DVD, Wide.** *IT* Claudine Auger, Chris Avran, Isa Miranda, Laura Betti, Luigi Pistilli, Sergio Canvari, Anna M. Rosati; ***D:*** Mario Bava; ***W:*** Mario Bava, Filippo Ottoni, Joseph McLee, Gene Luotto; ***C:*** Mario Bava; ***M:*** Stelvio Cipriano.

Two Bits 🦴🦴½ *A Day to Remember* **1996 (PG-13)** Depression-era drama tells the story of a 12-year-old boy and his emotional coming of age. Title refers to a quarter Gennaro (Barone, in his film debut) seeks in order to attend the grand opening of a glamorous, air-conditioned movie palace. A heavily made-up Pacino (looking suspiciously like Marlon Brando in the garden scene of "The Godfather"), co-stars as the boy's grandfather, who leaves him his last quarter. Gramps promises that he can collect later that day, when, he says, he will die. Fine performances all around and some powerful scenes go a long way toward masking the fact that the material is a bit too thin to stretch over an entire feature film. **85m/C VHS.** Al Pacino, Gerlando Barone, Mary Elizabeth Mastrantonio, Joe Grifasi, Joanna Merlin, Andy Romano, Ron McLarty, Donna Mitchell, Patrick Borriello, Mary Lou Rosato, Rosemary DeAngelis; ***D:*** James Foley; ***W:*** Joseph Stefano; ***C:*** Juan Ruiz-Anchia; ***M:*** Jane Musky; ***V:*** Alec Baldwin.

Two Bits & Pepper 🦴🦴½ **1995 (PG)** Bumbling criminals (both played by Piscopo) still manage to kidnap a a young girl and her friend and it's up to the title characters, a pet horse and a pony, to attempt a daring rescue. **90m/C VHS.** Joe Piscopo, Lauren Eckstrom, Rachel Crane, Perry Stephens, Kathrin Lautner, Dennis Weaver; ***D:*** Corey Michael Eubanks; ***W:*** Corey Michael Eubanks; ***C:*** Jacques Haitkin; ***M:*** Louis Febre.

Two by Forsyth 🦴🦴 **1986** Two short films based on stories by Frederick Forsyth, one dealing with a dying millionaire's clever efforts to prevent his fortune from being inherited by greedy relatives, the other about a mild-mannered stamp dealer who avenges himself on a nasty gossip columnist. **60m/C VHS.** Dan O'Herlihy, Cyril Cusack, Milo O'Shea, Shirley Anne Field.

2 by 4 🦴🦴 **1998** Johnnie (Smallhorne) is an Irish construction worker employed by his hard-living Uncle Trump (O'Neill) in New York. Though he's got a steady job, good friends, and a loving girlfriend in Maria (Topper), Johnnie's plagued by nightmares of something that happened in his childhood. And his apparent childhood abuse leads him to drugs, drink, and a certain sexual ambiguity as his repressed memories try to force their way to the surface. **90m/C VHS.** Jimmy Smallhorne, Chris O'Neill, Bradley Fitts, Joe Holyoake, Terrence McGoff, Michael Liebman, Ronan Carr, Leo Hamill, Seamus McDonagh, Kimberly Topper; ***D:*** Jimmy Smallhorne; ***W:*** Fergus Tighe, Jimmy Smallhorne, Terrence McGoff; ***C:*** Declan Quinn. Sundance '98: Cinematog.

Two Can Play That Game 🦴½ **2001 (R)** Upwardly mobile Shante (Fox) seems to be the fountain of knowledge for her romantically challenged girlfriends Diedre (Mo'Nique), Karen (Robinson) and Trayce (Jones) on the subject of how to keep a man in line. When she sees her boyfriend Keith (Chestnut) grinding on another woman at a nightclub, however, her credibility takes a blow. She decides on a ten-day plan of action to force Keith back under her thumb. Clued in by his worldly-wise buddy Tony (Anderson), however, Keith is well versed in the battle tactics of the opposite sex. Familiar material (director Brown also wrote "How to Be a Player"), spotty performances and the incessant narration by Fox's character make this a game you may want to quit halfway through. **90m/C VHS, DVD, Wide.** *US* Vivica A. Fox, Morris Chestnut, Anthony Anderson, Gabrielle Union, Wendy Raquel Robinson, Tamala Jones, Mo'Nique, Ray Wise, Bobby Brown, Dondre T. Whitfield; ***D:*** Mark Brown; ***W:*** Mark Brown; ***C:*** Alexander Grusynski; ***M:*** Marcus Miller.

Two Daughters 🦴🦴🦴 *Teen Kanya* **1961** Director Ray wrote the scripts for two stories based on the writings of Nobel Prize winner Rabindranath Tagore. "The Postmaster" covers the relationship between an ambitious young man who befriends his servant without realizing the consequences of his actions. "The Conclusion" finds a solemn young scholar declining to marry the girl arranged to be his intended and instead marrying a high-spirited young woman who doesn't want to give up her freedoms. Bengali with English subtitles. **114m/B VHS.** *IN* Chandana Banerjee, Anil Chatterjee, Soumitra Chatterjee; ***D:*** Satyajit Ray; ***W:*** Satyajit Ray; ***C:*** Soumendu Roy; ***M:*** Satyajit Ray.

Two Days in the Valley 🦴🦴🦴 **1996 (R)** Film adds two days with ten characters in one locale and one half dozen separate plots and tries to come up with a dark comedy/thriller and winning debut for Herzfeld. It succeeds, mostly. San Fernando Valley is the backdrop, with a diverse ensemble of disturbed characters thrown together by the murder of a philandering spouse. Disjointed, and some plot threads are left hanging, but there's some fine comic moments and interesting character development, especially Aiello's culinary hitman, Dosmo Pizzo. Theron's Helga adds eye candy. For those too young to remember "Dynasty," you may want to check out the intense cat-fight between Hatcher's Becky Foxx and Helga. **105m/C VHS, DVD.** Danny Aiello, Jeff Daniels, Marsha Mason, Teri Hatcher, Glenne Headly, James Spader, Eric Stoltz, Greg Cruttwell, Peter Horton, Charlize Theron, Keith Carradine, Louise Fletcher, Austin Pendleton, Paul Mazursky, Kathleen Luong; ***D:*** John Herzfeld; ***W:*** John Herzfeld; ***C:*** Oliver Wood; ***M:*** Anthony Marinelli.

Two Deaths 🦴🦴 **1994 (R)** Sex, brutality, power, madness, death, revolution—sounds like a Roeg concoction. In 1989 Romania, the Ceaucescu government is under siege and a civil war rages outside. But inside the opulent apartment of cynical Dr. Daniel Pavenic (Gambon) calmness prevails, as three longtime friends join him for their annual reunion dinner. Dinner is served by Pavenic's housekeeper Ana (Braga), who has a strange, disturbing relationship with the possessive doctor that he relates to his friends. His candor leads to similar revelations by his companions. Based on the novel "The Two Deaths of Senora Puccini" by Stephen Dobyns. **102m/C VHS, DVD.** *GB* Michael Gambon, Sonia Braga, Patrick Malahide, Nickolas Grace, John Shrapnel, Ion Caramitru; ***D:*** Nicolas Roeg; ***W:*** Allan Scott; ***C:*** Witold Stok; ***M:*** Hans Zimmer.

Two English Girls 🦴🦴🦴½ *Les Deux Anglaises et le Continent; Anne and Muriel* **1972 (R)** A pre-WWI French lad, with a possessive mother, loves two English sisters, one an impassioned, reckless artist, the other a repressed spinster. Tenderly delineates the triangle's interrelating love and friendship over seven years. Based on the novel "Les Deux Anglaises et le Continent" by Henri-Pierre Roche. In French with English subtitles. **130m/C VHS, DVD, Wide.** *FR* Jean-Pierre Leaud, Kika Markham, Stacey Tendeter, Sylvia Marriott, Marie Mansert, Philippe Leotard; ***D:*** Francois Truffaut; ***W:*** Francois Truffaut; ***C:*** Nestor Almendros; ***M:*** Georges Delerue.

Two Evil Eyes 🦴🦴 *Due Occhi Diabolici* **1990 (R)** Horror kings Romero and Argento each direct an Edgar Allan Poe tale in this release, hence the title. Barbeau, the scheming younger wife of a millionaire, hypnotizes her husband with the help of her lover in "The Facts in the Case of M. Valdemar." When hubby dies too soon to validate changes made in his will, the lovers decide to freeze him for two weeks in order that death can be recorded at the correct time. In "Black Cat" a crime photographer used to photographing gore adopts a feline friend and starts getting sick on the job. **121m/C VHS.** *IT* Adrienne Barbeau, Ramy Zada, Harvey Keitel, Madeleine Potter, Bingo O'Malley, E.G. Marshall, John Amos, Sally Kirkland, Kim Hunter, Martin Balsam, Tom Atkins; ***D:*** George A. Romero, Dario Argento; ***W:*** George A. Romero, Dario Argento, Franco Ferrini; ***C:*** Giuseppe Maccari, Peter Reniers; ***M:*** Pino Donaggio.

Two-Faced Woman 🦴🦴🦴 **1941** Garbo, in her last film, attempts a ruse when she finds her husband may be interested in an old flame. Pretending to be her twin sister in an attempt to lure Douglas away from the other woman, she's fooled a little herself. Romantic comedy unfortunately miscasts Garbo as an Americanized ski bunny. **90m/B VHS.** Greta Garbo, Melvyn Douglas, Constance Bennett, Roland Young, Ruth Gordon, Robert Sterling, George Cleveland, Frances Carson; ***D:*** George Cukor; ***C:*** Joseph Ruttenberg.

The Two Faces of Dr. Jekyll 🦴🦴½ *House of Fright; Jekyll's Inferno* **1960** Henry Jekyll's (Massie) experiments lead to the release of his suave alter ego Edward Hyde. When Hyde discovers that Jekyll's long-suffering wife has taken up with his best friend, Hyde pits everyone against each other, while Jekyll struggles to retain control over his insidious other half. **87m/C VHS.** *GB* Paul Massie, Dawn Addams, Christopher Lee, David Kossoff, Francis De Wolff, Oliver Reed, Norma Marla, Terry Quinn; ***D:*** Terence Fisher; ***W:*** Wolf Mankowitz; ***C:*** Jack Asher.

The Two Faces of Evil 🦴 **1982** A family's vacation turns into a night of unbearable terror when they pick up a sinister hitchhiker. **60m/C VHS.** Anna Calder-Marshall, Gary Raymond, Denholm Elliott, Pauline Delany, Philip Latham; ***D:*** Peter Sasdy, Alan Gibson.

Two Family House 🦴🦴½ **1999 (R)** The fifties aren't exactly a time of happiness and prosperity for factory worker Buddy Rispoli. He's a frustrated singer, still haboring dreams of the big time, with a number of failed moneymaking schemes behind him. His latest venture is buying a two-family house where he and his family can live upstairs while he turns the downstairs into a bar. But the current tenants, a pregnant Irish teen and her abusive husband, have other ideas. **109m/C VHS, DVD, Wide.** Michael Rispoli, Kelly Macdonald, Kathrine Narducci, Matt Servitto, Kevin Conway, Michele Santopietro; ***D:*** Raymond De Felitta; ***W:*** Raymond De Felitta; ***C:*** Mike Mayers; ***M:*** Stephen Endelman. Sundance '00: Aud. Award.

Two Fathers' Justice **1985** Two dads, one tough and one a wimp, seek revenge on the men who killed their kids. **100m/C VHS.** Robert Conrad, George Hamilton, Brooke Bundy, Catherine Corkill, Whitney Kershaw, Greg Terrell; ***D:*** Rod Holcomb. **TV**

Two Fisted Justice 🦴 **1931** A cowboy protects a town against a daring and deadly Indian attack. **45m/B VHS.** Tom Tyler.

Two-Fisted Justice 🦴 **1943** The Range Busters do their part to maintain law and order in the old West. **55m/B VHS.** John "Dusty" King, David Sharpe, Max Terhune.

Two-Fisted Law 🦴½ **1932** McCoy plays a rancher who borrows big bucks from the corrupt Oakman, who's actually a land grabber. McCoy then teams up with a posse to bring the evildoer to justice. Early (and small) screen roles for Wayne and Brennan. **58m/B VHS, DVD.** Tim McCoy, Tully Marshall, Wheeler Oakman, Alice Day, Wallace MacDonald, John Wayne, Walter Brennan; ***D:*** David Ross Lederman; ***W:*** Kurt Kempler; ***C:*** Benjamin (Ben H.) Kline.

Two for Texas 🦴🦴½ **1997** Young buck Holland (Bairstow) and grizzled adventurer Allison (Kristofferson) manage to escape from a Louisiana chain gang and decide to head to Texas so they can join in the Texas Volunteer Army under Sam Houston (Skerritt). Soon, they're part of a group sent to San Jacinto in order to avenge the massacre at the Alamo. Kind of plodding western based on the novel by James Lee Burke. **96m/C VHS.** Kris Kristofferson, Scott Bairstow, Tom Skerritt, Peter Coyote, Irene Bedard, Victor Rivers, Rodney A. Grant, Marco Rodriguez, Richard Jones; ***D:*** Rod Hardy; ***W:*** Larry Brothers; ***C:*** David Connell; ***M:*** Lee Holdridge. **CABLE**

Two for the Road 🦴🦴🦴½ **1967** On a road trip to the French Riviera, Mark (Finney) and Joanna (Hepburn) look back on more than a decade of marriage and find only fragments of their relationship. Flashbacks to their first meeting and subsequent vacations detail what when wrong and if their love is worth saving. Mancini score adds poignancy to the couple's reflections on their stormy life. Well-acted but the very sixties look has dated badly. **112m/C VHS, Wide.** *GB* Audrey Hepburn, Albert Finney, Eleanor Bron, William Daniels, Claude Dauphin, Nadia Gray, Jacqueline Bisset, Georges Descrieres, Gabrielle Middleton, Judy Cornwell, Irene Hilda, Roger Dann, Libby Morris, Yves Barsac; ***D:*** Stanley Donen; ***W:*** Frederic Raphael; ***C:*** Christopher Challis; ***M:*** Henry Mancini.

Two for the Seesaw 🦴🦴🦴 **1962** Mitchum stars as a Nebraska attorney who comes to New York and gets involved with MacLaine. Humorous and touching comedy-drama worked better on stage, because the large screen magnified the talkiness of Gibson's play. Unusual casting of Mitchum as a Midwest lawyer and MacLaine as a New York Jewish bohemian. **119m/B VHS, Wide.** Robert Mitchum, Shirley MacLaine, Edmon Ryan, Elisabeth Fraser, Eddie Firestone, Billy Gray, Vic Lundin; ***D:*** Robert Wise; ***W:*** Isobel Lennart; ***M:*** Andre Previn.

Two Friends 🦴🦴 **1986** Campion's first feature, made for Australian TV, depicts the severing of the friendship between 15-year-olds Kelly (Bidenko) and Louise (Coles). Separated physically and emotionally as they begin growing up and attending different schools, the film flashes back to moments in their once inseparable friendship. **76m/C VHS, DVD, Wide.** *AU* Kris Bidenko, Emma Coles, Peter Hehir, Kris McQuade; ***D:*** Jane Campion; ***W:*** Helen Garner; ***C:*** Julian Penney; ***M:*** Martin Armiger.

Two Girls and a Guy 🦴🦴🦴 **1998 (R)** Graham and Wagner find out that Downey's been two-timing them and they confront him at his apartment. Only don't expect the usual revenge scenario. Yeah, it's talky, but the dialogue (much of it improvised) is great. Downey is at his best, playing an irresistibly charismatic actor backed into a (real and figurative) corner by his lifestyle while Graham and Wagner avoid the wronged-woman cliches. In one of the all-time male fantasies ever, Downey's character still gets to have sex with one of the women even after his lie has been exposed. The MPAA had a little problem with that, since that scene, like most of the rest of the movie, was shot in real time. The uncut NC-17 version is also available. **92m/C VHS.** Robert Downey Jr., Heather Graham, Natasha Gregson Wagner, Angel David, Frederique van der Wal; ***D:*** James Toback; ***W:*** James Toback; ***C:*** Barry Markowitz.

Two Girls and a Sailor 🦴🦴🦴 **1944** Wartime musical revue loosely structured around a love triangle involving a sailor on leave. Vintage hokum with lots of songs. ♫Paper Doll; The Young Man with a Horn; Concerto for Index Finger; Take it Easy; Ritual Fire Dance; Inka Dinka Doo; My Mother Told Me; A Love Like Ours; In A Moment of Madness. **124m/B VHS.** June Allyson, Gloria De Haven, Van Johnson, Xavier Cugat, Jimmy Durante, Tom Drake, Lena Horne, Harry James, Gracie Allen, Virginia O'Brien, Jose Iturbi, Carlos Ramirez, Donald Meek, Ben Blue; ***Cameos:*** Buster Keaton; ***D:*** Richard Thorpe; ***C:*** Robert L. Surtees.

The Two Great Cavaliers 🦴 **1973** A Ming warrior has a hard time with the Manchurian army, fending it off as he must with only his bare instep, heel, and wrist. **95m/C VHS.** Chen Shing, Mao Ying; ***D:*** Yeung Ching Chen.

Two Gun Man 🦴½ **1931** America's first singing cowboy, Ken Maynard, performs hair-raising stunts in this old oater. One of the first "talkies!" **60m/B VHS.** Ken Maynard, Lafe (Lafayette) McKee, Charles "Blackie" King, Tom London, Lucille Powers; ***D:*** Phil Rosen.

Two-Gun Man from Harlem 1938 Big city guy travels to the wild West in search of a little truth. **60m/B VHS.** Herbert Jeffries, Marguerite Whitten, Mantan Moreland, Matthew "Stymie" Beard; ***D:*** Richard C. Kahn.

Two-Gun Troubador 🦴 *The Lone Troubador* **1937** A masked singing cowboy struggles to uncovers his father's murderer. **59m/B VHS.** Fred Scott, Claire Rochelle, John Merton.

Two Hands 🦴🦴🦴 **1998** Black comedy/thriller stars Aussie heartthrob Ledger as teen Jimmy who's got a nothing job in Sydney and would like to improve his prospects. So he agrees to deliver a cash-filled envelope for local gang boss, Pando (Brown), and then promptly loses the money. This sends Jimmy on the run to avoid Pando's retribution. (But the kid still finds some time to romance naive Alex (Byrne).) **104m/C VHS.** *AU* Heath Ledger, Bryan Brown, David Field, Rose Byrne, Susie Porter, Tom Long, Steven Vidler; ***D:*** Gregor Jordan; ***W:*** Gregor Jordan; ***C:*** Malcolm McCulloch; ***M:*** Chris Gough. Australian Film Inst. '99: Director (Jordan), Film, Film Editing, Orig. Screenplay, Support. Actor (Brown).

200 Cigarettes 🦴🦴 **1998 (R)** Directorial debut from former casting director Garcia follows the adventures of various self-absorbed hipsters on New Year's Eve in early '80s New York. The excellent ensemble cast is given spotty material, however. The primary goal of all these rather unlikable characters is to find someone (or anyone) to sleep with before the night is over. They all hook up in this ode to the high life of pre-AIDS promiscuity, but you don't really care about them at all. Chapelle provides the most entertainment as a philosophy-spouting disco cabbie who schleps the shallow partygoers to and fro. **101m/C VHS, DVD.** Ben Affleck, Casey Affleck, Jay Mohr, Dave Chappelle, Gaby Hoffman, Courtney Love, Christina Ricci, Paul Rudd, Catherine Kellner, Martha Plimpton, Janeane Garofalo, Guillermo Diaz, Angela Featherstone, Brian McCardie, Nicole Parker, Kate Hudson, Elvis Costello; ***D:*** Risa Bramon Garcia; ***W:*** Shana Larsen; ***C:*** Frank Prinzi; ***M:*** Mark Mothersbaugh, Bob Mothersbaugh.

200 Motels 🦴½ **1971 (R)** Rambling, non-narrative self-indulgent video album by and about Frank Zappa and the Mothers of Invention, as they document a long and especially grueling road tour. For fans only. **99m/C VHS.** Ringo Starr, Theodore Bikel, Keith Moon, Janet Ferguson, Lucy Offerall; ***D:*** Frank Zappa; ***W:*** Frank Zappa; ***C:*** Gillian Lynne; ***M:*** Frank Zappa.

Two If by Sea 🦴½ *Stolen Hearts* **1995 (R)** Small-time hood Frank (Leary) and his girlfriend Roz (Bullock) hole up in a New England mansion after Frank steals a valuable Matisse painting. Between verbal sparring matches, the two try to mingle with the upper crusty residents with predictable results. Pursuing the pair are the FBI, led by the deluded O'Malley (Kotto), and Frank's bonehead cousin Beano (Robson) and his trio of dim henchmen. Tries to be a caper/romantic comedy but fails to deliver on all fronts. The usually caustic Leary takes some of the edge off of his trademark bitter humor, and the alleged witty repartee is just plain annoying as a result. Nova Scotia turns in a fine performance as New England. **96m/C VHS, DVD, Wide.** Sandra Bullock, Denis Leary, Stephen (Dillon) Dillane, Yaphet Kotto, Wayne Robson, Jonathan Tucker, Mike Starr, Michael Badalucco, Lenny Clarke, John Friesen; ***D:*** Bill Bennett; ***W:*** Denis Leary, Mike Armstrong; ***C:*** Andrew Lesnie.

The Two Jakes 🦴🦴 **1990 (R)** Ten years have passed and Jake Gittes is still a private investigator in this sequel to 1974's "Chinatown." When a murder occurs while he's digging up dirt on an affair between the wife of a real estate executive and the executive's partner, Jake must return to Chinatown to uncover the killer and face the painful memories buried there. Despite solid dialogue and effective performances, it's unreasonably difficult to follow if you haven't seen "Chinatown." Outstanding photography by Vilmos Zsigmond. **137m/C VHS, DVD, Wide.** Jack Nicholson, Harvey Keitel, Meg Tilly, Madeleine Stowe, Eli Wallach, Ruben Blades, Frederic Forrest, David Keith, Richard Farnsworth, Tracey Walter; ***D:*** Jack Nicholson; ***W:*** Robert Towne; ***C:*** Vilmos Zsigmond; ***M:*** Van Dyke Parks.

Two Kinds of Love 🦴🦴 **1985** Adapted from Peggy Mann's novel "There Are Two Kinds of Terrible," this is the story of a young boy who learns to love his distant, workaholic father after his protective mother suddenly dies. **94m/C VHS.** Rick Schroder, Lindsay Wagner, Peter Weller; ***D:*** Jack Bender. **TV**

Two Lane Blacktop 🦴🦴🦴 **1971** Counterculture critics darling that failed at the box-office but has since developed a cult following. The Driver (Taylor) and the Mechanic (Wilson) are car freaks in a '55 Chevy, driving the southwestern backroads looking for a race. They meet up with Oates who's at the wheel of a brand-new G.T.O. He proposes they cross-country to D.C. and the winner gets the loser's car. Along the way, everyone's enthusiasm wanes and they part, with Wilson and Taylor driving down a two-lane blacktop as the film literally melts into a bright light. Music includes The Doors, Kris Kristofferson, and Ray Charles. **103m/C VHS, DVD.** James Taylor, Dennis Wilson, Warren Oates, Laurie Bird, Harry Dean Stanton; ***D:*** Monte Hellman; ***W:*** Rudy Wurlitzer, Will Corry; ***C:*** Jackson Deerson.

Two Lost Worlds woof! **1950** A young hero battles monstrous dinosaurs, pirates, and more in this cheapy when he and his shipmates are shipwrecked on an uncharted island. Don't miss the footage from "Captain Fury," "One Billion B.C.," and "Captain Caution" and Arness long before his Sheriff Dillon fame, and his "big" role in "The Thing." **63m/B VHS, DVD.** James Arness, Laura Elliott, Bill Kennedy; ***D:*** Norman Dawn; ***W:*** Tom Hubbard; ***C:*** Harry Neumann.

Two Men & a Wardrobe **1958** Polanski's project while a student at the Polish Film Institute. Consideration of modern man's lack of privacy and made without dialogue. Two men emerge from the sea carrying nothing but a large piece of furniture. Absurd and funny. **19m/B VHS.** ***D:*** Roman Polanski.

Two Minute Warning 🦴 **1976 (R)** A sniper plans to take out the president of the United States at an NFL playoff game in this boring, pointless, disaster film that goes on forever. Features all the ready-made characters inherent in the genre, but, until its too late, precious little of the mayhem. To get caught watching the TV version, which features more characters and an additional subplot, would be truly disastrous. **116m/C VHS, DVD, Wide.** Charlton Heston, John Cassavetes, Martin Balsam, Beau Bridges, Marilyn Hassett, David Janssen, Jack Klugman, Walter Pidgeon, Gena Rowlands; ***D:*** Larry Peerce; ***W:*** Ed Hume; ***C:*** Gerald Hirschfeld; ***M:*** Charles Fox.

The Two Mrs. Carrolls 🦴🦴½ **1947** Bogart is a psycho-killer/artist who paints portraits of his wives as the Angel of Death—and then kills them. The married Bogart falls for Stanwyck, poisons his current wife, and the two marry. After a few years, Bogart falls for Smith and decides to rid himself of Stanwyck in the same manner as his first killing. Stanwyck, however, becomes increasingly suspicious and calls on an old beau for help. Melodrama cast Bogart against type (not always successfully). Filmed in 1945, but was unreleased until 1947. **99m/B VHS.** Humphrey Bogart, Barbara Stanwyck, Alexis Smith, Nigel Bruce, Pat O'Moore, Ann Carter; ***D:*** Peter Godfrey.

Two Moon Junction 🦴½ **1988 (R)** A soon-to-be-wed Southern debutante enters into a wild love affair with a rough-edged carnival worker. Poorly acted, wildly directed, with many unintentional laughs. **104m/C VHS, DVD, Wide.** Sherilyn Fenn, Richard Tyson, Louise Fletcher, Burl Ives, Kristy McNichol, Millie Perkins, Don Galloway, Herve Villechaize, Dabbs Greer, Screamin' Jay Hawkins; ***D:*** Zalman King; ***W:*** Zalman King; ***C:*** Mark Plummer; ***M:*** Jonathan Elias. Golden Raspberries '88: Worst Support. Actress (McNichol).

Two Much 🦴½ **1996 (PG-13)** Banderas does double duty as a con man pretending to be twins in order to romance two sisters (Griffith and Hannah). Embarrassingly light comedy suffers from a complicated plot (which still manages to leave holes), weak or non-existent characterization, and a general lack of humor. About the only thing it has going for it is Cusack as a wisecracking secretary. It was on the set of this film that Banderas and Griffith started their real-life romance. While that may have helped the boxoffice and gossip columns in Banderas's homeland, the fireworks didn't find their way to the screen. **118m/C VHS.** Melanie Griffith, Antonio Banderas, Daryl Hannah, Joan Cusack, Danny Aiello, Eli Wallach, Vincent Schiavelli; ***D:*** Fernando Trueba; ***W:*** Fernando Trueba, David Trueba; ***C:*** Jose Luis Alcaine; ***M:*** Michel Camilo.

Two Mules for Sister Sara 🦴🦴🦴 **1970 (PG)** American mercenary in 19th century Mexico gets mixed up with a cigar-smoking nun and the two make plans to capture a French garrison. MacLaine and Eastwood are great together. Based on a Boetticher story. **105m/C VHS.** Clint Eastwood, Shirley MacLaine; ***D:*** Donald Siegel; ***W:*** Albert (John B. Sherry) Maltz; ***M:*** Ennio Morricone.

Two Nights with Cleopatra 🦴½ *Due Notti Con Cleopatra* **1954** A piece of Italian pizza involving Cleopatra's double (also played by Loren) falling in love with one of the guards. Notable only for the 19-year-old Sophia's brief nudity. **77m/C VHS.** *IT* Sophia Loren, Ettore Manni, Alberto Sordi, Paul Muller, Alberto Talegalli, Rolf Tasna, Gianni Cavalieri, Nando (Fernando) Bruno, Riccardo Garrone, Carlo Dale; ***D:*** Mario Mattoli; ***W:*** Nino Maccari, Ettore Scola.

Two Ninas 🦴½ **2000 (R)** Dreary romantic comedy finds mopey aspiring writer Marty (Livingston) meeting sarcastic Nina Cohen (Buono) at a party. The two hit it off but then Marty literally runs into Nina 2, i.e. wealthy Nina Harris (Peet), while rollerblading in Central Park. He starts dating her as well. Now Marty has to keep his stories straight and hope the two Ninas never meet, which, of course, they do. **90m/C VHS, DVD, Wide.** *US* Ron Livingston, Cara Buono, Amanda Peet, Bray Poor, Jill(ian) Hennessey; ***D:*** Neil Turitz; ***W:*** Neil Turitz; ***C:*** Joaquin Baca-Asay; ***M:*** Joseph Saba.

Two of a Kind 🦴🦴½ **1982** In his TV movie debut, Burns plays an elderly man whose mentally handicapped grandson helps him put the starch back in his shirt. Sensitively produced and performed. **102m/C VHS.** George Burns, Robby Benson, Cliff Robertson, Barbara Barrie, Frances Lee McCain, Geri Jewell, Ronny Cox; ***D:*** Roger Young. **TV**

Two of a Kind 🦴 **1983 (PG)** Angels make a bet with God—two selfish people will redeem themselves or God can blow up the Earth. Bad acting, awful direction, and the script needs divine intervention. **88m/C VHS.** John Travolta, Olivia Newton-John, Charles Durning, Beatrice Straight, Scatman Crothers, Oliver Reed; ***D:*** John Herzfeld; ***C:*** Fred W. Koenekamp.

The Two of Us 🦴🦴🦴½ *Le Vieil Homme Et L'Enfant; Claude; The Old Man and the Boy* **1968** Young Jewish boy flees Nazi-occupied Paris to live in the country with an irritable, bigoted guardian. Sensitive, eloquent movie about racial prejudice and anti-Semitism. In French with English subtitles. **86m/B VHS.** *FR* Michel Simon, Alain Cohen, Luce Fabiole, Roger Carel, Paul Preboist, Charles Denner; ***D:*** Claude Berri; ***W:*** Claude Berri; ***C:*** Jean Penzer; ***M:*** Georges Delerue.

Two or Three Things I Know about Her 🦴🦴 *Deux ou Trois Choses Que Je Sais d'Elle* **1966** Inspired by a magazine article about housewife-prostitutes, Godard takes on the bourgeoise. Juliette (Vlady) is a wife and mother who lives in the suburbs of Paris and goes into the city once a week to work as a prostitute in order to buy consumer goods. French with subtitles. **95m/C VHS.** *FR* Marina Vlady, Anny (Annie Legras) Duperey, Roger Montsoret, Jean Narboni, Raoul Levy; ***D:*** Jean-Luc Godard; ***W:*** Jean-Luc Godard; ***C:*** Raoul Coutard.

Two Plus One 🦴🦴 **1995** Triangular drama about Yuppie relationships, set in Philadelphia. Romantic couple searches for happiness and decides to invite a third person to join their relationship. Newcomer Lewis is the sister of actress Juliette. **85m/C VHS.** William Sage, Deirdre Lewis, Tony Vinto; ***D:*** Eugene Martian.

Two Rode Together 🦴🦴½ **1961** A Texas marshal and an army lieutenant negotiate with the Comanches for the return of captives, but complications ensue. **109m/C VHS.** James Stewart, Richard Widmark, Shirley Jones, Linda Cristal, Andy Devine, John McIntire; ***D:*** John Ford.

2 Seconds 🦴🦴 *Deux Secondes* **1998 (R)** Laurie (Laurier) has spent most of her life as a mountain bike racer but a two second hesitation costs her a race and forces her retirement. She returns to Montreal and meets Lorenzo (Tavarone), a cantankerous, elderly former racer who runs a bike shop. Laurie gets a job as a bike courier and begins to re-evaluate her life. French with subtitles. **101m/C VHS, DVD.** *CA* Charlotte Laurier, Suzanne Clement, Yves Pelletier, Dino Tavarone; ***D:*** Manon Briand; ***W:*** Manon Briand; ***C:*** Louise Archambault, Pierre Crepo; ***M:*** Dominic Grand, Sylvain-Charles Grand.

Two Shades of Blue 🦴½ **1998 (R)** Surprisingly dull erotic thriller. Writer Hunter is framed for the murder of fiancee Busey, so she assumes the alter ego identity of her novel's sexy heroine in order to hunt for the killer herself. She takes a job as a relay telephone operator for the deaf so she can contact deaf D.A. Matlin. But Matlin has a sexually obsessive relationship with boyfriend Roberts (who's in whacko mode) and Hunter begins to take a voyeuristic delight in their conversations. **103m/C VHS, DVD.** Rachel Hunter, Marlee Matlin, Eric Roberts, Gary Busey; ***D:*** James D. Deck; ***W:*** Ted Williams. **VIDEO**

The Two Sisters **1937** Goldstein, in her only film role, plays an older sister who sacrifices everything for the younger. The younger thanks her by stealing her fiance. In Yiddish with English subtitles. **70m/B VHS.** Jenney Goldstein, Michael Rosenberg.

Two Small Bodies 🦴🦴 **1993** Police detective Brann investigates the disappearance of two young children, suspecting their mother Eileen may have murdered them. Two character study set in Eileen's home with both verbally recreating versions of the possible crime. Based on the play by Neal Bell. **85m/C VHS.** *GE* Fred Ward, Suzy Amis; ***D:*** Beth B; ***W:*** Beth B, Neal Bell; ***C:*** Phil Parmet.

2000 Maniacs 🦴🦴½ **1964** One of cult director Lewis' most enjoyably watchable films. A literal Civil War "ghost town" takes its revenge 100 years after being slaughtered by renegade Union soldiers by luring unwitting "yankee" tourists to their centennial festival. The hapless Notherners are then chopped, crushed, ripped apart etc. while the ghostly rebels party. Quite fun in a cartoonishly gruesome sort of way. Filmed in St. Cloud, FL. **75m/C VHS, DVD.** Thomas Wood, Connie Mason, Jeffrey Allen, Ben Moore, Gary Bakeman, Jerome (Jerry Stallion) Eden, Shelby Livingston, Michael Korb, Yvonne Gilbert, Mark Douglas, Linda Cochran, Vincent Santo, Andy Wilson; ***D:*** Herschell Gordon Lewis; ***W:*** Herschell Gordon Lewis; ***C:*** Herschell Gordon Lewis; ***M:*** Herschell Gordon Lewis, Larry Wellington.

2001: A Space Odyssey 🦴🦴🦴🦴 **1968** Space voyage to Jupiter turns chaotic when a computer, HAL 9000, takes over. Seen by some as a mirror of man's historical use of machinery and by others as a grim vision of the future, the special effects and music are still stunning. Critically acclaimed and well accepted by some, simply confusing to others. Martin Balsam originally recorded the voice of HAL, but was replaced by Rain. From Arthur C. Clarke's short story "The Sentinel." Followed by a sequel "2010: The Year We Make Contact." **139m/C VHS, DVD, Wide.** *GB* Keir Dullea, Gary Lockwood, William Sylvester, Dan Richter, Leonard Rossiter, Margaret Tyzack, Robert Beatty, Vivian Kubrick; ***D:*** Stanley Kubrick; ***W:*** Stanley Kubrick, Arthur C. Clarke; ***C:*** Geoffrey Unsworth,

John Alcott; *V:* Douglas Rain. Oscars '68: Visual FX; AFI '98: Top 100, Natl. Film Reg. '91.

2001: A Space Travesty 🦴🦴½ **2000 (R)** Nielsen continues his tradition of parodies starring as none-too-bright Marshal "Dick" Dix who must rescue the U.S. president who has been kidnapped by aliens and replaced by a clone. He joins forces with sexy Cassandra (Winter) and heads to planet Vegan on his mission. **99m/C VHS, DVD.** Leslie Nielsen, Ezio Greggio, Peter Egan, Ophelie Winter; *D:* Allan Goldstein; *W:* Alan Shearman; *C:* Sylvain Brault; *M:* Claude Foisy.

2010: The Year We Make Contact 🦴🦴🦴 **1984 (PG)** Based on Arthur C. Clarke's novel, which is his sequel to "2001: A Space Odyssey." Americans and Russians unite to investigate the abandoned starship Discovery's decaying orbit around Jupiter and try to determine why the HAL 9000 computer sabotaged its mission years before, while signs of cosmic change are detected on and around the giant planet. **116m/C VHS, DVD, Wide.** Roy Scheider, John Lithgow, Helen Mirren, Bob Balaban, Keir Dullea, Madolyn Smith, Mary Jo Deschanel; *D:* Peter Hyams; *W:* Peter Hyams, Arthur C. Clarke; *C:* Peter Hyams; *M:* David Shire; *V:* Douglas Rain, Candice Bergen.

2020 Texas Gladiators woof! **1985 (R)** In the post-nuclear holocaust world, two groups, one good, one evil, battle for supremacy. **91m/C VHS.** *IT* Harrison Muller, Al Cliver, Daniel Stephen, Peter Hooten, Al Yamanouchi, Sabrina Santi; *D:* Kevin Mancuso.

2069: A Sex Odyssey 🦴½ **1978 (R)** Team of beautiful, sensuous astronauts are sent to Earth to obtain male sperm which they must bring back to Venus. Tongue-in-cheek soft core sci-fi spoof. **73m/C VHS, DVD.** Alena Penz, Nina Fredric, Gerti Sneider, Raul Retzer, Catherine Conti, Heidi Hammer, Michael Mein, Herb Heesel; *D:* George Keil; *W:* Willi Frisch; *C:* Michael Marszalek, Georg Mondi; *M:* Hans Hammerschmid.

Two Tickets to Broadway 🦴🦴½ **1951** A small-town singer and a crooner arrange a hoax to get themselves on Bob Crosby's TV show. Appealing but lightweight. ♫Let the Worry Bird Worry For You; Pagliacci; There's No Tomorrow; Manhattan; Big Chief Hole in the Ground; The Closer You Are; Baby, You'll Never Be Sorry; Pelican Falls High; It Began In Yucatan. **106m/C VHS.** Tony Martin, Janet Leigh, Gloria De Haven, Joi Lansing; *D:* James V. Kern; *M:* Leo Robin, Jule Styne.

Two to Tango 🦴½ **1988 (R)** A hired assassin goes to Buenos Aires to kill a crime boss, and falls in love with his tango-dancing mistress. Based on the novel by J.P. Feinman. **87m/C VHS.** *AR* Don Stroud, Adrienne Sachs; *D:* Hector Olivera.

Two-Way Stretch 🦴🦴½ **1960** Three prison inmates in a progressive jail plan to break out, pull a diamond heist, and break back in, all in the same night. Fast-paced slapstick farce. **84m/B VHS.** *GB* Peter Sellers, Wilfrid Hyde-White, Liz Fraser, David Lodge; *D:* Robert Day.

Two Weeks in Another Town 🦴🦴 **1962** Douglas and Robinson are a couple of Hollywood has-beens who set out to make a comeback picture but meet with adversity at every turn. Extremely sappy melodrama is based on Irwin Shaw's trashy novel and represents one of director Minnelli's poorer efforts. **107m/C VHS, Wide.** Kirk Douglas, Edward G. Robinson, Cyd Charisse, George Hamilton, Daliah Lavi, Claire Trevor, James Gregory, Rosanna Schiaffino, George Macready, Stefan Schnabel, Vito Scotti, Leslie Uggams; *D:* Vincente Minnelli; *C:* Milton Krasner.

Two Weeks to Live 🦴½ **1943** The comedy team inherits a railroad line, only to find it's a pile of junk. **60m/B VHS.** Lum & Abner, Franklin Pangborn.

Two Weeks with Love 🦴🦴 **1950** Reynolds and family wear funny bathing suits in the Catskills in the early 1900s while the Debster sings songs and blushes into young adulthood. ♫Aba Daba Honeymoon; The Oceana Roll; A Heart That's Free; By the Light of the Silvery Moon; My Hero; Row, Row, Row; That's How I Need You; Beautiful Lady. **92m/C VHS.** Debbie Reynolds, Jane Powell, Ricardo Montalban, Louis Calhern, Ann Harding, Phyllis Kirk, Carleton Carpenter, Clinton Sundberg, Gary Gray; *D:* Roy Rowland.

Two Women 🦴🦴🦴🦴 *La Ciociara* **1961** Widowed Cesira (Loren) and her 13-year-old daughter Rosetta (Brown) travel war-torn Italy during WWII and must survive lack of food, bombings, and brutal soldiers. Tragic, moving, well-directed. Loren received well-deserved Oscar. Based on the novel by Alberto Moravia. In Italian with English subtitles or dubbed. **99m/B VHS, DVD.** *IT* Sophia Loren, Raf Vallone, Eleonora Brown, Jean-Paul Belmondo; *D:* Vittorio De Sica; *W:* Cesare Zavattini, Vittorio De Sica; *C:* Gabor Pogany; *M:* Armando Trovajoli. Oscars '61: Actress (Loren); British Acad. '61: Actress (Loren); Cannes '61: Actress (Loren); Golden Globes '62: Foreign Film; N.Y. Film Critics '61: Actress (Loren).

The Two Worlds of Jenny Logan 🦴🦴½ **1979** A woman travels back and forth in time whenever she dons a 19th century dress she finds in her old house. She is also able to fall in love twice, in different centuries. Adapted from "Second Sight," a novel by David Williams. Stylish and well made. **97m/C VHS.** Lindsay Wagner, Marc Singer, Alan Feinstein, Linda Gray, Constance McCashin, Henry Wilcoxon, Irene Tedrow, Joan Darling, Allen Williams, Pat Corley, Gloria Stuart; *D:* Frank De Felitta. **TV**

Two Wrongs Make a Right 🦴 **1989** A quiet nightclub owner beats and clubs his way through his tough neighborhood to protect himself and his woman. Low budget actioner with standard plot and cool, atmospheric tone. **85m/C VHS.** Ivan Rogers, Ron Blackstone, Rich Komenich; *D:* Robert Brown; *W:* Ivan Rogers.

Two Years before the Mast 🦴🦴½ **1946** Charles Stewart (Ladd) is the privileged son of a ship owner who discovers just how difficult a sailor's life in the 1840s can be. Drinking in a Boston waterfront dive, he's shanghaied and pressed into service aboard the S.S. Pilgrim, which is bound for California. Sadistic Captain Thompson (da Silva) brutalizes the men in an effort to set a record time for the voyage. Stewart and the crew eventually mutiny and face trial back in Boston. Based on the novel by Richard Henry Dana. **98m/B VHS.** Alan Ladd, Howard da Silva, Brian Donlevy, William Bendix, Barry Fitzgerald, Albert Dekker, Darryl Hickman, Esther Fernandez; *D:* John Farrow; *W:* George Bruce, Seton I. Miller; *C:* Ernest Laszlo; *M:* Victor Young.

Twogether 🦴🦴½ **1994 (R)** Struggling artist John (Cassavettes) and environmentalist Allison (Bakke) have this lust thing going on. It leads to a drunken Las Vegas wedding and a quickie divorce but they still don't keep their hands off of each other (or any other body parts) and Allison gets pregnant. They decide to become partners in raising the baby but first they'll have to do some growing up of their own. Also available unrated. **108m/C VHS.** Brenda Bakke, Nick Cassavetes, Jeremy Piven, Jim Beaver; *D:* Andrew Chiaramonte; *W:* Andrew Chiaramonte; *C:* Eugene Shlugleit; *M:* Nigel Holton.

Tycoon 🦴🦴½ **1947** Wayne goes to Latin America to build a road for an American industrialist. When the industrialist insists on a shorter but more dangerous route, Wayne must satisfy his own sense of honor. Meanwhile, he's found romance with the industrialist's half-Spanish daughter. Long, but well-acted. **129m/C VHS.** John Wayne, Laraine Day, Cedric Hardwicke, Judith Anderson, James Gleason, Anthony Quinn; *D:* Richard Wallace.

Tycus 🦴🦴 **1998 (R)** Journalist Jake Lowe (Onorati) investigates a suspicious mining company and discovers that visionary Peter Crawford (Hopper) has been building his own vast underground city as a modern-day Noah's Ark. Seems the Tycus comet is on a destruco course with Earth and not much is expected to survive. And when the rest of the world finds out, it'll be a race against time. **94m/C VHS, DVD.** Dennis Hopper, Peter Onorati, Finola Hughes, Chick Vennera; *D:* John Putch; *W:* Michael C. Goetz, Kevin Goetz; *C:* Ross Berryman; *M:* Alexander Baker, Clair Marlo. **VIDEO**

Typhoon Treasure 🦴 **1939** Whilst recovering his sunken treasure, the hero battles bad guys, savage natives and a crocodile, all of whom could probably have made a more sophisticated film. **68m/B VHS.** *AU* Campbell Copelin, Gwen Munro, Joe Valli, Douglas Herald; *D:* Noel Monkman.

Tyson 🦴🦴 **1995** Based on the life of former World Heavyweight Champion, Mike Tyson (White) who rose from the streets of Brownsville to a million dollar lifestyle and a spectacular fall to a rape conviction and a prison term (which are handled in voiceover). Story begins with trainer Cus D'Amato (Scott) finding unpolished and troubled young Tyson and training him for the Junior Olympics. When promoter Don King (Winfield) enters the picture, Tyson's career really takes off. Pulls no punches about Tyson's short fuse and brutal abilities. Based on the book "Fire and Fear: The Inside Story of Mike Tyson" by Jose Torres. **90m/C VHS.** Michael Jai White, Paul Winfield, George C. Scott, Malcolm Jamal Warner, Tony LoBianco, James B. Sikking, Clark Gregg, Kristen Wilson, Sheila Wills, Holt McCallany, Lilyan Chauvin, Georg Stanford Brown, Joe Santos, Charles Napier; *D:* Uli Edel; *W:* Robert P. Johnson; *M:* Stewart Copeland.

U-Boat Prisoner 🦴 **1944** Bennett is an American sailor who's captured by a Nazi U-boat. He promptly defeats the crew, leaving the U-boat to the mercy of a U.S. destroyer. Silly, silly, silly. **65m/B VHS.** Bruce (Herman Brix) Bennett, John Abbott, John Wengraf, Kenneth MacDonald, Erik Rolf; *D:* Lew (Louis Friedlander) Landers.

U-571 🦴🦴½ **2000 (PG-13)** U.S sub crew is sent to steal an Enigma encryption device from a disabled Nazi U-boat before the Germans can send help. When their own sub is sunk, the Americans, led by Lt. Tyler (McConaughey), take over the German sub and try to make their way back home through enemy destroyers. Long on loud and impressive action sequences, but short on characterization and good dialogue, this one'll work best for adrenalin junkies and those with theater-quality entertainment systems. **116m/C VHS, DVD, Wide.** Matthew McConaughey, Bill Paxton, Harvey Keitel, Jon Bon Jovi, Jake Weber, David Keith, Terrence "T.C." Carson, Jack Noseworthy, Tom Guiry, Thomas Kretschmann, Erik Palladino, Will Estes, Matthew Settle, Dave Power, Derk Cheetwood; *D:* Jonathan Mostow; *W:* Jonathan Mostow, David Ayer, Sam Montgomery; *C:* Oliver Wood; *M:* Rick Marvin. Oscars '00: Sound FX Editing.

U-Turn 🦴🦴½ *Stray Dogs* **1997 (R)** Bobby (Penn) is a two-bit gambler on his way to pay off the balance of a debt in Las Vegas (the down payment was two of his fingers) when he is stranded in the town of Superior, Arizona. He becomes mixed up with a married couple (Nolte and Lopez), each of whom want Bobby to kill the other. Adding to the fun in this Mayberry on mescaline are the walking grease pit of a mechanic (Thornton) and a local tough guy named TNT (Phoenix), who thinks Bobby is making a play for his nymphet girlfriend (Danes). Also appearing is the stock issue Oliver Stone wise old Indian who dispenses wisdom, or something like it. The characters meet for the predestined showdown in the desert, with predictable results. Stone has a good time taking stereotypical noir characters and putting his unique twist on them, although you may not have as much fun watching them. **125m/C VHS, DVD.** Sean Penn, Jennifer Lopez, Claire Danes, Nick Nolte, Joaquin Rafael (Leaf) Phoenix, Powers Boothe, Billy Bob Thornton, Jon Voight, Abraham Benrubi, Julie Hagerty, Bo Hopkins, Valery (Valeri Nikolayev) Nikolaev, Aida Linares, Laurie Metcalf, Liv Tyler; *D:* Oliver Stone; *W:* John Ridley; *C:* Robert Richardson; *M:* Ennio Morricone.

UFO: Target Earth 🦴 **1974 (G)** Scientist attempts to fish flying saucer out of lake and costs studio $70,000. **80m/C VHS.** Nick Plakias, Cynthia Cline, Phil Erickson; *D:* Michael de Gaetano.

Uforia 🦴🦴🦴 **1981** Two rival evangelists meet up with a UFO-infatuated girl. Under her guidance, they wait for UFO encounters they intend to use to milk their revivalist audiences. Sometimes clumsy, but more often fun. **92m/C VHS.** Cindy Williams, Harry Dean Stanton, Fred Ward, Hank Worden, Beverly Hope Atkinson, Harry Carey Jr., Diane Adair, Robert Gray, Ted Harris; *D:* John Binder; *W:* John Binder; *C:* David Myers; *M:* Richard Baskin.

Ugetsu 🦴🦴🦴½ *Ugetsu Monogatari* **1953** The classic film that established Mizoguchi's reputation outside of Japan. Two 16th century Japanese peasants venture from their homes in pursuit of dreams, and encounter little more than their own hapless folly and a bit of the supernatural. A wonderful mix of comedy and action with nifty camera movement. Based on the stories of Akinara Ueda. In Japanese with English subtitles. **96m/B VHS, 8mm.** *JP* Machiko Kyo, Masayuki Mori, Kinuyo Tanaka, Eitaro (Sakae, Saka Ozawa) Ozawa; *D:* Kenji Mizoguchi; *W:* Yoshikata Yoda; *C:* Kazuo Miyagawa; *M:* Fumio Hayasaka. Venice Film Fest. '53: Silver Prize.

The Ugly 🦴🦴½ **1996** Confessed serial killer Simon (Rotondo) has celebrity shrink Karen (Hobbs) evaluate him to determine whether he's cured or has to stand trial for his crimes. Through flashbacks, dream sequences, and fantasies (both Simon's and the doc's), Simon's screwed-up past is revealed: mentally and physically abused by an unstable mother (Ward-Leeland) and picked on by bullies, he commits his first murder at 13. First-time director Reynolds' use of red herrings, alternate points of view, and mixing of perspectives can be hard to follow, but they do ratchet up the suspense. He also doesn't scrimp on the gore, which is highly stylized and effective. **93m/C VHS, DVD.** *NZ* Paolo Rotondo, Rebecca Hobbs, Jennifer Ward-Lealand, Roy Ward, Vanessa Byrnes; *D:* Scott Reynolds; *W:* Scott Reynolds; *C:* Simon Raby; *M:* Victoria Kelly.

The Ugly American 🦴🦴½ **1963** A naive American ambassador to a small, civil-war-torn Asian country fights a miniature Cold War against northern communist influence. Too preachy, and the "Red Menace" aspects are now very dated, but Brando's performance is worth watching. Based on the William J. Lederer novel. **120m/C VHS.** Marlon Brando, Sandra Church, Eiji Okada, Pat Hingle, Arthur Hill; *D:* George Englund; *W:* Stewart Stern.

The Ugly Dachshund 🦴🦴½ **1965** Jones and Pleshette are married dog lovers who raise Dachshunds. When Ruggles convinces them to take a Great Dane puppy, the fun begins! The Great Dane thinks he is a Dachshund because he has been raised with them—just imagine what happens when such a large dog acts as if he is small! Kids will love this wacky Disney film. **93m/C VHS.** Dean Jones, Suzanne Pleshette, Charlie Ruggles, Kelly Thordsen, Parley Baer; *D:* Norman Tokar; *C:* Edward Colman.

UHF 🦴🦴 **1989 (PG-13)** A loser is appointed manager of a bargain-basement UHF television station. He turns it around via bizarre programming ideas. Some fun parodies of TV enhance this minimal story. Developed solely as a vehicle for Yankovic. **97m/C VHS, DVD, Wide.** Weird Al Yankovic, Kevin McCarthy, Victoria Jackson, Michael Richards, David Bowe, Anthony Geary, Stan Brock, Trinidad Silva, Gedde Watanabe, Dr. Demento, Fran Drescher, John Paragon, Emo Phillips, Billy Barty; *D:* Jay Levey; *W:* Jay Levey, Weird Al Yankovic; *C:* David Lewis; *M:* John Du Prez.

Ulee's Gold 🦴🦴🦴 **1997 (R)** Slow-paced, deliberate character study, set in the Florida panhandle. Ulysses "Ulee" Jackson (Fonda) is a widowed, middle-aged Vietnam vet who puts most of his energies into his work as a beekeeper, much to the detriment of his family. Son Jimmy (Wood) is in prison and druggie daughter-in-law Helen (Dunford) has disappeared, leaving the taciturn Ulee to care for his troubled granddaughters, teenaged Casey (Biel) and nine-year-old Penny (Zima). But their ordinary lives change when Helen turns up in Orlando with two violent hoods from Jimmy's past and Ulee must not only rescue her but find the emotional release to make them all a home. Splendidly moving performance from Fonda. **111m/C VHS, DVD, Wide.** Peter Fonda, Tom Wood, Vanessa Zima, Jessica Biel, Christine Dunford, Patricia Richardson, Steve Flynn, Dewey Weber, J. Kenneth Campbell; *D:* Victor Nunez; *W:* Victor Nunez; *C:* Virgil Marcus Mirano; *M:* Charles

Engstrom. Golden Globes '98: Actor—Drama (Fonda); N.Y. Film Critics '97: Actor (Fonda).

Ulterior Motives 🦴½ 1992 (R) P.I. Jack Blaylock agrees to protect a pretty reporter from Japanese gangsters. He finds himself caught up in deception and betrayal and uses all his considerable, and violent, skills to make certain he does his job. **90m/C VHS.** Thomas Ian Griffith, Mary Page Keller, Joe Yamanaka, Ellen Crawford, Ken Howard, Tyra Ferrell; ***D:*** James Becket.

Ultimate Desires 🦴🦴 1991 (R) When a high class hooker is brutally killed, beautiful Scoggins puts on what there is of the victim's clothes in order to solve the mystery. But trouble lies in wait as she actually begins to enjoy her funky new double life. Can she solve the crime before becoming lost in her own hot fantasy world? **93m/C VHS.** Tracy Scoggins, Brion James, Marc Singer, Marc Baur, Marc Bennett, Suzy Joachim, Jason Scott, John Wood; ***D:*** Lloyd A. Simandl.

The Ultimate Imposter 🦴 1979 A secret agent acquires voluminous knowledge through a computer brain link-up, but can only retain the knowledge for 72 hours. In that timespan he has to rescue a defecting Russian from hordes of assassins. **97m/C VHS.** Keith Andes, Erin Gray, Joseph Hacker, Macon McCalman; ***D:*** Paul Stanley. **TV**

The Ultimate Thrill 🦴½ *The Ultimate Chase* 1974 (PG) Businessman's paranoia about his wife's affairs leads him to follow her to Colorado on a ski holiday and stalk her lovers. Well-filmed skiing scenes and not much else. **84m/C VHS.** Britt Ekland, Barry Brown, Michael Blodgett, John Davis Chandler, Eric (Hans Gudegast) Braeden; ***D:*** Robert Butler.

The Ultimate Warrior 🦴🦴½ 1975 (R) Yul Brynner must defend the plants and seeds of a pioneer scientist to help replenish the world's food supply in this thriller set in 2012. **92m/C VHS.** Yul Brynner, Max von Sydow, Joanna Miles, Richard Kelton, Lane Bradbury, William Smith; ***D:*** Robert Clouse; ***W:*** Robert Clouse.

Ultra Warrior 🦴½ *Welcome to Oblivion* 1992 (R) A basic post-apocalyptic adventure tale of a radioactive earth, mutants, and various battles by the good guys to save the planet. **80m/C VHS.** Dack Rambo, Meshach Taylor, Clare Beresford.

Ultraviolet 🦴½ 1991 (R) Another warning against playing the good samaritan. Young couple on vacation in Death Valley try to help a stranded stranger only to have him turn on them. **80m/C VHS.** Esai Morales, Stephen Meadows, Patricia Healy; ***D:*** Mark Griffiths.

Ultraviolet 🦴🦴½ 1998 Vampires walk among us. Humans are their food source and now they are threatened by humanity's ability to destroy itself and the vamps want to take control. The CIB, a secret government operation, is determined to prevent that situation. Atmospheric British miniseries in which the term "vampire" is never used—the bloodsuckers are referred to as Code Fives and the title refers to the ultraviolet light that the CIB uses in its work. **360m/C VHS, DVD.** *GB* Jack Davenport, Susannah Harker, Philip Quast, Idris Elba, Corin Redgrave, Stephen Moyer, Thomas Lockyer, Collette Brown, Fiona Dolman; ***D:*** Joe Ahearne; ***W:*** Joe Ahearne; ***C:*** Peter Greenhalgh; ***M:*** Sue Hewitt. **TV**

Ulysses 🦴🦴½ *Ulisse* 1955 An Italian made version of the epic poem by Homer, as the warrior returns to his homeland and the ever-faithful Penelope after the Trojan war. Ambitious effort provides for the ultimate mixed review. Douglas is good in the role and his stops along the ten-year way are well visualized. Sometimes sluggish with poor dubbing. Seven writers helped bring Homer to the big screen. **104m/C VHS, DVD.** *IT* Kirk Douglas, Silvana Mangano, Anthony Quinn, Rossana Podesta; ***D:*** Mario Camerini.

Ulysses 🦴🦴½ 1967 James Joyce's probably unfilmable novel was given a noble effort in this flawed film covering a day in the life of Leopold Bloom as he wanders through Dublin. Shot in Ireland with a primarily Irish cast. **140m/B VHS, DVD, Wide.** Milo O'Shea, Maurice Roeves, T.P. McKenna, Martin Dempsey, Sheila O'Sullivan, Barbara Jefford; ***D:*** Joseph Strick; ***W:*** Joseph Strick, Fred Haines; ***C:*** Wolfgang Suschitzky; ***M:*** Stanley Myers.

Ulysses' Gaze 🦴🦴 *The Look of Ulysses; To Vlemma Tou Odyssea; The Gaze of Ulysses* 1995 Nameless Greek-American filmmaker (Keitel) journeys across the Balkans from Athens to Sarajevo while making a documentary on pioneer filmmakers, the Manakia brothers, who ignored national and ethnic strife in order to record the lives of ordinary people. Keitel has heard that some undeveloped film shot by the brothers has turned up in Sarajevo and he's determined to see it despite the turmoil in Bosnia. Moving and pessimistic depiction of the Balkan conflict seen through a filmmaker's eyes. English and Greek with subtitles. **173m/C VHS, DVD, Wide.** *GR FR IT* Harvey Keitel, Maia Morgenstern, Erland Josephson, Thanassis Vengos, Yorgos Michalokopoulos, Dora Volonaki; ***D:*** Theo Angelopoulos; ***W:*** Theo Angelopoulos, Tonino Guerra, Petros Markaris; ***C:*** Yorgos Arvanitis; ***M:*** Eleni Karaindrou. Cannes '95: Grand Jury Prize.

Ulzana's Raid 🦴🦴🦴 1972 (R) An aging scout and an idealistic Cavalry lieutenant lock horns on their way to battling a vicious Apache chieftain. A violent, gritty western that enjoyed critical re-evaluation years after its first release. **103m/C VHS, DVD.** Burt Lancaster, Bruce Davison, Richard Jaeckel, Lloyd Bochner, Jorge Luke; ***D:*** Robert Aldrich; ***W:*** Alan Sharp; ***C:*** Joseph Biroc; ***M:*** Frank DeVol.

Umberto D 🦴🦴🦴🦴 1955 A government pensioner, living alone with his beloved dog, struggles to keep up a semblance of dignity on his inadequate pension. De Sica considered this his masterpiece. A sincere, tender treatment of the struggles involved with the inevitability of aging. In Italian with English subtitles. Laser edition features letterboxed print. **89m/B VHS, 8mm, Wide.** *IT* Carlo Battista, Maria Pia Casilio, Lina Gennari; ***D:*** Vittorio De Sica; ***W:*** Cesare Zavattini, Vittorio De Sica; ***M:*** Alessandro Cicognini. N.Y. Film Critics '55: Foreign Film.

Umbrellas of Cherbourg 🦴🦴🦴½ *Les Parapluies de Cherbourg; Die Regenschirme von Cherbourg* 1964 A bittersweet film operetta with no spoken dialog. Genevieve (Deneuve) is the teenaged daughter of a widow (Vernon) who owns an umbrella shop. She and her equally young boyfriend Guy (Castelnuovo) are separated by his military duty in Algeria. Finding she is pregnant, Genevieve marries the wealthy Roland (Michel), and when her former lover returns, he too marries someone else. But when they meet once again will their love be rekindled? Lovely photography and an evocative score enhance the story. French with subtitles; also available dubbed in English (not with the same effectiveness). **90m/C VHS, DVD, Wide.** *FR* Catherine Deneuve, Nino Castelnuovo, Anne Vernon, Ellen Farner, Marc Michel, Mireille Perrey, Jean Champion, Alfred Wolff, Dorothee Blanck; ***D:*** Jacques Demy; ***W:*** Jacques Demy; ***C:*** Jean Rabier; ***M:*** Michel Legrand. Cannes '64: Film.

Un Air de Famille 🦴🦴 *Respectable Families; Family Resemblances* 1996 Comedy, adapted from a play, about a dysfunctional family. They're meeting at the family's rundown bar to celebrate the birthday of son Philippe's (Yordanoff) silly wife, Yolande (Frot). The bar is run by his brother Henri (Bacri), whose wife calls to say she's left him, while their tactless mother (Maurier) frets over their sister, Betty (Jaoui), who's 30 and still single. What no one knows is that Betty has been secretly seeing Denis (Darroussin), the bartender, whom everyone thinks is simple but is actually the only one with any clue to the family's hypocrisy. French with subtitles. **107m/C VHS, DVD, Wide.** *FR* Jean-Pierre Bacri, Agnes Jaoui, Jean-Pierre Darroussin, Catherine Frot, Claire Maurier, Wladimir Yordanoff; ***D:*** Cedric Klapisch; ***W:*** Jean-Pierre Bacri, Agnes Jaoui, Cedric Klapisch; ***C:*** Benoit Delhomme. Cesar '97: Support. Actor (Darroussin), Support. Actress (Frot), Writing.

Un Chien Andalou 🦴🦴🦴🦴 *An Andalusian Dog* 1928 Masterful surrealist short features a host of classic sequences, including a razor across an eye, a severed hand lying in the street, ants crawling from a hole in a man's hand, priests, dead horses, and a piano dragged across a room. A classic. Score features both Wagner and tango. **20m/B VHS.** *FR* Pierre Batcheff, Simone Marevil, Jaime Miravilles, Luis Bunuel, Salvador Dali; ***D:*** Luis Bunuel, Salvador Dali; ***W:*** Luis Bunuel, Salvador Dali.

Un Coeur en Hiver 🦴🦴½ *A Heart in Winter* 1993 An anti-romance romantic drama where passion is frozen and real emotion is reserved for the inanimate. Serious Stephane (Auteuil) is a master craftsman at repairing violins; his partner Maxime (Dussollier) runs the business side and deals with the musicians, including beautiful violinist Camille (Beart) with whom he has fallen in love. Camille is single-mindedly fixated on her career and she recognizes a kindred spirit in Stephane but their calculated emotional seduction causes problems for all. Can be frustrating since the smooth surface of the characters is rarely cracked. In French with English titles. **100m/C VHS.** *FR* Emmanuelle Beart, Daniel Auteuil, Andre Dussollier, Elisabeth Bourgine, Brigitte Catillon, Maurice Garrel, Miriam Boyer; ***D:*** Claude Sautet; ***W:*** Jacques Fieschi, Jerome Tonnerre; ***C:*** Yves Angelo. Cesar '93: Director (Sautet), Support. Actor (Dussollier).

Un Singe en Hiver 🦴🦴½ *A Monkey in Winter; It's Hot in Hell* 1962 A young wanderer (Belmondo) befriends a crusty old alcoholic (Gabin) who has kept his vow to abstain since his village survived the German bombing of WWII. Moving tale of regret and the passage of time. In French with English subtitles. **105m/B VHS.** Jean-Paul Belmondo, Jean Gabin, Suzanne Flon, Paul Frankeur; ***D:*** Henri Verneuil.

The Unapproachable 🦴🦴½ 1982 A rendition of the Polish director's two one-act plays concerning a reclusive aging stage star being manipulated by her hangers-on. **92m/C VHS.** *PL* Leslie Caron, Daniel Webb, Leslie Malton; ***D:*** Krzysztof Zanussi.

The Unbearable Lightness of Being 🦴🦴🦴½ 1988 (R) Tomas (Day Lewis), a young Czech doctor in the late 1960s, leads a sexually and emotionally carefree existence with a number of women, including provocative artist Olin. When he meets the fragile Binoche, he may be falling in love for the first time. On the eve of the 1968 Russian invasion of Czechoslovakia the two flee to Switzerland, but Binoche can't reconcile herself to exile and returns, followed by the reluctant Tomas who has lost his position because of his new-found political idealism. They lead an increasingly simple life, drawn ever closer together. The haunting ending caps off superb performances. Based on the novel by Milan Kundera. **172m/C VHS, DVD.** Daniel Day-Lewis, Juliette Binoche, Lena Olin, Derek De Lint, Erland Josephson, Pavel Landovsky, Donald Moffat, Daniel Olbrychski, Stellan Skarsgard, Tormek Bork, Bruce Myers, Pavel Slaby, Pascale Kalensky, Jacques Ciron, Anne Lonnberg, Laszlo Szabo, Vladimir Valenta, Clovis Cornillac, Leon Lissek, Consuelo de Haviland; ***D:*** Philip Kaufman; ***W:*** Jean-Claude Carriere, Philip Kaufman; ***C:*** Sven Nykvist; ***M:*** Mark Adler, Ernie Fosselius, Leos Janacek. British Acad. '88: Adapt. Screenplay; Ind. Spirit '89: Cinematog.; Natl. Soc. Film Critics '88: Director (Kaufman), Film.

The Unbelievable Truth 🦴🦴½ 1990 (R) Ex-con Robocop-to-be Burke meets armageddon-obsessed model and sparks fly until bizarre murder occurs. Quirky black comedy shot in less than two weeks. **100m/C VHS, DVD, Wide.** Adrienne Shelly, Robert John Burke, Christopher Cooke, Julia Mueller, Julia McNeal, Mark Bailey, Gary Sauer, Kathrine Mayfield; ***D:*** Hal Hartley; ***W:*** Hal Hartley; ***C:*** Michael Spiller; ***M:*** Jim Coleman.

The Unborn 🦴½ 1991 (R) An infertile wife gets inseminated at unorthodox clinic. But once pregnant she suspects that her unborn baby is a monstrous being. Tasteless B-movie with an A-performance from Adams; if the rest had been up to her standard this could have been another "Stepford Wives." Instead it cops out with cheap gore. **85m/C VHS, DVD.** Brooke Adams, Jeff Hayenga, James Karen, K. Callan, Jane Cameron; ***D:*** Rodman Flender; ***W:*** Henry Dominic; ***C:*** Wally Pfister; ***M:*** Gary Numan, Michael R. Smith.

The Unborn 2 🦴 1994 (R) Greene's blood-craving baby thinks nothing of feasting off the babysitter until a gun-wielding avenger comes to the rescue. Some notably gross scenes. **84m/C VHS.** Michele Greene, Scott Valentine, Robin Curtis; ***D:*** Rick Jacobson.

Unbreakable 🦴🦴½ 2000 (PG-13) Willis reteams with "The Sixth Sense" writer/director Shyamalan for another spooky saga. He's not only the sole survivor of a train crash but he emerged without a scratch, which intrigues Jackson, who suffers from brittle bone disease. Shyamalan still knows how to hold attention, and the look and feel of the movie are mesmerizing, but this time the story doesn't quite hold up. You'll either find this one a keeper or a head-scratcher. **107m/C VHS, DVD, Wide.** Bruce Willis, Samuel L. Jackson, Robin Wright Penn, Spencer (Treat) Clark, Charlaine Woodard, James Handy, Elizabeth Lawrence, Leslie Stefanson, Eamonn Walker; ***D:*** M. Night Shyamalan; ***W:*** M. Night Shyamalan; ***C:*** Eduardo Serra; ***M:*** James Newton Howard.

The Unbreakable Alibi 🦴🦴 1983 A wealthy young man asks Tommy and Tuppence Beresford to help him prove that one of two alibis an Australian journalist created is false. Based on the mysteries by Agatha Christie. **51m/C VHS.** *GB* Francesca Annis, James Warwick. **TV**

Uncaged 🦴 *Angel in Red* 1991 (R) Five beautiful young prostitutes hit Sunset Strip, each of them dreaming of a better life. When a crazy pimp brutally murders one of their friends, they set out to avenge that girl, and her broken dreams. **78m/C VHS.** Leslie Bega, Jeffrey Dean Morgan, Pamella O'Pella, Gregory Millar, Henry Brown, Jason Oliver, Elena Sahagun; ***D:*** William Duprey; ***W:*** Robert Alden, Joan Freeman, Catherine Cyran.

The Uncanny woof! 1978 Horror anthology of three tales concerned with feline attempts to control the world. Waste of good cast and cats on silly stories. Not released in the U.S. **85m/C VHS.** *GB* Peter Cushing, Ray Milland, Samantha Eggar, Donald Pleasence; ***D:*** Denis Heroux.

Uncertain Glory 🦴🦴 1944 Errol plays a French thief who's willing to pretend to be a saboteur and die for his country. Based on a story by Joe May and Laszlo Vadnay. **102m/B VHS.** Errol Flynn, Paul Lukas, Jean Sullivan, Lucile Watson, Faye Emerson, James Flavin, Douglass Dumbrille, Dennis Hoey, Sheldon Leonard; ***D:*** Raoul Walsh; ***W:*** Laszlo Vadnay, Max Brand.

The Unchastened Woman 🦴🦴 1925 A married couple is torn apart by infidelity despite their impending parenthood, and wife Bara heads overseas to run wild and have the baby. She returns with a foreign flame, whom she dumps when erstwhile husband finds fatherly feelings in his heart. One of Bara's last films. **52m/B VHS.** Theda Bara, Wyndham Standing, Dale Fuller, John Miljan; ***D:*** James Young.

Uncivilized 🦴🦴 1994 Young couple, on a vacation in the mountains, run into a gang of drug runners who don't want their whereabouts revealed. So, the duo have to play a deadly game of hide-and-seek to survive. **90m/C VHS.** Martin Kove, Rick Aiello.

Uncle Buck 🦴🦴🦴 1989 (PG) When Mom and Dad have to go away suddenly, the only babysitter they can find is good ol' Uncle Buck, a lovable lout who spends much of his time smoking cigars, trying to make up with his girlfriend, and enforcing the teenage daughter's chastity. More intelligent than the average slob/teen comedy with a heart, due in large part to Candy's dandy performance. Memorable pancake scene. **100m/C VHS, DVD.** John Candy, Amy Madigan, Jean (Louisa) Kelly, Macaulay Culkin, Jay Underwood, Gaby Hoffman, Laurie Metcalf, Elaine Bromka, Garrett M. Brown; ***D:*** John Hughes; ***W:*** John Hughes; ***C:*** Ralf Bode; ***M:*** Ira Newborn.

Uncle Moses 🦴🦴½ **1932** The clash of old-world values and new-world culture in a story of East European Jewish immigrants transplanted to turn of the century New York's Lower East Side. Patriarch Uncle Moses struggles to keep traditional family values as romantic difficulties and labor union struggles intrude. Based on the novel by Sholem Asch. In Yiddish with English subtitles. **87m/B VHS.** Maurice Schwartz, Rubin Goldberg, Judith Abarbanel, Zvee Scooler; ***D:*** Sidney Goldin, Aubrey Scotto.

Uncle Sam 🦴 **1996 (R)** The box art is cool but this is basically a video horror. Desert Storm hero Sam Harper (Fralick) returns home—in a coffin. Only he doesn't stay dead and decides to liven up his small town's Fourth of July celebration by dressing up as Uncle Sam and going on a killing spree. **91m/C VHS, DVD.** David Fralick, Timothy Bottoms, Robert Forster, Isaac Hayes, Bo Hopkins; ***D:*** William Lustig; ***W:*** Larry Cohen; ***C:*** James Lebovitz; ***M:*** Mark Governor. **VIDEO**

Uncle Tom's Cabin 🦴🦴 **1914** Satisfying version of Harriet Beecher Stowe's tale from the view of a founder of the underground railroad. Lucas was the first black actor to garner a lead role. **54m/C VHS.** Mary Eline, Irving Cummings, Sam Lucas; ***D:*** William Robert Daly.

Uncle Tom's Cabin 🦴🦴½ **1927** Universal Studios' $2 million production was one of the costliest of the silent era, with more than 2400 actors, and a shooting schedule of 19 months. It follows Harriet Beecher Stowe's abolitionist novel about a black family torn apart by slavery. This version contains heroine Eliza's (Fischer) flight across the ice floes, which was borrowed by D.W. Griffith for his film "Way Down East." **112m/B VHS, DVD.** James B. Lowe, Margarita Fischer, George Siegmann, Virginia Grey; ***D:*** Harry Pollard; ***W:*** Harry Pollard, Harvey Thew; ***C:*** Charles Stumar, Jacob Kull; ***M:*** Erno Rapee.

Uncle Tom's Cabin 🦴½ *Onkel Toms Hutte; La Case de L'Oncle Tom; Cento Dollari D'Odio; Cica Tomina Koliba* **1969 (G)** Ambitious adaptation of Harriet Beecher Stowe's stirring book about the Southern slavery and the famous underground railroad devised to aid those most determined to reach freedom. The film has the habit of drifting away from the facts. Though set in Kentucky, the picture was filmed in Yugoslavia with an international cast. **120m/C VHS.** *FR IT YU GE* Herbert Lom, John Kitzmiller, O.W. Fischer, Eleanora Rossi-Drago, Mylene Demongeot, Juliette Greco; ***D:*** Geza von Radvanyi; ***V:*** Ella Fitzgerald.

Uncle Tom's Cabin 🦴🦴½ **1987** The first American sound version of this film. Excellent cast and interestingly adapted script are perfect for a message that is still socially relevant today. Based on the novel by Harriet Beecher Stowe. **110m/C VHS.** Avery Brooks, Kate Burton, Bruce Dern, Paula Kelly, Phylicia Rashad, Kathryn Walker, Edward Woodward, Frank Converse, George Coe, Albert Hall; ***D:*** Stan Lathan. **TV**

Uncle Was a Vampire 🦴🦴 *Tempi Duri per i Vampiri; Hard Times for Vampires* **1959** An impoverished Italian count has turned his castle into a hotel. But staying there could be hazardous to a guest's health since the count was bitten by a vampire. **85m/C VHS.** *IT* Christopher Lee, Kay Fisher, Renato Rascel, Sylva Koscina, Lia Zoppelli, Susanne Loret; ***D:*** Steno; ***W:*** Edoardo Anton; ***C:*** Marco Scarpelli.

Uncommon Valor 🦴🦴½ **1983 (R)** After useless appeals to the government for information on his son listed as "missing in action" in Vietnam, Colonel Rhodes takes matters into his own hands. Hackman is solid and believable as always, surrounded with good cast in generally well-paced film. **105m/C VHS, DVD, 8mm, Wide.** Gene Hackman, Fred Ward, Reb Brown, Randall "Tex" Cobb, Robert Stack, Patrick Swayze, Harold Sylvester, Tim Thomerson; ***D:*** Ted Kotcheff; ***C:*** Stephen Burum; ***M:*** James Horner.

Unconquered 🦴🦴½ **1947** Silly epic about America finds indentured servant Abby (Goddard), meeting Virignia militia man Christopher Holden (Cooper). He nobly buys her contract and frees her but scurvy trader Martin Garth (da Silva) manages to get Abby working in his saloon. Garth also illegally sells guns to the local Seneca Indian tribe and persuades their chief, Guyasuta (Karloff), to attack the colonists. Cooper has to keep rescuing Goodard throughout the movie, as well as battling da Silva and helping the settlers fight Indians. Based on the novel "The Judas Tree" by Neil H. Swanson. **147m/C VHS.** Gary Cooper, Paulette Goddard, Howard da Silva, Boris Karloff, Cecil Kellaway, Ward Bond, Katherine DeMille, Henry Wilcoxon, Sir C. Aubrey Smith, Victor Varconi, Virginia Grey, Mike Mazurki, Porter Hall; ***D:*** Cecil B. DeMille; ***W:*** Charles Bennett, Jesse Lasky Jr., Frederic M. Frank; ***C:*** Ray Rennahan; ***M:*** Victor Young.

Uncorked 🦴🦴½ *At Sachem Farm; Higher Love* **1998 (PG)** British ex-pats gather together in Simi Valley, California to essentially drive each other crazy. Ross (Sewell) is visiting his family in order to close a deal on selling some rare wines so he can get the money to support another get-rich-quick scheme. But he's thwarted by his eccentric Uncle Cullen (Hawthorne) who wants Ross to do something he passionately believes in (which happens to be music). Ross also has a reclusive, nutty brother Paul (Rodgers), and then there's his snooty girlfriend Kendal (Driver) who really wants her ex-boyfriend, Tom (Sporleder) back. It's predictable but pleasant. **95m/C VHS, DVD.** Rufus Sewell, Nigel Hawthorne, Minnie Driver, Michael E. Rodgers, Gregory Sporleder, Amelia Heinle, Keone Young; ***D:*** John Huddles; ***W:*** John Huddles; ***C:*** Mark Vicente; ***M:*** Jeff Danna.

The Undead 🦴🦴 **1957** A prostitute is accidentally sent back to the Middle Ages as the result of a scientific experiment and finds herself condemned to die for witchcraft. Early Corman script filled with convoluted storylines, laughable characters, violence, and heaving bosoms. **75m/B VHS.** Pamela Duncan, Richard Garland, Allison Hayes, Mel Welles, Richard Devon, Billy Barty, Dick Miller, Val Dufour, Dorothy Neumann, Aaron Saxon, Bruno VeSota; ***D:*** Roger Corman; ***W:*** Charles B. Griffith, Mark Hanna; ***C:*** William Sickner; ***M:*** Ronald Stein.

Undeclared War 🦴🦴 **1991 (R)** Suspenseful espionage thriller that takes you behind the scenes of an international terrorist plot, which has been cleverly disguised as a bloody global revolution. Intense action heightened by conflicts between worldwide intelligence networks, the news media and terrorist organizations. **103m/C VHS.** Vernon Wells, David Hedison, Olivia Hussey, Peter Lapis; ***D:*** Ringo Lam.

Undefeatable 🦴½ **1994 (R)** Rothrock is out to avenge the murder of her sister at the hands of a serial killer who, coincidentally, happens to be a martial arts expert. You watch for Cynthia to kick butt not for plot anyway. **88m/C VHS.** Cynthia Rothrock, Don Niam, John Miller, Donna Jason; ***D:*** Godfrey Hall.

The Undefeated 🦴🦴 **1969 (G)** A Confederate and Yankee find they must team up on the Rio Grande. They attempt to build new lives in the Spanish held Mexico territory, but are caught in the battle for Mexican independence. Standard fare made palatable only by Wayne and Hudson. **119m/C VHS.** John Agar, John Wayne, Rock Hudson, Lee Meriwether, Merlin Olsen, Bruce Cabot, Ben Johnson, Jan-Michael Vincent, Harry Carey Jr., Antonio Aguilar, Roman Gabriel; ***D:*** Andrew V. McLaglen; ***C:*** William Clothier.

Under California Stars 🦴🦴 *Under California Skies* **1948** Shady gang making a living rounding up wild horses decides they can make more money by capturing Rogers' horse, Trigger. **71m/C VHS.** Roy Rogers, Andy Devine, Jane Frazee; ***D:*** William Witney.

Under Capricorn 🦴🦴½ **1949** Bergman is an Irish lass who follows her convict husband Cotten out to 1830s Australia where he makes a fortune. She turns to drink, perhaps because of his neglect, and has her position usurped by a housekeeper with designs on her husband. When Bergman's cousin (Wilding) arrives, Cotten may have cause for his violent jealousy. There's a plot twist involving old family skeletons, but this is definitely lesser Hitchcock. Adapted from the Helen Simpson novel. Remade in 1982. **117m/C VHS.** *GB* Ingrid Bergman, Joseph Cotten, Michael Wilding, Margaret Leighton, Jack Watling, Cecil Parker, Denis O'Dea; ***D:*** Alfred Hitchcock; ***C:*** Jack Cardiff.

Under Capricorn 🦴🦴 **1982** An Australian remake of the 1949 Hitchcock film about family secrets, an unhappy marriage, and violence set in 1830s' Australia. **120m/C VHS.** *AU* Lisa Harrow, John Hallam, Peter Cousens, Julia Blake, Catherine Lynch; ***D:*** Rod Hardy.

Under Colorado Skies 🦴½ **1947** Medical student Hale is accused of robbery and escapes the law to clear his name. **65m/C VHS.** Monte Hale, Adrian (Lorna Gray) Booth, Paul Hurst, Tom London; ***D:*** R.G. Springsteen; ***W:*** Louise Rousseau; ***C:*** Alfred S. Keller.

Under Fire 🦴🦴🦴½ **1983 (R)** Three foreign correspondents, old friends from the past working together, find themselves in Managua, witnessing the 1979 Nicaraguan revolution. In a job requiring objectivity, but a situation requiring taking sides, they battle with their ethics to do the job right. Fine performances, including Harris as a mercenary. Interesting view of American media and its political necessities. **128m/C VHS, DVD, Wide.** Gene Hackman, Nick Nolte, Joanna Cassidy, Ed Harris, Richard Masur, Hamilton Camp, Jean-Louis Trintignant; ***D:*** Roger Spottiswoode; ***W:*** Clayton Frohman, Ron Shelton; ***C:*** John Alcott; ***M:*** Jerry Goldsmith.

Under Investigation 🦴🦴½ **1993 (R)** Burned out cop Hamlin is after a crazed killer. His cool lover Pacula turns out to be the prime suspect. Who's deceiving who? **94m/C VHS.** Harry Hamlin, Joanna Pacula, Ed Lauter, Richard Beymer, Lydie Denier; ***D:*** Kevin Meyer; ***W:*** Kevin Meyer.

Under Milk Wood 🦴🦴½ **1973 (PG)** An adaptation of the Dylan Thomas play about the lives of the residents of a village in Wales. Burton and O'Toole are wonderful in this uneven, but sometimes engrossing film. **90m/C VHS.** *GB* Richard Burton, Elizabeth Taylor, Peter O'Toole, Glynis Johns, Vivien Merchant; ***D:*** Andrew Sinclair.

Under Montana Skies 🦴½ **1930** An early talkie western features music and comedy in abundance, relegating the action to second place. A singing cowboy protects a travelling burlesque show from evildoers. **55m/B VHS.** Kenneth Harlan, Dorothy Gulliver, Lafe (Lafayette) McKee, Ethel Wales, Slim Summerville; ***D:*** Richard Thorpe.

Under Nevada Skies 🦴🦴½ **1946** Fairly good matinee-era western centers on a missing map to a uranium deposit, climaxing with Rogers heading a posse of Indian allies to the rescue. The Sons of the Pioneers contribute songs. **69m/B VHS.** Roy Rogers, George "Gabby" Hayes, Dale Evans, Douglass Dumbrille, Tristram Coffin, Rudolph Anders, Iron Eyes Cody; ***D:*** Frank McDonald.

Under Oath 🦴🦴 *Urban Justice; Blood Money* **1997 (R)** Financially strapped cops Scalia and Velez accidentally kill a drug runner in a shakedown and then learn he was an undercover ATF agent. Then they're assigned to investigate their own crime. Cast does good work in slick genre fare. **89m/C VHS, DVD.** Jack Scalia, James Russo, Eddie Velez, Richard Lynch, Abraham Benrubi, Beth Grant, Clint Howard, Robert LaSardo; ***D:*** Dave Payne; ***W:*** Scott Sandin; ***C:*** Mike Michiewicz; ***M:*** Roger Neil. **VIDEO**

Under Pressure 🦴🦴 **1998 (R)** What do you do when your neighbor tries to run your life? It's hot, the kids are cranky, you're cranky, and the guy next door comes over to complain about everything you do. Only he doesn't just complain—he threatens you, but the cops won't do anything to help. **88m/C VHS.** Charlie Sheen, Mare Winningham, John Ratzenberger, David Andrews; ***D:*** Craig R. Baxley; ***W:*** Betsey Giffen Nowrasteh.

Under Satan's Sun 🦴🦴🦴 *Under the Sun of Satan; Sous le Soleil de Satan* **1987** A rural priest is tortured by what he sees as his sins and failings to his parishioners. He is further tempted from the straight path by a beautiful murderess, a worldly priest, and, perhaps by Satan in disguise. Stylized film is not easily accessible, but Depardieu's performance is worth the effort. Based on the Georges Bernanos book "Diary of a Country Priest." In French with English subtitles. **97m/C VHS.** *FR* Gerard Depardieu, Sandrine Bonnaire, Yann Dedet, Alain Artur, Maurice Pialat; ***D:*** Maurice Pialat; ***W:*** Maurice Pialat. Cannes '87: Film.

Under Siege 🦴🦴 **1992 (R)** The USS Missouri becomes the battleground for good-guy-with-a-secret-past Seagal. He's up against the deranged Jones, as an ex-Special Forces leader, and Busey, a corrupt naval officer looking to steal the battleship's nuclear arsenal. May be predictable (especially the graphic violence) but the action is fast, the villains swaggering, and Seagal efficient at dispatching the enemy. Work for "Die Hard 3" was reportedly scrapped after Warner announced this film because DH's John McClane was supposed to save the passengers of a boat from terrorists. Sound familiar? **100m/C VHS, DVD, 8mm, Wide.** Steven Seagal, Tommy Lee Jones, Gary Busey, Patrick O'Neal, Erika Eleniak, Dale Dye, Richard Jones; ***D:*** Andrew Davis; ***W:*** J.F. Lawton; ***C:*** Frank Tidy; ***M:*** Gary Chang.

Under Siege 2: Dark Territory 🦴🦴 **1995 (R)** Kicking terrorists' butts and slinging hash have worn out ex-Navy SEAL and gourmet chef Casey Ryback (Seagal), so he takes a little vacation to the Rocky Mountains. By coincidence, the train he boards is command central for psychotic computer expert Dane's (Bogosian) scheme to control the world's deadliest satellite. Pretty familiar territory for Seagal, who's acting technique consists of "look mad and hurt poeple." Bigger budget means bigger, and more frequent, explosions. Bogosian takes over the Jones/Busey role of evil villain-talented actor. **100m/C VHS, DVD, Wide.** Steven Seagal, Eric Bogosian, Katherine Heigl, Morris Chestnut, Everett McGill, Andy Romano, Nick Mancuso, Brenda Bakke, Dale Dye; ***D:*** Geoff Murphy; ***W:*** Richard Hatem; ***C:*** Robbie Greenberg; ***M:*** Basil Poledouris.

Under Suspicion 🦴🦴½ **1992 (R)** Christmas 1959 in Brighton finds seedy private eye Tony Aaron and his wife faking adultery cases for those desperate to get around England's strict divorce laws. Sordid tale takes a turn when Tony bursts in to snap incriminating photos and finds both his wife and their client, a famous artist, murdered. Dark who-dunnit has some interesting twists that could have made it exceptional rather than the conventional melodrama it turned out to be. Neeson is very good as the charmingly sleazy Tony but nobody else stands out, except the unfortunately miscast San Giacomo. Theatrical feature debut for director Moore. **99m/C VHS.** *GB* Liam Neeson, Laura San Giacomo, Alphonsia Emmanuel, Kenneth Cranham, Maggie O'Neill, Martin Grace, Stephen Moore; ***D:*** Simon Moore; ***W:*** Simon Moore; ***C:*** Vernon Layton; ***M:*** Christopher Gunning. **TV**

Under Suspicion 🦴½ **2000 (R)** Not much tension in what aims to be a tension-filled thriller. Hackman is accused of raping and murdering several Puerto Rican women and spends the film being interrogated by detectives Freeman and Jane. Lots of talk but little to connect with in this remake of Claude Miller's very well respected "Garde a Vue." Both Hackman and Freeman co-executive produced. **111m/C VHS, DVD, Wide.** Morgan Freeman, Gene Hackman, Thomas Jane, Monica Bellucci; ***D:*** Stephen Hopkins; ***W:*** W. Peter Iliff, Tom Provost; ***C:*** Peter Levy.

Under the Biltmore Clock 🦴🦴 **1985** F. Scott Fitzgerald's story, "Myra Meets His Family," is the basis for this American Playhouse installment for PBS. It is outwit or be outwitted in this tale of a fortune-hunting '20s flapper who is outsmarted by the man she has set her sights on when he hires actors to play his eccentric "family." **80m/C VHS.** Sean Young, Lenny Von Dohlen, Barnard Hughes; ***D:*** Neal Miller. **TV**

Under the Boardwalk 🦴½ **1989 (R)** A pair of star-crossed teenage lovers struggle through familial and societal differences in 1980s California. This is, like, bogus, ya know. **102m/C VHS.** Keith Coogan, Danielle von Zerneck, Richard Joseph Paul, Hunter von Leer, Tracey Walter, Roxana Zal, Dick Miller, Sonny Bono, Corky Carroll; *D:* Fritz Kiersch; *C:* Don Burgess. **VIDEO**

Under the Cherry Moon ₰½ **1986 (PG-13)** Prince portrays a fictional musician of the 1940s who travels to the French Riviera, seeking love and money. Songs include "Under the Cherry Moon," "Kiss," "Anotherloverholeinyohead," "Sometimes It Snows in April," and "Mountains." A vanity flick down to its being filmed in black and white. **100m/B VHS.** Prince, Jerome Benton, Francesca Annis, Kristin Scott Thomas; *D:* Prince; *C:* Michael Ballhaus. Golden Raspberries '86: Worst Picture, Worst Actor (Prince), Worst Support. Actor (Benton), Worst Director (Prince), Worst Song ("Love or Money").

Under the Domim Tree ₰₰½ *Etz Hadomim Tafus* **1995** Sequel to "The Summer of Aviya," set in 1953, finds 15-year-old Aviya (Cohen) living in an Israeli community with other teenagers who were scarred by the Holocaust. As they get to know one another, each must deal with their own tormented memories. Based on a memoir by Almagor, who plays Aviya's institutionalized mother. Hebrew with subtitles. **102m/C VHS.** *IS* Kaipo Cohen, Julino Mer, Ohad Knoller, Orli Perl, Riki Blich, Gila Almagor; *D:* Eli Cohen; *W:* Gila Almagor, Eyal Sher; *C:* David Gurfinkel; *M:* Benny Nagari.

Under the Earth ₰₰₰ *Debajo del Mundo* **1986 (R)** An Argentine-Czech co-production, depicting the plight of a family of Polish Jews forced to live underground for two years to avoid the Nazis. Harrowing and critically well-received. In Spanish with subtitles. **100m/C VHS.** *SP* Victor Laplace; *D:* Beda Docampo Feijoo, Juan Bautista Stagnaro.

Under the Gun ₰₰ **1988 (R)** A cop recruits a lawyer to help him find the man who murdered his brother. Action drives this formulaic plot along. **89m/C VHS.** Sam Jones, Vanessa L(ynne) Williams, John Russell, Michael Halsey; *D:* James Sbardellati; *W:* James Sbardellati, Almer John Davis.

Under the Gun ₰½ **1995 (R)** Debt-ridden club owner Frank Torrance (Norton) is in trouble with everyone he knows. But he can't clear his debts just by quitting the business, so he decides to fight back. **90m/C VHS, DVD.** Jane Badler, Peter Lindsey, Richard Norton, Kathy Long; *D:* Matthew George; *W:* Matthew George; *C:* Dan Burstall; *M:* Frank Strangio.

Under the Hula Moon ₰₰½ **1995 (R)** Buzzard (Baldwin) and Betty (Lloyd) Wall are living unhappily in the charmless desert town of Cactus Gulch. Their trailer home is festooned in faux-Hawaiian finery and the duo dream of the day they can actually move to their island paradise. Buzz's invented an ultraprotective sunscreen that may be their ticket out, if his prison-escapee, trigger-happy half-brother Turk (Penn), who's also kidnapped Betty, doesn't get them all killed first. Charming lead performances—very lightweight story. **94m/C VHS.** Stephen Baldwin, Emily Lloyd, Christopher Penn, Musetta Vander, Edie McClurg, Pruitt Taylor Vince, Billy Campbell, Carel Struycken, R. Lee Ermey; *D:* Jeff Celentano; *W:* Jeff Celentano; *C:* Phil Parmet.

Under the Pear Tree ₰₰ *Unterm Birnbaum* **1973** Classic crime based on a novella by Theodor Fontane. Bankrupt restaurant owner Hradschek and his wife come up with a plan to foil the debt collector at their door. But when the man's carriage is found—empty—by the river, the neighbors remember Hradschek digging under the pear tree the night before. German with subtitles. **86m/C VHS.** *GE* Angelica Domrose, Manfred Karge, Erik S. Klein, Agnes Kraus, Norbert Christian; *D:* Ralf Kirsten; *W:* Ralf Kirsten.

Under the Rainbow woof! **1981 (PG)** Comic situations encountered by a talent scout and a secret service agent in a hotel filled with Munchkins during filming of "The Wizard of Oz." Features midgets, spies, and a prevailing lack of taste. International intrigue adds to the strange attempt at humor. **97m/C VHS.** Chevy Chase, Carrie Fisher, Eve Arden, Joseph Maher, Robert Donner, Mako, Pat McCormick, Billy Barty, Zelda Rubinstein; *D:* Steve Rash; *W:* Pat McCormick, Martin Smith, Harry Hurwitz, Fred Bauer, Pat Bradley.

Under the Red Robe ₰₰½ **1936** A French soldier of fortune is trapped into aiding Cardinal Richelieu in his persecution of the Huguenots and winds up falling in love with the sister of his intended victim. Good costume adventure-drama. Sjostrom's last film as a director. **82m/B VHS.** *GB* Raymond Massey, Conrad Veidt, Annabella, Romney Brent; *D:* Victor Sjostrom; *C:* James Wong Howe.

Under the Roofs of Paris ₰₰₰½ *Sous les Toits de Paris* **1929** An early French sound film about the lives of young Parisian lovers. A gentle, highly acclaimed melodrama. In French with English subtitles. **95m/B VHS.** *FR* Albert Prejean, Pola Illery, Gaston Modot, Edmond T. Greville; *D:* Rene Clair; *W:* Rene Clair; *C:* Georges Perinal; *M:* Armand Bernard.

Under the Sand ₰₰₰ *Sous le Sable* **2000** Middleaged Marie (Rampling) has been married for many years to Jean (Cremer). They are vacationing at their summer house and Jean goes for a swim while Marie takes a nap. When she awakens, he has disappeared. A search reveals nothing and Marie must eventually return to Paris and try to go on with her life. But Marie is deep in denial—she speaks as if Jean were still alive and, in fact, she continues to see and interact with—well, whatever spirit of Jean that she has conjured up. Bravura performance from Rampling. French with subtitles. **95m/C VHS, DVD, Wide.** *FR* Charlotte Rampling, Bruno Cremer, Jacques Nolot, Alexandra Stewart, Pierre Vernier, Andree Tainsey; *D:* Francois Ozon; *W:* Francois Ozon, Marina de Van, Emmanuele Bernheim, Marcia Romano; *C:* Jeanne Lapoirie, Antoine Heberle; *M:* Philippe Rombi.

Under the Skin ₰₰ **1997** After their mother's unexpected death, 19-year-old Iris (Morton) and her married, pregnant older sister Rose (Rushbrook) deal with their grief in very different ways. The dreamy Iris decides to explore all her sexual fantasies after she has a spontaneous sexual encounter with a stranger, Tom (Townsend), and drifts into promiscuity. The fragile Iris pushes her limits to find some kind of comfort while her remaining family ties steadily disintegrate. Astonishing no-holds-barred performance by Morton. **81m/C VHS.** *GB* Samantha Morton, Claire Rushbrook, Rita Tushingham, Stuart Townsend, Christine Tremarco, Mark Womack, Odette Springer; *D:* Carine Adler; *W:* Carine Adler; *C:* Barry Ackroyd; *M:* Ilona Sekacz.

Under the Sun ₰₰ *Under Solen* **1998** In 1956, 40-year-old virgin, Olof (Lassgard), lives on his rather rundown farm in western Sweden—his only friend being the younger Erik (Widerberg), who takes advantage of Olof's generosity. Then Ellen (Bergstrom) turns up in answer to Olof's ad for a housekeeper and the unlikely duo become a romantic couple much to Erik's dismay. So he decides to find out what a beautiful city girl is doing on a remote farm. Based on a short story by H.E. Bates. Swedish with subtitles. **118m/C VHS.** *SW* Rolf Lassgard, Helena Bergstrom, Johan Widerberg, Jonas Falk, Linda Ulvaeus; *D:* Colin Nutley; *W:* Colin Nutley; *C:* Jens Fischer; *M:* Paddy Maloney.

Under the Volcano ₰₰₰ **1984** An alcoholic British ex-consul finds his life further deteriorating during the Mexican Day of the Dead in 1939. His half-brother and ex-wife try to save him from himself, but their affair sends him ever-deeper into his personal hell. Finney's performance is pathetic and haunting. Adapted from the novel by Malcolm Lowry. **112m/C VHS.** Albert Finney, Jacqueline Bisset, Anthony Andrews, Katy Jurado; *D:* John Huston; *M:* John Beal, Alex North. L.A. Film Critics '84: Actor (Finney).

Under the Yum-Yum Tree ₰₰½ **1963** When womanizing landlord Hogan's (Lemmon) ex-fiance Irene (Adams) moves out, he doesn't pine. Instead he plots to romance her niece Robin (Lynley) who's just moved into his building. But his romantic shenanigans are thwarted by the presence of fiance David (Jones), who's living platonically with Robin to test their compatibility. Silly sex comedy based on the play by Roman. **110m/C VHS.** Jack Lemmon, Carol Lynley, Dean Jones, Edie Adams, Imogene Coca, Paul Lynde, Robert Lansing, Bill Bixby; *D:* David Swift; *W:* David Swift, Lawrence Roman; *C:* Joseph Biroc; *M:* Frank DeVol.

Under Western Stars ₰ **1945** Roy's first starring vehicle. A newly elected congressman goes to Washington and fights battles for his constituents, caught in the middle of the Dust Bowl and drought. **83m/B VHS.** Roy Rogers, Smiley Burnette; *D:* Jean Yarbrough.

The Underachievers ₰ **1988 (R)** A night school is the scene for typical libido-oriented gags, but this time instead of teenagers it's adult education providing the plot. Only a few real laughs in this one. **90m/C VHS.** Barbara Carrera, Edward Albert, Michael Pataki, Vic Tayback, Garrett Morris, Susan Tyrrell; *D:* Jackie Kong.

Undercover ₰½ **1987 (R)** Routine cop action film in which an eastern detective finds himself undercover in a southern high school in search of a cop-murdering drug ring. Plagued with cliches. Director Stockwell is appropriately better known for his role as "Cougar" in "Top Gun." **92m/C VHS.** David Neidorf, Jennifer Jason Leigh, Barry Corbin, David Harris, Kathleen Wilhoite; *D:* John Stockwell; *M:* Bruce Smeaton.

Undercover ₰½ **1994 (R)** Police detective (and hot babe) Cindy Hanen (Massey) gets an undercover assignment to capture a murderer who's targeted an upscale brothel. It's an excuse for interesting undies (or less). **93m/C VHS, DVD.** Athena Massey, Tom Tayback, Anthony Guidera, Rena Riffel, Jeffrey Dean Morgan, Meg Foster; *D:* Alexander Gregory (Gregory Dark) Hippolyte; *W:* Oola Bloome, Lalo Wolf; *C:* Philip Hurn; *M:* Ashley Irwin.

Undercover Angel ₰₰½ **1999 (PG-13)** Predictably cheesy but still entertaining movie that features the chubby-checked blonde girl from the Welch's Juice TV commercials. Six-year-old Young is left in the care of struggling writer Winters, her mom's old boyfriend. He's attracted to Bleeth and the little moppet charges into the woman's life in order to get the duo together. Oh yeah, and then Young and Winters discover that he's actually her biological father. **93m/C VHS, DVD.** Yasmine Bleeth, Dean Winters, Emily Mae Young, Lorraine Ansell, Casey Kasem, Richard Eden, James Earl Jones; *D:* Bryan Michael Stoller; *W:* Bryan Michael Stoller; *C:* Bruce Alan Greene; *M:* Greg Edmonson. **VIDEO**

Undercover Blues ₰₰½ **1993 (PG-13)** Comedy-thriller starring Turner and Quaid as married spies Jane and Jeff Blue, on parental leave from the espionage biz, who are on vacation with their 11-month-old daughter in New Orleans. But the holiday is interrupted when they're recruited by their boss to stop an old adversary from selling stolen weapons. The leads play cute together and the baby is adorable but this is strictly routine escapism. Stick with "The Thin Man" instead. **90m/C VHS, Wide.** Kathleen Turner, Dennis Quaid, Fiona Shaw, Stanley Tucci, Larry Miller, Obba Babatunde, Park Overall, Tom Arnold, Saul Rubinek, Michelle Schuelke; *D:* Herbert Ross; *W:* Ian Abrams; *M:* David Newman.

Undercover Brother ₰₰½ **2002 (PG-13)** Funny but padded spoof of secret agents and blaxploitation movies. Brother (Griffin) is a secret agent from the B.R.O.T.H.E.R.H.O.O.D. sent to rescue a black war hero turned presidential candidate (the always-cool Williams) who has been brainwashed in a plot by The Man to destroy African-American culture. More-hit-than-miss comedy finds many targets of all stripes to lampoon, and does so with just the right amount of funk. **85m/C VHS, DVD.** *US* Eddie Griffin, Chris Kattan, Denise Richards, Dave Chappelle, Chi McBride, Aunjanue Ellis, Neil Patrick Harris, Billy Dee Williams, Jack Noseworthy, Gary Anthony Williams, James Brown, Robert Trumbull; *D:* Malcolm Lee; *W:* John Ridley, Michael McCullers; *C:* Tom Priestley; *M:* Stanley Clarke; *Nar:* J.D. Hall.

Undercover Cop ₰₰ **1994** True story of Sergeant George Aguilar and the high-speed chase that left one dead and the police dealing their revenge on all the offenders. **90m/C VHS.** Danny Trejo, Kevin Anthony Cole; *D:* Martin Greene; *W:* Glenn A. Bruce; *M:* Randall Kent Heddon.

Undercover Man ₰½ **1936** A Wells Fargo agent goes undercover to expose a crooked sheriff. **57m/B VHS.** Johnny Mack Brown, Suzanne Kaaren, Ted Adams, Lloyd Ingraham, Horace Murphy; *D:* Albert Ray.

Undercurrent ₰₰½ **1946** Minnelli's only foray into film noir is high-gloss melodrama based on the novel "You Were There" by Thelma Strabel. Innocent Ann (Hepburn) marries Alan (Taylor) after a whirlwind romance and then discovers he's not the man she thinks. He may be a murderer and there's some chicanery involving his brother Michael (Mitchum) and the family business. Taylor's in a rare bad guy role while Hepburn seems too sophisticated for her naive wife and Mitchum just seems tired. **116m/B VHS.** Katharine Hepburn, Robert Taylor, Robert Mitchum, Edmund Gwenn, Marjorie Main, Clinton Sundberg, Dan Tobin, Jayne Cotter; *D:* Vincente Minnelli; *W:* Marguerite Roberts, Edward Chodorov, George Oppenheimer; *C:* Karl Freund; *M:* Herbert Stothart.

Undercurrent ₰₰ **1999 (R)** Ex-cop Lamas arrives in Puerto Rico to run a nightclub and is blackmailed into an affair with a mobster's wife. **99m/C VHS, DVD.** Lorenzo Lamas, Frank Vincent, Brenda Strong; *D:* Frank Kerr; *C:* Carlos Gaviria; *M:* Christopher Lennertz. **VIDEO**

The Underdog ₰½ **1943** After the bank forecloses, a farm family must move to the city. The family's young son has only his loyal dog to turn to for friendship, but the gallant animal proves his mettle by rounding up a gang of spies plotting some WWII sabotage. Believe it if you dare. **65m/B VHS, 8mm.** Barton MacLane, Bobby Larson, Jan Wiley; *D:* William Nigh.

Undergrads ₰₰₰ **1985** A bright generational Disney comedy with Carney, estranged from his stick-in-the-mud son, deciding to attend college with his free-thinking grandson. **102m/C VHS.** Art Carney, Chris Makepeace, Jackie Burroughs, Len Birman; *D:* Steven Hilliard Stern. **TV**

Underground ₰₰½ **1941** Eric (Dorn) is a member of the German underground working against the Nazis. But he must conceal his activities from his loyal solider brother Kurt (Lynn). Topical wartime drama still hits home with its story of divided loyalties. **95m/B VHS.** Philip Dorn, Jeffrey Lynn, Martin Kosleck, Karen Verne, Mona Maris, Peter Whitney, Ilka Gruning; *D:* Vincent Sherman; *W:* Charles Grayson; *C:* Sid Hickox; *M:* Adolph Deutsch.

Underground ₰₰₰ *Once Upon a Time There Was a Country; Il Etait une Fois un Pays* **1995** Exhausting black comedy, set in Yugoslavia from 1941 to 1992, follows the adventures of Marko (Manojlovic) and his best friend Blacky (Ristovski). They run a black-market operation and lead Communist Party meetings while trying to avoid the Gestapo in WWII Belgrade. Hiding out in a cellar, where refugees have put together a munitions factory, the treacherous Marko manages to convince everyone that the war is still going on—20 years later in fact—until the truth unexpectedly comes out (thanks to a pet monkey). The final section sees Marko unscrupulously dealing arms and drugs amidst the breakup of Yugoslavia in a civil war and the violence on all sides. **192m/C VHS.** *FR GE HU* Miki (Predrag) Manojlovic, Lazar Ristovski, Mirjana Jokovic, Slavko Stimac, Ernst Stotzner, Srdan Todorovic, Mirjana Karanovic, Milena Pavlovic, Danilo Stojkovic, Bora Todorovic, Davor Dujmovic, Branislav Lecic, Dragan Nikolic, Hark Bohm; *Cameos:* Emir Kusturica; *D:* Emir Kusturica; *W:* Emir Kusturica, Dusan Kovacevic; *C:* Vilko Filac; *M:* Goran Bregovic. Cannes '95: Film.

The Underground ₰₰ **1997 (R)** A rap artist is gunned down by a gang and Sgt. Brian Donnegan (Fahey) and his partner Scully (Tigar) are on the investigation. But when Scully is killed by the same scum, Donnegan is partnered with a rookie (McFall) and the duo must infiltrate

L.A.'s music scene to get their suspects. **92m/C VHS, DVD.** Jeff Fahey, Ken Tigar, Michael McFall.

Underground Aces woof! **1980 (PG)** A group of parking lot attendants transforms a sheik into an attendant in order to help him meet the girl of his dreams. A bad "Car Wash" spinoff. **93m/C VHS.** Dirk Benedict, Melanie Griffith, Frank Gorshin, Jerry Orbach, Robert Hegyes, Audrey Landers; ***D:*** Robert Butler; ***W:*** James (Jim) Carabatsos.

Underground Agent ½ **1942** Probably proved more exciting during its WWII release timeframe than it will for modern sensibilities. Government agent Lee Graham (Bennett) is hired to stop enemy eavesdropping at a defense plant. He invents a scrambler that confuses the Axis and then rounds up the saboteurs. Pretty standard B fare. **70m/B VHS.** Bruce (Herman Brix) Bennett, Leslie Brooks, Frank Albertson, Julian Rivero, Rhys Williams, Henry Victor, Addison Richards, Hans Conried; ***D:*** Michael Gordon; ***W:*** J. Robert Bren, Gladys Atwater; ***C:*** L.W. O'Connell.

Underground Rustlers **1941** The Range Busters are commissioned by the government to stop unscrupulous gold-marketeers. **58m/B VHS.** Ray Corrigan, Max Terhune, John "Dusty" King; ***D:*** S. Roy Luby.

Underground Terror **1988** A gang of murderers, organized by a psychopath, rampages through the New York City subway system. One cop enthusiastically tries to snuff out each one. **91m/C VHS.** Doc Dougherty, Lenny Y. Loftin; ***D:*** James McCalmont.

Underground U.S.A. **1984** Street hustler picks up a has-been underground movie star at the chic New York new wave disco, The Mudd Club. **85m/C VHS.** Patti Astor, Eric Mitchell; ***D:*** Eric Mitchell.

The Underneath **1995 (R)** Recovering gambling addict Michael Chambers (Gallagher) returns home after skipping out on his debts and his wife Rachel (sultry newcomer Elliott) several years before. Old passions ignite in more ways than one, and Michael's lust for his ex, now married to a hot-tempered hoodlum, leads him to risk it all for a final big score. Moody and tense study of the complexities of emotion is capped by smart lead performances but style wins out over substance and the finale definitely leaves more questions than answers. Remake of the 1949 film noir classic "Criss Cross," based on Don Tracy's novel of the same name. **99m/C VHS, DVD, Wide.** Shelley Duvall, Richard Linklater, Dennis Hill, Peter Gallagher, Alison Elliott, William Fichtner, Elisabeth Shue, Adam Trese, Paul Dooley, Joe Don Baker, Anjanette Comer, Harry Goaz, Vincent Gaskins, Tony Perenski, Helen Cates, John Martin, David Jensen, Joseph Chrest; ***D:*** Steven Soderbergh; ***W:*** Daniel Fuchs, Sam Lowry; ***C:*** Elliot Davis; ***M:*** Cliff Martinez.

Undersea Kingdom **1936** Adventure beneath the ocean floor. In 12 chapters of 13 minutes each; the first chapter runs 20 minutes. Later re-edited into one film, "Sharad of Atlantis." **226m/B VHS, DVD.** Ray Corrigan, Lon Chaney Jr., Lois Wilde, Monte Blue, William Farnum, Smiley Burnette; ***D:*** B. Reeves Eason.

Understudy: The Graveyard Shift 2 ½ **1988 (R)** Vampire survives poorly directed cliche-riddled original to be cast as a vampire cast as a vampire in a horror movie within a horrible sequel. **88m/C VHS.** *CA* Wendy Gazelle, Mark Soper, Silvio Oliviero, Ilse von Glatz, Tim Kelleher; ***D:*** Gerard Ciccoritti; ***C:*** Barry Stone.

The Undertaker and His Pals **1967** Undertaker teams up with diner owners in murder scheme to improve mortician's business and expand restaurateurs' menu. Pretty violent stuff, with some good laughs and a campy flare, but not for every one's palate. **70m/C VHS, DVD.** Ray Dannis, Brad Fulton, Larrene Ott, Robert Lowery, Sally Frei; ***D:*** David C. Graham; ***C:*** Andrew Janczak.

The Undertaker's Wedding **1997 (R)** Undertaker Mario Bellini (Brophy) fakes the death and burial of mob boss Rocco (Wincott) to stem a local mob war but then makes the big mistake of falling in love with the new "widow," Maria (Wuhrer). **90m/C VHS.** *CA* Adrien Brody, Jeff Wincott, Kari Wuhrer, Burt Young, Holly Gagnier, Nicholas Pasco; ***D:*** John Bradshaw; ***W:*** John Bradshaw; ***C:*** Edgar Egger.

Undertow **1995 (R)** Drifter Jack Ketchum (Phillips) loses control of his car in a storm and wakes up in the secluded cabin of paranoid Lyle Yates (Dance) and his terrified wife, Willie (Sara). Since the storm's worse, Jack can't leave—too bad for him that Willie's so darn attractive and Lyle's so crazy. **90m/C VHS.** Lou Diamond Phillips, Mia Sara, Charles Dance; ***D:*** Eric Red; ***W:*** Kathryn Bigelow, Eric Red; ***C:*** Geza Sinkovics; ***M:*** John (Gianni) Frizzell. **CABLE**

Underwater! **1955** A team of skin divers faces danger when they try to retrieve treasure from a Spanish galleon. The second film after "The Outlaw" masterminded by Howard Hughes, primarily to show off Russell's figure. **99m/C VHS.** Jane Russell, Richard Egan, Gilbert Roland, Jayne Mansfield; ***D:*** John Sturges.

Underworld **1927** Inspired gangster saga finds bank robber Bull Weed (Bancroft) befriending a genteel bum, known as Rolls Royce (Brook), and taking him into his gang. The bum has brains and soon makes Weed king of the underworld but there's jealousy when Weed's moll Feathers (Brent) falls for Royce. Climactic shootout set a standard for the genre. **85m/B VHS.** George Bancroft, Clive Brook, Evelyn Brent, Larry Semon, Fred Kohler Sr.; ***D:*** Josef von Sternberg. Oscars '28: Story.

Underworld **1996 (R)** Considering the on-screen talent, this crime comedy/thriller is a disappointment. Ex-wiseguy Johnny Crown (Leary) studied psychotherapy in the joint and, when he's released, decides to put his new knowledge to work on bossman Frank Gavilan (Mantegna), who may be behind the hit on Johnny's old man. Contrived dialogue and story but a sleek-looking production. **95m/C VHS, DVD.** Denis Leary, Joe Mantegna, Annabella Sciorra, Larry Bishop, Abe Vigoda, James Tolkan, Robert Costanzo; ***D:*** Roger Christian; ***W:*** Larry Bishop; ***C:*** Steven Bernstein; ***M:*** Anthony Marinelli.

Underworld Scandal *Big Town Scandal* **1947** An editor attempts to break up a ring of basketball game fixers. Based on the radio program "Big Town." **60m/C VHS.** Philip Reed, Hillary Brooke, Stanley Clements, Darryl Hickman, Carl "Alfalfa" Switzer; ***D:*** William C. Thomas; ***W:*** Milton Raison; ***C:*** Ellis W. Carter; ***M:*** Darrell Calker.

The Underworld Story ½ **1950** Big city journalist at large moves to smalltown New England after losing job for unethical reporting and uncovers scheme to frame innocent man for murder. Solid performances. **90m/B VHS.** Dan Duryea, Herbert Marshall, Gale Storm, Howard da Silva, Michael O'Shea, Mary Anderson, Gar Moore, Melville Cooper, Frieda Inescort, Art Baker, Harry Shannon, Alan Hale Jr., Steve (Stephen) Dunne, Roland Winters; ***D:*** Cy Endfield.

Underworld, U.S.A. **1960** A man infiltrates a tough crime syndicate to avenge his father's murder, which winds up with him caught between the mob and the feds. A well-acted and directed look at the criminal underworld. **99m/B VHS.** Cliff Robertson, Dolores Dorn, Beatrice Kay, Robert Emhardt, Larry Gates, Paul Dubov; ***D:*** Samuel Fuller; ***W:*** Samuel Fuller; ***C:*** Hal Mohr.

Undesirable *With a Vengeance* **1992** Dull thriller-wannabe. Amnesiac Jenna King (Gilbert) has no memory of her childhood and only knows that she alone survived the murder of her family. Now working as a nanny, Jenna's life is in danger when that same killer finally decides to finish the job. **93m/C VHS.** Melissa Gilbert, Jack Scalia, Matthew Lawrence, Michael Gross, Roger Aaron Brown, John Cullum, Russell Johnson, Robert Donner; ***D:*** Michael Switzer; ***W:*** Renee Longstreet; ***C:*** Rob Draper; ***M:*** J. Peter Robinson. **TV**

The Undying Monster ½ *The Hammond Mystery* **1942** Upper crusty Brit is werewolf with insatiable appetite. Familiar story with lots of atmosphere and style. **63m/B VHS.** James Ellison, Heather Angel, John Howard, Bramwell Fletcher, Heather Thatcher, Aubrey Mather, Halliwell Hobbes, Heather Wilde; ***D:*** John Brahm; ***C:*** Lucien Ballard.

Une Parisienne ½ **1958** Gallic fluff starring sex kitten Bardot finds her an unhappy newlywed whose husband (Vidal) is enjoying being a bon vivant a little too much. So she decides to make him jealous by heading off to the Riviera with an aging Prince (Boyer). French with subtitles. **85m/C VHS, Wide.** *FR* Brigitte Bardot, Charles Boyer, Henri Vidal, Andre Luguet, Nadia Gray, Madeleine LeBeau, Noel Roquevert; ***D:*** Michel Boisrond; ***W:*** Michel Boisrond, Annette Wademant, Jean Aurel; ***C:*** Marcel Grignon; ***M:*** Hubert Rostaing.

The Unearthing **1993 (R)** An unwanted pregnancy seems to find a happy solution when a woman decides to marry the heir to a wealthy estate and pass off her child as his. Only the family has some very strange tastes, including a taste for the blood of the unborn. Based on a Filipino vampire legend (!). **83m/C VHS.** Norman Moses, Tina Ona Paukstelis; ***D:*** Wyre Martin, Barry Poltermann; ***W:*** Wyre Martin, Barry Poltermann.

The Unearthly ½ **1957** A mad scientist is trying to achieve immortality through his strange experiments, but all he winds up with is a basement full of mutants. When his two latest about-to-be victims fall in love, the doctor's mutant assistant decides enough is enough and things come to an unpleasant end. Carradine is typecast. Absurd, but fun. **76m/B VHS.** John Carradine, Tor Johnson, Allison Hayes, Myron Healey; ***D:*** Brooke L. Peters.

The Unearthly Stranger ½ **1964** Earth scientist marries woman and decides she's from another planet. Not a nineties style gender drama; seems she's part of an invading alien force, but really does love her earth man. Surprisingly good low-budget sci-fi. **75m/B VHS.** *GB* John Neville, Gabriella Licudi, Philip Stone, Patrick Newell, Jean Marsh, Warren Mitchell; ***D:*** John Krish.

Uneasy Terms **1948** Rennie is a detective investigating the murder of one of his own clients. Evidence points to stepchildren and inheritance money but things may not be as they seem. Written for the screen by Peter Cheyney, adapted from his own novel. **91m/B VHS.** *GB* Michael Rennie, Moira Lister, Faith Brook, Joy Shelton, Patricia Goddard, Barry Jones, Nigel Patrick, Paul Carpenter, Marie Ney, Sydney Tafler, J.H. Roberts, John Robinson; ***D:*** Vernon Sewell; ***W:*** Peter Cheyney; ***C:*** Ernest Palmer.

An Unexpected Family ½ **1996 (PG)** Barbara Whitney (Channing) is a Manhattan career woman who is unwillingly thrust into the role of surrogate mom when her irresponsible sister, Ruth (Ebersole), dumps her two children at Barbara's door. Along with her friend Sam (Collins), Barbara and the children slowly make a new family but, after a year, Ruth returns, demanding her children back. Predictable plot is redeemed by good performances from Channing and Ebersole. **93m/C VHS.** Stockard Channing, Stephen Collins, Christine Ebersole, Noah Fleiss, Chelsea Russo; ***D:*** Larry Elikann; ***W:*** Lee Rose; ***C:*** Eric Van Haren Noman; ***M:*** Tom Scott. **CABLE**

An Unexpected Life ½ **1997 (PG)** Sequel to 1996's "An Unexpected Family." Barbara Whitney (Channing) has moved to the country and is raising her niece Megan (Russo) and nephew Matt (Fleiss) with the help of boyfriend Sam (Collins). Then Babs discovers she's pregnant—not altogether welcome news. Neither is Barbara's sister Ruth (Ebersole) deciding her life is back on track and she wants to regain custody of her kids or Sam's estrangement from his own visiting mother (Stritch). This blended family needs a good therapist. **92m/C VHS.** Stockard Channing, Stephen Collins, Christine Ebersole, Elaine Stritch, Noah Fleiss, Chelsea Russo, RuPaul Charles; ***D:*** David Hugh Jones; ***W:*** Lee Rose. **CABLE**

Unexplained Laughter **1989** A cynical journalist vacations in Wales with her timid vegetarian friend and stumbles across a mystery in this darkly comic British TV-movie. **85m/C VHS.** *GB* Diana Rigg, Elaine Page, Jon Finch.

Unfaithful ½ **2002 (R)** Director Lyne may be known for such hot-blooded features as "9 1/2 Weeks," "Fatal Attraction," and "Lolita" but he takes a cooler approach to adultery in this melodrama, which was inspired by Claude Chabrol's 1969 film "La Femme Infidele." Connie (a luscious Lane) is a suburban mom, complacently married to regular guy Edward (Gere), who cannot resist having a hot, hot, hot affair with French bookseller Paul (Martinez), whom Connie meets cute while shopping in New York. Edward gets suspicious, Connie tries to break things off, and it turns out there's nothing like a MAN who gets scorned to bring trouble. **123m/C VHS, DVD.** *US* Richard Gere, Diane Lane, Olivier Martinez, Erik Per Sullivan, Dominic Chianese, Zeljko Ivanek, Kate Burton, Chad Lowe, Gary Basaraba, Margaret Colin; ***D:*** Adrian Lyne; ***W:*** Alvin Sargent, William Broyles Jr.; ***C:*** Peter Biziou; ***M:*** Jan A.P. Kaczmarek.

Unfaithfully Yours ½ **1948** A conductor suspects his wife is cheating on him and considers his course of action. He imagines punishment scenarios while directing three classical works. Well-acted by all, but particularly by Harrison as the egotistical and jealous husband. Another of Sturges' comedic gems. Remade in 1984. **105m/B VHS.** Rex Harrison, Linda Darnell, Kurt Kreuger, Rudy Vallee, Lionel Stander, Edgar Kennedy; ***D:*** Preston Sturges; ***C:*** Victor Milner.

Unfaithfully Yours **1984 (PG)** A symphony conductor suspects his wife of fooling around with a musician; in retaliation, he plots an elaborate scheme to murder her with comic results. No match for the 1948 Preston Sturges film it's based on. **96m/C VHS.** Dudley Moore, Nastassia Kinski, Armand Assante, Albert Brooks, Cassie Yates, Richard Libertini, Richard B. Shull; ***D:*** Howard Zieff; ***W:*** Valerie Curtin, Barry Levinson, Robert Klane; ***M:*** Bill Conti.

The Unfaithfuls *Le Infedeli* **1960** Infidelity among upper-class Italian society couples leads to divorce, blackmail, suicide, and (amazingly enough) some laughs. One philandering husband tries to catch his wife fooling around so he can get a divorce and hook up with his girlfriend. **89m/B VHS.** *IT* Gina Lollobrigida, May Britt, Irene Papas, Pierre (Peter Cross) Cressoy, Marina Vlady, Franco Rossi; ***D:*** Mario Monicelli, Steno; ***W:*** Mario Monicelli, Steno, Franco Brusati, Ivo Perilli; ***C:*** Aldo Tonti; ***M:*** Armando Trovajoli.

Unfinished Business ½ **1989** A 17 year-old girl leads a troubled adolescent life with her divorced parents. She decides running away will ease her problems—not a smart move. Sequel to "Nobody Waved Goodbye." **88m/C VHS.** *CA* Isabelle Mejias, Peter Kastner, Leslie Toth, Peter Spence, Chuck Shamata, Julie Biggs; ***D:*** Don Owen.

An Unfinished Piece for a Player Piano ½ **1977** A general's widow invites family and friends to a weekend house party in 1910 Russia. Romantic and familial entanglements begin to intrude in a lyrical adaptation of Chekov's play "Platonov." In Russian with English subtitles. **100m/C VHS.** *RU* Alexander Kalyagin, Elena Solovei, Antonina Shuranova, Oleg Tabakov, Yuri Bogatyrev, Nikita Mikhalkov; ***D:*** Nikita Mikhalkov.

Unforgettable **1996 (R)** Unfortunately, the film doesn't live up to its title. On-the-edge medical examiner David Krane (Liotta) has barely escaped conviction for his wife's brutal murder. Living under a cloud of suspicion, he turns to university researcher Martha Briggs (Fiorentino, wasted as a nerdy scientist), whose experiments in memory transference lead David to believe he can uncover the killer. But, like a Chinese puzzle box, one discovery only leads to a further complication. Too many, in fact, for the story to stay focused (and the ending is less than satisfying). **116m/C VHS, DVD, Wide.** Ray Liotta, Linda Fiorentino, Peter Coyote, Christopher McDonald, Kim Cattrall, David Paymer, Kim Coates, Duncan Fraser, Garwin Sanford; ***D:*** John Dahl; ***W:*** Bill Geddie; ***C:*** Jeffrey Jur; ***M:*** Christopher Young.

An Unforgettable Summer 🦴🦴½ **1994** The elegant Marie-Therese Dumitriu (Scott Thomas) has married Army officer Petre (Bleont) and tried to focus on maintaining a serene life, following the Communist takeover of Romania. When Petre is transferred to an isolated border town, he and his family are caught between what the Army demands and what is just. The local Bulgarian peasants are accused of attrocities against the soldiers and Petre is ordered to execute a group of them as an example—guilty or not. Set in 1925 and based on the short story "La Salade" by Petru Dumitriu. English, French, and Romanian with subtitles. **82m/C VHS.** *RO* Kristin Scott Thomas, Claudiu Bleont, Olga Tudorache, George Constantin; ***D:*** Lucian Pintilie; ***W:*** Lucian Pintilie; ***C:*** Calin Ghibu; ***M:*** Anton Suteu.

The Unforgiven 🦴🦴🦴 **1960** A western family is torn asunder when it is suspected that the eldest daughter is of Indian birth. Film takes place in 1850s' Texas. One of Huston's weakest ventures, but viewed in terms of 1950s' prejudices it has more resonance. Fine acting from all the cast, especially Gish. Watch for the stunning Indian attack scene. **123m/C VHS, Wide.** Burt Lancaster, Audrey Hepburn, Lillian Gish, Audie Murphy, John Saxon, Charles Bickford, Doug McClure, Joseph Wiseman, Albert Salmi; ***D:*** John Huston.

Unforgiven 🦴🦴🦴½ **1992 (R)** Will Munny (Eastwood) lives a quiet life with his stepchildren on his failing pig farm, but his desperado past catches up with him when the Schofield Kid invites him to a bounty hunt. Munny reluctantly agrees, mistakenly believing that once the killing is through he can take up his peaceful ways again. Enter sadistic sheriff Little Bill Daggett (Hackman), who doesn't want any gunmen messing up his town. Eastwood uses his own status as a screen legend to full advantage as the aging gunman who realizes too late that his past can never be forgotten. Director Eastwood is also in top form with his well-seasoned cast and myth-defying Old West realism. Surprising critical and boxoffice hit. **131m/C VHS, DVD, Wide.** Clint Eastwood, Gene Hackman, Morgan Freeman, Richard Harris, Jaimz Woolvett, Saul Rubinek, Frances Fisher, Anna Thomson, David Mucci, Rob Campbell, Anthony James; ***D:*** Clint Eastwood; ***W:*** David Peoples; ***C:*** Jack N. Green; ***M:*** Lennie Niehaus. Oscars '92: Director (Eastwood), Film Editing, Picture, Support. Actor (Hackman); AFI '98: Top 100; British Acad. '92: Director (Eastwood), Film, Support. Actor (Hackman); Directors Guild '92: Director (Eastwood); Golden Globes '93: Director (Eastwood), Support. Actor (Hackman); L.A. Film Critics '92: Actor (Eastwood), Director (Eastwood), Film, Screenplay, Support. Actor (Hackman); N.Y. Film Critics '92: Support. Actor (Hackman); Natl. Soc. Film Critics '92: Director (Eastwood), Film, Screenplay, Support. Actor (Hackman).

The Unholy 🦴½ **1988 (R)** A New Orleans priest battles a demon that's killing innocent parishioners. Confusing and heavy-handed. **100m/C VHS.** Ben Cross, Hal Holbrook, Trevor Howard, Ned Beatty, William Russ, James Dennis (Jim) Carroll; ***D:*** Camilo Vila; ***W:*** Philip Yordan; ***M:*** Roger Bellon.

Unholy Four 🦴½ *A Stranger Came Home* **1954** An amnesiac returns home after three years to attempt to find out which of his three fishing buddies left him for dead. Confusing at times, but has some suspenseful moments. **80m/B VHS.** *GB* Paulette Goddard, Paul Carpenter, William Sylvester, Patrick Holt, Russell Napier; ***D:*** Terence Fisher; ***W:*** Michael Carreras.

Unholy Rollers 🦴 *Leader of the Pack* **1972 (R)** Jennings stars as a factory worker who makes it big as a tough, violent roller derby star. Typical "Babes-on-Wheels" film that promises nothing and delivers even less. **88m/C VHS.** Claudia Jennings, Louis Quinn, Betty Anne Rees, Roberta Collins, Alan Vint, Candice Roman; ***D:*** Vernon Zimmerman.

The Unholy Three 🦴🦴🦴½ **1925** Ventriloquist Chaney, working with other carnival cohorts, uses his talent to gain entrance to homes which he later robs. Things go awry when two of the gang strike out on their own and the victim is killed. When the wrong man is accused, his girl, one of Chaney's gang, begs Chaney to get him free, which he does by using his vocal talents. Chaney decides being a criminal is just too hard and goes back to his ventriloquism. **70m/B VHS.** Lon Chaney Sr., Harry Earles, Victor McLaglen, Mae Busch, Matt Moore, Matthew Betz, William Humphreys; ***D:*** Tod Browning.

The Unholy Three 🦴🦴🦴 **1930** Chaney remade his silent hit of 1925 for his first and only talking picture (he died before the film was released). The story is essentially the same. Chaney is a ventriloquist who, with his circus friends, work as scam artists and thieves. When an innocent man is accused of their crimes Chaney tries his ventriloquist tricks to come to his aid, only in this version Chaney is exposed as a fraud and is sent to prison. Rumors that Chaney was a mute had him agreeing to appear in a "talkie" and he actually used five different voices for his various roles. **75m/B VHS.** Lon Chaney Sr., Lila Lee, Elliott Nugent, Harry Earles, John Miljan; ***D:*** Jack Conway.

Unholy Wife 🦴½ **1957** A young woman plans to murder her wealthy husband, but her plan goes awry when she accidentally kills someone else. Muddled and heavy-handed, with Steiger chewing scenery. **94m/C VHS.** Rod Steiger, Diana Dors, Tom Tryon, Marie Windsor, Beulah Bondi; ***D:*** John Farrow.

Unhook the Stars 🦴🦴½ **1996 (R)** Director Cassavetes does mom Rowlands proud (and she him) with the lead role of widowed Mildred, who discovers there's life after the kids leave the nest. At loose ends, Mildred befriends her wild young neighbor Monica (Tomei), who conveniently needs a babysitter for her solemn six-year-old son, J.J. (Lloyd). Monica also tries to get Mildred to loosen up by taking her to a local joint, where French-Canadian trucker Tommy (Depardieu) knows a good woman when he sees one. Mildred makes some tentative steps towards independence and we get to enjoy the stellar Rowlands once again. **105m/C VHS.** Gena Rowlands, Marisa Tomei, Gerard Depardieu, Moira Kelly, Jake Lloyd, David Sherrill, David Thornton; ***D:*** Nick Cassavetes; ***W:*** Nick Cassavetes, Helen Caldwell; ***C:*** Phedon Papamichael; ***M:*** Steven Hufsteter.

Unicorn 🦴🦴 **1983** A small boy hears the legend that if one rubs the horn of a Unicorn his wishes will come true. Mistakenly he buys a one-horned goat and sets out to fulfill his dreams. **29m/C VHS.** *GB* Diana Dors, David Kossoff, Celia Johnson; ***D:*** Carol Reed.

Unidentified Flying Oddball 🦴🦴½ **1979 (G)** An astronaut and his robotic buddy find their spaceship turning into a time machine that throws them back into Arthurian times and at the mercy of Merlin the magician. Futuristic version of Twain's "A Connecticut Yankee at King Arthur's Court." **92m/C VHS, DVD.** Dennis Dugan, Jim Dale, Ron Moody, Kenneth More, Rodney Bewes; ***D:*** Russ Mayberry; ***W:*** Don Tait; ***C:*** Paul Beeson; ***M:*** Ronald Goodwin.

The Uninvited 🦴🦴🦴 **1944** Roderick Fitzgerald (Milland) and his sister Pamela (Hussey) buy a house in Cornwall, only to find it is haunted. Doors open and close by themselves, strange scents fill the air, and they hear sobbing during the night. Soon they are visited by a woman (Russell) with an odd link to the house—her mother is the spirit who haunts the house. Chilling and unforgettable, this is one of the first films to deal seriously with ghosts. Based on the novel by Dorothy Macardle. **99m/B VHS.** Ray Milland, Ruth Hussey, Donald Crisp, Cornelia Otis Skinner, Gail Russell, Alan Napier, Dorothy Stickney; ***D:*** Lewis Allen; ***W:*** Dodie Smith, Frank Partos; ***C:*** Charles B(ryant) Lang Jr.; ***M:*** Victor Young.

The Uninvited woof! **1988** A mutant cat goes berserk onboard a luxury yacht, killing the passengers one by one with big, nasty, pointy teeth. **89m/C VHS.** George Kennedy, Alex Cord, Clu Gulager, Toni Hudson, Eric Larson, Shari Shattuck, Austin Stoker; ***D:*** Greydon Clark.

Uninvited 🦴🦴½ **1993 (R)** Grady is a mysterious old man who leads eight misfits to the top of a sacred mountain with the promise of finding gold. But the fortune hunters have trespassed in a sacred Indian burial ground and find their nightmares becoming a violent reality. **90m/C VHS.** Jack Elam, Christopher Boyer, Erin Noble, Bari Buckner, Jerry Rector, Zane Paolo, Dennis Gibbs, Ted Haler, Eno Brutto; ***D:*** Michael Derek Bohusz; ***W:*** Michael Derek Bohusz.

Uninvited Guest 🦴🦴½ *An Invited Guest* **1999 (R)** Smooth-talking Silk (Phifer) comes to the suburban home of Howard (Jackson) and Debbie (Morrow) and asks to use their phone. The couple agree and let the stranger in and he promptly takes them and their friends captive. A twist comes unexpected early and takes a little away from the real ending. **103m/C VHS, DVD, Wide.** Mekhi Phifer, Mari Morrow, Mel Jackson, Kim Fields, Malinda Williams; ***D:*** Timothy Wayne Folsome; ***W:*** Timothy Wayne Folsome; ***C:*** Wayne Sells; ***M:*** Gregory Darryl Smith. **VIDEO**

Union City 🦴🦴 **1981 (R)** Deborah "Blondie" Harry's husband gets a little edgy when someone steals the milk. Murder ensues, and they're on the run from the law. Intended as a film noir spoof, and not without some good moments. **82m/C VHS, DVD.** Deborah Harry, Everett McGill, Dennis Lipscomb, Pat Benatar, Irina Maleeva, Terina Lewis, Sam McMurray, Paul Andor, Tony Azito, CCH Pounder; ***D:*** Mark Reichert; ***W:*** Mark Reichert; ***C:*** Edward Lachman; ***M:*** Chris Stein.

Union Pacific 🦴🦴🦴 **1939** Full DeMille treatment highlights this saga about the building of America's first transcontinental railroad. Jeff Butler (McCrea) is the construction overseer who must battle saboteurs and Indians (although the U.S. Cavalry does arrive to save the day). He also gets to fall for self-sufficient postmistress Mollie Monahan (Stanwyck). DeMille borrowed the actual golden spike used to drive in the last rail in 1869 for his reenactment of the completion celebration. Based on the book "Trouble Shooters" by Ernest Haycox. **136m/B VHS.** Joel McCrea, Barbara Stanwyck, Robert Preston, Brian Donlevy, Akim Tamiroff, Lynne Overman, Robert Barrat, Anthony Quinn, Stanley Ridges, Henry Kolker, Evelyn Keyes, Regis Toomey; ***D:*** Cecil B. DeMille; ***W:*** Walter DeLeon, Jesse Lasky Jr., C. Gardner Sullivan; ***C:*** Victor Milner.

Union Station 🦴🦴 **1950** Holden plays the chief of the railway police for Chicago's Union Station. He learns the station is to be used as a ransom drop in a kidnapping; but for all his security, the main thug gets away with the money, and the hunt is on. Good acting raises this film above the ordinary. **80m/B VHS.** William Holden, Barry Fitzgerald, Nancy Olson, Jan Sterling, Lee Marvin, Allene Roberts, Lyle Bettger; ***D:*** Rudolph Mate; ***C:*** Daniel F. Fapp.

U.S. Marshals 🦴🦴 **1998 (PG-13)** Jones reprises his Oscar-winning role from "The Fugitive" as the hound dog U.S. Marshal Sam Gerard in this lackluster sequel. Gerard tracks down Sheridan (Snipes) who is framed for a double homicide of two federal agents. Gerard's probing reveals that Sheridan really isn't the average Joe he seems, and the presence of shifty agent Downey Jr. further confirms Gerard's suspicions of a government cover-up. Jones remains solid in a popular role, supported well by his sidekick Cosmo (Pantolino). The stunts equal if not better its predecessor, yet a poorly developed Sheridan, compounded by Snipes's lack of intensity drag this chase movie down to a slow crawl. **133m/C VHS, DVD, Wide.** Tommy Lee Jones, Robert Downey Jr., Wesley Snipes, Joe Pantoliano, Kate Nelligan, Irene Jacob, Daniel Roebuck, Tom Wood, Latanya Richardson, Michael Paul Chan; ***D:*** Stuart Baird; ***W:*** John Pogue; ***C:*** Andrzej Bartkowiak; ***M:*** Jerry Goldsmith.

U.S. Seals 🦴🦴 **1998 (R)** Absolutely undistinguished action flick pits a team of Navy SEALs against pirates from Kazahkstan. The heroes are jut-jawed guys with crewcuts and cute kids. Lots of stuff blows up. Production values are strictly of the made-for-cable quality. **90m/C DVD.** Jim Fitzpatrick, Greg Collins, J. Kenneth Campbell; ***D:*** Yossi Wein.

Universal Soldier 🦴🦴 **1992 (R)** A reporter discovers a secret government project to design perfect robo-soldiers by using the bodies of dead GIs, including tough guys Lundgren and Van Damme who were killed in Vietnam. But the knowledge is going to get her killed until Van Damme has flashbacks of his past (the soldier's memories have supposedly been erased) and agrees to help her. Lundgren doesn't have the same compassion and goes after them both. Big-budget thriller with some good action sequences and a lot of violence. **98m/C VHS, DVD.** Jean-Claude Van Damme, Dolph Lundgren, Ally Walker, Ed O'Ross, Jerry Orbach; ***D:*** Roland Emmerich; ***W:*** Dean Devlin, Christopher Leitch, Richard Rothstein; ***C:*** Karl Walter Lindenlaub; ***M:*** Christopher Franke.

Universal Soldier 2: Brothers in Arms 🦴🦴 **1998 (R)** Cable actioner not to be confused with the 1999 big-screen sequel "Universal Soldier: The Return" starring Jean-Claude Van Damme. Here, Luc Devereaux (Battaglia), who works for the top-secret UniSol military operation, teams up with journalist Veronica Roberts (West) to expose UniSol's plan to re-animate dead soldiers into unstoppable killing machines. **93m/C VHS.** Matt Battaglia, Chandra West, Gary Busey, Jeff Wincott. **CABLE**

Universal Soldier 3: Unfinished Business 🦴½ **1998 (R)** An ex-soldier and a journalist try to stop a billion-dollar robbery and discover the deadly (and dead) military men are active once again. **95m/C VHS.** Matt Battaglia, Chandra West, Burt Reynolds, Jeff Wincott. **CABLE**

Universal Soldier: The Return 🦴🦴 **1999 (R)** The creators of superwarrior Van Damme have double-crossed him and he's out to get even in this sequel (although technically it's the fourth installment after two straight-to-cable releases). After Defense Department cutbacks short circuit the Universal Soldier program, the cyborgs start a rebellion led by an evil computer. Van Damme must battle the renegade warriors while attempting to not muss his hair. The Muscles from Brussels goes back to a proven winner after a series of box-office stinkers in hopes that he can kick-start his flagging career. **82m/C VHS, DVD.** Jean-Claude Van Damme, Michael Jai White, Daniel von Bargen, Heidi Schanz, Xander Berkeley, Justin Lazard; ***D:*** Mic Rodgers; ***W:*** John Fasano, William Malone; ***C:*** Michael A. Benson; ***M:*** Don Davis.

The Unkissed Bride 🦴 *Mother Goose A Go-Go* **1966 (PG)** A young newlywed couple are driven to distraction by the husband's inexplicable fainting spells and his strange obsession with Mother Goose. **82m/C VHS.** Tommy Kirk, Anne Helm, Danica D'Hondt, Henny Youngman; ***D:*** Jack H. Harris.

The Unknown 🦴🦴🦴½ **1927** Typically morbid Chaney fare has him working as a circus freak while trying to win the heart of his assistant. After drastic romancing he's still rejected by her, so he plots to kill the object of her intentions. Ghoulish as it is, the picture is really top-notch. **60m/B VHS.** Lon Chaney Sr., Norman Kerry, Joan Crawford, Nick De Ruiz, Frank Lanning, John St. Polis; ***D:*** Tod Browning.

Unknown Island 🦴½ **1948** Scientists travel to a legendary island where dinosaurs supposedly still exist. Bogus dinosaurs and cliche script. **76m/C VHS, DVD.** Virginia Grey, Philip Reed, Richard Denning, Barton MacLane; ***D:*** Jack Bernhard; ***W:*** Jack Harvey, Robert T. Shannon; ***C:*** Fred Jackman; ***M:*** Ralph Stanley.

Unknown Origin 🦴🦴 *The Alien Within; Roger Corman Presents: The Alien Within* **1995 (R)** Scientific crew is stuck in an underwater installation with a deadly parasite. It's "Aliens" under the sea but a few twists will tweak your interest. **75m/C VHS.** Roddy McDowall, Melanie Shatner, Alex Hyde-White, Don Stroud; ***D:*** Scott Levy; ***W:*** Alex Simon; ***M:*** Christopher Lennertz. **CABLE**

Unknown Powers woof! **1980 (PG)** Science and drama are combined to examine ESP and magic. Are they gifts or curses, and how are peoples' lives affected by them? Members of the cast introduce various sections of this totally inept film. **97m/C VHS.** Samantha Eggar, Jack Palance, Will Geer, Roscoe Lee Browne; ***D:*** Don Como.

The Unknown Ranger 🦴½ **1936** Allen's first cowboy role has him foiling a gang of rustlers. The real highlight turns out to be the battle between his horse and a wild stallion. Eat your heart out, Trigger! **57m/B VHS.** Robert "Tex" Allen, Harry Woods, Martha Tibbetts, Hal Taliaferro, Robert "Buzzy" Henry; ***D:*** Spencer Gordon Bennet.

The Unknown Soldier 🦴🦴½ **1998** Fine performances in an ultimately depressing drama, with some unexpected twists, focusing on the tragedy of war. When aristocratic Sophia Carey's (Aubrey) ancestral home is turned into a private hospital for WWI soldiers, she seriously takes up her nursing duties. One of her latest patients is an amnesiac, initially mute soldier nicknamed Angel (Mavers) by the men who rescued him in France. Sophia falls hopelessly in love with the traumatized Angel but the working-class Jenny (McGuckin) claims Angel is actually her fiance John and the military police believe he's a deserter wanted for murder. **180m/C VHS.** *GB* Juliet Aubrey, Gary Mavers, Aislin McGuckin; ***D:*** David Drury; ***W:*** Peter Barwood. **TV**

Unknown World 🦴 **1951** A group of scientists tunnel to the center of the Earth to find a refuge from the dangers of the atomic world. Big start winds down fast. Director Terry Morse sometimes credited as Terrell O. Morse. **73m/B VHS.** Bruce Kellogg, Marilyn Nash, Victor Kilian, Jim Bannon; ***D:*** Terry Morse; ***M:*** Ernest Gold.

Unlawful Entry 🦴🦴 **1992 (R)** After a break-in, Karen and Michael Carr naturally call the cops. Handsome, polite policeman Pete Davis responds to the call and agrees to help burglar-proof their home. But Pete has some definite quirks—he falls for the beauteous Karen and begins stalking the couple, deciding to get rid of Michael in order to have his wife. A lurid combination of the worst moments of "Internal Affairs" and "Fatal Attraction" undermines this usually talented cast. **107m/C VHS, DVD, Wide.** Kurt Russell, Ray Liotta, Madeleine Stowe, Roger E. Mosley, Ken Lerner, Deborah Offner, Carmen Argenziano, Andy Romano, Barry W. Blaustein, Dick Miller; ***D:*** Jonathan Kaplan; ***W:*** Lewis Colick; ***C:*** Jamie Anderson; ***M:*** James Horner.

Unlawful Passage **1994 (R)** Vacation turns into a nightmare when a man's wife is kidnapped. **?m/C VHS.** Lee Horsley, William Zabka, Felicity Waterman; ***D:*** Camilo Vila; ***W:*** Peter Dixon; ***C:*** Henry Vargas.

Unlikely Angel 🦴🦴½ **1997** Brassy singer Ruby Diamond (Parton) dies suddenly in an accident but is having some trouble entering heaven. St. Peter (McDowall) thinks she's a likely prospect but Ruby needs a few more good deeds before she can get her wings. So she's sent to help a frazzled widower (Kerwin) who's the father of two lonely preteens. **90m/C VHS, DVD.** Dolly Parton, Roddy McDowall, Brian Kerwin; ***D:*** Michael Switzer.

An Unmarried Woman 🦴🦴🦴 **1978 (R)** Suddenly divorced by her husband of 17 years, a woman deals with change. She enters the singles scene, copes with her daughter's growing sexuality, and encounters a new self-awareness. Mazursky puts real people on screen from start to finish. **124m/C VHS.** Jill Clayburgh, Alan Bates, Cliff Gorman, Michael Murphy; ***D:*** Paul Mazursky; ***W:*** Paul Mazursky; ***M:*** Bill Conti. Cannes '78: Actress (Clayburgh); L.A. Film Critics '78: Screenplay; N.Y. Film Critics '78: Screenplay; Natl. Soc. Film Critics '78: Screenplay.

Unmasked Part 25 🦴½ **1988** A second-generation serial killer takes up where dad left off. This one is intended to be a parody of slasher films, but it's still very bloody. **85m/C VHS.** *GB* Gregory Cox, Fiona Evans, Edward Brayshaw, Debbie Lee London; ***D:*** Anders Palm.

Unmasking the Idol 🦴 **1986** A suave hero with tongue firmly in check battles Ninja warlords. Sequel to "Order of the Black Eagle." **90m/C VHS.** *GB* Ian Hunter, William T. Hicks, Charles K. Bibby; ***D:*** Worth Keeter.

The Unnamable 🦴 **1988** The adaptation of the H.P. Lovecraft story about a particular New England ancestral home haunted by a typically Lovecraftian bloodthirsty demon borne of a woman hundreds of years before. College students, between trysts, investigate the myths about it. Uncut version, unseen in theatres, available only on video good for a few giggles and thrills. **87m/C VHS.** Charles King, Mark Kinsey Stephenson, Alexandra Durrell, Laura Albert, Eben Ham, Blane Wheatley, Mark Parra, Katrin Alexandre; ***D:*** Jean-Paul Ouellette; ***W:*** Jean-Paul Ouellette; ***C:*** Tom Fraser.

The Unnamable 2: The Statement of Randolph Carter 🦴½ *H.P. Lovecraft's The Unnamable Returns; The Unnamable Returns* **1992 (R)** Randolph Carter is investigating a series of murders at Miskatonic University. Evidence leads Carter back to a 17th-century warlock who had the misfortune to summon an evil creature known as Alyda. The half-demon, half-woman now wants to permanently return to the mortal plane and every new victim just helps her evil purpose along. Based on a story by H.P. Lovecraft. **104m/C VHS.** Mark Kinsey Stephenson, John Rhys-Davies, David Warner, Julie Strain, Maria Ford, Charles Klausmeyer; ***D:*** Jean-Paul Ouellette; ***W:*** Jean-Paul Ouellette; ***C:*** Greg Gardiner.

Unnatural 🦴🦴½ **1952** A mad scientist creates a souless child from the genes of a murderer and a prostitute. The child grows up to be the beautiful Neff, who makes a habit of seducing and destroying men. Dark, arresting film from a very popular German story. **90m/B VHS.** Hildegarde Neff, Erich von Stroheim, Karl-Heinz Boehm, Harry Meyen, Harry Helm, Denise Vernac, Julia Koschka; ***D:*** Arthur Maria Rabenalt.

Unnatural Causes 🦴🦴🦴 **1986** A dying Vietnam vet believes that his illness is the result of exposure to Agent Orange. With the help of a VA counselor, they lobby for national programs to assist other veterans who have been exposed to the chemical and together bring publicity to the issue. A TV drama that is exceptionally well-acted. **96m/C VHS.** John Ritter, Patti LaBelle, Alfre Woodard, John Sayles, Sean McCann, John Vargas, Gwen E. Davis; ***D:*** Lamont Johnson; ***W:*** John Sayles; ***M:*** Charles Fox. **TV**

Unnatural Pursuits 🦴🦴 **1991** Playwright Simon Gray's black comic look at a British playwright's sojourn from London to L.A., Dallas, and New York and the Broadway debut of his new work. Alcoholic Hamish Partt (Bates), in the throes of a midlife crisis, is plagued by ego, indignities, and hostile actors, audiences, and critics as he tries desperately to work. Made for British TV. **60m/C VHS.** *GB* Alan Bates, Keith Szarabajka, Deborah Rush, John Mahoney, Tom Hickey, Richard Wilson, David Healy, Jack Gilpin, Paul Zimet, Bob Balaban; ***W:*** Simon Gray. **TV**

An Unremarkable Life 🦴🦴 **1989 (PG)** Two aging sisters live symbiotically together, until one views the other's romantic attachment to a charming widower as destructive to her own life. **97m/C VHS.** Shelley Winters, Patricia Neal, Mako, Rochelle Oliver, Charles S. Dutton, Lily Knight; ***D:*** Amin Q. Chaudhri.

Unsane 🦴🦴½ *Shadow; Sotto gli Occhi dell'Assassino; Tenebrae; Tenebre* **1982** A mystery novelist realizes that a series of bizarre murders strangely resembles the plot of his latest book. Bloody fun from Argento. **91m/C VHS, DVD.** *IT* Anthony (Tony) Franciosa, John Saxon, Daria Nicolodi, Giuliano Gemma, Christian Borromeo, Mirella D'Angelo, Veronica Lario, Ania Pieroni, Carola Stagnaro, John Steiner, Lara Wendel; ***D:*** Dario Argento; ***W:*** Dario Argento; ***C:*** Luciano Tovoli; ***M:*** The Goblins, Claudio Simonetti.

The Unseen 🦴½ **1980** Three young women from a TV station are covering a story in a remote area of California. Before nightfall, two are horribly killed, leaving the third to come face to face with the terror. **91m/C VHS.** Barbara Bach, Sydney Lassick, Stephen Furst; ***D:*** Peter Foleg.

Unseen Evil 🦴 **1999 (R)** A group of archeological students accompany their professor to an ancient burial ground for a dig. Unfortunately, the prof wants to uncover a powerful alien force and is prepared to sacrifice anyone necessary. **90m/C VHS, DVD.** Richard Hatch, Tim Thomerson, Robbie (Reist) Rist, Cindi Braun, Frank Ruotolo, Jere Jon, Cindy Pena; ***D:*** Jay Woelfel; ***W:*** Scott Spears; ***C:*** Scott Spears. **VIDEO**

Unsettled Land 🦴🦴 **1988 (PG)** Young Israeli settlers try to survive the elements and Bedouin attackers in Palestine during the 1920s. **109m/C VHS, 8mm.** *IS* Kelly McGillis, John Shea, Arnon Zadok, Christine Boisson; ***D:*** Uri Barbash.

The Unsinkable Molly Brown 🦴🦴🦴 **1964** A spunky backwoods girl is determined to break into the upper crust of Denver's high society and along the way survives the sinking of the Titanic. This energetic version of the Broadway musical contains many Meredith Willson ("Music Man") songs and lots of hokey, good-natured fun. ♫Colorado Is My Home; Leadville Johnny Brown (Soliloquy); I Ain't Down Yet; Belly Up to the Bar, Boys; He's My Friend; I've Already Started; The Beautiful People of Denver; I May Never Fall in Love with You; Up Where the People Are. **128m/C VHS, DVD, Wide.** Debbie Reynolds, Harve Presnell, Ed Begley Sr., Martita Hunt, Hermione Baddeley; ***D:*** Charles Walters; ***C:*** Daniel F. Fapp; ***M:*** Meredith Willson.

Unspeakable 🦴🦴½ **2000** James (Cline) and Alice Fhelleps have a nasty, unsatisfying marriage until a car accident turns their life together into a true horror. From that premise, Chad Ferrin spins out a relatively realistic tale of madness and murder. For hard-core horror fans only. **81m/C DVD, Wide.** Robert Cline, Timothy Muskatell, Tina Birchfield, Wolf Dangler; ***D:*** Chad Ferrin; ***W:*** Chad Ferrin; ***C:*** Nicholas Loizides.

The Unstoppable Man 🦴½ **1959** The son of an American businessman is kidnapped while they are in London. No pushover he, dad develops his own plan to destroy the criminals, eventually pursuing them with a flame thrower. **68m/B VHS.** *GB* Cameron Mitchell, Marius Goring, Harry H. Corbett, Lois Maxwell, Denis Gilmore; ***D:*** Terry Bishop.

Unstrung Heroes 🦴🦴½ **1995 (PG)** Semi-autobiographical tale of Steven Lidz (Watt), growing up in 1960s California with a mother who is dying of cancer (MacDowell) and a nutty professor-type father (Turturro) who refuses to accept her illness. A desperate Steven goes to live with his two oddball uncles (Richards and Chaykin) who provide understanding and insight for the youngster, as well as a new name, Franz. Moving and quirky without being sappy, Keaton's feature debut avoids what would've been easy stereotypes. Based on the autobiography by Franz Lidz. **93m/C VHS.** Andie MacDowell, John Turturro, Michael Richards, Maury Chaykin, Nathan Watt, Kendra Krull; ***D:*** Diane Keaton; ***W:*** Richard LaGravenese; ***C:*** Phedon Papamichael; ***M:*** Thomas Newman.

Unsuitable Job for a Woman 🦴🦴½ **1982** Independent Cordelia Gray, following the death of her boss, takes over his detective agency and gets involved with murder. Based on the novel by P.D. James. **94m/C VHS.** *GB* Pippa Guard, Paul Freeman, Billie Whitelaw; ***D:*** Christopher Petit.

The Untamable 🦴🦴 **1923** Unusual silent about volatile woman suffering from schizophrenia. **65m/B VHS.** Gladys Walton, Malcolm McGregor, John St. Polis, Etta Lee; ***D:*** Herbert Blache.

Untamed Heart 🦴🦴½ **1993 (PG-13)** Adam (Slater), the painfully shy busboy with a heart condition, loves Caroline (Tomei), the bubbly waitress, from afar. She doesn't notice him until he saves her from some would-be rapists and their love blooms in the coffee shop where they both work. Tomei and Slater are both strong in the leads and Perez, as Caroline's best buddy Cindy, hurls comic barbs with ease. Charmingly familiar surroundings help set this formulaic romance apart. Filmed on location in Minneapolis. **102m/C VHS, DVD, Wide.** Christian Slater, Marisa Tomei, Rosie Perez, Kyle Secor, Willie Garson; ***D:*** Tony Bill; ***W:*** Tom Sierchio; ***C:*** Jost Vacano; ***M:*** Cliff Eidelman. MTV Movie Awards '93: Most Desirable Male (Slater), Kiss (Christian Slater/Marisa Tomei).

Until September 🦴🦴 **1984 (R)** An American tourist becomes stranded in Paris. She meets and falls in love with a married banker while she is stuck in her hotel. Routine romance. **96m/C VHS.** Karen Allen, Thierry Lhermitte, Christopher Cazenove, Johanna Pavlis; ***D:*** Richard Marquand; ***M:*** John Barry.

Until the End of the World 🦴🦴🦴½ *Bis ans Ende der Welt; Jusqu'au Bout du Monde* **1991 (R)** Convoluted road movie set in 1999 follows the travails of Sam Farber (Hurt) through 15 cities in eight countries on four continents as he is chased by Dommartin, her lover (Neill), a bounty hunter, a private detective, and bank robbers, until all wind up in the Australian outback. And this is only the first half of the movie. For true cinematic satisfaction, don't expect logic—just go with the flow. Visually stunning, unexpectedly humorous, with excellent performances from an international cast. Footage created with high definition (HDTV) video technology is a technological first. The soundtrack features Lou Reed, David Byrne, U2, and others. **158m/C VHS.** *AU GE FR* William Hurt, Solveig Dommartin, Sam Neill, Max von Sydow, Ruediger Vogler, Ernie Dingo, Jeanne Moreau, David Gulpilil; ***D:*** Wim Wenders; ***W:*** Wim Wenders, Peter Carey; ***C:*** Robby Muller; ***M:*** Graeme Revell.

Until They Get Me 🦴½ **1918** Northern Mountie rides horse in silence as he tracks criminal to the edge of the earth. **58m/B VHS.** Pauline Starke, Joe King, Jack Curtis, Wilbur Higby, Anna Dodge, Walter Perry; ***D:*** Frank Borzage; ***W:*** Kenneth B. Clarke; ***C:*** C.H. Wales.

Until They Sail 🦴🦴½ **1957** Soap opera set in New Zealand during WWII. Plot centers around the lives of four sisters involved in love and murder. Dee's film debut. Based on a story by James Michener. **95m/B VHS.** Jean Simmons, Joan Fontaine, Paul Newman, Piper Laurie, Charles Drake, Sandra Dee, Wally Cassell, Alan Napier; ***D:*** Robert Wise; ***W:*** Robert Anderson.

The Untold Story 🦴🦴 *The Untold Story: Human Meat Roast Pork Buns; Ba Xian Fan Dian Zhi Ren Rou Cha Shao Bao; Bunman; Human Meat Pies* **1993** New restaurant owner Wong discovers that the previous owner and his family mysteriously disappeared. Then the police detective (Lee) on the case makes a very shocking discovery. Modern cult classic includes footage cut from the original Hong Kong release and its violence is not for the squeamish. Cantonese with subtitles. **95m/C VHS, DVD, Wide.** *HK* Anthony Wong, Danny Lee, Emily Kwan, Fui-On Shing; ***D:*** Herman Yau, Danny Lee.

The Untouchables 🦴🦴🦴½ **1987 (R)** Big-budget, fast-paced, and exciting re-evaluation of the popular TV series about the real-life battle between Treasury officer Eliot Ness (Costner) and crime boss Al Capone (De Niro) in 1920s' Chicago. History sometimes takes a back seat to Hollywood's imagination in the screenplay, but it doesn't really matter since there are splendid performances by De Niro and Connery as Ness' mentor Jimmy Malone to help it look realistic. Costner does a fine job showing the change in Ness from naive idealism to steely conviction. Beautifully filmed with excellent special effects. Note DePalma's long train station/baby carriage scene that's an homage to the 1925 silent Russian classic, "Battleship Potemkin." **119m/C VHS, DVD, 8mm, Wide.** Kevin Costner, Sean Connery, Robert De Niro, Andy Garcia, Charles Martin Smith, Billy Drago, Richard Bradford, Jack Kehoe; ***D:*** Brian DePalma; ***W:*** David Mamet; ***C:*** Stephen Burum; ***M:*** Ennio Morricone. Oscars '87: Support. Actor (Connery); Golden Globes '88: Support. Actor (Connery); Natl. Bd. of Review '87: Support. Actor (Connery).

Unveiled 🦴🦴½ **1994 (R)** Stephanie Montgomery's (Zane) friend falls victim to a killer in Marrakesh. So Steph sets out to trap the killer, with the help of government offficial Peter (Hubley). **103m/C VHS.** Lisa

Zane, Whip Hubley, Nicholas Chinlund, Martha Gehman; *D:* William Cole; *W:* Michael Diamond, Roger Kumble; *M:* Christopher Tyng.

Unzipped 1994 (R) Witty, behind-the-scenes look at whiz-kid fashion designer Isaac Mizrahi as he prepares for the showing of his 1994 collection. Alternately filmed in black-and-white and color in a variety of film stocks, Keeve (Mizrahi's former lover) captures Mizrahi's varying moods, from his creative struggles to his unique sense of humor and gift for mimicry. Highlights include scenes with Mizrahi's doting mother. Fashionphiles will love every minute, and strictly off-the-rack viewers can enjoy the supermodels on parade. **76m/C VHS.** *D:* Douglas Keeve; *C:* Ellen Kuras. Sundance '95: Aud. Award.

Up Against the Wall 1991 (PG-13) A black kid from the Chicago projects attends school in the affluent suburbs, but there too he must resist temptation, crime and violence. A well-intentioned but didactic cautionary drama, adapted from the book by African-American author/commentator Dr. Jawanza Kunjufu. **103m/C VHS.** Marla Gibbs, Stoney Jackson, Catero Colbert, Ron O'Neal, Salli Richardson; *D:* Ron O'Neal.

Up at the Villa ½ 2000 (PG-13) The British and American expatriate community in 1938 Florence is the setting for the unlikely romantic travails of respectable British widow Mary Panton (Scott Thomas). She is courted by longtime (and older) friend/diplomat Sir Edgar (Fox) who will offer her a comfortable if dull life in India. But at a party, Mary is paired off with confident American Rowley Flint (Penn), who must unexpectedly help Mary out of a jam involving a dead body. However, politics also plays its part with the rise of fascism. Scott Thomas and Penn may not have any romantic sparks but they do well individually and Bancroft is an amusing scene stealer as a wealthy socialite. Based on a novella by W. Somerset Maugham. **115m/C VHS, DVD, Wide.** *GB* Kristin Scott Thomas, Sean Penn, Anne Bancroft, Derek Jacobi, Jeremy Davies, James Fox, Massimo Ghini; *D:* Philip Haas; *W:* Belinda Haas; *C:* Maurizio Calvesi; *M:* Pino Donaggio.

Up Close and Personal 1996 (PG-13) Ambitious Reno card dealer Tally Atwater (Pfeiffer) wants to get into broadcasting and finds her chance at a Miami TV station where she's mentored by successful veteran-reporter-turned-producer Warren Justice (Redford). They fall in love but find their careers clashing as Tally climbs the media success ladder. Originally inspired by the tragic life of NBC reporter Jessica Savitch, whose problems with drugs and abusive relationships led to a sad ending, film turned into a star-powered romance with media trappings and another variation of "A Star is Born." It's now "suggested" by Alanna Nash's book "Golden Girl." **124m/C VHS, DVD, Wide.** Michelle Pfeiffer, Robert Redford, Kate Nelligan, Stockard Channing, Joe Mantegna, Glenn Plummer, James Rebhorn, Noble Willingham, Scott Bryce, Raymond Cruz, Dedee Pfeiffer, Miguel (Michael) Sandoval, James Karen; *D:* Jon Avnet; *W:* Joan Didion, John Gregory Dunne; *C:* Karl Walter Lindenlaub; *M:* Thomas Newman.

Up/Down/Fragile *Haut Bas Fragile* 1995 New Wavish musical following the fortunes of three young women in Paris. Louise (Denicourt) has just emerged from a coma after several years and is living in a tiny apartment though she has inherited the antiques-filled home of an aunt; Ninon (Richard) has fled from her gangster boyfriend and gotten a job as a delivery girl; and the adopted Ida (Cote) has become obsessed with learning the identities of her biological parents. Their link is Roland (Marcon) who knows all three. The mood's more important than the plot anyway. French with subtitles. **169m/C VHS.** *FR* Marianne (Cuau) Denicourt, Laurence Cote, Nathalie Richard, Andre Marcon, Anna Karina; *D:* Jacques Rivette; *C:* Christophe Pollock; *M:* Francois Breant.

Up from the Depths ½ 1979 (R) Something from beneath the ocean is turning the paradise of Hawaii into a nightmare. Prehistoric fish are returning to the surface with one thing on their minds—lunch. "Jaws" rip-off played for humor. **85m/C VHS.** Sam Bottoms, Suzanne Reed, Virgil Frye; *D:* Charles B. Griffith; *W:* Alfred Sweeney; *M:* James Horner.

Up in Arms 1944 Danny Kaye's first film presents a typical Kaye scenario: he plays a twitching hypochondriac who is drafted into the Army and sneaks his girlfriend aboard the troopship bound for the Pacific. Features an appearance by the Goldwyn Girls. Remake of the film "The Nervous Wreck." ♫Theatre Lobby Number; Now I Know; All Out for Freedom; Tess's Torch Song; Melody in 4-F. **105m/C VHS.** Danny Kaye, Dinah Shore, Constance Dowling, Dana Andrews, Margaret Dumont, Lyle Talbot, Louis Calhern, Charles Halton; *D:* Elliott Nugent; *C:* Ray Rennahan.

Up in Central Park ½ 1948 Poor adaptation of the hit Broadway musical (the studio removed much of Romberg's score) about Irish immigrant lass Rosie Moore (Durbin), who teams up with New York reporter John Matthews (Haymes) to expose corrupt politician Boss Tweed (Price). Without the songs, the plot is shown to be wafer-thin. ♫When She Walks in the Room; Carousel in the Park; Oh Say Do You See What I See?; Pace, Pace Mio Dio. **88m/B VHS.** Deanna Durbin, Dick Haymes, Vincent Price, Albert Sharpe, Tom Powers, Hobart Cavanaugh, Thurston Hall; *D:* William A. Seiter; *W:* Dorothy Fields, Herbert Fields, Karl Tunberg; *C:* Milton Krasner; *M:* Sigmund Romberg.

Up in the Air 1940 Darro and Moreland have ambitions as radio comedians, and their friend Reynolds wants to be a singer. Their break comes when other performers are murdered on the air. First, though, they must solve the killings. **62m/B VHS.** Frankie Darro, Marjorie Reynolds, Mantan Moreland, Gordon Jones, Tristram Coffin, John Holland, Carleton Young; *D:* Howard Bretherton.

Up Periscope ½ 1959 Garner is a demolitions expert unwillingly assigned to a submarine commanded by O'Brien. His mission: to sneak onto a Japanese-held island and steal a top-secret code book. Trouble is, O'Brien may not wait for Garner to complete his mission before taking the sub back underwater. A routine submarine film. **111m/C VHS, Wide.** James Garner, Edmond O'Brien, Andra Martin, Alan Hale Jr., Carleton Carpenter, Frank Gifford, Richard Bakalyan; *D:* Gordon Douglas.

Up River 1979 Wealthy land baron rapes and murders the wife of a simple pioneer, who is beaten and whose homestead is burned by the baron as well. The pioneer lives to seek terrible vengeance. **90m/C VHS.** Jeff Corey, Morgan Stevens, Debbie AuLuce; *D:* Carl Kitt.

Up the Academy *Mad Magazine's Up the Academy; The Brave Young Men of Weinberg* 1980 (R) Four teenaged delinquents are sent to an academy for wayward boys where they encounter a sadistic headmaster and a gay dance instructor. Sometimes inventive, often tasteless fare from "Mad" magazine. **88m/C VHS.** Ron Leibman, Ralph Macchio, Barbara Bach, Tom Poston, Stacey Nelkin, Wendell Brown, Tom Citera; *D:* Robert Downey.

Up the Creek 1958 Crazy antics abound in this tale of an old British destroyer, a black-market scheme run by the crew, and the new skipper whose hobby is rocket building. Followed by "Further Up the River." **83m/B VHS.** *GB* David Tomlinson, Wilfrid Hyde-White, Peter Sellers, Vera Day, Michael Goodliffe, Lionel Jeffries; *D:* Val Guest.

Up the Creek ½ 1984 (R) Four college losers enter a whitewater raft race to gain some respect for their school. The soundtrack features songs by Heart, Cheap Trick and The Beach Boys. Routine. **95m/C VHS.** Tim Matheson, Jennifer Runyon, Stephen Furst, John Hillerman, James B. Sikking, Julia Montgomery, Jeana Tomasina; *D:* Robert Butler; *M:* William Goldstein.

Up the Down Staircase 1967 A naive, newly trained New York public school teacher is determined to teach the finer points of English literature to a group of poor students. She almost gives up until one student actually begins to learn. Good production and acting. Based on Bel Kaufman's novel. **124m/C VHS.** Sandy Dennis, Patrick Bedford, Eileen Heckart, Ruth White, Jean Stapleton, Sorrell Booke; *D:* Robert Mulligan.

Up the Sandbox 1972 (R) A bored housewife fantasizes about her life in order to avoid facing her mundane existence. Fine acting from Streisand, with real problems of young mothers accurately shown. **98m/C VHS.** Barbra Streisand, David Selby, Jane Hoffman, Barbara Rhoades; *D:* Irvin Kershner; *C:* Gordon Willis; *M:* Billy Goldenberg.

Up to a Certain Point *Up to a Point; Hasta Cierto Punto* 1983 Writer Oscar believes he has a liberal attitude (to go along with Cuban political ideology) but his belief is shaken when he interviews workers on the Havana docks about their notions of machismo. Seems when Oscar falls for a sexy dockworker his ideas of maleness and a woman's place are more traditional than he imagines. Spanish with subtitles. **70m/C VHS.** *CU* Oscar Alvarez, Mirta Ibarra, Omar Valdes, Coralia Veloz, Rogelio Blain, Ana Vina; *D:* Tomas Gutierrez Alea; *W:* Tomas Gutierrez Alea; *M:* Leo Brower.

Up Your Alley 1989 (R) A female reporter, pursuing a story on homelessness, and a skidrow bum find romance. Langston, who produced and cowrote the film, is better known as "The Unknown Comic." **90m/C VHS.** Linda Blair, Murray Langston, Ruth Buzzi, Johnny Dark, Bob Zany, Yakov Smirnoff; *D:* Bob Logan.

Uphill All the Way 1985 A couple of card-cheatin' good old boys are pursued by posses and cavalry alike, and end up killing real outlaws. **91m/C VHS.** Roy Clark, Mel Tillis, Glen Campbell, Trish Van Devere, Burl Ives, Burt Reynolds; *D:* Frank Q. Dobbs. **TV**

Upper Crust ½ 1988 Boring tale of corruption and greed that takes place at the highest levels of American business and government. **95m/C VHS.** Frank Gorshin, Broderick Crawford, Nigel Davenport.

The Uprising 1981 A Nicaraguan drama filmed just months after the 1979 Sandinista revolution, wherein a young guard of Somoza retains his job for the money, while his father is active in the revolutionary forces. In Spanish with English subtitles. **96m/C VHS.** *SP* *D:* Peter Lilienthal.

Uprising 2001 Well-done, realistic miniseries depicts the Warsaw Ghetto uprising of 1943, when Polish Jews, facing deportation to death camps, held off the Nazis for a month using guerilla tactics. Solid script, which avoids melodrama and over-sentimentality, leaves room to show the politics and motivations involved between the people who wanted to negotiate with the Nazis, those who collaborated for self-preservation, and the fighters. Though the whole cast is up to the task, Sobieski's performance stands out, and Schwimmer makes a better showing here than he did in "Band of Brothers." **177m/C VHS, DVD, Wide.** Leelee Sobieski, Hank Azaria, David Schwimmer, Jon Voight, Donald Sutherland, Cary Elwes, Stephen Moyer, Sadie Frost, Radha Mitchell, Mili Avital, Alexandra Holden, John Ales, Eric Lively, Jesper Christensen; *D:* Jon Avnet; *W:* Jon Avnet, Paul Brickman; *C:* Denis Lenoir; *M:* Maurice Jarre. **TV**

Uptown Angel 1990 (R) A young woman is determined to work her way out of her home on the wrong side of town. Black cast brings new life to old premise. **90m/C VHS.** Caron Tate, Cliff McMullen, Gloria Davis Hill, Tracy Hill; *D:* Joy Shannon; *W:* Joy Shannon.

Uptown New York 1932 A young man pressured by his family marries a rich girl instead of the woman he loves, who in turn marries a man she does not love. Routine melodrama. **81m/B VHS.** Jack Oakie, Shirley Green, Leon Ames, Shirley Grey, George Cooper, Raymond Hatton; *D:* Victor Schertzinger.

Uptown Saturday Night ½ 1974 (PG) Two working men attempt to recover a stolen lottery ticket from the black underworld after being ripped off at an illegal gambling place. Good fun, with nice performances from both leads and from Belafonte doing a black "Godfather" parody of Brando. Followed by "Let's Do It Again." **104m/C VHS.** Sidney Poitier, Bill Cosby, Harry Belafonte, Flip Wilson, Richard Pryor, Calvin Lockhart; *D:* Sidney Poitier; *W:* Richard Wesley; *C:* Fred W. Koenekamp.

The Uranium Conspiracy ½ 1978 (PG) A secret agent and a mercenary soldier try to stop a shipment of uranium out of Zaire from falling into enemy hands. It won't be easy. **100m/C VHS.** Fabio Testi, Janet Agren, Assaf Dayan.

Uranus 1991 (R) After WWII a French provincial town has been liberated from Nazi invaders—but not its own suspicions, as citizens try to rebuild knowing some of them collaborated with the enemy. An important subject is heavily talked over in static fashion, with a robust Depardieu either a standout or a ham as the earthy saloon-keeper. Based on a novel by Marcel Ayme, himself accused of pro-Vichy leanings during the era. In French with English subtitles. **100m/C VHS.** *FR* Gerard Depardieu, Michel Blanc, Jean-Pierre Marielle, Philippe Noiret, Gerard Desarthe, Michel Galabru, Fabrice Luchini, Daniel Prevost; *D:* Claude Berri; *W:* Claude Berri; *M:* Jean-Claude Petit.

Urban Cowboy ½ 1980 (PG) A young Texas farmer comes to Houston to work in a refinery. After work he hangs out at Gilley's, a roadhouse bar. Here he and his friends, dressed in their cowboy gear, drink, fight, and prove their manhood by riding a mechanical bull. Film made Winger a star, was an up in Travolta's roller coaster career, and began the craze for country western apparel and dance and them there mechanical bulls. Ride 'em, cowboy! **135m/C VHS.** John Travolta, Debra Winger, Scott Glenn, Madolyn Smith, Barry Corbin; *D:* James Bridges; *W:* James Bridges, Aaron Latham; *C:* Reynaldo Villalobos; *M:* Ralph Burns.

Urban Crossfire ½ 1994 (PG-13) Two veteran white Brooklyn detectives investigating gang violence are aided by a young black patrolman whose partner was killed by a gang leader. Solid cast, fast paced action. **95m/C VHS.** Mario Van Peebles, Ray Sharkey, Peter Boyle, Michael Boatman; *D:* Dick Lowry.

Urban Legend 1998 (R) Another in the nudge-and-wink genre of horror movies. Screen scream alumni litter the screen in this ode to modern tall tales that may have actually happened to the friend of a cousin of a friend of yours. Natalie (Watt) is the standard good girl who doesn't know why her friends are getting knocked off, even though her folklore prof (Englund) is the guy who played Freddy Krueger, and the voice of Chucky the evil doll is now coming out of her gas station attendant (Dourif). The killer uses urban legends as the theme of his crimes, but he never makes anyone eat Pop Rocks then drink Pepsi. Characters are so irritating you'll cheer when they die. **100m/C VHS, DVD, Wide.** Alicia Witt, Jared Leto, Rebecca Gayheart, Loretta Devine, Joshua Jackson, Tara Reid, John Neville, Robert Englund, Brad Dourif, Natasha Gregson Wagner, Danielle Harris, Michael Rosenbaum; *D:* Jamie Blanks; *W:* Silvio Horta; *C:* James Chressanthis; *M:* Christopher Young.

Urban Legends 2: Final Cut ½ 2000 (R) This entry in the current trend of tongue-in-cheek slasher flicks proves that the genre is like its crazed killer characters. It refuses to die and is getting really ugly. Nearly abandoning the urban legend aspect of the original, the "movie within a movie" schtick is stolen from the "Scream" series as film students compete for the career-starting Hitchcock award at a prestigious film school. Amy (Morrison) decides to base her movie on urban legends after a chat with Reese (Devine), the only returning cast member of the original. Soon, fellow students and their projects get killed in development. Composer and film editor Ottman, making his directorial debut, seems more intent on giving movie cliches a slight twist and making film industry inside jokes than actually delivering a coherent plot. **94m/C VHS, DVD, Wide.** Jenny Morrison, Anthony Anderson, Joseph Lawrence, Matthew Davis, Hart Bochner, Loretta Devine, Marco Hofschneider, Eva Mendez, Michael Bacall, Anson Mount, Jessica Cauffiel, Chas Lawther; ***D:*** John Ottman; ***W:*** Paul Harris Boardman, Scott Derrickson; ***C:*** Brian Pearson; ***M:*** John Ottman.

Urban Menace 🦴🦴 **1999 (R)** Another "the future sucks" urban nightmare. A quarantined wasteland known as "The Downs" is the killing ground for a serial maniac. Two men, Harper and Crow, try to stop the mayhem and discover their murderer isn't even human. Features a hardcore rap and hip-hop soundtrack. **73m/C VHS, DVD.** Snoop Dogg, Big Pun, Ice-T, Fat Joe, T.J. Storm, Vincent Klyn, Romany Malco, Tahitia, Karen Dyer, Ernie Hudson; ***D:*** Albert Pyun; ***W:*** Tim Story; ***C:*** Philip Alan Waters. **VIDEO**

Urban Warriors 🦴 **1975** Savage barbarians roam and pillage a post-nuclear war Earth, but one invincible warrior ushers them out. **90m/C VHS.** Karl Landgren, Alex Vitale, Deborah Keith; ***D:*** Joseph Warren.

Urbania 🦴🦴 **2000 (R)** Urban legends and painful flashbacks are plentifully featured in this disturbing film that finds Charlie (Futterman) restlessly wandering the streets of New York in search of the handsome homophobic stranger (Ball) who turns out to be responsible for the death of Charlie's boyfriend Chris (Keeslar). Directorial debut of Shear; based on Daniel Reitz's play "Urban Folk Tales." **104m/C VHS, DVD, Wide.** Dan Futterman, Matt Keeslar, Josh Hamilton, Samuel Ball, William Sage, Megan Dodds, Alan Cumming, Lothaire Bluteau, Barbara Sukowa, Paige Turco, Gabriel Olds; ***D:*** Jon Shear; ***W:*** Daniel Reitz; ***C:*** Shane Kelly; ***M:*** Marc Anthony Thompson.

Urge to Kill 🦴 **1984 (PG)** A man returning from a mental hospital after pleading temporary insanity to the murder of his girlfriend returns to her town and tries to uncover the truth, with the help of her younger sister. **96m/C VHS.** Karl Malden, Holly Hunter, William Devane, Alex McArthur; ***D:*** Mike Robe. **TV**

Ursus in the Valley of the Lions 🦴½ *The Mighty Ursus; Ursus* **1962** Ursus attempts to rescue his love from druids but is dismayed to find that she has taken up homicide in her free time. **92m/C VHS.** *IT SP* Ed Fury, Luis Prendes, Moira Orfei, Cristina Gajoni, Maria Luisa Merlo; ***D:*** Carlo Campogalliani.

Used Cars 🦴🦴🦴 **1980 (R)** A car dealer is desperate to put his jalopy shop competitors out of business. The owners go to great lengths to stay afloat. Sometimes too obnoxious, but often funny. **113m/C VHS, DVD, 8mm, Wide.** Kurt Russell, Jack Warden, Deborah Harmon, Gerrit Graham, Joe Flaherty, Michael McKean, David Lander, Al Lewis, Wendie Jo Sperber, Dick Miller, Rita Taggart; ***D:*** Robert Zemeckis; ***W:*** Robert Zemeckis, Bob Gale; ***C:*** Donald M. Morgan; ***M:*** Patrick Williams.

Used People 🦴🦴½ **1992 (PG-13)** A study in ethnicity and characterization, three Oscar-winning actresses lead a talented cast playing a Jewish family living in Queens in 1969. When the father dies, Joe (Mastroianni), an old friend with an old torch for the widow, Pearl (MacLaine), shows up at the funeral and manages to charm her into a date for coffee. Pearl's new relationship with her Italian suitor affects each of the somewhat off-balance family members and washes the whole clan with a sense of hope and renewal. Adpated from screenwriter Graff's play "The Grandma Plays" that was based on memories of his grandmother. Director Kidron's American debut. **116m/C VHS, Wide.** Shirley MacLaine, Marcello Mastroianni, Kathy Bates, Marcia Gay Harden, Jessica Tandy, Sylvia Sidney, Bob (Robert) Dishy, Joe Pantoliano, Matthew Branton, Louis Guff, Charles Cioffi, Doris Roberts, Helen Hanft; ***D:*** Beeban Kidron; ***W:*** Todd Graff; ***M:*** Rachel Portman.

Users 🦴🦴 **1978** Small-town girl who worked as a prostitute meets a faded film star and becomes involved in the movie business. Ode to decadent Hollywood. Based on the Joyce Haber novel. **125m/C VHS.** Jaclyn Smith, Tony Curtis, John Forsythe, Red Buttons, George Hamilton; ***D:*** Joseph Hardy; ***M:*** Maurice Jarre. **TV**

The Usual Suspects 🦴🦴🦴½ **1995 (R)** Twisted noir-thriller about some crooks, a $91 million heist, and mysterious crime lord Keyser Soze. Customs agent Kujan (Palminteri) tries to get a straight story out of small-time con man "Verbal" Kint (Spacey) about a burning tanker in the San Pedro harbor, 27 dead bodies, and the other four tempermental criminals involved: ex-cop-turned thief Keaton (Byrne), explosives expert Hockney (Pollak), and hot-headed partners McManus (Baldwin) and Fenster (Del Toro). Nothing is as it seems, and the ending keeps everyone guessing, right up to the final credits. Terrific performances from all complement the intelligent, humorous script. And yes, the title does come from the famous line in "Casablanca." **105m/C VHS, DVD.** Louis Lombardi, Kevin Spacey, Gabriel Byrne, Chazz Palminteri, Kevin Pollak, Stephen Baldwin, Benicio Del Toro, Giancarlo Esposito, Pete Postlethwaite, Dan Hedaya, Suzy Amis, Paul Bartel, Peter Greene; ***D:*** Bryan Singer; ***W:*** Christopher McQuarrie; ***C:*** Newton Thomas (Tom) Sigel; ***M:*** John Ottman. Oscars '95: Orig. Screenplay, Support. Actor (Spacey); British Acad. '95: Orig. Screenplay; Ind. Spirit '96: Screenplay, Support. Actor (Del Toro); Natl. Bd. of Review '95: Support. Actor (Spacey); N.Y. Film Critics '95: Support. Actor (Spacey); Broadcast Film Critics '95: Support. Actor (Spacey).

Utah 🦴🦴 **1945** A musical comedy star who inherits a ranch wishes to sell it to finance one of her shows. She is persuaded not to by Rogers, the ranch foreman. **54m/B VHS.** Roy Rogers, Dale Evans, George "Gabby" Hayes; ***D:*** John English.

Utah Trail 🦴 **1938** Lawman Ritter is hired to stop a gang of cattle rustlers. Cheapie oater made for Grand National, which went bankrupt soon after. **57m/B VHS.** Tex Ritter; ***D:*** Al(bert) Herman.

Utamaro and His Five Women 🦴🦴½ *Five Women Around Utamaro; Utamaro O Meguru Gonin No Onna* **1946** Utamaro is a legendary 19th-century Edo artist who gained inspiration from Tokyo's "floating world," of courtesans, brothels, drinking parties, and violent passions. His gorgeous portraits worship women but he dislikes the complications that flesh-and-blood females bring. Heavily stylized look at the artistic impulse. In Japanese with English subtitles. **89m/B VHS.** *JP* Minnosuke Bando, Kinuyo Tanaka, Kotaro Bando, Hisato Osawa, Tamezo Mochizuki, Hiroko Kawasaki; ***D:*** Kenji Mizoguchi; ***W:*** Yoshikata Yoda; ***C:*** Shigeto Miki; ***M:*** Hisato Osawa, Tamezo Mochizuki.

Utilities 🦴½ *Getting Even* **1983 (PG)** A frustrated social worker enlists the help of his friends in his efforts to impress an attractive policewoman by taking on a large corporate utility. **94m/C VHS.** *CA* Robert Hays, Brooke Adams, John Marley, Ben Gordon, Helen Burns; ***D:*** Harvey Hart.

Utopia 🦴🦴 *Atoll K; Robinson Crusoeland; Escapade* **1951** Laurel and Hardy inherit a paradisaical island, but their peace is disturbed when uranium is discovered. Final screen appearance of the team is diminished by poor direction and script. **82m/B VHS, DVD.** *FR* Stan Laurel, Oliver Hardy, Suzy Delair, Max Elloy; ***D:*** Leo Joannon; ***W:*** Rene Wheeler, Piero Tellini; ***C:*** Louis Nee, Armand Thirard; ***M:*** Paul Misraki.

Utu 🦴🦴🦴 **1983 (R)** A Maori tribesman serving with the colonizing British army in 1870 explodes into ritual revenge when his home village is slaughtered. Filmed in New Zealand. **122m/C VHS, DVD, Wide.** *NZ* Anzac Wallace, Kelly Johnson, Tim Elliot, Bruno Lawrence; ***D:*** Geoff Murphy; ***W:*** Geoff Murphy, Keith Aberdein; ***C:*** Graeme Cowley; ***M:*** John Charles.

U2: Rattle and Hum 🦴🦴½ **1988 (PG-13)** Very-well-done concert/documentary, focusing on the Irish band U2 and their 1988 U.S. tour. Filmed in black-and-white and color. **90m/C VHS, DVD, Wide.** ***D:*** Phil Joanou; ***C:*** Robert Brinkmann, Jordan Cronenweth.

Utz 🦴🦴½ **1993** The Baron von Utz (Mueller-Stahl) collects both women and priceless porcelain figures. When his friend, art dealer Marius Fischer (Riegert), travels to Prague for a visit he finds that both Utz's housekeeper (Fricker), who has suffered from unrequited love, and the porcelain have disappeared. So Marius teams up with the Baron's old friend Dr. Orlick (Scofield) to find out what's going on. Based on the novel by Bruce Chatwin. **95m/C VHS.** *GB GE IT* Armin Mueller-Stahl, Peter Riegert, Brenda Fricker, Paul Scofield; ***D:*** George Sluizer.

V 🦴🦴🦴 **1983** Very creepy sci-fi miniseries that spawned a short-lived TV show. Advanced aliens, known as the Visitors, come to Earth on a seemingly friendly quest. But their human-like appearance is a facade—as is their mission. Fake skin masks a repitilian hide and what they want is complete planetary control. Naturally, some earthlings don't fall for their smooth talk and a resistance movement is born. Followed by miniseries conclusion "V: The Final Battle." **190m/C VHS, DVD, Wide.** Marc Singer, Jane Badler, Faye Grant, Robert Englund, Michael Durrell, Peter Nelson, Neva Patterson, Andrew Prine, Richard Herd, Rafael Campos; ***D:*** Kenneth Johnson; ***W:*** Kenneth Johnson. **TV**

V: The Final Battle 🦴🦴½ **1984** It's four-months since the Visitors appeared on earth, proclaiming their false friendship. But a resistance movement knows these reptiles, who hide behind a human appearance, are only interested in harvesting earth's inhabitants as a new food source. Continuation of the TV miniseries "V." **285m/C VHS.** Marc Singer, Robert Englund, Michael Ironside; ***D:*** Richard T. Heffron.

Va Savoir 🦴🦴½ *Who Knows?* **2001 (PG-13)** Romantic farce involving theatre folk. French actress Camille (Balibar) returns to Paris as the star of an Italian theatrical company. She's involved with company director Ugo (Castellitto) but sees her ex, Pierre (Bonaffre), who has a new girlfriend, Sonia (Basler). Meanwhile, Ugo is searching for a lost play by 18th-century writer Goldoni, aided by grad student Do (de Fougerolles) who gets a crush on him, despite her half-brother Arthur's (Todeschini) dislike of the situation. That everyone will interact in each other's lives is a given. French with subtitles. **154m/C VHS, DVD, Wide.** *FR IT GE* Jeanne Balibar, Sergio Castellitto, Jacques Bonnaffe, Marianne Basler, Helene de Fougerolles, Bruno Todeschini, Catherine Rouvel, Claude Berri; ***D:*** Jacques Rivette; ***W:*** Jacques Rivette, Christine Laurent, Pascal Bonitzer; ***C:*** William Lubtchansky.

Vacas 🦴🦴 *Cows* **1991** The political and social climate of the Basque region of Spain is frequently dangerous but the region's cows (the "vacas" of the title) placidly continue as always despite what happens to the humans around them. Covering more than 50 years, from 1875 through the Spanish Civil War, the lives of two families are interwined in emotional conflict through three generations. Spanish with subtitles. **96m/C VHS, DVD.** *SP* Carmelo Gomez, Ana Torrent, Emma Suarez, Pilar Bardem, Kandito Uranga; ***D:*** Julio Medem; ***W:*** Julio Medem, Michel Gaztambide; ***C:*** Carles Gusi; ***M:*** Alberto Iglesias.

The Vacillations of Poppy Carew 🦴🦴½ **1994** Free-spirited Poppy is just trying to make funeral arrangements for her father when she becomes involved in a series of unexpected and complicated romances. Based on a novel by Mary Wesley. **109m/C VHS.** *GB* Tara Fitzgerald, Sian Phillips, Charlotte Coleman, Samuel West, Edward Atterton, Joseph Fiennes, Daniel Massey; ***D:*** James Cellan Jones; ***W:*** William Humble; ***C:*** David Feig; ***M:*** Richard Holmes. **TV**

The Vagabond **1916** The Little Tramp is a pathetic fiddler making a scanty living who rescues a damsel in distress. Silent with musical soundtrack added. **20m/B VHS.** Charlie Chaplin, Edna Purviance, Eric Campbell, Albert Austin; ***D:*** Charlie Chaplin.

Vagabond 🦴🦴🦴½ *Sans Toit Ni Loi* **1985** Bleak, emotionally shattering, powerful and compelling, this film traces the peripatetic life of an amoral and selfish young French woman who has no regard for social rules and tremendous fear of responsibility in her drifting yet inexorable journey into death. Told via flashbacks from the moment when she is found dead, alone, and unaccounted for by the roadside, this film will not leave you unscathed. Written by New Wave director Varda. In French with English subtitles. **105m/C VHS, DVD.** *FR* Sandrine Bonnaire, Macha Meril, Stephane Freiss, Elaine Cortadellas, Marthe Jarnias, Yolanda Moreau; ***D:*** Agnes Varda; ***W:*** Agnes Varda; ***C:*** Patrick Blossier; ***M:*** Joanne Bruzdowicz. Cesar '86: Actress (Bonnaire); L.A. Film Critics '86: Actress (Bonnaire), Foreign Film.

Vagabond Lover 🦴🦴½ **1929** The amusing tale of the loves, hopes, and dreams of an aspiring saxophone player. Rudy croons through his megaphone in his movie debut. Appealing, with Dressler sparkling in the role of the wealthy aunt. ♫If You Were the Only Girl in the World; A Little Kiss Each Morning; Heigh Ho Everybody; Piccolo Pete; I Love You; I'll Be Reminded of You; I'm Just a Vagabond Lover. **66m/B VHS.** Rudy Vallee, Sally Blane, Marie Dressler; ***D:*** Marshall Neilan.

The Vagrant 🦴 **1992 (R)** Run-of-the-mill creeper with a mind-game playing derelict inhabiting the home of a young exec. A series of murders has this wimp yuppie wondering how to get rid of his unwelcome intruder. **91m/C VHS.** Bill Paxton, Michael Ironside, Marshall Bell, Stuart Pankin; ***D:*** Chris Walas.

Valdez Is Coming 🦴🦴½ **1971 (PG-13)** Though not a world-class western, this filmed-in-Spain saga does feature a probing script (based on an Elmore Leonard novel) on the nature of race relations. Fine performance by Lancaster as a Mexican-American who ignites the passions of a town, and ultimately confronts the local land baron. **90m/C VHS.** Burt Lancaster, Susan Clark, Jon Cypher, Barton Heyman, Richard Jordan, Frank Silvera, Hector Elizondo; ***D:*** Edwin Sherin; ***W:*** David Rayfiel; ***M:*** Charles Gross.

Valentine 🦴 **2001 (R)** Slasher film with a former nerd of a killer in a Cupid mask wreaking revenge upon the snooty girls who dissed him in junior high. After one victim's funeral, the remaining four get some threatening Valentines, which they, of course, promptly ignore. Boreanaz is among the doomed babes' boyfriends and a prime suspect. After yet another of the girls falls victim to the demented deity-wannabe, the remaining three grieve by throwing a bash at a swanky mansion with rambling vacant rooms that just scream, well, you get it. Eye-candy cast with mild suspense mix with dubious scripting. The only real victim here is your precious time. **96m/C VHS, DVD, Wide.** *US* David Boreanaz, Denise Richards, Marley Shelton, Jessica Capshaw, Katherine Heigl, Johnny Whitworth, Hedy Burress, Jessica Cauffiel, Fulvio Cecere, Daniel Cosgrove; ***D:*** Jamie Blanks; ***W:*** Donna Powers, Wayne Powers, Gretchen J. Berg, Aaron Harberts; ***C:*** Rick Bota; ***M:*** Don Davis.

Valentino 🦴🦴 **1977 (R)** Another one of director Russell's flamboyantly excessive screen biographies, this time of silent screen idol Rudolph Valentino (Nureyev). The details hardly matter but the movie is told in flashback from Valentino's funeral to his beginnings as a dance instructor and his eventual success as a screen lover. Nureyev is noticeably stiff in his screen debut but at least he possesses some charisma. **127m/C VHS.** *GB* Rudolf Nureyev, Leslie Caron, Michelle Phillips, Carol Kane, Felicity Kendal, Seymour Cassel, Peter Vaughan, William Hootkins, Huntz Hall, David DeKeyser, Alfred Marks, Anton Diffring; ***D:*** Ken Russell; ***W:*** Mardik Martin, Ken Russell, John Byrum; ***C:*** Peter Suschitzky; ***M:*** Ferde Grofe Jr.

Valentino Returns 🦴🦴 **1988 (R)** A kid in 1955 California buys a pink Cadillac he nicknames "Valentino Returns," thinking it will help him meet girls, as his parents undergo a stormy divorce. Weak script fades fast from fine premise, good start. Nice period feel. **97m/C VHS.** Frederic Forrest, Veronica Cartwright, Jenny Wright, Barry Tubb; ***D:*** Peter Hoffman.

Valley Girl 🦴🦴½ *Bad Boyz* **1983 (R)** Slight but surprisingly likeable teen romantic-comedy inspired by Frank Zappa novelty tune. Title stereotype falls for a leather-jacketed rebel. Really. It may look like a music video, but the story is straight from "Romeo and Juliet" via Southern California. Helped launch Cage's career. Music by Men at Work, Culture Club, and others. **95m/C VHS.** Nicolas Cage, Deborah Foreman, Colleen Camp, Frederic Forrest, Lee Purcell, Elizabeth (E.G. Dailey) Daily, Michael Bowen, Cameron Dye, Heidi Holicker, Michelle Meyrink; ***D:*** Martha Coolidge; ***W:*** Wayne Crawford, Andrew Lane; ***C:*** Frederick Elmes; ***M:*** Marc Levinthal, Scott Wilk.

The Valley Obscured by the Clouds 🦴🦴 *La Vallee* **1972** A group of dropouts and seekers search for the valley of the gods in the wilds of New Guinea, and experience a sexual and spiritual metamorphosis. In French with English subtitles. **106m/C VHS.** *FR* Bulle Ogier, Michael Gothard, Jean-Pierre Kalfon, Jerome Beauvarlet, Monique Giraudy; ***D:*** Barbet Schroeder; ***W:*** Barbet Schroeder; ***C:*** Nestor Almendros; ***M:*** Pink Floyd.

The Valley of Decision 🦴🦴🦴 **1945** Entertaining poor-girl-meets-rich-boy story with Peck as a wealthy mill owner who falls in love with beautiful housemaid Garson (the Queen of MGM at the time). Set in 1870 Pittsburgh; based on Marcia Davenport's novel. **111m/B VHS.** Gregory Peck, Greer Garson, Donald Crisp, Lionel Barrymore, Preston Foster, Gladys Cooper, Marsha Hunt, Reginald Owen, Dan Duryea, Jessica Tandy, Barbara Everest; ***D:*** Tay Garnett; ***W:*** John Meehan, Sonya Levien; ***C:*** Joseph Ruttenberg.

Valley of Fire 🦴🦴 **1951** Autry is the mayor of a boom town that suffers from a lack of women. He decides to import a caravan of brides for the men in town but villains attempt to kidnap the women. **63m/B VHS.** Gene Autry, Gail Davis, Pat Buttram; ***D:*** John English.

The Valley of Gwangi 🦴🦴🦴 **1969 (G)** One of the best prehistoric-monster-westerns out there. Cowboys discover a lost valley of dinosaurs and try to capture a vicious, carnivorous allosaurus. Bad move, kemosabe! The creatures move via the stop-motion model animation by f/x maestro Ray Harryhausen, here at his finest. **95m/C VHS.** James Franciscus, Gila Golan, Richard Carlson, Laurence Naismith, Freda Jackson, Gustavo Rojo, Dennis Kilbane, Mario De Barros, Curtis Arden, Jose Burgos; ***D:*** James O'Connolly; ***W:*** William Bast, Julian More; ***C:*** Erwin Hillier; ***M:*** Jerome Moross.

Valley of Terror 🦴½ **1938** Maynard is framed for cattle rustling. Can he prove his innocence? **59m/B VHS.** Kermit Maynard, Harley Wood, John Merton, Jack Ingram, Dick Curtis, Roger Williams; ***D:*** Al(bert) Herman.

Valley of the Dolls 🦴🦴 **1967 (PG)** Camp/trash classic was rated as a bomb by many critics but is really of the so-bad-it's-good variety. Three beauties, Jennifer (Tate), Neely (Duke), and Anne (Parkins), dream of Hollywood stardom but fall victim to Hollywood excess, including drug dependency (the "dolls" of the title). There's unhappy love affairs, porno parts, health risks, and hysterics of various kinds—all designed to have you dropping your jaw in disbelief. The bathroom scene between Duke and Hayward involving a wig is not to be missed. Based on the novel by Jacqueline Susann who has a bit part as a reporter. Remade for TV as "Jacqueline Susann's Valley of the Dolls" in 1981. **123m/C VHS.** Barbara Parkins, Patty Duke, Sharon Tate, Paul Burke, Tony Scotti, Martin Milner, Susan Hayward, Charles Drake, Lee Grant, Alex Davion, Robert Harris, Robert Viharo, Joey Bishop, George Jessel, Richard Dreyfuss; ***Cameos:*** Jacqueline Susann; ***D:*** Mark Robson; ***W:*** Dorothy Kingsley, Helen Deutsch, Jacqueline Susann; ***C:*** William H. Daniels; ***M:*** John Williams.

Valley of the Eagles 🦴½ **1951** When his wife and partner take off into the Lapland wilderness with his new invention, a scientist leads the police across the tundra in pursuit. Setting is at least a plus. **83m/B VHS.** *GB* Jack Warner, Nadia Gray, John McCallum, Martin Boddey, Christopher Lee; ***D:*** Terence Young; ***M:*** Nino Rota.

Valley of the Kings 🦴🦴½ **1954** Corny big dig movie that does have some nice Egyptian scenery. Archeologist Mark Brandon (Taylor) is searching for the treasure of pharoah Ra-Hotep in 1900's Egypt. Ann (Parker) would like to prove that several Bible stories are, in fact, true while her husband Philip (Thompson) is supposed to be helping Mark but is only out for himself. Although he does seem a little upset when Mark and Ann begin making goo-goo eyes at each other. **86m/C VHS.** Robert Taylor, Eleanor Parker, Kurt Kasznar, Carlos Thompson, Victor Jory, Leon Askin, Aldo Silvani; ***D:*** Robert Pirosh; ***W:*** Robert Pirosh, Karl Tunberg; ***C:*** Robert L. Surtees; ***M:*** Miklos Rozsa.

Valley of the Lawless 🦴 **1936** A cowboy rides into trouble aplenty while out searching for treasure. A routine western for Brown fans only. **59m/B VHS.** Johnny Mack Brown; ***D:*** Robert North Bradbury; ***W:*** Robert North Bradbury.

Valley of the Sun 🦴🦴🦴 **1942** A government agent tracks a crooked Indian liaison to prevent an Indian uprising in Arizona. Ball, well before her "Lucy" days, plays the restaurant owner both men romance. Better than average, with good cast, some laughs, and lots of excitement. **84m/B VHS.** Lucille Ball, James Craig, Cedric Hardwicke, Dean Jagger, Peter Whitney, Billy Gilbert, Tom Tyler, Antonio Moreno, George Cleveland, Hank Bell; ***D:*** George Marshall.

Valley of Wanted Men 🦴½ **1935** Three cons escape during a jailbreak and one uses his wits and nerve to prove another was framed. **56m/B VHS, 8mm.** Frankie Darro.

Valmont 🦴🦴🦴 **1989 (R)** Another adaptation of the Choderlos de Laclos novel "Les Liaisons Dangereuses." Various members of the French aristocracy in 1782 mercilessly play each other for fools in a complex game of lust and deception. Firth and Bening are at first playfully sensual, then the stakes get too high. They share an interesting bathtub scene. Well-acted, the 1988 Frears version, "Dangerous Liaisons," is edgier. Seeing the two films together makes for interesting comparisons of characters and styles. **137m/C VHS.** Colin Firth, Meg Tilly, Annette Bening, Fairuza Balk, Sian Phillips, Jeffrey Jones, Fabia Drake, Henry Thomas, Vincent Schiavelli, T.P. McKenna, Ian McNeice; ***D:*** Milos Forman; ***W:*** Jean-Claude Carriere; ***M:*** Christopher Palmer. Cesar '90: Art Dir./Set Dec., Costume Des.

The Vals 🦴½ **1985 (R)** The glibly hip lethargy which is characteristic of four southern California teenaged girls turns to socially conscious resolve when a local orphanage is threatened. Like, for sure. **100m/C VHS.** Jill Carroll, Elana Stratheros, Gina Calabrese, Michelle Laurita, Chuck Connors, Sonny Bono, John Carradine, Michael Leon; ***D:*** James Polakof.

Vamp 🦴½ **1986 (R)** Two college freshmen encounter a slew of weird, semi-vampiric people in a seamy red-light district nightclub. Starts cute but goes kinky. Jones is great as the stripping vampire. **93m/C VHS, DVD, Wide.** Grace Jones, Chris Makepeace, Robert Rusler, Gedde Watanabe, Sandy Baron, Dedee Pfeiffer, Billy Drago, Lisa Lyons; ***D:*** Richard Wenk; ***W:*** Richard Wenk; ***C:*** Elliot Davis; ***M:*** Jonathan Elias.

Vamping 🦴½ **1984 (PG)** Struggling musician plans to burglarize a wealthy widow's home. Once inside, he finds himself attracted to his proposed victim. Tedious going. **110m/C VHS.** Patrick Duffy, Catherine Hyland, Rod Arrants, Fred A. Keller; ***D:*** Frederick King Keller.

The Vampire 🦴🦴 *Mark of the Vampire* **1957** Pale man with big teeth attempts to swindle a beautiful babe out of fortune. Followed by "The Vampire's Coffin." **95m/B VHS.** *MX* Abel Salazar, Ariadne Welter, German Robles, Carmen Montejo, Jose Luis Jimenez; ***D:*** Fernando Mendez.

Vampire at Midnight 🦴½ **1988** Fairly stupid homicide detective stalks a rampaging vampire in Los Angeles. Occasional moments of gratuitous sex thrown in for good measure. **93m/C VHS.** Jason Williams, Gustav Vintas, Jeanie Moore, Christina Whitaker, Leslie Milne; ***D:*** Gregory McClatchy.

The Vampire Bat 🦴🦴½ **1932** A mad scientist and a vampire bat and its supernatural demands set the stage for murders in a small town. Sets and actors borrowed from Universal Studios in this low-budget flick that looks and plays better than it should. Weird and very exploitative for 1932, now seems dated. **69m/B VHS, DVD.** Lionel Atwill, Fay Wray, Melvyn Douglas, Dwight Frye, Maude Eburne, George E. Stone; ***D:*** Frank Strayer; ***W:*** Edward T. Lowe; ***C:*** Ira Morgan.

Vampire Centerfolds 🦴🦴 **1998** Innocent college cheerleader (Williamson) seeks to try out her thespian skills when she's cast in a cult film about vampiric bloodlust. Then she discovers that the models and actresses involved are a secret coven of sex obsessed vamps! **125m/C VHS.** Elaine Juliette Williamson, Jasmine Jean, Tonya Qualls, Joan A. Teeter; ***D:*** Geoffrey de Valois. **VIDEO**

Vampire Circus 🦴🦴½ **1971 (R)** A circus appears in an isolated Serbian village in the 19th century but instead of bringing joy and happiness, this circus brings only death, mutilation and misery. It seems all the members are vampires who have the unique ability to transform themselves into animals. They intend to take revenge on the small town, whose inhabitants killed their evil ancestor 100 years previously. Excellent Hammer production. **84m/C** *GB* Adrienne Corri, Laurence Payne, Thorley Walters, John Moulder-Brown, Lynne Frederick, Elizabeth Seal, Anthony (Corlan) Higgins, Richard Owens, Domini Blythe, David Prowse; ***D:*** Robert W. Young; ***W:*** Judson Kinberg; ***C:*** Moray Grant.

Vampire Conspiracy 🦴🦴 **1996** Lisa Kirkpatrick and her sorority sister must prevent a fanatical vampires plot to repopulate the earth with brainwashed mutants. But they also have to overcome their own bloodlust to prevent the conspiracy. An adult erotic dark comedy. **90m/C VHS.** Heather LeMire, Floyd Irons, Jasmine Jean, Tonya Qualls, Joan A. Teeter; ***D:*** Geoffrey de Valois. **VIDEO**

Vampire Cop 🦴½ **1990 (R)** A vampire cop (not to be confused with zombie, maniac, midnight, psycho, future or Robo) teams up with a beautiful reporter to 'collar' a drug kingpin. **89m/C VHS.** Melissa Moore, Ed Cannon, Terence Jenkins; ***D:*** Donald Farmer.

The Vampire Happening 🦴½ **1971 (R)** An actress travels to Translyvania to sell the family castle and discovers to her chagrin that her ancestors were vampires after she unknowingly releases them to party hearty on the local villagers. **101m/C VHS, DVD, Wide.** *GE* Ferdinand "Ferdy" Mayne, Pia Degermark, Thomas Hunter, Yvor Murillo, Ingrid van Bergen, Raul Retzer; ***D:*** Freddie Francis; ***W:*** Karl Heinz Hummel, August Rieger; ***C:*** Gerard Vandenburg; ***M:*** Jerry Van Rooyen.

The Vampire Hookers 🦴 *Cemetery Girls; Sensuous Vampires; Night of the Bloodsuckers; Twice Bitten* **1978 (R)** Man in makeup recruits bevy of beautiful bloodsuckers to lure warm blooded victims to his castle. High ham performance by Carradine. **82m/C VHS.** *PH* John Carradine, Bruce Fairbairn, Trey Wilson, Karen Stride, Lenka Novak, Katie Dolan, Lex Winter; ***D:*** Cirio H. Santiago.

Vampire in Brooklyn 🦴 **1995 (R)** Murphy switches gears to play a Carribean vampire traveling to New York in search of his vampiric lady love—who turns out to be half-vamp-half-cop Bassett. As in "Coming to America," Murphy plays multiple characters, but that's three times the disappointment. Stale humor and cheap horror effects do little to break the zombie curse plaguing Murphy's career. Three days into filming, a stunt double for Bassett was killed after doing a routine jump on the set, providing a bad omen Murphy should have heeded. **103m/C VHS, DVD, Wide.** Eddie Murphy, Angela Bassett, Kadeem Hardison, Allen Payne, Zakes Mokae, John Witherspoon; ***D:*** Wes Craven; ***W:*** Charles Murphy, Christopher Parker, Michael Lucker; ***C:*** Mark Irwin; ***M:*** J. Peter Robinson.

Vampire Journals 🦴🦴½ **1996 (R)** Revenge-minded Zachary (Gunn) vows to destroy Ash (Morris), the ancient vampire who created him centuries before, especially when they both become interested in the same mortal woman, Sofia (Cerre). Shot on location in Transylvania. **82m/C VHS, DVD.** David Gunn, Jonathan Morris, Kirsten Cerre, Starr Andreeff; ***D:*** Ted Nicolaou; ***W:*** Ted Nicolaou; ***C:*** Adolfo Bartoli; ***M:*** Richard Kosinski.

The Vampire Lovers 🦴🦴½ **1970 (R)** An angry father goes after a lesbian vampire who has ravished his daughter and other young girls in a peaceful European village. Innovative story was soon used in countless other vampire vehicles. Hammer Studio's first horror film with nudity, another addition to the genre which spread rapidly. Based on the story "Carmilla" by Sheridan Le Fanu. Followed by "Lust for a Vampire." **91m/C VHS.** *GB* Ingrid Pitt, Pippa Steele, Madeleine Smith, Peter Cushing, George Cole, Dawn Addams, Kate O'Mara, Ferdinand "Ferdy" Mayne, Douglas Wilmer, Harvey Hall; ***D:*** Roy Ward Baker; ***W:*** Tudor Gates; ***C:*** Moray Grant.

The Vampire People 🦴½ *The Blood Drinkers* **1966 (PG)** A dwarf-assisted vampire attempts to save the life of his true love by transplanting her sister's heart. Typical Filipino vampire movie. In color and sepia-tone. **79m/C VHS.** *PH* Ronald Remy, Amalia Fuentes, Eddie Fernandez, Eva Montez; ***D:*** Gerardo (Gerry) De Leon.

Vampire Raiders—Ninja Queen woof! **1989** The white ninjas versus the black ninjas. The evil black ninjas are plotting to infiltrate the hotel industry. The white ninjas come to the rescue. **90m/C VHS.** Agnes Chan, Chris Petersen; ***D:*** Bruce Lambert.

Vampire Vixens from Venus 🦴 **1994** Three hideous drug smuggling aliens transform themselves into bodacious babes on earth so they can get what they came for. Seems their drug fix is derived from the life essence of men and they plan to drain every last drop they can. **90m/C VHS.** Michelle (McClellan) Bauer, Charlie Callas.

Vampirella 🦴½ *Roger Corman Presents: Vampirella* **1996 (R)** Inhabitants of the planet Drakulon use a synthetic concoction to quench their thirst for blood. When Vampirella's (Soto) stepfather is murdered by rebels, led by Vlad Tepes (Daltrey), she must pursue them to earth to get justice. There she finds two opposing forces—the vampires led by Tepes and a paramilitary group led by Adam Van Helsing (Paul), who's out to cleanse the planet of the interlopers. But it's Vampirella who wants a final confrontation with Tepes (in Las Vegas, no less). **90m/C VHS.** Talisa Soto, Roger Daltrey, Richard Joseph Paul, Angus Scrimm, Tom Deters, Cimna Harney, Brian Bloom; ***D:*** Jim Wynorski; ***W:*** Gary Gerani; ***C:*** Andrea V. Rossotto; ***M:*** Joel Goldsmith. **CABLE**

The Vampire's Coffin 🦴½ *El Ataud Del Vampiro; El Ataud Del Coffin* **1958** Count Lavud is relieved when faithful servant removes stake implanted in his heart. **86m/B VHS.** *MX* Abel Salazar, Ariadne Welter, German Robles; ***D:*** Fernando Mendez.

The Vampire's Ghost 🦴 **1945** A 400-hundred-year-old vampire/zombie, doomed to walk the earth forever, heads the African underworld. He can't be killed and can even go out during the day if he wears sunglasses. His future's so bright he's just gotta wear shades. **59m/B VHS.** John Abbott, Peggy Stewart; ***D:*** Lesley Selander.

Vampire's Kiss 🦴🦴🦴 **1988 (R)** Cage makes this one worthwhile; his twisted transformation from pretentious postval dude to psychotic yuppie from hell is inspired. If his demented torment of his secretary (Alonso) doesn't give you the creeps, his scene with the cockroach will. Cage fans will enjoy his facial aerobics; Beals fans will appreciate her extensive sucking scenes (she's the vamp of his dreams). More for psych majors than horror buffs. **103m/C VHS.** Nicolas Cage, Elizabeth Ashley, Jennifer Beals, Maria Conchita Alonso, Kasi Lemmons, Bob Lujan, David Hyde Pierce; ***D:*** Robert Bierman; ***W:*** Joe Minion; ***C:*** Stefan Czapsky; ***M:*** Colin Towns, Jessica Lundy.

Vampires of Sorority Row: Kickboxers From Hell 🦴 **1999** Trailer-trash princess Cindy (Glass) goes to college and pledges a sorority, only to find domineering pledge mistress Denise (Lydon) and a gaggle of vampires causing a commotion. T&A competes with kickboxing action and self-mocking humor (that really works!) for viewers' attention spans. You could do worse on a Saturday night when "Gandhi" is rented and you need a laugh. **80m/C VHS.** Christine Lydon, Rich Ward, Kathryn Glass, Rita Fiora, Erika Gardener, Christian Caitlin, Angelica Hayden; ***D:*** Dennis Devine, Kathryn Glass; ***W:*** Dennis Devine; ***M:*** Jonathan Price.

Vampyr 𝒮𝒮𝒮𝒮 *Vampyr, Ou l'Etrange Aventure de David Gray; Vampyr, Der Traum des David Gray; Not against the Flesh; Castle of Doom; The Strange Adventure of David Gray; The Vampire* **1931** Dreyer's classic portrays a hazy, dreamlike world full of chilling visions from the point of view of a young man who believes himself surrounded by vampires and who dreams of his own burial in a most disturbing way. Evil lurks around every corner as camera angles, light and shadow sometimes overwhelm plot. A high point in horror films based on a collection of horror stories by Sheridan Le Fanu. In German with English subtitles. **75m/B VHS, DVD.** *GE FR* Julian West, Sybille Schmitz, Henriette Gerard, Maurice Schutz, Rena Mandel, Jan Hieronimko, Albert Bras; ***D:*** Carl Theodor Dreyer; ***W:*** Carl Theodor Dreyer, Christen Jul; ***C:*** Rudolph Mate, Louis Nee; ***M:*** Wolfgang Zeller.

The Vampyr 𝒮𝒮 **1992** Uncut version of the BBC musical production about a lustful vampire. Text sets present-day lyrics to the 1827 opera by Heinrich Marschner. Vampire Ripley (Ebrahim) has just been set free in London after having been trapped in an underground tomb for 200 years. Unless he puts the bite on three lovely ladies within three days he will be condemned to eternal damnation. Everyone gets to sing in the nude. Surreally amusing. **115m/C VHS.** *GB* Omar Ebrahim, Willemijn Van Gent, Fiona O'Neill, Sally-Ann Shepherdson.

Vampyres 𝒮𝒮½ *Vampyres, Daughters of Dracula; Blood Hunger; Satan's Daughters; Daughters of Dracula; Vampire Orgy* **1974 (R)** Alluring female vampires coerce unsuspecting motorists to their castle for a good time, which ends in death. Anulka was the centerfold girl in "Playboy"'s May 1973 issue. **90m/C VHS, DVD, Wide.** *GB* Marianne Morris, Anulka, Murray Brown, Brian Deacon, Sally Faulkner, Michael Byrne, Karl Lanchbury, Bessie Love, Elliott Sullivan; ***D:*** Joseph (Jose Ramon) Larraz; ***W:*** Diane Daubeney; ***C:*** Harry Waxman; ***M:*** James Clark.

The Van 𝒮 *Chevy Van* **1977 (R)** A recent high school graduate passes on the college scene so he can spend more time picking up girls in his van. A lame sex (and sexist) comedy. **92m/C VHS, DVD.** Stuart Getz, Deborah White, Danny DeVito, Harry Moses, Maurice Barkin; ***D:*** Sam Grossman; ***W:*** Robert J. Rosenthal, Celia Susan Cotelo; ***C:*** Irv Goodnoff; ***M:*** Steve Eaton.

The Van 𝒮𝒮𝒮 **1995 (R)** The last of writer Roddy Doyle's Barrytown trilogy (following "The Commitments" and "The Snapper") is set in 1989-90, in Dublin, where baker Bimbo (O'Kelly) has just lost his job. Tired of sitting around the pub, he takes his redundancy money and buys a filthy, dilapidated fish 'n' chips van, which he decides to run with best friend Larry (Meany), with their families helping out. The months pass quickly and their venture turns out to be a big success but the close quarters puts a strain on the mens' friendship until Bimbo has another idea. **105m/C VHS, DVD.** *GB* Donal O'Kelly, Colm Meaney, Ger Ryan, Caroline Rotwell, Neili Conroy, Ruaidhri Conroy; ***D:*** Stephen Frears; ***W:*** Roddy Doyle; ***C:*** Oliver Stapleton; ***M:*** Eric Clapton, Richard Hartley.

Van Gogh 𝒮𝒮𝒮 **1992 (R)** "One doesn't produce 100 masterpieces in a state of depression—Van Gogh died from having had a glimpse of happiness." This is the way director Pialat sums up his approach to the last 67 days in the life of Vincent Van Gogh. Dutronc is skillful in portraying Van Gogh as a man with no excuses, and even a sense of humor. Not a psychological portrait and offers no answers—it's simply one artist's view of another. In French with English subtitles. **155m/C VHS.** *FR* Jacques Dutronc, Alexandra London, Gerard Sety, Bernard Le Coq, Corinne Bourdon; ***D:*** Maurice Pialat; ***W:*** Maurice Pialat; ***C:*** Gilles Henry, Emmanuel Machuel; ***M:*** Edith Vesperini. Cesar '92: Actor (Dutronc).

Van Nuys Blvd. 𝒮½ **1979 (R)** The popular boulevard is the scene where the cool southern California guys converge for cruising and girl watching, so naturally it's where a country hick comes to test his drag racing skills and check out the action. **93m/C VHS.** Bill Adler, Cynthia Wood, Dennis Bowen, Melissa Prophet; ***D:*** William Sachs.

Vanilla Sky 𝒮𝒮½ **2001 (R)** Director Crowe goes existential in this puzzling, surreal thriller, a remake of Alejandro Amenabar's 1997 Spanish film, "Abre los Ojos." Cruise plays David Aames, a publishing magnate and playboy who's got it all except for real love. Just when he thinks he's found it in the form of aspiring dancer Sofia (Cruz, reprising her role from the original), a bitter ex-lover (Diaz) changes the game by inadvertently changing David's pretty face. Fairly straightforward allegory becomes science fiction, where David (and the audience) can't tell dream from reality. Thought-provoking, even deliberately confusing plot may frustrate some. But for those who like to sink their brains into a film, it'll will be rewarding, whether you like the explain-it-all ending or not. Decent acting, dreamy cinematography, and an engaging soundtrack will provide entertainment at the very least. **135m/C VHS, DVD, Wide.** *US* Tom Cruise, Penelope Cruz, Cameron Diaz, Jason Lee, Kurt Russell, Noah Taylor, Timothy Spall, Tilda Swinton, Alicia Witt, Johnny Galecki, Michael Shannon; ***D:*** Cameron Crowe; ***W:*** Cameron Crowe; ***C:*** John Toll; ***M:*** Nancy Wilson.

Vanina Vanini 𝒮𝒮𝒮½ **1961** An acclaimed Rossellini historical drama about the daughter of an Italian aristocrat in 1824 who nurses and falls in love with a wounded patriot hiding in her house. Based on a Stendhal short story. In Italian with English subtitles. **113m/B VHS.** *IT* Sandra Milo, Laurent Terzieff; ***D:*** Roberto Rossellini.

The Vanishing 𝒮𝒮𝒮 *Spoorloos* **1988** When his wife suddenly disappears, a young husband finds himself becoming increasingly obsessed with finding her. Three years down the road, his world has become one big, mad nightmare. Then, just as suddenly, the answer confronts him, but the reality of it may be too horrible to face. Well-made dark thriller based on "The Golden Egg" by Tim Krabbe. In French and Dutch with English subtitles. Remade by Sluizer in 1992. **107m/C VHS, DVD, Wide.** *NL FR* Barnard Pierre Donnadieu, Johanna Ter Steege, Gene Bervoets, Gwen Eckhaus, Bernadette Le Sache, Tania Latarjet, Lucille Glenn, Roger Souza; ***D:*** George Sluizer; ***W:*** George Sluizer, Tim Krabbe; ***C:*** Toni Kuhn; ***M:*** Henry Vrienten.

The Vanishing 𝒮𝒮½ **1993 (R)** Director Sluizer remakes his own 1988 Dutch film "Spoorloos" to lesser effect. Tense thriller about the disappearance of a woman (Bullock) at a highway rest stop. Her boyfriend (Sutherland) becomes obsessed with locating her, searching for some three years as he is haunted by her memory. Unlike the Dutch original, the remake resorts to a clumsy ending designed for feel-good appeal. Based on the novel "The Golden Egg" by Tim Krabbe. **110m/C VHS, DVD.** Jeff Bridges, Kiefer Sutherland, Nancy Travis, Sandra Bullock, Park Overall, Lisa Eichhorn, George Hearn, Maggie Linderman, Lynn Hamilton; ***D:*** George Sluizer; ***W:*** Todd Graff; ***M:*** Jerry Goldsmith.

Vanishing Act 𝒮𝒮½ **1988 (PG)** While on his honeymoon, Harry Kenyon reports his wife missing to the local police. Within a short period of time his wife is found, but Harry says the woman is an impostor. This thriller follows Harry's desperate attempt to get to the truth. **94m/C VHS.** Mike Farrell, Margot Kidder, Elliott Gould, Fred Gwynne, Graham Jarvis; ***D:*** David Greene; ***W:*** Richard Levinson, William Link. **TV**

The Vanishing American 𝒮𝒮 **1925** The mistreatment of the American Indian is depicted in this sweeping Western epic that stars Dix as Navajo chieftain Nophaie. Nophaie must reconcile the heritage of his people with the 20th century and deal with a crooked government agent. Filmed in Monument Valley and the Betatkin Cliff Dwellings of Arizona. Based on the novel by Zane Grey. **109m/B VHS, DVD.** Richard Dix, Noah Beery Sr., Lois Wilson; ***D:*** George B. Seitz; ***W:*** Lucien Hubbard, Ethel Doherty; ***C:*** Harry Perry, Charles E. Schoenbaum.

Vanishing Legion **1931** Western serial with outdoor action and gunplay. Twelve chapters, 13 minutes each. **156m/B VHS.** Frankie Darro, Harry Carey Sr.; ***D:*** B. Reeves Eason.

Vanishing Point 𝒮𝒮 **1971 (R)** An ex-racer makes a bet to deliver a souped-up car from Denver to San Francisco in 15 hours. Taking pep pills along the way, he eludes police, meets up with a number of characters, and finally crashes into a roadblock. Rock score helps attract this film's cult following. **98m/C VHS.** Barry Newman, Cleavon Little, Gilda Texter, Dean Jagger, Paul Koslo, Robert Donner, Severn Darden, Victoria Medlin; ***D:*** Richard Sarafian; ***W:*** Guillermo Cain; ***C:*** John A. Alonzo; ***M:*** Jim Bowen, Peter Carpenter.

The Vanishing Westerner 𝒮𝒮 **1950** A cowboy, falsely accused of murder, works to vindicate himself and uncovers a series of robberies. This one has enough plot twists to take it out of the routine. **60m/B VHS.** Monte Hale, Arthur Space, Aline Towne, Paul Hurst, Roy Barcroft, Richard Anderson, William Phipps, Rand Brooks; ***D:*** Philip Ford.

Vanity Fair 𝒮𝒮 **1932** Loy stars in this tale of a wily and manipulative woman looking for the perfect marriage. This was the 58th film for the 27-year-old Loy, but even she couldn't save it. Of course, none of the three films based on the story by Thackeray have done it justice. **67m/B VHS.** Myrna Loy, Conway Tearle, Barbara Kent, Walter Byron, Anthony Bushell, Billy Bevan, Montagu Love, Mary Forbes; ***D:*** Chester M. Franklin.

Vanity Fair 𝒮𝒮½ **1967** BBC TV adaptation of William Makepeace Thackeray's satire on human folly in 19th-century England. Amoral governess (and anti-heroine) Becky Sharp (Hampshire) will stop at nothing to climb the social ladder, aided by a wealthy marriage and her own audacity, which ultimately leads to scandal. **250m/C VHS.** *GB* Susan Hampshire, Robert Flemyng, Richard Caldicot, Barbara Couper, Roy Marsden, Bryan Marshall; ***D:*** David Giles. **TV**

Vanity Fair 𝒮𝒮½ **1999** Orphaned Becky Sharp (Little) is beautiful, clever and, despite her poverty, determined to get ahead in society so she can enjoy the same privileges as her posh childhood friend, Amelia Sedley (Grey). And she's not too particular about how she stakes her claim. Based on the novel by William Makepeace Thackeray, this Brit miniseries loses the author's acerbic voice which makes for a bland, though typically lavish, production. **300m/C VHS.** Natasha Little, Frances Grey, Nathaniel Parker, Philip Glenister, Jeremy Swift, Roger Ashton-Griffiths, Eleanor Bron, Anton Lesser, Miriam Margolyes, Michele Dotrice, David Bradley; ***D:*** Marc Munden; ***W:*** Andrew Davies; ***C:*** Oliver Curtis. **TV**

Vanya on 42nd Street 𝒮𝒮𝒮½ **1994 (PG)** Group of actors in street clothes rehearse a workshop production of Chekhov's play, "Uncle Vanya," in New York's dilapidated New Amsterdam Theater. Theatrical director Gregory first gets his group together in 1989, with Mamet's contemporary adaptation, and they continue to work in private until Malle films their production some four years later before a small, select audience. Shawn, best known for "My Dinner with Andre" portrays Vanya with depth and complexity. The other actors shine as well, often against type, in this complex Russian drama of desperation. **119m/C VHS.** Wallace Shawn, Julianne Moore, Brooke Smith, Larry Pine, George Gaynes, Lynn Cohen, Madhur Jaffrey, Phoebe Brand, Jerry Mayer, Andre Gregory; ***D:*** Louis Malle; ***W:*** Andre Gregory, David Mamet; ***C:*** Declan Quinn; ***M:*** Joshua Redman.

Varan the Unbelievable 𝒮 *Daikaiju Baran; The Monster Baran* **1961** A chemical experiment near a small island in the Japanese archipelago disturbs a prehistoric monster beneath the water. The awakened monster spreads terror on the island. Most difficult part of this movie is deciding what the rubber monster model is supposed to represent. **70m/B VHS.** *JP* Myron Healey, Tsuruko Kobayashi; ***D:*** Inoshiro Honda.

Varian's War 𝒮𝒮½ **2001** Based on the true story of American Varian Fry (Hurt), who is the editor of a foreign affairs publication when he witnesses the Nazi rise in Berlin and decides he must help Europe's Jews despite American neutrality. He heads off to Marseilles where a number of artists and intellectuals wait to escape Vichy France and establishes an underground rescue organization. **120m/C VHS, DVD.** William Hurt, Julia Ormond, Matt Craven, Maury Chaykin, Alan Arkin, Lynn Redgrave, Remy Girard, Chris Heyerdahl, Vlasta Vrana, Gloria Carlin, John Dunn-Hill; ***D:*** Lionel Chetwynd; ***W:*** Lionel Chetwynd; ***C:*** Daniel Jobin; ***M:*** Neil Smolar. **CABLE**

Variety 𝒮𝒮𝒮𝒮 *Vaudeville; Variete* **1925** Simple and tragic tale of a scheming young girl and the two men of whom she takes advantage. The European circus in all its beautiful sadness is the setting. Extraordinary cast and superb cinematography. Silent. **104m/B VHS, DVD.** *GE* Emil Jannings, Lya de Putti, Warwick Ward, Werner Krauss; ***D:*** E.A. Dupont; ***W:*** E.A. Dupont; ***C:*** Karl Freund.

Variety 𝒮½ **1983** Christine (McLeod) gets a job selling tickets at a porno theatre near Times Square and starts getting curious about the milieu. Her relationships begin to change as her interest in pornography becomes all-consuming. **97m/C VHS.** Sandy McLeod, Will Patton, Richard Davidson; ***D:*** Bette Gordon; ***W:*** Kathy Acker; ***C:*** Tom DiCillo; ***M:*** John Lurie.

Variety Girl 𝒮𝒮½ **1947** More than 55 Paramount stars appear in this salute to the Variety Club charitable organization, so the plot is the least important element. Catherine (Hatcher) and Amber (San Juan) have both made their way to Hollywood with stars in their eyes and eventually find themselves on the studio lot. Your basic extravaganza-type show, benefitting the charity, concludes the picture. **93m/B VHS.** Mary Hatcher, Olga San Juan, DeForest Kelley; ***D:*** George Marshall; ***W:*** Edmund Hartmann, Frank Tashlin, Monte Brice, Robert L. Welch; ***C:*** Lionel Lindon, Stuart Thompson.

Variety Lights 𝒮𝒮𝒮½ *Luci del Varieta; Lights of Variety* **1951** Fellini's first (albeit joint) directorial effort, wherein a young girl runs away with a travelling vaudeville troupe and soon becomes its main attraction as a dancer. Filled with Fellini's now-familiar delight in the bizarre and sawdust/tinsel entertainment. In Italian with English subtitles. **93m/B VHS, DVD.** *IT* Giulietta Masina, Peppino de Filippo, Carla Del Poggio, Folco Lulli; ***D:*** Federico Fellini, Alberto Lattuada; ***W:*** Federico Fellini, Alberto Lattuada, Tullio Pinelli, Ennio Flaiano; ***C:*** Otello Martelli; ***M:*** Felice Lattuada.

Varsity Blues 𝒮𝒮½ **1998 (R)** After star quarterback Lance (Walker) goes down with an injury, backup Mox (Van Der Beek) learns the perks of stardom in a small Texas town obsessed with high school football. It's not all free six-packs and groupies in whipped cream bikinis, however. He butts heads with blood-and-guts Coach Kilmer (Voight), whose win-at-all-costs philosophy is injuring his players. Mox leads the players in a rebellion against the coach, leaving the usual doubts about the inevitable "big game." The young cast does an admirable job lifting the material above the average jock flick, but it lurches into the gutter a little too often for some tastes. **103m/C VHS, DVD.** James Van Der Beek, Jon Voight, Paul Walker, Ron Lester, Scott Caan, Richard Lineback, Amy Smart, Thomas F. Duffy, Tony Perenski, Tiffany C. Love, Eliel Swinton, Jill Parker Jones, Joe Pichler, Ali Larter; ***D:*** Brian Robbins; ***W:*** W. Peter Iliff; ***C:*** Charles Cohen; ***M:*** Mark Isham. MTV Movie Awards '99: Breakthrough Perf. (Van Der Beek).

Vasectomy: A Delicate Matter woof! *Vasectomy* **1986 (PG-13)** A mother of eight issues a final decree to her husband about their sex life. He must get a vasectomy or there won't be any. As good as it sounds. **92m/C VHS.** Paul Sorvino, Abe Vigoda, Cassandra Edwards, Lorne Greene, Ina Balin, June Wilkinson, William Marshall; ***D:*** Robert Burge; ***W:*** Robert Burge.

Vatel **2000 (PG-13)** Lavish period drama suffers from a dull screenplay and a lack of gusto. In 1671, Sun King Louis XIV (Sands) is ruling with the usual decadence when he and his court are invited to the country chateau of the Prince de Conde (Glover), who's hoping to curry favor. Conde leaves the plans for the the royal visit to his steward, Francois Vatel (Depardieu). He must supply food and entertainment to keep the court amused but Vatel provokes envy as well. Depardieu is efficient but the English language cast seems to be primping more than acting. **117m/C VHS, DVD.** *GB FR* Gerard Depardieu, Uma Thurman, Tim Roth, Julian Glover, Julian Sands, Timothy Spall, Arielle Dombasle, Hywel Bennett, Richard Griffiths, Feodor Atkine, Phillippe LeRoy, Murray Lachlan Young; ***D:*** Roland Joffe; ***W:*** Jeanne Labrune, Tom Stoppard; ***C:*** Robert Fraisse; ***M:*** Ennio Morricone.

Vatican Conspiracy ½ **1981** The members of the Vatican's College of Cardinals do everything in their power to discredit a newly appointed radical pontiff. **90m/C VHS.** Terence Stamp; ***D:*** Marcello Aliprandi.

The Vault **2000 (R)** Mr. Burnett (Lyde), a teacher, takes four students—Dezaray (Pride), Willy (Priester), Zipper (Walker), and Kyle (Davis) to visit an old high school, which is scheduled to be demolished. (The four kids fit the stereotypes of cheerleader, jock, nerd, and tough guy.) The school was originally a way-station for slaves and the group hopes to rescue some historical items (or something like that). Once they arrive at the school, they meet the eerie security guard Spangler (Papi), who warns them to not venture into the basement. You see, there's a very old locked door in the basement, and behind that door is...ultimate evil. Unfortunately, the film ends just as it's beginning to get interesting. **?m/C DVD, Wide.** Ted Lyde, Shani Pride, Austin Priester, Kyle Walker, Michael Cory Davis, Leopold Papi; ***D:*** James Black.

Vault of Horror ½ *Tales from the Crypt II* **1973 (R)** A collection of five terrifying tales based on original stories from the E.C. comic books of the 1950s. Stories include, "Midnight Mess," "Bargain in Death," "This Trick'll Kill You," "The Neat Job," and "Drawn and Quartered." **86m/C VHS.** *GB* Terry-Thomas, Curt Jurgens, Glynis Johns, Dawn Addams, Daniel Massey, Tom Baker, Michael Craig, Anna Massey, Denholm Elliott; ***D:*** Roy Ward Baker; ***W:*** Milton Subotsky.

Vegas **1978** A private detective, with Las Vegas beauties as assistants and pursuers, solves the murder of a teenage runaway girl. Pilot for a TV series. Scriptwriter Mann went on to do "Miami Vice." **74m/C VHS.** Robert Urich, June Allyson, Tony Curtis, Will Sampson, Greg Morris; ***D:*** Richard Lang; ***W:*** Michael Mann. **TV**

Vegas in Space woof! **1994** Four male astronauts take a secret mission to the planet Clitoris, the all-female pleasure plant where men are forbidden to trod. To capture a heinous villainous, they swallow gender-reversal pills in order to infiltrate the resort as show-girls. Typical Troma trash. Boasts an all-transvestite cast. **85m/C VHS.** Doris Fish, Miss X, Ginger Quest, Ramona Fischer, Lori Naslund, Timmy Spence, Silvana Nova, Sandelle Kincaid, Tommy Pace, Arturo Galster, Jennifer Blowdryer, Freida Lay, Tippi; ***D:*** Phillip R. Ford; ***W:*** Phillip R. Ford, Doris Fish, Miss X; ***C:*** Robin Clark; ***M:*** Ramona Fischer, Timmy Spence.

The Vegas Strip Wars *Las Vegas Strip War* **1984** Rival casino owners battle it out in the land of lady luck. Unmemorable except for Jones's Don King impersonation and the fact that it was Hudson's last TV movie. **100m/C VHS.** Rock Hudson, James Earl Jones, Noriyuki "Pat" Morita, Sharon Stone, Robert Costanzo; ***D:*** George Englund.

Vegas Vacation **1996 (PG)** It may not have come out under the "National Lampoon" banner but you'll recognize both the characters and the situations. The innocent Griswold clan head from their Chicago home to the bright lights and gambling temptations of Las Vegas. Clark (Chase) blows all their money, Ellen (D'Angelo) reveals a hidden passion for Wayne Newton, daughter Audrey (Nichols) decides to become a go-go dancer, and son Rusty (Embry) turns into a high roller who draws the attention of the mob. Oh yeah, dimwit cousin Eddie (Quaid) also tries to supply a few yucks. **98m/C VHS, DVD.** Chevy Chase, Beverly D'Angelo, Randy Quaid, Ethan (Randall) Embry, Miriam Flynn, Marisol Nichols, Shae D'Lyn, Wallace Shawn, Wayne Newton; ***Cameos:*** Sid Caesar, Julia Sweeney, Christie Brinkley; ***D:*** Stephen Kessler; ***W:*** Elisa Bell; ***C:*** William A. Fraker; ***M:*** Joel McNeely.

The Velocity of Gary ½ *The Velocity of Gary* (*Not His Real Name)* **1998 (R)** Melodrama about love, death, and what makes a family is undone by a weak script, strained humor, and a screechy performance by Hayek. Gary's (Jane) a hustler in New York City who's attracted to bisexual porn star Valentino (D'Onofrio). Valentino has a possessive waitress girlfriend, Mary Carmen (Hayek), and she and Gary immediately hate each other and constantly compete for Valentino's affections. But when Valentino falls ill with AIDS, the three move into together and try to put aside their differences. **98m/C VHS.** Vincent D'Onofrio, Salma Hayek, Thomas Jane, Olivia D'Abo; ***D:*** Dan Ireland; ***W:*** James Still; ***C:*** Claudio Rocha.

Velocity Trap **1999 (R)** In 2150, electronic crime and piracy run rampant throughout the galaxy. Cop Raymond Stokes (Gruner) is assigned to escort a federal banking ship through a section of space, known as the Velocity Run, that's equivalent to the Bermuda Triangle. Along with ship's navigator, Beth Sheffield (Coppola), Stokes must prevent thieves from grabbing the ship's loot and an asteroid from destroying the ship itself. **90m/C VHS, DVD, Wide.** Olivier Gruner, Alicia Coppola, Ken Olandt, Bruce Weitz, Craig Wasson; ***D:*** Phillip J. Roth; ***W:*** Phillip J. Roth. **VIDEO**

Velvet Goldmine **1998 (R)** Director Haynes takes on the excesses of the '70s British glam-rock era. In 1984, journalist Arthur Stuart (Bale) is assigned to write a "Whatever Happened to" article on the 10-year disappearance of vanished superstar Brian Slade (Rhys Meyers as a cross between T-Rex's Marc Bolan and a Ziggy Stardust-era David Bowie). This leads fan Arthur to Slade's viperish ex-wife Mandy (Collette) and his ex-manager Jerry Divine (Izzard). But Arthur discovers the most important relationship in Brian's life was to self-destructive cult idol Curt Wild (MacGregor, channelling Iggy Pop). The flamboyant duo had an equally flamboyant affair that eventual lead to a downward spiral for them both. The story might be average but the visuals are spectacular and MacGregor, especially, is mesmerizing. **120m/C VHS, DVD.** *GB* Ewan McGregor, Jonathan Rhys Meyers, Christian Bale, Toni Collette, Eddie Izzard, Emily Woof, Michael Feast; ***D:*** Todd Haynes; ***W:*** Todd Haynes; ***C:*** Maryse Alberti; ***M:*** Carter Burwell. British Acad. '98: Costume Des.; Ind. Spirit '99: Cinematog.

Velvet Smooth **1976 (R)** A protection agency's sultry boss, Velvet Smooth, gets involved solving the problems of a numbers racket. **89m/C VHS.** Johnnie Hill; ***D:*** Janace Fink.

Velvet Touch **1948** Well-engineered thriller about an actress who craftily murders her producer. A theatre-loving police detective winds up accusing the wrong woman—sending the overwrought murderess into a moral tailspin. Things don't work out as you may expect. Fine acting. **97m/B VHS.** Rosalind Russell, Leo Genn, Claire Trevor, Sydney Greenstreet, Leon Ames, Frank McHugh, Walter Kingsford, Dan Tobin, Lex Barker, Nydia Westman; ***D:*** John Gage; ***W:*** Leo Rosten.

The Velvet Vampire *Cemetery Girls; Through the Looking Glass; The Waking Hour* **1971 (R)** Yarnall is a sexy, sun-loving, dune buggy-riding vampiress who seduces a young, sexy, swinging, Southern California couple in her desert home. Lots of atmosphere to go along with the blood and nudity. **82m/C VHS.** Michael Blodgett, Sherry Miles, Celeste Yarnall, Gene Shane, Jerry Daniels, Sandy Ward, Paul Prokop, Chris Woodley, Robert Tessier; ***D:*** Stephanie Rothman; ***W:*** Stephanie Rothman, Maurice Jules, Charles S. Swartz; ***C:*** Daniel Lacambre.

Vendetta ½ **1985** A woman gets herself arrested and sent to the penitentiary in order to exact revenge there for her sister's death. Acting and pacing make this better than the average sexploitation flick. **89m/C VHS.** Karen Chase, Sandy Martin, Durga McBroom, Kin Shriner, Eugene Glazer; ***D:*** Bruce Logan; ***M:*** David Newman.

Vendetta **1999 (R)** Based on a true story. New Orleans politicians and businessman seek to wrest away control of the docks from the Italian family that controls it. An unleashed angry mob leads to the largest lynching in American history. Adapted from the book by Richard Gambino. **117m/C VHS, DVD.** Christopher Walken, Clancy Brown, Bruce Davison, Joaquim de Almeida, Edward Herrmann, Kenneth Welsh; ***D:*** Nicholas Meyer; ***W:*** Tim Prager; ***C:*** David Franco; ***M:*** John Altman. **CABLE**

Vendetta for the Saint **1968** A feature-length episode of the TV series "The Saint," in which Simon Templar pursues a Sicilian mobster on a personal vendetta. **98m/C VHS.** *GB* Roger Moore; ***D:*** James O'Connolly. **TV**

Vengeance **1937** A police officer resigns in shame after failing to thwart a holdup. He attempts to redeem himself by working on his own to infiltrate the same gang. **61m/B VHS.** Lyle Talbot, Wendy Barrie, Wally Albright, Marc Lawrence; ***D:*** Del Lord.

Vengeance **1980** Four burglars take hostages after their robbery is bungled, but they won't get away—especially after the hostages die. **92m/C VHS.** Sally Lockett, Nicholas Jacquez, Bob Elliott; ***D:*** Bob Blizz.

Vengeance **1986** A low-budget film about rebels fighting off an authoritarian government. **114m/C VHS.** Jason Miller, Lea Massari; ***D:*** Antonio (Isasi-Isasmendi) Isasi.

Vengeance *Vengeance: The Story of Tony Cimo* **1989 (R)** A bereaved young man strikes out against the injustice of his parents' murder. His revenge against the killers takes him several steps beyond the law, and he's not so sure it was the right idea. **90m/C VHS.** Brad Davis, Roxanne Hart, Brad Dourif, William Conrad; ***D:*** Marc Daniels. **TV**

Vengeance Is Mine *Fukusho Suruwa Ware Ni Ari* **1979** Told in flashbacks, the film focuses on the life of a habitual criminal whose life of deprivation leads to murder. Contains violence and nudity. Based on a true story. In Japanese with English subtitles. **129m/C VHS.** *JP* Ken Ogata, Rentaro Mikuni, Mitsuko Baisho, Chocho Miyako, Mayumi Ogawa, Nijiko Kiyokawa; ***D:*** Shohei Imamura; ***W:*** Masuru Baba; ***C:*** Sinsaku Himeda; ***M:*** Shinichiro Ikebe.

Vengeance Is Mine woof! **1984 (R)** A demented farmer captures three criminals and tortures them in horrifyingly sadistic ways. Gratuitously grisly. **90m/C VHS.** Ernest Borgnine, Michael J. Pollard, Hollis McLaren; ***D:*** John Trent.

The Vengeance of She *The Return of She* **1968** Carol (Berova) is taken for the reincarnation of 2,000-year-old queen, Ayesha, by her immortal lover, King Killikrates (Richardson). The king promises high priest Man Hari (Godfrey) immortality if he can restore Ayesha's soul. But Carol's shrink boyfriend (Judd) isn't crazy about the idea and tries to convince the king otherwise. **101m/C VHS, DVD.** *GB* Olinka (Schoberova) Berova, John Richardson, Derek Godfrey, Edward Judd, Colin Blakely; ***D:*** Cliff Owen; ***W:*** Peter O'Donnell; ***C:*** Peter Suschitzsky; ***M:*** Mario Nascimbene.

Vengeance of the Dead ½ **2001** This homegrown horror flick never manages to live up to the big ideas which it introduces. Eric (Galvin) journeys to the town of Harvest, to visit his Grandpa (Vollmers). (Although we're never told where he's been or given an idea of how long he's going to stay.) Once he's settled in, Eric has strange nightmares concerning a little girl, an act of violence, and a burning house. These dreams lead him to sleepwalk through the town and commit strange acts of vengeance. The dreams and Eric's behaviors are linked to a crime from many years ago, and a ghostly presence is seeking revenge on those responsible. Despite an interesting premise, but the film is slow, boring, and hard to follow at times. Kudos to filmmakers Adams and Picardi for squeezing as much as possible out of their limited budget, but this movie can't overcome its amateur roots. **85m/C DVD.** Michael Galvin, Mark Vollmers; ***D:*** Don Adams, Harry James Picardi.

Vengeance of the Zombies ½ **1972** A madman seeks revenge by setting an army of walking corpses to stalk the streets of London. **90m/C VHS.** *SP* Paul (Jacinto Molina) Naschy, Jacinto (Jack) Molina; ***D:*** Leon Klimovsky.

Vengeance Valley **1951** Lancaster and Walker are foster brothers with Walker being an envious weasel who always expects Lancaster to get him out of scrapes. Lancaster is even accused of a crime committed by Walker and must work to clear himself. Good cast is let down by uneven direction. **83m/C VHS, DVD.** Burt Lancaster, Joanne Dru, Robert Walker, Sally Forrest, John Ireland, Hugh O'Brian; ***D:*** Richard Thorpe; ***W:*** Irving Ravetch; ***C:*** George J. Folsey; ***M:*** Rudolph Kopp.

Venice, Venice ½ **1992 (R)** Alternately earnest and satirical, Jaglom pokes fun at himself and movie-making in a movie about, well, himself and movie-making. Consciously straddling the genre fence, he uses real people and events, but adopts a pseudonym, Dean. In Venice, Italy, young filmmaker Alard decides to make a film about Dean/Jaglom, a plot which creates the effect of two mirrors reflecting each other into infinity. Dean/Jaglom and Alard return to Venice, California, where he conducts auditions for a movie in which he will star and direct. Art imitating life or life imitating art? More importantly, does it really matter? **108m/C VHS.** Nelly Alard, Henry Jaglom, Suzanne Bertish, Melissa Leo, Daphna Kastner, David Duchovny, Diane Salinger, Zack Norman, Marshall Barer, John Landis, Pierre Cottrell, Edna Fainaru, Klaus Hellwig; ***D:*** Henry Jaglom; ***W:*** Henry Jaglom; ***C:*** Hanania Baer.

Venom woof! **1982 (R)** Deadly black mamba is loose in an elegant townhouse, terrorizing big-name cast. The snake continually terrorizes an evil kidnapper, his accomplices and his kidnapped victim. Participants walk through tired cliches with that far-away look in their eyes—like they wish they were anywhere else. Original director Tobe Hooper was replaced. **92m/C VHS.** *GB* Sterling Hayden, Klaus Kinski, Sarah Miles, Nicol Williamson, Cornelia Sharpe, Susan George, Michael Gough, Oliver Reed; ***D:*** Piers Haggard; ***W:*** Robert B. Carrington; ***M:*** Michael Kamen.

Venomous **2001 (PG-13)** Genetically altered poisonous snakes make their presence felt in a small town by spreading a deadly virus among the human population. To cover up the source of the disease, the military (the snakes are one of their experiments gone wrong) plans to blow up the town. **97m/C VHS, DVD, Wide.** Treat Williams, Mary Page Keller, Brian Poth, J.B. Gaynor, Hannes Jaenicke, Geoffrey Pierson, Catherine Dent; ***D:*** Fred Olen Ray; ***W:*** Dan Golden, Sean McGinley; ***C:*** Andrea V. Rossotto; ***M:*** Neal Acree. **VIDEO**

Venus Against the Son of Hercules *Marte, Dio Della Guerra* **1962** Our hero must use all his genetically procured musculature in his battle against the lovely but deadly Venus. **?m/C VHS.** *IT* Jackie Lane, Roger Browne, Massimo Serato, Linda Sini, Dante DiPaolo; ***D:*** Marcello Baldi; ***W:*** Ernesto Gastaldi.

Venus Beauty Institute ½ **1998 (R)** Fortyish Angele (Baye) works at a Paris beauty salon along with proprietor Nadine (Ogier) and younger colleagues Samantha (Seigner) and Marie (Tantou). Angele refuses to fall in love and picks up men strictly for sex—until she's pursued by Antoine (Le Bihan), a young sculptor who insists he fell in love with her at first sight. (He basically stalks her but Angele is intrigued rather than repulsed by his devotion.) The Institute also has a parade of frequently neurotic customers in romantic dilemmas. French with subtitles. **105m/C VHS, DVD.** *FR* Nathalie Baye, Bulle Ogier, Samuel Le Bihan, Jacques Bonnaffe, Mathilde Seigner, Robert Hossein, Claire Nebout, Audrey Tautou; ***D:*** Tonie Marshall; ***W:*** Tonie Marshall; ***C:*** Gerard de Battista; ***M:*** Khalil Chahine. Cesar '00: Director (Marshall), Film, Screenplay.

Venus in Furs ½ *Paroxismus; Puo Una Morta Rivivere Per Amore?; Venus in Peltz* **1970 (R)** Jazz musician working in Rio de Janeiro becomes obsessed with a mysterious woman; she resembles a murder victim whose body he discovered months earlier. Weird mix of horror, sadism, black magic, and soft porn. **70m/C VHS.** *GB IT GE* James Darren, Klaus Kinski, Barbara McNair, Dennis Price, Maria Rohm, Margaret Lee, Jess (Jesus) Franco; ***D:*** Jess (Jesus) Franco; ***W:*** Milo G. Cuccia, Malvin Wald, Jess (Jesus) Franco; ***C:*** Angelo Lotti.

Venus Rising **1995 (R)** In the year 2000, Eve and August manage to escape from the island prison on which they were raised. They discover that the mainland world features emotions that are controlled by drugs and love is only a game on the virtual reality network. Hunted, the fugitives try to fit in and figure out what's real and what's fantasy. Be forewarned—Fairchild's role is very small. **91m/C VHS.** Audie England, Costas Mandylor, Billy Wirth, Morgan Fairchild; ***D:*** Leora Barish; ***W:*** Leora Barish.

Vera Cruz ½ **1953** Two soldiers of fortune become involved in the Mexican Revolution of 1866, a stolen shipment of gold, divided loyalties, and gun battles. Less than innovative plot is made into an exciting action flick. **94m/C VHS, DVD, Wide.** Gary Cooper, Burt Lancaster, Denise Darcel, Cesar Romero, George Macready, Ernest Borgnine, Charles Bronson, Jack Elam; ***D:*** Robert Aldrich; ***W:*** Roland Kibbee, James R. Webb; ***C:*** Ernest Laszlo; ***M:*** Hugo Friedhofer.

Verboten! ½ **1959** In post-war occupied Berlin, an American G.I. falls in love with a German girl. Good direction maintains a steady pace. **93m/B VHS.** James Best, Susan Cummings, Tom Pittman, Paul Dubov; ***D:*** Samuel Fuller; ***W:*** Samuel Fuller; ***C:*** Joseph Biroc.

Verdi *The Life and Music of Giuseppe Verdi* **1953** The story of the Italian operatic composer and the loves of his life. Italian with subtitles. **80m/C VHS.** *IT* Pierre (Peter Cross) Cressoy, Gaby Andre; ***D:*** Raffaello Matarazzo; ***W:*** Leonardo Benvenuti; ***C:*** Tito Santoni.

The Verdict **1982 (R)** Frank Galvin (Newman) is an alcoholic failed attorney reduced to ambulance chasing. A friend gives him a supposedly easy malpractice case that pits Frank against a powerful establishment Catholic hospital in Boston in what turns out to be a last chance at redeeming himself and his career. Adapted from the novel by Barry Reed. One of Newman's finest performances. **122m/C VHS.** Paul Newman, James Mason, Charlotte Rampling, Jack Warden, Milo O'Shea, Lindsay Crouse, Edward Binns, Roxanne Hart, James Handy, Wesley Addy, Joe Seneca, Julie Bovasso; ***D:*** Sidney Lumet; ***W:*** David Mamet; ***C:*** Andrzej Bartkowiak; ***M:*** Johnny Mandel. Natl. Bd. of Review '82: Director (Lumet).

Vermont Is for Lovers ½ **1992** Pre-wedding jitters consume stressed-out Manhattanites Marya (Cohn) and George (Thrush) when they travel to bucolic Tunbridge, Vermont to get married on Marya's Aunt Ann's farm. After continuously arguing, they decide to spend the day before the wedding apart and George wanders around the community asking marriage advice from various old-timers. The Yuppie leads aren't terribly compelling and neither is the improvised dialogue. **86m/C VHS.** George Thrush, Marya Cohn, Ann O'Brien; ***D:*** John O'Brien; ***C:*** John O'Brien; ***M:*** Tony Silbert.

Verne Miller **1988 (R)** A film of the true story of Verne Miller, Al Capone's hit man. After rescuing a friend from the Feds, Miller is hunted down by both the cops and the mob. **95m/C VHS.** Scott Glenn, Barbara Stock, Thomas G. Waites, Lucinda Jenney, Sonny Carl Davis; ***D:*** Rod Hewitt.

The Vernonia Incident ½ **1989** Urban guerillas invade a small town, killing the police chief. The townspeople gather up their shotguns and fight back. That's entertainment. **95m/C VHS.** David Jackson, Shawn Stevens, Floyd Ragner, Ed Justice, Robert Louis Jakson; ***D:*** Ray Etheridge; ***W:*** Ray Etheridge.

Veronico Cruz ½ *La Dueda Interna; The Debt* **1987** Despite its sincerity, Pereira's feature debut offers muddled response to the human waste incurred by the Falklands War. Set in a tiny remote village in the Argentinean mountains, the film's narrative is derived from the growing friendship between a shepherd boy and a teacher from the city. Well-meaning antiwar movie. In Spanish with English subtitles. **96m/C VHS, DVD.** *AR GB* Juan Jose Camero, Gonzalo Morales, Rene Olaguivel, Guillermo Delgado; ***D:*** Miguel Pereira; ***W:*** Miguel Pereira, Eduardo Leiva Muller; ***C:*** Gerry Feeny; ***M:*** David Eppel, Jaime Torres.

Veronika Voss *Die Sehns Ucht Der Veronika Voss* **1982 (R)** Highlights the real life of fallen film star Sybille Schmitz who finally took her own life out of despair. Played by Zech, Voss is exploited by her physician to turn over all of her personal belongings for morphine. A lover discovers the corruption and reveals it to the authorities. This causes great upheaval resulting in Voss' suicide. Highly metaphoric and experimental in its treatment of its subject. In German with English subtitles. **105m/C VHS.** *GE* Rosel Zech, Hilmar Thate, Conny Froboess, Anna Marie Duringer, Volker Spengler; ***D:*** Rainer Werner Fassbinder; ***W:*** Pea Frolich, Peter Marthesheimer; ***C:*** Xaver Schwarzenberger; ***M:*** Peer. Raben.

Vertical Limit **2000 (PG-13)** Photographer O'Donnell joins a team of mountain climbers in order to rescue his sister Tunney, who is part of a group trapped on K2. Plot serves mainly as connective tissue for the numerous heart-stopping (and well-done) action sequences. Mountain-fodder cast has few standouts, except maybe Glenn in the crazy-but-wise-old-coot role. **126m/C VHS, DVD, Wide.** Chris O'Donnell, Robin Tunney, Bill Paxton, Scott Glenn, Izabela Scorupco, Temuera Morrison, Stuart Wilson, Nicholas Lea, Alexander Siddig, Robert Taylor, Roshan Seth, David Hayman, Ben Mendelsohn, Steve Le Marquand; ***D:*** Martin Campbell; ***W:*** Robert King, Terry Hayes; ***C:*** David Tattersall; ***M:*** James Newton Howard.

The Vertical Ray of the Sun ½ **2000 (PG-13)** Slow-moving visual treat set in Hanoi. Three sisters plan a commemorative meal in honor of the anniversary of their mother's death. The two eldest sisters have marital problems and the youngest is so close to their brother that many believe the twosome are sexually involved. Over the course of a month (which ends with the anniversary of their father's death), the women deal with their emotional entanglements. Vietnamese with subtites. **112m/C VHS, DVD, Wide.** *VT FR* Tran Nu Yen-Khe, Nguyen Nhu Quynh, Le Khanh, Tran Manh Cuong, Chu Ngoc Hung, Ngo Quang Hai; ***D:*** Tran Anh Hung; ***W:*** Tran Anh Hung; ***C:*** Mark Lee Ping-Bin; ***M:*** Ton That Tiet.

Vertigo **1958 (PG)** Hitchcock's romantic story of obsession, manipulation and fear. Stewart plays a detective forced to retire after his fear of heights causes the death of a fellow policeman and, perhaps, the death of a woman he'd been hired to follow. The appearance of her double (Novak), whom he compulsively transforms into the dead girl's image, leads to a mesmerizing cycle of madness and lies. Features Herrmann's haunting music. **126m/C VHS, DVD.** James Stewart, Kim Novak, Barbara Bel Geddes, Tom Helmore, Ellen Corby, Henry Jones, Raymond Bailey, Lee Patrick; ***D:*** Alfred Hitchcock; ***W:*** Samuel A. Taylor; ***C:*** Robert Burks; ***M:*** Bernard Herrmann. AFI '98: Top 100, Natl. Film Reg. '89.

Very Bad Things **1998 (R)** What begins as a not-so-innocent prenuptial bachelor party in Vegas quickly disintegrates into a murderous blood bath. Kyle (Favreau), the groom-to-be, escapes the clutches of his control-freak fiance Laura (Diaz) with some pals, including unscrupulous yuppie Boyd (Slater). When the hired "entertainment" is killed in a freak accident involving a towel hook, Boyd comes up with the idea of burying her body in the desert and going on with the wedding. A pitch-dark comedy of errors ensues. Peter Berg's first stab at writing and directing has some funny moments, mostly the kind you realize afterwards you shouldn't find funny, but relies too heavily on gratuitous gore and shock value. **100m/C VHS, DVD.** Jon Favreau, Christian Slater, Cameron Diaz, Jeremy Piven, Daniel Stern, Leland Orser, Jeanne Tripplehorn, Joey Zimmerman; ***D:*** Peter Berg; ***W:*** Peter Berg; ***C:*** David Hennings; ***M:*** Stewart Copeland.

A Very Brady Christmas **1988** Many of the original Bradys returned for this yuletide special. After Mike and Carol's vacation plans go awry, they decide to invite the whole bunch home for a family reunion. This was the highest rated TV movie in 1989. Spawned yet another unsuccessful "Brady" series sequel. **94m/C VHS.** Florence Henderson, Robert Reed, Ann B. Davis, Maureen McCormick, Eve Plumb, Jennifer Runyon, Barry Williams, Christopher Knight, Michael (Mike) Lookinland, Jerry Houser, Caryn Richman; ***D:*** Peter Baldwin. **TV**

A Very Brady Sequel ½ **1996 (PG-13)** They're back! The cast from the surprise hit "The Brady Bunch Movie" returns and Brady mom Carol (Long) is shocked when her presumed dead first husband Roy Martin (Matheson) suddenly appears on their doorstep. The Bradys must travel to Hawaii to attempt to save the family (based on a three-part episode from the original TV series). The stuck-in-the-'70s gang is still too far-out for the '90s, but in Hawaii it's always a sunshine day. Not as good as the first, but still worth a few laughs. **90m/C VHS.** Shelley Long, Gary Cole, Tim Matheson, Christopher Daniel Barnes, Christine Taylor, Paul Sutera, Jennifer Elise Cox, Henriette Mantel, Olivia Hack, Jesse Lee; ***D:*** Arlene Sanford; ***W:*** Harry Elfont, Deborah Kaplan, Stan Zimmerman, James Berg; ***C:*** Mac Ahlberg; ***M:*** Guy Moon.

A Very British Coup **1988** McAnally plays Harry Perkins, a former steelworker who gets involved in British politics. Although a left-wing radical, the charismatic Perkins is actually elected Prime Minister. However, his radical policies cause the entrenched government officials to conspire to bring him down. And you thought American politics were dirty! **180m/C VHS.** *GB* Ray McAnally, Alan MacNaughton, Keith Allen, Geoffrey Beevers, Jim Carter, Philip Madoc, Tim (McInnerny) McInnery; ***D:*** Mick Jackson; ***W:*** Alan Plater; ***C:*** Ernest Vincze; ***M:*** John Keane. **TV**

Very Close Quarters **1984** Thirty people face many trials and tribulations as they share an apartment in Moscow. Interesting cast is wasted in this mostly un-funny flick. **97m/C VHS.** Shelley Winters, Paul Sorvino, Theodore Bikel, Farley Granger; ***D:*** Vladmir Rif.

A Very Curious Girl ½ *La Fiancee du Pirate; Dirty Mary; Pirate's Fiancee* **1969 (R)** A peasant girl realizes she is being used by the male population of her village, and decides to charge them for sex, creating havoc. In French with English subtitles. **105m/C VHS.** *FR* Bernadette Lafont, Georges Geret, Michel Constantin, Julien Guiomar, Claire Maurier; ***D:*** Nelly Kaplan; ***W:*** Nelly Kaplan, Claude Makovski; ***C:*** Jean Badal; ***M:*** Georges Moustaki.

The Very Edge ½ **1963** A pregnant woman suffers a miscarriage after being brutally attacked. The repercussions nearly destroy her marriage until her attacker is caught. A disturbing psychodrama. **90m/B VHS.** *GB* Anne Heywood, Richard Todd, Jeremy Brett, Jack Hedley, Barbara Mullen, Maurice Denham, William Lucas, Gwen Watford, Patrick Magee; ***D:*** Cyril Frankel; ***W:*** Elizabeth Jane Howard; ***C:*** Robert Huke.

A Very Natural Thing **1973** Twenty-six-year-old Jason leaves the priesthood to pursue a gay lifestyle in New York. He becomes a teacher, meets ad exec David, and finds love. Considered to be the first film to explore homosexuality in a realistic manner, made by a gay director, and given national, commercial distribution. **85m/C VHS, DVD.** Robert Joel, Curt Gareth, Bo White; ***D:*** Christopher Larkin; ***W:*** Christopher Larkin, Joseph Coencas; ***C:*** C.H. Douglass; ***M:*** Gordon Gottlieb, Bert Lucarelli.

A Very Old Man with Enormous Wings *Un Senor Muy Viejo Con Unas Alas Enormes* **1988** An angel, battered during a hurricane, seeks refuge on a tiny Caribbean island. There, two men keep him and charge an increasingly curious world admission to view the creature. A colorful, musical expose of human failings based on a story by Gabriel Garcia Marquez. In Spanish with English subtitles. **90m/C VHS.** *SP IT* Daisy Granados, Asdrubal Melendez, Luis Alberto Ramirez, Fernando Birri; ***D:*** Fernando Birri.

A Very Private Affair ½ *La Vie Privee; Vita Privata* **1962** A movie star finds that she has no privacy from the hordes of fans and paparazzi who flock to her side. The glare of publicity helps to destroy her relationship with a married director, and to fuel her desire for privacy, a desire that ends tragically. An appealing, better-than-average Bardot vehicle, it is nonetheless below-average (early) Malle. In French with English subtitles. **95m/C VHS.** *FR* Marcello Mastroianni, Brigitte Bardot; ***D:*** Louis Malle.

The Very Thought of You ½ *Martha, Meet Frank, Daniel and Laurence* **1998 (PG-13)** Limp romantic comedy finds a trio of longtime London friends clashing over their interest in the same woman. Actor Frank (Sewell), music exec Daniel (Hollander), and painter Laurence (Fiennes) all separately encounter Martha (Potter) and pick her up—without anyone realizing (until late in the movie) how they're all connected. However, Martha's character comes across as a imperious nag, while the men are either petulant, arrogant, or wimpy. You won't care who Martha finally ends up with. **88m/C VHS, DVD.** *GB* Monica Potter, Rufus Sewell, Joseph Fiennes, Tom Hollander, Ray Winstone; ***D:*** Nick Hamm; ***W:*** Peter Morgan; ***C:*** David Johnson; ***M:*** Ed Shearmur.

V.I. Warshawski **1991 (R)** The filmmakers seem to think they can slum with the oldest cliches in detective shows just as long as the tough gumshoe is a woman. They're wrong. Turner is terrific as the leggy shamus of the title (from a popular series of books by Sara Paretsky), but the plot is nothing special, featuring stock characters in the killing of a pro athlete and a real-estate deal. **89m/C VHS.** Stephen (Steve) Root, Kathleen Turner, Jay O. Sanders, Angela Goethals, Charles Durning; ***D:*** Jeff Kanew; ***W:*** Nick Thiel, David Aaron Cohen; ***M:*** Randy Edelman.

Via Appia **1992** Fictional documentary about Frank, a German airline steward who brings a film crew with him when travels back to Rio de Janeiro in search of the street hustler who gave him AIDS. Grim guided tour of the city's gay subculture along the "Via Appia," the Rio district where the male prostitutes hang out. Film is firmly unapologetic for its sexual explicitness and lack of moralizing. In German and Portuguese with English subtitles. **90m/C VHS.** *GE BR* Peter Senner, Guilherme de Padua, Yves Jansen, Margarita Schmidt, Luiz Kleber; ***D:*** Jochen Hick; ***W:*** Jochen Hick.

Vibes **1988 (PG)** Two screwball psychics are sent on a wild goose chase through the Ecuadorean Andes in search of cosmic power and, of course, fall in love. Flat offering from the usually successful team of writers, Lowell Ganz and Babaloo Mandel ("Splash" and "Night Shift"). Lauper's first starring role (and so far, her last). **99m/C VHS.** Jeff Goldblum, Cyndi Lauper, Julian Sands, Googy Gress, Peter Falk, Elizabeth Pena; ***D:*** Ken Kwapis; ***W:*** Babaloo Mandel, Lowell Ganz; ***C:*** John Bailey; ***M:*** James Horner.

Vibration ♪♪ *Lejonsommar* **1968** Writer Mauritz (Taube) travels to an island off the Swedish coast to enjoy some fun in the sun and immediately becomes involved with the tempting Barbro (Sjodin). But she can't compete with sex kitten Eliza (Persson), a film star who says she wants to be alone—although her actions say something quite different. Sixties Swedish erotica. **84m/B VHS, DVD, Wide.** *SW* Sven-Bertil Taube, Essy Persson, Margareta Sjodin; ***D:*** Torbjorn Axelman; ***W:*** Torbjorn Axelman; ***C:*** Hans Dittmer; ***M:*** Ulf Bjorlin.

Vibrations ♪♪½ **1994 (R)** Anamika (Applegate), a dance club manager, befriends TJ (Marshall), a homeless, alcoholic, once-promising musician who lost his hands in a brutal attack. The duo find romance as Anamika encourages TJ to try again. **104m/C VHS.** James Marshall, Christina Applegate, Faye Grant, Paige Turco, Bruce Altman, David Burke, Scott Cohen, Shane Butterworth; ***D:*** Michael Paseornek; ***W:*** Michael Paseornek; ***M:*** Bob Christianson.

Vice Academy ♪½ **1988 (R)** Two females join the Hollywood vice squad. Allen was a former porn queen. **90m/C VHS.** Linnea Quigley, Ginger Lynn Allen, Karen Russell, Jayne Hamil, Ken Abraham, Stephen Steward, Jeannie Carol; ***D:*** Rick Sloane.

Vice Academy 2 ♪ **1990 (R)** Two vice cop babes try to stop a female crime boss from dumping aphrodesiacs in the city's water supply. **90m/C VHS.** Linnea Quigley, Ginger Lynn Allen, Jayne Hamil, Scott Layne, Jay Richardson, Joe Brewer, Marina Benvenga, Teagan Clive; ***D:*** Rick Sloane.

Vice Academy 3 woof! **1991 (R)** The worst of the series, and not just because cult actress Linnea Quigley is absent. Wit, pacing and even sets are nonexistent as the girls battle a toxic villainess called Malathion. **88m/C VHS.** Ginger Lynn Allen, Elizabeth Kaitan, Julia Parton, Jay Richardson, Johanna Grika, Steve Mateo; ***D:*** Rick Sloane; ***W:*** Rick Sloane.

Vice Girls ♪½ **1996 (R)** Three undercover female cops (all babes naturally) use their brains and bodies to capture a serial killer who gets his jollies by filming his victims before he kills them. Sexy fun. **85m/C VHS, DVD.** Lana Clarkson, Liat Goodson, Kimberly Roberts, A. Michael Baldwin, Richard Gabai, Caroline Keenan, Hoke Howell; ***D:*** Richard Gabai; ***W:*** A. Michael Baldwin; ***C:*** Gary Graver.

Vice Squad ♪♪ **1931** Lukas is forced to turn police informer to save his own neck, which almost ruins him. Just when he thinks he's free of the cops they come back threatening the woman he loves unless he plays stoolie again. Rather flat, but the different cop/criminal angle makes for some unusual twists. **80m/B VHS.** Paul Lukas, Kay Francis, Helen Johnson, William B. Davidson, Esther Howard; ***D:*** John Cromwell; ***C:*** Charles B(ryant) Lang Jr.

Vice Squad woof! **1982 (R)** Violent and twisted killer-pimp goes on a murderous rampage, and a hooker helps a vice squad plainclothesman trap him. Sleazy and disturbing, with little to recommend it. **97m/C VHS.** Wings Hauser, Season Hubley, Gary Swanson, Cheryl "Rainbeaux" Smith; ***D:*** Gary Sherman; ***W:*** Robert Vincent O'Neil.

Vice Versa ♪♪♪ **1988 (PG)** Another 80s comedy about a workaholic father and his 11-year-old son who switch bodies, with predictable slapstick results. Reinhold and Savage carry this, appearing to have a great time in spite of overdone story. **97m/C VHS.** Judge Reinhold, Fred Savage, Swoosie Kurtz, David Proval, Corinne Bohrer, Jane Kaczmarek, William Prince, Gloria Gifford; ***D:*** Brian Gilbert; ***W:*** Dick Clement, Ian La-Frenais; ***M:*** David Shire.

Vicious ♪ **1988** A bored young woman falls in with people your mother warned you about and soon their high school hijinks turn into murder. Graphic violence. **88m/C VHS.** Tamblyn Lord, Craig Pearce, Tiffany Dowe; ***D:*** Karl Zwicky.

The Vicious Circle ♪♪½ *The Circle* **1957** A prominent London physician becomes involved in murder and an international crime ring when he agrees to perform an errand for a friend. Good performances and tight pacing. **84m/B VHS.** *GB* John Mills, Wilfrid Hyde-White, Rene Ray, Lionel Jeffries, Noelle Middleton; ***D:*** Gerald Thomas.

Vicious Circles ♪♪ **1997 (R)** Decidedly kinky erotic thriller finds Dylan (Hipp) getting arrested for drug possession in Paris. So his half-sister and lover Andi (Lowery) decides to help raise the money for his release by working as a hooker for mystery man March (Gazzara). As Andi gets more involved in her new lifestyle, she also discovers that March was somehow connected to the death of a tycoon's daughter. **90m/C VHS.** Carolyn Lowery, Ben Gazzara, Paul Hipp; ***D:*** Alexander Whitelaw; ***W:*** Alexander Whitelaw; ***M:*** Robert Lockhart.

Victim ♪♪♪½ **1961** A successful married English barrister (Bogarde) with a hidden history of homosexuality is threatened by blackmail after the death of his ex-lover. When the blackmailers, who are responsible for his lover's suicide, are caught, Bogarde decides to prosecute them himself, even though it means revealing his hidden past. One of the first films to deal straightforwardly with homosexuality. Fine performances. **100m/B VHS.** *GB* Dirk Bogarde, Sylvia Syms, Dennis Price, Peter McEnery, Nigel Stock, Donald Churchill, Anthony Nicholls, Hilton Edwards, Norman Bird, Derren Nesbitt, Alan McNaughton, Noel Howlett, Charles Lloyd Pack, John Barrie, John Bennett; ***D:*** Basil Dearden; ***W:*** John McCormick, Janet Green; ***C:*** Otto Heller; ***M:*** Philip Green.

Victim of Beauty ♪♪ **1991** A small-town girl comes to the big city and becomes a successful model. However, she then becomes the victim of a fatal attraction killer as all her would-be suitors get killed off one by one. **90m/C VHS.** Jennifer Rubin, Sally Kellerman, Stephen Shellen, Peter Outerbridge; ***Cameos:*** Michael Ironside; ***D:*** Paul Lynch. **CABLE**

Victim of Desire ♪½ **1994 (R)** Mysterious death of an embezzler is investigated, only the investigator falls for the sexy widow and begins to doubt her innocence. Also available in an unrated version. **85m/C VHS.** Shannon Tweed, Julie Strain.

Victim of Love ♪♪ **1991 (PG-13)** A therapist doesn't know whom to believe when she finds out she and one of her more neurotic patients are sharing the same boyfriend. Only the patient claims the man murdered his wife to be with his lover. Who will be the next victim? **92m/C VHS, DVD.** Pierce Brosnan, JoBeth Williams, Virginia Madsen, Georgia Brown; ***D:*** Jerry London, James Desmarais; ***C:*** Billy Dickson; ***M:*** Richard Stone. **TV**

Victimless Crimes **1990 (R)** The seemingly victimless crime of robbing art galleries turns deadly when betrayal and murder enter the picture. **85m/C VHS.** Debra Sandlund, Craig Bierko, Larry Brandenburg, Peggy Dunne, Richard Redlin, Cheryl Lynn Bruce; ***D:*** Peter Hawley.

Victor/Victoria ♪♪♪ **1982 (PG)** Victoria (Andrews), an unsuccessful actress in Depression-era Paris, impersonates a man impersonating a woman and becomes a star. Luscious music and sets. Warren as confused showgirl Norma, and Preston as Andrews' gay mentor Toddy are right on target; Garner is charming as gangster King Marchan, who falls for the woman he thinks she is, with Karras amusing as his bodyguard with a secret, Squash. ♫You and Me; The Shady Dame from Seville; Le Jazz Hot; Crazy World; Chicago Illinois; Gay Paree. **133m/C VHS, DVD, Wide.** Julie Andrews, James Garner, Robert Preston, Lesley Ann Warren, Alex Karras, John Rhys-Davies, Norman Chancer, Peter Arne; ***D:*** Blake Edwards; ***W:*** Blake Edwards; ***C:*** Dick Bush; ***M:*** Henry Mancini. Oscars '82: Orig. Song Score and/or Adapt.; Cesar '83: Foreign Film; Golden Globes '83: Actress—Mus./Comedy (Andrews); Natl. Bd. of Review '82: Support. Actor (Preston); Writers Guild '82: Adapt. Screenplay.

Victoria & Albert ♪♪½ **2001** In this BBC production, fabulous sets and costumes frame the story of Victoria, the girl who would be Queen, and Albert, the husband she weds by arrangement. This is a romantic tale of two people who are put together through politics but come to depend on and love each other through trust and mutual respect. The story is historically accurate, but little things pertaining to the personal relationship and family life are painted a little too rosy. Literary license aside, this is a great, romantic, period drama that makes historical figures from a distant land accessible and friendly while teaching you a little about potentially dry English history. **200m/C VHS, DVD.** Victoria Hamilton, Jonathan Firth, David Suchet, Diana Rigg, Patrick Malahide, Penelope Wilton, Peter Ustinov, Nigel Hawthorne; ***D:*** John Erman; ***W:*** John Goldsmith; ***C:*** Tony Imi; ***M:*** Alan Parker. **TV**

Victoria Regina ♪♪ **1961** In a succession of vignettes, the life of Queen Victoria is viewed, from her ascension to the throne of England in 1837 through the celebration of her Diamond Jubilee. A presentation from "George Schaefer's Showcase Theatre." **76m/C VHS.** Julie Harris, James Donald, Felix Aylmer, Pamela Brown, Basil Rathbone; ***D:*** George Schaefer. **TV**

Victory ♪♪½ **1981 (PG)** Soccer match between WWII American prisoners of war and a German team is set up so that the players can escape through the sewer tunnels of Paris. Of course they want to finish the game first. Not particularly believable as either a soccer flick (even with Pele and other soccer stars) or a great escape, but watchable. **116m/C VHS, DVD, Wide.** Sylvester Stallone, Michael Caine, Max von Sydow, Pele, Carole Laure, Bobby Moore, Daniel Massey; ***D:*** John Huston; ***W:*** Jeff Maguire, Djordje Milicevic; ***C:*** Gerry Fisher; ***M:*** Bill Conti.

The Victory ♪♪ **1988 (PG)** In 1967 Montreal, an American college exchange student falls in love with a French-Canadian co-ed. Can love survive their different cultures? **95m/C VHS.** Vincent Van Patten, Cloris Leachman, Eddie Albert, Claire Pimpare, Nicholas (Nick) Campbell, Jack Wetherall, Jacques Godin, Marthe Mercure; ***D:*** Larry Kent.

The Video Dead woof! **1987 (R)** Gore-farce in which murderous zombies emerge from a possessed TV and wreak havoc. **90m/C VHS.** Roxanna Augesen, Rocky Duvall, Michael St. Michaels; ***D:*** Robert Scott.

Video Murders ♪ **1987** A police detective tracks down a rapist/murderer who tapes all his own crimes. **90m/C VHS.** Eric Brown, Virginia Loridans, John Ferita.

Video Violence ♪ **1987** A gory spoof about a video store owner who discovers that his customers have grown bored with the usual Hollywood horror movies and decide to shoot some flicks of their own. **90m/C VHS.** Art Neill, Jackie Neill, William Toddie, Bart Sumner; ***D:*** Gary P. Cohen.

Video Violence Part 2...The Exploitation! ♪ **1987** Two sickos named Howard and Eli run a cable TV network where talk show guests are spindled and mutilated. **90m/C VHS.** Uke, Bart Sumner, Lee Miller; ***D:*** Gary P. Cohen.

Video Wars woof! **1984** Video games explode randomly. A wicked computer whiz is behind it all in a blackmail scheme. **90m/C VHS.** George Diamond.

Videodrome ♪♪ **1983** Woods is a cable TV programmer with a secret yen for sex and violence, which he satisfies by watching a pirated TV show. "Videodrome" appears to show actual torture and murder, and also seems to control the thoughts of its viewers—turning them into human VCRs. Cronenberg's usual sick fantasies are definitely love 'em or leave 'em. Special effects by Rick Baker. **87m/C VHS, DVD, Wide.** *CA* James Woods, Deborah Harry, Sonja Smits, Peter Dvorsky; ***D:*** David Cronenberg; ***W:*** David Cronenberg; ***C:*** Mark Irwin; ***M:*** Howard Shore. Genie '84: Director (Cronenberg).

Vietnam, Texas ♪ **1990 (R)** Vietnam vet leaves his past to become a priest. But he returns to violence when he discovers his Vietnamese daughter is in the hands of Houston's most relentless gangster. **101m/C VHS.** Robert Ginty, Haing S. Ngor, Tamlyn Tomita, Tim Thomerson; ***D:*** Robert Ginty; ***W:*** C. Courtney Joyner, Tom Badal.

A View to a Kill ♪♪ **1985 (PG)** This James Bond mission takes him to the United States, where he must stop the evil Max Zorin from destroying California's Silicon Valley. Feeble and unexciting plot with unscary villain. Duran Duran performs the catchy title tune. Moore's last appearance as 007. **131m/C VHS, DVD, Wide.** *GB* Roger Moore, Christopher Walken, Tanya Roberts, Grace Jones, Patrick Macnee, Lois Maxwell, Dolph Lundgren, Desmond Llewelyn; ***D:*** John Glen; ***W:*** Michael G. Wilson; ***C:*** Alan Hume; ***M:*** John Barry.

Vigil ♪♪♪ **1984** A stark, dreamy parable about a young girl, living on a primitive farm in a remote New Zealand valley, who watches her family collapse after a stranger enters their territory. Visually ravishing and grim; Ward's first American import. Predecessor to "The Navigator." **90m/C VHS.** *NZ* Penelope Stewart, Bill Kerr, Fiona Kay, Gordon Shields, Frank Whitten; ***D:*** Vincent Ward; ***W:*** Vincent Ward.

Vigilante woof! *Street Gang* **1983 (R)** Frustrated ex-cop, tired of seeing criminals returned to the street, joins a vigilante squad dedicated to law and order. Often ridiculous and heavy handed. **91m/C VHS, DVD, Wide.** Robert Forster, Fred Williamson, Carol Lynley, Rutanya Alda, Richard Bright, Woody Strode, Donald Blakely, Joseph Carberry, Joe Spinell, Frank Pesce; ***D:*** William Lustig; ***W:*** Richard Vetere; ***C:*** James (Momel) Lemmo; ***M:*** Jay Chattaway.

The Vigilantes Are Coming ♪♪ **1936** "The Eagle" sets out to avenge his family and upsets a would-be dictator's plot to establish an empire in California. In 12 chapters; the first is 32 minutes, and additional chapters are 18 minutes each. **230m/B VHS.** Robert "Bob" Livingston, Kay Hughes, Guinn "Big Boy" Williams, Raymond Hatton, William Farnum; ***D:*** Mack V. Wright, Ray Taylor.

Vigilantes of Boom Town ♪½ **1946** A championship prize fight is the cover for a bank robbery which must be foiled by Red Ryder. **54m/B VHS.** Allan "Rocky" Lane, Robert (Bobby) Blake, Peggy Stewart, Martha Wentworth, Roscoe Karns, Roy Barcroft, George Turner, John Dehner; ***D:*** R.G. Springsteen; ***Nar:*** Leroy Mason.

The Viking Queen ♪♪ **1967** Babe and swordplay saga. After her father dies, Salina (Carita) becomes queen and must protect her British tribe from the Roman occupation. But after tribal rebels attack the Centurions, Roman commander Justinian (Murray) refuses her father a proper burial, even though he and Salina are getting romantic. Then Salina falls into the hands of the evil Octavian (Keir) and he begins a war against the tribes while Justinian is away. When Salina escapes, she joins the fighting. **91m/C VHS, DVD.** *GB* Carita, Don Murray, Andrew Keir, Donald Houston, Adrienne Corri, Niall MacGinnis, Nicola Pagett, Patrick Troughton; ***D:*** Don Chaffey; ***W:*** Clarke Reynolds; ***C:*** Stephen Dade; ***M:*** Gary Hughes.

The Viking Sagas ♪ **1995 (R)** Kjartan (Moeller) is the warrior who must avenge his father's execution, defend his people, and fight for his country's survival against evil oppressors. At least there's a beautiful babe around to offer him some comfort. The Icelandic scenery is the best thing about the movie. **83m/C VHS.** Ralph (Ralf) Moeller, Ingibjorg Stefansdottir, Sven-Ole Thorsen; ***D:*** Michael Chapman; ***W:*** Dale Herd, Paul R. Gurian; ***M:*** George S. Clinton.

The Vikings ♪♪½ **1958** A Viking king and his son kidnap a Welsh princess and hold her for ransom. Depicts the Vikings' invasion of England. Great location footage of both Norway and Brittany. Basic costume epic with good action scenes. Narrated by Welles. **116m/C VHS, DVD, Wide.** Kirk Douglas, Ernest Borgnine, Janet Leigh, Tony Curtis, James Donald, Alexander Knox; ***D:*** Richard Fleischer; ***W:*** Calder Willingham; ***C:*** Jack Cardiff; ***M:*** Mario Nascimbene, Gerard Schumann; ***Nar:*** Orson Welles.

Vile 21 ♪½ **1999** Let's see, a drug developed by Dr. Walter Hall on government orders turns an unsuspecting derelict into a part man/part reptile/part alien monster (the title character) that goes on a rampage. And now Hall must come up with a way to destroy the creature. **80m/C VHS.** Daniel Skinner, Ronnie Sortor, Steve Kelly, Byron Blakey, Brian Southwick, Tammi Strain; ***D:*** Mike Strain Jr.; ***W:*** Mike Strain Jr. **VIDEO**

Villa Rides **1968** A flying gunrunner aids Francisco "Pancho" Villa's revolutionary Mexican campaign. Considering the talent involved, this one is a disappointment. Check out Brynner's hair. **125m/C VHS.** Yul Brynner, Robert Mitchum, Charles Bronson, Herbert Lom, Jill Ireland, Robert Towne; ***D:*** Buzz Kulik; ***W:*** Robert Towne, Sam Peckinpah; ***C:*** Jack Hildyard; ***M:*** Maurice Jarre.

A Village Affair ½ **1995** Ward is a young wife and mother, living what appears to be a perfect life in a quiet English village, when she meets a neighbor's daughter (Fox) who's just returned from America. Fox makes her interests clear and soon the two women are having an affair that shatters the peacefulness around them. Based on a novel by Joanna Trollope. **108m/C VHS.** *GB* Sophie Ward, Kerry Fox, Nathaniel Parker, Claire Bloom, Michael Gough, Barbara Jefford, Jeremy Northam, Rosalie Crutchley; ***D:*** Moira Armstrong; ***W:*** Alma Cullen; ***C:*** John Else. **TV**

Village of Dreams **1997** Middle-aged identical twin brothers recall the sweetness of their childhood in a rural Japanese village in 1948. As mischievous eight-year-olds, the duo spend their time playing pranks, spying on their neighbors, and entertaining themselves in the woods and streams. Based on the memoir "The Village of My Paintings" by Seizo Tashima. Japanese with subtitles. **112m/C VHS, DVD, Wide.** *JP* Keigo Matsuyama, Shogo Matsuyama; ***D:*** Yoichi Higashi; ***W:*** Takehiro Nakajima, Yoichi Higashi; ***C:*** Yoshio Shimizu.

Village of the Damned **1960** A group of unusual children are born in a small English village. They avoid their fathers and other men, except for the one who is their teacher. He discovers they are the vanguard of an alien invasion and leads the counter-attack. Exciting and bone-chilling low-budget thriller. From the novel, "The Midwich Cuckoos," by John Wyndham. The sequel, "The Children of the Damned" (1964) is even better. **78m/B VHS.** *GB* George Sanders, Barbara Shelley, Martin Stephens, Laurence Naismith, Michael C. Goetz, Michael Gwynn, John Phillips, Richard Vernon, Jenny Laird, Richard Warner, Thomas Heathcote, Charlotte Mitchell, John Stuart, Bernard Archard; ***D:*** Wolf Rilla; ***W:*** Wolf Rilla, Stirling Silliphant, George Harley; ***C:*** Geoffrey Faithfull; ***M:*** Ronald Goodwin.

Village of the Damned ½ **1995 (R)** The quiet town of Midwich, California, has been enveloped by a strange force that seems to have impregnated the local women. The albino children born of this incident have disturbing telepathic powers that they display through their bright orange and red eyes—supposedly precipitating a plot to take control. A pale remake of the 1960 British horror classic, which was based on John Wyndham's novel "The Midwich Cuckoos." Fails to capture the eeriness of it's predecessor and is bogged down with awkward casting, absurd dialogue, and a brood of children with glowing eyes that make them less like a threat and more like Nintendo addicts. **98m/C VHS, DVD.** Christopher Reeve, Kirstie Alley, Linda Kozlowski, Mark Hamill, Meredith Salenger, Michael Pare, Peter Jason, Constance Forslund, Karen Kahn; ***D:*** John Carpenter; ***W:*** John Carpenter, David Himmelstein; ***C:*** Gary B. Kibbe; ***M:*** John Carpenter, Dave Davies.

Village of the Giants **1965** A group of beer-guzzling teenagers become giants after eating a mysterious substance invented by a 12-year-old genius. Fun to pick out all the soon-to-be stars. Totally silly premise with bad special effects and minimal plot follow-through. Based on an H.G. Wells story. **82m/C VHS, DVD.** Ron Howard, Johnny Crawford, Tommy Kirk, Beau Bridges, Freddy Cannon, Beau Brummel, Tisha Sterling, Tim Rooney, Charla Doherty, Joe Turkel; ***D:*** Bert I. Gordon; ***W:*** Alan Caillou; ***C:*** Paul Vogel; ***M:*** Jack Nitzsche.

The Villain ½ *Cactus Jack* **1979 (PG)** An unfunny spoof of "B" westerns that is almost like a live-action "Roadrunner" cartoon. Douglas plays Cactus Jack, a highwayman who keeps trying to kidnap fair damsel Ann-Margret. Hero Schwarzenegger keeps rescuing her. Lynde is amusing as the uptight Indian chief Nervous Elk. **93m/C VHS, DVD.** Kirk Douglas, Ann-Margret, Arnold Schwarzenegger, Paul Lynde, Foster Brooks, Ruth Buzzi, Jack Elam, Strother Martin, Robert Tessier, Mel Tillis; ***D:*** Hal Needham; ***W:*** Robert G. Kane; ***C:*** Bobby Byrne; ***M:*** Bill Justis.

The Villain Still Pursued Her **1941** A poor hero and rich villain vie for the sweet heroine in this satire of old-fashioned temperance melodrama. Keaton manages to shine as the hero's sidekick. **67m/B VHS.** Anita Louise, Alan Mowbray, Buster Keaton, Hugh Herbert; ***D:*** Edward F. (Eddie) Cline.

Vincent & Theo ½ **1990 (PG-13)** The story of Impressionist painter Vincent van Gogh (Roth), and his brother Theo (Rhys), a gallery owner who loved his brother's work, yet could not get the public to buy it. Increasing despair and mental illness traps both men, as each struggles to create beauty in a world where it has no value. Altman has created a stunning portrait of "the artist" and his needs. The exquisite cinematography will make you feel as if you stepped into van Gogh's work. **138m/C VHS.** Tim Roth, Paul Rhys, Johanna Ter Steege, Wladimir Yordanoff; ***D:*** Robert Altman; ***W:*** Julian Mitchell; ***C:*** Jean Lepine.

Vincent, Francois, Paul and the Others *Vincent, Francois, Paul et les Autres* **1976** Three middle-aged Frenchmen rely on their friendships to endure a host of mid-life crises. In French with English subtitles. **113m/C VHS, Wide.** *FR* Yves Montand, Gerard Depardieu, Michel Piccoli, Stephane Audran, Serge Reggiani, Marie DuBois; ***D:*** Claude Sautet; ***W:*** Claude Sautet, Jean-Loup Dabadie, Claude Neron; ***C:*** Jean Boffety; ***M:*** Philippe Sarde.

Vincent: The Life and Death of Vincent van Gogh **1987** Van Gogh's work and creativity is examined in a documentary manner through his life and his letters. Thoughtful and intriguing production. Narrated by John Hurt as van Gogh. **99m/C VHS.** *AU* ***D:*** Paul Cox; ***W:*** Paul Cox; ***M:*** Norman Kaye; ***V:*** John Hurt.

The Vindicator *Frankenstein '88* **1985 (R)** A scientist killed in a lab accident is transformed into a cyborg who runs amok and murders indiscriminately. A modernized Frankenstein, with interesting special effects and well drawn characters. **92m/C VHS.** *CA* Terri Austin, Richard Cox, David McIlwraith, Pam Grier; ***D:*** Jean-Claude Lord.

The Vineyard **1989 (R)** Hapless victims are lured to a Japanese madman's island, where he drinks their blood and maintains a questionable immortality. **95m/C VHS, DVD, Wide.** James Hong, Karen Witter, Michael Wong; ***D:*** James Hong, Bill Rice.

Violated **1953** Pathetic production about New York police attempting to track down a sex-maniac murderer who slays his victims and then gives them a haircut. Unbelievably bad. **78m/B VHS.** Wim Holland, Lili Dawn, Mitchell Kowal, Vicki Carlson, William Martell; ***D:*** Walter Strate.

Violated woof! **1984** A detective endeavors to implicate a local businessman in the rapes of two beautiful women. Exploitative and dreary. **88m/C VHS.** John Heard, J.C. Quinn, April Daisy White, Samantha Fox; ***D:*** Richard Cannistraro.

Violence at Noon **1966** Highly disturbing film in which two women protect a brutal sex murderer from the law. Living among a quiet community of intellectuals, this conspiracy ends in a shocking finale in Oshima's stylized masterpiece. In Japanese with English subtitles. **99m/B VHS.** *JP* Saeda Kawaguchi, Akiko Koyama; ***D:*** Nagisa Oshima.

Violent Breed **1983** A CIA operative is sent on a mission to put a black marketeer out of business. **91m/C VHS.** *IT* Henry Silva, Harrison Muller, Woody Strode; ***D:*** Fernando Di Leo.

Violent Cop *Sono Otoko, Kyobo ni Tsuki* **1989** Think "Dirty Harry" to the nth power and you'll have some idea of the kind of cop Detective Azuma (Kitano) is. However, he also gets results, so the boss is willing to overlook the violent way Azuma does his job. His latest case involves a drug-related murder, a sadistic killer, a corrupt friend, and the kidnapping of Azuma's own mentally unstable sister. Not for the squeamish. Japanese with subtitles. **103m/C VHS, DVD, Wide.** *JP* Takeshi "Beat" Kitano, Shiro Sano, Maiko Kawakami, Makoto Ashikawa, Shigeru Hiraizumi, Mikiko Otonashi; ***D:*** Takeshi "Beat" Kitano; ***W:*** Hisahi Nozawa; ***C:*** Yasushi Sakakibara; ***M:*** Daisaku Kume.

The Violent Men ½ *Rough Company* **1955** Big-time land baron Robinson is trying to push out all other landowners in the valley, including Ford. At first Ford refuses to fight back, but after one of Robinson's henchmen kills one of his hired hands, he starts an all-out war against Robinson to save his land. Stanwyck as Robinson's wife and Keith as his brother are wicked as the two urging him on and having an affair behind his back. Based on the novel "Rough Company" by Donald Hamilton. **95m/C VHS, Wide.** Glenn Ford, Barbara Stanwyck, Edward G. Robinson, Dianne Foster, Brian Keith, May Wynn; ***D:*** Rudolph Mate; ***C:*** Burnett Guffey.

Violent Ones woof! **1968** Three men who are suspected of raping a young girl are threatened with lynching by an angry mob of townspeople. Badly acted, poorly directed, uneven and feeble. **96m/C VHS.** Fernando Lamas, David Carradine; ***D:*** Fernando Lamas.

Violent Professionals ½ *La Polizia vuole Giustizia* **1973** Suspended cop runs into resistance inside and outside the force when he infiltrates the mob to get the goods on a crime boss. **100m/C VHS.** *IT* Richard Conte, Luc Merenda; ***D:*** Sergio Martino.

Violent Women **1959** Five female convicts escape and embark on a bloody journey through the countryside, pursued by the authorities. Shows women can be just as brutal as any man. **61m/C VHS.** Jennifer Slater, Jo Ann Kelly, Sandy Lyn, Eleanor Blair, Pati Magee; ***D:*** Barry Mahon.

The Violent Years woof! *Female* **1956** Spoiled high-school debutantes form a vicious all-girl gang and embark on a spree that includes murder, robbery, and male rape. Justice wins out in the end. Exploitive trash written by Wood, who directed the infamous "Plan 9 from Outer Space." **60m/B VHS, DVD.** Jean Moorehead, Barbara Weeks, Glenn Corbett, Theresa Hancock, I. Stanford Jolley, Arthur Millan; ***D:*** Edward D. Wood Jr., Franz Eichhorn, William M. Morgan; ***W:*** Edward D. Wood Jr.; ***C:*** William C. Thompson.

Violent Zone **1989** Mercenaries go on a supposed rescue mission in the wilderness. **92m/C VHS, DVD.** John Douglas, Chad Hayward, Christopher Weeks; ***D:*** John Garwood; ***W:*** David Pritchard, John Bushelman.

Violets Are Blue ½ **1986 (PG-13)** Two high-school sweethearts are reunited in their hometown years later and try to rekindle their romance—even though the man is married. **86m/C VHS.** Kevin Kline, Sissy Spacek, Bonnie Bedelia, John Kellogg, Augusta Dabney, Jim Standford; ***D:*** Jack Fisk; ***W:*** Naomi Foner; ***C:*** Ralf Bode; ***M:*** Patrick Williams.

Violette *Violette Noziere* **1978 (R)** Fascinating true-life account of a 19-year-old French girl in the 1930s who, bored with her life and wanting to be with her lover, decides to poison her parents so she can receive her inheritance. Her mother survives but her father dies, and the girl is sent to prison for murder. Extraordinary performance by Huppert and the film is visually stunning. **122m/C VHS.** *FR* Isabelle Huppert, Stephane Audran, Jean Carmet, Jean-Francoise Garreaud, Bernadette LaFont; ***D:*** Claude Chabrol; ***W:*** Odile Barski, Frederic Grendel; ***C:*** Jean Rabier; ***M:*** Pierre Jansen. Cannes '78: Actress (Huppert); Cesar '79: Support. Actress (Audran).

VIP, My Brother Superman **1990** The Vips are modern-day descendants of superbeings about to become legends in their own times. SuperVip is broad of chest and pure in spirit while his brother MiniVip possesses only limited powers. From the creator of "Allegro Non Troppo" comes this enticing, amusing piece of animation. **90m/C VHS.** ***D:*** Bruno Bozzetto.

Viper **1988** A woman battles a cryptic anti-terrorist band to avenge the murder of her husband. **96m/C VHS.** Linda Purl, Chris Robinson, James Tolkan; ***D:*** Peter Maris.

The V.I.P.'s **1963** Slick, sophisticated drama set in the V.I.P. lounge of a British airport. Trapped by fog, several of the passengers get acquainted and are forced to face their problems as they spend the night in the airport lounge. Taylor stars as Frances Andros, a wealthy young woman leaving her husband (Burton) for life in the U.S. with her lover, Jourdan. A movie tycoon, an Australian entrepreneur, his secretary, and a duchess are among the other passengers grounded by the fog. Both Rutherford and Smith give excellent performances and it was a toss-up as to which actress would be nominated for the Oscar. **119m/C VHS.** *GB* Elizabeth Taylor, Richard Burton, Louis Jourdan, Elsa Martinelli, Margaret Rutherford, Maggie Smith, Rod Taylor, Orson Welles, Linda Christian, Dennis Price; ***D:*** Anthony Asquith; ***W:*** Terence Rattigan; ***C:*** Jack Hildyard; ***M:*** Miklos Rozsa. Oscars '63: Support. Actress (Rutherford); Golden Globes '64: Support. Actress (Rutherford); Natl. Bd. of Review '63: Support. Actress (Rutherford).

Virgin among the Living Dead **1971 (R)** Young woman travels to remote castle when she hears of relative's death. Once there, she finds the residents a tad weird and has bad dreams in which zombies chase her. Bizarre even for Franco, who seems to have been going through a "Pasolini" phase while making this one. **90m/C VHS.** *SP* Christina von Blanc, Britt Nichols, Howard Vernon, Anne Libert, Rose Kiekens, Paul Muller; ***D:*** Jess (Jesus) Franco.

The Virgin and the Gypsy ½ **1970 (R)** An English girl brought up in a repressive household in 1920s England falls in love with a gypsy. Based on the novel by D.H. Lawrence. Directorial debut of Miles. **92m/C VHS.** *GB* Joanna Shimkus, Franco Nero, Honor Blackman, Mark Burns; ***D:*** Christopher Miles; ***W:*** Alan Plater.

Virgin High **1990 (R)** Three young men sneak into an all-girls Catholic boarding school with hilarious consequences. Ward (TV's Robin, from "Batman") makes a special appearance in bondage in this sex farce. **90m/C VHS.** Burt Ward, Linnea Quigley, Tracy Dali, Richard Gabai, Catherine McGuiness, Chris Dempsey; ***D:*** Richard Gabai; ***W:*** Richard Gabai, Jeff Neal.

Virgin Machine *Jungfrauenmaschine* **1988** Lesbian journalist Dorothy Muller (Blum) is unhappy in her native Hamburg and decides to move to California to pursue her idea of romantic love. English and German with English subtitles. **91m/B VHS.** *GE* Ina Blum, Susie Bright, Shelley Mars, Dominique Gaspar; ***D:*** Monika Treut; ***W:*** Monika Treut; ***C:*** Elfi Mikesch.

The Virgin of Nuremberg ½ *Horror Castle; Terror Castle; Castle of Terror; La Vergine de Norimberga* **1965** A young woman enters her new husband's ancestral castle and is stalked by the specter of a legendary sadist. **82m/C VHS.** *IT* Rossana Podesta, George Riviere, Christopher Lee, Jim Dolen; ***D:*** Anthony (Antonio Margheriti) Dawson.

The Virgin Queen **1955** Davis stars in this historical drama, which focuses on the stormy relationship between the aging Queen and Sir Walter Raleigh. Collins is the lady-in-waiting who is the secret object of Raleigh's true affections. Previously, Davis played Queen Elizabeth I in "Elizabeth and Essex." Davis holds things together. **92m/C VHS.** Bette Davis, Richard Todd, Joan Collins, Herbert Marshall, Dan O'Herlihy, Jay Robinson, Romney Brent; ***D:*** Henry Koster.

Virgin Queen of St. Francis High **1988 (PG)** Two high school foes make a bet that one of them can take the "virgin" title away from gorgeous Christensen by summer's end. She has to fight off their advances, but grows to like Straface. **89m/C VHS.** *CA* Joseph R. Straface, Stacy Christensen, J.T. Wotton; ***D:*** Francesco Lucente.

Virgin Sacrifice **1959** A great white hunter looking for zoo-bound jaguars confronts the virgin-sacrificing, Tiger God-revering natives of Guatemala. **67m/C**

VHS. David DaLie, Antonio Gutierrez, Angelica Morales, Fernando Wagner; *D:* Fernando Wagner.

The Virgin Soldiers 🦴🦴½ **1969 (R)** A British comedy about greenhorn military recruits stationed in Singapore, innocent of women as well as battle, and their struggles to overcome both situations. A good cast raises this above the usual low-brow sex farce. Based on the novel by Leslie Thomas. Followed by "Stand Up Virgin Soldiers." **96m/C VHS.** *GB* Hywel Bennett, Nigel Davenport, Lynn Redgrave, Nigel Patrick, Rachel Kempson, Jack Shepherd, Tsai Chin; *D:* John Dexter; *W:* John Hopkins.

The Virgin Spring 🦴🦴🦴½ *Jungfrukallan* **1959** Based on a medieval ballad and set in 14th-century Sweden. The rape and murder of young innocent Karin (Pattersson) spurs her father Tore (Van Sydow) to vengeance and he kills her attackers. Over the girl's dead body, the father questions how God could have let any of it happen, but he comes to find solace and forgiveness when a spring bursts forth from the spot. Stunning Bergman compositions. In Swedish with English subtitles; also available in dubbed version. **88m/B VHS.** *SW* Max von Sydow, Birgitta Valberg, Gunnel Lindblom, Brigitta Pattersson, Axel Duborg; *D:* Ingmar Bergman; *W:* Ulla Isaakson; *C:* Sven Nykvist; *M:* Erik Nordgren. Oscars '60: Foreign Film; Golden Globes '61: Foreign Film.

The Virgin Suicides 🦴🦴 **1999 (R)** The five teenaged Lisbon sisters are all blonde, lovely, and isolated in their 70s suburban life. Mom (Turner) is a rigid religious while Dad (Woods) is a wimpy math teacher. After 13-year-old Cecilia (Hall) ties to off herself, her parents are encouraged to let the girls socialize and the story becomes the recollections of the narrator (Ribisi), one of the boys fascinated by the quintet. Much of the movie focuses on sexually provocative Lux (Dunst) and her hunky would-be beau, Trip (Hartnett). There's a floaty, listlessly romantic air to the whole production (Coppola's directorial debut), which is based on the novel by Jeffrey Eugenides. **97m/C VHS, DVD, Wide.** Kirsten Dunst, Kathleen Turner, James Woods, Josh Hartnett, Hanna Hall, Chelse Swain, A.J. Cook, Leslie Hayman, Danny DeVito, Scott Glenn, Jonathan Tucker, Anthony DeSimone; *D:* Sofia Coppola; *W:* Sofia Coppola; *C:* Edward Lachman; *Nar:* Giovanni Ribisi.

The Virgin Witch 🦴½ *Lesbian Twins* **1970 (R)** Two beautiful sisters are sent to the British countryside, ostensibly for a modeling job. They soon find themselves in the midst of a witches' coven however, and discover one of them is to be sacrificed. The Michelles were "Playboy" magazine's first sister centerfolds. **89m/C VHS.** *GB* Anne Michelle, Vicki Michelle, Patricia Haines, Keith Buckley, James Chase, Neil Hallett; *D:* Ray Austin.

Virginia City 🦴🦴🦴 **1940** Action-packed western drama set during the Civil War. Flynn is a Union soldier who escapes from a Confederate prison run by Scott, after learning of a gold shipment being sent by Southern sympathizers to aid the Confederacy. He ends up in Virginia City (where the gold-laden wagon train is to leave from) and falls for a dance-hall girl (Hopkins) who turns out to be a Southern spy working for Scott but who falls for Flynn anyway. Bogart is miscast as a half-breed outlaw who aids Scott but wants the gold for himself. Considered a follow-up to "Dodge City." **121m/C VHS.** Errol Flynn, Miriam Hopkins, Randolph Scott, Humphrey Bogart, Frank McHugh, Alan Hale, Guinn "Big Boy" Williams, Douglass Dumbrille, Charles Halton; *D:* Michael Curtiz; *M:* Max Steiner.

The Virginia Hill Story 🦴🦴 **1976** Fictionalized biography of mobster Bugsy Siegel's girlfriend who, in the mid-'50s, was subpoenaed to appear before the Kefauver investigation on crime in the U.S. As the examining lawyer presents questions regarding her background and connections with the underworld, we see the story of her life. **90m/C VHS.** Dyan Cannon, Harvey Keitel, Robby Benson, Allen (Goorwitz) Garfield, John Vernon; *D:* Joel Schumacher. **TV**

The Virginian 🦴🦴½ **1923** The second silent version of Owen Wister's classic western novel, inferior to both the 1914 Cecil B. DeMille silent and the 1929 Victor Fleming talkie. Harlan plays the title role as the cowpoke who leads a posse against cattle rustlers and falls in love with a schoolteacher. **79m/B VHS.** Kenneth Harlan, Florence Vidor, Russell Simpson, Pat O'Malley, Raymond Hatton; *D:* Tom Forman.

The Virginian 🦴🦴🦴 **1929** A classic early-talkie western about a ranch-hand defeating the local bad guys. One line of dialogue has become, with modification, a standard western cliche: "If you want to call me that, smile." Based on the novel by Owen Wister. With this starring role, Cooper broke away from the juvenile lovers he had been playing to the laconic, rugged male leads he would be known for. Huston is perfectly cast as the outlaw leader. **95m/B VHS.** Gary Cooper, Walter Huston, Richard Arlen, Chester Conklin, Eugene Pallette; *D:* Victor Fleming.

The Virginian 🦴🦴½ **1946** Cowboy good guy, known as the Virginian (McCrea), and his best pal Steve (Tufts) both fall for Molly (Britton), the Eastern-bred schoolmarm who's come to their Wyoming town. Steve wants to make some quick money and joins up with leader Trampas' (Donlevy) cattle rustling gang. So the Virginian is forced to chose between friendship and the code of the west and Molly wonders if she can accepts the country's harsh ways. Based on Owen Wister's 1902 novel. **87m/C VHS.** Joel McCrea, Sonny Tufts, Barbara Britton, Brian Donlevy, Fay Bainter, Tom Tully, Henry O'Neill, William Frawley; *D:* Stuart Gilmore; *W:* Frances Goodrich, Albert Hackett; *C:* Harry Hallenberger; *M:* Daniele Amfitheatrof.

The Virginian 🦴🦴½ **1999** Yet another remake (this one unremarkable but watchable) of Owen Wister's 1902 novel. Pullman (who also directed) is the cowboy of the title, who is out for a brutal brand of justice against an unscupulous rancher. But his methods upset his schoolmarm sweetie (Lane). **95m/C VHS.** Bill Pullman, Diane Lane, John Savage, Dennis Weaver; *D:* Bill Pullman; *W:* Larry Gross. **CABLE**

Viridiana 🦴🦴🦴🦴 **1961** Innocent Viridiana (Pinal), with strong ideas about goodness, visits her worldly uncle, Don Jaime's (Rey), home before she takes her vows as a nun. He has developed a sick obsession for her, but after drugging Viridiana, Don Jaimefinds he cannot violate her purity. He tells her, however, she is no longer chaste so she will not join the church. After her uncle's suicide, Viridiana learns she and his illegitimate son Jorge (Rabal) have inherited her uncle's run-down estate. Viridiana opens the house to all sorts of beggars, who take shameless advantage, while Jorge works slowly to restore the estate and improve the lives of those around him. Considered to be one of Bunuel's masterpieces and a bitter allegory of Spanish idealism versus pragmatism and the state of the world. Spanish with subtitles. **90m/B VHS.** *SP MX* Silvia Pinal, Francesco Rabal, Fernando Rey, Margarita Lozano, Victoria Zinny; *D:* Luis Bunuel; *W:* Luis Bunuel, Julio Alajandro; *C:* Jose F. Aguayo. Cannes '61: Film.

Virtual Assassin 🦴🦴 *Cyberjack* **1995 (R)** 21st century sci-fi actioner finds the crooked Zef (James) leading his band of thugs into a research lab to steal a powerful computer virus. Naturally, the janitor (Dudikoff) just happens to be an ex-cop with a score to settle with Zef. Predictable but with decent special effects. **99m/C VHS.** *CA JP* Michael Dudikoff, Brion James, Jon Cuthbert, Suki Kaiser, James Thom; *D:* Robert Lee; *W:* Eric Poppen.

Virtual Combat 🦴🦴 **1995 (R)** Ex-cop Quarry (Wilson) teams up with some cyber-girls to stop a madman who's able to manipulate virtual reality programs into living beings and releases a killer who wants to lead a destructive virtual army. **97m/C VHS, DVD.** Don "The Dragon" Wilson, Athena Massey, Loren Avedon, Kenneth McLeod, Turhan Bey, Stella Stevens, Michael Bernardo; *D:* Andrew Stevens; *W:* William Martell; *C:* David J. Miller; *M:* Claude Gaudette.

Virtual Desire 🦴½ **1995 (R)** Brad Collins is bored with his marriage and finds some excitement via sexual games on the Internet. But someone is taking a very close interest in Brad's virtual amours and when his wife is murdered, Brad becomes the prime suspect. **92m/C VHS, DVD.** Michael Meyer, Julie Strain, Gail Harris; *D:* Noble Henri.

Virtual Encounters 🦴🦴½ **1996 (R)** Top-drawer soft-core fluff follows busy executive Amy (Elizabeth Kaitan), whose birthday present is a session of virtual wish fulfillment at a high-tech fantasyland. The fantasies involve masks, leather, desks, broccoli...well, O.K., the broccoli is an exaggeration. This is sexy and kinky, not sick. The action is slickly staged and well photographed by director Richards. Also available in an unrated version at 84 minutes. **80m/C VHS.** Elizabeth Kaitan, Taylore St. Claire, Rob Lee; *D:* Cybil Richards; *C:* Cybil Richards.

Virtual Girl 🦴🦴 **2000 (R)** Computer programmer John Lewis (Dixon) is working on an erotic virutal reality program that features a cyber-slut (Curtis). When said vixen gets rejected by her creator, she gets very, very angry. Erotica that makes the best use of its low-budget and Curtis' assets. **84m/C VHS.** Richard Gabai, Charlie Curtis, Max Dixon; *D:* Richard Gabai. **VIDEO**

Virtual Seduction 🦴🦴 **1996 (R)** Liam's (Fahey) taken a job testing a virtual reality pod that can interpret what the user wants—and Liam wants to see his dead girlfriend Paris (Genzel). Only he spends so much time with the virtual Paris, that his real-life gal Laura (Dolenz) is worried about his health and sanity—too bad project developer Grant (Novak) isn't so concerned. **84m/C VHS.** Jeff Fahey, Ami Dolenz, Carrie Genzel, Frank Novak, Meshach Taylor; *D:* Paul Ziller.

Virtual Sexuality 🦴🦴 **1999 (R)** Teen comedy, set in London, that has an amusing virtual reality plot. Cute 17-year-old Justine (Fraser) decides school stud Alex (O'Brien) is the perfect guy to lose her virginity to. But he's only interested in school vamp, "Hoover" (Bell). So Justine enters a virtual reality makeover machine at a technology fair in order to create an electronic facsimile of her perfect man. But a malfunction causes Justine to split in two—herself (with amnesia) and her perfect man, the bewildered male creation Jake (Penry-Jones). Based on the novel by Chloe Rayban. **92m/C VHS, DVD, Wide.** *GB* Laura Fraser, Rupert Penry-Jones, Kieran O'Brien, Luke De Lacey, Natasha Bell, Steve John Sheperd, Laura Macaulay, Marcelle Duprey; *D:* Nick Hurran; *W:* Nick Fisher; *C:* Brian Tufano; *M:* Rupert Gregson-Williams.

Virtue's Revolt 🦴½ **1924** A small-town girl is corrupted by the sleazy world of showbiz. Silent. **51m/B VHS.** Edith Thornton, Crauford Kent.

Virtuosity 🦴½ **1995 (R)** Ex-cop-with-a-tragic-past Parker Barnes (Washington) is sprung from prison to help capture computer-generated killer Sid 6.7 (Crowe), who escapes from cyberspace and goes on a rampage in 1997 Los Angeles. Seems this virtual reality bad guy has a personality composed of some 200 serial killers and criminal minds so Parker's got his work cut out for him. But criminal-behavior psychologist Madison Carter (Lynch) is around to lend her expert advice. Both the charismatically evil Crowe and the sufferingly noble Washington are wasted in this effects-laden thriller that sacrifices character for flash. **105m/C VHS, DVD, Wide.** Denzel Washington, Russell Crowe, Kelly Lynch, Stephen Spinella, William Forsythe, Louise Fletcher, William Fichtner, Costas Mandylor, Kevin J. O'Connor; *D:* Brett Leonard; *W:* Eric Bernt; *C:* Gale Tattersall; *M:* Christopher Young.

Virus 🦴🦴 *Fukkatsu no Hi* **1982 (PG)** After nuclear war and plague destroy civilization, a small group of people gather in Antarctica and struggle with determination to carry on life. A look at man's genius for self-destruction and his endless hope. **102m/C VHS.** *JP* George Kennedy, Sonny Chiba, Glenn Ford, Robert Vaughn, Stuart Gillard, Stephanie Faulkner, Ken Ogata, Bo Svenson, Olivia Hussey, Chuck Connors, Edward James Olmos; *D:* Kinji Fukasaku.

Virus 🦴½ **1996 (PG-13)** Secret Service agent Ken Fairchild (Bosworth) finds out that biological-warfare chemicals have been spilt in a national park that's the site for an ecological summit between the president and world leaders. It's up to Fairchild and a park ranger (Pinsent) to battle the minions of the chemical's manufacturer who wants to keep the whole thing quiet. **90m/C VHS.** Brian Bosworth, Leah K. Pinsent; *D:* Allan Goldstein.

Virus 🦴½ **1998 (R)** Curtis, Sutherland, and Baldwin are members of a tugboat crew whose boat has been wrecked by a typhoon. They take refuge aboard a Russian research ship only to discover the Russian crew has been eliminated by a strange life form. The electricity-based alien considers humanity a virus and begins making bizarre killing machines out of body parts and machinery. The plot also seems pieced together from other sci-fi horror movies that did it better. **100m/C VHS, DVD.** Jamie Lee Curtis, William Baldwin, Donald Sutherland, Joanna Pacula, Sherman Augustus, Clifford Curtis, Marshall Bell, Julio Mechoso, Yuri Chervotkin, Keith Flippen; *D:* John Bruno; *W:* Chuck Pfarrer, Dennis Feldman; *C:* David Eggby; *M:* Joel McNeely.

The Vision 🦴🦴 **1987** Suspenseful British production about televangelists who attempt to control their viewers' minds through worldwide satellite broadcasting. **103m/C VHS.** *GB* Lee Remick, Dirk Bogarde, Helena Bonham Carter, Eileen Atkins; *D:* Norman Stone.

Vision Quest 🦴🦴½ *Crazy for You* **1985 (R)** A high school student wants to win the Washington State wrestling championship and the affections of a beautiful older artist. He gives it his all as he trains for the meet and goes after his "visionquest." A winning performance by Modine raises this above the usual teen coming-of-age movie. Madonna sings "Crazy for You" in a nightclub. Based on novel by Terry Davis. **107m/C VHS, DVD.** Matthew Modine, Linda Fiorentino, Ronny Cox, Roberts Blossom, Daphne Zuniga, Charles Hallahan, Michael Schoeffling; *D:* Harold Becker; *W:* Darryl Ponicsan; *C:* Owen Roizman; *M:* Tangerine Dream.

Visions 🦴½ **1990** A man's ability to "see" murders before they happen leads police to suspect him of committing them, and he must clear himself. **90m/C VHS.** Joe Balogh, Alice Villarreal, Tom Taylor, A.R. Newman, J.R. Pella; *D:* Stephen E. Miller.

Visions of Evil 🦴 **1973** A young woman, recently released from a mental institution, is plagued by a series of terrifying visions when she moves into a house where a brutal axe murder took place. **85m/C VHS.** Lori Sanders, Dean Jagger.

Visions of Light: The Art of Cinematography 🦴🦴🦴 **1993** Excellent documentary on the way films look and how the art of photographing movies can contribute as much, if not more, than cast, director, and script. Scenes from 125 films, from "Birth of a Nation" to "Good-Fellas" are shown, with commentary from a number of cinematographers, including Gordon Willis, William A. Fraker, Conrad Hall, Ernest Dickerson, Vilmos Zsigmond, and Michael Chapman, on how they achieved certain effects and their collaborations with the director of the film. **95m/C VHS, DVD.** *D:* Arnold Glassman, Stuart Samuels, Todd McCarthy; *W:* Todd McCarthy; *C:* Nancy Schreiber. N.Y. Film Critics '93: Feature Doc.; Natl. Soc. Film Critics '93: Feature Doc.

The Visit 🦴🦴🦴 **2000 (R)** Harper leads an excellent cast in this story of Alex, a man imprisoned for a rape he may not have committed who only seeks the acceptance and love of his family. Through visits with his estranged, successful brother (Obatunde), his loving mother (Gibbs), and his disapproving father (Williams), as well as a prison psychiatrist (Rashad) and a childhood friend (Chong), Alex finds the peace he seeks. Yes, it sounds hokey, but the excellent performances and steady, subtle direction make it all work. The parole board scene is a highlight. **107m/C VHS, DVD, Wide.** *US* Hill Harper, Obba Babatunde, Billy Dee Williams, Marla Gibbs, Rae Dawn Chong, Phylicia Rashad, Talia Shire, David Clennon, Glynn Turman, Efrain Figueroa, Amy Stiller; ***D:*** Jordan Walker-Pearlman; ***W:*** Jordan Walker-Pearlman; ***C:*** John Ndiaga Demps; ***M:*** Michael Bearden.

Visitants 🦴 **1987** Aliens descend irreverently on a small town in the 1950s, with unexpected comedic results. **93m/C VHS.** Marcus Vaughter, Johanna Grika, Joel Hile, Nicole Rio; ***D:*** Rick Sloane.

Visiting Hours 🦴 *The Fright; Get Well Soon* **1982 (R)** Psycho-killer slashes his female victims and photographs his handiwork. Grant is one of his victims who doesn't die, so the killer decides to visit the hospital and finish the job. Fairly graphic and generally unpleasant. **101m/C VHS.** *CA* Lee Grant, William Shatner, Linda Purl, Michael Ironside; ***D:*** Jean-Claude Lord; ***W:*** Brian Taggert; ***M:*** Jonathan Goldsmith.

The Visitor 🦴½ **1980 (R)** Affluent handsome doctor and mate conspire with grisly devil worshippers to conceive devil child. **90m/C VHS.** Mel Ferrer, Glenn Ford, Lance Henriksen, John Huston, Shelley Winters, Joanne Nail, Sam Peckinpah; ***D:*** Giullo Paradisi.

Visitor from the Grave 🦴 **1981** When an American heiress and her boyfriend dispose of a dead man's body, his spirit comes back to haunt them. This annoys them. **60m/C VHS.** Simon MacCorkindale, Kathryn Leigh Scott, Gareth Thomas, Mia Nadasi.

The Visitors 🦴½ **1989 (R)** Ghosts come to stay at a young family's dream house in Sweden. Not exactly a novel treatment or a novel premise. **102m/C VHS.** *SW* Keith Berkeley, Lena Endre, John Force, John Olsen, Joanna Berg, Brent Landiss, Patrick Ersgard; ***D:*** Joakim (Jack) Ersgard.

The Visitors 🦴🦴 *Les Visiteurs* **1995 (R)** Time travel comedy features 12th-century knight Godefroy (Reno) and his vassal Jacquasse (Clavier) crossing paths with a powerful witch (and evidently pissing her off) since she casts a spell causing Godefroy to accidentally kill his father-in-law. So Godefroy contacts a wizard to give him a time travel potion so he can go back and stop the shooting. Too bad the potion hurls knight and vassal forward into present-day France. French with subtitles. **106m/C VHS.** *FR* Jean Reno, Christian Clavier, Mariann (Marie-Anne) Chazel, Valerie Lemercier, Christian Bujeau; ***D:*** Jean-Marie Poire; ***W:*** Christian Clavier, Jean-Marie Poire; ***C:*** Jean-Yves Le Mener; ***M:*** Eric Levi.

Vital Signs 🦴 **1990 (R)** Hackneyed drama about six medical students enduring the tribulations of their profession. **102m/C VHS.** Adrian Pasdar, Diane Lane, Jack Gwaltney, Laura San Giacomo, Jane Adams, Tim Ransom, Bradley Whitford, Lisa Jane Persky, William Devane, Norma Aleandro, Jimmy Smits, James Karen, Telma Hopkins; ***D:*** Marisa Silver; ***W:*** Jeb Stuart; ***M:*** Miles Goodman.

Viva Knievel woof! *Seconds to Live* **1977 (PG)** Crooks plan to sabotage Knievel's daredevil jump in Mexico and then smuggle cocaine back into the States in his coffin. Unintentionally campy. **106m/C VHS.** Evel Knievel, Gene Kelly, Lauren Hutton, Red Buttons, Leslie Nielsen, Cameron Mitchell, Marjoe Gortner, Albert Salmi, Dabney Coleman; ***D:*** Gordon Douglas; ***M:*** Charles Bernstein.

Viva Las Vegas 🦴🦴½ *Love in Las Vegas* **1963** Race car driver Elvis needs money to compete against rival Danova in the upcoming Las Vegas Grand Prix. He takes a job in a casino and romances fellow employee Ann-Margret, who turns out to be his rival for the grand prize in the local talent competition. Good pairing between the two leads, and the King does particularly well with the title song. ♫The Lady Loves Me; Viva Las Vegas; What'd I Say; I Need Somebody to Lean On; Come On, Everybody; Today, Tomorrow and Forever; If You Think I Don't Need You; Appreciation; My Rival. **85m/C VHS, DVD, Wide.** Elvis Presley, Ann-Margret, William Demarest, Jack Carter, Cesare Danova, Nicky Blair, Larry Kent; ***D:*** George Sidney; ***C:*** Joseph Biroc.

Viva Maria! 🦴🦴½ **1965 (R)** Tongue-in-cheek comedy with Bardot and Moreau as two dancers (both named Maria) in a show traveling through Mexico. The two become incensed by the poverty of the peasants and decide to turn revolutionary (especially after Moreau has an affair with revolutionary leader Hamilton, who promptly gets killed). The two French sex symbols are a fine match. **119m/C VHS.** *FR IT* Jeanne Moreau, Brigitte Bardot, George Hamilton, Paulette Dubost, Claudio Brook; ***D:*** Louis Malle; ***W:*** Louis Malle, Jean-Claude Carriere; ***C:*** Henri Decae; ***M:*** Georges Delerue.

Viva Max 🦴🦴½ **1969** A blundering modern-day Mexican general and his men recapture the Alamo, and an equally inept American force, headed by Winters, is sent to rout them out. Mostly works, with some very funny scenes. Ustinov is great. **93m/C VHS.** Peter Ustinov, Jonathan Winters, John Astin, Pamela Tiffin, Keenan Wynn; ***D:*** Jerry Paris.

Viva Villa! 🦴🦴🦴 **1934** Exciting action biography of Mexican revolutionary Pancho Villa, well-portrayed by the exuberant Beery. The film follows the early Robin Hood-like exploits of Villa and his men who soon join Walthall and his peasant army in overthrowing the government. But Villa's bandito instincts and ego cause problems and a power struggle ensues. Director Howard Hawks went uncredited for his work on the film, being fired by the studio after an incident while on location in Mexico. **115m/B VHS.** Wallace Beery, Fay Wray, Stuart Erwin, Leo Carrillo, Donald Cook, George E. Stone, Joseph Schildkraut, Henry B. Walthall, Katherine DeMille, David Durand, Frank Puglia; ***D:*** Jack Conway; ***W:*** Ben Hecht.

Viva Zapata! 🦴🦴🦴🦴 **1952** Chronicles the life of Mexican revolutionary Emiliano Zapata. Brando is powerful as he leads the peasant revolt in the early 1900s, only to be corrupted by power and greed. Quinn well deserved his Best Supporting Actor Oscar for his performance as Zapata's brother. Based on the novel "Zapata the Unconquered" by Edgcumb Pinchon. **112m/B VHS.** Marlon Brando, Anthony Quinn, Jean Peters, Margo, Arnold Moss, Joseph Wiseman, Mildred Dunnock; ***D:*** Elia Kazan; ***W:*** John Steinbeck; ***M:*** Alex North. Oscars '52: Support. Actor (Quinn); British Acad. '52: Actor (Brando); Cannes '52: Actor (Brando).

Vivacious Lady 🦴🦴🦴 **1938** Romantic comedy about a mild-mannered college professor who marries a chorus girl. Problems arise when he must let his conservative family and his former fiancee in on the marriage news. Good performances. Appealing. **90m/B VHS.** Ginger Rogers, James Stewart, James Ellison, Beulah Bondi, Charles Coburn, Jack Carson, Franklin Pangborn; ***D:*** George Stevens.

Vive l'Amour 🦴🦴 *Aiqing Wansui* **1994** A furnished Taipei luxury apartment is the setting for three characters who make use of the space but have little connection to each other. Guimei is the real estate agent who's trying to sell the apartment and uses it for casual sex, including an encounter with street vendor Zhaorong. The third part of the triangle is young salesman Kangsheng, who's broken into the place to commit suicide but is forestalled by Zhaorong, with whom Kangsheng then becomes sexually intrigued. The trio come and go, mostly alone, so dialogue is at a minimum. Taiwanese with subtitles. **118m/C VHS, DVD, Wide.** *TW* Yang Guimei, Chen Zhaorong, Li Kangsheng; ***D:*** Tsai Ming-Liang; ***W:*** Tsai Ming-Liang; ***C:*** Pen-jung Lioa, Ming-kuo Lin.

Vogues of 1938 🦴🦴 *All This and Glamour Too; Vogues* **1937** As a lark, a rich girl takes a job as a fashion model and incurs the displeasure of Baxter, the owner of the chic fashion house where she works. An early Technicolor fashion extravaganza. ♫That Old Feeling; Lovely One; Turn On the Red Hot Heat (Burn the Blues Away); King of Jam. **110m/C VHS.** Joan Bennett, Warner Baxter, Helen Vinson, Mischa Auer, Hedda Hopper, Penny Singleton, Alan Mowbray; ***D:*** Irving Cummings.

Voices from a Locked Room 🦴🦴 *Voices* **1995 (R)** Very loosely based on the life of British composer Peter Warlock (1894-1930) and music critic Philip Heseltine. Heseltine detests Warlock's music, Warlock threatens Heseltine, and Heseltine's fiancee (Bergen) is the girl in the middle. Of course, what's really bizarre is that Warlock is Heseltine's pseudonym. Film does have a nice period look. **93m/C VHS.** *GB* Jeremy Northam, Tushka Bergen, Allan Corduner, Hilton McRae; ***D:*** Malcolm Clarke; ***W:*** Peter Barnes; ***C:*** Ann T. Rossetti; ***M:*** Elliot Goldenthal.

Voices from Beyond 🦴½ *Voci dal Profondo* **1990** After wealthy Giorgio Mainardi hemorrhages to death, his daughter Rosy (Huff) returns home from college to attend the funeral. She soon begins to have strange dreams in which her father claims that he was murdered, and begs Rosy to discover the identity of the killer. In flashbacks, we learn that Giorgio did something to enrage everyone in the household before he died, so there are many suspects. While the revelation of the murderer is actually surprising, the rest of the film is a boring mess. While director Fulci is well-known for his liberal use of gore and his occasionally creepy visuals, this film has neither. The acting isn't very good, and the atrocious dubbing only makes matters worse. **91m/C DVD, Wide.** *IT* Dulio Del Prete, Karina Huff, Pascal Persiano, Lorenzo Flaherty, Bettina Giovannini, Damiano Azzos; ***D:*** Lucio Fulci; ***W:*** Piero Regnoli; ***M:*** Stelvio Cipriano.

The Void 🦴½ **2001 (R)** Physicist Eva Soderstrom (Tapping) discovers that industrialist Thomas Abernathy (McDowell) is experimenting with creating an artificial black hole on Earth. This isn't a good thing so Eva hooks up with Dr. Steven Price (Paul) to stop Abernathy. So-so thriller. **90m/C VHS, DVD.** Amanda Tapping, Adrian Paul, Malcolm McDowell, Andrew McIlroy; ***D:*** Gilbert M. Shilton; ***W:*** Gilbert M. Shilton, Geri Cudia Barger; ***C:*** Attila Szalay; ***M:*** Ross Vannelli.

Volcano 🦴🦴 **1997 (PG-13)** L.A. has already had to deal with earthquakes, mudslides, raging fires, riots and the acting career of Anna Nicole Smith. Now it's completely roasted by millions of gallons of molten lava. This overblown Rescue 911 has Mike Roark (Jones), the standard take-charge guy, trying to avert total destruction while being assisted by the brainy-but-beautiful seismologist Dr. Amy Barnes (Heche). Many tongue-in-cheek jokes about the general state of chaos in L.A. even on the best of days; but aside from these, the dialogue is cheesy beyond belief. The special effects are very impressive, however. Wilshire Blvd. was actually recreated on a 17-acre set (believed to be the biggest ever) in order to meet its fiery doom. **120m/C VHS, DVD, Wide.** Tommy Lee Jones, Anne Heche, Gaby Hoffman, Don Cheadle, Keith David, John Corbett, Michael Rispoli, John Carroll Lynch, Jacqueline Kim; ***D:*** Mick Jackson; ***W:*** Billy Ray, Jerome Armstrong; ***C:*** Theo van de Sande; ***M:*** Alan Silvestri.

Volcano: Fire on the Mountain 🦴½ *Fire on the Mountain* **1997 (PG)** Cheesy TV disaster flick finds geologist Peter Slater (Cortese) trying to convince both his boss and the residents of Angel Falls, California that a nearby volcano is about to blow. **99m/C VHS.** Dan Cortese, Cynthia Gibb, Brian Kerwin; ***D:*** Graeme Campbell; ***C:*** Tobias Schliessler; ***M:*** David Michael Frank.

Volere Volare 🦴🦴½ **1992 (R)** Shy sound engineer Nichetti shares a studio with his brother. The brother employs a bevy of beauties to dub sound effects onto soft-core porn films while Nichetti works on dubbing classic cartoons. He becomes so involved in his work he actually turns into a cartoon figure, which does nothing for his love life. Then he meets Martina, who's strangely attracted to this cartoon figure. Quirky comedy mixes animation and live action with too many gimmicks and not enough heart. In Italian with English subtitles. **92m/C VHS.** *IT* Maurizio Nichetti, Angela Finocchiaro, Mariella Valentini, Patrizio Roversi, Remo Remotti, Renato Scarpa; ***D:*** Maurizio Nichetti, Guido Manuli; ***W:*** Maurizio Nichetti, Guido Manuli. Montreal World Film Fest. '92: Director (Nichetti).

Volpone 🦴🦴🦴 **1939** A classic adaptation of Ben Jonson's famous tale. A greedy merchant pretends he is dying, leaving a fortune behind, in order see what his family will do to become his heir. In French with English subtitles. **95m/B VHS.** *FR* Harry Baur, Louis Jouvet, Fernand Ledoux; ***D:*** Maurice Tourneur.

Volunteers 🦴🦴 **1985 (R)** Ivy League playboy joins the newly formed Peace Corps to escape gambling debts and finds himself on a bridge-building mission in Thailand. Has its comedic moments, especially with Candy. **107m/C VHS, DVD, Wide.** Tom Hanks, John Candy, Rita Wilson, Tim Thomerson, Gedde Watanabe, George Plimpton, Ernest Harada; ***D:*** Nicholas Meyer; ***W:*** David Isaacs, Ken Levine; ***C:*** Ric Waite; ***M:*** James Horner.

Von Ryan's Express 🦴🦴🦴 **1965** An American Air Force colonel leads a group of prisoners-of-war in taking control of a freight train in order to make their exciting escape from a WWII P.O.W. camp in Italy. Strong cast. **117m/C VHS, DVD, Wide.** Frank Sinatra, Trevor Howard, Brad Dexter, Raffaella Carra, Sergio Fantoni, John Leyton, Vito Scotti, Edward Mulhare, Adolfo Celi, James Brolin, James B. Sikking, Wolfgang Preiss, John van Dreelen, Richard Bakalyan, Michael Goodliffe, Michael St. Clair, Ivan Triesault; ***D:*** Mark Robson; ***W:*** Wendell Mayes, Joseph Landon; ***C:*** William H. Daniels; ***M:*** Jerry Goldsmith.

Voodoo 🦴🦴 **1995 (R)** College student Andy (Feldman) must battle a fraternity, lead by an evil voodoo priest, when they decide to make his girlfriend their next human sacrifice. **91m/C VHS, DVD.** Corey Feldman, Sarah Douglas, Jack Nance, Joel J. Edwards; ***D:*** Rene Eram; ***W:*** Brian DiMuccio, Dino Vindeni; ***C:*** Dan Gillham; ***M:*** Keith Bilderbeck.

Voodoo Academy 🦴🦴 **2000** Imagine an episode of "Scooby Doo" crossed with a Calvin Klein ad and you'll get the idea of what video veteran Dave DeCoteau is doing in what he calls "the first horror film made for girls." A Bible college is a front for voodoo activity. The all-male students run around in their underwear trying to figure out what's going on. **100m/C DVD.** Riley Smith, Chad Burns, Debra Meyer; ***D:*** David DeCoteau.

Voodoo Black Exorcist 🦴 **1989** Some 3000 years ago, a black prince was buried alive for messin' with another man's woman. Now he's back...and he's mad—real mad. He's prepared to kill just about everyone. Can he be stopped before all in the modern world are dead?? **?m/C VHS.** Aldo Sambrel, Tenyeka Stadle, Fernando (Fernand) Sancho.

Voodoo Dawn 🦴🦴 **1989 (R)** Two New Yorkers travel to the Deep South to visit a friend who, it turns out, is the latest victim in a series of really gross voodoo murders. A beautiful girl is written into the plot, and the New York guys have an excuse to stay in voodooville, even though bimbolina's southern accent comes and goes for no discernable reason. Filmed near Charleston, South Carolina, and co-written by Russo of "Night of the Living Dead" fame. **83m/C VHS.** Raymond St. Jacques, Theresa Merritt, Gina Gershon, Kirk Baily, Billy "Sly" Williams, J. Grant Albrecht, Tony Todd; ***D:*** Steven Fierberg; ***W:*** John A. Russo, Jeffrey Delman.

Voodoo Dawn 🦴🦴½ **1999** Crazy con Frank Barlow (Madsen) has learned voodoo rites in prison and is using his power to get revenge on his brother's killer. Predictable crime drama despite the occult trappings. **93m/C VHS, DVD.** Michael Madsen, Rosanna Arquette, Balthazar Getty, Phillip Glasser, James Russo; ***D:*** Andrzej Sekula. **VIDEO**

Voodoo Woman 🦴 **1957** An innocent girl is lured into the jungle by an evil scientist who is trying to create the perfect woman to commit murders. He turns the girl into an ugly monster in an attempt to get her to obey his telepathic commands. A campy classic that's as bad as it sounds. **77m/B VHS.** Marla English, Tom Conway, Mike Connors, Lance Fuller; ***D:*** Edward L. Cahn.

Vortex ✓½ **1981** Punk/film noir style in which a female private eye becomes immersed in corporate paranoia and political corruption. **87m/C VHS.** Lydia Lunch, James Russo, Bill Rice, Richard France, Ann Magnuson, Haoui Montaug, Adele Bertei, Bill Landis; ***D:*** Scott B, Beth B; ***W:*** Scott B, Beth B; ***C:*** Steven Fierberg; ***M:*** Lydia Lunch, Adele Bertei.

Voulez-Vous Danser avec Moi? ✓✓ *Come Dance with Me; Do You Want to Dance with Me?* **1959** A young bride endeavors to clear her husband of murder charges and find the real killer. In French with English subtitles. **90m/C VHS, DVD.** *FR* Brigitte Bardot, Henri Vidal; ***D:*** Michel Boisrond.

A Vow to Kill ✓✓½ **1994 (PG-13)** Predictable cable thriller finds the wealthy Phillips marrying the charming Grieco after a whirlwind courtship. Then, on their honeymoon, she accidentally learns that her new husband has contacted her family and is masquerading as a kidnapper—demanding a large ransom for her safe release. But maybe it's not such a masquerade after all. **91m/C VHS.** Julianne Phillips, Richard Grieco, Gordon Pinsent, Peter MacNeill, Tom Cavanagh, Nicole Oliver; ***D:*** Harry S. Longstreet; ***W:*** Harry S. Longstreet, Sean Silas. **CABLE**

Voyage ✓½ **1993 (R)** Boring rip-off of "Dead Calm" and other couple-in-peril-from-psycho-on-boat films. Hauer and Allen are having marital problems and decide to sail away from their troubles with new-found friends Roberts and Nielson. Only their guests are sociopaths. Hauer takes a breather from his psycho roles for a turn as the good guy while Roberts could do his patented crazy act in his sleep. **88m/C VHS.** Rutger Hauer, Karen Allen, Eric Roberts, Connie Nielsen; ***D:*** John MacKenzie. **CABLE**

Voyage en Balloon ✓✓½ **1959** This is the delightful story of a young boy (played by the star of "The Red Balloon") who stows away on his grandfather's hot air balloon for an adventurous trip across France. **82m/C VHS.** *FR* Pascal Lamorisse, Andre Gille, Maurice Baquet; ***D:*** Albert Lamorisse; ***W:*** Albert Lamorisse; ***Nar:*** Jack Lemmon.

Voyage en Douce ✓✓ **1981** Helene and Lucie have been friends since childhood. Helene wants to rent a summer house, and Lucie, fed up with her marriage, agrees to join her on a leisurely journey through the south of France. Thoughtful look at friendship among women. French with subtitles. **95m/C VHS.** *FR* Dominique Sanda, Geraldine Chaplin; ***D:*** Michel DeVille.

Voyage in Italy ✓✓½ *Viaggio in Italia; Voyage to Italy; The Lonely Woman; Strangers* **1953** Narrative of a marriage finds unhappy English couple Bergman and Sanders travelling by car to Naples. However, various crises manage to reunite them. Critically mauled upon its release, this third collaboration between Bergman and Rossellini, following "Stromboli" and "Europa '51," later became a big hit with New Wave directors. **83m/B VHS.** *IT* Ingrid Bergman, George Sanders; ***D:*** Roberto Rossellini; ***W:*** Roberto Rossellini, Vitaliano Brancatti; ***C:*** Enzo Serafin; ***M:*** Renzo Rossellini.

Voyage of Terror: The Achille Lauro Affair ✓✓½ **1990** Recounting of the 1985 Italian cruise-ship hijacking by four Palestinians. Lancaster is the wheelchair-bound Leon Klinghoffer and Saint is wife Marilyn. Miniseries was shot on the actual ship and route where the tragedy occurred. **120m/C VHS.** Burt Lancaster, Eva Marie Saint, Robert Culp, Brian Bloom, Dominique Sanda, Rebecca Schaeffer, Joseph Nasser, Gabriele Ferzetti, Renzo Nontagnani; ***D:*** Alberto Negrin. **TV**

Voyage of the Damned ✓✓✓ **1976 (G)** The story of one of the most tragic incidents of WWII. In 1939, 1,937 German-Jewish refugees fleeing Nazi Germany are bound for Cuba aboard the Hamburg-America liner S.S. St. Louis. They are refused permission to land in Cuba (and everywhere else) and must sail back to Germany and certain death. Based on the novel by Gordon Thomas and Max Morgan-Witts. **155m/C VHS, DVD.** *GB* Faye Dunaway, Max von Sydow, Oskar Werner, Malcolm McDowell, Orson Welles, James Mason, Lee Grant, Katharine Ross, Ben Gazzara, Lynne Frederick, Wendy Hiller, Jose Ferrer, Luther Adler, Sam Wanamaker, Denholm Elliott, Nehemiah Persoff, Julie Harris, Maria Schell, Jonathan Pryce, Janet Suzman, Helmut Griem, Michael Constantine, Victor Spinetti; ***D:*** Stuart Rosenberg; ***W:*** Steve Shagan, David Butler; ***C:*** Billy Williams; ***M:*** Lalo Schifrin. Golden Globes '77: Support. Actress (Ross).

Voyage of the Heart ✓✓ **1990** An aging fisherman meets up with a sexy college girl and the passion begins. **88m/C VHS.** Bill Aldrij, Dunja Djordjenic.

Voyage of the Rock Aliens ✓ **1987** A quasi-satiric space farce about competing alien rock stars. **97m/C VHS.** Pia Zadora, Tom Nolan, Craig Sheffer, Rhema, Ruth Gordon, Michael Berryman, Jermaine Jackson, Alison La Placa; ***D:*** James Fargo; ***W:*** Edward Gold, S. James Guidotti; ***C:*** Gilbert Taylor; ***M:*** Jack White.

The Voyage of the Yes ✓✓ **1972 (PG)** Two teenagers, one white and one black, in a small sailboat hit rough weather and battle the elements while learning about themselves. Average TV movie. **100m/C VHS.** Desi Arnaz Jr., Mike Evans, Beverly Garland, Skip Homeier, Della Reese, Scoey Mitchell; ***D:*** Lee H. Katzin. **TV**

A Voyage 'Round My Father ✓✓✓ **1989** John Mortimer's adaptation of his semi-autobiographical stage play. Olivier is the eccentric, opinionated blind barrister-father and Bates the exasperated son as both try to come to terms with their stormy family relationship. Well-acted and directed. **85m/C VHS.** *GB* Laurence Olivier, Alan Bates, Jane Asher, Elizabeth Sellars; ***D:*** Alvin Rakoff. **TV**

Voyage Suprise ✓✓✓ **1946** A slapstick comedy about a crazy old man who runs a mystery tour from a dilapidated bus as he takes an unknowing mob of tourists on a cross-country escapade through a brothel, a wedding, criminals, police, terrorists and the Haute-Provence. In French with English subtitles. **108m/B VHS.** *FR* Martine Carol, Sioel; ***D:*** Pierre Prevert; ***C:*** Jean (Yves, Georges) Bourgoin.

Voyage to the Beginning of the World ✓✓✓ *Journey to the Beginning of the World; Viagem ao Principio do Mundo* **1996** Autobiographical piece by 88-year-old director de Oliveira, who has been making movies since the silent film era. Mastroianni, in his last role, plays the somewhat fictionalized director named Manoel who travels to Portugal to shoot a film. Along the way he points out crumbling landmarks that he remembers from his childhood, an apt metaphor for the memories where the majority of his life now resides. Along with him is French actor Afonso (Gautier), who makes a visit to an elderly aunt (de Castro) who poignantly tells Afonso about his father and the way things used to be. Slow moving but lyrical ode to aging and the changing perspective it gives. French and Portuguese with subtitles. **93m/C VHS, DVD.** *PT* Marcello Mastroianni, Jean-Yves Gautier, Leonor Silveira, Diogo Doria, Isabel de Castro; ***D:*** Manoel de Oliveira; ***W:*** Manoel de Oliveira; ***C:*** Renato Berta; ***M:*** Emmanuel Nunes.

Voyage to the Bottom of the Sea ✓✓✓ **1961** The crew of an atomic submarine must destroy a deadly radiation belt which has set the polar ice cap ablaze. Fun stuff, with good special effects and photography. Later became a TV series. **106m/C VHS, DVD, Wide.** Walter Pidgeon, Joan Fontaine, Barbara Eden, Peter Lorre, Robert Sterling, Michael Ansara, Frankie Avalon; ***D:*** Irwin Allen; ***W:*** Charles Bennett, Irwin Allen; ***C:*** Winton C. Hoch; ***M:*** Paul Sawtell, Bert Shefter.

Voyage to the Planet of Prehistoric Women woof! *Gill Woman; Gill Women of Venus* **1968** Astronauts journey to Venus, where they discover a race of gorgeous, sea-shell clad women led by Van Doren, as well as a few monsters. Incomprehensible but fun. The third film incorporating the Russian "Planeta Burg" footage. Directed (and narrated) by Bogdanovich under the pseudonym Derek Thomas. **78m/C VHS.** Mamie Van Doren, Mary Mark, Paige Lee, Aldo Roman, Margot Hartman; ***D:*** Peter Bogdanovich; ***W:*** Henry Ney; ***Nar:*** Peter Bogdanovich.

Voyage to the Prehistoric Planet ✓½ *Voyage to a Prehistoric Planet* **1965** In the year 2020, an expedition to Venus is forced to deal with dinosaurs and other perils. In the making of this movie, Roger Corman edited in special effects and additional footage from a recently acquired Russian film, "Planeta Burg," and his own "Queen of Blood." **80m/C VHS.** Basil Rathbone, Faith Domergue, Marc Shannon, Christopher Brand; ***D:*** Curtis Harrington.

Voyager ✓✓✓ **1991 (PG-13)** Restless, middle-aged engineer Walter Faber (Shepherd) tells his life story in a series of flashbacks. Twenty years before (the film starts in 1957) he abandons his pregnant girlfriend who promises to get an abortion. He laters hears she married, had a child, and divorced. While sailing to New York from France Walter falls in love with a young student and accompanies her to Greece to visit her mother. Only then does he realize her true identity, leading to a tragic conclusion. Shepherd's is a glum, repressed performance (in keeping with the character) while Delpy personifies youthful sweetness. Based on the novel "Homo Faber" by Max Frisch. **110m/C VHS.** *FR GE* Sam Shepard, Julie Delpy, Barbara Sukowa, Dieter Kirchlechner, Traci Lind, Deborra-Lee Furness, August Zirner, Thomas Heinze; ***D:*** Volker Schlondorff; ***W:*** Volker Schlondorff, Rudy Wurlitzer.

The Voyeur ✓ **1994** After ten years of marriage, a couple tries to ignite those sexual fires by spending a weekend in Napa Valley and indulging in erotic sexual games. Based on Lonnie Barbach's book "Erotic Edge." **80m/C VHS.** Al Sapienza, Kim (Kimberly Dawn) Dawson; ***D:*** Deborah Shames; ***W:*** Udana Power.

Vukovar ✓✓✓ **1994** Vukovar is a Croat town just across the Danube river from Serbia, in the former Yugoslavia, where different ethnic groups had managed to coexist peacefully. When Croatian Anna (Jokovic) marries her childhood sweetheart, the Serbian Toma (Isakovic), however, their celebration is marred by nationalist demonstrations. Soon Anna's pregnant, Toma has been drafted, and the town comes under siege, with Tomas' parents fleeing, Anna's family killed in a bombing, and Ann herself struggling to survive. Film was condemned by the Croatian government as pro-Serbian propaganda though director Draskovic, a Serbian whose parents are Croatian and Bosnian, strove to be nonpartisan. Serbo-Croatian with subtitles. **94m/C VHS.** *YU* Mirjana Jokovic, Boris Isakovic, Monica Romic; ***D:*** Boro Draskovic; ***W:*** Boro Draskovic, Maja Draskovic; ***C:*** Aleksandar Petkovic.

Vulcan God of Fire woof! *Vulcan, Son of Jupiter* **1962** Flash is a muscle-bound Vulcan fighting off cheesy monsters in an effort to win the hand of Venus. **76m/C VHS.** *IT* Rob Flash, Gordon Mitchell, Bella Cortez; ***D:*** Emmimo Salvi.

Vulture ✓ **1967** In an attempt to carry out a curse on the descendants of the man who killed his forefather, a scientist tries an atomic transmutation experiment and winds up combining himself with a bird. **91m/C VHS.** Robert Hutton, Akim Tamiroff, Broderick Crawford, Diane Clare, Philip Friend, Patrick Holt, Annette Carell; ***D:*** Lawrence Huntington.

Vultures ✓ **1984** A dying patriarch summons his predatory family to his home in order to straighten out the distribution of inheritance. One by one, they fall victim to a mysterious murderer. **101m/C VHS.** Yvonne De Carlo, Stuart Whitman, Jim Bailey, Meredith MacRae, Aldo Ray; ***D:*** Paul Leder.

W ✓½ *I Want Her Dead* **1974 (PG)** A woman and her husband are terrorized and must find out why. A single letter "W" is found at the scene of the crimes. Notable only as model Twiggy's first film. **95m/C VHS.** Twiggy, Dirk Benedict, John Vernon, Eugene Roche; ***D:*** Richard Quine.

Wackiest Ship in the Army ✓✓½ **1961** A completely undisciplined warship crew must smuggle an Australian spy through Japanese waters during WWII. Odd, enjoyable mixture of action and laughs. Became a TV series. In the middle of the war effort, Nelson straps on a guitar and sings "Do You Know What It Means to Miss New Orleans." **99m/C VHS.** Jack Lemmon, Ricky Nelson, Chips Rafferty, John Lund, Mike Kellin, Patricia Driscoll; ***D:*** Richard Murphy.

Wackiest Wagon Train in the West ✓ **1977 (G)** Hapless wagon master is saddled with a dummy assistant as they guide a party of five characters across the West. Based on the minor TV sitcom "Dusty's Trail." Produced by the same folks who delivered the similarly premised TV series "Gilligan's Island" and "The Brady Bunch." **86m/C VHS.** Bob Denver, Forrest Tucker, Jeannine Riley.

Wacko woof! **1983 (PG)** Group of nymphettes and tough guys get caught up in a wild Halloween-pumpkin-lawnmower murder. This spoof of the "Halloween" series works too hard for as few laughs as it gets. **84m/C VHS.** Stella Stevens, George Kennedy, Joe Don Baker, Andrew (Dice Clay) Silverstein; ***D:*** Greydon Clark.

The Wacky World of Wills & Burke ✓✓ **1985** Comedy based on the adventures of Wills and Burke, the two 19th-century explorers who led the first unsuccessful expedition across the outback—the Lewis and Clark of Australia, if you will. In real life they died during the adventure, a less than wacky finale. "Burke and Wills," out the same year, was a serious treatment of the same story. **102m/C VHS.** *AU* Garry McDonald, Kim Gyngell, Peter Collingwood, Jonathan Hardy, Mark Little; ***D:*** Bob Weis.

Wag the Dog ✓✓½ **1997 (R)** Based on the book "American Hero" by Larry Beinhart and adapted by Hilary Henkin and David Mamet. Over-the-top Hollywood producer (Hoffman) is hired by White House officials to stage a military attack against the U.S. to divert media attention from accusations that the President fondled a Girl Scout. Show biz insiders say Hoffman's Motss resembles one-time studio head Robert Evans; Washington insiders wonder if it's a documentary. In fact, the entire film is one big insider's joke. Luckily, it's smart enough, and short enough, to avoid becoming tiresome. Look for cameos by Woody Harrelson and Willie Nelson. Filmed in a speedy 29 days on a $15 million budget. **96m/C VHS, DVD.** Dustin Hoffman, Robert De Niro, Anne Heche, Woody Harrelson, Denis Leary, Willie Nelson, Andrea Martin, Suzanne Cryer, John Michael Higgins, Suzy Plakson, Kirsten Dunst, William H. Macy, Michael Belson; ***D:*** Barry Levinson; ***W:*** Hilary Henkin, David Mamet; ***C:*** Robert Richardson; ***M:*** Mark Knopfler. Natl. Bd. of Review '97: Support. Actress (Heche).

Wager of Love ✓✓ **1990** While vacationing on their annual pleasure cruise, four women bet on their individual power of seduction. They find themselves competing for passion as each woman's erotic adventure unravels in this exciting and sensual tale. **75m/C VHS.** Steve Landers, Shelly Johnson, Elliot Silverman, Lisa Cook; ***D:*** Jason Holt.

Wages of Fear ✓✓✓✓ *Le Salaire de la Peur* **1955** American oil company controls a desolate Central American town whose citizens desperately want out—so desperately that four are willing to try a suicide mission to deliver nitroglycerine to put out a well-fire raging 300 miles away. The company's cynical head has offered $2000 to each man, enough to finance escape from the hell-hole they live in. Complex, multi-dimensional drama concentrates on character development for the first half—crucial to the film's greatness. This is the restored version. Remade by William Friedkin as "Sorcerer" in 1977. Based on a novel by Georges Arnaud. In French with English subtitles. **138m/B VHS, DVD.** *FR* Yves Montand, Charles Vanel, Peter Van Eyck, Vera Clouzot, Folco Lulli, William Tubbs; ***D:*** Henri-Georges Clouzot; ***W:*** Henri-Georges Clouzot; ***C:*** Armand Thirard; ***M:*** Georges Auric. British Acad. '54: Film; Cannes '53: Actor (Vanel), Film.

Wagner: The Complete Epic 🦴🦴 **1985** The unedited version of the epic miniseries dramatizing the life of German composer Richard Wagner. The excellent photography does justice to the elaborate production, shot on some 200 different locations. The actors cringe in the presence of the subject's grandeur; Burton, a shell of his former cinematic self, is painful to watch in his last released film. Frankly, this is way too long. Also available in a edited 300-minute version, which is still too long. **540m/C VHS.** *GB HU* Richard Burton, Vanessa Redgrave, Ralph Richardson, John Gielgud, Laurence Olivier, Franco Nero; ***D:*** Tony Palmer. **TV**

Wagon Master 🦴🦴🦴 **1950** Two cowboys are persuaded to guide a group of Mormons, led by Bond, in their trek across the western frontier. They run into a variety of troubles, including a band of killers who joins the wagon train to escape a posse. Sensitively directed, realistic and worthwhile. Inspired the TV series "Wagon Train." Also available colorized. **85m/B VHS.** Ben Johnson, Joanne Dru, Harry Carey Jr., Ward Bond, Jane Darwell, James Arness; ***D:*** John Ford.

Wagon Tracks 🦴🦴½ **1919** Hart searches for the man responsible for his brother's death. **64m/B VHS.** William S. Hart, Jane Novak, Robert McKim, Lloyd Bacon; ***D:*** Lambert Hillyer.

Wagon Trail 🦴🦴½ **1935** The sheriff's son is blackmailed into helping a gang of robbers, with terrible consequences for himself and his father (Carey), who is fired from his job after the son breaks jail. The new sheriff is secretly chief of the outlaw band. Carey rides back into town and eventually virtue triumphs. Good, tense—but not too tense—western. **59m/B VHS.** Harry Carey Sr.; ***D:*** Harry Fraser.

Wagon Wheels 🦴🦴 *Caravans West* **1934** Recycling was in vogue in '34, when unused footage from "Fighting Caravans" (1931) with Gary Cooper was used to remake the very same plot. The result is biodegradable. Settlers heading to Oregon are ambushed by bad guy Blue, employed by fur traders. Blue sics Injuns on them too, but don't worry, they make it. Adapted from Zane Grey's novel "Fighting Caravans." **54m/B VHS.** Randolph Scott, Monte Blue, Gail Patrick, Billy Lee; ***D:*** Charles T. Barton.

Wagons East 🦴 **1994 (PG-13)** Fed up with prairie hardships, pioneers decide to hitch up to a wagon train and head east. Candy (who died during filming) plays the drunken former wagonmaster hired to get them back home, with Lewis (out of his depth) as a neurotic ex-doctor, and McGinley stuck in the role of a gay bookseller that reeks of stereotypical mannerisms. Script is desperate for humor, which it never finds, and it's hard to watch Candy's performance knowing this mess was his last role. **100m/C VHS.** John Candy, Richard Lewis, Ellen Greene, John C. McGinley, Robert Picardo, William Sanderson, Thomas F. Duffy, Russell Means, Rodney A. Grant, Michael Horse, Gailard Sartain, Lochlyn Munro, Stuart Proud Eagle Grant; ***D:*** Peter Markle; ***W:*** Matthew Carlson, Jerry Abrahamson.

The Wagons Roll at Night 🦴🦴½ **1941** The circus wagons that is. Remake of 1937's "Kid Galahad" transfers the action from the boxing arena to the circus arena. Nick Coster (Bogart) is the owner of the failing enterprise, romancing fortune teller Flo (Sidney) while trying to protect his innocent sister, Mary (Leslie) from the seedy side of life. This would have been easier if sis hadn't fallen for the new lion tamer, Matt Varney (Albert). Nick tries to break up the lovebirds with predictable results. Based on the novel by Francis Wallace. **84m/B VHS.** Humphrey Bogart, Sylvia Sidney, Eddie Albert, Joan Leslie, Sig Rumann, Cliff Clark, Charles Foy, Frank Wilcox; ***D:*** Ray Enright; ***W:*** Barry Trivers, Fred Niblo Jr.; ***C:*** Sid Hickox; ***M:*** Heinz Roemheld.

Wagon's Westward 🦴½ **1940** Good government agent Morris assumes identity of bad twin brother, who's in jail, in order to catch some outlaws. **53m/B VHS.** Chester Morris, Buck Jones, Guinn "Big Boy" Williams, Douglas Fowley, George "Gabby" Hayes, Anita Louise, Ona Munson; ***D:*** Lew (Louis Friedlander) Landers.

Waikiki 🦴½ **1980** Two private eyes set out to prove that their friend is not the "cane field murderer" who is terrorizing the Hawaiian island of Oahu. Harmless but pointless TV pilot. **96m/C VHS.** Dack Rambo, Steve Marachuk, Donna Mills, Cal Bellini, Darren McGavin; ***D:*** Ron Satlof. **TV**

Waikiki Wedding 🦴🦴🦴 **1937** Enjoyable musical about a scheming pineapple promoter (Crosby) who meets the woman of his dreams in a contest he concocted. Contest winner Ross dislikes Hawaii and wants to go home and Crosby must keep her from going...first for business reasons and later, for love. Supporting cast includes Hawaiian Prince Leilani and a pig. Lots of song and dance and Hawaiian sunsets, along with Burns and Raye, the other couple destined for love on the islands, keep the story moving. ♫Sweet Leilani; Sweet Is the Word for You; In a Little Hula Heaven; Blue Hawaii; Okolehao; Nani Ona Pua. **89m/B VHS.** Bing Crosby, Bob Burns, Martha Raye, Shirley Ross, George Barbier, Leif Erickson, Grady Sutton, Granville Bates, Anthony Quinn; ***D:*** Frank Tuttle; ***W:*** Frank Butler, Don Hartman, Walter DeLeon, Francis Martin; ***C:*** Karl Struss; ***M:*** Leo Robin, Ralph Rainger. Oscars '37: Song ("Sweet Leilani").

Wait Till Your Mother Gets Home 🦴🦴 **1983** "Mr. Mom"-like zaniness abounds as a football coach cares for the kids and does chores while his wife takes her first job in 15 years. Almost too darn cute, but well written. **97m/C VHS.** Paul Michael Glaser, Dee Wallace Stone, Peggy McKay, David Doyle, Raymond Buktenica, James Gregory, Joey Lawrence, Lynne Moody; ***D:*** Bill Persky. **TV**

Wait until Dark 🦴🦴🦴 **1967** A photographer unwittingly smuggles a drug-filled doll into New York, and his blind wife, alone in their apartment, is terrorized by murderous crooks in search of it. A compelling thriller based on the Broadway hit by Frederick Knott, who also wrote "Dial M for Murder." The individual actors' performances were universally acclaimed in this spinetingler. **105m/C VHS.** Audrey Hepburn, Alan Arkin, Richard Crenna, Efrem Zimbalist Jr., Jack Weston; ***D:*** Terence Young; ***W:*** Robert B. Carrington; ***C:*** Charles B(ryant) Lang Jr.; ***M:*** Henry Mancini.

Wait until Spring, Bandini 🦴🦴½ **1990 (PG-13)** A flavorful immigrant tale about a transplanted Italian family weathering the winter in 1925 Colorado, as seen through the eyes of a young son. Alternately funny and moving, with one of Dunaway's scenery-chewing performances as a local temptation for the father. Based on the autobiographical novel by John Fante, co-produced by Francis Ford Coppola. **104m/C VHS.** Joe Mantegna, Faye Dunaway, Burt Young, Ornella Muti, Alex Vincent, Renata Vanni, Michael Bacall, Daniel Wilson; ***D:*** Dominique Deruddere; ***M:*** Angelo Badalamenti.

Waiting 🦴🦴 **2000** Actor wannabe/slacker/waiter Sean (Keenan) is told by his dad that he has 30 days to find a job, an apartment, and something to do with his life. And dad doesn't mean that Sean should continue to wait tables at a South Philly mob-run Italian eatery—and maybe he could find a nice girl as well. **80m/C VHS, DVD, Wide.** Will Keenan, Hannah Dalton, Kerri Kenney, Harry Philabosian, Lloyd Kaufman, Ron Jeremy; ***D:*** Patrick Hasson; ***W:*** Patrick Hasson; ***C:*** Michael Pearlman.

Waiting for Guffman 🦴🦴 **1996 (R)** The eccentric citizens of Blaine, Missouri, plan an original musical ("Red, White, and Blaine") to celebrate the town's 150th anniversary with the aid of former New Yorker and semi-hysteric Corky St. Claire (Guest) as their director. Everyone's very game—and almost completely talentless. The Guffman of the title is the Broadway producer Corky knows and whom he's invited to see their disaster-in-the-making. A little too deliberately quirky for its own good. **84m/C VHS, DVD, Wide.** Bob Odenkirk, Christopher Guest, Eugene Levy, Catherine O'Hara, Parker Posey, Fred Willard, Lewis Arquette, Matt Keeslar, Paul Dooley, Paul Benedict, Bob Balaban, Larry Miller, Brian Doyle-Murray; ***D:*** Christopher Guest; ***W:*** Christopher Guest, Eugene Levy; ***C:*** Roberto Schaefer; ***M:*** Michael McKean, Harry Shearer, Christopher Guest.

Waiting for the Light 🦴🦴½ **1990 (PG)** When a woman takes over a small-town diner, she gets the surprise of her life. Seems an angel has made his home there and now the townsfolk are flocking to see him. MacLaine is wonderful and Garr is fetching and likeable. Set during the Cuban missile crisis. Enjoyable, tame comedy. **94m/C VHS, 8mm.** Shirley MacLaine, Teri Garr, Vincent Schiavelli, John Bedford Lloyd; ***D:*** Christopher Monger; ***W:*** Christopher Monger.

Waiting for the Moon 🦴½ **1987 (PG)** Hunt as Alice B. Toklas is a relative treat in this ponderous, frustrating biopic about Toklas and Gertrude Stein, her lover. Made for "American Playhouse" on PBS. **88m/C VHS.** Linda Hunt, Linda Bassett, Andrew McCarthy, Bruce McGill, Jacques Boudet, Bernadette LaFont; ***D:*** Jill Godmilow; ***W:*** Mark Magill; ***C:*** Andre Neau. Sundance '87: Grand Jury Prize. **TV**

The Waiting Game 🦴🦴 **1999** Group of actor wannabes are working in a New York restaurant while waiting for the proverbial big break. They fall in and out of lust and love and suffer audition humiliation and other trials. **81m/C VHS, DVD, Wide.** Michael Raynor, Will Arnett, Terumi Mathews, Dan Riordan, Debbon Ayer; ***D:*** Ken Liotti; ***W:*** Ken Liotti; ***C:*** Rich Eliano; ***M:*** Jim Farmer.

The Waiting Time 🦴🦴½ **1999** Post-Cold War thriller based on the novel by Gerald Seymour. Tracy Barnes (Turner) is a corporal in the British Intelligence Corps who makes a seemingly unprovoked attack on German politician Dieter Krause (Becker). Befriended by solicitor's clerk Joshua Mantle (Thaw), the duo travel to Berlin to make sense of things but Joshua finds himself involved in the decade-old murder of Tracy's German lover and with the dreaded East German secret police. **150m/C VHS.** *GB* John Thaw, Zara Turner, Hartmut Becker, Mark Pegg, Struan Rodger, Colin Baker, Christien Anholt; ***D:*** Stuart Orme; ***W:*** Patrick Harbinson; ***C:*** Peter Middleton; ***M:*** Colin Towns. **TV**

Waiting to Exhale 🦴🦴🦴 **1995 (R)** Adaptation of Terry McMillan's novel about four African-American women hoping to reach the point in their love lives when they can relax and stop waiting for the right man. After the string of dogs and users they choose, you want to tell them not to hold their breath. The women are supposed to be close friends, but all of their stories are broken up into vignettes. This erodes the ensemble feeling of the movie, but performances are strong all around. Retaining the book's feel of just-between-friends girl talk, it may be a little harsh for those who are, shall we say, estrogen-challenged. A lush R&B soundtrack is the perfect backdrop for the ladies' soulful yearning for real love. **120m/C VHS, DVD.** Whitney Houston, Angela Bassett, Loretta Devine, Lela Rochon, Gregory Hines, Dennis Haysbert, Mykelti Williamson, Michael Beach, Leon, Wendell Pierce, Donald Adeosun Faison, Jeffrey D. Sams, Toyomichi Kurita; ***Cameos:*** Wesley Snipes; ***D:*** Forest Whitaker; ***W:*** Ronald Bass; ***M:*** Kenneth "Babyface" Edmonds. MTV Movie Awards '96: Song ("Sittin' Up in My Room").

Waitress woof! *Soup to Nuts* **1981 (R)** Three beautiful girls are waitresses in a crazy restaurant where the chef gets drunk, the kitchen explodes, and the customers riot. Awful premise, worse production. **85m/C VHS, DVD.** Jim Harris, Carol Drake, Carol Bever; ***D:*** Lloyd Kaufman; ***W:*** Charles Kaufman, Michael Stone; ***C:*** Lloyd Kaufman.

Wake Island 🦴🦴🦴 **1942** After Pearl Harbor, a small group of Marines face the onslaught of the Japanese fleet on a small Pacific Island. Although doomed, they hold their ground for 16 days. Exciting, realistic, and moving. The first film to capitalize on early "last stands" of WWII; also among the most popular war movies. Shown to soldiers in training camps with great morale-raising success. **88m/B VHS.** Robert Preston, Brian Donlevy, William Bendix, MacDonald Carey, Albert Dekker, Walter Abel, Rod Cameron, Barbara Britton, Mikhail Rasumny, Bill Goodwin, Damian O'Flynn, Frank Albertson, Hugh Beaumont, Hillary Brooke, James Brown, Don Castle, Frank Faylen, Mary Field, William Forrest, Alan Hale Jr., Charles Trowbridge, Philip Van Zandt, Phillip Terry; ***D:*** John Farrow; ***W:*** W.R. Burnett, Frank Butler; ***C:*** William Mellor, Theodor Sparkuhl; ***M:*** David Buttolph. N.Y. Film Critics '42: Director (Farrow).

Wake of the Red Witch 🦴🦴½ **1949** Wayne captains the ship of the title and battles shipping tycoon Adler for a fortune in pearls and the love of a beautiful woman (Russell). Wayne shows impressive range in a non-gun-totin' role. **106m/B VHS.** John Wayne, Gail Russell, Gig Young, Luther Adler, Henry Daniell; ***D:*** Edward Ludwig.

Waking Life 🦴🦴½ **2001 (R)** Linklater's innovative and visually groundbreaking look at dreams, life, and philosophy doesn't really seem to have a plot. What it does have is several vignettes of people mostly just talking about the above subjects. What makes it stunning is the look of the project. Linklater "filmed" the scenes on digital video, then had a group of artists digitally "paint" over the footage, assigning different artists different scenes or actors so as to have a variety of styles. The result is a trippy experiment that might not appeal to many people except philosophy majors, computer geeks, or chemically altered college students. Film buffs looking for something new would do well to check it out. **99m/C VHS, DVD, Wide.** *US* Richard Linklater, Glover Gill, Julie Delpy, Wiley Wiggins, Ethan Hawke, Adam Goldberg, Nicky Katt, Steven Soderbergh; ***D:*** Richard Linklater; ***W:*** Richard Linklater; ***C:*** Richard Linklater, Tommy Pallotta; ***M:*** Glover Gill. N.Y. Film Critics '01: Animated Film.

Waking Ned Devine 🦴🦴🦴½ **1998 (PG)** Old Ned Devine has the winning ticket for the Irish National Lottery—unfortunately, the shock has killed him. Jackie O'Shea (Bannen) and the other 50 still-living residents of Tulaigh Morh conspire to fool a bored lottery official (Dempsey) into thinking that Michael O'Sullivan (Kelly) is Devine, so that they can share the wealth. As each obstacle to the payoff is overcome, a larger hurdle appears, and the comedy becomes more and more screwball until it reaches its darkly comic conclusion. Warm and full of blarney, but never becomes too sappy, or contrived. Filmed on the beautiful Isle of Man and accented with a fine score full of Celtic melodies. Veteran cast carries off even the most improbable gags (including Kelly's buck-naked motorcycle ride). **91m/C VHS, DVD.** Ian Bannen, David Kelly, Fionnula Flanagan, Susan Lynch, James Nesbitt, Maura O'Malley, Robert Hickey, Paddy Ward, James Ryland, Fintan McKeown, Matthew Devitt, Eileen Dromey, Dermot Kerrigan, Brendan F. Dempsey; ***D:*** Kirk Jones; ***W:*** Kirk Jones; ***C:*** Henry Braham; ***M:*** Shaun Davey.

Waking the Dead 🦴🦴½ **2000 (R)** Director Gordon's uneven but earnest adaptation of the Scott Spencer novel features Crudup as Fielding Pierce, an aspiring politician haunted by the death ten years earlier of his activist girlfriend Sarah (Connelly) in a car bombing. As Fielding begins a run at the Senate, he starts to see Sarah in crowds, wondering if the reports of her death were exaggerated, and doubting his sanity. The love story angle gets a lot of play, yet manages to be unconvincing, and the frequent jumps back and forth in time are jarring. Crudup and Connelly seem in over their heads at times. **105m/C VHS, DVD, Wide.** Billy Crudup, Jennifer Connelly, Molly Parker, Janet McTeer, Paul Hipp, Sandra Oh, Hal Holbrook, Lawrence Dane; ***D:*** Keith Gordon; ***W:*** Robert Dillon; ***C:*** Tom Richmond; ***M:*** Tomandandy.

Walk, Don't Run 🦴🦴½ **1966** Romantic comedy involving a British businessman (Grant) unable to find a hotel room in Tokyo due to the crowds staying for the 1964 summer Olympic Games. He winds up renting a room from an Embassy secretary (Eggar) and then meets and invites Hutton, a member of the U.S. Olympic walking team, also without a place to stay, to share it with him. Grant then proceeds to play matchmaker, despite the fact that Eggar has a fiance. Grant's last film. Innocuous, unnecessary remake of

"The More the Merrier." **114m/C VHS.** Cary Grant, Samantha Eggar, Jim Hutton, John Standing, Miiko Taka; *D:* Charles Walters; *M:* Quincy Jones.

A Walk in the Clouds 🦴🦴½ **1995 (PG-13)** Gorgeously photographed, if sappy, romantic fantasy finds WWII vet Paul Sutton (Reeves), returning to his unhappy marriage and salesman job. So when the good-hearted Paul meets beautiful Victoria (Sanchez-Gijon), the pregnant and unmarried daughter of a possessive Napa vineyard owner (Giannini), he's more than happy to help by posing as her husband. Naturally, dad is livid at their "marriage" and Paul falls in love with his sham bride. Quinn gets to do his part as wise family patriarch and yes, there's even a grape harvest (and some grape stomping) to put everyone in the proper romantic mood. Based on the 1942 Italian film "Four Steps in the Clouds." **103m/C VHS, DVD, Wide.** Keanu Reeves, Aitana Sanchez-Gijon, Giancarlo Giannini, Anthony Quinn, Angelica Aragon, Evangelina Elizondo, Freddy Rodriguez, Debra Messing; *D:* Alfonso Arau; *W:* Robert Mark Kamen; *C:* Emmanuel Lubezki; *M:* Leo Brower. Golden Globes '96: Score.

Walk in the Spring Rain 🦴🦴½ **1970 (PG)** The bored wife of a college professor follows him to rural Tennessee when he goes on sabbatical, where she meets the married Quinn and the two begin an affair. When Quinn's disturbed son learns of the affair, he attacks the woman, with tragic results. Fine cast should have had better effect on low-key script. **98m/C VHS.** Ingrid Bergman, Anthony Quinn, Fritz Weaver, Katherine Crawford, Tom Fielding, Virginia Gregg; *D:* Guy Green; *W:* Stirling Silliphant; *C:* Charles B(ryant) Lang Jr.; *M:* Elmer Bernstein.

A Walk in the Sun 🦴🦴🦴½ *Salerno Beachhead* **1946** The trials of a group of infantrymen in WWII from the time they land in Italy to the time they capture their objective, a farmhouse occupied by the Germans. Excellent ensemble acting shows well the variety of civilians who make up any fighting force and explores their fears, motivations, and weaknesses. Producer and director Milestone also made "All Quiet on the Western Front" and the Korean War masterpiece "Pork Chop Hill." Released in the final days of the war, almost concurrently with two other WWII films of the first echelon, "The Story of G.I. Joe" and "They Were Expendable." **117m/B VHS, DVD, 8mm.** Dana Andrews, Richard Conte, John Ireland, Lloyd Bridges, Sterling Holloway, George Tyne, Norman Lloyd, Herbert Rudley, Richard Benedict, Huntz Hall, James B. Cardwell, George Offerman Jr., Steve Brodie, Matt Willis, Alvin Hammer, Chris Drake, Victor Cutler, Jay Norris; *D:* Lewis Milestone; *W:* Robert Rossen, Harry Brown; *C:* Russell Harlan; *M:* Freddie Rich, Earl Robinson.

Walk into Hell 🦴🦴 **1957** A mining engineer and his assistant searching for oil meet the primitive natives of New Guinea. Tedious at times and dated, but pleasant enough. **91m/C VHS.** *AU* Chips Rafferty, Francoise Christophe, Reg Lye; *D:* Lee Robinson.

Walk Like a Man 🦴½ **1987 (PG)** In a take-off of Tarzan movies, Mandel plays a man raised by wolves. Comic problems arise when he is found by his mother and the family attempts to civilize him. Juvenile script wastes fine cast. **86m/C VHS.** Howie Mandel, Christopher Lloyd, Cloris Leachman, Colleen Camp, Amy Steel, George DiCenzo; *D:* Melvin Frank.

A Walk on the Moon 🦴🦴½ **1999 (R)** Goldwyn's promising directorial debut has 30-ish, vaguely restless Jewish housewife Pearl (Lane) vacationing in the Catskills in the summer of 1969 with her family: teenage daughter Alison (Paquin), son Daniel (Boriello), and intrusive mother-in-law Lillian (Feldshuh). Hubby Marty (Schreiber) is working in the city and visits on the weekends. When sensitive hippie blouse peddler Walker (Mortensen) catches her eye, she decides it's time to catch up on the '60s and her lost teenage years. When she takes off for Woodstock and happens upon her daughter, the family drama is intensified. Pearl's turmoil and motivations are handled well by Lane and the screenwriter Gray, and neither of the men vying for her are cardboard stereotypes, but the abruptly feel-good ending may not work for some. **107m/C VHS, DVD.** Diane Lane, Liev Schreiber, Viggo Mortensen, Anna Paquin, Tovah Feldshuh, Bobby Boriello; *D:* Tony Goldwyn; *W:* Pamela Gray; *C:* Anthony B. Richmond; *M:* Mason Daring.

Walk on the Wild Side 🦴🦴 **1962** In 1930s New Orleans, a man searches for his long-lost love, finds her working in a whorehouse and fights to save her from the lesbian madame Stanwyck. Melodrama, based only loosely on the Nelson Algren novel and adapted by cult novelist John Fante, with Edmund Morris. Much-troubled on the set, and it shows. **114m/B VHS.** Jane Fonda, Laurence Harvey, Barbara Stanwyck, Capucine, Anne Baxter; *D:* Edward Dmytryk; *M:* Elmer Bernstein.

Walk Softly, Stranger 🦴🦴 **1950** Two-bit crook is reformed by the love of an innocent peasant girl. If you can stand the cliche masquerading as a plot, the performances are good. **81m/B VHS.** Alida Valli, Joseph Cotten, Spring Byington, Paul Stewart, Jack Paar, Jeff Donnell, John McIntire; *D:* Robert Stevenson.

Walk the Proud Land 🦴🦴½ **1956** Story of Indian agent John Clum (Murphy), who fights for the rights of the Apache in 1870s Arizona and who convinces their leader Geronimo (Silverheels) to surrender to the authorities. Adapted from the biography "Apache Agent" by Woodworth Clum. **88m/C VHS.** Audie Murphy, Jay Silverheels, Anne Bancroft, Pat(ricia) Crowley, Charles Drake; *D:* Jesse Hibbs; *W:* Jack Sher, Gil Doud; *C:* Harold Lipstein.

A Walk to Remember 🦴🦴 **2002 (PG) 101m/C VHS, DVD.** *US* Mandy Moore, Shane West, Peter Coyote, Daryl Hannah, Lauren German, Clayne Crawford; *D:* Adam Shankman; *W:* Karen Janszen; *C:* Julio Macat; *M:* Mervyn Warren.

Walkabout 🦴🦴🦴½ **1971 (PG)** Beautifully told and filmed story (by Roeg in his debut) about a nameless young brother (John, Roeg's six-year-old son) and sister (Agutter), who are abandoned in the Australian outback when their father kills himself. The children wander, with little chance of survival, until a young aborigine (Gumpilil) finds them. He interrupts his own "walkabout," a rite of passage, to teach them to survive, leading to betrayal and tragedy. Based on a novel by James Vance Marshall. **100m/C VHS, DVD, Wide.** *AU* Jenny Agutter, Lucien John, David Gulpilil, John Meillon; *D:* Nicolas Roeg; *W:* Edward Bond; *C:* Nicolas Roeg; *M:* John Barry.

Walker 🦴🦴 **1987 (R)** Slapdash, tongue-in-cheek historical pastiche about the real-life American William Walker (played previously in "Burn!" by Marlon Brando), and how he led a revolution in Nicaragua in 1855 and became its self-declared president. A bitter, revisionist farce never for a moment attempting to be accurate. Matlin's unfortunate, though fortunately brief, follow-up to her Oscar-winning performance. **95m/C VHS.** Ed Harris, Richard Masur, Peter Boyle, Rene Auberjonois, Marlee Matlin, Miguel (Michael) Sandoval; *D:* Alex Cox; *W:* Rudy Wurlitzer; *M:* Joe Strummer.

Walker: Texas Ranger: One Riot, One Ranger 🦴🦴½ **1993 (PG-13)** Norris sticks with the action-adventure mode with this tv pilot movie about Cordell Walker, a good guy with a code and some martial arts skills, who teams up with an ex-gridiron star and a female district attorney to go after lawbreakers. This time its bank robbers and three hoods after a teenaged girl. **96m/C VHS.** Chuck Norris, Sheree J. Wilson, Clarence Gilyard Jr., Gailard Sartain, Floyd "Red Crow" Westerman, James Drury; *D:* Virgil W. Vogel; *W:* Louise McCarn. **TV**

Walking and Talking 🦴🦴½ **1996 (R)** Low-budget, lighthearted estrogen romp through the lives of two best friends in New York, Amelia (Keener) and Laura (Heche), going through commitment crises. Freshman writer/director Holofcener scores by making a lackluster story imminently watchable. Likable cast of mostly unknowns (Heche was deemed a rising star at a recent Cannes Festival) deliver Holofcener's clever and humorous exchanges. Corrigan's video store clerk and all-around "ugly guy" is a highlight. Brit Bragg brings in a worthy score. **86m/C VHS, DVD, Wide.** Anne Heche, Catherine Keener, Liev Schreiber, Todd Field, Kevin Corrigan, Randall Batinkoff, Joseph Siravo, Vincent Pastore, Lynn Cohen, Andrew Holofcener; *D:* Nicole Holofcener; *W:* Nicole Holofcener; *C:* Michael Spiller; *M:* Billy Bragg.

Walking Back 🦴🦴 **1926** Troubled teens go for joyride and bash mirthmobile to smithereens. The body shop agrees to give them a different car, but they find themselves in the middle of a heist at a plant belonging to the father of one of the boys. **53m/B VHS.** Sue Carol, Richard Walling, Ivan Lebedeff, Robert Edeson, Florence Turner, Arthur (L.) Rankin; *D:* Rupert Julian.

The Walking Dead 🦴🦴 **1994 (R)** Depicts the Vietnam War from the perspectives of four black and one white Marine assigned to rescue POWs from a North Vietnam camp in 1972. Fairly routine story with stock characters (by-the-book sergeant, family man, naive youngster, cynical hustler) and flashbacks to depict their back home struggles. Cast tries but is defeated by a one-dimensional script. **89m/C VHS.** Joe Morton, Eddie Griffin, Allen Payne, Vonte Sweet, Roger Floyd; *D:* Preston A. Whitmore II; *W:* Preston A. Whitmore II; *C:* John L. Demps Jr.; *M:* Gary Chang.

Walking on Air **1987** Ray Bradbury's story comes to life as a handicapped boy dreams of completing a real space walk. Originally aired on PBS as part of the "Wonderworks" series. **60m/C VHS.** Lynn Redgrave, Jordan Marder, James Treuer, Katheryn Trainor; *D:* Ed Kaplan.

Walking Tall 🦴🦴½ **1973 (R)** A Tennessee sheriff takes a stand against syndicate-run gambling and his wife is murdered in response. Ultra-violent crime saga wowed the movie going public and spawned several sequels and a TV series. Based on the true story of folk-hero Buford Pusser, admirably rendered by Baker. **126m/C VHS, DVD.** Joe Don Baker, Elizabeth Hartman, Noah Beery Jr., Gene Evans, Rosemary Murphy, Felton Perry; *D:* Phil Karlson; *W:* Mort Briskin; *C:* Jack Marta; *M:* Walter Scharf.

Walking Tall: Part 2 🦴🦴 **1975 (PG)** Club-wielding Tennessee sheriff Buford Pusser, this time played less memorably by Svenson, attempts to find the man who killed his wife. Even more violent than the original. **109m/C VHS.** Bo Svenson, Noah Beery Jr., Angel Tompkins, Richard Jaeckel; *D:* Earl Bellamy.

Walking Tall: The Final Chapter 🦴½ **1977 (PG)** The final months in the life of Tennessee sheriff Buford Pusser and the mystery surrounding his death. It wasn't the final chapter. Still to come: a TV flick and series. **112m/C VHS.** Bo Svenson, Forrest Tucker, Leif Garrett, Morgan Woodward; *D:* Jack Starrett; *C:* Robert B. Hauser.

Walking the Edge 🦴½ **1983 (R)** A widow hires a taxi driver to help her seek vengeance against the men who killed her husband and her son. Forster does what he can with the lousy story and script. **94m/C VHS, DVD, Wide.** Robert Forster, Nancy Kwan, Joe Spinell, Aarika Wells; *D:* Norbert Meisel; *W:* Curt Allen; *C:* Ernie Poulos; *M:* Jay Chattaway.

Walking Through the Fire 🦴🦴½ **1980** A young woman's real-life struggle with Hodgkin's disease. Her fight for her own and her unborn baby's survival is a stirring testament to the power of faith. Absorbing drama. **143m/C VHS.** Bess Armstrong, Tom Mason, Bonnie Bedelia, Richard Masur, Swoosie Kurtz, J.D. Cannon, June Lockhart; *D:* Robert Day. **TV**

Walking Thunder 🦴🦴½ **1994 (PG)** The McKay family are stranded in the Rocky Mountains in 1850 when their wagon is destroyed by a grizzly bear. But they're rescued by a mountain man (Read) and a Sioux medicine man (Thin Elk), who introduce young Jacob to a number of adventures. It's wholesome, old-fashioned kid entertainment. **95m/C VHS.** John Denver, James Read, David Tom, Chief Ted Thin Elk; *D:* Craig Clyde; *W:* Craig Clyde; *M:* John Scott; *Nar:* Brian Keith.

The Wall 🦴🦴🦴½ *Guney's The Wall; Le Mur; Duvar* **1983** The last film by Guney, author of "Yol," about orphaned boys in prison in the Turkish capitol of Ankara trying to escape and/or rebel after ceaseless rapings, beatings and injustice. An acclaimed, disturbing film made from Guney's own experience. He died in 1984, three years after escaping from prison. Brutal and horrifying. In Turkish with English subtitles. **117m/C VHS.** *TU* Ayse Emel Mesci, Saban, Sisko; *D:* Yilmaz Guney; *W:* Yilmaz Guney.

The Wall 🦴🦴🦴 **1999** Three stories that focus on the Vietnam Veterans Memorial and some of the objects left there. "The Pencil Holder" finds young Ben Holst (Blumas) living with his stiff-necked Army colonel father (Olmos) in Saigon in 1969 where he's mistaken by a dying soldier (Chevolleau) for his own son. "The Badge" is the good-luck toy sheriff's badge that black soldier Bracey Mitchell (Glover) clings to as he hides from the Vietcong and dreams of home. "The Player" is conniving wheeler-dealer Bishop (Whaley), who runs a base nightclub and gets his comeuppance from self-sacrificing soldier Luis (DeLorenzo), who's a guitar-playing whiz. **94m/C VHS, DVD.** Edward James Olmos, Richard Chevolleau, Trevor Blumas, Dean McDermott, Savion Glover, Ruby Dee, Martin Roach, Linette Robinson, Frank Whaley, Michael Delorenzo, Ron White, Matthew Ferguson; *D:* Joseph Sargent; *W:* Scott Abbott, Charles Fuller, Patrick Sheane Duncan; *C:* Donald M. Morgan; *M:* Larry Brown. **CABLE**

Wall Street 🦴🦴🦴 **1987 (R)** Stone's energetic, high-minded big business treatise in which naive, neophyte stockbroker Bud Fox (Charlie Sheen) is seduced into insider trading by sleek entrepreneur Gordon Gekko (Douglas), much to his blue-collar father's (Martin Sheen) chagrin. A fast-moving drama of '80s-style materialism with a mesmerizing, award-winning performance by Douglas as greed personified. Expert direction by Stone, who co-wrote the not-very-subtle script. His father, to whom this film is dedicated, was a broker. Look for Stone in a cameo. **126m/C VHS, DVD, Wide.** Paul Guilfoyle, Michael Douglas, Charlie Sheen, Martin Sheen, Daryl Hannah, Sean Young, James Spader, Hal Holbrook, Terence Stamp, Richard Dysart, John C. McGinley, Saul Rubinek, James Karen, Josh Mostel, Millie Perkins, Cecilia Peck, Grant Shaud, Franklin Cover, Oliver Stone; *D:* Oliver Stone; *W:* Stanley Weiser, Oliver Stone; *C:* Robert Richardson; *M:* Stewart Copeland. Oscars '87: Actor (Douglas); Golden Globes '88: Actor—Drama (Douglas); Natl. Bd. of Review '87: Actor (Douglas); Golden Raspberries '87: Worst Support. Actress (Hannah).

Wall Street Cowboy 🦴 **1939** When his land is threatened, a cowboy fights big business in the big city. **54m/B VHS.** Roy Rogers.

Wallaby Jim of the Islands 🦴🦴 **1937** The singing captain of a pearl fishing boat must protect his treasure from marauding pirates. Pleasant enough musical adventure. **61m/B VHS.** George Houston, Douglas Walton; *D:* Charles Lamont.

The Walloping Kid 🦴½ **1926** A B-western with photography done in Monument Valley. Silent with original organ music. **67m/B VHS, 8mm.** Kit Carson, Pauline Curley; *D:* Robert J. Horner.

Walls of Glass 🦴🦴½ *Flanagan* **1985 (R)** An aging New York cabby tries to make it as an actor. Effective performances by all override the thin plot. Slow and uneven, but involving. **85m/C VHS.** Geraldine Page, Philip Bosco, William Hickey, Olympia Dukakis, Brian Bloom, Linda Thorson; *D:* Scott Goldstein.

The Walls of Hell 🦴🦴 *Intramuros* **1964** Lt. Jim Sorenson (Mahoney) leads guerilla fighters into the city of Manila, aided by freedom fighter Nardo (Poe), to defeat desperate Japanese troops hold up in the city. **88m/B VHS, DVD.** *PH* Jock Mahoney, Fernando Poe Jr., Mike Parsons; *D:* Gerardo (Gerry) De Leon, Eddie Romero; *W:* Eddie Romero, Cesar Amigo, Ferde Grofe Jr.; *C:* F. Sacdalan; *M:* Tito Arevalo.

The Walls of Malapaga ☙☙ *Au-Dela des Grilles; Le Mura di Malapaga* **1949** Frenchman Gabin, who's killed his mistress, stows away aboard a ship to Italy. He arrives in Genoa only to have all his money and papers stolen. Gabin then meets Miranda, a lonely waitress with a young daughter, and the two fall in love. But it's only temporary as the authorities come closing in. French with subtitles. **91m/C VHS.** *FR IT* Jean Gabin, Isa Miranda, Vera Talchi, Andrea Checchi, Robert Dalban; ***D:*** Rene Clement; ***W:*** Jean Aurenche, Pierre Bost; ***M:*** Roman Vlad. Oscars '50: Foreign Film.

Walpurgis Night ☙☙☙ *Valborgmassoafton* **1941** Soapy Swedish drama about abortion was racy for its time. Office gal Bergman secretly loves her boss (Hanson). His wife refuses to have children and goes through an abortion. An unscrupulous fellow blackmails her with this knowledge. Bergman bides her time. Stay tuned... Interesting document on the mores of another time. In Swedish with English subtitles. **82m/B VHS.** *SW* Lars Hanson, Karin Carlsson, Victor Sjostrom, Ingrid Bergman, Erik "Bullen" Berglund, Sture Lagerwall, Georg Rydeberg, Georg Blickingberg; ***D:*** Gustaf Edgren.

Walter and Henry ☙☙☙ **2001** Walter (Larroquette) and his 12-year-old son Henry (Braun) live in a trailer in Brooklyn and (barely) make ends meet as street musicians in the city. However, after Walter has a psychotic breakdown and is institutionalized, Henry is forced to live with his rigid grandfather (Coburn) from whom Walter has been estranged for years. And slowly, Henry begins to adapt, and even enjoy, his new life. **90m/C VHS, DVD.** John Larroquette, James Coburn, Kate Nelligan, Nicholas Braun; ***D:*** Daniel Petrie; ***W:*** Geoffrey Sharp; ***C:*** Michael Storey; ***M:*** Christopher Dedrick. **CABLE**

The Waltons: The Christmas Carol ☙☙ **1980** The winter solstice brings no special joy to Walton's mountain; WWII has taken many men, with short wave reports indicating the Nazi terror spreading across Europe. But huddled in the glow of Walton's barn, the children rediscover the true meaning of Christmas. **94m/C VHS.** Judy Norton-Taylor, Jon Walmsley, Mary (Elizabeth) McDonough, Eric Scott, Kami Cotler, Joe Conley, Ronnie Clare, Leslie Winston, Peggy Rea; ***D:*** Lawrence (Larry) Dobkin. **TV**

Waltz across Texas ☙☙½ **1983** Young oil man Jastrow and good-lookin' rock scientist Archer at first don't take to each other, but there's something in the air, and romance blossoms. Jastrow and Archer cowrote and coproduced, and cohabitated as spouses in real-life. **100m/C VHS, DVD.** Terry Jastrow, Anne Archer, Mary Kay Place, Richard Farnsworth; ***D:*** Ernest Day; ***C:*** Robert Elswit.

Waltz King ☙☙ **1963** Typically hokey Disney biography of the young composer Johann Strauss during his Old Viennese heyday. Fine music, pretty German locations. Well-made family fare. **94m/C VHS.** Kerwin Mathews, Senta Berger, Brian Aherne; ***D:*** Steve Previn.

Waltz of the Toreadors ☙☙☙ *The Amorous General* **1962** Retired general Sellers doesn't care for his wealthy, shrewish wife and tries to re-kindle a 17-year-old romance with a French woman. It doesn't work out (seems his illegitimate son also has a soft spot for the lady), but the general decides to keep his eyes open for other possibilities. Interestingly cast adaptation of Jean Anouilh's play. Sellers is hilarious, as usual. **105m/C VHS, DVD.** *GB* Peter Sellers, Dany Robin, Margaret Leighton, Cyril Cusack; ***D:*** John Guillermin; ***W:*** Wolf Mankowitz; ***C:*** John Wilcox; ***M:*** Richard Addinsell.

A Waltz Through the Hills **1988** Two orphans head into the Australian outback and experience many adventures en route to the coast where they can set sail for England and their grandparents. Aired on PBS as part of the "Wonderworks" series. **116m/C VHS.** Tina Kemp, Andre Jansen, Ernie Dingo, Dan O'Herlihy; ***D:*** Frank Arnold.

Wanda Nevada ☙½ **1979 (PG)** Gambler Fonda wins nubile young Shields in a poker game, so he drags her with him to the Grand Canyon to look for gold. Director/star Fonda sure picked a lemon for his only screen appearance with dad Henry (a grizzled old varmint appearing briefly). Shields is in her usual form—stellar for a shampoo commercial. **105m/C VHS.** Peter Fonda, Brooke Shields, Henry Fonda, Fiona Lewis, Luke Askew, Ted Markland, Severn Darden, Paul Fix; ***D:*** Peter Fonda.

Wanda, the Sadistic Hypnotist ☙ **1967** A comely vixen hypnotizes an innocent pedestrian, ties him up and whips him to indulge her whims. Despite the "victim's" protests, she unleashes a gang of sexually playful women on him, and he is subjected to a multitude of "tortures." **70m/C VHS.** Katharine Shubeck, Janice Sweet, Dick Dangerfield, Daryl Cobinot; ***D:*** Gregory Corarito.

The Wanderer ☙☙ *Le Grand Meaulnes* **1967** Two friends fall in love—Frantz with Valentine and his friend Augustin with Frantz's sister, Yvonne. When the two women disappear on Frantz's wedding day, the two men begin a search to find both the women and the reasons for their disappearance. In French with English subtitles. **108m/C VHS.** *FR* Brigitte Fossey, Jean Blaise, Alain Noury, Juliette Villard; ***D:*** Jean-Gabriel Albicocco.

Wanderers ☙☙☙½ **1979 (R)** Richard Price's acclaimed novel about youth gangs coming of age in the Bronx in 1963. The "Wanderers," named after the Dion song, are a gang of Italian-American teenagers about to graduate high school, who prowl the Bronx with the feeling that something is slipping away from them. Fascinating, funny and touching. Manz is unforgettable as a scrappy gal. A wonderful 60s soundtrack (Dion, the Four Seasons) colors this "coming of age the hard way" film. **113m/C VHS.** Ken Wahl, John Friedrich, Karen Allen, Linda Manz, Richard Price, Toni Kalem, Tony Ganios, Alan Rosenberg, Jim Youngs, Val Avery, Dolph Sweet, Olympia Dukakis; ***D:*** Philip Kaufman; ***W:*** Philip Kaufman, Rose Kaufman; ***C:*** Michael Chapman.

Wandering Jew ☙☙½ **1920** An excellent print of the rare Austrian film version of the classic legend, one of at least three silent versions. A Jew is condemned to wander the earth for eternity. **65m/B VHS.** *AT* Rudolf Schildkraut, Joseph Schildkraut.

The Wannsee Conference ☙☙☙½ *Wannseekonferenz* **1984** A startling, important film depicting, in real time, the conference held at the Wannsee on January 20, 1942, during which 14 members of the Nazi hierarchy decided in 85 minutes the means and logistics of effecting the Final Solution. Recreated from the original secretary's notes. Horrifying and chilling. Along with "Shoah," a must-see for understanding the Holocaust and the psychology of genocide. In German with English subtitles. **87m/C VHS.** *GE* Dietrich Mattausch, Gerd Brockmann, Friedrich Beckhaus, Robert Atzorn, Jochen Busse, Hans-Werner Bussinger, Harald Dietl, Peter Fitz, Reinhard Glemnitz, Dieter Groest, Martin Luttge, Anita Mally, Gerd Riegauer; ***D:*** Heinz Schirk; ***W:*** Paul Mommertz; ***C:*** Horst Schier.

Wanted ☙½ **1998 (R)** Jimmy Scrico (Sutton) has accidentally shot a mob boss. Naturally, this means he's on the run from the vengeful wiseguys and he finds sanctuary in a Catholic school where Jimmy's befriended by Father Donnelly (Busfield). Then the bad guys catch up with him. **90m/C VHS, DVD.** Michael Sutton, Timothy Busfield, Robert Culp, Tracey Gold, James Quattrochi; ***D:*** Terence M. O'Keefe; ***W:*** Terence M. O'Keefe, Mark Evan Schwartz; ***C:*** Richard A. Jones.

Wanted: Babysitter woof! **1975** A young student accidentally becomes involved by her roommate in a plot to kidnap the child she is babysitting. Schneider is truly awful; Italian comic Pazzetto is at sea in a bad role as her boyfriend. Also released as "The Babysitter." **90m/C VHS.** Robert Vaughn, Vic Morrow, Maria Schneider, Renato Pozzetto, Nadja Tiller, Carl Mohner, Sydne Rome; ***D:*** Rene Clement.

Wanted Dead or Alive ☙½ **1986 (R)** Ex-CIA agent Hauer is now a high-tech bounty hunter assigned to bring in an international terrorist. When the terrorist kills Hauer's friend and girlfriend, he forgets the $50,000 bonus for bringing him in alive. Official "sequel" to the Steve McQueen TV series with Hauer as the McQueen character's great-grandson. The link is meaningless, and the plot is a thin excuse for much violence and anti-terrorist flag-waving. **104m/C VHS, DVD, Wide.** Rutger Hauer, Gene Simmons, Robert Guillaume, William Russ, Jerry Hardin, Mel Harris; ***D:*** Gary Sherman; ***W:*** Brian Taggert; ***C:*** Alex Nepomniaschy; ***M:*** Joe Renzetti.

Wanted: The Perfect Guy ☙☙½ **1990** Danny and Melanie try to find Mister Right for their divorced Mom (Kahn). An Emmy Award winner about single parents and their children. **45m/C VHS.** Madeline Kahn, Melanie Mayron.

The War ☙☙½ **1994 (PG-13)** Post-Vietnam war drama, set in 1970 Mississippi, centers on a children's battle over a treehouse but becomes a sermon on love, death, family values, pacifism, and the physical and spiritual wounds of war. After helping son Stu (Wood) and daughter Lidia (Randall) build their treehouse, troubled Vietnam vet Stephen Simmons (Costner) tries to coax Stu to make peace with the bullies trying to take it over. However cliched, director Avnet allows a talented cast of kids to thoughtfully express a child's view of the world but gosh-darn-it the preachy tone can get down-right annoying. **126m/C VHS, DVD.** Elijah Wood, Kevin Costner, Lexi (Faith) Randall, Mare Winningham, Christine Baranski, Bruce A. Young, Gary Basaraba, Raynor Scheine, Nick Searcy; ***D:*** Jon Avnet; ***W:*** Kathy McWorter; ***C:*** Geoffrey Simpson; ***M:*** Thomas Newman.

War & Love ☙☙ **1984 (PG-13)** Two Jewish teenagers in Warsaw are torn apart by WWII and Nazi persecution. After the war they search for each other. Sincere, but not adequately developed, drama based on the book "The Survivors" by film's producer Jack Eisner. **112m/C VHS.** Sebastian Keneas, Kyra Sedgwick; ***D:*** Moshe Mizrahi.

War and Peace ☙☙½ **1956** Lengthy adaptation of Tolstoy's great (and likewise lengthy) novel about three families caught up in Russia's Napoleonic Wars from 1805 to 1812; filmed in Rome. Bad casting and confused script (by six writers) are somewhat overcome by awesome battle scenes and Hepburn. Remade in 1968. **208m/C VHS.** Audrey Hepburn, Mel Ferrer, Henry Fonda, Anita Ekberg, Vittorio Gassman, John Mills, Oscar Homolka, Herbert Lom, Helmut Dantine, Tullio Carminati, Barry Jones, Milly Vitale, Maria Ferrero, Wilfred Lawson, May Britt, Jeremy Brett, Lea Seidl, Patrick Crean, Sean Barrett, Richard Dawson; ***D:*** King Vidor; ***W:*** King Vidor, Bridget Boland, Mario Camerini, Ennio de Concini, Ivo Perilli, Irwin Shaw, Robert Westerby; ***C:*** Jack Cardiff, Aldo Tonti; ***M:*** Nino Rota. Golden Globes '57: Foreign Film.

War and Peace ☙☙☙ **1968** The massive Russian production of Leo Tolstoy's masterpiece, adapting the classic tome practically scene by scene. All of the production took place in the Soviet Union. So painstaking that it took more than five years to finish, no other adaptation can touch it. Hugely expensive ($100 million, claimed the Russians), wildly uneven production. Great scenes of battle and aristocratic life. Though this version is far from perfect, one asks: Is it humanly possible to do screen justice to such a novel? In Russian with English subtitles. On four tapes. (Beware the two-part, poorly dubbed version that was also released.) **373m/C VHS.** *RU* Lyudmila Savelyeva, Sergei Bondarchuk, Vyacheslav Tihonor, Hira Ivanov-Golarko, Irina Gubanova, Antonina Shuranova; ***D:*** Sergei Bondarchuk; ***C:*** Jack Cardiff. Oscars '68: Foreign Film; Golden Globes '69: Foreign Film; N.Y. Film Critics '68: Foreign Film.

War and Peace ☙☙½ **1973** Lengthy BBC production of the lengthy Tolstoy masterpiece that follows the trials and triumphs of two Russian families whose lives intersect against a backdrop of the Napoleonic Wars. On 6 cassettes. **750m/C VHS.** *GB* Anthony Hopkins, Alan Dobie, Faith Brook, Morag Hood, Colin Baker, Neil Stacey; ***D:*** John (Howard) Davies; ***W:*** Jack Pulman.

War & Remembrance ☙½ **1988** Tedious sequel to the epic TV miniseries "The Winds of War," based on the novel by Herman Wouk. Historical fiction is created around the events of WWII, including Nazi persecution and naval battles in the Pacific. Followed by "War and Remembrance: The Final Chapter." On seven cassettes. **840m/C VHS.** Charles Lane, Robert Mitchum, Jane Seymour, Hart Bochner, Victoria Tennant, Barry Bostwick, Polly Bergen, David Dukes, Michael Woods, Sharon Stone, Robert Morley, Sami Frey, Chaim Topol, John Rhys-Davies, Ian McShane, William Schallert, Jeremy Kemp, Steven Berkoff, Robert Hardy, Ralph Bellamy, John Gielgud; ***D:*** Dan Curtis. **TV**

War & Remembrance: The Final Chapter ☙½ **1989** The final episodes of Herman Wouk's sweeping saga, following "The Winds of War" and "War and Remembrance," deal with the struggle of a Jewish family in war-torn Europe. Natalie and her son, Louis, are trapped in a ghetto under the reign of a vicious Nazi, who considers a bribe for the sake of the mother and son. On five cassettes. **600m/C VHS.** Robert Mitchum, Jane Seymour, Hart Bochner, Victoria Tennant, Polly Bergen, David Dukes, Michael Woods, Sharon Stone, Robert Morley, Sami Frey, Chaim Topol, John Rhys-Davies, Ian McShane, William Schallert, Jeremy Kemp, Steven Berkoff, Robert Hardy, Ralph Bellamy, John Gielgud; ***D:*** Dan Curtis. **TV**

War Arrow ☙☙ **1953** Army Major Howell Brady (Chandler) is sent by Washington to end the Kiowa uprisings in Texas in this cavalry vs. Indians western. Along the way, he tries to win the heart of O'Hara. **79m/C VHS.** Maureen O'Hara, Jeff Chandler, Suzan Ball, John McIntire, Noah Beery Jr., Henry (Kleinbach) Brandon, Dennis Weaver, Jay Silverheels; ***D:*** George Sherman; ***W:*** John Michael Hayes.

The War at Home ☙½ **1996 (R)** In 1972 Vietnam vet Jeremy Collier (Estevez) has been home in the Dallas suburbs for a year but the war and its effects still linger. Mom Maureen (Bates) is a conservative control freak and dad Bob (Sheen) just can't connect, while teenaged sis Karen (Williams) is going through her own rebellion. The tense situation comes to a bitter head over a Thanksgiving weekend. Based on the 1984 play "Home Front" by James Duff. **124m/C VHS.** Kathy Bates, Martin Sheen, Emilio Estevez, Kimberly Williams, Carla Gugino, Geoffrey Blake, Corin "Corky" Nemec, Ann Hearn; ***D:*** Emilio Estevez; ***W:*** James Duff; ***C:*** Peter Levy; ***M:*** Basil Poledouris.

War Between the Tates ☙☙ **1976** A college professor's affair with a female student is the basis for a tension filled stand-off with his wife. Mediocre adaptation of the Allison Lurie novel, somewhat redeemed by Ashley's performance. **90m/C VHS.** Mina (Badiyi) Badie, Ann Wedgeworth, Annette O'Toole, Colin Fox, Harvey Atkin, Michael J. Reynolds, Richard Crenna, Elizabeth Ashley, Granville Van Dusen; ***D:*** Lee Philips; ***W:*** Barbara Turner; ***M:*** John Barry. **TV**

The War Boy ☙☙½ **1985 (R)** Difficulties encountered by a young Canadian boy as he grows up in Central Europe during WWII. Not to be compared with "Empire of the Sun" or "Hope and Glory," both of which were released later; successful in its modest ambitions. Beautiful performance from 12-year-old star Hopely. **86m/C VHS.** *CA* Helen Shaver, Kenneth Welsh, Jason Hopely; ***D:*** Allan Eastman.

War Brides ☙ **1980** Civil War brides confront life after the war. Low-budget drama. **100m/C VHS.** *CA* Elizabeth Richardson, Sharry Fleet, Sonja Smits; ***D:*** Martin Lavut. **TV**

War Bus Commando ☙ **1989** A fully loaded bus is the only way out when soldiers are caught behind enemy lines in Afghanistan. A case of the spoof coming first: The plot is almost exactly the same as "Stripes"—only this one isn't funny. In Hi-Fi. **90m/C VHS.** *IT* Savina Gersak, Mark Gregory, John Vernon; ***D:*** Frank (Pierluigi Ciriaci) Valenti.

War in Space ✓ **1977** Powerful U.N. Space Bureau Starships and UFOs band together to battle alien invaders among the volcanoes and deserts of Venus. **91m/C VHS.** *JP* Kensaku Marita, Yuko Asano, Ryo Ikebe.

War in the Sky ✓✓✓ **1982** Director William Wyler's documentary account of the Army Air Corps in action. Extraordinary footage of the Thunderbolt, the P47 Fighter, and the B17 Bomber. **90m/C VHS.** ***D:*** William Wyler; ***Nar:*** Peter Lawford, James Stewart.

The War Lord ✓✓✓ **1965** Set in the 11th century, Heston stars as Chrysagon, a Norman knight and war lord who commands a peasant village. While battling his enemies, he becomes enamored of a peasant girl named Bronwyn (Forsyth), who is unfortunately engaged to someone else. Pulling rank, Chrysagon uses an ancient law that allows noblemen the first night with a bride and the two fall in love. The two vow to never part, but that sets the stage for even more bloody battles. Fine acting and great production values make this a well-adapted version of the play "The Lovers" by Leslie Stevens. **121m/C VHS, DVD, Wide.** Charlton Heston, Richard Boone, Rosemary Forsyth, Guy Stockwell, Niall MacGinnis, Henry Wilcoxon, James Farentino, Maurice Evans, Michael Conrad; ***D:*** Franklin J. Schaffner; ***W:*** John Collier, Millard Kaufman; ***C:*** Russell Metty.

War Lover ✓✓½ **1962** An American daredevil flying captain and his co-pilot find themselves vying for the affections of a woman during WWII in England. Seeks human frailty beneath surface heroism. McQueen is impressive, no thanks to mediocre script. Excellent aerial photography, and featuring one of only a very few serviceable WWII B-17s then remaining. Based on John Hersey's novel. **105m/B VHS.** *GB* Steve McQueen, Robert Wagner, Shirley Anne Field, Bill Edwards, Gary Cockrell; ***D:*** Philip Leacock; ***W:*** Howard Koch.

War of the Buttons ✓✓½ **1995 (PG)** Two sleepy Irish fishing villages provide childish battle grounds for two groups of local lads. The Ballys (Ballydowse village), lead by Fergus (Fitzgerald), and the Carricks (Carrickdowse), with leader Geronimo (Coffey), have an intense rivalry and capture by the other gang leads to the removal of every clothing button for the unfortunate captive. When Fergus becomes a Carrick victim, he organizes a retaliatory strike, and emotions threaten to overwhelm all concerned. Based on the French novel "La Guerre des Boutons" by Louis Pergaud. Filmed on location in West Cork, Ireland. **94m/C VHS.** Gregg Fitzgerald, John Coffey, Liam Cunningham, Paul Batt, Eveanna Ryan, Colm Meaney, Johnny Murphy; ***D:*** John Roberts; ***W:*** Colin Welland; ***C:*** Bruno de Keyzer; ***M:*** Rachel Portman.

The War of the Colossal Beast ✓½ *The Terror Strikes* **1958** This sequel to "The Amazing Colossal Man" finds the 70-foot Colonel Manning even angrier at the attempts to kill him than he was in the first film. So he wreaks more havoc until scolded by his sister into committing suicide for being such a troublemaker. Cheesy special effects but good for a laugh. **68m/B VHS.** Dean Parkin, Sally Fraser, Russ Bender, Roger Pace, Charles Stewart; ***D:*** Bert I. Gordon.

War of the Gargantuas ✓ *Duel of the Gargantuas; Frankenstein Monsters: Sanda vs. Gairath; Furankenshutain No Kaiju: Sanda tai Gailah; Sanda tai Gailah* **1970 (G)** Tokyo is once again the boxing ring for giant monsters. This time it's a good gargantua (half human, half monster) against a bad gargantua. This is a strange one. **92m/C VHS.** *JP* Russ Tamblyn, Kumi Mizuno, Kenji Sahara, Jun Tazaki, Kipp Hamilton, Haruo Nakajima, Nobuo Nakamura, Ikio Sawamura, Yoshifumi Tajima; ***D:*** Inoshiro Honda; ***W:*** Inoshiro Honda, Takeshi Kimura, Kaoru Mabuchi; ***C:*** Hajime Koizumi; ***M:*** Akira Ifukube.

War of the Robots ✓ **1978** A dying alien civilization kidnaps two brilliant Earth scientists in the hope that they'll help it survive. **99m/C VHS.** Antonio (Tony) Sabato, Melissa Long, James R. Stuart.

The War of the Roses ✓✓✓ **1989 (R)** Acidic black comedy about a well-to-do suburban couple who can't agree on a property settlement in their divorce so they wage unreserved and ever-escalating combat on each other, using their palatial home as a battleground. Expertly and lovingly (if that's the word) directed by DeVito, who plays the lawyer. Turner and Douglas are splendid. Adapted from the novel by Warren Adler. **116m/C VHS, DVD, Wide.** Michael Douglas, Kathleen Turner, Danny DeVito, Marianne Saegebrecht, Sean Astin, G.D. Spradlin, Peter Donat, Heather Fairfield, Dan Castellaneta, Danitra Vance, Tony Crane; ***D:*** Danny DeVito; ***W:*** Michael Leeson; ***C:*** Stephen Burum; ***M:*** David Newman.

War of the Wildcats ✓✓½ *In Old Oklahoma* **1943** Fast-moving western with Wayne as a tough cowboy battling a powerful land baron. They fight over land, oil and a woman. Unusual because Wayne's character acts on behalf of the Indians to drill and transport oil. **102m/B VHS.** John Wayne, Martha Scott, Albert Dekker, George "Gabby" Hayes, Sidney Blackmer; ***D:*** Albert Rogell.

War of the Wizards ✓½ *The Phoenix* **1981 (PG)** Low-budget sci-fi thriller about an alien woman with supernatural powers who comes to take over the Earth. But, lucky for all earthlings, she's challenged by a hero-type just in the nick of time. **90m/C VHS.** Richard Kiel; ***D:*** Richard Caan.

The War of the Worlds ✓✓✓½ **1953** H.G. Wells's classic novel of the invasion of Earth by Martians, updated to 1950s California, with spectacular special effects of destruction caused by the Martian war machines. Pretty scary and tense; based more on Orson Welles's radio broadcast than on the book. Still very popular; hit the top 20 in sales when released on video. Classic thriller later made into a TV series. Produced by George Pal, who brought the world much sci-fi, including "The Time Machine," "Destination Moon," and "When Worlds Collide," and who appears here as a street person. **85m/C VHS, DVD.** Gene Barry, Ann (Robin) Robinson, Les Tremayne, Lewis Martin, Robert Cornthwaite, Sandro Giglio, George Pal, Jack Kruschen, Carolyn Jones, Alvy Moore, William Phipps, Paul Frees; ***D:*** Byron Haskin; ***W:*** Barre Lyndon; ***C:*** George Barnes; ***M:*** Leith Stevens; ***V:*** Cedric Hardwicke.

War Party ✓✓ **1989 (R)** During a 100-year commemoration of an Indian massacre in the Midwest, a murder occurs and a lynch mob chases a pack of young Blackfeet into the mountains before the inevitable showdown. A feeble attempt at portraying the unfair treatment of Native Americans. Un-subtle, Hollywood style, this time in favor of the Indians, and therefore un-serious. Too bad; the premise had potential. **99m/C VHS.** Kevin Dillon, Billy Wirth, Tim Sampson, M. Emmet Walsh; ***D:*** Franc Roddam; ***C:*** Brian Tufano.

The War Room ✓✓✓ **1993 (PG)** Eye opening, sometimes disturbing documentary presents a behind the scenes peek at what really goes on during a Presidential campaign. When filming began in June '92 Bill Clinton was an unknown political quantity and advisors George Stephanopoulous and James Carville were masterminding his campaign. The "War Room" refers to the building in Little Rock where they struggled to organize a small army of volunteers into a winning team. Highlights include the Democratic National Convention, the North Carolina leg of Clinton's campaign bus tour, three Presidential debates, and the week leading up to election night. **93m/C VHS, DVD.** ***D:*** Chris Hegedus, D.A. Pennebaker; ***C:*** D.A. Pennebaker, Kevin Rafferty. Natl. Bd. of Review '93: Feature Doc.

The War Wagon ✓✓✓ **1967** The Duke plans revenge on Cabot, the greedy mine owner who stole his gold claim and framed him for murder for which he spent years in prison. He assembles a gang to aid him, including a wise-cracking Indian (Keel) and the man sent by Cabot to kill him (Douglas). Wayne's plan is to steal the gold being shipped in Cabot's armor-plated stagecoach, the "war wagon." Well-written, good performances, lots of action. Based on the book "Badman" by Clair Huffaker. **101m/C VHS, DVD, Wide.** John Wayne, Kirk Douglas, Howard Keel, Robert Walker Jr., Keenan Wynn, Bruce Dern, Bruce Cabot, Joanna Barnes; ***D:*** Burt Kennedy; ***W:*** Clair Huffaker; ***C:*** William Clothier; ***M:*** Dimitri Tiomkin.

The War Zone ✓✓ **1998 (R)** Harrowing and uncompromising look at a working class British family torn apart by incest and abuse. Dad (Winstone) has just moved the family to a small Devon town—a move resented by his children, 18-year-old Jessie (Belmont) and 15-year-old Tom (Cunliffe). Mum (Swinton) is too busy with a new baby to see what's going on but lonely Tom gradually (and later graphically) becomes aware that something not right is happening between Jessie and their father. Roth's disquieting directing debut; based on Stuart's novel. **98m/C VHS, DVD, Wide.** *GB* Ray Winstone, Tilda Swinton, Lara Belmont, Freddie Cunliffe, Aisling O'Sullivan, Colin Farrell, Annabelle Apsion, Kate Ashfield; ***D:*** Tim Roth; ***W:*** Alexander Stuart; ***C:*** Seamus McGarvey; ***M:*** Simon Boswell.

Warbirds ✓✓ **1988 (R)** American pilots are off to quell a revolution in a Middle East country. Too little action fails to support mediocre plot and characters. **88m/C VHS.** Jim Eldert, Cully Holland, Bill Brinsfield; ***D:*** Ulli Lommel; ***W:*** Ulli Lommel.

Warbus ✓✓ **1985 (R)** Marines lead a school bus load of Americans through war-torn Vietnam to safety. Decent action and surprisingly enjoyable characters. Otherwise mediocre. **90m/C VHS.** Daniel Stephen, Romano Kristoff, Urs Althaus; ***D:*** Ted Kaplan.

WarCat ✓ *Angel of Vengeance* **1988** The daughter of a green beret fights for her life against a blood-thirsty gang. **78m/C VHS.** Macka Foley, Jannina Poynter, David O'Hara, Carl Erwin; ***D:*** Ted V. Mikels.

Ward Six ✓✓ **19??** An insane asylum is the setting for various analogies regarding the perception of reality as defined by societal values. When it is felt that the residing physician is no more sane than his patients, he is placed among them, in Ward Six. Adapted from a story by Anton Chekhov. In Serbian with English subtitles. **93m/C VHS.** *YU* ***D:*** Lucian Pintilie.

Warden of Red Rock ✓✓½ **2001 (PG-13)** Ex-criminal John Flinders (Caan) has been an upstanding citizen a long time. In fact, he's now the warden of the Red Rock prison in Arizona, which is where his old partner, Mike Sullivan (Carradine), has just been sent to serve a life sentence. Instead, Sullivan engineers a bloody jail break and Flinders must set out with a posse to hunt them down. (And as expected, there's a final showdown between the two.) **89m/C VHS.** James Caan, David Carradine, Rachel Ticotin, Brian Dennehy; ***D:*** Stephen Gyllenhaal; ***W:*** James Lee Barrett; ***C:*** Henner Hofmann; ***M:*** Michel Colombier. **CABLE**

Wardogs ✓½ *The Assassination Team* **1987** A man tries to rescue his brother from becoming one of an elite, brainwashed group of ex-Vietnam vets trained by the government as professional assassins. Might not have been quite so bad; promising inversion of many 'Nam cliches wrecked by unnecessary violence and bad acting. **95m/C** *SW* Tim Earle, Bill Redvers; ***D:*** Daniel Hubenbecker.

WarGames ✓✓½ **1983 (PG)** A young computer whiz, thinking that he's sneaking an advance look at a new line of video games, breaks into the country's NORAD missile-defense system and challenges it to a game of Global Thermonuclear Warfare. The game might just turn out to be the real thing. Slick look at the possibilities of an accidental start to WWII. Entertaining and engrossing, but with a B-grade ending. **110m/C VHS, DVD.** Matthew Broderick, Dabney Coleman, John Wood, Ally Sheedy; ***D:*** John Badham; ***W:*** Walter F. Parkes, Lawrence Lasker; ***C:*** William A. Fraker; ***M:*** Arthur B. Rubinstein.

Warhead ✓½ **1996 (R)** Special Forces Ranger Tannen (Zagarino) has to stop a renegade military group, led by his former compatriot Craft (Lara), that have stolen a nuclear warhead and are threatening Washington. **97m/C VHS.** Frank Zagarino, Joe Lara, Elizabeth Giordano; ***D:*** Mark Roper; ***W:*** Jeff Albert; ***C:*** Rod Stewart; ***M:*** Robert O. Ragland.

Warkill ✓✓½ **1965** WWII action set in the jungles of the Philippines. Journalist who idolizes violent, hard-edged colonel, loses his illusions, but gains a more genuine respect for his men. Not-bad war flick. **99m/C VHS.** George Montgomery, Tom Drake, Eddie Infante; ***D:*** Ferde Grofe Jr.; ***W:*** Ferde Grofe Jr.

Warlock ✓✓✓ **1959** Claustrophic, resonant town-bound tale of a marshal (Fonda) and his adoring sidekick (Quinn) who clean up a town which then turns against him. Unusual story, fine performances carry this well beyond the run-of-the-mill cow flick. Fonda re-established himself at the box office as a western star, after "Stage Struck" and "Twelve Angry Men." From the novel by Oakley Hall. Look for "Bones" McCoy from "Star Trek" in a bit part. **122m/C VHS.** Henry Fonda, Anthony Quinn, Richard Widmark, Dorothy Malone, Wallace Ford, Richard Arlen, Regis Toomey, DeForest Kelley; ***D:*** Edward Dmytryk; ***W:*** Robert Alan Aurthur.

Warlock ✓✓½ **1991 (R)** It's 1691 and the most powerful warlock (Sands) in the New World is only hours away from execution. Luckily, his pal, Satan, whisks him (and witchhunter Grant, by mistake) three hundred years in the future to present-day Los Angeles, where he crash-lands in Singer's house. Surprisingly witty dialogue and neat plot twists outshine occasionally cheesy special effects. **103m/C VHS, DVD.** Richard E. Grant, Julian Sands, Lori Singer, Mary Woronov, Richard Kuss, Kevin O'Brien, Anna Levine, Allan Miller, David Carpenter; ***D:*** Steve Miner; ***W:*** David N. Twohy; ***C:*** David Eggby; ***M:*** Jerry Goldsmith.

Warlock 3: The End of Innocence ✓✓ **1998 (R)** Kris (Laurence) decides to spend a weekend in the abandoned 16th-century family manor that she has inherited. Disturbed by visions, she comes to realize that her family has a legacy of witchcraft and now she is the sacrifical target of a warlock (Payne). Predictable, although Payne is sufficiently chilling. **94m/C VHS, DVD.** Bruce Payne, Ashley Laurence, Angel Boris, Boti Ann Bliss, Paul Francis, Rick Hearst, Jan Schweiterman; ***D:*** Eric Freiser; ***W:*** Eric Freiser, Bruce David Eisen. **VIDEO**

Warlock Moon ✓½ **1973** Young woman is lured to a secluded spa and falls prey to a coven of witches. **75m/C VHS.** *MX* Laurie Walters, Joe Spano, Edna Macafee, Ray Goman, Steve Solinsky, Charles Raino; ***D:*** Bill Herbert.

Warlock: The Armageddon ✓✓½ **1993 (R)** Sequel finds Sands back again as the sinister Warlock. This time he's out to gather six Druidic rune stones which have the power to summon Satan's emissary (in the wrong hands) or to stop his nefarious activities (in the right ones). A sect in a small California town serves as the keeper of the stones, only their designated champions are two unprepared teenagers. Sands has all the fun, gleefully dispatching his would-be opponents with some good special effects. **93m/C VHS, DVD, Wide.** Julian Sands, Chris Young, Paula Marshall, Steve Kahan, Charles Hallahan, R.G. Armstrong, Bruce Glover, Zach Galligan, Dawn Ann Billings, Joanna Pacula; ***D:*** Anthony Hickox; ***W:*** Kevin Rock, Sam Bernard; ***C:*** Gerry Lively; ***M:*** Mark McKenzie.

Warlords ✓½ **1988 (R)** Lone soldier Carradine battles mutant hordes in a post-apocalyptic desert. Amateurish futuristic drivel. **87m/C VHS.** David Carradine, Sid Haig, Ross Hagen, Fox Harris, Robert Quarry, Victoria Sellers, Brinke Stevens, Dawn Wildsmith; ***D:*** Fred Olen Ray.

Warlords from Hell woof! **1987 (R)** Two young men motorcycling through Mexico are captured by a bloodthirsty gang and forced to do hard labor in the marijuana fields. We can only hope that they just learn to say no. **76m/C VHS.** Brad Henson, Jeffrey Rice; *D:* Clark Henderson.

Warlords of the 21st Century 🦴½ *Battletruck* **1982** Bandit gang speed around the galaxy in an indestructible battle cruiser. Then the boys are challenged by a space lawman. Gratuitously violent action pic lacking real action. Filmed on planet New Zealand. **91m/C VHS.** Michael Beck, Annie McEnroe, James Wainwright; *D:* Harley Cokliss; *W:* Harley Cokliss, Irving Austin, John Beech; *C:* Chris Menges.

Warlords 3000 🦴½ **1993 (R)** In the future, Earth is a barren wasteland ravaged by raging electrical storms. Deadly cancers are rampant and the few people who have survived take their comfort in a hallucinogenic drug that provides a temporary pleasure and a permanent madness. Drug lords control the planet but one man is out to eliminate the scum and save the future. **92m/C VHS.** Jay Roberts Jr., Denise Marie Duff, Steve Blanchard, Wayne Duvall; *D:* Faruque Ahmed; *W:* Ron Herbst, Faruque Ahmed.

Warm Nights on a Slow-Moving Train 🦴🦴 **1987 (R)** A hot-blooded schoolteacher turns tricks for cash to support her brother on the Sunday-night train to Melbourne, until she meets a stranger who has a deadly masquerade of his own. Interestingly different; much sex, as you can imagine. Australian-made. **90m/C VHS.** *AU* Wendy Hughes, Colin Friels, Norman Kaye, John Clayton, Peter Whitford; *D:* Bob Ellis; *W:* Bob Ellis, Denny Lawrence; *C:* Yuri Sokol.

Warm Summer Rain 🦴½ **1989 (R)** A young couple meet under unusual circumstances and develop a relationship in a desert cabin as they reflect on their unfulfilled pasts. Lust, self-doubt and longing for something to hold onto draw them together as the days pass. Thoroughly self-indulgent romantic comedy that's oddly self-pitying and poorly directed. **85m/C VHS.** Kelly Lynch, Barry Tubb; *D:* Joe Gayton.

The Warning 🦴 **1980** A pair of proverbial honest cops investigate ties between the mob and the police department. Hard to follow. **101m/C VHS.** *IT* Martin Balsam, Giuliano Gemma, Giancarlo Zanetti; *D:* Damiano Damiani.

Warning from Space 🦴½ *The Mysterious Satellite; The Cosmic Man Appears in Tokyo; Space Men Appear in Tokyo; Unknown Satellite Over Tokyo; Uchujin Tokyo Ni Arawaru* **1956** Aliens visit Earth to warn of impending cosmic doom. When it becomes apparent that the one-eyed starfish look is off-putting, they assume human form. Japanese sci fi. **87m/B VHS.** *JP* Toyomi Karita, Keizo Kawasaki, Isao Yamagata, Shozo Nanbu, Buntaro Miake, Mieko Nagai, Kiyoko Hirai; *D:* Koji Shima.

Warning Shadows 🦴🦴🦴 **1923** Classic example of interior German Expressionism. Brilliantly portrays a jealous husband's emotions and obsessions through shadows. Innocent events seem to reek of sin. A seldom-seen study of the oft-precarious distinction between love and obsession; directly influenced by the classic "The Cabinet of Dr. Caligari." Silent with German and English titles. **93m/B VHS, 8mm.** *GE* Fritz Kortner; *D:* Arthur Robison.

Warning Sign 🦴½ **1985 (R)** A high-tech thriller in which a small town is terrorized by the accidental release of an experimental virus at a research facility. Shades of "The Andromeda Strain" and "The China Syndrome," though less originality and quality. **99m/C VHS.** Sam Waterston, Kathleen Quinlan, Yaphet Kotto, Richard Dysart, Rick Rossovich; *D:* Hal Barwood; *W:* Hal Barwood, Matthew Robbins; *C:* Dean Cundey.

The Warrior & the Sorceress 🦴½ **1984 (R)** Mercenary Carradine offers his services to rival factions fighting for control of a water well in an impoverished desert village located on a planet with two suns. He attempts to aggravate the conflicts between the factions, playing the shifty go-between. The sorceress is topless throughout. "A Fistful of Dollars" goes to outer space. Inoffensive, except that better judgment is expected of Carradine. **81m/C VHS.** David Carradine, Luke Askew, Maria Socas, Harry Townes; *D:* John Broderick; *W:* John Broderick.

Warrior of Justice 🦴 **1996** Karate instructor has one of his students disappear after competing in a secret tournament. He then uncovers a black market ring specializing in selling human organs that's run by a former opponent. **90m/C VHS.** Richard Lynch, Jorge (George) Rivero, Nick (Nicholas, Niko) Hill, Ian Jacklin, Jorgo Ognenovski; *D:* Jorgo Ognenovski, Mike Tristano.

Warrior of the Lost World woof! **1984** A warrior must destroy the evil Omega Force who tyrannically rules the world in the distant future, etcetera, etcetera. One-size-fits-all premise; horrible special effects; miserably directed. Only for really hard-core Pleasence fans. **90m/C VHS.** Robert Ginty, Persis Khambatta, Donald Pleasence; *D:* David Worth.

Warrior Queen 🦴 **1987 (R)** Long ago in ancient Rome, overly histrionic mayor Pleasence married porn queen with a wandering eye Fox, and much gratuitous sex and erupting volcanoes resulted. Even the score blows. Also available in an "Unrated" version. Brit pop star Fox is billed as Stasia Micula. **69m/C VHS.** Sybil Danning, Donald Pleasence, Richard (Rick) Hill, Josephine Jacqueline Jones, Tally Chanel, Samantha Fox.

Warrior Spirit 🦴🦴½ **1994 (PG-13)** After getting kicked out of their prep school, two boys decide to head for the Yukon and search for gold. **94m/C VHS.** Lukas Haas, Jimmy Herman, Allan Musy; *D:* Rene Manzor.

The Warriors 🦴🦴½ *The Dark Avenger* **1955** Swashbuckling adventure about Prince Edward's valiant rescue of Lady Joan and her children from the clutches of the evil Count De Ville. Flynn looks old and pudgy, but buckles his way gallantly through intrepid adventure. Also the last Flynn to see: fun, but more or less completely derivative and familiar. Filmed in England. **85m/C VHS.** *GB* Errol Flynn, Peter Finch, Joanne Dru, Yvonne Furneaux, Noel Willman, Michael Hordern; *D:* Henry Levin.

The Warriors 🦴🦴½ **1979 (R)** Action story about a turf battle between NYC street gangs that rages from Coney Island to the Bronx. Silly plot works because of fine performances and direction, excellent use of action and color, and nonstop pace. Fight scenes are very carefully, even obviously, choreographed. **94m/C VHS, DVD, Wide.** Michael Beck, James Remar, Deborah Van Valkenburgh, Thomas G. Waites, David Patrick Kelly, Mercedes Ruehl, Dorsey Wright, David Harris, Brian Tyler, Tom McKitterick; *D:* Walter Hill; *W:* Walter Hill, David Shaber; *C:* Andrew Laszlo; *M:* Barry de Vorzon.

Warriors 🦴🦴 **1994 (R)** Col. Frank Vail (Busey) is the leader of a top secret government anti-terrorist hit squad, considered so deadly that its members are confined behind the walls of a military prison. But when Vail escapes, it's up to his lethal protege Colin Newl (Pare) to hunt him down. **100m/C VHS.** Gary Busey, Michael Pare; *D:* Shimon Dotan.

Warriors from Hell 🦴½ **1990 (R)** Western forces in a small African country battle rebel fighters who threaten the hapless native villagers. **90m/C VHS.** Deon Stewardson, Shayne Leith, Adrienne Pierce, Glen Gabela, Hector Manthanda, Ivan Dean, Connie Chume; *D:* Ronnie Isaacs; *W:* Ronnie Isaacs.

Warriors of the Apocalypse woof! *Searchers of the Voodoo Mountain; Time Raiders* **1985 (R)** After a nuclear holocaust, heavily sworded and loin-clothed men search for the secret of eternal life and instead find an Amazon realm in the jungle. A terrible waste of post-apocalyptic scenery. **96m/C VHS.** Michael James, Debrah Moore, Ken Metcalfe, Franco Guerrero; *D:* Bobby Suarez.

Warriors of the Wasteland woof! *The New Barbarians; I Nuovi Barbari* **1983 (R)** It's the year 2019, and the world has been devastated by a nuclear war. The few survivors try to reach a distant land which emits radio signals indicating the presence of human life. They are hindered by attacks from the fierce homosexual Templars, led by a self-proclaimed priest called One. Mindless rip-off of "Road Warrior" and obviously made on the proverbial shoestring budget. Dubbed. **92m/C VHS.** *IT* Fred Williamson, Giancarlo (Timothy Brent) Prete, Anna Kanakis; *D:* Enzo G. Castellari.

Warriors of Virtue 🦴🦴½ **1997 (PG)** Teenaged Ryan Jefers (Yedidia) is transported to the land of Tao where he learns the five virtues (righteousness, benevolence, integrity, wisdom, and loyalty) from the kangaroo-like Warmblood warriors, who live in harmony with humans. Then he must use his knowledge to fight the evil Komodo (MacFadyen), who wishes to steal the energy from Tao to make himself immortal. Nice message for the kids, with enough action to keep them interested, but the Warmbloods are dorky-looking. **101m/C VHS, DVD.** Mario Yedidia, Angus Macfadyen, Marley Shelton, Chao-Li Chi; *D:* Ronny Yu; *W:* Michael Vickerman, Hugh Kelley; *C:* Peter Pau; *M:* Don Davis.

The Wash 🦴🦴🦴 **1988** Quiet domestic drama about a couple who drift apart after 40 years of marriage. Set interestingly among Japanese-Americans in California; treats social and cultural factors with intelligence. Superb cast takes it a notch higher. **94m/C VHS.** Mako, Nobu McCarthy, Sab Shimono; *D:* Michael Toshiyuki Uno; *W:* Philip Kan Kotanda; *C:* Walt Lloyd.

The Wash 🦴🦴 **2001 (R)** Sean (Dre) loses his job and has his car booted, so pal Dee Loc (Snoop Dogg) helps him out by with some news about an opening at the car wash where he works. Soon Sean is assistant manager under crusty owner Mr. Washington (Wallace). Between dealing with the resentment of Loc, and the kidnapping of the boss, along with the usual supply of quirky characters and subplots, Sean has his hands full in this very laid-back, low-key tribute to 1977's "Car Wash." Appealling performances, moments of inspired comedy, and plenty of cameos to watch for make this a pleasant way to kill some time. **96m/C VHS, DVD, Wide.** Snoop Dogg, Dr. Dre, DJ Pooh, George Wallace, Tommy (Tiny) Lister, Alex Thomas, Arif S. Kinchen, Demetrius Navarro, Thomas Chong, Pauly Shore, Lamont Bentley, Bruce Bruce, Shari Watson, Shawn Fonteno, Angell Conwell; *D:* DJ Pooh; *W:* DJ Pooh; *C:* Keith L. Smith.

Washington Affair 🦴🦴 **1977 (PG)** A tale of intrigue in the nation's capital. Sullivan is a businessman who uses women and blackmail to capture government contracts. Selleck is the hapless bureaucrat he preys on. Remake of Stoloff's own "Intimacy" was not released until "Magnum P.I." became a hit. **90m/C VHS.** Tom Selleck, Carol Lynley, Barry Sullivan; *D:* Victor Stoloff.

Washington Mistress 🦴½ **1981** Emminently ordinary made-for-TV grist about Capitol Hill aide Arnaz, politician Jordan, and their affair. Listless performances. **96m/C VHS.** Lucie Arnaz, Richard Jordan, Tony Bill; *D:* Peter Levin.

Washington Square 🦴🦴🦴 **1997 (PG)** Adaptation of Henry James' novel, which was previously filmed as "The Heiress." Set in 19th-century New York City (filmed in Baltimore), wealthy spinster Catherine Sloper (Leigh), against the will of her overbearing father (Finney), is pursued by a handsome fortune hunter (Chaplin). Director Holland tends to bluntly simplify James' complex undertones, and Leigh's facial ticks can't equal "The Heiress'" Olivia de Havilland's painful plainness; nonetheless, definitely worth seeing. **115m/C VHS.** Jennifer Jason Leigh, Ben Chaplin, Albert Finney, Maggie Smith, Judith Ivey, Betsy Brantley, Jennifer Garner, Peter Maloney, Robert Stanton, Scott Jaeck; *D:* Agnieszka Holland; *W:* Carol Doyle; *C:* Jerzy Zielinski; *M:* Jan A.P. Kaczmarek.

The Wasp Woman 🦴½ **1959** In her quest for eternal beauty, a woman uses a potion made from wasp enzymes. Naturally, she turns into a wasp monster at night. Good fun, courtesy of Corman. **84m/B VHS, DVD.** Susan Cabot, Anthony Eisley, Barboura Morris, Michael Marks, William Roerick, Frank Gerstle, Bruno VeSota, Frank Wolff, Lynn Cartwright, Roy Gordon; *D:* Roger Corman; *W:* Leo Gordon; *C:* Harry Neumann; *M:* Fred Katz.

The Wasp Woman 🦴🦴 **1996 (R)** Equally campy cable remake of the 1959 flick finds ex-supermodel-turned-cosmetics company exec Janice Starlin (Rubin) discovering that her fading beauty is causing problems both with her company and her love life. So she turns to a mysterious doctor for help and injects herself with his untested serum, an experimental wasp hormone. She's hoping to discover a fountain of youth and is instead transformed into a nasty-tempered giant insect. Cool, disgusting makeup/costuming. **81m/C VHS.** Jennifer Rubin, Daniel J. Travanti, Maria Ford, Doug Wert; *D:* Jim Wynorski; *W:* Daniella Purcell; *M:* Terry Plumeri. **CABLE**

Watch It 🦴🦴🦴 **1993 (R)** Four self-absorbed 20-something guys share a house in Chicago for the summer. They pursue a post-adolescent game, consisting of increasingly complicated practical jokes, where the unsuspecting victim is set up for a "watch it" gag. The rivalry escalates, and turns increasingly unpleasant, when cousins John and Michael vie for the affections of Anne, who's wary of involvement because of male selfishness. A first-rate cast with recognizable situations and emotions. **102m/C VHS.** Jon Tenney, Peter Gallagher, Suzy Amis, John C. McGinley, Tom Sizemore, Lili Taylor, Cynthia Stevenson, Terri Hawkes, Jordanna Capra; *D:* Tom Flynn; *W:* Tom Flynn; *M:* Stanley Clarke.

Watch Me 🦴 **1996 (R)** Photog Paul (Medford) is inspired by new neighbor babe Elise (Burns) and secretly snaps her through the window. Meanwhile, Elise is peeking in on Paul's would-be gal Samantha (Burton) who's having sex with his best bud Alex (Sherwin). Paul of course wants to get more personally involved with Elise (especially after he finds out about Samantha). Lots of nudity—no heat. **90m/C VHS, DVD.** Robert Medford, Kelly Burns, Jennifer Burton, Steven Sherwin; *D:* Lipo Ching; *W:* Beth Salmon; *C:* Andreas Kossak; *M:* Yoav Goren.

Watch Me When I Kill 🦴 **1981 (R)** We'd rather not. A young nightclub dancer stops by a drugstore seconds after the owner was killed. She doesn't see the killer's face, but his rasping voice remains to torment her and the viewer. Dubbed. **95m/C VHS.** *IT* Richard Stewart, Sylvia Kramer, Anthony Bido.

Watch on the Rhine 🦴🦴🦴½ **1943** Couple involved with the anti-Nazi underground has escaped the country, but is pursued and harassed by Nazi agents. Adapted by Hammett and Hellman from her play. Performed on stage before the U.S. entered the war, it was the first American play and movie to portray the ugliness of fascism as an ideology, as opposed to the more devious evil of its practical side. The Production Code at the time required that a killer always be punished; the murderer (whose screen motives had been noble) refused to film the offending scene, which explains the tacked-on ending. Superb drama from a pair of highly gifted writers and a great cast. Shumlin also directed the play. **114m/B VHS.** Bette Davis, Paul Lukas, Donald Woods, Beulah Bondi, Geraldine Fitzgerald, George Coulouris, Henry Daniell, Helmut Dantine, Donald Buka, Anthony Caruso, Clyde Fillmore, Howard Hickman, Creighton Hale, Kurt Katch, Clarence Muse, Alan Hale Jr., Frank Reicher, Mary (Marsden) Young; *D:* Herman Shumlin; *W:* Lillian Hellman, Dashiell Hammett; *C:* Hal Mohr, Merritt B. Gerstad; *M:* Max Steiner. Oscars '43: Actor (Lukas); Golden Globes '44: Actor—Drama (Lukas); N.Y. Film Critics '43: Actor (Lukas), Film.

Watch the Birdie 🦴🦴½ **1950** It's Skelton three times over as cameraman, father, and grandfather! First, he accidentally films a scam that would send the lovely Miss Dahl filing for bankruptcy. Later a crazy chase scene unfolds, that will have viewers rolling, as Skelton the cameraman nabs the bad guys and turns them over to the cops. Light fun that will charm Skelton fans. **70m/B VHS.** Red Skelton, Arlene Dahl, Ann Miller, Leon Ames; *D:* Jack Donohue.

Watched 🦴🦴 **1973** A former U.S. attorney, gone underground, has a nervous breakdown and kills the narcotics agent who has him under surveillance. Self-important, too serious social/political conspiracy drama of the Watergate era. Keach and Yulin are good, but not good enough to save it. **95m/C VHS.** Stacy Keach, Harris Yulin, Bridgit Polk; ***D:*** John Parsons.

The Watcher 🦴🦴 **2000 (R)** Serial killer Reeves leaves clues for burned-out FBI agent Spader as to who his next victim will be so Spader will get back in the game. Start with a direct-to-video feel, add a plot cribbed from better serial killer thrillers, throw in a bunch of showy visual effects and Reeves' hysterical line readings, and you've got a night of talking back to the TV, MST3K-style. It's ridiculous, but that's half the fun. **97m/C VHS, DVD, Wide.** Keanu Reeves, James Spader, Marisa Tomei, Ernie Hudson, Chris Ellis, Robert Cicchini, Jenny McShane, Yvonne Niami, Gina Alexander, Joe Sikora, Rebekah Louise Smith; ***D:*** Joe Charbanic; ***W:*** Joe Charbanic, David Elliott, Clay Ayers; ***C:*** Michael Chapman; ***M:*** Marco Beltrami.

The Watcher in the Woods 🦴🦴 **1981 (PG)** When an American family rents an English country house, the children are haunted by the spirit of a long-missing young girl. A very bland attempt at a ghost story. **83m/C VHS, DVD.** Bette Davis, Carroll Baker, David McCallum, Ian Bannen, Lynn-Holly Johnson, Kyle Richards, Frances Cuka, Richard Pasco; ***D:*** John Hough; ***W:*** Brian Clemens; ***C:*** Alan Hume; ***M:*** Stanley Myers.

Watchers 🦴🦴 **1988 (R)** From the suspense novel by Dean R. Koontz, a secret experiment goes wrong, creating half-human monsters. A boy and his extremely intelligent dog are soon pursued. Low-budget, Corman-influenced production is tacky but effective. **99m/C VHS.** Barbara Williams, Michael Ironside, Corey Haim, Duncan Fraser, Blu Mankuma, Dale Wilson, Colleen Winton; ***D:*** Jon Hess; ***W:*** Bill Freed; ***C:*** Richard Leiterman; ***M:*** Joel Goldsmith.

Watchers 2 🦴🦴 **1990 (R)** Sequel to "Watchers" follows the further adventures of a super-intelligent golden retriever who leads a Marine to an animal psychologist and then attempts to warn them both of a mutant killer. The dog says woof, but this movie doesn't quite. Fun for lovers of hounds or horror flicks. **101m/C VHS.** Marc Singer, Tracy Scoggins; ***D:*** Thierry Notz; ***M:*** Rick Conrad.

Watchers 3 🦴½ **1994 (R)** A secret military outpost in the South American jungles is attacked by a carnivorous predator. Ex-military convicts are sent to rescue the remaining survivors and to make certain the government experiment that started the terror never comes to light. **95m/C VHS.** Wings Hauser, Gregory Scott Cummins, Daryl Roach, John K. Linton, Lolita Ronalds, Frank Novak; ***D:*** Jeremy Stanford.

Watchers Reborn 🦴🦴 **1998 (R)** Genetically-engineered mutants stalk the innocent with only a hyper-intelligent golden retreiver (of course!) able to stop them. Based on the novel "Watchers" by Dean R. Koontz. **83m/C VHS.** Mark Hamill, Lisa Wilcox, Stephen Macht, Lou Rawls, Floyd Levine, Gary Collins, Kane Hodder; ***D:*** John Carl Buechler; ***W:*** Sean Dash; ***M:*** Terry Plumeri.

Water 🦴 **1985 (PG-13)** The resident governor of a Caribbean British colony juggles various predatory interests when a valuable mineral water resource is found. The good cast is wasted in this all-too-silly effort. **89m/C VHS.** *GB* Michael Caine, Brenda Vaccaro, Leonard Rossiter, Valerie Perrine, Jimmie Walker; ***Cameos:*** Eric Clapton, George Harrison, Fred Gwynne, Ringo Starr; ***D:*** Dick Clement; ***W:*** Dick Clement, Ian LaFrenais, Bill Persky.

Water Babies 🦴🦴 *Slip Slide Adventures* **1979 (G)** When a chimney sweep's 12-year-old apprentice is wrongly accused of stealing silver, the boy and his dog fall into a pond and eventually rescue some of the characters they find there. Combination of live-action and animated fairy-tale story set in 19th-century London. Boring, unless you're a young child with equivalent standards. Based on the book by Charles Kingsley. **93m/C VHS.** *GB* James Mason, Billie Whitelaw, David Tomlinson, Paul Luty, Samantha Coates; ***D:*** Lionel Jeffries.

Water Drops on Burning Rocks 🦴🦴 *Gouttes d'Eau sur Pierres Brulantes* **1999** Director Ozon pays tribute to late German director Rainer Werner Fassbinder by resurrecting his unproduced play. In the '70s, 50-year-old businessman Leopold (Giraudeau) picks up 19-year-old Franz (Zidi), who winds up moving in, though the mismatched duo fight constantly. When Franz's former girlfriend, Anna (Sagnier), shows up, Leopold even begins seducing her. Then transexual Vera (Thomson), Leopold's ex-girlfriend, also comes back. And it's a very messy foursome, indeed. French with subtitles. **82m/C VHS, DVD, Wide.** *FR* Bernard Giraudeau, Anna Thomson, Malik Zidi, Ludivine Sagnier; ***D:*** Francois Ozon; ***W:*** Francois Ozon; ***C:*** Jeanne Lapoirie.

The Water Engine 🦴🦴½ **1992** Charles Lang (Macy) is a luckless machinist struggling to survive in Depression-era Chicago. Lang invents a remarkable engine, that runs on water, and holds the promise of limitless, cheap power. To protect his invention he finds a seedy patent attorney (Mahoney), which leads to the sinister Oberman (Mantegna), a mysterious and powerful figure who wants Lang's invention—at any cost. Based on the play by David Mamet. **110m/C VHS.** Charles Durning, Patti LuPone, William H. Macy, John Mahoney, Joe Mantegna, Joanna Miles, Mike Nussbaum, Treat Williams, Andrea Marcovicci, Peter Michael Goetz, David Mamet; ***D:*** Steven Schachter; ***W:*** David Mamet; ***C:*** Bryan England. CABLE

Water Rustlers 🦴½ **1939** Unscrupulous land baron builds a dam on his side of the creek with the intention of drying out the cattle pastures. Heroine Page, whose pop has been rubbed out by varmints, and good guy/lover O'Brien save her property and avenge her father. Second of three Page westerns. **55m/B VHS.** Dorothy Page, Dave O'Brien; ***D:*** Samuel Diege.

The Waterboy 🦴🦴 **1998 (PG-13)** Another in a continuing line of deliberately stupid comedies finds Sandler a not-too-bright, constantly picked-on waterboy for a lousy Louisiana college football team. After a player taunts him once too often, he tackles the big guy, and is suddenly promoted to player—much to the dismay of his over-protective mother, Bates. Loser player turns loser team into winners after some contrived obstacles: you've seen it before, but Sandler cultists (and less discerning football fans) will love it anyway. **90m/C VHS, DVD.** Adam Sandler, Kathy Bates, Henry Winkler, Fairuza Balk, Jerry Reed, Larry Gilliard Jr., Blake Clark, Rob Schneider, Clint Howard, Allen Whiting, Robert Kokol; ***D:*** Frank Coraci; ***W:*** Tim Herlihy, Adam Sandler; ***C:*** Steven Bernstein; ***M:*** Alan Pasqua.

The Waterdance 🦴🦴🦴 **1991 (R)** Autobiographical film based on the experiences of writer/co-director Jimenez. When writer Joel Garcia (Stoltz) is paralyzed in a hiking accident he finds himself dealing with not only the rehab process itself but his feelings, the feelings of his married lover, and those of his fellow patients. Deals unsentimentally with all the physical adjustments, including the sexual ones. Resolutions may be predictable but the performances rise above any script weaknesses. The title refers to Hill's dream of dancing on water—and the fear of drowning if he stops. **106m/C VHS.** Eric Stoltz, Wesley Snipes, William Forsythe, Helen Hunt, Elizabeth Pena, Grace Zabriskie; ***D:*** Neal Jimenez, Michael Steinberg; ***W:*** Neal Jimenez; ***C:*** Mark Plummer; ***M:*** Michael Convertino. Ind. Spirit '93: First Feature, Screenplay; Sundance '92: Screenplay, Aud. Award.

Waterfront 🦴½ **1939** Dreary dockside melodrama, with drinking and brawling longshoreman Jim (Morgan) avenging his brother's death. Based on the play "Blindspot" by Kenyon Nicholson. **59m/B VHS.** Dennis Morgan, Gloria Dickson, Marie Wilson, Larry Williams, Sheila (Manors) Mannors, Ward Bond, Frank Faylen; ***D:*** Terry Morse; ***W:*** Arthur Ripley, Lee Katz.

Waterfront 🦴🦴 **1944** Nazis coerce German-Americans into helping them in WWII-era San Francisco. Credulity defying spy doings, but that's okay. Fairly entertaining wartime drama about paranoia on the home front. **68m/B VHS.** John Carradine, J. Carrol Naish, Terry Frost, Maris Wrixon, Edwin Maxwell; ***D:*** Steve Sekely.

Waterfront 🦴🦴½ **1983** Effective romantic drama set in Melbourne, Australia. Australian workers strike after taking forced pay cuts. As a result, Italian immigrants are hired as scabs to keep the docks going. Despite the tension, an Italian woman and an Australian man fall deeply in love, only to find that they must struggle to keep that love alive. **294m/C VHS.** *AU* Jack Thompson, Greta Scacchi, Frank Gallacher, Tony Rickards, Mark Little, Jay Mannering, Ray Barrett, Chris Haywood, Warren Mitchell, Noni Hazlehurst, John Karlsen, Elin Jenkins; ***D:*** Chris Thomson.

Waterhole #3 🦴🦴½ **1967 (PG)** Three Confederate army buddies steal a fortune in gold bullion from the Union Army and hide it in a waterhole in the desert. One of the funnier entries in the Western comedy genre. **95m/C VHS.** James Coburn, Carroll O'Connor, Margaret Blye, Claude Akins, Bruce Dern, Joan Blondell, James Whitmore; ***D:*** William A. Graham; ***C:*** Robert Burks; ***M:*** Dave Grusin.

Waterland 🦴🦴 **1992 (R)** Meandering drama about a history teacher who tries to solve a personal crisis by using his class as a sounding board to describe his troubled past in England. Dark secrets abound, including incest, madness, murder, and the terrifying love between the teacher and his childhood bride. Melancholy, overwrought but partially redeemed by the lead performances of Irons and his (real-life and cinematic) wife, Cusack. The film's setting has been unfortunately moved from London to Pittsburgh, destroying story links. Based on the novel by Graham Swift. **95m/C VHS, Wide.** Jeremy Irons, Ethan Hawke, Sinead Cusack, John Heard, Grant Warnock, Lena Headey, Pete Postlethwaite, Cara Buono; ***D:*** Stephen Gyllenhaal; ***W:*** Peter Prince; ***C:*** Robert Elswit; ***M:*** Carter Burwell.

Waterloo 🦴🦴 **1971 (G)** Massive chronicle of Napoleon's European conquests and eventual defeat at the hands of Wellington. Filmed on location in Italy and the Ukraine, it bombed due largely to Steiger's bizarre rendition of Napoleon. **122m/C VHS.** *IT RU* Rod Steiger, Orson Welles, Virginia McKenna, Michael Wilding, Donal Donnelly, Christopher Plummer, Jack Hawkins, Dan O'Herlihy, Terence Alexander, Rupert Davies, Ivo Garrani, Gianni "John" Garko, Ian Ogilvy, Andrea Checchi, Jean Louis, Willoughby Gray, John Savident, Adrian Brine, Jeffrey Wickham, Sergei Zakariadze, Richard Heffer, Aldo Cecconi, Peter Davies, Eugene Samoilov; ***D:*** Sergei Bondarchuk; ***W:*** Sergei Bondarchuk, H.A.L. Craig, Vittorio Bonicelli; ***C:*** Armando Nannuzzi; ***M:*** Nino Rota.

Waterloo Bridge 🦴🦴🦴 **1940** In London during WWI, Capt. Roy Cronin (Taylor), a soldier from an aristocratic family, begins a tragic romance with ballet dancer Myra Lester (Leigh) when they meet by chance on the foggy Waterloo Bridge. She loses her job and when Roy is listed as dead, Myra's despair turns her to prostitution. But when Roy returns from POW camp, they once again meet by accident on Waterloo Bridge, and their romance resumes, with Myra struggling to conceal her shameful secret. Four-hanky drama with fine performances by Leigh (her first after "Gone with the Wind") and Taylor. Based on the play by Robert E. Sherwood. **109m/B VHS.** Vivien Leigh, Robert Taylor, Lucile Watson, Sir C. Aubrey Smith, Maria Ouspenskaya, Virginia Field; ***D:*** Mervyn LeRoy; ***W:*** S.N. Behrman, George Froeschel, Hans Rameau; ***C:*** Joseph Ruttenberg; ***M:*** Herbert Stothart.

Watermelon Man 🦴🦴 **1970 (R)** The tables are turned for a bigoted white guy when he wakes up one morning to discover he has become a black man. Broad comedy with not much place to go is still engaging. Cambridge takes on both roles, appearing in unconvincing white makeup. **97m/C VHS.** Godfrey Cambridge, Erin Moran, Estelle Parsons, Howard Caine, D'Urville Martin, Kay Kimberly, Paul Williams; ***D:*** Melvin Van Peebles; ***W:*** Herman Raucher; ***C:*** Herman Raucher; ***M:*** Melvin Van Peebles.

The Watermelon Woman 🦴🦴 **1997** Cheryl (Dunye) is a young, black, lesbian video store clerk who wants to be a documentary filmmaker. She becomes obsessed with a black actress seen in some 1930s black films, who was known only as the "Watermelon Woman." Doing research, Cheryl discovers the woman's name was Fae Richards (Bronson) and that she was a lesbian who had an affair with her white director. While deciding to film a documentary about Fae, Cheryl's personal life begins to parallel Fae's when she briefly falls for white customer, Diana (Turner). **85m/C VHS, DVD.** Cheryl Dunye, Valerie Walker, Guinevere Turner, Lisa Marie Bronson; ***D:*** Cheryl Dunye; ***W:*** Cheryl Dunye; ***C:*** Michelle Crenshaw; ***M:*** Bill Coleman.

Waterproof 🦴🦴🦴 **1999 (PG-13)** Reynolds is oddly cast but very effective as Eli, a Jewish shopkeeper who is shot by a young would-be robber, Thaniel (Dye). To protect him from prosecution, Thaniel's mother, Tyree (Grace), whisks her son and Eli to her childhood home in Waterproof, Louisiana. She's been away for 15 years and finds a great deal of tension with her family, but they are willing to take Tyree and Thaniel in to assist them. The film examines the struggles that exist between family members and individuals from differing ethnic backgrounds. Without becoming overwrought, the film delivers positive message while being entertaining. Special kudos to Jones, who overcomes his comic reputation by portraying a man with severe brain damage. **94m/C DVD, Wide.** Burt Reynolds, April Grace, Cordereau Dye, Whitman Mayo, Anthony Lee, Orlando Jones, Ja'net DuBois; ***D:*** Barry Berman.

Watership Down 🦴🦴½ **1978 (PG)** Wonderfully animated story based on Richard Adams's allegorical novel about how a group of rabbits escape fear and overcome oppression while searching for a new and better home. It's really an adult theme with sufficient violence to the poor wittle wabbits to scare the kiddies. **92m/C VHS, DVD, 8mm.** *GB* ***D:*** Martin Rosen; ***W:*** Martin Rosen; ***V:*** Richard Briers, Ralph Richardson, Zero Mostel, John Hurt, Denholm Elliott, Harry Andrews, Michael Hordern, Joss Ackland.

Waterworld 🦴🦴½ **1995 (PG-13)** "The Man From Atlantis" meets "Mad Max." Industry knives sharpened with glee before release, with some insiders calling this luck-impaired project "Fishtar" and "Kevin's Gate." With an estimated $150 million budget, the film must look to overseas sales and secondary markets to make any money. Most of said budget seems to have ended up on screen, which makes for a visually striking, and at times daunting, film. Costner, who did just about everything but cater the meals, stars as Mariner, a mutant man-fish who reluctantly helps human survivors search for the mythical Dryland since the polar ice caps melted, flooding the earth. The bad guys are the Smokers, led by the evil Hopper, who can play these roles in his sleep. Entertaining, but not riveting, as the budget and PR hype leads one to expect. The floating set was anchored (not very well, apparently) off the Hawaiian coast and was lost once during a tropical storm. Costner bet the boat on this one and stands to lose more than just money. With rumors of internal production battles, out of control budgets, and his other recent boxoffice disappointments, his star power is in question. **135m/C VHS, DVD, Wide.** Kevin Costner, Dennis Hopper, Jeanne Tripplehorn, Tina Majorino, Michael Jeter, R.D. Call, Robert Joy; ***D:*** Kevin Reynolds; ***W:*** Peter Rader, Marc Norman, David N. Twohy; ***C:*** Dean Semler; ***M:*** James Newton Howard. Golden Raspberries '95: Worst Support. Actor (Hopper).

Wavelength 🦴🦴½ **1983 (PG)** A rock star living in the Hollywood Hills with his girlfriend stumbles on an ultra-secret government project involving friendly aliens from outer space recovered from a recent UFO crash site. Fun, enthusiastically unoriginal cheap sci-fi. Soundtrack by Tangerine Dream. **87m/C VHS.** Bobby DiCicco, Robert

Carradine, Cherie Currie, Keenan Wynn; *D:* Mike Gray; *W:* Mike Gray; *M:* Tangerine Dream.

Wavelength ½ **1996 (R)** Physicist and Oxford professor Paul Higgins (Piven) has a few problems—a wife, Claire (Williams), a girlfriend, Lucy (Walker), Lucy's father who just happens to be the head of the physics department, and a mysterious presence (Attenborough) who's trying to help Paul with his research on nuclear fission. Piven's character is so selfish you'll wonder why either woman wants him and the happy ending feels contrived. **94m/C VHS.** *GB* Jeremy Piven, Kelli Williams, Liza Walker, James Villiers, James Faulkner, Richard Attenborough, Byrne Piven, Nicholas Marco, Dominic West; *D:* Benjamin Fry; *W:* Benjamin Fry; *C:* Chris Middleton; *M:* Michael Storey.

Wax Mask ½ *M.D.C. Maschera di Cera* **1997** Liner notes state that this loose remake of "House of Wax" was to have been directed by Lucio Fulci ("Zombie," "The Black Cat") who died before he could begin work. It was produced in part by Dario Argento, but the important thing for horror fans to know is that this one owes just as much to Stuart Gordon's "Re-Animator." It takes the same gleeful approach to outrageous medical horror and sex, though overall, it is a much more polished looking film with expensive production values, an attractive (if unknown in America) young cast, and a sharply focused image. The setting is Paris and Rome in the early 20th century. Sonia (Mondello) witnessed the brutal murder of her parents as a child. Years later, she goes to work for Boris Volkoff (Hossein), whose macabre wax museum hides terrible secrets. Director Sergio Stivaletti came to the job through special effects expertise and his work here (in both capacities) is very good. This is a man to watch. The plot goes much too far for the film ever to find a large mainstream audience, and that's the point of Grand Guignol horror. **98m/C DVD, Wide.** *IT FR* Robert Hossein, Romina Mondello, Ricardo Serventi Longhi; *D:* Sergio Stivaletti; *W:* Lucio Fulci; *C:* Sergio Salvati. **VIDEO**

Wax, or the Discovery of Television among the Bees **1993** Intricate and eccentric fable dealing with alternate realities and perceptions. Jacob Maker (Blair) keeps a hive of very unusual bees, a family legacy passed down from his grandfather. Jacob begins experiencing a eerie communication with his bees and suffering mysterious blackouts, which cause him to perceive the world through blurred bee vision. New Mexico desert setting provides a surreal and desolate landscape. **85m/C VHS.** David Blair, Meg Savlov, Florence Ormezzano, William S. Burroughs; *D:* David Blair; *W:* David Blair; *M:* Beo Morales, Brooks Williams.

Waxwork ½ **1988 (R)** A wax museum opens up, and it is soon evident that the dummies are not what they seem. Garbled nonthriller. Available in a 100-minute unrated version. **97m/C VHS.** Zach Galligan, Deborah Foreman, Michelle Johnson, Dana Ashbrook, Miles O'Keeffe, Patrick Macnee, David Warner, John Rhys-Davies; *D:* Anthony Hickox; *W:* Anthony Hickox; *C:* Gerry Lively; *M:* Roger Bellon.

Waxwork 2: Lost in Time ½ *Lost in Time* **1991 (R)** A young couple (Galligan and Schnarre) barely escape with their lives when the infamous waxworks museum burns down. A severed hand also gets loose and follows Schnarre home and murders her stepfather, leaving her to take the blame. In order to prove her innocence, the couple must travel through a bizarre time machine. Extraordinary special effects, strange plot twists, and recreations of scenes from past horror movies make this a highly entertaining sequel. **104m/C VHS.** Zach Galligan, Alexander Godunov, Bruce Campbell, Michael Des Barres, Monika Schnarre, Martin Kemp, Sophie Ward, Marina Sirtis, Juliet Mills, John Ireland, Patrick Macnee, David Carradine, Drew Barrymore; *D:* Anthony Hickox; *W:* Anthony Hickox; *C:* Gerry Lively.

Waxworks **1924** A major achievement in German Expressionism, in which a poet imagines scenarios in a wax museum fairground that involve Jack the Ripper, Ivan the Terrible, and Haroun al-Rashid. Influential and considered ahead of its time. Silent. **63m/B VHS.** *GE* William Dieterle, Emil Jannings, Conrad Veidt, Werner Krauss, John Gottowt, Olga Belajeff; *D:* Paul Leni; *W:* Henrik Galeen.

Way Back Home *Old Greatheart; Other People's Business* **1932** Man wants to adopt a boy to release him from the clutches of his cruel guardian. Minor role for the then unknown Davis. **81m/B VHS.** Phillips Lord, Frank Albertson, Bette Davis; *D:* William A. Seiter; *M:* Max Steiner.

Way Down East **1920** Melodramatic silent drama of a country girl who is tricked into a fake marriage by a scheming playboy. The famous final scene of Gish adrift on the ice floes is in color. One of Griffith's last critical and popular successes. This tape includes the original Griffith-approved musical score. Remade in 1935 with Henry Fonda. **107m/B VHS, DVD.** Lillian Gish, Richard Barthelmess, Lowell Sherman, Creighton Hale, Burr McIntosh, Kate Bruce, Florence Short; *D:* D.W. Griffith; *W:* D.W. Griffith, Joseph R. Grismer; *C:* Billy (G.W.) Bitzer, Hendrik Sartov.

Way Down South ½ **1939** The orphan son of a plantation owner tries to take over his father's estate, only to find out that the place has been run into the ground by a corrupt lawyer and a cruel slave driver. Black poet Hughes and actor Muse collaborated on the screenplay. German-born director Vorhaus was in his second year in Hollywood, after making his mark in Britain directing talkies. ♫Good Ground; Louisiana; Nobody Know De Trouble I See; Sometimes I Feel Like a Motherless Child; Lord I You Can't Come Send One Angel Down. **62m/B VHS.** Bobby Breen, Alan Mowbray, Ralph Morgan, Clarence Muse, Steffi Duna, Sally Blane, Edwin Maxwell; *D:* Bernard Vorhaus; *W:* Clarence Muse, Langston Hughes.

Way He Was **1976 (R)** A satirical re-enactment of the events that led up to the Watergate burglary and the coverup that followed. **87m/C VHS.** Steve Friedman, Al Lewis, Merrie Lynn Ross, Doodles Weaver.

Way of the Black Dragon **1981** When slave-trading drug traffickers threaten the moral fiber of our nation, two commandoes join forces to halt their operation. **88m/C VHS.** Ron Van Cliff, Carter Wang, Charles Bonet; *D:* Chan Wui Ngai.

Way of the Gun ½ **2000 (R)** Two unsuccessful career criminals (Phillippe and Del Toro) take up kidnapping and hold a surrogate mother (Lewis) for ransom. Only the parents-to-be are mobbed up and send two thugs (Diggs and Katt) and a philosophical enforcer (Caan) to get her back unharmed. McQuarrie shows that he still has the knack for twisty plots, surprise revelations, and cool dialogue, but he lets the proceedings drag on a little longer than they need to. He's also not shy about heaping on the violence and crude language (which isn't necessarily bad, just consider yourself forewarned). **118m/C VHS, DVD, Wide.** Ryan Phillippe, Benicio Del Toro, Juliette Lewis, James Caan, Taye Diggs, Nicky Katt, Scott Wilson, Kristen Lehman, Geoffrey Lewis, Dylan Kussman; *D:* Christopher McQuarrie; *W:* Christopher McQuarrie; *C:* Dick Pope; *M:* Joe Kraemer.

Way of the West ½ **1935** Them durn pesky sheepherders are up to it again! Okay, so the cow/sheep thing is a classic western plot, but here it's offered perfunctorily. **52m/B VHS.** Wally Wales, William Desmond, Art Mix, Jim Sheridan, Bobby Nelson; *D:* Robert Emmett Tansey.

The Way Out *Dial 999* **1956** Average crime drama starring Nelson as a fugitive accused of killing a bookie. **90m/C VHS.** *GB* Gene Nelson, Mona Freeman, John Bentley, Michael Goodliffe, Sydney Tafler; *D:* Montgomery Tully.

Way Out West **1937** The classic twosome journey way out west to deliver the deed to a gold mine to the daughter of their late prospector pal. The obligatory romance is missing, but you'll be laughing so hard you won't notice. One of Stan and Ollie's best. Score includes the song "Trail of the Lonesome Pine." Also included on this tape is a 1932 Todd and Pitts short, "Red Noses." Available colorized. **86m/B VHS.** Stan Laurel, Oliver Hardy, Rosina Lawrence, James Finlayson, Sharon Lynne, ZaSu Pitts, Thelma Todd, William Haines; *D:* James W. Horne.

The Way We Live Now ½ **2002** Based on the 1875 novel by Anthony Trollope, this adaptation centers around shady financier Augustus Melmotte (Suchet). An economic boom is sweeping through Europe in the 1870s and Melmotte arrives in London with a scheme to buy himself a place in Victorian society. Melmotte is even willing to sacrifice his daughter Marie (Henderson) who has developed an infatuation for debt-ridden but aristocratic Sir Felix Carbury (Macfadyen). The question for all this greedy bunch is who will get the better of whom? **300m/C VHS, DVD.** *GB* David Suchet, Shirley Henderson, Matthew MacFadyen, Cheryl Campbell, Paloma Baeza, Douglas Hodge, Miranda Otto, Cillian Murphy, Michael Riley, Allan Corduner, David Bradley, Jim Carter, Oliver Ford Davies, Joanna David; *D:* David Yates; *W:* Andrew Davies; *C:* Chris Seager; *M:* Nicholas Hooper. **TV**

The Way We Were **1973 (PG)** Big boxoffice hit follows a love story between opposites from the 1930s to the 1950s. Streisand is a Jewish political radical who meets the handsome WASP Redford at college. They're immediately attracted to one another, but it takes years before they act on it and eventually marry. They move to Hollywood where Redford is a screenwriter and left-wing Streisand becomes involved in the Red scare and the blacklist, much to Redford's dismay. Though always in love, their differences are too great to keep them together. An old-fashioned and sweet romance, with much gloss. Hit title song sung by Streisand. Adapted by Arthur Laurents from his novel. ♫The Way We Were. **118m/C VHS, DVD, Wide.** Barbra Streisand, Robert Redford, Bradford Dillman, Viveca Lindfors, Herb Edelman, Murray Hamilton, Patrick O'Neal, James Woods, Sally Kirkland; *D:* Sydney Pollack; *W:* Arthur Laurents; *C:* Harry Stradling Jr.; *M:* Marvin Hamlisch. Oscars '73: Song ("The Way We Were"), Orig. Dramatic Score; Golden Globes '74: Song ("The Way We Were").

The Way West ½ **1967** A wagon train heads to Oregon. A poor and muddled attempt at recreating the style of a John Ford western. What really galls is that it's based on the Pulitzer-winning novel by A.B. Guthrie Jr. Boy, is the book better than the movie. Field's first film. **122m/C VHS.** Kirk Douglas, Robert Mitchum, Richard Widmark, Lola Albright, Michael Witney, Stubby Kaye, Sally Field, Jack Elam; *D:* Andrew V. McLaglen; *C:* William Clothier.

Wayne Murder Case *Strange Adventure* **1938** A fast-moving, cleverly constructed murder mystery. A rich old man dies just as he is about to sign a new will. Though no one was standing near him, a knife is found stuck in his back. **61m/B VHS.** June Clyde, Regis Toomey, Jason Robards Sr.

Wayne's World **1992 (PG-13)** Destined to become one of the top movies of all time—Not! This "Saturday Night Live" skit proved to be so popular that it got its own movie, not unlike the plot, which has slimy producer Benjamin Oliver (Lowe) take the public access "Wayne's World" into the world of commercial television. The zany duo of Wayne (Myers) and Garth (Carvey) are as much fun on the big screen as they were on SNL and there are many funny moments, several of which are destined to become comedy classics. A huge boxoffice hit that spawned a sequel. It also spawned Lorne Michaels's desperate attempts to match its success with other non-bigscreen worthy skits from the show. **93m/C VHS, DVD, Wide.** Mike Myers, Dana Carvey, Rob Lowe, Tia Carrere, Brian Doyle-Murray, Lara Flynn Boyle, Kurt Fuller, Colleen Camp, Donna Dixon, Ed O'Neill, Alice Cooper, Meat Loaf Aday; *D:* Penelope Spheeris; *W:* Mike Myers, Bonnie Turner, Terry Turner; *C:* Theo van de Sande; *M:* J. Peter Robinson. MTV Movie Awards '92: On-Screen Duo (Mike Myers/Dana Carvey).

Wayne's World 2 **1993 (PG-13)** Good-natured rerun of the original has plenty of sophomoric gags, but feels tired. Wayne and Garth are on their own, planning a major concert, Waynestock. "If you book them they will come," Jim Morrison says in a dream. Meanwhile, Wayne's girlfriend (Carrere) is falling for slimeball record promoter Walken. Offers a few brilliantly funny segments. If you liked the "Bohemian Rhapsody" spot in the original, get ready for the Village People here. Heston has a funny cameo, and Walken and Basinger push the limits without going over the top. Feature film debut for director Surjik. **94m/C VHS, DVD, Wide.** Mike Myers, Dana Carvey, Tia Carrere, Christopher Walken, Ralph Brown, Kim Basinger, James Hong, Chris Farley, Ed O'Neill, Olivia D'Abo, Kevin Pollak, Drew Barrymore, Charlton Heston, Rip Taylor, Bob Odenkirk, Michael A. (M.A.) Nickles; *D:* Stephen Surjik; *W:* Bonnie Turner, Terry Turner, Mike Myers; *C:* Francis Kenny; *M:* Carter Burwell.

The Wayward Wife *La Provinciale* **1952** Young woman, married to a university professor, is blackmailed over her less-than-respectable past. Based on the novel by Alberto Moravia. Italian with subtitles. **92m/B VHS.** *IT* Gina Lollobrigida, Gabriele Ferzetti, Franco Interlenghi, Renato Baldini; *D:* Mario Soldati.

We All Loved Each Other So Much ½ **1977** Sensitive comedy follows three friends over 30 years, beginning at the end of WWII. All three have loved the same woman, an actress. Homage to friendship and to postwar Italian cinema. Includes a full-scale recreation of the fountain scene in "La Dolce Vita." In Italian with English subtitles. **124m/C VHS.** *IT* Vittorio Gassman, Nino Manfredi, Stefano Satta Flores, Stefania Sandrelli, Marcello Mastroianni, Federico Fellini, Anita Ekberg, Vittorio De Sica; *D:* Ettore Scola.

We Are the Children **1987** Cynical reporter covering the famine in Ethiopia meets an idealistic nurse who's been living there for years. Romance blossoms among the starving in made-for-TV drama co-produced by Danson. **92m/C VHS.** Ally Sheedy, Ted Danson, Judith Ivey, Zia Mohyeddin; *D:* Robert M. Young.

We Dive at Dawn **1943** Interesting, tense British submarine drama. The "Sea Tiger" attempts to sink the German battleship "Brandenburg" off Denmark. Good cast. Mills prepared for the role by riding an actual submarine, turning "a pale shade of pea-green" when it crash-dived. **98m/B VHS, DVD.** *GB* Eric Portman, John Mills; *D:* Anthony Asquith; *W:* Val Valentine; *C:* Jack Cox.

We of the Never Never **1982 (G)** In turn-of-the-century Australia a city-bred woman marries a cattle rancher and moves from civilized Melbourne to the barren outback of the Northern Territory. Based on the autobiographical story written by Jeannie Gunn, the first white woman to travel in the aboriginal wilderness. She finds herself fighting for her own rights as well as for those of the aborigines in this sincere, well-done film. **136m/C VHS.** *AU* Angela Punch McGregor, Arthur Dignam, Tony Barry; *D:* Igor Auzins.

We the Living ½ **1942** The torpid long-lost and restored Italian version of Ayn Rand's unique political tome. Deals with a young Soviet woman in revolutionary Petrograd who is slowly ruined by the system and her affair with a romantic counter-revolutionary. Made under the Fascists' nose during WWII. A fascinating dialectic between utopian melodrama and Rand dogma. In Italian with subtitles. **174m/B VHS.** *IT* Alida Valli, Rossano Brazzi, Fosco Giachetti; *D:* Goffredo Alessandrini.

We Think the World of You **1988 (PG)** When bisexual Oldman goes to prison, his lover Bates, whose feelings are unresolved and complex, finds friendship with Oldman's dog. Odd, oft-bitter comedy-drama of love and loyalty characterized by excellent acting and respectful, gentle direction. From the novel by Joseph R. Ackerly. **94m/C VHS.** *GB* Alan Bates, Gary Oldman, Frances Barber, Liz Smith, Max Wall, Kerry Wise; ***D:*** Colin Gregg.

We Were Soldiers 🦴🦴🦴½ **2002 (R)** Writer-director Wallace once again tackles the fact-based military epic, with outstanding results. Recounting the battle of the la Drang Valley in 1965, the first major land battle for U.S. troops in Vietnam, the story focuses on Lt. Col. Hal Moore (Gibson) and his leadership of the 7th Air Cavalry at LZ X-Ray. Moore's combination of experience, leadership, instinct, knowledge, and genuine concern for his men make him seem too good to be true, but Gibson's portrayal, and the fact that Moore is real, help to erase disbelief. Inevitable comparisons with "Black Hawk Down" are justified, as both pics deal with chaotic battlefields and the heroism of the soldiers who must fight their way out of situations they were trained, but not quite prepared, for. But this movie goes beyond the battle to show the impact to families back home, as well as giving a glimpe of the mindset of the enemy. Elliot stands out as Moore's right-hand man, as does Pepper as reporter Galloway, while Stein, Russell, and Kinnear do well playing against type. Based on the book "We Were Soldiers Once...and Young" by Lt. Gen. Harold G. Moore (Ret.) and Joseph L. Galloway. **137m/C VHS, DVD.** *US* Mel Gibson, Madeleine Stowe, Greg Kinnear, Sam Elliott, Chris Klein, Keri Russell, Barry Pepper, Don Duong, Ryan Hurst, Marc Blucas, Jsu Garcia, Clark Gregg, Desmond Harrington, Blake Heron, Dylan Walsh, Robert Bagnell, Josh Daugherty, Jon Hamm, Erik MacArthur; ***D:*** Randall Wallace; ***W:*** Randall Wallace; ***C:*** Dean Semler; ***M:*** Nick Glennie-Smith.

We Will Not Enter the Forest 🦴🦴🦴 **1979** Moral dilemmas afflict a group of French Resistance fighters during WWII when they must decide what to do with four German deserters they've captured. In French with subtitles. **88m/C VHS.** *FR* Marie-France Pisier; ***D:*** Georges Dumoulin.

The Weaker Sex 🦴🦴½ **1949** Typical patriotic British weepie finds a British widow and her daughters trying to hold on to hope as D-Day approaches. **89m/B VHS.** *GB* Ursula Jeans, Cecil Parker, Joan Hopkins, Derek Bond, Lana Morris; ***D:*** Roy Ward Baker.

Weapons of Mass Distraction 🦴🦴 **1997 (R)** Two megalomanical multimedia tycoons set out to destroy each other in this black comedy. Lionel Powers (Byrne) wants to buy pro football's Tucson Titans and so does his arch-rival Julian Messenger (Kingsley). So there's bribery and blackmail and airing of dirty family laundry all over the place. No heroes here but occasionally some sharp satire. **105m/C VHS.** Gabriel Byrne, Ben Kingsley, Mimi Rogers, Jeffrey Tambor, Illeana Douglas, Paul Mazursky, Kathy Baker, Chris Mulkey, R. Lee Ermey, Caroline Aaron, Jason Lee, Christina Pickles; ***D:*** Stephen Surjik; ***W:*** Larry Gelbart; ***C:*** Alar Kivilo; ***M:*** Don Davis. **CABLE**

Weather in the Streets 🦴½ **1984 (PG)** A young woman enters into an ill-fated love affair after spending a few moments with an aristocratic married man. Cliched drama set in England between the two world wars. **108m/C VHS.** Michael York, Joanna Lumley, Lisa Eichhorn, Isabel Dean, Norman Pitt; ***M:*** Carl Davis.

Web of Deceit 🦴🦴½ **1990 (PG-13)** Defense lawyer Purl returns to her Southern hometown to defend an unjustly accused teenager. She falls in love with the prosecutor, but could he be the killer? Shades of "Jagged Edge." Good, suspenseful made-for-TV movie. **93m/C VHS.** Linda Purl, James Read, Paul DeSouza, Larry Black, Len Birman, Barbara Rush; ***D:*** Sandor Stern; ***W:*** Sandor Stern.

Web of Deception 🦴 **1971 (R)** A jewel thief disappears with $5 million worth of jewels. When the case turns to murder, a private detective becomes the prime suspect. **90m/C VHS.** *SP* Thomas Hunter, Aelina Nathaniel, Gabriele Tinti, Marilia Branco.

Web of the Spider 🦴🦴 *Nella Stretta M Orsa Del Ragno; In the Grip of the Spider; Dracula in the Castle of Blood; And Comes the Dawn...But Colored Red* **1970** Kinski as Poe is really the only good thing about this run-of-the-mill horror outing. A man stays the night in a spooky house to prove it's not haunted. Remake of "Castle of Blood." **94m/C VHS.** *GE FR IT* Anthony (Tony) Franciosa, Klaus Kinski, Michele Mercier, Peter Carsten, Karin (Karen) Field; ***D:*** Anthony (Antonio Margheriti) Dawson.

Webmaster 🦴🦴 *Skyggen; The Shadow* **1998 (R)** The futureworld Technotropolis is run by tyrant industrialist Stoiss. Hacker JB is forced to work surveillance for Stoiss and when a thief breaks into Stoiss' cyber empire, JB is given a mechanical heart that will stop in 35 hours unless he finds the intruder first. Dubbed from Danish. **102m/C VHS, DVD.** *DK* Jorgen Kiil, Lars Bom, Puk Scharbau; ***D:*** Thomas Borch Nielsen; ***C:*** Lars Beyer.

A Wedding 🦴½ **1978 (PG)** The occasion of a wedding leads to complications galore for the relatives and guests on the happy day. Silent film legend Gish's 100th screen role. Miserable, self-indulgent outing for Altman, who went through quite a dry spell after "Nashville." **125m/C VHS.** Mia Farrow, Carol Burnett, Lillian Gish, Lauren Hutton, Viveca Lindfors, Geraldine Chaplin, Paul Dooley, Howard Duff, Dennis Christopher, Peggy Ann Garner, John Considine, Nina Van Pallandt, Dina Merrill, Pat McCormick, Vittorio Gassman, Desi Arnaz Jr.; ***D:*** Robert Altman; ***W:*** Robert Altman, Allan Nicholls, Patricia Resnick, John Considine.

Wedding Band 🦴🦴 **1989** Episodic comedy about a rock 'n' roll band that plays all sorts of weddings. Thin and lame but inoffensive. **95m/C VHS.** William Katt, Joyce Hyser, Tino Insana, Fran Drescher, David Rasche, Joe Flaherty, Tim Kazurinsky, James Belushi; ***D:*** Daniel Raskov.

The Wedding Banquet 🦴🦴🦴 *Xiyan; Hsi Yen* **1993 (R)** Charming story about a clash of customs and secrets. Naturalized American Wai Tung (Chao, in his film debut) lives comfortably with his lover Simon (Lichtenstein) while hiding the fact that he's gay from his Chinese parents. To appease his parents and get his "wife" (Chin) a green card, he marries for convenience and watches as the deception snowballs. Comedy of errors was shot on a small budget ($750,000) and examines small details with as much care as the larger ones. A fine effort from director Lee that's solidly humorous, but also poignant. In English and Chinese with subtitles. **111m/C VHS.** *TW* Winston Chao, May Chin, Mitchell Lichtenstein, Sihung Lung, Ah-Leh Gua, Michael Gaston, Jeffrey Howard; ***D:*** Ang Lee; ***W:*** Ang Lee, Neil Peng, James Schamus; ***C:*** Jong Lin.

Wedding Bell Blues 🦴🦴 **1996 (R)** Three 30ish single friends/roommates cope with a variety of crises. Pregnant Tanya (Porikova) learns that her boyfriend Tom (Edson) has no intention of marrying her, Micki's (Warner) fiance has just called off their wedding, and Jasmine's (Douglas) conservative parents are upset by their promiscuous daughter's approach to life. Stressed, the women decide to seek their fortunes in Vegas—preferably through some quickie marriages and even quickier divorces. Looks like it was shot on a shoestring budget and the lighting could be better, but the dialogue rings true and the actors do a decent job. Look for Seinfeld's TV mom as Micki's overbearing mother and Jackson as a disgruntled shopper. Reynolds plays herself. **100m/C VHS, DVD.** Illeana Douglas, Paulina Porizkova, Julie Warner, John Corbett, Jonathan Penner, Richard Edson, Charles Martin Smith, Stephanie Beacham, Carla Gugino, Leo Rossi, John Capodice, Victoria Jackson, Jeff Seymour; ***Cameos:*** Debbie Reynolds; ***D:*** Dana Lustig; ***W:*** Annette Goliti Gutierrez; ***C:*** Kent Wakeford; ***M:*** Paul Christian Gordon, Tal Bergman.

The Wedding Gift 🦴🦴🦴 *Wide-Eyed and Legless* **1993 (PG-13)** Offbeat charm and humor go a long way to overcome the inherent tragedy in this true story made for British TV. Longtime happily marrieds Diana (Walters) and Deric (Broadbent) Longden are struggling to cope with Diana's mysterious and increasingly debilitating illness, which causes blackouts, pain, and the inability to use her limbs. Diana comes to accept the fact that she's going to die and decides to find her hubby a new wife, aided by Deric's friendship with a blind novelist (Thomas). Terrific performances keep the mawkishness at bay. Based on Deric Longden's books "Diana's Story" and "Lost for Words." **87m/C VHS.** *GB* Julie Walters, Jim Broadbent, Sian Thomas, Thora Hird, Andrew Lancel, Anastasia Mulrooney; ***D:*** Richard Loncraine; ***W:*** Jack Rosenthal; ***C:*** Remi Adefarasin. **TV**

Wedding in Blood 🦴🦴🦴 **1974 (PG)** Two French lovers plot to kill their respective spouses, and proceed to do so amid calamity and much table-turning. Sharp social satire and suspenseful mystery. Based on a true story. In French with English subtitles. **98m/C VHS.** *FR IT* Claude Pieplu, Stephane Audran, Michel Piccoli; ***D:*** Claude Chabrol; ***W:*** Claude Chabrol; ***C:*** Jean Rabier.

A Wedding in Galilee 🦴🦴🦴 *Noce In Galilee* **1987** The elder of a Palestinian village is given permission to have a traditional wedding ceremony for his son if Israeli military officers can attend as the guests of honor. As the event approaches, conflicts arise among the villagers, the family, and the Israelis. Long but fascinating treatment of traditional culture in the modern world amidst political tension. In Arabic and Hebrew, with English subtitles. **113m/C VHS.** *BE FR* Ali M. El Aleili, Nazih Akleh, Anna Achdian; ***D:*** Michel Khleifi.

Wedding in White 🦴🦴 **1972 (R)** A rape and out-of-wedlock pregnancy trouble a poor British clan living in Canada during WWII. Sad, glum way to spend an evening. Kane is good in a non-comic role. Her screen father cares more for her honor than he does for her. **103m/C VHS.** *CA* Donald Pleasence, Carol Kane, Leo Phillips; ***D:*** William Fruet.

The Wedding March 🦴🦴🦴🦴 **1928** Von Stroheim's famous silent film about romantic couplings in pre-WWI Vienna. The director also stars as a prince preparing to marry for money, who falls in love with a beautiful, but poor woman. Romance and irony, with a memorable finale. Like many of his other great films, it was taken from him and re-edited. Initially the first of two halves; the second, "The Honeymoon," has been lost. Next to "Greed," his most successful film. **113m/B VHS.** Erich von Stroheim, Fay Wray, ZaSu Pitts, George Fawcett, Maud(e) (Ford) George, Matthew Betz, George Nicholls, Cesare Gravina; ***D:*** Erich von Stroheim; ***C:*** Hal Mohr; ***M:*** Gaylord Carter.

The Wedding Party 🦴½ **1969** Apprehensive groom is overwhelmed by his too-eager bride and her inquisitive relatives at a prenuptial celebration. Hokey, dull, would-be comedy. First screen appearances of both Clayburgh and De Niro (spelled DeNero in the credits). **90m/C VHS.** Jill Clayburgh, Robert De Niro, William Finley; ***D:*** Brian DePalma, Cynthia Munroe, Wilford Leach; ***W:*** Brian DePalma.

The Wedding Party 🦴🦴½ *Thank God He Met Lizzie* **1997 (R)** Predictable wedding comedy has thirty-something Guy (Roxburgh) searching for the perfect woman. Finally he meets Lizzie (Blanchett) and the twosome are soon involved in lavish wedding preparations before they really have a chance to get to know each other. In fact, Guy begins dreaming of former love, Jenny (O'Connor), in the middle of the ceremony! **91m/C VHS, DVD.** *AU* Richard Roxburgh, Cate Blanchett, Frances O'Connor, Linden Wilkinson, Michael Ross, John Gaden, Genevieve Mooy, Rhett Walton, Deborah Kennedy; ***D:*** Cherie Nowlan; ***W:*** Alexandra Long; ***C:*** Kathryn Milliss; ***M:*** Martin Armiger. Australian Film Inst. '97: Support. Actress (Blanchett).

The Wedding Planner 🦴🦴½ **2001 (PG-13)** A film that's a bridesmaid instead of a bride. Mary Fiore (Lopez) is a workaholic wedding planner in San Francisco who has no love life of her own. The driven Mary meets cute with aw-shucks doctor Steve Edison (McConaughey) who, naturally, turns out to be the fiance of Mary latest client, heiress Fran (Wilson). Not that the attractive duo can stay away from each other despite their good intentions. The leads nearly carry the film on charm alone before the script finally lets them down. **105m/C VHS, DVD, Wide.** *US* Jennifer Lopez, Matthew McConaughey, Bridgette Wilson, Justin Chambers, Alex Rocco, Judy Greer, Kevin Pollak, Joanna Gleason, Charles Kimbrough, Fred Willard, Kathy Najimy; ***D:*** Adam Shankman; ***W:*** Michael Ellis, Pamela Falk; ***C:*** Julio Macat; ***M:*** Mervyn Warren.

Wedding Rehearsal 🦴🦴½ **1932** A young nobleman thwarts his grandmother's plans to marry him off by finding suitors for all the young ladies offered to him until he finally succumbs to the charms of his mother's secretary. Enjoyable, fun comedy. First featured roles for actresses Oberon, Barrie, and Gardner. **84m/B VHS.** Merle Oberon, Roland Young, John Loder, Wendy Barrie, Maurice Evans, Joan Gardner; ***D:*** Alexander Korda.

The Wedding Singer 🦴🦴½ **1997 (PG-13)** Despite almost nonexistent pacing and a script full of holes, "Singer" is an enjoyably goofy look at the mid '80s. Surprisingly toned-down and appealing Sandler is Robbie Hart, wedding singer, ultimate nice guy, and rock-star wannabe, who's jilted at the altar. Waitress Barrymore is engaged to a skirt-chasing stock broker. It's immediately clear that they belong together, and the rest of the movie is spent on them chasing each other through various contrived obstacles, to the obvious ending. Features great cameos by punk-rocker Billy Idol, Jon Lovitz (as a rival wedding singer), and Steve Buscemi (excellent as the groom's jealous "dad always liked you best" brother). Musical highlight is Sandler's heartfelt rendition of the J. Geils Band's "Love Stinks." Isn't it a little scary that we're already spoofing the '80s? **96m/C VHS, DVD.** Adam Sandler, Drew Barrymore, Christine Taylor, Allen Covert, Matthew Glave, Ellen A. Dow, Angela Featherstone, Alexis Arquette, Christina Pickles, Jon Lovitz, Steve Buscemi, Kevin Nealon; ***Cameos:*** Billy Idol; ***D:*** Frank Coraci; ***W:*** Tim Herlihy; ***C:*** Tim Suhrstedt; ***M:*** Teddy Castellucci. MTV Movie Awards '98: Kiss (Adam Sandler/Drew Barrymore).

Wee Willie Winkie 🦴🦴🦴 **1937 (PG)** A precocious little girl is taken in by a British regiment in India. Sugar-coated. If you're a cinematic diabetic, be warned. If you're a Temple fan, you've probably already seen it. If not, you're in for a treat. Inspired by the Rudyard Kipling story. **99m/B VHS.** Shirley Temple, Victor McLaglen, Sir C. Aubrey Smith, June Lang, Michael Whalen, Cesar Romero, Constance Collier; ***D:*** John Ford; ***C:*** Arthur C. Miller.

Weeds 🦴🦴🦴 **1987 (R)** A highly fictionalized account of the career of Rick Cluchey, who, as a lifer in San Quentin federal prison, wrote a play. He was eventually paroled and went on to form a theatre group made up of ex-cons. Original and often enjoyable with a tight ensemble performance. Filmed on location at Stateville Correctional Center in Illinois, with inmates serving as extras. **115m/C VHS.** Nick Nolte, Rita Taggart, William Forsythe, Lane Smith, Joe Mantegna, Ernie Hudson, John Toles-Bey, Mark Rolston, Anne Ramsey, Charlie Rich; ***D:*** John Hancock; ***W:*** John Hancock, Dorothy Tristan; ***M:*** Angelo Badalamenti.

Week-End in Havana 🦴🦴½ **1941** Set in pre-revolution Cuba, this frothy musical finds salesgirl Faye on a long-awaited cruise when her ship gets stranded in Havana. She's escorted around town by shipping-official Payne and catches the eye of gambler-lothario Romero, who has a jealous girlfriend in Miranda. Fun fluff. ♫Romance and Rhumba; Tropical Magic; The Nango; A Weekend in Havana; When I Love, I Love; Maria Inez; Rebola a Bola. **80m/C VHS.** Alice Faye, John Payne, Cesar Romero, Carmen Miranda, Cobina Wright Jr., George Barbier, Sheldon Leonard, Billy Gilbert; ***D:*** Walter Lang; ***W:*** Karl Tunberg; ***M:*** Alfred Newman.

Weekend 🦴🦴🦴 **1967** A Parisian couple embark on a drive to the country. On the way they witness and are involved in horrifying highway wrecks. Leaving the road they find a different, equally grotesque kind of carnage. Godard's brilliant, surreal, hyper-paranoiac view of modern life was greatly influenced by the fact that his mother was killed in an auto accident in 1954 (he himself suffered a serious motorcycle mishap in 1975). In French with English subtitles. **105m/C VHS.** *FR IT* Mireille Darc, Jean Yanne, Jean-Pierre Kalfon, Valerie Lagrange, Jean-Pierre Leaud, Yves Beneyton; ***D:*** Jean-Luc Godard; ***W:*** Jean-Luc Godard; ***M:*** Antoine Duhamel.

The Weekend ✓✓½ **2000** Marian (Unger) and John (Harris) Kerr are hosting a weekend for family and friends at their upstate New York home to remember John's half-brother Tony (Sweeney) who died of AIDS a year before. Gathered are Tony's lover Lyle (Conrad) and his new boyfriend Robert (Duval) as well as neighbors Laura (Rowlands) and her daughter Nina (Shields). Turns out that mostly everybody was enamored of Tony and some unpleasant truths come out after too much wine. Good cast in a very gabby drama. Based on the novel by Peter Cameron. **97m/C VHS, DVD.** *GB US* Deborah Kara Unger, Jared Harris, Gena Rowlands, D.B. Sweeney, Brooke Shields, David Conrad, James Duval, Gary Jourdan; ***D:*** Brian Skeet; ***W:*** Brian Skeet; ***C:*** Ron Fortunato; ***M:*** Daniel Jones, Sarah Class.

Weekend at Bernie's ✓✓½ *Hot and Cold* **1989 (PG-13)** Two computer nerds discover embezzlement at their workplace after being invited to their boss's beach house for a weekend party. They find their host murdered. They endeavor to keep up appearances by (you guessed it) dressing and strategically posing the corpse during the party. Kiser as the dead man is memorable, and the two losers gamely keep the silliness flowing. Lots of fun. **101m/C VHS, DVD.** Andrew McCarthy, Jonathan Silverman, Catherine Mary Stewart, Terry Kiser, Don Calfa, Louis Giambalvo; ***D:*** Ted Kotcheff; ***W:*** Robert Klane; ***C:*** Francois Protat; ***M:*** Andy Summers.

Weekend at Bernie's 2 ✓½ **1993 (PG)** Unlikely but routine sequel to the original's cavorting cadaver slapstick, except now McCarthy and Silverman are frantically hunting for Bernie's (Kiser) cash stash, a quest that takes them and poor dead Bernie to the Caribbean. See Bernie get stuffed in a suitcase, see Bernie hang glide, see Bernie tango, see Bernie attract the opposite sex. Thin script with one-joke premise done to death but fun for those in the mood for the postmortem antics of a comedic stiff. Plenty of well-executed gags involving the well-preserved corpse (particularly one that's been dead for two films now) should lure back fans of the 1989 original. **89m/C VHS, DVD.** Andrew McCarthy, Jonathan Silverman, Terry Kiser, Steve James, Troy Beyer, Barry Bostwick; ***D:*** Robert Klane; ***W:*** Robert Klane; ***M:*** Peter Wolf.

Weekend at the Waldorf ✓✓✓ **1945** Glossy, americanized remake of "Grand Hotel" set at the famous Park Avenue hotel, the Waldorf-Astoria, in New York City. Turner and Rogers star in the roles originated by Joan Crawford and Greta Garbo. Johnson and Pidgeon play their love interests. Combining drawing room comedy with slapstick and a touch of romance proved to be a hit, as this film was one of the top grossers of 1945 and was just what war-weary moviegoers wanted to see. Based on the play "Grand Hotel" by Vicki Baum. **130m/B VHS.** Ginger Rogers, Walter Pidgeon, Van Johnson, Lana Turner, Robert Benchley, Edward Arnold, Leon Ames, Warner Anderson, Phyllis Thaxter, Keenan Wynn, Porter Hall, Samuel S. Hinds; ***D:*** Robert Z. Leonard; ***W:*** Samuel Spewack, Bella Spewack, Guy Bolton.

A Weekend in the Country ✓✓½ **1996 (R)** Ensemble comedy finds a varied group of couples and would-be couples traveling to California's wine country for a weekend of relaxation at a bed and breakfast inn. Nothing quite works out as planned but Cupid's arrow does strike. Filmed on location in Temecula, CA. **94m/C VHS.** Rita Rudner, Faith Ford, Christine Lahti, Jack Lemmon, Richard Lewis, Dudley Moore, Betty White, Dan Cortese, Jennifer Elise Cox; ***D:*** Martin Bergman; ***W:*** Rita Rudner, Martin Bergman; ***M:*** Patrick Williams. CABLE

Weekend of Shadows ✓✓✓ **1977** Confident, moralistic murder drama about a posse after an innocent immigrant they believe has killed a woman. Police sergeant Roberts is interested only in his reputation, not in justice. Posse member Waters begins to sympathize with the hunted man and defends his innocence. Intelligent, well-conceived, and professionally directed. **94m/C VHS.** John Waters, Melissa Jaffer, Graeme Blundell, Wyn Roberts, Barbara West, Graham Rouse; ***D:*** Tom Jeffrey.

Weekend Pass ✓ **1984 (R)** Moronic rookie sailors who have just completed basic training are out on a weekend pass, determined to forget everything they have learned. They find this surprisingly easy to do. **92m/C VHS.** D.W. Brown, Peter Ellenstein, Phil Hartman, Patrick Hauser, Chip McAllister; ***D:*** Lawrence Bassoff; ***W:*** Lawrence Bassoff; ***C:*** Bryan England.

Weekend War ✓✓½ **1988 (PG-13)** A group of National Guardsmen are sent to the Honduras for their annual tour of duty. But when a guerilla war between Honduras and Nicaragua breaks out, the Guardsmen are forced to fight for their lives. The "Bridge on the River Kwai" finale features the dilemma over a bridge linking the two countries. **96m/C VHS.** Daniel Stern, Stephen Collins, Charles Haid, Evan Mirand, Michael Beach, Scott Paulin, James Tolkan; ***D:*** Steven Hilliard Stern; ***M:*** Brad Fiedel. TV

Weekend Warriors ✓½ **1986 (R)** Young film-studio employees evade the draft in 1961 by enlisting for National Guard weekend duty. Grade "C" dumb comedy from professional celebrity and first-time director Convy. **88m/C VHS.** Chris Lemmon, Lloyd Bridges, Daniel Greene, Tom Villard, Vic Tayback; ***D:*** Bert Convy; ***W:*** Bruce Belland; ***M:*** Perry Botkin.

Weekend with the Babysitter woof! *Weekend Babysitter* **1970 (R)** Sordid teen drama about a weekend babysitter who goes to a film director's house and babysits everyone but the kids, running into a heroin-smuggling ring along the way. Casting-couch story with a twist. **93m/C VHS.** Susan (Suzan) Roman, George E. Carey, James Almanzar, Luanne Roberts; ***D:*** Don Henderson.

Weep No More My Lady ✓✓ **1993 (PG-13)** Suspense-filled whodunit about a wealthy businessman who comes between two sisters and a sibling rivalry that turns into a deadly game of murder. Based on the best-selling book by Mary Higgins Clark. **92m/C VHS.** Daniel J. Travanti, Shelley Winters, Kristin Scott Thomas.

Weird Science ✓✓ **1985 (PG-13)** Hall is appealing, and Hughes can write dialogue for teens with the best of them. However, many of the jokes are in poor taste, and the movie seems to go on forever. Hall and his nerdy cohort Mitchell-Smith use a very special kind of software to create the ideal woman who wreaks zany havoc in their lives from the outset. **94m/C VHS, DVD.** Kelly Le Brock, Anthony Michael Hall, Ilan Mitchell-Smith, Robert Downey Jr., Bill Paxton; ***D:*** John Hughes; ***W:*** John Hughes; ***C:*** Matthew F. Leonetti; ***M:*** Ira Newborn.

Weird Woman/Frozen Ghost **1944** In 1944's "Weird Woman" professor Chaney and his South Seas bride suffer the wrath of a jealous woman. In 1945's "The Frozen Ghost" hypnotist Chaney is ruined when a volunteer dies on stage. He relaxes at a friend's (who happens to own a wax museum) where he comes under a diabolical plot to drive him mad. Based on radio's "The Inner Sanctum Mysteries." **125m/B VHS.** Lon Chaney Jr., Evelyn Ankers, Ralph Morgan, Lois Collier, Douglass Dumbrille, Elena Verdugo, Anne Gwynne, Milburn Stone, Martin Kosleck; ***D:*** Harold Young, Reginald LeBorg; ***W:*** Brenda Weisberg, Bernard Schubert, Lucille Ward.

Weird World of LSD ✓½ **1967** Cheap exploitation film featuring the evil effects of LSD. **?m/C VHS.** Terry Tessem, Ann Lindsay, Yolanda Morino.

The Weirdo ✓ **1989** "The Jerk" meets Freddie Krueger. This film is absolutely wretched, even by horror movie standards. **91m/C VHS.** Steve Burlington, Jessica Straus; ***D:*** Andy Milligan.

Welcome Back Mr. Fox **1983** An award-winning science fiction short wherein an obnoxious movie producer cheats death by being cryogenically frozen, and then wakes up years later no wiser for the experience. Suitably, he receives his comeuppance. **21m/C VHS.** E.D. Phillips, Gustav Vintas; ***D:*** Walter W. Pitt III.

Welcome Home ✓✓ **1989 (R)** A missing-in-action Vietnam vet (Kristofferson) leaves his wife and children in Cambodia to return to America more than 15 years after he was reported dead. He finds his first wife remarried and discovers a teenaged son he unknowingly fathered. This plotless, sporadically moving film was Schaffner's last. **92m/C VHS.** Kris Kristofferson, JoBeth Williams, Sam Waterston, Brian Keith, Trey Wilson, Thomas Wilson Brown; ***D:*** Franklin J. Schaffner; ***C:*** Fred W. Koenekamp; ***M:*** Henry Mancini. CABLE

Welcome Home, Roxy Carmichael ✓✓ **1990 (PG-13)** Ryder, as a young misfit, is the bright spot in this deadpan, would-be satire. Hollywood star Roxy Charmichael returns to her small Ohio hometown and begins fantasizing that she is really her mother. It is obvious why this deadpan, hard-to-follow movie was a boxoffice flop. **98m/C VHS, 8mm.** Winona Ryder, Jeff Daniels, Laila Robins, Dinah Manoff, Ava Fabian, Robbie Kiger, Sachi (MacLaine) Parker; ***D:*** Jim Abrahams; ***C:*** Paul Elliott.

Welcome Stranger ✓✓½ **1947** New doctor's ideas clash with the old doctor's ways in a small town until the younger saves the live of the elder. Crosby and Fitzgerald star as the two clashing medics in this reunion of the cast of "Going My Way." He wins the heart of the town and the heart of local teacher Caulfield in the meantime. Sheekman's script calls for Marx Brothers'-like comedy and director Nugent appears in a cameo as another doctor. **107m/B VHS.** Bing Crosby, Barry Fitzgerald, Joan Caulfield, Wanda Hendrix, Frank Faylen, Elizabeth Patterson, Robert Shayne, Don Beddoe, Percy Kilbride, Larry Young; ***Cameos:*** Elliott Nugent; ***D:*** Elliott Nugent; ***W:*** Arthur Sheekman; ***C:*** Lionel Lindon; ***M:*** Johnny Burke, James Van Heusen.

Welcome to Blood City ✓½ **1977** An anonymous totalitarian organization kidnaps a man and transports him electronically to a fantasy western town where the person who murders the most people becomes the town's "kill master." Amateurish and low-budget. **96m/C VHS.** Jack Palance, Keir Dullea, Samantha Eggar, Barry Morse.

Welcome to 18 ✓ **1987 (PG-13)** Three girls, just out of high school, take summer jobs at a dude ranch, work a local casino, flirt, tease and get in trouble. The movie isn't funny in the least, and is filled with utter nonsense. Hargitay is the daughter of actress Jayne Mansfield. **91m/C VHS.** Courtney Thorne-Smith, Mariska Hargitay, Jo Ann Willette, Christine Kaufmann; ***D:*** Terry Carr.

Welcome to L.A. ✓✓✓ **1977 (R)** Rudolph's ambitious directorial debut focuses on the sexual escapades of a group of Southern Californians. Based on the music suite "City of the One Night Stands" by Baskin, which also (unfortunately) serves as the soundtrack. Rudolph improved greatly after this initial effort. **106m/C VHS.** Sissy Spacek, Sally Kellerman, Keith Carradine, Geraldine Chaplin, Lauren Hutton, Viveca Lindfors, Harvey Keitel, John Considine; ***D:*** Alan Rudolph; ***W:*** Alan Rudolph; ***M:*** Richard Baskin.

Welcome to Sarajevo ✓✓✓½ **1997 (R)** Fresh, unusual take on the siege of Sarajevo in 1992. A group of news correspondents, including British reporter Michael Henderson (Dillane), find themselves in the middle of the siege, and become disillusioned when the conflict is largely ignored by the rest of the world. Film sheds perspective when a particularly bloody massacre takes a backseat to the marital troubles of the royal family. Henderson becomes personally involved when his daily coverage of an orphanage sparks him to become a hero to the orphaned Emily (Sarajevan actress Nusevic). Intermingling actual news footage, Winterbottom shows the violence on a personal level. Solid supporting characters include Harrelson as the wonderfully egotistic American celeb journalist. Strong emotional content is tempered by the smart and savvy gallows humor, which keeps melodrama miles away. Loosely based on a true story by ITN reporter, Michael Nicholson. **102m/C VHS, Wide.** Stephen (Dillon) Dillane, Woody Harrelson, Marisa Tomei, Kerry Fox, Emily Lloyd, Goran Visnjic, Juliet Aubrey, Emira Nusevic, James Nesbitt, Igor Dzambazov, Gordana Gadzic, Drazen Sivak, Vesna Orel; ***D:*** Michael Winterbottom; ***W:*** Frank Cottrell-Boyce; ***C:*** Daf Hobson; ***M:*** Adrian Johnston.

Welcome to Spring Break ✓½ **1988 (R)** College co-eds are stalked by a killer on the beaches of Florida. **92m/C VHS.** John Saxon, Michael Parks.

Welcome to the Dollhouse ✓✓½ **1995 (R)** Eleven-year-old, glasses-wearing Dawn Wiener (Matarazzo) is the middle child of a middle-class family in an average New Jersey town. It's her first year in junior high and Dawn's bewildered—by school, by family, by life in general, and where she fits in. Puberty sucks. **87m/C VHS, DVD.** Heather Matarazzo, Brendan Sexton III, Daria Kalinina, Matthew Faber, Angela Pietropinto, Eric Mabius; ***D:*** Todd Solondz; ***W:*** Todd Solondz; ***C:*** Randy Drummond; ***M:*** Jill Wisoff. Ind. Spirit '97: Debut Perf. (Matarazzo); Sundance '96: Grand Jury Prize.

Welcome II the Terrordome ✓½ **1995 (R)** Yet another future apocalypse. Terrordome is a city collapsing under pollution, filled with corrupt police, where blacks are confined to ghettos with rampant gang violence and drugs. Spike's young nephew is killed in a police raid and his sister goes on a shooting spree, which draws more rage and has Spike being forced to choose between his homies and his preggers white girlfriend. **98m/C VHS, DVD.** *GB* Saffron Burrows, Valentine Nonyela, Suzette Llewellyn, Felix Joseph; ***D:*** Ngozi Onwurah; ***W:*** Ngozi Onwurah.

Welcome to Woop Woop ✓½ **1997 (R)** Hit-or-miss (mostly miss) comedy about a con man meeting his match in a small Australian town of redneck eccentrics. On the lam, Teddy (Schaech) nevertheless offers a ride to buxom blonde Angie (Porter), whom he meets at a gas station. The next thing he knows (having been drugged), Teddy wakes up in the nightmarish community of Woop Woop, where Angie announces they've gotten married. And Angie's violent father, Daddy-O (Taylor), makes it clear his new son-in-law has no chance of making it out alive. Based on the book "The Dead Heart" by Douglas Kennedy. **97m/C VHS.** *AU* Johnathon Schaech, Rod Taylor, Susie Porter, Dee Smart, Richard Moir, Rachel Griffiths, Barry Humphries; ***D:*** Stephan Elliott; ***W:*** Michael Thomas; ***C:*** Mike Molloy; ***M:*** Stewart Copeland.

The Well ✓✓✓ **1951** A young black girl disappears and a white man (Morgan) is accused of kidnapping her. When it is discovered that the girl is trapped in a deep well, Morgan's expertise is needed to help free her. **85m/B VHS.** Richard Rober, Harry (Henry) Morgan, Barry Kelley, Christine Larson; ***D:*** Leo Popkin, Russell Rouse; ***C:*** Ernest Laszlo.

The Well ✓✓ **1997** Repression, isolation, and tragedy set in barren rural Australia. Drab, middleaged Hester (Rabe) hires spirited teenager Katherine (Otto) to help out on her bleak farm. Hester soon becomes emotional dependent on Katherine, who eventually convinces her to sell the property so they can travel to Europe. (Yes, "The Servant" will come to mind.) But a car accident (caused by Katherine) claims the life of a mystery man and Hester decides to hide the body in an unused well. Then they discover all their money has been stolen, probably by their dead friend, and just who's going down the well to retrieve it? Based on a novel by Elizabeth Jolley. **101m/C VHS, DVD.** *AU* Pamela Rabe, Miranda Otto, Paul Chubb; ***D:*** Samantha Lang; ***W:*** Laura Jones; ***C:*** Mandy Walker; ***M:*** Stephen Rae. Australian Film Inst. '97: Actress (Rabe), Adapt. Screenplay, Art Dir./Set Dec.

Well-Digger's Daughter ☙☙☙ *La Fille Du Puisatier* **1946** As her lover goes off to war, a well-digger's daughter discovers that she is pregnant causing both sets of parents to feud over who's to blame. This is the first film made in France after the end of WWII and marks the return of the French film industry. In French with English subtitles. **142m/B VHS.** *FR* Raimu, Josette Day, Fernandel, Charpin; ***D:*** Marcel Pagnol.

We'll Meet Again ☙☙½ **1982** Cliched but touching miniseries set in a quiet English town in 1943. At least the town was quiet until the arrival of a bomber group from the U.S. Army Eighth Air Force. Soon the Yanks are chasing the local girls and getting into trouble while their commander (Shannon) finds himself falling for a married doctor (York). **690m/C VHS, DVD.** *GB* Michael J. Shannon, Susannah York, Ronald Hines, Ed Devereaux, Christopher Malcolm, Patrick O'Connell, Joris Stuyck; ***D:*** Christopher Hodson. **TV**

Wend Kuuni ☙☙ *God's Gift* **1982** A fable for modern times set in Burkina Faso before the coming of Islam or Christianity. A mute, memoryless child is found by a peddler and adopted by the peddler's village. One day the boy finds a body hanging from a tree. Shocked, he recovers his speech and tells the story of his tragic past, when he and his mother were cast out of their own village. When his mother dies, the boy is bereft of family and tradition. Without these ties to his history he loses both speech and memory. In More with English subtitles. **70m/C VHS.** ***D:*** Gaston Kabore.

Went to Coney Island on a Mission from God...Be Back by Five ☙☙ **1998 (R)** Daniel (Cryer), Stan (Stear), and Richie (Baez) were all best neighborhood friends while growing up in Brooklyn. Now it's years later and Stan and Daniel have lost touch with Richie, whom they hear is a mentally-ill vagrant living under the boardwalk at Coney Island. So they decide to ditch their boring lives and track him down. Flashbacks to earlier incidents get confusing if not tedious. **94m/C VHS, DVD.** Jon Cryer, Rick Stear, Rafael Baez, Ione Skye, Frank Whaley, Peter Gerety, Akili Prince, Aesha Waks, Dominic Chianese; ***D:*** Richard Schenkman; ***W:*** Richard Schenkman, Jon Cryer; ***C:*** Adam Beekman; ***M:*** Midge Ure.

We're Back! A Dinosaur's Story ☙☙½ **1993 (G)** Animated adventures of a pack of revived dinosaurs who return to their old stomping grounds—which are now modern-day New York City. Smart-mouth human boy Louie and his girlfriend Cecilia take the dinos under their wing (so to speak), wise them up to modern life, and try to prevent their capture by the evil Professor Screweyes. Slow-moving with some violence. Adapted from the book by Hudson Talbott. **78m/C VHS.** ***D:*** Dick Zondag, Ralph Zondag, Phil Nibbelink, Simon Wells; ***W:*** John Patrick Shanley; ***V:*** John Goodman, Felicity Kendal, Walter Cronkite, Joey Shea, Jay Leno, Julia Child, Kenneth Mars, Martin Short, Rhea Perlman, Rene LeVant, Blaze Berdahl, Charles Fleischer, Yeardley Smith.

We're in the Legion Now ☙½ **1937** Denny and Barnett star as a couple of American gangsters who join the French Foreign Legion to escape rival hoods from back home. **56m/B VHS, 8mm.** Reginald Denny, Vince Barnett, Esther Ralston.

We're in the Navy Now **1927** The famed comedy duo is back again with another armed forces farce. A mild successor to "Behind the Front." **60m/B VHS.** Wallace Beery, Raymond Hatton.

We're No Angels ☙☙½ **1955** Three escapees from Devil's Island hide out with the family of a kindly French storekeeper on Christmas Eve. Planning to rob the family, they end up helping them with various financial, romantic, and familial problems. Somewhat stagey, but great dialogue and excellent cast make for enjoyable holiday fare. One of Bogart's few comedies. From the French stage play of the same name, later remade with De Niro and Penn. **103m/C VHS.** Humphrey Bogart, Aldo Ray, Joan Bennett, Peter Ustinov, Basil Rathbone, Leo G. Carroll, Lea Penman, John Smith, Gloria Talbott, John Baer; ***D:*** Michael Curtiz; ***W:*** Ranald MacDougall; ***C:*** Loyal Griggs; ***M:*** Frederick "Friedrich" Hollander.

We're No Angels ☙☙½ **1989 (R)** Two escaped cons disguise themselves as priests and get in the appropriate series of jams. De Niro and Penn play off each other well, turning in fine comic performances. Distantly related to the 1955 film of the same name and the David Mamet play. **110m/C VHS.** Robert De Niro, Sean Penn, Demi Moore, Hoyt Axton, Bruno Kirby, James Russo, John C. Reilly, Ray McAnally, Wallace Shawn; ***D:*** Neil Jordan; ***W:*** David Mamet; ***C:*** Philippe Rousselot; ***M:*** George Fenton.

We're Not Dressing ☙☙☙ **1934** Loose musical adaptation of J.M. Barrie's "The Admirable Crichton" with the butler transformed into singing sailor Crosby. Fabulously wealthy heiress Lombard invites her pals for a South Seas yachting adventure. Only the ship gets wrecked and everyone winds up on a small island where the practical Crosby whips everyone into shape (and romances Lombard). Burns and Allen supply additional comedy as a pair of botanists who just happen to be studying the local fauna. ♫Good Night Lovely Little Lady; I'll Sing About the Birds and the Bees; It's Just a New Spanish Custom; Let's Play House; Love Thy Neighbor; May I?; Once in a Blue Moon; She Reminds Me of You. **74m/B VHS.** Bing Crosby, Carole Lombard, George Burns, Gracie Allen, Ethel Merman, Leon Errol, Ray Milland; ***D:*** Norman Taurog; ***W:*** Horace Jackson, Francis Martin; ***M:*** Harry Revel, Mack Gordon.

We're Not Married ☙☙☙ **1952** Five couples learn that they are not legally married when a judge realizes his license expired before he performed the ceremonies. The story revolves around this quintet of couples who now must cope with whether or not they really do want to be married. Although the episodes vary in quality, the Allen-Rogers sequence is excellent. Overall, the cast performs well in this lightweight comedy. **85m/B VHS.** Ginger Rogers, Fred Allen, Victor Moore, Marilyn Monroe, Paul Douglas, David Wayne, Eve Arden, Louis Calhern, Zsa Zsa Gabor, James Gleason, Jane Darwell, Eddie Bracken, Mitzi Gaynor; ***D:*** Edmund Goulding; ***W:*** Nunnally Johnson, Dwight Taylor.

We're Talkin' Serious Money ☙☙½ **1992 (PG-13)** Sal and Charlie are a couple of loser scam-artists always after the elusive big score. They borrow $10,000 from the mob for another get-rich-quick scheme and wind up over their heads with both the mob and the FBI out to get them. **92m/C VHS.** Dennis Farina, Leo Rossi, Fran Drescher, John Lamotta; ***D:*** James (Momel) Lemmo; ***W:*** Leo Rossi, James (Momel) Lemmo; ***M:*** Scott Grusin.

Werewolf ☙ **1995 (R)** A remote desert town is stricken by an ancient curse that turns its occupants into werewolves at the full moon. This doesn't help the tourism industry. **99m/C VHS, DVD.** Jorge (George) Rivero, Fred Cavalli, Adrianna Miles, Richard Lynch, Joe Estevez, R.C. Bates, Heidi Bjorn, Randall Oliver, Nena Belini, Tony Zarindast; ***D:*** Tony Zarindast; ***W:*** Tony Zarindast; ***C:*** Robert Hayes, Dan Gilman.

Werewolf in a Girl's Dormitory ☙ *Lycanthropus; The Ghoul in School* **1961** Girls' school headmaster undergoes dental transformation at night. Atrocious dubbing, with equally atrocious theme song "The Ghoul in School." **82m/B VHS.** *IT* Barbara Lass, Carl Schell, Curt Lowens, Maurice Marsac; ***D:*** Richard Benson.

Werewolf of London ☙☙½ **1935** A scientist searching for a rare Tibetan flower is attacked by a werewolf. He scoffs at the legend, but once he's back in London, he goes on a murderous rampage every time the moon is full. Dated but worth watching as the first werewolf movie made. **75m/B VHS, DVD.** Henry Hull, Warner Oland, Valerie Hobson, Lester Matthews, Spring Byington, Lawrence Grant, Zeffie Tilbury; ***D:*** Stuart Walker; ***W:*** Robert Harris, John Colton; ***C:*** Charles Stumar.

Werewolf of Washington ☙☙ **1973 (PG)** Stockwell is a White House press secretary with a problem—he turns into a werewolf. And bites the President, among others. Sub-plot involves a short mad scientist who operates a secret monster-making lab in a White House bathroom. Occasionally engaging horror spoof and political satire made during Watergate era. **90m/C VHS.** Dean Stockwell, Biff McGuire, Clifton James, Jane House, Beeson Carroll, Michael Dunn, Nancy Andrews, Stephen Cheng, Barbara Siegel; ***D:*** Milton Moses Ginsberg; ***W:*** Milton Moses Ginsberg; ***C:*** Robert M. "Bob" Baldwin Jr.; ***M:*** Arnold Freed.

The Werewolf vs. the Vampire Woman ☙½ *Shadow of the Werewolf; Blood Moon; Night of Walpurgis; La Noche de Walpurgis* **1970 (R)** Hirsute Spanish wolfman teams with two female students in search of witch's tomb. One is possessed by the witch, and eponymous title results. **82m/C VHS.** *SP GE* Paul (Jacinto Molina) Naschy, Jacinto (Jack) Molina, Gaby Fuchs, Barbara Capell, Patty (Patti) Shepard, Valerie Samarine, Julio Pena, Andres Resino; ***D:*** Leon Klimovsky; ***W:*** Jacinto (Jack) Molina; ***C:*** Leopoldo Villasenor; ***M:*** Anton Abril.

Werewolves on Wheels woof! **1971 (R)** A group of bikers are turned into werewolves due to a Satanic spell. A serious attempt at a biker/werewolf movie, however, too violent and grim, not at all funny, and painful to sit through. McGuire had a hit with "Eve of Destruction." **85m/C VHS.** Stephen Oliver, Severn Darden, D.J. Anderson, Duece Barry, Billy Gray, Barry McGuire; ***D:*** Michel Levesque.

Wes Craven Presents Mind Ripper ☙☙ *Mind Ripper* **1995 (R)** A top secret government experiment, intended to produce a superhuman, goes wrong and traps the scientists in a remote desert outpost with their deadly, pissed-off creation. **90m/C VHS.** Lance Henriksen, John Diehl, Natasha Gregson Wagner, Dan Blom, Claire Stansfield; ***D:*** Joe Gayton; ***W:*** Jonathan Craven, Phil Mittleman; ***C:*** Fernando Arguelles; ***M:*** J. Peter Robinson.

Wes Craven's New Nightmare ☙☙☙ *Nightmare on Elm Street 7* **1994 (R)** Seems the six previous conjurings of Freddy's tortured but fictional soul have inadvertently created a real supernatural force bent on tormenting the lives of retired scream queen Langenkamp, her son (Hughes), writer-director Craven, and surprisingly mild alter-ego Englund. Craven's solution is to write a script that reunites series principals for a final showdown with the slashmaster in Hell. Clever and original in a genre known for neither trait, this movie-in-a-movie-about-a-movie is equal parts playful gimmick and inspired terror that will give even the most seasoned Kruegerphile the heebie-jeebies. **112m/C VHS, DVD.** Robert Englund, Heather Langenkamp, Miko Hughes, David Newsom, Tracy Middendorf, Fran Bennett, John Saxon, Wes Craven, Robert Shaye, Sara Risher, Marianne Maddalena; ***D:*** Wes Craven; ***W:*** Wes Craven; ***C:*** Mark Irwin; ***M:*** J. Peter Robinson.

West Beirut ☙☙ *West Beyrouth* **1998** Muslim teenagers Tarek (Doueiri, the director's younger brother) and Omar (Chamas) and their new friend, the Christian May (Al Amin), live in an apartment complex in Muslim-controlled West Beirut in 1975. The date is significant since Muslim and Christian militias are battling for control of the Lebanese city and, since their school is closed, the teens have little better to do than to explore the forbidden. Arabic with subtitles. **105m/C VHS.** *FR* Rami Doueiri, Mohamad Chamas, Rola Al Amin, Leila Karam; ***D:*** Ziad Doueiri; ***W:*** Ziad Doueiri; ***C:*** Ricardo Jacques Gale; ***M:*** Stewart Copeland.

West-Bound Limited ☙☙½ **1923** A Romantic adventurer rescues a girl from certain death as a train is about to hit her, and the two fall in love. Lucky for him, she happens to be the boss' daughter. This film is a good example of classic silent melodrama with music score. **70m/B VHS.** John Harron, Ella Hall, Claire McDowell.

West Is West ☙☙ **1987** Vikram arrives in San Francisco from Bombay to attend university and discovers that his sponser has returned to India. With little money, he gets a room in a seedy hotel run by an Indian immigrant, who also gives Vikram a menial job. As he begins to explore the city Vikram meets arty punk Sue, but with his visa running out and the INS ready to deport him, Vikram needs to convince Sue to a green card marriage. **80m/C VHS.** Ashutosh Gowariker, Heidi Carpenter, Pearl Padamsee; ***D:*** David Rathod; ***W:*** David Rathod; ***C:*** Christopher Tufty.

West New York ☙☙ **1996 (R)** Ex-cop Tom Coletti (Vincent) has a job in Jersey, disposing of old bank bonds. He comes up with a scheme to skim some of the bonds but the news leaks to the local mob boss, Carmine (Pastore). He's unhappy he's not being cut in and decides to put out a hit to show his displeasure, so Coletti has to get to him first. **90m/C VHS, DVD.** Frank Vincent, Vincent Pastore, Victor Colicchio, Brian Burke, Gian DiDonna, Gloria Darpino, Brian McCormick; ***D:*** Phil Gallo.

West of Nevada ☙☙ **1936** A rare film, featuring the former Lieutenant Governor of Nevada (and Clara Bow's husband) in a fast-moving adventure about a band of Indians who must protect their gold from thieves. Bell is the good guy who aids the Indians. **59m/B VHS.** Rex Bell, Joan Barclay, Al "Fuzzy" St. John, Steve Clark.

West of Pinto Basin ☙☙ **1940** The Range Busters are riding around checking the territory for badmen in this tale of the old west. The music score includes "That Little Prairie Gal of Mine," "Rhythm of the Saddle," and "Ridin' the Trail Tonight." **60m/B VHS.** Ray Corrigan, Max Terhune, John "Dusty" King, Jack Perrin.

West of the Divide ☙☙½ **1933** A young cowboy (Wayne) impersonates an outlaw in order to hunt down his father's killer and find his missing younger brother. He saves a proud rancher and his feisty daughter along the way. A remake of "Partners of the Trail," and a solid early Wayne oater. **53m/B VHS, DVD.** John Wayne, George "Gabby" Hayes, Lloyd Whitlock, Yakima Canutt; ***D:*** Robert North Bradbury; ***W:*** Robert North Bradbury; ***C:*** Archie Stout.

West of the Law ☙☙ **1942** A group of ranchers turn to lawmen for protection from a band of outlaws. Part of the Rough Riders series. **60m/B VHS.** Buck Jones, Tim McCoy, Raymond Hatton; ***D:*** Howard Bretherton.

West of the Pecos ☙☙½ **1945** Rill (Hale) is a society gal on her way to the family ranch in Texas. She's disguised as a boy for safety, which turns out to be a smart idea when outlaws attack the stagecoach. Fortunately, Pecos Smith (Mitchum) is also around to lend a hand. Based on the novel by Zane Grey; first filmed in 1935. **66m/B VHS.** Robert Mitchum, Barbara Hale, Richard Martin, Thurston Hall, Rita (Paula) Corday, Russell Hopton, Harry Woods; ***D:*** Edward Killy; ***C:*** Russell Metty.

West of Zanzibar ☙☙½ **1928** Chaney plays an ivory trader, ruling a jungle kingdom, who lives for revenge on the man who left him a cripple. He decides to ruin the man's daughter and turn her into a prostitute but his plan backfires. Chaney and director Browning offer a steamy atmosphere amidst a number of script flaws. **63m/B VHS.** Lon Chaney Sr., Lionel Barrymore, Warner Baxter, Mary Nolan; ***D:*** Tod Browning.

The West Point Story ☙☙½ *Fine and Dandy* **1950** Cagney stars as an on-the-skids Broadway director offered a job staging a show at West Point. Seems cadet MacRae has written a musical and his uncle happens to be a producer. Cagney, with girlfriend Mayo, finds all the rules and regulations getting the better of his temper, so much so that he's told unless he can conform to academy standards the show won't go on! Day is the showgirl MacRae falls for. Cagney's energy and charm carry the too-long film but it's not one of his better musical efforts. ♫Ten Thousand Sheep; You Love Me; By the Kissing Rock; Long Before I Knew You; Brooklyn; It Could Only Happen in Brooklyn; Military Polka. **107m/B VHS.** James Cagney, Virginia Mayo, Gordon MacRae, Doris Day, Roland Winters, Gene Nelson, Alan Hale Jr., Wilton Graff, Jerome Cowan; ***D:*** Roy Del Ruth; ***W:*** John Monks Jr., Charles Hoffman, Irving Wallace; ***M:*** Sammy Cahn, Jule Styne.

West Side Story 🦴🦴🦴½ **1961** Gang rivalry and ethnic tension on New York's West Side erupts in a ground-breaking musical. Loosely based on Shakespeare's "Romeo and Juliet," the story follows the Jets and the Sharks as they fight for their turf while Tony and Maria fight for love. Features frenetic and brilliant choreography by co-director Robbins, who also directed the original Broadway show, and a high-caliber score by Bernstein and Sondheim. Wood's voice was dubbed by Marni Nixon and Jimmy Bryant dubbed Beymer's. ♫Prologue; Jet Song; Something's Coming; Dance at the Gym; Maria; America; Tonight; One Hand, One Heart; Gee, Officer Krupke. **151m/C VHS, DVD, Wide.** Yvonne Wilder, Natalie Wood, Richard Beymer, Russ Tamblyn, Rita Moreno, George Chakiris, Simon Oakland, Ned Glass; ***D:*** Robert Wise, Jerome Robbins; ***W:*** Ernest Lehman; ***C:*** Daniel F. Fapp; ***M:*** Leonard Bernstein, Stephen Sondheim. Oscars '61: Art Dir./Set Dec., Color, Color Cinematog., Costume Des. (C), Director (Wise), Film Editing, Picture, Sound, Support. Actor (Chakiris), Support. Actress (Moreno), Scoring/Musical; AFI '98: Top 100; Directors Guild '61: Director (Wise), Director (Robbins); Golden Globes '62: Film—Mus./Comedy, Support. Actor (Chakiris), Support. Actress (Moreno), Natl. Film Reg. '97;; N.Y. Film Critics '61: Film.

West to Glory 🦴½ **1947** Glory isn't necessarily exciting, as the hero helps a Mexican rancher save his gold and jewels from evildoers in this slow-paced oater. **61m/B VHS.** Eddie Dean, Roscoe Ates, Dolores Castle, Gregg Barton, Alex Montoya, Harry Vejar; ***D:*** Ray Taylor.

Western 🦴🦴 **1996** Spaniard Paco (Lopez), a traveling rep for a shoe manufacturer in France, picks up hitchhiking Russian emigre Nino (Bourdo) and soon finds himself minus car, shoe samples, and luggage. He's rescued by local beauty Marinette (Vitali) and, since he's been fired, decides to hang around the town where she lives. But when Paco spots Nino again, he promptly beats him up, sending the Russian to the hospital. Oddly, this serves as a bond for the two men and they decide to do a little traveling through Brittany together, with Paco trying to teach the naive Nino how to pick up pretty girls. Funny, if extended, French road trip. French with subtitles. **136m/C VHS.** *FR* Sergei Lopez, Sacha Bourdo, Elisabeth Vitali, Marie Matheron, Basile Siekoua; ***D:*** Manuel Poirier; ***W:*** Jean-Francois Goyet, Manuel Poirier; ***C:*** Nara Keo Kosal; ***M:*** Bernardo Sandoval. Cannes '97: Special Jury Prize.

Western Frontier 🦴🦴 **1935** Ordinary cowpoke Maynard is called on to lead the fight against a band of outlaws led by the Indian-raised sister he never knew he had. Action-packed, fast, and fun. Maynard's first outing for Columbia. **56m/B VHS.** Ken Maynard, Lucille Browne, Nora Lane, Robert "Buzzy" Henry, Frank Yaconelli; ***D:*** Al(bert) Herman.

Western Gold **1937** Western set during the Civil War in which the character played by Smith Ballew is sent west to stop thieves who are stealing gold from the Union. **57m/C VHS.** Smith Ballew, Heather Angel, Leroy Mason, Howard Hickman, Ben Alexander, Frank McGlynn, Otis Harlan, Tom London, Bud Osborne; ***D:*** Howard Bretherton.

Western Justice 🦴🦴 **1935** Good Guy Steele brings western-style justice to a lawless town. Ordinary oater with horses, etc., and a few chuckles on the side. **56m/B VHS.** Bob Steele; ***D:*** Robert North Bradbury.

Western Mail 🦴🦴 **1942** Yet another western in which the hero goes undercover so he can bring the bad guys to justice. Yaconelli plays a guitar tune, accompanied by his monkey. **54m/B VHS.** Tom (George Duryea) Keene, Frank Yaconelli, Leroy Mason, Jean Trent, Fred Kohler Jr.; ***D:*** Robert Emmett Tansey.

Western Pacific Agent 🦴🦴 **1951** A Western Pacific agent chases an outlaw who has committed robbery and murder. The agent falls in love with the victim's sister and, of course, prevails. Rather violent. **62m/B VHS.** Kent Taylor, Sheila Ryan, Mickey Knox, Robert Lowery; ***D:*** Sam Newfield; ***Nar:*** Jason Robards Sr.

Western Trails 🦴 **1938** Forgettable western about the clean-up of a Wild West town terrorized by outlaws. Thin script, bad acting, and a little singin' and funnin' around. **59m/B VHS.** Bob Baker, Marjorie Reynolds, Robert Burns; ***D:*** George Waggner.

Western Union 🦴🦴🦴½ **1941** A lavish, vintage epic romantically detailing the political machinations, Indian warfare, and frontier adventure that accompanied the construction of the Western Union telegraph line from Omaha, Nebraska, to Salt Lake City, Utah, during the Civil War. A thoroughly entertaining film in rich Technicolor. This was Lang's second western, following his personal favorite, "The Return of Frank James." Writer Carson utilized the title, but not the storyline, of a Zane Grey book. The German Lang showed himself a master of the most American of genres, yet made only one more western, "Rancho Notorious" (1952), another masterpiece. **94m/C VHS.** Randolph Scott, Robert Young, Dean Jagger, Slim Summerville, Virginia Gilmore, John Carradine, Chill Wills, Barton MacLane, Minor Watson, Charles Middleton, Irving Bacon; ***D:*** Fritz Lang.

The Westerner 🦴🦴🦴½ **1940** Cooper stars as Cole Hardin, a sly, soft-spoken drifter who champions Texas border homesteaders in a land war with the legendary Judge Roy Bean (Brennan). Known as "The Law West of the Pecos," Bean sentences Hardin hang as a horse thief, but he breaks out of jail. Hardin then falls for damsel Jane-Ellen (Davenport) and stays in the area, advocating the rights of homesteaders, and has to have a final confrontation with the judge. Brennan's Bean is unforgettable and steals the show from Cooper. Film debuts of actors Tucker and Andrews. Amazing cinematography; Brennan's Oscar was his third, making him the first performer to pull a hat trick. **100m/B VHS, DVD.** Gary Cooper, Walter Brennan, Doris Davenport, Fred Stone, Chill Wills, Dana Andrews, Forrest Tucker, Charles Halton, Lupita Tovar, Tom Tyler, Lillian Bond; ***D:*** William Wyler; ***W:*** Jo Swerling, Niven Busch; ***C:*** Gregg Toland; ***M:*** Dimitri Tiomkin. Oscars '40: Support. Actor (Brennan).

Westfront 1918 🦴🦴🦴 **1930** A dogmatic anti-war film by the German master (his first talkie), about German and French soldiers on the fields of WWI, dying together without victory. Stunning in its portrayal of war's futility, with excellent photography that achieves a palpable realism. In German with English subtitles. **90m/B VHS.** *GE* Gustav Diesl, Fritz Kampers, Claus Clausen, Hans Joachim Moebis; ***D:*** G.W. Pabst.

Westler: East of the Wall 🦴🦴 **1985** West Berliner Felix takes a day trip to East Berlin and falls in love with Thomas. Their time together is frustrating since Felix must return before the midnight curfew and the border guards become suspicious of his frequent trips. Eventually, Felix and Thomas decide that Thomas must escape to the west. German with subtitles. **94m/C VHS.** *GE* Sigurd Rachman, Rainer Strecker, Sasha Kogo, Andy Lucas; ***D:*** Wieland Speck; ***W:*** Wieland Speck; ***C:*** Klemens Becker; ***M:*** Engelbert Rehm.

Westward Ho 🦴½ **1935** Wayne is determined to bring to justice his parents' slayer. Haven't we seen this one before? Seems the bad guys have corrupted his brother. Wayne's group of vigilantes is called "The Singing Riders," so naturally he sings—or is made to appear to. He looks and sounds ridiculous. **55m/B VHS.** John Wayne, Sheila (Manors) Mannors; ***D:*** Robert North Bradbury.

Westward Ho, the Wagons! 🦴½ **1956** The promised land lies in the west, but to get there these pioneers must pass unfriendly savages, thieves, villains, and scoundrels galore. Suitable for family viewing, but why bother? Well, the cast does include four Mouseketeers. **94m/B VHS.** Fess Parker, Kathleen Crowley, Jeff York, Sebastian Cabot, George Reeves; ***D:*** William Beaudine; ***M:*** George Bruns.

Westward the Women 🦴🦴🦴 **1951** Buck Wyatt (Taylor) is a scout hired to wagon-train 150 mail-order brides from Chicago to California. When his lustful hired hands turn out to be all hands, Buck and the ladies must fight off attacking Indians on their own. Notable film allowing women to be as tough as men is not your typical western. Based on the Frank Capra story. **116m/C VHS.** Robert Taylor, Denise Darcel, Hope Emerson, John McIntire, Beverly Dennis, Lenore Lonergan, Marilyn Erskine, Julie (Jacqueline Wells) Bishop, Renata Vanni, Frankie Darro, George Chandler; ***D:*** William A. Wellman; ***W:*** Charles Schnee; ***C:*** William Mellor; ***M:*** Jeff Alexander.

Westworld 🦴🦴🦴 **1973 (PG)** Crichton wrote and directed this story of an adult vacation resort of the future which offers the opportunity to live in various fantasy worlds serviced by lifelike robots. Brolin and Benjamin are businessmen who choose a western fantasy world. When an electrical malfunction occurs, the robots begin to go berserk. Brynner is perfect as a western gunslinging robot whose skills are all too real. **90m/C VHS, DVD, Wide.** Yul Brynner, Richard Benjamin, James Brolin, Dick Van Patten, Majel Barrett; ***D:*** Michael Crichton; ***W:*** Michael Crichton; ***C:*** Gene Polito; ***M:*** Fred Karlin.

Wet and Wild Summer woof! **1992 (R)** Topless beach resort is the playground for stud lifeguards and sexy resort owners. **95m/C VHS.** Christopher Atkins, Elliott Gould, Julian McMahon, Rebecca Cross; ***D:*** Maurice Murphy.

Wet Gold 🦴 **1984** A beautiful young woman and three men journey to retrieve a sunken treasure. Nice scenery. Proves that it is possible to make "The Treasure of the Sierra Madre" without making a classic. John Huston, where are you? **90m/C VHS.** Brooke Shields, Brian Kerwin, Burgess Meredith, Tom Byrd; ***D:*** Dick Lowry. **TV**

Wet Hot American Summer 🦴🦴🦴 **2001 (R)** Send-up of late 70s/early 80s camp flicks like "Meatballs" and "Little Darlings" focuses on the counselors trying to get laid and/or stoned on the last weekend of a Maine summer camp in 1981 while the youngsters in their charge are thrown around like chew toys. Beth (Garofalo) is the camp director with the hots for an astrophysicist (Pierce) who finds that the camp is in danger of being crushed by Skylab. The plot also involves many other cast members trying to sleep with many other cast members, but to detail more of the story would take crucial print space away from the genius that is the Vietnam vet camp cook (Meloni), whose spiritual advisor is a can of mixed vegetables. Take that whatever way you want, but trust us, you really have to see it to believe it. **97m/C VHS, DVD, Wide.** *US* Janeane Garofalo, David Hyde Pierce, Michael Showalter, Marguerite Moreau, Paul Rudd, Zak Orth, Christopher Meloni, A.D. Miles, Molly Shannon, Ken Marino, Michael Ian Black, Marisa Ryan, Bradley Cooper; ***D:*** David Wain; ***W:*** Michael Showalter, David Wain; ***C:*** Ben Weinstein; ***M:*** Theodore Shapiro, Craig (Shudder to Think) Wedren.

Wetbacks 🦴🦴 **1956** Fishing boat skipper Jim Benson (Bridges) agrees to help the U.S. Immigration Department nab smugglers who want to use Benson's vessel to carry illegal immigrants from Mexico into the U.S. **89m/C VHS.** Lloyd Bridges, Nancy Gates, Barton MacLane, John Hoyt, Harold (Hal) Peary, Nacho Galindo; ***D:*** Hank McCune; ***W:*** Pete LaRoche; ***C:*** Brydon Baker; ***M:*** Les Baxter.

Wetherby 🦴🦴🦴 **1985 (R)** Playwright David Hare's first directorial effort, which he also wrote, about a Yorkshire schoolteacher whose life is shattered when a young, brooding stranger comes uninvited to a dinner party, and then shoots himself in her living room. Compelling but oh, so dark. Richardson, who plays a young Redgrave, is actually Redgrave's daughter. **97m/C VHS.** *GB* Vanessa Redgrave, Ian Holm, Judi Dench, Joely Richardson, Tim (McInnerny) McInnery, Suzanna Hamilton; ***D:*** David Hare; ***W:*** David Hare; ***M:*** Nick Bicat. Berlin Intl. Film Fest. '85: Golden Berlin Bear; Natl. Soc. Film Critics '85: Actress (Redgrave).

Whale for the Killing 🦴🦴½ **1981** An ecologist stranded in a remote Alaskan fishing village battles to save a beached humpbacked whale from a malicious Russian fisherman. Platitudinous and self-congratulatory, if well-meaning. From a book by Farley Mowat. **145m/C VHS.** Richard Widmark, Peter Strauss, Dee Wallace Stone, Bruce McGill, Kathryn Walker; ***D:*** Richard T. Heffron; ***M:*** Basil Poledouris. **TV**

Whale Music 🦴🦴 **1994** Off-beat saga of a burned-out rock star and the runaway who invades his life. Desmond Howl (Chaykin) has retreated to a tumble-down estate in the Pacific Northwest, tired of the music grind, and wanting to devote himself to his masterwork—a symphony for whales. Runaway Claire (Preston) provides a surprisingly welcome presence in contrast to Howl's other visitors—ex-wife Fay (Dale), who wants him to sell the estate, rapacious recording exec Kenneth (Welsh), and Howl's brother, singer Daniel (Gross), who happens to be dead and haunting his sibling. Haphazard direction helps dissipate powerful lead performances. Adapted from the novel by Paul Quarrington. **100m/C VHS.** *CA* Maury Chaykin, Cyndy Preston, Jennifer Dale, Kenneth Welsh, Paul Gross; ***D:*** Richard J. Lewis; ***W:*** Paul Quarrington, Richard J. Lewis; ***C:*** Vic Sarin; ***M:*** George Blondheim. Genie '94: Actor (Chaykin), Song ("Claire"), Sound.

Whale of a Tale 🦴 **1976 (G)** A young boy trains a killer whale to appear in the big show in the main tank at "Marineland." **90m/C VHS.** William Shatner, Marty Allen, Abby Dalton, Andy Devine, Nancy O'Conner; ***D:*** Ewing Miles Brown.

The Whales of August 🦴🦴🦴½ **1987** Based on the David Berry play, the story of two elderly sisters—one caring, the other cantankerous, blind, and possibly senile—who decide during a summer in Maine whether or not they should give up their ancestral house and enter a nursing home. Gish and Davis are exquisite to watch, and the all-star supporting cast is superb—especially Price as a suave Russian. Lovingly directed by Anderson in his first US outing. **91m/C VHS, 8mm.** Lillian Gish, Bette Davis, Vincent Price, Ann Sothern, Mary Steenburgen, Harry Carey Jr., Tisha Sterling, Margaret Ladd; ***D:*** Lindsay Anderson; ***W:*** David Berry; ***C:*** Mike Fash. Natl. Bd. of Review '87: Actress (Gish).

Wham-Bam, Thank You Spaceman 🦴½ **1975 (R)** Very silly stuff about aliens with fiberglass heads and balloon ears that inflate when they become excited. They transport themselves to Earth in a tiny set decorated with tinfoil where most of the action takes place. Their mission: to impregnate Earth women to save their race. Though the female nudity is abundant, the sexual action is pretty tame by today's standards. **79m/C DVD.** Jay Rasumny, Samuel Mann, Dyanne Thorne, Maria Arnold, Valda Hansen, Sandy Carey, John Ireland Jr.; ***D:*** William A. Levey; ***W:*** Shlomo D. Weinstein; ***C:*** David Platnik; ***M:*** Miles Goodman, David White.

The Wharf Rat **1995 (R)** Waterfront con man Petey Martin (Phillips) teams up with journalist Dexter Ireland (Ticotin) to avenge the murder of his policeman brother by a group of corrupt cops lead by the crazy Doc (Reinhold). **88m/C VHS.** Lou Diamond Phillips, Rachel Ticotin, Judge Reinhold, Rita Moreno, Scott Cohen; ***D:*** Jimmy Huston; ***W:*** Jimmy Huston; ***C:*** Levie Isaacks; ***M:*** Mervyn Warren. **CABLE**

What a Carve-Up! 🦴🦴 *No Place Like Homicide* **1962** A group of relatives gather in an old, spooky mansion to hear the reading of a will. Tries too hard. Remake of "The Ghoul." **87m/B VHS.** *GB* Kenneth Connor, Sidney James, Shirley Eaton, Donald Pleasence, Dennis Price, Michael Gough; ***D:*** Pat Jackson.

What a Way to Die 🦴½ **1970 (R)** An evil assassin plots dispatching with a difference. **87m/C VHS.** William Berger, Anthony Baker, Helga Anders, Georgia Moll; ***D:*** Helmut Foernbacher.

What a Woman! 🦴🦴½ *La Fortuna di Essere Donna; Lucky to Be a Woman* **1956** Shop girl Antonietta (Loren) becomes a star thanks to a sensational photo of her taken by a paparazzo (Mastroianni) that appears on the cover of a popular magazine. With the aid of a talent agent (Boyer), Antonietta becomes a famous fashion model. Only our photographer gets jealous when she ignores him for the debonair agent. **95m/B VHS.** *IT* Sophia Loren, Marcello Mastroianni, Charles Boyer, Elisa Cegan, Nino Besozzi; ***D:*** Alessandro Blasetti; ***W:*** Ennio Flaiano, Suso Cecchi D'Amico, Alessandro Continenza; ***C:*** Otello Martelli.

What about Bob? 🦴🦴🦴 **1991 (PG)** Bob, a ridiculously neurotic patient, follows his psychiatrist on vacation, turning his life upside down. The psychiatrist's family find Bob entertaining and endearing. Murray is at his comedic best; Dreyfuss's overly excitable characterization occasionally wears thin. **99m/C VHS, DVD, Wide.** Richard Dreyfuss, Bill Murray, Julie Hagerty, Charlie Korsmo, Tom Aldredge, Roger Bowen, Fran Brill, Kathryn Erbe, Doris Belack, Susan Willis; ***D:*** Frank Oz; ***W:*** Tom Schulman, Alvin Sargent; ***C:*** Michael Ballhaus; ***M:*** Miles Goodman.

What Comes Around 🦴🦴 **1985 (PG)** A good-ole-boy drama about a doped-up country singer who is kidnapped by his brother for his own good. The singer's evil manager sends his stooges out to find him. Might have been funny, but isn't. But is it meant to be? Good Reed songs; mildly interesting plot. **92m/C VHS.** Jerry Reed, Bo Hopkins, Arte Johnson, Barry Corbin; ***D:*** Jerry Reed.

What Did You Do in the War, Daddy? 🦴½ **1966** Unfunny comedy set in WWII about a group of weary American soldiers trying to get a small town in Sicily to surrender. Things don't go smoothly thanks to a combination soccer game/wine festival, not to mention the Germans deciding to attack. Director Edwards comedic verve deserted him. **119m/C VHS.** Dick Shawn, James Coburn, Sergio Fantoni, Giovanna Ralli, Aldo Ray, Harry (Henry) Morgan, Carroll O'Connor, Jay Novello, Vito Scotti; ***D:*** Blake Edwards; ***W:*** William Peter Blatty, Blake Edwards; ***M:*** Henry Mancini.

What Dreams May Come 🦴🦴 **1998 (PG-13)** Romantic idea and lushly colorful computer imagery combine with sappy dialogue to turn surreal fantasy into very average digital hocus-pocus. Dr. Chris Neilsen (Williams) and his artist-wife Annie (Sciorra) lose their two children to a traffic accident. Four years later the doctor himself is killed in a freak accident. He finds that his heaven is much like a painting done by his wife (or Monet or Van Gogh) of their dream cottage. Chris is just getting used to the "rules" when he learns that his wife has committed suicide, damning her to hell. Unable to accept eternal separation, he begins an odyssey to find her. For the first half hour, Williams alternates between a "Patch Adams" rehearsal and over-emoting into the tear-filled eyes of Sciorra. Very loosely adapted from a 20-year-old Richard Matheson novel. **113m/C VHS, DVD.** Rosalind Chao, Robin Williams, Annabella Sciorra, Cuba Gooding Jr., Max von Sydow, Jessica Brooks Grant, Josh Paddock; ***D:*** Vincent Ward; ***W:*** Ronald Bass; ***C:*** Eduardo Serra; ***M:*** Michael Kamen. Oscars '98: Visual FX.

What Ever Happened To... 🦴🦴½ **1993** Sisters play sisters as the Redgraves (in their first film together) tackle this remake of "What Ever Happened to Baby Jane?" in all its demented glory. Former actress Blanche (Vanessa) and former child star "Baby Jane" (Lynn) are living in a decaying mansion, which Blanche, confined to a wheelchair, is talking about selling. "Baby" snaps (not that she was ever very stable) and proceeds to torment her sis (now that's sibling rivalry!) **94m/C VHS.** Vanessa Redgrave, Lynn Redgrave, Bruce A. Young, Amy Steel, John Scott Clough, John Glover; ***D:*** David Greene; ***W:*** Brian Taggert.

What Ever Happened to Baby Jane? 🦴🦴🦴½ **1962** Davis and Crawford portray aging sisters and former child stars living together in a decaying mansion. When the demented Jane (Davis) learns of her now-crippled sister's (Crawford) plan to institutionalize her, she tortures the wheelchair-bound sis. Davis plays her part to the hilt, unafraid of Aldrich's unsympathetic camera, and the viciousness of her character. She received her 10th Oscar nomination for the role. **132m/B VHS, DVD, Wide.** Bette Davis, Joan Crawford, Victor Buono, Anna Lee, B.D. Merrill, Maidie Norman; ***D:*** Robert Aldrich; ***W:*** Lukas Heller; ***C:*** Ernest Haller; ***M:*** Frank DeVol.

What Happened to Rosa? 🦴🦴🦴 **1921** This early Goldwyn release, a whimsical Cinderella story, casts Normand as an endearing shop girl duped by a gypsy's bogus predictions. Believing herself to be the reincarnation of a Castillian noblewoman she dons a fancy gown, attends a fancy shipboard ball and captures the heart of the fancy doctor of her dreams. But fearing his rejection of her true identity she slips away during the chaos of a brawl, leading the good doctor to believe that she is dead. A comedy of errors unfolds before they meet again and live happily ever after. No doubt it jerked a few tears in its day. **42m/B VHS.** Mabel Normand, Hugh Thompson, Doris Pawn, Tully Marshall, Eugenie Besserer, Buster Trow; ***D:*** Victor Schertzinger.

What Happened Was... 🦴🦴 **1994 (R)** Two-character study about a weirdly nightmarish first date. Law secretary Jackie (Sillas) has been eyeing bookish paralegal Michael (Noonan) and finally invites him for dinner at her loft. The two struggle to relax and make small talk that turns into some unexpected soul baring. Emotionally distant Michael is unexpectedly hostile about his job and claims to be writing an expose of their law firm while overly friendly Jackie is writing a children's book, which turns out to be jarringly violent and apparently autobiographical. Provides an idiosyncratic, if limited, appeal thanks to a compelling performance by Sillas. **92m/C VHS.** Tom Noonan, Karen Sillas; ***D:*** Tom Noonan; ***W:*** Tom Noonan; ***C:*** Joe DeSalvo; ***M:*** Lodovico Sorret. Sundance '94: Screenplay, Grand Jury Prize.

What Have I Done to Deserve This? 🦴🦴🦴 *Que He Hecho Yo Para Merecer Esto!?* **1985** A savage parody on Spanish mores, about a speed-addicted housewife who ends up selling her son and killing her husband with a ham bone. Black, black comedy, perverse and funny as only Almodovar can be. In Spanish with subtitles. Nudity and profanity. **100m/C VHS.** Carmen Maura, Chus (Maria Jesus) Lampreave; ***D:*** Pedro Almodovar; ***W:*** Pedro Almodovar.

What Lies Beneath 🦴🦴 **2000 (PG-13)** Empty-nester Pfeiffer wanders around a seemingly haunted house suspecting neighbors of murder and finding out more about her scientist husband's past than she'd like. Zemeckis shoots for Hitchcockian suspense but manages mostly intermittent jolts and occasional wit. The "surprise" ending, telegraphed by the film's marketing campaign, has nothing to do with the film's first hour, which has everything to do with atmosphere and setting up distractions. **130m/C VHS, DVD, Wide.** Harrison Ford, Michelle Pfeiffer, Diana Scarwid, Joe Morton, James Remar, Miranda Otto, Amber Valletta, Katharine Towne, Victoria Birdwell; ***D:*** Robert Zemeckis; ***W:*** Clark Gregg; ***C:*** Don Burgess; ***M:*** Alan Silvestri.

What! No Beer? 🦴🦴 **1933** Two dim-bulb friends decide to put their money into a defunct brewery hoping for the end of Prohibition. They start up operations too soon and wind up attracting the unwelcome attentions of gangster bootleggers and the cops. Mediocre comedy and Keaton's last starring role as his own problems with alcohol affected his work. **66m/B VHS.** Buster Keaton, Jimmy Durante, Phyllis Barry, Roscoe Ates, John Miljan, Henry Armetta, Edward Brophy; ***D:*** Edward Sedgwick.

What Planet Are You From? 🦴🦴 **2000 (R)** Two jokes, no waiting! Shandling's feature film debut tries to be a comment on how differently men and women view sex and relationships, but it spends most of its time with a humming penis. Shandling is an alien sent from a planet of test tube people to impregnate an earth woman, once he's given the proper equipment (which has the previously mentioned unfortunate feature). He disguises himself as Harold, a bank executive, and gets dating tips from a philandering co-worker (Kinnear) who recommends AA meetings as a great pick-up place. His direct approach ("You smell nice") somehow attracts a recovering alcoholic (Bening) who's on the biological clock. The other joke (and better of the two) involves a hen-pecked FAA inspector who's suspicious of Harold's origins. Shandling's limited range is exposed, and the juvenile script doesn't do him any favors. **107m/C VHS, DVD, Wide.** Garry Shandling, Annette Bening, Greg Kinnear, Ben Kingsley, Linda Fiorentino, John Goodman, Richard Jenkins, Caroline Aaron, Judy Greer, Nora Dunn, Ann Cusack, Camryn Manheim, Janeane Garofalo; ***D:*** Mike Nichols; ***W:*** Garry Shandling, Michael Leeson, Edward Solomon, Peter Tolan; ***C:*** Michael Ballhaus; ***M:*** Carter Burwell.

What Price Glory? 🦴🦴🦴 **1952** Remake of the 1926 silent classic about a pair of comradely rivals for the affections of women in WWI France. Strange to have Ford directing an offbeat comedy, but it works: masterful direction, good acting. Demarest broke both legs in a motorcycle accident during shooting. **111m/C VHS.** James Cagney, Dan Dailey, Corinne Calvet, William Demarest, James Gleason, Robert Wagner, Max (Casey Adams) Showalter, Craig Hill, Marisa Pavan; ***D:*** John Ford.

What Price Hollywood? 🦴🦴🦴 **1932** Aspiring young starlet decides to crash film world by using an alcoholic director as her stepping stone. Bennett is lovely; Sherman is superb as an aging, dissolute man who watches his potential slip away. From a story by Adela Rogers St. Johns. Remade three times as "A Star is Born." **88m/B VHS.** Constance Bennett, Lowell Sherman, Neil Hamilton; ***D:*** George Cukor; ***C:*** Charles Rosher; ***M:*** Max Steiner.

What the Deaf Man Heard 🦴🦴🦴 **1998** Sly comedy starts off in the '40s with 10-year-old Sammy (Muniz) winding up alone in the small town of Barrington, Georgia after his single mother (Peters) vanishes. Since she told him to keep silent, Sammy continues to obey her—even when he's taken in by kindly bus station manager Norm (Skerritt). Soon everyone believes Sammy is deaf and mute and this doesn't change as Sammy grows to adulthood (Modine) as the local handyman. In fact, everyone is happy to confide in Sammy so he knows everyone's secrets—not always a happy situation. Based on the novel "What the Deaf-Mute Heard" by G.D. Gearino. **107m/C VHS, DVD.** Matthew Modine, Tom Skerritt, Judith Ivey, Claire Bloom, James Earl Jones, Jerry O'Connell, Anne Bobby, Stephen Spinella, Jake Weber, Bernadette Peters, Frankie Muniz; ***D:*** John Kent Harrison; ***W:*** Robert W. Lenski; ***C:*** Eric Van Haren Noman; ***M:*** J.A.C. Redford. **TV**

What the Moon Saw 🦴🦴½ **1990** When a young boy is confronted by a less than friendly theatre owner, he uses favorite scenes from "Sinbad" to deal with the aggressor. **86m/C VHS.** Pat Evison; ***D:*** Pino Amenta.

What the Peeper Saw 🦴🦴 *Night Hair Child; Child of the Night* **1972** The wife of a wealthy author finds her comfortable life turning into a terrifying nightmare when her young stepson starts acting funny. Juicy and terrifying. **97m/C VHS.** Britt Ekland, Mark Lester, Hardy Kruger, Lilli Palmer.

What Waits Below 🦴½ **1983 (PG)** A scientific expedition encounters a lost race living in caves in South America. Good cast, bad acting, and lousy script. Might have been much better. **88m/C VHS.** Dick Curtis, Timothy Bottoms, Robert Powell, Lisa Blount; ***D:*** Don Sharp.

What Women Want 🦴🦴½ **2000 (PG-13)** Male-chauvinist Gibson gets electrocuted in his bathroom and suddenly has the power to hear women's thoughts, which aren't very complimentary towards him. Gibson, obviously enjoying himself, shines in this intermittently funny, lightweight but enjoyable romantic comedy. Sublety and restraint are in short supply, but Gibson's performance, especially when he's doing his neo-Rat Pack act, makes up for the overindulgences. **123m/C VHS, DVD, Wide.** Mel Gibson, Helen Hunt, Marisa Tomei, Lauren Holly, Bette Midler, Mark Feuerstein, Ashley Johnson, Judy Greer, Alan Alda, Delta Burke, Valerie Perrine, Lisa Edelstein, Sarah Paulson, Ana Gasteyer, Loretta Devine; ***D:*** Nancy Meyers; ***W:*** Josh Goldsmith, Cathy Yuspa; ***C:*** Dean Cundey; ***M:*** Alan Silvestri.

What Your Eyes Don't See 🦴🦴 *Ojos Que No Ven* **1999** Abelardo Sachs is the owner/editor of a political magazine. He's murdered in his home by a masked gunman. As the police start investigating, everyone in Sachs's life has their own theory on whether the killing was political or personal. Spanish with subtitles. **90m/C VHS, DVD.** *AR* Mauricio Dayub, Luis Luque, Malena Solda, Gaston Pauls, Alejandra Flechner; ***D:*** Beda Docampo Feijoo; ***W:*** Beda Docampo Feijoo, Enrique Cortes; ***C:*** Ricardo Rodriguez; ***M:*** Ivan Wyszogrod.

Whatever 🦴🦴 **1998 (R)** Straightforward teenage coming of age story set in a small New Jersey town in the early 80s. Focuses on the friendship of two high school seniors, aspiring artist Anna (Weil) and party animal Brenda (Morgan). Anna copes with her bitter single mom (Rossetter) and bratty little brother and hopes to escape to a prestigious art school in New York, but is in danger of being dragged down by Brenda. The two girls numb their mostly grim home lives with drugs, alcohol and casual sex at joyless parties. The revelation that Brenda is being sexually abused at home moves the plot into the TV movie realm. **112m/C VHS.** Liza Weil, Chad Morgan, Kathryn Rossetter, Frederic Forrest; ***D:*** Susan Skoog; ***W:*** Susan Skoog; ***C:*** Michael Barrow, Mike Mayers.

Whatever Happened to Aunt Alice? 🦴🦴🦴 **1969 (PG)** After murdering her husband to inherit his estate, a poor, eccentric widow develops an awful habit: she hires maids, only to murder them and steal their savings. The only evidence is a growing number of trees by the drive. Sleuth Ruth Gordon (of "Harold and Maude" fame, acting here just as odd) takes the job in hopes of solving the mystery. Thoroughly amusing. **101m/C VHS, DVD, Wide.** Geraldine Page, Ruth Gordon, Rosemary Forsyth, Robert Fuller, Mildred Dunnock; ***D:*** Lee H. Katzin; ***W:*** Theodore Apstein; ***C:*** Joseph Biroc; ***M:*** Gerald Fried.

Whatever It Takes 🦴½ **2000 (PG-13)** Dopey teen romancer, with the usual attractive cast, that tries to be a modern version of "Cyrano de Bergerac." Ya got cutie boy-next-door-type Ryan (West) and his sensitive best pal Maggie (Sokoloff), who is, of course, his unknown soulmate. But Ryan pines for snobby hottie Ashley (O'Keefe). Meanwhile, Maggie has won the eye of jock Chris (Franco). So Chris and Ryan team up so that each can get their dream girl before the prom. You know how everything turns out. **94m/C VHS, DVD.** Marla Sokoloff, Jodi Lyn O'Keefe, Shane West, James Franco, Julia Sweeney, Richard Schiff, Aaron Paul, Colin Hanks; ***D:*** David Raynr; ***W:*** Mark Schwahn; ***C:*** Tim Suhrstedt; ***M:*** Ed Shearmur.

What's Cooking? 🦴🦴🦴 **2000 (PG-13)** Follows the Thanksgiving tradition of feasting amid household tension through the stories of four American families: one Jewish, one Latino, one Vietnamese, and one African American. Culture clashes, generation gaps, sexual identities, divorce, and other family flash points get addressed with sincere writing and delicate acting by all involved. Written by India-born English director Chadha and her Japanese-American husband Berges—you can't more all-American than that. **109m/C VHS, DVD, Wide.** Alfre Woodard, Joan Chen, Julianna Margulies, Mercedes Ruehl, Kyra Sedgwick, Lainie Kazan, Dennis Haysbert, Victor Rivers, Douglas Spain, A. Martinez, Maury Chaykin, Estelle Harris, Will Yun Lee, Kristy Wu; ***D:*** Gurinder Chadha; ***W:*** Gurinder Chadha, Paul Mayeda Berges; ***C:*** Jong Lin; ***M:*** Craig Preuss.

What's Eating Gilbert Grape *Gilbert Grape* **1993 (PG-13)** Offbeat is mildly descriptive. Depp stars as Gilbert Grape, the titular head of a very dysfunctional family living in a big house in a small Iowa town. His Momma (Cates) weighs more than 500 pounds and hasn't left the house in seven years, he has two squabbling teenage sisters, and 17-year-old brother Arnie (DiCaprio) is mentally retarded and requires constant supervision. What's a good-hearted grocery clerk to do? Well, when free-spirited Becky (Lewis) is momentarily marooned in town, Gilbert may have found a true soulmate. Performances, especially DiCaprio's, save this from the oddball/cute factor although flick would have benefitted from streamlining, particularly the scenes involving Depp and bad-haircut Lewis. Based on the novel by Hedges. **118m/C VHS, DVD, Wide.** Johnny Depp, Leonardo DiCaprio, Juliette Lewis, Mary Steenburgen, Darlene Cates, Laura Harrington, Mary Kate Schellhardt, Kevin Tighe, John C. Reilly, Crispin Glover, Penelope Branning; ***D:*** Lasse Hallstrom; ***W:*** Peter Hedges; ***C:*** Sven Nykvist; ***M:*** Alan Parker, Bjorn Isfalt. Natl. Bd. of Review '93: Support. Actor (DiCaprio).

What's Good for the Goose ½ **1969** Stuffy, married financial institution executive's lifestyle receives a major overhaul when he attends a banking conference and meets a beautiful and free-spirited young woman whom he takes as a lover. Unfortunately, he perpetually finds her in bed with other men, and then his wife gets in on the act, too. Classic British humor. **104m/C VHS.** *GB* Norman Wisdom, Sally Geeson, Sarah Atkinson, Sally Bazely; ***D:*** Menahem Golan; ***W:*** Norman Wisdom, Menahem Golan; ***M:*** Reg Tilsley.

What's Love Got to Do with It? ½ **1993 (R)** Energetic biopic of powerhouse songstress Tina Turner. Short sequences cover her early life before moving into her abusive relationship with Ike and solo comeback success. Bassett may not look like Tina, but her exceptionally strong performance leaves no question as to who she's supposed to be, even during on-stage Tina sequences. Some credibility is lost when Turner is shown in the final concert sequence—Gibson would have been wise to let Bassett finish what she started. Fishburne is a sympathetic but still chilling Ike, rising to the challenge of showing both Ike's initial charm and longtime cruelty. Based on "I, Tina" by Turner and Kurt Loder. **118m/C VHS, DVD.** Angela Bassett, Laurence "Larry" Fishburne, Vanessa Bell Calloway, Jenifer Lewis, Phyllis Stickney, Khandi Alexander, Pamela Tyson, Penny Johnson, Rae'ven (Alyia Larrymore) Kelly, Robert Miranda, Chi McBride; ***D:*** Brian Gibson; ***W:*** Kate Lanier; ***C:*** Jamie Anderson; ***M:*** Stanley Clarke. Golden Globes '94: Actress—Mus./Comedy (Bassett); Blockbuster '95: Female Newcomer, V. (Bassett).

What's New Pussycat? *Quoi De Neuf, Pussycat?* **1965** A young engaged man, reluctant to give up the girls who love him, seeks the aid of a married psychiatrist who turns out to have problems of his own. Allen's first feature as both actor and screenwriter. Oscar-nominated title song sung by Tom Jones. **108m/C VHS, Wide.** Peter Sellers, Peter O'Toole, Romy Schneider, Paula Prentiss, Woody Allen, Ursula Andress, Capucine; ***D:*** Clive Donner; ***W:*** Woody Allen; ***M:*** Burt Bacharach, Hal David.

What's the Matter with Helen? ½ **1971 (PG)** Two women, the mothers of murderous sons, move to Hollywood to escape their past and start a new life. They open a school for talented children, and seem to be adjusting to their new lives until strange things start happening. It is soon revealed that one of the mothers is a psychotic killer, and the other mother becomes part of an eerie finale. A fine starring vehicle for two aging actresses. Great score. **101m/C VHS.** Debbie Reynolds, Shelley Winters, Dennis Weaver, Agnes Moorehead, Michael MacLiammoir; ***D:*** Curtis Harrington.

What's the Worst That Could Happen? **2001 (PG-13)** Billionaire DeVito catches thief Lawrence robbing his mansion and, in retaliation, takes the man's lucky charm ring. Since Lawrence just received the ring from new girlfriend Ejogo, he'll do anything to get it back. It becomes an escalating, and ultimately tiresome, war of revenge and humiliation. The large and talented cast are given neither the script or the room to really shine, but some of the supporters fare well. Leguizamo, Fichtner, and Headly stand out, but Lawrence and DeVito should've been reined in a bit. **95m/C VHS, DVD, Wide.** *US* Martin Lawrence, Danny DeVito, Nora Dunn, William Fichtner, Glenne Headly, John Leguizamo, Bernie Mac, Carmen Ejogo, Larry Miller, Richard Schiff, Ana Gasteyer, Sascha Knopf, Siobhan Fallon, GQ, Lenny Clarke; ***D:*** Sam Weisman; ***W:*** Matthew Chapman; ***C:*** Anastas Michos; ***M:*** Tyler Bates.

What's Up, Doc? **1972 (G)** A shy musicologist from Iowa (Ryan) travels to San Francisco with his fiance (Kahn) for a convention. He meets the eccentric Streisand at his hotel and becomes involved in a chase to recover four identical flight bags containing top secret documents, a wealthy woman's jewels, the professor's musical rocks, and Streisand's clothing. Bogdanovich's homage to the screwball comedies of the '30s. Kahn's feature film debut. **94m/C VHS.** Barbra Streisand, Ryan O'Neal, Kenneth Mars, Austin Pendleton, Randy Quaid, Madeline Kahn; ***D:*** Peter Bogdanovich; ***W:*** David Newman, Buck Henry, Robert Benton; ***M:*** Artie Butler. Writers Guild '72: Orig. Screenplay.

What's Up Front ½ *The Fall Guy; A Fourth for Marriage* **1963** Occasionally funny '60s gag-fest about an ogle-eyed bra salesman who decides to sell door-to-door in order to save a failing brassiere company. Filmed in "Girl-O-Rama" by the young Vilmos Zsigmond. Dated and weird, with camp value. No nudity. Costumes were done by Frederick's of Hollywood. **90m/C VHS.** Tommy Holden, Marilyn Manning, Carolyn Walker, William Watters; ***D:*** Bob Wehling.

What's Up, Tiger Lily? **1966** This legitimate Japanese spy movie—"Kagi No Kag" (Key of Keys), a 1964 Bond imitation—was re-edited by Woody Allen, who added a new dialogue track, with hysterical results. Characters Terri and Suki Yaki are involved in an international plot to secure egg salad recipe; Allen's brand of Hollywood parody and clever wit sustain the joke. Music by the Lovin' Spoonful, who make a brief appearance. **90m/C VHS.** *JP* Tatsuya Mihashi, Mie Hama, Akiko Wakabayashi, China Lee, Eisei Amamoto, Kumi Mizuno, Tadao Nakamura, The Lovin' Spoonful; ***D:*** Senkichi Taniguchi, Woody Allen; ***W:*** Julie Bennett, Frank Buxton, Louise Lasser, Mickey Rose, Bryan Wilson, Kazuo Yamada, Woody Allen; ***C:*** Kazuo Yamada; ***M:*** Jack Lewis, The Lovin' Spoonful; ***Nar:*** Woody Allen.

Wheel of Fortune *A Man Betrayed; Citadel of Crime* **1941** A shrewd small-town lawyer, working on a case in the big city, is forced to expose his girlfriend's father as a crooked politician. Strange to see the Duke here in the lead, but what the hey. Not great, but interesting. **83m/B VHS.** John Wayne, Frances Dee, Edward Ellis, Ward Bond, Wallace Ford; ***D:*** John H. Auer.

The Wheeler Dealers *Separate Beds* **1963** Garner plays a supposedly penniless investor (actually a Texas millionaire) who comes to New York stock analyst Remick for investment advice. Her shyster boss (Backus) tells her to sell the aw-shucks cowboy worthless stock which turns out to be worth a fortune. Zany spoof of Wall Street ethics. **100m/C VHS.** James Garner, Lee Remick, Jim Backus, Phil Harris, Shelley Berman, Chill Wills, John Astin, Louis Nye; ***D:*** Arthur Hiller.

Wheels of Fire *Vindicator* **1984 (R)** The earth is a wasteland controlled by sadistic highway hoodlums. When they kidnap the hero's sister, he fights back in a flame-throwing car. Horrible "Road Warrior" rip-off. **81m/C VHS.** Gary Watkins, Lynda Wiesmeier; ***D:*** Cirio H. Santiago.

Wheels of Terror **1990 (R)** Possessed black car stalks children in isolated village. Bus driver Cassidy gets behind the wheel of V-8 super-charged school bus to initiate most interminable chase scene in screen history. **86m/C VHS.** Joanna Cassidy, Marcie Leeds, Carlos Cervantes, Arlen Dean Snyder; ***D:*** Christopher Cain; ***C:*** Rick Bota; ***M:*** Jay Gruska.

When a Man Loves a Woman ½ *To Have and to Hold; Significant Other* **1994 (R)** Time to get suspicious when song titles become film titles. Alice Green (Ryan) is the mother in a perfect little family, with a loving husband (Garcia), two little girls, and a satisfying career. She's also a closet alcoholic. Less about her alcoholism than the effect on her family and her hubby in particular, shown as a '90s sort of guy who allows Alice to keep her secret. Ryan's detox treatments and struggle back to sobriety are fertile ground for psycho-babble and 12-step cliches, but solid performances save this picture from drying out. **126m/C VHS, DVD.** Meg Ryan, Andy Garcia, Lauren Tom, Philip Seymour Hoffman, Tina Majorino, Mae Whitman, Ellen Burstyn, Eugene Roche, Latanya Richardson; ***D:*** Luis Mandoki; ***W:*** Ronald Bass, Al Franken; ***C:*** Lajos Koltai; ***M:*** Zbigniew Preisner. Blockbuster '95: Drama Actress, V. (Ryan).

When a Man Rides Alone **1933** Tyler relieves trains of their gold shipments in order to reimburse swindled investors. Lovely Lacey frowns on his initiative, so he kidnaps her to keep her quiet. The two fall in love, and the man who rides alone works beside his beloved. **60m/B VHS.** Tom Tyler, Adele Lacey, Alan Bridge, Robert Burns, Frank Ball, Alma Chester, Bud Osborne; ***D:*** J(ohn) P(aterson) McGowan.

When a Man Sees Red ½ **1934** Jones is a ranch foreman whose new boss is Campbell (she inherited the property). The two argue constantly but then come to realize all the fighting is just hiding true love. **60m/B VHS.** Buck Jones, Peggy Campbell, Dorothy Revier, Syd Saylor, Leroy Mason, Charles French, Robert F. (Bob) Kortman; ***D:*** Alan James.

When a Stranger Calls ½ **1979 (R)** Babysitter is terrorized by threatening phone calls and soon realizes that the calls are coming from within the house. Story was expanded from director Walton's short film "The Sitter." Distasteful and unlikely, though the first half or so is tight and terrifying. **97m/C VHS, DVD, Wide.** Carol Kane, Charles Durning, Colleen Dewhurst, Rachel Roberts, Rutanya Alda, Carmen Argenziano, Kirsten Larkin, Ron O'Neal, Tony Beckley; ***D:*** Fred Walton; ***W:*** Fred Walton, Steve Feke; ***C:*** Don Peterman.

When a Stranger Calls Back ½ **1993 (R)** Sequel to "When a Stranger Calls" finds college student Julia Jenz (Schoelen) still trying to put her life together five years after a terrifying ordeal with a stalker. She turns to her advisor Jill (Kane), who went through a similar fate, but once Jill becomes involved she again becomes the pawn of a psychopath. It's up to retired detective John Clifford (Durning), who saved Jill before, to do his heroics once again. Scary opening sequence but suspense peters out toward the end. **94m/C VHS, DVD.** Carol Kane, Charles Durning, Jill Schoelen, Gene Lythgow, Karen Austin; ***D:*** Fred Walton; ***W:*** Fred Walton; ***C:*** David Geddes; ***M:*** Dana Kaproff. **CABLE**

When a Woman Ascends the Stairs *Onna Ga Kaidan O Agaru Toki* **1960** A young widow with an elderly mother and a useless brother supports them all by working as a Ginza bar hostess. As she approaches the perilous professional age of 30, Keiko must decide whether to open her own bar or marry once again. In Japanese with English subtitles. **110m/B VHS.** *JP* Hideko Takamine, Tatsuya Nakadai, Masayuki Mori; ***D:*** Mikio Naruse.

When Angels Fly **1982** In this emotional tale of love and murder, a young woman sets out to find the exact circumstances surrounding the mysterious death of her sister. **96m/C VHS.** Jennifer Dale, Robin Ward.

When Brendan Met Trudy **2000** Irish romantic comedy by the writer of such standout novels as "The Commitments" and "The Snapper." Brendan (McDonald) is somewhat of a pansy-boy who attracts his polar opposite Trudy (Montgomery), a street-smart sort of girl and falls in love. Brendan, a straitlaced schoolteacher, soon learns that Trudy moonlights as a thief, and after the initial shock wears off, joins his outlaw honey in some good old-fashioned felonious fun. The true fun of the film, though, is its constant classic film references, such as when a misadventure lands Brendan in the gutter, he is reminded of William Holden in "Sunset Boulevard." Even if you're not a film buff, thought, you'll still enjoy this offbeat comic romp. **95m/C VHS, DVD.** *IR GB* Peter McDonald, Flora Montgomery, Marie Mullen, Pauline McLynn, Don Wycherley; ***D:*** Kieron J. Walsh; ***W:*** Roddy Doyle; ***C:*** Ashley Rowe; ***M:*** Richard Hartley.

When Danger Follows You Home ½ **1997 (PG-13)** Ann Werden (Williams), a psychologist at a county mental health facility, becomes interested in the case of a disturbed patient who calls himself Gogel, a computer genius with an FBI file. When Gogel mysteriously dies in Anne's home, she finds herself accused of manslaughter—and then her son is kidnapped. Anne's got a lot to figure out if she wants her life to go back to normal. **92m/C VHS.** JoBeth Williams, William Russ, Michael Manasseri, Vanessa King, Susan Hogan, Duncan Fraser, Nicolas Surovy; ***D:*** David Peckinpah; ***W:*** Sharon Elizabeth Doyle; ***C:*** Robert Hudececk; ***M:*** Charles Bernstein. **CABLE**

When Dinosaurs Ruled the Earth **1970 (G)** When "One Million Years B.C." ruled the boxoffice the Brits cranked out a few more lively prehistoric fantasies. A sexy cavegirl, exiled because of her blond hair, acquires a cave-beau and a dinosaur guardian. Stop-motion animation from Jim Danforth, story by J.G. Ballard. Under the name Angela Dorian, Vetri was Playmate of the Year in 1968 (A.D.). **96m/C VHS.** *GB* Victoria Vetri, Robin Hawdon, Patrick Allen, Drewe Henley, Sean Caffrey, Magda Konopka, Imogen Hassall, Patrick Holt, Jan Rossini; ***D:*** Val Guest; ***W:*** Val Guest; ***C:*** Dick Bush.

When Every Day Was the Fourth of July ½ **1978** A nine-year-old girl asks her father, a lawyer, to defend a mute handyman accused of murder, knowing this will bring on him the contempt of the community. Well handled, but see "To Kill a Mockingbird" first. Based on producer/director Curtis's childhood. Sequel: "The Long Days of Summer." **100m/C VHS.** Katy Kurtzman, Dean Jones, Louise Sorel, Harris Yulin, Chris Petersen, Geoffrey Lewis, Scott Brady, Henry Wilcoxon, Michael Pataki; ***D:*** Dan Curtis. **TV**

When Father Was Away on Business ½ **1985 (R)** Set in 1950s Yugoslavia. A family must take care of itself when the father is sent to jail for philandering with a woman desired by a Communist Party offical. The moving story of the family's day-to-day survival is seen largely through the eyes of the father's six-year-old son, who believes dad is "away on business." In Yugoslavian with English subtitles. **144m/C VHS.** *YU* Moreno D'E Bartolli, Miki (Predrag) Manojlovic, Mirjana Karanovic; ***D:*** Emir Kusturica. Cannes '85: Film.

When Gangland Strikes **1956** A country lawyer, blackmailed by the mob, tries to protect his family without caving in. Unexceptional remake of "Main Street Lawyer." **70m/B VHS.** Raymond Greenleaf, Marjie Millar, Anthony Caruso, Jack Perrin, John Hudson; ***D:*** R.G. Springsteen; ***M:*** Van Alexander.

When Good Ghouls Go Bad ½ **2001** Twelve-year-old Danny has just moved to a new town where he discovers that because of a town curse no one is allowed to celebrate Halloween. So Danny teams up with his recently departed Uncle Fred (Lloyd) to drive away the prankster ghouls who have been causing all the mischief. **93m/C VHS, DVD.** Christopher Lloyd, Tom Amandes, Joe Pichler; ***D:*** Patrick Read Johnson; ***W:*** Patrick Read Johnson; ***C:*** Brian J. Breheny; ***M:*** Christopher Gordon. **TV**

When Harry Met Sally... **1989 (R)** Romantic comedy follows the long relationship between two adults who try throughout the changes in their lives (and their mates) to remain platonic friends—and what happens when they don't. Wry and enjoyable script is enhanced by wonderful performances. Another directorial direct hit for "Meathead" Reiner, and a tour de force of comic screenwriting for Ephron, with improvisational help from Crystal. Great songs by Sinatra sound-alike Connick. **96m/C VHS, DVD, 8mm, Wide.** Billy Crystal, Meg Ryan, Carrie Fisher, Bruno Kirby, Steven Ford, Lisa Jane Persky, Michelle Nicastro, Harley Jane Kozak; ***D:*** Rob Reiner; ***W:*** Nora Ephron; ***C:*** Barry Sonnenfeld; ***M:*** Harry Connick Jr., Marc Shaiman. British Acad. '89: Orig. Screenplay.

When Hell Broke Loose 🦴½
1958 Routine WWII actioner about a small-time crook (Bronson) who joins the Army, changes his ways because of the love of a good woman, and gets a chance to be a hero when he stumbles upon a Nazi assassination plot against General Eisenhower. **78m/B VHS.** Charles Bronson, Violet Rensing, Richard Jaeckel, Arvid Nelson, Robert Easton; ***D:*** Kenneth Crane; ***W:*** Oscar Brodney.

When Hell Was in Session 🦴🦴🦴 **1982** In more than seven years as a prisoner of the Viet Cong, Holbrook is subjected to torture, starvation, and psychological warfare to break his will. Based on the true story of Navy Commander Jeremiah Denton. Painful and violent. **98m/C VHS.** Hal Holbrook, Eva Marie Saint, Ronny Cox; ***D:*** Paul Krasny. **TV**

When He's Not a Stranger 🦴🦴🦴 **1989** Lyn is a college freshman who goes to a campus party hosted by the football team. When Ron, the star quarterback, invites Lyn to his dorm room, the situation gets out of hand. Only Lyn calls it rape and Ron calls her a liar. Intense performances are a highlight of this well-done story. **100m/C VHS.** Annabeth Gish, John Terlesky, Kevin Dillon, Paul Dooley, Kim Meyers; ***D:*** John Gray. **TV**

When I Close My Eyes 🦴🦴
Ko Zaprem Oci **1993** First independent film from Slovenia is a thriller in which rural postal employee Ana uses one crime to cover another. When a motorcyclist robs the post office while Ana is working, she uses his crime to steal some money for herself. But then Ana becomes obsessed with the thief and decides to track him down. Slovenian with subtitles. **94m/C VHS.** Petra Govc, Mario Selih, Mira Sardo; ***D:*** Franci Slak; ***W:*** Franci Slak, Silvan Furlan; ***C:*** Sven Pepeonik.

When I Close My Eyes 🦴🦴
Love Letter **1995 (PG-13)** After attending a memorial service for her fiance, Hiroko (Nakayama) discovers his high school yearbook and an old address. She impulsively writes a letter to the address and is shocked to receive a reply from a young woman, Itsuki (also played by Nakayama), who bears the same name as her dead lover and even went to high school with him. The two women begin to correspond, as Hiroko asks what Itsuki remembers about the young man (Kashiwabara), and the mock resentment/friendship the two maintained in school. Eventually, Hiroko decides to meet Itsuki in person, hoping that she can get over the past that haunts her. Japanese with subtitles. **116m/C VHS.** *JP* Miho Nakayama, Takashi Kashiwabara, Etsushi Toyokawa; ***D:*** Shunji Iwai; ***W:*** Shunji Iwai; ***C:*** Noboru Shinoda.

When Justice Fails 🦴🦴 **1998 (R)**
Vigilante goes after rapists. **90m/C VHS, DVD.** Jeff Fahey, Marlee Matlin, Monique Mercure, Carl Marotte; ***D:*** Allan Goldstein; ***W:*** Tony Kayden; ***C:*** Barry Gravelle.

When Knights Were Bold 🦴🦴½ **1936** An English nobleman living in India inherits a castle in his native land. Returning home, he is knocked unconscious by a falling suit of armor while trying to impress a young lady and dreams himself back to medieval days. Enjoyable comedy about that ubiquitous British class hierarchy. **55m/B VHS.** Fay Wray, Jack Buchanan, Martita Hunt; ***C:*** Frederick A. (Freddie) Young.

When Ladies Meet 🦴🦴½
Strange Skirts **1941** Entertaining story of a love quadrangle that features several of MGM's top stars of the '40s. In this remake of the 1933 film, Crawford plays a novelist and an early proponent of the women's liberation movement. She falls in love with her publisher (Marshall), who just happens to be married to Garson. Meanwhile, Taylor, who is in love with Crawford, attempts to show her that he isa more suitable match for her than Marshall, but Crawford has yet to catch on.The lengthy dialogue on women's rights is badly dated, but the real-life rivalry between Crawford and Garson adds a certain bite to their witty exchanges. **105m/B VHS.** Joan Crawford, Robert Taylor, Greer Garson, Herbert Marshall, Spring Byington; ***D:*** Robert Z. Leonard; ***W:*** Anita Loos, S.K. Lauren.

When Lightning Strikes woof!
1934 Lightning the Wonder Dog prevents the owner of a rival lumber company from stealing his master's land. He gets to use his talents of running, swimming, barking, and smoking cigars. Proves that real woofers were made way back when, even though in 1934 they didn't feature scantily clad babes. Part of Video Yesteryear's Golden Turkey series. **51m/B VHS.** Francis X. Bushman.

When Love Comes 🦴🦴 **1998**
Katie Keen (Owen) is a fortyish one-hit pop singer who decides to return home to New Zealand to rethink her fading career and life with her manager/lover Eddie (Westaway). Her best pal is still Stephen (Prast) who is involved with the younger Mark (O'Gorman), a songwriter. Mark's friends Fig (Brunning) and Sally (Hawthorne) have a band and ask Katie to sing on a recording. Everyone eventually winds up at Katie's seaside home trying to make potentially life-altering decisions. **94m/C DVD.** *NZ* Rena Owen, Dean O'Gorman, Simon Prast, Nancy Brunning, Simon Westaway, Sally Hawthorne; ***D:*** Garth Maxwell; ***W:*** Garth Maxwell, Peter Wells, Rex Pilgrim; ***C:*** Darryl Ward; ***M:*** Chris Anderton.

When Nature Calls woof! **1985 (R)** A city family "gets back to nature" in this collection of mostly ineffective gags and poor satirical ideas. Probably your first and last chance to see Liddy and Mays on screen together. **76m/C VHS.** Davie Orange, Barbara Marineau, Nicky Beim, Tina Marie Staiano, Willie Mays, G. Gordon Liddy; ***D:*** Charles Kaufman.

When Night Is Falling 🦴🦴🦴
1995 (R) Camille (Bussieres) is a professor of mythology at a Calvinist college in Toronto and engaged to theologian Martin (Czerny). Vaguely unsatisfied, Camille meets Petra (Crawford), a trapeze artist in a traveling circus, gets drawn into her world, falls in love, and must decide what she wants from her life. Lots of yearning, romance, and fantasy. Lesbian lovemaking scenes caused a ratings problem (the MPAA originally deemed them worthy of NC-17). **96m/C VHS.** *CA* Pascale Bussieres, Rachel Crawford, Henry Czerny, David Fox, Don McKellar, Tracy Wright; ***D:*** Patricia Rozema; ***W:*** Patricia Rozema; ***C:*** Douglas Koch; ***M:*** Lesley Barber.

When Pigs Fly 🦴🦴 **1993** A story with two ghosts, a rocking chair, and a lonely, struggling musician. Lilly (Faithful) and young Ruthie (Bella) are the ghosts, who both happen to have died in the same rocking chair a century apart. The chair is now in the possession of down-and-out jazz musician Marty (Molina), who doesn't know how to react to his unworldly visitors. Whimsical but not cloying. **94m/C VHS.** Marianne Faithfull, Alfred Molina, Seymour Cassel, Rachael Bella; ***D:*** Sara Driver; ***W:*** Ray Dobbins; ***C:*** Robby Muller; ***M:*** Joe Strummer.

When Saturday Comes 🦴🦴½
1995 Feel-good working-class drama follows Sheffield-born Jimmy Muir (Bean), whose life revolves around a job in a brewery, the local pub, chasing girls, and playing football (soccer) on the weekends. He gets involved with co-worker Annie (Lloyd), whose Uncle Ken (Postlethwaite) coaches the local semi-pro team and who offers Jimmy a chance to play. His success leads to a trial with the pros, Sheffield United, which Jimmy blows by getting drunk. After losing his job, his girl, and having his brother die in an accident, Jimmy struggles to pull himself together, and maybe get a second chance. **97m/C VHS.** *GB* Sean Bean, Emily Lloyd, Pete Postlethwaite, John McEnery, Ann Bell, Craig Kelly; ***D:*** Maria Giese; ***W:*** Maria Giese; ***C:*** Gerry Fisher; ***M:*** Anne Dudley.

When Taekwondo Strikes 🦴
1983 (R) One brave Taekwondo master leads the Korean freedom fighters against the occupying army of WWII Japan. **95m/C VHS.** Jhoon Rhee, Ann Winton, Angela (Mao Ying) Mao, Huang Ing Sik; ***D:*** Raymond Chow.

When the Bough Breaks 🦴🦴
1986 A psychologist helps the police with the case of a murder-suicide witnessed by a child. He finds one sick secret society at work in this unkinder, ungentler TV thriller, based on the novel by Jonathan Kellerman. Danson co-produced. **100m/C VHS.** Ted Danson, Richard Masur, Rachel Ticotin, David Huddleston, James Noble, Kim Miyori, Merritt Butrick; ***D:*** Waris Hussein.

When the Bough Breaks 🦴🦴
1993 (R) A Texas police chief (Sheen) discovers seven severed hands and turns to a forensic expert (Walker) for help. But then the specialist discovers a psychic link between a mentally disturbed child and the serial killer. **103m/C VHS.** Ally Walker, Martin Sheen, Ron Perlman; ***D:*** Michael Cohn; ***W:*** Michael Cohn; ***C:*** Michael Bonvillain.

When the Bullet Hits the Bone 🦴 **1996 (R)** Particularly nasty vigilante flick as EMS doc Jack Davies (Wincott) decides to get even with a drug cartel, after being seriously wounded while trying to help drug-addicted hooker Lisa (Johnson) get away from her vicious pimp. **82m/C VHS.** Jeff Wincott, Michelle Johnson, Doug O'Keefe, Richard Fitzpatrick; ***D:*** Damian Lee; ***W:*** Damian Lee.

When the Cat's Away 🦴🦴🦴
Chacun Cherche Son Chat **1996 (R)** Touching Gallic frolic finds introverted Parisian make-up artist face-to-face with adventure while searching for her lost cat. Chloe (Clavel) eventually comes out of her shell, as the search for little Gris-Gris brings her into contact with a wide variety of characters, some lonely, like herself, played by real people and real cats. Best non-actor kudos to Renee Le Calm as Madame Renee, the kooky neighborhood cat lady, with her network of cat fanciers acting as the reconnaissance party for the runaway feline. Director Klapisch's comedy also tackles weightier topics along the way, including lonliness, homelessness, racism, and the moderization of a city steeped with history. Stylishly spare with adept photography, seems almost semi-documentary. **91m/C VHS.** *FR* Garance Clavel, Zinedine Soualem, Olivier Py, Renee Le Calm, Romain Duris; ***D:*** Cedric Klapisch; ***W:*** Cedric Klapisch; ***C:*** Benoit Delhomme.

When the Clouds Roll By 🦴🦴🦴½ **1919** Psycho-satire pits demented doctor against Fairbanks in experiment to make him suicidal basket case. Fairbanks seems to contract ferocious nightmares, passionate superstitions, a spurning lover, and a warrant for his arrest, none of which suppresses his penchant for acrobatics. **77m/B VHS.** Douglas Fairbanks Sr., Herbert Grimwood, Kathleen Clifford, Frank Campeau, Ralph Lewis, Daisy Robinson, Albert MacQuarrie; ***D:*** Victor Fleming.

When the Dark Man Calls 🦴🦴½ **1995 (R)** Shock ending and a strong lead performance by Van Ark enhance this cable mystery. Call-in radio shrink Julianne Kaiser (Van Ark) is stalked by ex-con Parmenter (Lewis). Twenty-five years ago she testified that he murdered her parents although the bitter man's always proclaimed his innocence. Now Kaiser is having grisly flashbacks to her childhood but can she figure out the truth before Parmenter kills her? Based on a novel by Stuart M. Kaminsky. **89m/C VHS.** Joan Van Ark, Geoffrey Lewis, Chris Sarandon, James Read, Frances Hyland, Janet-Laine Green; ***D:*** Nathaniel Gutman; ***W:*** Pablo F. Fenjves. **CABLE**

When the Greeks 🦴🦴 *Ton Kero Ton Hellinon* **1981** At the turn of the century, a rich young landowner is kidnapped by a group of nationalist bandits who demand a hefty ransom. But soon the young man realizes he's seeing his true Greek heritage for the first time and begins to identify with his captors. Greek with subtitles. **100m/C VHS.** *GR* Alexis Damianos, Kostas Arzoglou, George Sampanis, Stavros Mermighis; ***D:*** Lakis Papastathis; ***W:*** Lakis Papastathis; ***M:*** George Papadakis.

When the Legends Die 🦴🦴🦴
1972 (PG) A Ute Indian strives to preserve his heritage in an often harsh modern world. Recorded in hi-fi. **105m/C VHS.** Richard Widmark, Frederic Forrest; ***D:*** Stuart Millar.

When the Line Goes Through 🦴 **1971** A drifter arrives in a small West Virginia town and changes the lives of two pretty sisters. **90m/C VHS.** Martin Sheen, Davey Davidson, Beverly Washburn.

When the North Wind Blows 🦴🦴 **1974 (G)** An old, lone trapper hunts for and later befriends the majestic snow tiger of Siberia in the Alaskan wilderness. A good family film. **113m/C VHS.** Henry (Kleinbach) Brandon, Herbert Nelson, Dan Haggerty; ***D:*** Stewart Raffill.

When the Party's Over 🦴🦴½
1991 (R) Twenty-somethings share a southern California house and a hip—but ultimately empty—lifestyle. **114m/C VHS.** Rae Dawn Chong, Fisher Stevens, Elizabeth Berridge, Sandra Bullock, Brian McNamara, Kris Kramm; ***D:*** Matthew Irmas.

When the Screaming Stops 🦴 **1973 (R)** A hunter is hired to find out who has been cutting the hearts out of young women who reside in a small village near the Rhine River. Turns out it's a she-monster who rules a kingdom beneath the river. Bad effects; gory gore; outlandish plot. All the ingredients, in other words, of a classic dog. **86m/C VHS.** *SP* Tony Kendall, Helga Line, Sylvia Tortosa; ***D:*** Armando de Ossorio.

When the Sky Falls 🦴🦴 **1999**
Gritty bio loosely focuses on the last years of crusading Dublin journalist Veronica Gerin, who was murdered in 1996. Sinead Hamilton (Allen) has angered Dublin politicians, the IRA, police, and crime bosses with her investigation into the city's drug scene. She ticks off bad guy Dave Hackett (Flynn) and even tough detective Mackey (Bergin) tries to warn her but threats only make Hamilton more determined to do her expose. **107m/C VHS, DVD, Wide.** *IR* Joan Allen, Patrick Bergin, Liam Cunningham, Gerard Flynn, Kevin McNally, Jimmy Smallhorne, Jason Barry, Pete Postlethwaite, Des McAleer, Ruaidhri Conroy; ***D:*** John MacKenzie; ***W:*** Michael J. Sheridan, Ronan Gallagher, Colum McCann; ***C:*** Seamus Deasy; ***M:*** Pol Brennan.

When the Time Comes 🦴🦴
1991 (PG-13) A woman dying of cancer wants to take her own life, but when her husband refuses, she seeks the help of a male friend. Excellent acting doesn't provide the needed depth. Less a disease-of-the-week TV movie, more of an ethical-dilemma-of-the-week, and just as trivial. **94m/C VHS.** Bonnie Bedelia, Brad Davis, Terry O'Quinn, Karen Austin, Donald Moffat, Wendy Schaal; ***D:*** John Erman; ***M:*** Marvin Hamlisch.

When the West Was Young 🦴½ *Wild Horse Mesa* **1932** An outdoor adventure about rounding up horses in the Old West. Based on a novel by Zane Grey. **58m/B VHS.** Randolph Scott, Sally Blane, Guinn "Big Boy" Williams; ***D:*** Henry Hathaway.

When the Whales Came 🦴🦴½
1989 (PG) A conservationist fable about two children and a grizzled old codger living on a remote British isle during WWI. They try to avert disaster as mysterious narwhal whales descend on the island. Moralistic and uninvolving; poorly acted; slumber-inducing. Adapted from the novel by Morpugo. **100m/C VHS.** *GB* Paul Scofield, Helen Mirren, David Threlfall, David Suchet, Jeremy Kemp, Max Rennie, Helen Pearce, Barbara Jefford; ***D:*** Clive Rees; ***W:*** Michael Morpugo; ***M:*** Christopher Gunning, Ruth Rennie.

When the Wind Blows 🦴🦴🦴
1986 An animated feature about a retired British couple when their peaceful—and naive—life in the country is destroyed by nuclear war. Poignant, sad, and thought-provoking, and just a little scary. Features the voices of Ashcroft and Mills; Roger Waters, David Bowie, Squeeze, Genesis, Hugh Cornell, and Paul Hardcastle all contribute to the soundtrack. Based on the novel by Raymond Briggs. **80m/C VHS.** *GB* ***D:*** Jimmy T. Murakami; ***V:*** Peggy Ashcroft, John Mills.

When Thief Meets Thief 🦴½
1937 A cat burglar finds his world turned upside down when he begins to fall in love with one of his victims. Not much happening except a few nice stunts by Fairbanks. **85m/B VHS.** *GB* Douglas Fairbanks Jr., Valerie Hobson, Alan Hale, Jack Melford, Leo Genn, Ian Fleming; ***D:*** Raoul Walsh.

When Time Expires 🦴🦴 **1997**
(PG-13) Extraterrestrial scientist Travis Beck (Grieco) time travels from the future to present-day earth to stop the planet's destruction by evil forces. **93m/C VHS.** Richard Grieco, Cynthia Geary, Mark Hamill, Tim Thomerson, Chad Everett; ***D:*** David Bourla; ***W:*** David Bourla; ***C:*** Dean Lent; ***M:*** Todd Hayen. **CABLE**

When Time Ran Out 🦴 **1980**
(PG) A volcano erupts on a remote Polynesian island covered with expensive hotels and tourists with no way to escape. Contains scenes not seen in the theatrically released print of the film. A very good cast is wasted in this compilation of disaster film cliches. **144m/C VHS.** Paul Newman, Jacqueline Bisset, William Holden, Ernest Borgnine, Edward Albert, Barbara Carrera, Valentina Cortese, Burgess Meredith, Noriyuki "Pat" Morita, Red Buttons; ***D:*** James Goldstone; ***W:*** Stirling Silliphant; ***C:*** Fred W. Koenekamp; ***M:*** Lalo Schifrin.

When Trumpets Fade 🦴🦴½
1998 (R) Private Manning (Eldard) is the only survivor of his platoon, which is caught in the Battle of the Hurtgen Forest along the Belgian-German border in 1944. Manning is interested in nothing more than his own survival but his skills attract the attention of an officer (Donovan) who promptly promotes him to sgt. (and soon, lieutenant) and gives him his own platoon of raw recruits to whip into shape. **93m/C VHS, DVD, Wide.** Ron Eldard, Zak Orth, Frank Whaley, Dylan Bruno, Martin Donovan, Timothy Olyphant, Dan Futterman, Dwight Yoakam, Devon Gummersall, Jeffrey Donovan; ***D:*** John Irvin; ***W:*** W.W. Vought; ***C:*** Thomas Burstyn; ***M:*** Geoffrey Burgon. **CABLE**

When We Were Kings **1996 (PG)**
Chronicles the 1974 heavyweight championship fight, held in Zaire, between underdog Muhammad Ali and George Foreman. Gast uses original footage of the prefight hype as well as current interviews from George Plimpton and Norman Mailer (who covered the fight at the time) and Spike Lee. **94m/C VHS, DVD.** ***D:*** Leon Gast. Oscars '96: Feature Doc.; Broadcast Film Critics '96: Feature Doc.

When Wolves Cry 🦴½ *The Christmas Tree* **1969 (G)** Tearjerker about an estranged father and young son reunited on a Corsican vacation. Their newfound joy sours when the lad is diagnosed with a fatal illness. Hardly one of Holden's best films. **108m/C VHS.** William Holden, Virna Lisi, Brook Fuller, Andre Bourvil; ***D:*** Terence Young.

When Women Had Tails 🦴½
Quando De Donne Avevando La Coda **1970 (R)** A primitive comedy about prehistoric man's discovery of sex. And boy, did they ever discover it. Harmless (more or less), though not exactly cerebral. Followed by "When Women Lost Their Tails." **99m/C VHS.** *IT* Senta Berger, Frank Wolff; ***D:*** Pasquale Festa Campanile; ***M:*** Ennio Morricone.

When Women Lost Their Tails 🦴 **1975 (R)** Ostensible sequel to "When Women Had Tails" about prehistoric cavemen and their sexual habits. **94m/C VHS.** *IT* Senta Berger; ***D:*** Pasquale Festa Campanile; ***M:*** Ennio Morricone.

When Worlds Collide 🦴🦴½
1951 (G) Another planet is found to be rushing inevitably towards earth, but a select group of people attempt to escape in a spaceship; others try to maneuver their way on board. Oscar-quality special effects and plot make up for cheesy acting and bad writing. **81m/C VHS, DVD.** Richard Derr, Barbara Rush, Larry Keating, Peter Hanson; ***D:*** Rudolph Mate; ***W:*** Sydney Boehm; ***C:*** William Howard Greene; ***M:*** Leith Stevens.

When Your Lover Leaves 🦴
1983 Alleged comedy about a woman, dumped by her married boyfriend, who gets involved in a short-lived relationship with a neighbor. When that also doesn't work out, she decides she must first do something to please herself. Here endeth the lesson. Produced by Fonzie and Richie of "Happy Days." **100m/C VHS.** Valerie Perrine, Betty Thomas, David Ackroyd, Ed O'Neill, Dwight Schultz, Shannon Wilcox; ***D:*** Jeff Bleckner; ***M:*** Randy Edelman. **TV**

When's Your Birthday? 🦴🦴½
1937 Brown stars in this comedy about a prize-fighter who is working his way through astrology school with his fighting skills. The stars, in turn, tell him when to fight. Lame zaniness (what other kind is there?) meant as a vehicle for Brown, though Kennedy is funnier. The opening sequence, an animated cartoon showing the influence of the moon over the planets, was filmed in Technicolor. **77m/B VHS.** Joe E. Brown, Marian Marsh, Edgar Kennedy; ***D:*** Harry Beaumont.

Where 🦴🦴 **1994** Young man living in Budapest begins a psycho-sexual relationship with a young woman that explores the nature of domination and submission. After moving to Los Angeles, he subjects himself to the whims of a student. In English and Hungarian with subtitles. **?m/C VHS.** *HU* ***D:*** Gabor Zabo.

Where Angels Fear to Tread 🦴🦴🦴 **1991 (PG)** Another turn-of-the-century tale of the English in Italy from the pen of E.M. Forster. Widowed, 40ish Lilia (Mirren) is urged by her stuffy in-laws to spend some time in Italy. Much to everyone's dismay she impulsively marries a 21-year-old Italian—with disastrous consequences. Based on Forster's first novel, the characters are more stereotypical and the story less defined than his later works and the movies made from them. Impressive performances and beautiful settings make up for a somewhat lackluster direction that isn't up to the standards set by the team of Merchant Ivory, responsible for the Forster films "A Room with a View" and "Howard's End." **112m/C VHS.** *GB* Rupert Graves, Helena Bonham Carter, Judy Davis, Helen Mirren, Giovanni Guidelli, Barbara Jefford, Thomas Wheatley, Sophie Kullman; ***D:*** Charles Sturridge; ***W:*** Charles Sturridge, Tim Sullivan, Derek Granger; ***C:*** Michael Coulter; ***M:*** Rachel Portman.

Where Angels Go, Trouble Follows 🦴🦴½ **1968** Follow-up to "The Trouble with Angels," with Russell reprising her role as the wise Mother Superior challenged by her mischief loving students. Younger, modern nun Stevens tries to convince Russell to update her old-fashioned ways and persuades her to take the convent students on a bus trip to a California peace rally. A very young Saint James is one of the convent's irrepressible troublemakers. Very dated but still mildly amusing. **94m/C VHS.** Rosalind Russell, Stella Stevens, Binnie Barnes, Mary Wickes, Susan St. James, Dolores Sutton, Alice Rawlings; ***Cameos:*** Milton Berle, Arthur Godfrey, Van Johnson, Robert Taylor; ***D:*** James Neilson; ***W:*** Blanche Hanalis.

Where Are the Children? 🦴½
1985 (R) Based on Mary Higgins Clark's bestseller. A woman who was cleared of murdering the children from her first marriage remarries. Then the children from her second marriage are kidnapped. Sustains suspense completely, until it falls apart. **92m/C VHS.** Jill Clayburgh, Max Gail, Barnard Hughes, Clifton James, Harley Cross, Elisabeth Harnois, Elizabeth Wilson, Frederic Forrest; ***D:*** Bruce Malmuth.

Where Eagles Dare 🦴🦴🦴 **1968**
(PG) During WWII, a small group of Allied commandos must rescue an American general held by the Nazis in a castle in the Bavarian Alps. Relentless plot twists and action keep you breathless. Well-made suspense/adventure. Alistair MacLean adapted his original screenplay into a successful novel. **158m/C VHS, Wide.** *GB* Clint Eastwood, Richard Burton, Mary Ure, Michael Hordern, Anton Diffring, Ingrid Pitt, Patrick Wymark, Robert Beatty, Donald Houston, Derren Nesbitt, Ferdinand "Ferdy" Mayne, Peter Barkworth, William Squire, Neil McCarthy, Brook Williams, Vincent Ball; ***D:*** Brian G. Hutton; ***W:*** Alistair MacLean; ***C:*** Arthur Ibbetson; ***M:*** Ronald Goodwin.

Where East Is East 🦴🦴½ **1929**
In Indochina a badly scarred trapper (Chaney) lives with his daughter (Velez) and sells wild animals to circuses. Velez falls in love with a circus owner's son but finds out her own mother, seeking revenge on her ex-husband, trying to seduce the young man. A gorilla figures in the plot as well. Chaney's makeup, which contributed to his "Man of a Thousand Faces" nickname, highlights a contrived movie. **140m/B VHS.** Lon Chaney Sr., Lupe Velez, Estelle Taylor, Lloyd Hughes; ***D:*** Tod Browning.

Where Have All the People Gone? 🦴 **1974** Solar explosion turns most of Earth's inhabitants to dust while the Anders family vacations in a cave. The family tries to return home amid the devastation. Bad timing, bad acting, bad script. **74m/C VHS.** Peter Graves, Kathleen Quinlan, Michael-James Wixted, George O'Hanlon Jr., Verna Bloom; ***D:*** John Llewellyn Moxey. **TV**

Where Is My Child? 🦴🦴½ **1937**
Immigration to the New World brings only misfortune and betrayal in this tale of Jews in Eastern Europe between 1911 and 1937, as many experience the loss of family ties and religion. In Yiddish with English subtitles. **92m/B VHS.** Celia Adler, Anna Lillian, Morris Strassberg; ***D:*** Abraham Leff, Harry Lynn.

Where Is My Friend's House? 🦴🦴 *Where is the Friend's Home?; Khaneh-Je Doost Kojast?* **1987** At the village school, Mohamed is told by his teacher that he'll be expelled if he doesn't do his homework in the required exercise book. But that evening schoolmate Ahmed realizes he's taken Mohamed's book by mistake so he sets off to find his friend's house in a neighboring village. However, Ahmed gets lost and none of the adults he meets will help him. Farsi with subtitles. Followed by "Life and Nothing More..." and "Through the Olive Trees." **90m/C VHS.** *IA* Babek Ahmed Poor, Ahmed Ahmed Poor, Kheda Barech Defai; ***D:*** Abbas Kiarostami; ***W:*** Abbas Kiarostami; ***C:*** Farhad Saba.

Where Love Has Gone 🦴🦴½
1964 A soaper about a teenage daughter who kills her nympho mother's current boyfriend. Her divorced parents end up dragging the ordeal out in a murder trial/custody battle and a lot of family skeletons come out of their closets. Davis is the manipulative grand dame grandmother. Based on the novel by Harold Robbins. **114m/C VHS.** Bette Davis, Susan Hayward, Joey Heatherton, Jane Greer, George Macready; ***D:*** Edward Dmytryk; ***W:*** John Michael Hayes.

Where Sleeping Dogs Lie 🦴🦴
1991 (R) A struggling writer moves into an abandoned California home five years after a wealthy family was murdered there. While doing research for his novel on their brutal killings, he revives their ghosts as well as the very real presence of their killer. **92m/C VHS.** Dylan McDermott, Tom Sizemore, Sharon Stone; ***D:*** Charles Finch.

Where the Boys Are 🦴🦴½
1960 Four college girls go to Fort Lauderdale to have fun and meet boys during their Easter vacation. Features the film debuts of Francis, who had a hit single with the film's title song, and Prentiss. Head and shoulders above the ludicrous '84 remake. **99m/C VHS, Wide.** George Hamilton, Jim Hutton, Yvette Mimieux, Connie Francis, Paula Prentiss, Dolores Hart, Frank Gorshin, Barbara Nichols, Rory Harrity, Chill Wills, Jack Kruschen; ***D:*** Henry Levin; ***W:*** George Wells; ***C:*** Robert J. Bronner; ***M:*** Pete Rugolo, Georgie Stoll.

Where the Boys Are '84 woof! **1984 (R)** Horrible remake of the 1960 comedy still features girls searching for boys during spring break in Fort Lauderdale. Telling about its era: charm gives way to prurience. **95m/C VHS.** Lisa Hartman Black, Wendy Schaal, Lorna Luft, Lynn-Holly Johnson; ***D:*** Hy Averback; ***W:*** Jeff Burkhart. Golden Raspberries '84: Worst Support. Actress (Johnson).

Where the Buffalo Roam 🦴½
1980 (R) Early starring role for Murray as the legendary "gonzo" journalist Hunter S. Thompson. Meandering satire based on Thompson's books "Fear and Loathing in Las Vegas" and "Fear and Loathing on the Campaign Trail '72." Either confusing or offensively sloppy, depending on whether you've read Thompson. Music by Neil Young, thank goodness, or this might be a woof. **98m/C VHS, DVD, Wide.** Danny Goldman, Leonard Frey, Bill Murray, Peter Boyle, Susan Kellerman, Bruno Kirby, Rene Auberjonois, R.G. Armstrong, Rafael Campos, Craig T. Nelson; ***D:*** Art Linson; ***W:*** John Kaye; ***C:*** Tak Fujimoto; ***M:*** Neil Young.

Where the Bullets Fly 🦴🦴
1966 Fast-paced Bond spoof. A British spy takes on the intelligence forces of several governments in his search for a new fuel elixir. Fun, if not scintillating. **88m/C VHS.** *GB* Tom Adams, Dawn Addams, Michael Ripper, Tim Barrett; ***D:*** John Gilling.

Where the Day Takes You 🦴🦴½ **1992 (R)** Runaways on Hollywood Boulevard are depicted in an unfortunately heavy-handed drama. King (Mulroney) is the slightly older leader of a group of street kids who tries to discourage his friends from getting involved in the violence and drugs they see all around them. He falls in love with new runaway Heather (Boyle) but their love is blighted by the relentless bleakness of their lives. Among the other members of King's "family" are Astin, as a young druggie in thrall to his older dealer (MacLachlan) and Getty, as a young hustler drawn to violence. The story's predictability undercuts some convincing acting. **105m/C VHS, Wide.** Dermot Mulroney, Lara Flynn Boyle, Balthazar Getty, Sean Astin, James LeGros, Ricki Lake, Kyle MacLachlan, Rob Knepper, Peter Dobson, Stephen Tobolowsky, Will Smith, Adam Baldwin, Christian Slater, Nancy McKeon, Alyssa Milano, David Arquette, Leo Rossi, Rachel Ticotin; ***D:*** Marc Rocco; ***W:*** Michael Hitchcock, Kurt Voss, Marc Rocco; ***M:*** Mark Morgan; ***V:*** Laura San Giacomo.

Where the Eagle Flies 🦴🦴
Pickup on 101 **1972 (PG)** Ersatz '60s rock 'n' roll road movie shuffles together free spirited college coed, hobo with heart of gold, and rock and roller who's making a lane change out of the fast track. **93m/C VHS.** Jack Albertson, Lesley Ann Warren, Martin Sheen, Michael Ontkean; ***D:*** John Florea.

Where the Green Ants Dream 🦴🦴½ *Wo Die Grunen Ameisen Traumen* **1984** A mining excavation in the Outback is halted by Aborigines who declare ownership of the sacred place where the mythical green ants are buried. A minor entry in the Herzog vision of modern-versus-primal civilization. Too obvious and somehow unsure of itself artistically. **99m/C VHS.** *GE* Bruce Spence, Wandjuk Marika, Roy Marika, Ray Barrett, Norman Kaye, Colleen Clifford; ***D:*** Werner Herzog.

Where the Heart Is 🦴🦴 **1990 (R)**
Wealthy dad Coleman kicks his spoiled kids out on the streets to teach them the value of money. Meant as farce with a message. Flops in a big way; one senses it should have been much better. **111m/C VHS.** Dabney Coleman, Uma Thurman, Joanna Cassidy, Suzy Amis, Crispin Glover, Christopher Plummer; ***D:*** John Boorman; ***W:*** John Boorman, Telsche Boorman. Natl. Soc. Film Critics '90: Cinematog.

Where the Heart Is 🦴🦴 *Home Is Where the Heart Is* **2000 (PG-13)** Pregnant 17-year-old Novalee Nation (Portman) is on her way to California with her no-good boyfriend Willy Jack (Bruno), who abandons her at an Oklahoma WalMart. Without friends or funds, Novalee hides out in the store until she gives birth there. Suddenly a local celeb, Novalee finds shelter with eccentric Sister Husband (Channing) and becomes best pals with fecund single mom, Lexi (Judd). Novalee also gets a potential romance with shy librarian Forney (Frain). Superficially one-note sap and

Portman seems miscast. Based on the novel by Billie Letts. **115m/C VHS, DVD, Wide.** Natalie Portman, Ashley Judd, Stockard Channing, James Frain, Dylan Bruno, Joan Cusack, Keith David, Richard Jones, Sally Field; ***D:*** Matt Williams; ***W:*** Lowell Ganz, Babaloo Mandel; ***C:*** Richard Greatrex; ***M:*** Mason Daring.

Where the Hot Wind Blows ✐✐ *La Legge; La Loi; The Law* **1959** Marietta (Lollobrigida) is a poor girl in a Sicilian fishing village who's in love with Enrico (Mastroianni), an equally impoverished engineer. But she comes up with a unique way to get money for her dowry even as she's pursued by every male in town. Meanwhile, local mobster Brigante (Montand) wants to make sure than his son Francisco (Mattioli) doesn't get too involved with the unsuitable Lucrezia (Mercouri). Italian with subtitles. **120m/B VHS, DVD.** *FR IT* Gina Lollobrigida, Marcello Mastroianni, Yves Montand, Melina Mercouri, Raf Mattioli, Pierre Brasseur, Paolo Stoppa; ***D:*** Jules Dassin; ***W:*** Jules Dassin, Francoise Giroud; ***C:*** Otello Martelli; ***M:*** Roman Vlad.

Where the Lilies Bloom ✐✐✐ **1974 (G)** The touching story of four backwoods children who are left orphans when their father dies. They don't report his death to authorities, because they are afraid the family will be separated and sent to an orphanage. Stanton is great as the crusty landlord the children gradually accept as a friend. Based on the book by Vera and Bill Cleaver. **96m/C VHS.** Julie Gholson, Jan Smithers, Matthew Burrill, Helen Harmon, Harry Dean Stanton, Rance Howard, Sudie Bond, Tom Spratley, Helen Bragdon, Alice Beardsley; ***D:*** William A. Graham.

Where the Money Is ✐✐½ **2000 (PG-13)** Famed bank robber Henry (Newman) fakes a stroke so he can get transferred from prison to a nursing home. Carol (Fiorentino) is the bored former prom queen nurse who knows he's faking and enlists his help in pulling one more job. She also brings along dull but devoted hubby Wayne (Mulroney). The characters, and the superb actors playing them, are the main reasons to see this one. Newman is still more charismatic than 90% of the leading men around, while Fiorentino and Mulroney seem inspired just by being on the same set with him. The lightweight script depends heavily on the audience's knowledge of Newman's filmography and the standard caper comedy conventions, but still manages to entertain. **90m/C VHS, DVD, Wide.** Paul Newman, Linda Fiorentino, Dermot Mulroney, Susan Barnes, Bruce MacVittie, Dorothy Gordon, Anne Pioniak, Irma St. Paul; ***D:*** Marek Kanievska; ***W:*** E. Max Frye, Topper Lilien, Carroll Cartwright; ***C:*** Thomas Burstyn; ***M:*** Mark Isham.

Where the North Begins ✐ **1947** A Mountie ransacks the Canadian countryside in search of crime. **41m/B VHS.** Russell Hayden, Jennifer Holt, Tristram Coffin, Denver Pyle, Steve Barclay; ***D:*** Howard Bretherton; ***W:*** Betty Burbridge.

Where the Red Fern Grows ✐✐½ **1974 (G)** A young boy in Dust Bowl-era Oklahoma learns maturity from his love and responsibility for two Redbone hounds. Well produced, but tends to be hokey; good family fare. Followed by a sequel nearly 20 years later. **97m/C VHS, DVD.** James Whitmore, Beverly Garland, Jack Ging, Lonny (Loni) Chapman, Stewart Peterson; ***D:*** Norman Tokar; ***W:*** Douglas Day Stewart, Eleanor Lamb; ***C:*** Dean Cundey; ***M:*** Lex de Azevedo.

Where the Red Fern Grows: Part 2 ✐✐½ **1992 (G)** Sequel to one of the most popular family movies of all time starring Brimley as Grandpa Coleman. Set deep in the Louisiana woods, this magical coming of age tale will touch the hearts of young and old viewers alike. **105m/C VHS, DVD.** Wilford Brimley, Doug McKeon, Lisa Whelchel, Chad McQueen; ***D:*** Jim McCullough; ***W:*** Samuel Bradford; ***C:*** Joseph M. Wilcots; ***M:*** Robert Sprayberry.

Where the River Runs Black ✐✐ **1986 (PG)** An orphaned Indian child is raised in the Brazilian jungles by river dolphins. He is eventually befriended by a kindly priest who brings him into the modern world of violence and corruption. Slow pace is okay until the boy arrives at the orphanage, at which point the dolphin premise sadly falls by the wayside. **96m/C VHS.** Charles Durning, Peter Horton, Ajay Naidu, Conchata Ferrell, Alessandro Rabelo, Castulo Guerra; ***D:*** Christopher Cain; ***C:*** Juan Ruiz-Anchia; ***M:*** James Horner.

Where the Rivers Flow North ✐✐½ **1994 (PG-13)** Vermont logger Noel Lord (Torn) has lived on the land all his life and doesn't want to sell out to the power company. His blunt-talking Indian housekeeper/lover Bangor (Cardinal) knows it's best to take the money and move on. Set in 1927 and adapted from the novella by Howard Frank Mosher. Flat storytelling with a good performance by Cardinal. **104m/C VHS, DVD.** Rip Torn, Tantoo Cardinal, Bill Raymond, Mark Margolis, John Griesemer, Amy Wright, Dennis Mientka, Jusef Bulos, Michael J. Fox, Treat Williams; ***D:*** Jay Craven; ***W:*** Jay Craven, Don Bredos; ***C:*** Paul Ryan.

Where the Spirit Lives ✐✐½ **1989 (PG)** Native children kidnapped by Canadian government agents are forced to live in dreadful boarding schools where they are abused emotionally and physically. St. John is a new arrival who refuses to put up with it and tries to escape. Engrossing and moving. **97m/C VHS.** *CA* Michelle St. John; ***D:*** Bruce Pittman.

Where the Truth Lies ✐✐½ **1999** Dana Sue Lacey (Matlin) is the deaf campaign manager for a candidate who has just been murdered. When she becomes the prime suspect and goes to trial, attorney Lillian Rose Martin (King) has her work cut out for her since Dana refuses to cooperate. But the past and its secrets cannot stay hidden any longer. **92m/C VHS, DVD.** Marlee Matlin, Regina King, Philip Lester, Robert Blanche, Linden Ashby, Brian McNamara, Susan Walters; ***D:*** Nelson McCormick; ***W:*** Marshall Goldberg; ***C:*** Bill Roe; ***M:*** Peter Manning Robinson. CABLE

Where There's Life ✐✐½ **1947** Wisecracking Hope is a New York DJ about to be married to Marshe when he discovers he's the heir to the kingdom of Borovia (whose last king was assassinated). Hasso works her feminine wiles as the general who's guarding Hope when the assassins come after him. Oh, and Marshe and her cop brother Bendix are tracking him down to go through with the wedding ceremony. Frantic antics. **75m/B VHS.** Bob Hope, Signe Hasso, William Bendix, Vera Marshe, George Coulouris, George Zucco, Dennis Hoey, John Alexander; ***D:*** Sidney Lanfield; ***W:*** Melville Shavelson, Allen Boretz.

Where Time Began ✐✐ **1977 (G)** The discovery of a strange manuscript of a scientist's journey to the center of the earth leads to the decision to recreate the dangerous mission. Based on Jules Verne's classic novel "Journey to the Center of the Earth," but not anywhere near as fun or stirring. **87m/C VHS.** Kenneth More, Pep Munne, Jack Taylor; ***D:*** J(uan) Piquer Simon.

Where Trails Divide ✐½ **1937** Keene is a U.S. Marshal who poses as a lawyer to bring a gang of thieves to justice. Lacks action. **54m/B VHS.** Tom (George Duryea) Keene, Eleanor Stewart, Warner Richmond, David Sharpe, Charles French, Hal Price, Bud Osborne; ***D:*** Robert North Bradbury.

Where Trails End ✐✐ **1942** Novel sci-fi western set during WWII with just about everything, including phosphorescent-clothed good guys, Nazis, scoundrels, literate horses, and Gallic sidekicks. Interestingly different. **54m/B VHS.** Tom (George Duryea) Keene, Joan Curtis, Charles "Blackie" King; ***D:*** Robert Emmett Tansey.

Where Truth Lies ✐✐ **1996 (R)** After a severe breakdown, troubled psychiatrist Ian Lazarre (Savage) is sent to a clinic run by the sinister Dr. Renquist (McDowell). Lazarre's given an experimental drug that causes him to have visions of executed serial killer Jonas Keller (Forrest) and also to develop ESP. The plot doesn't make much sense in any case. **92m/C VHS.** John Savage, Kim Cattrall, Malcolm McDowell, Sam Jones, Eric Pierpont, Candice Daly, Dennis Forrest; ***D:*** William H. Molina; ***W:*** Ted Perkins; ***C:*** William H. Molina; ***M:*** David Wurst, Eric Wurst.

Where Were You When the Lights Went Out? ✐½ **1968 (PG)** A complicated, unsuccessful farce about a retiring Broadway actress, her jealous, possibly philandering husband, her greedy agent, an embezzler, and a citywide blackout. Film was actually not based on the 1965 New York City blackout but on a French play, "Monsieur Masure" by Claude Magnier, which was written nine years before. **94m/C VHS.** Doris Day, Patrick O'Neal, Robert Morse, Terry-Thomas, Lola Albright, Steve Allen, Jim Backus, Ben Blue, Pat Paulsen; ***D:*** Hy Averback.

Where's Marlowe? ✐✐ **1998 (R)** Sendup of both indie filming and the private eye genre in a b&w and color combo. NYU film school grads Crawley (Def) and Edison (Livingston) decide to make a documentary about private investigators and choose nearly bankrupt L.A. detectives Boone (Ferrer) and Murphy (Slattery) as their subjects. The dicks latest case seems to involve a wife, a mistress, and, soon, Murphy's demise and the two film students decide to lend a more active hand in solving the case. **99m/C VHS, DVD.** Miguel Ferrer, John Slattery, John Livingston, Mos Def, Allison Dean, Clayton Rohner, Barbara Howard, Elizabeth Schofield; ***D:*** Daniel Pyne; ***W:*** Daniel Pyne, John Mankiewicz; ***C:*** Greg Gardiner; ***M:*** Michael Convertino.

Where's Piccone ✐✐✐ **1984** A woman attempts, with the assistance of a two-bit hustler, to locate her missing husband, only to discover that he has led a double life in the Neapolitan underworld. Giannini as the sleazy hubby is perfectly cast. On-target social and political satire. In Italian with English subtitles. **110m/C VHS.** *IT* Giancarlo Giannini, Lina Sastri, Aldo Guiffre, Clelia Rondinelli; ***D:*** Nanni Loy.

Where's Poppa? ✐✐✐ *Going Ape* **1970** A Jewish lawyer's senile mother constantly ruins his love life, and he considers various means of getting rid of her, including dressing up as an ape to scare her to death. Filled with outlandish and often tasteless humor, befitting its reign as a black comedy cult classic. Adapted by Robert Klane from his novel. **84m/C VHS.** George Segal, Ruth Gordon, Trish Van Devere, Ron Leibman, Rae Allen, Vincent Gardenia, Barnard Hughes, Paul Sorvino, Rob Reiner, Garrett Morris; ***D:*** Carl Reiner; ***W:*** Robert Klane; ***C:*** Jack Priestley; ***M:*** Jack Elliott.

Where's the Money, Noreen? ✐✐½ **1995 (PG-13)** Noreen's (Phillips) out on parole and trailed by the police who believe she knows the whereabouts of the $3 million she helped to steal 12 years before. **93m/C VHS.** Julianne Phillips, A. Martinez, Nigel Bennett, Colm Feore; ***D:*** Artie Mandelberg; ***W:*** Carla Jean Wagner; ***C:*** Brenton Spencer; ***M:*** Richard Bellis. CABLE

Where's Willie? **1977 (G)** Willie is a very bright boy; perhaps a little too bright. When he reveals his latest invention to the folks in his small town, everyone is out to get him. **91m/C VHS.** Guy Madison, Henry Darrow, Kate Woodville, Marc Gilpin; ***D:*** John Florea.

Which Way Home ✐✐ **1990** A Red Cross nurse attempts to flee Cambodia with four young orphans. An Australian smuggler befriends and helps her. Way too long and wandering, though like many a TV movie, it means well. **141m/C VHS.** Cybill Shepherd, John Waters, Peta Toppano, John Ewart, Ruben Santiago-Hudson, Marc Gray; ***D:*** Carl Schultz; ***W:*** Michael Lawrence.

Which Way Is Up? ✐✐½ **1977 (R)** Pryor plays three roles in this story of an orange picker who accidentally becomes a union hero. He leaves his wife and family at home while he seeks work in Los Angeles. There he finds himself a new woman, starts a new family, and sells out to the capitalists. American version of the Italian comedy "The Seduction of Mimi" tries with mixed success for laughs. Pryor as a dirty old man is the high point. **94m/C VHS.** Richard Pryor, Lonette McKee, Margaret Avery, Morgan Woodward, Marilyn Coleman; ***D:*** Michael A. Schultz; ***W:*** Carl Gottlieb; ***C:*** John A. Alonzo.

Which Way to the Front? ✐½ **1970 (G)** Assorted Army rejects form a guerilla band and wage their own small-scale war during WWII. **96m/C VHS.** Jerry Lewis, Jan Murray, George L. Baxt, Steve Franken; ***D:*** Jerry Lewis; ***W:*** Dee Caruso.

Whiffs ✐ **1975 (PG)** A gullible man plays guinea pig in an Army experiment on germ warfare which leaves him with the intellect of a chimpanzee. Naturally, he then devises a plan to use the volatile gas in a chain of bank robberies. The title is appropriate—this movie is a stinker. **91m/C VHS.** Elliott Gould, Eddie Albert, Harry Guardino, Godfrey Cambridge, Jennifer O'Neill, Alan Manson; ***D:*** Ted Post; ***W:*** Malcolm Marmorstein.

While I Live ✐½ **1947** Woman meets female pianist with uncanny resemblance to sister who's been dead 25 years and rethinks her position on reincarnation. **85m/B VHS.** *GB* Tom Walls, Clifford Evans, Carole Raye, Patricia Burke, Sonia Dresdel, John Warwick; ***D:*** John Harlow; ***C:*** Frederick A. (Freddie) Young.

While the City Sleeps ✐✐✐ **1956** Three newspaper reporters vie to crack the case of a sex murderer known as "The Lipstick Killer" with the editorship of their paper the prize. Good thriller-plus with the emphasis on the reporters' ruthless methods of gaining information rather than on the killer's motivations. Lang's last big success. Based on "The Bloody Spur" by Charles Einstein. **100m/B VHS.** Dana Andrews, Rhonda Fleming, George Sanders, Howard Duff, Thomas Mitchell, Ida Lupino, Vincent Price, Mae Marsh; ***D:*** Fritz Lang; ***C:*** Ernest Laszlo.

While You Were Sleeping ✐✐✐ **1995 (PG)** Feel-good romantic comedy finds lonely Lucy Moderatz (Bullock) collecting tokens for the Chicago train system and admiring Yuppie lawyer Peter Callaghan (Gallagher) as he commutes to and fro. Fate conspires to throw them together when Lucy rescues Peter after a mugging. Trouble is, he's not conscious so Lucy goes to the hospital with him, where she's mistaken for his fiancee. She continues the charade and is warmly welcomed by the Callaghan family, with the exception of Peter's brother, Jack (Pullman), who smells a rat even as he falls under the token collector's spell. Meanwhile, Peter remains in a coma, allowing Jack and Lucy to supply romantic comedy. Gallagher brings a serenity to his role as the unconscious Peter, while Bullock and Pullman take the predictable plot and deliver performances that earn them another notch on the climb to stardom. **103m/C VHS, DVD.** Sandra Bullock, Bill Pullman, Peter Gallagher, Jack Warden, Peter Boyle, Glynis Johns, Micole Mercurio, Jason Bernard, Michael Rispoli, Ally Walker, Monica Keena; ***D:*** Jon Turteltaub; ***W:*** Fred Lebow, Daniel G. Sullivan; ***C:*** Phedon Papamichael; ***M:*** Randy Edelman. Blockbuster '96: Comedy Actress, V. (Bullock), Comedy Actress, T. (Bullock).

The Whip and the Body ✐✐½ *Night Is the Phantom; What* **1963** Mario Bava's 19th-century ghost/love/revenge story makes a belated arrival on home video. Nevena (Lavi) is about to be married when her ex-lover Kurt (Lee), soon to be her brother-in-law, shows up. The rest of the action is almost pure Gothic with a moody castle for setting, secret passages, ladies wandering the hallways late at night in their diaphanous gowns. Though the story doesn't quite live up to the title, it is very sexually charged for its time and Lee turns in an aggressive performance. **88m/C DVD, Wide.** *IT* Christopher Lee, Daliah Lavi, Tony Kendall, Harriet Medin, Isli Oberon; ***D:*** Mario Bava; ***W:*** Ernesto Gastaldi, Ugo Guerra, Luciano Martino; ***C:*** Ubaldo Terzano; ***M:*** Carlo Rustichelli.

Whipped ✐ **2000 (R)** It's probably aiming for sophisticated, adult romantic comedy but all it achieves is smut. Sexpot Mia (Peet) is forced to deal with the arrested development of three Manhattan yuppies (Van Holt, Domke, Abrahams) who have prehistoric attitudes towards women. They all discover they are dating her but none wants to give Mia up and they become rivals for her questionable affections. Very unlikeable characters; very unpleasant. **82m/C VHS, DVD, Wide.** Amanda Peet, Brian Van Holt, Judah Domke, Zorie Barber, Jonathan Abrahams, Callie (Calliope) Thorne; ***D:*** Peter M. Cohen; ***W:*** Peter M. Cohen; ***C:*** Peter B. Kowalsk; ***M:*** Michael Montes.

Whirlwind Horseman 🦴 **1938** Substandard horse opera. Maynard's search for a gold prospector friend leads him to a rancher and his pretty daughter. He beats up some bad guys, etcetera. **60m/B VHS.** Ken Maynard, Joan Barclay, Bill Griffith; ***D:*** Robert F. "Bob" Hill.

Whiskey Galore 🦴🦴🦴½ *Tight Little Island* **1948** During WWII, a whiskey-less Scottish island gets a lift when a ship, carrying 50,000 cases of spirits, wrecks off the coast. A full-scale rescue operation and the evasion of both local and British government authorities ensue. The classic Ealing studio comedy is based on the actual wreck of a cargo ship off the Isle of Eriskay in 1941. **81m/B VHS.** *GB* Basil Radford, Joan Greenwood, Gordon Jackson, James Robertson Justice; ***D:*** Alexander MacKendrick.

Whiskey Mountain 🦴 **1977 (PG)** Two couples go on a treasure hunt to Whiskey Mountain but instead find terror. **95m/C VHS.** Christopher George, Preston Pierce, Linda Borgeson, Roberta Collins, Robert Leslie; ***D:*** William Grefe.

A Whisper to a Scream 🦴🦴 **1988 (R)** An actress, in researching a film part, takes a job at a telephone sex service, creating different personas as she talks to keep herself interested. Soon, women resembling the personas are being murdered. Great premise fails to deliver fully, though there is some suspense. **96m/C VHS.** *CA* Nadia Capone, Yaphet Kotto, Lawrence Bayne, Silvio Oliviero; ***D:*** Robert Bergman; ***W:*** Robert Bergman, Gerard Ciccoritti.

The Whispering 🦴🦴 **1994 (R)** Scary little low-budget tale about an insurance investigator who's checking out several suicides and meets up with the Grim Reaper (who just happens to be female). **88m/C VHS.** Leif Garrett, Leslie Danon, Tom Patton, Maxwell Rutherford, Mette Holt; ***D:*** Gregory Gieras; ***W:*** Leslie Danon.

Whispering City 🦴🦴🦴 **1947** A female reporter receives an inside tip incriminating a prominent attorney in a murder committed several years earlier. She tries to get the evidence she needs before she becomes his latest victim. Highly suspenseful, thanks to competent scripting and directing. **89m/B VHS.** *CA* Helmut Dantine, Mary Anderson, Paul Lukas; ***D:*** Fedor Ozep.

Whispering Shadow **1933** Serial starring the master criminal known as the "faceless whisperer." Twelve chapters, 13 minutes each. **156m/B VHS.** Bela Lugosi, Robert Warwick; ***D:*** Al(bert) Herman, Colbert Clark.

Whispers 🦴🦴 **1989 (R)** Psycho Le Clerc repeatedly bothers writer Tennant even though she seems to have killed him. This dismays police guy Sarandon. Based on the novel by Dean R. Koontz. **96m/C VHS.** Victoria Tennant, Chris Sarandon, Jean LeClerc; ***D:*** Douglas Jackson; ***W:*** Anita Doohan, Don Carmody.

Whispers: An Elephant's Tale 🦴🦴½ **2000 (G)** Odd anthropomorphic film made up entirely of nature footage is similar in some respects to "The Adventures of Milo & Otis." As with that film, here we have animals photographed in the wilds of Africa, with various actors supplying voices for the animals. The film opens with the birth of Whispers (Derryberry), an elephant. While his herd is roaming, he gets lost and can't find his mother Gentle Heart (Archer). Wandering through the bush, he meets another elephant named Groove (Bassett). Groove isn't very fond of Whispers at first, but she ultimately decides to help him find his mom. Along the way, they meet a variety of interesting animals and encounter some evil poachers. An entertaining film, but it also feels very artificial. The end result is a film with some amazing photography, but a story which comes across as hollow. **72m/C DVD, Wide.** ***D:*** Dereck Joubert; ***W:*** Dereck Joubert, Jordan Moffet, Holly Goldberg Sloan; ***C:*** Dereck Joubert; ***M:*** Trevor Rabin; ***V:*** Debi Derryberry, Anne Archer, Angela Bassett, Joanna Lumley, Kevin M. Richardson, Alice Ghostley, Betty White, Kathryn Cressida, Joan Rivers.

Whispers in the Dark 🦴🦴 **1992 (R)** A psychiatrist counsels two odd patients—one is an ex-con turned painter with a violent streak, the other is a woman who reveals her kinky sexual experiences with a mystery man. Things get interesting when the doctor finds out her new lover is her patient's mystery man, and the patient turns up murdered. Confusing thriller seems forced but the experienced cast is worth watching. **103m/C VHS, Wide.** Annabella Sciorra, Jamey Sheridan, Anthony LaPaglia, Jill Clayburgh, John Leguizamo, Deborah Kara Unger, Alan Alda, Anthony Heald; ***D:*** Christopher Crowe; ***W:*** Christopher Crowe; ***C:*** Michael Chapman; ***M:*** Thomas Newman.

Whispers of White 🦴½ **1993 (R)** Bridgetown's mayor has been trying for years to put a stop to the drug dealing going on in his fair community. Finally, his new Chief of Police decides to deploy a special task force to clean-up the streets—using whatever methods are necessary (and they're all violent). **98m/C VHS.** Nicholette Goulet, Anthony De Sardo, Tony Craig, April Bransome, Ron Gorton Sr.; ***D:*** Ron Gorton Sr.; ***W:*** Ron Gorton Sr.

The Whistle Blower 🦴🦴🦴 **1987** A young government worker in England with a high-security position mysteriously dies. His father, a former intelligence agent, begins investigating his son's death and discovers sinister Soviet-related conspiracies. A lucid, complex British espionage thriller. Adapted from the John Hale novel by Julian Bond. **98m/C VHS.** *GB* Michael Caine, Nigel Havers, John Gielgud, James Fox, Felicity Dean, Gordon Jackson, Barry Foster, David Langton; ***D:*** Simon Langton; ***W:*** Julian Bond; ***C:*** Fred Tammes; ***M:*** John Scott.

Whistle down the Wind 🦴🦴🦴½ **1961** Three children of strict religious upbringing find a murderer hiding in their family's barn and believe him to be Jesus Christ. A well done and hardly grim or dull allegory of childhood innocence based on a novel by Mills's mother, Mary Hayley Bell. For a film relying heavily on child characters, it's important to portray childhood well and realistically. That is done here, as in "To Kill a Mockingbird." Mills is perfect. The film is Forbes's directorial debut and Richard Attenborough's second production. **99m/B VHS.** *GB* Hayley Mills, Bernard Lee, Alan Bates, Norman Bird, Elsie Wagstaff, Diane Holgate, Alan Barnes, Roy Holder, Barry Dean, Diane Clare, Patricia Heneghan; ***D:*** Bryan Forbes; ***W:*** Keith Waterhouse, Willis Hall; ***C:*** Arthur Ibbetson; ***M:*** Malcolm Arnold.

Whistle Stop 🦴🦴 **1946** A small-town girl divides her attentions between low-life gambler Raft, and villainous nightclub owner McLaglen, who plans a robbery-murder to get rid of any rivals. A forgettable gangster drama. **85m/B VHS.** George Raft, Ava Gardner, Victor McLaglen; ***D:*** Leonide Moguy; ***W:*** Philip Yordan.

Whistlin' Dan 🦴🦴 **1932** Yet another lead cowpoke sets out to avenge the murder of a close relative. Maynard whistles while he walks (and rides) woodenly through this one. **60m/B VHS.** Ken Maynard, Joyzelle Joyner, Lew Meehan, Georges Renavent, Dan Terry, Harlan E. Knight, Bud McClure, Hank Bell, Iron Eyes Cody, Frank Ellis; ***D:*** Phil Rosen.

Whistling Bullets 🦴🦴½ **1936** Action galore in the story of an undercover Texas Ranger infiltrating a gang of thieves. The low budget doesn't detract from an exciting script and tight direction. **58m/B VHS.** Kermit Maynard, Jack Ingram; ***D:*** John English.

Whistling in Brooklyn 🦴🦴½ **1943** Skelton again plays radio crime-solver Wally Benton in this third and last entry following "Whistling in the Dark" and "Whistling in Dixie." A cop-killer and the Brooklyn Dodgers baseball team figure in the mystery, which finds Skelton a suspect in the crimes. **87m/B VHS.** Red Skelton, Ann Rutherford, Jean Rogers, Rags Ragland, Ray Collins, Henry O'Neill, William Frawley, Sam Levene; ***D:*** Sylvan Simon; ***M:*** George Bassman.

Whistling in Dixie 🦴🦴½ **1942** The second appearance of Skelton as radio sleuth Wally "The Fox" Benton (following "Whistling in the Dark") finds him traveling to Georgia with girlfriend Carol (Rutherford). She's worried about an ex-sorority sister who knows the secret of a hidden Civil War treasure. When Wally gets involved, humorous trouble follows. Followed by "Whistling in Brooklyn." **73m/B VHS.** Red Skelton, Ann Rutherford, George Bancroft, Guy Kibbee, Diana Lewis, Peter Whitney, Rags Ragland; ***D:*** Sylvan Simon; ***W:*** Nat Perrin.

Whistling in the Dark 🦴🦴🦴 **1941** Skelton plays Wally Benton, a radio sleuth nicknamed "The Fox," in the first of a three-film series. Veidt (an always excellent villain) is the leader of a phony religious cult, after the money of one of his followers. He decides to kidnap Skelton and have him come up with a plan for the perfect murder but of course there are all sorts of comic complications. Skelton's first starring role is a clever comic mystery and a remake of the 1933 film. Followed by "Whistling in Dixie" and "Whistling in Brooklyn." **78m/B VHS.** Red Skelton, Ann Rutherford, Conrad Veidt, Virginia Grey, Rags Ragland, Eve Arden, Don Douglas, Don Costello, Paul Stanton, William Tannen, Reed Hadley; ***D:*** Sylvan Simon.

Whitcomb's War 🦴½ **1987** Small town becomes a battleground among a host of comic characters who are unaware who really is in charge. **67m/C VHS.** Patrick Pankhurst, Leon Charles, Bill Morey, Robert Denison, Garnett Smith; ***D:*** Russell S. Doughten Jr.

White Badge 🦴🦴 **1997** Kiju Han (Ahn) was a youthful infantry soldier in the South Korean Army's decorated White Horse Division, which fought alongside American troops in Vietnam. Now a writer, and having long suffered from post-tramatic stress, Han decides to use his experiences for his latest work. Flashbacks showcase a reconnaissance mission behind enemy lines that caused one of Han's men to go insane and in the present, Han has a reunion with this soldier in order to confront his own painful past. Korean with subtitles. **122m/C VHS, DVD, Wide.** *KN* Sung-Ki Ahn, Kyung-Young Lee, Hae-Jin Shim, Junho Huh, Sejun Kim, Yongjae Tokko; ***D:*** Ji-Yong Chung; ***W:*** Ji-Yong Chung.

The White Balloon 🦴🦴🦴½ *Badkonake Sefid* **1995** Beautifully told story from the viewpoint of determined seven-year-old Tehranian Razieh (Mohammadkhani), who wants to properly celebrate the Islamic New Year by buying a particularly plump goldfish (a symbol of harmony) from the pet shop. She manages to beg the money from her mother and sets off but, distracted by the street sights, Reziah loses the banknote, which falls into a street grate. Various characters seek to help her out but it's Reziah's resourceful brother Ali (Kafili) who gets a balloon seller to finally retrieve the money. Farsi with subtitles. **85m/C VHS.** *IA* Aida Mohammadkhani, Mohsen Kalifi, Fereshteh Sadr Ofrani, Anna Bourkowska, Mohammad Shahani, Mohammad Bahktiari; ***D:*** Jafar Panahi; ***W:*** Abbas Kiarostami; ***C:*** Farzad Jowdat. N.Y. Film Critics '96: Foreign Film.

White Boyz 🦴🦴 *Whiteboys* **1999 (R)** Flip (Hoch) and his friends long to be gangsta rappers, despite being white and from Iowa. He fantasizes about duets with his idol Snoop Doggy Dogg while dealing baking soda passed off as cocaine to dimwit yuppie disco patrons. He befriends recent Chicago transplant Khalid (Bird) and persuades him to take Flip and his poseur posse to the Cabrini Green projects, where Flip discovers his gangsta fantasy pales in comparison to the real thing. Uneven performances and a rather phat-free script water down an undeniably good premise. **92m/C VHS.** Danny Hoch, Dash Mihok, Eugene Bird, Mark Webber, Piper Perabo, Bonz Malone; ***D:*** Marc Levin; ***W:*** Danny Hoch, Marc Levin, Richard Stratton, Garth Belcon; ***C:*** Mark Benjamin.

The White Buffalo 🦴🦴 *Hunt to Kill* **1977 (PG)** A strange, semi-surreal western parable about the last days of Wild Bill Hickok (Bronson) and his obsession with a mythical white buffalo that represents his fear of mortality. Something of a "Moby Dick" theme set in the Wild West. Clumsy but intriguing. **97m/C VHS.** Charles Bronson, Jack Warden, Will Sampson, Kim Novak, Clint Walker, Stuart Whitman, John Carradine, Slim Pickens, Cara Williams, Douglas Fowley; ***D:*** J. Lee Thompson; ***M:*** John Barry.

White Cargo 🦴🦴½ **1942** Lamarr holds the corny story together with one of her best-known roles as sultry native girl Tondelayo. Pidgeon is a cynical African rubber planter who advises new assistant Carlson against Lamarr's sarong-clad charms. But hormones speak louder than warnings and Pidgeon has to take some strong action to save Carlson from this femme fatale. Based on the novel "Hell's Playground" by Ida Vera Simonton and adapted for both stage and screen by Gordon. **90m/B VHS.** Hedy Lamarr, Walter Pidgeon, Richard Carlson, Frank Morgan, Reginald Owen, Bramwell Fletcher, Henry O'Neill, Clyde Cook, Richard Ainley; ***D:*** Richard Thorpe; ***W:*** Leon Gordon; ***M:*** Bronislau Kaper.

White Cargo 🦴½ **1996** Detective Joe Hargatay is investigating a series of fashion model murders that lead him to Chinatown gangsters, corrupt cops, and the crazy world of model agencies. **92m/C VHS.** David Bradley, Shannon Tweed, Lydie Denier, Tommy (Tiny) Lister, David Groh; ***D:*** Daniel Reardon.

White Christmas 🦴🦴🦴 **1954** Two ex-army buddies become a popular comedy team and play at a financially unstable Vermont inn at Christmas for charity's sake. Many swell Irving Berlin songs rendered with zest. Paramount's first Vista Vision film. ♫The Best Things Happen While You're Dancing; Love, You Didn't Do Right By Me; Choreography; Count Your Blessings Instead of Sheep; What Can You Do With a General; Mandy; The Minstrel Show; Sisters; Heat Wave. **120m/C VHS, DVD, Wide.** Bing Crosby, Danny Kaye, Rosemary Clooney, Vera-Ellen, Dean Jagger; ***D:*** Michael Curtiz; ***W:*** Norman Panama; ***C:*** Loyal Griggs.

The White Cliffs of Dover 🦴🦴🦴 **1944** Prime example of a successful 40s "women's weepie." American Dunne goes to England in 1914, falls in love, and marries the British Marshal. He joins the WWI troops and is killed, without knowing he had a son. Dunne raises the boy in England as a new threat looms with the rise of Hitler. Now grown, he goes off to do his duty and she joins the Red Cross, where she sees him again among the wounded, another victim of the ravages of war. Dunne is fine in her noble, sacrificing role. McDowall is the young son with Taylor (with whom he'd already worked in "Lassie Come Home") as a childhood friend. Based on the poem by Alice Duer Miller. Bring the hankies. **126m/B VHS.** Irene Dunne, Alan Marshal, Frank Morgan, Peter Lawford, Gladys Cooper, May Whitty, Sir C. Aubrey Smith, Roddy McDowall, Van Johnson, Elizabeth Taylor, June Lockhart, John Warburton, Jill Esmond, Norma Varden, Tom Drake, Arthur Shields, Brenda Forbes, Edmund Breon, Clyde Cook, Isobel Elsom, Lumsden Hare, Miles Mander, Ian Wolfe; ***D:*** Clarence Brown; ***W:*** George Froeschel, Jan Lustig, Claudine West; ***C:*** George J. Folsey; ***M:*** Herbert Stothart.

White Comanche 🦴½ **1967** Half-breed twins battle themselves and each other to a rugged climax. **90m/C VHS.** William Shatner, Joseph Cotten, Perla Cristal, Rossana Yanni; ***D:*** Gilbert Kay.

The White Dawn 🦴🦴½ **1975 (PG)** Three whalers are stranded in the Arctic in the 1890s and are taken in by an Eskimo village. They teach the villagers about booze, gambling, and other modern amenities. Resentment grows until a clash ensues. All three leads are excellent, especally Oates. Much of the dialogue is in an Eskimo language, subtitled in English, as in "Dances with Wolves." **110m/C VHS.** Warren Oates, Timothy Bottoms, Louis Gossett Jr., Simonie Kopapik, Joanasie Salomonie; ***D:*** Philip Kaufman; ***C:*** Michael Chapman; ***M:*** Henry Mancini.

White Dwarf 🦴½ **1995** Confusing sci-fi adventure finds edgy Manhattan internist Driscoll Rampart (McDonough) serving his residency on Rusta, a war-torn planet located in a white-dwarf star system. The planet is divided into two hemispheres, one in perpetual darkness and the other in constant light. Rampart learns the ropes from mystical doc Akada (Winfield), who's also involved in a peace accord between Rusta's warring leaders. Visually striking but overly ambiguous—probably because it was intended as the pilot for a weekly series. **91m/C VHS.** Paul Winfield, Neal McDonough, CCH Pounder, Ele Keats, Michael McGrady, Katy Boyer; ***D:*** Peter Markle; ***W:*** Bruce Wagner; ***M:*** Stewart Copeland. **TV**

White Eagle 🦴🦴 **1932** A white man who believes himself to be an Indian gets a job as a Pony Express rider and gets mixed up with horse rustlers. When he finds out who he really is, he is free to marry the white woman he's had his eye on. Interesting plot twist caused by the narrow-mindedness of the Hays Office. **64m/B VHS.** Buck Jones, Barbara Weeks, Robert Ellis, Jason Robards Sr., Robert Elliott, Jim Thorpe, Ward Bond; ***D:*** Lambert Hillyer.

White Fang 🦴🦴🦴 **1991 (PG)** Boy befriends canine with big teeth and both struggle to survive in third celluloid rendition of Alaska during the Gold Rush. Beautiful cinematography. Fun for the entire family based on Jack London's book. Followed by "White Fang 2: The Myth of the White Wolf." **109m/C VHS.** Klaus Maria Brandauer, Ethan Hawke, Seymour Cassel, James Remar, Susan Hogan; ***D:*** Randal Kleiser; ***W:*** Jeanne Rosenberg, Nick Thiel, David Fallon; ***C:*** Tony Pierce-Roberts; ***M:*** Basil Poledouris.

White Fang 2: The Myth of the White Wolf 🦴🦴 **1994 (PG)** White boy and his wolf-dog lead starving Native American tribe to caribou during the Alaskan Gold Rush. Simplistic story with obvious heroes and villains, yes, but this is also wholesome (and politically correct) family fare compliments of Disney. Focuses less on the wolf, a flaw, and more on Bairstow and his love interest Craig, a Haida Indian princess, while exploring Native American mythology and dreams in sequences that tend to stop the action cold. Still, kids will love it, and there are plenty of puppies to achieve required awwww factor. Beautiful scenery filmed on location in Colorado and British Columbia. **106m/C VHS.** Scott Bairstow, Alfred Molina, Geoffrey Lewis, Charmaine Craig, Victoria Racimo, Paul Coeur, Anthony Michael Ruivivar, Al Harrington; ***Cameos:*** Ethan Hawke; ***D:*** Ken Olin; ***W:*** David Fallon; ***M:*** John Debney.

White Fang and the Hunter 🦴🦴 **1985 (G)** The adventures of a boy and his dog who survive an attack from wild wolves and then help to solve a murder mystery. Loosely based on the novel by Jack London. **87m/C VHS.** Pedro Sanchez, Robert Wood; ***D:*** Al (Alfonso Brescia) Bradley.

White Fire 🦴🦴 *Three Steps to the Gallows* **1953** Brady, in search of his lost brother, gets involved in a smuggling ring. Seems the brother is falsely accused of murder and about to hang. Brady and bar singer Castle solve the case. Good photography; bad script. **82m/C VHS.** *GB* Scott Brady, Mary Castle, Ferdinand "Ferdy" Mayne; ***D:*** John Gilling.

White Fire 🦴 **1983** Two jewel thieves will stop at nothing to own White Fire, a two hundred-carat diamond. **90m/C VHS.** Robert Ginty, Fred Williamson.

White Fury **1990** Couples on a campout are victimized by sleazy hoodlums during a snowstorm. **89m/C VHS.** Deke Anderson, Sean Holton, Douglas Hartier, Christine Shinn, Chastity Hammons; ***D:*** David A. Prior.

White Ghost 🦴 **1988 (R)** An Intelligence Officer who disappeared in the jungles of Asia 18 years ago is ready to come back to the United States, but not everyone wants to see him again. **90m/C VHS.** William Katt, Rosalind Chao, Martin Hewitt, Wayne Crawford, Reb Brown; ***D:*** B.J. Davis.

White Gold 🦴🦴🦴 **1928** Shepherd's son weds Mexican woman and his disgruntled father contrives apparent rendezvous between the wife and a ranch-hand, who's found dead in her bedroom. Seems no one believes the wife's story. Unprecedented, dark, silent drama. **73m/B VHS.** Jetta Goudal, Kenneth Thomson, George Bancroft, George Nicholls Jr., Clyde Cook; ***D:*** William K. Howard.

White Gorilla woof! **1947** A great white hunter sets out to kill a gigantic white gorilla that is terrorizing the black natives. Imperialist trash. On any informed person's list of all-time worst movies. **62m/B VHS.** Ray Corrigan, Lorraine Miller.

White Heat 🦴🦴🦴½ **1949** A classic gangster film with one of Cagney's best roles as a psychopathic robber/killer with a mother complex. The famous finale—perhaps Cagney's best-known scene—has Cagney trapped on top of a burning oil tank shouting "Made it, Ma! Top of the world!" before the tank explodes. Cagney's character is allegedly based on Arthur "Doc" Barker and his "Ma," and his portrayal is breathtaking. Also available colorized. **114m/B VHS.** James Cagney, Virginia Mayo, Edmond O'Brien, Margaret Wycherly, Steve Cochran, John Archer, Wally Cassell; ***D:*** Raoul Walsh; ***W:*** Ivan Goff, Ben Roberts; ***C:*** Sid Hickox; ***M:*** Max Steiner.

White Hot 🦴½ **1988 (R)** A young businessman loses his prestigious Wall Street job, and in order to live the good life, he resorts to selling drugs. Benson stars and directs. **95m/C VHS.** Robby Benson, Tawny Kitaen, Danny Aiello, Sally Kirkland, Judy Tenuta; ***D:*** Robby Benson.

White Hot: The Mysterious Murder of Thelma Todd 🦴🦴 **1991** Thelma Todd was a Hollywood starlet found dead under strange circumstances in 1935. Buffs have sought a solution to the maybe-murder ever since; this treatment (based on the book "Hot Toddy" by Andy Edmunds) leaves too many loose ends for purists and isn't sufficiently gripping for the uninitiated. **95m/C VHS.** Loni Anderson, Robert Davi, Paul Dooley, Lawrence Pressman; ***D:*** Paul Wendkos.

White Hunter, Black Heart 🦴🦴🦴 **1990 (PG)** Eastwood casts himself against type as Huston-esque director who is more interested in hunting large tusked creatures than shooting the film he came to Africa to produce. Based on Peter Viertel's 1953 account of his experiences working on James Agee's script for Huston's "African Queen." Eastwood's Huston impression is a highlight, though the story occasionally wanders off with the elephants. **112m/C VHS, 8mm.** Clint Eastwood, Marisa Berenson, George Dzundza, Jeff Fahey, Timothy Spall, Charlotte Cornwell, Mel Martin, Alun Armstrong, Richard Vanstone; ***D:*** Clint Eastwood; ***W:*** Peter Viertel, James Bridges, Burt Kennedy; ***C:*** Jack N. Green; ***M:*** Lennie Niehaus.

White Huntress 🦴½ *Golden Ivory* **1957** Two brothers venturing into the jungle encounter a beautiful young woman, the daughter of a settlement leader. Meanwhile, a killer is on the loose. **86m/C VHS.** *GB* Robert Urquhart, John Bentley, Susan Stephen; ***D:*** George Breakston.

The White Legion 🦴½ **1936** Workers and engineers push their way through steaming jungles and reeking swamps while building the Panama Canal. Many fall victim to yellow fever. Physician Keith does some medical sleuthing and saves the day. Plodding, predictable drama. **81m/B VHS.** Ian Keith, Tala Birell, Snub Pollard; ***D:*** Karl Brown.

White Lie 🦴🦴½ **1991 (PG-13)** Len Madison Jr. (Hines), a press secretary for the mayor of New York, receives an old photo of a lynched black man who he learns is his father, hung for raping a white woman. Madison returns to his Southern hometown to find out the truth behind his father's death, assisted by a white doctor (O'Toole) whose mother was a rape victim. They fall in love, adding to an already complicated situation, and incur the wrath of locals who are trying to keep the truth hidden. Based on the novel "Louisiana Black" by Samuel Charters. **93m/C VHS.** Gregory Hines, Annette O'Toole, Bill Nunn; ***D:*** Bill Condon.

White Lies 🦴🦴 **1998 (R)** Catherine (Polley), a freshman college student at a liberal university, feels alienated from her peers and finds solace in an online chat room. She becomes increasingly involved with the shadowy National Identity Movement and becomes their spokesperson before understanding what they really represent and that they're a group of neo-Nazis. **92m/C VHS, DVD.** *CA* Sarah Polley, Tanya Allen, Jonathan Scarfe, Lynn Redgrave, Joseph Kell, Albert Schultz; ***D:*** Keri Skogland; ***W:*** Dennis Foon. **TV**

White Light 🦴🦴 **1990 (R)** "Flatliners" with a flatfoot; after a near-death experience a cop returns with memories of a beautiful woman. He tries to find out who she is/was in plodding fashion. The voyage to the afterlife is represented by a jog through a storm sewer. **96m/C VHS.** Martin Kove, Allison Hossack, Martha Henry, Heidi von Palleske, James Purcell, Bruce Boa; ***D:*** Al Waxman.

White Lightning 🦴🦴½ *McKlusky* **1973 (PG)** Good ol' boy Reynolds plays a moonshiner going after the crooked sheriff who murdered his brother. Good stunt-driving chases enliven the formula. The inferior sequel is "Gator." **101m/C VHS.** Burt Reynolds, Ned Beatty, Bo Hopkins, Jennifer Billingsley, Louise Latham; ***D:*** Joseph Sargent; ***W:*** William W. Norton Sr.; ***M:*** Charles Bernstein.

White Line Fever 🦴🦴½ **1975 (PG)** A young trucker's search for a happy life with his childhood sweetheart is complicated by a corrupt group in control of the long-haul trucking business. Well-done action film of good triumphing over evil. **89m/C VHS.** Jan-Michael Vincent, Kay Lenz, Slim Pickens, L.Q. (Justus E. McQueen) Jones, John David Garfield; ***D:*** Jonathan Kaplan; ***W:*** Jonathan Kaplan, Ken Friedman; ***C:*** Fred W. Koenekamp.

The White Lioness 🦴🦴 *Den Vita Lejoninnan* **1996** A young woman is found murdered in the Swedish countryside and the small town cop investigating realizes it's a more complicated case than he can handle. Especially when the crime leads him to Russia and South Africa and an international terrorist organization. Based on the novel by Henning Mankell. Swedish with subtitles. **104m/C VHS, DVD, Wide.** *SW* Rolf Lassgard, Basil Appollis, Jesper Christensen, Nelson Mandela; ***D:*** Per (Pelle) Berglund; ***W:*** Lars Bjorkman; ***C:*** Tony Forsberg; ***M:*** Thomas Lindahl.

White Mama 🦴🦴🦴 **1980** A poor widow (Davis, in a splendid role) takes in a street-wise black kid (Harden) in return for protection from the neighborhood's dangers, and they discover friendship. Poignant drama, capably directed by Cooper, featuring sterling performances all around Made-for-TV drama at its best. **96m/C VHS.** Bette Davis, Ernest Harden, Eileen Heckart, Virginia Capers, Lurene Tuttle, Anne Ramsey; ***D:*** Jackie Cooper.

White Mane 🦴🦴🦴 **1952** The poignant, poetic story of a proud and fierce white stallion that continually eludes attempts by ranchers to capture it. In French with English subtitles. **38m/B VHS.** Alain Emery, Frank Silvera; ***D:*** Albert Lamorisse. Cannes '52: Film.

White Man's Burden 🦴🦴 **1995 (R)** In a world where blacks have all the wealth and power, and whites comprise the struggling underclasses, Caucasian factory worker Louis Pinnock (John Travolta) is fired by his bigoted black CEO (Belafonte) due to a misunderstanding. Driven by poverty-level financial strain, Louis kidnaps his wealthy boss to show him how the other half lives. Gimmicky premise is full of reversed stereotypes, such as black cops beating a white guy, and skinheads taking over as inner-city gangsters. Treads too lightly, and rehashes too many familiar stories, to make any real impact. Travolta had to be talked into this role by "Pulp Fiction" producer Lawrence Bender. **89m/C VHS, DVD.** John Travolta, Harry Belafonte, Kelly Lynch, Margaret Avery, Tom Bower, Carrie Snodgress, Sheryl Lee Ralph; ***D:*** Desmond Nakano; ***W:*** Desmond Nakano; ***C:*** Willy Kurant; ***M:*** Howard Shore.

White Men Can't Jump 🦴🦴 **1992 (R)** Sometimes they can't act either. Small-time con man Harrelson stands around looking like a big nerd until someone dares him to play basketball and he proves to be more adept than he looks. After he beats Snipes, they become friends and start hustling together. Harrelson lays to rest the rumor that he can't act; here, he proves it. Fast-paced, obscenity-laced dialogue does not cover up for the fact that the story hovers between dull and dismal, redeemed only by the surreal "Jeopardy" game show sequence and the convincing b-ball action. Snipes manages to rise above the material as well as the rim, while Perez, as wooden Woody's spitfire Hispanic girlfriend, is appropriately energetic. **115m/C VHS, DVD, Wide.** Wesley Snipes, Woody Harrelson, Rosie Perez, Tyra Ferrell, Cylk Cozart, Kadeem Hardison, Ernest Harden, John Jones; ***D:*** Ron Shelton; ***W:*** Ron Shelton; ***C:*** Russell Boyd; ***M:*** Bennie Wallace.

White Mile 🦴🦴½ **1994 (R)** Abusive L.A. advertising exec Dan Cutler (Alda) invites his top execs and important clients on a white-water rafting expedition along the Chilko River in the Canadian Rockies (filmed at Northern California's Russian River). But competition and arrogance causes the deaths of several participants and the widow of one sues the agency for damages. Alda excels in arrogant, self-serving nastiness. Fact-based TV movie based on court transcripts. **97m/C VHS.** Alan Alda, Peter Gallagher, Robert Loggia, Fionnula Flanagan, Dakin Matthews, Bruce Altman, Robert Picardo, Max Wright, Jack Gilpin, Ken Jenkins; ***D:*** Robert Butler; ***W:*** Michael Butler.

White Mischief 🦴🦴🦴 **1988 (R)** An alternately ghastly and hilarious indictment of the English upper class between the World Wars, and the decadence the British colonists perpetrated in Kenya, which came to world attention with the murder of the philandering Earl of Errol in 1941. Exquisitely directed and photographed. Acclaimed and grandly acted, especially by Scacchi; Howard's last appearance. **108m/C VHS, 8mm.** Greta Scacchi, Charles Dance, Joss Ackland, Sarah Miles, John Hurt, Hugh Grant, Geraldine Chaplin, Trevor Howard, Murray Head, Susan Fleetwood, Alan Dobie, Jacqueline Pearce; ***D:*** Michael Radford; ***W:*** Michael Radford; ***C:*** Roger Deakins; ***M:*** George Fenton.

White Nights 🦴🦴🦴 *Le Notti Bianche* **1957** Based on a love story by Dostoyevski. A young woman pines for the return of her sailor while a mild-mannered clerk is smitten by her. Both of their romantic fantasies are explored the dance-hall cadence is mixed with dreamy, fantastic flashbacks. In Italian with English subtitles. Equally good Soviet version made in 1959. **107m/C VHS.** *IT FR* Maria Schell, Jean Marais, Marcello Mastroianni, Clara Calamai, Giorgio Listuzzi; ***D:*** Luchino Visconti; ***W:*** Luchino Visconti, Suso Cecchi D'Amico; ***C:*** Giuseppe Rotunno; ***M:*** Nino Rota.

White Nights 🦴🦴½ **1985 (PG-13)** A Russian ballet dancer who defected to the U.S. (Baryshnikov) is a passenger on a jet that crashes in the Soviet Union. With the aid of a disillusioned expatriate tap dancer (Hines), he plots to escape again. The excellent dance sequences elevate the rather lame story. ♫Say You, Say Me. **135m/C VHS, Wide.** Mikhail Baryshnikov, Gregory Hines, Isabella Rossellini, Helen Mirren, Jerzy Skolimowski, Geraldine Page; ***D:*** Taylor Hackford; ***C:*** David Watkin; ***M:*** Michel Colombier. Oscars '85: Song ("Say You, Say Me"); Golden Globes '86: Song ("Say You, Say Me").

White of the Eye 🦴🦴🦴 **1988 (R)** A murdering lunatic is on the loose in Arizona, and an innocent man must find him to acquit himself of the murders. A tense, effective thriller; dazzling technique recalls the experimental films of the 1960s. **111m/C VHS.** David Keith, Cathy Moriarty, Art Evans, Alan Rosenberg, Michael Greene, Alberta Watson, Marc Hayashi; ***D:*** Donald Cammell; ***W:*** China Cammell, Donald Cammell; ***M:*** Nick Mason, Rick Fenn, George Fenton.

The White Orchid 🦴🦴 **1954** Romantic triangle ventures into the wilds of Mexico in search of Toltec ruins. Exceptional sets. **81m/C VHS.** William Lundigan, Peggy Castle, Armando Silvestre, Rosenda Monteros; ***D:*** Reginald LeBorg.

White Palace 🦴🦴½ **1990 (R)** Successful widowed Jewish lawyer Spader is attracted to older, less educated hamburger waitress Sarandon, and ethnic/cultural strife ensues, as does hot sex. Adapted from the Glenn Savan novel, it starts out with promise but fizzles toward the end. **103m/C VHS, DVD.** Susan Sarandon, James Spader, Jason Alexander, Eileen Brennan, Griffin Dunne, Kathy Bates, Steven Hill, Rachel Levin, Corey Parker, Spiros Focas, Renee Taylor, Kim Myers; *D:* Luis Mandoki; *W:* Alvin Sargent, Ted Tally; *C:* Lajos Koltai; *M:* George Fenton.

White Phantom: Enemy of Darkness 𝒮 **1987** Ninja warriors in modern day society battling against other evil ninjas. **89m/C VHS.** Page Leong, Jay Roberts Jr., Bo Svenson; *D:* Dusty Nelson; *W:* David Hamilton, Chris Gallagher.

White Pongo woof! **1945** A policeman goes undercover with a group of British biologists to capture a mythic white gorilla believed to be the missing link. A camp jungle classic with silly, cheap special effects. **73m/B VHS.** Richard Fraser, Maris Wrixon, Lionel Royce, Al Eben, Gordon Richards, Michael Dyne, George Lloyd; *D:* Sam Newfield; *W:* Raymond L. Schrock; *C:* Jack Greenhalgh.

The White Raven 𝒮𝒮 **1998 (R)** Nazi war criminal Markus Straud (Rubes) agrees to be interviewed only by Chicago journalist Tully Windsor (Silvers). During the war, Straud hid a priceless diamond and various factions think he's finally going to reveal where the stone is. But Straud only offers a series of cryptic clues that lead Windsor back home, with the bad guys in pursuit. **92m/C VHS.** Ron Silver, Jan Rubes, Joanna Pacula, Roy Scheider; *D:* Andrew Stevens; *W:* Michael Blodgett; *C:* Michael Slovis; *M:* David Wurst, Eric Wurst.

White River 𝒮 *The White River Kid* **1999 (R)** Embarassingly bad would-be comedy based on the book "The Little Brothers of St. Mortimer" by John Fergus Ryan. Broth Edgar (Hoskins) is a fake monk, teamed up with illegal immigrant Morales Pittman (Banderas), in a scam involving selling cheap "socks for God." Traveling through Arkansas they meet up with serial killer "The White River Kid" (Bentley), his girlfriend Apple Lisa Weed (Dickens) and her eccentric family, a blind prostitute (Barkin), and a singing, corrupt sheriff (Travis). Not that you'll be interested in any of them. **99m/C VHS, DVD, Wide.** Bob Hoskins, Antonio Banderas, Wes Bentley, Kim Dickens, Ellen Barkin, Randy Travis, Beau Bridges, Swoosie Kurtz; *D:* Arne Glimcher; *W:* David Leland; *C:* Michael Chapman; *M:* John (Gianni) Frizzell.

The White Rose 𝒮𝒮𝒮 **1923** An aspiring minister travels to see the world he intends to save, and winds up falling from grace. Complicated menage a trois is finally sorted out at the end. Silent. **120m/B VHS.** Mae Marsh, Carol Dempster, Ivor Novello, Neil Hamilton, Lucille LaVerne; *D:* D.W. Griffith.

The White Rose 𝒮𝒮𝒮 *Die Weisse Rose* **1983** The true story of a group of dissident students in Munich in 1942, who put their lives in danger by distributing leaflets telling the truth of what was going on in the concentration camps. Hans Scholl was an Army officer who discovered the truth and told the others. In the end, most of the students were captured by the Gestapo and executed. "The White Rose" was the name of the group, but none survived to tell where the name came from. Verhoeven's film telling is engrossing and compelling, with excellent acting from the young cast. In German with English subtitles. **108m/C VHS.** *GE* Lena Stolze, Wulf Kessler, Oliver Siebert, Ulrich Tucker, Werner Stocker, Martin Benrath, Anja Kruse, Ulf-Jurgen Wagner, Mechthild Reinders, Peter Kortenbach, Gerhard Friedrich, Sabine Kretzschmar, Heinz Keller, Suzanne Seuffert, Christina Schwartz; *D:* Michael Verhoeven; *W:* Michael Verhoeven, Mario Krebs; *C:* Axel de Roche; *M:* Konstantin Wecker.

White Sands 𝒮𝒮½ **1992 (R)** When a dead man's body is found at a remote Indian reservation clutching a gun and a briefcase filled with $500,000, the local sheriff (Dafoe) takes his identity to see where the money leads. Using a phone number found on a piece of paper in the dead man's stomach, the sheriff follows clues until he finds himself mixed up with a rich woman (Mastrantonio) who sells black market weapons and uses the money to support "worthy" causes, and an FBI man (Jackson) who uses him as bait to lure a CIA turncoat/arms dealer (Rourke). Sound confusing? It is, and despite the strong cast and vivid scenery of the southwest United States, this film just doesn't cut it. **101m/C VHS, DVD, Wide.** Willem Dafoe, Mary Elizabeth Mastrantonio, Mickey Rourke, Mimi Rogers, Samuel L. Jackson, M. Emmet Walsh, James Rebhorn, Maura Tierney, Beth Grant, Miguel (Michael) Sandoval, John Lafayette; *Cameos:* Fred Dalton Thompson, John P. Ryan; *D:* Roger Donaldson; *W:* Daniel Pyne; *C:* Peter Menzies Jr.; *M:* Patrick O'Hearn.

White Shadows in the South Seas 𝒮𝒮½ **1929** Alcohol, drugs, and prostitution take their toll on the native population of Tahiti in this early talkie. Blue plays a western doctor who marries the daughter of a native chief. However, he finds greed for the island's pearl treasures drawing other unscrupulous westerners to destroy the unspoiled paradise. **88m/B VHS.** Monte Blue, Robert Anderson, Raquel Torres; *D:* Woodbridge S. Van Dyke; *C:* Clyde De Vinna. Oscars '29: Cinematog.

The White Sheik 𝒮𝒮𝒮 *Lo Sceicco Bianco* **1952** Fellini's first solo effort. A newly wed bride meets her idol from the comic pages (made with photos, not cartoons; called fumetti) and runs off with him. She soon finds he's as ordinary as her husband. Brilliant satire in charming garb. Remade as "The World's Greatest Lover." Woody Allen's "The Purple Rose of Cairo" is in a similar spirit. In Italian with subtitles. **86m/B VHS.** *IT* Alberto Sordi, Giulietta Masina, Brunella Bova, Leopoldo Trieste; *D:* Federico Fellini; *W:* Federico Fellini, Tullio Pinelli, Ennio Flaiano; *C:* Arturo Galea; *M:* Nino Rota.

The White Sin 𝒮𝒮 **1924** An innocent country girl hires on as maid of a rich woman and is seduced and abandoned by the woman's profligate son, but everything turns out all right by the end of the third handkerchief. Silent with original organ music. **93m/B VHS, 8mm.** Madge Bellamy, John Bowers, Billy Bevan; *D:* William A. Seiter.

The White Sister 𝒮𝒮𝒮½ **1923** Gish is an Italian aristocrat driven from her home by a conniving sister. When her true love (Colman) is reported killed she decides to become a nun and enters a convent. When her lover does return he tricks her into leaving the convent but before he can persuade her to renounce her vows Vesuvius erupts and he goes off to warn the villagers, dying for his efforts. Gish then re-dedicates herself to her faith. Colman's first leading role, which made him a romantic star. Filmed on location in Italy. **108m/B VHS.** Lillian Gish, Ronald Colman, Gail Kane, J. Barney Sherry, Charles Lane; *D:* Henry King.

White Slave 𝒮 *Amazonia: The Catherine Miles Story* **1986 (R)** An Englishwoman is captured by bloodthirsty cannibals and, rather than being eaten, is tormented and made a slave. **90m/C VHS.** Elvive Avoray, Will Gonzales, Andrew Louis Coppola; *D:* Roy Garrett.

White Squall 𝒮𝒮½ **1996 (PG-13)** Based on the 1960 true story of 13 young men who become students at Ocean Academy, a year-long adventure spent aboard the brigantine Albatross. Bridges plays the ship's captain and surrogate dad. The boys agonize over their various crises, making the first half of the movie into a veritable "Dead Poets Yachting Society." However, a sudden storm overtakes the ship in the Caribbean and several crew members are killed. There's a shift to a "Caine Mutiny" type trial in which Bridges must prove the tragedy was not his fault while the survivors rally to his defense. Director Scott excels at showing the fury of nature in the prolonged storm scene, but takes his time getting there. **128m/C VHS, DVD, Wide.** Jeff Bridges, Scott Wolf, Caroline Goodall, Balthazar Getty, John Savage, Jeremy Sisto, Jason Marsden, David Selby, Zeljko Ivanek, Ryan Phillippe, David Lascher, Eric Michael Cole, Julio Mechoso, Ethan (Randall) Embry; *D:* Ridley Scott; *W:* Todd Robinson; *C:* Hugh Johnson; *M:* Jeff Rona.

White Tiger 𝒮𝒮½ **1923** Three crooks pull off a major heist and hide out in a mountain cabin where their mistrust of each other grows. **81m/C VHS.** Priscilla Dean, Matt Moore, Raymond Griffith, Wallace Beery; *D:* Tod Browning.

White Tiger 𝒮½ **1995 (R)** DEA agent Mike Ryan (Daniels) decides to take the law into his own fists when his partner Grogan (Craven) is murdered by Chinese gang/drug leader Victor Chow (Tagawa). **93m/C VHS.** Gary Daniels, Matt Craven, Cary-Hiroyuki Tagawa, Julia Nickson-Soul; *D:* Richard Martin; *W:* Gordon Melbourne; *C:* Gregory Middleton; *M:* Graeme Coleman.

The White Tower 𝒮𝒮𝒮 **1950** Five men and a woman set out to scale the infamous White Tower in the Alps. Each person's true nature is revealed as he or she scales the peak, which has defied all previous attempts. Slightly overwrought, but exciting. Filmed in Technicolor on location in the Swiss Alps. **98m/C VHS.** Glenn Ford, Claude Rains, Cedric Hardwicke, Oscar Homolka, Lloyd Bridges; *D:* Ted Tetzlaff; *W:* Paul Jarrico.

White Water Summer 𝒮½ *Rites of Summer* **1987 (PG)** A group of young adventurers trek into the Sierras, and find themselves struggling against nature and each other to survive. Bacon is the rugged outdoorsman (yeah, sure) who shows them what's what. Chances are it was never at a theatre near you, and with good reason. **90m/C VHS.** Kevin Bacon, Sean Astin, Jonathan Ward, Matt Adler, K.C. Martel; *D:* Jeff Bleckner; *M:* Michael Boddicker.

White Wolves 2: Legend of the Wild 𝒮𝒮½ **1994 (PG)** Troubled teens are on a school assignment involving a conservation foundation's rescue of a pair of young wolves. They must overcome lots of obstacles, including the fact that they can't stand each other. Average teens-in-the-woods adventure. **95m/C VHS, DVD.** Corin "Corky" Nemec, Justin Whalin, Jeremy London, Elizabeth Berkley, Ernie Reyes Jr., Ele Keats; *D:* Terence H. Winkless; *C:* John Aronson.

White Wolves 3: Cry of the White Wolf 𝒮𝒮½ **1998 (PG)** A plane crash strands three teens in the wilderness where they must depend on themselves, and the mystical white wolf, for survival. **82m/C VHS, DVD.** Rodney A. Grant, Mercedes McNab, Robin Clarke, Tracy Brooks Swope, Mick Cain, Margaret Howell; *D:* Victoria Muspratt.

The White Zombie 𝒮𝒮𝒮 **1932** Lugosi followed his success in "Dracula" with the title role in this low-budget horror classic about the leader of a band of zombies who wants to steal a beautiful young woman from her new husband. Set in Haiti; the first zombie movie. Rich and dark, though ludicrous. Based on the novel "The Magic Island" by William Seabrook. **73m/B VHS, DVD.** Bela Lugosi, Madge Bellamy, John Harron, Joseph Cawthorn, Robert Frazer, Brandon Hurst, George Burr Macannan, John Peters, Dan Crimmins, Clarence Muse; *D:* Victor Halperin; *W:* Garnett Weston; *C:* Arthur Martinelli; *M:* Xavier Cugat.

WhiteForce 𝒮 **1988 (R)** A secret agent tracks an enemy. His government tracks him. He runs around with a big machine gun and a couple of hand grenades. He fires the gun and throws the grenades. **90m/C** Sam Jones, Kimberly Pistone; *D:* Eddie Romero.

Whitewater Sam 𝒮𝒮½ **1978 (G)** Whitewater Sam and his Siberian Husky, Sybar, embark on an exciting trip through the uncharted wilds of the Great Northwest. The likeable, intelligent hound steals the show. Good family adventure. **87m/C VHS.** Keith Larsen; *D:* Keith Larsen; *W:* Keith Larsen.

Whity 𝒮𝒮 **1970** Whity (Kaufman) is the illegitimate mulatto son of the wealthy white man for whom he works. An equally exploited barmaid (Schygulla) convinces Whity his one chance for freedom is to murder his masters. Kaufman was one of Fassbinder's boyfriends and the personal tensions and obsessions of their relationship spilled onto the screen. German with subtitles. **102m/C DVD, Wide.** *GE* Rainer Werner Fassbinder, Gunther Kaufman, Hanna Schygulla, Ulli Lommel, Harry Baer; *D:* Rainer Werner Fassbinder; *W:* Rainer Werner Fassbinder; *C:* Michael Ballhaus; *M:* Peer Raben.

Who Am I This Time? 𝒮𝒮𝒮 **1982** Two shy people can express their love for each other only through their roles in a local theatre production of "A Streetcar Named Desire." Good cast responds well to competent direction from Demme; poignant, touching, and memorable. Based on a story by Kurt Vonnegut Jr. **60m/C VHS.** Susan Sarandon, Christopher Walken, Robert Ridgely, Mike Bacarella, Aaron Freeman, Caitlin Hart; *D:* Jonathan Demme; *M:* John Cale. **TV**

Who Done It? 𝒮𝒮 **1942** Average Abbott and Costello comedy about two would-be radio mystery writers, working as soda-jerks, who play detective after the radio station's president is murdered. **77m/B VHS.** Bud Abbott, Lou Costello, William Gargan, Patric Knowles, Louise Allbritton, Don Porter, Jerome Cowan, William Bendix, Mary Wickes; *D:* Erle C. Kenton.

Who Done It? 𝒮𝒮½ **1956** Film debut of the rakish Hill as ice-rink sweeper, Hugo Dill. When Dill comes into some money and a dog, he launches a private investigating firm. A woman enters the picture and Hugo discovers his sleuthing has gotten him in over his head. Lots of typical gags and car chases. **85m/B VHS.** *GB* Benny Hill, Belinda Lee, David Kossoff, Ernest Thesiger, Garry Marsh, George Margo, Denis Shaw, Fred Schiller, Jeremy Hawk, Thorley Walters, Philip Stainton, Stratford Johns; *D:* Basil Dearden; *W:* T.E.B. Clarke; *C:* Otto Heller; *M:* Philip Green.

Who Framed Roger Rabbit 𝒮𝒮𝒮½ **1988 (PG)** Technically marvelous, cinematically hilarious, eye-popping combination of cartoon and live action create a Hollywood of the 1940s where cartoon characters are real and a repressed minority working in films. A 'toon-hating detective is hired to uncover the unfaithful wife of 2-D star Roger, and instead uncovers a conspiracy to wipe out all 'toons. Special appearances by many cartoon characters from the past. Coproduced by Touchstone (Disney) and Amblin (Spielberg). Adapted from "Who Censored Roger Rabbit?" by Gary K. Wolf. **104m/C VHS, DVD, Wide.** Bob Hoskins, Christopher Lloyd, Joanna Cassidy, Alan Tilvern, Stubby Kaye; *D:* Robert Zemeckis; *W:* Jeffrey Price, Peter S. Seaman; *C:* Dean Cundey; *M:* Alan Silvestri; *V:* Charles Fleischer, Mae Questel, Kathleen Turner, Amy Irving, Mel Blanc, June Foray, Frank Sinatra. Oscars '88: Film Editing, Visual FX.

Who Has Seen the Wind? 𝒮𝒮 **1977** Two boys grow up in Saskatchewan during the Depression. So-so family viewing drama. Ferrer as a bootlegger steals the otherwise small-paced show. **102m/C VHS.** Jose Ferrer, Brian Painchaud, Charmion King, Helen Shaver.

Who Is Killing the Great Chefs of Europe? 𝒮𝒮𝒮 *Too Many Chefs; Someone is Killing the Great Chefs of Europe* **1978 (PG)** A fast-paced, lightly handled black comedy. When a gourmand, well-played by Morley, learns he must lose weight to live, a number of Europe's best chefs are murdered according to their cooking specialty. A witty, crisp, international mystery based on Ivan and Nan Lyon's novel. **112m/C VHS.** George Segal, Jacqueline Bisset, Robert Morley, Jean-Pierre Cassel, Philippe Noiret, Jean Rochefort, Joss Ackland, Nigel Havers; *D:* Ted Kotcheff; *M:* Henry Mancini. L.A. Film Critics '78: Support. Actor (Morley).

Who Is the Black Dahlia? 𝒮𝒮𝒮 **1975** In L.A. in 1947, a detective tries to find out who murdered a star-struck 22-year-old woman nicknamed "The Black Dahlia" (Arnaz). Based on a famous unsolved murder case which was later the basis for "True Confessions." Made for TV. **96m/C VHS.** Efrem Zimbalist Jr., Lucie Arnaz, Ronny Cox, MacDonald Carey, Linden Chiles; *D:* Joseph Pevney; *W:* Robert W. Lenski. **TV**

Who Killed Baby Azaria? 𝒮𝒮 **1983** Parents are arrested for infanticide after they claim their baby was stolen by a wild dog while vacationing on a supposedly haunted Australian mountain, or was it an aboriginal spirit that absconded with the tyke? Less compelling than the American remake, "A Cry in the Dark." Made for Australian TV. **96m/C VHS.** *AU* Elaine Hudson, John Hamblin, Peter Carroll; *D:* Judy Rymer. **TV**

Who Killed Doc Robbin? *Sinister House; Curley and His Gang in the Haunted Mansion* **1948** A group of youngsters try to clear their friend, Dan, the town handyman, when the sinister Dr. Robbin is murdered. The follow-up to "The Adventures of Curly and His Gang"; intended as part of a Roach kid-comedy series in the manner of "Our Gang." Fast pace and lots of slapstick give a first impression of spirited juvenile hijinks, but not much is genuinely funny. And the names of the two black kids—"Dis" and "Dat"—aren't funny either. **50m/C VHS.** Larry Olsen, Don Castle, Bernard Carr, Virginia Grey.

Who Killed Mary What's 'Er Name? 🦴🦴 *Death of a Hooker* **1971 (PG)** A diabetic ex-fighter tracks a prostitute's killer through Greenwich Village. Illogical, incredible and disjointed attempt at comedy/mystery. Odd, unsatisfying ending, with the boxer going into a coma. Good supporting cast. **90m/C VHS.** Red Buttons, Sylvia Miles, Conrad Bain, Ron Carey, David Doyle, Sam Waterston; *D:* Ernest Pintoff.

Who Shot Pat? 🦴🦴½ *Who Shot Patakango?; Brooklyn Love Story* **1992 (R)** Funny, nostalgic, coming of age story set in '50s Brooklyn. Knight stars as Bic Bickham, the leader of a clean-living "gang" of seniors at a Brooklyn vocational school. Memorable vintage soundtrack features hits by legendary artists Chuck Berry and Bo Diddly. **102m/C VHS, DVD.** David Edwin Knight, Sandra Bullock, Kevin Otto, Aaron Ingram, Brad Randall; *D:* Robert Brooks; *W:* Robert Brooks, Halle Brooks; *C:* Robert Brooks.

Who Slew Auntie Roo? 🦴🦴½ *Whoever Slew Auntie Roo?; Gingerbread House* **1971 (PG)** An updated twist on the Hansel and Gretel fairy tale. Features Winters as an odd, reclusive widow mistaken for the fairy tale's children-eating witch by one of the orphans at her annual Christmas party—with dire consequences. **90m/C VHS.** Shelley Winters, Ralph Richardson, Mark Lester, Lionel Jeffries, Hugh Griffith; *D:* Curtis Harrington; *W:* Robert Blees.

Whodunit 🦴 **1982 (R)** The bad horror flicks always seem to have (usually young) characters murdered one at a time, often on a remote island. This loser is no exception. **82m/C VHS.** Rick Bean, Gary Phillips; *D:* Bill Naud; *W:* Anthony Shaffer.

The Whole Nine Yards 🦴🦴½ **2000 (PG-13)** Wimpy dentist Oz (Perry) has his life turned to chaos when former hit man Jimmy (Willis) moves in next door, inspiring his wife Sophie (Arquette), who's bored and wants Oz dead for the insurance money, and Jill, Oz's receptionist, who aspires to be a hit woman herself. Sophie nags Oz into a plot to alert Jimmy's former employers of his whereabouts, which brings in a whole bunch of new over-the-top characters, all of whom want somebody dead. While it's true that most of the plot elements are not only ridiculous, but cribbed from other hit man movies, this one works because the actors all do fine jobs (except maybe Arquette), and seem to be having a good time. One of those movies that plays much better on video than on the big screen. **101m/C VHS, DVD, Wide.** Bruce Willis, Matthew Perry, Michael Clarke Duncan, Natasha Henstridge, Amanda Peet, Rosanna Arquette, Kevin Pollak, Harland Williams; *D:* Jonathan Lynn; *W:* Mitchell Kapner; *C:* David Franco; *M:* Randy Edelman.

The Whole Shootin' Match 🦴🦴🦴 **1979** Two 30-something Texas nobodies chase the American Dream via a sure-fire invention called the Kitchen Wizard, after failing in the small-animal biz and polyurethane. Offbeat, very low-budget independent feature shot interestingly in sepia tones. Sympathetic and human. **108m/C VHS.** Matthew Perry, Sonny Carl Davis, Doris Hargrave; *D:* Eagle Pennell.

The Whole Town's Talking 🦴🦴🦴 **1935** Meek clerk Arthur Jones (Robinson) usually leads an uneventful life, until the police arrest him, thinking he's escaped mobster Killer Mannion (Robinson again). Arthur manages to prove his identity and is issued an ID card to settle the confusion, but the mix-up has hit the papers and when Mannion finds out about his double, he steals the card and kidnaps Arthur's Aunt Agatha (Ellsler) and coworker Wilhelmina (Arhtur) to ensure his cooperation. Mannion goes on a crime spree and Arthur must figure a way out of his double trouble. Based on a novel by William R. Burnett. **95m/B VHS.** Edward G. Robinson, Jean Arthur, Arthur Hohl, Wallace Ford, Arthur Byron, Donald Meek, Paul Harvey, Effie Ellsler; *D:* John Ford; *W:* Jo Swerling, Robert Riskin; *C:* Joseph August.

The Whole Wide World 🦴🦴🦴 **1996 (PG)** Adaptation of Novalyne Price Ellis' memoirs about her friendship with "Conan the Barbarian" pulp writer Robert E. Howard. In 1933, proper young Cross Plains, Texas schoolteacher (and aspiring writer) Price (Zellweger) arranges an introduction to local eccentric Howard (D'Onofrio), who lives with his overprotective, dying mother (Wedgeworth) and respected doctor father (Presnell) while churning out his bloody tales. Howard has few, if any, social skills but his unpredictability appeals to the sensible Price and the two have a turbulent emotional relationship that never blooms into a full romance. Howard committed suicide in 1936 at the age of 30. **111m/C VHS.** Renee Zellweger, Vincent D'Onofrio, Ann Wedgeworth, Harve Presnell, Helen Cates, Benjamin Mouton, Michael Corbett, Marion Eaten, Leslie Berger, Chris Shearer, Sandy Walper, Dell Aldrich, Libby Villari, Antonia Bogdanovich, Elizabeth D'Onofrio, Stephen Marshall; *D:* Dan Ireland; *W:* Michael Scott Myers, Novalyne Price Ellis; *C:* Claudio Rocha; *M:* Hans Zimmer, Harry Gregson-Williams.

Who'll Save Our Children? 🦴🦴🦴 **1982** Two children are abandoned and left on the doorstep of a middle-aged, childless couple. Years later the natural parents, now reformed, attempt to reclaim their children. Well cast and topical. **96m/C VHS.** Shirley Jones, Len Cariou, Conchata Ferrell, Frances Sternhagen, Cassie Yates, David Hayward; *D:* George Schaefer. **TV**

Who'll Stop the Rain? 🦴🦴🦴½ *Dog Soldiers* **1978 (R)** A temperamental Vietnam vet (Nolte) is enlisted in a smuggling scheme to transport a large amount of heroin into California. An excellent blend of drama, comedy, action, suspense, and tragedy. Based on Robert Stone's novel "Dog Soldiers." Outstanding period soundtrack by Creedence Clearwater Revival, including title song. Violent and compelling tale of late-'60s disillusionment. **126m/C VHS, DVD, Wide.** Nick Nolte, Tuesday Weld, Michael Moriarty, Anthony Zerbe, Richard Masur, Ray Sharkey, David Opatoshu, Charles Haid, Gail Strickland; *D:* Karel Reisz; *W:* Judith Rascoe; *C:* Richard H. Kline; *M:* Laurence Rosenthal.

Wholly Moses! woof! **1980 (PG)** Set in biblical times, this alleged comedy concerns a phony religious prophet who begins to believe that his mission is to lead the chosen. Horrible ripoff of "Life of Brian," released the previous year. What a cast—what a waste! **125m/C VHS.** Dudley Moore, Laraine Newman, James Coco, Paul Sand, Dom DeLuise, Jack Gilford, John Houseman, Madeline Kahn, Richard Pryor, John Ritter; *D:* Gary Weis.

Whoopee! 🦴🦴 **1930** Cantor stars in his first sound picture as a rich hypochondriac sent out west for his health, where he encounters rugged cowboys and Indians. Filmed in two-color Technicolor and based on Ziegfeld's 1928 Broadway production with the same cast. Dances supervised by Busby Berkeley. ♫The Song of the Setting Sun; Mission Number; Makin' Whoopee; A Girlfriend of a Boyfriend of Mine; My Baby Just Cares for Me; I'll Still Belong to You; Stetson. **93m/C VHS.** Eddie Cantor, Ethel Shutta, Paul Gregory, Eleanor Hunt, Betty Grable; *D:* Thornton Freeland.

The Whoopee Boys 🦴 **1986 (R)** A New York lowlife in Palm Beach tries to reform himself by saving a school for needy children so his rich girlfriend will marry him. Full of unfunny jokes and very bad taste, with no redeeming qualities whatever. **89m/C VHS.** Michael O'Keefe, Paul Rodriguez; *D:* John Byrum; *W:* Jeff Buhai; *C:* Ralf Bode; *M:* Jack Nitzsche.

Whoops Apocalypse 🦴🦴½ **1983** T.V. series that offers a satiric account of events leading up to WWIII. Invasion in South America leads British prime minister to suggest nuclear retaliation. Uneven, lacking in the Strangelovian element, but funny in spots. **137m/C VHS.** *GB* John Cleese, John Barron, Richard Griffiths, Peter Jones, Bruce Montague, Barry Morse, Rik Mayall, Ian Richardson, Alexei Sayle, Herbert Lom, Joanne Pearce; *D:* John Reardon; *W:* Andrew Marshall, David Renwick.

Whore 🦴🦴 *If You Can't Say It, Just See It* **1991 (R)** Ken Russell's gritty night in the life of cynical prostitute Theresa Russell is strong medicine, a powerful antidote to sappy Hollywood films that glorify streetwalking. Also available in the 92-minute original uncut version, an 85-minute NC-17 version, and an alternate R-Rated version. **80m/C VHS.** Theresa Russell, Antonio Vargas; *D:* Ken Russell; *W:* Ken Russell, Deborah Dalton.

Whore 2 🦴½ *Bad Girls* **1994 (R)** Jack is a middle-aged writer who moves into Hell's Kitchen in order to do research for a book about prostitutes. Then Jack gets involved with two of the girls—the tough, jealous Lori and childlike Mary Lou. **85m/C VHS.** Amos Kollek, Marla Sucharetza, Mari Nelson; *D:* Amos Kollek; *W:* Amos Kollek.

Who's Afraid of Virginia Woolf? 🦴🦴🦴🦴 **1966 (R)** Nichols debuts as a director in this biting Edward Albee play. A teacher and his wife (Segal and Dennis) are invited to the home of a burned-out professor and his foul-mouthed, bitter, yet seductive wife (Burton and Taylor). The guests get more than dinner, as the evening deteriorates into brutal verbal battles between the hosts. Taylor and Dennis won Oscars; Burton's Oscar-nominated portrait of the tortured husband is magnificent. Richard and Liz's best film together. **127m/B VHS, DVD, Wide.** Richard Burton, Elizabeth Taylor, George Segal, Sandy Dennis; *D:* Mike Nichols; *W:* Ernest Lehman; *C:* Haskell Wexler; *M:* Alex North. Oscars '66: Actress (Taylor), Art Dir./Set Dec., B&W, B&W Cinematog., Costume Des. (B&W), Support. Actress (Dennis); British Acad. '66: Actor (Burton), Actress (Taylor), Film; Natl. Bd. of Review '66: Actress (Taylor); N.Y. Film Critics '66: Actress (Taylor).

Who's Got the Action? 🦴½ **1963** Martin and Turner are a husband and wife divided by his love of playing the ponies. In order to keep his gambling under control Turner schemes to become his new bookie. But when Martin suddenly goes on a winning streak, the new bookie is in trouble with her former competition, who just happen to be the Mob. Strained, flat comedy with Turner especially miscast. **93m/C VHS.** Lana Turner, Dean Martin, Walter Matthau, Eddie Albert, Nita Talbot, Margo, Paul Ford, John McGiver, Jack Albertson; *D:* Daniel Mann; *W:* Jack Rose.

Who's Harry Crumb? 🦴½ **1989 (PG-13)** Bumbling detective Candy can't even investigate a routine kidnapping! His incompetence is catching: the viewer can't detect a single genuinely funny moment. Candy is the only likeable thing in this all-around bad, mindless farce. **95m/C VHS, DVD.** John Candy, Jeffrey Jones, Annie Potts, Tim Thomerson, Barry Corbin, Shawnee Smith, Valri Bromfield, Renee Coleman, Joe Flaherty, Lyle Alzado, James Belushi, Stephen Young; *D:* Paul Flaherty; *W:* Robert Conte; *M:* Michel Colombier.

Who's Minding the Mint? 🦴🦴🦴 **1967** A money checker at the U.S. Mint must replace $50,000 he accidentally destroyed. He enlists a retired money printer and an inept gang to infiltrate the mint and replace the lost cash, with predictable chaos resulting. Non-stop zaniness in this wonderful comedy that never got its due when released. Thieves who befriend Hutton include Denver of "Gilligan's Island" and Farr, later of "M*A*S*H." **97m/C VHS.** Jim Hutton, Dorothy Provine, Milton Berle, Joey Bishop, Bob Denver, Walter Brennan, Jamie Farr; *D:* Howard Morris; *C:* Joseph Biroc.

Who's Minding the Store? 🦴🦴½ **1963** Well, it's certainly not Lewis, who plays poodle sitter Raymond Phiffier who's in love with rich girl Barbara (St. John). Barbara's imperious mother (Moorehead) is determined to break up the duo and hires Raymond to work at the family department store (hoping he'll be a disaster), instead he becomes a success in his own slapstick way. **90m/C VHS.** Jerry Lewis, Jill St. John, Agnes Moorehead, John McGiver, Ray Walston, Nancy Kulp; *D:* Frank Tashlin; *W:* Frank Tashlin, Harry Tugend; *C:* Wallace Kelley; *M:* Joseph J. Lilley.

Who's That Girl? 🦴 **1987 (PG)** A flighty, wrongly convicted parolee kidnaps her uptight lawyer and they have wacky adventures as she goes in search of the crumb that landed her in the pokey. Plenty of Madonna tunes, if that's what you like; they briefly keep you from wondering why you're not laughing. Kind of a remake (a bad one) of "Bringing Up Baby" (1938). **94m/C VHS, 8mm.** Madonna, Griffin Dunne, John Mills, Haviland (Haylie) Morris, Albert "Poppy" Popwell; *D:* James Foley; *C:* Jan De Bont. Golden Raspberries '87: Worst Actress (Madonna).

Who's That Knocking at My Door? 🦴🦴🦴 *J.R.; I Call First* **1968** Interesting debut for Scorsese, in which he exercises many of the themes and techniques that he polished for later films. An autobiographical drama about an Italian-American youth growing up in NYC, focusing on street life, Catholicism and adolescent bonding. Begun as a student film called "I Call First"; later developed into a feature. Keitel's film debut. **90m/B VHS.** Harvey Keitel, Zena Bethune; *D:* Martin Scorsese.

Who's the Man? 🦴🦴 **1993 (R)** Two clowning companions who work in a barbershop in Harlem get recruited onto the police force to investigate a murder. Doctor Dre and Ed Lover (themselves) make use of their hip-hop music connections and full-throttle slapstick humor to enliven the search. Salt of "Salt 'n' Pepa," is the female lead and Ice-T plays a gangster. First-time director Demme works his star duo for both foolish and vulgar humor. Filming done mostly on location in Harlem. Includes a lengthy list of cameo appearances by several hip-hop performers. For fans; based on a story by Dre, Lover, and Seth Greenland. **124m/C VHS.** Ed Lover, Cheryl "Salt" James, Ice-T, Jim Moody, Colin Quinn, Kim Chan, Rozwill Young, Badja (Medu) Djola, Richard Bright, Denis Leary, Andre B. Blake, Bill Bellamy; *D:* Ted (Edward) Demme; *W:* Seth Greenland; *M:* Michael Wolff.

Who's Who 🦴🦴 **1978** In a satire on climbing the British social ladder, workers in a London brokerage firm struggle with class issues and find the higher you climb, the more you find greed, pettiness, and stupidity. **75m/C VHS.** *GB* Bridget Kane, Simon Chandler, Adam Norton, Philip Davis, Joolia Cappleman; *D:* Mike Leigh; *W:* Mike Leigh. **TV**

Whose Child Am I? 🦴 **1975 (R)** A woman so desperately wants a child of her own that she doesn't mind who the father is. Ludicrous and vulgar. **90m/C VHS.** Kate O'Mara, Paul Freeman, Edward Judd, Felicity Devonshire; *D:* Lawrence Britten.

Whose Life Is It Anyway? 🦴🦴🦴½ **1981 (R)** Black humor abounds. Sculptor Dreyfuss is paralyzed from the neck down in an auto accident. What follows is his struggle to persuade the hospital authorities to let him die. Excellent cast headed impressively by Dreyfuss; Lahti as his doctor and hospital head Cassavetes also are superb. From Brian Clark's successful Broadway play. **118m/C VHS.** Richard Dreyfuss, John Cassavetes, Christine Lahti, Bob Balaban, Kenneth McMillan, Kaki Hunter, Thomas Carter; *D:* John Badham; *W:* Reginald Rose, Brian Clark.

Why Change Your Wife? 🦴🦴½ **1920** A rare, recently rediscovered silent comedy. Swanson and Meighan play married couple Beth and Robert who find themselves drifting apart after ten years of marriage. Robert becomes involved with someone else and Beth demands a divorce. After Robert remarries, Beth decides she wants him back and the real fun begins as she tries every trick in the book to regain her ex-husband. Piano scored. **100m/B VHS.** Gloria Swanson, Thomas Meighan, Bebe Daniels; ***D:*** Cecil B. DeMille.

Why Do Fools Fall in Love? **1998 (R)** Frankie Lymon was a teen do-wop singing sensation in the mid-fifties but a career slide led to heroin addiction and an OD death at the age of 25 in 1968. The other thing Frankie liked to do was marry—without bothering to get divorced. So there are three would-be widows battling for what's left of Lymon's estate: R&B singer Zola Taylor (Berry), goodtime girl and single mom Elizabeth Waters (Fox), and churchgoing schoolteacher Emira Eagle (Rochon). The ladies pull out of the stops but Lymon remains a mystery. **115m/C VHS, DVD.** Larenz Tate, Halle Berry, Lela Rochon, Vivica A. Fox, Paul Mazursky, Pamela Reed, Little Richard, Ben Vereen, Lane Smith, Alexis Cruz; ***D:*** Gregory Nava; ***W:*** Tina Andrews; ***C:*** Edward Lachman; ***M:*** Stephen James Taylor.

Why Do They Call It Love When They Mean Sex? *Por Que Lo Llaman Amor Cuando Quieren Decir Sexo?* **1992** Gloria (Forque) works in a live-sex act but is forced to change partners and work with inexperienced Manu (Sanz), who needs some quick cash because of gambling debts. But everything goes well until Manu's respectable parents meet Gloria and think the duo are just a nice conventional couple. **115m/C VHS, DVD, Wide.** *SP* Jorge Sanz, Veronica Forque, Fernando Colomo, Fernando Guillen, Rosa Maria Sarda, Alejandra Grepi, Elisa Matilla, Isabel Ordaz; ***D:*** Manuel Gomez Pereira; ***W:*** Manuel Gomez Pereira; ***C:*** Hans Burman; ***M:*** Manuel Tena.

Why Does Herr R. Run Amok? *Warum Lauft Herr R Amok?* **1969** Notorious Fassbinder black comedy about a middle-class man, unable to cope with the increasing problems of modern life, who suddenly murders his family. The characters are called by the actors' names to heighten the sense of reality. Film is based on a case history. In German with English subtitles. **88m/C VHS.** *GE* Kurt Raab, Lilith Ungerer, Amadeus Fengler, Hanna Schygulla, Franz Maron; ***D:*** Rainer Werner Fassbinder, Michael Fengler; ***W:*** Rainer Werner Fassbinder, Michael Fengler.

Why Has Bodhi-Darma Left for the East **1989** Set in a remote monastery in the Korean mountains, film follows an old master, close to death, who must lead his disciples in their search for spiritual freedom. The film's title is a Zen koan—an unanswerable riddle that serves as an aid on the path to enlightenment. Korean with subtitles. **135m/C VHS, DVD, Wide.** *KN* Hae-Jin Huang, Su-Myong Ko, Yi Pan-Yong, Sin Won-Sop; ***D:*** Bae Young-kyun; ***W:*** Bae Young-kyun; ***C:*** Bae Young-kyun.

Why Me? **1990 (R)** Two jewel thieves unknowingly steal an enormously valuable ruby ring and are in over their heads trying to evade the cops and everyone else. In the same vein as the much-funnier "Nuns on the Run," this caper is done in by bad acting and too much ill-conceived slapstick. Adapted by Donald E. Westlake from his own novel. **96m/C VHS.** Christopher Lambert, Christopher Lloyd, Kim Greist, J.T. Walsh, Michael J. Pollard, Tony Plana, John Hancock, Lawrence Tierney; ***D:*** Gene Quintano; ***W:*** Donald E. Westlake.

Why Shoot the Teacher **1979** A young teacher sent to a one-room schoolhouse in a small prairie town in Saskatchewan during the Depression gets a cold reception on the cold prairie. One of the more popular films at the Canadian box office. Cort was Harold in "Harold and Maude." Based on the novel by Max Braithwaite. **101m/C VHS.** *CA* Bud Cort, Samantha Eggar, Chris Wiggins; ***D:*** Silvio Narizzano; ***W:*** James DeFelice.

The Wicked *Outback Vampires* **1989** Though packaged as serious horror, this is a cheap, tacky spoof with folks stranded at the country residence of a vampire family. Sole point of interest: these Transylvanian cliches take place in the Australian outback. Kids might actually like this (gore isn't severe), if they can surmount the thick Down Under accents. **87m/C VHS.** Brett Cumo, Richard Morgan, Angela Kennedy, Maggie Blinco, John (Roy Slaven) Doyle; ***D:*** Colin Eggleston.

Wicked **1998 (R)** Fourteen-year-old Ellie (Stiles) has a big Electra complex—she's desperate to get Daddy Ben's (Moses) attention (he's too busy boffing their au pair) and get rid of Mom Karen (Field). Then Karen is murdered and Detective Boland (Parks) first suspects their sleazy neighbor, Lawson (Muldoon), with whom Karen had been carrying on. But Inger, Ellie's younger sister, notices that things aren't, well, normal between her sibling and their pop. But the twists aren't done yet. **87m/C VHS, DVD.** Julia Stiles, William R. Moses, Chelsea Field, Patrick Muldoon, Michael Parks, Vanessa Zima; ***D:*** Michael Steinberg; ***W:*** Eric Weiss; ***C:*** Bernd Heinl; ***M:*** Eric Martinez.

Wicked City **1989** Wild and woolly anime is similar in tone to a James Bond movie. In fact, the whole production has a mid-'60s look. A young man named Taki is picked up by a sexy woman in a bar and regrets his decision when she does one of those really icky transformations. Seems she's a visitor from the parallel Black World of monsters. He's an agent of the Black Guard, a secret intelligence organization that protects the Earth from these supernatural bad guys. The story revolves around Guiseppi Mayart, a strange little character who looks (and acts!) like an oversexed E.T., and is the key to a treaty between the two worlds. Taki and his reluctant female partner Makea are assigned to guard the debauched diplomat. **82m/C DVD.** *JP* ***D:*** Yoshiaki Kawajiri; ***W:*** Kisei Choo.

Wicked City **1992** Humans are uneasily coexisting with Reptoids (creatures that can assume human shape) in this sci-fi tale based on a Japanese comic strip. Then Hong Kong police discover a plot by the Reptoids to destroy mankind and rule the world (what else is new). Nifty special effects. Available dubbed or in Cantonese with subtitles. **88m/C VHS, DVD.** *HK* Tatsuya Nakadai, Yuen Woo Ping, Roy Cheung, Jacky Cheung, Leon Lai, Michelle Li; ***D:*** Peter Mak; ***W:*** Tsui Hark, Roy Szeto; ***C:*** Andrew Lau, Joe Chan; ***M:*** Richard Yuen.

The Wicked Lady **1945** Posh but lame costume drama about a bored 17th century noblewoman who takes to highway robbery to spice up her life. Credulity-stretcher extraordinaire. Based on "The Life and Death of Wicked Lady Skelton" by Magdalen King-Hall. Mason is cheeky as a fellow highwayman. Remade in 1983 with Faye Dunaway. **103m/B VHS.** *GB* James Mason, Margaret Lockwood, Patricia Roc, Michael Rennie, Felix Aylmer, Enid Stamp-Taylor, Griffith Jones; ***D:*** Leslie Arliss.

The Wicked Lady ½ **1983 (R)** Remake of the 1945 costumer about a 17th-century noblewoman trying her hand at highway robbery. More noted for its low-cut costumes and racy humor than any talent involved. **99m/C VHS.** *GB* Faye Dunaway, John Gielgud, Denholm Elliott, Alan Bates, Glynis Barber, Oliver Tobias, Prunella Scales; ***D:*** Michael Winner; ***W:*** Michael Winner; ***C:*** Jack Cardiff; ***M:*** Tony Banks.

Wicked Stepmother **1989 (PG-13)** A family discovers that an aged stepmother is actually a witch. Davis walked off the film shortly before she died, and was replaced by Carrera. Davis's move was wise; the result is dismal, and would have been had she stayed. As it is the viewer wonders: How come the stepmother isn't Davis anymore? Davis's unfortunate last role. **90m/C VHS.** Bette Davis, Barbara Carrera, Colleen Camp, Lionel Stander, David Rasche, Tom Bosley, Seymour Cassel, Evelyn Keyes, Richard Moll, Laurene Landon, James Dixon; ***D:*** Larry Cohen; ***W:*** Larry Cohen; ***C:*** Bryan England; ***M:*** Robert Folk.

Wicked Ways *A Table for One* **1999 (R)** Matt Draper (Rooker) is a bigamist. And when wife Ruth (De Mornay) discovers his other life, she becomes determined to make the vow "till death do us part" a reality. Watchable cast in a familiar storyline. **110m/C VHS, DVD.** Rebecca DeMornay, Michael Rooker, Lisa Zane, Mark Rolston, Peter Dobson; ***D:*** Ron Senkowski; ***W:*** Ron Senkowski; ***C:*** Chris Walling; ***M:*** Evan Evans. **VIDEO**

The Wicked, Wicked West *Painted Angels* **1997 (R)** Follows the desolate lives of several prostitutes and their pragmatic madam Annie Ryan (Fricker) in a prairie town bordello in the 1870s. **108m/C VHS, DVD.** Brenda Fricker, Kelly McGillis, Bronagh Gallagher, Meret Becker, Lisa Jakub; ***D:*** Jon Sanders; ***W:*** Jon Sanders; ***C:*** Gerald Packer.

The Wicker Man ½ **1975** The disappearance of a young girl leads a devoutly religious Scottish policeman to an island whose denizens practice bizarre pagan sexual rituals. An example of occult horror that achieves its mounting terror without gratuitous gore. The first original screenplay by playwright Shaffer. Beware shortened versions that may still lurk out there; the 103-minute restored director's cut is definitive. **103m/C VHS, DVD, Wide.** *GB* Edward Woodward, Christopher Lee, Britt Ekland, Diane Cilento, Ingrid Pitt, Lindsay Kemp, Irene Sunters, Walter Carr, Geraldine Cowper, Lesley Mackie; ***D:*** Robin Hardy; ***W:*** Anthony Shaffer; ***C:*** Harry Waxman; ***M:*** Paul Giovanni.

Wide Awake ½ **1997 (PG)** After the death of his beloved grandfather (Loggia), a young Catholic school boy (Cross) begins a mission to find God in order to find out if his grandpa is O.K. He asks difficult questions of his parents (Leary and Delaney) and teachers, including O'Donnell as a sports obsessed nun who compares Jesus and his disciples to a baseball team. He explores Judaism, Islam and Buddhism as well as Christianity. Finally he has an encounter with an angel that restores his faith. While Cross comes across well, the fellow youngsters in the movie have a stagy stiffness to their lines and expressions that lend the movie a hokey feel. **88m/C VHS, DVD, Wide.** Joseph Cross, Dana Delany, Rosie O'Donnell, Denis Leary, Robert Loggia, Dan Lauria, Timothy Reifsnyder, Camryn Manheim; ***D:*** M. Night Shyamalan; ***W:*** M. Night Shyamalan; ***C:*** Adam Holender; ***M:*** Edmund Choi.

Wide Open Faces **1938** Every crook in town is looking for some missing stolen loot. Soda jerk Brown outwits them all in his own inimitable way. The story may be predictable, but Brown's physical humor keeps things interesting. **67m/B VHS.** Joe E. Brown, Jane Wyman, Alison Skipworth, Alan Baxter, Lucien Littlefield, Sidney Toler, Berton Churchill, Barbara Pepper, Stanley Fields, Horace Murphy; ***D:*** Kurt Neumann; ***C:*** Paul Vogel.

Wide Sargasso Sea **1992 (NC-17)** Jamaica in the 1840s is a seething, mysterious paradise—a former British slave colony with a mix of powerful voodoo culture, beauty, and eroticism providing a very potent brew, a perfect setting for this soaper. Based on the novel by Jean Rhys, which is something of a prequel to Charlotte Bronte's "Jane Eyre." Properly English Edward Rochester meets and marries the tragic Antoinette—the same mad wife locked in the attic in the Bronte novel. Explicit nudity and sex earn the NC-17, but the film is tragic without being sensationalized. Also available in an edited R-rated and unrated versions. **98m/C VHS.** *AU* Karina Lombard, Nathaniel Parker, Rachel Ward, Michael York, Martine Beswick, Claudia Robinson, Rowena King, Huw Christie Williams; ***D:*** John Duigan; ***W:*** Jan Sharp, Carole Angier, John Duigan; ***C:*** Geoff Burton; ***M:*** Stewart Copeland.

The Widow **1976** A story about a woman slowly learning to deal with her own grief, her children's traumas, and monetary worries after the death of her husband. Straightforward, passable domestic drama based on Lynn Caine's best-selling novel. **99m/C VHS.** Michael Learned, Farley Granger, Bradford Dillman, Robert Lansing; ***D:*** J. Lee Thompson. **TV**

Widow Couderc **1974** A provincial widow unknowingly includes an escaped murderer among her liaisons. Based on a novel by Georges Simenon. In French with English subtitles. **92m/C VHS.** *FR* Simone Signoret, Alain Delon; ***D:*** Pierre Granier-Deferre.

The Widow of Saint-Pierre *La Veuve de Saint-Pierre* **2000 (R)** Saint-Pierre is a remote French-run island off the coast of Newfoundland. In 1849, drunken sailor Neel Auguste (Kusturica) is involved in a murder and condemned to death via guillotine—known as the "widow." But the island doesn't have one and it must be sent from another French colony. In the meantime, Auguste is in the custody of the local military officer, Le Capitaine (Auteuil), whose compassionate wife (Binoche) has a repentent Auguste released to do chores for the islanders. But the more Auguste becomes part of the community, the more the townspeople become uneasy about the rightness of his fate. French with subtitles. **112m/C VHS, DVD, Wide.** *FR* Juliette Binoche, Daniel Auteuil, Emir Kusturica, Michael Duchaussoy, Sylvie Moreau, Sarah McKenna, Reynald Bouchard, Philippe Magnan; ***D:*** Patrice Leconte; ***W:*** Claude Faraldo; ***C:*** Eduardo Serra; ***M:*** Pascal Esteve.

Widow's Kiss **1994 (R)** Sean Sager (Astin) is suspicious when his wealthy dad Justin (Davison) dies in the arms of sexy, widowed Vivian (D'Angelo). So he hires detective Eddie Costello (Haysbert), who learns that the widow has left a number of dead husbands behind. But Sean's in desperate trouble when he discovers Vivian gets dad's fortune if Sean should die. Rather dull cable drama wastes its talented cast. **103m/C VHS.** MacKenzie Astin, Beverly D'Angelo, Bruce Davison, Dennis Haysbert, Michael Woolson, Barbara Rush, Anna Maria Horsford, Michael Des Barres; ***D:*** Peter Foldy; ***W:*** Peter Foldy, Mark Donnelly; ***C:*** Doyle Smith; ***M:*** Robert Sprayberry. **CABLE**

Widow's Nest **1977** Three widowed sisters live in a bizarre fantasy world when they lock themselves in a dingy mansion in Cuba of the 1930s. Filmed in Spain. **90m/C VHS.** Patricia Neal, Susan Oliver, Lila Kedrova, Valentina Cortese; ***D:*** Tony Navarro.

Widow's Peak ½ **1994 (PG)** 1920s Irish community is run by a dictatorship of well-to-do widows with Mrs. Doyle-Counihan (Plowright) at the helm. Troubles begin for the town non-widow (Farrow) upon the arrival of recently widowed Broome (Richardson), who attracts Dunbar, the nitwit son of Plowright. Entertaining performances (Farrow shows that success is possible after the Wood-man) and beautiful scenery help boost a script that seems torn between whimsical comedy and dark drama. **102m/C VHS.** *GB* Mia Farrow, Joan Plowright, Natasha Richardson, Adrian Dunbar, Jim Broadbent, John Kavanagh, Gerard McSorley, Anne Kent, Rynagh O'Grady, Michael James Ford, Garrett Keogh; ***D:*** John Irvin; ***W:*** Hugh Leonard; ***C:*** Ashley Rowe; ***M:*** Carl Davis.

The Wife **1995 (R)** The routine of married psychotherapists Jack (Noonan) and Rita (Hagerty), who live in an isolated Vermont farmhouse, is disrupted by the unexpected (and unwelcome) appearance of Jack's patient Cosmo (Shawn), who's in crisis, and his wife Arlie (Young). Everyone's got secrets and marital dilemmas that come spilling out over too much wine. A variation on "Who's Afraid of Virginia Woolf?" **101m/C VHS, DVD, Wide.** Tom Noonan, Julie Hagerty, Karen Young, Wallace Shawn; ***D:*** Tom Noonan; ***W:*** Tom Noonan; ***C:*** Joe DeSalvo; ***M:*** Lodovico Sorret.

Wife Versus Secretary ½ **1936** Excellent acting against type creates a near-perfect picture of romantic relationships. Harlow and Gable play a secretary and her boss who have a wonderful professional relationship, but Loy worries something else is afoot. Could have been a heavy-handed soap opera, but the witty dialogue and Brown's fine pacing make it much more. Stewart later claimed that he purposely messed up his romantic scenes with Harlow in order to spend more time in her arms. **89m/B VHS.** Clark Gable, Jean Harlow, Myrna Loy, May Robson, Hobart Cavanaugh, James Stewart, George Barbier, Gilbert Emery; ***D:*** Clarence Brown.

Wifemistress 🦴🦴½ *Mogliamante; Lover, Wife* **1979 (R)** In the early 1900s, an invalid wife resents her neglectful husband. When he goes into hiding because of a murder he didn't commit, she begins to drift into a world of sexual fantasies. Fine performances. Italian dialogue with English subtitles. **101m/C VHS.** *IT* Marcello Mastroianni, Laura Antonelli; ***D:*** Marco Vicario.

Wigstock: The Movie 🦴🦴½ **1995 (R)** Documentary of the eponymous annual Labor Day event in Manhattan, billed as the Super Bowl of drag. Shils intercuts stage numbers with interviews from a variety of the talented, witty festival performers, such as Lypsinka, Mistress Formika, and RuPaul. One of the best numbers is performed by the Dueling Bankheads (as in Tallulah) singing "Born to Be Wild." Like the event itself, documentary is more a celebration than a probing, psychological look at drag. Won't appeal to everyone, but a lot of fun for those who can appreciate high hair and high fashion. **92m/C VHS.** RuPaul Charles, John (Lypsinka) Epperson, Alexis Arquette; ***D:*** Barry Shils; ***C:*** Wolfgang Held, Michael Barrow; ***M:*** Peter Fish, Robert Reale.

The Wilby Conspiracy 🦴🦴🦴 **1975 (PG)** A political activist and an Englishman on the wrong side of the law team up to escape the clutches of a prejudiced cop in apartheid Africa. The focus of the film is on the chase, not the political uprising taking place around it. Well-done chase film with fine performances throughout. **101m/C VHS.** Sidney Poitier, Michael Caine, Nicol Williamson, Prunella Gee, Persis Khambatta, Saeed Jaffrey, Rutger Hauer, Helmut Dantine; ***D:*** Ralph Nelson; ***W:*** Rod Amateau.

Wild America 🦴🦴🦴 **1997 (G)** Warner Bros. invades Disney's well-marked territory of family-friendly real-life adventure with this bio of famed nature documentarians Mark, Marty, and Marshall Stouffer. Pic focuses on the origins of the boys' fascination with animals, which started when their parents gave them a used 16mm camera to mess around with. After getting some footage of backyard wildlife, they're hooked, and hit the road to find more dangerous (and endangered) beasts to shoot (in the good way). As you would expect, the scenery and camera work are splendid, and any expected wild animal gore and violence has been toned way down. There's plenty to hold the interest of adults as well as children, with a big assist going to the clever script. Title is taken from Marty Stouffer's long-running PBS nature series. **105m/C VHS, DVD.** Sonny Shroyer, Jonathan Taylor Thomas, Devon Sawa, Scott Bairstow, Jamey Sheridan, Frances Fisher, Tracey Walter, Don Stroud; ***D:*** William Dear; ***W:*** David Michael Wieger; ***C:*** David Burr; ***M:*** Joel McNeely.

The Wild and the Free 🦴🦴 **1980** Light-hearted comedy about research chimps. The lab-raised bunch become the instruments for radioactive experimenting. Scheming scientists return the chimps to their home to save them from their demise. Made for TV. **100m/C VHS.** Granville Van Dusen, Linda Gray, Bill Gribble; ***D:*** James Hill. **TV**

Wild & Wooly 🦴½ **1978** In 1903, a tough cowgirl and her friends must prevent the assassination of the President. **120m/C VHS.** Chris DeLisle, Susan Bigelow, Elyssa Davalos, Jessica Walter, Doug McClure, David Doyle, Ross Martin, Vic Morrow, Charles Seibert, Sherry Bain, Paul Burke; ***D:*** Philip Leacock; ***M:*** Charles Bernstein. **TV**

The Wild Angels 🦴🦴½ **1966 (PG)** Excessively violent film but B-movie classic about an outlaw biker gang and the local townspeople. Typical Corman fodder was one of AIP's most successful productions. **124m/C VHS, DVD, Wide.** Peter Fonda, Nancy Sinatra, Bruce Dern, Diane Ladd, Michael J. Pollard, Gayle Hunnicutt, Peter Bogdanovich, Dick Miller; ***D:*** Roger Corman; ***W:*** Charles B. Griffith, Peter Bogdanovich; ***C:*** Richard Moore; ***M:*** Michael Curb.

Wild at Heart 🦴🦴🦴½ **1990 (R)** Dern and Cage are on the lam, going across country to escape her mother, his parole officer, and life. Humorous and frightening, sensual and evocative as only Lynch can be. Sweet love story of Sailor and Lula is juxtaposed with the violent and bizarre, obsessive brand of love of the people they encounter. Unmistakable Wizard of Oz imagery sprinkled throughout, as are some scenes of graphic violence. Ladd is unnerving as Dern's on-screen mother (she also has the role off-screen). **125m/C VHS, Wide.** Nicolas Cage, Laura Dern, Diane Ladd, Willem Dafoe, Isabella Rossellini, Harry Dean Stanton, Crispin Glover, Grace Zabriskie, J.E. Freeman, Freddie Jones, Sherilyn Fenn, Sheryl Lee, Albert "Poppy" Popwell, Jack Nance, Charlie Spradling; ***D:*** David Lynch; ***W:*** David Lynch; ***C:*** Frederick Elmes; ***M:*** Angelo Badalamenti. Cannes '90: Film; Ind. Spirit '91: Cinematog.

The Wild Beasts woof! *Savage Beasts* **1985** Children and animals clash violently after drinking water tainted with PCP. Disgusting premise; unredeemably violent. **92m/C VHS.** John Aldrich, Lorraine (De Sette) De Selle; ***D:*** Franco Prosperi.

Wild Bill 🦴🦴½ **1995 (R)** Realistic, un-heroic portrait of Wild Bill Hickok (Bridges), seen mostly in flashback. From trapper and lawman to his last days in Deadwood, South Dakota, focus is on the events haunting the glaucoma-stricken, opium-addicted legend in his later years, such as twice deserting his true love (Lane). Action packed first 20 minutes mellows along with the aging Hickok and the rest gets a bit talky for a Western, albeit an arty one. Bridges's Hickok is brilliant, but Barkin is given a somewhat tedious Calamity Jane. Based on the novel "Deadwood" by Pete Dexter and the play "Fathers and Sons" by Thomas Babe. **97m/C VHS, DVD, Wide.** Jeff Bridges, Ellen Barkin, John Hurt, Diane Lane, Keith Carradine, Christina Applegate, Bruce Dern, James Gammon, David Arquette, Marjoe Gortner; ***D:*** Walter Hill; ***W:*** Walter Hill; ***C:*** Lloyd Ahern; ***M:*** Van Dyke Parks.

The Wild Bunch 🦴🦴🦴🦴 **1969 (R)** Acclaimed western about a group of aging outlaws on their final rampage, realizing time is passing them by. Highly influential in dialogue, editing style, and lyrical slow-motion photography of violence; Peckinpah's main claim to posterity. Holden and Ryan create especially memorable characters. Arguably the greatest western and one of the greatest American films of all times. Beware of shortened versions; after a pre-release showing to the East Coast critics, producer Feldman cut key scenes without Peckinpah's knowledge or consent. **145m/C VHS, DVD.** William Holden, Ernest Borgnine, Robert Ryan, Warren Oates, Strother Martin, L.Q. (Justus E. McQueen) Jones, Albert Dekker, Bo Hopkins, Edmond O'Brien, Ben Johnson, Jaime Sanchez, Emilio Fernandez, Dub Taylor; ***D:*** Sam Peckinpah; ***W:*** Walon Green, Sam Peckinpah; ***C:*** Lucien Ballard; ***M:*** Jerry Fielding. AFI '98: Top 100, Natl. Film Reg. '99;; Natl. Soc. Film Critics '69: Cinematog.

Wild Cactus 🦴🦴 **1992 (R)** Philip and Alexandria Marcus decide to take a romantic vacation at a desert resort where they meet up with a homicidal ex-con and his seductive girlfriend. The two couples find themselves entangled in some violent and kinky games. An unrated version is also available. **92m/C VHS.** David Naughton, India Allen, Gary Hudson, Michelle Moffett, Kathy Shower, Robert Z'Dar, Paul Gleason, Anna Karin, David Wells; ***D:*** Jag Mundhra; ***W:*** Carl Austin.

The Wild Child 🦴🦴🦴½ *L'Enfant Sauvage* **1970 (G)** The brilliant film based on the journal of a 19th century physician who attempts to educate and civilize a young boy who has been found living in the wilderness, without any comprehension of human life. Tenderly told coming of age tale, with surprising sensitivity for its subject. In French with English subtitles. **85m/B VHS, DVD, Wide.** *FR* Jean-Pierre Cargol, Francois Truffaut, Jean Daste, Francoise Seigner, Paul Ville; ***D:*** Francois Truffaut; ***W:*** Jean Gruault, Francois Truffaut; ***C:*** Nestor Almendros; ***M:*** Antoine Duhamel. Natl. Bd. of Review '70: Director (Truffaut); Natl. Soc. Film Critics '70: Cinematog.

Wild Country 🦴½ **1947** Tame western. A U.S. Marshal races to stop the bad guy from killing the late sheriff's daughter and snatching her ranch. **57m/B VHS.** Eddie Dean, Roscoe Ates, Peggy Wynn, Douglas Fowley, I. Stanford Jolley, William "Bill" Fawcett; ***D:*** Ray Taylor.

The Wild Country 🦴🦴½ *The Newcomers* **1971 (G)** Children's fare detailing the trials and tribulations of a Pittsburgh family moving into an inhospitable Wyoming ranch in the 1880s. Based on the novel "Little Britches" by Ralph Moody. **92m/C VHS.** Steve Forrest, Ron Howard, Clint Howard, Rance Howard; ***D:*** Robert Totten; ***M:*** Robert F. Brunner.

The Wild Duck 🦴½ **1984 (PG)** A father discovers that his beloved daughter is illegitimate and turns against her. To regain his love, she plans to sacrifice her most prized possession. Irons overacts; Ullmann almost disappears into the woodwork. Child star Jones is insufferable, and the whole family squeaks with "literary" pomposity. A horrid adaptation of the classic Ibsen play. **96m/C VHS.** *AU* Jeremy Irons, Liv Ullmann, Lucinda Jones, Arthur Dignam; ***D:*** Henri Safran.

Wild Frontier 🦴🦴½ **1948** A rugged old lawman and his sons team up to rid a town of outlaws. Lane, playing a character with his own name for first time, takes over from his murdered father and roots out the evildoer (Holt). Decent, enjoyable, good-guys-win western. **59m/B VHS.** Allan "Rocky" Lane, Jack Holt.

Wild Geese 🦴🦴 **1978 (R)** The adventure begins when a veteran band of mercenaries land deep inside Africa to rescue the imprisoned leader of an emerging African nation, in the interest of protecting British commercial interest. Their mission meets an unexpected turn when they are betrayed by their financial backers. Too much training in the early part; too long; too much dialogue. Where's the action? **132m/C VHS.** *GB* Richard Burton, Roger Moore, Richard Harris, Hardy Kruger, Stewart Granger, Frank Finlay, Jeff Corey; ***D:*** Andrew V. McLaglen; ***W:*** Reginald Rose.

Wild Geese 2 🦴½ **1985 (R)** Lame sequel to the flamed and overlong "Wild Geese," which depended on its name stars. More of the same, this time sans Burton, Harris and Moore. Sure, it's got Olivier, but it still stinks. **124m/C VHS.** *GB* Laurence Olivier, Edward Fox, Scott Glenn, Barbara Carrera, Robert Webber; ***D:*** Peter Hunt; ***W:*** Reginald Rose.

Wild Grizzly 🦴🦴½ **1999 (PG)** A grizzly escapes from a mountain community and rampages through the small town of Pine Lake. Teenaged newcomer John Harding, Ranger Frank Bradford, wildlife tracker Jack Buck, and land developer Harlan Adams are all on a bear hunt for their own reasons. **100m/C VHS.** Daniel Baldwin, Fred (John F.) Dryer, Michele Greene, Steve Reevis, Brendan O'Brien, John Hurley, Courtney Peldon, Riley Smith; ***D:*** Sean McNamara. **VIDEO**

Wild Guitar woof! **1962** A swinging youth cycles into Hollywood and, improbably, becomes an instant teenidol. Considered a top contender for "Worst Picture of All Time" honors. **92m/B VHS, DVD.** Arch Hall Jr., Cash (Ray Dennis Steckler) Flagg, Ray Dennis Steckler, Carolyn Brandt, Bob Crumb, Nancy Czar, Marie Denn, Arch (Archie) Hall Sr.; ***D:*** Ray Dennis Steckler; ***W:*** Joe Thomas, Bob Wehling, Arch (Archie) Hall Sr.; ***C:*** Joseph Mascelli; ***M:*** Alan O'Day.

Wild Gypsies 🦴 **1969** A band of gypsies seek revenge against a renegade member who returned to rape and pillage. Without merit except for the good photography of Steven Burum, who has become respected doing cinematographically intriguing films like "Rumblefish." **85m/C VHS.** Todd Grange, Gayle Clark, Laurel Welcome.

Wild Hearts Can't Be Broken 🦴🦴🦴 **1991 (G)** Depicts the true-life story of Sonora Webster, a small town Georgia girl who runs away from a foster home to join a carnival in the early 1930s, hoping to become a stunt rider. She becomes a horse-diver (a Depression-era sideshow phenomena) and is blinded in a diving accident, but returns to find romance and ride again. Storyline has little screen tension, but it doesn't detract from this fresh family film with a feisty heroine, a sweet romance, and horses. Nice U.S. screen debut for British actress Anwar. **89m/C VHS.** Gabrielle Anwar, Cliff Robertson, Dylan Kussman, Michael Schoeffling, Kathleen York, Frank Renzulli; ***D:*** Steve Miner; ***W:*** Oley Sassone; ***M:*** Mason Daring.

Wild Horse 🦴½ *Silver Devil* **1931** Gibson is the lead (in his favorite talking role), but his magnificent mount Mut commands most of the attention. Interesting historically as an example of stars' (Gibson's in this case) difficulty adjusting to talking pictures. **68m/B VHS.** Hoot Gibson, Stepin Fetchit, Edmund Cobb, Alberta Vaughn; ***D:*** Richard Thorpe, Sidney Algier.

Wild Horse Canyon 🦴🦴 **1925** Yakima Canutt, the man credited with creating the profession of stunt man, stars in this tale about a lady rancher who requires saving from her evil foreman. The climactic stampede scene gives Yakima a chance to demonstrate a high dive off a cliff and a somersault onto his horse. Silent, with musical score. **68m/B VHS.** Yakima Canutt, Edward Cecil, Helene Rosson, Jay Talbet.

Wild Horse Canyon 🦴½ **1939** One of those westerns designed to run as half of a double-feature, this one's shorter than most, but hardly notable. The hero goes after a rustler who shot his brother. **57m/B VHS.** Addison "Jack" Randall, Dorothy Short, Frank Yaconelli, Dennis Moore, Warner Richmond, Charles "Blackie" King, Sherry Tansey; ***D:*** Robert F. "Bob" Hill.

Wild Horse Hank 🦴🦴 **1979** A young woman risks everything to save a herd of wild mustangs from being slaughtered for use as dog food. Creena is good; otherwise, it's sentimental family fare. Based on the novel "The Wild Horse Killers" by Mel Ellis. **94m/C VHS.** *CA* Linda Blair, Richard Crenna, Michael Wincott, Al Waxman; ***D:*** Eric Till.

Wild Horse Phantom 🦴🦴 **1944** A Wild West banker plans to fake a robbery in a diabolical deception to part honest ranchers from their lands. Surely this man's not a member of the F.D.I.C. Okay sagebrush saga. **56m/B VHS.** Buster Crabbe, Al "Fuzzy" St. John, Charles "Blackie" King, John Merton, Lane Chandler, Edward Cassidy, Bud Osborne; ***D:*** Sam Newfield.

Wild Horse Rodeo 🦴½ **1937** When a gunman appears at a rodeo, trouble starts. Part of "The Three Mesquiteers" series. Ordinary action-packed western, the good guys win. Actor Dick Weston, who sings, later gained fame as singing cowboy Roy Rogers. **53m/B VHS.** Ray Corrigan.

Wild Horses 🦴🦴 **1982** A man attempts to make a living by capturing and selling wild horses. Adventure fans will love this film which deals with the common theme of man against nature. **88m/C VHS.** *NZ* Keith Aberdein, John Bach, Robyn Gibbes; ***D:*** Derek Morton.

Wild Horses 🦴🦴 **1984** Ex-rodeo champ Rogers is hankering to escape his dull life. He joins a roundup of wild horses and with Dawber's help exposes a bureaucrat's scheme for them. Rogers is likable and sings, but the supporting cast carries this one. Made for TV. **90m/C VHS.** Kenny Rogers, Pam Dawber, Ben Johnson, Richard Masur, David Andrews, Karen Carlson; ***D:*** Dick Lowry. **TV**

Wild Horses 🦴🦴 *Caballos Salvajes* **1995** Elderly Jose (Alterio) resorts to bank robbery to recover his $15,000 nest egg. Young employee Pedro (Sbarablia) gives him $500,000 and offers to be the old man's hostage. The unlikely duo hit the road for Patagonia and send the press messages detailing the money's suspects origins and their own good intentions. Spanish with subtitles. **122m/C VHS, Wide.** *AR* Hector Alterio, Leonardo Sbaraglia, Cecilia Dopazo; ***D:*** Marcelo Pineyro; ***W:*** Marcelo Pineyro, Aida Bortnik; ***C:*** Alfredo Mayo; ***M:*** Andres Calamaro.

Wild in the Country 🦴🦴½ **1961** Backwoods delinquent Presley is aided in his literary aspirations by woman psychiatrist Lange. Okay, so that's fairly novel. Strange plot lines but in general Elvis is going to college and reading and writing and singing and playing his guitar. Meanwhile Weld wanders around seductively to provide that hint of Tennessee Williams ambience as interpreted by Odet but hey, who cares? Interesting if convoluted Elvis dramatic turn. ♫Wild in the Country; In My Way; I Slipped, I Stumbled, I Fell; Lonely Man. **114m/C VHS.** Elvis Presley, Hope Lange, Tuesday Weld, Millie Perkins, John Ireland, Gary Lockwood, Alan Napier; *D:* Philip Dunne; *W:* Clifford Odets; *C:* William Mellor.

Wild in the Streets ☙☙½ **1968** Satire set in the future, where a malcontent rock star becomes president after the voting age is lowered to 14. Adults over 30 are imprisoned and fed a daily dose of LSD. The president gets his comeuppance when challenged by even younger youths. Very groovy, very political in its own way, very funny. **97m/C VHS.** Christopher Jones, Shelley Winters, Hal Holbrook, Richard Pryor, Diane Varsi, Millie Perkins, Ed Begley Sr., Barry Williams, Dick Clark; *D:* Barry Shear; *W:* Robert Thom; *C:* Richard Moore; *M:* Les Baxter.

The Wild Life ☙ **1984 (R)** A recent high school graduate takes on a wild and crazy wrestler as his roommate in a swinging singles apartment complex. The same writer and producer as "Fast Times at Ridgemont High" but lacks that film's commercial success. Just as adolescent, though. **96m/C VHS.** Christopher Penn, Randy Quaid, Rick Moranis, Hart Bochner, Eric Stoltz, Jenny Wright, Lea Thompson, Sherilyn Fenn, Lee Ving, Ashley St. John, Francesca "Kitten" Natividad; *D:* Art Linson; *W:* Cameron Crowe.

Wild Man ☙ **1989** A Las Vegas gambling magnate with supernatural powers decides to avenge the murder of his friend and sets out on an adventure to find the killer. Crummy acting in yet another "ex-agent called back for one more mission" yarn. **106m/C VHS.** Ginger Lynn Allen, Michelle (McClellan) Bauer, Don Scribner, Kathleen Middleton; *D:* Fred J. Lincoln.

Wild Mustang ☙☙½ **1935** Sheriff's son (Gordon) joins some outlaws to help father (Carey) spring a trap. The plan is sidetracked, and Gordon is captured and nearly branded by the baddies. Don't worry, though; everything turns out all right. Good western. **62m/B VHS.** Harry Carey Sr., Robert F. (Bob) Kortman, George Chesebro, Del Gordon; *D:* Harry Fraser.

The Wild One ☙☙☙½ **1954** The original biker flick: two motorcycle gangs descend upon a quiet midwestern town and each other. Brando is the leader of one (Marvin leads the other), struggling against social prejudices and his own gang's lawlessness to find love and a normal life. The classic tribute to 1950s rebelliousness. Based vaguely on a real incident in California. Quaint after nearly 40 years, but still the touchstone for much that has come since, and still a central role in Brando's now-long career. Brando himself believes it failed to explore motivations for youth gangs and violence, only depicting them. Banned in Britain until 1967. **79m/B VHS, DVD.** Marlon Brando, Lee Marvin, Mary Murphy, Robert Keith, Jerry Paris, Alvy Moore, Jay C. Flippen, Peggy Maley, Bruno VeSota; *D:* Laslo Benedek; *W:* John Paxton; *C:* Hal Mohr; *M:* Leith Stevens.

Wild Ones on Wheels woof! *Drivers to Hell* **1962** A gang of teenage hotrod punks meet an ex-con in the Mojave desert who is searching for the half-a-million bucks he buried there years earlier. Before they find out where the money is, they kill him. In an attempt to find the stash, they kidnap the dead con's wife, hoping she'll sing like a bird. Plenty of unintended laughter. **92m/B VHS.** Francine York, Edmund Tontini, Robert Blair; *D:* Rudolph Cusumano.

Wild Orchid ☙ **1990 (R)** One of the most controversial theatrical releases of 1990. Rourke is a mystery millionaire involved with two beautiful women in lovely Rio de Janeiro. Bisset is strange as an international real estate developer with unusual sexual mores. Very explicit sex scenes, but otherwise mostly boring and unbelievable. Rourke allegedly took his method-acting technique to the limit in the last love scene with Otis. Available in an unrated version as well. From the producers of "9 1/2 Weeks." Followed by an unrelated sequel. **107m/C VHS, DVD, Wide.** Mickey Rourke, Jacqueline Bisset, Carre Otis, Assumpta Serna, Bruce Greenwood; *D:* Zalman King; *W:* Zalman King; *C:* Gale Tattersall; *M:* Simon Goldenberg, Geoff MacCormack.

Wild Orchid 2: Two Shades of Blue woof! **1992 (R)** Blue's jazz-musician, heroin-addict dad dies after a bad fix and she's sold into prostitution, until she runs away to find her true love and live a "normal" life. Effort from soft-core expert King has nothing to do with the first "Wild Orchid" and is almost laughably bad. Siemaszko is whiny, the plot is unbelievable, and the dialogue is unintentionally funny. Yes, you get sex, lots of it, but rather than passionate, it merely looks staged. Also available in an unrated version at 111 minutes. **105m/C VHS.** Nina Siemaszko, Wendy Hughes, Brent Fraser, Robert Davi, Tom Skerritt, Joe Dallesandro, Christopher McDonald, Liane (Alexandra) Curtis; *D:* Zalman King; *W:* Zalman King.

Wild Orchids ☙☙½ **1928** A husband suspects his wife of infidelity while they take a business cruise to Java. One of Garbo's earliest silent films. Garbo is lushly surrounded with great scenery, costumes and sets, making the best of her as she makes the best of a cheery tale. **119m/B VHS.** Greta Garbo, Lewis Stone, Nils Asther; *D:* Sidney Franklin; *C:* William H. Daniels.

The Wild Pair ☙½ *Hollow Point; Devil's Odds* **1987 (R)** Two cops track down a cocaine smuggling ring and uncover a private army planning to conquer the United States. Lloyd Bridges is memorable as a rabid right-winger, and the wild pairing of Bubba and Beau inspires head-scratching. Otherwise, what we have here is a typical action pic, complete with car chases. Beau Bridges' inauspicious feature directing debut. **89m/C VHS.** Beau Bridges, Bubba Smith, Lloyd Bridges, Gary Lockwood, Raymond St. Jacques; *D:* Beau Bridges; *M:* John Debney.

Wild Palms ☙☙ **1993** In 2007 Los Angeles, Harry (Belushi) takes a job at a TV station that offers virtual reality programming to viewers, only this isn't benign technology. Delany is stuck in a thankless role as his wife, Cattrall is his former lover, but Dickinson has the most fun as Harry's power-mad mother-in-law who's also a sadistic co-conspirator of a nasty senator (Loggia). Lesson in weird style over substance really doesn't make much sense, but unlike "Twin Peaks" (to which this TV miniseries was heavily compared) it at least has an ending. Executive producer Stone has a cameo which concerns the JFK conspiracy. Based on the comic strip by Wagner. In two parts. **300m/C VHS.** James Belushi, Robert Loggia, Dana Delany, Kim Cattrall, Angie Dickinson, Ernie Hudson, Bebe Neuwirth, Nick Mancuso, Charles Hallahan, Robert Morse, David Warner, Ben Savage, Bob Gunton, Brad Dourif, Charles Rocket; *Cameos:* Oliver Stone; *D:* Phil Joanou, Kathryn Bigelow, Keith Gordon, Peter Hewitt; *W:* Bruce Wagner; *C:* Phedon Papamichael; *M:* Ryuichi Sakamoto.

Wild Party ☙☙½ **1974 (R)** It's 1929, a year of much frivolity in Hollywood. Drinking, dancing, maneuvering and almost every sort of romance are the rule of the night at silent film comic Jolly Grimm's sumptuous, star-studded party that climaxes with, among other things, a murder. Well performed but somehow hollow; ambitious Ivory effort unfortunately falls short. Based on Joseph Moncure March's poem, and loosely on the Fatty Arbuckle scandal. **90m/C VHS.** Raquel Welch, James Coco, Perry King, David Dukes, Royal Dano, Tiffany Bolling; *D:* James Ivory; *C:* Walter Lassally.

Wild Pony ☙ **1983** A young boy spurns his new stepfather, preferring to live with his pony instead. Reversal of the evil-stepmother-and-girl-loves-horse theme. **87m/C VHS.** Marilyn Lightstone, Art Hindle, Josh Byrne; *D:* Kevin Sullivan; *M:* Hagood Hardy.

Wild Rebels ☙ **1971 (R)** A two-faced member of a ruthless motorcycle gang informs the police of the gang's plans to rob a bank. Lots of bullet-flying action. Dumb, ordinary biker flick; star Pastrano was a former boxing champ in real life. **90m/C VHS.** Steve Alaimo, Willie Pastrano, John Vella, Bobbie Byers; *D:* William Grefe.

Wild Reeds ☙☙☙ *Les Roseaux Sauvages* **1994** Emotional coming of age tale set in 1962 (at the end of the French war in Algeria) and focusing on three classmates at a French boarding school. Sensitive Francois (Morel) is just coming to the realization that he likes boys, particularly working-class Serge (Rideau) who's attracted to Francois's confidante Maite (Bouchez). The provocateur is Algerian-born Henri (Gorny), a bitter political militant who enjoys his battles with classmates and teachers alike. Politics and youthful passions are forced into crises. French historical/political context may prove a barrier. French with subtitles. **110m/C VHS, DVD, Wide.** *FR* Gael Morel, Stephane Rideau, Elodie Bouchez, Frederic Gorny, Michele Moretti; *D:* Andre Techine; *W:* Gilles Taurand, Olivier Massart, Andre Techine; *C:* Jeanne Lapoirie; *M:* Chubby Checker. Cesar '95: Director (Techine), Film, Writing; L.A. Film Critics '95: Foreign Film; Natl. Soc. Film Critics '95: Foreign Film.

The Wild Ride ☙☙ *Velocity* **1960** Nicholson, in an early starring role, portrays a rebellious punk of the Beat generation who hotrods his way into trouble and tragedy. He kidnaps now-straight ex-buddy Bean's squeeze (Carter); kills a few cops; then is killed. Interesting only if you're interested in Nicholson. **59m/B VHS.** Jack Nicholson, Georgianna Carter, Robert Bean; *D:* Harvey Berman; *W:* Marion Rothman.

Wild Riders woof! *Angels for Kicks* **1971 (R)** Two ruthless, amoral bikers molest, kidnap, rape, and beat two beautiful, naive young society ladies. Despicable story, with deplorable acting, but the ending, in which a husband slays a biker with a cello, surely is unique. **91m/C VHS.** Alex Rocco, Elizabeth Knowles, Sherry Bain, Arell Blanton; *D:* Richard Kanter.

Wild Rovers ☙☙ **1971 (PG)** An aging cowboy and his younger colleague turn to bank robbing and are pursued by a posse in a wacky comedy-adventure from director Edwards. Uneven script and too much referential baggage (faint shades of "Butch Cassidy") doom this valiant effort, with the two stars hanging right in there all the way. **138m/C VHS, Wide.** William Holden, Ryan O'Neal, Karl Malden, Lynn Carlin, Tom Skerritt, Joe Don Baker, Rachel Roberts, Moses Gunn; *D:* Blake Edwards; *W:* Blake Edwards; *M:* Jerry Goldsmith.

Wild Side ☙☙ **1995 (R)** Bank employee Alex (Heche) moonlights as a hooker and gets caught in a federal sting operation. Forced to inform on one of her clients, Bruno (Walken), who's involved in a money-laundering scheme, Alex complicates matters by falling in love with Bruno's mistress, Victoria (Chen). The unrated version is 96 minutes. Original director Cammell (who retained his screenwriter's credit) removed his name from the film after disagreeing with cuts made by the production company. **90m/C VHS, DVD.** Anne Heche, Christopher Walken, Joan Chen, Steven Bauer; *D:* Franklyn Brauner; *W:* Donald Cammell, China Cammell.

Wild Strawberries ☙☙☙☙ *Smultron-Stallet* **1957** Bergman's landmark film of fantasy, dreams and nightmares. An aging professor, on the road to accept an award, must come to terms with his anxieties and guilt. Brilliant performance by Sjostrom, Sweden's first film director and star. Excellent use of flashbacks and film editing. An intellectual and emotional masterpiece. In Swedish with English subtitles. **90m/B VHS, DVD, 8mm.** *SW* Victor Sjostrom, Bibi Andersson, Max von Sydow, Ingrid Thulin, Gunnar Bjornstrand, Folke Sundquist, Bjorn Bjelvenstam; *D:* Ingmar Bergman; *W:* Ingmar Bergman; *C:* Gunnar Fischer; *M:* Erik Nordgren. Golden Globes '60: Foreign Film.

Wild Style ☙☙ **1983** Zoro, a mild-mannered Bronx teenager, spends his evenings spray-painting subway cars. Intended as a depiction of urban street life, including graffiti, breakdancing and rap music. Mildly interesting social comment, but unconvincing as cinema. Too "realistic," with too little vision. **82m/C VHS.** Lee George Quinones, Fredrick Braithwaite, Dondi White; *D:* Charlie Ahearn; *M:* Fred Brathwaite.

Wild Thing ☙½ **1987 (PG-13)** A modern variation on the Wild Child/Tarzan myth, as a feral kid stalks a crime-ridden ghetto. Sayles, a usually imaginative writer and director, really takes a dive here. And of course, the Troggs' overplayed title hit is abused as the theme. **92m/C VHS.** Kathleen Quinlan, Rob Knepper, Robert Davi, Betty Buckley, Maury Chaykin; *D:* Max Reid, Ken Cameron; *W:* John Sayles; *M:* George S. Clinton, Guy Moon.

Wild Things ☙☙ **1998 (R)** Titillating pulp friction can't decide between modern noir and swampy spoof. Miami guidance counselor and high school heartthrob fodder Sam Lombardo (Dillon) lectures on sex crimes and gets accused of rape by two school girls: snotty rich Kelly (Richards) and trailer trash Suzie (Campbell). The seemingly upright investigator (Bacon) tries to figure out who's telling the truth. Murray pops up doing his best Bill Murray, but his hilarious presence doesn't play next to the oh-so-serious Dillon and gang. Even more out of place is Wagner's wooden cameo as Kelly's lawyer. Speaking of wooden, the normally fine Russell is reduced to similar stereotype as Kelly's vampy, conniving mother. Endless exercise in audience manipulation has plot twists and turns relentlessly continue through the credits for no apparent reason. **108m/C VHS, DVD.** Matt Dillon, Neve Campbell, Kevin Bacon, Denise Richards, Theresa Russell, Daphne Rubin-Vega, Bill Murray, Robert Wagner, Carrie Snodgress, Jeffery (Jeff) Perry, Marc Macaulay; *D:* John McNaughton; *W:* Steven Peters; *C:* Jeffrey L. Kimball; *M:* George S. Clinton. L.A. Film Critics '98: Support. Actor (Murray).

Wild Times ☙☙ **1979** Too long but pleasant rendition of the life of High Candill, early Wild West showman. Based on the novel by Brian Garfield. Made for TV, originally in two parts. **200m/C VHS.** Sam Elliott, Trish Stewart, Ben Johnson, Dennis Hopper, Pat Hingle; *D:* Richard Compton. **TV**

Wild West ☙☙ *Prairie Outlaws* **1946** The hero and loyal companions (with names like Skinny, Stormy, and Soapy) tackle desperadoes trying to stop telegraph line construction. More mild than wild, it was later trimmed and released under its alternate title, but here you're getting the original. **73m/C VHS.** Eddie Dean, Roscoe Ates, Lash LaRue, Robert "Buzzy" Henry, Sarah Padden, Louise Currie, Warner Richmond, Chief Yowlachie, Bud Osborne; *D:* Robert Emmett Tansey.

Wild West ☙☙ **1993** Three Pakistani brothers, living in London, decide to form an American-style country and western band they call the Honky Tonk Cowboys and dream of making it big in Nashville. A little romance, lots of energy, but too many gags leave the film unfocused. **83m/C VHS.** *GB* Naveen Andrews, Sarita Choudhury, Ronny Jhutti, Ravi Kapoor, Bhasker; *D:* David Attwood; *W:* Harwant Bains; *C:* Nicholas D. Knowland.

Wild Wheels woof! **1975 (PG)** A group of dune-buggy enthusiasts seek revenge against a gang of motorcyclists who have ravaged a small California beach town. **81m/C VHS.** Casey Kasem, Dovie Beams, Terry Stafford, Robert Dix.

Wild, Wild Planet ☙½ **1965** Alien beings from a distant planet are miniaturizing Earth's leaders in a bid to destroy our planet, and a dubbed, wooden hero comes to the rescue. A rarely seen Italian SF entry, great fun for genre fans. A must for "robot girls in skin tight leather outfits" completists. **93m/C VHS.** *IT* Tony Russell, Lisa Gastoni, Massimo Serato, Franco Nero; *D:* Anthony (Antonio Margheriti) Dawson.

Wild Wild West ☙ **1999 (PG-13)** A wild, wild waste of time, money, and star power that saw director Sonnenfeld and star Smith re-team (after "Men In Black") for this western spy spoof based on the 60s TV series. Government agents James T. West (Smith) and master-of-disguise Artemus Gordon (Kline) are sent to stop diabolical wheelchair-bound scientist, Dr. Arliss Loveless (Branagh), from assassinating President Ulysses S. Grant in 1867.

The budget was $100 million but the elaborate sets and effects are more hokey than cool and some money should have been spent on the script. And a black James West just doesn't work, no matter Smith's charm. **105m/C VHS, DVD.** Will Smith, Kevin Kline, Kenneth Branagh, Salma Hayek, M. Emmet Walsh, Ted Levine, Musetta Vander, Bai Ling, Rodney A. Grant, Frederique van der Wal, Garcelle Beauvais, Sofia Eng; ***D:*** Barry Sonnenfeld; ***W:*** Brent Maddock, S.S. Wilson, Jeffrey Price, Peter S. Seaman; ***C:*** Michael Ballhaus; ***M:*** Elmer Bernstein. Golden Raspberries '99: Worst Picture, Worst Director (Sonnenfeld), Worst Screenplay, Worst Song ("Wild Wild West").

Wild, Wild West Revisited 🦴🦴½ **1979** A feature-length reprise of the tongue-in-cheek western TV series. Irreverent and fun, in the spirit of its admirable predecessor—though it's probably just as well the proposed new series didn't see fruition. **95m/C VHS.** Robert Conrad, Ross Martin, Harry (Henry) Morgan, Rene Auberjonois; ***D:*** Burt Kennedy. **TV**

Wild Women 🦴 **1953** Extremely hilarious schlocker about a safari of white men captured by a savage tribe of jungle women. Total camp. **?m/C VHS.** Lewis Wilson, Frances Dubay, Dana Wilson.

Wild Women 🦴½ **1970** Five female convicts are released during the Texas/Mexico dispute to help smuggle arms to American forces. Innocuous western, original in a made-for-TV kind of way. **90m/C VHS.** Hugh O'Brian, Anne Francis, Marilyn Maxwell, Marie Windsor; ***D:*** Don Taylor. **TV**

Wild Women of Wongo 🦴½ **1959** The denizens of a primitive isle, essentially beautiful women and ugly men, meet the natives of a neighboring island, handsome men and ugly women. Not quite bad enough to be true camp fun, but stupidly silly in a low-budget way. **73m/C VHS.** Pat Crowley, Ed Fury, Adrienne Bourbeau, Jean Hawkshaw, Johnny Walsh; ***D:*** James L. Wolcott; ***W:*** Cedric Rutherford; ***C:*** Harry Walsh.

The Wild World of Batwoman 🦴🦴 *She Was a Hippy Vampire* **1966** A campy cult film in which Batwoman and a bevy of Bat Girls are pitted against an evil doctor in order to find the prototype of an atomic hearing aid/nuclear bomb. **70m/C VHS.** Katherine Victor, George Andre, Steve Brodie, Richard Banks, Lloyd Nelson, Steve Conte, Mel Oshins, Bruno VeSota, Bob Arbogast, Lucki Winn, Suzanne Lodge, Pam Garry, Sylvia Holiday, Francis Bryan, Leah London; ***D:*** Jerry Warren; ***W:*** Jerry Warren; ***C:*** William G. Troiano; ***M:*** Erich Bromberg.

Wild Zone 🦴 **1989 (R)** An American ex-soldier combats mercenaries in Africa in order to rescue his kidnapped father. **100m/C VHS.** Edward Albert, Philip Brown, Carla Herd; ***D:*** Percival Rubens.

Wildcard 🦴½ **1992 (PG-13)** When a veteran pilot is killed in a helicopter crash, a friend suspects foul play. He calls in Preacher, a special forces veteran, to investigate and what he discovers is murder, greed, and corruption. **86m/C VHS.** Powers Boothe, Cindy Pickett, Rene Auberjonois, Terry O'Quinn, M. Emmet Walsh, John Lacy; ***D:*** Mel Damski; ***W:*** Scobie Richardson.

The Wildcat 🦴🦴 **1926** Manager takes his fighter to an isolated ranch in order to recover from his boozing but the boxer winds up getting involved with a pretty girl and a robbery. **?m/B VHS.** Gordon Clifford, Charlotte Pierce, Frank Bond, Hooper Phillips, Ervin Renard, Arthur Millett; ***D:*** Harry Fraser.

Wildcat 🦴🦴 **1942** Crabbe, famous as the serials' Flash Gordon, is a villain in this petrochemical adventure. The hero overextends his credit when he buys an oil well and must produce a gusher or else. **73m/B VHS.** Richard Arlen, Arline Judge, Buster Crabbe, William Frawley, Arthur Hunnicutt, Elisha Cook Jr., William Benedict; ***D:*** Frank McDonald.

Wildcats 🦴🦴 **1986 (R)** A naive female phys-ed teacher (Hawn) is saddled with the job of coach for a completely undisciplined, inner city, high school football team. Formulaic, connect-the-dots comedy; moderately funny, and of course Hawn triumphs in adversity, but at nearly two hours a very long sitcom episode. **106m/C VHS.** Goldie Hawn, James Keach, Swoosie Kurtz, Bruce McGill, M. Emmet Walsh, Woody Harrelson, Wesley Snipes, Tab Thacker; ***D:*** Michael Ritchie; ***M:*** James Newton Howard.

Wilde 🦴🦴 **1997 (R)** The witty Wilde is making something of a resurgence in film, plays, and books. The Irish author/playwright (portrayed by look-alike Fry) is enjoying the London limelight and his family life with wife Constance (Ehle) and their two sons, while privately acknowledging his attraction to men. Unfortunately, this leads Oscar into a mad passion for sulky, neurotic pretty boy Bosie Douglas (Law), whose aristocratic father, the Marquess of Queensbury (Wilkinson), wants moral revenge on Wilde. His affair with Bosie leads to a celebrated trial for Oscar and a tragic outcome. Adapted from the biography by Richard Ellman. **115m/C VHS, DVD, Wide.** *GB* Stephen Fry, Jude Law, Vanessa Redgrave, Jennifer Ehle, Michael Sheen, Zoe Wanamaker, Tom Wilkinson, Gemma Jones, Judy Parfitt; ***D:*** Brian Gilbert; ***W:*** Julian Mitchell; ***C:*** Martin Fuhrer; ***M:*** Debbie Wiseman.

Wilder Napalm 🦴½ **1993 (PG-13)** Lame comedy about two at-odds brothers, the woman they both love, and their dangerous pyrokinetic abilities. Wilder (Howard) and Wallace (Quaid) Foudroyant have been feuding for years—and not just over the fact that Wallace is in love with Wilder's wife Vida (Winger). Wallace wants to use their family "gift" to become rich and famous but Wilder doesn't want them to exploit their fiery powers. They finally decide on an incendiary showdown to settle the score once and for all. Good actors lost in witless characters and a incoherent plot. **109m/C VHS, Wide.** Dennis Quaid, Arliss Howard, Debra Winger, M. Emmet Walsh, Jim Varney, Mimi Lieber, Marvin J. McIntyre; ***D:*** Glenn Gordon Caron; ***W:*** Vince Gilligan; ***M:*** Michael Kamen.

Wilderness 🦴🦴½ **1996 (R)** Quiet British librarian Alice White (Ooms) is keeping quite a secret. It seems when there's a full moon, she gets a little furry. She tries to cope with her affliction by seeing a shrink (Kitchen) but the weasel just wants to exploit her. And just try explaining you're a werewolf to the new guy (Teale) in your life. Think gothic romance more than straight horror. Made for British TV. **90m/C VHS, DVD.** *GB* Amanda Ooms, Michael Kitchen, Owen Teale, Gemma Jones; ***D:*** Ben Bolt; ***W:*** Andrew Davies, Bernadette Davis. **TV**

Wildest Dreams 🦴½ *Bikini Genie* **1990 (R)** Released from its bottle by a lovely nebbish, a genie puts a love spell on one beautiful girl after another in order to find him the right one, resulting in a bevy of women clamoring for our hero's attention. **84m/C VHS.** James Davies, Heidi Paine, Deborah (Tracey Adams) Blaisdell, Ruth (Coreen) Collins, Jane (Veronica Hart) Hamilton; ***D:*** Chuck Vincent.

Wildfire 🦴½ **1945** Two horse traders come to the aid of ranchers beset by horse thieves. Early color outing for Steele. Harmless, ordinary oater. **60m/C VHS.** Bob Steele, Sterling Holloway, John Miljan, William Farnum, Eddie Dean, Sarah Padden, Frank Ellis; ***D:*** Robert Emmett Tansey.

Wildfire 🦴🦴 **1988 (PG)** As teenagers, Frank and Kay run away to get married but Frank is sent to prison for robbing a bank and Kay winds up making a new life for herself. Released from prison after eight years, Frank discovers Kay is married with two children and doesn't want anything further to do with him. But when Frank violates his parole, Kay discovers she can't leave him again and the two go on the run together. **98m/C VHS.** Steven Bauer, Linda Fiorentino, Will Patton, Marshall Bell; ***D:*** Zalman King; ***W:*** Zalman King, Matthew Bright; ***C:*** Bill Butler; ***M:*** Maurice Jarre.

Wildflower 🦴🦴🦴 **1991** Set in the Depression-era South, Alice is a 17 year-old partially deaf girl who also suffers from epilepsy. Her stepfather believes she's possessed and confines her to a shed. Growing up ignorant and abused Alice is befriended by a neighboring brother and sister who decide to rescue her. A three-hankie family picture with moving performances and inspirational themes. Based on the novel "Alice" by Sara Flanigan. **94m/C VHS.** Patricia Arquette, Beau Bridges, Susan Blakely, William McNamara, Reese Witherspoon, Collin Wilcox-Paxton, Norman (Max) Maxwell, Heather Lynch, Allison Smith, Richard Olsen, Mary Page; ***D:*** Diane Keaton; ***W:*** Sara Flanigan; ***C:*** Janusz Kaminski; ***M:*** Jon Gilutin, Ken Edwards. **CABLE**

Wildflowers 🦴🦴½ *Wild Flowers* **1999 (R)** Cathy (DuVall) is a 17-year-old tomboy who lives on a houseboat with her single dad (Arana). Longing for a female role model, Cally stumbles across hippie artist Sabine (Hannah) and gets involved in her life and a past that has some secrets Cally may not want to uncover. Especially fine performance by DuVall. **98m/C VHS, DVD.** Clea DuVall, Daryl Hannah, Tomas Arana, Eric Roberts, Irene Bedard, James Gandolfini, Devin Crannell; ***D:*** Melissa Painter; ***W:*** Melissa Painter; ***C:*** Paul Ryan.

Wilding 🦴½ **1990** A pair of cops are on the trail of a gang of kids who go "wilding," which involves sprees of killing, raping and looting. Exploitive fare based on horrible, recent events in New York. The filmmakers skirt controversy by making the criminals rich suburban kids. **92m/C VHS.** Wings Hauser, Joey Travolta, Karen Russell, Steven Cooke; ***D:*** Eric Louzil.

Wildrose 🦴🦴🦴 **1985** Eichhorn is memorable as a recent divorcee who must assert herself among her otherwise all-male co-workers at a Minnesota strip mine. She finds a new love, and tries to put her life back together. Filmed on location. **96m/C VHS.** Lisa Eichhorn, Tom Bower, James Cada; ***D:*** John Hanson; ***W:*** John Hanson, Eugene Corr.

Will: G. Gordon Liddy 🦴🦴½ **1982** The life of the Watergate conspirator, based on his autobiography. Made for TV. Producer/star Conrad reportedly objected strongly to cuts from the original three-hour length, apparently with cause: the first half is superficial pap. The portrayal of Liddy's time in prison, though, is fascinating, and Conrad is excellent. **100m/C VHS.** Robert Conrad, Katherine (Kathy) Cannon, Gary Bayer, Peter Ratray, James Rebhorn, Red West, Maurice Woods, Danny Lloyd; ***D:*** Robert Lieberman. **TV**

Will It Snow for Christmas? 🦴🦴 *Y'aura t'il de la Niege a Noel?* **1996** A single mother and her seven children live in a drafty farmhouse in rural southern France. Their father is married, has another family, and uses his mistress and the children as cheap farm labor. He treats them all badly and their mother begins to sink into despair as the seasons pass. Finally, on Christmas Eve, everything comes to an unexpected conclusion. French with subtitles. **90m/C VHS.** *FR* Dominique Reymond, Daniel Duval; ***D:*** Sandrine Veysset; ***W:*** Sandrine Veysset; ***C:*** Helene Louvart.

Will Penny 🦴🦴🦴½ **1967** Just back from a cattle drive, a range-wandering loner looks for work in the wrong place and offends a family of outlaws who come after him. His escape from them leads to another kind of trap—one set by a love-hungry woman (Hackett, in a strong performance). Heston considers this film his personal best, and he's probably right. Superbly directed western, with excellent cinematography and professional, realistic portrayals, flopped in theatres, moviegoers preferring simultaneous Heston outing "Planet of the Apes." **109m/C VHS, DVD, Wide.** Charlton Heston, Joan Hackett, Donald Pleasence, Lee Majors, Bruce Dern, Anthony Zerbe, Ben Johnson, Clifton James, Jonathan (Jon Francis) Gries; ***D:*** Tom Gries; ***W:*** Tom Gries; ***C:*** Lucien Ballard; ***M:*** Elmer Bernstein.

Will Success Spoil Rock Hunter? 🦴🦴½ **1957** Dated advertising satire finds ad man Hunter (Randall) hoping to get the key to the executive washroom but he may instead find himself on the unemployment line unless he can convince the profitable Stay-Put lipstick account not to change agencies. One day Rock see movie star Rita Marlowe (Mansfield), and her kissable lips, on TV and tries to convince her to endorse the product but she'll only agree if he'll pose as her new boyfriend to make ex-beau Bobo (Mansfield's real-life hubby Hargitay) jealous. Naturally, the lipstick ads take off big-time but success does indeed spoil Rock (at least temporarily). Very slightly based on the play by George Axelrod. **94m/C VHS.** Tony Randall, Jayne Mansfield, Betsy Drake, Mickey Hargitay, John Williams, Henry Jones, Joan Blondell; ***Cameos:*** Groucho Marx; ***D:*** Frank Tashlin; ***W:*** Frank Tashlin; ***C:*** Joe MacDonald; ***M:*** Cyril Mockridge. Natl. Film Reg. '00.

Willa 🦴🦴 **1979** Raffin, a hash-joint waitress with two kids and one in the pipeline, is deserted by her husband and determines to get ahead by becoming a trucker. Okay made-for-TV drama. **95m/C VHS.** Cloris Leachman, Deborah Raffin, Clu Gulager, John Amos, Diane Ladd; ***D:*** Claudio Guzman, Joan Darling; ***M:*** John Barry.

Willard 🦴🦴 **1971 (PG)** Willard is a lonely, psychotic youngster who trains a group of rats, his only friends, to attack his enemies. Not as disgusting as it might have been (rated PG), but pretty weird and not redeemed by any sense of style or humor. Popular at the boxoffice; followed by inferior "Ben." Based on by Stephen Gilbert's novel "Ratman's Notebooks." **95m/C VHS.** Bruce Davison, Ernest Borgnine, Elsa Lanchester, Sondra Locke, Michael Dante, J. Pat O'Malley, Jody Gilbert, William Hansen; ***D:*** Daniel Mann; ***W:*** Gilbert Ralston; ***C:*** Robert B. Hauser; ***M:*** Alex North.

William Faulkner's Old Man 🦴🦴½ *Old Man* **1997 (PG)** TV adaptation of a part of Faulkner's 1939 novel "The Wild Palms" that is set in the '20s. The "Old Man" in question is the mighty Mississippi, which has flooded leaving a pregnant Addie (Tripplehorn), abandoned by her husband, stranded and about to give birth. But prison-farm inmate J.J. Taylor (Howard) is sent by the warden to row to her rescue, becoming a surrogate father when the baby is born, and traveling the river to New Orleans to get mother and child to safety. **98m/C VHS.** Jeanne Tripplehorn, Arliss Howard, Leo Burmester; ***D:*** John Kent Harrison; ***W:*** Horton Foote; ***C:*** Kees Van Oostrum; ***M:*** Lawrence Shragge. **TV**

William Shakespeare's A Midsummer Night's Dream 🦴🦴½ *A Midsummer Night's Dream* **1999 (PG-13)** Shakespeare's fantasy/romance/comedy is transported to turn-of-the-century Tuscany where Oberon (Everett), King of the Fairies, is fighting with his queen, Titania (Pfeiffer). Their spats lead to trouble for a variety of humans, including the hapless Bottom (Kline), who winds up with a donkey's head replacing his own. Kline is the most at ease with his role (Everett and Pfeiffer, primarily, have to look beautiful, which they do), while the younger foursome of would-be lovers (Flockhart, Bale, Friel, and West) prove to be less than memorable, as does the entire production. **115m/C VHS, DVD.** Rupert Everett, Michelle Pfeiffer, Kevin Kline, Stanley Tucci, Calista Flockhart, Dominic West, Christian Bale, David Strathairn, Sophie Marceau, John Sessions, Anna Friel, Roger Rees, Max Wright, Gregory Jbara, Bill Irwin, Sam Rockwell, Bernard Hill; ***D:*** Michael Hoffman; ***W:*** Michael Hoffman; ***C:*** Oliver Stapleton; ***M:*** Simon Boswell.

William Shakespeare's Romeo and Juliet 🦴🦴🦴 *Romeo and Juliet* **1996 (PG-13)** Bright, loud update of Shakespeare's tragedy of feuding families and first love. Contemporary fantasy setting, Verona Beach, and attitude (the Montagues and the Capulets are business rivals), with the 16th-century Elizabethan language intact, although Luhrmann's said to have cut half the text. Hot-blooded Romeo (DiCaprio) takes one look at angelic Juliet (Danes) and falls immediately in love/lust. This doesn't please Juliet's family, including quick-tempered cousin Tybalt (Leguizamo) who goes after Romeo with far-reaching consequences. DiCaprio's remarkable and the young duo look wonderful together. A big hit with the teens. Filmed in Mexico City. **120m/C VHS, DVD.** Leonardo DiCaprio, Claire Danes, John Leguizamo, Paul Sorvino, Brian Dennehy, Diane Venora, Pete Postlethwaite, Paul Rudd, Harold Perrineau Jr., Jesse Bradford, Miriam Margolyes, Vondie Curtis-Hall, Christina Pickles, M. Emmet Walsh; ***D:*** Baz Luhrmann; ***W:*** Baz Luhrmann, Craig Pearce; ***C:*** Donald McAlpine; ***M:*** Nellee

Hooper. British Acad. '97: Adapt. Screenplay, Art Dir./Set Dec., Director (Luhrmann), Score; MTV Movie Awards '97: Female Perf. (Danes).

Willie & Phil 🦴🦴½ **1980 (R)** At the start of the '70s, two buddies (Ontkean and Sharkey) fall for the same girl (Kidder). They become a threesome and are entangled in each other's lives for the rest of the decade. Insightful comedy-drama. **111m/C VHS.** Michael Ontkean, Margot Kidder, Ray Sharkey, Jan Miner, Julie Bovasso, Natalie Wood, Laurence "Larry" Fishburne, Louis Guss, Kaki Hunter, Kristine DeBell; ***D:*** Paul Mazursky; ***W:*** Paul Mazursky; ***C:*** Sven Nykvist; ***M:*** Claude Bolling.

The Willies 🦴🦴 **1990 (PG-13)** Three youngsters gross each other out with juvenile tales of horror and scariness while camping out in the backyard. Pointless but not without a few yuks (in both senses of the term). **120m/C VHS.** James Karen, Sean Astin, Kathleen Freeman, Jeremy Miller; ***D:*** Brian Peck.

Willow 🦴🦴½ **1988 (PG)** Blockbuster fantasy epic combines the story of Moses with "Snow White," dwarves and all. Willow is the little Nelwyn who finds the lost baby Daikini and is assigned the task of returning her safely to her people. Willow discovers that the girl is actually a sacred infant who is destined to overthrow the evil queen Bavmorda and rule the land. As you might expect from executive producer George Lucas, there is much action and plenty of clever, high-quality special effects. But the "Star Wars"-esque story (by Lucas) is strangely predictable, and a bit too action-packed. Not really for children. **118m/C VHS, DVD, Wide.** Warwick Davis, Val Kilmer, Jean Marsh, Joanne Whalley, Billy Barty, Pat Roach, Ruth Greenfield, Patricia Hayes, Gavan O'Herlihy, Kevin Pollak; ***D:*** Ron Howard; ***W:*** Bob Dolman; ***C:*** Adrian Biddle; ***M:*** James Horner.

Willy Wonka & the Chocolate Factory 🦴🦴🦴½ **1971 (G)** When the last of five coveted "golden tickets" falls into the hands of sweet but very poor Charlie, he and his Grandpa Joe get a tour of the most wonderfully strange chocolate factory in the world. The owner is the most curious hermit ever to hit the big screen. He leads the five young "winners" on a thrilling and often dangerous tour of his fabulous factory. Adapted from Roald Dahl's "Charlie and the Chocolate Factory." Without a doubt one of the best "kid's" movies ever made; a family classic worth watching again and again. ♫The Candy Man; Cheer Up, Charlie; (I've Got a) Golden Ticket; Pure Imagination; Oompa Loompa; I Want It Now. **100m/C VHS, DVD.** Gene Wilder, Jack Albertson, Denise Nickerson, Peter Ostrum, Roy Kinnear, Aubrey Woods, Michael Bollner, Ursula Reit, Leonard Stone, Dodo Denney, Julie Dawn Cole, Gunter Meisner; ***D:*** Mel Stuart; ***W:*** Roald Dahl; ***C:*** Arthur Ibbetson; ***M:*** Leslie Bricusse, Anthony Newley, Walter Scharf.

Wilma 🦴🦴 **1977** Based on the true story of Wilma Rudolph, a young black woman who overcame childhood illness to win three gold medals at the 1960 Olympics. Plodding made-for-TV biography suffers from sub-par script and acting. **100m/C VHS.** Joe Seneca, Cicely Tyson, Shirley Jo Finney; ***D:*** Bud Greenspan; ***M:*** Irwin Bazelon. **TV**

Wilson 🦴🦴🦴 **1944** Biography of Woodrow Wilson from his days as the head of Princeton University, to the governorship of New Jersey, and as U.S. President during WWI. After the war, Wilson conceives of the League of Nations but is unable to sell it to a U.S. still bent on isolationism. This lavish film won critical plaudits but was a major money-loser. **154m/C VHS.** Alexander Knox, Charles Coburn, Geraldine Fitzgerald, Thomas Mitchell, Ruth Nelson, Cedric Hardwicke, Vincent Price, William Eythe, Mary Anderson, Sidney Blackmer, Stanley Ridges, Eddie Foy Jr., Charles Halton; ***D:*** Henry King; ***W:*** Lamar Trotti; ***C:*** Leon Shamroy; ***M:*** Alfred Newman. Oscars '44: Color Cinematog., Film Editing, Orig. Screenplay, Sound; Golden Globes '45: Actor—Drama (Knox).

Wimps 🦴 **1987 (R)** A collegiate wimp is subjected to a brutal fraternity initiation, but eventually gets the girl. Cheap ripoff of Cyrano de Bergerac, turned into a teen sex flick. **94m/C VHS.** Louie Bonanno, Jim Abele, Deborah (Tracey Adams) Blaisdell; ***D:*** Chuck Vincent.

Win, Place, or Steal 🦴½ *The Big Payoff; Three For the Money; Just Another Day at the Races* **1972 (PG)** Lame comedy set at the racetrack about three grown men and their adolescent schemes to win big. Better you should scratch. **88m/C VHS.** McLean Stevenson, Alex Karras, Dean Stockwell; ***D:*** Richard Bailey.

Winchell 🦴🦴½ **1998 (R)** Flamboyant biopic of powerful journalist/radio personality Walter Winchell (Tucci), whose career stretched from the 1930s into the '50s. Winchell blurred the line between hard news and tabloid gossip and used his influence politically to re-elect President Roosevelt and get the U.S. involved in WWII. But he was also arrogant and mean-spirited and his grandiosity eventually proved to be his downfall. Based on the 1976 book "Walter Winchell: His Life and Times" by Winchell's longtime ghostwriter Herman Klurfeld. **105m/C VHS.** Stanley Tucci, Paul Giamatti, Glenne Headly, Christopher Plummer, Xander Berkeley, Kevin Tighe, Frank Medrano, Vic Polizos, Megan Mullally, Victoria Platt; ***D:*** Paul Mazursky; ***W:*** Scott Abbott; ***C:*** Robbie Greenberg; ***M:*** Bill Conti. **CABLE**

Winchester '73 🦴🦴🦴½ **1950** Superb acting and photography characterize this classic, landmark western. Simple plot—cowboy Stewart pursues his stolen state-of-the-art rifle as it changes hands—speeds along and carries the viewer with it, ending with an engrossing and unforgettable shoot-out. Almost singlehandedly breathed new life into the whole genre. Laser videodisc version contains a special narration track provided by Stewart. Mann's and Stewart's first teaming. **82m/C VHS.** James Stewart, Shelley Winters, Stephen McNally, Dan Duryea, Millard Mitchell, John McIntire, Will Geer, Jay C. Flippen, Rock Hudson, Tony Curtis, Charles Drake; ***D:*** Anthony Mann; ***C:*** William H. Daniels.

The Wind 🦴🦴🦴🦴 **1928** One of the last great silents still stands as a magnificent entertainment. Gish, in possibly her best role, is an innocent Easterner who finds herself married to a rough cowpoke and raped by a married man in a bleak frontier town. Director Sjostrom has a splendid feel for landscape, and the drama—climaxing with a tumultuous desert storm—is intense yet fully believable. Based on the novel by Dorothy Scarborough. **74m/B VHS.** Lillian Gish, Lars Hanson, Montagu Love, Dorothy (Dorothy G. Cummings) Cumming, Edward Earle, William Orlamond; ***D:*** Victor Sjostrom; ***W:*** Frances Marion. Natl. Film Reg. '93.

The Wind 🦴 **1987** Foster is terrorized by Hauser while attempting to write her next thriller in Greece. Let's hope her book is more exciting than this movie. Shot on location in Greece. **92m/C VHS, DVD.** Meg Foster, Wings Hauser, Steve Railsback, David McCallum, Robert Morley; ***D:*** Nico Mastorakis; ***W:*** Nico Mastorakis, Fred C. Perry; ***C:*** Andreas Bellis; ***M:*** Stanley Myers, Hans Zimmer.

Wind 🦴🦴½ **1992 (PG-13)** Sailor Will Parker (Modine) chooses the opportunity to be on the America's Cup team over girlfriend Grey and then has the dubious honor of making a technical error that causes their loss. Undaunted, he locates Grey and her new engineer boyfriend (Skarsgard) and convinces them to design the ultimate boat for the next set of races. ESPN carried extensive coverage of the America's Cup races for the first time in the summer of '92 and viewers discovered that a little goes a long way. The same holds true for "Wind" which has stunning race footage, but little else. The script lacks substance and was written as filming progressed, and it shows. **123m/C VHS, 8mm, Wide.** Matthew Modine, Jennifer Grey, Cliff Robertson, Jack Thompson, Stellan Skarsgard, Rebecca Miller, Ned Vaughn; ***D:*** Carroll Ballard; ***W:*** Rudy Wurlitzer, Mac Gudgeon; ***C:*** John Toll; ***M:*** Basil Poledouris.

The Wind and the Lion 🦴🦴🦴 **1975 (PG)** In turn-of-the-century Morocco, a sheik (Connery) kidnaps a feisty American woman (Bergen) and her children and holds her as a political hostage. President Teddy Roosevelt (Keith) sends in the Marines to free the captives, who are eventually released by their captor. Directed with venue and style by Milius. Highly entertaining, if heavily fictionalized. Based very loosely on a historical incident. **120m/C VHS, Wide.** Sean Connery, Candice Bergen, Brian Keith, John Huston, Geoffrey Lewis, Steve Kanaly, Vladek Sheybal, Nadim Sawalha, Roy Jenson, Larry Cross, Simon Harrison, Polly Gottesmann, Marc Zuber; ***D:*** John Milius; ***W:*** John Milius; ***C:*** Billy Williams; ***M:*** Jerry Goldsmith.

A Wind Named Amnesia **1993** A strange amnesia wind sweeps away all of mankind's knowledge and human civilization vanishes. Then a mysterious young man is miraculously re-educated and searches for those who destroyed man's memories. In Japanese with English subtitles. **80m/C VHS, DVD.** *JP* ***D:*** Kazuo Yamazaki; ***W:*** Hideyuki Kikuchi.

Wind River 🦴🦴½ **1998 (PG-13)** In 1855 Utah, there's trouble between the settlers and the Shoshone tribe. The wife of Chief Washakie (Means) dreams that a wolf threatens the tribe and a young blond warrior saves them. So the chief sends Moragoni (Martinez) to find the boy. Moragoni meets 15-year-old settler Nicolas Wilson (Heron) and believes him to be the dream warrior and Nicolas agrees to live with the Shoshone and learn their ways. But eventually, Nicolas must choose between his real and adopted families. Based on "The White Indian Boy" by Elijah Nicolas, which was inspired by actual events. **97m/C VHS, DVD.** Blake Heron, A. Martinez, Russell Means, Wes Studi, Karen Allen, Patricia Van Ingen, Joe Wandell; ***D:*** Tom Shell; ***W:*** Tom Shell, Elizabeth Hansen; ***C:*** Lawrence Schweich; ***M:*** Jeff Marsh. **VIDEO**

Windhorse 🦴🦴 **1998** In a Tibetan village in 1979, Dolkar and her brother Dorjee watch as two Chinese soldiers execute their grandfather for espousing Tibetan freedom. Eighteen years later, Dolkar has become a popular singing star by cooperating with the Chinese while her brother has become a sullen, cynical drunk. But as the Chinese initiate further crackdowns, the Tibetans decide to protest. Title refers to the prayers, written on bits of paper, that the Tibetans throw to the winds. Tibetan and Chinese with subtitles. **97m/C VHS.** Dadon, Jampa Kolsang, Richard Chang; ***D:*** Paul Wagner; ***W:*** Paul Wagner, Thupten Tsering, Julia Elliott; ***C:*** Steven Schecter; ***M:*** Tommy Hayes.

Windjammer 🦴🦴 **1937** Western star O'Brien took a break from the lone prairie to make this seafaring rescue drama. He is a deputy state's attorney who signs up for a yacht race in order to serve a subpoena. Bad guys arrive on the scene, and the initially moody yacht denizens rely on our trusty hero to save them. Decent adventure. **75m/B VHS.** George O'Brien, Constance Worth; ***D:*** Sam Newfield.

Windmills of the Gods 🦴🦴½ *Sidney Sheldon's Windmills of the Gods* **1988** Glamor, romance, intrigue, and politics all mixed together in eastern Europe. Smith is named ambassador to Romania, finds the suave Wagner in residence, and becomes the target of assassins. Based on the novel by Sidney Sheldon. **95m/C VHS.** Jaclyn Smith, Robert Wagner, Franco Nero, Christopher Cazenove, David Ackroyd, Jean-Pierre Aumont, Ruby Dee, Jeffrey DeMunn, Michael Moriarty, Ian McKellen, Susan Tyrrell; ***D:*** Lee Philips; ***W:*** John Gay; ***M:*** Perry Botkin. **TV**

Windom's Way 🦴🦴🦴 **1957** Finch, in a strong role in this intriguing political drama, is an idealistic doctor in a remote village in Malaysia. He juggles a failing marriage and a budding romance, then finds himself caught in a local labor dispute. He works for a peaceful solution, but is captured by an insurgent army. Disillusioned, he plans to leave the country, but his wife persuades him to stay and tend the wounded. Based on a novel by James Ramsey Ullman. **90m/B VHS.** *GB* Peter Finch, Mary Ure; ***D:*** Ronald Neame.

The Window 🦴🦴🦴½ **1949** A little boy (Disney star Driscoll, intriguingly cast by director, Tetzlaff) has a reputation for telling lies, so no one believes him when he says he witnessed a murder...except the killers. Almost unbearably tense, claustrophobic thriller about the helplessness of childhood. Tetzlaff clearly learned more than a thing or two from the master, Hitchcock, for whom he photographed "Notorious." Based on the novella "The Boy Who Cried Murder" by Cornell Woolrich. Driscoll was awarded a special miniature Oscar as Outstanding Juvenile for his performance. **73m/B VHS.** Bobby Driscoll, Barbara Hale, Arthur Kennedy, Ruth Roman; ***D:*** Ted Tetzlaff.

Window Shopping 🦴🦴½ **1986** Multiple, confusing romances occur at the "Toison d' Or" shopping mall in Paris. A modern, French homage to the classic Hollywood musical. In French with English subtitles. **96m/C VHS.** *FR* Delphine Seyrig, Charles Denner, Fanny Cottencon, Miriam Boyer, Lio, Pascale Salkin, Jean-Francois Balmer; ***D:*** Chantal Akerman; ***W:*** Chantal Akerman.

Window to Paris 🦴🦴 **1995 (PG-13)** East and West meet unexpectedly when a young music teacher (Dontsov) rents a room in St. Petersburg with a secret window that opens onto a Paris rooftop. Loony adventures ensue as Dontsov and his friends escape their dreary existence to exploit the bounties of Western capitalism in this sharp satire of Russian social ills. Relentless humor based on cross-cultural stereotypes wears thin (the Russians are cantankerous drunks; the Parisians, self-important snobs), but it keeps a sunny cast upon what could have been a scathing commentary. Russian and French with subtitles. **92m/C VHS.** *RU FR* Serguej Dontsov, Agnes Soral, Viktor Michailov, Nina Oussatova; ***D:*** Yuri Mamin; ***W:*** Arkadi Tigai, Yuri Mamin; ***M:*** Aleksei Zalivalov, Yuri Mamin.

Windows 🦴 **1980 (R)** A lonely lesbian (Ashley) becomes obsessed with her quiet neighbor (Shire) and concocts a plot to get close to her. Director Willis is known for his unbeatable cinematography, most notably for Woody Allen in "Manhattan." His debut in the chair is a miserable, offensive flop. **93m/C VHS.** Talia Shire, Joe Cortese, Elizabeth Ashley, Kay Medford, Linda Gillin; ***D:*** Gordon Willis; ***C:*** Gordon Willis; ***M:*** Ennio Morricone.

Windrider 🦴½ **1986** Simple love story made in Australia. A wind surfer and a rock star become lovers. Self-indulgent overwrought garbage with rare moments of promise. **83m/C VHS.** *AU* Tom Burlinson, Nicole Kidman, Charles Tingwell, Jill Perryman, Simon Chilvers; ***D:*** Vincent Monton.

Windrunner 🦴🦴½ **1994 (PG)** Angry at his football-star dad and rejected by the local high school team, Greg Cima (Wiles) finds an unlikely ally in the spirit of Native American Olympic hero Jim Thorpe (Means). Seems Thorpe needs some aid to return to the spirit world and, by coaching Cima, he'll also get the help he needs. Believable performances and an exploration of the power of Native American mysticism help the unlikely premise along. **110m/C VHS.** Russell Means, Jason Wiles, Amanda Peterson, Margot Kidder, Jake Busey, Max Casella, Bruce Weitz; ***D:*** William Clark; ***W:*** Mitch Davis; ***M:*** Arthur Kempel.

The Winds of Jarrah 🦴½ **1983** English woman runs from broken heart to Australia to become nanny for misogynist, and Harlequin code prevails. Based on a Harlequin romance novel. **78m/C VHS.** *AU* Terence Donovan, Susan Lyons; ***D:*** Mark Egerton; ***M:*** Bruce Smeaton.

The Winds of Kitty Hawk 🦴🦴 **1978** Visually interesting but talky account of the Wright brothers attempt to beat their rival Glenn Curtiss and his backer, phone man Alexander Graham Bell. Rule of thumb: Fast-forward through the parts when they are on the ground, or see Stacy Keach's public-TV version instead. **96m/C VHS.** Michael Moriarty, David Huffman, Kathryn Walker, Eugene Roche, John Randolph, Scott Hylands; ***D:*** E.W. Swackhamer; ***M:*** Charles Bernstein.

Winds of the Wasteland 🦴🦴½ **1936** Would-be Pony Express contractors, Wayne and Chandler, race rivals to land government work. Competent western that put Wayne on the Hollywood map. **54m/B VHS, DVD.** John Wayne, Phyllis Fraser,

Lane Chandler, Yakima Canutt; *D:* Mack V. Wright; *W:* Joseph Poland; *C:* William Nobles.

The Winds of War 🦴🦴 **1983** Excruciatingly long and dull miniseries based on Herman Wouk's bestseller about WWII. The book was much better; Mitchum appears to be fighting sleep unsuccessfully for much of the show. Two follow-ups were produced: "War and Remembrance" and "War and Remembrance: The Final Chapter." **900m/C VHS.** Charles Lane, Robert Mitchum, Ali MacGraw, Ralph Bellamy, Polly Bergen, Jan-Michael Vincent, David Dukes, John Houseman, Victoria Tennant, Peter Graves, Chaim Topol, Ben Murphy, Jeremy Kemp, Anton Diffring, Lawrence Pressman, Andrew Duggan, Barbara Steele; *D:* Dan Curtis. **TV**

Windtalkers **2002 (R)** Woo's long-awaited WW II drama has Navahos recruited by the Marines to use their native language as a code to fool the Japanese. Cage is a Marine assigned to protect one of these men, but he also has orders to kill him if capture is imminent to protect the secrets of the code. Not yet reviewed. **?m/C VHS, DVD.** Nicolas Cage, Adam Beach, Christian Slater, Noah Emmerich, Mark Ruffalo, Frances O'Connor; *D:* John Woo; *W:* John Rice, Joe Batteer.

Windwalker 🦴🦴🦴 **1981** Howard, the only cast member who is not a Native American, is an aged chief who shares the memories of his life with his grandchildren. Filmed in the Crow and Cheyenne Indian languages and subtitled in English throughout. A beautifully photographed, intelligent independent project. **108m/C VHS.** Trevor Howard, James Remar, Dusty Iron Wing McCrea; *D:* Keith Merrill.

Windy City 🦴🦴 **1984 (R)** A group of seven childhood friends must come to terms with the harsh realities of their failed ambitions when they meet for a weekend in Chicago. Told from the point of view of one of the group, recounting the sorts of memories we all prefer to forget. Typical and overwrought '80s yuppie reunion/regret drama. Aren't these people too young to be unhappy? **103m/C VHS.** John Shea, Kate Capshaw, Josh Mostel, Jeffrey DeMunn, Lewis J. Stadlen, James Sutorius; *D:* Armyan Bernstein; *W:* Armyan Bernstein; *M:* Jack Nitzsche.

A Wing and a Prayer 🦴🦴🦴 **1944** Better-than-average WWII Air Force action flick. Battles rage throughout the Pacific theater and the men aboard the aircraft carrier struggle to do their part to save the world for freedom. Fine cast receives Hathaway's excellent unsentimental direction. **97m/B VHS, DVD.** Don Ameche, Dana Andrews, William Eythe, Charles Bickford, Cedric Hardwicke, Kevin O'Shea, Richard Jaeckel, Harry (Henry) Morgan; *D:* Henry Hathaway; *W:* Jerome Cady; *C:* Glen MacWilliams; *M:* Hugo Friedhofer.

Wing Chun 🦴🦴 **1994** Wing Chun (Yeoh) battles horse stealing bandits and the male chauvinists around her that don't think a woman can be strong and independent (as well as a fighting expert). Chinese with subtitles or dubbed. **93m/C VHS, DVD.** *HK* Michelle Yeoh, Donnie Yan, Waise Lee; *D:* Yuen Woo Ping.

Wing Commander woof! **1999 (PG-13)** Unintentionally amusing sci-fi action flick combines elements from old WWII pilot movies, "Top Gun," and "Star Trek." Hot-shot space pilots (Prinz Jr. and Lillard) battle an evil race of aliens that resembles a heavily armed version of the cast of "Cats." Their real battle is with the heinous dialogue and techno-babble they are forced to regurgitate. Adapted from a video game. **105m/C VHS, DVD, Wide.** Freddie Prinze Jr., Matthew Lillard, Saffron Burrows, Tcheky Karyo, Juergen Prochnow, David Suchet, David Warner; *D:* Chris Roberts; *W:* Kevin Droney; *C:* Thierry Arbogast; *M:* Kevin Kiner.

Wings 🦴🦴½ **1927** The silent classic about friends, Rogers and Arlen, their adventures in the Air Corps during WWI, and their rivalry for the hand of a woman. Contains actual footage of combat flying from the Great War. Won the very first Best Picture Oscar. Too-thin plot hangs on (barely) to the stirring, intrepid dogfight scenes. **139m/B VHS.** Clara Bow, Charles "Buddy" Rogers, Richard Arlen, Gary Cooper, Jobyna Ralston, El Brendel, Richard Tucker, Henry B. Walthall, Roscoe Karns, Gunboat Smith, Julia Swayne Gordon, Arlette Marchal, Carl von Haartman, William A. Wellman; *D:* William A. Wellman; *W:* Hope Loring, John Monk Saunders, Louis D. Lighton; *C:* Harry Perry; *M:* J.S. Zamecnik. Oscars '27: Picture, Natl. Film Reg. '97.

Wings of Danger 🦴 *Dead on Course* **1952** A pilot tries to save his friend from blackmailing gold smugglers. **72m/B VHS.** *GB* Zachary Scott, Kay Kendall, Robert Beatty, Naomi Chance; *M:* Malcolm Arnold.

Wings of Desire 🦴🦴🦴½ *Der Himmel Uber Berlin* **1988 (PG-13)** An ethereal, haunting modern fable about angels Damiel (Ganz) and Cassiel (Sander), who observe human life in and above the broken existence of Berlin. Their attention is particularly focused on Homer (Bois), an elderly poet, American actor Peter Falk (playing himself), and a lovely French trapeze performer named marion (Dommartin). But the more Damiel observes, the more he longs to experience desire—emotional and physical—as humans do. A moving, unequivocable masterpiece, with as many beautiful things to say about spiritual need as about the schizophrenic emptiness of contemporary Germany; Wenders' magnum opus. German with subtitles, and with black-and-white sequences. **130m/C VHS.** *GE* Bruno Ganz, Peter Falk, Solveig Dommartin, Otto Sander, Curt Bois; *D:* Wim Wenders; *W:* Wim Wenders, Peter Handke; *C:* Henri Alekan; *M:* Jurgen Knieper. Ind. Spirit '89: Foreign Film; L.A. Film Critics '88: Cinematog., Foreign Film; N.Y. Film Critics '88: Cinematog.; Natl. Soc. Film Critics '88: Cinematog.

Wings of Eagles 🦴🦴½ **1957** Hollywood biography of Frank 'Spig' Wead, a famous WWI aviation pioneer turned screenwriter. Veers wildly from comedy to stolid drama, though Bond's lampoon of Ford as "John Dodge" is justly famous. **110m/C VHS.** John Wayne, Ward Bond, Maureen O'Hara, Dan Dailey, Edmund Lowe, Ken Curtis, Kenneth Tobey, Sig Rumann, Veda Ann Borg; *D:* John Ford; *C:* Paul Vogel.

Wings of Fame 🦴🦴½ **1993 (R)** Comic afterlife fantasy skewering celebrity status. Recently departed celebs check into a posh hotel, but as their fame on earth declines so do their afterlife accomodations, until they reach the state of oblivion. The latest hotel arrivals are a renowned, arrogant actor (O'Toole) and the frustrated writer (Firth) whose claim to fame has come from murdering him. **109m/C VHS.** Peter O'Toole, Colin Firth; *D:* Otakar Votocek; *W:* Herman Koch, Otakar Votocek.

The Wings of the Dove 🦴🦴🦴½ **1997 (R)** Beautifully acted and filmed romance "inspired by" Henry James's 1902 novel. Updated to 1910, this triangular tale focuses on well-bred-but-penniless Kate Croy (Bonham Carter), who's been taken in by her imperious Aunt Maude (Rampling) with the expectation that she marry well. And this doesn't mean Kate's present beau, poor journalist Milton Densher (Roache). But when Kate meets gentle American heiress Millie Theale (Elliott), learns she's dying, and that she's also intrigued by Merton, the wheels begin to turn. A trip to Venice sets Kate's plan in motion but leads to unexpected developments for all concerned. **101m/C VHS, DVD.** *GB* Helena Bonham Carter, Linus Roache, Alison Elliott, Elizabeth McGovern, Charlotte Rampling, Alex Jennings, Michael Gambon; *D:* Iain Softley; *W:* Hossein Amini; *C:* Eduardo Serra; *M:* Gabriel Yared. British Acad. '97: Cinematog., Makeup; L.A. Film Critics '97: Actress (Bonham Carter); Natl. Bd. of Review '97: Actress (Bonham Carter); Broadcast Film Critics '97: Actress (Bonham Carter).

Wings of the Morning 🦴🦴½ **1937** Maria (Annabella), a descendant of Spanish gypsies, comes to Ireland with her grandmother (Vanbrugh) who's entering a horse in the Epsom Downs Derby. Maria disguises herself as a boy so she can ride in the race but is discovered by Canadian horse-trainer Kerry (Fonda), who promptly falls in love with her. Legendary tenor John McCormack sings several songs. The first British movie to be filmed in Technicolor. **89m/C VHS.** *GB* Annabella, Henry Fonda, Edward Underdown, Irene Vanbrugh, Leslie Banks, Stewart Rome; *D:* Harold Schuster; *W:* Tom Geraghty; *C:* Jack Cardiff, Henry Imus, Ray Rennahan; *M:* Arthur Benjamin.

Wings over the Pacific 🦴½ **1943** Love and his daughter Cooper are living quietly on a Pacific island when a pair of pilots, American Norris and the Nazi Guttman, crash-land after a dogfight. The island is strategic because of its oil supply but Norris manages to prevent the Nazis from taking control and wins Cooper's love in the process. Veteran actor Love died shortly before the film's release. **60m/B VHS.** Montagu Love, Inez Cooper, Edward Norris, Henry Guttman, Robert Armstrong, Ernie Adams; *D:* Phil Rosen; *W:* George Wallace Sayre.

The Winner 🦴🦴 **1996 (R)** Philip (D'Onofrio) is on a winning streak at the Vegas Pair-A-Dice casino and the target of estranged brother Wolf (Madsen), tempermental lounge singer Louise (DeMornay), and various other con artists and thugs, all of whom want to separate him from his winnings. Lots of good actors but this Vegas story is nothing new. Based on the play "A Darker Purpose" by Riss. **90m/C VHS.** Vincent D'Onofrio, Michael Madsen, Rebecca DeMornay, Delroy Lindo, Frank Whaley, Billy Bob Thornton, Richard Edson; *D:* Alex Cox; *W:* Wendy Riss; *C:* Denis Maloney; *M:* Daniel Licht.

A Winner Never Quits 🦴🦴½ **1986 (PG)** A true story based on the life of 1940s baseball player Pete Gray. As a boy Gray lost his right arm above the elbow in an accident. He's determined to prove himself as a baseball player and during WWII is given a tryout, although his teammates consider him a sideshow freak. A Memphis sportswriter takes an interest in Pete's career and Gray's success on the field leads to a career with the St. Louis Browns. Along the way he becomes the inspiration to a young fan, who's also lost an arm. **96m/C VHS.** Keith Carradine, Mare Winningham, Huckleberry Fox, Dennis Weaver, Dana Delany, G.W. Bailey, Charles Hallahan, Fionnula Flanagan, Jack Kehoe; *D:* Mel Damski; *W:* Burt Prelutsky. **TV**

Winner Takes All 🦴🦴 **1986 (R)** A young college student during the Vietnam War comes to grips with maturity and growing pains. **94m/C VHS, DVD.** *GB* Jason Connery, Diane Cilento.

Winners of the West **1940** A landowner schemes to prevent a railroad from running through his property. The railroad's chief engineer leads the good guys in an attempt to prevent sabotage. A fun serial in 13 chapters, full of shooting, blown-up bridges, locomotives afire, etc., and, of course, the requisite damsel in distress. **250m/B VHS.** Anne Nagel, Dick Foran, James Craig, Harry Woods; *D:* Ray Taylor, Ford Beebe.

Winners Take All 🦴🦴 **1987 (PG-13)** A handful of friends compete in Supercross races. Spirited but thoroughly cliche sports flick. **103m/C VHS.** Gerardo Mejia, Don Michael Paul, Kathleen York, Robert Krantz; *D:* Fritz Kiersch.

Winning 🦴🦴🦴 **1969 (PG)** A race car driver (Newman) will let nothing, including his new wife (Woodward), keep him from winning the Indianapolis 500. Newman does his own driving. Thomas' film debut. **123m/C VHS, DVD, Wide.** Paul Newman, Joanne Woodward, Robert Wagner, Richard Thomas, Clu Gulager; *D:* James Goldstone; *W:* Howard A. Rodman; *C:* Richard Moore; *M:* Dave Grusin.

Winning of the West 🦴🦴 **1953** Yodelin' ranger Autry vows to protect a crusading publisher from unscrupulous crooks, including his own dog-gone brothers. The brothers see the light, and the two corral the varmints. Autry tunes include "Cowboy Blues," "Cowpoke Poking Along," and "Find Me My 45." **57m/B VHS.** Gene Autry, Smiley Burnette, Gail Davis, Richard Crane; *D:* George Archainbaud.

The Winning Team 🦴🦴½ **1952** Reagan stars in this biography of baseball legend Grover Cleveland Alexander and Day plays his dedicated wife. Some controversial issues were glossed over in the film, such as Alexander's real-life drinking problem and the fact that he had epilepsy. Although this was one of Reagan's favorite roles, he was upset by the studio's avoidance of all-too-human problems. Nonetheless, it's an entertaining enough movie about a very talented ballplayer. **98m/B VHS.** Doris Day, Ronald Reagan, Frank Lovejoy, Eve Miller, James Millican, Russ Tamblyn; *D:* Lewis Seiler.

The Winslow Boy 🦴🦴🦴½ **1948** A cadet at the Royal Naval College is wrongly accused of theft and expelled. Donat as the boy's lawyer leads a splendid cast. Despite consequences for his family, the boy's father (Hardwicke) sues the government and fights his son's battle, as the case makes the papers and he approaches bankruptcy. Plot would seem far-fetched if it weren't based on fact. Absorbing. Based on a play by Rattigan, who co-wrote the script. **112m/B VHS.** *GB* Robert Donat, Cedric Hardwicke, Margaret Leighton, Frank Lawton, Kathleen Harrison, Basil Radford; *D:* Anthony Asquith; *W:* Terence Rattigan; *C:* Frederick A. (Freddie) Young.

The Winslow Boy 🦴🦴🦴 **1998 (G)** Mamet successfully treads on unfamiliar ground with this English period piece in which young Ronnie Winslow (Edwards) is accused of stealing and expelled from military school. His father (Hawthorne) becomes determined to clear his name at whatever cost. And the cost is to be high, for his family, his health, and his moderate fortune. He hires renowned lawyer Sir Robert Morton (Northam), also with consequences for family and bank balance. Although based on a real case, the story largely ignores the main events of the scandal, focusing on its effects on the various family members. Strong performances are led by Northam and Hawthorne. Based on Terence Rattigan's play. **104m/C VHS, DVD, Wide.** Nigel Hawthorne, Jeremy Northam, Rebecca Pidgeon, Gemma Jones, Guy Edwards, Matthew Pidgeon, Colin Stinton, Aden (John) Gillett, Perry Fenwick, Sarah Flind, Sara Stewart, Alan Polanski, Neil North; *D:* David Mamet; *W:* David Mamet; *C:* Benoit Delhomme; *M:* Alaric Jans.

Winter Flight 🦴🦴 **1984** A small, gentle British drama about an RAF recruit and a barmaid who quickly become lovers, and then are confronted with her pregnancy. **105m/C VHS.** *GB* Reece Dinsdale, Nicola Cowper, Gary Olsen; *D:* Roy Battersby.

The Winter Guest 🦴🦴🦴 **1997 (R)** Rickman's directorial debut looks at the lives of eight people living in a remote and icy Scottish village, focusing on the fictional relationship between real-life mother and daughter Law and Thompson. Introspective and somewhat stagey, but fine performances and excellent use of the desolate landscape make this a worthwhile debut effort. Based on the play by Sharman Macdonald, which he and Rickman adapted for the screen. **106m/C VHS.** *GB* Emma Thompson, Phyllida Law, Sheila Reid, Sandra Voe, Gary Hollywood, Arlene Cockburn, Douglas Murphy, Sean Biggerstaff; *D:* Alan Rickman; *W:* Alan Rickman, Sharman MacDonald; *C:* Seamus McGarvey; *M:* Michael Kamen.

Winter Kills 🦴🦴🦴 **1979 (R)** Distinctive political black comedy suffers a hilariously paranoid version of American public life. Nick Kegan (Bridges) has been drifting through life ever since his older brother, a U.S. president, was assassinated 15 years earlier. His eccentric father (Huston) wants to draw Nick back into the family by claiming a conspiracy, but as Nick begins to dig into the past, he does uncover political machinations. Uneven, but well worth seeing; flopped at the boxoffice, but was re-edited (with the original ending restored) and re-released in 1983. Elizabeth Taylor (as Lola Comante) went unbilled. Based on the novel by Richard Condon. **97m/C VHS.** Jeff Bridges, John Huston, Anthony Perkins, Richard Boone, Sterling Hayden, Eli Wallach, Ralph Meeker, Belinda Bauer, Dorothy Malone, Toshiro Mifune, Elizabeth Taylor, Donald Moffat, Tisa Farrow, Brad Dexter, Joe Spinell; *D:* William Richert; *W:* William Richert; *C:* Vilmos Zsigmond; *M:* Maurice Jarre.

The Winter Light 🦴🦴🦴½ *Nattvardsgaesterna* **1962** The second film in Bergman's famous trilogy on the silence of God, preceded by "Through a Glass Darkly" and followed by "The Silence." Bleak and disturbing view of a tortured priest who searches for the faith and guidance he is unable to give his congregation. Hard to swallow for neophyte Bergmanites, but challenging, deeply serious and rewarding for those accustomed to the Swede's angst. Polished and personal. In Swedish with English subtitles. **80m/B VHS.** *SW* Gunnar Bjornstrand, Ingrid Thulin, Max von Sydow; ***D:*** Ingmar Bergman; ***W:*** Ingmar Bergman; ***C:*** Sven Nykvist.

Winter Meeting 🦴🦴 **1948** Overwrought drama with Bette Davis starring as a spinster poetess who falls in love with a war hero who wants to be a priest. Very talky script, of interest only as the sole romantic lead for James Davis, whose claim to fame was westerns and the TV series "Dallas." **104m/B VHS.** Bette Davis, Janis Paige, James Davis, John Hoyt, Florence Bates, Walter Baldwin, Ransom Sherman; ***D:*** Bretaigne Windust; ***M:*** Max Steiner.

The Winter of Our Dreams 🦴🦴½ **1982** Down Under slice of seamy life as a heroin-addicted prostitute becomes involved with an unhappy bookshop owner. Davis shines in otherwise slow and confusing drama. **89m/C VHS.** *AU* Judy Davis, Bryan Brown, Cathy Downes, Baz Luhrmann, Peter Mochrie, Mervyn Drak, Margie McCrae, Marcie Deane-Johns; ***D:*** John Duigan. Australian Film Inst. '81: Actress (Davis).

Winter People 🦴🦴½ **1989 (PG-13)** A clock-making widower and a woman living alone with her illegitimate son experience tough times together with feuding families in a Depression-era Appalachian community. Silly, rehashed premise doesn't deter McGillis, who gamely gives a fine performance. Based on the novel by John Ehle. **109m/C VHS, DVD, 8mm, Wide.** Kurt Russell, Kelly McGillis, Lloyd Bridges, Mitchell Ryan, Jeffrey Meek, Eileen Ryan, Amelia Burnette; ***D:*** Ted Kotcheff; ***W:*** Carol Sobieski; ***M:*** John Scott.

Winter Sleepers 🦴½ *Winterschlafer* **1997** Angsty and slow (completely unlike the director's breakthrough "Run Lola Run"). Rebecca (Daniel) is waiting at a mountain chalet for her boyfriend Marco (Ferch) to show up. When Marco leaves his keys in his car, Rene (Matthes) takes it for a joy ride and gets into an accident, eventually meeting Laura (Sellem) the nurse, who owns the chalet. The foursome wind-up together but nothing much matters. Based on the novel "Expense of the Spirit" by Pyszora, who co-wrote the screenplay. German with subtitles. **124m/C VHS, DVD, Wide.** *GE* Heino Ferch, Floriane Daniel, Ulrich Matthes, Marie-Lou Sellem, Josef Bierbichler; ***D:*** Tom Tykwer; ***W:*** Tom Tykwer, Anne-Francois Pyszora; ***C:*** Frank Griebe; ***M:*** Tom Tykwer, Johnny Klimek, Reinhold Heil.

A Winter Tan 🦴½ **1988** True story of New Yorker Maryse Holder (Burroughs), who's an alcoholic, drug-addicted, promiscuous one-time teacher who has decided to lose herself in the degradations Acapulco has to offer. Holder's eventually murdered by a pimp and her letters to a friend are posthumously published as "Give Sorrow Words." Self-destruction as its worst. **90m/C VHS.** *CA* Jackie Burroughs; ***D:*** Jackie Burroughs, John Frizzell, John Walker, Louise Clark; ***W:*** Jackie Burroughs; ***C:*** John Walker, Louise Clark. Genie '89: Actress (Burroughs).

Winterbeast 🦴 **1992** Winter resort community dwellers begin mysteriously disappearing until somebody remembers that the resort was built over a sacred Indian burial ground. Sgt. Bill Whitman, the valiant park ranger and his Barney Fife-like assistant Stillman, question the town's wise old sage, Sheldon, who's sitting on a secret that could threaten the entire community. **77m/C VHS.** Tim R. Morgan, Mike Magri.

Winterhawk 🦴🦴 **1976 (PG)** A Blackfoot Indian seeks smallpox serum from a nearby trapper camp for his stricken tribe. When he's attacked for his efforts, he takes revenge by kidnapping two of the settlement's children. Exceptional cinematography of the breathtaking scenery can't hide the cliched, melodramatic story and waste of a fine cast. This was Hunnicutt's last screen appearance. **98m/C VHS.** Leif Erickson, Woody Strode, Denver Pyle, L.Q. (Justus E. McQueen) Jones, Elisha Cook Jr., Arthur Hunnicutt, Dennis Fimple, Dawn Wells, Jimmy Clem, Michael Dante, Charles B. Pierce, Seamon Glass; ***D:*** Charles B. Pierce; ***W:*** Charles B. Pierce, Earl E. Smith; ***C:*** Jim Roberson; ***M:*** Lee Holdridge.

Winterset 🦴🦴½ **1936** A son seeks to clear his father's name of a falsely accused crime 15 years after his electrocution. Powerful at the time, though time has lessened its impact. Loosely based on the trial of Sacco and Vanzetti and adapted from Maxwell Anderson's Broadway play, with stars in the same roles. Meredith's film debut. **85m/B VHS.** Burgess Meredith, Margo, John Carradine; ***D:*** Alfred Santell.

Wintertime 🦴½ **1943** Forgettable and mindless Henie musical. Plot revolves around Henie travelling in Canada with her wealthy uncle, and saving an old, rundown hotel. An appearance by Woody Herman and his Orchestra give the film a much-needed boost. Based on a story by Arthur Kober. **82m/B VHS.** Sonja Henie, Jack Oakie, Cesar Romero, Carole Landis, S.Z. Sakall, Cornel Wilde, Woody Herman; ***D:*** John Brahm; ***W:*** E. Edwin Moran, Jack Jevne, Lynn Starling.

Wired 🦴 **1989 (R)** A justly lambasted, unintentionally hilarious biography of comic genius and overdose victim John Belushi, very loosely based on Bob Woodward's bestselling muckraking book. The chronicle of addiction and tragedy is tried here as a weird sort of comedy; was it meant as a tribute to its off-kilter subject? If so, it misses by a mile. And, we're sorry, but Chiklis doesn't cut it as Belushi—who would?! **112m/C VHS.** Michael Chiklis, Ray Sharkey, Patti D'Arbanville, J.T. Walsh, Gary Groomes, Lucinda Jenney, Alex Rocco, Jere Burns, Billy Preston; ***D:*** Larry Peerce; ***W:*** Earl MacRauch; ***C:*** Tony Imi; ***M:*** Basil Poledouris.

Wired to Kill woof! **1986 (R)** In a futuristic world, two teenagers seek justice for their parents' murder by building a remote-controlled erector set programmed for revenge. Laughably porous plot drops any pretence of credibility. Dizzyingly bad. **96m/C VHS.** Merritt Butrick, Emily Longstreth, Devin Hoelscher, Frank Collison; ***D:*** Francis Schaeffer.

Wirey Spindell 🦴 **1999** Self-indulgent clap-trap about a self-satisfied creep. The title character (Schaeffer) is engaged to beautiful Tabatha (Thorne) but has become suddenly impotent due to extreme premarital jitters. This little dilemma leads Wirey to explore his childhood and druggie high school/college years (when the character is played by Mabius), his first love, and his falling for Tabatha. Problem is Wirey isn't a very interesting character. **101m/C VHS, DVD, Wide.** Eric Schaeffer, Callie (Calliope) Thorne, Eric Mabius, Samantha Buck; ***D:*** Eric Schaeffer; ***W:*** Eric Schaeffer; ***C:*** Kramer Morgenthau; ***M:*** Amanda Kravat.

Wisdom 🦴½ **1987 (R)** Unemployed young guy (Estevez) becomes a bank robber with Robin Hood aspirations, coming to the aid of American farmers by destroying mortgage records. Estevez became the youngest person to star in, write, and direct a major motion picture. And, my goodness, it shows. **109m/C VHS.** Emilio Estevez, Demi Moore, Tom Skerritt, Veronica Cartwright; ***D:*** Emilio Estevez; ***M:*** Danny Elfman.

Wise Blood 🦴🦴🦴½ **1979 (PG)** Gothic drama about a drifter who searches for sin and becomes a preacher for a new religion, The Church Without Christ. Excellent cast in achingly realistic portrayal of ersatz religion, southern style. Many laughs are more painful than funny. Superb, very dark comedy from Huston. Adapted from the Flannery O'Connor novel. **106m/C VHS.** Brad Dourif, John Huston, Ned Beatty, Amy Wright, Harry Dean Stanton; ***D:*** John Huston; ***M:*** Alex North.

Wise Guys 🦴½ **1986 (R)** Two small-time hoods decide to rip off the mob. When their boss figures out their plan he decides to set them up instead. Lame black comedy that has too few moments. **100m/C VHS.** Joe Piscopo, Danny DeVito, Ray Sharkey, Captain Lou Albano, Dan Hedaya, Julie Bovasso, Patti LuPone; ***D:*** Brian DePalma; ***M:*** Ira Newborn.

Wisecracks 🦴🦴🦴 **1993** Women comics perform and talk about their work in this documentary directed by Gail Singer. The comics featured have, in some cases, little more in common than their work, but all share interesting perspectives on what they do. Interesting mix of performance clips and interviews sometimes includes banal comments about the nature of comedy, but is more often insightful, especially remarks by seasoned vet Phyllis Diller. Although there exists here the potential for an angry feminist diatribe on gender-based humor, the focus is more towards talented women who are just plain funny. **93m/C VHS.** ***D:*** Gail Singer.

Wish Me Luck 🦴½ **1995** A babe genie (Avalon) has a dilemma—unless she can make a man of a geek college student (Gesner) in 48 hours, she'll become the property of an evil sorcerer for a thousand years. She gets three equally bodacious college cheerleaders to help her out. Also available in an edited version that cuts six minutes worth of fleshy fantasies. **91m/C VHS.** Avalon Anders, Zen Gesner; ***D:*** Philip Jones.

Wish upon a Star 🦴🦴½ **1996 (PG)** Battling teenage sisters Alexia (Heigl) and Haley (Harris) wind up switching identities when bookish Haley wishes on a falling star to be like popular Alexia. Naturally, this confuses everyone but the sisters get to see how their other sibling feels. **90m/C VHS.** Katherine Heigl, Danielle Harris.

Wish You Were Dead 🦴🦴½ **2000 (R)** Schnook insurance adjuster MacBeth (Elwes) naively signs over his million dollar life insurance policy to slutty "girlfriend" Sally (Steenburgen), who promptly hires hit woman Jupiter (Hendrix) to get rid of the excess baggage. Only Jupiter can't get over what a nice guy MacBeth is and falls in love with him instead—which doesn't mean Sally is giving up. **89m/C VHS, DVD.** Cary Elwes, Mary Steenburgen, Elaine Hendrix, Christopher Lloyd, Billy Ray Cyrus, Robert Englund, Sally Kirkland, Gene Simmons, Shannon Tweed; ***D:*** Valerie McCaffrey; ***W:*** Scott Firestone; ***C:*** David Klein. **VIDEO**

Wish You Were Here 🦴🦴🦴 *Too Much* **1987** Poignant yet funny slice of British postwar life roughly based on the childhood memoirs of famous madame, Cynthia Payne. A troubled and freedom-loving teenager expresses her rebellion in sexual experimentation. Mum is dead and Dad just doesn't understand, so what's a girl to do, but get the boys excited? Lloyd, in her first film, plays the main character with exceptional strength and feistiness. Payne's later life was dramatized in the Leland-scripted "Personal Services." **92m/C VHS.** *GB* Emily Lloyd, Tom Bell, Clare Clifford, Barbara Durkin, Geoffrey Hutchings, Charlotte Barker, Chloe Leland, Trudy Cavanagh, Jesse Birdsall, Geoffrey Durham, Pat Heywood; ***D:*** David Leland; ***W:*** David Leland; ***C:*** Ian Wilson; ***M:*** Stanley Myers. British Acad. '87: Orig. Screenplay; Natl. Soc. Film Critics '87: Actress (Lloyd).

Wishful Thinking 🦴🦴 **1992** A lovelorn screenwriter rescues a peculiar man from mysterious assassins and receives a magical writing pad for his efforts. It seems that whatever Michael writes on the paper will come true, so he decides to write himself into the life of the luscious Diane. **94m/C VHS, DVD, Wide.** Murray Langston, Michelle Johnson, Ruth Buzzi, Billy Barty, Johnny Dark, Ray "Boom Boom" Mancini, Vic Dunlop, Kip Addotta; ***D:*** Murray Langston.

Wishful Thinking 🦴🦴½ **1996 (R)** Elizabeth (Beals) and Max (Le Gros) have been living together for four years. When Max doesn't want to get married, Elizabeth becomes withdrawn but Max decides she's having an affair. As he becomes more and more jealous, a third party enters the picture. Lena (Barrymore) decides she wants Max herself and devises a plan to get him at any cost. **89m/C VHS.** Drew Barrymore, Jennifer Beals, James LeGros, Mel Gorham, Eric Thal, Jon Stewart; ***D:*** Adam Park; ***W:*** Adam Park.

The Wishing Ring 🦴🦴🦴 **1914** Light and charming romance, beautifully filmed by Tourneur, based on Owen Davis' play. The son of an earl in Old England is expelled from college and told by his father he must earn half a crown on his own before the family will take him back. With the help of a minister's daughter, he sets things right. **50m/B VHS.** Vivian Martin, Alec B. Francis, Chester Barnett, Simeon Wiltsie, Walter Morton; ***D:*** Maurice Tourneur; ***W:*** Maurice Tourneur.

Wishman 🦴🦴½ **1993** Hollywood hustler Basie Banks (Le Mat) meets Hitch (Lewis), a two million-year-old genie whose magic bottle has been stolen. In exchange for Banks' help in recovering his home, Hitch agrees to help Banks get the girl of his dreams. **89m/C VHS.** Paul LeMat, Geoffrey Lewis, Paul Gleason, Quin Kessler, Nancy Parsons, Gailard Sartain, Brion James; ***D:*** Mike Marvin; ***W:*** Mike Marvin.

Wishmaster 🦴 *Wes Craven Presents Wishmaster* **1997 (R)** An evil genie grants wishes to those who stumble upon him, but he also gets his kicks by destroying the lives of those naive enough to play along. Anemic horror tale that's as thin on plot as it is on scares. Standard-issue exploding chest cavities and flying heads can't easily erase the boredom. Make-up artist turned director Kurtzman should have wished for some directorial skills, because he hasn't got a clue. Don't be misled by Wes Craven's name, his association with this dud is meant to lure the least discriminating of horror fans. **90m/C VHS, DVD.** Tammy Lauren, Andrew Divoff, Robert Englund, Chris Lemmon, Tony Crane, Wendy Benson, Jenny O'Hara, Tony Todd, Kane Hodder; ***D:*** Robert Kurtzman; ***W:*** Peter Atkins; ***C:*** Jacques Haitkin; ***M:*** Harry Manfredini.

Wishmaster 2: Evil Never Dies 🦴🦴 **1998 (R)** The Djinn is awakened by thief Morgana during a botched robbery and, in order to gain the souls he needs, the Djinn allows himself to be put in prison where he can offer wishes to the prisoners. But Morgana, aided by a priest, tries to stop him before the Djinn can destroy humanity. **96m/C VHS, DVD, Wide.** Andrew Divoff, Paul Johansson, Holly Fields, Bokeem Woodbine, Tommy (Tiny) Lister; ***D:*** Jack Sholder; ***W:*** Jack Sholder; ***C:*** Carlos Gonzalez; ***M:*** David Williams. **VIDEO**

Wishmaster 3: Beyond the Gates of Hell 🦴½ **2001 (R)** Baxter College history prof Joel Barash (Connery) has a crush on student Diana (Cook) who has been helping him out. Unfortunately, her help includes releasing the demonic Djinn from its puzzle box. The Djinn then possesses Barash and goes after Diana to grant her three wishes. Diana knows there's a trick but her fellow students aren't so smart and their wishes have nasty results. Diana can wish to spare her friends but the only thing that will really destroy the evil is the magical Sword of Justice. **92m/C VHS, DVD, Wide.** A.J. Cook, Jason Connery, Tobias Mehler, Aaron Smolinksi, Louisette Geiss, John Novak; ***D:*** Chris Angel; ***W:*** Alexander Wright. **VIDEO**

The Wistful Widow of Wagon Gap 🦴🦴 *The Wistful Widow* **1947** Lou, a traveling salesman, accidentally kills a man, and according to the law of the west he has to take care of the dead man's widow and children—all seven of them. Because the family is so unsavory, Lou knows that no other man will kill him, so he allows himself to be appointed sheriff and clears the town of lowlifes. Usual Abbott & Costello fare is highlighted with their zany antics. **78m/B VHS.** Bud Abbott, Lou Costello, Marjorie Main, George Cleveland, Gordon Jones, William Ching, Peter Thompson, Glenn Strange, Olin Howlin; ***D:*** Charles T. Barton.

Wit 🦴🦴🦴 **2001** A tough topic buoyed by Thompson's fierce performance and Nichols expert direction. Middleaged scholar Vivian Bearing (Thompson) has dedicated her work to studying the holy sonnets of John Donne. The poet's life-and-death issues take on new meaning when Vivian learns she has stage-four ovarian cancer and she agrees to undergo the most aggressive treatment available.

She puts herself in the care of veteran researcher Dr. Kelekian (Lloyd) and his internist Dr. Posner (Woodward), a former student of Vivian's. Their insensitivity sparks her bitter wit as Vivian realizes the inevitable truth. Based on the 1997 Pulitzer Prize-winning play by Margaret Edson. **98m/C VHS, DVD.** Emma Thompson, Christopher Lloyd, Audra McDonald, Jonathan M. Woodward, Eileen Atkins, Harold Pinter; ***D:*** Mike Nichols; ***W:*** Emma Thompson, Mike Nichols; ***C:*** Seamus McGarvey. CABLE

The Witch ½ *La Strega in Amore; Aura* **1966** Historian hired by family to assemble the late father's works falls in love with beautiful daughter. Seems she's no angel. **103m/B VHS.** *IT* Rosanna Schiaffino, Richard Johnson, Sarah Ferrati, Gian Marie Volonte, Margherita Guzzinati; ***D:*** Damiano Damiani.

Witch Hunt ½ **1994 (R)** Mock fantasy/mystery set in 1953 Hollywood. Private eye H. Phillip Lovecraft (Hopper) is hired by actress Kim Hudson (Miller) to shadow her philandering studio hubby Gottlieb (Rosenberg), who dies in an untimely fashion. The kicker is that witchcraft is commonplace, with the studio hiring witches and warlocks to cast spells. Also, a blowhard senator (Bogosian) is heading a McCarthy-like campaign to ban magic and Lovecraft fears his sorceress friend (Ralph) is going to be the scapegoat for Gottlieb's murder. Great special effects; fuzzy plot. **101m/C VHS.** Dennis Hopper, Penelope Ann Miller, Eric Bogosian, Sheryl Lee Ralph, Julian Sands, Alan Rosenberg, Valerie Mahaffey, Debi Mazar; ***D:*** Paul Schrader; ***W:*** Joseph Dougherty; ***M:*** Angelo Badalamenti.

Witch Who Came from the Sea ½ **1976 (R)** Witch terrorizes all the ships at sea, but doesn't exactly haunt the viewer. **98m/C VHS.** Millie Perkins, Lonny (Loni) Chapman, Vanessa Brown, Peggy (Margaret) Feury, Rick Jason; ***D:*** Matt Cimber.

A Witch Without a Broom ½ *Una Bruja Sin Escoba* **1968** Shoestring time travel fantasy. When an American professor catches the eye of a 15th century apprentice witch, the trip begins. Since the witch is only learning the ropes, they end up visiting a number of periods other than their own before the professor gets home. **78m/C VHS.** *SP* Jeffrey Hunter, Maria Perschy, Perla Cristal, Gustavo Rojo; ***D:*** Joe Lacy.

Witchboard ½ **1987 (R)** During a college party, a group of friends bring out the Ouija board and play with it for laughs. One of the girls discovers she can use the board to communicate with a small boy who died years before. In her effort to talk with him she unwittingly releases the evil spirit of an ax murderer who haunts and murders members of the group. An entertaining, relatively inoffensive member of its genre that displays some attention to characterization and plot. **98m/C VHS.** Todd Allen, Tawny Kitaen, Stephen Nichols, Kathleen Wilhoite, Burke Byrnes, Rose Marie, James W. Quinn, Judy Tatum, Gloria Hayes, J.P. Luebsen, Susan Nickerson; ***D:*** Kevin S. Tenney; ***W:*** Kevin S. Tenney; ***C:*** Roy Wagner; ***M:*** Dennis Michael Tenney.

Witchboard 2: The Devil's Doorway ½ **1993 (R)** There seem to be a lot of doorways to hell because someone is always finding a new one (and making a movie about it). This time it's the innocent Paige Benedict (Dolenz), who moves into an artist's loft and finds an old Ouija board in a closet. Through the board, Paige is contacted by a former tenant who claims to be a murder victim. Soon her fellow tenants are dying in violent and mysterious ways and Paige's dreams are haunted by evil. What hath she wrought—and can she get it back in the closet where it belongs. **98m/C VHS.** Ami Dolenz, Laraine Newman, Timothy Gibbs, John Gatins, Julie Michaels, Marvin Kaplan; ***D:*** Kevin S. Tenney; ***W:*** Kevin S. Tenney; ***C:*** David Lewis; ***M:*** Dennis Michael Tenney.

Witchboard 3: The Possession ½ **1995 (R)** A Ouija board opens the gates to hell (yet again or we wouldn't have a movie) and the board's spirit steals Brian's soul and takes control of his body—much to the bewilderment of his girlfriend Julie. **93m/C VHS.** David Nerman, Locky Lambert, Cedric Smith, Donna Sarrasin; ***D:*** Peter Svatek; ***W:*** Kevin S. Tenney, Jon Ezrine; ***C:*** Barry Gravelle.

Witchcraft woof! **1988 (R)** A young mother meets a couple killed three centuries ago for performing witchcraft. They want her baby, of course, to be the son of the devil. "Rosemary's Baby" rip-off, that is thoroughly predictable. **90m/C VHS, DVD.** Anat "Topol" Barzilai, Gary Sloan, Mary Shelley, Deborah Scott, Alexander Kirkwood, Lee Kisman, Edward Ross Newton; ***D:*** Robert Spera; ***W:*** Jody Savin; ***C:*** Jens Sturup; ***M:*** Randy Miller.

Witchcraft 2: The Temptress **1990 (R)** A sensuous woman seduces an innocent young man into the rituals of witchcraft and the occult. Sequel to "Witchcraft" does not succeed where original failed, but does have a fair share of sex and violence. **88m/C VHS, DVD.** Charles Solomon, Mia Ruiz, Delia Sheppard; ***D:*** Mark Woods; ***W:*** Jim Hanson, Sal Manna; ***C:*** Jens Sturup; ***M:*** Miriam Cutler.

Witchcraft 3: The Kiss of Death **1990 (R)** Once a master of the occult, William Spanner now seeks only to live a normal life. His plans are changed, however, when a sensual creature from Hell is sent to seduce him. More sex and violence, with an emphasis on sex. The best of the "Witchcraft" trio, for those trying to plan a festive evening. **85m/C VHS.** Charles Solomon, Lisa Toothman, William L. Baker, Lena Hall; ***D:*** R.L. Tillmanns.

Witchcraft 4: Virgin Heart **1992 (R)** Supernatural horror continues as attorney Will Spanner sinks even deeper into his enemy's satanic trap in this shocking sequel to the popular series. His only hope is to use his own black magic powers and to enlist the help of a seductive stripper (Penthouse Pet Strain). **92m/C VHS.** Charles Solomon, Julie Strain, Clive Pearson, Jason O'Gulihar, Lisa Jay Harrington, Barbara Dow; ***D:*** James Merendino.

Witchcraft 5: Dance with the Devil **1992 (R)** This undistinguished horror series continues with several successful people finding the unpleasant loopholes in their satanic contracts. A demon named Cain is behind all the trouble. The horror special effects are cheap but there are several soft-core sex scenes (pointless to the plot) which provide a minimal interest. An unrated version is also available. **94m/C VHS.** Marklen Kennedy, Carolyn Taye-Loren, Nicole Sassaman, Aysha Hauer; ***D:*** Talun Hsu.

Witchcraft 6: The Devil's Mistress **1994 (R)** Police detectives Lutz and Garner's new case involves young women turning up naked and dead. Turns out satanic disciple Savanti is expected to impress the boss with a virgin sacrifice before an impending eclipse. But since virgins are scarce, he's having a real tough time. Practically no gore but lots of skin, along with hit-or-miss humor. **86m/C VHS.** Kurt Alan, John E. Holiday, Bryan Nutter, Jerry Spicer, Shannon Lead; ***D:*** Julie Davis; ***W:*** Julie Davis.

Witchcraft 7: Judgement Hour **1995 (R)** Modern-day warlock must sacrifice his earthly existence to kill an evil vampire. **91m/C VHS.** David Byrnes, April Breneman, Alisa Christensen, John Cragen, Loren Schmalle; ***D:*** Michael Paul Girard; ***W:*** Peter Fleming; ***C:*** Denis Maloney; ***M:*** Miriam Cutler.

Witchcraft 8: Salem's Ghost *Salem's Ghost* **1995 (R)** Warlock Simon Winfrough (Van Landingham) was burned at the stake in 1692 but if you could keep a bad satanist in his grave there'd be no movie. So when Simon's spirit is accidentally awakened by the Dunaways (Grober and Korf) in their Salem home, they seek the help of exorcist McArthur (Overmyer). **90m/C VHS.** Lee Grober, Kim Kopf, Tom Overmyer, Jack Van Landingham, David Weills, Anthoni Stuart; ***D:*** Joseph John Barmettler Jr.; ***W:*** Joseph John Barmettler Jr.; ***C:*** Denis Maloney.

Witchcraft 9: Bitter Flesh **1996 (R)** Yet another sequel to the endless erotic horror series finds the LAPD investigating a series of murders. They get a tip from a strange call girl who claims to be chanelling the spirit of a warlock, who's about to open the gates to hell. **90m/C VHS, DVD.** Landon Hall, David Byrnes, Stephanie Beaton, Mikul Robins; ***D:*** Michael Paul Girard; ***W:*** Stephen J. Downing; ***C:*** Jeff Gateman; ***M:*** Michael Paul Girard.

Witchcraft 10: Mistress of the Craft **1998** Witch Celeste Sheridan has been hunting Raven and her band of vampires outside London. Meanwhile, LAPD detective Lucy Lutz arrives in London with an extradition order for Satanic serial killer, Hyde. But Raven and her vamps free Hyde in order to have him help in a ritual power-enhancing ceremony. After Celeste finds out, she teams up with Lucy and Interpol agent Chris Dixon to hunt down Raven and Hyde before they can finish their demonic work. **90m/C VHS, DVD.** Wendy Cooper, Eileen Daly, Stephanie Beaton, Kerry Knowlton, Sean Harry, Frank Scantori, Emily Bouffante, Lynn Michelle; ***D:*** Elisar Cabrera; ***W:*** Elisar Cabrera; ***C:*** Alvin Leong. VIDEO

Witchery *La Casa 4; Ghosthouse 2; Witchcraft* **1988** A photographer and his girlfriend vacation at a New England hotel where they discover a horrifying, satanic secret. One by one (as always, in this kind of bad flick, in the interest of "suspense"), people are killed off. Seems it's a witch, bent on revenge. Forget room service and bar the door. Laurenti used the pseudonym Martin Newlin. **96m/C VHS, DVD.** David Hasselhoff, Linda Blair, Catherine Hickland, Hildegarde Knef, Leslie Cumming, Bob Champagne, Richard Farnsworth, Michael Manches; ***D:*** Fabrizio Laurenti.

The Witches ½ *The Devil's Own* **1966** Gwen Mayfield (Fontaine) accepts a teaching position at Haddaby School. She wants to put terrifying memories of work in Africa behind her, but finds that the bucolic English country town is just as dangerous. The sense of menace isn't as strong as it is in the similar "Wicker Man," and the film isn't one of the strongest entries from the Hammer Studio, but it is up to their high standards in terms of production values and acting. **90m/C DVD, Wide.** Joan Fontaine, Kay Walsh, Alec McCowen, Ann Bell, John Collin, Michele Dotrice, Gwen Ffrangcon Davies, Ingrid Brett; ***D:*** Cyril Frankel; ***W:*** Nigel Kneale; ***C:*** Arthur Grant; ***M:*** Richard Rodney Bennett.

The Witches ½ **1990 (PG)** Nine-year-old boy on vacation finds himself in the midst of a witch convention, and grand high witch Huston plans to turn all children into furry little creatures. The boy, with the help of his good witch grandmother, attempts to prevent the mass transmutation of children into mice. Top-notch fantasy probably too spooky for the training wheel set. Wonderful special effects; the final project of executive producer Jim Henson. Based on Roald Dahl's story. **92m/C VHS, DVD.** Anjelica Huston, Mai Zetterling, Jasen Fisher, Rowan Atkinson, Charlie Potter, Bill Paterson, Brenda Blethyn, Jane Horrocks; ***D:*** Nicolas Roeg; ***W:*** Allan Scott; ***C:*** Harvey Harrison; ***M:*** Stanley Myers. L.A. Film Critics '90: Actress (Huston); Natl. Soc. Film Critics '90: Actress (Huston).

Witches' Brew **1979 (PG)** Three young women try to use their undeveloped skills in witchcraft and black magic to help Garr's husband get a prestigious position at a university, with calamitous results. Oft-funny spoof is silly and oft-predictable. Turner's role is small as an older, experienced witch. **98m/C VHS.** Teri Garr, Richard Benjamin, Lana Turner, Kathryn Leigh Scott; ***D:*** Richard Shorr, Herbert L. Strock.

Witches' Mountain **1971** A troubled couple is captured by a coven of witches in the Pyrenees. Dull and pointless. **98m/C VHS.** *MX* Patty (Patti) Shepard, John Caffari, Monica Randall; ***D:*** Raul Artigot.

The Witches of Eastwick ½ **1987 (R)** "Mad Max" director Miller meets Hollywood in this unrestrained, vomit-filled treatment of John Updike's novel about three lonely small-town New England women and their sexual liberation. A strange, rich, overweight and balding, but nonetheless charming man knows their deepest desires and makes them come true with decadent excess. Raunchy fun, with Nicholson over-acting wildly as the Mephisto. Miller lends a bombastic violent edge to the effort, sometimes at the expense of the story. Filmed on location in Cohasset, Massachusetts. **118m/C VHS, DVD, 8mm.** Jack Nicholson, Cher, Susan Sarandon, Michelle Pfeiffer, Veronica Cartwright, Richard Jenkins, Keith Joakum, Carel Struycken; ***D:*** George Miller; ***W:*** Michael Cristofer; ***C:*** Vilmos Zsigmond; ***M:*** John Williams. L.A. Film Critics '87: Actor (Nicholson); N.Y. Film Critics '87: Actor (Nicholson).

Witchfire **1986 (R)** After their pyschiatrist dies in an automobile accident, three maniacal women escape from an asylum and hide out in the woods. Winters then holds seances to contact the dead doctor, but instead captures a young, very much alive hunter. For dedicated fans of Winters. **92m/C VHS.** Shelley Winters, Gary Swanson, David Mendenhall, Corinne Chateau; ***D:*** Vincent J. Privitera; ***W:*** Vincent J. Privitera.

The Witching woof! *Necromancy* **1972** Poorly made story of man's continuing quest for supernatural power. Welles slums as the high priest out to get victim Franklin. **90m/C VHS.** Orson Welles, Pamela Franklin, Michael Ontkean, Lee Purcell, Lisa James, Harvey Jason, Terry Quinn; ***D:*** Bert I. Gordon; ***W:*** Bert I. Gordon, Gail March; ***C:*** Winton C. Hoch.

The Witching of Ben Wagner ½ **1995 (G)** Strange occurrences have Ben believing his friend Regina and her grandmother may be witches. But, if so, they're friendly ones as they help Ben adjust to a new home and neighborhood. **96m/C VHS.** Justin Gocke, Harriet Hall, Sam Bottoms; ***D:*** Paul Annett.

Witching Time ½ **1984** Elvira presents this film, in which a young composer is visited by a horny 17th-century witch while his wife is away from home. When the wife returns, both women fight to possess him. **60m/C VHS.** Jon Finch, Prunella Gee, Patricia Quinn, Ian McCulloch; ***D:*** Don Leaver.

The Witchmaker *Legend of Witch Hollow; Witchkill* **1969** Remote, crocodile-infested bayou in Louisiana is the scene of witchcraft and the occult as young girls are murdered in order for a group of witches to become youthful again. **101m/C VHS.** John Lodge, Alvy Moore, Thordis Brandt, Anthony Eisley, Shelby Grant, Robyn Millan; ***D:*** William O. Brown; ***W:*** William O. Brown.

Witchouse **1999 (R)** Elizabeth (McKinney), a modern-day witch, invites some fellow college students to an off-campus party at her creepy mansion. But it turns out they are all descendants of witch-hunters who burned Elizabeth's ancestor at the stake. And now it's time for revenge. **90m/C VHS, DVD.** David Oren Ward, Ashley Mckinney, Matt Raftery, Monica Serene Garnich, Brooke Muller, Ariauna Albright, Marissa Tait, Dane Northcutt, Kimberly Pullis; ***D:*** Jack Reed; ***W:*** Matthew Jason Walsh; ***C:*** Viorel Sergovici Jr. VIDEO

Witchouse 3: Demon Fire **2001 (R)** Stevie (Rochon) and Rose (Krause) are filming a documentary on witchcraft, when their old friend Annie (Dempsey) comes to visit. Annie is seeking refuge from her abusive boyfriend and her buddies are glad to oblige. As part of the documentary, the three women conduct a mock seance, and inadvertently raise the spirit of the evil witch Lilith (Stevens). Soon, strange things happen and the corpses start piling up. Is Lilith real, or has one of the girls gone insane? As with the other films in this series, director Bookwalter is able to put every nickel up onscreen and create an interesting movie. This one isn't great art, nor does it want to be. It's simply a horror film that offers cheap thrills, attractive ladies, and a brief escape from reality. **77m/C DVD, Wide.** Debbie Rochon, Tanya Dempsey, Tina Krause, Brinke Stevens; ***D:*** J.R. Bookwalter.

The Witch's Mirror **1960** A sorceress plots to destroy the murderer of her god- daughter. The murderer, a surgeon, begins a project to restore the disfigured face and hands of his burned second wife, and he doesn't care how he gets the materials. For true fans of good bad horror flicks. Badly dubbed (which adds to the charm); dark (of course); and offbeat (naturally). **75m/B VHS.** *MX* Rosita (Rosa) Arenas, Armando Calvo, Isabela Corona, Dina De Marco; ***D:*** Chano Urueto.

WitchTrap **1989 (R)** Lame sequel to "Witchboard." A mansion's new owner hires psychics to exorcise the disturbed ghost of his predecessor. **87m/C VHS.** James W. Quinn, Kathleen Bailey, Linnea Quigley; ***D:*** Kevin S. Tenney.

With a Friend Like Harry *Harry, He's Here to Help; Harry, un Ami Qui Vous Veut du Bien; Harry, A Friend Who Wishes You Well* **2000 (R)** Twisted, surprisingly funny black comedy about a sociopath. Michel (Lucas), wife Claire (Seigner), and their three young daughters have embarked on the vacation from hell as they head to their summer home. At a rest stop, Michel happens to meet Harry (Lopez), a high school acquaintance who remembers Michel very well. Before they know it, Claire and Michel are sharing their farmhouse with Harry and his sexy girlfriend, the aptly named Plum (Guillemin). Harry's a very, very generous (if offkilter) guy—in fact, he'll do anything to make Michel's life better, even kill. French with subtitles. **117m/C VHS, DVD, Wide.** *FR* Sergei Lopez, Laurent Lucas, Mathilde Seigner, Sophie Guillemin; ***D:*** Dominik Moll; ***W:*** Dominik Moll, Gilles Marchand; ***C:*** Mathieu Poirot-Delpech; ***M:*** David Whitaker. Cesar '01: Actor (Lopez), Director (Moll), Film Editing, Sound.

With Friends Like These **1998 (R)** Four buddies, who are all smalltime character actors, find their friendship put to the test when they realize they're all up for the same part in a Martin Scorsese gangster movie. Johnny (Costanza), Steve (Arkin), Dorian (Tenney), and Armand (Strathairn) all want that proverbial big break and if it means backstabbing a best friend, well that's showbiz. Good ensemble cast. **105m/C VHS.** Robert Costanzo, Adam Arkin, Jon Tenney, David Strathairn, Amy Madigan, Laura San Giacomo, Elle Macpherson, Lauren Tom, Beverly D'Angelo, Garry Marshall, Michael McKean, Jon Polito, Ashley Peldon, Bill Murray, Carmine Costanzo; ***Cameos:*** Martin Scorsese; ***D:*** Philip Frank Messina; ***W:*** Philip Frank Messina; ***C:*** Brian Reynolds; ***M:*** John Powell, Hans Zimmer.

With Honors **1994 (PG-13)** Pesci is a bum who finds desperate Harvard student Fraser's Honors thesis, and, like any quick-witted bum with a yen for literature, holds it for ransom. Desperate to salvage his future gold card, Fraser and his roommates agree to fix Joe's homeless state. Self-involved students learn something about love and life while Madonna drones in the background. Fraser is believable as the ambitious student about to endure Pesci's enlightenment. Pesci is Pesci, doing his best to overcome numerous script difficulties. **100m/C VHS, DVD.** Joe Pesci, Brendan Fraser, Moira Kelly, Patrick Dempsey, Josh Hamilton, Gore Vidal; ***D:*** Alek Keshishian; ***W:*** William Mastrosimone; ***C:*** Sven Nykvist; ***M:*** Patrick Leonard.

With Kit Carson over the Great Divide **1925** A large-scale silent western about a doctor's family gone asunder and then reunited during the Fremont expeditions out of St. Louis in the 1840s. Snow's final screen appearance. Recently refound. Fun cinematic history (in two senses of the phrase). Beautiful landscape. **72m/B VHS, 8mm.** Roy Stewart, Henry B. Walthall, Marguerite Snow, Sheldon Lewis, Earl Metcalfe; ***D:*** Frank S. Mattison.

With Six You Get Eggroll *A Man in Mommy's Bed* **1968 (G)** A widow with three sons and a widower with a daughter elope and then must deal with the antagonism of their children and even their dogs. Brady Bunch-esque family comedy means well, but doesn't cut it. Hershey's debut. Jamie Farr, William Christopher, and Vic Tayback have small parts. To date, Day's last big-screen appearance. **95m/C VHS.** Doris Day, Brian Keith, Pat Carroll, Alice Ghostley, Vic Tayback, Jamie Farr, William (Bill) Christopher, Barbara Hershey; ***D:*** Howard Morris; ***C:*** Harry Stradling Jr.

Within the Rock **1996 (R)** Space crew must shift a wandering moon before it collides with earth but beyond that problem they've got an alien predator that's escaped. **91m/C VHS, DVD.** Xander Berkeley, Bradford Tatum, Brian Krause, Caroline Barclay, Calvin Levels, Earl Boen, Dale Dye; ***D:*** Gary J. Tunnicliffe; ***W:*** Gary J. Tunnicliffe; ***C:*** Adam Kane; ***M:*** Tony Fennell, Rod Gammons.

Withnail and I **1987 (R)** A biting and original black comedy about a pair of unemployed, nearly starving English actors during the late 1960s. They decide to retreat to a country house owned by Withnail's uncle, for a vacation and are beset by comic misadventures, particularly when the uncle, who is gay, starts to hit on his nephew's friend. Robinson, who scripted "The Killing Fields," makes his successful directorial debut, in addition to drafting the screenplay from his own novel. Co-produced by George Harrison and Richard Starkey (Ringo Starr). **108m/C VHS, DVD, Wide.** *GB* Richard E. Grant, Paul McGann, Richard Griffiths, Ralph Brown, Michael Elphick; ***D:*** Bruce Robinson; ***W:*** Bruce Robinson; ***C:*** Peter Hannan; ***M:*** David Dundas.

Without a Clue **1988 (PG)** Spoof of the Sherlock Holmes legend, in which Holmes is actually portrayed by a bumbling, skirt-chasing actor, and Watson is the sole crime-solving mastermind, hiring the actor to impersonate the character made famous by the doctor's published exploits. The leads have some fun and so do we; but laughs are widely spaced. **107m/C VHS.** *GB* Michael Caine, Ben Kingsley, Jeffrey Jones, Lysette Anthony, Paul Freeman, Nigel Davenport, Peter Cook, Pat Keen; ***D:*** Thom Eberhardt; ***W:*** Gary Murphy, Larry Strawther; ***M:*** Henry Mancini.

Without a Trace **1983 (PG)** One morning, a six-year-old boy is sent off to school by his loving mother, never to return. The story of the mother's relentless search for her son. Cardboard characters, wildly unrealistic ending that is different from the real-life incident on which it's based. Scripted by Gutcheon from her book "Still Missing." Jaffe's directorial debut. **119m/C VHS.** Kate Nelligan, Judd Hirsch, Stockard Channing, David Dukes; ***D:*** Stanley R. Jaffe; ***C:*** John Bailey; ***M:*** Jack Nitzsche.

Without Anesthesia *Rough Treatment; Bez Znieczulenia* **1978** Journalist Jerzy returns from a trip abroad to discover his wife has left him for an obnoxious young writer. Against advice, Jerzy fights the divorce and searches for an explanation. Meanwhile, he has mysteriously fallen out of political favor and finds his career falling apart as well. Polish with English subtitles. **111m/C VHS.** *PL* Zbigniew Zapasiewicz, Ewa Dalkowska, Krystyna Janda, Andrzej Seweryn; ***D:*** Andrzej Wajda; ***W:*** Agnieszka Holland, Andrzej Wajda.

Without Evidence **1996** When Oregon correctional director Michael Francke (Garrett) is visiting younger brother Kevin (Plank) in Florida, he mentions his suspicions about an operation within his department involving drugs in prison. Then the next phone call Kevin gets is that Michael's been murdered. When he heads to Oregon, Kevin seems to be getting the official runaround and becomes increasingly suspicious about a coverup. A tension-building true story that remains unsolved. **90m/C VHS, DVD.** Scott Plank, Anna Gunn, Andrew Prine, Angelina Jolie, Paul Perri, Allen Nause, Ernie Garrett; ***D:*** Gill Dennis; ***W:*** Gill Dennis, Phil Stanford; ***C:*** Victor Nunez; ***M:*** Franco Piersanti.

Without Honors **1932** A man seeks to restore the reputation of his dead brother, accused of murder and theft. He joins the Texas Rangers and brings the real criminals to justice. Excellent location shooting lifts ordinary early western. **62m/B VHS.** Harry Carey Sr., Mae Busch, Gibson Gowland, George "Gabby" Hayes; ***D:*** William Nigh.

Without Limits *Pre* **1997 (PG-13)** Second biopic about '70s long-distance runner Steve Prefontaine (after 1996's "Prefontaine") focuses mainly on Prefontaine's (Crudup) relationship with his University of Oregon coach Bill Bowerman (Sutherland), who later was a co-founder of Nike. Also explores the heartbreak of the 1972 Olympics. Crudup does a fine job exploring the runner's playful arrogance, fearlessness, and iconoclasm (especially when dealing with the corrupt AAU). Sutherland, playing a three-dimensional character for the first time in a while, gives a fine performance. Kenny Moore, a close friend and fellow '72 Olympian, wrote the script with director Towne, with the full cooperation of Bowerman and Prefontaine's girlfriend. **117m/C VHS, DVD.** Billy Crudup, Donald Sutherland, Monica Potter, Jeremy Sisto, Matthew Lillard, Billy Burke, Dean Norris, Gabriel Olds, Judith Ivey; ***D:*** Robert Towne; ***W:*** Robert Towne, Kenny Moore; ***C:*** Conrad L. Hall; ***M:*** Randy Miller.

Without Love **1945** Tracy is a scientist, Hepburn, a woman with an empty basement for his laboratory. Since the neighbors would be scandalized by the idea of unmarried people living together, however platonically, they decide to get married, although each has sworn off romance. Snappy dialogue, expertly rendered by the Tracy/Hepburn team. Terrific supporting cast keeps this minimally plotted outing afloat. Adapted from the play of the same name by Philip Barry. **113m/B VHS.** Spencer Tracy, Katharine Hepburn, Lucille Ball, Keenan Wynn, Carl Esmond, Patricia Morison, Felix Bressart; ***D:*** Harold Bucquet; ***W:*** Donald Ogden Stewart; ***C:*** Karl Freund.

Without Love **1980** Ambitious young journalist experiences resentment from her peers because of her aggressive methods, and they decide to teach her a lesson by drawing her into a situation destined for disaster. In Polish with English subtitles. **104m/C VHS.** *PL* ***D:*** Barbara Sass.

Without Mercy **1995 (R)** Marine platoon is shafted by the government when they're left to die while on a U.N. peacekeeping mission in Africa. POW survivor John Carter (Zagarino) then winds up in Asia and gets set up by ex-soldier and general bad guy Larsen (Kove), who he must constantly battle in order to survive. **88m/C VHS.** Frank Zagarino, Martin Kove, Ayu Azhari, Frans Tumbuan; ***D:*** Robert Anthony; ***W:*** Robert Anthony.

Without Reservations **1946** Hollywood-bound novelist Colbert encounters Marine flyer Wayne and his pal (DeFore) aboard a train. She decides he would be perfect for her newest movie. They both dislike her famous book and don't realize they're traveling with the renowned author. Misadventures and misunderstandings abound as this trio make their way to Tinseltown. Of course, Colbert and Wayne fall in love. Boxoffice success with a tired script and too few real laughs. The Duke is interesting but miscast. Based on the novel "Thanks, God, I'll Take It From Here" by Jane Allen. **101m/B VHS.** Claudette Colbert, John Wayne, Don DeFore, Phil Brown, Frank Puglia; ***Cameos:*** Louella Parsons, Cary Grant, Jack Benny; ***D:*** Mervyn LeRoy; ***C:*** Milton Krasner.

Without Warning *The Story Without A Name* **1952** Inexperienced director and actors pull out a minor success in this fairly ordinary murder mystery, about a serial killer of beautiful blondes. **75m/C VHS.** *FR* Maurice Ronet, Adam Williams, Gloria Franklin, Edward Binns; ***D:*** Arnold Laven.

Without Warning: The James Brady Story **1991 (R)** White House Press Secretary Brady took a bullet in the brain during the 1981 shooting of President Reagan, and made a slow, grueling recovery. This fine cable film spares none of it, concentrating on the stricken man and his family, and opting out of disease-of-the-week cliches (though the pic's politics won't please the gun-adorers). Based on Mollie Dickinson's biography "Thumbs Up." **120m/C VHS.** Beau Bridges, Joan Allen, David Strathairn, Christopher Bell, Gary Grubbs, Bryan Clark, Steve Flynn, Christine Healy, Susan Brown; ***D:*** Michael Toshiyuki Uno; ***W:*** Robert Bolt. **CABLE**

Witness **1985 (R)** A young Amish boy, Samuel Lapp (Haas), traveling from his father's funeral witnesses a murder in a Philadelphia bus station. Investigating detective John Book (Ford, in one of his best roles) soon discovers the killing is part of a conspiracy involving corruption in his department. He follows the child and his young widowed mother, Rachel (McGillis) to their home in the country. A thriller with a difference, about the encounter of alien worlds, with a poignant love story. McGillis, in her first major role, is luminous as the Amish mother, while Ford is believable as both a cop and a sensitive man. An artfully crafted drama, richly focusing on the often misunderstood Amish lifestyle. **112m/C VHS, DVD.** Harrison Ford, Kelly McGillis, Alexander Godunov, Lukas Haas, Josef Sommer, Danny Glover, Patti LuPone, Viggo Mortensen; ***D:*** Peter Weir; ***W:*** William P. Kelley, Earl W. Wallace; ***C:*** John Seale; ***M:*** Maurice Jarre. Oscars '85: Film Editing, Orig. Screenplay; Writers Guild '85: Orig. Screenplay.

The Witness Files **2000 (R)** Sandy (Butler) has been imprisoned for the murder of her abusive husband. Corrupt politician Frank Sutton (Flatman) arranges for her release so he can use her special talents (she does makeup special effects) for his own nefarious ends. But Sandy hooks up with a detective (Nerman) to doublecross Sutton. Watch "F/X" instead unless you're a particular fan of Butler. **97m/C VHS, DVD.** Yancy Butler, David Nerman, Barry Flatman, Matthew Harbour; ***D:*** Douglas Jackson. **VIDEO**

Witness for the Prosecution **1957** An unemployed man is accused of murdering a wealthy widow whom he befriended. Ailing defense attorney Laughton can't resist taking an intriguing murder case, and a straitforward court case becomes increasingly complicated in this energetic adaptation of an Agatha Christie story and stage play. Outstanding performances by Laughton, with excellent support by real life wife, Lanchester, as his patient nurse. Power, as the alleged killer, and Dietrich as a tragic woman are top-notch (see if you can detect Dietrich in an unbilled second role). **116m/B VHS, DVD, Wide.** Charles Laughton, Tyrone Power, Marlene Dietrich, Elsa Lanchester, John Williams, Henry Daniell, Una O'Connor; ***D:*** Billy Wilder; ***W:*** Billy Wilder, Harry Kurnitz; ***C:*** Russell Harlan; ***M:*** Matty Malneck. Golden Globes '58: Support. Actress (Lanchester).

Witness Protection **1999** Highly watchable performances raise this cable movie about mobsters above the average. Boston goodfella Bobby Batton (Sizemore) turns state's evidence after he's betrayed by his cronies. He and his family are placed in the witness protection program under the eye of a U.S. marshal (Whitaker) but living as a regular mook proves difficult. Bobby's wife (Mastrantonio) is bitter, his kids are angry and confused, and there are no easy endings. Based on a 1996 New York Times Magazine article by Robert Sabbag. **105m/C VHS, DVD.** Tom Sizemore, Forest Whitaker, Mary Elizabeth Mastrantonio, Shawn Hatosy, Richard Portnow; ***D:*** Richard Pearce; ***W:*** Daniel Therriault; ***C:*** Fred Murphy; ***M:*** Cliff Eidelman. **CABLE**

Witness to the Execution **1994 (PG-13)** It's 1999 and Tycom Entertainment, a pay-per-view network, is looking for some hot entertainment. Top exec Jessica (Young) decides to televise the electric chair execution of convicted criminal Dennis Casterline (Daly). But Casterline claims to be innocent and as the execution date nears Jessica is unsettled by new evidence that may supports his claim. The cutthroat TV execs provide amusement but this TV movie fare quickly becomes muddled. **92m/C VHS.** Sean Young, Timothy Daly, Len Cariou, George Newbern; ***D:*** Tommy Lee Wallace; ***W:*** Thomas Baum.

Witness to the Mob **1998 (R)** Originally an NBC miniseries, this mob saga tells the true story of Sammy "The Bull" Gravano (Turturro), who turned state's evidence against his boss, John Gotti. Manages to hit every cliche and stereotype along the way. **172m/C VHS.** Nicholas Turturro, Tom Sizemore, Debi Mazar, Frankie Valli, Abe Vigoda, Philip Baker Hall, Frank Vincent, Michael Imperioli, Lenny Venito, Vincent Pastore, Kirk Acevedo; ***D:*** Thaddeus O'Sullivan; ***W:*** Stanley Weiser; ***C:*** Frank Prinzi; ***M:*** Stephen Endelman. **TV**

Wittgenstein 🦴🦴 **1993** Complicated, experimental portrait of Viennese-born philosopher Ludwig Wittgenstein (Johnson), executed as a series of blackout sketches (that feature a green Martian dwarf and such friends as Bertrand Russell and Ottoline Morrell). Assumes a familiarity with the eccentric Wittgenstein's ideas but does manage to convey some emotion and wit. **75m/C VHS.** *GB* Karl Johnson, Michael Gough, Tilda Swinton, John Quentin, Nabil Shaban; ***D:*** Derek Jarman; ***W:*** Derek Jarman, Terry Eagleton, Ken Butler.

Wives and Daughters 🦴🦴½ **2001** Charming adaptation of Elizabeth Gaskell's 1864 chronicle of family ties, romance, and scandal set in an 1820s English country town. Our heroine is modest Molly Gibson (Waddell), whose widower doctor father (Paterson) marries ambitious Hyacinth (Annis), who has a beautiful daughter, Cynthia (Hawes), who's Molly's age. Then there's the local gentry, Squire Hamley (Gambon), and his two sons, the poetic Osborne (Hollander) and the scientific Roger (Howell). Molly becomes everyone's confidante, but also has her own secrets. **300m/C VHS, DVD.** *GB* Justine Waddell, Keeley Hawes, Francesca Annis, Bill Paterson, Michael Gambon, Penelope Wilton, Tom Hollander, Anthony Howell, Ian Carmichael, Iain Glen, Barbara Leigh-Hunt, Tonia Chauvet, Shaughan Seymour, Barbara Flynn, Deborah Findlay; ***D:*** Nicholas Renton; ***W:*** Andrew Davies. **TV**

Wives under Suspicion 🦴🦴½ **1938** While prosecuting a man who murdered his wife out of jealousy, a district attorney finds his own home life filled with similar tension. Director Whale's unnecessary remake of his own earlier film, "The Kiss Before the Mirror." He is best known for "Frankenstein." **75m/B VHS.** Warren William, Gail Patrick, Constance Moore, William Lundigan; ***D:*** James Whale.

The Wiz 🦴🦴 **1978 (G)** Black version of the long-time favorite "The Wizard of Oz," based on the Broadway musical. Ross plays a Harlem schoolteacher who is whisked away to a fantasy version of NYC in a search for her identity. Some good character performances and musical numbers, but generally an overblown and garish effort with Ross too old for her role. Pryor is poorly cast, but Jackson is memorable as the Scarecrow. High-budget ($24 million) production with a ton of name stars, lost $11 million, and cooled studios on black films. Horne's number as the good witch is the best reason to sit through this one. ♫The Feeling That We Have; Can I Go On Not Knowing; Glinda's Theme; He's the Wizard; Soon as I Get Home; You Can't Win; Ease on Down the Road; What Would I Do If I Could Feel?; Slide Some Oil to Me. **133m/C VHS, DVD, Wide.** Diana Ross, Michael Jackson, Nipsey Russell, Ted Ross, Mabel King, Thelma Carpenter, Richard Pryor, Lena Horne; ***D:*** Sidney Lumet; ***W:*** Joel Schumacher; ***C:*** Oswald Morris; ***M:*** Quincy Jones.

The Wizard 🦴½ **1989 (PG)** Facing the dissolution of his dysfunctional family, a youngster decides to take his autistic, video game-playing little brother across the country to a national video competition. Way too much plot in pretentious, blatantly commercial feature-length Nintendo ad, featuring the kid from "The Wonder Years." For teen video addicts only. **99m/C VHS.** Fred Savage, Beau Bridges, Christian Slater, Luke Edwards, Jenny Lewis; ***D:*** Todd Holland; ***W:*** David Chisholm.

The Wizard of Gore 🦴 **1970 (R)** The prototypical Lewis splatter party, about a magician whose on-stage mutilations turn out to be messily real. High camp and barrels of bright movie blood. **96m/C VHS, DVD.** Ray Sager, Judy Cler, Wayne Ratay, Phil Lauenson, Jim Rau, Don Alexander, Monika Blackwell, Corinne Kirkin, John Elliott; ***D:*** Herschell Gordon Lewis; ***W:*** Allen Kahn; ***C:*** Alex Ameri, Daniel Krogh; ***M:*** Larry Wellington.

The Wizard of Loneliness 🦴🦴½ **1988 (PG-13)** A disturbed young boy goes to live with his grandparents during WWII, and slowly discovers family secrets centering on his aunt. Excellent performances barely save an aimless plot with an overdone denouement. Based on the novel by John Nichols. **110m/C VHS.** Lukas Haas, Lea Thompson, John Randolph, Lance Guest, Anne Pitoniak, Jeremiah Warner, Dylan Baker; ***D:*** Jenny (H. Anne Riley) Bowen; ***W:*** Nancy Larson; ***C:*** Richard Bowen; ***M:*** Michel Colombier.

The Wizard of Oz 🦴🦴½ **1925** An early silent version of the L. Frank Baum fantasy, with notable plot departures from the book and later 1939 adaptation, starring long-forgotten comedian Semon as the Scarecrow, supported by a pre-Laurel Hardy as the Tin Woodman. With music score. **96m/B VHS, DVD, 8mm.** Larry Semon, Dorothy Dwan, Bryant Washburn, Charles Murray, Oliver Hardy, Josef Swickard, Virginia Pearson; ***D:*** Larry Semon; ***W:*** L. Frank Baum Jr., Larry Semon; ***C:*** Leonard Smith, Frank Good, Hans Koenekamp.

The Wizard of Oz 🦴🦴🦴🦴 **1939** From the book by L. Frank Baum. Fantasy about a Kansas farm girl (Garland, in her immortal role) who rides a tornado to a brightly colored world over the rainbow, full of talking scarecrows, munchkins and a wizard who bears a strange resemblance to a Kansas fortune-teller. She must outwit the Wicked Witch if she is ever to go home. Delightful performances from Lahr, Bolger, and Hamilton; King Vidor is uncredited as co-director. Director Fleming originally wanted Deanna Durbin or Shirley Temple for the role of Dorothy, but settled for Garland who made the song "Over the Rainbow" her own. She received a special Academy Award for her performance. For the 50th anniversary of its release, "The Wizard of Oz" was restored and includes rare film clips of Bolger's "Scarecrow Dance" and the cut "Jitterbug" number, and shots by Buddy Ebsen as the Tin Man before he became ill and left the production. Another special release of the film, "The Ultimate Oz," contains a documentary on the making of the film, a reproduction of the original script, still photos, and liner notes. ♫Munchkinland; Ding Dong the Witch is Dead; Follow the Yellow Brick Road; If I Only Had a Brain/a Heart/the Nerve; If I Were the King of the Forest; The Merry Old Land of Oz; Threatening Witch; Into the Forest of the Wild Beast; The City Gates are Open. **101m/C VHS, DVD.** Judy Garland, Margaret Hamilton, Ray Bolger, Jack Haley, Bert Lahr, Frank Morgan, Charley Grapewin, Clara Blandick, Mitchell Lewis, Billie Burke; ***D:*** Victor Fleming; ***W:*** Noel Langley; ***C:*** Harold Rosson; ***M:*** Herbert Stothart. Oscars '39: Song ("Over the Rainbow"), Orig. Score; AFI '98: Top 100, Natl. Film Reg. '89.

The Wizard of Speed and Time 🦴🦴½ **1988 (PG)** A special-effects wizard gets the break of his life when he's hired by a movie studio, but there's more to this particular studio than he realizes. Jittlov, a real special-effects expert, plays himself in this personally financed production. Although brimming with inside jokes and references, this self-indulgence succeeds with its enthusiasm and ambition, despite being rather obviously self-produced. Unique special effects make it memorable. **95m/C VHS.** Mike Jittlov, Richard Kaye, Page Moore, David Conrad, Steve Brodie, John Massari, Frank Laloggia, Philip Michael Thomas, Angelique Pettyjohn, Arnetia Walker, Paulette Breen, Forrest J Ackerman; ***D:*** Mike Jittlov; ***W:*** Deven Chierighino, Mike Jittlov, Richard Kaye; ***C:*** Russell Carpenter; ***M:*** John Massari.

Wizards 🦴🦴½ **1977 (PG)** A good, bumbling sorcerer battles for the sake of a magic kingdom and its princess against his evil brother who uses Nazi propaganda films to inspire his army of mutants. Profane, crude, & typically Bakshian fantasy with great graphics. Animated. **81m/C VHS.** ***D:*** Ralph Bakshi; ***W:*** Ralph Bakshi; ***M:*** Andrew Belling; ***V:*** Bob Holt, Jesse Wells, Richard Romanus, David Proval.

Wizards of the Demon Sword 🦴 **1994 (R)** Group of warriors battle over a sword with the power to control the world. **90m/C VHS.** Lawrence Tierney, Michael Berryman, Russ Tamblyn, Lyle Waggoner, Blake Bahner, Heidi Paine, Dan Speaker, Jay Richardson, Dawn Wildsmith; ***D:*** Fred Olen Ray; ***W:*** Dan Golden, Ernest Farino.

Wizards of the Lost Kingdom 🦴½ **1985 (PG)** A boy magician, aided by various ogres and swordster Svenson battles an all-powerful wizard for control of his kingdom. Family fare a bit too clean and harmless. **76m/C VHS.** Bo Svenson, Vidal Peterson, Thom Christopher; ***D:*** Hector Olivera.

Wizards of the Lost Kingdom 2 🦴 **1989 (PG)** A boy wizard is charged with vanquishing the evil tyrants from three kingdoms. Barely a sequel; no plot continuation or cast from earlier kiddie sword epic. **80m/C VHS.** David Carradine, Bobby Jacoby, Lana Clarkson, Mel Welles, Susan Lee Hoffman, Sid Haig; ***D:*** Charles B. Griffith.

Wolf 🦴 **1986** To everyone's lasting regret, an ex-Vietnam POW strives to rescue an American ambassador kidnapped by Central American rebels. **95m/C VHS.** J. Antonio Carreon, Ron Marchini; ***D:*** Charlie Ordonez.

Wolf 🦴🦴½ **1994 (R)** Harrison's original script is massaged by Nichols into an upscale new age men's movement horror spectacle lacking a suitable climax. Stressed out Manhattan book editor Will Randall's (Nicholson) car hits a wolf on a country road and he's bitten when he tries to help the animal. Normally a wishy-washy guy, he notices some distinctly hairy changes to both his body and personality, leading him to make some drastic changes at work by knocking off his firm's greedy honchos and taking over. Talk about being ruthless in business. Boss' daughter Pfeiffer takes a shine to Randall's new animal magnetism, but is just visual candy. Walks a fine line between black comedy, camp, romance, and horror, though Jack baying at the moon seems sort of campy. **125m/C VHS, DVD, 8mm, Wide.** Osgood Perkins II, Jack Nicholson, Michelle Pfeiffer, James Spader, Kate Nelligan, Christopher Plummer, Richard Jenkins, Om Puri, Eileen Atkins, David Hyde Pierce, Ron Rifkin, Prunella Scales; ***D:*** Mike Nichols; ***W:*** Wesley Strick, Jim Harrison; ***C:*** Giuseppe Rotunno; ***M:*** Ennio Morricone.

The Wolf at the Door 🦴🦴½ **1987 (R)** A well-appointed, sincere biography of impressionist Paul Gauguin in the middle period of life, during his transition from the petty demands of his Parisian life to the freedom of Tahiti. Not definitive or compelling, but serves the purpose of a biography—arousing interest in the subject's life and art. **90m/C VHS.** *DK FR* Donald Sutherland, Jean Yanne, Sofie Graboel, Ghita Norby, Max von Sydow, Merete Voldstedlund, Fanny Bastien, Valerie Morea; ***D:*** Henning Carlsen; ***W:*** Christopher Hampton; ***M:*** Roger Bourland.

Wolf Blood 🦴🦴½ **1925** When Dick (Chesebro) is hurt in an accident, Dr. Horton uses wolf's blood for a transfusion. Soon there are unexplained deaths and Dick fears he's becoming a man-beast. Early precursor to the wolfman films. **68m/B VHS.** George Chesebro, Marguerite Clayton, Ray Hanford, Roy Watson, Milburn (Milt) Morante; ***D:*** George Chesebro, George Mitchell.

Wolf Call 🦴½ **1939** Carroll plays the son of a miner who travels with his devoted hound to see his father's old mine and start it working again. Gangsters and a beautiful Indian maiden get in his way. Master and pooch both find romance, and both sing. From the Jack London novel. **62m/B VHS, 8mm.** John Carroll, Movita, Wheeler Oakman, Peter George Lynn; ***D:*** George Waggner.

Wolf Dog **1933** A boy and his dog. Outdoor action and adventure. Twelve chapters, 13 minutes each. **156m/B VHS.** Frankie Darro, Patricia "Boots" Mallory; ***D:*** Harry Fraser, Colbert Clark.

Wolf Lake 🦴½ **1979** WWII veteran, whose son was killed in Vietnam, and a Vietnam army deserter clash with tragic consequences during their stay at a Canadian hunting lodge. Steiger gives it a go, but overwrought revenge pic resists quality upgrade. **90m/C VHS.** Rod Steiger, David Hoffman, Robin Mattson, Jerry Hardin, Richard Herd, Paul Mantu; ***D:*** Burt Kennedy.

The Wolf Man 🦴🦴🦴½ **1941** Fun, absorbing classic horror with Chaney as a man bitten by werewolf Lugosi. His dad thinks he's gone nuts, his screaming gal pal just doesn't understand, and plants on the Universal lot have no roots. Ouspenskaya's finest hour as the prophetic gypsy woman. Ow-ooo! Chilling and thrilling. **70m/B VHS, DVD.** Lon Chaney Jr., Claude Rains, Maria Ouspenskaya, Ralph Bellamy, Bela Lugosi, Warren William, Patric Knowles, Evelyn Ankers, Forrester Harvey, Fay Helm; ***D:*** George Waggner; ***W:*** Curt Siodmak; ***C:*** Joseph Valentine; ***M:*** Charles Previn, Hans J. Salter, Frank Skinner.

Wolf Trap 🦴🦴 *Vlci Jama* **1957** Trapped indeed—small town veterinarian is suffocating in a marriage to an older, domineering and needy wife. The two adopt an orphaned teenager, which turns out to be a big mistake as the unhappy husband gradually falls in love with the girl. Czech with subtitles. **95m/C VHS.** *CZ* Jirinaova Sejbalova, Jana Brecjchova, Miroslav Dolezal, Jaroslav Pucha; ***D:*** Jiri Weiss; ***W:*** Jiri Weiss; ***C:*** Vaclav Hanus.

Wolfen 🦴🦴🦴 **1981 (R)** Surrealistic menace darkens this original and underrated tale of super-intelligent wolf creatures terrorizing NYC. Police detective Finney tries to track down the beasts before they kill again. Notable special effects in this thriller, which covers environmental and Native American concerns while maintaining the tension. Feature film debuts of Hines and Venora. Based on the novel by Whitley Strieber. **115m/C VHS, Wide.** Albert Finney, Gregory Hines, Tom Noonan, Diane Venora, Edward James Olmos, Dick O'Neill, Dehl Berti, Peter Michael Goetz, Sam Gray, Ralph Bell; ***D:*** Michael Wadleigh; ***W:*** Michael Wadleigh, David Eyre; ***C:*** Gerry Fisher; ***M:*** James Horner.

Wolfheart's Revenge **1925** An honest cowboy, helped by Wolfheart the Wonder Dog, steps in when a sheep rancher is murdered. Silent film with original organ score. **64m/B VHS, 8mm.** Guinn "Big Boy" Williams.

The Wolfman 🦴 **1982** Colin Glasgow is summoned back to his family manor to attend the funeral of his father. Unbeknownst to Colin, his father was actually murdered by his children who are in thrall to a Satanist priest. The family stalls Colin, hoping their father's "curse" will be passed on to him at the next full moon. It does, and Colin turns into a werewolf and begins a small rural rampage. Extremely amateurish gothic horror attempt in the Universal/"Dark Shadows" vein. The sets and models look flimsy and the acting is like that of a bad stage-play. **102m/C VHS, DVD.** Earl Owensby, Kristina Reynolds, Sid Rancer, Julian Morton; ***D:*** Worth Keeter; ***W:*** Worth Keeter; ***C:*** Darrell Cathcart; ***M:*** David Floyd, Arthur Smith.

Wolverine 🦴🦴 *Code Name: Wolverine* **1996 (R)** Former Navy SEAL Harry Gordini (Sabato Jr.) and his family are vacationing in Italy where he becomes an unwitting drug smuggler. After the drug cartel kidnaps his wife and son, Harry uses his training to attempt a rescue before the authorities intervene. Based on the book by Frederick Forsyth. Supplies the required action quotient. **91m/C VHS, DVD.** Antonio Sabato Jr., Richard Brooks, Traci Lind, Daniel Quinn; ***D:*** David S. Jackson; ***W:*** Robert T. Megginson; ***C:*** Denis Maloney; ***M:*** Christopher Franke. **TV**

The Wolves 🦴🦴🦴 **1982** Gosha shows the world of the yakuza (gangster) during the 1920s. Reminiscent of the samurai, the movie combines ancient Japanese culture with the rapidly changing world of 20th century Japan. In Japanese with English subtitles. **131m/C VHS, Wide.** *JP* Tatsuya Nakadai; ***D:*** Hideo Gosha.

The Wolves 🦴🦴 **1995 (PG-13)** Blackie (Dalton) and his sister Barbara (Hocking) have inherit some land in the Alaskan wilderness that evil businessman King (Harmstorf) wants to use as a toxic waste dump. But when Blackie befriends native guide Chilkoot (Cardinal) and rescues an injured wolf, he decides to fight King and his henchmen. **87m/C VHS.** Darren Dalton, Kristen Hocking, Raymond Harmstorf, Ben Cardinal, John Furey; ***D:*** Steve Carver; ***W:*** Steven Peters, Art Bernd; ***C:*** Eugene Shugleit.

The Wolves of Kromer 🦴🦴 **1998** A modern-day fairytale set in the rural English town of Kromer. The hypocritical townspeople are mean-spirited gossips who look down upon the local wolf population (in this case very attractive young human/beasts in fur coats and long tails). Seth (Williams) has just "come out" as a wolf and fallen for promiscuous Gabriel (Layton). Meanwhile, two servants are poisoning their cruel mistress and plan to point accusing fingers at the wolves, giving the human populace the excuse they need for violence. Based on the play by Lambert, who wrote the screenplay. **77m/C VHS, DVD, Wide.** *GB* Lee Williams, James Layton, Rita Davies, Margaret Towner, Rosemary Dunham, Angharad Rees, Kevin Moore, Leila Lloyd-Evelyn, Matthew Dean, David Prescott; ***D:*** Will Gould; ***W:*** Charles Lambert, Matthew Read; ***C:*** Laura Remacha; ***M:*** Basil Moore-Asfouri; ***Nar:*** Boy George.

A Woman and a Woman **1980** Covers a ten-year period in the friendship of Barbara and Irena and how it survives their professional and personal conflicts. In Polish with English subtitles. **99m/C VHS.** *PL* Halina Labonarska, Anna Romantowska; ***D:*** Richard Bugajski.

A Woman at Her Window ½ *Une Femme a sa Fentre* **1977** Aristocratic, jaded Margot (Schneider), the wife of dissolute nobleman Rico (Orsini), is pursued by capitalistic businessman Raoul (Noiret). But Margot herself is taken by idealistic Michel (Lanoux), a communist evading the secret police in 1936 Greece, and has a daughter from their brief and ultimately tragic union. Years later, Margot's now-grown daughter returns to Greece to learn more about her parents. Adapted from the novel by Pierre Drieu La Rochelle. French with subtitles. **110m/C VHS.** *FR* Romy Schneider, Philippe Noiret, Victor Lanoux, Umberto Orsini, Delia Boccardo, Gastone Moschin, Carl Mohner; ***D:*** Pierre Granier-Deferre; ***W:*** Pierre Granier-Deferre, Jorge Semprun.

A Woman at War ½ **1994 (PG-13)** True-story of a young woman's heroic fight against the Nazis. Nineteen-year-old Helene Moskiewicz (Plimpton) has had her parents arrested by the Gestapo in occupied Brussels, Belgium. She joins the resistance and falls for Franz Boehler (Stoltz), a young businessman who is not above lining his pockets with Nazi profits. When persecution of the Jews intensifies, Helene risks infiltrating Gestapo headquarters in order to save lives. **115m/C VHS.** Martha Plimpton, Eric Stoltz; ***D:*** Edward Bennett; ***W:*** Edward Bennett.

A Woman Called Golda **1982** Political drama following the life and career of Golda Meir, the Israeli Prime Minister and one of the most powerful political figures of the 20th century. Davis portrays the young Golda, Bergman taking over as she ages. Superior TV bio-epic. **192m/C VHS.** Ingrid Bergman, Leonard Nimoy, Anne Jackson, Ned Beatty, Robert Loggia, Judy Davis; ***D:*** Alan Gibson; ***W:*** Steven Gethers, Howard Gast. **TV**

A Woman Called Moses ½ **1978** The story of Harriet Ross Tubman, who bought her freedom from slavery, founded the underground railroad, and helped lead hundreds of slaves to freedom before the Civil War. Wonderful performance by Tyson but the telefilm is bogged down by a so-so script. Based on the novel by Marcy Heldish. **200m/C VHS, DVD.** Cicely Tyson, Dick Anthony Williams, Will Geer, Robert Hooks, Hari Rhodes, James Wainwright; ***D:*** Paul Wendkos; ***W:*** Lonnie Elder III; ***M:*** Coleridge-Taylor Perkinson. **TV**

Woman Condemned ½ **1933** A reporter tries to clear a woman's name of murder. **58m/B VHS.** Mischa Auer, Lola Lane, Claudia Dell, Richard Hemingway.

Woman Hater **1949** Delightful farce about the belief in the single life. Confirmed bachelor plays games with a single woman. They eventually disregard their solitary ways in favor of romance. **101m/B VHS.** Stewart Granger, Edwige Feuillere, Ronald Squire, Mary Jerrold; ***D:*** Terence Young.

The Woman He Loved ½ **1988** The infamous romance of Edward VIII, who gave up the throne of England for American divorcee, Wallis Warfield Simpson. Seymour and Andrews are fine in their roles but the drama is slow-going. **100m/C VHS.** Anthony Andrews, Jane Seymour, Olivia de Havilland, Lucy Gutteridge, Julie Harris, Robert Hardy, Phyllis Calvert; ***D:*** Charles Jarrott. **TV**

A Woman, Her Men and Her Futon **1992 (R)** A beautiful woman tries to find her identity by having a number of lovers but none can satisfy her every need. **90m/C VHS, DVD.** Jennifer Rubin, Lance Edwards, Grant Show, Michael Ceveris, Delaune Michel, Robert Lipton; ***D:*** Mussef Sibay; ***W:*** Mussef Sibay; ***C:*** Michael J. Davis; ***M:*** Joel Goldsmith.

Woman Hunt woof! *The Highest Bidder* **1972 (R)** Men kidnap women, then hunt them in the jungle for fun. So deeply offensive, we would give it negative bones if we could. "Hee Haw" bimbo Todd plays a sadistic lesbian. **81m/C VHS.** John Ashley, Lisa Todd, Eddie Garcia, Laurie Rose; ***D:*** Eddie Romero.

The Woman Hunter ½ **1972** A wealthy woman recovering from a traffic accident in Mexico believes someone is after her for her jewels and possibly her life. Eden dressed well, if nothing else; suspense builds ploddingly to a "Yeah, sure" climax. **73m/C VHS.** Barbara Eden, Robert Vaughn, Stuart Whitman, Sydney Chaplin, Larry Storch, Enrique Lucero; ***D:*** Bernard L. Kowalski. **TV**

Woman in Black ½ **1989** Chilling ghost story set in 1925 and adapted from the novel by Susan Hill. Soliciter Arthur Kidd is sent to a remote house to settle the estate of a client. He's haunted by the mysterious figure of a woman in black, who according to the locals, has put a curse on the village. Arthur's driven close to the edge of sanity by the ghostly figure and the tragedy that haunts the past. **100m/C VHS, DVD.** *GB* Adrian Rawlins, Bernard Hepton, David Daker, Pauline Moran; ***D:*** Herbert Wise; ***W:*** Nigel Kneale. **TV**

Woman in Brown ½ *The Vicious Circle; The Circle* **1948** It's Hungary, 1882, and five Jewish men are on trial for the murder of a man who actually committed suicide. Despite the prejudice and hatred from the locals, their lawyer believes in and fights for their innocence. **77m/B VHS.** Conrad Nagel, Fritz Kortner, Reinhold Schunzel, Philip Van Zandt, Eddie LeRoy, Edwin Maxwell; ***D:*** W. Lee Wilder.

A Woman in Flames *Die Flambierte Frau* **1984 (R)** A bored middle-class housewife leaves her overbearing husband and becomes a high-priced prostitute. She has a passionless affair with an aging bisexual gigolo. Dark and dreary tale of human relationships and the role of sex in people's lives. Interesting but depressing. **106m/C VHS.** *GE* Gudrun Landgrebe, Robert Van Ackeren, Matthieu Carriere, Gabriele Lafari, Hanns Zischler; ***D:*** Robert Van Ackeren.

The Woman in Green *Sherlock Holmes and the Woman in Green* **1945** Murder victims are found with missing index fingers, and it's up to Holmes and Watson to try to solve this apparently motiveless crime. Available colorized. **68m/B VHS, DVD.** Basil Rathbone, Nigel Bruce, Hillary Brooke, Henry Daniell, Paul Cavanagh, Frederick Worlock, Mary Gordon, Billy Bevan; ***D:*** Roy William Neill; ***W:*** Bertram Millhauser; ***C:*** Virgil Miller.

Woman in Grey **1919** A man and a woman battle wits when they attempt to locate and unravel the Army Code while staying one step ahead of J. Haviland Hunter, a suave villain after the same fortune. Silent. **205m/B VHS.** Arline Pretty, Henry Sell.

The Woman in Question ½ *Five Angles on Murder* **1950** When carnival fortune teller Astra (Kent) is murdered, Police Inspector Lodge (MacRae) finds that all her acquaintances have differing views about her character, making his investigation even more difficult. **82m/B VHS.** *GB* Jean Kent, Dirk Bogarde, Susan Shaw, Duncan MacRae, John McCallum, Hermione Baddeley, Charles Victor, Lana Morris, Vida Hope, Joe Linnane, Duncan Lament, Bobbie Scroggins, Anthony Dawson, John Boxer, Julian D'Albie, Josephine Middleton, Everley Gregg, Albert Chevalier, Richard Pearson; ***D:*** Anthony Asquith; ***W:*** John Cresswell; ***C:*** Desmond Dickinson; ***M:*** John Wooldridge.

The Woman in Red ½ **1984 (PG-13)** Executive Wilder's life unravels when he falls hard for stunning Le Brock. Inferior Hollywood-ized remake of the ebulliant "Pardon Mon Affaire." Somehow the French seem to do the sexual force thing with more verve, but this one has its moments, and Wilder is likeable. Music by Stevie Wonder. ♫I Just Called to Say I Love You; Don't Drive Drunk; It's More Than You; It's You; Love Light in Flight; Moments Aren't Moments; Weakness; Woman in Red. **87m/C VHS.** Gene Wilder, Charles Grodin, Kelly Le Brock, Gilda Radner, Judith Ivey, Joseph Bologna; ***D:*** Gene Wilder; ***W:*** Gene Wilder; ***M:*** John Morris. Oscars '84: Song ("I Just Called to Say I Love You"); Golden Globes '85: Song ("I Just Called to Say I Love You").

Woman in the Dunes *Suna No Onna; Woman of the Dunes* **1964** Splendid, resonant allegorical drama. A scientist studying insects in the Japanese sand dunes finds himself trapped with a woman in a hut at the bottom of a pit. Superbly directed and photographed (by Hiroshi Segawa). Scripted by Kobo Abe from his acclaimed novel. In Japanese with English subtitles. **123m/B VHS, DVD.** *JP* Eiji Okada, Kyoko Kishida, Koji Mitsui, Hiroko Ito, Sen Yano; ***D:*** Hiroshi Teshigahara; ***W:*** Kobe Abe; ***C:*** Hiroshi Segawa; ***M:*** Toru Takemitsu. Cannes '64: Grand Jury Prize.

Woman in the Moon ½ *By Rocket to the Moon; Girl in the Moon* **1929** Assorted people embark on a trip to the moon and discover water, and an atmosphere, as well as gold. Lang's last silent outing is nothing next to "Metropolis," with a rather lame plot (greedy trip bashers seek gold), but interesting as a vision of the future. Lang's predictions about space travel often hit the mark. Silent with music. **115m/B VHS.** *GE* Klaus Pohl, Willy Fritsch, Gustav von Wagenheim, Gerda Maurus; ***D:*** Fritz Lang.

Woman in the Shadows **1934** A ex-con retreats to the woods for serenity and peace, but is assaulted by mysterious women, jealous lovers, and gun-slinging drunks, until he explodes. A man can only take so much. From a Dashiell Hammett story. **70m/B VHS.** Fay Wray, Ralph Bellamy, Melvyn Douglas, Roscoe Ates, Joe King.

Woman in the Window **1944** Psycho-melodrama finds staid college professor Richard Wanley straying off the straight and narrow into a world of trouble—thanks to beautiful model Alice (Bennett). She invites him over but when her jealous boyfriend Claude (Loft) arrives unexpectedly, he attacks them both and Richard kills Claude in self-defense. Thinking no one will believe them, and afraid of scandal, the inept duo bury the body in the woods. Too bad Richard's best friend Frank (Massey) is the D.A. and there's a blackmailer around. Or is there? Surprise ending. Based on the novel "Once Off Guard" by J.H. Wallis. **99m/B VHS.** Edward G. Robinson, Joan Bennett, Raymond Massey, Arthur Loft, Dan Duryea, Edmund Breon, Dorothy Peterson, Robert (Bobby) Blake; ***D:*** Fritz Lang; ***W:*** Nunnally Johnson; ***C:*** Milton Krasner; ***M:*** Arthur Lange.

The Woman in White ½ **1997** The happy hours half-sisters, outgoing Marian (Fitzgerald) and shy Laura (Waddell), spend with their eccentric Uncle Fairlie (Richardson) soon turn sinister when Laura is married off to the seemingly charming Sir Percival Glyde (Wilby). Sir Percival quickly appears to be conspiring with the suspicious Count Fosco (Callow) to take control of Laura's money. When Marian visits her sister, she's alarmed by Laura's decline and equally unnerved by the mysterious woman in white, Anne (Vidler), who seems to know Glyde and tries to warn the sisters of impending danger. Based on the novel by Wilkie Collins, who also wrote "The Moonstone." **120m/C VHS.** *GB* Tara Fitzgerald, Justine Waddell, James Wilby, Simon Callow, Ian Richardson, Andrew Lincoln, Susan Vidler, John Standing, Corin Redgrave; ***D:*** Tim Fywell; ***W:*** David Pirie; ***M:*** David Ferguson. **TV**

The Woman Inside ½ **1983 (R)** Low-budget gender-bender depicts the troubled life of a Vietnam veteran who decides on a sex-change operation to satisfy his inner yearnings. Blondell's unfortunate last role as his/her aunt. Cheesy like Limburger; almost too weird and boring even for camp buffs. **94m/C VHS.** *CA* Gloria Manon, Dave Clark, Joan Blondell; ***D:*** Joseph Van Winkle.

A Woman Is a Woman *Une Femme Est une Femme; La Donna E Donna* **1960** Godard's affectionate sendup of Hollywood musicals is a hilarious comedy about a nightclub dancer (Karina) who desperately wants a baby. When boyfriend Belmondo balks, she asks his best friend Brialy. Much ado is had, with the three leads all splendid. Godard's first film shot in color and cinemascope, with great music. In French with English subtitles. **88m/C VHS, DVD.** *FR* Jean-Claude Brialy, Jean-Paul Belmondo, Anna Karina, Marie DuBois; ***D:*** Jean-Luc Godard; ***W:*** Jean-Luc Godard; ***C:*** Raoul Coutard; ***M:*** Michel Legrand.

A Woman Named Jackie ½ **1991 (PG)** Three-part TV miniseries covering the life of Jacqueline Bouvier Kennedy Onassis. Downey offers a pretty picture as the enigmatic and beleagured heroine but this version is simplistic at best. Based on the book by C. David Heymann. On three cassettes. **246m/C VHS.** Roma Downey, Stephen Collins, William Devane, Joss Ackland, Rosemary Murphy, Wendy Hughes, Josef Sommer; ***D:*** Larry Peerce; ***W:*** Roger O. Hirson. **TV**

The Woman Next Door *La Femme d'a Cote* **1981 (R)** One of Truffaut's last films before his sudden death in 1984. The domestic drama involves a suburban husband who resumes an affair with a tempestuous now-married woman after she moves next door, with domestic complications all around. An insightful, humanistic paean to passion and fidelity by the great artist, though one of his lesser works. Supported by strong outings from the two leads. In French with English subtitles. **106m/C VHS, DVD.** *FR* Gerard Depardieu, Fanny Ardant, Michele Baumgartner, Veronique Silver, Roger Van Hool; ***D:*** Francois Truffaut; ***W:*** Suzanne Schiffman; ***C:*** William Lubtchansky; ***M:*** Georges Delerue.

A Woman Obsessed **1988 (R)** Pathetic, over-cooked drama about a woman obsessed with her long-lost son. "Ruth Raymond" is really porn-flick vet Georgina Spelvin. Soon-to-be camp classic takes itself with utter seriousness. **105m/C VHS, VHS.** Ruth Raymond, Gregory Patrick, Troy Donahue, Linda Blair; ***D:*** Chuck Vincent.

A Woman of Affairs **1928** Garbo, who can't have the guy she really loves (Gilbert), marries scoundrel. When she finds out husband's true profession, he kills himself and Gilbert comes back. In order to preclude happy ending, she decides the affair wasn't meant to be and expires. Tragically. Silent. **90m/B VHS.** Greta Garbo, John Gilbert, Lewis Stone, Johnny Mack Brown, Douglas Fairbanks Jr., Hobart Bosworth, Dorothy Sebastian; ***D:*** Clarence Brown.

Woman of Desire **1993 (R)** Christina Ford (Derek) is a femme fatale who is yachting with rich boyfriend Ted when there is a terrible storm. Christina, Ted, and yacht captain Jack are washed overboard and Jack is found washed ashore with no memory. When Christina turns up she claims Jack killed Ted. So Jack gets a lawyer, Walter J. Hill (played by the redoubtable Mitchum) but is he wily enough to discredit the deceitful Christina? Bo's body is once again on display. Also available in an unrated version. **97m/C VHS, DVD.** Bo Derek, Jeff Fahey, Steven Bauer, Robert Mitchum.

A Woman of Distinction **1950** Slapstick comedy with potential to be ordinary is taken over the top by a good, vivacious cast. Russell, the stuffy Dean of a women's college, is driven to distraction by a reporter linking her romantically to Milland, a visiting professor. **85m/C VHS.** Ray Milland, Rosalind Russell, Edmund Gwenn, Francis Lederer; ***Cameos:*** Lucille Ball; ***D:*** Edward Buzzell.

A Woman of Rome ♪♪ *La Romana* **1956** Standard Italian star vehicle, with Lollobrigida portraying a successful prostitute in Rome who decides to change her life. Dubbed. **93m/B VHS.** *IT* Gina Lollobrigida, Daniel Gelin, Franco Fabrizi, Raymond Pellegrin; *D:* Luigi Zampa.

A Woman of Substance ♪♪½ **1984** The woman of the title, Emma Harte, rises from poverty to wealth and power through self-discipline, enduring various romantic disappointments and tragedies along the way. Based on the novel by Barbara Taylor Bradford. Followed by "Hold the Dream." **300m/C VHS.** Jenny Seagrove, Barry Bostwick, Deborah Kerr, Liam Neeson, Diane Baker, George Baker, Peter Chelsom, Peter Egan, Christopher Gable, Christopher Guard, Gayle Hunnicutt, John Mills, Nicola Pagett, Saskia Reeves, Miranda Richardson; *D:* Don Sharp; *W:* Lee Langley; *C:* Ernest Vincze; *M:* Nigel Hess. **TV**

The Woman of the Town ♪♪½ **1944** Frontier marshal and newspaperman Bat Masterson is portrayed convincingly by Dekker as a very human hero who seeks justice when the woman he loves, a dance hall girl who works in the town for social causes, is killed by an unscrupulous rancher. Fictionalized but realistic western shows "heroes" as good, ordinary people. **90m/B VHS.** Claire Trevor, Albert Dekker, Barry Sullivan, Henry Hull, Porter Hall, Percy Kilbride; *D:* George Archainbaud; *M:* Miklos Rozsa.

Woman of the Year ♪♪♪♪ **1942** First classic Tracy/Hepburn pairing concerns the rocky marriage of a renowned political columnist and a lowly sportswriter. Baseball scene with Hepburn at her first game is delightful. Hilarious, rich entertainment that tries to answer the question "What really matters in life?" Tracy and Hepburn began a close friendship that paralleled their quarter-century celluloid partnership. Hepburn shepherded Kamin and Lardner's Oscar-winning script past studio chief Louis B. Mayer, wearing four-inch heels to press her demands. Mayer caved in, Tracy was freed from making "The Yearling," and the rest is history. **114m/B VHS, DVD.** Spencer Tracy, Katharine Hepburn, Fay Bainter, Dan Tobin, Reginald Owen, Roscoe Karns, William Bendix, Minor Watson; *D:* George Stevens; *W:* Ring Lardner Jr., Michael Kanin; *C:* Joseph Ruttenberg; *M:* Franz Waxman. Oscars '42: Orig. Screenplay, Natl. Film Reg. '99.

Woman on Top ♪♪½ **2000 (R)** Mildly amusing romantic comedy that's held together by the charm of its lead. Beautiful Brazilian Isabella (Cruz) suffers from extreme motion sickness, which means she must always be in control. She's a whiz in the kitchen and her talents make her husband's (Benicio) restaurant a big success. But Izzie takes off for San Francisco when she discovers Toninho with another gal. Thanks to her culinary skills (and some magical realism), Isabella soon has her own cable cooking show and men (literally) falling at her feet. First there's "Like Water for Chocolate," then there's "Simply Irresistible," and now "Woman" completes the trifecta of food overwhelming the emotions. **93m/C VHS, DVD, Wide.** Penelope Cruz, Harold Perrineau Jr., Mark Feuerstein, Murilo Benicio, John de Lancie; *D:* Fina Torres; *W:* Vera Blasi; *C:* Thierry Arbogast; *M:* Luis Bacalov.

A Woman Rebels ♪♪½ **1936** A young Victorian woman challenges Victorian society by fighting for women's rights. Excellent performance from Hepburn lifts what might have been a forgettable drama. Screen debut of Van Heflin. Based on Netta Syrett's "Portrait of a Rebel." **88m/B VHS.** Katharine Hepburn, Herbert Marshall, Elizabeth Allan, Donald Crisp, Van Heflin; *D:* Mark Sandrich.

Woman Times Seven ♪♪½ *Sept Fois Femme; Sette Volte Donna* **1967 (PG)** Italian sexual comedy: seven sketches, each starring MacLaine with a different leading man. Stellar cast and good director should have delivered more, but what they have provided has its comedic moments. **99m/C VHS.** *IT FR* Shirley MacLaine, Peter Sellers, Rossano Brazzi, Vittorio Gassman, Lex Barker, Elsa Martinelli, Robert Morley, Alan Arkin, Michael Caine, Patrick Wymark, Anita Ekberg, Philippe Noiret, Elspeth March; *D:* Vittorio De Sica.

A Woman under the Influence ♪♪♪ **1974 (R)** Strong performances highlight this overlong drama about a family's disintegration. Rowlands is the lonely, middle-aged housewife who's having a breakdown and Falk is her blue-collar husband who can't handle what's going on. **147m/C VHS, DVD.** Gena Rowlands, Peter Falk, Matthew Cassel, Matthew Laborteaux, Christina Grisanti; *D:* John Cassavetes; *W:* John Cassavetes; *C:* Caleb Deschanel, Mitch Breit. Golden Globes '75: Actress—Drama (Rowlands); Natl. Bd. of Review '74: Actress (Rowlands), Natl. Film Reg. '90.

Woman Undone ♪♪½ *Joshua Tree* **1995 (R)** Husband Allen Hansen (Quaid) and wife Terri (McDonnell) are involved in a car crash on a lonely stretch of desert highway. He dies, she's thrown clear, but an autopsy reveals he was actually shot in the head before the accident. Then attorney Ross Bishop (Elliott) gets involved and in a California courtroom Terri must prove that her unhappy marriage wasn't ended by murder. **91m/C VHS.** Mary McDonnell, Randy Quaid, Sam Elliott, Benjamin Bratt; *D:* Evelyn Purcell; *W:* William Mickelberry; *C:* Toyomichi Kurita; *M:* Daniel Licht.

Woman Wanted ♪♪ **1998 (R)** Vivacious Emma Riley (Hunter) is hired by as a live-in housekeeper by widowed professor Richard Goddard (Moriarty) and his troubled son Wendell (Sutherland). Both men fall in love with her and Emma, who loves Richard, nevertheless has a one-nighter with Wendell. Then she winds up pregnant. Rather yakky but these are actors who are worth watching. Based on the novel by Glass, who also wrote the screenplay. **110m/C VHS.** Holly Hunter, Michael Moriarty, Kiefer Sutherland; *D:* Kiefer Sutherland; *W:* Joanna McClelland Glass. **CABLE**

The Woman Who Came Back ♪♪ **1945** A young woman who believes she suffers from a witch's curse returns to her small hometown with unhappy results. Good cast; bad script. Indifference inducing. **69m/B VHS, DVD.** Nancy Kelly, Otto Kruger, John Loder, Ruth Ford, Jeanne Gail; *D:* Walter Colmes; *W:* Dennis J. Cooper, Lee Willis; *C:* Henry Sharp; *M:* Edward Plumb.

The Woman Who Loved Elvis ♪½ **1993 (PG-13)** TV movie about an obsessive fan who converts her home into an Elvis shrine. **?m/C VHS.** Roseanne, Tom Arnold, Cynthia Gibb, Sally Kirkland, Danielle Harris, Joe Guzaldo; *D:* Bill Bixby.

The Woman Who Willed a Miracle ♪♪ **1983** TV drama has a devoted mother encouraging her mentally retarded son to pursue his interest in the piano. **72m/C VHS.** Cloris Leachman, James Noble; *D:* Sharron Miller. **TV**

Woman with a Past ♪♪½ **1992 (PG-13)** Reed gets out of an abusive marriage only to have her ex kidnap their kids. Since the law's no help she hires a bounty hunter to find them—committing armed robbery to pay the fees. Caught and imprisoned, Reed escapes, changes her identity, remarries, and even is reunited with her sons. Then she's suddenly arrested when her fugitive status comes to light 10 years later. Based on a true story; made for TV melodrama. **95m/C VHS.** Pamela Reed, Dwight Schultz, Paul LeMat, Carrie Snodgress, Richard Lineback; *D:* Mimi Leder. **TV**

A Woman Without Love ♪♪♪ **1951** A rarely seen film from Bunuel's Mexican period based on a classic Guy de Maupassant tale about a forbidden romance. Family tragedy results later when the husband "misbequeaths" his fortune. Minor but fascinating bug-the-bourgeoisie Bunuel. In Spanish with English subtitles. **91m/C VHS.** *MX* Rosario Granados, Julio Villareal, Tito Junco; *D:* Luis Bunuel.

The Womaneater ♪♪ **1959** This '50s oddity makes a belated appearance on home video. Dr. James Moran (Coulouris) returns from the depths of the Amazon jungle (obviously a set filled with plastic plants) with a miraculous tree that's a close cousin of "Audrey" in the original "Little Shop of Horrors." To maintain its healing powers, the doctor must feed it a steady diet of young women. Not a good sign for his sexy housekeeper Sally (Day). It's every bit as silly as it sounds, swiftly paced and short. **71m/B VHS, DVD, Wide.** *GB* Vera Day, George Coulouris, Robert MacKenzie, Norman Claridge, Marpessa Dawn, Jimmy Vaughan; *D:* Charles Saunders; *W:* Brandon Fleming; *C:* Ernest Palmer; *M:* Edwin Astley.

A Woman's Face ♪♪♪ *En Kvinnas Ansikte* **1938** An unpleasant, bitter woman with a hideous scar on her face blackmails illicit lovers as a form of revenge for a happiness she doesn't know. She even plots to murder a child for his inheritance. But after plastic surgery, she becomes a nicer person and doubts her plan. Lean, tight suspense with a bang-up finale. In Swedish with English subtitles. Remade in Hollywood in 1941. **100m/B VHS.** *SW* Ingrid Bergman, Anders Henrikson, Karin Carlsson, Georg Rydeberg, Goran Bernhard, Tore Svennberg; *D:* Gustaf Molander.

A Woman's Face ♪♪♪ **1941** A physically and emotionally scarred woman becomes part of a blackmail ring. Plastic surgery restores her looks and her attitude. Begins with a murder trial and told in flashbacks; tight, suspenseful remake of the 1938 Swedish Ingrid Bergman vehicle. Climax will knock you out of your chair. **107m/B VHS.** Joan Crawford, Conrad Veidt, Melvyn Douglas, Osa Massen, Reginald Owen, Albert Bassermann, Marjorie Main, Donald Meek, Charles Quigley, Henry Daniell, George Zucco, Robert Warwick; *D:* George Cukor.

A Woman's Guide to Adultery ♪♪½ **1993** Four female friends, living and working in London, find their lives turned upside down by their passions for unavailable men. Political advisor Jo (Donohoe) is involved with married politician Martin (McElhinney) while art tutor Jennifer (Gillies) wants her student David (Morrissey), despite his having a live-in girlfriend. Ad execs Helen (Lacey) and Michael (Dunbar) find their marriage in tatters when Helen admits to an affair with their boss and photographer Rose (Russell) breaks her own rule about adultery by getting involved with married university instructor Paul (Bean). Based on the novel by Carol Clewlow. Made for TV. **145m/C VHS.** *GB* Theresa Russell, Amanda Donohoe, Sean Bean, Adrian Dunbar, Ingrid Lacey, Fiona Gillies, Neil Morrissey, Danny Webb, Ian McElhinney, Julie Peasgood, Caroline Lee-Johnson; *D:* David Hayman; *W:* Frank Cottrell-Boyce; *C:* Graham Frake; *M:* Daemion Barry. **TV**

A Woman's Secret ♪♪ **1949** O'Hara admits to murder she didn't commit. Why? It's as indiscernible as why the plot should be muddled by flashbacks. RKO lost big bucks on this one. **85m/B VHS.** Maureen O'Hara, Melvyn Douglas, Gloria Grahame, Bill Williams, Victor Jory, Jay C. Flippen; *D:* Nicholas Ray; *W:* Herman J. Mankiewicz.

A Woman's Tale ♪♪♪ **1992 (PG-13)** The superlative performance of Florence highlights this look at aging and death. Martha, 78, has been diagnosed with terminal lung cancer. She is looked after by a much-younger nurse and in turn looks after the older friends who share her apartment house. This gentle story quietly depicts the feisty, joyous Martha's last days and the simple pleasures she derives from her remaining time. Florence herself died from cancer not long after completing the film. **94m/C VHS.** *AU* Sheila Florance, Gosia Dobrowolska, Norman Kaye, Chris Haywood, Myrtle Woods, Ernest Gray, Monica Maughan, Bruce Myles, Alex Menglet; *D:* Paul Cox; *W:* Paul Cox. Australian Film Inst. '91: Actress (Florance).

A Woman's World ♪♪♪ **1954** Slick, sophisticated look at big business in the '50s, with Webb as the boss who chooses his next general manager based on the suitability of the executive's wives. Beautiful costumes, witty dialogue, and good acting make this worthwhile viewing. Plus, film offers a nostalgic look at New York in the '50s, with several shots of Fifth Avenue, Macy's, Park Avenue, and the long-gone Stork Club. Based on a story by Mona Williams. **94m/C VHS.** Clifton Webb, June Allyson, Van Heflin, Lauren Bacall, Fred MacMurray, Arlene Dahl, Cornel Wilde, Elliott Reid, Margalo Gillmore, Alan Reed, David Hoffman, George Melford; *D:* Jean Negulesco; *W:* Claude Binyon, Richard Sale, Mary Loos, Howard Lindsay, Russel Crouse.

Wombling Free ♪♪ **1977** An English girl makes friends with a race of tiny, litter-hating furry creatures called Wombles. The creatures are visible only to the little girl because she is the only one who believes. Together they try to clean up a dirty world. British society is less cutting-edge about social roles, etc. than our enlightened one; be prepared for retrograde characterizations. Fun scene with Kelly/Astaire-style dance number. **86m/C VHS.** *GB* Bonnie Langford, David Tomlinson; *D:* Lionel Jeffries; *M:* George Bassman.

The Women ♪♪♪½ **1939** A brilliant adaptation of the Clare Boothe Luce stage comedy about a group of women who destroy their best friends' reputations at various social gatherings. Crawford's portrayal of the nasty husband-stealer is classic, and the fashion-show scene in Technicolor is one not to miss. Hilarious bitchiness all around. Remade semi-musically as "The Opposite Sex." Another in that long list of stellar 1939 pics. **133m/B VHS.** Norma Shearer, Joan Crawford, Rosalind Russell, Joan Fontaine, Mary Boland, Lucile Watson, Margaret Dumont, Paulette Goddard, Ruth Hussey, Marjorie Main; *D:* George Cukor; *W:* Anita Loos; *C:* Joseph Ruttenberg.

The Women ♪♪½ *Les Femmes; The Vixen* **1969** Sexy secretary seduces a world-weary writer. French with subtitles. **86m/C VHS, DVD.** *FR* Brigitte Bardot, Maurice Ronet, Anny (Annie Legras) Duperey, Jean-Pierre Marielle; *D:* Jean Aurel; *W:* Jean Aurel.

Women ♪♪½ *Elles* **1997** Linda (Maura) is a journalist who asks her equally middleaged female friends what they would do with three wishes. Wishes may not help as the ladies suffer through career and family crises, infidelity, affairs, and aging. French with subtitles. **94m/C VHS, DVD, Wide.** *FR* Carmen Maura, Miou-Miou, Marthe Keller, Marisa Berenson, Guesch Patti, Joaquim de Almeida, Didier Flamand, Morgan Perez; *D:* Luis Galvao Teles; *W:* Don Bohlinger, Luis Galvao Teles; *C:* Alfredo Mayo; *M:* Alejandro Masso.

Women & Men: In Love There Are No Rules ♪♪½ **1991 (R)** Extravaganza chronicling the relationships of three couples, each adapted from the short story of a renowned author. Irwin Shaw's "Return to Kansas City" tells of a young boxer who is prematurely pushed into a match by his ambitious wife. In Carson McCullers' "A Domestic Dilemma," a marriage begins to crumble thanks to an alcoholic wife. Finally, Henry Miller's "Mara" has an aging man and a young Parisian prostitute spending a revealing evening together. **90m/C VHS.** Matt Dillon, Kyra Sedgwick, Ray Liotta, Andie MacDowell, Scott Glenn, Juliette Binoche, Jerry Stiller; *D:* Kristi Zea, Walter Bernstein, Mike Figgis. **CABLE**

Women & Men: Stories of Seduction ♪♪½ **1990** Three famous short stories are brought to the screen in this made-for-TV collection. Mary McCarthy's "The Man in the Brooks Brothers Shirt," Dorothy Parker's "Dusk Before Fireworks," and Hemingway's "Hills Like White Elephants" between them cover every aspect of male-female relationships. Since there are three casts and three directors, there is little to join the stories in style, calling attention to some flaws in pacing and acting ability; still, worth watching. **90m/C VHS.** James Woods, Melanie Griffith, Peter Weller, Elizabeth McGovern, Beau Bridges, Molly Ringwald; *D:* Ken Russell, Tony Richardson, Frederic Raphael.

Women from the Lake of Scented Souls ♪♪ **1994** Mournful film, set in a rural Chinese village, focuses on matriarchal businesswoman Xiang (Gaowa), who runs the local sesame oil making factory that has just attracted the attention of Japanese investors. Seems the water of the nearby lotus-covered lake, scene of local tragedies, is Xiang's special ingredient. With her new-found wealth, Xiang is able to purchase a very reluctant bride, Huanhuan (Yujuan), for her mentally retarded son—a disaster in the making. Rich detail and nuanced performances; Chinese with subtitles. **105m/C VHS.** *CH* Siqin Gaowa, Wu Yujuan, Lei Luosheng, Chen Baoguo; ***D:*** Xie Fei; ***W:*** Xie Fei; ***C:*** Bao Xianran; ***M:*** Wang Liping.

Women in Cell Block 7 woof! *Diario Segreto Di Un Carcere Femminele* **1977 (R)** Exploitative skinfest about women in prison suffering abuse from their jailers and each other. Seems that one of the prisoners knows the location of massive heroin stash. Badly dubbed. **100m/C VHS.** *IT* Anjta Strindberg, Eve Czemeys, Olga Bisera, Jane Avril, Valeria Fabrizi, Jenny Tamburi; ***D:*** Rino Di Silvestro.

Women in Fury woof! **1984** A woman is sentenced to imprisonment in a mostly lesbian Brazilian jail, and subsequently leads a breakout. **94m/C VHS.** *BR* Suzanne Carvalno, Gloria Cristal, Zeni Pereira, Leonardo Jose.

Women in Love 🦴🦴🦴 **1970 (R)** Atmospheric drama of two steamy affairs, based on D.H. Lawrence's classic novel. Forward-thinking artist Gudrun (Jackson) and her teacher sister Ursula (Linden) are introduced to Gerald (Reed) and Rupert (Bates). The more conventional Ursual and Rupert marry while Gudrun and Gerald have an affair that ends violently when Gudrun takes up with another man. Deservedly Oscar-winning performance by Jackson; controversial nude wrestling scene with Bates and Reed is hard to forget. Followed nearly two decades later (1989) by a "prequel": "The Rainbow," also from Lawrence, also directed by Russell and featuring Jackson. **129m/C VHS.** *GB* Glenda Jackson, Jennie Linden, Alan Bates, Oliver Reed, Michael Gough, Eleanor Bron, Vladek Sheybal; ***D:*** Ken Russell; ***W:*** Larry Kramer; ***C:*** Billy Williams; ***M:*** Georges Delerue. Oscars '70: Actress (Jackson); Golden Globes '71: Foreign Film; Natl. Bd. of Review '70: Actress (Jackson); N.Y. Film Critics '70: Actress (Jackson); Natl. Soc. Film Critics '70: Actress (Jackson).

Women in Prison 🦴🦴 *Women without Names* **1949** A pseudo-documentary style expose of the hardships endured by women in Italian detention camps following WWII. Controversial for its examination of such themes as human rights, abortion, lesbianism, and sexuality. English, French, Italian, with English subtitles. **94m/C VHS.** *IT* Simone Simon; ***D:*** Geza Radvanyi; ***W:*** Geza Radvanyi.

The Women of Brewster Place 🦴🦴🦴 **1989** Seven black women living in a tenement fight to gain control of their lives. (Men in general don't come out too well.) Excellent, complex script gives each actress in a fine ensemble headed by Winfrey (in her TV dramatic debut) time in the limelight. Pilot for the series "Brewster Place." Based on the novel by Gloria Naylor. Winfrey was executive producer. **180m/C VHS, DVD.** Oprah Winfrey, Mary Alice, Olivia Cole, Robin Givens, Moses Gunn, Jackee, Paula Kelly, Lonette McKee, Paul Winfield, Cicely Tyson; ***D:*** Donna Deitch; ***W:*** Karen Hall; ***C:*** Alexander Grusynski; ***M:*** David Shire. **TV**

Women of the Prehistoric Planet woof! **1966** On a strange planet, the members of a space rescue mission face deadly perils. Typical bad sci-fi of its era, with horrid special effects, including "giant" lizards. Get this: there's one woman, and she's not of the planet in question. See if you can last long enough to catch the amazing plot twist at the end. **87m/C VHS.** John Agar, Wendell Corey, Irene Tsu, Robert Ito, Stuart Margolin, Lyle Waggoner, Adam Roarke, Merry Anders; ***D:*** Arthur C. Pierce.

Women of Valor 🦴½ **1986** During WWII, a band of American nurses stationed in the Philippines are captured by the Japanese and struggle to survive in a brutal POW camp. TV feature was made 40 years too late, adding up to a surreal experience. **95m/C VHS, DVD.** Susan Sarandon, Kristy McNichol, Alberta Watson, Valerie Mahaffey, Suzanne Lederer, Pat Bishop, Terry O'Quinn, Neva Patterson; ***D:*** Buzz Kulik; ***C:*** Mike Fash; ***M:*** Georges Delerue. **TV**

The Women on the Roof 🦴🦴 *Kvinnorna pa Taket* **1989** Naive Linnea (Ooms) rents an attic apartment in Stockholm, just before the start of WWI. Her neighbor is Anna (Bergstrom), an artist working on a tableaux that soon involves Linnea, as the women become friends and then lovers. The reappearance of Anna's former boyfriend Willy (Skarskard) leads to a menage a trois until an accident compels Anna to reveal secrets that alter their lives. Swedish with subtitles. **86m/C VHS.** *SW* Helena Bergstrom, Amanda Ooms, Stellan Skarsgard; ***D:*** Carl-Gustaf Nykvist; ***W:*** Carl-Gustaf Nykvist, Lasse Summanen; ***C:*** Jorgen Persson, Ulf Brantas.

Women on the Verge of a Nervous Breakdown 🦴🦴🦴½ *Mujeres al Borde de un Ataque de Nervios* **1988 (R)** Surreal and hilarious romp through the lives of film dubber Maura, her ex-lover, his crazed wife, his new lover, his son, and his son's girlfriend. There's also Maura's friend Barranco, who inadvertantly lent her apartment to Shiite terrorists and now believes the police are after her as an accomplice in an airline hijacking. They meet in a comedy of errors, missed phone calls, and rental notices, while discovering the truth and necessity of love. Fast-paced and full of black humor, with loaded gazpacho serving as a key element. Introduced Almodovar to American audiences. In Spanish with English subtitles. **88m/C VHS, DVD, Wide.** *SP* Carmen Maura, Fernando Guillen, Julieta Serrano, Maria Barranco, Rossy de Palma, Antonio Banderas; ***D:*** Pedro Almodovar; ***W:*** Pedro Almodovar; ***C:*** Jose Luis Alcaine; ***M:*** Bernardo Bonazzi. N.Y. Film Critics '88: Foreign Film.

Women Unchained woof! **1972 (R)** Five women escape from a maximum security prison and make a run for the Mexican border, shunning civilized behavior along the way. Much less-than-honorable entry in desperate women genre. **82m/C VHS.** Carolyn Judd, Teri Guzman, Darlene Mattingly, Angel Colbert, Bonita Kalem; ***D:*** Kent Osborne; ***W:*** Kent Osborne.

Women's Club 🦴½ **1987 (R)** Table-turning sex comedy about a wealthy matron who patronizes a talented (?) young movie writer, but really wants—you know what. She begins lending his services to friends—and does he ever get worn out! This excuse may be intended to be uproarious, but it's hard to tell. And all that sex gets very perfunctory after awhile. **89m/C VHS.** Michael Pare, Maud Adams, Eddie Velez; ***D:*** Sandra Weintraub; ***M:*** Paul Antonelli.

Women's Prison Escape 🦴½ *Cell Block Girls; Thunder County* **1974** Four tough broads blow the pen and are forced to high-tail it through the Everglades. They can't decide which is worse, the snakes and 'gators, or the corrupt and sleazy life they left behind. Only cinematic pairing of Rooney and Lurch. **90m/C VHS.** Ted Cassidy, Chris Robinson, Mickey Rooney; ***D:*** Chris Robinson.

Women's Prison Massacre woof! **1985** Four male convicts temporarily detained at a woman's prison (why?) violently take hostages and generally make trouble for the authorities and the women. Horribly dubbed. **89m/C VHS.** *IT* Laura Gemser, Lorraine (De Sette) De Selle, Francois Perrot, Ursula Flores, Gabriele Tinti; ***D:*** Gilbert Roussel.

Wonder Boys 🦴🦴🦴 **2000 (R)** Curis Hanson's excellent follow up to "L.A. Confidential" pits professor and former literary star Grady (Douglas in his finest performance in years) against a strange case of writer's block, his flamboyant New York editor (Downey), an approaching literary festival, and several converging mid-life crises. His wife's just left, he's having an affair with the school chancellor (McDormand), who's the wife of his boss and has just informed him that she's pregnant, and his prize pupil is a death-obsessed compulsive liar (Maguire) who shoots his boss's dog and steals a valuable piece of memorabilia. On paper it seems chaotic, but the screwball comedy manages to be subtle and understated. Based on Michael Chambon's novel. **112m/C VHS, DVD, Wide.** Michael Douglas, Tobey Maguire, Frances McDormand, Katie Holmes, Robert Downey Jr., Richard Thomas, Rip Torn, Philip Bosco, Jane Adams; ***D:*** Curtis Hanson; ***W:*** Steven Kloves; ***C:*** Dante Spinotti; ***M:*** Christopher Young. Oscars '00: Song ("Things Have Changed"); Golden Globes '01: Song ("Things Have Changed").

Wonder Man 🦴🦴½ **1945** When a brash nightclub entertainer (Kaye) is killed by gangsters, his mild-mannered twin brother (Kaye) takes his place to smoke out the killers. One of Kaye's better early films. The film debuts of Vera-Ellen and Cochran. Look for Mrs. Howell of "Gilligan's Island." ♫So In Love; Bali Boogie; Ortchi Chornya; Opera Number. **98m/C VHS, DVD.** Danny Kaye, Virginia Mayo, Vera-Ellen, Steve Cochran, S.Z. Sakall, Otto Kruger, Natalie Schafer; ***D:*** H. Bruce Humberstone; ***W:*** Jack Jevne, Eddie Moran, Don Hartman, Melville Shavelson, Philip Rapp; ***C:*** Victor Milner; ***M:*** Ray Heindorf.

The Wonderful Ice Cream Suit 🦴½ **1998 (PG)** Slapstick hokum based on Bradbury's 1957 story "The Magic White Suit." Cash-poor barrio sharpster Gomez (Mantegna) would like to buy a flashy white suit he sees in a shop window and manages to convince four more men of roughly the same size to pony up some money and have shares in the suit. Each take a turn wearing the garment and find their various dreams coming true. **77m/C VHS.** Joe Mantegna, Esai Morales, Edward James Olmos, Clifton (Gonzalez) Collins Jr., Gregory Sierra, Liz Torres, Sid Caesar, Howard Morris, Lisa Vidal, Mike Moroff; ***D:*** Stuart Gordon; ***W:*** Ray Bradbury; ***C:*** Mac Ahlberg.

The Wonderful World of the Brothers Grimm 🦴🦴½ **1962** Big-budget fantasy based very loosely on the Grimm Brothers' lives and three of their stories: "The Dancing Princesses," "The Cobbler and the Elves," and "The Singing Bone." Good, fun Puppetoon scenes, but leaves much else to be desired. A mega-watt cast and the ubiquitous hand of producer-director Pal are not enough to cover the flaws. The biographical parts are hokey, and the tales used are the wrong ones. Disappointing but historically interesting. The second-ever story film done in Cinerama. ♫The Theme From the Wonderful World of the Brothers Grimm; Gypsy Rhapsody; Christmas Land; Ah-Oom; Above the Stars; Dee-Are-A-Gee-O-En (Dragon). **134m/C VHS, Wide.** Laurence Harvey, Karl-Heinz Boehm, Claire Bloom, Buddy Hackett, Terry-Thomas, Russ Tamblyn, Yvette Mimieux, Oscar Homolka, Walter Slezak, Beulah Bondi, Martita Hunt, Otto Kruger, Barbara Eden, Jim Backus, Arnold Stang; ***D:*** Henry Levin, George Pal; ***W:*** William Roberts; ***C:*** Paul Vogel. Oscars '62: Costume Des. (C).

Wonderland 🦴🦴🦴 *The Fruit Machine* **1988** Campy thriller follows two young gay boys in England, inadvertent witnesses to a murder, who find themselves on the run. Fast paced, dreamy atmosphere makes up for the sometimes confusing plot. Often overlooked British import. **103m/C VHS.** *GB* Emile Charles, Tony Forsyth, Robert Stephens, Clare Higgins, Bruce Payne, Robbie Coltrane; ***D:*** Philip Saville; ***W:*** Frank Clarke; ***C:*** Dick Pope; ***M:*** Hans Zimmer.

Wonderland 🦴🦴 **1999** Slice of London pic covers four November days in the lives of sisters Debbie (Henderson), Nadia (McKee), and Molly (Parker) and their daily struggles—single parenthood, bad dates, pregnancy, separation, unemployment, and their equally frustrated parents. Yet the film is about the ability to survive rather than about succumbing to despair. **108m/C VHS, DVD, Wide.** *GB* Shirley Henderson, Gina McKee, Molly Parker, Ian Hart, John Simm, Stuart Townsend, Kika Markham, Jack Shepherd; ***D:*** Michael Winterbottom; ***W:*** Laurence Coriat; ***C:*** Sean Bobbitt; ***M:*** Michael Nyman.

Wonderland Cove 🦴 **1975** Seafaring adventurer adopts five orphan children and embarks on journeys to exotic locales. **78m/C** Clu Gulager, Sean Marshall, Randi Kiger, Lori Walsh; ***D:*** Jerry Thorpe.

The Wonders of Aladdin 🦴½ *Les Mille Et Une Nuits; Le Meraviglie Di Aladino* **1961** Slapstick comedy based on the ancient rubbed-lamp-and-genie chestnut. Kids'll love it; adults will yawn. **93m/C VHS.** *IT FR* Donald O'Connor, Vittorio De Sica; ***D:*** Henry Levin, Mario Bava.

Wonderwall: The Movie 🦴½ **1969** Bizarre characters trip over themselves in love while groovy music plays in background. **82m/C VHS, DVD.** *GB* Jack MacGowran, Jane Birkin, Irene Handl; ***D:*** Joe Massot; ***C:*** Harry Waxman; ***M:*** George Harrison, Eric Clapton, Ravi Shankar.

Wonsan Operation 🦴 **1978** U.N. soldiers plunge into the muddy depths of enemy territory in search of secret information that would end the Korean War. Dubbed. **100m/C VHS.** Lew Montania, Frederick Hill; ***D:*** Terrence Sul.

Woo 🦴🦴 **1997 (R)** Knock-out party girl Darlene "Woo" Bates (Pinkett Smith) agrees to a blind date with nice-guy law student Tim (Davidson) on the advice of her cross-dressing psychic. Tim wants to do the right thing and be honorable, but Woo seduces, endangers, and humiliates him at every turn. When Tim finally stands up for himself, she has a change of heart and appreciates his better qualities. Somewhat mean-spirited comedy trods familiar urban cliches and blind-date disaster territory, but Pinkett Smith's turn could be a star-maker. **80m/C VHS.** Jada Pinkett Smith, Tommy Davidson, Duane Martin, Dave Chappelle, L.L. Cool J., Paula Jai Parker, Darrell Heath, Pam Grier, Isaac Hayes; ***D:*** Daisy von Scherler Mayer; ***W:*** David Johnson; ***C:*** Jean Lepine; ***M:*** Michel Colombier.

The Wood 🦴🦴½ **1999 (R)** Follows the friendship of three young black men growing up together during the 80s in Inglewood, California. Through the use of flashbacks, their lives are traced from junior high to the imminent wedding day of one of the trio. Mike (Epps) and Slim (Jones) are also forced to track down reluctant groom Roland (Diggs), sober him up, and get him to the church on time. Newcomer Famuyiwa based the script on his own life. Good cast is left with little interesting to do in this likable, but bland, nostalgia-fest. **107m/C VHS, DVD, Wide.** Omar Epps, Sean Nelson, Richard T. Jones, Taye Diggs, Trent Cameron, Malinda Williams, Duane Finley, Sanaa Lathan, De'Aundre Bonds, (Lisa Ray McCoy) LisaRaye, Cynthia Martells, Tamala Jones, Elayne J. Taylor; ***D:*** Rick Famuyiwa; ***W:*** Rick Famuyiwa; ***C:*** Steven Bernstein; ***M:*** Robert Hurst.

Woodchipper Massacre woof! **1989** Aunt Tess is frozen in the freezer, waiting to be turned into whatever the fleshy equivalent of woodchips is by her three unloving relations, and her totally evil son has just broken out of prison looking to retrieve his inheritance. You think you have problems? You'll have one less if you leave this one on the shelf. **90m/C VHS.** Jon McBride, Patricia McBride; ***D:*** Jon McBride.

The Wooden Gun 🦴🦴½ *Roveh Huliot* **1979** Conflicts arise between two teenage factions in 1950s Tel Aviv: native Israelis, and the children of Jews arrived from Europe since WWII. In Hebrew with English subtitles. **91m/C VHS.** *IS* Nadav Brenner, Nissim Eliaz, Michael Kafir, Arik Rosen, Louis Rosenberg; ***D:*** Ilan Moshenson; ***W:*** Ilan Moshenson; ***C:*** Gadi Danzig; ***M:*** Yossi Mar-Haim.

Wooden Horse 🦴🦴 **1950** Lean thriller of British POWs escaping a Nazi camp through a tunnel beneath their exercise horse. Based on a true incident in 1943 and on "The Tunnel Escape" by Eric Williams; set the tone for all British prison-camp movies to follow: stiff upper lip and all that, and adolescent-style trickery reminiscent of English boarding schools. **98m/C VHS.** Anthony Steel, Leo Genn, David Tomlinson, Bryan Forbes, Peter Finch; ***D:*** Jack Lee.

The Wooden Man's Bride 🦴🦴 **1994** The inhabitants of this austere 1920s, northwest Chinese community live in stone fortresses, fearful of being attacked by roving armed bandits. Which is what happens to the bridal party of Young Mistress (Lan), who's kidnapped by bandit leader Tang (Mingjun). She's released unharmed when her servant Kui (Shih) impresses Tang with his bravery but her bridegroom has been killed in a freak accident and formidable Madame Liu (Yumei), who runs the fortress, forces her to marry a wooden likeness of the deceased. Despairing Young Mistress begins an affair with Kui, which can only end badly. Mandarin with subtitles. **114m/C VHS.** *CH* Wang Lan, Chang Shih, Wang Yu-mei, Kao Mingjun; ***D:*** Huang Jianxin; ***W:*** Yang Zhengguang; ***C:*** Zhang Xiaoguang; ***M:*** Zhang Dalong.

Woodstock 🦴🦴🦴🦴 **1970 (R)** Step into the way-back machine and return to the times of luv, peace, and understanding. Powerful chronicle of the great 1969 Woodstock rock concert celebrates the music and lifestyle of the late '60s. More than 400,000 spectators withstood lack of privacy, bathrooms, parking, and food while wallowing in the mud for four days to catch classic performances by a number of popular performers and groups. Martin Scorcese helped edit the documentary, trail-blazing in its use of split-screen montage. A director's cut is available at 225 minutes. **180m/C VHS, DVD, Wide.** ***D:*** Michael Wadleigh. Oscars '70: Feature Doc., Natl. Film Reg. '96.

Woodstock '94 **1994** The 25th anniversary of the original festival was celebrated with a three-day music explosion (complete with mud). Includes backstage footage and interviews with some of the 30 acts, including Aerosmith, Peter Gabriel, Blind Melon, Metallica, and the Red Hot Chili Peppers. **165m/C VHS.**

The Word 🦴🦴½ **1978** Intriguing premise has an archeologist finding a perviously unknown text purporting to be written by the younger brother of Jesus. If authentic and publicized, it would wreak theological havoc. Janssen is off to Italy to check up; he finds murder and skullduggery. Well-acted, interesting story. **300m/C VHS.** David Janssen, James Whitmore, Florinda Bolkan, Eddie Albert, Geraldine Chaplin, Hurd Hatfield, John Huston, Kate Mulgrew, Janice Rule, Nicol Williamson; ***D:*** Richard Lang; ***M:*** Alex North.

Words and Music 🦴🦴½ **1948** Plot based on the careers of Rodgers and Hart is little more than a peg on which to hang lots of classic songs, sung by a parade of MGM stars. Also includes Kelly's dance recreation of "Slaughter on Tenth Avenue." Good advice: if no one's singing or dancing, fast forward. **122m/C VHS.** Mickey Rooney, Tom Drake, Judy Garland, Gene Kelly, Lena Horne, Mel Torme, Cyd Charisse, Marshall Thompson, Janet Leigh, Betty Garrett, June Allyson, Perry Como, Vera-Ellen, Ann Sothern; ***D:*** Norman Taurog; ***M:*** Richard Rodgers, Lorenz Hart.

Words by Heart **1984** An African American family in turn of the century Missouri faces issues of discrimination and prejudice. Twelve-year-old Lena wins a speech contest and begins to question their place in the community and their aspirations for a better life. Based on a book by Ouida Sebestyen. Aired by PBS as part of the "Wonderworks" family movie series. **116m/C VHS.** Charlotte Rae, Robert Hooks, Alfre Woodard; ***D:*** Robert Thompson.

The Worker and the Hairdresser 🦴🦴 *Metalmeccanico e Parrucchiera in un Turbine di Sesso e di Politica* **1996** Married Tunin is a leftist labor organizer who falls instantly into lust with right-wing business zealot Rossella when he spots her at a political rally. The opposites may attract but Rosella is determined to put the would-be Lothario in his place. Italian with subtitles. **104m/C VHS.** *IT* Tullio Solenghi, Gene Gnocchi, Veronica Pivetti, Cyrielle Claire; ***D:*** Lina Wertmuller; ***W:*** Lina Wertmuller, Leonardo Benvenuti, Piero De Bernardi; ***C:*** Basco Giurato.

Working Girl 🦴🦴🦴 **1988 (R)** Romantic comedy set in the Big Apple has secretary Tess McGill (Griffith) working her way to the top in spite of her manipulative boss Katherine Parker (Weaver in a powerful parody). Tess gets her chance to shine when Katherine breaks a leg and she strikes a business deal with Jack Trainer (Ford)that turns to romance. A 1980s Cinderella story that's sexy, funny, and sharply written and directed. Nice work by Ford, but this is definitely Griffith's movie. And keep an eye on Tess's gal pal Cynthia (Cusack). ♫Let the River Run. **115m/C VHS, DVD, Wide.** Melanie Griffith, Harrison Ford, Sigourney Weaver, Joan Cusack, Alec Baldwin, Philip Bosco, Ricki Lake, Nora Dunn, Olympia Dukakis, Oliver Platt, James Lally, Kevin Spacey, Robert Easton; ***D:*** Mike Nichols; ***W:*** Kevin Wade; ***C:*** Michael Ballhaus; ***M:*** Carly Simon, Rob Mounsey. Oscars '88: Song ("Let the River Run"); Golden Globes '89: Actress—Mus./Comedy (Griffith), Film—Mus./Comedy, Song ("Let the River Run"), Support. Actress (Weaver).

Working Girls 🦴 **1975 (R)** Three girls who share an apartment in Los Angeles are willing to do anything for money. And they do. For lack of anything else to recommend, watch for the striptease by Peterson, better known as Elvira on TV. **80m/C VHS.** Sarah Kennedy, Laurie Rose, Mark Thomas, Cassandra Peterson; ***D:*** Stephanie Rothman.

Working Girls 🦴🦴🦴 **1987** An acclaimed, controversial look by independent filmmaker Borden into lives of modern brothel prostitutes over the period of one day. The sex is realistically candid and perfunctory; the docudrama centers on a prostitute who is a Yale graduate and aspiring photographer living with a female lover. Compelling, touching, and lasting, with sexually candid language and scenery. **93m/C VHS, DVD, Wide.** Amanda Goodwin, Louise Smith, Ellen McElduff, Maurisia Zach, Janne Peters, Helen Nicholas; ***D:*** Lizzie Borden; ***W:*** Sandra Kay, Lizzie Borden; ***C:*** Judy Irola; ***M:*** David Van Tiegham.

The World According to Garp 🦴🦴🦴 **1982 (R)** Comedy turns to tragedy in this relatively faithful version of John Irving's popular (and highly symbolic) novel, adapted by Steve Tesich. Chronicles the life of T.S. Garp, a struggling everyman beset by the destructive forces of modern society. Nevertheless, Garp maintains his optimism even as his life unravels around him. At the core of the film is a subplot involving a group of extreme feminists inspired in part by Garp's mother, the author of "A Sexual Suspect." Close and Lithgow (as a giant transsexual) are spectacular, while Williams is low-key and tender as the beleagured Garp. Ultimately pointless, perhaps, but effectively and intelligently so. **136m/C VHS, DVD, Wide.** Robin Williams, Mary Beth Hurt, John Lithgow, Glenn Close, Hume Cronyn, Jessica Tandy, Swoosie Kurtz, Amanda Plummer, Warren Berlinger, Brandon Maggart, George Roy Hill; ***D:*** George Roy Hill; ***W:*** Steve Tesich; ***C:*** Miroslav Ondricek; ***M:*** David Shire. L.A. Film Critics '82: Support. Actor (Lithgow), Support. Actress (Close); Natl. Bd. of Review '82: Support. Actress (Close); N.Y. Film Critics '82: Support. Actor (Lithgow).

The World Accuses 🦴½ **1935** A woman takes a job in a nursery, unaware that one child is her own, put up for adoption after her wealthy husband died. Then, her ex-lover shows up in her attic after escaping from prison and takes her hostage. Whew! Everything works out, except that the viewer is left confused and incredulous. **62m/B VHS.** Vivian Tobin, Dickie Moore, Russell Hopton, Cora Sue Collins, Mary Carr; ***D:*** Charles Lamont.

World and Time Enough 🦴½ **1995** Sculptor Mark's (Guidry) father compulsively designed Gothic cathedrals and after his death Mark decides to build his own version in a field belonging to a sympathetic cleric. Meanwhile, his equally eccentric lover, garbage-collector Joey (Giles), goes on a search for his birth parents. Lots of symbols, not much sense. **90m/C VHS.** Matt Guidry, Gregory G. Giles, Kraig Swartz, Peter Macon; ***D:*** Eric Mueller; ***W:*** Eric Mueller; ***C:*** Kyle Bergersen; ***M:*** Eugene Huddleston.

A World Apart 🦴🦴🦴½ **1988 (PG)** Cinematographer Menges' first directoral effort is a blistering, insightful drama told from the point of view of a 13-year-old white girl living in South Africa, oblivious to apartheid until her crusading journalist mother is arrested under the 90-Day Detention Act, under which she might remain in prison permanently. Political morality tale is also a look at the family-vs-cause choices activists must make. Heavily lauded, with good reason; the autobiographical script is based on Slovo's parents, persecuted South African journalists Joe Slovo and Ruth First. **114m/C VHS.** *GB* Barbara Hershey, Jodhi May, Linda Mvusi, David Suchet, Jeroen Krabbe, Paul Freeman, Tim Roth, Jude Akuwidike, Albee Lesotho; ***D:*** Chris Menges; ***W:*** Shawn Slovo; ***C:*** Peter Biziou; ***M:*** Hans Zimmer. British Acad. '88: Orig. Screenplay; Cannes '88: Actress (Hershey), Actress (May, Mvusi), Grand Jury Prize; N.Y. Film Critics '88: Director (Menges).

The World Gone Mad 🦴🦴½ *The Public Be Hanged; Public Be Damned* **1933** During Prohibition, a tough reporter discovers the district attorney is the intended victim of a murder plot involving crooked Wall Street types. Full circle: this interesting drama of white-collar crime is again topical, though dialogue heavy and desultory. **70m/B VHS.** Pat O'Brien, Louis Calhern, J. Carrol Naish; ***D:*** Christy Cabanne.

World Gone Wild 🦴½ **1988 (R)** Action yarn about a post-apocalyptic world of the future where an evil cult leader brainwashes his disciples. Together they battle a small band of eccentrics for the world's last water source. Stale rehash (with ineffective satiric elements) of the Mad Max genre, served with Ant for campy appeal. **95m/C VHS.** Bruce Dern, Michael Pare, Adam Ant, Catherine Mary Stewart, Rick Podell; ***D:*** Lee H. Katzin; ***C:*** Don Burgess.

The World in His Arms 🦴🦴½ **1952** Action and romance, circa 1850. Seal hunter Jonathan Clark (Peck) and his crew are in San Francisco when he meets beautiful Countess Marina Selanova (Blyth), who's fleeing an arranged marriage and is anxious to join her Uncle (Rumann), who happens to be the Governor General of Alaska (which is under Russian control). The twosome fall quickly in love but Marina's kidnapped by her would-be fiance, Prince Semyon (Esmond), who takes off for Alaska and Clark must go to rescue his love. Based on the book by Rex Beach. **104m/C VHS.** Gregory Peck, Ann Blyth, Anthony Quinn, Carl Esmond, Sig Rumann, John McIntire, Hans Conried, Andrea King; ***D:*** Raoul Walsh; ***W:*** Borden Chase; ***C:*** Russell Metty; ***M:*** Frank Skinner.

The World Is Full of Married Men woof! **1980 (R)** A philandering ad exec gets involved with a reckless model, inspiring his fed-up wife also to look for extramarital sex. Promiscuously raunchy melodrama was written by the queen of sleaze, Jackie Collins, based on her novel. **106m/C VHS.** *GB* Anthony (Tony) Franciosa, Carroll Baker, Sherrie Croon, Gareth Hunt, Paul Nicholas; ***D:*** Robert W. Young; ***W:*** Jackie Collins.

The World Is Not Enough 🦴🦴½ **1999 (PG-13)** Brosnan returns in the 19th James Bond adventure in which 007 is sent to protect Elektra King (Marceau), the daughter of a murdered oil tycoon who was also an old friend of M's (Dench). The threat appears to come from terrorist Renard (Carlyle), who has a bullet in the brain courtesy of MI6 that has made him impervious to pain. Renard's playing the nuclear explosion card, which leads to this episode's Bond girl, nuclear weapons expert (!) Dr. Christmas Jones (Richards), who has minimal impact but looks fetching and (of course) falls for the dashing spy's charms. The numerous action sequences overwhelm the characters and Bond has little to pit himself against since the villains are so low-key. There is a welcome darker edge to both Bond's character and the plot that the franchise should build on, rather than trying to top its death-defying stunts each time. **125m/C VHS, DVD, Wide.** Pierce Brosnan, Sophie Marceau, Denise Richards, Robert Carlyle, Judi Dench, John Cleese, Desmond Llewelyn, Robbie Coltrane, Samantha Bond, Michael Kitchen, Colin Salmon, Maria Grazia Cucinotta, David Calder, Serena Scott Thomas, Ulrich Thomsen, Goldie; ***D:*** Michael Apted; ***W:*** Neal Purvis, Robert Wade, Bruce Feirstein; ***C:*** Adrian Biddle; ***M:*** David Arnold. Golden Raspberries '99: Worst Support. Actress (Richards).

The World of Apu 🦴🦴🦴🦴 *Apu Sansat; Apur Sansar* **1959** Finale of director Ray's acclaimed Apu trilogy (following "Pather Panchali" and "Aparajito"). Aspiring writer Apu drops out of the university for want of money and takes up with an old chum. An odd circumstance leads him to marry his friend's cousin, whom he comes to love. She dies in childbirth (though her baby boy lives); Apu is deeply distraught, destroys the novel he was working on, and becomes a wanderer. His friend finds him five years later and helps him begin again with his young son. Wonderfully human, hopeful story told by a world-class director. From the novel "Aparajito" by B. Bandopadhaya. In Bengali with English subtitles. **103m/B VHS.** *IN* Soumitra Chatterjee, Sharmila Tagore, Alok Charkravarty, Swapan Makerji; ***D:*** Satyajit Ray; ***W:*** Satyajit Ray; ***M:*** Ravi Shankar.

The World of Henry Orient 🦴🦴🦴½ **1964** Charming, eccentric comedy about two 15-year-old girls who, madly in love with an egotistical concert pianist, pursue him all around New York City. Sellers is hilarious, Walker and Spaeth are adorable as his teen groupies; Bosley and Lansbury are great as Walker's indulgent parents. For anyone who has ever been uncontrollably infatuated. Screenplay by the father/daughter team, Nora and Nunnally Johnson, based on Nora Johnson's novel. **106m/C VHS, Wide.** Peter Sellers, Tippy Walker, Merrie Spaeth, Tom Bosley, Angela Lansbury, Paula Prentiss, Phyllis Thaxter, Bibi Osterwald; ***D:*** George Roy Hill; ***W:*** Nunnally Johnson, Nora Johnson; ***C:*** Boris Kaufman; ***M:*** Elmer Bernstein.

A World of Strangers 🦴🦴🦴 **1962** A harsh look at apartheid through the eyes of an Englishman who has traveled to South Africa to manage a publishing house. Filmed in strict secrecy in Johannesburg due to the film's aggressive condemnation of the practice. Based on a novel by Nadine Gordimer. **89m/B VHS.** *DK* Ivan Jackson, Zakes Mokae; ***D:*** Henning Carlsen.

The World of Suzie Wong 🦴🦴 **1960** Asian prostitute Kwan plays cat-and-mouse with American painter Holden. She lies to him about her profession, her family, and herself. His association with her ruins relationships in his life. Why, then, does he not get a clue? Good question, not answered by this soap opera that would be a serious drama. Offensively sanitized picture of the world of prostitution in an Asian metropolis. On the other hand, it's all nicely shot, much of it on location in Hong Kong. Based on Paul Osborn's play which was taken from Richard Mason's novel. **129m/C VHS.** *GB* William Holden, Nancy Kwan, Sylvia Syms, Michael Wilding, Laurence Naismith, Jacqueline "Jackie" Chan; ***D:*** Richard Quine; ***C:*** Geoffrey Unsworth.

World of the Depraved 🦴 **1967** Tango (Storm) runs an exercise club for young lovelies that are systematically being stalked by the mysterious full moon sex killer. Enter police detectives Riley and Hamilton (Decker, Reed), joking types who peep on their charges through keyholes, etc. When the plot finally gets around to the issue of the killer, the point of the movie has already been made clear. Silly, trivial, sophomoric humor lacking a trace of sincerity. Volume 6 of Frank Henenlotter's Sexy Shockers series. **73m/C VHS.** Tempest Storm, Johnnie Decker, Larry Reed; ***D:*** Herbert Jeffries; ***W:*** Herbert Jeffries.

The World Owes Me a Living 🦴🦴 **1947** Melodrama about pilot Farrar losing his memory in a plane crash and Campbell trying to spark his recollection of the past. **91m/B VHS.** *GB* David Farrar, Judy Campbell, Jack Livesey, John Laurie; ***D:*** Vernon Sewell; ***W:*** Vernon Sewell.

World Traveler 🦴🦴½ **2001 (R)** One day, thirtysomething NYC architect Cal (Crudup) leaves his wife and son, gets into the family station wagon, and hits the road to drive cross country in this frustrating film. Although Crudup is a fine actor, the viewer never learns Cal's motives for leaving his life behind except that he's not the nicest guy around, considering the way he treats some of the people he meets on his trip, including construction worker Carl (Derricks) whose marriage Cal damages, and various female hitchhikers. Not a lot really happens as Cal searches for himself (apparently) and the film ultimately falls flat. **104m/C VHS, DVD.** *US CA* Billy Crudup, Julianne Moore, Cleavant Derricks, David Keith, Mary McCormack, James LeGros, Karen Allen, Liane Balaban; ***D:*** Bart

Freundlich; *W:* Bart Freundlich; *C:* Terry Stacey; *M:* Clint Mansell.

World War II: When Lions Roared 🦴🦴½ **1994** The "Lions" are Franklin Delano Roosevelt, Winston Churchill, and Joseph Stalin. The three Allied leaders formed an uneasy alliance to crush Hitler and Mussolini, all against much internal treachery. Uses lots of WWII newsreel footage. **186m/C VHS.** John Lithgow, Bob Hoskins, Michael Caine, Ed Begley Jr., Jan Tiska; *D:* Joseph Sargent; *W:* David W. Rintels; *C:* John A. Alonzo. **TV**

World War III 🦴🦴½ **1986** How's that for a title? A Russian plot is afoot to seize and destroy the Alaskan pipeline. When the plot is discovered, negotiation is needed to prevent world war. Executive branch showdown ensues between U.S. prez Hudson and Soviet chief Keith. Director Boris Sagal was killed on location, whereupon Greene took over, and shooting was moved indoors with dramatic tension lost in the transition. **186m/C VHS.** Brian Keith, David Soul, Rock Hudson, Cathy Lee Crosby, Katherine Helmond, Robert Prosky, James Hampton, Richard Yniguez, Herbert Jefferson Jr.; *D:* David Greene; *W:* Robert L. Joseph. **TV**

The Worldly Madonna 🦴🦴½ **1922** Young plays two roles as Janet, a convent novitiate, and her cabaret dancer sister, Lucy. Lucy thinks she's killed a man and Janet agrees to change places with her. **47m/B VHS.** Clara Kimball Young, Richard Tucker, George Hackathorne, William P. Carleton, Jean De Limur, William Marion, Milla Davenport; *D:* Harry Garson.

The World's Greatest Athlete 🦴🦴 **1973 (G)** Lame Disney comedy about a Tarzan-like jungle-man (Vincent) recruited by an unsuccessful American college coach (Amos) and his bumbling assistant (Conway). Fun special effects, weak script add up to mediocre family fare. Cameo by Howard Cosell as—who else?—himself. **89m/C VHS.** Jan-Michael Vincent, Tim Conway, John Amos, Roscoe Lee Browne, Dayle Haddon; ***Cameos:*** Howard Cosell; *D:* Robert Scheerer; *W:* Dee Caruso; *M:* Marvin Hamlisch.

World's Greatest Lover 🦴🦴½ **1977 (PG)** Milwaukee baker Rudi Valentine, played oft-hilariously by Wilder, tries to make it big in 1920s Hollywood. He has a screen test as a Hollywood movie sheik, but his wife (Kane) leaves him for the real McCoy. Episodic and uneven, it's alternately uproarious, touching and downright raunchy. **89m/C VHS.** Gene Wilder, Carol Kane, Dom DeLuise, Fritz Feld, Carl Ballantine, Michael Huddleston, Matt Collins, Ronny Graham; *D:* Gene Wilder; *W:* Gene Wilder.

The World's Oldest Living Bridesmaid 🦴🦴½ **1992** Hokey romantic comedy about a successful woman attorney who just can't find Mr. Right. Brenda feels even worse when she attends yet another friend's wedding. However, when she hires a younger, male secretary (former model Wimmer) the romantic sparks fly. An appealing and attractive cast helps this TV fare. **100m/C VHS.** Donna Mills, Brian Wimmer, Beverly Garland, Winston Rekert, Art Hindle, Laura Press; *D:* Joseph L. Scanlan. **TV**

The Worm Eaters woof! **1977 (PG)** Mean developers want to take over a reclusive worm farmer's land. He unleashes his livestock on them. The bad guys turn into—eeck!—"worm people." A truck runs over our hero nearly 75 minutes too late to save the viewer. **75m/C VHS, DVD, Wide.** Herb Robins, Barry Hostetler, Lindsay Armstrong Black, Joseph Sacket, Robert Garrison, Mike Garrison; *D:* Herb Robins; *W:* Herb Robins; *C:* Willis Hawkins; *M:* Theodore Stern.

The Worst Witch 🦴🦴½ **1986 (G)** Fantasy about a school for young witches where the educational lessons never go quite as planned. Adapted from the children's book "The Worst Witch" by Jill Murphy. **70m/C VHS.** Diana Rigg, Charlotte Rae, Tim Curry, Fairuza Balk; *D:* Robert M. Young.

Worth Winning 🦴½ **1989 (PG-13)** A notoriously eligible Philadelphia bachelor takes a bet to become engaged to three women within three months, and finds himself in hot water. A critically dead-in-the-water chucklefest. **103m/C VHS.** Mark Harmon, Lesley Ann Warren, Madeleine Stowe, Maria Holvoe, Mark Blum, Andrea Martin, Alan Blumenfeld, Brad Hall, Tony Longo; *D:* Will MacKenzie; *W:* Sara Parriott, Josann McGibbon.

The Would-Be Gentleman 🦴🦴½ **1958** The Comedie Francaise troupe performs Moliere's famous farce-comedy. Valuable as a record of the famous troupe on stage. When they're long gone, our grandkids can enjoy this. We can too (if we can't afford the trip to France), though it's less a film than a filming of a play. In French with English subtitles. **93m/C VHS.** *FR* Louis Seigner, Jean Meyer, Jean Piat.

Wounded 🦴🦴 **1997 (R)** Game warden Julie Clayton (Amick) vows to get even with poacher Hanghan (Pasdar) after he murders her fiance and assaults her. The FBI tell her to stay clear but Julie is determined to track Hanaghan down. **91m/C VHS.** Madchen Amick, Adrian Pasdar, Graham Greene, Richard Joseph Paul, Daniel Kash; *D:* Richard Martin; *W:* Harry S. Longstreet, Lindsay Bourne; *C:* Gregory Middleton; *M:* Ross Vannelli. **CABLE**

The Wounds 🦴🦴 *Rane* **1998** In 1991, 16-year-old Pinki (Pekic) and Kraut (Maric) are two relatively innocent Serbians who, by 1996, have fallen under the pernicious influence of Dickie (Bjelogrlic), a flashy black marketeer. With brutality everywhere in their war-torn country, the young men have become amoral brutes who only understand an eye-for-an-eye—even with each other. Serbo-Croatian with subtitles. **103m/C VHS, DVD.** Dragan Bjelogric, Dusan Pekic, Milan Maric, Branka Katic; *D:* Srdjan Dragojevic; *W:* Srdjan Dragojevic; *C:* Dusan Joksimovic; *M:* Aleksandar Habic.

Woyzeck 🦴🦴🦴 **1978** Chilling portrayal of a man plunging into insanity. Mired in the ranks of the German Army, Woyzeck is harassed by his superiors and tortured in scientific experiments, gradually devolving into homicidal maniac. Based on Georg Buchner play. In German with English subtitles. **82m/C VHS, DVD, Wide.** *GE* Klaus Kinski, Eva Mattes, Wolfgang Reichmann, Josef Bierbichler; *D:* Werner Herzog; *W:* Werner Herzog; *C:* Jorge Schmidt-Reitwein.

Woyzeck 🦴🦴 **1994** Woyzeck (Kovacs) is a flagman in a decaying trainyard—caught between his cruel employer, poverty, and his distant wife. In order to make a little extra money, he agrees to take part in a bizarre medical experiment. Increasingly pushed to the edge, Woyzeck snaps when he learns his wife is having an affair. Based on the play by Georg Buchner. Hungarian with subtitles. **93m/B VHS.** *HU* Lajos Kovacs, Diana Vacaru, Aleksandr Porokhovshchikov, Sandor Gaspar; *D:* Janos Szasz; *W:* Janos Szasz; *C:* Tibor Mathe.

Wozzeck 🦴🦴 **1947** The corpse of murderer Franz Wozzeck (Meisel) is being used in an anatomy lecture, while medical student Buchner (Eckard) tells Wozzeck's tragic story in flashbacks. A soldier, Wozzeck endures humiliation in order to barely support his wife Marie (Zulch) and their child. The beautiful Marie allows herself to be seduced by another soldier (Haussler), as Wozzeck's physical and mental health declines. And then Franz learns of her infidelity. Based on the drama by Georg Buchner. German with subtitles. **94m/B VHS.** Kurt Meisel, Helga Zulch, Richard Haussler, Max Eckard; *D:* Georg C. Klaren; *W:* Georg C. Klaren; *C:* Bruno Mondi; *M:* Herbert Trantow.

WR: Mysteries of the Organism 🦴🦴🦴 **1971** Makavejev's breakthrough film, a surreal, essayist exploration of the conflict/union between sexuality and politics—namely, Wilheim Reich and Stalin. A raunchy, bitterly satiric non-narrative that established the rule-breaking Yugoslav internationally. In Serbian with English subtitles. **84m/C VHS.** Milena Dravic, Jagoda Kaloper, Tuli Kupferberg, Jackie Curtis; *D:* Dusan Makavejev; *W:* Dusan Makavejev.

The Wraith 🦴½ **1987 (PG-13)** Drag-racing Arizona teens find themselves challenged by a mysterious, otherworldly stranger. Hot cars; cool music; little else to recommend it. Lousy script; ludicrous excuse for a premise. Most of the stars herein are related to somebody famous. **92m/C VHS.** Charlie Sheen, Nick Cassavetes, Sherilyn Fenn, Randy Quaid, Matthew Barry, Clint Howard, Griffin O'Neal; *D:* Mike Marvin; *W:* Mike Marvin.

Wrangler 🦴🦴½ **1988** When an Australian rancher dies his daughter tries to hang on to the family ranch from a ruthless creditor. She also has to deal with the attentions of two men—one a businessman and the other a cattleman, both equally dashing and handsome. Beautiful scenery of the Australian Outback as well as romance and adventure. **93m/C VHS, Wide.** Jeff Fahey, Tushka Bergen, Steven Vidler, Richard Moir, Shane Briant, Drew Forsythe, Cornelia Frances, Sandy Gore, Frederick Parslow; *D:* Ian Barry; *W:* John Sexton; *M:* Mario Millo.

The Wreck of the Mary Deare 🦴🦴½ **1959** Slow-moving adventure drama focusing on the wreck of the freighter called the Mary Deare. Heston plays a ship salvager who comes upon a seemingly empty ship one night and Cooper is the only crew member on board. Special effects are the main attraction in this interesting sea drama. Film originally was to be directed by Hitchcock, but he turned down the offer to do "North by Northwest." **105m/C VHS, Wide.** *GB* Gary Cooper, Charlton Heston, Michael Redgrave, Emlyn Williams, Cecil Parker, Alexander Knox, Virginia McKenna, Richard Harris; *D:* Michael Anderson Sr.; *W:* Eric Ambler.

The Wrecking Crew 🦴🦴 **1968** The fourth and final of Martin's Matt Helm spy spoof series. Matt and bumbling babe Freya (Tate) must save the world from economic doom when evildoer Massimo (Green) steals $1 billion in gold. Tate was murdered several months after the film's release. **105m/C VHS.** Dean Martin, Sharon Tate, Nigel Green, Elke Sommer, Nancy Kwan, Tina Louise, John Larch; *D:* Phil Karlson; *W:* William McGivern; *C:* Sam Leavitt; *M:* Hugo Montenegro.

The Wrecking Crew 🦴½ **1999 (R)** Ice-T heads the title "crew," a government-sponsored (secret) hit squad that's sent to the Motor City to clean up the mess made by gangmaster Snoop Dogg. **81m/C VHS, DVD, Wide.** Ice-T, Snoop Dogg, David Askew, Ernie Hudson Jr.; *D:* Albert Pyun; *W:* Hannah Blue. **VIDEO**

The Wrestler 🦴 **1973** All-star wrestling, which is fictional anyway, gets said treatment in the appropriate way. Honest promoter (yeah, sure) bumps heads with bad-guy crooks who want in on the action. Made-for-TV opportunity for Asner to slum. **103m/C VHS.** Ed Asner, Elaine Giftos, Verne Gagne, Harold Sakata.

Wrestling Ernest Hemingway 🦴🦴 **1993 (PG-13)** A shy barber and a rollicking sea captain, both 75 and retired, form an unlikely companionship in a Florida retirement mecca. Duvall is the persnickety introvert who quietly follows routine and Harris is the would-be ladies' man whose endless tall tales include having tangled with Papa Hemingway in his youth. They share walks in the park, little league baseball from the bleachers, and coffee klatches that reveal the emptiness of their lives. Director Haines' focus on the principals' emotional baggage considerably dampens the proceedings. Depression in the elderly may be a topic that is not quite ready to come out of Hollywood's closet. **123m/C VHS.** Robert Duvall, Richard Harris, Piper Laurie, Shirley MacLaine, Sandra Bullock; *D:* Randa Haines; *W:* Steve Conrad; *C:* Lajos Koltai; *M:* Michael Convertino.

Wrestling Women vs. the Aztec Mummy woof! *Las Luchadoras Contra la Momia; Rock and Roll Wrestling Women vs. the Aztec Mummy* **1959** Women, broad of shoulder, wrestle an ancient Aztec wrestler who comes to life. Furnished with a new rock soundtrack. **88m/C VHS.** *MX* Lorena Lalazquez, Armando Silvestre, Elizabeth Campbell, Maria Eugenia San Martin, Ramon Bugarini, Victor Velaquez, Chabela Romero; *D:* Rene Cardona Sr.; *W:* Alfredo Salazar, Guillermo Calderon; *C:* E. Carrasco.

Write to Kill 🦴½ **1991 (R)** A young mystery writer seeks revenge when his brother is murdered by a ring of counterfeiters. **120m/C VHS.** Scott Valentine, Chris Mulkey, Joan Severance, G.W. Bailey, Ray Wise; *D:* Ruben Preuss.

Writer's Block 🦴🦴 **1991 (R)** Fairchild is a successful thriller writer whose latest books feature a serial killer. She decides to kill the character off and is soon stalked by a psycho who is using her plots for some copy-cat killings. Tepid cable movie with San Diego locations the only highlight. **90m/C VHS.** Morgan Fairchild, Joe Regalbuto, Michael Praed, Cheryl Anderson, Mary Ann Pascal, Douglas Rowe, Ned Bellamy; *D:* Charles Correll; *W:* Elisa Bell. **CABLE**

Written on the Wind 🦴🦴🦴½ **1956** Sirk's frenzied, melodrama-as-high-art dissection of both the American Dream and American movies follows a Texas oil family's self-destruction through wealth, greed and unbridled lust. Exaggerated depiction of and comment on American ambition and pretension, adapted from Robert Wilder's novel. **99m/C VHS, DVD, Wide.** Lauren Bacall, Rock Hudson, Dorothy Malone, Robert Stack, Robert Keith, Grant Williams, Edward Platt, Harry Shannon; *D:* Douglas Sirk; *W:* George Zuckerman; *C:* Russell Metty. Oscars '56: Support. Actress (Malone).

The Wrong Arm of the Law 🦴🦴🦴 **1963** Loopy gangster yarn about a trio of Aussie gangsters who arrive in London and upset the local crime balance when they dress up as cops and confiscate loot from apprehended robbers. General confusion erupts among the police, the local crooks, and the imposters. Riotous and hilarious, with Sellers leading a host of familiar faces. **94m/B VHS.** *GB* Peter Sellers, Lionel Jeffries, Nanette Newman, Bernard Cribbins, Dennis Price; *D:* Cliff Owen; *M:* Richard Rodney Bennett.

The Wrong Box 🦴🦴🦴 **1966** Two elderly Victorian brothers try to kill each other so that one of them may collect the large inheritance left to them. Based on a Robert Louis Stevenson novel. Well-cast black comedy replete with sight gags, many of which flop. **105m/C VHS.** *GB* Peter Sellers, Dudley Moore, Peter Cook, Michael Caine, Ralph Richardson, John Mills; *D:* Bryan Forbes; *W:* Larry Gelbart; *M:* John Barry.

The Wrong Guys 🦴 **1988 (PG)** Five giants of stand-up comedy star as a group of men who reunite their old boy scout pack and go camping. A crazed convict mistakes them for FBI agents. It's supposed to get zany after that, but succeeds only in being clumsy and embarassing. **86m/C VHS.** Richard Lewis, Richard Belzer, Louie Anderson, Tim Thomerson, Franklin Ajaye, John Goodman, Ernie Hudson, Timothy Van Patten; *D:* Danny Bilson; *W:* Danny Bilson, Paul DeMeo.

Wrong Is Right 🦴🦴 *The Man With The Deadly Lens* **1982 (R)** A black action comedy about international terrorism, news reporting and the CIA. Connery is terrific, as usual, as a TV reporter in a head-scratching attempt at satire of our TV-influenced society. **117m/C VHS.** Sean Connery, Katharine Ross, Robert Conrad, George Grizzard, Henry Silva, G.D. Spradlin, John Saxon, Leslie Nielsen, Robert Webber, Rosalind Cash, Hardy Kruger, Dean Stockwell, Ron Moody, Jennifer Jason Leigh; *D:* Richard Brooks; *W:* Richard Brooks; *C:* Fred W. Koenekamp.

The Wrong Man 🦴🦴🦴½ **1956** Nightclub musician Fonda is falsely accused of a robbery and his life is destroyed. Taken almost entirely from the real-life case of mild-mannered bass player "Manny" Balestrero; probes his anguish at being wrongly accused; and showcases Miles (later to appear in "Psycho") and her character's agony. Harrowing, especially following more lighthearted Hitchcock fare such as "The Trouble with Harry." Part of the "A Night at the Movies" series, this tape simulates a 1956 movie evening with a color Bugs Bunny cartoon, "A Star Is Bored," a newsreel and coming attractions for "Toward the Unknown." **126m/B VHS.** Henry Fonda, Vera Miles, Anthony Quayle, Nehemiah Persoff; *D:* Alfred Hitchcock; *C:* Robert Burks.

The Wrong Man 🦴🦴½ **1993 (R)** American sailor Alex Walker (Anderson) is framed for the murder of a Mexican smuggler. He eludes the police and winds up hitching a ride from wacko couple Phillip (Lithgow) and Missy Mills (Arquette). Missy does topless table dancing and is very interested in their fugitive passenger. Alex may be better off with the police. **98m/C VHS.** Kevin Anderson, John Lithgow, Rosanna Arquette, Robert Harper; ***D:*** Jim McBride; ***C:*** Alfonso Beato. **CABLE**

The Wrong Move 🦴🦴½ **1978** A loose adaptation of Goethe's "Sorrows of Young Werther" by screenwriter Peter Handke. Justly acclaimed and engrossing, though slow. Kinski's first film. A young poet, searching for life's meaning, wanders aimlessly through Germany. In German with English subtitles. **103m/C VHS.** *GE* Nastassia Kinski, Hanna Schygulla, Ruediger Vogler, Hans-Christian Blech; ***D:*** Wim Wenders.

The Wrong Road 🦴½ **1937** A young couple embark on a robbery spree, and subsequently end up in prison. On their release, they search for the loot they had previously hidden, but find the man who was holding it for them has died. Will they ever recover their ill-gotten stash? **62m/B VHS.** Richard Cromwell, Helen Mack, Lionel Atwill, Horace McMahon, Russ Powell, Billy Bevan, Marjorie Main, Rex Evans; ***D:*** James Cruze.

The Wrong Woman 🦴🦴½ **1995 (PG-13)** When Melanie Brooke's (McKeon) boss is murdered, she's framed to take by rap by the company's sleazy comptroller (Field). Melanie begins a desperate hunt for the real culprit with the killer and the cops both after her. **90m/C VHS.** Nancy McKeon, Chelsea Field.

Wrongfully Accused 🦴½ **1998 (PG-13)** Yet another Nielsen spoof, with "The Fugitive" (along with several other movies) the target this time around. He's violinist Ryan Harrison who has a tryst with socialite Lauren Goodhue (Le Brock) and then gets convicted of her husband Hibbing's (York) murder. Harrison escapes, determined to find the actual killer—the one-armed, one-legged, and one-eyed man—while being hunted by Marshal Fergus Falls (Crenna). This is one genre that's definitely had its day, with more clunkers than chuckles. **85m/C VHS, DVD.** Leslie Nielsen, Richard Crenna, Kelly Le Brock, Melinda McGraw, Michael York, Sandra Bernhard; ***D:*** Pat Proft; ***W:*** Pat Proft; ***C:*** Glen MacPherson; ***M:*** Bill Conti.

Wuthering Heights 🦴🦴🦴🦴 **1939** The first screen adaptation of Emily Bronte's romantic novel about the doomed love between Heathcliff and Cathy on the Yorkshire moors. Dynamically captures the madness and ferocity of the classic novel, remaining possibly the greatest romance ever filmed. Excellent performances from Wyler's sure direction, particularly Olivier's, which made him a star, and Oberon in her finest hour as the exquisite but selfish Cathy. Remade twice, in 1953 (by Luis Bunuel) and in 1970. **104m/B VHS, DVD.** Laurence Olivier, Merle Oberon, David Niven, Geraldine Fitzgerald, Flora Robson, Donald Crisp, Cecil Kellaway, Leo G. Carroll, Miles Mander, Hugh Williams; ***D:*** William Wyler; ***W:*** Ben Hecht, Charles MacArthur; ***C:*** Gregg Toland; ***M:*** Alfred Newman. Oscars '39: B&W Cinematog.; AFI '98: Top 100; N.Y. Film Critics '39: Film.

Wuthering Heights 🦴🦴½ *Abismos de Pasion; Cumbres Borrascosas* **1953** Bunuel tackles the Bronte classic during his Mexican period, and comes up with a film containing little passion, but much of the customary Bunuel manic cynicism. The 1939 version is far superior, but fans of Bunuel will probably enjoy this one. Loosely adapted; in Spanish with English subtitles. Remade in another English-language version in 1970. **90m/B VHS.** *MX* Irasema Dilian, Jorge Mistral, Lilia Prado, Ernesto Alonso; ***D:*** Luis Bunuel.

Wuthering Heights 🦴🦴½ **1970 (G)** The third screening of the classic Emily Bronte romance about two doomed lovers. Fuest's version features excellent photography, and Calder-Marshall's and Dalton's performances are effective, but fail even to approach the intensity and pathos of the 1939 film original (or of the book). Filmed on location in Yorkshire, England. **105m/C VHS, DVD, Wide.** *GB* Anna Calder-Marshall, Timothy Dalton, Harry Andrews, Pamela Brown, Judy Cornwell, James Cossins, Rosalie Crutchley, Hilary Dwyer, Hugh Griffith, Ian Ogilvy; ***D:*** Robert Fuest; ***W:*** Patrick Tilley; ***C:*** John Coquillon; ***M:*** Michel Legrand.

Wuthering Heights 🦴🦴½ **1998** Yet another adaptation of Emily Bronte's 1847 gothic romance. Cavanah plays the embittered Heathcliff while Brady is the wilfull Cathy, whose desire for a life of ease places them both on a tragic path that haunts them even after death. **120m/C VHS.** *GB* Robert Cavanah, Orla Brady, Crispin Bonham Carter, Peter Davison. **TV**

Wyatt Earp 🦴🦴½ **1994 (PG-13)** Revisionist epic suffers from bad timing as it follows "Tombstone" in telling the story of tarnished badge Earp (Costner), his brothers, and tubercular friend Doc Holliday (Quaid). Costner is barely believable as a 20-something lad, but fares better as he ages. Forty pounds lighter and likely delusional from lack of food, Quaid is unrecognizable but terrific, hacking his way to supporting Oscar territory. 'Course, Val Kilmer got there first. Huge cast finds screen time precious, even though film is some 40 minutes too long, due to prolonged intro to early Wyatt life. Originally envisioned as a TV miniseries till sheriff Costner took a hankering to bring tall tale to the big screen. Filmed on location in Sante Fe, New Mexico. For the full Earp effect, see it with "Tombstone" and relive the legend. **191m/C VHS, Wide.** James Gammon, Randle Mell, Lewis Smith, Ian Bohen, Alison Elliott, MacKenzie Astin, John Dennis Johnston, Jack Kehler, Kris Kamm, Michael Huddleston, John Doe, Kevin Costner, Dennis Quaid, Gene Hackman, Jeff Fahey, Mark Harmon, Michael Madsen, Catherine O'Hara, Bill Pullman, Isabella Rossellini, Tom Sizemore, JoBeth Williams, Mare Winningham, Betty Buckley, Adam Baldwin, Rex Linn, Todd Allen, David Andrews, Linden Ashby, Annabeth Gish, Joanna Going, Martin Kove, Tea Leoni, James Caviezel, Karen Grassle, Owen Roizman; ***D:*** Lawrence Kasdan; ***W:*** Dan Gordon, Lawrence Kasdan; ***C:*** Owen Roizman; ***M:*** James Newton Howard. Golden Raspberries '94: Worst Remake/Sequel, Worst Actor (Costner).

Wyatt Earp: Return to Tombstone 🦴🦴½ **1994** O'Brian, who starred in TV's "The Life and Legend of Wyatt Earp" from 1955 to 1961, returns to Tombstone in 1914. Colorized clips from the series are used for flashbacks. Filmed on location in Tombstone, Arizona. **94m/C VHS.** Hugh O'Brian, Bruce Boxleitner, Paul Brinegar, Harry Carey Jr., Bo Hopkins, Martin Kove, Don Meredith, Alex Hyde-White, Jay Underwood. **TV**

Wyoming Outlaw 🦴🦴 **1939** Based on an actual incident, the story revolves around a small-town man who kills an outlaw. Barry, in the role that made him a western star, is forced into crime after a corrupt politician extorts money from him in exchange for a job. Lincoln, the screen's first Tarzan, appears in a supporting role. **62m/B VHS.** John Wayne, Ray Corrigan, Raymond Hatton, Donald (Don "Red") Barry, Adele Pearce, Leroy Mason, Charles Middleton, Elmo Lincoln, Jack Ingram, Yakima Canutt, Curly Dresden; ***D:*** George Sherman.

The X-Files 🦴🦴½ *The X-Files: Fight the Future* **1998 (PG-13)** The TV series' fifth-season cliffhanger continues in the big screen adaptation, which supposedly has a plot clear enough so viewers unfamiliar with the series can still figure out what's going on. Creator Chris Carter uses the show's "mythology" episodes to have FBI agents Mulder (Duchovny) and Scully (Anderson) battling a global conspiracy involving the Cigarette-Smoking Man (Davis) and an international syndicate, colonizing aliens, and related paranormal perplexities. The big budget allows for some big action sequences and special effects and the two leads have a comfortable partnership. **120m/C VHS, DVD.** David Duchovny, Gillian Anderson, Martin Landau, William B. Davis, John Neville, Armin Mueller-Stahl, Blythe Danner, Mitch Pileggi, Terry O'Quinn, Jeffrey DeMunn, Lucas Black, Glenne Headly; ***D:*** Rob Bowman; ***W:*** Chris Carter, Frank Spotnitz; ***C:*** Ward Russell; ***M:*** Mark Snow.

X from Outer Space 🦴 **1967 (PG)** A space voyage to Mars brings back a giant rampaging creature. Badly dubbed. **85m/C VHS.** *JP* Eiji Okada, Peggy Neal, Toshiya Wazaki, Itoko Harada, Shinichi Yanagisawa, Franz Gruber, Keisuke Sonoi, Mike Daning, Torahiko Hamada; ***D:*** Nazui Nihonmatsu.

X Marks the Spot 🦴🦴 **1942** When a police sergeant is killed, his detective son investigates his murder. He's drawn into a crime ring which smuggles rubber (a scarce commodity during WWII). Quick pacing enlivens standard cliches. **55m/B VHS.** Damian O'Flynn, Helen Parrish, Dick Purcell, Jack LaRue, Neil Hamilton, Robert E. Homans, Anne Jeffreys, Dick Wessel, Vince Barnett; ***D:*** George Sherman.

X-Men 🦴🦴½ **2000 (PG-13)** The Marvel Comics characters, who were born with genetic mutations that give them superpowers, get their shot at the big screen. Wheelchair-bound telepath Charles Xavier (Stewart), AKA Professor X, runs a school to help others learn to use their mutant powers. The good guys, who seeks to work with humans, fight against the Magneto (McKellen)-led Brotherhood, who feel mankind is expendable. The story is simple enough for newbies to follow and takes itself seriously (no camp allowed) but doesn't have a lot of surprises and, except for Wolverine (Jackman), the characters aren't very involving. The setup calls for a sequel, which may flesh things out. **104m/C VHS, DVD, Wide.** Patrick Stewart, Ian McKellen, Famke Janssen, Hugh Jackman, James Marsden, Halle Berry, Rebecca Romijn-Stamos, Ray Park, Tyler Mane, Anna Paquin, Bruce Davison, Shawn Ashmore; ***D:*** Bryan Singer; ***W:*** David Hayter; ***C:*** Newton Thomas (Tom) Sigel; ***M:*** Michael Kamen.

X: The Man with X-Ray Eyes 🦴🦴🦴 *The Man with the X-Ray Eyes; X* **1963** First-rate Corman has Milland gain power to see through solid materials. Predates Little Caesars campaign. **79m/C VHS, DVD, Wide.** Ray Milland, Diana Van Der Vlis, Harold J. Stone, John Hoyt, Don Rickles, Dick Miller, Jonathan Haze, Morris Ankrum, Barboura Morris; ***D:*** Roger Corman; ***W:*** Ray Russell, Robert Dillon; ***C:*** Floyd Crosby; ***M:*** Les Baxter.

X The Unknown 🦴½ **1956** Geologist Adam Royston (Jagger) is sent to investigate a radioactive spot where a mysterious and deadly fissure has appeared. Seems a mud something that feeds on radiation bursts out of the Earth's surface every 50 years or so and kills. Now, it's expanding its territory. **78m/B VHS, DVD.** Dean Jagger, Leo McKern, Edward Chapman, John Harvey, William Lucas, Anthony Newley; ***D:*** Leslie Norman; ***W:*** Jimmy Sangster; ***C:*** Gerald Gibbs; ***M:*** James Bernard.

X, Y & Zee 🦴½ *Zee & Co* **1972 (R)** A brassy, harsh version of the menage a trois theme, wherein the vicious wife (Taylor) of a philanderer (Caine) decides to avenge herself by seducing his mistress. An embarrassment for everyone involved. **110m/C VHS.** Michael Caine, Elizabeth Taylor, Susannah York, Margaret Leighton; ***D:*** Brian G. Hutton; ***W:*** Edna O'Brien; ***C:*** Billy Williams.

Xanadu woof! **1980 (PG)** Dorky star-vehicle remake (of 1947's "Down to Earth") eminently of its era, which is now better forgotten. Newton-John is a muse who descends to Earth to help two friends open a roller disco. In the process she proves that as an actor, she's a singer. Kelly attempts to soft shoe some grace into the proceedings, though he seems mystified as anyone as to why he's in the movie. Don Bluth adds an animated sequence. ♫I'm Alive; The Fall; Don't Walk Away; All Over the World; Xanadu; Magic; Suddenly; Dancing; Suspended in Time. **96m/C VHS, DVD.** Olivia Newton-John, Michael Beck, Gene Kelly, Sandahl Bergman; ***D:*** Robert Greenwald; ***W:*** Richard Danus; ***C:*** Victor Kemper; ***M:*** Barry de Vorzon. Golden Raspberries '80: Worst Director (Greenwald).

Xchange 🦴🦴🦴 *X Change* **2000 (R)** In the near future, bio-technology advances allow people to transfer their minds into the bodies of others. The process called "floating" lets anyone "travel" by having his or her consciousness transmitted anywhere in the world. When anti-corporate terrorists assassinate a powerful CEO, Baldwin is called in to investigate the murder. He is transported to San Francisco, where he ends up occupying the body of the lead terrorist (MacLachlan). Then he must fight to reclaim his body. The concept is more than compelling, and the action sequences generally overcome the relative low budget of the production. **110m/C VHS, DVD, Wide.** *CA* Stephen Baldwin, Kyle MacLachlan, Kim Coates, Pascale Bussieres; ***D:*** Allan Moyle. **VIDEO**

Xica 🦴🦴🦴 **1976** A diamond rush in 18th century Brazil transformed that country's interior into a place of undreamed wealth and excess. Black slave Xica uses her sexual allure to rise out of poverty and capture the attentions of Joao, the governor of the diamond-mining town. She gleefully wields her increasing wealth and power, becoming the unofficial Empress of Brazil. Reportedly based on a real-life character. In Portuguese with English subtitles. **109m/C VHS.** *BR* Zeze Motta, Walmor Chagas, Altair Lima, Jose Wilker, Marcus Vinicius, Elke Maravilha; ***D:*** Carlos Diegues; ***W:*** Joao Felicio.

Xiu Xiu: The Sent Down Girl 🦴🦴🦴 *Tian Yu* **1997 (R)** To foil Chinese censors, first-time director Chen was forced into guerilla filmmaking (accounting for the film's somewhat rough look) in this moving effort set during the Cultural Revolution. In 1975, teenaged city girl Xiu-Xiu (Lu Lu) is sent down to a remote corner of Tibet to learn horse training from peasant Lao Jin (Lopsang). She expects only to be gone six-months but is instead stuck, forgotten, on the plains. In desperation, Xiu-Xiu begins to trade sexual favors in exchange for the chance to return home. Based on the novel "Tian Yu" (Heavenly Bath) by co-writer Geling. Mandarin with subtitles. **99m/C VHS, DVD.** Lu Lu, Lopsang; ***D:*** Joan Chen; ***W:*** Joan Chen, Yan Geling; ***C:*** Lu Yue; ***M:*** Johnny Chen.

Xtro woof! **1983 (R)** An Englishman, abducted by aliens three years before, returns to his family with a deadly, transforming disease. Slime-bucket splatter flick notable for the scene where a woman gives birth to a full-grown man, and various sex slashings. **80m/C VHS.** *GB* Philip Sayer, Bernice Stegers, Danny Brainin, Simon Nash, Maryam D'Abo, David Cardy, Anna Wing, Peter Mandell, Robert Fyfe; ***D:*** Harry Bromley Davenport; ***W:*** Robert Smith, Iain Cassie; ***C:*** John Metcalfe; ***M:*** Harry Bromley Davenport.

Xtro 2: The Second Encounter 🦴🦴 **1991 (R)** Research facility conducts an experiment to transfer people to a parallel dimension. Out of the three researchers sent to the other side, only one returns, unconscious. Turns out that he is playing host to a biohazardous creature brought over from the other dimension who escapes into the air shafts and threatens to kill everyone in the building. One more problem: if the creature isn't killed, the computer system will fill the building with radiation. Sound familiar? It should, because this is a low-budget remake of "Alien." Good photography, adequate acting, but Vincent just isn't credible as a brilliant scientist. A sequel to "Xtro" in name only. **92m/C VHS.** *CA* Jan-Michael Vincent, Paul Koslo, Tara Buckman, Jano Frandsen, Nicholas Lea, W.F. Wadden, Rolf Reynolds, Nic Amoroso, Tracy Westerholm; ***D:*** Harry Bromley Davenport.

Xtro 3: Watch the Skies 🦴🦴 **1995 (R)** Military unit arrives at a remote island where the government has covered up a UFO landing. However, the island is now inhabited by a pissed-off alien whose mate has been killed. **90m/C VHS, DVD.** Sal Landi, Jim Hanks, Robert Culp, Andrew Divoff, Karen Moncrieff; ***D:*** Harry Bromley Davenport; ***W:*** Daryl Haney.

XXX **2002** Xander "XXX" Cage (Diesel) is a former extreme athlete who is recruited by the NSA for a covert op. Cohen and Diesel previously teamed up on the unexpected hit "The Fast and the Furious" and are no doubt hoping boxoffice magic will strike twice. Not yet reviewed. **?m/C VHS, DVD.** Vin Diesel, Samuel L. Jackson, Asia Argento, Marton Csokas; ***D:*** Rob Cohen; ***W:*** Rich Wilkes.

Y Tu Mama Tambien 🦴🦴½ *And Your Mother Too* **2001** Mexican teenagers Julio (Bernal) and Tenoch (Luna) envision a guilt-free, sex-filled summer when their girlfriends go to Europe on vacation. At a wedding, they meet Luisa (Verdu), the wife of Tenoch's cousin, and begin a flirtation, telling her of their planned trip to a secluded (and non-existent) beach. When Luisa discovers her husband's infidelity, she decides to join the boys on their trip, and their adolescent sexual fantasies turn to emotional upheaval when she seduces them separately. Believe it or not, this is a comedy (and a funny one), with "American Pie" type jokes and shenanigans sprinkled throughout. But since this movie has a brain, and something of a soul, the consequences aren't always slapstick-funny. Spanish with subtitles. **105m/C VHS, DVD.** *MX* Gael Garcia Bernal, Diego Luna, Maribel Verdu; ***D:*** Alfonso Cuaron; ***W:*** Alfonso Cuaron, Carlos Cuaron; ***C:*** Emmanuel Lubezki.

Y2K 🦴½ **1999 (R)** The gimmick of the Y2K bug is what this tame actioner hangs its plot on. A secret U.S. nuclear facility, estabished by the CIA in the Colombian jungle 30 years ago, is becoming destablized because its computer thinks it's 1969 and that the U.S. is under nuclear attack. A Y2K expert (Woolvett), a crazy general (McDowell), a CIA officer (O'Ross), and the facility's designer (Gossett), among others, all try to head off disaster. **103m/C VHS.** Jaimz Woolvett, Louis Gossett Jr., Ed O'Ross, Malcolm McDowell, Sarah Chalke, Ismael Carlo; ***D:*** Richard Pepin; ***W:*** Terry Cunningham, Mick Dalrymple; ***C:*** Ronald Orieux; ***M:*** John Sponsler.

The Yakuza 🦴🦴½ *Brotherhood of the Yakuza* **1975 (R)** An ex G.I. (Mitchum) returns to Japan to help an old army buddy find his kidnapped daughter. He learns the daughter has been kidnapped by the Japanese version of the Mafia (the Yakuza) and he must call on old acquaintances to help free her. A westernized oriental gangster drama with a nice blend of buddy moments, action, ancient ritual, and modern Japanese locations. **112m/C VHS, Wide.** Robert Mitchum, Richard Jordan, Ken Takakura, Brian Keith, Herb Edelman; ***D:*** Sydney Pollack; ***W:*** Paul Schrader, Leonard Schrader, Robert Towne; ***M:*** Dave Grusin.

Yanco 🦴🦴 **1964** A young Mexican boy makes visits to an island where he plays his homemade violin. Unfortunately, no one can understand or tolerate his love for music, save for an elderly violinist, who gives him lessons on an instrument known as "Yanco." No dialogue. Not exactly riveting, but sensitively played. **95m/B VHS.** *MX* Ricardo Ancona, Jesus Medina, Maria Bustamante.

A Yank in Australia 🦴🦴 **1943** Australian farce/war mystery/romance/documentary tells the story of two WWII newspaper reporters whose ship gets torpedoed, stranding them in the Australian outback, where they manage to foil a Japanese invasion. **56m/B VHS, 8mm.** *AU*

Yank in Libya 🦴½ **1942** No, not the American bombing raid of Khadafy, rather a low-budget WWII adventure pitting an American man and an English girl against Libyan Arabs and Nazis. **65m/B VHS.** Walter Woolf King, Joan Woodbury, H.B. Warner, Parkyakarkus (Harry Einstein).

A Yank in the R.A.F. 🦴🦴½ **1941** Power's enthusiastic performance as a brash American pilot boosts this dated WWII adventure. He and his British allies seem more concerned over who gets showgirl Betty Grable than in the Nazis, but climactic air attacks retain excitement. Produced by Darryl F. Zanuck to drum up American support for embattled Britain and France. **98m/B VHS.** Tyrone Power, Betty Grable, John Sutton, Reginald Gardiner; ***D:*** Henry King.

Yankee Clipper 🦴🦴½ **1927** Deceit, treachery, and romance are combined in this depiction of a fierce race from China to New England between the American ship Yankee Clipper, and the English ship Lord of the Isles. Silent. **68m/B VHS.** William Boyd, Elinor Fair, Frank "Junior" Coghlan, John Miljan, Walter Long; ***D:*** Rupert Julian.

Yankee Doodle Dandy 🦴🦴🦴🦴 **1942** Nostalgic view of the Golden Era of show business and the man who made it glitter—George M. Cohan. His early days, triumphs, songs, musicals and romances are brought to life by the inexhaustible Cagney in a rare and wonderful song-and-dance performance. Told in flashback, covering the Irishman's struggling days as a young song writer and performer to his salad days as the toast of Broadway. Cagney, never more charismatic, dances up a storm, reportedly inventing most of the steps on the spot. ♫Give My Regards to Broadway; Yankee Doodle Dandy; You're a Grand Old Flag; Over There; I Was Born in Virginia; Off the Record; You're a Wonderful Girl; Blue Skies, Grey Skies; Oh You Wonderful Girl. **126m/B VHS.** James Cagney, Joan Leslie, Walter Huston, Richard Whorf, Irene Manning, Rosemary DeCamp, Jeanne Cagney, S.Z. Sakall, Walter Catlett, Frances Langford, Eddie Foy Jr., George Tobias, Michael Curtiz; ***D:*** Michael Curtiz; ***W:*** Robert Buckner; ***C:*** James Wong Howe. Oscars '42: Actor (Cagney), Sound, Scoring/Musical; AFI '98: Top 100, Natl. Film Reg. '93;; N.Y. Film Critics '42: Actor (Cagney).

Yankee Doodle in Berlin 🦴🦴½ **1919** A spoof of WWI dramas, with the hero dressing up as a woman and seducing the Kaiser into giving up his war plans. Typical Sennett slapstick with a music and effects score added to the silent film. **60m/B VHS.** Ford Sterling, Ben Turpin, Marie Prevost, Bothwell Browne.

Yankee Zulu 🦴🦴 **1995 (PG)** A young black boy, Zulu, and a young white boy, Rhino, begin a friendship in their South African homeland that is torn apart by apartheid. Twenty-five years later, they are reunited by chance and forced into race-reversal roles that lead to a number of comedic disasters and a renewal of their boyhood friendship. **89m/C VHS.** *SA* Leon Schuster, John Matshikiza, Wilson Dunster, Terri Treas; ***D:*** Gray Hofmeyr; ***W:*** Leon Schuster, Gray Hofmeyr.

Yanks 🦴🦴 **1979** An epic-scale but uneventful drama depicts the legions of American soldiers billeted in England during WWII, and their impact—mostly sexual—on the staid Britons. No big story, no big deal, despite a meticulous recreation of the era. **139m/C VHS.** Richard Gere, Vanessa Redgrave, William Devane, Lisa Eichhorn, Rachel Roberts, Chick Vennera, Arlen Dean Snyder, Annie Ross; ***D:*** John Schlesinger; ***W:*** Colin Welland, Walter Bernstein; ***C:*** Dick Bush; ***M:*** Richard Rodney Bennett. British Acad. '79: Support. Actress (Roberts); Natl. Bd. of Review '79: Director (Schlesinger).

The Yards 🦴🦴½ **2000 (R)** Director James Gray presents a gloomy, tragic New York story once again in his follow-up to "Little Odessa." Just out of the joint, Leo (Wahlberg) returns home to find that his mother Val (Burstyn) is suffering from a heart condition and his girl Erica (Theron) has taken up with his best friend Willie (Phoenix). Deciding to do right by mom, Leo decides to get a job with his Uncle Frank (Caan), whose company makes and repairs New York City trains. He discovers that his uncle isn't as squeaky clean as he thought when he joins Willie's crew, running highly illegal errands for Frank. On a sabotage mission to a competing company, Willie murders a security guard and tries to pin the crime on Leo. Leo is now chased by the cops and Uncle Frank's "family." Gray's writing is superb and the cast turns in good performances as well, although Theron's Noo Yawk accent tends to grate. **115m/C VHS, DVD, Wide.** Mark Wahlberg, James Caan, Charlize Theron, Joaquin Rafael (Leaf) Phoenix, Ellen Burstyn, Faye Dunaway, Tony Musante, Steve Lawrence, Victor Argo, Tomas Milian, Victor Arnold, Chad Aaron, Andrew Davoli, Robert Montano; ***D:*** James Gray; ***W:*** James Gray, Matt Reeves; ***C:*** Harris Savides; ***M:*** Howard Shore. Natl. Bd. of Review '00: Support. Actor (Phoenix).

The Yarn Princess 🦴🦴½ **1994** With her family threatened by separation, mentally retarded Marjorie Thomas (Smart) must prove to state authorities that she has the ability to take care of her six sons when husband Jake (Pastorelli) falls victim to severe schizophrenia. Boutsikaris plays Smart's defense lawyer. Average made for TV movie about a handicapped woman beating the odds. **92m/C VHS.** Jean Smart, Robert Pastorelli, Dennis Boutsikaris, Peter Crook; ***D:*** Tom McLoughlin; ***W:*** Dalene Young. **TV**

A Year in Provence 🦴🦴🦴 **1989** Retired London executive Peter Mayle and his wife Annie decide to leave England to live in the south of France. They buy a 200-year-old farmhouse and experience all the trials and amusements of forging a new life in a different country, complete with different language and customs. They hoped for tranquility and what they got were eccentric neighbors, endless renovations, lots of company, and a taste for good food and drink. Based on Mayle's autobiographical novels "A Year in Provence" and "Tonjours Provence" and filmed on location. **360m/C VHS.** *GB* John Thaw, Lindsay Duncan, Bernard Spiegel, Jean-Pierre Delage, Maryse Kuster, Louis Lyonnet; ***D:*** David Tucker; ***W:*** Michael Sadler. **TV**

The Year My Voice Broke 🦴🦴🦴 **1987 (PG-13)** Above-average adolescent drama: a girl breaks a boy's heart by getting pregnant by a tougher, older boy, then leaves town. Blues-inducing, explicit, and not pleasant, but good acting from newcomers carries the day. Followed by "Flirting." **103m/C VHS, DVD.** *AU* Noah Taylor, Leone Carmen, Ben Mendelsohn, Graeme Blundell, Lynette Curran, Malcolm Robertson, Judi Farr, Bruce Spence; ***D:*** John Duigan; ***W:*** John Duigan; ***C:*** Geoff Burton; ***M:*** Christine Woodruff. Australian Film Inst. '87: Film.

The Year of Living Dangerously 🦴🦴🦴½ **1982 (PG)** Political thriller features Gibson as immature, impulsive Australian journalist Guy Hamilton, who's covering a political story in Indonesia, circa 1965. During the coup against President Sukarno, he becomes involved with British attache Jill Bryant (Weaver) at the height of the bloody fighting and rioting in Jakarta. Hunt is excellent as male photographer Billy Swan, central to the action as the moral center. Rumored to be based on the activities of CNN's Peter Arnett, although the original source is a novel by C.J. Koch, who reportedly collaborated/battled with Weir on the screenplay. Fascinating, suspenseful film, set up brilliantly by Weir, with great romantic chemistry between Gibson and Weaver. Shot on location in the Philippines (then moved to Sydney after cast and crew were threatened). First Australian movie financed by a U.S. studio. **114m/C VHS, DVD, Wide.** *AU* Mel Gibson, Sigourney Weaver, Linda Hunt, Michael Murphy, Noel Ferrier, Bill Kerr; ***D:*** Peter Weir; ***W:*** Peter Weir, David Williamson; ***C:*** Russell Boyd; ***M:*** Maurice Jarre. Oscars '83: Support. Actress (Hunt); L.A. Film Critics '83: Support. Actress (Hunt); Natl. Bd. of Review '83: Support. Actress (Hunt); N.Y. Film Critics '83: Support. Actress (Hunt).

Year of the Comet 🦴🦴 **1992 (PG-13)** Amusing adventure/romantic comedy throws straightlaced Maggie (Miller) together with carefree Oliver (Daly) in a quest for a rare bottle of wine. Fine wine is Maggie's passion, and snagging this particular bottle will boost her status in the family business. Oliver is a pretzels and beer kind of guy, but his boss wants this bottle and will pay a lot to get it. Wants to be another "Romancing the Stone," but plot and characters are too thin. Nice chemistry between Miller and Daly sort of saves this one despite a disappointing script. Beautiful location shots of Scotland. **135m/C VHS.** Penelope Ann Miller, Timothy Daly, Louis Jourdan, Art Malik, Ian Richardson, Ian McNeice, Timothy Bentinck, Julia McCarthy, Jacques Mathou; ***D:*** Peter Yates; ***W:*** William Goldman; ***M:*** Hummie Mann.

Year of the Dragon 🦴🦴½ **1985 (R)** Polish police Captain Stanley White of the NYPD vows to neutralize the crime lords running New York's Chinatown. Brilliant cinematography, well-done action scenes with maximum violence, a racist hero you don't want to root for, murky script, and semi-effective direction are the highlights of this tour through the black market's underbelly and hierarchy. Based on Robert Daley's novel. **136m/C VHS.** Mickey Rourke, John Lone, Ariane, Leonard Termo, Raymond J. Barry; ***D:*** Michael Cimino; ***W:*** Oliver Stone, Michael Cimino.

Year of the Gun 🦴🦴½ **1991 (R)** McCarthy is an American journalist in Rome who begins a novel based on the political instability around him, using the names of real people in his first draft. Soon, ambitious photojournalist Stone wants to collaborate with him, and the Red Brigade terrorist group wants to "remove" anyone associated with the book. Although failing on occasion to balance the thin line it establishes between reality and perception, "Gun" aspires to powerful drama, offering a realistic look at the lives and priorities of political terrorists. Love scenes between Stone and McCarthy are torrid. **111m/C VHS, DVD.** Andrew McCarthy, Sharon Stone, Valeria Golino, John Pankow, Mattia Sbragia, George Murcell; ***D:*** John Frankenheimer; ***W:*** David Ambrose, Jay Presson Allen; ***M:*** Bill Conti.

Year of the Horse 🦴🦴 **1997 (R)** Jarmusch's documentary on the nearly 30-year rock phenomenon of Neil Young & Crazy Horse. Looking as gritty as some of Horse's riffs sound, pic intercuts footage of the band's performances in '76, '86, and the latest '96 European and U.S. tours shot on Super-8, High Fi-8 video, and 16 mm. Jarmusch wisely lets songs run full-length with complete performances intact, though lesser fans of the band may not be as thrilled about that. Falls short in capturing the spirit and essence of the band and their drive to stay together after all these years, but does show some cool behind-the-scenes moments that make it worthwhile to rock fans. **107m/C VHS, DVD, Wide.** ***D:*** Jim Jarmusch.

Year of the Quiet Sun 🦴🦴🦴½ **1984 (PG)** A poignant, acclaimed love story about a Polish widow and an American soldier who find each other in the war-torn landscape of 1946 Europe. Beautifully rendered, with a confident sense of time and place, making this much more than a simple love story. In Polish with English subtitles. **106m/C VHS.** *PL GE* Scott Wilson, Maja Komorowska; ***D:*** Krzysztof Zanussi. Venice Film Fest. '84: Film.

The Yearling 🦴🦴🦴½ **1946** This family classic is a tear-jerking adaptation of the Marjorie Kinnan Rawlings novel about a young boy's love for a yearling fawn during the post Civil-War era. His father's encouragement and his mother's bitterness play against the story of unqualified love amid poverty and the boy's coming of age. Wonderful footage of Florida. Jarman was awarded a special Oscar as outstanding child actor. **128m/C VHS.** Gregory Peck, Jane Wyman, Claude Jarman Jr., Chill Wills, Henry Travers, Jeff York, Forrest Tucker, June Lockhart, Margaret Wycherly; ***D:*** Clarence Brown; ***C:*** Charles Rosher. Oscars '46: Color Cinematog.; Golden Globes '47: Actor—Drama (Peck).

The Yearling 🦴🦴½ **1994** TV remake of the classic Marjorie Kinnan Rawlings novel about a boy and his orphaned fawn. The Baxters are struggling in '30s Florida: Pa Penny (Strauss) is a hard-scrabble farmer and severe Ma Ora (Smart) has lost three of her four children. Surviving son, 12-year-old Jody (Horneff), gets more than his share of life's hard lessons—with even his adored pet causing problems. On the cloying side, the 1946 big-screen version is still the one to watch. Filmed in South Carolina. **98m/C VHS.** Peter Strauss, Jean Smart, Wil Horneff, Brad Greenquist, Jarred Blanchard, Philip Seymour Hoffman, Nancy Moore Atchison; ***D:*** Rod Hardy; ***W:*** Joe Wiesenfeld; ***M:*** Lee Holdridge.

Yellow 🦴🦴 **1998** Eight Korean-American teens have big plans for their graduation night in L.A. but they didn't originally include trying to help Sin Lee (Chung) recover the large sum of his dad's dough that he lost. They get into more trouble trying to round up the cash and Sin reacts to their friendly efforts by running away and making things worse for himself. **90m/C VHS, DVD, Wide.** Soon-Teck Oh, Amy Hill, Michael Chung, Burt Bulos, Angie Suh, Mia Suh, Jason J. Tobin, Lela Lee, Mary Chen, John Cho; ***D:***

Chris Chan Lee; *W:* Chris Chan Lee; *C:* Ted Cohen; *M:* John Oh.

The Yellow Cab Man 🦴🦴½ **1950** Skelton plays a cab driver who is also an inventor of safety gadgets. When he invents unbreakable elastic glass he finds various crooks after him for the formula. Skelton's wacky inventions are amusing and the movie culminates in a breakneck chase through a home show exposition. **85m/B VHS.** Red Skelton, Gloria De Haven, Walter Slezak, Edward Arnold, James Gleason, Jay C. Flippen, Paul Harvey; *D:* Jack Donohue.

Yellow Cargo 🦴🦴 **1936** Ingenious "B" movie about a pair of undercover agents who blow the lid off a smuggling scam. It seems that the smugglers have been masquerading as a movie crew, and use disguised Chinese "extras" to transport their goods. The agents pose as actors to infiltrate the gang. **70m/B VHS.** Conrad Nagel, Eleanor Hunt, Vince Barnett, Jack LaRue, Claudia Dell; *D:* Crane Wilbur; *W:* Crane Wilbur.

Yellow Dust 🦴½ **1936** Dull story of a gold miner (Dix) who hits a big strike but before he can make good on it he's accused of a series of stagecoach robberies. So he goes undercover to clear his name. Based on the play "Mother Lode" by Dan Totheroh and George O'Neil. **68m/B VHS.** Richard Dix, Leila Hyams, Andy Clyde, Onslow Stevens, Moroni Olsen, Jessie Ralph; *D:* Wallace Fox.

Yellow Earth 🦴🦴½ *Huang Tudi* **1989** In 1939 a soldier arrives in a small Chinese village to research folk songs. He becomes involved in the lives of a local peasant family, including a 14-year-old girl who wishes to escape from a pre-arranged marriage. Mixture of poetry, dance, music, and drama set against the barren landscape of the title. In Mandarin Chinese with English subtitles. **89m/C VHS.** *CH* Xue Bai, Wang Xueqi, Tan Tuo, Liu Qiang; *D:* Chen Kaige; *W:* Zhang Ziliang.

The Yellow Fountain 🦴🦴 *La Fuente Amarilla* **1999** Following the mysterious suicide of her boyfriend, Lola (Abascal) heads for Madrid to research the Chinese side of her family, and to get clues surrounding her beau's strange behavior. There, she meets Sergio (Noriega), a nerdy government employee whose hobby is collecting data on Chinese immigrants. Together, they uncover an illegal immigrant smuggling ring, and Lola decides to take on the ruthless Triads. Director Santesmases allows the film to unfold at a deliberate pace, as another piece of the puzzle is revealed every few minutes. The problem is that most of the story seems very hackneyed. We've all seen the movie where the fearless girl influences the bookish guy, and the image of Chinese only being gangsters is getting very old. The bright spot in the film is Noriega, who sheds his playboy image and is quite good as the quiet Sergio. **94m/C DVD, Wide.** *SP* Silvia Abascal, Eduardo Noriega, Carlos Wu, Chuen Lam; *D:* Miguel Santesmases; *W:* Miguel Santesmases; *C:* Javier Aguirresarobe.

Yellow Hair & the Fortress of Gold 🦴½ *Yellow Hair and the Pecos Kid* **1984 (R)** Princess who's part Indian and her sidekick fight bad guys and seek gold. Well-meaning, self-conscious parody. **102m/C VHS.** *SP* Laurene Landon, Ken Robertson; *D:* Matt Cimber; *W:* Matt Cimber.

The Yellow Rose of Texas 🦴🦴 **1944** Rogers works as an undercover insurance agent (he's singing on a river boat) to clear the name of an old man falsely accused of a stagecoach robbery. The usual melodious Rogers lead. **55m/B VHS.** Roy Rogers, Dale Evans, Grant Withers, Harry Shannon; *D:* Joseph Kane.

Yellow Submarine 🦴🦴🦴½ **1968 (G)** The acclaimed animated fantasy based on a plethora of mid-career Beatles songs, sees the Fab Four battle the Blue Meanies for the sake of Sgt. Pepper, the Nowhere Man, Strawberry Fields, and Pepperland. The first full-length British animated feature in 14 years features a host of talented cartoonists. Fascinating LSD-esque animation and imagery. Speaking voices provided by John Clive (John), Geoff Hughes (Paul), Peter Batten (George), and Paul Angelis (Ringo). The Beatles themselves do appear in a short scene at the end of the film. Martin fills in as music director, and Segal of "Love Story" fame co-scripts. ♫Yellow Submarine; All You Need is Love; Hey, Bulldog; When I'm Sixty Four; Nowhere Man; Lucy in the Sky With Diamonds; Sgt. Pepper's Lonely Hearts Club Band; A Day in the Life; All Together Now. **87m/C VHS, DVD.** *GB* *D:* George Duning, Dick Emery; *W:* Erich Segal, Al Brodax, Jack Mendelsohn, Lee Minoff; *M:* George Martin, George Harrison, John Lennon, Paul McCartney, Ringo Starr; *V:* John Clive, Geoff Hughes, Peter Batten, Paul Angelis, Dick Emery, Lance Percival, George Harrison, John Lennon, Paul McCartney, Ringo Starr.

Yellowbeard 🦴🦴 **1983 (PG)** An alleged comedy with a great cast who wander about with little direction. Follows the efforts of an infamous pirate (Chapman) to locate a buried treasure using the map tattooed on the back of his son's head. Final role for Feldman, who died during production. **97m/C VHS.** Graham Chapman, Peter Boyle, Richard "Cheech" Marin, Thomas Chong, Peter Cook, Marty Feldman, Martin Hewitt, Michael Hordern, Eric Idle, Madeline Kahn, James Mason, John Cleese, Susannah York, David Bowie, Monte Landis, Kenneth Mars, Ferdinand "Ferdy" Mayne, Beryl Reid; *D:* Mel Damski; *W:* Bernard McKenna, Graham Chapman, Peter Cook; *C:* Gerry Fisher; *M:* John Morris.

Yellowneck 🦴🦴 **1955** A handful of Confederate Army soldiers desert, hoping to cross the Florida Everglades and eventually reach Cuba. The swamp takes its toll, however, and one by one the men fall by the wayside. A sole survivor reaches the coast. Will the escape boat be waiting for him? **83m/C VHS.** Lin McCarthy, Stephen Courtleigh, Berry Kroeger, Harold Gordon, Bill Mason; *D:* R. John Hugh.

Yellowstone 🦴🦴 **1936** An ex-con is murdered at Yellowstone National Park, at the site of a hidden cache of money, of which assorted folks are in search. Uncomplicated, well-meaning mystery. **65m/B VHS, 8mm.** Andy Devine, Ralph Morgan, Judith Barrett; *D:* Arthur Lubin.

Yentl 🦴🦴½ **1983 (PG)** The famous Barbra adaptation of Isaac Bashevis Singer's story set in 1900s Eastern Europe about a Jewish girl who masquerades as a boy in order to study the Talmud, and who becomes enmeshed in romantic miscues. Lushly photographed, with a repetitive score that nevertheless won an Oscar. Singer was reportedly appalled by the results of Streisand's hyper-controlled project. ♫A Piece of Sky; No Matter What Happens; This Is One of Those Moments; Tomorrow Night; Where Is It Written; No Wonder; The Way He Makes Me Feel; Papa, Can You Hear Me; Will Someone Ever Look at Me That Way?. **134m/C VHS.** Barbra Streisand, Mandy Patinkin, Amy Irving, Nehemiah Persoff, Steven Hill, Allan Corduner, Ruth Goring, David DeKeyser, Bernard Spear; *D:* Barbra Streisand; *C:* David Watkin; *M:* Michel Legrand, Alan Bergman, Marilyn Bergman. Oscars '83: Orig. Song Score and/or Adapt.; Golden Globes '84: Director (Streisand), Film—Mus./Comedy.

Yes, Giorgio 🦴🦴 **1982 (PG)** Opera singer Pavarotti in his big-screen debut. He has an advantage over other non-actors trapped in similar situations (e.g., Hulk Hogan): He can sing (but of course, not wrestle). Lame plot (famous opera star falls for lady doctor) is the merest excuse for the maestro to belt out "If We Were in Love," "I Left My Heart in San Francisco," and arias by Verdi, Donizetti, and Puccini. **111m/C VHS.** Luciano Pavarotti, Kathryn Harrold, Eddie Albert, James Hong; *D:* Franklin J. Schaffner; *W:* Norman Steinberg; *M:* John Williams.

Yes, Sir, Mr. Bones 🦴½ **1951** Entertaining but dated musical about a boy who wanders into a rest home and inspires the old folks there to reminisce about their days as riverboat minstrels. ♫I Want to Be a Minstrel Man; Stay Out of the Kitchen; Is Your Rent Paid Up in Heaven?; Flying Saucers; Memphis Bill; Southland. **60m/B VHS.** Pete Daily, Jimmy O'Brien, Sally Anglim, Cotton Watts, Chick Watts, Chet Davis, F.E. (Flourney) Miller, Scatman Crothers; *D:* Ron Ormond; *W:* Ron Ormond.

The Yesterday Machine woof! **1963** Camp sci-fi: A mad doctor tries to bring back Hitler. Don't worry, though: the good guys win. Predictable, dumb drivel. **85m/B VHS.** Tim Holt, James Britton, Jack Herman; *D:* Russ Marker.

Yesterday, Today and Tomorrow 🦴🦴🦴½ *Ieri, Oggi E Domani; She Got What She Asked For* **1964** Trilogy of comic sexual vignettes featuring Loren and her many charms. She plays a black marketeer, a wealthy matron, and a prostitute. Funny, and still rather racy. Loren at her best, in all senses; includes her famous striptease for Mastroianni. **119m/C VHS.** *IT FR* Sophia Loren, Marcello Mastroianni, Tony Pica, Giovanni Ridolfi; *D:* Vittorio De Sica. Oscars '64: Foreign Film; British Acad. '64: Actor (Mastroianni).

Yesterday's Hero 🦴½ **1979** A fading soccer star finds his career and love-life on the upswing. Poor production with equally lame pop music score. **95m/C VHS.** *GB* Ian McShane, Suzanne Somers, Adam Faith, Paul Nicholas, Glynis Barber, Sandy Ratcliff; *D:* Neil Leifer; *W:* Jackie Collins.

Yesterday's Target 🦴🦴 **1996 (R)** Paul (Baldwin), Jessica (Haiduk), and Carter (Carter) all possess special psychic powers in their future society, which is on the verge of destruction. They're sent back in time to rescue a young boy who may hold the key to saving their world but a glitch leaves them with collective amnesia and ruthless hunter Holden (McDowell) on their trail. **80m/C VHS.** Daniel Baldwin, Stacy Haiduk, T.K. Carter, LeVar Burton, Malcolm McDowell, Trevor Goddard; *D:* Barry Samson.

Yi Yi 🦴🦴 *A One and a Two* **2000** N.J. Jian is a middle-aged partner in a Taipei computer firm that needs to innovate if the business is to stay profitable. NJ thinks about teaming up with Japanese games designer, Ota, but a number of family difficulties begin to distract him and things unravel even more while NJ is on a business trip to Japan. Japanese and Mandarin with subtitles. **173m/C VHS, DVD, Wide.** *JP TW* Elaine Jin, Nianzhen Wu, Kelly Lee, Jonathan Chang, Issey Ogata, Suyun Ke; *D:* Edward Yang; *W:* Edward Yang; *C:* Weihan Yang; *M:* Kai-li Peng. Cannes '00: Director (Yang); L.A. Film Critics '00: Foreign Film; N.Y. Film Critics '00: Foreign Film; Natl. Soc. Film Critics '00: Film.

Yidl Mitn Fidl 🦴🦴 *Yiddle with a Fiddle; Castle in the Sky* **1936** Disguised as a man, a young woman travels about the countryside with a group of musicians, revealing her female identity only after falling for a man. One of Picon's finest roles and Green's biggest successes. Vaudevillian fare in Yiddish with English subtitles. ♫Yiddle With His Fiddle; Arye With His Bass. **92m/B VHS.** *PL* Molly Picon, Simche Fostel, Max Bozyk, Leon Liebgold; *D:* Joseph Green.

Yin & Yang of Mr. Go 🦴 **1971 (R)** A CIA operative must retrieve the stolen plans of an awesome weapons system. Set in Hong Kong, features a strong cast in a tangled tale of no particular merit. Unworthy spoof of Oriental intrigue flicks. **89m/C VHS.** Jeff Bridges, James Mason, Broderick Crawford, Burgess Meredith; *D:* Burgess Meredith; *W:* Burgess Meredith.

Yodelin' Kid from Pine Ridge 🦴½ *The Hero of Pine Ridge* **1937** Autry tries to stop a war between cattlemen and woodsmen in Georgia. Standard horse opera notable for its location. **59m/B VHS.** Gene Autry, Smiley Burnette, Betty Bronson, Charles Middleton, Art Mix; *D:* Joseph Kane.

Yog, Monster from Space 🦴 *Kessen Nankai No Daikaiju; Nankai No Daikaiju; The Space Amoeba* **1971 (G)** When a spaceship crashes somewhere near Japan, the aliens in it create monsters out of ordinary critters in order to destroy all the cities. A promoter gets a gleam in his eye and sees the potential for a vacation spot featuring the viscious creatures. Standard Japanese monster flick utilizing the usual out-of-synch dub machine. Dubbed. **105m/C VHS.** *JP* Akira Kubo, Yoshio Tsuchiya, Kenji Sahara, Atsuko Takohashi, Yukiko Kobayashi, Yu Fujiki, Noritake Saito; *D:* Inoshiro Honda; *W:* Ei Ogawa; *C:* Taiichi Kankura; *M:* Akira Ifukube.

Yojimbo 🦴🦴🦴🦴 **1961** Two clans vying for political power bid on the services of a laconic masterless samurai Sanjuro (Mifune), who comes to their small town in 1860. The samurai sells his services to both parties, with devastating results for all. Japanese with subtitles or dubbed. Re-made by Sergio Leone as the 1964 western "A Fist Full of Dollars." **110m/B VHS, DVD, Wide.** *JP* Toshiro Mifune, Eijiro Tono, Isuzu Yamada, Seizaburo Kawazu, Kamatari (Keita) Fujiwara, Takashi Shimura, Tatsuya Nakadai, Daisuke Kato, Yoshio Tsuchiya, Susumu Fujita, Hiroshi Tachikawa, Kyu Sazanka, Ko Nishimura, Ikio Sawamura, Yoko Tsukasa; *D:* Akira Kurosawa; *W:* Akira Kurosawa, Hideo Oguni, Ryuzo Kikushima; *C:* Kazuo Miyagawa; *M:* Masaru Sato.

Yol 🦴🦴🦴½ *The Way* **1982 (PG)** Five Turkish prisoners are granted temporary leave to visit their families. An acclaimed, heartfelt film, written by Guney while he himself was in prison. A potent protest against totalitarianism. In Turkish with English subtitles. **126m/C VHS.** *TU* Tarik Akan, Serif Sezer; *D:* Yilmaz Guney, Serif Goren; *W:* Yilmaz Guney; *M:* Sebastian Argol. Cannes '82: Film.

Yolanda and the Thief 🦴🦴½ **1945** A charming, forgotten effort from the Arthur Freed unit about a con man who convinces a virginal South American heiress that he is her guardian angel. Songs include a lengthy Dali-esque ballet built around "Will You Marry Me?" ♫This is the Day for Love; Angel; Yolanda; Coffee Time; Will You Marry Me. **109m/C VHS.** Fred Astaire, Lucille Bremer, Leon Ames, Mildred Natwick; *D:* Vincente Minnelli; *C:* Charles Rosher; *M:* Arthur Freed, Harry Warren.

Yongkari Monster of the Deep 🦴 *Dai Koesu Yongkari; Monster Yongkari; Great Monster Yongkari* **1967 (PG)** A giant burrowing creature is causing earthquakes and generally ruining scores of Japanese models. Dubbed. **79m/C VHS.** *KN* Oh Young Il, Nam Chung-Im; *D:* Kim Ki-dak.

Yor, the Hunter from the Future 🦴 *Il Mondo Di Yor; The World of Yor* **1983 (PG)** Lost in a time warp where the past and the future mysteriously collide, Yor sets out on a search for his real identity, with his only clue a golden medallion around his neck. **88m/C VHS.** *IT* Reb Brown, Corinne Clery, John Steiner; *D:* Anthony (Antonio Margheriti) Dawson; *W:* Anthony (Antonio Margheriti) Dawson, Robert Bailey.

You and Me 🦴🦴½ **1938** Joe Dennis (Raft) is an ex-con now employed at the same department store as Helen (Sidney). They fall in love and marry without Helen admitting she's on parole herself and the rules forbid her to wed. When Joe realizes his marriage is illegal (and his wife's a liar), he picks up with his old gang and plans a robbery but Helen intervenes before any damage is done, except to Joe's ego. The duo finally manage to work out their problems and later get married for real. Schizophrenic film is an uneasy mixture of comedy, pathos, romance, crime, and even some songs by Lang's associate Kurt Weill. **90m/B VHS.** George Raft, Sylvia Sidney, Harry Carey Sr., Robert Cummings, Barton MacLane, Warren Hymer, Roscoe Karns, George E. Stone; *D:* Fritz Lang; *W:* Virginia Van Upp; *C:* Charles B(ryant) Lang Jr.; *M:* Boris Morros.

You Are Here * 🦴🦴 **2000 (R)** You are a big loser. (Well, maybe not you personally but you get the idea.) Your job sucks, your love life sucks, life sucks in general. So you decide to quit your job and do what you've always wanted to do. And then your boss comes along and offers you a promotion. Now what? This indie feature gives you some possibilities. **86m/C VHS, DVD, Wide.** Todd Peters, Randall Jaynes, Ajay Naidu, Caroline Hall, Larry Fessenden, Heather Burns; *D:* Jeff Winner; *W:* Jeff Winner; *C:* Bryan Pryzpek; *M:* Byron Estep.

You Can Count On Me 🦴🦴🦴 **1999 (R)** Sammy (Linney) is a single mom who works at the local bank in her small hometown. Orphaned at an early age, she has grown apart from her younger brother Terry (Ruffalo), who's become a self-destructive wanderer. When Terry comes for a visit, the love they still share as siblings conflicts with their unease over their adult selves and what they now expect from each other. Great performances and no pat resolutions. **109m/C VHS, DVD.** Laura Linney, Mark Ruffalo, Matthew Broderick, Jon Tenney, Rory Culkin; ***Cameos:*** Kenneth Lonergan; ***D:*** Kenneth Lonergan; ***W:*** Kenneth Lonergan; ***C:*** Stephen Kazmierski; ***M:*** Lesley Barber. Ind. Spirit '01: First Feature, Screenplay; L.A. Film Critics '00: Screenplay; N.Y. Film Critics '00: Actress (Linney), Screenplay; Natl. Soc. Film Critics '00: Actress (Linney), Screenplay; Sundance '00: Screenplay, Grand Jury Prize; Writers Guild '00: Orig. Screenplay.

You Can't Cheat an Honest Man **1939** The owner of a misfit circus suffers a variety of headaches including the wisecracks of Charlie McCarthy. Contains Field's classic ping-pong battle and some of his other best work. **79m/B VHS.** W.C. Fields, Edgar Bergen, Constance Moore, Eddie Anderson, Mary Forbes, Thurston Hall; ***D:*** George Marshall; ***C:*** Milton Krasner.

You Can't Fool Your Wife **1940** Ball in two roles gives zip to this otherwise ordinary marital comedy. Previously blah hubby has a fling; previously blah better half wins him back with glamour. **69m/C VHS.** Lucille Ball, James Ellison, Robert Coote, Emma Dunn, Nita Naldi; ***D:*** Ray McCarey.

You Can't Hurry Love **1988 (R)** A jilted-at-the-altar Ohio bachelor moves to Los Angeles and flounders in the city's fast-moving fast lane. A dull film with Fonda, daughter of "Easy Rider" Peter, playing a minor role. **92m/C VHS.** David Leisure, Scott McGinnis, Sally Kellerman, Kristy McNichol, Charles Grodin, Anthony Geary, Bridget Fonda, David Packer, Frank Bonner; ***D:*** Richard Martini; ***C:*** Peter Collister.

You Can't Take It with You **1938** The Capra version of the Kaufman-Hart play about an eccentric New York family and their non-conformist houseguests. Alice Sycamore (Arthur), the stable family member of an offbeat clan of free spirits, falls for Tony Kirby (Stewart), the down-to-earth son of a snooty, wealthy and not always quite honest family. Amidst the confusion over this love affair, the two families rediscover the simple joys of life. **127m/B VHS.** James Stewart, Jean Arthur, Lionel Barrymore, Spring Byington, Edward Arnold, Mischa Auer, Donald Meek, Samuel S. Hinds, Ann Miller, H.B. Warner, Halliwell Hobbes, Dub Taylor, Mary Forbes, Eddie Anderson, Harry Davenport, Lillian Yarbo; ***D:*** Frank Capra; ***W:*** Robert Riskin. Oscars '38: Director (Capra), Picture.

You Can't Take It with You **1984** Taped performance of the Kaufman and Hart comedy about the strange pastimes of the Sycamore family who must behave themselves to impress their daughter's boyfriend's stuffy family. **116m/C VHS.** Colleen Dewhurst, James Coco, Jason Robards Jr., Elizabeth Wilson, George Rose; ***D:*** Ellis Raab.

You Gotta Stay Happy **1948** Heiress Dee Dee Dillwood (Fontaine) marries the man (Parker) her family approves of and realizes her mistake on their wedding night honeymoon in New York. Distraught, she manages to hide out in the room of failing airplane cargo company owner Marvin Payne (Stewart). He takes her with him on a California-bound cargo flight that winds up crashlanding in a field. By this time Dee Dee and Marvin are in love but then he finds out the truth about his would-be fiancee. **101m/B VHS.** James Stewart, Joan Fontaine, Eddie Albert, Willard Parker, Roland Young, Halliwell Hobbes, Stanley Prager, Mary Forbes, Percy Kilbride, William "Billy" Bakewell; ***D:*** H.C. Potter; ***W:*** Karl Tunberg; ***C:*** Russell Metty; ***M:*** Daniele Amfitheatrof.

You Know My Name **1999** Elliott is perfectly cast in this true story of legendary lawman-turned-moviemaker Bill Tilghman. Tilghman was connected to the Earp Brothers and then segued into early filmmaking, trying to produce authentic silent westerns in what turned out to be an ill-fated venture. In 1924, toward the end of his life, Tilghman is called upon by the law-abiding citizens of oil-rich boomtown Cromwell, Oklahoma to clean up its dens of iniquity. But Tilghman finds himself unexpectedly opposed by corrupt federal agent Wiley (Howard). **94m/C VHS.** Sam Elliott, Arliss Howard, Carolyn McCormick, James Gammon, R. Lee Ermey, Sheila McCarthy, Jonathan Young, Nataalia Rey, James Parks; ***D:*** John Kent Harrison; ***W:*** John Kent Harrison; ***C:*** Kees Van Oostrum; ***M:*** Lawrence Shragge. **CABLE**

You Light Up My Life woof! **1977 (PG)** Sappy sentimental story of a young singer trying to break into the music business. Debbie Boone's version of the title song was a radio smash, the constant playing of which drove many people over the edge. ♫You Light Up My Life. **91m/C VHS, DVD, Wide.** Didi Conn, Michael Zaslow, Melanie Mayron, Joe Silver, Stephen Nathan; ***D:*** Joseph Brooks; ***W:*** Joseph Brooks; ***C:*** Eric Saarinen; ***M:*** Joseph Brooks. Oscars '77: Song ("You Light Up My Life"); Golden Globes '78: Song ("You Light Up My Life").

You Must Remember This **1992** When Uncle Buddy (Guillaume) receives a mysterious trunk, Ella's curiosity gets the best of her. She opens the trunk to discover a number of old movies made by W.B. Jackson—Uncle Buddy. Ella takes the films to a movie archive to find out about her uncle's past as an independent black filmmaker. After researching the history of black cinema, Ella convinces her uncle to be proud of his contribution to the film world. Includes a viewers' guide. Part of the "Wonderworks" series. **110m/C VHS.** Robert Guillaume, Tim Reid, Daphne Maxwell Reid, Vonetta McGee.

You Only Live Once **1937** Ex-con Fonda wants to mend his ways and tries to cross into Canada with his girlfriend in tow. Impressively scripted, but a glum and dated Depression-era tale. **86m/B VHS.** Henry Fonda, Sylvia Sidney, Ward Bond, William Gargan, Barton MacLane, Margaret Hamilton, Jean Dixon, Warren Hymer, Charles "Chic" Sale, Guinn "Big Boy" Williams, Jerome Cowan, John Wray, Jonathan Hale, Ben Hall, Jean Stoddard, Wade Boteler, Henry Taylor, Walter DePalma; ***D:*** Fritz Lang; ***W:*** C. Graham Baker, Gene Towne; ***C:*** Leon Shamroy.

You Only Live Twice **1967 (PG)** 007 travels to Japan to take on arch-nemesis Blofeld, who has been capturing Russian and American spacecraft in an attempt to start WWIII. Great location photography; theme sung by Nancy Sinatra. Implausible plot, however, is a handicap, even though this is Bond. **125m/C VHS, DVD, Wide.** *GB* Sean Connery, Mie Hama, Akiko Wakabayashi, Tetsuro Tamba, Karin Dor, Charles Gray, Donald Pleasence, Tsai Chin, Bernard Lee, Lois Maxwell, Desmond Llewelyn; ***D:*** Lewis Gilbert; ***W:*** Roald Dahl; ***C:*** Frederick A. (Freddie) Young; ***M:*** John Barry.

You So Crazy *Martin Lawrence You So Crazy* **1994** Scandalous star of TV show "Martin" and host of HBO's "Def Comedy Jam" follows in the footsteps of raunchy humorists Richard Pryor and Eddie Murphy. Threatened with an NC-17 rating, Lawrence refused to edit and Miramax, the original distributor, dropped it. It was picked up by Samuel Goldwyn, who released the original version, uncut and unrated. Filmed live at the Brooklyn Academy of Music, Lawrence displays too little of his considerable talent, and too much vulgarity and poor taste. **85m/C VHS, DVD.** Martin Lawrence; ***D:*** Thomas Schlamme; ***W:*** Martin Lawrence; ***C:*** Arthur Albert.

You Talkin' to Me? **1987 (R)** Fledgling actor who idolizes De Niro moves to the West Coast for his big break. He fails, so he dyes his hair blond and digs the California lifestyle. Embarrassingly bad. **97m/C VHS.** Chris Winkler, Jim Youngs, Faith Ford; ***D:*** Charles Winkler; ***W:*** Charles Winkler.

You Were Never Lovelier **1942** Charming tale of a father who creates a phony Romeo to try to interest his daughter in marriage. Astaire appears and woos Hayworth in the flesh. The dancing, of course, is superb, and Hayworth is stunning. ♫Dearly Beloved; I'm Old Fashioned; Shorty George; Wedding in the Spring; You Were Never Lovelier. **98m/B VHS.** Fred Astaire, Rita Hayworth, Leslie Brooks, Xavier Cugat, Adolphe Menjou, Larry Parks; ***D:*** William A. Seiter; ***M:*** Jerome Kern, Johnny Mercer.

You'll Find Out **1940** A comic mix of music and mystery as Kay Kyser and his Band, along with a debutante in distress, are terrorized by Lugosi, Karloff, and Lorre. ♫The Bad Humor; I'd Know You Anywhere; You've Got Me This Way; Like the Fella Once Said; I've Got a One-Track Mind; Don't Think it Ain't Been Charming. **97m/B VHS.** Peter Lorre, Kay Kyser, Boris Karloff, Bela Lugosi, Dennis O'Keefe, Helen Parrish; ***D:*** David Butler.

You'll Like My Mother **1972 (PG)** Surprisingly tense thriller finds preggers Francesca (Duke) traveling to Minnesota to meet the family of her recently deceased husband. Mrs. Kinsolving (Murphy) refuses to acknowledge her but Fran is forced to stay the night because of a snowstorm. She meets the rest of the clan, including mentally retarded Kathleen (Allen) and homicidal Kenny (Thomas). When she learns the truth about these various relations, all the strain pushes Fran into labor and no one's about to let her go to the hospital. Adapted from the novel by Naomi A. Hintze. **92m/C VHS.** Patty Duke, Rosemary Murphy, Richard Thomas, Sian Barbara Allen; ***D:*** Lamont Johnson; ***W:*** Jo Heims; ***C:*** Jack Marta; ***M:*** Gil Melle.

You'll Never Get Rich **1941** A Broadway dance director is drafted into the Army, where his romantic troubles cause him to wind up in the guardhouse more than once. He of course gets the girl. Exquisitely funny. ♫Since I Kissed My Baby Goodbye; The A-stairable Rag; Shootin' the Works for Uncle Sam; Wedding Cake Walk; Dream Dancing; Boogie Barcarolle; So Near and Yet So Far. **88m/B VHS.** Fred Astaire, Rita Hayworth, Robert Benchley; ***D:*** Sidney Lanfield.

The Young Americans **1993 (R)** Tough New York cop John Harris (Keitel) is sent to London to aid the police with their investigations into a series of killings related to a drug smuggling operation working out of the club scene. Harris wants to tie everything to the sleazeball gangster Carl Frazer (Mortensen) that he's been trailing. Slick formula with hard-working cast. Debut for 25-year-old director Cannon. **108m/C VHS.** *GB* Harvey Keitel, Viggo Mortensen, Iain Glen, John Wood, Keith Allen, Craig Kelly, Thandie Newton, Terence Rigby; ***D:*** Danny Cannon; ***W:*** Danny Cannon, David Hilton; ***M:*** David Arnold.

Young & Free **1978** Following the death of his parents, a young man must learn to face the perils of an unchartered wilderness alone. Ultimately he must choose between returning to civilization, or remain with his beloved wife and life in the wild. **87m/C VHS.** Erik Larsen; ***D:*** Keith Larsen.

Young and Innocent *The Girl Was Young* **1937** Somewhat uneven thriller about a police constable's daughter who helps a fugitive prove he didn't strangle a film star. **80m/B VHS, DVD.** *GB* Derrick DeMarney, Nova Pilbeam, Percy Marmont, Edward Rigby, Mary Clare, John Longden, George Curzon, Basil Radford, Pamela Carme, George Merritt, J.H. Roberts, Jerry Verno, H.F. Maltby, Beatrice Varley, Syd Crossley, Frank Atkinson, Torin Thatcher; ***D:*** Alfred Hitchcock; ***W:*** Charles Bennett, Alma Reville, Gerald Savory, Antony Armstrong, Edwin Greenwood; ***C:*** Bernard Knowles; ***M:*** Louis Levy.

The Young and the Guilty **1958** Two star-crossed teenagers are frustrated in their romance when their parents find one of their love letters and hit the ceiling. Told not to see each other again, the two take to sneaking around, which adds an edge to their relationship. Moving performances by the two young leads. **65m/B VHS.** Phyllis Calvert, Andrew Ray, Edward Chapman, Janet Munro, Campbell Singer; ***D:*** Peter Cotes.

Young & Willing **1942** A group of struggling actors gets hold of a terrific play and tries various schemes to get it produced. Based on the Broadway Play "Out of the Frying Pan" by Francis Swann. Unexceptional but enjoyable comedy. **83m/B VHS.** William Holden, Susan Hayward, Eddie Bracken, Robert Benchley, Martha O'Driscoll, Barbara Britton; ***D:*** Edward H. Griffith; ***W:*** Virginia Van Upp.

Young Aphrodites *Mikres Aphrodites* **1963** Two young teenagers of a primitive Greek tribe discover sexuality. An acclaimed film retelling the myth of Daphnis and Chloe. Narrated in English. **87m/B VHS.** *GR* ***D:*** Nikos Koundouros. Berlin Intl. Film Fest. '63: Director (Koundouros).

Young at Heart **1954** Fanny Hurst's lighthearted tale of a cynical hard-luck musician who finds happiness when he falls for a small town girl. A remake of the 1938 "Four Daughters." ♫Young at Heart; Someone to Watch Over Me; One for My Baby; Hold Me in Your Arms; Ready, Willing and Able; Till My Love Comes Back to Me; There's a Rising Moon For Every Falling Star; You, My Love. **117m/C VHS.** Frank Sinatra, Doris Day, Gig Young, Ethel Barrymore, Dorothy Malone, Robert Keith, Elisabeth Fraser, Alan Hale Jr.; ***D:*** Gordon Douglas; ***W:*** Julius J. Epstein, Liam O'Brien.

Young Bess **1953** Simmons and real-life husband Granger star in this splashy costume drama about 16th century England's young Queen. Features outstanding performances by Simmons as Elizabeth I and Laughton (repeating his most famous role) as Henry VIII. Based on the novel by Margaret Irwin. **112m/C VHS.** Jean Simmons, Stewart Granger, Deborah Kerr, Charles Laughton, Kay Walsh, Guy Rolfe, Kathleen Byron, Cecil Kellaway, Rex Thompson; ***D:*** George Sidney; ***W:*** Jan Lustig, Arthur Wimperis; ***C:*** Charles Rosher; ***M:*** Miklos Rozsa.

Young Bill Hickok **1940** A Rogers vehicle in the form of a very fictionalized biography of the famous gunfighter. **54m/B VHS.** Roy Rogers, George "Gabby" Hayes, Julie (Jacqueline Wells) Bishop, John Miljan, Sally Payne, Monte Blue, Archie Twitchell; ***D:*** Joseph Kane; ***W:*** Olive Cooper, Norton S. Parker; ***C:*** William Nobles.

Young Blood **1933** A cowboy robs from the rich to help the poor. He's also interested in a foreign actress having trouble bonding with the townfolk. Lots of old fashioned western violence. **61m/B VHS.** Bob Steele, Charles "Blackie" King, Helen Foster; ***D:*** Phil Rosen.

The Young Bruce Lee **1980** A young boy named Bruce Lee and his friend both learn the martial arts in order to defend themselves from bullies. As they grow up Lee sets his sights on becoming a movie star while his friend performs in acrobatic stage shows. Though Lee achieves stardom, he finds himself hounded by martial artists that want to challenge him. This unauthorized biopic follows the major events in Bruce Lee's life but most of it is cliched fabrication. The film is cheap and poorly crafted, but Lung (AKA Bruce Li) does a fairly successful job of mimicking Lee and he's helped by an accurate hairdo and wardrobe. As far as Bruce Lee wannabe films, you could do a lot worse. Despite the packaging, there is no Lee footage in the film—only a newsphoto of his body. **80m/C VHS, DVD.** Bruce Li.

Young Buffalo Bill **1940** Buffalo Bill battles the Spanish land-grant patrons. **54m/B VHS.** Roy Rogers, George "Gabby" Hayes, Pauline Moore; ***D:*** Joseph Kane.

Young Caruso **1951** Dramatic biography of legendary tenor Enrico Caruso, following his life from childhood poverty in Naples to the beginning of his rise to fame. Dubbed in English. **78m/B VHS.** Gina Lollobrigida, Ermanno Randi, Mario del Monaco.

Young Catherine **1991** Made-for-TV account of Russia's strongest female ruler, the girl who would be Catherine the Great. Star-studded cast and excellent production values. Script and strong cast make Ormond look like a lightweight. Filmed in Leningrad. Also available in 186-minute version. **150m/C VHS.** Vanessa Redgrave, Christopher Plummer, Marthe Keller, Franco Nero, Julia Ormond, Maximilian Schell, Reece Dinsdale, Mark Frankel; ***D:*** Michael Anderson Sr.; ***W:*** Chris Bryant.

Young Charlie Chaplin 🦴🦴
1988 A British-made TV biography of the legendary silent screen comic. **160m/C VHS.** Ian McShane, Twiggy; ***M:*** Rachel Portman.

A Young Connecticut Yankee in King Arthur's Court 🦴🦴½
1995 A modern-day teenager timetravels back to the court of King Arthur and Camelot. Based on the book by Mark Twain. **93m/C VHS.** Michael York, Theresa Russell, Nick Mancuso, Philippe Ross, Jack Langedijk, Polly Shannon, Paul Hopkins; ***D:*** Ralph L. (R.L.) Thomas; ***W:*** Ralph L. (R.L.) Thomas, Frank Encarnacao; ***C:*** John Berrie; ***M:*** Alan Reeves.

Young Doctors in Love 🦴🦴
1982 (R) Spoof of medical soap operas features a chaotic scenario at City Hospital, where the young men and women on the staff have better things to do than attend to their patients. Good cast keeps this one alive, though many laughs are forced. Includes cameos by real soap star, including then-General Hospital star Moore. **95m/C VHS.** Dabney Coleman, Sean Young, Michael McKean, Harry Dean Stanton, Hector Elizondo, Patrick Macnee, Pamela Reed, Saul Rubinek; ***Cameos:*** Demi Moore, Janine Turner; ***D:*** Garry Marshall; ***W:*** Michael Elias, Rich Eustis; ***M:*** Maurice Jarre.

Young Einstein 🦴🦴 **1989 (PG)** A goofy, irreverent Australian farce starring, directed, co-scripted and co-produced by Serious, depicting Einstein as a young Outback clod who splits beer atoms and invents rock and roll. Winner of several Aussie awards. Fun for the kids. **91m/C VHS.** *AU* Yahoo Serious, Odile Le Clezio, John Howard, Pee Wee Wilson, Su Cruickshank, Lulu Pinkus, Kaarin Fairfax, Jonathan Coleman; ***D:*** Yahoo Serious; ***W:*** David Roach, Yahoo Serious; ***C:*** Jeff Darling; ***M:*** Martin Armiger, William Motzig, Tommy Tycho.

Young Frankenstein 🦴🦴🦴🦴
1974 (PG) Young Dr. Frankenstein (Wilder), a brain surgeon, inherits the family castle back in Transylvania. He's skittish about the family business, but when he learns his grandfather's secrets, he becomes obsessed with making his own monster. Wilder and monster Boyle make a memorable song-and-dance team to Irving Berlin's "Puttin' on the Ritz," and Hackman's cameo as a blind man is inspired. Garr ("What knockers!" "Oh, sank you!") is adorable as a fraulein, and Leachman ("He's vass my—boyfriend!") is wonderfully scary. Wilder saves the creature with a switcheroo, in which the doctor ends up with a certain monster-sized body part. Hilarious parody. **108m/B VHS, DVD, Wide.** Peter Boyle, Gene Wilder, Marty Feldman, Madeline Kahn, Cloris Leachman, Teri Garr, Kenneth Mars, Richard Haydn, Gene Hackman, Liam Dunn, Monte Landis; ***D:*** Mel Brooks; ***W:*** Mel Brooks, Gene Wilder; ***C:*** Gerald Hirschfeld; ***M:*** John Morris.

The Young Girls of Rochefort 🦴🦴½ *Les Demoiselles de Rochefort* **1968** Twins sisters Delphine and Solange (played by sisters Deneuve and Dorleac) dream of romance, which first appears in the forms of salesmen Etienne (Chakiris) and Bill (Dale), who are minor distractions for the real thing—artistic sailor Maxence (Perrin) and concert pianist Andy (Kelly). Demy's followup to the more compelling "The Umbrellas of Cherbourg" is still an equally candy-colored musical fantasy. Rochefort (like Cherbourg) is an actual town that Demy took over for filming. **125m/C VHS, DVD, Wide.** *FR* Catherine Deneuve, Francoise Dorleac, George Chakiris, Grover Dale, Gene Kelly, Jacques Perrin, Danielle Darrieux, Michel Piccoli, Pamela Hart, Jacques Riberolles, Leslie North; ***D:*** Jacques Demy; ***W:*** Jacques Demy; ***C:*** Ghislan Cloquet; ***M:*** Michel Legrand.

The Young Graduates 🦴 **1971 (PG)** Hormonally imbalanced teens come of age in spite of meandering plot. Features "Breaking Away" star Christopher in big screen debut. **99m/C VHS.** Patricia Wymer, Steven Stewart, Gary Rist, Bruce Kirby, Jennifer Ritt, Dennis Christopher; ***D:*** Robert Anderson.

Young Guns 🦴🦴½ **1988 (R)** A sophomoric Wild Bunch look-alike that ends up resembling a western version of the Bowery Boys. Provides a portrait of Billy the Kid and his gang as they move from prairie trash to demi-legends. Features several fine performances by a popular group of today's young stars. **107m/C VHS, DVD.** Emilio Estevez, Kiefer Sutherland, Lou Diamond Phillips, Charlie Sheen, Casey Siemaszko, Dermot Mulroney, Terence Stamp, Terry O'Quinn, Jack Palance, Brian Keith, Patrick Wayne, Sharon Thomas; ***D:*** Christopher Cain; ***W:*** John Fusco; ***C:*** Dean Semler; ***M:*** Anthony Marinelli, Brian Backus, Brian Banks.

Young Guns 2 🦴🦴 **1990 (PG-13)** Brat Pack vehicle neo-Western sequel about Billy the Kid (Estevez) and his gang. Told as an account by Brushy Bill Roberts who, in 1950, claims to be the real Billy the Kid and recounts his continuing adventures with Doc (Sutherland), Chavez (Phillips) and Pat Garrett (Petersen). Not bad for a sequel, thanks mostly to Petersen. **105m/C VHS, DVD, Wide.** Emilio Estevez, Kiefer Sutherland, Lou Diamond Phillips, Christian Slater, William L. Petersen, Alan Ruck, R.D. Call, James Coburn, Balthazar Getty, Jack Kehoe, Rob Knepper, Jenny Wright, Tracey Walter, Ginger Lynn Allen, Jon Bon Jovi, Viggo Mortensen, Leon Rippy, Bradley Whitford, Scott Wilson, John Hammil; ***D:*** Geoff Murphy; ***W:*** John Fusco; ***C:*** Dean Semler; ***M:*** Alan Silvestri. Golden Globes '91: Song ("Blaze of Glory").

Young Hercules 🦴🦴½ **1997 (PG-13)** Seventeen-year-old Herc (Bohen) is a confused teen, torn between his mortal and immortal sides. So concerned mom Alcmene sends the kid to Cherion's academy where Herc can learn to be a warrior and where he'll meet friends and rivals Iolus (O'Gorman), Prince Jason (Conrad), and the beautiful Yvenna (Stewart). Oh yes, war god Ares (Smith) also shows up, trying to prevent half-brother Herc and his friends from obtaining the golden fleece for Jason's dying father. **93m/C VHS, DVD.** Ian Bohen, Dean O'Gorman, Johna Stewart, Chris Conrad, Kevin Smith; ***D:*** T.J. Scott; ***W:*** Robert Tapert, Andrew Dettmann, Daniel Truly; ***C:*** John Mahaffie; ***M:*** Joseph LoDuca. **VIDEO**

The Young in Heart 🦴🦴🦴 **1938** A lonely, old woman allows a family of con-artists into her life for companionship. Impressed by her sweet nature, the parasitic brood reforms. The cute comedy was a real crowd-pleaser in its day, especially after the bittersweet ending was replaced with a happier variety. Based on the novel "The Gay Banditti" by I.A.R. Wylie. **90m/C VHS.** Janet Gaynor, Douglas Fairbanks Jr., Paulette Goddard, Roland Young, Billie Burke, Minnie Dupree, Richard Carlson, Charles Halton; ***D:*** Richard Wallace; ***W:*** Charles Bennett, Paul Osborn.

Young Ivanhoe 🦴🦴½ **1995** Ivanhoe learns how to be a warrior, with some help from Robin Hood and the Black Knight, inspiring others to follow him into battle to save their land from seizure by the Norman invaders. **96m/C VHS.** Stacy Keach, Nick Mancuso, Margot Kidder, Kris Holdenried, Rachel Blanchard, Matthew Daniels; ***D:*** Ralph L. (R.L.) Thomas; ***W:*** Ralph L. (R.L.) Thomas, Frank Encarnacao; ***C:*** John Berrie; ***M:*** Alan Reeves.

Young Lady Chatterly 2 🦴½
1985 A poor sequel to the popular MacBride film, with only the name of the Lawrence classic. Chatterly inherits the family mansion and fools around with the servants and any one else who comes along. Unrated version with 13 minutes of deleted footage is also available. **87m/C VHS.** Sybil Danning, Adam West, Harlee MacBride; ***D:*** Alan Roberts.

The Young Land 🦴½ **1959** Less-than-inspiring western does feature a good performance by Hopper as malcontent bully Hatfield Carnes. Carnes kills a respected Mexican in a barroom gunfight in 1848 California and sheriff Jim Ellison (Wayne) is quick to call territorial judge Isham (O'Herlihy) to ensure a fair trial—with the rest of the Spanish-speaking town looking on in skepticism. Based on the story "Frontier Frenzy" by John Reese. **88m/C VHS, DVD.** Dennis Hopper, Patrick Wayne, Dan O'Herlihy, Yvonne Craig, Ken Curtis, Pedro Gonzalez-Gonzalez; ***D:*** Ted Tetzlaff; ***W:*** Norman S. Hall; ***C:*** Winton C. Hoch, Henry Sharp; ***M:*** Dimitri Tiomkin.

The Young Lions 🦴🦴🦴 **1958** A cynical WWII epic following the experiences of a young American officer and a disillusioned Nazi in the war's last days. Martin does fine in his first dramatic role. As the Nazi, Brando sensitively considers the belief that Hitler would save Germany. A realistic anti-war film. **167m/B VHS, DVD, Wide.** Marlon Brando, Montgomery Clift, Dean Martin, Hope Lange, Barbara Rush, Lee Van Cleef, Maximilian Schell, May Britt, Dora Doll, Liliane Montevecchi, Parley Baer, Arthur Franz, Hal Baylor, Richard Gardner, Herbert Rudley, L.Q. (Justus E. McQueen) Jones; ***D:*** Edward Dmytryk; ***W:*** Edward Anhalt; ***C:*** Joe MacDonald; ***M:*** Hugo Friedhofer.

Young Love, First Love 🦴½
1979 TV movie about a young woman who must decide whether to have sex with her boyfriend. Sound familiar? Pretty blah, earnest story, though well cast. **100m/C VHS.** Valerie Bertinelli, Leslie Ackerman, Timothy Hutton, Arlen Dean Snyder, Fionnula Flanagan; ***D:*** Steven Hilliard Stern. **TV**

Young Love—Lemon Popsicle 7 🦴 **1987 (R)** Three hunks stalk the beaches in search of babes. **91m/C VHS.** Yftach Katzur, Zachi Noy, Jonathan Segall, Sonja Martin; ***D:*** Walter Bennett.

Young Man with a Horn 🦴🦴🦴 **1950** Dorothy Baker's novel, which was loosely based on the life of jazz immortal Bix Beiderbecke, was even more loosely adapted for this film, featuring Kirk as an angst-ridden trumpeter who can't seem to hit that mystical "high note." ♫The Very Thought of You; I May be Wrong; The Man I Love; Too Marvelous for Words; With a Song in My Heart; Pretty Baby; I Only Have Eyes for You; Limehouse Blues; Melancholy Rhapsody. **112m/B VHS.** Kirk Douglas, Doris Day, Lauren Bacall, Hoagy Carmichael; ***D:*** Michael Curtiz.

Young Master 🦴🦴 **1980** Chan, searching for his missing brother, is mistaken for a fugitive and has to save himself from bounty hunters and police. Oh, and get the real bad guys so he can clear his name. Chinese with subtitles or dubbed. **90m/C VHS.** *HK* Jackie Chan; ***D:*** Jackie Chan.

Young Mr. Lincoln 🦴🦴🦴½
1939 A classy Hollywood biography of Lincoln in his younger years from log-cabin country boy to idealistic Springfield lawyer. A splendid drama, and one endlessly explicated as an American masterpiece by the French auteur critics in "Cahiers du Cinema." **100m/B VHS.** Henry Fonda, Alice Brady, Marjorie Weaver, Arleen Whelan, Eddie Collins, Ward Bond, Donald Meek, Richard Cromwell, Eddie Quillan, Charles Halton; ***D:*** John Ford; ***W:*** Lamar Trotti.

The Young Nurses 🦴🦴 *Nightingale; Young L.A. Nurses 3* **1973 (R)** The fourth entry in the Roger Corman produced "nurses" series. Three sexy nurses uncover a drug ring run from their hospital, headed by none other than director Fuller. Also present is Moreland, in his last role. Preceded by "The Student Nurses," "Private Duty Nurses," "Night Call Nurses," followed by "Candy Stripe Nurses." Also on video as "Young L.A. Nurses 3." **77m/C VHS.** Jean Manson, Ashley Porter, Angela Gibbs, Zack Taylor, Dick Miller, Jack LaRue, William Joyce, Sally Kirkland, Allan Arbus, Mary Doyle, Don Keefer, Nan Martin, Mantan Moreland, Samuel Fuller; ***D:*** Clinton Kimbrough; ***W:*** Howard R. Cohen; ***M:*** Greg Prestopino.

Young Nurses in Love 🦴 **1989 (R)** Low-budget sex farce in which a foreign spy poses as a nurse to steal sperm from a sperm bank donated by world leaders, celebrities and geniuses. **82m/C VHS.** Jeanne Marie, Alan Fisher, Barbra Robb, James Davies; ***D:*** Chuck Vincent.

The Young One 🦴🦴½ *La Joven; Island of Shame* **1961** Traver (Hamilton) is a black jazz musician who escapes from his southern town when he's wrongly accused of raping a white woman. He hides out on a small island which is used as a private hunting ground for rich sportsmen, overseen by Miller (Scott), the game keeper. Hamilton gets work as the new handyman and becomes close to the young Evalyn (Meersman). When Miller rapes Evalyn, it's Traver who's once again accused until things can be put right. Racist elements are heavy-handed; one of Bunuel's lesser efforts. Based on the story "Travelin' Man" by Peter Matthiessen. **94m/B VHS.** *MX* Bernie Hamilton, Zachary Scott, Kay Meersman, Claudio Brook, Graham Denton; ***D:*** Luis Bunuel; ***W:*** Hugo Butler, Luis Bunuel.

Young People 🦴🦴½ **1940 (G)**
Temple's 12 in this lesser vehicle and almost-adolescence doesn't serve her well with this tired plot. She's an orphan adopted by showbiz team Oakie and Greenwood who've decided to retire to rural life. They even get to put on a show to prove to the small-minded small-towners what a swell trio they are. Temple's last film for 20th-Century Fox does include nostalgic clips from earlier Shirley hits, including "Stand Up and Cheer" and "Curly Top," to explain her character's background. ♫Tra-La-La; Fifth Avenue; I Wouldn't Take a Million; The Mason-Dixon Line; Young People. **78m/C VHS.** Shirley Temple, Jack Oakie, Charlotte Greenwood, Arleen Whelan, George Montgomery, Kathleen Howard; ***D:*** Allan Dwan; ***W:*** Edwin Blum, Don Ettlinger.

The Young Philadelphians 🦴🦴🦴 *The City Jungle* **1959** Ambitious young lawyer Newman works hard at making an impression on the snobbish Philadelphia upper crust. As he schemes and scrambles, he woos debutante Rush and defends buddy Vaughn on a murder charge. Long, but worth it. Part of the "A Night at the Movies" series, this package simulates a 1959 movie evening with a Bugs Bunny cartoon, "People Are Bunny," a newsreel and coming attractions for "The Nun's Story" and "The Hanging Tree." **136m/B VHS.** Paul Newman, Barbara Rush, Alexis Smith, Billie Burke, Brian Keith, John Williams, Otto Kruger, Robert Vaughn; ***D:*** Vincent Sherman; ***C:*** Harry Stradling Sr.; ***M:*** Ernest Gold.

The Young Pioneers 🦴🦴½
1976 Teenaged newlyweds David and Molly Beaton head for the Dakota Territory in the 1870s to secure a homestead. They're faced with a blizzard, an army of grasshoppers that destroy their crop, and Molly's pregnancy and find their survival harder than expected. Pilot TV movie for the brief 1978 series. **96m/C VHS.** Linda Purl, Roger Kern, Robert Donner, Mare Winningham, Robert Hays; ***D:*** Michael O'Herlihy. **TV**

The Young Poisoner's Handbook 🦴🦴🦴 **1994 (R)** Based on the true story of London teenager Graham (O'Conor), who's obsessed with chemistry and at odds with his stepmother. So, he poisons her chocolates and she dies. Sent to Broadmoor prison for the criminally insane, Graham comes under the care of Dr. Ziegler (Sher), who, eight years later, recommends Graham for parole. Now working in a photographic lab, Graham decides to experiment with doctoring his co-workers tea—which results in eight more deaths before Graham is caught. Locked up again, Graham spends his time writing a poisoner's handbook for Dr. Ziegler. Be warned that the sufferings of the poisoned victims are gruesome. **99m/C VHS.** *GB* Hugh O'Conor, Anthony Sher, Ruth Sheen, Charlotte Coleman, Roger Lloyd Pack, Paul Stacey, Samantha Edmonds, Charlie Creed-Miles; ***D:*** Benjamin Ross; ***W:*** Benjamin Ross, Jeff Rawle; ***C:*** Hubert Taczanowski; ***M:*** Robert Lane, Frank Strobel.

Young Sherlock Holmes 🦴🦴
1985 (PG-13) Holmes and Watson meet as schoolboys. They work together on their first case, solving a series of bizarre murders gripping London. Watch through the credits for an interesting plot twist. Promising "what if" sleuth tale crashes and burns, becoming a typical high-tech Spielberg film. Second half bears too strong a resemblance to "Indiana Jones and the Temple of Doom." **109m/C VHS, 8mm.** Nicholas (Nick) Rowe, Alan Cox, Sophie Ward, Freddie Jones, Michael Hordern; ***D:*** Barry Levinson; ***W:*** Chris Columbus; ***M:*** Bruce Broughton.

Young Tiger 1980 (R) First a 90-minute movie never before seen in the U.S. featuring an expert in martial arts who is accused of murder. Next is a 12-minute documentary featuring Jackie Chan, kung-fu sensation, demonstrating his skills. What an evening. **102m/C VHS.** Jackie Chan.

Young Tom Edison 1940 Two teenaged years in the life of Thomas Alva Edison, as he drives his family crazy with his endless experiments on his way to becoming the famed inventor. Rooney manages to be enthusiastic without being overwhelming. Followed by "Edison the Man," with Spencer Tracy in the adult role. **82m/B VHS.** Mickey Rooney, Fay Bainter, George Bancroft, Virginia Weidler, Eugene Pallette, Victor Kilian, Bobby Jordan, Lloyd Corrigan; ***D:*** Norman Taurog; ***W:*** Dore Schary, Bradbury Foote, Hugo Butler.

Young Warlord 1975 Arthur roams western England in 500 AD, leading a band of guerrilla cavalrymen. When the Saxons invade, Arthur unites the tribe, holds off the attack and becomes king. **97m/C VHS.** Oliver Tobias, Michael Gothard, Jack Watson, Brian Blessed; ***D:*** Peter Sasdy.

Young Warriors 1983 (R) Frat boys turn vigilante to avenge a street gang murder. Weird mix of teen sex comedy, insufferable self-righteous preachiness, and violence. **104m/C VHS.** Ernest Borgnine, James Van Patten, Richard Roundtree, Lynda Day George, Dick Shawn; ***D:*** Lawrence Foldes; ***W:*** Lawrence Foldes, Richard Matheson, Russell W. Colgin; ***C:*** Mac Ahlberg.

Young Winston 1972 (PG) Based on Sir Winston Churchill's autobiography "My Early Life: A Roving Commission." Follows him through his school days, journalistic career in Africa, early military career, and his election to Parliament at the age of 26. Ward is tremendous as the prime minister-to-be. **145m/C VHS.** *GB* Simon Ward, Robert Shaw, Anne Bancroft, John Mills, Jack Hawkins, Ian Holm, Anthony Hopkins, Patrick Magee, Edward Woodward, Jane Seymour; ***D:*** Richard Attenborough. Golden Globes '73: Foreign Film.

Youngblood 1986 (R) An underdog beats the seemingly insurmountable odds and becomes a hockey champion. Some enjoyable hockey scenes although the success storyline is predictable. **111m/C VHS, DVD, Wide.** Rob Lowe, Patrick Swayze, Cynthia Gibb, Ed Lauter, George Finn, Fionnula Flanagan, Keanu Reeves; ***D:*** Peter Markle.

Younger & Younger 1994 (R) Jonathan Younger (Sutherland) is forced to run the family storage business after his long-suffering wife Penny (Davidovich) dies. The business starts to fail, even after Jonathan's son (Fraser) arrives to help out, and the widower begins having visions of the woman he mistreated. And each time he sees her she looks younger and more beautiful than ever. **97m/C VHS.** Donald Sutherland, Brendan Fraser, Lolita (David) Davidovich, Sally Kellerman, Julie Delpy, Linda Hunt; ***D:*** Percy Adlon; ***W:*** Percy Adlon, Felix Adlon; ***C:*** Bernd Heinl; ***M:*** Hans Zimmer.

Your Friends & Neighbors 1998 (R) If these are your friends and neighbors, you should reconsider your decisions and address. Six yuppies lie, cheat and deceive their way around the block in La Bute's tale of modern suburban immorality. Weasel Jerry (Stiller) sleeps with Mary (Brenneman), the supposedly happy wife of his old friend Barry (Eckhart). Meanwhile, his live-in girlfriend (Keener) is having a lesbian affair with art gallery employee Cheri (Kinski), and chilly misogynist Cary (Patric) seduces and discards a string of women. Excellent performances by the entire cast bring this nasty group to life and La Bute provides riveting if unsettling material for them. **99m/C VHS, DVD.** Jason Patric, Nastassia Kinski, Ben Stiller, Catherine Keener, Aaron Eckhart, Amy Brenneman; ***D:*** Neil LaBute; ***W:*** Neil LaBute; ***C:*** Nancy Schreiber.

Your Place or Mine 1983 Self-indulgent yuppie pap about middle-aged singles trying to find the right mate. **100m/C VHS.** Bonnie Franklin, Robert Klein, Peter Bonerz, Tyne Daly, Penny Fuller; ***D:*** Robert Day; ***M:*** Gerald Alters. **TV**

Your Ticket Is No Longer Valid 1984 (R) Prurient excuse for a serious drama. Impotent failed businessman has disturbing erotic dreams about his girlfriend. Adapted from a novel by Romain Gary. **96m/C VHS.** *CA* Richard Harris, George Peppard, Jeanne Moreau; ***D:*** George Kaczender.

Your Turn Darling *A Toi de Faire, Mignonne; L'Agente Federale Lemmy Caution; Ladies Man* 1963 French espionage thriller with Constantine once again playing Lemmy Caution, a U.S. secret agent involved with a gang of spies. **93m/B VHS.** *FR* Eddie Constantine, Gaia Germani, Elga Andersen; ***D:*** Bernard Borderie; ***W:*** Bernard Borderie; ***C:*** Henri Persin; ***M:*** Paul Misraki.

You're a Big Boy Now 1966 Kastner, a virginal young man working in the New York Public Library, is told by his father to move out of his house and grow up. On his own, he soon becomes involved with man-hating actress Hartman and a discotheque dancer. A wild and weird comedy. Coppola's commercial directorial debut. **96m/C VHS.** Elizabeth Hartman, Geraldine Page, Peter Kastner, Julie Harris, Rip Torn, Michael Dunn, Tony Bill, Karen Black; ***D:*** Francis Ford Coppola; ***W:*** Francis Ford Coppola.

You're Jinxed, Friend, You've Met Sacramento 1970 The tongue-in-cheek adventures of a cool-headed cowboy as he passes from town to colorful town. Great title, too. **99m/C VHS.** *IT* Ty Hardin, Christian Hay, Jenny Atkins; ***D:*** George Cristallini.

Yours, Mine & Ours 1968 Bigger, better, big screen version of "The Brady Bunch." It's the story of a lovely lady (Ball) with eight kids who marries a a widower (Fonda) who has ten. Imagine the zany shenanigans! Family comedy manages to be both wholesome and funny. Based on a true story. **114m/C VHS, DVD.** Lucille Ball, Henry Fonda, Van Johnson, Tim Matheson, Tom Bosley, Tracy Nelson, Morgan Brittany; ***D:*** Melville Shavelson; ***W:*** Melville Shavelson; ***C:*** Charles F. Wheeler; ***M:*** Fred Karlin.

Youth Aflame woof! *Hoodlum Girls* 1959 Trash film that tells the tale of two sisters—one good, one bad. Poor dialogue and weak performances do, however, make for some great camp. Based on a story by Helen Kiedy. **61m/B VHS.** Joy Reese, Warren Burr, Kay Morley, Michael Owen, Rod Rogers; ***D:*** Elmer Clifton; ***W:*** Elmer Clifton.

Youth of the Beast *Yaju No Seishun* 1963 A cop in disgrace plots to avenge the murder of a friend by infiltrating two rival yakuza gangs and having them destroy each other. Flamboyant visuals and filled with Suzuki's soon-to-be trademarked sex and violence. Japanese with subtitles. **91m/C VHS, Wide.** *JP* Joe Shishido, Shoji Kobayashi, Ichiro Kijima, Misako Suzuki; ***D:*** Seijun Suzuki.

Youth on Parole 1937 Same old story: Boy gets paroled. Girl gets paroled. Parolee meets parolette and romance blossoms as they beat a further rap. **60m/B VHS.** Marian Marsh, Gordon Oliver.

You've Got Mail 1998 (PG) Third remake of "The Shop Around the Corner" ("In the Good Old Summertime" was number 2) finds independent bookstore owner Ryan battling Hank's bookstore conglomerate to stay in business. How does this qualify as a romantic comedy? Because they're flirting with each other anonymously by e-mail. Third teaming of Ryan and Hanks relies, almost too much, on their considerable chemistry. Soundtrack music was chosen for maximum on-screen and record store effect. Must-see for hopeless romantics and fans of Hanks and/or Ryan. Others must decide based on tolerance for meet-cute situations and lightweight romantic comedy. **119m/C VHS, DVD.** Meg Ryan, Tom Hanks, Parker Posey, Greg Kinnear, Jean Stapleton, Steve Zahn, Dave Chappelle, Dabney Coleman, John Randolph, Michael Badalucco, Heather Burns, Hallee Hirsh; ***D:*** Nora Ephron; ***W:*** Nora Ephron; ***C:*** John Lindley; ***M:*** George Fenton.

You've Got to Have Heart *La Moglie Vergine; The Virgin Wife* 1977 (R) A young bridegroom's life gets complicated after he does not sexually satisfy his bride on their wedding night. **98m/C VHS.** *IT* Carroll Baker, Edwige Fenech, Ray Lovelock, Renzo Montagnani; ***D:*** Marino Girolami; ***W:*** Marino Girolami.

You've Ruined Me, Eddie *The Touch of Flesh* 1958 A spoiled rich girl gets knocked up and her boyfriend will never know peace again. Meanwhile, their once quiet town is outraged. **76m/B VHS.** Charles Martin, Robert Cannon, Ted Marshall, Jeanne Rainer, Sue Ellis, Josie Hascall; ***D:*** R. John Hugh; ***C:*** Charles T. O'Rork.

Yukon Flight 1940 A Renfrew of the Mounties adventure. The hero finds illegal gold mining operations and murder in the Yukon. **57m/B VHS.** James Newill, Dave O'Brien, Louise Stanley, Warren Hull, Karl Hackett, Roy Barcroft; ***D:*** Ralph Staub; ***W:*** Edward Halperin; ***C:*** Mack Stengler.

The Yum-Yum Girls 1978 (R) Pair of innocent girls arrive in NYC to pursue their dreams. Gives an inside looks at the fashion industry. Not as funny or as cute as it wants to be. **89m/C VHS.** Judy Landers, Tanya Roberts, Barbara Tully, Michelle Daw; ***D:*** Barry Rosen.

Yuma 1970 An old-style Western about a sheriff (Walker) who rides into town, cleans it up, and saves his own reputation from a plot to discredit him. Dull in places, but action-packed ending saves the day. **73m/C VHS.** Clint Walker, Barry Sullivan, Edgar Buchanan; ***D:*** Ted Post; ***M:*** George Duning. **TV**

Yuri Nosenko, KGB 1986 Fact-based account of a KGB defector and the CIA agent who must determine if he's on the up-and-up. **85m/C VHS.** *GB* Tommy Lee Jones, Oleg Rudnik, Josef Sommer, Ed Lauter, George Morfogen, Stephen D. Newman; ***D:*** Mick Jackson. **TV**

Z 1969 The assassination of a Greek nationalist in the 1960s and its aftermath are portrayed by the notorious political director as a gripping detective thriller. Excellent performances, adequate cinematic techniques, and important politics in this highly acclaimed film. **128m/C VHS.** *FR* Yves Montand, Jean-Louis Trintignant, Irene Papas, Charles Denner, Georges Geret, Jacques Perrin, Francois Perier, Marcel Bozzuffi; ***D:*** Constantin Costa-Gavras; ***W:*** Constantin Costa-Gavras; ***M:*** Mikis Theodorakis. Oscars '69: Film Editing, Foreign Film; Cannes '69: Special Jury Prize, Actor (Trintignant); Golden Globes '70: Foreign Film; N.Y. Film Critics '69: Director (Costa-Gavras), Film; Natl. Soc. Film Critics '69: Film.

Zabriskie Point 1970 (R) Antonioni's first U.S. feature. A desultory, surreal examination of the American way of life. Worthy but difficult. Climaxes with a stylized orgy in Death Valley. **112m/C VHS.** Mark Frechette, Daria Halprin, Paul Fix, Rod Taylor, Harrison Ford, G.D. Spradlin; ***D:*** Michelangelo Antonioni; ***W:*** Michelangelo Antonioni, Sam Shepard, Fred Gardner, Tonino Guerra, Clare Peploe.

Zachariah 1970 (PG) A semi-spoof '60s rock western, wherein two gunfighters given to pursuing wealth-laden bands of outlaws separate and experience quixotic journeys through the cliched landscape. Scripted by members of The Firesign Theater and featuring appearances by Country Joe and The Fish, The New York Rock Ensemble, and The James Gang. **93m/C VHS, DVD, Wide.** Don Johnson, John Rubinstein, Pat Quinn, Dick Van Patten, William Challee, Country Joe McDonald, Elvin Jones, Doug Kershaw, Lawrence Kubik, Hank Worden; ***D:*** George Englund; ***W:*** Peter Bergman, Joe Massot, Phil(ip) Proctor, Philip Austin, David Ossman; ***C:*** Jorge Stahl Jr.; ***M:*** Jimmie Haskell.

Zack & Reba 1998 (R) When Reba (Murphy) calls off her wedding a week before the ceremony, her fiance commits suicide. Guilt-ridden, Reba returns to her hometown of Spooner and its eccentric residents, which include shotgun-toting grandma, Beulah (Reynolds), and her grief-stricken grandson Zack (Flanery), who can't seem to get over the death of his wife. Naturally, Beulah thinks Zack and Reba are just made for each other. **91m/C VHS, DVD.** Sean Patrick Flanery, Brittany Murphy, Debbie Reynolds, Kathy Najimy, Martin Mull, Michael Jeter; ***D:*** Nicole Bettauer; ***W:*** Jay Stapleton; ***C:*** Mark Irwin; ***M:*** Joel McNeely.

Zafarinas *Moriras en Chafarinas* 1994 (R) Zafarinas is an ancient walled city on the island of Melilla that houses a military barracks. Two suspicious deaths force Commander Contreras (Ladoire) to release zealous corporal Jaime (Sanz) and Corporal Cidraque (Albala) from the stockades to investigate. Then there's a third death and things just aren't what they seem. Spanish with subtitles. **85m/C VHS.** *SP* Jorge Sanz, Javier Albala, Oscar Ladoire, Maria Barranco; ***D:*** Pedro Olea; ***W:*** Pedro Olea, Fernando Lalana; ***C:*** Paco Femenia.

Zalmen or the Madness of God 1975 Elie Wiesel's mystical story about a rabbi's struggle against religious persecution in post-Stalin Russia. **120m/C VHS.** Joseph Wiseman.

Zandalee woof! 1991 (R) The sexual adventures of a bored sexy young woman who has a fling with her husband's friend. Bad script, graphic sex. Also available in an unrated version. **100m/C VHS.** Nicolas Cage, Judge Reinhold, Erika Anderson, Viveca Lindfors, Aaron Neville, Joe Pantoliano, Ian Abercrombie, Marisa Tomei, Zach Galligan; ***D:*** Sam Pillsbury; ***W:*** Mari Kornhauser.

Zandy's Bride 1974 (PG) Basic story about a rancher who sents for a mail-order bride. She's shocked by his ill-treatment of her and stands up to his bullying, thus winning his respect and love. Beautiful scenery, courtesy of Big Sur, California, but predictable all-around and essentially a waste of an experienced cast. Based on the novel "The Stranger" by Lillian Bos Ross. **97m/C VHS.** Gene Hackman, Liv Ullmann, Eileen Heckart, Harry Dean Stanton, Joe Santos, Sam Bottoms, Susan Tyrrell, Frank Cady; ***D:*** Jan Troell; ***W:*** Marc Norman; ***C:*** Jordan Cronenweth; ***M:*** Michael Franks.

The Zany Adventures of Robin Hood 1984 Hackneyed spoof of the Robin Hood legend. Medieval man robs from the rich to help the poor. Not nearly as funny as. Mel Brooks' TV series that spoofed "Robin Hood." **95m/C VHS.** George Segal, Morgan Fairchild, Roddy McDowall, Roy Kinnear, Janet Suzman, Tom Baker; ***D:*** Ray Austin.

Zapped! 1982 (R) Teen genius discovers he possesses telekinetic powers. He does the natural thing, using his talent to remove clothing from nearby females. A teen boy's dream come true. **98m/C VHS.** Scott Baio, Willie Aames, Robert Mandan, Felice Schachter, Scatman Crothers, Roger Bowen, Marya Small, Greg Bradford, Hilary Beane, Sue Ane Langdon, Heather Thomas, Merritt Butrick, LaWanda Page, Rosanne Katon; ***D:*** Robert J. Rosenthal; ***M:*** Charles Fox.

Zapped Again 1989 (R) The lame-brained sequel to 1982's "Zapped" about a high schooler who has telekinetic powers and lust on his mind. **93m/C VHS, 8mm.** Todd Eric Andrews, Kelli Williams, Reed Rudy, Linda Blair, Karen Black, Lyle Alzado; ***D:*** Doug Campbell.

Zardoz 1973 A surreal parable of the far future (2293), when Earth society is broken into strict classes: a society of intellectuals known as the Eternals, a society of savages called the Brutals, and an elite unit of killers, naturally named the Exterminators, who keep the order. The Exterminators worship a stone god named Zardoz, but killer Zed (Connery) discovers that it's merely a futuristic version of "The Wizard of Oz" and that the Eternals have been manipulating the social order. His presence causes chaos and destruction (but he does get all the babes). Visually interesting but pretentious. **105m/C VHS, DVD, Wide.** *GB* Sean Connery, Charlotte Rampling, John Alderton, Sara Kestelman, Sally Anne Newton, Niall Buggy, Christopher Casson, Bosco Hogan, Jessica Swift; ***D:*** John Boorman; ***W:*** John Boorman; ***C:*** Geoffrey Unsworth; ***M:*** David Munrow.

Zarkorr! The Invader 1996 (PG) Aliens studying earth decide humans need a challenge (like we don't have enough problems of our own) so they send a 185-foot tall, laser-eyed monster to crush (American) cities and cause general terror in the population. And who's our hero? A postal worker—aided by a five-inch tall alien girl. Low-budget spoof has its moments, but eventually wears thin. **80m/C VHS.** Rhys Pugh, Deprise Grossman, Mark Hamilton, Charles Schneider, Eileen Wesson; ***D:*** Aaron Osborne; ***W:*** Benjamin Carr; ***C:*** Joe C. Maxwell; ***M:*** Richard Band.

Zatoichi: Master Ichi and a Chest of Gold 🦴🦴 **1964** A violent thriller about a blind gambler and former samurai who tries to clear his name after being framed for a gold robbery. Adapted from a novel by Kazuo Miyagawa. In Japanese with English subtitles. **83m/C VHS.** *JP* Shintaro Katsu; ***D:*** Kazuo Ikehiro.

Zatoichi: The Blind Swordsman and the Chess Expert 🦴🦴 **1965** Zatoichi, the blind gambler and former samurai, befriends a master chess player and gets involved with Japanese gangsters. In Japanese with English subtitles. **87m/C VHS.** *JP* Shintaro Katsu; ***D:*** Kenji Misumi.

Zatoichi: The Blind Swordsman and the Fugitives 🦴🦴 **1968** This time Zatoichi, the blind masseur and master swordsman, is pitted against a band of outlaws. When the local bandits brutalize the countryside Zatoichi steps in to defend the weak and faces a showdown with outlaw leader Genpachiro. In Japanese with English subtitles. **82m/C VHS.** *JP* Shintaro Katsu, Yumiko Nogawa, Kayo Mikimoto, Kyosuke Machida; ***D:*** Kimiyoshi Yasuda.

Zatoichi: The Blind Swordsman's Vengeance 🦴🦴 **1966** Zatoichi defends a dying man against a group of gangsters who have taken over an isolated village. In Japanese with English subtitles. **83m/C VHS.** *JP* Shintaro Katsu, Shigeru Amachi, Kei Sato, Mayumi Ogawa; ***D:*** Tokuzo Tanaka.

Zatoichi: The Life and Opinion of Masseur Ichi 🦴🦴 **1962** The first film in the action series about the Zen-like blind masseur, gambler, and swordsman. Zatoichi is drawn into a revenge match between two ruthless gangs. When one gang tries to hire him the other hires a savage killer. This sets in motion a war between the yakuza gangs and mercenary samurai. In Japanese with English subtitles. **96m/C VHS.** *JP* Shintaro Katsu, Masayo Mari, Ryuzo Shimada, Gen Mitamura, Shigeru Amachi; ***D:*** Kenji Misumi.

Zatoichi vs. Yojimbo 🦴🦴🦴½ *Zatoichi Meets Yojimbo; Zato Ichi To Yojimbo* **1970** The legendary blind warrior-samurai, Zatoichi, wants to retire, but his village is being held captive by outlaws. He is forced to fight Yojimbo, the crude wandering samurai without a master, and the sparks really fly! This was a comic send-up of Akiro Kurosawa's "Yojimbo" with Mifune recreating his role here and playing it for laughs. Subtitled. **90m/C VHS.** *JP* Toshiro Mifune, Shintaro Katsu, Osamu Takizawa; ***D:*** Kihachi Okamoto.

Zatoichi: Zatoichi's Flashing Sword 🦴🦴 **1964** Blind swordsman Zatoichi gets caught up in a feud between two competing yakuza bosses. When Zatoichi declares his alliegence to Tsumugi, the unhappy Yasu tries to get his revenge. In Japanese with English subtitles. **82m/C VHS.** *JP* Shintaro Katsu, Mayumi Nagisa, Naoko Kubo, Ryutaro Gami, Yutaka Nakamura; ***D:*** Kazuo Ikehiro.

Zazie dans le Metro 🦴🦴🦴½ *Zazie in the Underground; Zazie in the Subway* **1961** One of Malle's early movies, this is one of the best of the French New Wave comedies. A young girl, wise beyond her years, visits her drag queen uncle in Paris. She wants to ride the subway, but the ensuing hilarious adventures keep her from her goal. In French with English subtitles. **92m/C VHS.** *FR* Catherine Demonget, Philippe Noiret, Carla Marlier; ***W:*** Louis Malle.

Zebra Force 🦴 **1976 (R)** Group of army veterans embark on a personal battle against organized crime, using their military training with deadly precision. Non-distinguished substandard action-adventure. **81m/C VHS.** Mike Lane, Richard X. Slattery, Rockne Tarkington, Glenn Wilder, Anthony Caruso; ***D:*** Joe Tornatore.

Zebra in the Kitchen 🦴🦴½ **1965** A 12-year-old boy living in a small town is upset when he sees the run-down condition of the local zoo. So he decides to set all the animals free, which causes pandemonium in the town. Pleasant family fare. **92m/C VHS.** Jay North, Martin Milner, Andy Devine, Joyce Meadows, Jim Davis; ***D:*** Ivan Tors.

Zebra Lounge 🦴🦴 **2001** Wendy (Swanson) and Alan (Baldwin) Barnet feel their marriage has gotten dull, so they place an ad in a swingers' magazine that leads them to the Zebra Lounge. There they meet the more experienced Jack (Daddo) and Louise (Ledford) Bauer who take them on a new sexual trip. But the Barnets soon discover that their new partners are not the emotionally stable people to get involved with. **92m/C VHS, DVD, Wide.** *CA* Stephen Baldwin, Kristy Swanson, Cameron Daddo, Brandy Ledford; ***D:*** Keri Skogland; ***W:*** Claire Montgomery, Monte Montgomery; ***C:*** Barry Parrell. **VIDEO**

Zebrahead 🦴🦴🦴 **1992 (R)** Zack and Nikki are two high schoolers in love—which would be okay except Zack's white and Nikki's black. Writer/director Drazan's expressive debut features one of last appearances by Sharkey as Zack's dad. Outstanding performances by the young and largely unknown cast, particularly Rapaport and Wright, and a great musical score enrich the action. Filmed on location in Detroit, with plenty of authentic Motown scenery to chew on, including Cody High School and a shootout at the eastside Skateland. Developed with assistance by the Sundance Institute. **102m/C VHS, DVD.** Michael Rapaport, N'Bushe Wright, Ray Sharkey, DeShonn Castle, Ron Johnson, Marsha Florence, Paul Butler, Abdul Hassan Sharif, Dan Ziskie, Candy Ann Brown, Helen Shaver, Luke Reilly, Martin Priest, Kevin Corrigan; ***D:*** Tony Drazan; ***W:*** Tony Drazan; ***C:*** Maryse Alberti; ***M:*** Taj Mahal. Sundance '92: Filmmakers Trophy.

A Zed & Two Noughts 🦴🦴🦴 **1988** A serio-comic essay by the acclaimed British filmmaker. Twin zoologists, after their wives are killed in an accident, explore their notions of death by, among other things, filming the decay of animal bodies absconded from the zoo. Heavily textured and experimental; Greenaway's second feature film. **115m/C VHS, DVD, Wide.** *GB* Eric Deacon, Brian Deacon, Joss Ackland, Andrea Ferreol, Frances Barber; ***D:*** Peter Greenaway; ***W:*** Peter Greenaway; ***C:*** Sacha Vierny; ***M:*** Michael Nyman.

Zeder 🦴🦴½ *Revenge of the Dead; Zeder: Voices from Beyond* **1983** A young novelist (Lavia) discovers fragments of curious documents on the ribbon of a used typewriter bought by his wife (Canovas). He comes to think that they suggest research into immortality. The rest of the film combines elements of suspense with horror in a fairly slow-moving, serious plot with references to Val Lewton's "Cat People." **98m/C VHS, DVD.** *IT* Gabriele Lavia, Anne Canovos; ***D:*** Pupi Avati; ***W:*** Pupi Avati, Antonio Avati, Maurizio Costanzo.

Zelig 🦴🦴🦴½ **1983 (PG)** Documentary spoof stars Allen as Leonard Zelig, the famous "Chameleon Man" of the 1920s, whose personality was so vague he would assume the characteristics of those with whom he came into contact, and who had a habit of showing up among celebrities and at historic events. Filmed in black-and-white; intersperses bits of newsreel and photographs with live action. Allen-style clever filmmaking at its best. **79m/B VHS, DVD, Wide.** Woody Allen, Mia Farrow, Susan Sontag, Saul Bellow, Irving Howe; ***D:*** Woody Allen; ***W:*** Woody Allen; ***C:*** Gordon Willis. N.Y. Film Critics '83: Cinematog.

Zelly & Me 🦴🦴🦴 *Phoebe* **1988 (PG)** A strange little drama about a young orphan living with her maniacally possessive grandmother, who forces the child into her own interior life through humiliation and isolation from anyone she cares for. Well-acted and interesting film that suffers from an overly introspective plot and confusing gaps in the narrative. Look for director Lynch on the other side of the camera. **87m/C VHS.** Isabella Rossellini, Alexandra Johnes, David Lynch, Glynis Johns, Kaiulani Lee, Joe Morton; ***D:*** Tina Rathborne; ***W:*** Tina Rathborne; ***C:*** Mikael Salomon; ***M:*** Pino Donaggio.

Zentropa 🦴🦴 **1992 (R)** Clever cinematic allusions and visuals aside, this is essentially a conventional thriller. German-American pacifist Leopold travels to Germany in 1945 to help in the postwar rebuilding. He finds work as a sleeping-car conductor for a giant railway system called Zentropa and finds himself romancing the mysterious Katharina, who draws the hapless Leopold into an intrigue involving Nazi sympathizers. Director von Trier uses the voice of Von Sydow as an omniscient narrator to address the audience and move the story along. Filmed primarily in black-and-white with bursts of color denoting dramatic moments. In English and German with English subtitles. **112m/C VHS.** *GE* Jean-Marc Barr, Barbara Sukowa, Udo Kier, Eddie Constantine; ***D:*** Lars von Trier; ***W:*** Niels Vorsel, Lars von Trier; ***Nar:*** Max von Sydow.

Zeppelin 🦴🦴½ **1971 (G)** During WWI, the British enlist the aid of York as a double agent. His mission is to steal Germany's plans for a super-dirigible. Accompanying the Germans on the craft's maiden voyage, York discovers they are actually on a mission to steal British treasures. Although the script is poor, the battle scenes and the airship itself are very impressive. **102m/C VHS.** *GB* Michael York, Elke Sommer, Peter Carsten,. Marius Goring, Anton Diffring, Andrew Keir, Rupert Davies, Alexandra Stewart; ***D:*** Etienne Perier.

Zeram 🦴🦴 *Zeiram; Zeiramu* **1991** Zeram is a giant renegade space alien lured to earth by a female bounty hunter. How does she expect to capture it? Why with a warp machine, space bazooka, electric shield, and a computer named Bob, of course. Dubbed. **92m/C VHS, DVD.** *JP* Yuko Moriyama, Yukihiro Hotaru, Kunihiko Ida; ***D:*** Keita Amemiya; ***W:*** Hajime Matsumoto; ***C:*** Hiroshi Kidokoro; ***M:*** Hirokazu Ohta.

Zeram 2 🦴🦴🦴 *Zeiram 2; Zeiramu* **1994** Moriyama returns to play Investigator Iria, an intergalactic bounty hunter, who is assisted by her computer, Bob. Iria has been given a new android as a trainee, but it malfunctions during a battle and turns on her. The android is infected with a Zeram, an evil alien force. To make matters worse, Iria's partner Fujikuro (Sabu) has betrayed her and is trying to steal an ancient artifact which Iria possesses. Trapped and in need of assistance, Iria calls on her old friends Teppei (Iida) and Kamiya (Hotaru), two bumbling electricians to help her. The film is non-stop fun, as it mixes amazing action scenes, gross monsters, and slapstick comedy seamlessly to create an entertaining sci-fi treat. **100m/C DVD, Wide.** *JP* Yukihiro Hotaru, Kunihiko Iida, Yuko Moriyama; ***D:*** Keito Amamiya.

Zero **1984** WWII story about the building of the zero fighter that was used to devastating effect in the invasion of Pearl Harbor. **128m/C VHS.** Yuzo Kayama, Tetsuro Tamba; ***D:*** Toshio Masuda.

Zero Boys woof! **1986 (R)** Teenage survivalists in the Californian wilderness are stalked by a murderous lunatic. Exploitative and mean-spirited. **89m/C VHS, DVD.** Daniel Hirsch, Kelli Maroney, Nicole Rio, Joe Phelan; ***D:*** Nico Mastorakis; ***W:*** Nico Mastorakis, Fred C. Perry; ***C:*** Steve Shaw; ***M:*** Stanley Myers, Hans Zimmer.

Zero Degrees Kelvin 🦴🦴½ *Zero Kelvin; Kjaerlighetens Kjotere* **1995** Brrrr! Get the ice scraper ready, because you may have to clear off your TV screen in this chilly tale of trappers in 1920s Greenland. Henrik Larsen (Eidsvold), a poet living in Oslo, decides to join the band of trappers after his girlfriend Gertrude (Martens) spurns his marriage proposal. On his arrival in the stark and frozen landscape, he is forced to share a cabin with the stoic, silent Holm (Sundquist) and the lewd, violent Randbaek (Skarsgard). Randbaek holds the newcomer and his city-boy ways in disdain, creating an air of tension and menace that inevitably results in a clash between the two. Instead of dwelling on the action aspect, director Moland uses the minimalist landscape to echo the psychological battles the men must face with the frigid terrain and between themselves. Norwegian with subtitles. **113m/C VHS, DVD, Wide.** *NO* Gard B. Eidsvold, Stellan Skarsgard, Bjorn Sundquist, Camilla Martens; ***D:*** Hans Petter Moland; ***W:*** Hans Petter Moland, Lars Bill Lundheim; ***C:*** Philip Ogaard; ***M:*** Terje Rypdal.

Zero Effect 🦴🦴½ **1997 (R)** A cross between Howard Hughes and Sherlock Holmes, brilliant, eccentric detective Daryl Zero (Pullman), who, along with his harried helper Steve Arlo (Stiller), takes on the case of a blackmailed timber tycoon (O'Neal) in this comedic whodunit. The normally reclusive sleuth bites the bullet and agrees to trek to Oregon to personally investigate the particularly intriguing case, which also involves an attractive paramedic (Dickens). Pullman pulls off another quirky leading man performance with flair. Stiller is stellar as the exasperated assistant. Fresh idea and hip humor mark this debut for 22-year-old writer/director Kasdan, son of director Lawrence Kasdan. **150m/C VHS, DVD.** Bill Pullman, Ben Stiller, Ryan O'Neal, Kim Dickens, Angela Featherstone; ***D:*** Jake Kasdan; ***W:*** Jake Kasdan; ***C:*** Bill Pope.

Zero for Conduct 🦴🦴🦴🦴 *Zero de Conduit* **1933** Vigo's classic French fantasy about an outrageous rebellion of schoolboys against bureaucratic adults. More of a visual poem than a drama, it inspired Lindsay Anderson's "If...." One of only four films created by Vigo before his early death. Banned across Europe at release. In French with English subtitles. **49m/B VHS.** *FR* Jean Daste, Robert Le Flon, Louis Lef'evre, Constantin Kelber, Gerard de Bedarieux; ***D:*** Jean Vigo; ***W:*** Jean Vigo; ***C:*** Boris Kaufman.

Zero Patience 🦴🦴 **1994** Yes, it's an audacious film musical about AIDS myths and ghosts and Victorian explorers—among other things. Infamous Patient Zero (Fauteux) is the Canadian flight attendant reputed to have carried the virus to North America. Ghostly Zero pleads for someone to tell his story and his cause is taken up by Victorian explorer Sir Richard Francis Burton (Robinson), who happens to have achieved eternal life after an encounter with the Fountain of Youth, and who is also preparing an exhibit on contagious diseases. Sharp mix of politics, humor, and fantasy. **100m/C VHS.** *CA* John Robinson, Normand Fauteux, Dianne Heatherington, Ricardo Keens-Douglas; ***D:*** John Greyson; ***W:*** John Greyson; ***M:*** Glenn Schellenberg.

Zero Population Growth 🦴½ *Z.P.G* **1972** In the 21st century the government has decreed that no babies may be born for a 30-year span in order to control the population. But Chaplin and Reed secretly have a child and when they are discovered are sent to be executed. Can they escape? Maudlin and simplistic. **95m/C VHS.** Oliver Reed, Geraldine Chaplin, Diane Cilento, Don Gordon; ***D:*** Michael Campus; ***W:*** Frank De Felitta, Max Ehrlich.

Zero to Sixty 🦴 **1978 (PG)** Newly divorced man finds his car has been repossessed for nonpayment. Seeking out the manager of the finance company, he gets a job as a repo man with a sassy 16-year-old girl as his assistant. Repartee develops, stuff happens, and the movie ends. **96m/C VHS.** Darren McGavin, Sylvia Miles, Denise Nickerson, Joan Collins; ***D:*** Don Weis; ***M:*** John Beal.

Zero Tolerance 🦴🦴½ **1993 (R)** FBI agent Jeff Douglas (Patrick) is assigned to travel to Mexico and pick up a drug-runner who works for the White Hand cartel, whose latest product is liquid heroin. When they are ambushed Douglas is forced to carry a shipment of drugs across the border—the lives of his wife and child hang in the balance. But after the dirty deed is done, Douglas finds his family has been murdered anyway. So he sets out to execute the cartel druglords. **92m/C VHS.** Robert Patrick, Miles O'Keeffe, Mick Fleetwood, Titus Welliver, Jeffrey Anderson-Gunter, Gustav Vintas, Michael Gregory, Maurice Lamont; ***D:*** Joseph Merhi; ***W:*** Jacobsen Hart.

Zertigo Diamond Caper ☾ 1982 Utilizing his heightened senses, a blind boy solves a diamond caper and proves his mother's innocence. **50m/C VHS.** Adam Rich, David Groh, Jane Elliot.

Zeta One ☾ *Alien Women; The Love Factor* **1969** A soft-core British science fiction yarn about scantily clad alien babes and the special agent who's trying to uncover their secret. It's all very sketchy, silly and campy, though pleasantly cast with plenty of lovely British actresses. **86m/C VHS, DVD.** *GB* James Robertson Justice, Charles Hawtrey, Robin Hawdon, Anna Gael, Brigitte Skay, Dawn Addams, Valerie Leon, Yutte Stensgaard, Wendy Lingham, Rita Webb, Caroline Hawkins; ***D:*** Michael Cort; ***W:*** Michael Cort, Christopher Neame, Alistain McKenzie; ***C:*** Jack Atcheler; ***M:*** John Hawksworth.

Zeus and Roxanne ☾☾ **1996 (PG)** Hey, I know! Let's combine "Flipper" and "Benji" with "The Parent Trap!" You know, for the kids! Marine biologist and single mom Mary Beth (Quinlan) meets her unconventional (and conveniently widowed) new neighbor Terry (Guttenberg) and his dog Zeus. Cuteness ensues. Mary Beth's daughters and Terry's young son go about getting the two adults together. Meanwhile, Zeus and Roxanne, Mary Beth's dolphin, strike up a unique friendship of their own. Showing up to provide drama is evil guy Claude (Vosloo), who is vying for the same grant as Mary Beth. Unlikely animal couple steals the show, and the story would have benefitted from focusing on the entertaining bond between those two and less on the human romance. Not much appeal for anyone over the age of nine. **98m/C VHS, DVD, Wide.** Kathleen Quinlan, Steve Guttenberg, Arnold Vosloo, Miko Hughes, Dawn McMillan, Majandra Delfino; ***D:*** George Miller; ***W:*** Tom Benedek; ***C:*** David Connell; ***M:*** Bruce Rowland.

Ziegfeld Follies ☾☾½ **1946** A lavish revue of musical numbers and comedy sketches featuring many MGM stars of the WWII era. Highlights include Astaire and Kelly's only duet and a Astaire-Bremer ballet number. ♫Bring on Those Wonderful Men; Bring on Those Beautiful Girls; The Drinking Song; La Traviata; This Heart is Mine; Love; When Television Comes; There's Beauty Everywhere; The Babbitt and the Bromide. **115m/C VHS.** Fred Astaire, Judy Garland, Gene Kelly, Red Skelton, Fanny Brice, William Powell, Jimmy Durante, Edward Arnold, Lucille Bremer, Hume Cronyn, Victor Moore, Lena Horne, Lucille Ball, Esther Williams; ***D:*** Vincente Minnelli; ***C:*** Charles Rosher.

Ziegfeld Girl ☾☾☾ **1941** Three star-struck girls are chosen for the Ziegfeld follies and move on to success and heartbreak. Lavish costumes and production numbers in the MGM style. ♫You Stepped Out of a Dream; I'm Always Chasing Rainbows; Minnie from Trinidad; Mr. Gallagher & Mr. Shean; You Never Looked So Beautiful. **131m/B VHS.** James Stewart, Judy Garland, Hedy Lamarr, Lana Turner, Tony Martin, Jackie Cooper, Ian Hunter, Charles Winninger, Al Shean, Edward Everett Horton, Philip Dorn, Paul Kelly, Eve Arden, Dan Dailey, Fay Holden, Felix Bressart, Mae Busch, Reed Hadley; ***D:*** Robert Z. Leonard.

ZigZag ☾☾☾ **2002 (R)** Louis "ZigZag" Fletcher (Jones) is an autistic 15-year-old who lives in fear of his dad Fletcher (Sniper), an abusive drug addict. ZigZag works after school as a dishwasher for the foul-mouthed Toad (Platt) and his one caring friend is his volunteer Big Brother, Dean (Leguizamo), who has cancer. As if things are bad enough, after a confrontation with Fletcher, ZigZag steals $9,000 from Toad to give to his dad and Dean goes to a loan shark (Goss) to get the money to return to Toad's safe before he realizes it's missing. Based on the novel by Landon J. Napoleon; Goyer's directorial debut. The sort of story that can easily descend into sap but doesn't thanks to some fearless performances and Goyer's tight control. **101m/C VHS, DVD.** Sam Jones III, John Leguizamo, Wesley Snipes, Oliver Platt, Natasha Lyonne, Sherman Augustus, Luke Goss, Michael Greyeyes, Elizabeth Pena; ***D:*** David S. Goyer; ***W:*** David S. Goyer; ***C:*** James L. Carter; ***M:*** Grant Lee Phillips.

Zipperface ☾ **1992** A Palm Beach serial killer is making mincemeat of the local prostitutes. In order to capture the scum, the prerequisite beautiful police detective goes undercover only to find herself the killer's biggest thrill. **90m/C VHS.** Dona Adams, Jonathan Mandell, David Clover, Trisha Melynkov, Richard Vidan, Harold Cannon, Bruce Brown, Rikki Brando, Timothy D. Lechner, John Dagnen; ***D:*** Mansour Pourmand; ***W:*** Barbara Bishop; ***C:*** F. Smith Martin; ***M:*** Jim Halfpenny.

Zis Boom Bah ☾½ **1942** Musical-comedy star buys a cafe for her college son. He and his friends transform the place into a restaurant-theatre with predictable results. ♫Annabella; It Makes No Difference When You're In the Army; Put Your Trust in the Moon; Zis Boom Bah; Good News Tomorrow; I've Learned to Smile Again. **61m/B VHS.** Peter Lind Hayes, Mary Healy, Grace Hayes, Huntz Hall, Benny Rubin.

The Zodiac Killer ☾½ **1971 (R)** Based on a true story, this tells the violent tale of the San Francisco murders that occurred in the late 1960s. Doesn't have the suspense it should. **87m/C VHS.** Tom Pittman, Hal Reed, Bob Jones, Ray Lynch; ***D:*** Tom Hanson.

Zoltan...Hound of Dracula ☾½ *Dracula's Dog* **1978** The vampire and his bloodthirsty dog go to Los Angeles to find the last of Count Dracula's living descendants. Campy and just original enough to make it almost worth watching. **85m/C VHS.** Michael Pataki, Reggie Nalder, Jose Ferrer, Jan Shutan, Libbie Chase, John Levin, Cleo Harrington, Simmy Bow, JoJo D'Amore; ***D:*** Albert Band; ***W:*** Frank Ray Perilli; ***C:*** Bruce Logan; ***M:*** Andrew Belling.

Zombie ☾ *Zombie Flesh-Eaters; Island of the Living Dead; Zombi 2* **1980** Italian-made white-men-in-the-Caribbean-with-flesh-eating-zombies cheapie. **91m/C VHS, DVD.** *IT* Tisa Farrow, Ian McCulloch, Richard Johnson, Al Cliver, Auretta Gay, Olga Karlatos, Stefania D'Amario, Lucio Fulci, Ugo Bologna, Monica Zanchi; ***D:*** Lucio Fulci; ***W:*** Elisa Briganti, Dardano Sacchetti; ***C:*** Sergio Salvati; ***M:*** Fabio Frizzi, Giorgio Tucci.

Zombie and the Ghost Train ☾☾ *Zombie ja Kummitusjuna* **1991** Absurdist punk comedy about the vicissitudes of a down-and-out bass player. Finnish with subtitles. **88m/C VHS.** *FI* ***D:*** Mika Kaurismaki; ***W:*** Mika Kaurismaki; ***C:*** Olli Varja; ***M:*** Mauri Sumen.

The Zombie Army ☾ **1993** Tough drill sergeant tries to whip a bunch of raw female recruits up to muster for a special mission. Toward that end, the government has conveniently bought a defunct lunatic asylum as a training ground. Only problem is that a few of the former inmates have been left behind and are able to menace the troops with their penchant for psychotic weirdness. **80m/C VHS.** Eileen Saddow.

Zombie High ☾ *The School That Ate My Brain* **1987 (R)** Students at a secluded academy are being lobotomized by the school president. Mindless, in two senses of the word. **91m/C VHS.** Virginia Madsen, Richard Cox, Kay E. Kuter, James Wilder, Sherilyn Fenn, Paul Williams, Scott Coffey, Clare Carey, Walter Addison; ***D:*** Ron Link; ***W:*** Aziz Ghazal, Tim Doyle, Elizabeth Passerelli; ***C:*** Brian Coyne, David Lux; ***M:*** Daniel May.

Zombie Island Massacre ☾ **1984 (R)** In this trying film, tourists travel to see a voodoo ritual, and then are systematically butchered by the rite-inspired zombies. Featuring former congressional wife and "Playboy" magazine model Jenrette. **89m/C VHS.** Rita Jenrette, David Broadnax; ***D:*** John N. Carter.

Zombie Lake ☾ *El Lago de los Muertos Vivientes; The Lake of the Living Dead* **1980** Killed in an ambush by villagers during WWII, a group of Nazi soldiers turned zombies reside in the town's lake, preying on unsuspecting swimmers, especially dog paddling nude young women. Laughable FX, almost bad enough to be good. From the team that produced "Oasis of the Zombies." **90m/C VHS, DVD, Wide.** *FR SP* Howard Vernon, Pierre Escourrou, Anouchka, Anthony (Jose, J. Antonio, J.A.) Mayans, Nadine Pascale, Jean Rollin; ***D:*** J.A. Laser, Jean Rollin; ***W:*** A. L. Mariaux, Julian Esteban.

Zombie Nightmare woof! **1986 (R)** A murdered teenager is revived by a voodoo queen and slaughters his punk-teen assailants. Cheap and stupid just about sums this one up. Music by Motorhead, Death Mask, Girlschool, and Thor. **89m/C VHS.** Adam West, Jon Mikl Thor, Tia Carrere, Frank Dietz, Linda Singer, Mandn E. Turbride, Hamibh McEwen; ***D:*** John Bravman.

Zombies of Moratau woof! **1957** A diver and his girlfriend seek to retrieve an undersea treasure of diamonds protected by zombies. So boring you'll want to die. **70m/B VHS.** Gregg (Hunter) Palmer, Allison Hayes, Jeff Clark, Autumn Russel, Joel Ashley; ***D:*** Edward L. Cahn.

Zombies of the Stratosphere *Satan's Satellites* **1952** A serial in 12 chapters in which a cosmic policeman fights Zombies attempting to blow the Earth out of orbit. Also available in a 93-minute, colorized version. **152m/B VHS.** Judd Holdren, Aline Towne, Leonard Nimoy, John Crawford, Ray Boyle; ***D:*** Fred Brannon.

Zombies on Broadway ☾☾½ *Loonies on Broadway* **1944** Two press agents travel to the Caribbean in search of new talent, but find Lugosi performing experiments on people and turning them into sequel material. RKO hoped this would be equally successful follow-up to "I Walked with a Zombie." **68m/B VHS.** Wally Brown, Alan Carney, Bela Lugosi, Anne Jeffreys, Sheldon Leonard, Frank Jenks, Russell Hopton, Joseph (Joe) Vitale, Ian Wolfe, Louis Jean Heydt, Darby Jones, Sir Lancelot; ***D:*** Gordon Douglas; ***W:*** Robert Kent, Lawrence Kimble; ***C:*** Jack MacKenzie; ***M:*** Roy Webb.

Zone of the Dead ☾ **1978** A mortician is using his morgue for other than embalming—and it isn't pretty! **81m/C VHS.** John Ericson, Ivor Francis, Charles Aidman, Bernard Fox.

Zone 39 ☾☾ **1996** Sci-fi thriller vibrates with impending doom. A 40-year war results in an uneasy peace between two rival factions. Guard Leo (Phelps) has gone a little loopy after the death of his wife and is assigned to patrol the remote outpost of Zone 39, where a severe contamination is spreading. Thanks to the illegal drug Novan that Leo keeps taking, he's also experiencing flashbacks of his wife and other ghostly figures. The spectacularly desolate setting is a dry salt lake located in Woomera, Australia. **93m/C VHS.** *AU* Peter Phelps, William Zappa, Caroline Beck, Brad Byquar, Alex Menglet, Jeff Kovski; ***D:*** John Tatoulis; ***W:*** Deborah Parsons; ***C:*** Peter Zakhavor; ***M:*** Burkhard Dallwitz.

Zone Troopers ☾½ **1984 (PG)** Five American G.I.'s in WWII-ravaged Europe stumble upon a wrecked alien spacecraft and enlist the extraterrestrial's help in fending off the Nazis. **86m/C VHS.** Timothy Van Patten, Tim Thomerson, Art LaFleur, Biff Manard; ***D:*** Danny Bilson; ***W:*** Danny Bilson, Paul DeMeo; ***C:*** Mac Ahlberg; ***M:*** Richard Band.

Zontar, the Thing from Venus ☾ **1966** Scientist is taken over by alien batlike thing from Venus, and attempts to take over the Earth. A parody of itself. **68m/C VHS.** John Agar, Anthony Huston, Susan Bjorman, Pat Delaney, Warren Hammack, Neil Fletcher; ***D:*** Larry Buchanan; ***W:*** Larry Buchanan, Hillman Taylor; ***C:*** Robert Alcott. **TV**

The Zoo Gang ☾½ **1985 (PG-13)** A group of teens want to open a nightclub. Will they bring their dream to fruition, or will the mean rival gang foil their plans? **96m/C VHS.** Jackie Earle Haley, Tiffany Helm, Ben Vereen, Jason Gedrick, Eric Gurry; ***D:*** John Watson, Pen Densham; ***W:*** John Watson, Pen Densham; ***M:*** Patrick Gleeson.

Zoolander ☾☾½ **2001 (PG-13)** Stiller plays Derek Zoolander, an absurdly vacuous and successful male model who's brainwashed into becoming an assassin by over-the-top designer Mugatu (Ferrell). It seems that a foreign prime minister is committed to cutting off the supply of cheap third world labor for the fashion industry, and Zoolander is the only model stupid enough to have his noggin scrubbed clean. He develops a friendship with arch-rival model Hansel (Wilson), and the dim duo try to stop the nefarious plot. Packed to the gills with celebrity cameos, including Heidi Klum, Donald Trump and, yes, Fabio. Ran into unexpected controversy because the intended target is the prime minister of Malaysia (and the Malaysians naturally objected). **89m/C VHS, DVD, Wide.** *US* Ben Stiller, Owen C. Wilson, Christine Taylor, Will Ferrell, Milla Jovovich, Jerry Stiller, Jon Voight, David Duchovny; ***D:*** Ben Stiller; ***W:*** Ben Stiller, John Hamburg, Drake Sather; ***C:*** Barry Peterson; ***M:*** David Arnold.

Zooman ☾☾☾ **1995 (R)** Hard-hitting message on violence and responsibility. Gang member Zooman (Kain) spots members of a rival gang in a Brooklyn neighborhood, whips out his gun, and begins firing. When the shooting stops, a little girl sitting on her stoop is dead—what's even worse for her estranged parents is the fact that obvious witnesses refuse to identify the gunman for fear of their own safety. So father Reuben (Gossett Jr.) puts up a sign about their plight, attracting lots of media attention, and neighborhood hostility. Based on Fuller's 1978 play "Zooman and the Sign." **95m/C VHS.** Louis Gossett Jr., Charles S. Dutton, Khalil Kain, Cynthia Martells, CCH Pounder, Vondie Curtis-Hall, Hill Harper; ***D:*** Leon Ichaso; ***W:*** Charles Fuller. **CABLE**

Zoot Suit ☾☾☾ **1981 (R)** Based on Luis Valdez' play, this murder mystery/musical is rooted in the historical Sleepy Lagoon murder in the 1940s. Valdez plays a Mexican-American accused of the crime. His friends (and defense lawyers) rally around him to fight this travesty of justice. Lots o'music and dancing. **104m/C VHS.** Edward James Olmos, Daniel Valdez, Tyne Daly, Charles Aidman, John Anderson; ***D:*** Luis Valdez; ***W:*** Luis Valdez.

Zora Is My Name! ☾☾½ **1990** The funny, moving story of Zora Neal Hurston, a Black writer known for her stories and folklore of the rural South of the '30s and '40s. From PBS's American Playhouse. **90m/C VHS.** Ruby Dee, Louis Gossett Jr.

Zorba the Greek ☾☾☾½ *Zormba* **1964** A young British writer (Bates) comes to Crete to find himself by working his father's mine. He meets Zorba, an itinerant Greek laborer (Quinn), and they take lodgings together with an aging courtesan, who Zorba soon romances. The writer, on the other hand, is attracted to a lovely young widow. When she responds to him, the townsmen jealously attack her. Zorba teaches the young man the necessary response to life and its tragedies. Based on a novel by Nikos Kazantzakis. Masterpiece performance from Quinn. Beautifully photographed, somewhat overlong. Film later written for stage production. **142m/B VHS.** Anthony Quinn, Alan Bates, Irene Papas, Lila Kedrova; ***D:*** Michael Cacoyannis; ***C:*** Walter Lassally. Oscars '64: Art Dir./Set Dec., B&W, B&W Cinematog., Support. Actress (Kedrova); Natl. Bd. of Review '64: Actor (Quinn).

Zorro ☾☾½ *El Zorro la belva del Colorado; El Zorro* **1974 (G)** Italian take on the Zorro legend is a light romp, with Delon as the masked one careful not to take the proceedings too seriously. Recently arrived California governor Diego runs afoul of corrupt officials and dons the famous cape and mask to help the peasants. Mostly aims to please the kids but should keep adults interested, too. **120m/C VHS.** *IT FR* Alain Delon, Stanley Baker, Adriana Asti, Marino (Martin) Mase, Giacomo "Jack" Rossi-Stuart, Moustache, Ottavia Piccolo, Giampiero Albertini, Enzo Cerusico; ***D:*** Duccio Tessari; ***W:*** Giorgio Arlorio; ***C:*** Giulio Albonico; ***M:*** Guido de Angelis, Maurizio de Angelis.

Zorro Rides Again **1937** Zorro risks his life to outwit gangsters endeavoring to secure ancestor's property. In 12 chapters; the first runs 30 minutes, the rest 17. **217m/B VHS.** John Carroll, Helen Christian, Noah Beery Sr., Duncan Renaldo; ***D:*** William Witney, John English.

Zorro, the Gay Blade ☾☾½ **1981 (PG)** Tongue-in-cheek sword play with Hamilton portraying the swashbuckling crusader and his long-lost brother, Bunny Wigglesworth, in this spoof of the Zorro legend. The fashion-conscious hero looks his best in plum. Leibman is fun to watch. **96m/C VHS, DVD, Wide.** George Hamilton, Lauren Hutton, Brenda Vaccaro, Ron Leibman, Donovan Scott, James Booth, Helen Burns, Clive Revill; *D:* Peter Medak; *W:* Greg Alt; *C:* John A. Alonzo; *M:* Ian Fraser.

Zorro's Black Whip **1944** A young girl dons the mask of her murdered brother (Zorro) to fight outlaws in the old West. Serial in 12 episodes. **182m/B VHS.** George Lewis, Linda Stirling, Lucien Littlefield, Francis McDonald, Tom London; *D:* Spencer Gordon Bennet; *W:* Wallace Grissell.

Zorro's Fighting Legion **1939** Zorro forms a legion to help the president of Mexico fight a band of outlaws endeavoring to steal gold shipments. A serial in 12 chapters. **215m/B VHS.** Reed Hadley, Sheila (Rebecca Wassem) Darcy; *D:* William Witney, John English.

Zotz! 🦴🦴 **1962** The holder of a magic coin can will people dead by uttering "zotz"; spies pursue the mild-mannered professor who possesses the talisman. Adapted from a Walter Karig novel. Typical William Castle fare; his gimic in the theatrical release of the movie was to distribute plastic "zotz" coins to the theatre patrons. **87m/B VHS.** Tom Poston, Julia Meade, Jim Backus, Fred Clark, Cecil Kellaway, Margaret Dumont, Jimmy Hawkins; *D:* Ray Russell, William Castle; *W:* Ray Russell; *C:* Gordon Avil; *M:* Bernard Green.

Zou Zou 🦴🦴½ **1934** Lavish backstage musical/drama of a laundress who fills in for the leading lady on opening night and becomes a hit. Baker's talking picture debut. In French with English subtitles. **92m/B VHS.** *FR* Josephine Baker, Jean Gabin; *D:* Marc Allegret.

Zu: Warriors from the Magic Mountain 🦴🦴 *Shu Shan* **1983** The forces of evil are plotting to take over the world and a warrior endures the perils of the Zu Mountains in order to find the Twin Swords, the only weapons capable of defeating the demons. Cantonese with subtitles or dubbed. **98m/C VHS, DVD, Wide.** *HK* Adam Cheng, Yuen Biao, Brigitte (Lin Chinag-hsia) Lin, Sammo Hung, Moon Lee; *D:* Tsui Hark; *C:* Bill Wong.

Zulu 🦴🦴½ **1964** In 1879, a small group of British soldiers try to defend their African outpost from attack by thousands of Zulu warriors. Amazingly, the British win. Dated colonial epic based on an actual incident; battle scenes are magnificent. Prequel "Zulu Dawn" (1979) depicts British mishandling of the situation that led to the battle. **139m/C VHS, Wide.** Michael Caine, Jack Hawkins, Stanley Baker, Nigel Green, Ulla Jacobsson, James Booth, Paul Daneman, Neil McCarthy, Gary Bond, Patrick Magee, Dickie Owen, Larry Taylor, Dennis Folbigge, Ivor Emmanuel, Glynn Edwards, David Kernan; *D:* Cy Endfield; *W:* Cy Endfield, John Prebble; *C:* Stephen Dade; *M:* John Barry; *Nar:* Richard Burton.

Zulu Dawn 🦴🦴🦴 **1979 (PG)** An historical epic about British troops fighting the Zulus at Ulandi in 1878. Shows the increasing tensions between the British colonial government and the Zulus. Stunning landscapes unfortunately don't translate to the small screen. Good but unoriginal colonial-style battle drama. **117m/C VHS.** Burt Lancaster, Peter O'Toole, Denholm Elliott, Nigel Davenport, John Mills, Simon Ward, Bob Hoskins, Freddie Jones; *D:* Douglas Hickox; *M:* Elmer Bernstein.

Zvenigora 🦴🦴🦴🦴 **1928** Dovzhenko's first major film, and a lyrical revelation in the face of Soviet formality: a passionate, funny fantasy tableaux of 1,000 years of Ukrainian history, encompassing wild folk myths, poetic drama, propaganda and social satire. Silent. **73m/B VHS.** *RU* Mikola Nademsy, Alexander Podorozhny, Semyon Svashenko; *D:* Alexander Dovzhenko.

Category List

The **Category Index** contains genre, sub-genre, thematic, or significant scene classifications, ranging from the very general terms (Western, Sports Comedies) to the fairly particular (Heists: Casinos, Ninjas, Grandparents). The terms are defined (more or less) below. We've done our best to provide serious subject references while also including fun categories and lists to make your video viewing experience a little more enjoyable. No one list is all-inclusive. We are continuously reclassifying, adding, and subtracting movies. Many of the categories in this list are new, and therefore represent only a beginning. We're also trying to pare down some of the bigger categories, like Cops, by creating more focused subject categories, such as **Comic Cops** or **Police Detectives**. *VideoHound* invites readers to participate in this pastime by sending in suggestions for new categories and adding movies to existing ones. **An asterisk (*) denotes a new category for this edition.**

Adoption & Orphans: Cute kids lacking permanent authority figures, ranging from *Annie* to *Wild Hearts Can't Be Broken*

***Adultery:** Gettin' a little on the side; usually ends badly

Adventure Drama: Action with more attention to dramatic content—*Apocalypse Now* to *Robin Hood, Prince of Thieves*

Advertising: Corporate shenanigans at the agency—*How to Get Ahead in Advertising* to *The Horse in the Gray Flannel Suit*

Africa: *Out of Africa* to *Zulu Dawn*

African America: Dominant African American themes

AIDS: Someone usually dies; *An Early Frost* to *Longtime Companion*

Air Disasters: Contraptions up in the sky, but not for long

Airborne: Contraptions up in the sky

Alaska: The 49th state, home of the Iditarod and site of many manly Jack London adventures

Alcatraz: Prison island off San Francisco, aka *The Rock*

Alien Babes: Women who possess otherworldly beauty (and appetites)

Alien Beings—Benign: Friendly space visitors, including *Howard the Duck* and little buddy *E.T.*

Alien Beings—Vicious: Not-so-friendly space visitors, notably the multi-jawed *Alien* continually harassing Sigourney Weaver

Aliens Are People, Too: Space visitors pretend to be human, or just take over the bodies—*Invasion of the Body Snatchers* kinda stuff

Amateur Sleuths: ...and I woulda gotten away with it, too, if it weren't for those meddling kids!

American South: Theatrics amid much brow mopping and drawling; *A Streetcar Named Desire* rattling down *Flamingo Road*

Amnesia: Phone call for *Anastasia*

Amusement Parks: Cotton candy, ferris wheels, Coney Island, *Godzilla on Monster Island*, *Rollercoaster*

Angels: Benevolent winged visitors from above: *Wings of Desire*

Animated Musicals: Boys, girls, dogs, ducks, birds, mice, and monkeys croon; many of Disney vintage, including *Aladdin* and *Sleeping Beauty*

Animated Sci-Fi: To boldly go where no cartoon has gone before!

Animation & Cartoons: Antics of Daffy, Donald, Bugs, Mickey, Chip, Dale, Tom, Jerry, Fred, Wilma, Charlie, and the rest of the gang

Anime: Animated cartoons from Japan with cult following

Anthology: More than one story to a cassette

Anti-Heroes: From *Billy Jack* to *Dirty Harry* to *Thelma & Louise*

Anti-War War Movies: Recognizes that war really is hell—from *All Quiet on the Western Front* to *Paths of Glory*

Apartheid: Afrikaans term for racial segregation in South Africa

***Army Training, Sir** Tales of basic training, or boot camp, if you prefer. Are those *Stripes* on your *Full Metal Jacket?*

Art & Artists: They paint, pause, and propagate with equal passion

Asia: *China White, Red Dust, Sand Pebbles*

Asian America: Asian experience in the US—*The Joy Luck Club, Come See the Paradise*

Assassinations: Lincoln, *JFK, La Femme Nikita, Times of Harvey Milk*, and more

Astronauts: Houston, we have a problem.

At the Drive-In: Scenes in which people watch movies...at the drive-in.

At the Movies: The movie within a movie or movies about watching the movies, from *The Purple Rose of Cairo* to *Last Action Hero* to *Matinee*

At the Video Store: Scenes from a video store, *Clerks, Remote Control*

Atlanta: Home of the Braves, Ted Turner, CNN, and that annoying Tomahawk Chop. Sherman dropped in a while back with some rowdy friends.

Atlantic City: Gambling mecca of the East Coast, aka Trumptown

Babysitting: Supervision of small-fry pranksters not your own; *Uncle Buck* to *The Hand that Rocks the Cradle*

Bachelor Party: The groom's last foray into debauchery before the big day; all hell generally breaks loose

***Bad Bosses:** When he says he wants that report by 5:00 or heads will roll...it may not be a figure of speech

Bad Dads: Daddy-Os with unpredictable mean streak:*The Shining, Kiss Daddy Goodbye*

Ballet: On your toes—*The Turning Point*

Ballooning: Up, up and away, or *Around the World in 80 Days*

Baltimore: Take a look at the Maryland city, hometown of director Barry Levinson and favorite digs of John Waters

Bar & Grill: Most, if not all, of the action takes place in a drinking establishment.

Baseball: Action on the diamond, ranging from *Bull Durham* to *A League of Their Own* to *Rookie of the Year*

Basketball: Roundball thrillers, including the memorable *The Fish that Saved Pittsburgh* and *White Men Can't Jump*

Beach Blanket Bingo: Annette, Frankie, sand, surf, bikinis

Bears: Most of 'em are looking for more than just pic-i-nic baskets

Beatniks: Jazz beards, bongos, poetry that doesn't rhyme, berets

Beauty Pageants: From the heartless to the hilarious, beauty is a big business—*Smile* girls!

Behind the Scenes: Peek behind show business curtain, from *A Chorus Line* to *Truth or Dare*

Belfast: Northern Ireland city, Van Morrison's hometown (but that's not what it's famous for)

Berlin: City in Germany divided after WWII, now it's one big happy city again

***Betrayal:** Somebody done somebody wrong. Could be a spouse, could be a partner, could be the intelligence agency that used to employ you that now wants you dead

Beverly Hills: Fancy-pants area of L.A., home of Cops, Troops, Vamps, and 30-year-old teenagers

Bicycling: Two wheels, no motor, much leg action and sweating

Big Battles: Big-budget (or at least illusion of such) clash of large, opposing military forces, from *Cromwell* to *Ran*

Big Budget Bombs: Millions spent for no apparent reason

Big Digs: Anthropology and archaeology, from Indiana Jones to various mummy on-the-loose stories

Big Ideas: Philosophy, ideology and other semi-mental pursuits somehow translated to film

Big Rigs: *Smokey and the Bandit* speed down *Thieves' Highway* in a *Convoy*

Bigfoot/Yeti: Large, hairy, seldom-seen beast with really big feet

Bikers: Usually with a mean streak and traveling in leather-clad packs

***Biopics—Artists:** True stories of artists' lives. Find out if they were really starving or not

***Biopics—Cops & Robbers:** True stories of real life criminals and the real life cops who arrested 'em

***Biopics—Military:** True stories of the men and women who fought this (and other) country's wars

***Biopics—Musicians:** From European composers to punk rock icons, they usually end up being tales of over-indulgence and others ripping them off

***Biopics—Politics:** True stories of the politicians who lead counries, states, and municipalities

***Biopics—Religious:** Life stories of church leaders, reformers, saints, and the occasional deity

***Biopics—Royalty:** Life stories of kings, queens, czars. They ran things before politicians were invented

***Biopics—Science/Medical:** Life stories of the people who invented the medicine and products that make modern life...modern

***Biopics—Showbiz:** Life stories of those who entertain us. It ain't always all glamour and happy endings

***Biopics—Sports:** Life stories of those we admire for their athletic prowess

***Biopics—Writers:** Life stories of those who put thoughts, stories, or manifestoes to paper and became famous for it

Birds: Beaks, feathers, talons, bird #%!; *The Birds, Beaks: The Movie, Howard the Duck*

Birthdays: Congratulations on making it through another year!

Bisexuality: Going both ways—*Basic Instinct, Three of Hearts*

Black Comedy: Funny in a biting or despairing sort of way, from *The Addams Family* to *The Hospital*

Black Gold: Oil, that is; aka *Oklahoma Crude*

Blackmail: I'm gonna tell, unless... *The Last Seduction, Letter to My Killer*

Blaxploitation: '70s remakes of horror classics, as well as B-movies made with the black audience in mind

Blindness: Can't see or sight impaired; *Afraid of the Dark*

Blizzards: Big snow storms, usually overblown by over-excited local weather people.

Bloody Messages: Cryptic warnings to the living written in the blood of the poor slob who was just killed—Redrum

Bodyguards: Costner looks after Whitney's personal business

Books: As a major plot device: *La Lectrice* to *Crossing Delancey*

Bookstores: Very nice places where fine literary works (such as this) can be found

Boom!: Really big explosions, bombs, and other noisy or fiery messes popular in big budget action flicks

Boomer Reunions: thirtysomethings gather and reminisce: *The Big Chill*

Bosnia: Has played host to Olympics and ethnic strife

Boston: Beantown, where everybody knows your name.

Bounty Hunters: Bring 'em back dead or alive—for a price

Bowling: Heavy round ball is thrown down waxed alley toward club-like pins; all fall down

Boxing: Yo, Adrian!

Bridges: For crossing, or if you're in a war movie, defending and/or blowing up

Bringing Up Baby: *Look Who's Talking* to *Raising Arizona*, plus infants with that little something different—*Alien 3, Enemy Mine, Basket Case 3: The Progeny*

Brothers & Sisters: Siblings getting along and sometimes not

Buddhism: Eastern religion with bald guys

Buddies: Butch and Sundance, Bill and Ted, Rubin and Ed, *Thelma and Louise*

Buddy Cops: Couple of police hanging together, usually practicing limited repartee at a donut shop; *Lethal Weapon, Tango and Cash*

Buried Alive: I'm not quite dead, yet! Hello, Mr. grave digger person, hello!

Buses: Large truck-like passenger vehicles—*Speed, The Big Bus, The Trip to Bountiful*

Cabbies: Where to, Mac?

Calcutta: Big, overpopulated city in India

Camelot (New): The exploits of JFK, Jackie, and various relatives and hangers-on

Camelot (Old): The exploits of King Arthur and his *Knights of the Round Table*

Campus Capers: What really goes on at college—*Assault of the Party Nerds*

Canada: Renfrew of the Mounties plus lots of wilderness and the occasional hockey puck

Canadian Mounties: The Great White North version of cops. They always get their man

Cannibalism: People who eat people are the luckiest people; *Alive, Rabid Grannies, Cannibal Women in the Avocado Jungle of Death, The Cook, the Thief, His Wife & Her Lover*

Capitol Capers: Hollywood versions of hijinks in Washington, D.C.—*Dave, Mr. Smith Goes to Washington, All the President's Men*

Carnivals & Circuses: Big top, little top, domes: *Shakes the Clown* to *Rollercoaster*, plus *Big Top Pee Wee, State Fair*, and metaphoric circuses: *Brewster McCloud, La Strada*

Cats: Lesser vertebrate nonetheless much beloved by Hollywood

Cave People: From the most primitive (*The Clan of the Cave Bear*) to the fairly modernized (*The Flintstones*)

Checkered Flag: *Eat My Dust*; racing in the street or on the track; *The Last American Hero*

Cheerleaders: Give me an A! *The Positively True Adventures of the Alleged Texas Cheerleader-Murdering Mom* meets *Revenge of the Cheerleaders*

Chicago: City in Illinois, right at the bottom of Lake Michigan

Child Abuse: Not very funny at all—*Mommie Dearest, Fallen Angel*

***Childhood Buddies:** The pals we hang around with before puberty hits

Childhood Visions: Stories dominated by the kid point of view, or by an adult flashbacking to childhood; *Au Revoir Les Enfants, Home Alone*

China: *The Last Emperor* to *Red Sorghum* to *The World of Suzie Wong*

Christmas: Reindeer, Santa, children make appearance amid much sentimentality

Cinderella Stories: Gal down on her luck meets fairy godmother (or father) and finds true love—*Pretty Woman, Flashdance, Cinderella*

Civil Rights: Fighting for equality—*The Autobiography of Miss Jane Pittman, Mississippi Burning*

Civil War: The Yankees against the Confederates; aka *The Blue and the Gray*

Classic Horror: Boris Karloff, Vincent Price, piercing screams

Cloning Around: Makin' copies—of people or animals. *Multiplicity* to *Jurassic Park*

Clowns: Big red noses, huge feet, painted smiles frighten many

Cockroaches: Creepy crawlies signifying the work of the supernatural, or a lack of housekeeping skills

Cold Spots: Set in a frostbitten locale with lots of shivering; *Ice Station Zebra, Never Cry Wolf, Quest for Fire*

Comedy Anthologies: More than one yuk fest on a cassette

Comedy Drama: Drama with a comedic touch or comedy underwired with drama—*Avalon, The Big Chill, Fried Green Tomatoes, One Flew Over the Cuckoo's Nest, Tootsie*

Comedy Mystery: Wacky whodunits like *Murder by Death, Clue*

Comedy Sci-Fi: Laughs in space! *Spaceballs*

Comic Adventure: Adventurous romps liberally laced with humor: *Romancing the Stone* to *Bird on a Wire* to *Crocodile Dundee*

***Comic Cops:** Police officers that catch laughs as they catch the bad guys. Think Axel Foley or those cut-ups from the *Police Academy* series

Coming of Age: Hard-fought adolescent battle for adulthood, led by *American Graffiti, The Apprenticeship of Duddy Kravitz, The Karate Kid*

***Communists & Communism:** Way left-wingers politically. They used to run Eastern Europe, but now they just rant in coffeehouses. The ones in Asia are still around, though

Computers: Bits and bytes play major role

Concentration/Internment Camps: Nazis used them for their "final solution" while the U.S. used them to imprison Japanese-Americans

Concert Films: Rock or comedy concerts—from *Woodstock* to *Divine Madness* to *Eddie Murphy: Raw*

Contemporary Musicals: Thematically modern and made during last 20 years; *All That Jazz*

Contemporary Noir: Dark and moody or tributes to dark and moody that pay homage to the original Film Noir genre—*Blue Velvet, 92 Weeks, sex, lies, and videotape, Wild Orchid*

Cops: Police and pseudo-police work, including *Action Jackson, Blue Steel, The Choirboys, RoboCop, Lethal Weapon, National Lampoon's Loaded Weapon 1*

Corporate Shenanigans: Big Business runs amuck—*Barbarians at the Gate, Wall Street*

Creepy Houses: Scary dwellings—*Amityville Horror* 1 through 33

Crime Drama: Gangster family dysfunction, heists gone awry, packin' pathos with your piece. *The Godfather, Goodfellas, Reservior Dogs.*

Crime Sprees: Bad guy, gal or couple goes on a crime binge and other tales of obsessive criminal activity, including *Bonnie & Clyde, The Boys Next Door*

Crimes of Passion: Love, sex, and death

***Criminally Insane:** They don't really care if crime pays, they're just following orders from the voices.

Crop Dusters: Down on the farm: *Bitter Harvest, Pelle the Conqueror, Jean de Florette, The River*

Cuba: Fidel's Island, where the survivors vote themselves off and the winners make it 90 miles north to become high-priced baseball players.

Cults: Something like a gang but more intense and usually governed by a state of mind similar to irrationality—*Helter Skelter*

Culture Clash: Hilarity ensues (or sometimes not) as people from vastly different backgrounds try to interact. *Deliverance, Witness, George of the Jungle*

***Custody Battles:** People, mostly divorced couples, fight over who keeps the kids. *Kramer vs. Kramer, Losing Isaiah*

Cuttin' Heads: Barber shops and Beauty salons are the scenes of all or most of the "action"

Cyberpunk: Dark, moody, futuristic flicks—*Blade Runner, Freejack, Tank Girl*

Dads: Fathers play a major role

Dance Fever: Whole lotta foot-tapping going on, including *An American in Paris, Daddy Long Legs*, and *Dirty Dancing*

Dates from Hell: Fun evening for two singles turns into a nightmare for one of them—*Bye Bye Love, Singles, Something Wild*

A Day In The Life: All the action takes place within a 24-hour period

Deadly Implants: Where is that ticking coming from?

Deafness: Can't hear or hearing impaired; *Bridge to Silence, The Miracle Worker*

Death & The Afterlife: Could be ghosts, could be voices from the beyond, could be any number of post-dead things—*Beetlejuice, Carnival of Souls, Flatliners, Poltergeist, Weekend at Bernie's*

Death Row: Waitin' for a call from the Governor; *Dead Man Walking, Angels with Dirty Faces*

Dedicated Teachers: From *The Dead Poet's Society* to *The Blackboard Jungle* to *The Miracle Worker*

Deep Blue: The sea around us, including *ffolkes* and *Splash*

Demons & Wizards: Swords, sorcery and wrinkled old men with wands—*The Alchemist, The Hobbit, The Sword & the Sorcerer*

Dental Mayhem: Tooth-pickin' uproars; *Marathon Man, The Dentist*

Desert War/Foreign Legion: Big battles among the dunes

Deserts: Endless beach minus the water—*Ishtar, Lawrence of Arabia*

Detective Spoofs: Putting together clues in humorous fashion—*The Adventures of Sherlock Holmes' Smarter Brother, The Naked Gun*

Detroit: The Motor City, home of Motown, lots of cars, the Stanley Cup Champion Red Wings, and...VideoHound

Devils: Some may meet on *Judgment Day*

Devil's Island: French Island prison in the South Atlantic

Dinosaurs: *Jurassic Park* and other less animated thundering lizards

Disaster Flicks: Natural and man-made, including 47 *Airport* sequels

Disco Musicals: '70s tackiness reigns supreme, from *Saturday Night Fever* to *Xanadu*

Disease of the Week: Bulimia, anorexia, polio, cancer, and so on

Disorganized Crime: Stupid crime, including *Amos and Andrew, Dog Day Afternoon, Home Alone, Quick Change*

Divorce: Breaking up is hard to do; *Accidental Tourist, Heartburn, Kramer vs. Kramer*

Doctors & Nurses: Men and women in scrubs concerned about health of complete strangers for profit, often to the dismay of the patient—*Autopsy, Candy Stripe Nurses, Dead Ringers*

Docudrama: *The Thin Blue Line* between documentaries and drama

Documentary: Real life manipulated on film—*A Brief History of Time, The Last Waltz, Paris Is Burning, Roger and Me*

Dogs In Peril: Manipulative plot device, usually in disaster flicks, where things blow up just as Fido high-tails it out of there.

***Doublecross!:** Usually happens when there's no more honor among thieves, like in *Payback*

Down Under: Australian, New Zealand settings—*The Rescuers Down Under, Gallipoli, The Man from Snowy River, The Thorn Birds*

Dragons: Legendary medieval lizards, usually with fiery dispositions; *Dragonheart, Pete's Dragon*

Dream Girls: Product of male mid-life crisis; *Battling Amazons, Cycle Vixens, The Doll Squad, The Woman in Red*

Drug Abuse: Life with a drugstore cowboy; consumption of drugs, mostly illegal or in extra-large dosages

Dublin: Irish capitol city, home to *The Committments*

***Dying for a Promotion:** ...or killing for one. Guess those business ethics seminars were a waste of money

Ears!: Bloody detachment and general maiming of...

Earthquakes: The Earth moved! Common occurrence in California

***Eastern Europe:** Basically everything east of Germany and west of Asia

Eat Me: Characters end up as food. *Jurassic Park, Soylent Green, Alive*

Eco-Vengeance!: Nature wreaks havoc on man—watch out for *Alligators, Frogs* and *Piranhas*

Edibles: Something's cooking—*Babette's Feast, Like Water for Chocolate*

Edinburgh: Scottish town. They pronounce it "Goff" instead of "Golf" according to Judge Smails.

Egypt–Ancient: Mummies, Pharoahs, Pyramids, when they were brand new

Elephants: Pachyderms play a BIG part in the plot—*Dumbo, Larger Than Life*

Elevators: Sometimes the oddest things happen in them...

Emerging Viruses: Deadly virus spreads like wildfire as frantic medical personnel search for a cure; think ebola

* = new to this edition

The Empire State Building: Used to be the tallest building in NYC, still the most famous

Erotic Thrillers: Hot sex and murder, including *Basic Instinct, Body of Evidence*

***Errant Educators:** Teachers, coaches, or principals who may not have the kids' best interests in mind, maybe because they're aliens (*The Faculty*), or they're just mean (*Teaching Mrs. Tingle*)

Escaped Cons: They busted outta the joint, now they're makin' a run for it. *Con Air, We're No Angels, Papillon, Fled*

Ethics & Morals: Examination of values (or lack of)—*Crimes & Misdemeanors, Judgment at Nuremberg*

Etiquette: Usually comedy of manners: *Educating Rita, My Fair Lady* **Evil Doctors:** Don't go to these guys for a checkup—*Malice, Dead Ringers*, and *Doctor X*

Executing Revenge: Bad guys come back from being executed to cause more trouble. *Fallen, Shocker*

Exploitation: Rigged to take advantage of viewer, including historic treats like *Reefer Madness* and more recent ventures such as *Sleazemania*

Explorers: Going boldly where no man or woman has regularly gone before

Extraordinary Pairings: Jesse James meets Frankenstein's Daughter

Eyeballs!: Unnerving scenes involving pupils, irises, lids, and occasionally, lashes

Fairs & Expositions: Short term amusement parks: *State Fair*

Family Ties: Blood runs deep—*Back to the Future, Five Easy Pieces, The Godfather, Homeward Bound, Lorenzo's Oil, The Mosquito Coast, Rocket Gibraltar*

Fantasy: Tales of the imagination, including *Alice* and her looking glass, *E.T., Ladyhawke, My Stepmother Is an Alien*

Feds: Men and women of the Bureau, the Agency, or any national police organization with an acronym and a dress code

Female Bonding: Women get together, usually to the men's dismay; *Waiting to Exhale*

Femme Fatale: She done him and him and him wrong

Fencing: En garde, dude

Film History: *America at the Movies;* includes movies important to film history

Film Noir: Dark and moody or tributes to dark and moody—*Farewell, My Lovely, The Postman Always Ring Twice, The Third Man, Who Framed Roger Rabbit?*

Filmmaking: The making of a film within a film: *The Player*

Firemen: *Backdraft, Frequency*, and other tales of brave people with hoses

Fires: *Frankenstein, Quest for Fire, Pyrates*

***The First Time:** Y'know, the first time you had...when you broke your...when you made...when you first...uh, did it...with another person

Flashback: Why, I remember like it was yesterday. It all started when...*The Usual Suspects, Casablanca*

Flatulence: Embarrassing gaseous emissions

Floods: Water, water everywhere

Florida: Beaches, retirement communities, swamps, Spring Training, Disney World.

Florence: Not Alice's grits-kissing pal, but the city in Italy.

Folklore & Legend: Age-old adult tales covering Atlantis, little people, faeries, Paul Bunyan, and the like

Football: Everything from terrorist attacks on the Superbowl (*Black Sunday*) to prison competition (*The Longest Yard*) plus *Diner*

Foreign Intrigue: Overseas mystery, with emphasis on accent and location

Frame-ups: Someone's set up to take the rap: *My Cousin Vinny* to *Consenting Adults*

France: From *Dirty Rotten Scoundrels* to *The Moderns* to *Gigi* to *The Last Metro* to *Killer Tomatoes Eat France*

Fraternities & Sororities: Those fun-lovin' campus cut-ups who're always pulling pranks or getting offed in bad slasher flicks

Front Page: *Citizen Kane, All the President's Men, The Philadelphia Story*, and other journalistic stories

Fugitives: Running from the law; *Breathless, Nowhere to Hide, Posse*

Funerals: The final good-bye—*Four Weddings and a Funeral, Gardens of Stone, The Big Chill*

***Funny Money:** Counterfeiting, and all the action movie stuff that goes with it

Future Cop: The future of law enforcement

***Future Shock:** Someone from our past comes to our present, or someone from our present goes to our future; *Sleeper, Just Visiting*

Gambling: Aces and Eights, *The Color of Money, Eight Men Out, Honeymoon in Vegas*

Game Shows: *The Running Man* and *Queen for a Day*

Gangs: Criminally enterprising teens and adults running in packs: *State of Grace, Miller's Crossing, Public Enemy, The Wanderers*

Gays: Gay themes—*Kiss of the Spider Woman, The Hunger*

Gender Bending: *The Crying Game, La Cage aux Folles, Her Life as a Man* and other instances of boys becoming girls and vice versa

Generation X: Slacking in the '90s—*Reality Bites, Singles*

Genetics: Fooling with the double helix—*The Fly*

Genies: *Aladdin* finds magic lamp filled with compressed Robin Williams

Genre Spoofs: Wacky takes on serious films, starting with the granddaddy of them all: *Airplane!*

Germany: *The Blue Angel, Wings of Desire*

Ghosts, Ghouls, & Goblins: *Ghostbusters, Topper, Poltergeist*

Giants: *The Amazing Colossal Man* visits *Village of the Giants*

Gifted Children: Kids show amazing talents that astound adults, from *Rookie of the Year* to *Little Man Tate*

Glasgow: Scottish capitol city.

Go Fish: Casting a line in the river that runs through it; *Man of Aran, A Fish Called Wanda, Captains Courageous*

Going Native: Outsiders try to blend in; *Dances with Wolves, The Swiss Family Robinson*

Going Postal: Neither rain, snow, sleet, nor dead of night....Hello, Newman

Golf: Slow boring game best experienced on screen ('Be the ball, Danny')

Grand Hotel: Checkout time is noon; *Blame It on the Bellboy*

***Grand Theft Auto:** Boosting cars for fun and/or profit. Just like on *Cops*, chases usually ensue

***Grandparents:** Your parents' parents, the ones who spoil you and drive your folks crazy

Great Britain: Thwarted royals (*Charles & Diana: A Palace Divided, Edward and Mrs. Simpson*), kings (*King Ralph*), queens (*The Naked Civil Servant*), class distinctions (*The Ruling Class*), vanished empires (*Cromwell, A Man for All Seasons*), criminals (*The Krays, The Long Good Friday*) plus multiple stiff upper lips, the Brontes, and Dickens

Great Death Scenes: Signing off with style or elaboration; *Buffy the Vampire Killer, Bonnie and Clyde, Breaker Morant*

Great Depression: The era, not the state of mind—*Bound for Glory, Of Mice and Men, The Grapes of Wrath, Rambling Rose*

Great Escapes: Seizing the day for freedom—*The Big Doll House, Escape from Alcatraz, Papillon*

Greece—Ancient: In the immortal words of Socrates, "I drank what?"

***Greece—Modern:** They don't walk around in sheets and philosophize anymore, at least not in public

Growing Older: *On Golden Pond, *batteries not included, Cocoon, Driving Miss Daisy, The Shootist, The Wild Bunch*

Gymnastics: Human pretzels like *Nadia*

***Gypsies:** Fortune tellers with scarves around their heads and vaguely—European accents, or modern day con men are the two basic movie types

Hackers: Computer whiz kids cause havoc—or just change their grades

Halloween: *Trick or Treat!*

***Hallucinations/Illusions:** Stuff looks real, but it's all in yer head, man!

Hard Knock Life: Poverty and bad luck; *City of Joy, The Match Factory Girl*

Harlem: Part of New York City you don't see in the tourism brochures

Hawaii: The 50th state, fun in the sun, if the volcanoes are behaving.

Hearts!: Unnerving scenes involving human hearts, generally seen by the audience and almost always still pumping

Heaven Sent: Visits or returns from the place where good souls and all dogs go—*Field of Dreams* to *Made in Heaven* to *Oh God!*

Heists: The big lift

* **Heists—Armored Car:** Crooks plan and carry out jobs on armored cars

* **Heists—Art:** Crooks plan and carry out jobs to steal works of art, *The Thomas Crown Affair*

* **Heists—Bank:** Crooks plan and carry out early withdrawals, sometimes incurring substantial penalties

* **Heists—Casinos:** Crooks plan to steal from the one-armed bandits; *Oceans's Eleven* are *3000 Miles From Graceland*

* **Heists—Gold/Precious Metals:** Elaborate plans to go for the gold, or silver, or platinum. Bronze isn't that valuable in this game

* **Heists—Jewels:** Ya gotta be cool to get the ice, just ask the *Reservior Dogs*

***Heists—Trains:** Not the whole train, just the good stuff inside it. *Butch Cassidy and the Sundance Kid* liked the choo-choos

Hell: Not a place you wanna end up. The forecast calls for continued hot, with a 0% chance of freezing over.

Hell High School: Place where adolescents gather against their will; also known as *Rock 'n' Roll High School*

The Help—Female: Maids, nannies, governesses, cooks, housekeepers

The Help—Male: Butlers, chauffeurs, manservants, valets

Hide the Dead Guy: What to do with those pesky bodies after the killing's done?

***High School:** This is for those few movies where high school isn't treated like the hellish experience we all seem to remember it being

High School Reunions: Adults gather to impress other adults they didn't like as adolescents

Hispanic America: Dominant Hispanic American themes (*Salsa, Mi Vida Loca*)

Historical Detectives: It's elementary! Sherlock, meet Elliot Ness.

Historical Drama: Usually at least loosely based on a real incident or personality

Hit Men: Boys and girls armed with silencers; *Prizzi's Honor, Romeo is Bleeding*

Hockey: *Slap Shot* and other icy tales of passing the puck

Holidays: Easter, Thanksgiving, New Year's, Halloween, but generally not Christmas

Holocaust: *Playing for Time, Schindler's List*

Home Alone: Kids find themselves without adult supervision—*Adventures in Babysitting* to *Young Sherlock Holmes*

The Homefront—England: Air raids, stiff upper lips, they were a lot closer to the action, and were just as worried about their sons and husbands.

The Homefront—U.S./ Canada: The war at home during WWII—looking for spies, rationing, waiting for word about 'the boys.'

Homeless: Street people with no homes

***Homicide:** Murder most foul! It's what usually gets those wacky buddy-cop movies started

Hong Kong: Land of the really cool action flick; Chow Yun-Fat and Jackie Chan became stars there. Great Britain gave it back to the Chinese

Horrible Holidays: Holidays with a ghoulish twist—*Bloody New Year, Halloween, My Bloody Valentine, Silent Night, Bloody Night*

Horror: Modern cut 'em up scare theater

Horror Anthologies: More than one scarefest on a cassette

Horror Comedy: Tongue-in-bloody cheek—*The Fearless Vampire Killers, Piranha, Sorority Babes in the Slimeball Bowl-A-Rama*

Horses: Can you say *Black Beauty?*

Hospitals & Medicine: Dysfunctional institutional health care—*Article 99, The Hospital, One Flew Over the Cuckoo's Nest, Young Doctors in Love*

Hostage!: People held against their will for bargaining purposes

Houston: That big city in Texas where J.R. didn't live, but Roger Clemens did.

Hunted!: Humans tracking humans for trophy purposes

Hunting: Where's dat wascally wabbit? *Caddyshack, The Bear, White Hunter, Black Heart*

Hurling: What goes down sometimes comes back up—*The Exorcist, Parenthood*

I'm Not Dead, Yet! Reports of their demise have been greatly exaggerated

Immigration: Melting pot stories—*Avalon, Far and Away, Living on Tokyo Time*

Impending Retirement: Gold watch, a party, some tearful goodbyes...but there's always those darn loose ends to tie up first

In-Laws: The family you marry into; usually a source of conflict and punchlines

Incest: Implied or actual relationships among family members—*The Grifters, Spanking the Monkey*

India: On the road to *Bombay*

Insomnia: Can't sleep at night

Interracial Affairs: Couple from different racial backgrounds cause trauma for family and friends—*Mississippi Masala, Jungle Fever*

Interviews: When asked questions, people talk

Inventors & Inventions: Those wacky folks and their newfangled machines; *Chitty Chitty Bang Bang*

Invisibility: Now you see 'em, now you don't

Ireland: Aye, make that a pint for take away; *The Field, Cal, The Playboys*

Islam: Religious themes

Island Fare: Thin, isolated stretch of land surrounded by water notorious for encouraging natural appetites in men and women

Israel: *Cast a Giant Shadow, Exodus*

Istanbul, not Constantinople: Former seat of the Eastern Roman Empire, now the Turks run things.

Italy: Passion, vino, lust, vino, Sophia Loren

It's a Conspiracy, Man!: Just because you're paranoid doesn't mean they're not out to get you

Japan: *Land of the Rising Sun, Godzilla, Hiroshima, Mon Amour*

Jerusalem: Much-fought-over Holy City, it's ground zero for much of the world's religious population.

Judaism: *Fiddler on the Roof* meets *Funny Girl*

Jungle Stories: Tarzan, tribes, trees, treasure, temperature, temptresses, tigers

Justice Prevails?: The verdict's in, but is it fair? *And Justice for All, In the Name of the Father, Presumed Innocent*

Karaoke: This Japanese import usually runs best on alcohol

***Kiddie Viddy:** Stuff aimed at kids that's actually suitable for the little nippers to watch

** = new to this edition*

Kidnapped!: Held for ransom or just for the heck of it—*A Perfect World, Raising Arizona*

Killer Apes and Monkeys: *King Kong* lives on *The Planet of the Apes*

Killer Appliances: Defrosted refrigerator goes on killing binge

Killer Beasts: Cloned dinosaurs run amuck in backyard, destroying patio

Killer Brains: Literally has a mind of its own, i.e., *The Brain That Wouldn't Die*

Killer Bugs: Giant and/or miserably mean spiders, ants, bees, worms, flies, slugs, tarantulas, wasps, and other creepy things

Killer Cars: You should have changed *Christine*'s oil

Killer Dogs: Fido takes a walk on the wild side—*Cujo*, baby

Killer Dreams: More like nightmares on elm street

Killer Kats: Kitties with a killer instinct

Killer Pigs: Evil swine

Killer Plants: Too much fertilizer produces killer tomatoes (stewed)

Killer Reptiles: *Godzilla* and pals, not rampaging lawyers

Killer Rodents: Nasty mice, rats, bats, and shrews

Killer Sea Critters: Just when you thought it was safe to go back in the water; formerly **Sea Critter Attack**

***Killer Spouses:** Watch their eyes very closely when you get to the "...until death do you part" portion of the vows

Killer Toys: Demented play things develop homicidal urges; why hello, Chucky

Kindness of Strangers: Baffling altruistic behavior

King of Beasts (Dogs): Need we say more?

Korean War: *M*A*S*H* and friends

L.A.: Smoggy city in California also known as Los Angeles or the City of Angels; includes Hollywood & Beverly Hills

Labor & Unions: *Hoffa* and other working stiffs

Late Bloomin' Love: Better late than not blooming at all

Law & Lawyers: Tom Cruise joins *The Firm* and other realistic legal adventures

Leprechauns: The wee mischievous people of Irish lore who carry around pots o' gold

Lesbians: Lesbian themes—*Lianna, Bar Girls*

Libraries & Librarians: Important things happen where you can't talk—sometimes people even read!

Lifeguards: Rescuers of the swimming-challenged

London: City in merry old England, home to many generations of the most famous royals

Loner Cops: *Dirty Harry* Syndrome

Look Ma! I'm on TV!: TV becomes real life—*The Truman Show*, live from *Pleasantville*

Lost Worlds: From *Brigadoon* to *The People That Time Forgot*

Lottery Winners: Ordinary schmoes get rich quick. Be careful what you wish for...

Lovable Loonies: Crazy, but not Norman Bates crazy; *Crazy People, Benny & Joon*

Lovers on the Lam: Couples commit crimes and find themselves on the run—*Badlands, Natural Born Killers, True Romance*

Mad Scientists: *The Brain That Wouldn't Die* spends an evening with *Frankenhooker*

Magic: Hocus pocus, often with evil intent

Magic Carpet Rides: *Aladdin* joins *Sinbad the Sailor* for *The Golden Voyage of Sinbad*

Mail-Order Brides: Shipping is okay, but I've got a problem with this handling charge!

Marriage: Wedding bells, honeymoons, affairs, divorce, and growing old together, as well as the occasional unfortunate marital union with a blood-sucking vampire or knife-wielding satanist

***Marriages of Convenience:** Will you marry me so I can inherit boatloads of cash or not get deported? Oh, how romantic!

Mars: The Red Planet, which gave us (supposedly) little green men and the Illudium-Q Explosive Space Modulator.

Martial Arts: Fists of Aluminum Foil; much head-kicking, rib-crunching, chop-socky action

Martyred Pop Icons: For us, they gave their all; Buddy Holly, Elvis, Marilyn, James Dean, *Stardust Memories*

Mass Media: From *Network* to *Broadcast News* to *My Favorite Year*

Masseurs: People who knead people...

May-December Romance: Older people meet younger people and the romantic sparks fly; *Harold and Maude* visit *Atlantic City.*

The Meaning of Life: The search for the elusive answer—*My Life, The Remains of the Day, Shadowlands*

Medieval Romps: Dirty peasants, deodorized and glorified kings and queens, splendid knights in shining armor, and one for all and all for one

Meltdown: Or how I learned to stop worrying and love the bomb; also bad wiring at local nuclear plants

Memphis: The other city in Tennessee; Elvis' home

Men: What is man? Is he neither fish nor fowl? Or perhaps linoleum?

Men in Prison: Working on a chain gang; what we have here is a failure to communicate

***Mental Hospitals:** Storage area for those not on speaking terms with Mr. Reality

Mental Retardation: *Bill, Charly*, Dominick, Lenny, Raymond (definitely)

***Mermaids:** Half woman, half fish, alright! *The Little Mermaid* makes a big *Splash*

Metamorphosis: Ch-ch-ch-changes—From *The Fly* to *Wolf*

Meteors, Asteroids & Comets: Chunks of stuff wizzing through space, sometimes they land and cause problems

Mexico: *South of Sante Fe* and *Against All Odds*

Miami: Extremely warm coastal city in southern Florida

Middle East: Desert fare and camel close-ups ranging from *Ishtar* to *Lawrence of Arabia* to *The Jewel of the Nile*

Military: Air Force: Flyboys fight America's aerial battles

Military: Army: GIs, Grunts, Dogfaces

Military Comedy: Marching to a different drummer, including *Stripes, M*A*S*H* and *No Time for Sergeants*

***Military Crimes & Trials:** Courtroom drama in the Armed Forces; *A Few Good Men* didn't follow the *Rules of Engagement* on their *Paths to Glory*

Military: Foreign: Armed forces of other nations are the focus

Military: Marines: Jarheads. The first ones in and the last ones out.

Military: Navy: Fighting on the high seas and in the air

Miners & Mining: Helmets with the little flashlights are nifty; *Matewan* and *McCabe & Mrs. Miller*

Minnesota: Northern state that makes Michigan seem like the tropics. Home of theTwin cities and Prince, eh?

Missing Persons: People who disappear for a variety of reasons, sometimes because other people have taken them away

Missionaries: On a mission from God to save native populations

Mistaken Identity: You mean to say you're not the King of France?

***Mockumentary:** Movies in which actors pretend to be real people being followed around by fake documentary crews that are actually real filmmaking crews; *This is Spinal Tap*'s genre, and they're still *Best in Show* at it.

Model Behavior: Fashion and models are the center of attention—but isn't that the point? *Looker, Gia, Unzipped, Ready to Wear*

Modern Cowboys: Fun-lovin' rascals adept at riding horses through busy city streets or with a yen to experience mid-life crisis by doing a rodeo

Moms: Maternal figures have a prominent role

Monkeyshines: Critters from the jungle, sometimes cute and fluffy, often wreaking havoc—*Congo, Monkey Trouble, Outbreak*

Monster Moms: Loving on the outside, evil on the inside—*Mommie Dearest, Serial Mom*

***Monster Yuks:** Monster movies where the creatures are more funny, or cuddly, than scary

Montreal: Cosmopolitan city of francophones currently in Canada

Moscow: City in Russia (the country formerly known as USSR)

***Moscow Mafia:** The Russian Mob

Motor Vehicle Dept.: *Chitty Chitty Bang Bang* at the *Car Wash*, plus *Tucker, Herbie*, and the *Repo Man*

Mountaineering: *Cliffhangers*

Mummies: Dead guys with leather-like skin, often wrapped in sheets

Murderous Children: *Children of the Corn* hang out on the outskirts of the *Village of the Damned*...isn't that near the 7-Eleven of Doom?

Museums: Big buildings that contain old paintings, sculptures, treasures...and the occasional ancient man-eating beastie

Musical Comedy: Laughter, singing, and dancing

Musical Drama: Singing and dancing, less laughter, more tension

Musical Fantasy: Singing and dancing in a figment of someone's imagination

Musicals: High-energy singing and dancing, often for no particular reason

Mutiny: Gang of disgruntled sailors takes over the ship

Mystery & Suspense: Edge-of-the-couch thrillers and whodunits

Nannies & Governesses: Musically-inclined women raise kids for rich people too busy to do it themselves

Nashville: Tennessee city that country music and Robert Altman made famous

Nashville Narratives: *Honkytonk Man* elopes with the *Coal Miner's Daughter*

Native America: Dancing with the wolves on *Pow Wow Highway*

Nazis & Other Paramilitary Slugs: *The Boys from Brazil* and *The Dirty Dozen* plus SS she-wolf *Ilsa* and modern David Duke adaptations

***Near-Death Experiences:** Brushes with the Reaper, usually resulting in some extra powers upon the victim's return

Negative Utopia: Things seemed so perfect until...

New Black Cinema: Spike is Godfather

New Orleans: City in Louisiana that boasts the Mardi Gras and cajun cookin'

New Year's Eve: Stay up late, count down with Dick Clark, drink too much, greet the New Year feeling like...

New York, New York: It's a hell of a town...

***Newlyweds:** Ah, the first year of marriage; the honeymoon, settling into your new life together, hanging out with Bob Eubanks...

Niagara Falls: Little upstate New York border town where honeymooners and barrel riders gather. Oh yeah, they have some water thing there, too...

Nice Mice: Cute anthropomorphic or cartoon rodents, rather than the disease-carrying vermin variety

Nightclubs: *Casablanca*, of course

***Ninjas:** Stealthy martial arts assassins in pajamas

No-Exit Motel: Sleazy motels with extremely lenient late-checkout policies

Not-So-True Identity: People pass themselves off as something else; *Soul Man, Gentleman's Agreement*

Nuns & Priests: Collars and habits; *Agnes of God, The Cardinal, Going My Way, Nuns on the Run, Sister Act*

Nuns With Guns: Sister Mary Margaret has traded up from the ol' yardstick. Better practice that penmanship.

Nursploitation!: *Night Call Nurses* offer *Tender Loving Care* in *The Hospital of Terror*

Obsessive Love: You like me. You really, really, *really* like me.

Occult: Witches, warlocks, devil worshippers, spell makers, spell breakers, haunted houses, and so on

Office Surprise: Office supplies used as weapons

Oldest Profession: It's not accounting

The Olympics: *Chariots of Fire* and other tales of athletic discipline

On the Rocks: Alcoholism, alcohol, barflies, moonshining, Prohibition—*Arthur, Days of Wine and Roses, Papa's Delicate Condition, My Favorite Year*

***One Last Job:** Crooks just wanna retire to a warm climate and enjoy their ill-gotten booty, but someone is always pullin' 'em back in!

Only the Lonely: 50 ways to play solitaire—*The Cemetery Club, The Heart Is a Lonely Hunter, Sleepless in Seattle*

Opera: Shouting in a melodic way while in costume

Order in the Court: Courtroom tales, including *The Accused, And Justice for All, A Few Good Men, Witness for the Prosecution*

Organized Crime: Gangsters with Franklin Planners

Otherwise Engaged: Couple buys ring, sets date, and gets ready to march down the aisle, sometimes with a new fiancee—*Moonstruck, Only You, Sleepless in Seattle*

Pacific Islands: Hawaii, Tahiti, Philippines, etc.

Paperboys: Kids who toss papers everywhere but your front porch

Parades & Festivals: *Animal House* and *Ferris Bueller's Day Off*

Paradise Gone Awry: You'd think it'd be perfect, but you'd be mistaken

Parallel Universes: There's a whole other world out there—*Cool World, Who Framed Roger Rabbit?*

***Pardners:** Buddies in the Old West; Butch & Sundance, Wyatt Earp & Doc Holliday, the guys from *Silverado*

Paramedics: Part doctor, part fireman, part delivery driver. Cool!

Parenthood: Moms, dads, substitutes—*Dutch, Ma Barker's Killer Brood, Father of the Bride, Three Men and a Baby, Yours, Mine, and Ours, Raising Arizona*

Paris: Ze city in France with rude occupants and ze Eiffel Tower

Party Hell: *Psycho Girls* have fun at a sleepover until *Monsters Crash the Pajama Party* and it becomes *The Slumber Party Massacre*

Patriotism & Paranoia: Run the flag up the pole and salute it—Rambo, Patton, Norris, etc.

Peace: *Friendly Persuasion, Gandhi*

Period Piece: Costume epics or evocative of a certain time and place; now divided into eras for your time traveling pleasure

15th Century—*Braveheart* and other tales of the end of the Middle Ages

16th Century—The Renaissance; rebirth of culture, art, science

17th Century—The Enlightenment, or Age of Reason

18th Century—Revolutions all over the place

19th Century—more war, plus the Industrial Revolution

20th Century—Epics that span more than one decade

1900s—the decade that began the now-completed 20th century

1910s—stories not involving World War I

1930s—stories not involving the Depression

1940s—stories not involving World War II

1950s—Rock 'n' Roll, Elvis, Eisenhower, McCarthyism, Civil Rights movement begins

1960s—assassinations, hippies, Vietnam, along with more mundane concerns

* = new to this edition

1970s—bad clothes, Watergate, disco, Elvis dies...let's just forget this decade happened

1980s—Reagan, Iran-Contra, John Hughes angst-fests, big hair, and greed

Persian Gulf War: Smart bombs away

Philadelphia: Famous Pennsylvania city that's home to *Rocky*, the Liberty Bell, cheesesteaks, and M. Night Shamamlayan films

Phobias!: Eeeeeeeeeeeeeeek!

Phone Sex: Is it really the next best thing to being there?

Phone Terror: *Don't Answer the Phone*

Physical Problems: *My Left Foot, Coming Home, The Elephant Man, The Other Side of the Mountain, Untamed Heart, The Waterdance*

Pigs: Loveable swine—*Gordy, Babe the Gallant Pig*

Pirates: Avast, ye scurvy dogs! *Captain Blood* drops in on *Treasure Island*

Pittsburgh: City in western Pennsylvania, home of sports teams fond of the colors black and yellow.

Poetry: Not exactly a booming category, but think of *Poetic Justice*

Poisons: *Arsenic and Old Lace* and *D.O.A.*

Police Detectives: They get paid to bust open the big cases amid wild car chases and gunplay.

Politics: *Bob Roberts, Mandela, Whoops Apocalypse*

Pool: *The Hustler*

Pornography: *Hardcore, Body Double*

Post Apocalypse: No more convenience stores

Postwar: After effects of war, generally WWI or WWII but sometimes the Civil War, the War of 1812, the Revolutionary War, and the Ohio Automobile Dealers War

POW/MIA: Captured by the enemy

Pregnant Men: Ahh-nuld fails the *Rabbit Test*

Pregnant Pauses: Humorous takes on pregnancy and birth—*Nine Months, She's Having a Baby*

***Prep School:** Where the children of the elite meet to learn how to be upper-crusty

Presidency: Mr. Lincoln, *JFK*, LBJ, FDR, and, of course, *Dave*

Price of Fame: What goes up...

Private Eyes: There's no such thing as a simple little case...

Prom: A night you'll always remember,..which isn't necessarily a good thing. Right, *Carrie*?

Propaganda: Deliberately stretching the truth in order to persuade

Protests: Hell no, we won't go (to bad movies)! Make popcorn, not war!

***Psychic Abilities:** I see dead people! Or the future, or read minds, or have telekenesis...

Psycho-Thriller: It's all in your mind—*Bad Influence, House of Games, The Silence of the Lambs*

Psychotics/Sociopaths: *Killer Inside Me, Reservoir Dogs, The Stepfather*

***Punk Rock:** Anarchic semi-musical revolution of the late 70s, where the message (if you could decipher it) was more important that the melody. Way more important.

Puppets: Usually with strings, but also muppets

Pure Ego Vehicles: Big stars doing their big star thing—*Hudson Hawk, Harlem Nights, Yes, Giorgio*

Rabbits: *Harvey* has a *Fatal Attraction* for the *Nasty Rabbit*

Race Against Time: Tick, tock, tick, tock—*China Syndrome, Lorenzo's Oil*

Radio: Over the airwaves—*Choose Me, The Fisher King, Radio Days, Sleepless in Seattle*

Rags to Riches: Grit, determination, and hustling (or just pure dumb luck) lead to fortune—*Trading Places, Working Girls*

Rape: Victims and often their revenge

Rebel With a Cause: Bucking the establishment for a reason

Rebel Without a Cause: Bucking the establishment just because it's the establishment

The Red Cross: Organization that helps those in need of blood, disaster relief, and war relief; also monitors treatment of POWs

Red Scare: Cold War and Communism—*The Commies Are Coming, The Commies Are Coming, Reds*

Reefer Madness: Tales of the demon weed.

Rehab: Drying out, sobering up...walking around in bathrobes.

Reincarnation: Why is everyone somebody famous in a past life?

Religion: *Witness, The Last Temptation of Christ*

Religious Epics: Charlton Heston parts the Red Sea—religion on a really big scale

Renegade Body Parts: Hands, fingers, eyes, brains with a life of their own

Repressed Men: Often British (*see* Anthony Hopkins or Hugh Grant), always with plenty of stiffness in upper lip and little elsewhere

Rescue Missions: I'll save you—*The Searcher, Free Willy*

Rescue Missions Involving Time Travel: I'll save you in another dimension—*Back to the Future*

The Resistance: WWII rebels with an anti-Nazi cause

Revenge: A key motivation—*Death and the Maiden, Death Wish*

Revolutionary War: Fought over tea

Rio: As in de Janeiro—that swingin' South American party town.

Road Trip: Escapism courtesy of two- and four-wheel vehicles—*Easy Rider, Coupe de Ville, Pee Wee's Big Adventure, Wild at Heart*

Roaring '20s: Flappers, prohibition, bobbed hair

Robots/Androids: Mechanical but fascinating; *Blade Runner* and *The Terminator*

***Rock Flicks:** Movies about real or made up rockers, starring rock stars, or featuring bands in concert; *Eddie & the Cruisers, The Last Waltz, Almost Famous*

Rock Stars on Film: But can they act? Prince (Symbol), Sting, Elvis, Lennon, The Monkees, Whitney, and so on

Rodeos: Rope tricks with steers

***Rogue Cops:** Corruption in the PD, cops on the take, etc. Usually, *Internal Affairs* gets involved

Role Reversal: Vice versa; empathy test—*Freaky Friday, My Fair Lady, Switch, Soul Man*

Romantic Adventures: Love among the chases and explosions—*The African Queen, Romancing the Stone*

Romantic Comedy: Falling in love has its hilarious moments—*French Kiss, Crossing Delancey, Modern Romance, Much Ado About Nothing*

Romantic Drama: Love thing leads to tension and anxiety—*Cyrano de Bergerac, Far and Away, Sommersby, Tender Mercies*

Romantic Triangles: Three where there's only room for two—*The Age of Innocence, Casablanca, Three of Hearts*

Rome—Ancient Emperors ran the show, feeding Christians to the lions, using V for U, having orgies, and throwing up on purpose...those were the days!

Rome—Modern: Capital city of Italy. The Pope has a little place there

Roommates from Hell: Sometimes they won't do the dishes, sometimes they're homicidal—*Single White Female*

Royalty: Emperors, kings, queens, princes, princesses, crowns, scepters

Royalty, British: Emperors, kings, queens, etc in Merry Olde England

Royalty, Russian: Emperors, czars, and czarinas who ran things in Moscow till those mean old Bolsheviks showed up

Running: Jogging, panting, collapsing

Russia/USSR: Back in what used to be the USSR

Sail Away: Vessels on the water—*Mutiny on the Bounty, Erik the Viking, Mister Roberts*

St. Petersburg: The one in Russia, seat of the old monarchy. You wouldn't wanna have spring break here

Saints: *Bernadette, Saint Joan, A Time for Miracles*

Salespeople: Have I got a deal for you...

***Samurai:** Bodyguards to royalty and nobility in ancient Japan, sometimes they had to freelance

San Francisco: Set in the Northern California city known for hills and sourdough bread

Sanity Check: Inmates running the asylum; also deviant mental states

Satanism: *Speak of the Devil*

Satire & Parody: Biting social commentary or genre spoofs, including *Being There, Airplane!, Down and Out in Beverly Hills, I'm Gonna Git You Sucka, Monty Python's The Meaning of Life, The Player*

Savannah: the city in Georgia, with the southern belles and the big social events

Savants: Half-minded geniuses; *Rain Man, Forrest Gump*

Scams, Stings & Cons: The hustle—*The Billionaire Boys Club, The Color of Money, A Fish Called Wanda, The Grifters, The Sting*

Scared 'Chuteless: Jumping out of airplanes without the proper equipment. Good candidates for a bad case of cement poisoning

School Daze: Education, school, and teachers, generally grammar school days—*Lean on Me, Dead Poet's Society, To Sir, with Love, Teachers*

Sci Fi: Imagination fueled by science and a vision of the future

Sci-Fi Westerns: You ain't from around heah, is ya?

Science & Scientists: *Altered States, Darkman, Them, They, Son of Flubber, The Story of Louis Pasteur*

Scotland: Lush hills, thick brogues, kilts, bagpipes, and *Whiskey Galore*

Screwball Comedy: Snappy repartee between a man and a woman dealing with an impossibly silly situation

Scuba: Wet suits, including *The Abyss, Navy SEALS*

Sculptors: Artists who like to work with clay, rock, hammers, and chisels

Sea Disasters: We've sprung a leak—*The Poseidon Adventure*

Seattle: Showcases the city in Washington state where it rains a lot; the home of grunge rock

***Second Chance:** Another opportunity to set things right, fix mistakes, redeem yourself, or all of the above

Serial Killers: They just won't stop—*Henry: Portrait of a Serial Killer, The Rosary Murders*

Serials: Segmented adventures; Heyday was in the 1930s-*The Adventures of Red Ryder, The Little Rascals, Flash Gordon*

Sex & Sexuality: Focus is on lust, for better or worse—*Alfie, Barbarella, Emmanuelle, Looking for Mr. Goodbar, Rambling Rose, She's Gotta Have It*

Sex on the Beach: Flashing the fish and getting sand in the darndest places; the most famous couple was in *From Here to Eternity* and *Airplane!* lost no time making fun of them

Sexcapades: The wilder edge of the whole sex thing

Sexploitation: Softcore epics usually lacking in plot but not skin—*The Erotic Adventures of Pinocchio*

Sexual Abuse: Victims and their stories—*Twin Peaks, Fire Walk with Me*

Sexual Harassment: When I say no, I mean it

Shipwrecked: Stranded on an island when your boat sinks

Shops & Shopping: When commerce at the mall is a major plot point.

Showbiz Comedies: Laughter behind the scenes in Hollywood or on Broadway

Showbiz Dramas: Tension behind the scenes in Hollywood or on Broadway

Showbiz Musicals: Singing and dancing behind the scenes in Hollywood or on Broadway

Showbiz Thrillers: Screaming behind the scenes in Hollywood or on Broadway

Shrinks: Psychiatry or equivalent, with *The Prince of Tides, One Flew Over the Cuckoo's Nest*

Shutterbugs: Photographers and their pictures—*The Public Eye, The Eyes of Laura Mars, Peeping Tom*

Silent Films: No small talk/no big talk/no talk talk

Silent Horror/Fantasy Classics: Silent screams, expressions of terror

Single Parents: Divorced or widowed, they're doing the work of two—and they're back in the dating scene, usually assisted by match-making kids

Singles: Not always swinging but still solidly single—*About Last Night, Singles, When Harry Met Sally*

Skateboarding: Teens on wheels—*Gleaming the Cube*

Skating: Roller and ice, including *The Cutting Edge, Xanadu*

Skiing: Slap on a couple of waxed boards and off you go—*Downhill Racer, Swinging Ski Girls*

Skinheads: Nazi wannabes wreak havok and cause trouble

Skydiving: Jumping from a plane with a polyester slip

Slapstick Comedy: Humor of the physical sort, including Abbott and Costello, the Marx Brothers, sports comedies, Ernest, Pink Panther, Home Alone, the Three Stooges

Slavery: *Roots, Spartacus*

***Small-Town Sheriffs:** Think Sly in *Cop Land*, or Buford Pusser of *Walking Tall* fame

Smuggler's Blues: Making, transporting, and selling the drugs. Don't *Blow* your cool in the *Traffic*.

Snakes: Slithering creatures who frighten many—*Raiders of the Lost Ark* **Soccer:** Known as football outside of the USA—*Victory, Ladybugs*

South America: Right below North America—*Aguirre, the Wrath of God, The Mission*

Southern Belles: Southern gals ooze charm—*Blaze, Driving Miss Daisy, Steel Magnolias*

Space Operas: Going where no spam has gone before—*Alien, Star Trek, 2001: A Space Odyssey, Apollo 13*

Spaghetti Western: Clint with a squint, *A Fistful of Dollars, My Name is Nobody, Once Upon a Time in the West*

Spain: Siesta

***Spanish Civil War:** Franco and the Fascists vs. the defenders of the newly-elected Socialist government. A preview of how WWII would be fought

Spies & Espionage: Trench coats, dark glasses, Bond, *North by Northwest*

Sports Comedies: Humorous athletic tales, generally not based on a true story

Sports Dramas: Intense athletic tales, often based on a true story

Spousal Abuse: *The Burning Bed, What's Love Got to Do With It?*

Stagestruck: Stories of the theatre; *Broadway Melody* sung at the *Stage Door* by *The Dolly Sisters*

Stalked: No, I do not want to switch to MCI

Star Gazing: Not Hollywood stars, astrology/astronomy type stars

Stepparents: New spouse hiding either alien origins or sociopathic tendencies greets existing clan

Stewardesses: *Three Guys Named Mike* go to *Stewardess School* and meet *Blazing Stewardesses*

Stolen from Asia: American remakes of Asian classics—usually Kurosawa's; *Seven Samurai* becomes *The Magnificent Seven*

Stolen from Europe: American remakes of European fare; *A Walk in the Clouds, The Vanishing, Scent of a Woman*

Stolen From France: Hollywood goes to its favorite remake well; *Diabolique, Cousins, Nine Months, Three Men and a Baby*

** = new to this edition*

Storytelling: *Amazing Stories, Grim Prairie Tales*

Strained Suburbia: Neighborhood is not what it seems—*Dennis the Menace, Neighbors, Edward Scissorhands*

Strippers: Take it off, take it all off

***Struggling Artists:** It's hard not to struggle when your work only becomes valuable after you're dead

Struggling Musicians: Talented, but still reaching for the top

Stupid Is...: Stupidity on purpose—*Billy Madison, Dumb and Dumber,* or dumbness as a plot device—*Being There, Forrest Gump*

Submarines: Deep sea diving; *Das Boot, Up Periscope, Run Silent, Run Deep, Hunt for Red October*

Subways: A train for shorter trips—*Speed, The Taking of Pelham One Two Three*

Suicide: Self-inflicted premature ends—*The Big Chill, Scent of a Woman, Romeo and Juliet*

Summer Camp: Where children go to misbehave, including *Meatballs* and *Sleepaway Camp*

Super Heroes: Men and women of extraordinary strength and abilities wearing silly-looking costumes

Supernatural Comedies: *Beetlejuice* marries *She-Devil* and they take *The Ghost Train* to their *Haunted Honeymoon*

Supernatural Horror: Forces from beyond terrorize those who are here

Supernatural Martial Arts: Kung fu *From Beyond the Grave*

Supernatural Westerns: Forces from beyond terrorize cowboys in the Old West

Surfing: Awesome wave, dude! *Mad Wax, The Surf Movie, Surf Nazis Must Die, Endless Summer*

Survival: *Alive, The Bridge over the River Kwai, Testament*

Suspended Animation: Frozen in time—*Coma, Late for Dinner*

Swashbucklers: Crossed swords and rope swinging, including *Robin Hood,* Zorro, various Musketeers, *Captain Blood, The Three Amigos*

Swimming: Ranging from *Gremlins* to *Jaws* to *The Swimmer* to *Cocoon*

Swingers: *Bob & Carol & Ted & Alice* try *Group Marriage* and Carol and Alice become *Swinging Wives*

Sword & Sandal: *See* Arnold Schwarzenegger's early career

Sydney: Big Aussie city; recent site of Olympic glory

Talking Animals: *Dr. Doolittle* treats *Babe*

Tattoos: *The Illustrated Man* visits *Cape Fear* to do battle with *Cyber Bandits*

Team Efforts: Working together pays off—*Hoosiers, Memphis Belle, Renaissance Man*

Tearjerkers: Crying fests—*Love Story, Steel Magnolias, Old Yeller*

Technology—Rampant: Machines that wreak havoc—*Metropolis, Death Ray 2000, Blade Runner*

Teen Angst: Adolescent anxieties, including *Baby It's You* and almost everything produced or directed by John Hughes

***Teen Horror:** Horror flicks where the body count is skewed toward the 15-19 demographic (isn't that pretty much all of 'em?)

Tennis: Anyone?

Terminal Confusion: Luggage gets mixed up at the airport, bus station, etc. Trouble usually follows

Terminal Illness: Someone's gonna die a tragic death from a horrible disease, but probably not before falling on love or doing something inspirational. Usually not considered comedy premise

Terror in Tall Buildings: From *Die Hard* to *Speed* to *The Towering Inferno*

Terrorism: Love affairs with hidden bombs

Thanksgiving: Huge dinner, football, familial angst, turkey coma, Christmas shopping may now commence

The Third Degree: Where were you on the night of...

This Is My Life: Autobiographies starring the subject—Muhammed Ali in *The Greatest,* Audie Murphy goes *To Hell and Back*

This Is Your Life: Biography and autobiography, including *The Babe Ruth Story, Amazing Howard Hughes, Amadeus, Catherine the Great, Great Balls of Fire, Raging Bull, What's Love Got to Do With It?*

3-D Flicks: Bring your special glasses

Thumbs Up: Hitchin' a ride—*Even Cowgirls Get the Blues, The Hitcher*

Tibet: So I says "Hey, Lama, how's about a little somethin' for the effort..."

Time Travel: Fast forward or reverse with Bill and Ted, *Dr. Who, Back to the Future,* and *Peggy Sue Got Married*

Time Warped: You wake up in an era not your own; *Austin Powers,* the Bradys and the Cleavers coping with the '90s

Titanic: The unsinkable ship that hit an iceberg its first time out...and sunk. It was in all the papers

***To the Moon!:** *Apollo 13, From the Earth to the Moon*

Tokyo: Crowded city in Japan terrorized by Godzilla

Torn in Two (or More): *Sybil* and *Dr. Jekyll and Mr. Hyde* are *Raising Cain* leading *Separate Lives* on the *Edge of Sanity*

Toronto: Big city in Canada where they don't make you speak French. Home of Skydome and the Hockey Hall of Fame

Torrid Love Scenes: Steamy and/or sticky—*Angel Heart, Bull Durham, From Here to Eternity, Risky Business, The Unbearable Lightness of Being*

Toys: *Babes in Toyland, The Toy, Toys*

Tragedy: The fate of humankind, magnified—*King Lear, Madame Bovary, Tess, The World According to Garp*

Trains: Rhythm of the clackity clack—*Romance on the Orient Express, Throw Momma from the Train, Running Scared, The Silver Streak*

Trapped with a Killer!: And there's no escape—*Dead Calm, Misery, The Shining*

Treasure Hunt: Looking for hidden riches—*Klondike Fever, Treasure of Sierra Madre, Romancing the Stone*

Trees & Forests: Can't see one for the other, that wilderness paradox—includes *Mr. Sycamore* and *The Wizard of Oz*

***Triads:** Chinese organized crime outfit. Chow-Yun Fat is always shooting it out with 'em in John Woo flicks

True Crime: Based on fact, including *The Boston Strangler, The Executioner's Song, Helter Skelter*

True Stories: Approximations of real-life events often significantly fictionalized for the screen, including *All The President's Men, Chariots of Fire, Cry Freedom, Heart Like a Wheel, The Killing Fields, Silkwood*

TV Pilot Movies: Some became series; some did not

TV Series: Collections, anthologies, and individual episodes of memorable shows—*I Love Lucy, Star Trek, The Fugitive*

Twins: *Double Trouble, Double Vision, Mirror Images*

Twister!: The big wind not caused by Mexican food that picks up heavy things (houses, cows, trucks) and deposits them elsewhere

***Under My Skin:** People (or cartoon characters) get inside a guy's pelt, and crawl around for a little while

***Undercover Cops:** Cops pretend they're bad guys to catch more bad guys, but sometimes they get *In Too Deep*

Unexplained Phenomena: No apparent reason for an event

U.S. Marshals: Law enforcement branch that transports prisoners, hunts down fugitives, and in the Old West, handled the showdown duties

Up All Night: Movie takes place mostly after the sun goes down and *Before Sunrise*

Urban Drama: *American Me* to *Boyz N the Hood* to *Grand Canyon* to *Zebrahead*

***Urban Gangstas:** Gangs fight it out for their piece of the mean streets of the inner city; *Colors, New Jack City*

The USO: Entertained the troops through two world wars and a variety of police actions—with Bob Hope usually leading the way

Vacations: From *City Slickers* to *Deliverance* to *Fraternity Vacation*

Vampire Babes: Blood sucking dames—*The Brides of Dracula*

Vampire Spoof: Comedic blood suckers, including *Buffy, Andy Warhol's Dracula, Dracula Sucks*

Vampires: More serious vein of blood sucking varmint, including *Dracula* in his many manifestations

Venice: Italian city of gondolas

Veterans: Retired fighting men (and women)—*Alamo Bay* to *Who'll Stop the Rain*

Vietnam War: *Platoon, Hamburger Hill, Apocalypse Now, Good Morning, Vietnam*

Vigilantes: Individuals take the law into their own hands—*Death Wish, The Outlaw Josey Wales*

Virtual Reality: High-tech video game that seems real...to computer geeks

Viva Las Vegas!: Celebrating America's tackiest city—*Honeymoon in Vegas, Sister Act*

Volcanoes: Mountain blowing off steam, including *Joe Versus the Volcano*

Volleyball: *Side Out* used to be the only one till we remembered the barechested boys from *Top Gun*

Voodoo: From *Angel Heart* to *How to Stuff a Wild Bikini* to *Weekend at Bernie's 2*

Vote for Me!: Political campaigns for various offices, from student council (*Election*) to U.S. President (*The Candidate*)

Waitresses: *Alice Doesn't Live Here Anymore,* she went to *Atlantic City* to get some *Mystic Pizza*

War Between the Sexes: Men and women battle for supremacy—*It Happened One Night, The King and I, He Said, She Said, Romancing the Stone, When Harry Met Sally, The War of the Roses, Thelma & Louise*

War, General: Generally any conflict that defies other classification—*The Alamo, Gunga Din, The Last of the Mohicans*

Wedding Bells: Memorable weddings; *Father of the Bride, Four Weddings and a Funeral, Sixteen Candles, The Wedding*

Wedding Hell: Horror-filled or anxiety-ridden weddings; *The Blood Spattered Bride, The Brides Wore Blood, The Graduate, Wedding Banquet*

Werewolves: Full moon wonders, like *Wolf*

Western Comedy: Gags and horses—*Ballad of Cable Hogue, Blazing Saddles, Rancho Deluxe, Support Your Local Sheriff*

Westerns: Cowboys, cowgirls, horses and jingle jangling spurs on the frontier

Westrogens: The Old West through women's eyes

Whales: Really big sea-faring mammals. It's best to just stay out of their way...Just ask *Pinocchio*

Whitewater Rafting: Wild ride down a raging river, often in the company of a psycho

***Widows & Widowers:** The one who's left when a spouse dies; *Dragonfly, Sleepless in Seattle*

Wild Kingdom: Animals on their own and interacting with confused humans, including *The Bear, Dumbo, Born Free, Free Willy, Never Cry Wolf*

Wilderness: More trees than a forest, plus wild critters—*The Life and Times of Grizzly Adams*

Witchcraft: From *Hocus Pocus* to *Three Sovereigns for Sarah* to *The Wizard of Oz*

Witness Protection Program: Rat out your "associates," get a new identity

Women: Impressive women, less than impressive women, and issues concerning women—*Crimes of the Heart, My Brilliant Career, Passion Fish, Working Girls*

Women Cops: Female officers of the law

Women in Prison: The things that go on in the big doll house

Women in War: Nurses, WACs, WAVES, USO performers, sometimes prisoners—they also served...

Wonder Women: *Attack of the 50-Foot Woman, Ripley, La Femme Nikita, Supergirl*

World War I: The First Big One, including *African Queen, Gallipoli, Grand Illusion*

World War II: The Last Big One, including *A Bridge Too Far, Guadalcanal Diary, The Guns of Navarone, Hope and Glory, Memphis Belle, Tora! Tora! Tora!*

***World War II Spies:** British and American agents who used stealth and deception to fight the Nazis

Wrestling: Choreographed sport involving men and women—*No Holds Barred, All the Marbles, Wrestling Women vs. the Aztec Ape*

Writers: Tortured souls who put pen to paper when they're not putting bottle to lips. Does not include the ink-stained wretches of the journalistic trade

The Wrong Man: ...has been accused or convicted. *The Fugitive* is in a *Frenzy* because *Jack's Back.*

Wrong Side of the Tracks: Often involves relationship with someone on the right side—*Cannery Row, The Flamingo Kid, Pretty in Pink, White Palace*

Yakuza: Japanese version of the Mafia, very organized crime

You Lose, You Die: Sports goes nuts—only the winner survives; *Arena, Rollerball, Tron*

Yuppie Nightmares: Young adults find best-laid plans for attaining wealth and privilege going astray—*Baby Boom, Desperately Seeking Susan, The Mighty Ducks, Pacific Heights, Something Wild, Wall Street*

Zombie Soldiers: Recently undead in the army—*They Saved Hitler's Brain*

Zombies: Recently undead everywhere—*I Walked with a Zombie, Night of the Living Dead*

* = new to this edition

The **Category Index** includes subject terms ranging from straight genre descriptions (Drama, Comedy, etc.) to more off-the-wall themes (Nuns with Guns, Eyeballs!). These terms can help you identify unifying themes (Baseball, Heists), settings (Miami, Nifty '50s), events (The Great Depression, World War II), occupations (Clowns, Cops, Doctors & Nurses), or suddenly animate objects (Killer Appliances, Killer Cars). Category definitions and cross-references precede the index; category terms are listed alphabetically. **A tipped triangle indicates a video rated three bones or higher.**

Abortion

The Choice
Choices
The Cider House Rules▲
Citizen Ruth
Critical Choices
Daddy's Gone A-Hunting▲
Dogma
Eye of God▲
Family Life
If These Walls Could Talk
Listen to Me
Maria's Child
Panic in Needle Park▲
A Private Matter▲
Rain Without Thunder
Roe vs. Wade▲
Rude
Signs & Wonders
Silent Victim
The Story of Women▲
Things You Can Tell Just by Looking at Her
Walpurgis Night▲

Action-Adventure

***see** Adventure Drama; Boom!; Comic Adventure; Disaster Flicks; Martial Arts; Romantic Adventures; Swashbucklers*

Action-Comedy

***see also** Action-Adventure; Comedy*

Bait
Bounty Hunters 2: Hardball
Camouflage
Charlie's Angels
Chill Factor
Double Agent 73
Double Take
Gorgeous
Kelly's Heroes
Meltdown
Miracles
Partners
Project A
Project A: Part 2
Rush Hour

Adolescence

***see** Coming of Age; Hell High School; Summer Camp; Teen Angst*

Adoption & Orphans

***see also** Hard Knock Life; Only the Lonely*

A la Mode
Across the Great Divide
Adoption▲
The Affair of the Necklace
Aladdin▲
All Mine to Give
The Amazing Mrs. Holiday
Anastasia
Andre
Angel in a Taxi
Anne of Green Gables▲
Annie
Annie▲
Babes on Broadway
Bachelor Mother▲
Back to the Secret Garden
Bambi▲
Batman Forever▲
Battle Hymn
The Beniker Gang
Beshkempir the Adopted Son
Big Daddy
Big Red
Blossoms in the Dust
Blues Brothers 2000
Bogus
Born Free▲
Born in America
The Boy with the Green Hair▲
The Breaks
Catfish in Black Bean Sauce
The Children of An Lac
Children of the Corn 3: Urban Harvest
Christmas Lilies of the Field
Chronicle of a Boy Alone
The Cider House Rules▲
City Boy▲
A Cry from the Streets
Crystalstone
Daddy Long Legs
Daddy Long Legs▲
Dangerous Orphans
D.A.R.Y.L.
David Copperfield▲
David Copperfield
Deadly Sanctuary
Defiant
The Devil's Backbone
Dick Tracy▲
Don't Cry, It's Only Thunder
Eagle's Shadow
Earthling
The Education of Little Tree▲
Escape to Witch Mountain▲
The Father Clements Story
Fighting Father Dunne
First Love
The Flamingo Rising
Flirting with Disaster▲
Free Willy
Gloria
Great Expectations
Great Expectations▲
Great Expectations
Great Expectations▲
Great Expectations
Great Expectations: The Untold Story
Heaven on Earth
Home at Last
A Home of Our Own
Hoodoo Ann
Immediate Family
Intimate Relations
The Jack Knife Man▲
James and the Giant Peach▲
Jane Eyre
Jane Eyre▲
Jane Eyre
The Kid▲
The Kid Who Loved Christmas
King, Queen, Knave▲
Korczak▲
La Passante▲
Lady from Yesterday
The Lady Is Willing
The Land Before Time▲
Like Mike
The Little Kidnappers
Little Men
Little Orphan Annie
The Little Princess
A Long Way Home
Losing Isaiah▲
The Lost Child
Love Come Down
Love Without Fear
The Loves of Edgar Allen Poe
Mad Max: Beyond Thunderdome
Madeline
The Magic Christian▲
Major Payne
Man, Woman & Child
Manny's Orphans
Mercury Rising
Mighty Aphrodite
Mighty Joe Young
Min & Bill
Moll Flanders
Mon Amie Max
Mondo
My Dog Shep
My Little Girl
Mystery of the Million Dollar Hockey Puck
Napoleon and Samantha▲
Nice Girl Like Me
Nothing But the Night
The Odyssey of the Pacific
The Official Story▲
Oliver!▲
Oliver & Company
Oliver Twist▲
Oliver Twist
Oliver Twist▲
Oliver Twist
Oliver Twist▲
On the Right Track
One Good Cop
The Orphan
Orphan Train▲
Orphans▲
Orphans of the Storm▲
Our Very Own
Paper Moon▲
Peck's Bad Boy
Penny Serenade▲
Pixote▲
A Place for Annie
Pollyanna
Pollyanna▲
The Poor Little Rich Girl
The Prince of Central Park▲
Prison for Children
Problem Child
Queen Kelly▲
The Quest
Rags to Riches
Raising Heroes
Rebecca of Sunnybrook Farm
Record of a Tenement Gentleman
Red Cherry
Redwood Curtain
Rent-A-Kid
The Revolt of Job▲
Rikisha-Man▲
The Road Home
The Road to Life
The Royal Tenenbaums▲
Sally of the Sawdust
Samantha
Santa with Muscles
Scout's Honor
The Sea Serpent
Second Best▲
The Secret Garden▲
The Secret Garden
The Secret Garden▲
The Secret Garden
Secrets and Lies
Shep Comes Home
Shooting Fish
Sidewalks of London▲
A Simple Twist of Fate
Sioux City
Snow Dogs
Snow White and the Seven Dwarfs▲
Sois Belle et Tais-Toi
A Soldier's Daughter Never Cries
The Stranger Who Looks Like Me
Streetwise▲
Stuart Little
Sugar Cane Alley▲
The Sugarland Express▲
Sundays & Cybele▲
Superman: The Movie▲
Susannah of the Mounties
Tarzan Finds a Son▲
They Still Call Me Bruce
Three Secrets
The Tie That Binds
To Each His Own▲
Tom Jones▲
The Tunnel of Love
Twisted
Up/Down/Fragile
Way Back Home
Welcome to Sarajevo▲
Where the River Runs Black
Which Way Home
Who'll Save Our Children?▲
Wild Hearts Can't Be Broken▲
The World Accuses
Young & Free
Young People

Adultery

Bed and Board▲
Bread and Tulips▲
The Bridges of Madison County▲
Darkness Falls
The Decalogue▲
Fatal Attraction▲

Adultery

The Golden Bowl
The Good Girl
Heart
Hitched
The Ice Storm➚
In the Mood for Love
Lantana➚
The Man Who Wasn't There➚
The Monkey's Mask
Nina Takes a Lover
The Scarlet Letter
The Scarlet Letter➚
The Scarlet Letter
The Shooting Party➚
Sidewalks of New York
Signs & Wonders
Steam: A Turkish Bath➚
A Summer Place
Town and Country
The Two Jakes
Unfaithful
Unfaithfully Yours➚
Unfaithfully Yours
The Unfaithfuls
Y Tu Mama Tambien

Adventure Drama

***see also** Action-Adventure; Boom!; Drama*

Abandon Ship
Ace of Aces
Act of Piracy
Action in the North Atlantic
The Admirable Crichton
The Adventures of Frontier Fremont
The Adventures of Huck Finn➚
The Adventures of Huckleberry Finn➚
The Adventures of Huckleberry Finn
The Adventures of Milo & Otis➚
The Adventures of Robin Hood➚
The Adventures of the Wilderness Family
The Adventures of Tom Sawyer➚
Air Force➚
Air Force One➚
Alaska
Alexander Nevsky➚
Ali Baba and the Forty Thieves
All the Rivers Run
Allan Quatermain and the Lost City of Gold
Alligator Alley
Aloha, Bobby and Rose
The Amazing Panda Adventure
Amazon
The Amazons
America
American Empire
American Roulette
The American Scream
American Tiger
And I Alone Survived
Angels of the City
Anzacs: The War Down Under➚
Apocalypse Now➚
Apollo 13➚
Appointment with Crime
The Arab Conspiracy
Archer's Adventure
Arctic Blue
Arizona Heat
Around the World in 80 Days➚
Around the World in 80 Days
The Ascent
Assassination
The Aviator
Back in the USSR
Backdraft
Backlash
Barbary Coast➚
The Baron
Bataan
Battle Hell
The Battle of El Alamein
Battle of the Eagles
The Battle of the Japan Sea
Battleforce
Bear Island
Beau Geste➚
The Beloved Rogue➚
Beneath the 12-Mile Reef
Benji the Hunted
The Berlin Conspiracy
Between Heaven and Hell➚
Beyond Rangoon
Big Bad Mama
The Big Push
The Big Scam
Bigfoot: The Unforgettable Encounter
Billy Budd➚
Black Arrow➚
The Black Arrow
Black Bikers from Hell
Black Moon Rising
Blackout
Blood and Sand➚
Blood Debts
Blowing Wild
Blown Away
The Blue and the Gray
Blue Fin
The Blue Lamp➚
Blue Thunder
The Bodyguard from Beijing
Bomb at 10:10
Bombardier
Born Wild
Botany Bay
The Bounty
Breakdown➚
The Breed
Brighty of the Grand Canyon
Brotherhood of Death
A Bullet Is Waiting
Burke & Wills
By Way of the Stars
Cadence
California Gold Rush
Call of the Wild
Camel Boy
Casablanca Express
The Castilian
Casualties of War➚
The Cat
Chain Reaction
Chains of Gold
The Challenge➚
Challenge of a Lifetime
The Charge of the Light Brigade➚
Children of the Wild
China Gate➚
Chrome Soldiers
Clarence, the Cross-eyed Lion➚
Claws
Clear and Present Danger
The Climb
The Coast Patrol
Code Name: Emerald
Cold Heat
Cold Justice
Command Decision
Commando Attack
Con Air➚
Con Man
Conspiracy Theory➚
Contagious
Coogan's Bluff➚
The Cop & the Girl
Cop-Out
The Corruptor➚
Corsair
The Count of Monte Cristo
The Count of Monte Cristo➚
The Count of Monte Cristo
Courage Mountain
Courage of Black Beauty
Courage of Rin Tin Tin
Crimebusters
Crimson Romance
Crimson Tide➚
Dam Busters➚
Danger Beneath the Sea
Dangerous Ground
Dangerous Moonlight➚
Dangerous Passage
Daring Game
Dark Before Dawn
Dark Mountain
Dark Tide
The Darkside
The Dawson Patrol
The Day Will Dawn➚
Days of Thunder
Deadlock
Deadlock 2
Deadly Sanctuary
Death in the Garden
The Death Merchant
Death Stalk
The Deceivers
Deliverance➚
Desert Warrior
Destination Tokyo
Dick Tracy➚
Dick Turpin
Die Hard➚
Die Hard 2: Die Harder➚
Die Hard: With a Vengeance
Dinosaur Island
Diplomatic Immunity
Dive Bomber➚
Down to the Sea in Ships
Dragonfly Squadron
Dust➚
Each Dawn I Die
The Eagle Has Landed➚
East of Borneo
Edge of Honor
84 Charlie MoPic➚
The Elusive Pimpernel
The Emerald Forest➚
Enchanted Island
Enemy Below➚
Enemy of the State
The Enforcer
Eraser
Escape to Witch Mountain➚
Evel Knievel
Executive Decision
The Expendables
Eye of the Wolf
Fangs of the Wild
Fantastic Balloon Voyage
Fantastic Seven
Far from Home: The Adventures of Yellow Dog
A Far Off Place
Farewell to the King
The Fencing Master
Ferry to Hong Kong
55 Days at Peking➚
The Fighting Prince of Donegal
Fire Alarm
Fire in the Night
Firepower
Flame of Araby
Flame Over India➚
The Flash
Flight of the Grey Wolf
Flipper➚
Flying Leathernecks➚
Flying Tigers
Follow Me
For Whom the Bell Tolls➚
Fort Saganne
Fortunes of War
Forty Thousand Horsemen
The Four Feathers➚
The Four Feathers
F.P. 1
F.P. 1 Doesn't Answer
Free Grass
Free Willy
Free Willy 2: The Adventure Home
Free Willy 3: The Rescue
The Fugitive➚
Fugitive Champion
Full Eclipse
Fury to Freedom: The Life Story of Raul Ries
Future Zone
Game for Vultures
The Gaucho➚
The Ghost and the Darkness
Glory & Honor
God's Country
Goldrush: A Real Life Alaskan Adventure
Goliath Awaits
Gone in 60 Seconds
Great Adventure
The Great Elephant Escape
The Great Escape➚
The Great Escape 2: The Untold Story
The Great Locomotive Chase
The Great Train Robbery➚
The Green Glove
Greystoke: The Legend of Tarzan, Lord of the Apes
Grizzly Mountain
Guadalcanal Diary
Gun Cargo
Gunblast
Gunga Din➚
The Gunrunner
Hackers
The Halls of Montezuma
Hamlet➚
Hangfire
Hard Knocks
Harley
Hawk and Castile
Hell Commandos
Hell in the Pacific➚
Hell River
Hell Squad
Hell to Eternity
Hellcats of the Navy
Hellfighters
Hell's Angels➚
Hell's Brigade: The Final Assault
Here Come the Littles: The Movie
The Heroes of Desert Storm
Heroes Three
Himalaya➚
Himatsuri➚
Hired to Kill
Hiroshima: Out of the Ashes➚
Hit!
Homeward Bound: The Incredible Journey➚
Horatio Hornblower➚
Horatio Hornblower: The Adventure Continues➚
Hostile Waters
Huck and the King of Hearts
The Hunt for Red October➚
Hurricane Smith
Hustler Squad
Immortal Sergeant
In Harm's Way
In Love and War
In Search of a Golden Sky
In Which We Serve➚
The Indian Tomb➚
Indiana Jones and the Last Crusade➚
Indiana Jones and the Temple of Doom➚
Inferno in Paradise
Into Thin Air: Death on Everest
The Iron Mask
Iron Will
Island of the Blue Dolphins
Island Trader
Islands
Isle of Forgotten Sins
Istanbul
It Rained All Night the Day I Left
Jack London's The Call of the Wild
JAG
Jaguar
Jamaica Inn
Jason and the Argonauts
Jaws of Justice
Jenny's War
Jet Pilot
Joey
Johnny Mnemonic
The Journey of Natty Gann➚
Journey to the Center of the Earth
Joy Ride to Nowhere
Juggernaut➚
Jungle
Jungle Goddess
Jurassic Park➚
Jurassic Park 3
Kamikaze '89➚
The Karate Kid➚
The Karate Kid: Part 2
The Karate Kid: Part 3
Kashmiri Run
Kavik the Wolf Dog
Keeper of the City
Keeping Track
Kid Colter
Kidnapped
The Killer➚
The Killer Elite
Killer Instinct
King of New York➚
King Solomon's Mines➚
King Solomon's Mines
King Solomon's Treasure
Kingfisher Caper
Kiss and Kill
Klondike Fever
Knives of the Avenger
Kojiro➚
K2: The Ultimate High
La Guerre Est Finie➚
Lady Avenger
Lady Cocoa
Landslide
Lassie: Adventures of Neeka
Lassie, Come Home
Lassie: Well of Love
Lassiter
The Last Hunter
Last Man Standing
The Last of the Finest
The Last of the Mohicans
The Last of the Mohicans➚
The Last Place on Earth
The Last Riders
The Last Season
Legend of Billie Jean
Legend of Lobo
The Legend of Sea Wolf
The Legend of the Sea Wolf
The Legend of Wolf Mountain
Lethal Pursuit
Liana, Jungle Goddess
Life & Times of Grizzly Adams
The Lion Man
Lion of the Desert➚
The Live Wire
Loaded Guns
Lockdown
Lost
The Lost World: Jurassic Park 2
Lost Zeppelin
Macao➚
The Mad Bomber
Made for Love
Magnificent Adventurer
The Man from Beyond
The Man in the Iron Mask➚
The Man in the Iron Mask
The Man in the Iron Mask➚
Man of Legend
Manhunt for Claude Dallas
The Mask of Zorro➚
Massacre in Dinosaur Valley
The Master of Ballantrae
The McConnell Story
Memphis Belle➚
Men in War
Men of Steel
Merlin and the Sword
Miami Vice
Midnight Crossing
Midway
Milo & Otis
Ms. 45➚
Mission Phantom
Mr. Kingstreet's War
Moby Dick➚
Moby Dick
Money Movers
Money Train
The Moon-Spinners
Moran of the Lady Letty
Mountain Family Robinson
Mountain of the Cannibal God
Moving Target
Murder Without Motive
The Mutiny of the Elsinore
My Dog Shep
Naked Jungle➚
The Navy Comes Through
The Negotiator
Night Crossing
The Night Train to Kathmandu
Nightstick
No Greater Love
No Time to Die
Noon Sunday
Norseman
The North Star➚
Northern Pursuit
Northwest Passage➚
Number One with a Bullet
Objective, Burma!➚
Obsessed
Oceans of Fire
The Odyssey
Omega Syndrome
On Wings of Eagles
One Armed Executioner
One Man Force
One Minute to Zero
One of Our Aircraft Is Missing➚
One That Got Away➚
Operation Cross Eagles
Operation Haylift
Operation Julie
Operation 'Nam
Operation Thunderbolt
Operation Warzone
Opposing Force
Oubliette
Outbreak➚
Outlaw Blues
Outlaw Force
The Package
Paco
Palais Royale
Papillon➚
Party Line
Passenger 57
Passion
Pathfinder➚
The Patriot
Patriot Games➚
Payoff
The Peacemaker
Penitentiary
Penitentiary 2
Penitentiary 3
The Perils of Gwendoline
Permission To Kill
The Phantom
Pharaoh
Pirates of the High Seas
Place in Hell
Platoon➚
Platoon Leader
Plunder Road
Plunge Into Darkness
Policewomen
Pork Chop Hill➚
Portrait of a Hitman
Pray for the Wildcats
The Presidio
Prime Target
Prince Brat and the Whipping Boy➚
Prisoner in the Middle
Private Investigations
PT 109
Pursuit of the Graf Spee
Radio Patrol
Raid on Entebbe➚
Raid on Rommel
Raiders of the Lost Ark➚
Rainbow Warrior
Ran➚
Raw Courage
The Real Glory➚
Reap the Wild Wind
Red Barry
Red Flag: The Ultimate Game
Renegades
The Replacement Killers
Report to the Commissioner➚
The Rescue
Retreat, Hell!
Revelation
Revenge
Riot in Cell Block 11➚
The River Pirates
The River Wild
Robbery
Robin Hood: Prince of Thieves
RoboCop➚

➚ *= rated three bones or higher*

Ronin
Rudyard Kipling's The Jungle Book
Runaway Train▲
Running out of Time▲
The Saint
The St. Valentine's Day Massacre
San Demetrio, London
The Sand Pebbles▲
Sands of Iwo Jima▲
Sardinia Kidnapped
Savage Hunger
Savage Justice
Savage Sam
Savage Streets
Scaramouche▲
The Scarlet Car
Scarlet Spear
Scorchy
Scott of the Antarctic
Sea Chase
Sea Devils
Sea Gypsies
The Sea Hawk▲
The Sea Shall Not Have Them
Sea Wolves
Search and Destroy
Secret Weapon
Self-Defense
Sell Out
Sergeant York▲
Seven Alone
Sex Crimes
The Shadow
Shadow Force
Shame
Shark!
She
She Came to the Valley
Shell Shock
Shogun Assassin
Shooting Stars
Shout at the Devil
The Siege
The Siege of Firebase Gloria
The Silent Enemy
Silent Raiders
Silk
The Silver Stallion: King of the Wild Brumbies
Sinai Commandos
The Sinister Urge
Sink the Bismarck▲
Sins of Rome
Six Pack
Sky Riders
Slow Moves
Smugglers
The Sniper
Sniper
Sno-Line
Sodom and Gomorrah
Soldier of Fortune
Sonny Boy
Sorcerer
Soul Vengeance
Souls at Sea
South of Hell Mountain
Spawn of the North
Special Forces
The Specialist
Speed▲
Spirit of the Eagle
The Spring
Squanto: A Warrior's Tale▲
Stanley and Livingstone▲
Star Trek: Insurrection
The Starfighters
The Steel Claw
The Steel Helmet▲
Steele Justice
Steele's Law
The Sting▲
The Stone Killer
Strange Days▲
Street Crimes
Street War
Streets of Fire
Strike Force
Striker
Striker's Mountain
Sub Down
Submarine Seahawk
Sudden Death
Sundown
Sunset Grill
Sunset Heat
Surabaya Conspiracy
Surfacing
Survival Run
The Swiss Family Robinson▲
Switchback
The Taking of Pelham One Two Three▲
Tank
Taps
The Ten Million Dollar Getaway
Thelma & Louise▲
They Were Expendable▲
Thirty-Six Hours of Hell
Those Calloways
The 317th Platoon▲
The Three Musketeers
The Three Musketeers▲
Three the Hard Way
Throw Down
Thunderground
Tides of War
Tiger Fangs
A Tiger Walks
Tim Tyler's Luck
Tom Sawyer
Top Gun
Tour of Duty
Toy Soldiers
Tribulation
Triple Cross▲
Trouble in Paradise
True Blood
True Heart
Truth or Die
Turnaround
Twisted Justice
Two Years before the Mast
Unconquered
Underworld▲
U.S. Marshals
U.S. Seals
Up Periscope
Valley of Wanted Men
Violent Breed
Von Ryan's Express▲
Wake Island▲
A Walk in the Sun▲
Walking Back
A Waltz Through the Hills
The War Boy
Warkill
We Dive at Dawn▲
Weekend War
What a Way to Die
Wheel of Fortune
Where the Spirit Lives
White Fire
White Fury
White Hot
White Squall
The White Tower▲
White Wolves 2: Legend of the Wild
The Wicked Lady
The Wild Pair
Wild Riders
Wild Thing
A Wing and a Prayer▲
Winning▲
Wooden Horse▲
The World in His Arms
World War III
The Year of Living Dangerously▲
Yellowneck
Young & Free
A Young Connecticut Yankee in King Arthur's Court
Young Warlord
Young Warriors
Zafarinas
Zeppelin
Zulu
Zulu Dawn▲

Advertising

***see also** Front Page; Mass Media*

Advertising Rules!
The Agency
Beauty School
Beer
Bliss▲
Bounce
C.O.D.
Crazy People
DROP Squad
A Fool and His Money
The Girl Can't Help It
Her Husband's Affairs
The Horse in the Gray Flannel Suit
How to Get Ahead in Advertising▲
The Hucksters▲
I Married a Woman
Image of Passion
Kids in the Hall: Brain Candy
Kramer vs. Kramer▲
Lost in America▲
Lover Come Back
The Man in the Gray Flannel Suit
Mr. Blandings Builds His Dream House▲
Mr. Mom▲
Mr. Write
Nothing in Common
Nothing to Lose
One Night Stand▲
Pray for the Wildcats
Putney Swope▲
Renaissance Man
Santa Claus: The Movie
Sweet November
Ten Speed
Think Dirty
The Thrill of It All!
Thunder in the City▲
Transformers: The Movie
Waikiki Wedding▲
What Women Want
White Mile
Will Success Spoil Rock Hunter?

Africa

***see also** Apartheid*

Abdulla the Great
Ace Ventura: When Nature Calls
The Adventurers
Africa Screams
An African Dream
African Journey
The African Queen▲
African Rage
The Air Up There
Albino
Algiers▲
Allan Quatermain and the Lost City of Gold
Amin: The Rise and Fall
Amistad▲
The Ascent
Black Force
Black Hawk Down▲
Black Jesus
Black Terrorist
Boesman & Lena
Bophal▲
Born Wild
The Bushbaby
Call Me Bwana
Cheetah
Chocolat▲
City of Blood
The Claw
Cobra Verde
Coming to America▲
Congo
Curse 3: Blood Sacrifice
Dangerous Ground
Dark of the Sun
Darkest Africa
The Desert Fox▲
Dingaka
The Dogs of War
A Dry White Season▲
East of Kilimanjaro
The Egyptian
An Elephant Called Slowly
Ernest Goes to Africa
Eyes of a Witness
Faces of Women
A Far Off Place
The Fighting Rats of Tobruk
Firefall
Five Weeks in a Balloon
The Flame Trees of Thika▲
Fort Saganne
Friends
Ganja and Hess
The Garden of Allah▲
George of the Jungle▲
The Ghost and the Darkness
The Gods Must Be Crazy▲
The Gods Must Be Crazy 2
The Golden Salamander
A Good Man in Africa
Gorillas in the Mist▲
The Great Elephant Escape
Greystoke: The Legend of Tarzan, Lord of the Apes
Guns at Batasi
Hatari!▲
Heat of the Sun▲
Hideous Kinky
I Dreamed of Africa
In Desert and Wilderness
In the Army Now
In the Shadow of Kilimanjaro
Inside▲
It Rained All Night the Day I Left
Ivory Hunters
Jaguar
Jericho
The Jewel of the Nile
Jit
Jungle Drums of Africa
Jungle Master
The Key to Rebecca
Killers
King Kong▲
King Solomon's Mines▲
King Solomon's Mines
The Kitchen Toto▲
La Vie Est Belle
The Last Safari
The Leopard Son
Les Aventuriers
The Light in the Jungle
The Lion King: Simba's Pride
The Lion of Africa
The Lost Patrol▲
The Lost World
Made for Love
Mandela▲
Mandela and de Klerk
Manhattan Baby
Manhunt in the African Jungle
March or Die
The Mark of the Hawk▲
Master Harold and the Boys▲
Men of Two Worlds
Mercenary Fighters
Mighty Joe Young
Mines of Kilimanjaro
Mister Johnson▲
Mr. Kingstreet's War
Mogambo▲
Monster from Green Hell
Mountains of the Moon▲
My African Adventure
Nairobi Affair
The Naked Prey▲
Night of the Sorcerers
Notes for an African Orestes
Oddball Hall
One Step to Hell
Operation: Delta Force
Options
Out of Africa▲
Over Indulgence
Overseas: Three Women with Man Trouble▲
The Passenger▲
Pepe Le Moko▲
Place of Weeping
Quartier Mozart
Red Scorpion
Return to Africa
Rhodes
Running Wild
Sanders of the River▲
Sarafina!▲
Satan's Harvest
Secret Obsession
Shaft in Africa
Shaka Zulu▲
The Sheltering Sky▲
Simba▲
Skeleton Coast
The Snows of Kilimanjaro▲
Something of Value▲
Song of Freedom
Sundown
Tarzan▲
Tarzan and the Lost City
Tilai
Time to Kill
To Walk with Lions
Tobruk
Touki Bouki
Trader Horn
The Treasure of Bengal
Tuxedo Warrior
Warriors from Hell
We Are the Children
Wend Kuuni
White Cargo
White Hunter, Black Heart▲
White Mischief▲
Wild Geese
A World Apart▲
Yankee Zulu
Zulu
Zulu Dawn▲

African America

***see also** New Black Cinema*

Aaron Loves Angela
Above the Rim
The Affair
Ali
All About the Benjamins
Always Outnumbered Always Outgunned▲
America's Dream▲
The Angel Levine
Ashes and Embers
Assault at West Point: The Court-Martial of Johnson Whittaker
The Autobiography of Miss Jane Pittman▲
Baby Boy
Bamboozled
B.A.P.'s
Bebe's Kids
Beloved
The Best Man▲
Beware
The Big Dis
Bingo Long Traveling All-Stars & Motor Kings▲
Bird▲
Black and White▲
Black Brigade
Black Godfather
The Black King
Black Knight
Black Like Me
Black Sister's Revenge
Blade
Blind Faith
Blood Brothers
Blue Collar▲
Boardinghouse Blues
Body and Soul
Boesman & Lena
Boycott▲
Boyz N the Hood▲
The Breaks
Broken Strings
Bronze Buckaroo
The Brother from Another Planet▲
Brother John▲
The Brothers▲
Bucktown
Buffalo Soldiers▲
Bulworth▲
Cabin in the Sky▲
Carmen Jones▲
Catfish in Black Bean Sauce
Caught Up
CB4: The Movie
Charlotte Forten's Mission: Experiment in Freedom▲
The Cherokee Kid
Chuck Berry: Hail! Hail! Rock 'n' Roll
Class Act
Clockers▲
The Color of Courage
Color of Justice
The Color Purple▲
Conrack▲
Cooley High▲
Cora Unashamed
Corrupt
Cosmic Slop
Cotton Comes to Harlem▲
The Court Martial of Jackie Robinson▲
Crooklyn▲
Dancing in September
Dangerous Evidence: The Lori Jackson Story
Darktown Strutters
Daughters of the Dust▲
Dead Presidents
The Defiant Ones▲
Devil in a Blue Dress▲
The Devil's Daughter
Dirty Gertie from Harlem U.S.A.
Disappearing Acts
Disorderlies
Divided We Stand
Do the Right Thing▲
Don't Be a Menace to South Central While Drinking Your Juice in the Hood
Don't Look Back: The Story of Leroy "Satchel" Paige
Double Deal
Double Take
Down to Earth
A Dream for Christmas▲
DROP Squad
Drums O'Voodoo
Dynamite Chicken
The Ernest Green Story
Eubie!
Eve's Bayou▲
A Family Thing▲
Fear of a Black Hat
Final Comedown
Final Exam
Finding Buck McHenry
Firehouse
The Five Heartbeats▲
Fly by Night
Foolish
For Us, the Living▲
48 Hrs.▲
Foxy Brown
Free of Eden
Freedom Song▲
Fresh
Friday
Gang in Blue
Get On the Bus▲
Ghosts of Mississippi
Girl from Chicago
The Glass Shield
Glory▲
Glory & Honor
Go Down Death
Go Tell It on the Mountain
The Golden Child
A Good Day to Die
Graffiti Bridge
Greased Lightning
The Great White Hope
The Greatest
The Green Mile
Green Pastures▲
Guess Who's Coming to Dinner▲
The Guy from Harlem
Half Slave, Half Free
Hallelujah!▲
Hangin' with the Homeboys▲
Hank Aaron: Chasing the Dream▲
Hard Lessons
Harlem Nights
Harlem on the Prairie
Hav Plenty▲
Having Our Say: The Delany Sisters' First 100 Years
He Got Game
Hendrix
A Hero Ain't Nothin' but a Sandwich
Hi-De-Ho
Higher Learning
Hollywood Shuffle
Home of the Brave▲

Hoodlum
Hoop Dreams▲
A House Divided
House Party▲
House Party 2: The Pajama Jam
House Party 3
How High
How I Spent My Summer Vacation
How Stella Got Her Groove Back
How U Like Me Now?▲
The Hurricane▲
I Got the Hook-Up
I Know Why the Caged Bird Sings▲
Identity Crisis
I'm Gonna Git You Sucka▲
Imitation of Life
Imitation of Life▲
In His Father's Shoes
In the Heat of the Night▲
The Inkwell
Introducing Dorothy Dandridge▲
Intruder in the Dust▲
The Jackie Robinson Story▲
Jason's Lyric
J.D.'s Revenge
The Jesse Owens Story
Jo Jo Dancer, Your Life Is Calling
The Joe Louis Story
Joe's Bed-Stuy Barbershop: We Cut Heads
Joey Breaker▲
The Josephine Baker Story▲
Juice
Juke Joint
Junior's Groove
Just Another Girl on the I.R.T.
Kansas City▲
Keep Punching
The Keeper
Killer Diller
Killing Floor
King▲
Kingdom Come
The Klansman
Krush Groove
Lady Sings the Blues
The Last Dragon
Laurel Avenue
Lean on Me▲
The Learning Tree
A Lesson Before Dying▲
Let's Do It Again
Liberty Heights
Lilies of the Field▲
Lily in Winter
Little John
Livin' for Love: The Natalie Cole Story
Livin' Large
The Long Walk Home▲
Look Out Sister▲
The Loretta Claiborne Story
Losing Isaiah▲
Lost Boundaries
The Lost Man
Lotto Land
Love Jones▲
Love Song
Love Songs
Love Your Mama
A Low Down Dirty Shame
Lying Lips
Machine Gun Blues
Mahogany
Malcolm X▲
Mama Flora's Family
Mama, There's a Man in Your Bed▲
A Man Called Adam
Mandela and de Klerk
Menace II Society▲
Miracle in Harlem
Miss Evers' Boys
Miss Melody Jones
Mississippi Burning▲
Mississippi Masala▲
Mr. & Mrs. Loving▲
Mister Johnson▲
Mixing Nia
Mo' Better Blues
Mo' Money
Monster's Ball▲
Moon over Harlem
Ms. Scrooge
The Murder of Stephen Lawrence▲
Murder on Lenox Avenue
Mutiny
Native Son
New Jack City
New Jersey Drive
Next Friday
Nightjohn
No Time for Romance
No Way Back
No Way Out
Nothing but a Man
The Old Settler
Once Upon a Time ... When We Were Colored▲
One False Move▲
Original Gangstas
Othello▲
The Other Brother
Our Song▲
Out of Sync
Panther
Parallel Sons
Paris Is Burning▲
Passing Glory▲
Pastime▲
A Patch of Blue
Paul Robeson
Penitentiary
Perfume
Personals
Phat Beach
The Piano Lesson▲
Pinky▲
Poetic Justice
Pootie Tang
The Preacher's Wife
Purple Rain
Putney Swope▲
Quartier Mozart
Quiet Fire
Race to Freedom: The Story of the Underground Railroad
A Rage in Harlem▲
A Raisin in the Sun▲
Raising the Heights
Rappin'
Rebound: The Legend of Earl "The Goat" Manigault
Return of Superfly
Ricochet▲
Ride
The River Niger
Rockwell: A Legend of the Wild West
Roll of Thunder, Hear My Cry
Romeo Must Die
Roots▲
Roots: The Gift
Roots: The Next Generation▲
Rosewood▲
Ruby Bridges
Rude
Scar of Shame
School Daze▲
Selma, Lord, Selma
Separate but Equal▲
Sepia Cinderella
Sergeant Rutledge▲
Set It Off
Seventeen Again
The '70s
Shadows▲
Shaft▲
Shaft's Big Score
Shanty Tramp
Sheba, Baby
She's Gotta Have It▲
The Show
The Simple Life of Noah Dearborn
Six Degrees of Separation
The '60s
Slam
Small Time
Snow Dogs
A Soldier's Story▲
Song of Freedom
Sophisticated Gents▲
Soul Food
Soul of the Game▲
Soul Survivor
Soul Vengeance
Sounder▲
South Central
Sparkle
Sprung
Straight out of Brooklyn
Strange Justice: The Clarence Thomas and Anita Hill Story
A Stranger in the Kingdom
Strapped
Sudie & Simpson▲
Sugar Hill
Summer's End
Sun Ra & His Intergalactic Solar Arkestra: Space Is the Place
Superfly
Superfly T.N.T.
Sweet Love, Bitter
Sweet Sweetback's Baadasssss Song▲
Tales from the Hood
Tap
Tar
The Temptations
They Call Me Sirr
A Thin Line Between Love and Hate
Three Strikes
Three the Hard Way
The Tiger Woods Story
A Time to Kill▲
To Sir, with Love
To Sleep with Anger▲
Tougher Than Leather
Trippin'
Truck Turner
Turn It Up
The Tuskegee Airmen▲
Two Can Play That Game
Tyson
Uncle Tom's Cabin
Undercover Brother
Uptown Angel
Waiting to Exhale▲
The Walking Dead
The Wash
Watermelon Man
The Watermelon Woman
Way Down South
What's Love Got to Do with It?
When We Were Kings
White Man's Burden
White Men Can't Jump
The Wiz
The Women of Brewster Place▲
The Wood
Words by Heart
You Must Remember This
You So Crazy
Zebrahead▲
Zooman▲
Zora Is My Name!

AIDS

***see also** Disease of the Week*

Alive and Kicking
All About My Mother▲
Amazing Grace
And the Band Played On▲
As Is
Because of You
Before Night Falls▲
Blue
Boys on the Side
The Cure
An Early Frost▲
Forrest Gump▲
Gia
Heaven's a Drag
In the Gloaming▲
Intimate Contact▲
It's My Party
Jeanne and the Perfect Guy
Jeffrey
Joey Breaker▲
Kids
Les Nuits Fauves▲
Life
Longtime Companion▲
Love! Valour! Compassion!
Love Without Fear
Men in Love
A Mother's Prayer
My Own Country
No One Sleeps
One Night Stand▲
Our Sons
Parting Glances▲
Peter's Friends
Philadelphia▲
A Place for Annie
Playing by Heart
Postcards from America
Remembering the Cosmos Flower
Sweet Jane
The Velocity of Gary
Via Appia
The Visit▲
Zero Patience

Air Disasters

***see also** Airborne; Disaster Flicks; Sea Disasters*

Air Force One▲
Airport▲
Airport '75
Airport '77
Alaska
Alive
Apollo 13▲
Bounce
Broken Arrow
The Buddy Holly Story▲
Cast Away▲
Con Air▲
The Concorde: Airport '79
The Crash of Flight 401
Die Hard 2: Die Harder▲
Escape from Wildcat Canyon
Executive Decision
Extreme Limits
Fearless▲
Fire and Rain
Flight to Fury
Get Shorty▲
Ground Control
Heaven's Prisoners
Hero▲
The Hindenburg
Jet Over the Atlantic
Jurassic Park 3
Madam Satan
Mercy Mission
Nowhere to Land
Operation Intercept
Ordeal in the Arctic
Panic in the Skies
Restless Spirits
Sole Survivor
Submerged
Survivor
Tailspin: Behind the Korean Airline Tragedy
A Thousand Heroes
The Ticket
Tragedy of Flight 103: The Inside Story▲
Turbulence
Turbulence 2: Fear of Flying
U.S. Marshals

Airborne

***see also** Air Disasters*

Above and Beyond▲
Ace Drummond
Ace of Aces
Aces: Iron Eagle 3
Active Stealth
Adventures of Smilin' Jack
Afterburn▲
Air America
Air Force▲
Air Force One▲
Air Hawk
Air Rage
Airborne
Airboss
Airplane!▲
Airplane 2: The Sequel
Airport▲
Airport '75
Airport '77
Always
Amelia Earhart: The Final Flight
And I Alone Survived
Angels One Five
Attack Squadron
The Aviator
Bail Out at 43,000
Battle of Britain
Battle of the Eagles
Beyond the Time Barrier
Biggles
Birds of Prey
Black Box Affair
Black Thunder
The Blue Max
Blue Thunder
Blue Tornado
Boeing Boeing
Bombardier
Brewster McCloud▲
Bulldog Drummond at Bay
Bulletproof
Bush Pilot
By Dawn's Early Light
Captains of the Clouds
Ceiling Zero▲
Chain Lightning
Christopher Strong
Con Air▲
The Concorde: Airport '79
The Crash of Flight 401
Crimson Romance
Danger in the Skies
Dangerous Moonlight▲
Dark Blue World
Dawn Patrol▲
Deadly Encounter▲
Delta Force
Desert Thunder
Devil Dogs of the Air
Die Hard 2: Die Harder▲
Dive Bomber▲
Dr. Strangelove, or: How I Learned to Stop Worrying and Love the Bomb▲
The Dogfighters
The Doomsday Flight
Dragonfly Squadron
Drop Zone
Dumbo▲
The Eagle and the Hawk▲
Enola Gay: The Men, the Mission, the Atomic Bomb
Executive Decision
Fighter Attack
Fighting Pilot
Final Approach
Final Destination
Final Mission
Fire Birds
Firefox
Five Came Back
Five Weeks in a Balloon
Flaming Signal
Flat Top
Flight from Glory
Flight from Singapore
Flight of Black Angel
Flight of the Intruder
The Flight of the Phoenix▲
Flight to Fury
Fly Away Home▲
Fly Boy
Flying Blind
The Flying Deuces▲
Flying Down to Rio
Flying Leathernecks▲
Flying Tigers
For the Moment
Forget Paris
Freedom Strike
French Kiss
The Great Skycopter Rescue
The Great Waldo Pepper▲
A Guy Named Joe
Gypsy Angels
Hell's Angels▲
High Road to China
Hostage
Hot Shots!▲
The Hunters
Independence Day▲
Interceptor
Into the Sun
Iron Eagle
Iron Eagle 2
Iron Eagle 4
The Island at the Top of the World
It Happened at the World's Fair
Jet Over the Atlantic
Jet Pilot
Keep 'Em Flying
La Bamba▲
La Grande Vadrouille▲
Lafayette Escadrille
L'Anne Sainte
The Left Hand of God▲
The Lion Has Wings
Look Who's Talking Now
Lost Squadron
Love Affair
Mach 2
Malta Story
The Man with the Golden Gun
The McConnell Story
Memphis Belle▲
Men of Steel
Men of the Fighting Lady▲
Mercy Mission
Millennium
Moon Pilot
Murder on Flight 502
Mystery Squadron
1941
No Highway in the Sky▲
October Sky▲
One of Our Aircraft Is Missing▲
Only Angels Have Wings▲
Operation Dumbo Drop
Out of Control
Pancho Barnes
Paradise, Hawaiian Style
Party Plane
Passenger 57
Pearl Harbor
The Phantom
Phantom of the Air
Phone Call from a Stranger
Piece of Cake
The Pursuit of D.B. Cooper
Pushing Tin▲
Reach for the Sky
Red Flag: The Ultimate Game
Return to Earth
Revenge of the Red Baron
The Right Stuff▲
Robot Pilot
Sabre Jet
Saint-Ex: The Story of the Storyteller
Savage Hunger
Shadow of the Eagle
Shadow on the Sun
Six Days, Seven Nights
633 Squadron
Sky Hei$t
Sky Liner
Sky Riders
Spirit of St. Louis▲
Spitfire▲
The Starfighters
Starflight One
Steal the Sky
Stealth Fighter
Stephen King's The Langoliers
Stephen King's The Night Flier
Strategic Air Command
Stunt Pilot
Survivor
Tactical Assault
Tailspin: Behind the Korean Airline Tragedy
The Taking of Flight 847: The Uli Derickson Story▲
Tarnished Angels▲
Task Force
Terminal Velocity
Test Pilot▲
Texas Buddies
Those Endearing Young Charms
Those Magnificent Men in Their Flying Machines▲
Today We Live
Top Gun
Tragedy of Flight 103: The Inside Story▲
Turbulence

The Tuskegee Airmen▲
Twelve o'Clock High▲
War in the Sky▲
War Lover
Warbirds
We'll Meet Again
The Winds of Kitty Hawk
A Wing and a Prayer▲
Wings
Wings of Danger
Wings of Eagles
The World Owes Me a Living
You Gotta Stay Happy
Zeppelin
Zero

Airplanes

see ***Air Disasters; Airborne***

Alaska

see also ***Cold Spots***

Alaska
Avalanche
Balto
Call of the Wild
Cry Vengeance
Dead Ahead: The Exxon Valdez Disaster▲
The Edge
Extreme Limits
Eye of the Beholder
The Gold Rush▲
Goldrush: A Real Life Alaskan Adventure
Insomnia▲
Jack London's The Call of the Wild
Klondike Annie
Klondike Fever
Limbo
Mystery, Alaska
Never Cry Wolf▲
North to Alaska▲
On Deadly Ground
The Road to Utopia▲
Runaway Train▲
Spawn of the North
The Spoilers
The Spoilers▲

Alcatraz

see also ***Great Escapes; Men in Prison***

Birdman of Alcatraz▲
Dark Passage
Escape from Alcatraz▲
Murder in the First
Point Blank
The Rock▲

Alcoholism

see ***On the Rocks***

Alien Babes

see also ***Alien Beings—Benign; Alien Beings—Vicious; Aliens Are People, Too***

Alien Visitor
Beach Babes 2: Cave Girl Island
Beach Babes from Beyond Infinity
Cat Women of the Moon
Cocoon▲
Last Exit to Earth
Leprechaun 4: In Space
Mars Attacks!
Men in Black 2
My Stepmother Is an Alien
Planet of Blood
Queen of Outer Space
The Sender
Species
Species 2
Star Portal
Star Trek: First Contact▲
Starlight
Vampire Vixens from Venus
Vampirella

Alien Beings—Benign

see also ***Alien Beings—Vicious; Aliens Are People, Too; Space Operas***

The Abyss▲
Aftershock
Alien from L.A.
Alien Nation
Alien Nation: Dark Horizon
Alien Private Eye
Amanda and the Alien
The Aurora Encounter
*batteries not included
Big Meat Eater
The Brother from Another Planet▲
Can of Worms
The Cat from Outer Space
Close Encounters of the Third Kind▲
Cocoon▲
Cocoon: The Return
Communion
Coneheads
The Cosmic Eye▲
The Cosmic Man
Dark City
The Day the Earth Stood Still▲
Doctor Who
Doin' Time on Planet Earth
Earth Girls Are Easy
Earth vs. the Flying Saucers
The Empire Strikes Back▲
Enemy Mine
Escape to Witch Mountain▲
E.T.: The Extra-Terrestrial▲
The Ewok Adventure
The Ewoks: Battle for Endor
Explorers
Femalien
Fire in the Sky
Flight of the Navigator
Galaxy Quest
Gremlins▲
Gremlins 2: The New Batch▲
The Hidden▲
Howard the Duck
Hyper-Sapien: People from Another Star
Intruders
It Came from Outer Space▲
Josh Kirby...Time Warrior: Chapter 5, Journey to the Magic Cavern
Labyrinth▲
The Last Starfighter
Lilo & Stitch
Mac and Me
Man Facing Southeast▲
The Man from Atlantis
The Man Who Fell to Earth▲
Martians Go Home!
Masters of Venus
The Mating Habits of the Earthbound Human
Men in Black▲
Missile to the Moon
Moon Pilot
Morons from Outer Space
Munchie
Muppets from Space
My Favorite Martian
My Stepmother Is an Alien
My Uncle: The Alien
Mysterious Two
Nukie
Official Denial
Pajama Party
Pet Shop
The Phantom Planet
Project: Genesis
Purple People Eater
Real Men
Repo Man▲
Return of the Jedi▲
Search for the Gods
Simon
Spaced Invaders
Star Knight
Star Trek 3: The Search for Spock
Star Trek 4: The Voyage Home▲
Star Trek: First Contact▲
Star Wars▲
Star Wars: Episode 1—The Phantom Menace▲
Stardust Memories
Starlight
Starman▲
Starship Invasions
Suburban Commando
Super Mario Bros.
Supergirl
Superman: The Movie▲
Superman 2▲
Superman 3
Superman 4: The Quest for Peace
Teenage Mutant Ninja Turtles 2: The Secret of the Ooze
The Terronauts
The 27th Day
UFO: Target Earth
Vegas in Space
Voyage of the Rock Aliens
War of the Robots
Warning from Space
Wavelength
What Planet Are You From?
When Time Expires
Zarkorr! The Invader
Zeta One

Alien Beings—Vicious

see also ***Alien Beings—Benign; Aliens Are People, Too; Space Operas***

The Adventures of Buckaroo Banzai Across the Eighth Dimension▲
Alien▲
Alien 3
The Alien Agenda: Endangered Species
The Alien Agenda: Out of the Darkness
The Alien Agenda: Under the Skin
Alien Cargo
Alien Contamination
Alien Dead
The Alien Factor
Alien Fury: Countdown to Invasion
Alien Massacre
Alien Nation: Dark Horizon
Alien Predators
Alien Prey
Alien: Resurrection▲
Alien Seed
Alien Space Avenger
Alien Terminator
Alienator
Aliens▲
Aliens Are Coming
The Alpha Incident
The Ambushers
The Angry Red Planet
The Arrival
The Arrival 2
The Astounding She-Monster
The Astro-Zombies
Atomic Submarine
Attack from Mars
Backlash: Oblivion 2
Bad Channels
Bad Taste▲
Battle Beyond the Stars
Battle of the Worlds
Battlefield Earth
Battlestar Galactica
Beware! The Blob
Bio Hazard
The Blob
The Blob▲
Bloodsuckers from Outer Space
Blue Flame
Blue Monkey
Body Snatchers
The Borrower
The Brain
The Brain Eaters
The Brain from Planet Arous
Breeders
Cat Women of the Moon
Class of Nuke 'Em High 3: The Good, the Bad and the Subhumanoid
The Colony
The Cosmic Monsters
Creature
Creeping Terror
The Cremators
Critters
Critters 2: The Main Course
Critters 3
Critters 4
Crossworlds
The Curse
D-Day on Mars
The Dark
Dark Breed
Dark Star▲
Dark Universe
Day the World Ended
Day Time Ended
Dead Space
Dead Weekend
Deceit
Deep Red
Deep Space
Destroy All Planets
Devil Girl from Mars
Dr. Alien
Doctor Who
Dollman
Dracula vs. Frankenstein
Earth vs. the Flying Saucers
Eat and Run
The Empire Strikes Back▲
Encounter at Raven's Gate
End of the World
Escape from Galaxy Three
Escapes
Evils of the Night
Evolution
The Eye Creatures
Eyes Behind the Stars
The Faculty
The Fear Chamber
The Fifth Element
Final Fantasy: The Spirits Within
First Man into Space
Flight to Mars
Forbidden World
Forbidden Zone: Alien Abduction
Frankenstein Meets the Space Monster
From Beyond▲
Galaxy Invader
Galaxy of Terror
Galaxy Quest
Gamera vs. Guiron
Gamera vs. Zigra
Ghidrah the Three Headed Monster
The Giant Claw
The Giant Spider Invasion
God Told Me To
Godzilla vs. King Ghidora
Godzilla vs. the Cosmic Monster
Grand Tour: Disaster in Time
The Green Slime
Gremlins▲
Gremlins 2: The New Batch▲
The Guyver
Guyver 2: Dark Hero
Hands of Steel
The Hidden▲
The Hidden 2
The High Crusade
High Desert Kill
Horror of the Blood Monsters
The Human Duplicators
Hybrid
I Come in Peace
I Married a Monster from Outer Space
Imposter
Independence Day▲
Inseminoid
Interceptor Force
Invader
The Invaders
Invaders from Mars
Invasion
Invasion!
Invasion: Earth
Invasion Earth: The Aliens Are Here!
Invasion of the Animal People
Invasion of the Bee Girls▲
Invasion of the Body Snatchers▲
Invasion of the Body Stealers
Invasion of the Girl Snatchers
Invasion of the Saucer Men
Invasion of the Space Preachers
Invisible Adversaries
Invisible Invaders
Island of the Burning Doomed
It Came from Outer Space▲
It Came from Outer Space 2
It Conquered the World
It! The Terror from Beyond Space
J-Men Forever!▲
Jimmy Neutron: Boy Genius
John Carpenter's Ghosts of Mars
Killer Klowns from Outer Space
Killer Tongue
Killers from Space
Killings at Outpost Zeta
Kronos
Laboratory
Laserhawk
Leviathan
Lifeform
Liquid Sky▲
Lords of the Deep
Lost in Space
Mars Attacks!
Mars Needs Women
The Martian Chronicles: Part 3
Masters of Venus
Men in Black▲
Men in Black 2
Metallica
Mindwarp
Mission Mars
Mom and Dad Save the World
Monolith
The Monolith Monsters
Monster
Monster a Go-Go!
Monster High
Moontrap
Munchies
The Mysterians
Night Beast
Night Caller from Outer Space
Night of the Blood Beast
Night of the Creeps
No Survivors, Please
Not of This Earth
Oblivion
The Outer Limits: Sandkings▲
The P.A.C.K.
Peacemaker
Pet Shop
Phantom from Space
The Phantom Planet
The Pink Chiquitas
Pitch Black▲
Plan 9 from Outer Space
Plan 10 from Outer Space
Planet of Blood
Planets Against Us
Predator
Predator 2
Progeny
The Puppet Masters
Quatermass 2▲
Quatermass and the Pit
The Quatermass Experiment▲
Radar Men from the Moon
Reactor
Remote Control
Reptilian
The Return
Return of the Aliens: The Deadly Spawn
Return of the Jedi▲
Revenge of the Teenage Vixens from Outer Space
Robot Monster
Rock 'n' Roll Nightmare
Scared to Death
Sci-Fighters
The Silencers
The Sinister Invasion
Slapstick of Another Kind
Slaughterhouse Five
Space Jam
Species
Species 2
Specimen
Split
Split Second
Star Crystal
Star Hunter
Star Trek: The Motion Picture
Star Trek 3: The Search for Spock
Star Trek: First Contact▲
Star Wars▲
Star Wars: Episode 1—The Phantom Menace▲
Stargate
Starship Invasions
Stephen King's The Langoliers
Stephen King's The Tommyknockers
Strange Invaders▲
The Stranger from Venus
Super Mario Bros.
Superman 2▲
Supernova
A Taste for Flesh and Blood
Teen Alien
Teenagers from Outer Space
Terror of Mechagodzilla
They
They Came from Beyond Space
They Live
The Thing▲
The Thing
This Island Earth
Thrill Seekers
Time Runner
Time Walker
Tripods: The White Mountains
20 Million Miles to Earth
2001: A Space Travesty
The Unearthly Stranger
Unknown Origin
Unseen Evil
V▲
V: The Final Battle
Vampire Vixens from Venus
Village of the Damned▲
Village of the Damned
Virus
War in Space
War of the Wizards
The War of the Worlds▲
When Time Expires
Wicked City
Wild, Wild Planet
Within the Rock
Women of the Prehistoric Planet
The X-Files
X from Outer Space
Xtro
Xtro 2: The Second Encounter
Xtro 3: Watch the Skies
Zarkorr! The Invader
Zeram
Zeram 2▲
Zombies of the Stratosphere
Zontar, the Thing from Venus

Aliens Are People, Too

see also ***Alien Babes; Alien Beings—Benign; Alien Beings—Vicious***

Alien▲
Alien 3
The Alien Agenda: Under the Skin
Alien: Resurrection▲

▲ = rated three bones or higher

Aliens▲
The Arrival
The Astronaut's Wife
Body Snatchers
The Hidden▲
The Hidden 2
I Married a Monster
Imposter
The Invader
The Invaders
Invaders from Mars
Invasion of the Body Snatchers▲
K-PAX
Mars Attacks!
Men in Black▲
Men in Black 2
My Favorite Martian
My Stepmother Is an Alien
Not Like Us
Planet of the Vampires
The Puppet Masters
Species 2
Specimen
Star Portal
Starlight
Starman▲
The Thing▲
The Thing
Thrill Seekers
V▲
V: The Final Battle

Amateur Sleuths

After the Thin Man▲
The Body in the Library
Clubhouse Detectives
The Crackler
Deathmask
The Detective▲
Dirkham Detective Agency
Emil and the Detectives
Ex-Mrs. Bradford▲
Fletch
Fletch Lives
Footsteps in the Dark
Frog and Wombat
The Glass Key▲
Gumshoe
Hard-Boiled Mahoney
Irish Luck
Killing 'Em Softly
The Lady in Question
Lying Lips
Man from Cairo
The Mandarin Mystery
Manhattan Murder Mystery▲
Messenger of Death
Mr. Arkadin▲
Murder Ahoy
Murder at the Gallop▲
Murder by the Book
Murder in a Small Town
A Murder Is Announced
Murder Most Foul▲
Murder She Purred: A Mrs. Murphy Mystery
Murder She Said
Mystery Kids
Mystery Liner
Nancy Drew, Reporter
Shadow of the Thin Man▲
Sherlock's Rivals & Where's My Wife
Shooting Stars
A Shot in the Dark
The Silent Passenger
Song of the Thin Man
Speedy Death▲
Star of Midnight
They Might Be Giants▲
The Thin Man▲
The Thin Man Goes Home
13th Guest
Tomorrow at Seven
The Unbreakable Alibi
Whistling in Brooklyn
Whistling in Dixie
Whistling in the Dark▲

American Indians

***see** Native America*

American South

***see also** Atlanta; Memphis; Miami; Nashville; Nashville Narratives; New Orleans; Savannah; Southern Belles*

Ain't No Way Back
Alligator Alley
Andersonville▲
Angel Baby
Angel City
Angel Heart
The Apostle▲
As Summers Die
The Autobiography of Miss Jane Pittman▲
The Baby Dance▲
Baby Doll▲
Bad Georgia Road
The Ballad of the Sad Cafe
Bandwagon
Bastard out of Carolina
The Beguiled▲
Belizaire the Cajun
Between Heaven and Hell▲
Beulah Land
The Big Easy▲
Big Momma's House
Black Like Me
Blind Vengeance
Blue Ridge Fall
Boxcar Bertha
Boycott▲
Bucktown
Camilla
Cape Fear▲
Cat on a Hot Tin Roof▲
Cat on a Hot Tin Roof
The Chamber
Chiefs
Christy
Cold Sassy Tree▲
The Color Purple▲
The Con
Cookie's Fortune▲
Crazy in Alabama
Cries of Silence
Crossroads
Cypress Edge
Dancer, Texas—Pop. 81▲
Dead Right
The Delta
Delta Heat
Divine Secrets of the Ya-Ya Sisterhood
Dixiana
Down in the Delta▲
Driving Miss Daisy▲
The Drowning Pool
Drum
Eve's Bayou▲
A Family Thing▲
Final Cut
Fire in the Night
First Love, Last Rites
Flamingo Road▲
Fled
Fletch Lives
Follow That Car
Forrest Gump▲
Foxfire▲
Frailty▲
Freedom Song▲
Fried Green Tomatoes▲
The Fugitive Kind
The General's Daughter
George Wallace
Gettysburg▲
The Ghost of Fletcher Ridge
Ghosts of Mississippi
The Gift
The Gingerbread Man
The Girl from Tobacco Row
The Glass Menagerie▲
God's Little Acre▲
Gone with the Wind▲
A Good Baby
The Grass Harp
The Grave
Great Balls of Fire
The Great Santini▲
The Green Mile
Hard Drivin'
Harlan County War
The Heart of Dixie
Heroes of the Heart
Home from the Hill▲
Hooch
Hootch Country Boys
Hope
Hot Spell
A House Divided
The Hunley
Hunter's Blood
Hunter's Moon
Hush, Hush, Sweet Charlotte▲
I Know Why the Caged Bird Sings▲
I'd Climb the Highest Mountain▲
In a Shallow Grave
In the Flesh
In the Heat of the Night▲
Inherit the Wind
Intruder in the Dust▲
Invitation to a Gunfighter
Jezebel▲
John Grisham's The Rainmaker
The Journey of August King
Judge Horton and the Scottsboro Boys
Judge Priest▲
Kentucky Kernels
Kiss of Fire
The Klansman
Lady for a Night
Lady from Louisiana
Last Dance
The Legend of Gator Face
A Lesson Before Dying▲
Life
The Life and Assassination of the Kingfish
Lily in Winter
A Lion Is in the Streets▲
The Little Colonel▲
The Lords of Discipline
Louisiana
Louisiana Story▲
Macon County Line
Mandingo
Meeting Daddy
The Member of the Wedding
Midnight in the Garden of Good and Evil
Miss Evers' Boys
Miss Firecracker▲
Mississippi Burning▲
Mississippi Masala▲
Mr. & Mrs. Loving▲
Monster's Ball▲
Moonshine Highway
Moonshine Mountain
Morning Glory
The Mothman Prophecies
Murder in Coweta County
The Murder of Mary Phagan▲
Murder on the Bayou▲
Murder She Purred: A Mrs. Murphy Mystery
My Cousin Vinny▲
My Dog Skip▲
My Louisiana Sky
My Own Country
My Sweet Charlie
Mystery of the Riverboat
The Neon Bible
Netherworld
No Mercy
Norma Rae▲
North and South Book 1▲
North and South Book 2▲
Nothing but a Man
O Brother Where Art Thou?
An Occasional Hell
Ode to Billy Joe
On the Run
On Valentine's Day
Once Upon a Time ... When We Were Colored▲
One False Move▲
100 Proof
The Only Thrill
Orpheus Descending
Other Voices, Other Rooms
Outside Chance
Paradise▲
Paris Trout
Passion Fish▲
The Patriot
Perfect Harmony
The Ponder Heart
Poor Pretty Eddie
Poor White Trash
Poor White Trash 2
Primary Colors
The Prince of Tides▲
Psycho from Texas
Queen Bee
Rambling Rose▲
A Real American Hero
Red Dirt
Reflections in a Golden Eye
The Relic
Return to Mayberry
Return to Two Moon Junction
Rich in Love
Ride the Wild Fields
Ride with the Devil
Ripe
Riverbend
Road to Nashville
Roll of Thunder, Hear My Cry
Rooster: Spurs of Death!
Roots▲
Roots: The Next Generation▲
The Rose Tattoo▲
Rosewood▲
Ruby Gentry
The Runaway
Running Mates▲
The St. Francisville Experiment
Saratoga Trunk
Scarlett
Scorchers
Selma, Lord, Selma
Shadrach
Shag: The Movie▲
Shanty Tramp
Shy People▲
The Simple Life of Noah Dearborn
Sins of the Father▲
Sister, Sister
Sixteen
Sling Blade▲
Smokey Bites the Dust
Snuffy Smith, Yard Bird
Something to Talk About
Sounder▲
Southern Comfort▲
The Southerner▲
Sparrows▲
Stormswept
Storyville
A Streetcar Named Desire▲
A Streetcar Named Desire
Summer and Smoke
The Summer of Ben Tyler
Summer's End
The Supernaturals
Swamp Fire
Sweet Bird of Youth▲
Sweet Bird of Youth
Sweet Country Road
Tammy and the Bachelor
Tammy and the Doctor
Tank
The Tempest
Texasville
They Won't Forget▲
This Stuff'll Kill Ya!
Tigerland▲
A Tiger's Tale
A Time to Kill▲
To Kill a Mockingbird▲
The Trail of the Lonesome Pine▲
The Trip to Bountiful▲
Tune in Tomorrow
Two Moon Junction
2000 Maniacs
Uncle Tom's Cabin
Uphill All the Way
Voodoo Dawn
Walk in the Spring Rain
A Walk to Remember
Walking Tall
Walking Tall: Part 2
Walking Tall: The Final Chapter
The War
The Waterboy
What Comes Around
Where the Lilies Bloom▲
White Lie
The White Rose▲
Wild Things
Wildflower▲
William Faulkner's Old Man
Wise Blood▲
A Woman Called Moses

Amnesia

Amateur▲
Amnesia
Anastasia▲
Anastasia: The Mystery of Anna
Armistead Maupin's More Tales of the City
As You Desire Me▲
Black Out
Blackout
The Blonde
The Bourne Identity▲
The Bourne Identity
The Bumblebee Flies Anyway
Clean Slate
Crack-Up
Dead Again▲
Desperately Seeking Susan
Diabolically Yours
Final Approach
Forger of London
The Great Dictator▲
Gypsy Angels
Hellhole
High Stakes
Hysteria
I Love You Again▲
Identity Unknown
The Immoral One
Inferno
Istanbul
Jackie Chan's Who Am I
Jane Doe
The Killing Jar
Landslide
Last Rites
The Lazarus Man
The Long Kiss Goodnight
Lost Honeymoon
Love Letters
The Majestic
Memories of Murder
Mirage▲
Moment to Moment
Mulholland Drive▲
Murder by Night
Overboard
Palombella Rossa
The Perfect Daughter
A Pure Formality
Random Harvest▲
The Red Squirrel
Regarding Henry▲
Return of the Soldier▲
The Road to Hong Kong
Santa with Muscles
The Second Woman
The Sender
Shattered
Shock
Siesta
Singapore
Someone Behind the Door
Spellbound▲
Strange Awakening
The Stranger▲
Summer's Children
Sundays & Cybele▲
36 Hours▲
The Three Lives of Karen
Time Lapse
Total Recall▲
Twice a Judas
Undesirable
Unholy Four
The Unknown Soldier
Virtual Sexuality
While I Live

Amusement Parks

***see also** Carnivals & Circuses; Fairs & Expositions*

The Beast from 20,000 Fathoms
Bebe's Kids
Beverly Hills Cop 3
Big▲
Carnival of Blood
Carnival of Souls▲
The Crying Game▲
Curse of the Headless Horseman
Dr. Giggles
Dragonworld
Fatal Attraction▲
Funland
Gangster World
Getting Even with Dad
Godzilla on Monster Island
KISS Meets the Phantom of the Park
The Lady from Shanghai▲
Luv
Mighty Joe Young
My Life
National Lampoon's Vacation▲
1941
Omega Doom
Rollercoaster
Scooby-Doo
Strangers on a Train▲
Strike Me Pink
The Third Man▲
3 Ninjas: High Noon at Mega Mountain
Tremors 3: Back to Perfection

Angels

***see also** Heaven Sent*

Always
The Angel Levine
Angels in the Endzone
Angels in the Infield
Angels in the Outfield▲
Angels in the Outfield
The Bishop's Wife▲
Cabin in the Sky▲
The Christmas Box
City of Angels
Clarence
Creation of Adam
Date with an Angel
Defending Your Life▲
Dogma
Down to Earth
Fallen
Faraway, So Close!
Fear No Evil
Field of Dreams▲
For Heaven's Sake
Forever Darling
Gabriel Over the White House▲
Green Pastures▲
A Guy Named Joe
Heart and Souls
Heaven Can Wait▲
The Heavenly Kid
Here Comes Mr. Jordan▲
The Horn Blows at Midnight▲
I Married an Angel
It Came Upon a Midnight Clear
It's a Wonderful Life▲
The Kid with the Broken Halo
La Merveilleuse Visite
Levitation
A Life Less Ordinary
The Littlest Angel
Lover's Knot
Made in Heaven
Michael
Miracle in Milan▲
One Magic Christmas
The Preacher's Wife
The Prophecy
The Prophecy 2: Ashtown
The Prophecy 3: The Ascent
Raging Angels
A Season for Miracles
Slam Dunk Ernest
Soultaker
Stairway to Heaven▲
Two of a Kind
Unlikely Angel
Waiting for the Light
Wide Awake

Wings of Desire▲

Animals

see *Birds; Cats; Horses; King of Beasts (Dogs); Wild Kingdom*

Animated Musicals

see also *Animation & Cartoons; Musicals*

Aladdin▲
All Dogs Go to Heaven
All Dogs Go to Heaven 2
American Pop
An American Tail
An American Tail: Fievel Goes West
Anastasia
Beauty and the Beast▲
Cats Don't Dance
Charlotte's Web
Cinderella▲
Fantasia/2000
Gay Purr-ee
Hercules▲
The Hunchback of Notre Dame▲
The Jungle Book▲
The King and I
Lady and the Tramp▲
The Lion King▲
The Little Mermaid▲
The Magic Voyage
Melody Time
Mulan
The Nightmare before Christmas▲
The Pebble and the Penguin
Pink Floyd: The Wall
Pinocchio▲
Pocahontas▲
Prince of Egypt▲
Quest for Camelot
The Return of Jafar
The Road to El Dorado
Robin Hood▲
Rock-a-Doodle
Shinbone Alley
Sleeping Beauty▲
Snow White and the Seven Dwarfs▲
South Park: Bigger, Longer and Uncut
The Swan Princess
The Swan Princess 2: Escape from Castle Mountain
The Thief and the Cobbler▲
Thumbelina
The Trumpet of the Swan
The Tune
Water Babies
Yellow Submarine▲

Animated Sci-Fi

Final Fantasy: The Spirits Within
Heavy Metal▲
Iron Giant▲
Jimmy Neutron: Boy Genius
Pokemon 3: The Movie
Titan A.E.
Transformers: The Movie

Animation & Cartoons

see also *Animated Musicals*

The Adventures of Ichabod and Mr. Toad▲
The Adventures of Mark Twain▲
Aladdin and the King of Thieves
Alice in Wonderland
Alice in Wonderland▲
Allegro Non Troppo▲
Animal Farm▲
Antz▲
The Aristocats▲
Atlantis: The Lost Empire
Babar: The Movie
Balto
Bambi▲
Batman: Mask of the Phantasm
Beavis and Butt-Head Do America
Bebe's Kids
The Black Cauldron
A Bug's Life▲
Butterfly Ball
Chicken Run▲
Cool World
The Cosmic Eye▲
The Dagger of Kamui▲
Dinosaur
Doug's 1st Movie▲
DuckTales the Movie: Treasure of the Lost Lamp
Dumbo▲
Evil Toons
Fantasia▲
Fantastic Planet▲
Felix the Cat: The Movie
Ferngully: The Last Rain Forest
Fire and Ice
Flight of Dragons
The Fox and the Hound▲
Freddie the Frog
Fritz the Cat▲
Gargoyles, The Movie: The Heroes Awaken
Ghost in the Shell▲
The Good, the Bad, and Huckleberry Hound
A Goofy Movie
The Great Mouse Detective▲
Grendel, Grendel, Grendel
Gulliver's Travels
Gumby: The Movie
Happily Ever After
Heavy Metal 2000
Heavy Traffic▲
Here Come the Littles: The Movie
Hey Good Lookin'
Hey There, It's Yogi Bear
The Hobbit▲
Hoppity Goes to Town
Huckleberry Finn
Hugo the Hippo
Ice Age▲
Jetsons: The Movie
Journey Back to Oz
The Land Before Time▲
The Land Before Time 2: The Great Valley Adventure
The Land Before Time 3: The Time of the Great Giving
The Land Before Time 4: Journey Through the Mists
The Land Before Time 5: The Mysterious Island
Land Before Time 7: The Stone of Cold Fire
The Last Unicorn
The Legend of Sleepy Hollow
Lensman
Light Years
The Little Mermaid
Little Nemo: Adventures in Slumberland
Looney Looney Looney Bugs Bunny Movie▲
The Lord of the Rings
Mad Monster Party
Man from Button Willow
The Many Adventures of Winnie the Pooh
Marco Polo, Jr.
Marquis
The Miracle Maker: The Story of Jesus
Monsters, Inc.▲
Mouse and His Child
Nine Lives of Fritz the Cat
The Nutcracker Prince
The Old Curiosity Shop
Oliver & Company
Once Upon a Forest
101 Dalmatians▲
1001 Arabian Nights
Peter Pan▲
Phantom Tollbooth▲
Phantom 2040 Movie: The Ghost Who Walks
The Plague Dogs
Pogo for President: "I Go Pogo"
The Point
Pound Puppies and the Legend of Big Paw
The Princess and the Goblin
The Puppetoon Movie
Race for Your Life, Charlie Brown
The Rescuers▲
The Rescuers Down Under
The Return of the King
Return to Never Land
Rock & Rule
Rover Dangerfield
Rugrats in Paris: The Movie▲
The Rugrats Movie▲
Scruffy
The Secret of NIMH▲
Shame of the Jungle
Shrek▲
Sinbad and the Eye of the Tiger
Spirit: Stallion of the Cimarron
Starchaser: The Legend of Orin
Streetfight
The Sword in the Stone▲
Tarzan▲
The Three Caballeros
Tiny Toon Adventures: How I Spent My Vacation▲
Todd McFarlane's Spawn
Tom and Jerry: The Movie
Tom Thumb▲
Toy Story▲
Toy Story 2▲
A Troll in Central Park
VIP, My Brother Superman
Waking Life
Watership Down
We're Back! A Dinosaur's Story
When the Wind Blows▲
Wizards

Anime

see also *Animation & Cartoons*

Akira
The Castle of Cagliostro
The Dagger of Kamui▲
Grave of the Fireflies▲
GUY: Awakening of the Devil
Lensman
My Neighbor Totoro
Otaku No Video▲
Pokemon: The First Movie
Pokemon the Movie 2000: The Power of One
Princess Mononoke▲
Toward the Terra
Twilight of the Cockroaches
Wicked City▲
A Wind Named Amnesia

Anthology

see also *Comedy Anthologies; Horror Anthologies; Serials*

The Acid House
Actors and Sin
America at the Movies
American Tickler
America's Dream▲
Amore▲
Beyond the Clouds
Black Sabbath▲
Boys in Love
Boys in Love 2
Boys Life
Cat's Eye
The Chaplin Revue
Charade
Common Ground
Cosmic Slop
Dark Eyes▲
Deadtime Stories
The Decameron▲
Decameron Nights
The Discovery Program
Erotique
Escapes
Fallen Angels 1▲
Fallen Angels 2▲
Fantasia/2000
Four Rooms
From Beyond the Grave
A Girl Thing
Halfmoon
Hotel Room
If These Walls Could Talk
If These Walls Could Talk 2
Kaos▲
Kisses in the Dark
Kurt Vonnegut's Monkey House
Kwaidan▲
Le Plaisir
Letters from My Windmill▲
The Little Theatre of Jean Renoir▲
Love in the City▲
Love Songs
Melody Time
Mickey the Great
More American Graffiti
Mystery Train▲
Night Gallery▲
Night on Earth▲
Nightmares
Once Upon a Midnight Scary
Paisan▲
Picture Windows
Prison Stories: Women on the Inside▲
Pulp Fiction▲
Red Shoe Diaries
Red Shoe Diaries 2: Double Dare
Red Shoe Diaries 3: Another Woman's Lipstick
Red Shoe Diaries 4: Auto Erotica
Red Shoe Diaries 5: Weekend Pass
Red Shoe Diaries 6: How I Met My Husband
Red Shoe Diaries 7: Burning Up
Red Shoe Diaries 8: Night of Abandon
Red Shoe Diaries: Four on the Floor
Red Shoe Diaries: Luscious Lola
Red Shoe Diaries: Strip Poker
Red Shoe Diaries: Swimming Naked
Rendezvous in Paris
Renoir Shorts▲
RoGoPaG
Seven Deadly Sins▲
Sherlock's Rivals & Where's My Wife
Short Cuts▲
The Silent Mr. Sherlock Holmes
Six in Paris
Slacker▲
Strictly G.I.
Subway Stories
Tales from the Crypt
Tales of Erotica
Tales of Manhattan▲
Tales of the Unexpected
Tales That Witness Madness
Terrorgram
That's Dancing!
That's Entertainment
That's Entertainment, Part 2
That's Entertainment, Part 3
Things 2
Three Cases of Murder▲
Twice-Told Tales▲
Twilight Zone: The Movie
Twisted
Two Days in the Valley▲
The Unapproachable
The Uncanny
Vanishing Legion
The Wall▲
Women & Men: In Love There Are No Rules
Women & Men: Stories of Seduction

Anti-Heroes

see also *Rebel With a Cause*

The Adventures of Robin Hood▲
Belly
Billy Jack
Blade
Bonnie & Clyde▲
Born Losers
Butch Cassidy and the Sundance Kid▲
Casino▲
A Civil Action
The Dead Pool
Dirty Harry▲
Easy Rider▲
The Enforcer
Gang Related
H
Hero▲
In a Lonely Place▲
Last Man Standing
Lock, Stock and 2 Smoking Barrels▲
Magnum Force
Niagara, Niagara
Palookaville▲
Playing God
Rebel without a Cause▲
Robin Hood: Prince of Thieves
The Secret Agent
Set It Off
Steal This Movie!
Sudden Impact
Surviving Picasso
Ten Benny
Thelma & Louise▲
Things to Do in Denver When You're Dead▲
To Wong Foo, Thanks for Everything, Julie Newmar
Traveller▲
The Trial of Billy Jack
Trojan Eddie▲
True Crime
12 Monkeys▲
Twin Town
U-Turn
Wisdom
Yojimbo▲

Anti-War War Movies

see also *Satire & Parody*

The Adventures of Werner Holt
All Quiet on the Western Front▲
All Quiet on the Western Front
Amazing Grace & Chuck
Apocalypse Now▲
The Big Parade▲
Born on the Fourth of July▲
The Bridge
The Bridges at Toko-Ri▲
The Burmese Harp▲
Catch-22▲
The Charge of the Light Brigade
Civilization▲
Come and See▲
Coming Home▲
Cup Final
Dr. Strangelove, or: How I Learned to Stop Worrying and Love the Bomb▲
The Eagle and the Hawk▲
Field of Honor
Fiesta
Fires on the Plain▲
Forbidden Games▲
The Four Horsemen of the Apocalypse▲
The Four Horsemen of the Apocalypse
Gallipoli▲
Glory▲
Grand Illusion▲
Hamburger Hill
Hell in the Pacific▲
Henry V▲
Hombres Armados▲
J'Accuse▲
Jud
King and Country▲
The King of Hearts▲
La Guerre Est Finie▲
The Last Bridge
Latino
Les Carabiniers▲
The Line
M*A*S*H▲
M*A*S*H: Goodbye, Farewell & Amen▲
Master of the World
A Midnight Clear▲
Mission to Death
No Man's Land
Nurse Edith Cavell▲
Paths of Glory▲
Platoon▲
Pretty Village, Pretty Flame▲
Prisoner of the Mountains▲
The Red Badge of Courage▲
Revolution
San Demetrio, London
She Goes to War
The Steel Helmet▲
A Time to Love & a Time to Die
The Tin Drum▲
Too Late the Hero▲
Twilight's Last Gleaming
Veronico Cruz
Vukovar▲
Wackiest Ship in the Army
Westfront 1918▲
What Price Glory?▲
The Young Lions▲

Apartheid

see also *Africa; Civil Rights*

An African Dream
Boesman & Lena
Bopha!▲
City of Blood
Cry Freedom
Cry, the Beloved Country▲
Dangerous Ground
A Dry White Season▲
Funeral for an Assassin
Inside▲
Mandela▲
Mandela and de Klerk
Master Harold and the Boys▲
Place of Weeping
The Power of One
The Quarry
Sarafina!▲
The Wilby Conspiracy▲
A World Apart▲
A World of Strangers▲
Yankee Zulu

Archaeology

see *Big Digs*

Army Training, Sir!

Band of Brothers▲
Biloxi Blues
The Boys in Company C
Buck Privates
D.I.
Full Metal Jacket▲
In the Army Now
Stripes
Tigerland▲

Art & Artists

see also *Biopics: Musicians; Sculptors; Struggling Musicians; This Is Your Life; Writers*

The Adventures of Picasso
Advertising Rules!
The Agony and the Ecstasy
All the Vermeers in New York▲
An American in Paris▲
Andrei Rublev▲
Artemisia
Artists and Models
Back in the USSR
Backbeat▲
Basquiat▲

Bean▸
The Belly of an Architect▸
Bergonzi Hand
Big Eden
Black Magic Woman
The Blue Light▸
Bluebeard
Body Strokes
Boricua's Bond
Bride of the Wind
A Bucket of Blood▸
Camille Claudel▸
Canvas: The Fine Art of Crime
Caravaggio▸
Carrington
Cauldron of Blood
Changing Habits
Chasing Amy
Circle of Two
Color Me Blood Red
The Color of Evening
The Competition▸
Crucible of Terror
Crumb
Dante's Inferno: Life of Dante Gabriel Rossetti
Dark Side of Genius
The Death Artist
Death in Venice▸
The Designated Mourner
Detonator 2: Night Watch
Dirty Pictures
Dishonored Lady
A Dog of Flanders
Driller Killer
Ebony Tower
Echoes
Edie in Ciao! Manhattan
Edvard Munch
Empty Canvas
Entre-Nous▸
Escapade in Florence
Evil Has a Face
Fear and Loathing in Las Vegas
Femme Fatale
Fleshtone
Framed
Frida
From the Mixed-Up Files of Mrs. Basil E. Frankweiler
Frozen
Frozen in Fear
Gothic▸
Goya in Bordeaux
Great Expectations
Headless Eyes
The Hideaways
Hip Hip Hurrah!▸
The Horse's Mouth▸
Horsey
Hot Touch
Hour of the Wolf▸
House of Horrors
House of Wax▸
How to Steal a Million▸
Hullabaloo over Georgie & Bonnie's Pictures
Hunger
The Hypothesis of the Stolen Painting
I Shot Andy Warhol▸
If Lucy Fell
In the Land of the Owl Turds
Incognito
I've Heard the Mermaids Singing▸
Jimmy Zip
A Kink in the Picasso
La Belle Noiseuse▸
La Vie de Boheme▸
The Life of Emile Zola▸
Little Noises
Love & Sex
Love Is the Devil▸
Love Play
The Low Down
Luscious
Lust and Revenge
Lust for Life▸
Men...▸
Milo Milo
Mirror, Mirror 3: The Voyeur
Missing Pieces
Mistral's Daughter
The Moderns▸
Modigliani
Moll Flanders
The Moon and Sixpence▸
Morgan: A Suitable Case for Treatment
Moulin Rouge▸
Murder by Numbers
My Left Foot▸
The Naked Maja
Never Met Picasso
New York Stories▸
The Object of Beauty▸
Out of the Shadows
Paint It Black
The Painted Lady▸
A Perfect Murder
Picture Windows
Pollock▸
Portrait in Terror
Portrait of Jennie▸
Postcards from America
Prick Up Your Ears▸
Primal Secrets
Pucker Up and Bark Like a Dog
A Question of Attribution
Rembrandt▸
Rembrandt—1669
Rendezvous in Paris
Retribution
Salut l'Artiste▸
The Sandpiper
Savage Messiah▸
Scenario du Film Passion▸
Scream, Baby, Scream
The Seventh Veil▸
Sheer Madness▸
Shifting Sands
The Silver Chalice
Sirens
Slaves of New York
Starry Night
Stars and Bars
Stealing Beauty
Still Life
Strange Fruit
A Sunday in the Country▸
Sunday in the Park with George▸
Superstar: The Life and Times of Andy Warhol▸
Surviving Picasso
Sweet Thing▸
Tainted Image
The Tenant of Wildfell Hall
The Testament of Orpheus▸
The Thomas Crown Affair▸
Track of the Vampire
Trespasser
Trust Me
200 Cigarettes
Two If by Sea
The Two Mrs. Carrolls
Two Much
Utamaro and His Five Women
Utz
Van Gogh▸
Victimless Crimes
Vincent & Theo▸
Vincent: The Life and Death of Vincent van Gogh▸
What Dreams May Come
The Wolf at the Door
The Women on the Roof
World and Time Enough
The World of Suzie Wong

Asia

***see also** China; Japan*

Anna and the King
Beyond Rangoon
Bloodsport 2: The Next Kumite
Brokedown Palace
A Bullet in the Head▸
Catfish in Black Bean Sauce
Chaos Factor
China White
Eat Drink Man Woman▸
Emmanuelle
Emmanuelle, the Joys of a Woman
Entrapment
Escape to Burma
Far East
Flight from Singapore
Flower Drum Song
Fortunes of War
Indochine▸
Inn of Temptation
Jackie Chan's First Strike▸
Jakarta
The Kill
The Killing Beach
The Killing Fields▸
K2: The Ultimate High
Lara Croft: Tomb Raider
Little Buddha
Lost Horizon▸
Love Is a Many-Splendored Thing
Malaya
The Man with the Golden Gun
The Mongols
Natural Causes
The Quest
Red Dust▸
Rogue Trader
The Sand Pebbles▸
The Scent of Green Papaya▸
Shanghai Surprise
Singapore
That's the Way I Like It
The 13th Mission
Three Seasons
Tigershark
The Two Great Cavaliers
The Ugly American
The Vertical Ray of the Sun
Wake Island▸
White Ghost

Asian America

Chan Is Missing▸
Color of a Brisk and Leaping Day
Combination Platter
Come See the Paradise▸
Dim Sum: A Little Bit of Heart▸
Double Happiness▸
Eat a Bowl of Tea▸
Golden Gate
The Joy Luck Club▸
Living on Tokyo Time
Romeo Must Die
Strawberry Fields
The Wedding Banquet▸
Yellow

Assassinations

***see also** Camelot (New); Foreign Intrigue; Hit Men/Women; Spies & Espionage*

Abraham Lincoln
Ace of Hearts
Act of Vengeance
An Affair in Mind
African Rage
All the King's Men▸
The American Friend▸
The American Soldier
Antonio Das Mortes
The Arab Conspiracy
Ashes and Diamonds▸
Assassination
The Assassination Bureau▸
The Assassination File
The Assassination Game
The Assignment
Beautiful Beast
Beautiful Hunter
Belfast Assassin
Black Sunday
Blood for Blood
Blow Out▸
The Bourne Identity
Brass Target
The Break
Brother Orchid▸
The Brotherhood of the Rose
The Burning Season▸
Cal▸
Caracara
Center of the Web
Cleopatra
The Clockmaker▸
Cold Front
Coming Out Alive
The Criminal Mind
Dagger Eyes
The Dallas Connection
Dangerous Pursuit
The Day of the Dolphin
The Day of the Jackal▸
The Day That Shook the World
Dead Zone▸
Deadly Exposure
Death Force
Death to Smoochy
The Destructors
Diamond Run
The Dirty Dozen: The Next Mission
Disappearance
The Domino Principle
The Eagle Has Landed▸
The Eagle Has Two Heads▸
Elizabeth▸
Emmanuelle, the Queen
The Emperor and the Assassin
Enigma
Equalizer 2000
The Evil That Men Do
Excellent Cadavers
Excessive Force 2: Force on Force
Executive Action
Expert Weapon
F/X▸
Fatal Justice
Flashpoint
Flirting with Fate▸
Foul Play▸
Friday Foster
From Russia with Love▸
Funeral for an Assassin
Ghosts of Mississippi
Godson▸
Hangmen Also Die
Hard Way
Harum Scarum
Hidden Assassin
Hit Lady
The Hunted
I Spit on Your Corpse
In the Line of Fire▸
The Informant▸
Invitation to a Gunfighter
Jack Higgins' Midnight Man
Jack Higgins' On Dangerous Ground
The Jackal
JFK▸
Judgment Night
Kill Castro
The Killer Elite
Killer Likes Candy
The Killing Device
King Richard and the Crusaders
Kingfish: A Story of Huey P. Long
La Femme Nikita▸
La Passante▸
La Scorta▸
The Long Kiss Goodnight
Love and Anarchy▸
Love Kills
Loves & Times of Scaramouche
Malcolm X▸
The Man Who Knew Too Much▸
The Man Who Knew Too Much
The Man with the Golden Gun
The Manchurian Candidate▸
Maniac
Mark of the Beast
The Mercenaries
Mercury Rising
Michael Collins▸
Most Wanted
Murder of a Moderate Man
My Little Assassin
Nashville▸
Nick of Time
A Night of Love
Night of the Assassin
Ninja Death Squad
November Conspiracy
The November Men
Nowhere to Hide
The Odd Job
Omar Khayyam
One Man Out
Operation C.I.A.
The Ordeal of Dr. Mudd▸
The Parallax View▸
Paris Belongs to Us
Point of No Return
Programmed to Kill
PT 109
Quicker Than the Eye
Quiet Thunder
Red King, White Knight
Red Scorpion
Revenge of the Pink Panther
Rogue Male
Ruby
Running Against Time
Russian Roulette
Scorpio
Seven Days in May▸
Silent Trigger
Snake Eyes
Stalking Danger
State of Siege▸
Steele's Law
Suddenly▸
Supreme Sanction
Target: Favorite Son
Taxi Driver▸
The Terminator▸
The Terrorist
This Gun for Hire
Times of Harvey Milk
Two Minute Warning
Wardogs
What a Way to Die
When Hell Broke Loose
Where There's Life
Windmills of the Gods
Winter Kills▸
Without Warning: The James Brady Story▸
Xchange▸
Yojimbo▸
Z▸
Zoolander

Astronauts

***see also** Space Operas*

Apollo 13▸
Armageddon
The Astronaut's Wife
Beneath the Planet of the Apes
Capricorn One▸
Countdown
Deep Impact
Escape from Mars
From the Earth to the Moon▸
Gattaca▸
Marooned
Mission to Mars
Planet of the Apes▸
Red Planet
The Reluctant Astronaut
The Right Stuff▸
RocketMan
Space Cowboys▸
Species 2
2001: A Space Odyssey▸
2010: The Year We Make Contact▸

Astronomy & Astrology

***see** Star Gazing*

At the Drive-In

***see also** At the Movies*

Dead End Drive-In
Drive-In
Drive-In Massacre
The Flamingo Rising
Grease▸
Lone Star▸
Pee-wee's Big Adventure▸
Targets▸
Twister

At the Movies

***see also** Behind the Scenes*

Anguish
Apartment Zero▸
Attack from Mars
Bonnie & Clyde▸
Boogie Nights▸
Cinema Paradiso▸
Come See the Paradise▸
Coming Up Roses
The Creeps
Day for Night▸
Demons
Desperately Seeking Susan
Entropy
For Ever Mozart
Get Shorty▸
Gremlins 2: The New Batch▸
The Hard Way▸
In and Out▸
The Inner Circle▸
Into the West▸
Invasion Earth: The Aliens Are Here!
Johnny Dangerously
Last Action Hero
The Last Picture Show▸
The Long Day Closes▸
Love and Death on Long Island
Matinee
Merton of the Movies
The Movie House Massacre
A Nightmare on Elm Street 4: Dream Master
One Summer Love
Passion
Polyester
Popcorn
The Projectionist▸
The Proprietor
The Purple Rose of Cairo▸
The Real Blonde
The Replacement Killers
Rorret▸
Sabotage▸
Scenes from a Mall
Scream▸
Scream 2▸
Scream 3
Shadow of the Vampire▸
Something Short of Paradise
South Park: Bigger, Longer and Uncut
Tampopo▸
Things to Do in Denver When You're Dead▸
Trailer, the Movie
Trojan Eddie▸
Two Bits
Variety
Venice, Venice
Wes Craven's New Nightmare▸
White Heat▸
Who Framed Roger Rabbit▸

At the Video Store

***see also** At the Drive-In; At the Movies*

Clerks▸
EDtv
The Fisher King▸
Love and Death on Long Island
Remote Control
Scream▸
Tainted
Video Violence
The Watermelon Woman

Atlanta

***see also** American South*

Blast
Cyborg
Driving Miss Daisy▸
Echo of Murder
Gone with the Wind▸
In the Flesh
Let's Do It Again
Midnight Blue
The Murder of Mary Phagan▸
Run for the Dream: The Gail Devers Story
Scarlett
Sharky's Machine

Atlantic City

Atlantic City▲
Beaches▲
Gunshy▲
The King of Marvin Gardens
The Lemon Sisters
Snake Eyes
Sour Grapes

Australia

see *Down Under*

Automobiles

see *Checkered Flag; Motor Vehicle Dept.*

Babysitting

see also *Bringing Up Baby; Parenthood*
Adventures in Babysitting
Angel Blue
Are You in the House Alone?
The Baby-Sitters' Club
The Babysitter
Battling for Baby
Bebe's Kids
The Crazysitter
Don't Bother to Knock
Don't Tell Mom the Babysitter's Dead
Fright
A Global Affair
The Guardian
Halloween▲
Implicated
Laurel & Hardy: Brats
Look Who's Talking▲
Rita, Sue & Bob Too▲
Rock-A-Bye Baby
See Spot Run
Three's Trouble
Trick or Treats
Uncle Buck▲
Unhook the Stars
Wanted: Babysitter
Weekend with the Babysitter
When a Stranger Calls
When a Stranger Calls Back

Bachelor Party

see also *Up All Night*
Bachelor Party
The Best Man▲
A Guy Thing
House Party 3
In and Out▲
Intimate Betrayal
Laurel & Hardy: Be Big
Psycho Cop 2
Revenge of the Nerds 4: Nerds in Love
Stag
Very Bad Things

Bad Bosses

see also *Corporate Shenanigans; Dying for a Promotion; Office Surprise*
Antitrust
Clockwatchers
Joe Somebody
Kate & Leopold
A Matter of Taste
9 to 5
Office Space
Swimming with Sharks▲

Bad Dads

see also *Dads; Monster Moms; Parenthood*
Aberdeen
Affliction▲
Alice et Martin
American Beauty▲
American Virgin
At Close Range▲
The Attic
The Audrey Hepburn Story
Basil
Bastard out of Carolina
Beatrice▲
Benefit of the Doubt
Blade II
The Break
Broken English
The Brothers Karamazov▲
Buddy's Song
Buffalo 66▲
The Butcher Boy▲
The Celebration
Character
The Claim
Conseil de Famille
Crime and Punishment in Suburbia
Croupier▲
Dad Savage
Daddy's Boys
Damage▲
Dangerous Relations
Deconstructing Harry
Die Screaming, Marianne
Dolores Claiborne▲
Dracula Father and Son
East of Eden▲
East of Eden
Edwin
Elisa
The Empire Strikes Back▲
Farmer & Chase
Father Hood
Fear Strikes Out▲
Finish Line
Flesh and Bone▲
Four Days
Frailty▲
Freddy Got Fingered
The General's Daughter
Getting Even with Dad
Goldengirl
Grave of the Vampire
The Great Santini▲
Hand Gun
Hanging Up
He Got Game
Heart of the Stag
The Heiress▲
The Horror Chamber of Dr. Faustus▲
Hunter's Moon
Joe the King
Julien Donkey-boy
Kiss Daddy Goodbye
Kiss Daddy Goodnight
La Promesse
Last Time Out
L.I.E.
Life as a House
Lilian's Story
Little Boy Blue
Love and Basketball▲
Love Come Down
Luckytown
Magnolia▲
Monster's Ball▲
The Myth of Fingerprints
Natural Born Killers
Niagara, Niagara
No Looking Back
One True Thing▲
Opposite Corners
The Other Side of the Law
Panic
Parents▲
Price of Glory
Red River▲
Riding in Cars with Boys
Rites of Passage
River Red
Romeo Must Die
The Rookie▲
The Royal Tenenbaums▲
Sarah, Plain and Tall: Winter's End▲
Shine▲
The Shining
Sins of the Father▲
The Spanish Gardener▲
Spare Me
Spider-Man▲
Star Maps
The Stepfather▲
Stepfather 2: Make Room for Daddy
Stepfather 3: Father's Day
This Boy's Life▲
A Thousand Acres
Toll of the Desert
Turn It Up
U-Turn
The War Zone
Washington Square▲
Where the Hot Wind Blows
ZigZag▲

Ballet

see also *Dance Fever*
Alive and Kicking
An American in Paris▲
Angel in a Taxi
The Bacchantes
Black Tights
Body Beat
Brain Donors
Center Stage
The Children of Theatre Street
The Cowboy & the Ballerina
Dance
Dance, Girl, Dance
Dancers
George Balanchine's The Nutcracker
Grand Hotel▲
Invitation to the Dance
Limelight▲
Little Ballerina
Meet Me in Las Vegas
Mirrors
Never Let Me Go
Nijinsky
Nine Months
Nutcracker Sweet
Nutcracker: The Motion Picture
The Red Shoes▲
Shadow Dancing▲
Shall We Dance▲
Spectre of the Rose
Summer Interlude▲
Suspiria▲
Tales of Beatrix Potter▲
The Tales of Hoffmann
The Turning Point
Waterloo Bridge▲

Ballooning

The Adventures of Baron Munchausen▲
Around the World in 80 Days▲
Around the World in 80 Days
Charlie and the Great Balloon Chase
Cloud Waltzing
Fantastic Balloon Voyage
Five Weeks in a Balloon
Flight of the Eagle
Frankenstein Island
The Great Race
Lost Zeppelin
Men Don't Leave
Mysterious Island▲
Night Crossing
Octopussy
Olly Olly Oxen Free
Police Academy 4: Citizens on Patrol
Queen of the Jungle
The Red Balloon▲
Those Magnificent Men in Their Flying Machines▲
Voyage en Balloon
The Wizard of Oz▲

Baltimore

The Alien Factor
And Justice for All
Avalon▲
Breathing Lessons▲
The Climb
Diner▲
Hairspray▲
He Said, She Said
Homicide: The Movie
Liberty Heights
Pecker
Polyester
Sleepless in Seattle▲
The Sum of All Fears
Tin Men

Bar & Grill

see also *Nightclubs*
Albino Alligator
Bar Girls
Barb Wire
Barfly▲
Before Sunrise
The Broken Hearts Club▲
Bucktown
Burnzy's Last Call
Cocktail
Coyote Ugly
Death in Brunswick
Deterrence
The Florentine
From Dusk Till Dawn
From Dusk Till Dawn 2: Texas Blood Money
From Dusk Till Dawn 3: The Hangman's Daughter
Headless Body in Topless Bar
Hedwig and the Angry Inch▲
Hi-Life
John Carpenter's Vampires
The Last Time I Committed Suicide
Lemonade Joe
Little Boy Blue
Luminarias
Money Kings
Nobody
One Night at McCool's
Rare Birds
Restaurant
Stand-Ins
The Tavern
Time Served
Tree's Lounge
Twice upon a Yesterday
Two Family House
Un Air de Famille
Urbania

Baseball

Air Bud 4: Seventh Inning Fetch
Amazing Grace & Chuck
Angels in the Infield
Angels in the Outfield▲
Angels in the Outfield
The Babe
Babe Ruth Story
The Bad News Bears▲
The Bad News Bears Go to Japan
The Bad News Bears in Breaking Training
Bang the Drum Slowly
Bang the Drum Slowly▲
Battling Orioles
Bingo Long Traveling All-Stars & Motor Kings▲
Blood Games
Blue Skies Again
Brewster's Millions
Bull Durham▲
The Busher
Casey at the Bat
The Catcher
Chasing Dreams
Chu Chu & the Philly Flash
Cobb▲
Comeback Kid
The Comrades of Summer
Cooperstown
Damn Yankees▲
Don't Look Back: The Story of Leroy "Satchel" Paige
Ed
Eight Men Out▲
The Fan
Fear Strikes Out▲
Field of Dreams▲
Finding Buck McHenry
For Love of the Game
Frequency
Hank Aaron: Chasing the Dream▲
Hardball
Headin' Home
Ironweed▲
It Happens Every Spring▲
It's Good to Be Alive
It's My Turn
The Jackie Robinson Story▲
Jim Thorpe: All American
Joe Torre: Curveballs Along the Way
The Kid from Left Field
A League of Their Own▲
Life
The Life and Times of Hank Greenberg▲
Little Big League
Long Gone
Love Affair: The Eleanor & Lou Gehrig Story▲
Major League
Major League 2
Major League 3: Back to the Minors
The Man from Left Field
Mean Streak
Mr. Baseball
Mr. Destiny
The Natural▲
Night Game
One in a Million: The Ron LeFlore Story
Past the Bleachers
Pastime▲
Perfect Game
Pride of St. Louis
The Pride of the Yankees▲
The Rookie▲
Rookie of the Year
The Sandlot▲
The Scout
61*▲
The Slugger's Wife
Soul of the Game▲
Squeeze Play
Stealing Home
The Stratton Story▲
Summer Catch
Take Me Out to the Ball Game
Taking Care of Business
Talent for the Game
Three Wishes
Tiger Town
Trading Hearts
Wait until Spring, Bandini
Whistling in Brooklyn
Wide Awake
A Winner Never Quits
The Winning Team
Woman of the Year▲

Basketball

Above the Rim
The Absent-Minded Professor▲
Air Bud
The Air Up There
Annie O
The Basket
The Basketball Diaries
Big and Hairy
Big Mo
Black and White▲
Blue Chips
Celtic Pride
Coach
Cornbread, Earl & Me
Eddie
Fast Break
Final Exam
Final Shot: The Hank Gathers Story
Finding Forrester
The Fish that Saved Pittsburgh
For Heaven's Sake
Forget Paris
He Got Game
Heaven Is a Playground
Hoop Dreams▲
Hoosiers▲
Inside Moves
King of the Jungle
Like Mike
Love and Basketball▲
O▲
One on One
Passing Glory▲
Pistol: The Birth of a Legend
Porky's Revenge
Rebound: The Legend of Earl "The Goat" Manigault
The St. Tammany Miracle
The Sixth Man
Slam Dunk Ernest
Space Jam
Sunset Park
Tall Story
Teen Wolf
That Championship Season
White Men Can't Jump

Beach Blanket Bingo

see also *Lifeguards; Sex on the Beach; Surfing; Swimming*
Back to the Beach
Baywatch the Movie: Forbidden Paradise
Beach Babes from Beyond Infinity
Beach Blanket Bingo▲
Beach Girls
The Beach Girls and the Monster
Beach House
Beach Party
Bikini Beach
Bikini Summer
Bikini Summer 3: South Beach Heat
Body Waves
California Dreaming
Computer Beach Party
Horror of Party Beach
How to Stuff a Wild Bikini
Kill Shot
Love! Valour! Compassion!
Malibu Beach
Muscle Beach Party
Nico and Dani
Pajama Party
Phat Beach
Psycho Beach Party
Ride the Wild Surf
Seaside Swingers
Shag: The Movie▲
South Beach Academy
A Summer's Tale
Surf Party
A Swingin' Summer
Too Good to Be True
Wet and Wild Summer
Where the Boys Are

Bears

see also *Wild Kingdom*
Almost Heroes
The Bear▲
The Bears & I
Berserker
The Capture of Grizzly Adams
Claws
Deadtime Stories
Dr. Dolittle 2
The Edge
Gentle Giant
The Great Outdoors
Grizzly
Grizzly Adams: The Legend Continues
Grizzly Falls
The Hotel New Hampshire
The Jungle Book▲
King of the Grizzlies
Legends of the Fall
Life & Times of Grizzly Adams
Ms. Bear
The Parent Trap
The Polar Bear King
Rudyard Kipling's The Jungle Book
Rudyard Kipling's the Second Jungle Book: Mowgli and Baloo
Starbird and Sweet William
True Heart
Wild Grizzly

Beatniks

Beat Girl
A Bucket of Blood▲
Expresso Bongo
Funny Face▲
Hairspray▲
The Last Time I Committed Suicide

▲ = rated three bones or higher

The Prime Time
The Sleazy Uncle
So I Married an Axe Murderer

Beauty Pageants

see also Dream Girls
Beautiful
The Case of the Lucky Legs
Drop Dead Gorgeous
The Duchess of Idaho
Happy, Texas▲
I Wanna Be a Beauty Queen
Miss All-American Beauty
Miss Congeniality
Miss Firecracker▲
No Contest
Shag: The Movie▲
Smile▲
Waikiki Wedding▲

Behind Bars

see Great Escapes; Men in Prison; Women in Prison

Behind the Scenes

see also At the Movies; Film History
Abuse
Actors and Sin
The Affairs of Annabel
An Alan Smithee Film: Burn, Hollywood, Burn
Alexandria Again and Forever
American Virgin
America's Sweethearts
Anaconda
...And God Spoke
The Audrey Hepburn Story
Augustin
The Bad and the Beautiful▲
Beaumarchais the Scoundrel
Behind the Planet of the Apes▲
Best Friends
Beware of a Holy Whore
Big Fat Liar
The Big Knife▲
The Big Picture
Big Show
Bloodbath
Body Chemistry 3: Point of Seduction
The Bodyguard
Bombay Talkie
Boy Meets Girl▲
Broadway Rhythm
Bullets over Broadway▲
Cannes Man
Cats Don't Dance
Cecil B. Demented
Celebrity▲
Chaplin▲
The Chaplin Revue
A Chorus Line
A Chorus of Disapproval
Chuck Berry: Hail! Hail! Rock 'n' Roll
The Confessional▲
Contempt▲
Cosi▲
Crimetime
Crocodile Dundee in Los Angeles
Crossover Dreams
Cut
Dames▲
Dance of Life
Dancing in September
Dancing Lady
Dangerous Game
Darlings of the Gods
Day at the Beach
Day for Night▲
The Death Kiss
Delirious
The Disappearance of Kevin Johnson
Don't Let Your Meat Loaf
Double Threat
The Dresser▲
Ed Wood▲
The End of Violence
Entropy
Evil Ed
Expresso Bongo
Face the Music
5 Dark Souls
The Fluffer
Footlight Parade▲
For Ever Mozart
Free and Easy
Free Enterprise
The Freeway Maniac
French Exit
The French Lieutenant's Woman▲
Full Tilt Boogie
Get Shorty▲
The Ghost Walks
Give a Girl a Break
Glam
Gods and Monsters▲
Going Hollywood▲
The Goldwyn Follies
Good Times
Goodbye, Norma Jean
Goodnight, Sweet Marilyn
The Grace Kelly Story
Grief
Grunt! The Wrestling Movie
The Hard Way▲
He Said, She Said
The Hearst and Davies Affair
Hearts of Darkness: A Filmmaker's Apocalypse▲
Help!▲
Hijacking Hollywood
Hindsight
Hollywood Boulevard
Hollywood Confidential
Hollywood Ending
Hollywood Man
Hollywood Mystery
Hollywood Shuffle
Hooper
Hughes & Harlow: Angels in Hell
The Ice Rink
Identification of a Woman
I'll Do Anything
In a Moment of Passion
In the Shadows
In the Soup
Inside Daisy Clover
Into the Sun
Introducing Dorothy Dandridge▲
Irma Vep
James Dean
The Jayne Mansfield Story
Joey Breaker▲
The Killing of Sister George
L.A. Confidential▲
La Dolce Vita▲
L.A. Goddess
The Last Don 2
The Last Word
Le Polygraphe
Le Schpountz
The Leading Man
Legs
Lies
Lisbon Story
Living in Oblivion▲
Lobster Man from Mars
The Lonely Lady
Make a Wish
A Man in Love▲
Man of a Thousand Faces▲
Matinee
Meet the Feebles
A Midwinter's Tale
Miss All-American Beauty
Mistress
Modern Romance▲
Movie Maker
Movies Money Murder
The Mozart Brothers▲
Mulholland Drive▲
The Muppets Take Manhattan▲
The Muse
My Life's in Turnaround
Naked in New York
New Faces of 1952
A Night for Crime
Night of the Living Dead, 25th Anniversary Documentary
Nixon▲
Noises Off
Notting Hill▲
The November Men
On an Island with You
Open Season
Opening Night
The Oscar
Paris When It Sizzles
Passion
Pastime▲
The Perils of Pauline
The Phantom Lover
Pick a Star
The Pickle
The Player▲
Portraits Chinois
Postcards from the Edge▲
Rave Review
Ready to Wear
Rented Lips
Return to Cabin by the Lake
Rhythm on the River
Ringmaster
RKO 281▲
Roadie
Rorret▲
Scream 3
Search and Destroy
Secret Honor▲
Sex Is Crazy
Shadow of the Vampire▲
The Shot
The Show
Silent Motive
Simone
Sioux City Sue
Slaves of Hollywood
S.O.B.
Somewhere in Time
Son of Gascogne
Spice World: The Movie
Stage Door▲
Stand-In
Stand-Ins
The Star Maker
Star Spangled Rhythm▲
State and Main▲
State of Things▲
The Stranger: Kabloonak
The Stunt Man▲
Stunts
The Suburbans
Sugar Town
Sullivan's Travels▲
Summer Stock▲
Sunset
Sunset Boulevard▲
Sweet Liberty
Sweet Perfection
Swimming with Sharks▲
Tango
Teenager
That Thing You Do!▲
These Old Broads
They Bite
Through the Olive Trees▲
Tie Me Up! Tie Me Down!
Time Code
Tootsie▲
The Travelling Players
Truth or Dare
Ulysses' Gaze
Under the Rainbow
Users
Valley of the Dolls
Velvet Touch▲
Venice, Venice
A Very Private Affair
Wag the Dog
Waiting for Guffman
The Waiting Game
The Watermelon Woman
Wes Craven's New Nightmare▲
The West Point Story
What Price Hollywood?▲
Where's Marlowe?
White Hunter, Black Heart▲
Whodunit
Wild Party
Witch Hunt
With Friends Like These
Zou Zou

Belfast

see also Ireland
Belfast Assassin
Cal▲
Circle of Deceit
The Devil's Own▲
An Everlasting Piece
Four Days in July
Hennessy
In the Name of the Father▲
The Informant▲
Mad About Mambo
Nothing Personal▲
Quiet Day in Belfast▲
Resurrection Man
This Is the Sea

Berlin

see also Germany
Aimee & Jaguar
The Alley Cats
Anita, Dances of Vice
The Apple
The Assignment
Bent
Berlin Alexanderplatz▲
The Berlin Conspiracy
Berlin Tunnel 21
The Blue Hour
Cabaret▲
The Captain from Koepenick
Chinese Boxes
Club Extinction
Cold Room
David▲
Demons
Faraway, So Close!
Fatherland
Forbidden
A Foreign Affair▲
Funeral in Berlin▲
Hidden Agenda
I Am a Camera▲
Indiana Jones and the Last Crusade▲
The Innocent
Judgment in Berlin
Kamikaze '89▲
The Legend of Rita
Lola and Billy the Kid
The Looking Glass War
Mother Night▲
The Murderers Are Among Us
The Murderers are Among Us
The Oppermann Family
The Promise
Run Lola Run▲
Salmonberries
The Search▲
The Serpent's Egg
Shining Through
Solo Sunny
The Song of Songs
The Third Sex
The Tigress
The Truce▲
Verboten!
The Waiting Time
Wings of Desire▲

Betrayal

Amores Perros▲
Blade II
The Business of Strangers
Chill Factor
The Count of Monte Cristo
The Devil's Backbone
Enigma
Extremely Dangerous
Heart
Heist▲
In the Mood for Love
Mindstorm
Signs & Wonders
Star Wars: Episode 2—Attack of the Clones▲

Beverly Hills

Anywhere But Here
B.A.P.'s
Beverly Hills Cop
Beverly Hills Cop 2
Beverly Hills Cop 3
Beverly Hills Madam
Clueless▲
Down and Out in Beverly Hills
The Hollywood Knights
Housewife
Legally Blonde
Pretty Woman▲
Scenes from the Class Struggle in Beverly Hills
Slums of Beverly Hills▲
Troop Beverly Hills

Bicycling

American Flyers
And Soon the Darkness
The Bicycle Thief▲
BMX Bandits
Breaking Away▲
Butch Cassidy and the Sundance Kid▲
E.T.: The Extra-Terrestrial▲
Isn't Life Wonderful▲
Off the Mark
Pee-wee's Big Adventure▲
Quicksilver
Rad
Rush It
Ten Speed
2 Seconds
The Wizard of Oz▲

Big Battles

see also Civil War; Korean War; Korean War; Persian Gulf War; Revolutionary War; Vietnam War; World War I; World War II
The Alamo▲
Alexander Nevsky▲
Alexander the Great
Aliens▲
Anzio
Apocalypse Now▲
The Arena
Arena
Attila
Back to Bataan
Barry Lyndon▲
Battle Beyond the Sun
Battle of Britain
The Battle of El Alamein
Battle of the Bulge
The Battle of the Japan Sea
Battle of the Worlds
Battleground▲
The Battleship Potemkin▲
Ben-Hur▲
The Big Parade▲
The Big Red One▲
The Birth of a Nation▲
Braveheart▲
A Bridge Too Far
The Bruce
Cage 2: The Arena of Death
Captain Caution
The Castilian
Chasing the Deer
Crazy Horse▲
Cromwell
Cross of Iron
The Crossing
The Crusades
Das Boot▲
Diamonds Are Forever▲
Dragonheart
Dragonslayer▲
Druids
El Cid▲
The Emperor and the Assassin
The Empire Strikes Back▲
Enemy Below▲
Excalibur▲
The Fall of the Roman Empire▲
The Fighting Sullivans▲
First Knight
Gallipoli▲
Gettysburg▲
The Giant of Marathon
Giants of Rome
Gladiator▲
Gladiators 7
Glory▲
Godzilla vs. the Smog Monster
Goldfinger▲
The Guns of Navarone▲
Heaven & Earth▲
Henry V▲
Hercules vs. the Sons of the Sun
Highlander▲
I Bombed Pearl Harbor
Independence Day▲
Jeanne la Pucelle
Joan of Arc
John Paul Jones
The King of the Kickboxers
The Last Command
The Lighthorsemen▲
The Long Riders▲
The Longest Day▲
Lord of the Rings 1: The Fellowship of the Rings▲
The Magical Legend of the Leprechauns
The Man Who Would Be King▲
Mars Attacks!
Memphis Belle▲
The Messenger: The Story of Joan of Arc
Midway
Mists of Avalon▲
The Mongols
Monty Python and the Holy Grail▲
Moonraker
Motel Hell
Mulan
The Mummy Returns
A Nightmare on Elm Street
The Odyssey
The Patriot
Patton▲
Pearl
Raiders of the Lost Ark▲
Ran▲
Rawhide▲
Red Dawn
Return of the Jedi▲
Revolution
Ring of Fire
Rob Roy▲
Robo Warriors
Robot Jox
Samson and His Mighty Challenge
The Sand Pebbles▲
Sands of Iwo Jima▲
Saving Private Ryan▲
The Siege of Firebase Gloria
The Silk Road
Soldier
Son of the Morning Star▲
Stalingrad
Star Crash
Star Wars▲
Star Wars: Episode 1—The Phantom Menace▲
Star Wars: Episode 2—Attack of the Clones▲
Street Hunter
Tales from a Parallel Universe: I Worship His Shadow
Ten Days That Shook the World▲
They Died with Their Boots On▲
The 13th Warrior
Thunderball
To Hell and Back
Tora! Tora! Tora!
The Trojan Horse
Twelve o'Clock High▲
Two for Texas
The Viking Queen
War and Peace
War and Peace▲
War and Peace
The War Lord▲
The Wild Bunch▲
Zulu
Zulu Dawn▲

▲ = rated three bones or higher

Big-Budget Bombs

see also *Pure Ego Vehicles*

The Adventurers
Alexander the Great
American Anthem
Annie
The Bonfire of the Vanities
Boom!
Christopher Columbus: The Discovery
Cleopatra
The Conqueror
The Cotton Club▸
Dune
Harlem Nights
Heaven's Gate
Howard the Duck
Hudson Hawk
I'll Do Anything
Ishtar
Last Action Hero
The Long Ships
The Lovers on the Bridge
Midway
Money Train
Moon in the Gutter
1941
One from the Heart
Pirates
Rambo 3
Santa Claus: The Movie
The Scarlet Letter
The Shoes of the Fisherman
The Silver Chalice
Sphere
Summer Holiday
Supergirl
Tora! Tora! Tora!
Toys
Two Minute Warning
Two of a Kind
Waterloo

Big Digs

Ancient Evil: Scream of the Mummy
Blood from the Mummy's Tomb
The Body
The Curse of King Tut's Tomb
Dead Are Alive
Deadly Intent
The Golden Salamander
Indiana Jones and the Last Crusade▸
Indiana Jones and the Temple of Doom▸
King of the Forest Rangers
Legend of the Lost Tomb
March or Die
The Mask
The Mole People
The Mummy▸
The Mummy
The Mummy's Hand
The Mummy's Shroud
Pimpernel Smith
Raiders of the Lost Ark▸
Russell Mulcahy's Tale of the Mummy
Search for the Gods
Secre of the Andes
Sound of Horror
Specters
Stargate
Tomb
Unseen Evil
Valley of the Kings
The Word

Big Rigs

see also *Motor Vehicle Dept.; Road Trip*

Big Trouble in Little China
Black Dog
Breakdown▸
Breaker! Breaker!
California Straight Ahead
Citizens Band▸
Coast to Coast
Convoy
Desperate
Driving Force
Duel▸
Every Which Way But Loose
F.I.S.T.
Flatbed Annie and Sweetiepie: Lady Truckers
Great Smokey Roadblock
High Ballin'
Joy Ride▸
Larger Than Life
The Long Haul
Maximum Overdrive
The Other Side of the Mountain, Part 2
Pee-wee's Big Adventure▸
Road Games
Rolling Vengeance
Smokey and the Bandit
Smokey and the Bandit 2
Smokey and the Bandit, Part 3
Sorcerer
Steel Cowboy
The Sure Thing▸
They Drive by Night▸
Think Big
Trucks
Wages of Fear▸
White Line Fever
Willa

Bigfoot/Yeti

The Abominable Snowman
Big and Hairy
Big Foot
Bigfoot: The Unforgettable Encounter
The Capture of Bigfoot
Frostbiter: Wrath of the Wendigo
Half Human
Harry and the Hendersons
Legend of Big Foot
Legend of Boggy Creek
Little Bigfoot
Man Beast
Night of the Demon
Night of the Howling Beast
Return to Boggy Creek
Sasquatch
Shriek of the Mutilated
The Snow Creature
Snowbeast
To Catch a Yeti

Bikers

The Acid Eaters
Adventures Beyond Belief
Angel Unchained
Angels Die Hard
Angels from Hell
Angels Hard As They Come
Angels' Wild Women
Beach Party
Beyond the Law
Black Bikers from Hell
Blonde in Black Leather
Born Losers
Born to Ride
Breaking Loose
Bury Me an Angel
C.C. & Company
Chopper Chicks in Zombietown
Chrome and Hot Leather
Chrome Soldiers
City Limits
Cleopatra Jones
Club Life
Crossing the Line
Cycle Psycho
Cycle Vixens
Cyclone
Danger Zone
Danger Zone 2
Danger Zone 3: Steel Horse War
Dark Rider
Darktown Strutters
Deadly Reactor
Devil's Angels
Dirt Bike Kid
Dirt Gang
Easy Rider▸
Easy Wheels
Eat the Peach
Electra Glide in Blue▸
Evel Knievel
Every Which Way But Loose
Eye of the Tiger
The Final Alliance
Fugitive Champion
The Girl on a Motorcycle
The Glory Stompers
The Great Escape▸
Great Ride
The Great Skycopter Rescue
Greedy Terror
The Hard Ride
Harley
Harley Davidson and the Marlboro Man
Hellblock 13
Hellcats
Hellriders
Hell's Angels Forever
Hell's Angels on Wheels
Hell's Angels '69
Hell's Belles
Hog Wild
Hollywood Chaos
In Your Face
Iron Horsemen
The Jesus Trip
Knightriders
Lone Hero
Loners
The Losers
Loveless
Mad Max▸
Mask▸
The Masters of Menace
Master's Revenge
Me & Will
Motor Psycho
Motorcycle Gang
The Naked Angels
Nam Angels
Nomad Riders
Northville Cemetery Massacre
The Only Way Home
The Outlaw Bikers—Gang Wars
Outlaw Riders
Peacekillers
Pee-wee's Big Adventure▸
Pray for the Wildcats
Psychomania
Punk Vacation
Race for Glory
Raising Arizona▸
Raw Courage
Rebel Rousers
Return of the Rebels
Riding High
The Road
Roadside Prophets
Run, Angel, Run!
Running Cool
Satan's Sadists
Savage Dawn
The Savage Seven
Savages from Hell
Shame
She-Devils on Wheels
The Shrieking
Sidewinder One
Silver Dream Racer
Sinner's Blood
Space Riders
Spetters
Stone Cold
Street Hawk
Streets of Fire
Survival Zone
Timerider
Viva Knievel
Warlords from Hell
Werewolves on Wheels
The Wild Angels
Wild Guitar
The Wild One▸
Wild Rebels
Wild Riders
Wild Wheels
Winners Take All

Biography

see *This Is Your Life*

Biopics: Artists

see also *Art & Artists*

Basquiat▸
Camille Claudel▸
Caravaggio▸
Carrington
Crumb
Dante's Inferno: Life of Dante Gabriel Rossetti
Edvard Munch
Frida
Goya in Bordeaux
Love Is the Devil▸
Lust for Life▸
Magnificent Adventurer
Modigliani
Moulin Rouge▸
The Naked Maja
Pollock▸
Postcards from America
Rembrandt▸
Rembrandt—1669
Savage Messiah▸
Surviving Picasso
Van Gogh▸
Vincent & Theo▸
Vincent: The Life and Death of Vincent van Gogh▸
The Wolf at the Door

Biopics: Cops & Robbers

see also *Crime Drama; True Crime*

Al Capone▸
Bandit Queen
Bonanno: A Godfather's Story
Bonnie & Clyde▸
The Buccaneer
Bugsy▸
Butch Cassidy and the Sundance Kid▸
Chopper
Dick Turpin
Dillinger▸
Dillinger
The Elegant Criminal
The General▸
Goodfellas▸
Gore Vidal's Billy the Kid
Gotti
Great Missouri Raid
The Grey Fox▸
I Am a Fugitive from a Chain Gang▸
I Shot Billy the Kid
I Shot Jesse James▸
J. Edgar Hoover
The King of the Roaring '20s: The Story of Arnold Rothstein
Lansky
Last Days of Frank & Jesse James
The Left-Handed Gun▸
Lepke
Lucky Luciano
Mafia Princess
McVicar
Melvin Purvis: G-Man
Ned Kelly
The Outlaw
A Real American Hero
The Rise and Fall of Legs Diamond
Sugartime
Walking Tall
Walking Tall: Part 2
Walking Tall: The Final Chapter
Weeds▸
Wild Bill
Wyatt Earp
You Know My Name▸

Biopics: Military

see also *Civil War; Korean War; Military: Air Force; Military: Army; Military: Foreign; Military: Marines; Military: Navy; True Stories; Vietnam War; World War I; World War II*

Alexander the Great
Attila
Battle Hymn
The Big Red One▸
Breaking the Code
A Bright Shining Lie
Cast a Giant Shadow
Chapayev▸
Churchill and the Generals
Cromwell
The Desert Fox▸
The Gallant Hours▸
George Washington
Geronimo▸
Ike
The Iron Duke
John Paul Jones
The Last Days of Patton
Lawrence of Arabia▸
The Long Gray Line▸
MacArthur
Men of Honor
Napoleon▸
Napoleon
Patton▸
PT 109
To Hell and Back
We Were Soldiers▸

Biopics: Musicians

see also *Nashville Narratives*

Amadeus▸
Backbeat▸
Bandwagon
Beethoven
Beethoven Lives Upstairs
The Benny Goodman Story
Bird▸
Bix
Bound for Glory▸
Bride of the Wind
The Buddy Holly Story▸
Coal Miner's Daughter▸
Deep in My Heart
The Doors
The Eddy Duchin Story
Edith & Marcel
Elvis and Me
Elvis: The Movie
The Eternal Waltz
Eubie!
The Fabulous Dorseys
Farinelli
The Five Pennies
For Love or Country: The Arturo Sandoval Story
The Gene Krupa Story
The Glenn Miller Story▸
Great Balls of Fire
The Great Caruso
The Great Waltz▸
The Harmonists
Harmony Lane
Hendrix
Hilary and Jackie▸
The Hours and Times▸
I Dream of Jeannie
I'll See You in My Dreams
Immortal Beloved
Impromptu▸
In His Life: The John Lennon Story
Interrupted Melody▸
The Jacksons: An American Dream
John & Yoko: A Love Story
La Bamba▸
Lady Sings the Blues
Let's Get Lost
The Life and Loves of Mozart
Life of Verdi
Lisztomania
Living Proof: The Hank Williams Jr. Story
Love Me or Leave Me▸
Madonna: Innocence Lost
The Magic Bow
Mahler▸
Meat Loaf: To Hell and Back
Melody Master
Mo' Better Blues
Mozart: A Childhood Chronicle▸
The Mozart Story
The Music Lovers
Nico Icon▸
Night and Day
Passion
Piaf
The Rat Pack
Rhapsody in Blue▸
Selena
Shine▸
Sid & Nancy▸
Song of Norway
Song of Scheherazade
A Song to Remember▸
Song Without End
Spring Symphony
The Strauss Family
Sweet and Lowdown
Sweet Dreams
Sweet Love, Bitter
Tchaikovsky
The Temptations
32 Short Films about Glenn Gould▸
This Is Elvis
Three Little Words
Till the Clouds Roll By
Tous les Matins du Monde▸
Verdi
Voices from a Locked Room
Wagner: The Complete Epic
Waltz King
Whale Music
What's Love Got to Do with It?
Why Do Fools Fall in Love?
Words and Music
Young Caruso

Biopics: Politics

see also *Capitol Capers; Politics; True Stories; Vote for Me!*

Abe Lincoln in Illinois▸
Abraham Lincoln
Amin: The Rise and Fall
Barefoot in Athens
Blaze
Blind Ambition
The Burning Season▸
Cesare Borgia
Churchill and the Generals
Citizen Cohn
The Courageous Mr. Penn
A Dangerous Man: Lawrence after Arabia▸
The Death of Adolf Hitler
Disraeli▸
Eleanor & Franklin▸
Eleanor: First Lady of the World
Enemy of Women
Gandhi▸
The Gathering Storm
George Washington: The Forging of a Nation
Give 'Em Hell, Harry!
Gore Vidal's Lincoln
Hitler
Imperial Venus
Inside the Third Reich
Invincible Mr. Disraeli
Jackie, Ethel, Joan: The Kennedy Women
Jefferson in Paris
The Jesse Ventura Story
JFK: Reckless Youth
Johnny We Hardly Knew Ye
Juarez
The Kennedys of Massachusetts
Kingfish: A Story of Huey P. Long
Kissinger and Nixon
Kundun▸
The Last Emperor▸
Last Four Days
LBJ: The Early Years▸
The Life and Assassination of the Kingfish
Magnificent Doll
The Magnificent Yankee▸
Mandela▸
Michael Collins▸
Mosley
Mussolini & I
Nixon▸
Prince Jack
Robert Kennedy and His Times
Sadat
Sakharov▸

▸ = rated three bones or higher

Secret Honor▲
The Sicilian
Simon Bolivar
Stalin
Sunrise at Campobello▲
Truman
Viva Zapata!▲
Will: G. Gordon Liddy
Wilson▲
Without Warning: The James Brady Story▲
A Woman Called Golda▲
Young Mr. Lincoln▲

Biopics: Religious

see also *Islam; Judaism; Religion*

The Courageous Mr. Penn
Kundun▲

Biopics: Royalty

see also *Politics; Royalty; Royalty, British; Royalty, Russian; True Stories*

Bonnie Prince Charlie
Catherine the Great
Charlemagne
Diana: Her True Story
Edward and Mrs. Simpson
Elizabeth R▲
Elizabeth, the Queen
Lady Jane▲
Ludwig
Marie Antoinette
Mary of Scotland▲
Nicholas and Alexandra
Peter the Great▲
The Rise of Louis XIV▲
Six Wives of Henry VIII▲
Victoria Regina
The Virgin Queen▲
The Woman He Loved

Biopics: Science/ Medical

see also *This Is My Life; This Is Your Life*

A Beautiful Mind▲
Bethune
Breaking the Code
The Doctor
Dr. Bethune▲
The Elephant Man▲
The Five of Me
The Great Moment
Holy Terror
Infinity
Korczak▲
Lamp at Midnight
Long Journey Back
Madame Curie▲
A Matter of Life and Death
The Miracle Worker▲
The Miracle Worker
Nurse Edith Cavell▲
Sakharov▲
The Secret Diary of Sigmund Freud
The Sound and the Silence
The Story of Alexander Graham Bell▲
The Story of Dr. Wassell
The Story of Louis Pasteur▲
Theremin: An Electronic Odyssey▲
Young Tom Edison

Biopics: Showbiz

see also *Price of Fame*

Actor: The Paul Muni Story
Alex in Wonderland
All That Jazz▲
The Amazing Howard Hughes
The Ann Jillian Story
The Audrey Hepburn Story
The Bodyguard
Bogie: The Last Hero
Bojangles
Bruce Lee: Curse of the Dragon▲
Bud and Lou
Can You Hear the Laughter? The Story of Freddie Prinze
The Cat's Meow
Cecil B. Demented
Chaplin▲
Darlings of the Gods
Dear Brigitte
The Dolly Sisters
Dragon: The Bruce Lee Story▲
Ed Wood▲
Enter Laughing
Ernie Kovacs: Between the Laughter
F. Scott Fitzgerald in Hollywood
Flynn
Frances▲
From the Journals of Jean Seberg
Funny Girl▲
Funny Lady
Go West, Young Man
The Goddess▲
Gods and Monsters▲
Goodbye, Norma Jean
Goodnight, Sweet Marilyn
The Grace Kelly Story
The Great Ziegfeld▲
Gypsy▲
Gypsy
Harlow
Hughes & Harlow: Angels in Hell
In Person
The Incredible Sarah
Introducing Dorothy Dandridge▲
Isadora▲
James Dean
James Dean: Live Fast, Die Young
The Jayne Mansfield Story
Jolson Sings Again
The Jolson Story▲
The Josephine Baker Story▲
Legend of Valentino
Lenny▲
Life with Judy Garland—Me and My Shadows▲
Lillie▲
Livin' for Love: The Natalie Cole Story
Look for the Silver Lining
The Love Goddesses
Lucy and Desi: Before the Laughter
Mae West
Man of a Thousand Faces▲
Man on the Moon
Marilyn & Bobby: Her Final Affair
Marilyn: The Untold Story▲
Merton of the Movies
Mommie Dearest
My Favorite Year▲
My Wicked, Wicked Ways
Nijinsky
Norma Jean and Marilyn
Paul Robeson
The Perils of Pauline
Queenie
Quiet Days in Hollywood
Rainbow
Rascal Dazzle
Rita Hayworth: The Love Goddess
RKO 281▲
Rock Hudson's Home Movies
Roseanne: An Unauthorized Biography
Rosie: The Rosemary Clooney Story
The Seven Little Foys▲
Sinatra
Sophia Loren: Her Own Story
Star!
The Story of Vernon and Irene Castle▲
Superstar: The Life and Times of Andy Warhol▲
Taxi zum Klo▲
That's Entertainment
That's Entertainment, Part 2
That's Entertainment, Part 3
This Is Elvis
Thursday's Child
Topsy Turvy▲
Valentino
Veronika Voss▲
What Ever Happened to Baby Jane?▲
White Hot: The Mysterious Murder of Thelma Todd
White Hunter, Black Heart▲
Wired
Yankee Doodle Dandy▲
Young Charlie Chaplin

Biopics: Sports

see also *Baseball; Basketball; Football; Hockey; The Olympics; Running; Soccer; Sports Dramas; Team Efforts*

Ali
Babe!▲
The Babe
Babe Ruth Story
Big Mo
Boy in Blue
Breaking the Surface: The Greg Louganis Story
Brian's Song▲
Brian's Song
Champions
Chariots of Fire▲
Cobb▲
Dempsey
Don King: Only in America
Don't Look Back: The Story of Leroy "Satchel" Paige
Fallen Champ: The Untold Story of Mike Tyson▲
Fast Company
Final Shot: The Hank Gathers Story
Gentleman Jim▲
Going for the Gold: The Bill Johnson Story
Grambling's White Tiger
Greased Lightning
The Great White Hope
The Greatest
Harmon of Michigan
Headin' Home
Heart Like a Wheel
Heart of a Champion: The Ray Mancini Story
It's Good to Be Alive
The Jackie Robinson Story▲
The Jesse Owens Story
Jim Thorpe: All American
The Joe Louis Story
Joe Torre: Curveballs Along the Way
Knute Rockne: All American▲
The Loneliest Runner
Marciano
One in a Million: The Ron LeFlore Story
Pistol: The Birth of a Legend
Prefontaine
Pride of St. Louis
The Pride of the Yankees▲
Raging Bull▲
Rebound: The Legend of Earl "The Goat" Manigault
Richard Petty Story
Rocky Marciano
The Rookie▲
Run for the Dream: The Gail Devers Story
61*▲
Somebody Up There Likes Me▲
The Tiger Woods Story
Tyson
Wilma
A Winner Never Quits
The Winning Team
Without Limits▲

Biopics: Writers

The Adventures of Mark Twain▲
Agatha
Almost Famous▲
An Angel at My Table▲
Balzac: A Life of Passion▲
The Barretts of Wimpole Street▲
Becoming Colette
Before Night Falls▲
Celeste▲
Coming Through
Cross Creek
Dash and Lilly
The Disappearance of Garcia Lorca
Forbidden Passion: The Oscar Wilde Movie
Goldeneye: The Secret Life of Ian Fleming
Gothic▲
Hammett
Hans Christian Andersen
Haunted Summer
Heart Beat
Henry & June▲
I Shot Andy Warhol▲
Iris
Iris▲
Isn't She Great
Jack London
James Joyce: A Portrait of the Artist as a Young Man
James Joyce's Women▲
The Loves of Edgar Allen Poe
Meteor & Shadow
Mishima: A Life in Four Chapters▲
Mrs. Parker and the Vicious Circle
My Apprenticeship▲
My Childhood▲
My Left Foot▲
My Universities▲
Nerolio
Nora
The Passion of Ayn Rand
Pinero
Postcards from America
The Road from Coorain
Saint-Ex: The Story of the Storyteller
Shadowlands▲
The Spectre of Edgar Allen Poe
Spymaker: The Secret Life of Ian Fleming
Stevie
Swann
Tom & Viv▲
Total Eclipse
The Trials of Oscar Wilde▲
Wilde
The Wonderful World of the Brothers Grimm
Zora Is My Name!

Birds

Batman Returns
Beaks: The Movie
Birdman of Alcatraz▲
The Birds▲
The Birds 2: Land's End
Blade Master
Blood Freak
A Breed Apart
Brewster McCloud▲
Chicken Run▲
Cockfighter▲
Continental Divide
The Crow
The Crow 2: City of Angels
Cry of the Penguins
Fly Away Home▲
The Giant Claw
The Goodbye Bird
High Anxiety
Howard the Duck
Magic in the Mirror: Fowl Play
Mating Season
Million Dollar Duck
No Fear, No Die
Paulie
The Pebble and the Penguin
Rare Birds
The Real Macaw
The Rescuers Down Under
Rooster: Spurs of Death!
Sesame Street Presents: Follow That Bird
Spirit of the Eagle
Stuart Little 2
The Trumpet of the Swan
Vulture

Birthdays

Bloody Birthday
The Boys in the Band
Cat on a Hot Tin Roof▲
Cat on a Hot Tin Roof
The Celebration
City Slickers▲
The Game▲
Happy Birthday, Gemini
Happy Birthday to Me
Meet Joe Black
Mrs. Doubtfire
Mob Queen
On Golden Pond▲
Rabid Grannies
Sitcom
Sixteen Candles▲
10
That's Life!
To Gillian on Her 37th Birthday
Un Air de Famille
What's Eating Gilbert Grape▲

Bisexuality

see also *Gays; Lesbians*

Basic Instinct
Bedrooms and Hallways
California Suite▲
Change of Heart
The Crying Game▲
Dog Day Afternoon▲
Dona Herlinda & Her Son
Dry Cleaning
Female Perversions
Happily Ever After
Les Biches▲
Liquid Sky▲
Mary, Mary, Bloody Mary
Pas Tres Catholique
The Scorpion Woman
Showgirls
Sunday, Bloody Sunday▲
Those Who Love Me Can Take the Train
Three of Hearts
Threesome
The Trio
The Velocity of Gary
Velvet Goldmine
A Woman in Flames▲

Black Comedy

see also *Comedy; Comedy Drama; Satire & Parody*

Abigail's Party
The Acid House
The Addams Family
Addams Family Values
The Advocate▲
After Hours▲
Age Isn't Everything
The Alarmist
Alberto Express
Alice▲
Alone in the T-Shirt Zone
American Strays
The Americanization of Emily▲
America's Deadliest Home Video
Angels Over Broadway▲
The Anniversary
The Applegates
Ariel▲
Army Brats
Arnold
Arrivederci, Baby!
Arsenic and Old Lace▲
The Assassination Bureau▲
Assault of the Killer Bimbos
At Home with the Webbers
The Atomic Kid
Baby Face Morgan
Baby Love
Bad Boy Bubby
Bad Charleston Charlie
Barjo
Barton Fink▲
Battle of the Bullies
Beat the Devil▲
Beautiful People
Being John Malkovich▲
Bizarre Bizarre▲
Bliss▲
Brazil▲
Bread and Chocolate▲
Brewster McCloud▲
Bringing Out the Dead
Buddy Buddy
Buffalo 66▲
Buffet Froid▲
Cabaret Balkan
The Cable Guy
Canadian Bacon
Careful
The Cars That Ate Paris▲
Catch-22▲
Celine and Julie Go Boating
Checking Out
Choice of Weapons
The Choirboys
City Unplugged
Clay Pigeons
Clerks▲
Coldblooded
The Comic▲
Consuming Passions
The Cook, the Thief, His Wife & Her Lover▲
Coup de Torchon▲
Crimes of the Heart
The Criminal Life of Archibaldo de la Cruz▲
Critical Care
Crocodile Tears
Crocodiles in Amsterdam
Curdled
The Curve
The Dark Backward
Day at the Beach
A Day in the Death of Joe Egg▲
Dead Husbands
Dead Silence
Deadly Advice
Death Becomes Her▲
Death in Brunswick
Death to Smoochy
Delicatessen▲
Delivered
Divine
Dr. Strangelove, or: How I Learned to Stop Worrying and Love the Bomb▲
Don's Party▲
The Doom Generation▲
The Dress
Drop Dead Gorgeous
Eat the Rich
Eating Raoul▲
8 Heads in a Duffel Bag
El
Ellie
The End▲
Enid Is Sleeping
Entertaining Mr. Sloane
eXistenZ
Exquisite Corpses
The Exterminating Angel▲
Fargo▲
Female Trouble
A Fine Madness▲
The Firemen's Ball▲
A Fish Called Wanda▲
Four Bags Full
Four Rooms
Freaked
Frogs for Snakes
The Funeral▲
Funny Bones▲
Funny, Dirty Little War
The Garden of Delights▲
Gas-s-s-s!
The Gazebo▲
Genghis Cohn
Getting Away With Murder
Ghost Chase
Goodbye Cruel World
Grace Quigley
Grave Indiscretions
Gravesend
The Great Madcap
Greetings▲
Gridlock'd▲
Grosse Pointe Blank▲
Guilty as Charged
Happiness▲
Harold and Maude▲
Hawks
Head Above Water
Headless Body in Topless Bar

Heart Condition
Heathers▲
Henry Fool▲
Hexed
Hi, Mom!▲
High Heels
High Heels▲
Highway 61
Hold Me, Thrill Me, Kiss Me
Hombres Complicados
Home Sweet Home
Homebodies
The Honey Pot
The Hospital▲
The Hot Rock▲
The House of Yes
How Tasty Was My Little Frenchman
How to Get Ahead in Advertising▲
The Hudsucker Proxy▲
Husbands, Wives, Money, and Murder
I Love You to Death
I Ought to Be in Pictures
In the Company of Men
The Infernal Trio
Intimate Relations
Into the Night
Jawbreaker
Junk Mail
Killing Grandpa
The Killing of Sister George
Kind Hearts and Coronets▲
King of Comedy▲
King, Queen, Knave▲
Kiss & Tell
Kiss of Death
The Ladykillers▲
The Laserman
The Last Dance
The Last Supper
Leolo▲
Life Is Sweet▲
Like It Never Was Before
Little Murders▲
Loot ... Give Me Money, Honey!
Love and Action in Chicago
The Loved One▲
Lucky Stiff
L'Udienza
Mad Dog and Glory▲
Man Bites Dog
Matador
A Matter of WHO
Max, Mon Amour
Meet the Feebles
Miracle Mile▲
Mixed Blood
Mojave Moon
Mondo Balordo
Monsieur Verdoux▲
Montenegro▲
Mortuary Academy
Mother, Jugs and Speed
Movies Money Murder
Murder Czech Style
Muriel's Wedding▲
Murphy's Fault
My New Gun
My Sweet Suicide
Mystery Train▲
The Natural History of Parking Lots
No Problem
No Surrender▲
Novocaine
Nurse Betty▲
Nuts in May
O Lucky Man!▲
The Oak
The Odd Job
Of Freaks and Men
Office Killer
Oh Dad, Poor Dad (Momma's Hung You in the Closet & I'm Feeling So Sad)
The Operator
The Opposite of Sex
Orphans
Out Cold
Pain in the A—▲
Panic
Parents▲
Passed Away
Paul Bartel's The Secret Cinema
Penn and Teller Get Killed
Permanent Midnight
The Pornographers▲
Private Parts
Raising Arizona▲
Ravenous
Reckless
Red Earth
The Red Inn
The Ref▲
Repo Man▲
Reuben, Reuben▲
Riff Raff▲
Rubin & Ed
St. Patrick's Day
Salvation!
The Scent of a Woman
Schtonk
The Second Civil War
Serial Mom▲
Seven Beauties▲
Shadey
Shakes the Clown
Shallow Grave
She-Devil
Shoot Loud, Louder, I Don't Understand!
A Sinful Life
So I Married an Axe Murderer
Some Girls
Something for Everyone
Something Wild
Spanking the Monkey▲
Stars and Bars
The Steagle
Sticky Fingers
The Story of Fausta
Stuart Bliss
Sudden Manhattan
Suicide Kings
Sweet Movie
Sweet Revenge
Sweethearts
Swimming with Sharks▲
Tatie Danielle▲
A Texas Funeral
That Obscure Object of Desire▲
There Was a Crooked Man▲
Throw Momma from the Train▲
Tie Me Up! Tie Me Down!
To Be or Not to Be▲
To Die For▲
Toto le Heros▲
Touch
Trainspotting▲
Transylvania Twist
Trigger Happy
Trois Couleurs: Blanc▲
The Trouble with Harry▲
Twin Town
Two Days in the Valley▲
Two Hands▲
The Unbelievable Truth
Underground▲
Unexplained Laughter
Unnatural Pursuits
Vampire's Kiss▲
Very Bad Things
The War of the Roses▲
Weapons of Mass Distraction
What Have I Done to Deserve This?▲
Where's Piccone▲
Where's Poppa?▲
Who Is Killing the Great Chefs of Europe?▲
The Whole Nine Yards
Why Does Herr R. Run Amok?
Wilder Napalm
Wise Guys
Wish You Were Dead
The Witches of Eastwick
With a Friend Like Harry▲
Withnail and I▲
Women on the Verge of a Nervous Breakdown▲
World of the Depraved
The Wrong Box▲
Zombie and the Ghost Train

Black Gold

The Abyss▲
The Beverly Hillbillies
Black Gold
Blowing Wild
Boom Town
Breaking the Waves▲
Chain of Command
Comes a Horseman
Country Gentlemen
Crossfire Trail▲
The Crude Oasis
Dead Ahead: The Exxon Valdez Disaster▲
Devil's Crude
The Dive
Double Deal
Fighting Texans
Five Easy Pieces▲
The Formula
Gas Pump Girls
Giant▲
The Guns and the Fury
Hellfighters
Intruder Within
Legend of Frenchie King
Lie Down with Lions
Local Hero▲
Louisiana Story▲
The Madwoman of Chaillot
Mission in Morocco
Naked Gun 2 1/2: The Smell of Fear
'Neath the Arizona Skies
Oceans of Fire
Oklahoma Crude
On Deadly Ground
Red Rock West▲
Roughnecks
The Stars Fell on Henrietta
Thunder Bay▲
Tulsa▲
Waltz across Texas
War of the Wildcats
Wildcat
The World Is Not Enough
Written on the Wind▲

Blackmail

***see also** Corporate Shenanigans; Crime & Criminals; Disorganized Crime; Organized Crime*

The Art of Murder
Barocco
The Big Brass Ring
Blackmale
Captives
Choke
Clue
The Deep End▲
Devil in the Flesh
Feeling Minnesota
First Degree
The First Wives Club
A Gentleman After Dark
The Golden Spiders: A Nero Wolfe Mystery
Goodbye, Lover
The Guilty
Hard Evidence
High Heels and Low Lifes
An Ideal Husband▲
The Immoral One
The Informant▲
Johnny Skidmarks
Keys to Tulsa
Kiss Tomorrow Goodbye
Legal Deceit
Letter to My Killer
Love Walked In
Lucky Numbers
Mrs. Winterbourne
Mulholland Falls
The Opposite of Sex
Perfect Lies
A Perfect Murder
The Player▲
Portrait in Black
The Silent Partner▲
Slackers
A Slight Case of Murder
Twilight▲
Undercurrent
Victim▲
Zero Effect

Blaxploitation

***see also** African America; New Black Cinema*

Across 110th Street
Avenging Disco Godfather
Big Score
Black Belt Jones
Black Caesar
Black Gestapo
Black Godfather
Blackenstein
Blacula
Bones
Bucktown
Cleopatra Jones
Cleopatra Jones & the Casino of Gold
Coffy
Cotton Comes to Harlem▲
Detroit 9000
Dr. Black, Mr. Hyde
Dolemite
Dolemite 2: Human Tornado
Foxy Brown
Friday Foster
Ganja and Hess
The Guy from Harlem
Hell Up in Harlem
Hot Potato
J.D.'s Revenge
Let's Do It Again
The Mack
Mean Johnny Barrows
Miracle in Harlem
Monkey Hustle
Moon over Harlem
No Way Back
One Down, Two to Go!
Return of Superfly
Savage!
Scream Blacula Scream
Shaft▲
Shaft in Africa
Shaft's Big Score
Sheba, Baby
Slaughter
Slaughter's Big Ripoff
Soul Vengeance
Superfly
Superfly T.N.T.
Sweet Sweetback's Baadasssss Song▲
That Man Bolt
Three the Hard Way
Top of the Heap
Truck Turner
Undercover Brother

Blindness

***see also** Physical Problems*

Afraid of the Dark
Alligator Eyes
Amy
At First Sight
Aurora
Ballad in Blue
Blacklight
Blackout
Blind Date
Blind Fear
Blind Fury
Blind Justice
Blind Man's Bluff
Blind Witness
Blink
Breaking Free
Butterflies Are Free▲
Cactus
Can You Feel Me Dancing?
City for Conquest▲
City Lights▲
The Color of Paradise
Crimes & Misdemeanors▲
Dancer in the Dark
Don't Look Now▲
Eight Witnesses
Elmer
Eye on the Sparrow
A Family Thing▲
Good Luck
Hollywood Ending
The Human Monster
Ice Castles
If You Could See What I Hear
Jennifer 8
The Killer▲
La Symphonie Pastorale▲
Last Game
Life on a String
Lost for Words▲
Love at First Sight
Love Leads the Way
Mask▲
Minnesota Clay
The Miracle Worker▲
The Miracle Worker
Mr. Magoo
Night Gallery▲
Night Is My Future
Nowhere in Sight
Octavia
On Dangerous Ground▲
Ordinary Heroes
A Patch of Blue
People Who Own the Dark
Places in the Heart▲
Proof▲
Return of the Evil Dead
The Scent of a Woman
Scent of a Woman▲
Schlock
Second Sight▲
See No Evil▲
See No Evil, Hear No Evil
Sketch Artist 2: Hands That See
Sneakers
Someone Else's America▲
They Watch
Things You Can Tell Just by Looking at Her
To Race the Wind
The Toxic Avenger
Until the End of the World▲
A Voyage 'Round My Father▲
Wait until Dark▲
The Whales of August▲
Wild Hearts Can't Be Broken▲
Young Frankenstein▲
Zatoichi: The Blind Swordsman and the Chess Expert
Zatoichi: The Blind Swordsman's Vengeance
Zertigo Diamond Caper

Blizzards

***see also** Cold Spots*

Babes in Toyland
Cold Comfort
Donner Pass: The Road to Survival
The Last Stop
Ravenous
The Shining
Snow Day
Snowbound: The Jim and Jennifer Stolpa Story
Stephen King's The Storm of the Century
Trapped in Paradise
You'll Like My Mother

Bloody Messages

Die Hard▲
Fatal Vision
Harold and Maude▲
Helter Skelter
The Jagged Edge
Seven▲
The Shining
Stephen King's The Night Flier
The Untouchables▲

Boating

***see** Sail Away*

Bodyguards

Absolute Power
Assassination
Black Belt
Blackjack
The Bodyguard
The Bodyguard from Beijing
The Chase
Fatal Beauty
Fatal Past
Final Voyage
First Kid
Genuine Risk
Get Shorty▲
Guarding Tess
Half a Loaf of Kung Fu
Heat
His Bodyguard
In the Line of Fire▲
La Scorta▲
Man on Fire
Mr. Nanny
My Bodyguard▲
Night Eyes 4: Fatal Passion
Pushed to the Limit
Time and Tide
The Tsar's Bride▲

Books

***see also** Storytelling*

Cross Creek
Crossing Delancey▲
Fahrenheit 451▲
Falling in Love
I, Madman
In the Mouth of Madness
La Lectrice
The NeverEnding Story▲
A Night to Remember▲
The Ninth Gate
The Paper Chase▲
Priest of Love
Providence▲
QB VII▲
The Russia House
The Seven Year Itch▲

Bookstores

Ambition
Better Than Chocolate
Burglar
84 Charing Cross Road▲
Funny Face▲
The Love Letter
Notting Hill▲
You've Got Mail

Boom!

***see also** Action-Adventure; Fires*

Airport▲
Arlington Road
Armageddon
Atomic Train
Bad Company
Black Dog
Blown Away
Broken Arrow
Casino▲
Chain Reaction
Chill Factor
Clear and Present Danger
Collateral Damage
Con Air▲
Crackerjack 2
Cutthroat Island
Dante's Peak
The Day After▲
Daylight
Die Hard▲
Die Hard 2: Die Harder▲
Die Hard: With a Vengeance
Dr. Strangelove, or: How I Learned to Stop Worrying and Love the Bomb▲
Earthquake
Enemy of the State
The English Patient▲
Eraser
Extreme Limits
Face/Off▲
Fight Club: °▲
The Final Cut
Fire Down Below
Firestorm
Friends
From Dusk Till Dawn
The Fugitive▲
Goldeneye▲
Gone Fishin'
Grosse Pointe Blank▲
Hiroshima: Out of the Ashes▲
Hoodlum
Human Bomb
Independence Day▲

The Inspectors
Lethal Weapon 3
Lethal Weapon 4
Live Wire: Human Timebomb
Nowhere to Land
Path to Paradise
The Peacemaker
Pearl Harbor
Riot
The Rock▲
Sabotage▲
Sea of Sand
The Secret Agent
Serial Bomber
The Siege
Simon Sez
The Specialist
Speed▲
Spider-Man▲
Stealth Fighter
Steel
Sudden Death
The Sum of All Fears
Sweepers
Swordfish
The Terminator▲
Testament▲
Thirty Seconds Over Tokyo▲
Ticker
Total Recall▲
True Lies
The Usual Suspects▲
The X-Files

Boomer Reunions

***see also** Period Piece: 1960s*

The Big Chill▲
The Brutal Truth
Everything Relative
Far Harbor
I Think I Do
Indian Summer
Lifeguard
Parallel Lives
Peter's Friends
Return of the Secaucus 7▲
Spin the Bottle
That Championship Season

Bosnia

Beautiful People
Behind Enemy Lines
For Ever Mozart
Harrison's Flowers
No Man's Land
Pretty Village, Pretty Flame▲
Savior▲
Shot Through the Heart▲
Ulysses' Gaze
Underground▲
Vukovar▲
Welcome to Sarajevo▲
The Wounds

Boston

Adrenalin: Fear the Rush
Athena
Bad Manners
A Beautiful Mind▲
Before and After
Blown Away
Body Count
Boondock Saints
The Boston Strangler
Breeders
A Case of Deadly Force▲
Celtic Pride
Coma▲
Criminal Law
Fear Strikes Out▲
Fuzz
Gentleman Bandit
Good Will Hunting
The Great Moment
Jill the Ripper
Johnny We Hardly Knew Ye
Little Men
Little Shots of Happiness
Love Story▲
The Matchmaker
Money Kings
Monument Ave.
Never Met Picasso
Next Stop, Wonderland
The Proposition
The Scarlet Letter
The Scarlet Letter▲
The Scarlet Letter
Sci-Fighters
See How She Runs▲
The Seekers
Small Vices: A Spenser Mystery
Southie
Spenser: Ceremony
Spenser: Pale Kings & Princes
Spraggue
Squeeze
Tuesdays with Morrie
Two Years before the Mast
The Verdict▲
What's the Worst That Could Happen?
Witness Protection▲

Bounty Hunters

All About the Benjamins
American Streetfighter 2: The Full Impact
Bounty Hunter 2002
Bounty Hunters
Bounty Hunters 2: Hardball
The Bounty Man
Bounty Tracker
Cold Harvest
Critters
Critters 2: The Main Course
The Empire Strikes Back▲
A Fistful of Dollars▲
For a Few Dollars More
The Good, the Bad and the Ugly▲
Home for Christmas
The Hunter
Midnight Run▲
Most Wanted
Moving Target
Past Perfect
Return of the Jedi▲
Slipstream
Star Wars▲
Star Wars: Episode 2—Attack of the Clones▲
Terminal Impact
The Tracker
True Vengeance
Wanted Dead or Alive

Bowling

Alley Cats Strike
The Big Lebowski▲
Dream with the Fishes
Dreamer
Fright Night 2
Grease 2
Kingpin
Mr. Wonderful
Spare Me
Uncle Buck▲

Boxing

Abbott and Costello Meet the Invisible Man▲
Ali
Any Which Way You Can
Arena
Back Roads
Battling Bunyon
Battling Butler
Be Yourself
Belle of the Nineties
Best of the Best
The Big Man: Crossing the Line▲
Blade Boxer
Body and Soul▲
Body & Soul
Body and Soul
Bowery Blitzkrieg
Boxcar Blues
The Boxer
The Boxer and Death▲
Breakdown
Brutal Glory
The Cage
The Champ▲
The Champ
Champion▲
Circle Man
City for Conquest▲
Confessions of Tom Harris
Counter Punch
Dempsey
Diggstown
Don King: Only in America
Dynamite Dan
Fallen Champ: The Untold Story of Mike Tyson▲
Far and Away
Fat City▲
Fight Club: °▲
Fight for the Title
The Fighter▲
Fighting Champ
Firepower
Fist Fighter
Gentleman Jim▲
Girlfight▲
Gladiator
Golden Boy▲
Great Guy
The Great White Hope
The Great White Hype
The Greatest
Hard Times▲
The Harder They Fall▲
Heart
Heart of a Champion: The Ray Mancini Story
Here Comes Mr. Jordan▲
The Hitter
Hollywood Stadium Mystery
Homeboy
Honeyboy
The Hurricane▲
The Joe Louis Story
Keep Punching
Kelly the Second
The Kid
Kid Dynamite
Kid from Brooklyn
Kid Galahad▲
Kid Galahad
Kid Monk Baroni
Killer's Kiss
The Last Fight
Last Man Standing
Les Miserables
Like It Is▲
Love Come Down
Love Songs
Made
The Main Event
Marciano
Matilda
Meatballs 2
Milky Way
Miracle Kid
Movie, Movie
Navy Way
Night and the City▲
Ocean's Eleven▲
Off Limits
On the Waterfront▲
One-Punch O'Day
The Opponent
Opposite Corners
Palooka
Penitentiary
Penitentiary 2
Penitentiary 3
Percy & Thunder
Play It to the Bone
The Power of One
Price of Glory
Pride of the Bowery
Prison Shadows
Prize Fighter
The Prizefighter and the Lady▲
Pulp Fiction▲
The Quest
The Quiet Man▲
Raging Bull▲
Requiem for a Heavyweight▲
Ricky 1
The Ring
Ringside
Rip Roarin' Buckaroo
Roaring City
Rocky▲
Rocky 2
Rocky 3
Rocky 4
Rocky 5
Rocky Marciano
Rude
The Set-Up▲
Snake Eyes
Snatch▲
Somebody Up There Likes Me▲
Spike of Bensonhurst
The Spirit of Youth
Split Decisions
The Sting 2
Street Crimes
Streets of Gold
Teen Wolf Too
They Made Me a Criminal
They Never Come Back
Thunderground
Title Shot
Tough Enough
Tough Kid
Triumph of the Spirit▲
24-7
Tyson
Vigilantes of Boom Town
When We Were Kings
When's Your Birthday?
The Wildcat

Bridges

Bataan
The Bridge
The Bridge at Remagen
The Bridge of San Luis Rey▲
The Bridge on the River Kwai▲
Bridge to Hell
A Bridge Too Far
The Bridges at Toko-Ri▲
The Bridges of Madison County▲
Carnival of Souls▲
Crossing the Bridge
Dream with the Fishes
For Whom the Bell Tolls▲
George of the Jungle▲
The Ghost and the Darkness
The Girl on the Bridge▲
Graffiti Bridge
It's a Wonderful Life▲
The Longest Day▲
The Lovers on the Bridge
Ode to Billy Joe
Saving Private Ryan▲
Tarzan's New York Adventure
Volunteers
Waterloo Bridge▲

Bringing Up Baby

***see also** Parenthood; Pregnant Men; Pregnant Pauses*

Addams Family Values
And Baby Makes Six
Angie
Baby
The Baby and the Battleship
Baby Boom
Baby Boy
Baby Geniuses
Babyfever
Baby's Day Out
Bachelor Mother▲
Basket Case 3: The Progeny
Being Two Isn't Easy
Blondie Brings Up Baby
Brink of Life
The Brood
Bundle of Joy
By Design
Cotton Mary
Eye on the Sparrow
Fanny▲
For Keeps
Four Days in July
Fran
From Here to Maternity
The Girls of Huntington House
A Good Baby
Grave of the Vampire
The Great Lie▲
Growing Pains
A Hole in the Head
I Don't Want to Be Born
In Search of a Golden Sky
It's Alive▲
It's Alive 2: It Lives Again
It's Alive 3: Island of the Alive
Jack and Sarah
The Lightning Incident
Little Man Tate▲
Look Who's Talking▲
Look Who's Talking, Too
Mamele
Monika
Night Cries
Paternity
Penny Serenade▲
Problem Child 2
Psycho 4: The Beginning
Raising Arizona▲
Rock-A-Bye Baby
Rosemary's Baby▲
The Rugrats Movie▲
Rumpelstiltskin
Sacred Ground
The Saga of the Draculas
Sarah's Child
Scarred
Secrets
She's So Lovely
The Snapper▲
Son of Godzilla
A Stranger in Town
The Sugarland Express▲
Table for Five
The Tender Years
The Terminator▲
Test Tube Babies
That's My Baby!
The 13th Floor
Thomas Graal's First Child▲
Three Men and a Baby▲
Three Men and a Cradle▲
Tomorrow's Child
Tomorrow's Children
The 24 Hour Woman
The Unborn 2
Unnatural
The War Zone
Willa
A Woman Is a Woman▲

Brothers & Sisters

***see also** Twins*

About Adam
Above Suspicion
The Accidental Tourist▲
Adam Had Four Sons
Alaska
All Fall Down
All My Sons▲
All the Brothers Were Valiant
Alpine Fire
American Flyers
American History X
American Outlaws
American Samurai
American Streetfighter
America's Sweethearts
Amores Perros▲
And You Thought Your Parents Were Weird!
Angela
Angels in the Endzone
The Anniversary
Arabian Nights
The Aristocrats
Ask Any Girl
At Any Cost
At Close Range▲
Autumn Sonata▲
The Avenging
Backdraft
Bad Blood
Bare Knees
Barjo
Based on an Untrue Story
The Basket
Basket Case▲
Basket Case 2
Beau Geste▲
Behind the Sun
Belle Epoque▲
Benny & Joon
Better Than Chocolate
Big Brother Trouble
Big Business
Big Night
The Black Room▲
Black Sheep
Blinded by the Light
Blood Rage
Blood Relatives
Bloodlink
Blue River
The Bodyguard
The Book of Stars
Boondock Saints
Born to Run
Bread and Roses
Breathing Fire
Brilliant Lies
Broadway Melody
Broken Trust
The Brontes of Haworth
Brother
The Brothers Karamazov▲
Brother's Keeper▲
A Brother's Kiss
The Brothers McMullen▲
Bush Pilot
Bye-Bye
Cadillac Ranch
The Captive: The Longest Drive 2
Carolina Skeletons
Carry Me Back
Cat People▲
Cat People
Catherine Cookson's The Dwelling Place
Catherine Cookson's The Fifteen Streets
Catherine Cookson's The Wingless Bird
Cavalcade of the West
Cavalry Charge
Cellblock Sisters: Banished Behind Bars
The Cement Garden
Chameleon 3: Dark Angel
Cheetah
Children of Heaven
Children of the Corn 3: Urban Harvest
Christmas Comes to Willow Creek
Chutney Popcorn
City of Industry
Come Undone
The Confession
The Confessional▲
Cookie's Fortune▲
Corky Romano
Coupe de Ville
Cracker: Brotherly Love▲
Cries and Whispers▲
Crimes of the Heart
The Criminal Mind
Cruel and Unusual
Curly Top
Cyclo
Dancing at Lughnasa
Dangerous Ground
A Dangerous Place
Daniel
Danielle Steel's Kaleidoscope
Dark Mirror▲
Dark Odyssey
Deathfight
December Bride
Delightfully Dangerous
Demons in the Garden▲
Desperate Remedies
Deuces Wild
The Devil's Daughter
The Devil's Web
Diamonds
Dick Tracy
Die Sister, Die!
Dinotopia
Dixie Dynamite
The Dolly Sisters
Dominick & Eugene▲
Double Dragon
Dream Street
Driven
Duel in the Sun▲
East of Eden▲
East of Eden
East Side Kids
EDtv
El Norte▲
Endplay
Enid Is Sleeping

Entertaining Mr. Sloane
Erskinville Kings
Experiment in Terror▲
Eye of the Storm
Eyes of a Stranger
The Fabulous Baker Boys▲
The Fabulous Dorseys
The Fall of the House of Usher
The Fall of the House of Usher▲
The Fall of the House of Usher
Fanny and Alexander▲
Farinelli
Fatal Passion
The Favorite Son▲
Feeling Minnesota
Female Perversions
The Fighting Sullivans▲
Final Analysis
Final Appeal
The Florentine
Flowers in the Attic
The Flying Fool
Fool for Love
For Better or Worse
Force of Evil▲
40 Days and 40 Nights
Four Daughters▲
Frailty▲
Frank and Jesse
Freddy Got Fingered
Freud Leaving Home
From Dusk Till Dawn
The Game▲
Gas Food Lodging▲
Georgia▲
Get Over It!
Ginger Snaps
The Girl with a Suitcase
Give Me a Sailor
Gladiator▲
The Glass House
God Said "Ha!"▲
Gone in 60 Seconds
Good Morning, Babylon▲
The Good Old Boys
Goodbye, Lover
Grave of the Fireflies▲
Green Dolphin Street
Grind
Gun Play
Halloween: H20▲
Hanging Up
Hannah and Her Sisters▲
Hard Luck
Having Our Say: The Delany Sisters' First 100 Years
Head of the Family
Heart of Dragon
Hell on Wheels
Her First Romance
The Hiding Place
Hilary and Jackie▲
Hombres Complicados
The Hoodlum
Horizons West
Hot Lead & Cold Feet
The House of Eliott
House of Strangers▲
The House of the Seven Gables
The House of Usher
Howard's End▲
The Human Shield
I Sent a Letter to My Love▲
Igby Goes Down
In Celebration▲
In Dark Places
In Search of the Castaways▲
In the Flesh
In the Time of the Butterflies
Incubus
The Indian Runner
Innocents
Institute Benjamenta or This Dream People Call Human Life
Interiors▲
Invasion!
Inventing the Abbotts
Invisible Circus
It Could Happen to You
Jack Be Nimble
Jacob Have I Loved
Jason's Lyric
Jeepers Creepers
Joe Torre: Curveballs Along the Way
Josh and S.A.M.
Joy Ride▲
Julien Donkey-boy
Jumpin' at the Boneyard
The Juniper Tree
Kate & Leopold
Kidnapped in Paradise
Kill by Inches
Kill or Be Killed
The King of Marvin Gardens
La Bamba▲
La Buche
La Chute de la Maison Usher▲
Labyrinth▲
Landscape in the Mist▲
The Last Days of Chez Nous
The Last Five Days
Law of Desire▲
Legends of the Fall
Les Enfants Terrible▲
Les Voleurs▲
Light of Day
Limbo
Little Giants
Little Nicky
Lola and Billy the Kid
The Long Riders▲
A Long Way Home
Looking for Miracles
The Lost Capone▲
Love Come Down
Lovely & Amazing
Luminarias
Lush
Ma Saison Preferee▲
Mac▲
Mad at the Moon
Maids of Wilko
The Makioka Sisters▲
A Man About the House
The Man in the Moon▲
Manny & Lo▲
Marianne and Juliane▲
Martial Outlaw
Me & Veronica
Meantime
Mexico City
Midnight Dancers
Midnight Warning
Mifune
Miles from Home
The Mill on the Floss
Mirror, Mirror 2: Raven Dance
Miss Rose White▲
Mr. Saturday Night
Molly
Moondance
Mouse Hunt▲
Murder One
My Brother's War
My Outlaw Brother
My Sister Eileen▲
My Sister, My Love
My Sister's Keeper
Nenette and Boni▲
The Newton Boys
A Night at the Roxbury
Nightstalker
No Alibi
No Way Home
The Old Settler
On the Waterfront▲
Once in the Life
One Way Out
The Opposite of Sex
Orange County
Orphans▲
Orphans
Orphans of the Storm▲
The Other Brother
Over the Wire
Pandaemonium
Paradise Alley
Paranoiac
Paris, Texas▲
Peppermint Soda▲
Persons Unknown
Phantasm 4: Oblivion
Phantom Brother
The Pianist
The Pit and the Pendulum▲
The Pit & the Pendulum
Plucking the Daisy
Pola X
Power of Attorney
Practical Magic
Price of Glory
Psycho Girls
The Quiet Man▲
Radio Inside
Rain Man▲
Rated X
The Real Thing
Relative Values
Return of Wildfire
Rich Man, Poor Man▲
The Right Hand Man
Rikky and Pete
Risk▲
River Red
A River Runs Through It▲
The Road Home
Rocco and His Brothers▲
Romeo Must Die
Row Your Boat
The Royal Tenenbaums▲
The Rugrats Movie▲
Rumble Fish▲
Sabrina▲
Sabrina
The Sacketts
Say It Isn't So
The Secret Rapture
Seducing Maarya
Sense & Sensibility
Sense and Sensibility▲
Sensuous Summer
Seven Alone
Seven Beauties▲
Seventeen Again
The Shadow Riders
Shadows▲
Shark River
The Sheep Has Five Legs
She's the One
The Shining Hour
Shot in the Heart▲
Shower
The Sibling
Sibling Rivalry
The Sicilian Connection
Sidewalks of New York
Signs
The Silence▲
Simple Men▲
Sister My Sister
The Sisters▲
Sisters▲
Sisters of the Gion
Sisters, Or the Balance of Happiness
The Sixth Man
Slap Shot 2: Breaking the Ice
Slums of Beverly Hills▲
Smiling Fish & Goat on Fire
Soft Fruit
A Soldier's Daughter Never Cries
The Son of the Shark
Sons of Katie Elder▲
Sons of Steel
Sorrento Beach
Soul Food
South of Hell Mountain
Spy Kids▲
State of Grace▲
The Stolen Children▲
The Story of Jacob & Joseph▲
Strapless
Street Hitz
A Streetcar Named Desire▲
A Streetcar Named Desire
Suffering Bastards
Sugar Hill
Surface to Air
Suture
Sweet Smell of Success▲
Sweetie▲
The Tempest
Tex
Texas Jack
That Was Then...This Is Now
Things You Can Tell Just by Looking at Her
Thirteen Days▲
A Thousand Acres
Three Brothers▲
3 Ninjas
3 Ninjas Kick Back
The Three Sisters
Three Smart Girls▲
Three Smart Girls Grow Up▲
Three Violent People
The Three Weird Sisters
Thrillkill
Till Marriage Do Us Part
Till There Was You
Time Stands Still▲
'Tis a Pity She's a Whore
To All My Friends on Shore▲
Tombstone▲
Tortilla Soup
Trained to Kill
Trapped in Paradise
The Triumph of Love
Troublemakers
True Blood
True Confessions▲
True West▲
Twelfth Night
The Twilight of the Ice Nymphs
Two Much
The Two Sisters
Under the Hula Moon
Under the Skin
Under the Volcano▲
Undercurrent
Underground
An Unremarkable Life
Until They Sail
Vengeance Valley
Vertical Limit
The Vertical Ray of the Sun
Vincent & Theo▲
Violent Cop
The Virgin Suicides
The Visit▲
The Wagons Roll at Night
Walkabout▲
The War Zone
Weep No More My Lady
Whale Music
The Whales of August▲
What Ever Happened To...
What Ever Happened to Baby Jane?▲
When Brendan Met Trudy▲
Where the Lilies Bloom▲
Wild America▲
Wild West
Wilder Napalm
Windhorse
Wish upon a Star
Without Evidence
The Wizard
The Wolves
The Woman in White
Wonderland
Wyatt Earp
You Can Count On Me▲
The Young Girls of Rochefort

Buddhism

The Cup
Green Snake
Kundun▲
Little Buddha
Omaha (the movie)
Raw Force
Seven Years in Tibet
Temptation of a Monk
Why Has Bodhi-Darma Left for the East
Windhorse

Buddies

see also ***Buddy Cops***

Abbott and Costello Meet Frankenstein▲
Adios Amigo
The Adventures of Huck Finn▲
The Adventures of Huckleberry Finn
The Adventures of Milo & Otis▲
The Adventures of Rusty
Ain't No Way Back
The Alamo▲
All Saint's Day
American Pie▲
An American Story
Amongst Friends
Andre
Another 48 Hrs.
Another You
Anzacs: The War Down Under▲
At First Sight
The Baby-Sitters' Club
Babyfever
Bachelor Party
Backbeat▲
Bad Company▲
Bad Girls
Band of Brothers▲
BASEketball
The Basketball Diaries
The Battle of Blood Island
The Bear▲
Beautiful Girls
Belly
A Better Tomorrow, Part 1
A Better Tomorrow, Part 2
Between Heaven and Hell▲
The Big Chill▲
Big Deadly Game
Big Eden
Big Mo
Big Shots
The Big Slice
Bigfoot: The Unforgettable Encounter
Bill & Ted's Bogus Journey
Birdy▲
Black Beauty
Black Fox: The Price of Peace
Blackrock
Blonde in Black Leather
Blowin' Smoke
Blue De Ville
Blue Juice
The Blue Lamp▲
Blue Ridge Fall
Blue Skies▲
Body Shots
Bogus
Boot Hill
Boots Malone
Born to Be Wild
Boston Kickout
A Boy and His Dog
The Boy Who Could Fly▲
The Boys in the Band
The Boys Next Door
Branded Men
Breaking the Rules
Breakout
Brian's Song
Bride of Killer Nerd
Broadway Melody of 1940
The Brothers▲
The Buddy System
A Bullet in the Head▲
Bulletproof
The Bumblebee Flies Anyway
Bundle of Joy
Butch Cassidy and the Sundance Kid▲
The Cable Guy
The Caddy
Calendar Girl
The Campus Corpse
Campus Man
Capitaine Conan▲
Captive Hearts
The Cat
Celtic Pride
Charlie's Ghost: The Secret of Coronado
Chasing Amy
Cheap Shots
Chill Factor
Circle of Two
The Cisco Kid
City Slickers▲
City Slickers 2: The Legend of Curly's Gold
Class Act
Class of '61
Clay Pigeons
Clayton County Line
Clerks▲
Clown Murders
The Color Purple▲
Colorado Serenade
Company Business
The Concrete Cowboys
Convict Cowboy
Cops and Robbers
Corleone
Country Gentlemen
Courage of Black Beauty
The Cowboy Way
Crack Up
Crime Busters
Crime Lords
Cross My Heart
Crossfire
Crossing the Bridge
Cry Freedom
The Cure
Curtis's Charm
Cycle Vixens
Dancer, Texas—Pop. 81▲
Dark Blue World
Dead Presidents
Dead Reckoning▲
Deadlock
Deadly Surveillance
December
The Deer Hunter▲
Defenseless
The Defiant Ones▲
The Desperadoes
Detroit Rock City
Die Hard: With a Vengeance
Digger
Diner▲
Dirty Work
Dish Dogs
Dogfight▲
Donnie Brasco▲
Donovan's Reef▲
Don't Look Back▲
Double Down
Double Team
Down Under
Downtown
Dragonheart
Dragonworld
Dream a Little Dream 2
Dream with the Fishes
The Dresser▲
Driving Miss Daisy▲
Drop Dead Fred
Drums in the Deep South
Dumb & Dumber
The Eagle and the Hawk▲
Easy Rider▲
Eat the Peach
Ed's Next Move
The Eighth Day
El Dorado▲
Elmer
The Emperor's New Groove▲
Enemy Mine
Enemy of the State
Entre-Nous▲
Every Which Way But Loose
Extreme Prejudice
Extremedays
F/X 2: The Deadly Art of Illusion
The Falcon and the Snowman▲
Far from Home: The Adventures of Yellow Dog
Father's Day
Federal Hill
Fight Club: °▲
First Kid
The Five Heartbeats▲
Fled
The Flintstones
The Flintstones in Viva Rock Vegas
Floating
For the Moment
Forgive and Forget
Forsaking All Others
Francis in the Navy
Free Enterprise
Free Willy
Free Willy 2: The Adventure Home
Free Willy 3: The Rescue
Freeze-Die-Come to Life▲
The Frisco Kid
Frontier Fugitives
The Full Monty▲
Galaxies Are Colliding
Gallipoli▲
Get Over It!

Getting Even
A Girl, 3 Guys and a Gun
Glory Daze
Going All the Way
Going Back
Gold Diggers: The Secret of Bear Mountain
Gone Fishin'
Good Luck
Good Will Hunting
Goodfellas ▲
Gordy
Gossip
Grand Illusion ▲
Gridlock'd ▲
Grumpier Old Men
Grumpy Old Men ▲
Guarding Tess
Gunga Din ▲
Gunmen
Halfmoon
Hangin' with the Homeboys ▲
Hard Core Logo
Hard Eight ▲
Hard Luck
Harley Davidson and the Marlboro Man
Harriet the Spy
The Hasty Heart
Hate ▲
Hats Off
Hawaii Calls
Heartaches ▲
Heartbreakers ▲
Heavenly Creatures ▲
Henry & Verlin
Hercules ▲
The Hi-Lo Country
The Highest Honor
Highway
Hired Hand
Hollywood or Bust
Home Free All
Homeward Bound 2: Lost in San Francisco
Hong Kong Nights
Hong Kong 1941
Huck and the King of Hearts
The Hunters
Hurlyburly
Hurricane Streets
Husbands
I Shot a Man in Vegas
I Went Down ▲
If Lucy Fell
I'll Remember April
I'm Not Rappaport
The In-Laws ▲
In the Navy
Indian Summer
Inn of Temptation
Intimate Lighting
Iron Giant ▲
Ishtar
Ivan and Abraham
Jay and Silent Bob Strike Back
Jimmy Hollywood
Johnny Come Lately
Johnny Holiday
Joy Ride to Nowhere
Joyride
Judgment Night
Juice
Jules and Jim ▲
Just a Little Harmless Sex
Just Between Friends
K-9000
The Kansas Terrors
The Karate Kid ▲
The Karate Kid: Part 2
The Karate Kid: Part 3
Kazaam
Keeping the Faith
Killer Bud
The Killing Fields ▲
King of the Mountain
Kingpin
Kings of the Road—In the Course of Time ▲
Knock Off
K2: The Ultimate High
Ladies on the Rocks
The Land Before Time 5: The Mysterious Island
Lansky
Larry McMurtry's Dead Man's Walk
Last American Virgin
The Last Boy Scout
Last Summer
The Last Time I Committed Suicide
Late Last Night
Lawn Dogs
Le Beau Serge ▲
Le Doulos ▲
Leaving Normal
Les Comperes ▲
The Lesser Evil
Let 'er Go Gallegher
Let's Do It Again
L.I.E.
Life
The Life of Jesus
Little City
The Littlest Outlaw
The Lives of a Bengal Lancer ▲
The Long Voyage Home ▲
Looking for Miracles
The Lords of Flatbush
Lost in the Barrens
Love Letters
Love! Valour! Compassion!
Lovelife
Love's Labour's Lost
The Low Down
Macaroni
Mad Dog and Glory ▲
Made
Mallrats
The Man Who Would Be King ▲
Managua
Manhattan Melodrama ▲
March or Die
McHale's Navy
Me and Him
Mean Frank and Crazy Tony
Meet Danny Wilson
Men Men Men
The Men's Club
Metroland
Midnight Cowboy ▲
Midnight Run ▲
The Mighty ▲
The Mighty Quinn
Mikey & Nicky
Mina Tannenbaum
Misunderstood
Molly and Gina
Money Talks
Money to Burn
Monsters, Inc. ▲
Monument Ave.
Moon over Miami ▲
Moonlight and Valentino
Mortal Thoughts
The Mosaic Project
My Beautiful Laundrette ▲
My Best Friend's Girl
My Best Friend's Wedding
My Dinner with Andre ▲
My First Mister
My Giant
My Girl
My Name Is Joe
Mystic Pizza ▲
Naked Youth
The Naughty Nineties
Neil Simon's The Odd Couple 2
Night Beat
Nightforce
The Nightingale
Nothing to Lose
Ocean's Eleven ▲
The Odd Couple ▲
Old Explorers
Oliver & Company
On the Fiddle
On the Line
Once Upon a Time in America ▲
One Crazy Summer
100 Days Before the Command
One Sings, the Other Doesn't
The Opposite Sex and How to Live With Them
Out to Sea
Palookaville ▲
Pals
Papillon ▲
Parallel Lives
Past the Bleachers
Peck's Bad Boy with the Circus
The Penitent
Perfectly Normal
Peter's Friends
Petits Freres
The Phantom of 42nd Street
Phat Beach
Piece of Cake
P.K. and the Kid
Plan B
Platoon ▲
Play It to the Bone
Playmates
A Pleasure Doing Business
Plunder Road
The Pompatus of Love
Portrait of a Showgirl
Psycho Cop 2
P.U.N.K.S.
Racing with the Moon ▲
Rafferty & the Gold Dust Twins
Rape
The Rat Pack
Ready to Rumble
The Red Balloon ▲
The Reivers ▲
Relax... It's Just Sex!
Reno and the Doc
Requiem for Dominic ▲
The Return of Grey Wolf
The Return of the Musketeers
Return of the Secaucus 7 ▲
Return to Paradise ▲
Revenge of the Nerds
Revenge of the Nerds 2: Nerds in Paradise
Rich and Famous
Ride the High Country ▲
Ride with the Devil
Rio Conchos ▲
The Road to El Dorado
The Road to Hong Kong
The Road to Morocco ▲
Road Trip
Roadside Prophets
Robby
Robert et Robert ▲
Roommates
Rubin & Ed
Rules of Engagement
The Run of the Country ▲
Running Scared
Russkies
Rusty's Birthday
St. Elmo's Fire
The Saint of Fort Washington
Saints and Sinners
Salut l'Artiste ▲
Same River Twice
The Sandlot ▲
Saving Silverman
The Search for One-Eyed Jimmy
The Seventh Veil ▲
Shag: The Movie ▲
Shaking the Tree
She Gods of Shark Reef
The Shot
Shot Through the Heart ▲
Showdown in Little Tokyo
Silence Like Glass
Slackers
Slappy and the Stinkers
Sleepers
Sling Blade ▲
Snow White and the Seven Dwarfs
So This Is Washington
Some Like It Hot ▲
Someone Else's America ▲
Something of Value ▲
Son of Rusty
Songwriter
Sophisticated Gents ▲
The Souler Opposite
Souls at Sea
Sparkler
Spawn of the North
Spies Like Us
Spittin' Image
Spotlight Scandals
Sprung
Stag
Stand by Me ▲
Star Trek 4: The Voyage Home ▲
Starbird and Sweet William
State of Grace ▲
Stealing Home
Steaming
The Steel Helmet ▲
Sticks and Stones
The Stoned Age
Stranger than Fiction
Strawberry and Chocolate ▲
Stuckey's Last Stand
The Substitute 3: Winner Takes All
subUrbia
Sudden Death
Summer City
Sunny Skies
The Sunshine Boys ▲
Swingers ▲
Tape ▲
The Tavern
Ten Benny
Ten Who Dared
Tequila Sunrise
Terminal Bliss
That Championship Season
That Sinking Feeling ▲
Thelma & Louise ▲
Three Amigos
Three Legionnaires
Three Men and a Baby ▲
Three Men and a Cradle ▲
The Three Musketeers
The Three Musketeers ▲
The Three Musketeers
Thunder in the Pines
Thursday's Game ▲
Tin Cup ▲
To Forget Venice
To Wong Foo, Thanks for Everything, Julie Newmar
Tombstone ▲
Tomcats
Top Dog
Top Gun
Tough Guys
Tour of Duty
Toy Story ▲
Toy Story 2 ▲
Trainspotting ▲
Tree's Lounge
The Triangle
Trippin'
True Colors
True Friends
The Turning Point
Twin Warriors
Two Weeks to Live
Ugetsu ▲
Under the Sun
Underworld ▲
Unholy Four
The Van ▲
Veronico Cruz
Very Bad Things
The Very Thought of You
Vincent, Francois, Paul and the Others ▲
The Virginian
Walking and Talking
Warrior Spirit
Wayne's World ▲
Wayne's World 2
Went to Coney Island on a Mission from God...Be Back by Five
We're in the Legion Now
Western
What Price Glory? ▲
Where Is My Friend's House?
Where the River Runs Black
Whipped
White Christmas ▲
White Mama ▲
White Men Can't Jump
White Nights
Who's the Man?
Why Me?
Wild Horses
The Wild Life
Wild Rovers
Windy City
Winners Take All
With a Friend Like Harry ▲
With Friends Like These
Withnail and I ▲
The Wood
Wrestling Ernest Hemingway
The Wrong Guys
The Wrong Road
Y Tu Mama Tambien
The Yakuza
Yankee Zulu
You Are Here *
Young Guns 2
Young Hercules
Zorba the Greek ▲

Buddy Cops

***see also** Cops; Women Cops*

Another 48 Hrs.
Another Stakeout
Arizona Heat
Bad Boys
Blue Streak
Car 54, Where Are You?
City Heat
Collision Course
Cop Land ▲
The Corruptor ▲
Exit to Eden
48 Hrs. ▲
Gang Related
The Glimmer Man
The Hard Way ▲
Internal Affairs
La Chevre ▲
Lethal Weapon ▲
Lethal Weapon 2 ▲
Lethal Weapon 3
Lethal Weapon 4
Liberty & Bash
Men in Black ▲
Metro
Money Train
Mulholland Falls
National Lampoon's Loaded Weapon 1
Night Children
Nighthawks
The Presidio
Red Heat
Renegades
The Rookie
Rush Hour 2
Shakedown
Shoot to Kill ▲
Simon Sez
Speed ▲
Stakeout
Tango and Cash

Buried Alive

Buried Alive
Buried Alive 2
The Fall of the House of Usher
The Fall of the House of Usher ▲
The Fall of the House of Usher
The House of Usher
La Chute de la Maison Usher ▲
The Oblong Box
Oxygen
Premature Burial

Buses

The Adventures of Priscilla, Queen of the Desert ▲
All God's Children
Almost Famous ▲
Beavis and Butt-Head Do America
The Big Bus
Boycott ▲
Bull Durham ▲
Bus Stop ▲
Dirty Harry ▲
Forrest Gump ▲
The Fugitive ▲
The Gauntlet
Get On the Bus ▲
Heart and Souls
Incident at Deception Ridge
Lady on the Bus
The Laughing Policeman
A League of Their Own ▲
Long Journey Back
Love Field
Magical Mystery Tour
A Man of No Importance ▲
Mexican Bus Ride
National Lampoon's Senior Trip
Pardon My Sarong
Planes, Trains & Automobiles
Ride
The Runaway Bus
Siam Sunset
The Siege
Speed ▲
Spice World: The Movie
Still Crazy ▲
The Sweet Hereafter ▲
Swordfish
The Trip to Bountiful ▲
Wheels of Terror
Where Angels Go, Trouble Follows

Cabbies

The Bishop's Wife ▲
Blood & Donuts
Born Romantic
Chicago Cab
Claire Dolan
Conspiracy Theory ▲
Crossing Delancey ▲
Daylight
D.C. Cab
Escape from New York
Extremely Dangerous
Fall
The Fifth Element
For Hire
Look Who's Talking ▲
Mexico City
My Son the Fanatic ▲
Nick and Jane
Night on Earth ▲
Pulp Fiction ▲
Scrooged
She's the One
Taxi Blues ▲
Taxi Driver ▲
The Taxi Mystery
3 A.M. ▲
200 Cigarettes
The Yellow Cab Man

Calcutta

***see also** India*

The Adversary
Baraka ▲
City of Joy
Days and Nights in the Forest
The Quest

Camelot (New)

***see also** Assassinations; Presidency*

Jackie, Ethel, Joan: The Kennedy Women
Jacqueline Bouvier Kennedy
JFK ▲
The JFK Conspiracy
JFK: Reckless Youth
Kennedy
Prince Jack
PT 109
Robert Kennedy and His Times
Ruby
Thirteen Days ▲

Camelot (Old)

***see also** Medieval Romps; Swashbucklers*

Arthur's Quest
Camelot
A Connecticut Yankee ▲
A Connecticut Yankee in King Arthur's Court
Excalibur ▲
First Knight
A Kid in King Arthur's Court

▲ = rated three bones or higher

Kids of the Round Table
King Arthur, the Young Warlord
A Knight in Camelot
Knights of the Round Table
Merlin▲
Merlin and the Sword
Mists of Avalon▲
Monty Python and the Holy Grail▲
Prince Valiant
Quest for Camelot
The Sword in the Stone▲
Sword of Lancelot
Sword of the Valiant
A Young Connecticut Yankee in King Arthur's Court

Campus Capers

***see also** Fraternities & Sororities; Hell High School; School Daze*

Accident
The Affairs of Dobie Gillis
All-American Murder
American Psycho 2: All American Girl
American Tiger
Animal Behavior
Assault of the Party Nerds
Attack of the Killer Refrigerator
Baby Love
Bachelor of Hearts
Back to School
A Beautiful Mind▲
Beware
Beyond Dream's Door
Big Man on Campus
Black Christmas
Black Tower
Blondie Goes to College
Blood Cult
Blood Sisters
Blue Chips
Boys and Girls
Breeders
Bride of Killer Nerd
The Campus Corpse
Campus Knights
Campus Man
Carnal Knowledge▲
The Cheerleaders
Cheers for Miss Bishop
A Chump at Oxford
Circle of Friends
College▲
College Swing
Computer Beach Party
The Computer Wore Tennis Shoes
Confessions of Sorority Girls
The Cousins▲
The Crimson Rivers
The Curve
Dead Man on Campus
Deadly Lessons
Deadly Obsession
Deadly Possession
Death Screams
Defying Gravity
Devil in the Flesh 2
Didn't You Hear?
Divided We Stand
Doctor in the House▲
Dorm That Dripped Blood
Down to You
The Duke of West Point
Ernest Rides Again
Escapade in Florence
Father Was a Fullback
Final Exam
First Affair
First Love
First Time
Foreign Student
Francis Goes to West Point
Fraternity Vacation
The Freshman▲
The Freshman
Fright Night 2
Getting Away With Murder
Getting In
Ghoulies 3: Ghoulies Go to College
Girl Crazy▲
Girls Night Out
The Gladiator▲
Glory Daze
Good News
Good Will Hunting
Gossip
Gotcha!
Gross Anatomy
Gross Misconduct
Hamburger...The Motion Picture
Harmon of Michigan
Harrad Experiment
Harrad Summer
HauntedWeen
The Heart of Dixie
Hell Night
Higher Education
Higher Learning
Horse Feathers▲
H.O.T.S.
The House on Sorority Row
House Party 2: The Pajama Jam
How High
How I Got into College
How I Spent My Summer Vacation
I Don't Buy Kisses Anymore
I'll Be Home for Christmas
The Initiation
Initiation of Sarah
I.Q.
Iris▲
Is There Life Out There?
Jock Petersen
Kicking and Screaming▲
The Kid with the 200 I.Q.
A Killer in Every Corner
Killer Party
Knock Outs
Lady Killer
Legally Blonde
Let's Go Collegiate
Life 101
Little Sister
A Little Stiff
Loser
Love and Basketball▲
Love and Other Catastrophes
Lover's Knot
Lucky Jim
Maker of Men
Malice
A Matter of Degrees
Mazes and Monsters
Midnight Madness
The Mirror Has Two Faces
The Misadventures of Merlin Jones
The Monkey's Mask
Monkey's Uncle
Monster on the Campus
Mortuary Academy
Mugsy's Girls
Murder on the Campus
My Lucky Star
My Sex Life...Or How I Got into an Argument
National Lampoon's Animal House▲
National Lampoon's Van Wilder
Navy Blue and Gold
Necessary Roughness
New Best Friend
A Night in the Life of Jimmy Reardon
Night of the Creeps
Nightwish
The Nutty Professor▲
Nutty Professor 2: The Klumps
An Occasional Hell
Odd Jobs
Oleanna
100 Girls
The Paper Chase▲
Parallel Lives
Party Animal
P.C.U.
Pieces
Pigskin Parade
The Plastic Age
Pledge Night
Preppies
The Prodigy
The Program
A Reason to Believe
Red Letters
Return Engagement
Revenge of the Nerds
Revenge of the Nerds 2: Nerds in Paradise
Revenge of the Nerds 3: The Next Generation
Ring of Terror
Ripper: Letter from Hell
Road Trip
Roommate
Roommates
Rosalie
R.P.M.* (* Revolutions Per Minute)
Rudy
Rush Week
Scent of a Woman▲
School Daze▲
School Spirit
Scream 2▲
The Secret Life of Girls
The Seniors
Sensation
Senseless
Shallow Grave
Silent Madness
Silent Scream
The Sixth Man
The Skulls
The Skulls 2
Sky High
Slackers
Slipping into Darkness
A Small Circle of Friends
Sniper▲
Sorority Babes in the Slimeball Bowl-A-Rama
Sorority Boys
Sorority Girl
Sorority House Massacre
Sorority House Massacre 2: Nighty Nightmare
Sorority House Party
Sorority House Vampires
Soul Man
Soul Survivors
South Beach Academy
Spellbound
The Spirit of West Point
Splatter University
Splitz
Spring Break
Stitches
Stonebrook
Storytelling▲
The Student Affair
The Substitute 3: Winner Takes All
The Sure Thing▲
Surviving Desire▲
Sweet Young Thing
Tag: The Assassination Game
Talking Walls
Tall Lie
Tall Story
Teen Wolf Too
Thesis
Three in the Attic
Three in the Cellar
Threesome
Toga Party
Undergrads▲
Unforgettable
The Unnamable
The Unnamable 2: The Statement of Randolph Carter
Up the Creek
Urban Legend
Urban Legends 2: Final Cut
Vampires of Sorority Row: Kickboxers From Hell
The Victory
Voodoo
Voodoo Academy
Waking the Dead
War Between the Tates
The Waterboy
Wavelength
What Lies Beneath
When He's Not a Stranger▲
The Wild Life
Wish Me Luck
Wishmaster 3: Beyond the Gates of Hell
Witchboard
Witches' Brew
With Honors
Wonder Boys▲
Zis Boom Bah

Canada

***see also** Cold Spots; Hockey*

Abducted
The Adjuster
The Agency
American Boyfriends
The Amityville Curse
And Then You Die▲
Angel Square
Angela
Anne of Avonlea▲
Anne of Green Gables▲
The Apprenticeship of Duddy Kravitz▲
Atlantic City▲
The Bay Boy
Beautiful Dreamers
Big Bear
The Big Crimewave
Big Meat Eater
Big Red
Black Christmas
Black Robe▲
Blades of Courage
Blood Clan
Blood of the Hunter
Blood Relations
The Bloody Brood
Boy in Blue
The Boys
The Boys Club
The Boys of St. Vincent▲
Breaking All the Rules
The Brood
Buffalo Jump▲
Bullies
Bush Pilot
Busted Up
By Design
By Way of the Stars
Bye Bye Blues
Cafe Romeo
Camilla
Canada's Sweetheart: The Saga of Hal C. Banks
Canadian Bacon
Candy Mountain
The Cariboo Trail
Cathy's Curse
The Changeling
Christina
Circle of Two
City on Fire
Class of 1984
Clean, Shaven
Clearcut
Close to Home
Cold Comfort
Concrete Angels
The Confessional▲
Confidential
Conquest
Covergirl
Cross Country
A Cry in the Wild▲
Curtains
Dan Candy's Law
Dance Me Outside
Dancing in the Dark
Danger Ahead
Daughter of Death
The Dawson Patrol
Dead Ringers▲
Death Ship
Death Weekend
Deathdream
The Decline of the American Empire▲
Decoy
Deranged▲
The Deserters
Dirty Tricks
Disappearance
Distant Thunder
Dog Pound Shuffle▲
The Dog Who Stopped the War
A Doll's House▲
The Double Negative
Drying Up the Streets
Dudley Do-Right
Eddie and the Cruisers 2: Eddie Lives!
The Enemy
Explosion
Fighting Mad
The Fishing Trip
Fly Away Home▲
For the Moment
Ginger Snaps
Going Home
Grey Owl
Grizzly Falls
Hard Core Logo
Heaven on Earth
Heck's Way Home
Henry & Verlin
Holy Matrimony
House of the Living Dead
The Incredible Journey
Intersection
Invasion!
Jaws of Justice
La Deroute
Ladies of the Lotus
Lassie's Great Adventure
The Little Kidnappers
The Lotus Eaters
Love and Human Remains▲
Magic in the Water
Margaret's Museum▲
Maria Chapdelaine
Men of Steel
Murder on the Yukon
My American Cousin▲
Mystery Trooper
A Name for Evil
Narrow Margin
'Neath Canadian Skies
New Waterford Girl
The Newton Boys
90 Days▲
No
Nomads of the North
Northern Extremes
Obsessed
Phantom Patrol
Renfrew of the Royal Mounted
Renfrew on the Great White Trail
Restless Spirits
The Return of Grey Wolf
Riel
Rose Marie▲
Rupert's Land
The Shipping News
Silent Code
Slipstream
Some Girls
South Park: Bigger, Longer and Uncut
Spirit Rider▲
Strange Brew
Strangers in Good Company▲
The Sweet Hereafter▲
Tail Lights Fade
Tales of the Klondike: In a Far Country
Tales of the Klondike: Race for Number One
Tales of the Klondike: The Unexpected
Termini Station
Time Lock
Tokyo Cowboy
Torso
Trail of the Mounties
Wedding in White
Where the North Begins
Who Has Seen the Wind?
The Widow of Saint-Pierre▲
Yukon Flight

Canadian Mounties

***see also** Canada; Cops*

Canadian Bacon
Courage of the North
Danger Ahead
Death Hunt
Dudley Do-Right
Fighting Mad
Mrs. Mike
Murder on the Yukon
'Neath Canadian Skies
Northern Pursuit
Renfrew of the Royal Mounted
Renfrew on the Great White Trail
Rose Marie▲
Silent Code
Sky Bandits
Susannah of the Mounties
Until They Get Me
Where the North Begins
Yukon Flight

Cannibalism

***see also** Edibles*

Adrenalin: Fear the Rush
Adventures of Eliza Fraser
The Alien Agenda: Out of the Darkness
Alien Prey
Alive
Auntie Lee's Meat Pies
Back from Eternity
Bad Taste▲
The Beast Must Die
Beast of the Yellow Night
Beware! Children at Play
Bleeders
Blood Clan
Blood Diner
Blood Feast
Blood Hook
Blood Sisters
Blood Tracks
Bloodsucking Freaks
Bloodsucking Pharoahs of Pittsburgh
Body Count
A Boy and His Dog
The 'Burbs
Buried Alive
Cannibal Apocalypse
Cannibal Campout
Cannibal! The Musical
Cannibal Women in the Avocado Jungle of Death
The Chilling
C.H.U.D.
C.H.U.D. 2: Bud the Chud
Consuming Passions
The Cook, the Thief, His Wife & Her Lover▲
The Corpse Grinders
Crazy Fat Ethel II
Criminally Insane
Dawn of the Dead▲
Dawn of the Mummy
Delicatessen▲
Demon Barber of Fleet Street
Deranged▲
Doctor X
Donner Pass: The Road to Survival
Eat the Rich
Eating Raoul▲
Ed Gein
Emerald Jungle
Enchanted Island
Fiend
Flesh Eating Mothers
Freakshow
Frightmare
The Further Adventures of Tennessee Buck
Gore-Met Zombie Chef from Hell
Grim Reaper
Gruesome Twosome
Hannibal
Hell of the Living Dead
The Hills Have Eyes
How Tasty Was My Little Frenchman
Human Beasts
I Drink Your Blood
I Eat Your Skin
Igor & the Lunatics
Incredible Melting Man
Jeepers Creepers
Leatherface: The Texas Chainsaw Massacre 3
The Mad Butcher
A Man Called Rage
Mom
The Monster Club

▲ = rated three bones or higher

Motel Hell
Mountain of the Cannibal God
Murderer's Keep
Night of the Living Dead ▲
Night of the Living Dead
Night of the Zombies
Nightstalker
The Offspring
Parents ▲
The Perverse Countess
Porcile
Rabid Grannies
Ravenous
Raw Force
Redneck Zombies
The Severed Arm
The Silence of the Lambs ▲
Slaughterhouse
Slaughterhouse Rock
Slave Girls from Beyond Infinity
Society
Soylent Green
Tales from the Darkside: The Movie
Tenderness of the Wolves
Terror at Red Wolf Inn
The Texas Chainsaw Massacre
The Texas Chainsaw Massacre 2
The 13th Warrior
Three on a Meathook
The Time Machine
The Undertaker and His Pals
The Untold Story
Warlock Moon
The Womaneater
Zombie
Zombie Island Massacre
Zombie Lake

Capitol Capers

Abraham Lincoln
Absolute Power
All the President's Men ▲
An American Affair
The American President ▲
Born Yesterday ▲
Born Yesterday
Bulworth ▲
The Capitol Conspiracy
The Contender
Cupid & Cate
Dave ▲
Dick ▲
The Distinguished Gentleman
Enemy of the State
Eraser
First Kid
Get On the Bus ▲
Image of Death
In the Line of Fire ▲
J. Edgar Hoover
JFK ▲
Malevolence
The Manchurian Candidate ▲
Mars Attacks!
Minority Report
Mr. Smith Goes to Washington ▲
Most Wanted
Murder at 1600
My Fellow Americans
National Lampoon's Senior Trip
Nixon ▲
Primary Colors
Random Hearts
The Seduction of Joe Tynan
1776 ▲
The Shadow Conspiracy
Sherlock Holmes in Washington
Three Days of the Condor ▲
Traffic ▲
Trial by Media
Wag the Dog
Washington Affair
Washington Mistress
Without Love

Carnivals & Circuses

***see also** Amusement Parks; Clowns; Fairs & Expositions*

Arizona Mahoney
At the Circus
Ava's Magical Adventure
Bad Man of Deadwood
Barney's Great Adventure
Barnum
Batman Forever ▲
Behind the Sun
Bells of Rosarita
Berserk!
Betrayal from the East
Big Top Pee-wee
Billy Rose's Jumbo ▲
Black Orpheus ▲
Boca
Brewster McCloud ▲
The Cabinet of Dr. Caligari ▲
Candyman 2: Farewell to the Flesh
Captive Wild Woman
Carnival Lady
Carnival of Souls ▲
Carnival Story
Carny ▲
Carousel ▲
Castle of the Living Dead
The Circus ▲
Circus of Fear
Circus of Horrors
Circus World
Cloud Dancer
Clowning Around
Clowning Around 2
The Clowns ▲
Court Jester ▲
Death Mask
Dixiana
Dual Alibi
Dumbo ▲
Elvira Madigan ▲
Encore ▲
The Fantasticks
Flamingo Road ▲
Fox and His Friends ▲
Frankenstein and Me
Freaked
Freaks ▲
Freakshow
The Funhouse
Glass Tomb
The Great Wallendas
The Greatest Show on Earth ▲
He Who Gets Slapped ▲
Hoopla
Incredibly Strange Creatures Who Stopped Living and Became Mixed-Up Zombies
Julia Misbehaves ▲
Killer Klowns from Outer Space
La Strada ▲
Larger Than Life
Lili ▲
Lola Montes ▲
Looking for Trouble
Love in Bloom
Luther the Geek
Make-Up
The Man Who Laughs ▲
Moscow on the Hudson ▲
Multiple Maniacs
One Arabian Night ▲
Outrage
Parade ▲
Peck's Bad Boy with the Circus
Portrait of an Assassin
P.T. Barnum
The Red Dwarf
The Road to Zanzibar ▲
Roustabout
The Rousters
Sally of the Sawdust
Santa Sangre ▲
Sawdust & Tinsel ▲
The Serpent's Egg
7 Faces of Dr. Lao ▲
Shakes the Clown
She Creature
She-Freak
Side Show
So Dear to My Heart ▲
Something Wicked This Way Comes
Spangles
State Fair
Strong Man ▲
Texas Carnival
Three Texas Steers
Tillie Wakes Up
Toby Tyler ▲
Trapeze ▲
Tromba, the Tiger Man
Two Moon Junction
The Unholy Three ▲
The Unknown ▲
Vampire Circus
Variety ▲
Variety Lights ▲
The Wagons Roll at Night
When Night Is Falling ▲
Where East Is East
Wild Hearts Can't Be Broken ▲
Wilder Napalm
The Woman in Question
You Can't Cheat an Honest Man ▲

Cats

***see also** Killer Kats*

The Adventures of Milo & Otis ▲
After the Revolution
The Aristocats ▲
Babe: Pig in the City
Batman Returns
The Big Cat
The Black Cat ▲
The Black Cat
Black Cat
The Cat
The Cat from Outer Space
Cat Girl
Cat People
Cats & Dogs
Cats Don't Dance
Cat's Eye
The Corpse Grinders
Felix the Cat: The Movie
Fritz the Cat ▲
Gay Purr-ee
Harry and Tonto ▲
Homeward Bound 2: Lost in San Francisco
Homeward Bound: The Incredible Journey ▲
The Incredible Journey
The Late Show ▲
Le Chat ▲
Milo & Otis
Murder She Purred: A Mrs. Murphy Mystery
Night of a Thousand Cats
Oliver & Company
Pet Sematary
Puss 'n Boots
Return of Chandu
Rubin & Ed
Seven Deaths in the Cat's Eye
The Stars Fell on Henrietta
Stuart Little 2
That Darn Cat
The Three Lives of Thomasina ▲
Tom and Jerry: The Movie
Two Evil Eyes
The Uncanny
The Uninvited
When the Cat's Away ▲

Cave People

Beach Babes 2: Cave Girl Island
Being Human
Cave Girl
Caveman
The Clan of the Cave Bear
Creatures the World Forgot
Encino Man
The Flintstones
The Flintstones in Viva Rock Vegas
History of the World: Part 1
Iceman ▲
One Million B.C.
Prehistoric Women
Quest for Fire ▲
Teenage Caveman
When Dinosaurs Ruled the Earth
When Women Had Tails
When Women Lost Their Tails

Central America

***see also** Mexico; South America*

Appointment in Honduras
Carla's Song
Cyclone Cavalier
Delta Force Commando
Devil Wears White
El Norte ▲
The Evil That Men Do
Exiled in America
The Firing Line
Hombres Armados ▲
Last Plane Out
Latino
Marie Galante ▲
The Mosquito Coast
Noriega: God's Favorite
Panama Menace
Panama Patrol
Romero
Salvador ▲
The Silence of Neto
Solo
The Tailor of Panama ▲
Toy Soldiers
Under Fire ▲
Virgin Sacrifice
Wages of Fear ▲

Checkered Flag

***see also** Motor Vehicle Dept.*

American Graffiti ▲
Baffled
Banzai Runner
The Big Wheel
Bobby Deerfield
Born to Race
Born to Run
Brewster McCloud ▲
Bullitt ▲
Cannonball
Cannonball Run
Cannonball Run 2
Car Crash
Catch Me ... If You Can
The Checkered Flag
Daddy-O
Days of Thunder
Death Driver
Death Race 2000
Death Sport
Desert Steel
The Devil on Wheels
Diamonds Are Forever ▲
Dirty Mary Crazy Larry ▲
Dragstrip Girl
Driven
Eat My Dust
The Fast and the Furious
Fast Company
Faster, Pussycat! Kill! Kill!
Fury on Wheels
Genevieve ▲
Goldfinger ▲
Grand Prix
Grandview U.S.A.
Greased Lightning
The Great Race
Gumball Rally
Hard Drivin'
Heart Like a Wheel
The Heavenly Kid
Hell on Wheels
Herbie Goes Bananas
Herbie Goes to Monte Carlo
High Gear
Hot Rod
Hot Rod Girl
King of the Mountain
The Last American Hero ▲
Last Chase
Le Mans ▲
The Love Bug
A Man and a Woman: 20 Years Later
Pit Stop ▲
Private Road: No Trespassing
Race for Life
Race the Sun
The Racers
Rebel without a Cause ▲
Red Line
Red Line 7000
Return to Macon County
Richard Petty Story
Road Racers
Roaring Roads
Safari 3000
Sahara
Shaker Run
Six Pack
Smash Palace
Smokey and the Bandit
Speed Zone
Speedway
Spinout
Stroker Ace
Those Daring Young Men in Their Jaunty Jalopies
To Please a Lady
Van Nuys Blvd.
Vanishing Point
Viva Las Vegas
Winning ▲
The Wraith

Cheerleaders

***see also** Campus Capers; Hell High School*

Bring It On
Buffy the Vampire Slayer ▲
But I'm a Cheerleader
Cheering Section
Cheerleader Camp
The Cheerleaders
Cheerleaders' Wild Weekend
Flesh Gordon 2: Flesh Gordon Meets the Cosmic Cheerleaders
Gimme an F
Grease ▲
The Majorettes
National Lampoon's Animal House ▲
The New Guy
Pandemonium
Pom Pom Girls
The Positively True Adventures of the Alleged Texas Cheerleader-Murdering Mom ▲
The Replacements
Revenge of the Cheerleaders
Satan's Cheerleaders
Sugar & Spice ▲
The Swinging Cheerleaders
Varsity Blues

Chicago

Adventures in Babysitting
The Alien Agenda: Under the Skin
Angel Eyes
Baby Face Nelson
Big Town
The Blues Brothers ▲
Blues Brothers 2000
Call Northside 777 ▲
Candyman
Chain Reaction
Chicago Cab
City That Never Sleeps
Code of Silence
Deadline
Down in the Delta ▲
Dragonfly
A Family Thing ▲
Ferris Bueller's Day Off ▲
First Time Felon
The Fixer
For Hire
The Front Page
The Fugitive ▲
Hardball
High Fidelity ▲
Holiday Heart
Home Alone ▲
Home Alone 3
Hoopla
Jerry and Tom
John Q
Just Visiting
Keeper of the City
Kissing a Fool
Let No Man Write My Epitaph
Lethal Tender
Love and Action in Chicago
Love Jones ▲
Mad Dog and Glory ▲
Mercury Rising
Mickey One
My Best Friend's Wedding
My Big Fat Greek Wedding
The Negotiator
Never Been Kissed
The Newton Boys
Next of Kin
On the Line
Primal Fear
The Relic
Resurrection
Return to Me
Risky Business ▲
Running Scared
Save the Last Dance
The Song of the Lark
Stir of Echoes
Straight Talk
Taking Care of Business
The Third Miracle
Three to Tango
Uncle Buck ▲
U.S. Marshals
The Watcher
The Water Engine
While You Were Sleeping ▲
The White Raven
The Whole Nine Yards

Child Abuse

Abuse
Any Place But Home
Bastard out of Carolina
Blind Fools
The Boys of St. Vincent ▲
A Brother's Kiss
Close to Home
Cries of Silence
Dolores Claiborne ▲
Ellen Foster
Evil Has a Face
Fallen Angel
Fatal Confinement
Father Hood
The Hanging Garden
Hollow Reed ▲
Hush Little Baby, Don't You Cry
Impulse
Indictment: The McMartin Trial ▲
Joe the King
Johnny Belinda
Judgment ▲
Lamb
The Lost Son
Mommie Dearest
Monsoon Wedding ▲
Monster's Ball ▲
The Offence ▲
Postcards from America
Psychopath
A Question of Guilt
Radio Flyer
Raising Cain
Ripe
River Red
Seeing Red
Short Eyes ▲
Shot in the Heart ▲
Sleepers
South Bronx Heroes
The Stepdaughter
The Stolen Children ▲
This Boy's Life ▲
2 by 4
Where the Spirit Lives
Who Killed Baby Azaria?
Wildflower ▲
ZigZag ▲

Childhood Buddies

***see also** Childhood Visions*

Lilo & Stitch

Childhood Visions

see also *Home Alone*

A. I.: Artificial Intelligence
About a Boy▲
Afraid of the Dark
Alice in Wonderland
All I Want for Christmas
Alone in the Woods
Alsino and the Condor▲
The Amazing Mrs. Holiday
American Heart▲
Amy
And Now Miguel
Andre
Angela
Angela's Ashes
Angels in the Outfield
Army Brats
Au Revoir les Enfants▲
The Baby-Sitters' Club
Back to the Secret Garden
Balloon Farm
Bastard out of Carolina
Beethoven Lives Upstairs
The Beniker Gang
Beyond Silence
Big▲
Big Bully
Big Daddy
Big Fella
Billy Elliot▲
Black Beauty▲
The Black Stallion▲
Blank Check
Bless the Child
Bogus
The Borrowers
Boys Will Be Boys
Breakout
Brighton Beach Memoirs
Broken Harvest
But Where Is Daniel Wax?
The Butcher Boy▲
Butterfly▲
Cameron's Closet
Camp Nowhere
Captain January
Careful, He Might Hear You▲
Casey's Shadow
Casper▲
The Cat
Catherine Cookson's The Rag Nymph
Cathy's Curse
Celia: Child of Terror
The Cellar
Central Station▲
Child in the Night
Child Star: The Shirley Temple Story
The Children Are Watching Us▲
Children of Divorce
Children of Heaven▲
Child's Play
China, My Sorrow
Chocolat▲
The Christmas Box
A Christmas Reunion
A Christmas Story▲
Chronicle of a Boy Alone
Cider with Rosie
Cinema Paradiso▲
The Client
Clifford
Clubhouse Detectives
The Color of Paradise
Cria▲
Crooklyn▲
Cross My Heart and Hope to Die
Crows
Curly Sue
Curly Top
D.A.R.Y.L.
David Copperfield▲
David Copperfield
Days of Heaven▲
Dead Silent
Deadly Game
A Death in the Family
Demons in the Garden▲
Dennis the Menace
Dennis the Menace Strikes Again
Desert Bloom▲
Deutschland im Jahre Null▲
The Devil's Backbone
The Diary of Anne Frank▲
Digger
Digging to China
Disney's The Kid
Diva▲
Domestic Disturbance
Don't Tell Mom the Babysitter's Dead
The Dress Code
D3: The Mighty Ducks
Earth
The Education of Little Tree▲
The Elementary School
Ellen Foster
Emma's Shadow▲
Empire of the Sun▲
Escapade▲
E.T.: The Extra-Terrestrial▲
Eternity and a Day
Eve's Bayou▲
Eye Witness
FairyTale: A True Story
The Fallen Idol▲
Family Tree
Fanny and Alexander▲
Far Away and Long Ago
Father▲
Finding Buck McHenry
The Flame Trees of Thika▲
Flight of the Grey Wolf
Flight of the Innocent
Flowers in the Attic
Fly Away Home▲
For a Lost Soldier
Forbidden Games▲
Forever Together
Freedom Song▲
Fresh
Girl from Hunan▲
A Girl of the Limberlost
The Golden Seal
Goodnight, Mr. Tom
The Goonies
The Green House
Grizzly Falls
Grizzly Mountain
Gypsy Colt
Happiness▲
Hardball
Harriet the Spy
Hearts in Atlantis
Heavyweights
Heidi
Heidi▲
Heidi
Heidi▲
Home Alone▲
Home Alone 2: Lost in New York
Home for Christmas
Home of Angels
Homecoming
Honey, I Shrunk the Kids
Hook
Hope
Hope and Glory▲
House Arrest
House of Cards
How Green Was My Valley▲
How to Kill Your Neighbor's Dog
Huck and the King of Hearts
Hue and Cry▲
I Was Born But...▲
I'll Remember April
The Indian in the Cupboard
Into the West▲
Invaders from Mars
Iron Giant▲
Jack
Jack Be Nimble
Jacob Two Two Meets the Hooded Fang
Jacquot
James and the Giant Peach▲
Jimmy the Kid
Joey
John and Julie
Josh and S.A.M.
Journey for Margaret▲
Kazaam
The Kid from Left Field
The Kid with the Broken Halo
The Kid with the X-Ray Eyes
Kids of the Round Table
Kikujiro
The King of Masks▲
King of the Hill▲
The Kitchen Toto▲
Kolya▲
The Lady in White▲
Lamb
Landscape in the Mist▲
Lassie's Great Adventure
Last Action Hero
The Last Winter
Lawn Dogs
Lawnmower Man 2: Beyond Cyberspace
Lazarillo
Le Grand Chemin▲
Leave It to Beaver
Leolo▲
Les Violons du Bal
Lies My Father Told Me▲
Life According to Muriel
Life-Size
Little Big League
Little Buddha
Little Fugitive▲
Little Lord Fauntleroy
Little Man Tate▲
Little Monsters
The Little Princess▲
A Little Princess▲
The Little Rascals
The Littlest Horse Thieves
Lloyd
Locked in Silence
Look Who's Talking▲
Look Who's Talking, Too
Lord of the Flies▲
Lord of the Flies
Lost in Yonkers
Louisiana Story▲
Love Film
Luminous Motion
Ma Vie en Rose▲
Madeline
Magic in the Mirror: Fowl Play
Magic in the Water
Magic of Lassie
Man of the House
Matilda▲
The Member of the Wedding
Mendel▲
Mermaid
The Mighty▲
Miracle in Lane Two
The Miracle Maker: The Story of Jesus
The Miracle of Marcelino
The Mirror▲
Ms. Bear
Mrs. Doubtfire
Mr. Rice's Secret
Misty
Mom, Can I Keep Her?
Mommie Dearest
Mondo
Mosby's Marauders
My Childhood▲
My Dog Skip▲
My Friend Flicka▲
My Life As a Dog▲
My Life So Far
My Louisiana Sky
My Mother's Castle▲
My Name Is Ivan▲
Mystery Kids
National Velvet▲
The Neon Bible
New York Stories▲
The Night of the Shooting Stars▲
North
Not One Less
Nothing Personal▲
Now and Then
Old Swimmin' Hole
Oliver!▲
Oliver Twist
Oliver Twist▲
One Christmas
One Little Indian
One Small Hero
An Orphan Boy of Vienna
The Orphans▲
The Other▲
Other Voices, Other Rooms
The Others▲
The Pagemaster
Paradise▲
The Parent Trap
Parents▲
Paulie
Pay It Forward
Peck's Bad Boy
Pelle the Conqueror▲
Perfect Game
Peter Pan
The Pillow Book
Pixote▲
Pokemon 3: The Movie
Pollyanna▲
Poltergeist▲
Poltergeist 2: The Other Side
Poltergeist: The Legacy
Ponette
A Poor Little Rich Girl▲
The Poor Little Rich Girl
Possessed
Powder
Prancer Returns
Prince of Central Park
Psycho 4: The Beginning
The Quest
The Quiet Room
Radio Flyer
The Railway Children▲
Ratcatcher
Real Genius▲
The Real Howard Spitz
The Red Balloon▲
The Red Pony▲
The Reflecting Skin
Return from Witch Mountain
Return to Never Land
Richie Rich
Ride the Wild Fields
Rock-a-Doodle
Roll of Thunder, Hear My Cry
Ruby Bridges
Running Free
Safety Patrol
Salaam Bombay!▲
Savage Sam
Searching for Bobby Fischer▲
Second Chances
The Secret Garden▲
The Secret Garden
The Secret Garden▲
The Secret Garden
Selma, Lord, Selma
The Seven Little Foys▲
Shiloh 2: Shiloh Season
Sidekicks
The Silence of Neto
The Silences of the Palace▲
Simon Birch
The Sixth Sense▲
The Skateboard Kid 2
Slappy and the Stinkers
Sling Blade▲
The Slingshot▲
Small Change▲
Snap Decision
Snow Day
Sounds of Silence
South Park: Bigger, Longer and Uncut
Sparrows▲
Spirit of the Beehive▲
Spy Kids▲
Square Shoulders
Star Kid▲
Star Wars: Episode 1—The Phantom Menace▲
Stealing Home
Stephen King's It
Stir
Stir of Echoes
Sudie & Simpson▲
The Summer of Aviya
A Summer to Remember▲
Sunday Daughters▲
Sunday's Children▲
Taps
Tea with Mussolini
Three Wishes
The Tin Drum▲
Tito and Me▲
To Kill a Mockingbird▲
Toothless
Toto le Heros▲
Toy Story▲
Trading Mom
Train to Hollywood▲
Treasure Island▲
Treasure Island
Treehouse Hostage
Turf Boy
The Turn of the Screw
12 Monkeys▲
Twisted
Undercover Angel
An Unexpected Family
Unicorn
Village of Dreams
Wait until Spring, Bandini
Walkabout▲
Walking Thunder
The War
The War Boy
Welcome to Sarajevo▲
Welcome to the Dollhouse
What the Moon Saw
When Father Was Away on Business▲
Where's Willie?
Whistle down the Wind▲
White Fang▲
Wide Awake
The Wild Country
Will It Snow for Christmas?
Willy Wonka & the Chocolate Factory▲
The Witching of Ben Wagner
The Wizard of Loneliness
Wombling Free
A World Apart▲
The Yearling▲
Yes, Sir, Mr. Bones
Zazie dans le Metro▲
Zero for Conduct▲
Zeus and Roxanne

Children

see *Animated Musicals; Animation & Cartoons; Childhood Visions; Storytelling*

China

see also *Asia*

Adventures of Smilin' Jack
The Amazing Panda Adventure
Bethune
Beyond the Next Mountain
The Bitter Tea of General Yen▲
Black Mask
The Blue Kite▲
Blush
China
China Cry
China, My Sorrow
Chinese Box
Crows and Sparrows▲
The Day the Sun Turned Cold▲
Deadly Target
Dragon Seed
East Palace, West Palace
The Emperor and the Assassin
The Emperor's Shadow
Empire of the Sun▲
Ermo
Farewell My Concubine
Flowers of Shanghai
The General Died at Dawn▲
Girl from Hunan▲
The Good Earth▲
A Great Wall▲
The Horse Thief▲
The Inn of the Sixth Happiness▲
Iron & Silk
The Joy Luck Club▲
Ju Dou▲
Kashmiri Run
The Keys of the Kingdom▲
The Killer▲
The King of Masks▲
The Last Emperor▲
The Leatherneck
The Lost Empire
M. Butterfly
The Mountain Road
Mulan
Not One Less
Once Upon a Time in China▲
Once Upon a Time in China III▲
Pavilion of Women
Princess Yang Kwei Fei▲
Raise the Red Lantern▲
Red Corner
Red Firecracker, Green Firecracker
Red Sorghum▲
The Red Violin
The Reincarnation of Golden Lotus▲
The Road Home▲
The Sand Pebbles▲
Shadow Magic
Shadows of the Orient
Shadows over Shanghai
Shanghai Express▲
Shanghai Triad▲
The Silk Road
Soldier of Fortune
Song of the Exile
Spy Game
The Story of Qiu Ju▲
The Story of Xinghua
Tai-Pan
Temptation of a Monk
Temptress Moon
To Live▲
Windhorse
Women from the Lake of Scented Souls
The Wooden Man's Bride
The World of Suzie Wong
Xiu Xiu: The Sent Down Girl▲

Christmas

see also *Holidays; Horrible Holidays*

ABC Stage 67: Truman Capote's A Christmas Memory
All I Want for Christmas
An American Christmas Carol
Babes in Toyland
Batman Returns
Bernard and the Genie
The Bishop's Wife▲
Black Christmas
Bloodbeat
Breathing Room
Call Me Claus
Cast Away▲
The Christmas Box
A Christmas Carol▲
A Christmas Carol
A Christmas Carol▲
A Christmas Carol
The Christmas Coal Mine Miracle
Christmas Comes to Willow Creek
Christmas Evil
Christmas in Connecticut▲
Christmas in Connecticut
Christmas in July▲
The Christmas Kid
Christmas Lilies of the Field
A Christmas Reunion
A Christmas Story▲
The Christmas That Almost Wasn't
A Christmas to Remember
The Christmas Wife
A Christmas Without Snow
The Crossing
The Day of the Beast
The Dead▲
Die Hard▲
Diner▲
Dr. Seuss' How the Grinch Stole Christmas
Don't Open Till Christmas
Dorm That Dripped Blood
A Dream for Christmas▲
Ebenezer
Elves
Ernest Saves Christmas
Friends & Lovers
Funny Farm

The Gathering
The Gathering: Part 2
George Balanchine's The Nutcracker
The Gift of Love
Go▲
Gremlins▲
Here Comes Santa Claus
Hi-Life
Hobo's Christmas
Holiday Affair
Holiday Inn▲
Home Alone▲
Home Alone 2: Lost in New York
Home Alone 3
Home for Christmas
Home of Angels
Homecoming: A Christmas Story
A House without a Christmas Tree
I'll Be Home for Christmas
It Came Upon a Midnight Clear
It's a Bundyful Life
It's a Wonderful Life▲
Jack Frost
Jingle All the Way
The Kid Who Loved Christmas
Kramer vs. Kramer▲
La Buche
Lady on a Train▲
The Lemon Drop Kid
Lethal Weapon▲
Lily in Winter
The Lion in Winter▲
The Little Drummer Girl▲
The Little Match Girl
Little Women▲
The Long Kiss Goodnight
Ma Saison Preferee▲
The Man in the Santa Claus Suit
The Man Upstairs
March of the Wooden Soldiers▲
A Matter of Principle
Merry Christmas, Mr. Lawrence▲
A Midnight Clear▲
A Midwinter's Tale
Miracle Down Under
Miracle in the Wilderness
Miracle on 34th Street▲
Miracle on 34th Street
Mrs. Santa Claus
Mr. Corbett's Ghost
Mixed Nuts
Ms. Scrooge
The Muppet Christmas Carol
Must Be Santa
My Uncle: The Alien
The Mystery of Edwin Drood
Naked City: A Killer Christmas
National Lampoon's Christmas Vacation
Nativity
The Night of the Hunter▲
The Night They Saved Christmas
The Nightmare before Christmas▲
The Nutcracker Prince
Nutcracker: The Motion Picture
One Christmas
One Magic Christmas
Parental Guidance
Prancer
Prancer Returns
The Preacher's Wife
The Railway Children▲
Reckless
The Ref▲
Reindeer Games
Remember the Night▲
Riot
The Robe
Roots: The Gift
Santa Claus
Santa Claus Conquers the Martians
Santa Claus: The Movie
The Santa Clause
Santa with Muscles
Scrooge▲
Scrooge
Scrooged
A Season for Miracles
Silent Night, Deadly Night
Silent Night, Deadly Night 2
Silent Night, Deadly Night 3: Better Watch Out!
Silent Night, Deadly Night 5: The Toymaker
Silent Night, Lonely Night
Sleepless in Seattle▲
A Smoky Mountain Christmas
Stalag 17▲
The Sum of Us▲
Susan Slept Here
A Tale of Winter
Thirteenth Day of Christmas
Three Godfathers▲
A Time to Remember
To All a Goodnight
To Grandmother's House We Go
Trading Places
Trail of Robin Hood
Trapped in Paradise
Turbulence
24 Nights
Untamed Heart
A Very Brady Christmas
The Waltons: The Christmas Carol
While You Were Sleeping▲
White Christmas▲
Who Slew Auntie Roo?
Will It Snow for Christmas?

CIA

see *Feds; Spies & Espionage*

Cinderella Stories

Angus
Arthur▲
B.A.P.'s
Boogie Nights▲
Born Yesterday▲
Born Yesterday
Celestial Clockwork
Cinderella▲
Cinderfella
Ever After: A Cinderella Story▲
Evita
First Love
Flashdance
Heaven or Vegas
Hero▲
The Little Mermaid▲
Milk Money
The Mirror Has Two Faces
Mrs. Winterbourne
My Fair Lady▲
Once Around
Pretty Woman▲
The Princess Diaries
Pygmalion▲
She's All That
The Slipper and the Rose
Splash
A Star Is Born▲
Stroke of Midnight
Up Close and Personal▲
Working Girl▲
The World of Suzie Wong

Circuses

see *Carnivals & Circuses; Clowns*

Cities

see *Urban Drama*

City Lights

see *Baltimore; Berlin; Boston; Calcutta; Capitol Capers; Chicago; Detroit; L.A.; London; Miami; Moscow; New Orleans; New York, New York; Paris; San Francisco; Seattle; Tokyo; Urban Drama; Venice; Viva Las Vegas!*

Civil Rights

see also *Apartheid; Slavery*

An African Dream
Ali
As Summers Die
The Autobiography of Miss Jane Pittman▲
Boycott▲
Bucktown
The Bus Is Coming
The Color of Courage
The Color Purple▲
The Conversation▲
Crazy in Alabama
Crisis at Central High▲
Dangerous Evidence: The Lori Jackson Story
Driving Miss Daisy▲
A Dry White Season▲
The Ernest Green Story
Final Comedown
For Us, the Living▲
Free, White, and 21
Freedom Road
Freedom Song▲
The Fringe Dwellers
Game for Vultures
Gang in Blue
George Wallace
Get On the Bus▲
Ghosts of Mississippi
Half Slave, Half Free
Hank Aaron: Chasing the Dream▲
Hawmps!
The Heart of Dixie
Hidden Agenda
Home of the Brave▲
King▲
The Kitchen Toto▲
Long Shadows
The Long Walk Home▲
Malcolm X: Make It Plain
The McMasters
Mean Streak
Mississippi Burning▲
Mr. & Mrs. Loving▲
A Nation Aflame
Panther
The Red Fury
The Ring
Rosewood▲
Ruby Bridges
Selma, Lord, Selma
A Soldier's Story▲
The Two of Us▲
We of the Never Never▲

Civil War

see also *American South; Southern Belles*

Abraham Lincoln
Alvarez Kelly
Andersonville▲
The Andersonville Trial▲
Bad Company▲
Band of Angels
The Beguiled▲
The Birth of a Nation▲
Blood at Sundown
Bloody Trail
The Blue and the Gray
The Bushwackers
Cavalry
Cavalry Charge
Charlotte Forten's Mission: Experiment in Freedom▲
Civil War Diary
Class of '61
Colorado
Copper Canyon
Dark Command▲
Drums in the Deep South
Escape from Fort Bravo
Finger on the Trigger
The Fool Killer
Friendly Persuasion▲
Frontier Pony Express
Frontier Scout
The General▲
General Spanky
Gettysburg▲
The Ghost Brigade
Glory▲
Gone with the Wind▲
The Good, the Bad and the Ugly▲
Gore Vidal's Lincoln
Great Day in the Morning
The Great Locomotive Chase
Hangman's Knot
Hellbenders
The Horse Soldiers
How the West Was Won▲
The Hunley
Ironclads
It Happened in New Orleans
Johnny Shiloh
Kansas Pacific
Last Stand at Saber River
Little Women▲
Little Women
Little Women▲
The Littlest Rebel
Louisiana
The Love Letter
Love Me Tender
Love's Savage Fury
Macho Callahan
The McMasters
Menace on the Mountain
Mosby's Marauders
Mysterious Island▲
No Drums, No Bugles
North and South Book 1▲
North and South Book 2▲
Of Human Hearts
The Old Maid▲
Oldest Confederate Widow Tells All▲
The Ordeal of Dr. Mudd▲
The Outlaw Josey Wales▲
Pharoah's Army
The Private History of a Campaign That Failed
Queen▲
Raiders of Ghost City
Raintree County
Rebel Love
Rebel Vixens
The Red Badge of Courage▲
Ride with the Devil
The Rose and the Jackal
Run of the Arrow
The Sacketts
Shadow of Chikara
The Shadow Riders
Shenandoah▲
Sommersby
South of St. Louis
A Southern Yankee
The Supernaturals
The Tempest
Tramplers
True Women
The Undefeated
Virginia City▲
War Brides
Way Down South
Western Gold
Yellowneck

Classic Horror

see also *Horror Anthologies*

The Abominable Dr. Phibes▲
And Now the Screaming Starts
The Ape
The Ape Man
The Appointment
Asylum
Asylum of Satan
Atom Age Vampire
Attack of the Beast Creatures
Attack of the Mayan Mummy
Attack of the Swamp Creature
Avenging Conscience
The Awakening
Barn of the Naked Dead
The Bat▲
The Bat
The Bat People
The Beast from Haunted Cave
The Beast Must Die
Bedlam▲
Before I Hang▲
The Birds▲
The Black Cat▲
The Black Room▲
Black Sabbath▲
The Black Scorpion
Black Sunday▲
Blood and Roses
Blood Beast Terror
Blood Island
Blood of Dracula
Blood of Dracula's Castle
Blood of the Vampire
The Bloodsuckers
Bluebeard
The Body Snatcher▲
The Bride
The Bride of Frankenstein▲
Bride of the Gorilla
Bride of the Monster
The Brute Man
Burn Witch, Burn!▲
The Cabinet of Dr. Caligari▲
Carnival of Souls▲
Castle of Blood
Castle of Evil
Castle of the Living Dead
Cat Girl
Cat in the Cage
Cat People▲
Cat People
Cauldron of Blood
Cave of the Living Dead
Chamber of Horrors
The Changeling
Circus of Fear
Condemned to Live
The Conqueror Worm▲
Corridors of Blood
Count Dracula
Count Yorga, Vampire
The Crawling Eye
Creature from the Black Lagoon▲
Creature of Destruction
Creature of the Walking Dead
The Creature Walks among Us
Creature with the Blue Hand
The Creeper
The Creeping Flesh
Creeping Terror
Creepshow
Creepshow 2
The Crime of Dr. Crespi
Crimes at the Dark House▲
Crimes of Dr. Mabuse▲
The Crimes of Stephen Hawke
The Crimson Cult
Crucible of Horror
Cry of the Banshee
Cry of the Werewolf
Crypt of the Living Dead
The Curse of Frankenstein
Curse of the Devil
Curse of the Swamp Creature
Cyclops
Dance of the Damned
Daughters of Darkness▲
Dementia 13
Demon Barber of Fleet Street
Demons of the Mind
The Devil Bat
The Devil Bat's Daughter
Devil Doll▲
Dr. Death, Seeker of Souls
Dr. Jekyll and Mr. Hyde▲
Dr. Jekyll and Mr. Hyde
Doctor X
Dolly Dearest
Dorian Gray
Dracula (Spanish Version)
Dracula▲
Dracula
Dracula A.D. 1972
Dracula/Garden of Eden
Dracula 2000
Dracula vs. Frankenstein
Dracula's Daughter▲
Dracula's Great Love
Dracula's Last Rites
Dracula's Widow
The Evil of Frankenstein
The Exorcist▲
Eye of the Demon
Eyes of Fire
Eyes of the Panther
The Fall of the House of Usher
The Fall of the House of Usher▲
The Fall of the House of Usher
Fangs of the Living Dead
The Fear Chamber
Fear No Evil
The Fog
Frankenstein▲
Frankenstein
Frankenstein and the Monster from Hell
Frankenstein Created Woman▲
Frankenstein '80
Frankenstein Island
Frankenstein Meets the Wolfman▲
Frankenstein Must Be Destroyed
Frankenstein Unbound▲
Frankenstein's Daughter
Fright Night
Fright Night 2
The Fury
The Fury of the Wolfman
Genie of Darkness
The Ghost of Frankenstein
The Ghoul
The Gorgon
Gothic▲
Grave of the Vampire
Graveyard Shift
The Greed of William Hart
Growing Pains
Guardian of the Abyss
Halloween Night
The Hanging Woman
The Haunted
The Haunted Strangler
Haunted Summer
The Haunting▲
Haunting Fear
The Haunting of Morella
Haxan: Witchcraft through the Ages▲
The Head
The Horror of Dracula▲
House of Dark Shadows▲
House of Dracula
House of Frankenstein
House of the Black Death
The House of Usher
House of Wax▲
House on Haunted Hill
The House that Dripped Blood
How to Make a Monster
The Hunchback of Notre Dame▲
The Hunger
I Walked with a Zombie▲
I Was a Teenage Werewolf
Invasion of the Vampires
The Invisible Dr. Mabuse▲
The Invisible Man▲
The Invisible Ray
The Island of Dr. Moreau
Island of Lost Souls▲
Isle of the Dead

Jaws▲
Jaws 2
Jaws 3
Jaws: The Revenge
King of the Zombies
La Chute de la Maison Usher▲
Lady Frankenstein
The Lair of the White Worm▲
The Legend of Blood Castle
Legend of the Werewolf
The Legend of the Wolf Woman
Lemora, Lady Dracula
The Living Coffin
The Mad Monster
The Man They Could Not Hang
Mark of the Vampire▲
Martin▲
Mary Shelley's Frankenstein
Masque of the Red Death▲
Masque of the Red Death
Miami Horror
Mirrors
The Mummy▲
Mummy & Curse of the Jackal
The Mummy's Curse
The Mummy's Ghost
The Mummy's Hand
The Mummy's Tomb
Murders in the Rue Morgue
Mystery of the Wax Museum▲
Night of Dark Shadows▲
Nosferatu▲
Once Upon a Midnight Scary
Pandora's Box▲
The Phantom of the Opera▲
The Phantom of the Opera
Picture of Dorian Gray▲
The Pit and the Pendulum▲
The Pit & the Pendulum
Psycho▲
The Raven▲
Return of the Vampire
Revenge of the Creature
Revenge of the Zombies
Scared to Death
The Snow Creature
Son of Dracula▲
Son of Frankenstein▲
Teenage Frankenstein
The Undying Monster
The Vampire
The Vampire Bat
The Vampire People
The Vampire's Coffin
The Vampire's Ghost
Vampyr▲
Werewolf of London
The Werewolf vs. the Vampire Woman
The White Zombie▲
The Wolf Man▲

Cloning Around

Alien: Resurrection▲
The Boys from Brazil
The Clones
The Clonus Horror
Jurassic Park▲
The Lost World: Jurassic Park 2
Multiplicity
Replicant
Resurrection of Zachary Wheeler
The 6th Day
Species 2
Spy Kids▲
Star Wars: Episode 2—Attack of the Clones▲
2001: A Space Travesty

Clowns

see also ***Carnivals & Circuses***

Clown House
Clown Murders
Clowning Around
Clowning Around 2
The Clowns▲
Court Jester▲
The Funhouse
Funland
He Who Gets Slapped▲
Killer Klowns from Outer Space
Make-Up
The Man Who Laughs▲
Painted Hero
Poltergeist▲
Quick Change
Shakes the Clown
Stephen King's It
To Catch a Killer▲

Cockroaches

see also ***Killer Bugs and Slugs***

Addicted to Love
The Craft
Creepshow
Joe's Apartment
Mimic
The Nest
Pacific Heights▲
Twilight of the Cockroaches
Vampire's Kiss▲

Cold Spots

The Abominable Snowman
Alaska
Antarctica
Arctic Blue
Atomic Submarine
Avalanche
Balto
The Big Push
Bog
Call of the Wild
Challenge To Be Free
Christmas Comes to Willow Creek
Cold Fever
Cool Runnings
Courage Mountain
Crackerjack
The Crimson Rivers
Cry of the Penguins
The Day the Earth Froze
Dead Ahead: The Exxon Valdez Disaster▲
Dead of Winter▲
Devil's Island
Doctor Zhivago▲
Downhill Willie
The Eiger Sanction
The Empire Strikes Back▲
Firefox
The Forbidden Quest
Friends & Lovers
Glory & Honor
Heart of Light
The Heroes of Telemark
Ice Age▲
Ice Palace
The Ice Runner
Ice Station Zebra
Into Thin Air: Death on Everest
Intruder Within
Iron Will
Jack Frost
Jack Frost 2: Revenge of the Mutant Killer Snowman
Jack London's The Call of the Wild
The Juniper Tree
Kavik the Wolf Dog
Klondike Annie
The Last Place on Earth
The Last Stop
Lost in Alaska
Lost Zeppelin
Lovers of the Arctic Circle
Map of the Human Heart
Mystery, Alaska
Never Cry Wolf▲
North Star
North to Alaska▲
Operation Haylift
Ordeal in the Arctic
Out Cold
Pathfinder▲
The Pebble and the Penguin
Pipe Dreams
Quest for Fire▲
Reindeer Games
Salmonberries
Shackleton▲
Shadow of the Wolf
She
The Shining
Silent Hunter
A Simple Plan▲
Smilla's Sense of Snow
Snow Day
Snow Dogs
Snowboard Academy
Snowbound: The Jim and Jennifer Stolpa Story
Sometimes They Come Back ... For More
Spawn of the North
The Spoilers▲
Spy Games
The Stranger: Kabloonak
Sub Down
Tentacles of the North
The Thing▲
The Thing
Vertical Limit
The Viking Sagas
Virus
The White Dawn
White Fang 2: The Myth of the White Wolf
White Wolves 3: Cry of the White Wolf
Winter People
Winter Sleepers
You'll Like My Mother
Zero Degrees Kelvin

Cold War

see ***Red Scare***

Comedy

see ***Black Comedy; Comedy Anthologies; Comedy Drama; Comedy Mystery; Comedy Sci-Fi; Comic Adventure; Detective Spoofs; Disorganized Crime; Genre Spoofs; Horror Comedy; Military Comedy; Musical Comedy; Romantic Comedy; Satire & Parody; Screwball Comedy; Showbiz Comedies; Slapstick Comedy; Sports Comedies; Stupid Is...; Western Comedy***

Comedy Anthologies

see also ***Comedy***

Amazon Women on the Moon
And Now for Something Completely Different▲
Boccaccio '70
Everything You Always Wanted to Know about Sex (But Were Afraid to Ask)▲
Foreplay
The Groove Tube
Hollywood Boulevard
Kentucky Fried Movie▲
Kid 'n' Hollywood and Polly Tix in Washington
Laurel & Hardy and the Family
Laurel & Hardy: At Work
Laurel & Hardy On the Lam
Laurel & Hardy Spooktacular
Laurel & Hardy: Stan "Helps" Ollie
Looney Looney Looney Bugs Bunny Movie▲
The Lost Stooges
Love Notes
Mack & Carole
The Marx Brothers in a Nutshell▲
Monty Python's The Meaning of Life▲
National Lampoon Goes to the Movies
National Lampoon's Favorite Deadly Sins
New York Stories▲
Oldest Profession
Parade▲
Plaza Suite▲
Pop Goes the Cork
Queen for a Day
Rascal Dazzle
Really Weird Tales
Sex and Buttered Popcorn
Tigers in Lipstick
Tunnelvision
Woman Times Seven
Yours, Mine & Ours

Comedy Drama

see also ***Black Comedy; Comedy***

Adventure
Alice Doesn't Live Here Anymore
Alice's Restaurant
All I Want for Christmas
All My Good Countrymen
All Screwed Up▲
An Almost Perfect Affair
Aloha Summer
Always▲
Amarcord▲
The Amazing Mrs. Holiday
American Boyfriends
American Graffiti▲
Amy
And Baby Makes Six
Androcles and the Lion
Andy Hardy Gets Spring Fever
Andy Hardy's Double Life
Andy Hardy's Private Secretary
Angel in a Taxi
Angie
The Anniversary Party▲
Antonia's Line
The Apprenticeship of Duddy Kravitz▲
Arabian Nights▲
Arizona Dream
Armistead Maupin's More Tales of the City
Armistead Maupin's Tales of the City
Article 99
Author! Author!
Autumn Marathon
Avalon▲
Awakenings▲
Ay, Carmela!▲
Babette's Feast▲
Baby It's You▲
The Baby-Sitters' Club
Baby, Take a Bow
Back Roads
Bad Behavior
Bail Jumper
The Baker's Wife▲
The Ballad of Paul Bunyan
Band of Outsiders
Barcelona▲
Bartleby
Baxter
Beautiful Girls
Beautiful Thing▲
Bed and Board▲
Being Human
Being Two Isn't Easy
The Bells of St. Mary's▲
Benji▲
Best Men
The Best Way
Bhaji on the Beach
Big▲
The Big Chill▲
Big Eden
Big Girls Don't Cry...They Get Even
Big Night
Big Wednesday
Billy Liar▲
The Bishop's Wife▲
The Black King
Bleak Moments
Blueberry Hill
Blues Busters
Blume in Love▲
Bogus
Bongwater
Boogie Nights▲
Born to Win
Borsalino▲
Box of Moonlight
The Boys Next Door
The Breakfast Club▲
Breaking Away▲
Breaking the Rules
Breaking Up Is Hard to Do
The Bretts▲
Bright Eyes
Brighton Beach Memoirs
Broadcast News▲
Bud and Lou
The Buddha of Suburbia▲
The Buddy System
Buddy's Song
A Bunny's Tale
Bureau of Missing Persons
Butterflies Are Free▲
Cadillac Ranch
Caesar and Cleopatra
Cafe Express
Calendar Girl
Candy Mountain
Cannery Row
Captain Newman, M.D.
Carbon Copy
Carnal Knowledge▲
Carnival in Flanders▲
Caro Diario▲
Carried Away
Casey's Shadow
Celestial Clockwork
Cesar▲
Cesar & Rosalie▲
The Challengers
Charles et Lucie▲
Charlie and the Great Balloon Chase
Cheaper to Keep Her
A Chef in Love
Chicago Cab
Children of the Revolution
Chimes at Midnight▲
China, My Sorrow
Chips, the War Dog
Chloe in the Afternoon▲
Choose Me▲
A Chorus of Disapproval
The Christmas Wife
Chungking Express▲
City Lights▲
City of Women
Claire's Knee▲
Clara's Heart
Class Reunion
Cleo from 5 to 7▲
Clipped Wings
Coast to Coast
Cocoon: The Return
Combination Platter
Come to the Stable▲
Commandments
Comment Ca Va?
Conspiracy of Terror
Cookie's Fortune▲
Cooperstown
Corvette Summer
Country Life
Coupe de Ville
The Courtship of Eddie's Father▲
Cousin, Cousine▲
Cousins▲
Crazy from the Heart▲
Crimes & Misdemeanors▲
Crooklyn▲
Cruel Intentions
Danny Boy
David Holzman's Diary▲
The Decameron▲
The Decline of the American Empire▲
Deconstructing Harry
Deep in the Heart (of Texas)
Der Purimshpiler
Destiny Turns on the Radio
Details of a Duel: A Question of Honor
Detour to Danger
The Devil & Daniel Webster▲
Devil on Horseback
The Devil's Eye
Diary of a Chambermaid▲
Diary of a Mad Housewife▲
Diary of a Young Comic
Diary of Forbidden Dreams▲
Different for Girls▲
Digger
Dim Sum: A Little Bit of Heart▲
The Dining Room
Dinner at Eight▲
Dinner at Eight
The Discovery Program
Dixie Lanes
Do the Right Thing▲
Doctor at Sea
Dr. Christian Meets the Women
Dog Eat Dog
Don Quixote▲
Don Quixote
Don't Drink the Water
Double Happiness▲
Down by Law▲
Dream Chasers
The Dream Team
Dream with the Fishes
The Dress Code
DROP Squad
Drugstore Cowboy▲
D2: The Mighty Ducks
Duets
Earthly Possessions
Eat a Bowl of Tea▲
Eat Drink Man Woman▲
Eat My Dust
Eat the Peach
Eating
Educating Rita▲
El Cochecito▲
The Elementary School
Eli Eli
Elizabeth of Ladymead▲
Elmore Leonard's Gold Coast
Emanon
End of the Line
Enemies, a Love Story▲
Enormous Changes▲
Ermo
Even Cowgirls Get the Blues
The Evening Star
Extra Girl
Eyes Right!
The Fabulous Baker Boys▲
Faithful
Family Business
Fandango
Far North
Fast Talking
Fatso
Feeling Minnesota
The Fifth Monkey
First Name: Carmen▲
The Fisher King▲
Five Corners▲
The Five Heartbeats▲
The Flamingo Kid▲
Flesh▲
Flirting▲
Floundering
FM
Follow the Leader
Foolish
For Keeps
For the Love of Benji
A Foreign Field
Forrest Gump▲
Four Adventures of Reinette and Mirabelle▲
Four Days in July
Four Deuces
Four Friends▲
The Four Musketeers▲
The Four Seasons
Freud Leaving Home
Fried Green Tomatoes▲
From the Hip
From the Mixed-Up Files of Mrs. Basil E. Frankweiler
Full Moon in Blue Water
Fuzz
Garbo Talks
Generation
George!
Georgy Girl▲
Get Shorty▲
Getting Over
Getting Straight
Ghost Chasers

▲ = rated three bones or higher

The Gig
Gin Game▲
Ginger & Fred▲
The Girl with the Hat Box
Girlfriends▲
A Girl's Folly
Go▲
Go Now▲
The Gold of Naples▲
Gone Are the Days
Good Luck
A Good Man in Africa
Good Morning, Vietnam▲
Good Sam
The Goodbye Bird
Goodbye Columbus▲
The Goodbye People
Goodnight, Michelangelo
The Gospel According to Vic
The Graduate▲
Grandview U.S.A.
The Great Man Votes▲
The Great McGinty▲
The Great Moment
A Great Wall▲
The Great War
Gregory's Girl▲
Grief
Gross Anatomy
Grown Ups
Grumpy Old Men▲
Guess What We Learned in School Today?
Guess Who's Coming to Dinner▲
Half a Sixpence
Hangin' with the Homeboys▲
Hannah and Her Sisters▲
Happily Ever After
Happy Since I Met You▲
Hard Promises
The Hard Way▲
Harlem Nights
The Hawks & the Sparrows
Head Winds
The Heartbreak Kid▲
Heartburn▲
Here Come the Marines
Hero▲
Hero of the Year
Hey, Babu Riba
The Hideaways
Hideous Kinky
His Double Life
His First Command
Hold Your Man▲
A Hole in the Head
Hollywood Heartbreak
Hollywood Vice Sqaud
Holy Man
Home for the Holidays
Home Free All
Homegrown
Homer and Eddie
Horsemasters
The Hot Line
The Hotel New Hampshire
House of Angels
Household Saints▲
The Householder
Housekeeping▲
I Live My Life
I Live with Me Dad
I Vitelloni▲
The Ice Flood
If You Could See What I Hear
Il Sorpasso
I'll Never Forget What's 'Isname▲
Illuminata
I'm Not Rappaport
Immediate Family
Impure Thoughts
In Praise of Older Women
In the Land of the Owl Turds
In the Mood
In the Soup
Indian Summer
Inside Monkey Zetterland
Insignificance▲
International Lady
It Couldn't Happen Here
It Started in Naples▲
It's a Wonderful Life▲
Jack and Sarah
Jailbird's Vacation
Jamon, Jamon
The January Man
Jazzman▲
Jimmy Hollywood
Jo Jo Dancer, Your Life Is Calling
Joe
Joe's Bed-Stuy Barbershop: We Cut Heads
Johnny Suede
The Jolly Paupers
Joshua Then and Now▲
Judge Priest▲
Judy Berlin
Just Another Pretty Face
Kicking and Screaming▲
The Kid▲
Kid Dynamite
The Kid from Left Field
The Killing Game
A King in New York
Kingdom Come
Kisses in the Dark
Knights & Emeralds
Kolya▲
Kostas
Kotch▲
La Discrete▲
La Dolce Vita▲
La Ronde▲
Lady by Choice
Lady for a Day▲
The Lady Says No
Larks on a String▲
The Last American Hero▲
The Last Days of Chez Nous
The Last Detail▲
Last Holiday▲
Last Night▲
The Last of Mrs. Cheyney▲
Last Summer In the Hamptons▲
Law and Disorder▲
Le Beau Serge▲
Le Petit Amour▲
A League of Their Own▲
Leap of Faith
Leave 'Em Laughing
The Lemon Sisters
Let's Talk About Sex
Letter to Brezhnev▲
Letters from My Windmill▲
Letting Go
Life
Life 101
Like Water for Chocolate▲
Lily in Love
Little Annie Rooney
Little Red Schoolhouse
A Little Sex
The Little Theatre of Jean Renoir▲
The Little Thief▲
Little Vegas
Little Voice▲
Live Nude Girls
Living Out Loud
Local Hero▲
Loch Ness
Long Shot
Loose Connections
The Lovable Cheat
Love and Human Remains▲
Love Finds Andy Hardy▲
Love in the City▲
Love! Valour! Compassion!
Lover Girl
Lovers and Other Strangers▲
Loves of a Blonde▲
The Low Life
Lucas▲
Ma Vie en Rose▲
Mac and Me
Madame Sousatzka▲
Made for Each Other▲
Made in USA
Magic Town
Make Room for Tomorrow
Mama Turns a Hundred▲
The Man Upstairs
Manny's Orphans
Mantrap
Marathon
Maria's Child
Marius▲
The Marriage of Maria Braun▲
Marry Me, Marry Me▲
The Marrying Kind
Masala
M*A*S*H▲
M*A*S*H: Goodbye, Farewell & Amen▲
Mauvaise Graine
Max Dugan Returns
May Fools▲
Maybe Baby
Me Myself I
Meantime
Mediterraneo▲
Memories of Me
Men at Work
Men Don't Leave
Mermaids▲
Metropolitan▲
Mexican Bus Ride
Middle Age Crazy
Midnight Auto Supply
Mifune
The Mighty Ducks
The Mighty Quinn
The Milagro Beanfield War▲
Million Dollar Kid
Min & Bill
Miracle on 34th Street
Mischief
The Misfit Brigade
Miss Annie Rooney
Mrs. 'Arris Goes to Paris
Mrs. Wiggs of the Cabbage Patch
Mr. Deeds Goes to Town▲
Mr. Mom▲
Mr. North
Mr. Saturday Night
Mr. Winkle Goes to War
M'Lady's Court
Mom, the Wolfman and Me
Money for Nothing
The Moneytree
Moon over Parador
Moonlighting
More American Graffiti
Morgan Stewart's Coming Home
Moscow on the Hudson▲
Mother
The Mozart Brothers▲
Murmur of the Heart▲
My Beautiful Laundrette▲
My Bodyguard▲
My Dinner with Andre▲
My Girl
My Life As a Dog▲
My Other Husband
My Therapist
My Twentieth Century▲
My Wonderful Life
Mystic Pizza▲
Nadine
The Nasty Girl▲
Nasty Rabbit
Nea
'Neath Brooklyn Bridge
Never Let Go
The New Age
A New Life
New Year's Day▲
Next Stop, Greenwich Village▲
Next Summer▲
Night on Earth▲
1969▲
1999
90 Days▲
The Ninth Configuration▲
No Man of Her Own
No Small Affair
Nobody's Fool▲
Norman, Is That You?
North
North Dallas Forty▲
Nothing in Common
Nueba Yol
Nurse on Call
The Object of Beauty▲
The Object of My Affection
Oblomov▲
Off Your Rocker
Oh, Alfie
Oh, What a Night
Olly Olly Oxen Free
Omaha (the movie)
Once Around
One Arabian Night▲
One Flew Over the Cuckoo's Nest▲
Only One Night
Only When I Laugh▲
Orphans▲
Other People's Money
Our Little Girl
Out
Outrageous!▲
Outside Chance of Maximillian Glick
Over the Brooklyn Bridge
Paddy
Padre Nuestro
Palm Springs Weekend
Palooka
The Paper▲
The Paper Chase▲
Parental Guidance
Parenthood▲
Patch Adams
Patti Rocks▲
The Pentagon Wars
People Will Talk▲
Peppermint Soda▲
Perfect Timing
Perfumed Nightmare▲
Period of Adjustment▲
Pete 'n' Tillie
Peter's Friends
The Philadelphia Story▲
The Pickle
Pictures
Ping Pong
Pink Cadillac
Pink Nights
P.K. and the Kid
Playboy of the Western World
The Players Club▲
Pocketful of Miracles▲
The Pointsman
Pollyanna
Pollyanna▲
Pontiac Moon
Popi▲
Portnoy's Complaint
Power
Powwow Highway▲
The Preacher's Wife
Pretty in Pink
Pride of the Bowery
The Prime of Miss Jean Brodie▲
Primrose Path
Prisoner of Second Avenue
Prisoners of Inertia
The Private History of a Campaign That Failed
Prizzi's Honor▲
Problem Child
Promised Land▲
Pronto
Provincial Actors
Punchline
Purple People Eater
Pushing Hands
Pushing Tin▲
Queen of Hearts▲
The Rachel Papers▲
Racquet
Rafferty & the Gold Dust Twins
Rags to Riches
Raining Stones
The Rascals
Ratboy
Reckless▲
Reckless: The Sequel▲
The Red Light Sting
Remedy for Riches
Reno and the Doc
Return of the Secaucus 7▲
Rich and Famous
Ride the Wild Surf
Robert et Robert▲
Rocket Gibraltar▲
Romance of a Horsethief
Roommate
Roommates
The Rules of the Game▲
The Runnin' Kind
Rupert's Land
Sadie McKee▲
Saving Grace
Say Anything▲
Scenes from a Mall
Scoumoune
Second Thoughts
Secrets of Women▲
Seduced and Abandoned▲
The Seducer
A Self-Made Hero▲
The Seven-Per-Cent Solution▲
Seven Thieves▲
Shadows and Fog
Shag: The Movie▲
She Must Be Seeing Things
Shirley Valentine▲
A Shock to the System▲
Shooters
Short Cuts▲
Side Out
Signs of Life
Simon Birch
Simon, King of the Witches
A Simple Twist of Fate
Single Bars, Single Women
Six in Paris
Six Weeks
Sizzle Beach U.S.A.
Skin Game▲
Slap Shot▲
Slaves of New York
SLC Punk!
Sliding Doors
Slightly Honorable
The Slingshot▲
The Slugger's Wife
Smart Alecks
Smoke Signals
Smugglers' Cove▲
The Snapper▲
Soldier in the Rain
Some Kind of Hero
Some Kind of Wonderful
Someone Else's America▲
Something in Common
Something Special
Something to Talk About
Song of the Thin Man
Soul Food
Soul Man
Spencer's Mountain
Spike of Bensonhurst
Spitfire▲
Spoiled Children
Spook Busters
Spy Games
Stage Door▲
Star Maps
Star of Midnight
Star Spangled Girl
Stardust Memories
Starlight Hotel
The Stars Fell on Henrietta
Starting Over▲
Staying Together
Stealing Beauty
Steamboat Bill, Jr.▲
Stoogemania
Storm in a Teacup
The Story of Seabiscuit
Strange Fits of Passion
Stranger than Paradise▲
Strawberry Blonde▲
Street Music
Striptease
Strong Man▲
Stroszek▲
Stuck on You
Student Confidential
Sugarbaby▲
The Sugarland Express▲
Summer Fantasy
Summer Snow
The Sunshine Boys▲
Suppose They Gave a War and Nobody Came?
Swedenhielms
Sweet Adeline
Sweet Hearts Dance
Sweet Lorraine▲
Sweet William▲
Sweetie▲
Swept Away...▲
Swing Shift
Sylvia Scarlett
T Bone N Weasel
Table Settings
Take Down
Take This Job & Shove It
Take Your Best Shot
A Tale of Springtime
Tales of Manhattan▲
Talk
Talking Walls
Taxi Blues▲
A Taxing Woman▲
Teachers
Teacher's Pet▲
Teddy at the Throttle
10
Ten Things I Hate about You▲
Teresa Venerdi▲
Texasville
That Thing You Do!▲
That's Life!
That's My Baby!
There Goes My Baby
They Might Be Giants▲
The Thin Man Goes Home
Things Change▲
This Is My Life
Those Lips, Those Eyes
A Thousand Clowns▲
Three for the Road
Three in the Attic
Three Men and a Baby▲
Three Men and a Cradle▲
Three Men and a Little Lady
Thunder in the City▲
Thursday's Child
Thursday's Game▲
A Tiger's Tale
The Time of Your Life▲
Tin Men
The Tip-Off
Tito and Me▲
To Please a Lady
To Sleep with Anger▲
Toby Tyler▲
Tom Brown's School Days
Tom Brown's School Days▲
Tom Sawyer▲
Tony Draws a Horse
Too Pretty to Be Honest
Tootsie▲
Topaze▲
Torch Song Trilogy
Toys
Trading Hearts
The Tragedy of a Ridiculous Man
Train to Hollywood▲
Traveller▲
Travels with My Aunt
Trouble along the Way
Trouble in the Glen
True Love▲
Truly, Madly, Deeply▲
The Truman Show▲
Trust
Truth about Women
Turk 182!
Turkish Delight
Twenty Bucks▲
Twenty-One
The 24 Hour Woman
29th Street
Twister
Two for the Road▲
Two for the Seesaw▲
Twogether
Ugetsu▲
Under the Biltmore Clock
Under the Boardwalk
Underworld
The Unfaithfuls
An Unfinished Piece for a Player Piano▲
Up the Down Staircase▲
Up the Sandbox
Used People
The Vals
The Van▲
Varsity Blues
Venice, Venice
Very Close Quarters
The Virgin Soldiers
Volpone▲
Wait until Spring, Bandini
Walls of Glass
We Think the World of You▲
Weekend at the Waldorf▲
Welcome Home, Roxy Carmichael
Went to Coney Island on a Mission from God...Be Back by Five

▲ = rated three bones or higher

We're No Angels
West Is West
What's Cooking?▲
When Your Lover Leaves
Where the Heart Is
Whitcomb's War
The Whole Shootin' Match▲
The Whole Town's Talking▲
Who's Who
Whose Life Is It Anyway?▲
Widow's Peak
The Wife
Wild in the Streets
Willie & Phil
Wings of Eagles
Winter Kills▲
Wired
Wise Blood▲
Wish upon a Star
Wish You Were Here▲
With Honors
The Wizard
The Women▲
The World According to Garp▲
The World of Henry Orient▲
WR: Mysteries of the Organism▲
The Wrong Arm of the Law▲
A Yank in Australia
A Year in Provence▲
The Year My Voice Broke▲
Yesterday, Today and Tomorrow▲
You and Me
You Are Here *
The Young in Heart▲
You're a Big Boy Now▲
A Zed & Two Noughts▲

Comedy Mystery

see also *Black Comedy; Comedy; Comedy Drama; Genre Spoofs; Horror Comedy; Satire & Parody*

Charade▲
Clubhouse Detectives
Clue
Curse of the Pink Panther
Deathtrap
Goodbye, Lover
Hard-Boiled Mahoney
High Anxiety
Lady on a Train▲
Murder by Death
Mystery Kids
Off and Running
The Pink Panther▲
The Pink Panther Strikes Again▲
The Princess Comes Across▲
Return of the Pink Panther
Revenge of the Pink Panther
Safe House
A Shot in the Dark▲
Trail of the Pink Panther
Trixie
Whistling in Brooklyn
Whistling in Dixie
Whistling in the Dark▲
Zero Effect

Comedy Performance

see *Concert Films*

Comedy Sci-Fi

see also *Comedy; Comic Adventure; Genre Spoofs; Satire & Parody; Sci Fi*

The Absent-Minded Professor▲
Beach Babes 2: Cave Girl Island
Beach Babes from Beyond Infinity
Bug Buster
Can of Worms
Class of Nuke 'Em High
Class of Nuke 'Em High 2: Subhumanoid Meltdown
Class of Nuke 'Em High 3: The Good, the Bad and the Subhumanoid
Clockstoppers
Coneheads
Dinosaur Valley Girls
Doin' Time on Planet Earth
Earth Girls Are Easy
Evolution
Galaxy Quest
Hell Comes to Frogtown
Honey, I Shrunk the Kids
Honey, We Shrunk Ourselves
Howard the Duck
Ice Pirates
Invasion!
Invasion of the Saucer Men
Men in Black▲
Men in Black 2
My Favorite Martian
My Uncle: The Alien
Out There
Sleeper▲
Son of Flubber
Spaceballs
Star Kid▲
Theodore Rex
Wham-Bam, Thank You Spaceman

Comic Adventure

see also *Action-Adventure; Comedy*

Adventures Beyond Belief
Adventures in Babysitting
Adventures in Spying
Adventures of a Private Eye
Adventures of a Taxi Driver
The Adventures of Bullwhip Griffin
Air America
Alien from L.A.
All the Lovin' Kinfolk
All the Way, Boys
The Amazing Dobermans
The Ambushers
The Americano
Andy and the Airwave Rangers
Angel of H.E.A.T.
Angels Hard As They Come
Another 48 Hrs.
Another Stakeout
Avenging Disco Godfather
Baby on Board
Back Roads
Back to the Future▲
Back to the Future, Part 2
Back to the Future, Part 3▲
Bad Guys
Bagdad Cafe▲
The Baltimore Bullet
Bananas Boat
Behind the Front
Beverly Hills Cop
Beverly Hills Cop 2
Beverly Hills Cop 3
The Big Lebowski▲
The Big Slice
Big Zapper
Bingo
Bird on a Wire
Black Tight Killers▲
Bloodstone
Blue Iguana
Body Trouble
Boris and Natasha: The Movie
Brink's Job▲
Brothers O'Toole
Burglar
Butler's Dilemma
California Straight Ahead
Campus Knights
Cannibal Women in the Avocado Jungle of Death
Cannonball Run
Cannonball Run 2
The Captain from Koepenick
Captain Swagger
Cartouche▲
Chan Is Missing▲
Chasers
Chu Chu & the Philly Flash
City Heat
Club Med
Collision Course
The Concrete Cowboys
Crocodile Dundee▲
Crocodile Dundee 2
Dirt Bike Kid
Doctor Detroit
Dog Pound Shuffle▲
Dolemite 2: Human Tornado
The Double O Kid
Down to Earth▲
Every Girl Should Have One
Explosion
Fast Getaway
Feds
The Fifth Musketeer
The Fighting American
Flatfoot
Flipper▲
Flirting with Fate▲
Forever Young
48 Hrs.▲
Foul Play▲
Free Ride
The Further Adventures of Tennessee Buck
Ghostbusters▲
Ghostbusters 2
Go for It
The Golden Child
The Gumshoe Kid
Gunmen
Hambone & Hillie
Harriet the Spy
Hawthorne of the USA
Here We Go Again!
High Road to China
High Voltage
Highpoint
Hudson Hawk
In Like Flint
In 'n Out
It's in the Bag
Jackie Chan's Who Am I
Jake Speed
Jane & the Lost City
The Jewel of the Nile
Just Tell Me You Love Me
Kazaam
Kindergarten Cop
King Kung Fu
Kiss My Grits
Kuffs
Landlord Blues
Last Action Hero
Leonard Part 6
Looking for Trouble
A Low Down Dirty Shame
Lucky Devil
Lunch Wagon
Lust in the Dust▲
Mad About Money
Madigan's Millions
Magic Island
Magic Kid
A Man Called Sarge
The Man in the Raincoat
The Man Who Wasn't There
The Man with One Red Shoe
Master Mind
The Masters of Menace
Memoirs of an Invisible Man
Miami Supercops
Midnight Madness
Midnight Run▲
Miracles
Mr. Billion
Mr. Nanny
Mr. Nice Guy
Mr. Robinson Crusoe
Mr. Superinvisible
Mitchell
Mo' Money
Mob Story
Mom and Dad Save the World
The Money
Money Talks
Monkey Hustle
Monkey's Uncle
Muppet Treasure Island
Mutants In Paradise
My African Adventure
My Dog, the Thief
My Science Project
The Naked Sword of Zorro
No Deposit, No Return
O Brother Where Art Thou?
Oddball Hall
Odds and Evens
Operation Condor 2: The Armour of the Gods
Operation Dumbo Drop
Our Man Flint
Over the Hill
Palookaville▲
Pippi Goes on Board
Pippi in the South Seas
Pippi Longstocking
Pippi on the Run
Pirates
Pootie Tang
Prehysteria
The Prince of Thieves
Red Lion
Reggie Mixes In▲
The Reivers▲
Rescue Me
The Return of the Musketeers
Return of the Rebels
Riff-Raff
Romancing the Stone▲
Round Trip to Heaven
Royal Flash▲
Rumble in the Bronx
Running Scared
Rush Hour
Russkies
Seven
Sherlock: Undercover Dog
Sherlock's Rivals & Where's My Wife
She's Back
Shoot
Short Time▲
Shredder Orpheus
Silver Streak▲
Ski Patrol
Sky High
Slither▲
Smokey and the Bandit
Smokey and the Bandit 2
Smokey and the Bandit, Part 3
Smokey & the Judge
Smokey Bites the Dust
Spaghetti House
Special Delivery
Speed Zone
Speedy▲
Spies, Lies and Naked Thighs
Spy Trap
Spy with a Cold Nose
S*P*Y*S
The Squeeze
Stakeout
Stand-In
Steelyard Blues
Stepmonster
The Stick-Up
The Sting 2
Stingray
Stop! or My Mom Will Shoot
Stop That Cab
Stuntwoman
Suburban Commando
Suffering Bastards
The Suitors
Summer Night with Greek Profile, Almond Eyes & Scent of Basil
Sunburn
Super Fuzz
Surf Nazis Must Die
Surf Ninjas
Survivors
Swashbuckler
The Tall Blond Man with One Black Shoe▲
Tall, Tan and Terrific
A Taxing Woman's Return▲
Teenage Mutant Ninja Turtles: The Movie
Teenage Mutant Ninja Turtles 2: The Secret of the Ooze
Teenage Mutant Ninja Turtles 3
Terminal Exposure
That Man from Rio
That Sinking Feeling▲
They Met in Bombay
The Thief Who Came to Dinner
Think Big
This Time I'll Make You Rich
Those Daring Young Men in Their Jaunty Jalopies
Those Fantastic Flying Fools
Those Magnificent Men in Their Flying Machines▲
Three Amigos
Three Fugitives
Three Kinds of Heat
The Three Musketeers▲
3 Ninjas
3 Ninjas Kick Back
3 Ninjas Knuckle Up
Thunder and Lightning
Thunder in the Pines
Thursday
Title Shot
Toga Party
Tom and Huck▲
Too Hot to Handle▲
Top Dog
Topkapi▲
Tough Guys
Treasure of the Moon Goddess
Trenchcoat
TripleCross
Trouble in Store
The Trouble with Spies
True Lies
12 Plus 1▲
Twin Dragons
Twins
Under the Hula Moon
Under the Rainbow
Up the Creek
Uphill All the Way
Uptown Saturday Night
Van Nuys Blvd.
Vice Academy
Vice Academy 2
Vice Academy 3
Viva Maria!
Wackiest Ship in the Army
We're No Angels
When the Clouds Roll By▲
Who Killed Mary What's 'Er Name?
The Wild and the Free
Wishman
World Gone Wild
Wrong Is Right
Year of the Comet
The Yum-Yum Girls

Comic Cops

see also *Disorganized Crime*

Big Trouble
Dragnet
Freebie & the Bean
K-9
Me, Myself, and Irene▲
The Naked Gun: From the Files of Police Squad▲
Naked Gun 33 1/3: The Final Insult
Naked Gun 2 1/2: The Smell of Fear
National Lampoon's Loaded Weapon 1
Police Academy
Police Academy 2: Their First Assignment
Police Academy 3: Back in Training
Police Academy 4: Citizens on Patrol
Police Academy 5: Assignment Miami Beach
Police Academy 6: City under Siege
Police Academy 7: Mission to Moscow
Rush Hour
Rush Hour 2
Turner and Hooch

Coming of Age

see also *Teen Angst*

A la Mode
A Nos Amours▲
The Abe Lincoln of Ninth Avenue
Across the Great Divide
The Affairs of Annabel
Ah, Wilderness!▲
Alan & Naomi
Alexandria...Why?
All Fall Down
All I Wanna Do
All Over Me▲
All the Right Moves
All Things Fair
Aloha Summer
Alpine Fire
Amarcord▲
American Boyfriends
American Graffiti▲
An American Rhapsody▲
An American Summer
Among the Cinders
... And the Earth Did Not Swallow Him
Angele▲
Angelo My Love▲
Anne of Green Gables▲
Anthony Adverse
Anywhere But Here
Aparajito▲
The Apprenticeship of Duddy Kravitz▲
Au Revoir les Enfants▲
An Awfully Big Adventure
Babe▲
Baby It's You▲
Back Door to Heaven▲
Battling Bunyon
Beautiful Thing▲
Beshkempir the Adopted Son
Big▲
The Big Bet
The Big Red One▲
Billy Bathgate
The Birch Interval
Blue Fin
Blue Jeans
The Blue Kite▲
The Blue Lagoon
Blue River
Blue Velvet▲
Boss' Son▲
The Boys in Company C
Boys Life
Breaking Away▲
Breaking Home Ties
Brighton Beach Memoirs
A Bronx Tale▲
The Buddha of Suburbia▲
Buddy's Song
Butterfly▲
By Way of the Stars
Calendar Girl
Can You Feel Me Dancing?
Can't Buy Me Love
Carnal Knowledge▲
Catherine Cookson's The Cinder Path
Catherine Cookson's The Dwelling Place
Catherine Cookson's The Glass Virgin
The Chicken Chronicles
China, My Sorrow
Christy
The Cider House Rules▲
Circle of Friends
City Boy▲
Civil War Diary
Class
Class of '44
The Claw
Closely Watched Trains▲
Clowning Around 2
Cocktail
Cold Sassy Tree▲
The Color of Money▲
Come and See▲
Come Undone
Coming Home
Coming Soon
Courage Mountain
Courtship▲
Crazy Moon
Cria▲
The Crossing
Crossing the Bridge
A Cry in the Wild▲
Cry of Battle

▲ = *rated three bones or higher*

Culpepper Cattle Co.
Dakota
Damien: Omen 2
Dancer, Texas—Pop. 81▸
David Copperfield
David Holzman's Diary▸
Dead Beat
Dead Poets Society▸
December
The Deer Hunter▸
Desert Bloom▸
The Devil's Playground▸
Diner▸
Dirty Dancing▸
Dogfight▸
Dragstrip Girl
D3: The Mighty Ducks
Dutch Girls
Eat Drink Man Woman▸
Edge of Seventeen
The Education of Little Tree▸
Edward Scissorhands▸
Ellen Foster
Emanon
Ernesto
Experience Preferred... But Not Essential
The Eyes of Youth
Eyes Right!
Family Prayers
Fandango
Fast Times at Ridgemont High▸
Father▸
Feelin' Screwy
Fellini Satyricon▸
Fiesta
The Fire in the Stone
First Affair
First Love
The First Time
The Flamingo Kid▸
For a Lost Soldier
For Love Alone
Forever
Forever Young
The 400 Blows▸
Foxes
Freedom Is Paradise▸
Freud Leaving Home
Friends Forever▸
A Friendship in Vienna
Gas Food Lodging▸
A Generation▸
Get Real
The Getting of Wisdom
Gidget
Ginger Snaps
Girl
A Girl of the Limberlost
Girlfight▸
Go Tell It on the Mountain
Going All the Way
The Gold & Glory
Goodbye Columbus▸
Goodbye, Miss 4th of July
Goodbye, My Lady
The Graduate▸
The Grass Harp
The Great Outdoors
The Great Santini▸
Gregory's Girl▸
Grown Ups
Hairspray▸
Hammers over the Anvil
Hangin' with the Homeboys▸
Happy Birthday, Gemini
Hard Choices▸
Hearts in Atlantis
Heathers▸
Heaven Help Us
A Hero Ain't Nothin' but a Sandwich
Higher Education
Hole in the Sky
Holy Matrimony
Homeboy
Homework
The Horse▸
The Horsemen
Hot Moves
The Hour of the Star▸
How I Learned to Love Women
Huck and the King of Hearts
The Human Comedy▸
Hurricane Streets
I Don't Want to Talk About It
I Know Why the Caged Bird Sings▸
I Love You, I Love You Not
I Vitelloni▸
If Looks Could Kill
Il Sorpasso
In Praise of Older Women
In the Custody of Strangers▸
Indian Paint
The Inheritors
Inventing the Abbotts
Invisible Circus
The Islander
Jacob Have I Loved
Jerry Maguire▸
Joe the King
Joey
Johnny Be Good
Jory
The Journey of Jared Price
The Journey of Natty Gann▸
Just Looking
The Karate Kid▸
The Karate Kid: Part 2
The Karate Kid: Part 3
Kicking and Screaming▸
King of the Gypsies
King of the Hill▸
Kings Row▸
Kipperbang
The Kitchen Toto▸
La Boum
La Symphonie Pastorale▸
Labyrinth▸
The Last Prostitute
Late Summer Blues
The Lawrenceville Stories
Le Grand Chemin▸
Le Sexe des Etoiles
The Learning Tree
Les Mistons▸
L'Homme Blesse▸
Liam
L.I.E.
Life 101
The Lion King▸
Little Ballerina
A Little Romance▸
Little Women▸
Little Women
The Littlest Viking
The Long Day Closes▸
The Lords of Flatbush
Lost Legacy: A Girl Called Hatter Fox
Love Film
Lover Girl
Lucas▸
Maid to Order
Malena
The Man from Snowy River
The Man in the Moon▸
A Man of Passion
The Man Without a Face
The Mango Tree
Martha and I▸
Matinee
Mean Streets▸
The Member of the Wedding▸
The Member of the Wedding
Men of Ireland
Metropolitan▸
Mickey
A Midnight Clear▸
Milk Money
Mirrors
Mischief
Monika
More American Graffiti
Mosby's Marauders
Murmur of the Heart▸
My American Cousin▸
My Apprenticeship▸
My Bodyguard▸
My Brilliant Career▸
My Girl
My Girl 2
My Life As a Dog▸
My Tutor
My Universities▸
Mystic Pizza▸
New Waterford Girl
Next Stop, Greenwich Village▸
Nicholas Nickleby▸
Nico and Dani
A Night in the Life of Jimmy Reardon
1969▸
No Regrets for Our Youth▸
No Secrets
No Time for Sergeants▸
Norman Loves Rose
The Nostradamus Kid
Now and Then
Odd Birds
Oddballs
Ode to Billy Joe
Oh, What a Night
Old Enough
One on One
Only the Brave
Oranges Are Not the Only Fruit
The Other Side of Sunday
Other Voices, Other Rooms
Out of the Blue▸
Outside Providence
The Outsiders
Over the Edge▸
Over the Summer
The Pallbearer
Palm Beach
Palookaville▸
The Paper Chase▸
Paradise
The Passing of Evil
Pather Panchali▸
Pauline at the Beach▸
P.C.U.
Peck's Bad Boy
Peppermint Soda▸
Peter Lundy and the Medicine Hat Stallion
A Place in the World▸
Platoon▸
Portrait of a Lady
Portrait of a Lady▸
The Power of One
The Prodigal
Promised Land▸
Quadrophenia▸
Racing with the Moon▸
Rambling Rose▸
Ramparts of Clay▸
The Rascals
The Razor's Edge▸
The Razor's Edge
A Real Young Girl
Red Dirt
The Red Fury
Red Kiss▸
Red Nights
The Reivers▸
Restless Spirits
Reunion▸
Ride with the Devil
Risky Business▸
The River▸
A River Runs Through It▸
The Road from Coorain
A Room with a View▸
Rudyard Kipling's The Jungle Book
Rumble Fish▸
A Rumor of Angels
The Run of the Country▸
Rushmore▸
St. Elmo's Fire
Samurai 1: Musashi Miyamoto▸
The Sandlot▸
Sands of Iwo Jima▸
Sarafina!▸
Savage Is Loose
Say Anything▸
Scent of a Woman▸
The Scent of Green Papaya▸
Season of Change
A Secret Space
Secrets
A Separate Peace
Set Me Free
Seven Minutes in Heaven
Shaking the Tree
Sharma & Beyond
She's Out of Control
Shipwrecked
Shout
Showgirls
Side Show
The Silence of Neto
The Silences of the Palace▸
Simon Birch
Sixteen
Skipped Parts
The Slingshot▸
Slums of Beverly Hills▸
Small Faces▸
Smooth Talk▸
Snow: The Movie
Soldier of Orange▸
A Soldier's Daughter Never Cries
Some Kind of Wonderful
Sons of Steel
Sounder▸
Sous Sol
SpaceCamp
Spanking the Monkey▸
Spy of Napoleon
Square Dance
Stacking
Star Wars▸
Star Wars: Episode 1—The Phantom Menace▸
Starlight Hotel
The Stripper
Stuckey's Last Stand
Studs Lonigan
Summer Affair
Summer Fantasy
Summer Holiday
Summer Interlude▸
Summer of '42▸
Summer Vacation: 1999
Summer's End
Sunnyside
Sweet 15
Swing Kids
The Sword in the Stone▸
Teenage Mutant Ninja Turtles 2: The Secret of the Ooze
Telling Lies in America
Tex
That Brennan Girl
That Naughty Girl
That Night
That Was Then...This Is Now
There Goes My Baby
36 Fillete▸
This Boy's Life▸
Those Glory, Glory Days
Thunder Alley
A Tiger's Tale
Time of the Gypsies▸
Time Stands Still▸
A Time to Remember
Toby Tyler▸
Tomboy & the Champ
Tonio Kroger
Top Gun
Totally F***ed Up
A Tree Grows in Brooklyn▸
Tumbleweeds
Twenty-One
Twist & Shout▸
Two Bits
Two Daughters▸
Unstrung Heroes
Vision Quest
Walking and Talking
Wanderers▸
West Beirut
Whatever
What's Eating Gilbert Grape▸
Where the Red Fern Grows: Part 2
Who Has Seen the Wind?
Who Shot Pat?
Who's That Knocking at My Door?▸
Why Shoot the Teacher▸
Wide Awake
Wild America▸
The Wild Child▸
Wild Reeds▸
Winner Takes All
The Wishing Ring▸
With Honors
Wonder Boys▸
Y Tu Mama Tambien
The Year My Voice Broke▸
The Yearling▸
The Yearling
The Young and the Guilty
The Young Graduates
Young Guns 2
Young Love, First Love
Young Sherlock Holmes
Young Tom Edison
Youngblood
You're a Big Boy Now▸
Zapped!

Communists & Communism

***see also** Red Scare; Russia/USSR*

Dark Blue World
The Seventh Dawn

Computers

***see also** Robots & Androids; Technology—Rampant*

Antitrust
The Computer Wore Tennis Shoes
Conceiving Ada
Cyberstalker
Dangerous Game
Dean Koontz's Black River
Dee Snider's Strangeland
Demon Seed▸
Desk Set▸
The Double O Kid
Electric Dreams
Entrapment
Every Mother's Worst Fear
Evilspeak
Fair Game
Hackers
Hard Drive
Homewrecker
The Honeymoon Machine
Hostile Intent
How to Make a Monster
The Human Factor
Interface
Johnny Mnemonic
Jumpin' Jack Flash
Jurassic Park▸
The Lawnmower Man
Lawnmower Man 2: Beyond Cyberspace
The Matrix▸
Menno's Mind
Mission: Impossible▸
The Net
New World Disorder
Pi
The Pirates of Silicon Valley
Playing Dangerous
Prime Risk
Resident Evil
The Scorpio Factor
Silicon Towers
Superman 3
Tin Man
Tom Clancy's Netforce
Twilight Man
Virtual Assassin
Virtual Desire
WarGames
Y2K
You've Got Mail

Concentration/ Internment Camps

***see also** Nazis & Other Paramilitary Slugs; POW/MIA*

Bent
The Boxer and Death▸
Come See the Paradise▸
The Devil's Arithmetic
Forced March
The Hiding Place
Holocaust▸
I Love You, I Love You Not
The Last Butterfly
Life Is Beautiful▸
Merry Christmas, Mr. Lawrence▸
One Day in the Life of Ivan Denisovich▸
Paradise Road
Playing for Time▸
Schindler's List▸
Seven Beauties▸
The Siege
Snow Falling on Cedars
Sophie's Choice▸
A Town Like Alice
Triumph of the Spirit▸
The Truce▸

Concert Films

***see also** Rock Stars on Film*

Clark & McCullough
Gimme Shelter
Jo Jo Dancer, Your Life Is Calling
John Cleese on How to Irritate People
The Last Waltz▸
Lenny▸
Mr. Mike's Mondo Video
Monster in a Box▸
Monterey Pop▸
National Lampoon's Class of '86
Punchline
Queens of Comedy
Search for Signs of Intelligent Life in the Universe▸
The Secret Policeman's Other Ball▸
Secret Policeman's Private Parts
Sex, Drugs, Rock & Roll: Eric Bogosian
Spalding Gray: Terrors of Pleasure
Stop Making Sense▸
U2: Rattle and Hum
Wisecracks▸
Woodstock▸
Year of the Horse
You Can't Take It with You▸
You So Crazy

Contemporary Musicals

***see also** Musicals*

Absolute Beginners
All That Jazz▸
The Apple
Blame It on the Night
Body Beat
Breakin'
Breakin' 2: Electric Boogaloo
Breakin' Through
Breaking Glass
A Chorus Line
Fame▸
The Josephine Baker Story▸
One from the Heart

Contemporary Noir

***see also** Film Noir*

After Dark, My Sweet▸
After Hours▸
After the Storm
Against All Odds
Albino Alligator
The American Friend▸
Angel Dust
Angel Heart
Barocco
Best Laid Plans
Betty Blue▸
The Big Easy▸
The Big Empty▸
Blade Runner▸
Blood Simple▸
Blue Velvet▸
Bodies, Rest & Motion
Bodily Harm
Body Double▸
Body Heat▸
Bring Me the Head of Alfredo Garcia
Bringing Out the Dead
Bulletproof Heart▸
Cafe Society
Cape Fear▸
Chinatown▸
Choose Me▸
City of Industry
Croupier▸
The Crude Oasis
Cutter's Way

Dance with a Stranger▲
Dark City
Deceiver
Detour
Devil in a Blue Dress▲
D.O.A.
Dogwatch
Dressed to Kill
The Driver
Experiment in Terror▲
Eyes of Laura Mars
Fatal Attraction▲
52 Pick-Up
First Degree
Flypaper
Following
Forever Mine
The Girl in a Swing
Goodbye, Lover
The Grifters▲
Guncrazy
Hammett
Hard Eight▲
The Hi-Lo Country
The Horseplayer
The Hot Spot
Husbands and Lovers
The Hustle
I Want You
Jigsaw
Kill Me Again
The Kill-Off
Killing Zoe
Kiss of Death
Kiss Tomorrow Goodbye
L.A. Confidential▲
The Last Seduction▲
Le Samouraï▲
Let the Devil Wear Black
The Limey▲
Live Flesh▲
The Locusts
The Long Goodbye▲
Love Walked In
The Manchurian Candidate▲
Manhunter▲
Marlowe
The Million Dollar Hotel
Mirage
Mulholland Falls
The Music of Chance
Narrow Margin
Night Moves▲
9 1/2 Weeks
No Way Out▲
Novocaine
One False Move▲
Palmetto
Payback
Performance▲
Place Vendome▲
Promised Land▲
The Public Eye▲
Pulp Fiction▲
Purple Noon▲
Red Rock West▲
Reservoir Dogs▲
The Rich Man's Wife
River of Grass
Romeo Is Bleeding
The Salton Sea
sex, lies and videotape▲
Shattered
The Silence of the Lambs▲
Simpatico
A Slight Case of Murder
So Close to Paradise
Something Wild
The Spanish Prisoner▲
Spare Me
Sticks
Stormy Monday
Taxi Driver▲
Tequila Sunrise
Things to Do in Denver When You're Dead▲
This World, Then the Fireworks
To Live & Die in L.A.
Track 29
Trouble in Mind▲
True Believer
True Confessions▲
Twilight▲
Two Days in the Valley▲
The Two Jakes
U-Turn
The Underneath▲
Union City
The Usual Suspects▲
Who'll Stop the Rain?▲
Wild at Heart▲
Wild Orchid
Wild Orchid 2: Two Shades of Blue
Wild Things

Cooking

see Edibles

Cops

see also Buddy Cops; Detectives; Future Cop; Historical Detectives; Loner Cops; Police Detectives; Private Eyes; Women Cops

Above Suspicion
Abraxas: Guardian of the Universe
Absence of the Good
Across 110th Street
Across the Line
Adrenalin: Fear the Rush
The Adventures of a Gnome Named Gnorm
Affliction▲
Against the Law
Alien Nation
Alone in the Neon Jungle
American Cop
American Justice
The Amsterdam Kill
Angel Eyes
The Animal
Animal Instincts
Apartment Complex
Assault on Precinct 13▲
At Gunpoint
Back in Action
Back in Business
Backlash
Backstreet Justice
B.A.D. Cats
Badge 373
Ballbuster
Band of the Hand
Bandits
Bang
Before Morning
Belfast Assassin
Bellamy
Beretta's Island
Best Kept Secrets
Best Seller▲
Beverly Hills Cop
Beverly Hills Cop 2
Beverly Hills Cop 3
Beyond Forgiveness
Big Chase
Big Combo▲
The Big Easy▲
The Big Heat▲
Big Momma's House
Big Score
The Big Slice
Bitter Sweet
Black and White▲
Black & White
Black Day Blue Night
Black Eliminator
The Black Marble▲
Black Mask
Black Rain
Blacklight
Blackout
Blade
Blade Boxer
Blind Faith
Blink
Blood for Blood
Blood on the Badge
Blood Relatives
Bloodfist 7: Manhunt
Bloodhounds
Blowback
Blown Away
Blue Desert▲
Blue Flame
The Blue Lamp▲
Blue Thunder
Blues Brothers 2000
Bodily Harm
The Bone Collector
Bopha!▲
The Boston Strangler
Brainscan
Brannigan
Brass
Breach of Trust
Breaking Point
Broken Badge▲
Bulletproof
Bullets or Ballots▲
Bunco
Busting
Cafe Society
Captive
Carmen, Baby
Caroline at Midnight
The Carpathian Eagle
Carpool
A Case of Deadly Force▲
The Caveman's Valentine
Cement
The Chase
Chiefs
China Moon
Chinatown Connection
The Chinatown Murders: Man against the Mob
Choice of Weapons
The Choirboys
Chungking Express▲
City Hall▲
City That Never Sleeps
Clayton County Line
Clockers▲
Cobra
Cold Blooded
Cold Front
Cold Light of Day
Cold Steel
Coldfire
Colors▲
Confessions of a Police Captain
Conflict of Interest
Coogan's Bluff▲
Cop
Cop and a Half
Cop-Out
Cops and Robbersons
Cornbread, Earl & Me
Cotton Comes to Harlem▲
Coup de Torchon▲
Cover Me
Cracker: Brotherly Love▲
Cracker: Men Should Weep
Cracker: To Be a Somebody
Crime Busters
Crime Story
The Crimson Rivers
The Crow
The Custodian
Danger Ahead
The Dark
Dark Before Dawn
Dark City
Dead Badge
Dead End
Dead Heart▲
Dead Heat
Dead to Rights
Deadly Breed
Deadly Conspiracy
Deadly Diamonds
Deadly Game
Deadly Hero▲
Deadly Sins
Deadly Surveillance
Death Shot
The Death Squad
Deceiver
Deceptions
Deep Cover
Deep Space
The Delicate Delinquent
Delta Heat
Demolition Man
The Designated Mourner
Detroit 9000
Devil in a Blue Dress▲
Devil's Angels
The Devil's Own▲
The Devil's Undead
Devlin
Distant Justice
Diva▲
Dogwatch
Dollman
Dollman vs Demonic Toys
Double Edge
Double Take
Double Trouble
Drop Zone
Drowning Mona
Drying Up the Streets
Dying Game
East Palace, West Palace
Electra Glide in Blue▲
Evil Has a Face
Ex-Cop
Exorcist 3: Legion
Extreme Justice
Extreme Prejudice
Extreme Vengeance
An Eye for an Eye
Eyes of Laura Mars
Eyewitness
Eyewitness to Murder
Fair Game
Fallen
Family of Cops
Family of Cops 2: Breach of Faith
Family of Cops 3
The Fast and the Furious
Fatal Chase
Fatal Error
Fatal Instinct
Feeling Minnesota
The Female Jungle
Fever
15 Minutes
Final Embrace
Final Equinox
Find the Lady
Firepower
Fireworks
The First Deadly Sin
First Degree
Flashpoint
Flatfoot
Flipping
The Formula
Fort Apache, the Bronx▲
Fortune Dane
Foul Play
Frame by Frame
Frame Up
Framed▲
The French Connection▲
French Connection 2▲
French Quarter Undercover
French Silk
Frequency
From Dusk Till Dawn 2: Texas Blood Money
Full Eclipse
Full Exposure: The Sex Tape Scandals
Future Cop
Future Force
Fuzz
Gambler's Choice
Gang in Blue
Gen-X Cops
Get On the Bus▲
The Glass Shield
The Glitter Dome
Glitz
Go▲
Go for It
Gone Are the Days
Goodbye, Lover
Gorky Park▲
The Guardian
Hands of a Stranger
The Happy Face Murders
Hard-Boiled
Hard Justice
Hard Rain
The Hard Truth
Hard Vice
Hardcase and Fist
Hate▲
Hawkeye
He Walked by Night▲
Hear No Evil
Heart of Dragon
Heaven's Heroes
Hellbound
Heroes in Blue
The Hidden▲
The Hidden 2
High & Low▲
High Crime
Highway Patrolman
Hollywood Vice Sqaud
Hologram Man
Homicide▲
Homicide: The Movie
The Hot Rock▲
Hot Stuff
Humanity
The Hunted Lady
I Take This Oath
The Ice House▲
Illegal in Blue
Illtown
In the Kingdom of the Blind the Man with One Eye Is King
Indecent Behavior
The Indian Runner
Indiscreet
The Informant▲
Innocent Blood
The Innocent Sleep
Inside Information
Interpol Connection
It Could Happen to You
It's the Rage
Jackie Brown▲
Jailbait
The January Man
Jennifer 8
Jet Li's The Enforcer
Jigsaw
John Carpenter's Ghosts of Mars
Johnny Skidmarks
Jungleground
Just Cause
K-911
K-9000
Kamikaze '89▲
Karate Cop
Keaton's Cop
Keeper of the City
Kidnapped
The Kill Reflex
Killer Condom
The Killer's Edge
The Killing Mind
The Killing Time
Killing Time
Kiss & Tell
Kiss of Death▲
Kiss or Kill
The Klansman
Knife in the Head
Kuffs
L.627▲
La Balance▲
L.A. Bounty
L.A. Confidential▲
L.A. Heat
La Scorta▲
L.A. Vice
L.A. Wars
Ladykiller
Laguna Heat
Laser Moon
Last Man Standing
The Last Marshal
The Last of the Finest
The Last Stop
The Laughing Policeman
Law and Disorder▲
Le Samouraï▲
Legacy of Lies
Les Miserables
Les Miserables▲
Les Voleurs▲
Lethal Obsession
Lethal Seduction
Lightblast
The Limbic Region
Lockdown
Lone Star Law Men
Love and Bullets
Love on the Run
Mad Dog and Glory▲
Mad Max▲
Madigan▲
Magic Hunter
Magnolia▲
Malarek
Man from Mallorca
A Man in Uniform
The Man Inside
Man on a String
The Man on the Roof
Manhunt
Mardi Gras for the Devil
Martial Law
Martial Law 2: Undercover
Martial Outlaw
Mask of Death
Matter of Trust
Maximum Force
Maximum Risk
Miami Beach Cops
Miami Blues
Miami Cops
Miami Vice
Midnight Ride
Midnight Witness
Mimic 2
Mind, Body & Soul
A Mind to Kill
Mind Twister
Mission of Justice
Mr. Inside, Mr. Outside
Mr. Reliable: A True Story
Mistrial
Mitchell
Model by Day
Money to Burn
Monolith
Moonshine Highway
Mortal Challenge
Motor Patrol
Moving Violations
Murder at 1600
The Murder of Stephen Lawrence▲
Murder Without Motive
Murdered Innocence
My Husband's Secret Life
Mystery Date
Nails
The Naked City▲
The Narrow Margin▲
Navajo Blues
The New Centurions
New Jack City
New Jersey Drive
New York Cop
New York Ripper
Next of Kin
Night Game
Night of the Cyclone
Night Partners
The Night Patrol
Night Patrol
Night Vision
Nightmare
Nightwatch
Ninja Vengeance
No Code of Conduct
No Escape, No Return
No Place to Hide
Off the Wall
The Offence▲
One Man Force
One Man Jury
One Night at McCool's
One Tough Cop
The Onion Field▲
Organized Crime & Triad Bureau
Othello▲
Out in Fifty
Outside the Law
The Painted Lady▲
Pair of Aces
Paper Bullets
Past Perfect
Past Tense
Pendulum
Phoenix
P.I. Private Investigations
Piece of the Action
Point of Impact
Police
Police Story
Portraits of a Killer
Post Mortem
Practical Magic
Prime Suspect▲
Prime Target
Prince of the City▲
Private Investigations
Probable Cause
Profile for Murder
Pronto
The Prophecy
The Proposal
Protector
Provoked
Prowler
Puppet on a Chain
A Pure Formality
Q & A

▲ = rated three bones or higher

The Quarry
Question of Honor
Rage and Honor 2: Hostile Takeover
Rainbow Drive
Random Hearts
Rapid Fire
Raw Nerve
Raw Target
The Razor: Sword of Justice
Reach the Rock
Recruits
Red Sun Rising
Renfrew of the Royal Mounted
The Replacement Killers
Replicant
Resurrection
Return to Macon County
Return to Mayberry
Ricochet ▲
The Right to Remain Silent
Ring of Death
Riot in the Streets
Rising Sun ▲
The Road
Rock House
Rogue Force
Roots of Evil
Route 9
Rumble in the Streets
The Runaway
The Rutherford County Line
Sands of Sacrifice
Santa Fe
The Satan Killer
Sawbones
Scanner Cop
Scanner Cop 2: Volkin's Revenge
Scanners: The Showdown
Scarred City
Sci-Fighters
Scream 3
Season for Assassins
Self-Defense
Sgt. Kabukiman N.Y.P.D.
Serial Killer
Shadow Force
Shadow of a Scream
Shadowhunter
Shameless
Sharon's Secret
Shoot It Black, Shoot It Blue
Shoot to Kill
Shootfighter 2: Kill or Be Killed!
Short Time ▲
The Shot
Sirens
Siringo
Sketch Artist
Sketch Artist 2: Hands That See
Skull: A Night of Terror
Slipstream
Slow Burn
A Small Killing
Smokey & the Judge
Snake Eyes
Snapdragon
Soggy Bottom U.S.A.
Solar Force
Son of the Pink Panther
Soul Patrol
South Seas Massacre
Speed 2: Cruise Control
Speedtrap
The Spree
Stamp of a Killer
Stand Off
Steele's Law
The Stendahl Syndrome
Stephano Quantestorie
The Stone Killer
Stonewall ▲
Stop! or My Mom Will Shoot
Strange Days ▲
Stranger by Night
Street Asylum
Street Crimes
Street War
Strike Force
Strip Search
The Substitute 4: Failure is Not an Option
Super Force
Super Fuzz
Supercop
Supercop 2
Supervixens
Suspicious Agenda
Sweet Trash
Sword of Honor
T-Force
The Take
Taking the Heat
Tar
The Taxman
Terminal Justice: Cybertech P.D.
Terror Stalks the Class Reunion
Theodore Rex
They Only Kill Their Masters
The Thomas Crown Affair ▲
Three Strikes
Tightrope ▲
Till Death Do Us Part
A Time to Die
Timecop
To Protect and Serve
Too Fast, Too Young
Top of the Heap
Total Recall 2070: Machine Dreams
Touch of Evil ▲
Traces of Red
Traffic ▲
Trancers
Trancers 2: The Return of Jack Deth
Trancers 3: Deth Lives
Trancers 4: Jack of Swords
Trancers 5: Sudden Deth
True Romance
Truth or Consequences, N.M.
Tunnel Vision
Twin Sisters
Twisted Justice
Two Days in the Valley ▲
Two Small Bodies
Ultraviolet
Under Investigation
Under Oath
Undercover
Undercover Cop
The Underground
Underground Terror
Unforgettable
Union Station
The Untold Story
Urban Crossfire
Vampire Cop
Vampire in Brooklyn
Vengeance
Vice Academy
Vice Academy 2
Vice Academy 3
Virtuosity
Walker: Texas Ranger: One Riot, One Ranger
The Warning
The Wharf Rat
When Danger Follows You Home
Where's the Money, Noreen?
Whispers of White
White Cargo
The White Lioness
The Wild Pair
Witchcraft 6: The Devil's Mistress
The Young Americans
Youth of the Beast
Zipperface

Corporate Shenanigans

***see also** Advertising; Salespeople*

The Abduction of Allison Tate
Ablaze
Acceptable Risks
The Alarmist
The Alchemists
All in a Night's Work
All My Sons ▲
And Nothing But the Truth
Antitrust
Any Wednesday
The Apartment ▲
April Fools
As Young As You Feel ▲
Ask Any Girl
The Associate
Avalanche
Baby Geniuses
Bad Company
The Bad Sleep Well ▲
Barbarians at the Gate ▲
BASEketball
The Battle of the Sexes ▲
Beggars in Ermine
Behind Office Doors
The Best of Everything ▲
The Bible and Gun Club
Big Business
Big Business Girl
The Big One
Big Trees ▲
The Bikini Car Wash Company
The Bikini Car Wash Company 2
Blood Red
Body & Soul ▲
Body Language
Boiler Room ▲
Bombshell
Boom Town
Boomerang
Boys Will Be Boys
Burning Daylight
The Business of Strangers
Buy & Cell
The Capture of Bigfoot
The Carpetbaggers
Cash McCall
Catherine & Co.
Chairman of the Board
Changing Lanes ▲
The China Syndrome ▲
China White
C.H.O.M.P.S.
Circle of Power
A Civil Action
Class of Nuke 'Em High 2: Subhumanoid Meltdown
Clockwatchers
The Closet
The Coca-Cola Kid ▲
The Colombian Connection
The Colony
Consuming Passions
Corporate Affairs
The Corporate Ladder
The Corporation
Crime of Honor
The Crime of Monsieur Lange ▲
Cyborg 2
Dark River: A Father's Revenge
The Daydreamer
Deadly Business ▲
Deadly Conspiracy
Dealers
Death Chase
Death Collector
Death Machine
The Devil & Miss Jones ▲
The Devil's Advocate
Devil's Crude
Disclosure
Dr. Dolittle
Dodsworth ▲
Double Play
Dragonfight
Dutch Treat
Ebbtide
The Efficiency Expert
Empire Records
The Empty Beach
End of the Line
Erin Brockovich ▲
Escape: Human Cargo ▲
Eternity
Executive Suite ▲
Fatal Confinement
Fatal Skies
Feel the Motion
Fierce Creatures
Fire Down Below
Firetrap
First Degree
The Flintstones
FM
For Love or Money
Ford: The Man & the Machine
Forest Warrior
Freaked
Frozen Assets
Gas
Gas Pump Girls
Glengarry Glen Ross ▲
Good Burger
Good Neighbor Sam ▲
Goodfellas ▲
Gorgeous
Gremlins 2: The New Batch ▲
Gung Ho
Hackers
Haiku Tunnel
Halloween 3: Season of the Witch
Hamlet ▲
Happy Hour
The Harder They Come
Head Office
Her Husband's Affairs
Herbie Rides Again
His Girl Friday ▲
Hold the Dream
Home Town Story
Hot Chocolate
How the West Was Fun
How to Get Ahead in Advertising ▲
How to Succeed in Business without Really Trying ▲
The Hucksters ▲
The Hudsucker Proxy ▲
I Love Trouble
If I Were Rich
In the Company of Men
Indio 2: The Revolt
The Insider ▲
Ivory Tower
Jack and the Beanstalk: The Real Story
Joe Somebody
John Grisham's The Rainmaker
Johnny Mnemonic
Journey to Spirit Island
Kids in the Hall: Brain Candy
A Kiss Before Dying
La Truite ▲
Ladies Who Do
Land of Promise
The Last Hour
The Late Shift
The Lavender Hill Mob ▲
Lawnmower Man 2: Beyond Cyberspace
Le Bonheur Est Dans le Pre
Legal Deceit
Let the Devil Wear Black
Letter to My Killer
Life Stinks
Limit Up
Little Bigfoot
Little Giant
Lloyds of London ▲
Local Hero ▲
Love or Money?
Ma and Pa Kettle at Waikiki
Major League
Mama, There's a Man in Your Bed ▲
The Man in the Gray Flannel Suit
The Man in the White Suit ▲
The Man Inside
Married to It
A Matter of WHO
Meet Joe Black
Megaville
Millions
Miss Grant Takes Richmond
Mr. Accident
Mo' Money
Monkey Hustle
Monsters, Inc. ▲
Moon 44
Morals for Women
Naked Gun 2 1/2: The Smell of Fear
Network ▲
Never 2 Big
New Rose Hotel
The Night They Saved Christmas
9 to 5
No Room to Run
No Time to Die
Noble House
Nowhere to Run
Office Killer
Office Space
One, Two, Three ▲
Open Season
Other People's Money
The Other Side of Midnight
Out Cold
Outland
Overdrawn at the Memory Bank
The Pajama Game ▲
The Paper ▲
Parrish
Patterns ▲
Perfume
The Pirates of Silicon Valley
Playback
The Player ▲
Pootie Tang
Power
Primal Scream
The Prime Gig
The Prince
Private Parts
Private Wars
A Public Affair
P.U.N.K.S.
Putney Swope ▲
The Queen of Mean
Quicksand: No Escape
Race the Sun
Rancid Aluminium
Ravenhawk
The Reluctant Agent
Return Fire
Richie Rich
Rising Sun ▲
RoboCop ▲
RoboCop 2
RoboCop 3
Roger & Me ▲
Rogue Trader
Rollover
Sabrina
Santa with Muscles
Scrooged
The Secret of My Success
The Secretary
Secretary
Sensations of 1945
Shadow of China ▲
The Shawshank Redemption ▲
Shining Star
A Shock to the System ▲
Silicon Towers
The Silver Horde
The Simple Life of Noah Dearborn
Sins
The 6th Day
Ski Bum
Skyscraper Souls ▲
Smilla's Sense of Snow
Solid Gold Cadillac ▲
The Spanish Prisoner ▲
Stand-In ▲
Stormy Monday
The Story of O, Part 2
Strange Bedfellows
Strange Brew
Swimming with Sharks ▲
Switching Channels
Synapse
Taffin
Take This Job & Shove It
A Taxing Woman ▲
The Temp
They All Kissed the Bride
They Drive by Night ▲
3 Ninjas Knuckle Up
Tiger Heart
Tin Men
Tommy Boy
Topaze ▲
The Toxic Avenger, Part 3: The Last Temptation of Toxie
Toys
Trading Places
Tucker: The Man and His Dream ▲
Undercurrent
Upper Crust
Utilities
Vendetta
Virus
The Void
Vortex
Wall Street ▲
Wall Street Cowboy
Washington Affair
The Way We Live Now
Weapons of Mass Distraction
Weekend at Bernie's
Weekend at Bernie's 2
The Wheeler Dealers ▲
Which Way Is Up?
White Mile
Who's Who
Wolf
A Woman's World ▲
Working Girl ▲
The World Gone Mad
The Wrong Woman
You've Got Mail

Courtroom Drama

***see** Order in the Court*

Creepy Houses

An American Werewolf in Paris
The Amityville Horror
Amityville 2: The Possession
Amityville 3: The Demon
Amityville 4: The Evil Escapes
The Amityville Curse
Amityville 1992: It's About Time
Angel of the Night
The Bat Whispers
Believe
Beyond Darkness
Beyond Evil
The Black Castle
The Black Cat
Black Cat
Blondie Has Trouble
Blood Island
Blood Legacy
Blue Blood
Bones
Burnt Offerings
Candles at Nine
Carnage
Casper ▲
Castle Freak
Castle in the Desert
Castle of Blood
Castle of the Living Dead
The Cat and the Canary
Celine and Julie Go Boating
Cellar Dweller
The Changeling
Chasing Sleep
The Colony
Contagion
The Craft
Crazed
Cthulhu Mansion
Demon Seed ▲
Demon Wind
Die Sister, Die!
Dolls
Don't Be Afraid of the Dark
The Doorway
Dream Demon
Dream House
Endless Night
The Evictors
The Evil
Evil Laugh
Evil Toons
The Fall of the House of Usher
The Fall of the House of Usher ▲
Fatally Yours
Fear in the Night ▲
Flowers in the Attic
Forever: A Ghost of a Love Story
Francis in the Haunted House
Fright House
Fright Night

▲ = rated three bones or higher

Funnyman
The Ghastly Ones
The Ghost and Mr. Chicken
The Ghost Breakers▲
Girls School Screamers
The Glass House
Goblin
Great Expectations
Halloween: Resurrection
Haunted
The Haunting▲
The Haunting
The Haunting of Hell House
House▲
House 2: The Second Story
House 4: Home Deadly Home
House of Mystery
The House of Secrets
House of the Dead
House of the Living Dead
House of the Long Shadows
House of the Rising Sun
The House of the Seven Gables
The House of Usher
House on Haunted Hill
The House on Tombstone Hill
The House that Bled to Death
The House that Dripped Blood
The House that Vanished
House Where Evil Dwells
The Innocents▲
Knocking on Death's Door
La Chute de la Maison Usher▲
The Legend of Hell House▲
Malice
The Mephisto Waltz▲
Monsters Crash the Pajama Party
Mother's Day
Mouse Hunt▲
Munster, Go Home!
Murder Mansion
The Nesting
Next of Kin
Night Nurse
Night of the Demons 2
Office Killer
The Old Dark House▲
The Others▲
Panic Room
Paperhouse▲
Paranoiac
The People under the Stairs
The Perverse Countess
The Phantom
Psycho▲
Psycho
Psycho 2
Psycho 3
Psycho 4: The Beginning
Rest in Pieces
Revenge in the House of Usher
The Rocky Horror Picture Show▲
The St. Francisville Experiment
Salem's Lot
Scary Movie 2
The Screaming Skull
Seven Days to Live
The Shining
Shock
Silent Scream
Sister, Sister
Smart House
Spectre
Spirit Lost
Spookies
Stephen King's Rose Red
Stormswept
A Strange and Deadly Occurrence
Superstition
Tangled Destinies
Teenage Exorcist
Terror in the Haunted House
Terror Tract
Things 2
13 Ghosts
Three Cases of Murder▲
Treasure of Fear

The Uninvited▲
Visions of Evil
Warlock 3: The End of Innocence
Web of the Spider
What a Carve-Up!
Who Killed Doc Robbin?
Witchouse

Crime & Criminals

***see** Crime Drama; Crime Sprees; Crimes of Passion; Disorganized Crime; Frame-Ups; Fugitives; Gangs; Heists; Hit Men/Women; Organized Crime; Scams, Stings & Cons; Serial Killers; Smuggler's Blues; True Crime; Urban Drama; Vigilantes*

Crime Drama

***see also** Drama*

The Abduction of Allison Tate
The Abduction of Kari Swenson
Against the Law
Al Capone▲
Albino Alligator
Alibi
American Me▲
Angels with Dirty Faces▲
Another Day in Paradise
Another Man's Poison
Assault on Precinct 13▲
At Close Range▲
Baby Face Nelson
Backlash
Bad Boys▲
Bad Lieutenant▲
Bandits
Belly
Best Laid Plans
A Better Way to Die
Billionaire Boys Club
Billy Bathgate
Bitter Sweet
The Black Legion▲
Black Rain
Blackrock
Blink
Blood & Wine
Blood, Guts, Bullets and Octane
Blood In ... Blood Out: Bound by Honor
Blood Money
Blood Vows: The Story of a Mafia Wife
Blue Ridge Fall
Body Count
Bodywork
Boiling Point
Bonanno: A Godfather's Story
Bonnie's Kids
Born to Run
A Bronx Tale▲
A Brooklyn State of Mind
Brother
Brother▲
Bugsy▲
B.U.S.T.E.D.
Bye-Bye
Capone
Carbon Copy
Casino▲
Cement
Children of Fury
Cop Land▲
Crime and Punishment in Suburbia
Dad Savage
Dead Presidents
The Deliberate Stranger▲
Detour
Dilemma
Dillinger▲
Dillinger
Dillinger and Capone
Doctor Chance
Donnie Brasco▲
Dostoevsky's Crime and Punishment

Double Edge
Element of Doubt
Entrapment
Essex Boys
Fallen Angels
Family of Cops 2: Breach of Faith
Family of Cops 3
15 Minutes
Final Appeal
Fingers▲
Flypaper
For Which He Stands
Force of Evil▲
Foreign Land
Four Days
"G" Men▲
Gang Busters
Gang Related
Genealogies of a Crime
The General▲
A Gentleman After Dark
Get Carter▲
Get Carter
Ghost Dog: The Way of the Samurai
Gloria
The Godfather▲
The Godfather 1902-1959: The Complete Epic▲
The Godfather, Part 2▲
The Godfather, Part 3▲
Gone in 60 Seconds
Goodfellas▲
Gunshy▲
Heat▲
High & Low▲
The Highway Man
Honor Thy Father
Honor Thy Father and Mother: The True Story of the Menendez Brothers
The Hoodlum
Hoodlum
I Met a Murderer
I Went Down▲
Illtown
In Cold Blood▲
In Cold Blood
In the Line of Duty: A Cop for the Killing
In the Line of Duty: Ambush in Waco
In the Line of Duty: The FBI Murders▲
In Too Deep
Incognito
Inferno
The Innocent Sleep
Internal Affairs
Jackie Brown▲
Judas Kiss
Juice
Kalifornia
Kansas City▲
Key Largo▲
Kidnap Syndicate
The Killers▲
The Killing of a Chinese Bookie
Killing Zoe
The King of the Roaring '20s: The Story of Arnold Rothstein
Kiss or Kill
Kiss the Girls
The Krays▲
Lansky
The Last Don
The Last Don 2
Last Man Standing
Le Samourai▲
The Life Before This
The Limey▲
Little Caesar▲
Little Odessa
The Long Good Friday▲
The Lost Capone▲
The Lost Man
Love to Kill
Lucky Luciano
M▲
Mafia Princess
Malevolence
The Maltese Falcon▲
Mam'zelle Pigalle
Man from Mallorca
Mean Streets▲

Memento▲
Men of Means
Men of Respect
Menace II Society▲
Midnight Murders
Miller's Crossing▲
Mobsters
Money Kings
Montana
Monument Ave.
Murder in New Hampshire: The Pamela Smart Story
Naked City: Justice with a Bullet
Natural Born Killers
New Blood
New Jack City
Night Falls on Manhattan▲
The Night Heaven Fell
No Alibi
No Tomorrow
Normal Life
Once Upon a Time in America▲
One False Move▲
One of Her Own
One Tough Cop
Out of Sight▲
The Outfit
Outside Ozona
The Painted Lady▲
Pale Saints
The Palermo Connection
Palmetto
Paper Bullets
Parisian Love
Party Girl▲
Payback
Persons Unknown
Phantom Lady▲
Phoenix
Pigalle
Playing God
The Pope of Greenwich Village
Post Mortem
The Prince
Prince of Poisoners: The Life and Crimes of William Palmer
Public Enemy▲
Pulp Fiction▲
Purple Noon▲
Pusher
Q & A
Railroaded
Ratas, Ratones, Rateros
Raven's Ridge
Reindeer Games
Reservoir Dogs▲
Road Ends
The Roaring Twenties▲
Romeo Must Die
Row Your Boat
A Scandal in Paris
Scarface▲
Scarface Mob
The Score
Seven▲
Sexy Beast▲
Shoot to Kill▲
Showdown
The Sicilian Connection
A Simple Plan▲
Six Ways to Sunday
Smalltime
Soft Deceit
Sonatine▲
Spanish Judges
The Spree
State of Grace▲
Straight out of Compton
Stray Bullet
Street Gun
Sworn Enemies
They Made Me a Fugitive
Thick as Thieves
Things to Do in Denver When You're Dead▲
Third World Cop
The Thomas Crown Affair▲
Tight Spot▲
Tom Clancy's Netforce
Trojan Eddie▲
True Friends
Turn It Up
The Underneath▲
The Untouchables▲

Way of the Gun
West New York
Wetbacks
When the Sky Falls
Without Evidence
Witness to the Mob
The Wounds
Wozzeck
The Yards
The Young Americans

Crime Sprees

***see also** Fugitives; Lovers on the Lam*

America's Deadliest Home Video
Baise Moi
Bonnie & Clyde▲
Border Radio
The Boys Next Door
Butterfly Kiss
Copkillers
Crackers
Enemy Gold
Explosion
Fatal Bond
15 Minutes
Flash & Firecat
Heat▲
High Rolling in a Hot Corvette
Idiot Box
In Cold Blood
Jessi's Girls
Lewis and Clark and George
Love and a .45
Marshal Law
Messidor
Murder One
Naked Youth
Natural Born Killers
Normal Life
The One
One Way Out
Public Enemies
Rampage
Road Kill USA
Set It Off
She Came on the Bus
Shopping
Steelyard Blues
Sworn Enemies
That Sinking Feeling▲
Thieves Like Us▲
The Tie That Binds
Too Fast, Too Young
Twin Town
Virtuosity
When Brendan Met Trudy▲
The Whole Town's Talking▲
Why Does Herr R. Run Amok?
The Wrong Road

Crimes of Passion

The Amy Fisher Story
Backfire
Bad Boy Bubby
Being at Home with Claude
The Big Clock▲
Bizarre
Blood Vows: The Story of a Mafia Wife
The Blue Dahlia▲
Born to Kill▲
Casque d'Or▲
Casualties of Love: The "Long Island Lolita" Story
China Moon
Concealed Weapon
Crime of Passion
The Crucible▲
A Dark Adapted Eye▲
Deadbolt
Deception▲
Dupont Lajoie
Fatal Attraction▲
For Your Love Only
The Gingerbread Man
The Girl
Homicidal Impulse
I Love You to Death
Intimate Relations
Jade
The Last Dance
Lethal Lolita—Amy Fisher: My Story

Love and Hate: A Marriage Made in Hell
The Love Flower
Make Haste to Live
The Man in the Attic
The Mask of Diijon
Men Are Not Gods
Murder in New Hampshire: The Pamela Smart Story
Murder Rap
Niagara
Passion
The People vs. Jean Harris▲
The Preppie Murder
Roadhouse Girl
Secret Beyond the Door
Sex Crimes
Sharon's Secret
The Shooting Party
Single White Female
This World, Then the Fireworks
To Die For▲
Tomorrow Never Comes
Victim of Beauty
The Walls of Malapaga
Woman in the Window▲
The Worldly Madonna
Wozzeck

Criminally Insane

***see also** Crime Sprees; Sanity Check; Torn in Two (or More)*

Unbreakable

Crop Dusters

... And the Earth Did Not Swallow Him
Animal Farm
Balloon Farm
Bitter Harvest▲
Blessing
Bloodsuckers from Outer Space
Boy Takes Girl
The Bridges of Madison County▲
Broken Harvest
Buffalo Jump▲
The Cabin in the Cotton
Captain Boycott
The Castaway Cowboy
Chicken Run▲
The Cider House Rules▲
City Girl
Clodhopper
Cold Comfort Farm
Cold Comfort Farm▲
Country▲
Country Life
The Curse
Curse of the Starving Class
Dark Before Dawn
Days of Heaven▲
Deadly Stranger
December Bride
Demon Wind
Desire Under the Elms
The Devil & Daniel Webster▲
Doc Hollywood
Dog Day
Earth▲
Earthworm Tractors
The Echo of Thunder
Egg and I▲
Eli Eli
Far from the Madding Crowd▲
The Farmer Takes a Wife
The Farmer's Other Daughter
The Field▲
The General Line▲
Giant▲
God's Little Acre▲
The Good Old Boys
The Grapes of Wrath▲
The Green Promise
Harvest▲
Harvest
Harvest of Fire
Horton Foote's Alone
In the Winter Dark
The Inheritors
Jean de Florette▲

The Kettles in the Ozarks
Kings in Grass Castles
The Land Girls
Little John
Ma and Pa Kettle at Home
The Mating Game▲
Mifune
The Milagro Beanfield War▲
Missouri Traveler▲
Morning Glory
My Antonia
Northern Lights▲
Nowhere to Run
Oklahoma Bound
Our Daily Bread▲
Pelle the Conqueror▲
Places in the Heart▲
The Proposition
The Purchase Price
Rachel and the Stranger▲
Rage
Ride the Wild Fields
The River
The Road from Coorain
Rock-a-Doodle
Ruggles of Red Gap▲
Sarah, Plain and Tall: Skylark
Sarah, Plain and Tall: Winter's End▲
Signs
Sommersby
Son-in-Law
Sounder▲
The Southerner▲
Stacking
The Stars Fell on Henrietta
Steal Big, Steal Little
The Stone Boy▲
The Story of Xinghua
Summer of the Monkeys
Sunday Too Far Away▲
The Sundowners▲
Sunrise▲
This Is My Father
A Thousand Acres
Tomboy & the Champ
The Tree of Wooden Clogs▲
Under the Sun
Vacas
The Well
Will It Snow for Christmas?
Wisdom
The Yearling
The Young Pioneers

Cuba

***see also** Red Scare*
Assault of the Rebel Girls
Before Night Falls▲
Company Man
Cuba▲
Dance with Me
Death of a Bureaucrat▲
A Few Good Men▲
Fidel▲
For Love or Country: The Arturo Sandoval Story
The Godfather, Part 2▲
Guantanamera▲
Havana
Key Largo▲
Lansky
The Last Supper▲
Letters from the Park▲
Memories of Underdevelopment
The Old Man and the Sea▲
The Old Man and the Sea
Original Sin
A Paradise Under the Stars
The Perez Family
Plato's Run
Rough Riders
Ruby
Scarface▲
Strawberry and Chocolate▲
Tamango
Thirteen Days▲
Up to a Certain Point

Cults

***see also** Occult; Satanism*
Bad Dreams
The Believers
Beware! Children at Play
Blinded by the Light
Blood Clan
Bloodbath
Burial of the Rats
Children of the Corn 2: The Final Sacrifice
Cobra Woman
Cult of the Cobra
The Dark Secret of Harvest Home
Deadly Blessing
Death of an Angel
The Deceivers
The Devil's Prey
Divided by Hate
Fatal Passion
Force: Five
Forever Evil
The Guyana Tragedy: The Story of Jim Jones
Helter Skelter
Helter Skelter Murders
Holy Smoke
The House on Todville Road
In the Line of Duty: Ambush in Waco
Isaac Asimov's Nightfall
The Lightning Incident
Lord of Illusions
The Mephisto Waltz▲
Mind, Body & Soul
Mindstorm
Next One
The Night God Screamed
Night of the Death Cult
Putney Swope▲
The Pyx▲
Raging Angels
The Reincarnate
Rest in Pieces
Revenge
Sabaka
Safe▲
Servants of Twilight
Shock 'Em Dead
The Snake Hunter Strangler
The Snake People
The Spellbinder
Split Image▲
Steps from Hell
Thou Shalt Not Kill...Except
Ticket to Heaven▲
Treasure of the Four Crowns
Withnail and I▲

Culture Clash

An American Rhapsody▲
At Play in the Fields of the Lord▲
Babe: Pig in the City
The Baby Dance▲
The Beverly Hillbillies
Black Robe▲
The Brother from Another Planet▲
Brothers in Trouble
Cabaret▲
Carla's Song
Catfish in Black Bean Sauce
Chutney Popcorn
City of Joy
The Comfort of Strangers▲
Coneheads
Conrack▲
crazy/beautiful
Crocodile Dundee in Los Angeles
Dead Heart▲
Deliverance▲
Down in the Delta▲
East Is East▲
The Emerald Forest▲
Encino Man
The Europeans▲
For Richer or Poorer
George of the Jungle▲
Gorillas in the Mist▲
Greystoke: The Legend of Tarzan, Lord of the Apes
Heart of Light
Heat and Dust▲
Holy Man
Hotel Colonial
House of Angels
Just Visiting
Lawrence of Arabia▲
Leningrad Cowboys Go America
The Lost Child
Meet the Parents▲
The Mission▲
Mississippi Masala▲
Mister Johnson▲
Mixing Nia
Moonlighting▲
Moscow on the Hudson▲
The Nephew
A Passage to India▲
Pizzicata
Quigley Down Under
Rescue from Gilligan's Island
Rodgers & Hammerstein's South Pacific
Rush Hour
Shadow Magic
Shanghai Noon
The Sheltering Sky▲
Shogun▲
Snow Dogs
Someone Else's America▲
Songcatcher▲
South Pacific▲
Splash
Starman▲
Swept from the Sea
Thunderheart▲
Tokyo Cowboy
West Is West
Witness▲
Zorba the Greek▲

Custody Battles

***see also** Divorce; Order in the Court; Single Parents*
Changing Lanes▲

Cuttin' Heads

Abbott and Costello in Hollywood
The Barber Shop▲
The Beautician and the Beast
The Big Tease
Black Shampoo
Blow Dry
Born to Win
Claire Dolan
The Crying Game▲
Demon Barber of Fleet Street
Earth Girls Are Easy
Educating Rita▲
An Everlasting Piece
The French Touch
Frolics on Ice
The Hairdresser's Husband
Hairspray▲
Joe's Bed-Stuy Barbershop: We Cut Heads
The Man Who Wasn't There▲
Mississippi Burning▲
Poetic Justice
Shampoo
Spotlight Scandals
Steel Magnolias▲
Stigmata
Sweeney Todd: The Demon Barber of Fleet Street
Venus Beauty Institute

Cyberpunk

Arcade
Blade Runner▲
The Crow 2: City of Angels
Cyborg
Cyborg 2
Cyborg Cop
Cyborg Soldier
Demolition Man
Escape from L.A.
Escape from New York
The Fifth Element
Freejack
Hackers
Johnny Mnemonic
The Lawnmower Man
Lawnmower Man 2: Beyond Cyberspace
Mad Max▲
Mad Max: Beyond Thunderdome
Megaville
Nemesis
Overdrawn at the Memory Bank
The Road Warrior▲
RoboCop▲
RoboCop 2
RoboCop 3
Tank Girl
TekWar
The Terminator▲
Terminator 2: Judgment Day▲
Tetsuo: The Iron Man
Tetsuo 2: Body Hammer
Total Recall▲
Tron
Universal Soldier
Universal Soldier 2: Brothers in Arms
Universal Soldier 3: Unfinished Business
Universal Soldier: The Return
Virtual Combat
Virtuosity
Webmaster

Dads

***see also** Bad Dads; Moms; Monster Moms; Parenthood*
Address Unknown
The Adventures of Pinocchio
Alice et Martin
All My Sons▲
American Heart▲
April Fool
Armageddon
Artemisia
Author! Author!
Autumn Marathon
Bandits
The Baron and the Kid
Beat Girl
The Bed You Sleep In
Behind Prison Walls
Between Men
Beyond Obsession
Big Daddy
A Bill of Divorcement
Billy Elliot▲
Billy Galvin
Billy Madison
The Birdcage▲
Black Eyes
Bloodfist 4: Die Trying
Bloodfist 8: Hard Way Out
Blue Fin
Boiler Room▲
Bonjour Tristesse▲
Boomerang
Bopha!▲
Boss' Son▲
The Brady Bunch Movie▲
Broken Angel
A Bronx Tale▲
The Buddha of Suburbia▲
Butterfly
Bye Bye, Love
Cal▲
Call of the Forest
The Capture of Grizzly Adams
Carbon Copy
Carousel▲
Carpool
Casanova Brown
Casper▲
Catherine Cookson's The Glass Virgin
Celine and Julie Go Boating
The Champ▲
The Champ
Chasing Destiny
Chasing the Deer
Class Action▲
The Climb
Clown
Cody
Cold Comfort
The Color of Paradise
Come and Get It▲
Common Ground
Complex World
Cookie
A Cool, Dry Place
Cop-Out
Corky Romano
The Courtship of Eddie's Father▲
crazy/beautiful
Crush
A Cry from the Mountain
Cry, the Beloved Country▲
Da
Dad
Daddy Nostalgia▲
The Dance Goes On
Daughter of Don Q
David
Dead to Rights
Deadlocked
The Death of Richie
Demonstrator
Desert Blue
Diamonds
Distant Thunder
Django Strikes Again
Domestic Disturbance
Donkey Skin▲
Donovan's Reef▲
A Dream of Kings▲
Dreaming of Rita
Drifting Weeds▲
Duets
East and West▲
Eat Drink Man Woman▲
Eden Valley▲
Elisa, Vida Mia
The Emerald Forest▲
The Enemy
Escape from Atlantis
Everybody's Famous!
Everybody's Fine
Eyes of a Witness
Eyes of an Angel
Family Tree
The Fantasticks
Fast Getaway 2
Fatal Justice
Father
Father and Scout
Father Figure
Father of the Bride▲
Father Was a Fullback
Fathers and Sons
Father's Day
A Father's Revenge
The Favorite Son▲
Fear
Fingers▲
Five Easy Pieces▲
Floating
For Richer, for Poorer
Force on Thunder Mountain
Fourth Wish
Free Willy 3: The Rescue
Freedom Is Paradise▲
Freedom Song▲
Frequency
Friends & Lovers
Gepetto
Ghost Dad
The Golden Bowl▲
The Golden Bowl
A Goofy Movie
Green Eyes▲
The Green Promise
Grizzly Falls
Gunman's Walk
Harry & Son
Heaven Tonight
Hidden Guns▲
Hidden in America
High & Low▲
High Command
Hobson's Choice▲
Hobson's Choice
A Hole in the Head
Holiday in Mexico
Home from the Hill▲
Home Is Where the Hart Is
Honey, We Shrunk Ourselves
The Horse▲
The Horse in the Gray Flannel Suit
The Horsemen
House Arrest
A House Divided
A House without a Christmas Tree
Hud▲
I Am Sam
I Live with Me Dad
I Ought to Be in Pictures
I Was Born But...▲
Il Grido
I'll Do Anything
I'm Not Rappaport
Imaginary Crimes▲
In His Father's Shoes
In the Gloaming▲
In the Name of the Father▲
Indiana Jones and the Last Crusade▲
Invisible Dad
It's a Date
Jack Frost
Jack the Bear
Jet Li's The Enforcer
Jingle All the Way
Joe Somebody
Joey
John Q
Johnny's Girl
Jungle 2 Jungle
Just Write
Kolya▲
La Deroute
The Lady Eve▲
The Lady Refuses
Lamb
Lara Croft: Tomb Raider
The Last Hit
Late Spring▲
Laughing at Life
Le Sexe des Etoiles
Leon the Pig Farmer
Les Comperes▲
Letter of Introduction
Liar Liar
Life Is Beautiful▲
Life with Father▲
Like Father, Like Son
The Limey▲
Little Dorrit, Film 1: Nobody's Fault▲
Little Dorrit, Film 2: Little Dorrit's Story▲
Little Indian, Big City
Little John
A Little Princess▲
The Lives of a Bengal Lancer▲
Lone Star▲
Looking for an Echo
Luna Park
Lust and Revenge
Magic in the Water
Maker of Men
The Marshal's Daughter
The Mask of Zorro▲
Meet the Parents▲
Meeting Daddy
Memories of Me
Missing Pieces
Mr. Mom▲
Misunderstood
Mom and Dad Save the World
Mulan
Must Be Santa
Mutual Respect
My Date with the President's Daughter
My Father Is Coming
My Father the Hero
My Old Man
My Son the Fanatic▲
My Stepmother Is an Alien
National Lampoon's Christmas Vacation
National Lampoon's Dad's Week Off
National Lampoon's European Vacation
National Lampoon's Vacation▲
Nick of Time
Night Falls on Manhattan▲
Night Zoo
No Way Back
Noah
Nobody's Fool▲
Nothing in Common
Oldest Living Graduate▲
On the Edge

On the Third Day
One Christmas
Our Vines Have Tender Grapes▸
Over the Top
The Patriot
The Pillow Book
Platinum High School
Pokemon 3: The Movie
Ponette
Pontiac Moon
Pop Always Pays
Popi▸
Princess of Thieves
Proud Men
Raining Stones
Return to Lonesome Dove
Revenge of the Musketeers
Revolution
The River Rat
A River Runs Through It▸
Rugrats in Paris: The Movie▸
The Run of the Country▸
The Santa Clause
Sea Devils
Second Best▸
Secre of the Andes
The Secret Agent Club
The Secret Passion of Robert Clayton
The Sender
Severance
Shattered▸
The Shepherd of the Hills▸
She's the One
Shower
Signs
A Simple Wish
Skeletons in the Closet
Slaughter of the Innocents
Sleepless in Seattle▸
Slums of Beverly Hills▸
Snow Dogs
So I Married an Axe Murderer
A Soldier's Daughter Never Cries
Special Olympics
The Spring
Star Spangled Rhythm▸
The Stupids
The Sum of Us▸
Superdad
Tank
The Tempest
The Tempest▸
The Tempest
The 10th Kingdom
Texas Lightning
The Three Lives of Thomasina▸
Three Men and a Baby▸
Three Men and a Cradle▸
Three Men and a Little Lady
The Tiger Woods Story
A Time to Kill▸
Time Without Pity
To Gillian on Her 37th Birthday
The Tomorrow Man
Tortilla Soup
The Tracker
Two Kinds of Love
Undercover Angel
A Very Brady Sequel
A Voyage 'Round My Father▸
Wait Till Your Mother Gets Home
Walter and Henry▸
The War at Home
When Wolves Cry
Woman Wanted

Dance Fever

see also ***Ballet; Disco Musicals***

Alive and Kicking
All That Jazz▸
An American in Paris▸
Anchors Aweigh▸
April in Paris
Babes in Arms
The Bacchantes
The Band Wagon▸
The Barefoot Contessa▸
The Barkleys of Broadway▸
Beat Street
Because of You
The Belle of New York
Bert Rigby, You're a Fool
Billy Elliot▸
Billy Rose's Jumbo▸
Black Orpheus▸
Blood Wedding▸
Body Moves
Body Rock
Bojangles
Boogie Nights▸
Bootmen
Born to Dance
Breakin'
Breakin' 2: Electric Boogaloo
Breakin' Through
Broadway Melody of 1940
Cabin in the Sky▸
Can-Can
Captain January
Carefree▸
Carmen▸
Center Stage
Charleston▸
A Chorus Line
Chu Chu & the Philly Flash
Cover Girl▸
Curdled
Daddy Long Legs▸
Dames▸
Dance or Die
Dance with Me
Dancing Lady
Danzon▸
Deadly Dancer
Delightfully Dangerous
Delivery Boys
Dirty Dancing▸
The Discovery Program
Doll Face
The Eighties
El Amor Brujo▸
Everybody's Dancin'
Everyone Says I Love You▸
Faith
Fame▸
Fass Black
Fast Forward
Faster, Pussycat! Kill! Kill!
Femmes de Paris
Flashdance
Flower Drum Song
Flying Down to Rio
Follies Girl
Follow the Fleet▸
Footlight Parade▸
Footloose
The Forbidden Dance
42nd Street▸
French Can-Can▸
The Gay Divorcee▸
Ginger & Fred▸
Girl in Gold Boots
Girls Just Want to Have Fun
Give a Girl a Break
The Glass Slipper
Gold Diggers of 1933▸
Gold Diggers of 1935▸
Grease▸
Grease 2
Groove▸
The Harvey Girls▸
Heavenly Bodies
Hit the Deck
Holiday in Havana
Human Traffic
Idiot's Delight▸
The In Crowd
Isadora▸
It Started in Naples▸
Kiss Me Kate▸
Lambada
Last Dance
The Last Dance
The Last Days of Disco▸
Le Bal▸
Legs
Les Girls
Let's Dance
Liquid Dreams
Little Ballerina
Mad About Mambo
Mad Youth
Manhattan Merenque!
Mantis in Lace
Meet Me in Las Vegas
Michael
Midnight Dancer
Music in My Heart
Neurotic Cabaret
The Next Step
No Time for Romance
Nutcracker: The Motion Picture
Orgy of the Dead
Out to Sea
Paris Is Burning▸
Party Girl▸
Pennies from Heaven▸
The Pirate▸
Pizzicata
Portrait of a Showgirl
Portrait of a Stripper
Queen of the Stardust Ballroom▸
Rhythm Romance
Risky Business▸
Roberta▸
Romance in Manhattan
Rooftops
Roseland▸
Salome, Where She Danced
Salsa
Saturday Night Fever
Save the Last Dance
Scent of a Woman▸
Second Chorus
Seven Brides for Seven Brothers▸
Shag: The Movie▸
Shall We Dance▸
Shall We Dance?▸
Showgirls
Silk Stockings▸
Singin' in the Rain▸
Slashdance
So This Is Paris▸
Spirit of '76
Staying Alive
Stepping Out▸
The Story of Vernon and Irene Castle▸
Strictly Ballroom▸
Stripped to Kill II: Live Girls
Summer Stock▸
Sunset Strip
Sweet Charity▸
Swing Kids
Swing Time▸
Take Me Out to the Ball Game
Tango
Tango Bar
The Tango Lesson
Tap
Taxi Dancers
Teen Wolf
Thank God It's Friday
That's Dancing!
That's Entertainment, Part 2
That's Entertainment, Part 3
That's the Way I Like It
They Shoot Horses, Don't They?▸
Those Lips, Those Eyes
Top Hat▸
The Turning Point
Urban Cowboy
What's the Matter with Helen?
Words and Music
Yankee Doodle Dandy▸
You Were Never Lovelier▸
You'll Never Get Rich▸
Ziegfeld Follies
Ziegfeld Girl▸
Zou Zou

Dates from Hell

see also ***Singles***

After Hours▸
Blind Date
Body Shots
Bride of Chucky
Bye Bye, Love
Ed's Next Move
Harold and Maude▸
Night of the Creeps
The Personals
Reality Bites
Singles▸
Something Wild
20 Dates
Walking and Talking
What Happened Was...
Woo

A Day in the Life...

see also ***Up All Night***

Before Sunrise
The Best Man
The Boys▸
The Breakfast Club▸
The Daytrippers
Deadlocked
Flypaper
Full Frontal
Groundhog Day▸
Head On▸
Interceptor Force
Judy Berlin
Killing Time
Last Night▸
The Life Before This
Love and Other Catastrophes
Magnolia▸
Midaq Alley▸
Mrs. Dalloway
My Mother's Courage
North Shore Fish
Nothing Personal▸
Nowhere
One Fine Day
100 Proof
Orphans
Radiance
Say Hello to Yesterday
Spy Game
Sunday
Time Code
Training Day
Trojan War
True Crime
12:01
Ulysses
Working Girls▸

Deadly Implants

Alien: Resurrection▸
Blind Date
Bombshell
Drive
Escape from L.A.
Escape from New York
Fortress
King of Kong Island
Live Wire: Human Timebomb
The Mosaic Project
Star Trek: First Contact▸
Street Asylum
Synapse
Terminal Impact
The Terminal Man
Total Recall▸

Deafness

see also ***Physical Problems***

Amy
Beyond Silence
Bridge to Silence
Children of a Lesser God▸
Cop Land▸
Crazy Moon
Dead Silence
For the First Time
Goya in Bordeaux
Hear No Evil
The Heart Is a Lonely Hunter▸
His Bodyguard
Immortal Beloved
In the Company of Men
Johnny Belinda▸
Johnny Belinda
Mandy▸
The Miracle Worker▸
The Miracle Worker
Mr. Holland's Opus▸
Murderer's Keep
Psych-Out
Secret of Yolanda
See No Evil, Hear No Evil
Silent Victory: The Kitty O'Neil Story▸
Sincerely Yours
The Sound and the Silence
Sound of Love
The Sphinx
The Story of Alexander Graham Bell▸
A Summer to Remember
Suspect
Tin Man
Two Shades of Blue
Where the Truth Lies

Death & the Afterlife

see also ***Angels; Funerals; Ghosts, Ghouls, & Goblins; Great Death Scenes; Heaven Sent; Occult; Suicide***

After Life
The Alchemist
Alive and Kicking
All About My Mother▸
All of Me
All That Jazz▸
Always
The Amityville Horror
Amityville 2: The Possession
Amityville 3: The Demon
Amityville 4: The Evil Escapes
The Amityville Curse
Amityville 1992: It's About Time
Angel Eyes
Angel Heart
Angel on My Shoulder▸
Angel on My Shoulder
Another Chance
The Asphyx▸
Audrey Rose
Avanti!
Baby Girl Scott
Backwoods
Beetlejuice▸
Beyond Tomorrow
Bill & Ted's Bogus Journey
Black Force 2
Black Magic
Bliss▸
Blithe Spirit▸
Blood of the Vampire
Bloody New Year
The Bone Yard
Bowery at Midnight
Boys on the Side
The Bramble Bush
Breaking the Rules
Bulletproof Heart▸
Burnt Offerings
The Canterville Ghost
Carnival of Souls▸
Carousel▸
Carry Me Back
Castle of the Creeping Flesh
The Cat and the Canary▸
Cathy's Curse
Cemetery Man
The Chair
Chances Are▸
The Changeling
The Child
A Christmas Carol▸
A Christmas Carol
A Christmas Carol▸
A Christmas Carol
City of Angels
Cold Heaven
The Corridor: Death
Courage Under Fire▸
The Crow
The Crow 2: City of Angels
Curse of the Cat People▸
Curse of the Living Corpse
Da
Daddy's Dyin'...Who's Got the Will?
Dark of the Night
Dark Tower
Dark Victory▸
Daughter of Horror
The Day It Came to Earth
Dead Heat
Dead Mate
Death Be Not Proud▸
Death Becomes Her▸
The Death Curse of Tartu
Death Row Diner
Death Takes a Holiday▸
Defending Your Life▸
Deja Vu
The Devil & Max Devlin
The Diabolical Dr. Z
Diary of the Dead
Digging Up Business
D.O.A.▸
D.O.A.
Dr. Death, Seeker of Souls
Dr. Hackenstein
Doctor Phibes Rises Again
Dominique Is Dead
Dona Flor and Her Two Husbands▸
Donkey Skin▸
Donovan's Brain▸
Don't Go in the House
Don't Let Me Die on a Sunday
Doomed Love
Down to Earth
Dragonfly
The Duellists▸
Early Days
Earthling
Eleni
Emerald of Artama
Encounter with the Unknown
The End▸
The English Patient▸
Enrapture
The Entertainer▸
Estate of Insanity
Eternity and a Day
Evil Spirits
Executive Suite▸
The Eyes, the Mouth
Fearless▸
The Fig Tree
Flatliners
Fluke
For Roseanna
The Forgotten One
Friendly Fire▸
Frightmare
Frisk
From the Dead of Night▸
The Funeral▸
Funeral Home
Garbo Talks
Gates of Hell
The Ghost
Ghost▸
The Ghost and Mrs. Muir▸
Ghost Writer
Ghosts Can Do It
Ghosts Can't Do It
Ghosts of Berkeley Square
Go Down Death
Gotham▸
The Granny
Grave Secrets
The Green Room
Griffin and Phoenix: A Love Story
Hawks
Heart and Souls
Heart Condition
Heaven
Heaven Can Wait▸
The Heavenly Kid
Heaven's a Drag
Hello Again
Hercules the Legendary Journeys, Vol. 4: In the Underworld
Here Comes Mr. Jordan▸
Hideaway
High Plains Drifter
High Spirits
Highlander: Endgame
Highway 61
Hocus Pocus
Hold That Ghost▸
Hollow Gate
Homeward Bound
Human Nature
I Bury the Living▸
I Married a Witch▸
I Walked with a Zombie▸
I'm Losing You
Impure Thoughts
In an Old Manor House

▸ = *rated three bones or higher*

In Between
In the Gloaming▲
The Indestructible Man
Infinity
Into the West▲
Intruso
It Came Upon a Midnight Clear
It Could Happen to You
It's a Wonderful Life▲
It's My Party
Jacob's Ladder
Judge & Jury
The Kid with the Broken Halo
Killing Grandpa
Kiss Me Goodbye
Kiss of Death
Kissed
La Vie Continue
The Lady in White▲
The Last Best Year
Last Light
The Legend of Hell House▲
Liliom▲
Loot ... Give Me Money, Honey!
The Loved One▲
Macbeth▲
Macbeth
Made in Heaven
Magnolia▲
The Man with Two Lives
Mannequin
Marvin's Room
Mausoleum
Maxie
Meet Joe Black
Mermaid
The Midnight Hour
The Miracle of the Bells
Mr. Corbett's Ghost
Monkeybone
Monty Python's The Meaning of Life▲
Moonlight and Valentino
Mortuary Academy
Mother and Son
A Mother's Prayer
My Life
Necropolis
The Newlydeads
Night of the Death Cult
Night of the Demons
Night of the Demons 2
Night of the Living Dead▲
Night of the Living Dead
Night Shift
The Nightcomers
Nightmare Castle
Oh Dad, Poor Dad (Momma's Hung You in the Closet & I'm Feeling So Sad)
Oh, Heavenly Dog!
On Borrowed Time▲
The Oracle
Our Sons
Out of the Rain
Passed Away
The Peanut Butter Solution
Pet Sematary
Phantasm
Phantasm 2
Phantasm 3: Lord of the Dead
The Phantom Chariot
Phantom of the Ritz
The Plague
Playroom
Poltergeist▲
Poltergeist 2: The Other Side
Poltergeist 3
Ponette
Portrait of Jennie▲
The Possessed
Premonition
The Premonition
Prison
Promises in the Dark
The Prophecy
The Psychic
Psychomania
The Reincarnation of Peter Proud
Resurrection of Zachary Wheeler
Retribution
Return
Revenge of the Dead
Riders to the Sea
Rimfire
The Rue Morgue Massacres
Savage Hearts
Saved by the Light
Scared Stiff▲
School Spirit
Scrooge▲
Scrooge
Scrooged
Seven Days to Live
The Seventh Seal▲
Shadow Play
She Waits
Shock Waves
Sibling Rivalry
Silence Like Glass
The Sixth Man
The Sixth Sense▲
Sole Survivor
Sometimes They Come Back
Somewhere Tomorrow
Soultaker
South Park: Bigger, Longer and Uncut
Spawn▲
Stand by Me▲
Star Trek 3: The Search for Spock
Stones of Death
Strangers of the Evening
The Substitute Wife
Supernatural
Tell Me a Riddle
Tequila Body Shots
Terror Eyes
They Watch
Things to Do in Denver When You're Dead▲
13 Ghosts
To Dance with the White Dog▲
To Forget Venice
To Gillian on Her 37th Birthday
Tomb of Torture
Topper▲
Topper Returns▲
Topper Takes a Trip▲
Trick or Treat
Truly, Madly, Deeply▲
Truth or Dare?
Twice Dead
Two of a Kind
Under the Sand▲
Under the Skin
The Undertaker's Wedding
The Unnamable
Unnatural
Unstrung Heroes
The Vacillations of Poppy Carew
The Vampire's Ghost
Vengeance
Visitor from the Grave
The Visitors
Weekend at Bernie's
Weekend at Bernie's 2
Welcome Back Mr. Fox
What Dreams May Come
Where the Lilies Bloom▲
Whispers
White Light
The Widow
Wings of Fame
A Woman's Tale▲
A Zed & Two Noughts▲
Zone of the Dead

Death Row

***see also** Men in Prison; Women in Prison*

Angels with Dirty Faces▲
Beyond the Call
The Chamber
Crime of the Century
Daniel
A Dark Adapted Eye▲
Dead Man Out▲
Dead Man Walking▲
The Detective▲
The Executioner's Song
The Green Mile
Hellblock 13
I Want to Live!▲
In Cold Blood▲
In Cold Blood
Killer: A Journal of Murder
Last Dance
Last Rites
A Lesson Before Dying▲
Let Him Have It▲
Letters from a Killer
Live! From Death Row
Lost Highway
Mommy 2: Mommy's Day
Monster's Ball▲
A Place in the Sun▲
The Seventh Sign
Shot in the Heart▲
The Thin Blue Line▲
True Crime
Under Suspicion
The Widow of Saint-Pierre▲

Dedicated Teachers

***see also** Hell High School; School Daze*

Amy
Anna and the King
Balance of Power
Blackboard Jungle▲
Born Yesterday▲
Born Yesterday
Bossa Nova
The Browning Version
Burn Witch, Burn!▲
Butterfly▲
Carried Away
Cheaters
Cheers for Miss Bishop
A Child Is Waiting▲
Children of a Lesser God▲
Christy
Ciao, Professore!
Coming Out
Conrack▲
The Corn Is Green▲
Dangerous Minds
Dead Poets Society▲
Eden
Educating Rita▲
Election▲
The Elementary School
Forever Mary▲
Goodbye, Mr. Chips▲
Goodbye, Mr. Chips
High School High
Homework
If Lucy Fell
Inherit the Wind
Institue Benjamenta or This Dream People Call Human Life
Johnny Tiger
Kindergarten Cop
Lean on Me▲
L'Eleve
A Lesson Before Dying▲
Lovey: A Circle of Children 2
Luna e L'Altra
Madame Sousatzka▲
Matilda▲
The Miracle Worker▲
The Miracle Worker
Mr. Holland's Opus▲
Music of the Heart
Necessary Roughness
The Next Karate Kid
Night Visitor
Not One Less
October Sky▲
187
The Paper Chase▲
Passion for Life
Powder
The Prime of Miss Jean Brodie▲
The Principal
Race the Sun
Rachel, Rachel▲
Renaissance Man
The Road Home▲
The Rookie▲
Stand and Deliver▲
The Substitute
Summer School
Sunset Park
Teachers
To Sir, with Love
Twenty-Four Eyes▲
Up the Down Staircase▲

Deep Blue

***see also** Go Fish; Sail Away; Shipwrecked; Submarines*

The Abyss▲
Andre
Assault on a Queen
Baywatch the Movie: Forbidden Paradise
The Beast
The Big Blue
Crimson Tide▲
Danger Beneath the Sea
Deep Blue Sea
ffolkes
Flipper▲
1492: Conquest of Paradise
Free Willy
Free Willy 2: The Adventure Home
Free Willy 3: The Rescue
Lords of the Deep
Men of Honor
Mission of the Shark▲
Moby Dick
Namu, the Killer Whale
Pirates
Shipwrecked
The Silent Enemy
Splash
The Spy Who Loved Me
Waterworld
Whale of a Tale
Wind

Demons & Wizards

***see also** Occult*

The Alchemist
Archer: The Fugitive from the Empire
Army of Darkness▲
Arthur's Quest
Beyond Darkness
Bloodlust: Subspecies 3
Bloodstone: Subspecies 2
Blue Blood
Born of Fire
Bram Stoker's Shadowbuilder
The Church▲
Conan the Barbarian▲
Conan the Destroyer
The Convent
Cthulhu Mansion
Curse 4: The Ultimate Sacrifice
Dead Waters
Deathstalker
Deathstalker 3
Deathstalker 4: Match of Titans
Demon Rage
Demon Wind
Demonoid, Messenger of Death
The Demons
Demons
Demons of Ludlow
Demonstone
Demonwarp
Devil Woman
The Devil's Web
El Barbaro
Ernest Scared Stupid
Evil Dead
Evil Dead 2: Dead by Dawn
Evil Toons
Excalibur▲
Fantasia▲
Fire and Ice
Funnyman
The Gate
Gate 2
Ghosts That Still Walk
The Giants of Thessaly
Gor
The Guardian
Guardian
Hellraiser
Hellraiser 4: Bloodline
The Heroic Trio
The Hobbit▲
Jack-O
Just Visiting
The King and I
Krull
Ladyhawke
The Legacy
Lord of the Rings 1: The Fellowship of the Rings▲
The Mephisto Waltz▲
The Minion
Mirror, Mirror
Natas ... The Reflection
Night of the Demons 3
Outlaw of Gor
Possessed
Pumpkinhead
Pumpkinhead 2: Blood Wings
Quest for the Mighty Sword
The Raven▲
Rawhead Rex
Red Sonja
The Return of the King
Rock & Rule
Seizure
Silent Night, Deadly Night 4: Initiation
Sinthia: The Devil's Doll
Sorceress
Spellcaster
Stay Awake
Supergirl
Sword & the Sorcerer
The Sword in the Stone▲
Tales from the Crypt Presents Demon Knight
Talisman
Terror Eyes
Trancers 4: Jack of Swords
Troll
Troll 2
The Unholy
The Unnamable 2: The Statement of Randolph Carter
Warlock
Warlock: The Armageddon
Willow
Witchcraft 5: Dance with the Devil
The Witchmaker
Wizards of the Lost Kingdom
Wizards of the Lost Kingdom 2
Zu: Warriors from the Magic Mountain

Dental Mayhem

***see also** Doctors & Nurses; Evil Doctors*

Almost Heroes
Brazil▲
Captives
Compromising Positions
The Dentist▲
The Dentist
The Dentist 2: Brace Yourself
Dentist In the Chair
Diabolique▲
Don't Raise the Bridge, Lower the River
Eversmile New Jersey
Houseguest
The In-Laws▲
Little Shop of Horrors▲
Marathon Man▲
Novocaine
The Paleface▲
Poltergeist 2: The Other Side
Reuben, Reuben▲
Serial Mom▲
The Shakiest Gun in the West
Snow Dogs
Strawberry Blonde▲
Toothless
12 Monkeys▲
The Whole Nine Yards

Desert War/Foreign Legion

***see also** Deserts; Persian Gulf War*

Abbott and Costello in the Foreign Legion
Beau Geste▲
Delta Force 3: The Killing Game
The Flying Deuces▲
Follow That Camel
Gunga Din▲
The Last Remake of Beau Geste
Lionheart
Man of Legend
March or Die
Morocco▲
Outpost in Morocco
Sahara▲

Deserts

***see also** Desert War/ Foreign Legion*

The Adventures of Priscilla, Queen of the Desert▲
American Strays
Back of Beyond
Baja
Beavis and Butt-Head Do America
Broken Arrow
Desert Blue
The Desert Fox▲
Desert Gold
Desert Hearts▲
Desert Heat
The Desert Rats▲
The Desert Song
Desert Winds
Dune
Dune Warriors
The English Patient▲
Evolution
A Far Off Place
Faster, Pussycat! Kill! Kill!
Five Graves to Cairo▲
Flame of Araby
The Forsaken
Frankenstein and Me
In the Army Now
Indiana Jones and the Last Crusade▲
Ishtar
It Came from Outer Space 2
The Jewel of the Nile
Larry McMurtry's Dead Man's Walk
Lawrence of Arabia▲
Legend of the Lost Tomb
Legionnaire
Mad Max▲
Mad Max: Beyond Thunderdome
Mojave Moon
Morocco▲
The Mummy
Natural Born Killers
New Eden
Operation Condor
The Passenger▲
Passion in the Desert
Patriot Games▲
Picking Up the Pieces
The Road to Morocco▲
The Road Warrior▲
Sahara▲
Sahara
Samson and Delilah
Scorpion Spring
Sea of Sand
The Sheik▲
The Sheltering Sky▲
Slow Burn
Son of the Sheik▲
Star Wars▲
Stargate
Strawberry Fields
Tremors
Tremors 2: Aftershocks
White Sands
The Wind and the Lion▲

Detective Spoofs

***see also** Detectives*

Ace Ventura: Pet Detective
Ace Ventura: When Nature Calls
The Adventures of Sherlock Holmes' Smarter Brother▲
Assault of the Party Nerds 2: Heavy Petting Detective

▲ = rated three bones or higher

Blondes Have More Guns
Camouflage
Carry On Dick
Carry On Screaming
The Cheap Detective▲
Clean Slate
Clue
The Crooked Circle
Cry Uncle
The Curse of the Jade Scorpion
Curse of the Pink Panther
Dead Men Don't Wear Plaid
Detective School Dropouts
Dragnet
Fatal Instinct
Gumshoe
The Hollywood Detective
Hollywood Harry
The Hound of the Baskervilles
How to Kill 400 Duponts
Inspector Gadget
Inspector Hornleigh
Love Happy
The Man with Bogart's Face
Master Mind
Murder by Death
My Favorite Brunette
The Naked Gun: From the Files of Police Squad▲
Naked Gun 33 1/3: The Final Insult
Naked Gun 2 1/2: The Smell of Fear
Night Patrol
Oh, Heavenly Dog!
One Body Too Many
The Pink Chiquitas
The Pink Panther▲
The Pink Panther Strikes Again▲
The Private Eyes
Pure Luck
Rentadick
Return of the Pink Panther
Revenge of the Pink Panther
Ryder P.I.
Second Sight
Secret Agent 00-Soul
A Shot in the Dark▲
The Strange Case of the End of Civilization As We Know It
Terror 2000
Trail of the Pink Panther
Who Done It?
Who's Harry Crumb?
Without a Clue
Zero Effect

Detectives

***see also** Cops; Detective Spoofs; Feds*

Sleepless

Detroit

***see also** Checkered Flag; Motor Vehicle Dept.*

Aspen Extreme
Beverly Hills Cop
Beverly Hills Cop 2
Beverly Hills Cop 3
Bird on a Wire
Chameleon Street▲
Collision Course
The Color of Courage
Coupe de Ville
Crimewave
Crossing the Bridge
Detroit 9000
Detroit Rock City
The Dollmaker
Exit Wounds
Gridlock'd▲
Grosse Pointe Blank▲
Hoffa▲
Indian Summer
The Last Word
Let's Kill All the Lawyers
The Life and Times of Hank Greenberg▲
Mirrors
Mr. Mom▲
One in a Million: The Ron LeFlore Story

Paper Lion
Presumed Innocent▲
Private Parts
Renaissance Man
Ringmaster
RoboCop▲
RoboCop 2
RoboCop 3
Roger & Me▲
The Rosary Murders
Scarecrow
Tainted
Tiger Town
True Romance
Tucker: The Man and His Dream▲
The Wrecking Crew
Zebrahead▲

Devils

Beauty and the Devil
The Craft
Crocodile Tears
Damn Yankees▲
Dark Angel: The Ascent
Deal of a Lifetime
The Devil & Max Devlin
The Devils▲
The Devil's Advocate
End of Days
Faust▲
Gates of Hell 2: Dead Awakening
God, Man and Devil
Guardian of the Abyss
Haunted Symphony
Hell's Belles
High Strung
Highway to Hell
Judgment Day
Legend
Les Visiteurs du Soir▲
Little Nicky
Lost Souls
Magic Hunter
The Mangler
Mr. Frost
Mother Joan of the Angels▲
Needful Things
The Prophecy
Second Time Lucky
The Sorrows of Satan▲
South Park: Bigger, Longer and Uncut
Stephen King's The Stand
Tales from the Hood
The Witches of Eastwick

Devil's Island

***see also** Great Escapes; Men in Prison*

The Life of Emile Zola▲
Papillon▲
Passage to Marseilles▲
Strange Cargo
We're No Angels

Dinosaurs

***see also** Killer Beasts*

Adventures in Dinosaur City
At the Earth's Core
Baby ... Secret of the Lost Legend
Barney's Great Adventure
Carnosaur
Carnosaur 2
Carnosaur 3: Primal Species
Caveman
Clifford
The Crater Lake Monster
Dennis the Menace: Dinosaur Hunter
Dinosaur
Dinosaur Island
Dinosaur Valley Girls
Dinosaurus!
Dinotopia
Ganjasaurus Rex
Josh Kirby...Time Warrior: Chapter 1, Planet of the Dino-Knights
Jurassic Park▲
Jurassic Park 3
King Dinosaur
The Land Before Time▲
The Land Before Time 2: The Great Valley Adventure
The Land Before Time 3: The Time of the Great Giving
The Land Before Time 4: Journey Through the Mists
The Land Before Time 5: The Mysterious Island
Land Before Time 7: The Stone of Cold Fire
The Land That Time Forgot
The Land Unknown
The Lost Continent
The Lost World
The Lost World: Jurassic Park 2
Massacre in Dinosaur Valley
My Science Project
A Nymphoid Barbarian in Dinosaur Hell
One Million B.C.
One Million Years B.C.
One of Our Dinosaurs Is Missing
The People That Time Forgot
Planet of the Dinosaurs
Prehysteria
Prehysteria 2
Prehysteria 3
Pterodactyl Woman from Beverly Hills
Return to the Lost World
Sir Arthur Conan Doyle's The Lost World
Sound of Horror
Super Mario Bros.
Tammy and the T-Rex
Teenage Caveman
Theodore Rex
Toy Story▲
Two Lost Worlds
Unknown Island
The Valley of Gwangi▲
We're Back! A Dinosaur's Story
When Dinosaurs Ruled the Earth

Disaster Flicks

***see also** Action-Adventure; Air Disasters; Meltdown; Sea Disasters*

Accident
After the Shock
Aftershock: Earthquake in New York
Airport▲
Airport '75
Airport '77
Alive
Armageddon
Assignment Outer Space
Asteroid
Atomic Train
Avalanche
Avalanche Express
Beyond the Poseidon Adventure
The Big Bus
Britannic
The Cassandra Crossing
The China Syndrome▲
The Christmas Coal Mine Miracle
City on Fire
The Concorde: Airport '79
The Crash of Flight 401
Dante's Peak
The Day the Sky Exploded
Daybreak
Daylight
Dead Ahead: The Exxon Valdez Disaster▲
Deep Core
Deep Impact
The Doomsday Flight
Earthquake
Falling Fire
Fallout
Final Warning
Fire
Fire and Rain
Firestorm
Firestorm: 72 Hours in Oakland
Firetrap
Flood!
Flood: A River's Rampage
Gale Force
Gray Lady Down
Hard Rain
The Hindenburg
The Hurricane▲
Hurricane
In Old Chicago▲
Independence Day▲
Judgment Day
Last Days of Pompeii
The Last Voyage
The Last Warrior
The Last Woman on Earth
The Lost Missile
Meteor
A Night to Remember▲
Panic in the Skies
The Perfect Storm
Planet on the Prowl
The Poseidon Adventure
The Rains Came
Raise the Titanic
Red Alert
Red Planet
St. Helen's, Killer Volcano
Snowblind
Snowbound: The Jim and Jennifer Stolpa Story
S.O.S. Titanic
The Survivalist
Survivor
Tailspin: Behind the Korean Airline Tragedy
Terror on the 40th Floor
Tidal Wave
Titanic▲
The Towering Inferno
Tragedy of Flight 103: The Inside Story▲
Twister
Two Minute Warning
Tycus
Velocity Trap
Volcano
Volcano: Fire on the Mountain
When Time Ran Out
White Squall
Y2K

Disco Musicals

***see also** Musicals*

Can't Stop the Music
Car Wash
KISS Meets the Phantom of the Park
Pirate Movie
The Rocky Horror Picture Show▲
Saturday Night Fever
Thank God It's Friday
The Wiz
Xanadu

Disease of the Week

***see also** AIDS; Emerging Viruses*

The Affair▲
The Ann Jillian Story
Bang the Drum Slowly
Beaches▲
Bear Ye One Another's Burden...
The Best Little Girl in the World▲
Between Two Women
Bobby Deerfield
The Book of Stars
The Boy in the Plastic Bubble
Brian's Song▲
Brian's Song
Bubble Boy
Camille▲
The Carrier
The Cassandra Crossing
Champions
Checking Out
Children of the Corn 4: The Gathering
Chinese Box
C.H.U.D.
Cleo from 5 to 7▲
Cold Harvest
Contagious
The Contaminated Man
Crash Course
Cries and Whispers▲
Crystal Heart
The Curse
Damien: The Leper Priest
Daybreak
Dead Man Walking
Dead Space
Dick Barton, Special Agent
The Doctor
Dr. Akagi
Down in the Delta▲
A Dream of Kings▲
Duet for One
Dying Young
An Early Frost▲
East of Kilimanjaro
The End▲
Eric▲
Erin Brockovich▲
The First Deadly Sin
First Do No Harm
Fourth Wish
Gaby: A True Story▲
Germicide
Girls' Night
Glory Enough for All: The Discovery of Insulin
Go Now▲
Griffin and Phoenix: A Love Story
Here on Earth
Hilary and Jackie▲
Incredible Melting Man
Interrupted Melody▲
Intimate Contact▲
Iris▲
Isle of the Dead
Isn't She Great
Jack
Jericho Fever
John Grisham's The Rainmaker
Killer on Board
L.A. Bad
The Last Best Year
Last Breath
The Last Man on Earth
Lorenzo's Oil▲
Love Affair: The Eleanor & Lou Gehrig Story▲
Love Story▲
Mad Death
Marvin's Room
A Matter of WHO
Miles to Go
Miss Evers' Boys
Molokai: The Story of Father Damien
A Mother's Prayer
My Father's House
My Life
Nasty Rabbit
Niagara, Niagara
On Her Majesty's Secret Service▲
One True Thing▲
Osmosis Jones
Panic in Echo Park
Parting Glances▲
Philadelphia▲
Pilgrim, Farewell
The Plague
The Plague Dogs
The Pride of the Yankees▲
Princes in Exile
Project: Alien
Promises in the Dark
The Proud Ones
Quarantine
Question of Faith
A Quiet Duel
Rabid
Rasputin: Dark Servant of Destiny▲
Reborn
Right of Way
The Road to Galveston▲
The Road to Wellville
Safe House
The Shadow Box▲
Shadowlands▲
A Shining Season▲
Silence Like Glass
The Silver Streak
Simon Birch
Six Weeks
Stepmom▲
Stigma
Sunchaser
Terms of Endearment▲
Terror Creatures from the Grave
The Theory of Flight
The Tic Code
A Time to Live
Venomous
Walking Through the Fire
The Wedding Gift▲
When the Time Comes
When Wolves Cry
The White Legion
Xtro
ZigZag▲

Disorganized Crime

***see also** Comic Cops; Organized Crime*

The Adventures of Rocky & Bullwinkle
Airheads
Albino Alligator
All About the Benjamins
All Saint's Day
Amos and Andrew
The Apple Dumpling Gang
The Apple Dumpling Gang Rides Again
Armed and Dangerous
Baby on Board
Baby's Day Out
Bait
Bandits
Beautiful Creatures
Big Trouble
Born Bad
Bottle Rocket
Buffalo 66▲
Cop and a Half
Crackers
Disorganized Crime
Dr. Otto & the Riddle of the Gloom Beam
Drowning Mona
Dying to Get Rich
8 Heads in a Duffel Bag
Ernest Goes to Jail
Everybody's Famous!
Face
Fargo▲
Finders Keepers
A Fine Mess
Get Shorty▲
Glitch!
Goodbye South, Goodbye
Gravesend
Gridlock'd▲
The Gun in Betty Lou's Handbag
Gun Shy
Happy New Year
Headless Body in Topless Bar
Held Up
Her Alibi
Herbie Goes Bananas
High Heels and Low Lifes
Home Alone▲
Home Alone 2: Lost in New York
Hoods
I Wonder Who's Killing Her Now?
Idiot Box
In the Country Where Nothing Happens
Inside the Law
The Italian Job
The Jerky Boys
Keys to Tulsa
Kicked in the Head
Kill Me Later
Killing Zoe
The League of Gentlemen▲
Leather Jackets
L.I.E.

Lock, Stock and 2 Smoking Barrels▲
Love, Honour & Obey
Lucky Numbers
Lunch Wagon
Mad Dog and Glory▲
A Man, a Woman, and a Bank
Man of the House
Menage▲
The Mexican
Mexican Hayride
Milo Milo
Miss Grant Takes Richmond
Mixed Nuts
Mutant on the Bounty
The Night They Robbed Big Bertha's
Ocean's 11
Once in the Life
Once Upon a Crime
101 Dalmatians
102 Dalmatians
Oscar
Out on a Limb
Palookaville▲
Partners
Perpetrators of the Crime
Picking Up the Pieces
Poor White Trash
Pouvoir Intime
Quick Change
Ransom Money
Reservoir Dogs▲
River Red
Round Trip to Heaven
Ruthless People▲
Safe Men
St. Benny the Dip
See No Evil, Hear No Evil
See Spot Run
Shake Hands with Murder
The Shot
Silver Bears
Sister Act
Sitting Ducks▲
A Slight Case of Murder
Small Time Crooks
Snatch▲
Stop! or My Mom Will Shoot
Stop That Cab
Suicide Kings
The Super
Survivors
Tall, Tan and Terrific
The Thief Who Came to Dinner
Things to Do in Denver When You're Dead▲
Three Kinds of Heat
Thrilled to Death
Too Many Crooks
Trapped in Paradise
Truth or Consequences, N.M.
Two If by Sea
We're Talkin' Serious Money
What's the Worst That Could Happen?
The Wrong Arm of the Law▲
The Young in Heart▲
Zoolander

Divorce

see also *Marriage; Single Parents; Singles; Stepparents*
The Accidental Tourist▲
All I Want for Christmas
Alpha Beta
The Awful Truth▲
Between Friends
A Bill of Divorcement
Breaking Up
Breaking Up Is Hard to Do
Bye Bye, Love
California Suite▲
Can She Bake a Cherry Pie?
Celebrity▲
Cheaper to Keep Her
Children of Divorce
Clara's Heart
Cold Heat
A Conspiracy of Love
A Cooler Climate
Cross My Heart
Desert Hearts▲
Divorce American Style
Divorce His, Divorce Hers
Divorce—Italian Style▲
The Divorcee
Dying to Get Rich
Early Frost
Edie & Pen
Escapade▲
E.T.: The Extra-Terrestrial▲
Every Other Weekend▲
The Ex
Expectations
Face the Music
Faces▲
Falling Down
Family Pictures▲
Father Figure
Fergie & Andrew: Behind the Palace Doors
A Fight for Jenny
The First Wives Club
For Richer or Poorer
Found Alive
The Fury Within
The Good Father▲
The Good Mother
Goodbye Love
Hard Promises
Heartbreakers
Heartburn▲
High Society▲
History Is Made at Night▲
Hollow Reed▲
Hope Floats
House Arrest
How to Break Up a Happy Divorce
How to Commit Marriage
Husbands and Wives▲
Interiors▲
Irreconcilable Differences
The Kiss You Gave Me
Kramer vs. Kramer▲
Let's Make It Legal
Liar Liar
The Liberation of L.B. Jones
Living Out Loud
Love and Hate: A Marriage Made in Hell
Love Matters
Marie▲
The Marrying Kind
Melanie
Misbehaving Husbands
The Misfits▲
Mrs. Doubtfire
Mr. Skeffington▲
Mr. Wonderful
Mother
Nadine
Naked Paradise
Necessary Parties
Never Say Goodbye
A New Life
Night Life in Reno
Nothing in Common
Now and Then
Ocean's Eleven▲
The Odd Couple▲
The Odd Job
One Cooks, the Other Doesn't
The Parent Trap
Patti Rocks▲
Peggy Sue Got Married
The Personals
Petulia▲
Pilgrim, Farewell
Play It Again, Sam▲
The Prize Pulitzer
Reckless▲
Rich in Love
Rich Kids
Riptide▲
Scenes from a Marriage▲
Second Chance
See You in the Morning
Serving Sara
Sex and the Single Parent
Shattered Silence
Signs & Wonders
The Solitary Man
Starting Over▲
Stepmom▲
Strange Bedfellows
Sweet Revenge
Table for Five
Tattle Tale
Tell It to the Judge
Tell Me That You Love Me
Tenth Month
That Old Feeling
Till Murder Do Us Part
Town and Country
Twister
An Unmarried Woman▲
Valentino Returns
Wanted: The Perfect Guy
The War of the Roses▲
Without Anesthesia

Doctors & Nurses

see also *AIDS; Dental Mayhem; Disease of the Week; Emerging Viruses; Evil Doctors; Hospitals & Medicine; Nursploitation!; Sanity Check; Shrinks*
All Creatures Great and Small▲
Alone in the Dark
And the Band Played On▲
The Android Affair
Anne of Green Gables: The Continuing Story
Any Given Sunday▲
Armistead Maupin's More Tales of the City
Arrowsmith
Ashanti, Land of No Mercy
The Asphyx▲
At First Sight
Awakenings▲
Baby Girl Scott
Bad Medicine
Battle Circus
Beautiful People
Bethune
Between Wars
Bikini House Calls
Bikini Med School
The Black Dragons
Black Friday
Blade
Bless the Child
Blind Justice
Bliss
Blood Mania
Bloodlink
Body Parts
Bone Daddy
Botany Bay
Brain Dead▲
The Bramble Bush
Breast Men
Broken Glass
The Broken Mask
The Bumblebee Flies Anyway
Calling Paul Temple
Candy Stripe Nurses
Carry On Doctor▲
Castle of the Creeping Flesh
Caught▲
Century
Children of Rage
Children of the Corn 4: The Gathering
China Beach▲
The Cider House Rules▲
Circus of Horrors
The Citadel▲
City of Angels
City of Joy
The Clonus Horror
Club Havana
Coma▲
Contagious
Corregidor
Corridors of Blood
Courageous Dr. Christian
Cries of Silence
Crimes & Misdemeanors▲
Critical Care
Critical Choices
Crossover
Dark City
Dead Ringers▲
Dead Sleep
Death Becomes Her▲
Death by Prescription
Death Nurse
The Devil's Web
Doc Hollywood
The Doctor
Dr. Akagi
Dr. Alien
The Doctor and the Devils
Doctor at Large
Doctor at Sea
Dr. Bethune▲
Dr. Black, Mr. Hyde
Doctor Blood's Coffin
Doctor Butcher M.D.
Dr. Caligari
Dr. Christian Meets the Women
Dr. Cyclops
Dr. Death, Seeker of Souls
Doctor Detroit
Doctor Dolittle
Dr. Dolittle
Dr. Dolittle 2
Doctor Faustus
Dr. Frankenstein's Castle of Freaks
Dr. Heckyl and Mr. Hype
Doctor in Distress
Doctor in the House▲
Dr. Jekyll and Mr. Hyde
Dr. Jekyll & Mr. Hyde
Dr. Kildare's Strange Case
Dr. Mabuse, The Gambler▲
Dr. Mabuse vs. Scotland Yard
Dr. Petiot
Doctor Satan's Robot
Doctor Takes a Wife▲
Dr. Tarr's Torture Dungeon
Dr. Terror's House of Horrors
Doctor Who
Doctor X
Doctors and Nurses
Doctors' Wives
Donor Unknown
Don't Cry, It's Only Thunder
Don't Look in the Basement
Dragonfly
Drunken Angel▲
East of Borneo
The Egyptian
The Elephant Man▲
Emmanuelle in the Country
The English Patient▲
Extreme Measures
Eyes Wide Shut
False Faces
Fantastic Voyage▲
Fatal Error
First Do No Harm
Flatliners
The Flesh and the Fiends
Flesh Feast
Foreign Body
The Fortune Cookie▲
The Fugitive▲
Girl, Interrupted
Glory Enough for All: The Discovery of Insulin
The Great Moment
Gross Anatomy
Guest in the House
Gun Shy
Halloween 2: The Nightmare Isn't Over!
Hands Up▲
Healer
High Heels
Holy Terror
Hombres Armados▲
The Horrible Dr. Hichcock
The Horror Chamber of Dr. Faustus▲
Horror Hospital
The Hospital▲
Hospital of Terror
House Calls▲
I Love My...Wife
I Never Promised You a Rose Garden▲
In Dreams
The In-Laws▲
In Love and War
The Incredible Journey of Dr. Meg Laurel▲
An Indecent Obsession
Internes Can't Take Money
The Interns
Invasion
Jesse
Johnny Belinda▲
Johnny Belinda
Junior
Kidnapping of Baby John Doe
Korczak▲
La Sentinelle
The Last Angry Man▲
The Last Bridge
The Lazarus Syndrome
Le Cas du Dr. Laurent▲
Lie Down with Lions
Life Is a Long Quiet River▲
The Light in the Jungle
Like Father, Like Son
Looking for an Echo
Love Is a Many-Splendored Thing
Lover's Knot
Mad Love▲
The Mad Monster
The Madness of King George▲
Make-Up
Malice
Maniac Nurses Find Ecstasy
Marvin's Room
M*A*S*H▲
M*A*S*H: Goodbye, Farewell & Amen▲
The Mask of Fu Manchu
A Matter of Life and Death
Matter of Trust
Maze
Meet Dr. Christian
Memories of Me
Men of Ireland
Mesmer
Metamorphosis: The Alien Factor
The Millionairess
Miss Evers' Boys
Mr. North
Molly
Monty Python's The Meaning of Life▲
Murder in Texas▲
Murder Once Removed
Murder or Mercy
The Murderers are Among Us
My Own Country
Nell
Night Call Nurses
Night Monster
Night Nurse▲
Night Nurse
Nightbreaker▲
Nine Months
No Way Out
Nomads
Not as a Stranger
Not of This Earth
Nurse
The Nurse
Nurse Betty▲
Nurse Edith Cavell▲
Nurse Marjorie
Nurse on Call
Old Swimmin' Hole
One Flew Over the Cuckoo's Nest▲
Only Love
The Ordeal of Dr. Mudd▲
Outbreak▲
Panic in Echo Park
Panic in the Streets▲
Paper Mask
Patch Adams
The Patriot
Pearl Harbor
People Will Talk▲
Persona▲
Petulia▲
A Place for Annie
The Plague
Playing God
Praying Mantis
The Princess and the Warrior▲
Private Duty Nurses
Promises in the Dark
Purple Hearts
A Quiet Duel
The Raven▲
The Real Glory▲
Reckless▲
Reckless Disregard
Reckless: The Sequel▲
Red Beard▲
Restoration▲
Riot Squad
The Road to Wellville
Rodgers & Hammerstein's South Pacific
Roommates
Sawbones
Say Goodbye, Maggie Cole
Scalpel
Series 7: The Contenders
Serving in Silence: The Margarethe Cammermeyer Story▲
Sister Dora
Sister Kenny▲
Skeezer
Slaughter Hotel
So Proudly We Hail▲
Sour Grapes
South Pacific▲
Spraggue
The Spring
State of Emergency
Stigma
Stitches
The Story of Dr. Wassell
The Student Nurses
Sunchaser
The Surgeon
Teenage Frankenstein
Tender Loving Care
Testament of Youth
Things You Can Tell Just by Looking at Her
Torture Ship
Trial by Media
Tundra
The Twilight of the Ice Nymphs
The Unbearable Lightness of Being▲
The Unknown Soldier
The Vicious Circle
Vital Signs
We Are the Children
Welcome Stranger
What Dreams May Come
When the Bullet Hits the Bone
Where the Money Is
White Dwarf
Wit▲
Women of Valor
Young Doctors in Love
The Young Nurses

Docudrama

see also *Documentary*
Above Us the Waves▲
Adam▲
After the Shock
Al Capone▲
Alexandria Again and Forever
The Amy Fisher Story
And the Band Played On▲
Babyfever
The Battle of Algiers▲
Beefcake
Blind Ambition
The Boston Strangler
Bound for Glory▲
Boycott▲
Call Northside 777▲
Casualties of Love: The "Long Island Lolita" Story
Christian the Lion
Close to Home
Cocaine: One Man's Seduction
Conspiracy: The Trial of the Chicago Eight▲
The Cool World
Countdown
The Courtesans of Bombay▲
The Cruel Sea▲
A Cry in the Dark▲
Edge of the World▲
8-A
The Flaming Teen-Age
Free, White, and 21
The General Line▲

▲ = rated three bones or higher

H
Helter Skelter Murders
Henry: Portrait of a Serial Killer▸
Hiroshima▸
Hostages▸
Immortal Battalion▸
In Cold Blood▸
Inside the Third Reich
Iron & Silk
James Dean
The Jayne Mansfield Story
JFK: Reckless Youth
Journey Through Rosebud
Kamikaze Hearts
Kids
King▸
Lethal Lolita—Amy Fisher: My Story
The Lion Has Wings
Looking for Richard▸
Mandela and de Klerk
Miss Evers' Boys
Murder in Texas▸
The Naked City▸
Panther
Pickpocket▸
The Poppy Is Also a Flower
Prince of the City▸
Qui Etes Vous, Mr. Sorge?
Real Life▸
The Red Menace
Shaka Zulu▸
S.O.S. Titanic
Special Bulletin▸
The Spy Who Came in from the Cold▸
Tailspin: Behind the Korean Airline Tragedy
Take the Money and Run▸
Teenage Devil Dolls
Ten Days That Shook the World▸
That's Adequate
The Thin Blue Line▸
32 Short Films about Glenn Gould▸
Times of Harvey Milk
Uprising▸
Women in Prison
Working Girls▸

Documentary

***see also** Docudrama*
American Fabulous
Assassination of Trotsky
The Atomic Cafe▸
Behind the Planet of the Apes▸
The Big One
Born to Boogie
A Brief History of Time▸
Brother's Keeper▸
Bruce Lee: Curse of the Dragon▸
Burden of Dreams
The Celluloid Closet▸
The Children of Theatre Street
Chuck Berry: Hail! Hail! Rock 'n' Roll
Ciao Federico! Fellini Directs Satyricon
The Clowns▸
Crumb
Dance Hall Racket
December 7th: The Movie
Decline of Western Civilization 1▸
Decline of Western Civilization 2: The Metal Years
Derby▸
Ebony Dreams
Elvis in Hollywood▸
Encounter with the Unknown
The Endless Summer▸
The Endless Summer 2▸
Fallen Champ: The Untold Story of Mike Tyson▸
Fast, Cheap & Out of Control▸
The Filth and the Fury
Full Tilt Boogie
Germany in Autumn
Gray's Anatomy
Guilty of Treason
Hank Aaron: Chasing the Dream▸
Harlan County, U.S.A.
Haxan: Witchcraft through the Ages▸
Hearts of Darkness: A Filmmaker's Apocalypse▸
Heavy Petting
Hell's Angels Forever
The Hellstrom Chronicle▸
Hide and Seek
Hoop Dreams▸
Hugh Hefner: Once Upon a Time
I Wanna Be a Beauty Queen
Incident at Oglala: The Leonard Peltier Story▸
It Happened in the Park
It's All True
The JFK Conspiracy
Kidco
The Last Waltz▸
LBJ: A Biography
Le Joli Mai
The Leopard Son
Let It Be
Let's Get Lost
The Life and Times of Hank Greenberg▸
Long Shadows
Louisiana Story▸
The Love Goddesses
Love Meetings
Love Without Fear
Malcolm X: Make It Plain
Man in the Silk Hat▸
Man of Aran▸
The Man with the Movie Camera▸
Many Faces of Sherlock Holmes
Marjoe
Microcosmos▸
Moana, a Romance of the Golden Age▸
Mondo Cane
Mondo Cane 2
Moon over Broadway
Nico Icon▸
Night of the Living Dead, 25th Anniversary Documentary
Paris Is Burning▸
Prelude to War
Punk Rock Movie
Rascal Dazzle
Rock Hudson's Home Movies
Roger & Me▸
Sasquatch
Sex and Buttered Popcorn
The Show
Soft and Hard
The Sorrow and the Pity▸
Streetwise▸
Stripper
Superstar: The Life and Times of Andy Warhol▸
Swimming to Cambodia▸
Thank You & Good Night
Theremin: An Electronic Odyssey▸
The Thin Blue Line▸
Tokyo-Ga▸
Tokyo Olympiad
Triumph of the Will
Truth or Dare
20 Dates
Unzipped▸
Visions of Light: The Art of Cinematography▸
War in the Sky▸
The War Room▸
When We Were Kings
Wigstock: The Movie
Wisecracks▸
Year of the Horse

Dogs

***see** King of Beasts (Dogs)*

Dolls That Kill

***see** Killer Toys*

Doublecross!

***see also** Crime Drama; Heists; Revenge; Scams, Stings & Cons*
Circus
Four Days
Heist▸
Partners
Payback

Down Under

The Adventures of Priscilla, Queen of the Desert▸
Alien Visitor
Alvin Purple
Anzacs: The War Down Under▸
Around the World in 80 Ways
Back of Beyond
Barry McKenzie Holds His Own
Between Wars
Blackrock
Blackwater Trail
Blood Surf
The Blue Lightning
Bootmen
Botany Bay
Boulevard of Broken Dreams
The Boys▸
Brides of Christ
Broken English
Burke & Wills
Caddie
The Cars That Ate Paris▸
Cass
The Castle
Children of the Revolution
Chopper
Country Life
Crocodile Dundee▸
Crocodile Dundee 2
Crocodile Dundee in Los Angeles
The Crocodile Hunter: Collision Course
A Cry in the Dark▸
The Custodian
Dark Age
Dead Alive
Dead Easy
Dead Heart▸
Death of a Soldier
The Desert Rats▸
Dingo
The Dish▸
Down Under
The Dunera Boys▸
Dusty
The Echo of Thunder
Erskinville Kings
Eureka Stockade
Fair Game
Fast Talking
Fierce Creatures
Forty Thousand Horsemen
Freedom
The Fringe Dwellers
Gallagher's Travels
Gallipoli▸
The Getting of Wisdom
The Good Wife
Great Gold Swindle
Ground Zero▸
Hammers over the Anvil
Head On▸
Heavenly Creatures▸
Heaven's Burning
Holy Smoke
Howling 3: The Marsupials
Hurricane Smith
The Irishman
Jackie Chan's First Strike▸
Kings in Grass Castles
Kitty and the Bagman
Lantana▸
The Lighthorsemen▸
A Little Bit of Soul
Little Boy Lost
Love Serenade
Mad Dog Morgan
The Man from Snowy River
Miracle Down Under
Mission: Impossible 2▸
Mr. Nice Guy
Mr. Reliable: A True Story
Money Movers
Monkey Grip▸
Moving Out
Muriel's Wedding▸
My Brilliant Career▸
The Naked Country
Ned Kelly
Nevil Shute's The Far Country
On the Beach▸
On the Beach
Once Were Warriors▸
One Crazy Night
Only the Brave
Oscar and Lucinda
Overlanders▸
Palm Beach
Passion
Phar Lap
Praise▸
Prince and the Great Race
Prisoners of the Sun▸
The Quest
Quigley Down Under
Race the Sun
Rebel
Reckless Kelly
The Rescuers Down Under
Return to Snowy River▸
Ride a Wild Pony▸
The Right Hand Man
The Road from Coorain
Robbery under Arms
Run, Rebecca, Run
Sara Dane
Savage Attraction
Shine▸
The Shrimp on the Barbie
Siam Sunset
Silver City
The Silver Stallion: King of the Wild Brumbies
Sirens
Sister Kenny▸
Soft Fruit
Sorrento Beach
Squizzy Taylor
Stones of Death
Strange Fits of Passion
Strictly Ballroom▸
Summer City
The Sundowners▸
Sweet Talker
Talk
The Thorn Birds▸
Tim
Two Hands▸
Under Capricorn
The Wacky World of Wills & Burke
Walkabout▸
A Waltz Through the Hills
Waterfront
We of the Never Never▸
Welcome to Woop Woop
Where the Green Ants Dream
The Winds of Jarrah
The Winter of Our Dreams
Wrangler

Dragons

***see also** Medieval Romps*
Captain Sinbad
Dragonheart
Dragonheart: A New Beginning
Dragonslayer▸
Dragonworld
Dungeons and Dragons
Erik the Viking
Ghidrah the Three Headed Monster
Goliath and the Dragon
Jabberwocky
Jack the Giant Killer▸
Jason and the Argonauts▸
The Magic Sword
Mulan
The NeverEnding Story▸
Pete's Dragon
Pufnstuf
Quest for Camelot
Reign of Fire
The Seventh Voyage of Sinbad▸
Shrek▸
Sleeping Beauty▸
Sword & the Dragon
The Wonderful World of the Brothers Grimm

Drama

***see** Adventure Drama; Comedy Drama; Crime Drama; Historical Drama; Musical Drama; Romantic Drama; Sports Dramas; Tearjerkers; Tragedy*

Dream Girls

***see also** Beauty Pageants*
A la Mode
American Graffiti▸
Angus
The Arena
Barb Wire
The Barbarians
Baywatch the Movie: Forbidden Paradise
Beauties of the Night
Beautiful Girls
Beauty School
Bikini Bistro
The Bikini Car Wash Company
The Bikini Car Wash Company 2
Bikini Drive-In
Bikini Island
Bikini Summer
Bikini Summer 3: South Beach Heat
Blondes Have More Guns
Bluebeard
Bolero
Burial of the Rats
Calendar Girl Murders
California Girls
Cannonball Run
Cannonball Run 2
Can't Buy Me Love
Cheerleader Camp
The Chosen One: Legend of the Raven
City of Women
Cover Me
Creatures the World Forgot
Cupid
Cycle Vixens
Daddy-O
Day of the Warrior
Deadly Weapons
Def Jam's How to Be a Player
Desperate Cargo
Desperate Moves
Devil Girl from Mars
The Devil's Hand
Diamonds Are Forever▸
Dinosaur Valley Girls
Divine Nymph
Do or Die
Dr. Alien
Dr. Goldfoot and the Bikini Machine
Dr. No▸
The Doll
The Doll Squad
The Dolls
Domino
Downhill Willie
Dracula: Dead and Loving It
Dream Trap
Dreaming of Rita
Dumb & Dumber
Emmanuelle
Emmanuelle 4
Emmanuelle & Joanna
Emmanuelle in the Country
Emmanuelle on Taboo Island
Emmanuelle, the Joys of a Woman
Emmanuelle, the Queen
Emmanuelle's Daughter
Enchanted Island
Evil Toons
Exotica▸
Fair Game
Fate
Femme Fontaine: Killer Babe for the C.I.A.
Fire Maidens from Outer Space
Fireballs
Forbidden Planet▸
Forbidden Zone: Alien Abduction
Gamera vs. Guiron
Gator Bait
Ghosts Can't Do It
Girl Shy▸
Gold of the Amazon Women
Goldeneye▸
The Grace Kelly Story
Great Bikini Off-Road Adventure
Guns
Hard Hunted
Helen of Troy
Hell's Belles
Hercules and the Princess of Troy
Hired to Kill
Hollywood Boulevard 2
Hollywood or Bust
How I Learned to Love Women
How to Succeed with Girls
I, a Woman
I Married a Centerfold
I Posed for Playboy
It Takes a Thief
Junk Mail
Just Looking
Kiss and Kill
La Collectioneuse
Last Dance
Les Girls
Les Mistons▸
The Lion of Thebes▸
Lost and Found
The Loves of Hercules
Malena
A Man with a Maid
Masseuse
The Mermaids of Tiburon
Mirror Images
Mirror Images 2
Mirror, Mirror 3: The Voyeur
Missile to the Moon
Mysterious Island of Beautiful Women
Mystery Date
Naked Souls
National Lampoon's Vacation▸
Never Say Never Again
Nine Ages of Nakedness
A Nymphoid Barbarian in Dinosaur Hell
Oxford Blues
Panther Squad
Party Incorporated
Phat Beach
Pin-Up Girl
Posed for Murder
Priceless Beauty
Princess Daisy
Private Affairs
Queen of Outer Space
Queen of the Jungle
The Reckless Way
Return to Savage Beach
Revenge of the Cheerleaders
Round Trip to Heaven
Savage Beach
Seduce Me: Pamela Principle 2
The Seven Year Itch▸
She Gods of Shark Reef
She's Dressed to Kill
Sidekicks
Silk 'n' Sabotage
Sizzle Beach U.S.A.
Ski School 2
Slumber Party Massacre
Some Like It Hot▸

Sorceress
Soup for One
South Beach Academy
Spinout
The Spring
Star Crash
The Story of a Love Story
Strawberry Blonde▲
The Sure Thing▲
Swimsuit
The Swinging Cheerleaders
Tammy and the Doctor
Tanya's Island
Tarzan, the Ape Man
Telling Lies in America
10
Ten Things I Hate about You▲
There's Something about Mary▲
Thieves of Fortune
Thunder & Mud
To the Limit
Tomorrow Never Dies
Too Shy to Try
Total Exposure
Trojan War
Undercover
Underground Aces
Vampire Vixens from Venus
Vampire's Kiss▲
Vice Academy 3
Voyage to the Planet of Prehistoric Women
Wayne's World▲
Wayne's World 2
Weird Science
Wet and Wild Summer
When Dinosaurs Ruled the Earth
Will Success Spoil Rock Hunter?
Wish Me Luck
Wishful Thinking
The Woman in Red
Woo
You Only Live Twice
Young Nurses in Love
Zeta One

Drug Abuse

***see also** On the Rocks*

Above the Law
Aces: Iron Eagle 3
The Acid Eaters
Across the Tracks
Adventures in Spying
Air America
All That Jazz▲
Alphabet City
Altered States▲
American Fabulous
Amongst Friends
The Amsterdam Connection
The Amsterdam Kill
And Then You Die▲
Angel's Brigade
The Anniversary Party▲
Another Day in Paradise
Armistead Maupin's Tales of the City
Around the Fire
Assassin of Youth
At Any Cost
Avenging Disco Godfather
Awakenings of the Beast
B. Monkey
Back in Action
Bad Boys
Bad Lieutenant▲
Bad Medicine
Baja
The Basketball Diaries
Basquiat▲
The Beach
Belly
Beretta's Island
Best Revenge
The Big Lebowski▲
Bird▲
Black Circle Boys
Black Snow
Black Starlet
The Blackout
Blast-Off Girls
Blind Spot
Blindside
Blood & Concrete: A Love Story
Blood Freak
Blood In ... Blood Out: Bound by Honor
Bloodbath
The Bloody Brood
Blow
Blowin' Smoke
Blue Sunshine
Bongwater
Boogie Boy
Boogie Nights▲
The Boost
Borderline
Born to Win
Bright Lights, Big City
Bringing Out the Dead
Broken Vessels▲
Brotherhood of Justice
A Brother's Kiss
Bully
Busting
Bye-Bye
Capital Punishment
Captain Blackjack
Captive Rage
Carlito's Way▲
Caroline at Midnight
Cartel
Casino▲
Catch the Heat
Caught
Cause of Death
Cement
Chained Heat 2
Chains of Gold
Cheech and Chong: Still Smokin'
Cheech and Chong: Things Are Tough All Over
Cheech and Chong's Next Movie
Cheech and Chong's Nice Dreams
Cheech and Chong's Up in Smoke
Chelsea Walls
The Children of Times Square
China White
Chinatown Connection
Christiane F.▲
Chrome Soldiers
Chungking Express▲
The Cider House Rules▲
Circuit
Class of 1984
Clean and Sober▲
Clockers▲
Club Life
Cocaine Cowboys
Cocaine Fiends
Cocaine: One Man's Seduction
Cocaine Wars
Codename: Wildgeese
Coffy
Coldfire
The Colombian Connection
Commando Squad
Comrades in Arms
Confessions of a Vice Baron
The Connection▲
Contraband
The Cool World
Corridors of Blood
Countryman
Courage▲
Covert Action
Crack House
crazy/beautiful
Crossing the Bridge
The Crow 2: City of Angels
A Cry for Love
The Curfew Breakers
Curtis's Charm
Cut and Run
Dance or Die
Dangerous Game
Dangerous Heart
Darkman 3: Die Darkman Die
Day of Atonement
Day of the Cobra
Day of the Maniac
Dazed and Confused▲
Dead Aim
Dead Presidents
Dead Ringers▲
Deadly Surveillance
Death Drug
The Death of Richie
Death Shot
Death Wish 4: The Crackdown
Deep Cover
Delta Heat
Desert Snow
Desperado▲
Desperate Lives
The Destructors
The Devil's Sleep
Dirty Laundry
Distant Justice
Dr. Jekyll and Mr. Hyde▲
Dr. Jekyll and Mr. Hyde
Dogs in Space
Don't Look Back▲
The Doom Generation▲
Double-Crossed
Down & Dirty▲
Down in the Delta▲
Dream with the Fishes
Drug Wars 2: The Cocaine Cartel
Drugstore Cowboy▲
Drunks
Drying Up the Streets
Easy Kill
Easy Rider▲
Ed Wood▲
Edge of Sanity
Edie in Ciao! Manhattan
8 Million Ways to Die
The End of Innocence
Enter the Dragon▲
Exposure
Extreme Prejudice
Fall from Innocence
Fast Money
Fatal Beauty
Fatal Fix
Fear and Loathing in Las Vegas
Federal Hill
Feelin' Screwy
Fever
The Fifth Floor
54
Fiona
Fire Birds
First Born
The Five Heartbeats▲
The Fix
The Flaming Teen-Age
Flashback▲
Flatfoot
Flesh▲
Fletch
Four Friends▲
Foxes
Frances▲
The French Connection▲
French Connection 2▲
French Intrigue
Fresh
Fresh Kill
Friday
The Fury of the Wolfman
Ganjasaurus Rex
The Gene Krupa Story
Georgia▲
Gia
Go▲
Godmoney
Goodfellas▲
Gordon's War
Gothic▲
Gridlock'd▲
Gunmen
H
Half-Baked
Hallucination
Hard Evidence
Haunted Summer
Heat▲
Heaven's Prisoners
Hell's Kitchen NYC
Help Wanted Female
Hendrix
A Hero Ain't Nothin' but a Sandwich
Heroes for Sale▲
High Art
High Crime
High Risk
High School Confidential
Hit!
Holiday Heart
Homegrown
The Hooked Generation
Horsey
How Come Nobody's On Our Side?
Hugo Pool
Human Traffic
Hussy
I Come in Peace
I Drink Your Blood
I Love You, Alice B. Toklas!
Idle Hands
Illtown
I'm Dancing as Fast as I Can
The Imposter
In Hot Pursuit
In the Flesh
In the Line of Duty: A Cop for the Killing
Inside Edge
Iron Horsemen
Island Monster
Jaguar Lives
Jane Doe
Jekyll and Hyde
Jekyll & Hyde...Together Again
Jesus' Son
Jo Jo Dancer, Your Life Is Calling
Jumpin' at the Boneyard
Kamikaze Hearts
Kandyland
Kemek
Keys to Tulsa
Kickboxer the Champion
Kicked in the Head
Kids
Kids in the Hall: Brain Candy
Kill or Be Killed
Killing Zoe
The Killing Zone
L.627▲
La Bamba▲
L.A. Wars
Lady Sings the Blues
Last Flight to Hell
The Last of the Finest
Lenny▲
Less Than Zero
Let No Man Write My Epitaph
Lethal Obsession
Lethal Weapon▲
Let's Get Harry
Let's Get Lost
License to Kill▲
Light Sleeper
Live and Let Die
Livin' for Love: The Natalie Cole Story
Loaded
Loaded Guns
London Kills Me
Long Day's Journey into Night▲
Long Day's Journey into Night
Long Day's Journey Into Night▲
Loser
Lost Angels
Love Come Down
Lovely ... But Deadly
Magnolia▲
Mainline Run
The Man Inside
The Man with the Golden Arm▲
Marihuana
Marked for Death
Martial Outlaw
Maybe I'll Be Home in the Spring
McBain▲
McQ
The Messenger
Miami Vendetta
Midnight Cop
Midnight Express▲
Mike's Murder
Mindfield
Mission Manila
Mrs. Parker and the Vicious Circle
Mixed Blood
Mob War
The Mod Squad
The Moneytree
Monkey Grip▲
More
My Life and Times with Antonin Artaud▲
The Mystery of Edwin Drood
Naked Lunch▲
The Narcotics Story
National Lampoon's Senior Trip
New Best Friend
New Jack City
Newman's Law
Nico Icon▲
Night Friend
The Night of the Iguana▲
Night Zoo
Nil by Mouth
Ninja in the U.S.A.
No Escape, No Return
Not My Kid
Nowhere
Olga's Girls
On the Edge: The Survival of Dana
One False Move▲
100 Proof
One Man's Justice
The Organization▲
Out of Sync
Out of the Rain
Over the Edge▲
Pace That Kills
The Palermo Connection
Pandaemonium
Panic in Needle Park▲
Passion for Power
The People Next Door
The People vs. Larry Flynt▲
The Perfect Daughter
Performance▲
Permanent Midnight
Pharmacist
Pigalle
Pinero
Platoon the Warriors
Playing with Fire
Point of No Return
Police
The Poppy Is Also a Flower
Postcards from the Edge▲
Pot, Parents, and Police
Praise▲
Premonition
Pretty Smart
Prime Cut
Private Investigations
Protector
Psych-Out
Pulp Fiction▲
Puppet on a Chain
Pusher
Question of Honor
Quiet Cool
Rage and Honor
Rapid Fire
Rated X
Raw Target
Rebound: The Legend of Earl "The Goat" Manigault
Reckless Disregard
Red Blooded American Girl
Red Heat
Red Surf
Requiem for a Dream▲
Resurrection Man
Retribution
Return of the Tiger
Return to Paradise▲
Revenge of the Ninja
Revenge of the Stepford Wives
Riding in Cars with Boys
Rip-Off
River's Edge▲
Rock House
Rodrigo D.: No Future
The Rose▲
The Royal Tenenbaums▲
Rude
Running Out of Time
Running Scared
Rush▲
Saigon Commandos
Saints and Sinners
The Salton Sea
Satan's Harvest
Savage Instinct
Scarface▲
Schnelles Geld
Scorchy
Scorpion Spring
Secret Agent Super Dragon
The Seducers
The Seven-Per-Cent Solution▲
The '70s
Severance
Shameless
She Shoulda Said No
The Show
Showdown in Little Tokyo
Sicilian Connection
Sid & Nancy▲
Silk
The '60s
SLC Punk!
The Slender Thread▲
The Snake People
SnakeEater 2: The Drug Buster
Sno-Line
Sorry, Wrong Number
Spenser: Pale Kings & Princes
Stand Alone
Stella Does Tricks
Still Crazy▲
The Stoned Age
Straight Up
Strange Days▲
Street Girls
Street Hawk
Street Wars
Streetwalkin'
Strike Force
The Substitute
The Substitute 3: Winner Takes All
Sugar Hill
Suicide Kings
Sunset Heat
Sunset Strip
Super Bitch
Superfly
Surrender Dorothy
The Sweet Hereafter▲
Sweet Jane
Sweet Nothing▲
The Take
Talons of the Eagle
Target Eagle
Tchao Pantin▲
Teenage Devil Dolls
TekWar
The Temptations
Temptress Moon
Tequila Sunrise
The Third Man▲
This Time I'll Make You Rich
Thunder Alley
The Tingler▲
To Die Standing
Tombstone▲
The Tong Man
Tongs: An American Nightmare
Too Young to Die
Torchlight
Tough and Deadly
Toughlove
Traffic▲
Traffik▲
Trainspotting▲
Transmutations
Trash
Trespass
The Trip
Tropical Snow
Trouble in Paradise
True Romance
Twenty-One
24-7
Twin Peaks: Fire Walk with Me
Twin Town
Twisted
Ulee's Gold▲
Undercover

Valley of the Dolls
Vanishing Point
Velvet Goldmine
Vicious Circles
Wait until Dark ▲
Wanda, the Sadistic Hypnotist
Warlords from Hell
Warlords 3000
Watched
Weekend with the Babysitter
Weird World of LSD
What Have I Done to Deserve This? ▲
Whispers of White
Who'll Stop the Rain? ▲
Why Do Fools Fall in Love?
Wild Bill
Wild in the Streets
The Wild Pair
The Winter of Our Dreams
A Winter Tan
Wired
Withnail and I ▲
Women on the Verge of a Nervous Breakdown ▲
Wonder Boys ▲
Woodstock ▲
The Young Americans
Zero Tolerance
ZigZag ▲
Zone 39

Drugs

see Drug Abuse

Dublin

see also Ireland
About Adam
Agnes Browne
Circle of Friends
The Commitments ▲
The Dead ▲
Echoes
Frankie Starlight
The General ▲
Girl with Green Eyes
The Informer ▲
Into the West ▲
The Lonely Passion of Judith Hearne ▲
A Man of No Importance ▲
Michael Collins ▲
My Left Foot ▲
Nora
Shake Hands with the Devil ▲
The Snapper ▲
Ulysses
The Van ▲
When Brendan Met Trudy ▲
When the Sky Falls

Dying for a Promotion

see also Bad Bosses; Corporate Shenanigans; Office Surprise
A Shock to the System ▲
The Temp

Ears!

see also Eyeballs!; Renegade Body Parts
Blue Velvet ▲
Django
Feeling Minnesota
High Plains Drifter
I, Madman
Lust for Life ▲
Reservoir Dogs ▲
Say It Isn't So
Van Gogh ▲
Vincent & Theo ▲
White Mischief ▲

Earthquakes

see also Disaster Flicks; L.A.; San Francisco
After the Shock
Aftershock: Earthquake in New York
Black Scorpion 2: Ground Zero
Daybreak
Earthquake
Escape from L.A.
The Great Los Angeles Earthquake
The Last Warrior
Life and Nothing More ...
Marshal Law
Quake
The Rains Came
San Francisco ▲
Shakedown

Eastern Europe

Dark Blue World
Divided We Fall
Dracula: The Dark Prince

Eat Me

see also Cannibalism; Eco-Vengeance!; Killer Beasts; Killer Bugs and Slugs; Killer Plants
Alive
Auntie Lee's Meat Pies
Deep Blue Sea
Deep Rising
Eating Raoul ▲
Event Horizon
Invasion!
Lake Placid
Little Shop of Horrors ▲
The Lost World: Jurassic Park 2
Mimic
Motel Hell
Ravenous
The Relic
Soylent Green
Starship Troopers ▲

Eating

see Cannibalism; Edibles

Eco-Vengeance!

see also Killer Bugs and Slugs
Aberration
Alligator ▲
Anaconda
Ants
The Applegates
Arachnophobia
Ben
Body Snatchers
The Crawlers
Day of the Animals
Deadly Harvest
Falling Fire
Fangs
Ferngully: The Last Rain Forest
The Fire Next Time
Food of the Gods
Frogs
Grizzly
Habitat
Idaho Transfer
Jaws ▲
Jaws 2
Jaws 3
Jaws: The Revenge
Jurassic Park ▲
Kingdom of the Spiders
Last Days of Planet Earth
Magic in the Water
On Deadly Ground
Phantom 2040 Movie: The Ghost Who Walks
Piranha
Piranha 2: The Spawning
Prophecy
Savage Capitalism
Squirm
The Swarm
Thunder Bay ▲
Ticks
The Toxic Avenger
Virus
Willard

Edibles

see also Cannibalism
The Age of Innocence ▲
Babette's Feast ▲
Bar-B-Q
Big Eden
The Big Hit
Big Night
Bikini Bistro
Blood Diner
A Chef in Love
Chocolat ▲
Combination Platter
Consuming Passions
The Cook, the Thief, His Wife & Her Lover ▲
The Deli
Dim Sum: A Little Bit of Heart ▲
The Dinner Game
The Duchess of Duke Street ▲
Eat a Bowl of Tea ▲
Eat Drink Man Woman ▲
Eat the Rich
Eat Your Heart Out
Far Harbor
Felicia's Journey ▲
Gabriela
The Godfather ▲
The Godfather, Part 2 ▲
The Godfather, Part 3 ▲
God's Comedy
Good Burger
Goodfellas ▲
Grave Indiscretions
Hamburger...The Motion Picture
Home Fries
Hot Chocolate
Ice Cream Man
Just Your Luck
La Grande Bouffe ▲
The Last Supper
Life Is Sweet ▲
Like Water for Chocolate ▲
Love Is All There Is
Mambo Cafe
A Matter of Taste
Men
Monty Python's The Meaning of Life ▲
My Big Fat Greek Wedding
9 1/2 Weeks
Palmy Days
Scotland, PA
Simply Irresistible
Small Time Crooks
Soul Food
The Spitfire Grill
The Story of Boys & Girls ▲
Tales from a Parallel Universe: Eating Pattern
Tampopo ▲
301, 302
Tom Jones ▲
Tortilla Soup
The Untold Story
The Van ▲
The Waiting Game
What's Cooking? ▲
Who Is Killing the Great Chefs of Europe? ▲
Willy Wonka & the Chocolate Factory ▲
Woman on Top

Edinburgh

see also Scotland
The Body Snatcher ▲
Greyfriars Bobby
The Prime of Miss Jean Brodie ▲
Terror by Night
Trainspotting ▲

Egypt—Ancient

Cleopatra
Land of the Pharaohs
The Mummy ▲
The Mummy
The Mummy Returns
Prince of Egypt ▲
The Scorpion King
Two Nights with Cleopatra

Elephants

see also Carnivals & Circuses; Wild Kingdom
Babar: The Movie
Billy Rose's Jumbo ▲
Dumbo ▲
Ele, My Friend
Elephant Boy ▲
An Elephant Called Slowly
Elephant Walk
Fantasia ▲
Freddy Got Fingered
George of the Jungle ▲
Jupiter's Darling
Larger Than Life
Looking for Trouble
Maya
Operation Dumbo Drop
Pardon My Trunk
Smokey and the Bandit 2
Whispers: An Elephant's Tale
White Hunter, Black Heart ▲

Elevators

see also Terror in Tall Buildings
Basic Instinct
The Client
Die Hard ▲
Fatal Attraction ▲
In the Line of Fire ▲
The Lift
The Man with Two Brains ▲
Mixed Nuts
Nick of Time
The Omen
Poltergeist 3
Pretty Woman ▲
The Secret of My Success
The Silence of the Lambs ▲
Sleepless in Seattle ▲
Speed ▲
Terminator 2: Judgment Day ▲
Thoroughly Modern Millie
The Towering Inferno
True Lies
The Untouchables ▲
What about Bob? ▲

Emerging Viruses

see also Disease of the Week
Adrenalin: Fear the Rush
And the Band Played On ▲
The Andromeda Strain
Body Armor
Escape from L.A.
Fatal Error
Future Fear
Jericho Fever
Mimic
Mission: Impossible 2 ▲
Outbreak ▲
Panic in the Streets ▲
The Patriot
Resident Evil
Sci-Fighters
Shakedown
Stephen King's The Stand
Terminal Virus
12 Monkeys ▲
Zero Patience

The Empire State Building

see also New York, New York
An Affair to Remember
King Kong ▲
King Kong
Love Affair ▲
Love Affair
On the Town ▲
The Shadow
Sleepless in Seattle ▲

Erotic Thrillers

see also Sex & Sexuality
Animal Instincts 2
Animal Instincts 3: The Seductress
Basic Instinct
Baton Rouge
Beyond Desire
Bitter Harvest
Blindfold: Acts of Obsession
Blown Away
Body Chemistry 3: Point of Seduction
Body Chemistry 4: Full Exposure
Body of Evidence
Body of Influence
Body of Influence 2
Body Shot
Body Strokes
Broken Trust
Business for Pleasure
Caroline at Midnight
Chain of Desire
Cold Sweat
Color of Night
Cover Story
The Crush
The Dangerous
Dangerous Indiscretion
Dangerous Touch
The Dark Dancer
Dark Secrets
Dark Tide
Dead Cold
Dead On
Dead Sexy
Deadly Past
Death and Desire
Deceptions 2: Edge of Deception
Desire
Die Watching
Disclosure
Discretion Assured
Double Cross
Double Threat
Ebbtide
Embrace of the Vampire
Entangled
The Escort
Every Breath
Evil Obsession
Exit
Extramarital
Fatal Bond
Fatal Instinct
Fatal Past
Final Judgment
Flinch
The Girl Next Door
Hard Drive
Hourglass
I Like to Play Games
Illegal in Blue
Illicit Behavior
Illicit Dreams
Improper Conduct
In a Moment of Passion
In Dark Places
In the Heat of Passion 2: Unfaithful
Indecent Behavior
Indecent Behavior 2
Indecent Behavior 3
Inner Sanctum 2
Invasion of Privacy
Kept
Killer Looks
Killing for Love
Lady in Waiting
The Last Seduction 2
Lethal Seduction
Lipstick Camera
Listen
The Little Death
Lonely Hearts
Love Is a Gun
The Man in the Attic
Maniac Nurses Find Ecstasy
Mercy
Midnight Blue
Midnight Confessions
Midnight Tease
Midnight Tease 2
Mind Twister
Mirror Images
Mirror Images 2
Motel Blue
Night Eyes
Night Eyes 2
Night Eyes 3
Night Eyes 4: Fatal Passion
Night Fire
The Nightman
Notorious ▲
Object of Obsession
Outside the Law
Over the Wire
Payback
A Place Called Truth
Playback
Playmaker
Poison Ivy 2: Lily
Poison Ivy 3: The New Seduction
Possessed by the Night
Private Obsession
Rubdown
Running Wild
Saturday Night Special
Save Me
Scorned
Scorned 2
Secret Games
Secret Games 2: The Escort
Secret Games 3
The Seductress
Sexual Malice
Sexual Roulette
Shadow Dancer
Shame, Shame, Shame
The Showgirl Murders
Sins of Desire
Sins of the Night
Sliver
Snapdragon
Spirit Lost
Stolen Hearts
Stormswept
Stormy Nights
Strike a Pose
Suite 16
Sunset Grill
Sweet Evil
Sweet Killing
Temptation
Temptress
Terrified
Trade Off
Tryst
Turn of the Blade
Two Shades of Blue
Under Investigation
Undercover
Vicious Circles
Victim of Desire
Virtual Desire
Virtual Girl
Wild Cactus

Errant Educators

see also Dedicated Teachers; Hell High School
Disturbing Behavior
The Faculty
Teaching Mrs. Tingle
When Brendan Met Trudy ▲

Escaped Cons

see also Great Escapes; Men in Prison
Another Man's Poison
Bandits
Big Momma's House
Black Cat Run
Chasers
Con Air ▲
Cool Hand Luke ▲
Dark Passage
Dead of Night
Deadlock
Deadlock 2
The Defiant Ones ▲
Destiny Turns on the Radio
Double Jeopardy
Duets
The Escape
Escape from Alcatraz ▲
Face/Off ▲
Firestorm
Fled
From Dusk Till Dawn
The Fugitive ▲
Gang Busters
A Gentleman After Dark
Great Expectations
Great Expectations ▲
Great Expectations

▲ = rated three bones or higher

Great Expectations: The Untold Story
Happy, Texas▲
I Am a Fugitive from a Chain Gang▲
Jailbreakers
Jailbreakin'
The Last Marshal
Lewis and Clark and George
Lonely Are the Brave▲
The Man Who Broke 1,000 Chains
The Mighty▲
Moonbase
Next Friday
O Brother Where Art Thou?
Out of Sight▲
Papillon▲
Parallel Sons
Passage to Marseilles▲
Passenger 57
A Perfect World
Point Blank
Prison on Fire 2
Proximity
Raising Arizona▲
Red Letters
Rites of Passage
Runaway Train▲
A Scandal in Paris
Slow Burn
Soft Deceit
Stakeout
The Stunt Man▲
Two for Texas
Warden of Red Rock
We're No Angels
Where the Money Is
The Wrong Guys
Wrongfully Accused

Ethics & Morals

All the King's Men▲
And Justice for All
Any Man's Death
The Assault▲
Barbarians at the Gate▲
The Best Man▲
Blame It on Rio
Blue Chips
Boiler Room▲
The Border▲
The Boy with the Green Hair▲
The Bridge on the River Kwai▲
Casualties of War▲
Changing Lanes▲
Chinese Roulette
Chloe in the Afternoon▲
Circle of Power
The Citadel▲
City Hall▲
A Civil Action
Commandments
The Contender
The Conversation▲
The Corruptor▲
Crime and Punishment in Suburbia
Crimes & Misdemeanors▲
Cruel Intentions
Cutter's Way
A Dangerous Woman
The Deep End▲
Deep Six
The Defiant Ones▲
The Doctor
Double Identity
The Dreamlife of Angels▲
Election▲
The Elephant Man▲
Elmer Gantry▲
Extreme Measures
Fifth Day of Peace
The Fifth Seal
Force of Evil▲
Fortunes of War
The Funeral▲
Fury▲
Getting Away With Murder
Gossip
Harriet the Spy
The Ice Storm▲
The Image
It Could Happen to You
Jerry Maguire▲
Jezebel▲
The Judge and the Assassin▲
Judgment at Nuremberg▲
The Juggler of Notre Dame
Keys to Tulsa
Kings Row▲
Knocks at My Door
La Ronde▲
La Truite▲
The Last of England▲
L'Avventura▲
The Lazarus Syndrome
License to Kill
Love with the Proper Stranger▲
Malicious
The Man Inside
The Man Who Shot Liberty Valance▲
Manhattan Melodrama▲
Marihuana
A Matter of Dignity
Midnight
The Millionairess
Mindwalk: A Film for Passionate Thinkers▲
Mr. Smith Goes to Washington▲
Mom & Dad
Muriel▲
Network▲
News at Eleven
The Next Voice You Hear
Nixon▲
No Man's Land
Oedipus Rex▲
One Flew Over the Cuckoo's Nest▲
Other People's Money
Overture to Glory
The Ox-Bow Incident▲
Paris Trout
Penalty Phase
A Place in the Sun▲
Platoon▲
Playing God
The Ploughman's Lunch▲
Prime Suspect
Private Hell 36
The Proposition
Quiz Show▲
Ran▲
Reckless Disregard
Return to Paradise▲
Riel
The Sacrifice▲
Scandal Man
The Scarlet Letter
The Scarlet Letter▲
Shampoo
The Shootist▲
Silent Witness
Soul Man
S*P*Y*S
SS Girls
The Star Chamber
The Story of Women▲
Strangers When We Meet
Survival of Spaceship Earth
Sweet Smell of Success▲
Test Tube Babies
The Things of Life▲
To Live & Die in L.A.
A Touch of Class▲
The Toy
Tulsa▲
Twelve Angry Men▲
Twelve Angry Men
Twenty-One
Tycoon
Under Fire▲
Viridiana▲
Wall Street▲
The Wheeler Dealers▲
With Honors
Zabriskie Point▲
Zero Degrees Kelvin

Etiquette

Born Yesterday▲
Educating Rita▲
My Fair Lady▲
Papa's Delicate Condition▲
Phantom of Liberty▲
Pleasure
Pygmalion▲
The Ruling Class▲
True Love▲

Evil Doctors

***see also** Doctors & Nurses; Mad Scientists*

The Abominable Dr. Phibes▲
Anatomy▲
The Awful Dr. Orloff
Baby Geniuses
Blackmale
Body Melt
The Curious Dr. Humpp
Curse of the Puppet Master: The Human Experiment
Dead Ringers▲
Death and the Maiden▲
The Dentist
Dr. Alien
The Doctor and the Devils
Dr. Black, Mr. Hyde
Doctor Blood's Coffin
Doctor Butcher M.D.
Dr. Caligari
Dr. Cyclops
Dr. Death, Seeker of Souls
Dr. Frankenstein's Castle of Freaks
Dr. Giggles
Dr. Goldfoot and the Bikini Machine
Dr. Hackenstein
Dr. Jekyll and Mr. Hyde▲
Dr. Jekyll and Mr. Hyde
Dr. Jekyll and Sister Hyde
Dr. Jekyll and the Wolfman
Dr. Jekyll's Dungeon of Death
Dr. Mabuse, The Gambler▲
Dr. Mabuse vs. Scotland Yard
Dr. No▲
Dr. Orloff's Invisible Horror
Dr. Otto & the Riddle of the Gloom Beam
Doctor Phibes Rises Again
Doctor Satan's Robot
Dr. Tarr's Torture Dungeon
Dr. Terror's House of Horrors
Doctor X
Extreme Measures
Feast for the Devil
Jekyll and Hyde
Mad Doctor of Blood Island
Malice
Night of the Bloody Apes
Night of the Bloody Transplant
Prince of Poisoners: The Life and Crimes of William Palmer
Slaughter Hotel
Strange World of Coffin Joe
The Two Faces of Dr. Jekyll

Executing Revenge

***see also** Death & the Afterlife; Death Row; Men in Prison; Revenge*

Before I Hang▲
Blowback
Destroyer
Exorcist 3: Legion
Fallen
The First Power
The Horror Show
I Know What You Did Last Summer▲
The Indestructible Man
Judge & Jury
The Man They Could Not Hang
Prison
Shocker
Soldier

Existentialism

***see** The Meaning of Life*

Exploitation

***see also** Sexploitation*

Abduction
Agony of Love
American Nightmare
Angel of H.E.A.T.
Angels of the City
Armed Response
Assassin of Youth
Bad Girls from Mars
Barn of the Naked Dead
Basic Training
Beatrice▲
Betrayal
Beyond the Valley of the Dolls
Black Shampoo
Blackenstein
Blood Games
The Bloody Brood
Blue Movies
Boss
The Cage
Caged Terror
Certain Sacrifice
Chained for Life
Common Law Wife
Confessions of a Vice Baron
Cover Girl Models
The Curfew Breakers
The Cut Throats
Cycle Psycho
Cycle Vixens
Dance Hall Racket
Dangerous Obsession
The Dark Side of Love
Deadly Sanctuary
Death of a Centerfold
Def Jam's How to Be a Player
Devil's Wedding Night
Escape from Safehaven
Exterminator 2
Five Minutes to Love
The Flaming Teen-Age
For Ladies Only
Fox and His Friends▲
Foxy Brown
Ghoulies 3: Ghoulies Go to College
Girl on a Chain Gang
Gun Girls
Heat of the Flame
High School Caesar
Hitler's Children▲
Hollywood after Dark
Hollywood Dreams
The Hollywood Strangler Meets the Skid Row Slasher
House of Whipcord
In Trouble
Island of Lost Girls
Jock Petersen
Kidnapped
Kinjite: Forbidden Subjects
L.A. Heat
L.A. Vice
Last Call
Little Girl ... Big Tease
Little Miss Innocence
The Lonely Sex
Love Camp
The Mack
Malibu Express
Mandinga
M'Lady's Court
My Wonderful Life
The Naked Flame
Naked in the Night
Naked Vengeance
The Narcotics Story
Night Friend
Night of Evil
Nomugi Pass
One Down, Two to Go!
One Night Only
One Plus One
One Too Many
Overexposed
Paradise Motel
Party Incorporated
Pin Down Girls
Policewoman Centerfold
Poor Pretty Eddie
Reefer Madness
Ringmaster
The Road to Ruin
Satan's Cheerleaders
Savages from Hell
Secrets of Sweet Sixteen
Sensual Partners
Sex Adventures of the Three Musketeers
She Shoulda Said No
Sin You Sinners
Single Room Furnished
Slaughter
Slaughter's Big Ripoff
Slaves in Bondage
S.O.B.
Something Weird
SS Girls
Star 80
Street of Forgotten Women
Student Confidential
Suite 16
Summer School Teachers
Sunset Strip
Swamp Women
Sweet Spirits
Taxi Dancers
The Teacher
Teenage Doll
Test Tube Babies
They're Playing with Fire
Three in the Attic
Thunder & Mud
Tomorrow's Children
Violated
Warrior Queen
Weekend with the Babysitter
Weird World of LSD
Woman Hunt
Women's Club
Yesterday's Hero
Young Lady Chatterly 2
Youth Aflame

Explorers

The Adventures of Marco Polo
Almost Heroes
Apollo 13▲
Atlantis: The Lost Empire
Cabeza de Vaca▲
Call Me Bwana
Christopher Columbus
Christopher Columbus: The Discovery
Congo
The Conqueror & the Empress
The Forbidden Quest
Forgotten City
1492: Conquest of Paradise
Glory & Honor
How Tasty Was My Little Frenchman
King Solomon's Mines▲
King Solomon's Mines
The Last Place on Earth
The Live Wire
The Lost World
The Magic Voyage
Mountains of the Moon▲
Shackleton▲
She
Sir Arthur Conan Doyle's The Lost World
The Sky Above, the Mud Below
The Valley Obscured by the Clouds
The Wacky World of Wills & Burke
Wagon Wheels
Wake of the Red Witch

Extraordinary Pairings

Abbott and Costello Meet Frankenstein▲
All About the Benjamins
Almost Heroes
Bela Lugosi Meets a Brooklyn Gorilla
Billy the Kid Versus Dracula
The Breed
Doctor of Doom
Dracula vs. Frankenstein
Frankenstein Meets the Space Monster
Frankenstein Meets the Wolfman▲
The Hollywood Strangler Meets the Skid Row Slasher
Jesse James Meets Frankenstein's Daughter
King Kong vs. Godzilla
Living Out Loud
My Giant
Santa Claus Conquers the Martians
Wrestling Women vs. the Aztec Mummy

Eyeballs!

***see also** Hearts!*

Anguish
The Birds▲
A Clockwork Orange▲
The Crawling Eye
Damien: Omen 2
Demolition Man
Die Hard 2: Die Harder▲
Evil Dead 2: Dead by Dawn
The Eye Creatures
Eyeball
Eyes of Laura Mars
Friday the 13th, Part 3
The Fury
The Godfather▲
Halloween 2: The Nightmare Isn't Over!
Headless Eyes
Idle Hands
Nightwatch
Peeping Tom▲
The Phantom
Pitch Black▲
Rocky▲
Scanners
Silver Bullet
Strange Behavior
Summer School
The Terminator▲
True Lies
Un Chien Andalou▲
Wild Palms
X: The Man with X-Ray Eyes▲
Zombie

Fairs & Expositions

***see also** Amusement Parks; Carnivals & Circuses*

Howling 6: The Freaks
It Happened at the World's Fair
Ma and Pa Kettle at the Fair
My Girl
Shag: The Movie▲
State Fair▲
Swap Meet

Family Ties

***see also** Dads; Moms; Parenthood*

A. I.: Artificial Intelligence
ABC Stage 67: Truman Capote's A Christmas Memory
Abraham
The Addams Family
Addams Family Values
The Adventures of Felix
The Adventures of the Wilderness Family
After Julius
Air Force One▲
Alberto Express
Alice▲
Alice et Martin
All I Desire
All I Want for Christmas
All Mine to Give
All the Kind Strangers
American Beauty▲
An American Christmas Carol
American Dream▲
American Gothic
American Pop
An American Rhapsody▲
Amityville Dollhouse
And Baby Makes Six
... And the Earth Did Not Swallow Him

▲ = rated three bones or higher

▲ = rated three bones or higher

Les Violons du Bal
Let the Devil Wear Black
Lethal Weapon▲
Lethal Weapon 4
Let's Dance
The Letter▲
Letting the Birds Go Free
Liam
Liar's Edge
Liar's Moon
Liberty Heights
License to Kill
The Lickerish Quartet
Lies My Father Told Me▲
Life and Nothing More ...
Life Is a Long Quiet River▲
Life Is Sweet▲
Like Water for Chocolate▲
Lily Dale
Lily in Winter
The Lion in Winter▲
The Lion King▲
The List of Adrian Messenger▲
Little Bigfoot
Little Buddha
The Little Death
Little House on the Prairie▲
Little Indian, Big City
The Little Kidnappers
Little Lord Fauntleroy
Little Nellie Kelly
Little Nicky
Little Odessa
The Little Vampire
Little Women▲
Little Women
Little Women▲
The Littlest Viking
Locked in Silence
Lone Star▲
The Long Day Closes▲
Long Day's Journey into Night▲
Long Day's Journey into Night
Long Day's Journey Into Night▲
The Long, Hot Summer▲
The Long Kiss Goodnight
Look Who's Talking Now
Lorenzo's Oil▲
Lorna Doone
Lorna Doone▲
Lost Boundaries
The Lost Boys
The Lost Child
Lost Honeymoon
Lost in Space
Lost in Yonkers
The Lost Language of Cranes▲
Lots of Luck
Lotto Land
The Lotus Eaters
Love Finds Andy Hardy▲
Love, Honour & Obey
Love Kills
Love Laughs at Andy Hardy
Love Me Tender
Love on the Dole▲
Love Under Pressure
Love Without Fear
Love Your Mama
Lover Girl
Lovers and Other Strangers▲
The Low Life
Lucky Stiff
Ma and Pa Kettle
Ma and Pa Kettle at Home
Ma and Pa Kettle at the Fair
Ma and Pa Kettle at Waikiki
Ma and Pa Kettle Back On the Farm
Ma and Pa Kettle Go to Town
Ma and Pa Kettle on Vacation
Ma Barker's Killer Brood
Ma Vie en Rose▲
Mad Max▲
M.A.D.D.: Mothers Against Drunk Driving
Made in America
The Madness of King George▲
Mafia!
Mafia Princess
Magenta
Magic Kid
The Magnificent Ambersons▲
The Magnificent Ambersons
Make Room for Tomorrow
The Maker
Mama Turns a Hundred▲
Mame
Man & Boy
The Man from Laramie▲
The Man in the Gray Flannel Suit
The Man in the Santa Claus Suit
A Man of Passion
Man of the House
Man, Woman & Child
Mandy▲
Maniac
Mansfield Park
Margaret's Museum▲
Maria's Day▲
Martha and I▲
Martin Chuzzlewit
Marvin's Room
Masala
Masterminds
The Mating Game▲
A Matter of Principle
Maverick
May Fools▲
Maybe I'll Be Home in the Spring
Me and the Mob
Meet Me in St. Louis▲
Meet the Hollowheads
Meet the Parents
Meet the Parents▲
The Member of the Wedding▲
The Member of the Wedding
Memory of Us
Menace on the Mountain
Merlin
Miami Rhapsody
Midnight
The Migrants▲
Milk Money
The Million Dollar Kid
Min & Bill
Mind Games
The Miniver Story
Miracle at Midnight
Miracle Down Under
Miracle on 34th Street▲
Miracle on 34th Street
The Mirror Has Two Faces
Mississippi Masala▲
Missouri Traveler▲
Mrs. Doubtfire
Mrs. Miniver▲
Mrs. Parkington
Mr. & Mrs. Bridge▲
Mr. Hobbs Takes a Vacation▲
Mr. Skitch
Mob Boss
Model Behavior
Mom & Dad
Mom, Can I Keep Her?
Mon Oncle▲
Mon Oncle Antoine▲
A Mongolian Tale
Monkey Trouble
Monsieur Verdoux▲
Monsoon Wedding▲
Moonstruck▲
The Mortal Storm▲
The Mosquito Coast
Mother▲
Mother
Mother & Daughter: A Loving War
Mother and Son
Mother Doesn't Always Know Best
Mother Wore Tights▲
Mother's Boys
Mouchette▲
Moving
Multiplicity
The Mummy Returns
Murder, He Says
Murder in the Doll House
Music from Another Room
My Best Girl▲
My Big Fat Greek Wedding
My Daughter's Keeper
My Family▲
My Father's Glory▲
My Friend Walter
My Girl 2
My Grandpa Is a Vampire
My Heroes Have Always Been Cowboys
My Life
My Life So Far
My Mother's Castle▲
My Other Husband
My Son, My Son
My Summer Story
My Twentieth Century▲
My Uncle Silas▲
The Myth of Fingerprints
Nadja▲
Naked Paradise
National Lampoon's Christmas Vacation
National Lampoon's European Vacation
National Lampoon's Last Resort
National Lampoon's The Don's Analyst
Natural Enemies
The Natural History of Parking Lots
The Neon Bible
The Nephew
New Blood
The New Land▲
New Waterford Girl
New York Stories▲
Next of Kin
Next Stop, Greenwich Village▲
Next Summer▲
Nice Girl?
Nicholas Nickleby▲
Night Crossing
Night Moves▲
Night Must Fall▲
Night of Terror
The Night of the Hunter▲
Night of the Twisters
Nights and Days
Nil by Mouth
Nine Months
1900▲
No End
No Laughing Matter
No Place to Hide
No Place to Run
Noah's Ark
Noon Wine▲
The Norman Conquests, Part 1: Table Manners▲
The Norman Conquests, Part 2: Living Together▲
The Norman Conquests, Part 3: Round and Round the Garden▲
North
Not in This Town
Not My Kid
Not Quite Human
Not Quite Human 2
Now and Forever
Numero Deux
The Nutty Professor▲
Nutty Professor 2: The Klumps
The Object of My Affection
Of Human Hearts
Oh Dad, Poor Dad (Momma's Hung You in the Closet & I'm Feeling So Sad)
O'Hara's Wife
The Old Curiosity Shop
The Old Dark House▲
Old Yeller▲
Olivier, Olivier▲
Ollie Hopnoodle's Haven of Bliss
Olly Olly Oxen Free
On Golden Pond▲
On Moonlight Bay
On Valentine's Day
Once Around
Once Upon a Time ... When We Were Colored▲
Once Were Warriors▲
The One and Only, Genuine, Original Family Band▲
One Cooks, the Other Doesn't
One Good Cop
One More Chance
The Only Thrill
Only You
Orange County
Ordet▲
Ordinary People▲
The Other Sister
Other Voices, Other Rooms
Our Little Girl
Our Mother's Murder
Our Mutual Friend
Our Town▲
Our Very Own
Out of the Blue▲
Out of Time
Out on a Limb
Outcasts of the Trail
Outside Chance of Maximillian Glick
Overboard
Overture to Glory
The Ox
Paco
Padre Nuestro
Padre Padrone▲
The Painted Lady▲
Panic in the Year Zero!
Paradise▲
A Paradise Under the Stars
The Parent Trap
Parental Guidance
Parrish
Passed Away
Passion
Pecker
Peg o' My Heart
Peggy Sue Got Married
The Perez Family
The Perfect Daughter
Perfect Family
A Perfect Little Murder
Personal Exemptions
Persuasion
Persuasion▲
Pet Sematary
Phaedra
Phedre
Philadelphia▲
The Piano Lesson▲
Ping Pong
Pinocchio's Revenge
Pitfall▲
A Place in the World▲
Please Don't Eat the Daisies
Poil de Carotte
Poison Ivy
Poldark▲
Poldark
Poldark 2▲
Polish Wedding
Pollyanna▲
Poltergeist: The Legacy
The Pope of Greenwich Village
The Portrait▲
Prehysteria
Prehysteria 3
Pride and Prejudice▲
Pride and Prejudice
Pride and Prejudice▲
Prince of Pennsylvania
The Prince of Tides▲
The Princess Diaries
Prizzi's Honor▲
The Prodigal
Promised a Miracle
The Proposition
Psycho Sisters
Pushing Hands
Queen Margot▲
Queen of Hearts▲
Quiz Show▲
Radiance
Radio Flyer
Rage of Angels: The Story Continues
Raging Bull▲
The Railway Children▲
Rainbow's End
A Raisin in the Sun▲
Ran▲
Ransom▲
Ratcatcher
The Real Charlotte
Rebecca of Sunnybrook Farm
Red Dirt
Red Firecracker, Green Firecracker
The Red Pony▲
Redwood Curtain
The Ref▲
Regarding Henry▲
Regina
Relative Fear
Remember the Night▲
Return
The Return of the Borrowers▲
Return to Africa
Return to Me
Rhapsody in August
Rich in Love
Rich, Young and Pretty
Richie Rich
Riders of the Purple Sage
Riot in the Streets
Rivals
The River Niger
The River Wild
Road Racers
Road to Salina▲
Robert Kennedy and His Times
Rocket Gibraltar▲
The Rocking Horse Winner
RoGoPaG
Roll of Thunder, Hear My Cry
Rolling Home
Romeo and Juliet
Romeo and Juliet▲
Romola
Ronnie and Julie
Roommates
Roosters
The Royal Bed
Royal Deceit
Ruby Bridges
A Rumor of Angels
Runaway Father
Running Mates▲
Running on Empty▲
Running Wild
Rupert's Land
Safe Passage
Saint Maybe▲
St. Patrick's Day
A Saintly Switch
Sallah▲
Samantha
Same Old Song▲
Sand
Sandra of a Thousand Delights
The Saphead
Sarah, Plain and Tall: Skylark
Sarah, Plain and Tall: Winter's End▲
Sardinia Kidnapped
Satan in High Heels
Savage Is Loose
Say Anything▲
Scarlett
Scent of a Woman▲
Scott Turow's The Burden of Proof
Scream for Help
The Sculptress
The Search▲
Searching for Bobby Fischer▲
A Season for Miracles
Season of Change
Season of Fear
The Secret
The Secret Garden▲
The Secret of Roan Inish▲
Secrets
Secrets and Lies
Seduced and Abandoned▲
The Seducers
See You in the Morning
The Seekers
Selena
Separate Vacations
Set Me Free
7 Faces of Dr. Lao▲
Shadow of a Doubt▲
Shameless
The Shanghai Gesture
The Shell Seekers
Shenandoah▲
The Shepherd of the Hills▲
Sherman's March: An Improbable Search for Love
She's So Lovely
Shiloh
The Shipping News
Shock
Shoot the Moon
Shot Through the Heart▲
Showdown
Shy People▲
Siberiade▲
Silence
The Silence of Neto
The Silences of the Palace▲
Silent Rebellion
Silent Tongue
The Silver Stallion: King of the Wild Brumbies
Simple Justice
A Simple Plan▲
Since You Went Away▲
Sinners
Sins of the Mind
Sioux City
Sitcom
Six in Paris
Sixteen Candles▲
The '60s
'68
Skag▲
Skeletons
Skin Game
The Sleazy Uncle
The Slingshot▲
Smart House
Smilin' Through▲
Smoke
Smoke Signals
The Snapper▲
Snow Day
Snowbound: The Jim and Jennifer Stolpa Story
Sofie
The Solitary Man
Something in the Wind
Something to Talk About
Sometimes a Great Notion▲
Sometimes They Come Back ... Again
Son-in-Law
Son of Flubber
Son of Frankenstein▲
Son of Fury▲
The Song of Songs
Song of the Exile
Song of the Islands
Sons
Sorceress
Sorrows of Gin
The Sound of Music▲
Sous Sol
South Central
South Riding
The Southerner▲
Southie
Souvenir
Spectre
Spencer's Mountain
Spider Baby
Spirit Rider▲
Spitfire
Splendor
Split Decisions
Split Image▲
Splitting Heirs
Spraggue
Spy Kids▲
Star Maps
State Fair▲
State Fair
Steal This Movie!
Stealing Beauty
Stella Dallas▲
Stepmonster
Stepsisters
Still Not Quite Human
Stir of Echoes
The Stone Boy▲
The Storm Within▲
The Story of Boys & Girls▲
Storytelling▲
Storyville

▲ = rated three bones or higher

The Strange Door
Strange Interlude▲
Strange Interlude
The Stranger
Strangers in the City
Strangers: The Story of a Mother and Daughter▲
The Strauss Family
Street Girls
Street Hero
Street Justice
Striking Distance
Struggle
Stuart Little
Stuck on You
The Stupids
The Subject Was Roses▲
The Substance of Fire
The Substitute Wife
Such a Long Journey▲
Suddenly, Last Summer▲
Sugar Cane Alley▲
Summer Holiday
Summer Magic
The Summer of Aviya
Summer of Fear
Summer of the Monkeys
A Sunday in the Country▲
Sunday's Children▲
The Sundowners▲
Sunshine
Sure Fire
Susan and God▲
Susana▲
Suzanne
Swedenhielms
The Sweeper
The Sweet Hereafter▲
Sweet Nothing▲
Sweet Thing▲
The Swiss Family Robinson▲
Switched at Birth
Table Settings
The Tale of Ruby Rose▲
A Tale of Winter
Tarantella
Tatie Danielle▲
Tears in the Rain
Teenage Exorcist
Temptress Moon
Ten Days Wonder
The Tenant of Wildfell Hall
Teorema
Termini Station
Terranova
Testament▲
Tevye
Tex
A Texas Funeral
Thank You & Good Night
That Eye, the Sky
There's No Business Like Show Business▲
They Call Me Sirr
They Watch
The Thief
Things in Their Season
The Third Sex
This Boy's Life▲
This Happy Breed▲
This Is My Father
This Is My Life
This Is the Sea
This Property Is Condemned
Those Who Love Me Can Take the Train
A Thousand Clowns▲
Threads▲
Three Daring Daughters
The Three Lives of Karen
Three Wishes
Three's Trouble
Through a Glass Darkly▲
Thursday's Child
The Ticket
Ticket to Heaven▲
The Tie That Binds
Tieta of Agreste
Tiger Warsaw
Time Indefinite
A Time to Live
A Time to Live and a Time to Die
Timemaster
Tito and Me▲
T.N.T.
To Dance with the White Dog▲
To Die For 2: Son of Darkness
To Gillian on Her 37th Birthday
To Live▲
To Paris with Love
To Sleep with Anger▲
Toby McTeague
Tokyo Cowboy
Tokyo Story▲
Tollbooth
Tommy Boy
Toughlove
Tourist Trap
Toys
Toys in the Attic
Track 29
Trade Secrets
Traffic Jam
The Trail of the Lonesome Pine▲
Tramp at the Door
Traps
Traveller▲
Travels with My Aunt
Treasure of the Sierra Madre▲
The Tree of Wooden Clogs▲
Trois Couleurs: Blanc▲
Trois Couleurs: Bleu▲
Tromeo & Juliet
True Love▲
True Women
Trusting Beatrice
The Turning
The Tuttles of Tahiti▲
29th Street
Twice in a Lifetime▲
The Twilight of the Golds
Twister
2 by 4
Two Small Bodies
Ulee's Gold▲
Un Air de Famille
Uncle Buck▲
Uncle Moses
Uncommon Valor
Uncorked
Under the Boardwalk
Undergrads▲
Uneasy Terms
An Unexpected Family
An Unexpected Life
The Unforgiven▲
Unstrung Heroes
Up/Down/Fragile
Up the Sandbox
The Uprising▲
Used People
Vacas
Vegas Vacation
A Very Brady Christmas
A Very Brady Sequel
Vigil▲
Village of Dreams
Violette▲
Viridiana▲
The Visit▲
Voyage en Balloon
Voyager▲
Vultures
Wait Till Your Mother Gets Home
A Walk in the Clouds
Walk in the Spring Rain
Walking Thunder
The Wall▲
The Waltons: The Christmas Carol
The War
War & Remembrance
War & Remembrance: The Final Chapter
The War at Home
Waterproof▲
The Way We Live Now
The Wedding Banquet▲
Wedding Bell Blues
Wedding in White
The Weekend
Welcome Home
Welcome to the Dollhouse
What about Bob?▲
What the Peeper Saw
What's Cooking?▲
What's Eating Gilbert Grape▲
When Nature Calls
When Saturday Comes
Where East Is East
Where Have All the People Gone?
Where Love Has Gone
Where the Heart Is
While You Were Sleeping▲
The White Balloon▲
The White Cliffs of Dover▲
Whity
Why Do They Call It Love When They Mean Sex?
Why Does Herr R. Run Amok?
Wicked
Wicked Stepmother
Wide Awake
Widow's Kiss
The Wild Country
The Wild Duck
Wild Pony
Wild Zone
Wildflower▲
William Shakespeare's Romeo and Juliet▲
The Winds of War
The Wings of the Dove▲
The Winner
The Winslow Boy▲
The Winter Guest▲
Winter Kills▲
Winter People
The Wistful Widow of Wagon Gap
With Six You Get Eggroll
Witness Protection▲
Wives and Daughters
The Wizard of Loneliness
A Woman under the Influence▲
Women on the Verge of a Nervous Breakdown▲
Woodchipper Massacre
The World Accuses
World and Time Enough
A World Apart▲
The World of Apu▲
The Yards
The Yarn Princess
The Yearling
Yellow Earth
Yi Yi
You Can't Take It with You▲
You'll Like My Mother
Younger & Younger
Yours, Mine & Ours
Zack & Reba
Zertigo Diamond Caper
Zooman▲

Fantasy

***see also** Animation & Cartoons; Musical Fantasy*

A Nous la Liberte▲
The Acid Eaters
Adventures in Dinosaur City
The Adventures of a Gnome Named Gnorm
The Adventures of Baron Munchausen▲
The Adventures of Mark Twain▲
The Adventures of Pinocchio
Aladdin
Aladdin and His Wonderful Lamp
Alice▲
Alice in Wonderland
Alice Through the Looking Glass
Alien from L.A.
...Almost
Alone Against Rome
Amazing Mr. Blunden
The Amazing Spider-Man
Amazing Stories
Amazons
America 3000
The Amphibian Man
Angel on My Shoulder▲
Angel on My Shoulder
Ashik Kerib▲
Atlantis, the Lost Continent
Atlantis: The Lost Empire
Atlas
Atlas in the Land of the Cyclops
Ator the Fighting Eagle
Babe▲
Babe: Pig in the City
Baby ... Secret of the Lost Legend
Barbarella
Barbarian Queen
Baron Munchausen▲
Batman▲
Batman and Robin
Batman Forever▲
Batman Returns
*batteries not included
Beanstalk
Beastmaster
Beastmaster 2: Through the Portal of Time
Beastmaster 3: The Eye of Braxus
Beauties of the Night
Beauty and the Devil
Bernard and the Genie
Between Heaven and Earth
Beyond Atlantis
Beyond Tomorrow
Big▲
Big Top Pee-wee
Biggles
Bill & Ted's Excellent Adventure
The Bishop's Wife▲
The Black Cauldron
Blithe Spirit▲
The Blood of a Poet
The Blue Bird▲
Blue Monkey
The Borrowers▲
The Boy Who Could Fly▲
The Boy Who Loved Trolls
Brothers Lionheart
Cabin Boy
The Canterville Ghost
The Cat from Outer Space
Celine and Julie Go Boating
The Challenge
Charleston▲
Charley and the Angel
The Children of Noisy Village
The Christmas That Almost Wasn't
The Chronicles of Narnia
Cinderella 2000
Circus Angel▲
The City of Lost Children▲
The Clan of the Cave Bear
Clarence
Clash of the Titans
Cocoon▲
Cocoon: The Return
The Company of Wolves▲
Conan the Barbarian▲
Conan the Destroyer
A Connecticut Yankee▲
A Connecticut Yankee in King Arthur's Court
Conquest
Conquest of Mycene
Coriolanus, Man without a Country
The Crazy Ray▲
Crossworlds
The Crow
The Crow 2: City of Angels
Curse of the Cat People▲
Darby O'Gill & the Little People▲
The Dark Crystal▲
The Day the Earth Froze
Death Takes a Holiday▲
Deathstalker
Deathstalker 2: Duel of the Titans
Deathstalker 3
Deathstalker 4: Match of Titans
Desperate Living
The Devil & Max Devlin
Devil of the Desert Against the Son of Hercules
Diary of Forbidden Dreams▲
Digby, the Biggest Dog in the World
Dinotopia
Donkey Skin▲
Dragonheart
Dragonheart: A New Beginning
Dragonslayer▲
Dragonworld
Dream a Little Dream
Dream a Little Dream 2
Dreamchild▲
Dreamscape
Drop Dead Fred
Dungeonmaster
Dungeons and Dragons
Edward Scissorhands▲
Emmanuelle 4
The Enchanted Cottage
The Enchantress
Endgame
Eraserhead▲
Erotic Escape
Erotic Touch of Hot Skin
Escape from Atlantis
Escapes
E.T.: The Extra-Terrestrial▲
Eternal Return
The Ewok Adventure
The Ewoks: Battle for Endor
Excalibur▲
Explorers
Falcon
The Fantastic Night▲
Fantasy Island
Faraway, So Close!
Field of Dreams▲
The Final Programme
Fire and Ice
Flight of Dragons
Flight of the Navigator
Fluke
Francis Goes to the Races
Francis the Talking Mule▲
Frankenstein and Me
Freddie the Frog
French Quarter
From the Earth to the Moon
Galgameth
George's Island▲
The Ghost and Mrs. Muir▲
Ghost Chase
Ghost Writer
Ghosts Can't Do It
Ghostwarrior
The Giants of Thessaly
Gladiators 7
The Glass Slipper
The Gnome-Mobile
Golden Voyage of Sinbad
The Golem▲
Goliath Against the Giants
Goliath and the Barbarians
Goliath and the Dragon
Goliath and the Sins of Babylon
Gor
The Great Land of Small
Grendel, Grendel, Grendel
Gryphon
Gulliver's Travels
A Gun, a Car, a Blonde
A Guy Named Joe
The Hanged Man
Harry Potter and the Sorcerer's Stone▲
Harvey▲
Hawk the Slayer
Heartbreak Hotel
Hearts & Armour
Heaven Can Wait▲
Heavy Metal▲
Helen of Troy
Herbie Rides Again
Hercules
Hercules and the Captive Women
Hercules and the Princess of Troy
Hercules in the Haunted World
Hercules, Prisoner of Evil
Hercules Unchained
Here Come the Littles: The Movie
Here Comes Mr. Jordan▲
Hey There, It's Yogi Bear
Highlander 2: The Quickening
Highlander: Endgame
Highlander: The Final Dimension
The Hobbit▲
Hobgoblins
The Holes
Hook
Hoppity Goes to Town
Horrors of the Red Planet
A Hungarian Fairy Tale▲
Hyper-Sapien: People from Another Star
I Married a Witch▲
The Incredible Mr. Limpet
Incubus
The Indian in the Cupboard
Indiana Jones and the Last Crusade▲
Inhibition
The Invasion of Carol Enders
The Invincible Gladiator
Invisible Agent
The Invisible Kid
Invisible: The Chronicles of Benjamin Knight
Irish Cinderella
The Iron Crown
Iron Warrior
Ironmaster
It Happened Tomorrow
It's a Wonderful Life▲
Jack Frost
Jack the Giant Killer▲
Jacob Two Two Meets the Hooded Fang
James and the Giant Peach▲
Jason and the Argonauts▲
Jason and the Argonauts
Jimmy, the Boy Wonder
Jonathan Livingston Seagull
Josh Kirby...Time Warrior: Chapter 1, Planet of the Dino-Knights
Josh Kirby...Time Warrior: Chapter 2, The Human Pets
Josh Kirby...Time Warrior: Chapter 3, Trapped on Toyworld
Josh Kirby...Time Warrior: Chapter 4, Eggs from 70 Million B.C.
Josh Kirby...Time Warrior: Chapter 5, Journey to the Magic Cavern
Journey Beneath the Desert
Journey to the Center of the Earth▲
Journey to the Center of the Earth
Journey to the Lost City
Julia and Julia
Julia Has Two Lovers
Jumanji
The Jungle Book
Jungle Boy
Jungle Hell
Kazaam
A Kid for Two Farthings
A Kid in Aladdin's Palace
Kids of the Round Table
King Kong▲
King Kong
Kiss Me Goodbye
Kriemhilde's Revenge▲
Krull
Kull the Conqueror
La Merveilleuse Visite
L.A. Story▲
Labyrinth▲
Ladyhawke
Land of Doom
The Land of Faraway
The Last Days of Pompeii
The Last Unicorn
Le Magnifique
Leapin' Leprechauns
Legend
The Legend of Suram Fortress
Legion of Iron
Leprechaun 2
Les Visiteurs du Soir▲
The Lickerish Quartet
Like Father, Like Son
The Lion of Thebes▲
The Little Mermaid

Little Monsters
Little Nemo: Adventures in Slumberland
Little Red Riding Hood
Logan's Run
The Lord of the Rings
Lord of the Rings 1: The Fellowship of the Rings▲
Lords of Magick
The Lost Continent
The Lost Empire
Love Notes
The Loves of Hercules
Maciste in Hell
Made in Heaven
The Magic Fountain
Magic Hunter
Magic in the Mirror: Fowl Play
Magic in the Water
Magic Island
Magic Serpent▲
The Magic Voyage of Sinbad
The Magical Legend of the Leprechauns
The Magician▲
Making Contact
The Man in the Santa Claus Suit
The Man Who Could Work Miracles▲
The Man Who Wagged His Tail
Mannequin 2: On the Move
Marco Polo, Jr.
The Martian Chronicles: Part 1
The Martian Chronicles: Part 2
The Martian Chronicles: Part 3
Master of the World
Masters of the Universe
Maxie
Mazes and Monsters
Medusa Against the Son of Hercules
Meet Joe Black
Merlin
Merlin▲
Merlin and the Sword
Messalina vs. the Son of Hercules
Michael
A Midsummer Night's Dream▲
Mighty Joe Young
Mighty Morphin Power Rangers: The Movie
Million Dollar Duck
Miracle Beach
Miracle in Milan▲
Mr. Destiny
Mr. Rice's Secret
Mr. Sycamore
Mists of Avalon▲
Mole Men Against the Son of Hercules
Monkeybone
The Moon Stallion
More about the Children of Noisy Village
Mortal Kombat 1: The Movie
Mortal Kombat 2: Annihilation
Mouse and His Child
Munchie
My Friend Walter
My Neighbor Totoro
My Science Project
My Stepmother Is an Alien
The Mysterious Stranger
Mystery Island
Natas ... The Reflection
The Navigator▲
Neutron vs. the Amazing Dr. Caronte
Neutron vs. the Death Robots
Neutron vs. the Maniac
The NeverEnding Story▲
NeverEnding Story 2: The Next Chapter
The NeverEnding Story 3: Escape from Fantasia
Night Tide
The Nightmare before Christmas▲
Nine Lives of Fritz the Cat
Nutcracker: The Motion Picture
The Ogre
Once a Hero
One Magic Christmas
1001 Arabian Nights
One Wish Too Many
The Original Fabulous Adventures of Baron Munchausen
Orpheus
Outlaw of Gor
The Pagemaster
Painted Skin
Pandora and the Flying Dutchman
Paperhouse▲
Patchwork Girl of Oz
The Peanut Butter Solution
Peau D'Ane▲
Peter Pan
Peter Pan▲
Pete's Dragon
The Phantom Chariot
Phantom Tollbooth▲
The Phoenix and the Magic Carpet
The Plague Dogs
Pleasantville▲
The Point
The Polar Bear King
Powder
Prancer
Prehistoric Bimbos in Armageddon City
Prehistoric Women
Prehysteria
Prehysteria 2
Prehysteria 3
Prelude to a Kiss
Private Passions
Pufnstuf
The Puppetoon Movie
Quest for the Mighty Sword
Quest of the Delta Knights
Radio Flyer
Ratboy
Real Men
Reckless
The Red Balloon▲
Red Sonja
Renoir Shorts▲
The Rescuers Down Under
Restless Spirits
Return from Witch Mountain
The Return of Jafar
The Return of Peter Grimm
The Return of the Borrowers▲
Return of the Fly
The Return of the King
Return to Fantasy Island
Return to Never Land
Return to Oz
Return to the Lost World
Revolt of the Barbarians
The Rise & Rise of Daniel Rocket
Rock & Rule
Roland the Mighty
Rookie of the Year
Salome's Last Dance
Samson
Samson Against the Sheik
Samson and His Mighty Challenge
Samson and the 7 Miracles of the World
Santa Claus
Santa Claus Conquers the Martians
Santa Claus: The Movie
The Saragossa Manuscript
The Scalawag Bunch
Sea of Dreams
Sea People
The Sea Serpent
Search for the Gods
The Secret of NIMH▲
The Secret of Roan Inish▲
Serpent Island
7 Faces of Dr. Lao▲
Seven Magnificent Gladiators
The Seventh Voyage of Sinbad▲
The Shaggy Dog
She
She Gods of Shark Reef
Shredder Orpheus
Shrek▲
Siegfried▲
A Simple Wish
Simply Irresistible
Sinbad and the Eye of the Tiger
Sinbad of the Seven Seas
Slave Girls from Beyond Infinity
Sleepwalk
Snow White: A Tale of Terror
Snow White: The Fairest of Them All
Solarbabies
Some Call It Loving
Something Wicked This Way Comes
Son of Hercules in the Land of Darkness
Son of Kong
Son of Samson
Son of Sinbad
Song Spinner
Sorceress
Space Raiders
Space Soldiers Conquer the Universe
Spellbreaker: Secret of the Leprechauns
Splash
The Spring
Stairway to Heaven▲
Stalker▲
Stand Up and Cheer
Starry Night
The Steagle
Steel Dawn
Story of a Cowboy Angel
Storybook
Student of Prague▲
Super Mario Bros.
Supergirl
Superman: The Movie▲
Superman 2▲
Superman 3
Superman 4: The Quest for Peace
Superman & the Mole Men
Sword & the Dragon
Sword & the Sorcerer
The Sword in the Stone▲
Sword of the Valiant
Sylvia and the Phantom▲
Tales of Beatrix Potter▲
Tall Tale: The Unbelievable Adventures of Pecos Bill
Tammy and the T-Rex
Tank Girl
Tanya's Island
Teenage Mutant Ninja Turtles: The Movie
The Tempest
The 10th Kingdom
Terror of Rome Against the Son of Hercules
Terror of the Steppes
Test Tube Teens from the Year 2000
The Testament of Dr. Cordelier▲
The Testament of Orpheus▲
The Thief and the Cobbler▲
The Thief of Bagdad▲
The Thief of Baghdad▲
Thief of Baghdad
The Thief of Baghdad
Thor and the Amazon Women
A Thousand and One Nights
Three Wishes
The Three Worlds of Gulliver
Throne of Fire
Thumbelina
Time Bandits
The Time of Their Lives
Timestalkers
Tobor the Great
Tom Thumb▲
Toy Story▲
Toy Story 2▲
Trading Mom
Train to Hollywood▲
Transformers: The Movie
The Trip
A Troll in Central Park
Trouble in Mind▲
The Tune
Turbo: A Power Rangers Movie
20,000 Leagues under the Sea▲
20,000 Leagues Under the Sea
The Twilight of the Ice Nymphs
Twisted
The Two Worlds of Jenny Logan
Undersea Kingdom
Unidentified Flying Oddball
Ursus in the Valley of the Lions
The Valley of Gwangi▲
Venus Against the Son of Hercules
A Very Old Man with Enormous Wings
Vibes
Vice Versa▲
Vulcan God of Fire
Walking on Air
The Warrior & the Sorceress
Warrior Queen
Warriors of Virtue
Watership Down
Wax, or the Discovery of Television among the Bees
Waxworks▲
What Dreams May Come
The White Sheik▲
Wild Women of Wongo
Wildest Dreams
William Shakespeare's A Midsummer Night's Dream
Willow
Window to Paris
Wings of Desire▲
Wings of Fame
Witch Hunt
A Witch Without a Broom
The Witching of Ben Wagner
The Wizard of Oz
The Wizard of Speed and Time
Wizards
Wizards of the Demon Sword
Wizards of the Lost Kingdom
Wizards of the Lost Kingdom 2
The Wolves of Kromer
Wombling Free
The Wonderful World of the Brothers Grimm
The Worst Witch
Yor, the Hunter from the Future
Zapped!
Zardoz
Zero for Conduct▲
Zone Troopers
Zu: Warriors from the Magic Mountain

Farming

see *Crop Dusters*

Fashion

A la Mode
The Bitter Tears of Petra von Kant
Chanel Solitaire
The Dress
Fashions of 1934
Fernandel the Dressmaker
Hourglass
The House of Eliott
I'm Dangerous Tonight
Intern
Kill by Inches
A Life of Her Own
Lovely to Look At▲
Maytime in Mayfair
Mrs. 'Arris Goes to Paris
My Lucky Star
102 Dalmatians
Perfume
Portraits Chinois
Princess Daisy
Ready to Wear
Scruples
Sins
Stroke of Midnight
Tales of Manhattan▲
Unzipped▲
Vogues of 1938

Feds

see also *Detectives; Spies & Espionage*

Absolute Power
Airboss
Aldrich Ames: Traitor Within
Along Came a Spider
American Yakuza
Analyze This▲
Assassin
The Assassination File
The Assignment
Bad Company
Bait
A Beautiful Mind▲
Beavis and Butt-Head Do America
Best Men
Betrayed
A Better Way to Die
Big Trouble
Black Dog
Black Widow▲
Bless the Child
Blink of an Eye
Blood, Guts, Bullets and Octane
Blood Work
Bloodfist 5: Human Target
Bloodfist 8: Hard Way Out
Boiling Point
Boondock Saints
Boss of Bosses
The Breed
Broken Trust
The Capitol Conspiracy
Capone
Captain Nuke and the Bomber Boys
Caracara
The Cell
Chain of Command
Chain Reaction
Children of Fury
Chu Chu & the Philly Flash
C.I.A.: Code Name Alexa
C.I.A. 2: Target Alexa
Class of 1999 2: The Substitute
Clay Pigeons
Clear and Present Danger
The Client
Code Name Alpha
Conspiracy Theory▲
Corky Romano
Crackerjack 3
Crash & Byrnes
Crime Killer
The Crimson Code
Daughter of the Tong
Dead Silence
Deadly Spygames
Dillinger and Capone
Diplomatic Siege
Divided by Hate
Donnie Brasco▲
Double Team
D.R.E.A.M. Team
The Eiger Sanction
Eraser
Exterminator
Extreme Limits
Face/Off▲
Fast Getaway 2
FBI Girl
The FBI Story▲
Federal Agents vs. Underworld, Inc.
Feds
Femme Fontaine: Killer Babe for the C.I.A.
First Kid
The Fix
Flashback▲
Flight to Nowhere
Follow That Car
Frailty▲
Full Disclosure
"G" Men▲
G-Men Never Forget
The Glass Jungle
The Glimmer Man
Golden Gate
Government Agents vs. Phantom Legion
Grosse Pointe Blank▲
Guarding Tess
Gun Grit
Hannibal
Hard Cash
Hit Woman: The Double Edge
Hollow Point
Honor and Glory
House on 92nd Street▲
I Was a Zombie for the FBI
I'll Get You
In the Line of Duty: The FBI Murders▲
In the Line of Fire▲
J. Edgar Hoover
The Jackal
Johnnie Gibson F.B.I.
Judas Kiss
Kelly of the Secret Service
Kill Castro
Kill Me Later
Killer Likes Candy
Knock Off
Let 'Em Have It
Live Wire
Live Wire: Human Timebomb
The Long Kiss Goodnight
Lure of the Islands
Mach 2
Manhunter▲
Mankillers
Married to the Mob▲
Me and the Mob
Mean Streak
Melvin Purvis: G-Man
Memoirs of an Invisible Man
Men in Black▲
Mercury Rising
Midnight Murders
Militia
Mindstorm
Miss Congeniality
Mission: Impossible▲
Mission: Impossible 2▲
Mississippi Burning▲
Most Wanted
Murder at 1600
My Brother's War
My Little Assassin
Naked Lies
Nixon▲
No Safe Haven
No Way Back
Nowhere Land
The Outfit
The P.A.C.K.
Panther
Paradise Canyon
Partners in Crime
Path to Paradise
Patriot Games▲
The Peacemaker
Perfect Lies
Plughead Rewired: Circuitry Man 2
Point Break
President's Target
The Private Files of J. Edgar Hoover
Pups
The Rage
Raiders of Ghost City
Ransom▲
Raw Deal
The Reluctant Agent
The Return of Eliot Ness
Revolver
Road Ends
Robin of Locksley
The Rock▲
Rosebud
Royce
Rush Hour
S.A.S. San Salvador

Scam
See Spot Run
Serial Bomber
The Shadow Conspiracy
Shattered Image
Silence of the Hams
The Silence of the Lambs▲
The Silencers
Silk Degrees
Sky High
Slaughter of the Innocents
The Spanish Prisoner▲
Special Investigator
The Spook Who Sat by the Door
Standoff
Sticks
Street Hawk
Street Justice
Sugartime
The Sum of All Fears
Switchback
Swordfish
T-Men▲
Target
That Darn Cat
357 Magnum
Thunderheart▲
Time Lapse
To Live & Die in L.A.
To the Limit
Traffic▲
Trail of a Serial Killer
Triplecross
The Untouchables▲
The Usual Suspects▲
Violent Breed
The Watcher
White Ghost
White Sands
Wounded
The X-Files
Zero Tolerance

Female Bonding

***see also** Women; Wonder Women*

Across the Moon
All I Wanna Do
Antonia's Line
Autumn Tale
Bandits
B.A.P.'s
Beaches▲
Beautiful Creatures
Berkeley Square
Blush
Boys on the Side
The Buccaneers▲
The Business of Strangers
Cadillac Ranch
Camilla
The Cemetery Club
Clockwatchers
Collected Stories▲
The Color of Courage
Coming Soon
A Cooler Climate
The Craft
Crossroads
Crush
Dancing at the Blue Iguana
Daughters of the Dust▲
Desert Hearts▲
Divine Secrets of the Ya-Ya Sisterhood
The Dreamlife of Angels▲
Emma▲
Everything Relative
The First Wives Club
Foxfire
Freeway 2: Confessions of a Trickbaby
Fried Green Tomatoes▲
Girl, Interrupted
A Girl Thing
Girls' Night
Girls Town
Grace & Glorie
The Heidi Chronicles
High Heels and Low Lifes
Hilary and Jackie▲
How to Make an American Quilt
The Ice House▲
It's My Turn, Laura Cadieux
Jackie, Ethel, Joan: The Kennedy Women
The Joy Luck Club▲
Just a Little Harmless Sex
The Land Girls
The Last of the Blonde Bombshells
The Lemon Sisters
Let's Talk About Sex
Little Witches
Live Nude Girls
Living Out Loud
Losing Chase
Love and Other Catastrophes
Lover Girl
Luminarias
Manny & Lo▲
Me & Will
Mists of Avalon▲
Moonlight and Valentino
My Very Best Friend
Nevada
9 to 5
Now and Then
One True Thing▲
Our Song▲
Passion Fish▲
Private Benjamin
Radiance
The Road to Galveston▲
Romy and Michele's High School Reunion
Set It Off
The Smokers
Some Mother's Son▲
Stand-Ins
Steel Magnolias▲
Stepmom▲
Sugar & Spice▲
The Sweetest Thing
Talk
Tea with Mussolini
Terranova
Thelma & Louise▲
These Old Broads
Things You Can Tell Just by Looking at Her
Two Can Play That Game
Two Friends
Unhook the Stars
Waiting to Exhale▲
Walking and Talking
Wedding Bell Blues
The Well
Where the Heart Is
Wildflowers
A Woman's Guide to Adultery
Women

Feminism

***see** Women; Wonder Women*

Femme Fatale

***see also** Wonder Women*

The Accused
Addams Family Values
Algiers▲
All About Eve▲
The Amy Fisher Story
Armored Command
Auntie Lee's Meat Pies
Austin Powers: International Man of Mystery▲
Austin Powers 2: The Spy Who Shagged Me▲
Backstab
Basic Instinct
Batman and Robin
Beautiful Beast
Beautiful Hunter
The Beneficiary
Beverly Hills Ninja
Beverly Hills Vamp
Big Town
Bitter Harvest
Black Magic Woman
Black Widow▲
Blood of Dracula
The Blood Spattered Bride
Blown Away
The Blue Angel▲
Body Heat▲
Body of Evidence
Body Trouble
Bound
Bulletproof Heart▲
The Cabin in the Cotton
Caesar and Cleopatra
Carried Away
Casque d'Or▲
Casualties of Love: The "Long Island Lolita" Story
Champagne for Caesar▲
Clash by Night▲
Clean Slate
Cleopatra
Crime of Passion
Cruel Intentions
Crush
The Crush
The Dallas Connection
Dance Hall
Dangerous Ground
Dangerous Liaisons▲
Daughter of the Tong
Dead Reckoning▲
Deadly Past
Death in Deep Water
Deceptions
Detour▲
Detour
The Devil's Daughter
Disclosure
Dishonored Lady
Dr. Caligari
Dr. Jekyll and Sister Hyde
Double Indemnity▲
Double Jeopardy
Dream Lover
Drowning by Numbers▲
Emmanuelle, the Queen
Eve of Destruction
Eye of the Beholder
The Fall
Fangs of the Living Dead
Far from the Madding Crowd▲
Faster, Pussycat! Kill! Kill!
Federal Agents vs. Underworld, Inc.
Final Analysis
First Name: Carmen▲
Flame of the Islands
The Flesh and the Devil▲
A Fool There Was
A Foreign Affair▲
Frankenhooker
The Gingerbread Man
The Girl from Tobacco Row
Girl Hunters
Girl in His Pocket
A Girl to Kill For
Girlfriend from Hell
Great Flamarion
Grievous Bodily Harm
The Grifters▲
Hedda
Hellgate
Hoopla
Human Desire
I Spit on Your Corpse
I Want You
Illusions
Impact▲
Impulse
Inner Sanctum
Innocents with Dirty Hands
International Lady
Intersection
Into the Fire
Invasion of the Bee Girls▲
Irresistible Impulse
Jay and Silent Bob Strike Back
The Jayne Mansfield Story
Jezebel▲
Kill Cruise
The Killers▲
L'Addition
Lady and the Tramp▲
Lady for a Night
Lady Frankenstein
The Lady from Shanghai▲
The Lair of the White Worm▲
The Last Seduction▲
The Last Seduction 2
Leave Her to Heaven▲
The Legend of the Wolf Woman
Lemora, Lady Dracula
The Leopard Woman
Les Vampires
Lethal Lolita—Amy Fisher: My Story
Lethal Seduction
The Lifetaker
Linda
The Little Death
Love Is a Gun
Love Walked In
Mado▲
The Malibu Beach Vampires
Malice
Malicious
The Maltese Falcon▲
Mantis in Lace
Married to the Mob▲
Mata Hari▲
Mata Hari
Medusa Against the Son of Hercules
Mesa of Lost Women
Mirage
Ms. 45▲
Mountaintop Motel Massacre
Nana▲
Nana
The Natural▲
Night Angel
The Night Evelyn Came Out of the Grave
Night of the Cobra Woman
Night Tide
The Ninth Gate
No Way Out▲
Novocaine
An Occasional Hell
Of Human Bondage▲
Of Human Bondage
On Her Majesty's Secret Service▲
One Night at McCool's
The Opposite of Sex
Out Cold
Out of the Past▲
Palmetto
The Pamela Principle
Party Girls
Pepe Le Moko▲
Perfect Alibi
Planet of Blood
Play Murder for Me
Playing God
Point of No Return
Poison Ivy
Poison Ivy 2: Lily
Possession: Until Death Do You Part
The Postman Always Rings Twice▲
Praying Mantis
Prey of the Chameleon
Queen Bee
The Quick and the Dead
The Rage: Carrie 2
A Rage in Harlem▲
Ran▲
Range Renegades
Reckless
Ring of Steel
Roadhouse Girl
Salome
Samson and Delilah▲
Samson and Delilah
Sand Trap
Satanik
Scandal▲
Scarlet Street▲
Schemes
Scorned
Sea of Love▲
Second Skin
Secret Weapons
The Secretary
Serpent's Lair
Seven Sinners▲
Sexpot
Shadows in the Storm
The Showgirl Murders
Sins of Jezebel
Sleep of Death
Sleepy Eyes of Death: The Chinese Jade
Snow White and the Seven Dwarfs▲
Some Came Running▲
Something Wild
The Specialist
Stormy Nights
The Strange Woman
Sunrise▲
Sunset Boulevard▲
Suspicious Minds
The Temp
The Temptress
A Thin Line Between Love and Hate
Third Degree Burn
Tomb
Too Late for Tears▲
Torso
Trading Favors
Truth or Dare
U-Turn
Under Suspicion
The Untamable
Valmont▲
Vanity Fair
The Velvet Vampire
Venus Against the Son of Hercules
Venus in Furs
Victim of Desire
The Wasp Woman
White Cargo
Who Framed Roger Rabbit▲
Wicked Ways
Widow's Kiss
Witchcraft 3: The Kiss of Death
Woman of Desire
The Women
Wrongfully Accused

Fencing

***see also** Swashbucklers*

By the Sword
Court Jester▲
Dangerous Beauty▲
The Fencing Master
Ring of Steel
Rob Roy▲

Fifties

***see** Period Piece: 1950s*

Film History

America at the Movies
Burden of Dreams
The Cat's Meow
The Celluloid Closet▲
Forgotten Silver
Heavy Petting
Intervista▲
A Kiss for Mary Pickford
The Little Theatre of Jean Renoir▲
Lost Squadron
The Love Goddesses
Many Faces of Sherlock Holmes
Scenario du Film Passion▲
Sex and Buttered Popcorn
Shadow Magic
A Star Is Born▲
That's Dancing!
That's Entertainment
That's Entertainment, Part 2
That's Entertainment, Part 3
Visions of Light: The Art of Cinematography▲

Film Noir

***see also** Contemporary Noir*

The Accused
Al Capone▲
Amateur▲
The Asphalt Jungle▲
Beware, My Lovely
Beyond a Reasonable Doubt
The Big Clock▲
Big Combo▲
The Big Heat▲
The Big Sleep▲
Black Angel▲
Black Lizard
The Blue Dahlia▲
Bob le Flambeur▲
Boomerang▲
Born to Kill▲
Cornered▲
Crack-Up
Criss Cross▲
Crossfire▲
Dark Corner▲
Dark Mirror▲
Dark Passage
Dead Again▲
Dead Silence
Deadline at Dawn
Delusion
Desperate
Detour▲
The Devil Thumbs a Ride▲
D.O.A.▲
Don't Bother to Knock
Double Indemnity▲
The Element of Crime
The Enforcer
Fallen Angels 1▲
Fallen Angels 2▲
Farewell, My Lovely▲
Force of Evil▲
Frantic▲
Gilda▲
The Glass Key▲
Gotham▲
Gun Crazy▲
He Walked by Night▲
High & Low▲
High Sierra▲
The Hitch-Hiker▲
Human Desire
In a Lonely Place▲
Jigsaw▲
Johnny Angel▲
Key Largo▲
The Killers▲
Killer's Kiss
The Killing▲
King Creole
Kiss Me Deadly▲
Kiss of Death▲
The Lady from Shanghai▲
Lady in the Death House
Lady in the Lake
The Las Vegas Story
Laura▲
Le Doulos▲
Leave Her to Heaven▲
The Long Night
Macao▲
The Maltese Falcon▲
The Mask of Dimitrios▲
Mikey & Nicky
Mildred Pierce▲
Ministry of Fear▲
Murder, My Sweet▲
The Naked City▲
Naked Kiss
The Narrow Margin▲
Niagara
Night and the City▲
Nightfall▲
Nocturne
Odds Against Tomorrow▲
On Dangerous Ground▲
Out of the Past▲
Panic in the Streets▲
Phantom Lady▲
Pickup on South Street▲
Pitfall▲
Plunder Road
Portrait of an Assassin
The Postman Always Rings Twice▲
The Postman Always Rings Twice
Prowler
Railroaded
Raw Deal▲
The Red House▲
Rendez-vous▲
Rope▲
The Scar
Scarlet Street▲
The Set-Up▲
Shoot to Kill
Signal 7
Slow Moves
Sorry, Wrong Number▲
Station
Strange Illusion
Strange Impersonation
The Strange Love of Martha Ivers▲
Sudden Fear▲
Sunset Boulevard▲
Sweet Smell of Success▲

▲ = rated three bones or higher

T-Men▲
Tchao Pantin▲
They Live by Night▲
The Third Man▲
This Gun for Hire▲
Too Late for Tears▲
Touch of Evil▲
Undercurrent
Vortex
While the City Sleeps▲
White Heat▲
The Window▲
A Woman's Secret
The Wrong Man▲

Filmmaking

***see also** At the Movies; Behind the Scenes*

Abbott and Costello Meet the Keystone Kops
The Adjuster
An Alan Smithee Film: Burn, Hollywood, Burn
Alexandria Again and Forever
An Almost Perfect Affair
...And God Spoke
Art House
Barton Fink▲
Beyond the Clouds
Big Show
Black Cat
The Blair Witch Project
Bloodbath in Psycho Town
Body Chemistry 3: Point of Seduction
Bombay Talkie
Bowfinger▲
Cannes Man
Cass
Children Shouldn't Play with Dead Things
Ciao Federico! Fellini Directs Satyricon
Comment Ca Va?
Contempt▲
The Cool Surface
Dangerous Game
David Holzman's Diary▲
Dead Silence
Deep in the Heart (of Texas)
Drifting
Dubeat-E-O
Ed Wood▲
84 Charlie MoPic▲
Elsa, Elsa
Elvis in Hollywood▲
F/X 2: The Deadly Art of Illusion
Final Cut
Finnegan's Wake
Full Tilt Boogie
Get Shorty▲
Good Morning, Babylon▲
Gosford Park▲
Hearts of Darkness: A Filmmaker's Apocalypse▲
Hi, Mom!▲
Hollywood Chaos
Hollywood Mystery
The House of Seven Corpses
How to Make a Monster
Identification of a Woman
I'll Do Anything
In a Moment of Passion
Intervista▲
Invasion Force
Iron Cowboy
Island of Blood
It's All True
Jacquot
Kamikaze Hearts
The King of the Kickboxers
The Last Porno Flick
Les Violons du Bal
Living in Oblivion▲
Loaded
A Man, a Woman and a Killer
A Man Like Eva▲
The Mirror Crack'd
Mistress
Movies Money Murder
Mute Witness
My Dream Is Yours
My Life's in Turnaround
Nightmare in Blood
Nightmare in Wax
Notes for an African Orestes
Nudity Required
On an Island with You
Once in Paris...
One Hundred and One Nights
Passion
The Pickle
Pictures
The Player▲
The Pornographer
The Red Raven Kiss-Off
RKO 281▲
Secret File of Hollywood
She Must Be Seeing Things
Silent Motive
Skin Deep
A Slave of Love▲
Slaves of Hollywood
Special Effects
Stand-In
Storytelling▲
The Stunt Man▲
Sullivan's Travels▲
The Swap
Sweet Liberty
Swimming with Sharks▲
The Tango Lesson
Two Weeks in Another Town
Ulysses' Gaze
Understudy: The Graveyard Shift 2
Venice, Venice
Visions of Light: The Art of Cinematography▲
Voyage to the Beginning of the World▲
Wes Craven's New Nightmare▲
Where's Marlowe?
White Hunter, Black Heart▲
The Wizard of Speed and Time
You Know My Name▲
You Must Remember This

Firemen

***see also** Fires*

Ablaze
Always
Backdraft
Backfire!
Club Paradise
Collateral Damage
Evolution
Fahrenheit 451▲
Fire Alarm
Fireballs
Firehouse
The Fireman
The Firemen's Ball▲
Firestorm
Frequency
Hellfighters
Inferno in Paradise
Just One Time
Reign of Fire
Roxanne▲
Trespass
Turk 182!

Fires

***see also** Boom!; Disaster Flicks; Firemen*

Ablaze
Always
Backdraft
Burning Rage
City on Fire
The Claim
The Cremators
Dinosaurus!
Don't Go in the House
Endless Love
Erendira
Fire
Fire Alarm
Firehead
The Fireman
Firestarter
Firestarter 2: Rekindled
Firestorm
Firestorm: 72 Hours in Oakland
Firetrap
The Flaming Urge
Flashfire
Frankenstein▲
In Old Chicago▲
Inferno
Island of the Burning Doomed
Little Men
The Michigan Kid
Mighty Joe Young
Nice Girls Don't Explode
Oil
Pretty Poison▲
Pyrates
A Pyromaniac's Love Story
Quest for Fire▲
Rosewood▲
Save the Tiger▲
Sounds of Silence
Specimen
Speeding Up Time
Spontaneous Combustion
Terror on the 40th Floor
Ticks
The Towering Inferno
The Triangle Factory Fire Scandal
Twin Town
Volcano
Wilder Napalm

The First Time

***see also** Sex & Sexuality; Teen Angst*

American Pie▲
Biloxi Blues
Fast Times at Ridgemont High▲
Little Darlings
Losin' It
My Tutor
Nico and Dani
Porky's
Pretty Baby▲
Risky Business▲
Skipped Parts

Flashback

All Over the Guy
American Beauty▲
Amores Perros▲
Antonia's Line
Back of Beyond
Bandits
Beau Geste▲
Being at Home with Claude
Beloved
Best Laid Plans
Betrayal
Blind Faith
Bonanno: A Godfather's Story
Boondock Saints
Boss of Bosses
Boys
Breaking Up
Broken Harvest
The Brutal Truth
Carried Away
Casablanca▲
Catfish in Black Bean Sauce
Cement
Character
Charming Billy
Citizen Kane▲
Come Undone
Company Man
The Confessional▲
Courage Under Fire▲
Dad Savage
Dark Blue World
Deeply
The Devil Is a Woman▲
The Disappearance of Garcia Lorca
Dogfight▲
Dolores Claiborne▲
Don Juan (Or If Don Juan Were a Woman)
Drowning Mona
Eddie and the Cruisers
Edward Scissorhands▲
The Escape
Eternity and a Day
Eve's Bayou▲
Exotica▲
Eye of God▲
A Family Thing▲
Fear and Loathing in Las Vegas
Fever Pitch
Fight Club▲
Final
The Forbidden Quest
Frailty▲
Frankie Starlight
Frozen
Genealogies of a Crime
The General▲
The General's Daughter
Godmoney
Gods and Monsters▲
Grey Owl
Grizzly Falls
The Hanging Garden
Heart
Hearts in Atlantis
Hedwig and the Angry Inch▲
Helas pour Moi
Hellraiser 4: Bloodline
The Hi-Lo Country
High Fidelity▲
Highlander: Endgame
Hiroshima, Mon Amour▲
Horatio Hornblower: The Adventure Continues▲
Houdini
A House Divided
I Shot a Man in Vegas
In His Life: The John Lennon Story
Inferno
Instinct
Jackie's Back
Jacob's Ladder
Jerry and Tom
Johnny Dangerously
Jungle Woman
Kicking and Screaming▲
Lansky
The Lawless Breed▲
Leave Her to Heaven▲
The Legend of Bagger Vance
The Legend of 1900
Les Voleurs▲
The Lesser Evil
Liebestraum
Life
The Life Before This
Lone Star▲
The Long Night
The Loss of Sexual Innocence
Love Come Down
The Marrying Kind
A Matter of Taste
Memento▲
Mrs. Dalloway
Mother Night▲
Murder in Mind
The Neon Bible
Never Been Kissed
New Blood
Nina Takes a Lover
The Ninth Configuration▲
Now and Then
One Kill▲
Only Love
Oscar and Lucinda
Passage to Marseilles▲
Passenger▲
Perfect Crime
Permanent Midnight
Post Mortem
Pretty Village, Pretty Flame▲
The Proposition
A Rather English Marriage
The Razor's Edge▲
The Razor's Edge
The Red Violin
Reservoir Dogs▲
The Road Home▲
Rosie
Saint-Ex: The Story of the Storyteller
The Salton Sea
Sergeant Rutledge▲
Shattered
Shining Through
Shot in the Heart▲
The Silences of the Palace▲
Simon Birch
Simpatico
SLC Punk!
Smoke Signals
Snow Falling on Cedars
A Soldier's Sweetheart
Spy Game
Steal This Movie!
Stealing Home
Stella Does Tricks
Stephen King's It
The Stranger: Kabloonak
Sweet and Lowdown
Sweet Nothing▲
Sweetwater: A True Rock Story
Swept from the Sea
T-Men▲
The Tenant of Wildfell Hall
A Texas Funeral
This Is My Father
The Three Lives of Karen
301, 302
To Each His Own▲
Total Eclipse
Two for the Road▲
Two Friends
The Ugly
The Underneath▲
Urbania
The Usual Suspects▲
Valentino
Velvet Goldmine
Walkabout▲
The Wedding Party
The Weekend
Went to Coney Island on a Mission from God...Be Back by Five
When I Close My Eyes
White Badge
Why Do Fools Fall in Love?
Wild Bill
The Wild Bunch▲
The Wood
Wozzeck
Zone 39

Flatulence

Blazing Saddles▲
Dr. Dolittle
Dr. Dolittle 2
Dumb & Dumber
Ed
Grumpier Old Men
Lost and Found
National Lampoon's Senior Trip
The Nutty Professor▲
Osmosis Jones
The Road to Wellville
RocketMan

Flight

***see** Airborne*

Flood

***see also** Disaster Flicks*

Flood!
Flood: A River's Rampage
Hard Rain
Heroes of the Heart
The Last Wave▲
Noah's Ark
The Rains Came
The River
Waterworld
William Faulkner's Old Man

Florence

***see also** Italy*

Obsession
Romola
A Room with a View▲
Tea with Mussolini
Up at the Villa

Florida

***see also** American South; Miami*

The Alien Agenda: Endangered Species
Blue City
Body Heat▲
Bully
The Devil's Advocate
Elmore Leonard's Gold Coast
The Flamingo Rising
A Flash of Green
Gal Young 'Un▲
Great Expectations
Heartbreakers
Illtown
Just Cause
Last Rites
Miami Blues
Palmetto
Porky's
Porky's 2: The Next Day
Porky's Revenge
River of Grass
Rosewood▲
Ruby in Paradise▲
Sunshine State
The Sweetest Gift
Tollbooth
Trading Hearts
Ulee's Gold▲
Wild Things
The Yearling▲
The Yearling

Flying Saucers

***see** Alien Beings—Benign; Alien Beings—Vicious; Space Operas*

Folklore & Legends

***see also** Storytelling*

Antonio Das Mortes
Atlantis, the Lost Continent
Atlas in the Land of the Cyclops
The Ballad of Paul Bunyan
Beauty and the Devil
Black Cat, White Cat▲
Black Orpheus▲
The Blair Witch Project
Brotherhood of the Wolf
Candyman
Candyman 2: Farewell to the Flesh
Chunhyang
Clash of the Titans
Colossus and the Amazon Queen
Crossroads
Darby O'Gill & the Little People▲
Donkey Skin▲
Down to Earth
Erik the Viking
Faust▲
The Fool Killer
Force on Thunder Mountain
The Fury of Hercules
Gabbeh▲
The Giant of Marathon
The Giant of Metropolis
The Giants of Thessaly
Golden Voyage of Sinbad
Goliath Against the Giants
Goliath and the Barbarians
Goliath and the Dragon
Goliath and the Sins of Babylon
The Gorgon
Grendel, Grendel, Grendel
Heart of Glass▲
Helen of Troy
Hercules
Hercules▲
Hercules 2
Hercules against the Moon Men
Hercules and the Captive Women
Hercules in the Haunted World
Hercules the Legendary Journeys, Vol. 1: And the Amazon Women
Hercules the Legendary Journeys, Vol. 2: The Lost Kingdom
Hercules the Legendary Journeys, Vol. 3: The Circle of Fire
Hercules the Legendary Journeys, Vol. 4: In the Underworld
Hercules Unchained

Into the West▲
Invincible Gladiators
Invitation to the Dance
Iphigenia▲
Jason and the Argonauts▲
Johnny Appleseed
Kismet▲
Kriemhilde's Revenge▲
Leapin' Leprechauns
The Legend of Gator Face
The Legend of Sleepy Hollow
The Legend of Suram Fortress
Leprechaun 2
Life on a String
The Lost Empire
The Loves of Hercules
Magic in the Water
Merlin and the Sword
Messalina vs. the Son of Hercules
A Midsummer Night's Dream
Monty Python and the Holy Grail▲
Mulan
The Odyssey
Out of Time
Pancho Villa Returns
Pandora and the Flying Dutchman
Pathfinder▲
Pecos Bill
Phedre
Phoenix
The Phoenix and the Magic Carpet
The Relic
The Secret of Navajo Cave
The Secret of Roan Inish▲
The Secret of the Loch
The Seventh Stream
Siegfried▲
Son of Hercules in the Land of Darkness
Son of Samson
Tall Tale: The Unbelievable Adventures of Pecos Bill
Terror of Rome Against the Son of Hercules
Thor and the Amazon Women
Ulysses
Urban Legend
Ursus in the Valley of the Lions
Vulcan God of Fire
Wend Kuuni
The Wonderful World of the Brothers Grimm
Young Aphrodites
Zvenigora▲

Food

***see** Edibles*

Football

Ace Ventura: Pet Detective
Air Bud 2: Golden Receiver
All the Right Moves
Angels in the Endzone
Any Given Sunday▲
Backfield in Motion
The Best of Times
Black Sunday
Blue Ridge Fall
Brian's Song▲
Brian's Song
Buffalo 66▲
Cheering Section
Cheerleaders' Wild Weekend
Diner▲
The Dropkick▲
Easy Living
Everybody's All American
Father Was a Fullback
First & Ten
First & Ten: The Team Scores Again
The Fortune Cookie▲
The Freshman▲
The Galloping Ghost
The Garbage-Picking, Field Goal-Kicking Philadelphia Phenomenon
Good Luck
Good News
Grambling's White Tiger
Gus
The Halfback of Notre Dame
Harmon of Michigan
Heaven Can Wait▲
Hold 'Em Jail
Horse Feathers▲
Jerry Maguire▲
Jim Thorpe: All American
Johnny Be Good
Knute Rockne: All American▲
The Last Boy Scout
Last Game
Last Time Out
Little Giants
The Longest Yard▲
Maker of Men
Midnight Heat
Navy Blue and Gold
Necessary Roughness
North Dallas Forty▲
The O.J. Simpson Story
One Night Only
Paper Lion
Pigskin Parade
The Program
Quarterback Princess
Remember the Titans▲
The Replacements
Roberta▲
Rudy
A Saintly Switch
School Ties▲
Semi-Tough
The Spirit of West Point
They Call Me Sirr
Trouble along the Way
Two Minute Warning
Varsity Blues
The Waterboy
Wildcats
Windrunner

Foreign Intrigue

***see also** Spies & Espionage*

Above Suspicion▲
Ambassador Bill
American Roulette
Anne of Green Gables: The Continuing Story
Austin Powers: International Man of Mystery▲
Battle Beneath the Earth
Bulldog Drummond at Bay
Call Him Mr. Shatter
Catch Me a Spy
Chinese Boxes
Chinese Web
Cover-Up
Crimson Tide▲
The Day of the Jackal▲
Deadly Alliance
Defense Play
The Destructors
Devil Wears White
Diamonds Are Forever▲
Diplomatic Courier▲
Dr. No▲
The Dogs of War
Don't Drink the Water
The Eiger Sanction
An Englishman Abroad▲
Enigma
Erik
Escapade in Florence
Escape from the KGB
Escape to Love
Escape to the Sun
The Executioner
The Experts
Exposed
Exposure
Eye of the Needle
Federal Agent
Foreign Correspondent▲
The Fourth Protocol▲
The Glimmer Man
A Global Affair
Gunpowder
Half Moon Street
Hamlet▲
The Human Factor
The Hunt for Red October▲
In the Company of Spies
Jaguar Lives
Jumpin' Jack Flash
The Key to Rebecca
La Passante▲
Lady L
License to Kill▲
The Little Drummer Girl▲
Man from Headquarters
The Man Who Knew Too Little
The Man Who Knew Too Much▲
The Man Who Knew Too Much
Marathon Man▲
The Mask of Dimitrios▲
Natural Causes
The Odessa File
Overthrow
Panama Hattie
Postmark for Danger
Puzzle
Reilly: Ace of Spies▲
Return of the Man from U.N.C.L.E.
Return of the Tall Blond Man with One Black Shoe
Return to Paradise▲
Rollover
The Russia House
Saigon: Year of the Cat
Sebastian
The Secret Agent
The Spy Who Came in from the Cold▲
Strangers
Sweet Country
They Met in Bombay
The Third Man▲
Tokyo Joe
Topaz▲
Torn Curtain
Undeclared War
The Wind and the Lion▲
Windmills of the Gods

Foreign Legion

***see** Desert War/Foreign Legion*

Foreign: United States

Fanny Hill: Memoirs of a Woman of Pleasure
Nam Angels

Frame-Ups

Abbott and Costello Meet the Invisible Man▲
Agatha Christie's The Pale Horse
Another Pair of Aces: Three of a Kind▲
The Art of War
Backfire
Bedroom Eyes
Below the Deadline
Best Revenge
The Big Clock▲
Big Score
The Big Sweat
The Big Switch
Bitter Vengeance
Blind Man's Bluff
The Blum Affair
Breakdown
Buried Alive
Caged Fear
Candyman 3: Day of the Dead
Capital Punishment
Caught in the Act
Chain Reaction
A Challenge for Robin Hood
City Hall▲
Class of Fear
Consenting Adults
Cop-Out
Covered Wagon Days
Crime and Punishment in Suburbia
Cry Vengeance
Dancing Man
Deadline at Dawn
Death Sentence
The Disappearance of Christina
Double Take
Escape from DS-3
Exit in Red
Extremely Dangerous
F/X▲
A Face to Kill For
Family of Cops
Fast Getaway 2
The Fighting Rookie
Final Payback
Fingerprints Don't Lie
Fleshtone
Frame by Frame
Framed
Framed▲
Free to Love
The Fugitive▲
Gang Related
Get Rita
The Ghost Camera
The Gilded Cage
Girls in Prison
The Glimmer Man
Hi-Jacked
How to Frame a Figg
The Inner Circle
An Innocent Man
Judicial Consent
Kentucky Blue Streak
Killing 'Em Softly
Kiss of the Dragon
The Lady Confesses
Lady in the Death House
Left for Dead
Legacy of Rage
Les Miserables
Letters from a Killer
The Life & Times of the Chocolate Killer
The Life of Emile Zola▲
Linda
Louisiana Purchase
Macon County Line
Malevolence
Man Outside
The Manhunt
The Mighty Quinn
Mr. Wise Guy
Most Wanted
Motel Blue
Moving Target
Murder▲
Murphy's Law
My Cousin Vinny▲
My Fellow Americans
Nasty Hero
Never 2 Big
Nightmare in Badham County
Nightwatch
No Escape, No Return
North by Northwest▲
Now and Forever
The Obsessed
Off the Wall
Old Mother Riley's New Venture
Palmetto
Phantom Lady▲
Plato's Run
Powder Burn
Presumed Innocent▲
Prime Suspect
Prison Break
Prison on Fire
Red Corner
The Rich Man's Wife
Rubdown
The Shadow Conspiracy
Shakes the Clown
Shelter
The Sphinx
Stir Crazy
Storm Catcher
Sunset Heat
Suspended Alibi
Tank
TekWar
Thick as Thieves
Today I Hang
U.S. Marshals
Voulez-Vous Danser avec Moi?
White Fire
Wild Things
The Wrong Man
The Wrong Woman
The Yards

France

***see also** Paris*

A la Mode
The Accompanist
The Adventures of Felix
The Advocate▲
The Affair of the Necklace
Alice et Martin
The Ambassador's Daughter
An American in Paris▲
An American Werewolf in Paris
And Soon the Darkness
Arch of Triumph▲
Arch of Triumph
Becoming Colette
Bedtime Story
Big Fella
Bluebeard's Eighth Wife
Borsalino▲
Breathless▲
Brotherhood of the Wolf
Buffet Froid▲
Can-Can
Cannes Man
Captain Scarlett
Carnival in Flanders▲
Carve Her Name with Pride
Catherine & Co.
Cesar▲
Charade▲
Charlotte Gray
Chasing Butterflies
Chocolat▲
Cloud Waltzing
Come Undone
The Count of Monte Cristo
Danton▲
Desiree
Diane
Dirty Rotten Scoundrels▲
Dr. Petiot
The Dreamlife of Angels▲
Dubarry
The Duellists▲
Dupont Lajoie
The Elusive Corporal▲
Ever After: A Cinderella Story▲
Fanfan la Tulipe▲
The Fatal Image
The Foreman Went to France
Forget Paris
Frantic▲
French Connection 2▲
French Intrigue
French Kiss
The French Lesson
French Postcards
The French Woman
Full Speed
Gentlemen Prefer Blondes▲
Gigi▲
Goya in Bordeaux
Harvest▲
Hate▲
Heart of a Nation▲
Hellraiser 4: Bloodline
The Horseman on the Roof
How to Steal a Million▲
I Stand Alone
Impromptu▲
Is Paris Burning?▲
Jeanne la Pucelle
Jefferson in Paris
Joan of Arc
Joan of Paris▲
The Josephine Baker Story▲
Just Visiting
Killer Tomatoes Eat France
Killing Zoe
Kings Go Forth
A Knight's Tale
La Ceremonie▲
La Collectionneuse
La Marseillaise▲
La Passante▲
La Silence de la Mer▲
La Vie de Boheme▲
The Lacemaker▲
Lafayette Escadrille
The Last Metro▲
Last Tango in Paris▲
The Last Time I Saw Paris
The Last Train
Le Bal▲
Le Complot▲
Le Corbeau▲
Le Gendarme de Saint-Tropez
Le Joli Mai
Le Million▲
Les Grandes Manoeuvres▲
Les Miserables▲
The Life of Emile Zola▲
The Longest Day▲
Lovely to Look At▲
Loves & Times of Scaramouche
Lucie Aubrac
Ma and Pa Kettle on Vacation
Madame Bovary▲
Madame Bovary
Mademoiselle Fifi
The Man in the Iron Mask▲
The Man in the Iron Mask
The Man in the Iron Mask▲
Man on the Eiffel Tower▲
Maniac
Manon
Marie Antoinette
Marie Baie des Anges
Marius▲
A Matter of Taste
Maximum Risk
May Fools▲
Me and the Colonel
Mr. Klein▲
The Moderns▲
Moment to Moment
Mondo
Monkeys, Go Home!
Monsieur Beaucaire
Monsieur Beaucaire▲
Monsieur Verdoux▲
The Moon and Sixpence▲
The Moonraker
Moulin Rouge▲
The Mountain
My Father's Glory▲
Napoleon▲
Napoleon
A New Kind of Love
The Night and the Moment
The Old Lady Who Walked in the Sea
O.S.S.▲
Passion
Passion of Joan of Arc▲
Passion of Mind
Paths of Glory▲
Piaf
Prisoner of Honor▲
The Proprietor
Quality Street
Quatorze Juliet
Queen Margot▲
Ready to Wear
The Red Inn
Reign of Terror
Reunion in France
Revenge of the Musketeers
Ridicule▲
Round Midnight▲
The Rover
The Rules of the Game▲
Saint Joan
The Scarlet Pimpernel▲
The Scarlet Pimpernel
The Scarlet Pimpernel 2: Mademoiselle Guillotine
The Scarlet Pimpernel 3: The Kidnapped King
Silk Stockings▲
Sister My Sister
A Soldier's Daughter Never Cries
Spy of Napoleon
Suite 16
A Summer's Tale
Surviving Picasso
Sweet Ecstasy
A Tale of Two Cities▲
A Tale of Two Cities
A Tale of Winter
Theatre of Death
This Land Is Mine▲
Those Magnificent Men in Their Flying Machines▲

▲ = rated three bones or higher

To Catch a Thief▲
Tous les Matins du Monde▲
Tropic of Cancer▲
True Colors
Uncertain Glory
Until September
Uranus▲
Valmont▲
Varian's War
Vatel
Waterloo
Western
What Price Glory?▲
Will It Snow for Christmas?
Window to Paris
With a Friend Like Harry▲
A Year in Provence▲

Fraternities & Sororities

***see also** Campus Capers*
Black Christmas
The Campus Corpse
Confessions of Sorority Girls
Dead Man on Campus
Defying Gravity
Funny About Love
Hell Night
H.O.T.S.
The Initiation
Initiation of Sarah
Little Sister
Midnight Madness
Monsters Crash the Pajama Party
National Lampoon's Animal House▲
National Lampoon's Van Wilder
Revenge of the Nerds
Ring of Terror
Scream 2▲
Senseless
The Skulls 2
Sorority Babes in the Slimeball Bowl-A-Rama
Sorority Boys
Sorority Girl
Sorority House Massacre
Sorority House Massacre 2: Nighty Nightmare
Sorority House Party
Sorority House Vampires
Urban Legend
Vampire Conspiracy
Wimps

Friendship

***see** Buddies*

Front Page

***see also** Mass Media; Shutterbugs*
Absence of Malice
Act of Passion: The Lost Honor of Kathryn Beck
Action in Arabia
The Adventures of Nellie Bly
Alice in the Cities▲
All the President's Men▲
American Autobahn
America's Sweethearts
AngKor: Cambodia Express
Anima
Another Time, Another Place
Anzio
The Average Woman
The Barcelona Kill
The Beniker Gang
Between the Lines▲
The Big Hurt
Big News
Big Town
Big Town After Dark
Blessed Event▲
Bloody Proof▲
Boca
Boeing Boeing
Brenda Starr
Broadway Melody of 1936▲
Bulldog Edition
A Bunny's Tale
Call Northside 777▲
Caroline at Midnight
Chinese Box
Circumstantial Evidence
Citizen Kane▲
City in Fear▲
Close to Home
Cobb▲
Cold Blooded
Concrete Beat
Continental Divide
Cover Story
Criminal Act
Crocodile Dundee in Los Angeles
Cry Freedom
Cut and Run
Dark Secrets
Dark Side of Genius
Dead Air
Dead Connection
Deadline
Deadly Exposure
Deep Impact
Defense of the Realm▲
Diamond Trail
Diary of a Serial Killer
The Disappearance of Garcia Lorca
Don't Torture a Duckling
Double Cross
Double Edge
Double Exposure
Down Came a Blackbird
Echo of Murder
Everything Happens at Night▲
Extramarital
Eyes Behind the Stars
Eyes of a Stranger
A Face in the Fog
Far East
Fast Money
Father Hood
Fatherland
Fever Pitch
Finnegan Begin Again
Fit for a King
A Flash of Green
Fletch
Fletch Lives
Footsteps
The Forbidden Quest
Foreign Correspondent▲
Francis Covers the Big Town
Freeze Frame
The Front Page▲
The Front Page
Full Disclosure
Fun
Gentleman's Agreement▲
The Ghost and Mr. Chicken
Good Advice
The Great Muppet Caper▲
Grown Ups
Gunshy▲
Harrison's Flowers
Headline Woman
Heads
Heat Wave▲
Her Life as a Man
Hero▲
His Girl Friday▲
Hit the Ice
Hour of Decision
The Hudsucker Proxy▲
Hue and Cry▲
Hustling▲
I Cover the Waterfront
I Love Trouble
I Vampiri
The Image
In and Out▲
An Inconvenient Woman
The Infiltrator
The Innocent Sleep
The Insider▲
Invasion of Privacy
Istanbul
It Happened Tomorrow
Joe Gould's Secret
Johnny Come Lately
Journey for Margaret▲
Just One of the Guys
Keeper of the City
Keeper of the Flame
Kid from Not-So-Big
Kill Slade
The Killing Beach
The Killing Device
The Killing Fields▲
Killing Stone
L.A. Confidential▲
La Dolce Vita▲
Lana in Love
The Last Word
Late Extra
Legalese
Let 'er Go Gallegher
Lethal Charm
Libeled Lady▲
Lip Service▲
L'Odeur des Fauves
Lonelyhearts
Love Is a Many-Splendored Thing
The Love Machine
Malarek
The Man Inside
Man of Iron▲
Mean Season
Meet John Doe▲
Message in a Bottle
Midnight Edition
Midnight in the Garden of Good and Evil
Midnight Warrior
Mrs. Parker and the Vicious Circle
Mr. Deeds
Mr. Deeds Goes to Town▲
Mr. Nice Guy
Money Talks
The Mothman Prophecies
Murder on the Campus
Murrow
Mystic Circle Murder
Natas ... The Reflection
Never Been Kissed
News at Eleven
Newsbreak
Newsfront▲
Newsies
Night Hunter
The Night Stalker
The Night Strangler
The Nightmare Years
Nina Takes a Lover
No Man's Land
No Time to Die
Not for Publication
Nothing Sacred▲
Notting Hill▲
Novel Desires
November Conspiracy
The Odessa File
On Our Merry Way
One Fine Day
One Man Out
One True Thing▲
The Other Woman
The Outlaws Is Coming!
The Paper▲
Paper Lion
Paralyzed
The Payoff
The Pelican Brief
Perfect
The Philadelphia Story▲
Platinum Blonde▲
The Ploughman's Lunch▲
Premonition
Primary Motive
Private Investigations
Profile
Qui Etes Vous, Mr. Sorge?
Reckless Disregard
Reed: Insurgent Mexico
Resurrection Man
Resurrection of Zachary Wheeler
Retribution
Revenge of the Radioactive Reporter
Riding on Air
Roman Holiday▲
Roxie Hart
The Rumor Mill
Runaway Bride▲
Safari 3000
Salome, Where She Danced
Salvador▲
Savage Capitalism
Scandal
Scream 2▲
The Secrets of Wu Sin
Seeds of Doubt
Sex & Mrs. X
Sex and the Single Girl
Sex Through a Window
The Shadow Conspiracy
The Shipping News
Shock Corridor▲
Short Fuse
Shriek in the Night
Shy People▲
The Sixth Man
61*▲
Skeletons
Snake Eyes
Snow Falling on Cedars
Somewhere I'll Find You▲
Soul Patrol
Special Bulletin▲
Speed Reporter
Spice World: The Movie
Star Reporter
Stavisky▲
Stay Tuned for Murder
Stephen King's The Night Flier
The Story of G.I. Joe▲
Straight Talk
The Strange Love of Molly Louvain
Stranger on the Third Floor▲
Street Smart
Sucker Money
Superman: The Movie▲
Sweet Rosie O'Grady
Sweet Smell of Success▲
Sweetwater: A True Rock Story
Switching Channels
Tainted Blood
Tarnished Angels▲
Teacher's Pet▲
Texas Lady
That Certain Age
That Lucky Touch
They All Kissed the Bride
They Got Me Covered
The Thirteenth Man
Thirteenth Reunion
Those Glory, Glory Days
Three Kings▲
Three o'Clock High
Tomorrow at Seven
Too Hot to Handle▲
Tough Assignment
Tower of Terror
Trahir▲
Transylvania 6-5000
Traps
True Crime
Under Fire▲
The Underworld Story
Unexplained Laughter
Universal Soldier 2: Brothers in Arms
Universal Soldier 3: Unfinished Business
Up in Central Park
Up to a Certain Point
Up Your Alley
Velvet Goldmine
Virgin Machine
Welcome to Sarajevo▲
The Wharf Rat
When the Sky Falls
Where the Buffalo Roam
While the City Sleeps▲
Whispering City▲
The White Raven
Winchell
Without Love
Woman Condemned
Woman of the Year▲
A World Apart▲
The World Gone Mad
The Year of Living Dangerously▲

Fugitives

***see also** Lovers on the Lam*
Agent on Ice
Bad Girls
Bail Jumper
Ball of Fire▲
Ballad of Gregorio Cortez▲
Bandits of Orgosolo
Bed & Breakfast
The Big Fix▲
Bloodfist 7: Manhunt
Bobbie Jo and the Outlaw
The Boldest Job in the West
A Boy Called Hate
Boys on the Side
Brannigan
Breathless
Bushwhacked
Butch and Sundance: The Early Days
Butch Cassidy and the Sundance Kid▲
Cadillac Ranch
Captured in Chinatown
Chain Reaction
The Chase
Cyber-Tracker 2
Danger: Diabolik
Dead Easy
The Deserters
Desperate
Desperate Measures
The Desperate Trail
Eddie Macon's Run
Eight on the Lam
The Escape
Escape 2000
Father Hood
Fled
Frank and Jesse
Free Grass
The Fugitive▲
Fugitive Among Us
Good Girls Don't
The Great Texas Dynamite Chase
Gridlock'd▲
Hard Knocks
Hiding Out
Hold Me, Thrill Me, Kiss Me
Hollow Point
I Died a Thousand Times
I Met a Murderer
The Jesus Trip
Jungle Inferno
Keeping Track
Kiss of Death▲
Klondike Annie
Le Doulos▲
Leather Jackets
Liberators
Loners
Long Pants▲
The Love Flower
The Man Upstairs
Manhunt
Marked Man
Miami Cops
Miles from Home
Moving Target
Moving Violation
North by Northwest▲
Northwest Trail
Nowhere to Hide
On the Run
One Away
The Outlaw and His Wife
Outlaw Riders
Paris Express
A Perfect World
Posse▲
The Pursuit of D.B. Cooper
The Quarry
The Red Half-Breed
Rider on the Rain▲
Rough Cut
The Savage Woman
Scorpion Spring
Sea Devils
The Second Awakening of Christa Klages
The Secret Agent
Shallow Grave
Shoot to Kill▲
Simple Men▲
Slate, Wyn & Me
Sonny and Jed
The Spy Within
Storm Catcher
Stray Dog▲
Strike Back
Suspect Device
Teenage Bonnie & Klepto Clyde
Three Days of the Condor▲
Three Fugitives
Three Strikes
Thunder County
Truth or Consequences, N.M.
Twilight Man
U.S. Marshals
The Walls of Malapaga
The Way Out
Woman with a Past
The Wrong Man
Wrongfully Accused

Funerals

***see also** Death & the Afterlife*
The Addams Family
The Big Chill▲
Big Eden
Blackwater Trail
City Hall▲
Dangerous Ground
A Death in the Family
Erskinville Kings
The Evening Star
First Knight
The Flamingo Rising
Four Weddings and a Funeral▲
The Funeral▲
Funeral Home
Gardens of Stone
Guantanamera▲
Harold and Maude▲
Hearts in Atlantis
Heathers▲
High Fidelity▲
Himalaya▲
Hope Floats
Jack and Sarah
Kingdom Come
Kissed
La Buche
Mr. Saturday Night
My Girl
My Girl 2
One Night Stand▲
Only the Lonely
Orphans
The Pallbearer
The Road Home▲
Roommates
Rupert's Land
Simon Birch
Sleepless in Seattle▲
Steel Magnolias▲
Terms of Endearment▲
A Texas Funeral
Those Who Love Me Can Take the Train
Tom and Huck▲
24-7
What's Eating Gilbert Grape▲
The Wings of the Dove▲
The Winter Guest▲

Funny Money

***see also** Crime Drama; Disorganized Crime; Organized Crime*
Bad Men of the Border
Beverly Hills Cop 3
Fighting Caballero
Honeymoon Academy
Kounterfeit
Lethal Weapon 4
Murder on the Yukon
Naked Lies
Paradise Canyon
Phantom Ranger
Playing God
Renfrew of the Royal Mounted
Rush Hour 2
T-Men▲
To Live & Die in L.A.
Treehouse Hostage
Twilight in the Sierras

Future Cop

***see also** Cops*
Apprentice to Murder
The Believers
The Dying Truth
The Fifth Element
The First Power
God Told Me To

Future Shock

***see also** Post Apocalypse; Time Travel; Time Warped*

Gambling

***see also** Viva Las Vegas!*

Game Shows

Gangs

***see also** Crime & Criminals; Organized Crime*

Small Faces▸
Smart Alecks
SnakeEater 3: His Law
Sno-Line
Some Like It Hot▸
South Central
Speedy▸
Spike of Bensonhurst
Spook Busters
Star Reporter
Stavisky▸
Steel
Sticky Fingers
Stingray
Stone Cold
Straight Line
Street Corner Justice
Street Crimes
Street Hitz
The Street King
Street Knight
Street Soldiers
Street Warriors
Street Warriors, Part 2
The Street with No Name▸
The Streets of L.A.
The Substitute
The Substitute 2: School's Out
Sunnyside
The Sun's Burial▸
Switchblade Sisters
T-Bird Gang
Teenage Doll
Teenage Gang Debs
Teenage Wolfpack
This Time I'll Make You Rich
Three Strikes
Timber Queen
The Tin Soldier
The Tip-Off
Tongs: An American Nightmare
Too Late for Tears▸
Topaze▸
Tough Assignment
Tough Kid
Tough to Handle
Tropical Snow
Trouble in Store
Truck Stop Women
True Believer
True Blood
Tuff Turf
Two to Tango
The Underground
Underground Terror
The Underworld Story
Urban Crossfire
Vengeance
Verne Miller
Vietnam, Texas
Violent Professionals
The Violent Years
The Virginia Hill Story
Wanderers▸
The Warriors
West Side Story▸
When Gangland Strikes
The Wild One▸
Wilding
Wonder Man
Wonderland▸
The Wrecking Crew
The Wrong Arm of the Law▸
Year of the Dragon
Young Warriors
Zooman▸

Gays

***see also** Bisexuality; Gender Bending; Lesbians*

Abuse
The Adventures of Felix
Alive and Kicking
All Over the Guy
Amazing Grace
American Beauty▸
American Fabulous
And the Band Played On▸
Angel
Another Country
Apart from Hugh
Arabian Nights▸
Armistead Maupin's More Tales of the City
Armistead Maupin's Tales of the City
As Good As It Gets▸
As Is
B. Monkey
Beautiful Thing▸
Bedrooms and Hallways
Before Night Falls▸
Beloved/Friend
Bent
The Best Way
The Big Brass Ring
Big Eden
The Big Tease
Billy's Hollywood Screen Kiss
The Birdcage▸
Blast from the Past
Blue
Boondock Saints
Boyfriends
Boys in Love
Boys in Love 2
The Boys in the Band
Boys Life
Breaking the Code
Breaking the Surface: The Greg Louganis Story
Broadway Damage
The Broken Hearts Club▸
B.U.S.T.E.D.
Cabaret▸
Caresses
Carrington
The Celluloid Closet▸
Chuck & Buck
Circuit
City in Panic
The Closet
Colonel Redl▸
Come Undone
Coming Out
Common Ground
The Conformist▸
Consenting Adult
Crocodile Tears
Cruising
The Crying Game▸
Curse of the Queerwolf
David Searching
Dear Boys
Death in Venice▸
The Deep End▸
Defying Gravity
The Delta
The Detective▸
Different Story
Dress Gray▸
Drift
Drifting
An Early Frost▸
East Palace, West Palace
Eban and Charley
Eclipse
Edge of Seventeen
Edward II
El Diputado▸
An Empty Bed▸
Entertaining Mr. Sloane
Ernesto
The Everlasting Secret Family
Execution of Justice
Finding North
First Love and Other Pains / One of Them
Flipping
Flirt
Floating
The Fluffer
For a Lost Soldier
Forbidden Passion: The Oscar Wilde Movie
Forgive and Forget
Fortune and Men's Eyes
Four Weddings and a Funeral▸
Fox and His Friends▸
Friends & Lovers
Frisk
Full Speed
Fun Down There
The Garden
The Gay Deceivers
Get Real
Go Fish▸
Gods and Monsters▸
Gorgeous
Grief
The Hanging Garden
Happy Together
Head On▸
Hearing Voices
Heaven's a Drag
Her and She and Him
Hollow Reed▸
The Hours and Times▸
Hustler White
I Can't Sleep
I Think I Do
If You Only Knew
Illuminata
In and Out▸
In the Flesh
It's In the Water
It's My Party
It's the Rage
Jeffrey
Joey Breaker▸
The Journey of Jared Price
Just One Time
Killer Condom
Kiss Me, Guido
Kiss of the Spider Woman▸
La Cage aux Folles▸
La Cage aux Folles 2
La Cage aux Folles 3: The Wedding
The Laramie Project▸
The Leather Boys
Leather Jacket Love Story
Les Nuits Fauves▸
L'Escorte
L'Homme Blesse▸
L.I.E.
Lie Down with Dogs
Like It Is▸
Like It Never Was Before
Lilies
Lisa Picard Is Famous
The Living End
Lola and Billy the Kid
Longtime Companion▸
The Lost Language of Cranes▸
Love and Death on Long Island
Love and Human Remains▸
Love Is the Devil▸
Love Kills
Love! Valour! Compassion!
Ludwig
Luminarias
Madagascar Skin
Making Love
A Man of No Importance▸
Maurice▸
Maybe ... Maybe Not
Men in Love
Men Men Men
Menage▸
Meteor & Shadow
The Mexican
Midnight Cowboy▸
Midnight Dancers
Midnight in the Garden of Good and Evil
Mouth to Mouth
The Music Lovers
My Beautiful Laundrette▸
My Best Friend's Wedding
My Father Is Coming
My Own Private Idaho▸
The Naked Civil Servant▸
Naked Lunch▸
Nerolio
Never Met Picasso
The Next Best Thing
Next Year in Jerusalem
Nico and Dani
Nighthawks
Nijinsky
No One Sleeps
Norman, Is That You?
Nowhere
The Object of My Affection
Okoge
The Opposite of Sex
Other Voices, Other Rooms
Our Lady of the Assassins
Our Sons
The Painted Lady▸
Parallel Sons
Paris Is Burning▸
Parting Glances▸
Partners
Pedale Douce
Perfume
Philadelphia▸
The Pillow Book
Postcards from America
Prick Up Your Ears▸
Priest
Querelle
Quiet Days in Hollywood
Raising Heroes
Ready to Wear
Red Dirt
Reflections in a Golden Eye
Relax... It's Just Sex!
Rites of Passage
The Ritz▸
Rock Hudson's Home Movies
The Rocky Horror Picture Show▸
Rope▸
Rude
Sand and Blood
Satan's Brew
The Sculptress
Seducing Maarya
Sergeant Matlovich vs. the U.S. Air Force
Sitcom
Smoke
Speedway Junky
Spent
The Sprinter
Steam: A Turkish Bath▸
Stonewall▸
Straight for the Heart
Strange Fits of Passion
Strawberry and Chocolate▸
The Sum of Us▸
Sunday, Bloody Sunday▸
Sweet November
Swoon▸
The Talented Mr. Ripley
Taxi zum Klo▸
The Third Sex
This Special Friendship
Those Who Love Me Can Take the Train
Three to Tango
Threesome
Tidy Endings
Times of Harvey Milk
To Forget Venice
To Play or to Die
The Toilers and the Wayfarers
Tomcats
Too Much Sun
Torch Song Trilogy
Total Eclipse
Totally F***ed Up
Trick▸
The Trio
24 Nights
The Twilight of the Golds
Twisted
Urbania
A Very Natural Thing
Via Appia
Victim▸
Victor/Victoria▸
Vive l'Amour
Water Drops on Burning Rocks
We Think the World of You▸
The Wedding Banquet▸
The Weekend
Westler: East of the Wall
When Love Comes
Wild Reeds▸
Wilde
Withnail and I▸
Wittgenstein
The Wolves of Kromer
Wonderland▸
World and Time Enough
Zero Patience

Gender Bending

***see also** Gays; Lesbians; Role Reversal*

Abroad with Two Yanks
The Adventures of Priscilla, Queen of the Desert▸
The Adventures of Sebastian Cole
All About My Mother▸
Angel
Anything for Love
At War with the Army
The Ballad of Little Jo
Better Than Chocolate
Blue Murder at St. Trinian's▸
Boy! What a Girl
The Crying Game▸
The Damned
Desperate Living
Different for Girls▸
Divine
Dr. Jekyll and Ms. Hyde
Dressed to Kill
Ed Wood▸
First a Girl
Flawless
Forever Mary▸
Glen or Glenda?
Hairspray▸
Happily Ever After
Hedwig and the Angry Inch▸
Her Life as a Man
He's My Girl
Holiday Heart
I Like It Like That▸
I Shot Andy Warhol▸
I Wanna Be a Beauty Queen
I Want What I Want
I Was a Male War Bride▸
In a Year of 13 Moons
It's Pat: The Movie
Just Like a Woman
Just One of the Girls
Just One of the Guys
La Cage aux Folles▸
La Cage aux Folles 2
La Cage aux Folles 3: The Wedding
Law of Desire▸
Le Sexe des Etoiles
Lilies
Lola and Billy the Kid
Lust in the Dust▸
M. Butterfly
Ma Vie en Rose▸
Mascara
Mrs. Doubtfire
Mr. Headmistress
Mixed Nuts
Mob Queen
Mutant on the Bounty
My Son, the Vampire
Myra Breckinridge
The Mystery of Alexina
The Newlydeads
Nobody's Perfect
Nowhere
Nuns on the Run
Old Mother Riley's Ghosts
Outrageous!▸
Paris Is Burning▸
Pink Flamingos
Polyester
Psycho▸
The Rocky Horror Picture Show▸
Shadey
The Silence of the Lambs▸
Skin Deep
Some Like It Hot▸
Sonny Boy
Sorority Boys
Stonewall▸
Surrender Dorothy
Switch▸
Those Who Love Me Can Take the Train
To Wong Foo, Thanks for Everything, Julie Newmar
Tootsie▸
Torch Song Trilogy
Trash
Twelfth Night
Twisted
Vegas in Space
Velvet Goldmine
Victor/Victoria▸
Water Drops on Burning Rocks
Wigstock: The Movie
The Woman Inside
Woman on Top
The World According to Garp▸
The Year of Living Dangerously▸
Yentl
Zazie dans le Metro▸

Generation X

Bandwagon
The Beach
Beautiful Girls
Before Sunrise
Blade
Bodies, Rest & Motion
Bottle Rocket
Chasing Amy
Clerks▸
Don't Do It
Dream for an Insomniac
Ed's Next Move
Empire Records
Floundering
Gen-X Cops
Glory Daze
Half-Baked
Keys to Tulsa
Kicked in the Head
Kicking and Screaming▸
A Little Stiff
Live Bait
Loaded
Love and Other Catastrophes
The Low Life
Mallrats
Meet the Deedles
Nowhere
Omaha (the movie)
Party Girl
Reality Bites
S.F.W.
Singles▸
Slacker▸
Sleep with Me
Something More
Strange Fits of Passion
subUrbia
When the Party's Over

Genetics

***see also** Mad Scientists; Metamorphosis*

Biohazard: The Alien Force
The Boys from Brazil
Ed's Next Move
The Fly▸
The Fly▸
The Fly 2
Forbidden World
Gattaca▸
The Island of Dr. Moreau
Metamorphosis: The Alien Factor
Mimic
Rats
The Sender
Species 2
Tomcat: Dangerous Desires
The Twilight of the Golds
Wes Craven Presents Mind Ripper

Genies

***see also** Magic Carpet Rides*

Aladdin▸
Aladdin and His Wonderful Lamp
Aladdin and the King of Thieves
Arabian Nights
Bernard and the Genie
The Brass Bottle
Kazaam
A Kid in Aladdin's Palace
Miracle Beach
Naked Wishes
The Outing
Priceless Beauty
The Return of Jafar
The Thief of Bagdad▸
The Thief of Bagdad▸
The Thief of Baghdad
A Thousand and One Nights
Three Wishes
Wildest Dreams
Wish Me Luck
Wishman
Wishmaster
The Wonders of Aladdin

▸ = rated three bones or higher

▸ = rated three bones or higher

The Legend of Bagger Vance
The Man with the Perfect Swing
My Favorite Brunette
National Lampoon's Golf Punks
Pat and Mike▲
Prehysteria 3
Space Jam
The Tiger Woods Story
Tin Cup▲

Governesses

***see** The Help: Female; Nannies & Governesses*

Grand Hotel

***see also** No-Exit Motel*

An Affair of Love
Agent of Death
America's Sweethearts
Ants
Appetite
The Avenging Hand
The Big Kahuna
Billy Madison
Blame It on the Bellboy
Blondie Takes a Vacation
Bloody Wednesday
Bugsy▲
The Business of Strangers
Chelsea Walls
Come September
Crawlspace
Detective
Dirty Dancing▲
The Duchess of Duke Street▲
Dunston Checks In
Eden
Eden 2
Eden 3
Eden 4
Five Graves to Cairo▲
For Love or Money
40 Pounds of Trouble
Four Rooms
French Kiss
Girl in Black Stockings
The Girl with the Hungry Eyes
Grand Hotel▲
The Green Man▲
Holiday Hotel
Holiday Inn▲
Home Alone 2: Lost in New York
Hook, Line and Sinker
Hostage Hotel
Hotel
Hotel de Love
Hotel du Lac
Hotel Imperial
Hotel Room
It Happened at Nightmare Inn
Italian for Beginners
The Last Stop
Meltdown
The Million Dollar Hotel
Mistaken Identity
Mystery Train▲
New Rose Hotel
Nick of Time
A Night in Casablanca▲
The Night Porter
Nightmare on the 13th Floor
Old Mother Riley's New Venture
One Crazy Night
The Out-of-Towners
Plaza Suite▲
Pretty Woman▲
Psycho▲
Psycho 2
Psycho 3
The Queen of Mean
The Red Inn
Roadside Prophets
Room Service
Rosebud Beach Hotel
Secret of the Black Trunk
Separate Tables▲
Separate Tables
The Shining
A Single Girl
Sleeping with Strangers
Snowball Express
Somewhere in Time
Spare Parts
Stir
Suite 16
Sweet Lorraine▲
The Terror
Terror at Red Wolf Inn
This Property Is Condemned
Three Strikes
Tower of Terror
Twin Falls Idaho▲
Weekend at the Waldorf▲
A Weekend in the Country
Witchery

Grand Theft Auto

B.A.D. Cats
Black Moon Rising
Eat My Dust
The Fast and the Furious
Gone in 60 Seconds
Grand Theft Auto
Kiss of Death
New Jersey Drive
No Man's Land
Rat Race
The Rookie
Twin Town

Grandparents

All I Want for Christmas
An American Rhapsody▲
Anastasia
Big Eden
By Dawn's Early Light
The Chalk Garden▲
The Chamber
The Company of Wolves▲
A Dog of Flanders
The Education of Little Tree▲
18 Again!
Father's Little Dividend▲
Flowers in the Attic
Happenstance
Heidi
Heidi▲
Heidi
Heidi▲
The Little Colonel▲
My Louisiana Sky
The Night of the Iguana▲
On Borrowed Time▲
Pinky▲
Powder
The Princess Bride▲
The Princess Diaries
The Red Stallion
Restless Spirits
The Secret of Roan Inish▲
Sixteen Candles▲
Tammy and the Bachelor
Tell Me a Riddle
Two Bits
Walter and Henry▲
Wee Willie Winkie▲
Where the Red Fern Grows: Part 2
Willy Wonka & the Chocolate Factory▲
Zelly & Me▲

Great Britain

***see also** Ireland; London; Scotland*

The Affair
Alien Prey
Amazing Mr. Blunden
American Friends
Among Giants
And a Nightingale Sang
Angels and Insects▲
Angels One Five
Anne of the Thousand Days▲
August
An Awfully Big Adventure
Back Home
Back to the Secret Garden
Band of Gold▲
Barry Lyndon▲
Basil
Bean▲
Beau Brummel▲
Bhaji on the Beach
The Big Scam
Billy Elliot▲
Birthday Girl
Black Panther
The Black Windmill
Blue Jeans
Bonnie Prince Charlie
The Borrowers
Boston Kickout
Brassed Off
Brighton Rock▲
The Brontes of Haworth
The Browning Version
The Buccaneers▲
Bullshot
Camelot
The Canterville Ghost
Carrington
Catherine Cookson's Colour Blind
Catherine Cookson's The Black Velvet Gown
Catherine Cookson's The Cinder Path
Catherine Cookson's The Dwelling Place
Catherine Cookson's The Fifteen Streets
Catherine Cookson's The Round Tower
Catherine Cookson's Tilly Trotter
The Charge of the Light Brigade
Charles & Diana: A Palace Divided
Chicago Joe & the Showgirl
Chicken Run▲
A Chump at Oxford
Cider with Rosie
Circus
Cold Comfort Farm
Cold Comfort Farm▲
Cold Light of Day
Coming Home
The Corn Is Green▲
The Courtney Affair
Cromwell
Crush
A Cry from the Streets
Dad Savage
Danger UXB
Dark Blue World
Deja Vu
Devices and Desires▲
Devotion
Diana: Her True Story
Dick Turpin
Disraeli▲
Distant Voices, Still Lives▲
The Duke
The Eagle Has Landed▲
Eden Valley▲
Edge of the World▲
Edward and Mrs. Simpson
Elizabeth of Ladymead▲
Elizabeth R▲
Elizabeth, the Queen
Emma▲
The Englishman Who Went up a Hill But Came down a Mountain▲
Enigma
Everybody Wins
Excalibur▲
FairyTale: A True Story
Fame Is the Spur
Far from the Madding Crowd▲
Feast of July
Fergie & Andrew: Behind Palace Doors
The Final Cut▲
Firelight
Flambards
Foreign Affairs▲
Forever and a Day▲
Four Weddings and a Funeral▲
Framed▲
Frenchman's Creek
Funny Bones▲
Gallowglass▲
Go Now▲
Goodbye, Mr. Chips
Goodnight, Mr. Tom
Gosford Park▲
Grave Indiscretions
Great Expectations: The Untold Story
The Great Muppet Caper▲
The Green Man▲
Greenfingers
Gulliver's Travels
Harnessing Peacocks
Haunted
The Hellfire Club
High Hopes▲
House of Cards▲
The House of Eliott
The House of Secrets
How Green Was My Valley▲
The Importance of Being Earnest
In His Life: The John Lennon Story
The Innocents▲
Intimate Relations
Invincible Mr. Disraeli
Iris▲
The Iron Duke
Jack Higgins' On Dangerous Ground
Jamaica Inn
Jane Eyre▲
Jane Eyre
Jude▲
Killing Time
King Ralph
The King's Thief
Lady Jane▲
The Lady's Not for Burning
The Land Girls
Lara Croft: Tomb Raider
The Last of England▲
Lillie▲
The Lion in Winter▲
Lipstick on Your Collar
Lloyds of London▲
Lock, Stock and 2 Smoking Barrels▲
The Long Day Closes▲
The Long Good Friday▲
Looking for Richard▲
Lorna Doone
Lorna Doone▲
Love for Lydia▲
Madagascar Skin
Made in Heaven
The Madness of King George▲
A Man for All Seasons▲
The Man from the Pru
The Man in Grey▲
The Man Who Knew Too Little
Mapp & Lucia
Mary of Scotland▲
Merlin▲
A Midwinter's Tale
The Mill on the Floss
A Mind to Murder
Mrs. Brown▲
Mrs. Miniver▲
Mister Drake's Duck
Mr. Toad's Wild Ride
The Moonraker
Mosley
Munster, Go Home!
Murder Elite
My Brother Tom
My Uncle Silas▲
Naked▲
The Naked Civil Servant▲
Night Must Fall▲
Nine Days a Queen▲
No Surrender▲
None But the Lonely Heart▲
Pandaemonium
Passport to Pimlico
Persuasion▲
Pictures
Pink String and Sealing Wax
Plenty
Poldark▲
Portrait of a Lady▲
Pride and Prejudice▲
Prince of Poisoners: The Life and Crimes of William Palmer
Princess Caraboo
The Proposition
A Question of Attribution
Raffles▲
The Railway Children▲
Reckless▲
Reckless: The Sequel▲
The Red Violin
A Respectable Trade
The Return of the Native
Rhodes
Richard III
Richard III▲
The Riddle of the Sands
Riders
Riff Raff▲
Robbery
Room to Let
A Royal Scandal
Royal Wedding▲
The Ruling Class▲
The Saint
Say Hello to Yesterday
Scandal▲
The Scarlet Tunic
The Secret Garden▲
Secret of the Black Trunk
Sense and Sensibility▲
The Serpent's Kiss
The Servant▲
Shadowlands▲
Shopping
Silver Dream Racer
Six Wives of Henry VIII▲
Soldier in Love
South Riding
Speedy Death▲
Split Second
The Stick-Up
Stiff Upper Lips
Still Crazy▲
Sweet Revenge
Swept from the Sea
Testament of Youth
That Sinking Feeling▲
This England
Those Magnificent Men in Their Flying Machines▲
To Play the King▲
Tom Jones▲
A Touch of Class▲
Tunes of Glory▲
Under the Skin
Velvet Goldmine
A Very British Coup▲
Victoria Regina
A Village Affair
The Virgin Queen▲
We Think the World of You▲
We'll Meet Again
When Saturday Comes
Whiskey Galore▲
The Whistle Blower▲
The White Cliffs of Dover▲
Wives and Daughters
The Wolves of Kromer
The Woman He Loved
Woman in Black
A Woman of Substance
Wuthering Heights▲
Yanks
Year of the Comet
The Young Americans
Young Bess▲
Young Winston▲

Great Death Scenes

***see also** Death & the Afterlife; Funerals*

Bonnie & Clyde▲
Breaker Morant▲
Bring Me the Head of Alfredo Garcia
Buffy the Vampire Slayer▲
Butch Cassidy and the Sundance Kid▲
Camille▲
The Champ
Coquette
Dangerous Liaisons▲
Dark Victory▲
Die Hard: With a Vengeance
Evita
Face/Off▲
From Dusk Till Dawn
Gallipoli▲
Gettysburg▲
Glory▲
The Godfather▲
The Green Mile
Highlander▲
Highlander: The Gathering
Jeanne la Pucelle
Joan of Arc
Johnny Mnemonic
Jude▲
Julius Caesar▲
Jurassic Park▲
The Last Temptation of Christ▲
The Lost World: Jurassic Park 2
Mimi
Monty Python and the Holy Grail▲
Pat Garrett & Billy the Kid▲
Psycho▲
Public Enemy▲
Shadowlands▲
A Song to Remember▲
Strangers on a Train▲
Things to Do in Denver When You're Dead▲
Valmont▲
The Wizard of Oz▲

Great Depression

***see also** Hard Knock Life; Homeless*

After the Promise
All the King's Men▲
Angela's Ashes
Annie▲
The Assistant
Baby Face Nelson
The Ballad of the Sad Cafe
Big Bad Mama
Big Bad Mama 2
Billy Bathgate
Bloody Mama
Bonnie & Clyde▲
Bound for Glory▲
Boxcar Bertha
Catherine Cookson's The Man Who Cried
Charley and the Angel
Chinatown▲
A Christmas to Remember
The Cradle Will Rock
Dance Fools Dance▲
Dillinger▲
Dillinger
Dillinger and Capone
Dream Chasers
Eleanor & Franklin▲
Emperor of the North Pole▲
Falling for a Dancer
Fatty Finn
Four Deuces
Fresh Horses
The Funeral▲
The Grapes of Wrath▲
The Green Mile
The Group
Hallelujah, I'm a Bum
Hard Times▲
Hard Traveling
Henry & Verlin
Hit the Dutchman
Homecoming: A Christmas Story
Honkytonk Man
Hoodlum
Hunter's Moon
In a Savage Land
The Inheritors
Inside Daisy Clover
Ironweed▲
It Happened One Night▲
The Journey of Natty Gann▲
Just Around the Corner
Kansas City▲
The King of Masks▲
King of the Hill▲
Kingfish: A Story of Huey P. Long
The Lady in Question
Last Man Standing
Laurel & Hardy: Below Zero
Life
The Life and Times of Hank Greenberg▲
Long Road Home
Love on the Dole▲
Melvin Purvis: G-Man
Modern Times▲
Morning Glory

- Idle Hands
- I've Been Waiting for You
- Jack-O
- KISS Meets the Phantom of the Park
- The Legend of Sleepy Hollow
- The Midnight Hour
- Night of the Demons
- Night of the Demons 2
- Night of the Demons 3
- The Nightmare before Christmas▲
- Revenge of the Living Zombies
- Spaced Invaders
- Teen Alien
- Trick or Treat
- Trick or Treats
- Twin Falls Idaho▲
- Wacko
- When Good Ghouls Go Bad

Hallucinations/ Illusions

- A Beautiful Mind▲
- Buried Alive
- The Caveman's Valentine
- Final
- Imposter
- Mirrors
- Monkeybone
- The Mothman Prophecies
- Naked Lunch▲
- Nightwish
- Operation Sandman: Warriors in Hell
- Pi
- Repulsion▲
- Waking Life

Hard Knock Life

see also Great Depression; Homeless

- Agnes Browne
- Always Outnumbered Always Outgunned▲
- American Buffalo
- Angel
- Angela's Ashes
- The Assistant
- The Baby Dance▲
- Beggars in Ermine
- Black Tower
- Blessing
- Boesman & Lena
- A Brivele der Mamen▲
- Broken Blossoms▲
- Cafe Express
- Captain Scarlett
- Carrie▲
- Catherine Cookson's The Rag Nymph
- Children of Heaven
- City of Joy
- Clockers▲
- Crisscross
- Crows and Sparrows▲
- Dancing at Lughnasa
- Daughters of the Sun
- David Copperfield
- Devil's Island
- A Dog of Flanders
- Dolores Claiborne▲
- The Dreamlife of Angels▲
- Elena and Her Men▲
- Entertaining Angels: The Dorothy Day Story
- Extreme Measures
- Eye of God▲
- Foolish
- Forbidden Choices
- The Full Monty▲
- The Good Earth▲
- Gridlock'd▲
- The Grim Reaper▲
- Here Comes Cookie
- Heroes of the Heart
- Hidden in America
- Hideous Kinky
- A Home of Our Own
- The Inheritors
- The Italian
- Joe Dirt
- Jude▲
- Jude the Obscure
- Juno and the Paycock
- The King of Masks▲
- Lamerica▲
- Laughing Sinners
- Les Miserables▲
- Liam
- Lies My Father Told Me▲
- Little Dorrit, Film 1: Nobody's Fault▲
- Little Dorrit, Film 2: Little Dorrit's Story▲
- Little Heroes
- Little Women▲
- Lolo
- Mama Flora's Family
- Marius and Jeannette
- The Match Factory Girl▲
- Me You Them
- Meantime
- Moll Flanders
- Monster's Ball▲
- Monument Ave.
- Mother Teresa: In the Name of God's Poor
- My Name Is Joe
- None But the Lonely Heart▲
- Not One Less
- The Old Curiosity Shop
- Oliver Twist
- Oliver Twist▲
- 100 Proof
- One Third of a Nation
- Pay It Forward
- Petits Freres
- Pocketful of Miracles▲
- The Pope of Greenwich Village
- Ratas, Ratones, Rateros
- Ratcatcher
- Restoration▲
- The Road Home▲
- Rosetta
- Salaam Bombay!▲
- Set It Off
- Shadrach
- Small Faces▲
- Sparrows▲
- The Stars Fell on Henrietta
- The Story of Fausta
- Street Scene▲
- The Super
- The Sweetest Gift
- Tess▲
- Tess of the D'Urbervilles
- Tess of the Storm Country
- They Call Me Sirr
- This Is My Father
- Vagabond▲
- Where the Hot Wind Blows
- White Man's Burden
- Will It Snow for Christmas?
- Woyzeck
- Yellow Earth

Hard Knuckle Sandwich

see Boxing

Harlem

see also New York, New York

- A Brother's Kiss
- The Cotton Club▲
- Hoodlum
- Machine Gun Blues
- The Old Settler
- A Rage in Harlem▲
- Ride

Hawaii

see also Island Fare

- Blue Crush
- Blue Hawaii
- Hawaii▲
- Hercules
- In God's Hands
- Lilo & Stitch
- Magnum P.I.: Don't Eat the Snow in Hawaii
- Paradise, Hawaiian Style
- Pearl
- Pearl Harbor
- Picture Bride
- Race the Sun
- Silk 2
- A Very Brady Sequel
- Waikiki
- Waikiki Wedding▲

Hearts!

see also Eyeballs!

- An American Werewolf in Paris
- Angel Heart
- Brainstorm
- Dumb & Dumber
- Heart
- Indiana Jones and the Temple of Doom▲
- John Q
- The Last of the Mohicans▲
- Legends of the Fall
- Mary Shelley's Frankenstein
- My Bloody Valentine
- The Prophecy
- The Prophecy 2: Ashtown
- Pulp Fiction▲
- Return to Me
- Split Second
- Tales from the Crypt▲
- Tales from the Crypt Presents Bordello of Blood
- The Terminator▲

Heaven Sent

see also Angels

- All Dogs Go to Heaven
- All Dogs Go to Heaven 2
- All of Me
- Almost an Angel
- Always
- Angel on My Shoulder▲
- Angel on My Shoulder
- The Bishop's Wife▲
- Brewster McCloud▲
- Brother John▲
- Carousel▲
- Chances Are▲
- Charley and the Angel
- Clarence
- Date with an Angel
- Defending Your Life▲
- Dogma
- Down to Earth
- Field of Dreams▲
- Forever Darling
- Ghost▲
- Ghost Dad
- A Guy Named Joe
- Heading for Heaven
- Heart Condition
- Heaven
- Heaven Can Wait▲
- The Heavenly Kid
- Hello Again
- Here Comes Mr. Jordan▲
- The Horn Blows at Midnight▲
- I Married an Angel
- It Came Upon a Midnight Clear
- It's a Wonderful Life▲
- Kiss Me Goodbye
- Liliom▲
- The Littlest Angel
- Made in Heaven
- Miracle in Milan▲
- Mr. Destiny
- The Next Voice You Hear
- Noah
- Oh, God!
- Oh, God! Book 2
- Oh, God! You Devil
- One Magic Christmas
- The Preacher's Wife
- The Return of Peter Grimm
- Stairway to Heaven▲
- Static
- The Three Lives of Thomasina▲
- To Gillian on Her 37th Birthday
- Toothless
- Truly, Madly, Deeply▲
- Two of a Kind
- What Dreams May Come
- White Light
- Wide Awake
- Xanadu

Heists

see also Scams, Stings & Cons

- Aladdin and the King of Thieves
- Alberto Express
- Almost Partners
- The Amazing Transparent Man
- The Anderson Tapes▲
- The Apple Dumpling Gang
- Armored Car Robbery
- Army of One
- The Asphalt Jungle▲
- Assault of the Rebel Girls
- At Gunpoint
- Back in the USSR
- Bad Boys
- The Badlanders▲
- Bandits
- The Bank Dick▲
- Bank Robber
- Bank Shot▲
- Bellman and True
- Bells of Coronado
- Belly
- Best Men
- Beyond Fear
- The Bicycle Thief▲
- Big Chase
- Big Deal on Madonna Street▲
- The Big Scam
- Bitter Vengeance
- The Black Lash
- Blind Justice
- Blood & Wine
- The Boatniks
- Body Count
- Bonnie & Clyde▲
- Born Bad
- Bottle Rocket
- Bound
- The Brain
- Breathing Fire
- Butch and Sundance: The Early Days
- Canvas: The Fine Art of Crime
- Captain Blackjack
- Casino▲
- The Catamount Killing
- C.I.A. 2: Target Alexa
- City of Industry
- City Unplugged
- The Cobra Strikes
- Cold Around the Heart
- Crack Up
- Crackerjack
- Crime Broker
- Crooks & Coronets
- Croupier▲
- The Curse of Inferno
- The Curse of the Jade Scorpion
- Danger: Diabolik
- Daring Dobermans
- Dead Presidents
- Deadly Diamonds
- Death Tide
- The Deputy Drummer
- Desperate Cargo
- The Desperate Trail
- Destiny Turns on the Radio
- Diamond Fleece
- Diamond Trail
- The Diamond Trap
- Die Hard: With a Vengeance
- Dillinger and Capone
- Dog Eat Dog
- Dollars▲
- Double Deal
- Double Trouble
- Dunston Checks In
- 11 Harrowhouse▲
- Entrapment
- Extreme Honor
- Face
- Fast Money
- Firetrap
- Five Golden Dragons
- The Florida Connection
- Four Ways Out
- Free Ride
- French Kiss
- Gambit
- The Getaway
- Getting Even with Dad
- Going in Style▲
- Grand Larceny
- Great Bank Hoax
- Great Gold Swindle
- The Great St. Louis Bank Robbery
- The Great Train Robbery▲
- The Green Glove
- Grisbi
- Gun Crazy▲
- Gun Girls
- Guns Don't Argue
- Gypsy
- Hand Gun
- Happy New Year
- Happy, Texas▲
- Hard Cash
- Hard Hunted
- Hard Rain
- The Hard Truth
- Harley Davidson and the Marlboro Man
- Heat▲
- The Heist
- High Risk
- Holy Matrimony
- The Hoodlum
- The Horse Without a Head
- Hot Money
- Hot Target
- Hot Touch
- How to Steal a Million▲
- I Died a Thousand Times
- Ice
- The Immortals
- Incident at Deception Ridge
- Inside Information
- Interceptor
- The Italian Job
- Joy Ride to Nowhere
- Kansas City Confidential▲
- Kelly's Heroes
- Killer
- Killer Force
- The Killing▲
- Killing in the Sun
- Killing Zoe
- King's Ransom
- Lassiter
- The Last of Mrs. Cheyney▲
- Late Extra
- The Lavender Hill Mob▲
- The League of Gentlemen▲
- Letting the Birds Go Free
- A Life Less Ordinary
- Lightning Jack
- The Lion's Share
- Lock, Stock and 2 Smoking Barrels▲
- Loophole
- Mad Mission 3
- A Man, a Woman, and a Bank
- Man Trouble
- Marbella
- Marked Money
- Master Touch
- Midnight Limited
- Million Dollar Haul
- Mission Batangas
- Money Movers
- Money to Burn
- Motor Patrol
- Motorama
- Murph the Surf
- My Dog, the Thief
- Normal Life
- Ocean's 11
- Odds Against Tomorrow▲
- The Old Lady Who Walked in the Sea
- Old Mother Riley's New Venture
- On the Border
- Once a Thief▲
- Operation Amsterdam
- Operation Condor 2: The Armour of the Gods
- Out of Sight▲
- Palookaville▲
- Pardon My Sarong
- Passionate Thief
- Persons Unknown
- The Pink Panther▲
- Point Break
- Queen of Diamonds
- The Real McCoy
- The Real Thing
- The Rebel Set
- Reindeer Games
- The Return of Boston Blackie
- Rififi▲
- The Rip Off
- Robbery
- Rough Cut
- R.P.M.
- Scarlet Street▲
- The Score
- Set It Off
- Seven Thieves▲
- Sexy Beast▲
- Shadow Man
- Slaughterday
- Sneakers
- The Spree
- The Squeaker
- The Squeeze
- Stranger in the House
- Styx
- They Met in Bombay
- Thick as Thieves
- Thief▲
- The Thief Who Came to Dinner
- The Thomas Crown Affair▲
- Three Kings▲
- To Catch a Thief▲
- Too Many Crooks
- Topkapi▲
- Tough Guys
- Trapped in Paradise
- Truth or Consequences, N.M.
- Two If by Sea
- Two-Way Stretch
- The Underneath▲
- The Usual Suspects▲
- Velocity Trap
- When I Close My Eyes
- Where the Money Is
- White Fire
- White Tiger
- Who'll Stop the Rain?▲
- The Wrong Arm of the Law▲
- The Wrong Road
- X Marks the Spot

Heists: Armored Car

- Raven's Ridge

Heists: Art

- Four Dogs Playing Poker

Heists: Banks

- Bandits
- Four Days
- Kill Me Later
- Pups
- Shakedown
- Sugar & Spice▲

Heists: Casinos

- Any Number Can Win
- Bob le Flambeur▲
- Ocean's Eleven▲
- 3000 Miles to Graceland

Heists: Gold/ Precious Metals

- Heist▲

Heists: Jewels

- All About the Benjamins
- Fathom
- Modesty Blaise
- Place Vendome▲
- Reservoir Dogs▲
- Snatch▲

Heists: Trains

- The Grey Fox▲
- Money Train

Hell

- All Dogs Go to Heaven
- Bill & Ted's Bogus Journey
- Bliss▲

▲ = rated three bones or higher

Dark Angel: The Ascent
The Doorway
Faust: Love of the Damned
Heaven Can Wait▲
Hellbound: Hellraiser 2
Hellraiser
Hellraiser 3: Hell on Earth
Hellraiser 4: Bloodline
Hellraiser 5: Inferno
Highway to Hell
Little Nicky
South Park: Bigger, Longer and Uncut
Spawn▲
What Dreams May Come
Witchery

Hell High School

***see also** Campus Capers; School Daze; Teen Angst*

Angus
Animal Room
Anything for Love
The Beat
Big Bully
Bill & Ted's Excellent Adventure
Billy Madison
Black Circle Boys
Blackboard Jungle▲
Blood of Dracula
Bloodmoon
Boltneck
Born Innocent
Boy's Reformatory
The Brady Bunch Movie▲
Brutal Fury
Buffy the Vampire Slayer▲
Carrie▲
Catch Me ... If You Can
Cemetery High
Cheaters
Cheering Section
Cherry Hill High
The Chicken Chronicles
Class
Class Act
Class of Fear
Class of '44
The Class of Miss MacMichael
Class of 1984
Class of 1999
Class of 1999 2: The Substitute
Class of Nuke 'Em High
Class of Nuke 'Em High 2: Subhumanoid Meltdown
Class of Nuke 'Em High 3: The Good, the Bad and the Subhumanoid
Class Reunion Massacre
The Club
Clueless▲
Coach
Coneheads
Cooley High▲
The Craft
Creepers
Crisis at Central High▲
Cruel Intentions 2
Cry-Baby▲
Cutting Class
Dangerously Close
Dazed and Confused▲
Deadly Fieldtrip
Deal of a Lifetime
Death Goes to School
Demolition High
Disturbing Behavior
Echoes in the Darkness
Ernest Goes to School
The Ernest Green Story
Fast Times at Ridgemont High▲
Fear
Ferris Bueller's Day Off▲
Finishing School
5 Dark Souls
Ginger Snaps
The Girl, the Body and the Pill
Girls in Chains
Girls Town
Grad Night
Graduation Day
Grease 2
Great Love Experiment
The Great St. Trinian's Train Robbery
Hadley's Rebellion
Halloween: H20▲
Hard Knox
Hard Lessons
Heathers▲
Hell High
Hide and Go Shriek
Hiding Out
High School Caesar
High School Confidential
High School High
High School USA
Hollywood High
Homework
Hoosiers▲
Hostage High
I Was a Teenage Werewolf
I Was a Teenage Zombie
If...▲
The Imposter
The Invisible Kid
The Invisible Maniac
Joy of Sex
Just One of the Girls
Killing Mr. Griffin
The Lawrenceville Stories
Light It Up
Little Witches
Lone Wolf
Loose Screws
Lust for a Vampire
Major Payne
The Majorettes
Making the Grade
Massacre at Central High
Maya
Mirror, Mirror
Monster High
My Bodyguard▲
National Lampoon's Senior Trip
Night Visitor
Nowhere to Run
On the Edge: The Survival of Dana
187
One Night Only
Only the Strong
Pandemonium
Peggy Sue Got Married
Platinum High School
Porky's
Porky's 2: The Next Day
The Positively True Adventures of the Alleged Texas Cheerleader-Murdering Mom▲
Princess Academy
Prison for Children
Prom Night
Prom Night 3: The Last Kiss
Prom Night 4: Deliver Us from Evil
Pump Up the Volume
The Rage: Carrie 2
Rebel High
Return to Horror High
Rock 'n' Roll High School▲
Rock 'n' Roll High School Forever
Rock, Pretty Baby
Satan's Cheerleaders
Satan's School for Girls
School Ties▲
Screwballs
Senior Trip
Show Me Love
Showdown
Shriek If You Know What I Did Last Friday the 13th
Sidekicks
Sister Act 2: Back in the Habit
Sixteen Candles▲
Slaughter High
Some Kind of Wonderful
Stay Awake
Student Affairs
Student Bodies
The Substitute
Summer School
Sunset Park
Superstar
Teaching Mrs. Tingle
Teenage Strangler
Terror Squad
3:15—The Moment of Truth
Three o'Clock High
Tom Brown's School Days▲
Trick or Treat
Twisted Brain
Undercover
Valentine
Wanderers▲
Werewolf in a Girl's Dormitory
White Squall
Zero for Conduct▲
Zombie High

The Help: Female

The Beautician and the Beast
The Brady Bunch Movie▲
Cora Unashamed
Cotton Mary
Diary of a Chambermaid▲
End of Desire
The Farmer's Daughter▲
For Love of Ivy
Gaslight▲
Gone with the Wind▲
Gosford Park▲
Grave Indiscretions
His Butler's Sister
Houseboat
The Housekeeper
I Can't Sleep
Imitation of Life
Imitation of Life▲
In the White City▲
Kama Sutra: A Tale of Love
The King and I
La Ceremonie▲
The Long Walk Home▲
Loyalties
The Maid
Maid to Order
Maid's Night Out
A Matter of Time
The Member of the Wedding
Mrs. Parkington
My Chauffeur
The Others▲
Plain Jane
Private Lessons
Rebecca▲
The Remains of the Day▲
The Rules of the Game▲
The Silences of the Palace▲
Sister My Sister
That Obscure Object of Desire▲
Under the Sun
A Very Brady Sequel
The Well
A Woman of Substance
Woman Wanted

The Help: Male

The Admirable Crichton
Arthur▲
Arthur 2: On the Rocks
B.A.P.'s
Batman▲
Batman and Robin
Batman Forever▲
Batman Returns
Blue Blood
Candleshoe
Catherine Cookson's The Moth
Clue
Driving Miss Daisy▲
The Duke
The Fallen Idol▲
Fancy Pants
Gosford Park▲
Grave Indiscretions
Institue Benjamenta or This Dream People Call Human Life
Lady Chatterley's Lover
Lara Croft: Tomb Raider
A Matter of Taste
Maurice▲
Miss Julie
Mrs. Brown▲
My Man Godfrey▲
My Man Godfrey
Nothing But Trouble
Private Lessons
The Remains of the Day▲
Ruggles of Red Gap▲
Screwed
The Servant▲
Stiff Upper Lips

Hide the Dead Guy

Arsenic and Old Lace▲
Black Cat, White Cat▲
Blue Ridge Fall
Enid Is Sleeping
Head Above Water
Jawbreaker
The Last Supper
Pulp Fiction▲
Shallow Grave
The Trouble with Harry▲
Up at the Villa
Very Bad Things
Waking Ned Devine▲

High School

***see also** Hell High School; Teen Angst*

The New Guy
Not Another Teen Movie
Orange County
Seventeen Again
They Call Me Sir

High School Reunions

***see also** School Daze*

Archie: Return to Riverdale
Beautiful Girls
Class Reunion
Class Reunion Massacre
Grosse Pointe Blank▲
National Lampoon's Class Reunion
Peggy Sue Got Married
Romy and Michele's High School Reunion
Since You've Been Gone
Something Wild
Terror Stalks the Class Reunion

Hispanic America

crazy/beautiful
Dragstrip Girl
Fools Rush In
Gabriela
Hitz
I Like It Like That▲
Lone Star▲
Lotto Land
Luminarias
Mambo Cafe
Maricela
Mi Vida Loca
Miami Rhapsody
My Family▲
Our Song▲
Pinero
The Ring
Roosters
Salsa
Selena
Stand and Deliver▲
Steal Big, Steal Little
The Street King
Sweet 15
Tortilla Soup
Zoot Suit▲

Historical Detectives

The Adventures of Sherlock Holmes
The Alphabet Murders
Appointment with Death
The Barbary Coast
The Crucifer of Blood
Death on the Nile
Dressed to Kill
Evil under the Sun
Great K & A Train Robbery
The Great Mouse Detective▲
Hands of a Murderer
Heat of the Sun▲
The Hound of the Baskervilles▲
The Hound of the Baskervilles
House of Fear
Masks of Death
Murder at the Baskervilles
Murder by Decree▲
Murder on Approval
Murder on the Orient Express▲
The Name of the Rose
The Pearl of Death
The Private Life of Sherlock Holmes▲
Pursuit to Algiers
The Ripper
The Rose and the Jackal
Scarlet Claw▲
The Seven-Per-Cent Solution▲
Sherlock Holmes and the Deadly Necklace
Sherlock Holmes and the Incident at Victoria Falls
Sherlock Holmes and the Secret Weapon▲
Sherlock Holmes Faces Death▲
Sherlock Holmes in Washington
Sherlock Holmes: The Voice of Terror
The Sign of Four
The Silent Mr. Sherlock Holmes
The Speckled Band▲
Spider Woman▲
A Study in Scarlet
A Study in Terror▲
Terror by Night
The Triumph of Sherlock Holmes
The Woman in Green
Young Sherlock Holmes

Historical Drama

***see also** Medieval Romps*

Abe Lincoln in Illinois▲
Across the Wide Missouri
A.D.
The Adventures of Tom Sawyer
The Affair of the Necklace
The Agony and the Ecstasy
The Alamo▲
The Alamo: Thirteen Days to Glory
Alexander the Great
Alone Against Rome
Amadeus▲
Anastasia▲
Anastasia: The Mystery of Anna
Andrei Rublev▲
Anne of the Thousand Days▲
Antony and Cleopatra
Artemisia
Assassination of Trotsky
The Attic: The Hiding of Anne Frank
Attila
Augustine of Hippo▲
The Autobiography of Miss Jane Pittman▲
The Ballad of Narayama▲
Barabbas
Barefoot in Athens
The Bastard
The Battle of Algiers▲
Battle of Britain
Battle of the Bulge
Battle of Valiant
The Battleship Potemkin▲
Beau Brummel▲
Becket▲
Beethoven's Nephew
Ben-Hur▲
Bhowani Junction
The Big Red One▲
The Birth of a Nation▲
Black Robe▲
Blaise Pascal▲
The Blue Yonder
Bonnie Prince Charlie
The Bounty
Braveheart▲
A Bridge Too Far
Brigham Young: Frontiersman
Brother Sun, Sister Moon
The Bruce
The Bushido Blade
Cabeza de Vaca▲
Cabiria
Caesar and Cleopatra
Captain Caution
Captain from Castile▲
Carthage in Flames
Catherine Cookson's The Rag Nymph
Catherine the Great
Centennial▲
The Charge of the Light Brigade▲
The Charge of the Light Brigade
Chasing the Deer
Children of Paradise▲
Christopher Columbus
Christopher Columbus: The Discovery
Cleopatra
Condemned to Live
A Connecticut Yankee▲
Conquest▲
The Court Martial of Billy Mitchell▲
Crazy Horse▲
Crisis at Central High▲
Cromwell
The Crossing
The Crucible▲
The Crusades
Dances with Wolves▲
A Dangerous Man: Lawrence after Arabia▲
Danton▲
David and Bathsheba▲
David Copperfield▲
David Copperfield
The Day That Shook the World
De Mayerling a Sarajevo
Demetrius and the Gladiators
Desiree
The Devils▲
The Devil's Disciple▲
Diane
Doctor Zhivago▲
Druids
Drums in the Deep South
Dynasty
Edward II
El Cid▲
Eleanor & Franklin▲
Eleanor: First Lady of the World
Elizabeth▲
Elizabeth R▲
Elizabeth, the Queen
The Emperor and the Assassin
The Emperor's Shadow
Erik, the Viking
The Eternal Waltz
Eureka Stockade
Extramuros
Fabiola▲
FairyTale: A True Story
The Fall of the Roman Empire▲
Fellini Satyricon▲
Fiesta
Fire Over England▲
The First Olympics: Athens 1896
Forever and a Day▲
Forty Days of Musa Dagh
47 Ronin, Part 1▲
47 Ronin, Part 2▲
1492: Conquest of Paradise
Freedom Road
Gallipoli▲
Gate of Hell▲
The Gathering Storm
Geheimakte WB1
Geronimo: An American Legend
Gettysburg▲
Giants of Rome
Gladiator of Rome
Glory▲
Gonza the Spearman
The Great Commandment

The Greatest Story Ever Told
Guilty by Suspicion
Hawaii▲
The Hellfire Club
Henry V▲
Hill Number One
Hiroshima▲
Hitler
The Horseman on the Roof
The Howards of Virginia
The Hunchback
The Hunchback of Notre Dame
The Hunchback of Notre Dame▲
Hunter in the Dark
I Beheld His Glory
I Shot Andy Warhol▲
Imperial Venus
In Old Chicago▲
The Iron Crown
The Iron Duke
Ironclads
Ivan the Terrible, Part 1▲
Ivan the Terrible, Part 2▲
Ivanhoe▲
Ivanhoe
Ivanhoe▲
Jakob the Liar▲
Jeanne la Pucelle
Jefferson in Paris
Jesus of Nazareth▲
The Jew
The Jewel in the Crown▲
JFK▲
Joan of Arc
Johnny Tremain & the Sons of Liberty
Judith of Bethulia▲
Julius Caesar▲
Justin Morgan Had a Horse
Kama Sutra: A Tale of Love
Kaspar Hauser
Khartoum
King David
King Richard and the Crusaders
Kolberg
Kundun▲
La Marseillaise▲
La Nuit de Varennes▲
The Lady and the Highwayman
Lady Godiva
Lady Jane▲
Last Days of Pompeii
The Last Emperor▲
Last Four Days
The Last of the Mohicans
The Last Valley
Lawrence of Arabia▲
Le Complot▲
The Lighthorsemen▲
The Lindbergh Kidnapping Case▲
The Lion in Winter▲
The Lion of Thebes▲
Lionheart
Little House on the Prairie▲
Lloyds of London▲
Long Shadows
Ludwig
Luther
The Magician of Lublin
The Mahabharata
Mahler▲
A Man for All Seasons▲
Mandela▲
Marie Antoinette
The Marquise of O
Martin Luther
Mary of Scotland▲
Mary, Queen of Scots
Masada▲
Mata Hari
Mayerling
Mayflower: The Pilgrims' Adventure
The Messenger: The Story of Joan of Arc
Michael Collins▲
Missiles of October▲
The Mission▲
Mrs. Brown▲
Mockery
Moll Flanders
The Moonraker
Moses
Mountain Man
Mountbatten: The Last Viceroy
Mutiny on the Bounty▲
Mutiny on the Bounty
Napoleon▲
Nefertiti, Queen of the Nile
Nicholas and Alexandra
Nightjohn
Nine Days a Queen▲
Nixon▲
Norseman
Omar Khayyam
The Ordeal of Dr. Mudd▲
Orphan Train▲
Orphans of the Storm▲
Overlanders▲
Passion in the Desert
Passion of Joan of Arc▲
The Passover Plot
The Pathfinder
The Patriot
Peter and Paul
Peter the First: Part 1
Peter the First: Part 2
Peter the Great▲
Pharoah's Army
Portrait of a Lady▲
Portrait of a Rebel: Margaret Sanger
The Power of One
Pride and Prejudice▲
The Private Life of Henry VIII▲
The Private Lives of Elizabeth & Essex▲
Queen Christina▲
Queen Margot▲
Quo Vadis
Quo Vadis▲
Quo Vadis
Ragtime▲
Raintree County
Rasputin▲
Rasputin and the Empress▲
Rasputin: Dark Servant of Destiny▲
The Rebels
The Red and the Black▲
Reign of Terror
A Respectable Trade
Restoration▲
Revolt of the Barbarians
Revolution
Richard III▲
The Right Stuff▲
Rikyu▲
The Rise of Louis XIV▲
Roanoak
Rob Roy—The Highland Rogue
The Robe
Robin and Marian
Roots▲
Roots: The Gift
Roots: The Next Generation▲
Rosewood▲
Royal Deceit
A Royal Scandal
Saint Joan
St. Michael Had a Rooster
St. Patrick: The Irish Legend
Salome
Samson and Delilah
Samurai Reincarnation
Scarlet Empress▲
The Scarlet Letter
The Scarlet Pimpernel▲
The Scarlet Pimpernel
The Scarlet Pimpernel 2: Mademoiselle Guillotine
The Scarlet Pimpernel 3: The Kidnapped King
The Scarlet Tunic
Sebastiane▲
The Seekers
Senso▲
Separate but Equal▲
Shaka Zulu▲
Shenandoah▲
Shin Heike Monogatari▲
The Sicilian
The Sign of the Cross
The Silk Road
Sins of Rome
Six Wives of Henry VIII▲
Soldier in Love
Soldier of Orange▲
Soul of the Game▲
Spartacus▲
Spy of Napoleon
Sunrise at Campobello▲
Surviving Picasso
The Sword of El Cid
Tai-Pan
A Tale of Two Cities▲
Tamango
The Ten Commandments
The Ten Commandments▲
Ten Days That Shook the World▲
Ten Who Dared
Tharus Son of Attila
That Hamilton Woman▲
Therese▲
They Died with Their Boots On▲
Thirteen Days▲
'38: Vienna before the Fall
This England
The Thorn Birds▲
Three Sovereigns for Sarah
The Tower of London
Tower of London
Tower of Screaming Virgins
The Triangle Factory Fire Scandal
The Truce▲
True Women
Uncle Tom's Cabin
Uranus▲
Vanina Vanini▲
Victoria Regina
The Virgin Queen▲
Viva Zapata!▲
The Wannsee Conference▲
The War Lord▲
The Warriors
Waterloo
The White Rose▲
Who Has Seen the Wind?
The Winds of Kitty Hawk
A Woman Called Golda▲
A Woman Called Moses
Young Bess▲
Young Catherine▲
Young Mr. Lincoln▲

Hit Men/Women

see also *Assassinations; Organized Crime*

African Rage
Amateur▲
Amores Perros▲
Angel's Dance
Assassins
Back to Back
Baja
Big City Blues
The Big Hit
Big Trouble
Blackjack
Body Count
The Bodyguard
The Bourne Identity
Breakaway
Brother
Bulletproof Heart▲
Bulworth▲
Chameleon
Codename: Jaguar
Cold Sweat
The Collectors
Confessions of a Hit Man
The Contract
Cybercity
DaVinci's War
Deja Vu
Deliberate Intent
Desperado▲
Destination Vegas
Devils on the Doorstep
Diary of a Hitman
Direct Hit
Dumb & Dumber
8 Heads in a Duffel Bag
El Mariachi▲
Elmore Leonard's Gold Coast
Escape Clause
Faithful
Fallen Angels
The Family
Fatal Chase
Fatal Justice
Final Mission
Firepower
Full Disclosure
The Funeral▲
Ghost Dog: The Way of the Samurai
Goodbye, Lover
Grosse Pointe Blank▲
Hard-Boiled
Her Name Is Cat
Hidden Agenda
The Hit List
Hit Woman: The Double Edge
Hitman's Journal
Hitman's Run
Honor and Glory
In the Shadows
The Jackal
Jerry and Tom
Joyride
The Killer▲
The Killers▲
Killing Time
La Femme Nikita▲
The Last Hit
Le Samourai▲
Lethal Panther
Life Without Dick
Little Odessa
Love and Action in Chicago
Made Men
The Man Who Knew Too Little
Man with a Gun
The Manchurian Candidate▲
Mean Johnny Barrows
The Mechanic
The Mexican
Mr. Nice Guy
Montana
The Naked City▲
Nemesis 4: Cry of Angels
Night of the Running Man
Nurse Betty▲
One Night at McCool's
Our Lady of the Assassins
The Outside Man
Over the Wire
The Pact
Paid to Kill
Panic
Perfect Killer
Point of No Return
Portrait of a Hitman
The Positively True Adventures of the Alleged Texas Cheerleader-Murdering Mom▲
Prisoner of Love
Prizzi's Honor▲
The Professional
Project: Kill!
Pulp Fiction▲
Quick
Raising Heroes
Razor Blade Smile
Red King, White Knight
Red Rock West▲
The Replacement Killers
Road to Perdition
Sanctuary
Savage Hearts
Season for Assassins
The Shadow Conspiracy
Shattered Image
The Silencer
Six Ways to Sunday
Sleepers
The Specialist
Stiletto
Strangers on a Train▲
Suddenly▲
Suicide Ride
Things to Do in Denver When You're Dead▲
Thrill Seekers
Too Hot to Handle
Two Days in the Valley▲
U-Turn
The Whole Nine Yards
Wish You Were Dead
The Wrecking Crew

Hitchhikers

The Adventures of Felix
World Traveler

Hockey

see also *Skating*

Accident
The Boys
The Cutting Edge
D3: The Mighty Ducks
D2: The Mighty Ducks
The Duke of West Point
Dutch Girls
Happy Gilmore
Hockey Night
The Ice Rink
Jack Frost
Lethal Weapon 3
Love Story▲
The Mighty Ducks
Miracle on Ice
MVP (Most Valuable Primate)
Mystery, Alaska
Mystery of the Million Dollar Hockey Puck
Paperback Hero
Slap Shot▲
Slap Shot 2: Breaking the Ice
Strange Brew
Sudden Death
Touch and Go
Youngblood

Holidays

see also *Christmas; Horrible Holidays*

Carry On Behind
Easter Parade▲
Fourth Wise Man
Groundhog Day▲
Jack Frost
Plan B
Strange Days▲
Turumba▲
Two Weeks with Love
The White Balloon▲

The Holocaust

see also *Germany; Judaism; Nazis & Other Paramilitary Slugs; World War II*

Alan & Naomi
The Assault▲
The Assisi Underground
The Attic: The Hiding of Anne Frank
Au Revoir les Enfants▲
The Boxer and Death▲
A Call to Remember
Charlie Grant's War
Christabel
Cold Days
Conspiracy
David▲
A Day in October
The Devil's Arthmetic
Diamonds of the Night▲
The Diary of Anne Frank▲
Enemies, a Love Story▲
Era Notte a Roma▲
Europa, Europa▲
The Execution
Forced March
The Garden of the Finzi-Continis▲
Genghis Cohn
Getting Away With Murder
Good Evening, Mr. Wallenberg
Hanna's War
The Hiding Place
Hitler
The Holcroft Covenant
Holocaust▲
Holocaust Survivors...Remembrance of Love
I Love You, I Love You Not
In a Glass Cage
In the Presence of Mine Enemies
Jacob the Liar
Jakob the Liar▲
Kanal▲
Kapo▲
Korczak▲
The Last Butterfly
The Last Metro▲
Les Miserables
Les Violons du Bal
Max and Helen
Mendel▲
Murderers Among Us: The Simon Wiesenthal Story▲
The Murderers Are Among Us
Never Forget
Passenger▲
The Pawnbroker▲
Playing for Time▲
Rescuers: Stories of Courage—Two Couples▲
Reunion▲
The Revolt of Job▲
The Rose Garden
Schindler's List▲
The Shop on Main Street▲
Sophie's Choice▲
Speak Up! It's So Dark
The Substance of Fire
Sunshine
Transport from Paradise
Triumph of the Spirit▲
The Truce▲
Uprising▲
The Wannsee Conference▲
War & Love
The White Rose▲

Home Alone

see also *Childhood Visions*

Adventures in Babysitting
And You Thought Your Parents Were Weird!
Anything for a Thrill
The Apple Dumpling Gang
Baby's Day Out
Blank Check
Bless the Beasts and Children
The Blue Lagoon
Boys Will Be Boys
Camp Nowhere
Cloak & Dagger
Cohen and Tate
Courage Mountain
Cross My Heart
Dirkham Detective Agency
Dirt Bike Kid
Don't Tell Mom the Babysitter's Dead
Explorers
Famous Five Get into Trouble
Fatal Skies
Four Rooms
Gleaming the Cube
The Goonies
He Is My Brother
Home Alone▲
Home Alone 2: Lost in New York
Home Alone 3
Honey, I Shrunk the Kids
Honey, We Shrunk Ourselves
Hook
The Horse Without a Head
House Arrest
Invaders from Mars
Island Trader
Just William's Luck
Legend of Billie Jean
The Littlest Horse Thieves
Lord of the Flies▲
Lord of the Flies
Mr. Wise Guy
Monkey Trouble
The Monster Squad
Paradise
Playing Dangerous
The Rescue
Return to the Blue Lagoon
Scream▲
Shipwrecked
Snow Treasure
3 Ninjas
3 Ninjas Kick Back

▲ = rated three bones or higher

A Waltz Through the Hills
The Window▲
Young Sherlock Holmes

The Homefront: England

***see also** World War II*
The Affair
And a Nightingale Sang
Hope and Glory▲
The Land Girls
The Last of the Blonde Bombshells
Mrs. Miniver▲
The Weaker Sex
The White Cliffs of Dover▲

The Homefront: U.S./Canada

***see also** World War II*
Blondie for Victory
Bye Bye Blues
Come See the Paradise▲
For the Moment
The Human Comedy▲
I'll Remember April
In Love and War
In the Mood
A League of Their Own▲
The More the Merrier▲
1941
Racing with the Moon▲
Raggedy Man▲
Ride the Wild Fields
Saboteur▲
Since You Went Away▲
The Summer of My German Soldier▲
Swing Shift
Wedding in White

Homeless

***see also** Great Depression; Hard Knock Life; Yuppie Nightmares*
Accatone!▲
All Mine to Give
Amores Perros▲
The Billion Dollar Hobo
Billy: Portrait of a Street Kid
Bums
Caught
The Caveman's Valentine
Children of Sanchez
City Lights▲
Curly Sue
Distant Thunder▲
Dodes 'ka-den▲
Down, Out and Dangerous
Emanon
Emperor of the North Pole▲
The Fisher King▲
God Bless the Child▲
The Grapes of Wrath▲
Home for Christmas
Home of Angels
Homecoming
The Innocent Sleep
Into the West▲
Joe Gould's Secret
Kanal▲
The Kid▲
Life Stinks
Los Olvidados▲
The Lovers on the Bridge
The Lower Depths▲
The Man from Left Field
Midnight Cowboy▲
Mon Homme
Mondo
None But the Lonely Heart▲
Oliver!▲
Oliver Twist▲
Oliver Twist
Oliver Twist▲
Oliver Twist
Oliver Twist▲
Original Intent
An Orphan Boy of Vienna
Pardon My Trunk
Pinero
The Prince of Central Park▲
The Saint of Fort Washington
Salaam Bombay!▲
Samaritan: The Mitch Snyder Story▲
Scarecrow
Silas Marner▲
Sounder▲
The Stray
Streetwise▲
Sullivan's Travels▲
Summer Magic
They Shall Have Music
Times Square
Up Your Alley
The Vagrant
Where the Day Takes You
With Honors

Homicide

Behind the Sun
The Cat's Meow
The Caveman's Valentine
Eye of the Storm
Gosford Park▲
In the Bedroom▲
Insomnia▲
Lola and Billy the Kid
The Man Who Wasn't There▲
A Matter of Taste
Memento▲
Murder by Numbers
The Murder of Stephen Lawrence▲
One Kill▲
Our Lady of the Assassins
Series 7: The Contenders
Signs & Wonders
Sudden Manhattan
Torso
Unfaithful
Valentine
What Your Eyes Don't See
With a Friend Like Harry▲

Homosexuality

***see** Bisexuality; Gays; Lesbians*

Hong Kong

***see also** Asia; China*
The Amsterdam Kill
The Art of War
Autumn Moon
A Better Tomorrow, Part 1
Black Mask
Blade in Hong Kong
Bloodsport
Chinese Box
Chungking Express▲
Cleopatra Jones & the Casino of Gold
Crime Lords
Detonator 2: Night Watch
Dr. Jekyll & Mr. Hyde
Double Impact
Dream Lovers
Enter the Dragon▲
Fallen Angels
First Love and Other Pains / One of Them
Five Golden Dragons
Forced Vengeance
Gen-X Cops
Hong Kong 1941
Hong Kong '97
In the Mood for Love
Just Like Weather▲
Knock Off
Koroshi
Noble House
Once a Thief▲
Romeo Must Die
Rush Hour 2
Shadow of China▲
Tai-Pan
That Man Bolt
TNT Jackson
To Live and Die in Hong Kong
Twin Dragons
Yin & Yang of Mr. Go

Horrible Holidays

***see also** Christmas; Holidays*
April Fool's Day
Black Christmas
Bloodbeat
Bloody New Year
Christmas Evil
Don't Open Till Christmas
Dorm That Dripped Blood
Frankenstein Sings...The Movie
Gremlins▲
Halloween▲
Halloween 2: The Nightmare Isn't Over!
Halloween 3: Season of the Witch
Halloween 4: The Return of Michael Myers
Halloween 5: The Revenge of Michael Myers
Halloween 6: The Curse of Michael Myers
Halloween: H20▲
Halloween Night
Happy Birthday to Me
Home for the Holidays
Home Sweet Home
I Still Know What You Did Last Summer
Jack-O
Mixed Nuts
Mother's Day
My Bloody Valentine
The Myth of Fingerprints
New Year's Evil
The Night After Halloween
Night of the Demons
Night of the Demons 2
Night of the Demons 3
Reckless
The Ref▲
Resurrection
Silent Night, Bloody Night
Silent Night, Deadly Night
Silent Night, Deadly Night 2
Silent Night, Deadly Night 3: Better Watch Out!
Silent Night, Deadly Night 4: Initiation
Silent Night, Deadly Night 5: The Toymaker
Teen Alien
Trick or Treats
Uncle Sam
Valentine
Wacko

Horror Anthologies

Alien Massacre
Asylum
Body Bags
Creepshow
Creepshow 2
Cremains▲
The Dark Dealer
Dead of Night▲
Dead of Night
Deadtime Stories
Dr. Terror's House of Horrors
Escapes
Freakshow
Fright House
Future Shock
Grim Prairie Tales
Hellblock 13
The House that Dripped Blood
H.P. Lovecraft's Necronomicon: Book of the Dead
Into the Badlands
The Monster Club
Night Gallery▲
Nightmares
The Offspring
Once Upon a Midnight Scary
Quicksilver Highway
Screamtime
Spirits of the Dead▲
Tales from the Crypt▲
Tales from the Darkside: The Movie
Tales from the Hood
Tales of Terror
Tales That Witness Madness
Terror Tract
Things
Torture Garden
Trilogy of Terror
Trilogy of Terror 2
Twice-Told Tales▲
Twilight Zone: The Movie
Twists of Terror
Two Evil Eyes
The Uncanny
Vault of Horror
The Willies

Horror Comedy

Adventures of Eliza Fraser
American Vampire
An American Werewolf in Paris
Andy Warhol's Dracula▲
Andy Warhol's Frankenstein
April Fool's Day
Arachnophobia
Army of Darkness▲
Atomic Dog
Attack of the Killer Refrigerator
Attack of the Killer Tomatoes
Attack of the Robots
Auntie Lee's Meat Pies
Autopsy of a Ghost
Bad Channels
Bad Taste▲
Beauty on the Beach
Beetlejuice▲
Bela Lugosi Meets a Brooklyn Gorilla
Beverly Hills Bodysnatchers
Big Meat Eater
Billy the Kid Versus Dracula
Biozombie
Black Magic
Blood & Donuts
Blood Beach
Blood Hook
Bloodbath at the House of Death
Body Bags
The Bogus Witch Project
The Bone Yard
Bowery Boys Meet the Monsters
Brain Damage
Bride of Chucky
Bride of Re-Animator
A Bucket of Blood▲
Bugged!
Carry On Screaming
Christmas Evil
C.H.U.D.
C.H.U.D. 2: Bud the Chud
The Comedy of Terrors▲
Creature from the Haunted Sea
The Creeps
Critters
Critters 2: The Main Course
Critters 3
Critters 4
Curse of the Queerwolf
Cutting Class
Dead Alive
Dead Heat
Dr. Jekyll and Sister Hyde
Dolls
Doom Asylum
Dracula & Son
Dracula Blows His Cool
Dracula: Dead and Loving It
Dracula: Up in Harlem
Eat and Run
Ed and His Dead Mother
Elvira, Mistress of the Dark
Evil Spawn
Face of the Screaming Werewolf
The Fearless Vampire Killers▲
Frankenhooker
Frankenstein Sings...The Movie
Frankenstein's Great Aunt Tillie
The Frighteners
From Beyond▲
Funnyman
The Ghost Breakers▲
Ghoulies
Ghoulies 2
Ghoulies 3: Ghoulies Go to College
Ghoulies 4
Goblin
Gore-Met Zombie Chef from Hell
The Granny
Gremlins▲
Gremlins 2: The New Batch▲
Hard to Die
Head of the Family
Highway to Hell
Hillbillies in a Haunted House
The Horror of Frankenstein
House▲
House 2: The Second Story
House of the Long Shadows
Human Beasts
Hysterical
I Married a Vampire
I Was a Teenage Zombie
Idle Hands
Incredibly Strange Creatures Who Stopped Living and Became Mixed-Up Zombies
The Invisible Maniac
Jack Frost 2: Revenge of the Mutant Killer Snowman
Killer Condom
Killer Klowns from Outer Space
Killer Tomatoes Eat France
Killer Tomatoes Strike Back
Killer Tongue
The Kingdom▲
The Kingdom 2▲
Little Shop of Horrors▲
Mama Dracula
A Man with a Maid
The Mask▲
Matinee
Microwave Massacre
Mindkiller
Mr. Vampire
Mom
Monster in the Closet
Motel Hell
Munchies
My Boyfriend's Back
My Demon Lover
My Grandpa Is a Vampire
My Mom's a Werewolf
My Son, the Vampire
Near Dark▲
Night of a Thousand Cats
Night of the Creeps
Night of the Laughing Dead
Nightlife
Nocturna
Nothing But Trouble
The Old Dark House▲
Old Mother Riley's Ghosts
Once Bitten
Out of the Dark
Phantom Brother
Phantom Empire
Piranha
Piranha 2: The Spawning
Psycho Girls
Psychos in Love
Q (The Winged Serpent)▲
Rabid Grannies
Re-Animator▲
Redneck Zombies
The Refrigerator
Return of the Killer Tomatoes!
Return of the Living Dead
Return of the Living Dead 2
Return of the Living Dead 3
Revenge of the Red Baron
Saturday the 14th
Saturday the 14th Strikes Back
Scary Movie 2
Schlock
Shrunken Heads
Son of Ingagi
Sorority Babes in the Slimeball Bowl-A-Rama
Speak of the Devil
Spider Baby
Spooks Run Wild
Strangers of the Evening
Street Trash
Student Bodies
The Stuff
Tainted
Tales from the Crypt Presents Bordello of Blood
Tales from the Crypt Presents Demon Knight
Teenage Exorcist
Tequila Body Shots
Terror Tract
Terrorvision
Theatre of Blood▲
There's Nothing out There
The Thing with Two Heads
The Thrill Killers
The Toxic Avenger
The Toxic Avenger, Part 2
The Toxic Avenger, Part 3: The Last Temptation of Toxie
Treasure of Fear
Tremors
Tremors 2: Aftershocks
Tremors 3: Back to Perfection
The Undertaker and His Pals
Vamp
The Vampire Happening
Vampire in Brooklyn
Vampires of Sorority Row: Kickboxers From Hell
When Good Ghouls Go Bad
Zombies on Broadway

Horse Racing

***see** Gambling; Horses*

Horses

The Adventures of Gallant Bess
All the Pretty Horses
The Appaloosa
Archer's Adventure
The Bashful Bachelor
Bells of San Angelo
Bite the Bullet▲
Black Beauty
Black Beauty▲
The Black Stallion▲
The Black Stallion Returns
Blue Fire Lady
Boots Malone
Broadway Bill▲
By Dawn's Early Light
Call of the Forest
Casey's Shadow
Champions
Chino
City Slickers 2: The Legend of Curly's Gold
Cold Feet
Come on Tarzan
Courage of Black Beauty
Courage of the North
Danielle Steel's Palomino
Danny
Dark Horse
A Day at the Races▲
Day the Bookies Wept
Devil Horse
Devil on Horseback
The Devil's Cargo
Duke of the Derby
Eagle's Wing
Eden Valley▲
The Electric Horseman
Equus
Ex-Mrs. Bradford▲
Far North
The Fighting Stallion▲
A Fine Mess
Flame of Araby
Flash
The Flying Deuces▲
Forbidden Trails
Francis Goes to the Races
A Girl in Every Port
Glory
The Golden Stallion
Great Dan Patch
The Great Mike
Gypsy Colt
Half-Baked

Horses

Heart of the Rockies
Hell's Hinges
Hit the Saddle
A Horse for Danny
The Horse in the Gray Flannel Suit
The Horse Whisperer
Horsemasters
The Horsemen
Hot to Trot!
In Pursuit of Honor
Indian Paint
International Velvet
Into the West▲
It Ain't Hay
Italian Straw Hat▲
It's a Great Life
Justin Morgan Had a Horse
Kentucky Blue Streak
King of the Sierras
King of the Stallions
King of the Wild Horses▲
King of the Wind
Law of the Wild
Le Gentleman D'Epsom
The Lemon Drop Kid
The Lighthorsemen▲
Lightning: The White Stallion
The Littlest Horse Thieves
The Littlest Outlaw
The Longshot
Lotna
Lucky Luke
Ma and Pa Kettle at the Fair
The Man from Snowy River
Marshal of Cedar Rock
Meet Wally Sparks
The Miracle of the White Stallions
The Misfits▲
Misty
My Friend Flicka▲
My Old Man
My Pal Trigger
National Lampoon's Animal House▲
National Velvet▲
Off and Running
On the Right Track
Phar Lap
Prince and the Great Race
The Quiet Man▲
Racing Luck
A Rare Breed
The Red Fury
The Red Pony▲
The Red Stallion
Return of Wildfire
Return to Snowy River▲
Ride a Wild Pony▲
Ride Him, Cowboy▲
Riders
Riding High
Rolling Home
The Rounders
Run for the Roses
Running Wild
Saddle Buster
Saratoga
Second Chances
Shooting Fish
Silver Stallion
The Silver Stallion: King of the Wild Brumbies
Simpatico
Something to Talk About
Speedy▲
Spirit: Stallion of the Cimarron
The Story of Seabiscuit
Sundown Saunders
Sylvester
Tennessee Stallion
Texas to Bataan
Thoroughbreds Don't Cry
Three Men on a Horse▲
Trail to San Antone
Turf Boy
Two Bits & Pepper
The Undefeated
When the West Was Young
White Mane▲
Wild Hearts Can't Be Broken▲
Wild Horse Hank
Wild Horses
Wild Pony
Win, Place, or Steal
Winds of the Wasteland
Wings of the Morning

Hospitals & Medicine

see also Disease of the Week; Doctors & Nurses; Emerging Viruses; Sanity Check; Shrinks

Article 99
BASEketball
B.O.R.N.
Bringing Out the Dead
Britannia Hospital
Carry On Nurse
A Child Is Waiting▲
China Beach▲
City of Joy
The Clonus Horror
Coma▲
Come to the Stable▲
Critical Care
Critical Condition
Dead Ringers▲
Desperate Measures
Disorderlies
Disorderly Orderly
Doctor at Large
Dr. Kildare's Strange Case
Doctors' Wives
East of Kilimanjaro
The Egyptian
Extreme Measures
For Roseanna
Frankenstein General Hospital
The Fugitive▲
Green for Danger
Gross Anatomy
Halloween 2: The Nightmare Isn't Over!
Hard-Boiled
The Hasty Heart
Horror Hospital
The Hospital▲
Hospital Massacre
Hospital of Terror
In for Treatment▲
In Love and War
The Interns
Invasion
John Q
Junior
The Kingdom▲
The Kingdom 2▲
Lifespan
Like Father, Like Son
Miss Evers' Boys
Naked Is Better
Nine Months
Nurse
One Flew Over the Cuckoo's Nest▲
Open Your Eyes▲
Patch Adams
Range of Motion
The Red Squirrel
State of Emergency
A Stolen Face
The Surgeon
Take Down
Tales from the Gimli Hospital
Tender Loving Care
Threshold
12 Monkeys▲
28 Days
The Ugly
Vital Signs
Welcome Stranger
Where Truth Lies
While You Were Sleeping▲
Whose Life Is It Anyway?▲
Young Doctors in Love

Hostage!

see also Kidnapped!; Missing Persons

The Abduction
Against the Wall▲
Air Force One▲
Air Rage
Airheads
Albino Alligator
Amos and Andrew
Autumn Born
Bandits
Black Cobra 2
Black Fox: Good Men and Bad
Blackout
Blast
Blood of the Hunter
Body Count
Born Bad
The Boys Club
Cadillac Man
Carpool
Chameleon 2: Death Match
Codename: Vengeance
Cold Sweat
Crackerjack 2
Cube
Cul de Sac▲
Days of Hell
Dead Ahead
Dead Silence
Deadlocked
Deadly Outbreak
Death and the Maiden▲
Death Stalk
Demolition High
Die Hard▲
Die Hard 2: Die Harder▲
Diplomatic Siege
Distortions
Dog Day Afternoon▲
Door to Door Maniac
Escape from New York
Face the Evil
Fall Time
Fatal Mission
Field of Fire
Firestorm
For Which He Stands
48 Hours to Live
Funny Games
Headless Body in Topless Bar
The Heist
Held Up
Hostage High
Hostage Hotel
Hostages▲
Housewife
Human Bomb
Iron Eagle
The Jesus Trip
John Q
Johnny 100 Pesos
Kill Me Later
King of Comedy▲
The Last Samurai
The Legend of Wolf Mountain
Lethal Tender
Light It Up
Live! From Death Row
Mad City
Masterminds
Meltdown
Midnight Fear
Mr. Reliable: A True Story
Mistrial
The Negotiator
Nick of Time
No Contest
Nothing to Lose
One Way Out
Open Fire
Operation Thunderbolt
A Perfect World
Peril
A Prayer in the Dark
Provoked
Pups
Quake
Quick Change
Raising the Heights
The Ref▲
Rock All Night
The Seventh Floor
Sex and the Other Man
S.F.W.
The Shot
Skyscraper
Snatched
Space Marines
Spaghetti House
Speed 2: Cruise Control
Split Second
Stand Off
A Stranger Is Watching
Stranglehold
Stripteaser
Sudden Death
Suddenly▲
Sweet Hostage
Take Down
The Taking of Pelham One Two Three▲
Terror Stalks the Class Reunion
3 Ninjas: High Noon at Mega Mountain
The Trap
Truth or Consequences, N.M.
12 Monkeys▲
Uninvited Guest
Vengeance

Housekeepers

see The Help: Female

Houston

Apollo 13▲
The Bad News Bears in Breaking Training
Brewster McCloud▲
Dance with Me
The Evening Star
Full Fathom Five
Jason's Lyric
Last Night at the Alamo▲
Night Game
Reality Bites
The Swarm
Terms of Endearment▲
Thursday
Urban Cowboy
Vietnam, Texas

Hunted!

see also Survival

Arctic Blue
Beyond Fear
Beyond Rangoon
Bigfoot: The Unforgettable Encounter
Bounty Hunter 2002
The Cursed Mountain Mystery
Cyborg 2
Damned River
Deadly Game
Death Hunt
Decoy
Deliverance▲
Desperate Prey
Diary of a Hitman
Dominion
Ex-Cop
Eyes of the Beholder
Fair Game
Final Round
5 Dark Souls
Fortress
Freejack
Fugitive X
The Ghost of Fletcher Ridge
The Good Guys and the Bad Guys
Hard Target
The Hunted
Hunter's Blood
Illegal Entry: Formula for Fear
Incident at Deception Ridge
Jungleground
Killing at Hell's Gate
Ladykillers
The Last of the Dogmen
Last Witness
Little Bigfoot
Maximum Risk
Midnight Murders
Montana
The Most Dangerous Game▲
The Naked Prey▲
Nemesis 2: Nebula
Nightmare at Bittercreek
Overkill
The Pest
Prey for the Hunter
Project Shadowchaser 3000
Rumble in the Streets
Shadowhunter
Shoot to Kill▲
Solo
Southern Comfort▲
Star Hunter
Survival Quest
Surviving the Game
Tracked
Trial and Error
Uncivilized
Warriors
Wild Grizzly
Wounded
Yesterday's Target

Hunting

see also Go Fish

The Amazing Panda Adventure
The Bear▲
The Belstone Fox
The Bridge to Nowhere
Caddyshack▲
Dan Candy's Law
Deadly Prey
Escanaba in da Moonlight
First Blood
Forest of Little Bear
Frostbiter: Wrath of the Wendigo
The Ghost and the Darkness
Git!
Harry Black and the Tiger
The Hunt▲
The Last Hunt
The Last Safari
Mogambo▲
Night of the Grizzly
Shoot
Shooting
Those Calloways
To Catch a Yeti
White Hunter, Black Heart▲

Hurling

Ace Ventura: When Nature Calls
Anaconda
BASEketball
Blood Simple▲
Car Wash
The Crying Game▲
The Cutting Edge
Dogfight▲
Eating Raoul▲
The Exorcist▲
Fear and Loathing in Las Vegas
52 Pick-Up
Heathers▲
Jaws▲
Kingpin
Monty Python's The Meaning of Life▲
My Giant
National Lampoon's Animal House▲
Osmosis Jones
Parenthood▲
Poltergeist 2: The Other Side
The Sandlot▲
Sirens
Stand by Me▲
This Is Spinal Tap▲
The Verdict▲
The Witches of Eastwick

I'm Not Dead, Yet!

Blackout
Hello Again
The Lazarus Man
My Favorite Wife▲
The Return of Martin Guerre▲
Sommersby
Three for the Show
A Very Brady Sequel

Immigration

The Adventures of Felix
An American Rhapsody▲
An American Tail
Arizona
Avalon▲
Blood Red
Borderline
Bread and Chocolate▲
Bread and Roses
Break of Dawn
Brothers in Trouble
Buck Privates Come Home▲
Bye-Bye
Combination Platter
Coming to America▲
The Cowboy Way
Dancer in the Dark
Does This Mean We're Married?
Drachenfutter▲
Driving Me Crazy
East Is East▲
El Super▲
The Emigrants▲
Enemies, a Love Story▲
Far and Away
Floating Life
Green Card
Heaven Before I Die
Hester Street▲
I Can't Sleep
I Cover the Waterfront
The Immigrant▲
The Italian
Journey of Hope▲
A King in New York
Kings in Grass Castles
La Promesse
Letters from Alou
Liam
Living on Tokyo Time
Manhattan Merenque!
The Manions of America
Maricela
Miami Rhapsody
Midnight Auto Supply
Monkey Business▲
Moscow on the Hudson▲
My Girl Tisa
My Sweet Victim
The New Land▲
Nueba Yol
O Quatrilho
Pelle the Conqueror▲
Sky High
Skyline▲
Someone Else's America▲
Tarantella
Wait until Spring, Bandini
West Is West
Wetbacks
Where Is My Child?

Impending Retirement

The Blue Knight
Crackerjack 3
Falling Down
Firetrap
Hitman's Journal
K-911
Lethal Weapon▲
Love to Kill
Major League 3: Back to the Minors
The Mask of Zorro▲
Must Be Santa
The Pledge▲
Seven▲
She Wore a Yellow Ribbon▲
Sonatine▲
Spy Game
Suicide Ride

In-Laws

Affair in Trinidad
August
Between Two Women
Bittersweet Love
Blacksnake!
Blood Relations
Cal▲
Commandments
Deadly Blessing
Diary of a Mad Old Man
Diary of the Dead
Die! Die! My Darling!
For Better or Worse
Free Money
The Grandfather

▲ = rated three bones or higher

Hush
I Met a Murderer
The In-Laws▲
The Inheritance
The Last Days of Chez Nous
Leila
Love▲
Love Crazy▲
Love Songs
Madame X
Meet the Parents▲
Mirele Efros
Murder-in-Law
Mussolini & I
My Brother's Wife
Norman Loves Rose
Onibaba▲
Passion in Paradise
Portrait of a Stripper
Secrets of Women▲
Silent Witness
The Sister-in-Law
Son-in-Law
Stir of Echoes
Summer Snow
A Time of Destiny

Incest

***see also** Family Ties*

Against the Wind
Andy Warhol's Frankenstein
Angels and Insects▲
Blood Relatives
The Cement Garden
The Cider House Rules▲
The Fishing Trip
Flowers in the Attic
The Grifters▲
The House of Yes
I Stand Alone
Innocent Lies
Little Boy Blue
My Sister, My Love
Natural Born Killers
Novocaine
Pola X
Ringmaster
Say It Isn't So
Seducing Maarya
Sitcom
Spanking the Monkey▲
The Sweet Hereafter▲
This World, Then the Fireworks
A Thousand Acres
'Tis a Pity She's a Whore
U-Turn
Vicious Circles
The War Zone
Waterland
Wicked

India

***see also** Calcutta*

The Adversary
Aparajito▲
Autobiography of a Princess
Bandit Queen
Bhowani Junction
The Big City
The Black Devils of Kali
Black Narcissus▲
Charulata
City of Joy
Conduct Unbecoming
Cotton Mary
The Courtesans of Bombay▲
The Deceivers
Distant Thunder▲
Drums
Earth
Ele, My Friend
The Far Pavilions
Fire
Flame Over India▲
Gandhi▲
Gunga Din▲
Heat and Dust▲
The Home and the World▲
Hullabaloo over Georgie & Bonnie's Pictures
In Custody
The Indian Tomb
Jalsaghar
The Jewel in the Crown▲
Journey to the Lost City
Jungle Boy
Jungle Hell
Kama Sutra: A Tale of Love
Kim▲
Kim
The Lives of a Bengal Lancer▲
The Mahabharata
The Man Who Would Be King▲
Masala
Maya
The Middleman
Mission Kashmir
Monsoon
Monsoon Wedding▲
Mother Teresa: In the Name of God's Poor
Mountbatten: The Last Viceroy
Octopussy
A Passage to India▲
Pather Panchali▲
The Rains Came
The Razor's Edge▲
The River▲
Rudyard Kipling's The Jungle Book
Sabaka
Shakespeare Wallah▲
Spices▲
Staying On
Stiff Upper Lips
Such a Long Journey▲
Tales of the Kama Sutra: The Perfumed Garden
Two Daughters▲
Wee Willie Winkie▲
The World of Apu▲

Inheritance

The Aristocats▲
The Bachelor
Billy Madison
Black Widow▲
Brewster's Millions
The Cheyenne Social Club
Daddy's Dyin'...Who's Got the Will?
Easy Money
Freaks▲
The Glass House
Greedy
Hot to Trot!
In the Heat of Passion 2: Unfaithful
La Cage aux Folles 3: The Wedding
Larger Than Life
Little Big League
Lord of the Rings 1: The Fellowship of the Rings▲
Mr. Deeds
Mr. Deeds Goes to Town▲
Scavenger Hunt
Seven Chances▲
Snow Dogs
Splitting Heirs

Insomnia

***see also** Up All Night*

Bringing Out the Dead
Dream for an Insomniac
Fight Club: °
The Haunting
I Can't Sleep
Taxi Driver▲

Interracial Affairs

Ali: Fear Eats the Soul▲
Bleeding Hearts
The Bodyguard
Broken Blossoms▲
Bulworth▲
Cafe au Lait▲
Chinese Box
Colorz of Rage
Come See the Paradise▲
Corrina, Corrina
The Delta
Driving Miss Daisy▲
A Fight for Jenny
Guess Who's Coming to Dinner▲
Heaven and Earth
Jungle Fever▲
The Liberation of L.B. Jones
Love Field
Love Is a Many-Splendored Thing
Love Song
Machine Gun Blues
Made in America
Miami Rhapsody
Mississippi Masala▲
Mr. & Mrs. Loving▲
Monster's Ball▲
My Beautiful Laundrette▲
The Nephew
Norman, Is That You?
One Night Stand▲
Othello
Othello▲
Parallel Sons
A Patch of Blue
The Pianist
Pinky▲
Pocahontas▲
Relax... It's Just Sex!
A Respectable Trade
Restaurant
Romeo Must Die
The Royal Tenenbaums▲
Save the Last Dance
Shadows▲
Snow Falling on Cedars
The Story of a Three Day Pass
Storytelling▲
Taxi Blues▲
The Tic Code
The Watermelon Woman
The Wedding Banquet▲
Welcome II the Terrordome
Zebrahead▲

Interviews

***see also** This Is Your Life*

Chuck Berry: Hail! Hail! Rock 'n' Roll
Dirty Pictures
The Filth and the Fury
Having Our Say: The Delany Sisters' First 100 Years
Hearts of Darkness: A Filmmaker's Apocalypse▲
The JFK Conspiracy
La Salamandre
The Laramie Project▲
Roger & Me▲
Stripper
The Thin Blue Line▲
When We Were Kings
Wisecracks▲

Inventors & Inventions

***see also** Mad Scientists; Science & Scientists*

Chairman of the Board
Chitty Chitty Bang Bang
C.H.O.M.P.S.
The Demi-Paradise▲
Edison the Man
The Great Moment
Hidden Enemy
Homewrecker
Honey, I Blew Up the Kid
Honey, I Shrunk the Kids
Honey, We Shrunk Ourselves
Invisible Mom
Longitude▲
The Machine
The Man in the White Suit▲
The Man Who Fell to Earth▲
Mom's Outta Sight
The Mosquito Coast
Mystery Plane
Not Quite Human
Not Quite Human 2
The Nut
Orgazmo
P.U.N.K.S.
Roaring Speedboats
Rogue's Gallery
So This Is Washington
The Sound and the Silence
The Spanish Prisoner▲
Spitfire▲
Still Not Quite Human
The Story of Alexander Graham Bell▲
Strange Impersonation
Theremin: An Electronic Odyssey▲
Time Chasers
Under the Hula Moon
The Water Engine
Where's Willie?
The Whole Shootin' Match▲
The Yellow Cab Man
Young Tom Edison

Invisibility

Abbott and Costello Meet the Invisible Man▲
The Amazing Transparent Man
Clash of the Titans
The Dancing Princesses
Dick Tracy vs. Crime Inc.
Doctor Faustus
Dr. Orloff's Invisible Horror
Golden Voyage of Sinbad
The Hollow Man
Invisible Agent
The Invisible Avenger
Invisible Dad
The Invisible Dr. Mabuse▲
Invisible Invaders
The Invisible Kid
The Invisible Man▲
The Invisible Man Returns▲
The Invisible Maniac
The Invisible Man's Revenge
Invisible Mom
The Invisible Monster
The Invisible Strangler
The Invisible Terror
Invisible: The Chronicles of Benjamin Knight
The Invisible Woman▲
Leapin' Leprechauns
Mad Monster Party
The Man Who Wasn't There
Memoirs of an Invisible Man
Mr. Superinvisible
Mom's Outta Sight
My Magic Dog
The New Invisible Man
Now You See Him, Now You Don't
Orloff and the Invisible Man
Panama Menace
The Phantom Creeps
Phantom from Space
Phantom 2040 Movie: The Ghost Who Walks
Return of Chandu
Riding with Death
Sound of Horror

Ireland

***see also** Great Britain*

American Women
Angela's Ashes
Beloved Enemy▲
Blown Away
The Boxer
The Break
Broken Harvest
The Brylcreem Boys
The Butcher Boy▲
Captain Boycott
Children in the Crossfire
The Crying Game▲
Dancing at Lughnasa
Danny Boy▲
Darby O'Gill & the Little People▲
The Dawning
December Bride
Durango
Echoes
The Eternal
The External
Falling for a Dancer
Far and Away
The Field▲
The Fighting Prince of Donegal
Fools of Fortune
Hear My Song▲
I See a Dark Stranger▲
I Went Down▲
The Informer
Irish Cinderella
James Joyce: A Portrait of the Artist as a Young Man
Johnny Nobody
Lamb
The Last of the High Kings
The Last September
Leprechaun
Love and Rage
The Magical Legend of the Leprechauns
Man of Aran▲
The Manions of America
The Matchmaker
Men of Ireland
Moondance
My Brother's War
The Nephew
Odd Man Out▲
Oh, Mr. Porter
The Playboys▲
Poltergeist: The Legacy
Prayer for the Dying
The Purple Taxi
The Quiet Man▲
Rawhead Rex
The Real Charlotte
River of Unrest
The Run of the Country▲
Ryan's Daughter
St. Patrick: The Irish Legend
Scarlett
The Secret of Roan Inish▲
The Seventh Stream
She Creature
Snatch▲
Some Mother's Son▲
Song o' My Heart▲
Spectre
Spellbreaker: Secret of the Leprechauns
Taffin
This Is My Father
Trojan Eddie▲
Troubles
Waking Ned Devine▲
War of the Buttons
Widow's Peak
Wings of the Morning

Islam

***see also** Middle East*

Hamsin▲
Honey & Ashes
Leila
Malcolm X: Make It Plain
The Message
My Son the Fanatic▲
The Suitors

Island Fare

***see also** Pacific Islands; Sex on the Beach*

The Admirable Crichton
The Adventures of Sadie
Affair in Trinidad
All the Brothers Were Valiant
Arachnid
Atlantis, the Lost Continent
Bare Essentials
Baywatch the Movie: Forbidden Paradise
The Beach
Beverly Hills Family Robinson
Bikini Island
Bird of Paradise
Blacksnake!
Bleeders
The Blue Lagoon
Body Trouble
Boom!
The Bounty
Cabin Boy
Captain Corelli's Mandolin
Captain Ron
Cast Away▲
The Castaway Cowboy
Chandu on the Magic Island
Club Paradise
The Conqueror & the Empress
The Cover Girl Murders
Crusoe
Cutthroat Island
Cyber Bandits
Dark Harbor
Dead of Night
Dead Waters
Deadly Currents
Deeply
Dinosaur Island
Dinotopia
Doomsdayer
Dungeon of Harrow
The Ebb-Tide
Echoes of Paradise
Emmanuelle on Taboo Island
Escape from Atlantis
Exit to Eden
Father Goose
Flipper▲
F.P. 1
Gale Force
Gargantua
Girl in Black
Hawk of the Wilderness
Head Above Water
Heaven Knows, Mr. Allison▲
Horrors of Spider Island
Hurricane
The Idol Dancer
In a Savage Land
The Island
Island in the Sun
The Island of Dr. Moreau
Island of Lost Souls▲
Island of the Blue Dolphins
Island of the Dead
Island of the Lost
Jack Frost 2: Revenge of the Mutant Killer Snowman
Jacob Two Two Meets the Hooded Fang
Joe Versus the Volcano
Jurassic Park▲
Jurassic Park 3
Kidnapped in Paradise
Kilma, Queen of the Amazons
King of the Damned
Kiss the Sky
L'Enfant d'Eau
The Lost World: Jurassic Park 2
The Lunatic
Ma and Pa Kettle at Waikiki
Magic on Love Island
A Man of Passion
Mararia
McHale's Navy
Mediterraneo▲
Melody in Love
Men of War
Molokai: The Story of Father Damien
Mutiny on the Bounty▲
Mutiny on the Bounty
My Father the Hero
My Little Assassin
Mysterious Island▲
Mysterious Island of Beautiful Women
National Lampoon's Last Resort
No Escape
No Man Is an Island
Northern Extremes
Old Mother Riley's Jungle Treasure
On an Island with You
One Night in the Tropics
The Other Side of Heaven
The Others▲
Pagan Island
Paradise
Passion in Paradise
The Passion of Anna▲
Pearl of the South Pacific
Pippi in the South Seas
The Postman▲
PT 109
Pufnstuf
The Quest
Rapa Nui
The Ravagers
The Real Macaw
Rescue from Gilligan's Island
Return to Paradise

▲ = rated three bones or higher

Return to the Blue Lagoon
Savage Is Loose
The Seducers
The Seventh Dawn
Shadow Warriors
Signs of Life
Six Days, Seven Nights
The Snake People
Somewhere in Time
Son of Fury▲
Speed 2: Cruise Control
Spy Kids 2: The Island of Lost Dreams
Stephen King's The Storm of the Century
The Story of Dr. Wassell
Summer Affair
Swept Away...▲
A Swingin' Summer
Tales of the Kama Sutra 2: Monsoon
The Tempest▲
Terror in Paradise
Third World Cop
Trouble in Paradise
The Tuttles of Tahiti▲
Undercurrent
Utopia
Vibration
Waikiki Wedding▲
Week-End in Havana
We're Not Dressing▲
When Time Ran Out
Wide Sargasso Sea
The Widow of Saint-Pierre▲
Wings over the Pacific
Xtro 3: Watch the Skies

Israel

see also ***The Holocaust; Judaism***
Amazing Grace
Cast a Giant Shadow
Children of Rage
Cup Final
Diamonds
Double Edge
Eagles Attack at Dawn
Exodus▲
Hide and Seek
Hill 24 Doesn't Answer▲
Intimate Story
Kippur▲
Late Summer Blues
The Little Drummer Girl▲
The Man Who Captured Eichmann
Mother Night▲
Operation Thunderbolt
The Seventh Coin
Sinai Commandos
Soldier of the Night
Under the Domim Tree

Istanbul, not Constantinople

From Russia with Love▲
Istanbul
The Mask of Dimitrios▲
Steam: A Turkish Bath▲
Topkapi▲
The World Is Not Enough

Italy

see also ***Venice***
Accatone!▲
Acla's Descent into Floristella
Acqua e Sapone
All Screwed Up▲
Amarcord▲
The Assisi Underground
Avanti!
Beyond the Clouds
The Bicycle Thief▲
A Blade in the Dark
Blame It on the Bellboy
Blood Feud
Cemetery Man
The Children
Christ Stopped at Eboli▲
Ciao, Professore!
Cinema Paradiso▲
Cobra
Come September
The Conformist▲
Cry of a Prostitute: Love Kills
Death Takes a Holiday▲
Divorce—Italian Style▲
Don't Torture a Duckling
Double Team
1860
The Eighteenth Angel
Elective Affinities
Enchanted April
Escapade in Florence
Europa '51
Excellent Cadavers
Executioner of Venice
A Face in the Rain
Fellini's Roma
Fiances
Final Justice
For Roseanna
The Forbidden Christ
Francesco
Gallowglass▲
The Garden of Redemption
The Garden of the Finzi-Continis▲
The Godfather, Part 3▲
Hornet's Nest
In Love and War
It Started in Naples▲
Italian for Beginners
Kaos▲
La Chartreuse de Parme
La Dolce Vita▲
La Scorta▲
La Terra Trema▲
The Lickerish Quartet
Life Is Beautiful▲
Lost Moment
Love and Anarchy▲
Love in the City▲
The Love Light
The Luzhin Defence
Macaroni
Malena
Mamma Roma▲
A Man About the House
Massacre in Rome
A Month by the Lake
Mussolini & I
Night Sun
1900▲
Nora
Nostalghia
Only You
Open City▲
Orchestra Rehearsal
The Organizer
Ossessione▲
Paisan▲
Passion of Love▲
Pizzicata
The Postman▲
Pronto
A Rare Breed
The Red Violin
Rome Adventure
St. Michael Had a Rooster
The Scent of a Woman
Screw Loose
Season for Assassins
The Secret of Santa Vittoria
The Seven Hills of Rome
Shoeshine▲
The Sicilian
Spice World: The Movie
Stealing Beauty
Stiff Upper Lips
The Story of G.I. Joe▲
The Talented Mr. Ripley
That Long Night in '43
Three Coins in the Fountain
The Tree of Wooden Clogs▲
The Truce▲
Two Women▲
Von Ryan's Express▲
Voyage in Italy
The Walls of Malapaga
What Did You Do in the War, Daddy?
Where Angels Fear to Tread▲
William Shakespeare's A Midsummer Night's Dream
Wolverine
Women in Prison
Year of the Gun

It's a Conspiracy, Man!

see also ***Capitol Capers; Mystery & Suspense***
Absolute Power
The Alchemists
All the President's Men▲
Anatomy▲
The Arrival
The Arrival 2
The Assassination File
Backlash
The Capitol Conspiracy
Chain Reaction
City Hall▲
Company Business
Conspiracy Theory▲
Cop Land▲
Dead Bang
Echo of Murder
The End of Violence
Enemy of the State
Eraser
Executive Action
Final Payback
Flashpoint
The Fourth Protocol▲
The Game▲
The Jackal
JFK▲
Looking for Richard▲
Malevolence
Man from Mallorca
The Manchurian Candidate▲
The Matrix▲
Mulholland Falls
Muppets from Space
Murder at 1600
Nixon▲
No Way Out▲
November Conspiracy
The Package
The Parallax View▲
Rangers
Red Corner
Rush Hour 2
Seven Days in May▲
The Shadow Conspiracy
Sneakers
The Star Chamber
Storm Catcher
Storm Tracker
They Live
Three Days of the Condor▲
Tom Clancy's Netforce
Venomous
Winter Kills▲
The X-Files

Jail

see ***Great Escapes; Men in Prison; Women in Prison***

Japan

see also ***Asia; Tokyo***
Akira
The Ballad of Narayama▲
Barbarian and the Geisha
The Battle of the Japan Sea
Behind the Rising Sun
Black Rain▲
Black Rain
Blood on the Sun
Captive Hearts
Cold Fever
The Cruel Story of Youth▲
Destination Tokyo
Dr. Akagi
Dodes 'ka-den▲
The Eel▲
Eijanaika▲
Enjo
Escapade in Japan
Flirt
Force of the Ninja
47 Ronin, Part 1▲
47 Ronin, Part 2▲
The Geisha Boy
Geisha Girl
Girls of the White Orchid
Gung Ho
Heaven & Earth▲
Hiroshima▲
Hiroshima Maiden
Hiroshima, Mon Amour▲
House Where Evil Dwells
The Hunted
The Idiot▲
The Imperial Japanese Empire
Journey of Honor
Kikujiro
King's Ransom
Life of Oharu▲
Love and Faith▲
MacArthur's Children▲
Madame Butterfly
A Majority of One
The Makioka Sisters▲
The Men Who Tread on the Tiger's Tail
Midway
Minbo—Or the Gentle Art of Japanese Extortion
Mishima: A Life in Four Chapters▲
Mr. Baseball
Mother▲
No
No Regrets for Our Youth▲
Nomugi Pass
Objective, Burma!▲
Okoge
Osaka Elegy
Otaku No Video▲
The Pillow Book
Prisoners of the Sun▲
Professional Killers 1
Ran▲
Rashomon▲
Red Beard▲
Rikyu▲
Rising Sun▲
Saga of the Vagabond
Samurai Cowboy
Samurai Rebellion▲
Samurai Reincarnation
Sansho the Bailiff▲
Sayonara▲
Seven Samurai▲
Shall We Dance?▲
She and He
Shin Heike Monogatari▲
Shogun▲
Showdown in Little Tokyo
Sisters of the Gion
Snow Country
Sonatine▲
The Sun's Burial▲
Thirty Seconds Over Tokyo▲
3 Ninjas Kick Back
Tokyo Decadence
Tokyo-Ga▲
Tokyo Pop
Tora! Tora! Tora!
Traffic Jam
Twenty-Four Eyes▲
Ugetsu▲
Utamaro and His Five Women
Village of Dreams
Walk, Don't Run
What's Up, Tiger Lily?▲
When I Close My Eyes
The Wolves▲
The Yakuza
You Only Live Twice
Zatoichi vs. Yojimbo▲

Jealousy

Amores Perros▲
Crush
The Devil's Backbone
Enigma
Fast Sofa
Gosford Park▲
Heart
A Matter of Taste
Nora
Othello▲
Pandaemonium
Signs & Wonders

Jerusalem

Appointment with Death
Ben-Hur▲
The Body
The Crusades
Every Time We Say Goodbye
Kadosh
The Silver Chalice

Journalism

see ***Front Page***

Judaism

see also ***The Holocaust; Israel***
Aimee & Jaguar
American Matchmaker
The Angel Levine
Angry Harvest▲
The Apprenticeship of Duddy Kravitz▲
The Assisi Underground
The Assistant
Atalia
The Attic: The Hiding of Anne Frank
Au Revoir les Enfants▲
Autumn Sun▲
The Blum Affair
A Brivele der Mamen▲
Broken Glass
The Cantor's Son
Charlie Grant's War
The Chosen▲
Commissar▲
Conspiracy of Hearts▲
The Corridor: Death
Crossfire▲
Crossing Delancey▲
David▲
David
A Day in October
Deconstructing Harry
The Devil's Arithmetic
The Diary of Anne Frank▲
Disraeli▲
Divided We Fall
Drifting
The Dunera Boys▲
The Dybbuk▲
East and West▲
Eli Eli
Enemies, a Love Story▲
Esther
Every Time We Say Goodbye
Exodus▲
Fiddler on the Roof▲
The Fixer▲
Freud Leaving Home
A Friendship in Vienna
The Frisco Kid
Funny Girl▲
The Garden of the Finzi-Continis▲
Gentleman's Agreement▲
God, Man and Devil
The Golem▲
Good Evening, Mr. Wallenberg
Goodbye, New York
Green Fields
Hamsin▲
Hanna's War
The Harmonists
Hester Street▲
Hill 24 Doesn't Answer▲
Holocaust▲
Homicide▲
The House on Chelouche Street
I Love You, Alice B. Toklas!
I Love You, I Love You Not
I Love You Rosa
In the Presence of Mine Enemies
The Infiltrator
Ivan and Abraham
Jacob the Liar
The Jazz Singer
Jeremiah
The Jew
Jew-boy Levi
Jud Suess▲
Kadosh
Keeping the Faith
King David
Kuni Lemel in Tel Aviv
Lansky
The Last Metro▲
The Last Winter
Left Luggage
Leon the Pig Farmer
Les Violons du Bal
Liberty Heights
Lies My Father Told Me▲
The Life and Times of Hank Greenberg▲
The Light Ahead
Madman
The Man Who Captured Eichmann
The Man Who Cried
Martha and I▲
Masada▲
Me and the Colonel
Mendel▲
Miracle at Midnight
Miracle at Moreaux
Miss Rose White▲
Mr. Emmanuel
Moses
The Murder of Mary Phagan▲
My Michael▲
My Mother's Courage
Next Year in Jerusalem
No Way to Treat a Lady▲
Noa at Seventeen▲
November Moon
The Only Way
Outside Chance of Maximillian Glick
Over the Brooklyn Bridge
The Pawnbroker▲
Playing Mona Lisa
Power
A Price above Rubies
The Proprietor
The Quarrel
Radio Days▲
Rescuers: Stories of Courage—Two Couples▲
Rescuers: Stories of Courage "Two Women"▲
The Revolt of Job▲
Safe Men
Sallah▲
Schindler's List▲
School Ties▲
A Secret Space
The Serpent's Egg
The Shop on Main Street▲
Sofie
Solomon
Solomon and Gaenor
The Sorrow and the Pity▲
A Stranger Among Us
The Substance of Fire
The Summer of Aviya
The Summer of My German Soldier▲
Sunshine
Table Settings
The Taxman
Tevye
They Were Ten
'38: Vienna before the Fall
Train of Life
Transport from Paradise
The Twilight of the Golds
The Two of Us▲
Uncle Moses
Under the Domim Tree
Under the Earth▲
Unsettled Land
Unstrung Heroes
Uprising▲
Used People
Voyage of the Damned▲
Wandering Jew
War & Love
Where Is My Child?
Where's Poppa?▲
The Wooden Gun
Yentl
Zalmen or the Madness of God

Jungle Stories

see also ***Monkeyshines; Treasure Hunt***
Ace Ventura: When Nature Calls
Active Stealth
Africa Screams
Aguirre, the Wrath of God▲
All the Way, Boys
Amazon
Amazon Jail
Anaconda
At Play in the Fields of the Lord▲

▲ = rated three bones or higher

Baby ... Secret of the Lost Legend
Back from Eternity
Bat 21
Bela Lugosi Meets a Brooklyn Gorilla
Beyond Rangoon
Black Cobra 3: The Manila Connection
The Black Devils of Kali
Blonde Savage
Brenda Starr
Bride of the Gorilla
Cannibal Women in the Avocado Jungle of Death
Cobra Woman
Codename: Terminate
The Colombian Connection
Commando Invasion
Congo
Death in the Garden
Delta Force Commando
The Diamond of Jeru
Diplomatic Immunity
DNA
Dr. Cyclops
East of Borneo
Elephant Boy▲
Elephant Walk
The Emerald Forest▲
Emerald Jungle
Emmanuelle 6
Enemy Unseen
Escape from Hell
Escape to Burma
Escape 2000
Farewell to the King
Fatal Mission
Field of Fire
Field of Honor
Final Mission
Fire on the Amazon
Firehawk
Firewalker
Fitzcarraldo▲
Five Came Back
Flight from Singapore
Found Alive
The Further Adventures of Tennessee Buck
Fury
George of the Jungle▲
Gold of the Amazon Women
Gold Raiders
Gorillas in the Mist▲
Green Fire
Green Inferno
Green Mansions
Greystoke: The Legend of Tarzan, Lord of the Apes
Harry Black and the Tiger
Heart of Darkness
Hell's Headquarters
How Tasty Was My Little Frenchman
Indio
Indio 2: The Revolt
Instinct
Invincible Barbarian
Jane & the Lost City
Jumanji
Jungle
The Jungle Book
The Jungle Book▲
Jungle Boy
Jungle Bride
Jungle Drums of Africa
Jungle Goddess
Jungle Heat
Jungle Hell
Jungle Inferno
Jungle Master
Jungle Patrol
Jungle Raiders
Jungle Siren
Jungle Warriors
Killers
Killing Heat
King of the Kongo
King Solomon's Treasure
Krippendorf's Tribe
The Land Unknown
Law of the Jungle
Liana, Jungle Goddess
The Lion King▲
The Lion Man
Lion Man
The Lost City
Lost City of the Jungle
The Lost Continent
The Lost Jungle
The Lost Tribe
Lure of the Islands
Managua
Medicine Man
Mercenary 2: Thick and Thin
Merrill's Marauders
Mighty Jungle
The Mighty Peking Man
Miracles
Missing in Action
The Mission▲
Mistress of the Apes
Mogambo▲
The Mosquito Coast
The Muthers
Mysterious Island of Beautiful Women
Nabonga
Naked Jungle▲
The Naked Prey▲
The New Adventures of Tarzan
Night Creature
Nightforce
No Man Is an Island
Objective, Burma!▲
Omoo Omoo, the Shark God
Operation Dumbo Drop
Options
Overkill
Perils of the Darkest Jungle
The Phantom
The Pink Jungle
Predator
Prehistoric Women
Queen of the Amazons
Queen of the Jungle
The Real Glory▲
Red Dust▲
Revenge of Doctor X
River of Death
River of Evil
The Road to Zanzibar▲
Robbers of the Sacred Mountain
Romancing the Stone▲
Rudyard Kipling's The Jungle Book
Rudyard Kipling's the Second Jungle Book: Mowgli and Baloo
Samar
The Savage Girl
Shame of the Jungle
Sheena
Sniper
Solo
Son of Kong
Stormquest
Sweet Revenge
Tarzan▲
Tarzan and His Mate▲
Tarzan and the Green Goddess
Tarzan and the Lost City
Tarzan and the Trappers
Tarzan Escapes▲
Tarzan Finds a Son▲
Tarzan of the Apes
Tarzan, the Ape Man▲
Tarzan, the Ape Man
Tarzan the Fearless
Tarzan the Tiger
Tarzana, the Wild Girl
Tarzan's Revenge
Tarzan's Secret Treasure
Terror in the Jungle
Terror of the Bloodhunters
The Thin Red Line▲
The Thirsty Dead
Tiger Fangs
Trader Horn
Trap Them & Kill Them
The Treasure of the Amazon
Troma's War
Tropical Heat
Typhoon Treasure
Virgin Sacrifice
Volunteers
Voodoo Woman
Wages of Fear▲
Warkill
Warriors of the Apocalypse
Watchers 3
West of Zanzibar
Where the River Runs Black
White Cargo
White Ghost
White Gorilla
White Huntress
The White Legion
The White Orchid
White Pongo
Wild Women
Woman Hunt
The World's Greatest Athlete
Y2K
Zombie Island Massacre

Justice Prevails...?

***see also** Order in the Court*

Above Suspicion
Absence of Malice
The Accused▲
The Advocate▲
All-American Murder
And Justice for All
Assault at West Point: The Court-Martial of Johnson Whittaker
The Avenging Angel
Beau Geste▲
Better Off Dead
Beyond Reasonable Doubt
The Burning Season▲
A Case for Murder
Cause Celebre▲
A Certain Justice
The Chamber
Circumstantial Evidence
A Civil Action
Color of Justice
The Confession
Crash Course
Creature with the Blue Hand
Crime of the Century
Cross Examination
The Crucible▲
A Cry in the Dark▲
Cyber-Tracker
Dangerous Evidence: The Lori Jackson Story
Dark Justice
The Day the Sun Turned Cold▲
Dead Right
Deadlocked
Dingaka
A Dry White Season▲
Eddie Macon's Run
Edwin
8-A
Erin Brockovich▲
Excellent Cadavers
Execution of Justice
The Execution of Private Slovik▲
An Eye for an Eye
False Arrest
Final Justice
Forgotten Prisoners
Ghosts of Mississippi
The Good Fight
Guilty as Charged
Guilty as Sin
A Gun in the House
The Hanging Tree▲
Hollow Reed▲
Honor Thy Father and Mother: The True Story of the Menendez Brothers
I Am Sam
In Self Defense
In the Name of the Father▲
Indictment: The McMartin Trial▲
Invasion of Privacy
The Jack Bull
The Jagged Edge
JFK▲
Judge Dredd
Judicial Consent
Jury Duty
Just Cause
Last Dance
Lawman▲
Laws of Deception
Let Him Have It▲
Life & Times of Judge Roy Bean
Losing Isaiah▲
The Magnificent Yankee▲
Man in the Shadow
Melanie Darrow
Mr. & Mrs. Loving▲
Mother Night▲
Murder in the First
The Murder of Mary Phagan▲
The Murder of Stephen Lawrence▲
Music Box
Mutiny
Night Falls on Manhattan▲
Nuremberg
Nuts▲
One Kill▲
The Paper▲
Presumed Innocent▲
Prisoners of the Sun▲
The Quarry
Restraining Order
Reversal of Fortune▲
Roe vs. Wade▲
Rules of Engagement
The Runaway
Separate but Equal▲
Shoot to Kill
The Shooting Party
Showdown
Sins of the Father▲
Sirens
Skin
Sleepers
Snap Decision
The Story of Qiu Ju▲
The Summer of Ben Tyler
A Time to Kill▲
A Town Has Turned to Dust
Trial & Error
Trial and Error
The Trials of Oscar Wilde▲
An Unforgettable Summer
The Verdict▲
Weekend of Shadows▲
White Lie
Wilde
The Winslow Boy▲
Woman Undone
The Wrong Man▲
The Young Land
The Young One

Karaoke

The Astronaut's Wife
The Cable Guy
Crossroads
Duets
I Still Know What You Did Last Summer
Jackpot
Junk Mail
A Life Less Ordinary
Love, Honour & Obey
Pushing Tin▲
Rush Hour 2
A Smile Like Yours
The Watermelon Woman
When Harry Met Sally...▲

Kiddie Viddy

***see also** Animation & Cartoons*

Monsters, Inc.▲

Kidnapped!

***see also** Hostage!; Missing Persons*

Abducted
Abducted 2: The Reunion
Abduction
The Abduction of Allison Tate
The Abduction of Kari Swenson
Ace Ventura: Pet Detective
Act of Piracy
Adam▲
African Rage
Against a Crooked Sky
Agent of Death
An Alan Smithee Film: Burn, Hollywood, Burn
All Over Town
Alone in the Woods
Along Came a Spider
American Kickboxer 2: To the Death
And Hope to Die
Any Place But Home
The Art of War
Ashanti, Land of No Mercy
The Atomic City
Autumn Born
Baby's Day Out
Beach Blanket Bingo▲
Beethoven's 2nd
Benji▲
Best Revenge
Beverly Hills Brats
Beyond Fear
Beyond Justice
Big Brother Trouble
The Big Hit
The Big Lebowski▲
Black Cat Run
Black Samurai
Blacklight
Bless the Child
Blind Heat
Blink of an Eye
Blood at Sundown
Blown Away
Bound and Gagged: A Love Story
Buffalo 66▲
Burial of the Rats
B.U.S.T.E.D.
Cecil B. Demented
Celtic Pride
Charlie's Angels
The Chase
The City of Lost Children▲
Cohen and Tate
Cold Blood
Commando▲
The Concentratin' Kid
Contraband
Crime of the Century
Crime Story
Crimebusters
Crows
The Crying Game▲
Dance with the Devil
Dead Air
The Deep End of the Ocean
Dirty Little Secret
Distant Justice
Django Strikes Again
Don't Say a Word
Door to Door Maniac
Double Play
Dumb & Dumber
Earthly Possessions
Emma's Shadow▲
The End of Violence
Ernest Goes to Africa
Ernie Kovacs: Between the Laughter
Everybody's Famous!
Excess Baggage
Executive Target
Eye
Fargo▲
Fatal Combat
Final Justice
Fire in the Sky
Fireback
First Daughter
Follow the River
Force of the Ninja
Four Days in September
Fugitive Champion
Gallowglass▲
The Gay Desperado
The Gingerbread Man
A Girl, 3 Guys and a Gun
The Grissom Gang▲
Guarding Tess
Gun Fury
Hangfire
Harem
Hearts & Armour
Hide and Seek
Hollywood Cop
Hostage for a Day
Implicated
In a Stranger's Hand
In the Country Where Nothing Happens
In the Doghouse
Incident at Deception Ridge
Invasion of Privacy
Island Monster
Jack and His Friends
Jailbait
Judas Kiss
Judgment Day
Kansas City▲
Kickboxer 3: The Art of War
Kid Colter
Kidnap Syndicate
Kidnapped
Kidnapped in Paradise
Lake Consequence
The Last Assassins
Last Lives
A Life Less Ordinary
The Light in the Forest
The Lightning Incident
The Lindbergh Kidnapping Case▲
Lorna Doone
Ma and Pa Kettle at Waikiki
The Man Who Captured Eichmann
Manipulator
Manny & Lo▲
Martin's Day
Memphis
Mercy
Midnight in Saint Petersburg
The Mighty▲
Mr. Nanny
The Money
Moran of the Lady Letty
The Mummy Returns
Mystery Men
National Lampoon's The Don's Analyst
Never Say Die
New Blood
Nick of Time
The Night of the Following Day
The Nightmare before Christmas▲
Nightstick
No
No Deposit, No Return
No Way Back
Omega Syndrome
101 Dalmatians
One Small Hero
The Only Way Home
Operation Condor 2: The Armour of the Gods
Operation Delta Force 2: Mayday
Orphans▲
Out of Sight▲
Outlaw Force
Paper Bullets
Parker
A Perfect World
Perpetrators of the Crime
Prince of Pennsylvania
Private Obsession
Proof of Life
Public Enemies
The Quest
Rage of Wind
Raising Arizona▲
Ransom▲
Ransom Money
A Rare Breed
The Real McCoy
Remote Control
Rescue Me
Return to Never Land
The Revenger
Riders of the Purple Sage
Ring of Fire 2: Blood and Steel
Ring of the Musketeers
Rio Diablo
Riot
The Road Killers
Rockabye
Rosebud
Rumpelstiltskin
Runaway Nightmare
Rush Hour
Ruthless People▲
Sahara
Savage Abduction
Screwed
Second Sight
Seven Hours to Judgment
Sexus

▲ = rated three bones or higher

Shanghai Noon
Sharpe's Enemy
Shattered Image
Singapore
Slate, Wyn & Me
Sloane
SnakeEater
So Close to Paradise
Soldier Boyz
Son of the Pink Panther
Son of the Sheik▲
The Squeeze
Starved
Still Not Quite Human
Street Fighter
Suicide Kings
Sunchaser
Sunstroke
Sweet Poison
Switchback
Taken
Tar
Tarzan's New York Adventure
Teaching Mrs. Tingle
Teresa's Tattoo
Terror Stalks the Class Reunion
Terror 2000
That Darn Cat
That Man from Rio
Thou Shalt Not Kill...Except
Three Days to a Kill
3 Ninjas
3 Ninjas Knuckle Up
Tie Me Up! Tie Me Down!
Till the End of the Night
To Grandmother's House We Go
Toy Story 2▲
The Trap
Trapped Alive
TripFall
Try and Get Me
Twinsitters
Two Bits & Pepper
Under the Hula Moon
Unlawful Passage
The Vanishing
A Vow to Kill
Waikiki Wedding▲
The Wash
Way of the Gun
When Danger Follows You Home
When the Greeks
Whistling in the Dark▲
The Wind and the Lion▲
Winterhawk
Wolverine
The World in His Arms

Killer Apes and Monkeys

see also Monkeyshines

The Ape
A*P*E*
The Ape Man
Battle for the Planet of the Apes
The Beast That Killed Women
Beneath the Planet of the Apes
The Bride & the Beast
Congo
Conquest of the Planet of the Apes
Doctor of Doom
Dr. Orloff's Invisible Horror
Gorilla
In the Shadow of Kilimanjaro
Jungle Captive
Jungle Woman
King Kong▲
King Kong
King Kong Lives
King Kong vs. Godzilla
King of Kong Island
Link
Mighty Joe Young
The Mighty Peking Man
Monkey Boy
Monkey Shines
Planet of the Apes▲
Primal Rage
Rat Pfink a Boo-Boo
Return of the Ape Man
Son of Ingagi
Son of Kong

Killer Appliances

see also Technology—Rampant

Attack of the Killer Refrigerator
Ghost in the Machine
The Mangler
Microwave Massacre
The Refrigerator

Killer Beasts

see also Killer Apes and Monkeys; Killer Dogs; Killer Kats; Killer Pigs; Killer Rodents

The Abomination
Attack of the Beast Creatures
Beaks: The Movie
Berserker
Bog
The Brain Eaters
Creepshow
Day of the Animals
Food of the Gods
Grizzly
In the Shadow of Kilimanjaro
Island of Terror▲
Jabberwocky
Jaws of Satan
Jurassic Park▲
The Lost World: Jurassic Park 2
Mad Death
The Monster Walks
Monty Python and the Holy Grail▲
Night of the Grizzly
The Rats Are Coming! The Werewolves Are Here!
Return to Boggy Creek
Rodan
Shakma
Shriek of the Mutilated
Sleepwalkers
The Slime People
Snowbeast
Subspecies
Swamp of the Lost Monster
Vulture
The Wild Beasts
Winterbeast

Killer Brains

see also Renegade Body Parts

Black Friday
Blood of Ghastly Horror
Boltneck
The Brain
Brain Damage
The Brain from Planet Arous
Brain of Blood
The Brain that Wouldn't Die
Donovan's Brain▲
Fiend without a Face
The Machine
Mindkiller

Killer Bugs and Slugs

Ants
The Applegates
Arachnid
Arachnophobia
Attack of the Giant Leeches
The Bees
Beginning of the End
The Black Scorpion
Blood Beast Terror
Blue Monkey
Bug
Bug Buster
Bugged!
The Cosmic Monsters
Creepers
Creepshow
Curse of the Black Widow
The Deadly Mantis
DNA
Earth vs. the Spider
Earth Vs. the Spider
Eight Legged Freaks
Empire of the Ants
Evil Spawn
Food of the Gods
The Giant Spider Invasion
Godzilla vs. Megalon
Godzilla vs. Mothra
Horrors of Spider Island
Island of the Dead
Kingdom of the Spiders
Kiss of the Tarantula
The Lair of the White Worm▲
Last Days of Planet Earth
Man of the House
Mimic 2
Monster from Green Hell
The Monster That Challenged the World
Mosquito
Mothra▲
Mysterious Island▲
Naked Jungle▲
The Nest
Parasite
Phase 4
Return of the Fly
The Savage Bees
The Scorpion's Tail
Skeeter
Slugs
Son of Godzilla
Spider Woman▲
Spiders
Squirm
Starship Troopers▲
The Swarm
Tarantula▲
Tarantulas: The Deadly Cargo
Terror out of the Sky
Them!▲
They Came from Within
Ticks
Tremors
Tremors 2: Aftershocks
Tremors 3: Back to Perfection
The Wasp Woman
The Worm Eaters

Killer Cars

see also Motor Vehicle Dept.

The Cars That Ate Paris▲
Christine
Dark of the Night
Death Race 2000
Death Sport
Duel▲
The Hearse
Mad Max▲
Mad Max: Beyond Thunderdome
Maximum Overdrive
One Deadly Owner
The Road Warrior▲
Wheels of Terror

Killer Dogs

see also King of Beasts (Dogs)

Atomic Dog
Cujo
Devil Dog: The Hound of Hell
Dogs of Hell
The Hound of the Baskervilles▲
The Hound of the Baskervilles
Man's Best Friend
Mongrel
Monster Dog
The Omen
The Pack
Pet Sematary 2
Play Dead
Revenge
Zoltan...Hound of Dracula

Killer Dreams

Alias John Preston
Bad Dreams
Blood Rage
Dario Argento's Trauma
Dead of Night▲
Deadly Dreams
Dream No Evil
Freddy's Dead: The Final Nightmare
In Dreams
Mirrors
A Nightmare on Elm Street
A Nightmare on Elm Street 2: Freddy's Revenge
A Nightmare on Elm Street 3: Dream Warriors
A Nightmare on Elm Street 4: Dream Master
A Nightmare on Elm Street 5: Dream Child
Paperhouse▲
Phantasm
Strange Impersonation
Twisted Nightmare
Waking Life
Wes Craven's New Nightmare▲

Killer Kats

see also Cats

Batman Returns
The Black Cat
Cat People▲
Cat People
Cat Women of the Moon
Claws
The Corpse Grinders
The Creeper
Curse of the Cat People▲
The Leopard Man
Mutator
Night Creature
Night of a Thousand Cats
Pet Sematary
Seven Deaths in the Cat's Eye
Strays
Tromba, the Tiger Man
The Uncanny
The Uninvited

Killer Kiddies

see also Childhood Visions

Alice Sweet Alice
The Bad Seed
Before and After
The Child
The Children
Children of the Corn
Children of the Corn 2: The Final Sacrifice
Children of the Corn 3: Urban Harvest
Children of the Corn 5: Fields of Terror
Children of the Corn: Revelation
Children of the Damned
Daddy's Girl
Damien: Omen 2
Don't Go to Sleep
The Good Son
Gummo
The Little Girl Who Lives down the Lane
Milo
The Omen
The Other▲
Relative Fear
Village of the Damned▲
Village of the Damned

Killer Pigs

see also Pigs

The Amityville Horror
Evilspeak
Pigs
Razorback

Killer Plants

Attack of the Killer Tomatoes
Attack of the Mushroom People
Body Snatchers
Day of the Triffids▲
Dr. Terror's House of Horrors
The Freakmaker
Godzilla vs. Biollante
Invasion of the Body Snatchers▲
It Conquered the World
Killer Tomatoes Eat France
Killer Tomatoes Strike Back
Little Shop of Horrors▲
Navy vs. the Night Monsters
Please Don't Eat My Mother
Return of the Killer Tomatoes!
Seedpeople
Seeds of Evil
The Womaneater
Yog, Monster from Space

Killer Reptiles

Alligator▲
Alligator 2: The Mutation
Copperhead
Crocodile
Dark Age
Destroy All Monsters
Dinosaurus!
Dragonslayer▲
Fangs
Frogs
Gamera, the Invincible
Gamera vs. Barugon
Gamera vs. Gaos
Gamera vs. Guiron
Gamera vs. Zigra
Gargantua
Gator King
The Giant Gila Monster
Godzilla
Godzilla, King of the Monsters
Godzilla 1985
Godzilla on Monster Island
Godzilla Raids Again
Godzilla 2000▲
Godzilla vs. Biollante
Godzilla vs. King Ghidora
Godzilla vs. Mechagodzilla II
Godzilla vs. Megalon
Godzilla vs. Monster Zero
Godzilla vs. Mothra
Godzilla vs. the Cosmic Monster
Godzilla vs. the Sea Monster
Godzilla vs. the Smog Monster
Godzilla's Revenge
Hell Comes to Frogtown
King Kong vs. Godzilla
Komodo
Lake Placid
The Mole People
Mothra▲
Q (The Winged Serpent)▲
Rana: The Legend of Shadow Lake
Rattlers
The Relic
Reptilian
Reptilicus
Return to Frogtown
Slithis
Spasms
Stanley
Venom
Yongkari Monster of the Deep

Killer Rodents

The Bat
The Bat People
Bats
Ben
Burial of the Rats
Deadly Eyes
The Devil Bat
Food of the Gods
Food of the Gods: Part 2
The Killer Shrews
Nightwing
Of Unknown Origin
Rats
The Rats Are Coming! The Werewolves Are Here!
Trilogy of Terror 2
Willard

Killer Sea Critters

see also Deep Blue; Go Fish; Killer Beasts

Alligator▲
Around the World Under the Sea
Attack of the Giant Leeches
Attack of the Swamp Creature
Barracuda
The Beach Girls and the Monster
The Beast
The Beast from 20,000 Fathoms
Beyond Atlantis
Blood Beach
Blood Surf
Bloodstalkers
Creature from Black Lake
Creature from the Black Lagoon▲
Creature from the Haunted Sea
Creature of Destruction
The Creature Walks among Us
Curse of the Swamp Creature
Deep Blue Sea
Deep Rising
Deepstar Six
Demon of Paradise
Devil Monster
Devilfish
Fer-De-Lance
The Flesh Eaters
Godzilla vs. Mothra
Godzilla vs. the Sea Monster
Gorgo
The Great Alligator
Horror of Party Beach
Humanoids from the Deep
Island Claw
It Came from Beneath the Sea▲
Jason and the Argonauts▲
Jaws▲
Jaws 2
Jaws 3
Jaws of Death
Jaws: The Revenge
Killer Fish
The Loch Ness Horror
The Man from Atlantis
The McConnell Story
Mean Streets▲
Memphis Belle▲
Monster from the Ocean Floor
The Monster of Piedras Blancas
The Monster That Challenged the World
Mysterious Island▲
New York, New York▲
None But the Brave
Obsession
Octaman
Octopus
Orca
The Phantom from 10,000 Leagues
Piranha
Piranha
Piranha 2: The Spawning
Reap the Wild Wind
Revenge of the Creature
Scorpion with Two Tails
Screams of a Winter Night
The Sea Serpent
Serpent Island
Shark!
Shark Attack
She Creature
The Spawning
Sphere
Swamp Thing
Tentacles
Terror in the Swamp
They Bite
Tintorera...Tiger Shark

▲ = rated three bones or higher

20,000 Leagues under the Sea▲
20,000 Leagues Under the Sea
Up from the Depths
War of the Gargantuas
What Waits Below

Killer Spouses

***see also** Wedding Hell*

Black Widow▲
Deliberate Intent
High Stakes
Sleeping with the Enemy
What Lies Beneath

Killer Toys

Amityville Dollhouse
Black Devil Doll from Hell
Bride of Chucky
Child's Play
Child's Play 2
Child's Play 3
Dance of Death
Demonic Toys
Devil Doll▲
Devil Doll
Devil's Gift
Dollman vs Demonic Toys
Dolls
Dolly Dearest
Halloween 3: Season of the Witch
Magic
Pinocchio's Revenge
Poltergeist▲
The Preacher's Wife
Puppet Master
Puppet Master 2
Puppet Master 3: Toulon's Revenge
Puppet Master 4
Puppet Master 5: The Final Chapter
Retro Puppet Master
Silent Night, Deadly Night 5: The Toymaker
Small Soldiers
Tales from the Hood
Trilogy of Terror
Trilogy of Terror 2
Wired to Kill

Kindness of Strangers

Amelie▲
Angels Over Broadway▲
The Big Push
Dear God
Forrest Gump▲
Good Sam
Lilies of the Field▲
Major Barbara▲
The Matchmaker
Mr. Deeds
Mr. Deeds Goes to Town▲
Mr. Lucky▲
Mr. North
Powder
The Rich Man's Wife
She Couldn't Say No
Sincerely Yours
The Toll Gate
Touch & Go
The Vals

King of Beasts (Dogs)

***see also** Killer Dogs*

The Accidental Tourist▲
Across the Bridge
The Adventures of Milo & Otis▲
The Adventures of Rusty
After the Thin Man▲
Air Bud
Air Bud 2: Golden Receiver
Air Bud 3: World Pup
Air Bud 4: Seventh Inning Fetch
All Dogs Go to Heaven
All Dogs Go to Heaven 2
The Amazing Dobermans
Amores Perros▲
Antarctica
As Good As It Gets▲
Atomic Dog
The Awful Truth▲
Babe: Pig in the City
Bad Moon
Balto
Baxter
Beautiful Creatures
Beethoven
Beethoven's 2nd
Beethoven's 3rd
Behave Yourself!
Benji▲
Benji the Hunted
Best in Show▲
Big Red
Bingo
Blondie Brings Up Baby
Blondie in Society
A Boy and His Dog
Buck and the Magic Bracelet
Call of the Wild
Captured in Chinatown
Cats & Dogs
Challenge To Be Free
Challenge to Lassie
Challenge to White Fang
Children of the Wild
Chips, the War Dog
C.H.O.M.P.S.
Clean Slate
Cool Hand Luke▲
Courage of Lassie
Courage of Rin Tin Tin
Courage of the North
A Cry in the Dark▲
Cujo
Danny Boy
Daring Dobermans
The Dawson Patrol
Devil Dog: The Hound of Hell
Digby, the Biggest Dog in the World
Dirkham Detective Agency
The Doberman Gang
Dr. Seuss' How the Grinch Stole Christmas
A Dog of Flanders
Dog Park
Dog Pound Shuffle▲
The Dog Who Stopped the War
Dogs of Hell
Down and Out in Beverly Hills
The Duke
Dumb & Dumber
Dusty
The Echo of Thunder
Elmer
Eyes of an Angel
Eyes of Texas
Fabulous Joe
Famous Five Get into Trouble
Fangs of the Wild
Far from Home: The Adventures of Yellow Dog
Flaming Signal
Fluke
For the Love of Benji
The Fox and the Hound▲
Frankenweenie
George!
Git!
God's Country
The Good, the Bad, and Huckleberry Hound
Goodbye, My Lady
A Goofy Movie
Great Adventure
Greyfriars Bobby
Hambone & Hillie
Heart of the Rockies
Heck's Way Home
The Hills Have Eyes
Hollow Gate
Homeward Bound 2: Lost in San Francisco
Homeward Bound: The Incredible Journey▲
The Hound of the Baskervilles
In the Doghouse
The Incredible Journey
Inside Information
Iron Will
It's a Dog's Life
Jack London's The Call of the Wild
K-9
K-911
K-9000
Kavik the Wolf Dog
Lady and the Tramp▲
Lassie
Lassie: Adventures of Neeka
Lassie, Come Home
Lassie: Well of Love
Lassie's Great Adventure
Laurel & Hardy: Laughing Gravy
Legend of the Northwest
Lightning Warrior
Little Heroes
The Lone Defender
Look Who's Talking Now
Lost and Found
Love Leads the Way
Magic of Lassie
Man Trouble
The Man Who Wagged His Tail
Man's Best Friend
The Mask▲
The Mexican
Michael
Million Dollar Haul
Milo & Otis
Mrs. Brown, You've Got a Lovely Daughter
Mr. Superinvisible
Mom, the Wolfman and Me
Mongrel
Monster Dog
Murder She Purred: A Mrs. Murphy Mystery
My Dog Shep
My Dog Skip▲
My Dog, the Thief
My Magic Dog
Napoleon
The Night Cry
Nikki, the Wild Dog of the North
Oh, Heavenly Dog!
Old Yeller▲
Oliver & Company
101 Dalmatians▲
101 Dalmatians
The Pack
The Painted Hills
The Plague Dogs
Play Dead
Poco
Pound Puppies and the Legend of Big Paw
The Return of Grey Wolf
Reuben, Reuben▲
Rin Tin Tin, Hero of the West
Rough Magic
Rover Dangerfield
Rusty's Birthday
The Sandlot▲
Savage Sam
Scooby-Doo
Screwed
Scruffy
Shadow of the Thin Man▲
The Shaggy D.A.
The Shaggy Dog
Shep Comes Home
Sherlock: Undercover Dog
Shiloh
Shiloh 2: Shiloh Season
Silver Stallion
Six of a Kind▲
Skeezer
Skull & Crown
Smoke
Snow Dogs
Soccer Dog: The Movie
Son of Lassie
Son of Rusty
Song of the Thin Man
Sputnik
Spy with a Cold Nose
Storm in a Teacup
Summerdog
Sweet November
Teddy at the Throttle
The Tender Years
There's Something about Mary▲
They Only Kill Their Masters
The Thin Man▲
The Thin Man Goes Home
Three Wishes
To Dance with the White Dog▲
Toby McTeague
Tom and Jerry: The Movie
Top Dog
Tracked
The Truth about Cats and Dogs▲
Turner and Hooch
Twin Town
The Ugly Dachshund
Umberto D▲
The Underdog
Watchers
Watchers 2
Watchers Reborn
We Think the World of You▲
When Lightning Strikes
Where the Red Fern Grows
Where the Red Fern Grows: Part 2
White Fang 2: The Myth of the White Wolf
White Fang and the Hunter
Whitewater Sam
The Wizard of Oz▲
Wolf Dog
Wolfheart's Revenge
Wonder Boys▲
Zeus and Roxanne
Zoltan...Hound of Dracula

Kings

***see** Royalty*

Korean War

All the Young Men▲
Battle Circus
Battle Hymn
The Bridges at Toko-Ri▲
Dragonfly Squadron
Field of Honor
For the Boys
The Hunters
I Want You
Iron Angel
The Last Picture Show▲
MacArthur
The Manchurian Candidate▲
M*A*S*H▲
M*A*S*H: Goodbye, Farewell & Amen▲
Men in War
Men of the Fighting Lady▲
Mr. Walkie Talkie
One Minute to Zero
Operation Dames
Pork Chop Hill▲
Retreat, Hell!
Sabre Jet
Sayonara▲
Sergeant Ryker
The Steel Helmet▲
Torpedo Alley
Wonsan Operation

Kung Fu

***see** Martial Arts*

L.A.

***see also** Earthquakes*

Abbott and Costello in Hollywood
Against the Law
Agent of Death
An Alan Smithee Film: Burn, Hollywood, Burn
The Alarmist
All Over the Guy
Always Outnumbered Always Outgunned▲
An American Rhapsody▲
American Virgin
Angel's Dance
The Anniversary Party▲
Apartment Complex
Assault on Precinct 13▲
At Any Cost
Baby Boy
Bad Influence
Bandits
Bang
Barton Fink▲
Bean▲
Beefcake
Bellyfruit
Best of the Best: Without Warning
The Beverly Hillbillies
Beverly Hills Bodysnatchers
Beverly Hills Brats
Beverly Hills Ninja
Beyond Suspicion
The Big Fall
Big Fat Liar
The Big Lebowski▲
The Big Picture
The Big Tease
Billy's Hollywood Screen Kiss
Black Scorpion 2: Ground Zero
Blast from the Past
Blow
Blue Streak
Body Double▲
Bowfinger▲
A Boy Called Hate
The Boys Next Door
Bread and Roses
Break of Dawn
The Breaks
The Broken Hearts Club▲
Broken Vessels▲
Brown's Requiem
Bulletproof
Candyman 3: Day of the Dead
Celebrity▲
Cement
Circuit
City of Angels
City of Industry
Cleopatra's Second Husband
Collateral Damage
Color of a Brisk and Leaping Day
Come See the Paradise▲
Cool Blue
Cover Me
The Craft
crazy/beautiful
Crimes of Passion▲
Crocodile Dundee in Los Angeles
The Crow 2: City of Angels
Crystal's Diary
The Day of the Locust▲
Daybreak
Dead Again▲
Dead Bang
Dead Sexy
Dear God
Defying Gravity
Delta Heat
The Dentist
The Destiny of Marty Fine
Devil in a Blue Dress▲
Die Hard▲
The Disappearance of Kevin Johnson
Don't Be a Menace to South Central While Drinking Your Juice in the Hood
The Doom Generation▲
Double Down
Drift
Dunston Checks In
Eastside
8mm
Encino Man
The End of Violence
Escape from L.A.
Face/Off▲
Falling Down
The Fast and the Furious
Fast Sofa
Fast Times at Ridgemont High▲
Female Perversions
52 Pick-Up
The Fluffer
Four Dogs Playing Poker
Four Rooms
Free Enterprise
Freeway
French Exit
Frisk
Full Contact
Gang Boys
Get On the Bus▲
Get Shorty▲
Glam
The Glass House
The Glimmer Man
Go▲
Gods and Monsters▲
Goodbye, Lover
Grand Canyon▲
The Guardian
Hanging Up
He Walked by Night▲
Heat▲
Hijacking Hollywood
Hindsight
How to Kill Your Neighbor's Dog
Hugo Pool
Hurlyburly
Hustler White
I Love You, Don't Touch Me!
In God We Trust
Internal Affairs
It's My Party
Jackie Brown▲
Jack's Back▲
Jimmy Hollywood
johns
The Journey of Jared Price
Just Write
K-911
Kate's Addiction
Kiss & Tell
Kiss Tomorrow Goodbye
L.A. Bad
L.A. Bounty
L.A. Confidential▲
L.A. Crackdown
L.A. Crackdown 2
L.A. Goddess
L.A. Law▲
L.A. Story▲
L.A. Vice
The Last Days of Frankie the Fly
Late Last Night
Lawnmower Man 2: Beyond Cyberspace
The Learning Curve
Let the Devil Wear Black
Lethal Weapon 4
The Limey▲
Living in Peril
Lost Angels
Lover Girl
The Low Life
Luminarias
Marshal Law
Matter of Trust
Memento▲
Men
The Mexican
Midnight Blue
The Mod Squad
Modern Vampires
Mommie Dearest
Mortal Challenge
Mulholland Drive▲
The Muse
My Uncle: The Alien
Nails
Neil Simon's The Odd Couple 2
The New Age
The Next Best Thing
Nick of Time
A Night at the Roxbury
Night Hunter
Night on Earth▲
1941
Nowhere
187
Paper Bullets
Parental Guidance
Paulie
Permanent Midnight
Phat Beach
Pie in the Sky
The Player▲
Point Blank
Quiet Days in Hollywood
Raging Angels
Rave Review
Recoil

▲ = rated three bones or higher

Relax... It's Just Sex!
Relentless
The Replacement Killers
Repo Man▲
Revenge Quest
Riot
Riot in the Streets
Rumpelstiltskin
Running Mates
Running Woman
Rush Hour
Ruthless People▲
Safe House
Save the Tiger▲
Scream 3
Serpent's Lair
Set It Off
Shadow Dancer
Shadow of Doubt
Shakedown
Short Cuts▲
The Shot
Showtime
Sink or Swim
Skyscraper
Slaves of Hollywood
Smiling Fish & Goat on Fire
Somebody to Love
The Souler Opposite
Spanish Judges
Speed▲
Spent
Splendor
Stand and Deliver▲
Stand-Ins
Star Maps
Starry Night
Steel
Sticks
Still Breathing
Storm Tracker
Strange Days▲
Street Corner Justice
The Street King
The Streets of L.A.
Sugar Town
Sunset Boulevard▲
Swimming with Sharks▲
Swingers▲
Swordfish
Talking about Sex
Telling You
They Call Me Sirr
This World, Then the Fireworks
Three Strikes
Time Code
Tinseltown
To Live & Die in L.A.
Too Fast, Too Young
Tortilla Soup
Totally F***ed Up
Touch
The Towering Inferno
Training Day
The Trigger Effect
20 Dates
Twilight▲
Two Days in the Valley▲
The Two Jakes
The Underground
Unlawful Entry
Virtuosity
Volcano
The Wash
Whatever It Takes
Where's Marlowe?
Witchcraft 9: Bitter Flesh
With Friends Like These
Yellow

Labor & Unions

***see also** Miners & Mining*

Act of Vengeance
Black Fury▲
Blue Collar▲
Boxcar Bertha
Bread and Roses
Brother John▲
The Burning Season▲
Canada's Sweetheart: The Saga of Hal C. Banks
Daens
Deadly Stranger
The Devil & Miss Jones▲
The End of St. Petersburg▲
End of the Line
Fame Is the Spur
F.I.S.T.
The $5.20 an Hour Dream
Gung Ho
Harlan County War
Hoffa▲
I'm All Right Jack▲
Joyride
Keeping On
Killing Floor
Land of Promise
Last Exit to Brooklyn▲
Liam
Long Road Home
Mac▲
Man of Iron▲
Man of Marble▲
Matewan▲
Molly Maguires
Moonlighting▲
Never Steal Anything Small
Newsies
Norma Rae▲
North Dallas Forty▲
On the Waterfront▲
The Organizer
The Pajama Game▲
Riff Raff▲
Salt of the Earth▲
Silkwood▲
Singleton's Pluck▲
Sons of Steel
Strike▲
Take This Job & Shove It
Teamster Boss: The Jackie Presser Story▲
The Triangle Factory Fire Scandal
Waterfront
Which Way Is Up?

Las Vegas

***see** Viva Las Vegas!*

Late Bloomin' Love

***see also** Growing Older*

Adorable Julia
The African Queen▲
Ali: Fear Eats the Soul▲
Atlantic City▲
Autumn Sun▲
Bed & Breakfast
Breakfast in Paris
The Bridges of Madison County▲
Brief Encounter▲
Camilla
Cass Timberlane
Charly▲
Children of Nature
The Christmas Wife
Circle of Two
Cold Sassy Tree▲
Crazy from the Heart▲
Devil in the Flesh▲
Digger
Doctor in Distress
End of August
A Fine Romance
Finnegan Begin Again
Forbidden Love
Foreign Affairs▲
Forty Carats
Gal Young 'Un▲
Gin Game▲
Grumpy Old Men▲
Harold and Maude▲
If Ever I See You Again
La Symphonie Pastorale▲
The Last Winters
Lonely Hearts▲
The Lonely Passion of Judith Hearne▲
Love Among the Ruins▲
Macaroni
A Majority of One
A Man and a Woman▲
Mrs. 'Arris Goes to Paris
A Month by the Lake
The Night of the Iguana▲
Other People's Money
The Pamela Principle
Players
Queen of the Stardust Ballroom▲
The Rainmaker▲
Roman Spring of Mrs. Stone▲
San Antonio
Shadowlands▲
Shirley Valentine▲
The Shock
The Shop Around the Corner▲
Shore Leave▲
A Small Killing
Something in Common
Stay As You Are
Stormy Waters
Stroszek▲
Summertime▲
To Love Again
Travelling North
24 Hours in a Woman's Life
Twice in a Lifetime▲
Used People
With Six You Get Eggroll

Law & Lawyers

***see also** Order in the Court*

Adam's Rib▲
The Advocate▲
Afterburn▲
American Tragedy
Amistad▲
Anatomy of a Murder▲
And Justice for All
Angel on My Shoulder
Assault at West Point: The Court-Martial of Johnson Whittaker
Before and After
Better Off Dead
Beyond a Reasonable Doubt
Beyond the Silhouette
Big Daddy
Bleak House
Blind Faith
Blood Brothers
Body Chemistry 4: Full Exposure
Body Language
Boomerang▲
Brain Donors
Brothers in Law
Brother's Keeper▲
The Candidate▲
Cape Fear▲
Carlito's Way▲
A Case for Murder
A Case of Libel
A Certain Justice
The Chamber
Changing Lanes▲
Character
Chase
Circonstances Attenuantes
Citizen Cohn
A Civil Action
Class Action▲
The Client
Color of Justice
Compulsion▲
The Confession
The Conqueror Worm▲
Conspiracy Theory▲
Cop-Out
Criminal Law
Critical Care
Dark Justice
Death and the Maiden▲
Death Benefit
Death of a Soldier
Defenders of the Law
The Defenders: Payback
The Defenders: Taking the First
Deliberate Intent
Destination Vegas
The Devil's Advocate
Dirty Mary Crazy Larry▲
Disorganized Crime
The Divorce of Lady X
Dr. Dolittle 2
Down the Drain
Dragons Forever
Ebbtide
Enemy of the State
The Enforcer
Erin Brockovich▲
Evelyn Prentice
Eye Witness
Fair Game
False Witness
Father's Day
Fear and Loathing in Las Vegas
Female Perversions
A Few Good Men▲
Final Appeal
Final Justice
Final Verdict
The Firm▲
First Monday in October
The Fixer
For Roseanna
Forbidden Sins
Force of Evil▲
The Franchise Affair
A Free Soul
From the Hip
Genealogies of a Crime
Georgia
Getting Gotti
The Ghost of Spoon River
Ghosts of Mississippi
Gideon's Trumpet
The Glass Shield
The Good Fight
The Great American Sex Scandal
The Guilty
Guilty as Sin
High Crimes
Honor Thy Father and Mother: The True Story of the Menendez Brothers
I Am Sam
I Am the Law▲
Illegal
Illegal Affairs
I'm No Angel▲
In Pursuit
In the Name of the Father▲
The Incident▲
Inherit the Wind
The Island of Dr. Moreau
It's the Rage
JAG
The Jagged Edge
John Grisham's The Rainmaker
The Judge
Judge Dredd
Judge Priest▲
Judicial Consent
The Juror
Jury Duty
Just Cause
Justice
King and Country▲
L.A. Law▲
Last Dance
The Last Innocent Man
Laws of Deception
Legal Deceit
Legal Eagles
Legalese
Legally Blonde
Legend of Billie Jean
Let Freedom Ring
Let's Kill All the Lawyers
Liar Liar
Life & Times of Judge Roy Bean
Losing Isaiah▲
Love Among the Ruins▲
Love Crimes
Love Stinks
Loved
Luminarias
Madame X
The Magnificent Yankee▲
Man from Colorado
Man of the House
Manhattan Melodrama▲
Marked Woman▲
Matter of Trust
Melanie Darrow
Minbo—Or the Gentle Art of Japanese Extortion
Misbehaving Husbands
Mr. & Mrs. Loving▲
Murder in the First
A Murder of Crows
My Cousin Vinny▲
The Narrow Margin▲
Night and the City▲
Night Falls on Manhattan▲
Nixon▲
North
Nuremberg
One Night at McCool's
Ordeal by Innocence
Original Intent
Our Mutual Friend
The Paper Chase▲
Party Girl▲
The Pelican Brief
Penthouse▲
The People vs. Larry Flynt▲
Perfect Witness
Perry Mason Returns▲
Philadelphia▲
Physical Evidence
Pinocchio's Revenge
Portraits of a Killer
Power of Attorney
Presumed Innocent▲
Primal Fear
Promised a Miracle
Psychopath
Red Corner
Reet, Petite and Gone▲
Regarding Henry▲
Restraining Order
Return to Paradise▲
Road Agent
Rounders
Roxie Hart
Runaway Father
Rustler's Valley
Scandal
Scott Turow's The Burden of Proof
Shadow of Doubt
Shakedown
Sharon's Secret
Shoot to Kill
A Simple Twist of Fate
Sleepers
Slightly Honorable
The Star Chamber
State's Attorney
Stephen King's Thinner
A Stranger in the Kingdom
The Summer of Ben Tyler
The Sun Shines Bright
The Sweet Hereafter▲
Swoon▲
A Time to Kill▲
To Kill a Mockingbird▲
Too Young to Die
Town without Pity
The Trial
Trial & Error
Trial and Error
Trial by Jury
Trois Couleurs: Rouge▲
True Believer
True Colors
Truth or Die
Twelve Angry Men▲
Twelve Angry Men
The Verdict▲
Victim▲
Web of Deceit
Where the Truth Lies
Wild Things
The Winslow Boy▲
The Wistful Widow of Wagon Gap
Woman of Desire
The World's Oldest Living Bridesmaid
The Young Philadelphians▲

Leprechauns

Darby O'Gill & the Little People▲
Finian's Rainbow▲
Leprechaun
Leprechaun 2
Leprechaun 3
Leprechaun 4: In Space
Leprechaun 5: In the Hood
The Magical Legend of the Leprechauns
Spellbreaker: Secret of the Leprechauns

Lesbians

***see also** Bisexuality; Gays; Gender Bending*

Aimee & Jaguar
Alien Prey
All Over Me▲
The Alley Cats
Another Way▲
Bar Girls
The Berlin Affair
Better Than Chocolate
The Bitter Tears of Petra von Kant
Black Cobra
The Blood Spattered Bride
Blow Dry
Bound
Boys on the Side
But I'm a Cheerleader
Butterfly Kiss
Carmilla
The Celluloid Closet▲
Chasing Amy
The Children's Hour
Chuck & Buck
Chutney Popcorn
Claire of the Moon
Common Ground
Crocodiles in Amsterdam
Daughters of Darkness▲
Desert Hearts▲
Desperate Remedies
Different Story
Double Face
Entre-Nous▲
Even Cowgirls Get the Blues
Everything Relative
Extramuros
Fanci's Persuasion
Fire
The Fourth Sex
Foxfire
French Twist
Gia
Her and She and Him
High Art
Higher Learning
The Hunger
If These Walls Could Talk 2
The Incredibly True Adventure of Two Girls in Love
It's In the Water
I've Heard the Mermaids Singing▲
Just One Time
Kamikaze Hearts
The Killing of Sister George
Late Bloomers
Law of Desire▲
Le Jupon Rouge
Les Voleurs▲
Lianna▲
Listen
Little City
Lost and Delirious
Love and Other Catastrophes
Maedchen in Uniform▲
The Monkey's Mask
My Father Is Coming
My Sister, My Love
Nadja▲
November Moon
Nowhere
Only the Brave
Oranges Are Not the Only Fruit
Personal Best▲
A Question of Love▲
The Rainbow▲
Relax... It's Just Sex!
The Scorpion Woman
Seducers
Serving in Silence: The Margarethe Cammermeyer Story▲
Set It Off
Shades of Black
She Must Be Seeing Things
Show Me Love
The Silence▲
Simone Barbes
Skin Deep
Slaves to the Underground
The Souler Opposite
The Sticky Fingers of Time
Sugar Cookies
Therese & Isabelle
These Three▲
Things You Can Tell Just by Looking at Her

▲ = rated three bones or higher

Three of Hearts
Tokyo Cowboy
Totally F***ed Up
The Truth About Jane
The Twilight Girls
The Vampire Lovers
Vampyres
A Village Affair
Virgin Machine
Walk on the Wild Side
The Watermelon Woman
When Love Comes
When Night Is Falling ▶
Wild Side
Windows
The Women on the Roof
X, Y & Zee

Libraries and Librarians

Adventure
Black Mask
The Breakfast Club ▶
Desk Set ▶
Foul Play ▶
Fright Night 2
Ghostbusters ▶
Good News
Goodbye Columbus ▶
The Gun in Betty Lou's Handbag
Hard-Boiled
It's a Wonderful Life ▶
Kicking and Screaming ▶
Mr. Sycamore
The Mummy
The Music Man ▶
The Name of the Rose
No Man of Her Own
Off Beat
Only Two Can Play ▶
The Pagemaster
Party Girl
7 Faces of Dr. Lao ▶
The Shawshank Redemption ▶
Shooting the Past
Something Wicked This Way Comes
With Honors

Lifeguards

***see also** Beach Blanket Bingo; Swimming*

Baywatch the Movie: Forbidden Paradise
Caddyshack ▶
Fun in Acapulco
Lifeguard
The Sandlot ▶
That Summer of White Roses
Wet and Wild Summer

London

***see also** Great Britain; Royalty*

Abbott and Costello Meet Dr. Jekyll and Mr. Hyde
About a Boy ▶
Alfie ▶
American Roulette
An American Werewolf in London ▶
Annie: A Royal Adventure
The Assassination Bureau ▶
Autobiography of a Princess
The Avengers
B. Monkey
Bad Behavior
Beat Girl
Beautiful People
Beautiful Thing ▶
Bedlam ▶
Bedrooms and Hallways
Berkeley Square
Betrayal
Born Romantic
Bridget Jones's Diary ▶
Broken Blossoms ▶
The Buddha of Suburbia ▶
Carpet of Horror
Century
A Certain Justice
Chicago Joe & the Showgirl
Claudia
Comic Act ▶
Contraband
Croupier ▶
Curse of the Yellow Snake
Danger UXB
Dick Barton, Special Agent
Different for Girls ▶
Disraeli ▶
Double Vision
Dracula's Daughter ▶
Dream Street
The Duchess of Duke Street ▶
An Egyptian Story
84 Charing Cross Road ▶
The Elephant Man ▶
11 Harrowhouse ▶
Elizabeth ▶
End of the Affair
The End of the Affair ▶
Entrapment
Expresso Bongo
Face
Fanny Hill: Memoirs of a Woman of Pleasure
Fever Pitch
Fierce Creatures
Foreign Affairs ▶
Foreign Correspondent ▶
Forever and a Day ▶
Forgive and Forget
Frenzy ▶
The Frightened City
From Hell ▶
Full Moon in Paris
The Gambler & the Lady
Gaslight ▶
The Gay Lady
The Golden Bowl ▶
The Golden Bowl
Great Expectations
The Great Muppet Caper ▶
Hands of a Murderer
Heaven's a Drag
High Heels and Low Lifes
Hope and Glory ▶
The Horse's Mouth ▶
The House of Eliott
Husbands
I, Monster ▶
An Ideal Husband ▶
Immortality
In the Name of the Father ▶
Incognito
The Innocent Sleep
John and Julie
Journey for Margaret ▶
Just Like a Woman
The Knack ▶
The Krays ▶
The L-Shaped Room ▶
Lady L
Lamb
The Leading Man
Like It Is ▶
The Little Princess ▶
The Long Good Friday ▶
The Lost Language of Cranes ▶
The Lost Son
Love Among the Ruins ▶
Love and Death on Long Island
Love Is the Devil ▶
The Low Down
Lured
The Man Who Knew Too Little
The Man Who Made Husbands Jealous
Mary Poppins ▶
Mary Reilly
Maybe Baby
Meantime
A Merry War ▶
Metroland
Midnight Lace
Ministry of Fear ▶
The Missionary
Mrs. 'Arris Goes to Paris
Mrs. Dalloway
Moll Flanders
Moonlighting ▶
The Mummy Returns
The Murder of Stephen Lawrence ▶
Murder on Line One
My Beautiful Laundrette ▶
My Friend Walter
The Mysterious Magician
Naked ▶
National Lampoon's European Vacation
Night and the City ▶
Nighthawks
Nil by Mouth
Notting Hill ▶
The Old Curiosity Shop
Oliver Twist
Oliver Twist ▶
101 Dalmatians
One Wish Too Many
Othello ▶
Our Mutual Friend
The Painted Lady ▶
The Parent Trap
Phantom Fiend
The Phantom of the Opera
Photographing Fairies
Plain Jane
Plunkett & Macleane
Poldark
Priest
Quatermass and the Pit
Rancid Aluminium
Razor Blade Smile
Return to Never Land
The Ripper
Robert Louis Stevenson's The Game of Death
Rough Cut
Royal Wedding ▶
Sabotage ▶
The Saint in London
Sammy & Rosie Get Laid ▶
Say Hello to Yesterday
The Secret Agent
Secrets and Lies
Seeing Red
Sexy Beast ▶
Shakespeare in Love ▶
She Wolf of London
Shine ▶
Shooting Fish
Shooting the Past
Snatch ▶
Solitaire for 2
Spice World: The Movie
Split Second
Stella Does Tricks
Strange Bedfellows
Strapless
Tale of a Vampire
The Tall Guy ▶
They Made Me a Fugitive
The Three Penny Opera ▶
Time After Time ▶
To Each His Own ▶
To Sir, with Love
Topsy Turvy ▶
Touching Evil ▶
Turtle Diary ▶
Twice upon a Yesterday
Ultraviolet
Vanity Fair
The Very Thought of You
Virtual Sexuality
Water Babies
Waterloo Bridge ▶
The Way We Live Now
Werewolf of London
Wild West
Wilde
The Wings of the Dove ▶
The Winslow Boy ▶
Witchcraft 10: Mistress of the Craft
A Woman's Guide to Adultery
Wonderland
The Young Americans
The Young Poisoner's Handbook ▶
Young Sherlock Holmes

Loneliness

***see** Only the Lonely*

Loner Cops

***see also** Cops*

Above the Law
Action Jackson
Bad Attitude
Bad Lieutenant ▶
The Blue Knight
The Breed
Code of Silence
The Cop & the Girl
Cop in Blue Jeans
Dead Bang
The Dead Pool
Deadly Dancer
Die Hard ▶
Die Hard 2: Die Harder ▶
Die Hard: With a Vengeance
Dirty Harry ▶
The Enforcer
Excessive Force
Exit Wounds
Force of One
The Gauntlet
Heat
Heat ▶
In the Heat of the Night ▶
Judge Dredd
Klute ▶
Magnum Force
McQ
Minority Report
Murder by Numbers
Nightstick
Northwest Trail
One Good Cop
One Man Jury
The Pledge ▶
Rent-A-Cop
RoboCop ▶
Serpico ▶
Sharky's Machine
SnakeEater
SnakeEater 2: The Drug Buster
SnakeEater 3: His Law
Speed ▶
Stick
Stone Cold
The Street King
Striking Distance
Sudden Impact
Ten to Midnight
Top Dog
Year of the Dragon

Look Ma! I'm on TV!

***see also** Mass Media*

At Home with the Webbers
Death to Smoochy
Eat Your Heart Out
EDtv
15 Minutes
Gale Force
Magnolia ▶
The New Gladiators
Paul Bartel's The Secret Cinema
Pleasantville ▶
Series 7: The Contenders
Showtime
Sink or Swim
Stay Tuned
The Truman Show ▶
The 24 Hour Woman
Woman on Top

Lost Worlds

***see also** Parallel Universes*

At the Earth's Core
Beyond Atlantis
Brigadoon ▶
Creatures the World Forgot
Gold of the Amazon Women
Jane & the Lost City
Journey to the Center of the Earth ▶
Journey to the Center of the Earth
Jumanji
The Land That Time Forgot
The Land Unknown
The Lost Continent
Lost Horizon ▶
The Lost World
Mysterious Island ▶
Mysterious Island of Beautiful Women
The People That Time Forgot
Warriors of Virtue
What Waits Below
When Dinosaurs Ruled the Earth
Where Time Began

Lottery Winners

Antoine et Antoinette
Babette's Feast ▶
Dual Alibi
Fox and His Friends ▶
It Could Happen to You
Just Your Luck
Le Million ▶
Lots of Luck
Lottery Bride
Lucky Numbers
Lucky Partners
The Million Dollar Kid
Next Friday
The Squeeze
The Ticket
29th Street
Uptown Saturday Night
Waking Ned Devine ▶
The Wrong Box ▶

Lovable Loonies

***see also** Shrinks*

Bean ▶
Benny & Joon
Best in Show ▶
Beyond Therapy
Box of Moonlight
The Couch Trip
Crazy People
David and Lisa ▶
The Eighth Day
The Fisher King ▶
Ghost World ▶
Gridlock'd ▶
Julian Po
The King of Hearts ▶
Meet Wally Sparks
The Ninth Configuration ▶
One Flew Over the Cuckoo's Nest ▶
Patch Adams
The Ruling Class ▶
Superstar
What about Bob? ▶

Lovers on the Lam

***see also** Fugitives*

Badlands ▶
Blood & Wine
Bonnie & Clyde ▶
Boys
The Getaway
Gun Crazy ▶
Guncrazy
Heaven's Burning
Jailbreakers
Kalifornia
Kill Me Later
Kiss or Kill
Love and a .45
Mad Love
Natural Born Killers
Niagara, Niagara
River of Grass
The Road
Rough Magic
The Sugarland Express ▶
Trojan Eddie ▶
True Romance
Two If by Sea
When Brendan Met Trudy ▶
Wild at Heart ▶

Mad Scientists

***see also** Inventors & Inventions; Science & Scientists*

Alien Terminator
The Amazing Transparent Man
The Animal
The Ape
The Ape Man
Atom Age Vampire
Attack of the Puppet People
Attack of the 60-Foot Centerfold
Attack of the Swamp Creature
The Avengers
Before I Hang ▶
Bela Lugosi Meets a Brooklyn Gorilla
Beverly Hills Bodysnatchers
Bloodbath at the House of Death
Bloodlust
Bloodstorm: Subspecies 4
Body Armor
The Body Shop
Bowery Boys Meet the Monsters
The Brain that Wouldn't Die
Brenda Starr
Bride of Re-Animator
Bride of the Monster
Bug Buster
Captain America
Captive Wild Woman
The Cars That Ate Paris ▶
Castle of Evil
Castle of the Creeping Flesh
The City of Lost Children ▶
Clockstoppers
The Cobweb
The Corpse Vanishes
Creator
Creature of the Walking Dead
The Creeper
The Creeping Flesh
The Creeps
The Crime of Dr. Crespi
Crimes of Dr. Mabuse ▶
The Curse of the Aztec Mummy
Cyborg Cop
Darkman ▶
Darkman 2: The Return of Durant
Darkman 3: Die Darkman Die
The Dead Next Door
Dead Pit
Dead Sleep
Death Warmed Up
Deep Red
Devil Doll ▶
Dr. Black, Mr. Hyde
Doctor Blood's Coffin
Doctor Butcher M.D.
Dr. Caligari
Dr. Cyclops
Dr. Death, Seeker of Souls
Dr. Frankenstein's Castle of Freaks
Dr. Goldfoot and the Bikini Machine
Dr. Jekyll and Mr. Hyde ▶
Dr. Jekyll and Mr. Hyde
Dr. Jekyll and Sister Hyde
Dr. Jekyll and the Wolfman
Dr. Jekyll's Dungeon of Death
Dr. No ▶
Dr. Orloff's Monster
Doctor X
Donovan's Brain ▶
The Double O Kid
Embryo
Evil Town
The Fear Chamber
Firestarter 2: Rekindled
The Flesh Eaters
Frankenhooker
Frankenstein ▶
Frankenstein
Frankenstein and the Monster from Hell
Frankenstein '80
Frankenstein General Hospital
Frankenstein Must Be Destroyed
Frankenstein Reborn
Frankenstein Unbound ▶
Frankenstein's Daughter
Freaked
The Freakmaker
Geisha Girl
The Giant Spider Invasion
Girl in His Pocket
The Head
Hellmaster
Hideous Sun Demon
The Hollow Man
House of Frankenstein
Hyena of London
I, Monster ▶

▶ = rated three bones or higher

The Immortalizer
The Incredible Two-Headed Transplant
The Indestructible Man
Invasion!
Invasion of the Zombies
The Invisible Dr. Mabuse▲
The Invisible Man▲
The Invisible Ray
The Invisible Terror
The Island of Dr. Moreau
Island of Lost Souls▲
Jekyll and Hyde
Jungle Captive
Jungle Woman
Jurassic Park▲
Kids in the Hall: Brain Candy
The Killing Device
King of Kong Island
King of the Zombies
Lady Frankenstein
The Lawnmower Man
Lawnmower Man 2: Beyond Cyberspace
Lightblast
The Living Dead
The Lost City
The Mad Ghoul
Man Made Monster
The Man They Could Not Hang
The Man Who Lived Again
The Man with Two Lives
Mandroid
Maniac
The Manster
Mary Shelley's Frankenstein
Master Minds
Metamorphosis
Miami Horror
Mr. Stitch
Mom's Outta Sight
The Monster▲
The Monster Maker
Monsters Crash the Pajama Party
The Mosaic Project
The Munsters' Revenge
Murders in the Rue Morgue
Mystery Science Theater 3000: The Movie
Naked Souls
Nightmare Castle
Nightmare Weekend
Orloff and the Invisible Man
The Outer Limits: Sandkings▲
Philadelphia Experiment 2
The Pink Panther Strikes Again▲
Proteus
Re-Animator▲
Red Blooded American Girl
Retroactive
Return of the Killer Tomatoes!
Revenge of the Zombies
Revolt of the Zombies
The Robot vs. the Aztec Mummy
Samson in the Wax Museum
Savage
Scanner Cop
Science Crazed
Screamers
Severed Ties
Shadow Creature
Shadow of Chinatown
She Demons
Shock Waves
Silent Killers
Spider-Man▲
Star Trek: Generations▲
Strange Behavior
Strange Case of Dr. Jekyll & Mr. Hyde
Superargo
Supersonic Man
Tammy and the T-Rex
Teenage Zombies
Terror Is a Man
Testament of Dr. Mabuse
The Tingler▲
Torture Ship
Transmutations
The Unearthly
The Vampire Bat
Vile 21
Virtual Seduction
Vulture
The Wasp Woman
Werewolf of London
Wes Craven Presents Mind Ripper
Wild Wild West

Made for Television

see TV Pilot Movies; TV Series

Mafia

see Organized Crime

Magic

see also Genies; Magic Carpet Rides; Occult

Alabama's Ghost
The Alchemist
Arabian Nights
Balloon Farm
Bedknobs and Broomsticks
The Black Cauldron
Black Magic Terror
Bogus
The Butcher's Wife
Celine and Julie Go Boating
Chandu on the Magic Island
Chandu the Magician
The Craft
Cthulhu Mansion
The Day the Earth Froze
Death Magic
Deathstalker 3
Doctor Mordrid: Master of the Unknown
Don't Torture a Duckling
Dream a Little Dream 2
Dungeons and Dragons
Escape to Witch Mountain▲
Eternally Yours
FairyTale: A True Story
Gryphon
Harry Potter and the Sorcerer's Stone▲
Houdini
Kids of the Round Table
Killing Grandpa
Lady in Distress
The Linguini Incident
Lord of Illusions
Lord of the Rings 1: The Fellowship of the Rings▲
Luna e L'Altra
Magic Moments
Magic Serpent▲
The Magician▲
The Magician of Lublin
The Man in the Santa Claus Suit
Mary, My Dearest
Merlin
Merlin▲
My Chauffeur
The Mysterious Stranger
Penn and Teller Get Killed
Pick a Card
Prospero's Books▲
Pufnstuf
Quicker Than the Eye
Ratz
Rough Magic
A Simple Wish
Stephen King's Thinner
The Swan Princess 2: Escape from Castle Mountain
Sword & the Sorcerer
Teen Witch
The Tempest
Turnaround
Tut & Tuttle
Wedding Band
The Wizard of Gore
Wizards of the Demon Sword
Zotz!

Magic Carpet Rides

see also Genies

Aladdin▲
Aladdin and the King of Thieves
Arabian Nights
Golden Voyage of Sinbad
1001 Arabian Nights
The Seventh Voyage of Sinbad▲
Sinbad and the Eye of the Tiger
Sinbad of the Seven Seas
Sinbad, the Sailor▲
The Thief of Bagdad▲
The Thief of Baghdad▲
Thief of Baghdad
The Thief of Baghdad

Mail-Order Brides

see also Marriage; Wedding Bells

Birthday Girl
Mississippi Mermaid▲
Naked Jungle▲
Original Sin
The Purchase Price
Zandy's Bride

Marriage

see also Divorce; Otherwise Engaged; War Between the Sexes; Wedding Bells; Wedding Hell

Above Suspicion
Abraham's Valley
Absent Without Leave
Accused
Across the Wide Missouri
The Adjuster
The Adultress
The Adventures of Mark Twain▲
An Affair in Mind
Affairs of Anatol
After Sex
Afterglow
The Age of Innocence▲
Alfredo, Alfredo
All Things Fair
All This and Heaven Too▲
Almost You
Always▲
American Beauty▲
American Matchmaker
America's Sweethearts
Amnesia
Angel
The Anniversary Party▲
Antoine et Antoinette
Any Wednesday
Arabian Nights
The Aristocrats
Arnold
Arrivederci, Baby!
As You Desire Me▲
Ash Wednesday
Ask Any Girl
Assault and Matrimony
The Astronaut's Wife
Asunder
Attack of the 50 Ft. Woman
Autumn Leaves
Autumn Marathon
Baby Doll▲
The Baby Maker
Bachelor in Paradise
Bachelor Party
Back to the Wall
Backstreet Dreams
Bad Behavior
Bad Manners
Barefoot in the Park▲
Barjo
The Barkleys of Broadway▲
The Bat People
Battle of the Sexes
Battle Shock
A Beautiful Mind▲
Because of You
Bed and Board▲
Bedroom Eyes 2
Being John Malkovich▲
The Beneficiary
Best Enemies
Best Friends
The Best Intentions▲
The Best Man
Betrayal
Betsy's Wedding
Big Business Girl
The Big Squeeze
A Black Veil for Lisa
Blanche Fury
Blindfold: Acts of Obsession
Bliss
The Bliss of Mrs. Blossom▲
Blonde Venus▲
Blondie
Blondie Hits the Jackpot
Blondie in Society
Blondie Knows Best
Blondie Plays Cupid
Blood of Jesus
The Blood Oranges
Blood Wedding▲
Blue Heaven
Blue in the Face
Blue Moon
Blue Sky▲
Bluebeard's Eighth Wife
Blume in Love▲
Body Chemistry
Body Strokes
Boulevard of Broken Dreams
Brand New Life
Bread and Tulips▲
Breaking the Waves▲
Breaking Up
Breathing Lessons▲
The Bride & the Beast
Bride of the Wind
The Bride Walks Out
Broken Glass
The Browning Version
The Buccaneers▲
Bulldog Drummond's Bride
Bullwhip
Burn Witch, Burn!▲
The Burning Bed▲
A Business Affair
The Butcher's Wife
By Love Possessed
By the Light of the Silvery Moon
Calendar▲
Captain's Paradise▲
Car Trouble
Casanova Brown
Cast a Dark Shadow▲
Catherine Cookson's Colour Blind
Catherine Cookson's The Man Who Cried
Catherine Cookson's The Round Tower
Caught
Cause for Alarm
Chained
Change of Heart
A Change of Seasons
Charles & Diana: A Palace Divided
Charulata
Cheaters
Cheatin' Hearts
Child Bride of Short Creek
China Moon
Chinese Roulette
Chloe in the Afternoon▲
The Chocolate Soldier
Choices
Christina
Circumstances Unknown
Circus
Claire's Knee▲
Clash by Night▲
Coast to Coast
Cold Heaven
Come Back, Little Sheba▲
The Comfort of Strangers▲
Coming to America▲
Committed
Common Law Wife
Company Man
Conflict▲
Consenting Adults
Consolation Marriage
Conspiracy of Terror
The Convent
Cosmic Slop
Cotton Mary
Country Girl▲
Country Girl
The Cowboy and the Lady
Crash
Crazy in Love
Creation of Adam
Crime & Passion
A Cry in the Night
The Crying Child
Cul de Sac▲
Damage▲
Dancing in the Dark
Dangerous Game
Dangerous Liaisons
Danielle Steel's Changes
Darlings of the Gods
The Daytrippers
De Mayerling a Sarajevo
The Dead▲
Dead Husbands
Dead in the Water
Dead Mate
Dead On
Death Kiss
Deception
Deep in the Heart (of Texas)
Deja Vu
Designing Woman▲
Desire and Hell at Sunset Motel
Desire Under the Elms
Desperate Characters▲
Desperate Hours
Desperate Remedies
The Devil in Silk
The Devil's Advocate
Diabolically Yours
Dial "M" for Murder▲
Diary of a Mad Housewife▲
Diary of the Dead
Dinner with Friends
Dirty Hands
The Disappearance of Christina
The Disciple
Divided We Fall
Divorce American Style
Divorce—Italian Style▲
The Divorce of Lady X
Doctors' Wives
Dodsworth▲
Dollar
A Doll's House
A Doll's House▲
Dominique Is Dead
Don Juan DeMarco
Dona Flor and Her Two Husbands▲
Donkey Skin▲
Don't Raise the Bridge, Lower the River
Don't Say a Word
Don't Talk to Strangers
Doomsday
Double Deal
Double Exposure
Double Indemnity▲
Double Standard
Doubting Thomas
Dream Lover
Dressmaker
Drifting Souls
Drowning by Numbers▲
Drums Along the Mohawk▲
Dry Cleaning
East Is East▲
East Side, West Side
East-West
Easy Living▲
Easy Living
Eat a Bowl of Tea▲
Ecstasy
Edward and Mrs. Simpson
Effi Briest▲
Egg and I▲
El
Elective Affinities
Element of Doubt
Elizabeth of Ladymead▲
Ellie
Elvis and Me
Emissary
Emmanuelle
Emmanuelle, the Queen
Encore▲
End of Desire
The End of the Affair▲
End of the Road
Enemies, a Love Story▲
Enormous Changes▲
Enough
The Entertainer▲
Entre-Nous▲
Ernie Kovacs: Between the Laughter
Erotic Images
Escapade▲
Escape Clause
Estate of Insanity
Eternally Yours
Ethan Frome
Eureka!
Evelyn Prentice
Every Breath
Every Girl Should Be Married
Everybody's All American
Everyone Says I Love You▲
Eve's Bayou▲
The Ex
Ex-Lady
Experiment Perilous▲
The Eyes of Youth
Eyes Wide Shut
Faces▲
The Facts of Life
Faithful
Falling for a Dancer
Falling from Grace
Family Upside Down▲
Far Cry from Home
The Farmer's Wife
Fatal Attraction▲
Father of the Bride▲
Fearless▲
Femme Fatale
Fergie & Andrew: Behind Palace Doors
Fever
Fictitious Marriage
A Fine Romance
Fireworks
First Affair
Flirt
The Flower of My Secret▲
Follow the Boys▲
Fools
Fools Rush In
For Keeps
For Love or Country: The Arturo Sandoval Story
For Love or Money
For Pete's Sake
Forbidden Fruit▲
Forever Love
Forget Paris
Fortune's Fool
Fortunes of War▲
Four Daughters▲
Four Days in July
Four Rooms
The Four Seasons
Fourth Story▲
Free Money
French Twist
Frieda
From the Terrace
Fulfillment
Full of Life
Fun with Dick and Jane
Funny About Love
Gabbeh▲
Games
Gaslight▲
A Gathering of Eagles
A Gentle Woman
George Washington
George Washington: The Forging of a Nation
Gertrud▲
Get Out Your Handkerchiefs▲
Getting Up and Going Home
The Ghost and the Guest
Giant▲
The Gift of Love
Girl from Hunan▲
Goin' to Town
The Golden Bowl▲
The Golden Bowl
The Good Girl
The Good Wife
Gore Vidal's Lincoln
Gosford Park▲
Grace of My Heart
Grand Isle
Grand Theft Auto
The Grass Is Greener
Greed▲
The Greek Tycoon

Grievous Bodily Harm
Group Marriage
Grown Ups
Grumpier Old Men
The Guardsman▲
Guess Who's Coming to Dinner▲
Guest Wife
A Guide for the Married Man▲
A Guide for the Married Woman
The Hairdresser's Husband
Halfmoon
Hammers over the Anvil
Hamsun
A Handful of Dust
Happiness▲
Hard Promises
Harlan County War
Harriet Craig▲
Harrison's Flowers
The Hawk
Head Above Water
Heartburn▲
Heaven
Heaven's Prisoners
Heist▲
Helas pour Moi
Hell-Ship Morgan
Here We Go Again!
High Crimes
High Heels
High Society▲
Highway Patrolman
Hilary and Jackie▲
Hindsight
Hitched
Homecoming▲
Hope Floats
The Horrible Dr. Hichcock
Hostage for a Day
Hot Spell
Hotel Room
Houdini
House of Mirth▲
The Householder
How to Be a Woman and Not Die in the Attempt
How to Break Up a Happy Divorce
How to Commit Marriage
How to Kill Your Neighbor's Dog
How to Make an American Quilt
How to Marry a Millionaire
How to Murder Your Wife▲
Howard's End▲
The Howards of Virginia
Hurry, Charlie, Hurry
Husbands
Husbands and Lovers
Husbands and Wives▲
Hush
I Do! I Do!
I Dood It
I Like It Like That▲
I Love My...Wife
I Love You Again▲
I Love You ... Goodbye
I Love You Rosa
I Love You to Death
I Married a Vampire
I Married a Woman
I Only Want You to Love Me
I Was a Male War Bride▲
I Will, I Will for Now
I Wonder Who's Killing Her Now?
An Ideal Husband▲
Il Bell'Antonio
Il Grido
I'll See You in My Dreams
Illicit
Illusions
Immortal Bachelor
The Imported Bridegroom
In a Savage Land
In Celebration▲
In Name Only
In the Bedroom▲
In the Mood for Love
Indecent Proposal
Infinity
The Innocent▲
Intersection
Intimate Story
Intimate Strangers
Intruso
The Invasion of Carol Enders
The Invisible Ghost
Iris▲
Isn't She Great
It Came from the Sky
It Started with a Kiss
It Takes Two
It's the Rage
Jackie, Ethel, Joan: The Kennedy Women
Java Head▲
Jenny
The Jeweller's Shop
Josepha▲
Ju Dou▲
Jubal
Jubilee Trail
Jude▲
Jude the Obscure
Juliet of the Spirits▲
Just a Little Harmless Sex
Just Like Weather▲
Kadosh
The Keeper
Keeper of the Flame
The Kettles on Old MacDonald's Farm
The Kill-Off
Killing Heat
A Kind of Loving▲
Kiss and Be Killed
Kuni Lemel in Tel Aviv
La Bete Humaine▲
La Chienne▲
La Deroute
La Vengeance d'une Femme
La Vie Continue
Lady Audley's Secret
Lady Chatterley's Lover
Lady Godiva
Lady L
Lady Windermere's Fan
Lantana▲
Last Breath
The Last Dance
The Last Days of Chez Nous
The Last Married Couple in America
L'Atalante▲
Late Spring▲
Laurel & Hardy: Be Big
Le Beau Mariage▲
Le Bonheur
Le Bonheur Est Dans le Pre
Le Chat▲
Lea
The Leather Boys
Leila
L'Enfer▲
Leo Tolstoy's Anna Karenina
Lesson in Love
Let's Get Married
A Letter to Three Wives▲
Lianna▲
The Liars
Liar's Moon
Lie Down with Lions
Life of Oharu▲
Like It Never Was Before
Linda
The Lion in Winter▲
Listen, Darling
A Little Sex
Lonely Wives
The Long Haul
Losing Chase
Lost Highway
Lost Honeymoon
The Lotus Eaters
Loulou▲
Love, Cheat & Steal
Love, etc.
Love from a Stranger
Love Matters
Love Walked In
The Lovers▲
Lovers and Other Strangers▲
Loving Couples
Lucie Aubrac
Lucy and Desi: Before the Laughter
Lured Innocence
Lust and Revenge
The Luzhin Defence
Ma Saison Preferee▲
Maborosi▲
Mad at the Moon
Madame Bovary▲
Madame Bovary▲
Madame Butterfly
Made in Heaven
Magnificent Doll
Magnolia▲
Making Love
The Makioka Sisters▲
Man from Nowhere
Man of the House
The Man Who Made Husbands Jealous
The Man Who Wasn't There▲
Manhattan Murder Mystery▲
A Map of the World
Maria Chapdelaine▲
The Marquise of O
The Marriage Circle▲
Marriage Is Alive and Well
Marriage Italian Style▲
The Marriage of Maria Braun▲
Married?
Married People, Single Sex 2: For Better or Worse
Married to It
Married Too Young
A Married Woman▲
The Marrying Kind
Martha and I▲
Marty▲
Mary, Queen of Scots
Matrimaniac
A Matter of Dignity
Max, Mon Amour
Maybe Baby
McLintock!▲
Me Myself I
Me You Them
The Member of the Wedding
Memories of a Marriage▲
Memory of Us
Men...▲
The Merry Widow
Metroland
Mexican Spitfire at Sea
Miami Rhapsody
Microwave Massacre
Mid-Channel
Midnight▲
Midnight Crossing
Mighty Aphrodite
The Millionairess
Miracle of Morgan's Creek▲
The Mirror Has Two Faces
Misbehaving Husbands
Mrs. Dalloway
Mrs. Mike
Mr. & Mrs. Smith▲
Mr. Love
Mr. Mom▲
Mr. Skeffington▲
Mr. Sycamore
Mr. Wonderful
Mistress▲
Modern Love
Moment to Moment
The Money Pit
Montana
Moon over Harlem
The Moon's Our Home
Mouth to Mouth
Multiplicity
Murder at 45 R.P.M.
Murder Czech Style
Murder So Sweet
Murders in the Zoo
Muriel's Wedding▲
The Music Lovers
My Dear Secretary
My First Wife
My 5 Wives
My Husband's Double Life
My Life So Far
My Little Chickadee▲
My Michael▲
My New Gun
My Other Husband
My Sweet Victim
Naked Jungle▲
Never Say Die
The New Age
Niagara
Night Ride Home
Nightkill
Nina Takes a Lover
Nora
Normal Life
Not Tonight Darling
The Notorious Lady
Nouvelle Vague
Now and Forever
Nudo di Donna▲
Nurse Marjorie
O Quatrilho
Odd Obsession
O'Hara's Wife
The O.J. Simpson Story
Oldest Confederate Widow Tells All▲
On Approval▲
On Golden Pond▲
On Her Majesty's Secret Service▲
On Valentine's Day
One Good Turn
One Hour Photo
One Night in the Tropics
One of My Wives Is Missing
One Trick Pony
Only with Married Men
Orchestra Wives▲
Othello▲
Overnight Sensation
The Paint Job
Paint Your Wagon
The Painted Veil
Pajama Tops
The Palm Beach Story▲
Pandaemonium
Panic
Paper Marriage
Paradise▲
Pardon Mon Affaire▲
Pardon Mon Affaire, Too!
Paris, France
Party
Passion in Paradise
The Passion of Ayn Rand
A Passion to Kill
Pavilion of Women
Pedale Douce
Peggy Sue Got Married
The Penitent
Pennies from Heaven▲
Perfect Alibi
The Perfect Bride
Perfect Crime
The Perfect Marriage
A Perfect Murder
Period of Adjustment▲
Persuasion
Pete 'n' Tillie
Petulia▲
Phaedra
Phffft!
The Philadelphia Story▲
The Piano▲
Picture Bride
A Piece of Pleasure▲
Pipe Dreams
Platinum Blonde▲
Playing Dead
Pollock▲
Portrait of a Lady▲
Portrait of an Assassin
Portrait of Teresa▲
The Postman Always Rings Twice▲
The Postman Always Rings Twice
Praying Mantis
Prelude to a Kiss
Primary Colors
The Primitive Lover
Prisoner of Second Avenue
Prisoners of Inertia
Private Confessions
Private Life
Private Lives▲
Promises! Promises!
Provincial Actors
Prowler
The Pumpkin Eater▲
The Purchase Price
Pushing Hands
Quartet▲
Queen Bee
Queen Margot▲
Question of Faith
Race for Life
Raging Bull▲
Raise the Red Lantern▲
Range of Motion
Rape and Marriage: The Rideout Case
Rebecca▲
Reckless▲
The Rector's Wife
Red Rock West▲
Remember Me
A Respectable Trade
Return to Me
Revenge of the Stepford Wives
Reversal of Fortune▲
Rich and Famous
Rich and Strange
The Rich Man's Wife
Rider from Tucson
Riptide▲
Risky Business
Rocky 2
Romantic Englishwoman▲
The Roof
Rose of Washington Square
Roseanne: An Unauthorized Biography
A Royal Scandal
The Royal Tenenbaums▲
Runaways
Ryan's Daughter
Safe Passage
The Sandy Bottom Orchestra
Santa Fe
Sarah's Child
Satan's Black Wedding
Saturday Night and Sunday Morning▲
Savage Attraction
Say Yes!
Scar of Shame
Scarlet Dawn
Scenes from a Mall
Scenes from a Marriage▲
Scorchers
Score
Scotland, PA
Season of Fear
Second Chance
Secret Beyond the Door
The Secret Life of Girls
Secrets of Women▲
Seems Like Old Times
Send Me No Flowers▲
Separate Vacations
Separate Ways
Seven Chances▲
The Seven Year Itch▲
The Seventeenth Bride
Seventh Heaven
Sex and the Single Girl
Sexpot
Sexual Malice
Shadowlands▲
The Shakiest Gun in the West
The Shame▲
Shattered
She and He
She-Devil
She Waits
She's So Lovely
She's the One
Shoot the Moon
Shooting Elizabeth
The Show Off
Sibling Rivalry
Sidewalks of New York
Signs & Wonders
Silent Tongue
Silent Victim
Sin and Redemption
Sin Takes a Holiday
The Singing Blacksmith
The Single Standard
The Sisters▲
Sketch Artist
Skinner's Dress Suit
The Slugger's Wife
Small Time Crooks
Smash Palace
Smash-Up: The Story of a Woman▲
Smoking/No Smoking
Smouldering Fires
Snow White: A Tale of Terror
So This Is Paris▲
Sofie
The Soft Skin▲
Something About Sex
Something to Talk About
Soul Food
Sound of Murder
Splendor
The Stationmaster's Wife
Steam: A Turkish Bath▲
The Stepford Wives▲
The Story of Boys & Girls▲
The Story of Esther Costello
The Story of Us
The Story of Xinghua
Strange Bedfellows
Stromboli
The Student Affair
The Substitute Wife
Sudden Fear▲
Summer Wishes, Winter Dreams
Suspicion▲
Sweet Hearts Dance
Sweet Movie
Sweet Nothing▲
Sweet Poison
Sweet Revenge
Sweethearts▲
The Tailor of Panama▲
Tarnished Angels▲
Tell Me a Riddle
Tell Me That You Love Me
The Tenant of Wildfell Hall
Tender Is the Night
The Tender Trap
Tess of the D'Urbervilles
Test Pilot▲
Thanks for the Memory
That Certain Thing
That Old Feeling
That Uncertain Feeling
Thicker Than Water
The Third
Third Walker▲
30 Is a Dangerous Age, Cynthia
Three Broadway Girls▲
Three Daring Daughters
Three for the Show
Three Husbands
Three Smart Girls▲
Thursday's Game▲
Till Death Do Us Part
Till Marriage Do Us Part
Till Murder Do Us Part
Till the End of the Night
Tin Men
To Joy▲
Tom & Viv▲
Too Beautiful for You
Too Far to Go▲
Torchlight
The Torture of Silence
A Touch of Class▲
Town and Country
Trade Off
Traps
Tricks of the Trade
True Lies
True Love▲
The Truman Show▲
The Tunnel
The Tunnel of Love
Turn of the Blade
Twice a Woman
Twilight▲
The Twilight of the Golds
Two Family House
Two for the Road▲
The Two Mrs. Carrolls
Ulysses
The Unchastened Woman
Under Capricorn
Under the Sand▲
Under the Volcano▲
Undercover Blues
Undercurrent
Une Parisienne
Unfaithfully Yours▲
Unfaithfully Yours
Unholy Wife
The Unkissed Bride
Until September
Uptown New York
The Van▲

▲ = rated three bones or higher

Vanishing Act
Vanity Fair
Vasectomy: A Delicate Matter
Velvet Goldmine
The Vertical Ray of the Sun
Victoria & Albert
A Village Affair
Violets Are Blue
The Virgin of Nuremberg
Vivacious Lady ▲
Voulez-Vous Danser avec Moi?
A Vow to Kill
Voyage in Italy
Vukovar ▲
W
A Walk in the Clouds
Walk in the Spring Rain
Walking and Talking
Waltz of the Toreadors ▲
War Brides
The Wash ▲
Waterland
Way Down East ▲
The Wayward Wife
A Wedding
The Wedding Gift ▲
Wedding in Blood ▲
A Wedding in Galilee ▲
We're Not Married ▲
What Lies Beneath
What's Good for the Goose
When a Man Loves a Woman
Where Angels Fear to Tread ▲
Where Were You When the Lights Went Out?
White Gold ▲
White Mischief ▲
Who's Afraid of Virginia Woolf? ▲
Who's Got the Action?
Why Do Fools Fall in Love?
Wicked Ways
The Widow of Saint-Pierre ▲
Widow's Kiss
The Wife
Wife Versus Secretary ▲
Wifemistress
Wilde
With a Friend Like Harry ▲
Without Anesthesia
Wolf Trap
The Woman in White
A Woman Named Jackie
The Woman Next Door ▲
Woman of the Year ▲
Woman on Top
A Woman under the Influence ▲
Woman Undone
Woman with a Past
A Woman's Guide to Adultery
A Woman's World ▲
The Women ▲
Women from the Lake of Scented Souls
The Wooden Man's Bride
The World Is Full of Married Men
World's Greatest Lover
Worth Winning
Woyzeck
X, Y & Zee
A Year in Provence ▲
You and Me
You Can't Fool Your Wife
You Gotta Stay Happy
The Young Pioneers
Younger & Younger
Yours, Mine & Ours
You've Got to Have Heart
Zandy's Bride
Zebra Lounge

Marriages of Convenience

The Great McGinty ▲
Green Card
Honeymoon
A Paper Wedding ▲
Rachel and the Stranger ▲
Seducing Maarya
The Wedding Banquet ▲

Mars

see also Space Operas

Abbott and Costello Go to Mars
The Angry Red Planet
Buck Rogers in the 25th Century
Capricorn One ▲
Escape from Mars
Flight to Mars
Frankenstein Meets the Space Monster
The Invader
It! The Terror from Beyond Space
John Carpenter's Ghosts of Mars
Mars Attacks!
The Martian Chronicles: Part 1
The Martian Chronicles: Part 2
The Martian Chronicles: Part 3
Martians Go Home!
Mission to Mars
My Favorite Martian
Planet of Blood
Project Shadowchaser 3000
Red Planet
Red Planet Mars
RocketMan
Rocketship X-M
Santa Claus Conquers the Martians
Species 2
Total Recall ▲
Zombies of the Stratosphere

Martial Arts

Above the Law
Alley Cat
Aloha Summer
American Chinatown
American Kickboxer 1
American Kickboxer 2: To the Death
American Ninja
American Ninja 2: The Confrontation
American Ninja 3: Blood Hunt
American Ninja 4: The Annihilation
American Samurai
American Shaolin: King of the Kickboxers 2
American Streetfighter
The Amsterdam Connection
Angel of Fury
Angel Town
Baby Cart 1: Lend a Child...Lend an Arm
Baby Cart at the River Styx
Back in Action
Balance of Power
Bells of Death
Best of the Best
Best of the Best 2
Best of the Best 3: No Turning Back
Best of the Best: Without Warning
Beverly Hills Ninja
The Big Brawl
Big Trouble in Little China
Black Belt
Black Belt Jones
Black Eagle
Black Mask
Black Samurai
Blackbelt 2: Fatal Force
Blind Fury
Blind Rage
Blood for Blood
Blood Ring
Blood Warriors
Bloodfist
Bloodfist 2
Bloodfist 3: Forced to Fight
Bloodfist 4: Die Trying
Bloodfist 5: Human Target
Bloodfist 6: Ground Zero
Bloodfist 7: Manhunt
Bloodfist 8: Hard Way Out
Bloodmatch
Bloodsport
Bloodsport 2: The Next Kumite
Bloodsport 3
The Bodyguard
Born Losers
Bounty Tracker
Braddock: Missing in Action 3
Brain Smasher...A Love Story
Breaker! Breaker!
Breathing Fire
The Bride with White Hair
The Bride with White Hair 2
The Bronx Executioner
Bruce Lee: Curse of the Dragon ▲
Bruce Lee Fights Back from the Grave
The Bushido Blade
Cage 2: The Arena of Death
Capital Punishment
Catch the Heat
Challenge of the Masters
China O'Brien
China O'Brien 2
China White
The Chinatown Kid
Chinese Connection
Chinese Connection 2
Circle of Iron
Clash of the Ninja
Cleopatra Jones
Cleopatra Jones & the Casino of Gold
Clones of Bruce Lee
The Cobra
Counter Attack
Crack Shadow Boxers
Crime Story
The Crippled Masters
Crouching Tiger, Hidden Dragon ▲
Cyber Ninja
A Dangerous Place
Day of the Panther
Deadly Bet
Deadly Target
Death Challenge
Death Machines
Death Match
Death Ring
Death Warrant
Deathfight
Desert Kickboxer
The Divine Enforcer
Dolemite
Double Dragon
Double Impact
Dragon Fury
Dragon Lord
Dragon: The Bruce Lee Story ▲
Dragons Forever
Duel of Fists
The Dynamite Brothers
Dynasty
Eagle's Shadow
The Eliminators
Enter the Dragon ▲
Enter the Ninja
The Executioners
An Eye for an Eye
Fantasy Mission Force
Fatal Combat
Fearless Tiger
Ferocious Female Freedom Fighters
The Fighter
Fighting Black Kings
Final Impact
Firecracker
Fist of Fear, Touch of Death
Fist of Glory
Fist of Legend
Fist of Steel
Fists of Blood
Fists of Fury ▲
Fists of Fury 2
Fists of Iron
Force of One
Force of the Ninja
Forced Vengeance
Forgotten Warrior
Four Robbers
Full Contact
Full Metal Ninja
Futurekick
G2: Mortal Conquest
The Gambling Samurai
Game of Death
Gang Justice
Gang Wars
Ghostwarrior
Gladiator Cop: The Swordsman 2
The Glimmer Man
Goldfinger ▲
Good Guys Wear Black
Green Dragon Inn
Guardian Angel
Gymkata
Half a Loaf of Kung Fu
Hard to Kill
Hawk's Vengeance
Heart of Dragon
Heatseeker
Hero and the Terror
The Heroic Trio
Hot Potato
Immortal Combat
In Your Face
The Instructor
Invasion U.S.A.
Invincible
Iron Monkey
Iron Thunder
Ironheart
Jackie Chan's First Strike ▲
Jaguar Lives
Jet Li's The Enforcer
Joe Somebody
Karate Cop
The Karate Kid ▲
The Karate Kid: Part 2
The Karate Kid: Part 3
Karate Warrior
The Kick Fighter
Kick of Death: The Prodigal Boxer
Kickboxer
Kickboxer 2: The Road Back
Kickboxer 3: The Art of War
Kickboxer 4: The Aggressor
Kickboxer the Champion
Kill and Kill Again
Kill Line
Kill or Be Killed
Kill Squad
Kill the Golden Goose
Killer Elephants
The King of the Kickboxers
Kingfisher the Killer
Kiss of the Dragon
Knights
Knock Off
Kung Fu
Kung Fu: The Movie
Lady Dragon
Lady Dragon 2
The Last Dragon
Last Hurrah for Chivalry
Legacy of Rage
The Legend of Drunken Master ▲
The Legend of the 7 Golden Vampires
Lethal Ninja
Lethal Panther
Lionheart
Little Dragons
Little Ninjas
Mafia vs. Ninja
Magic Kid
Magic Kid 2
Magnum Killers
Manchurian Avenger
Marked for Death
Martial Law
Martial Law 2: Undercover
Martial Outlaw
Master with Cracked Fingers
Master's Revenge
Maximum Risk
Meltdown
The Millionaire's Express
Mission of Justice
Mr. Nice Guy
Mortal Kombat 1: The Movie
Mortal Kombat 2: Annihilation
The Mosaic Project
Moving Target
My Samurai
Naked Killer
New Fist of Fury
New York Cop
The Next Karate Kid
Night Hunter
Night Master
Night of the Kickfighters
Night of the Warrior
9 1/2 Ninjas
Nine Deaths of the Ninja
Ninja 3: The Domination
Ninja Academy
Ninja: American Warrior
Ninja Brothers of Blood
Ninja Champion
Ninja Commandments
Ninja Condors
Ninja Connection
Ninja Death Squad
Ninja Destroyer
Ninja Fantasy
Ninja Hunt
Ninja in the U.S.A.
Ninja Masters of Death
Ninja Mission
Ninja of the Magnificence
Ninja Operation: Licensed to Terminate
Ninja Phantom Heroes
Ninja Powerforce
Ninja Showdown
Ninja Strike Force
Ninja the Battalion
Ninja, the Violent Sorcerer
Ninja Vengeance
No Retreat, No Surrender
No Retreat, No Surrender 2
No Retreat, No Surrender 3: Blood Brothers
Octagon
Omega Cop
Once Upon a Time in China ▲
Once Upon a Time in China II ▲
Once Upon a Time in China III ▲
The One
One Down, Two to Go!
One-Eyed Swordsman
One Man Army
Only the Strong
Open Fire
Operation Condor
Operation Golden Phoenix
Operation Orient
Out for Blood
Out for Justice
Overkill
The Perfect Weapon
The Power of the Ninjitsu
The Power Within
Pray for Death
The Prisoner
The Prodigal Son
Professional Killers 1
Project A
Project A: Part 2
Protector
Pursuit
Pushed to the Limit
The Quest
Rage and Honor
Rage and Honor 2: Hostile Takeover
Rage of Honor
Rage of Wind
Ragin' Cajun
Rapid Fire
Raw Force
Raw Target
Red Sun Rising
Redemption: Kickboxer 5
Remo Williams: The Adventure Begins
Retrievers
Return of the Dragon
Return of the Street Fighter
Return of the Tiger
Revenge of the Ninja
Ring of Fire
Ring of Fire 2: Blood and Steel
Ring of Fire 3: Lion Strike
Ring of Steel
Riot
Roller Blade
Romeo Must Die
Rumble in the Bronx
Sanshiro Sugata ▲
Scorpion
Shogun's Ninja
Shootfighter: Fight to the Death
Shootfighter 2: Kill or Be Killed!
Showdown
Showdown in Little Tokyo
Sidekicks
Silent Assassins
Silent Rage
Sister Street Fighter
Slaughter in San Francisco
Sleepy Eyes of Death: The Chinese Jade
Sloane
Snuff-Bottle Connection
Stickfighter
The Stranger and the Gunfighter
Stranglehold
The Street Fighter
The Street Fighter's Last Revenge
Street Hunter
Street Soldiers
Supercop
Supercop 2
Surf Ninjas
Survival Game
Sword of Doom ▲
Sword of Honor
Swords of Death
Sworn to Justice
Talons of the Eagle
Teenage Mutant Ninja Turtles: The Movie
Teenage Mutant Ninja Turtles 2: The Secret of the Ooze
They Call Me Bruce?
They Still Call Me Bruce
The Three Avengers
3 Ninjas
3 Ninjas: High Noon at Mega Mountain
3 Ninjas Kick Back
3 Ninjas Knuckle Up
Throw Down
Tiger Claws
Tiger Heart
Tigershark
Timecop
TNT Jackson
To Be the Best
To the Death
Tokyo Raiders ▲
Tongs: An American Nightmare
Top Dog
Tough Guy
Trancers 3: Deth Lives
Triple Impact
24 Hours to Midnight
Twin Dragons
Twin Warriors
The Two Great Cavaliers
Undefeatable
Unmasking the Idol
Vampire Raiders—Ninja Queen
Warrior of Justice
Way of the Black Dragon
When Taekwondo Strikes
White Phantom: Enemy of Darkness
White Tiger
Wing Chun
Without Mercy
The Young Bruce Lee
Young Master
Young Tiger
Zatoichi: Master Ichi and a Chest of Gold
Zatoichi: The Blind Swordsman and the Chess Expert
Zatoichi: The Blind Swordsman's Vengeance
Zatoichi vs. Yojimbo ▲

Martyred Pop Icons

see also Rock Stars on Film

Beatlemania! The Movie
Blue Hawaii

▲ = *rated three bones or higher*

The Buddy Holly Story▲
Bus Stop▲
Clambake
The Doors
Elvis and Me
Elvis: The Movie
Fun in Acapulco
Highway
I Shot Andy Warhol▲
John & Yoko: A Love Story
King Creole
Kissin' Cousins
La Bamba▲
Lenny▲
Live a Little, Love a Little
Love Me Tender
Marilyn: The Untold Story▲
Norma Jean and Marilyn
Paradise, Hawaiian Style
Rebel without a Cause▲
The Rose▲
Roustabout
Sgt. Pepper's Lonely Hearts Club Band
The Seven Year Itch▲
Speedway
Spinout
Stardust Memories
Stay Away, Joe
This Is Elvis
Train to Hollywood▲
The Trouble with Girls (and How to Get into It)▲

Mass Media

***see also** Front Page; Radio*

Against the Law
America
American Tragedy
And Nothing But the Truth
At Home with the Webbers
Behind the Rising Sun
Bigfoot: The Unforgettable Encounter
Blankman
Broadcast Bombshells
Broadcast News▲
A Case of Libel
Chill Factor
The China Syndrome▲
Color of Justice
Crimetime
A Cry in the Dark▲
Dead Men Don't Die
Death Watch▲
Demonstone
E. Nick: A Legend in His Own Mind
Eternity
Exiled to Shanghai
Eyewitness
A Face in the Crowd▲
The Gladiators
The Groove Tube
Groundhog Day▲
Hero▲
Holy Man
I Was a Teenage TV Terrorist
The Image
In and Out▲
Indictment: The McMartin Trial▲
The Insider▲
Intern
International House
King of the Airwaves
The Late Shift
Life or Something Like It
Lipstick Camera
Live! From Death Row
Livin' Large
The Lost Honor of Katharina Blum▲
Love and a .45
Mad City
Medium Cool▲
Meet Wally Sparks
Mr. Reliable: A True Story
My Favorite Year▲
Naked City: A Killer Christmas
National Lampoon's Attack of the 5 Ft. 2 Women
Natural Born Killers
Network▲
News at Eleven
No Such Thing
Nothing Sacred▲
The Passenger▲
Pray TV
Primary Colors
Prime Suspect
Prime Time Murder
Private Parts
Quiz Show▲
Raising the Heights
Ratings Game
Ready to Wear
Riders of the Storm
RKO 281▲
Scrooged
The Second Civil War
The Seduction
Serving in Silence: The Margarethe Cammermeyer Story▲
Sex Through a Window
S.F.W.
Showtime
Soft and Hard
Stardom
The Story of Esther Costello
The Stuff
Superstar: The Life and Times of Andy Warhol▲
Switching Channels
Tabloid!
The Thrill of It All!
To Die For▲
Tomorrow Never Dies
Trial by Media
The Truman Show▲
Tunnelvision
UHF
Up Close and Personal▲
Videodrome
Wayne's World▲
Weapons of Mass Distraction
Welcome to Sarajevo▲
Wild Horses
Witness to the Execution
Zelig▲

Masseurs

At First Sight
Breathtaking
Living Out Loud
Love Kills
Never Say Never Again

May-December Romance

***see also** Coming of Age; Growing Older; Romantic Adventures; Romantic Comedy; Romantic Drama*

After Sex
All That Heaven Allows▲
Atlantic City▲
Autumn in New York
Cass Timberlane
The Cat's Meow
The Color of Evening
Crush
Georgy Girl▲
Girl with Green Eyes
Goodbye Again
The Graduate▲
Guinevere▲
Harold and Maude▲
Live Bait
Lolita▲
Lolita
Love in the Afternoon
The Love Letter
Lured Innocence
Nelly et Monsieur Arnaud▲
Our Lady of the Assassins
The Pallbearer
Perfect Love
Reckless▲
Reckless: The Sequel▲
Roman Spring of Mrs. Stone▲
Sabrina▲
Seducing Maarya
Six Days, Seven Nights
That Obscure Object of Desire▲
Tim
Trojan Eddie▲

The Meaning of Life

The Apostle▲
At Home with the Webbers
Badlands▲
Being Human
The Blood of Others
Breathing Lessons▲
The Castle▲
The Collector▲
The Designated Mourner
End of the Road
Field of Dreams▲
The French Lieutenant's Woman▲
Full Body Massage
Funny Face▲
Galaxies Are Colliding
Gospa
Heaven Can Wait▲
Here Comes Mr. Jordan▲
Joey Breaker▲
Julian Po
Land and Freedom▲
Life Upside Down
Love and Death▲
Monty Python's The Meaning of Life▲
My Life
My Own Private Idaho▲
The Razor's Edge▲
The Razor's Edge
The Remains of the Day▲
Shadowlands▲
The Sheltering Sky▲
The Trial
Why Has Bodhi-Darma Left for the East
Wings of Desire▲
Zabriskie Point▲

Medieval Romps

***see also** Camelot (Old); Historical Drama; Swashbucklers*

The Adventures of Marco Polo
The Adventures of Robin Hood▲
Army of Darkness▲
Beatrice▲
Becket▲
Being Human
The Beloved Rogue▲
Black Knight
Braveheart▲
Brothers Lionheart
Camelot
The Canterbury Tales
The Castilian
A Challenge for Robin Hood
Choice of Weapons
Chunhyang
The Company of Wolves▲
Conquest of the Normans
Deathstalker
Deathstalker 2: Duel of the Titans
The Decameron▲
Decameron Nights
Destiny
Diane
Don Quixote▲
Don Quixote
Donkey Skin▲
Dragonheart: A New Beginning
Dragonslayer▲
El Cid▲
Excalibur▲
The Fighting Prince of Donegal
Fire and Sword
First Knight
The Flame & the Arrow▲
Flesh and Blood
Francesco
Galgameth
Gate of Hell▲
Hamlet▲
Hawk and Castile
Hawk the Slayer
Inquisition
Ivanhoe▲
Ivanhoe
Ivanhoe▲
Jabberwocky
Jack the Giant Killer▲
The Juniper Tree
Just Visiting
King Arthur, the Young Warlord
A Knight in Camelot
Knights of the Round Table
A Knight's Tale
Kojiro▲
Kristin Lavransdatter
Ladyhawke
The Lady's Not for Burning
Lancelot of the Lake
Legend
Leonor
The Lion in Winter▲
Lionheart
Magdalene
Magic Serpent▲
The Magic Stone
The Magic Sword
Mark of the Devil
Mark of the Devil 2
Masque of the Red Death▲
Masque of the Red Death
The Mongols
Monty Python and the Holy Grail▲
The Name of the Rose
Naughty Knights
The Navigator▲
Omar Khayyam
Onibaba▲
Passion of Joan of Arc▲
Perceval
Pippin▲
The Prince of Thieves
Prince Valiant
Princess of Thieves
Quest for Camelot
Ran▲
Rashomon▲
The Return of Martin Guerre▲
Richard III▲
Robin and Marian
Robin Hood▲
Robin Hood: Men in Tights
Robin Hood: Prince of Thieves
Robin Hood...The Legend: Herne's Son
Robin Hood...The Legend: Robin Hood and the Sorcerer
Robin Hood...The Legend: The Swords of Wayland
Robin Hood...The Legend: The Time of the Wolf
Ruyblas
Sansho the Bailiff▲
The Scalawag Bunch
The Secret of El Zorro
Seven Samurai▲
The Seventh Seal▲
Skullduggery
Sorceress▲
Star Knight
Stealing Heaven
Sword & the Dragon
Sword & the Sorcerer
The Sword in the Stone▲
Sword of Lancelot
Sword of Sherwood Forest
Sword of the Valiant
Tales of Robin Hood
Temptation of a Monk
Tharus Son of Attila
The 13th Warrior
Throne of Blood▲
Time Bandits
Time Trackers
Tor
The Undead
Unidentified Flying Oddball
The Vikings
The Warrior & the Sorceress
When Knights Were Bold
Wholly Moses!
Wizards of the Demon Sword
Wizards of the Lost Kingdom
Young Ivanhoe
Young Warlord
The Zany Adventures of Robin Hood

Meltdown

***see also** Disaster Flicks*

Above and Beyond▲
Access Code
Amazing Grace & Chuck
Atomic Attack
The Atomic Cafe▲
The Atomic Kid
Black Rain▲
Bloodfist 6: Ground Zero
Bombs Away!
Broken Arrow
Chain Reaction
The China Syndrome▲
Cloak and Dagger
Control
Crimson Tide▲
Cyclotrode "X"
Danger Beneath the Sea
The Day After▲
The Day the Earth Caught Fire▲
The Death Merchant
Desert Bloom▲
Dick Barton Strikes Back
Disaster at Silo 7
Dr. Strangelove, or: How I Learned to Stop Worrying and Love the Bomb▲
Doomsdayer
Enola Gay: The Men, the Mission, the Atomic Bomb
Fail-Safe▲
Fat Man and Little Boy
Final Sanction
First Spaceship on Venus▲
First Strike
First Yank into Tokyo
Flight of Black Angel
The Fourth Protocol▲
Freedom Strike
Full Fathom Five
Future Kill
Geisha Girl
Glen and Randa
Ground Zero▲
H-Man
Hiroshima▲
Hiroshima Maiden
Hiroshima: Out of the Ashes▲
I Live in Fear▲
In the King of Prussia
Invasion U.S.A.
Jackie Chan's First Strike▲
A Man Called Rage
The Manhattan Project
Massive Retaliation
Miracle Mile▲
Modern Problems
Night Siege Project: Shadowchaser 2
Nuclear Conspiracy
A Nymphoid Barbarian in Dinosaur Hell
Omega Man
On the Beach▲
On the Beach
One Night Stand▲
Panic in the Year Zero!
The Patriot
The Peacekeeper
The Peacemaker
Plutonium Incident
Prisoner in the Middle
Radioactive Dreams
Rats
Reactor
The Reflecting Skin
Rhapsody in August
Rocket Attack U.S.A.
The Sacrifice▲
Seven Days in May▲
The Shoes of the Fisherman
Silkwood▲
Slugs
Special Bulletin▲
Split Second
The Spy Who Loved Me
State of Things▲
Superman 4: The Quest for Peace
TC 2000
Testament▲
This Is Not a Test
Threads▲
True Lies
The 27th Day
Unknown World
Utopia
Voyage to the Bottom of the Sea▲
WarGames
Warhead
When the Wind Blows▲
The World Is Not Enough
Young Lady Chatterly 2

Memphis

***see also** American South; Nashville Narratives*

The Client
Elvis and Me
Elvis: The Movie
Finding Graceland
The Firm▲
John Grisham's The Rainmaker
Mystery Train▲
The Silence of the Lambs▲

Men

***see also** Dads; Repressed Men; War Between the Sexes*

Bachelor Apartment
Beefcake
The Bible and Gun Club
Carnal Knowledge▲
City Hall▲
City Slickers▲
Escanaba in da Moonlight
The Full Monty▲
Good Luck
Hurlyburly
Hustler White
In the Company of Men
The Incredible Shrinking Man▲
La Grande Bouffe▲
The Men's Club
Mr. Mom▲
90 Days▲
Patti Rocks▲
Planet of the Apes▲
Raging Bull▲
The Saint of Fort Washington
Swingers▲
Three Men and a Baby▲
Three Men and a Cradle▲
Thursday's Game▲
Truth or Die
Twelve Angry Men
Up to a Certain Point
Watch It▲
The Wonderful Ice Cream Suit
The Young Poisoner's Handbook▲

Men in Prison

***see also** Fugitives; Great Escapes; POW/MIA; Women in Prison*

Against the Wall▲
Alias, La Gringa
All the Pretty Horses
American History X
American Me▲
Andersonville▲
Angels with Dirty Faces▲
Animal Factory
Appointment with Crime
Attica▲
Baba▲
Bad Boys▲
Bait
Band of the Hand
Beaumarchais the Scoundrel
Before Night Falls▲
Behind Prison Walls
Beyond the Call
Beyond the Walls
Birdman of Alcatraz▲
Black Lemons
Blind Faith
Bloodsport 2: The Next Kumite

▲ = rated three bones or higher

Blow
Blues Brothers 2000
Botany Bay
Boy's Reformatory
The Break
Break of Dawn
Breaker Morant▲
Breakout
The Brig▲
Broken Melody
Brubaker▲
Buried Alive
Buy & Cell
The Cable Guy
Caged Heat 2: Stripped of Freedom
Caged in Paradiso
Call Northside 777▲
Captives
Chain Gang Killings
The Chair
The Chamber
Chopper
City Without Men
Club Fed
Colonel Chabert
Coming Out of the Ice▲
Con Air▲
Convict Cowboy
Cool Hand Luke▲
The Count of Monte Cristo
The Count of Monte Cristo▲
The Count of Monte Cristo
Crashout
Criminal Code
Cry Danger▲
Dangerous Relations
Dark Blue World
Darkdrive
Dead Man Out▲
Dead Right
Deadlock
Deadlock 2
Death House
Death Warrant
Deathrow Gameshow
The Defiant Ones▲
Devil's Canyon
The Devil's Cargo
The Dirty Dozen▲
The Dirty Dozen: The Deadly Mission
The Dirty Dozen: The Fatal Mission
The Dirty Dozen: The Next Mission
Doin' Time
Doing Time for Patsy Cline▲
The Domino Principle
Double Team
Down by Law▲
Each Dawn I Die
Eagles Attack at Dawn
Embassy
Empire of the Sun▲
Ernest Goes to Jail
Escape from Alcatraz▲
Escape from Death Row
Escape from DS-3
Escape from El Diablo
Escape from New York
Execution of Raymond Graham
The Executioner's Song
Face/Off▲
Fast Walking
The Fence
First Time Felon
Fled
Fortress
Fortress 2: Re-Entry
Framed
Freedom Is Paradise▲
Gang Busters
Gideon's Trumpet
The Glass House▲
The Grave
The Green Mile
Greenfingers
Gulag
Half-Baked
Hangfire
Hard Frame
Hard Justice
He Got Game
Hold 'Em Jail
House Across the Bay
The Hurricane▲
I Am a Fugitive from a Chain Gang▲
I Killed That Man
In God's Hands
In Hot Pursuit
In the Name of the Father▲
An Innocent Man
Inside▲
Instinct
Invasion
The Invisible Strangler
Jailbreakin'
Jailhouse Rock▲
The Jericho Mile
John Carpenter's Ghosts of Mars
Johnny Handsome▲
Kansas City Confidential▲
The Keeper
Killer: A Journal of Murder
King of the Damned
Kiss of the Spider Woman▲
L'Addition
The Last Castle
The Last Detail▲
The Last Mile
Last Rites
Le Trou▲
Les Miserables
Les Miserables▲
A Lesson Before Dying▲
Life
The Life of Emile Zola▲
Lilies
The Line
Little Red Schoolhouse
Live Flesh▲
Live! From Death Row
Lock Up
The Longest Yard▲
Lost Highway
Lucie Aubrac
A Man Escaped▲
Man of La Mancha
The Man Who Broke 1,000 Chains
Maximum Security
McKenzie Break▲
McVicar
Mean Frank and Crazy Tony
Mean Machine
Midnight Express▲
Mrs. Soffel
Mr. Frost
Monster's Ball▲
Moon 44
Most Wanted
Murder in the First
Mutiny in the Big House
My Boys Are Good Boys
New Crime City: Los Angeles 2020
New Eden
The New Guy
The Night and the Moment
The Night Visitor
984: Prisoner of the Future
No Escape
Ocean's Eleven▲
Off the Wall
On the Yard
Out in Fifty
Out of Sight▲
Papillon▲
Pardon Us
Payback
Penitentiary
Penitentiary 2
Penitentiary 3
Phantom Empire
Pressure Point▲
Prison
Prison Break
Prison on Fire
Prison on Fire 2
Prison Planet
Prison Train
The Prisoner
Proximity
The Pursuit of Happiness
Real Bullets
Return to Paradise▲
Riot
Riot in Cell Block 11▲
The Rock▲
Runaway Train▲
St. Michael Had a Rooster
Samar
Scum▲
A Sense of Freedom▲
The Shawshank Redemption▲
Shoeshine▲
Shooting Fish
Short Eyes▲
Shot in the Heart▲
Slam
Slaughterhouse Rock
Some Mother's Son▲
Soul Vengeance
Space Rage
Spy Game
Stir Crazy
The Survivor
Taking Care of Business
Tank
Terminal Island
Terror of the Bloodhunters
Terror on Alcatraz
There Was a Crooked Man▲
They Never Come Back
They Went That-a-Way & That-a-Way
Timelock
Tomb of the Undead
Torture Ship
Tracked
Triumph of the Spirit▲
The Truce▲
True Crime
Truth or Die
Two-Way Stretch
Ulee's Gold▲
The Visit▲
Warden of Red Rock
Weeds▲
William Faulkner's Old Man
Wishmaster 2: Evil Never Dies
Without Evidence
Women's Prison Massacre
Yol▲

Mental Hospitals

***see also** Doctors & Nurses; Sanity Check; Shrinks*

Final
On the Edge
Session 9

Mental Retardation

***see also** Physical Problems; Savants*

All the Little Animals
Bill▲
Bill: On His Own▲
Charly▲
A Child Is Waiting▲
A Dangerous Woman
Dark Night of the Scarecrow
A Day in the Death of Joe Egg▲
Digging to China
Dominick & Eugene▲
The Eighth Day
Family Pictures▲
Heart of Dragon
Homer and Eddie
I Am Sam
It Came from the Sky
King of the Jungle
Larry
L'Enfant d'Eau
Lovey: A Circle of Children 2
Malcolm
Mifune
Molly
My Louisiana Sky
Of Mice and Men▲
The Other Sister
Rain Man▲
The Rain People▲
Shooting Fish
Sling Blade▲
Slipping into Darkness
Some Folks Call It a Sling Blade▲
Square Dance
Sweetie▲
Tim
Two of a Kind
What's Eating Gilbert Grape▲
The Wizard
The Woman Who Willed a Miracle
The Yarn Princess
ZigZag▲

Mermaids

***see also** Folklore & Legends*

Beach Blanket Bingo▲
La Petite Sirene
The Little Mermaid
The Little Mermaid▲
Mr. Peabody & the Mermaid
Night Tide
Sea People
She Creature
Splash

Metamorphosis

***see also** Genetics; Werewolves*

An American Werewolf in London▲
Boogie Nights▲
Cat People▲
Cat People
The Company of Wolves▲
The Curse of the Werewolf
Earth Vs. the Spider
The Fly▲
The Fly▲
The Fly 2
The Howling▲
I Was a Teenage Werewolf
Jack Frost
Jungle Captive
Jungle Woman
The Lair of the White Worm▲
Miss Congeniality
Naked Lunch▲
The Nutty Professor▲
Nutty Professor 2: The Klumps
Silver Bullet
Species
Stephen King's Thinner
Vampire in Brooklyn
The Wasp Woman
When the Cat's Away▲
Wolfen▲
The Wolfman

Meteors, Asteroids, and Comets

***see also** Alien Beings—Vicious; Disaster Flicks; Space Operas*

Alien Dead
Armageddon
The Blob
The Blob▲
Creepshow
The Day It Came to Earth
Day of the Triffids▲
Deep Impact
Die, Monster, Die!
Dinosaur
Falling Fire
The Invisible Ray
Judgment Day
Lifeforce
Meteor
The Meteor Man
The Monolith Monsters
Night of the Comet
The Phantom Creeps
The Pink Chiquitas
Return of the Aliens: The Deadly Spawn
Stalker▲
Teenage Monster
Trapped in Space
Tycus

Mexico

***see also** Central America*

Across the Bridge
Against All Odds
All the Pretty Horses
Amores Perros▲
The Black Scorpion
Bloody Proof▲
The Border▲
Borderline
Breakout
A Bullet for the General
Bullfighter & the Lady
Bullfighters
Captain from Castile▲
The Cisco Kid
Commando Squad
Companeros
Crazy from the Heart▲
Danzon▲
Deep Crimson
Desperado▲
Django
Double Take
8 Heads in a Duffel Bag
El Mariachi▲
Escape from Cell Block 3
The Falcon in Mexico
Five Giants from Texas
Found Alive
Frida
From Dusk Till Dawn
From Dusk Till Dawn 3: The Hangman's Daughter
Fun in Acapulco
Highway Patrolman
His Kind of Woman▲
Holiday in Mexico
A Home of Our Own
In 'n Out
In Pursuit
Interval
Juarez
Kid from Spain
La Cucaracha
Lolo
Los Olvidados▲
Love Has Many Faces
The Magnificent Seven▲
The Masked Rider
The Mexican
Mexican Hayride
Mexico City
Midaq Alley▲
Missing Pieces
The Night of the Iguana▲
Octaman
Old Gringo
On the Line
One Man's Hero
Out to Sea
Outta Time
The Pearl▲
The Professionals▲
The Proud Ones
Pure Luck
Que Viva Mexico▲
Red Salute
Reed: Insurgent Mexico
The Road to El Dorado
Rough Magic
Santitos
The Scout
Shoot the Living, Pray for the Dead
Sonny and Jed
South of Santa Fe
Survival Run
Three Amigos
The Torch
Touch of Evil▲
Traffic▲
Treasure of the Sierra Madre▲
Two Mules for Sister Sara▲
Under the Volcano▲
Valdez Is Coming
Vera Cruz
Villa Rides
Viva Villa!▲
Viva Zapata!▲
Warlords from Hell
Way of the Gun
The White Orchid
Wild Rovers
A Winter Tan
Y Tu Mama Tambien

Miami

***see also** American South*

Ace Ventura: Pet Detective
All About the Benjamins
Analyze This▲
Any Given Sunday▲
Band of the Hand
Big Trouble
The Birdcage▲
The Blackout
Blood & Wine
Catherine's Grove
The Crew
Curdled
Elmore Leonard's Gold Coast
Fair Game
Fires Within
Forever Mine
Get Shorty▲
Illtown
In the Shadows
Instinct
Lansky
The Last Marshal
Laws of Deception
Let's Talk About Sex
Miami Beach Cops
Miami Blues
Miami Cops
Miami Horror
Miami Hustle
Miami Rhapsody
Miami Supercops
Miami Vendetta
Miami Vice
Off and Running
Out of Sight▲
The Perez Family
The Pest
Pronto
Ride
Scarface▲
There's Something about Mary▲
Tony Rome
Two Much
Wild Things

Middle East

***see also** Desert War/ Foreign Legion; Deserts; Genies; Islam; Israel; Persian Gulf War; Terrorism*

Abbott and Costello Meet the Mummy
A.D.
Ali Baba and the Forty Thieves
Ali Baba and the 40 Thieves▲
All the King's Men
The Ambassador
The Arab Conspiracy
Arabian Nights
The Assignment
Bagdad
Black Thunder
Bloodstone
A Casualty of War
Chain of Command
Chronicle of a Disappearance
Counterforce
The Crusades
Cup Final
Desert Thunder
Eagles Attack at Dawn
The Egyptian
Escape: Human Cargo▲
Fictitious Marriage
Five Graves to Cairo▲
Flame of Araby
The Flight of the Phoenix▲
Gabbeh▲
The Glory Boys
The Great Armored Car Swindle
The Guns and the Fury
Halfmoon
Hamsin▲
Hanna K.
Harum Scarum
Held Hostage
Honeybaby
Hostages▲
Ilsa, Harem Keeper of the Oil Sheiks
The Invincible Six
Iran: Days of Crisis
Iron Eagle
Iron Eagle 2
Ishtar
The Jewel of the Nile

▲ = *rated three bones or higher*

▲ = *rated three bones or higher*

AngKor: Cambodia Express
Big Jake
Breakdown▲
Bureau of Missing Persons
Cavalcade of the West
Chasing Sleep
Christina
Coming Out Alive
Curse of the Pink Panther
Disappearance
Dying Room Only
The Emerald Forest▲
Empire State
The Empty Beach
Equinox▲
Escapade in Japan
Experiment in Terror▲
Eye Witness
Final Cut
Foxtrap
Frantic▲
From Hollywood to Deadwood
Girl Hunters
Grayeagle
Green Eyes▲
Grievous Bodily Harm
Harem
Harper▲
Harrison's Flowers
Heading for Heaven
Hell Squad
Hide in Plain Sight▲
High Road to China
The Hit List
Hollywood Chaos
Home for Christmas
Home Is Where the Hart Is
Hurricane Smith
In the Mouth of Madness
Into Thin Air▲
The Island at the Top of the World
Jungle Goddess
Kentucky Jubilee
Kidnap Syndicate
The Lady Vanishes▲
The Lady Vanishes
The Last Winter
A Low Down Dirty Shame
Mexico City
Midnight Warning
Misery▲
Missing▲
The Missing Corpse
Murder, My Sweet▲
Nickel & Dime
Night of the Cyclone
Norseman
Old Gringo
Picnic at Hanging Rock▲
The Port of Missing Girls
Prisoner of Zenda▲
The Professionals▲
Psych-Out
Psycho from Texas
Pure Luck
Raising Arizona▲
Romancing the Stone▲
Scandalous
Seance on a Wet Afternoon▲
The Search for One-Eyed Jimmy
The Searchers▲
Skull: A Night of Terror
Stark
Street Girls
Street Justice
Surfacing
Tarzan the Fearless
Terminal Force
Tokyo Joe
Tony Rome
The Vanishing▲
Wanted: Where Are the Children?
Where's Piccone▲
White Fire
The Wicker Man▲
Without a Trace

Missionaries

***see also** Nuns & Priests; Religion; Religious Epics*

The African Queen▲
At Play in the Fields of the Lord▲
Beyond the Next Mountain
Black Robe▲
Ethan
Hawaii▲
The Inn of the Sixth Happiness▲
The Keys of the Kingdom▲
The Mission▲
Mission to Glory
The Missionary
The Other Side of Heaven
Paradise Road

Mistaken Identity

***see also** Amnesia; Gender Bending; Role Reversal*

Across the Bridge
The Adventurer
The Adventures of Bullwhip Griffin
Along Came Jones▲
Alvin Rides Again
American Cop
Amore!
Amos and Andrew
Another You
As Good as Dead
As You Desire Me▲
As You Like It
As Young As You Feel▲
The Assignment
The Associate
Bachelor Mother▲
The Ballad of Little Jo
Barocco
The Beautician and the Beast
The Beautiful Blonde from Bashful Bend
Being There▲
Betrayed▲
A Better Way to Die
Beyond Suspicion
The Big Lebowski▲
Big Mouth
Billy the Kid Returns
Bittersweet Love
Black Glove
Blackjack
Blame It on the Bellboy
Blind Justice
Blondie Knows Best
Body Snatchers
Borderline
Boy's Reformatory
Brighton Strangler
Broadway Limited
Broken Melody
Bullets or Ballots▲
Bullseye!
Bundle of Joy
Buona Sera, Mrs. Campbell
Bushwhacked
Butler's Dilemma
Camp Cucamonga: How I Spent My Summer Vacation
The Capture▲
Caroline?▲
Carry On Admiral
A Case of Deadly Force▲
CB4: The Movie
Center of the Web
The Challengers
Chameleon Street▲
Charade▲
Charley's Aunt
The Chase
The Closet
Colonel Chabert
Company Man
Convicted
Convicts at Large
Cornbread, Earl & Me
A Couch in New York
The Couch Trip
Counterblast
Court Jester▲
Daughters of the Sun
Dave▲
Deadwood
Deconstructing Sarah
The Desert Song
Don Juan DeMarco
Don't Tell Her It's Me
Double Play
Double Take
Double Vision
El Mariachi▲
Ernest Goes to Jail
Erotic Touch of Hot Skin
Evergreen
Every Man's Law
Execution of Raymond Graham
F/X 2: The Deadly Art of Illusion
Family Reunion
Fargo Express
Fatal Exposure
Father
Feet First
Fighting Parson
Five Graves to Cairo▲
The Flame of New Orleans▲
Focus
Gangway
The Gay Divorcee▲
Generale Della Rovere▲
Gentleman Bandit
Get That Man
The Glass Bottom Boat
Good Neighbor Sam▲
The Great Dictator▲
Grosse Fatigue▲
The Gun in Betty Lou's Handbag
Gunfire
Gunsmoke Trail
Hell on Frisco Bay
Her Life as a Man
Hero▲
High & Low▲
High Lonesome
Highway 13
His Brother's Ghost
His Wife's Lover▲
Hittin' the Trail
Hollywood Chaos
Hometown Boy Makes Good
Honolulu
A House in the Hills
Houseguest
I Love You
I Want to Live!▲
I Will, I Will for Now
If Looks Could Kill
The Imposter
The Imposters
In Person
In Society
The Inspector General▲
Invasion of the Body Snatchers▲
It Started with Eve▲
It Takes Two
It! The Terror from Beyond Space
Jade
Johnny Handsome▲
Johnny Stecchino▲
Junk Mail
Just Write
Kansas City Confidential▲
Keaton's Cop
Kid from Spain
Killer Dill
The Killing Time
The King of Masks▲
A Kiss Before Dying
Lady Killer
Landslide
The Last Contract
The Last Winter
Laughing at Danger
Laurel & Hardy: The Hoose-Gow
Law of the Underworld
Le Bonheur Est Dans le Pre
Life Is a Long Quiet River▲
Lisa
The Little Drummer Girl▲
Little Sister
The Lookalike
Lost Highway
Love at Large▲
Lucky Cisco Kid
Mad About Music▲
Made in America
Maid's Night Out
The Majestic
The Man in the Raincoat
The Man on the Box
Man on the Run
The Man Who Knew Too Little
The Man with One Red Shoe
Manhandled
The Mark of Zorro▲
McHale's Navy Joins the Air Force
Meet the Deedles
Meet the Mob
Memento▲
Miami Hustle
Mickey Blue Eyes
The Misadventures of Mr. Wilt
Mississippi Mermaid▲
Mistaken Identity
Mr. Headmistress
Mr. Klein▲
Monsieur Beaucaire▲
Monsignor Quixote
The Monster
Monte Carlo Nights
My Geisha
My Man Godfrey▲
My Outlaw Brother
My Twentieth Century▲
Mystery Date
Naked Tango
Naughty Marietta
Never a Dull Moment
Next of Kin
Nick and Jane
The Night We Never Met
Nightfall▲
Nobody's Perfect
North by Northwest▲
The Nutt House
The Obsessed
Obsession
One Body Too Many
Only You
Opportunity Knocks
Oscar
Out of Bounds
Out on a Limb
Pale Saints
Palmy Days
Paper Mask
Paperback Hero
Pardon My Sarong
The Passenger▲
Phantom Fiend
Phantom Killer
Picture Perfect
Pier 23
The Player▲
The Pope Must Diet
Prelude to a Kiss
The Princess Comes Across▲
Private Life of Don Juan
The Private Secretary
Profile
Purple Noon▲
Ranson's Folly
Rattler Kid
Red Firecracker, Green Firecracker
The Red Half-Breed
Red Heat
Red Rock West▲
Reindeer Games
The Reluctant Agent
The Reluctant Astronaut
Return of Jesse James
The Return of Martin Guerre▲
Return of the Tall Blond Man with One Black Shoe
River Beat
Romance on the High Seas▲
Running Hot
Ruyblas
Safe Men
St. Benny the Dip
The Santa Clause
Santa with Muscles
Say It Isn't So
The Scar
Scream of Fear▲
Seconds▲
The Secret of My Success
A Self-Made Hero▲
The 7th Commandment
She Must Be Seeing Things
The Sinister Invasion
Sister Act
Sister Act 2: Back in the Habit
Six Gun Gospel
Six of a Kind▲
Small Kill
Smokey and the Bandit, Part 3
Social Error
Soldat Duroc...Ca Va Etre Ta Fete!
Someone at the Door
Something in the Wind
Splitting Heirs
Stolen Identity
A Stolen Life
Straight Talk
Stray Bullet
The Stupids
The Suitors
Sunday
Supergrass
Support Your Local Gunfighter▲
Suture
Switched at Birth
Tattle Tale
10 Rillington Place▲
The Tenth Man
Texas Carnival
Texas Cyclone
They Knew What They Wanted▲
The Thin Blue Line▲
Things Change▲
The 39 Steps▲
Tombstone Terror
Top Hat▲
Toto le Heros▲
True Identity
The Truth about Cats and Dogs▲
Twelfth Night
Twin Dragons
Two Much
The Unholy Three▲
The Well▲
We're No Angels
West of the Pecos
While You Were Sleeping▲
White Eagle
White of the Eye▲
Who's Harry Crumb?
Wings of the Morning
Withnail and I▲
The Worldly Madonna
The Wrong Guys
Young Master
Zertigo Diamond Caper

Mockumentary

***see also** Documentary; Genre Spoofs*

All You Need Is Cash▲
...And God Spoke
Best in Show▲
The Blair Witch Project
Bob Roberts▲
Drop Dead Gorgeous
Elvis Meets Nixon
Fear of a Black Hat
Glen or Glenda?
Grunt! The Wrestling Movie
Hard Core Logo
Jackie's Back
The Last Polka▲
Lisa Picard Is Famous
The Return of Spinal Tap
Stardom
This Is Spinal Tap▲
Waiting for Guffman
Zelig▲

Model Citizens

Blackjack
The Bride Is Much Too Beautiful
Cover Girl▲
Cover Girl Models
The Cover Girl Murders
Covergirl
Daniella by Night
Darling▲
Designing Woman▲
D.R.E.A.M. Team
The Eighteenth Angel
Eyes of Laura Mars
Fall
Funny Face▲
Gia
Head Over Heels
Human Desires
In and Out▲
Intimate Deception
Looker
Mahogany
Model Behavior
Model by Day
Nothing Underneath
Obsession: A Taste for Fear
The Pink Jungle
Portfolio
Ready to Wear
Slaves of New York
So Fine
Stardom
Tight Spot▲
Unzipped▲
What a Woman!
What's New Pussycat?▲
When the Cat's Away▲
Zoolander

Modern Cowboys

***see also** Western Comedy; Westerns*

All the Pretty Horses
Another Pair of Aces: Three of a Kind▲
Barbarosa▲
Bronco Billy
By Dawn's Early Light
City Slickers▲
City Slickers 2: The Legend of Curly's Gold
Coogan's Bluff▲
The Cowboy Way
Dudes
8 Seconds
The Electric Horseman
Fool for Love
The Hi-Lo Country
The Horse Whisperer
The Last of the Dogmen
Lonely Are the Brave▲
My Heroes Have Always Been Cowboys
Rhinestone
Ruby Jean and Joe
Samurai Cowboy
Sweet Creek County War
Toy Story▲
Toy Story 2▲
True West▲
Wild Horses

Moms

***see also** Bad Dads; Dads; Monster Moms; Parenthood*

Above the Rim
Agnes Browne
Alice Doesn't Live Here Anymore
All About My Mother▲
All That Heaven Allows▲
Amazing Grace
Antonia's Line
Anywhere But Here
Applause▲
Aurora
Autumn Sonata▲
Baby
Baby Boom
Bad Boy
The Bad Seed
Bastard out of Carolina
Beautiful
Beautiful Thing▲
Beloved
Better Than Chocolate
Bogus
The Brady Bunch Movie▲
Bridge to Silence
A Brivele der Mamen▲
Cadillac Girls
A Call to Remember
Carnegie Hall
Children of the Revolution
Chocolat▲
Cider with Rosie
Cinderella Liberty▲

▲ = rated three bones or higher

Monkeyshines

Monster Moms

Monster Yuks

Monsters, General

Montreal

Moscow

Moscow Mafia

Motor Vehicle Dept.

Mountaineering

Mummies

Museums

▲ = rated three bones or higher

- Ghostbusters 2
- The Hideaways
- House of Wax▲
- Mad City
- Midnight at the Wax Museum
- The Mummy Returns
- Mystery of the Wax Museum▲
- Nightmare in Wax
- The Outing
- Paul Bartel's The Secret Cinema
- The Pick-Up Artist
- The Relic
- Terror in the Wax Museum
- The Thomas Crown Affair▲
- Topkapi▲
- Vibes
- Waxwork
- Waxwork 2: Lost in Time
- Waxworks▲
- Weird Woman/Frozen Ghost

Musical Comedy

see also Musicals

- The Adventures of Priscilla, Queen of the Desert▲
- The Affairs of Dobie Gillis
- Almost Angels
- Amateur Night
- Andy Hardy Meets Debutante
- April in Paris
- Around the World
- Artists and Models
- Athena
- Babes in Arms
- Babes on Broadway
- Bathing Beauty
- Be Yourself
- Beach Blanket Bingo▲
- Beach Party
- Because You're Mine
- Bert Rigby, You're a Fool
- Best Foot Forward
- The Best Little Whorehouse in Texas
- The Big Broadcast of 1938
- Bikini Beach
- Billy Rose's Jumbo▲
- Birth of the Blues
- The Blues Brothers▲
- Blues Brothers 2000
- Boardinghouse Blues
- The Boy Friend▲
- Boy! What a Girl
- Broadway Melody of 1936▲
- Broadway Rhythm
- Bundle of Joy
- Bye, Bye, Birdie▲
- Cairo
- Call Out the Marines
- Cannibal! The Musical
- Captain January
- Carefree▲
- The Cocoanuts
- College Swing
- Copacabana
- Court Jester▲
- Cover Girl▲
- Cry-Baby▲
- Dames▲
- Dance, Girl, Dance
- Dangerous When Wet
- Darling Lili
- Delightfully Dangerous
- The Devil's Brother
- Diplomaniacs
- Disorderlies
- Dixiana
- Dixie Jamboree
- Doll Face
- DuBarry Was a Lady
- The Duchess of Idaho
- Easy Come, Easy Go
- The Eighties
- Escape to Paradise
- Evergreen
- Everybody Sing
- Everyone Says I Love You▲
- Fashions of 1934
- Feel the Motion
- Femmes de Paris
- Finian's Rainbow▲
- The First Nudie Musical
- Flirtation Walk
- Flower Drum Song
- Follow That Dream
- Follow That Rainbow
- Four Jacks and a Jill
- Frankie and Johnny
- The French Line
- The French Way
- Frolics on Ice
- Fun in Acapulco
- Funny Face▲
- A Funny Thing Happened on the Way to the Forum▲
- The Gay Desperado
- The Gay Divorcee▲
- Gentlemen Prefer Blondes▲
- George White's Scandals
- G.I. Blues
- Gigi▲
- The Girl Can't Help It
- Girl Crazy▲
- Girl Happy
- The Girl Most Likely
- Girl of the Golden West
- Girl Rush
- Girls! Girls! Girls!
- Give a Girl a Break
- Give Me a Sailor
- Glorifying the American Girl
- Godspell
- Going Hollywood▲
- Going My Way▲
- Gold Diggers of 1933▲
- Gold Diggers of 1935▲
- The Goldwyn Follies
- Good News
- Grease▲
- Grease 2
- The Great American Broadcast▲
- Guys and Dolls▲
- Gypsy▲
- Gypsy
- Hairspray▲
- Hallelujah, I'm a Bum
- The Happiest Millionaire
- Happy Go Lovely
- The Harvey Girls▲
- Head▲
- The Heat's On
- Hello, Dolly!
- Help!▲
- Here Come the Girls
- Here Come the Waves▲
- Here Comes the Groom
- High Society▲
- Hips, Hips, Hooray
- His Butler's Sister
- Hit the Deck
- Holiday in Havana
- Holiday in Mexico
- Holiday Inn▲
- Hollywood Canteen▲
- Honolulu
- How to Stuff a Wild Bikini
- How to Succeed in Business without Really Trying▲
- Huckleberry Finn
- I Do! I Do!
- I Dood It
- I Dream of Jeannie
- I Dream Too Much
- I Love Melvin
- I Married an Angel
- I'll Be Yours
- In the Good Old Summertime▲
- In the Navy
- International House
- It Happened in Brooklyn
- It's a Date
- It's a Great Feeling
- It's Love Again
- Jive Junction
- Juke Joint
- Jupiter's Darling
- Just for You
- Keep 'Em Flying
- Kid from Spain
- Kid Galahad
- Kid Millions
- King Kelly of the U.S.A.
- King of Jazz
- Kiss Me Kate▲
- Kissin' Cousins
- Lady Be Good
- Latin Lovers
- Le Million▲
- Les Girls
- Let's Dance
- Let's Go Collegiate
- Life Begins for Andy Hardy▲
- Li'l Abner
- Lili▲
- Lily of Killarney
- Little Nellie Kelly
- Little Shop of Horrors▲
- Live a Little, Love a Little
- Look Out Sister▲
- Louisiana Purchase
- Lovely to Look At▲
- Lucky Me
- Lullaby of Broadway
- Make a Wish
- Mame
- Mamele
- A Matter of Degrees
- Maytime in Mayfair
- Meet Me in Las Vegas
- Melody Cruise
- The Merry Widow▲
- The Merry Widow
- Mr. Music
- The Muppet Christmas Carol
- The Muppet Movie▲
- The Muppets Take Manhattan▲
- Muscle Beach Party
- My Dream Is Yours
- My Sister Eileen▲
- My Song Goes Round the World
- Nancy Goes to Rio
- Naughty Marietta
- Neptune's Daughter
- Never a Dull Moment
- New Faces of 1952
- Newsies
- Nice Girl?
- No Time for Romance
- On a Clear Day You Can See Forever
- On the Avenue▲
- One from the Heart
- One in a Million▲
- One Night in the Tropics
- One Touch of Venus
- The Opposite Sex
- Paint Your Wagon
- The Pajama Game▲
- Pajama Party
- Pal Joey▲
- Palmy Days
- Panama Hattie
- The Perils of Pauline
- Phantom of the Paradise
- Pigskin Parade
- Pin-Up Girl
- The Pirate▲
- The Pirates of Penzance
- Popeye
- Presenting Lily Mars
- Rebecca of Sunnybrook Farm
- Rhythm on the Range
- Rhythm on the River
- Rhythm Romance
- Riding High
- The Road to Bali▲
- The Road to Lebanon
- The Road to Morocco▲
- Road to Nashville
- The Road to Rio▲
- The Road to Singapore
- The Road to Utopia▲
- The Road to Zanzibar▲
- Roadie
- Roberta▲
- Robin and the 7 Hoods
- Rock 'n' Roll High School▲
- Rock 'n' Roll High School Forever
- Roman Scandals
- Romance on the High Seas▲
- Royal Wedding▲
- Running out of Luck
- Second Fiddle
- Sensations of 1945
- Sgt. Pepper's Lonely Hearts Club Band
- Seven Brides for Seven Brothers▲
- Seven Days' Leave
- The Seven Little Foys▲
- 1776▲
- Sextette
- Shake, Rattle and Rock
- Shake, Rattle & Rock!
- Shall We Dance▲
- Ship Ahoy
- Shock Treatment
- Show Business▲
- Silk Stockings▲
- Sing Your Worries Away
- Singin' in the Rain▲
- Sioux City Sue
- The Sky's the Limit
- Small Town Girl
- A Song Is Born▲
- Song of the Islands
- Speedway
- Spice World: The Movie
- Spinout
- Spotlight Scandals
- Springtime in the Rockies
- Star Spangled Rhythm▲
- Starstruck
- State Fair▲
- State Fair
- Step Lively
- The Stooge
- The Stork Club
- Strike Me Pink
- Strike Up the Band
- Summer Holiday
- Summer Stock▲
- Sun Valley Serenade
- Sunny
- Sunny Skies
- Sweet Rosie O'Grady
- Sweethearts▲
- Swing
- Swing It, Professor
- Swing Time▲
- Take Me Out to the Ball Game
- Tea for Two▲
- Texas Carnival
- That Certain Age
- That Girl from Paris
- There's No Business Like Show Business▲
- Thin Ice▲
- Thoroughly Modern Millie
- Three Daring Daughters
- Three for the Show
- The Three Musketeers
- Three Smart Girls▲
- Tickle Me
- Tokyo Pop
- Too Many Girls
- Top Hat▲
- 23 1/2 Hours Leave
- Two Girls and a Sailor▲
- Two Tickets to Broadway
- Two Weeks with Love
- The Unsinkable Molly Brown▲
- Up in Arms
- Up in Central Park
- Vogues of 1938
- Waikiki Wedding▲
- Wallaby Jim of the Islands
- We're Not Dressing▲
- The West Point Story
- White Christmas▲
- Whoopee!
- A Woman Is a Woman▲
- Wonder Man
- Yes, Giorgio
- Yidl Mitn Fidl
- Yolanda and the Thief
- You Were Never Lovelier▲
- You'll Find Out
- You'll Never Get Rich▲
- Ziegfeld Follies
- Zis Boom Bah

Musical Drama

see also Musicals

- Actor: The Paul Muni Story
- The Band Wagon▲
- The Barkleys of Broadway▲
- Beatlemania! The Movie
- The Belle of New York
- Bells Are Ringing▲
- Beware
- Big Fella
- Blonde Venus▲
- Blue Hawaii
- Body Moves
- Body Rock
- Broadway Serenade
- The Buddy Holly Story▲
- Cabaret▲
- Camelot
- Can-Can
- The Cantor's Son
- Carmen Jones▲
- Carnegie Hall
- Carnival Rock
- Casbah▲
- The Cat and the Fiddle▲
- The Chocolate Soldier
- A Christmas Carol
- Clambake
- Club Havana
- Coal Miner's Daughter▲
- Concrete Angels
- Congress Dances
- Cool Mikado
- The Cotton Club▲
- Crossover Dreams
- Curly Top
- Daddy Long Legs▲
- A Damsel in Distress▲
- Dance Hall
- Dance of Life
- Dancing Lady
- Dancing Pirate
- A Date with Judy
- Deadman's Curve
- The Deputy Drummer
- Dimples
- Dogs in Space
- Don Quixote▲
- Double Trouble
- Down Argentine Way▲
- The Duke Is Tops
- Evita
- Expresso Bongo
- The Farmer Takes a Wife
- Fast Forward
- Fiddler on the Roof▲
- The Firefly
- Fisherman's Wharf
- The Five Pennies
- Flashdance
- Follow the Boys▲
- Footloose
- The Forbidden Dance
- 42nd Street▲
- Frankie and Johnny
- Funny Girl▲
- Funny Lady
- Gangway
- George Balanchine's The Nutcracker
- The Glenn Miller Story▲
- Go, Johnny Go!
- Goodbye, Mr. Chips
- Graffiti Bridge
- Great Balls of Fire
- The Great Caruso
- The Great Waltz▲
- The Great Ziegfeld▲
- Greek Street
- Hard to Hold
- The Harder They Come
- Harmony Lane
- Harum Scarum
- Heart's Desire
- Hello, Frisco, Hello
- Honeysuckle Rose
- Honkytonk Nights
- I Could Go on Singing
- Idolmaker
- If You Knew Susie
- I'll Cry Tomorrow▲
- I'll See You in My Dreams
- The In Crowd
- It Happened at the World's Fair
- It's Always Fair Weather
- Jailbird Rock
- Jailhouse Rock▲
- The Jazz Singer
- Jeanne and the Perfect Guy
- Jesus Christ, Superstar▲
- Jesus Christ Superstar
- Jolson Sings Again
- The Jolson Story▲
- The Josephine Baker Story▲
- Jungle Patrol
- Just Around the Corner
- The King and I▲
- King Creole
- Knights of the City
- La Bamba▲
- Ladies of the Chorus
- Lady Sings the Blues
- Lambada
- Life of Verdi
- Light of Day
- The Little Colonel▲
- Little Miss Broadway
- The Littlest Angel
- The Littlest Rebel
- Lottery Bride
- Love Me or Leave Me▲
- Love Me Tender
- Mack the Knife
- The Mambo Kings▲
- The Man I Love▲
- Man of La Mancha
- Marco
- A Matter of Time
- Meet Danny Wilson
- Melody Master
- Miss Sadie Thompson▲
- Murder at the Vanities
- Murder with Music
- The Music Lovers
- The Music Man▲
- Musica Proibita
- My Fair Lady▲
- Never Steal Anything Small
- New Moon
- New Orleans
- New York, New York▲
- Night and Day
- No, No Nanette
- Northwest Outpost
- The Old Curiosity Shop
- Oliver!▲
- The One and Only, Genuine, Original Family Band▲
- One Night of Love▲
- One Trick Pony
- Opera do Malandro
- Orchestra Wives▲
- Orfeu
- An Orphan Boy of Vienna
- Paradise, Hawaiian Style
- Paradise in Harlem
- Paradise Island
- Paris Blues
- Pennies from Heaven▲
- Pete Kelly's Blues
- Piaf
- The Poor Little Rich Girl
- Princess Tam Tam▲
- Purple Rain
- Quadrophenia▲
- Rainbow
- Rappin'
- Reckless
- The Red Shoes▲
- Rhapsody in Blue▲
- Rock, Baby, Rock It
- Rock, Rock, Rock
- Rooftops
- The Rose▲
- Rose Marie▲
- Rose of Washington Square
- Roustabout
- Sailing Along
- Salsa
- Same Old Song▲
- Sarafina!▲
- Satisfaction
- Scrooge
- Senora Tentacion
- Shining Star
- Shout
- Show Boat▲
- Show Boat
- Sincerely Yours
- Sing
- The Singing Detective
- Smilin' Through
- Something to Sing About
- Song o' My Heart▲
- Song of Freedom
- Song of Norway
- Song of Scheherazade
- Song Without End
- Songwriter
- The Sound of Music▲
- Sparkle
- Star!
- Stars and Stripes Forever▲
- Stay Away, Joe
- Stepping Out▲
- Stowaway▲

▲ = rated three bones or higher

Sunday in the Park with George▲
Sweet Charity▲
Sweet Dreams
Sweetheart of the Navy
Tap
They Shall Have Music
This Is the Army
The Three Penny Opera▲
Thunder Alley
Tommy
Transatlantic Merry-Go-Round
Umbrellas of Cherbourg▲
Up/Down/Fragile
Waltz King
Way Down South
West Side Story▲
What's Love Got to Do with It?
Yankee Doodle Dandy▲
Yentl
Young at Heart
Young Caruso
Young Man with a Horn▲
Ziegfeld Girl▲
Zoot Suit▲
Zou Zou

Musical Fantasy

***see also** Musicals*

Alice
Babes in Toyland
Bedknobs and Broomsticks
Brigadoon▲
Butterfly Ball
Cabin in the Sky▲
Carousel▲
Chitty Chitty Bang Bang
Cinderella
Cinderella 2000
Comic Book Kids
A Connecticut Yankee in King Arthur's Court
Damn Yankees▲
Dancer in the Dark
Doctor Dolittle
Down to Earth
Fairy Tales
The 5000 Fingers of Dr. T▲
Gepetto
Kismet
Labyrinth▲
The Little Match Girl
The Little Prince
Magical Mystery Tour
March of the Wooden Soldiers▲
Mary Poppins▲
Moulin Rouge
The New Adventures of Pippi Longstocking
Once Upon a Brothers Grimm
Peter Pan▲
Rumpelstiltskin
Sleeping Beauty
The Slipper and the Rose
Willy Wonka & the Chocolate Factory▲
The Wizard of Oz▲
Wonderwall: The Movie
Zero Patience

Musicals

***see also** Animated Musicals; Contemporary Musicals; Disco Musicals; Musical Comedy; Musical Drama; Musical Fantasy*

Alexander's Ragtime Band▲
An American in Paris▲
Anchors Aweigh▲
Annie
Annie▲
Annie Get Your Gun▲
Babes in Toyland
Balalaika
Beat Street
Billy's Holiday
Bitter Sweet
Black Tights
Blue Skies▲
Born to Dance
Breaking the Ice
Broadway Melody
Broadway Melody of 1938
Broadway Melody of 1940
Bugsy Malone
By the Light of the Silvery Moon
Calamity Jane▲
Can't Help Singing
Charm of La Boheme
Deep in My Heart
The Desert Song
Dogs in Space
The Dolly Sisters
Easter Parade▲
Easy to Love
Emperor Waltz
The Fantasticks
Flying Down to Rio
Follies Girl
Follies in Concert
Follow the Fleet▲
Footlight Parade▲
Footlight Serenade
For Me and My Gal
For the First Time
Frankenstein Sings...The Movie
Hair▲
Half a Sixpence
Hands Across the Border
Hans Brinker
Hans Christian Andersen
Happy Landing
Harlem on the Prairie
Harvest Melody
Hats Off
Hawaii Calls
Hi-De-Ho
Higher and Higher
Hillbillies in a Haunted House
Hot Summer
Iceland
Incident at Channel Q
Invitation to the Dance
Joseph and the Amazing Technicolor Dreamcoat▲
Junction 88
Killer Diller
Krush Groove
Let Freedom Ring
Let's Sing Again
A Little Night Music
London Melody
Look for the Silver Lining
Love's Labour's Lost
Madam Satan
Manhattan Merry-Go-Round
The Marriage of Figaro
Maytime▲
Meet Me in St. Louis▲
Meet the Navy
Mrs. Brown, You've Got a Lovely Daughter
Mrs. Santa Claus
Moon over Harlem
Moon over Miami▲
Music in My Heart
Music Shoppe
My Lucky Star
Oh! Calcutta!
Oklahoma!▲
On Moonlight Bay
On the Town
100 Men and a Girl▲
Pagan Love Song
Pippin▲
Private Buckaroo
Rainbow over Broadway
Red Garters
Reet, Petite and Gone▲
Rhapsody
Rhythm Parade
Rich, Young and Pretty
Rodgers & Hammerstein's South Pacific
Rosalie
Second Chorus
Sepia Cinderella
The Seven Hills of Rome
She Shall Have Music
Something in the Wind
South Pacific▲
Stage Door Canteen
Stormy Weather
The Story of Vernon and Irene Castle▲
The Student Prince
Sweeney Todd: The Demon Barber of Fleet Street
Sweet Adeline
Swing Parade of 1946
Take It Big
Terror of Tiny Town
Thank Your Lucky Stars▲
That Midnight Kiss
That's Dancing!
That's Entertainment
That's Entertainment, Part 2
That's Entertainment, Part 3
Thousands Cheer
The Threepenny Opera
Thrill of a Romance
Tin Pan Alley
The Toast of New Orleans
Tonight and Every Night
The Trouble with Girls (and How to Get into It)▲
Under the Cherry Moon
Vagabond Lover
The Vampyr
Viva Las Vegas
Week-End in Havana
Welcome Stranger
Wigstock: The Movie
Window Shopping
Wintertime
Words and Music
Yes, Sir, Mr. Bones
The Young Girls of Rochefort
Young People

Mutiny

***see also** Deep Blue; Sail Away; Sea Disasters; Shipwrecked*

Amistad▲
The Bounty
Crimson Tide▲
The Legend of the Sea Wolf
Mutiny
The Mutiny of the Elsinore
Mutiny on the Bounty▲
Mutiny on the Bounty
Pirate Ship
The Sea Wolf▲
The Sea Wolf

Mystery & Suspense

***see also** Psycho-Thriller*

Abduction of St. Anne
Above Suspicion▲
Above Suspicion
Absolution
Accidental Meeting
Accidents
Accomplice
Accused
Ace Drummond
Ace of Hearts
Across the Bridge
Across the Pacific▲
Acting on Impulse
Address Unknown
Adrift
Adventures of a Private Eye
The Adventures of Sherlock Holmes
An Affair in Mind
African Rage
After Dark, My Sweet▲
After Pilkington
After the Thin Man▲
Agatha
Agatha Christie's The Pale Horse
Alias John Preston
All-American Murder
All the Kind Strangers
Alligator Eyes
Almost Partners
The Alphabet Murders
Alphaville▲
The Amateur
Amazing Mr. Blunden
The Amazing Mr. X
The Ambassador
The American Friend▲
American Gigolo
Amnesia
Amsterdamned
And Soon the Darkness
And Then There Were None▲
The Anderson Tapes▲
Android
The Andromeda Strain
Angel Dust
Angel Heart
Animal Instincts
Animal Instincts 2
Another Thin Man
Any Man's Death
Any Number Can Win
Apology
Appointment with Death
Appointment with Fear
Apprentice to Murder
Arabesque
Are You in the House Alone?
Arizona Stagecoach
The Arsenal Stadium Mystery
The Art of Crime
As Good as Dead
Assassin
The Assassination File
The Assassination Run
Assault
The Atomic City
Autopsy
The Avenging Hand
The Baby Doll Murders
The Babysitter
Back from Eternity
Back to Hannibal: The Return of Tom Sawyer and Huckleberry Finn
Back to the Wall
Backfire
Backstab
Backstreet Justice
Backtrack▲
B.A.D. Cats
Bad Company
Bad Ronald▲
The Banker
The Barcelona Kill
Basic Instinct
The Bat Whispers
Battle Shock
Bedford Incident
Bedroom Eyes
Bedroom Eyes 2
The Bedroom Window
Before Morning
Behind Locked Doors
Bell from Hell
Bellamy
The Beneficiary
Benefit of the Doubt
Berlin Express▲
Berserk!
Best Seller▲
Betrayal of the Dove
Betrayed
Beyond a Reasonable Doubt
Beyond the Bermuda Triangle
Beyond the Silhouette
Big Deadly Game
The Big Easy▲
The Big Fall
The Big Fix▲
The Big Heat▲
The Big Hurt
Big News
The Big Sleep▲
The Big Sleep
The Big Switch
Big Town After Dark
Bikini Island
The Bird with the Crystal Plumage
Birgitt Haas Must Be Killed
Bitter Harvest
Bitter Vengeance
The Black Abbot
Black Bird
Black Box Affair
The Black Cat
Black Cobra
Black Glove
Black Gold
The Black Hand▲
Black Hand
Black Ice
Black Limelight
Black Magic Woman
Black Panther
Black Rainbow▲
The Black Raven
Black Sunday
Black Tide
Black Tower
A Black Veil for Lisa
Black Water
Black Widow▲
The Black Windmill
Blackmail▲
Blackout
Blackwater Trail
Blind Date
Blind Fear
Blind Justice
Blind Man's Bluff
Blind Side
Blind Vision
Blind Witness
Blindfold: Acts of Obsession
Blindside
Blindsided
Blitz
Blonde Blackmailer
Blood Frenzy
Blood on the Sun
Blood Relations
Blood Relatives
Blood Simple▲
Bloodhounds
Bloodhounds 2
Bloody Avenger
Blow Out▲
Blown Away
Blue City
Blue Desert▲
Blue Ice
Blue Steel
Blue Tornado
Blue Velvet▲
Bodily Harm
Body Chemistry
Body Chemistry 3: Point of Seduction
Body Double▲
Body Heat▲
The Body in the Library
Body Language
Body of Influence
Body Parts
Body Shot
The Body Vanished
Boomerang▲
Borderline
B.O.R.N.
Born to Kill▲
The Boston Strangler
Bounty Hunters
The Bourne Identity▲
The Boys from Brazil
Brass Target
Breakdown▲
Breakheart Pass
Breaking All the Rules
The Bride Wore Black▲
Brighton Strangler
Broken Vows
Brotherly Love
Bulldog Drummond
Bulldog Drummond at Bay
Bulldog Drummond Comes Back
Bulldog Drummond's Bride
Bulldog Drummond's Peril
Bulldog Drummond's Revenge
Bulldog Drummond's Secret Police
Bullet to Beijing
Bulletproof Heart▲
Bums
Burndown
Buying Time
By Dawn's Early Light
By the Blood of Others▲
Calendar Girl Murders
The Caller
Calling Paul Temple
Candles at Nine
Caper of the Golden Bulls
Cardiac Arrest
Caribe
Carnival Lady
Caroline at Midnight
A Case for Murder
The Case of the Lucky Legs
Cast a Dark Shadow▲
Cast a Deadly Spell▲
Castle in the Desert
Cat and Mouse▲
The Cat and the Canary▲
The Cat and the Canary
Cat Chaser
The Cat o' Nine Tails
Catacombs
The Catamount Killing
Catch Me a Spy
Catherine's Grove
Caught in the Act
Cause for Alarm
Center of the Web
The Centerfold Girls
Chain of Desire
Challenge of McKenna
Charlie Chan and the Curse of the Dragon Queen
Charlie Chan at the Opera▲
Charlie Chan at the Wax Museum
Charlie Chan in Paris
Charlie Chan in Rio
Charlie Chan in the Secret Service
Charlie Chan's Secret
Child in the Night
Child of Glass
Chill Factor
The China Lake Murders
China Moon
Chinatown▲
The Chinese Cat
Choice of Arms
Christina
City in Panic
City Killer
City of Blood
City of Shadows
City on Fire
The Clay Pigeon
A Climate for Killing
Cloak and Dagger
The Clouded Yellow▲
Clouds over Europe▲
Clown Murders
The Clutching Hand
The Cobra Strikes
The Cobweb
Code Name Alpha
Code Name: Diamond Head
Codename: Foxfire
Codename: Icarus
Cohen and Tate
Cold Comfort
Cold Eyes of Fear
Cold Sweat
The Colony
Color Me Dead
Color of Night
Columbo: Murder by the Book
Columbo: Prescription Murder
Coma▲
Coming Out Alive
Compromising Positions
Concealed Weapon
Concrete Beat
The Confession
Confessions of a Hit Man
Confidentially Yours▲
Consenting Adults
The Conversation▲
Convicted
The Corpse Vanishes
Counter Punch
The Cover Girl Murders
Cover Me
Cover Story
Crack-Up
The Crackler
The Cradle Will Fall
Crime Broker
Criminal Court
Criminal Law
Criminals Within
Criss Cross▲
Cross Country
Crow Hollow
The Crucifer of Blood
The Crude Oasis
Cruise into Terror
Cruise Missile
Cruising
Cry Danger▲

▲ = *rated three bones or higher*

A Cry in the Night
The Cry of the Owl
Cry Panic
Cry Terror
Cry Wolf
The Crying Child
Curiosity Kills
Curse of the Yellow Snake
Cutter's Way
Cycle Psycho
Dagger Eyes
The Dain Curse
Damned River
Dance Macabre
Dance with Death
Dancing with Danger
Danger of Love
Danger on the Air
Danger Zone
The Dangerous
Dangerous Appointment
Dangerous Game
Dangerous Heart
Dangerous Love
Dangerous Mission
Dangerous Obsession
Dangerous Summer
Danielle Steel's Kaleidoscope
The Dark Angel▲
Dark Corner▲
Dark Forces
Dark Night of the Scarecrow
Dark of the Night
Dark Passage
Dark Side of Genius
Dark Side of Midnight
The Dark Wind
Darker than Amber
The Darkside
Daughter of Horror
The Day of the Jackal▲
Day of the Maniac
Dead Again▲
Dead Air
Dead Certain
Dead Cold
Dead Connection
Dead Eyes of London
Dead Funny
Dead Heat on a Merry-Go-Round▲
Dead in the Water
Dead Lucky
Dead of Winter▲
Dead On
Dead on Sight
Dead on the Money
Dead Pigeon on Beethoven Street
Dead Reckoning▲
Dead Reckoning
Dead Women in Lingerie
Dead Zone▲
Deadfall
Deadline
Deadline Assault
Deadline at Dawn
Deadly Business
Deadly Currents
Deadly Dancer
Deadly Embrace
Deadly Exposure
Deadly Fieldtrip
Deadly Force
The Deadly Game
Deadly Games
Deadly Illusion
Deadly Impact
Deadly Innocence
Deadly Intent
Deadly Passion
Deadly Possession
Deadly Rivals
The Deadly Secret
Deadly Sins
Deadly Spygames
Deadly Sting
Deadly Strangers
Deadly Surveillance
Dear Dead Delilah
Dear Detective
Death at Love House
Death by Prescription
Death Cruise
Death Dreams
Death from a Distance
Death Games
Death Goes to School
The Death Kiss
Death Kiss
Death Magic
Death of a Scoundrel
Death on the Nile
Death Rage
Death Ray 2000
Death Sentence
Death Train
Death Valley
Death Warrant
Death Weekend
Deathmask
Deceived
December Flower
Deception
Deceptions
The Deep
Deep Cover
Defense of the Realm▲
Defenseless
Deja Vu
Delusion
Deranged
Descending Angel▲
Desire and Hell at Sunset Motel
Desperate
Desperate Hours▲
Desperate Hours
Desperate Motives
The Detective▲
Detective
Devices and Desires▲
Devil Diamond
Devil in a Blue Dress▲
The Devil Thumbs a Ride▲
The Devil's Cargo
Devil's Party
The Devil's Undead
Devlin
Diabolically Yours
Dial Help
Dial "M" for Murder▲
Diamond Run
The Diamond Trap
Diamonds
Diamond's Edge
Dick Tracy
Dick Tracy, Detective
Dick Tracy Meets Gruesome
Dick Tracy Returns
Dick Tracy vs. Crime Inc.
Dick Tracy vs. Cueball
Dick Tracy's Dilemma
Die! Die! My Darling!
Die Screaming, Marianne
Die Sister, Die!
Die Watching
Dinner at the Ritz
Diplomatic Courier▲
Dirkham Detective Agency
Dirty Hands
Dirty Harry▲
Disappearance
The Disappearance of Christina
Disconnected
Discretion Assured
Dishonored Lady
Distortions
Disturbance
Diva▲
The Dive
D.O.A.▲
D.O.A.
Dr. Mabuse vs. Scotland Yard
Dr. Tarr's Torture Dungeon
Dog Day
Dog Day Afternoon▲
Dominique Is Dead
The Domino Principle
Donor Unknown
Don't Bother to Knock
Don't Go in the House
Don't Look in the Attic
Don't Look Now▲
Don't Open the Door!
Don't Torture a Duckling
Doomed to Die
The Doomsday Flight
Door with the Seven Locks
Double Agents
Double Cross
Double Exposure
Double Face
Double Identity
Double Indemnity▲
Double Jeopardy
The Double McGuffin
The Double Negative
Double Obsession
Double Threat
Double Vision
The Draughtsman's Contract▲
Dream Lover
Dream Man
Dream No Evil
Dress Gray▲
Dressed for Death
Dressed to Kill
Driven to Kill
Driver's Seat
The Dropkick▲
The Drowning Pool
Drums of Jeopardy
Duel▲
The Dummy Talks
Dust to Dust
Dying Game
Dying Room Only
Dying to Remember
The Dying Truth
Dynasty of Fear
Early Frost
Ebbtide
Echo Murders
Echoes
Edge of Darkness
The Eiger Sanction
Eight Witnesses
Embassy
Emil and the Detectives
Emissary
The Empty Beach
Endangered Species
Endless Night
Enigma
Enrapture
Equus
Escapade in Florence
Escape
Escape Clause
Escapist
Estate of Insanity
Evelyn Prentice
Even Angels Fall
Everybody Wins
Everybody's Dancin'
Evidence of Blood
Evil under the Sun
Ex-Mrs. Bradford▲
The Executioner
Exit in Red
Experiment in Terror▲
Experiment Perilous▲
The Expert
Exposed
Exposure
Express to Terror
Exterminator
Extreme Measures
Eye of the Needle
Eye Witness
Eyes of Laura Mars
Eyewitness
Eyewitness to Murder
F/X▲
The Face at the Window
A Face in the Fog
Fade to Black
Fail-Safe▲
Fake Out
The Falcon and the Snowman▲
The Falcon in Hollywood
The Falcon in Mexico
The Falcon's Brother
False Faces
False Identity
Family of Cops
Family Plot
The Fan
The Fantasist
Far from Home
Farewell, My Lovely▲
Fatal Bond
Fatal Charm
Fatal Exposure
Fatal Games
The Fatal Hour
The Fatal Image
Fatal Instinct
Fatal Past
Fatherland
FBI Girl
Fear
Fear City
Fear in the Night▲
Fearless
Fearmaker
The Female Jungle
Femme Fatale
Fer-De-Lance
Fever
Fiction Makers
The Fifth Floor
52 Pick-Up
The Fighting Westerner
Final Analysis
Final Assignment
Final Cut
Final Embrace
Final Judgment
Final Notice
The Final Option
Fingerprints Don't Lie
The Finishing Touch
The Firm▲
First Degree
Five Dolls for an August Moon
Five Graves to Cairo▲
Flashfire
Flashpoint
Flatliners
Fleshtone
Flowers in the Attic
Flying from the Hawk
Fog Island
Follow Me Quietly▲
The Fool Killer
Footsteps in the Dark
For Hire
Forbidden Sun
The Force
Foreign Correspondent▲
Forger of London
Forget Mozart
The Forgotten One
The Formula
Formula for a Murder
Fortress
The Fourth Protocol▲
Fourth Story▲
Frame by Frame
The Franchise Affair
Frantic▲
The French Detective▲
French Intrigue
French Silk
Frenzy
Frenzy▲
Fresh Kill
Fright
From Hollywood to Deadwood
From the Dead of Night▲
Frozen Alive
Fugitive Among Us
Full Circle
Full Exposure: The Sex Tape Scandals
Full Fathom Five
Funeral in Berlin▲
The Game
Game of Seduction
Gangbusters
Gaslight▲
Georgia
Get That Man
Getting Even
The Ghost Camera
Ghost Ship
The Ghost Walks
Girl Hunters
The Girl in a Swing
The Girl in Lover's Lane
A Girl to Kill For
Girls Night Out
Glass
The Glass Cage
The Glass Key▲
Glass Tomb
Go-Get-'Em-Haines
Golden Lady
Golden Rendezvous
The Golden Spiders: A Nero Wolfe Mystery
Gone to Ground
Gorky Park▲
Gotham▲
The Grave
The Great Riviera Bank Robbery
The Great St. Louis Bank Robbery
Green Archer
Green Eyes
Green for Danger
Green Ice
The Green Man▲
Grievous Bodily Harm
Ground Zero
Guest in the House
Guilty as Sin
Gunpowder
Half a Soldier
Hammett
Hand Gun
Hands of a Stranger
Hanky Panky
Happily Ever After
Hard Drive
Hard Evidence
The Hard Truth
Harper▲
The Harvest
Hat Box Mystery
The Haunted Castle▲
The Haunted Sea
Haunted: The Ferryman
Haunting of Harrington House
The Haunting Passion
The Hawk
He Lives: The Search for the Evil One
Heads
Hear No Evil
Heartaches
The Heat of the Day
Heat of the Sun▲
Heat Wave
Heatwave▲
Heaven's Prisoners
The Heist
Hell Harbor
Hell's Headquarters
Help!▲
Hi-Jacked
Hidden Agenda
Hidden City
Hidden Fears
Hidden Obsession
The Hidden Room▲
Hide in Plain Sight▲
High Frequency
High Stakes
Highway 13
The Hillside Strangler
The Hit List
The Hitman
The Holcroft Covenant
Hollywood Confidential
Hollywood Stadium Mystery
Home for the Holidays
Homicide▲
The Hooded Terror
The Horse Without a Head
The Horseplayer
Hostage
Hostages
Hot Child in the City
Hotel Colonial
Hotel Reserve▲
Hotline
The Hound of London
The Hound of the Baskervilles▲
The Hound of the Baskervilles
Hour of Decision
A House in the Hills
House of Fear
House of Mystery
The House of Secrets
House of Shadows
The House of the Arrow▲
House of the Damned
House of the Rising Sun
The House on Carroll Street
The Housekeeper
Human Desires
Human Gorilla
The Human Monster
Hunt the Man Down
Hunter
The Hunting
The Hustle
Hysteria
I Am the Cheese
I Bury the Living▲
I Confess
I Killed That Man
I, Madman
I See a Dark Stranger▲
I Stand Condemned
I, the Jury
I Wake Up Screaming▲
The Ice House▲
I'd Give My Life
If It's a Man, Hang Up
If Looks Could Kill
I'll Get You
I'll Name the Murderer
Illegal
Illegal in Blue
Illicit Behavior
Illicit Dreams
Illusions
I'm the Girl He Wants to Kill
I'm the One You're Looking For
Image of Death
Impact▲
Improper Conduct
Impulse
In a Lonely Place▲
In a Moment of Passion
In a Stranger's Hand
In an Old Manor House
In Self Defense
In the Cold of the Night
In the Deep Woods
In the Heat of the Night▲
In the Kingdom of the Blind the Man with One Eye Is King
In the Line of Fire▲
In the Secret State
In the Spirit
Indecency
Indecent Behavior
Indecent Behavior 2
The Indian Scarf
Indiscreet
Infamous Crimes
Inheritance▲
The Inheritor
The Inner Circle
Inner Sanctum
Inner Sanctum 2
The Innocent
Innocent Lies
Innocent Victim
The Inquiry
Insanity
The Inside Man
The Instructor
Interface
International Crime
Internecine Project
Interrupted Journey
Intimate Stranger
Into the Blue
Into the Fire
Intrigue
Intruder
Invasion of Privacy
Investigation
The Invisible Avenger
The Invisible Killer
Invitation to Hell
The Ipcress File▲
Irish Luck
Island Monster
Istanbul
It Could Happen to You
It Happened at Nightmare Inn
Jack's Back▲
The Jade Mask
The Jagged Edge
Jane Doe
Jaws of Death
Jennifer 8
Jenny Lamour
Jezebel's Kiss
Jigsaw
The Jigsaw Man
Jigsaw Murders
Johnny Angel▲
Johnny Nobody
Johnny Skidmarks
Journey into Fear▲

Journey into Fear
Joy House
Judicial Consent
Juggernaut▲
Jungle Bride
The Junkman
Just Another Pretty Face
Just Cause
Kafka
Kemek
The Kennel Murder Case
Kentucky Jubilee
Keys to Tulsa
The KGB: The Secret War
Kid
Kidnapped
The Kidnapping of the President
Kill Cruise
The Kill-Off
Killer Fish
Killer Image
A Killer in Every Corner
Killer Likes Candy
Killer Looks
Killer with Two Faces
The Killers
A Killing Affair
The Killing Game
Killing Hour
The Killing Jar
The Killing Kind
The Killing Mind
Killing Obsession
Killing Stone
The Killing Time
Killjoy
Killpoint
The King Murder
A Kiss Before Dying
Kiss Daddy Goodnight
Kiss Me a Killer
Kiss Me, Kill Me
Klute▲
La Ceremonie▲
L.A. Confidential▲
L.A. Goddess
La Passante▲
Lady Audley's Secret
Lady Beware
The Lady Confesses
The Lady from Shanghai▲
Lady in a Cage▲
Lady in Cement
The Lady in Question
Lady in the Death House
The Lady in White▲
Lady of Burlesque
Lady Scarface
The Lady Vanishes▲
The Lady Vanishes
Ladykiller
Ladykillers
Laguna Heat
Last Dance
Last Embrace▲
The Last of Philip Banter
The Last of Sheila
Last Rites
Last Song
The Late Show▲
The Laughing Policeman
Laura▲
Le Corbeau▲
Le Magnifique
Le Polygraphe
Le Secret▲
Left for Dead
Legacy of Lies
Legal Deceit
Letter to My Killer
The Liars
Liar's Edge
Lie Down with Lions
Liebestraum
Lies
Lies Before Kisses
Lifespan
The Lift
The Lightning Incident
Lights! Camera! Murder!
Lily Was Here
The Limping Man
Linda
Lipstick Camera
Lisa
Lisbon
The List of Adrian Messenger▲
The Little Drummer Girl▲
The Little Girl Who Lives down the Lane
Little Nikita
Living to Die
The Lodger▲
Lonely Hearts
The Long Goodbye▲
Long Time Gone
Loose Cannons
The Lost Jungle
The Lost Tribe
Love and Hate: A Marriage Made in Hell
Love & Murder
Love at Large▲
Love Camp
Love from a Stranger
Love Kills
Love on the Run
Lower Level
Lure of the Islands
Lying Lips
Mackintosh Man
The Mad Executioners
Madame Sin
Madeleine
Madigan▲
Magic Moments
Malibu Express
Malice
Malicious
A Man About the House
Man Bait
Man from Headquarters
The Man from the Pru
The Man Inside
Man on Fire
The Man on the Roof
Man on the Run
Man Outside
The Man Who Haunted Himself
The Man Who Knew Too Much▲
The Man Who Knew Too Much
The Man Who Would Not Die
Man with a Gun
The Manchurian Candidate▲
The Mandarin Mystery
Manfish
The Manhattan Project
Manhunter▲
Maniac
Marathon Man▲
Margin for Murder
Marie Galante▲
Mark of Cain
Mark of the Beast
Marked for Murder
Marlowe
Marnie▲
Maroc 7
Mascara
Mask of the Dragon
Masks of Death
Masquerade▲
Master Touch
A Matter of WHO
Maya
The Maze▲
Mazes and Monsters
The McGuffin
Medusa
Meeting at Midnight
Memories of Murder
Men at Work
Messenger of Death
Miami Blues
Midnight
Midnight at the Wax Museum
Midnight Faces
Midnight Girl
Midnight Heat
Midnight in Saint Petersburg
Midnight Limited
Midnight Warning
Midnight Witness
Mike's Murder
Million Dollar Haul
Million Dollar Mystery
Mind, Body & Soul
A Mind to Kill
A Mind to Murder
Mind Twister
Mindfield
Mirage▲
Mirage
The Mirror Crack'd
Mirror Images
Mirror Images 2
Missing Pieces
Mistaken Identity
Mr. Frost
Mr. Moto's Last Warning▲
Mr. Reeder in Room 13
Mr. Scarface
Mr. Wong, Detective
Mr. Wong in Chinatown
Money Madness
Monique
The Monster Walks
Moon in Scorpio
Moonlighting
The Moonstone▲
The Morning After
Mortal Passions
The Most Dangerous Game▲
Mother's Boys
Motor Patrol
Motorcycle Squad
Murder▲
Murder Ahoy
Murder at 45 R.P.M.
Murder at Midnight
Murder at 1600
Murder at the Baskervilles
Murder at the Gallop▲
Murder by Decree▲
Murder by Natural Causes▲
Murder by Night
Murder by Numbers
Murder by Phone
Murder by Television
Murder by the Book
Murder in a Small Town
Murder in Mind
Murder in Space
Murder in the Doll House
Murder in the Footlights
A Murder Is Announced
Murder Most Foul▲
Murder, My Sweet▲
Murder of a Moderate Man
A Murder of Crows
A Murder of Quality
Murder on Approval
Murder on the Campus
Murder on the High Seas
Murder on the Midnight Express
Murder on the Orient Express▲
Murder Once Removed
Murder 101
Murder over New York
Murder Rap
Murder She Purred: A Mrs. Murphy Mystery
Murder She Said
Murder So Sweet
Murder Story
Murder: Ultimate Grounds for Divorce
Murdered Innocence
Murderers' Row
Murderlust
Murderous Vision
Murders at Lynch Cross
Murders in the Rue Morgue
The Murders in the Rue Morgue▲
Mute Witness
My Man Adam
My Sister, My Love
My Sweet Victim
Mysterious Doctor Satan
The Mysterious Magician
Mysterious Mr. Wong
Mystery at Fire Island
Mystery in Swing
Mystery Liner
The Mystery Man
Mystery Mansion
The Mystery of Edwin Drood
Mystery of Mr. Wong
The Mystery of Rampo▲
The Mystery of the Mary Celeste
Mystery of the Riverboat
Mystery Plane
Mystic Circle Murder
The Naked Edge
The Naked Face
Naked Obsession
The Name of the Rose
Nancy Drew, Reporter
The Narrow Margin▲
Narrow Margin
Natural Causes
Natural Enemy
Nature's Playmates
The Neighbor
Neutron vs. the Maniac
Never Say Die
New Year's Evil
New York Ripper
Newman's Law
The Next Victim
Next Victim
Niagara
Night and the City▲
Night Angel
Night Birds
Night Cries
Night Eyes
Night Eyes 2
Night Eyes 3
Night Fire
A Night for Crime
The Night Has Eyes
Night Moves▲
Night of Terror
Night of the Assassin
Night of the Cyclone
The Night of the Hunter▲
Night of the Juggler
Night Rhythms
Night School
Night Shadow
Night Stalker
Night Terror
A Night to Remember▲
Night Train to Munich▲
The Night Visitor
Night Watch
The Nightcomers
Nighthawks
Nightkill
The Nightman
Nightmare in Badham County
Nightwing
No Comebacks
No Mercy
No Place to Hide
No Problem
No Secrets
No Way Out▲
No Way to Treat a Lady▲
Nocturne
Non-Stop New York
Norman Conquest
North by Northwest▲
Nothing Underneath
Notorious▲
November Conspiracy
Nowhere to Hide
Nuclear Conspiracy
No. 17▲
The Oblong Box
The Obsessed
Obsession
Obsession: A Taste for Fear
Obsessive Love
An Occasional Hell
Octagon
The October Man▲
The Odessa File
On Dangerous Ground▲
One Frightened Night
One Night Stand
One of My Wives Is Missing
One Shoe Makes It Murder
Open House
Open Secret
Operation Amsterdam
Ordeal by Innocence
The Osterman Weekend
The Other Woman
Out of Annie's Past
Out of Bounds
Out of Order
Out of Sight, Out of Her Mind
Out of the Darkness▲
Out of the Past▲
Out of the Shadows
Out on Bail
The Outside Man
Outside the Law
The Oval Portrait
Over Indulgence
Overexposed
Paid to Kill
Paint It Black
Painted Hero
The Pamela Principle
Panic in the Streets▲
Panic on the 5:22
Panique▲
The Panther's Claw
Paperhouse▲
The Parallax View▲
Paranoia
Paris Belongs to Us
Paris Express
Parker
Party Girls for Sale
Party Line
Passion Flower
Passion in Paradise
Past Midnight
Past Tense
Payback
The Payoff
The Pearl of Death
The Pelican Brief
Pendulum
Penthouse▲
The Perfect Bride
Perfect Crime
Perfect Family
A Perfect Murder
A Perfect Spy
Perfect Strangers
Perfect Victims
Peril
Perry Mason Returns▲
Perry Mason: The Case of the Lost Love
Personals
Peter Gunn
The Phantom Broadcast
The Phantom Creeps
Phantom Express
Phantom Fiend
Phantom Killer
The Phantom Light
Phantom of Chinatown
The Phantom of 42nd Street
The Phantom of Soho
Phobia
Phoenix Team
The Phone Call
Photographer
Physical Evidence
Picnic at Hanging Rock▲
Picture Mommy Dead
Pier 23
Plain Clothes
Play Misty for Me▲
Play Nice
The Pledge▲
Plumber
A Pocketful of Rye
Poor Girl, a Ghost Story
Portrait in Black
Portraits of a Killer
Posed for Murder
Positive I.D.
Power of Attorney
Power Play
The Practice of Love
Praying Mantis
President's Mistress
The President's Mystery
The Presidio
Presumed Innocent▲
Prey of the Chameleon
Primal Secrets
Prime Suspect
Prime Suspect▲
Prime Time Murder
Prison Shadows
The Private Life of Sherlock Holmes▲
Private Obsession
The Prize▲
Probable Cause
Probe
Project: Eliminator
Project X
Promise to Murder
Prowler
Psychic
Psycho▲
Psycho 2
Psycho 3
Psychomania
Pulp
Pursuit▲
Pursuit to Algiers
Puzzle
Quake
Quicker Than the Eye
Quicksand: No Escape
The Quiller Memorandum▲
Radioland Murders
Rage
The Rain Killer
Raw Nerve
Rear Window▲
Rebecca▲
Reckless Moment▲
Red Corner
The Red House▲
Red King, White Knight
Red Lights Ahead
The Red Raven Kiss-Off
Red Rock West▲
Red Wind
Redneck
Reflections of Murder
Regina
Rehearsal for Murder
Reilly: Ace of Spies▲
The Reincarnation of Peter Proud
Relentless 3
Relentless 4
Remember Me
Return
The Return of Boston Blackie
Return of Chandu
The Return of Dr. Mabuse
Return of Frank Cannon
Revenge
Revenge of the Stepford Wives
Rich and Strange
The Rich Man's Wife
Rider on the Rain▲
Riders to the Sea
Rififi▲
Ring of Death
Rising Sun▲
Road Games
Road to Salina▲
Roaring City
Rogue's Gallery
Rogue's Tavern
Rogue's Yarn
Romeo Is Bleeding
Room 43
Roots of Evil
Rope▲
The Rosary Murders
R.S.V.P.
Rude Awakening
Rule #3
Run If You Can
Runaways
Russian Roulette
Saboteur▲
The Saint
The Saint in London
The Saint in New York
The Saint Strikes Back
The Saint Strikes Back: Criminal Court
The Saint Takes Over
The Saint's Double Trouble
The Salamander
The Salzburg Connection
Sanctuary of Fear
Sanders of the River▲
Savage Hearts
Savages
Save Me
Scalp Merchant
Scam
Scandal Man
Scandalous
Scarlet Claw▲
The Scarlet Clue
Scarlet Street▲
Scavengers
Scene of the Crime
Scene of the Crime▲
Scenes from a Murder
Schemes
Schnelles Geld

▲ = rated three bones or higher

Scissors
Scorned
Scorpio
The Scorpio Factor
Scotland Yard Inspector
Scream
Scream Bloody Murder
Scream for Help
Screamer
The Sculptress
Sea of Love ▲
Seance on a Wet Afternoon ▲
Season of Fear
The Second Woman
Secret Agent 00
Secret of the Black Trunk
The Secret Passion of Robert Clayton
The Set Up
Seven Doors to Death
Seven Hours to Judgment
The Seven-Per-Cent Solution ▲
The Seventh Sign
Sexpot
Sexton Blake and the Hooded Terror
Sexual Intent
Sexual Malice
Sexual Response
Shades of Fear
The Shadow
The Shadow Conspiracy
Shadow Dancing ▲
The Shadow Man
Shadow of a Doubt ▲
Shadow of a Scream
Shadow of Doubt
Shadow of the Thin Man ▲
Shadow Play
The Shadow Strikes
Shadows on the Stairs
Shaft ▲
Shallow Grave
The Shanghai Cobra
Shattered
Shattered Image
Shattered Silence
She Waits
Sherlock Holmes and the Deadly Necklace
Sherlock Holmes and the Incident at Victoria Falls
Sherlock Holmes and the Secret Weapon ▲
Sherlock Holmes Faces Death ▲
Sherlock Holmes in Washington
Sherlock Holmes: The Voice of Terror
She's Dressed to Kill
Shock!
Shoot to Kill
A Shot in the Dark
The Shout ▲
A Show of Force
Show Them No Mercy ▲
Shriek in the Night
Side Show
Sidney Sheldon's Bloodline
The Sign of Four
The Silencer
Silent Assassins
Silent Fall
Silent Killers
The Silent Mr. Sherlock Holmes
Silent Motive
The Silent Partner ▲
The Silent Passenger
Silhouette
Sins of Desire
Sins of the Night
Sioux City
The Sister-in-Law
Sister, Sister
Sisters of Death
Skeletons
Sketch Artist
Sketch Artist 2: Hands That See
Sketches of a Strangler
Sky Liner
Slamdance
The Slasher
Slaughter of the Innocents
Slayground
Sleeping Car to Trieste
Sleepwalk
Sleuth ▲
Slightly Honorable
Slightly Scarlet
Slipping into Darkness
Sliver
Slow Burn
Small Kill
Smile, Jenny, You're Dead
Smilla's Sense of Snow
Smooth Talker
Snatched
Sneakers
Snow Kill
Snowblind
Sois Belle et Tais-Toi
Soldier of the Night
Somebody Has to Shoot the Picture ▲
Someone Behind the Door
Someone to Watch Over Me ▲
Song of the Thin Man
Sound of Murder
Spaceways
The Spaniard's Curse
Spare Parts
Special Police
The Specialist
The Speckled Band ▲
Spectre of the Rose
Speedy Death ▲
Spellbound ▲
Spenser: Ceremony
Spenser: Pale Kings & Princes
The Sphinx
Sphinx
The Spider and the Fly
Spider Woman ▲
Spiders ▲
The Spider's Stratagem ▲
Spraggue
Sputnik
The Spy Who Came in from the Cold ▲
The Spy Within
S*P*Y*S
The Squeaker
The Squeeze
Stacey
Stage Fright ▲
Stamp of a Killer
Star of Midnight
Star Time
State Department File 649
State of Things ▲
Station
Stay Tuned for Murder
The Stepmother
The Stepsister
Stick
Still Life
Still of the Night
Stir
A Stolen Face
Stone Cold Dead
Stormy Monday
The Strange Affair of Uncle Harry
Strange Confession
The Strange Countess
Strange Shadows in an Empty Room
The Stranger ▲
A Stranger Among Us
Stranger in the House
Stranger in Town
A Stranger Is Watching
Stranger on the Third Floor ▲
The Stranger Within
Strangers
Strangers on a Train ▲
The Strangler
Strangler of Blackmoor Castle
Strangler of the Swamp
Stray Dog ▲
Strike Force
Stripped to Kill
Stripped to Kill II: Live Girls
A Study in Scarlet
A Study in Terror ▲
The Substitute
Subterfuge
Sucker Money
Sudden Fear ▲
Suddenly ▲
Summer Heat
Summer's Children
Sunstroke
Surrogate
Suspect
Suspicion ▲
Suspicion
Svengali
Sweet Murder
Swiss Conspiracy
Tag: The Assassination Game
Taggat
Tainted Blood
Take Two
Taking the Heat
Tale of a Vampire
Tales of the Unexpected
The Tall Blond Man with One Black Shoe ▲
Tangiers
Tangled Destinies
Target
The Tattered Web
The Taxi Mystery
The Teacher
Telefon
Temptation
Ten Days Wonder
Ten Little Indians
10 Rillington Place ▲
Tequila Sunrise
Tereza ▲
Terminal Choice
Terminal Entry
The Terror
Terror at London Bridge
Terror by Night
Terror Stalks the Class Reunion
Terror Street
Terrorists
There Goes Kelly
They Call Me Mr. Tibbs!
They Meet Again
They Only Kill Their Masters
They Watch
They Won't Believe Me ▲
They're Playing with Fire
Thief
Thief ▲
Thief of Hearts
The Thin Man ▲
The Thin Man Goes Home
Third Degree Burn
The Third Key
The Third Man ▲
Third Solution
13th Guest
The Thirteenth Man
The 39 Steps ▲
The Thirty-Nine Steps
This Is a Hijack
This Lightning Always Strikes Twice
This Man Must Die ▲
This Sweet Sickness
Threat
Three by Hitchcock
Three Cases of Murder ▲
Three Days of the Condor ▲
Thrilled to Death
Thrillkill
Through Naked Eyes
Thundersquad
Tiara Tahiti
The Ticket
Ticket of Leave Man
Tiger Bay ▲
Tightrope ▲
Till Death Do Us Part
Till There Was You
Time for Revenge
A Time to Die
Time Without Pity
Times to Come ▲
To Catch a King
To Catch a Thief ▲
To Kill a Clown
To Kill a Stranger
The Todd Killings
Tomorrow at Seven
Tony Rome
Too Scared to Scream
Topaz ▲
Torment
Torn Curtain
Total Exposure
Touch Me Not
Touch of Evil ▲
Touching Evil ▲
Tough Assignment
Tough Guys Don't Dance
Tourist Trap
Tower of Terror
Town That Dreaded Sundown
Traces of Red
Track 29
Trade Secrets
The Train Killer
The Trap
Trapped
Trauma
Treacherous Crossing
Trial and Error
Trial by Jury
The Triumph of Sherlock Holmes
Tropical Heat
The Trouble with Harry ▲
True Believer
True Crime
True Lies
Twenty Dollar Star
Twilight ▲
Twilight Man
Twin Sisters
Twisted Obsession
Two by Forsyth
Two Fathers' Justice
The Two Jakes
Two Minute Warning
Ultimate Desires
The Ultimate Imposter
The Ultimate Thrill
Ultraviolet
The Unbreakable Alibi
Under Capricorn
Under Investigation
Under Suspicion
Undercover
Uneasy Terms
Unholy Four
Unholy Wife
Union City
Union Station
Unsane
Unsuitable Job for a Woman
Unveiled
Up in the Air
Urge to Kill
The Usual Suspects ▲
Utz
The Vagrant
Vamping
The Vanishing ▲
The Vanishing
Vanishing Act
Vatican Conspiracy
Vegas
Velvet Touch ▲
Vertigo ▲
The Very Edge
Vicious
The Vicious Circle
Victim of Beauty
Victim of Desire
Victim of Love
Video Murders
Violette ▲
The Vision
Visions
Visiting Hours
Voulez-Vous Danser avec Moi?
A Vow to Kill
Vultures
W
Waikiki
Wanted: Babysitter
Warm Nights on a Slow-Moving Train
Warning Sign
Watched
The Way Out
Wayne Murder Case ▲
Weep No More My Lady
Whatever Happened to Aunt Alice? ▲
When a Stranger Calls
When a Stranger Calls Back
When Angels Fly
When I Close My Eyes
When the Bough Breaks
Where Are the Children?
Where Sleeping Dogs Lie
Where's the Money, Noreen?
A Whisper to a Scream
Whispering City ▲
Whispering Shadow
Whispers in the Dark
The Whistle Blower ▲
White Fire
White Hot: The Mysterious Murder of Thelma Todd
White Mischief ▲
White of the Eye ▲
The White Raven
White Sands
Who Is the Black Dahlia? ▲
Who Killed Baby Azaria?
Who Killed Mary What's 'Er Name?
Whodunit
Widow Couderc ▲
Widow's Kiss
Widow's Nest
Wild Cactus
Wild Things
Wild West
Wildcard
The Wind
The Window ▲
Witch Hunt
Witchfire
Without Warning
Witness for the Prosecution ▲
Woman Condemned
Woman Hunt
The Woman Hunter
Woman in Black
The Woman in Green
The Woman in Question
The Woman in White
Woman of Desire
Woman Undone
The Woman Who Came Back
A Woman's Face ▲
Wonderland ▲
The Word
Writer's Block
The Wrong Man ▲
The Wrong Man
The Wrong Woman
Yellowstone
Young and Innocent ▲
Young Sherlock Holmes
Z ▲
Zentropa
Zero Boys
Zertigo Diamond Caper
The Zodiac Killer

Nannies & Governesses

see also ***Babysitting; Bringing Up Baby; The Help: Female; Parenthood***

Adam Had Four Sons
Addams Family Values
All This and Heaven Too ▲
Anna and the King of Siam ▲
Baby Monitor: Sound of Fear
Berkeley Square
Blanche Fury
Blue Blood
The Chalk Garden ▲
Corrina, Corrina
Cousin Bette
The Devil's Own ▲
Flame Over India ▲
Friend of the Family 2
The Governess
The Hand that Rocks the Cradle
The Haunting of Morella
The Innocents ▲
Jack and Sarah
Jane Eyre
Jane Eyre ▲
Jane Eyre
The King and I ▲
The King and I
Lady Audley's Secret
Left Luggage
Lily in Winter
Mary Poppins ▲
Midnight's Child
Miss Mary
Mrs. Doubtfire
Mr. Nanny
My Daughter's Keeper
The Nanny
The Nightcomers
Perfect Family
The Perfect Nanny
Peter Pan ▲
Provocateur
Rescuers: Stories of Courage "Two Women" ▲
The Sound of Music ▲
The Turn of the Screw
Undesirable
Vanity Fair

Nashville

see also ***American South; Nashville Narratives***

The Concrete Cowboys
Honkytonk Man
Nashville ▲
Nashville Beat
Nashville Girl
The Night the Lights Went Out in Georgia
Sweet Country Road
The Thing Called Love

Nashville Narratives

see also ***American South; Biopics: Musicians; Southern Belles***

Baja Oklahoma
Cassie
The City
Coal Miner's Daughter ▲
Doing Time for Patsy Cline ▲
Falling from Grace
Hard Part Begins
Honeysuckle Rose
Honkytonk Man
Honkytonk Nights
Jackpot
Lady Grey
Living Proof: The Hank Williams Jr. Story
Nashville ▲
Nashville Girl
The Night the Lights Went Out in Georgia
Paradise Park
Payday
Pure Country
Rhinestone
Rikky and Pete
Road to Nashville
Saturday Night Special
A Smoky Mountain Christmas
Songwriter
Sweet Dreams
Tender Mercies ▲
The Thing Called Love
Wild West

Native America

The Abduction of Allison Tate
Across the Wide Missouri
Angry Joe Bass
Apache Blood
Apache Chief
Apache Woman
The Avenging
Bad Lands
The Bears & I
Big Bear
Big Eden
Billy Jack
Billy Two Hats
Black Fox: Blood Horse
Black Fox: The Price of Peace
Black Robe ▲
Born Losers
Braveheart
Broken Arrow
The Broken Chain
Buck and the Magic Bracelet

▲ = rated three bones or higher

Buffalo Bill Rides Again
Buffalo Heart: The Pain of Death
Buffalo Soldiers ▲
Bugles in the Afternoon
Canyon Passage ▲
Captain Apache
The Captive: The Longest Drive 2
Cavalier of the West
Cavalry Charge
Centennial ▲
Chato's Land
Cheyenne Autumn
Cheyenne Warrior
Chuka
Circle of Death
Clearcut
The Comancheros ▲
Conquest of Cochise
Cotter
Crazy Horse ▲
Crazy Horse and Custer: "The Untold Story"
Crypt of Dark Secrets
Custer's Last Fight
Dakota Incident
Dalva
Dan Candy's Law
Dance Me Outside
Dances with Wolves ▲
The Dark Wind
Dead Man
Diplomaniacs
The Education of Little Tree ▲
Escape from Fort Bravo
Eyes of Fire
Fish Hawk
Flaming Star ▲
Fleshburn
Follow the River
The Gatling Gun
Geronimo
Geronimo ▲
Geronimo: An American Legend
Ghost Dance
The Glory Trail
A Good Day to Die
Gunman's Walk
Hondo ▲
I Heard the Owl Call My Name
I Will Fight No More Forever ▲
Incident at Oglala: The Leonard Peltier Story ▲
The Indian Fighter ▲
The Indian in the Cupboard
Island of the Blue Dolphins
Jim Thorpe: All American
Joe Panther ▲
Johnny Firecloud
Johnny Tiger
Journey Through Rosebud
Journey to Spirit Island
Lakota Woman: Siege at Wounded Knee
The Last of His Tribe
The Last of the Dogmen
The Last of the Mohicans ▲
The Last of the Mohicans
The Last of the Mohicans ▲
The Last of the Redmen
Legend of Walks Far Woman
The Legend of Wolf Mountain
The Light in the Forest
Little Big Man ▲
The Lost Child
Lost Legacy: A Girl Called Hatter Fox
The Magic Stone
The Magnificent Seven
A Man Called Horse ▲
Man of the House
The Manitou
Map of the Human Heart
Mission to Glory
A Mormon Maid
Naked in the Sun
Natas ... The Reflection
Navajo Blues
Northern Passage
On Top of the Whale
One Little Indian
The Pathfinder
Pocahontas ▲
Pocahontas: The Legend
Poltergeist 2: The Other Side
Powwow Highway ▲
The Prophecy
Ravenhawk
The Red Fury
The Red Half-Breed
Renegades
Requiem for a Heavyweight ▲
Roanoak
Running Brave
Savage Sam
The Savage Seven
Savage Wilderness
The Secret of Navajo Cave
Shadow of the Wolf
Shadowhunter
Silent Tongue
Sioux City
Skipped Parts
Smith!
Smoke Signals
Spirit Rider ▲
Spirit: Stallion of the Cimarron
Squanto: A Warrior's Tale ▲
Sunchaser
Tecumseh: The Last Warrior
Tell Them Willie Boy Is Here ▲
Terror in the Jungle
Texas John Slaughter: Geronimo's Revenge
3 Ninjas Knuckle Up
Three Warriors
Thunder Warrior
Thunder Warrior 2
Thunderheart ▲
Tomahawk
Tonka
Track of the Moonbeast
True Heart
True Women
Unconquered
Uninvited
The Vanishing American
The Villain
Wagon Wheels
Walk the Proud Land
War Party
Where the Spirit Lives
White Fang 2: The Myth of the White Wolf
Wind River
Windrunner
Windtalkers
Windwalker ▲
Winterhawk

Nazis & Other Paramilitary Slugs

see also *Germany; The Holocaust; Judaism; World War II*

All Through the Night ▲
Angel of Death
Angel with the Trumpet
Angry Harvest ▲
Anima
Any Man's Death
Apt Pupil
Ark of the Sun God
The Assisi Underground
Background to Danger ▲
Bedknobs and Broomsticks
The Berlin Affair
Berlin Express ▲
Betrayed ▲
The Black Klansman
The Blues Brothers ▲
The Boxer and Death ▲
The Boys from Brazil
Brady's Escape
Brainwashed
Broken Glass
Cabaret ▲
Cabo Blanco
Casablanca ▲
Casablanca Express
Charlie Grant's War
Clipped Wings
Closet Land
Cold Days
Commandos Strike at Dawn
The Conformist ▲
Conspiracy
Contraband
Cottage to Let
Counterblast
The Counterfeit Traitor ▲
The Coward
The Cut Throats
Dam Busters ▲
Dawn Express
A Day in October
Dead Bang
Death Is Called Engelchen ▲
The Death of Adolf Hitler
Descending Angel ▲
Desert Commandos
The Desert Fox ▲
Despair ▲
The Devil's Brigade
The Diary of Anne Frank ▲
The Dirty Dozen ▲
The Dirty Dozen: The Deadly Mission
The Dirty Dozen: The Fatal Mission
The Dirty Dozen: The Next Mission
Dirty Heroes
Divided We Fall
Edge of Darkness ▲
Elves
The Empty Mirror
Enemy at the Gates
Enemy of Women
Enigma Secret
Equalizer 2000
Escape from Sobibor ▲
Europa, Europa ▲
The Execution
Eye of the Needle
A Face in the Rain
The Fallen Sparrow ▲
Father
Fatherland
Firewalker
Five Fingers ▲
Five Graves to Cairo ▲
The Flesh Eaters
Flesh Feast
Forbidden
Force 10 from Navarone
Foreign Correspondent ▲
The Forty-Ninth Parallel ▲
Four Bags Full
The Four Horsemen of the Apocalypse
A Friendship in Vienna
Genghis Cohn
Getting Away With Murder
Ghost on the Loose
Goldengirl
Good Evening, Mr. Wallenberg
The Great Dictator ▲
The Great Escape ▲
Hamsun
Hangmen Also Die
Hanna's War
Hanussen ▲
The Harmonists
Hart's War
He Lives: The Search for the Evil One
Hell Commandos
Hell Hunters
Hell River
Hell Squad
Heroes in Hell
The Heroes of Telemark
The Hiding Place
Higher Learning
Hitler
Hitler: Dead or Alive
Hitler's Children ▲
Hitler's Daughter
Holocaust ▲
Hornet's Nest
Hotel Reserve ▲
The House on Carroll Street
The House on Garibaldi Street
House on 92nd Street ▲
Ilsa, Harem Keeper of the Oil Sheiks
Ilsa, She-Wolf of the SS
In a Glass Cage
In the Presence of Mine Enemies
The Incredible Mr. Limpet
Indiana Jones and the Last Crusade ▲
Indiana Jones and the Temple of Doom ▲
The Infiltrator
Inside Out
Inside the Third Reich
Into the Homeland
Invisible Agent
Jack Higgins' The Windsor Protocol
Jacob the Liar
Jakob the Liar ▲
Jenny's War
Jew-boy Levi
Judgment at Nuremberg ▲
Julia ▲
Jungle Siren
Kanal ▲
Kapo ▲
The Keep
The Key to Rebecca
The Klansman
Kojak: The Belarus File
Korczak ▲
La Passante ▲
Lassiter
The Last Butterfly
The Last Five Days
The Last Metro ▲
The Last Train
Law of the Jungle
Les Miserables
Les Violons du Bal
Life Is Beautiful ▲
Lifeboat ▲
The Longest Day ▲
Lucie Aubrac
The Lucifer Complex
Madame Rosa ▲
A Man Escaped ▲
The Man in the Glass Booth ▲
The Man Who Captured Eichmann
Marathon Man ▲
Martha and I ▲
Massacre in Rome
Master Key
Master Race
Me and the Colonel
The Mediterranean in Flames
Mephisto ▲
Ministry of Fear ▲
Miracle at Midnight
Miracle at Moreaux
Mr. Klein ▲
The Mortal Storm ▲
Mosley
Mother Night ▲
Music Box
My Mother's Courage
The Nasty Girl ▲
Night Ambush
A Night in Casablanca ▲
Night of the Fox
Night of the Generals ▲
The Night Porter
Night Train to Munich ▲
Night Train to Venice
No Dead Heroes
The North Star ▲
Northern Pursuit
Notorious ▲
November Moon
Nuremberg
Oasis of the Zombies
The Odessa File
The Ogre
Old Gun ▲
Once Upon a Honeymoon
One of Our Aircraft Is Missing ▲
The Only Way
Open City ▲
Operation Amsterdam
Operation Crossbow ▲
O.S.S. ▲
Passage to Marseilles ▲
The Pedestrian ▲
Pimpernel Smith
Porcile
A Prayer for Katarina Horovitzova ▲
Prayer of the Rollerboys
Pressure Point ▲
Puppet Master 3: Toulon's Revenge
The Quiller Memorandum ▲
Raid on Rommel
Raiders of the Lost Ark ▲
Rescuers: Stories of Courage "Two Women" ▲
Reunion in France
The Revolt of Job ▲
Richard III ▲
Rio Rita
River of Death
River of Diamonds
The Rocketeer ▲
The Rose Garden
The Salzburg Connection
Savage Attraction
The Scarlet & the Black
Schindler's List ▲
Schtonk
Scream and Scream Again
Sea of Sand
The Secret Code
Secret Mission
The Secret War of Harry Frigg
The Seventh Cross ▲
Severed Ties
She Demons
Shining Through
Shock Waves
Silent Scream
633 Squadron
Skinheads: The Second Coming of Hate
Snow Treasure
So Ends Our Night ▲
Soldier of Orange ▲
A Soldier's Tale
Son of Lassie
The Sorrow and the Pity ▲
The Sound of Music ▲
Stalag 17 ▲
Stalag Luft
The Stranger ▲
Strangers in Paradise
Sundown
Surf Nazis Must Die
Sweet Light in a Dark Room ▲
Swing Kids
A Taxing Woman's Return ▲
That Summer of White Roses
They Saved Hitler's Brain
13 Rue Madeleine ▲
'38: Vienna before the Fall
This Land Is Mine ▲
Tiger Fangs
Tigershark
To Be or Not to Be ▲
To Be or Not to Be
To Catch a King
Tomorrow the World
Top Dog
Top Secret! ▲
The Tormentors
Train of Life
Transport from Paradise
Triumph of the Spirit ▲
Triumph of the Will
True Colors
U-Boat Prisoner
Underground
Uprising ▲
Uranus ▲
War & Love
War & Remembrance
War & Remembrance: The Final Chapter
Watch on the Rhine ▲
Waterfront
Where Eagles Dare ▲
Where Trails End
Wild Geese 2
The Winds of War
Wings over the Pacific
Wizards
A Woman at War
Wooden Horse ▲
Yank in Libya
The Yesterday Machine
Zentropa
Zombie Lake
Zone Troopers

Near-Death Experiences

see also *Death & the Afterlife*

Dead Zone ▲
Fearless ▲
Flatliners
The Princess and the Warrior ▲

Negative Utopia

see also *Post Apocalypse; Technology—Rampant*

Alphaville ▲
Animal Farm ▲
Brazil ▲
El Norte ▲
Futureworld
Gattaca ▲
Metropolis ▲
Moonraker
The Mosquito Coast
984: Prisoner of the Future
1984 ▲
Rollerball
Soylent Green
10th Victim ▲
THX 1138 ▲
Whodunit
Zardoz

New Black Cinema

see also *African America; Blaxploitation*

Bamboozled
Belly
Boyz N the Hood ▲
Clockers ▲
Crooklyn ▲
Do the Right Thing ▲
The Five Heartbeats ▲
Get On the Bus ▲
Girl 6
Hangin' with the Homeboys ▲
Hollywood Shuffle
I'm Gonna Git You Sucka ▲
Joe's Bed-Stuy Barbershop: We Cut Heads
Jungle Fever ▲
Just Another Girl on the I.R.T.
Livin' Large
Menace II Society ▲
The Meteor Man
Mo' Better Blues
The Players Club ▲
Poetic Justice
Posse ▲
A Rage in Harlem ▲
School Daze ▲
Set It Off
She's Gotta Have It ▲
Straight out of Brooklyn
To Sleep with Anger ▲

New Orleans

see also *American South*

Albino Alligator
Angel Heart
Band of Angels
The Big Easy ▲
Birth of the Blues
Blues Brothers 2000
Boxcar Blues
Candyman 2: Farewell to the Flesh
Child of Glass
The Cincinnati Kid
Crazy in Alabama
Cry of the Werewolf
The Cure
The Dangerous
The Dark Side of Love
Dead Man Walking ▲
Dixie: Changing Habits ▲
Double Jeopardy
Easy Rider ▲
End of August
False Witness
The Family
The First 9 1/2 Weeks
The Flame of New Orleans ▲
French Quarter
French Quarter Undercover

▲ = rated three bones or higher

French Silk
The Glass Cage
Hard Target
Heaven's Prisoners
Hotel
Interview with the Vampire
The Invisible Avenger
It Happened in New Orleans
J.D.'s Revenge
Judas Kiss
King Creole
Lush
Mardi Gras for the Devil
Mardi Gras Massacre
Mirrors
A Murder of Crows
My Forbidden Past
New Orleans
New Orleans After Dark
Night of the Strangler
One Christmas
Panic in the Streets▲
Passing Glory▲
Pretty Baby▲
Ruby Bridges
A Saintly Switch
Saratoga Trunk
The Savage Bees
Storyville
A Streetcar Named Desire▲
A Streetcar Named Desire
Suddenly, Last Summer▲
Thunderground
Tightrope▲
Toys in the Attic
Tune in Tomorrow
Undercover Blues
The Unholy
Vendetta
Walk on the Wild Side

New Year's Eve

see also Christmas; Holidays; Horrible Holidays

About Last Night...▲
The Art of War
The Best Man
Bloodhounds of Broadway
Bloody New Year
Century
Doctor Who
End of Days
The Enforcer
Entrapment
Gridlock'd▲
Happy New Year▲
A Happy New Year!
Happy New Year
Hav Plenty▲
Holiday Affair
The Hudsucker Proxy▲
The January Man
More about the Children of Noisy Village
New Year's Day▲
New Year's Evil
1999
Peter's Friends
Plan B
The Poseidon Adventure
The Real Thing
Strange Days▲
The Sum of Us▲
200 Cigarettes
Virtual Seduction
Waiting to Exhale▲
When Harry Met Sally...▲

New York, New York

see also The Empire State Building

Across 110th Street
Addicted to Love
Addicted to Murder 2: Tainted Blood
Addicted to Murder 3: Bloodlust
The Addiction
An Affair to Remember
After Hours▲
Aftershock: Earthquake in New York
Alice▲
All About Eve▲
All Over Me▲
All That Jazz▲
All the Vermeers in New York▲
Alphabet City
Amarilly of Clothesline Alley
American Psycho
Analyze This▲
The Anderson Tapes▲
Angelo My Love▲
Angels with Dirty Faces▲
Anne of Green Gables: The Continuing Story
Annie
Annie▲
Annie Hall▲
Another Woman▲
The Apartment▲
Armageddon
The Art of War
Arthur▲
Arthur 2: On the Rocks
As Good As It Gets▲
The Astronaut's Wife
At First Sight
Autumn in New York
Awakenings▲
Bad Lieutenant▲
Barefoot in the Park▲
The Basketball Diaries
Basquiat▲
The Beautician and the Beast
The Beautiful, the Bloody and the Bare
Because of Him
Because of You
Bed of Roses
Before Night Falls▲
Being John Malkovich▲
Big▲
The Big Bus
Big Business
Big Night
Big Street
Blackboard Jungle▲
The Blackout
Blade
Bless the Child
Blink
Bloodhounds of Broadway
Bloodmoon
Blue in the Face
Blue Skies▲
Blue Steel
Boiler Room▲
Bonanno: A Godfather's Story
The Bone Collector
The Bonfire of the Vanities
Booty Call
Boricua's Bond
Born to Win
Boss of Bosses
The Bostonians
The Break
Breakfast at Tiffany's▲
Breathing Room
Bright Lights, Big City
Brighton Beach Memoirs
Bringing Out the Dead
Broadway Bound
Broadway Damage
Broadway Danny Rose▲
The Broadway Drifter
Broadway Limited
Broadway Melody
Broadway Melody of 1936▲
Broadway Melody of 1938
Broadway Melody of 1940
Broadway Rhythm
Broadway Serenade
The Bronx Executioner
A Bronx Tale▲
The Bronx War
The Brother from Another Planet▲
A Brother's Kiss
Bullet
Bullets over Broadway▲
Burnzy's Last Call
Cafe Society
Carlito's Way▲
Carnal Knowledge▲
Carnegie Hall
Cat People
The Caveman's Valentine
Center Stage
Chain of Desire
Changing Lanes▲
Chelsea Walls
A Chorus Line
Chutney Popcorn
City Hall▲
City Slickers▲
Claire Dolan
Clockers▲
Cocktail
The Cocoanuts
Codename: Jaguar
Collected Stories▲
The Collectors
Color of Justice
Coming Soon
Coming to America▲
Compromising Positions
Conspiracy Theory▲
Coogan's Bluff▲
Corrupt
The Corruptor▲
The Cotton Club▲
A Couch in New York
The Cowboy Way
Coyote Ugly
The Cradle Will Rock
Crimes & Misdemeanors▲
Crocodile Dundee▲
Crocodile Dundee 2
Crooklyn▲
Crossing Delancey▲
Crossroads
The Crowd▲
Cruel Intentions
Cruising
The Curse of the Jade Scorpion
Dark Odyssey
David Searching
Day at the Beach
Daylight
The Daytrippers
Dead Funny
Dead Presidents
Death to Smoochy
The Deli
Desolation Angels
Desperate Characters▲
Desperately Seeking Susan
Detective Story▲
The Devil's Advocate
The Devil's Own▲
Die Hard: With a Vengeance
Disappearing Acts
Do the Right Thing▲
Dog Day Afternoon▲
Donnie Brasco▲
Don't Say a Word
The Doorbell Rang: A Nero Wolfe Mystery
Double Edge
Down to Earth
Down to You
The Dream Team
Dressed to Kill
Drunks
Easy Living▲
Eddie
Ed's Next Move
84 Charing Cross Road▲
End of Days
Entertaining Angels: The Dorothy Day Story
Escape from New York
Everyone Says I Love You▲
Eyes of Laura Mars
Eyes Wide Shut
Eyewitness
F/X▲
Face Down
Fall
Falling in Love
Fame▲
Fatal Attraction▲
Fear, Anxiety and Depression
Fever
15 Minutes
The Fifth Element
54
Finding Forrester
Fingers▲
Fiona
First Love
The First Wives Club
The Fisher King▲
Flawless
Fleshpot on 42nd Street
Flirt
Focus
For Love or Money
The Foreigner
Fort Apache, the Bronx▲
42nd Street▲
Frankie and Johnny▲
The French Connection▲
Frequency
The Freshman
Frogs for Snakes
The Funeral▲
Funny Girl▲
Games
Get Well Soon
Ghost▲
Ghostbusters▲
Ghostbusters 2
Glitter
Gloria
The Godfather▲
The Godfather, Part 2▲
The Godfather, Part 3▲
Godspell
Godzilla
The Golden Spiders: A Nero Wolfe Mystery
The Goodbye Girl▲
Goodbye, New York
Goodfellas▲
Gossip
Gotti
Grace of My Heart
Gravesend
Great Expectations
The Great Gatsby
Green Card
Greetings▲
The Guardian
Guys and Dolls▲
Habit
Hair▲
Hamlet▲
Hangin' with the Homeboys▲
Hanging Up
Hannah and Her Sisters▲
Happy Accidents
Harlem Nights
Harry and Tonto▲
Hav Plenty▲
Head Over Heels
Headless Body in Topless Bar
Heartburn▲
Heartstrings
Heaven Help Us
Hello Again
Henry Fool▲
Hester Street▲
Hi-Life
Hi, Mom!▲
High Art
Highlander▲
Highlander: Endgame
His Butler's Sister
His Girl Friday▲
Home Alone 2: Lost in New York
Hoodlum
House of Mirth▲
The Hunger
Hurricane Streets
Husbands and Wives▲
If You Only Knew
Igby Goes Down
I'll Be Yours
Illuminata
I'm Not Rappaport
Intern
It Could Happen to You
It Happened in Brooklyn
It Should Happen to You▲
Italian Movie
It's My Turn
Jane Doe
The January Man
Jeffrey
Joe
Joe Gould's Secret
Joe's Apartment
Joe's Bed-Stuy Barbershop: We Cut Heads
Johnny Suede
Juice
Jumpin' Jack Flash
Jungle Fever▲
Jungle 2 Jungle
Just One Time
Just the Ticket
K-PAX
Kate & Leopold
Keeping the Faith
Key Exchange
Kicked in the Head
Kids
Kill by Inches
Killer Condom
King Kong▲
King of Comedy▲
King of New York▲
King of the Gypsies
King of the Jungle
Kiss Me, Guido
Klute▲
Kramer vs. Kramer▲
Lady on a Train▲
The Last Days of Disco▲
Last Exit to Brooklyn▲
The Last Seduction▲
Laws of Gravity▲
Legal Eagles
Let It Snow
The Life and Times of Hank Greenberg▲
A Life of Her Own
Light Sleeper
Liquid Sky▲
Lisa Picard Is Famous
Little Miss Marker▲
Living in Oblivion▲
Living Out Loud
Lonely in America
Look Who's Talking, Too
Looking for Richard▲
The Lords of Flatbush
Loser
Lost in Yonkers
Lotto Land
Love Affair
Love at First Bite
Love Is Better Than Ever
Love Story▲
Lullaby of Broadway
Lulu on the Bridge
Ma and Pa Kettle Go to Town
Made
Malcolm X▲
Mambo Cafe
Man of the Century
The Manchurian Candidate▲
Manhattan▲
Manhattan Melodrama▲
Manhattan Merenque!
Manhattan Merry-Go-Round
Manhattan Murder Mystery▲
Marathon Man▲
Marty▲
Maximum Risk
Maze
Mean Streets▲
Mercy
Metropolitan▲
Mickey Blue Eyes
Midnight Cowboy▲
Mighty Aphrodite
Mimic
Mimic 2
The Minion
Minnie and Moskowitz
Miracle on 34th Street▲
Miracle on 34th Street
The Mirror Has Two Faces
Mirrors
Misery▲
Mrs. Parker and the Vicious Circle
Mrs. Santa Claus
Mr. Blandings Builds His Dream House▲
Mr. Jealousy
Mixing Nia
Mo' Better Blues
Money Train
Moon over Broadway
Morning Glory
Mortal Thoughts
Moscow on the Hudson▲
The Muppets Take Manhattan▲
Music of the Heart
My Favorite Year▲
My Little Assassin
My Man Godfrey▲
My Sister Eileen▲
Nadja▲
The Naked City▲
Naked City: A Killer Christmas
Naked City: Justice with a Bullet
Naked in New York
The Natural▲
Network▲
New Jack City
New York Cop
New York, New York▲
New York Nights
New York Ripper
New York Stories▲
New York's Finest
News from Home
Next Stop, Greenwich Village▲
Next Year in Jerusalem
Nick and Jane
Nico Icon▲
Night and the City▲
Night Falls on Manhattan▲
Night on Earth▲
The Night They Raided Minsky's▲
The Night We Never Met
9 1/2 Weeks
1931: Once Upon a Time in New York
The Ninth Gate
No Such Thing
Nueba Yol
The Object of My Affection
The Odd Couple▲
Off Beat
Olga's Girls
Oliver & Company
On the Town▲
On the Waterfront▲
Once in the Life
Once Upon a Time in America▲
One Fine Day
One Tough Cop
Only When I Laugh▲
Our Song▲
The Out-of-Towners▲
The Out-of-Towners
Outrageous!▲
The Painted Lady▲
Panic in Needle Park▲
Panic Room
The Paper▲
Paradise Alley
Paradise in Harlem
Paris Is Burning▲
The Park Is Mine
Party Girl
Passion of Mind
Path to Paradise
The Peacemaker
A Perfect Murder
Permanent Vacation
Personals
The Phantom
Pi
The Pick-Up Artist
Pillow Talk▲
Pinero
Plaza Suite▲
Pollock▲
The Pompatus of Love
The Pope of Greenwich Village
Portrait of Jennie▲
Postcards from America
A Price above Rubies
The Prince of Central Park▲
Prince of Central Park
Prince of the City▲
The Prince of Tides▲
The Princess & the Call Girl
Prisoner of Second Avenue
Private Parts
The Public Eye▲
Pushing Tin▲
The Quest
Quick Change
Radio Days▲
A Rage in Harlem▲
Rage of the Werewolf
Raging Bull▲
Ragtime▲
A Raisin in the Sun▲
Ransom▲

▲ = rated three bones or higher

The Rat Race▲
A Rat's Tale
Ready to Wear
The Real Blonde
Rear Window▲
Return to Paradise▲
Ride
Rift
Risk▲
The Roaring Twenties▲
Rockabye
Rosemary's Baby▲
Rounders
The Royal Tenenbaums▲
Rumble in the Bronx
Runaway Bride▲
The Saint in New York
Saturday Night Fever
Scent of a Woman▲
Scrooged
Searching for Bobby Fischer▲
Serendipity
Serpico▲
Seven▲
The Seven-Ups
The Seven Year Itch▲
Shadows and Fog
ShadowZone: The Undead Express
Shaft▲
She-Devil
She's Gotta Have It▲
She's the One
Shining Star
Sidewalks of New York
The Siege
Single White Female
Six Degrees of Separation
61*▲
Slaves of New York
Sleepers
Sliver
Small Time Crooks
Smithereens
Someone Else's America▲
Someone Like You
Something Short of Paradise
Something Wild
Somewhere in the City
Sophie's Choice▲
The Spanish Prisoner▲
Speedy▲
Spider-Man▲
Splash
Stage Door▲
State of Grace▲
Staying Alive
Stepmom▲
Stepping Out▲
The Sticky Fingers of Time
Still of the Night
Stonewall▲
Straight out of Brooklyn
Stranger than Paradise▲
Street Scene▲
Street Smart
Street Trash
Stuart Little 2
The Substance of Fire
The Substitute 2: School's Out
Subway Stories
Sudden Manhattan
Sugar Hill
Summer of Sam
Sunday
Sunset Park
The Super
Superfly
Sweet Charity▲
Sweet Nothing▲
Sweet Smell of Success▲
Tadpole
The Taking of Pelham One Two Three▲
Talk to Me
Tart
Tarzan's New York Adventure
The Tavern
Taxi Driver▲
The 10th Kingdom
They Call It Sin
The Thomas Crown Affair▲
3 A.M.▲
Three Days of the Condor▲
Three Men and a Baby▲
Through the Eyes of a Killer
The Tic Code
Timeless
Times Square
To Catch a Yeti
Tootsie▲
Torch Song Trilogy
Town and Country
Trash
A Tree Grows in Brooklyn▲
Trick▲
A Troll in Central Park
True Blue
The 24 Hour Woman
29th Street
Twisted
2 by 4
Two Girls and a Guy▲
200 Cigarettes
Two Ninas
Underground U.S.A.
Unfaithful
An Unmarried Woman▲
Untamed Heart
Unzipped▲
Up in Central Park
Uptown New York
Urbania
Vampire in Brooklyn
Vanilla Sky
Vanya on 42nd Street▲
Variety
The Velocity of Gary
A Very Natural Thing
The Waiting Game
Walking and Talking
Wall Street▲
Walls of Glass
Washington Square▲
The Way We Were▲
The Wedding Party
We're Back! A Dinosaur's Story
West Side Story▲
When Harry Met Sally...▲
Where Were You When the Lights Went Out?
Whipped
Who's That Knocking at My Door?▲
Wild Style
Wirey Spindell
Wise Guys
Witness to the Mob
Wolf
Wolfen▲
Working Girl▲
X-Men
The Yards
Year of the Dragon
You've Got Mail

New Zealand

see Down Under

Newlyweds

see also Wedding Bells

Chunhyang
The Heartbreak Kid▲
Honeymoon Academy
Honeymoon Horror
The Long, Long Trailer
Made for Each Other▲
Mannequin
Mr. & Mrs. Loving▲
The Ponder Heart
She's Having a Baby
10

Newspapers

see Front Page

Niagara Falls

The Long Kiss Goodnight
Niagara
Niagara, Niagara

Nice Mice

An American Tail
An American Tail: Fievel Goes West
Babe▲
Babe: Pig in the City
Escape from Alcatraz▲
The Great Mouse Detective▲
The Green Mile
Mouse and His Child
Mouse Hunt▲
A Rat's Tale
Ratz
The Rescuers▲
The Rescuers Down Under
Road Trip
The Secret of NIMH▲
Sitcom
Stuart Little
Stuart Little 2

Nightclubs

The Adventures of Pluto Nash
Amateur Night
Animal Instincts
Backbeat▲
Be Yourself
Berlin Blues
Better Than Chocolate
Birth of the Blues
Black Angel▲
Black Glove
The Blue Angel▲
Body Shots
Born Romantic
The Bride Wore Red
A Bunny's Tale
Bus Stop▲
Cabaret▲
Cabaret Balkan
Cafe Society
Can-Can
Carnival Rock
Casablanca▲
CB4: The Movie
Chameleon 2: Death Match
Club Havana
Copacabana
The Cotton Club▲
Dance, Girl, Dance
Dance Hall Racket
Dancing at the Blue Iguana
Dark Secrets
Deadly Revenge
Desperate Cargo
Dick Tracy▲
Dracula Blows His Cool
The Dreamlife of Angels▲
The Fabulous Baker Boys▲
Fake Out
Femmes de Paris
54
Flaming Lead
Foxstyle
Framed
French Can-Can▲
The French Way
Fun in Acapulco
G.I. Blues
Girls! Girls! Girls!
Harlem Nights
It Started in Naples▲
Jive Junction
The Killing of a Chinese Bookie
King Creole
La Cage aux Folles▲
La Cage aux Folles 2
La Cage aux Folles 3: The Wedding
Lady on a Train▲
Lambada
The Last Days of Disco▲
Last Night at the Alamo▲
Le Samourai▲
Lenny▲
Like It Is▲
Liquid Dreams
Little Shots of Happiness
Love Come Down
Love Jones▲
Lullaby of Broadway
Lured
Machine Gun Blues
Mad Dog and Glory▲
The Mambo Kings▲
Marked Woman▲
Martial Law 2: Undercover
Mickey One
Midnight Warrior
Mighty Joe Young
Miracles
Morocco▲
Moulin Rouge
New Orleans
Night After Night
A Night at the Roxbury
A Night in Heaven
The Night They Raided Minsky's▲
No Surrender▲
The Nutty Professor▲
Pandora and the Flying Dutchman
A Paradise Under the Stars
Party Girl▲
Party Girl
Pecker
Pete Kelly's Blues
Play Murder for Me
Playing by Heart
The Public Eye▲
Rebel
Ripper Man
Ruby
Ruby's Dream
The Score
Sea Racketeers
Sex, Drugs, and Rock-n-Roll
Shanghai Triad▲
The Shining Hour
Showgirls
Smash-Up: The Story of a Woman▲
So Close to Paradise
Stonewall▲
Suffering Bastards
Sweet Evil
Swingers▲
That Naughty Girl
30 Is a Dangerous Age, Cynthia
To Catch a King
Treasure of the Moon Goddess
Trigger Happy
200 Cigarettes
Undercurrent
Underground U.S.A.
Uptown Saturday Night
Vamp
Whistle Stop
A Woman Is a Woman▲
Wonderland▲
Woo
Xanadu
The Zoo Gang

Ninjas

see also Martial Arts

Black Tight Killers▲
Ninja in the U.S.A.
3 Ninjas Kick Back

Ninjitsu

see Martial Arts

No-Exit Motel

see also Grand Hotel

Cheap Shots
Dead Simple
Eaten Alive
Memento▲
Motel Hell
Mountaintop Motel Massacre
The Newlydeads
Pink Motel
Poor Pretty Eddie
Psycho▲
Psycho
Psycho 2
Psycho 3
Psycho 4: The Beginning
Slaughter Hotel
Tape▲

Not-So-True Identity

Above Suspicion
Albino Alligator
The Amazing Mrs. Holiday
Apt Pupil
Armistead Maupin's Tales of the City
The Associate
Autumn Sun▲
Big Momma's House
Black Like Me
Blue Streak
Boys Don't Cry▲
The Breaks
Catherine's Grove
Charlotte Gray
The Claim
Corky Romano
The Cotton Club▲
The Count of Monte Cristo
Deceived
Defying Gravity
Devil in the Flesh 2
Europa, Europa▲
Exit Wounds
Face/Off▲
For Richer or Poorer
Forever Mine
Gattaca▲
Gentleman's Agreement▲
Good Advice
Gosford Park▲
The Governess
Grey Owl
Gun Shy
Happy, Texas▲
Head Over Heels
High Crimes
Homegrown
I Married a Dead Man
If You Only Knew
Imitation of Life
Imitation of Life▲
The Importance of Being Earnest
Imposter
A Knight's Tale
The Lady Eve▲
The Legend of Rita
Les Miserables▲
The Long Kiss Goodnight
Lost Boundaries
The Major and the Minor▲
Mask of Death
The Mask of Zorro▲
Master of Disguise
Mrs. Winterbourne
Model Behavior
Mother Night▲
Mulan
Mulholland Drive▲
Mumford▲
Never Been Kissed
Nevil Shute's The Far Country
Olivier, Olivier▲
Orlando▲
Our Mutual Friend
Out to Sea
The Painted Lady▲
A Paradise Under the Stars
The Parent Trap
Pinky▲
The Prince and the Surfer
Princess of Thieves
The Principal Takes a Holiday
The Quarry
The Rowdy Girls
The Saint
The Scarlet Pimpernel▲
The Scarlet Pimpernel
The Scarlet Pimpernel 2: Mademoiselle Guillotine
The Scarlet Pimpernel 3: The Kidnapped King
The Secret Agent
Shadows▲
Shallow Hal
The Silencer
Soul Man
The Tailor of Panama▲
Taking Care of Business
The Talented Mr. Ripley
Texas Trouble
The Thief
Three to Tango
Train of Life
Trial and Error
The Triumph of Love
True Identity
The Truman Show▲
Twin Dragons
Two Shades of Blue
Virtual Sexuality
What the Deaf Man Heard▲
The Witness Files

Nuclear Disaster

see Disaster Flicks; Meltdown

Nuns & Priests

see also Missionaries; Religion; Religious Epics

Absolution
Agnes of God
The Agony and the Ecstasy
All About My Mother▲
Amateur▲
The American
Angels with Dirty Faces▲
Anna
The Apostate
The Assisi Underground
The Atonement of Gosta Berling▲
Beautiful Hunter
Becket▲
The Bells of St. Mary's▲
Black Narcissus▲
Black Robe▲
Blues Brothers 2000
The Body
Body & Soul▲
The Boys of St. Vincent▲
Brides of Christ
The Bridge of San Luis Rey▲
Camila▲
The Cardinal
Change of Habit
Changing Habits
Child of Darkness, Child of Light
Chocolat▲
Cold Justice
Come to the Stable▲
The Confession
The Confessional
The Confessional▲
Conspiracy of Hearts▲
The Cross & the Switchblade
Cry, the Beloved Country▲
Curse 4: The Ultimate Sacrifice
Daens
Damien: The Leper Priest
The Dangerous Lives of Altar Boys
The Day of the Beast
Dead Man Walking▲
Dead Waters
Death of an Angel
Demonia
The Detective▲
The Devils▲
The Devil's Playground▲
Diary of a Country Priest▲
The Divine Enforcer
Dixie: Changing Habits▲
The Eighteenth Angel
Elmer Gantry▲
End of Days
The End of the Affair▲
End of the World
The Exorcist▲
The Exorcist 2: The Heretic
Extramuros
The Father Clements Story
Fighting Father Dunne
First Legion
For Better and for Worse
Forever Young
40 Days and 40 Nights
The Fugitive▲
The Garden of Redemption
Gentleman Bandit
Going My Way▲
Gospa
Heaven Knows, Mr. Allison▲
Hideous Kinky
A Home of Our Own
Hot Under the Collar
I Confess
I Heard the Owl Call My Name
I, the Worst of All
In the Region of Ice▲
In This House of Brede▲
Jesus of Montreal▲

▲ = rated three bones or higher

Judgment▲
Keeping the Faith
Kid Monk Baroni
Knocks at My Door
Lamb
The Last Don 2
Last Rites
The Left Hand of God▲
Leon Morin, Priest
Liam
Lilies of the Field▲
Los Locos Posse
Loyola, the Soldier Saint
Madeline
Mass Appeal
Massacre in Rome
Mission to Glory
Molokai: The Story of Father Damien
Monsignor
Mortal Sins
Most Wanted
Mother Joan of the Angels▲
The Name of the Rose
Nasty Habits
Nazarin▲
Night of the Assassin
Night of the Demons 2
Night Sun
The Nun
Nuns on the Run
The Nun's Story▲
Oscar and Lucinda
Passing Glory▲
Pier 23
Pope John Paul II
The Pope Must Diet
The Possessed
Possessed
Prayer for the Dying
Priest
Primal Fear
Prince of Darkness
The Prisoner▲
The Private War of Major Benson
The Proposition
The Ravagers
The Red Inn
Revenge of the Musketeers
Romance
The Rosary Murders
The Runner Stumbles
Sanctuary
Saving Grace
The Scarlet & the Black
Scary Movie 2
Second Sight
Secret Ingredient
September Gun
Shattered Vows
The Shoes of the Fisherman
Silver Bullet
The Singing Nun
Sister Act
Sister Act 2: Back in the Habit
Sisters of Satan
Sleepers
Sorceress▲
Soul Survivors
The Sound of Music▲
Spirits
Stigmata
Therese▲
The Third Miracle
To Kill a Priest
Trouble along the Way
The Trouble with Angels
True Confessions▲
Under Satan's Sun▲
Under the Red Robe
The Unholy
Vatican Conspiracy
Wanted
We're No Angels
Where Angels Go, Trouble Follows
The White Sister▲
Wide Awake

Nuns with Guns

The Enforcer
Girlfriend from Hell
Ms. 45▲
Nuns on the Run
Two Mules for Sister Sara▲
We're No Angels

Nursploitation!

see also *Doctors & Nurses; Sexploitation*

Candy Stripe Nurses
Emmanuelle in the Country
Hospital of Terror
Inner Sanctum
Naked Massacre
Night Call Nurses
Nurse on Call
Private Duty Nurses
The Sensuous Nurse
The Student Nurses
Tender Loving Care
The Young Nurses
Young Nurses in Love

Obsessive Love

Aaron Loves Angela
Addicted to Love
After Sex
Against All Odds
Anna Karenina▲
Anna Karenina
The Aviator's Wife▲
The Best Man
Betty Blue▲
Beyond the Clouds
Brief Encounter▲
Can't Buy Me Love
Cause Celebre▲
The Center of the World
Chungking Express▲
The Climax
Crazy Moon
The Crush
Cupid
Cyrano de Bergerac▲
Cyrano de Bergerac
Cyrano de Bergerac▲
Damage▲
Danger of Love
Death and Desire
Deceptions 2: Edge of Deception
Deep Crimson
Devil in the Flesh
Devil in the Flesh 2
8 1/2 Women
El
Emily Bronte's Wuthering Heights
End of the Affair
The End of the Affair▲
Endless Love
The English Patient▲
Eva
The Ex
Eye of God▲
Eye of the Beholder
Far from the Madding Crowd▲
Fatal Attraction▲
Fear
First Love, Last Rites
For Sale
Ghost▲
The Heartbreak Kid▲
Her and She and Him
Homage
Hush
I Want You
Jealousy
Junk Mail
Kama Sutra: A Tale of Love
Last Breath
L'Ennui
Leo Tolstoy's Anna Karenina
Letters from a Killer
Live Flesh▲
Lost and Delirious
Love and Death on Long Island
Love and Rage
Loved
Mad Love
Mararia
Midnight Blue
Mr. Wrong
The Mystery of Edwin Drood
One Kill▲
Only Love
Our Mutual Friend
The Phantom of the Opera▲
The Phantom of the Opera
A Place in the Sun▲
Plain Jane
Romeo and Juliet▲
Romeo and Juliet
Romeo and Juliet▲
Roxanne▲
Sabrina▲
Sabrina
Sea of Love▲
Shades of Black
Show Boat▲
Show Boat
Skin Deep
Some Kind of Wonderful
Temptress Moon
10
A Thin Line Between Love and Hate
To Gillian on Her 37th Birthday
Truly, Madly, Deeply▲
Twisted Love
Twisted Obsession
West Side Story▲
Wilde
Wuthering Heights▲
Wuthering Heights

Occult

see also *Demons & Wizards; Satanism; Witchcraft*

Alabama's Ghost
The Amazing Mr. X
The American Scream
Amityville Dollhouse
Apprentice to Murder
Army of Darkness▲
Bad Dreams
Barbarian Queen
Because of the Cats
The Believers
Beyond Dream's Door
Beyond Evil
Beyond the Door 3
The Black Cat
Black Circle Boys
Black Magic Terror
Black Magic Woman
Blackbeard's Ghost
Bless the Child
Blood Diner
The Blood on Satan's Claw▲
Blood Orgy of the She-Devils
Bloodspell
Born of Fire
The Brainiac
Brimstone & Treacle▲
The Brotherhood of Satan
The Burning Court
Cabin in the Sky▲
Cat Girl
Cat in the Cage
The Cellar
Chandu on the Magic Island
Child of Glass
Children Shouldn't Play with Dead Things
Come Along with Me
The Craft
Craze
The Curse of the Crying Woman
Curse of the Demon▲
Curse of the Devil
Damien: Omen 2
Damn Yankees▲
Dance with the Devil
The Dark Secret of Harvest Home
Dead Men Don't Die
Deathstalker 4: Match of Titans
Deep Red: Hatchet Murders
Demon Possessed
Demon Rage
Demon Wind
Demonoid, Messenger of Death
Demons 2
Demons of Ludlow
The Devil & Daniel Webster▲
Devil Dog: The Hound of Hell
Devil Doll▲
Devil Doll
The Devils▲
The Devil's Daughter
The Devil's Eye
Devil's Gift
The Devil's Hand
The Devil's Mistress
The Devil's Nightmare
Devil's Rain
Devil's Son-in-Law
Diary of a Madman
Dick Tracy, Detective
Doctor Faustus
Dr. Strange
Dominique Is Dead
Dona Flor and Her Two Husbands▲
Donovan's Brain▲
Don't Be Afraid of the Dark
Dream Man
Dreamscape
The Dunwich Horror
The Dybbuk▲
The Dying Truth
Encounter with the Unknown
The Entity
Equinox▲
Eternal Evil
The Evictors
The Evil
Evil Altar
Evil Dead
Evil Dead 2: Dead by Dawn
The Evil Mind
Evilspeak
Excalibur▲
Exorcism
The Exorcist▲
The Exorcist 2: The Heretic
Exorcist 3: Legion
Eye of the Demon
Eyes of Fire
Fallen
Feast for the Devil
The First Power
The Fish that Saved Pittsburgh
Four Rooms
Fright House
Full Circle
Gates of Hell 2: Dead Awakening
Genie of Darkness
Ghosts That Still Walk
The Girl in a Swing
God Told Me To
Grave Secrets
The Guardian
Half of Heaven▲
Hanussen▲
Haunted Symphony
Haxan: Witchcraft through the Ages▲
The Hearse
Horror Hotel
House of the Yellow Carpet
The House on Skull Mountain
The House that Bled to Death
I Don't Want to Be Born
I'm Dangerous Tonight
Inferno
Inner Sanctum
Into the Badlands
The Invasion of Carol Enders
Invasion of the Blood Farmers
Kill, Baby, Kill▲
Killing Hour
The Kingdom▲
The Kingdom 2▲
The Kiss
KISS Meets the Phantom of the Park
Lady Terminator
Land of the Minotaur
The Legacy
The Legend of Hell House▲
Leonor
Life-Size
The Living Head
Lost Souls
The Magician▲
Making Contact
The Mangler
Manos, the Hands of Fate
Mardi Gras for the Devil
Mardi Gras Massacre
Maxim Xul
Medea
Men of Two Worlds
Midnight
Midnight Cabaret
Mirror, Mirror
Mirror, Mirror 2: Raven Dance
Mirror of Death
Mirrors
Mists of Avalon▲
The Monster Demolisher
Mystic Circle Murder
Natas ... The Reflection
Necromancer: Satan's Servant
Necropolis
The Night Stalker
The Night Strangler
Ninja, the Violent Sorcerer
The Occultist
Omen 3: The Final Conflict
Omoo Omoo, the Shark God
Only You
The Oracle
Orgy of the Dead
Out on a Limb
Phantasm
Phantasm 2
Phantasm 3: Lord of the Dead
Poltergeist▲
Poltergeist 2: The Other Side
Poltergeist 3
Possession: Until Death Do You Part
The Power
The Psychic
Psychic
Psychic Killer
Psychomania
Puppet Master
Quest of the Delta Knights
Race with the Devil
The Raven▲
A Reflection of Fear
The Reincarnate
Rendez-Moi Ma Peau
Repossessed
Rest in Pieces
Retribution
Return
Return from Witch Mountain
Return of Chandu
Rosemary's Baby▲
Ruby
Run If You Can
The Runestone
Sabaka
Satan's Princess
Satan's Touch
Scared Stiff
Season of the Witch
Second Sight
Seduced by Evil
Seizure
Sensation
The Sentinel
The Seventh Sign
The Seventh Victim▲
The Shaman
Shock 'Em Dead
Silent Night, Deadly Night 3: Better Watch Out!
Sorceress
The Spaniard's Curse
Speak of the Devil
The Spellbinder
Spellbound
Spiritism
Student of Prague▲
Summer of Fear
Supergirl
Teen Witch
The Tempter
Temptress
Terror Beach
Terror Creatures from the Grave
That Darn Sorceress
Three Sovereigns for Sarah
To the Devil, a Daughter
The Torture Chamber of Dr. Sadism
The Touch of Satan
Treasure of the Four Crowns
The Undead
Unknown Powers
Venus in Furs
Vibes
The Visitor
Warlock Moon
White Gorilla
Who Killed Doc Robbin?
The Wicker Man▲
Wild Man
Wishmaster
Witch Hunt
Witch Who Came from the Sea
Witchboard
Witchboard 2: The Devil's Doorway
Witchboard 3: The Possession
Witchcraft 2: The Temptress
Witchcraft 4: Virgin Heart
Witchcraft 5: Dance with the Devil
The Witches of Eastwick
The Witching
Witching Time
The Witchmaker
The Witch's Mirror
The Wizard of Oz▲
Wizards
The Woman Who Came Back
Zapped Again
The Zodiac Killer

Oceans

see *Deep Blue; Go Fish; Killer Sea Critters; Mutiny; Scuba; Shipwrecked; Submarines*

Office Surprise

Casino▲
Dead Again▲
Dial "M" for Murder▲
Die Hard▲
Goldeneye▲
Grosse Pointe Blank▲
Henry: Portrait of a Serial Killer▲
La Femme Nikita▲
Misery▲
Mission: Impossible▲
9 to 5
Office Killer
Point of No Return
The Temp

Oil

see *Black Gold*

Oldest Profession

see also *Women in Prison*

Accatone!▲
Alexander: The Other Side of Dawn
Alien Warrior
The Allnighter
American Gigolo
American Justice
American Nightmare
American Psycho
Amor Bandido
The Amsterdam Connection
Angel
Angel 3: The Final Chapter
Anna Christie▲
Anna Christie
Armistead Maupin's More Tales of the City
Aroused
Avenging Angel
Back Roads
Bad Girls
The Balcony▲
Band of Gold▲
Being at Home with Claude
Belle de Jour▲

▲ = rated three bones or higher

Beloved/Friend
The Best Little Whorehouse in Texas
Beverly Hills Madam
Beverly Hills Vamp
Beyond Desire
Big City Blues
Blood Money: The Story of Clinton and Nadine
Blow Out▲
The Blue Hour
Blush
Boiling Point
The Book of Stars
Bordello
Boulevard
Broken Mirrors
Butterfield 8▲
Cafe Society
Candy Tangerine Man
Caravaggio▲
Carmen, Baby
Casino▲
Catherine & Co.
Celebrity▲
Chained Heat 2
The Cheyenne Social Club
Christiane F.▲
Cinderella Liberty▲
The Claim
Claire Dolan
Class of 1984
Club Life
Coffy
The Confessional▲
Confessions of a Vice Baron
The Courtesans of Bombay▲
Cracker: Brotherly Love▲
Crimes of Passion▲
Cross Country
Cry of a Prostitute: Love Kills
Cry, the Beloved Country▲
Cyclo
Dangerous Beauty▲
The Dark Side of the Heart
Dead End Street
Deadly Sanctuary
Death Shot
Death Target
Deceiver
Deconstructing Harry
Dedee d'Anvers
Desperate Crimes
The Desperate Trail
Deuce Bigalow: Male Gigolo
Diamonds
Diary of a Lost Girl▲
The Dirty Girls
Diva▲
Dixie: Changing Habits▲
Doctor Detroit
Dr. Jekyll and Sister Hyde
Double Cross
Dressed to Kill
Drying Up the Streets
8 Million Ways to Die
Elmer Gantry▲
Emily
Emmanuelle & Joanna
Erendira
Eva
Everybody Wins
Fall from Innocence
Fiona
Firepower
Flesh▲
Fleshpot on 42nd Street
Flowers of Shanghai
For Sale
Forbidden Fruit▲
Forever Amber
Foxy Brown
Frankenhooker
Frankie and Johnny
French Quarter
From Hell▲
From the Edge of the City
Full Exposure: The Sex Tape Scandals
Fyre
Gate of Flesh
Get Rita
The Gift
Gigi▲
Girls of the White Orchid
Half Moon Street
The Happy Hooker
The Happy Hooker Goes Hollywood
The Happy Hooker Goes to Washington
Hard Bounty
Hard Vice
Harnessing Peacocks
He Got Game
Heaven or Vegas
Help Wanted Female
High Stakes
Highway
Highway Patrolman
Hindsight
Hollywood Chainsaw Hookers
Hollywood Vice Sqaud
Hot Blooded
Hotel Room
Hurlyburly
The Hustle
Hustler Squad
Hustler White
Hustling▲
I Am Frigid...Why?
I Want to Live!▲
The Immoral One
Impulse
In the Flesh
Intimate Betrayal
Irma La Douce
Italian Movie
Jack's Back▲
Jade
Jamon, Jamon
John Carpenter's Vampires
johns
Just a Gigolo
Justine
Katie Tippel
Killing Zoe
Kinjite: Forbidden Subjects
Kiss of the Dragon
Kiss the Night
Kitty and the Bagman
Klute▲
La Chienne▲
L.A. Confidential▲
L.A. Crackdown
L.A. Crackdown 2
Ladies of the Lotus
Lady in Waiting
Lady of the Evening
Lady of the House
The Last Prostitute
The Last Temptation of Christ▲
Leaving Las Vegas▲
Les Miserables▲
Life of Oharu▲
A Life of Sin
The List
Little Ladies of the Night
Lola Montes▲
Love by Appointment
Love Strange Love
The Mack
Madame Rosa▲
Magdalene
Malibu High
Mamma Roma▲
Man of Flowers
The Man Who Knew Too Little
Mandragora
Manon
Marriage Italian Style▲
Mayflower Madam
McCabe & Mrs. Miller▲
Miami Blues
Mid Knight Rider
Midnight Auto Supply
Midnight Cop
Midnight Cowboy▲
Midnight Dancers
Mifune
The Million Dollar Hotel
Miss Sadie Thompson▲
The Missionary
Mob Queen
Moll Flanders
Mon Homme
Mona Lisa▲
Moulin Rouge
Murderlust
Murphy's Law
My Life to Live▲
My Mother's Secret Life
My Own Private Idaho▲
My Pleasure Is My Business
My Son the Fanatic▲
Naked Kiss
Naked Tango
Nana▲
Nana
Never on Sunday▲
New York's Finest
Night Friend
Night of the Generals▲
Night Shift
Night Slasher
The Night They Robbed Big Bertha's
Nightmare in Badham County
Nights of Cabiria▲
Nightwatch
No One Cries Forever
No Prince for My Cinderella
The Nun
Nuts▲
Off Limits
Oldest Profession
Olivia
One Night Only
Out of the Dark
Padre Nuestro
Pandora's Box▲
Panic in Needle Park▲
Party Girls
The Passing of Evil
Pennies from Heaven▲
Personal Services
Pigalle
Play for Me
The Players Club▲
Poker Alice
Postcards from America
Pretty Baby▲
Pretty Woman▲
Prettykill
Prime Cut
The Princess & the Call Girl
Prison of Secrets
The Pyx▲
Queen Kelly▲
Quick, Let's Get Married
Quiet Days in Hollywood
Rain
Raw Justice
Reason to Die
Red Kimono
Rent-A-Cop
The Ripper
Risky Business▲
Road Movie
Roman Spring of Mrs. Stone▲
Room 43
Roots of Evil
Running Out of Time
Saint Jack▲
Sandakan No. 8▲
Sansho the Bailiff▲
Santitos
Scarred
Schnelles Geld
Scorchers
Secret Games
Secrets of a Married Man
Sessions
Sex, Love and Cold Hard Cash
Shadow of Angels
Sharky's Machine
The Silencer
Single Room Furnished
Sketches of a Strangler
Skin Art
Slaves in Bondage
Speedway Junky
Spenser: Ceremony
SS Girls
Star Maps
Stella Does Tricks
Stone Cold Dead
Story of a Prostitute
Storyville
Street Girls
Street of Forgotten Women
Street of Shame▲
Street Smart
Streetwalkin'
The Substitute Wife
The Sun's Burial▲
Sweet Charity▲
Sweet Revenge
Sweet Sweetback's Baadasssss Song▲
Sweet Trash
The Sword and the Cross
Talons of the Eagle
Taxi Driver▲
They Were So Young
Things
Things to Do in Denver When You're Dead▲
Thousand Pieces of Gold▲
Three Seasons
Tightrope▲
The Toilers and the Wayfarers
Tokyo Decadence
Too Young to Die
Trading Places
Traffic in Souls▲
Train Station Pickups
Tricks
Tricks of the Trade
Truck Stop Women
Twenty Dollar Star
Twin Falls Idaho▲
Twin Peaks: Fire Walk with Me
Twin Sisters
Twisted
Two or Three Things I Know about Her
Ultimate Desires
Uncaged
Utamaro and His Five Women
The Vampire Hookers
Via Appia
Vice Squad
Vicious Circles
Walk on the Wild Side
Warm Nights on a Slow-Moving Train
Warrior Queen
Waterloo Bridge▲
Whore
Whore 2
The Wicked, Wicked West
Wild Bill
Wild Orchid 2: Two Shades of Blue
Wild Side
The Winter of Our Dreams
A Woman in Flames▲
A Woman of Rome
Working Girls
Working Girls▲
The World of Suzie Wong

The Olympics

***see also** Sports Dramas*

Alex
American Anthem
Best of the Best
Blades of Courage
Blast
Breaking the Surface: The Greg Louganis Story
Chariots of Fire▲
Cool Runnings
Crossbar
The Cutting Edge
The First Olympics: Athens 1896
Going for the Gold: The Bill Johnson Story
International Velvet
The Jesse Owens Story
The Loretta Claiborne Story
A Million to One
Miracle on Ice
Pentathlon
Personal Best▲
Prefontaine
Rowing Through
Run for the Dream: The Gail Devers Story
Running Brave
Special Olympics
Sword of Gideon
Tokyo Olympiad
21 Hours at Munich▲
Walk, Don't Run
Wilma
Without Limits▲

On the Rocks

***see also** Drug Abuse*

Aberdeen
Affliction▲
Angela's Ashes
Arthur▲
Arthur 2: On the Rocks
Barfly▲
Betty
The Big Hangover
The Big Lebowski▲
Black Angel▲
Blue Heaven
Bounce
Break of Hearts
The Butcher Boy▲
Casino▲
Cat on a Hot Tin Roof▲
Cat on a Hot Tin Roof
The Chamber
Chelsea Walls
Clean and Sober▲
Cocktail
Come Back, Little Sheba▲
Cop-Out
Country Girl▲
Country Girl
Country Life
crazy/beautiful
The Crossing Guard▲
A Cry for Love
Dance of Life
Dancer, Texas—Pop. 81▲
Danger in the Skies
Dangerous
Dash and Lilly
Days of Wine and Roses
Days of Wine and Roses▲
Desert Bloom▲
The Devil at 4 O'Clock
The Devil Thumbs a Ride▲
Dona Flor and Her Two Husbands▲
Drunken Angel▲
Drunks
Educating Rita▲
8 Heads in a Duffel Bag
El Dorado▲
The Electric Horseman
The Entertainer▲
Eye of the Killer
F. Scott Fitzgerald in Hollywood
Fat City▲
The Fire Within▲
Fish Hawk
The Flaming Teen-Age
Flesh and Bone▲
Floating
Frances▲
A Free Soul
Georgia▲
Gervaise▲
The Great Man Votes▲
The Green Man▲
Heaven's Prisoners
Honkytonk Man
Hot Summer in Barefoot County
I Live with Me Dad
I'll Cry Tomorrow▲
The Informer▲
Ironweed▲
Izzy & Moe
Jack and Sarah
Jack the Bear
Joe the King
Kill Cruise
La Cucaracha
The Last American Hero▲
Last Time Out
Le Beau Serge▲
Leaving Las Vegas▲
License to Kill
Little Boy Blue
Little Voice▲
Living Proof: The Hank Williams Jr. Story
Long Day's Journey into Night▲
Long Day's Journey into Night
Long Day's Journey Into Night▲
The Lost Weekend▲
Lush
M.A.D.D.: Mothers Against Drunk Driving
Marvin & Tige
Matter of Trust
Mean Dog Blues
Mrs. Parker and the Vicious Circle
The Morning After
My Favorite Year▲
My Name Is Joe
No Laughing Matter
No Such Thing
Once Were Warriors▲
One for the Road
100 Proof
One Too Many
Only When I Laugh▲
Papa's Delicate Condition▲
Place Vendome▲
Police Court
Pollock▲
Pushing Tin▲
Reuben, Reuben▲
River Red
The Robe
Rosetta
Scent of a Woman▲
The Secret Rapture
Shakes the Clown
She's So Lovely
The Sin of Harold Diddlebock
The Singing Blacksmith
Skin Deep
Sling Blade▲
Smash-Up: The Story of a Woman▲
Somebody Is Waiting
Spent
A Star Is Born▲
A Star Is Born
Straight Up
Stranded
Strange Brew
Struggle
Stuart Saves His Family
Tales of Ordinary Madness
Ten Nights in a Bar Room
Ten Nights in a Bar-Room
The Tenant of Wildfell Hall
Termini Station
Tree's Lounge
True Crime
24-7
28 Days
Under Capricorn
Under the Volcano▲
Unnatural Pursuits
The Verdict▲
Wagons East
What Price Hollywood?▲
When a Man Loves a Woman
Whiskey Galore▲
White Lightning
Willa
The Winning Team
A Winter Tan

One Last Job

***see also** Crime Drama; Heists; Hit Men/Women; Organized Crime; Scams, Stings & Cons*

Dillinger and Capone
Entrapment
Going in Style▲
Gone in 60 Seconds
Heat▲
Heist▲
Out of Sight▲
The Ref▲
Reindeer Games
The Score
Sexy Beast▲
Small Time Crooks
The Squeeze
Things to Do in Denver When You're Dead▲
Tough Guys
Two If by Sea
The Usual Suspects▲

Only the Lonely

Abducted
The Abduction of Kari Swenson
All That Heaven Allows▲
Amelie▲

▲ = *rated three bones or higher*

An Autumn Afternoon▲
Autumn Tale
The Ballad of Little Jo
Bed of Roses
Besieged
Betrayal
Birdman of Alcatraz▲
The Body Shop
Born Romantic
Bossa Nova
Bread and Tulips▲
Breakfast in Paris
The Browning Version▲
The Business of Strangers
The Cemetery Club
The Center of the World
Central Station▲
Choose Me▲
A Chorus of Disapproval
A Christmas Without Snow
Citizen Kane▲
The Closet
Cotter
Cowboys Don't Cry
Cyrano de Bergerac▲
Cyrano de Bergerac
Cyrano de Bergerac▲
A Day in the Country▲
Dead Letter Office
Desperately Seeking Susan
Didn't You Hear?
Dirty Dishes▲
Distant Thunder
Docks of New York▲
Doin' Time on Planet Earth
The Doll
A Doll's House
A Doll's House▲
Eat Drink Man Woman▲
The Eclipse▲
84 Charing Cross Road▲
El Super▲
An Empty Bed▲
The Enchanted Cottage
Escapade in Japan
E.T.: The Extra-Terrestrial▲
Every Man for Himself & God Against All▲
Eye of the Needle
Fanatic
Felicia's Journey▲
Fever
Fiances
The Final Alliance
Fire
Full Moon in Blue Water
Full Moon in Paris
The Game of Love
Ginger Snaps
The Gun in Betty Lou's Handbag
Harold and Maude▲
The Heart Is a Lonely Hunter▲
Heavy▲
Hell Hounds of Alaska
High Country
Hiroshima, Mon Amour▲
The Hunchback of Notre Dame▲
The Hunchback of Notre Dame
Husband Hunting
Husbands and Wives▲
I Don't Give a Damn
I Sent a Letter to My Love▲
In the White City▲
In the Winter Dark
Inside Out
Kaspar Hauser
La Petite Sirene
La Vie Continue
Lana in Love
The Last Best Year
The Legend of 1900
Les Bons Debarras
Les Voleurs▲
The Lonely Guy
Lonely Hearts▲
The Lonely Passion of Judith Hearne▲
Lonelyhearts
Looking for Mr. Goodbar
Lulu on the Bridge
Lunatics: A Love Story▲
Luther the Geek
Madagascar Skin
Man of Flowers
Marty▲
The Match Factory Girl▲
Men Don't Leave
Miles to Go Before I Sleep
Minnie and Moskowitz
Mr. Kingstreet's War
Mouchette▲
My First Mister
976-EVIL
Ninotchka▲
None But the Lonely Heart▲
Notes from Underground
Once Around
Only the Lonely
Only You
Our Miss Brooks
Panic Station
The Passion of Anna▲
Persona▲
Pi
A Price above Rubies
Priest of Love
Primal Secrets
The Prime of Miss Jean Brodie▲
The Prince of Central Park▲
The Pursuit of Happiness
Queen of the Stardust Ballroom▲
The Rachel Papers▲
Rachel, Rachel▲
The Red Desert▲
Red Kimono
Restless
Return Engagement
Rhythm Thief
Richie Rich
Risk▲
Robert et Robert▲
Roseland▲
Samurai 2: Duel at Ichijoji Temple▲
Scene of the Crime▲
The Seagull▲
Secret Life of an American Wife
Seize the Day▲
Separate Tables▲
Separate Tables
September
Shadows in the Storm
Single Bars, Single Women
Sleepless in Seattle▲
Slipstream
The Solitary Man
Someone to Love
South of Reno
Street Heart
Stuart Saves His Family
Summer▲
Sunday
Tales of the Klondike: The Scorn of Women
Tenth Month
That Cold Day in the Park
Til There Was You
Tomorrow▲
Too Shy to Try
Turtle Diary▲
Twin Falls Idaho▲
Under the Skin
Vagabond▲
The Walls of Malapaga
The War Zone
What Happened Was...
When the Cat's Away▲
When Your Lover Leaves
While You Were Sleeping▲
Wildest Dreams
Woman in the Shadows
World Traveler
The Young in Heart▲
Zelly & Me▲

Opera

see also *Musicals*

The Climax
Cosi▲
Farinelli
Interrupted Melody▲
Madame Butterfly
The Man Who Cried
Musica Proibita
Naughty Marietta
A Night at the Opera▲
Opera
The Perfect Husband
The Phantom of the Opera
Romance
Tonight or Never

Order in the Court

see also *Justice Prevails...?; Law & Lawyers*

Absence of Malice
The Accused
The Accused▲
Action for Slander
Adam's Rib▲
All God's Children
Amazing Dr. Clitterhouse▲
The Ambush Murders
American Tragedy
Anatomy of a Murder▲
And Justice for All
The Andersonville Trial▲
Artemisia
As Summers Die
Assault at West Point: The Court-Martial of Johnson Whittaker
Beefcake
Before and After
Beyond a Reasonable Doubt
Big Daddy
The Black Legion▲
Blind Faith
Body Chemistry 4: Full Exposure
Body of Evidence
Boomerang▲
Bounce
The Bramble Bush
Breaker Morant▲
Broken Trust
The Burning Bed▲
The Caine Mutiny Court Martial▲
Carrington, V.C.▲
A Case of Libel
The Castle
Cause Celebre▲
The Chamber
A Civil Action
Class Action▲
Clearcut
The Client
Cold Days
Color of Justice
Compulsion▲
Conduct Unbecoming
The Confession
Conspiracy: The Trial of the Chicago Eight▲
Convicted
The Court Martial of Billy Mitchell▲
Crazy in Alabama
Crime Broker
Crime of the Century
Criminal Court
Cross Examination
The Crucible▲
A Cry in the Dark▲
Dancer in the Dark
Dangerous Beauty▲
Dangerous Evidence: The Lori Jackson Story
Deacon Brodie
Deadlocked
Dear God
Death of a Soldier
Death Sentence
The Defenders: Payback
The Defenders: Taking the First
Defenseless
Deliberate Intent
Delinquent Parents
The Devil & Daniel Webster▲
The Devil's Advocate
Dirty Pictures
Disclosure
Dishonored Lady
The Drake Case
A Dry White Season▲
8-A
Ernest Goes to Jail
Eureka!
Evelyn Prentice
Execution of Justice
A Few Good Men▲
Final Appeal
Final Justice
Final Verdict
A Free Soul
From the Hip
Getting Gotti
Ghosts of Mississippi
Gideon's Trumpet
The Gift
The Good Father▲
The Good Fight
The Good Mother
Gospa
The Great American Sex Scandal
Guilty as Sin
Guilty of Innocence
Hard Traveling
Hitz
Honor Thy Father and Mother: The True Story of the Menendez Brothers
A House Divided
How Many Miles to Babylon?
The Hurricane▲
I Want to Live!▲
Illegally Yours
In the Name of the Father▲
Indictment: The McMartin Trial▲
Inherit the Wind▲
Inherit the Wind
Invasion of Privacy
It Could Happen to You
Jaded
The Jagged Edge
Jailbait: Betrayed By Innocence
Jeanne la Pucelle
Joan of Arc
John Grisham's The Rainmaker
The Judge
The Judge and the Assassin▲
Judge Horton and the Scottsboro Boys
Judgment at Nuremberg▲
Judgment in Berlin
Judicial Consent
Jungle Woman
The Juror
Jury Duty
Justice
A Killing in a Small Town▲
King and Country▲
King of the Pecos
Knock on Any Door
L.A. Law▲
The Last Innocent Man
The Last Wave▲
Legalese
Legally Blonde
Les Assassins de L'Ordre
Liar Liar
The List
Little Gloria... Happy at Last
The Long Dark Hall
The Love God?
Loved
Lured Innocence
Madame X
Madeleine
The Man in the Glass Booth▲
A Map of the World
Melanie Darrow
Midnight
Midnight in the Garden of Good and Evil
Miracle on 34th Street
Mrs. R's Daughter
Mr. Deeds Goes to Town▲
Mistrial
Monsieur Beaucaire
Murder▲
Murder in the First
Murder or Mercy
Music Box
Mutiny
My Cousin Vinny▲
Naked Lie
Never Forget
The Next Best Thing
Night Falls on Manhattan▲
Nuremberg
Nuts▲
One of Her Own
Outrage!
The Paradine Case
Passion of Joan of Arc▲
Penalty Phase
The People vs. Larry Flynt▲
Perfect Crime
Perry Mason Returns▲
Perry Mason: The Case of the Lost Love
Philadelphia▲
The Ponder Heart
Presumed Innocent▲
Primal Fear
Prisoners of the Sun▲
Psychopath
Question of Silence▲
Rampage
Red Corner
Red Kimono
Remember the Night▲
The Respectful Prostitute
Return to Paradise▲
Reversal of Fortune▲
The Rite
River Red
Riverbend
Roe vs. Wade▲
The Rose Garden
Roxie Hart
Rules of Engagement
The Runner Stumbles
Sacco & Vanzetti
The Scorpion Woman
The Secret Passion of Robert Clayton
Separate but Equal▲
Sergeant Rutledge▲
Sergeant Ryker
Shadow of Doubt
Silent Victim
A Simple Twist of Fate
Skullduggery
Sleepers
Small Sacrifices
Snow Falling on Cedars
Souls at Sea
Stairway to Heaven▲
The Star Chamber
State's Attorney
A Stranger in the Kingdom
Stuck on You
Suspect
Swoon▲
They Won't Believe Me▲
A Time to Kill▲
To Kill a Mockingbird▲
Tom and Huck▲
Too Young to Die
Town without Pity
The Trial▲
The Trial
Trial & Error
Trial and Error
Trial by Jury
The Trial of Lee Harvey Oswald
Trial of the Catonsville Nine
The Trials of Oscar Wilde▲
Twelve Angry Men▲
Twelve Angry Men
Two Years before the Mast
The Verdict▲
When Every Day Was the Fourth of July
When Thief Meets Thief
Where Love Has Gone
Where the Truth Lies
White Mischief▲
White Squall
Why Do Fools Fall in Love?
Wilde
The Winslow Boy▲
Witness for the Prosecution▲
Wives under Suspicion
Woman in Brown
Woman Undone
A Woman's Face▲
The Young Philadelphians▲

Organized Crime

see also *Crime & Criminals; Disorganized Crime; Gangs*

Absence of Malice
Across 110th Street
Action U.S.A.
Agent on Ice
Alibi
The Alien Agenda: Under the Skin
Almost Human
Alphabet City
American Born
American Chinatown
American Cop
American Justice
The American Soldier
American Yakuza
Analyze This▲
Angel's Dance
Angels with Dirty Faces▲
Another Stakeout
Armed for Action
Armed Response
Atlantic City▲
Avenging Disco Godfather
Baby Face Nelson
Baby on Board
Back to Back
Backtrack▲
Bad Charleston Charlie
Bad Georgia Road
Ball of Fire▲
Ballistic
The Barber Shop▲
The Barcelona Kill
Beautiful Hunter
Beautiful Joe
Bella Mafia
Best of the Best: Without Warning
A Better Way to Die
Beverly Hills Bodysnatchers
Beverly Hills Cop 3
Big Bad Mama 2
Big Boss
Big Combo▲
The Big Hit
Big News
The Big Slice
The Big Sweat
The Big Switch
Big Town After Dark
Billy Bathgate
Birth of the Blues
Bitter Sweet
Black Belt Jones
Black Caesar
Black Godfather
Black Lemons
Black Lizard
Black Shampoo
Black Snow
Blackjack
Blank Check
Blind Fury
Blood Brothers
Blood Money
Blood Ties
Blood Vows: The Story of a Mafia Wife
Blown Away
Blue Money
Boca
Body Trouble
Bonanno: A Godfather's Story
Boondock Saints
Born to Run
Boss of Bosses
Bound
The Boys
Branded to Kill
Breach of Trust
Breakaway
Brighton Rock▲
A Bronx Tale▲
A Brooklyn State of Mind
Brother
The Brotherhood
Bugsy▲
Bugsy Malone
Bullets over Broadway▲
B.U.S.T.E.D.
California Casanova
Camorra: The Naples Connection
Capone
Car Crash
Car 54, Where Are You?
Casino▲

▲ = rated three bones or higher

Otherwise Engaged

***see also** Romantic Triangles; Wedding Bells; Wedding Hell*

Pacific Islands

***see also** Island Fare*

▲ = rated three bones or higher

The Last Flight of Noah's Ark
The Last Warrior
Lt. Robin Crusoe, U.S.N.
Mad Doctor of Blood Island
The Mermaids of Tiburon
Miss Sadie Thompson▲
Mission Manila
Mr. Robinson Crusoe
Moana, a Romance of the Golden Age▲
Mysterious Island▲
Noon Sunday
Paradise, Hawaiian Style
Paradise Road
Pardon My Sarong
Rain
Rodgers & Hammerstein's South Pacific
South Pacific▲
Tabu: A Story of the South Seas▲
Till There Was You
Tora! Tora! Tora!
Wackiest Ship in the Army
Wake Island▲
White Shadows in the South Seas
Windom's Way▲
The Year of Living Dangerously▲

Painting

see *Art & Artists*

Paperboys

Better Off Dead
Newsies
The Paper Brigade
While You Were Sleeping▲
Willy Wonka & the Chocolate Factory▲

Parades & Festivals

see also *Carnivals & Circuses*
Barney's Great Adventure
Doc Hollywood
Easter Parade▲
Ferris Bueller's Day Off▲
The Fugitive▲
The Matchmaker
Miracle on 34th Street▲
Miracle on 34th Street
National Lampoon's Animal House▲
State of Grace▲
Sweet Beat

Paradise Gone Awry

The Beach
Club Paradise
Kiss the Sky
The Mosquito Coast
Six Days, Seven Nights

Parallel Universes

see also *Lost Worlds*
Alice in Wonderland
Alice in Wonderland▲
Alice in Wonderland
Blue Flame
Cool World
Crossworlds
Dark City
Journey to the Center of the Earth▲
Journey to the Center of the Earth
Julia and Julia
Jumanji
Last Action Hero
Last Lives
The Little Mermaid▲
Logan's Run
Lost in the Bermuda Triangle
Magic in the Mirror: Fowl Play
Me Myself I
Mortal Kombat 2: Annihilation
The One
Passion of Mind
The Purple Rose of Cairo▲
Splash
Super Mario Bros.
The 10th Kingdom
The Thirteenth Floor
Twisted
Who Framed Roger Rabbit▲

Paramedics

Bringing Out the Dead
Broken Vessels▲
Mother, Jugs and Speed
Paramedics

Pardners

see also *Buddies; Westerns*
Silverado▲
Texas Rangers

Parenthood

see also *Bad Dads; Bringing Up Baby; Dads; Moms; Monster Moms; Stepparents*
Adam▲
Addams Family Values
The Adventures of Rusty
The Adventures of Sebastian Cole
Afraid of the Dark
Alice in the Cities▲
Aliens▲
All the Kind Strangers
Alpha Beta
Amazing Grace
American Heart▲
An Autumn Afternoon▲
Baby Boom
Baby Girl Scott
Bachelor Mother▲
Back to the Beach
Backfield in Motion
The Ballad of Narayama▲
Basket Case 3: The Progeny
Battling for Baby
Being Two Isn't Easy
Between Two Women
Beyond Silence
Big Daddy
Big Fella
Big Girls Don't Cry...They Get Even
The Big Wheel
Blind Fools
Blondie's Blessed Event
Blow
Boys Town▲
Bye Bye, Love
Cahill: United States Marshal
A Call to Remember
Careful, He Might Hear You▲
Casanova Brown
Casey's Shadow
Cheaper by the Dozen▲
The Children of Times Square
Cody
Cold River
Commissar▲
A Cool, Dry Place
The Courtship of Eddie's Father▲
Cowboys Don't Cry
Crisscross
Crooklyn▲
A Cry in the Dark▲
Da
Daddy Nostalgia▲
Danielle Steel's Daddy
Danielle Steel's Fine Things
The Day My Parents Ran Away
The Deep End of the Ocean
Distant Voices, Still Lives▲
Dona Herlinda & Her Son
Drop-Out Mother
Duplicates
Dutch
Eat Drink Man Woman▲
The Emerald Forest▲
Endless Love
Enormous Changes▲
Ernie Kovacs: Between the Laughter
Every Other Weekend▲
Family Life
Fatal Confinement
Father Figure
Father of the Bride▲
Father of the Bride Part II
A Fight for Jenny
Firelight
Flirting with Disaster▲
Follow That Rainbow
Follow the Stars Home
Forbidden Planet▲
40 Pounds of Trouble
Ghost Dad
A Global Affair
God Bless the Child▲
The Good Father▲
The Good Mother
A Goofy Movie
Growing Pains
Guess What We Learned in School Today?
Gypsy▲
Gypsy
Harry & Son
Held for Murder
High Tide▲
A Hole in the Head
Holiday Heart
Hollow Reed▲
Home from the Hill▲
A Home of Our Own
Hope Floats
House Arrest
Houseboat
I Accuse My Parents
I Live with Me Dad
I Never Sang for My Father▲
I Ought to Be in Pictures
I Remember Mama▲
I'll Do Anything
I'll Take Sweden
Immediate Family
In the Bedroom▲
Innocent Victim
Irreconcilable Differences
Jack and Sarah
Journey for Margaret▲
Judy Berlin
Jungle 2 Jungle
Jurassic Park 3
Kiss Daddy Goodbye
The Kiss You Gave Me
Kolya▲
The Lady Is Willing
Ladybird, Ladybird▲
Les Bons Debarras
Liar Liar
Life as a House
Long Time Gone
Losing Isaiah▲
Lost Angels
Love Is All There Is
Love Under Pressure
Ma and Pa Kettle Back On the Farm
Ma Barker's Killer Brood
Mad Youth
M.A.D.D.: Mothers Against Drunk Driving
Magic in the Water
Mama Flora's Family
Mamma Roma▲
Matilda▲
Max Dugan Returns
Memory of Us
Men Don't Leave
Mermaids▲
Miracle on 34th Street
Mirele Efros
Mrs. Doubtfire
Mrs. R's Daughter
Mr. Mom▲
Misunderstood
Mom
Mom & Dad
Monkey Grip▲
Mother & Daughter: A Loving War
Mother and Son
My Life
My Mom's a Werewolf
National Lampoon's European Vacation
Natural Enemies
The Next Best Thing
Next of Kin
Night Cries
No Dessert Dad, 'Til You Mow the Lawn
North
Nothing in Common
On Golden Pond▲
On the Third Day
One Fine Day
One Man's War
Only the Lonely
Only When I Laugh▲
The Others▲
Padre Padrone▲
The Parent Trap
Parenthood▲
Parents▲
Paris, Texas▲
Penny Serenade▲
A Place for Annie
Poil de Carotte
Psycho 4: The Beginning
The Quiet Room
Raising Arizona▲
The Red House▲
Red River▲
The Reluctant Debutante▲
Rent-A-Kid
Revenge
The Revolt of Job▲
Riding in Cars with Boys
Rising Son▲
The River Rat
Runaway Father
Saint Maybe▲
The Sandy Bottom Orchestra
The Santa Clause
Sarah's Child
Scream for Help
Secret Ceremony
Secrets and Lies
Sex and the Single Parent
The Shaggy D.A.
Silence of the Heart▲
Silent Witness
A Simple Twist of Fate
A Slightly Pregnant Man
Somebody Is Waiting
Son of Godzilla
Special Olympics
Speeding Up Time
Stella
Stella Dallas▲
The Storm Within▲
The Strange Love of Molly Louvain
Sunstroke
Superdad
Suzanne
Taken Away
Target
Tea with Mussolini
Teenage Bad Girl
Tequila Sunrise
Terms of Endearment▲
This Property Is Condemned
Three Fugitives
Three Men and a Baby▲
Three Men and a Cradle▲
Throw Momma from the Train▲
Trading Mom
Tumbleweeds
The Turning Point
Ulee's Gold▲
The Unborn 2
Undercover Blues
An Unexpected Family
Unfinished Business
The Unstoppable Man
Wanted: The Perfect Guy
When Wolves Cry
Where Are the Children?
Where's Poppa?▲
Without a Trace
The Woman Who Willed a Miracle
Yours, Mine & Ours

Paris

see also *France*
A la Mode
The Accompanist
Accused
An Affair of Love
After Sex
Alberto Express
Alice et Martin
Alphaville▲
The Ambassador's Daughter
Amelie▲
The American
American Dreamer
An American in Paris▲
An American Werewolf in Paris
Angel
Another 9 1/2 Weeks
Antoine et Antoinette
April in Paris
Arch of Triumph▲
Arch of Triumph
The Assignment
Augustin
The Aviator's Wife▲
Baise Moi
Balzac: A Life of Passion▲
Beau Pere▲
Beaumarchais the Scoundrel
Bed and Board▲
Belle Americaine
Beyond the Clouds
Boeing Boeing
Boy Meets Girl▲
Breakfast in Paris
Breathless▲
The C-Man
Camille▲
Cartouche▲
Casque d'Or▲
Catherine & Co.
Celestial Clockwork
Charade▲
Chariots of Fire▲
Charlie Chan in Paris
Children of Paradise▲
China White
Circle of Love
Circle of Passion
Cleo from 5 to 7▲
Clowning Around
Cousin Bette
The Cousins▲
Crainquebille▲
The Crazy Ray▲
A Dangerous Man: Lawrence after Arabia▲
Daniella by Night
Dear Brigitte
Delicatessen▲
Delta of Venus
The Destructors
Detective
The Devil, Probably
Diary of a Seducer
Dingo
The Dirty Girls
The Disenchanted
Diva▲
Does This Mean We're Married?
Dracula Father and Son
Elisa
Entangled
Everyone Says I Love You▲
The Face at the Window
The Fall
The Fantastic Night▲
Fashions of 1934
The Fatal Image
The Favor, the Watch, & the Very Big Fish
A Fine Romance
Forget Paris
The Fourth Sex
Frantic▲
French Can-Can▲
French Kiss
The French Lesson
French Postcards
The French Touch
The French Way
From Hell to Victory
Funny Face▲
Gentlemen Prefer Blondes▲
Gigi▲
A Girl on Her Own
The Girl on the Bridge▲
The Green House
Half-Shot at Sunrise
Happenstance
Heartbeat
Henry & June▲
Her and She and Him
The Holes
How to Steal a Million▲
The Hunchback
The Hunchback of Notre Dame▲
The Hunchback of Notre Dame
The Hunchback of Notre Dame▲
I Am Frigid...Why?
I Can't Sleep
I Vampiri
If I Were King▲
If Looks Could Kill
The Immoral One
Incognito
Innocents in Paris
Interview with the Vampire
Intolerance▲
Invisible Circus
Irma Vep
Is Paris Burning?▲
Jeanne and the Perfect Guy
Jefferson in Paris
Killing Zoe
Kiss of the Dragon
La Boum
La Marseillaise▲
La Sentinelle
La Separation▲
La Vie de Boheme▲
Lady L
The Last Metro▲
Last Tango in Paris▲
The Last Time I Saw Paris
Le Joli Mai
Le Samourai▲
Le Schpountz
Le Trou▲
Les Miserables
Les Miserables▲
Les Vampires
Little Indian, Big City
A Little Romance▲
Love After Love
Love Play
The Lovers on the Bridge
Ma and Pa Kettle on Vacation
Ma Vie en Rose▲
Madeline
The Madwoman of Chaillot
The Man in the Iron Mask▲
The Man Who Cried
Marquis de Sade
Mauvaise Graine
Max, Mon Amour
Mesmer
Metroland
Mina Tannenbaum
Mrs. 'Arris Goes to Paris
The Moderns▲
Mon Oncle d'Amerique▲
Moulin Rouge
Murders in the Rue Morgue
The Murders in the Rue Morgue▲
My Life and Times with Antonin Artaud▲
My Sex Life...Or How I Got into an Argument
Nelly et Monsieur Arnaud▲
The New Eve▲
A New Kind of Love
Night on Earth▲
Ninotchka▲
November Moon
Now and Forever
Oliver Twist
Once in Paris...
One Against the Wind▲
Orpheus
Panique▲
Paris Blues
Paris Holiday
Paris When It Sizzles
Parisian Love
Pedale Douce
Peppermint Soda▲
The Perfect Furlough
Perfumed Nightmare▲
Petits Freres
The Phantom of the Opera▲

▲ = *rated three bones or higher*

The Phantom of the Opera
Pigalle
Place Vendome▲
Plucking the Daisy
Pola X
Portraits Chinois
The Private Affairs of Bel Ami▲
Ready to Wear
Red Kiss▲
Rendez-vous de Juillet
Rendezvous in Paris
Rich, Young and Pretty
Ridicule▲
Ronin
Round Midnight▲
Rugrats in Paris: The Movie▲
Same Old Song▲
A Scandal in Paris
A Self-Made Hero▲
Sex & Mrs. X
Shoot the Piano Player▲
Simone Barbes
The Sin of Madelon Claudet▲
Sin Takes a Holiday
A Single Girl
Six in Paris
Son of Gascogne
The Story of a Three Day Pass
The Street
Subway
Summer▲
The Tango Lesson
Target
The Testament of Dr. Cordelier▲
Theatre of Death
13 Rue Madeleine▲
Time Out for Love
To Paris with Love
Total Eclipse
Tropic of Cancer▲
Two or Three Things I Know about Her
Under the Roofs of Paris▲
Under the Sand▲
Until September
Up/Down/Fragile
Va Savoir
Venus Beauty Institute
Vicious Circles
Victor/Victoria▲
Victory
When the Cat's Away▲
Window Shopping
Zazie dans le Metro▲

Party Hell

The Anniversary Party▲
April Fool's Day
Carrie▲
The Club
Happy Birthday to Me
Hell Night
Hello Mary Lou: Prom Night 2
Killer Party
Meet Wally Sparks
Monsters Crash the Pajama Party
Night of the Demons
Prom Night
Prom Night 3: The Last Kiss
Prom Night 4: Deliver Us from Evil
Psycho Girls
Rabid Grannies
The Rage: Carrie 2
Slumber Party Massacre
Slumber Party Massacre 2
Slumber Party Massacre 3
Twilight Zone: The Movie

Patriotism & Paranoia

***see also** Propaganda*

Amber Waves
Born on the Fourth of July▲
The Chase
The Commies Are Coming, the Commies Are Coming
The Cosmic Man
Death of a Bureaucrat▲
Delta Force
Dress Gray▲
F/X▲
Fellow Traveler▲
Firefox
First Blood
Guilty by Suspicion
Harry's War
Heroes for Sale▲
Ivan the Terrible, Part 1▲
Ivan the Terrible, Part 2▲
Keeper of the Flame
Missing in Action
Mom & Dad
Murrow
Nixon▲
Panama Patrol
Paris Belongs to Us
Patton▲
The Prisoner▲
Radar Patrol vs. Spy King
Rambo: First Blood, Part 2
Rambo 3
Red Dawn
The Red Menace
Red Nightmare
Reunion in France
The Sea Hawk▲
The Secret Four
The Siege
Skinheads: The Second Coming of Hate
Sky High
So Proudly We Hail▲
The Spider's Stratagem▲
Strictly G.I.
Taps
Thirty Seconds Over Tokyo▲
The 27th Day

Peace

The Day the Earth Stood Still▲
The Deserters
Destry Rides Again▲
Diplomaniacs
Firehead
Friendly Persuasion▲
Gandhi▲
A Midnight Clear▲
Sadat
War and Peace
War and Peace▲

Peculiar Partners

***see also** Buddies; Buddy Cops; Cops*

Alien Nation
Alien Nation: Dark Horizon
The Beautician and the Beast
Cop and a Half
Dead Heat
Dollman
Dream with the Fishes
The Glimmer Man
Gridlock'd▲
The Hard Way▲
The Hidden▲
The Hidden 2
Judge Dredd
K-9
K-911
Stop! or My Mom Will Shoot
Theodore Rex
Top Dog
Turner and Hooch

Period Piece: 15th Century

The Advocate▲
Cesare Borgia
Christopher Columbus
Dracula: The Dark Prince
If I Were King▲
Jeanne la Pucelle
Joan of Arc
The Messenger: The Story of Joan of Arc

Period Piece: 16th Century

Dangerous Beauty▲
Elizabeth▲
Elizabeth, the Queen
Henry V▲
Highlander: Endgame
Ivan the Terrible, Part 1▲
Ivan the Terrible, Part 2▲
Kagemusha▲
Kama Sutra: A Tale of Love
Love and Faith▲
A Man for All Seasons▲
Mary of Scotland▲
The Merry Wives of Windsor
Orlando▲
The Prince and the Pauper
The Private Life of Henry VIII▲
The Private Lives of Elizabeth & Essex▲
Queen Margot▲
Rikyu▲
The Road to El Dorado
The Sea Hawk▲
Seven Samurai▲
Shakespeare in Love▲
Taras Bulba
The Virgin Queen▲
Young Bess▲

Period Piece: 17th Century

At Sword's Point
Black Robe▲
Carnival in Flanders▲
The Conqueror Worm▲
The Crucible▲
The Deluge
Delusions of Grandeur
The Devils▲
Ever After: A Cinderella Story▲
Forever Amber
The Four Musketeers▲
Frenchman's Creek
Highlander: Endgame
I, the Worst of All
The Iron Mask
Journey of Honor
The King's Thief
The King's Whore
Lazarillo
Lorna Doone
Lorna Doone▲
The Man in the Iron Mask▲
The Man in the Iron Mask
The Man in the Iron Mask▲
Marquis de Sade
Mayflower: The Pilgrims' Adventure
Monsieur Vincent▲
Mother Joan of the Angels▲
The Musketeer
The Night and the Moment
Queen Christina▲
Rapa Nui
Rembrandt▲
Rembrandt—1669
Restoration▲
The Return of the Musketeers
Revenge of the Musketeers
Samurai Reincarnation
The Scarlet Letter
The Scarlet Letter▲
The Scarlet Letter
The Serpent's Kiss
Squanto: A Warrior's Tale▲
The Three Musketeers
The Three Musketeers▲
The Three Musketeers
The Three Musketeers▲
The Three Musketeers
Tous les Matins du Monde▲
Vatel
The Wicked Lady

Period Piece: 18th Century

The Affair of the Necklace
Amadeus▲
The Amorous Adventures of Moll Flanders
The Aristocrats
Barry Lyndon▲
Beaumarchais the Scoundrel
The Black Castle
Botany Bay
The Bounty
The Broken Chain
Brotherhood of the Wolf
Cartouche▲
Casanova
Casanova's Big Night
Catherine the Great
The Crossing
Dangerous Liaisons▲
Danton▲
Deacon Brodie
DuBarry Was a Lady
Fanny Hill: Memoirs of a Woman of Pleasure
Farinelli
Follow the River
Forget Mozart
George Washington
George Washington: The Forging of a Nation
Gulliver's Travels
Haunted Symphony
Highlander: Endgame
Immortal Beloved
Interview with the Vampire
Joseph Andrews
Kidnapped
La Marseillaise▲
La Nuit de Varennes▲
The Last of the Mohicans▲
The Last of the Mohicans
The Last of the Mohicans▲
The Last of the Redmen
The Last Supper▲
Les Miserables▲
Les Miserables
Les Miserables▲
Longitude▲
Loves & Times of Scaramouche
The Madness of King George▲
Marie Antoinette
The Marquise of O
Mesmer
Minna von Barnhelm or The Soldier's Fortune
Moll Flanders
Monsieur Beaucaire▲
Mutiny on the Bounty▲
Mutiny on the Bounty
Night Sun
Orlando▲
Pandaemonium
Passion
The Patriot
Plunkett & Macleane
Poldark▲
Poldark 2▲
Power
Prince Brat and the Whipping Boy▲
Princess Yang Kwei Fei▲
Ridicule▲
The Road to Yesterday
Rob Roy▲
Rob Roy—The Highland Rogue
Sally Hemings: An American Scandal
Samurai Rebellion▲
The Scarlet Pimpernel▲
The Scarlet Pimpernel
The Scarlet Pimpernel 2: Mademoiselle Guillotine
The Scarlet Pimpernel 3: The Kidnapped King
School for Scandal
The Seekers
Shogun▲
Sleepy Hollow▲
Son of Fury▲
A Tale of Two Cities▲
A Tale of Two Cities
A Tale of Two Cities▲
Tom Jones▲
The Triumph of Love
Valmont▲
Xica▲

Period Piece: 19th Century

The Adventures of Mark Twain▲
The Age of Innocence▲
All the Brothers Were Valiant
Allonsanfan▲
The American
American Outlaws
Angels and Insects▲
Anna and the King
Anna and the King of Siam▲
Anna Karenina▲
Anna Karenina
Anthony Adverse
The Assassination Bureau▲
Assault at West Point: The Court-Martial of Johnson Whittaker
August
The Avenging Angel
Back to Hannibal: The Return of Tom Sawyer and Huckleberry Finn
The Ballad of Little Jo
Balzac: A Life of Passion▲
Band of Angels
The Barbary Coast
The Barretts of Wimpole Street▲
Beau Brummel
Beau Brummel▲
Beautiful Dreamers
Becoming Colette
Belizaire the Cajun
Belle of the Nineties
The Best Man
Beulah Land
Big Bear
Blacksnake!
Blanche Fury
Bleak House
Blood Red
The Bostonians
Bram Stoker's Dracula
The Brontes of Haworth
Brother of Sleep▲
The Brothers Karamazov▲
The Buccaneers▲
Buffalo Girls
By Way of the Stars
Call of the Wild
Camille Claudel▲
Captain Boycott
Catherine Cookson's The Black Velvet Gown
Catherine Cookson's The Dwelling Place
Catherine Cookson's The Fifteen Streets
Catherine Cookson's The Glass Virgin
Catherine Cookson's Tilly Trotter
The Charge of the Light Brigade▲
The Charge of the Light Brigade
A Christmas Carol▲
A Christmas Carol
A Christmas Carol▲
A Christmas Carol
The Cisco Kid
The Claim
Cobra Verde
Colonel Chabert
Conceiving Ada
Conduct Unbecoming
Conquest▲
Conquest of Cochise
The Count of Monte Cristo
Cousin Bette
The Covered Wagon
Daisy Miller
Damn the Defiant▲
Dante's Inferno: Life of Dante Gabriel Rossetti
The Dark Angel▲
David Copperfield
Dead Man
The Deceivers
Demons of the Mind
Desiree
Desperate Remedies
Disraeli▲
A Dog of Flanders
A Doll's House
A Doll's House▲
Dostoevsky's Crime and Punishment
Duel of Hearts
Edvard Munch
Effi Briest▲
1860
Eijanaika▲
Elective Affinities
The Elegant Criminal
The Elephant Man▲
Elvira Madigan▲
The Emigrants▲
Emma
Emma▲
End of Summer
Ethan Frome
The Europeans▲
Every Day's a Holiday
Far and Away
Far from the Madding Crowd▲
The Far Pavilions
The Farmer Takes a Wife
Feast of July
The Fighting Kentuckian
Fiorile▲
Firelight
The First Olympics: Athens 1896
Five Weeks in a Balloon
The Flame of New Orleans▲
The Flesh and the Fiends
Flight of the Eagle
Flowers of Reverie
Flowers of Shanghai
The Four Feathers▲
The Four Feathers
Frankenstein▲
Frankenstein
Frankie and Johnny
Freedom Road
The French Lieutenant's Woman▲
From Hell▲
The Gambler
Gaslight▲
Germinal▲
Geronimo
Geronimo▲
Geronimo: An American Legend
Gervaise▲
The Getting of Wisdom
The Golden Bowl▲
Goldrush: A Real Life Alaskan Adventure
The Gorgeous Hussy
Gothic▲
The Governess
Goya in Bordeaux
Great Expectations
Great Expectations▲
Great Expectations
Great Expectations▲
Great Expectations
Great Expectations: The Untold Story
The Great Moment
The Great Train Robbery▲
Green Dolphin Street
Greyfriars Bobby
Hamlet▲
Hands of a Murderer
Harmony Lane
Haunted Summer
Hawaii▲
The Heiress▲
Hip Hip Hurrah!▲
Hobson's Choice▲
Hobson's Choice
Horatio Hornblower▲
Horatio Hornblower: The Adventure Continues▲
The Horse Soldiers
The Hound of the Baskervilles▲
The Hound of the Baskervilles
The House of the Seven Gables
Hunger
I Dream of Jeannie
I, Monster▲
Immortal Beloved
The Importance of Being Earnest
Impromptu▲
In Old Chicago▲
Interview with the Vampire
The Jack Bull
Jamaica Inn
Jane Eyre
Jane Eyre▲
Jane Eyre
Java Head▲

▲ = rated three bones or higher

Jezebel▲
The Journey of August King
Journey to the Center of the Earth
Jude▲
Jude the Obscure
Kaspar Hauser
Kate & Leopold
Katie Tippel
Kim▲
Kim
The King and I▲
The King and I
Kings in Grass Castles
La Chartreuse de Parme
La Grande Bourgeoise
Lady Audley's Secret
Lady Caroline Lamb
Lady for a Night
Lady from Louisiana
The Lawless Breed▲
Leo Tolstoy's Anna Karenina
The Life and Adventures of Nicholas Nickleby▲
Life with Father▲
Lisztomania
The Little Colonel▲
Little Dorrit, Film 1: Nobody's Fault▲
Little Dorrit, Film 2: Little Dorrit's Story▲
Little House on the Prairie▲
Little Men
The Little Princess▲
The Little Princess
Little Women▲
Little Women
Little Women▲
The Lives of a Bengal Lancer▲
Lloyds of London▲
Love and Death▲
Love and Rage
The Loves of Edgar Allen Poe
Madame Bovary▲
Madame Bovary
Mademoiselle Fifi
Magnificent Doll
The Magnificent Seven
The Man from Snowy River
The Man in Grey▲
Mansfield Park
The Mark of Zorro▲
Mary Reilly
Mayerling▲
Mayerling
Melody Master
Mesmerized
Middlemarch▲
The Mill on the Floss
Miss Julie
Mrs. Brown▲
Modigliani
Molokai: The Story of Father Damien
The Moonstone▲
Moulin Rouge
My Antonia
My Apprenticeship▲
My Childhood▲
My Universities▲
The Mystery of Edwin Drood
The New Land▲
Newsies
Nicholas Nickleby▲
Northanger Abbey
Oliver!▲
Oliver Twist▲
Oliver Twist
Oliver Twist▲
Oliver Twist
Oliver Twist▲
Once Upon a Time in China▲
One Man's Hero
Onegin
The Organizer
Original Sin
Orlando▲
Oscar and Lucinda
The Ox
Pandaemonium
Pelle the Conqueror▲
The Perfect Husband
Persuasion
Persuasion▲
The Phantom of the Opera▲
The Phantom of the Opera
The Piano▲
Pink String and Sealing Wax
Poldark
Portrait of a Lady
Portrait of a Lady▲
The Possessed
Possession
Pride and Prejudice▲
Pride and Prejudice
Pride and Prejudice▲
Prince of Poisoners: The Life and Crimes of William Palmer
Princess Caraboo
The Private Affairs of Bel Ami▲
P.T. Barnum
Race to Freedom: The Story of the Underground Railroad
Ravenous
The Real Charlotte
The Return of the Native
The Right Hand Man
The Ripper
Robert Louis Stevenson's St. Ives
Robert Louis Stevenson's The Game of Death
The Rover
Rowing with the Wind
Saratoga Trunk
A Scandal in Paris
Scarlett
Sea Devils
The Secret Garden▲
The Secret Garden
The Secret Garden▲
The Secret Garden
Sense & Sensibility
Sense and Sensibility▲
Senso▲
Sergeant Rutledge▲
Shanghai Noon
Sharpe's Battle
Sharpe's Company
Sharpe's Eagle
Sharpe's Enemy
Sharpe's Gold
Sharpe's Honour
Sharpe's Justice
Sharpe's Legend
Sharpe's Mission
Sharpe's Regiment
Sharpe's Revenge
Sharpe's Rifles
Sharpe's Siege
Sharpe's Sword
Sharpe's Waterloo
Show Boat▲
Show Boat
The Sign of Four
Silas Marner▲
Sister Dora
Skin Game▲
Sofie
Sommersby
A Song to Remember▲
Song Without End
Souls at Sea
The Sound and the Silence
Spirit: Stallion of the Cimarron
Spring Symphony
The Story of Alexander Graham Bell▲
The Strauss Family
The Substitute Wife
Swept from the Sea
Tai-Pan
Tamango
Tchaikovsky
The Tenant of Wildfell Hall
Tess▲
Tess of the D'Urbervilles
The Texans
Texas Rangers
That Forsyte Woman
Tom and Huck▲
Tom Sawyer▲
Tom Sawyer
Topsy Turvy▲
Torrents of Spring
Total Eclipse
Twelfth Night
Two Years before the Mast
Under Capricorn
Utamaro and His Five Women
Vacas
The Valley of Decision▲
Van Gogh▲
Vanity Fair
Victoria & Albert
Victoria Regina
Vincent & Theo▲
Waltz King
War and Peace
War and Peace▲
War and Peace
Washington Square▲
The Way We Live Now
Wide Sargasso Sea
The Widow of Saint-Pierre▲
Wild Bill
Wild Wild West
Wilde
Wind River
Wives and Daughters
The Wolf at the Door
The Woman in White
A Woman Rebels
The World in His Arms
The Young Pioneers
Young Sherlock Holmes

Period Piece: 20th Century

America's Dream▲
The Babe
Bride of the Wind
Carrington
Century
Cobb▲
Coming Through
Dash and Lilly
Gypsy▲
Gypsy
Hold the Dream
Indochine▲
Interview with the Vampire
Iris▲
Lansky
The Last Emperor▲
The Legend of 1900
Legends of the Fall
Lillie▲
Malcolm X▲
Mama Flora's Family
Nicholas and Alexandra
O Pioneers!
Orlando▲
Rasputin▲
Rasputin and the Empress▲
Rasputin: Dark Servant of Destiny▲
Rasputin the Mad Monk
Rich Man, Poor Man▲
The Sexual Life of the Belgians
The Song of the Lark
Star!
Sunshine
Tom & Viv▲
Trahir▲
The Travelling Players
Winchell
A Woman of Substance

Period Piece: 1900s

Anne of Green Gables▲
The Bachelor▲
Berkeley Square
The Best Intentions▲
Cheaper by the Dozen▲
City Boy▲
Cold Sassy Tree▲
Colonel Redl▲
Daens
Daughters of the Dust▲
The Dead▲
December Bride
The Dolly Sisters
Fanny and Alexander▲
Fiddler on the Roof▲
55 Days at Peking▲
The Flame Is Love
The Forbidden Quest
Fulfillment
Glory & Honor
The Go-Between▲
The Golden Bowl
The Good Old Boys
Grand Isle
The Guns and the Fury
Hamlet
Harem
Heart of Darkness
Hester Street▲
Home at Last
House of Mirth▲
I Remember Mama▲
Illuminata
The Imported Bridegroom
Institue Benjamenta or This Dream People Call Human Life
It's a Dog's Life
La Ronde▲
Lady L
Land of Promise
Liebelei
Like Water for Chocolate▲
Love Among the Ruins▲
Madame Butterfly
The Magician of Lublin
The Magnificent Ambersons▲
The Magnificent Ambersons
The Man in the Attic
Man of Evil
Meet Me in St. Louis▲
A Midsummer Night's Sex Comedy▲
Mrs. Mike
Mrs. Soffel
Mr. Toad's Wild Ride
Mother Wore Tights▲
My Fair Lady▲
My Twentieth Century▲
My Uncle Silas▲
Nora
Of Freaks and Men
Our Town▲
Our Town
The Railway Children▲
A River Runs Through It▲
The Road to Wellville
A Room with a View▲
San Francisco▲
Secrets
Shadow Magic
She Creature
A Summer Story▲
Tales from the Gimli Hospital
Valley of the Kings
Viva Zapata!▲
We of the Never Never▲
When the Greeks
Where Angels Fear to Tread▲
William Shakespeare's A Midsummer Night's Dream
Yentl

Period Piece: 1910s

Abbott and Costello Meet the Keystone Kops
Anne of Avonlea▲
Atlantis: The Lost Empire
The Basket
Britannic
Brutal Glory
Catherine Cookson's Colour Blind
The Chambermaid on the Titanic
Christy
Cider with Rosie
Country Life
Courage Mountain
A Death in the Family
Doctor Zhivago▲
Eight Men Out▲
The Englishman Who Went up a Hill But Came down a Mountain▲
FairyTale: A True Story
The Fixer▲
Flambards
The Flame Trees of Thika▲
From Dusk Till Dawn 3: The Hangman's Daughter
Good Morning, Babylon▲
Goodbye, Miss 4th of July
Grizzly Falls
Heartland▲
Hole in the Sky
Howard's End▲
Iron Will
Lady Chatterley
Lady Chatterley's Lover
The Last of His Tribe
The Last Place on Earth
The Lawrenceville Stories
Lily Dale
A Little Princess▲
Michael Collins▲
Mrs. Santa Claus
The Murder of Mary Phagan▲
O Quatrilho
Old Gringo
On Moonlight Bay
On Valentine's Day
Peg o' My Heart
Picture Bride
Plain Jane
Red Firecracker, Green Firecracker
Rosa Luxemburg
Sarah, Plain and Tall▲
Sarah, Plain and Tall: Skylark
Sarah, Plain and Tall: Winter's End▲
Savage Messiah▲
Shackleton▲
The Shooting Party▲
Shopworn Angel▲
Solomon and Gaenor
Stiff Upper Lips
Sunday's Children▲
They Came to Cordura
Troubles
An Unfinished Piece for a Player Piano▲
Warden of Red Rock
The Wings of the Dove▲
The Winslow Boy▲
The Women on the Roof

Period Piece: 1930s

Acla's Descent into Floristella
The Bay Boy
Belle Epoque▲
Break of Dawn
Broken Glass
Burnt by the Sun▲
Butterfly▲
Cause Celebre▲
The Charmer
Child Star: The Shirley Temple Story
Cora Unashamed
Crime of the Century
The Devil's Backbone
Durango
The Education of Little Tree▲
Emma's Shadow▲
The Field▲
Go Tell It on the Mountain
Gosford Park▲
The Grass Harp
The Habitation of Dragons
The Harmonists
Heat of the Sun▲
The Hindenburg
I Don't Want to Talk About It
The Imposters
In Pursuit of Honor
In the Realm of the Senses▲
The Inheritors
Innocent Lies
Ivan and Abraham
Jew-boy Levi
Liam
Love's Labour's Lost
The Man from the Pru
The Man Who Cried
A Merry War▲
Miracles
The Mummy Returns
Murder in a Small Town
Out of the Cold
Pandora and the Flying Dutchman
Pavilion of Women
The Phantom Lover
The Proposition
Radioland Murders
The Remains of the Day▲
Richard III▲
The Rocketeer▲
Shadow on the Sun
Shanghai Triad▲
Sirens
The Stick-Up
Swing Kids
Tea with Mussolini
The Thirteenth Floor
This Is My Father
Under the Volcano▲
Up at the Villa
The Whole Wide World▲
A Woman at Her Window
Yellow Earth

Period Piece: 1940s

Aimee & Jaguar
All the Pretty Horses
All Things Fair
An American Story
Back Home
Back to the Secret Garden
Barton Fink▲
Batman: Mask of the Phantasm
Bugsy▲
Bye Bye Blues
Catherine Cookson's The Round Tower
The Chosen▲
The Cider House Rules▲
Color of a Brisk and Leaping Day
The Color of Courage
Confessing to Laura
The Curse of the Jade Scorpion
A Dark Adapted Eye▲
Deep Crimson
Delta of Venus
Devil in a Blue Dress▲
The Dollmaker
The Doorbell Rang: A Nero Wolfe Mystery
Earth
East of Elephant Rock
East-West
Farewell, My Lovely▲
Focus
For a Lost Soldier
The Forbidden Quest
The Franchise Affair
Gate of Flesh
The Golden Spiders: A Nero Wolfe Mystery
Good Evening, Mr. Wallenberg
Goodbye, Mr. Chips
Goodnight, Mr. Tom
The Grass Harp
Hong Kong 1941
In the Mood
Joe Gould's Secret
The Last Time I Committed Suicide
A League of Their Own▲
Les Miserables
A Lesson Before Dying▲
Lost in Yonkers
Malena
The Man Who Wasn't There▲
Maria
Margaret's Museum▲
The McCullochs
The Member of the Wedding▲
The Member of the Wedding
Miss Rose White▲
My Dog Skip▲
The Mystery of Rampo▲
The Neon Bible
Nuremberg
The Old Settler
Other Voices, Other Rooms
The Others▲
Passion in Paradise
Pizzicata
Pollock▲
Possessed
The Power of One
The Public Eye▲

▲ = rated three bones or higher

The Quarrel
Racing with the Moon▸
The Return of Eliot Ness
Ride the Wild Fields
RKO 281▸
The Road from Coorain
Rocky Marciano
The Runaway
Salome
Season of Change
The Seventh Dawn
Snow Falling on Cedars
Something for Everyone
Stand-Ins
Sudie & Simpson▸
The Summer of Ben Tyler
Surviving Picasso
Swing Shift
Three Comrades▸
A Time to Live and a Time to Die
Torso
The Two Jakes
Village of Dreams
A Winner Never Quits

Period Piece: 1950s

Absolute Beginners
The Affairs of Dobie Gillis
Alex
An American Rhapsody▸
As Summers Die
The Audrey Hepburn Story
Austin Powers In Goldmember
Back to the Future▸
Back to the Future, Part 2
Badlands▸
Bear Ye One Another's Burden...
A Beautiful Mind▸
Beefcake
Big Night
Big Town
Blind Faith
The Blue Kite▸
Book of Love
Born Reckless
Boycott▸
The Buddy Holly Story▸
Bye, Bye, Birdie▸
Cafe Society
Calendar Girl
Celia: Child of Terror
Chicken Run▸
Child Bride of Short Creek
Chocolat▸
Circle of Friends
The Climb
Common Ground
The Confessional▸
Corrina, Corrina
Cotton Mary
Crazy Mama
Cry-Baby▸
Dance with a Stranger▸
Daniel Takes a Train
Dark Blue World
Dark of the Sun
Dead Poets Society▸
Desire and Hell at Sunset Motel
Deuces Wild
Devil's Island
Diner▸
Dirty Dancing▸
Dreaming of Joseph Lees
Echoes
Elvis: The Movie
The Ernest Green Story
Fall Time
Father of the Bride▸
Fellow Traveler▸
For the Boys
The Front▸
Girls' Town
Going All the Way
Golden Gate
Grease▸
Grease 2
Ground Zero▸
Guilty by Suspicion
A Gun, a Car, a Blonde
The Heart of Dixie
Hometown U.S.A.
The House on Carroll Street
Housekeeping▸
The Hudsucker Proxy▸
In His Life: The John Lennon Story
Intimate Relations
Introducing Dorothy Dandridge▸
Inventing the Abbotts
I.Q.
Jailbreakers
James Dean
James Dean: Live Fast, Die Young
Just Looking
A King in New York
The Kitchen Toto▸
La Bamba▸
L.A. Confidential▸
Last Exit to Brooklyn▸
The Last Picture Show▸
Liberty Heights
Lily in Winter
The Long Day Closes▸
Long Gone
The Long Walk Home▸
The Lords of Flatbush
Lost, Lonely, and Vicious
Loveless
Lovers: A True Story▸
Mac▸
The Majestic
The Mambo Kings▸
The Man in the Moon▸
Mendel▸
Mischief
Mrs. 'Arris Goes to Paris
Mr. Rock 'n' Roll: The Alan Freed Story
Mob Queen
Monaco Forever
Moscow Does Not Believe in Tears▸
Mulholland Falls
My American Cousin▸
My Favorite Year▸
My Michael▸
Newsfront▸
Nightbreaker▸
Oh, What a Night
Once Upon a Time ... When We Were Colored▸
One Plus One
Ordeal by Innocence
The Other Side of Heaven
The Other Side of Sunday
Our Time
Palais Royale
Parents▸
The Passion of Ayn Rand
Peggy Sue Got Married
Perfect Harmony
Pillow Talk▸
The Playboys▸
Pollock▸
Porky's
Quiz Show▸
A Rage in Harlem▸
A Raisin in the Sun▸
Red Hot
Red Kiss▸
The Reflecting Skin
Relative Values
The Road Home▸
Roadracers
Rock All Night
Rock, Baby, Rock It
Rocky Marciano
Round Midnight▸
The Scent of Green Papaya▸
School Ties▸
Shadowlands▸
Shake, Rattle and Rock
Shake, Rattle & Rock!
Shout
The Silence of Neto
Snow Falling on Cedars
Sparkle
Stacking
The Star Maker
The Sticky Fingers of Time
Strange Invaders▸
A Stranger in the Kingdom
The Summer House
Superdad
Suzanne
The Talented Mr. Ripley
Teenage Doll
Terranova
That'll Be the Day
The Thief
This Boy's Life▸
This World, Then the Fireworks
Three Wishes
Tito and Me▸
Trading Hearts
Traps
Tune in Tomorrow
Two Family House
Valentino Returns
Visitants
The War of the Worlds▸
The Way We Were▸
When Father Was Away on Business▸
Who Shot Pat?
The Wild One▸
Witch Hunt
The Wooden Gun
You've Ruined Me, Eddie

Period Piece: 1960s

see also Boomer Reunions

A la Mode
Adam at 6 a.m.
Agnes Browne
Ali
Alice's Restaurant
All I Wanna Do
American Blue Note
American Graffiti▸
Angels Hard As They Come
Austin Powers 2: The Spy Who Shagged Me▸
Awakenings of the Beast
Backbeat▸
The Beautiful, the Bloody and the Bare
Best Enemies
Best Revenge
The Big Chill▸
The Big Fix▸
Blast-Off Girls
The Blue Kite▸
Blue Sky▸
Bob & Carol & Ted & Alice
Born on the Fourth of July▸
Brian's Song
The Bridges of Madison County▸
A Bronx Tale▸
Children Shouldn't Play with Dead Things
Company Man
Confessions of Sorority Girls
Conspiracy: The Trial of the Chicago Eight▸
Crazy in Alabama
The Crimson Cult
Dead Beat
Dead Presidents
Digging to China
The Dish▸
Dogfight▸
The Doors
Dynamite Chicken
Easy Rider▸
Even Cowgirls Get the Blues
Family Prayers
Fatherland
First Love and Other Pains / One of Them
Five Corners▸
The Flamingo Rising
Flashback▸
Four Friends▸
Free Grass
Freedom Song▸
Fritz the Cat▸
From the Earth to the Moon▸
Gimme Shelter
Girl, Interrupted
The Glory Stompers
Godspell
Grace of My Heart
Greetings▸
Hair▸
Head▸
Hearts in Atlantis
Help Wanted Female
Hendrix
Hideous Kinky
High Hopes▸
The Hollywood Knights
Hope
The Hours and Times▸
I Drink Your Blood
I Love You, Alice B. Toklas!
I Shot Andy Warhol▸
If These Walls Could Talk 2
Imaginary Crimes▸
In His Father's Shoes
In His Life: The John Lennon Story
In the Mood for Love
Isn't She Great
K-19: The Widowmaker
The Krays▸
The Locusts
The Lords of Discipline
The Lotus Eaters
Love Field
M. Butterfly
Malevolence
Mantis in Lace
Married to It
Matinee
Metroland
The Milky Way
More
More American Graffiti
My Little Assassin
Odd Birds
Off Limits
One Crazy Night
The Only Thrill
Out
Passing Glory▸
Peppermint Soda▸
A Perfect World
Petit Con
Psych-Out
Psycho Beach Party
Rainbow Bridge
The Rebel Set
Riding in Cars with Boys
R.P.M.* (* Revolutions Per Minute)
Ruby Bridges
Rude Awakening
Saint Maybe▸
The Sandlot▸
The Sandpiper
Satan's Sadists
Sea Devils
Second Thoughts
Selma, Lord, Selma
Set Me Free
Shag: The Movie▸
The '60s
61* ▸
'68
Skipped Parts
Slashed Dreams
A Small Circle of Friends
The Snake People
The Speed Lovers
Steal This Movie!
The Stoned Age
The Strawberry Statement
Sugartime
Sweetwater: A True Rock Story
Telling Lies in America
A Texas Funeral
That Night
That Thing You Do!▸
There Goes My Baby
There's a Girl in My Soup
Thirteen Days▸
Thumb Tripping
The Trip
Used People
A Walk on the Moon
Where Angels Go, Trouble Follows
Where the Eagle Flies
Who'll Stop the Rain?▸
Wild in the Streets
Wild Reeds▸
Woodstock▸
Yellow Submarine▸

Period Piece: 1970s

Ali
Almost Famous▸
Armistead Maupin's More Tales of the City
Armistead Maupin's Tales of the City
Austin Powers In Goldmember
Blow
Boogie Nights▸
Casino▸
Chopper
Common Ground
Crooklyn▸
Crossing the Bridge
The Dangerous Lives of Altar Boys
Dazed and Confused▸
Detroit Rock City
Dick▸
Donnie Brasco▸
Drugstore Cowboy▸
East Is East▸
Escape: Human Cargo▸
Execution of Justice
Fear and Loathing in Las Vegas
54
Forever Mine
Frailty▸
From the Earth to the Moon▸
Gia
Hedwig and the Angry Inch▸
Hideous Kinky
The Ice Storm▸
If These Walls Could Talk 2
The Inkwell
Invisible Circus
Isn't She Great
Jesus' Son
Jill the Ripper
Joe the King
The Killing Beach
Kippur▸
The Ladies Man
The Last of the High Kings
Left Luggage
The Legend of Rita
The Lesser Evil
Man on the Moon
Meat Loaf: To Hell and Back
Metroland
New Waterford Girl
No
Nothing Personal▸
Of Love and Shadows
Pinero
Prefontaine
Ratcatcher
Rated X
Resurrection Man
Riding in Cars with Boys
The Royal Tenenbaums▸
Scotland, PA
Seeing Red
The '70s
Shot in the Heart▸
Slums of Beverly Hills▸
Spirit of '76
Spy Game
Steal This Movie!
Strawberry and Chocolate▸
Such a Long Journey▸
Summer of Sam
That's the Way I Like It
The Third Miracle
Tigerland▸
Velvet Goldmine
The Virgin Suicides
Waking the Dead
The War
Water Drops on Burning Rocks
West Beirut
Without Limits▸
Xiu Xiu: The Sent Down Girl▸

Period Piece: 1980s

The Adventures of Sebastian Cole
American Psycho
Apt Pupil
The Assignment
Billy Elliot▸
Blow
Cherish
The Confessional▸
Dangerous Evidence: The Lori Jackson Story
Donnie Darko▸
Edge of Seventeen
An Everlasting Piece
Fever Pitch
Forever Mine
Hurlyburly
The Informant▸
The Last Days of Disco▸
The Legend of Rita
The Lovers on the Bridge
Man on the Moon
Noriega: God's Favorite
The Perez Family
Pinero
The Replacements
Riding in Cars with Boys
Rock Star
Safe Men
SLC Punk!
Spy Game
Summer's End
To Walk with Lions
24-7
200 Cigarettes
Valentine
Velvet Goldmine
Waking the Dead
The Wedding Singer
Wet Hot American Summer▸
Whatever
The Wood

Persian Gulf War

see also Desert War/ Foreign Legion

Courage Under Fire▸
The Heroes of Desert Storm
The Human Shield
Tactical Assault
Three Kings▸

Philadelphia

Birdy▸
Blow Out▸
Downtown
The Garbage-Picking, Field Goal-Kicking Philadelphia Phenomenon
Happy Birthday, Gemini
I Don't Buy Kisses Anymore
Kitty Foyle▸
Like Mike
Mannequin
Mannequin 2: On the Move
Marnie▸
Money for Nothing
My Little Girl
Nasty Habits
Philadelphia▸
The Philadelphia Story▸
Rocky▸
Rocky 2
Rocky 3
Rocky 4
Rocky 5
The Sixth Sense▸
Stonewall▸
Time at the Top
Trading Places
12 Monkeys▸
Two Bits
Two Plus One
Unbreakable
Up Close and Personal▸
Waiting
The Watermelon Woman
Winter Kills▸
Witness▸
The Young Philadelphians▸

Philanthropy

see Kindness of Strangers

Phobias!

Arachnophobia
Blackjack
Body Double▸
Copycat
High Anxiety
Home Remedy

▸ = rated three bones or higher

- Inside Out
- Pontiac Moon
- Vertigo▸

Phone Sex

see also Sex & Sexuality; Sexploitation

- Denise Calls Up
- Girl 6
- Happiness▸
- Listen
- Mouth to Mouth
- 1-900
- Short Cuts▸
- The Truth about Cats and Dogs▸
- Walking and Talking
- A Whisper to a Scream

Phone Terror

- Are You Lonesome Tonight
- Black Sabbath▸
- Call Me
- Dead Connection
- Dial Help
- Don't Answer the Phone
- The Jerky Boys
- Lady Beware
- Lisa
- Listen
- Midnight Lace
- The Night Caller
- 976-EVIL
- 976-EVIL 2: The Astral Factor
- Party Line
- Scream▸
- Scream 2▸
- Scream 3
- Smooth Talker
- Sorry, Wrong Number▸
- Sorry, Wrong Number
- Telefon
- When a Stranger Calls
- When a Stranger Calls Back

Photography

see Shutterbugs

Physical Problems

see also Blindness; Deafness; Mental Retardation; Savants

- Acorn People
- The Affair▸
- An Affair to Remember
- Amy
- Autumn Sonata▸
- The Big Lebowski▸
- Big Street
- The Bone Collector
- Born on the Fourth of July▸
- Breaking the Waves▸
- A Brief History of Time▸
- Broken Strings
- The Brute Man
- Catherine Cookson's The Wingless Bird
- Chained for Life
- Chinese Roulette
- Choices
- Closer and Closer
- Coming Home▸
- Cries of Silence
- The Crippled Masters
- Crossbar
- Dance Me to My Song
- A Day in the Death of Joe Egg▸
- Dead Silent
- Diamonds
- Don't Say a Word
- Double Parked
- Eden
- El Cochecito▸
- The Elephant Man▸
- Endgame
- Even Cowgirls Get the Blues
- Everything That Rises
- Fallen Angels
- Fireworks
- Flawless
- Floating
- Follow the Stars Home
- Frankie Starlight
- Freddy Got Fingered
- George Wallace
- The Glass Menagerie▸
- Go Now▸
- Good Luck
- Gray's Anatomy
- A Gun, a Car, a Blonde
- Hearing Voices
- Hugo Pool
- The Hunchback
- The Hunchback of Notre Dame▸
- The Hunchback of Notre Dame
- The Hunchback of Notre Dame▸
- I Don't Want to Talk About It
- I Want You
- Inside Moves
- It's Good to Be Alive
- Joni
- Knife in the Head
- Lea
- Lewis and Clark and George
- Lightning Jack
- Locked in Silence
- Long Journey Back
- Looking for Richard▸
- The Loretta Claiborne Story
- Love Affair▸
- Love Affair
- Mac and Me
- The Man with the Golden Arm▸
- The Man Without a Face
- Mask▸
- The Men▸
- Miracle in Lane Two
- The Miracle Worker▸
- The Miracle Worker
- Mrs. Munck
- Monkey Shines
- Mute Witness
- My Left Foot▸
- Next Victim
- Niagara, Niagara
- Night Monster
- Night Must Fall▸
- Of Human Bondage▸
- Off the Mark
- One-Eyed Swordsman
- Orphans
- The Other Side of the Mountain
- The Other Side of the Mountain, Part 2
- Paperback Romance
- Passion Fish▸
- The Penalty
- The People vs. Larry Flynt▸
- Persons Unknown
- The Phantom of the Opera▸
- The Pit
- Portrait of an Assassin
- Powder
- Ratboy
- Reach for the Sky
- Rear Window▸
- Rear Window
- The Red Dwarf
- Regarding Henry▸
- Revolver
- Richard III▸
- Ride a Wild Pony▸
- The River▸
- Roxanne▸
- Rumble in the Bronx
- Scent of a Woman▸
- Second Chances
- The Secret
- Seizure: The Story of Kathy Morris
- The Seventh Veil▸
- Shallow Hal
- Silence
- Silence Like Glass
- Silent Witness
- Silver Bullet
- Sitcom
- Skag▸
- The Sky Pilot
- The Small Back Room▸
- Sound of Love
- Special Olympics
- The Spiral Staircase▸
- Spiral Staircase
- Steel
- The Steel Claw
- Stella Maris▸
- The Story of Esther Costello
- The Stratton Story▸
- Suite 16
- The Sum of Us▸
- Sweet and Lowdown
- Talk to Me
- The Terry Fox Story▸
- A Test of Love
- Things to Do in Denver When You're Dead▸
- To All My Friends on Shore▸
- Twin Falls Idaho▸
- Untamed Heart
- Vibrations
- Walking on Air
- The Waterdance▸
- What Ever Happened to Baby Jane?▸
- What the Deaf Man Heard▸
- What's Eating Gilbert Grape▸
- Whose Life Is It Anyway?▸
- Wild Wild West
- A Winner Never Quits
- A Woman's Face▸
- X-Men

Pigs

see also Killer Pigs

- The Advocate▸
- Animal Farm
- Babe▸
- Babe: Pig in the City
- The Black Cauldron
- Charlotte's Web
- Doc Hollywood
- Gordy
- Leon the Pig Farmer
- A Private Function
- Waikiki Wedding▸

Pirates

see also Island Fare; Sail Away; Swashbucklers

- Abbott and Costello Meet Captain Kidd
- Against All Flags▸
- The Black Pirate▸
- The Black Swan▸
- Blackbeard the Pirate
- Blackbeard's Ghost
- The Buccaneer
- Captain Blood▸
- Captain Kidd
- Captain Ron
- Crimson Pirate▸
- Cutthroat Island
- Dancing Pirate
- Frenchman's Creek
- His Majesty O'Keefe
- Hook
- Ice Pirates
- Long John Silver
- The Master of Ballantrae
- Morgan the Pirate
- Muppet Treasure Island
- New Moon
- Old Ironsides▸
- Peter Pan▸
- The Phantom
- The Pirate▸
- Pirate Movie
- The Pirates of Penzance
- The Princess and the Pirate▸
- The Princess Bride▸
- Return to Never Land
- The Sea Hawk▸
- Shipwrecked
- Six Days, Seven Nights
- Son of Captain Blood
- Space Marines
- Space Truckers
- The Spanish Main
- Swashbuckler
- The Swiss Family Robinson▸
- Tiger of the Seven Seas
- Treasure Island▸
- Treasure Island
- Yellowbeard

Pittsburgh

- Alone in the Neon Jungle
- Angels in the Outfield▸
- Angels in the Outfield
- Backstreet Justice
- Bloodsucking Pharoahs of Pittsburgh
- Bob Roberts▸
- The Cemetery Club
- Diabolique
- Dominick & Eugene▸
- The Fish that Saved Pittsburgh
- Flashdance
- Houseguest
- Innocent Blood
- Lady Beware
- Mrs. Soffel
- The Piano Lesson▸
- Roommates
- Silent Witness
- Stigmata
- Striking Distance
- Sudden Death
- The Valley of Decision▸
- Wonder Boys▸

Poetry

- The Barretts of Wimpole Street▸
- Before Night Falls▸
- The Color of Pomegranates▸
- Hedd Wyn
- Henry Fool▸
- I, the Worst of All
- In Custody
- Lady Caroline Lamb
- My Life and Times with Antonin Artaud▸
- Pinero
- Poetic Justice
- The Postman▸
- Satan's Brew
- Stevie
- Swann
- Tales of Ordinary Madness
- Tom & Viv▸
- Total Eclipse

Poisons

- Arsenic and Old Lace▸
- Barracuda
- Color Me Dead
- The Crazies
- D.O.A.▸
- D.O.A.
- Doomwatch
- The Invisible Killer
- Juggernaut
- Kiss and Kill
- Safe▸
- Surf 2
- The Young Poisoner's Handbook▸

Police Detectives

- Abduction of St. Anne
- Above the Law
- All-American Murder
- Along Came a Spider
- Angels Don't Sleep Here
- Another Stakeout
- Beautiful Creatures
- Below the Deadline
- Blackmail▸
- Bloodbath
- Bloody Avenger
- Bloody Proof▸
- Bullitt▸
- Cat and Mouse▸
- Catherine's Grove
- Columbo: Murder by the Book
- Columbo: Prescription Murder
- Cookie's Fortune▸
- Criminals Within
- Curse of the Pink Panther
- Cyberstalker
- Dead Connection
- Dead Sexy
- Death from a Distance
- The Deep End of the Ocean
- The Detective▸
- Detective
- Detective Story▸
- Dick Tracy
- Dick Tracy▸
- Dick Tracy, Detective
- Dick Tracy Meets Gruesome
- Dick Tracy Returns
- Dick Tracy vs. Crime Inc.
- Dick Tracy vs. Cueball
- Dick Tracy's Dilemma
- Dragnet
- Edge of Darkness
- The Element of Crime
- The Enforcer
- Escape Clause
- Falling Down
- Final Notice
- Follow Me Quietly▸
- The Force
- The French Detective▸
- From Hell▸
- Fugitive Among Us
- The Gore-Gore Girls
- Green Eyes
- Green for Danger
- Guardian Angel
- Heat▸
- Hellraiser 5: Inferno
- Hitched
- Hollywood Stadium Mystery
- House of Mystery
- The House of the Arrow▸
- The Human Monster
- The Hunt for the Night Stalker
- The Hustle
- Innocent Lies
- Insomnia▸
- The Invisible Killer
- Jill the Ripper
- Just Another Pretty Face
- K-9
- K-911
- Kept
- Kiss the Girls
- Kojak: The Belarus File
- Lantana▸
- Laura▸
- Loose Cannons
- The Mad Bomber
- Magnum Force
- Man on the Eiffel Tower▸
- Mean Streak
- Mercy
- Midnight 2: Sex, Death, and Videotape
- The Million Dollar Hotel
- A Mind to Murder
- Murder at the Vanities
- Murder by Numbers
- My New Partner
- Naked City: A Killer Christmas
- Naked City: Justice with a Bullet
- New Orleans After Dark
- Newman's Law
- Nick Knight
- Night School
- Night Stalker
- No One Sleeps
- No Way to Treat a Lady▸
- Nocturne
- Number One with a Bullet
- On Dangerous Ground▸
- One Good Cop
- Operation Julie
- The Organization▸
- Out of the Darkness▸
- Out of the Shadows
- Partners in Crime
- The Phantom Light
- The Phantom of Soho
- Play Nice
- Postmark for Danger
- The Presidio
- Prettykill
- Private Hell 36
- The Prophet's Game
- Relentless
- Relentless 2: Dead On
- Relentless 3
- Relentless 4
- The Return of Dr. Mabuse
- Revenge Quest
- Rough Cut
- Sapphire▸
- Scotland, PA
- Sea of Love▸
- Second Sight▸
- Seeds of Doubt
- Seven▸
- The Seven-Ups
- Shadows of the Orient
- Showtime
- Silk
- Someone to Watch Over Me▸
- The Squeeze
- Stakeout
- Station
- Stray Dog▸
- Strike a Pose
- Tales from the Crypt Presents Bordello of Blood
- They Call Me Mr. Tibbs!
- The Third Key
- Third World Cop
- Ticker
- To Catch a Killer▸
- Touching Evil▸
- True Blue
- Vertigo▸
- Video Murders
- Violated
- What Your Eyes Don't See
- When the Sky Falls
- Who Is the Black Dahlia?▸
- Wild Things
- Witchcraft 10: Mistress of the Craft
- Witness▸
- World of the Depraved
- X Marks the Spot

Politics

see also Presidency

- Absolute Power
- The Act
- The American President▸
- An American Story
- The Americano
- Americathon
- And the Band Played On▸
- Angi Vera▸
- Animal Instincts
- Antonio Das Mortes
- The Art of War
- Article 99
- Attila
- Bear Ye One Another's Burden...
- Beggars in Ermine
- Being There▸
- Beyond Obsession
- Beyond Rangoon
- The Big Brass Ring
- The Big Hurt
- The Birdcage▸
- Bitter Sugar▸
- Black Ice
- Black Jesus
- Black Sheep
- Blaze
- Blood Money: The Story of Clinton and Nadine
- The Blue Kite▸
- Bob Roberts▸
- Bopha!▸
- The Break
- Break of Dawn
- Bulworth▸
- Buried Alive
- The Burning Season▸
- Burnt by the Sun▸
- Call Him Mr. Shatter
- Canadian Bacon
- The Candidate▸
- Carla's Song
- Carry On Emmanuelle
- Casino▸
- Chain of Command
- Children of the Revolution
- China Gate▸
- Citizen Cohn
- City Hall▸
- Clear and Present Danger
- Code Name: Chaos
- The Colombian Connection
- The Comedians
- Complex World
- Confessing to Laura
- Conspiracy
- Conspiracy: The Trial of the Chicago Eight▸
- The Contender

▸ = rated three bones or higher

Pool

Pornography

Post Apocalypse

Postwar

Rambo: First Blood, Part 2
Random Harvest▲
The Razor's Edge▲
Rendez-vous de Juillet
Reunion▲
Rich Man, Poor Man▲
Rio Conchos▲
Robin Hood of the Pecos
The Rose Garden
Savage Dawn
The Search▲
A Self-Made Hero▲
Sergeant Ryker
Shoeshine▲
Something for Everyone
Sommersby
Sophie's Choice▲
Souvenir
Strategic Air Command
The Subject Was Roses▲
Sunshine
The Teahouse of the August Moon
The Texans
They Made Me a Fugitive
The Third Man▲
Three Comrades▲
Till the End of Time
Time of Indifference
Torpedo Alley
Trained to Kill, U.S.A.
The Truce▲
Uranus▲
Verboten!
Vietnam, Texas
A Walk in the Clouds
We All Loved Each Other So Much▲
Who'll Stop the Rain?▲
Wish You Were Here▲
Wolf Lake
Women in Prison
The Yakuza
Year of the Quiet Sun▲
Zentropa

POW/MIA

see also *War, General; Vietnam War; World War II*

Against the Wind
All My Sons▲
American Commandos
Andersonville▲
The Andersonville Trial▲
Another Time, Another Place▲
The Ascent
Au Revoir les Enfants▲
Ay, Carmela!▲
Bat 21
The Beast
Blockhouse
Bomb at 10:10
The Boxer and Death▲
Brady's Escape
Brainwashed
The Bridge on the River Kwai▲
Bridge to Hell
The Brylcreem Boys
Bye Bye Blues
Captive Heart▲
Captive Hearts
Charlie Bravo
Codename: Terminate
The Colditz Story
Come See the Paradise▲
Cornered▲
Crossfire
Devils on the Doorstep
Dirty Heroes
The Dunera Boys▲
The Elusive Corporal▲
Empire of the Sun▲
Era Notte a Roma▲
Escape
Escape from Sobibor▲
Escape to Athena
Fighting Mad
The Forgotten
Generale Della Rovere▲
Grand Illusion▲
The Great Escape▲
The Great Escape 2: The Untold Story
The Hand
Hanoi Hilton
Hart's War
Hell to Eternity
Heroes in Hell
Homecoming▲
The Human Condition: A Soldier's Prayer▲
Hunted
In Gold We Trust
In Love and War
The Incident▲
The Iron Triangle
Jenny's War
King Rat▲
A Love in Germany
McKenzie Break▲
Merry Christmas, Mr. Lawrence▲
Mine Own Executioner▲
Missing in Action
Nam Angels
Night Wars
Objective, Burma!▲
On Wings of Eagles
One That Got Away▲
Operation 'Nam
Operation Warzone
Pacific Inferno
Paradise Road
Porridge
P.O.W. Deathcamp
The P.O.W. Escape
Prisoners of the Sun▲
The Purple Heart
Raiders of Leyte Gulf
Robert Louis Stevenson's St. Ives
Rolling Thunder
Seven Years in Tibet
The Seventh Cross▲
Some Kind of Hero
Stalag 17▲
Stalag Luft
The Summer of My German Soldier▲
Three Came Home▲
Three Wishes
Victory
Von Ryan's Express▲
When Hell Was in Session▲
Women of Valor
Wooden Horse▲

Pregnant Men

Enemy Mine
Junior
Rabbit Test

Pregnant Pauses

see also *Bringing Up Baby*

Alien 3
All About My Mother▲
Almost Pregnant
Alternative
Angel Baby▲
Angie
Armistead Maupin's More Tales of the City
The Astronaut's Wife
The Baby Dance▲
The Baby Maker
Baby of the Bride
Babyfever
Beautiful People
Bed and Board▲
Bellyfruit
Beloved/Friend
Between Heaven and Earth
Billy: Portrait of a Street Kid
Bleeding Hearts
Brand New Life
Butterfly Wings
Cafe au Lait▲
Cast the First Stone
Catherine Cookson's The Dwelling Place
Catherine Cookson's The Round Tower
Catherine Cookson's The Wingless Bird
Cheyenne Warrior
Child of Darkness, Child of Light
Choices
Chutney Popcorn
The Circle
Citizen Ruth
Cocktail
Coming Out
Conceiving Ada
The Confessional▲
Crossroads
Dancing at the Blue Iguana
Danielle Steel's Heartbeat
Demon Seed▲
Divided We Fall
Down, Out and Dangerous
Earthly Possessions
Eraserhead▲
Everything Put Together
The Evil Within
Falling for a Dancer
Fargo▲
Father of the Bride Part II
Father's Little Dividend▲
Felicia's Journey▲
Fools Rush In
Friends
Generation
Hell Comes to Frogtown
Help Wanted: Male
Hide and Seek
Home Fries
Hush
I Married a Dead Man
If These Walls Could Talk
Immediate Family
Interlocked
The Invader
Invasion of Privacy
Jailbait!
Julien Donkey-boy
Just Another Girl on the I.R.T.
A Kind of Loving▲
The L-Shaped Room▲
La Buche
Labor Pains
Le Cas du Dr. Laurent▲
Lethal Weapon 4
Let's Get Married
Levitation
Lily Was Here
Love Child
Lucie Aubrac
Manny & Lo▲
The Marquise of O
The Match Factory Girl▲
Maternal Instincts
Maybe Baby
Maybe ... Maybe Not
Maze
Me You Them
Micki & Maude
The Miracle▲
Misbegotten
Mists of Avalon▲
A Modern Affair
Mom & Dad
Morning Glory
My Life
My Little Assassin
Nenette and Boni▲
The New Eve▲
Nickel Mountain
Nine Months
No Alibi
No Laughing Matter
North Shore Fish
The Object of My Affection
The Opposite of Sex
Our Song▲
Our Time
Outrageous!▲
Parenthood▲
Polish Wedding
Progeny
Promises! Promises!
The Prophecy 2: Ashtown
Riding in Cars with Boys
A Saintly Switch
Saturday Night and Sunday Morning▲
Savior▲
Seducing Maarya
Series 7: The Contenders
She's Having a Baby
A Single Girl
Skipped Parts
A Smile Like Yours
Solomon and Gaenor
Spice World: The Movie
Splendor
The Stranger Within
Sugar & Spice▲
Sweet Evil
A Taste of Honey▲
Tenth Month
Tess of the Storm Country
Time and Tide
Tomorrow▲
Turn It Up
The 24 Hour Woman
The Twilight of the Golds
Two Family House
Twogether
The Unborn
Under the Skin
The Unearthing
An Unexpected Life
The Unknown Soldier
The Very Edge
A Walk in the Clouds
Way of the Gun
Wedding Bell Blues
A Weekend in the Country
What Planet Are You From?
Where the Heart Is
William Faulkner's Old Man
Winter Flight
Woman Wanted
Wonder Boys▲
You'll Like My Mother
The Young Pioneers
You've Ruined Me, Eddie
Zero Population Growth

Prep School

see also *Hell High School; Teen Angst*

Brotherhood 2: The Young Warlocks
Chasing Holden
Harry Potter and the Sorcerer's Stone▲
Lost and Delirious
Making the Grade
O▲
Scent of a Woman▲
School Ties▲
The Smokers
Tart

Presidency

see also *Camelot (New); Politics*

Abe Lincoln in Illinois▲
Absolute Power
Advise and Consent▲
Agent of Death
Air Force One▲
All the President's Men▲
The American President▲
Amistad▲
Assassination
The Assassination File
The Best Man▲
Black Sunday
Dave▲
Deep Impact
Deterrence
Dick▲
Dirty Tricks
Eleanor & Franklin▲
Eleanor: First Lady of the World
Elvis Meets Nixon
The Enemy Within
Escape from New York
Executive Action
Executive Target
The Final Days
First Daughter
First Family
First Kid
For the Love of Mary
Foreplay
Forrest Gump▲
Gabriel Over the White House▲
Gore Vidal's Lincoln
Guarding Tess
Hail
Imagemaker
In the Line of Fire▲
Independence Day▲
Jefferson in Paris
JFK▲
The JFK Conspiracy
JFK: Reckless Youth
Kennedy
The Kennedys of Massachusetts
The Kidnapping of the President
Kisses for My President
Kissinger and Nixon
The Last Bastion
LBJ: A Biography
LBJ: The Early Years▲
Magnificent Doll
Mars Attacks!
Meteor
Missiles of October▲
Murder at 1600
My Date with the President's Daughter
My Fellow Americans
My Uncle: The Alien
Nixon▲
The President's Analyst▲
President's Mistress
The President's Plane Is Missing
Primary Colors
Prince Jack
The Rat Pack
Ruby
Sadat
Sally Hemings: An American Scandal
The Second Civil War
Secret Honor▲
The Shadow Conspiracy
Suddenly▲
The Sum of All Fears
Sunrise at Campobello▲
Thirteen Days▲
Truman
The War Room▲
Wild in the Streets
Wilson▲
Winter Kills▲
Young Mr. Lincoln▲

Price of Fame

see also *Rags to Riches*

Abraham Lincoln
All About Eve▲
All That Jazz▲
American Blue Note
At Any Cost
The Bad and the Beautiful▲
Bank Robber
Bert Rigby, You're a Fool
Beyond the Valley of the Dolls
The Big Knife▲
Black Starlet
The Bodyguard
The Buddy Holly Story▲
By the Sword
The Cantor's Son
Cassie
Champion▲
A Chorus Line
Citizen Kane▲
Coal Miner's Daughter▲
Comeback
The Comic▲
The Commitments▲
The Cotton Club▲
Country Girl
Covergirl
Crossover Dreams
Darling▲
Dead Ringers▲
Echo Park
Eddie and the Cruisers
Eddie and the Cruisers 2: Eddie Lives!
Edie in Ciao! Manhattan
EDtv
Elmer Gantry▲
Elvis and Me
Elvis: The Movie
Eureka!
Extra Girl
Fame▲
The Fan
Fellow Traveler▲
The Five Heartbeats▲
Flashdance
Frances▲
Gemini Affair
The Gene Krupa Story
The Goddess▲
Goodbye, Norma Jean
Goodnight, Sweet Marilyn
Gore Vidal's Lincoln
Grosse Fatigue▲
The Gunfighter▲
Hail Caesar
A Hard Day's Night▲
Hard Part Begins
Harvest Melody
Hero at Large
Hollywood Heartbreak
I Ought to Be in Pictures
Idolmaker
I'll Cry Tomorrow▲
Imitation of Life
Imitation of Life▲
Inside Daisy Clover
Irreconcilable Differences
It Could Happen to You
It Should Happen to You▲
The Jacksons: An American Dream
Jacqueline Bouvier Kennedy
James Dean
The Jayne Mansfield Story
The Jazz Singer
Jimmy Hollywood
Jo Jo Dancer, Your Life Is Calling
John & Yoko: A Love Story
Keep Punching
King of Comedy▲
La Bamba▲
La Dolce Vita▲
Lady Grey
Lady Jane▲
Lady Sings the Blues
The Lady Without Camelias
Lenny▲
Let It Rock
Little Caesar▲
The Lonely Lady
Love Me or Leave Me▲
Lucy and Desi: Before the Laughter
The Magnificent Ambersons▲
The Magnificent Ambersons
Mahogany
The Main Event
The Man Who Would Be King▲
Marilyn: The Untold Story▲
Meat Loaf: To Hell and Back
Mephisto▲
Miss All-American Beauty
Mistress
Mommie Dearest
My Fair Lady▲
My Favorite Year▲
Naked in New York
Oh, God! You Devil
The One and Only
One Trick Pony
The Oscar
Payday
Pecker
Police Court
Postcards from the Edge▲
Prisoner of Rio
Provincial Actors
Pure Country
Purple Rain
The Queen of Mean
Raging Bull▲
Ransom▲
Rocky▲
Rocky 2
Rocky 3
Rocky 4
Rocky 5
The Rose▲
The Seduction
Shadow of China▲
Shakes the Clown
Shop Angel
Show People▲
Sins
Small Town Boy
Smash-Up: The Story of a Woman▲
Smithereens
S.O.B.
Soldier in Love
Solo Sunny
Star 80
A Star Is Born▲
Stardom

Stardust Memories
Sunset Boulevard▲
Svengali
Sweet Dreams
Sweet Love, Bitter
Sweet Perfection
Sweethearts▲
The Thing Called Love
The Tiger Woods Story
True Colors
Tucker: The Man and His Dream▲
Twenty Dollar Star
Two Weeks in Another Town
Valley of the Dolls
Velvet Goldmine
A Very Private Affair
What Ever Happened to Baby Jane?▲
What Price Hollywood?▲
What's Love Got to Do with It?
While the City Sleeps▲
Winning▲
Wired
A Woman Named Jackie
You Light Up My Life
Ziegfeld Girl▲

Princes/Princesses
see *Royalty*

Prison
see *Great Escapes; Men in Prison; POW/MIA; Women in Prison*

Private Eyes
Abbott and Costello Meet the Invisible Man▲
Accomplice
Adventures of a Private Eye
Alphaville▲
Angel Heart
Are You Lonesome Tonight
Arrest Bulldog Drummond
The Art of Crime
Asylum
Backstreet Justice
Bad Seed
The Big Empty▲
The Big Fall
The Big Sleep▲
The Big Sleep
Big Store
Black Bird
Blackout
Blade in Hong Kong
Bloodhounds 2
The Blue Lightning
Bootleg
Brown's Requiem
Bulldog Drummond
Bulldog Drummond at Bay
Bulldog Drummond Comes Back
Bulldog Drummond Escapes
Bulldog Drummond's Bride
Bulldog Drummond's Peril
Bulldog Drummond's Revenge
Bulldog Drummond's Secret Police
Bulldog Jack▲
Calling Paul Temple
Camouflage
The Case of the Lucky Legs
Cast a Deadly Spell▲
Castle in the Desert
Charlie Chan and the Curse of the Dragon Queen
Charlie Chan at the Opera▲
Charlie Chan at the Wax Museum
Charlie Chan in Paris
Charlie Chan in Rio
Charlie Chan in the Secret Service
Charlie Chan's Secret
Chinatown▲
The Chinese Cat
Clean Slate
Conspiracy of Terror
Cry Uncle
The Curse of the Jade Scorpion
The Dain Curse
Dancing with Danger
Dark Corner▲
The Dark Hour
Dark Side of Midnight
Dead Again▲
Dead Men Don't Wear Plaid
Dead Pigeon on Beethoven Street
Deadly Force
Deadly Illusion
Deadly Passion
Deadly Sins
Death Train
Deceptions 2: Edge of Deception
Detective Sadie & Son
Devil in a Blue Dress▲
The Devil's Cargo
Diabolique
The Doorbell Rang: A Nero Wolfe Mystery
The Drowning Pool
8mm
The Empty Beach
The End of the Affair▲
Entangled
Everybody Wins
Eye of the Killer
Face Down
The Falcon in Hollywood
The Falcon in Mexico
The Falcon's Brother
False Witness
Farewell, My Lovely▲
Fearless
Fiction Makers
For Sale
Fourth Story▲
From Hollywood to Deadwood
Ginger
Girl Hunters
The Golden Spiders: A Nero Wolfe Mystery
Gotham▲
The Gumshoe Kid
A Gun, a Car, a Blonde
Hat Box Mystery
Hollywood Confidential
House of Mystery
Human Desires
I, the Jury
In the Deep Woods
Indiscreet
Infamous Crimes
The Inner Circle
The Invisible Avenger
The Jade Mask
The Kennel Murder Case
The Kill
Kill Me Again
The King Murder
Kiss Me Deadly▲
La Rupture
Lady in Cement
Lady in the Lake
The Late Show▲
The Long Goodbye▲
The Long Kiss Goodnight
Long Time Gone
Lord of Illusions
The Lost Son
Love at Large▲
Love Walked In
A Low Down Dirty Shame
Magnum P.I.: Don't Eat the Snow in Hawaii
The Maltese Falcon▲
The Man Who Would Not Die
The Man with Bogart's Face
Margin for Murder
Marlowe
Meet Sexton Blake
Meeting at Midnight
Midnight Limited
Mindstorm
Mirage
Missing Pieces
Mr. Moto's Last Warning▲
Mr. Wong, Detective
Mr. Wong in Chinatown
The Monkey's Mask
Moonlighting
Mortal Sins
Murder by Death
Murder in the Doll House
Murder, My Sweet▲
Murder over New York
Murderous Vision
Mystery of Mr. Wong
Nature's Playmates
Night Moves▲
One of My Wives Is Missing
One Shoe Makes It Murder
Out of the Past▲
The Panther's Claw
Pas Tres Catholique
Perfect Lies
Peter Gunn
Phantom of Chinatown
Pier 23
Powder Burn
Radioactive Dreams
The Red Raven Kiss-Off
The Return of Boston Blackie
Return of Frank Cannon
The Right Temptation
Roaring City
Ryder P.I.
Satan Met a Lady
Satan's Harvest
Scalp Merchant
The Scarlet Clue
Sexton Blake and the Hooded Terror
Shaft▲
Shaft in Africa
Shaft's Big Score
Shamus
The Shanghai Cobra
Sheba, Baby
The Singing Detective
Slow Burn
Small Vices: A Spenser Mystery
Smile, Jenny, You're Dead
The Soft Kill
South Beach
Speedtrap
Spenser: Ceremony
Spenser: Pale Kings & Princes
Stolen Kisses▲
Strange Shadows in an Empty Room
Sunset Grill
Suspicious Minds
Sweet Lies
TekWar
There's Something about Mary▲
They All Laughed
Third Degree Burn
Tony Rome
TripleCross
Trixie
Twilight▲
The Two Jakes
Ulterior Motives
Under Suspicion
Uneasy Terms
Unsuitable Job for a Woman
Vegas
V.I. Warshawski
Victim of Desire
Vortex
Waikiki
Web of Deception
Where's Marlowe?
Who Framed Roger Rabbit▲
Witch Hunt
Zero Effect

Prom
see also *Hell High School; School Daze*
Carrie▲
The Club
Drive Me Crazy
Footloose
Hello Mary Lou: Prom Night 2
Jawbreaker
Never Been Kissed
The Night Before
Peggy Sue Got Married
Pretty in Pink
Prom Night
Prom Night 3: The Last Kiss
Prom Night 4: Deliver Us from Evil
The Rage: Carrie 2
Rock, Rock, Rock
She's All That
The Texas Chainsaw Massacre 4: The Next Generation
Trippin'
Whatever It Takes

Propaganda
see also *Patriotism & Paranoia; Politics*
Air Force▲
Alfred Hitchcock's Aventure Malgache
Alfred Hitchcock's Bon Voyage
Arsenal▲
The Atomic Cafe▲
Baltic Deputy▲
Behind the Rising Sun
The Black King
Blood on the Sun
Born American
Chapayev▲
China
The Commies Are Coming, the Commies Are Coming
Corregidor
Dangerous Hours
Desperate Journey
The End of St. Petersburg▲
Fighting Seabees
The General Line▲
The Green Berets
Guadalcanal Diary
Hangmen Also Die
Invasion U.S.A.
Jud Suess▲
Mrs. Miniver▲
A Mormon Maid
No Greater Love
Passage to Marseilles▲
Que Viva Mexico▲
The Red Menace
Red Nightmare
Reefer Madness
Reunion in France
Rocket Attack U.S.A.
Shack Out on 101▲
Strike▲
Teenage Devil Dolls
Ten Days That Shook the World▲
Ten Nights in a Bar-Room
The Thief
Threads▲
To the Shores of Tripoli
Tomorrow's Children
Trapped by the Mormons
Zvenigora▲

Prostitutes
see *Oldest Profession*

Protests
see also *Rebel With a Cause*
Born on the Fourth of July▲
Forrest Gump▲
Hairspray▲
In the Name of the Father▲
The Long Walk Home▲
Malcolm X▲
Matewan▲
Michael Collins▲
Norma Rae▲
Panther
Red Kiss▲
Silkwood▲

Psychiatry
see *Shrinks*

Psychic Abilities
see also *Mystery & Suspense; Supernatural Comedies; Supernatural Horror*
After Midnight
Blink of an Eye
Carrie▲
The Dark
Dark Sanity
Dead Zone▲
Deathtrap
Don't Look Now▲
Dream Man
Dreamscape
Fear
Final Destination
Firestarter
Firestarter 2: Rekindled
Friday the 13th, Part 7: The New Blood
The Frighteners
From Hell▲
Ghost▲
The Gift
The Haunting▲
Hearts in Atlantis
Last Rites
The Legend of Hell House▲
Life Without Dick
Love and Human Remains▲
Mindstorm
The Mothman Prophecies
Poltergeist▲
Poltergeist 2: The Other Side
Poltergeist 3
The Psychic
Scanner Cop
Scanner Cop 2: Volkin's Revenge
Scanners
Scanners 2: The New Order
Scanners 3: The Takeover
Scanners: The Showdown
Seance on a Wet Afternoon▲
Second Sight
The Shining
The Sixth Sense▲
Stephen King's Rose Red
Trancers
Vibes

Psycho-Thriller
see also *Mystery & Suspense*
Absolute Power
Afraid of the Dark
After Darkness
After Midnight
Alligator Eyes
Almanac of Fall
Almost Dead
Ambition
Anatomy of a Psycho
Apartment Complex
Apartment Zero▲
Apology
Are You Lonesome Tonight
The Arousers
The Art of Dying▲
The Astronaut's Wife
Asunder
Asylum
The Attic
Awakening of Candra
Baby Monitor: Sound of Fear
The Babysitter
Bad Influence
The Bad Seed
Baffled
Being at Home with Claude
The Berlin Affair
Betrayal
Beware, My Lovely
Beyond Erotica
Bird of Prey
Bitter Moon
Bizarre
Black and White As Day and Night
Black Day Blue Night
Blacklight
Bloodknot
Blow-Up▲
Body Chemistry 2: Voice of a Stranger
Bone Daddy
Bound
The Boys Club
Breach of Conduct
The Break Up
Breaking Point
Brighton Strangler
A Brilliant Disguise
Brimstone & Treacle▲
By the Blood of Others▲
Call Me
Cape Fear▲
Captive
The Case of the Frightened Lady
Cat's Play
Cause for Alarm
Circumstances Unknown
Closer and Closer
Cold Heaven
Cold Light of Day
Cold Room
The Collector▲
The Comfort of Strangers▲
Conflict▲
The Corporate Ladder
The Courtyard
The Crew
Crimetime
The Crush
Cul de Sac▲
Cupid
Curse of the Stone Hand
Cyberstalker
Daddy's Gone A-Hunting▲
Dangerous Pursuit
Dangerous Touch
A Dark Adapted Eye▲
Dark Mirror▲
The Dark Past▲
The Dark Ride
Dark Waters
Darkroom
Day of Wrath▲
The Day the Sun Turned Cold▲
Dead As a Doorman
Dead Calm▲
Deadbolt
Deadly Daphne's Revenge
Deadly Game
Deadly Hero▲
Deadly Lessons
Deadly Sunday
Death Benefit
Deceiver
Deconstructing Sarah
Deep Down
Depraved
Deranged
Desperate Measures
Desperate Prey
Devil in the Flesh
Diabolique▲
Diabolique
Diary of a Serial Killer
Disturbance
Disturbed
Dolores Claiborne▲
The Donor
Don't Answer the Phone
Don't Talk to Strangers
Doppelganger: The Evil Within
Down, Out and Dangerous
Dream Lover
Dressed for Death
The Drifter
Dynasty of Fear
8mm
Entangled
Every Breath
Evil Has a Face
Evil Judgment
The Ex
Eye of the Beholder
Eye of the Storm
Eyes of the Beholder
Facade
Facing the Enemy
Fair Game
The Fall
Fallen
Falling Down
The Fan
Fatal Attraction▲
A Fatal Inversion
Fatally Yours
Fear
The Fear Inside
Final Approach
The Flaming Urge
Flinch
Force of Evil

▲ = rated three bones or higher

Psycho-Thriller

The 4th Floor
Freeway
Frenchman's Farm
Fright
Funny Games
Gallowglass▲
The Game▲
Gaslight▲
The Gingerbread Man
Girl in Black Stockings
Girly
The Glass House
Gross Misconduct
Hallucination
The Hand
The Hand that Rocks the Cradle
Haunted
Hellbent
Highway Hitcher
The Hitch-Hiker▲
Honeymoon
House of Games▲
The House on Todville Road
Hush
Hush, Hush, Sweet Charlotte▲
I Never Promised You a Rose Garden▲
In a Glass Cage
In Dreams
In the Heat of Passion
In the Heat of Passion 2: Unfaithful
In the Realm of Passion
In the Winter Dark
The Incident
Innocent Prey
Intimate Stranger
Invasion of Privacy
Investigation
The Invisible Ghost
Jack Be Nimble
Jacob's Ladder
Jade
Jealousy
Joy Ride▲
Joyride
Juggernaut
Julia and Julia
The Juror
Kill by Inches
The Killer Inside Me
The Killing Mind
A Kiss Goodnight
Kiss of a Killer
Knife in the Water▲
Knight Moves
La Rupture
La Vengeance d'une Femme
Lady in Waiting
Laser Moon
Last Breath
The Last of Sheila
The Last Seduction▲
Le Boucher▲
Leave Her to Heaven▲
Les Bonnes Femmes▲
Letters from a Killer
The Limbic Region
Living in Peril
Love, Cheat & Steal
Love Crimes
Love Is a Gun
Love, Lies and Murder
The Machine
The Maddening
Magic
Make Haste to Live
Man on the Eiffel Tower▲
The Man Who Haunted Himself
The Mark▲
Marnie▲
Maternal Instincts
Mayalunta
The Meal
Mean Season
Memories of Murder
Midnight Edition
Midnight Fear
Midnight Lace
Midnight Tease
Mind Games
Misbegotten
Misery▲
Mrs. Munck
Mortal Sins
The Most Dangerous Game▲
Mother
Moving Targets
Murder by Numbers
Murphy's Law
My Brother Has Bad Dreams
My Very Best Friend
Naked Massacre
A Name for Evil
Nature of the Beast
The Net
Never Talk to Strangers
The Night Caller
The Night of the Following Day
Night Train to Venice
The Night Walker
Nightmare at Bittercreek
Nightwatch
Number One Fan
The Offence▲
One Good Turn
One Night Stand
Opposing Force
Outrage
Pacific Heights▲
The Paint Job
Panic Station
The Paperboy
Paranoia
The Passion of Anna▲
A Passion to Kill
Peephole
Peeping Tom▲
The Penthouse
Perfect Alibi
Perfect Tenant
Performance▲
Play Misty for Me▲
Playgirl Killer
Playmaker
Poison Ivy
Portrait in Terror
Posed for Murder
Postmortem
Powder Burn
Power 98
Praying Mantis
Pretty Poison▲
Prey of the Chameleon
Profile for Murder
Psycho 3
Psychomania
A Pure Formality
Rage
Raising Cain
Ransom▲
Reason to Die
A Reflection of Fear
Relentless
Repulsion▲
Requiem for Murder
Ricochet▲
Rituals
Room to Let
Rorret▲
Sabotage▲
Savage Abduction
Seconds▲
Secret Beyond the Door
Secret Ceremony
Secret Games
Secret Games 2: The Escort
Secret Games 3
The Secretary
Secrets of Three Hungry Wives
Seduced
Seduced by Evil
The Seduction
Sensation
Separate Lives
Serial Killer
Seven▲
The Seventh Floor
Shadows in the Storm
Shallow Grave
Sharon's Secret
Shattered Image
Siesta
The Silence of the Lambs▲
Single White Female
The Sister-in-Law
The Sixth Sense▲
Sleeping with the Enemy
A Small Killing
Snapdragon
The Soft Kill
Someone to Die For
Sorry, Wrong Number▲
Sorry, Wrong Number
The Spiral Staircase▲
Spiral Staircase
Stalked
Stalking Laura
Stardust Memories
The Stepfather▲
Stepfather 2: Make Room for Daddy
Stepfather 3: Father's Day
Stigmata
Storm
Strange Illusion
The Stranger▲
Stranger by Night
A Stranger in Town
Striking Distance
Stripteaser
Suture
Svengali▲
Svengali
Sweet Killing
Tails You Live, Heads You're Dead
Tall, Dark and Deadly
A Taste for Killing
Tattoo
The Temp
The Tenant▲
Terrified
Thesis
Thicker Than Water
36 Hours▲
The Three Lives of Karen
Through a Glass Darkly▲
Through the Eyes of a Killer
The Tie That Binds
Till the End of the Night
Timebomb
To Play or to Die
Tower of Terror
Trapped
Trauma
Tryst
Tunnel Vision
Twisted Love
The Two Mrs. Carrolls
Undertow
Unforgettable
Unlawful Entry
The Vanishing▲
Vengeance Is Mine▲
Vengeance of the Dead
Victim of Love
Violated
Voyage
Wait until Dark▲
Web of Deceit
What Ever Happened To...
When Hell Was in Session▲
When the Bough Breaks
When the Dark Man Calls
Where Are the Children?
While I Live
Wicked
Wicked Ways
Wild Side
The Wind
Woman in the Window▲
You'll Like My Mother
The Young Poisoner's Handbook▲

Psychotics/ Sociopaths

see also Roommates from Hell

Accidental Meeting
Albino Alligator
Apartment Zero▲
The Avenger
Bad Ronald▲
The Bad Seed
Badlands▲
Bellamy
Berserk!
Black Eliminator
Black Panther
Black Pit of Dr. M
Blind Side
Blind Vision
Blue Steel
Body Bags
Bone Daddy
The Boston Strangler
Boxing Helena
The Boys▲
The Boys Next Door
Breakdown▲
Broken Arrow
The Butcher Boy▲
The Cable Guy
Cape Fear▲
The Centerfold Girls
City Killer
Clay Pigeons
Cold Eyes of Fear
Cold Steel
Con Air▲
Consenting Adults
Crimes of Dr. Mabuse▲
The Crush
Damned River
Dario Argento's Trauma
The Dark Past▲
The Dark Ride
Dead As a Doorman
Dead Boyz Can't Fly
Deadbolt
Deadly Daphne's Revenge
Deadly Game
Death Benefit
Death of a Soldier
Death Sentence
Dee Snider's Strangeland
Demolition Man
Demon Hunter
The Dentist
Deranged▲
Deranged
Desperate Measures
Desperate Motives
Diary of a Teenage Hitchhiker
Dr. Giggles
Don't Answer the Phone
Don't Talk to Strangers
Doppelganger: The Evil Within
Down, Out and Dangerous
The Drifter
Escape Velocity
The Escort
Ex-Cop
Eye of God▲
Eyes of the Beholder
Fade to Black
Fair Game
Falling Down
The Fan
Fast Gun
Fatal Attraction▲
Fear
Fear City
The Fear Inside
The Fiance
The Fool Killer
Force of Evil
From Dusk Till Dawn
Gallowglass▲
The Gingerbread Man
Girl in Black Stockings
The Glimmer Man
Gloria
Guardian Angel
Guilty as Sin
Halloween: H20▲
Headless Body in Topless Bar
Heat▲
Helter Skelter
Helter Skelter Murders
Highway Hitcher
Homage
Homer and Eddie
Honeymoon
The Hostage
Hot Potato
Hot Touch
House of Terror
The Housekeeper
Hush
Hush Little Baby, Don't You Cry
I Know What You Did Last Summer▲
I Still Know What You Did Last Summer
In Dreams
In the Line of Fire▲
In the Mouth of Madness
Invasion of Privacy
The Invisible Terror
Kalifornia
Keys to Tulsa
The Killer Inside Me
Killing Obsession
Killing Zoe
Killzone
Kiss the Girls
Lightning Bolt
The Lightship
The Little Girl Who Lives down the Lane
Live Wire
Lunatic
The Machine
The Mad Bomber
The Mad Executioners
Mademoiselle
A Man in Uniform
Maniac Warriors
Maternal Instincts
Meet the Deedles
Metro
Midnight 2: Sex, Death, and Videotape
Midnight Edition
Midnight Fear
Midnight Ride
Misbegotten
Mommie Dearest
Mondo Balordo
Most Wanted
Mother's Boys
Moving Targets
Murder by Numbers
Murder Elite
Murderlust
The Naked Flame
Naked Massacre
Natural Enemy
The Neighbor
Office Killer
One Good Turn
Pacific Heights▲
The Paperboy
Past Midnight
Perfect Family
Perfect Victims
Play Nice
Playgirl Killer
Poison Ivy
Pretty Poison▲
Prime Time Murder
Psycho▲
Psycho 2
Psycho 3
Psycho 4: The Beginning
Psycho Girls
Psychos in Love
Quake
The Rage
Rampage
Relentless
Repulsion▲
Reservoir Dogs▲
Resurrection Man
Retroactive
The Rich Man's Wife
Ricochet▲
The River Wild
The Road Killers
Roadkill
The Sadist
Sarah's Child
Savage Abduction
Scream▲
Scream 2▲
Scream 3
The Sea Wolf▲
The Secretary
The Seduction
Seven Hours to Judgment
The Seventh Floor
The Shining
The Silencer
Single White Female
The Sister-in-Law
Skinner
Small Kill
Speed▲
Speed 2: Cruise Control
Stalked
Starved
The Stepfather▲
Stepfather 2: Make Room for Daddy
Stepfather 3: Father's Day
Still Life
Stripped to Kill
Stripteaser
Sweet Hostage
Tainted Blood
The Taking of Beverly Hills
The Talented Mr. Ripley
Tall, Dark and Deadly
Ted & Venus
The Temp
The Tenant▲
Tetsuo: The Iron Man
A Thin Line Between Love and Hate
Thirteenth Day of Christmas
Three the Hard Way
3000 Miles to Graceland
Through the Eyes of a Killer
To Die For▲
Truth or Consequences, N.M.
Turbulence
Twin Peaks: Fire Walk with Me
The Two Mrs. Carrolls
U-Turn
Ultraviolet
Unlawful Entry
Urban Legend
The Vanishing
Vice Squad
Violence at Noon▲
Voyage
What Ever Happened to Baby Jane?▲
When a Stranger Calls Back
Whispers
White Heat▲
With a Friend Like Harry▲
Writer's Block
The Young Poisoner's Handbook▲
Zero Degrees Kelvin
The Zombie Army

Puerto Rico

The Apostate
Assassins
D.R.E.A.M. Team
Frankenstein Meets the Space Monster
Ship Ahoy

Punk Rock

see also Rock Flicks

Decline of Western Civilization 1▲
The Filth and the Fury
Hard Core Logo
Punk Rock Movie
Repo Man▲
Rock 'n' Roll High School▲
Rock 'n' Roll High School Forever
Sid & Nancy▲
Times Square

Puppets

see also Killer Toys; Toys

The Adventures of Pinocchio
Alice in Wonderland
Curse of the Puppet Master: The Human Experiment
The Dark Crystal▲
Devil Doll
Gepetto
The Great Gabbo
The Great Rupert▲
Lili▲
Magic
Meet the Feebles
Pinocchio▲
Puppet Master
Puppet Master 2
Puppet Master 4
Puppet Master 5: The Final Chapter
A Rat's Tale
Retro Puppet Master
The Sound of Music▲

Pure Ego Vehicles

see also ***Big-Budget Bombs; Rock Stars on Film***

The Adventures of Ford Fairlane
Air America
Assault of the Rebel Girls
The Big One
Boom!
Charade
Conan the Destroyer
The Dead Pool
Dee Snider's Strangeland
Fire Down Below
Foolish
Get Carter
Gummo
Harlem Nights
Hello, Dolly!
Hudson Hawk
I Got the Hook-Up
The Jazz Singer
Last Action Hero
Le Repos du Guerrier
Marie Antoinette
Modern Love
On Deadly Ground
Private Parts
Purple Rain
Rambo 3
Richard Petty Story
Running out of Luck
The Scarlet Letter
Sidekicks
SnakeEater
Sophia Loren: Her Own Story
Staying Alive
Sweet Country Road
Tarzan, the Ape Man
Thank Your Lucky Stars ▲
A Thin Line Between Love and Hate
Torch Song
200 Motels
Under the Cherry Moon
Vampire in Brooklyn
Waterworld
What Comes Around
Wildcats
The Wizard of Speed and Time
Yes, Giorgio

Queens

see ***Royalty***

Rabbits

Alice ▲
Alice in Wonderland ▲
Alice in Wonderland
Donnie Darko ▲
Fatal Attraction ▲
Harvey ▲
Mona Lisa ▲
Monty Python and the Holy Grail ▲
Nasty Rabbit
Roger & Me ▲
Space Jam
Watership Down
Who Framed Roger Rabbit ▲

Race Against Time

Acceptable Risks
Alien Space Avenger
The Andromeda Strain
Apollo 13 ▲
Balto
Bitter Harvest ▲
Blown Away
The Borrowers
Broken Arrow
Chain Reaction
The China Syndrome ▲
Coma ▲
The Corporation
Daylight
D.O.A. ▲
D.O.A.
Escape from L.A.
Fail-Safe ▲
Free Willy 2: The Adventure Home
Free Willy 3: The Rescue
Germicide
Grand Tour: Disaster in Time
Hell Commandos
I'll Be Home for Christmas
In Pursuit of Honor
Independence Day ▲
Jet Over the Atlantic
Killer on Board
Last Dance
Last Flight Out: A True Story
Lorenzo's Oil ▲
Nick of Time
Octopussy
Once Upon a Forest
Outbreak ▲
Panic in Echo Park
Panic in the Streets ▲
The Peacemaker
Prisoner in the Middle
Pursuit ▲
Race Against Time
A Rat's Tale
Return to Paradise ▲
Robot in the Family
The Silver Streak
Somebody Has to Shoot the Picture ▲
Sudden Death
The Taking of Beverly Hills
Things to Do in Denver When You're Dead ▲
Time Lock
Time Without Pity
TripFall
True Crime
Twister
Tycus
WarGames

Radio

see also ***Mass Media***

Airheads
American Nightmare
Bad Channels
Break of Dawn
Breakfast in Hollywood
Bye Bye, Love
Carefree ▲
Choose Me ▲
Citizens Band ▲
City in Panic
Comfort and Joy ▲
The Couch Trip
Danger on the Air
The Day Silence Died
Dead Air
The Fisher King ▲
FM
Freeway
Girls Night Out
Good Morning, Vietnam ▲
The Great American Broadcast ▲
The Hucksters ▲
The Jackpot
Joe Dirt
The Key Man
Laser Moon
Look Who's Laughing
Love Serenade
The Man Who Came to Dinner ▲
Midnight Confessions
Mr. Rock 'n' Roll: The Alan Freed Story
My Dream Is Yours
The Next Voice You Hear
The Night Caller
Night Rhythms
No Trace
Old Barn Dance
On the Air Live with Captain Midnight
Once Upon a Honeymoon
Open House
Outside Ozona
People Are Funny
People's Choice
The Phantom Broadcast
Play Misty for Me ▲
Pot o' Gold
Power 98
Private Parts
Psycho 4: The Beginning
Pump Up the Volume
Rachel River
Radio Days ▲
Radioland Murders
Rebecca of Sunnybrook Farm
Requiem for Murder
Rude
Sexual Response
Sleepless in Seattle ▲
Straight Talk
Strike Up the Band
Talk Radio ▲
Telling Lies in America
There Goes Kelly
The Truth about Cats and Dogs ▲
Tune in Tomorrow
Up in the Air
Whistling in Brooklyn
Who Done It?
Winchell

Rags to Riches

see also ***Price of Fame; Wrong Side of the Tracks***

The Abe Lincoln of Ninth Avenue
Aladdin ▲
All the King's Men ▲
The Amorous Adventures of Moll Flanders
Annie
B.A.P.'s
Better Late Than Never
The Beverly Hillbillies
Blank Check
Body Slam
Boogie Nights ▲
Breaking Glass
Brewster's Millions
The Buddy Holly Story ▲
Callie and Son
Can You Hear the Laughter? The Story of Freddie Prinze
Christmas in July ▲
Citizen Kane ▲
Coal Miner's Daughter ▲
Covergirl
Craig's Wife ▲
Daddy Long Legs ▲
Dangerous When Wet
Darling ▲
Dodsworth ▲
Dreamer
Drifting Souls
EDtv
Emperor Jones
Evita
Fifth Avenue Girl
Footlight Parade ▲
For Richer, for Poorer
Forever Amber
Give a Girl a Break
Great Expectations
The Great Rupert ▲
Hero ▲
Honeyboy
The Hudsucker Proxy ▲
I Love Melvin
It Could Happen to You
Jailhouse Rock ▲
The Jerk
Jimmy Hollywood
Joseph Andrews
Kept Husbands
A Kid for Two Farthings
Kipps ▲
La Vie Est Belle
Lady for a Day ▲
Lady Grey
The Last American Hero ▲
The Last Laugh ▲
Laurel & Hardy: Below Zero
Lenny ▲
Lili ▲
Little Lord Fauntleroy ▲
Little Lord Fauntleroy
Livin' Large
Lots of Luck
Love Nest
Lucky Partners
The Mambo Kings ▲
The Manions of America
Mannequin
Meet John Doe ▲
A Million to Juan
Miss Melody Jones
Mrs. Parkington
Mrs. Winterbourne
Mr. Billion
Money for Nothing
My Fair Lady ▲
New York's Finest
The Object of Beauty ▲
One in a Million: The Ron LeFlore Story
Only One Night
The Patsy
The Pearl ▲
Peddlin' in Society
Possessed
Power
Pride of the Clan
The Prince and the Pauper ▲
The Prince and the Pauper
The Prince and the Showgirl
Princess Tam Tam ▲
Pygmalion ▲
Rebecca of Sunnybrook Farm
Rocky ▲
Scarlet Dawn
Scruples
The Secret of My Success
Sepia Cinderella
The Sin of Harold Diddlebock
The Sin of Madelon Claudet ▲
Sing Your Worries Away
Speak Easily
The Stars Fell on Henrietta
The Stork Club
Straight Talk
Striker's Mountain
Sweet Adeline
Sweet Hearts Dance
The Tall Guy ▲
Tennessee Stallion
Three Coins in the Fountain
The Toast of New Orleans
Toast of New York ▲
Trading Places
Trois Couleurs: Blanc ▲
The Unsinkable Molly Brown ▲
Up Close and Personal ▲
What Price Hollywood? ▲
A Woman of Substance
Working Girl ▲
Ziegfeld Girl ▲

Rape

see also ***Sexual Abuse***

The Accused ▲
Act of Vengeance
The Adventurers
American Commandos
And Justice for All
Awakening of Candra
Backlash
Bad Lieutenant ▲
Baise Moi
Bandit Queen
Bastard out of Carolina
The Beast Within
Blackrock
Blind Justice
Blue Desert ▲
Body Shots
Born Innocent
Boys Don't Cry ▲
Broken Badge ▲
A Brother's Kiss
Bullies
Caged Heat 2: Stripped of Freedom
Caged Terror
Cast the First Stone
Casualties of War ▲
The Center of the World
Certain Sacrifice
Chain Gang Women
Class of 1984
Code of Honor
Convicted
Coward of the County
Cracker: Men Should Weep
Dead Man Walking ▲
Deadline Assault
Deadly Daphne's Revenge
Deadly Darling
Deadly Twins
Death and the Maiden ▲
Death Blow
Death Wish
Deep in the Heart
Deliverance ▲
Demented
Demon Seed ▲
Desolation Angels
The Desperados
Diary of a Lost Girl ▲
Diary of a Teenage Hitchhiker
Divided We Stand
Emmanuelle's Daughter
The Entity
Extremities
An Eye for an Eye
Final Justice
Flesh and Blood
Forbidden Sun
Forced Entry
Free, White, and 21
From the Life of the Marionettes ▲
Fugitive Among Us
The General's Daughter
Gentle Savage
Girls Town
Gossip
Guncrazy
Hands of a Stranger
Hannie Caulder
Heat of the Flame
His Name Was King
Home Before Midnight
The Hooked Generation
The Hotel New Hampshire
I Am Frigid...Why?
I Spit on Your Grave
I'm the One You're Looking For
In Trouble
It's Alive ▲
Jackson County Jail
Jaded
Jailbait: Betrayed By Innocence
Judge Horton and the Scottsboro Boys
Kika
Kiss of a Killer
The Ladies Club
Landscape in the Mist ▲
Lethal Woman
Lipstick
Liquid Sky ▲
The Marquise of O
Ms. 45 ▲
Mrs. R's Daughter
Most Wanted
Motor Psycho
Multiple Maniacs
Naked Vengeance
Necromancer: Satan's Servant
Night of the Demon
Northville Cemetery Massacre
Olivier, Olivier ▲
One of Her Own
One Tough Cop
Open Doors ▲
Outrage
A Passage to India ▲
The Phantom of Soho
Positive I.D.
Postcards from America
Purgatory
Quiet Days in Hollywood
Rage ▲
Rape and Marriage: The Rideout Case
Rape of Love
Rashomon ▲
A Reason to Believe
Rider on the Rain ▲
Rob Roy ▲
Sci-Fighters
Screamer
Sex Crimes
Shame
The Shaming
She Came on the Bus
Short Fuse
Showgirls
Silent Witness
Sin and Redemption
Sketch Artist 2: Hands That See
Slashed Dreams
The Story of Esther Costello
A Stranger Is Watching
Straw Dogs ▲
Streets
Sudden Death
Sudden Impact
Tainted
Time to Kill
A Time to Kill ▲
Titus
To Kill a Mockingbird ▲
To Kill a Stranger
The Tormentors
Town without Pity
Trespasses
Violated
Violent Ones
The Violent Years
Vukovar ▲
When He's Not a Stranger ▲
When Justice Fails
Wild Riders
The Wind ▲
The Young One

Rebel With a Cause

see also ***Rebel Without a Cause; The Resistance***

Acceptable Risks
The Accused ▲
Ace High
The Adventures of Robin Hood ▲
Afterburn ▲
Alice's Restaurant
American Tiger
Ann Vickers
The Applegates
Armageddon: The Final Challenge
As Young As You Feel ▲
The Attic: The Hiding of Anne Frank
Basquiat ▲
Billy Jack
The Blob
Blue Collar ▲
Born Losers
Boyz N the Hood ▲
Braveheart ▲
Brubaker ▲
Burglar ▲
The Burmese Harp ▲
The China Syndrome ▲
Courage ▲
Courageous Dr. Christian
Crime of Honor
Dark Rider
Daybreak
Dead Poets Society ▲
Deadly Business ▲
Deadly Stranger
Demolition High
Die Hard ▲
Die Hard 2: Die Harder ▲
Disturbing Behavior
Dragon Fury
A Dream for Christmas ▲
Dust ▲
East of Eden ▲
East of Eden
Easy Wheels
Exiled in America
The Fighter ▲
The Fighter
The Final Alliance
The Firing Line
The $5.20 an Hour Dream
Flesh and the Spur
Flight of the Intruder
Foxfire
The Fugitive ▲
The Gambling Samurai
Game of Survival
Gandhi ▲
Gorillas in the Mist ▲
Guess Who's Coming to Dinner ▲
Hair ▲
Hardcore
Hidden City
In the Name of the Father ▲
Iron Horsemen
Iron Thunder

James Dean: Live Fast, Die Young
Jesse
Joe Kidd
Johnny Firecloud
Katherine
Kidnapped
Killing of Randy Webster
Knights of the City
Kung Fu
La Marseillaise▲
The Last American Hero▲
Lawrence of Arabia▲
Legend of Billie Jean
Legend of Earl Durand
Legend of the Lone Ranger
Light It Up
Little Tough Guys
Lois Gibbs and the Love Canal
The Loneliness of the Long Distance Runner▲
Lust for Life▲
Luther
Man of Marble▲
The Manhattan Project
Marie▲
Memories of Underdevelopment
Michael Collins▲
Mr. Smith Goes to Washington▲
Mountain Man
Network▲
Night of Evil
Norma Rae▲
Northern Lights▲
Odd Man Out▲
One-Eyed Jacks▲
One Man Jury
One Man's War
Original Intent
Outbreak▲
Overdrawn at the Memory Bank
Patch Adams
Paths of Glory▲
Patty Hearst
Plutonium Baby
Prefontaine
The Principal
Private Parts
Project X
Punk Rock Movie
Quarantine
A Raisin in the Sun▲
Rob Roy▲
Robin Hood: Prince of Thieves
The Rock▲
Roe vs. Wade▲
Rooster: Spurs of Death!
Sakharov▲
Samaritan: The Mitch Snyder Story▲
The Sand Pebbles▲
Sansho the Bailiff▲
Save the Lady
The Scarlet Pimpernel▲
The Scarlet Pimpernel
The Scarlet Pimpernel 2: Mademoiselle Guillotine
The Scarlet Pimpernel 3: The Kidnapped King
The Secret Agent
Serpico▲
The Shock
Silkwood▲
Sins of Rome
Solo
Somebody Has to Shoot the Picture▲
Stay Away, Joe
Steel Frontier
The Stranger
The Stranger Wore a Gun
Sympathy for the Devil
Taffin
Tank Girl
The Texican
This Land Is Mine▲
The Tin Star▲
To Kill a Priest
Trial of the Catonsville Nine
True Believer
Under Western Stars
V: The Final Battle
Vengeance
WarGames
The Westerner▲
When a Man Rides Alone
Wisdom
Without Limits▲

Rebel Without a Cause

see also *Rebel With a Cause*

Across the Tracks
All Night Long▲
Badlands▲
A Boy and His Dog
The Boys Next Door
Breathless▲
Breathless
Cheech and Chong's Up in Smoke
A Clockwork Orange▲
Cool As Ice
The Cruel Story of Youth▲
Dino
Easy Rider▲
The Electric Horseman
The Fence
Ferris Bueller's Day Off▲
Five Easy Pieces▲
The Fugitive Kind
Fury to Freedom: The Life Story of Raul Ries
Girls' Town
Going Places▲
Gore Vidal's Billy the Kid
Great Missouri Raid
Guncrazy
Heart Beat
Hud▲
I Was a Teenage Werewolf
If...▲
Inventing the Abbotts
Just for the Hell of It
Kicked in the Head
Leather Jackets
The Little Valentino
Loser
Lost Angels
Niagara, Niagara
On the Edge: The Survival of Dana
Over the Edge▲
Petit Con
Presumed Guilty
Pump Up the Volume
Rambo: First Blood, Part 2
Rambo 3
Rebel High
Rebel Rousers
Rebel without a Cause▲
Reckless
Road House
Roadracers
Rocky 4
September 30, 1955
sex, lies and videotape▲
Shopping
SLC Punk!
Snow Kill
Suburbia
Summer Camp Nightmare
That Was Then...This Is Now
3:15—The Moment of Truth
Thunder Road▲
Top Gun
The Violent Years
West Side Story▲
The Wild Angels
The Wild One▲
The Wild Ride

Red Cross

China Beach▲
One Against the Wind▲
So Proudly We Hail▲
The White Cliffs of Dover▲

Red Scare

see also *Politics; Russia/USSR*

Arsenal▲
Baltic Deputy▲
The Bamboo Saucer
Battle Beneath the Earth
A Beautiful Mind▲
Chapayev▲
China Cry
China, My Sorrow
Coming Out of the Ice▲
Comment Ca Va?
The Commies Are Coming, the Commies Are Coming
Commissar▲
Comrade X
Conspirator
Dash and Lilly
Death of a Bureaucrat▲
Earth▲
Eminent Domain
Fellow Traveler▲
Golden Gate
The Great Armored Car Swindle
Guilty by Suspicion
Guilty of Treason
Hands Up▲
Hawthorne of the USA
Indochine▲
The Inner Circle▲
The Interrogation▲
Invasion U.S.A.
Jet Pilot
Little World of Don Camillo▲
Man of Iron▲
Man of Marble▲
The Manchurian Candidate▲
Mandela▲
Mother Kusters Goes to Heaven▲
Mother of Kings
Never Let Me Go
Nicholas and Alexandra
Night Crossing
Night Flight from Moscow
The Oak
Oh, Bloody Life!
Open Doors▲
Red Dawn
The Red Menace
Red Nightmare
Reds▲
Requiem for Dominic▲
Revolution! A Red Comedy▲
The She-Beast
Sideburns
Strike▲
The Theme▲
Thoughts Are Free▲
Tito and Me▲
Tobor the Great
Trahir▲
The Ugly American
Uranus▲
When Father Was Away on Business▲

Reefer Madness

How High
Reefer Madness
Saving Grace
The Wash

Rehab

see also *Drug Abuse; On the Rocks*

Bounce
Clean and Sober▲
Gridlock'd▲
Jesus' Son
28 Days
When a Man Loves a Woman

Reincarnation

see also *Death & the Afterlife*

Angel on My Shoulder▲
Angel on My Shoulder
Audrey Rose
Bram Stoker's The Mummy
Chances Are▲
Cleo/Leo
Creature of Destruction
Dead Again▲
Devi▲
Down to Earth
Fluke
Goodbye Charlie
Heart and Souls
Heaven Can Wait▲
Here Comes Mr. Jordan▲
I Married a Witch▲
Little Buddha
The Mummy
The Mummy Returns
Oh, Heavenly Dog!
On a Clear Day You Can See Forever
The Reincarnation of Peter Proud
The Robot vs. the Aztec Mummy
The Search for Bridey Murphy
Switch▲
Tales of the Kama Sutra 2: Monsoon
Tequila Body Shots
The Vengeance of She

Religion

see also *Buddhism; Islam; Judaism; Missionaries; Nuns & Priests; Religious Epics; Saints*

Abduction of St. Anne
Absolution
The Addiction
Alice Sweet Alice
Androcles and the Lion
Angel Baby
Angela
Anna
The Apostle▲
Augustine of Hippo▲
The Avenging Angel
Bear Ye One Another's Burden...
Before the Rain▲
Bernadette
The Big Squeeze
The Birch Interval
Blood of Jesus
The Body
Body and Soul
Breaking the Waves▲
Brides of Christ
Brigham City
Brigham Young: Frontiersman
Broken Vows
Brother Sun, Sister Moon
Brothers in Arms
The Butcher Boy▲
Camila▲
Catholics▲
Chariots of Fire▲
Children of Fury
Chocolat▲
The Church▲
Citizen Ruth
Come to the Stable▲
Commandments
Conquest of Space
Contact
The Convent
Cosmic Slop
The Courageous Mr. Penn
Cracker: The Big Crunch
Crimes of Passion▲
Critical Choices
The Crucible▲
A Cry from the Mountain
Day of Judgment
Day of Triumph
Dead Man Walking▲
Def by Temptation
Destiny
Devi▲
The Devil at 4 O'Clock
The Disappearance of Aimee▲
Divided by Hate
Dr. Syn
Dr. Syn, Alias the Scarecrow
Dogma
A Dream for Christmas▲
Earth
El Cid▲
Elizabeth▲
Emanon
The End of the Affair▲
Enjo
Entertaining Angels: The Dorothy Day Story
An Everlasting Piece
Extramuros
Eye of God▲
The Favor, the Watch, & the Very Big Fish
The Fiend
Final Judgment
The Flowers of St. Francis▲
A Fool and His Money
Francesco
Friendly Persuasion▲
From a Far Country: Pope John Paul II
The Garden
The Gaucho▲
The Ghoul
Glory! Glory!▲
Go Down Death
The Godfather, Part 3▲
God's Gun
Godspell
Gospa
Greaser's Palace
The Greatest Story Ever Told
Green Pastures▲
The Guyana Tragedy: The Story of Jim Jones
Hail Mary
Hallelujah!▲
Harvest of Fire
Hazel's People
Heavens Above▲
Helas pour Moi
Hellfire
Holy Man
Holy Matrimony
The Hoodlum Priest▲
Household Saints▲
The Hunchback
I, the Worst of All
I'd Climb the Highest Mountain▲
In God We Trust
In the Line of Duty: Ambush in Waco
Inherit the Wind▲
The Inquiry
Invasion of the Space Preachers
Iron Horsemen
Jeanne la Pucelle
Jerusalem
Jesus
Jesus Christ, Superstar▲
Jesus Christ Superstar
Jesus of Nazareth
Jesus of Nazareth▲
The Jesus Trip
The Jew
Joan of Arc
Joni
The Judas Project: The Ultimate Encounter
Klondike Annie
Knock's at My Door
Kristin Lavransdatter
La Chartreuse de Parme
The Last Temptation of Christ▲
Laughing Sinners
Leap of Faith
Leaves from Satan's Book
Left Behind: The Movie
The Light of Faith
Lilies
Little Buddha
Little Church Around the Corner
The Littlest Angel
The Loss of Sexual Innocence
Love and Faith▲
Lust and Revenge
Luther
Major Barbara▲
A Man Called Peter▲
A Man for All Seasons▲
Marjoe
Martin Luther
Mary, Mother of Jesus
Mary, Queen of Scots
Mayflower: The Pilgrims' Adventure
The Message
The Milky Way▲
The Milky Way
The Miracle▲
Miracle in Rome
The Miracle of Marcelino
Miracle of Our Lady of Fatima
The Miracle Woman
Monsieur Vincent▲
Monsignor Quixote
Monty Python's Life of Brian▲
A Mormon Maid
Mother Joan of the Angels▲
Mother Teresa: In the Name of God's Poor
The Neon Bible
The Next Voice You Hear
The Night of the Iguana▲
Nostalghia
One Man's Way
Oranges Are Not the Only Fruit
Ordet▲
The Other Side of Heaven
The Other Side of Sunday
Padre Nuestro
Pass the Ammo
The Passion of Darkly Noon
Passion of Joan of Arc▲
The Passover Plot
The Penitent
Peter and Paul
Pi
Picking Up the Pieces
Pray TV
A Prayer in the Dark
Preacherman
The Preacher's Wife
Priest
Prisoner of Rio
Private Confessions
The Private Secretary
The Prodigal Planet
Promised a Miracle
The Quarry
Queen Margot▲
Quo Vadis▲
Quo Vadis
Rain
The Rapture
The Rector's Wife
Red Planet Mars
Resurrection▲
Resurrection
Return to Paradise
Revelation
RoGoPaG
Romero
Sacrilege
St. Benny the Dip
Saint Joan
Saint Maybe▲
St. Patrick: The Irish Legend
Salome
Salvation!
Sanctuary of Fear
The Scarlet Letter▲
Sebastiane▲
Shadowlands▲
The Sky Pilot
The Song of Bernadette▲
Stigmata
A Stranger in the Kingdom
Susan and God▲
Tales from the Crypt Presents Bordello of Blood
That Eye, the Sky
The Third Miracle
This Stuff'll Kill Ya!
Through a Glass Darkly▲
Touch
Tournament
Trapped by the Mormons
Tribulation
The Vision
A Walk to Remember
West Beirut
When Night Is Falling▲
Where Angels Go, Trouble Follows
Whistle down the Wind▲
Whistling in the Dark▲
Whitcomb's War
The White Rose▲
Wholly Moses!
Why Has Bodhi-Darma Left for the East
Wide Awake
The Winter Light▲
Wise Blood▲
Witness▲

▲ = rated three bones or higher

The Word
The Worldly Madonna

Religious Epics

***see also** Religion*
Abraham
A.D.
The Agony and the Ecstasy
...And God Spoke
Barabbas
Ben-Hur▸
The Bible
Cleopatra
David
David and Bathsheba▸
Demetrius and the Gladiators
The Egyptian
El Cid▸
From the Manger to the Cross
The Gospel According to St. Matthew▸
In the Name of the Pope-King▸
Jacob
Jesus
Jesus of Nazareth
Joseph
Judith of Bethulia▸
The King of Kings▸
The Messiah▸
Moses
Noah's Ark
Prince of Egypt▸
The Prodigal
The Robe
Samson and Delilah
The Sign of the Cross
Sodom and Gomorrah
The Song of Bernadette▸
The Story of David▸
The Story of Jacob & Joseph▸
The Story of Ruth
The Sword and the Cross
The Ten Commandments
The Ten Commandments▸

Renegade Body Parts

***see also** Killer Brains*
The Addams Family
Addams Family Values
And Now the Screaming Starts
The Animal
The Beast with Five Fingers
Blood of Ghastly Horror
Body Parts
The Brain that Wouldn't Die
The Crawling Eye
The Crawling Hand
Demonoid, Messenger of Death
Doctor Butcher M.D.
Dr. Terror's House of Horrors
8 Heads in a Duffel Bag
Evil Dead 2: Dead by Dawn
Gravesend
The Hand▸
Hands of a Stranger
The Hands of Orlac
How to Get Ahead in Advertising▸
Idle Hands
The Incredible Two-Headed Transplant
Killer Tongue
The Kingdom▸
The Kingdom 2▸
Mad Love▸
The Man with Two Brains▸
Mindkiller
Picking Up the Pieces
Quicksilver Highway
Severed Ties
The Thing with Two Heads
Tomcats
Virus
Waxwork 2: Lost in Time

Rent-a-Cop

Above the Rim
Armed and Dangerous
Cyber-Tracker
End of Days
The Heist
Hobgoblins
Inspector Gadget
Light It Up
Mannequin
Rent-A-Cop
Star Spangled Rhythm▸
Tapeheads
Trixie
Unbreakable
Urban Legend

Repressed Men

***see also** Men*
The Age of Innocence▸
American Beauty▸
Beloved/Friend
Bitter Moon
Bleak Moments
The Bodyguard
Box of Moonlight
Creation of Adam
The Eighth Day
El
Falling Down
Felicia's Journey▸
Fight Club: °▸
The Game▸
Howard's End▸
In and Out▸
Kiss the Sky
Like It Never Was Before
The Little Kidnappers
Love and Death on Long Island
Maurice▸
The Preacher's Wife
A Rather English Marriage
The Red Dwarf
The Remains of the Day▸
Shadowlands▸
Sirens
Yi Yi
Zero Degrees Kelvin

Rescue Missions

***see also** Rescue Missions Involving Time Travel*
Agent of Death
Air Rage
Alaska
Alone in the Woods
The Amazing Panda Adventure
Any Place But Home
Apollo 13▸
Balto
Behind Enemy Lines
Berlin Tunnel 21
Black Hawk Down▸
Blade II
Blind Heat
Boomerang
Born to Be Wild
Breakout
A Bug's Life▸
Caged Fear
The Chamber
The Children
The City of Lost Children▸
Comanche Station
Commando▸
Con Air▸
Courage Under Fire▸
Crossfire
Dante's Peak
Daredevils of the Red Circle
Dark Mountain
Daylight
Dead Ahead
Desperate Women
The Diamond of Jeru
Die Hard▸
Die Hard 2: Die Harder▸
Die Hard: With a Vengeance
The Dirty Dozen: The Deadly Mission
Django Strikes Again
Dragonworld
Ernest Scared Stupid
Escape from L.A.
Event Horizon
The Ewok Adventure
Executioner of Venice
Executive Decision
Expect No Mercy
Far from Home: The Adventures of Yellow Dog
First Daughter
Force: Five
Free Willy
Free Willy 2: The Adventure Home
Free Willy 3: The Rescue
Grizzly Mountain
Hard Ticket to Hawaii
The Hidden Fortress▸
High Velocity
Hired to Kill
Honeybaby
Ice Age▸
In the Company of Spies
Independence Day▸
The Inn of the Sixth Happiness▸
Jenny's War
Joey
Journey to the Center of the Earth
Jurassic Park 3
Kidnapped in Paradise
Kids of the Round Table
Killing Streets
Legend of the Lost Tomb
The Lone Runner
The Losers
Losing Isaiah▸
Lucie Aubrac
The Magnificent Seven▸
Managua
Master of Disguise
Mercenary 2: Thick and Thin
Mercy Mission
Miracle at Midnight
Ms. Bear
Missing in Action
Missing in Action 2: The Beginning
Mission to Mars
Naked Souls
Navy SEALS
Oliver & Company
One Small Hero
Operation Delta Force 2: Mayday
Operation Dumbo Drop
Ordeal in the Arctic
Outbreak▸
Pray for Death
Prince Valiant
Raid on Entebbe▸
Rambo: First Blood, Part 2
Red Planet
The Rescue
Rescue Me
The Rescuers▸
The Rescuers Down Under
Rescuers: Stories of Courage—Two Couples▸
Return of Chandu
Revenge of the Barbarians
Revenge of the Musketeers
Riot
The Rock▸
Rules of Engagement
Saving Private Ryan▸
The Sea Shall Not Have Them
The Searchers▸
The Secret Agent Club
Seven Samurai▸
Shadow Warriors 2: Hunt for the Death Merchant
Shanghai Noon
Shrek▸
The Slender Thread▸
Soldier Boyz
Soldier of Fortune Inc.
Space Marines
Spy Game
Spy Kids▸
Star Trek: Insurrection
Steel Sharks
The Story of Dr. Wassell
Stranglehold
Street Fighter
Submarine Attack
Submerged
Sudden Death
Supernova
Surface to Air
The Survivor
The Taking of Flight 847: The Uli Derickson Story▸
A Thousand Heroes
Three Days to a Kill
Thunder in Paradise
Thunder in Paradise 2
Toy Story▸
Toy Story 2▸
Two Bits & Pepper
2001: A Space Travesty
Uncommon Valor
Varian's War
Vertical Limit
Volcano
Waikiki Wedding▸
Welcome to Sarajevo▸
William Faulkner's Old Man
Wolverine
The World in His Arms
The World Is Not Enough
The Yakuza

Rescue Missions Involving Time Travel

***see also** Rescue Missions*
Back to the Future▸
Back to the Future, Part 2
Back to the Future, Part 3▸
Bill & Ted's Excellent Adventure
Disney's The Kid
Frequency
Jumanji
Lost in Space
Maximum Breakout
Millennium
The Navigator▸
Star Trek 4: The Voyage Home▸
Star Trek: First Contact▸
Superman: The Movie▸
The Terminator▸
Terminator 2: Judgment Day▸
Time After Time▸
Timemaster
Trancers 2: The Return of Jack Deth
When Time Expires
Yesterday's Target

The Resistance

***see also** World War II*
Action in the North Atlantic
Alfred Hitchcock's Bon Voyage
Carve Her Name with Pride
Casablanca▸
Charlotte Gray
A Day in October
Hangmen Also Die
The Heroes of Telemark
Holocaust▸
Julia▸
The Last Lieutenant
The Last Metro▸
Les Miserables
Lucie Aubrac
Manon
One Against the Wind▸
Passage to Marseilles▸
Soldier of Orange▸
That Summer of White Roses
This Land Is Mine▸
To Be or Not to Be▸
To Be or Not to Be
The Train▸
Underground
Watch on the Rhine▸
The White Rose▸
A Woman at War

Revealing Swimwear

The American Angels: Baptism of Blood
Beach Babes from Beyond Infinity
Beach Girls
The Bikini Car Wash Company
The Bikini Car Wash Company 2
Bikini Island
Bikini Summer
Bikini Summer 2
Blood of Dracula's Castle
Body Waves
Buford's Beach Bunnies
California Girls
The Cover Girl Murders
Dark Tide
The Dolls
Fit to Kill
Frankenstein Island
Fun in Acapulco
Girls Next Door
Great Bikini Off-Road Adventure
Hardbodies
Hollywood High, Part 2
Hollywood Hot Tubs
Hollywood Hot Tubs 2: Educating Crystal
Horrors of Spider Island
Hot Resort
The House that Vanished
Island of Lost Girls
L'Annee des Meduses
Malibu Beach
The Malibu Beach Vampires
Malibu Bikini Shop
Malibu Express
Mugsy's Girls
Ocean Drive Weekend
Our Man Flint
Pauline at the Beach▸
Pin-Up Girl
Playgirl Killer
Private Lessons, Another Story
Slumber Party Massacre 2
Sorority House Party
Starhops
Summer City
Summer Fantasy
Swimsuit
Tarzan, the Ape Man
They Were So Young
Tintorera...Tiger Shark
Vice Academy 3
Welcome to Spring Break
When Dinosaurs Ruled the Earth

Revenge

***see also** Vigilantes*
Act of Aggression
Act of Passion: The Lost Honor of Kathryn Beck
Act of Vengeance
An Actor's Revenge
Addicted to Love
Adios, Hombre
The Adventurers
The Alchemist
Alien Seed
All Dogs Go to Heaven
Amazon Warrior
Ambush▸
American Buffalo
American Commandos
American Eagle
American Samurai
Anatomy of a Psycho
Angel and the Badman▸
Angel of Destruction
Angel Square
Angels from Hell
Appointment with Crime
Archer: The Fugitive from the Empire
Arizona Terror
Asylum
Attack of the 50 Ft. Woman
The Avenging
Avenging Angel
Avenging Force
Back in Action
Back to Back
Bad Blood
Ballad of Cable Hogue▸
The Ballad of the Sad Cafe
Bandits
Bang
Banzai Runner
The Baron
Basket Case▸
The Beast with Five Fingers
The Beguiled▸
Behind the Sun
Bell from Hell
Bella Mafia
Benefit of the Doubt
Best of the Best 2
Beyond Forgiveness
Big Bully
Big Jake
Bird of Prey
Bitter Sweet
Bitter Vengeance
Black Arrow▸
The Black Arrow
Black Cobra
Black Fox: Good Men and Bad
The Black Hand▸
The Black Klansman
The Black Pirate▸
The Black Raven
Black Scorpion
The Black Six
Black Sunday▸
A Black Veil for Lisa
Blackbelt 2: Fatal Force
Blind Vengeance
Blood and Guns
Blood for a Silver Dollar
Blood on the Mountain
Blood Red
Blood Ring
Bloodfist
Bloodknot
Bloodmatch
Bloody Birthday
Blue City
The Blue Knight
The Blue Lamp▸
Blue Tiger
Body Count
Boiling Point
Bones
Border Rangers
Bounty Hunters
Bounty Tracker
Branded a Coward
Breakdown▸
Bride of Killer Nerd
Broken Harvest
Bronze Buckaroo
Brotherhood of Justice
Bruiser
The Brute Man
Buffalo Heart: The Pain of Death
Bulldance
Bulldog Courage
Bullet
Bullet for Sandoval
Bullies
Buried Alive 2
The Burning
Bury Me an Angel
Cadillac Man
Caged Heat 2: Stripped of Freedom
Caged Terror
Cape Fear▸
The Caravan Trail
Carolina Skeletons
Carson City Kid
Cartouche▸
Cellblock Sisters: Banished Behind Bars
Certain Sacrifice
Chain Gang Women
The Chair
Challenge
Chameleon
Chan Is Missing▸
Changing Lanes▸
The Chase
Chisum
The Chosen One: Legend of the Raven
Chrome and Hot Leather
Circumstances Unknown
Class of 1984
Clayton County Line
Cobra
Code Name: Zebra
Code of Honor
Coffy
Cold Eyes of Fear
Cold Justice
Cold Steel
Cold Sweat
Cole Justice

Collateral Damage
Commando Invasion
Conflict of Interest
The Conqueror & the Empress
The Contract
Cornered▲
The Corsican Brothers
The Count of Monte Cristo
The Count of Monte Cristo▲
The Count of Monte Cristo
The Count of the Old Town
The Courier
Cousin Bette
Covert Assassin
The Cowboys▲
Crack House
The Craft
Crazed Cop
Creepers
Creepshow 2
Crimebusters
The Crippled Masters
The Crossing Guard▲
The Crow
The Crow 2: City of Angels
The Crow: Salvation
The Crucible▲
Cry Danger▲
Cry of the Innocent▲
The Cry of the Owl
Cry Vengeance
Curse of the Devil
Cybercity
Daddy-O
Daddy's Gone A-Hunting▲
Danger Zone 2
Dangerous Obsession
Dangerous Orphans
Dark August
Dark River: A Father's Revenge
Darkman▲
Darkness Falls
Daughter of the Dragon
DaVinci's War
Dawn Rider
The Day the Women Got Even
Dead Boyz Can't Fly
Dead Man's Revenge
Dead on the Money
Dead Silence
Deadly Daphne's Revenge
Deadly Darling
Deadly Game
Deadly Lessons
Deadly Reactor
The Deadly Secret
Deadly Sting
The Deadly Trackers
Deadly Twins
Deadly Vengeance
Deadly Weapon
Death and the Maiden▲
Death Blow
Death Magic
Death Row Diner
Death to Smoochy
Death Wish
Death Wish 2
Death Wish 3
Deep in the Heart
The Defenders: Payback
Demented
The Demons
Demonwarp
Desert Heat
Desolation Angels
Desperado▲
The Desperados
Desperate Crimes
Devastator
Devil Times Five
Devil Woman
Devil's Canyon
The Devil's Mistress
The Devil's Possessed
Devonsville Terror
The Diabolical Dr. Z
Die! Die! My Darling!
Die Hard: With a Vengeance
Dingaka
Dinner at the Ritz
Diplomatic Immunity
Dirty Harry▲
Dirty Little Secret
Dirty Work
Disclosure
The Divine Enforcer
Dixie Dynamite
Do or Die
Dr. Jekyll & Mr. Hyde
Dr. Syn, Alias the Scarecrow
Dr. Terror's House of Horrors
Dogwatch
Dolemite
Double Exposure
Double Jeopardy
The Double Negative
Double Revenge
Driven to Kill
Drop Zone
Drums of Jeopardy
Dudes
Duel at Silver Creek
Dynasty
Eagles Attack at Dawn
Easy Kill
Edge of Darkness
The Eiger Sanction
El Barbaro
Election▲
The Eliminators
Emmanuelle, the Queen
The Empire of Passion▲
Escape
The Evil That Men Do
Evilspeak
The Ex
Ex-Cop
The Execution
The Executioner, Part 2: Frozen Scream
The Expert
Exterminator
Exterminator 2
Extreme Vengeance
Extremely Dangerous
Extremities
An Eye for an Eye
Eye of the Eagle 2
Eye of the Tiger
Face/Off▲
A Face to Kill For
Facing the Enemy
Fair Game
Faithful
The Fall of the House of Usher
The Fall of the House of Usher▲
The Fall of the House of Usher
Falling Down
Far Country▲
Faust: Love of the Damned
Fight for Us
Fight for Your Life
The Fighter▲
Fighting Back
The Fighting Legion
Fighting Mad
Final Impact
Final Mission
Fine Gold
Fiorile▲
Firecracker
The First Wives Club
Fist Fighter
Fist of Honor
Fists of Blood
Fists of Iron
Flesh and Blood
Flesh and the Spur
Flesh Feast
Fleshburn
Fog Island
For Which He Stands
For Your Eyes Only▲
The Forbidden Christ
Forbidden Sun
Force of Evil
Forced Vengeance
Forgotten Warrior
The Four Musketeers▲
Frame Up
Framed
Freaks▲
Freakshow
Freeway
Friend of the Family 2
Frightmare
Frogs
Full Contact
Full Metal Ninja
The Funeral▲
Funland
Future Kill
"G" Men▲
Galloping Dynamite
The Gambling Samurai
Gang Boys
Gangs, Inc.
Garringo
Gator Bait 2: Cajun Justice
Genghis Cohn
Gentleman from Dixie
Get Carter▲
Get Carter
Getting Even
The Ghost
Ghost Dance
The Ghost of Yatsuya
Ghostriders
The Girl with the Hungry Eyes
Gladiator▲
The Godfather▲
The Godfather 1902-1959: The Complete Epic▲
The Godfather, Part 2▲
God's Gun
Gone with the West
Grave of the Vampire
The Graveyard
Green Mansions
Gunfighter
Gunplay
Gunsmoke: Return to Dodge
Halloween▲
Halloween 6: The Curse of Michael Myers
Hamlet▲
Hamlet
Hang 'Em High
Hannibal
Hannie Caulder
Hard Bounty
Hard to Kill
Hardcase and Fist
Harold Robbins' Body Parts
The Haunted Palace
HauntedWeen
Hawkeye
He Who Gets Slapped▲
Headless Eyes
Heat Street
Heavy Metal 2000
The Heist
Hell Hunters
Hell on Frisco Bay
Hellbent
Hello Mary Lou: Prom Night 2
Hell's Angels '69
Hell's Belles
Hennessy
Hi-Riders
The Hidden Room▲
High Command
High Noon▲
High Noon
Highlander: Endgame
The Highway Man
Hired Hand
Hit!
Hit & Run
Hitched
Hog Wild
Homeboy
Hornet's Nest
Horror Rises from the Tomb
The Horror Show
Hostage Hotel
Hot Lead
Hour of the Gun
Hourglass
House Across the Bay
A House in the Hills
House of Horrors
House of Strangers▲
The House of Usher
Housewife
How to Make a Monster
Human Beasts
The Human Factor
Hunter
I Drink Your Blood
I Married a Witch▲
I Met a Murderer
I Spit on Your Grave
If I Die Before I Wake
Igor & the Lunatics
Illicit Behavior
Illtown
I'm the One You're Looking For
In a Glass Cage
In Deadly Heat
In the Bedroom▲
In the Line of Duty: A Cop for the Killing
In the Presence of Mine Enemies
In the Realm of Passion
In Your Face
The Indestructible Man
The Indian Tomb
Inn of the Damned
An Innocent Man
Innocent Victim
Inquisition
Instant Justice
The Invisible Man's Revenge
Ironheart
Jack Frost 2: Revenge of the Mutant Killer Snowman
The Jayhawkers
Jenny Lamour
Jessi's Girls
The Jitters
Joe Somebody
Johnny Handsome▲
Joshua
Jubal
Kansas City Confidential▲
The Karate Kid: Part 2
Karate Warrior
Kemek
Keys to Tulsa
Kickboxer 2: The Road Back
Kickboxer 4: The Aggressor
Kid
Kid Colter
Kid Vengeance
Kidnap Syndicate
Kill Alex Kill
Kill Line
Killcrazy
The Killing Kind
Killing Time
The Killing Zone
The King of the Kickboxers
King of the Pecos
Kingfisher the Killer
Kiss Daddy Goodbye
Kiss of Death
Kuffs
L.A. Bounty
L.A. Crackdown
L.A. Heat
La Passante▲
La Vengeance d'une Femme
L.A. Vice
The Ladies Club
The Ladies of the Bois de Bologne
Lady Avenger
Lady Dragon
Lady Dragon 2
The Lady in White▲
Lady Mobster
Lady Street Fighter
L'Annee des Meduses
Laserblast
Last Bullet
The Last Days of Dolwyn
The Last Don 2
The Last Hour
Last House on the Left
Last Hurrah for Chivalry
The Last Reunion
Last Train from Gun Hill▲
The Late Show▲
Law of the Sea
Legacy of Rage
Legend of the Northwest
License to Kill▲
The Limey▲
Lionheart
The Lion's Share
Lip Service
Lipstick
Little Boy Blue
Little Moon & Jud McGraw
Live Flesh▲
Lorna Doone
Lorna Doone▲
Lovely ... But Deadly
Lure of the Sila
Lust and Revenge
Macbeth▲
Macbeth
Macho Callahan
Mad Dog
Mad Max▲
Magdalene
Make a Million
Make Haste to Live
Malicious
The Man from Laramie▲
The Man in the Iron Mask▲
The Man in the Iron Mask
The Man in the Iron Mask▲
Man in the Wilderness
The Man They Could Not Hang
The Manhandlers
Manhunt
Maniac
Manon of the Spring▲
Marathon Man▲
Mars
The Mask▲
Mask of Death
Massacre at Central High
The Match Factory Girl▲
Maternal Instincts
McBain▲
McQ
Mean Machine
Memento▲
Memories of Murder
Men...▲
Mercenary
Mercy
The Messenger
Metro
Miami Cops
Miami Vendetta
Midnite Spares
Millie
Mind Trap
Mindstorm
Ms. 45▲
Missing Pieces
Mission Kashmir
Mrs. Munck
Model by Day
Molly and Gina
The Monster and the Girl
Monte Walsh▲
Monument Ave.
Mooncussers
Moonshine County Express
Motor Psycho
The Mummy▲
Murder on Lenox Avenue
Murdered Innocence
The Murderers Are Among Us
Murphy's Law
Murphy's War
Nails
The Naked Angels
Naked Vengeance
Nasty Hero
Navajo Joe
Necromancer: Satan's Servant
The Nesting
Nevada Smith
Never Pick Up a Stranger
Never Say Die
The New Frontier
The New Kids
The Newlydeads
Next of Kin
Night Creature
Night Hunter
The Night Visitor
Nightmare Castle
Nightmare in Wax
No Name on the Bullet▲
No Safe Haven
Nomad Riders
Nowhere to Run
The Nurse
Object of Obsession
Obsessed
Offerings
Office Killer
Oklahoma Kid▲
Old Boyfriends
Old Gun▲
Olivia
On Dangerous Ground▲
One Arabian Night▲
One Armed Executioner
One Deadly Summer▲
One-Eyed Jacks▲
One Man Army
One Man's Justice
One Man's War
One Russian Summer
Operation Intercept
The Operator
Orca
Original Gangstas
Othello▲
The Other Side of Midnight
Out for Blood
Out for Justice
Outlaw Force
The Outlaw Josey Wales▲
Outrage!
Outrage
Overkill
Paper Bullets
Pathfinder▲
The Patriot
Patriot Games▲
Pay Off
Payback
Payoff
Pecos Kid
The Penalty
Pepi, Luci, Bom and Other Girls on the Heap
The Perfect Bride
The Perfect Weapon
The Perfect Wife
The Phantom Bullet
The Phantom of Soho
Phantom of the Paradise
The Pit
Platoon the Warriors
Play Dead
Pledge Night
Plutonium Baby
Point Blank
Poison Ivy 3: The New Seduction
Positive I.D.
Posse▲
Possession: Until Death Do You Part
The Power of the Ninjitsu
Premature Burial
President's Target
Prison
The Professional
Prom Night
The Prowler
Psychic Killer
Psycho Girls
Psychopath
Pumpkinhead
The Punisher
Puppet Master 3: Toulon's Revenge
Pursued▲
Pushed to the Limit
The Quick and the Dead
Quiet Cool
Quiet Fire
Rage
Rainbow Ranch
Rapid Fire
The Raven▲
Raven
Raw Deal▲
Raw Target
Recoil
Redline
Relentless
Renegades
The Replacement Killers
Reservoir Dogs▲
The Restless Breed
Retribution
Return of Frank James▲
Return of the Evil Dead
Return of the Magnificent Seven
The Return of the Musketeers
Return of the Vampire
Return of Wildfire
Return to Macon County
Revenge

Revenge of the Barbarians
Revenge of the Nerds
Revenge of the Nerds 2: Nerds in Paradise
Revenge of the Radioactive Reporter
Revenge of the Red Baron
The Revenge Rider
Revolt of the Zombies
Revolver
Ricco
Ricochet▸
Ride Clear of Diablo
Ride Lonesome
Ride to Glory
Ride with the Devil
Ringside
Rio Lobo
Rip Roarin' Buckaroo
Road to Perdition
Rock House
Rolling Thunder
Rolling Vengeance
Romola
Rose of Rio Grande
Rosewood▸
Round Numbers
Royal Deceit
Ruby Gentry
Rulers of the City
Runaways
Rushmore▸
Rustler's Paradise
Ruyblas
Sacrifice
Sacrilege
Samurai Reincarnation
The Satan Killer
Savage Drums
Savage Instinct
Savage Justice
Savage Run▸
Savage Streets
Scam
Scanner Cop 2: Volkin's Revenge
Scorned
Scorned 2
Scream Dream
Screamer
Search and Destroy
Second Victory
The Secret Four
Serial Bomber
Seven Hours to Judgment
The Seven-Ups
Severed Ties
Sex Crimes
The Shadow Man
Shame
Sharpe's Eagle
The She-Beast
She-Devil
She Devils in Chains
She-Freak
Shoot Out
Shootfighter 2: Kill or Be Killed!
The Shooting▸
Shooting Fish
Short Eyes▸
The Showdown
Showdown
Silent Night, Deadly Night 2
Simba▸
Simple Justice
The Sin of Harold Diddlebock
The Sister-in-Law
Sisters of Death
Six Shootin' Sheriff
Sizzle
Slaughter
Slaughter's Big Ripoff
Slayground
Sleepers
Sleeping with the Enemy
Sloane
A Small Town in Texas
Smart Money
Smoke in the Wind
The Smokers
SnakeEater
SnakeEater 3: His Law
Soldier Blue
Soldier's Fortune
Sometimes They Come Back
Sons of Katie Elder▸
Sorority Girl
Soul Vengeance
Sound of Murder
Sour Grapes
Special Investigator
The Specialist
Speed 2: Cruise Control
Speeding Up Time
The Spoilers▸
Stanley
Star Trek 2: The Wrath of Khan▸
Star Trek: First Contact▸
Steel and Lace
Steele Justice
The Sting 2
Straight Shooter
Strange Shadows in an Empty Room
Stranger in Paso Bravo
Strangler of the Swamp
Straw Dogs▸
Street Hunter
Street War
Street Wars
Striker
The Substitute
The Substitute 2: School's Out
Sudden Death
Sudden Impact
Super Force
The Supernaturals
Sweet Justice
Sweet Poison
Sweet Revenge
Swift Justice
Sword of Gideon
Sword of Venus
Sworn Enemies
Tactical Assault
Take Two
Talion
Taste the Blood of Dracula
Terror Creatures from the Grave
Terror in a Texas Town
Texas Kid
Texas Payback
The Texican
Theatre of Blood▸
They Made Me a Fugitive
Things
This Gun for Hire▸
This Man Must Die▸
Thou Shalt Not Kill...Except
Threat
Three Husbands
Three in the Cellar
Thunder in the Desert
Thunder Warrior 3
Tillie's Punctured Romance
A Time of Destiny
Time to Die
A Time to Kill▸
Titus
To Be the Best
Today We Kill, Tomorrow We Die
Tombs of the Blind Dead
Top of the Heap
Tormented
The Tormentors
The Torture Chamber of Dr. Sadism
Toy Soldiers
The Trackers
Trained to Kill
Trapper County War
Trick or Treat
Tricks
Trigger Tricks
Trois Couleurs: Blanc▸
Truck Turner
Turk 182!
24 Hours to Midnight
Twice a Judas
Twilight People
Twin Town
Twisted Brain
Twisted Nightmare
Two by Forsyth
Two Fathers' Justice
2000 Maniacs
Undefeatable
Under the Gun
Underworld
Underworld, U.S.A.▸
Unfaithfully Yours▸
Unfaithfully Yours
Unholy Four
Universal Soldier: The Return
The Unstoppable Man
Until They Get Me
Up River
Utu▸
Valentine
Valmont▸
Vampire Journals
Vendetta
Vengeance
Vengeance of the Zombies
The Vernonia Incident
Vietnam, Texas
The Vigilantes Are Coming
Viper
The Virgin Spring▸
Voodoo Black Exorcist
Voodoo Dawn
Walking Tall
Walking Tall: Part 2
Walking the Edge
The War Wagon▸
Water Rustlers
Waterfront
Weekend of Shadows▸
The Weirdo
West of Zanzibar
The Wharf Rat
What's the Worst That Could Happen?
The White Sheik▸
Wild Bill
Wild Gypsies
Wild Man
Wild Wheels
Wired to Kill
Witchouse
Without Honors
Wolf
Wolf Lake
The Women▸
Wonder Man
Wounded
Write to Kill
X Marks the Spot
Xtro 3: Watch the Skies
Young Warriors
Youth of the Beast
Yuma
Zero Tolerance
Zombie Lake
Zombie Nightmare

Revolutionary War

America
The Bastard
George Washington
The Howards of Virginia
John Paul Jones
Johnny Tremain & the Sons of Liberty
The Patriot
The Rebels
Revolution
The Seekers
1776▸
Sweet Liberty
The Time of Their Lives

Rio

Amor Bandido
Black Orpheus▸
Blame It on Rio
Boca
Bossa Nova
Central Station▸
Exposure
Flying Down to Rio
Herbie Goes Bananas
Kickboxer 3: The Art of War
Orfeu
Party Girls for Sale
The Road to Rio▸
The Story of Fausta
Subway to the Stars
Venus in Furs
Via Appia
Wild Orchid

Road Trip

***see also** Bikers; Checkered Flag; Motor Vehicle Dept.*

Aberdeen
The Acid Eaters
Across the Great Divide
Across the Moon
Adrenaline Drive
The Adventures of Felix
The Adventures of Huck Finn▸
The Adventures of Milo & Otis▸
The Adventures of Priscilla, Queen of the Desert▸
Alice Doesn't Live Here Anymore
Alligator Eyes
Almost Famous▸
Aloha, Bobby and Rose
Along for the Ride
American Autobahn
American Fabulous
Another Day in Paradise
Ariel▸
Armed for Action
Around the World in 80 Days▸
Around the World in 80 Days
Ashik Kerib▸
Bad Company▸
Bandwagon
Beautiful Joe
Beavis and Butt-Head Do America
Because of You
Beethoven's 3rd
The Big Crimewave
Bingo
Black Day Blue Night
Black Dog
Blue De Ville
Blue Murder at St. Trinian's▸
Blues Brothers 2000
Bolero
Boogie Boy
Born to Be Wild
Bound for Glory▸
Box of Moonlight
Boxcar Blues
A Boy Called Hate
Boys on the Side
Breaking the Rules
Breathing Lessons▸
Bright Angel
Bronson's Revenge
Bubble Boy
Buck and the Preacher
Bustin' Loose▸
Butch Cassidy and the Sundance Kid▸
Butterfly Kiss
By Dawn's Early Light
Bye Bye Brazil
Calendar Girl
Camilla
Candy Mountain
Cannonball
Cannonball Run
Cannonball Run 2
A Canterbury Tale▸
Central Station▸
Changes
The Chase
Chasers
Cheech and Chong: Things Are Tough All Over
Clodhopper
Coast to Coast
Cold Around the Heart
Cold Fever
Committed
The Concrete Cowboys
Cooperstown
Coupe de Ville
Crazy in Alabama
Crazy Mama
Crossroads
The Cure
Cycle Vixens
Danzon▸
The Daytrippers
The Delivery
Delusion
Der Purimshpiler
Detour▸
The Devil Thumbs a Ride▸
Diamonds
Doctor Chance
Doing Time for Patsy Cline▸
The Doom Generation▸
Down by Law▸
Dream with the Fishes
Dreaming of Rita
Drive
Dumb & Dumber
Dutch
Earthly Possessions
The Easy Life▸
Easy Rider▸
End of the Line
Endplay
Eternity and a Day
Every Other Weekend▸
Every Which Way But Loose
Extremedays
Eye of the Beholder
Fandango
Far Out Man
Fast Sofa
Father Hood
Fear and Loathing in Las Vegas
Finders Keepers
Finding Graceland
Finding North
Flash & Firecat
Flight of the Innocent
Flim-Flam Man
Flirting with Disaster▸
Forces of Nature
The Forsaken
Four Days
Freeway 2: Confessions of a Trickbaby
From Dusk Till Dawn
Get On the Bus▸
Girl in the Cadillac
Goodbye Pork Pie
A Goofy Movie
The Grapes of Wrath▸
Great Smokey Roadblock
The Great Texas Dynamite Chase
Greedy Terror
Guantanamera▸
Hard Core Logo
Hard Luck
Harry and Tonto▸
Having Wonderful Crime
Heart Beat
Heaven's Burning
Heck's Way Home
Hedwig and the Angry Inch▸
Hell's Angels on Wheels
High Rolling in a Hot Corvette
Highway
Highway Hitcher
The Highway Man
Highway 61
The Hitcher
Hitchhikers
Hollywood or Bust
Hombres Complicados
Home of Angels
Homecoming
Homer and Eddie
Homeward Bound 2: Lost in San Francisco
Homeward Bound: The Incredible Journey▸
Honkytonk Man
Hot Blooded
Huck and the King of Hearts
Il Sorpasso
I'll Be Home for Christmas
The Incredible Journey
Innocents
Into the Night
Into the West▸
It Takes Two
Jackpot
Jay and Silent Bob Strike Back
Jeepers Creepers
Jerome▸
Joe Dirt
Jon Jost's Frameup
Josh and S.A.M.
The Journey of Natty Gann▸
Joy Ride▸
Joy Ride to Nowhere
Joyride
The Judge Steps Out
Kalifornia
Kandahar
Kikujiro
Killer Bud
Kingpin
Kings of the Road—In the Course of Time▸
Kiss My Grits
Kiss or Kill
La Strada▸
Ladies on the Rocks
Lamerica▸
Landscape in the Mist▸
Larger Than Life
Leaving Normal
Leningrad Cowboys Go America
Les Rendez-vous D'Anna
Lewis and Clark and George
A Life Less Ordinary
The Lion of Africa
Lisboa
The Living End
Lolita
Loners
The Long Haul
The Long, Long Trailer
Loose Connections
Lord of the Rings 1: The Fellowship of the Rings▸
Los Locos Posse
Lost in America▸
Love and a .45
Luminous Motion
Mad Love
Made in USA
Me and the Kid
Me & Will
Me, Myself, and Irene▸
The Mexican
Michael
Midnight Run▸
Mob Story
More
The Muppet Movie▸
The Music of Chance
My Fellow Americans
My Own Private Idaho▸
National Lampoon's Vacation▸
Natural Born Killers
Neil Simon's The Odd Couple 2
Neon City
Never on Tuesday
Niagara, Niagara
Night on Earth▸
No Place to Run
Nurse Betty▸
The Odyssey
Omaha (the movie)
One Way Out
The Opposite of Sex
Out
Outside Ozona
Over the Hill
Overnight Delivery
Paper Moon▸
The Passing of Evil
Patti Rocks▸
Paulie
Pee-wee's Big Adventure▸
Phat Beach
Pierrot le Fou▸
Pink Cadillac
Planes, Trains & Automobiles
Play for Me
Play It to the Bone
Pontiac Moon
Powwow Highway▸
Prime Target
Prison Train
The Raffle
Rain Man▸
The Rain People▸
Rainbow Bridge
Rat Race
Reckless
The Reivers▸
Rescue Me
Retroactive
Ride
Ride in the Whirlwind
The Road
Road Games
Road Kill USA

The Road Killers
Road Movie
The Road to Bali▲
The Road to El Dorado
The Road to Galveston▲
The Road to Hong Kong
The Road to Lebanon
The Road to Morocco▲
Road to Perdition
The Road to Rio▲
The Road to Singapore
The Road to Utopia▲
The Road to Zanzibar▲
Road Trip
The Road Warrior▲
Roadie
Roadkill
Roadside Prophets
Rockin' Road Trip
Rough Magic
Round Trip to Heaven
Rubin & Ed
The Runaway Bus
Running Hot
Running Wild
The Saragossa Manuscript
Sawdust & Tinsel▲
Say It Isn't So
Scarecrow
September Gun
A Shadow You Soon Will Be
Sincerely Charlotte▲
Six of a Kind▲
Six-String Samurai
Slither▲
Smoke Signals
Something Wild
Sorcerer
Spare Me
Sparkler
Spies Like Us
Starlight Hotel
Starman▲
Stay As You Are
The Straight Story▲
Strawberry Fields
Summer City
Sunchaser
The Sure Thing▲
The Sweetest Thing
Thelma & Louise▲
Those Magnificent Men in Their Flying Machines▲
Three for the Road
Thumb Tripping
Tilt
To Wong Foo, Thanks for Everything, Julie Newmar
Tokyo Pop
Tommy Boy
Tourist Trap
Trading Favors
Traveling Man
Trouble Bound
The Truce▲
True Romance
Truth or Consequences, N.M.
Twentieth Century▲
Two for the Road▲
Until the End of the World▲
Voyage in Italy
Wagons East
The Way West
Wedding Bell Blues
Weekend▲
Western
Where the Eagle Flies
White Line Fever
White River
Wild America▲
Wild at Heart▲
Wild Horses
The Wizard
The Wizard of Oz▲
World Traveler
The Wrong Man
Y Tu Mama Tambien

Roaring '20s

Al Capone▲
Balto
Bare Knees
Bix
The Bretts▲
Bullets over Broadway▲
By the Light of the Silvery Moon
The Cat's Meow
Character
Cold Comfort Farm
Cold Comfort Farm▲
The Cotton Club▲
Deja Vu
The Disappearance of Aimee▲
Dr. Bethune▲
Ele, My Friend
Enchanted April
Entertaining Angels: The Dorothy Day Story
Forest of Little Bear
The Front Page
The Great Gatsby
The Great Waldo Pepper▲
The Grissom Gang▲
The Harmonists
Haunted
The Hearst and Davies Affair
High Road to China
Hit the Dutchman
The House of Eliott
I'll See You in My Dreams
Inherit the Wind
The Jazz Singer
Jazzman▲
Johnny Dangerously
Killer: A Journal of Murder
The Last September
The Legend of Bagger Vance
Legend of Valentino
Legionnaire
Longitude▲
Love for Lydia▲
The Lover
The Luzhin Defence
Maids of Wilko
Man of the Century
Mapp & Lucia
Mrs. Dalloway
Mrs. Parker and the Vicious Circle
Mister Johnson▲
The Moderns▲
The Mummy
My Life So Far
Naked Tango
The Newton Boys
Once Upon a Time in America▲
Pancho Barnes
Party Girl▲
A Passage to India▲
Pictures
Private Confessions
The Quest
Red Sorghum▲
Return to Paradise
The Roaring Twenties▲
Rosewood▲
Roxie Hart
The St. Valentine's Day Massacre
Shadow of the Vampire▲
Shake Hands with the Devil▲
The Slingshot▲
Speedy Death▲
Splendor in the Grass▲
The Stationmaster's Wife
The Stranger: Kabloonak
Swoon▲
Temptress Moon
Tenderness of the Wolves
Theremin: An Electronic Odyssey▲
Thoroughly Modern Millie
The Tigress
Twenty-Four Eyes▲
Under the Biltmore Clock
Underworld▲
An Unforgettable Summer
The Untouchables▲
Valentino
Where the Rivers Flow North
Wild Party
The Wolves▲
Woman in Black
The Wooden Man's Bride
You Know My Name▲

Robots & Androids

***see also** Technology—Rampant*

A. I.: Artificial Intelligence
Alien▲
Alien Chaser
Alien: Resurrection▲
Aliens▲
American Cyborg: Steel Warrior
And You Thought Your Parents Were Weird!
Android
The Android Affair
A.P.E.X.
Assassin
The Astro-Zombies
Automatic
Bicentennial Man
Bill & Ted's Bogus Journey
The Black Hole
Blade Runner▲
Carver's Gate
Chopping Mall
Circuit Breaker
Circuitry Man
Class of 1999
Class of 1999 2: The Substitute
The Companion
The Creation of the Humanoids
Cyber-Tracker
Cyber-Tracker 2
Cyberzone
Cyborg
Cyborg 2
Cyborg 3: The Recycler
Cyborg Cop
Cyborg Soldier
Daleks—Invasion Earth 2150 A.D.
D.A.R.Y.L.
The Day the Earth Stood Still▲
Devil Girl from Mars
Digital Man
Dr. Goldfoot and the Bikini Machine
Doctor of Doom
Doctor Satan's Robot
Downdraft
Edward Scissorhands▲
The Eliminators
The Empire Strikes Back▲
Eve of Destruction
Evolver
The Fifth Element
Forbidden Planet▲
Future Cop
Ghost in the Shell▲
Heartbeeps
Heatseeker
The Hitchhiker's Guide to the Galaxy
How to Make a Doll
The Human Duplicators
Humanoid Defender
The Invisible Boy
Iron Giant▲
K-9000
Knights
Kronos
Light Years
Lost in Space
Mac and Me
Mandroid
Megaville
Metropolis▲
Mortal Challenge
Mystery Science Theater 3000: The Movie
Nemesis
Nemesis 2: Nebula
Nemesis 3: Time Lapse
Night Siege Project: Shadowchaser 2
Not Quite Human
Not Quite Human 2
Omega Doom
Planets Against Us
Plughead Rewired: Circuitry Man 2
Programmed to Kill
Project: Shadowchaser
Project Shadowchaser 3000
Prototype▲
Prototype X29A
Return of the Jedi▲
Robo Warriors
RoboCop▲
RoboCop 2
RoboCop 3
Roboman
Robot Holocaust
Robot in the Family
Robot Jox
Robot Monster
The Robot vs. the Aztec Mummy
Robot Wars
R.O.T.O.R.
Runaway
Running Delilah
Shadow Warriors
Short Circuit
Short Circuit 2
Silent Running▲
Solo
Space Truckers
Star Crash
Star Trek: Generations▲
Star Wars▲
Star Wars: Episode 1—The Phantom Menace▲
Star Wars: Episode 2—Attack of the Clones▲
Starship
Steel and Lace
Still Not Quite Human
Storm Trooper
Suspect Device
T-Force
TC 2000
The Terminator▲
Terminator 2: Judgment Day▲
Terror of Mechagodzilla
Tobor the Great
Total Recall 2070: Machine Dreams
Universal Soldier: The Return
The Vindicator
Virus
Voyage of the Rock Aliens
War of the Robots
Westworld▲

Rock Flicks

The Adventures of Buckaroo Banzai Across the Eighth Dimension▲
Almost Famous▲
American Pop
At Any Cost
Backbeat▲
Beat Street
Beyond the Valley of the Dolls
Blame It on the Night
The Blues Brothers▲
Blues Brothers 2000
Born to Boogie
Bummer
Burglar▲
Chuck Berry: Hail! Hail! Rock 'n' Roll
The Commitments▲
The Courier
Cry-Baby▲
Dead Girls
Decline of Western Civilization 1▲
Decline of Western Civilization 2: The Metal Years
Detroit Rock City
Disorderlies
The Doors
Double Trouble
Eddie and the Cruisers
Eddie and the Cruisers 2: Eddie Lives!
Elvis and Me
Elvis: The Movie
The Filth and the Fury
The Five Heartbeats▲
FM
Follow That Dream
Frankie and Johnny
Get Crazy
Gimme Shelter
The Girl Can't Help It
Give My Regards to Broad Street
Grace of My Heart
Great Balls of Fire
Hail Caesar
Hard Core Logo
A Hard Day's Night▲
Head▲
Heaven Tonight
Hedwig and the Angry Inch▲
Help!▲
Horsey
In His Life: The John Lennon Story
Incident at Channel Q
It Couldn't Happen Here
The Jacksons: An American Dream
Jailhouse Rock▲
Johnny Suede
Josie and the Pussycats
The Kids Are Alright▲
KISS Meets the Phantom of the Park
La Bamba▲
The Last Waltz▲
Leningrad Cowboys Go America
Let It Be
Light of Day
Loving You
A Matter of Degrees
Meat Loaf: To Hell and Back
Monterey Pop▲
Netherworld
Nico Icon▲
1991: The Year Punk Broke
Party! Party!
Quadrophenia▲
Queen of the Damned
Red Hot
The Return of Spinal Tap
Rock & Roll Cowboys
Rock & Rule
Rock, Baby, Rock It
Rock 'n' Roll High School▲
Rock 'n' Roll High School Forever
Rock 'n' Roll Nightmare
Rock, Pretty Baby
Rock Star
Rocktober Blood
Running out of Luck
Satisfaction
Scenes from the Goldmine
Shock 'Em Dead
Shout
Sid & Nancy▲
Six-String Samurai
Spellcaster
Spice World: The Movie
Still Crazy▲
Streets of Fire
The Suburbans
Sugar Town
Sunset Strip
Sweetwater: A True Rock Story
Tapeheads
Terror on Tour
That Thing You Do!▲
Theremin: An Electronic Odyssey▲
This Is Elvis
This Is Spinal Tap▲
Thunder Alley
Thunder & Mud
Tokyo Pop
Tommy
Trick or Treat
U2: Rattle and Hum
Velvet Goldmine
Vibrations
Voyage of the Rock Aliens
When Love Comes
Wild Guitar
Woodstock▲
Yellow Submarine▲
Zombie and the Ghost Train

Rock Stars on Film

***see also** Concert Films; Martyred Pop Icons; Pure Ego Vehicles*

Absolute Beginners
All You Need Is Cash▲
Backbeat▲
Bill & Ted's Excellent Adventure
Black Dog
Blow-Up▲
Blue Hawaii
The Blues Brothers▲
Blues Brothers 2000
The Bodyguard
Breaking Glass
The Bride
B.U.S.T.E.D.
Carny▲
Caveman
Charro!
Chuck Berry: Hail! Hail! Rock 'n' Roll
Clambake
Coal Miner's Daughter▲
The Crossing Guard▲
Crossroads
Detroit Rock City
Double Trouble
Dune
Easy Come, Easy Go
End of the Line
Fire Down Below
Flaming Star▲
Follow That Dream
Frankie and Johnny
Freddy's Dead: The Final Nightmare
Fun in Acapulco
G.I. Blues
The Girl Can't Help It
Girl Happy
Girls! Girls! Girls!
Give My Regards to Broad Street
Go, Johnny Go!
A Hard Day's Night▲
The Harder They Come
Harum Scarum
Head▲
Heat▲
Help!▲
How I Won the War
The Hunger
It Happened at the World's Fair
Jailhouse Rock▲
Jawbreaker
Johnny Mnemonic
Kid Galahad
King Creole
KISS Meets the Phantom of the Park
Kissin' Cousins
La Bamba▲
Labyrinth▲
The Last Temptation of Christ▲
The Leading Man
The Legacy
Let It Be
Lisztomania
Live a Little, Love a Little
Lock, Stock and 2 Smoking Barrels▲
Love Me Tender
Loving You
The Magic Christian▲
Magical Mystery Tour
The Man Who Fell to Earth▲
McVicar
Merry Christmas, Mr. Lawrence▲
Mrs. Brown, You've Got a Lovely Daughter
Monster Dog
Moonlight and Valentino
No Looking Back
Nomads
One Trick Pony
Paradise, Hawaiian Style
Pat Garrett & Billy the Kid▲
Performance▲
Pink Floyd: The Wall
The Players Club▲
Poetic Justice
The Postman
The Preacher's Wife
Quadrophenia▲
Rock 'n' Roll High School▲
Roustabout
Runaway
The Running Man
Sgt. Pepper's Lonely Hearts Club Band

▲ = rated three bones or higher

▲ = rated three bones or higher

For Better or Worse
For Heaven's Sake▲
For Love of Ivy
For Love or Money
For Roseanna
For the Love of Mary
A Foreign Affair▲
Forever Together
Forget Paris
A Forgotten Tune for the Flute▲
Forty Carats
40 Days and 40 Nights
Four Weddings and a Funeral▲
Framed
Frankie and Johnny▲
French Exit
French Kiss
The French Lesson
French Twist
Fridays of Eternity
Friends & Lovers
Friends, Lovers & Lunatics
Full of Life
Funny About Love
Gabriela
The Gay Lady
Get Out Your Handkerchiefs▲
Get Over It!
Get Well Soon
Getting It Right
The Ghost and the Guest
Gidget
Gidget Goes Hawaiian
Gidget Goes to Rome
Ginger in the Morning
A Girl, a Guy and a Gob
The Girl from Missouri▲
The Girl from Petrovka
The Girl in the Picture
Girl Shy▲
Girl Under the Sheet
The Glass Bottom Boat
Go Fish▲
The Gold of Naples▲
Good Advice
The Goodbye Girl▲
Goodbye, New York
The Grand Duchess and the Waiter▲
The Grass Is Greener
The Great Gildersleeve
Green Card
Groundhog Day▲
A Guy Thing
The Halfback of Notre Dame
Hammersmith Is Out
Hanky Panky
Happy Accidents
Happy New Year▲
Happy Together
Hardhat & Legs
Hav Plenty▲
Having It All
Having Wonderful Crime
Having Wonderful Time
He Said, She Said
Head Over Heels
Hear My Song▲
Heartaches▲
Heartbeat
Heartbeeps
Heartstrings
Heaven Before I Die
Heaven or Vegas
Heaven's a Drag
Her Alibi
Her First Romance
Herbie Goes to Monte Carlo
Hi Diddle Diddle
Hi-Life
High Fidelity▲
High Spirits
Higher Education
His First Flame▲
His Wife's Lover▲
Hobson's Choice▲
Hobson's Choice
Home Fries
Honeymoon Academy
Honeymoon in Vegas
Hook, Line and Sinker
The Horizontal Lieutenant
Hot Chocolate
Hotel de Love
House Calls▲
Houseboat
Housesitter
How I Spent My Summer Vacation
How to Marry a Millionaire
How to Steal a Million▲
How U Like Me Now?▲
Hurry, Charlie, Hurry
Hurry Up or I'll Be Thirty
I Don't Buy Kisses Anymore
I Know Where I'm Going▲
I Love Trouble
I Love You, Don't Touch Me!
I Married a Centerfold
I Married a Witch▲
I Married a Woman
I Will, I Will for Now
Idiot's Delight▲
If Lucy Fell
If You Only Knew
Il Bell'Antonio
I'll Take Sweden
The Importance of Being Earnest
Imposters
Impromptu▲
In Love with an Older Woman
In Person
The Incredible Mr. Limpet
The Incredibly True Adventure of Two Girls in Love
Indiscreet
Indiscreet▲
Indiscreet
Innerspace
Instant Karma
Invitation to the Wedding
I.Q.
Iris Blond
Irma La Douce
It
It Could Happen to You
It Happened One Night▲
It Should Happen to You▲
It Started with a Kiss
It Started with Eve▲
It Takes Two
Italian for Beginners
It's My Turn
I've Heard the Mermaids Singing▲
Jeffrey
Jerry Maguire▲
Jersey Girl
Jit
Jock Petersen
Joe Versus the Volcano
Joey Breaker▲
The Judge Steps Out
Julia Has Two Lovers
June Bride▲
Jupiter's Thigh
Just a Little Harmless Sex
Just Like a Woman
Just Me & You
Just One Night
Just One of the Girls
Just One Time
Just Tell Me What You Want
Just the Ticket
Just the Way You Are
Just Write
Kate & Leopold
Keeping the Faith
Key Exchange
Key to the City
Kill Me Later
The King on Main Street
King Ralph
A Kiss for Mary Pickford
Kiss Me Goodbye
Kiss Shot
Kissing a Fool
Kuni Lemel in Tel Aviv
La Collectionneuse
La Lectrice
L.A. Story▲
La Vie de Boheme▲
Labor Pains
The Lady Eve▲
The Lady Is Willing
Lady L
Lady on a Train▲
Lady Takes a Chance▲
The Lady's Not for Burning
L'Annee des Meduses
Lassie from Lancashire
The Last Fling
The Last Married Couple in America
The Last of the High Kings
Late Bloomers
Late for Dinner
Le Beau Mariage▲
Le Magnifique
The Leading Man
Legal Eagles
Lena's Holiday
Les Grandes Manoeuvres▲
Let It Snow
Let's Make It Legal
Let's Make Love
Lt. Robin Crusoe, U.S.N.
Life in the Fast Lane
Life or Something Like It
Life Without Dick
The Linguini Incident
Listen to Your Heart
Little City
Little Noises
A Little Romance▲
Little Sister
A Little Stiff
Little White Lies
Live Bait
The Lonely Guy
Lonely Hearts▲
Lonely in America
Look Who's Talking▲
Look Who's Talking, Too
Loose in New York
Lost and Found
Lost in Yonkers
The Love Affair, or The Case of the Missing Switchboard Operator▲
Love Among the Ruins▲
Love & Sex
Love at First Sight
Love by Appointment
Love Can Seriously Damage Your Health
Love Hurts
Love in the Afternoon
Love Is All There Is
Love Is Better Than Ever
Love Jones▲
Love Laughs at Andy Hardy
Love on the Run
Love or Money?
Love Potion #9
Love Stinks
Lovelife
Lovelines
Lover Come Back
Loverboy
Lovers and Liars
Lover's Knot
Lovers Like Us
Lovers' Lovers
Loves & Times of Scaramouche
Love's Labour's Lost
Loving Couples
Loving Jezebel
The Low Down
Luminarias
The Lunatic
Lunatics: A Love Story▲
Made in America
Made in Heaven
Magic on Love Island
The Magnificent Dope
The Maid
Maid's Night Out
The Main Event
Main Street to Broadway
A Majority of One
Making Mr. Right
Male and Female▲
Mama, There's a Man in Your Bed▲
A Man, a Woman, and a Bank
Man Trouble
The Man Who Loved Women▲
The Man Who Loved Women
The Man Who Made Husbands Jealous
Manhattan▲
Manhattan Merenque!
Mannequin
Marius and Jeannette
Marriage Italian Style▲
The Marriage of Figaro
Married?
Married to the Mob▲
The Marrying Man
The Matchmaker▲
The Matchmaker
The Mating Habits of the Earthbound Human
Matrimaniac
May Wine
Me, Myself & I
Me, Myself, and Irene▲
Meeting Daddy
Meeting Venus
Miami Rhapsody
Michael
Mickey Blue Eyes
Micki & Maude
A Midsummer Night's Dream▲
A Midsummer Night's Dream
Milk Money
The Millionairess
Minnie and Moskowitz
Miracle Beach
The Mirror Has Two Faces
The Misadventures of Merlin Jones
Miss Right
Mrs. Winterbourne
Mr. Boggs Steps Out
Mr. Jealousy
Mr. Love
Mr. Lucky▲
Mr. Peabody & the Mermaid
Mr. Wonderful
Mr. Write
A Modern Affair
Modern Love
Modern Romance▲
Monaco Forever
Money Buys Happiness
Monsoon Wedding▲
A Month by the Lake
The Moon Is Blue
Moon Pilot
Moonstruck▲
Morgan: A Suitable Case for Treatment
Mouth to Mouth
Much Ado about Nothing▲
Murphy's Romance▲
Music from Another Room
My Best Friend's Girl
My Best Friend's Wedding
My Brother's Wife
My Dear Secretary
My Girl 2
My Love For Yours
My Man Godfrey
My Night at Maud's▲
My Sex Life...Or How I Got into an Argument
My Stepmother Is an Alien
My Tutor
Mystery Date
The Mystery Man
Naked in New York
Never Been Kissed
Never Met Picasso
Never on Sunday▲
The New Eve▲
A New Kind of Love
A New Leaf
Next Stop, Wonderland
Next Time I Marry
Next Year If All Goes Well
Nice Girl Like Me
Nice Girls Don't Explode
Nice Guys Sleep Alone▲
Nick and Jane
Night and Day▲
The Night Club
The Night We Never Met
Nina Takes a Lover
Ninotchka▲
Nobody's Fool
The Norman Conquests, Part 1: Table Manners▲
The Norman Conquests, Part 2: Living Together▲
The Norman Conquests, Part 3: Round and Round the Garden▲
North to Alaska▲
Nothin' 2 Lose
Nothing Personal
Notting Hill▲
Off Beat
Okoge
On Approval▲
On the Line
On the Sunny Side
Once Around
One Fine Day
One Rainy Afternoon
One, Two, Three▲
One Wild Moment
Only the Lonely
Only with Married Men
Only You
The Opposite Sex and How to Live With Them
The Other Brother
The Other Sister
Our Miss Brooks
Outrageous Fortune
Overboard
Overnight Delivery
The Owl and the Pussycat▲
The Pallbearer
Panama Lady
Pantaloons
Paper Marriage
Paperback Hero
Paperback Romance
A Paradise Under the Stars
Pardon Mon Affaire▲
Paris Holiday
Party
Pat and Mike▲
Pedale Douce
Peggy Sue Got Married
The Perfect Gift
Perfect Match
Perfectly Normal
Personal Property
The Personals
Personals
Phffft!
Pick a Card
The Pick-Up Artist
Picture Perfect
Pie in the Sky
Pillow Talk▲
Play It Again, Sam▲
Playing Mona Lisa
Playmates
Please Not Now!
The Pompatus of Love
Pool Hustlers
Pool Sharks
Pop Always Pays
Practical Magic
Prelude to a Kiss
Pretty Woman▲
Priceless Beauty
The Prince and the Showgirl
The Princess and the Pirate▲
Prisoner of Zenda
Private Lives▲
Probation
Promise Her Anything
Promises! Promises!
Protocol
The Purple Rose of Cairo▲
A Pyromaniac's Love Story
Quackser Fortune Has a Cousin in the Bronx▲
Queens Logic
Quick Change
The Quiet Man▲
The Raffle
The Rage of Paris▲
The Ranch
The Rat Race▲
Rattle of a Simple Man
Reaching for the Moon
Reality Bites
Relative Values
Relax... It's Just Sex!
The Reluctant Debutante▲
Remember the Night▲
Rendez-vous de Juillet
Return to Me
Rich in Love
The Ritz▲
River Street
Road to Ruin
Roads to the South
The Roaring Road
Robert Louis Stevenson's St. Ives
Roman Holiday▲
Romantic Comedy
Roses Bloom Twice
Round Numbers
Roxanne▲
Roxie Hart
Runaway Bride▲
Running Mates▲
Sabrina▲
Sabrina
Saratoga
Scorchers
Seaside Swingers
Secret Admirer
Secret Ingredient
Secret Life of an American Wife
The Secret of My Success
See You in the Morning
Seems Like Old Times
Send Me No Flowers▲
The Sensual Man
The Sensuous Nurse
Separate Vacations
Serendipity
Serving Sara
Seven Girlfriends
Seven Minutes in Heaven
The Seven Year Itch▲
Sex and the Single Girl
Sex and the Single Parent
Shadow of the Thin Man▲
Shakespeare in Love▲
Shallow Hal
Shanghai Surprise
She Done Him Wrong▲
She's All That
She's Gotta Have It▲
She's Having a Baby
She's the One
The Shop Around the Corner▲
Shore Leave▲
Short Circuit
The Shrimp on the Barbie
Sibling Rivalry
Sidewalks of New York
Silver Streak▲
Simply Irresistible
Singles▲
Sixteen Candles▲
Skin Deep
Sleepless in Seattle▲
A Smile Like Yours
Smiles of a Summer Night▲
Smiling Fish & Goat on Fire
Smokescreen
Snow: The Movie
Snowballin'
So This Is Paris▲
Soapdish▲
The Social Secretary
Soldat Duroc...Ca Va Etre Ta Fete!
Solitaire for 2
Someone Like You
Something About Sex
Something More
Something Short of Paradise
Son of Gascogne
The Souler Opposite
Soup for One
Speechless
Spite Marriage▲
Splash
Splendor
Sprung
Stand-In▲
State of the Union▲
The Station
The Sterile Cuckoo▲
Still Breathing
Stolen Kisses▲
The Story of Boys & Girls▲
The Story of Us
Straight Talk
Strange Bedfellows
Strictly Ballroom▲
Strictly Business
Stroke of Midnight
The Student Affair
Summer School
A Summer's Tale
Sunset Limousine
Surf Party

Surrender
Surviving Desire▲
Suzy
The Swan
The Swan▲
Sweet Lies
Sweet Talker
The Sweetest Thing
Tadpole
The Tall Guy▲
The Taming of the Shrew
The Taming of the Shrew▲
Tammy and the Bachelor
Tammy and the Doctor
The Tao of Steve▲
The Teahouse of the August Moon
Ted & Venus
The Tender Trap
Thanks for the Memory
That Certain Thing
That Lucky Touch
That Old Feeling
That Touch of Mink
That Uncertain Feeling
Theodora Goes Wild▲
There's a Girl in My Soup
There's Something about Mary▲
They All Kissed the Bride
They All Laughed
They Got Me Covered
The Thing Called Love
The Things of Life▲
30 Is a Dangerous Age, Cynthia
This Could Be the Night
This Happy Feeling
Thomas Graal's Best Film▲
Thomas Graal's First Child▲
Those Endearing Young Charms
Three Broadway Girls▲
Three Coins in the Fountain
Three for Bedroom C
Three Guys Named Mike
Three Husbands
Three of Hearts
Three Smart Girls Grow Up▲
Three to Tango
Three Way Weekend
Threesome
Tieta of Agreste
Tiger and the Pussycat
Til There Was You
Till Marriage Do Us Part
Tillie's Punctured Romance
Time of the Gypsies▲
Tin Cup▲
To Cross the Rubicon
To Paris with Love
Togetherness
Tokyo Cowboy
Tom, Dick, and Harry
Tom Jones▲
Tomboy
Too Beautiful for You
Too Smooth
Topsy Turvy
A Touch of Class▲
Town and Country
Trick▲
Trippin'
The Triumph of Love
Trojan War
The Truth about Cats and Dogs▲
Tulips
Tune in Tomorrow
Twelfth Night
24 Nights
Twice upon a Yesterday
Two-Faced Woman▲
Two If by Sea
Two Much
Two Nights with Cleopatra
Two Ninas
Two of a Kind
Undercover Angel
Underground Aces
The Undertaker's Wedding
Une Parisienne
The Unkissed Bride
Up Your Alley
Utilities
The Vacillations of Poppy Carew
Valley Girl
Venus Beauty Institute
The Very Thought of You
Victor/Victoria▲
Vivacious Lady▲
Waiting for the Light
Walk, Don't Run
Warm Summer Rain
Watch It▲
Wavelength
We All Loved Each Other So Much▲
The Wedding Banquet▲
Wedding Bell Blues
The Wedding Party
The Wedding Planner
The Wedding Singer
A Weekend in the Country
We're Not Married▲
What a Woman!
What Happened to Rosa?▲
What Women Want
Whatever It Takes
What's Good for the Goose
What's New Pussycat?▲
When Brendan Met Trudy▲
When Harry Met Sally...▲
When Ladies Meet
While You Were Sleeping▲
Whipped
Who Am I This Time?▲
The Whoopee Boys
Why Change Your Wife?
Wildest Dreams
William Shakespeare's A Midsummer Night's Dream
Wimps
Wishful Thinking
With Six You Get Eggroll
Without Love
Without Reservations
Woman Hater
The Woman in Red
Woman of the Year▲
Woman on Top
The Women
Working Girl▲
World and Time Enough
The World's Oldest Living Bridesmaid
Worth Winning
You Can't Fool Your Wife
You Gotta Stay Happy
Younger & Younger
Your Place or Mine
You've Got Mail
You've Got to Have Heart
Zack & Reba
Zeus and Roxanne

Romantic Drama

A Coeur Joie
Aaron Loves Angela
Absent Without Leave
The Accidental Tourist▲
The Accompanist
The Adorable Cheat
The Affair▲
The Affair
An Affair of Love
An Affair to Remember
The African Queen▲
After Julius
After Midnight
After Sex
Afterglow
Against All Odds
Against the Wind
The Age of Innocence▲
Aimee & Jaguar
Algiers▲
Ali: Fear Eats the Soul▲
Alice▲
Alice Adams
Alice et Martin
Alive and Kicking
All That Heaven Allows▲
All the Pretty Horses
All the Vermeers in New York▲
All This and Heaven Too▲
Almost Blue
Always
The American
Anatomy of a Seduction
And a Nightingale Sang
And Now My Love
Angel
Angel Baby▲
Angel Eyes
Angel Square
Angels and Insects▲
The Animal Kingdom▲
Ann Vickers
Anna
Anna Christie▲
Anna Karenina
Annapolis
The Annapolis Story
Anne of Avonlea▲
Another Time, Another Place▲
Another Way▲
Anthony Adverse
Apart from Hugh
Arch of Triumph▲
Arch of Triumph
As Is
Aspen Extreme
At First Sight
Atalia
The Atonement of Gosta Berling▲
Autumn Moon
The Average Woman
Back Street
Backstreet Dreams
Bad Love
The Ballad of the Sad Cafe
Band of Angels
Barbarian and the Geisha
The Barretts of Wimpole Street▲
Basil
Bayou Romance
The Beast
Beau Revel▲
Beauty and the Beast▲
Because of You
Bed of Roses
Before Sunrise
Before the Rain▲
Beloved Enemy▲
Beloved Infidel
Berlin Blues
Besieged
The Best Intentions▲
The Best of Everything▲
Betty Blue▲
Beware of Pity
Beyond the Clouds
The Big Parade▲
Big Street
The Bigamist
Bird of Paradise
Bitter Sugar▲
Bitter Sweet
The Bitter Tea of General Yen▲
The Bitter Tears of Petra von Kant
The Black Marble▲
Black Orchid
Bleeding Hearts
Blind Husbands▲
The Blonde
Blood and Sand
Blood Feud
The Blood of Others
The Blue Hour
The Blue Light▲
Blush
Bolero
Bombay Talkie
Born to Be Bad
The Boss Is Served
Bounce
The Boxer
Boy Takes Girl
Boys
Breakfast in Paris
Breathless▲
Bride of the Wind
The Bride Wore Red
The Bridge▲
The Bridges of Madison County▲
Brief Encounter▲
The Brylcreem Boys
Buffalo Jump▲
Bullfighter & the Lady
Burning Secret
Buster and Billie
By Love Possessed
Bye Bye Blues
Cabiria
Cabo Blanco
Cactus
Cactus in the Snow
Caddie
Calendar▲
Camila▲
Camille▲
Camille Claudel▲
Captive Hearts
Captives
Carla's Song
Carmen▲
Carnival Story
The Carpetbaggers
Carrington
Casablanca▲
Cash McCall
Casino
Cass Timberlane
Castaway
The Castaway Cowboy
Catherine Cookson's The Fifteen Streets
Catherine Cookson's The Moth
Catherine Cookson's The Secret▲
Catherine Cookson's The Wingless Bird
Catherine Cookson's Tilly Trotter
Caught▲
Chain Lightning
Chained
The Chambermaid on the Titanic
Chanel Solitaire
Chapter Two
Charles & Diana: A Palace Divided
Charlotte Gray
Charulata
The Children
Children of a Lesser God▲
Christopher Strong
Chunhyang
Cinderella Liberty▲
Circle of Friends
Circle of Love
Circle of Passion
Circle of Two
Circus World
City for Conquest▲
City Girl
Claire of the Moon
Clash by Night▲
Close My Eyes
Cloud Waltzing
Cobra
Cocktail
Cold Sassy Tree▲
Collector's Item▲
The Color of Evening
Come and Get It▲
Come See the Paradise▲
Coming Home
The Coming of Amos▲
Coming Through
The Competition▲
Conquest▲
Consolation Marriage
Corregidor
Corrina, Corrina
The Cousins▲
The Cowboy & the Ballerina
The Cranes Are Flying▲
crazy/beautiful
The Crossing
Crystal Heart
The Cutting Edge
Cyrano de Bergerac▲
Daddy Long Legs
Dalva
Damage▲
Dance
Dancers
Dangerous Beauty▲
Dangerous Liaisons▲
Danielle Steel's Changes
Danielle Steel's Daddy
Danielle Steel's Heartbeat
Danielle Steel's Palomino
Danielle Steel's Star
Dark Eyes▲
Dark Journey▲
Dark Odyssey
Dash and Lilly
The Dawning
A Day in October
Daybreak
Days and Nights in the Forest
Dead Beat
Deadly Desire
Death Takes a Holiday▲
December Bride
Deception▲
A Dedicated Man
Deja Vu
The Delta
The Deluge
Desert Hearts▲
Desert Winds
Desire▲
Desire
Desperate Remedies
Devil in the Flesh▲
Devil in the Flesh
The Devil Is a Woman▲
Devil's Wanton
Devotion
Die Grosse Freiheit Nr. 7
Disappearing Acts
The Divorcee
Doctor Zhivago▲
Dogfight▲
Dogtown
The Dolls
The Dolphin
Don Juan DeMarco
Doomsday
A Dream of Kings▲
Dreams Lost, Dreams Found
The Dressmaker
Dubarry
Duel of Hearts
Dying Young
Dynasty
The Eagle Has Two Heads▲
East Side, West Side
Echoes
Ecstasy
Edward and Mrs. Simpson
Effi Briest▲
8 Seconds
84 Charing Cross Road▲
El Diputado▲
Elective Affinities
Elena and Her Men▲
Elephant Walk
Eliza's Horoscope
Emily Bronte's Wuthering Heights
Emma
Emma▲
Empty Canvas
Enchanted April
End of August
End of Summer
End of the Affair
The End of the Affair▲
Endless Love
The English Patient▲
Entropy
Escape to Love
Ethan
Ethan Frome
Evangeline
Every Time We Say Goodbye
Everybody's All American
Everything Happens at Night▲
Ex-Lady
The Eyes, the Mouth
The Fable of the Beautiful Pigeon Fancier
Falling for a Dancer
Falling in Love
The Family Man
Fanny▲
The Fantastic Night▲
Far and Away
Far from the Madding Crowd▲
The Far Pavilions
A Farewell to Arms▲
The Farmer Takes a Wife
Fatal Attraction
Feast of July
Fergie & Andrew: Behind Palace Doors
Fiances
Fire
Fire and Ice
Fire and Sword
Fire with Fire
Firelight
Fires Within
First Affair
First Knight
First Love
First Love and Other Pains / One of Them
First Love, Last Rites
Five Days One Summer
The Flame Is Love
Flor Silvestre
The Flying Fool
Fool for Love
Fools
For Love Alone
For Love or Money
For the Love of Angela
For the Moment
Forbidden
Forbidden Fruit▲
Foreign Affairs▲
Foreign Student
Forever
Forever: A Ghost of a Love Story
Forever Emmanuelle
Foxfire Light
Franz
The French Lieutenant's Woman▲
French Postcards
Fresh Horses
The Fugitive Kind
Fulfillment
Full Moon in Paris
Gabriela
Gal Young 'Un▲
Gamble on Love
The Game of Love
A Gentle Woman
Georgia, Georgia
Ghost▲
The Gift of Love
Girl in Black
The Girl in Blue
The Girl with a Suitcase
Girl with Green Eyes
Glitter
The Go-Between▲
Golden Demon
Golden Gate
Gone with the Wind▲
Goodbye Again
The Gorgeous Hussy
The Governess
Grand Isle
The Great Gatsby
The Great Lie▲
Green Dolphin Street
Green Fields
Green Fire
Green Mansions
Griffin and Phoenix: A Love Story
Guinevere▲
The Hairdresser's Husband
Hammers over the Anvil
Hanover Street
Harem
Harnessing Peacocks
Havana
Head Over Heels▲
Hearing Voices
The Hearst and Davies Affair
Heart of Humanity
Heartbreakers▲
Heartwood
Heat and Dust▲
The Heiress▲
Here on Earth
Heroes
Hide-Out
High Art
His Private Secretary
History Is Made at Night▲
Hold the Dream
Holiday Affair
Holocaust Survivors...Remembrance of Love
The Home and the World▲
Home Before Midnight
Home Sweet Home
Homecoming

Romantic

Hong Kong 1941
Honky
Hope Floats
The Horse Whisperer
Horsey
Hotel Room
Humoresque▸
Husbands and Wives▸
I Can't Escape
I Conquer the Sea
I Live in Grosvenor Square
I Love All of You
I Love N.Y.
I Love You
I Never Sang for My Father▸
Ice Castles
Iguana
Image of Passion
In a Shallow Grave
In Dangerous Company
In Love and War
In Search of Anna
In the Mood for Love
In the Shadows
In Too Deep
An Indecent Obsession
Indecent Proposal
Independence Day
Indiscretion of an American Wife
Indochine▸
Infinity
Interval
Intrigue and Love
Intruso
Inventing the Abbotts
Invisible Circus
Iron Cowboy
Island of Desire
Isle of Secret Passion
Istanbul
It's My Party
I've Always Loved You
Jacko & Lise
Jailbreakers
Jane Doe
Jane Eyre
Jane Eyre▸
Jane Eyre
Jason's Lyric
Jenny
Johnny Frenchman
Jon Jost's Frameup
Josepha▸
Jude▸
Jude the Obscure
Jules and Jim▸
Jungle Fever▸
Just Between Friends
Kept Husbands
The Key
Killing Heat
Kings Go Forth
The King's Rhapsody
The King's Whore
Kipperbang
Kiss of Fire
Kissed
Kitty Foyle▸
Knight Without Armour▸
Knights of the Round Table
Kristin Lavransdatter
The L-Shaped Room▸
La Chartreuse de Parme
La Grande Bourgeoise
La Petite Sirene
La Separation▸
La Strada▸
The Ladies of the Bois de Bologne
Lady Chatterley
Lady Chatterley's Lover
Lady from Louisiana
The Lady in Question
The Lady Refuses
The Lady with the Dog▸
L'Amour en Herbe
Lana in Love
The Land Girls
The Last Prostitute
The Last Ride
The Last Time I Saw Paris
The Last Train
The Last Winters
Le Bonheur
Le Jupon Rouge
Le Petit Soldat▸
Le Repos du Guerrier
A Legacy for Leonette
The Legend of Paul and Paula
Legends of the Fall
Leo Tolstoy's Anna Karenina
Leon Morin, Priest
Leopard in the Snow
Letters from the Park▸
Lianna▸
Liebelei
Lies of the Twins
The Life and Loves of Mozart
Life and Nothing But▸
A Life of Her Own
Lilith▸
Limbo
Linda
Listen to Me
The Little American
Little Dorrit, Film 2: Little Dorrit's Story▸
Little Minister▸
Lola▸
Lola
Long Ago Tomorrow
The Long, Hot Summer▸
Lorna Doone
Lorna Doone▸
Louisiana
Loulou▸
Love Affair▸
Love Affair
Love Affair: The Eleanor & Lou Gehrig Story▸
Love After Love
Love and Basketball▸
Love and Faith▸
Love and the Frenchwoman▸
Love at the Top
Love in Bloom
A Love in Germany
Love Is a Many-Splendored Thing
The Love Letter
Love Letters
Love Letters▸
The Love Light
The Love of Jeanne Ney
The Love of Three Queens
Love on the Run▸
Love Play
Love Songs
Love Streams
Love with a Perfect Stranger
Love with the Proper Stranger▸
Love Without Pity
The Lover
The Lovers▸
Lovers: A True Story▸
Lovers of the Arctic Circle
The Lovers on the Bridge
The Loves of Carmen
Love's Savage Fury
Lovespell
Lulu on the Bridge
The Luzhin Defence
Lydia▸
Machine Gun Blues
Mad Bull
Mad Love
Madagascar Skin
Madame Bovary▸
Madame Bovary
Magenta
The Magnificent Matador
Maids of Wilko
Mambo
A Man and a Woman▸
The Man in Grey▸
The Man in the Moon▸
Man Is Not a Bird
The Man Who Cried
The Man Who Guards the Greenhouse
Mannequin
Manon
Mansfield Park
Map of the Human Heart
Margaret's Museum▸
Maria Chapdelaine▸
Maria Chapdelaine
Marilyn & Bobby: Her Final Affair
Marjorie Morningstar
Martha and I▸
Marty▸
A Matter of Love
Mayerling▸
Mayerling
Medicine Man
Melody
Men
Merry-Go-Round▸
Message in a Bottle
Middlemarch▸
The Mill on the Floss
The Million Dollar Hotel
A Million to One
Minna von Barnhelm or The Soldier's Fortune
Mirrors
Mississippi Masala▸
Mississippi Mermaid▸
Mrs. Mike
Mrs. Soffel
Mr. & Mrs. Loving▸
Mr. Jones
Model Behavior
Mogambo▸
Monsoon
Moondance
Moonlight Sonata
Morning Glory
Morocco▸
Mouvements du Desir
My Antonia
My Brother Tom
My Champion
My Forbidden Past
My Man Adam
My Name Is Joe
Mysteries
Nairobi Affair
Nais▸
Naked Tango
Nativity
Nelly et Monsieur Arnaud▸
The Nest
Nevil Shute's The Far Country
New York Nights
Nicole
The Night and the Moment
A Night Full of Rain
Night Games
A Night in Heaven
Night Is My Future
No Looking Back
North Shore
Northanger Abbey
Not Quite Paradise
Nouvelle Vague
November Moon
Now and Forever
O Pioneers!
O Quatrilho
Of Human Bondage▸
Of Love and Shadows
Of Mice and Men▸
An Officer and a Gentleman▸
Old Gringo
Oliver's Story
Once in Paris...
One Brief Summer
One Summer Love
Only Love
Only Once in a Lifetime
The Only Thrill
The Other Side of the Mountain
The Other Side of the Mountain, Part 2
Our Modern Maidens
Our Mutual Friend
Our Time
Out of Season
Outcasts of the City
Over the Summer
Oxford Blues
A Paper Wedding▸
Parrish
Passion of Love▸
A Patch of Blue
Paul and Michelle
Pay It Forward
Pepe Le Moko▸
The Perfect Husband
Perfect Love
Persuasion
Persuasion▸
The Phantom of the Opera
The Pianist
The Piano▸
Picnic▸
Pittsburgh
Pizzicata
The Playboys▸
Playing by Heart
Pleasure
Poetic Justice
Poor White Trash
Port of Call▸
Portrait of Jennie▸
Portraits Chinois
Possessed
Possession
Pride and Prejudice▸
Pride of the Clan
Princess Yang Kwei Fei▸
Private Confessions
The Private Lives of Elizabeth & Essex▸
The Prizefighter and the Lady▸
The Promise
Proof of Life
The Proposition
The Proud Ones
The Public Eye▸
Pure Country
Purple Hearts
The Purple Taxi
Quality Street
Quatorze Juliet
Queen Bee
Queen Christina▸
Queen of the Stardust Ballroom▸
Rachel, Rachel▸
Rachel's Man
Racing with the Moon▸
Raffles▸
Rage of Angels
Rage of Angels: The Story Continues
The Railway Station Man▸
The Rainmaker▸
Random Hearts
Reach the Rock
The Real Charlotte
Rebel
Rebel Love
Reckless
Red Firecracker, Green Firecracker
Red Headed Woman▸
Red Kiss▸
Red Sorghum▸
The Red Squirrel
Regeneration
Rendezvous in Paris
Return Engagement
The Return of Martin Guerre▸
The Return of the Native
Return of the Soldier▸
Return to Paradise
Return to the Blue Lagoon
Return to Two Moon Junction
Reunion in France
The Ring
Risk▸
The Road Home▸
The Road to Yesterday
Rob Roy▸
Roman Spring of Mrs. Stone▸
Romance
Romance in Manhattan
Romance on the Orient Express
Romantic Englishwoman▸
Rome Adventure
Romeo and Juliet▸
Romeo and Juliet
Romeo and Juliet▸
Romper Stomper
Room at the Top▸
A Room with a View▸
The Rose Tattoo▸
The Rover
Rowing with the Wind
The Run of the Country▸
Running Away
Running Out of Time
Ruyblas
Ryan's Daughter
Sadie Thompson▸
The Sailor Who Fell from Grace with the Sea
Sally Hemings: An American Scandal
Same Time, Next Year▸
San Francisco▸
Sand and Blood
The Sandpiper
Santa Fe
Sarah, Plain and Tall▸
Saratoga Trunk
Savage Capitalism
Savage Messiah▸
Say Hello to Yesterday
Sayonara▸
Scarlet Dawn
Scarlett
Scenes from the Goldmine
Second Wind
Secret Obsession
Secret of Yolanda
Secret Passions
Sense & Sensibility
Sense and Sensibility▸
The Separation
September Affair
The Serpent's Kiss
The Seventh Stream
Shadow of China▸
Shadowlands▸
The Shining Hour
Shining Through
Shoot the Piano Player▸
Shop Angel
Shopworn Angel▸
Silver City
The Silver Horde
Silver Strand
Sin Takes a Holiday
Sincerely Charlotte▸
Singapore
Sister Dora
A Slave of Love▸
Sleep with Me
Slipstream
Smilin' Through▸
Snow Country
The Soft Skin▸
A Soldier's Tale
Solomon and Gaenor
Somewhere I'll Find You▸
Somewhere in Time
Somewhere Tomorrow
Sommersby
The Song of Songs
A Song to Remember▸
Sooner or Later
The Sorrows of Satan▸
South Riding
Souvenir
A Special Day▸
Splendor
Stanley and Iris
Stealing Heaven
Stella
The Stilts▸
Stolen Hours
Stormy Waters
The Story of a Three Day Pass
The Story of the Late Chrysanthemum▸
The Story of Xinghua
The Strange Love of Molly Louvain
Strangers Kiss
Strangers When We Meet
Strapless
Street Scene▸
The Student Prince in Old Heidelberg
Sugartime
Summer Affair
Summer Lovers
A Summer Story▸
Summertime▸
Sweet Bird of Youth
Sweet Light in a Dark Room▸
Sweet November
Swept from the Sea
Swimming Pool
A Tale of Two Cities
A Tale of Winter
Talk of Angels
Talk to Me
Tango
Tango Bar
Tarzan Escapes▸
Tears in the Rain
The Tempest▸
The Tempest
The Tenant of Wildfell Hall
Tender Mercies▸
Tess▸
Tess of the D'Urbervilles
Tess of the Storm Country
Test Pilot▸
That Long Night in '43
That Night
That Summer of White Roses
The Theory of Flight
They Call It Sin
36 Fillete▸
This Is My Father
This Is the Sea
Three Comrades▸
Through the Olive Trees▸
Tilai
Tim
Time Out for Love
A Time to Love & a Time to Die
Timeless
To Gillian on Her 37th Birthday
To Have & Have Not▸
To Love Again
Today We Live
Together?
Tomorrow▸
Tomorrow Is Forever
Tonight or Never
The Torch
Torn Apart
Torn Between Two Lovers
Torrents of Spring
The Torture of Silence
The Touch
A Town Like Alice
Trapeze▸
Tristana▸
Trouble in Mind▸
True Heart Susie
True Romance
The Tsar's Bride▸
The Tunnel
21 Days
24 Hours in a Woman's Life
Twin Falls Idaho▸
Twist & Shout▸
Two Daughters▸
Two English Girls▸
Two Moon Junction
Two Plus One
Un Coeur en Hiver
The Unbearable Lightness of Being▸
Under the Sun
The Unknown Soldier
An Unremarkable Life
Untamed Heart
Up Close and Personal▸
The Valley of Decision▸
Vanity Fair
Verboten!
Vibrations
The Victory
The Virgin and the Gypsy
Virgin Machine
Vive l'Amour
Voyage of the Heart
Voyager▸
A Walk in the Clouds
Walk in the Spring Rain
A Walk on the Moon
Walk Softly, Stranger
A Walk to Remember
The Walls of Malapaga
Waltz across Texas
The Wanderer
War & Love
War and Peace
War and Peace▸
War and Peace
War Lover
Washington Mistress
Waterfront
The Way We Were▸
We the Living
Weather in the Streets
Wedding in Blood▸
The Wedding March▸
We'll Meet Again
West Side Story▸

▸ = *rated three bones or higher*

What Dreams May Come
When I Close My Eyes
When Love Comes
When Night Is Falling➚
When the Time Comes
When Thief Meets Thief
Where the Boys Are
Which Way Home
Whistle Stop
White Cargo
White Light
White Nights➚
White Palace
The White Sister➚
Wide Sargasso Sea
Wife Versus Secretary➚
Wild at Heart➚
Wild Hearts Can't Be Broken➚
Wildfire
William Shakespeare's Romeo and Juliet➚
Wind
The Wind and the Lion➚
Windmills of the Gods
Windrider
The Winds of Jarrah
Wings
Wings of Desire➚
The Wings of the Dove➚
Wings of the Morning
Winter Flight
Winter People
Wives and Daughters
A Woman at Her Window
A Woman at War
The Woman He Loved
The Woman Next Door➚
A Woman of Substance
A Woman Without Love➚
A Woman's Guide to Adultery
The Women on the Roof
The World of Suzie Wong
Wuthering Heights➚
Wuthering Heights
Yanks
Year of the Quiet Sun➚
Yesterday's Hero
You Light Up My Life
The Young and the Guilty
Young Lady Chatterly 2
Youth on Parole

Romantic Triangles

see also *Otherwise Engaged*

The Age of Innocence➚
Aladdin➚
All Things Fair
The Alley Cats
Amateur➚
Amnesia
Among Giants
Amores Perros➚
Angie
Anna
Another Woman's Husband
The Art of Murder
The Aviator's Wife➚
Baby Monitor: Sound of Fear
Baja
Bandits
Baton Rouge
The Best Man
A Better Tomorrow, Part 3
Bitter Moon
Black Day Blue Night
Blue Skies➚
Blush
Body Heat➚
Bride of the Wind
Broadcast News➚
The Brylcreem Boys
Bull Durham➚
A Business Affair
Business for Pleasure
Cactus Flower
Cafe au Lait➚
Calendar➚
Canyon Passage➚
Captain Corelli's Mandolin
Carnal Knowledge➚
Carny➚
Carried Away
Carrington
Casablanca➚
Casino➚
Caught
Celine and Julie Go Boating
Circle of Passion
Cleopatra's Second Husband
The Color of Evening
Coming Out
Condition Red
The Cook, the Thief, His Wife & Her Lover➚
Country Life
The Crucible➚
Dalva
Damage➚
The Dangerous
Dangerous Indiscretion
Dangerous Passion
Dark Blue World
Dark Harbor
Dead Beat
Dead in the Water
Dead Ringers➚
Death in Brunswick
December Bride
The Devil Is a Woman➚
Diabolique
The Doom Generation➚
Dreaming of Joseph Lees
Drift
Driven
Dry Cleaning
Elephant Walk
Emma➚
End of the Affair
The End of the Affair➚
The English Patient➚
Ethan Frome
Everyone Says I Love You➚
The Ex
The Favor
Feast of July
First Knight
The First Wives Club
The Flame of New Orleans➚
Flirt
The Fluffer
A Foreign Affair➚
Forever Mine
Foxfire Light
French Kiss
French Twist
The Getaway
The Girl with a Suitcase
The Golden Bowl➚
The Golden Bowl
Goodbye, Lover
The Great Gatsby
Grind
Gunshy➚
Hard Evidence
The Hard Truth
Henry & June➚
Here on Earth
The Hi-Lo Country
High Art
High Society➚
Hilary and Jackie➚
Hindsight
Homage
Hong Kong 1941
In the Shadows
Indecent Proposal
Indiscreet
Innocents with Dirty Hands
Interlocked
Intersection
Intimate Betrayal
Intimate Relations
Intruso
Is Money Everything?
It Could Happen to You
Jason's Lyric
Jules and Jim➚
Keeping the Faith
Killer Looks
Kiss the Sky
Kissing a Fool
The Ladies of the Bois de Bologne
Lady Chatterley
The Last Days of Chez Nous
The Last of the Mohicans➚
Le Jupon Rouge
The Leading Man
Legends of the Fall
Les Voleurs➚
L'Escorte
Liebelei
Lloyds of London➚
Love, etc.
Love Play
Love Serenade
Love Walked In
The Lovers➚
Lured Innocence
Magenta
Making Love
The Man in the Attic
Man in the Saddle
Mararia
The Married Virgin
Matter of Trust
Maybe ... Maybe Not
Maze
Mildred Pierce➚
Miller's Crossing➚
Mr. Jealousy
Mists of Avalon➚
Mo' Better Blues
Mojave Moon
Moment to Moment
Mon Homme
Money Train
Moondance
Moonshine Highway
The Mother and the Whore➚
Mouth to Mouth
Murder Czech Style
My Best Friend's Wedding
My Favorite Wife➚
My Husband's Secret Life
Never Say Die
Nick and Jane
No Way Home
On the Beach
Once a Thief➚
One Night Stand➚
Only You
The Opposite of Sex
Out of Africa➚
The Pallbearer
Palmetto
Pearl Harbor
Pedale Douce
The Perfect Gift
The Philadelphia Story➚
The Pianist
Play It to the Bone
Playing by Heart
Polish Wedding
Portrait in Black
Portraits Chinois
Possessed by the Night
A Price above Rubies
Private Confessions
Pushing Tin➚
Quiet Days in Hollywood
Radio Inside
Reality Bites
Reckless➚
Reckless: The Sequel➚
Restoration➚
Revenge
Riders
Rift
Risk
Robin Hood: Prince of Thieves
A Room with a View➚
Sabrina➚
Sabrina
Sand and Blood
Saturday Night and Sunday Morning➚
Saturday Night Special
Savage Capitalism
Scorned 2
The Separation
The Serpent's Kiss
Sex and the Other Man
She's Gotta Have It➚
She's So Lovely
Simpatico
Slaves to the Underground
Sleep with Me
Sleepless in Seattle➚
Sliding Doors
Something More
Sommersby
The Song of Songs
Splendor
Stella
Stella Maris➚
Stonewall➚
Stormy Nights
Story of a Prostitute
The Story of Xinghua
The Student Affair
Summer Catch
Summer Lovers
A Tale of Winter
Talk of Angels
Tango
Tape➚
The Tenant of Wildfell Hall
Tequila Sunrise
Tess➚
Tess of the D'Urbervilles
There's Something about Mary➚
A Thin Line Between Love and Hate
Three for the Show
Three of Hearts
Three to Tango
Threesome
Tilai
Tin Cup➚
Tollbooth
Torrents of Spring
Town and Country
Trace of Stones
The Trio
Trojan War
The Truth about Cats and Dogs➚
Twice upon a Yesterday
Twister
Two Girls and a Guy➚
Two Much
Two Ninas
Two Plus One
Two Shades of Blue
U-Turn
The Unbearable Lightness of Being➚
The Underneath➚
Unfaithful
The Unknown Soldier
Valley of the Kings
The Velocity of Gary
A Village Affair
Vive l'Amour
Waiting to Exhale➚
A Walk on the Moon
Wavelength
The Wedding Banquet➚
What a Woman!
While You Were Sleeping➚
White Mischief➚
The Whole Nine Yards
Wild Things
Willie & Phil
The Wings of the Dove➚
Wishful Thinking
Wolf Trap
A Woman at Her Window
Woman Wanted
The Women on the Roof
X, Y & Zee
You Gotta Stay Happy

Rome—Ancient

see also *Historical Drama; Italy*

A.D.
Alone Against Rome
Attila
Battle of Valiant
Ben-Hur➚
Caesar and Cleopatra
Caligula
Cleopatra
Demetrius and the Gladiators
Druids
Duel of Champions
Fabiola➚
The Fall of the Roman Empire➚
Fellini Satyricon➚
A Funny Thing Happened on the Way to the Forum➚
Gladiator➚
Julius Caesar➚
Julius Caesar
Last Days of Pompeii
The Last Days of Pompeii
Quo Vadis
Quo Vadis➚
Quo Vadis
The Robe
Roman Scandals
Rome '78
The Sign of the Cross
Spartacus➚
Three Ages➚
Titus

Rome—Modern

see also *Italy*

Artemisia
Bellissima➚
The Belly of an Architect➚
Besieged
Camille 2000
Daniella by Night
Fellini's Roma
The Frightened Woman
Ginger & Fred➚
The Godfather, Part 3➚
Hudson Hawk
Indiscretion of an American Wife
La Dolce Vita➚
My Own Private Idaho➚
National Lampoon's European Vacation
Night on Earth➚
Portrait of a Lady➚
Roman Holiday➚
Roman Spring of Mrs. Stone➚
The Scarlet & the Black
A Special Day➚
Steam: A Turkish Bath➚
The Stendahl Syndrome
The Talented Mr. Ripley
The Unfaithfuls
The White Sheik➚

Roommates from Hell

see also *Psychotics/ Sociopaths*

Deadbolt
The Fear Inside
The Last Supper
Lip Service
Malice
The Night We Never Met
Pacific Heights➚
Perfect Tenant
Shallow Grave
Single White Female
Sweet Murder
Zero Degrees Kelvin

Royalty

see also *Historical Drama; Medieval Romps; Royalty, British; Royalty, Russian*

Abdulla the Great
The Adventures of Marco Polo
The Affair of the Necklace
Aladdin➚
Ali Baba and the Forty Thieves
Ali Baba and the 40 Thieves➚
Anna and the King
Anna and the King of Siam➚
Annie: A Royal Adventure
Arabian Nights
Atlantis: The Lost Empire
Autobiography of a Princess
Bagdad
Balalaika
Barbarian Queen 2: The Empress Strikes Back
Beaumarchais the Scoundrel
The Beautician and the Beast
The Black Cauldron
Bonnie Prince Charlie
Boots & Saddles
Caligula
Carlton Browne of the F.O.
Carry On Henry VIII
Charlemagne
Charles & Diana: A Palace Divided
Chimes at Midnight➚
Cinderella
Cleopatra
Cobra Woman
The Coming of Amos➚
Coming to America➚
A Connecticut Yankee in King Arthur's Court
Conquest of the Normans
Court Jester➚
The Crusades
David
De Mayerling a Sarajevo
Desiree
Dr. Syn, Alias the Scarecrow
Donkey Skin➚
Dracula: The Dark Prince
Dragonheart
DuBarry Was a Lady
Dune
The Eagle Has Two Heads➚
East of Borneo
The Egyptian
Elena and Her Men➚
The Emperor and the Assassin
Emperor Jones
Emperor Waltz
The Emperor's New Clothes
The Emperor's New Groove➚
The Emperor's Shadow
Esther
Ever After: A Cinderella Story➚
Excalibur➚
Fairy Tales
Fanfan la Tulipe➚
Farinelli
Fergie & Andrew: Behind Palace Doors
The Fifth Musketeer
The Fighting Prince of Donegal
First Knight
Fit for a King
Flame of Araby
Forever Amber
Galgameth
Gladiator➚
The Grace Kelly Story
The Grand Duchess and the Waiter➚
Hamlet➚
Hamlet
Hennessy
Hercules the Legendary Journeys, Vol. 2: The Lost Kingdom
His Majesty, the American
If I Were King➚
The Indian Tomb
The Iron Mask
Jason and the Argonauts
Jeanne la Pucelle
Joan of Arc
Joseph
Julius Caesar➚
Julius Caesar
Just Suppose
Kama Sutra: A Tale of Love
Kaspar Hauser
A Kid in Aladdin's Palace
A Kid in King Arthur's Court
Kind Hearts and Coronets➚
The King and I➚
The King and I
A King in New York
King Lear➚
The King on Main Street
King Ralph
The King's Guard
The King's Rhapsody
The King's Thief
The King's Whore
La Nuit de Varennes➚
Lancelot of the Lake
The Last Emperor➚
Lillie➚
Lion Man
Lorna Doone
Lost in a Harem
Love's Labour's Lost
Ludwig
Macbeth➚
Macbeth
The Magic Fountain

The Man in the Iron Mask▲
The Man in the Iron Mask
The Man in the Iron Mask▲
The Man Who Would Be King▲
Mannequin 2: On the Move
Marbella
Marie Antoinette
The Master of Ballantrae
Mayerling▲
Mayerling
A Midsummer Night's Dream▲
A Midsummer Night's Dream
Mom and Dad Save the World
Monsieur Beaucaire
Monsieur Beaucaire▲
Moses
Mulan
The Musketeer
My Pal, the King
A Night of Love
Nostradamus
Options
Passion
Phedre
Phoenix
The Polar Bear King
Power
The Prince and the Pauper▲
The Prince and the Pauper
The Prince and the Showgirl
The Prince and the Surfer
Prince Brat and the Whipping Boy▲
The Princess and the Pea
Princess Caraboo
The Princess Comes Across▲
The Princess Diaries
Princess Tam Tam▲
Princess Yang Kwei Fei▲
Prisoner of Zenda▲
Prisoner of Zenda
Queen Christina▲
Queen Kelly▲
Queen Margot▲
Quest for Camelot
The Rape of the Sabines
The Return of the Musketeers
Return to Oz
Revenge of the Musketeers
Ridicule▲
The Rise of Louis XIV▲
Roman Holiday▲
The Royal Bed
Royal Deceit
Ruyblas
The Saragossa Manuscript
Shanghai Noon
Shin Heike Monogatari▲
Shrek▲
The Sign of the Cross
The Silences of the Palace▲
Snow White and the Seven Dwarfs▲
Snow White and the Seven Dwarfs
Snow White: The Fairest of Them All
Soldier in Love
Solomon
Solomon and Sheba
Son of Ali Baba
Song Spinner
Splitting Heirs
Spy of Napoleon
Star Knight
Start the Revolution without Me▲
Storm over Asia▲
The Story of David▲
Storybook
Surf Ninjas
The Swan
The Swan▲
The Swan Princess 2: Escape from Castle Mountain
The Sword & the Rose
Sword & the Sorcerer
The Sword of El Cid
The 10th Kingdom
The Thief and the Cobbler▲
A Thousand and One Nights
The Three Musketeers▲
Throne of Blood▲
Titus
To Play the King▲
The Tower of London
Tower of London
Tower of Screaming Virgins
The Triumph of Love
Two Nights with Cleopatra
Vatel
The War Lord▲
The Warriors
The Wedding March▲
Where There's Life
Willow

Royalty, British

***see also** Great Britain; Historical Drama; Medieval Romps; Royalty*

All the King's Men
Anne of the Thousand Days▲
Becket▲
Black Knight
The Black Shield of Falworth
Braveheart▲
The Bruce
Chasing the Deer
Diana: Her True Story
Edward and Mrs. Simpson
Edward II
Edward the King
Elizabeth▲
Elizabeth R▲
Elizabeth, the Queen
Henry IV
Henry V▲
Ivanhoe▲
Jack Higgins' Midnight Man
John and Julie
King Lear▲
King Richard and the Crusaders
A Knight in Camelot
Lady Godiva
Lady Jane▲
The Lion in Winter▲
Looking for Richard▲
The Madness of King George▲
A Man for All Seasons▲
Mary of Scotland▲
Mary, Queen of Scots
Merlin▲
Mrs. Brown▲
Mists of Avalon▲
Nine Days a Queen▲
Orlando▲
The Prince and the Pauper
Prince Valiant
Princess of Thieves
The Private Life of Henry VIII▲
The Private Lives of Elizabeth & Essex▲
Restoration▲
Richard III
Richard III▲
The Ripper
A Royal Scandal
Shakespeare in Love▲
Six Wives of Henry VIII▲
Victoria & Albert
Victoria Regina
The Virgin Queen▲
The Woman He Loved
Young Bess▲

Royalty, Russian

***see also** Historical Drama; Medieval Romps; Royalty; Russia/USSR*

Alexander Nevsky▲
Anastasia▲
Anastasia
Anastasia: The Mystery of Anna
Catherine the Great
I Killed Rasputin
Ivan the Terrible, Part 1▲
Ivan the Terrible, Part 2▲
Never Say Die
Nicholas and Alexandra
Peter the Great▲
Rasputin▲
Rasputin and the Empress▲
Rasputin: Dark Servant of Destiny▲
Rasputin the Mad Monk
Scarlet Empress▲
Young Catherine▲

Running

Across the Tracks
Billie
Chariots of Fire▲
College▲
Finish Line
Forrest Gump▲
The Four Minute Mile
Go for the Gold
The Gold & Glory
Goldengirl
The Jericho Mile
The Jesse Owens Story
Jim Thorpe: All American
The Loneliest Runner
The Loneliness of the Long Distance Runner▲
The Loretta Claiborne Story
Marathon
Marathon Man▲
Off the Mark
On the Edge
Prefontaine
Raw Courage
Run for the Dream: The Gail Devers Story
Running Brave
Sam's Son
See How She Runs▲
A Shining Season▲
The Sprinter
The Terry Fox Story▲
Without Limits▲

Russia/USSR

***see also** Moscow; Red Scare*

American Cop
Anastasia▲
Anastasia
Anastasia: The Mystery of Anna
The Ascent▲
Assassination of Trotsky
Back in the USSR
Balalaika
Baltic Deputy▲
The Battleship Potemkin▲
The Brothers Karamazov▲
Burglar▲
Burnt by the Sun▲
Children of the Revolution
Citizen X▲
Come and See▲
Coming Out of the Ice▲
The Commies Are Coming, the Commies Are Coming
Commissar▲
Comrade X
Creation of Adam
Crimson Tide▲
Days of Glory
Dersu Uzala▲
Doctor Zhivago▲
Don't Drink the Water
Dostoevsky's Crime and Punishment
Drums of Jeopardy
The Eagle▲
East-West
The End of St. Petersburg▲
Enemy at the Gates
The Extraordinary Adventures of Mr. West in the Land of the Bolsheviks
Final Assignment
Final Warning
First Strike
The Fixer▲
Freeze-Die-Come to Life▲
The Gambler
The Girl from Petrovka
Goldeneye▲
Gorky Park▲
Gulag
The Hunt for Red October▲
I Killed Rasputin
The Ice Runner
The Inner Circle▲
Ivan the Terrible, Part 1▲
Ivan the Terrible, Part 2▲
The Jackal
K-19: The Widowmaker
Kindergarten▲
Laser Mission
Last Command▲
The Light Ahead
Little Vera▲
Love and Death▲
The Man with the Movie Camera▲
The Mirror▲
Moscow Does Not Believe in Tears▲
Mother▲
Mother and Son
Mute Witness
My Family Treasure
My Name Is Ivan▲
Never Let Me Go
Nicholas and Alexandra
Nostalghia
One Day in the Life of Ivan Denisovich▲
100 Days Before the Command
One Russian Summer
The Peacemaker
Peter the Great▲
The Possessed
Prisoner of the Mountains▲
Rasputin▲
Rasputin and the Empress▲
Rasputin the Mad Monk
The Red and the White▲
Red Cherry
Red Heat
Red Hot
Reds▲
The Road to Life
The Russia House
Russian Roulette
The Saint
Sakharov▲
Scarlet Dawn
Scarlet Empress▲
The Seagull▲
Siberiade▲
Sideburns
A Slave of Love▲
Solo Voyage: The Revenge
Stalin
Stalingrad
Taxi Blues▲
Terminal Velocity
Theremin: An Electronic Odyssey▲
The Thief
The Three Sisters
Torrents of Spring
The Truce▲
The Ultimate Imposter
War and Peace
War and Peace▲
War and Peace
We the Living
White Nights
Window to Paris
World War III
Young Catherine▲

Sail Away

***see also** Deep Blue; Go Fish; Killer Sea Critters; Mutiny; Scuba; Shipwrecked; Submarines*

Abandon Ship
Adrift
Adventure Island
The Adventures of Huckleberry Finn▲
An Affair to Remember
The African Queen▲
All the Brothers Were Valiant
And the Ship Sails On▲
Anna Christie
Annapolis
Assault on a Queen
Away All Boats
The Baby and the Battleship
The Battleship Potemkin▲
Beat the Devil▲
Beyond the Poseidon Adventure
The Big Broadcast of 1938
Billy Budd▲
Bitter Moon
Blondie Goes Latin
Blood Voyage
The Boatniks
Botany Bay
The Bounty
Boy in Blue
Britannic
Cabin Boy
The Caine Mutiny▲
The Caine Mutiny Court Martial▲
Captain Caution
Captain Horatio Hornblower▲
Captain Jack
Captain Ron
Captains Courageous▲
Captains Courageous
Captain's Paradise▲
The Captain's Table
Carry On Admiral
Carry On Cruising
The Cat's Meow
China Seas▲
Christopher Columbus
The Coast Patrol
Convoy
A Countess from Hong Kong
The Crew
Crimson Tide▲
Cruise into Terror
Damn the Defiant▲
Danger Beneath the Sea
Dangerous Charter
Dangerous Passage
Dark Tide
Das Boot▲
Day of the Assassin
The Day Will Dawn▲
Dead Ahead: The Exxon Valdez Disaster▲
Dead Calm▲
Dead in the Water
Dead Reckoning
Dead Tides
Deadly Voyage
Death Cruise
Death Ship
Death Tide
The Deep
Deep Rising
Destroyer▲
Die Hard: With a Vengeance
Dixie Jamboree
Doctor at Sea
Don Winslow of the Coast Guard
The Dove
Down Periscope
Down to the Sea in Ships
The Ebb-Tide
Ensign Pulver
Erik, the Viking
Escape from Atlantis
Escape under Pressure
The Evil Below
Far from Home: The Adventures of Yellow Dog
Feet First
Ferry to Hong Kong
The Fighting Sullivans▲
The Final Countdown▲
Final Voyage
Flat Top
Flight of the Intruder
Flipper▲
Francis in the Navy
Friday the 13th, Part 8: Jason Takes Manhattan
Gangway
Geheimakte WB1
Ghost Ship
The Gift Horse
A Girl in Every Port
Give Me a Sailor
Going Overboard
Going Under
Golden Rendezvous
Goliath Awaits
Gone Fishin'
Gray Lady Down
The Great Lover
Gun Cargo
The Hairy Ape
Haunted Harbor
The Haunted Sea
Hawaii Calls
He Is My Brother
Hell-Ship Morgan
History Is Made at Night▲
Horatio Hornblower▲
Horatio Hornblower: The Adventure Continues▲
Horror of the Zombies
The Hunt for Red October▲
I Conquer the Sea
The Imposters
In Which We Serve▲
The Incredible Mr. Limpet
The Incredible Petrified World
Ironclads
Isle of Forgotten Sins
JAG
Jason and the Argonauts
Jaws▲
Jaws 2
The Jewel of the Nile
Johnny Angel▲
Juggernaut▲
Kill Cruise
Killer on Board
King Kelly of the U.S.A.
Knife in the Water▲
The Last of Sheila
The Last Voyage
Law of the Sea
Le Crabe Tambour▲
The Legend of 1900
The Legend of Sea Wolf
The Legend of the Sea Wolf
Lifeboat▲
Light at the Edge of the World
The Lightship
Live and Let Die
Loch Ness
Long John Silver
The Long Ships
The Long Voyage Home▲
Longitude▲
Lord Jim▲
Lost in the Bermuda Triangle
Love Affair▲
The Magic Stone
A Majority of One
Manfish
Mayflower: The Pilgrims' Adventure
McHale's Navy
The Mermaids of Tiburon
Message in a Bottle
Mister Roberts▲
Monkey Business▲
Moon in Scorpio
Moran of the Lady Letty
Muppet Treasure Island
Murder on the High Seas
Mutiny
The Mutiny of the Elsinore
Mutiny on the Bounty▲
Mutiny on the Bounty
Mystery Liner
The Mystery of the Mary Celeste
The Navigator▲
The Navy Comes Through
New Moon
A Night to Remember▲
The Odyssey
Old Ironsides▲
One Crazy Summer
Operation Petticoat▲
Out to Sea
Oxford Blues
Passenger▲
The Perfect Storm
Pirate Ship
The Port of Missing Girls
The Poseidon Adventure
The Princess Comes Across▲
Pueblo Affair▲
Pursuit of the Graf Spee
Rainbow Warrior
Reaching for the Moon
Reap the Wild Wind
Rich and Strange
Roaring Speedboats
Romancing the Stone▲
Run Silent, Run Deep▲
The Sand Pebbles▲

▲ = rated three bones or higher

The Incredible Two-Headed Transplant
Innocent Victim
Innocents
Insanity
Instinct
Interiors▸
The Invisible Ghost
Irma Vep
It Happened at Nightmare Inn
It's Alive!
Jekyll and Hyde
Joe Gould's Secret
Juggernaut
Julien Donkey-boy
K-PAX
Keeper
King Lear▸
The King of Hearts▸
Lassie from Lancashire
The Last Don 2
The Last of Philip Banter
The Last Ride
The Last Seduction▸
Leave Her to Heaven▸
Lethal Weapon▸
Lethal Weapon 2▸
Let's Scare Jessica to Death
Life Upside Down
Lilian's Story
Lilith▸
Little Boy Blue
The Locusts
The Lonely Sex
Los Locos Posse
Lost Angels
Lower Level
Ludwig
Lunatics: A Love Story▸
Luther the Geek
Macabre
Mad Love▸
Mad Love
Man Facing Southeast▸
Manhunter▸
Mary, My Dearest
A Matter of Taste
Midnight Warning
Mind Games
Mine Own Executioner▸
Ministry of Fear▸
Mr. Deeds Goes to Town▸
Mr. Jones
Mixed Nuts
Morgan: A Suitable Case for Treatment
Mother Kusters Goes to Heaven▸
Murder in Mind
Murder in the First
My First Wife
My Sister's Keeper
My Very Best Friend
Network▸
Night of Bloody Horror
Night of Terror
The Night Visitor
Night Wars
Night Watch
Nijinsky
1941
The Ninth Configuration▸
Nobody's Perfekt
Nurse Betty▸
Nuts▸
The October Man▸
Offerings
Office Killer
One Flew Over the Cuckoo's Nest▸
One Hour Photo
125 Rooms of Comfort
One Summer Love
The Onion Field▸
Open Your Eyes▸
The Others▸
Out of Sight, Out of Her Mind
Overexposed
Pale Blood
Paperback Hero
Passion of Mind
Pay Off
Pecker
Peeping Tom▸
The Perfect Nanny
Performance▸
Peril
A Piano for Mrs. Cimino▸
Picture Mommy Dead
Pigs
The Pink Panther Strikes Again▸
The Pit and the Pendulum▸
The Pit & the Pendulum
Play Misty for Me▸
Poison▸
The Possessed▸
The President's Analyst▸
Prettykill
Prime Suspect
Private Parts
Psychic Killer
Psycho▸
Psycho
Psycho 2
Psycho Cop
Psycho Cop 2
Psychos in Love
Question of Silence▸
Raising Cain
Rasputin▸
The Red Desert▸
The Rejuvenator
Remember Me
Return of the Ape Man
Return to Cabin by the Lake
Revenge in the House of Usher
Revolt of the Zombies
Richard III▸
Room to Let
The Ruling Class▸
Scarlet Empress▸
Scissors
The Scout
Scream Bloody Murder
Scream for Help
Screamer
Screw Loose
Seance on a Wet Afternoon▸
Secret Beyond the Door
The Sender
Session 9
Sessions
Seven Days in May▸
Seventh Heaven
Shades of Black
Shadow Play
Shattered
Shattered Image
Shattered Silence
Shattered Spirits
The Shining
Shock Corridor▸
The Silence of the Lambs▸
Silent Night, Bloody Night
Sisters▸
Sisters, Or the Balance of Happiness
Skeletons in the Closet
Sketches of a Strangler
Slaughter Hotel
Sledgehammer
Sling Blade▸
Sniper▸
Solaris
Some Folks Call It a Sling Blade▸
Sophie's Choice▸
Soul Survivors
South of Reno
Spectre of the Rose
Spellbound▸
Star Maps
The Story of Adele H.▸
Strait-Jacket
Strange Illusion
Strangers on a Train▸
Street Asylum
A Streetcar Named Desire▸
Strong Medicine
Stuart Bliss
Stuart Saves His Family
The Substance of Fire
The Survivalist
Svengali
Sweethearts
Sybil▸
Tainted Image
Teenage Frankenstein
The Tenant▸
The Testament of Dr. Cordelier▸
They Might Be Giants▸
The Thin Red Line
The Three Faces of Eve
The 300 Year Weekend
Three Nuts in Search of a Bolt
Titus
Torture Train
Touched
Tracks
Trapped in Silence
The Turn of the Screw
12 Monkeys▸
Twilight Man
Twin Peaks: Fire Walk with Me
Twinsanity
Twister
The Two Faces of Dr. Jekyll
The Ugly
Under the Sand▸
Under the Skin
Urge to Kill
Vampire's Kiss▸
Vengeance Is Mine▸
Vincent & Theo▸
Violated
Virtual Seduction
Walter and Henry▸
Ward Six
Watched
What about Bob?▸
What Ever Happened to Baby Jane?▸
What's the Matter with Helen?
While I Live
White Badge
White Heat▸
The Wind
Witchfire
Woman in Black
The Woman in White
A Woman under the Influence▸
Woyzeck

Satanism

***see also** Demons & Wizards; Devils; Occult*

Alison's Birthday
Amazon Jail
Angel on My Shoulder
Asylum of Satan
Bad Dreams
Beast of the Yellow Night
Beyond the Door 3
The Black Cat▸
Black Roses
Black Sunday▸
Bless the Child
The Blood on Satan's Claw▸
Blood Orgy of the She-Devils
The Bloodsuckers
The Brotherhood of Satan
Child of Darkness, Child of Light
The Chosen
The Convent
The Crimson Cult
Damien: Omen 2
The Day of the Beast
The Demon Lover
Demonoid, Messenger of Death
The Devil & Daniel Webster▸
The Devil Rides Out▸
The Devils▸
The Devil's Daughter
The Devil's Eye
The Devil's Mistress
The Devil's Nightmare
The Devil's Partner
The Devil's Possessed
The Devil's Prey
Devil's Rain
Devil's Son-in-Law
The Devil's Web
Disciple of Death
Doctor Faustus
Equinox▸
Eternal Evil
Evil Altar
Evilspeak
Exorcism
The Exorcist▸
The Exorcist 2: The Heretic
Eye of the Demon
Family Reunion
Fear No Evil
Ghoulies 4
Guardian of the Abyss
Hack O'Lantern
Halloween Night
Highway to Hell
House of the Black Death
I Don't Want to Be Born
I Drink Your Blood
Inferno
Invitation to Hell
Jaws of Satan
Land of the Minotaur
Leaves from Satan's Book
The Legend of Hillbilly John
Leonor
A Little Bit of Soul
Lost Souls
The Man and the Monster
The Mangler
Maxim Xul
The Mephisto Waltz▸
Midnight
Midnight Cabaret
Midnight's Child
Mind, Body & Soul
Mysterious Doctor Satan
Necromancer: Satan's Servant
Night Visitor
976-EVIL
976-EVIL 2: The Astral Factor
The Ninth Gate
The Occultist
Oh, God! You Devil
The Omen
Omen 3: The Final Conflict
Other Hell
Prime Evil
Prince of Darkness
The Pyx▸
Race with the Devil
Raging Angels
The Relic
Rest in Pieces
Revenge
Rosemary's Baby▸
The Satanic Rites of Dracula
Satan's Black Wedding
Satan's Cheerleaders
Satan's Princess
Satan's School for Girls
Satan's Touch
Satanwar
The Sentinel
Servants of Twilight
The Seventh Victim▸
Shock 'Em Dead
Sisters of Satan
Speak of the Devil
Specters
The Spellbinder
Sugar Cookies
The Tempter
Terror Beach
To the Devil, a Daughter
Tombs of the Blind Dead
The Visitor
Warlock
Warlock: The Armageddon
Witchcraft
Witchcraft 3: The Kiss of Death
Witchcraft 5: Dance with the Devil
Witchcraft 6: The Devil's Mistress
Witchcraft 10: Mistress of the Craft
WitchTrap

Satire & Parody

***see also** Black Comedy; Comedy; Genre Spoofs*

A Propos de Nice▸
Abbott and Costello Go to Mars
Abduction
The Act
The Adventures of Picasso
The Adventures of Sherlock Holmes' Smarter Brother▸
The Affairs of Annabel
Aftershock
Airplane!▸
Airplane 2: The Sequel
An Alan Smithee Film: Burn, Hollywood, Burn
Alex in Wonderland
All Through the Night▸
All You Need Is Cash▸
The Alphabet Murders
Amazing Dr. Clitterhouse▸
Amazon Women on the Moon
America 3000
American Psycho
American Tickler
America's Deadliest Home Video
Americathon
...And God Spoke
Andy Warhol's Dracula▸
Andy Warhol's Frankenstein
Animal Farm▸
Animal Farm
Any Wednesday
The Apartment▸
As Young As You Feel▸
The Associate
Attack of the Robots
Auntie Mame▸
Austin Powers: International Man of Mystery▸
Austin Powers 2: The Spy Who Shagged Me▸
Backfire!
Bad Manners
Bad Medicine
Bamboozled
Bananas▸
Bank Robber
Barjo
Barry McKenzie Holds His Own
Based on an Untrue Story
Basic Training
The Bawdy Adventures of Tom Jones
Beautiful
Being There▸
Best in Show▸
The Best Man▸
Beyond the Valley of the Dolls
Beyond Therapy
The Big Bus
Big Deal on Madonna Street▸
The Big Picture
The Big Tease
Big Trouble in Little China
Bill & Ted's Bogus Journey
Bill & Ted's Excellent Adventure
Black and White in Color▸
Black Bird
Bob & Carol & Ted & Alice
Bob Roberts▸
The Bogus Witch Project
The Bonfire of the Vanities
Born in East L.A.
Boss
Boy Meets Girl▸
The Brady Bunch Movie▸
Bread and Chocolate▸
Breakfast of Champions
Bring It On
Britannia Hospital
Bullshot
Bulworth▸
The 'Burbs
But I'm a Cheerleader
Camera Buff
Canadian Bacon
The Candidate▸
Candy
Carry On Cleo
Carry On Dick
Casino Royale
Caveman
CB4: The Movie
Cecil B. Demented
Champagne for Caesar▸
The Cheap Detective▸
Cherry Falls
Children of the Revolution
Citizen Ruth
Clockwise
A Clockwork Orange▸
The Coca-Cola Kid▸
Code Name: Chaos
Cold Turkey▸
The Committee
Contract▸
Coup de Grace
Crainquebille▸
Creature from the Haunted Sea
Crimewave
Curtain Up
Dark Habits
Dark Star▸
Darktown Strutters
Darling Lili
Dead Men Don't Die
Dead Men Don't Wear Plaid
Deal of the Century
Death of a Bureaucrat▸
Deathrow Gameshow
Diary of a Chambermaid▸
Dick▸
Dirty Dishes▸
The Disappearance of Kevin Johnson
The Discreet Charm of the Bourgeoisie▸
Dr. Heckyl and Mr. Hype
Doctors and Nurses
Don't Be a Menace to South Central While Drinking Your Juice in the Hood
Down & Dirty▸
Down and Out in Beverly Hills
Down to Earth
Down Under
Dracula: Dead and Loving It
Dracula Sucks
Dragnet
Drop Dead Gorgeous
E. Nick: A Legend in His Own Mind
Easy Wheels
EDtv
Election▸
11 Harrowhouse▸
Ella Cinders▸
Erik the Viking
Evil Roy Slade▸
The Extraordinary Adventures of Mr. West in the Land of the Bolsheviks
The Family Game▸
Fatal Instinct
Fear of a Black Hat
Ferocious Female Freedom Fighters
First Family
The Flaming Teen-Age
Flesh Gordon
Flicks
Floundering
Footlight Frenzy
Forgotten Silver
The Fortune Cookie▸
Frankenstein General Hospital
Frankenstein Sings...The Movie
Frankenweenie
The French Touch
The Freshman
From Here to Maternity
The Front▸
Funny Money
Gabriel Over the White House▸
Galactic Gigolo
Galaxina
Ganjasaurus Rex
Gas
Geek Maggot Bingo
Genevieve▸
Gentlemen Prefer Blondes▸
Girls in Prison
Glory! Glory!▸
Going Berserk
Going Places▸
Gosford Park▸
Greaser's Palace
Great American Traffic Jam
The Great Dictator▸
The Great Madcap
Great McGonagall

▸ = rated three bones or higher

Savannah

Savants

***see also** Mental Retardation*

Scams, Stings & Cons

***see also** Heists*

Nothing Sacred▲
Now and Forever
Office Space
The Old Lady Who Walked in the Sea
Old Spanish Custom
On the Fiddle
One Christmas
One of My Wives Is Missing
Opportunity Knocks
Ossessione▲
Out to Sea
Pale Saints
Palmetto
Panic Button
Paper Man
Paper Moon▲
The Parallax View▲
Parole, Inc.
Pass the Ammo
The Pest
Phantom Gold
Piece of the Action
The Pope Must Diet
Popi▲
Portrait of a Lady▲
The President's Plane Is Missing
The Prime Gig
Prisoner of Rio
The Producers▲
The Promoter▲
The Quest
Quiz Show▲
Reborn
The Red Light Sting
Remedy for Riches
Risk
Risky Business▲
The Road to El Dorado
The Road to Zanzibar▲
Roaring Speedboats
Rule #3
Ruthless People▲
Sands of Sacrifice
Save the Tiger▲
Scam
Scandalous
Schemes
Schtonk
Sgt. Bilko
The Settlement
Sexual Intent
Shattered Image
Shooting Fish
Silk 'n' Sabotage
Silver Bears
Simpatico
Six Degrees of Separation
Skin Game▲
Sky Hei$t
Slackers
Slither▲
Small Hotel
Something for Everyone
South Riding
The Spanish Prisoner▲
The Squeeze
Stacy's Knights
Stagecoach to Denver
The Star Maker
Stavisky▲
Still Breathing
The Sting▲
The Sting 2
Stolen Hearts
The Story of a Cheat▲
The Story of Esther Costello
Sucker Money
Suicide Kings
Sunburn
Support Your Local Gunfighter▲
Sweet Talker
Swindle
The Swindle
The Switch
Tall in the Saddle
A Taste for Killing
Tax Season
The Taxman
The Ten Million Dollar Getaway
Tequila Sunrise
Things Change▲
Things to Do in Denver When You're Dead▲
The Third Key
36 Hours▲
This Is a Hijack
This World, Then the Fireworks
Thrilled to Death
The Tigress
Title Shot
Too Pretty to Be Honest
Tootsie▲
Touch
Train Robbers
Traveller▲
Tricheurs
Trojan Eddie▲
Trust Me
Two Much
Underworld Scandal
The Unholy Three▲
Walpurgis Night▲
The Warrior & the Sorceress
Watch the Birdie
We're Talkin' Serious Money
The Wharf Rat
Where the Money Is
White Men Can't Jump
White River
Why Me?
Wild Things
The Winner
Wish You Were Dead
Write to Kill

Scared 'Chuteless

***see also** Airborne; Skydiving*

Con Air▲
Double Team
Eraser
Goldeneye▲
Point Break
Terminal Velocity

School Daze

***see also** Campus Capers; Hell High School*

Absolution
Accident
The Adventures of Sebastian Cole
All God's Children
All I Wanna Do
All Things Fair
Alley Cats Strike
American Friends
American Pie▲
Amy
Angels in the Endzone
Anna and the King of Siam▲
Apt Pupil
Around the Fire
Au Revoir les Enfants▲
Back to School
Backfield in Motion
The Basket
The Beguiled▲
The Belles of St. Trinian's▲
The Bells of St. Mary's▲
Big and Hairy
Billy Madison
Black Narcissus▲
Blue Jeans
Blue Ridge Fall
Bluffing It
Boarding School
Boys
The Broadway Drifter
The Browning Version▲
The Browning Version
Brutal Fury
Buried Alive
Can't Hardly Wait
Cheaters
Cheers for Miss Bishop
Children of a Lesser God▲
The Children's Hour
The Chocolate War▲
Christy
Ciao, Professore!
Common Ground
The Convent
The Corn Is Green▲
The Craft
crazy/beautiful
Crazy for Love
Crazy from the Heart▲
Cruel Intentions
Dangerous Minds
Dead Poets Society▲
Deadly Sins
The Devil's Backbone
The Devil's Playground▲
Diabolique
Doctor Dolittle
Dream to Believe
Dress Gray▲
Drive Me Crazy
D3: The Mighty Ducks
Eden
Educating Rita▲
Election▲
The Elementary School
Encino Man
The Ernest Green Story
Europa, Europa▲
Eyes Right!
The Faculty
Fame▲
Final Exam
Finding Forrester
Flirting▲
Flubber
Forever Mary▲
Free of Eden
The French Lesson
French Postcards
Frog and Wombat
Games Girls Play
Get Over It!
Get Real
Getting It On
The Getting of Wisdom
Getting Straight
Getting Wasted
The Girl, the Body and the Pill
The Girl Who Spelled Freedom▲
The Girls of Huntington House
The Goodbye Bird
Goodbye, Mr. Chips▲
Goodbye, Mr. Chips
The Gospel According to Vic
Grease▲
Grown Ups
Guess What We Learned in School Today?
The Guinea Pig
The Halfback of Notre Dame
The Happiest Days of Your Life▲
Hard Knox
Hard Lessons
Heavenly Creatures▲
Here Come the Co-Eds
High School High
High School USA
Homework
Horsemasters
How I Got into College
Idle Hands
Impure Thoughts
In a Class of His Own
Iron & Silk
Is There Life Out There?
Jack
Jawbreaker
Johnny Holiday
Johnny Tiger
Judy Berlin
The Kid with the 200 I.Q.
Kindergarten Cop
Kurt Vonnegut's Harrison Bergeron
Lambada
Last Time Out
Late Bloomers
Leader of the Band
Lean on Me▲
Liberty Heights
Little Men
The Little Princess▲
A Little Princess▲
Little Red Schoolhouse
Lloyd
The Long Gray Line▲
The Lords of Discipline
Luna e L'Altra
Maedchen in Uniform▲
The Major and the Minor▲
Major Payne
Married to It
Masterminds
Matilda▲
Max Keeble's Big Move
A Minor Miracle
Mr. Headmistress
Murder in New Hampshire: The Pamela Smart Story
A Murder of Quality
Murder 101
Music of the Heart
My Teacher's Wife
National Lampoon's Class Reunion
National Lampoon's Senior Trip
Never Been Kissed
The NeverEnding Story▲
Nighthawks
Not Quite Human 2
Old Mother Riley, Headmistress
Oleanna
187
Our Time
Outside Providence
Oxford Blues
Passing Glory▲
Passion for Life
The People
Perfect Harmony
Platinum High School
Porky's
Porky's Revenge
The Possessed
Powder
Prep School
Pride of Jesse Hallum
The Prime of Miss Jean Brodie▲
The Principal
The Principal Takes a Holiday
The Private War of Major Benson
The Pure Hell of St. Trinian's
Rachel, Rachel▲
The Rage: Carrie 2
The Rascals
Real Genius▲
Rebel
Renaissance Man
Robin of Locksley
Ruby Bridges
Rushmore▲
Sabrina the Teenage Witch
Safety Patrol
The St. Tammany Miracle
The Sandpiper
Satan's School for Girls
Save the Last Dance
Secret Places
A Separate Peace
September Gun
She's All That
Shout
Sing
The Sixth Sense▲
Stand and Deliver▲
Stanley and Iris
Star Kid▲
The Strange One
Student Confidential
The Student Teachers
The Substitute
The Substitute 2: School's Out
The Substitute 4: Failure is Not an Option
Sugar & Spice▲
Summer School
Summer School Teachers
Tea and Sympathy▲
Teachers
Ten Things I Hate about You▲
There Goes My Baby
To Sir, with Love
Tom Brown's School Days
Tom Brown's School Days▲
Tommy Boy
Topaze▲
Toy Soldiers
Treehouse Hostage
Trippin'
The Trouble with Angels
Twenty-Four Eyes▲
The Twilight Girls
The Underachievers
Undergrads▲
Up the Academy
Up the Down Staircase▲
Varsity Blues
Virgin Queen of St. Francis High
Vital Signs
Waterland
Whatever It Takes
Where Is My Friend's House?
Why Shoot the Teacher▲
Wild Reeds▲
The Winslow Boy▲
With Honors
The Worst Witch
Yentl
Zebrahead▲

Sci Fi

***see also** Fantasy*

A. I.: Artificial Intelligence
Abbott and Costello Go to Mars
Abraxas: Guardian of the Universe
The Abyss▲
Access Code
Adrenalin: Fear the Rush
Aelita: Queen of Mars
After the Fall of New York
Aftermath
Aftershock
Akira
The Alchemists
Alien▲
Alien 3
The Alien Agenda: Out of the Darkness
Alien Chaser
Alien Contamination
The Alien Factor
Alien from L.A.
Alien Intruder
Alien Nation
Alien Nation: Dark Horizon
Alien Predators
Alien Private Eye
Alien: Resurrection▲
Alien Space Avenger
Alien Terminator
Alien Warrior
Alienator
Aliens▲
Aliens Are Coming
Aliens from Spaceship Earth
The Alpha Incident
Alphaville▲
Altered States▲
The Amazing Colossal Man
Amazing Stories
American Cyborg: Steel Warrior
Android
The Android Affair
The Angry Red Planet
Anna to the Infinite Power
A.P.E.X.
The Apocalypse
Arcade
Arena
Armageddon: The Final Challenge
Around the World Under the Sea
The Arrival
The Arrival 2
The Asphyx▲
Assassin
Assignment Outer Space
The Astounding She-Monster
The Astro-Zombies
At the Earth's Core
Atom Man vs. Superman
The Atomic Brain
The Atomic Man
Atomic Submarine
Attack from Mars
Attack of the 50 Foot Woman
Attack of the 50 Ft. Woman
Attack of the Giant Leeches
Attack of the Killer Tomatoes
Attack of the Mushroom People
The Aurora Encounter
Automatic
Backlash: Oblivion 2
Bad Channels
Bad Girls from Mars
The Bamboo Saucer
Barb Wire
Barbarella
* batteries not included
Battle Beneath the Earth
Battle Beyond the Stars
Battle Beyond the Sun
Battle for the Planet of the Apes
Battle of the Worlds
Battle Queen 2020
Battlestar Galactica
The Beast from 20,000 Fathoms
The Beast of Yucca Flats
The Bees
Beginning of the End
Beneath the Planet of the Apes
Beware! The Blob
Beyond the Stars
Beyond the Time Barrier
Bicentennial Man
Biohazard: The Alien Force
The Black Hole
Black Scorpion
Blade Runner▲
Blake of Scotland Yard
The Blob
The Blob▲
The Blood of Heroes
Blue Flame
Blue Monkey
Body Melt
Body Snatchers
Bog
Bombshell
Boom in the Moon
Bounty Hunter 2002
A Boy and His Dog
The Brain Eaters
The Brain from Planet Arous
Brainstorm
Brainwaves
The Bronx Executioner
The Brother from Another Planet▲
Buck Rogers Conquers the Universe
Buck Rogers in the 25th Century
Bug
Caged Heat 3000
Capricorn One▲
Captive Planet
Carver's Gate
The Castle of Fu Manchu
Cat Women of the Moon
Chameleon
Chameleon 2: Death Match
Chameleon 3: Dark Angel
Charly▲
Cherry 2000
Children of the Damned
Cinderella 2000
Circuit Breaker
Circuitry Man
City Limits
Class of 1999
Class of 1999 2: The Substitute
The Clones
The Clonus Horror
Close Encounters of the Third Kind▲
Club Extinction
Cocoon▲
The Colony
Colossus: The Forbin Project▲
Communion
The Companion
Conquest of Space
Conquest of the Planet of the Apes
Contact
The Cosmic Man
The Cosmic Monsters
Cosmic Slop
Cosmos: War of the Planets
Crash and Burn
The Crazies
The Creation of the Humanoids

▲ = rated three bones or higher

▸ = *rated three bones or higher*

Replicilus
Resistance
Resurrection of Zachary Wheeler
The Return
Return from Witch Mountain
Return of Chandu
The Return of Swamp Thing
Return of the Aliens: The Deadly Spawn
Return of the Fly
Return of the Jedi▲
Return to Frogtown
Revenge of the Teenage Vixens from Outer Space
Revenge Quest
Riding with Death
Robinson Crusoe on Mars
Robo-Chic
Robo Warriors
Roboman
Robot Holocaust
Robot Jox
Robot Monster
Robot Wars
Rock & Roll Cowboys
Rocket Attack U.S.A.
Rocketship
Rocketship X-M
Rocky Jones, Space Ranger: Renegade Satellite
Roller Blade
Roller Blade Warriors: Taken By Force
Rollerball
R.O.T.O.R.
Runaway
Running Against Time
Running Delilah
The Running Man
Rush
Saturn 3
Savage
Scanner Cop
Scanner Cop 2: Volkin's Revenge
Sci-Fighters
Scream and Scream Again
Screamers
The Sea Serpent
Search and Destroy
The Secret of the Golden Eagle
The Secret of the Telegian
The Sender
The Sex Machine
Shadow Warriors
Shadowzone
She
Shepherd
The Silencers
Silent Running▲
The Sisterhood
Skeeter
Sky Pirates
Slaughterhouse Five
Slave Girls from Beyond Infinity
The Slime People
Slipstream
Solar Crisis
Solar Force
Solarbabies
Solaris
Soldier
Son of Godzilla
Soylent Green
Space Marines
Space Monster
Space Mutiny
Space Rage
Space Raiders
Space Soldiers Conquer the Universe
Space Truckers
SpaceCamp
Spaced Invaders
Spacehunter: Adventures in the Forbidden Zone
Spacejacked
Spaceship
Species
Species 2
Specimen
Sphere
Split
Split Second
Sputnik
Stalker▲
Star Crash
Star Crystal
Star Hunter
Star Knight
Star Portal
Star Quest
Star Slammer
Star Trek: The Motion Picture
Star Trek 2: The Wrath of Khan▲
Star Trek 3: The Search for Spock
Star Trek 4: The Voyage Home▲
Star Trek 5: The Final Frontier
Star Trek 6: The Undiscovered Country
Star Trek: First Contact▲
Star Trek: Generations▲
Star Trek: Insurrection
Star Wars▲
Star Wars: Episode 1—The Phantom Menace▲
Starchaser: The Legend of Orin
Starflight One
Stargate
Starlight
Starman▲
Starship
Starship Invasions
Starship Troopers▲
Steel and Lace
Steel Frontier
Stephen King's The Langoliers
Storm Trooper
Stranded
Strange New World
The Stranger
The Stranger from Venus
Strangers in Paradise
Stryker
Sun Ra & His Intergalactic Solar Arkestra: Space Is the Place
Super Force
Survival Zone
Survivor
The Survivor
Suspect Device
Swamp Thing
Synapse
Syngenor
T-Force
Tales from a Parallel Universe: Eating Pattern
Tales from a Parallel Universe: Giga Shadow
Tales from a Parallel Universe: I Worship His Shadow
Tales from a Parallel Universe: Super Nova
Tarantula▲
A Taste for Flesh and Blood
Teen Alien
Teenage Caveman
Teenage Monster
Teenagers from Outer Space
TekWar
10th Victim▲
Terminal Impact
Terminal Justice: Cybertech P.D.
The Terminal Man
Terminal Virus
The Terminator▲
Terminator 2: Judgment Day▲
Terror Beneath the Sea
Terror Is a Man
Terror of Mechagodzilla
The Terror Within
The Terror Within 2
The Terrornauts
Test Tube Teens from the Year 2000
Tetsuo: The Iron Man
Tetsuo 2: Body Hammer
Them!▲
They
They Came from Beyond Space
The Thing▲
The Thing
Things to Come▲
This Is Not a Test
This Island Earth
Those Fantastic Flying Fools
The Three Worlds of Gulliver
THX 1138▲
Ticks
Time After Time▲
Time Chasers
The Time Guardian
The Time Machine▲
Time Machine
Time Runner
Time Tracers
Time Trackers
The Time Travelers
Time Troopers
Time Walker
Timecop
Timelock
Timemaster
Timerider
Timestalkers
Tobor the Great
Total Recall▲
Total Recall 2070: Machine Dreams
Toward the Terra
A Town Has Turned to Dust
Trancers
Trancers 2: The Return of Jack Deth
Trancers 3: Deth Lives
Trancers 4: Jack of Swords
Trancers 5: Sudden Deth
Transatlantic Tunnel
Transformations
Trapped in Space
The Trial of the Incredible Hulk
Tripods: The White Mountains
Tron
The Trouble with Dick
12 Monkeys▲
12:01
20 Million Miles to Earth
The 27th Day
Two Lost Worlds
2001: A Space Odyssey▲
2010: The Year We Make Contact▲
2069: A Sex Odyssey
UFO: Target Earth
Uforia
The Ultimate Warrior
Undersea Kingdom
The Unearthly Stranger
Unknown Origin
Unknown World
Unnatural
Until the End of the World▲
Urban Menace
V▲
V: The Final Battle
The Valley of Gwangi▲
Vampire Vixens from Venus
Vampirella
Vegas in Space
Velocity Trap
Venus Rising
Village of the Damned▲
Village of the Damned
Village of the Giants
Virtual Assassin
Virtual Combat
Virtual Seduction
Virtuosity
Virus
Visitants
The Void
Voyage of the Rock Aliens
Voyage to the Bottom of the Sea▲
Voyage to the Planet of Prehistoric Women
Voyage to the Prehistoric Planet
War in Space
The War of the Colossal Beast
War of the Gargantuas
War of the Robots
War of the Wizards
The War of the Worlds▲
Warlords
Warlords of the 21st Century
Warning from Space
Warrior of the Lost World
Waterworld
Wavelength
Waxwork 2: Lost in Time
Webmaster
Weird Science
Welcome Back Mr. Fox
Wes Craven Presents Mind Ripper
Westworld▲
What Waits Below
When Dinosaurs Ruled the Earth
When Time Expires
When Worlds Collide
Where Time Began
White Dwarf
Wicked City
Wild Palms
Wild, Wild Planet
A Wind Named Amnesia
Wing Commander
Wired to Kill
Within the Rock
Woman in the Moon
The Womaneater
Women of the Prehistoric Planet
World Gone Wild
The X-Files
X from Outer Space
X: The Man with X-Ray Eyes▲
Xchange▲
Xtro
Xtro 2: The Second Encounter
Xtro 3: Watch the Skies
The Yesterday Machine
Yesterday's Target
Yongkari Monster of the Deep
Zardoz
Zarkorr! The Invader
Zeram
Zeram 2▲
Zero Population Growth
Zeta One
Zombies of the Stratosphere
Zone 39
Zone Troopers
Zontar, the Thing from Venus

Sci-Fi Westerns

***see also** Sci Fi; Supernatural Westerns; Westerns*

Back to the Future, Part 3▲
Backlash: Oblivion 2
Battle Beyond the Stars
Ghost Patrol
Neon City
Oblivion
Outland
The Phantom Empire
Teenage Monster
Welcome to Blood City
Westworld▲

Science & Scientists

***see also** Genetics; Inventors & Inventions; Mad Scientists*

The Alien Agenda: Under the Skin
Altered States▲
Android
The Andromeda Strain
Around the World Under the Sea
Arrowsmith
Assassin
The Atomic City
The Atomic Man
Attack of the Robots
Beach Party
A Beautiful Mind▲
Bombshell
A Brief History of Time▲
Brotherhood of the Wolf
Caravan to Vaccares
Chain Reaction
Children of the Damned
Chill Factor
Contact
The Dallas Connection
Dam Busters▲
Dark Star▲
Darkman▲
The Day of the Dolphin
Day One▲
Dead Men Don't Wear Plaid
The Dead Next Door
Deadly Friend
Deadly Outbreak
Deep Blue Sea
Deep Core
Demon Seed▲
Dick Barton, Special Agent
Die Laughing
Die, Monster, Die!
Dirty Games
The Dish▲
Dr. Alien
Doctor Dolittle
Dr. Jekyll and Ms. Hyde
Dragon Fury 2
Electra
The Eliminators
Evolution
Fantastic Voyage▲
Fat Man and Little Boy
The Fly▲
The Fly▲
The Fly 2
Forbidden World
Forever Darling
Four Sided Triangle
The 4D Man
From the Earth to the Moon
Gattaca▲
Geheimakte WB1
Glory Enough for All: The Discovery of Insulin
Habitat
The Henderson Monster
How to Make a Doll
Human Gorilla
Human Nature
Humanoid Defender
Illegal Entry: Formula for Fear
Illumination
The Incredible Hulk Returns
Infinity
International House
The Invisible Man Returns▲
I.Q.
Junior
Jurassic Park▲
Kate & Leopold
Last Day of the War
Laughing at Danger
Lifeform
Link
A Little Bit of Soul
The Lost World
The Lost World: Jurassic Park 2
Love Potion #9
The Man with Two Brains▲
Mary Reilly
Medicine Man
Mimic
Miracle Mile▲
Mr. Superinvisible
Monkey Boy
Monkey Business▲
Monkey's Uncle
My Science Project
My Stepmother Is an Alien
Neptune Factor
October Sky▲
Outbreak▲
Phantom Empire
Project X
Prototype X29A
The Quiet Earth▲
Real Genius▲
Return of Captain Invincible
Return of the Ape Man
Return of the Fly
The Rocky Horror Picture Show▲
The Secret of the Telegian
Senseless
The Sex Machine
Shaker Run
Shakma
Simon
Sir Arthur Conan Doyle's The Lost World
Smilla's Sense of Snow
Son of Flubber
Spaceways
Species
Stephen King's Golden Years
The Story of Louis Pasteur▲
The Structure of Crystals
Sub Down
Surf 2
Swamp Thing
The Thing
Things to Come▲
This Island Earth
Threshold
Tidal Wave
Time Trackers
The Time Travelers
Tomcat: Dangerous Desires
12:01
Ultraviolet
Unforgettable
Unknown Island
Unknown World
Virus
The Void
Where Time Began
The Wild and the Free
Woman in the Dunes▲
The Yesterday Machine

Scotland

***see also** Great Britain*

Aberdeen
The Acid House
Another Time, Another Place▲
Behind the Lines
The Big Man: Crossing the Line▲
Blood Clan
Bonnie Prince Charlie
Bonnie Scotland
Braveheart▲
Breaking the Waves▲
Brigadoon▲
The Bruce
Challenge to Lassie
Chasing the Deer
Deacon Brodie
Devil Girl from Mars
The Devil's Undead
Dragonworld
Dreams Lost, Dreams Found
Entrapment
Escape
The Gospel According to Vic
The Governess
Gregory's Girl▲
Greystoke: The Legend of Tarzan, Lord of the Apes
Highlander: Endgame
I Know Where I'm Going▲
Kidnapped
Lady of the Lake
Little Minister▲
Local Hero▲
Loch Ness
Madeleine
Mary of Scotland▲
Mary, Queen of Scots
The Master of Ballantrae
The Match
My Life So Far
The Pointsman
Pride of the Clan
Ratcatcher
Ring of Bright Water▲
Rob Roy▲
Rob Roy—The Highland Rogue
Robert Louis Stevenson's St. Ives
The Secret of the Loch
The Three Lives of Thomasina▲
Tragedy of Flight 103: The Inside Story▲
Trouble in the Glen

▲ = rated three bones or higher

Whiskey Galore▸
Year of the Comet

Screwball Comedy

see also Comedy; Romantic Comedy; Slapstick Comedy

All in a Night's Work
Amazing Adventure
Ambassador Bill
America
And Baby Makes Six
Antonio
As You Like It
As You Were
Assault of the Party Nerds
Attention Shoppers
The Awful Truth▸
The Baby and the Battleship
The Bachelor and the Bobby-Soxer▸
Bachelor Mother▸
Bachelor of Hearts
Back to School
Bank Shot▸
Bedazzled▸
Bedtime Story
Beer
Big Business
Blame It on the Bellboy
The Bliss of Mrs. Blossom▸
Blue Murder at St. Trinian's▸
Boeing Boeing
Bringing Up Baby▸
Bullseye!
Buona Sera, Mrs. Campbell
Camp Cucamonga: How I Spent My Summer Vacation
Carry On Admiral
The Chaplin Revue
Charlie Chaplin: Night at the Show▸
Charlie Chaplin ... Our Hero!
The Circus▸
Combat Academy
The Couch Trip
The Count
Crackers
Days of Thrills and Laughter▸
Doctor in the House▸
Dr. Otto & the Riddle of the Gloom Beam
Doctor Takes a Wife▸
Don Juan, My Love▸
Double Wedding▸
Doubting Thomas
Down Among the Z Men
Down the Drain
Dude, Where's My Car?
Easy Living▸
Easy Money
Easy Street▸
Egg and I▸
Everything You Always Wanted to Know about Sex (But Were Afraid to Ask)▸
The Favor, the Watch, & the Very Big Fish
Fireballs
The Fireman
Fit for a King
The Floorwalker▸
Forces of Nature
Forever Darling
Forsaking All Others
The Gay Deceivers
The Geisha Boy
Get Crazy
Hands Across the Table▸
A Hard Day's Night▸
Harvey▸
Her Husband's Affairs
He's My Girl
Holiday▸
How I Learned to Love Women
How Sweet It Is!
I Love My...Wife
I Love You Again▸
Inspector Hornleigh
Italian Straw Hat▸
It's the Old Army Game
Joy of Living▸
La Chevre▸
Labyrinth of Passion
The Ladies Man
The Lady Eve▸
Libeled Lady▸
A Life Less Ordinary
Life Stinks
Lobster Man from Mars
The Long, Long Trailer
Lots of Luck
The Love Bug
Love Crazy▸
Lucky Partners
Lunatics & Lovers
Madhouse
The Major and the Minor▸
Make Mine Mink▸
Malibu Beach
Malibu Bikini Shop
The Marriage Circle▸
The Marx Brothers in a Nutshell▸
The Mating Game▸
Me and Him
Meatballs
Meatballs 2
Meet the Parents▸
A Midsummer Night's Sex Comedy▸
Miracle of Morgan's Creek▸
Mr. & Mrs. Smith▸
Mr. Deeds
Modern Girls
The Money Pit
Monkey Business▸
Monkeys, Go Home!
The Moon's Our Home
The More the Merrier▸
Morons from Outer Space
Mugsy's Girls
The Munsters' Revenge
My American Cousin▸
My Chauffeur
My Favorite Brunette
My Favorite Wife▸
My Man Godfrey▸
Naked Is Better
National Lampoon's Christmas Vacation
National Lampoon's European Vacation
National Lampoon's Vacation▸
Nervous Ticks
Noises Off
Not for Publication
Nothing Sacred▸
The Nude Bomb
Ollie Hopnoodle's Haven of Bliss
One Woman or Two
The Palm Beach Story▸
Pink Flamingos
Platinum Blonde▸
Police Academy 3: Back in Training
Polyester
Reaching for the Moon
Recruits
The Rink▸
Romance with a Double Bass▸
Running Wild
See No Evil, Hear No Evil
Simon
The Smallest Show on Earth▸
Social Intercourse
Some Like It Hot▸
Somewhere in the City
A Southern Yankee
Spaced Invaders
Spring Break
Starhops
Start the Revolution without Me▸
The Statue
Stewardess School
Still Not Quite Human
Stir Crazy
Stitches
Strange Brew
Stroker Ace
Stuckey's Last Stand
Student Affairs
The Student Teachers
Summer School Teachers
Superdad
Supergrass
Swap Meet
Sweet Revenge
Sweet Young Thing
Swing It, Sailor!
The Swinging Cheerleaders
Switching Channels
Talk of the Town▸
Teen Vamp
Teen Witch
Tell It to the Judge
That Naughty Girl
They Went That-a-Way & That-a-Way
Three in the Cellar
Thunder & Mud
Tigers in Lipstick
Tramp & a Woman
Tricks of the Trade
Truck Stop
Twin Beds
Twist
Two Weeks to Live
The Underachievers
The Vagabond
Vibes
Vice Versa▸
Waitress
Waltz of the Toreadors▸
Watch the Birdie
What's Up, Doc?▸
When Women Had Tails
When Women Lost Their Tails
Where Were You When the Lights Went Out?
Which Way Is Up?
Whoops Apocalypse
Who's That Girl?
Wild Women of Wongo
Witches' Brew
Wonder Boys▸
World's Greatest Lover
You Can't Cheat an Honest Man▸
You Can't Take It with You▸
Zotz!

Scuba

see also Deep Blue

The Abyss▸
Beneath the 12-Mile Reef
The Big Blue
Daring Game
The Deep
Easy Come, Easy Go
The Evil Below
ffolkes
Flipper▸
Flipper's New Adventure▸
Full Fathom Five
Isle of Forgotten Sins
Leviathan
The Man from Atlantis
Men of Honor
Navy SEALS
Neptune Factor
Never Say Never Again
Night of the Sharks
Oceans of Fire
The Sea Serpent
Thunderball
The Treasure Seekers
Underwater!

Sculptors

see also Art & Artists

The Agony and the Ecstasy
Before and After
A Bucket of Blood▸
Camille Claudel▸
Fly Away Home▸
House of Wax▸
The Juror
The Silver Chalice
The Song of Songs

Sea Disasters

see also Air Disasters; Deep Blue; Disaster Flicks; Shipwrecked

The Abyss▸
Airport '77
Beyond the Poseidon Adventure
Das Boot▸
Deep Rising
Deepstar Six
Far from Home: The Adventures of Yellow Dog
Goliath Awaits
Juggernaut▸
K-19: The Widowmaker
The Last Voyage
Leviathan
Men of Honor
A Night to Remember▸
The Poseidon Adventure
Raise the Titanic
The Seducers
S.O.S. Titanic
Souls at Sea
Titanic▸
The Unsinkable Molly Brown▸
Waterworld

Seattle

Bombs Away!
Breaking Point
Dream Man
Georgia▸
The Hitman
It Happened at the World's Fair
Little Buddha
My Own Private Idaho▸
Shattered Image
Singles▸
Slaves to the Underground
Sleepless in Seattle▸
The Slender Thread▸
Stakeout
Streetwise▸

Second Chance

Chances Are▸
Life as a House
Mr. Destiny
Place Vendome▸
The Princess and the Warrior▸
The Rookie▸
Seventeen Again

Serial Killers

see also Crime & Criminals; Crime Sprees

Addams Family Values
Addicted to Murder
Addicted to Murder 2: Tainted Blood
Addicted to Murder 3: Bloodlust
Along Came a Spider
Ambition
American Nightmare
American Psycho
American Psycho 2: All American Girl
American Strays
American Streetfighter 2: The Full Impact
Amsterdamned
Angel Dust
The Apostate
Aroused
Asylum
The Awful Dr. Orloff
The Baby Doll Murders
Band of Gold▸
The Banker
Beyond Redemption
Black & White
Blackwater Trail
Blondes Have More Guns
Bloodhounds 2
Bloodmoon
Bloody Proof▸
Blowback
Bluebeard▸
Body Parts
The Bone Collector
The Boston Strangler
Breaking Point
Bride of Chucky
Brigham City
Broken Mirrors
Bums
Butterfly Kiss
Cabin by the Lake
The Cell
Cherry Falls
The China Lake Murders
Citizen X▸
Clay Pigeons
Closer and Closer
Cold Blooded
Cold Front
Cold Light of Day
Con Air▸
Confessions of a Serial Killer
Cop
Copycat
Cosh Boy
Crimetime
The Crimson Code
The Crimson Rivers
Cruel and Unusual
Curdled
Cyberstalker
Dancing with Danger
Dangerous Love
Dark Asylum
The Dark Ride
Dead Certain
Dead Girls
Dead on Sight
Dead to Rights
Deadly Force
Deadly Games
Deadly Neighbor
The Deliberate Stranger▸
Delivered
A Demon in My View
Desire
Destroyer
Diary of a Serial Killer
Dirty Harry▸
Ed Gein
The Element of Crime
Evil Laugh
Evil Obsession
Exorcist 3: Legion
Eye of the Beholder
Eye of the Killer
Eyes of a Stranger
Eyes of Laura Mars
Eyes of the Beholder
Fallen
Fatal Charm
Fathers and Sons
Fear
The Fear: Halloween Night
Felicia's Journey▸
Final Notice
The First Power
Frailty▸
Freeway
Freeway 2: Confessions of a Trickbaby
The Freeway Maniac
Frequency
The Frighteners
Ghost in the Machine
The Girl Who Knew Too Much
The Glimmer Man
Hangman
Hannibal
The Hawk
Henry: Portrait of a Serial Killer▸
Henry: Portrait of a Serial Killer 2: Mask of Sanity
Hidden Obsession
Hideaway
The Hillside Strangler
Honeymoon Killers▸
The Horror Show
The Hunt for the Night Stalker
I Can't Sleep
Impulse
In Dreams
In the Deep Woods
Inhumanity
Inn on the River
The Invisible Strangler
Jack Frost
Jack the Ripper
Jack the Ripper▸
Jack's Back▸
The January Man
Jason X
Jennifer 8
Kalifornia
Kiss the Girls
L.A. Crackdown 2
Lady in Waiting
Lady Killer
Laser Moon
The Laughing Policeman
The Limbic Region
Listen
Love and Human Remains▸
Lured
M▸
The Mad Executioners
Man Bites Dog
Maniac Cop
Mean Streak
Mercy
A Mind to Kill
The Minus Man
Mr. Frost
Mixed Nuts
The Monster
Mortal Sins
Naked City: A Killer Christmas
Natural Born Killers
Nature of the Beast
Never Talk to Strangers
Night Shadow
Night Stalker
Night Vision
Nightscare
Nightwatch
No One Sleeps
No Way to Treat a Lady▸
Office Killer
Outside Ozona
The Paint Job
Pale Blood
The Pledge▸
Portraits of a Killer
Postmortem
Power 98
Prey of the Chameleon
Prime Suspect▸
Probable Cause
Profile for Murder
The Prophet's Game
Psychic
Psychopath
The Rain Killer
Ravenous
The Reaper
Relentless
Relentless 3
Relentless 4
Replicant
Resurrection
Retribution
Return to Cabin by the Lake
Revenge Quest
The Rosary Murders
Sacrifice
The Satan Killer
Scary Movie
Scream▸
Scream 2▸
Scream 3
Serial Killer
Serial Mom▸
Seven▸
Shadow of a Scream
The Silence of the Lambs▸
Slaughter of the Innocents
Sleepless
Sleepstalker: The Sandman's Last Rites
Snapdragon
So I Married an Axe Murderer
Split Second
Stagefright
Stamp of a Killer
Star Time
The Stendahl Syndrome
Still Life
Stranger by Night
Strangler of Blackmoor Castle
Striking Distance
Summer of Sam
Switchback
Tails You Live, Heads You're Dead
10 Rillington Place▸
Ten to Midnight
Tenderness of the Wolves
Terror at London Bridge
Things 2
3 A.M.▸
Tinseltown
To Catch a Killer▸

The Todd Killings
Trail of a Serial Killer
True Crime
Tunnel Vision
Turbulence
The Ugly
Undefeatable
Urban Menace
Valentine
Vice Girls
The Watcher
When the Bough Breaks
While the City Sleeps▸
White River
Witchcraft 10: Mistress of the Craft
Without Warning
Writer's Block
Zipperface

Serials

Ace Drummond
The Adventures of Captain Marvel
The Adventures of Frank and Jesse James
Adventures of Red Ryder
Adventures of Smilin' Jack
The Adventures of Tarzan
Amazing Stories
Atom Man vs. Superman
Battling with Buffalo Bill
The Black Widow
Blake of Scotland Yard
Captain America
Cheyenne Rides Again
The Clutching Hand
Custer's Last Stand
Cyclotrode "X"
D-Day on Mars
Daredevils of the Red Circle
Darkest Africa
Daughter of Don Q
Destination Saturn
Devil Horse
Dick Tracy
Dick Tracy Returns
Dick Tracy vs. Crime Inc.
Doctor Satan's Robot
Don Daredevil Rides Again
Don Winslow of the Coast Guard
Don Winslow of the Navy
Drums of Fu Manchu▸
Federal Agents vs. Underworld, Inc.
Federal Operator 99
Fighting Devil Dogs
Fighting Marines
Fighting with Kit Carson
Flaming Frontiers
Flash Gordon Conquers the Universe
Flash Gordon: Mars Attacks the World
Flash Gordon: Rocketship
G-Men Never Forget
G-Men vs. the Black Dragon
The Galloping Ghost
Genie of Darkness
Government Agents vs. Phantom Legion
Green Archer
The Green Hornet
Haunted Harbor
Hawk of the Wilderness
Holt of the Secret Service
Hurricane Express
In Old New Mexico
The Invisible Monster
The Ivory Handled Gun
Jesse James Rides Again
Jungle Drums of Africa
Junior G-Men
Junior G-Men of the Air
King of the Congo
King of the Forest Rangers
King of the Kongo
King of the Rocketmen
King of the Texas Rangers
Last Frontier
The Last of the Mohicans
Law for Tombstone
Law of the Wild
A Lawman Is Born▸
Les Vampires
Lightning Warrior
The Lone Defender
The Lone Ranger
Lone Ranger
The Lost City
Lost City of the Jungle
The Lost Jungle
Lost Planet Airmen
Manhunt in the African Jungle
Manhunt of Mystery Island
The Masked Marvel
Master Key
Masters of Venus
The Miracle Rider
The Monster Demolisher
Mysterious Doctor Satan
Mystery Mountain
Mystery of the Riverboat
Mystery Squadron
Mystery Trooper
The New Adventures of Tarzan
Nyoka and the Tigermen
Oregon Trail
Overland Mail
The Painted Stallion
The Perils of Pauline
Perils of the Darkest Jungle
The Phantom Creeps
The Phantom Empire
Phantom of the Air
Phantom of the West
The Phantom Rider
Pirates of the High Seas
The Purple Monster Strikes
Queen of the Jungle
Radar Men from the Moon
Radar Patrol vs. Spy King
Radio Patrol
Raiders of Ghost City
Red Barry
Return of Chandu
Riders of Death Valley
Robinson Crusoe of Clipper Island
Robinson Crusoe of Mystery Island
Rustlers of Red Dog
Savage Fury
Sea Hound
The Secret Code
Shadow of Chinatown
Shadow of the Eagle
Son of Zorro
S.O.S. Coast Guard
Space Soldiers Conquer the Universe
Spy Smasher
Spy Smasher Returns
Stone Cold Dead
Stone of Silver Creek
Sunset on the Desert
Tailspin Tommy
Tarzan the Fearless
Tarzan the Tiger
Texas to Bataan
The Three Musketeers
Tim Tyler's Luck
Trader Tom of the China Seas
Trail of the Silver Spurs
Trail Riders
Tumbledown Ranch in Arizona
Undersea Kingdom
Vanishing Legion
The Vigilantes Are Coming
Whispering Shadow
Winners of the West
Wolf Dog
Woman in Grey
Zombies of the Stratosphere
Zorro Rides Again
Zorro's Black Whip
Zorro's Fighting Legion

Sex & Sexuality

***see also** Crimes of Passion; Erotic Thrillers; Pornography; Sex on the Beach; Sexploitation*

About Adam
Accident
Acting on Impulse
The Adjuster
The Adultress
Adventures of a Private Eye
Adventures of a Taxi Driver
The Adventures of Sadie
The Advocate▸
An Affair of Love
Affairs of Anatol
Afterglow
Alfie▸
All Things Fair
The Alley Cats
The Allnighter
Almost Pregnant
Alpine Fire
Alvin Purple
Alvin Rides Again
The Amazing Transplant
American Beauty▸
American Gigolo
American Pie▸
American Pie 2
American Virgin
The Amorous Adventures of Moll Flanders
The Amy Fisher Story
And God Created Woman
Angel Blue
Angel of H.E.A.T.
Angels and Insects▸
Animal Instincts
Animal Instincts 2
Animal Instincts 3: The Seductress
Any Wednesday
The Apartment▸
Armistead Maupin's More Tales of the City
Armistead Maupin's Tales of the City
The Arousers
Arrivederci, Baby!
Art for Teachers of Children
Assault
Baby Doll▸
The Baby Doll Murders
Baby Face
Baby Love
The Baby Maker
The Bachelor▸
Bachelor in Paradise
Bachelor Party
Bad Company
Bad Girls from Mars
Bank Robber
Barbarella
Basic Training
Baton Rouge
Battle of the Sexes
The Bawdy Adventures of Tom Jones
Beach Girls
The Beast
Beau Pere▸
Becoming Colette
Bedroom Eyes
Bedroom Eyes 2
Before Sunrise
Belle Epoque▸
Belle of the Nineties
Beneath the Valley of the Ultra-Vixens
Bent
The Best Little Whorehouse in Texas
Betrayal
Better Than Chocolate
Beverly Hills Madam
Beyond Erotica
Beyond the Silhouette
The Big Bet
The Big Dis
Bikini House Calls
Bikini Med School
Bilitis
The Bitch
Bitter Harvest
Bitter Rice▸
Black & White
The Black Room
Black Starlet
Blind Vision
Blindfold: Acts of Obsession
Bliss
Blood and Sand▸
The Blood Oranges
Bloodbath
Blown Away
The Blue Angel▸
Blue Jeans
The Blue Lagoon
Blue Movies
Boarding School
Bob & Carol & Ted & Alice
Boccaccio '70
Bodily Harm
Body Chemistry
Body Chemistry 2: Voice of a Stranger
Body Chemistry 3: Point of Seduction
Body Double▸
Body Language
Body of Influence 2
Body Shots
Body Waves
Boeing Boeing
Bonjour Tristesse▸
Booty Call
Born Romantic
The Boss' Wife
Boxing Helena
A Boy and His Dog
Boys' Night Out▸
Bram Stoker's Dracula
Breaking the Waves▸
Breathless
The Bride Is Much Too Beautiful
Brides of the Beast
Broken Trust
Buford's Beach Bunnies
Bully
Business As Usual
Business for Pleasure
Butterfield 8▸
Butterfly
Bye Bye Baby
Cactus in the Snow
Cal▸
Camille 2000
Can I Do It...Till I Need Glasses?
The Canterbury Tales
Captives
Caresses
Carmen, Baby
Carnal Crimes
Carnal Knowledge▸
Carnival in Flanders▸
Carried Away
Carry On Camping
Carry On Emmanuelle
Carry On Henry VIII
Casanova
Casanova '70
Casual Sex?
Cat on a Hot Tin Roof▸
Cat on a Hot Tin Roof
Cat People
Cave Girl
Cesar & Rosalie▸
Chain of Desire
Champagne for Breakfast
Chasing Amy
Chatterbox
Cheaters
Cheech and Chong's Up in Smoke
Cherry Falls
Cherry 2000
The Chicken Chronicles
Chinese Roulette
Choose Me▸
Chuck & Buck
Cinderella 2000
Claire's Knee▸
Class
Class of '63
Class Reunion
Cleo/Leo
Cleopatra
Close My Eyes
Closely Watched Trains▸
Cold Sweat
Collector's Item▸
Color of Night
Come Undone
Coming Apart
Coming Soon
Compromising Positions
Conspiracy
Contagion
The Cool Surface
Cool World
The Courtesans of Bombay▸
Cruel Intentions
Cruel Intentions 2
The Cruel Story of Youth▸
Crush
Cry Uncle
Crystal's Diary
Damage▸
Dance with the Devil
Dangerous Game
Dangerous Indiscretion
Dangerous Liaisons▸
Dangerous Touch
The Dark Side of Love
The Dark Side of the Heart
Dark Tide
Daughters of Satan
David Searching
Dead On
Dead Weekend
Dear Boys
Death and Desire
Death of a Centerfold
The Decameron▸
Decameron Nights
Deceit
Deceptions
The Decline of the American Empire▸
Deep Down
Def Jam's How to Be a Player
Denial: The Dark Side of Passion
Depraved
Desire
Desire and Hell at Sunset Motel
Desk Set▸
Devil in the Flesh▸
The Devils▸
The Devil's Eye
The Devil's Nightmare
The Devil's Playground▸
Devil's Wedding Night
Diary of a Chambermaid▸
Diary of a Mad Housewife▸
Diary of a Mad Old Man
Die Watching
Diner▸
The Dirty Girls
Discretion Assured
The Disenchanted
Divine Nymph
Divorce—Italian Style▸
Dr. Alien
Dr. Caligari
Dog Day Afternoon▸
Doll Face
Dollar
Domino
Don Juan (Or If Don Juan Were a Woman)
Don's Party▸
Double Cross
Double Suicide▸
Dracula Sucks
Dreams
Dreams Come True
Driver's Seat
Drum
Dry Cleaning
Eating Raoul▸
Ebbtide
Ebony Tower
Echoes of Paradise
The Eclipse▸
Eclipse
Ecstasy
Eden
Eden 2
Eden 3
Eden 4
Edge of Seventeen
El
Electra
Elizabeth▸
Elmer Gantry▸
Elvira, Mistress of the Dark
Embrace of the Vampire
Emily
Emmanuelle
Emmanuelle 4
Emmanuelle & Joanna
Emmanuelle in the Country
Emmanuelle, the Joys of a Woman
Emmanuelle, the Queen
Emmanuelle's Daughter
End of August
Endless Love
Enemies, a Love Story▸
Enormous Changes▸
Enrapture
Ernesto
Erotic Escape
Erotic House of Wax
Erotic Images
Erotic Touch of Hot Skin
Erotique
The Escape
Every Breath
Everything You Always Wanted to Know about Sex (But Were Afraid to Ask)▸
Evils of the Night
Expose
Extramarital
Eyes Wide Shut
Fairy Tales
Fall
Fanny Hill
Fanny Hill: Memoirs of a Woman of Pleasure
The Fantasist
Farinelli
Fast Food
Fast Times at Ridgemont High▸
Fatal Attraction
Fatal Attraction▸
Fatal Bond
Fatal Charm
Fatal Instinct
Fatal Past
The Favor
Federal Protection
Feelin' Screwy
Female Perversions
Female Trouble
Female Vampire
Femalien
54
Final Judgment
The Finishing Touch
Fire
First Affair
The First Time
First Time
Flesh▸
Flesh Gordon
A Flight of Rainbirds
Flirt
Forbidden Sins
Forbidden Zone: Alien Abduction
Foreign Body
Foreplay
Forever Emmanuelle
40 Days and 40 Nights
The 4th Man▸
The Fourth Sex
Foxes
Frankenstein Unbound▸
Frasier the Sensuous Lion
Fraternity Vacation
French Fried Vacation
The French Woman
Frenzy▸
Friend of the Family
Friend of the Family 2
Friends & Lovers
Fritz the Cat▸
The Fugitive Kind
Full Exposure: The Sex Tape Scandals
Gabriela
Galactic Gigolo
The Game Is Over
Games Girls Play
The Garden
Gas Pump Girls
Gate of Flesh
The General's Daughter
Gentlemen Prefer Blondes▸
Genuine Risk
Georgy Girl▸
Get Out Your Handkerchiefs▸
Get Real
Ghosts Can Do It
The Gift
Gilda▸
Ginger Ale Afternoon
The Girl
Girl
The Girl Next Door
The Girl on a Motorcycle

▲ = rated three bones or higher

Under Investigation
Under Suspicion
Under the Skin
Under the Yum-Yum Tree
The Underachievers
The Valley Obscured by the Clouds
Valmont▸
Vanilla Sky
Variety
A Very Curious Girl
Via Appia
Vibration
Vicious Circles
A View to a Kill
Virgin Queen of St. Francis High
The Virgin Soldiers
Virtual Encounters
Virtual Girl
Virtual Sexuality
The Voyeur
Wager of Love
Watch Me
Water Drops on Burning Rocks
Wedding in Blood▸
Weekend Pass
Welcome to L.A.▸
What Planet Are You From?
What's Good for the Goose
What's Up Front
When Women Had Tails
Where
Where the Boys Are '84
Where the Hot Wind Blows
A Whisper to a Scream
Whispers in the Dark
Wide Sargasso Sea
Wild at Heart▸
Wild Things
Winter Sleepers
A Winter Tan
Wish Me Luck
Wish You Were Here▸
The Witches of Eastwick
A Woman, Her Men and Her Futon
A Woman in Flames▸
The Woman Next Door▸
Woman of Desire
Woman Times Seven
Women in Love▸
Women on the Verge of a Nervous Breakdown▸
Women's Club
The Worker and the Hairdresser
Working Girls
Working Girls▸
The World Is Full of Married Men
The Wrong Man
X, Y & Zee
Xica▸
Yanks
Yesterday, Today and Tomorrow▸
Young Aphrodites
Young Lady Chatterly 2
Young Love, First Love
Young Nurses in Love
Your Friends & Neighbors▸
Your Ticket Is No Longer Valid
You've Got to Have Heart
The Yum-Yum Girls
Zabriskie Point▸
Zandalee
Zapped!
Zombie Island Massacre

Sex on the Beach

***see also** Island Fare*

Against All Odds
Airplane!▸
The Beach
The Blue Lagoon
Come Undone
The Firm▸
From Here to Eternity▸
Kiss Tomorrow Goodbye
Mixed Nuts
Phat Beach
Sweet Ecstasy
Swept Away...▸
Swept from the Sea
Tales of the Kama Sutra 2: Monsoon
Vibration

Sexcapades

Andy Warhol's Dracula▸
Andy Warhol's Frankenstein
Angel Heart
Another 9 1/2 Weeks
Bad Lieutenant▸
Basic Instinct
Being at Home with Claude
Belle de Jour▸
Betty Blue▸
Bitter Moon
The Blackout
Blue Velvet▸
Body of Evidence
Caligula
Candy
The Center of the World
Circuit
Cleopatra's Second Husband
The Comfort of Strangers▸
The Cook, the Thief, His Wife & Her Lover▸
Crash
Crimes of Passion▸
Cruising
Delta of Venus
Devil in the Flesh
Dona Herlinda & Her Son
Don't Let Me Die on a Sunday
8 1/2 Women
8mm
Exit to Eden
Exotica▸
Fellini Satyricon▸
The First 9 1/2 Weeks
First Turn On
Four Times That Night
The Frightened Woman
Frisk
God's Comedy
Henry & June▸
Husbands and Lovers
I Am Frigid...Why?
In the Realm of the Senses▸
Jade
Jill the Ripper
Just One Time
Kama Sutra: A Tale of Love
Kill Me Tomorrow
Kiss the Sky
Kissed
Lake Consequence
Little Shots of Happiness
Love and Human Remains▸
Love and Rage
Love Is the Devil▸
Maitresse
Marquis de Sade
Men Cry Bullets
The Monkey's Mask
Naked Lunch▸
The New Eve▸
The Night Porter
9 1/2 Weeks
One Night at McCool's
Paris, France
Payback
Peeping Tom▸
The Pillow Book
Return to Two Moon Junction
Secretary
sex, lies and videotape▸
Simone Barbes
Sitcom
The Story of O
The Story of O, Part 2
Suite 16
The Sweetest Thing
Teenage Caveman
Tie Me Up! Tie Me Down!
Tokyo Decadence
Tomcats
The Trio
Two Moon Junction
Unfaithful
Whipped
White Mischief▸
Whore
Why Do They Call It Love When They Mean Sex?
Wild Orchid
Wild Orchid 2: Two Shades of Blue
Y Tu Mama Tambien
Zebra Lounge

Sexploitation

***see also** Erotic Thrillers; Exploitation*

The Abductors
The Acid Eaters
Agony of Love
Amazon Jail
Angel 3: The Final Chapter
Aroused
Baby Love
Bad Girls Do Cry
Bad Girls Go to Hell
Barbarian Queen 2: The Empress Strikes Back
The Bawdy Adventures of Tom Jones
Beach Babes 2: Cave Girl Island
Beach Babes from Beyond Infinity
The Beast That Killed Women
Bedroom Eyes
The Bellboy and the Playgirls
Beneath the Valley of the Ultra-Vixens
The Big Bust Out
The Big Doll House
The Bikini Car Wash Company
The Bikini Car Wash Company 2
Black Venus
Blazing Stewardesses
Bolero
Broadcast Bombshells
Caged Fury
Candy Stripe Nurses
Candy Tangerine Man
Carnal Crimes
Chain Gang Women
Champagne for Breakfast
Cheering Section
The Cheerleaders
Cheerleaders' Wild Weekend
Cherry Hill High
Chesty Anderson USN
Class Reunion
Cleo/Leo
The Curious Dr. Humpp
Dandelions
Deadly Embrace
Def Jam's How to Be a Player
Delinquent School Girls
Devil's Wedding Night
Dinosaur Island
Domino
Dracula Sucks
Ecstasy
Emily
Emmanuelle
Emmanuelle 4
Emmanuelle 5
Emmanuelle 6
Emmanuelle & Joanna
Emmanuelle in the Country
Emmanuelle on Taboo Island
Emmanuelle, the Joys of a Woman
Erotic Escape
Erotic Touch of Hot Skin
Fanny Hill: Memoirs of a Woman of Pleasure
Fantasies
Feelin' Up
Firehouse
The First Nudie Musical
Flesh Gordon
Flesh Gordon 2: Flesh Gordon Meets the Cosmic Cheerleaders
Fleshpot on 42nd Street
Forever Emmanuelle
The French Woman
Ghosts Can't Do It
Gimme an F
Ginger
The Girl, the Body and the Pill
Goodbye Emmanuelle
Great Bikini Off-Road Adventure
The Happy Hooker
The Happy Hooker Goes to Washington
Hard Ticket to Hawaii
Hard to Die
Hardbodies
Help Wanted Female
Hollywood Boulevard 2
Hollywood High
Hollywood High, Part 2
Hollywood Hot Tubs
Hollywood Hot Tubs 2: Educating Crystal
Homework
Honkytonk Nights
Hot Moves
Hot T-Shirts
H.O.T.S.
How to Make a Doll
Ilsa, She-Wolf of the SS
Ilsa, the Tigress of Siberia
Ilsa, the Wicked Warden
Inferno in Paradise
Inhibition
Inn of Temptation
Invasion of the Girl Snatchers
The Invisible Maniac
Joy of Sex
Kandyland
Knock Outs
Lady Godiva Rides
Last Dance
Liana, Jungle Goddess
Lips of Blood
Liquid Dreams
Little Miss Innocence
The Living Dead Girl
Love Desperados
The Love Factor
Love Notes
Lust for Freedom
Mistress Pamela
Modern Girls
Mondo Balordo
My Pleasure Is My Business
My Therapist
Mysterious Jane
Naked Killer
The Naked Sword of Zorro
Naked Venus
Nature's Playmates
Naughty Knights
Night Call Nurses
The Night Evelyn Came Out of the Grave
Nine Ages of Nakedness
Nude on the Moon
Nurse on Call
Olga's Girls
Orgy of the Dead
Pagan Island
Paranoia
Party Favors
Party Plane
Perfect Timing
The Perverse Countess
Please Don't Eat My Mother
Prehistoric Bimbos in Armageddon City
Preppies
The Prime Time
Private Duty Nurses
Private Passions
Profile for Murder
Rebel Vixens
Red Shoe Diaries 2: Double Dare
Return to the Blue Lagoon
Revenge of the Cheerleaders
Revenge of the Virgins
Sacrilege
Screen Test
Scum of the Earth
Sea of Dreams
The Seducers
Sensual Partners
The Sensuous Teenager
Sex Adventures of the Three Musketeers
Sex and Buttered Popcorn
Sex and Zen
Sex Is Crazy
Sex Through a Window
Shanty Tramp
She Came on the Bus
She Devils in Chains
Slammer Girls
Slumber Party Massacre 3
Snapshot
Snowballing
Sorority Babes in the Slimeball Bowl-A-Rama
Sorority House Party
Spaced Out
The Speed Lovers
Strange World of Coffin Joe
The Student Nurses
The Student Teachers
Submission
Suburban Roulette
Sugar Cookies
Superchick
Supervixens
Sweater Girls
Sweet Georgia
Sweet Young Thing
The Swinging Cheerleaders
Tarzana, the Wild Girl
Tender Flesh
Tender Loving Care
Test Tube Teens from the Year 2000
Texas Layover
Thinkin' Big
Tomcat: Dangerous Desires
Train Station Pickups
Truck Stop
Truck Stop Women
2069: A Sex Odyssey
Ultimate Desires
The Vampire Hookers
Venus in Furs
Vice Academy
Vice Academy 2
Vice Academy 3
Wanda, the Sadistic Hypnotist
Wham-Bam, Thank You Spaceman
Witchcraft 2: The Temptress
Witchcraft 3: The Kiss of Death
Witchcraft 5: Dance with the Devil
World of the Depraved
The Young Nurses
The Zombie Army

Sexual Abuse

***see also** Rape; Spousal Abuse*

The Accused▸
The Bed You Sleep In
Boxing Helena
The Boys of St. Vincent▸
Breathtaking
The Devils▸
Fall from Innocence
Fortune and Men's Eyes
Heart of the Stag
Ilsa, Harem Keeper of the Oil Sheiks
Loved
Man of Ashes
Mesmerized
The Night Porter
Priest
Romper Stomper
Twin Peaks: Fire Walk with Me
Whatever

Sexual Harrassment

Brilliant Lies
Disclosure
Foxfire
G.I. Jane
Improper Conduct
Oleanna
Strange Justice: The Clarence Thomas and Anita Hill Story

Ships

***see** Deep Blue; Mutiny; Sail Away; Shipwrecked; Submarines*

Shipwrecked

***see also** Sea Disasters*

Adventures of Eliza Fraser
Benji the Hunted
The Black Pirate▸
The Black Stallion▸
Blue Fin
The Blue Lagoon
Cabeza de Vaca▸
Dead of Night
Dungeon of Harrow
Eye of the Needle
Far from Home: The Adventures of Yellow Dog
Greystoke: The Legend of Tarzan, Lord of the Apes
Hawk of the Wilderness
He Is My Brother
Humongous
The Island of Dr. Moreau
Island of Lost Souls▸
Island of the Lost
Jungle Bride
Kilma, Queen of the Amazons
The Legend of the Sea Wolf
Light at the Edge of the World
Male and Female▸
The Most Dangerous Game▸
Mutiny on the Bounty▸
Mutiny on the Bounty
My Favorite Wife▸
Pardon My Sarong
Princess Caraboo
Project: Genesis
Revenge of Doctor X
Rich and Strange
Robby
Robinson Crusoe
Robinson Crusoe & the Tiger
Sea Gypsies
The Sea Wolf▸
The Sea Wolf
She Gods of Shark Reef
Shogun▸
Summer Affair
Swept Away...▸
Swept from the Sea
The Swiss Family Robinson▸
Trader Tom of the China Seas
20,000 Leagues under the Sea▸
Two Lost Worlds

Shops & Shopping

Attention Shoppers
Clueless▸
Holy Man
Pretty Woman▸
Scenes from a Mall
Seven Doors to Death
Shopping
Where the Heart Is
Who's Minding the Store?

Showbiz Comedies

Alex in Wonderland
America's Sweethearts
Art House
Bamboozled
Because of Him
Being John Malkovich▸
The Big Broadcast of 1938
Big Fat Liar
The Big Picture
Blazing Saddles▸
Bloodhounds of Broadway
Boardinghouse Blues
Bowfinger▸
The Boy Friend▸
Broadway Melody
Broadway Melody of 1936▸
Broadway Melody of 1938
Broadway Melody of 1940
Bullets over Broadway▸

 ▸ = *rated three bones or higher*

Cannes Man
Cats Don't Dance
Celebrity▲
The Comic▲
Comic Act▲
The Dark Backward
The Day the Women Got Even
Delirious
Dog Pound Shuffle▲
EDtv
Ella Cinders▲
The Errand Boy
Everybody Sing
Everybody's Famous!
Extra Girl
The Final Hit
Forever Female▲
Free and Easy
Funny Bones▲
Galaxy Quest
George White's Scandals
Get Shorty▲
Glam
Good Times
Goodbye Charlie
Grave Secrets
Gypsy▲
Gypsy
The Hard Way▲
Hear My Song▲
Here Comes Cookie
Hollywood Boulevard 2
Hollywood Chaos
Hollywood Ending
Hollywood in Trouble
Hollywood Party
Hollywood Shuffle
Hooper
I'll Do Anything
In the Doghouse
It's a Date
It's a Great Feeling
Jackie's Back
Jay and Silent Bob Strike Back
Joey Breaker▲
Josie and the Pussycats
Just Write
Lady Killer▲
Let's Make Love
Life with Mikey
Lisa Picard Is Famous
Main Street to Broadway
Merton of the Movies
A Midwinter's Tale
Mr. Saturday Night
Movies Money Murder
The Muppet Movie▲
The Muppets Take Manhattan▲
The Muse
My Dream Is Yours
My Favorite Year▲
Nancy Goes to Rio
The Night They Raided Minsky's▲
Notting Hill▲
Nudity Required
Panama Hattie
Panic Button
The Party▲
Pick a Star
Postcards from the Edge▲
The Prince and the Showgirl
The Producers▲
Ratings Game
The Real Blonde
Rock-A-Bye Baby
Rubberface
Salut l'Artiste▲
Second Fiddle
The Shot
Silent Movie
Sink or Swim
Soapdish▲
S.O.B.
The Souler Opposite
Star Spangled Rhythm▲
Still Crazy▲
Swingers▲
Tapeheads
There's No Business Like Show Business▲
These Old Broads
Tinseltown
Too Smooth
Tune in Tomorrow
The 24 Hour Woman
Wag the Dog
Waiting for Guffman
Who Framed Roger Rabbit▲
With Friends Like These
The Wizard of Speed and Time
World's Greatest Lover
Young & Willing
Young People

Showbiz Dramas

Actors and Sin
All About Eve▲
American Blue Note
The Ann Jillian Story
Anna▲
The Anniversary Party▲
The Audrey Hepburn Story
The Barefoot Contessa▲
The Beatniks
The Big Knife▲
Blast-Off Girls
The Bodyguard
Boogie Nights▲
Can You Hear the Laughter? The Story of Freddie Prinze
Cassie
The Cat's Meow
Child Star: The Shirley Temple Story
A Chorus Line
The Comic
Concrete Angels
The Cradle Will Rock
Dancing in September
Dangerous
Day for Night▲
The Day of the Locust▲
Doll Face
Double Platinum
Dragon: The Bruce Lee Story▲
The Dresser▲
Entropy
Ernie Kovacs: Between the Laughter
F. Scott Fitzgerald in Hollywood
The Fabulous Dorseys
Fame▲
Flynn
For Ever Mozart
For the Boys
Frances▲
From the Journals of Jean Seberg
Funny Girl▲
Funny Lady
The Girl Said No
The Goddess▲
Gods and Monsters▲
Goodbye, Norma Jean
Goodnight, Sweet Marilyn
Grace of My Heart
Happily Ever After
Hard Part Begins
Harlow
Hollywood Dreams
Hollywood Heartbreak
Hollywood Mystery
Hughes & Harlow: Angels in Hell
I'm Losing You
The Incredible Sarah
Introducing Dorothy Dandridge▲
Isn't She Great
The Jacksons: An American Dream
James Dean
James Dean: Live Fast, Die Young
King of Comedy▲
La Dolce Vita▲
The Last Metro▲
Last Summer In the Hamptons▲
The Last Tycoon▲
Lenny▲
Little Voice▲
Livin' for Love: The Natalie Cole Story
The Lonely Lady
Lucy and Desi: Before the Laughter
Madonna: Innocence Lost
Mae West
A Man Called Adam
Man of a Thousand Faces▲
Man on the Moon
Marilyn: The Untold Story▲
Max
Mickey One
Mommie Dearest
My Wicked, Wicked Ways
Network▲
The Next Step
Night and Day
Norma Jean and Marilyn
Once in Paris...
Out of the Cold
Payday
Permanent Midnight
The Player▲
Postcards from the Edge▲
Pure Country
Rainbow over Broadway
Rhapsody in Blue▲
Rita Hayworth: The Love Goddess
RKO 281▲
Sam's Son
Second Coming of Suzanne
Shadow of the Vampire▲
Shakespeare Wallah▲
Sidewalks of London▲
Sinatra
Smash-Up: The Story of a Woman▲
Somebody to Love
Something to Sing About
Sparkle
Stage Struck
Stand-Ins
Star!
Star 80
A Star Is Born▲
A Star Is Born
State and Main▲
Sugar Town
Sunset Boulevard▲
Targets▲
They Call It Sin
Time Code
Topsy Turvy▲
What's Love Got to Do with It?
Why Do Fools Fall in Love?
Wired

Showbiz Musicals

see also *Musical Fantasy; Musicals; Showbiz Comedies*

All That Jazz▲
Bloodhounds of Broadway
Broadway Serenade
Bye Bye Birdie
Cats Don't Dance
A Chorus Line
Glitter
Hedwig and the Angry Inch▲
Kiss Me Kate▲
Ladies of the Chorus
Moulin Rouge
Noises Off
Singin' in the Rain▲
The Suburbans
The Temptations
There's No Business Like Show Business▲
Three for the Show
Three Little Words
Till the Clouds Roll By
Variety Girl
Yankee Doodle Dandy▲

Showbiz Thrillers

Children Shouldn't Play with Dead Things
Dead of Winter▲
The Dead Pool
Destroyer
F/X▲
F/X 2: The Deadly Art of Illusion
The House of Seven Corpses
Kiss Tomorrow Goodbye
Lady of Burlesque
Number One Fan
Return to Cabin by the Lake
Return to Horror High
Satan in High Heels
Stage Fright
Strangers Kiss
The Stunt Man▲
Up in the Air
What Ever Happened To...
What Ever Happened to Baby Jane?▲
The Wizard of Speed and Time

Shrinks

see also *Doctors & Nurses*

Agnes of God
Almost Dead
Analyze This▲
Angel Dust
Batman Forever▲
Baton Rouge
A Beautiful Mind▲
Beauty on the Beach
Behind the Lines
Betrayal
Beyond Reason
Beyond Therapy
Bliss
Blood Frenzy
Body Chemistry 2: Voice of a Stranger
Body of Influence
Body of Influence 2
The Brain
Breathtaking
A Brilliant Disguise
Captain Newman, M.D.
The Cell
The Cobweb
Color of Night
Coming Apart
Conspiracy Theory▲
A Couch in New York
The Couch Trip
Cracker: Brotherly Love▲
Cracker: Men Should Weep
Cracker: The Big Crunch
Cracker: To Be a Somebody
Cruel Intentions
Dark Asylum
Dark Mirror▲
Dead Man Out▲
Deconstructing Harry
Disturbing Behavior
Don Juan DeMarco
Don't Say a Word
The Dream Team
The Evening Star
Exit in Red
Face to Face▲
Faithful
Fear
The Fear
Female Perversions
Final
Final Analysis
Final Approach
A Fine Madness▲
Future Shock
Genealogies of a Crime
A Girl Thing
Good Will Hunting
Grosse Pointe Blank▲
Gun Shy
Halloween▲
Hangman
Happiness▲
Heaven
Hell's Gate
High Anxiety
Home Movies
Hometown Boy Makes Good
House of Games▲
Human Experiments
I Don't Buy Kisses Anymore
I Never Promised You a Rose Garden▲
If Lucy Fell
The Impossible Years
Indecent Behavior 2
Instinct
Jade
K-PAX
Lantana▲
Last Rites
Lies of the Twins
Locked in Silence
Lovesick
Lovey: A Circle of Children 2
The Machine
The Man Who Loved Women
Mercy
A Mind to Murder
Mine Own Executioner▲
Mr. Frost
Mr. Jones
Mr. Stitch
Moment to Moment
Monkeybone
Mulholland Falls
Mumford▲
Murder in Mind
The Myth of Fingerprints
National Lampoon's The Don's Analyst
Nell
The Night Caller
Night Eyes 4: Fatal Passion
On a Clear Day You Can See Forever
On the Edge
One Fine Day
One Flew Over the Cuckoo's Nest▲
Open Your Eyes▲
Panic
Passion of Mind
A Passion to Kill
Peephole
Pressure Point▲
Primal Fear
The Prince of Tides▲
Profile for Murder
Progeny
Red Wind
The Royal Tenenbaums▲
The Scar
Schizoid
Seventh Heaven
Sharon's Secret
Shock!
Silent Fall
The Sixth Sense▲
The Sleeping Tiger
Sometimes They Come Back ... Again
Speak Up! It's So Dark
Spellbound▲
Sphere
Still of the Night
The Stranger▲
Stuart Saves His Family
The Student Affair
Sybil▲
They Might Be Giants▲
36 Hours▲
The Three Faces of Eve
The 300 Year Weekend
Tin Cup▲
12 Monkeys▲
The Ugly
Underworld
Victim of Love
The Visit▲
The Watcher
What's New Pussycat?▲
When Danger Follows You Home
When the Dark Man Calls
Where Truth Lies
Whispers in the Dark
The Wife
Wild in the Country
Wilderness
The Young Poisoner's Handbook▲

Shutterbugs

see also *Front Page*

Addicted to Love
Adventures in Spying
Amelie▲
Art for Teachers of Children
Backbeat▲
The Beautiful, the Bloody and the Bare
Beefcake
Bikini Island
Billy's Hollywood Screen Kiss
Blondie Meets the Boss
Blow-Up▲
Body Shot
The Bridges of Madison County▲
Calendar▲
Camera Buff
The Caveman's Valentine
The Corrupt Ones
Dagger Eyes
Darkroom
Death and Desire
Dr. Mabuse vs. Scotland Yard
The Dolls
Don't Answer the Phone
Don't Change My World
Double Exposure
Double Exposure: The Story of Margaret Bourke-White
The Double Negative
Down in the Delta▲
Eyes Behind the Stars
Eyes of Laura Mars
Fatal Exposure
Fatal Images
The Favor, the Watch, & the Very Big Fish
Fire on the Amazon
Firefall
Footsteps
Funny Face▲
The Governess
Guinevere▲
Harrison's Flowers
Heat and Sunlight
High Art
High Season
I Love Melvin
Joe Gould's Secret
Johnny Skidmarks
Journey
Killer Image
Love & Murder
Love Crimes
Love Is a Gun
Machine to Kill Bad People
Mad Dog and Glory▲
Memento▲
Model Behavior
Not for Publication
Of Love and Shadows
One Hour Photo
Out There
The Outcasts▲
Pecker
Peeping Tom▲
Perfect Timing
Perfume
Photographer
Photographing Fairies
The Pink Jungle
The Portrait
Portraits of a Killer
Pretty Baby▲
Private Lessons, Another Story
Proof▲
The Public Eye▲
Rear Window▲
Return to Boggy Creek
Secret File of Hollywood
Seduce Me: Pamela Principle 2
Shadow Magic
Shoot
Shoot It Black, Shoot It Blue
Shooting the Past
Smoke
Snap Decision
Snapshot
Somebody Has to Shoot the Picture▲
Spice World: The Movie
Stephen King's The Night Flier
Stepmom▲
Straight for the Heart
Sunset Heat
Sunset Strip
Temptress
A Time to Die
The Truth about Cats and Dogs▲
The Unbearable Lightness of Being▲
Until the End of the World▲
Watch Me
Watch the Birdie
The Watcher

▲ = rated three bones or higher

What a Woman!
Wild America▲
The Winter Guest▲

Silent Films

***see also** Silent Horror/ Fantasy Classics*

A Propos de Nice▲
The Adorable Cheat
The Adventurer
The Adventures of Tarzan
Aelita: Queen of Mars
Amarilly of Clothesline Alley
American Aristocracy
American Pluck
The Americano
Anna Christie▲
Annapolis
April Fool
Are Parents People?
Arsenal▲
The Atonement of Gosta Berling▲
Avenging Conscience
The Average Woman
Backfire
Backstairs
Bare Knees
The Bargain
The Bat▲
Battle of Elderbush Gulch
The Battleship Potemkin▲
Battling Bunyon
Battling Butler
Beau Brummel
Beau Revel▲
Bed and Sofa▲
Behind the Front
The Bells▲
The Beloved Rogue▲
Below the Deadline
Ben-Hur▲
The Big Parade▲
Big Stakes
The Birth of a Nation▲
The Black Pirate▲
Blind Husbands▲
Blood and Sand
The Blot
Body and Soul
The Broadway Drifter
Broken Blossoms▲
Broken Hearts of Broadway
The Broken Mask
Burlesque on Carmen
Burning Daylight
The Busher
The Cabinet of Dr. Caligari▲
Cabiria
California Straight Ahead
The Cameraman▲
Camille
Campus Knights
Captain Swagger
The Cat and the Canary▲
Cesare Borgia
Champagne
The Chaplin Revue
Charleston▲
Charley's Aunt
Charlie Chaplin: Night at the Show▲
Charlie Chaplin ... Our Hero!
The Cheat▲
The Cheerful Fraud
Child of the Prairie
The Cigarette Girl of Mosselprom
The Circus▲
City Girl
City Lights▲
Civilization▲
Clodhopper
Cobra
College▲
The Coming of Amos▲
The Confession
The Count
The Count of Monte Cristo
The Country Kid▲
County Fair
The Covered Wagon
Crainquebille▲
The Crazy Ray▲
Cricket on the Hearth
The Crowd▲
The Cure
Custer's Last Fight
Cyclone Cavalier
Daddy Long Legs
Dames Ahoy
Dancing Mothers
Dangerous Hours
Dante's Inferno▲
Days of Thrills and Laughter▲
Desert of the Lost
Destiny▲
Diary of a Lost Girl▲
The Disciple
Discontent
Docks of New York▲
Dr. Jekyll and Mr. Hyde▲
Dr. Mabuse, The Gambler▲
Dog Star Man▲
Don Juan▲
Don Q., Son of Zorro
Doomsday
Down to Earth▲
Down to the Sea in Ships
Dracula/Garden of Eden
The Drake Case
Dream Street
The Dropkick▲
Dynamite Dan
The Eagle▲
Earth▲
East and West▲
Easy Street▲
Easy Virtue
Ella Cinders▲
The End of St. Petersburg▲
Entr'acte
Evangeline
Extra Girl
The Extraordinary Adventures of Mr. West in the Land of the Bolsheviks
Eyes of Julia Deep
The Eyes of Youth
Eyes Right!
False Faces
Fangs of Fate
The Farmer's Wife
Faust▲
Feel My Pulse
The Fighting American
Fighting Jack
The Fighting Stallion▲
The Fireman
Flesh and Blood
The Flesh and the Devil▲
Flirting with Fate▲
The Floorwalker▲
The Flying Scotsman
A Fool There Was
Foolish Wives▲
For Heaven's Sake▲
The Forbidden City
Fortune's Fool
The Four Horsemen of the Apocalypse▲
Free to Love
The Freshman▲
From the Manger to the Cross
The Fugitive: Taking of Luke McVane
The Garden of Eden▲
The Gaucho▲
The General▲
The General Line▲
Girl Shy▲
The Girl with the Hat Box
A Girl's Folly
The Gold Rush▲
The Golem▲
The Grand Duchess and the Waiter▲
Great K & A Train Robbery
The Greatest Question
Greed▲
Gypsy Blood
The Hands of Orlac
Hands Up
Happiness
The Haunted Castle▲
Hawthorne of the USA
Haxan: Witchcraft through the Ages▲
He Who Gets Slapped▲
Head Winds
Headin' Home
Heart of Humanity
Heart of Texas Ryan
Heart's Haven
Hearts of the World▲
Her Silent Sacrifice
His First Flame▲
His Majesty, the American
His Picture in the Papers
Home Sweet Home
Homecoming▲
Hoodoo Ann
Hotel Imperial
Hula
Human Hearts
The Hunchback of Notre Dame▲
The Ice Flood
The Idol Dancer
The Immigrant▲
In the Days of the Thundering Herd & the Law & the Outlaw
Intolerance▲
Irish Cinderella
The Iron Mask
The Island▲
Isn't Life Wonderful▲
It
The Italian
Italian Straw Hat▲
It's the Old Army Game
The Jack Knife Man▲
Jesse James Under the Black Flag
Jesus of Nazareth
Joyless Street▲
Judith of Bethulia▲
Just Suppose
The Kid▲
The Kid Brother▲
King of Kings
King of the Kongo
King of the Rodeo
King of the Wild Horses▲
The King on Main Street
Kismet▲
The Kiss▲
Kriemhilde's Revenge▲
La Chute de la Maison Usher▲
Lady of the Lake
Lady Windermere's Fan
The Lamb
Last Command▲
The Last Laugh▲
The Last of the Mohicans▲
The Last Outlaw
Laughing at Danger
Leap Year
The Leatherneck
Leaves from Satan's Book
The Leopard Woman
Let 'er Go Gallegher
Let's Go!
The Light of Faith
Linda
The Little American
Little Annie Rooney
Little Church Around the Corner
The Lodger▲
Long Pants▲
The Lost World
Love 'Em and Leave 'Em▲
The Love Flower
The Love of Jeanne Ney
Lucky Devil
Mabel & Fatty
Mack & Carole
The Mad Whirl
Male and Female▲
The Man from Beyond
The Man from Painted Post
Man in the Silk Hat
Man in the Silk Hat▲
The Man on the Box
The Man Who Laughs▲
The Man with the Movie Camera▲
Manhandled
Mantrap
The Manxman
Mark of Zorro▲
Marked Money
The Marriage Circle▲
Married?
Master of the House▲
Matrimaniac
Merry-Go-Round▲
Metropolis▲
The Michigan Kid
Mickey
Mid-Channel
Midnight Faces
Moana, a Romance of the Golden Age▲
Modern Times▲
The Mollycoddle
Monsieur Beaucaire
Moran of the Lady Letty
A Mormon Maid
Mother▲
My Best Girl▲
My Boy
My Lady of Whims
The Mysterious Lady
Napoleon▲
Narrow Trail▲
The Navigator▲
The Nervous Wreck▲
Nevada
The Night Club
The Night Cry
The Night Patrol
No Man's Law
Nomads of the North
Nosferatu▲
The Notorious Lady
Nurse Marjorie
The Nut
Old Ironsides▲
Oliver Twist▲
On the Night Stage
One A.M.
One Arabian Night▲
One-Punch O'Day
Orphans of the Storm▲
Othello
Our Dancing Daughters
Our Hospitality▲
The Outlaw and His Wife
Outside the Law
Pace That Kills
Pandora's Box▲
Passion
Passion of Joan of Arc▲
Patchwork Girl of Oz
Paths to Paradise▲
Pawnshop
The Peacock Fan
Peck's Bad Boy
Peg o' My Heart
Peter Pan
The Phantom Chariot
The Phantom Flyer
The Phantom of the Opera▲
The Plastic Age
Playing Dead
Pollyanna
The Pony Express
Pool Sharks
A Poor Little Rich Girl▲
Pop Goes the Cork
Power
The Prairie King
The Prairie Pirate
Pride of the Clan
The Primitive Lover
Q Ships
Queen Kelly▲
Quo Vadis
Ranson's Folly
The Raven
Reaching for the Moon
Rebecca of Sunnybrook Farm
Red Kimono
Red Signals
Regeneration
Reggie Mixes In▲
Renoir Shorts▲
The Return of Boston Blackie
Return of Draw Egan
The Return of Grey Wolf
Riders of the Purple Sage
Riders of the Range
The Ring
The Rink▲
Risky Business
The Road to Ruin
The Road to Yesterday
The Roaring Road
Robin Hood▲
Robinson Crusoe
Romola
Rounding Up the Law
Running Wild
Sadie Thompson▲
Safety Last▲
Salammbo
Sally of the Sawdust
Salome
Sands of Sacrifice
The Saphead
Scar of Shame
The Scarlet Car
Sea Lion
Secrets of a Soul
Seven Chances▲
Seven Years Bad Luck▲
Sex
Shadows
Shattered▲
She
The Sheik▲
Shifting Sands
Ships in the Night
The Shock
Show People▲
Siegfried▲
The Silent Mr. Sherlock Holmes
Silent Movie
The Single Standard
Skinner's Dress Suit
Sky High
So This Is Paris▲
The Social Secretary
Son of a Gun
The Sorrows of Satan▲
Soul-Fire
Soul of the Beast
Spangles
Sparrows▲
The Speed Spook
Spiders▲
Spies▲
Spite Marriage▲
The Spoilers
Square Shoulders
Stand and Deliver
Steamboat Bill, Jr.▲
Stella Maris▲
Storm over Asia▲
Straight Shootin'
The Street
Street of Forgotten Women
Strike▲
Student of Prague▲
The Student Prince in Old Heidelberg
Suds
Sunny Side Up
Sunrise▲
The Swan
Sweet Adeline
Tabu: A Story of the South Seas▲
Tarzan of the Apes
Tarzan the Tiger
The Taxi Mystery
Teddy at the Throttle
The Tempest▲
The Ten Commandments
Ten Days That Shook the World▲
Ten Nights in a Bar Room
Tentacles of the North
Tess of the Storm Country
Test of Donald Norton
That Certain Thing
These Girls Won't Talk
The Thief
The Thief of Baghdad▲
Thomas Graal's Best Film▲
Thomas Graal's First Child▲
Three Ages▲
Three Charlies and One Phoney!
The Three Musketeers
The Three Musketeers▲
Three Word Brand
Through the Breakers
Tillie Wakes Up
Tillie's Punctured Romance
Tol'able David
The Toll Gate
The Tomboy
The Tong Man
Too Wise Wives
The Torture of Silence
Tournament
Traffic in Souls▲
Trailin'
Tramp & a Woman
The Trap
Trapped by the Mormons
Treasure of Arne
True Heart Susie
20,000 Leagues under the Sea▲
Two Men & a Wardrobe
Un Chien Andalou▲
The Unchastened Woman
Uncle Tom's Cabin
Underworld▲
The Unholy Three▲
The Unknown▲
The Untamable
Until They Get Me
The Vagabond
The Vanishing American
Variety▲
The Virginian
Virtue's Revolt
Wagon Tracks
Walking Back
The Walloping Kid
Warning Shadows▲
Waxworks▲
Way Down East▲
The Wedding March▲
We're in the Navy Now
West-Bound Limited
West of Zanzibar
What Happened to Rosa?▲
When the Clouds Roll By▲
Where East Is East
White Gold▲
The White Rose▲
The White Sin
The White Sister▲
White Tiger
Why Change Your Wife?
Wild Horse Canyon
Wild Orchids
The Wind▲
Wings
The Wishing Ring▲
With Kit Carson over the Great Divide
The Wizard of Oz
Wolf Blood
Wolfheart's Revenge
Woman in Grey
Woman in the Moon
A Woman of Affairs
The Worldly Madonna
Yankee Clipper
Yankee Doodle in Berlin
Zvenigora▲

Silent Horror/ Fantasy Classics

***see also** Silent Films*

Aelita: Queen of Mars
The Cabinet of Dr. Caligari▲
Dante's Inferno▲
Dr. Jekyll and Mr. Hyde▲
The Golem▲
The Hunchback of Notre Dame▲
La Chute de la Maison Usher▲
Les Vampires
Metropolis▲
The Monster▲
Nosferatu▲
The Penalty
The Phantom of the Opera▲
The Thief of Baghdad▲
20,000 Leagues under the Sea▲
Vampyr▲
The Wizard of Oz

Single Parents

***see also** Bringing Up Baby; Parenthood*

About a Boy▲
Air Bud 2: Golden Receiver
All About My Mother▲
American History X
Anywhere But Here
Baby Boom
Beautiful
Bogus
Boricua's Bond
Bye Bye, Love
Crows

Dancer in the Dark
Double Parked
Erin Brockovich▲
Girlfight▲
Hearts in Atlantis
Hideous Kinky
How Stella Got Her Groove Back
I Am Sam
Kramer vs. Kramer▲
Life According to Muriel
Limbo
Message in a Bottle
Music of the Heart
One Fine Day
Pay It Forward
The Players Club▲
Rugrats in Paris: The Movie▲
The Shipping News
The Sixth Sense▲
Skeletons in the Closet
Sleepless in Seattle▲
The Spring
The Sweetest Gift
Ten Things I Hate about You▲
Things You Can Tell Just by Looking at Her
The Tic Code
A Walk to Remember
Where the Heart Is
Wildflowers
You Can Count On Me▲
Zeus and Roxanne

Singles

***see also** Dates from Hell*

About a Boy▲
About Last Night...▲
Beautiful Girls
Before Sunrise
Boys' Night Out▲
Breakfast at Tiffany's▲
Bridget Jones's Diary▲
Bye Bye, Love
Crossing Delancey▲
Ed's Next Move
Everyone Says I Love You▲
Everything Relative
Forget Paris
He Said, She Said
Kicking and Screaming▲
Love & Sex
Metropolitan▲
Mr. Wonderful
Mr. Wrong
Mystic Pizza▲
The Opposite Sex and How to Live With Them
The Personals
Pillow Talk▲
Reality Bites
St. Elmo's Fire
Singles▲
Sleepless in Seattle▲
Sliding Doors
That Touch of Mink
The Thing Called Love
Trial and Error
Wedding Bell Blues
When Harry Met Sally...▲
When the Cat's Away▲
The Wild Life

Sixties

***see** Period Piece: 1960s*

Skateboarding

Above and Beyond▲
Gleaming the Cube
Gummo
MVP2: Most Vertical Primate
Skateboard
The Skateboard Kid 2

Skating

***see also** Hockey*

Airborne
Blades of Courage
Breaking the Ice
Brink
The Cutting Edge
Death to Smoochy
Derby▲
Everything Happens at Night▲
Frolics on Ice
Hans Brinker
Happy Landing
Ice Castles
Ice Pawn
The Ice Rink
Iceland
My Lucky Star
One in a Million▲
Roller Boogie
Schizo
Sun Valley Serenade
Unholy Rollers
Wintertime
Xanadu

Skiing

Aspen Extreme
Avalanche
Better Off Dead
Club Med
Downhill Racer
Downhill Willie
Dumb & Dumber
Fire and Ice
Fire, Ice and Dynamite
For Your Eyes Only▲
Going for the Gold: The Bill Johnson Story
Hot Dog ... The Movie!
Iced
Lost and Found
On Her Majesty's Secret Service▲
One Last Run
The Other Side of the Mountain
The Other Side of the Mountain, Part 2
Out Cold
Red Snow
Reno and the Doc
Ski Bum
Ski Patrol
Ski School
Ski School 2
Ski Troop Attack
Skier's Dream
Snow: The Movie
Snowball Express
Snowballin'
Snowballing
Snowblind
Striker's Mountain
Tales from the Snow Zone

Skinheads

***see also** Nazis & Other Paramilitary Slugs*

American History X
An American Werewolf in Paris
Brotherhood of Murder
Cracker: To Be a Somebody
The Infiltrator
Lola and Billy the Kid
Luna Park
Meantime
The Murder of Stephen Lawrence▲
Red Scorpion 2
Romper Stomper
Skin
Speak Up! It's So Dark
The Substitute 4: Failure is Not an Option
Surf Nazis Must Die
Terror 2000
The Turning
White Lies

Skydiving

Cutaway
Drop Zone
Fandango
Honeymoon in Vegas
Point Break
Terminal Velocity

Slapstick Comedy

***see also** Comedy; Screwball Comedy*

Abbott and Costello Go to Mars
Abbott and Costello in Hollywood
Abbott and Costello in the Foreign Legion
Abbott and Costello Meet Captain Kidd
Abbott and Costello Meet Dr. Jekyll and Mr. Hyde
Abbott and Costello Meet Frankenstein▲
Abbott and Costello Meet the Invisible Man▲
Abbott and Costello Meet the Keystone Kops
Abbott and Costello Meet the Killer, Boris Karloff
Abbott and Costello Meet the Mummy
Abroad with Two Yanks
Ace Ventura: Pet Detective
Ace Ventura: When Nature Calls
The Adventurer
The Adventures of Buckaroo Banzai Across the Eighth Dimension▲
Africa Screams
After the Fox
Air Raid Wardens
All New Adventures of Laurel and Hardy: For Love or Mummy
All of Me
All Over Town
Alvin Purple
Alvin Rides Again
American Aristocracy
American Pluck
Amos and Andrew
The Animal
Animal Crackers▲
Any Which Way You Can
Armed and Dangerous
Around the World in 80 Ways
Around the World in a Daze
Assault and Matrimony
At the Circus
At War with the Army
Baby's Day Out
The Bad News Bears▲
The Bad News Bears Go to Japan
The Bad News Bears in Breaking Training
The Bank Dick▲
The Barber Shop▲
The Barefoot Executive
The Battle of the Sexes▲
Bean▲
Bedtime for Bonzo
Beethoven
Beethoven's 2nd
The Bellboy
Beverly Hills Ninja
Big Mouth
Big Store
Black Cat, White Cat▲
Block-heads▲
Bohemian Girl▲
Bonnie Scotland
Bowery Boys Meet the Monsters
Boy, Did I Get a Wrong Number!
Boys Will Be Boys
Brain Donors
Buck Privates
Buck Privates Come Home▲
Bullfighters
The Caddy
Caddyshack▲
Caddyshack 2
Candleshoe
Carry On at Your Convenience
Carry On Behind
Carry On Camping
Carry On Cruising
Carry On Doctor▲
Carry On Emmanuelle
Carry On England
Carry On Henry VIII
Carry On Nurse
Casanova's Big Night
The Case of the Mukkinese Battle Horn
Cheech and Chong: Still Smokin'
Cheech and Chong: Things Are Tough All Over
Cheech and Chong's Next Movie
Cheech and Chong's The Corsican Brothers
Cheech and Chong's Up in Smoke
Christmas in July▲
A Chump at Oxford
Cinderfella
Cockeyed Cavaliers
College▲
Comin' Round the Mountain
Corky Romano
Cracking Up
The Cure
Dance with Me, Henry
A Day at the Races▲
The Delicate Delinquent
The Dentist▲
Detective School Dropouts
Disorderly Orderly
Don't Raise the Bridge, Lower the River
Double Trouble
Doughboys
Dragons Forever
Duck Soup▲
Dumb & Dumber
Ernest Goes to Africa
Ernest Goes to Camp
Ernest Goes to Jail
Ernest Goes to School
Ernest Rides Again
Ernest Scared Stupid
The Errand Boy
Family Jewels
The Feud
Finders Keepers
A Fine Mess
Flim-Flam Man
Flubber
The Flying Deuces▲
Folks!
Follow That Camel
Francis Covers the Big Town
Francis Goes to the Races
Francis Goes to West Point
Francis in the Haunted House
Francis in the Navy
Francis Joins the WACs
Francis the Talking Mule▲
Freddy Got Fingered
Free and Easy
The Fuller Brush Girl
The Fuller Brush Man
Funny Farm
George Washington Slept Here▲
Get Smart, Again!
The Ghost and Mr. Chicken
Ghost in the Noonday Sun
Ghost on the Loose
A Girl in Every Port
The Gods Must Be Crazy▲
The Gods Must Be Crazy 2
Going Bananas
The Gorilla
Great Guns
The Great Lover
The Great Race
A Guide for the Married Man▲
Gus
Half-Shot at Sunrise
Hands Up
Hardly Working
Have Rocket Will Travel
Here Come the Co-Eds
Hold That Ghost▲
Hollywood or Bust
Home Alone▲
Home Alone 2: Lost in New York
Home Alone 3
The Horn Blows at Midnight▲
Horse Feathers▲
Hot Lead & Cold Feet
I Hate Blondes
The Imposters
In Society
Ishtar
It's a Mad, Mad, Mad, Mad World
Jack & the Beanstalk
The Jerk
Jingle All the Way
Jour de Fete▲
Julia Misbehaves▲
Jumping Jacks
Kentucky Kernels
The Kettles in the Ozarks
The Kettles on Old MacDonald's Farm
The Klutz
The Last Remake of Beau Geste
Laurel & Hardy and the Family
Laurel & Hardy: Another Fine Mess
Laurel & Hardy: At Work
Laurel & Hardy: Be Big
Laurel & Hardy: Below Zero
Laurel & Hardy: Berth Marks
Laurel & Hardy: Blotto
Laurel & Hardy: Brats
Laurel & Hardy: Chickens Come Home
Laurel & Hardy: Hog Wild
Laurel & Hardy: Laughing Gravy
Laurel & Hardy: Men O'War
Laurel & Hardy: Night Owls
Laurel & Hardy On the Lam
Laurel & Hardy: Perfect Day
Laurel & Hardy Spooktacular
Laurel & Hardy: Stan "Helps" Ollie
Laurel & Hardy: The Hoose-Gow
Let's Go!
Little Giant
Long Pants▲
Lost in a Harem
Lost in Alaska
The Lost Stooges
Love Happy
Ma and Pa Kettle
Ma and Pa Kettle at the Fair
Ma and Pa Kettle at Waikiki
Ma and Pa Kettle Back On the Farm
Ma and Pa Kettle Go to Town
Man of the House
Man's Favorite Sport?
Matilda
Meatballs 3
Meatballs 4
Menage▲
Mexican Hayride
Milky Way
Mr. Hulot's Holiday▲
Mr. Magoo
Monkey Business▲
Monkey Trouble
The Monster
My Friend Irma
The Naughty Nineties
The Navigator▲
Never Give a Sucker an Even Break▲
A Night at the Opera▲
A Night in Casablanca▲
The Noose Hangs High▲
The North Avenue Irregulars
Not Quite Human
Not Quite Human 2
Nothing But Trouble
Nuns on the Run
Odd Jobs
Off Limits
Off the Wall
One A.M.
Our Relations▲
Out of the Blue
The Out-of-Towners
The Outlaws Is Coming!
Pack Up Your Troubles
Pardon My Sarong
Pardon My Trunk
Pardon Us
The Party▲
The Patsy
Pawnshop
Pharmacist
Playtime▲
Police Academy
Police Academy 2: Their First Assignment
Police Academy 4: Citizens on Patrol
Police Academy 5: Assignment Miami Beach
Police Academy 6: City under Siege
Police Academy 7: Mission to Moscow
Problem Child 2
Quick, Let's Get Married
Railrodder▲
Reckless Kelly
Red Salute
Rescue from Gilligan's Island
Rio Rita
The Road to Hong Kong
Robin Hood: Men in Tights
RocketMan
Rockin' Road Trip
Room Service
Saps at Sea
Say It Isn't So
Seven Years Bad Luck▲
Show People▲
Sidewalks of New York
Slapstick of Another Kind
Snow White and the Three Stooges
Son of the Pink Panther
Sons of the Desert▲
The Speed Spook
Spies Like Us
Stripes
The Stupids
Superstar
Swiss Miss
Take the Money and Run▲
Tanks a Million
The 30-Foot Bride of Candy Rock
Three Charlies and One Phoney!
Three Stooges in Orbit
The Three Stooges Meet Hercules
Tillie Wakes Up
Too Shy to Try
Trial and Error
Two-Way Stretch
Up the Creek
Utopia
Voyage Suprise▲
Walk Like a Man
Weekend at Bernie's
Weekend at Bernie's 2
What! No Beer?
Who Done It?
Who Killed Doc Robbin?
The Whole Nine Yards
Who's Minding the Store?
Why Me?
Wide Open Faces
A Woman of Distinction▲
The Wonders of Aladdin
Yankee Doodle in Berlin
The Yellow Cab Man
Yellowbeard

Slavery

***see also** Civil Rights*

The Abductors
Acla's Descent into Floristella
The Adventures of Huckleberry Finn
Amistad▲
Angel City
The Arena
Band of Angels
Beloved
The Big Bust Out
Black Fox: The Price of Peace
Blacksnake!
Brother Future
Buck and the Preacher
Burn!▲
Candyman 2: Farewell to the Flesh
Cobra Verde

The Colombian Connection
Dragonard
Gladiator▲
Gone Are the Days
Half Slave, Half Free
A House Divided
The House of Dies Drear
The House of 1000 Dolls
Intimate Power
Island of Lost Girls
Jefferson in Paris
Joseph
The Journey of August King
The King and I▲
Kull the Conqueror
The Last Supper▲
Lust for Freedom
The Magic Stone
Man Friday
Man from Deep River
Mandinga
Mandingo
Moses
Naked in the Sun
Nightjohn
Olga's Girls
Once Upon a Time in China▲
Planet of the Apes▲
Pudd'nhead Wilson
Queen▲
Quilombo
Race to Freedom: The Story of the Underground Railroad
A Respectable Trade
Ride with the Devil
The Road to Morocco▲
The Robe
Roots▲
Roots: The Gift
St. Patrick: The Irish Legend
Sally Hemings: An American Scandal
Sansho the Bailiff▲
Shadrach
Shaft in Africa
The Silencer
Skin Game▲
Slavers
Souls at Sea
Spartacus▲
Sunshine Run
Tamango
Traffic in Souls▲
True Women
Uncle Tom's Cabin
Wanda, the Sadistic Hypnotist
White Slave
A Woman Called Moses
Xica▲

Small-Town Sheriffs

Blue Ridge Fall
Brigham City
Cherry Falls
Cop Land▲
Eight Legged Freaks
Eye of the Storm
Hard Luck
In the Heat of the Night▲
Lone Star▲
The Mothman Prophecies
A Real American Hero
Red Rock West▲
Silverado▲
Sudden Impact
Walking Tall
Walking Tall: Part 2
Walking Tall: The Final Chapter

Smuggler's Blues

see also *Crime & Criminals; Drug Abuse*

Blow
Brother▲
Cutaway
Deuces Wild
Essex Boys
Exit Wounds
The Guardian
In Too Deep
Jimmy Zip
Memento▲
Once in the Life
Our Lady of the Assassins
Outta Time
Rare Birds
Requiem for a Dream▲
Shaft▲
The Street Fighter's Last Revenge
Time and Tide
Training Day

Snakes

see also *Wild Kingdom*

Anaconda
Black Cobra
Copperhead
The Craft
Curse 2: The Bite
Fer-De-Lance
Green Snake
Halfmoon
Indiana Jones and the Last Crusade▲
Indiana Jones and the Temple of Doom▲
Jennifer
Journey to the Lost City
King Cobra
Lewis and Clark and George
Natural Born Killers
Python
Raiders of the Lost Ark▲
Rattled
Rattlers
The Reptile
The Road Warrior▲
Silent Predators
Silver Stallion
The Snake People
Spasms
Sssssss
Stanley
Venomous
Women's Prison Escape

Soccer

Air Bud 3: World Pup
Big Brother Trouble
The Big Green
Bossa Nova
The Club▲
Cracker: To Be a Somebody
The Cup
Cup Final
Fever Pitch
The Final Goal
Go Now▲
The Goalie's Anxiety at the Penalty Kick▲
Gregory's Girl▲
The Hero
Home Team
Hot Shot
Hothead
Ladybugs
Long Shot
The Match
Mean Machine
Soccer Dog: The Movie
Those Glory, Glory Days
Victory
When Saturday Comes
Yesterday's Hero

South America

see also *Central America*

Aguirre, the Wrath of God▲
Amazon
The Americano
Americano
Apartment Zero▲
At Play in the Fields of the Lord▲
Bananas▲
Behind the Sun
Black Orpheus▲
Boca
Burden of Dreams
The Burning Season▲
Bye Bye Brazil
Catch the Heat
Clear and Present Danger
Cobra Verde
Collateral Damage
The Colombian Connection
The Dark Side of the Heart
Death and the Maiden▲
Death in the Garden
Diplomatic Immunity
Doctor Chance
800 Leagues Down the Amazon
El Muerto
The Emerald Forest▲
Evita
Far Away and Long Ago
Fitzcarraldo▲
Five Came Back
Four Days in September
The Fugitive▲
Funny, Dirty Little War
Fury
Green Fire
Green Mansions
Happy Together
Hercules vs. the Sons of the Sun
The Hour of the Star▲
The House of the Spirits
I Don't Want to Talk About It
It's All True
Johnny 100 Pesos
Knocks at My Door
Last Flight to Hell
The Last Movie
Latin Lovers
Let's Get Harry
Little Mother
Managua
Max Is Missing
Me You Them
Mighty Jungle
Miracles
Miss Mary
Missing▲
The Mission▲
Monster
Moon over Parador
The Muthers
Naked Jungle▲
Naked Tango
Nancy Goes to Rio
Night Gallery▲
Nostromo
O Quatrilho
Of Love and Shadows
One Man Out
Only Angels Have Wings▲
Our Lady of the Assassins
Overkill
The Pink Jungle
A Place in the World▲
The Plague
Play for Me
Quilombo
Ratas, Ratones, Rateros
Rodrigo D.: No Future
Romancing the Stone▲
Secre of the Andes
A Shadow You Soon Will Be
Shoot to Kill
Simon Bolivar
The Story of Fausta
Sweet Country
Tango
Terranova
Terror in the Jungle
The Three Caballeros
To Kill a Stranger
Veronico Cruz
What Your Eyes Don't See
Wild Orchid
Xica▲
You Were Never Lovelier▲

Southern Belles

see also *American South; Nashville Narratives*

Blaze
Cat on a Hot Tin Roof▲
Cat on a Hot Tin Roof
Crimes of the Heart
Dear Dead Delilah
Driving Miss Daisy▲
The Glass Menagerie▲
Gone with the Wind▲
Hush, Hush, Sweet Charlotte▲
Jezebel▲
Miss Firecracker▲
Nashville▲
North and South Book 1▲
North and South Book 2▲
Other Voices, Other Rooms
Queen Bee
Rich in Love
Scarlett
Scorchers
Steel Magnolias▲
A Streetcar Named Desire▲
A Streetcar Named Desire
The Trip to Bountiful▲

Space Operas

see also *Alien Beings—Benign; Alien Beings—Vicious*

Alien▲
Alien Cargo
The Apocalypse
Apollo 13▲
Assignment Outer Space
Battle Beyond the Stars
Battle Beyond the Sun
Battlestar Galactica
The Black Hole
Buck Rogers Conquers the Universe
Capricorn One▲
Cat Women of the Moon
Conquest of Space
Contact
Countdown
Creature
Dark Breed
Dark Side of the Moon
Dark Star▲
The Day the Sky Exploded
Dead Fire
Destination Moon
Destination Moonbase Alpha
Destination Saturn
The Dish▲
Escape from Mars
Escape from Planet Earth
Escape Velocity
Event Horizon
Explorers
Fire Maidens from Outer Space
First Encounter
First Men in the Moon
First Spaceship on Venus▲
Flight to Mars
Forbidden Planet▲
From the Earth to the Moon
From the Earth to the Moon▲
Galaxy of Terror
Gattaca▲
The Green Slime
Hangar 18
Have Rocket Will Travel
Heavens Above▲
Hellraiser 4: Bloodline
Horrors of the Red Planet
In the Dead of Space
Inseminoid
John Carpenter's Ghosts of Mars
Journey to the Far Side of the Sun▲
Killings at Outpost Zeta
Laser Mission
The Last Starfighter
Lifepod
Lost in Space
Marooned
Megaforce
Mission Galactica: The Cylon Attack
Mission Mars
Mission to Mars
Mom and Dad Save the World
Moon 44
Moonraker
Moontrap
The Mouse on the Moon▲
Murder in Space
Mutant on the Bounty
Mystery Science Theater 3000: The Movie
Nude on the Moon
Outland
Planet Burg
Planet of the Apes▲
Planet of the Dinosaurs
Planet of the Vampires
Precious Find
Project Moon Base
PSI Factor
Red Planet
The Reluctant Astronaut
Return of the Jedi▲
Return to Earth
The Right Stuff▲
Robinson Crusoe on Mars
RocketMan
Rocketship X-M
Silent Running▲
Solar Crisis
Solaris
Space Cowboys▲
Space Mutiny
Space Rage
Space Raiders
Spaceballs
SpaceCamp
Spacejacked
Star Crash
Star Slammer
Star Trek: The Motion Picture
Star Trek 2: The Wrath of Khan▲
Star Trek 3: The Search for Spock
Star Trek 4: The Voyage Home▲
Star Trek 5: The Final Frontier
Star Trek 6: The Undiscovered Country
Star Trek: First Contact▲
Star Trek: Generations▲
Star Trek: Insurrection
Star Wars▲
Star Wars: Episode 2—Attack of the Clones▲
Starship
Supernova
Tales from a Parallel Universe: Eating Pattern
Tales from a Parallel Universe: Giga Shadow
The Terrornauts
Three Stooges in Orbit
Titan A.E.
Transformations
Trapped in Space
2001: A Space Odyssey▲
2001: A Space Travesty
2010: The Year We Make Contact▲
Vegas in Space
Velocity Trap
Voyage to the Planet of Prehistoric Women
Voyage to the Prehistoric Planet
Walking on Air
Warlords of the 21st Century
Wing Commander
Woman in the Moon
Women of the Prehistoric Planet

Spaghetti Western

see also *Western Comedy; Westerns*

Ace High
Adios, Hombre
And God Said to Cain
Any Gun Can Play
Apache's Last Battle
Belle Starr
Beyond the Law
Blood for a Silver Dollar
The Boldest Job in the West
Boot Hill
Bullet for Sandoval
A Bullet for the General
Chino
Django Shoots First
A Fistful of Dollars▲
A Fistful of Dynamite▲
Five Giants from Texas
For a Few Dollars More
Garringo
The Good, the Bad and the Ugly▲
The Grand Duel
Gun Fight at Red Sands
Gunfire
Hang 'Em High
Hellbenders
His Name Was King
The Last Tomahawk
Minnesota Clay
A Minute to Pray, a Second to Die
My Name Is Nobody
Navajo Joe
Once Upon a Time in the West▲
Red Sun
Rough Justice
The Ruthless Four
Spaghetti Western
The Stranger and the Gunfighter
Stranger in Paso Bravo
Take a Hard Ride
Tramplers
Trinity Is Still My Name
Twice a Judas
You're Jinxed, Friend, You've Met Sacramento

Spain

Against the Wind
Ay, Carmela!▲
Barcelona▲
The Barcelona Kill
Behold a Pale Horse
Belle Epoque▲
Blood and Sand▲
Butterfly▲
Caper of the Golden Bulls
Carmen, Baby
The Castilian
Desire▲
Destiny
The Devil Is a Woman▲
The Devil's Backbone
The Disappearance of Garcia Lorca
Extramuros
Fiesta
For Whom the Bell Tolls▲
The Grandfather
I'm the One You're Looking For
Kevin & Perry Go Large
Land and Freedom▲
The Last Seduction 2
Lazarillo
Letters from Alou
Live Flesh▲
Love Can Seriously Damage Your Health
Marbella
The Naked Maja
Nico and Dani
Pandora and the Flying Dutchman
The Pride and the Passion
Running Out of Time
Sand and Blood
Sexy Beast▲
Siesta
The Spanish Gardener▲
Surprise Attack
The Sword of El Cid
Talk of Angels
Tierra
A Touch of Class▲
Vacas

Spanish Civil War

Behold a Pale Horse
The Devil's Backbone
The Disappearance of Garcia Lorca
For Whom the Bell Tolls▲
Land and Freedom▲
The Night Has Eyes
Vacas

Spies & Espionage

see also *Feds; Foreign Intrigue; Terrorism*

Above Suspicion▲
Access Code
Across the Pacific▲
Act of War
Action in Arabia
Adventures in Spying

The Adventures of Rocky & Bullwinkle
The Adventures of Tartu
Against the Wind
Agent on Ice
Air Raid Wardens
Alamut Ambush
Aldrich Ames: Traitor Within
Alfred Hitchcock's Aventure Malgache
Alfred Hitchcock's Bon Voyage
All Through the Night▲
The Amateur
The Apocalypse Watch
Arabesque
Armored Command
The Art of War
Artists and Models
As If It Were Raining
Assassin
The Assassination Game
The Assassination Run
The Atomic Kid
Attack of the Robots
Austin Powers: International Man of Mystery▲
Austin Powers 2: The Spy Who Shagged Me▲
Austin Powers In Goldmember
Avalanche Express
The Avengers
Background to Danger▲
Bad Company
Bear Island
Beaumarchais the Scoundrel
Behind Enemy Lines
The Berlin Conspiracy
Berlin Express▲
Betrayed▲
Big Deadly Game
Big Jim McLain
The Big Lift
Black Box Affair
Black Brigade
The Black Dragons
Black Eagle
The Black Windmill
Blue Ice
Boris and Natasha: The Movie
The Bourne Identity▲
British Intelligence
Bulldog Drummond at Bay
Bulldog Drummond Escapes
Bullet to Beijing
Bulletproof
Cairo
Call Me Bwana
Call Out the Marines
Caravan to Vaccares
Carve Her Name with Pride
Casablanca▲
Casino Royale
A Casualty of War
Charge of the Model T's
Chu Chu & the Philly Flash
Clear and Present Danger
Clipped Wings
Cloak and Dagger
Cloak & Dagger
Code Name Alpha
Code Name: Chaos
Code Name: Dancer
Code Name: Diamond Head
Code Name: Emerald
Codename: Foxfire
Codename: Icarus
Codename Kyril
Codename: Wildgeese
Cold War Killers
Company Business
Company Man
Comrades in Arms
Condorman
Conspirator
Contraband
Counterblast
The Counterfeit Traitor▲
Cowboy Commandos
Criminals Within
Dandy in Aspic
Daniel
Daniella by Night
Dark Journey▲
Darling Lili
Dawn Express
The Day and the Hour
The Day of the Dolphin
The Day of the Jackal▲
The Day Will Dawn▲
Dead Aim
Deadly Currents
The Deadly Game
Deadly Recruits
Deadly Rivals
Deadly Spygames
The Deadly Trap
Death Ray 2000
Death Rides the Range
Deathcheaters
Defense Play
Delta Force Commando 2
Desperate Cargo
Diamonds Are Forever▲
Diplomatic Courier▲
Dishonored
Dr. No▲
The Doll Squad
Don't Drink the Water
Don't Raise the Bridge, Lower the River
Doomsday Gun
Double Agents
Double Deal
The Double O Kid
Down Among the Z Men
Duck Soup▲
The Dunera Boys▲
Edge of Darkness▲
Edge of Darkness
The Eiger Sanction
Elizabeth▲
Embassy
Emissary
The Endless Game
Enforcer from Death Row
The English Patient▲
An Englishman Abroad▲
Enigma
Erik
Escape from Fort Bravo
Escape from the KGB
The Executioner
The Experts
Extremely Dangerous
Eye of the Needle
Eyewitness
A Face in the Rain
The Falcon and the Snowman▲
The Falcon's Brother
Fall from Grace
The Fallen Sparrow▲
False Faces
The Fantastic World of D.C. Collins
Fathom
Federal Agent
Final Assignment
The Final Option
Fire Over England▲
Firefall
Firefox
Firehead
First Yank into Tokyo
Five Fingers▲
Five for Hell
Five Graves to Cairo▲
Flight from Vienna
Flight to Nowhere
Flying Blind
For Your Eyes Only▲
Foreign Correspondent▲
The Foreigner
The Formula
The Fourth Protocol▲
Francis Gary Powers: The True Story of the U-2 Spy
French Intrigue
From Russia with Love▲
Funeral in Berlin▲
The General Died at Dawn▲
A Generation▲
Get Smart, Again!
Girl Hunters
Girls Are for Loving
The Glass Bottom Boat
Golden Earrings
Goldeneye▲
Goldeneye: The Secret Life of Ian Fleming
Goldfinger▲
Gotcha!
The Great Armored Car Swindle
Green Inferno
The Groundstar Conspiracy▲
Gunpowder
Hanky Panky
Hard Ticket to Hawaii
Harriet the Spy
Head Over Heels
The Heat of the Day
Heroes in Hell
Heroes Stand Alone
Hidden Agenda
Hidden Enemy
Hillbillies in a Haunted House
The Holcroft Covenant
Holt of the Secret Service
Honeybaby
Honeymoon Academy
Hopscotch▲
Hostage
The Hot Line
Hotel Reserve▲
Hour of the Assassin
The House on Carroll Street
The House on Garibaldi Street
House on 92nd Street▲
The Human Factor
The Hunt for Red October▲
Hunter
I Dood It
I See a Dark Stranger▲
I Stand Condemned
The Ice Runner
Ice Station Zebra
If Looks Could Kill
The Impossible Spy▲
The In-Laws▲
In the Company of Spies
In the Secret State
The Innocent
The Inside Man
Inside the Lines
International Lady
Internecine Project
Intrigue
Invisible Agent
The Ipcress File▲
Ishtar
It Means That to Me
J-Men Forever!▲
Jack Higgins' The Windsor Protocol
Jack Higgins' Thunder Point
Jackie Chan's First Strike▲
Jakarta
Jet Pilot
The Jigsaw Man
Joan of Paris▲
Journey into Fear▲
Journey into Fear
Jumpin' Jack Flash
Jungle Drums of Africa
Keep Talking Baby
The KGB: The Secret War
The Kid with the X-Ray Eyes
Kill Castro
Kill Factor
Kim▲
Kim
Koroshi
La Cage aux Folles 2
Laser Mission
Last Embrace▲
Le Magnifique
Le Professionnel▲
License to Kill
License to Kill▲
Lie Down with Lions
Lightning Bolt
Lipstick Camera
Lisbon
The Little Drummer Girl▲
Live and Let Die
The Living Daylights▲
Loaded Guns
The Looking Glass War
Lost Diamond
The Lost One
The Love Light
Love on the Run
M. Butterfly
Ma and Pa Kettle on Vacation
Mackintosh Man
Madame Sin
Malone
Man from Headquarters
The Man on the Box
The Man Outside
The Man Who Knew Too Little
The Man Who Never Was▲
The Man Who Wasn't There
The Man with One Red Shoe
The Man with the Golden Gun
Marie Galante▲
Maroc 7
The Mask of Dimitrios▲
Mata Hari▲
Mata Hari
The Mediterranean in Flames
The Mercenaries
Midnight in Saint Petersburg
Mind Trap
Mindfield
Ministry of Fear▲
Mission: Impossible▲
Mission: Impossible 2▲
Mission Phantom
Mission to Venice
Mr. Superinvisible
Modesty Blaise
The Monocle
Monte Carlo
Moonraker
Morituri▲
Mother Night▲
Murder for Sale
Murder on the Midnight Express
Murderers' Row
My Favorite Blonde▲
My Favorite Brunette
My Name Is Ivan▲
The Mysterious Lady
Mystery Plane
Nasty Rabbit
Never Say Never Again
Never Too Young to Die
Night Flight from Moscow
A Night in Casablanca▲
Night Train to Munich▲
Ninja Champion
No Dead Heroes
No Way Out▲
North by Northwest▲
Notorious▲
The Nude Bomb
Number 1 of the Secret Service
Octopussy
The Odessa File
Old Mother Riley's Ghosts
On Her Majesty's Secret Service▲
Once Upon a Honeymoon
One Armed Executioner
One of Our Dinosaurs Is Missing
Operation C.I.A.
Operation Crossbow▲
O.S.S.▲
The Osterman Weekend
Overture
The Package
Panama Hattie
Panama Menace
Panama Patrol
Paper Tiger
Paradisio
Pascali's Island▲
Patriot Games▲
The Peking Blond
A Perfect Spy
Permission To Kill
Philby, Burgess and MacLean: Spy Scandal of the Century
Phoenix Team
Picasso Trigger
Pickup on South Street▲
President's Mistress
Prime Risk
The Prize▲
Protocol
Provocateur
Pueblo Affair▲
A Question of Attribution
Qui Etes Vous, Mr. Sorge?
The Quiller Memorandum▲
Ravishing Idiot
Rebel Love
Reilly: Ace of Spies▲
Rescue from Gilligan's Island
Retrievers
Return of the Man from U.N.C.L.E.
Return to Savage Beach
Rio Rita
Robinson Crusoe of Mystery Island
Roboman
Robot Pilot
The Rocketeer▲
Ronin
Running Blind
Running Delilah
Running Scared
The Russia House
Russian Roulette
The Rutanga Tapes
Sabotage▲
Saboteur▲
The Saint
S.A.S. San Salvador
Scorpio
Sea Devils
Sebastian
Second Best Secret Agent in the Whole Wide World
The Secret Agent▲
The Secret Agent
Secret Agent 00
The Secret Agent Club
Secret Agent 00-Soul
Secret Agent Super Dragon
Secret Mission
Secret Weapon
Secret Weapons
Sell Out
Shack Out on 101▲
Shadows over Shanghai
The Shakiest Gun in the West
S*H*E
Shining Through
Ship Ahoy
A Show of Force
The Silencers
Sky High
Sky Liner
Sneakers
Snuff-Bottle Connection
The Soldier
A Southern Yankee
The Spanish Prisoner▲
Spies▲
Spies, Lies and Naked Thighs
Spitfire
Spy
Spy Game
Spy Games
Spy Hard
Spy in Black▲
Spy Kids▲
Spy Kids 2: The Island of Lost Dreams
Spy of Napoleon
Spy Smasher
Spy Smasher Returns
Spy Trap
The Spy Who Came in from the Cold▲
The Spy Who Loved Me
Spy with a Cold Nose
The Spy Within
Spymaker: The Secret Life of Ian Fleming
S*P*Y*S
Stalag 17▲
State Department File 649
Steal the Sky
Stopover Tokyo
The Stranger▲
Strike Commando
Subterfuge
Swordfish
The Tailor of Panama▲
The Tall Blond Man with One Black Shoe▲
The Tamarind Seed
Tangiers
Target for Killing
Telefon
Terminal Entry
Terminal Velocity
Texas to Bataan
There Goes Barder
They Got Me Covered
The Thief
The Third Man▲
13 Rue Madeleine▲
The 39 Steps▲
The Thirty-Nine Steps
Three Days in Beirut
Three Days of the Condor▲
Three Kinds of Heat
Thunderball
Tiffany Jones
To Live and Die in Hong Kong
Tokyo Joe
Tomorrow Never Dies
Top Secret!▲
Topaz▲
Torn Curtain
Trader Tom of the China Seas
Trenchcoat
Trident Force
Triple Cross▲
Tripwire
The Trouble with Spies
True Lies
The Ultimate Imposter
Undeclared War
Under the Rainbow
Undercover Blues
Undercover Brother
Underground Agent
Up Periscope
The Uranium Conspiracy
A View to a Kill
Viper
Virginia City▲
The Waiting Time
Wanted Dead or Alive
Watch on the Rhine▲
Waterfront
What's Up, Tiger Lily?▲
Where Eagles Dare▲
Where the Bullets Fly
The Whistle Blower▲
White Ghost
White Nights
WhiteForce
Wild Wild West
Wonsan Operation
The Wrecking Crew
XXX
Yin & Yang of Mr. Go
You Only Live Twice
Young Nurses in Love
Your Turn Darling
Yuri Nosenko, KGB
Zeppelin
Zeta One
Zotz!

Sports

see ***Baseball; Basketball; Bicycling; Boxing; Football; Golf; Hockey; The Olympics; Running; Scuba; Skating; Skiing; Skydiving; Soccer; Sports Comedies; Sports Dramas; Surfing; Swimming; Tennis; Volleyball***

Sports Comedies

Air Bud
Air Bud 2: Golden Receiver
Air Bud 3: World Pup
Air Bud 4: Seventh Inning Fetch
The Air Up There
Angels in the Infield
Angels in the Outfield
The Bad News Bears▲
The Bad News Bears Go to Japan
The Bad News Bears in Breaking Training
BASEketball
The Best of Times
Big and Hairy
The Big Green

▲ = rated three bones or higher

Billie
Bingo Long Traveling All-Stars & Motor Kings▲
Blue Juice
Blue Skies Again
Body Slam
Bowery Blitzkrieg
The Boys
Bull Durham▲
Celtic Pride
Comeback Kid
The Comrades of Summer
Cool Runnings
The Cup
Day the Bookies Wept
Diggstown
Downhill Willie
D3: The Mighty Ducks
D2: The Mighty Ducks
Ed
Eddie
Fast Break
Fever Pitch
First & Ten
First & Ten: The Team Scores Again
The Fish that Saved Pittsburgh
For Heaven's Sake
The Freshman▲
Goof Balls
The Great White Hype
Happy Gilmore
Hold 'Em Jail
Home Team
Hot Dog ... The Movie!
Hothead
It Happens Every Spring▲
Jerry Maguire▲
Jocks
Johnny Be Good
Kingpin
Ladybugs
A League of Their Own▲
Little Big League
Little Giants
The Longest Yard▲
The Longshot
Major League
Major League 2
Major League 3: Back to the Minors
The Man with the Perfect Swing
The Match
The Mighty Ducks
Mr. Baseball
Monty Python's The Meaning of Life▲
MVP (Most Valuable Primate)
Mystery, Alaska
National Lampoon's Golf Punks
Necessary Roughness
North Dallas Forty▲
Off the Mark
The One and Only
One-Punch O'Day
Paper Lion
Pat and Mike▲
Perfect Game
Prehysteria 3
Prize Fighter
The Replacements
Rookie of the Year
The St. Tammany Miracle
The Sandlot▲
The Scout
Semi-Tough
The Sixth Man
Ski School
Slam Dunk Ernest
Slap Shot▲
Slap Shot 2: Breaking the Ice
Soccer Dog: The Movie
Space Jam
Splitz
Spring Fever
Squeeze Play
Sunset Park
Swim Team
Tin Cup▲
Trading Hearts
The Waterboy
White Men Can't Jump
Wildcats
The World's Greatest Athlete

Sports Dramas

Above the Rim
Airborne
Alex
All the Right Moves
American Anthem
American Flyers
American Kickboxer 1
Any Given Sunday▲
Babe!▲
The Babe
Babe Ruth Story
Bang the Drum Slowly
Bang the Drum Slowly▲
The Big Blue
Big Mo
Blades of Courage
Blue Chips
Body and Soul▲
Body & Soul
Boy in Blue
The Break
Breaking Away▲
Breaking Free
Brian's Song▲
Brutal Glory
Challenge of a Lifetime
Champion▲
Champions
Chariots of Fire▲
Chasing Dreams
The Club▲
Coach
Cobb▲
The Color of Money▲
Crossbar
The Cutting Edge
Dawn!
Days of Thunder
Dempsey
Diving In
Don't Look Back: The Story of Leroy "Satchel" Paige
Downhill Racer
Dream to Believe
Dreamer
Dynamite Dan
Eight Men Out▲
8 Seconds
The Fan
Fat City▲
Field of Dreams▲
Fight for the Title
Final Shot: The Hank Gathers Story
Finish Line
The First Olympics: Athens 1896
For Love of the Game
The Four Minute Mile
Futuresport
Gentleman Jim▲
Girlfight▲
Gladiator
Go for the Gold
Going for the Gold: The Bill Johnson Story
The Gold & Glory
Goldengirl
Grambling's White Tiger
He Got Game
Heart Like a Wheel
Heaven Is a Playground
The Hero
Hockey Night
Honeyboy
Hoosiers▲
Hot Shot
The Hustler▲
Ice Castles
Ice Pawn
International Velvet
The Jericho Mile
The Jesse Owens Story
Jim Thorpe: All American
The Joe Louis Story
Joe Torre: Curveballs Along the Way
Kid Galahad▲
Kid Monk Baroni
Knute Rockne: All American▲
The Last American Hero▲
The Last Fight
Last Time Out
The Legend of Bagger Vance
The Loneliest Runner
Long Gone
Love and Basketball▲
Maker of Men
Marciano
A Matter of Honor
Miracle on Ice
My Champion
Nadia
The Natural▲
O▲
On the Edge
One in a Million: The Ron LeFlore Story
One Last Run
One on One
Opposite Corners
Over the Top
Paperback Hero
Passing Glory▲
Pastime▲
Personal Best▲
Pistol: The Birth of a Legend
Players
Prefontaine
Price of Glory
Pride of St. Louis
The Pride of the Yankees▲
The Program
Pulsebeat
Raging Bull▲
Rebound: The Legend of Earl "The Goat" Manigault
Red Line 7000
Red Surf
Remember the Titans▲
Requiem for a Heavyweight▲
Rocky▲
Rocky 2
Rocky 3
Rocky 4
Rocky 5
Rocky Marciano
Rollerball
Rowing Through
Rudy
Run for the Dream: The Gail Devers Story
Running Brave
School Ties▲
Side Out
61*▲
Skier's Dream
Soul of the Game▲
The Spirit of West Point
The Sprinter
The Stratton Story▲
Summer Catch
Talent for the Game
That Championship Season
They Call Me Sirr
This Sporting Life▲
Tiger Town
The Tiger Woods Story
Touch and Go
21 Hours at Munich▲
Varsity Blues
Victory
Vision Quest
When Saturday Comes
Wilma
Wind
A Winner Never Quits
The Winning Team
Without Limits▲
Youngblood

Spousal Abuse

***see also** Sexual Abuse*
The Abduction
Angel Eyes
The Break Up
The Burning Bed▲
Casualties
Dangerous Game
Enough
Falling Down
Far Cry from Home
The Gift
Honey & Ashes
The Ice House▲
In the Bedroom▲
Independence Day
Intimate Strangers
Lea
Love Come Down
Love Letters
Mesmerized
Mortal Thoughts
Nil by Mouth
Olivia
The Opponent
Our Mother's Murder
Perfect Crime
Remember Me
Shattered Dreams
Sleeping with the Enemy
The Tenant of Wildfell Hall
This Boy's Life▲
What's Love Got to Do with It?
Woman Undone
Woman with a Past

Stagestruck

***see also** Showbiz Comedies; Showbiz Dramas; Showbiz Thrillers*
All About Eve▲
Applause▲
Because of Him
Bloodhounds of Broadway
Broadway Damage
Broadway Danny Rose▲
Broadway Limited
Broadway Melody
Broadway Melody of 1938
Broadway Rhythm
Bullets over Broadway▲
Carnegie Hall
The Cradle Will Rock
The Dolly Sisters
Fame▲
First a Girl
Frogs for Snakes
The Great Ziegfeld▲
Gypsy▲
Gypsy
Haunted
Illuminata
Interview with the Vampire
Jesus of Montreal▲
The King of Masks▲
Kiss Me, Guido
The Lady in Question
The Leading Man
Let's Make Love
Lillie▲
Look for the Silver Lining
A Midwinter's Tale
Morning Glory
Mother Wore Tights▲
The Next Step
No
The Phantom Lover
Shakespeare in Love▲
Stage Door▲
Stage Struck
Stagefright
Star!
Tea for Two▲
Topsy Turvy▲
Va Savoir
Vanya on 42nd Street▲
William Shakespeare's A Midsummer Night's Dream
Yankee Doodle Dandy▲

Stalked!

***see also** Obsessive Love*
Addicted to Love
Backwoods
Breach of Conduct
The Cable Guy
Chuck & Buck
Circuit Breaker
Copycat
Dying Game
Evil Obsession
The Fan
Fatal Attraction▲
The Gingerbread Man
Kill Shot
A Kiss Goodnight
Klute▲
Living in Peril
Mr. Wrong
Number One Fan
The Seduction
Stalked
Stalker
Stalking Laura
Taxi Driver▲
Turn of the Blade
Twilight Man

Star Gazing

The Arrival
Eliza's Horoscope
The Fish that Saved Pittsburgh
How Come Nobody's On Our Side?
Lamp at Midnight
Local Hero▲
My Stepmother Is an Alien
Roxanne▲

Stepparents

***see also** Family Ties; Parenthood*
The Adventures of Rusty
The Adventures of Sebastian Cole
All the Little Animals
Beat Girl
Beau Pere▲
Big Girls Don't Cry...They Get Even
Cinderella▲
Cinderella
Domestic Disturbance
Electra
Ellie
Ever After: A Cinderella Story▲
Everyone Says I Love You▲
Fear
Hard Frame
Home for Christmas
Lassie
Lost
Night of the Twisters
The Orphan
Out on a Limb
Petits Freres
Private Passions
Rivals
Second Sight▲
Snow White: A Tale of Terror
Snow White: The Fairest of Them All
The Stepdaughter
The Stepfather▲
Stepfather 2: Make Room for Daddy
Stepfather 3: Father's Day
Stepmom▲
The Stepmother
The Stepsister
A Summer to Remember▲
Tadpole
This Boy's Life▲

Stewardesses

***see also** Airborne*
Airplane!▲
Black Tight Killers▲
Blazing Stewardesses
Boeing Boeing
Executive Decision
Jackie Brown▲
Passenger 57
Stewardess School
Three Guys Named Mike
Turbulence

Stolen from Asia

A Fistful of Dollars▲
Last Man Standing
The Magnificent Seven▲
Reservoir Dogs▲
Star Wars▲
Tortilla Soup

Stolen from Europe

Babycakes
Dirty Rotten Scoundrels▲
Head Above Water
Insomnia▲
Jakob the Liar▲
Kiss Me Goodbye
Last House on the Left
Nightwatch
Scent of a Woman▲
Vanilla Sky
The Vanishing
A Walk in the Clouds

Stolen from France

The Associate
The Birdcage▲
Blame It on Rio
Breathless
Buddy Buddy
Cactus Flower
Casbah▲
Cousins▲
Diabolique
Down and Out in Beverly Hills
Father's Day
Happy New Year
Intersection
Jungle 2 Jungle
Just Visiting
The Long Night
The Man Who Loved Women
The Man with One Red Shoe
Men Don't Leave
The Mirror Has Two Faces
Mixed Nuts
My Father the Hero
Nine Months
Paradise▲
Point of No Return
Pure Luck
Quick Change
Return to Paradise▲
Scenes from the Class Struggle in Beverly Hills
Sommersby
Sorcerer
Three Fugitives
Three Men and a Baby▲
The Toy
12 Monkeys▲
Under Suspicion
Unfaithful
The Woman in Red

Storytelling

Babyfever
The Company of Wolves▲
Grim Prairie Tales
Monster in a Box▲
My Dinner with Andre▲
The NeverEnding Story 3: Escape from Fantasia
Paper Tiger
The Princess Bride▲
The Story Lady
The Willies
Windwalker▲

Strained Suburbia

***see also** Yuppie Nightmares*
Adventures in Spying
American Beauty▲
The Amityville Horror
Amongst Friends
Amos and Andrew
Arlington Road
Beavis and Butt-Head Do America
Blue Velvet▲
The Brady Bunch Movie▲
The 'Burbs
Clown House
Coneheads
Consenting Adults
Crime and Punishment in Suburbia
The Crude Oasis
Deadly Neighbor
Dennis the Menace
Dennis the Menace Strikes Again
Desperate Hours▲
Desperate Hours
Don't Talk to Strangers
Don't Tell Mom the Babysitter's Dead

▲ = rated three bones or higher

Edward Scissorhands▲
Faithful
Godmoney
The Graduate▲
Grand Canyon▲
The Grass Is Always Greener Over the Septic Tank
Gummo
Hocus Pocus
Home Alone▲
Home Alone 3
House▲
How to Beat the High Cost of Living
Hugo Pool
Hush Little Baby, Don't You Cry
I Love My...Wife
Jaws▲
Jaws 2
Krippendorf's Tribe
Madhouse
Marked for Death
The Meal
Mr. Blandings Builds His Dream House▲
The Money Pit
My Blue Heaven
My New Gun
Neighbors
Next Friday
1941
Opportunity Knocks
The Osterman Weekend
Over the Edge▲
Parents▲
The People Next Door
Please Don't Eat the Daisies
Polyester
The Positively True Adventures of the Alleged Texas Cheerleader-Murdering Mom▲
Return of the Living Dead 2
Revenge of the Stepford Wives
Serial Mom▲
Shattered Spirits
Short Cuts▲
The Stepford Wives▲
The Stranger▲
The Swimmer▲
Terrorvision
Three Wishes
The Trigger Effect
Twice in a Lifetime▲
The Underworld Story
A Very Brady Sequel
The Virgin Suicides
The War of the Roses▲
When Every Day Was the Fourth of July
The Whole Nine Yards
Your Friends & Neighbors▲

Strippers

Blaze
Blood Money
Body Language
Breakdown▲
Cadillac Ranch
The Center of the World
Club Vampire
Crystal's Diary
Dance of the Damned
Dancing at the Blue Iguana
Dangerous Ground
The Dark Dancer
Day of the Warrior
Dogma
Exit
Exotica▲
The Fluffer
For Ladies Only
From Dusk Till Dawn
The Full Monty▲
The Glass Cage
Gypsy▲
Gypsy
Headless Body in Topless Bar
Heaven
Keys to Tulsa
Kiss of Death
Kiss of Fire
Lady of Burlesque
Lap Dancing
The Last Word
Laws of Deception
Lenny▲
Made
Miami Hustle
Midnight Tease
Midnight Tease 2
A Night in Heaven
Overnight Delivery
Pecker
Pigalle
The Players Club▲
Plucking the Daisy
Shadow Dancer
The Showgirl Murders
Showgirls
Sparkler
Stag
Strip Search
The Stripper
Stripper
Stripshow
Striptease
Stripteaser
Sweet Evil
Time Served
Tin Cup▲
True Lies
Under Siege
Working Girls

Struggling Artists

see also Art & Artists; Biopics: Artists

Maze

Struggling Musicians

The Adventures of Buckaroo Banzai Across the Eighth Dimension▲
American Blue Note
Backbeat▲
Beyond the Valley of the Dolls
Bikini Summer
Blast-Off Girls
The Brady Bunch Movie▲
Breaking Glass
Bye Bye Blues
The Competition▲
Cotton Candy
Crossover Dreams
Crossroads
Dangerous Holiday
Dangerous Moonlight▲
Dogs in Space
Eddie and the Cruisers
Eddie and the Cruisers 2: Eddie Lives!
The Eternal Waltz
The Fabulous Dorseys
Falling from Grace
Fear of a Black Hat
The Five Heartbeats▲
Gridlock'd▲
Heaven Tonight
Jack Frost
Killing 'Em Softly
Knights of the City
Light of Day
Love Song
A Man Called Adam
Mo' Better Blues
Murder Rap
Oh, God! You Devil
One Trick Pony
Purple Rain
The Return of Spinal Tap
Rhinestone
Rock & Rule
Rock Star
The Rose▲
Satisfaction
Sparkle
A Star Is Born
Streets of Fire
subUrbia
Tender Mercies▲
This Is Spinal Tap▲
Vibrations
You Light Up My Life

Stupid Is...

Bean▲
Beavis and Butt-Head Do America
Being There▲
Big Top Pee-wee
Bill & Ted's Bogus Journey
Bill & Ted's Excellent Adventure
Billy Madison
Bio-Dome
Black Sheep
Caddyshack▲
Chairman of the Board
The Curse of Inferno
The Dinner Game
Drowning Mona
Dudley Do-Right
Dumb & Dumber
The Extreme Adventures of Super Dave
Fast Times at Ridgemont High▲
Forrest Gump▲
Half-Baked
Happy Gilmore
Idiot Box
Idle Hands
In God We Trust
The Jerk
The Jerky Boys
Joe Dirt
Killer Bud
Little Nicky
Lock, Stock and 2 Smoking Barrels▲
Meet the Deedles
Mr. Accident
National Lampoon's Animal House▲
The Nutty Professor▲
Orgazmo
Pee-wee's Big Adventure▲
Ready to Rumble
Road Trip
Romy and Michele's High School Reunion
Son-in-Law
The Stupids
Tommy Boy
The Waterboy
Wayne's World▲
White Mile
Young Einstein
Zoolander

Submarines

see also Deep Blue

Above Us the Waves▲
The Abyss▲
Action in the North Atlantic
Agent Red
Assault on a Queen
Atlantis: The Lost Empire
Atomic Submarine
Crash Dive
Crimson Tide▲
Danger Beneath the Sea
Das Boot▲
The Day Will Dawn▲
Destination Tokyo
Down Periscope
Enemy Below▲
Fer-De-Lance
First Strike
For Your Eyes Only▲
Full Fathom Five
Going Under
Hostile Waters
The Hunley
The Hunt for Red October▲
Ice Station Zebra
The Incredible Mr. Limpet
The Inside Man
K-19: The Widowmaker
Leviathan
Mysterious Island▲
1941
Octopus
On the Beach
Operation Delta Force 2: Mayday
Operation Delta Force 3: Clear Target
Operation Petticoat▲
Q Ships
Raise the Titanic
Run Silent, Run Deep▲
The Spy Who Loved Me
Steel Sharks
Sub Down
Submarine Attack
Submarine Seahawk
Torpedo Alley
Torpedo Attack
Torpedo Run
20,000 Leagues under the Sea▲
20,000 Leagues Under the Sea
U-571
Up Periscope
Voyage to the Bottom of the Sea▲
We Dive at Dawn▲
Yellow Submarine▲
You Only Live Twice

Subways

see also Trains

Adventures in Babysitting
Angel Dust
Carlito's Way▲
Daybreak
Die Hard: With a Vengeance
Eve of Destruction
The French Connection▲
The Fugitive▲
Highlander 2: The Quickening
The Incident
The Jackal
Lethal Weapon 3
Mimic
Money Train
Next Stop, Wonderland
On the Line
Predator 2
Quatermass and the Pit
Risky Business▲
ShadowZone: The Undead Express
Sliding Doors
Speed▲
Subway
Subway Stories
The Taking of Pelham One Two Three▲
Trick▲
The Warriors
Zazie dans le Metro▲

Suicide

see also Death & the Afterlife

Absence of Malice
Alien 3
All My Sons▲
American Strays
Angels Over Broadway▲
The Arrangement
Asylum
Attack Squadron
Autopsy
Bad Girls Dormitory
Bedazzled▲
The Bell Jar
Better Off Dead
The Big Chill▲
Blacklight
Body & Soul▲
Buddy Buddy
Can You Hear the Laughter? The Story of Freddie Prinze
Cause Celebre▲
Club Extinction
Come Undone
Cookie's Fortune▲
Courage Under Fire▲
Crimes of the Heart
The Crude Oasis
Crumb
The Curve
Dead Man on Campus
Dead Poets Society▲
Death Wish Club
Delicatessen▲
Delinquent Daughters
Deutschland im Jahre Null▲
The Devil in Silk
Divine
Docks of New York▲
Dominique Is Dead
Double Suicide▲
Dream with the Fishes
The Eagle and the Hawk▲
Elisa
The End▲
Europa '51
Eva
The Eyes, the Mouth
Faithful
Father's Day
The Fire Within▲
The First Wives Club
From the Journals of Jean Seberg
Frozen
Fuzz
A Gentle Woman
The Girl on the Bridge▲
Golden Gate
Goodbye Cruel World
The Guyana Tragedy: The Story of Jim Jones
The Hanging Garden
Harold and Maude▲
Heading for Heaven
Heat▲
Heathers▲
The Hudsucker Proxy▲
The Hustle
Iris
It's a Wonderful Life▲
Julian Po
Junk Mail
Kill Me Later
Last Cry for Help
Last Tango in Paris▲
The Last Time I Committed Suicide
Le Corbeau▲
Leaving Las Vegas▲
Maborosi▲
Madame Bovary
Maedchen in Uniform▲
Memorial Day
Missing Pieces
Mrs. Dalloway
Mixed Nuts
Monster's Ball▲
Mortal Danger
Mother Kusters Goes to Heaven▲
Mouchette▲
My Sweet Suicide
Nais▲
Natural Enemies
'night, Mother
The Odd Job
Ode to Billy Joe
On the Edge
One Flew Over the Cuckoo's Nest▲
Ordinary People▲
Pain in the A—▲
The Pallbearer
Peeping Tom▲
Permanent Record
Primary Colors
Remolino de Pasiones
Retribution
Return of Frank Cannon
Reuben, Reuben▲
Right of Way
Robert Louis Stevenson's The Game of Death
Romeo and Juliet▲
Romeo and Juliet
Romeo and Juliet▲
Scent of a Woman▲
Silence of the Heart▲
Sisters, Or the Balance of Happiness
The Slender Thread▲
Solo Sunny
Stealing Home
Stella Maris▲
The Taste of Cherry
The Tenant▲
The Unknown Soldier
The Virgin Suicides
Warm Summer Rain
Wetherby▲
Whale Music
What Dreams May Come
Whose Life Is It Anyway?▲

Summer Camp

Addams Family Values
Backwoods
Berserker
The Best Way
Bloody Murder
The Burning
Bushwhacked
But I'm a Cheerleader
Camp Cucamonga: How I Spent My Summer Vacation
Camp Nowhere
Cannibal Campout
A Cry from the Mountain
Deliverance▲
Don't Go in the Woods
Ernest Goes to Camp
Escanaba in da Moonlight
Evil Dead
Evils of the Night
Father and Scout
The Final Terror
First Turn On
Forever Evil
Friday the 13th
Friday the 13th, Part 2
Friday the 13th, Part 3
Friday the 13th, Part 4: The Final Chapter
The Ghost of Fletcher Ridge
Gimme an F
Gorp
The Great Outdoors
Grim Prairie Tales
Grizzly
Happy Campers
Heavyweights
The Hills Have Eyes
Hot Resort
Indian Summer
Little Darlings
Man of the House
Meatballs
Meatballs 2
Meatballs 3
Meatballs 4
Memorial Valley Massacre
Mother's Day
Nuts in May
Oddballs
One Small Hero
The Parent Trap
Party Camp
A Pig's Tale
Poison Ivy
The Prey
Princes in Exile
Race for Your Life, Charlie Brown
Race with the Devil
Redwood Forest Trail
Rituals
The River Wild
Sleepaway Camp
Sleepaway Camp 2: Unhappy Campers
Sleepaway Camp 3: Teenage Wasteland
Storm
Stuckey's Last Stand
Summer Camp Nightmare
There's Nothing out There
Three Way Weekend
Ticks
Troop Beverly Hills
Wet Hot American Summer▲
The Willies

Super Heroes

The Amazing Spider-Man
Batman
Batman▲
Batman and Robin
Batman Forever▲
Batman: Mask of the Phantasm
Batman Returns
Black Mask
Black Scorpion
Blankman
Captain America
Captain America 2: Death Too Soon
Chinese Web
The Chosen One: Legend of the Raven
Cloak & Dagger▲
Death of the Incredible Hulk
Dr. Strange

▲ = rated three bones or higher

The Flash
Flash Gordon
Freddie the Frog
Howard the Duck
The Incredible Hulk
The Incredible Hulk Returns
Infra-Man
The Mask▲
The Meteor Man
Mighty Morphin Power Rangers: The Movie
Mystery Men
Orgazmo
The Phantom
Phantom 2040 Movie: The Ghost Who Walks
Phenomenal and the Treasure of Tutankamen
Pootie Tang
The Puma Man
The Punisher
Rat Pfink a Boo-Boo
Return of Captain Invincible
Sgt. Kabukiman N.Y.P.D.
The Shadow
Spawn▲
The Specials▲
Spider-Man▲
Spiderman: The Deadly Dust
Steel
Super Fuzz
Supergirl
Superman: The Movie▲
Superman 2▲
Superman 3
Superman 4: The Quest for Peace
Superman & the Mole Men
Supersonic Man
3 Ninjas: High Noon at Mega Mountain
Todd McFarlane's Spawn
The Toxic Avenger, Part 2
The Trial of the Incredible Hulk
Turbo: A Power Rangers Movie
Unbreakable
VIP, My Brother Superman
The Wild World of Batwoman
X-Men
Zorro

Supernatural Comedies

***see also** Comedy*

Angels in the Outfield
Bedazzled
Beetlejuice▲
Bell, Book and Candle
Bernard and the Genie
Blackbeard's Ghost
The Craft
Dead Heat
The Devil & Max Devlin
Fridays of Eternity
The Frighteners
Ghost Chasers
Ghost Dad
Ghost Fever
The Ghost Goes West▲
The Ghost Train
Ghost Writer
Ghostbusters▲
Ghostbusters 2
Ghosts Can Do It
Ghosts of Berkeley Square
Haunted Honeymoon
Heart and Souls
High Spirits
Hillbillies in a Haunted House
Hocus Pocus
Limit Up
Love at Stake
The Man in the Santa Claus Suit
Matilda▲
Michael
My Best Friend Is a Vampire
Oh, God!
Oh, God! Book 2
Oh, God! You Devil
Rockula
Saturday the 14th
Saturday the 14th Strikes Back
She-Devil
The Sixth Man
Spook Busters
Spooks Run Wild
Teen Wolf
Teen Wolf Too
Topper▲
Topper Returns▲
Topper Takes a Trip▲
When Pigs Fly
Who Killed Doc Robbin?
Wicked Stepmother
Wishful Thinking
A Witch Without a Broom

Supernatural Horror

***see also** Classic Horror*

Alabama's Ghost
Alison's Birthday
The Amityville Horror
Amityville 2: The Possession
Amityville 3: The Demon
Amityville 4: The Evil Escapes
Amityville: A New Generation
Amityville 1992: It's About Time
The Appointment
Attack of the Puppet People
Audrey Rose
Bad Dreams
The Believers
Beyond Evil
The Black Cat
Bless the Child
Blood from the Mummy's Tomb
Blood Orgy of the She-Devils
Bloodbeat
Bloodlust
Bones
Book of Shadows: Blair Witch 2
Born of Fire
The Brainiac
Bruiser
Candyman
Cassandra
Charlie Boy
The Child
Children of the Night
Christine
Crimes of Dr. Mabuse▲
The Crow: Salvation
Crypt of Dark Secrets
Curse of the Black Widow
Curse of the Blue Lights
The Curse of the Crying Woman
Curse of the Demon▲
Curse of the Headless Horseman
Curse of the Living Corpse
Curse of the Stone Hand
The Curse of the Werewolf
The Cursed Mountain Mystery
Damien: Omen 2
Dance of Death
The Dark
Dark Places
The Dark Secret of Harvest Home
Dark Tower
The Daughter of Dr. Jekyll
Daughters of Satan
Dawn of the Mummy
Dead and Buried
Dead Are Alive
The Dead Don't Die
The Death Curse of Tartu
Death Mask
Death Ship
Deathdream
Deathhead Virgin
Deathmoon
Deep Red: Hatchet Murders
Def by Temptation
The Demon Lover
Demon of Paradise
Demon Rage
Demon Wind
Demonia
Demonoid, Messenger of Death
The Demons
Demons
Demons 2
Demons of Ludlow
Demonstone
Demonwarp
Destroyer
Devil Dog: The Hound of Hell
Devil Doll
The Devil Rides Out▲
Devil Woman
The Devil's Daughter
Devil's Gift
The Devil's Hand
The Devil's Nightmare
The Devil's Partner
The Devil's Possessed
Devil's Rain
The Devil's Web
Devil's Wedding Night
Devonsville Terror
The Diabolical Dr. Z
Diary of a Madman
Diary of the Dead
Die, Monster, Die!
Disciple of Death
The Doctor and the Devils
Doctor Butcher M.D.
Dr. Frankenstein's Castle of Freaks
Doctor Phibes Rises Again
Dr. Tarr's Torture Dungeon
Dr. Terror's House of Horrors
Don't Be Afraid of the Dark
Don't Go to Sleep
The Dunwich Horror
Dust Devil
Edge of Sanity
The Eighteenth Angel
Embrace of the Vampire
Equinox▲
The Evil
Evil Altar
Evil Dead Trap▲
Evil Town
Evilspeak
Exorcism
The Exorcist▲
The Exorcist 2: The Heretic
Fallen
Feast for the Devil
Female Vampire
Firestarter
The First Power
Fright House
From Beyond the Grave
From Dusk Till Dawn
The Fury Within
The Gate
Gate 2
Gates of Hell 2: Dead Awakening
The Ghastly Ones
The Ghost
The Ghost Brigade
Ghost Dance
Ghost Keeper
The Ghost of Rashmon Hall
The Ghost of Yatsuya
Ghost Story
Ghosthouse
Ghostriders
The Ghosts of Hanley House
Ghosts That Still Walk
Giant from the Unknown
God Told Me To
Grave Secrets: The Legacy of Hilltop Drive
The Haunted Palace
The Hearse
Hellbound: Hellraiser 2
Hellraiser
Hellraiser 3: Hell on Earth
Hellraiser 4: Bloodline
The Horrible Dr. Bones
The Horrible Dr. Hichcock
Horror Express
Horror Hotel
Horror of the Blood Monsters
Horror Rises from the Tomb
The House by the Cemetery
The House in Marsh Road
The House of Seven Corpses
House of the Yellow Carpet
The House on Skull Mountain
The House that Bled to Death
House Where Evil Dwells
The Howling▲
Howling 2: Your Sister Is a Werewolf
Howling 3: The Marsupials
Howling 4: The Original Nightmare
Howling 5: The Rebirth
Howling 6: The Freaks
Immortal Sins
The Indestructible Man
Inferno
Initiation of Sarah
Inquisition
Invasion of the Blood Farmers
Invasion of the Zombies
Invitation to Hell
It's Alive!
Jaws of Satan
J.D.'s Revenge
Jennifer
Judgment Day
Kill, Baby, Kill▲
The Kiss
Kiss Daddy Goodbye
Knocking on Death's Door
Kwaidan▲
Land of the Minotaur
The Last Gasp
The Last Man on Earth
The Legacy
The Legend of Hell House▲
Let's Scare Jessica to Death
Lisa and the Devil
The Living Head
Lord of Illusions
Lost Souls
Lurkers
Lust for a Vampire
The Man and the Monster
Manhattan Baby
Maniac
The Manitou
Manos, the Hands of Fate
Mardi Gras for the Devil
Mardi Gras Massacre
Mark of the Devil
Mark of the Devil 2
Mary, Mary, Bloody Mary
Maxim Xul
The Medusa Touch
The Mephisto Waltz▲
Meridian: Kiss of the Beast
Messiah of Evil
Midnight
Midnight Cabaret
Midnight's Child
Mirror, Mirror
Mirror of Death
The Monster Demolisher
The Mummy's Revenge
The Mummy's Shroud
Necromancer: Satan's Servant
Necropolis
Neon Maniacs
The Nesting
Netherworld
The Night Evelyn Came Out of the Grave
Night Life
Night Nurse
Night of Horror
Night of the Death Cult
Night of the Demons
Night of the Demons 2
Night of the Ghouls
Night of the Sorcerers
Night Orchid▲
The Night Stalker
The Night Strangler
Night Vision
Night Visitor
Nightmare Castle
Nightmare in Blood
Nightmare Sisters
Nightmare Weekend
Nightstalker
Nightwish
Nomads
Nothing But the Night
The Occultist
Of Unknown Origin
The Offspring
The Omen
Omen 3: The Final Conflict
Omen 4: The Awakening
The Oracle
Orgy of the Dead
Orgy of the Vampires
The Other▲
Other Hell
The Others▲
Out of the Body
The Outing
Patrick
Pet Sematary
Pet Sematary 2
Phantasm
Phantasm 2
Phantom of the Ritz
Phantoms
Poltergeist▲
Poltergeist 2: The Other Side
Poltergeist 3
Poltergeist: The Legacy
The Possessed
The Possession of Joel Delaney
The Premonition
Premonition
The Prophecy
The Psychic
Psychomania
Pumpkinhead
Rawhead Rex
The Relic
Revolt of the Zombies
Route 666
Sarah's Child
Scream of the Wolf
Session 9
Signs
The Sleeping Car
Sleepstalker: The Sandman's Last Rites
Sorceress
Soul Survivors
Specters
Spooky Encounters
Stephen King's Rose Red
Stephen King's The Storm of the Century
Stephen King's Thinner
Stir of Echoes
Supernatural
The Supernaturals
Terror Creatures from the Grave
They Watch
13 Ghosts
The Turn of the Screw
Unseen Evil
Unspeakable
The Vault
The Visitors
Voices from Beyond
Voodoo Academy
The Whip and the Body
Witchcraft 4: Virgin Heart
Witchcraft 10: Mistress of the Craft
The Witches
The Wraith

Supernatural Martial Arts

Baby Cart at the River Styx
Baby Cart to Hades
The Crow
Hellbound
The Heroic Trio
The Legend of the 7 Golden Vampires
Ninja, the Violent Sorcerer
Remo Williams: The Adventure Begins
Sgt. Kabukiman N.Y.P.D.
Vampire Raiders—Ninja Queen
Zu: Warriors from the Magic Mountain

Supernatural Westerns

Billy the Kid Versus Dracula
Curse of the Undead
The Devil's Mistress
Ghostriders
Grim Prairie Tales
The Hitcher
Into the Badlands
Jesse James Meets Frankenstein's Daughter
John Carpenter's Vampires
Mad at the Moon
Near Dark▲
Sundown
Timerider

Surfing

***see also** Beach Blanket Bingo*

Aloha Summer
Beach Blanket Bingo▲
Beach Party
Big Wednesday
Bikini Beach
Blackrock
Blood Surf
Blue Crush
Blue Juice
California Dreaming
Chairman of the Board
Computer Beach Party
The Endless Summer▲
The Endless Summer 2▲
Escape from L.A.
Follow Me
Gidget
How to Stuff a Wild Bikini
In God's Hands
Lauderdale
Mad Wax: The Surf Movie
Meet the Deedles
Muscle Beach Party
North Shore
Point Break
Psycho Beach Party
Puberty Blues
Red Surf
Ride the Wild Surf
South Beach Academy
Summer City
Surf Nazis Must Die
Surf Party
Surf 2

Survival

***see also** Hunted!; Negative Utopia; Post Apocalypse*

Abandon Ship
The Admirable Crichton
Adrift
Adventure Island
Adventures of Eliza Fraser
Alive
Alpine Fire
And I Alone Survived
Antarctica
Arctic Blue
Attack of the Beast Creatures
The Aviator
Back from Eternity
Bat 21
Battlefield Earth
Beverly Hills Family Robinson
Black Rain▲
Born Killer
Born Wild
The Bridge on the River Kwai▲
Buffalo Rider
A Bullet Is Waiting
Cage 2: The Arena of Death
Caged in Paradiso
Captain January
A Captive in the Land
Cast Away▲
Challenge To Be Free
Cheyenne Warrior
Clearcut
Cliffhanger▲
Clown
Cold River
The Colony

▲ = rated three bones or higher

Cool Hand Luke▲
Courage Under Fire▲
Damned River
Das Boot▲
The Dawson Patrol
The Day After▲
Daylight
Dead Calm▲
Deadly Harvest
Deadly Prey
Death Hunt
Def-Con 4
Deliverance▲
Delos Adventure
Delusion
Desperate Target
The Devil at 4 O'Clock
Diamonds of the Night▲
The Dive
Dust Devil
Earthling
Edge of Honor
Empire of the Sun▲
Endangered
Endgame
Enemy Mine
Enemy Territory
Erendira
Eric▲
Escape from Hell
Escape from Mars
Escape from Wildcat Canyon
Escapist
Far from Home: The Adventures of Yellow Dog
Fight for Your Life
Firehawk
Five Came Back
Flight from Glory
Flight from Singapore
Flight of the Eagle
The Flight of the Phoenix▲
The Forbidden Quest
Fortress
Found Alive
Gas-s-s-s!
Germany, Pale Mother
The Ghost of Fletcher Ridge
Grave of the Fireflies▲
He Is My Brother
Heaven and Earth
Heaven Knows, Mr. Allison▲
Heck's Way Home
Heroes for Sale▲
High Ice
High Noon▲
High Noon
Hunter's Blood
The Incredible Journey
The Interrogation▲
Into Thin Air: Death on Everest
The Island▲
The Island at the Top of the World
Island of the Blue Dolphins
Island of the Lost
Jeremiah Johnson▲
Jungle Inferno
Just Before Dawn
Kameradschaft▲
Killing at Hell's Gate
The Killing Fields▲
King Rat▲
The Land That Time Forgot
The Last Chance▲
Last Exit to Brooklyn▲
The Last Flight of Noah's Ark
Le Dernier Combat▲
Legend of Alfred Packer
The Legend of Wolf Mountain
Legionnaire
L'Enfant d'Eau
The Leopard Son
The Life and Death of Colonel Blimp▲
Lifeboat▲
Lily Was Here
Limbo
Little Dorrit, Film 1: Nobody's Fault▲
Little Dorrit, Film 2: Little Dorrit's Story▲
Lord of the Flies▲
Lord of the Flies
Lost
Love on the Dole▲
Male and Female▲
Man in the Wilderness
Manon
Melody
Merry Christmas, Mr. Lawrence▲
Mr. Robinson Crusoe
The Mosquito Coast
The Most Dangerous Game▲
My Side of the Mountain
Mysterious Island▲
The Naked Prey▲
Nightmare at Bittercreek
Nightmare at Noon
Objective, Burma!▲
On the Beach▲
On the Beach
Once Before I Die
Ordeal in the Arctic
Osa
Out of Control
Packin' It In
Pagan Island
Panic in the Year Zero!
Panic Room
Paradise
Passion in the Desert
Perfect Witness
Phone Call from a Stranger
Pioneer Woman
Pitch Black▲
The Poseidon Adventure
Proteus
Quest for Fire▲
Ravager
The Return of Grey Wolf
Return of the Jedi▲
The Revolt of Job▲
The Ride Back
Robby
Robinson Crusoe
Sahara▲
Savage Hunger
Savage Is Loose
Sea Gypsies
The Sea Shall Not Have Them
Seven Days in May▲
Shackleton▲
Shadow of the Wolf
She'll Be Wearing Pink Pajamas
Silence
Silence of the North
Six Days, Seven Nights
Skyline▲
Sniper
Snowbound: The Jim and Jennifer Stolpa Story
S.O.S. Pacific
Sourdough
SpaceCamp
Stagecoach▲
Standoff
Starbird and Sweet William
Storm and Sorrow
Sub Down
Survival of Spaceship Earth
Survival Quest
Survival Run
The Survivalist
Sweet Sweetback's Baadasssss Song▲
The Swiss Family Robinson▲
The Terror
Testament▲
Thief▲
Three Came Home▲
The Ticket
Titanic
Trouble in Paradise
Trucks
True Heart
Tundra
Two Women▲
Unsettled Land
Voyage
The Voyage of the Yes
Vukovar▲
Wagon Master▲
Walkabout▲
Walking Thunder
Warriors of the Apocalypse
Waterworld
When Trumpets Fade
The White Dawn
White Fang and the Hunter
White Water Summer
White Wolves 3: Cry of the White Wolf
Wild America▲
Zarkorr! The Invader

Suspended Animation

Alien 3
Aliens▲
Austin Powers: International Man of Mystery▲
Buck Rogers in the 25th Century
Chances Are▲
Coma▲
Dragon Fury 2
Encino Man
Forever Young
Late for Dinner

Suspense

***see also** Mystery & Suspense*
Arlington Road
The Devil's Advocate
Lady Killer
Panic Room
Sphere
Trail of a Serial Killer
The Well
Zeder

Swashbucklers

***see also** Action-Adventure; Fencing; Medieval Romps*
Abbott and Costello Meet Captain Kidd
Adventures of Captain Fabian
Adventures of Don Juan▲
The Adventures of Robin Hood▲
Against All Flags▲
Ali Baba and the Forty Thieves
Ali Baba and the 40 Thieves▲
Anthony Adverse
Arabian Nights
At Sword's Point
The Black Pirate▲
The Black Shield of Falworth
The Black Swan▲
Blackbeard the Pirate
Blackbeard's Ghost
Bluebeard
The Bold Caballero
The Buccaneer
Captain Blood▲
Captain Horatio Hornblower▲
Captain Kidd
Captain Kronos: Vampire Hunter▲
Captain Ron
Cartouche▲
The Challenge
Cheech and Chong's The Corsican Brothers
China Seas▲
The Conqueror & the Empress
Corsair
The Corsican Brothers
The Count of Monte Cristo
The Count of Monte Cristo▲
The Count of Monte Cristo
Court Jester▲
Crimson Pirate▲
Cutthroat Island
Dancing Pirate
Dr. Syn
Dr. Syn, Alias the Scarecrow
Don Juan DeMarco
Don Q., Son of Zorro
The Elusive Pimpernel
Executioner of Venice
Fanfan la Tulipe▲
Fearless Tiger
The Fencing Master
The Fifth Musketeer
Fighting Marines
The Fighting Prince of Donegal
The Flame & the Arrow▲
The Four Musketeers▲
Frenchman's Creek
Ghost in the Noonday Sun
Gun Cargo
Gypsy
Hawk of the Wilderness
Hell Ship Mutiny
Highlander: The Gathering
His Majesty O'Keefe
Hook
If I Were King▲
The Iron Mask
The Island
Island Trader
The King's Guard
The King's Thief
Kojiro▲
The Lady and the Highwayman
The Lamb
The Lives of a Bengal Lancer▲
Long John Silver
Magic Island
The Man in the Iron Mask▲
The Man in the Iron Mask
The Man in the Iron Mask▲
Marauder
Mark of Zorro▲
The Mark of Zorro▲
The Mask of Zorro▲
The Master of Ballantrae
Master of Dragonard Hill
Monty Python's The Meaning of Life▲
Mooncussers
Moonfleet
Moran of the Lady Letty
Morgan the Pirate
Muppet Treasure Island
The Musketeer
My Favorite Year▲
My Wicked, Wicked Ways
The Naked Sword of Zorro
Nate and Hayes
Naughty Marietta
New Moon
Old Ironsides▲
The Phantom
The Pirate▲
Pirate Movie
Pirate Warrior
Pirates
The Pirates of Penzance
Pirates of the Coast
Pirates of the Seven Seas
The Princess and the Pirate▲
The Princess Bride▲
Princess of Thieves
Prisoner of Zenda▲
Prisoner of Zenda
Project A
Project A: Part 2
Quest of the Delta Knights
The Return of the Musketeers
Revenge of the Musketeers
Ring of the Musketeers
Robin Hood▲
Romola
Royal Flash▲
Scaramouche▲
The Scarlet Pimpernel▲
The Scarlet Pimpernel
The Scarlet Pimpernel 2: Mademoiselle Guillotine
The Scarlet Pimpernel 3: The Kidnapped King
The Sea Hawk▲
Sea Hound
The Secret of El Zorro
Shipwrecked
The Sign of Zorro
Sinbad and the Eye of the Tiger
Sinbad, the Sailor▲
Son of Ali Baba
Son of Captain Blood
Son of Fury▲
The Son of Monte Cristo
Son of Zorro
South of Pago Pago
South Seas Massacre
The Spanish Main
The Story of Robin Hood & His Merrie Men▲
Swashbuckler
The Swiss Family Robinson▲
Sword & the Sorcerer
Sword of Sherwood Forest
The Swordsman
Tharus Son of Attila
Three Amigos
The Three Musketeers
The Three Musketeers▲
The Three Musketeers
The Three Musketeers▲
The Three Musketeers
Tiger of the Seven Seas
Treasure Island▲
Treasure Island
Treasure of the Golden Condor
Treasure of the Moon Goddess
Two Lost Worlds
Under the Red Robe
Wallaby Jim of the Islands
The Warriors
The Wicked Lady
Yellowbeard
Zorro
Zorro, the Gay Blade

Swimming

***see also** Deep Blue; Go Fish; Island Fare; Killer Sea Critters; Lifeguards; Pacific Islands*
Alex
Barracuda
Bathing Beauty
The Bridges at Toko-Ri▲
Cocoon▲
Dangerous When Wet
Dawn!
Easy to Love
Gremlins▲
Jaws▲
The Man from Atlantis
Million Dollar Mermaid
Neptune's Daughter
Off the Mark
Sea People
Splash
Swim Team
The Swimmer▲
Thrill of a Romance

Swingers

Barfly▲
Bob & Carol & Ted & Alice
A Change of Seasons
Eating Raoul▲
Group Marriage
Invasion of the Bee Girls▲
Looking for Mr. Goodbar
9 1/2 Weeks
The Party▲
The Swap
The Swinging Cheerleaders
The Unfaithfuls
Your Friends & Neighbors▲

Sword & Sandal

Ali Baba and the Forty Thieves
Ali Baba and the 40 Thieves▲
Alone Against Rome
Arabian Nights
The Avenger
Battle of Valiant
Colossus and the Amazon Queen
Colossus of the Arena
Coriolanus, Man without a Country
Duel of Champions
Fabiola▲
Fire Monsters Against the Son of Hercules
Giants of Rome
Gladiator▲
Gladiator of Rome
Gladiators 7
Goliath Against the Giants
Goliath and the Barbarians
Goliath and the Dragon
Goliath and the Sins of Babylon
Gor
Hercules
Hercules against the Moon Men
Hercules and the Captive Women
Hercules and the Princess of Troy
Hercules in the Haunted World
Hercules, Prisoner of Evil
Hercules Unchained
Hercules vs. the Sons of the Sun
Hero of Rome
The Invincible Gladiator
The Last Days of Pompeii
Revenge of the Barbarians
Revolt of the Barbarians
Roland the Mighty
Samson
Samson Against the Sheik
Samson and His Mighty Challenge
Samson and the 7 Miracles of the World
The Scorpion King
Sins of Rome
Son of Ali Baba
Son of Hercules in the Land of Darkness
Sword of Venus
Terror of the Steppes
Thor and the Amazon Women
The Triumph of Hercules
The Trojan Horse

Sydney

***see also** Down Under*
Cosi▲
Don's Party▲
Floating Life
Joey
The Last Wave▲
Lilian's Story
Me Myself I
Napoleon
Out of the Body
Over the Hill
Paperback Hero
The Road from Coorain
The Sum of Us▲
Young Einstein

Talking Animals

***see also** Wild Kingdom*
Animal Farm
Babe▲
Babe: Pig in the City
Cats & Dogs
Dinotopia
Dr. Dolittle
Dr. Dolittle 2
Francis Covers the Big Town
Francis Goes to the Races
Francis Goes to West Point
Francis in the Haunted House
Francis in the Navy
Francis Joins the WACs
Francis the Talking Mule▲
George of the Jungle▲
Homeward Bound 2: Lost in San Francisco
Homeward Bound: The Incredible Journey▲
Paulie
The Real Macaw
Sherlock: Undercover Dog
Stuart Little

Tattoos

Blue Tiger
Cape Fear▲
The Crow 2: City of Angels
Cyber Bandits
Down Periscope
Escape from L.A.
Foxfire

Tattoos

The Illustrated Man►
Lust in the Dust►
Memento►
The Night of the Hunter►
Skin Deep
Son-in-Law
Tattoo
Teresa's Tattoo
Waterworld
The Yakuza

Team Efforts

The Alamo►
The Bad News Bears Go to Japan
The Bad News Bears in Breaking Training
Breaking Away►
The Club►
Coach
Codename: Foxfire
Codename: Wildgeese
Crossfire
The Cutting Edge
The Dirty Dozen►
The Dirty Dozen: The Deadly Mission
The Dirty Dozen: The Fatal Mission
The Dirty Dozen: The Next Mission
Dirty Hands
The Doll Squad
D3: The Mighty Ducks
D2: The Mighty Ducks
Eddie
Finger on the Trigger
Force Five
Force 10 from Navarone
The Guns of Navarone►
Hoosiers►
Kill and Kill Again
Ladybugs
Let's Get Harry
The Losers
The Magnificent Seven►
Major League 3: Back to the Minors
Memphis Belle►
The Mighty Ducks
Miracle on Ice
The Mod Squad
Necessary Roughness
Race the Sun
Remember the Titans►
Renaissance Man
Seven Magnificent Gladiators
Seven Samurai►
Silverado►
The Sixth Man
Soldier Boyz
Space Jam
Steel
Sunset Park
That Thing You Do!►
Three the Hard Way
Twister
Uncommon Valor
The Untouchables►
Varsity Blues
Victory
White Squall
Wild Geese
Wild Geese 2
Wind

Tearjerkers

Acorn People
An Affair to Remember
After the Promise
All About My Mother►
All Dogs Go to Heaven
All Fall Down
All Mine to Give
Another Time, Another Place
Autumn in New York
Baby Face
Back Street
Balboa
Ballad in Blue
Bang the Drum Slowly
Bang the Drum Slowly►
Beaches►
Because of You
Big Bluff
Bittersweet Love
Black Eyes
Blind Spot
Blood of Jesus
Blossoms in the Dust
Bonjour Tristesse►
Bouquet of Barbed Wire
Breaking the Rules
Brian's Song►
The Cabin in the Cotton
Camille
Carrie►
Carry On Cruising
Cast the First Stone
The Champ►
The Champ
Change of Heart
Chantilly Lace
The Cheat►
Chinatown After Dark
Choices
Christmas Comes to Willow Creek
City That Never Sleeps
City Without Men
Claudia
Clown
Coquette
The Country Kid►
The Courtney Affair
Craig's Wife►
Crawlspace
Curly Sue
Dance Fools Dance►
Danielle Steel's Fine Things
Dead Wrong
Death Be Not Proud►
Dedee d'Anvers
Delinquent Parents
A Dog of Flanders
Dog Pound Shuffle►
An Early Frost►
Easy Virtue
The Eddy Duchin Story
Eric►
Escape Me Never
The Evening Star
Fire Down Below
Flamingo Road►
The Forbidden City
Forever Love
Fortune's Fool
Found Alive
Fourth Wish
Fulfillment
Gangs, Inc.
The Garden of Allah►
The Gathering
The Gathering: Part 2
Ghost►
Girl from Chicago
The Girl Who Had Everything
Goodbye, Mr. Chips►
Goodbye, My Lady
Great Day
The Greatest Question
Griffin and Phoenix: A Love Story
Harlow
Hearts of Humanity
Heaven and Earth
Heaven's a Drag
Hell-Ship Morgan
Her Silent Sacrifice
Here on Earth
High Gear
A Home of Our Own
Honky Tonk►
Hot Spell
Human Desire
Human Hearts
I Conquer the Sea
I Sent a Letter to My Love►
Ice Castles
If Ever I See You Again
Imitation of Life
In This Our Life
Inside Daisy Clover
Intermezzo►
Introducing Dorothy Dandridge►
Jack the Bear
Johnny Belinda►
Johnny Belinda
Johnny Eager►
Journey for Margaret►
Keep Punching
The Kid with the Broken Halo
La Bete Humaine►
La Chienne►
Lady Caroline Lamb
The Lady Without Camelias
The Last Best Year
Le Jour Se Leve►
Legends of the Fall
Leopard in the Snow
Leper
Letter from an Unknown Woman►
The Little Match Girl
The Little Princess►
A Little Princess►
Look Who's Talking Now
Looking for an Echo
Love Affair►
Love Affair
Love Affair: The Eleanor & Lou Gehrig Story►
Love Butcher
The Love Flower
Love Has Many Faces
The Love Light
Love Songs
Love Story►
Lovers of Their Time
Loving
Lure of the Sila
Madame Butterfly
Madame X
Magnificent Obsession
Man of Evil
The Manxman
Marvin's Room
Matters of the Heart
Mayerling
Mildred Pierce►
Miles to Go
Millie
Mimi
The Miniver Story
Miss Julie
Mrs. Silly
Mr. Holland's Opus►
Mr. Skeffington►
Mistress
Moon over Harlem
A Mormon Maid
Mother and Son
Murder on Lenox Avenue
The Nest
The Night Cry
Night Life in Reno
Nomads of the North
Now, Voyager►
Old Yeller►
One True Thing►
Only Angels Have Wings►
An Orphan Boy of Vienna
The Other Side of the Mountain
The Other Side of the Mountain, Part 2
Our Sons
Our Time
Paradise Road
The Passing of the Third Floor Back
Pattes Blanches
Peg o' My Heart
Penny Serenade►
A Place in the Sun►
The Pride of the Yankees►
The Promise
Question of Faith
A Question of Guilt
Quicksand
The Racket►
Rage of Angels
The Rains Came
Random Harvest►
Rebecca of Sunnybrook Farm
Red Kimono
Remolino de Pasiones
Rikisha-Man►
The Road to Ruin
Romola
Scar of Shame
Secrets of a Married Man
Seizure: The Story of Kathy Morris
Sex
Shadowlands►
She Goes to War
A Shining Season►
The Shock
Shopworn Angel►
Silent Night, Lonely Night
The Sin of Madelon Claudet►
Since You Went Away►
Six Weeks
Smilin' Through►
Sommersby
Sooner or Later
Sparrows►
Steel Magnolias►
Stella
Stella Dallas►
Stella Maris►
Stolen Hours
The Story of Esther Costello
Strangers: The Story of a Mother and Daughter►
Stromboli
Struggle
Suds
Summer and Smoke
A Summer Place
Sunny
Sunny Skies
Susan Lenox: Her Fall and Rise
Sweet November
Tango
Tell Me That You Love Me
Tender Comrade
Terms of Endearment►
Test Tube Babies
That Certain Woman
They Drive by Night►
Things in Their Season
This Boy's Life►
Three Secrets
Thursday's Child
Tiefland
A Time to Live
To Gillian on Her 37th Birthday
Tomorrow's Children
The Tong Man
Torch Song
Toute Une Nuit►
Traffic in Souls►
Trapped by the Mormons
Under the Roofs of Paris►
The Underdog
The Unholy Three►
Untamed Heart
Uptown New York
The Visit►
Walk on the Wild Side
Walpurgis Night►
Waterfront
Waterloo Bridge►
Waterproof►
Way Down East►
The Weaker Sex
Welcome Home
West-Bound Limited
West of Zanzibar
When Wolves Cry
Where East Is East
Where the Red Fern Grows
The White Cliffs of Dover►
The White Rose►
Wide Sargasso Sea
Winter Meeting
Without a Trace
A Woman of Affairs
The World Accuses
The World Is Full of Married Men
The World Owes Me a Living
Written on the Wind►
X, Y & Zee
The Yarn Princess
The Yearling►

Technology—Rampant

see also *Computers; Killer Appliances; Robots & Androids*

A Nous la Liberte►
The Android Affair
Armageddon: The Final Challenge
Assassin
Attack of the Killer Refrigerator
Attack of the Robots
Baby Girl Scott
Back to the Future►
Batman Forever►
Best Defense
Bicentennial Man
The Bionic Woman
Black Cobra 3: The Manila Connection
The Black Hole
Blade Runner►
Blades
Bloodlust
Brainscan
Breakout
Bullet to Beijing
Chameleon
Chameleon 2: Death Match
Chameleon 3: Dark Angel
Chandu the Magician
Charly►
Chopping Mall
Circuitry Man
Colossus: The Forbin Project►
The Companion
Computer Beach Party
Computer Wizard
The Corporation
Crash and Burn
The Creation of the Humanoids
Cyber Bandits
Cyber-Tracker 2
Dean Koontz's Black River
Dean Koontz's Mr. Murder
Death Ray 2000
Defense Play
Demon Seed►
Denise Calls Up
Detonator 2: Night Watch
Diamonds Are Forever►
Digital Man
Dr. Goldfoot and the Bikini Machine
Doctor of Doom
Doomsdayer
Downdraft
Dream House
Dungeonmaster
Duplicates
Electric Dreams
The Eliminators
Enemy of the State
Eve of Destruction
Evolver
Fail-Safe►
Fair Game
Family Viewing►
Fatal Error
The Fifth Element
Final Mission
The Final Programme
The Fly►
The Fly►
The Fly 2
Fugitive Mind
Future Cop
Futureworld
Geheimakte WB1
Ghost in the Machine
Goldeneye►
Hackers
Hide and Seek
Hologram Man
Hostile Intent
How to Make a Monster
Improper Channels
Interface
The Invisible Boy
Johnny Mnemonic
Johnny 2.0
A Joke of Destiny, Lying in Wait Around the Corner Like a Bandit
Judge Dredd
A King in New York
Lawnmower Man 2: Beyond Cyberspace
The Lift
Live Wire: Human Timebomb
Lost in Space
Lost Legacy: A Girl Called Hatter Fox
The Matrix►
Maximum Overdrive
Metropolis►
Microwave Massacre
Mr. Toad's Wild Ride
Modern Times►
Mon Oncle►
Moonraker
The Mosaic Project
The Munsters' Revenge
Murder by Phone
Murder by Television
Mutant Hunt
Mutant Species
The Net
New Crime City: Los Angeles 2020
Night of the Kickfighters
Nightflyers
One Deadly Owner
Out of Order
Panique►
The Philadelphia Experiment
The Pirates of Silicon Valley
Plughead Rewired: Circuitry Man 2
The Power Within
Project: Eliminator
Project: Shadowchaser
The Quiet Earth►
Rage
Ravager
Redline
Remote
Replikator: Cloned to Kill
Resident Evil
RoboCop►
RoboCop 2
RoboCop 3
Robot Holocaust
Robot Jox
Rock & Roll Cowboys
R.O.T.O.R.
Runaway
Screamers
Search and Destroy
The Seventh Floor
Shadowzone
Shaker Run
Shocker
Short Circuit
Short Circuit 2
Small Soldiers
Smart House
Sneakers
Soldier
Solo
Speaking Parts►
Speed 2: Cruise Control
The Spy Who Loved Me
Stay Tuned
Steel and Lace
Strange New World
Terminal Choice
Terminal Entry
Terminal Impact
The Terminal Man
The Terminator►
Terrorvision
Things to Come►
The Thirteenth Floor
Thrillkill
Tom Clancy's Netforce
Touki Bouki
Tron
12:01
Twisted
2001: A Space Odyssey►
The Ultimate Imposter
The Unborn
Under Siege 2: Dark Territory
The Vindicator
Virtual Sexuality
Virtuosity
WarGames
Warning Sign
Webmaster
Weird Science
Westworld►
Wild Palms
Wired to Kill
Zardoz

Teen Angst

see also *Coming of Age; Hell High School*

Above the Rim
Abuse
Across the Tracks
Address Unknown
Adventures in Dinosaur City
The Adventures of Sebastian Cole
The Adventures of Werner Holt
Age Isn't Everything
Ah, Wilderness!▲
Airborne
Alex
All Over Me▲
All Things Fair
American Beauty▲
American Graffiti▲
American Pie▲
American Pie 2
An American Rhapsody▲
An American Summer
American Virgin
Amor Bandido
Andy Hardy Gets Spring Fever
Andy Hardy Meets Debutante
Andy Hardy's Double Life
Andy Hardy's Private Secretary
Angel
Angels with Dirty Faces▲
Angus
Annie O
Anything for Love
Anywhere But Here
Apt Pupil
Around the Fire
Art for Teachers of Children
Arthur's Quest
Autumn Moon
Baby It's You▲
The Baby-Sitters' Club
The Bachelor and the Bobby-Soxer▲
Backstreet Dreams
Bad Boys▲
Bad Ronald▲
The Basketball Diaries
Battle of the Bullies
The Bay Boy
Beach Blanket Bingo▲
Beach House
Beach Party
The Beat
Beau Pere▲
Beautiful Thing▲
Before and After
Bellyfruit
The Beniker Gang
Berserker
The Best Little Girl in the World▲
Better Off Dead
Beyond Innocence
The Big Bet
Big Bully
Big Fat Liar
Big Girls Don't Cry...They Get Even
Big Town
Bikini Beach
Bill & Ted's Excellent Adventure
Blackboard Jungle▲
Bleeding Hearts
Blood of Dracula
BMX Bandits
Body Snatchers
Book of Love
Born Bad
Born Innocent
Born to Be Wild
Boston Kickout
A Boy Called Hate
Boys
The Boys Club
Boys Life
Boy's Reformatory
Boyz N the Hood▲
The Brady Bunch Movie▲
Brainscan
The Break
The Breakfast Club▲
Breaking All the Rules
Breaking Away▲
Breaking Free
The Bridge
Brotherhood of Justice
Buck and the Magic Bracelet
Buffy the Vampire Slayer▲
Bully
The Bumblebee Flies Anyway
Burglar▲
Buster and Billie
But I'm a Cheerleader
Buying Time
By Dawn's Early Light
Bye, Bye, Birdie▲
Cadillac Girls
Can You Feel Me Dancing?
Candy
Can't Buy Me Love
Can't Hardly Wait
The Canterville Ghost
Captain Nuke and the Bomber Boys
Career Opportunities
Carrie▲
Carried Away
Cave Girl
The Cement Garden
The Chalk Garden▲
Cherry Falls
The Chicken Chronicles
Children of the Corn 2: The Final Sacrifice
China, My Sorrow
Choices
The Choppers
The Chosen▲
Christine
Class
The Class of Miss MacMichael
Clayton County Line
Clockstoppers
The Club
Clueless▲
Condemned to Hell
Coneheads
The Cool World
Cooley High▲
Corvette Summer
Cotton Candy
The Craft
crazy/beautiful
Cries of Silence
Crime and Punishment in Suburbia
Cruel Intentions
Cruel Intentions 2
The Cruel Story of Youth▲
The Crush
Cry-Baby▲
A Cry in the Wild▲
The Cure
The Curfew Breakers
Dance Me Outside
Dancer, Texas—Pop. 81▲
A Dangerous Age
Dangerous Curves
The Dangerous Lives of Altar Boys
Dangerous Minds
A Dangerous Place
Dangerous Youth
Dangerously Close
Dario Argento's Trauma
Dark Horse
Date Bait
A Date with Judy
Daughter of Death
The Day My Parents Ran Away
Dazed and Confused▲
Dead Beat
Dead End▲
Dead Poets Society▲
Deadly Weapon
Deal of a Lifetime
Death Wish Club
The Deep End▲
Defense Play
The Defilers
Delinquent Daughters
Delivery Boys
Desert Bloom▲
Desert Blue
Desperate Lives
Detroit Rock City
The Devil on Wheels
The Devil's Arithmetic
The Devil's Sleep
The Diary of Anne Frank▲
Dick▲
Diner▲
Dino
The Disenchanted
Diving In
Dogs in Space
Doin' Time on Planet Earth
Donnie Darko▲
Don't Tell Mom the Babysitter's Dead
The Doom Generation▲
Double Platinum
Double Play
Dracula A.D. 1972
Dream Date
Dream Machine
Dream to Believe
Drive-In
Drive Me Crazy
Dudes
Dutch
Dutch Girls
East of Eden▲
East of Eden
East Side Kids
Eban and Charley
The Echo of Thunder
Eden Valley▲
Edge of Seventeen
The Effect of Gamma Rays on Man-in-the-Moon Marigolds▲
Eight Days a Week
Empire Records
Encino Man
Endless Love
The Ernest Green Story
The Escape Artist▲
Escape from El Diablo
E.T.: The Extra-Terrestrial▲
Every Mother's Worst Fear
Evils of the Night
Eyes of the Panther
Eyes Right!
The Faculty
Fall Time
Fame▲
Family Life
Fast Talking
Fast Times at Ridgemont High▲
Father's Day
Fear
Fear No Evil
Fear Runs Silent
Fellini's Roma
Ferris Bueller's Day Off▲
Fighting Elegy
Final Destination
Final Exam
Fire with Fire
First Daughter
The First Time
5 Dark Souls
The Flamingo Kid▲
Flash
Flipper▲
Flirting▲
The Fly 2
Fly with the Hawk
Footloose
For Keeps
Force of Impulse
Forever
Four Days
Foxes
Foxfire
The Franchise Affair
Frankenstein Reborn
Free of Eden
Freeway
Freeze Frame
Friends
Friends Forever▲
A Friendship in Vienna
From the Edge of the City
Fun
Galgameth
Gas Food Lodging▲
Gate 2
Get Over It!
Get Real
Ghost World▲
Girl
Girl from Hunan▲
Girl, Interrupted
A Girl of the Limberlost
The Girl, the Body and the Pill
Girlfriend from Hell
Girls Just Want to Have Fun
Girls Town
Gleaming the Cube
Good Burger
The Goodbye Bird
Goodbye, Miss 4th of July
A Goofy Movie
Grease▲
Grease 2
Gregory's Girl▲
The Guinea Pig
Gummo
Hackers
Hadley's Rebellion
Hairspray▲
The Halfback of Notre Dame
Halloween▲
Halloween 6: The Curse of Michael Myers
The Hanging Garden
Hard Knocks
Hardcore
Harley
He Got Game
Head On▲
Heathers▲
Heavenly Creatures▲
The Heavenly Kid
Heavyweights
Here on Earth
Hide and Go Shriek
High School Caesar
High School Confidential
High School USA
Hollywood High
Hollywood High, Part 2
The Hollywood Knights
A Home of Our Own
Hometown U.S.A.
Homework
Hoop Dreams▲
Hoosiers▲
Hornet's Nest
The Horse Whisperer
Hot Bubblegum
Hot Summer
Hot Times
How I Got into College
How to Stuff a Wild Bikini
Hurricane Streets
I Accuse My Parents
I Am the Cheese
I Never Promised You a Rose Garden▲
I Wanna Hold Your Hand
I Was a Teenage Werewolf
I Was a Teenage Zombie
If....▲
If Looks Could Kill
I'll Be Home for Christmas
Imaginary Crimes▲
The Impossible Years
The In Crowd
In His Father's Shoes
In the Land of the Owl Turds
The Incredibly True Adventure of Two Girls in Love
The Inkwell
The Invisible Kid
Iron Eagle 4
It Came from the Sky
I've Been Waiting for You
Jailbait!
Jailbreakers
Jawbreaker
Jennifer
Jimmy Zip
Joe the King
Johnny 100 Pesos
Just Another Girl on the I.R.T.
Just for the Hell of It
Just Looking
Just One of the Girls
Kansas
Kevin & Perry Go Large
The Kid
Kid Dynamite
A Kid in King Arthur's Court
Kids
Kill Me Tomorrow
Kim
King Creole
Kitten with a Whip
Knights & Emeralds
La Bamba▲
La Petite Sirene
La Promesse
L'Amour en Herbe
Lantern Hill
The Last Best Sunday
Last Cry for Help
The Last of the High Kings
Last Summer
Lauderdale
The Lawrenceville Stories
L'Eleve
Les Enfants Terrible▲
Les Mistons▲
Liar's Edge
License to Drive
L.I.E.
Life as a House
Life Begins for Andy Hardy▲
Light It Up
Limbo
Lisa
Little Darlings
Little Men
The Little Mermaid▲
A Little Romance▲
Little Sweetheart
The Little Thief▲
The Little Valentino
Little Witches
The Loneliest Runner
The Loneliness of the Long Distance Runner▲
Loners
Looking for Miracles
Loose Screws
Losin' It
Lost and Delirious
Lost Angels
The Lost Boys
Love Laughs at Andy Hardy
Love Under Pressure
Lovelines
Lover Girl
Lucas▲
Mad About You
Mad Love
Mad Youth
Made in USA
Magenta
Magic Kid 2
Major Payne
Making the Grade
Malibu Beach
Man from Texas
The Man in the Attic
The Man in the Moon▲
Mandragora
The Manhattan Project
Manny & Lo▲
Marie Baie des Anges
Married Too Young
Marvin's Room
Masterminds
Meatballs
Meatballs 2
Meatballs 3
Meatballs 4
The Member of the Wedding▲
The Member of the Wedding
Mermaids▲
Metropolitan▲
Min & Bill
The Miracle
Mirror, Mirror
Mischief
Misfits of Science
Miss A & Miss M
Miss Annie Rooney
Model Behavior
Mommy 2: Mommy's Day
Mon Oncle Antoine▲
Monika
Monkey Business▲
Morgan Stewart's Coming Home
Mortal Danger
Motorcycle Gang
Mouchette▲
Murder in New Hampshire: The Pamela Smart Story
Muscle Beach Party
My American Cousin▲
My Antonia
My Best Friend Is a Vampire
My Boyfriend's Back
My Boys Are Good Boys
My Date with the President's Daughter
My Father, My Rival
My Father the Hero
My First Mister
My Girl 2
My Own Private Idaho▲
My Science Project
My Teacher's Wife
My Uncle: The Alien
Mystery Date
Mystic Pizza▲
Naked Youth
National Lampoon's Senior Trip
Nenette and Boni▲
The Neon Bible
Never Been Kissed
New Jersey Drive
New Waterford Girl
The Next Karate Kid
Nice Girls Don't Explode
Nickel Mountain
The Night Before
Night Friend
A Night in the Life of Jimmy Reardon
Night Life
Night of Evil
Night of the Twisters
Nightbreed
A Nightmare on Elm Street 2: Freddy's Revenge
A Nightmare on Elm Street 3: Dream Warriors
A Nightmare on Elm Street 4: Dream Master
A Nightmare on Elm Street 5: Dream Child
1969▲
No Big Deal
No Laughing Matter
Nobody's Perfect
Not Another Teen Movie
Not My Kid
Now and Then
Nowhere
Nowhere to Run
O.C. and Stiggs
October Sky▲
Odd Birds
Ode to Billy Joe
On My Own
On the Edge
On the Edge: The Survival of Dana
One Crazy Night
One Crazy Summer
One Dark Night
Only the Brave
Only the Strong
Ordinary Magic
The Other Side of Sunday
Our Song▲
Our Time
Our Very Own
Outside Chance of Maximillian Glick
Outside Providence
The Outsiders
Over the Edge▲
Over the Summer
The Pact
Pajama Party
Palm Springs Weekend
The Paper Brigade
Paradise Motel
Parenthood▲
Party! Party!
Pathfinder▲
Pecker
Peggy Sue Got Married
The People Next Door
Peppermint Soda▲
Petits Freres
Phantom 2040 Movie: The Ghost Who Walks
Phat Beach
A Pig's Tale
Pin...
Pippin▲
Platypus Cove
Playing for Keeps
Playing with Fire

Poison Ivy
Pom Pom Girls
Porky's
Porky's 2: The Next Day
The Positively True Adventures of the Alleged Texas Cheerleader-Murdering Mom▲
Pot, Parents, and Police
Powder
The Power Within
Prayer of the Rollerboys
Pretty in Pink
Pretty Smart
The Prime of Miss Jean Brodie▲
The Prime Time
The Prince and the Surfer
Princes in Exile
The Princess Diaries
Prison for Children
Psycho Beach Party
Puberty Blues
Pump Up the Volume
Pups
Quarterback Princess
Race the Sun
Racing with the Moon▲
Rad
The Rage: Carrie 2
Rambling Rose▲
Ratz
Rebel without a Cause▲
Reckless
Red Kiss▲
Remembering the Cosmos Flower
Return to Horror High
Return to the Blue Lagoon
Revenge of the Living Zombies
Ripe
River's Edge▲
Roadhouse 66
Robin of Locksley
Rock 'n' Roll High School Forever
Rock, Rock, Rock
Rockula
Rodrigo D.: No Future
Romeo and Juliet
Romeo and Juliet▲
Ronnie and Julie
Rooftops
Rosetta
Rosie
Roustabout
Ruby Jean and Joe
The Run of the Country▲
Running Mates▲
Rushmore▲
Sabrina the Teenage Witch
Save the Last Dance
Say Anything▲
Scarred
Scary Movie
Scream for Help
Screen Test
Screwballs
Season of Change
Secret Admirer
The Secret Life of Girls
Secrets of Sweet Sixteen
Seizure: The Story of Kathy Morris
Senior Trip
Set Me Free
Seven Minutes in Heaven
Seventeen Again
The Seventh Coin
S.F.W.
ShadowZone: The Undead Express
Shag: The Movie▲
Shake, Rattle and Rock
Shake, Rattle & Rock!
Sharma & Beyond
Sharon's Secret
She's All That
She's Out of Control
Shine▲
Shooting
Shout
Show Me Love
Shriek If You Know What I Did Last Friday the 13th
Silence of the Heart▲
The Silent One
Sing
Sixteen Candles▲
Skateboard
Skeletons in the Closet
Skipped Parts
SLC Punk!
Sleepers
Small Faces▲
Small Soldiers
Smokey Bites the Dust
Smugglers' Cove▲
Snowballing
Social Misfits
Solarbabies
Some Kind of Wonderful
Somebody Is Waiting
Something Special
Sooner or Later
The Spell
Spetters
Spirit Rider▲
Splendor in the Grass▲
Spring Fever
Squeeze
Stand and Deliver▲
Starchaser: The Legend of Orin
State and Main▲
Stealing Beauty
Stella Does Tricks
Sticks and Stones
Sticky Fingers
Still Not Quite Human
Stones of Death
Straight out of Brooklyn
Straight Up
Strange Illusion
Strawberry Fields
Streets
The Stripper
Student Bodies
Suburbia
Sugar & Spice▲
Summer Camp Nightmare
Summer Holiday
Summer of '42▲
The Summer of My German Soldier▲
Summer School
Sunchaser
Sunnyside
Swap Meet
Sweet Jane
Sweet 16
Swim Team
Swing Kids
A Swingin' Summer
Tadpole
Tainted Blood
Take It to the Limit
Talisman
Tammy and the T-Rex
Tearaway
Teen Wolf
Teenage
Teenage Bad Girl
Teenage Bonnie & Klepto Clyde
Teenage Caveman
Teenage Crime Wave
Teenage Doll
Teenage Mother
Teenage Mutant Ninja Turtles 2: The Secret of the Ooze
Teenage Strangler
Teenage Wolfpack
Teenager
Teenagers from Outer Space
Telling Lies in America
The Tender Age
Terminal Bliss
Tex
That Certain Age
That Darn Cat
That Night
That Thing You Do!▲
That Was Then...This Is Now
There Goes My Baby
Therese & Isabelle
They Made Me a Criminal
36 Fillete▲
This Boy's Life▲
This Special Friendship
Thrashin'
3:15—The Moment of Truth
Three o'Clock High
Tiger Heart
Time at the Top
Time Stands Still▲
Timeless
Times Square
To Die For▲
To Gillian on Her 37th Birthday
To Play or to Die
The Toilers and the Wayfarers
Tom Brown's School Days▲
Too Young to Die
Totally F***ed Up
Toughlove
Toy Soldiers
Trading Favors
Treasure Island
Trojan War
Troop Beverly Hills
The Trouble with Angels
True Crime
Trust
The Truth About Jane
24-7
Twirl
Twist & Shout▲
Twisted
Twisted Love
Two Friends
Two Hands▲
Uncle Buck▲
Under the Boardwalk
Under the Domim Tree
Unfinished Business
Unstrung Heroes
Up Against the Wall
Uptown Angel
Valley Girl
The Vals
The Van
Varsity Blues
A Very Brady Sequel
Village of the Giants
Virgin High
The Virgin Suicides
Virtual Sexuality
Vision Quest
The Voyage of the Yes
A Walk to Remember
Walking Back
Wanderers▲
The War Zone
Warriors of Virtue
Weird Science
Welcome Home, Roxy Carmichael
Welcome to 18
West Beirut
Whatever
Whatever It Takes
Where Angels Go, Trouble Follows
Where the Boys Are '84
Where the Day Takes You
White Squall
White Wolves 2: Legend of the Wild
White Wolves 3: Cry of the White Wolf
The Wild Life
Wild Ones on Wheels
Wild Pony
Wildflowers
William Shakespeare's Romeo and Juliet▲
Windrunner
Wish upon a Star
Wish You Were Here▲
The Wooden Gun
The Wounds
The Wraith
X-Men
Xiu Xiu: The Sent Down Girl▲
The Year My Voice Broke▲
Yellow
A Young Connecticut Yankee in King Arthur's Court
The Young Graduates
Young Guns
Young Hercules
Young Love, First Love
The Young Poisoner's Handbook▲
Youngblood
Youth Aflame
Youth on Parole
You've Ruined Me, Eddie
Zebrahead▲
Zero Boys
Zombie Nightmare
The Zoo Gang

Teen Horror

***see also** Hell High School; Horror Comedy; Teen Angst*

Cherry Falls
Dead Silence
Disturbing Behavior
Ginger Snaps
The Glass House
I Know What You Did Last Summer▲
I Still Know What You Did Last Summer
Scream▲
Wishmaster 3: Beyond the Gates of Hell

Television

***see** Mass Media; TV Pilot Movies; TV Series*

Tennis

The Break
Jocks
Nobody's Perfect
Players
Racquet
Spring Fever
The Witches of Eastwick

Terminal Confusion

Big Trouble
Dumb & Dumber
8 Heads in a Duffel Bag
Home Alone 3
The Out-of-Towners
Wait until Dark▲
What's Up, Doc?▲

Terminal Illness

***see also** Disease of the Week*

Beaches▲
Because of You
Blow Dry
Boom!
The Bumblebee Flies Anyway
Chinese Box
The Claim
Dying Young
The End of the Affair▲
Girls' Night
Hard Luck
Here on Earth
Hong Kong 1941
Igby Goes Down
In the Shadows
Late August, Early September
Life as a House
Magnolia▲
Mr. Rice's Secret
Moulin Rouge
My First Mister
Never Say Die
One True Thing▲
Perfume
The Settlement
Soft Fruit
Stealing Beauty
Stepmom▲
Sweet November
Terms of Endearment▲
The Theory of Flight
Things You Can Tell Just by Looking at Her
Tuesdays with Morrie
The Visit▲
A Walk to Remember
The Wings of the Dove▲
Wit▲

Terror in Tall Buildings

***see also** Elevators; Mystery & Suspense*

Blackout
Die Hard▲
Firetrap
Hard to Die
Poltergeist 3
Project: Shadowchaser
Skyscraper
Speed▲
Terror on the 40th Floor
Tower of Terror
The Towering Inferno

Terrorism

***see also** Crime & Criminals; Foreign Intrigue; Spies & Espionage*

Act of Passion: The Lost Honor of Kathryn Beck
Act of Piracy
Act of War
Active Stealth
Agent Red
Air Force One▲
Airborne
Airboss
Airheads
The Amateur
Angel of Fury
The Applegates
Arlington Road
The Assassination Run
The Assignment
Bad Company
Barcelona▲
Belfast Assassin
Black Cobra 2
Black Cobra 3: The Manila Connection
Black Sunday
Black Terrorist
Blast
Blink of an Eye
Blood on the Badge
Bloodfist 6: Ground Zero
Blown Away
Bombshell
Captain America 2: Death Too Soon
Captive
Captive Rage
The Cassandra Crossing
Children of Rage
C.I.A. 2: Target Alexa
Circle of Deceit
Codename: Vengeance
Collateral Damage
Commando▲
Could It Happen Here?
Cover-Up
Covert Assassin
Crackerjack 2
Crash and Burn
Crash & Byrnes
Crash Dive
Cry of the Innocent▲
The Crying Game▲
Dark Rider
Deadline
Deadly Heroes
Deadly Outbreak
Death Before Dishonor
The Death Merchant
Death of the Incredible Hulk
Death Ray
Delta Force
Delta Force 3: The Killing Game
Delta Force Commando
Delta Force Commando 2
Demolition High
Desert Thunder
The Devil's Own▲
Dick Barton, Special Agent
Die Hard▲
Die Hard 2: Die Harder▲
Die Hard: With a Vengeance
Diplomatic Siege
Dirty Games
Dr. Otto & the Riddle of the Gloom Beam
Dog Day Afternoon▲
The Dogfighters
Double Team
D.R.E.A.M. Team
The Enforcer
Eraser
Escape under Pressure
The Evil That Men Do
Executive Decision
Exposed
Extreme Limits
Face/Off▲
Falling Fire
Fast Kill
A Father's Revenge
ffolkes
The Final Cut
The Final Option
Final Voyage
Flashpoint Africa
Fortress of Amerikka
48 Hours to Live
Freedom Strike
French Quarter Undercover
Full Disclosure
Full Fathom Five
Futuresport
Galyon
Germicide
The Glass Jungle
The Glory Boys
Held Hostage
Hell Squad
Hidden Agenda
Hologram Man
Hostage
Human Bomb
In the Name of the Father▲
Invasion Force
Invasion U.S.A.
Invisible Circus
Iran: Days of Crisis
Jericho Fever
Judgment in Berlin
Juggernaut▲
July Group
Jungle Assault
Kamikaze '89▲
Katherine
The Kidnapping of the President
Kings and Desperate Men
Knock Off
Land of the Free
L'Anne Sainte
The Legend of Rita
Lethal Tender
The Little Drummer Girl▲
Live Wire
The Lost Command
The Mad Bomber
The Man Who Knew Too Little
Marianne and Juliane▲
McHale's Navy
Memorial Day
Merchants of War
Michael Collins▲
Midnight in Saint Petersburg
Molly Maguires
Murder on Flight 502
My Brother's War
Naked Gun 33 1/3: The Final Insult
Navy SEALS
Night of the Assassin
Nighthawks
Nightstick
Ninja Connection
Ninja the Battalion
No
No Contest
No Dead Heroes
Odd Man Out▲
Omega Syndrome
Once Upon a Time in China II▲
Open Fire
Operation Thunderbolt
Panic in the Streets▲
Panic on the 5:22
The Passenger▲
Passenger 57
Path to Paradise
The Patriot
Patriot Games▲
Patty Hearst
The Peacekeeper
The Peacemaker
Programmed to Kill

▲ = rated three bones or higher

Teenage Mutant Ninja Turtles 3
The Terminator▲
Terminator 2: Judgment Day▲
Test Tube Teens from the Year 2000
The Thirteenth Floor
The Three Stooges Meet Hercules
Thrill Seekers
Time After Time▲
Time at the Top
Time Bandits
Time Chasers
The Time Guardian
The Time Machine▲
Time Machine
The Time Machine
Time Runner
Time Tracers
Time Trackers
The Time Travelers
Timecop
Timemaster
Timerider
Timestalkers
The Tomorrow Man
Total Reality
Trancers
Trancers 2: The Return of Jack Deth
Trancers 3: Deth Lives
Trancers 4: Jack of Swords
Trancers 5: Sudden Deth
12 Monkeys▲
12:01
Twice upon a Yesterday
Unidentified Flying Oddball
The Visitors
Warlock
Waxwork 2: Lost in Time
When Time Expires
A Witch Without a Broom
Yor, the Hunter from the Future
A Young Connecticut Yankee in King Arthur's Court

Time Warped

Austin Powers: International Man of Mystery▲
Austin Powers 2: The Spy Who Shagged Me▲
Black Knight
Blast from the Past
The Brady Bunch Movie▲
Demolition Man
Disney's The Kid
Encino Man
Forever Young
Groundhog Day▲
Kate & Leopold
Late for Dinner
Leave It to Beaver
Peggy Sue Got Married
Pleasantville▲
Retroactive
The Two Worlds of Jenny Logan
A Very Brady Sequel

Titanic

The Chambermaid on the Titanic
A Night to Remember▲
Raise the Titanic
S.O.S. Titanic
Titanic▲
Titanic
Titanic▲
The Unsinkable Molly Brown▲

To the Moon!

***see also** Space Operas*
The Adventures of Baron Munchausen▲
The Adventures of Pluto Nash
Alien Fury: Countdown to Invasion
Apollo 13▲
Beyond the Stars
Cat Women of the Moon
Countdown
Dark Side of the Moon
Destination Moon
Destination Moonbase Alpha
The Dish▲
First Men in the Moon
From the Earth to the Moon
From the Earth to the Moon▲
Missile to the Moon
Moon Pilot
The Mouse on the Moon▲
Project Moon Base
Quatermass 2▲
Radar Men from the Moon
They Came from Beyond Space

Tokyo

***see also** Japan*
Akira
Angel Dust
An Autumn Afternoon▲
The Bad News Bears Go to Japan
Black Lizard
Black Rain
Dodes 'ka-den▲
Escapade in Japan
Gamera vs. Barugon
Gappa the Trifibian Monster
Ghidrah the Three Headed Monster
Godzilla, King of the Monsters
Godzilla 2000▲
Godzilla vs. King Ghidora
Godzilla vs. Megalon
H-Man
Mothra▲
Okoge
One Wonderful Sunday
Otaku No Video▲
Proof of the Man
Running Brave
Street of Shame▲
A Taxing Woman's Return▲
Thirty Seconds Over Tokyo▲
Tokyo Decadence
Tokyo-Ga▲
Tokyo Joe
Tokyo Pop
Tokyo Story▲
War of the Gargantuas

Torn in Two (or More)

Abbott and Costello Meet Dr. Jekyll and Mr. Hyde
Batman Forever▲
Carbon Copy
Color of Night
Dr. Heckyl and Mr. Hype
Dr. Jekyll and Ms. Hyde
Dr. Jekyll and Mr. Hyde▲
Dr. Jekyll and Mr. Hyde
Dr. Jekyll and Sister Hyde
Edge of Sanity
Exorcist 3: Legion
The Five of Me
I, Monster▲
Jekyll and Hyde
Luna e L'Altra
Mary Reilly
Me, Myself, and Irene▲
Mirage
Multiplicity
Never Talk to Strangers
The Nutty Professor▲
Nutty Professor 2: The Klumps
Passion of Mind
Primal Fear
Psycho Beach Party
Raising Cain
Separate Lives
Shattered Image
Spider-Man▲
Sybil▲
The Three Faces of Eve
Three Lives and Only One Death
The Three Lives of Karen
Tierra
Voices from a Locked Room

Toronto

***see also** Canada*
Exotica▲
Last Night▲
The Life Before This
The Newton Boys
Paris, France
Rude
Skin Deep
Soul Survivor

Torrid Love Scenes

***see also** Sex & Sexuality; Sex on the Beach; Sexploitation*
The Adventurers
Against All Odds
Alien Prey
Angel Heart
Atlantic City▲
Basic Instinct
The Berlin Affair
Betty Blue▲
The Big Easy▲
Bitter Moon
Black Ice
Blue Velvet▲
Body Double▲
Body Heat▲
Body of Evidence
Bram Stoker's Dracula
Breathless
Broken English
Bull Durham▲
Cat Chaser
Cat on a Hot Tin Roof▲
Close My Eyes
Color of Night
The Cook, the Thief, His Wife & Her Lover▲
Crimes of Passion▲
Dark Obsession
Deadly Desire
The Dolphin
Dona Flor and Her Two Husbands▲
Don't Look Now▲
Everything Relative
The Executioner's Song
Exit to Eden
The Fabulous Baker Boys▲
Fatal Attraction▲
Five Easy Pieces▲
From Here to Eternity▲
Green Fire
The Harvest
Heat of Desire
Henry & June▲
The Hunting
In the Realm of the Senses▲
Jason's Lyric
Kiss Me a Killer
Lady Godiva Rides
Last Tango in Paris▲
Law of Desire▲
The Lawnmower Man
Live Flesh▲
The Lover
The Lovers▲
Mad Dog and Glory▲
The Mambo Kings▲
Men in Love
Moon in the Gutter
Moonstruck▲
Night Eyes 2
Night Eyes 3
9 1/2 Weeks
1900▲
An Officer and a Gentleman▲
The Pamela Principle
The Postman Always Rings Twice
Prizzi's Honor▲
Pyrates
Rage of Angels
Revenge
Risky Business▲
Sea of Love▲
Secrets
Sexual Response
Siesta
Sliver
Something Wild
The Story of O
Swept Away...▲
Tattoo
Tequila Sunrise
Threesome
The Unbearable Lightness of Being▲
White Palace
Wide Sargasso Sea
Wild at Heart▲
Wild Orchid
Wild Orchid 2: Two Shades of Blue
The Woman Next Door▲
Women & Men: In Love There Are No Rules
Women in Love▲
Year of the Gun
Zandalee

Toys

***see also** Killer Toys*
Babes in Toyland
Big▲
Child's Play
Child's Play 2
Dance of Death
Demonic Toys
Dolls
Dolly Dearest
Home Alone 3
Jingle All the Way
Josh Kirby...Time Warrior: Chapter 3, Trapped on Toyworld
Life-Size
Not Quite Human
Silent Night, Deadly Night 5: The Toymaker
The Toy
Toy Story▲
Toy Story 2▲
Toys
Wired to Kill

Tragedy

***see also** Drama; Tearjerkers*
Against the Wind
All the King's Men
Angel with the Trumpet
Anna Karenina▲
Baba▲
Bitter Sweet
Camille
Camille▲
Catherine Cookson's The Fifteen Streets
Celebrity
Charly▲
The Crucified Lovers▲
Damage▲
Danielle Steel's Palomino
Dark Odyssey
Deadman's Curve
Deep End▲
The Discovery Program
Dream Lovers
Dreaming of Joseph Lees
Dying Young
East of Eden▲
East of Eden
Effi Briest▲
El Amor Brujo▲
El Bruto
End of the Road
Enemies, a Love Story▲
Ernie Kovacs: Between the Laughter
Ethan Frome
Evangeline
Everybody's All American
The Fighting Sullivans▲
First Knight
Flowers of Reverie
Forbidden Choices
Franz
The French Lieutenant's Woman▲
From the Journals of Jean Seberg
Gandhi▲
Gate of Hell▲
Girl in Black
Golden Boy▲
A Good Day to Die
Hamlet▲
Hamlet
Hamlet▲
Hamlet
Harmony Lane
Henry IV
Hong Kong 1941
House of Cards
Howard's End▲
The Hunchback of Notre Dame
I Dreamed of Africa
Il Grido
In Memoriam
In the Bedroom▲
Intrigue and Love
Jalsaghar
Jude▲
Jude the Obscure
Jules and Jim▲
Julius Caesar▲
Julius Caesar
King Lear▲
King Lear
King Lear▲
Law of Desire▲
Leo Tolstoy's Anna Karenina
Love Is a Many-Splendored Thing
Love Story▲
Lovespell
Lush Life▲
Macbeth▲
Macbeth
Madame Bovary▲
Madame Butterfly
A Map of the World
Margaret's Museum▲
Maria Candelaria
Marilyn & Bobby: Her Final Affair
Martha and I▲
Mary of Scotland▲
The Merchant of Venice▲
Mother Night▲
The Mummy▲
The Nest
Night Ride Home
Nothing Personal▲
The Notorious Lady
O▲
Oedipus Rex▲
Onegin
Othello
Othello▲
Our Time
Pennies from Heaven▲
The Perfect Storm
Phaedra
Piece of Cake
A Place in the Sun▲
Princess Yang Kwei Fei▲
Queen Bee
Ran▲
The Red Violin
The Return of the Native
Romeo and Juliet▲
Romeo and Juliet
Romeo and Juliet▲
Savior▲
The Scarlet Tunic
The Secret Agent
Selena
Shadowlands▲
Shadows of Forgotten Ancestors▲
Shattered▲
The Shooting Party
Silent Tongue
Solomon and Gaenor
Stag
Stella
Sure Fire
The Sweet Hereafter▲
Swept from the Sea
Tess▲
Tess of the D'Urbervilles
Three Comrades▲
Throne of Blood▲
Tilai
Titanic▲
Tragedy of Flight 103: The Inside Story▲
Trois Couleurs: Bleu▲
Trojan Women
Turkish Delight
The Unknown Soldier
Variety▲
A Very Private Affair
The Virgin Spring▲
Voyager▲
The Walls of Malapaga
The War Zone
The Wedding Gift▲
Where Angels Fear to Tread▲
The White Cliffs of Dover▲
White Mile
The White Sister▲
William Shakespeare's Romeo and Juliet▲
A Woman at Her Window
The Woman Next Door▲
The Wooden Man's Bride
The World According to Garp▲
Wuthering Heights

Trains

***see also** Subways*
Across the Bridge
Alberto Express
Atomic Train
Avalanche Express
Before Sunrise
Berlin Express▲
Blood and Steel
Boxcar Bertha
The Brain
Breakheart Pass
Broken Arrow
Bullet to Beijing
Cafe Express
The Cassandra Crossing
Chattanooga Choo Choo
Closely Watched Trains▲
Color of a Brisk and Leaping Day
Courage Under Fire▲
Crackerjack 2
Dakota
Danger Lights
Daniel Takes a Train
Death Train
The Denver & Rio Grande
Detonator
The Dirty Dozen: The Fatal Mission
Emperor of the North Pole▲
End of the Line
Express to Terror
Finders Keepers
Flame Over India▲
The Flying Scotsman
Free Money
From Russia with Love▲
The Fugitive▲
The General▲
The Ghost and the Darkness
The Ghost Train
The Glory Trail
Go Kill and Come Back
Great K & A Train Robbery
The Great Locomotive Chase
The Great Train Robbery▲
The Grey Fox▲
The Harvey Girls▲
Horror Express
Hot Lead & Cold Feet
The Illusion Travels by Streetcar▲
Indiscretion of an American Wife
Inner Sanctum
Interrupted Journey
Jesse James at Bay
The Journey of Natty Gann▲
La Bete Humaine▲
The Lady Eve▲
Lady on a Train▲
The Lady Vanishes▲
The Lady Vanishes
The Major and the Minor▲
Malcolm
Man Who Loved Cat Dancing
Man Without a Star▲
Midnight Limited
The Millionaire's Express
Mrs. Winterbourne
Mouvements du Desir
Murder on the Midnight Express
Murder on the Orient Express▲
My Twentieth Century▲

 ▲ = rated three bones or higher

Mystery Mountain
Narrow Margin
The Newton Boys
Night Train to Munich➚
Night Train to Terror
Night Train to Venice
No. 17➚
The Odyssey of the Pacific
Oh, Mr. Porter
Once Upon a Time in the West➚
The Out-of-Towners
Panic on the 5:22
Paris Express
The Peacemaker
Phantom Express
Plunder Road
Prison Train
Railrodder➚
Red Signals
The Return of Casey Jones
Rhythm on the Range
The Road Home
The Road to Yesterday
Robbery
Romance on the Orient Express
Runaway Train➚
Running Scared
Saratoga Trunk
Shanghai Express➚
The Silver Streak
Silver Streak➚
The Sleeping Car
Sleeping Car to Trieste
Some Like It Hot➚
Strangers on a Train➚
Subway
Switchback
A Tale of Winter
Terror Train
Thomas and the Magic Railroad
Those Who Love Me Can Take the Train
Three for Bedroom C
3:10 to Yuma➚
Throw Momma from the Train➚
Thunder Over Texas
Torture Train
Tough Guys
Tracks
Trading Places
The Trail of the Lonesome Pine➚
The Train➚
The Train Killer
Train of Life
Train Robbers
Train to Tombstone
The Truce➚
Two Weeks to Live
Unbreakable
Under Siege 2: Dark Territory
Union Pacific➚
Von Ryan's Express➚
Warm Nights on a Slow-Moving Train
Without Reservations
Zentropa

Transvestites & Transsexuals

***see** Gender Bending*

Trapped with a Killer!

***see also** Psychotics/ Sociopaths*

Adrift
Air Force One➚
Alien Terminator
Blind Witness
Blink
Blood at Sundown
Blood Bride
Clue
Con Air➚
Copycat
Dead Calm➚
Deadbolt
Extremities
Eye of the Needle
Eyes of the Beholder
Fatal Attraction➚
Final Justice
Headless Body in Topless Bar
Hider in the House
Kalifornia
Kiss the Girls
Lifepod
The Maddening
Manhunter➚
Misery➚
Mute Witness
Narrow Margin
Pacific Heights➚
The Penthouse
The Shining
The Silence of the Lambs➚
Slaughter of the Innocents
Ten Little Indians
The Terror
Terror Train
Through the Eyes of a Killer
The Tie That Binds
Tracks of a Killer
Turbulence
Undertow
Unveiled
Virus
Voyage
Wait until Dark➚
What's the Matter with Helen?
When a Stranger Calls
When a Stranger Calls Back

Treasure Hunt

Abbott and Costello Meet the Mummy
Adventure of the Action Hunters
The Adventurers
After the Storm
All the Brothers Were Valiant
Big Mouth
Blue Jeans and Dynamite
Cabo Blanco
Call of the Wild
City Slickers 2: The Legend of Curly's Gold
Comin' Round the Mountain
Curse of the Crystal Eye
Cutthroat Island
The Diamond of Jeru
Diamonds
Double Trouble
Enemy Gold
Ernest Rides Again
Escape under Pressure
Finger on the Trigger
Forgotten City
Girls in Prison
Gold Diggers: The Secret of Bear Mountain
The Goonies
The Grave
Greedy
Green Fire
The Haunted Sea
Hear No Evil
Hunters of the Golden Cobra
Inside Out
The Jewel of the Nile
Kelly's Heroes
The Killing Grounds
Klondike Fever
Kull the Conqueror
Lara Croft: Tomb Raider
Legends of the North
Les Aventuriers
Lewis and Clark and George
Lust in the Dust➚
Max Is Missing
The Mermaids of Tiburon
Missing Pieces
The Mummy
Muppet Treasure Island
My Family Treasure
Naked Hills
Old Mother Riley's Jungle Treasure
One-Eyed Soldiers
Operation Condor
Operation Golden Phoenix
Pattern for Plunder
The Phantom of the Range
The Pink Jungle
Rat Race
The Ravagers
The Real Macaw
Romancing the Stone➚
Rudyard Kipling's The Jungle Book
Russell Mulcahy's Tale of the Mummy
Secre of the Andes
The Secret of the Golden Eagle
Secret of the Ice Cave
Shadow of Chikara
Slow Burn
Tarzan's Secret Treasure
Terror on Alcatraz
That Man from Rio
There Goes the Neighborhood
Thieves of Fortune
Tom and Huck➚
Treasure Island➚
Treasure Island
The Treasure of Jamaica Reef
The Treasure of Matecumbe
The Treasure of the Amazon
Treasure of the Four Crowns
Treasure of the Golden Condor
Treasure of the Sierra Madre➚
Treasure of the Yankee Zephyr
The Treasure Seekers
Trespass
The Triangle
Uninvited
Warrior Spirit
Whistling in Dixie
The Wrong Road

Trees & Forests

***see also** Wilderness*

Big Trees➚
The Burning Season➚
A Crack in the Floor
Crosscut
Dr. Dolittle 2
Dr. Tarr's Torture Dungeon
Equinox➚
Evil Dead
Family Tree
Fatal Passion
Fear Runs Silent
Ferngully: The Last Rain Forest
5 Dark Souls
Forest Warrior
Heartwood
Himatsuri➚
Hole in the Sky
The Ice Flood
Inferno
Jailbird's Vacation
King of the Forest Rangers
Lassie: Adventures of Neeka
Lunatic
The Many Adventures of Winnie the Pooh
Mrs. Mike
Mr. Sycamore
The Night Brings Charlie
Out of Time
The Passion of Darkly Noon
Poltergeist 2: The Other Side
Redwood Curtain
Redwood Forest Trail
Return of the Jedi➚
Surfacing
Vertigo➚
The Watcher in the Woods
Where the Rivers Flow North
William Shakespeare's A Midsummer Night's Dream
The Wizard of Oz➚
Wounded

Triads

***see also** China; Gangs*

Time and Tide

True Crime

***see also** Crime & Criminals; This Is Your Life; True Stories*

American Tragedy
At Close Range➚
Ballad of Gregorio Cortez➚
Beyond Reasonable Doubt
Billionaire Boys Club
Black Oak Conspiracy
Black Panther
Blackrock
Blanche Fury
Bluebeard➚
Boomerang➚
The Boston Strangler
Boys Don't Cry➚
Bully
The Cat's Meow
Cause Celebre➚
Chicago Joe & the Showgirl
Chopper
Citizen X➚
Compulsion➚
Crime of the Century
Danger of Love
Deadly Voyage
Death Scream
Deep Crimson
The Deliberate Stranger➚
Dick Turpin
Dillinger
Dr. Petiot
Double-Crossed
Echo of Murder
Echoes in the Darkness
Ed Gein
The Elegant Criminal
Essex Boys
Excellent Cadavers
Execution of Justice
The Executioner's Song
The Falcon and the Snowman➚
Final Appeal
From Hell➚
The General➚
Getting Gotti
Gotti
Great Gold Swindle
The Great St. Louis Bank Robbery
The Happy Face Murders
Headless Body in Topless Bar
Helter Skelter
Helter Skelter Murders
The Hillside Strangler
Honor Thy Father and Mother: The True Story of the Menendez Brothers
I Can't Sleep
In Cold Blood
Johnny 100 Pesos
Killer: A Journal of Murder
L'Appat
The Laramie Project➚
The Life Before This
Mad Dog Morgan
The Man from the Pru
The Man in the Attic
McVicar
Midnight in the Garden of Good and Evil
Mrs. Soffel
Money Movers
Murder in Coweta County
Murder in New Hampshire: The Pamela Smart Story
Murder in Texas➚
The Murder of Stephen Lawrence➚
Murder So Sweet
Murph the Surf
The Newton Boys
Normal Life
Nowhere to Run
The O.J. Simpson Story
100 Proof
One Kill➚
One of Her Own
The Onion Field➚
Our Mother's Murder
Path to Paradise
The People vs. Jean Harris➚
Perfect Crime
The Preppie Murder
Prince of Poisoners: The Life and Crimes of William Palmer
Prince of the City➚
The Pursuit of D.B. Cooper
Rainbow Warrior
Rampage
Rule #3
Sister My Sister
Squizzy Taylor
Stalking Laura
Stand Off
Summer of Sam
Swoon➚
Till Murder Do Us Part
Too Young to Die
Triple Cross➚
Under the Pear Tree
Undercover Cop
The Untouchables➚
Verne Miller
When the Sky Falls
A Winter Tan
Without Evidence
Witness to the Mob
The Zodiac Killer

True Stories

***see also** This Is Your Life; True Crime*

The Abduction
The Abduction of Kari Swenson
Above and Beyond➚
The Accused➚
Act of Vengeance
Adam➚
The Adventures of Nellie Bly
The Affair of the Necklace
After the Promise
After the Shock
Afterburn➚
Against the Wall➚
Aimee & Jaguar
Al Capone➚
The Alamo➚
Alamo Bay
Aldrich Ames: Traitor Within
Alive
All Mine to Give
All the King's Men
All the President's Men➚
Alvarez Kelly
The Ambush Murders
Amelia Earhart: The Final Flight
An American Story
The Amityville Horror
Amor Bandido
The Amy Fisher Story
And I Alone Survived
And the Band Played On➚
Andersonville➚
Andre
Angel
The Ann Jillian Story
Anna and the King of Siam➚
Apollo 13➚
Apprentice to Murder
Archer's Adventure
The Aristocrats
Art for Teachers of Children
Artemisia
The Ascent
Assault at West Point: The Court-Martial of Johnson Whittaker
The Assisi Underground
The Attic: The Hiding of Anne Frank
Attica➚
Au Revoir les Enfants➚
Awakening of Candra
Awakenings➚
Away All Boats
Backbeat➚
Bad Blood
Badge of the Assassin
Badlands➚
Ballad in Blue
Ballad of Gregorio Cortez➚
The Ballad of Little Jo
Balto
The Basketball Diaries
Bataan
Battle Hell
Battle Hymn
Battle of the Eagles
Beautiful Dreamers
Beloved Infidel
Beyond Reasonable Doubt
Beyond the Next Mountain
Big Mo
The Big Red One➚
Bill➚
Bill: On His Own➚
Bitter Harvest➚
Black Hawk Down➚
Black Oak Conspiracy
Black Panther
Blind Ambition
Blood Clan
Blow
Bonanno: A Godfather's Story
Bonnie & Clyde➚
The Boston Strangler
The Bounty
The Boys of St. Vincent➚
Breast Men
Brian's Song➚
The Bridge
The Bridge at Remagen
Brink's Job➚
Britannic
Brotherhood of Murder
Brutal Glory
Buddy
Burke & Wills
The Burning Bed➚
The Burning Season➚
Cabeza de Vaca➚
Cafe Society
Call Northside 777➚
Camel Boy
Camila➚
Can You Hear the Laughter? The Story of Freddie Prinze
Canada's Sweetheart: The Saga of Hal C. Banks
The Cantor's Son
The Captain from Koepenick
Carve Her Name with Pride
A Case of Deadly Force➚
Cast the First Stone
Castaway
Casualties of Love: The "Long Island Lolita" Story
Casualties of War➚
Chameleon Street➚
Champions
Chariots of Fire➚
Charlie Grant's War
Charlotte Forten's Mission: Experiment in Freedom➚
The Chase
Chattahoochee
Cheaper by the Dozen➚
Cheaters
Cheyenne Autumn
The Children of An Lac
Children of Fury
China Cry
Christabel
Christian the Lion
Christiane F.➚
Churchill and the Generals
Circle of Power
Citizen X➚
A Civil Action
The Climb
The Color of Courage
Coming Out of the Ice➚
Coming Through
Communion
Confessions of a Serial Killer
Confessions of Tom Harris
Conrack➚
Convicted
Cool Runnings
The Counterfeit Traitor➚
Courage➚
The Court Martial of Billy Mitchell➚
The Court Martial of Jackie Robinson➚
Cowboy➚
The Cradle Will Rock

➚ = rated three bones or higher

Crash Course
The Crash of Flight 401
Crime of Honor
The Crossing
Cry Freedom
A Cry in the Dark▲
Dance with a Stranger▲
Dangerous Life
Dangerous Minds
David and Lisa▲
Dawn!
Day One▲
Dead Ahead: The Exxon Valdez Disaster▲
Dead Ringers▲
Deadly Business▲
Death of a Centerfold
Death of a Soldier
The Death of Adolf Hitler
The Death of Richie
Death Scream
The Deliberate Stranger▲
Delta Force
Deranged▲
The Diary of Anne Frank▲
Dillinger▲
Dillinger
Dirty Pictures
The Dish▲
Divided by Hate
The Doctor
Dr. Bethune▲
Dog Day Afternoon▲
Donner Pass: The Road to Survival
Donnie Brasco▲
Don't Cry, It's Only Thunder
Doomsday Gun
Double-Crossed
Double Exposure: The Story of Margaret Bourke-White
The Dove
Drugstore Cowboy▲
Drum Beat
East-West
Echoes in the Darkness
Eddie Macon's Run
Edie in Ciao! Manhattan
Edison the Man
The Education of Sonny Carson
Edward and Mrs. Simpson
Egg and I▲
8-A
Eight Men Out▲
8 Seconds
84 Charing Cross Road▲
Eleni
The Elephant Man▲
Elvira Madigan▲
Elvis and Me
Elvis Meets Nixon
Elvis: The Movie
The Emerald Forest▲
Eminent Domain
Empire of the Sun▲
Encounter with the Unknown
Endangered Species
Enemy at the Gates
Enemy of Women
The Enforcer
An Englishman Abroad▲
Enigma Secret
Enjo
Enola Gay: The Men, the Mission, the Atomic Bomb
Enter Laughing
Entertaining Angels: The Dorothy Day Story
The Entity
Eric▲
Erin Brockovich▲
The Ernest Green Story
Escape from Sobibor▲
Escape: Human Cargo▲
Europa, Europa▲
Evel Knievel
Every Man for Himself & God Against All▲
The Execution of Private Slovik▲
Execution of Raymond Graham
The Executioner's Song
Exodus▲
Extreme Justice
Eye on the Sparrow
The Falcon and the Snowman▲
False Arrest
Farinelli
Fast Company
Fat Man and Little Boy
Fatal Vision
The Father Clements Story
The FBI Story▲
Fear Strikes Out▲
Fifth Day of Peace
Fighting Father Dunne
Fighting Seabees
The Fighting Sullivans▲
The Final Days
Final Warning
Fire and Rain
Fire in the Sky
First Time Felon
Fitzcarraldo▲
The Fixer▲
Flight of the Eagle
For Love or Country: The Arturo Sandoval Story
The Forbidden Christ
Forever Love
Forty Days of Musa Dagh
Foul Play
Four Days in September
Frances▲
Francis Gary Powers: The True Story of the U-2 Spy
Gaby: A True Story▲
Gentleman Bandit
George Wallace
Geronimo▲
The Ghost and the Darkness
Ghosts of Mississippi
Gia
Gideon's Trumpet
The Girl Who Spelled Freedom▲
Girls of the White Orchid
Glory Enough for All: The Discovery of Insulin
Going for the Gold: The Bill Johnson Story
Going Home
Goldrush: A Real Life Alaskan Adventure
Good Evening, Mr. Wallenberg
Goodbye, Miss 4th of July
Goodfellas▲
Gospa
Grain of Sand▲
Grambling's White Tiger
Grave Secrets: The Legacy of Hilltop Drive
The Great Escape▲
Great Gold Swindle
The Great Impostor
The Great Locomotive Chase
The Great Riviera Bank Robbery
The Great Train Robbery▲
The Great Wallendas
The Greek Tycoon
Greenfingers
The Grey Fox▲
Grey Owl
Gross Misconduct
Guilty of Innocence
The Guyana Tragedy: The Story of Jim Jones
Hanna's War
Hard Choices▲
Hard Lessons
Harlan County War
The Harmonists
The Hatfields & the McCoys
He Walked by Night▲
He Who Walks Alone
Heart Like a Wheel
Heartland▲
Heavenly Creatures▲
Heaven's Heroes
Hedd Wyn
Held Hostage
Hell to Eternity
Hellcats of the Navy
Helter Skelter
Helter Skelter Murders
Henry & June▲
Henry: Portrait of a Serial Killer▲
Hide in Plain Sight▲
The Hiding Place
The Highest Honor
Hilary and Jackie▲
The Hindenburg
Holy Terror
A Home of Our Own
Honeymoon Killers▲
Honor Thy Father
Honor Thy Father and Mother: The True Story of the Menendez Brothers
Hoodlum Empire
The Hoodlum Priest▲
The Horse Soldiers
Hostage High
Hostages▲
Hostile Waters
A House Divided
The House on Garibaldi Street
The House on Todville Road
The Hunley
The Hunt for the Night Stalker
The Hunter
The Hurricane▲
I Am a Fugitive from a Chain Gang▲
I Dreamed of Africa
I Love You to Death
I Only Want You to Love Me
I Shot Andy Warhol▲
I, the Worst of All
I Will Fight No More Forever▲
If You Could See What I Hear
I'm Dancing as Fast as I Can
The Impossible Spy▲
In a Class of His Own
In Cold Blood▲
In Love and War
In Pursuit of Honor
In the Line of Duty: Ambush in Waco
In the Line of Duty: The FBI Murders▲
In the Mood
In the Name of the Father▲
In the Time of the Butterflies
In Which We Serve▲
Indictment: The McMartin Trial▲
The Infernal Trio
The Infiltrator
Infinity
Inherit the Wind▲
Inherit the Wind
The Inn of the Sixth Happiness▲
The Inner Circle▲
Inside the Third Reich
The Insider▲
Interrupted Melody▲
Intimate Relations
Into Thin Air: Death on Everest
Iron Will
Ironclads
Island of the Blue Dolphins
It's Good to Be Alive
It's My Party
Izzy & Moe
The Jayne Mansfield Story
Jenny's War
Jerusalem
The Jesse Owens Story
The Jesse Ventura Story
Jesus Christ, Superstar▲
The Jew
JFK▲
Jo Jo Dancer, Your Life Is Calling
Joe Torre: Curveballs Along the Way
Joni
Journey of Hope▲
Judge Horton and the Scottsboro Boys
Judgment in Berlin
Julia▲
Justin Morgan Had a Horse
K-19: The Widowmaker
Kaspar Hauser
Kidco
Killer: A Journal of Murder
The Killing Fields▲
A Killing in a Small Town▲
King of the Wind
Knute Rockne: All American▲
Korczak▲
The Krays▲
Kundun▲
Ladies They Talk About
Lady Jane▲
Lady of the House
Ladybird, Ladybird▲
Larry
The Last American Hero▲
The Last Days of Dolwyn
The Last Five Days
Last Flight Out: A True Story
The Last Place on Earth
The Last Supper▲
The Late Shift
Lean on Me▲
The Legend of Blood Castle
Legend of Boggy Creek
Let Him Have It▲
Lethal Lolita—Amy Fisher: My Story
Life & Times of Grizzly Adams
Little Boy Lost
Little Gloria... Happy at Last
Little Heroes
Little Laura & Big John
A Little Stiff
Locked in Silence
Lone Star Kid
Longitude▲
Lorenzo's Oil▲
The Loretta Claiborne Story
Lost
Lost Battalion
Lost Boundaries
The Lost Child
The Lost One
Love and Rage
Love Leads the Way
Love, Lies and Murder
Lovey: A Circle of Children 2
Lucie Aubrac
M. Butterfly
Ma Barker's Killer Brood
Machine Gun Kelly
Mad Dog Morgan
M.A.D.D.: Mothers Against Drunk Driving
Madeleine
Madman
Malaya
A Man Escaped▲
The Man Who Captured Eichmann
The Man Who Never Was▲
Mandela and de Klerk
Manhunt for Claude Dallas
Marciano
Marianne and Juliane▲
Marie▲
Mark Twain and Me
Marked Woman▲
Mary White
Mask▲
Massacre in Rome
Mata Hari▲
Matewan▲
A Matter of Life and Death
Mayerling▲
Mayerling
The McConnell Story
Melvin and Howard▲
Memphis Belle▲
Men of Honor
Michael Collins▲
Midnight Express▲
Miracle in Lane Two
Miracle of Our Lady of Fatima
The Miracle Worker▲
The Miracle Worker
Miss Evers' Boys
Missing▲
Mission of the Shark▲
Mrs. R's Daughter
Mrs. Soffel
Mr. & Mrs. Loving▲
Mr. Horn
Mr. Reliable: A True Story
Molly Maguires
Molokai: The Story of Father Damien
Money for Nothing
Money Movers
Mother Joan of the Angels▲
Mother Teresa: In the Name of God's Poor
A Mother's Prayer
The Mothman Prophecies
Mountain Man
Murder in Coweta County
Murder in the First
Murder in the Old Red Barn
The Murder of Mary Phagan▲
Murder One
Murder Ordained
Murph the Surf
Music of the Heart
Mutiny
Mutiny on the Bounty▲
Mutiny on the Bounty
My Darling Clementine▲
My Husband's Double Life
My Left Foot▲
My Mother's Courage
My Own Country
My Pleasure Is My Business
My Sister's Keeper
The Mystery of Alexina
The Mystery of the Mary Celeste
Naked in the Sun
The Nasty Girl▲
The Neon Empire
The Newton Boys
Night Ambush
Night Crossing
A Night to Remember▲
Nightmare at 43 Hillcrest
Nitti: The Enforcer
No Man Is an Island
Norma Rae▲
Normal Life
Not in This Town
Not Without My Daughter
Nowhere to Run
Nuremberg
Nurse Edith Cavell▲
October Sky▲
Old Gringo
Olivier, Olivier▲
On Wings of Eagles
One Against the Wind▲
One in a Million: The Ron LeFlore Story
One Man's Hero
One That Got Away▲
The Onion Field▲
Operation Amsterdam
Operation Haylift
Operation Thunderbolt
Opposing Force
The Ordeal of Dr. Mudd▲
The Other Side of the Mountain
The Other Side of the Mountain, Part 2
The Ox
Pancho Barnes
Passion in Paradise
Passion of Joan of Arc▲
Pat Garrett & Billy the Kid▲
Paths of Glory▲
Patton▲
Patty Hearst
The Pentagon Wars
The People vs. Larry Flynt▲
The Perfect Storm
Phar Lap
Philby, Burgess and MacLean: Spy Scandal of the Century
A Place for Annie
Playing for Time▲
Portrait of a Rebel: Margaret Sanger
The Positively True Adventures of the Alleged Texas Cheerleader-Murdering Mom▲
Possessed
The Preppie Murder
Pressure Point▲
Pretty Village, Pretty Flame▲
Prick Up Your Ears▲
Prince of the City▲
Princess Caraboo
A Private Matter▲
The Prize Pulitzer
Promised a Miracle
PT 109
Quarterback Princess
A Question of Attribution
Question of Faith
Question of Honor
Qui Etes Vous, Mr. Sorge?
Quilombo
Raid on Entebbe▲
Rainbow Drive
Rape and Marriage: The Rideout Case
Rasputin: Dark Servant of Destiny▲
Rated X
Reach for the Sky
A Real American Hero
Rebound: The Legend of Earl "The Goat" Manigault
Reckless Disregard
Red Cherry
Reds▲
Reilly: Ace of Spies▲
Rescuers: Stories of Courage—Two Couples▲
Rescuers: Stories of Courage "Two Women"▲
The Return of Martin Guerre▲
Reversal of Fortune▲
Rhodes
Riding in Cars with Boys
Ring of Bright Water▲
Ring of Terror
Riot in Cell Block 11▲
Riot in the Streets
River's Edge▲
The Road to Galveston▲
Rodeo Girl
Roe vs. Wade▲
Rogue Trader
Rosewood▲
Roswell: The U.F.O. Cover-Up
Rough Riders
A Royal Scandal
Ruby
Ruby Bridges
Rudy
The Rumor Mill
A Rumor of War▲
Run for the Dream: The Gail Devers Story
Runaway Father
The Runner Stumbles
Running Brave
Sacco & Vanzetti
Sadat
St. Helen's, Killer Volcano
The St. Valentine's Day Massacre
Sakharov▲
Samaritan: The Mitch Snyder Story▲
Samurai 1: Musashi Miyamoto▲
Samurai 2: Duel at Ichijoji Temple▲
Samurai 3: Duel at Ganryu Island▲
Savage Attraction
Saved by the Light
Scandal▲
A Scandal in Paris
The Scarlet & the Black
Schindler's List▲
Sea Gypsies
Sea Wolves
The Search for Bridey Murphy
Searching for Bobby Fischer▲
Secret Weapon
Seeing Red
Seizure: The Story of Kathy Morris
Selena
Selma, Lord, Selma
Separate but Equal▲
Sergeant Matlovich vs. the U.S. Air Force
Sergeant York▲
Serpico▲
Serving in Silence: The Margarethe Cammermeyer Story▲
Seven Years in Tibet

Sexual Intent
Shackleton➶
Shadow on the Sun
Shadowlands➶
Shattered Dreams
Shattered Vows
Shine➶
A Shining Season➶
Shot in the Heart➶
Shot Through the Heart➶
Shout at the Devil
The Sicilian
Sid & Nancy➶
Silence of the North
Silent Victim
Silent Victory: The Kitty O'Neil Story➶
Silkwood➶
The Singing Nun
Sins of the Father➶
Six Degrees of Separation
633 Squadron
Skeezer
Skin
The Slender Thread➶
Small Sacrifices
Snap Decision
Sniper➶
Snowbound: The Jim and Jennifer Stolpa Story
So Proudly We Hail➶
Soldier Blue
The Son of the Shark
Soul of the Game➶
The Sound of Music➶
Spartacus➶
Spirit of St. Louis➶
The Spirit of West Point
Springfield Rifle
Squizzy Taylor
Stand and Deliver➶
Star 80
Starved
Stealing Heaven
Stonewall➶
Storm and Sorrow
The Story of Dr. Wassell
The Straight Story➶
Strange Justice: The Clarence Thomas and Anita Hill Story
The Stratton Story➶
Street Smart
The Sugarland Express➶
Sugartime
Sweetwater: A True Rock Story
Switched at Birth
The Taking of Flight 847: The Uli Derickson Story➶
Teamster Boss: The Jackie Presser Story➶
The Ten Million Dollar Getaway
10 Rillington Place➶
Ten Who Dared
Tenderness of the Wolves
The Terry Fox Story➶
They Call Me Sirr
The Thin Blue Line➶
Thirteen Days➶
Thirty Seconds Over Tokyo➶
A Thousand Heroes
Thousand Pieces of Gold➶
Three Came Home➶
The Three Faces of Eve
The Tiger Woods Story
Till Death Do Us Part
Titanic➶
Titanic
Titanic➶
To Catch a Killer➶
To Heal a Nation
To Kill a Priest
Toast of New York➶
Torso
Touched by Love
Town That Dreaded Sundown
Tragedy of Flight 103: The Inside Story➶
The Triangle Factory Fire Scandal
Triple Cross➶
Triumph of the Spirit➶
True Confessions➶
The Truth About Jane
Tuesdays with Morrie
The Tuskegee Airmen➶
29th Street
Tyson
Varian's War
Vendetta
Vengeance Is Mine➶
Violette➶
Voyage of Terror: The Achille Lauro Affair
Voyage of the Damned➶
Walk the Proud Land
Walking Tall
Walking Tall: Part 2
Walking Tall: The Final Chapter
Walking Through the Fire
The Wall➶
The Wannsee Conference➶
The Wedding Gift➶
Wedding in Blood➶
Weeds➶
Welcome to Sarajevo➶
What's Love Got to Do with It?
When Hell Was in Session➶
White Mile
White Mischief➶
The White Rose➶
The Whole Wide World➶
Wild America➶
The Wild Child➶
Wild Hearts Can't Be Broken➶
Will: G. Gordon Liddy
A Winner Never Quits
Without a Trace
A Woman at War
A Woman Called Golda➶
The Woman He Loved
Woman with a Past
Wooden Horse➶
A World Apart➶
The Wrong Man➶
You Know My Name➶
The Young Poisoner's Handbook➶
Yours, Mine & Ours
Yuri Nosenko, KGB
The Zodiac Killer
Zoot Suit➶
Zulu

TV Pilot Movies

Africa Texas Style
American Dream➶
The Art of Crime
Balboa
Battlestar Galactica
The Bionic Woman
Blade in Hong Kong
Blue De Ville
Brass
Buck Rogers in the 25th Century
Call to Glory
China Beach➶
Christy
Columbo: Prescription Murder
The Concrete Cowboys
Conspiracy of Terror
Cruel Intentions 2
Daring Game
Death Ray 2000
Destination Moonbase Alpha
Dr. Strange
Evil Roy Slade➶
Express to Terror
Fantasy Island
The Flash
Force Five
The Gunfighters
Hercules and the Princess of Troy
Hercules the Legendary Journeys, Vol. 1: And the Amazon Women
Highlander: The Gathering
The Hunted Lady
Hunter
The Incredible Hulk
JAG
Jigsaw
The Kid with the Broken Halo
Kung Fu
L.A. Law➶
The Lazarus Man
Little House on the Prairie➶
Loving
The Magnificent Seven
Magnum P.I.: Don't Eat the Snow in Hawaii
Miami Vice
Misfits of Science
Moonlighting
Nick Knight
Night Gallery➶
The Night Stalker
Our Family Business
Poltergeist: The Legacy
Probe
Rags to Riches
Riding with Death
Sabrina the Teenage Witch
Sanctuary of Fear
Scarface Mob
Search for the Gods
She's in the Army Now
Skag➶
Smile, Jenny, You're Dead
Soldier of Fortune Inc.
Spraggue
Stalk the Wild Child
Stark
Strange New World
The Streets of San Francisco➶
Strike Force
Superman & the Mole Men
TekWar
Terraces
Thunder in Paradise
Tour of Duty
V➶
Vegas
Waikiki
Walker: Texas Ranger: One Riot, One Ranger
White Dwarf
The Women of Brewster Place➶
The Young Pioneers

TV Series

And Now for Something Completely Different➶
Dark Justice
Davy Crockett and the River Pirates
Davy Crockett, King of the Wild Frontier➶
Queen for a Day
Requiem for a Heavyweight➶
Robin Hood: The Movie
Rocky Jones, Space Ranger: Renegade Satellite
Wild, Wild West Revisited

Twins

***see also** Family Ties*

After Darkness
Angels Don't Sleep Here
Bad Company
Basket Case➶
Basket Case 2
Basket Case 3: The Progeny
Big Business
Billboard Dad
Bloodlink
The Bride with White Hair
Brotherly Love
Campus Knights
Chained for Life
City of Shadows
Class of Nuke 'Em High 3: The Good, the Bad and the Subhumanoid
Cobra Woman
The Corsican Brothers
The Crazysitter
Dead Men Walk
Dead Ringers➶
Deadly Twins
Devil's Wedding Night
Double Double Toil and Trouble
The Double Life of Veronique
Double Trouble
Double Vision
Dual Alibi
Equinox
The Eyes, the Mouth
Freaks➶
Here Come the Waves➶
Hotel de Love
How the West Was Fun
Invitation au Voyage
It Takes Two
Jack's Back➶
Killer with Two Faces
The Krays➶
Lies of the Twins
Lost Honeymoon
Love! Valour! Compassion!
Madhouse
Major League 3: Back to the Minors
The Man in the Iron Mask➶
The Man in the Iron Mask
The Man in the Iron Mask➶
Man with a Gun
Maximum Risk
Mirror Images
Mirror Images 2
Mother Lode
Nukie
The Nutt House
The Other➶
Out on a Limb
The Parent Trap
The Prince and the Surfer
Raising Cain
The Reluctant Agent
Ripe
Schizopolis
Second Sight➶
Sisters➶
The Sphinx
Start the Revolution without Me➶
Steal Big, Steal Little
A Stolen Life
Thicker Than Water
This World, Then the Fireworks
To Grandmother's House We Go
Twin Dragons
Twin Falls Idaho➶
Twin Sisters
Twin Town
Twins
Twins of Evil
Twinsanity
Twinsitters
Two Much
Urban Legends 2: Final Cut
Village of Dreams
Wagon's Westward
The Worldly Madonna
The Young Girls of Rochefort

Twister!

***see also** Disaster Flicks*

Eye of the Storm
Night of the Twisters
Places in the Heart➶
Storm Chasers: Revenge of the Twister
Storm Tracker
Tornado!
Twister
The Wizard of Oz
The Wizard of Oz➶

UFOs

***see** Alien Beings—Benign; Alien Beings—Vicious; Space Operas*

Under My Skin

Fantastic Voyage➶
Innerspace
Osmosis Jones

Undercover Cops

***see also** Crime Drama; Organized Crime*

Angel of Destruction
Ballistic
Beyond Suspicion
Beyond the Law
Cruising
Cutaway
Donnie Brasco➶
The Finishing Touch
Get Christie Love!
Hellcats
Idiot Box
Impulse
In the Flesh
In the Line of Duty: A Cop for the Killing
In the Shadows
In Too Deep
Kindergarten Cop
Kiss of Death
The Mod Squad
The Naked Gun: From the Files of Police Squad➶
No Man's Land
Raw Deal
Reservoir Dogs➶
Rush➶
Saints and Sinners
Serpico➶
Sharky's Machine
Small Kill
Stiletto Dance
Stone Cold
A Stranger Among Us
The Sweeper
TekWar
Training Day
Witness➶

Unexplained Phenomena

The Amityville Curse
Angel Baby
Beyond the Bermuda Triangle
The Birds➶
Black Rainbow➶
Blue Tornado
Book of Shadows: Blair Witch 2
The Carpathian Eagle
The Carpenter
Carrie➶
Catacombs
Cube
Dead Again➶
Dead Zone➶
Delusion
Destiny Turns on the Radio
Die, Monster, Die!
Dream a Little Dream 2
Dying to Remember
Encounter with the Unknown
Endgame
The Entity
Escapes
E.S.P.
Eternal Evil
The Evil Mind
Eyes of Laura Mars
Fallen
Fire in the Sky
Firestarter
The 4D Man
The Fury
Ghost Chasers
Ghost Town
The Ghosts of Hanley House
Grandma's House
Hangar 18
The Haunting Passion
The House of Seven Corpses
In Dreams
Lisa and the Devil
Lurkers
Maximum Overdrive
Michael
Miracle in Rome
Miracle of Our Lady of Fatima
Mondo Balordo
Murphy's Fault
A Name for Evil
Nomads
Out There
Phenomenon
Psychic
The Psychotronic Man
The Rage: Carrie 2
Retribution
Return from Witch Mountain
Roswell: The U.F.O. Cover-Up
Salem's Lot
Scared Stiff➶
Shattered Silence
The Sleeping Car
Spook Busters
The Stranger
Things Happen at Night
The Three Lives of Thomasina➶
The Tin Drum➶
Truly, Madly, Deeply➶
Unbreakable
The Undead
Visions
Visions of Evil
Waiting for the Light
Wavelength
Web of the Spider
The X-Files
X: The Man with X-Ray Eyes➶

U.S. Marshals

***see also** Loner Cops; Westerns*

Cahill: United States Marshal
Con Air➶
The Fugitive➶
Gunfight at the O.K. Corral➶
Heaven's Gate
My Darling Clementine➶
Out of Sight➶
Outland
Rooster Cogburn
South of Heaven, West of Hell
Texas Rangers
Tombstone➶
True Grit➶
U.S. Marshals
The Usual Suspects➶
Witness Protection➶
Wyatt Earp

Up All Night

***see also** Vampire Babes; Vampires*

After Hours➶
Albino Alligator
American Graffiti➶
The Anniversary Party➶
Batman➶
Before Sunrise
Big City Blues
The Big Kahuna
Blade Runner➶
Cabaret Balkan
Caresses
Chicago Cab
Dazed and Confused➶
East Palace, West Palace
Escape from New York
54
The French Connection➶
From Dusk Till Dawn
Go➶
Gone in 60 Seconds
Groove➶
Head On➶
Hocus Pocus
Into the Night
Judgment Night
Just One Night
The Last Days of Disco➶
Late Last Night
Little Nemo: Adventures in Slumberland
Mannequin
Miracle Mile➶
Miss Julie
Nightwatch
Panic Room
Pitch Black➶
Reach the Rock
Rites of Passage
Simone Barbes
Swingers➶
Tainted
Trick➶
200 Cigarettes
Woo
Yellow

➶ = rated three bones or higher

Urban Drama

Above the Rim
American Heart▲
American Me▲
The Asphalt Jungle▲
Baby Boy
Bad Attitude
Bad Lieutenant▲
Belly
Black and White▲
Blood Brothers
Boricua's Bond
Boston Kickout
Boyz N the Hood▲
The Bronx War
A Brother's Kiss
Bullet
Carlito's Way▲
Caught Up
Changing Lanes▲
City Hall▲
Colors▲
Cooley High▲
Corrupt
Crossing the Bridge
Cry, the Beloved Country▲
Curtis's Charm
Dangerous Minds
Dead Boyz Can't Fly
Deep Trouble
Do the Right Thing▲
Dope Case Pending
Erskinville Kings
The Fence
Final Exam
Fly by Night
Free of Eden
Fresh
Gang Related
Grand Canyon▲
Hard Lessons
Head On▲
Heaven Is a Playground
Hell's Kitchen NYC
Jason's Lyric
Juice
Jungleground
Junior's Groove
Just Another Girl on the I.R.T.
Light It Up
Loser
Love Your Mama
Menace II Society▲
Mi Vida Loca
Money for Nothing
Naked▲
New Jack City
New Jersey Drive
Night Falls on Manhattan▲
Once Were Warriors▲
Original Gangstas
Out of Sync
Poetic Justice
Raising the Heights
Rude
Slam
Soul Survivor
South Central
Southie
Squeeze
Straight out of Brooklyn
Strange Days▲
Strapped
Street Wars
Sugar Hill
Tar
Ten Benny
Training Day
Turn It Up
Urban Crossfire
White Man's Burden
Zebrahead▲
Zooman▲

Urban Gangstas

see also *Gangs; Urban Drama*
Colors▲
In Too Deep

The USO

see also *World War II*
China Beach▲
For the Boys
Stage Door Canteen

Vacations

American Gothic
American Pie 2
The American Scream
An American Werewolf in London▲
Backwoods
Beethoven's 3rd
Beverly Hills Family Robinson
Beyond the Door 3
Blame It on Rio
Blondie Takes a Vacation
Body Trouble
Bread and Tulips▲
Brokedown Palace
Cabin Boy
California Suite▲
Camilla
Cancel My Reservation
Captain Ron
Casual Sex?
City Slickers▲
Claire's Knee▲
Cold Fever
Come September
The Comfort of Strangers▲
Crackerjack
Dangerous Prey
Dead Cold
Deadly Intruder
Death Stalk
Death Weekend
Deliverance▲
Devil Wears White
Dirty Dancing▲
Don't Drink the Water
8 Heads in a Duffel Bag
Enchanted April
End of Summer
Family Reunion
Far from Home
A Far Off Place
The Fatal Image
A Fatal Inversion
The First to Go
Frantic▲
Fraternity Vacation
Funny Games
Gidget Goes Hawaiian
Gidget Goes to Rome
The Girl Getters
Grotesque
Harry and the Hendersons
Head Above Water
The Hills Have Eyes
Home Alone▲
Home Alone 2: Lost in New York
Hot Pursuit
Hot Summer
The Hours and Times▲
How Stella Got Her Groove Back
The Inkwell
Jack Frost 2: Revenge of the Mutant Killer Snowman
Judgment Day
Just Looking
Kevin & Perry Go Large
Killing at Hell's Gate
La Collectionneuse
The Last of the High Kings
Last Summer In the Hamptons▲
Lena's Holiday
Lie Down with Dogs
Like It Never Was Before
Little Bigfoot
The Long, Long Trailer
Love! Valour! Compassion!
The Lunatic
Magic in the Water
Magic Kid
The Man Who Knew Too Much▲
The Man Who Knew Too Much
The Mask of Dimitrios▲
Mr. Hobbs Takes a Vacation▲
Mr. Hulot's Holiday▲
A Month by the Lake
My Father the Hero
My Grandpa Is a Vampire
My Uncle Silas▲
National Lampoon's Christmas Vacation
National Lampoon's Dad's Week Off
National Lampoon's European Vacation
National Lampoon's Vacation▲
Nico and Dani
Nightmare at Bittercreek
Ollie Hopnoodle's Haven of Bliss
The Out-of-Towners▲
Overkill
Pauline at the Beach▲
Poor White Trash 2
Red Salute
Ring of Fire 3: Lion Strike
The River Wild
Russian Roulette
Siam Sunset
Six Days, Seven Nights
Spellbreaker: Secret of the Leprechauns
Spring Break
Stealing Beauty
The Sucker
Summer Rental
A Summer's Tale
A Tale of Winter
Target
Terror at Red Wolf Inn
Terror at Tenkiller
Tourist Trap
Tracks of a Killer
TripFall
Twitch of the Death Nerve
The Two Faces of Evil
Two for the Road▲
Two If by Sea
Uncivilized
Unlawful Passage
Vegas Vacation
Vibration
A Walk on the Moon
Week-End in Havana
Weekend at Bernie's
A Weekend in the Country
Welcome to Spring Break
Where the Boys Are '84
The Wild Life
Witchery
With a Friend Like Harry▲

Vampire Babes

see also *Up All Night; Vampires*
Addicted to Murder
Addicted to Murder 2: Tainted Blood
Addicted to Murder 3: Bloodlust
The Addiction
American Vampire
Blade II
The Brides of Dracula
Buffy the Vampire Slayer▲
Captain Kronos: Vampire Hunter▲
Cold Hearts
The Craving
Crypt of the Living Dead
Daughters of Darkness▲
Demon Queen
Dracula's Daughter▲
Fangs of the Living Dead
The Fearless Vampire Killers▲
The Forsaken
Fright Night
From Dusk Till Dawn
From Dusk Till Dawn 3: The Hangman's Daughter
The Girl with the Hungry Eyes
Habit
Interview with the Vampire
John Carpenter's Vampires
Karmina
The Kiss
Lemora, Lady Dracula
Lips of Blood
Lust for a Vampire
Mary, Mary, Bloody Mary
The Midnight Hour
Nadja▲
Night of the Sorcerers
Night Shade
Nightlife
Once Bitten
Queen of the Damned
Razor Blade Smile
Samson vs. the Vampire Women
Saturday the 14th Strikes Back
Sergio Lapel's Drawing Blood
Sorority House Vampires
Stephen King's The Night Flier
Tales from the Crypt Presents Bordello of Blood
Twins of Evil
Vamp
Vampire Centerfolds
The Vampire Lovers
Vampires of Sorority Row: Kickboxers From Hell
Vampyres
The Velvet Vampire
Witchcraft 10: Mistress of the Craft

Vampire Spoof

see also *Horror Comedy; Vampires*
Andy Warhol's Dracula▲
Beverly Hills Vamp
Buffy the Vampire Slayer▲
Dracula & Son
Dracula Blows His Cool
Dracula: Dead and Loving It
Dracula Father and Son
Dracula Sucks
Dracula: Up in Harlem
Dracula vs. Frankenstein
The Fearless Vampire Killers▲
Gore-Met Zombie Chef from Hell
I Married a Vampire
Karmina
The Little Vampire
Love at First Bite
The Malibu Beach Vampires
Mr. Vampire
My Best Friend Is a Vampire
My Grandpa Is a Vampire
Near Dark▲
Once Bitten
A Polish Vampire in Burbank
Rockula
Teen Vamp
Vamp
The Vampire Happening

Vampires

see also *Up All Night; Vampire Babes; Vampire Spoof*
Addicted to Murder
Addicted to Murder 2: Tainted Blood
Addicted to Murder 3: Bloodlust
The Addiction
Alien Massacre
Angel of the Night
Attack from Mars
The Bat People
Beast of Morocco
Billy the Kid Versus Dracula
The Black Room
Black Sabbath▲
Blacula
Blade
Blade II
Blood & Donuts
Blood and Roses
Blood Freak
Blood of Dracula's Castle
Blood of the Vampire
The Blood Spattered Bride
Blood Thirst
Blood Ties
Bloodbath
Bloodlust: Subspecies 3
Bloodstone: Subspecies 2
Bloodstorm: Subspecies 4
The Bloodsuckers
Bloodsuckers from Outer Space
Body Snatcher from Hell
Bram Stoker's Dracula
The Breed
The Brides of Dracula
Buffy the Vampire Slayer▲
Captain Kronos: Vampire Hunter▲
Carmilla
Cave of the Living Dead
Children of the Night
Club Vampire
Condemned to Live
Count Dracula
Count Yorga, Vampire
The Craving
Cronos
Crypt of the Living Dead
Curse of the Undead
Dance of the Damned
Daughter of Darkness
Daughters of Darkness▲
Dead Men Walk
Demon Queen
The Devil Bat
The Devil Bat's Daughter
Devil's Wedding Night
Dr. Terror's House of Horrors
Dracula (Spanish Version)
Dracula▲
Dracula
Dracula A.D. 1972
Dracula: Dead and Loving It
Dracula/Garden of Eden
Dracula Has Risen from the Grave
Dracula Rising
Dracula 2000
Dracula vs. Frankenstein
Dracula's Daughter▲
Dracula's Great Love
Dracula's Last Rites
Dracula's Widow
Elvira, Mistress of the Dark
Embrace of the Vampire
Evil's Commandment
Evils of the Night
Fangs of the Living Dead
Female Vampire
The Forsaken
Fright Night
Fright Night 2
From Dusk Till Dawn
From Dusk Till Dawn 2: Texas Blood Money
Ganja and Hess
Genie of Darkness
Grave of the Vampire
Graveyard Shift
Habit
Heartstopper
The Horror of Dracula▲
Horror of the Blood Monsters
House of Dark Shadows▲
House of Dracula
House of Frankenstein
The House that Dripped Blood
Howling 6: The Freaks
The Hunger
I Like Bats
Immortality
Innocent Blood
Interview with the Vampire
Invasion of the Vampires
Isle of the Dead
John Carpenter's Vampires
Karmina
Kiss of the Vampire
The Last Man on Earth
The Legend of the 7 Golden Vampires
Lemora, Lady Dracula
Les Vampires
Let's Scare Jessica to Death
Lifeforce
Lips of Blood
The Lost Boys
The Lost Platoon
Lust for a Vampire
Mark of the Vampire▲
Martin▲
Mary, Mary, Bloody Mary
The Midnight Hour
Midnight Kiss
Modern Vampires
The Monster Club
The Monster Demolisher
The Monster Squad
My Grandpa Is a Vampire
My Son, the Vampire
Nadja▲
Near Dark▲
Nick Knight
Night Hunter
Night of Dark Shadows▲
Night of the Sorcerers
The Night Stalker
Nightlife
Nightmare in Blood
Ninja, the Violent Sorcerer
Nocturna
Nosferatu▲
Nosferatu the Vampyre
Not of This Earth
Once Bitten
Orgy of the Vampires
Pale Blood
Planet of Blood
Planet of the Vampires
Project Vampire
Queen of the Damned
Rabid
Red Blooded American Girl
The Reflecting Skin
The Return of Count Yorga
Return of the Vampire
Return to Salem's Lot
The Saga of the Draculas
Salem's Lot
Samson vs. the Vampire Women
The Satanic Rites of Dracula
The Scars of Dracula
Scream Blacula Scream
Shadow of the Vampire▲
ShadowZone: The Undead Express
The Slaughter of the Vampires
Sleepwalkers
Son of Dracula▲
Sorority House Vampires
Stephen King's The Night Flier
Subspecies
Sundown
Tainted
Tale of a Vampire
Tales from the Crypt Presents Bordello of Blood
A Taste of Blood
Taste the Blood of Dracula
Theatre of Death
Thirst
The Thirsty Dead
To Die For
To Die For 2: Son of Darkness
To Sleep with a Vampire
Track of the Vampire
Transylvania Twist
Twins of Evil
Ultraviolet
Uncle Was a Vampire
Understudy: The Graveyard Shift 2
The Unearthing
Vamp
The Vampire
Vampire at Midnight
The Vampire Bat
Vampire Circus
Vampire Conspiracy
Vampire Cop
The Vampire Happening
The Vampire Hookers
Vampire in Brooklyn
Vampire Journals
The Vampire Lovers
The Vampire People
Vampirella
The Vampire's Coffin
The Vampire's Ghost
Vampire's Kiss▲
Vampyr▲
The Vampyr
Vampyres
The Velvet Vampire
The Werewolf vs. the Vampire Woman

The Wicked
Witchcraft 7: Judgement Hour
Zoltan...Hound of Dracula

Venice

see also Italy

Betrayal
Blame It on the Bellboy
Bread and Tulips▲
The Children
The Comfort of Strangers▲
Dangerous Beauty▲
Death in Venice▲
Don't Look Now▲
Everyone Says I Love You▲
Indiana Jones and the Last Crusade▲
A Little Romance▲
Night Train to Venice
Only You
Othello▲
Panic Button
Summertime▲
Tonight or Never
Venice, Venice
Walk, Don't Run
The Wings of the Dove▲

Veterans

see also Postwar

Air Force One▲
Alamo Bay
American Eagle
Americana
Anatomy of Terror
Angels from Hell
The Annihilators
Article 99
Ashes and Embers
Backfire
Bad Company▲
The Ballad of Andy Crocker
The Best Years of Our Lives▲
Billy Jack
Birds of Prey
Birdy▲
The Black Six
Braddock: Missing in Action 3
The Bushwackers
The Cage
Cannibal Apocalypse
Cease Fire
Chattahoochee
Child Bride of Short Creek
Chrome Soldiers
Combat Shock
Cry of the Innocent▲
Dark Before Dawn
Distant Thunder
The Enchanted Cottage
Fear
Fireback
First Blood
Fleshburn
Forced Vengeance
The Forgotten
Ghetto Revenge
G.I. Executioner
The Great American Broadcast▲
Heated Vengeance
Heroes
Heroes for Sale▲
House▲
Identity Unknown
In a Shallow Grave
In Country
Jud
Jungle Assault
Kill Alex Kill
Killcrazy
The Killer's Edge
Killzone
Last Mercenary
Lethal Weapon▲
Liberty & Bash
The Line
Memorial Day
Mr. Majestyk
Moon in Scorpio
The Park Is Mine
Rambo 3
Red, White & Busted
Redwood Curtain
Ride in a Pink Car
Riders of the Storm
Robbery
Rolling Thunder
Savage Dawn
Scent of a Woman▲
Shark River
Skin Art
Soldier's Revenge
Stand Alone
Stanley
Steele Justice
Tagget
To Heal a Nation
To Kill a Clown
Tracks
The War
The War at Home
Who'll Stop the Rain?▲
The Woman Inside

Vietnam War

see also Postwar; POW/MIA

Air America
American Commandos
Americana
The Annihilators
Apocalypse Now▲
Ashes and Embers
The Ballad of Andy Crocker
Bat 21
Beyond the Call of Duty
Birdy▲
The Black Six
Born on the Fourth of July▲
The Boys in Company C
Braddock: Missing in Action 3
A Bright Shining Lie
Cactus in the Snow
Cannibal Apocalypse
Casualties of War▲
Cease Fire
Charlie Bravo
The Children of An Lac
China Beach▲
China Gate▲
Combat Shock
Coming Home▲
Commando Invasion
Conspiracy: The Trial of the Chicago Eight▲
Crossfire
Dead Presidents
Deathdream
The Deer Hunter▲
The Deserters
Dogfight▲
Don't Cry, It's Only Thunder
Eastern Condors
84 Charlie MoPic▲
Explosion
Eye of the Eagle
Eye of the Eagle 2
Eye of the Eagle 3
Fatal Mission
Fear
Fighting Mad
Firehawk
First Blood
Fist of Glory
Flight of the Intruder
For the Boys
The Forgotten
Forgotten Warrior
Forrest Gump▲
Four Friends▲
Friendly Fire▲
Full Metal Jacket▲
Gardens of Stone
Ghetto Revenge
Go Tell the Spartans▲
Good Morning, Vietnam▲
The Green Berets
Green Eyes▲
Hail, Hero!
Hair▲
Hamburger Hill
Hanoi Hilton
The Hard Ride
Heated Vengeance
Heaven and Earth
In Country
In Gold We Trust
In Love and War
The Iron Triangle
Jacknife▲
Jacob's Ladder
Jenny
Jud
Jungle Assault
Kent State
The Killing Fields▲
Kissinger and Nixon
Lady from Yesterday
Last Flight Out: A True Story
The Last Hunter
Memorial Day
Missing in Action
Missing in Action 2: The Beginning
More American Graffiti
Nam Angels
Night Wars
1969▲
No Dead Heroes
The Odd Angry Shot
Off Limits
Operation C.I.A.
Operation Dumbo Drop
Operation 'Nam
Operation Warzone
Ordinary Heroes
Platoon▲
Platoon Leader
P.O.W. Deathcamp
The P.O.W. Escape
Primary Target
Private War
Purple Hearts
Rambo: First Blood, Part 2
Rambo 3
Red, White & Busted
Return of the Secaucus 7▲
Ride in a Pink Car
Rolling Thunder
A Rumor of War▲
Running on Empty▲
Saigon Commandos
Saigon: Year of the Cat
Search and Destroy
The Siege of Firebase Gloria
The '60s
Skin Art
Soldier's Revenge
A Soldier's Sweetheart
Some Kind of Hero
Streamers
Strike Commando
Summertree
Thou Shalt Not Kill...Except
The 317th Platoon▲
Tigerland▲
To Heal a Nation
To the Shores of Hell
Tornado
Tour of Duty
Trial of the Catonsville Nine
Twilight's Last Gleaming
Uncommon Valor
Unnatural Causes▲
The Walking Dead
The Wall▲
The War
The War at Home
Warbus
Wardogs
We Were Soldiers▲
Welcome Home
When Hell Was in Session▲
Which Way Home
White Badge
Winner Takes All
Woodstock▲

Vigilantes

see also Revenge

American Commandos
The Avenging Angel
Best of the Best 3: No Turning Back
Black Fox: Blood Horse
Boondock Saints
Brutal Fury
Combat Shock
Dark Angel: The Ascent
The Death Squad
Death Wish
Death Wish 2
Death Wish 3
Death Wish 5: The Face of Death
Defiance
Dirty Harry▲
DROP Squad
An Eye for an Eye
Falling Down
Force Five
Gang Boys
Jimmy Hollywood
Keeper of the City
One Man Jury
Original Gangstas
Out for Blood
The Outlaw Josey Wales▲
Quiet Cool
Ransom▲
Raw Deal
Rogue Force
Self-Defense
Shadows and Fog
SnakeEater
SnakeEater 2: The Drug Buster
The Sniper
Soldier of the Night
Steele Justice
The Stranger Wore a Gun
Street Corner Justice
Street Hunter
Swordfish
Target Eagle
To Protect and Serve
Trespasses
When Justice Fails
When the Bullet Hits the Bone
Zebra Force

Virtual Reality

see also Computers; Technology—Rampant

Arcade
Brainstorm
Carver's Gate
Conceiving Ada
Cyber Bandits
Cybercity
Darkdrive
eXistenZ
Future Shock
Hologram Man
How to Make a Monster
The Lawnmower Man
Lawnmower Man 2: Beyond Cyberspace
Looker
The Matrix▲
Megaville
TekWar
Terminal Justice: Cybertech P.D.
The Thirteenth Floor
Total Recall 2070: Machine Dreams
Venus Rising
Virtual Assassin
Virtual Combat
Virtual Desire
Virtual Encounters
Virtual Girl
Virtual Seduction
Virtual Sexuality
Virtuosity
Wild Palms

Viva Las Vegas!

see also Gambling

Beautiful Joe
Beavis and Butt-Head Do America
Beyond Desire
The Bible and Gun Club
Blackjack
Bodily Harm
Bogus
Casino▲
The Center of the World
Con Air▲
The Corporation
Crazy in Alabama
Dance with Me
Destination Vegas
Destiny Turns on the Radio
Diamonds Are Forever▲
Fear and Loathing in Las Vegas
Feeling Minnesota
The Flintstones in Viva Rock Vegas
Fools Rush In
For Which He Stands
Gamble on Love
Get Shorty▲
Girls' Night
Go▲
The Great White Hype
Happily Ever After
Hard Vice
Heaven or Vegas
Hell Squad
High Stakes
Honeymoon in Vegas
I Shot a Man in Vegas
Indecent Proposal
Jinxed
Jocks
Kingpin
Kiss Me, Stupid!
Lady Cocoa
Las Vegas Hillbillys
Las Vegas Lady
Las Vegas Serial Killer
The Las Vegas Story
Las Vegas Weekend
Leaving Las Vegas▲
Leprechaun 3
Luckytown
The Marrying Man
Meet Me in Las Vegas
The Mexican
Nature of the Beast
The Night Stalker
Ocean's Eleven▲
Play It to the Bone
Rain Man▲
The Rat Pack
Rat Race
Rock-a-Doodle
The Runner
Rush Hour 2
The Showgirl Murders
Showgirls
Sister Act
Six-String Samurai
Sparkler
Stripshow
Sugartime
Swingers▲
Sword of Honor
Texas Payback
3000 Miles to Graceland
Tomcats
Tricks
Vampirella
The Vegas Strip Wars
Vegas Vacation
Very Bad Things
Viva Las Vegas
Wedding Bell Blues
The Winner

Volcanos

see also Disaster Flicks

Dante's Peak
The Devil at 4 O'Clock
Joe Versus the Volcano
Last Days of Pompeii
The Last Days of Pompeii
Nutcase
St. Helen's, Killer Volcano
Volcano
Volcano: Fire on the Mountain
Waikiki Wedding▲
When Time Ran Out

Volleyball

Kill Shot
Side Out
South Beach Academy
Top Gun

Voodoo

see also Occult

Angel Heart
Asylum
Black Devil Doll from Hell
Black Magic Woman
Blues Brothers 2000
Caribe
Curse 3: Blood Sacrifice
Curtis's Charm
The Devil's Daughter
Dr. Terror's House of Horrors
Eve's Bayou▲
Headhunter
The House on Skull Mountain
Household Saints▲
How to Stuff a Wild Bikini
I Eat Your Skin
I Walked with a Zombie▲
Jungle Drums of Africa
Live and Let Die
Macumba Love
The Offspring
Plague of the Zombies
The Possession of Joel Delaney
Scared Stiff
Scream Blacula Scream
The Serpent and the Rainbow
Shrunken Heads
The Snake People
Tales from the Hood
Theatre of Death
Voodoo
Voodoo Academy
Voodoo Black Exorcist
Voodoo Dawn
Weekend at Bernie's 2

Vote for Me!

see also Capitol Capers

The Big Brass Ring
Bulworth▲
The Candidate▲
The Contract
Deterrence
Election▲
Homicide: The Movie
The Manchurian Candidate▲
Menno's Mind
My Date with the President's Daughter
Primary Colors
Random Hearts
Running Mates
The Seduction of Joe Tynan
Waking the Dead

Waiters & Waitresses

About Adam
Alice Doesn't Live Here Anymore
Amelie▲
As Good As It Gets▲
Atlantic City▲
Bikini Bistro
Broken English
Cafe Romeo
Celebrity▲
Come Back to the Five & Dime Jimmy Dean, Jimmy Dean▲
Coyote Ugly
Dancer, Texas—Pop. 81▲
Dream for an Insomniac
Duets
Fear and Loathing in Las Vegas
Five Easy Pieces▲
Frankie and Johnny▲
Hard Eight▲
Heavy▲
Highway Hitcher
It Could Happen to You
Joey Breaker▲
Just Your Luck
Monster's Ball▲
Mystic Pizza▲
No Looking Back
Nurse Betty▲
The Postman Always Rings Twice▲
The Postman Always Rings Twice
Pure Danger
Quiet Days in Hollywood
Restaurant
Return to Me
The Runner
A Season for Miracles
Shaft▲
Skipped Parts
Spare Me

▲ = rated three bones or higher

The Spitfire Grill
A Summer's Tale
Thelma & Louise▲
Untamed Heart
Waiting
The Waiting Game
Waitress
The Wedding Singer
White Palace
Willa

War Between the Sexes

***see also** Divorce; Marriage; Singles*

About Last Night...▲
Adam's Rib▲
Addicted to Love
The Adventures of Robin Hood▲
The African Queen▲
All of Me
All Tied Up
All's Fair
Alternative
Always▲
America 3000
Annie Hall▲
Around the World Under the Sea
Autumn Marathon
The Awful Truth▲
The Ballad of the Sad Cafe
Bare Essentials
Basic Training
Battle of the Sexes
Behind Office Doors
The Best Intentions▲
Beware of Pity
The Bigamist
Blood and Sand▲
The Bodyguard
Bonnie's Kids
Boomerang
The Bride Walks Out
Bringing Up Baby▲
Buffalo Jump▲
Bull Durham▲
Cannibal Women in the Avocado Jungle of Death
Carmen▲
Carmen Jones▲
Carrington, V.C.▲
Carry On Nurse
Casablanca▲
Casanova's Big Night
Castaway
Casual Sex?
Chained
Cold Heat
Concrete Beat
Cruel Intentions
The Cry of the Owl
The Cutting Edge
Dangerous Liaisons
Dating the Enemy
Dear Murderer
Dear Wife
Def Jam's How to Be a Player
Designing Woman▲
Disclosure
Divorce His, Divorce Hers
Divorce—Italian Style▲
Dogfight▲
Don Juan, My Love▲
Easy Wheels
Far and Away
The Favor
The Female Bunch
Fever
The Fighting Sheriff
First Monday in October
The First to Go
The First Wives Club
Forever Darling
Forget Paris
Frankie and Johnny▲
A Girl in a Million
Gone with the Wind▲
The Good Father▲
Goodbye Love
Guarding Tess
The Happy Ending
Hardhat & Legs
Having It All
He Said, She Said
Hearing Voices
Heartburn▲
His Girl Friday▲
Hot Summer
Hotel Room
Housesitter
I Live My Life
I Love All of You
I Love My...Wife
I Love Trouble
I Love You
In the Good Old Summertime▲
In the Line of Fire▲
Intimate Story
Irreconcilable Differences
It Happened One Night▲
The Jewel of the Nile
Juliet of the Spirits▲
June Bride▲
Just Tell Me What You Want
Key Exchange
Kill My Wife...Please!
The King and I▲
Kiss Me Kate▲
Kramer vs. Kramer▲
La Discrete▲
L.A. Story▲
The Lady Says No
The Last Woman on Earth
Le Chat▲
Legion of Iron
Letters to an Unknown Lover
Lily in Love
The Lion in Winter▲
Love Crazy▲
Love in the Afternoon
Love Nest
Lover Come Back
Loyalties
Lucky Partners
Man of Destiny
The Man Who Guards the Greenhouse
Manhattan▲
Maria's Lovers
The Marriage of Maria Braun▲
The Marrying Man
A Matter of Love
Maverick
McLintock!▲
Men...▲
A Midsummer Night's Dream▲
A Midsummer Night's Dream
Moonlighting
Moonstruck▲
Mortal Thoughts
Much Ado about Nothing▲
Murphy's Law
My Brilliant Career▲
Near Misses
A New Leaf
9 to 5
Nothing in Common
One Woman or Two
The Opposite Sex and How to Live With Them
Pajama Tops
Pat and Mike▲
Patti Rocks▲
Pauline at the Beach▲
A Piece of Pleasure▲
Pillow Talk▲
Places in the Heart▲
Portrait of Teresa▲
The Practice of Love
Private Lives▲
Prizzi's Honor▲
Public Enemy▲
Queen of Outer Space
Question of Silence▲
The Quiet Man▲
Ramrod
The Ref▲
Romancing the Stone▲
Rooster Cogburn
Running Mates▲
Sabrina▲
Sabrina
Scenes from a Mall
Seance on a Wet Afternoon▲
The Sensual Man
Sex and the College Girl
She-Devil
Shore Leave▲
Siberian Lady Macbeth▲
The Single Standard
The Social Secretary
Solitaire for 2
Someone Like You
Sotto, Sotto
Speechless
Speedtrap
Spies, Lies and Naked Thighs
Star 80
The Story of Fausta
Summer Night with Greek Profile, Almond Eyes & Scent of Basil
Switch▲
Switching Channels
The Taming of the Shrew
The Taming of the Shrew▲
A Taxing Woman▲
Teacher's Pet▲
Ted & Venus
That Old Feeling
That's My Baby!
Thelma & Louise▲
The Thing▲
Thor and the Amazon Women
Three of Hearts
Thunder in the Pines
Tiger and the Pussycat
To Have & Have Not▲
To Wong Foo, Thanks for Everything, Julie Newmar
Tony Draws a Horse
True Love▲
Two-Faced Woman▲
Vasectomy: A Delicate Matter
War Between the Tates
The War of the Roses▲
When Harry Met Sally...▲
When Ladies Meet
When Women Lost Their Tails
Who's Afraid of Virginia Woolf?▲
Wife Versus Secretary▲
The Witches of Eastwick
Without Love
A Woman of Distinction▲
Woman of the Year▲
Women & Men: In Love There Are No Rules
Women & Men: Stories of Seduction
Women on the Verge of a Nervous Breakdown▲
The World According to Garp▲
Year of the Comet
Yesterday, Today and Tomorrow▲
Your Friends & Neighbors▲
You're a Big Boy Now▲

War, General

***see also** Anti-War War Movies; Big Battles; Civil War; Korean War; Persian Gulf War; Postwar; POW/MIA; Revolutionary War; Terrorism; Veterans; Vietnam War; World War I; World War II*

The Alamo▲
The Alamo: Thirteen Days to Glory
Alexander Nevsky▲
Alexander the Great
Alone Against Rome
Alsino and the Condor▲
Anna Karenina
Atlas
The Avenger
Ay, Carmela!▲
Ballad of a Soldier▲
Barb Wire
Battle Hell
The Battle of Algiers▲
The Battle of Austerlitz
The Beast
Beau Geste▲
Before the Rain▲
Behind the Front
The Bitter Tea of General Yen▲
Braveheart▲
The Buccaneer
Bugles in the Afternoon
A Bullet for the General
By Dawn's Early Light
Captain Caution
Captain Horatio Hornblower▲
Carthage in Flames
Cast a Giant Shadow
Cavalry Command
Chapayev▲
The Charge of the Light Brigade▲
The Charge of the Light Brigade
Civilization▲
Codename: Terminate
Colonel Chabert
Colonel Wolodyjowski
The Conqueror
Conquest of the Normans
Coup de Grace
The Court Martial of Billy Mitchell▲
Cromwell
Cup Final
Danton▲
Days of Hell
Deadline
The Deluge
The Desert of the Tartars
Devil Wears White
Distant Drums
Doctor Zhivago▲
Dragon Seed
Eagles Attack at Dawn
1860
El Cid▲
El Paso Stampede
Elizabeth of Ladymead▲
Emissary
The Enchanted Cottage
The End of St. Petersburg▲
The Expendables
The Fall of the Roman Empire▲
Field of Honor
Fiesta
The Fighter▲
Fighting Marines
Fighting Pilot
The Fighting Prince of Donegal
The Finest Hour
Fire Over England▲
The Firing Line
Flor Silvestre
Flowers of Reverie
Forever and a Day▲
Fort Apache▲
Forty Days of Musa Dagh
The Four Feathers▲
The Four Feathers
F.P. 1
Funny, Dirty Little War
Guerilla Brigade
Gunga Din▲
Guns at Batasi
Hail the Conquering Hero▲
Harry's War
Heart of a Nation▲
Heartbreak Ridge▲
Hearts & Armour
Heaven & Earth▲
Hell in the Pacific▲
Hell on the Battleground
Hell Raiders
Henry V▲
Hero Bunker
The Hidden Fortress▲
Hill 24 Doesn't Answer▲
Holy Terror
Hombres Armados▲
Homecoming▲
How I Won the War
In the Name of the Pope-King▲
The Informer▲
The Invincible Gladiator
Johnny Got His Gun▲
Judith of Bethulia▲
Khartoum
Killers
Kippur▲
Kolberg
La Marseillaise▲
La Nuit de Varennes▲
The Last Command
The Last of the Mohicans▲
The Last of the Mohicans
The Last of the Mohicans▲
The Last Valley
Late Summer Blues
Latino
Laughing at Life
Le Petit Soldat▲
Legion of Missing Men
The Life and Death of Colonel Blimp▲
Lion of the Desert▲
Lipstick on Your Collar
The Longest Day▲
The Lost Command
Mademoiselle Fifi
Man from the Alamo▲
Man with a Cross
Massive Retaliation
Megaforce
Mercenary Fighters
Mission Kashmir
Mission to Glory
Mission to Kill
The Mongols
The Moonraker
Mother▲
The Mouse That Roared▲
Mulan
Napoleon▲
No Man's Land
Old Gringo
One Night Stand▲
Orphans of the Storm▲
The Phantom Planet
Planet of the Apes▲
Prehistoric Bimbos in Armageddon City
The Pride and the Passion
Prisoner of the Mountains▲
Project: Alien
Rage to Kill
The Rape of the Sabines
The Real Glory▲
A Reason to Live, a Reason to Die
The Red and the Black▲
The Red and the White▲
Red Dawn
Reds▲
Reed: Insurgent Mexico
Reign of Terror
Revenge of the Barbarians
Rhodes
Richard III
Richard III▲
Ride to Glory
River of Unrest
Rough Riders
Ryan's Daughter
Saga of the Vagabond
Salome, Where She Danced
Sanders of the River▲
Scarlet Dawn
Senso▲
The Seventeenth Bride
Shake Hands with the Devil▲
The Shame▲
Sharpe's Battle
Sharpe's Company
Sharpe's Eagle
Sharpe's Enemy
Sharpe's Gold
Sharpe's Honour
Sharpe's Justice
Sharpe's Legend
Sharpe's Mission
Sharpe's Regiment
Sharpe's Revenge
Sharpe's Rifles
Sharpe's Siege
Sharpe's Sword
Sharpe's Waterloo
Shot Through the Heart▲
Simon Bolivar
Sinai Commandos
Smugglers
Something of Value▲
South Park: Bigger, Longer and Uncut
Starship Troopers▲
Storm over Asia▲
Striker
Surprise Attack
Taras Bulba
This England
This Island Earth
The 317th Platoon▲
Tiger Joe
Time to Kill
The Torch
Treasure of the Lost Desert
The Ugly American
Ulysses' Gaze
Under Fire▲
The Uprising▲
Vera Cruz
Villa Rides
Walker
War and Peace
War and Peace▲
War and Peace
War Bus Commando
Warbirds
Waterloo
Weekend War
Welcome to Sarajevo▲
White Dwarf
Wild Geese 2
Wing Commander
The World Owes Me a Living
World War III
Yank in Libya
Young Winston▲
Zulu Dawn▲

Washington, DC

***see** Capitol Capers*

Wedding Bells

***see also** Marriage; Otherwise Engaged; Wedding Hell*

Aladdin and the King of Thieves
Anne of Green Gables: The Continuing Story
The Arrangement▲
The Bachelor
The Best Man▲
Betsy's Wedding
Blind Date
The Bride Came C.O.D.
The Bride Walks Out
Common Ground
Date Bait
The Duke
Easy Money
8 Seconds
Emma▲
Esmeralda Comes by Night
Everyone Says I Love You▲
Fanci's Persuasion
Fandango
Father of the Bride▲
Father of the Bride
Foolin' Around
For Better and for Worse
Forget Paris
Four Weddings and a Funeral▲
Full of Life
Give Me a Sailor
Hard Promises
Heartbreakers
Holy Matrimony
Honeymoon in Vegas
House Party 3
Housesitter
It Started with Eve▲
Jack and Sarah
Jerry Maguire▲
The Jewel of the Nile
Kissing a Fool
Love, etc.
Lovers and Other Strangers▲
Ma Vie en Rose▲
The Marriage of Figaro
The Marrying Man
The Member of the Wedding
Miami Rhapsody
Mickey Blue Eyes
Minnie and Moskowitz
The Mirror Has Two Faces
Mrs. Winterbourne
Monsoon Wedding▲
Moonstruck▲

▲ = rated three bones or higher

Murders in the Rue Morgue
Muriel's Wedding▲
My Best Friend's Wedding
My Big Fat Greek Wedding
My Favorite Wife▲
Neil Simon's The Odd Couple 2
Nine Months
Notting Hill▲
Only You
The Philadelphia Story▲
Polish Wedding
Prelude to a Kiss
Reckless: The Sequel▲
Revenge of the Nerds 4: Nerds in Love
Rhythm on the Range
Ride with the Devil
Roommates
Royal Wedding▲
She's Having a Baby
Sixteen Candles▲
Splendor
The Summer House
That Old Feeling
The 30-Foot Bride of Candy Rock
Three Smart Girls Grow Up▲
To Each His Own▲
Two Moon Junction
Waikiki Wedding▲
A Wedding
Wedding Band
Wedding Bell Blues
The Wedding March▲
The Wedding Party
Wedding Rehearsal
West Is West
When Harry Met Sally...▲
Where There's Life
The Wood
The World's Oldest Living Bridesmaid

Wedding Hell

see also *Marriage; Otherwise Engaged; Wedding Bells*

Analyze This▲
The Best Man
Best Men
The Big Day
Blood Bride
The Blood Spattered Bride
The Bride
The Bride & the Beast
The Bride of Frankenstein▲
Bride of Killer Nerd
Bride of Re-Animator
Bride of the Gorilla
Bride of the Monster
The Bride with White Hair
The Bride Wore Black▲
Brides of the Beast
Captive
The Catered Affair▲
Cheatin' Hearts
Contract▲
Feeling Minnesota
The Flame of New Orleans▲
Forces of Nature
Ganja and Hess
The Graduate▲
The Hanging Garden
He Knows You're Alone
Highway to Hell
Honeymoon
Honeymoon Killers▲
I Married a Monster from Outer Space
I Think I Do
In and Out▲
Last Lives
Love Stinks
Meet the Parents▲
My New Gun
The Newlydeads
Niagara
The Perfect Bride
Riding in Cars with Boys
River Street
Runaway Bride▲
Saving Silverman
The Sweetest Thing
That Old Feeling
Tomcats
Trojan Eddie▲
True Love▲
28 Days
The Undertaker's Wedding
Very Bad Things
The Wedding Banquet▲
Wedding in Blood▲
Wedding in White
The Wedding Planner
The Wedding Singer

Werewolves

see also *Metamorphosis*

An American Werewolf in London▲
An American Werewolf in Paris
Bad Moon
The Beast Must Die
Blood of Dracula's Castle
Bride of the Gorilla
Brotherhood of the Wolf
Children of the Full Moon
The Company of Wolves▲
The Craving
The Creeps
Cry of the Werewolf
Curse of the Devil
Curse of the Queerwolf
The Curse of the Werewolf
Deathmoon
Dr. Jekyll and the Wolfman
Dr. Terror's House of Horrors
Dracula vs. Frankenstein
Face of the Screaming Werewolf
Frankenstein Meets the Wolfman▲
Full Eclipse
The Fury of the Wolfman
Ginger Snaps
Hercules, Prisoner of Evil
House of Dracula
House of Frankenstein
The Howling▲
Howling 2: Your Sister Is a Werewolf
Howling 3: The Marsupials
Howling 4: The Original Nightmare
Howling 6: The Freaks
The Howling: New Moon Rising
I Was a Teenage Werewolf
Legend of the Werewolf
The Legend of the Wolf Woman
Lone Wolf
Mad at the Moon
The Mad Monster
Meridian: Kiss of the Beast
Monster Dog
The Monster Squad
Moon of the Wolf
My Mom's a Werewolf
Night of the Howling Beast
Orgy of the Dead
Project Metalbeast: DNA Overload
Rage of the Werewolf
The Rats Are Coming! The Werewolves Are Here!
Return of the Vampire
Scream of the Wolf
She Wolf of London
Silver Bullet
The Strangers
Teen Wolf
Teen Wolf Too
The Undying Monster
Waxwork
Werewolf
Werewolf in a Girl's Dormitory
Werewolf of London
Werewolf of Washington
The Werewolf vs. the Vampire Woman
Werewolves on Wheels
Wilderness
Wolf
Wolf Blood
The Wolf Man▲
Wolfen▲
The Wolfman
The Wolves of Kromer

Western Comedy

see also *Comedy; Westerns*

Adios Amigo
Alias Jesse James
Along Came Jones▲
The Apple Dumpling Gang
The Apple Dumpling Gang Rides Again
Bad Man's River
Ballad of Cable Hogue▲
Bang Bang Kid
The Beautiful Blonde from Bashful Bend
Beyond the Trail
Blazing Saddles▲
Bordello
Border Phantom
Boss
Bowery Buckaroos
Branded Men
Bronco Billy
Brothers O'Toole
Bus Stop▲
Carry On Cowboy
Cat Ballou▲
Catlow
Check & Double Check
The Cherokee Kid
The Cheyenne Social Club
The Cisco Kid
City Slickers▲
City Slickers 2: The Legend of Curly's Gold
Cold Feet
Companeros
The Cowboy Way
Desperate Women
Destry Rides Again▲
The Duchess and the Dirtwater Fox
Ebenezer
El Diablo Rides
Evil Roy Slade▲
Four Eyes and Six Guns
Four for Texas
The Frisco Kid
From Noon Till Three
Go West
Goin' South▲
Gold Raiders
The Good Guys and the Bad Guys
Greaser's Palace
Great Scout & Cathouse Thursday
Gun Crazy
The Hallelujah Trail
Hangman's Knot
Hearts of the West▲
How the West Was Fun
I'm from Arkansas
The Incredible Rocky Mountain Race
The Kid Brother▲
Lemonade Joe
Life & Times of Judge Roy Bean
Lightning Jack
Local Badman
Lucky Luke
Maverick
McLintock!▲
More Wild, Wild West
The Nervous Wreck▲
Oklahoma Kid▲
The Outlaws Is Coming!
Over the Hill Gang
The Paleface▲
Pardners
Pocket Money
Rachel and the Stranger▲
Rancho Deluxe▲
Red Garters
Rhythm on the Range
Ride 'Em Cowboy
The Rounders
Rustler's Rhapsody
Samurai Cowboy
The Scalphunters
Scandalous John
September Gun
The Shakiest Gun in the West
Shame, Shame on the Bixby Boys
Shanghai Noon
Sodbusters
Son of Paleface▲
Sons of Trinity
Sting of the West
Straight to Hell
Sunset
Support Your Local Gunfighter▲
Support Your Local Sheriff▲
Take Me Back to Oklahoma
Texas▲
Texas across the River
Texas Layover
There Was a Crooked Man▲
They Call Me Trinity
Three Godfathers▲
Ticket to Tomahawk
Trinity Is Still My Name
Troublemakers
Under Montana Skies
The Villain
Wackiest Wagon Train in the West
Wagons East
Waterhole #3
Way Out West▲
Wild & Wooly
Wild Horse Phantom
Wild Rovers
Wild, Wild West Revisited
The Wistful Widow of Wagon Gap
Yellow Hair & the Fortress of Gold
Zachariah

Westerns

see also *Sci-Fi Westerns; Spaghetti Western; Supernatural Westerns; Western Comedy; Westrogens*

Abilene Town▲
Aces and Eights
Aces Wild
Across the Line
Across the Plains
The Adventures of Gallant Bess
Adventures of Red Ryder
Against a Crooked Sky
The Alamo▲
Alias Billy the Kid
Alias John Law
All the Pretty Horses
Allegheny Uprising
Along the Great Divide
Along the Navaho Trail
Along the Sundown Trail
Alvarez Kelly
Ambush at Tomahawk Gap
Ambush Trail
American Empire
American Outlaws
Americano
Angel and the Badman▲
Animal Called Man
Another Man, Another Chance
Another Pair of Aces: Three of a Kind▲
Apache
Apache Blood
Apache Chief
Apache Kid's Escape
Apache Rose
Apache Uprising
Apache Woman
The Appaloosa
Arizona
Arizona Bound
Arizona Bushwackers
Arizona Cowboy
Arizona Days
Arizona Gangbusters
Arizona Gunfighter
Arizona Kid
Arizona Mahoney
Arizona Raiders
Arizona Roundup
Arizona Stagecoach
Arizona Terror
Arizona Whirlwind
Arrowhead
At Gunpoint
The Avenging
The Avenging Angel
Back in the Saddle
Backfire
Bad Company▲
Bad Day at Black Rock▲
Bad Guys
Bad Jim
Bad Lands
Bad Man of Deadwood
Bad Men of the Border
The Badlanders▲
Badman's Territory▲
Badmen of Nevada
Ballad of a Gunfighter
Ballad of Gregorio Cortez▲
Bandit King of Texas
Bandit Queen
Bandits
Bandolero!
Barbarosa▲
The Bargain
Baron of Arizona▲
Battle of Elderbush Gulch
Battling Marshal
Battling Outlaws
Battling with Buffalo Bill
Bells of Capistrano
Bells of Coronado
Bells of Rosarita
Bells of San Angelo
Bells of San Fernando
Below the Border
Bend of the River▲
Best of the Badmen
Between Fighting Men
Between God, the Devil & a Winchester
Between Men
Beyond the Rockies
Big Calibre
The Big Cat
The Big Country
A Big Hand for the Little Lady
Big Jake
Big Show
The Big Sky▲
The Big Sombrero
Big Stakes
The Big Stampede
Big Trail▲
Billy the Kid
Billy the Kid in Texas
Billy the Kid Returns
Billy the Kid Trapped
Billy Two Hats
Bite the Bullet▲
Black Fox: Blood Horse
Black Fox: Good Men and Bad
Black Fox: The Price of Peace
Black Hills
The Black Lash
Black Market Rustlers
Blazing Across the Pecos
Blazing Guns
Blind Justice
Blood at Sundown
Blood on the Moon
Bloody Trail
Blue
Blue Canadian Rockies
Blue Steel
Boiling Point
Bonanza: The Return
Bonanza Town
Boot Hill Bandits
Boothill Brigade
Boots & Saddles
Boots of Destiny
Border Badmen
Border Bandits
Border Caballero
Border Devils
Border Feud
Border Law
The Border Legion
Border Patrol
Border Rangers
Border Romance
Border Roundup
Border Saddlemates
Border Shootout
Border Vengeance
Border Vigilantes
Bordertown Gunfighters
Born in America
Boss Cowboy
Boss of Bullion City
Boss of Rawhide
The Bounty Man
Brand of Fear
Brand of Hate
Brand of the Outlaws
Branded
Branded a Bandit
Branded a Coward
The Bravados▲
Breakheart Pass
Breed of the Border
Broadway to Cheyenne
Broken Arrow
Broken Lance▲
Bronson's Revenge
Bronze Buckaroo
Brothers of the West
Buck and the Preacher
Buckeye and Blue
Buckskin
Buckskin Frontier
Buffalo Bill
Buffalo Bill & the Indians▲
Buffalo Bill Rides Again
Buffalo Rider
Buffalo Soldiers▲
Buffalo Stampede
Bugles in the Afternoon
Bull of the West
Bulldog Courage
Bullet Code
Bullwhip
The Burning Hills
Bury Me Not on the Lone Prairie
The Bushwackers
Butch and Sundance: The Early Days
Butch Cassidy and the Sundance Kid▲
Buzzy Rides the Range
Cahill: United States Marshal
Cain's Cutthroats
California Joe
Call of the Canyon
Call of the Forest
Call of the Rockies
Calling Wild Bill Elliott
Can't Help Singing
Canyon Passage▲
Captain Apache
The Captive: The Longest Drive 2
The Capture▲
The Caravan Trail
The Cariboo Trail
Carson City Kid
Cattle Queen of Montana
Cavalcade of the West
Cavalier of the West
Cavalry
Cavalry Charge
Cavalry Command
Challenge of McKenna
Charro!
Chato's Land
Check Your Guns
Cheyenne Autumn
Cheyenne Kid
Cheyenne Rides Again
Cheyenne Takes Over
Cheyenne Warrior
Child of the Prairie
The Chisholms
Chisum
The Christmas Kid
Chuka
Cimarron
Circle Canyon
Circle of Death
The Claim
Clearing the Range
Code of the Fearless
Colorado
Colorado Serenade
Colorado Sundown
Colt Comrades
Comanche Station
Comanche Territory
The Comancheros▲
Come on, Cowboys
Come on Danger!
Come on Rangers
Come on Tarzan
Conagher
The Concentratin' Kid
Conquest of Cochise

Westerns

Convict Cowboy
Copper Canyon
Cornered
Coroner Creek
Cotter
Courageous Avenger
Courtin' Wildcats
The Covered Wagon
Covered Wagon Days
Covered Wagon Trails
Cow Town
Cowboy▲
Cowboy & the Bandit
Cowboy & the Senorita
Cowboy Commandos
Cowboy Counselor
Cowboy Millionaire
The Cowboys▲
Cowboys from Texas
Coyote Trails
Crazy Horse and Custer: "The Untold Story"
The Crimson Trail
Crooked Trail
Crossfire
Crossfire Trail▲
Cry Blood, Apache
Culpepper Cattle Co.
Custer's Last Fight
Custer's Last Stand
Cyclone of the Saddle
Dakota
Dakota Incident
Dan Candy's Law
Danger Trails
Daniel Boone
Daniel Boone: Trail Blazer
Daring Danger
Dark Command▲
Dawn on the Great Divide
Dawn Rider
Days of Jesse James
Dead for a Dollar
Dead Man
Dead Man's Revenge
Dead or Alive
Deadly Companions
The Deadly Trackers
Deadwood
Deadwood Pass
Death of a Gunfighter
Death Rides the Plains
Death Rides the Range
Death Valley
Death Valley Manhunt
Death Valley Rangers
The Deerslayer
Demon for Trouble
The Denver & Rio Grande
Deputy Marshal
Desert Gold
Desert Phantom
Desert Snow
Desert Trail
The Desperadoes
Desperados
The Desperados
The Desperate Trail
Devil & Leroy Basset
Devil Horse
Devil Riders
Devil's Canyon
Diamond Trail
The Disciple
Distant Drums
Django
Dodge City▲
Don Daredevil Rides Again
Donner Pass: The Road to Survival
Don't Fence Me In
The Doolins of Oklahoma
Doomed at Sundown
Doomed Caravan▲
Down Dakota Way
Down Mexico Way
Down Texas Way
Down the Wyoming Trail
Draw!
Drift Fence
The Drifter
The Driftin' Kid
Driftin' River
Drum Beat
Drum Taps
Drums Along the Mohawk▲
Dude Bandit
Dude Ranger
Duel at Diablo▲
Duel at Silver Creek
Duel in the Sun▲
Durango Valley Raiders
Dynamite and Gold
Dynamite Canyon
Dynamite Pass
Dynamite Ranch
Eagle's Wing
El Condor
El Diablo
El Dorado▲
El Paso Stampede
The Electric Horseman
Enemy of the Law
Escape from Fort Bravo
Every Man's Law
Everything That Rises
Extreme Prejudice
Eyes of Texas
False Colors
Fangs of Fate
Far Country▲
Far Frontier
Fargo Express
Fast Bullets
Fastest Guitar Alive
Fastest Gun Alive▲
Feud Maker
Feud of the Trail
Feud of the West
The Fiddlin' Buckaroo
$50,000 Reward
Fight for Gold
The Fighter
Fightin' Ranch
Fighting Caballero
Fighting Caravans
Fighting Champ
Fighting Cowboy
Fighting Fists of Shanghai Joe
Fighting Fool
Fighting Jack
The Fighting Kentuckian
The Fighting Legion
The Fighting Marshal
Fighting Parson
The Fighting Redhead
Fighting Renegade
Fighting Shadows
The Fighting Sheriff
The Fighting Stallion▲
Fighting Texans
Fighting Thru
The Fighting Trooper
Fighting Valley
Fighting Vigilantes
Fighting with Kit Carson
Finger on the Trigger
Firecreek
Fistful of Death
Five Card Stud
Flame of the Barbary Coast
Flaming Bullets
Flaming Frontiers
Flaming Lead
Flaming Star▲
Flesh and the Spur
Forbidden Trails
Forlorn River
Fort Apache▲
The Forty-Niners
Four Faces West
Four Rode Out
Frank and Jesse
Frontier Days
Frontier Fugitives
Frontier Horizon
Frontier Justice
Frontier Law
Frontier Outlaws
Frontier Pony Express
Frontier Scout
Frontier Uprising
Frontier Vengeance
The Frontiersmen
The Fugitive: Taking of Luke McVane
Fugitive Valley
The Gallant Fool
Galloping Dynamite
Galloping Romeo
The Gambler Returns: The Luck of the Draw
The Gambling Terror
Gangster's Den
Gangsters of the Frontier
The Gatling Gun
Gaucho Serenade
The Gay Ranchero
Gentle Savage
The Gentleman from California
Gentleman from Dixie
Gentleman from Texas
The Gentleman Killer
Geronimo
Geronimo: An American Legend
Geronimo's Revenge
Get That Girl
Ghost City
Ghost Rider
Ghost Town
Ghost Town Gold
Ghost Town Law
Ghost Town Renegades
Ghost Town Riders
Ghost Valley
Girl of the Golden West
Git Along Little Dogies
The Glory Trail
God's Country and the Man
God's Gun
The Golden Stallion
Gone with the West
Good Day for a Hanging
A Good Day to Die
The Good Old Boys
Gore Vidal's Billy the Kid
Grand Canyon Trail
Grayeagle
Great Day in the Morning
The Great Gundown
Great Jesse James Raid
Great Missouri Raid
The Great Northfield Minnesota Raid
Great Treasure Hunt
Gun Code
Gun Fury
Gun Glory
Gun Grit
Gun Law
Gun Lords of Stirrup Basin
Gun Packer
Gun Play
The Gun Ranger
Gun Riders
A Gunfight
Gunfight at the O.K. Corral▲
The Gunfighter▲
Gunfighter
The Gunfighters
Gunfighter's Moon
Gunfire
Gunman from Bodie
Gunman's Walk
Gunners & Guns
Gunplay
Guns for Dollars
Guns in the Dark
Guns of Diablo
Guns of Fury
Guns of Justice
Guns of the Law
Guns of the Magnificent Seven
Gunslinger
Gunsmoke
Gunsmoke: Return to Dodge
Gunsmoke Trail
The Half-Breed
Hands Across the Border
The Hanged Man
The Hanging Tree▲
Hannie Caulder
Hard Bounty
Hard Hombre
Harlem on the Prairie
Harlem Rides the Range
Harry Tracy
The Harvey Girls▲
Haunted Gold
Haunted Ranch
Hawaiian Buckaroo
The Hawk of Powder River
Hawken's Breed
Headin' for the Rio Grande
Heart of Texas Ryan
Heart of the Golden West
Heart of the Rio Grande
Heart of the Rockies
Heaven's Gate
Hell Fire Austin
Helldorado
Heller in Pink Tights
Hellfire
Hello Trouble
Hell's Hinges
Helltown
Heritage of the Desert
Heroes of the Alamo
Heroes of the Hills
Hidden Gold
Hidden Guns▲
Hidden Valley
High Lonesome
High Noon▲
High Noon
High Noon: Part 2
High Plains Drifter
Hills of Oklahoma
Hills of Utah
Hired Hand
His Brother's Ghost
His Fighting Blood
Hit the Saddle
Hittin' the Trail
Hole in the Sky
Hombre▲
Home in Oklahoma
Homesteaders of Paradise Valley
Hondo▲
Honor of the Range
Hopalong Cassidy▲
Hopalong Cassidy: Borrowed Trouble
Hopalong Cassidy: Dangerous Venture
Hopalong Cassidy: False Paradise
Hopalong Cassidy: Hoppy's Holiday
Hopalong Cassidy: Renegade Trail
Hopalong Cassidy Returns
Hopalong Cassidy: Riders of the Deadline
Hopalong Cassidy: Silent Conflict
Hopalong Cassidy: Sinister Journey
Hopalong Cassidy: The Dead Don't Dream
Hopalong Cassidy: The Devil's Playground
Hopalong Cassidy: The Marauders
Hopalong Cassidy: Unexpected Guest
Hoppy Serves a Writ
Horizons West
Hostile Guns
Hot Lead
Hour of the Gun
How the West Was Won▲
Hurricane Express
I Shot Billy the Kid
I Shot Jesse James▲
I Will Fight No More Forever▲
Idaho
In Old Caliente
In Old California
In Old Cheyenne
In Old Colorado
In Old Montana
In Old New Mexico
In Old Santa Fe
In the Days of the Thundering Herd & the Law & the Outlaw
The Indian Fighter▲
Indian Paint
Indian Uprising
Invitation to a Gunfighter
Iron Mountain Trail
The Ivory Handled Gun
The Jack Bull
The Jayhawkers
Jeepers Creepers
Jeremiah Johnson▲
Jesse James▲
Jesse James at Bay
Jesse James Rides Again
Jesse James Under the Black Flag
Joe Kidd
Johnny Reno
Jory
Joshua
Jubal
Jubilee Trail
Junior Bonner▲
Justice of the West
Justice Rides Again
The Kansan
Kansas Pacific
The Kansas Terrors
Keep the Change
Kenny Rogers as the Gambler
Kenny Rogers as the Gambler, Part 2: The Adventure Continues
Kenny Rogers as the Gambler, Part 3: The Legend Continues
The Kentuckian
Kentucky Rifle
Kid Courageous
Kid from Gower Gulch
Kid Ranger
Kid Vengeance
Kid's Last Ride
The King and Four Queens
King of the Bullwhip
King of the Cowboys
King of the Grizzlies
King of the Pecos
King of the Rodeo
King of the Sierras
King of the Stallions
King of the Texas Rangers
King of the Wild Horses▲
Kit Carson
Knights of the Range
The Lamb
Land of Hunted Men
Land of the Lawless
Land Raiders
Laramie Kid
Larry McMurtry's Dead Man's Walk
Larry McMurtry's Streets of Laredo▲
Last Bullet
The Last Command
Last Days of Frank & Jesse James
Last Frontier
Last Gun
The Last Hunt
Last of the Clintons
Last of the Comanches
The Last of the Dogmen
Last of the Pony Riders
Last of the Warrens
Last of the Wild Horses
The Last Outlaw
Last Outlaw
The Last Outlaw
The Last Ride of the Dalton Gang
Last Stand at Saber River
Last Train from Gun Hill▲
The Law and Jake Wade
Law and Lawless
Law and Order
Law for Tombstone
Law of the Land
Law of the Lash
Law of the Pampas
Law of the Saddle
Law of the Texan
The Law Rides
The Law Rides Again
Law West of Tombstone
The Lawless Breed▲
Lawless Frontier
Lawless Range
A Lawless Street
Lawman▲
A Lawman Is Born▲
Lawmen
The Lazarus Man
Leather Burners
The Left-Handed Gun▲
Legend of Alfred Packer
Legend of Earl Durand
The Legend of Frank Woods
Legend of Frenchie King
The Legend of Jedediah Carver
Legend of the Lone Ranger
Legend of Tom Dooley
Legion of the Lawless
The Light of Western Stars
Lightnin' Carson Rides Again
Lightning Bill
Lightning Bill Crandall
Lightning Raiders
Lightning Range
Lightning Strikes West
Lightning Warrior
Lights of Old Santa Fe
Lion's Den
Little Big Horn
Little Big Man▲
Little Moon & Jud McGraw
Loaded Pistols
The Lone Avenger
Lone Bandit
The Lone Defender
Lone Justice
Lone Justice 2
Lone Justice 3: Showdown at Plum Creek
The Lone Ranger
Lone Ranger
The Lone Rider in Cheyenne
The Lone Rider in Ghost Town
Lone Star
Lone Star▲
Lone Star Law Men
The Lone Star Ranger
Lone Wolf McQuade
Lonely Are the Brave▲
Lonely Man
Lonesome Dove▲
Lonesome Trail
The Long Riders▲
The Longest Drive
Los Locos Posse
Lost Canyon
Love Desperados
Lucky Cisco Kid
Lucky Terror
Lucky Texan
Lust for Gold
The Lusty Men▲
Macho Callahan
MacKenna's Gold
Madron
The Magnificent Seven▲
Major Dundee
A Man Alone
Man & Boy
A Man Called Horse▲
A Man Called Sledge
Man from Button Willow
Man from Cheyenne
Man from Colorado
The Man from Gun Town
The Man from Hell
Man from Hell's Edges
The Man from Laramie▲
Man from Montana
Man from Monterey
The Man from Music Mountain
The Man from Painted Post
The Man from Snowy River
Man from Texas
Man from the Alamo▲
Man from Thunder River
Man from Utah
Man in the Saddle
Man in the Shadow
Man of Action
Man of the Forest
Man of the West
Man or Gun
Man Who Loved Cat Dancing
The Man Who Shot Liberty Valance▲
Man Without a Star▲
Manchurian Avenger
The Manhunt
Man's Country
Man's Land
Mark of the Spur
Marked for Murder
Marked Trails
Marshal of Cedar Rock
Marshal of Heldorado
The Marshal's Daughter
The Masked Rider
Mason of the Mounted
McCabe & Mrs. Miller▲
The McMasters

▸ = rated three bones or higher

The Virginian
The Virginian▲
The Virginian
Wagon Master▲
Wagon Tracks
Wagon Trail
Wagon Wheels
Wagon's Westward
Walk the Proud Land
Walking Thunder
Wall Street Cowboy
The Walloping Kid
Wanda Nevada
War Arrow
War of the Wildcats
The War Wagon▲
Warden of Red Rock
Warlock▲
Water Rustlers
Way of the West
The Way West
West of Nevada
West of Pinto Basin
West of the Divide
West of the Law
West of the Pecos
West to Glory
Western Frontier
Western Gold
Western Justice
Western Mail
Western Pacific Agent
Western Trails
Western Union▲
The Westerner▲
Westward Ho
Westward Ho, the Wagons!
Westward the Women▲
When a Man Rides Alone
When a Man Sees Red
When the Legends Die▲
When the West Was Young
Where Trails Divide
Where Trails End
Whirlwind Horseman
Whistlin' Dan
Whistling Bullets
The White Buffalo
White Comanche
White Eagle
White Gold▲
Wild Bill
The Wild Bunch▲
Wild Country
The Wild Country
Wild Frontier
Wild Horse
Wild Horse Canyon
Wild Horse Rodeo
Wild Mustang
Wild Times
Wild West
Wild Wild West
The Wildcat
Wildfire
Will Penny▲
Winchester '73▲
The Wind▲
Wind River
Winds of the Wasteland
Winners of the West
Winning of the West
With Kit Carson over the Great Divide
Without Honors
Wolf Call
Wolfheart's Revenge
The Woman of the Town
Wrangler
Wyatt Earp
Wyatt Earp: Return to Tombstone
Wyoming Outlaw
Yellow Dust
The Yellow Rose of Texas
Yodelin' Kid from Pine Ridge
You Know My Name▲
Young Bill Hickok
Young Blood
Young Buffalo Bill
Young Guns
Young Guns 2
The Young Land
The Young Pioneers
Yuma
Zandy's Bride
Zorro Rides Again
Zorro's Fighting Legion

Westrogens

see also ***Westerns; Wonder Women***

Angel and the Badman▲
Annie Get Your Gun▲
Annie Oakley▲
Bad Girls
The Ballad of Little Jo
The Beautiful Blonde from Bashful Bend
Belle Starr
A Big Hand for the Little Lady
Buffalo Girls
Calamity Jane▲
Calamity Jane
Cat Ballou▲
Comes a Horseman
Even Cowgirls Get the Blues
Girl from Calgary
The Gunslinger
Hannie Caulder
Heartland▲
Johnny Guitar▲
The Maverick Queen
McCabe & Mrs. Miller▲
Nevada
Poker Alice
The Quick and the Dead
Raiders of Sunset Pass
Ramrod
Riders of the Purple Sage
The Rowdy Girls
Texas Lady
Tulsa▲
Two Mules for Sister Sara▲
The Wicked, Wicked West
Wild Women
Zorro's Black Whip

Whales

see also ***Deep Blue; Wild Kingdom***

The Adventures of Baron Munchausen▲
The Adventures of Pinocchio
Free Willy
Free Willy 2: The Adventure Home
Free Willy 3: The Rescue
Moby Dick▲
Moby Dick
Namu, the Killer Whale
Orca
Pinocchio▲
Star Trek 4: The Voyage Home▲
Whale for the Killing
Whale Music
Whale of a Tale
The Whales of August▲
When the Whales Came
The White Dawn

Whitewater Rafting

A Cry from the Mountain
Deliverance▲
Good Luck
Race for Your Life, Charlie Brown
The River Wild
Same River Twice
Scream
White Water Summer

Widows & Widowers

see also ***Single Parents; Stepparents***

Dragonfly
First Degree
Frailty▲
Love and Rage
Monster's Ball▲
The Mothman Prophecies
The Road Home▲
St. Patrick's Day
The Salton Sea
The Shipping News
Signs
Witness▲

Wild Kingdom

see also ***Bears; Birds; Cats; Dinosaurs; Elephants; Killer Apes and Monkeys; Killer Beasts; Killer Bugs and Slugs; Killer Dogs; Killer Kats; Killer Pigs; Killer Sea Critters; King of Beasts (Dogs); Monkeyshines; Nice Mice; Pigs; Rabbits; Talking Animals; Whales; Wilderness***

Ace Ventura: When Nature Calls
The Adventures of Tarzan
Africa Texas Style
Alaska
All Creatures Great and Small▲
All Dogs Go to Heaven 2
The Amazing Panda Adventure
Andre
The Animal
Animal Farm▲
Ava's Magical Adventure
Bambi▲
The Barefoot Executive
The Bear▲
The Bears & I
The Beast That Killed Women
Beastmaster
Beastmaster 2: Through the Portal of Time
Beasts
Bedtime for Bonzo
The Belstone Fox
Black Cobra
Bless the Beasts and Children
Born Free▲
Born to Be Wild
Born Wild
The Brave One▲
A Breed Apart
Bringing Up Baby▲
Buddy
Buffalo Rider
Call of the Wild
Captive Wild Woman
Catch as Catch Can
Charlie, the Lonesome Cougar
Cheetah
Christian the Lion
The Chronicles of Narnia
Clarence, the Cross-eyed Lion▲
Courage of the North
A Cry in the Dark▲
A Cry in the Wild▲
Dark Age
Darkest Africa
Day of the Animals
The Day of the Dolphin
Doctor Dolittle
Dr. Dolittle
Dr. Dolittle 2
Dumbo▲
Dunston Checks In
Eaten Alive
Ed
The Edge
Ele, My Friend
The Electric Horseman
Elephant Boy▲
An Elephant Called Slowly
The Emperor's New Groove▲
Every Which Way But Loose
Eye of the Wolf
Eyes of the Panther
Far from Home: The Adventures of Yellow Dog
Fierce Creatures
The Fifth Monkey
Flight of the Grey Wolf
Flipper▲
Fly Away Home▲
The Fox and the Hound▲
Francis Covers the Big Town
Francis Goes to the Races
Francis Goes to West Point
Francis in the Haunted House
Francis in the Navy
Francis Joins the WACs
Francis the Talking Mule▲
Frasier the Sensuous Lion
Futz
Gentle Giant
George of the Jungle▲
The Ghost and the Darkness
Gladiator▲
Going Ape!
Going Bananas
The Golden Seal
Gordy
Gorilla
Gorillas in the Mist▲
The Great Adventure▲
The Great Elephant Escape
The Great Rupert▲
Grizzly Adams: The Legend Continues
Gus
Harry and the Hendersons
Hatari!▲
Hawmps!
Hollywood Safari
Homeward Bound 2: Lost in San Francisco
I Dreamed of Africa
Ice Age▲
In the Shadow of Kilimanjaro
The Island of Dr. Moreau
Island of Lost Souls▲
Island of the Blue Dolphins
Joey
Jumanji
Jungle
The Jungle Book▲
Jungle Boy
Jungle Drums of Africa
King Kung Fu
King of the Grizzlies
Lassie, Come Home
The Last Safari
Legend of Lobo
Leonard Part 6
The Leopard Son
The Lion King▲
The Lion King: Simba's Pride
Living Free
The Many Adventures of Winnie the Pooh
Matilda
Max, Mon Amour
The Mighty Peking Man
The Misadventures of Merlin Jones
Mr. Kingstreet's War
Mr. Toad's Wild Ride
Monkey Trouble
Monkeys, Go Home!
Monkey's Uncle
The Monster and the Girl
Mountain Family Robinson
Mountain Man
Murders in the Rue Morgue
My Sister, My Love
Napoleon
Napoleon and Samantha▲
Never Cry Wolf▲
Night of the Grizzly
Nikki, the Wild Dog of the North
Noah's Ark
Once Upon a Forest
Operation Dumbo Drop
Operation Haylift
Pardon My Trunk
Passion in the Desert
Paulie
Pet Sematary 2
Pippi Longstocking
Planet of the Apes▲
Project X
Razorback
Red Earth
The Rescuers▲
The Rescuers Down Under
Ring of Bright Water▲
Rock-a-Doodle
Rudyard Kipling's The Jungle Book
Rudyard Kipling's the Second Jungle Book: Mowgli and Baloo
The Runaways
Running Free
Running Wild
Sammy, the Way-Out Seal
The Secret of NIMH▲
Shakma
Silver Streak▲
Slappy and the Stinkers
Soul of the Beast
Stalk the Wild Child
A Summer to Remember
Super Seal
Survival of Spaceship Earth
The Tender Warrior
Those Calloways
Thumbelina
A Tiger Walks
To Walk with Lions
Tomboy & the Champ
Trap on Cougar Mountain
Vampire Circus
The Wagons Roll at Night
Walk Like a Man
Watership Down
When the North Wind Blows
Whispers: An Elephant's Tale
The White Buffalo
White Gorilla
White Pongo
White Wolves 2: Legend of the Wild
Wild America▲
Wild Horses
The Yearling▲
The Yearling
Zebra in the Kitchen
Zeus and Roxanne

Wilderness

see also ***Trees & Forests***

Abducted
Across the Great Divide
The Adventures of Frontier Fremont
The Adventures of the Wilderness Family
Alaska
All Mine to Give
Almost Heroes
Arctic Blue
Backwoods
The Bear▲
Beyond Fear
Black Robe▲
Blood of the Hunter
The Bridge to Nowhere
Bullies
Bushwhacked
Cannibal! The Musical
The Capture of Grizzly Adams
Claws
Clearcut
Cold River
Continental Divide
Cross Creek
Davy Crockett and the River Pirates
Davy Crockett, King of the Wild Frontier▲
Dead Ahead
Death Hunt
Decoy
Dominion
Earthling
The Edge
Edge of Honor
Endangered
Eyes of Fire
Far from Home: The Adventures of Yellow Dog
Father and Scout
Ferngully: The Last Rain Forest
Flight from Glory
Further Adventures of the Wilderness Family, Part 2
God's Country
Great Adventure
The Great Outdoors
Grizzly
Grizzly Adams: The Legend Continues
Grizzly Falls
Grizzly Mountain
Heaven on Earth
Hunter's Blood
Ice Palace
Jeremiah Johnson▲
Just Before Dawn
Kid Colter
The Legend of Wolf Mountain
Life & Times of Grizzly Adams
Little Bigfoot
Lost
Lost in the Barrens
Man in the Wilderness
Man of the House
The Many Adventures of Winnie the Pooh
Mountain Charlie
Mountain Family Robinson
Mountain Man
Napoleon
Napoleon and Samantha▲
Never Cry Wolf▲
Northwest Passage▲
Northwest Trail
Orphans of the North
Quest for Fire▲
Shoot to Kill▲
Silence
Silence of the North
Slashed Dreams
Sourdough
Spirit of the Eagle
Starbird and Sweet William
The Tale of Ruby Rose▲
Tales of the Klondike: In a Far Country
Tales of the Klondike: Race for Number One
Tales of the Klondike: The Scorn of Women
Tales of the Klondike: The Unexpected
The Ticket
Timber Queen
True Heart
Tundra
Violent Zone
Warrior Spirit
White Fang▲
White Fang and the Hunter
The White Tower▲
White Water Summer
White Wolves 2: Legend of the Wild
White Wolves 3: Cry of the White Wolf
Whitewater Sam
The Wolves
Young & Free
Zero Degrees Kelvin

Witchcraft

see also ***Demons & Wizards; Occult***

Bell, Book and Candle
Beyond Darkness
Black Magic
Black Sunday▲
Book of Shadows: Blair Witch 2
The Bride with White Hair
The Bride with White Hair 2
Brotherhood 2: The Young Warlocks
Burn Witch, Burn!▲
Cast a Deadly Spell▲
The Conqueror Worm▲
The Craft
The Crucible▲
Cry of the Banshee
The Curse of the Crying Woman
Curse of the Devil
Daughters of Satan
Day of Wrath▲
The Day the Earth Froze
The Demons
The Devil Rides Out▲
The Devils▲
Devonsville Terror
Dr. Strange
Double Double Toil and Trouble
The Eternal

 ▲ = rated three bones or higher

Eye of the Demon
Eyes of Fire
Four Rooms
Fright House
The Haunted Palace
The Haunting of Morella
Hellblock 13
Hercules, Prisoner of Evil
Hocus Pocus
Horror Hotel
Horror Rises from the Tomb
The Hospital▸
House of the Black Death
I Married a Witch▸
Inquisition
I've Been Waiting for You
The Juniper Tree
Kill, Baby, Kill▸
Kill Me Tomorrow
The Lady's Not for Burning
Lisa and the Devil
Little Witches
Lost Legacy: A Girl Called Hatter Fox
Love at Stake
Maciste in Hell
Mark of the Devil
Mark of the Devil 2
Netherworld
Night of the Scarecrow
The Polar Bear King
Practical Magic
Pufnstuf
Quartier Mozart
Rendez-Moi Ma Peau
The Resurrected
Return to Oz
Sabrina the Teenage Witch
Season of the Witch
The She-Beast
The Shrieking
Sleepy Hollow▸
Snow White: A Tale of Terror
Snow White: The Fairest of Them All
Something Weird
Sorceress▸
Sorceress
Spellbreaker: Secret of the Leprechauns
Summer of Fear
The Terror
Terror Beach
That Darn Sorceress
Three Sovereigns for Sarah
The Touch of Satan
Troll 2
The Undead
The Virgin Witch
Warlock
Warlock 3: The End of Innocence
Warlock Moon
Warlock: The Armageddon
The Werewolf vs. the Vampire Woman
Wicked Stepmother
The Witch
Witch Who Came from the Sea
A Witch Without a Broom
Witchcraft
Witchcraft 3: The Kiss of Death
Witchcraft 4: Virgin Heart
Witchcraft 7: Judgement Hour
Witchcraft 8: Salem's Ghost
Witchcraft 9: Bitter Flesh
Witchcraft 10: Mistress of the Craft
Witchery
The Witches
The Witches▸
Witches' Brew
Witches' Mountain
The Witches of Eastwick
The Witching of Ben Wagner
The Witchmaker
Witchouse
Witchouse 3: Demon Fire
The Witch's Mirror
WitchTrap
The Wizard of Oz▸
The Woman Who Came Back
The Worst Witch

Witness Protection Program

***see also** Organized Crime; U.S. Marshals*

Ballistic
Eraser
Federal Protection
The Godfather, Part 2▸
Goodfellas▸
Hide in Plain Sight▸
Lethal Weapon 2▸
My Blue Heaven
Nowhere Land
The Pact
Romeo Is Bleeding
Sister Act
The Whole Nine Yards
Witness Protection▸

Women

***see also** Dream Girls; Femme Fatale; Moms; Westrogens; Women in Prison; Wonder Women*

Absolutely Fabulous: The Last Shout
Accidental Meeting
Alice Doesn't Live Here Anymore
Amelia Earhart: The Final Flight
Anna▸
Another Way▸
Another Woman▸
Antonia and Jane▸
Arizona
Artemisia
The Astounding She-Monster
Babyfever
Bachelor Mother▸
Backstreet Justice
Bandit Queen
Bang
Bar Girls
Beaches▸
Bella Mafia
Betty
Bhaji on the Beach
The Big City
Black Day Blue Night
Black Scorpion
Blood and Sand▸
Blood Games
Blue De Ville
The Bostonians
Boulevard
Boys on the Side
The Buccaneers▸
A Bunny's Tale
Business As Usual
Camilla
Certain Fury
Challenge of a Lifetime
Chantilly Lace
The Children's Hour
China Beach▸
The Circle
Citizen Ruth
City Without Men
Claire of the Moon
The Color Purple▸
Come Back to the Five & Dime Jimmy Dean, Jimmy Dean▸
Commissar▸
Conceiving Ada
Courage Under Fire▸
Crazy Mama
Cry of the Werewolf
Daisy Miller
The Dallas Connection
Dames Ahoy
Dangerous Prey
A Dangerous Woman
Darktown Strutters
The Day the Women Got Even
Dead Men Can't Dance
Deconstructing Harry
Defenseless
The Desperate Trail
Dirty Dishes▸
Dogs: The Rise and Fall of an All-Girl Bookie Joint
A Doll's House
A Doll's House▸
Double Obsession
The Dreamlife of Angels▸
Dreams
The Duchess of Duke Street▸
Early Summer▸
Easy Virtue
Eating
Ebony Dreams
Eddie
8 1/2 Women
Eleanor: First Lady of the World
Elizabeth R▸
Enchanted April
Enid Is Sleeping
Enormous Changes▸
Entertaining Angels: The Dorothy Day Story
Erotique
Even Cowgirls Get the Blues
Evita
The Execution
An Eye for an Eye
Faces of Women
Family Secrets
Feast of July
Feds
Female Perversions
Fire
Fire in the Night
The First Wives Club
Flatbed Annie and Sweetiepie: Lady Truckers
The Flower of My Secret▸
Follow the River
Fran
Fried Green Tomatoes▸
Friends
From the Journals of Jean Seberg
Gangs, Inc.
A Geisha▸
Gentlemen Prefer Blondes▸
G.I. Jane
Girl 6
A Girl Thing
Girlfriends▸
Good Girls Don't
Grace of My Heart
The Great Man's Lady
The Group
Guardian Angel
The Happy Ending
Hard Country
Harvest of Fire
Head of the Family
Heat and Dust▸
Heaven and Earth
The Heidi Chronicles
Hellcats
The Heroic Trio
Hidden Assassin
Honey & Ashes
Horror of the Zombies
House of Whipcord
Household Saints▸
How to Be a Woman and Not Die in the Attempt
How to Make an American Quilt
How to Marry a Millionaire
I Dreamed of Africa
I Like It Like That▸
If These Walls Could Talk
In This House of Brede▸
The Insect Woman▸
Introducing Dorothy Dandridge▸
Is There Life Out There?
Island of Lost Girls
Isn't She Great
Jaded
James Joyce's Women▸
Jamon, Jamon
Je Tu Il Elle
The Joy Luck Club▸
Joy Ride to Nowhere
Judicial Consent
Juliet of the Spirits▸
Just Another Girl on the I.R.T.
Kamikaze Hearts
Kandahar
Katie Tippel
The Ladies Club
Ladies on the Rocks
Ladybird, Ladybird▸
The Last Best Year
Late Chrysanthemums
A League of Their Own▸
Leaving Normal
The Legend of Blood Castle
Les Bonnes Femmes▸
Little Mother
Little Women▸
Little Women
Little Women▸
Live Nude Girls
Lola Montes▸
Losing Isaiah▸
Love After Love
Love and Basketball▸
The Love Goddesses
Lumiere
Madame Bovary▸
Madame Bovary
Madonna: Innocence Lost
Maedchen in Uniform▸
The Magic Bubble
Magnificent Doll
Malou
Mapp & Lucia
Marianne and Juliane▸
Marilyn: The Untold Story▸
Mars Needs Women
Mary, Queen of Scots
Memories of Murder
Messidor
Mi Vida Loca
Miles to Go
Mina Tannenbaum
Miss Firecracker▸
Moll Flanders
Monkey Grip▸
Moonlight and Valentino
Mortal Thoughts
Moscow Does Not Believe in Tears▸
Mother & Daughter: A Loving War
Mother Teresa: In the Name of God's Poor
My Brilliant Career▸
My Twentieth Century▸
9 to 5
Nomugi Pass
Norma Jean and Marilyn
Now and Then
The Nun
One Sings, the Other Doesn't
One True Thing▸
The Opposite Sex
Oriane
Osaka Elegy
Overseas: Three Women with Man Trouble▸
Pancho Barnes
Passenger▸
Passion Fish▸
Patti Rocks▸
Perfume
The Pillow Book
Poetic Justice
Poor Little Rich Girl: The Barbara Hutton Story
Portrait of a Lady▸
Portrait of a Showgirl
Portrait of Teresa▸
A Price above Rubies
Prime Suspect▸
Quartier Mozart
Queen of Diamonds
Question of Silence▸
The Rector's Wife
Rescuers: Stories of Courage "Two Women"▸
Revenge of the Teenage Vixens from Outer Space
Rich and Famous
Rosa Luxemburg
Roseanne: An Unauthorized Biography
Ruby in Paradise▸
Run for the Dream: The Gail Devers Story
Running Mates
Salmonberries
Samson vs. the Vampire Women
Sandra of a Thousand Delights
The Scent of Green Papaya▸
Set It Off
The '70s
Sexual Intent
Shadow on the Sun
She-Devil
The Silences of the Palace▸
A Single Girl
Sister Street Fighter
The Sisterhood
Sisters of the Gion
Sisters, Or the Balance of Happiness
Snapdragon
Sorceress▸
Spices▸
The Spitfire Grill
Stage Door▸
Star!
Steaming
Steel and Lace
Steel Magnolias▸
The Story of Qiu Ju▸
The Story of Women▸
The Stranger
Strangers in Good Company▸
Strangers: The Story of a Mother and Daughter▸
Street of Shame▸
Stripper
Sudden Death
Sunset Strip
Swann
Talk
Talking about Sex
The Tango Lesson
The Taxi Mystery
Tell Me Where It Hurts
Tender Comrade
The Terrorist
Testament of Youth
301, 302
Three Secrets
Tomorrow's Children
Trojan Women
True Women
Trumps
Twenty-One
Unhook the Stars
An Unmarried Woman▸
Unnatural
Up/Down/Fragile
Utamaro and His Five Women
Visiting Hours
Viva Maria!
Voyage en Douce
Waiting to Exhale▸
Walpurgis Night▸
Washington Square▸
Westward the Women▸
What's Love Got to Do with It?
When a Woman Ascends the Stairs
Whose Child Am I?
Widow's Peak
Wildrose▸
Wing Chun
Witchfire
A Woman and a Woman
A Woman Named Jackie
A Woman Rebels
The Women▸
Women from the Lake of Scented Souls
Women in Prison
The Women of Brewster Place▸
Women on the Verge of a Nervous Breakdown▸
Working Girl▸
Working Girls▸
The Wrong Woman

Women Cops

***see also** Cops*

Arizona Heat
Black Widow▸
Blue Steel
China O'Brien
Copycat
Corky Romano
Dear Detective
The Deep End of the Ocean
Do or Die
The Enforcer
Fargo▸
Fatal Beauty
Get Christie Love!
Impulse
L.A. Crackdown
L.A. Crackdown 2
Miss Congeniality
The Mod Squad
One of Her Own
Policewoman Centerfold
Policewomen
Prey of the Chameleon
Scorchy
The Silence of the Lambs▸
Silk 2
A Stranger Among Us
Tereza▸
V.I. Warshawski
Vice Girls

Women in Prison

***see also** Exploitation; Men in Prison; Sexploitation*

Alien 3
Amazon Jail
Bad Girls Dormitory
Bandits
Better Off Dead
The Big Bird Cage
The Big Bust Out
The Big Doll House
Born Innocent
Brokedown Palace
Caged Fear
Caged Fury
Caged Hearts
Caged Heat
Caged Heat 2: Stripped of Freedom
Caged Heat 3000
Caged in Paradiso
Caged Women
Cellblock Sisters: Banished Behind Bars
Chained Heat
Chained Heat 2
Chasers
The Circle
The Concrete Jungle
Condemned to Hell
Condition Red
Convicted: A Mother's Story
Deadlock
Deadlock 2
Desperate Women
East-West
Escape from Cell Block 3
Escape from Hell
False Arrest
Fugitive Rage
Fun
Getting Out
Girl on a Chain Gang
Girls in Chains
Girls in Prison
Girls Riot
Hellblock 13
Hot Box
Human Experiments
I Want to Live!▸
Ilsa, the Wicked Warden
Jailbird Rock
Ladies They Talk About
Lady in the Death House
Last Dance
Love Child
Lust for Freedom
A Map of the World
Me & Veronica
Midnight
Mommy 2: Mommy's Day
The Muthers
Naked Cage
Nightmare in Badham County
99 Women
Off the Wall
Outside Chance
Paradise Road
Playing for Time▸

Prison of Secrets
Prison Stories: Women on the Inside▲
Purgatory
Red Heat
Red Letters
Reflections in the Dark
Reform School Girl
Reform School Girls
Savage Island
Scrubbers
Slammer Girls
Star Slammer
Sweet Sugar
10 Violent Women
Terminal Island
Time Served
Vendetta
Violent Women
Women in Cell Block 7
Women in Fury
Women Unchained
Women's Prison Escape
Women's Prison Massacre

Women in War

see also *Doctors & Nurses; Korean War; Vietnam War; Women; Wonder Women; World War I; World War II*

China Beach▲
Courage Under Fire▲
The English Patient▲
A Farewell to Arms▲
G.I. Jane
A Guy Named Joe
Hanna's War
In Love and War
Nurse Edith Cavell▲
Paradise Road
Purple Hearts
Rodgers & Hammerstein's South Pacific
She Goes to War
So Proudly We Hail▲
South Pacific▲
A Town Like Alice

Wonder Women

see also *Dream Girls*

The Abductors
Act of Vengeance
Alien▲
Alien 3
Alien: Resurrection▲
Aliens▲
Alley Cat
Amazon Warrior
The Amazons
Amazons
The American Angels: Baptism of Blood
Angel's Brigade
Angel's Dance
The Associate
Attack of the 50 Foot Woman
Attack of the 50 Ft. Woman
Attack of the 60-Foot Centerfold
Bad Georgia Road
Barbarian Queen
Barbarian Queen 2: The Empress Strikes Back
Basic Training
Batman and Robin
Batman Returns
Battle Queen 2020
Beauty for the Asking
Big Bad Mama 2
The Big Bust Out
Billie
Bimini Code
The Bionic Woman
Black Scorpion 2: Ground Zero
Blonde in Black Leather
Blonde Savage
Blue Tiger
Buffy the Vampire Slayer▲
Bury Me an Angel
Business As Usual
Chameleon
Chameleon 2: Death Match
Chameleon 3: Dark Angel
Charlie's Angels
China O'Brien 2
Chopper Chicks in Zombietown
The Clan of the Cave Bear
Cleopatra
Cleopatra Jones
Coffy
Colossus and the Amazon Queen
Crouching Tiger, Hidden Dragon▲
Cutthroat Island
Danger Zone
The Deadly and the Beautiful
Deadly Weapons
The Demolitionist
Do or Die
Doctor of Doom
Dragon Fury 2
Evita
The Executioners
The $5.20 an Hour Dream
Fugitive Rage
Galaxis
Get Christie Love!
G.I. Jane
God Said "Ha!"▲
Golden Lady
The Great Texas Dynamite Chase
Heartland▲
Heavy Metal 2000
Hercules the Legendary Journeys, Vol. 1: And the Amazon Women
Hot Box
Hundra
I Spit on Your Grave
Invincible Barbarian
Kilma, Queen of the Amazons
Kisses for My President
L.A. Crackdown
La Femme Nikita▲
Lady Scarface
Lara Croft: Tomb Raider
Lethal Panther
Lethal Woman
The Long Kiss Goodnight
The Lost Empire
Mame
Mankillers
Marie▲
The Messenger: The Story of Joan of Arc
Mind Trap
Mission of Justice
Mistress of the Apes
Moonshine County Express
Nancy Drew, Reporter
Night Partners
Not Without My Daughter
Nyoka and the Tigermen
One Million Years B.C.
Panther Squad
The Perils of Pauline
Phoenix the Warrior
Pocahontas▲
Point of No Return
Prehistoric Women
Queen of the Road
Ravenhawk
Resurrection▲
The River Wild
Roller Blade
Runaway Nightmare
Running Delilah
Sara Dane
Savage Beach
The Savage Girl
Savage Streets
See How She Runs▲
S*H*E
Sheena
She'll Be Wearing Pink Pajamas
She's in the Army Now
The Silence of the Lambs▲
Sister Kenny▲
Skyscraper
Speed 2: Cruise Control
Spice World: The Movie
Stormquest
Superchick
Supergirl
Sweet Revenge
Switchblade Sisters
Terminal Velocity
Thor and the Amazon Women
Tiffany Jones
Trapped
Tulsa▲
The 24 Hour Woman
Uncaged
Velvet Smooth
Waiting to Exhale▲
The Wild World of Batwoman
The Wind and the Lion▲
A Woman Rebels
The World Is Not Enough
Wrestling Women vs. the Aztec Mummy
Zorro's Black Whip

World War II Spies

see also *Spies & Espionage; World War II*

36 Hours▲

World War I

Ace of Aces
The African Queen▲
All Quiet on the Western Front▲
All Quiet on the Western Front
All the King's Men
Anne of Green Gables: The Continuing Story
Anzacs: The War Down Under▲
Arsenal▲
Behind the Lines
The Big Parade▲
Biggles
The Blue Max
Capitaine Conan▲
Catherine Cookson's The Cinder Path
Catherine Cookson's The Wingless Bird
The Chaplin Revue
Charge of the Model T's
Crimson Romance
Dark Journey▲
Darling Lili
Dawn Patrol▲
The Day That Shook the World
Devil in the Flesh▲
Dishonored
Dr. Mabuse, The Gambler▲
Doughboys
The Eagle and the Hawk▲
Elizabeth of Ladymead▲
The End of St. Petersburg▲
FairyTale: A True Story
False Faces
A Farewell to Arms▲
Fifth Day of Peace
The Fighting 69th▲
Flambards
For Me and My Gal
Fort Saganne
The Four Horsemen of the Apocalypse▲
Gallipoli▲
Gods and Monsters▲
Going Home
Grand Illusion▲
The Great War
Half-Shot at Sunrise
Heart of Humanity
Hearts of the World▲
Hedd Wyn
Hell's Angels▲
Hotel Imperial
How Many Miles to Babylon?
In Love and War
An Indecent Obsession
Inside the Lines
The Iron Major
Isn't Life Wonderful▲
Jericho
Killing Floor
King and Country▲
The King of Hearts▲
Lafayette Escadrille
The Land That Time Forgot
Lawrence of Arabia▲
The Legend of Bagger Vance
Legends of the Fall
The Life and Death of Colonel Blimp▲
Life and Nothing But▲
The Lighthorsemen▲
The Little American
Lost Battalion
The Lost Patrol▲
The Love Light
Man of Legend
Mata Hari▲
Mata Hari
Miracle of Our Lady of Fatima
My Son, My Son
Nicholas and Alexandra
1918
Nurse Edith Cavell▲
Paths of Glory▲
The Patriots▲
Photographing Fairies
Q Ships
Return of the Soldier▲
Revolt of the Zombies
She Goes to War
Shopworn Angel▲
Shout at the Devil
Spy in Black▲
Suzy
Testament of Youth
Three Legionnaires
Tin Pan Alley
Today We Live
Tomorrow Is Forever
The Unknown Soldier
Waterloo Bridge▲
Westfront 1918▲
What Price Glory?▲
When the Whales Came
The White Cliffs of Dover▲
Wilson▲
Wings
Wings of Eagles
Yankee Doodle in Berlin
Zeppelin

World War II

see also *The Holocaust; Postwar; POW/MIA; The Resistance*

Above and Beyond▲
Above Suspicion▲
Above Us the Waves▲
Abroad with Two Yanks
Absent Without Leave
The Accompanist
Across the Pacific▲
Action in Arabia
Action in the North Atlantic
Adventures of Smilin' Jack
The Adventures of Werner Holt
The Affair
Against the Wind
Air Force▲
Air Raid Wardens
Alan & Naomi
Alexandria...Why?
Alfred Hitchcock's Aventure Malgache
Alfred Hitchcock's Bon Voyage
All Through the Night▲
Ambush▲
The Americanization of Emily▲
And a Nightingale Sang
Angels One Five
Angry Harvest▲
The Annapolis Story
Another Time, Another Place
Another Time, Another Place▲
Anzio
Arch of Triumph▲
Arch of Triumph
Armored Command
Around the World
The Ascent▲
The Ascent
Ashes and Diamonds▲
The Assault▲
Assault on Agathon
The Assisi Underground
Attack!▲
Attack Force Z
Attack Squadron
The Attic: The Hiding of Anne Frank
Au Revoir les Enfants▲
The Audrey Hepburn Story
Away All Boats
Back Home
Back to Bataan
Background to Danger▲
Band of Brothers▲
Bataan
Battle Cry▲
The Battle of Blood Island
Battle of Britain
The Battle of El Alamein
Battle of Neretva
Battle of the Bulge
Battle of the Commandos
Battle of the Eagles
The Battle of the Japan Sea
Battleforce
Battleground▲
Bear Island
Bedknobs and Broomsticks
Behind Enemy Lines
Berlin Express▲
The Best Years of Our Lives▲
Betrayal from the East
Betrayed▲
Between Heaven and Hell▲
The Big Lift
The Big Red One▲
Black Brigade
The Black Dragons
Black Rain▲
Blockhouse
The Blood of Others
Blood on the Sun
The Boat Is Full▲
Bomb at 10:10
Bombardier
The Boxer and Death▲
Brady's Escape
Brainwashed
Brass Target
The Brave Bunch
Breaking the Code
Breakthrough
The Bridge
The Bridge at Remagen
The Bridge on the River Kwai▲
Bridge to Hell
A Bridge Too Far
Brief Encounter▲
The Brylcreem Boys
The Burmese Harp▲
The Caine Mutiny▲
Cairo
A Canterbury Tale▲
The Canterville Ghost
Captain Corelli's Mandolin
Captain Newman, M.D.
Captains of the Clouds
Captive Heart▲
Captive Hearts
Carry On England
Carve Her Name with Pride
Casablanca▲
Casablanca Express
Catch-22▲
Caught in the Draft▲
Chain Lightning
Charlie Grant's War
Charlotte Gray
Chicago Joe & the Showgirl
China
China Sky
Chips, the War Dog
Christ Stopped at Eboli▲
Christabel
Churchill and the Generals
Class of '44
Cloak and Dagger
The Clock▲
Closely Watched Trains▲
Code Name: Emerald
Cold Days
The Colditz Story
Combat Killers
Come and See▲
Come See the Paradise▲
Coming Home
Command Decision
Commando Attack
Commando Squad
Commandos
Commandos Strike at Dawn
Conspiracy
Conspiracy of Hearts▲
Contraband
Convoy
Cornered▲
Corregidor
Cottage to Let
The Counterfeit Traitor▲
The Coward
Cowboy Commandos
The Cranes Are Flying▲
Crash Dive
Cross of Iron
The Cruel Sea▲
Cry of Battle
D-Day, the Sixth of June▲
Dam Busters▲
Danger UXB
Dangerous Moonlight▲
Darby's Rangers
Dark Blue World
Das Boot▲
David▲
Dawn Express
The Day and the Hour
A Day in October
Day One▲
The Day Will Dawn▲
Days of Glory
Deadly Mission
Death Is Called Engelchen▲
Death of a Soldier
The Death of Adolf Hitler
December
December 7th: The Movie
Deep Six
Desert Commandos
The Desert Fox▲
The Desert Rats▲
Despair▲
Desperate Journey
Destination Tokyo
Destroyer▲
The Devil's Brigade
Devils on the Doorstep
Diamonds of the Night▲
The Diary of Anne Frank▲
The Dirty Dozen▲
The Dirty Dozen: The Deadly Mission
The Dirty Dozen: The Fatal Mission
The Dirty Dozen: The Next Mission
Dirty Heroes
Distant Thunder▲
Distant Voices, Still Lives▲
Dive Bomber▲
Divided We Fall
Dr. Akagi
Dr. Petiot
The Dresser▲
The Dressmaker
The Dunera Boys▲
The Eagle Has Landed▲
Ebony Dreams
Edge of Darkness▲
Elizabeth of Ladymead▲
The Elusive Corporal▲
Empire of the Sun▲
The Empty Mirror
End of the Affair
The End of the Affair▲
Enemy at the Gates
Enemy Below▲
Enemy of Women
The English Patient▲
Enigma
Enigma Secret
Enola Gay: The Men, the Mission, the Atomic Bomb
Ensign Pulver
Era Notte a Roma▲
Escape from Sobibor▲
Escape to Athena
Europa, Europa▲
Every Time We Say Goodbye
The Execution
The Execution of Private Slovik▲
Eye of the Needle
A Face in the Rain
Fall from Grace
Farewell to the King

Wrestling

▲ = rated three bones or higher

Writers

see also *This Is Your Life*

The Adventures of Mark Twain ▲
Agatha
Ambition
American Dreamer
Amuck!
An Angel at My Table ▲
Anne of Green Gables: The Continuing Story
Another Man's Poison
As Good As It Gets ▲
Author! Author!
Balzac: A Life of Passion ▲
Bamboozled
Barton Fink ▲
The Basketball Diaries
Beautiful Dreamers
Becoming Colette
Before Night Falls ▲
Behind the Lines
Beloved Infidel
The Best Man ▲
Best Seller ▲
The Big Slice
Bloodhounds
Bloodhounds 2
Bone Daddy
Boom!
Breakfast at Tiffany's ▲
Breakfast of Champions
The Brontes of Haworth
Burial of the Rats
A Business Affair
Cabin by the Lake
Celebrity ▲
Celeste ▲
Chapter Two
Chelsea Walls
Closer and Closer
Collected Stories ▲
Coming Through
Cross Creek
Croupier ▲
Dante's Inferno: Life of Dante Gabriel Rossetti
The Dark Half
The Dark Side of the Heart
Dash and Lilly
Dead Husbands
Dean Koontz's Mr. Murder
Deathtrap
Deconstructing Harry
Delirious
The Disappearance of Garcia Lorca
Divine Secrets of the Ya-Ya Sisterhood
The End of the Affair ▲
Eternity and a Day
Eva
Evidence of Blood
Evil Lives
F. Scott Fitzgerald in Hollywood
Fall
Father's Day
Fear and Loathing in Las Vegas
Finding Forrester
The Flower of My Secret ▲
For Hire
Forbidden Passion: The Oscar Wilde Movie
Full Speed
The Gambler
Ghostwriter
Glam
Goldeneye: The Secret Life of Ian Fleming
Gothic ▲
Hamsun
Harriet the Spy
Haunted Summer
Hav Plenty ▲
Heart Beat
Heartburn ▲
Henry & June ▲
Her Alibi
House of the Long Shadows
How to Kill Your Neighbor's Dog
Hustler White
Impromptu ▲
In the Deep Woods
In the Mouth of Madness
Iris ▲
Isn't She Great
Jack London
James Joyce: A Portrait of the Artist as a Young Man
James Joyce's Women ▲
Jane Doe
The Jew
Joe Gould's Secret
Joshua Then and Now ▲
Just Write
Kafka
Kissing a Fool
Lady on a Train ▲
The Last Days of Chez Nous
Late August, Early September
Letters from a Killer
The Life of Emile Zola ▲
The Lonely Lady
Long Day's Journey Into Night ▲
Love and Death on Long Island
The Loves of Edgar Allen Poe
The Majestic
The Mask of Dimitrios ▲
Maybe Baby
A Merry War ▲
Meteor & Shadow
Misery ▲
Mrs. Parker and the Vicious Circle
Mr. Jealousy
Mixing Nia
Mother
Moulin Rouge
Murder by the Book
A Murder of Crows
The Muse
My Apprenticeship ▲
My Brilliant Career ▲
My Childhood ▲
My Left Foot ▲
My Universities ▲
The Mystery of Rampo ▲
Naked Lunch ▲
Nerolio
The Night and the Moment
Our Lady of the Assassins
Out of Africa ▲
Pandaemonium
Paperback Hero
Paperback Romance
The Passion of Ayn Rand
Personals
The Pillow Book
Portraits Chinois
Possession
Postmortem
The Prize ▲
The Proprietor
Quills
The Real Howard Spitz
The Reaper
Reds ▲
Restaurant
Romancing the Stone ▲
Romantic Comedy
Rowing with the Wind
The Royal Tenenbaums ▲
Saint-Ex: The Story of the Storyteller
The Sculptress
Shadowlands ▲
Shakespeare in Love ▲
Sink or Swim
Slam
The Snows of Kilimanjaro ▲
Spymaker: The Secret Life of Ian Fleming
The Sticky Fingers of Time
Storytelling ▲
Street Smart
Swann
Sweet and Lowdown
Teach Me
Thanks for the Memory
Theodora Goes Wild ▲
Things 2
The Third Man ▲
301, 302
Tom & Viv ▲
The Trials of Oscar Wilde ▲
Two Ninas
Two Shades of Blue
Undercover Angel
Unsane
White Badge
The Whole Wide World ▲
Wilde
Wonder Boys ▲
The Wonderful World of the Brothers Grimm
The World According to Garp ▲
Zeder
Zora Is My Name!
Zorba the Greek ▲

The Wrong Man

see also *Frame-Ups; Mistaken Identity*

Absolute Power
Bad Seed
The Bedroom Window
Black Angel ▲
Bloodfist 7: Manhunt
Body Heat ▲
Chain Reaction
Codename: Jaguar
Consenting Adults
Cookie's Fortune ▲
Cop-Out
The Crow: Salvation
Dangerous Evidence: The Lori Jackson Story
Dead End
Deadline
Deadlocked
Delivered
Double Jeopardy
Double Take
Extremely Dangerous
Fallen
Frenzy ▲
The Fugitive ▲
Girls in Prison
The House of the Seven Gables
I Confess
In Pursuit
In the Name of the Father ▲
Jack's Back ▲
Jennifer 8
Kept
Kiss of the Dragon
Life
Life & Times of Grizzly Adams
The Man Who Knew Too Much ▲
The Man Who Knew Too Much
Marked Man
Ministry of Fear ▲
Most Wanted
The Negotiator
Partners in Crime
Perfect Target
Phantom Lady ▲
Plato's Run
Presumed Innocent ▲
Red Corner
Running Woman
Seven Doors to Death
Small Vices: A Spenser Mystery
Storm Catcher
A Stranger in the Kingdom
They Made Me a Criminal
The 39 Steps ▲
Three Days of the Condor ▲
Time Served
Under Suspicion
U.S. Marshals
When Danger Follows You Home
The Whole Town's Talking ▲
The Winslow Boy ▲
Winterset
The Wrong Man ▲
The Wrong Man
Wrongfully Accused

Wrong Side of the Tracks

see also *Rags to Riches*

Aaron Loves Angela
Algiers ▲
Alice Adams
Amarilly of Clothesline Alley
Angel and the Badman ▲
Angels with Dirty Faces ▲
Anna Christie
Bachelor Party
Back Door to Heaven ▲
Breaking Away ▲
The Bride Wore Red
Camille ▲
Cannery Row
Captains Courageous ▲
Captives
Carbon Copy
Careful, He Might Hear You ▲
Carrie ▲
Cat Ballou ▲
Chains
China Girl
Claudia
Cool As Ice
The Courtney Affair
Courtship ▲
crazy/beautiful
The Crucified Lovers ▲
Cry-Baby ▲
The Dark Side of Love
Diary of a Chambermaid ▲
Dirty Dancing ▲
Dragstrip Girl
Eegah!
Far and Away
Federal Hill
The Fence
Fire with Fire
The Flamingo Kid ▲
Foxfire Light
Fresh Horses
Future Kill
Grease ▲
Great Expectations
The Great Gatsby
The Hairy Ape
Hearts of Humanity
Here on Earth
Hush
Iron Maze
It
It Could Happen to You
It Happened One Night ▲
Jailbait!
Jersey Girl
Jungle Fever ▲
King Ralph
The Lacemaker ▲
Last Exit to Brooklyn ▲
Liar's Moon
Little Minister ▲
The Loves of Carmen
Luzia
Mad About Mambo
The Man from Snowy River
Manhattan Melodrama ▲
Masquerade ▲
A Million to One
Min & Bill
My Forbidden Past
My Man Godfrey ▲
Naked Youth
Night Beat
Off Beat
Outpost in Morocco
Over the Brooklyn Bridge
The Phantom in the House
The Phantom of the Opera ▲
Picnic on the Grass
A Place in the Sun ▲
The Pope of Greenwich Village
Port of New York
Pretty in Pink
Primrose Path
Princess Tam Tam ▲
Probation
Pygmalion ▲
The Rage: Carrie 2
Reckless
Reform School Girl
Return to Snowy River ▲
Rich Girl
Riff Raff ▲
Rocky ▲
Room at the Top ▲
Rosewood ▲
Ruby Gentry
Rumble Fish ▲
San Francisco ▲
The Servant ▲
Set It Off
sex, lies and videotape ▲
She's All That
Show People ▲
Small Faces ▲
Snow Country
Some Kind of Wonderful
Somebody Up There Likes Me ▲
Stay Hungry ▲
The Story of the Late Chrysanthemum ▲
Suburbia
The Swan
The Swan ▲
Sweet Light in a Dark Room ▲
The Tamarind Seed
Tango
That Night
This Sporting Life ▲
Tortilla Flat ▲
A Tree Grows in Brooklyn ▲
Under the Boardwalk
Uptown Angel
Valley Girl
The Valley of Decision ▲
Virtue's Revolt
Vivacious Lady ▲
Waterloo Bridge ▲
White Palace
The White Sin
The World of Suzie Wong
The Young Philadelphians ▲

Yakuza

see also *Crime & Criminals; Japan; Organized Crime*

Adrenaline Drive
American Yakuza
Beautiful Beast
Black Rain
The Bodyguard
Boiling Point
Brother ▲
Double Edge
Girls of the White Orchid
Johnny Mnemonic
Minbo—Or the Gentle Art of Japanese Extortion
No Way Back
Organized Crime & Triad Bureau
Overkill
Showdown in Little Tokyo
Sonatine ▲
The Street Fighter's Last Revenge
Tokyo Drifter
Wicked City
The Wolves ▲
The Yakuza
Youth of the Beast
Zatoichi: The Life and Opinion of Masseur Ichi
Zatoichi: Zatoichi's Flashing Sword

You Lose, You Die

see also *Post Apocalypse*

Arcade
The Arena
Arena
Blade Boxer
Death Race 2000
Deathrow Gameshow
Dominion
Fatal Combat
Futuresport
The Game ▲
Mad Max: Beyond Thunderdome
Mean Guns
Mortal Challenge
Prayer of the Rollerboys
Robot Jox
Roller Blade
Roller Blade Warriors: Taken By Force
Rollerball
The Running Man
Solarbabies
Star Hunter
Tron
Webmaster

Yuppie Nightmares

see also *Strained Suburbia*

Addams Family Values
Alice ▲
Almost You
Amos and Andrew
Baby Boom
Bad Influence
Barbarians at the Gate ▲
Bare Essentials
Bedroom Eyes
Beetlejuice ▲
The Big Chill ▲
Blind Date
Blind Side
Boiler Room ▲
The Bonfire of the Vanities
The Boost
Bright Lights, Big City
Cape Fear ▲
City of Hope ▲
Clara's Heart
Clean and Sober ▲
Cold Fever
Coma ▲
Consenting Adults
Curly Sue
Dead Calm ▲
Denise Calls Up
Desperately Seeking Susan
Diary of a Mad Housewife ▲
Down and Out in Beverly Hills
Drop Dead Fred
Edge of Honor
The End of Innocence
Eye of the Demon
Fatal Attraction ▲
The First Wives Club
The Fisher King ▲
Folks!
Fun with Dick and Jane
The Further Adventures of Tennessee Buck
The Game ▲
Goodbye, New York
The Guardian
The Hand that Rocks the Cradle
Happiness ▲
The Hard Way ▲
He Said, She Said
Heartburn ▲
Hiding Out
In the Company of Men
In the Spirit
Indian Summer
Jungle Fever ▲
Key Exchange
Kicks
L.A. Story ▲
Let's Kill All the Lawyers
Limit Up
Looking for Mr. Goodbar
Lost in America ▲
Love or Money?
Madhouse
Maid to Order
The Malibu Beach Vampires
Maniac
Micki & Maude
Mifune
The Mighty Ducks
The Money Pit
Mother's Boys
Moving
My Daughter's Keeper
My New Gun
Neighbors
New Year's Day ▲
Next Door
Night of the Living Babes
Nothing But Trouble
Nothing in Common
Oasis of the Zombies
The Object of Beauty ▲
Pacific Heights ▲
Perfect Family
Permanent Vacation
Preppies
Private Benjamin
Quicksilver
Reversal of Fortune ▲
Roadhouse 66
Rude Awakening
Ruthless People ▲
St. Elmo's Fire

The Secret of My Success
The Secretary
September
sex, lies and videotape ▸
Shattered
A Shock to the System ▸
Six Degrees of Separation
A Smile Like Yours
Something Wild
Stay Tuned
Straw Dogs ▸
Summer Rental
Taking Care of Business
Taking the Heat
The Temp
Three Men and a Little Lady
Through the Eyes of a Killer
The Tie That Binds
The Toxic Avenger, Part 3: The Last Temptation of Toxie
Trading Places
Trapped
The Trigger Effect
Truth or Consequences, N.M.
Under Pressure
Unlawful Entry
The Vagrant
Voodoo Dawn
Wall Street ▸
The War of the Roses ▸
Westworld ▸
What about Bob? ▸
When a Man Loves a Woman
Windy City
Wolf
Your Friends & Neighbors ▸

Zombie Soldiers

see also *Zombies*
Akira Kurosawa's Dreams
Army of Darkness ▸
The Dark Power
Deathdream
Hard Rock Zombies
House ▸
Oasis of the Zombies
Revenge of the Zombies
Revolt of the Zombies
Scream and Scream Again
She Demons
Shock Waves
The Supernaturals
They Saved Hitler's Brain
The Zombie Army
Zombie Lake

Zombies

see also *Death & the Afterlife; Ghosts, Ghouls, & Goblins; Zombie Soldiers*
The Alchemist
Alien Dead
Alien Massacre
Almost Dead
The Astro-Zombies
The Beyond
Biozombie
Bowery at Midnight
Bride of Re-Animator
Carnival of Souls ▸
Cast a Deadly Spell ▸
Cemetery Man
Children Shouldn't Play with Dead Things
The Chilling
Chopper Chicks in Zombietown
C.H.U.D. 2: Bud the Chud
City of the Walking Dead
Creature of the Walking Dead
The Curse of the Aztec Mummy
Dawn of the Dead ▸
Dawn of the Mummy
Day of the Dead
Dead Alive
Dead Creatures
The Dead Don't Die
Dead Heat
Dead Men Don't Die
The Dead Next Door
Dead Pit
Death Becomes Her ▸
The Death Curse of Tartu
Deathdream
Demon Wind
Destroyer
Ed and His Dead Mother
Evil Town
The Ghost Brigade
The Ghoul
The Granny
The Hanging Woman
Haunting Fear
Hellgate
Horror of the Zombies
Horror Rises from the Tomb
The House of Seven Corpses
House of the Dead
I Eat Your Skin
I Walked with a Zombie ▸
I Was a Teenage Zombie
Invisible Invaders
Isle of the Dead
The Jitters
John Carpenter's Ghosts of Mars
King of the Zombies
Kiss Daddy Goodbye
The Legend of the 7 Golden Vampires
Let Sleeping Corpses Lie
The Mad Ghoul
Messiah of Evil
The Mummy ▸
The Mummy
Mummy & Curse of the Jackal
The Mummy's Revenge
My Boyfriend's Back
Neon Maniacs
Night Life
Night of Horror
Night of the Comet
Night of the Creeps
Night of the Death Cult
Night of the Ghouls
Night of the Living Babes
Night of the Living Dead ▸
Night of the Living Dead
Night of the Living Dead, 25th Anniversary Documentary
Nightmare Weekend
Oasis of the Zombies
Orgy of the Dead
The Outing
Pet Sematary 2
Phantasm 3: Lord of the Dead
Plague of the Zombies
Plan 9 from Outer Space
Prison
Quatermass 2 ▸
Re-Animator ▸
Redneck Zombies
Resident Evil
Return of the Evil Dead
Return of the Living Dead
Return of the Living Dead 2
Return of the Living Dead 3
Revenge of the Dead
Revenge of the Living Zombies
Revenge of the Zombies
Revolt of the Zombies
Seedpeople
Shock Waves
Sole Survivor
Steps from Hell
The Stuff
Svengali ▸
Teenage Zombies
Tomb of the Undead
Tombs of the Blind Dead
Torture Chamber of Baron Blood
The Vampire's Ghost
Vengeance of the Zombies
Virgin among the Living Dead
Voodoo Dawn
Voodoo Woman
The White Zombie ▸
Winterbeast
Zombie
The Zombie Army
Zombie High
Zombie Island Massacre
Zombie Lake
Zombie Nightmare
Zombies of Moratau
Zombies of the Stratosphere
Zombies on Broadway

Kibbles and Series List

The **Kibbles** and **Series** indexes have been combined into one index. This is where you'll find info on where your favorite movies came from—literary, theatrical, cartoon, and television adaptations to name a few, as well as the behind the scenes talents that make movies possible, such as producers and special effects wizards. Another important feature of this index is the quality check it provides with categories like **Woofs!**, **4 Bones**, and **Top Grossing Films** by year. This index also provides information on recurring characters like James Bond, Jack Ryan, or Mike Hammer, as well as notable screen partnerships. Some examples include Abbott & Costello, Hope & Crosby, and De Niro & Scorsese. **A tipped triangle denotes a three-bone or higher rating.** The categories are as follows, with an asterisk (*) denoting a new category:

* = *new to this edition*

Hammer Films: Horror

Hammer Films: Sci Fi & Fantasy

Hercule Poirot

Hercules

Highest Grossing Films of All Time

Hopalong Cassidy

Indiana Jones

Jack Ryan

Jack the Ripper

James Bond

James Bond Spoofs

Jesse James

Lassie

Live Action/Animation Combos

The Lone Rider

Ma & Pa Kettle

The Marx Brothers

MGM Musicals

Mike Hammer

Miss Marple

Mr. Wong

Modern Shakespeare

Modern Updates

Monty Python

The Muppets

National Lampoon

Our Gang

The Pink Panther

The Planet of the Apes

Plays to Film:
- Maxwell Anderson
- James M. Barrie
- Anton Chekov
- Noel Coward
- Horton Foote
- Beth Henley
- Arthur Miller
- Eugene O'Neill
- Rodgers & Hammerstein
- Arthur Schnitzler
- William Shakespeare
- George Bernard Shaw
- Sam Shepard
- *Robert E. Sherwood
- Neil Simon
- Tom Stoppard
- Tennessee Williams

Producers:
- Robert Altman
- Bruckheimer/Simpson
- William Castle
- Coppola/American Zoetrope
- Roger Corman/New World
- Val Lewton
- George Lucas
- Merchant Ivory
- George Pal
- Steven Spielberg
- Andy Warhol

Rambo

The Rangebusters

Recycled Footage/ Redubbed Dialogue

Renfrew of the Mounties

Restored Footage

The Ritz Brothers

Robin Hood

The Rough Riders

Rusty the Dog

The Saint

Screen Teams:
- Abbott & Costello
- Allen & Farrow
- Allen & Keaton
- Astaire & Rogers
- Belushi & Aykroyd
- Bogart & Bacall
- Burton & Taylor
- Cagney & O'Brien
- Cheech & Chong
- Cusack & Robbins
- De Niro & Pesci
- Douglas & Lancaster
- *Eastwood & Locke
- Eddy & McDonald
- Farley & Spade
- Flynn & de Havilland
- Gable & Crawford
- Garland & Rooney
- Garson & Pidgeon
- Gibson & Glover
- Hawn & Russell
- Hepburn & Grant
- Hepburn & Tracy
- Hope & Crosby
- Ladd & Lake
- Laurel & Hardy
- *Lee & Cushing
- Lemmon & Matthau
- Loy & Powell
- Martin & Lewis
- Newman & Woodward
- Redford & Newman
- *Reynolds & DeLuise
- *Reynolds & Field
- Rogers & Evans
- Snipes & Harrelson
- Stewart & Sullavan
- Turner & Douglas
- Wilder & Pryor

Scrooge

Sexton Blake

Sherlock Holmes

Special FX Extravaganzas

Special FX Extravaganzas: Make-Up

Special FX Wizards:
- Rick Baker
- Rob Bottin
- Anton Furst
- Ray Harryhausen
- Herschell Gordon Lewis
- Tom Savini
- Dick Smith
- Douglas Trumball

Star Wars

Tarzan

The Texas Rangers

The Thin Man

The Three Mesquiteers

The Three Musketeers

Three Stooges

Top Grossing Films: 1939-2001

The Trail Blazers

Trash

Troma Films

Universal Studios' Classic Horror

Wild Bill Hickok

The Wolfman

Wyatt Earp

Zorro

Zucker/Abrahams/Zucker

* = *new to this edition*

Kibbles and Series Index

Recurrent characters, cinematic collaborations, various adaptations, and important behind-the-scenes personnel information is the focus of the **Kibbles and Series Index**. These categories are listed alphabetically. **A tipped triangle indicates a video rated three bones or higher**.

Adapted from a Cartoon

The Addams Family
Addams Family Values
The Adventures of Captain Marvel
Adventures of Red Ryder
Adventures of Smilin' Jack
The Amazing Spider-Man
Barbarella
The Belles of St. Trinian's▲
Big Zapper
Blondie
Blondie Brings Up Baby
Blondie for Victory
Blondie Goes Latin
Blondie Goes to College
Blondie Has Trouble
Blondie Hits the Jackpot
Blondie in Society
Blondie Knows Best
Blondie Meets the Boss
Blondie On a Budget
Blondie Plays Cupid
Blondie Takes a Vacation
Blondie's Blessed Event
Casper▲
Cool World
Crimewave
Dennis the Menace
Dennis the Menace: Dinosaur Hunter
Dennis the Menace Strikes Again
Dick Tracy
Dick Tracy vs. Cueball
Dick Tracy's Dilemma
Dr. Strange
Dudley Do-Right
Edward Scissorhands▲
Elvira, Mistress of the Dark
Fatty Finn
The Fighting Redhead
The Flash
Flash Gordon
Flesh Gordon 2: Flesh Gordon Meets the Cosmic Cheerleaders
The Flintstones
The Flintstones in Viva Rock Vegas
Footlight Glamour
Friday Foster
Frostbiter: Wrath of the Wendigo
George of the Jungle▲
The Great St. Trinian's Train Robbery
The Guyver
Guyver 2: Dark Hero
Heavy Metal▲
Hillbilly Blitzkrieg
Inspector Gadget
It's a Great Life
Jane & the Lost City
Josie and the Pussycats
Li'l Abner
Little Nemo: Adventures in Slumberland
Little Orphan Annie
The Mask▲
Masters of the Universe
Maybe ... Maybe Not
Mighty Morphin Power Rangers: The Movie
Mr. Magoo
Office Space
The Perils of Gwendoline
Petit Con
Phantom 2040 Movie: The Ghost Who Walks
The Pink Panther▲
The Pink Panther Strikes Again▲
Prince Valiant
The Pure Hell of St. Trinian's
Reg'lar Fellers
The Return of Swamp Thing
Richie Rich
The Sad Sack
Scooby-Doo
Supergirl
Superman 2▲
Tank Girl
Teenage Mutant Ninja Turtles: The Movie
Teenage Mutant Ninja Turtles 2: The Secret of the Ooze
Teenage Mutant Ninja Turtles 3
Timecop
Tom and Jerry: The Movie
Turbo: A Power Rangers Movie
The Villain
Wild Palms
The Wild World of Batwoman

Adapted from a Game

Clue
Double Dragon
Dungeons and Dragons
Final Fantasy: The Spirits Within
Lara Croft: Tomb Raider
Mortal Kombat 1: The Movie
Mortal Kombat 2: Annihilation
Resident Evil
Street Fighter
Super Mario Bros.
Tag: The Assassination Game
Wing Commander

Adapted from a Musical

Annie
Annie▲
Babes in Arms
Babes in Toyland
Beatlemania! The Movie
Bells Are Ringing▲
Best Foot Forward
The Best Little Whorehouse in Texas
Brigadoon▲
Bye, Bye, Birdie▲
Bye Bye Birdie
Cabaret▲
Can-Can
Charm of La Boheme
A Chorus Line
Cool Mikado
Damn Yankees▲
The Desert Song
Evita
The Fantasticks
Fiddler on the Roof▲
Finian's Rainbow▲
Flower Drum Song
Follies in Concert
Footlight Serenade
A Funny Thing Happened on the Way to the Forum▲
The Gay Divorcee▲
Gentlemen Prefer Blondes▲
George White's Scandals
Godspell
Grease▲
Grease 2
The Guardsman▲
Gypsy▲
Gypsy
Hair▲
Hello, Dolly!
I Do! I Do!
Irma La Douce
The King and I▲
Kiss Me Kate▲
Lady Be Good
A Little Night Music
Mame
Maytime▲
The Merry Widow▲
The Merry Widow
The Music Man▲
My Fair Lady▲
Oh! Calcutta!
On a Clear Day You Can See Forever
Opera do Malandro
Paint Your Wagon
The Pajama Game▲
1776▲
Show Boat▲
Show Boat
Sweeney Todd: The Demon Barber of Fleet Street
Sweet Charity▲
The Three Penny Opera▲
The Threepenny Opera
West Side Story▲
The Wiz

Adapted from a Play

Abe Lincoln in Illinois▲
The Admirable Crichton
The Adventures of Robin Hood▲
Aelita: Queen of Mars
Age Old Friends▲
Agnes of God
Ah, Wilderness!▲
Alfie▲
Alice
All My Sons▲
All Over the Guy
Amadeus▲
American Buffalo
Anastasia▲
Animal Crackers▲
The Animal Kingdom▲
Anna Christie▲
Anna Christie
Annie Get Your Gun▲
The Anniversary
Another Country
Another Man's Poison
Any Wednesday
Arsenic and Old Lace▲
As Is
As You Desire Me▲
The Avenger
The Awful Truth▲
Babes in Toyland
The Baby Dance▲
Baby Doll▲
Baby, the Rain Must Fall
The Bacchantes
Bad Manners
The Balcony▲
The Ballad of the Sad Cafe
Bar Girls
Barefoot in the Park▲
Beau Brummel
Beau Brummel▲
Beautiful Thing▲
Becket▲
Becky Sharp
Being at Home with Claude
The Bells▲
Bent
The Best Man▲
Betrayal
Beyond Therapy
The Big Kahuna
The Big Knife▲
Big News
Billie
Biloxi Blues
The Birth of a Nation▲
Bitter Sweet
Black Limelight
Black Lizard
Black Orpheus▲
Blessed Event▲
Blithe Spirit▲
Blood Wedding▲
Bluebeard's Eighth Wife
Bodies, Rest & Motion
Boesman & Lena
Bopha!▲
Born Yesterday▲
Born Yesterday
Boy Meets Girl▲
The Boys▲
The Boys in the Band
The Boys Next Door
Breaking the Code
Breaking Up
Breath of Scandal
The Brig▲
Brighton Beach Memoirs
Brilliant Lies
Broadway Bound
Broken Glass
A Bronx Tale▲
A Brother's Kiss
The Browning Version▲
The Browning Version
Bus Stop▲
Butterflies Are Free▲
Cabaret Balkan
Cactus Flower

Adapted

Caesar and Cleopatra
California Suite▸
Can-Can
Caresses
Casablanca▸
Casanova Brown
Cast a Dark Shadow▸
Casual Sex?
The Cat and the Canary
The Cat's Meow
Cavalcade▸
Cease Fire
Ceiling Zero▸
The Chalk Garden▸
Chapter Two
The Chase
The Cheap Detective▸
Chelsea Walls
Children of a Lesser God▸
The Children's Hour
Chimes at Midnight▸
China
A Chorus of Disapproval
Clarence, the Cross-eyed Lion▸
Clash by Night▸
The Climax
Cold Comfort
Collected Stories▸
Columbo: Prescription Murder
Come Back, Little Sheba▸
Come Back to the Five & Dime Jimmy Dean, Jimmy Dean▸
Come Blow Your Horn▸
Command Decision
Conduct Unbecoming
The Connection▸
Coquette
The Corn Is Green▸
Cosi▸
The Count of the Old Town
Country Girl▸
County Fair
Craig's Wife▸
Crimes of the Heart
The Crucible▸
Curse of the Starving Class
Cyrano de Bergerac
Cyrano de Bergerac▸
Da
Daddy Long Legs
Daddy's Dyin'...Who's Got the Will?
Dancing at Lughnasa
Dangerous Liaisons▸
A Day in the Death of Joe Egg▸
Day of Wrath▸
Daybreak
Dead End▸
Dead Heart▸
Death and the Maiden▸
Death of a Salesman▸
Death Takes a Holiday▸
Deathtrap
The Designated Mourner
Desire Under the Elms
Desk Set▸
Desperate Hours▸
Detective Story▸
Devil Girl from Mars
The Devils▸
The Devil's Brother
The Devil's Disciple▸
Dial "M" for Murder▸
Diary of a Hitman
The Dining Room
Dinner at Eight▸
Dinner with Friends
Disraeli▸
The Divorce of Lady X
The Doctor and the Devils
Doctor X
Doll Face
A Doll's House
A Doll's House▸
Don't Drink the Water
Double Wedding▸
Dracula▸
The Dresser▸
Driving Miss Daisy▸
Drunks
DuBarry Was a Lady
Duet for One
Dumb Waiter
The Eagle Has Two Heads▸
East Is East▸
Easy Virtue
Educating Rita▸
Edward II
The Effect of Gamma Rays on Man-in-the-Moon Marigolds▸
84 Charing Cross Road▸
Emperor Jones
Employees' Entrance▸
The Enchanted Cottage
Ensign Pulver
The Entertainer▸
Entertaining Mr. Sloane
Equus
Escanaba in da Moonlight
Escapade▸
Escape Me Never
Execution of Justice
Extremities
Eye of the Storm
Faithful
The Farmer Takes a Wife
The Farmer's Wife
A Few Good Men▸
The Field▸
A Fine Romance
Five Graves to Cairo▸
Fog Island
Fool for Love
Footsteps in the Dark
Forbidden Planet▸
Forever Female▸
Fortune and Men's Eyes
Forty Carats
Foxfire▸
Frankenstein Sings...The Movie
Frankie and Johnny▸
The Front Page▸
The Fugitive Kind
Fun
Futz
Gaslight▸
The Gazebo▸
Generation
George Washington Slept Here▸
Get Real
Getting Out
The Ghost Breakers▸
Give Me a Sailor
The Glass Menagerie▸
Glengarry Glen Ross▸
God Said "Ha!"▸
Golden Boy▸
The Golden Coach▸
Gone Are the Days
Goodbye Charlie
The Goodbye Girl▸
The Gorilla
Grace & Glorie
The Great White Hope
Green Pastures▸
Grown Ups
The Hairy Ape
Hamlet▸
Hamlet
Hamlet▸
The Happiest Days of Your Life▸
Happy Birthday, Gemini
Harriet Craig▸
Having Our Say: The Delany Sisters' First 100 Years
He Who Gets Slapped▸
Heartbreak House
Heaven Can Wait▸
Hedda
The Heidi Chronicles
Henry IV
Henry V▸
His Double Life
His Girl Friday▸
Hit the Deck
Holiday▸
Holiday Heart
Homage
Home of the Brave▸
The Honey Pot
Hoopla
Hotel Paradiso
The Hound of London
House of the Long Shadows
The House of Yes
Hurlyburly
I Confess
I Love You, I Love You Not
I Married an Angel
I Never Sang for My Father▸
I Ought to Be in Pictures
I Remember Mama▸
An Ideal Husband▸
Idiot's Delight▸
I'll Be Yours
Illicit
Illuminata
Illusions
I'm Not Rappaport
The Importance of Being Earnest
The Impossible Years
In Celebration▸
In Search of the Castaways▸
In the Good Old Summertime▸
Indiscreet
Inherit the Wind▸
Inherit the Wind
Intrigue and Love
Iphigenia▸
Italian Straw Hat▸
It's the Rage
Jacknife▸
Jeffrey
Jesus Christ, Superstar▸
Johnny Belinda
Jubal
Julius Caesar▸
Julius Caesar
Key Exchange
The Killing of Sister George
King and Country▸
The King and I
King Lear▸
King Lear
King Lear▸
Kingdom Come
Kiss Me, Stupid!
The Knack▸
Knocks at My Door
K2: The Ultimate High
La Cage aux Folles▸
La Cage aux Folles 2
La Cage aux Folles 3: The Wedding
Ladies They Talk About
The Lady's Not for Burning
Lantana▸
The Laramie Project▸
The Last of Mrs. Cheyney▸
Last of the Red Hot Lovers
Laughing Sinners
Lenny▸
Les Enfants Terrible▸
Life
A Life in the Theater
Li'l Abner
Lilies
Lily Dale
The Lion in Winter▸
The Little Foxes▸
Little Murders▸
Little Shop of Horrors▸
Little Voice▸
Long Day's Journey into Night▸
Long Day's Journey into Night
Long Day's Journey Into Night▸
The Long Voyage Home▸
Look Back in Anger▸
Look Back in Anger
Look Back in Anger▸
Looking for Richard▸
Loot ... Give Me Money, Honey!
Lost in Yonkers
Louisiana Purchase
The Lovable Cheat
Love and Human Remains▸
Love! Valour! Compassion!
The Lower Depths▸
M. Butterfly
Macbeth▸
Macbeth
Madame X
The Madwoman of Chaillot
The Magnificent Yankee▸
The Mahabharata
Major Barbara▸
A Majority of One
Male and Female▸
A Man for All Seasons▸
The Man in the Glass Booth▸
Man of La Mancha
The Man Who Came to Dinner▸
Marius▸
Marriage Italian Style▸
Marvin's Room
Mass Appeal
Master Harold and the Boys▸
The Matchmaker▸
Me and the Colonel
Medea
Merton of the Movies
Mexican Hayride
Midnight Lace
A Midsummer Night's Dream▸
A Midsummer Night's Dream
The Migrants▸
The Millionairess
Minna von Barnhelm or The Soldier's Fortune
The Miracle Woman
The Miracle Worker▸
The Miracle Worker
Miss Evers' Boys
Miss Firecracker▸
Miss Julie
Miss Rose White▸
Mister Drake's Duck
Mr. Music
Mister Roberts▸
Mr. Write
Monster in a Box▸
Morning Glory
Much Ado about Nothing▸
Murder▸
Murder at the Vanities
Murder by Death
My Big Fat Greek Wedding
My Brother's Wife
My Sister Eileen▸
Nell
Never Say Die
Never Steal Anything Small
Never Too Late to Mend
New Faces of 1952
New Moon
Nico and Dani
Night Must Fall▸
The Night of the Iguana▸
No
No, No Nanette
No Sex Please—We're British
No Time for Sergeants▸
Noises Off
The Norman Conquests, Part 1: Table Manners▸
The Norman Conquests, Part 2: Living Together▸
The Norman Conquests, Part 3: Round and Round the Garden▸
Norman, Is That You?
North Shore Fish
No. 17▸
Nurse Marjorie
The Obsessed
The Odd Couple▸
Oedipus Rex▸
Oh Dad, Poor Dad (Momma's Hung You in the Closet & I'm Feeling So Sad)
Oklahoma!▸
The Old Settler
Oleanna
On Approval▸
On Borrowed Time▸
On Golden Pond▸
On the Town▸
Once in the Life
1-900
One of My Wives Is Missing
One Touch of Venus
One Trick Pony
The Only Thrill
Only When I Laugh▸
Ordet▸
Orfeu
Orphans▸
Orphans of the Storm▸
Orpheus Descending
Oscar
Othello
Othello▸
Other People's Money
Our Town▸
Our Town
Out of Season
The Owl and the Pussycat▸
Panama Hattie
The Passing of the Third Floor Back
Patterns▸
Peephole
People Will Talk▸
The Perfect Marriage
A Perfect Murder
Period of Adjustment▸
Personal Property
Petrified Forest▸
Phaedra
The Phantom of the Opera
Phantom of the Paradise
The Philadelphia Story▸
The Piano Lesson▸
Pippin▸
The Pirates of Penzance
Play It Again, Sam▸
Playboy of the Western World
Plaza Suite▸
Plenty
The Portrait▸
Portrait in Black
Prelude to a Kiss
The Prime of Miss Jean Brodie▸
Prince of Central Park
Princess Tam Tam▸
Prisoner of Second Avenue
Private Lives▸
The Private Secretary
Privates on Parade
Psycho Beach Party
Purlie Victorious
Pygmalion▸
A Question of Attribution
Quiet Day in Belfast▸
A Quiet Duel
Quills
Radiance
The Rainmaker▸
A Raisin in the Sun▸
Ran▸
Reckless
Red Planet Mars
Redwood Curtain
The Return of Peter Grimm
Rhythm Romance
Richard III▸
Ride the Wild Fields
Riders to the Sea
The Right to Remain Silent
The Ritz▸
River Red
Rodgers & Hammerstein's South Pacific
Roman Spring of Mrs. Stone▸
Romance
Romantic Comedy
Romeo and Juliet▸
Romeo and Juliet
Romeo and Juliet▸
Romy and Michele's High School Reunion
The Room
Roosters
Rope▸
Rosencrantz & Guildenstern Are Dead▸
Roxie Hart
Ruby
The Runner Stumbles
Sabrina▸
Sabrina
Saint Joan
Same Time, Next Year▸
The Saphead
Sarafina!▸
School for Scandal
Scorchers
Scum▸
The Seagull▸
Search and Destroy
Secret Honor▸
The Secret Rapture
Separate Tables▸
Separate Tables
Seven Chances▸
Sex and the Other Man
Sextette
The Shadow Box▸
Shadow of Angels
Shadowlands▸
The Shanghai Gesture
Shirley Valentine▸
The Shop Around the Corner▸
Short Eyes▸
The Shot
The Show-Off
Siberian Lady Macbeth▸
The Sicilian
The Sign of the Cross
Silent Night, Lonely Night
Silk Stockings▸
A Sinful Life
The Singing Blacksmith
Six Degrees of Separation
Skin Game
Sleuth▸
Small Hotel
Smoking/No Smoking
So Ends Our Night▸
A Soldier's Story▸
Solid Gold Cadillac▸
The Song of Songs
Sorrento Beach
South Pacific▸
Stage Door▸
Stand-Ins
Star Spangled Girl
State of the Union▸
Stevie
Stolen Hours
The Storm Within▸
Strange Interlude▸
Strange Interlude
The Strange Love of Molly Louvain
Streamers
Street Scene▸
A Streetcar Named Desire▸
A Streetcar Named Desire
The Stripper
The Student Affair
The Subject Was Roses▸
The Substance of Fire
subUrbia
Suddenly, Last Summer▸
The Sum of Us▸
Summer and Smoke
Summertime▸
Summertree
Sunday in the Park with George▸
Sunrise at Campobello▸
The Sunshine Boys▸
Susan Slept Here
Sweet Bird of Youth▸
Sweet Bird of Youth
Sweet Revenge
Sylvia and the Phantom▸
Talk Radio▸
Tall Story
The Taming of the Shrew
The Taming of the Shrew▸
Tape▸
Tartuffe
A Taste of Honey▸
Tea and Sympathy▸
Tea for Two▸
The Teahouse of the August Moon
The Tempest
The Tempest▸
The Terror
That Championship Season
There's a Girl in My Soup
These Three▸
They Knew What They Wanted▸
Thin Ice▸
This Happy Breed▸
This Is the Army
This Property Is Condemned
Thoroughly Modern Millie
Those Endearing Young Charms
A Thousand Clowns▸
Three Daring Daughters
Three for the Show
Three Men on a Horse▸
Throne of Blood▸
Tidy Endings

▸ = rated three bones or higher

Adapted from a Poem

Adapted from a Song

Adapted from a Story

Women & Men: Stories of Seduction
The Wonderful Ice Cream Suit
Young at Heart
The Young Land
The Young One
Youth Aflame

Adapted from an Article

All Mine to Give
Christiane F.▲
Coyote Ugly
The Insider▲
Isn't She Great
Joe Gould's Secret
The Last American Hero▲
Olivier, Olivier▲
Pushing Tin▲
Streetwise▲
Two or Three Things I Know about Her
Witness Protection▲

Adapted from an Opera

Aria
Balalaika
Baritone
Broken Melody
Burlesque on Carmen
Carmen▲
Carmen, Baby
Carmen Jones▲
The Chocolate Soldier
Farewell My Concubine
Fitzcarraldo▲
For the First Time
The Great Caruso
The Great Waltz▲
Gypsy Blood
I Dream Too Much
Jesus Christ, Superstar▲
La Grande Vadrouille▲
Life of Verdi
The Magic Flute▲
The Marriage of Figaro
The Medium
Meeting Venus
Midnight Girl
The Mozart Brothers▲
Otello▲
The Panther's Claw
The Phantom of the Opera▲
Rose Marie▲
The Tales of Hoffmann
The Toast of New Orleans
The Tsar's Bride▲
The Vampyr
Verdi
Wagner: The Complete Epic

Adapted from Comics

Annie
Archie: Return to Riverdale
Barb Wire
Batman
Batman▲
Batman and Robin
Batman Forever▲
Batman Returns
Black Mask
Blade
Blade II
Brenda Starr
Captain America
Captain America 2: Death Too Soon
Casper▲
Creepshow
The Crow
The Crow 2: City of Angels
The Crow: Salvation
Dennis the Menace
Dennis the Menace Strikes Again
Dick Tracy▲
Faust: Love of the Damned
Fist of the North Star
Ghost in the Shell▲
Ghost World▲
Howard the Duck
The Incredible Hulk
The Incredible Hulk Returns
Josie and the Pussycats
Judge Dredd
Killer Condom
Kull the Conqueror
The Mask▲
Men in Black▲
Modesty Blaise
Monkeybone
Mystery Men
The Phantom
Prince Valiant
Richie Rich
Sabrina the Teenage Witch
Spawn▲
Spider-Man▲
Steel
Superman: The Movie▲
Superman 2▲
Superman 3
Superman 4: The Quest for Peace
Superman & the Mole Men
Swamp Thing
Tales from the Crypt▲
Tales from the Crypt
Tales from the Crypt Presents Bordello of Blood
Tales from the Crypt Presents Demon Knight
Todd McFarlane's Spawn
Vampirella
Vault of Horror
Virus
Wicked City
X-Men

Adapted from a Fairy Tale

The Adventures of Pinocchio
Aladdin
Aladdin▲
Aladdin and His Wonderful Lamp
Alice in Wonderland
Beanstalk
Beauty and the Beast▲
Beauty and the Beast
Beauty and the Beast▲
The Blue Light▲
The Boy Who Left Home to Find Out About the Shivers
Butterfly Ball
Casey at the Bat
Cinderella▲
Cinderella
Cinderella 2000
Cinderfella
The Company of Wolves▲
The Dancing Princesses
Deadtime Stories
Donkey Skin▲
The Emperor's New Clothes
Ever After: A Cinderella Story▲
Fairy Tales
Freeway
Fun & Fancy Free▲
George Balanchine's The Nutcracker
The Glass Slipper
Goldilocks & the Three Bears
Green Snake
Hans Christian Andersen
Hansel and Gretel
Happily Ever After
A Hungarian Fairy Tale▲
Irish Cinderella
Jack & the Beanstalk
Jack and the Beanstalk: The Real Story
La Petite Sirene
Les Visiteurs du Soir▲
The Little Match Girl
The Little Mermaid
The Little Mermaid▲
Little Red Riding Hood
The Magic Fountain
The Magic Sword
March of the Wooden Soldiers▲
Mother Goose Rock 'n' Rhyme
The NeverEnding Story▲
The NeverEnding Story 3: Escape from Fantasia
The Nightingale
The Nutcracker Prince
Nutcracker: The Motion Picture
Once Upon a Brothers Grimm
Peau D'Ane▲
Peter Pan▲
The Pied Piper of Hamelin
Pin...
Pinocchio▲
Pinocchio
Pinocchio's Revenge
The Princess and the Pea
The Princess Bride▲
Princess Cinderella
The Princess Who Never Laughed
Puss 'n Boots
Rapunzel
Red Riding Hood
Rip van Winkle
Rumpelstiltskin
The Scalawag Bunch
Sleeping Beauty▲
Sleeping Beauty
The Slipper and the Rose
The Snow Queen
Snow White
Snow White: A Tale of Terror
Snow White and the Seven Dwarfs
Snow White and the Three Stooges
Snow White: The Fairest of Them All
The Swan▲
The Swan Princess
The Tale of the Frog Prince▲
The Three Little Pigs
Thumbelina
The Tin Soldier
Tom Thumb▲
Who Slew Auntie Roo?
The Witches▲
The Wonderful World of the Brothers Grimm
The Wonders of Aladdin

Adapted from Memoirs or Diaries

Angela's Ashes
Anna and the King
At First Sight
Bandit Queen
The Basketball Diaries
A Business Affair
Caro Diario▲
Celeste▲
Churchill and the Generals
Cowboy▲
Danger UXB
The Diary of Anne Frank▲
Edvard Munch
The Elegant Criminal
The Flame Trees of Thika▲
A Free Soul
The Gathering Storm
Girl, Interrupted
Goodbye, Miss 4th of July
Gypsy▲
The Happy Hooker
The Happy Hooker Goes Hollywood
The Happy Hooker Goes to Washington
Heart Beat
Heartland▲
Henry & June▲
I Remember Mama▲
I Was Nineteen
I'll Cry Tomorrow▲
I'm Dancing as Fast as I Can
In Love and War
In the Name of the Father▲
Inside the Third Reich
Iris▲
Jacquot
Julia▲
Just Like a Woman
Kings in Grass Castles
The Lawless Breed▲
Lost for Words▲
Maids of Wilko
Meetings with Remarkable Men
Mommie Dearest
My Life and Times with Antonin Artaud▲
My Own Country
My Sister's Keeper
October Sky▲
The Other Side of Heaven
Our Lady of the Assassins
The Passion of Ayn Rand
The Pillow Book
The Road from Coorain
Seven Years in Tibet
Shot in the Heart▲
Sister Kenny▲
Stars and Stripes Forever▲
The Summer of Aviya
Sweet Nothing▲
This Boy's Life▲
Under the Domim Tree
Village of Dreams
What's Love Got to Do with It?
The Whole Wide World▲
Wish You Were Here▲

Adapted from Saturday Night Live

The Blues Brothers▲
Blues Brothers 2000
It's Pat: The Movie
The Ladies Man
A Night at the Roxbury
Stuart Saves His Family
Superstar
Wayne's World▲
Wayne's World 2

Adapted from Television

Absolutely Fabulous: The Last Shout
The Addams Family
Addams Family Values
The Adventures of Rocky & Bullwinkle
Alien Nation: Dark Horizon
The Avengers
Batman
Batman: Mask of the Phantasm
Baywatch the Movie: Forbidden Paradise
Bean▲
Beavis and Butt-Head Do America
The Beverly Hillbillies
Big Top Pee-wee
Bonanza: The Return
Boris and Natasha: The Movie
The Brady Bunch Movie▲
Car 54, Where Are You?
Charlie's Angels
Coneheads
The Crawling Eye
Days of Wine and Roses▲
The Defenders: Payback
Dennis the Menace
Dennis the Menace Strikes Again
Doctor Who
Dragnet
Dudley Do-Right
The Extreme Adventures of Super Dave
The Flintstones
The Flintstones in Viva Rock Vegas
Flipper▲
The Fugitive▲
Gargoyles, The Movie: The Heroes Awaken
George of the Jungle▲
Get Smart, Again!
Good Burger
Here Come the Littles: The Movie
The Invaders
Jetsons: The Movie
Joe's Apartment
Kevin & Perry Go Large
The Key to Rebecca
Kids in the Hall: Brain Candy
Lassie
Leave It to Beaver
The Left-Handed Gun▲
Lost in Space
Maverick
McHale's Navy
McHale's Navy Joins the Air Force
Mission: Impossible▲
Mission: Impossible 2▲
The Mod Squad
Munster, Go Home!
My Favorite Martian
Mystery Science Theater 3000: The Movie
The Naked Gun: From the Files of Police Squad▲
Naked Gun 33 1/3: The Final Insult
Naked Gun 2 1/2: The Smell of Fear
The Nude Bomb
One Night Stand
Our Miss Brooks
Pee-wee's Big Adventure▲
Pennies from Heaven▲
The People Next Door
Phantom 2040 Movie: The Ghost Who Walks
Pokemon: The First Movie
Pootie Tang
Pufnstuf
Queen for a Day
Requiem for a Heavyweight▲
Rescue from Gilligan's Island
Ringmaster
Rugrats in Paris: The Movie▲
The Rugrats Movie▲
The Saint
Sgt. Bilko
Sergeant Ryker
South Park: Bigger, Longer and Uncut
Star Trek: The Motion Picture
Star Trek 2: The Wrath of Khan▲
Star Trek 3: The Search for Spock
Star Trek 4: The Voyage Home▲
Star Trek 5: The Final Frontier
Star Trek 6: The Undiscovered Country
Star Trek: First Contact▲
Star Trek: Generations▲
Star Trek: Insurrection
Tales from the Crypt Presents Bordello of Blood
Tales from the Crypt Presents Demon Knight
Thomas and the Magic Railroad
Thunder in Paradise 2
Thunder in Paradise 3
Twin Peaks: Fire Walk with Me
The Untouchables▲
A Very Brady Sequel
Wackiest Wagon Train in the West
Wild Wild West
The X-Files

Adapted from the Bible

Abraham
A.D.
The Bible
David
David and Bathsheba▲
The Decalogue▲
Esther
Godspell
The Gospel According to St. Matthew▲
Jacob
Jeremiah
Jesus
Jesus Christ, Superstar▲
Jesus Christ Superstar
Joseph
Joseph and the Amazing Technicolor Dreamcoat▲
King David
King of Kings
The King of Kings▲
The Last Supper▲
Mary and Joseph: A Story of Faith
Mary, Mother of Jesus
The Messiah▲
The Miracle Maker: The Story of Jesus
Moses
Noah
Noah's Ark
Peter and Paul
Prince of Egypt▲
Salome
Samson and Delilah▲
Samson and Delilah
Solomon
The Story of Jacob & Joseph▲
The Ten Commandments
The Ten Commandments▲

Adapted from the Radio

Behind the Mask
Big Town
Calling Dr. Death/Strange Confession
Check & Double Check
Dead Man's Eyes/Pillow of Death
The Devil's Eye
Dreaming Out Loud
Gang Busters
Gangbusters
Going to Town
Goon Movie
The Great Gildersleeve
Here Come the Nelsons
Here We Go Again!
Inner Sanctum
International Crime
The Invisible Avenger
Mr. Arkadin▲
My Friend Irma
Queen for a Day
Renfrew of the Royal Mounted
The Shadow
The Shadow Strikes
Sorry, Wrong Number▲
Treacherous Crossing
The War of the Worlds▲
Weird Woman/Frozen Ghost

Andy Hardy

Andy Hardy Gets Spring Fever
Andy Hardy Meets Debutante
Andy Hardy's Double Life
Andy Hardy's Private Secretary
Life Begins for Andy Hardy▲
Love Finds Andy Hardy▲
Love Laughs at Andy Hardy

B/W & Color Combos

Amazon Women on the Moon
And Now My Love
Andrei Rublev▲
Awakenings of the Beast
The Blue Bird▲
Dead Again▲
Dixiana
D.O.A.
Gods and Monsters▲
If...▲
JFK▲
Kafka
Kiss of the Spider Woman▲
Made in Heaven
A Man and a Woman▲
Martin▲
Mishima: A Life in Four Chapters▲
The Moon and Sixpence▲
Movie, Movie
Natural Born Killers

▲ = rated three bones or higher

A Nightmare on Elm Street 4: Dream Master
Nixon▲
Portrait of Jennie▲
Rumble Fish▲
Schindler's List▲
She's Gotta Have It▲
Stalker▲
Transylvania Twist
Truth or Dare
Unzipped▲
Wings of Desire▲
The Wizard of Oz▲
The Women▲
Zelig▲

Beach Party

Back to the Beach
Beach Blanket Bingo▲
Beach Party
Bikini Beach
How to Stuff a Wild Bikini
Muscle Beach Party
Pajama Party

Billy the Kid

Billy the Kid
Billy the Kid in Texas
Billy the Kid Returns
Billy the Kid Trapped
Billy the Kid Versus Dracula
Border Badmen
Deadwood
Devil Riders
Frontier Outlaws
Gangster's Den
Gore Vidal's Billy the Kid
I Shot Billy the Kid
Law and Order
The Left-Handed Gun▲
The Mysterious Rider
Oath of Vengeance
The Outlaw
Outlaw of the Plains
Pat Garrett & Billy the Kid▲
Prairie Badmen
Rustler's Hideout
Shadows of Death
Texas Trouble
Thundering Gunslingers
Trigger Men
Wild Horse Phantom
Young Guns
Young Guns 2

Blondie

Blondie
Blondie Brings Up Baby
Blondie for Victory
Blondie Goes Latin
Blondie Goes to College
Blondie Has Trouble
Blondie Hits the Jackpot
Blondie in Society
Blondie Knows Best
Blondie Meets the Boss
Blondie On a Budget
Blondie Plays Cupid
Blondie Takes a Vacation
Blondie's Blessed Event
Footlight Glamour
It's a Great Life

Books to Film: Louisa May Alcott

Little Men
Little Women▲
Little Women
Little Women▲

Books to Film: Eric Ambler

Background to Danger▲
Hotel Reserve▲
Journey into Fear▲
The Mask of Dimitrios▲

Books to Film: Kingsley Amis

Lucky Jim
That Uncertain Feeling

Books to Film: Hans Christian Andersen

The Red Shoes▲

Books to Film: Maya Angelou

Georgia, Georgia
I Know Why the Caged Bird Sings▲

Books to Film: Isaac Asimov

Bicentennial Man
Isaac Asimov's Nightfall
Nightfall

Books to Film: Jane Austen

Emma
Emma▲
Mansfield Park
Northanger Abbey
Persuasion
Persuasion▲
Pride and Prejudice▲
Pride and Prejudice
Pride and Prejudice▲
Sense & Sensibility
Sense and Sensibility▲

Books to Film: Honore de Balzac

Colonel Chabert
Cousin Bette
Passion in the Desert

Books to Film: Russell Banks

Affliction▲
The Sweet Hereafter▲

Books to Film: Clive Barker

Candyman
Candyman 2: Farewell to the Flesh
Hellbound: Hellraiser 2
Hellraiser
Hellraiser 3: Hell on Earth
Hellraiser 4: Bloodline
Lord of Illusions
Nightbreed
Rawhead Rex
Transmutations

Books to Film: Peter Benchley

The Beast
The Deep
Jaws▲

Books to Film: Thomas Berger

The Feud
Little Big Man▲
Neighbors

Books to Film: Ambrose Bierce

Eyes of the Panther

Books to Film: Maeve Binchy

Circle of Friends

Books to Film: Robert Bloch

The Skull
Torture Garden

Books to Film: Judy Blume

Forever

Books to Film: Ray Bradbury

The Beast from 20,000 Fathoms
Fahrenheit 451▲
The Illustrated Man▲
It Came from Outer Space▲
The Martian Chronicles: Part 1
The Martian Chronicles: Part 2
The Martian Chronicles: Part 3
Something Wicked This Way Comes
Walking on Air

Books to Film: Barbara Taylor Bradford

Hold the Dream
A Woman of Substance

Books to Film: The Brontes

Emily Bronte's Wuthering Heights
Jane Eyre
Jane Eyre▲
Jane Eyre
The Tenant of Wildfell Hall
Wuthering Heights▲
Wuthering Heights

Books to Film: Pearl S. Buck

China Sky
Dragon Seed
The Good Earth▲
Pavilion of Women

Books to Film: Frances Hodgson Burnett

Little Lord Fauntleroy▲
Little Lord Fauntleroy
The Little Princess▲
The Little Princess
A Little Princess▲
The Secret Garden▲
The Secret Garden
The Secret Garden▲
The Secret Garden

Books to Film: Edgar Rice Burroughs

At the Earth's Core
Greystoke: The Legend of Tarzan, Lord of the Apes
The Land That Time Forgot
The People That Time Forgot
Tarzan▲
Tarzan and His Mate▲
Tarzan and the Green Goddess
Tarzan and the Trappers
Tarzan Escapes▲
Tarzan Finds a Son▲
Tarzan, the Ape Man▲
Tarzan, the Ape Man
Tarzan the Fearless
Tarzan's New York Adventure
Tarzan's Revenge
Tarzan's Secret Treasure

Books to Film: William Burroughs

Naked Lunch▲

Books to Film: James M. Cain

Butterfly
Double Indemnity▲
Girl in the Cadillac
Mildred Pierce▲
The Postman Always Rings Twice▲
The Postman Always Rings Twice
Slightly Scarlet

Books to Film: Truman Capote

ABC Stage 67: Truman Capote's A Christmas Memory
Breakfast at Tiffany's▲
The Glass House▲
The Grass Harp
In Cold Blood▲
In Cold Blood
Other Voices, Other Rooms

Books to Film: Barbara Cartland

Duel of Hearts
The Flame Is Love
The Lady and the Highwayman

Books to Film: Willa Cather

My Antonia
O Pioneers!
The Song of the Lark

Books to Film: Raymond Chandler

The Big Sleep▲
The Big Sleep
Farewell, My Lovely▲
The Finger Man
Lady in the Lake
The Long Goodbye▲
Marlowe
Murder, My Sweet▲

Books to Film: Paddy Chayefsky

Altered States▲
As Young As You Feel▲
The Catered Affair▲

Books to Film: John Cheever

Sorrows of Gin
The Swimmer▲

Books to Film: Agatha Christie

Agatha Christie's The Pale Horse
The Alphabet Murders
And Then There Were None▲
Appointment with Death
The Body in the Library
The Crackler
Death on the Nile
Endless Night
Evil under the Sun
Love from a Stranger
The Mirror Crack'd
Murder Ahoy
Murder at the Gallop▲
A Murder Is Announced
Murder Most Foul▲
Murder on the Orient Express▲
Murder She Said
Ordeal by Innocence
A Pocketful of Rye
Ten Little Indians
The Unbreakable Alibi
Witness for the Prosecution▲

Books to Film: Tom Clancy

Clear and Present Danger
The Hunt for Red October▲
Patriot Games▲
The Sum of All Fears

Books to Film: Mary Higgins Clark

The Cradle Will Fall
A Cry in the Night
Double Vision
Terror Stalks the Class Reunion

Books to Film: Arthur C. Clarke

Trapped in Space
2001: A Space Odyssey▲
2010: The Year We Make Contact▲

Books to Film: James Clavell

King Rat▲
Noble House
Shogun▲
Tai-Pan

Books to Film: Jackie Collins

The Bitch
The World Is Full of Married Men
Yesterday's Hero

Books to Film: Wilkie Collins

Basil
The Moonstone▲
The Woman in White

Books to Film: Richard Condon

Gun Crazy
The Manchurian Candidate▲
Prizzi's Honor▲
Winter Kills▲

Books to Film: Joseph Conrad

Apocalypse Now▲
The Duellists▲
Face to Face
Heart of Darkness
Lord Jim▲
Nostromo
The Rover
Sabotage▲
The Secret Agent
Swept from the Sea

Books to Film: Pat Conroy

Conrack▲
The Great Santini▲
The Lords of Discipline
The Prince of Tides▲

Books to Film: Robin Cook

Coma▲
Sphinx

Books to Film: Catherine Cookson

Catherine Cookson's Colour Blind
Catherine Cookson's The Black Velvet Gown
Catherine Cookson's The Cinder Path
Catherine Cookson's The Dwelling Place
Catherine Cookson's The Fifteen Streets
Catherine Cookson's The Gambling Man
Catherine Cookson's The Girl
Catherine Cookson's The Glass Virgin
Catherine Cookson's The Man Who Cried
Catherine Cookson's The Moth
Catherine Cookson's The Rag Nymph
Catherine Cookson's The Round Tower
Catherine Cookson's The Secret▲
Catherine Cookson's The Tide of Life
Catherine Cookson's The Wingless Bird
Catherine Cookson's Tilly Trotter

Books to Film: James Fenimore Cooper

The Deerslayer
The Last of the Mohicans▲
The Last of the Mohicans
The Last of the Mohicans▲
The Last of the Redmen
The Pathfinder

Books to Film: Stephen Crane

Face to Face
The Red Badge of Courage▲

Books to Film: Michael Crichton

The Andromeda Strain
Congo
The Great Train Robbery▲
Jurassic Park▲
The Lost World: Jurassic Park 2
Rising Sun▲
Sphere
The Terminal Man
The 13th Warrior
Westworld▲

Books to Film: Clive Cussler

Raise the Titanic

Books to Film: Roald Dahl

James and the Giant Peach▲
Matilda▲
Willy Wonka & the Chocolate Factory▲
The Witches▲

Books to Film: Miguel de Cervantes

Don Quixote▲
Man of La Mancha

Books to Film: Guy de Maupassant

A Day in the Country▲
Diary of a Madman
Le Plaisir
The Private Affairs of Bel Ami▲
A Woman Without Love▲

Books to Film: Daniel Defoe

The Amorous Adventures of Moll Flanders
Crusoe
Man Friday
Moll Flanders
Robinson Crusoe
Robinson Crusoe on Mars

Books to Film: Len Deighton

Bullet to Beijing
Funeral in Berlin▲
The Ipcress File▲
Midnight in Saint Petersburg

Books to Film: Phillip K. Dick

Barjo
Blade Runner▲
Imposter
Minority Report
Screamers
Total Recall▲
Total Recall 2070: Machine Dreams

Books to Film: Charles Dickens

An American Christmas Carol
Bleak House
A Christmas Carol▲
A Christmas Carol
A Christmas Carol▲
A Christmas Carol
Cricket on the Hearth
David Copperfield▲
David Copperfield
Great Expectations
Great Expectations▲
Great Expectations
Great Expectations▲
Great Expectations
Great Expectations: The Untold Story
The Life and Adventures of Nicholas Nickleby▲
Little Dorrit, Film 1: Nobody's Fault▲
Little Dorrit, Film 2: Little Dorrit's Story▲
Martin Chuzzlewit
Ms. Scrooge
The Muppet Christmas Carol
The Mystery of Edwin Drood
Nicholas Nickleby▲
The Old Curiosity Shop
Oliver!▲
Oliver & Company
Oliver Twist▲
Oliver Twist
Oliver Twist▲
Oliver Twist
Oliver Twist▲
Our Mutual Friend
The Pickwick Papers
Scrooge▲
Scrooge
A Tale of Two Cities▲
A Tale of Two Cities
A Tale of Two Cities▲
Twisted

Books to Film: E.L. Doctorow

Billy Bathgate
Daniel
Ragtime▲

Books to Film: Fyodor Dostoyevski

The Brothers Karamazov▲
Crime and Punishment▲
Crime and Punishment
Crime and Punishment in Suburbia
Dostoevsky's Crime and Punishment
The Gambler
A Gentle Woman
La Vengeance d'une Femme
L'Idiot
Notes from Underground
The Possessed
White Nights▲

Books to Film: Sir Arthur Conan Doyle

The Adventures of Sherlock Holmes
The Crucifer of Blood
Dressed to Kill
The Hound of the Baskervilles▲
The Hound of the Baskervilles
House of Fear
The Lost World
Masks of Death
Murder at the Baskervilles
The Pearl of Death
Return to the Lost World
Robbers of the Sacred Mountain
Scarlet Claw▲
Sherlock Holmes and the Deadly Necklace
Sherlock Holmes and the Secret Weapon▲
The Sign of Four
The Silent Mr. Sherlock Holmes
Tales from the Darkside: The Movie
The Triumph of Sherlock Holmes
The Woman in Green

Books to Film: Daphne Du Maurier

The Birds▲
Don't Look Now▲
Frenchman's Creek
Jamaica Inn
Rebecca▲

Books to Film: Alexandre Dumas

At Sword's Point
Black Magic
Camille
Camille▲
The Corsican Brothers
The Count of Monte Cristo
The Count of Monte Cristo▲
The Count of Monte Cristo
The Four Musketeers▲
The Iron Mask
The Man in the Iron Mask▲
The Man in the Iron Mask
The Man in the Iron Mask▲
The Musketeer
The Prince of Thieves
Queen Margot▲
The Return of the Musketeers
Robin Hood▲
Sword of Monte Cristo
The Three Musketeers
The Three Musketeers▲
The Three Musketeers
The Three Musketeers▲

Books to Film: Lois Duncan

I Know What You Did Last Summer▲
I've Been Waiting for You
Killing Mr. Griffin
Summer of Fear

Books to Film: Dominick Dunne

An Inconvenient Woman

Books to Film: George Eliot

Middlemarch▲
The Mill on the Floss
Silas Marner▲
A Simple Twist of Fate

Books to Film: Bret Easton Ellis

American Psycho
Less Than Zero

Books to Film: James Ellroy

Brown's Requiem
Cop
L.A. Confidential▲

Books to Film: Howard Fast

The Crossing
Freedom Road

Books to Film: William Faulkner

Intruder in the Dust▲
Land of the Pharaohs
The Long, Hot Summer▲
The Reivers▲
Tarnished Angels▲
Today We Live
Tomorrow▲
William Faulkner's Old Man

Books to Film: Edna Ferber

Cimarron
Come and Get It▲
Dinner at Eight▲
Dinner at Eight
Giant▲
Saratoga Trunk
Show Boat▲
Show Boat
Stage Door▲

Books to Film: Henry Fielding

Joseph Andrews
Tom Jones▲

Books to Film: F. Scott Fitzgerald

The Great Gatsby
The Last Time I Saw Paris
The Last Tycoon▲
Tender Is the Night

Books to Film: Gustov Flaubert

Madame Bovary▲
Madame Bovary
Salammbo

Books to Film: Ian Fleming

Casino Royale
Chitty Chitty Bang Bang
Diamonds Are Forever▲
Dr. No▲
For Your Eyes Only▲
From Russia with Love▲
Goldfinger▲
License to Kill▲
Live and Let Die
The Living Daylights▲
The Man with the Golden Gun
Moonraker
Never Say Never Again
Octopussy
On Her Majesty's Secret Service▲
The Poppy Is Also a Flower
The Spy Who Loved Me
Thunderball
A View to a Kill
You Only Live Twice

Books to Film: Ken Follett

Capricorn One▲
Eye of the Needle
The Key to Rebecca
Lie Down with Lions

Books to Film: E.M. Forster

Howard's End▲
Maurice▲
A Passage to India▲
A Room with a View▲
Where Angels Fear to Tread▲

Books to Film: Frederick Forsyth

The Day of the Jackal▲
The Dogs of War
The Fourth Protocol▲
No Comebacks
The Odessa File
Two by Forsyth
Wolverine

Books to Film: Rumer Godden

Black Narcissus▲
In This House of Brede▲
The River▲

Books to Film: Nikolai Gogol

The Overcoat▲
Taras Bulba

Books to Film: William Goldman

Heat
Magic
Marathon Man▲
The Princess Bride▲

Books to Film: David Goodis

Dark Passage
Moon in the Gutter
Nightfall▲
Shoot the Piano Player▲

Books to Film: Elizabeth Goudge

Green Dolphin Street

Books to Film: Kenneth Grahame

The Adventures of Ichabod and Mr. Toad▲

Books to Film: Graham Greene

Across the Bridge
Beyond the Limit
Brighton Rock▲
End of the Affair
The End of the Affair▲
The Fallen Idol▲
The Fugitive▲
The Human Factor
Ministry of Fear▲
Monsignor Quixote
Strike It Rich
The Tenth Man
The Third Man▲
This Gun for Hire▲
This Gun for Hire
Travels with My Aunt

Books to Film: Zane Grey

Arizona Mahoney
The Border Legion
Desert Gold
Drift Fence
Dude Ranger
Fighting Caravans
Forlorn River
Helltown
The Light of Western Stars
Man of the Forest
Nevada
Riders of the Purple Sage
Roll Along Cowboy
Thunder Mountain
Thunder Pass
To the Last Man
The Vanishing American
Wagon Wheels
West of the Pecos
When the West Was Young

Books to Film: John Grisham

The Chamber
The Client
The Firm▲
John Grisham's The Rainmaker
The Pelican Brief
A Time to Kill▲

Books to Film: H. Rider Haggard

Allan Quatermain and the Lost City of Gold
King Solomon's Mines▲
King Solomon's Mines
She

Books to Film: Arthur Hailey

Airport▲
Hotel
Time Lock

Books to Film: Alex Haley

Malcolm X▲
Mama Flora's Family
Queen▲
Roots▲
Roots: The Gift
Roots: The Next Generation▲

Books to Film: Dashiell Hammett

After the Thin Man▲
Another Thin Man
The Dain Curse
The Glass Key▲
Hammett
The Maltese Falcon▲
Satan Met a Lady
Shadow of the Thin Man▲
Song of the Thin Man
The Thin Man▲
The Thin Man Goes Home
Woman in the Shadows

Books to Film: Thomas Hardy

The Claim
Far from the Madding Crowd▲
Jude▲
Jude the Obscure
The Return of the Native
The Scarlet Tunic
Tess▲
Tess of the D'Urbervilles

Books to Film: Harlequin Romances

Dreams Lost, Dreams Found
Love with a Perfect Stranger
The Winds of Jarrah

Books to Film: Thomas Harris

Hannibal
Manhunter▲
The Silence of the Lambs▲

Books to Film: Jim Harrison

Carried Away
Dalva
Legends of the Fall
Revenge
Wolf

Books to Film: Nathaniel Hawthorne

The House of the Seven Gables
The Scarlet Letter
The Scarlet Letter▲
The Scarlet Letter
Twice-Told Tales▲

Books to Film: Ernest Hemingway

After the Storm
A Farewell to Arms▲
For Whom the Bell Tolls▲
Islands in the Stream
The Killers▲
The Killers
My Old Man
The Old Man and the Sea▲
The Old Man and the Sea
The Snows of Kilimanjaro▲
To Have & Have Not▲
Women & Men: Stories of Seduction

Books to Film: O. Henry

The Cisco Kid
The Gift of Love
Ruthless People▲

Books to Film: Patricia Highsmith

The American Friend▲
Purple Noon▲
Strangers on a Train▲
The Talented Mr. Ripley

Books to Film: James Hilton

Lost Horizon▲
Random Harvest▲
The Story of Dr. Wassell

Books to Film: S.E. Hinton

The Outsiders
Rumble Fish▲
Tex
That Was Then...This Is Now

Books to Film: Nick Hornby

About a Boy▲
Fever Pitch
High Fidelity▲

Books to Film: Victor Hugo

Delusions of Grandeur
The Halfback of Notre Dame
The Hunchback
The Hunchback of Notre Dame▲
The Hunchback of Notre Dame
The Hunchback of Notre Dame▲
Les Miserables▲
Les Miserables
Les Miserables▲
Les Miserables
Les Miserables▲
Ruyblas

Books to Film: Evan Hunter (aka Ed McBain)

Blackboard Jungle▲
Blood Relatives
The Chisholms
Fuzz
High & Low▲
Last Summer
Strangers When We Meet

Books to Film: Fanny Hurst

Back Street
Four Daughters▲
Imitation of Life
Imitation of Life▲
Young at Heart

Books to Film: John Irving

The Cider House Rules▲
The Hotel New Hampshire
The World According to Garp▲

Books to Film: Washington Irving

The Adventures of Ichabod and Mr. Toad▲
The Legend of Sleepy Hollow
Rip van Winkle
Sleepy Hollow▲

Books to Film: Susan Isaacs

Compromising Positions
Shining Through

Books to Film: Rona Jaffe

Mazes and Monsters

Books to Film: John Jakes

The Bastard
North and South Book 1▲
North and South Book 2▲

▲ = rated three bones or higher

The Rebels
The Seekers

Books to Film: Henry James

The American
The Bostonians
Celine and Julie Go Boating
Daisy Miller
The Europeans➶
The Golden Bowl➶
The Golden Bowl
The Green Room
The Haunting of Hell House
The Heiress➶
In the Shadows
The Innocents➶
L'Eleve
Lost Moment
The Nightcomers
Portrait of a Lady
Portrait of a Lady➶
The Turn of the Screw
Washington Square➶
The Wings of the Dove➶

Books to Film: P.D. James

A Certain Justice
Devices and Desires➶
A Mind to Murder
Unsuitable Job for a Woman

Books to Film: James Jones

From Here to Eternity➶
From Here to Eternity
Some Came Running➶
The Thin Red Line
The Thin Red Line➶

Books to Film: James Joyce

The Dead➶
James Joyce: A Portrait of the Artist as a Young Man
Ulysses

Books to Film: Franz Kafka

The Castle➶
The Trial➶
The Trial

Books to Film: Stephen King

Apt Pupil
Carrie➶
Cat's Eye
Children of the Corn
Christine
Creepshow
Creepshow 2
Cujo
The Dark Half
Dead Zone➶
Dolores Claiborne➶
Firestarter
Graveyard Shift
The Green Mile
Hearts in Atlantis
The Lawnmower Man
The Mangler
Maximum Overdrive
Misery➶
Needful Things
Pet Sematary
Return to Salem's Lot
The Running Man
Salem's Lot
The Shawshank Redemption➶
The Shining
Silver Bullet
Sleepwalkers
Sometimes They Come Back
Sometimes They Come Back ... Again
Stand by Me➶
Stephen King's Golden Years
Stephen King's It
Stephen King's Rose Red
Stephen King's The Langoliers
Stephen King's The Night Flier
Stephen King's The Stand
Stephen King's The Storm of the Century
Stephen King's The Tommyknockers
Stephen King's Thinner
Tales from the Darkside: The Movie
Trucks

Books to Film: Rudyard Kipling

Captains Courageous➶
Captains Courageous
A Fool There Was
Gunga Din➶
The Jungle Book
Kim➶
Kim
The Man Who Would Be King➶
Rudyard Kipling's The Jungle Book
Rudyard Kipling's the Second Jungle Book: Mowgli and Baloo
They Watch
Wee Willie Winkie➶

Books to Film: Dean R. Koontz

Dean Koontz's Black River
Dean Koontz's Mr. Murder
Demon Seed➶
Hideaway
Phantoms
Servants of Twilight
Watchers
Watchers Reborn
Whispers

Books to Film: Judith Krantz

Mistral's Daughter
Princess Daisy
Scruples

Books to Film: Louis L'Amour

The Burning Hills
Cancel My Reservation
Conagher
Crossfire Trail➶
The Diamond of Jeru
Heller in Pink Tights
Hondo➶
The Quick and the Dead
The Sacketts
The Shadow Riders
Shalako

Books to Film: D.H. Lawrence

Kangaroo➶
Lady Chatterley
Lady Chatterley's Lover
The Rainbow➶
The Rocking Horse Winner
Trespasser
The Virgin and the Gypsy
Women in Love➶
Young Lady Chatterly 2

Books to Film: John Le Carre

The Little Drummer Girl➶
The Looking Glass War
A Murder of Quality
A Perfect Spy
The Russia House
The Spy Who Came in from the Cold➶
The Tailor of Panama➶

Books to Film: Harper Lee

To Kill a Mockingbird➶

Books to Film: Elmore Leonard

The Ambassador
Cat Chaser
Elmore Leonard's Gold Coast
52 Pick-Up
Get Shorty➶
Glitz
Hombre➶
Jackie Brown➶
Last Stand at Saber River
Mr. Majestyk
Out of Sight➶
Pronto
Stick
3:10 to Yuma➶
Touch
Valdez Is Coming

Books to Film: Ira Levin

The Boys from Brazil
A Kiss Before Dying
Rosemary's Baby➶
Sliver
The Stepford Wives➶

Books to Film: Sinclair Lewis

Ann Vickers
Arrowsmith
Dodsworth➶
Elmer Gantry➶

Books to Film: Astrid Lindgren

Brothers Lionheart
The Children of Noisy Village
The Land of Faraway
More about the Children of Noisy Village
The New Adventures of Pippi Longstocking
Pippi Goes on Board
Pippi in the South Seas
Pippi Longstocking
Pippi on the Run

Books to Film: Jack London

The Assassination Bureau➶
Burning Daylight
Call of the Wild
The Fighter➶
Great Adventure
Jack London's The Call of the Wild
The Legend of Sea Wolf
The Legend of the Sea Wolf
Legends of the North
The Mutiny of the Elsinore
The Sea Wolf➶
The Sea Wolf
Tales of the Klondike: In a Far Country
Tales of the Klondike: Race for Number One
Tales of the Klondike: The Scorn of Women
Tales of the Klondike: The Unexpected
Torture Ship
White Fang➶
White Fang and the Hunter
Wolf Call

Books to Film: H.P. Lovecraft

Blood Island
Bride of Re-Animator
Cthulhu Mansion
The Curse
Die, Monster, Die!
The Dunwich Horror
From Beyond➶
The Haunted Palace
H.P. Lovecraft's Necronomicon: Book of the Dead
Lurking Fear
Re-Animator➶
The Resurrected
The Sinister Invasion
The Unnamable
The Unnamable 2: The Statement of Randolph Carter

Books to Film: Robert Ludlum

The Apocalypse Watch
The Bourne Identity➶
The Bourne Identity
The Holcroft Covenant
The Osterman Weekend

Books to Film: Peter Maas

King of the Gypsies
Marie➶
Serpico➶

Books to Film: Alistair MacLean

Bear Island
Breakheart Pass
Caravan to Vaccares
Detonator
Detonator 2: Night Watch
Force 10 from Navarone
Golden Rendezvous
The Guns of Navarone➶
Ice Station Zebra
Puppet on a Chain
River of Death
Where Eagles Dare➶

Books to Film: Norman Mailer

The Executioner's Song
Marilyn: The Untold Story➶
The Naked and the Dead
Pursuit➶
Tough Guys Don't Dance

Books to Film: Richard Matheson

Cold Sweat
Icy Breasts➶
The Incredible Shrinking Man➶
The Last Man on Earth
The Legend of Hell House➶
Omega Man
Somewhere in Time
Stir of Echoes
What Dreams May Come
Young Warriors

Books to Film: W. Somerset Maugham

Adorable Julia
Beachcomber➶
Dirty Gertie from Harlem U.S.A.
Encore➶
The Letter➶
Miss Sadie Thompson➶
The Moon and Sixpence➶
Of Human Bondage➶
Of Human Bondage
Overnight Sensation
The Painted Veil
Rain
The Razor's Edge➶
The Razor's Edge
Sadie Thompson➶
Trio➶
Up at the Villa

Books to Film: Colleen McCullough

An Indecent Obsession
The Thorn Birds➶
Tim

Books to Film: Ian McEwan

The Cement Garden
The Comfort of Strangers➶
The Innocent

Books to Film: Terry McMillan

Disappearing Acts
How Stella Got Her Groove Back
Waiting to Exhale➶

Books to Film: Larry McMurtry

The Best Little Whorehouse in Texas
Hud➶
Larry McMurtry's Dead Man's Walk
The Last Picture Show➶
Lonesome Dove➶
Terms of Endearment➶
Texasville

Books to Film: Herman Melville

Bartleby
Enchanted Island
Moby Dick➶
Moby Dick
Pola X

Books to Film: James Michener

The Bridges at Toko-Ri➶
Centennial➶
Dynasty
Hawaii➶
Return to Paradise
Sayonara➶
Texas
Until They Sail

Books to Film: L.M. Montgomery

Anne of Avonlea➶
Anne of Green Gables➶
Lantern Hill

Books to Film: Brian Moore

Black Robe➶
Catholics➶
Cold Heaven
The Lonely Passion of Judith Hearne➶

Books to Film: Vladimir Nabokov

Despair➶
Lolita➶
Lolita
The Luzhin Defence

Books to Film: Joyce Carol Oates

Foxfire
Smooth Talk➶

Books to Film: John O'Hara

Butterfield 8➶
From the Terrace
Pal Joey➶
Ten North Frederick

Books to Film: George Orwell

Animal Farm
A Merry War➶
1984➶

Books to Film: Marcel Pagnol

The Baker's Wife➶
Fanny➶
Jean de Florette➶
Manon of the Spring➶
Marius➶
My Father's Glory➶
My Mother's Castle➶
Topaze➶

Books to Film: Nicholas Pileggi

Casino➶
Goodfellas➶

Books to Film: Edgar Allan Poe

The Bells➶
The Black Cat➶
The Black Cat
Dr. Tarr's Torture Dungeon
The Fall of the House of Usher
The Fall of the House of Usher➶
The Fall of the House of Usher
The Haunted Palace
Haunting Fear
The Haunting of Morella
The House of Usher
Jaws of Justice
La Chute de la Maison Usher➶
The Living Coffin
Manfish
Masque of the Red Death➶
Masque of the Red Death
Murders in the Rue Morgue
The Murders in the Rue Morgue➶
The Oblong Box
The Oval Portrait
The Pit and the Pendulum➶
The Pit & the Pendulum
Premature Burial
The Raven
The Raven➶
The Spectre of Edgar Allen Poe
Spirits of the Dead➶
Tales of Terror
The Tell-Tale Heart
Tomb of Ligeia➶
The Torture Chamber of Dr. Sadism
Two Evil Eyes
Web of the Spider

Books to Film: Katherine Anne Porter

Noon Wine➶
Ship of Fools➶

Books to Film: Mario Puzo

The Godfather➶
The Godfather, Part 2➶
The Godfather, Part 3➶
The Last Don
The Sicilian

Books to Film: Ruth Rendell

A Dark Adapted Eye➶
A Demon in My View
A Fatal Inversion
Gallowglass➶
La Ceremonie➶
Live Flesh➶

Books to Film: Anne Rice

Exit to Eden
Interview with the Vampire
Queen of the Damned

Books to Film: Harold Robbins

The Adventurers
The Betsy
The Carpetbaggers
King Creole
The Lonely Lady
Nevada Smith
Never Love a Stranger
Stiletto
Where Love Has Gone

Books to Film: Damon Runyon

Big Street

➶ = *rated three bones or higher*

Bloodhounds of Broadway
40 Pounds of Trouble
Guys and Dolls ▲
It Ain't Hay
Lady for a Day ▲
The Lemon Drop Kid
Little Miss Marker ▲
Little Miss Marker
Pocketful of Miracles ▲
Sorrowful Jones

Books to Film: Sir Walter Scott

Ivanhoe ▲
Ivanhoe
Ivanhoe ▲
King Richard and the Crusaders

Books to Film: Sidney Sheldon

The Naked Face
The Other Side of Midnight
Rage of Angels
Rage of Angels: The Story Continues
Sidney Sheldon's Bloodline
Windmills of the Gods

Books to Film: Mary Shelley

The Bride of Frankenstein ▲
Frankenstein ▲
Frankenstein
Frankenstein Unbound ▲
Mary Shelley's Frankenstein

Books to Film: Jean Shepherd

A Christmas Story ▲
My Summer Story
Ollie Hopnoodle's Haven of Bliss

Books to Film: Georges Simenon

Betty
Cop-Out
Man on the Eiffel Tower ▲
Monsieur Hire ▲
Paris Express

Books to Film: Danielle Steel

Danielle Steel's Changes
Danielle Steel's Daddy
Danielle Steel's Fine Things
Danielle Steel's Heartbeat
Danielle Steel's Kaleidoscope
Danielle Steel's Palomino
Danielle Steel's Star
Now and Forever
The Promise

Books to Film: John Steinbeck

Cannery Row
East of Eden ▲
East of Eden
The Grapes of Wrath ▲
Lifeboat ▲
Of Mice and Men ▲
The Pearl ▲
The Red Pony ▲
Tortilla Flat ▲

Books to Film: Stendhal

La Chartreuse de Parme
The Red and the Black ▲
Vanina Vanini ▲

Books to Film: Robert Louis Stevenson

Abbott and Costello Meet Dr. Jekyll and Mr. Hyde
Adventure Island
Black Arrow ▲
The Body Snatcher ▲
Dr. Jekyll and Mr. Hyde ▲
Dr. Jekyll and Mr. Hyde
Dr. Jekyll and Sister Hyde
The Ebb-Tide
I, Monster ▲
Jekyll and Hyde
Jekyll & Hyde...Together Again
Kidnapped
Man with Two Heads
The Master of Ballantrae
Muppet Treasure Island
Robert Louis Stevenson's St. Ives
Robert Louis Stevenson's The Game of Death
Strange Case of Dr. Jekyll & Mr. Hyde
The Strange Door
Treasure Island ▲
Treasure Island
The Wrong Box ▲

Books to Film: Bram Stoker

Blood from the Mummy's Tomb
Bram Stoker's Dracula
Bram Stoker's Shadowbuilder
Bram Stoker's The Mummy
Burial of the Rats
Count Dracula
Dracula (Spanish Version)
Dracula ▲
Dracula
The Horror of Dracula ▲
The Lair of the White Worm ▲
Nosferatu ▲
Nosferatu the Vampyre
Tomb

Books to Film: Harriet Beecher Stowe

Uncle Tom's Cabin

Books to Film: Jacqueline Susann

The Love Machine
Once Is Not Enough

Books to Film: Jonathan Swift

Gulliver's Travels
The Three Worlds of Gulliver

Books to Film: Paul Theroux

Half Moon Street
The Mosquito Coast
Saint Jack ▲

Books to Film: Jim Thompson

After Dark, My Sweet ▲
Coup de Torchon ▲
The Getaway
The Grifters ▲
The Kill-Off
This World, Then the Fireworks

Books to Film: James Thurber

The Battle of the Sexes ▲
Billy Liar ▲
The Secret Life of Walter Mitty ▲

Books to Film: J.R.R. Tolkien

The Hobbit ▲
The Lord of the Rings
Lord of the Rings 1: The Fellowship of the Rings ▲
The Return of the King

Books to Film: Leo Tolstoy

Anna Karenina ▲
Anna Karenina
Leo Tolstoy's Anna Karenina
Night Sun
Prisoner of the Mountains ▲
War and Peace
War and Peace ▲
War and Peace

Books to Film: Scott Turow

Presumed Innocent ▲

Books to Film: Mark Twain

The Adventures of Huck Finn ▲
The Adventures of Huckleberry Finn ▲
The Adventures of Huckleberry Finn
The Adventures of Tom Sawyer ▲
The Adventures of Tom Sawyer
Arthur's Quest
Ava's Magical Adventure
A Connecticut Yankee ▲
A Connecticut Yankee in King Arthur's Court
Huck and the King of Hearts
Huckleberry Finn
The Innocents Abroad
A Kid in King Arthur's Court
A Knight in Camelot
A Million to Juan
The Mysterious Stranger
The Prince and the Pauper ▲
The Prince and the Pauper
The Prince and the Surfer
The Private History of a Campaign That Failed
Pudd'nhead Wilson
Tom and Huck ▲
Tom Sawyer ▲
Tom Sawyer
Unidentified Flying Oddball
A Young Connecticut Yankee in King Arthur's Court

Books to Film: Anne Tyler

The Accidental Tourist ▲
Breathing Lessons ▲
Earthly Possessions
Saint Maybe ▲

Books to Film: John Updike

Roommate
Too Far to Go ▲
The Witches of Eastwick

Books to Film: Leon Uris

Battle Cry ▲
Exodus ▲
QB VII ▲
Topaz ▲

Books to Film: Jules Verne

Around the World in 80 Days ▲
Around the World in 80 Days
Around the World in a Daze
800 Leagues Down the Amazon
Five Weeks in a Balloon
From the Earth to the Moon
In Search of the Castaways ▲
Journey to the Center of the Earth ▲
Journey to the Center of the Earth
Light at the Edge of the World
Master of the World
Mysterious Island ▲
On the Comet ▲
Those Fantastic Flying Fools
20,000 Leagues under the Sea ▲
20,000 Leagues Under the Sea
Where Time Began

Books to Film: Kurt Vonnegut

Breakfast of Champions
D.P.
Kurt Vonnegut's Harrison Bergeron
Mother Night ▲
Slapstick of Another Kind
Slaughterhouse Five
Who Am I This Time? ▲

Books to Film: Alice Walker

The Color Purple ▲

Books to Film: Edgar Wallace

The Black Abbot
Chamber of Horrors
Creature with the Blue Hand
Curse of the Yellow Snake
Dead Eyes of London
Door with the Seven Locks
Forger of London
The Human Monster
The Indian Scarf
Mr. Reeder in Room 13
The Mysterious Magician
The Secret Four
Secret of the Black Trunk
The Squeaker
The Strange Countess
The Terror

Books to Film: Joseph Wambaugh

The Black Marble ▲
The Choirboys
Echoes in the Darkness
The Glitter Dome
The New Centurions
The Onion Field ▲

Books to Film: Evelyn Waugh

Brideshead Revisited ▲
A Handful of Dust
The Loved One ▲

Books to Film: H.G. Wells

Empire of the Ants
First Men in the Moon
Food of the Gods
Food of the Gods: Part 2
Half a Sixpence
The Invisible Man ▲
The Invisible Man's Revenge
The Island of Dr. Moreau
Island of Lost Souls ▲
Kipps ▲
La Merveilleuse Visite
The Man Who Could Work Miracles ▲
The New Invisible Man
Terror Is a Man
Things to Come ▲
The Time Machine ▲
Time Machine
The Time Machine
Village of the Giants
The War of the Worlds ▲

Books to Film: Donald Westlake (aka Richard Stark)

Bank Shot ▲
Cops and Robbers
The Hot Rock ▲
Made in USA
Payback
Point Blank
Slayground
A Slight Case of Murder
Two Much
What's the Worst That Could Happen?
Why Me?

Books to Film: Edith Wharton

The Age of Innocence ▲
The Buccaneers ▲
The Children
Ethan Frome
House of Mirth ▲
The Old Maid ▲

Books to Film: William Wharton

Birdy ▲
Dad
A Midnight Clear ▲

Books to Film: E(lwyn) B(rooks) White

Charlotte's Web
Stuart Little
Stuart Little 2
The Trumpet of the Swan

Books to Film: Oscar Wilde

The Canterville Ghost
Dorian Gray
An Ideal Husband ▲
The Importance of Being Earnest ▲
The Importance of Being Earnest
Lady Windermere's Fan
Picture of Dorian Gray ▲
Salome
The Sins of Dorian Gray

Books to Film: Thornton Wilder

The Bridge of San Luis Rey ▲
Hello, Dolly!
The Matchmaker ▲
Mr. North
Our Town ▲
Our Town

Books to Film: Virginia Woolf

Mrs. Dalloway
To the Lighthouse

Books to Film: Cornell Woolrich

Black Angel ▲
The Bride Wore Black ▲
I Married a Dead Man
Mississippi Mermaid ▲
Mrs. Winterbourne
Original Sin
Phantom Lady ▲
Rear Window ▲
The Window ▲

Books to Film: Herman Wouk

The Caine Mutiny ▲
The Caine Mutiny Court Martial ▲
Marjorie Morningstar
War & Remembrance
War & Remembrance: The Final Chapter
The Winds of War

The Bowery Boys

Angels with Dirty Faces ▲
Blues Busters
Bowery Blitzkrieg
Bowery Boys Meet the Monsters
Bowery Buckaroos
Boys of the City
Clipped Wings
Dead End ▲
East Side Kids
Flying Wild
Follow the Leader
Ghost Chasers
Ghost on the Loose
Hard-Boiled Mahoney
Here Come the Marines
Kid Dynamite
Let's Get Tough
Little Tough Guys
Master Minds
Million Dollar Kid
Mr. Wise Guy
'Neath Brooklyn Bridge
Pride of the Bowery
Smart Alecks
Smugglers' Cove ▲
Spook Busters
Spooks Run Wild
That Gang of Mine
They Made Me a Criminal

Buffalo Bill Cody

Annie Oakley ▲
Buffalo Bill
Buffalo Bill & the Indians ▲
Buffalo Bill Rides Again
The Plainsman
Pony Express ▲
Young Buffalo Bill

Bulldog Drummond

Arrest Bulldog Drummond
Bulldog Drummond
Bulldog Drummond at Bay
Bulldog Drummond Comes Back
Bulldog Drummond Escapes
Bulldog Drummond's Bride
Bulldog Drummond's Peril
Bulldog Drummond's Revenge
Bulldog Drummond's Secret Police
Bulldog Jack ▲

Carry On

Carry On at Your Convenience
Carry On Behind
Carry On Camping
Carry On Cleo
Carry On Cowboy
Carry On Cruising
Carry On Dick
Carry On Doctor ▲
Carry On Emmanuelle
Carry On England
Carry On Henry VIII
Carry On Nurse
Carry On Screaming
Follow That Camel

Charlie Brown and the Peanuts Gang

Race for Your Life, Charlie Brown

Charlie Chan

Castle in the Desert
Charlie Chan and the Curse of the Dragon Queen
Charlie Chan at the Opera ▲
Charlie Chan at the Wax Museum
Charlie Chan in Paris
Charlie Chan in Rio
Charlie Chan in the Secret Service
Charlie Chan's Secret
The Chinese Cat
The Jade Mask
Meeting at Midnight
Murder over New York
The Scarlet Clue
The Shanghai Cobra

Corman's Mama

Big Bad Mama
Big Bad Mama 2
Bloody Mama
Crazy Mama

 ▲ = *rated three bones or higher*

Director/Star Teams: Boetticher & Scott

Comanche Station
Ride Lonesome
The Tall T

Director/Star Teams: Burton & Depp

Ed Wood▲
Edward Scissorhands▲
Sleepy Hollow▲

Director/Star Teams: Capra & Stewart

It's a Wonderful Life▲
Mr. Smith Goes to Washington▲
You Can't Take It with You▲

Director/Star Teams: Carpenter & Russell

Big Trouble in Little China
Elvis: The Movie
Escape from L.A.
Escape from New York
The Thing

Director/Star Teams: Cukor & Hepburn

Adam's Rib▲
A Bill of Divorcement
Holiday▲
Keeper of the Flame
Little Women▲
Love Among the Ruins▲
Pat and Mike▲
The Philadelphia Story▲
Sylvia Scarlett

Director/Star Teams: Donner & Gibson

Conspiracy Theory▲
Lethal Weapon▲
Lethal Weapon 2▲
Lethal Weapon 3
Lethal Weapon 4
Maverick

Director/Star Teams: Ford & Wayne

Donovan's Reef▲
Fort Apache▲
The Horse Soldiers
How the West Was Won▲
The Long Voyage Home▲
The Man Who Shot Liberty Valance▲
The Quiet Man▲
Rio Grande▲
The Searchers▲
She Wore a Yellow Ribbon▲
Stagecoach▲
They Were Expendable▲
Three Godfathers▲
Wings of Eagles

Director/Star Teams: Hawks & Wayne

El Dorado▲
Hatari!▲
Red River▲
Rio Bravo▲
Rio Lobo

Director/Star Teams: Hill & Newman

Butch Cassidy and the Sundance Kid▲
Slap Shot▲
The Sting▲

Director/Star Teams: Hitchcock & Stewart

The Man Who Knew Too Much
Rear Window▲
Rope▲
Vertigo▲

Director/Star Teams: Huston & Bogart

Across the Pacific▲
The African Queen▲
Beat the Devil▲
Key Largo▲
The Maltese Falcon▲
Treasure of the Sierra Madre▲

Director/Star Teams: Jordan & Rea

The Butcher Boy▲
The Company of Wolves▲
The Crying Game▲
Danny Boy▲
The End of the Affair▲
In Dreams
Interview with the Vampire
Michael Collins▲

Director/Star Teams: King & Peck

Beloved Infidel
The Bravados▲
The Gunfighter▲
The Snows of Kilimanjaro▲
Twelve o'Clock High▲

Director/Star Teams: Kurosawa & Mifune

The Bad Sleep Well▲
Drunken Angel▲
The Hidden Fortress▲
High & Low▲
A Quiet Duel
Rashomon▲
Red Beard▲
Sanjuro▲
Scandal
Seven Samurai▲
Stray Dog▲
Throne of Blood▲
Yojimbo▲

Director/Star Teams: Lee & Washington

He Got Game
Malcolm X▲
Mo' Better Blues

Director/Star Teams: Mann & Stewart

Bend of the River▲
Far Country▲
The Man from Laramie▲
The Naked Spur▲
Winchester '73▲

Director/Star Teams: Needham & Reynolds

Cannonball Run
Cannonball Run 2
Hooper
Smokey and the Bandit
Smokey and the Bandit 2
Stroker Ace

Director/Star Teams: Newman & Woodward

The Effect of Gamma Rays on Man-in-the-Moon Marigolds▲
The Glass Menagerie▲
Harry & Son
Rachel, Rachel▲
The Shadow Box▲

Director/Star Teams: Pollack & Redford

The Electric Horseman
Havana
Jeremiah Johnson▲
Out of Africa▲
This Property Is Condemned
Three Days of the Condor▲
The Way We Were▲

Director/Star Teams: Rafelson & Nicholson

Blood & Wine
Five Easy Pieces▲
Head▲
The King of Marvin Gardens
Man Trouble
The Postman Always Rings Twice

Director/Star Teams: Raimi & Campbell

Army of Darkness▲
Crimewave
Darkman▲
Evil Dead
Evil Dead 2: Dead by Dawn
Spider-Man▲

Director/Star Teams: Raimi & 1973 Oldsmobile Delta 88

Army of Darkness▲
Crimewave
Darkman▲
Evil Dead
Evil Dead 2: Dead by Dawn
For Love of the Game
The Gift
A Simple Plan▲
Spider-Man▲

Director/Star Teams: Reiner & Martin

All of Me
Dead Men Don't Wear Plaid
The Jerk
The Man with Two Brains▲

Director/Star Teams: Ritt & Newman

Hombre▲
Hud▲
The Long, Hot Summer▲
Paris Blues

Director/Star Teams: Sayles & Strathairn

The Brother from Another Planet▲
City of Hope▲
Eight Men Out▲
Limbo
Matewan▲
Passion Fish▲
Return of the Secaucus 7▲

Director/Star Teams: Scorsese & De Niro

Cape Fear▲
Casino▲
Goodfellas▲
King of Comedy▲
Mean Streets▲
New York, New York▲
Raging Bull▲
Taxi Driver▲

Director/Star Teams: Sheridan & Day-Lewis

The Boxer
In the Name of the Father▲
My Left Foot▲

Director/Star Teams: Siegel & Eastwood

The Beguiled▲
Coogan's Bluff▲
Dirty Harry▲
Escape from Alcatraz▲
Two Mules for Sister Sara▲

Director/Star Teams: Truffault & Leaud

Bed and Board▲
Day for Night▲
The 400 Blows▲
Stolen Kisses▲
Two English Girls▲

Director/Star Teams: von Sternberg & Dietrich

Blonde Venus▲
The Blue Angel▲
Dishonored
Morocco▲
Scarlet Empress▲
Shanghai Express▲

Director/Star Teams: Walsh & Bogart

The Enforcer
High Sierra▲
The Roaring Twenties▲
They Drive by Night▲

Director/Star Teams: Woo & Fat

A Better Tomorrow, Part 1
A Better Tomorrow, Part 2
A Bullet in the Head▲
Hard-Boiled
The Killer▲

Dirty Harry

The Dead Pool
Dirty Harry▲
The Enforcer
Magnum Force
Sudden Impact

Disney Animated Movies

Aladdin▲
Aladdin and the King of Thieves
Alice in Wonderland▲
The Aristocats▲
Bambi▲
Beauty and the Beast▲
The Black Cauldron
Cinderella▲
Dinosaur
Doug's 1st Movie▲
DuckTales the Movie: Treasure of the Lost Lamp
Dumbo▲
The Emperor's New Groove▲
Fantasia▲
Fantasia/2000
The Fox and the Hound▲
A Goofy Movie
The Great Mouse Detective▲
Hercules▲
The Hunchback of Notre Dame▲
The Jungle Book▲
Lady and the Tramp▲
Lilo & Stitch
The Lion King▲
The Lion King: Simba's Pride
The Little Mermaid▲
The Many Adventures of Winnie the Pooh
Melody Time
Mulan
The Nightmare before Christmas▲
Oliver & Company
101 Dalmatians▲
Peter Pan▲
Pinocchio▲
Pocahontas▲
The Rescuers▲
The Rescuers Down Under
The Return of Jafar
Return to Never Land
Robin Hood▲
Sleeping Beauty▲
Snow White and the Seven Dwarfs▲
The Sword in the Stone▲
Tarzan▲
The Three Caballeros
Toy Story▲
Toy Story 2▲

Disney Family Movies

The Absent-Minded Professor▲
The Adventures of Bullwhip Griffin
The Adventures of Huck Finn▲
The Adventures of Ichabod and Mr. Toad▲
The Air Up There
Almost Angels
Amy
Angels in the Endzone
Angels in the Outfield
The Apple Dumpling Gang
The Apple Dumpling Gang Rides Again
Babes in Toyland
The Barefoot Executive
The Bears & I
Bedknobs and Broomsticks
Benji the Hunted
Big Red
Black Arrow▲
The Black Arrow
The Black Hole
Blackbeard's Ghost
Blank Check
The Blue Yonder
Bon Voyage!
Breakin' Through
Candleshoe
The Castaway Cowboy
The Cat from Outer Space
Charley and the Angel
Charlie, the Lonesome Cougar
Cheetah
Child of Glass
The Computer Wore Tennis Shoes
Condorman
Darby O'Gill & the Little People▲
Davy Crockett and the River Pirates
Davy Crockett, King of the Wild Frontier▲
The Devil & Max Devlin
Dr. Syn, Alias the Scarecrow
D3: The Mighty Ducks
Emil and the Detectives
Escapade in Florence
Escape to Witch Mountain▲
A Far Off Place
The Fighting Prince of Donegal
Flight of the Grey Wolf
Flight of the Navigator
Flubber
Freaky Friday
Fun & Fancy Free▲
The Girl Who Spelled Freedom▲
The Gnome-Mobile
Gone Are the Days
A Goofy Movie
The Great Locomotive Chase
Greyfriars Bobby
Gus
Heavyweights
Herbie Goes Bananas
Herbie Goes to Monte Carlo
Herbie Rides Again
Homeward Bound: The Incredible Journey▲
Honey, I Blew Up the Kid
Honey, I Shrunk the Kids
Honey, We Shrunk Ourselves
The Horse in the Gray Flannel Suit
The Horse Without a Head
Horsemasters
Hot Lead & Cold Feet
The Hunchback of Notre Dame▲
In Search of the Castaways▲
The Incredible Journey
Iron Will
The Island at the Top of the World
Johnny Shiloh
Johnny Tremain & the Sons of Liberty
The Journey of Natty Gann▲
Justin Morgan Had a Horse
King of the Grizzlies
The Last Flight of Noah's Ark
Lt. Robin Crusoe, U.S.N.
The Light in the Forest
The Littlest Horse Thieves
The Littlest Outlaw
Lots of Luck
The Love Bug
Love Leads the Way
Mary Poppins▲
Menace on the Mountain
Million Dollar Duck
Miracle Down Under
The Miracle of the White Stallions
The Misadventures of Merlin Jones
Monkeys, Go Home!
Monkey's Uncle
Moon Pilot
The Moon-Spinners
Mooncussers
Mosby's Marauders
My Dog, the Thief
My Favorite Martian
Napoleon and Samantha▲
Never a Dull Moment
Newsies
Night Crossing
Nikki, the Wild Dog of the North
The Nine Lives of Elfego Baca
No Deposit, No Return
The North Avenue Irregulars
Now You See Him, Now You Don't
Old Yeller▲
The One and Only, Genuine, Original Family Band▲
101 Dalmatians
102 Dalmatians
One Little Indian
One Magic Christmas
One of Our Dinosaurs Is Missing
The Parent Trap
Pete's Dragon
Pocahontas▲
Pollyanna▲
Return from Witch Mountain
Return to Oz
Ride a Wild Pony▲
Rob Roy—The Highland Rogue
The Rocketeer▲
Sammy, the Way-Out Seal
Savage Sam
Scandalous John
The Secret of El Zorro
The Shaggy D.A.
The Shaggy Dog
The Sign of Zorro
Smith!
Smoke
Snow Dogs
Snowball Express

So Dear to My Heart➚
Son of Flubber
The Story of Robin Hood & His Merrie Men➚
Summer Magic
Summer of the Monkeys
Superdad
The Swiss Family Robinson➚
The Sword & the Rose
Tall Tale: The Unbelievable Adventures of Pecos Bill
Ten Who Dared
That Darn Cat
Third Man on the Mountain
Those Calloways
The Three Lives of Thomasina➚
3 Ninjas
3 Ninjas Kick Back
A Tiger Walks
Toby Tyler➚
Tom and Huck➚
Tonka
Toothless
Toy Story➚
Treasure Island➚
The Treasure of Matecumbe
20,000 Leagues under the Sea➚
The Ugly Dachshund
Undergrads➚
Unidentified Flying Oddball
Waltz King
The Watcher in the Woods
Westward Ho, the Wagons!
White Fang➚
White Fang 2: The Myth of the White Wolf
The Wild Country
Wild Hearts Can't Be Broken➚
The World's Greatest Athlete

Doc Holliday

Cheyenne Autumn
Gunfight at the O.K. Corral➚
Hour of the Gun
My Darling Clementine➚
Tombstone➚
Wyatt Earp

Dr. Christian

Courageous Dr. Christian
Dr. Christian Meets the Women
Meet Dr. Christian
Melody for Three
Remedy for Riches
They Meet Again

Dr. Mabuse

Dr. Mabuse, The Gambler➚
Dr. Mabuse vs. Scotland Yard
The Invisible Dr. Mabuse➚
The Return of Dr. Mabuse
The Thousand Eyes of Dr. Mabuse

Dr. Seuss

Dr. Seuss' How the Grinch Stole Christmas
The 5000 Fingers of Dr. T.➚

Dracula

Abbott and Costello Meet Frankenstein➚
Blood of Dracula
Blood of Dracula's Castle
Bram Stoker's Dracula
The Brides of Dracula
Count Dracula
The Creeps
Dracula (Spanish Version)
Dracula➚
Dracula
Dracula A.D. 1972
Dracula & Son
Dracula: Dead and Loving It
Dracula Father and Son
Dracula/Garden of Eden
Dracula Has Risen from the Grave
Dracula, Prince of Darkness
Dracula Rising
Dracula Sucks
Dracula: The Dark Prince
Dracula 2000
Dracula: Up in Harlem
Dracula vs. Frankenstein
Dracula's Daughter➚
Dracula's Great Love
Dracula's Last Rites
Dracula's Widow
The Horror of Dracula➚
House of Dracula
House of Frankenstein
Hysterical
The Legend of the 7 Golden Vampires
Love at First Bite
Mad Monster Party
The Monster Squad
Nocturna
Return of Dracula
Return of the Vampire
The Satanic Rites of Dracula
The Scars of Dracula
The Screaming Dead
Son of Dracula➚
Taste the Blood of Dracula
To Die For
Transylvania 6-5000
Vampire Circus
Waxwork
Zoltan...Hound of Dracula

Elvisfilm

Blue Hawaii
Change of Habit
Charro!
Clambake
Double Trouble
Easy Come, Easy Go
Elvis and Me
Elvis in Hollywood➚
Elvis Meets Nixon
Elvis: The Movie
Finding Graceland
Flaming Star➚
Follow That Dream
Frankie and Johnny
Fun in Acapulco
G.I. Blues
Girl Happy
Girls! Girls! Girls!
Harum Scarum
Heartbreak Hotel
Honeymoon in Vegas
It Happened at the World's Fair
Jailhouse Rock➚
Kid Galahad
King Creole
Kissin' Cousins
Live a Little, Love a Little
Love Me Tender
Loving You
Paradise, Hawaiian Style
Rock-a-Doodle
Roustabout
Six-String Samurai
Speedway
Spinout
Stay Away, Joe
This Is Elvis
3000 Miles to Graceland
Tickle Me
Top Secret!➚
The Trouble with Girls (and How to Get into It)➚
True Romance
Viva Las Vegas
Wild in the Country
The Woman Who Loved Elvis

The Falcon

The Amityville Curse
The Devil's Cargo
The Falcon in Hollywood
The Falcon in Mexico
The Falcon's Brother

4 Bones

A Nous la Liberte➚
Abe Lincoln in Illinois➚
Adam's Rib➚
The Adventures of Robin Hood➚
The African Queen➚
All About Eve➚
All Quiet on the Western Front➚
All the King's Men➚
An American in Paris➚
Anatomy of a Murder➚
Andrei Rublev➚
An Angel at My Table➚
Angels with Dirty Faces➚
Annie Hall➚
Apocalypse Now➚
The Asphalt Jungle➚
Au Revoir les Enfants➚
The Awful Truth➚
The Ballad of Narayama➚
Bambi➚
The Bank Dick➚
The Battleship Potemkin➚
Beauty and the Beast➚
Ben-Hur➚
The Best Years of Our Lives➚
The Bicycle Thief➚
The Big Parade➚
The Big Sleep➚
The Birth of a Nation➚
The Blue Angel➚
The Boys of St. Vincent➚
Breathless➚
Brian's Song➚
The Bride of Frankenstein➚
The Bridge on the River Kwai➚
Brief Encounter➚
Bringing Up Baby➚
The Burmese Harp➚
Butch Cassidy and the Sundance Kid➚
The Cabinet of Dr. Caligari➚
The Caine Mutiny➚
The Cameraman➚
Casablanca➚
Cesar➚
Children of Paradise➚
Chimes at Midnight➚
Chinatown➚
Christ Stopped at Eboli➚
A Christmas Carol➚
Citizen Kane➚
City Lights➚
A Clockwork Orange➚
Close Encounters of the Third Kind➚
Colonel Redl➚
Come and See➚
Commissar➚
The Conformist➚
Crime and Punishment➚
The Crowd➚
Cyrano de Bergerac➚
Danton➚
Das Boot➚
David Copperfield➚
Day for Night➚
Day of Wrath➚
Dead of Night➚
The Deer Hunter➚
Deliverance➚
Destry Rides Again➚
Diamonds of the Night➚
Dinner at Eight➚
The Discreet Charm of the Bourgeoisie➚
Dr. Strangelove, or: How I Learned to Stop Worrying and Love the Bomb➚
Don Quixote➚
Double Indemnity➚
Duck Soup➚
Dumbo➚
The Earrings of Madame De...➚
Earth➚
East of Eden➚
8 1/2➚
El Norte➚
The Elephant Man➚
The Empire Strikes Back➚
E.T.: The Extra-Terrestrial➚
Every Man for Himself & God Against All➚
Fanny➚
Fanny and Alexander➚
Fantasia➚
Fitzcarraldo➚
Five Easy Pieces➚
Forbidden Games➚
Foreign Correspondent➚
Forever and a Day➚
Forrest Gump➚
42nd Street➚
The Four Feathers➚
The 400 Blows➚
Frankenstein➚
The Freshman➚
From Here to Eternity➚
The Fugitive➚
Gallipoli➚
The Garden of the Finzi-Continis➚
The General➚
The General Line➚
Gigi➚
The Godfather➚
The Godfather 1902-1959: The Complete Epic➚
The Godfather, Part 2➚
The Gold Rush➚
Gone with the Wind➚
Goodfellas➚
The Gospel According to St. Matthew➚
The Graduate➚
Grand Illusion➚
The Great Dictator➚
Great Expectations➚
Greed➚
Gunga Din➚
Hamlet➚
Harold and Maude➚
Harvest➚
Hearts of Darkness: A Filmmaker's Apocalypse➚
Henry V➚
Henry: Portrait of a Serial Killer➚
Here Comes Mr. Jordan➚
High Noon➚
Hiroshima, Mon Amour➚
His Girl Friday➚
Hollywood Canteen➚
Hoop Dreams➚
How Green Was My Valley➚
Howard's End➚
Hud➚
The Hunchback of Notre Dame➚
The Hustler➚
I Am a Fugitive from a Chain Gang➚
The Idiot➚
If...➚
Ikiru➚
The Informer➚
Intolerance➚
The Invisible Man➚
Isn't Life Wonderful➚
It Happened One Night➚
It's a Wonderful Life➚
Ivan the Terrible, Part 1➚
Ju Dou➚
Judgment at Nuremberg➚
Jules and Jim➚
The King and I➚
King Kong➚
Knife in the Water➚
Koyaanisqatsi➚
Kriemhilde's Revenge➚
Kwaidan➚
La Chienne➚
La Dolce Vita➚
La Strada➚
Lady and the Tramp➚
The Lady Eve➚
The Lady Vanishes➚
L'Age D'Or➚
Last Command➚
The Last Detail➚
The Last Emperor➚
The Last Picture Show➚
The Last Seduction➚
Late Spring➚
Laura➚
Lawrence of Arabia➚
Les Miserables➚
The Letter➚
A Letter to Three Wives➚
The Life and Death of Colonel Blimp➚
The Lion in Winter➚
The Lion King➚
Little Women➚
The Lives of a Bengal Lancer➚
Local Hero➚
Lola Montes➚
Long Day's Journey into Night➚
Lost Horizon➚
The Lost Weekend➚
M➚
The Magnificent Ambersons➚
The Magnificent Seven➚
Male and Female➚
The Maltese Falcon➚
A Man for All Seasons➚
The Man Who Would Be King➚
The Manchurian Candidate➚
Manhattan➚
Marius➚
The Marriage of Maria Braun➚
M*A*S*H➚
McCabe & Mrs. Miller➚
Mean Streets➚
Metropolis➚
Miracle of Morgan's Creek➚
Miracle on 34th Street➚
Mrs. Miniver➚
Mr. & Mrs. Bridge➚
Mister Roberts➚
Mr. Smith Goes to Washington➚
Modern Times➚
Mon Oncle➚
Monster's Ball➚
The Music Man➚
Mutiny on the Bounty➚
My Left Foot➚
My Life As a Dog➚
My Life to Live➚
My Man Godfrey➚
Napoleon➚
Nashville➚
National Velvet➚
A Night at the Opera➚
The Night of the Hunter➚
The Night of the Shooting Stars➚
North by Northwest➚
Nosferatu➚
Notorious➚
O Lucky Man!➚
Objective, Burma!➚
Of Mice and Men➚
Oliver Twist➚
On the Waterfront➚
One Flew Over the Cuckoo's Nest➚
Only Angels Have Wings➚
Open City➚
Our Hospitality➚
The Ox-Bow Incident➚
Pandora's Box➚
Pather Panchali➚
Paths of Glory➚
Pelle the Conqueror➚
Persona➚
Petulia➚
The Philadelphia Story➚
Pinocchio➚
Pixote➚
Poltergeist➚
The Private Life of Henry VIII➚
Psycho➚
Pulp Fiction➚
The Quiet Man➚
Quiz Show➚
Raging Bull➚
Raiders of the Lost Ark➚
A Raisin in the Sun➚
Ran➚
Rashomon➚
Rear Window➚
Rebecca➚
Rebel without a Cause➚
Red River➚
The Red Shoes➚
The Reincarnation of Golden Lotus➚
The Report on the Party and the Guests➚
Ride the High Country➚
The River➚
A Room with a View➚
Roots➚
Rosemary's Baby➚
Ruggles of Red Gap➚
The Rules of the Game➚
Sansho the Bailiff➚
Scenes from a Marriage➚
Schindler's List➚
The Searchers➚
Sergeant York➚
Seven Beauties➚
Seven Samurai➚
The Seventh Seal➚
Shane➚
Shin Heike Monogatari➚
Shoeshine➚
Shoot the Piano Player➚
The Shop on Main Street➚
Show Boat➚
Siegfried➚
Singin' in the Rain➚
Small Change➚
Snow White and the Seven Dwarfs➚
Some Like It Hot➚
The Sound of Music➚
Sounder➚
The Southerner➚
Spartacus➚
Stagecoach➚
Stalag 17➚
Star Wars➚
Storm over Asia➚
Strangers on a Train➚
A Streetcar Named Desire➚
The Stunt Man➚
Sullivan's Travels➚
Sunrise➚
A Tale of Two Cities➚
The Third Man➚
The 39 Steps➚
Throne of Blood➚
The Tin Drum➚
To Kill a Mockingbird➚
To Live➚
Tokyo Story➚
Tom Jones➚
Tootsie➚
Top Hat➚
Touch of Evil➚
The Train➚
Treasure of the Sierra Madre➚
Tristana➚
Twelve Angry Men➚
Twentieth Century➚
2001: A Space Odyssey➚
Two Women➚
Umberto D➚
Un Chien Andalou➚
Vampyr➚
Variety➚
Vertigo➚
Viridiana➚
Viva Zapata!➚
Wages of Fear➚
The Wedding March➚
Who's Afraid of Virginia Woolf?➚
The Wild Bunch➚
Wild Strawberries➚
The Wind➚
The Wizard of Oz➚
Woman in the Dunes➚
Woman of the Year➚
Woodstock➚
The World of Apu➚
Wuthering Heights➚
Yankee Doodle Dandy➚
Yojimbo➚
Young Frankenstein➚
Z➚
Zero for Conduct➚
Zvenigora➚

Francis the Talking Mule

Francis Covers the Big Town
Francis Goes to the Races
Francis Goes to West Point
Francis in the Haunted House
Francis in the Navy
Francis Joins the WACs
Francis the Talking Mule➚

Frankenstein

Abbott and Costello Meet Frankenstein➚

➚ = rated three bones or higher

Andy Warhol's Frankenstein
Blackenstein
Boltneck
The Bride
The Bride of Frankenstein➚
The Creeps
The Curse of Frankenstein
Dr. Frankenstein's Castle of Freaks
Dracula vs. Frankenstein
The Evil of Frankenstein
Frankenstein➚
Frankenstein
Frankenstein and Me
Frankenstein and the Monster from Hell
Frankenstein Created Woman➚
Frankenstein '80
Frankenstein General Hospital
Frankenstein Island
Frankenstein Meets the Space Monster
Frankenstein Meets the Wolfman➚
Frankenstein Must Be Destroyed
Frankenstein Reborn
Frankenstein Sings...The Movie
Frankenstein Unbound➚
Frankenstein's Daughter
Frankenstein's Great Aunt Tillie
Frankenweenie
The Ghost of Frankenstein
Gothic➚
The Horror of Frankenstein
House of Dracula
House of Frankenstein
Jesse James Meets Frankenstein's Daughter
Lady Frankenstein
Mad Monster Party
Mary Shelley's Frankenstein
Mr. Stitch
The Munsters' Revenge
Nosferatu➚
Prototype➚
The Revenge of Frankenstein
The Screaming Dead
Son of Frankenstein➚
Teenage Frankenstein
The Vindicator
Young Frankenstein➚

Godzilla and Friends

Dagora, the Space Monster
Destroy All Monsters
Destroy All Planets
Gamera vs. Barugon
Gamera vs. Gaos
Gamera vs. Guiron
Gamera vs. Zigra
Gappa the Trifibian Monster
Ghidrah the Three Headed Monster
Godzilla
Godzilla, King of the Monsters
Godzilla 1985
Godzilla on Monster Island
Godzilla Raids Again
Godzilla 2000➚
Godzilla vs. Biollante
Godzilla vs. King Ghidora
Godzilla vs. Mechagodzilla II
Godzilla vs. Megalon
Godzilla vs. Monster Zero
Godzilla vs. Mothra
Godzilla vs. the Cosmic Monster
Godzilla vs. the Sea Monster
Godzilla vs. the Smog Monster
Godzilla's Revenge
King Kong vs. Godzilla
Mothra➚
Rodan
Son of Godzilla
Terror of Mechagodzilla
Varan the Unbelievable
War of the Gargantuas
X from Outer Space
Yog, Monster from Space
Yongkari Monster of the Deep

Hallmark Hall of Fame

An American Story
Blind Spot
The Boys Next Door
Breathing Lessons➚
Calm at Sunset
Caroline?➚
Cupid & Cate
Decoration Day➚
Durango
The Echo of Thunder
Ellen Foster
The Flamingo Rising
Follow the Stars Home
Foxfire➚
Grace & Glorie
Harvest of Fire
In Love and War
Journey
Little John
The Lost Child
The Love Letter
Miss Rose White➚
Missing Pieces
My Sister's Keeper
Night Ride Home
O Pioneers!
One Against the Wind➚
The Piano Lesson➚
A Place for Annie
Redwood Curtain
The Return of the Native
The Runaway
Saint Maybe➚
Sarah, Plain and Tall➚
Sarah, Plain and Tall: Skylark
Sarah, Plain and Tall: Winter's End➚
A Season for Miracles
The Secret Garden➚
The Seventh Stream
The Shell Seekers
The Summer of Ben Tyler
To Dance with the White Dog➚
20,000 Leagues Under the Sea
What the Deaf Man Heard➚
William Faulkner's Old Man

Hammer Films: Horror

The Abominable Snowman
Asylum
Blood of the Vampire
The Blood on Satan's Claw➚
The Brides of Dracula
Captain Kronos: Vampire Hunter➚
The Creeping Flesh
The Curse of Frankenstein
The Curse of the Werewolf
The Devil Rides Out➚
Die Screaming, Marianne
Dr. Jekyll and Sister Hyde
Dr. Terror's House of Horrors
Dracula A.D. 1972
Dracula Has Risen from the Grave
Dracula, Prince of Darkness
Dynasty of Fear
The Evil of Frankenstein
Frankenstein and the Monster from Hell
Frankenstein Created Woman➚
Frankenstein Must Be Destroyed
The Ghoul
The Gorgon
Hands of the Ripper
The Horror of Dracula➚
The Horror of Frankenstein
The Hound of the Baskervilles
Hysteria
Kiss of the Vampire
The Legend of the 7 Golden Vampires
Lust for a Vampire
Maniac
The Mummy➚
The Mummy's Shroud
The Nanny
Nightmare
Paranoiac
The Phantom of the Opera
Plague of the Zombies
Rasputin the Mad Monk
The Reptile
The Revenge of Frankenstein
The Satanic Rites of Dracula
The Scars of Dracula
Tales from the Crypt➚
Tales That Witness Madness
Taste the Blood of Dracula
Theatre of Blood➚
To the Devil, a Daughter
Twins of Evil
The Two Faces of Dr. Jekyll
Vampire Circus
The Vampire Lovers
Vault of Horror
The Witches

Hammer Films: Sci Fi & Fantasy

Creatures the World Forgot
Four Sided Triangle
Men of Sherwood Forest
One Million Years B.C.
Prehistoric Women
Quatermass 2➚
Quatermass and the Pit
The Quatermass Experiment➚
Spaceways
Sword of Sherwood Forest
The Vengeance of She
The Viking Queen
When Dinosaurs Ruled the Earth
X The Unknown

Hercule Poirot

The Alphabet Murders
Appointment with Death
Death on the Nile
Murder on the Orient Express➚

Hercules

Conquest of Mycene
The Fury of Hercules
Hercules
Hercules➚
Hercules 2
Hercules against the Moon Men
Hercules and the Captive Women
Hercules in New York
Hercules in the Haunted World
Hercules, Prisoner of Evil
Hercules the Legendary Journeys, Vol. 1: And the Amazon Women
Hercules the Legendary Journeys, Vol. 2: The Lost Kingdom
Hercules the Legendary Journeys, Vol. 3: The Circle of Fire
Hercules the Legendary Journeys, Vol. 4: In the Underworld
Hercules Unchained
Hercules vs. the Sons of the Sun
Jason and the Argonauts➚
The Loves of Hercules
Samson and His Mighty Challenge
The Three Stooges Meet Hercules
The Triumph of Hercules
Young Hercules

Highest Grossing Films of All Time

Aladdin➚
Back to the Future➚
Batman➚
Beverly Hills Cop
The Empire Strikes Back➚
E.T.: The Extra-Terrestrial➚
Forrest Gump➚
Ghost➚
Ghostbusters➚
Gone with the Wind➚
Home Alone➚
Indiana Jones and the Last Crusade➚
Jaws➚
Jurassic Park➚
The Lion King➚
Mrs. Doubtfire
Raiders of the Lost Ark➚
Return of the Jedi➚
Star Wars➚
Terminator 2: Judgment Day➚
Titanic➚

Hopalong Cassidy

Border Patrol
Border Vigilantes
Colt Comrades
Doomed Caravan➚
False Colors
The Frontiersmen
Hopalong Cassidy➚
Hopalong Cassidy: Borrowed Trouble
Hopalong Cassidy: Dangerous Venture
Hopalong Cassidy: False Paradise
Hopalong Cassidy: Hoppy's Holiday
Hopalong Cassidy: Renegade Trail
Hopalong Cassidy Returns
Hopalong Cassidy: Riders of the Deadline
Hopalong Cassidy: Silent Conflict
Hopalong Cassidy: Sinister Journey
Hopalong Cassidy: The Dead Don't Dream
Hopalong Cassidy: The Devil's Playground
Hopalong Cassidy: The Marauders
Hopalong Cassidy: Unexpected Guest
Hoppy Serves a Writ
In Old Colorado
Law of the Pampas
Leather Burners
Lost Canyon
Mystery Man
Outlaws of the Desert
Renegade Trail
Riders of the Timberline
Rustler's Valley
Santa Fe Marshal
The Showdown
Texas Masquerade
Twilight on the Trail
Undercover Man

Indiana Jones

Indiana Jones and the Last Crusade➚
Indiana Jones and the Temple of Doom➚
Raiders of the Lost Ark➚

Jack Ryan

Clear and Present Danger
The Hunt for Red October➚
Patriot Games➚
The Sum of All Fears

Jack the Ripper

Cosh Boy
Deadly Advice
Fatal Exposure
From Hell➚
Hands of the Ripper
He Kills Night After Night After Night
Hell's Gate
Jack the Ripper
Jack the Ripper➚
Jack's Back➚
The Lodger➚
A Man with a Maid
The Monster of London City
Murder by Decree➚
Night Ripper
Phantom Fiend
The Ripper
Ripper: Letter from Hell
Room to Let
A Study in Terror➚
Terror at London Bridge
Terror in the Wax Museum
Time After Time➚
Waxworks➚

James Bond

Diamonds Are Forever➚
Dr. No➚
For Your Eyes Only➚
From Russia with Love➚
Goldeneye➚
Goldfinger➚
License to Kill➚
Live and Let Die
The Living Daylights➚
The Man with the Golden Gun
Moonraker
Never Say Never Again
Octopussy
On Her Majesty's Secret Service➚
The Spy Who Loved Me
Thunderball
Tomorrow Never Dies
A View to a Kill
The World Is Not Enough
You Only Live Twice

James Bond Spoofs

The Ambushers
Austin Powers: International Man of Mystery➚
Austin Powers 2: The Spy Who Shagged Me➚
Casino Royale
If Looks Could Kill
In Like Flint
Murderers' Row
Number 1 of the Secret Service
Our Man Flint
Second Best Secret Agent in the Whole Wide World
Where the Bullets Fly

Jesse James

American Outlaws
Days of Jesse James
Frank and Jesse
I Shot Jesse James➚
Jesse James➚
Jesse James at Bay
Jesse James Meets Frankenstein's Daughter
Jesse James Rides Again
Last Days of Frank & Jesse James
The Long Riders➚
Return of Jesse James

Lassie

Challenge to Lassie
Courage of Lassie
The Hills of Home➚
Lassie: Adventures of Neeka
Lassie, Come Home
Lassie: Well of Love
Lassie's Great Adventure
Magic of Lassie
The Painted Hills
Son of Lassie
The Sun Comes Up

Laurel & Hardy

Air Raid Wardens
Block-heads➚
Bohemian Girl➚
Bonnie Scotland
Bullfighters
A Chump at Oxford
The Devil's Brother
The Flying Deuces➚
Great Guns
Hollywood Party
Laurel & Hardy and the Family
Laurel & Hardy: Another Fine Mess
Laurel & Hardy: At Work
Laurel & Hardy: Be Big
Laurel & Hardy: Below Zero
Laurel & Hardy: Berth Marks
Laurel & Hardy: Blotto
Laurel & Hardy: Brats
Laurel & Hardy: Chickens Come Home
Laurel & Hardy: Hog Wild
Laurel & Hardy: Laughing Gravy
Laurel & Hardy: Men O'War
Laurel & Hardy: Night Owls
Laurel & Hardy On the Lam
Laurel & Hardy: Perfect Day
Laurel & Hardy Spooktacular
Laurel & Hardy: Stan "Helps" Ollie
Laurel & Hardy: The Hoose-Gow
Nothing But Trouble
Our Relations➚
Pack Up Your Troubles
Pardon Us
Pick a Star
Saps at Sea
Sons of the Desert➚
Swiss Miss
Utopia
Way Out West➚

Live Action/ Animation Combos

The Adventures of Rocky & Bullwinkle
Alice➚
Alice in Wonderland
Anchors Aweigh➚
Bedknobs and Broomsticks
Butterfly Ball
Cats & Dogs
Cool World
Dangerous When Wet
Fabulous Adventures of Baron Munchausen
Fun & Fancy Free➚
Hollywood Party
The Incredible Mr. Limpet
James and the Giant Peach➚
Mary Poppins➚
Monkeybone
Osmosis Jones
The Pagemaster
Pete's Dragon
Small Soldiers
So Dear to My Heart➚
Space Jam
Stuart Little
Tank Girl
Thomas and the Magic Railroad
The Three Caballeros
Tron
Volere Volare
Who Framed Roger Rabbit➚
Xanadu

The Lone Rider

Border Roundup
Death Rides the Plains
Law of the Saddle
The Lone Rider in Cheyenne
The Lone Rider in Ghost Town
Raiders of Red Gap
Rangeland Racket

Ma and Pa Kettle

Egg and I➚
The Kettles in the Ozarks

➚ = rated three bones or higher

The Kettles on Old MacDonald's Farm
Ma and Pa Kettle
Ma and Pa Kettle at Home
Ma and Pa Kettle at the Fair
Ma and Pa Kettle at Waikiki
Ma and Pa Kettle Back On the Farm
Ma and Pa Kettle Go to Town
Ma and Pa Kettle on Vacation

The Marx Brothers

Animal Crackers▲
At the Circus
Big Store
The Cocoanuts
A Day at the Races▲
Duck Soup▲
Go West
Horse Feathers▲
Love Happy
The Marx Brothers in a Nutshell▲
Monkey Business▲
A Night at the Opera▲
A Night in Casablanca▲
Room Service

MGM Musicals

An American in Paris▲
Anchors Aweigh▲
Annie Get Your Gun▲
Athena
The Band Wagon▲
The Barkleys of Broadway▲
Because You're Mine
Bells Are Ringing▲
Big Store
Born to Dance
Broadway Melody
Broadway Melody of 1936▲
Broadway Melody of 1938
Broadway Melody of 1940
Broadway Rhythm
Broadway Serenade
The Chocolate Soldier
Dancing Lady
Deep in My Heart
Double Trouble
The Duchess of Idaho
Easter Parade▲
Easy to Love
Everybody Sing
The Firefly
For Me and My Gal
Gigi▲
Girl of the Golden West
Give a Girl a Break
Going Hollywood▲
Good News
Goodbye, Mr. Chips
The Great Ziegfeld▲
Harum Scarum
Holiday in Mexico
Honolulu
I Love Melvin
I Married an Angel
In the Good Old Summertime▲
It Happened at the World's Fair
It Happened in Brooklyn
Lady Be Good
Les Girls
Little Nellie Kelly
Live a Little, Love a Little
Love Me or Leave Me▲
Lovely to Look At▲
Madam Satan
Maytime▲
Meet Me in Las Vegas
Meet Me in St. Louis▲
The Merry Widow▲
The Merry Widow
Million Dollar Mermaid
Mrs. Brown, You've Got a Lovely Daughter
On an Island with You
On the Town▲
Pagan Love Song
Rich, Young and Pretty
Rosalie
Rose Marie▲
Royal Wedding▲
Seven Brides for Seven Brothers▲
Ship Ahoy
Show Boat
Singin' in the Rain▲
Skirts Ahoy!
Small Town Girl
Spinout
Stay Away, Joe
Strike Up the Band
The Student Prince
Summer Stock▲
Sweethearts▲
Take Me Out to the Ball Game
Texas Carnival
That Midnight Kiss
That's Dancing!
That's Entertainment
That's Entertainment, Part 2
That's Entertainment, Part 3
Three Little Words
Thrill of a Romance
Till the Clouds Roll By
The Toast of New Orleans
The Trouble with Girls (and How to Get into It)▲
The Unsinkable Molly Brown▲
Viva Las Vegas
The Wizard of Oz▲
Words and Music
Yankee Doodle Dandy▲
Yolanda and the Thief
Ziegfeld Follies
Ziegfeld Girl▲

Mike Hammer

Girl Hunters
I, the Jury
Kiss Me Deadly▲
Margin for Murder

Miss Marple

The Body in the Library
Murder Ahoy
Murder at the Gallop▲
A Murder Is Announced
Murder She Said

Mr. Wong

Doomed to Die
The Fatal Hour
Mr. Wong, Detective
Mr. Wong in Chinatown
Mysterious Mr. Wong
Mystery of Mr. Wong
Phantom of Chinatown

Modern Shakespeare

Chimes at Midnight▲
A Double Life▲
Forbidden Planet▲
The Godfather▲
The Godfather, Part 2▲
The Godfather, Part 3▲
Hamlet▲
Jubal
King Lear
Kiss Me Kate▲
Let the Devil Wear Black
Looking for Richard▲
Love Is All There Is
Men Are Not Gods
Men of Respect
A Midsummer Night's Sex Comedy▲
My Own Private Idaho▲
O▲
Otello▲
Othello▲
Prospero's Books▲
Ran▲
Richard III▲
Ring of Fire
Ronnie and Julie
Rosencrantz & Guildenstern Are Dead▲
Scotland, PA
Shakespeare Wallah▲
Siberian Lady Macbeth▲
The Street King
The Tempest▲
The Tempest
Ten Things I Hate about You▲
Theatre of Blood▲
The Three Weird Sisters
Throne of Blood▲
Tromeo & Juliet
West Side Story▲
William Shakespeare's Romeo and Juliet▲

Modern Updates

An American Christmas Carol
Arthur's Quest
Carmen, Baby
Clueless▲
Crime and Punishment in Suburbia
Cruel Intentions
Double Play
Ebenezer
Great Expectations
In the Shadows
King Lear
Les Miserables
Ms. Scrooge
The Prince and the Surfer
Scrooged
Ten Things I Hate about You▲
Twisted
Whatever It Takes
William Shakespeare's Romeo and Juliet▲

Monty Python

The Adventures of Baron Munchausen▲
All You Need Is Cash▲
And Now for Something Completely Different▲
Brazil▲
Clockwise
Consuming Passions
Down Among the Z Men
Erik the Viking
A Fish Called Wanda▲
The Fisher King▲
Jabberwocky
The Missionary
Monty Python and the Holy Grail▲
Monty Python's Life of Brian▲
Monty Python's The Meaning of Life▲
Nuns on the Run
The Odd Job
Personal Services
A Private Function
Privates on Parade
Rentadick
Romance with a Double Bass▲
The Secret Policeman's Other Ball▲
Secret Policeman's Private Parts
Time Bandits
Yellowbeard

The Muppets

The Adventures of a Gnome Named Gnorm
The Great Muppet Caper▲
Labyrinth▲
The Muppet Christmas Carol
The Muppet Movie▲
Muppet Treasure Island
Muppets from Space
The Muppets Take Manhattan▲
Sesame Street Presents: Follow That Bird

National Lampoon

National Lampoon's Animal House▲
National Lampoon's Attack of the 5 Ft. 2 Women
National Lampoon's Christmas Vacation
National Lampoon's Class of '86
National Lampoon's Class Reunion
National Lampoon's European Vacation
National Lampoon's Favorite Deadly Sins
National Lampoon's Golf Punks
National Lampoon's Last Resort
National Lampoon's Loaded Weapon 1
National Lampoon's Senior Trip
National Lampoon's The Don's Analyst
National Lampoon's Vacation▲
National Lampoon's Van Wilder

Our Gang

General Spanky
The Little Rascals
Rascal Dazzle

The Pink Panther

Curse of the Pink Panther
The Pink Panther▲
The Pink Panther Strikes Again▲
Return of the Pink Panther
Revenge of the Pink Panther
A Shot in the Dark▲
Son of the Pink Panther
Trail of the Pink Panther

The Planet of the Apes

Battle for the Planet of the Apes
Behind the Planet of the Apes▲
Beneath the Planet of the Apes
Conquest of the Planet of the Apes
Escape from the Planet of the Apes▲
Planet of the Apes▲

Plays to Film: Maxwell Anderson

Anne of the Thousand Days▲
The Bad Seed
The Guardsman▲
Joan of Arc
Key Largo▲
Mary of Scotland▲
Meet Joe Black
The Private Lives of Elizabeth & Essex▲
What Price Glory?▲
Winterset

Plays to Film: James M. Barrie

The Admirable Crichton
Hook
Little Minister▲
Peter Pan
Peter Pan▲
Quality Street
Seven Days' Leave

Plays to Film: Anton Chekhov

August
Country Life
The Lady with the Dog▲
The Seagull▲
The Shooting Party
The Three Sisters
An Unfinished Piece for a Player Piano▲
Vanya on 42nd Street▲
Ward Six

Plays to Film: Noel Coward

Bitter Sweet
Blithe Spirit▲
Brief Encounter▲
Cavalcade▲
Private Lives▲
Relative Values
This Happy Breed▲

Plays to Film: Horton Foote

Baby, the Rain Must Fall
The Chase
Courtship▲
Lily Dale
1918
The Trip to Bountiful▲

Plays to Film: Beth Henley

Crimes of the Heart
Miss Firecracker▲
Nobody's Fool
True Stories▲

Plays to Film: Arthur Miller

All My Sons▲
Broken Glass
The Crucible▲
Death of a Salesman▲
Everybody Wins
Focus

Plays to Film: Eugene O'Neill

Ah, Wilderness!▲
Anna Christie▲
Anna Christie
Desire Under the Elms
Emperor Jones
The Hairy Ape
Long Day's Journey into Night▲
Long Day's Journey into Night
Long Day's Journey Into Night▲
The Long Voyage Home▲
On Borrowed Time▲
Strange Interlude▲
Strange Interlude
Summer Holiday

Plays to Film: Rodgers & Hammerstein

Carousel▲
Flower Drum Song
The King and I▲
Oklahoma!▲
Rodgers & Hammerstein's South Pacific
The Sound of Music▲
South Pacific▲

Plays to Film: Arthur Schnitzler

Affairs of Anatol
Circle of Love
Eyes Wide Shut
La Ronde▲
Liebelei

Plays to Film: William Shakespeare

Antony and Cleopatra
As You Like It
Carry On Cleo
Hamlet▲
Hamlet
Hamlet▲
Hamlet
Henry V▲
Julius Caesar▲
Julius Caesar
King Lear▲
King Lear
King Lear▲
Looking for Richard▲
Love's Labour's Lost
Macbeth▲
Macbeth
The Merchant of Venice▲
The Merry Wives of Windsor
A Midsummer Night's Dream▲
A Midsummer Night's Dream
Much Ado about Nothing▲
Othello
Othello▲
Prospero's Books▲
Ran▲
Richard III
Richard III▲
Romeo and Juliet▲
Romeo and Juliet
Romeo and Juliet▲
Shakespeare in Love▲
The Taming of the Shrew
The Taming of the Shrew▲
The Tempest
The Tempest▲
The Tempest
Ten Things I Hate about You▲
Titus
Tromeo & Juliet
Twelfth Night
William Shakespeare's A Midsummer Night's Dream
William Shakespeare's Romeo and Juliet▲

Plays to Film: George Bernard Shaw

Androcles and the Lion
Caesar and Cleopatra
The Devil's Disciple▲
Heartbreak House
Major Barbara▲
The Millionairess
Pygmalion▲
Saint Joan

Plays to Film: Sam Shepard

Curse of the Starving Class
Fool for Love
Simpatico
True West▲

Plays to Film: Neil Simon

Barefoot in the Park▲
Biloxi Blues
Brighton Beach Memoirs
Broadway Bound
California Suite▲
Chapter Two
The Cheap Detective▲
Come Blow Your Horn▲
The Goodbye Girl▲
The Heartbreak Kid▲
I Ought to Be in Pictures
Last of the Red Hot Lovers
Lost in Yonkers
The Marrying Man
Max Dugan Returns
Murder by Death
The Odd Couple▲
One Trick Pony
Only When I Laugh▲
The Out-of-Towners▲
Plaza Suite▲
Prisoner of Second Avenue
Seems Like Old Times
The Slugger's Wife
Star Spangled Girl
The Sunshine Boys▲
Sweet Charity▲

Plays to Film: Tom Stoppard

Rosencrantz & Guildenstern Are Dead▲

Plays to Film: Tennessee Williams

Baby Doll▲
Boom!
Cat on a Hot Tin Roof▲
Cat on a Hot Tin Roof
The Fugitive Kind
The Glass Menagerie▲

The Migrants➚
The Night of the Iguana➚
Orpheus Descending
Period of Adjustment➚
Roman Spring of Mrs. Stone➚
The Rose Tattoo➚
A Streetcar Named Desire➚
A Streetcar Named Desire
Suddenly, Last Summer➚
Summer and Smoke
Sweet Bird of Youth➚
Sweet Bird of Youth
This Property Is Condemned

Producers: Robert Altman

Buffalo Bill & the Indians➚
Kansas City➚
The Late Show➚
Nashville➚
Quintet
Rich Kids
A Wedding
Welcome to L.A.➚

Producers: Bruckheimer/ Simpson

Bad Boys
Beverly Hills Cop
Beverly Hills Cop 2
Crimson Tide➚
Dangerous Minds
Days of Thunder
Flashdance
The Ref➚
The Rock➚
Thief of Hearts
Top Gun

Producers: William Castle

Bug
House on Haunted Hill
Macabre
Riot
Rosemary's Baby➚
Strait-Jacket
13 Ghosts
Zotz!

Producers: Coppola/American Zoetrope

American Graffiti➚
The Black Stallion➚
The Conversation➚
The Escape Artist➚
The Godfather, Part 2➚
Hammett

Producers: Roger Corman/New World

Atlas
Attack of the Giant Leeches
Avalanche
Battle Beyond the Stars
Battle Beyond the Sun
Beyond the Call of Duty
Big Bad Mama
Big Bad Mama 2
The Big Bird Cage
The Big Doll House
Bloodfist
Bloodfist 2
Bloody Mama
Body Waves
Boxcar Bertha
A Bucket of Blood➚
Caged Heat
Candy Stripe Nurses
Carnival Rock
Cocaine Wars
Cockfighter➚
The Corporation
Crazy Mama
Daddy's Boys
Day the World Ended
Death Race 2000
Death Sport
Dementia 13
Dinosaur Island
The Dunwich Horror
Eat My Dust
Eye of the Eagle 3
The Fall of the House of Usher➚
Field of Fire
Fighting Mad
Firehawk
Forbidden World
Futurekick
Galaxy of Terror
Gas-s-s-s!
Grand Theft Auto
The Gunslinger
The Haunted Palace
Humanoids from the Deep
I, Mobster
I Never Promised You a Rose Garden➚
In the Heat of Passion
It Conquered the World
Jackson County Jail
Lady in Red
The Last Woman on Earth
Little Shop of Horrors➚
Lords of the Deep
Lumiere
Machine Gun Kelly
Masque of the Red Death➚
Masque of the Red Death
Monster from the Ocean Floor
Munchies
Nam Angels
Night of the Blood Beast
Not of This Earth
Piranha
The Pit and the Pendulum➚
Premature Burial
Primary Target
Private Duty Nurses
Raiders of the Sun
The Raven➚
Rock 'n' Roll High School Forever
The St. Valentine's Day Massacre
Ski Troop Attack
Small Change➚
Smokey Bites the Dust
Stripped to Kill
The Student Nurses
T-Bird Gang
Tales of Terror
Targets➚
Teenage Caveman
The Terror
Thunder and Lightning
Time Trackers
Tomb of Ligeia➚
Too Hot to Handle
The Trip
The Undead
Unholy Rollers
Voyage to the Planet of Prehistoric Women
The Wasp Woman
The Wild Angels
The Wild Ride
X: The Man with X-Ray Eyes➚
The Young Nurses

Producers: Val Lewton

Bedlam➚
The Body Snatcher➚
Cat People➚
Isle of the Dead
The Leopard Man

Producers: George Lucas

The Empire Strikes Back➚
The Ewok Adventure
More American Graffiti
Raiders of the Lost Ark➚
Return of the Jedi➚

Producers: Merchant Ivory

Autobiography of a Princess
The Ballad of the Sad Cafe
Bombay Talkie
The Courtesans of Bombay➚
The Europeans➚
Fast Talking
Feast of July
The Golden Bowl
Howard's End➚
Hullabaloo over Georgie & Bonnie's Pictures
Jane Austen in Manhattan
Jefferson in Paris
Maurice➚
Mr. & Mrs. Bridge➚
The Remains of the Day➚
A Room with a View➚
Roseland➚
Shakespeare Wallah➚
A Soldier's Daughter Never Cries
Surviving Picasso

Producers: George Pal

Atlantis, the Lost Continent
Conquest of Space
Destination Moon
Doc Savage
The Great Rupert➚
Naked Jungle➚
7 Faces of Dr. Lao➚
Time Machine
The War of the Worlds➚
When Worlds Collide

Producers: Steven Spielberg

Amazing Stories
An American Tail
An American Tail: Fievel Goes West
Back to the Future➚
The Color Purple➚
Empire of the Sun➚
The Goonies
Gremlins➚
Honey, I Shrunk the Kids
Innerspace
Jurassic Park➚
Poltergeist➚
Twilight Zone: The Movie
Who Framed Roger Rabbit➚
Young Sherlock Holmes

Producers: Andy Warhol

Andy Warhol's Bad➚
Cocaine Cowboys
Flesh➚
Heat➚
Trash

Rambo

First Blood
Rambo: First Blood, Part 2
Rambo 3

The Rangebusters

Arizona Stagecoach
Black Market Rustlers
Boot Hill Bandits
Cowboy Commandos
Fugitive Valley
Haunted Ranch
Kid's Last Ride
Land of Hunted Men
Range Busters
Rock River Renegades
Saddle Mountain Round-Up
Texas to Bataan
Thunder River Feud
Tonto Basin Outlaws
Trail of the Silver Spurs
Trail Riders
Trailing Double Trouble
Tumbledown Ranch in Arizona
Two-Fisted Justice
Underground Rustlers
West of Pinto Basin

Recycled Footage/ Redubbed Dialogue

Battle Beyond the Sun
Contact
Dead Men Don't Wear Plaid
Fast, Cheap & Out of Control➚
Ferocious Female Freedom Fighters
Forrest Gump➚
J-Men Forever!➚
Last Action Hero
The Legend of Drunken Master➚
Mystery Science Theater 3000: The Movie
Planet of Blood
Twin Dragons
Voyage to the Planet of Prehistoric Women
Voyage to the Prehistoric Planet
What's Up, Tiger Lily?➚
Zelig➚

Renfrew of the Mounties

Danger Ahead
Fighting Mad
Murder on the Yukon
Renfrew of the Royal Mounted
Renfrew on the Great White Trail
Sky Bandits
Yukon Flight

Restored Footage

Beau Revel➚
Crimes of Passion➚
Dr. Jekyll and Mr. Hyde➚
Foolish Wives➚
Frankenstein➚
Isadora➚
Lawrence of Arabia➚
Lost Horizon➚
The Lost World
New York, New York➚
Othello➚
Que Viva Mexico➚
Red River➚
The Rules of the Game➚
Sadie Thompson➚
Spartacus➚
Spiders➚
A Star Is Born➚
Star Trek: The Motion Picture
Sunny Side Up
Tarzan and His Mate➚
Twelve o'Clock High➚
Two English Girls➚
Wages of Fear➚
When Time Ran Out

The Ritz Brothers

Blazing Stewardesses
The Goldwyn Follies
The Gorilla

Robin Hood

The Adventures of Robin Hood➚
A Challenge for Robin Hood
Men of Sherwood Forest
The Prince of Thieves
Princess of Thieves
Robin and Marian
Robin Hood➚
Robin Hood: Men in Tights
Robin Hood: Prince of Thieves
Robin Hood: The Movie
Robin Hood...The Legend: Herne's Son
Robin Hood...The Legend: Robin Hood and the Sorcerer
Robin Hood...The Legend: The Swords of Wayland
Robin Hood...The Legend: The Time of the Wolf
Robin of Locksley
The Story of Robin Hood & His Merrie Men➚
Sword of Sherwood Forest
Tales of Robin Hood
Time Bandits
Young Ivanhoe
The Zany Adventures of Robin Hood

The Rough Riders

Arizona Bound
Below the Border
Dead Man
Down Texas Way
Forbidden Trails
Ghost Town Law
Gunman from Bodie
Riders of the West

Rusty the Dog

The Adventures of Rusty
Rusty's Birthday
Son of Rusty

The Saint

The Saint
The Saint in London
The Saint in New York
The Saint Strikes Back
The Saint Takes Over
The Saint's Double Trouble
Vendetta for the Saint

Screen Teams: Abbott & Costello

Abbott and Costello Go to Mars
Abbott and Costello in Hollywood
Abbott and Costello in the Foreign Legion
Abbott and Costello Meet Captain Kidd
Abbott and Costello Meet Dr. Jekyll and Mr. Hyde
Abbott and Costello Meet Frankenstein➚
Abbott and Costello Meet the Invisible Man➚
Abbott and Costello Meet the Keystone Kops
Abbott and Costello Meet the Killer, Boris Karloff
Abbott and Costello Meet the Mummy
Africa Screams
Buck Privates
Buck Privates Come Home➚
Comin' Round the Mountain
Dance with Me, Henry
Here Come the Co-Eds
Hit the Ice
Hold That Ghost➚
In Society
In the Navy
It Ain't Hay
Jack & the Beanstalk
Keep 'Em Flying
Little Giant
Lost in a Harem
Lost in Alaska
Mexican Hayride
The Naughty Nineties
The Noose Hangs High➚
One Night in the Tropics
Pardon My Sarong
Ride 'Em Cowboy
Rio Rita
The 30-Foot Bride of Candy Rock
The Time of Their Lives
Who Done It?
The Wistful Widow of Wagon Gap

Screen Teams: Allen & Farrow

Alice➚
Another Woman➚
Broadway Danny Rose➚
Crimes & Misdemeanors➚
Hannah and Her Sisters➚
Husbands and Wives➚
A Midsummer Night's Sex Comedy➚
New York Stories➚
The Purple Rose of Cairo➚
Radio Days➚
September
Shadows and Fog
Zelig➚

Screen Teams: Allen & Keaton

Annie Hall➚
Interiors➚
Love and Death➚
Manhattan➚
Manhattan Murder Mystery➚
Play It Again, Sam➚
Sleeper➚

Screen Teams: Astaire & Rogers

The Barkleys of Broadway➚
Carefree➚
Flying Down to Rio
Follow the Fleet➚
The Gay Divorcee➚
Roberta➚
Shall We Dance➚
The Story of Vernon and Irene Castle➚
Swing Time➚
Top Hat➚

Screen Teams: Belushi & Aykroyd

The Blues Brothers➚
Neighbors
1941

Screen Teams: Bogart & Bacall

The Big Sleep➚
Dark Passage
To Have & Have Not➚

Screen Teams: Burton & Taylor

Boom!
Cleopatra
The Comedians
Divorce His, Divorce Hers
Doctor Faustus
Hammersmith Is Out
The Sandpiper
The Taming of the Shrew➚
Under Milk Wood
The V.I.P.'s➚
Who's Afraid of Virginia Woolf?➚

Screen Teams: Cagney & O'Brien

Angels with Dirty Faces➚
Boy Meets Girl➚
Ceiling Zero➚
The Fighting 69th➚
Ragtime➚

Screen Teams: Cheech & Chong

After Hours➚
Cheech and Chong: Still Smokin'
Cheech and Chong: Things Are Tough All Over
Cheech and Chong's Next Movie
Cheech and Chong's Nice Dreams
Cheech and Chong's The Corsican Brothers
Cheech and Chong's Up in Smoke

Screen Teams: Cusack & Robbins

Bob Roberts➚
The Cradle Will Rock
High Fidelity➚
The Player➚
The Sure Thing➚
Tapeheads

Screen Teams: De Niro & Pesci

A Bronx Tale➚
Casino➚
Goodfellas➚
Once Upon a Time in America➚
Raging Bull➚

Screen Teams: Eastwood & Locke

Any Which Way You Can
Bronco Billy
Every Which Way But Loose
The Gauntlet
The Outlaw Josey Wales▲
Sudden Impact

Screen Teams: Eddy & McDonald

Bitter Sweet
Girl of the Golden West
I Married an Angel
Maytime▲
Naughty Marietta
New Moon
Rose Marie▲
Sweethearts▲

Screen Teams: Farley & Spade

Black Sheep
Coneheads
Tommy Boy

Screen Teams: Flynn & de Havilland

The Adventures of Robin Hood▲
Captain Blood▲
The Charge of the Light Brigade▲
Dodge City▲
The Private Lives of Elizabeth & Essex▲
Santa Fe Trail
They Died with Their Boots On▲

Screen Teams: Gable & Crawford

Chained
Dance Fools Dance▲
Dancing Lady
Forsaking All Others
Laughing Sinners
Love on the Run
Possessed
Strange Cargo

Screen Teams: Garland & Rooney

Andy Hardy Meets Debutante
Babes in Arms
Babes on Broadway
Girl Crazy▲
Life Begins for Andy Hardy▲
Love Finds Andy Hardy▲
Strike Up the Band
Thoroughbreds Don't Cry
Thousands Cheer
Words and Music

Screen Teams: Garson & Pidgeon

Blossoms in the Dust
Julia Misbehaves▲
Madame Curie▲
The Miniver Story
Mrs. Miniver▲
Mrs. Parkington
That Forsyte Woman

Screen Teams: Gibson & Glover

Lethal Weapon▲
Lethal Weapon 2▲
Lethal Weapon 3
Lethal Weapon 4
Maverick

Screen Teams: Hepburn & Grant

Bringing Up Baby▲
Holiday▲
The Philadelphia Story▲
Sylvia Scarlett

Screen Teams: Hepburn & Tracy

Adam's Rib▲
Desk Set▲
Guess Who's Coming to Dinner▲
Pat and Mike▲
State of the Union▲
Without Love
Woman of the Year▲

Screen Teams: Hope & Crosby

Cancel My Reservation
My Favorite Blonde▲
My Favorite Brunette
The Princess and the Pirate▲
The Road to Bali▲
The Road to Hong Kong
The Road to Morocco▲
The Road to Rio▲
The Road to Singapore
The Road to Utopia▲
The Road to Zanzibar▲
Scared Stiff▲
Star Spangled Rhythm▲

Screen Teams: Ladd & Lake

The Blue Dahlia▲
The Glass Key▲
This Gun for Hire▲

Screen Teams: Lancaster & Douglas

The Devil's Disciple▲
Gunfight at the O.K. Corral▲
The List of Adrian Messenger▲
Seven Days in May▲
Tough Guys

Screen Teams: Lee & Cushing

The Creeping Flesh
The Curse of Frankenstein
The Devil's Undead
Dr. Terror's House of Horrors
Dracula A.D. 1972
The Gorgon
Hamlet▲
Horror Express
The Horror of Dracula▲
The Hound of the Baskervilles
The House that Dripped Blood
Island of the Burning Doomed
Moulin Rouge▲
The Mummy▲
Nothing But the Night
The Satanic Rites of Dracula
Scream and Scream Again
The Skull

Screen Teams: Lemmon & Matthau

Buddy Buddy
The Fortune Cookie▲
The Front Page
Grumpier Old Men
Grumpy Old Men▲
JFK▲
Neil Simon's The Odd Couple 2
The Odd Couple▲
Out to Sea

Screen Teams: Loy & Powell

After the Thin Man▲
Another Thin Man
Double Wedding▲
Evelyn Prentice
The Great Ziegfeld▲
I Love You Again▲
Libeled Lady▲
Love Crazy▲
Manhattan Melodrama▲
Shadow of the Thin Man▲
Song of the Thin Man
The Thin Man▲
The Thin Man Goes Home

Screen Teams: Martin & Lewis

Artists and Models
At War with the Army
The Caddy
Hollywood or Bust
Jumping Jacks
My Friend Irma
Pardners
The Road to Bali▲
Scared Stiff▲
The Stooge

Screen Teams: Newman & Woodward

The Drowning Pool
From the Terrace
The Long, Hot Summer▲
Mr. & Mrs. Bridge▲
A New Kind of Love
Paris Blues

Screen Teams: Redford & Newman

Butch Cassidy and the Sundance Kid▲
The Sting▲

Screen Teams: Reynolds & DeLuise

The Best Little Whorehouse in Texas
Cannonball Run
Cannonball Run 2
The End▲
Smokey and the Bandit 2

Screen Teams: Reynolds & Field

The End▲
Hooper
Smokey and the Bandit
Smokey and the Bandit 2

Screen Teams: Rogers & Evans

Along the Navaho Trail
Apache Rose
Bells of Coronado
Bells of Rosarita
Bells of San Angelo
Cowboy & the Senorita
Don't Fence Me In
Down Dakota Way
The Golden Stallion
Helldorado
Home in Oklahoma
My Pal Trigger
Rainbow over Texas
Roll on Texas Moon
Song of Arizona
Sunset in El Dorado
Susanna Pass
Trigger, Jr.
Twilight in the Sierras
Under Nevada Skies
Utah

Screen Teams: Snipes & Harrelson

Money Train
White Men Can't Jump
Wildcats

Screen Teams: Stewart & Sullavan

The Mortal Storm▲
The Shop Around the Corner▲
Shopworn Angel▲

Screen Teams: Turner & Douglas

The Jewel of the Nile
Romancing the Stone▲
The War of the Roses▲

Screen Teams: Wilder & Pryor

Another You
See No Evil, Hear No Evil
Silver Streak▲
Stir Crazy

Scrooge

An American Christmas Carol
A Christmas Carol▲
A Christmas Carol
A Christmas Carol▲
A Christmas Carol▲
A Christmas Carol
Ms. Scrooge
Scrooged

Sexton Blake

Echo Murders
Meet Sexton Blake
Sexton Blake and the Hooded Terror
Stage Struck

Sherlock Holmes

The Adventures of Sherlock Holmes
The Adventures of Sherlock Holmes' Smarter Brother▲
The Crucifer of Blood
Dressed to Kill
Hands of a Murderer
The Hound of London
The Hound of the Baskervilles▲
The Hound of the Baskervilles
House of Fear
Masks of Death
Murder at the Baskervilles
Murder by Decree▲
The Pearl of Death
The Private Life of Sherlock Holmes▲
Pursuit to Algiers
Scarlet Claw▲
The Seven-Per-Cent Solution▲
Sherlock Holmes and the Deadly Necklace
Sherlock Holmes and the Incident at Victoria Falls
Sherlock Holmes and the Secret Weapon▲
Sherlock Holmes Faces Death▲
Sherlock Holmes in Washington
Sherlock Holmes: The Voice of Terror
The Sign of Four
The Silent Mr. Sherlock Holmes
The Speckled Band▲
Spider Woman▲
The Strange Case of the End of Civilization As We Know It
A Study in Scarlet
A Study in Terror▲
Terror by Night
They Might Be Giants▲
The Triumph of Sherlock Holmes
Without a Clue
The Woman in Green
Young Sherlock Holmes

Special FX Extravaganzas

The Abyss▲
Alien: Resurrection▲
Aliens▲
An American Werewolf in Paris
Anaconda
The Arrival
Baby Geniuses
Batman▲
Batman and Robin
Batman Forever▲
Beetlejuice▲
Big Trouble in Little China
The Black Hole
Blithe Spirit▲
The Borrowers
Captain Sinbad
Crash Dive
Dante's Peak
Daylight
Dragonheart
Event Horizon
The Ewok Adventure
The Exorcist▲
The Exorcist 2: The Heretic
FairyTale: A True Story
Fantastic Voyage▲
The Fifth Element
Forbidden Planet▲
Hideaway
Highlander: The Final Dimension
Independence Day▲
Innerspace
Judge Dredd
Jumanji
Jurassic Park▲
Lifeforce
The Lost World: Jurassic Park 2
Mars Attacks!
Mary Shelley's Frankenstein
The Mask▲
My Favorite Martian
Poltergeist▲
The Rains Came
Return of the Jedi▲
The Shadow
Small Soldiers
Solar Crisis
Spawn▲
Species
Species 2
Star Trek 2: The Wrath of Khan▲
Star Trek 4: The Voyage Home▲
Star Trek: Generations▲
Superman 2▲
The Terminator▲
Terminator 2: Judgment Day▲
The Thing
Total Recall▲
Twister
2001: A Space Odyssey▲
2010: The Year We Make Contact▲
Virtuosity
Virus
Volcano
Who Framed Roger Rabbit▲
Wolfen▲

Special FX Extravaganzas: Make-Up

An American Werewolf in London▲
The Associate
Bad Moon
Batman and Robin
Battle for the Planet of the Apes
Beetlejuice▲
Beneath the Planet of the Apes
Body Melt
Conquest of the Planet of the Apes
Darkman 2: The Return of Durant
Darkman 3: Die Darkman Die
Dawn of the Dead▲
Day of the Dead
Escape from the Planet of the Apes▲
The Exorcist▲
The Fly▲
The Fly 2
Freaked
Hocus Pocus
The Howling▲
The Island of Dr. Moreau
The Man Without a Face
Mary Shelley's Frankenstein
The Nutty Professor▲
Nutty Professor 2: The Klumps
Planet of the Apes▲
Scanner Cop
Scanners
Sssssss
The Thing
Vampire in Brooklyn
Warriors of Virtue
Wolf

Special FX Wizards: Rick Baker

An American Werewolf in London▲
Food of the Gods
The Funhouse
The Fury
Greystoke: The Legend of Tarzan, Lord of the Apes
Harry and the Hendersons
Incredible Melting Man
The Incredible Shrinking Woman
It's Alive▲
King Kong
Men in Black▲
Mighty Joe Young
The Nutty Professor▲
Octaman
Planet of the Apes▲
Schlock
Squirm
Star Wars▲
Tanya's Island
Track of the Moonbeast
Videodrome
Wolf

Special FX Wizards: Rob Bottin

Bugsy▲
Explorers
Fear and Loathing in Las Vegas
The Fog
The Howling▲
Humanoids from the Deep
Innerspace
Legend
Mission: Impossible▲
RoboCop▲
Tanya's Island
The Thing
Total Recall▲
Twilight Zone: The Movie
The Witches of Eastwick

Special FX Wizards: Anton Furst

Alien▲
Batman▲
The Company of Wolves▲
Full Metal Jacket▲
Moonraker
Star Wars▲

Special FX Wizards: Ray Harryhausen

The Beast from 20,000 Fathoms
Clash of the Titans
Earth vs. the Flying Saucers
First Men in the Moon
Golden Voyage of Sinbad
It Came from Beneath the Sea▲
Jason and the Argonauts▲
Mighty Joe Young
Mysterious Island▲
One Million Years B.C.
The Seventh Voyage of Sinbad▲
Sinbad and the Eye of the Tiger
The Three Worlds of Gulliver
20 Million Miles to Earth
The Valley of Gwangi▲

Special FX Wizards: Herschell Gordon Lewis

Blood Feast

▲ = rated three bones or higher

Color Me Blood Red
Gruesome Twosome
Just for the Hell of It
Moonshine Mountain
The Psychic
She-Devils on Wheels
Suburban Roulette
This Stuff'll Kill Ya!
2000 Maniacs
The Wizard of Gore

Special FX Wizards: Tom Savini

Creepshow
Dawn of the Dead▲
Day of the Dead
Deathdream
Deranged▲
Friday the 13th
Friday the 13th, Part 4: The Final Chapter
Knightriders
Maniac
Martin▲
Midnight
Monkey Shines
The Prowler
The Ripper
The Texas Chainsaw Massacre 2

Special FX Wizards: Dick Smith

Altered States▲
Amadeus▲
The Exorcist▲
Ghost Story
The Godfather▲
House of Dark Shadows▲
Little Big Man▲
Marathon Man▲
Midnight Cowboy▲
Scanners
The Sentinel
Spasms
The Stepford Wives▲
The Sunshine Boys▲
Taxi Driver▲
The World of Henry Orient▲

Special FX Wizards: Douglas Trumball

The Andromeda Strain
Blade Runner▲
Brainstorm
Close Encounters of the Third Kind▲
Silent Running▲
Star Trek: The Motion Picture
2001: A Space Odyssey▲

Star Wars

The Empire Strikes Back▲
The Ewok Adventure
The Ewoks: Battle for Endor
Return of the Jedi▲
Star Wars▲
Star Wars: Episode 1—The Phantom Menace▲
Star Wars: Episode 2—Attack of the Clones▲

Tarzan

Greystoke: The Legend of Tarzan, Lord of the Apes
The New Adventures of Tarzan
Tarzan▲
Tarzan and His Mate▲
Tarzan and the Green Goddess
Tarzan and the Lost City
Tarzan and the Trappers
Tarzan Escapes▲
Tarzan Finds a Son▲
Tarzan of the Apes
Tarzan, the Ape Man▲
Tarzan, the Ape Man
Tarzan the Fearless
Tarzan the Tiger
Tarzan's New York Adventure
Tarzan's Revenge
Tarzan's Secret Treasure
Walk Like a Man

The Texas Rangers

Boss of Rawhide
Dead or Alive
Enemy of the Law
Fighting Valley
Flaming Bullets
Frontier Fugitives
Gangsters of the Frontier
Guns of the Law
Marked for Murder
Outlaw Roundup
Ranger's Roundup
Rangers Take Over
Three in the Saddle
Wild West

The Thin Man

After the Thin Man▲
Another Thin Man
Shadow of the Thin Man▲
Song of the Thin Man
The Thin Man▲
The Thin Man Goes Home

The Three Mequiteers

Come on, Cowboys
Covered Wagon Days
Cowboys from Texas
Frontier Horizon
Ghost Town Gold
Heart of the Rockies
Heroes of the Hills
Hit the Saddle
The Kansas Terrors
Outlaws of Sonora
Overland Stage Raiders▲
Pals of the Saddle
Powdersmoke Range
Purple Vigilantes
Riders of the Whistling Skull
Roarin' Lead
Rocky Mountain Rangers
Santa Fe Stampede
Three Texas Steers
The Trigger Trio
Wild Horse Rodeo
Wyoming Outlaw

The Three Musketeers

The Four Musketeers▲
The Man in the Iron Mask▲
The Musketeer
Ring of the Musketeers
The Three Musketeers
The Three Musketeers▲
The Three Musketeers
The Three Musketeers▲
The Three Musketeers

3 Stooges

Around the World in a Daze
Dancing Lady
Gold Raiders
Have Rocket Will Travel
Hollywood Party
It's a Mad, Mad, Mad, Mad World
The Lost Stooges
The Outlaws Is Coming!
Snow White and the Three Stooges
Stoogemania
Three Stooges in Orbit
The Three Stooges Meet Hercules

Top Grossing Films of 1939

Gone with the Wind▲
The Hunchback of Notre Dame▲
Jesse James▲
Mr. Smith Goes to Washington▲
The Wizard of Oz▲

Top Grossing Films of 1940

Boom Town
Fantasia▲
Pinocchio▲
Rebecca▲
Santa Fe Trail

Top Grossing Films of 1941

Honky Tonk▲
The Philadelphia Story▲
Sergeant York▲
A Yank in the R.A.F.

Top Grossing Films of 1942

Bambi▲
Casablanca▲
Mrs. Miniver▲
Random Harvest▲
Yankee Doodle Dandy▲

Top Grossing Films of 1943

The Outlaw
The Song of Bernadette▲
Stage Door Canteen
This Is the Army

Top Grossing Films of 1944

Going My Way▲
Meet Me in St. Louis▲
Since You Went Away▲
Thirty Seconds Over Tokyo▲

Top Grossing Films of 1945

Anchors Aweigh▲
The Bells of St. Mary's▲
Spellbound▲
Weekend at the Waldorf▲

Top Grossing Films of 1946

The Best Years of Our Lives▲
Duel in the Sun▲
The Jolson Story▲

Top Grossing Films of 1947

Egg and I▲
Life with Father▲

Top Grossing Films of 1948

Johnny Belinda▲
On an Island with You
The Paleface▲
Red River▲
The Red Shoes▲
The Three Musketeers

Top Grossing Films of 1949

Battleground▲
Jolson Sings Again
Samson and Delilah▲
Sands of Iwo Jima▲

Top Grossing Films of 1950

Annie Get Your Gun▲
Cinderella▲
Father of the Bride▲
King Solomon's Mines▲

Top Grossing Films of 1951

Alice in Wonderland▲
David and Bathsheba▲
The Great Caruso
Quo Vadis▲
Show Boat

Top Grossing Films of 1952

The Greatest Show on Earth▲
Hans Christian Andersen
Ivanhoe▲
The Snows of Kilimanjaro▲

Top Grossing Films of 1953

From Here to Eternity▲
How to Marry a Millionaire
Peter Pan▲
The Robe
Shane▲

Top Grossing Films of 1954

The Caine Mutiny▲
The Glenn Miller Story▲
Rear Window▲
20,000 Leagues under the Sea▲
White Christmas▲

Top Grossing Films of 1955

Battle Cry▲
Lady and the Tramp▲
Mister Roberts▲
Oklahoma!▲

Top Grossing Films of 1956

Around the World in 80 Days▲
Giant▲
The King and I▲
The Ten Commandments▲

Top Grossing Films of 1957

The Bridge on the River Kwai▲
Old Yeller▲
Peyton Place▲
Raintree County
Sayonara▲

Top Grossing Films of 1958

Auntie Mame▲
Cat on a Hot Tin Roof▲
Gigi▲
No Time for Sergeants▲
South Pacific▲

Top Grossing Films of 1959

Ben-Hur▲
Darby O'Gill & the Little People▲
Operation Petticoat▲
The Shaggy Dog
Sleeping Beauty▲

Top Grossing Films of 1960

The Alamo▲
Exodus▲
Psycho▲
Spartacus▲
The Swiss Family Robinson▲

Top Grossing Films of 1961

The Absent-Minded Professor▲
El Cid▲
The Guns of Navarone▲
West Side Story▲

Top Grossing Films of 1962

How the West Was Won▲
In Search of the Castaways▲
Lawrence of Arabia▲
The Longest Day▲
The Music Man▲

Top Grossing Films of 1963

Cleopatra
Irma La Douce
It's a Mad, Mad, Mad, Mad World
The Sword in the Stone▲
Tom Jones▲

Top Grossing Films of 1964

The Carpetbaggers
From Russia with Love▲
Goldfinger▲
Mary Poppins▲
My Fair Lady▲

Top Grossing Films of 1965

Doctor Zhivago▲
The Sound of Music▲
That Darn Cat
Those Magnificent Men in Their Flying Machines▲
Thunderball

Top Grossing Films of 1966

Hawaii▲
Lt. Robin Crusoe, U.S.N.
A Man for All Seasons▲
Who's Afraid of Virginia Woolf?▲

Top Grossing Films of 1967

Bonnie & Clyde▲
The Dirty Dozen▲
The Graduate▲
Guess Who's Coming to Dinner▲
The Jungle Book▲

Top Grossing Films of 1968

Bullitt▲
Funny Girl▲
The Odd Couple▲
Romeo and Juliet▲
2001: A Space Odyssey▲

Top Grossing Films of 1969

Butch Cassidy and the Sundance Kid▲
Easy Rider▲
Hello, Dolly!
The Love Bug
Midnight Cowboy▲

Top Grossing Films of 1970

Airport▲
Love Story▲
M*A*S*H▲
Patton▲

Top Grossing Films of 1971

Billy Jack
Diamonds Are Forever▲
Fiddler on the Roof▲
The French Connection▲
Summer of '42▲

Top Grossing Films of 1972

Deliverance▲
The Godfather▲
Jeremiah Johnson▲
The Poseidon Adventure
What's Up, Doc?▲

Top Grossing Films of 1973

American Graffiti▲
The Exorcist▲
Papillon▲
The Sting▲
The Way We Were▲

Top Grossing Films of 1974

Blazing Saddles▲
Earthquake
The Towering Inferno
The Trial of Billy Jack
Young Frankenstein▲

Top Grossing Films of 1975

Dog Day Afternoon▲
Jaws▲
One Flew Over the Cuckoo's Nest▲

Top Grossing Films of 1976

All the President's Men▲
King Kong
Rocky▲
Silver Streak▲
A Star Is Born

Top Grossing Films of 1977

Close Encounters of the Third Kind▲
The Goodbye Girl▲
Saturday Night Fever
Smokey and the Bandit
Star Wars▲

Top Grossing Films of 1978

Every Which Way But Loose
Grease▲
Jaws 2
National Lampoon's Animal House▲
Superman: The Movie▲

Top Grossing Films of 1979

Alien▲
The Jerk
Kramer vs. Kramer▲
Rocky 2
Star Trek: The Motion Picture

Top Grossing Films of 1980

Airplane!▲
Any Which Way You Can
The Empire Strikes Back▲
9 to 5
Stir Crazy

Top Grossing Films of 1981

Arthur▲
Cannonball Run
On Golden Pond▲
Raiders of the Lost Ark▲
Stripes
Superman 2▲

Top Grossing Films of 1982

E.T.: The Extra-Terrestrial▲
An Officer and a Gentleman▲
Porky's
Rocky 3

Top Grossing Films of 1983

Return of the Jedi▲
Superman 3
Terms of Endearment▲
Trading Places
WarGames

Top Grossing Films of 1984

Beverly Hills Cop
Ghostbusters▲
Gremlins▲
Indiana Jones and the Temple of Doom▲
The Karate Kid▲

▲ = rated three bones or higher

Top Grossing Films of 1985

Back to the Future▲
The Color Purple▲
Out of Africa▲
Rambo: First Blood, Part 2
Rocky 4

Top Grossing Films of 1986

Crocodile Dundee▲
The Karate Kid: Part 2
Platoon▲
Star Trek 4: The Voyage Home▲
Top Gun

Top Grossing Films of 1987

Beverly Hills Cop 2
Fatal Attraction▲
Good Morning, Vietnam▲
Lethal Weapon▲
Three Men and a Baby▲
The Untouchables▲

Top Grossing Films of 1988

Coming to America▲
Crocodile Dundee 2
Die Hard▲
Rain Man▲
Twins
Who Framed Roger Rabbit▲

Top Grossing Films of 1989

Batman▲
Driving Miss Daisy▲
Ghostbusters 2
Honey, I Shrunk the Kids
Indiana Jones and the Last Crusade▲
Lethal Weapon 2▲

Top Grossing Films of 1990

Dances with Wolves▲
Dick Tracy▲
Die Hard 2: Die Harder▲
Ghost▲
Home Alone▲
The Hunt for Red October▲
Pretty Woman▲
Teenage Mutant Ninja Turtles: The Movie
Total Recall▲

Top Grossing Films of 1991

The Addams Family
Backdraft
Boyz N the Hood▲
City Slickers▲
Doc Hollywood
Dying Young
Hot Shots!▲
Naked Gun 2 1/2: The Smell of Fear
New Jack City
101 Dalmatians▲
Robin Hood: Prince of Thieves
The Rocketeer▲
The Silence of the Lambs▲
Sleeping with the Enemy
Teenage Mutant Ninja Turtles 2: The Secret of the Ooze
Terminator 2: Judgment Day▲
What about Bob?▲

Top Grossing Films of 1992

Aladdin▲
Alien 3
Basic Instinct
Batman Returns
The Bodyguard
Boomerang
Bram Stoker's Dracula
Fried Green Tomatoes▲
The Hand that Rocks the Cradle
Home Alone 2: Lost in New York
The Last of the Mohicans▲
A League of Their Own▲
Lethal Weapon 3
Patriot Games▲
Sister Act
Under Siege
Unforgiven▲
Wayne's World▲
White Men Can't Jump

Top Grossing Films of 1993

Aladdin▲
Cliffhanger▲
A Few Good Men▲
The Firm▲
Free Willy
The Fugitive▲
In the Line of Fire▲
Indecent Proposal
Jurassic Park▲
Sleepless in Seattle▲

Top Grossing Films of 1994

Ace Ventura: Pet Detective
Clear and Present Danger
The Client
The Flintstones
Forrest Gump▲
The Lion King▲
The Mask▲
Maverick
Speed▲
True Lies

Top Grossing Films of 1995

Ace Ventura: When Nature Calls
Apollo 13▲
Batman Forever▲
Casper▲
Die Hard: With a Vengeance
Goldeneye▲
Jumanji
Pocahontas▲
Seven▲
Toy Story▲

Top Grossing Films of 1996

The Birdcage▲
Broken Arrow
The Cable Guy
Courage Under Fire▲
Eraser
The First Wives Club
The Hunchback of Notre Dame▲
Independence Day▲
Jack
Jerry Maguire▲
Mission: Impossible▲
The Nutty Professor▲
101 Dalmatians
Phenomenon
Ransom▲
The Rock▲
Space Jam
Star Trek: First Contact▲
A Time to Kill▲
Twister

Top Grossing Films of 1997

Air Force One▲
Batman and Robin
Con Air▲
Conspiracy Theory▲
Contact
Face/Off▲
Flubber
George of the Jungle▲
Hercules▲
I Know What You Did Last Summer▲
Jerry Maguire▲
Liar Liar
The Lost World: Jurassic Park 2
Men in Black▲
My Best Friend's Wedding
Scream▲
Scream 2▲
Star Wars▲
Titanic▲
Tomorrow Never Dies

Top Grossing Films of 1998

Antz▲
Armageddon
As Good As It Gets▲
A Bug's Life▲
Deep Impact
Dr. Dolittle
Enemy of the State
Godzilla
Good Will Hunting
Lethal Weapon 4
The Mask of Zorro▲
Mulan
The Rugrats Movie▲
Saving Private Ryan▲
There's Something about Mary▲
Titanic▲
The Truman Show▲
The Waterboy
The X-Files

Top Grossing Films of 1999

American Pie▲
Analyze This▲
Austin Powers 2: The Spy Who Shagged Me▲
Big Daddy
The Blair Witch Project
A Bug's Life▲
Entrapment
The Matrix▲
The Mummy
Notting Hill▲
Runaway Bride▲
Shakespeare in Love▲
The Sixth Sense▲
Star Wars: Episode 1—The Phantom Menace▲
Tarzan▲
Toy Story 2▲
Wild Wild West
The World Is Not Enough
You've Got Mail

Top Grossing Films of 2000

Big Momma's House
Cast Away▲
Charlie's Angels
Chicken Run▲
Dinosaur
Dr. Seuss' How the Grinch Stole Christmas
Erin Brockovich▲
George Wallace
Gladiator▲
Gone in 60 Seconds
Me, Myself, and Irene▲
Meet the Parents▲
Mission: Impossible 2▲
Nutty Professor 2: The Klumps
The Patriot
The Perfect Storm
Remember the Titans▲
Scary Movie
What Women Want
X-Men

Top Grossing Films of 2001

American Pie 2
Cast Away▲
Crouching Tiger, Hidden Dragon▲
Dr. Dolittle 2
The Fast and the Furious
Hannibal
Harry Potter and the Sorcerer's Stone▲
Jurassic Park 3
Lara Croft: Tomb Raider
Lord of the Rings 1: The Fellowship of the Rings▲
Monsters, Inc.▲
The Mummy Returns
Pearl Harbor
Planet of the Apes▲
Rush Hour 2
Shrek▲
Traffic▲

The Trail Blazers

Arizona Whirlwind
Death Valley Rangers
The Law Rides Again
Outlaw Trail

Troma Films

Beware! Children at Play
Blades
Blondes Have More Guns
Bloodsucking Freaks
Bugged!
Cannibal! The Musical
Chopper Chicks in Zombietown
The Chosen One: Legend of the Raven
Christmas Evil
Class of Nuke 'Em High
Class of Nuke 'Em High 2: Subhumanoid Meltdown
Class of Nuke 'Em High 3: The Good, the Bad and the Subhumanoid
Combat Shock
Cry Uncle
Deadly Daphne's Revenge
Escape from Hell
Evil Clutch
Fat Guy Goes Nutzoid
Ferocious Female Freedom Fighters
Frostbiter: Wrath of the Wendigo
Girls School Screamers
I Married a Vampire
I Was a Teenage TV Terrorist
Invasion of the Space Preachers
Maniac Nurses Find Ecstasy
A Nymphoid Barbarian in Dinosaur Hell
Preacherman
Rabid Grannies
Redneck Zombies
Sgt. Kabukiman N.Y.P.D.
Sergio Lapel's Drawing Blood
Sizzle Beach U.S.A.
Splatter University
Squeeze Play
Stuck on You
Student Confidential
Surf Nazis Must Die
Teenage Catgirls in Heat
The Toxic Avenger
The Toxic Avenger, Part 2
The Toxic Avenger, Part 3: The Last Temptation of Toxie
Troma's War
Tromeo & Juliet
Unspeakable
Vegas in Space
Wizards of the Demon Sword
Zombie Island Massacre

Universal Studios' Classic Horror

Abbott and Costello Meet Dr. Jekyll and Mr. Hyde
Abbott and Costello Meet Frankenstein▲
Abbott and Costello Meet the Killer, Boris Karloff
The Black Cat▲
The Bride of Frankenstein▲
Creature from the Black Lagoon▲
The Creature Walks among Us
Dracula (Spanish Version)
Dracula▲
Dracula's Daughter▲
Frankenstein▲
Frankenstein Meets the Wolfman▲
The Ghost of Frankenstein
House of Dracula
House of Frankenstein
The Hunchback of Notre Dame▲
Invisible Agent
The Invisible Man▲
The Invisible Man Returns▲
The Invisible Woman▲
Island of Lost Souls▲
The Mummy▲
The Mummy's Curse
The Mummy's Ghost
The Mummy's Hand
The Mummy's Tomb
Murders in the Rue Morgue
The Phantom of the Opera▲
The Raven▲
Revenge of the Creature
Son of Dracula▲
Son of Frankenstein▲
Werewolf of London
The Wolf Man▲

Wild Bill Hickok

Buffalo Girls
Calamity Jane▲
Calamity Jane
Little Big Man▲
The Plainsman
Pony Express▲
The White Buffalo
Wild Bill
Young Bill Hickok

The Wolfman

Frankenstein Meets the Wolfman▲
House of Dracula
House of Frankenstein
Mad Monster Party
The Monster Squad
The Wolf Man▲
The Wolfman

Wyatt Earp

Cheyenne Autumn
Four Eyes and Six Guns
Gunfight at the O.K. Corral▲
Hour of the Gun
My Darling Clementine▲
Sunset
Tombstone▲
Wyatt Earp
Wyatt Earp: Return to Tombstone

Zorro

The Bold Caballero
Don Q., Son of Zorro
Mark of Zorro▲
The Mark of Zorro▲
The Mask of Zorro▲
The Naked Sword of Zorro
The Secret of El Zorro
Son of Zorro
Zorro
Zorro Rides Again
Zorro, the Gay Blade
Zorro's Black Whip
Zorro's Fighting Legion

Zucker/Abrahams/Zucker

Airplane!▲
Kentucky Fried Movie▲
The Naked Gun: From the Files of Police Squad▲
Naked Gun 33 1/3: The Final Insult
Naked Gun 2 1/2: The Smell of Fear
Top Secret!▲

▲ = rated three bones or higher

The **Awards Index** lists films honored (or dishonored, in some cases) by over 10 national and international award bodies, representing over 100 categories of recognition. This information can also be found in the reviews, following the credits. **Only features available on video and reviewed in the main section are listed in this index; movies not yet released on video are not covered here.** As award-winning and nominated films find their way to video, they will be added to the review section and covered in this index. **Nominations are once again covered in this index; they are not covered in the individual reviews.** The awards covered include:

Academy Awards
British Academy of Film and Television Arts
Broadcast Film Critics Awards
Cannes Film Festival
Directors Guild of America
Genie Awards (Canadian)
Golden Globe
Golden Raspberries
Independent Spirit Awards
National Film Registry
Screen Actors Guild Awards
Writers Guild of America

ACADEMY AWARDS

ACTOR

1928
★ **Emil Jannings**/*Last Command*
Charlie Chaplin/*The Circus*

1929
Chester Morris/*Alibi*

1930
★ **George Arliss**/*Disraeli*
Wallace Beery/*The Big House*
Ronald Colman/*Bulldog Drummond*

1931
★ **Lionel Barrymore**/*A Free Soul*
Richard Dix/*Cimarron*
Adolphe Menjou/*The Front Page*

1932
★ **Wallace Beery**/*The Champ*
★ **Fredric March**/*Dr. Jekyll and Mr. Hyde*
Alfred Lunt/*The Guardsman*

1933
★ **Charles Laughton**/*The Private Life of Henry VIII*
Paul Muni/*I Am a Fugitive from a Chain Gang*

1934
★ **Clark Gable**/*It Happened One Night*
William Powell/*The Thin Man*

1935
★ **Victor McLaglen**/*The Informer*
Clark Gable/*Mutiny on the Bounty*
Charles Laughton/*Mutiny on the Bounty*
Franchot Tone/*Mutiny on the Bounty*

1936
★ **Paul Muni**/*The Story of Louis Pasteur*
Gary Cooper/*Mr. Deeds Goes to Town*
Walter Huston/*Dodsworth*
William Powell/*My Man Godfrey*
Spencer Tracy/*San Francisco*

1937
★ **Spencer Tracy**/*Captains Courageous*
Charles Boyer/*Conquest*
Fredric March/*A Star Is Born*
Robert Montgomery/*Night Must Fall*
Paul Muni/*The Life of Emile Zola*

1938
★ **Spencer Tracy**/*Boys Town*
Charles Boyer/*Algiers*
James Cagney/*Angels with Dirty Faces*
Robert Donat/*The Citadel*
Leslie Howard/*Pygmalion*

1939
★ **Robert Donat**/*Goodbye, Mr. Chips*
Clark Gable/*Gone with the Wind*
Laurence Olivier/*Wuthering Heights*
Mickey Rooney/*Babes in Arms*
James Stewart/*Mr. Smith Goes to Washington*

1940
★ **James Stewart**/*The Philadelphia Story*
Charlie Chaplin/*The Great Dictator*
Henry Fonda/*The Grapes of Wrath*
Raymond Massey/*Abe Lincoln in Illinois*
Laurence Olivier/*Rebecca*

1941
★ **Gary Cooper**/*Sergeant York*
Cary Grant/*Penny Serenade*
Walter Huston/*The Devil & Daniel Webster*
Robert Montgomery/*Here Comes Mr. Jordan*
Orson Welles/*Citizen Kane*

1942
★ **James Cagney**/*Yankee Doodle Dandy*
Ronald Colman/*Random Harvest*
Gary Cooper/*The Pride of the Yankees*
Walter Pidgeon/*Mrs. Miniver*

1943
★ **Paul Lukas**/*Watch on the Rhine*
Humphrey Bogart/*Casablanca*
Gary Cooper/*For Whom the Bell Tolls*
Walter Pidgeon/*Madame Curie*
Mickey Rooney/*The Human Comedy*

1944
★ **Bing Crosby**/*Going My Way*
Charles Boyer/*Gaslight*
Barry Fitzgerald/*Going My Way*
Cary Grant/*None But the Lonely Heart*
Alexander Knox/*Wilson*

1945
★ **Ray Milland**/*The Lost Weekend*
Bing Crosby/*The Bells of St. Mary's*
Gene Kelly/*Anchors Aweigh*
Gregory Peck/*The Keys of the Kingdom*
Cornel Wilde/*A Song to Remember*

1946
★ **Fredric March**/*The Best Years of Our Lives*
Laurence Olivier/*Henry V*
Larry Parks/*The Jolson Story*
Gregory Peck/*The Yearling*
James Stewart/*It's a Wonderful Life*

1947
★ **Ronald Colman**/*A Double Life*
John Garfield/*Body and Soul*
Gregory Peck/*Gentleman's Agreement*
William Powell/*Life with Father*

1948
★ **Laurence Olivier**/*Hamlet*
Lew Ayres/*Johnny Belinda*
Montgomery Clift/*The Search*

1949
★ **Broderick Crawford**/*All the King's Men*
Kirk Douglas/*Champion*
Gregory Peck/*Twelve o'Clock High*
John Wayne/*Sands of Iwo Jima*

1950
★ **Jose Ferrer**/*Cyrano de Bergerac*
Louis Calhern/*The Magnificent Yankee*
William Holden/*Sunset Boulevard*
James Stewart/*Harvey*
Spencer Tracy/*Father of the Bride*

1951
★ **Humphrey Bogart**/*The African Queen*
Marlon Brando/*A Streetcar Named Desire*
Montgomery Clift/*A Place in the Sun*

1952
★ **Gary Cooper**/*High Noon*
Marlon Brando/*Viva Zapata!*
Kirk Douglas/*The Bad and the Beautiful*
Jose Ferrer/*Moulin Rouge*
Alec Guinness/*The Lavender Hill Mob*

1953
★ **William Holden**/*Stalag 17*
Marlon Brando/*Julius Caesar*
Richard Burton/*The Robe*
Montgomery Clift/*From Here to Eternity*
Burt Lancaster/*From Here to Eternity*

1954
★ **Marlon Brando**/*On the Waterfront*
Humphrey Bogart/*The Caine Mutiny*
Bing Crosby/*Country Girl*
James Mason/*A Star Is Born*

1955
★ **Ernest Borgnine**/*Marty*
James Cagney/*Love Me or Leave Me*
James Dean/*East of Eden*
Frank Sinatra/*The Man with the Golden Arm*
Spencer Tracy/*Bad Day at Black Rock*

1956
★ **Yul Brynner**/*The King and I*
James Dean/*Giant*
Kirk Douglas/*Lust for Life*
Rock Hudson/*Giant*
Laurence Olivier/*Richard III*

1957
★ **Alec Guinness**/*The Bridge on the River Kwai*
Marlon Brando/*Sayonara*
Charles Laughton/*Witness for the Prosecution*

1958
★ **David Niven**/*Separate Tables*
Tony Curtis/*The Defiant Ones*
Paul Newman/*Cat on a Hot Tin Roof*
Sidney Poitier/*The Defiant Ones*

1959
★ **Charlton Heston**/*Ben-Hur*
Laurence Harvey/*Room at the Top*
Jack Lemmon/*Some Like It Hot*
Paul Muni/*The Last Angry Man*
James Stewart/*Anatomy of a Murder*
Spencer Tracy/*The Old Man and the Sea*

1960
★ **Burt Lancaster**/*Elmer Gantry*
Jack Lemmon/*The Apartment*
Laurence Olivier/*The Entertainer*
Spencer Tracy/*Inherit the Wind*

1961
★ **Maximilian Schell**/*Judgment at Nuremberg*
Charles Boyer/*Fanny*
Paul Newman/*The Hustler*
Spencer Tracy/*Judgment at Nuremberg*
Stuart Whitman/*The Mark*

★ = winner

ACTOR *cont.*

1962
★ **Gregory Peck**/*To Kill a Mockingbird*
Burt Lancaster/*Birdman of Alcatraz*
Jack Lemmon/*Days of Wine and Roses*
Marcello Mastroianni/*Divorce—Italian Style*
Peter O'Toole/*Lawrence of Arabia*

1963
★ **Sidney Poitier**/*Lilies of the Field*
Albert Finney/*Tom Jones*
Richard Harris/*This Sporting Life*
Rex Harrison/*Cleopatra*
Paul Newman/*Hud*

1964
★ **Rex Harrison**/*My Fair Lady*
Richard Burton/*Becket*
Peter O'Toole/*Becket*
Anthony Quinn/*Zorba the Greek*
Peter Sellers/*Dr. Strangelove, or: How I Learned to Stop Worrying and Love the Bomb*

1965
★ **Lee Marvin**/*Cat Ballou*
Richard Burton/*The Spy Who Came in from the Cold*
Laurence Olivier/*Othello*
Rod Steiger/*The Pawnbroker*
Oskar Werner/*Ship of Fools*

1966
★ **Paul Scofield**/*A Man for All Seasons*
Alan Arkin/*The Russians Are Coming, the Russians Are Coming*
Richard Burton/*Who's Afraid of Virginia Woolf?*
Michael Caine/*Alfie*
Steve McQueen/*The Sand Pebbles*

1967
★ **Rod Steiger**/*In the Heat of the Night*
Warren Beatty/*Bonnie & Clyde*
Dustin Hoffman/*The Graduate*
Paul Newman/*Cool Hand Luke*
Spencer Tracy/*Guess Who's Coming to Dinner*

1968
★ **Cliff Robertson**/*Charly*
Alan Arkin/*The Heart Is a Lonely Hunter*
Alan Bates/*The Fixer*
Ron Moody/*Oliver!*
Peter O'Toole/*The Lion in Winter*

1969
★ **John Wayne**/*True Grit*
Richard Burton/*Anne of the Thousand Days*
Dustin Hoffman/*Midnight Cowboy*
Peter O'Toole/*Goodbye, Mr. Chips*
Jon Voight/*Midnight Cowboy*

1970
★ **George C. Scott**/*Patton*
Melvyn Douglas/*I Never Sang for My Father*
James Earl Jones/*The Great White Hope*
Jack Nicholson/*Five Easy Pieces*
Ryan O'Neal/*Love Story*

1971
★ **Gene Hackman**/*The French Connection*
Peter Finch/*Sunday, Bloody Sunday*
Walter Matthau/*Kotch*
George C. Scott/*The Hospital*
Chaim Topol/*Fiddler on the Roof*

1972
★ **Marlon Brando**/*The Godfather*
Michael Caine/*Sleuth*
Peter O'Toole/*The Ruling Class*
Laurence Olivier/*Sleuth*
Paul Winfield/*Sounder*

1973
★ **Jack Lemmon**/*Save the Tiger*
Marlon Brando/*Last Tango in Paris*
Jack Nicholson/*The Last Detail*
Al Pacino/*Serpico*
Robert Redford/*The Sting*

1974
★ **Art Carney**/*Harry and Tonto*
Albert Finney/*Murder on the Orient Express*
Dustin Hoffman/*Lenny*
Jack Nicholson/*Chinatown*
Al Pacino/*The Godfather, Part 2*

1975
★ **Jack Nicholson**/*One Flew Over the Cuckoo's Nest*
Walter Matthau/*The Sunshine Boys*
Al Pacino/*Dog Day Afternoon*
Maximilian Schell/*The Man in the Glass Booth*
James Whitmore/*Give 'Em Hell, Harry!*

1976
★ **Peter Finch**/*Network*
Robert De Niro/*Taxi Driver*
Giancarlo Giannini/*Seven Beauties*
William Holden/*Network*
Sylvester Stallone/*Rocky*

1977
★ **Richard Dreyfuss**/*The Goodbye Girl*
Woody Allen/*Annie Hall*
Richard Burton/*Equus*
Marcello Mastroianni/*A Special Day*
John Travolta/*Saturday Night Fever*

1978
★ **Jon Voight**/*Coming Home*
Warren Beatty/*Heaven Can Wait*
Gary Busey/*The Buddy Holly Story*
Robert De Niro/*The Deer Hunter*
Laurence Olivier/*The Boys from Brazil*

1979
★ **Dustin Hoffman**/*Kramer vs. Kramer*
Jack Lemmon/*The China Syndrome*
Al Pacino/*And Justice for All*
Roy Scheider/*All That Jazz*
Peter Sellers/*Being There*

1980
★ **Robert De Niro**/*Raging Bull*
Robert Duvall/*The Great Santini*
John Hurt/*The Elephant Man*
Jack Lemmon/*Tribute*
Peter O'Toole/*The Stunt Man*

1981
★ **Henry Fonda**/*On Golden Pond*
Warren Beatty/*Reds*
Burt Lancaster/*Atlantic City*
Dudley Moore/*Arthur*
Paul Newman/*Absence of Malice*

1982
★ **Ben Kingsley**/*Gandhi*
Dustin Hoffman/*Tootsie*
Jack Lemmon/*Missing*
Paul Newman/*The Verdict*
Peter O'Toole/*My Favorite Year*

1983
★ **Robert Duvall**/*Tender Mercies*
Michael Caine/*Educating Rita*
Tom Conti/*Reuben, Reuben*
Tom Courtenay/*The Dresser*
Albert Finney/*The Dresser*

1984
★ **F. Murray Abraham**/*Amadeus*
Jeff Bridges/*Starman*
Albert Finney/*Under the Volcano*
Tom Hulce/*Amadeus*
Sam Waterston/*The Killing Fields*

1985
★ **William Hurt**/*Kiss of the Spider Woman*
Harrison Ford/*Witness*
James Garner/*Murphy's Romance*
Jack Nicholson/*Prizzi's Honor*
Jon Voight/*Runaway Train*

1986
★ **Paul Newman**/*The Color of Money*
Dexter Gordon/*Round Midnight*
Bob Hoskins/*Mona Lisa*
William Hurt/*Children of a Lesser God*
James Woods/*Salvador*

1987
★ **Michael Douglas**/*Wall Street*
William Hurt/*Broadcast News*
Marcello Mastroianni/*Dark Eyes*
Jack Nicholson/*Ironweed*
Robin Williams/*Good Morning, Vietnam*

1988
★ **Dustin Hoffman**/*Rain Man*
Gene Hackman/*Mississippi Burning*
Tom Hanks/*Big*
Edward James Olmos/*Stand and Deliver*
Max von Sydow/*Pelle the Conqueror*

1989
★ **Daniel Day-Lewis**/*My Left Foot*
Kenneth Branagh/*Henry V*
Tom Cruise/*Born on the Fourth of July*
Morgan Freeman/*Driving Miss Daisy*
Robin Williams/*Dead Poets Society*

1990
★ **Jeremy Irons**/*Reversal of Fortune*
Kevin Costner/*Dances with Wolves*
Robert De Niro/*Awakenings*
Gerard Depardieu/*Cyrano de Bergerac*
Richard Harris/*The Field*

1991
★ **Anthony Hopkins**/*The Silence of the Lambs*
Warren Beatty/*Bugsy*
Robert De Niro/*Cape Fear*
Nick Nolte/*The Prince of Tides*
Robin Williams/*The Fisher King*

1992
★ **Al Pacino**/*Scent of a Woman*
Robert Downey, Jr./*Chaplin*
Clint Eastwood/*Unforgiven*
Stephen Rea/*The Crying Game*
Denzel Washington/*Malcolm X*

1993
★ **Tom Hanks**/*Philadelphia*
Daniel Day-Lewis/*In the Name of the Father*
Laurence "Larry" Fishburne/*What's Love Got to Do with It?*
Anthony Hopkins/*The Remains of the Day*
Liam Neeson/*Schindler's List*

1994
★ **Tom Hanks**/*Forrest Gump*
Morgan Freeman/*The Shawshank Redemption*
Nigel Hawthorne/*The Madness of King George*
Paul Newman/*Nobody's Fool*
John Travolta/*Pulp Fiction*

1995
★ **Nicolas Cage**/*Leaving Las Vegas*
Richard Dreyfuss/*Mr. Holland's Opus*
Anthony Hopkins/*Nixon*
Sean Penn/*Dead Man Walking*
Massimo Troisi/*The Postman*

1996
★ **Geoffrey Rush**/*Shine*
Tom Cruise/*Jerry Maguire*
Ralph Fiennes/*The English Patient*
Woody Harrelson/*The People vs. Larry Flynt*
Billy Bob Thornton/*Sling Blade*

1997
★ **Jack Nicholson**/*As Good As It Gets*
Matt Damon/*Good Will Hunting*
Robert Duvall/*The Apostle*
Peter Fonda/*Ulee's Gold*
Dustin Hoffman/*Wag the Dog*

1998
★ **Roberto Benigni**/*Life Is Beautiful*
Tom Hanks/*Saving Private Ryan*
Ian McKellen/*Gods and Monsters*
Nick Nolte/*Affliction*
Edward Norton/*American History X*

1999
★ **Kevin Spacey**/*American Beauty*
Russell Crowe/*The Insider*
Richard Farnsworth/*The Straight Story*
Sean Penn/*Sweet and Lowdown*
Denzel Washington/*The Hurricane*

2000
★ **Russell Crowe**/*Gladiator*
Javier Bardem/*Before Night Falls*
Ed Harris/*Pollock*
Geoffrey Rush/*Quills*

2001
★ **Denzel Washington**/*Training Day*
Russell Crowe/*A Beautiful Mind*
Sean Penn/*I Am Sam*
Will Smith/*Ali*
Tom Wilkinson/*In the Bedroom*

ACTOR—SUPPORTING

1936
★ **Walter Brennan**/*Come and Get It*
Mischa Auer/*My Man Godfrey*
Stuart Erwin/*Pigskin Parade*
Basil Rathbone/*Romeo and Juliet*
Akim Tamiroff/*The General Died at Dawn*

1937
★ **Joseph Schildkraut**/*The Life of Emile Zola*
Ralph Bellamy/*The Awful Truth*
Thomas Mitchell/*The Hurricane*
H.B. Warner/*Lost Horizon*
Roland Young/*Topper*

1938
John Garfield/*Four Daughters*
Gene Lockhart/*Algiers*
Robert Morley/*Marie Antoinette*

1939
★ **Thomas Mitchell**/*Stagecoach*
Brian Aherne/*Juarez*
Harry Carey, Sr./*Mr. Smith Goes to Washington*
Brian Donlevy/*Beau Geste*
Claude Rains/*Mr. Smith Goes to Washington*

1940
★ **Walter Brennan**/*The Westerner*
Albert Bassermann/*Foreign Correspondent*
William Gargan/*They Knew What They Wanted*
Jack Oakie/*The Great Dictator*
James Stephenson/*The Letter*

1941
★ **Donald Crisp**/*How Green Was My Valley*
Walter Brennan/*Sergeant York*
Charles Coburn/*The Devil & Miss Jones*
James Gleason/*Here Comes Mr. Jordan*
Sydney Greenstreet/*The Maltese Falcon*

1942
★ **Van Heflin**/*Johnny Eager*
William Bendix/*Wake Island*
Walter Huston/*Yankee Doodle Dandy*
Frank Morgan/*Tortilla Flat*
Henry Travers/*Mrs. Miniver*

1943
★ **Charles Coburn**/*The More the Merrier*
Charles Bickford/*The Song of Bernadette*
J. Carrol Naish/*Sahara*
Claude Rains/*Casablanca*
Akim Tamiroff/*For Whom the Bell Tolls*

1944
★ **Barry Fitzgerald**/*Going My Way*
Hume Cronyn/*The Seventh Cross*
Claude Rains/*Mr. Skeffington*
Clifton Webb/*Laura*
Monty Woolley/*Since You Went Away*

1945
★ **James Dunn**/*A Tree Grows in Brooklyn*
Michael Chekhov/*Spellbound*
John Dall/*The Corn Is Green*

1946
★ **Harold Russell**/*The Best Years of Our Lives*
William Demarest/*The Jolson Story*
Claude Rains/*Notorious*
Clifton Webb/*The Razor's Edge*

1947
★ **Edmund Gwenn**/*Miracle on 34th Street*
Charles Bickford/*The Farmer's Daughter*
Robert Ryan/*Crossfire*
Richard Widmark/*Kiss of Death*

1948
★ **Walter Huston**/*Treasure of the Sierra Madre*
Charles Bickford/*Johnny Belinda*
Jose Ferrer/*Joan of Arc*
Oscar Homolka/*I Remember Mama*

1949
★ **Dean Jagger**/*Twelve o'Clock High*
John Ireland/*All the King's Men*
Arthur Kennedy/*Champion*
Ralph Richardson/*The Heiress*
James Whitmore/*Battleground*

1950
★ **George Sanders**/*All About Eve*
Jeff Chandler/*Broken Arrow*
Sam Jaffe/*The Asphalt Jungle*
Erich von Stroheim/*Sunset Boulevard*

1951
★ **Karl Malden**/*A Streetcar Named Desire*
Leo Genn/*Quo Vadis*
Peter Ustinov/*Quo Vadis*

1952
★ **Anthony Quinn**/*Viva Zapata!*
Arthur Hunnicutt/*The Big Sky*
Victor McLaglen/*The Quiet Man*
Jack Palance/*Sudden Fear*

1953
★ **Frank Sinatra**/*From Here to Eternity*
Eddie Albert/*Roman Holiday*
Jack Palance/*Shane*
Robert Strauss/*Stalag 17*
Brandon de Wilde/*Shane*

1954
★ **Edmond O'Brien**/*The Barefoot Contessa*
Lee J. Cobb/*On the Waterfront*
Karl Malden/*On the Waterfront*
Rod Steiger/*On the Waterfront*
Tom Tully/*The Caine Mutiny*

1955
★ **Jack Lemmon**/*Mister Roberts*
Joe Mantell/*Marty*
Sal Mineo/*Rebel without a Cause*
Arthur O'Connell/*Picnic*

1956
★ **Anthony Quinn**/*Lust for Life*
Don Murray/*Bus Stop*
Anthony Perkins/*Friendly Persuasion*
Robert Stack/*Written on the Wind*

1957
★ **Red Buttons**/*Sayonara*
Sessue Hayakawa/*The Bridge on the River Kwai*
Arthur Kennedy/*Peyton Place*
Russ Tamblyn/*Peyton Place*

1958
★ **Burl Ives**/*The Big Country*
Theodore Bikel/*The Defiant Ones*

★ = winner

Lee J. Cobb/*The Brothers Karamazov*
Arthur Kennedy/*Some Came Running*
Gig Young/*Teacher's Pet*

1959

★ Hugh Griffith/*Ben-Hur*
Arthur O'Connell/*Anatomy of a Murder*
George C. Scott/*Anatomy of a Murder*
Robert Vaughn/*The Young Philadelphians*
Ed Wynn/*The Diary of Anne Frank*

1960

★ Peter Ustinov/*Spartacus*
Jack Kruschen/*The Apartment*
Sal Mineo/*Exodus*
Chill Wills/*The Alamo*

1961

★ George Chakiris/*West Side Story*
Montgomery Clift/*Judgment at Nuremberg*
Peter Falk/*Pocketful of Miracles*
Jackie Gleason/*The Hustler*
George C. Scott/*The Hustler*

1962

★ Ed Begley, Sr./*Sweet Bird of Youth*
Victor Buono/*What Ever Happened to Baby Jane?*
Telly Savalas/*Birdman of Alcatraz*
Omar Sharif/*Lawrence of Arabia*
Terence Stamp/*Billy Budd*

1963

★ Melvyn Douglas/*Hud*
Bobby Darin/*Captain Newman, M.D.*
Hugh Griffith/*Tom Jones*
John Huston/*The Cardinal*

1964

★ Peter Ustinov/*Topkapi*
John Gielgud/*Becket*
Stanley Holloway/*My Fair Lady*
Edmond O'Brien/*Seven Days in May*
Lee Tracy/*The Best Man*

1965

★ Martin Balsam/*A Thousand Clowns*
Ian Bannen/*The Flight of the Phoenix*
Tom Courtenay/*Doctor Zhivago*
Michael Dunn/*Ship of Fools*
Frank Finlay/*Othello*

1966

★ Walter Matthau/*The Fortune Cookie*
Mako/*The Sand Pebbles*
James Mason/*Georgy Girl*
George Segal/*Who's Afraid of Virginia Woolf?*
Robert Shaw/*A Man for All Seasons*

1967

★ George Kennedy/*Cool Hand Luke*
John Cassavetes/*The Dirty Dozen*
Gene Hackman/*Bonnie & Clyde*
Cecil Kellaway/*Guess Who's Coming to Dinner*
Michael J. Pollard/*Bonnie & Clyde*

1968

★ Jack Albertson/*The Subject Was Roses*
Seymour Cassel/*Faces*
Daniel Massey/*Star!*
Jack Wild/*Oliver!*
Gene Wilder/*The Producers*

1969

★ Gig Young/*They Shoot Horses, Don't They?*
Rupert Crosse/*The Reivers*
Elliott Gould/*Bob & Carol & Ted & Alice*
Jack Nicholson/*Easy Rider*
Anthony Quayle/*Anne of the Thousand Days*

1970

★ John Mills/*Ryan's Daughter*
Richard S. Castellano/*Lovers and Other Strangers*
Chief Dan George/*Little Big Man*
Gene Hackman/*I Never Sang for My Father*
John Marley/*Love Story*

1971

★ Ben Johnson/*The Last Picture Show*
Jeff Bridges/*The Last Picture Show*
Leonard Frey/*Fiddler on the Roof*
Richard Jaeckel/*Sometimes a Great Notion*
Roy Scheider/*The French Connection*

1972

★ Joel Grey/*Cabaret*
Eddie Albert/*The Heartbreak Kid*
James Caan/*The Godfather*
Robert Duvall/*The Godfather*
Al Pacino/*The Godfather*

1973

★ John Houseman/*The Paper Chase*
Vincent Gardenia/*Bang the Drum Slowly*
Jack Gilford/*Save the Tiger*
Jason Miller/*The Exorcist*
Randy Quaid/*The Last Detail*

1974

★ Robert De Niro/*The Godfather, Part 2*
Fred Astaire/*The Towering Inferno*
Jeff Bridges/*Thunderbolt & Lightfoot*
Michael V. Gazzo/*The Godfather, Part 2*
Lee Strasberg/*The Godfather, Part 2*

1975

★ George Burns/*The Sunshine Boys*
Brad Dourif/*One Flew Over the Cuckoo's Nest*
Burgess Meredith/*The Day of the Locust*
Chris Sarandon/*Dog Day Afternoon*
Jack Warden/*Shampoo*

1976

★ Jason Robards, Jr./*All the President's Men*
Ned Beatty/*Network*
Burgess Meredith/*Rocky*
Laurence Olivier/*Marathon Man*
Burt Young/*Rocky*

1977

★ Jason Robards, Jr./*Julia*
Mikhail Baryshnikov/*The Turning Point*
Peter Firth/*Equus*
Alec Guinness/*Star Wars*
Maximilian Schell/*Julia*

1978

★ Christopher Walken/*The Deer Hunter*
Bruce Dern/*Coming Home*
Richard Farnsworth/*Comes a Horseman*
John Hurt/*Midnight Express*
Jack Warden/*Heaven Can Wait*

1979

★ Melvyn Douglas/*Being There*
Robert Duvall/*Apocalypse Now*
Frederic Forrest/*The Rose*
Justin Henry/*Kramer vs. Kramer*
Mickey Rooney/*The Black Stallion*

1980

★ Timothy Hutton/*Ordinary People*
Judd Hirsch/*Ordinary People*
Michael O'Keefe/*The Great Santini*
Joe Pesci/*Raging Bull*
Jason Robards, Jr./*Melvin and Howard*

1981

★ John Gielgud/*Arthur*
James Coco/*Only When I Laugh*
Ian Holm/*Chariots of Fire*
Jack Nicholson/*Reds*
Howard E. Rollins, Jr./*Ragtime*

1982

★ Louis Gossett, Jr./*An Officer and a Gentleman*
Charles Durning/*The Best Little Whorehouse in Texas*
John Lithgow/*The World According to Garp*
James Mason/*The Verdict*
Robert Preston/*Victor/Victoria*

1983

★ Jack Nicholson/*Terms of Endearment*
Charles Durning/*To Be or Not to Be*
John Lithgow/*Terms of Endearment*
Sam Shepard/*The Right Stuff*
Rip Torn/*Cross Creek*

1984

★ Haing S. Ngor/*The Killing Fields*
Adolph Caesar/*A Soldier's Story*
John Malkovich/*Places in the Heart*
Noriyuki "Pat" Morita/*The Karate Kid*
Ralph Richardson/*Greystoke: The Legend of Tarzan, Lord of the Apes*

1985

★ Don Ameche/*Cocoon*
Klaus Maria Brandauer/*Out of Africa*
William Hickey/*Prizzi's Honor*
Robert Loggia/*The Jagged Edge*
Eric Roberts/*Runaway Train*

1986

★ Michael Caine/*Hannah and Her Sisters*
Tom Berenger/*Platoon*
Willem Dafoe/*Platoon*
Denholm Elliott/*A Room with a View*
Dennis Hopper/*Hoosiers*

1987

★ Sean Connery/*The Untouchables*
Albert Brooks/*Broadcast News*
Morgan Freeman/*Street Smart*
Vincent Gardenia/*Moonstruck*
Denzel Washington/*Cry Freedom*

1988

★ Kevin Kline/*A Fish Called Wanda*
Alec Guinness/*Little Dorrit, Film 1: Nobody's Fault*
Martin Landau/*Tucker: The Man and His Dream*
River Phoenix/*Running on Empty*
Dean Stockwell/*Married to the Mob*

1989

★ Denzel Washington/*Glory*
Danny Aiello/*Do the Right Thing*
Dan Aykroyd/*Driving Miss Daisy*
Marlon Brando/*A Dry White Season*
Martin Landau/*Crimes & Misdemeanors*

1990

★ Joe Pesci/*Goodfellas*
Bruce Davison/*Longtime Companion*
Andy Garcia/*The Godfather, Part 3*
Graham Greene/*Dances with Wolves*
Al Pacino/*Dick Tracy*

1991

★ Jack Palance/*City Slickers*
Tommy Lee Jones/*JFK*
Harvey Keitel/*Bugsy*
Ben Kingsley/*Bugsy*
Michael Lerner/*Barton Fink*

1992

★ Gene Hackman/*Unforgiven*
Jaye Davidson/*The Crying Game*
Jack Nicholson/*A Few Good Men*
Al Pacino/*Glengarry Glen Ross*
David Paymer/*Mr. Saturday Night*

1993

★ Tommy Lee Jones/*The Fugitive*
Leonardo DiCaprio/*What's Eating Gilbert Grape*
Ralph Fiennes/*Schindler's List*
John Malkovich/*In the Line of Fire*
Pete Postlethwaite/*In the Name of the Father*

1994

★ Martin Landau/*Ed Wood*
Samuel L. Jackson/*Pulp Fiction*
Chazz Palminteri/*Bullets over Broadway*
Paul Scofield/*Quiz Show*
Gary Sinise/*Forrest Gump*

1995

★ Kevin Spacey/*The Usual Suspects*
James Cromwell/*Babe*
Ed Harris/*Apollo 13*
Brad Pitt/*12 Monkeys*
Tim Roth/*Rob Roy*

1996

★ Cuba Gooding, Jr./*Jerry Maguire*
William H. Macy/*Fargo*
Armin Mueller-Stahl/*Shine*
Edward Norton/*Primal Fear*
James Woods/*Ghosts of Mississippi*

1997

★ Robin Williams/*Good Will Hunting*
Robert Forster/*Jackie Brown*
Anthony Hopkins/*Amistad*
Greg Kinnear/*As Good As It Gets*
Burt Reynolds/*Boogie Nights*

1998

★ James Coburn/*Affliction*
Robert Duvall/*A Civil Action*
Ed Harris/*The Truman Show*
Geoffrey Rush/*Shakespeare in Love*
Billy Bob Thornton/*A Simple Plan*

1999

★ Michael Caine/*The Cider House Rules*
Tom Cruise/*Magnolia*
Michael Clarke Duncan/*The Green Mile*
Jude Law/*The Talented Mr. Ripley*
Haley Joel Osment/*The Sixth Sense*

2000

★ Benicio Del Toro/*Traffic*
Jeff Bridges/*The Contender*
Willem Dafoe/*Shadow of the Vampire*
Albert Finney/*Erin Brockovich*
Joaquin Rafael (Leaf) Phoenix/*Gladiator*

2001

★ Jim Broadbent/*Iris*
Ethan Hawke/*Training Day*
Ben Kingsley/*Sexy Beast*
Ian McKellen/*Lord of the Rings 1: The Fellowship of the Rings*
Jon Voight/*Ali*

ACTRESS

1928

★ Janet Gaynor/*Sunrise*
Gloria Swanson/*Sadie Thompson*

1929

★ Mary Pickford/*Coquette*
Bessie Love/*Broadway Melody*

1930

★ Norma Shearer/*The Divorcee*
Greta Garbo/*Anna Christie*
Greta Garbo/*Romance*

1931

★ Marie Dressler/*Min & Bill*
Marlene Dietrich/*Morocco*
Irene Dunne/*Cimarron*
Norma Shearer/*A Free Soul*

1932

★ Helen Hayes/*The Sin of Madelon Claudet*
Lynn Fontanne/*The Guardsman*

1933

★ Katharine Hepburn/*Morning Glory*
May Robson/*Lady for a Day*
Diana Wynyard/*Cavalcade*

1934

★ Claudette Colbert/*It Happened One Night*
Grace Moore/*One Night of Love*
Norma Shearer/*The Barretts of Wimpole Street*

1935

★ Bette Davis/*Dangerous*
Katharine Hepburn/*Alice Adams*
Miriam Hopkins/*Becky Sharp*

1936

★ Luise Rainer/*The Great Ziegfeld*
Irene Dunne/*Theodora Goes Wild*
Carole Lombard/*My Man Godfrey*
Norma Shearer/*Romeo and Juliet*

1937

★ Luise Rainer/*The Good Earth*
Irene Dunne/*The Awful Truth*
Greta Garbo/*Camille*
Janet Gaynor/*A Star Is Born*
Barbara Stanwyck/*Stella Dallas*

1938

★ Bette Davis/*Jezebel*
Wendy Hiller/*Pygmalion*
Norma Shearer/*Marie Antoinette*
Margaret Sullavan/*Three Comrades*

1939

★ Vivien Leigh/*Gone with the Wind*
Bette Davis/*Dark Victory*
Irene Dunne/*Love Affair*
Greta Garbo/*Ninotchka*
Greer Garson/*Goodbye, Mr. Chips*

1940

★ Ginger Rogers/*Kitty Foyle*
Bette Davis/*The Letter*
Joan Fontaine/*Rebecca*
Katharine Hepburn/*The Philadelphia Story*
Martha Scott/*Our Town*

1941

★ Joan Fontaine/*Suspicion*
Bette Davis/*The Little Foxes*
Greer Garson/*Blossoms in the Dust*
Barbara Stanwyck/*Ball of Fire*

1942

★ Greer Garson/*Mrs. Miniver*
Bette Davis/*Now, Voyager*
Katharine Hepburn/*Woman of the Year*
Teresa Wright/*The Pride of the Yankees*

1943

★ Jennifer Jones/*The Song of Bernadette*
Jean Arthur/*The More the Merrier*
Ingrid Bergman/*For Whom the Bell Tolls*
Greer Garson/*Madame Curie*

1944

★ Ingrid Bergman/*Gaslight*
Claudette Colbert/*Since You Went Away*
Bette Davis/*Mr. Skeffington*
Greer Garson/*Mrs. Parkington*
Barbara Stanwyck/*Double Indemnity*

1945

★ Joan Crawford/*Mildred Pierce*
Ingrid Bergman/*The Bells of St. Mary's*
Greer Garson/*The Valley of Decision*
Gene Tierney/*Leave Her to Heaven*

1946

★ Olivia de Havilland/*To Each His Own*
Celia Johnson/*Brief Encounter*
Jennifer Jones/*Duel in the Sun*
Rosalind Russell/*Sister Kenny*
Jane Wyman/*The Yearling*

1947

★ Loretta Young/*The Farmer's Daughter*
Joan Crawford/*The Possessed*
Susan Hayward/*Smash-Up: The Story of a Woman*
Dorothy McGuire/*Gentleman's Agreement*

1948

★ Jane Wyman/*Johnny Belinda*
Ingrid Bergman/*Joan of Arc*
Irene Dunne/*I Remember Mama*
Barbara Stanwyck/*Sorry, Wrong Number*
Olivia de Havilland/*The Snake Pit*

★ = winner

ACTRESS *cont.*

1949
★ **Olivia de Havilland/***The Heiress*
Jeanne Crain/*Pinky*
Loretta Young/*Come to the Stable*

1950
★ **Judy Holliday/***Born Yesterday*
Anne Baxter/*All About Eve*
Bette Davis/*All About Eve*
Gloria Swanson/*Sunset Boulevard*

1951
★ **Vivien Leigh/***A Streetcar Named Desire*
Katharine Hepburn/*The African Queen*
Eleanor Parker/*Detective Story*
Shelley Winters/*A Place in the Sun*

1952
★ **Shirley Booth/***Come Back, Little Sheba*
Joan Crawford/*Sudden Fear*
Julie Harris/*The Member of the Wedding*

1953
★ **Audrey Hepburn/***Roman Holiday*
Leslie Caron/*Lili*
Ava Gardner/*Mogambo*
Deborah Kerr/*From Here to Eternity*
Maggie McNamara/*The Moon Is Blue*

1954
★ **Grace Kelly/***Country Girl*
Dorothy Dandridge/*Carmen Jones*
Judy Garland/*A Star Is Born*
Audrey Hepburn/*Sabrina*
Jane Wyman/*Magnificent Obsession*

1955
★ **Anna Magnani/***The Rose Tattoo*
Susan Hayward/*I'll Cry Tomorrow*
Katharine Hepburn/*Summertime*
Jennifer Jones/*Love Is a Many-Splendored Thing*
Eleanor Parker/*Interrupted Melody*

1956
★ **Ingrid Bergman/***Anastasia*
Carroll Baker/*Baby Doll*
Katharine Hepburn/*The Rainmaker*
Nancy Kelly/*The Bad Seed*
Deborah Kerr/*The King and I*

1957
★ **Joanne Woodward/***The Three Faces of Eve*
Deborah Kerr/*Heaven Knows, Mr. Allison*
Elizabeth Taylor/*Raintree County*
Lana Turner/*Peyton Place*

1958
★ **Susan Hayward/***I Want to Live!*
Deborah Kerr/*Separate Tables*
Shirley MacLaine/*Some Came Running*
Rosalind Russell/*Auntie Mame*
Elizabeth Taylor/*Cat on a Hot Tin Roof*

1959
★ **Simone Signoret/***Room at the Top*
Doris Day/*Pillow Talk*
Audrey Hepburn/*The Nun's Story*
Katharine Hepburn/*Suddenly, Last Summer*
Elizabeth Taylor/*Suddenly, Last Summer*

1960
★ **Elizabeth Taylor/***Butterfield 8*
Greer Garson/*Sunrise at Campobello*
Deborah Kerr/*The Sundowners*
Shirley MacLaine/*The Apartment*
Melina Mercouri/*Never on Sunday*

1961
★ **Sophia Loren/***Two Women*
Audrey Hepburn/*Breakfast at Tiffany's*
Piper Laurie/*The Hustler*
Geraldine Page/*Summer and Smoke*
Natalie Wood/*Splendor in the Grass*

1962
★ **Anne Bancroft/***The Miracle Worker*
Bette Davis/*What Ever Happened to Baby Jane?*
Katharine Hepburn/*Long Day's Journey into Night*
Geraldine Page/*Sweet Bird of Youth*
Lee Remick/*Days of Wine and Roses*

1963
★ **Patricia Neal/***Hud*
Shirley MacLaine/*Irma La Douce*
Rachel Roberts/*This Sporting Life*
Natalie Wood/*Love with the Proper Stranger*

1964
★ **Julie Andrews/***Mary Poppins*
Anne Bancroft/*The Pumpkin Eater*
Sophia Loren/*Marriage Italian Style*
Debbie Reynolds/*The Unsinkable Molly Brown*
Kim Stanley/*Seance on a Wet Afternoon*

1965
★ **Julie Christie/***Darling*
Julie Andrews/*The Sound of Music*
Samantha Eggar/*The Collector*
Elizabeth Hartman/*A Patch of Blue*
Simone Signoret/*Ship of Fools*

1966
★ **Elizabeth Taylor/***Who's Afraid of Virginia Woolf?*
Anouk Aimee/*A Man and a Woman*
Ida Kaminska/*The Shop on Main Street*
Lynn Redgrave/*Georgy Girl*
Vanessa Redgrave/*Morgan: A Suitable Case for Treatment*

1967
★ **Katharine Hepburn/***Guess Who's Coming to Dinner*
Anne Bancroft/*The Graduate*
Faye Dunaway/*Bonnie & Clyde*
Audrey Hepburn/*Wait until Dark*

1968
★ **Katharine Hepburn/***The Lion in Winter*
★ **Barbra Streisand/***Funny Girl*
Patricia Neal/*The Subject Was Roses*
Vanessa Redgrave/*Isadora*
Joanne Woodward/*Rachel, Rachel*

1969
★ **Maggie Smith/***The Prime of Miss Jean Brodie*
Genevieve Bujold/*Anne of the Thousand Days*
Jane Fonda/*They Shoot Horses, Don't They?*
Liza Minnelli/*The Sterile Cuckoo*
Jean Simmons/*The Happy Ending*

1970
★ **Glenda Jackson/***Women in Love*
Jane Alexander/*The Great White Hope*
Ali MacGraw/*Love Story*
Sarah Miles/*Ryan's Daughter*
Carrie Snodgress/*Diary of a Mad Housewife*

1971
★ **Jane Fonda/***Klute*
Julie Christie/*McCabe & Mrs. Miller*
Glenda Jackson/*Sunday, Bloody Sunday*
Vanessa Redgrave/*Mary, Queen of Scots*
Janet Suzman/*Nicholas and Alexandra*

1972
★ **Liza Minnelli/***Cabaret*
Diana Ross/*Lady Sings the Blues*
Maggie Smith/*Travels with My Aunt*
Cicely Tyson/*Sounder*
Liv Ullmann/*The Emigrants*

1973
★ **Glenda Jackson/***A Touch of Class*
Ellen Burstyn/*The Exorcist*
Marsha Mason/*Cinderella Liberty*
Barbra Streisand/*The Way We Were*
Joanne Woodward/*Summer Wishes, Winter Dreams*

1974
★ **Ellen Burstyn/***Alice Doesn't Live Here Anymore*
Faye Dunaway/*Chinatown*
Valerie Perrine/*Lenny*
Gena Rowlands/*A Woman under the Influence*

1975
★ **Louise Fletcher/***One Flew Over the Cuckoo's Nest*
Isabelle Adjani/*The Story of Adele H.*
Ann-Margret/*Tommy*
Glenda Jackson/*Hedda*
Carol Kane/*Hester Street*

1976
★ **Faye Dunaway/***Network*
Marie-Christine Barrault/*Cousin, Cousine*
Talia Shire/*Rocky*
Sissy Spacek/*Carrie*
Liv Ullmann/*Face to Face*

1977
★ **Diane Keaton/***Annie Hall*
Anne Bancroft/*The Turning Point*
Jane Fonda/*Julia*
Shirley MacLaine/*The Turning Point*
Marsha Mason/*The Goodbye Girl*

1978
★ **Jane Fonda/***Coming Home*
Ingrid Bergman/*Autumn Sonata*
Ellen Burstyn/*Same Time, Next Year*
Jill Clayburgh/*An Unmarried Woman*
Geraldine Page/*Interiors*

1979
★ **Sally Field/***Norma Rae*
Jill Clayburgh/*Starting Over*
Jane Fonda/*The China Syndrome*
Marsha Mason/*Chapter Two*
Bette Midler/*The Rose*

1980
★ **Sissy Spacek/***Coal Miner's Daughter*
Ellen Burstyn/*Resurrection*
Goldie Hawn/*Private Benjamin*
Mary Tyler Moore/*Ordinary People*
Gena Rowlands/*Gloria*

1981
★ **Katharine Hepburn/***On Golden Pond*
Diane Keaton/*Reds*
Marsha Mason/*Only When I Laugh*
Susan Sarandon/*Atlantic City*
Meryl Streep/*The French Lieutenant's Woman*

1982
★ **Meryl Streep/***Sophie's Choice*
Julie Andrews/*Victor/Victoria*
Jessica Lange/*Frances*
Sissy Spacek/*Missing*
Debra Winger/*An Officer and a Gentleman*

1983
★ **Shirley MacLaine/***Terms of Endearment*
Jane Alexander/*Testament*
Meryl Streep/*Silkwood*
Julie Walters/*Educating Rita*
Debra Winger/*Terms of Endearment*

1984
★ **Sally Field/***Places in the Heart*
Judy Davis/*A Passage to India*
Jessica Lange/*Country*
Vanessa Redgrave/*The Bostonians*
Sissy Spacek/*The River*

1985
★ **Geraldine Page/***The Trip to Bountiful*
Anne Bancroft/*Agnes of God*
Whoopi Goldberg/*The Color Purple*
Jessica Lange/*Sweet Dreams*
Meryl Streep/*Out of Africa*

1986
★ **Marlee Matlin/***Children of a Lesser God*
Jane Fonda/*The Morning After*
Sissy Spacek/*Crimes of the Heart*
Kathleen Turner/*Peggy Sue Got Married*
Sigourney Weaver/*Aliens*

1987
★ **Cher/***Moonstruck*
Glenn Close/*Fatal Attraction*
Holly Hunter/*Broadcast News*
Sally Kirkland/*Anna*
Meryl Streep/*Ironweed*

1988
★ **Jodie Foster/***The Accused*
Glenn Close/*Dangerous Liaisons*
Melanie Griffith/*Working Girl*
Meryl Streep/*A Cry in the Dark*
Sigourney Weaver/*Gorillas in the Mist*

1989
★ **Jessica Tandy/***Driving Miss Daisy*
Isabelle Adjani/*Camille Claudel*
Pauline Collins/*Shirley Valentine*
Jessica Lange/*Music Box*
Michelle Pfeiffer/*The Fabulous Baker Boys*

1990
★ **Kathy Bates/***Misery*
Anjelica Huston/*The Grifters*
Julia Roberts/*Pretty Woman*
Meryl Streep/*Postcards from the Edge*
Joanne Woodward/*Mr. & Mrs. Bridge*

1991
★ **Jodie Foster/***The Silence of the Lambs*
Geena Davis/*Thelma & Louise*
Laura Dern/*Rambling Rose*
Bette Midler/*For the Boys*
Susan Sarandon/*Thelma & Louise*

1992
★ **Emma Thompson/***Howard's End*
Catherine Deneuve/*Indochine*
Mary McDonnell/*Passion Fish*
Michelle Pfeiffer/*Love Field*
Susan Sarandon/*Lorenzo's Oil*

1993
★ **Holly Hunter/***The Piano*
Angela Bassett/*What's Love Got to Do with It?*
Stockard Channing/*Six Degrees of Separation*
Emma Thompson/*The Remains of the Day*
Debra Winger/*Shadowlands*

1994
★ **Jessica Lange/***Blue Sky*
Jodie Foster/*Nell*
Miranda Richardson/*Tom & Viv*
Winona Ryder/*Little Women*
Susan Sarandon/*The Client*

1995
★ **Susan Sarandon/***Dead Man Walking*
Elisabeth Shue/*Leaving Las Vegas*
Sharon Stone/*Casino*
Meryl Streep/*The Bridges of Madison County*
Emma Thompson/*Sense and Sensibility*

1996
★ **Frances McDormand/***Fargo*
Brenda Blethyn/*Secrets and Lies*
Diane Keaton/*Marvin's Room*
Kristin Scott Thomas/*The English Patient*
Emily Watson/*Breaking the Waves*

1997
★ **Helen Hunt/***As Good As It Gets*
Helena Bonham Carter/*The Wings of the Dove*
Julie Christie/*Afterglow*
Judi Dench/*Mrs. Brown*
Kate Winslet/*Titanic*

1998
★ **Gwyneth Paltrow/***Shakespeare in Love*
Cate Blanchett/*Elizabeth*
Fernanda Montenegro/*Central Station*
Meryl Streep/*One True Thing*
Emily Watson/*Hilary and Jackie*

1999
★ **Hilary Swank/***Boys Don't Cry*
Annette Bening/*American Beauty*
Janet McTeer/*Tumbleweeds*
Julianne Moore/*The End of the Affair*
Meryl Streep/*Music of the Heart*

2000
★ **Julia Roberts/***Erin Brockovich*
Joan Allen/*The Contender*
Juliette Binoche/*Chocolat*
Ellen Burstyn/*Requiem for a Dream*
Laura Linney/*You Can Count On Me*

2001
★ **Halle Berry/***Monster's Ball*
Judi Dench/*Iris*
Nicole Kidman/*Moulin Rouge*
Sissy Spacek/*In the Bedroom*
Renee Zellweger/*Bridget Jones's Diary*

ACTRESS—SUPPORTING

1936
★ **Gale Sondergaard/***Anthony Adverse*
Beulah Bondi/*The Gorgeous Hussy*
Alice Brady/*My Man Godfrey*
Bonita Granville/*These Three*
Maria Ouspenskaya/*Dodsworth*

1937
★ **Alice Brady/***In Old Chicago*
Andrea Leeds/*Stage Door*
Anne Shirley/*Stella Dallas*
Claire Trevor/*Dead End*
May Whitty/*Night Must Fall*

1938
★ **Fay Bainter/***Jezebel*
Beulah Bondi/*Of Human Hearts*
Spring Byington/*You Can't Take It with You*
Milza Korjus/*The Great Waltz*

1939
★ **Hattie McDaniel/***Gone with the Wind*
Geraldine Fitzgerald/*Wuthering Heights*
Edna May Oliver/*Drums Along the Mohawk*
Maria Ouspenskaya/*Love Affair*
Olivia de Havilland/*Gone with the Wind*

1940
★ **Jane Darwell/***The Grapes of Wrath*
Judith Anderson/*Rebecca*
Ruth Hussey/*The Philadelphia Story*
Barbara O'Neil/*All This and Heaven Too*
Marjorie Rambeau/*Primrose Path*

1941
★ **Mary Astor/***The Great Lie*
Sara Allgood/*How Green Was My Valley*
Patricia Collinge/*The Little Foxes*
Teresa Wright/*The Little Foxes*
Margaret Wycherly/*Sergeant York*

1942
★ **Teresa Wright/***Mrs. Miniver*
Gladys Cooper/*Now, Voyager*
Agnes Moorehead/*The Magnificent Ambersons*
Susan Peters/*Random Harvest*
May Whitty/*Mrs. Miniver*

1943
★ **Katina Paxinou/***For Whom the Bell Tolls*

★ = winner

Gladys Cooper/*The Song of Bernadette*
Paulette Goddard/*So Proudly We Hail*
Anne Revere/*The Song of Bernadette*
Lucile Watson/*Watch on the Rhine*

1944
★ **Ethel Barrymore**/*None But the Lonely Heart*
Jennifer Jones/*Since You Went Away*
Angela Lansbury/*Gaslight*
Aline MacMahon/*Dragon Seed*
Agnes Moorehead/*Mrs. Parkington*

1945
★ **Anne Revere**/*National Velvet*
Eve Arden/*Mildred Pierce*
Ann Blyth/*Mildred Pierce*
Angela Lansbury/*Picture of Dorian Gray*
Joan Lorring/*The Corn Is Green*

1946
★ **Anne Baxter**/*The Razor's Edge*
Ethel Barrymore/*The Spiral Staircase*
Lillian Gish/*Duel in the Sun*
Flora Robson/*Saratoga Trunk*
Gale Sondergaard/*Anna and the King of Siam*

1947
★ **Celeste Holm**/*Gentleman's Agreement*
Ethel Barrymore/*The Paradine Case*
Gloria Grahame/*Crossfire*
Marjorie Main/*Egg and I*
Anne Revere/*Gentleman's Agreement*

1948
★ **Claire Trevor**/*Key Largo*
Barbara Bel Geddes/*I Remember Mama*
Ellen Corby/*I Remember Mama*
Agnes Moorehead/*Johnny Belinda*
Jean Simmons/*Hamlet*

1949
★ **Mercedes McCambridge**/*All the King's Men*
Ethel Barrymore/*Pinky*
Celeste Holm/*Come to the Stable*
Elsa Lanchester/*Come to the Stable*
Ethel Waters/*Pinky*

1950
★ **Josephine Hull**/*Harvey*
Celeste Holm/*All About Eve*
Nancy Olson/*Sunset Boulevard*
Thelma Ritter/*All About Eve*

1951
★ **Kim Hunter**/*A Streetcar Named Desire*
Lee Grant/*Detective Story*

1952
★ **Gloria Grahame**/*The Bad and the Beautiful*
Jean Hagen/*Singin' in the Rain*
Colette Marchand/*Moulin Rouge*
Terry Moore/*Come Back, Little Sheba*

1953
★ **Donna Reed**/*From Here to Eternity*
Grace Kelly/*Mogambo*
Marjorie Rambeau/*Torch Song*
Thelma Ritter/*Pickup on South Street*

1954
★ **Eva Marie Saint**/*On the Waterfront*
Nina Foch/*Executive Suite*
Katy Jurado/*Broken Lance*

1955
★ **Jo Van Fleet**/*East of Eden*
Betsy Blair/*Marty*
Peggy Lee/*Pete Kelly's Blues*
Marisa Pavan/*The Rose Tattoo*
Natalie Wood/*Rebel without a Cause*

1956
★ **Dorothy Malone**/*Written on the Wind*
Mildred Dunnock/*Baby Doll*
Eileen Heckart/*The Bad Seed*
Mercedes McCambridge/*Giant*
Patty McCormack/*The Bad Seed*

1957
★ **Miyoshi Umeki**/*Sayonara*
Elsa Lanchester/*Witness for the Prosecution*
Hope Lange/*Peyton Place*
Diane Varsi/*Peyton Place*

1958
★ **Wendy Hiller**/*Separate Tables*
Peggy Cass/*Auntie Mame*
Martha Hyer/*Some Came Running*
Maureen Stapleton/*Lonelyhearts*
Cara Williams/*The Defiant Ones*

1959
★ **Shelley Winters**/*The Diary of Anne Frank*
Hermione Baddeley/*Room at the Top*
Susan Kohner/*Imitation of Life*
Juanita Moore/*Imitation of Life*
Thelma Ritter/*Pillow Talk*

1960
★ **Shirley Jones**/*Elmer Gantry*
Glynis Johns/*The Sundowners*
Janet Leigh/*Psycho*

1961
★ **Rita Moreno**/*West Side Story*
Fay Bainter/*The Children's Hour*
Judy Garland/*Judgment at Nuremberg*
Lotte Lenya/*Roman Spring of Mrs. Stone*
Una Merkel/*Summer and Smoke*

1962
★ **Patty Duke**/*The Miracle Worker*
Mary Badham/*To Kill a Mockingbird*
Shirley Knight/*Sweet Bird of Youth*
Angela Lansbury/*The Manchurian Candidate*
Thelma Ritter/*Birdman of Alcatraz*

1963
★ **Margaret Rutherford**/*The V.I.P.'s*
Diane Cilento/*Tom Jones*
Edith Evans/*Tom Jones*
Joyce Redman/*Tom Jones*
Lilia Skala/*Lilies of the Field*

1964
★ **Lila Kedrova**/*Zorba the Greek*
Gladys Cooper/*My Fair Lady*
Edith Evans/*The Chalk Garden*
Grayson Hall/*The Night of the Iguana*
Agnes Moorehead/*Hush, Hush, Sweet Charlotte*

1965
★ **Shelley Winters**/*A Patch of Blue*
Ruth Gordon/*Inside Daisy Clover*
Joyce Redman/*Othello*
Maggie Smith/*Othello*
Peggy Wood/*The Sound of Music*

1966
★ **Sandy Dennis**/*Who's Afraid of Virginia Woolf?*
Wendy Hiller/*A Man for All Seasons*
Jocelyn Lagarde/*Hawaii*
Vivien Merchant/*Alfie*
Geraldine Page/*You're a Big Boy Now*

1967
★ **Estelle Parsons**/*Bonnie & Clyde*
Carol Channing/*Thoroughly Modern Millie*
Mildred Natwick/*Barefoot in the Park*
Beah Richards/*Guess Who's Coming to Dinner*
Katharine Ross/*The Graduate*

1968
★ **Ruth Gordon**/*Rosemary's Baby*
Lynn Carlin/*Faces*
Sondra Locke/*The Heart Is a Lonely Hunter*
Kay Medford/*Funny Girl*
Estelle Parsons/*Rachel, Rachel*

1969
★ **Goldie Hawn**/*Cactus Flower*
Cathy Burns/*Last Summer*
Dyan Cannon/*Bob & Carol & Ted & Alice*
Sylvia Miles/*Midnight Cowboy*
Susannah York/*They Shoot Horses, Don't They?*

1970
★ **Helen Hayes**/*Airport*
Karen Black/*Five Easy Pieces*
Sally Kellerman/*M*A*S*H*
Maureen Stapleton/*Airport*

1971
★ **Cloris Leachman**/*The Last Picture Show*
Ann-Margret/*Carnal Knowledge*
Ellen Burstyn/*The Last Picture Show*
Margaret Leighton/*The Go-Between*

1972
★ **Eileen Heckart**/*Butterflies Are Free*
Jeannie Berlin/*The Heartbreak Kid*
Geraldine Page/*Pete 'n' Tillie*
Susan Tyrrell/*Fat City*
Shelley Winters/*The Poseidon Adventure*

1973
★ **Tatum O'Neal**/*Paper Moon*
Linda Blair/*The Exorcist*
Candy Clark/*American Graffiti*
Madeline Kahn/*Paper Moon*
Sylvia Sidney/*Summer Wishes, Winter Dreams*

1974
★ **Ingrid Bergman**/*Murder on the Orient Express*
Valentina Cortese/*Day for Night*
Madeline Kahn/*Blazing Saddles*
Diane Ladd/*Alice Doesn't Live Here Anymore*
Talia Shire/*The Godfather, Part 2*

1975
★ **Lee Grant**/*Shampoo*
Ronee Blakley/*Nashville*
Sylvia Miles/*Farewell, My Lovely*
Lily Tomlin/*Nashville*
Brenda Vaccaro/*Once Is Not Enough*

1976
★ **Beatrice Straight**/*Network*
Jane Alexander/*All the President's Men*
Jodie Foster/*Taxi Driver*
Lee Grant/*Voyage of the Damned*
Piper Laurie/*Carrie*

1977
★ **Vanessa Redgrave**/*Julia*
Leslie Browne/*The Turning Point*
Quinn Cummings/*The Goodbye Girl*
Melinda Dillon/*Close Encounters of the Third Kind*
Tuesday Weld/*Looking for Mr. Goodbar*

1978
★ **Maggie Smith**/*California Suite*
Dyan Cannon/*Heaven Can Wait*
Penelope Milford/*Coming Home*
Maureen Stapleton/*Interiors*
Meryl Streep/*The Deer Hunter*

1979
★ **Meryl Streep**/*Kramer vs. Kramer*
Jane Alexander/*Kramer vs. Kramer*
Barbara Barrie/*Breaking Away*
Candice Bergen/*Starting Over*
Mariel Hemingway/*Manhattan*

1980
★ **Mary Steenburgen**/*Melvin and Howard*
Eileen Brennan/*Private Benjamin*
Eva LeGallienne/*Resurrection*
Cathy Moriarty/*Raging Bull*
Diana Scarwid/*Inside Moves*

1981
★ **Maureen Stapleton**/*Reds*
Melinda Dillon/*Absence of Malice*
Jane Fonda/*On Golden Pond*
Joan Hackett/*Only When I Laugh*
Elizabeth McGovern/*Ragtime*

1982
★ **Jessica Lange**/*Tootsie*
Glenn Close/*The World According to Garp*
Teri Garr/*Tootsie*
Kim Stanley/*Frances*
Lesley Ann Warren/*Victor/Victoria*

1983
★ **Linda Hunt**/*The Year of Living Dangerously*
Cher/*Silkwood*
Glenn Close/*The Big Chill*
Amy Irving/*Yentl*
Alfre Woodard/*Cross Creek*

1984
★ **Peggy Ashcroft**/*A Passage to India*
Glenn Close/*The Natural*
Lindsay Crouse/*Places in the Heart*
Christine Lahti/*Swing Shift*
Geraldine Page/*The Pope of Greenwich Village*

1985
★ **Anjelica Huston**/*Prizzi's Honor*
Margaret Avery/*The Color Purple*
Amy Madigan/*Twice in a Lifetime*
Meg Tilly/*Agnes of God*
Oprah Winfrey/*The Color Purple*

1986
★ **Dianne Wiest**/*Hannah and Her Sisters*
Tess Harper/*Crimes of the Heart*
Piper Laurie/*Children of a Lesser God*
Mary Elizabeth Mastrantonio/*The Color of Money*
Maggie Smith/*A Room with a View*

1987
★ **Olympia Dukakis**/*Moonstruck*
Norma Aleandro/*Gaby: A True Story*
Anne Archer/*Fatal Attraction*
Anne Ramsey/*Throw Momma from the Train*
Ann Sothern/*The Whales of August*

1988
★ **Geena Davis**/*The Accidental Tourist*
Joan Cusack/*Working Girl*
Frances McDormand/*Mississippi Burning*
Michelle Pfeiffer/*Dangerous Liaisons*
Sigourney Weaver/*Working Girl*

1989
★ **Brenda Fricker**/*My Left Foot*
Anjelica Huston/*Enemies, a Love Story*
Lena Olin/*Enemies, a Love Story*
Julia Roberts/*Steel Magnolias*
Dianne Wiest/*Parenthood*

1990
★ **Whoopi Goldberg**/*Ghost*
Annette Bening/*The Grifters*
Lorraine Bracco/*Goodfellas*
Diane Ladd/*Wild at Heart*
Mary McDonnell/*Dances with Wolves*

1991
★ **Mercedes Ruehl**/*The Fisher King*
Diane Ladd/*Rambling Rose*
Juliette Lewis/*Cape Fear*
Kate Nelligan/*The Prince of Tides*
Jessica Tandy/*Fried Green Tomatoes*

1992
★ **Marisa Tomei**/*My Cousin Vinny*
Judy Davis/*Husbands and Wives*
Joan Plowright/*Enchanted April*
Vanessa Redgrave/*Howard's End*
Miranda Richardson/*Damage*

1993
★ **Anna Paquin**/*The Piano*
Holly Hunter/*The Firm*
Rosie Perez/*Fearless*
Winona Ryder/*The Age of Innocence*
Emma Thompson/*In the Name of the Father*

1994
★ **Dianne Wiest**/*Bullets over Broadway*
Rosemary Harris/*Tom & Viv*
Helen Mirren/*The Madness of King George*
Uma Thurman/*Pulp Fiction*
Jennifer Tilly/*Bullets over Broadway*

1995
★ **Mira Sorvino**/*Mighty Aphrodite*
Joan Allen/*Nixon*
Kathleen Quinlan/*Apollo 13*
Mare Winningham/*Georgia*
Kate Winslet/*Sense and Sensibility*

1996
★ **Juliette Binoche**/*The English Patient*
Joan Allen/*The Crucible*
Lauren Bacall/*The Mirror Has Two Faces*
Barbara Hershey/*Portrait of a Lady*
Marianne Jean-Baptiste/*Secrets and Lies*

1997
★ **Kim Basinger**/*L.A. Confidential*
Joan Cusack/*In and Out*
Minnie Driver/*Good Will Hunting*
Julianne Moore/*Boogie Nights*
Gloria Stuart/*Titanic*

1998
★ **Judi Dench**/*Shakespeare in Love*
Kathy Bates/*Primary Colors*
Brenda Blethyn/*Little Voice*
Rachel Griffiths/*Hilary and Jackie*
Lynn Redgrave/*Gods and Monsters*

1999
★ **Angelina Jolie**/*Girl, Interrupted*
Toni Collette/*The Sixth Sense*
Catherine Keener/*Being John Malkovich*
Samantha Morton/*Sweet and Lowdown*
Chloe Sevigny/*Boys Don't Cry*

2000
★ **Marcia Gay Harden**/*Pollock*
Judi Dench/*Chocolat*
Kate Hudson/*Almost Famous*
Frances McDormand/*Almost Famous*
Julie Walters/*Billy Elliot*

2001
★ **Jennifer Connelly**/*A Beautiful Mind*
Helen Mirren/*Gosford Park*
Maggie Smith/*Gosford Park*
Marisa Tomei/*In the Bedroom*
Kate Winslet/*Iris*

ART DIRECTION

1957
★ *Sayonara*
Funny Face
Les Girls
Pal Joey
Raintree County

1958
★ *Gigi*
Auntie Mame
Bell, Book and Candle
Vertigo

1967
★ *Camelot*
Doctor Dolittle
Guess Who's Coming to Dinner
The Taming of the Shrew
Thoroughly Modern Millie

1968
★ *Oliver!*
The Shoes of the Fisherman
Star!
2001: A Space Odyssey

★ = winner

ART DIRECTION cont.

War and Peace

1969
★ Hello, Dolly!
Anne of the Thousand Days
Sweet Charity
They Shoot Horses, Don't They?

1970
★ Patton
Airport
Molly Maguires
Scrooge
Tora! Tora! Tora!

1971
★ Nicholas and Alexandra
The Andromeda Strain
Bedknobs and Broomsticks
Fiddler on the Roof
Mary, Queen of Scots

1972
★ Cabaret
Lady Sings the Blues
The Poseidon Adventure
Travels with My Aunt
Young Winston

1973
★ The Sting
Brother Sun, Sister Moon
The Exorcist
Tom Sawyer
The Way We Were

1974
★ The Godfather, Part 2
Chinatown
Earthquake
The Island at the Top of the World
The Towering Inferno

1975
★ Barry Lyndon
The Hindenburg
The Man Who Would Be King
Shampoo
The Sunshine Boys

1976
★ All the President's Men
The Incredible Sarah
The Last Tycoon
Logan's Run
The Shootist

1977
★ Star Wars
Airport '77
Close Encounters of the Third Kind
The Spy Who Loved Me
The Turning Point

1978
★ Heaven Can Wait
Brink's Job
California Suite
Interiors
The Wiz

1979
★ All That Jazz
Alien
Apocalypse Now
The China Syndrome
Star Trek: The Motion Picture

1980
★ Tess
Altered States
Coal Miner's Daughter
The Elephant Man
The Empire Strikes Back
Kagemusha

1981
★ Raiders of the Lost Ark
The French Lieutenant's Woman
Heaven's Gate
Ragtime
Reds

1982
★ Gandhi
Annie
Blade Runner
Victor/Victoria

1983
★ Fanny and Alexander
Return of the Jedi
The Right Stuff
Terms of Endearment
Yentl

1984
★ Amadeus
The Cotton Club
The Natural
A Passage to India
2010: The Year We Make Contact

1985
★ Out of Africa
Brazil
The Color Purple
Ran
Witness

1986
★ A Room with a View
Aliens
The Color of Money
Hannah and Her Sisters
The Mission

1987
★ The Last Emperor
Empire of the Sun
Hope and Glory
Radio Days
The Untouchables

1988
★ Dangerous Liaisons
Beaches
Rain Man
Tucker: The Man and His Dream
Who Framed Roger Rabbit

1989
★ Batman
The Abyss
The Adventures of Baron Munchausen
Driving Miss Daisy
Glory

1990
★ Dick Tracy
Cyrano de Bergerac
Dances with Wolves
The Godfather, Part 3
Hamlet

1991
★ Bugsy
Barton Fink
The Fisher King
Hook
The Prince of Tides

1992
★ Howard's End
Bram Stoker's Dracula
Chaplin
Toys
Unforgiven

1993
★ Schindler's List
Addams Family Values
The Age of Innocence
Orlando
The Remains of the Day

1994
★ The Madness of King George
Bullets over Broadway
Forrest Gump
Interview with the Vampire
Legends of the Fall

1995
★ Restoration
Apollo 13
Babe
A Little Princess
Richard III

1996
★ The English Patient
The Birdcage
Evita
Hamlet
William Shakespeare's Romeo and Juliet

1997
★ Titanic
Gattaca
Kundun
L.A. Confidential
Men in Black

1998
★ Shakespeare in Love
Elizabeth
Pleasantville
Saving Private Ryan
What Dreams May Come

1999
★ Sleepy Hollow
Anna and the King
The Cider House Rules
The Talented Mr. Ripley
Topsy Turvy

2000
★ Crouching Tiger, Hidden Dragon
Dr. Seuss' How the Grinch Stole Christmas
Gladiator
Quills

2001
★ Moulin Rouge
Amelie
Gosford Park
Harry Potter and the Sorcerer's Stone
Lord of the Rings 1: The Fellowship of the Rings

ART DIRECTION (B&W)

1946
★ Anna and the King of Siam

1947
★ Great Expectations

1948
★ Hamlet
Johnny Belinda

1949
★ The Heiress
Come to the Stable
Madame Bovary

1950
★ Sunset Boulevard
All About Eve

1951
★ A Streetcar Named Desire
La Ronde

1952
★ The Bad and the Beautiful
Carrie
Rashomon
Viva Zapata!

1953
★ Julius Caesar
Martin Luther
Roman Holiday
Titanic

1954
★ On the Waterfront
Country Girl
Executive Suite
Le Plaisir
Sabrina

1955
★ The Rose Tattoo
Blackboard Jungle
I'll Cry Tomorrow
The Man with the Golden Arm
Marty

1956
★ Somebody Up There Likes Me
Seven Samurai
Solid Gold Cadillac

1959
★ The Diary of Anne Frank
Career
The Last Angry Man
Some Like It Hot
Suddenly, Last Summer

1960
★ The Apartment
The Facts of Life
Psycho

1961
★ The Hustler
The Absent-Minded Professor
The Children's Hour
Judgment at Nuremberg
La Dolce Vita

1962
★ To Kill a Mockingbird
Days of Wine and Roses
The Longest Day
Period of Adjustment

1963
8 1/2
Hud
Love with the Proper Stranger

1964
★ Zorba the Greek
The Americanization of Emily
Hush, Hush, Sweet Charlotte
The Night of the Iguana
Seven Days in May

1965
★ Ship of Fools
King Rat
A Patch of Blue
The Slender Thread
The Spy Who Came in from the Cold

1966
★ Who's Afraid of Virginia Woolf?
The Fortune Cookie
The Gospel According to St. Matthew
Is Paris Burning?

ART DIRECTION (COLOR)

1947
★ Black Narcissus
Life with Father

1948
★ The Red Shoes
Joan of Arc

1949
★ Little Women
Adventures of Don Juan

1950
★ Samson and Delilah
Annie Get Your Gun
Destination Moon

1951
★ An American in Paris
David and Bathsheba
Quo Vadis
The Tales of Hoffmann

1952
★ Moulin Rouge
Hans Christian Andersen
The Merry Widow
The Quiet Man
The Snows of Kilimanjaro

1953
★ The Robe
Knights of the Round Table
Lili
Young Bess

1954
★ 20,000 Leagues under the Sea
Brigadoon
Desiree
Red Garters
A Star Is Born

1955
★ Picnic
Daddy Long Legs
Guys and Dolls
Love Is a Many-Splendored Thing
To Catch a Thief

1956
★ The King and I
Around the World in 80 Days
Giant
Lust for Life
The Ten Commandments

1959
★ Ben-Hur
Journey to the Center of the Earth
North by Northwest
Pillow Talk

1960
★ Spartacus
Cimarron
It Started in Naples
Sunrise at Campobello

1961
★ West Side Story
Breakfast at Tiffany's
El Cid
Flower Drum Song
Summer and Smoke

1962
★ Lawrence of Arabia
The Music Man
Mutiny on the Bounty
That Touch of Mink
The Wonderful World of the Brothers Grimm

1963
★ Cleopatra
The Cardinal
Come Blow Your Horn
How the West Was Won
Tom Jones

1964
★ My Fair Lady
Becket
Mary Poppins
The Unsinkable Molly Brown

1965
★ Doctor Zhivago
The Agony and the Ecstasy
The Greatest Story Ever Told
Inside Daisy Clover
The Sound of Music

1966
★ Fantastic Voyage
Gambit
Juliet of the Spirits
The Oscar
The Sand Pebbles

CINEMATOGRAPHY

1928
★ Sunrise
My Best Girl
Sadie Thompson
The Tempest

1929
★ White Shadows in the South Seas
Our Dancing Daughters

1930
All Quiet on the Western Front
Anna Christie
Hell's Angels

1931
★ Tabu: A Story of the South Seas
Cimarron
Morocco
Svengali

1932
★ Shanghai Express
Arrowsmith
Dr. Jekyll and Mr. Hyde

1933
★ A Farewell to Arms
The Sign of the Cross

1934
★ Cleopatra

1935
★ A Midsummer Night's Dream
Barbary Coast
The Crusades
Les Miserables

1936
★ Anthony Adverse
The General Died at Dawn
The Gorgeous Hussy

1937
★ The Good Earth
Dead End

1938
★ The Great Waltz
Algiers
Jezebel
Mad About Music
Vivacious Lady
You Can't Take It with You
The Young in Heart

1957
★ The Bridge on the River Kwai
An Affair to Remember
Funny Face
Peyton Place
Sayonara

1959
James Wong Howe/The Old Man and the Sea

1967
★ Bonnie & Clyde
Camelot
Doctor Dolittle
The Graduate
In Cold Blood

1968
★ Romeo and Juliet
Funny Girl
Ice Station Zebra
Oliver!
Star!

1969
★ Butch Cassidy and the Sundance Kid
Anne of the Thousand Days
Bob & Carol & Ted & Alice
Hello, Dolly!
Marooned

1970
★ Ryan's Daughter
Airport
Patton
Tora! Tora! Tora!
Women in Love

1971
★ Fiddler on the Roof
The French Connection
The Last Picture Show
Nicholas and Alexandra
Summer of '42

1972
★ Cabaret
Butterflies Are Free
The Poseidon Adventure
1776
Travels with My Aunt

1973
★ Cries and Whispers
The Exorcist
Jonathan Livingston Seagull
The Sting
The Way We Were

1974
★ The Towering Inferno
Chinatown
Earthquake
Lenny
Murder on the Orient Express

1975
★ Barry Lyndon
The Day of the Locust
Funny Lady
The Hindenburg
One Flew Over the Cuckoo's Nest

1976
★ Bound for Glory
King Kong
Logan's Run
Network
A Star Is Born

1977
★ Close Encounters of the Third Kind
Islands in the Stream
Julia
Looking for Mr. Goodbar
The Turning Point

1978
★ Days of Heaven
The Deer Hunter
Heaven Can Wait
Same Time, Next Year
The Wiz

1979
★ Apocalypse Now
All That Jazz
The Black Hole
Kramer vs. Kramer
1941

★ = winner

1980
★ Tess
The Blue Lagoon
Coal Miner's Daughter
The Formula
Raging Bull

1981
★ Reds
Excalibur
On Golden Pond
Ragtime
Raiders of the Lost Ark

1982
★ Gandhi
Das Boot
E.T.: The Extra-Terrestrial
Sophie's Choice
Tootsie

1983
★ Fanny and Alexander
Flashdance
The Right Stuff
WarGames
Zelig

1984
★ The Killing Fields
Amadeus
The Natural
A Passage to India
The River

1985
★ Out of Africa
The Color Purple
Murphy's Romance
Ran
Witness

1986
★ The Mission
Peggy Sue Got Married
Platoon
A Room with a View
Star Trek 4: The Voyage Home

1987
★ The Last Emperor
Broadcast News
Empire of the Sun
Hope and Glory
Matewan

1988
★ Mississippi Burning
Rain Man
Tequila Sunrise
The Unbearable Lightness of Being
Who Framed Roger Rabbit

1989
★ Glory
The Abyss
Blaze
Born on the Fourth of July
The Fabulous Baker Boys

1990
★ Dances with Wolves
Avalon
Dick Tracy
The Godfather, Part 3
Henry & June

1991
★ JFK
Bugsy
The Prince of Tides
Terminator 2: Judgment Day
Thelma & Louise

1992
★ A River Runs Through It
Hoffa
Howard's End
The Lover
Unforgiven

1993
★ Schindler's List
Farewell My Concubine
The Fugitive
The Piano
Searching for Bobby Fischer

1994
★ Legends of the Fall
Forrest Gump
The Shawshank Redemption
Trois Couleurs: Rouge
Wyatt Earp

1995
★ Braveheart
Batman Forever
A Little Princess
Sense and Sensibility
Shanghai Triad

1996
★ The English Patient
Evita
Fargo
Fly Away Home
Michael Collins

1997
★ Titanic
Amistad
Kundun
L.A. Confidential
The Wings of the Dove

1998
★ Saving Private Ryan
A Civil Action
Elizabeth
The Thin Red Line

1999
★ American Beauty
The End of the Affair
The Insider
Sleepy Hollow
Snow Falling on Cedars

2000
★ Crouching Tiger, Hidden Dragon
Gladiator
O Brother Where Art Thou?
The Patriot

2001
★ Lord of the Rings 1: The Fellowship of the Rings
Amelie
Black Hawk Down
The Man Who Wasn't There
Moulin Rouge

CINEMATOGRAPHY (B&W)

1939
★ Wuthering Heights
First Love
Gunga Din
Intermezzo
Juarez
Only Angels Have Wings
The Rains Came
Stagecoach

1940
★ Rebecca
Abe Lincoln in Illinois
All This and Heaven Too
Boom Town
Foreign Correspondent
The Letter
The Long Voyage Home
Waterloo Bridge

1941
★ How Green Was My Valley
The Chocolate Soldier
Citizen Kane
Dr. Jekyll and Mr. Hyde
Here Comes Mr. Jordan
Sergeant York
Sun Valley Serenade
Sundown
That Hamilton Woman

1942
★ Mrs. Miniver
Kings Row
The Magnificent Ambersons
The Pride of the Yankees
Talk of the Town

1943
★ The Song of Bernadette
Air Force
Casablanca
Five Graves to Cairo
The Human Comedy
Madame Curie
The North Star
Sahara
So Proudly We Hail

1944
★ Laura
Double Indemnity
Dragon Seed
Gaslight
Going My Way
Lifeboat
Since You Went Away
Thirty Seconds Over Tokyo
The Uninvited
The White Cliffs of Dover

1945
★ Picture of Dorian Gray
The Keys of the Kingdom
The Lost Weekend
Mildred Pierce
Spellbound

1946
★ Anna and the King of Siam

1947
★ Great Expectations
The Ghost and Mrs. Muir
Green Dolphin Street

1948
★ The Naked City
I Remember Mama
Johnny Belinda
Portrait of Jennie

1949
★ Battleground
Champion
Come to the Stable
The Heiress

1950
★ The Third Man
All About Eve
The Asphalt Jungle
Sunset Boulevard

1951
★ A Place in the Sun
Strangers on a Train
A Streetcar Named Desire

1952
★ The Bad and the Beautiful
The Big Sky
Sudden Fear

1953
★ From Here to Eternity
Julius Caesar
Martin Luther
Roman Holiday

1954
★ On the Waterfront
Country Girl
Executive Suite
Sabrina

1955
★ The Rose Tattoo
Blackboard Jungle
I'll Cry Tomorrow
Marty
Queen Bee

1956
★ Somebody Up There Likes Me
Baby Doll
The Bad Seed
The Harder They Fall

1958
★ The Defiant Ones
Desire Under the Elms
I Want to Live!
Separate Tables
The Young Lions

1959
★ The Diary of Anne Frank
Anatomy of a Murder
Career
The Gazebo
Some Like It Hot
The Young Philadelphians

1960
The Apartment
The Facts of Life
Inherit the Wind
Psycho

1961
★ The Hustler
The Absent-Minded Professor
The Children's Hour
Judgment at Nuremberg
One, Two, Three

1962
★ The Longest Day
Birdman of Alcatraz
To Kill a Mockingbird
Two for the Seesaw
What Ever Happened to Baby Jane?

1963
★ Hud
The Balcony
Lilies of the Field
Love with the Proper Stranger

1964
★ Zorba the Greek
The Americanization of Emily
Hush, Hush, Sweet Charlotte
The Night of the Iguana

1965
★ Ship of Fools
In Harm's Way
King Rat
Morituri
A Patch of Blue

1966
★ Who's Afraid of Virginia Woolf?
The Fortune Cookie
Georgy Girl
Is Paris Burning?
Seconds

CINEMATOGRAPHY (COLOR)

1939
★ Gone with the Wind
Drums Along the Mohawk
The Four Feathers
The Private Lives of Elizabeth & Essex
The Wizard of Oz

1940
★ The Thief of Bagdad
Bitter Sweet
The Blue Bird
Down Argentine Way
Northwest Passage

1941
★ Blood and Sand
Billy the Kid
Blossoms in the Dust
Dive Bomber
Louisiana Purchase

1942
★ The Black Swan
Arabian Nights
Captains of the Clouds
The Jungle Book
Reap the Wild Wind
To the Shores of Tripoli

1943
★ The Phantom of the Opera
For Whom the Bell Tolls
Heaven Can Wait
Hello, Frisco, Hello
Lassie, Come Home
Thousands Cheer

1944
★ Wilson
Cover Girl
Meet Me in St. Louis

1945
★ Leave Her to Heaven
Anchors Aweigh
National Velvet
A Song to Remember
The Spanish Main

1946
★ The Yearling
The Jolson Story

1947
★ Black Narcissus
Life with Father
Mother Wore Tights

1948
★ Joan of Arc
The Loves of Carmen
The Three Musketeers

1949
★ She Wore a Yellow Ribbon
The Barkleys of Broadway
Jolson Sings Again
Little Women

1950
★ King Solomon's Mines
Annie Get Your Gun
Broken Arrow
The Flame & the Arrow
Samson and Delilah

1951
★ An American in Paris
David and Bathsheba
Quo Vadis
Show Boat
When Worlds Collide

1952
★ The Quiet Man
Hans Christian Andersen
Ivanhoe
Million Dollar Mermaid
The Snows of Kilimanjaro

1953
★ Shane
All the Brothers Were Valiant
Beneath the 12-Mile Reef
Lili
The Robe

1954
★ Three Coins in the Fountain
The Egyptian
Rear Window
Seven Brides for Seven Brothers
The Silver Chalice

1955
★ To Catch a Thief
Guys and Dolls
Love Is a Many-Splendored Thing
A Man Called Peter
Oklahoma!

1956
★ Around the World in 80 Days
The Eddy Duchin Story
The King and I
The Ten Commandments
War and Peace

1958
★ Gigi
Auntie Mame
Cat on a Hot Tin Roof
South Pacific

1959
★ Ben-Hur
The Five Pennies
The Nun's Story

1960
★ Spartacus
The Alamo
Butterfield 8
Exodus

1961
★ West Side Story
Fanny
Flower Drum Song
One-Eyed Jacks

1962
★ Lawrence of Arabia
Gypsy
Hatari!
Mutiny on the Bounty
The Wonderful World of the Brothers Grimm

1963
★ Cleopatra
The Cardinal
How the West Was Won
Irma La Douce
It's a Mad, Mad, Mad, Mad World

1964
★ My Fair Lady
Becket
Cheyenne Autumn
Mary Poppins
The Unsinkable Molly Brown

1965
★ Doctor Zhivago
The Agony and the Ecstasy
The Great Race
The Greatest Story Ever Told
The Sound of Music

1966
★ A Man for All Seasons
Fantastic Voyage
Hawaii
The Professionals
The Sand Pebbles

COSTUME DESIGN

1957
★ Les Girls
An Affair to Remember
Funny Face
Pal Joey
Raintree County

1958
★ Gigi
Bell, Book and Candle
The Buccaneer
Some Came Running

1967
★ Camelot
Bonnie & Clyde
The Happiest Millionaire
The Taming of the Shrew
Thoroughly Modern Millie

1968
★ Romeo and Juliet
The Lion in Winter
Oliver!
Planet of the Apes
Star!

1969
★ Anne of the Thousand Days
Hello, Dolly!
Sweet Charity
They Shoot Horses, Don't They?

1970
★ Cromwell
Airport
Darling Lili
Scrooge

1971
★ Nicholas and Alexandra
Bedknobs and Broomsticks
Death in Venice
Mary, Queen of Scots
What's the Matter with Helen?

1972
★ Travels with My Aunt
The Godfather
Lady Sings the Blues
The Poseidon Adventure
Young Winston

1973
★ The Sting
Cries and Whispers
Tom Sawyer
The Way We Were

1974
★ The Great Gatsby
Chinatown
Daisy Miller
The Godfather, Part 2
Murder on the Orient Express

1975
★ Barry Lyndon
The Four Musketeers
Funny Lady
The Magic Flute
The Man Who Would Be King

1976
Bound for Glory
The Incredible Sarah
The Passover Plot
The Seven-Per-Cent Solution

1977
★ Star Wars
Airport '77
Julia
A Little Night Music
The Other Side of Midnight

1978
★ Death on the Nile
Days of Heaven
The Swarm
The Wiz

1979
★ All That Jazz
Agatha
Butch and Sundance: The Early Days
The Europeans

★ = winner

COSTUME DESIGN *cont.*

La Cage aux Folles

1980

★ Tess
The Elephant Man
My Brilliant Career
Somewhere in Time
When Time Ran Out

1981

★ Chariots of Fire
The French Lieutenant's Woman
Pennies from Heaven
Ragtime
Reds

1982

★ Gandhi
Sophie's Choice
Tron
Victor/Victoria

1983

★ Fanny and Alexander
Cross Creek
Heart Like a Wheel
The Return of Martin Guerre
Zelig

1984

★ Amadeus
The Bostonians
A Passage to India
Places in the Heart
2010: The Year We Make Contact

1985

★ Ran
The Color Purple
The Journey of Natty Gann
Out of Africa
Prizzi's Honor

1986

★ A Room with a View
The Mission
Otello
Peggy Sue Got Married
Pirates

1987

★ The Last Emperor
The Dead
Empire of the Sun
Maurice
The Untouchables

1988

★ Dangerous Liaisons
Coming to America
A Handful of Dust
Sunset
Tucker: The Man and His Dream

1989

★ Henry V
The Adventures of Baron Munchausen
Driving Miss Daisy
Harlem Nights
Valmont

1990

★ Cyrano de Bergerac
Avalon
Dances with Wolves
Dick Tracy
Hamlet

1991

★ Bugsy
The Addams Family
Barton Fink
Hook
Madame Bovary

1992

★ Bram Stoker's Dracula
Enchanted April
Howard's End
Malcolm X
Toys

1993

★ The Age of Innocence
Orlando
The Piano
The Remains of the Day
Schindler's List

1994

★ The Adventures of Priscilla, Queen of the Desert
Bullets over Broadway
Little Women
Maverick
Queen Margot

1995

★ Restoration
Braveheart
Richard III
Sense and Sensibility
12 Monkeys

1996

★ The English Patient
Angels and Insects
Emma
Hamlet
Portrait of a Lady

1997

★ Titanic
Amistad
Kundun
Oscar and Lucinda
The Wings of the Dove

1998

★ Shakespeare in Love
Beloved
Elizabeth
Pleasantville
Velvet Goldmine

1999

★ Topsy Turvy
Anna and the King
The Talented Mr. Ripley
Titus

2000

★ Gladiator
Crouching Tiger, Hidden Dragon
Dr. Seuss' How the Grinch Stole Christmas
102 Dalmatians
Quills

2001

★ Moulin Rouge
The Affair of the Necklace
Gosford Park
Harry Potter and the Sorcerer's Stone
Lord of the Rings 1: The Fellowship of the Rings

COSTUME DESIGN (B&W)

1948

★ Hamlet

1949

★ The Heiress

1950

★ All About Eve
Born Yesterday
The Magnificent Yankee

1951

★ A Place in the Sun
A Streetcar Named Desire

1952

★ The Bad and the Beautiful
Affair in Trinidad
Carrie
Sudden Fear

1953

★ Roman Holiday
From Here to Eternity

1954

★ Sabrina
The Earrings of Madame De...
Executive Suite
Indiscretion of an American Wife
It Should Happen to You

1955

★ I'll Cry Tomorrow
The Pickwick Papers
Queen Bee
The Rose Tattoo
Ugetsu

1956

★ Solid Gold Cadillac
Seven Samurai

1959

★ Some Like It Hot
Career
The Diary of Anne Frank
The Young Philadelphians

1960

★ The Facts of Life
Never on Sunday
The Rise and Fall of Legs Diamond
Seven Thieves
The Virgin Spring

1961

★ La Dolce Vita
The Children's Hour
Judgment at Nuremberg
Yojimbo

1962

Days of Wine and Roses
The Man Who Shot Liberty Valance
The Miracle Worker
Phaedra
What Ever Happened to Baby Jane?

1963

★ 8 1/2
Love with the Proper Stranger
The Stripper
Toys in the Attic

1964

★ The Night of the Iguana
Hush, Hush, Sweet Charlotte
Kisses for My President

1965

★ Darling
Morituri
Ship of Fools
The Slender Thread

1966

★ Who's Afraid of Virginia Woolf?
The Gospel According to St. Matthew
Morgan: A Suitable Case for Treatment

COSTUME DESIGN (COLOR)

1948

★ Joan of Arc

1949

★ Adventures of Don Juan

1950

★ Samson and Delilah
That Forsyte Woman

1951

★ An American in Paris
David and Bathsheba
The Great Caruso
Quo Vadis
The Tales of Hoffmann

1952

★ Moulin Rouge
The Greatest Show on Earth
Hans Christian Andersen
The Merry Widow

1953

★ The Robe
The Band Wagon
How to Marry a Millionaire
Young Bess

1954

★ Gate of Hell
Brigadoon
Desiree
A Star Is Born
There's No Business Like Show Business

1955

★ Love Is a Many-Splendored Thing
Guys and Dolls
Interrupted Melody
To Catch a Thief
The Virgin Queen

1956

★ The King and I
Around the World in 80 Days
Giant
The Ten Commandments
War and Peace

1959

★ Ben-Hur
The Best of Everything
The Five Pennies

1960

★ Spartacus
Can-Can
Midnight Lace
Sunrise at Campobello

1961

★ West Side Story
Babes in Toyland
Back Street
Flower Drum Song
Pocketful of Miracles

1962

★ The Wonderful World of the Brothers Grimm
Bon Voyage!
Gypsy
The Music Man
My Geisha

1963

★ Cleopatra
The Cardinal
How the West Was Won
A New Kind of Love

1964

★ My Fair Lady
Becket
Mary Poppins
The Unsinkable Molly Brown

1965

★ Doctor Zhivago
The Agony and the Ecstasy
The Greatest Story Ever Told
Inside Daisy Clover
The Sound of Music

1966

★ A Man for All Seasons
Gambit
Hawaii
Juliet of the Spirits
The Oscar

DIRECTOR

1928

Charlie Chaplin/*The Circus*
King Vidor/*The Crowd*
Ted Wilde/*Speedy*

1929

Harry Beaumont/*Broadway Melody*

1930

★ **Lewis Milestone/***All Quiet on the Western Front*
Clarence Brown/*Anna Christie*
Clarence Brown/*Romance*
Robert Z. Leonard/*The Divorcee*
King Vidor/*Hallelujah!*

1931

Clarence Brown/*A Free Soul*
Lewis Milestone/*The Front Page*
Wesley Ruggles/*Cimarron*
Josef von Sternberg/*Morocco*

1932

King Vidor/*The Champ*
Josef von Sternberg/*Shanghai Express*

1933

★ **Frank Lloyd/***Cavalcade*
Frank Capra/*Lady for a Day*
George Cukor/*Little Women*

1934

★ **Frank Capra/***It Happened One Night*
Victor Schertzinger/*One Night of Love*
Woodbridge S. Van Dyke/*The Thin Man*

1935

★ **John Ford/***The Informer*
Henry Hathaway/*The Lives of a Bengal Lancer*
Frank Lloyd/*Mutiny on the Bounty*

1936

★ **Frank Capra/***Mr. Deeds Goes to Town*
Gregory La Cava/*My Man Godfrey*
Robert Z. Leonard/*The Great Ziegfeld*
Woodbridge S. Van Dyke/*San Francisco*
William Wyler/*Dodsworth*

1937

★ **Leo McCarey/***The Awful Truth*
William Dieterle/*The Life of Emile Zola*
Sidney Franklin/*The Good Earth*
Gregory La Cava/*Stage Door*
William A. Wellman/*A Star Is Born*

1938

★ **Frank Capra/***You Can't Take It with You*
Michael Curtiz/*Angels with Dirty Faces*
Michael Curtiz/*Four Daughters*
Norman Taurog/*Boys Town*
King Vidor/*The Citadel*

1939

★ **Victor Fleming/***Gone with the Wind*
Frank Capra/*Mr. Smith Goes to Washington*
John Ford/*Stagecoach*
Sam Wood/*Goodbye, Mr. Chips*
William Wyler/*Wuthering Heights*

1940

★ **John Ford/***The Grapes of Wrath*
George Cukor/*The Philadelphia Story*
Alfred Hitchcock/*Rebecca*
Sam Wood/*Kitty Foyle*
William Wyler/*The Letter*

1941

★ **John Ford/***How Green Was My Valley*
Alexander Hall/*Here Comes Mr. Jordan*
Howard Hawks/*Sergeant York*
Orson Welles/*Citizen Kane*
William Wyler/*The Little Foxes*

1942

★ **William Wyler/***Mrs. Miniver*
Michael Curtiz/*Yankee Doodle Dandy*
John Farrow/*Wake Island*
Mervyn LeRoy/*Random Harvest*
Sam Wood/*Kings Row*

1943

★ **Michael Curtiz/***Casablanca*
Clarence Brown/*The Human Comedy*
Henry King/*The Song of Bernadette*
Ernst Lubitsch/*Heaven Can Wait*
George Stevens/*The More the Merrier*

1944

★ **Leo McCarey/***Going My Way*
Alfred Hitchcock/*Lifeboat*
Henry King/*Wilson*
Otto Preminger/*Laura*
Billy Wilder/*Double Indemnity*

1945

★ **Billy Wilder/***The Lost Weekend*
Clarence Brown/*National Velvet*
Alfred Hitchcock/*Spellbound*
Leo McCarey/*The Bells of St. Mary's*
Jean Renoir/*The Southerner*

1946

★ **William Wyler/***The Best Years of Our Lives*
Clarence Brown/*The Yearling*
Frank Capra/*It's a Wonderful Life*
David Lean/*Brief Encounter*
Robert Siodmak/*The Killers*

1947

★ **Elia Kazan/***Gentleman's Agreement*
George Cukor/*A Double Life*
Edward Dmytryk/*Crossfire*
Henry Koster/*The Bishop's Wife*
David Lean/*Great Expectations*

1948

★ **John Huston/***Treasure of the Sierra Madre*
Anatole Litvak/*The Snake Pit*
Jean Negulesco/*Johnny Belinda*
Laurence Olivier/*Hamlet*
Fred Zinnemann/*The Search*

1949

★ **Joseph L. Mankiewicz/***A Letter to Three Wives*
Carol Reed/*The Fallen Idol*
Robert Rossen/*All the King's Men*
William A. Wellman/*Battleground*
William Wyler/*The Heiress*

1950

★ **Joseph L. Mankiewicz/***All About Eve*
George Cukor/*Born Yesterday*
John Huston/*The Asphalt Jungle*
Carol Reed/*The Third Man*
Billy Wilder/*Sunset Boulevard*

1951

★ **George Stevens/***A Place in the Sun*
John Huston/*The African Queen*
Elia Kazan/*A Streetcar Named Desire*
Vincente Minnelli/*An American in Paris*
William Wyler/*Detective Story*

1952

★ **John Ford/***The Quiet Man*
Cecil B. DeMille/*The Greatest Show on Earth*
John Huston/*Moulin Rouge*
Joseph L. Mankiewicz/*Five Fingers*
Fred Zinnemann/*High Noon*

1953

★ **Fred Zinnemann/***From Here to Eternity*
George Stevens/*Shane*
Charles Walters/*Lili*
Billy Wilder/*Stalag 17*
William Wyler/*Roman Holiday*

1954

★ **Elia Kazan/***On the Waterfront*
Alfred Hitchcock/*Rear Window*
George Seaton/*Country Girl*
Billy Wilder/*Sabrina*

1955

★ **Delbert Mann/***Marty*
Elia Kazan/*East of Eden*
David Lean/*Summertime*
Joshua Logan/*Picnic*

★ = winner

John Sturges/*Bad Day at Black Rock*
1956
★ George Stevens/*Giant*
Michael Anderson, Sr./*Around the World in 80 Days*
Walter Lang/*The King and I*
King Vidor/*War and Peace*
William Wyler/*Friendly Persuasion*
1957
★ David Lean/*The Bridge on the River Kwai*
Joshua Logan/*Sayonara*
Sidney Lumet/*Twelve Angry Men*
Mark Robson/*Peyton Place*
Billy Wilder/*Witness for the Prosecution*
1958
★ Vincente Minnelli/*Gigi*
Richard Brooks/*Cat on a Hot Tin Roof*
Stanley Kramer/*The Defiant Ones*
Mark Robson/*The Inn of the Sixth Happiness*
Robert Wise/*I Want to Live!*
1959
★ William Wyler/*Ben-Hur*
Jack Clayton/*Room at the Top*
George Stevens/*The Diary of Anne Frank*
Billy Wilder/*Some Like It Hot*
Fred Zinnemann/*The Nun's Story*
1960
★ Billy Wilder/*The Apartment*
Jules Dassin/*Never on Sunday*
Alfred Hitchcock/*Psycho*
Fred Zinnemann/*The Sundowners*
1961
★ Robert Wise/*West Side Story*
Federico Fellini/*La Dolce Vita*
Stanley Kramer/*Judgment at Nuremberg*
Robert Rossen/*The Hustler*
J. Lee Thompson/*The Guns of Navarone*
1962
★ David Lean/*Lawrence of Arabia*
Pietro Germi/*Divorce—Italian Style*
Robert Mulligan/*To Kill a Mockingbird*
Arthur Penn/*The Miracle Worker*
Frank Perry/*David and Lisa*
1963
★ Tony Richardson/*Tom Jones*
Federico Fellini/*8 1/2*
Otto Preminger/*The Cardinal*
Martin Ritt/*Hud*
1964
★ George Cukor/*My Fair Lady*
Michael Cacoyannis/*Zorba the Greek*
Peter Glenville/*Becket*
Stanley Kubrick/*Dr. Strangelove, or: How I Learned to Stop Worrying and Love the Bomb*
Robert Stevenson/*Mary Poppins*
1965
★ Robert Wise/*The Sound of Music*
David Lean/*Doctor Zhivago*
John Schlesinger/*Darling*
Hiroshi Teshigahara/*Woman in the Dunes*
William Wyler/*The Collector*
1966
★ Fred Zinnemann/*A Man for All Seasons*
Michelangelo Antonioni/*Blow-Up*
Richard Brooks/*The Professionals*
Claude Lelouch/*A Man and a Woman*
Mike Nichols/*Who's Afraid of Virginia Woolf?*
1967
★ Mike Nichols/*The Graduate*
Richard Brooks/*In Cold Blood*
Norman Jewison/*In the Heat of the Night*
Stanley Kramer/*Guess Who's Coming to Dinner*
Arthur Penn/*Bonnie & Clyde*
1968
★ Carol Reed/*Oliver!*
Anthony Harvey/*The Lion in Winter*
Stanley Kubrick/*2001: A Space Odyssey*
Gillo Pontecorvo/*The Battle of Algiers*
Franco Zeffirelli/*Romeo and Juliet*
1969
★ John Schlesinger/*Midnight Cowboy*
Constantin Costa-Gavras/*Z*
George Roy Hill/*Butch Cassidy and the Sundance Kid*
Arthur Penn/*Alice's Restaurant*
Sydney Pollack/*They Shoot Horses, Don't They?*
1970
★ Franklin J. Schaffner/*Patton*
Robert Altman/*M*A*S*H*
Federico Fellini/*Fellini Satyricon*
Arthur Hiller/*Love Story*
Ken Russell/*Women in Love*
1971
★ William Friedkin/*The French Connection*
Peter Bogdanovich/*The Last Picture Show*
Norman Jewison/*Fiddler on the Roof*
Stanley Kubrick/*A Clockwork Orange*
John Schlesinger/*Sunday, Bloody Sunday*
1972
★ Bob Fosse/*Cabaret*
John Boorman/*Deliverance*
Francis Ford Coppola/*The Godfather*
Joseph L. Mankiewicz/*Sleuth*
Jan Troell/*The Emigrants*
1973
★ George Roy Hill/*The Sting*
Ingmar Bergman/*Cries and Whispers*
Bernardo Bertolucci/*Last Tango in Paris*
William Friedkin/*The Exorcist*
George Lucas/*American Graffiti*
1974
★ Francis Ford Coppola/*The Godfather, Part 2*
John Cassavetes/*A Woman under the Influence*
Bob Fosse/*Lenny*
Roman Polanski/*Chinatown*
Francois Truffaut/*Day for Night*
1975
★ Milos Forman/*One Flew Over the Cuckoo's Nest*
Robert Altman/*Nashville*
Federico Fellini/*Amarcord*
Stanley Kubrick/*Barry Lyndon*
Sidney Lumet/*Dog Day Afternoon*
1976
★ John G. Avildsen/*Rocky*
Ingmar Bergman/*Face to Face*
Sidney Lumet/*Network*
Alan J. Pakula/*All the President's Men*
Lina Wertmuller/*Seven Beauties*
1977
★ Woody Allen/*Annie Hall*
George Lucas/*Star Wars*
Herbert Ross/*The Turning Point*
Steven Spielberg/*Close Encounters of the Third Kind*
Fred Zinnemann/*Julia*
1978
★ Michael Cimino/*The Deer Hunter*
Woody Allen/*Interiors*
Hal Ashby/*Coming Home*
Warren Beatty/*Heaven Can Wait*
Buck Henry/*Heaven Can Wait*
Alan Parker/*Midnight Express*
1979
★ Robert Benton/*Kramer vs. Kramer*
Francis Ford Coppola/*Apocalypse Now*
Bob Fosse/*All That Jazz*
Edouard Molinaro/*La Cage aux Folles*
Peter Yates/*Breaking Away*
1980
★ Robert Redford/*Ordinary People*
David Lynch/*The Elephant Man*
Roman Polanski/*Tess*
Richard Rush/*The Stunt Man*
Martin Scorsese/*Raging Bull*
1981
★ Warren Beatty/*Reds*
Hugh Hudson/*Chariots of Fire*
Louis Malle/*Atlantic City*
Mark Rydell/*On Golden Pond*
Steven Spielberg/*Raiders of the Lost Ark*
1982
★ Richard Attenborough/*Gandhi*
Sidney Lumet/*The Verdict*
Wolfgang Petersen/*Das Boot*
Sydney Pollack/*Tootsie*
Steven Spielberg/*E.T.: The Extra-Terrestrial*
1983
★ James L. Brooks/*Terms of Endearment*
Bruce Beresford/*Tender Mercies*
Ingmar Bergman/*Fanny and Alexander*
Mike Nichols/*Silkwood*
Peter Yates/*The Dresser*
1984
★ Milos Forman/*Amadeus*
Woody Allen/*Broadway Danny Rose*
Robert Benton/*Places in the Heart*
Roland Joffe/*The Killing Fields*
David Lean/*A Passage to India*
1985
★ Sydney Pollack/*Out of Africa*
Hector Babenco/*Kiss of the Spider Woman*
John Huston/*Prizzi's Honor*
Akira Kurosawa/*Ran*
Peter Weir/*Witness*
1986
★ Oliver Stone/*Platoon*
Woody Allen/*Hannah and Her Sisters*
James Ivory/*A Room with a View*
Roland Joffe/*The Mission*
David Lynch/*Blue Velvet*
1987
★ Bernardo Bertolucci/*The Last Emperor*
John Boorman/*Hope and Glory*
Lasse Hallstrom/*My Life As a Dog*
Norman Jewison/*Moonstruck*
Adrian Lyne/*Fatal Attraction*
1988
★ Barry Levinson/*Rain Man*
Charles Crichton/*A Fish Called Wanda*
Mike Nichols/*Working Girl*
Alan Parker/*Mississippi Burning*
Martin Scorsese/*The Last Temptation of Christ*
1989
★ Oliver Stone/*Born on the Fourth of July*
Woody Allen/*Crimes & Misdemeanors*
Kenneth Branagh/*Henry V*
Jim Sheridan/*My Left Foot*
Peter Weir/*Dead Poets Society*
1990
★ Kevin Costner/*Dances with Wolves*
Francis Ford Coppola/*The Godfather, Part 3*
Stephen Frears/*The Grifters*
Barbet Schroeder/*Reversal of Fortune*
Martin Scorsese/*Goodfellas*
1991
★ Jonathan Demme/*The Silence of the Lambs*
Barry Levinson/*Bugsy*
Ridley Scott/*Thelma & Louise*
John Singleton/*Boyz N the Hood*
Oliver Stone/*JFK*
1992
★ Clint Eastwood/*Unforgiven*
Robert Altman/*The Player*
Martin Brest/*Scent of a Woman*
James Ivory/*Howard's End*
Neil Jordan/*The Crying Game*
1993
★ Steven Spielberg/*Schindler's List*
Robert Altman/*Short Cuts*
Jane Campion/*The Piano*
James Ivory/*The Remains of the Day*
Jim Sheridan/*In the Name of the Father*
1994
★ Robert Zemeckis/*Forrest Gump*
Woody Allen/*Bullets over Broadway*
Krzysztof Kieslowski/*Trois Couleurs: Rouge*
Robert Redford/*Quiz Show*
Quentin Tarantino/*Pulp Fiction*
1995
★ Mel Gibson/*Braveheart*
Mike Figgis/*Leaving Las Vegas*
Chris Noonan/*Babe*
Michael Radford/*The Postman*
Tim Robbins/*Dead Man Walking*
1996
★ Anthony Minghella/*The English Patient*
Joel Coen/*Fargo*
Milos Forman/*The People vs. Larry Flynt*
Scott Hicks/*Shine*
Mike Leigh/*Secrets and Lies*
1997
★ James Cameron/*Titanic*
Peter Cattaneo/*The Full Monty*
Atom Egoyan/*The Sweet Hereafter*
Curtis Hanson/*L.A. Confidential*
Gus Van Sant/*Good Will Hunting*
1998
★ Steven Spielberg/*Saving Private Ryan*
Roberto Benigni/*Life Is Beautiful*
John Madden/*Shakespeare in Love*
Terrence Malick/*The Thin Red Line*
Peter Weir/*The Truman Show*
1999
★ Sam Mendes/*American Beauty*
Lasse Hallstrom/*The Cider House Rules*
Spike Jonze/*Being John Malkovich*
Michael Mann/*The Insider*
M. Night Shyamalan/*The Sixth Sense*
2000
★ Steven Soderbergh/*Traffic*
Stephen Daldry/*Billy Elliot*
Ang Lee/*Crouching Tiger, Hidden Dragon*
Ridley Scott/*Gladiator*
Steven Soderbergh/*Erin Brockovich*
2001
★ Ron Howard/*A Beautiful Mind*
Robert Altman/*Gosford Park*
Peter Jackson/*Lord of the Rings 1: The Fellowship of the Rings*
David Lynch/*Mulholland Drive*
Ridley Scott/*Black Hawk Down*

FILM

1927
★ *Wings*
1928
Last Command
1929
★ *Broadway Melody*
Alibi
1930
★ *All Quiet on the Western Front*
The Big House
Disraeli
The Divorcee
1931
★ *Cimarron*
The Front Page
Trader Horn
1932
★ *Grand Hotel*
Arrowsmith
The Champ
Shanghai Express
1933
★ *Cavalcade*
A Farewell to Arms
42nd Street
I Am a Fugitive from a Chain Gang
Lady for a Day
Little Women
The Private Life of Henry VIII
She Done Him Wrong
Smilin' Through
1934
★ *It Happened One Night*
The Barretts of Wimpole Street
Cleopatra
Flirtation Walk
The Gay Divorcee
Imitation of Life
One Night of Love
The Thin Man
Viva Villa!
1935
★ *Mutiny on the Bounty*
Alice Adams
Broadway Melody of 1936
Captain Blood
David Copperfield
The Informer
Les Miserables
The Lives of a Bengal Lancer
A Midsummer Night's Dream
Naughty Marietta
Ruggles of Red Gap
Top Hat
1936
★ *The Great Ziegfeld*
Anthony Adverse
Dodsworth
Libeled Lady
Mr. Deeds Goes to Town
Romeo and Juliet
San Francisco
The Story of Louis Pasteur
A Tale of Two Cities
Three Smart Girls
1937
★ *The Life of Emile Zola*
The Awful Truth
Captains Courageous
Dead End
The Good Earth
In Old Chicago
Lost Horizon
100 Men and a Girl
Stage Door
A Star Is Born
1938
★ *You Can't Take It with You*
The Adventures of Robin Hood
Alexander's Ragtime Band
Boys Town
The Citadel
Four Daughters
Grand Illusion
Jezebel
Pygmalion
Test Pilot
1939
★ *Gone with the Wind*
Dark Victory
Goodbye, Mr. Chips
Love Affair
Mr. Smith Goes to Washington
Ninotchka
Of Mice and Men
Stagecoach
The Wizard of Oz
Wuthering Heights
1940
★ *Rebecca*
All This and Heaven Too
Foreign Correspondent
The Grapes of Wrath
The Great Dictator
Kitty Foyle
The Letter
The Long Voyage Home
Our Town
The Philadelphia Story
1941
★ *How Green Was My Valley*
Blossoms in the Dust
Citizen Kane
Here Comes Mr. Jordan
The Little Foxes
The Maltese Falcon
Sergeant York
Suspicion
1942
★ *Mrs. Miniver*
Kings Row

★ = winner

FILM cont.

The Magnificent Ambersons
The Pride of the Yankees
Random Harvest
Talk of the Town
Wake Island
Yankee Doodle Dandy

1943
★ Casablanca
For Whom the Bell Tolls
Heaven Can Wait
The Human Comedy
In Which We Serve
Madame Curie
The More the Merrier
The Ox-Bow Incident
The Song of Bernadette
Watch on the Rhine

1944
★ Going My Way
Double Indemnity
Gaslight
Since You Went Away
Wilson

1945
★ The Lost Weekend
Anchors Aweigh
The Bells of St. Mary's
Mildred Pierce
Spellbound

1946
★ The Best Years of Our Lives
Henry V
It's a Wonderful Life
The Razor's Edge
The Yearling

1947
★ Gentleman's Agreement
The Bishop's Wife
Crossfire
Great Expectations
Miracle on 34th Street

1948
★ Hamlet
Johnny Belinda
The Red Shoes
The Snake Pit
Treasure of the Sierra Madre

1949
★ All the King's Men
Battleground
The Heiress
A Letter to Three Wives
Twelve o'Clock High

1950
★ All About Eve
Born Yesterday
Father of the Bride
King Solomon's Mines
Sunset Boulevard

1951
★ An American in Paris
A Place in the Sun
Quo Vadis
A Streetcar Named Desire

1952
★ The Greatest Show on Earth
High Noon
Ivanhoe
Moulin Rouge
The Quiet Man

1953
★ From Here to Eternity
Julius Caesar
The Robe
Roman Holiday
Shane

1954
★ On the Waterfront
The Caine Mutiny
Country Girl
Seven Brides for Seven Brothers
Three Coins in the Fountain

1955
★ Marty
Love Is a Many-Splendored Thing
Mister Roberts
Picnic
The Rose Tattoo

1956
★ Around the World in 80 Days
Friendly Persuasion
Giant
The King and I
The Ten Commandments

1957
★ The Bridge on the River Kwai
Peyton Place
Sayonara
Twelve Angry Men
Witness for the Prosecution

1958
★ Gigi
Auntie Mame
Cat on a Hot Tin Roof
The Defiant Ones
Separate Tables

1959
★ Ben-Hur
Anatomy of a Murder
The Diary of Anne Frank
The Nun's Story
Room at the Top

1960
★ The Apartment
The Alamo
Elmer Gantry
The Sundowners

1961
★ West Side Story
Fanny
The Guns of Navarone
The Hustler
Judgment at Nuremberg

1962
★ Lawrence of Arabia
The Longest Day
The Music Man
Mutiny on the Bounty
To Kill a Mockingbird

1963
★ Tom Jones
Cleopatra
How the West Was Won
Lilies of the Field

1964
★ My Fair Lady
Becket
Dr. Strangelove, or: How I Learned to Stop Worrying and Love the Bomb
Mary Poppins
Zorba the Greek

1965
★ The Sound of Music
Darling
Doctor Zhivago
Ship of Fools
A Thousand Clowns

1966
★ A Man for All Seasons
Alfie
The Russians Are Coming, the Russians Are Coming
The Sand Pebbles
Who's Afraid of Virginia Woolf?

1967
★ In the Heat of the Night
Bonnie & Clyde
Doctor Dolittle
The Graduate
Guess Who's Coming to Dinner

1968
★ Oliver!
Funny Girl
The Lion in Winter
Rachel, Rachel
Romeo and Juliet

1969
★ Midnight Cowboy
Anne of the Thousand Days
Butch Cassidy and the Sundance Kid
Hello, Dolly!
Z

1970
★ Patton
Airport
Five Easy Pieces
Love Story
M*A*S*H

1971
★ The French Connection
A Clockwork Orange
Fiddler on the Roof
The Last Picture Show
Nicholas and Alexandra

1972
★ The Godfather
Cabaret
Deliverance
The Emigrants
Sounder

1973
★ The Sting
American Graffiti
Cries and Whispers
The Exorcist
A Touch of Class

1974
★ The Godfather, Part 2
Chinatown
The Conversation
Lenny
The Towering Inferno

1975
★ One Flew Over the Cuckoo's Nest
Barry Lyndon
Dog Day Afternoon
Jaws
Nashville

1976
★ Rocky
All the President's Men
Bound for Glory
Network
Taxi Driver

1977
★ Annie Hall
The Goodbye Girl
Julia
Star Wars
The Turning Point

1978
★ The Deer Hunter
Coming Home
Heaven Can Wait
Midnight Express
An Unmarried Woman

1979
★ Kramer vs. Kramer
All That Jazz
Apocalypse Now
Breaking Away
Norma Rae

1980
★ Ordinary People
Coal Miner's Daughter
The Elephant Man
Raging Bull
Tess

1981
★ Chariots of Fire
Atlantic City
On Golden Pond
Raiders of the Lost Ark
Reds

1982
★ Gandhi
E.T.: The Extra-Terrestrial
Missing
Tootsie
The Verdict

1983
★ Terms of Endearment
The Big Chill
The Dresser
The Right Stuff
Tender Mercies

1984
★ Amadeus
The Killing Fields
A Passage to India
Places in the Heart
A Soldier's Story

1985
★ Out of Africa
The Color Purple
Kiss of the Spider Woman
Prizzi's Honor
Witness

1986
★ Platoon
Children of a Lesser God
Hannah and Her Sisters
The Mission
A Room with a View

1987
★ The Last Emperor
Broadcast News
Fatal Attraction
Hope and Glory
Moonstruck

1988
★ Rain Man
The Accidental Tourist
Dangerous Liaisons
Mississippi Burning
Working Girl

1989
★ Driving Miss Daisy
Born on the Fourth of July
Dead Poets Society
Field of Dreams
My Left Foot

1990
★ Dances with Wolves
Awakenings
Ghost
The Godfather, Part 3
Goodfellas

1991
★ The Silence of the Lambs
Beauty and the Beast
Bugsy
JFK
The Prince of Tides

1992
★ Unforgiven
The Crying Game
A Few Good Men
Howard's End
Scent of a Woman

1993
★ Schindler's List
The Fugitive
In the Name of the Father
The Piano
The Remains of the Day

1994
★ Forrest Gump
Four Weddings and a Funeral
Pulp Fiction
Quiz Show
The Shawshank Redemption

1995
★ Braveheart
Apollo 13
Babe
The Postman
Sense and Sensibility

1996
★ The English Patient
Fargo
Jerry Maguire
Secrets and Lies
Shine

1997
★ Titanic
As Good As It Gets
The Full Monty
Good Will Hunting
L.A. Confidential

1998
★ Shakespeare in Love
Elizabeth
Life Is Beautiful
Saving Private Ryan
The Thin Red Line

1999
★ American Beauty
The Cider House Rules
The Green Mile
The Insider
The Sixth Sense

2000
★ Gladiator
Chocolat
Crouching Tiger, Hidden Dragon
Erin Brockovich
Traffic

2001
★ A Beautiful Mind
Gosford Park
In the Bedroom
Lord of the Rings 1: The Fellowship of the Rings

FEATURE DOCUMENTARY

1942
★ Prelude to War

1961
★ The Sky Above, the Mud Below

1970
★ Woodstock

1971
★ The Hellstrom Chronicle

1972
★ Marjoe

1976
★ Harlan County, U.S.A.

1977
The Children of Theatre Street

1983
★ Times of Harvey Milk

1988
Let's Get Lost

1993
The War Room

1996
★ When We Were Kings

FILM EDITING

1934
Cleopatra
One Night of Love

1935
★ A Midsummer Night's Dream
David Copperfield
The Informer
Les Miserables
The Lives of a Bengal Lancer
Mutiny on the Bounty

1936
★ Anthony Adverse
Come and Get It
The Great Ziegfeld
Lloyds of London
A Tale of Two Cities
Theodora Goes Wild

1937
★ Lost Horizon
The Awful Truth
Captains Courageous
The Good Earth
100 Men and a Girl

1938
★ The Adventures of Robin Hood
Alexander's Ragtime Band
The Great Waltz
Test Pilot
You Can't Take It with You

1939
★ Gone with the Wind
Goodbye, Mr. Chips
Mr. Smith Goes to Washington
The Rains Came
Stagecoach

1940
The Grapes of Wrath
The Letter
The Long Voyage Home
Rebecca

1941
★ Sergeant York
Citizen Kane
Dr. Jekyll and Mr. Hyde
How Green Was My Valley
The Little Foxes

1942
★ The Pride of the Yankees
Mrs. Miniver
Talk of the Town
Yankee Doodle Dandy

1943
★ Air Force
Casablanca
Five Graves to Cairo
For Whom the Bell Tolls
The Song of Bernadette

1944
★ Wilson
Going My Way
None But the Lonely Heart
Since You Went Away

1945
★ National Velvet
The Bells of St. Mary's
The Lost Weekend
Objective, Burma!
A Song to Remember

1946
★ The Best Years of Our Lives
It's a Wonderful Life
The Jolson Story
The Killers
The Yearling

1947
★ Body and Soul
The Bishop's Wife
Gentleman's Agreement
Green Dolphin Street
Odd Man Out

1948
★ The Naked City
Joan of Arc
Johnny Belinda
Red River
The Red Shoes

1949
★ Champion
All the King's Men
Battleground
Sands of Iwo Jima
The Window

1950
★ King Solomon's Mines
Annie Get Your Gun
Sunset Boulevard
The Third Man

1951
★ A Place in the Sun
An American in Paris
Quo Vadis
The Well

1952
★ High Noon
Come Back, Little Sheba
Flat Top
The Greatest Show on Earth
Moulin Rouge

1953
★ From Here to Eternity
The Moon Is Blue
Roman Holiday
The War of the Worlds

1954
★ On the Waterfront
The Caine Mutiny
Seven Brides for Seven Brothers
20,000 Leagues under the Sea

1955
★ Picnic
Blackboard Jungle
The Bridges at Toko-Ri
Oklahoma!
The Rose Tattoo

1956
★ Around the World in 80 Days
The Brave One
Giant
Somebody Up There Likes Me
The Ten Commandments

1957
★ The Bridge on the River Kwai
Gunfight at the O.K. Corral
Pal Joey
Sayonara

★ = winner

Witness for the Prosecution

1958

★ Gigi
Auntie Mame
Cowboy
The Defiant Ones
I Want to Live!

1959

★ Ben-Hur
Anatomy of a Murder
North by Northwest
The Nun's Story
On the Beach

1960

★ The Apartment
The Alamo
Inherit the Wind
Spartacus

1961

★ West Side Story
Fanny
The Guns of Navarone
Judgment at Nuremberg
The Parent Trap

1962

★ Lawrence of Arabia
The Longest Day
The Manchurian Candidate
The Music Man
Mutiny on the Bounty

1963

★ How the West Was Won
The Cardinal
Cleopatra
The Great Escape
It's a Mad, Mad, Mad, Mad World

1964

★ Mary Poppins
Becket
Father Goose
Hush, Hush, Sweet Charlotte
My Fair Lady

1965

★ The Sound of Music
Cat Ballou
Doctor Zhivago
The Flight of the Phoenix
The Great Race

1966

★ Grand Prix
Fantastic Voyage
The Russians Are Coming, the Russians Are Coming
The Sand Pebbles
Who's Afraid of Virginia Woolf?

1967

★ In the Heat of the Night
The Dirty Dozen
Doctor Dolittle
Guess Who's Coming to Dinner

1968

★ Bullitt
Funny Girl
The Odd Couple
Oliver!
Wild in the Streets

1969

★ Z
Hello, Dolly!
Midnight Cowboy
They Shoot Horses, Don't They?

1970

★ Patton
Airport
M*A*S*H
Tora! Tora! Tora!
Woodstock

1971

★ The French Connection
The Andromeda Strain
A Clockwork Orange
Kotch
Summer of '42

1972

★ Cabaret
Deliverance
The Godfather
The Hot Rock
The Poseidon Adventure

1973

★ The Sting
American Graffiti
The Day of the Jackal
The Exorcist
Jonathan Livingston Seagull

1974

★ The Towering Inferno
Blazing Saddles
Chinatown
Earthquake
The Longest Yard

1975

★ Jaws
Dog Day Afternoon
The Man Who Would Be King
One Flew Over the Cuckoo's Nest
Three Days of the Condor

1976

★ Rocky
All the President's Men
Bound for Glory
Network
Two Minute Warning

1977

★ Star Wars
Close Encounters of the Third Kind
Julia
Smokey and the Bandit
The Turning Point

1978

★ The Deer Hunter
The Boys from Brazil
Coming Home
Midnight Express
Superman: The Movie

1979

★ All That Jazz
Apocalypse Now
The Black Stallion
Kramer vs. Kramer
The Rose

1980

★ Raging Bull
Coal Miner's Daughter
The Competition
The Elephant Man
Fame

1981

★ Raiders of the Lost Ark
Chariots of Fire
The French Lieutenant's Woman
On Golden Pond
Reds

1982

★ Gandhi
Das Boot
E.T.: The Extra-Terrestrial
An Officer and a Gentleman
Tootsie

1983

★ The Right Stuff
Blue Thunder
Flashdance
Silkwood
Terms of Endearment

1984

★ The Killing Fields
Amadeus
The Cotton Club
A Passage to India
Romancing the Stone

1985

★ Witness
A Chorus Line
Out of Africa
Prizzi's Honor
Runaway Train

1986

★ Platoon
Aliens
Hannah and Her Sisters
The Mission
Top Gun

1987

★ The Last Emperor
Broadcast News
Empire of the Sun
Fatal Attraction
RoboCop

1988

★ Who Framed Roger Rabbit
Die Hard
Gorillas in the Mist
Mississippi Burning
Rain Man

1989

★ Born on the Fourth of July
The Bear
Driving Miss Daisy
The Fabulous Baker Boys
Glory

1990

★ Dances with Wolves
Ghost
The Godfather, Part 3
Goodfellas
The Hunt for Red October

1991

★ JFK
The Commitments
The Silence of the Lambs
Terminator 2: Judgment Day
Thelma & Louise

1992

★ Unforgiven
Basic Instinct
The Crying Game
A Few Good Men
The Player

1993

★ Schindler's List
The Fugitive
In the Line of Fire
In the Name of the Father
The Piano

1994

★ Forrest Gump
Hoop Dreams
Pulp Fiction
The Shawshank Redemption
Speed

1995

★ Apollo 13
Babe
Braveheart
Crimson Tide
Seven

1996

★ The English Patient
Evita
Fargo
Jerry Maguire
Shine

1997

★ Titanic
Air Force One
As Good As It Gets
Good Will Hunting
L.A. Confidential

1998

★ Saving Private Ryan
Life Is Beautiful
Out of Sight
Shakespeare in Love
The Thin Red Line

1999

★ The Matrix
American Beauty
The Cider House Rules
The Insider
The Sixth Sense

2000

★ Traffic
Almost Famous
Crouching Tiger, Hidden Dragon
Gladiator
Wonder Boys

2001

★ Black Hawk Down
A Beautiful Mind
Lord of the Rings 1: The Fellowship of the Rings
Memento
Moulin Rouge

MAKEUP

1981

★ An American Werewolf in London

1982

★ Quest for Fire
Gandhi

1984

★ Amadeus
Greystoke: The Legend of Tarzan, Lord of the Apes
2010: The Year We Make Contact

1985

★ Mask
The Color Purple
Remo Williams: The Adventure Begins

1986

★ The Fly
The Clan of the Cave Bear
Legend

1987

★ Harry and the Hendersons
Happy New Year

1988

★ Beetlejuice

1989

★ Driving Miss Daisy
The Adventures of Baron Munchausen
Dad

1990

★ Dick Tracy
Cyrano de Bergerac
Edward Scissorhands

1991

★ Terminator 2: Judgment Day
Hook
Star Trek 6: The Undiscovered Country

1992

★ Bram Stoker's Dracula
Batman Returns
Hoffa

1993

★ Mrs. Doubtfire
Philadelphia
Schindler's List

1994

★ Ed Wood
Forrest Gump
Mary Shelley's Frankenstein

1995

★ Braveheart
My Family
Roommates

1996

★ The Nutty Professor
Ghosts of Mississippi
Star Trek: First Contact

1997

★ Men in Black
Mrs. Brown
Titanic

1998

★ Elizabeth
Saving Private Ryan
Shakespeare in Love

1999

★ Topsy Turvy
Austin Powers 2: The Spy Who Shagged Me
Bicentennial Man
Life

2000

The Cell
Dr. Seuss' How the Grinch Stole Christmas
Shadow of the Vampire

2001

A Beautiful Mind
Lord of the Rings 1: The Fellowship of the Rings
Moulin Rouge
Moulin Rouge

ADAPTED SCORE

1962

★ The Music Man
Billy Rose's Jumbo
Gypsy
The Wonderful World of the Brothers Grimm

1963

★ Irma La Douce
Bye, Bye, Birdie
A New Kind of Love
Sundays & Cybele
The Sword in the Stone

1964

★ My Fair Lady
A Hard Day's Night
Robin and the 7 Hoods
The Unsinkable Molly Brown

1965

★ The Sound of Music
Cat Ballou
A Thousand Clowns

1966

★ A Funny Thing Happened on the Way to the Forum
The Gospel According to St. Matthew
Return of the Magnificent Seven
The Singing Nun

1967

★ Camelot
Guess Who's Coming to Dinner
Valley of the Dolls

1968

★ Oliver!
Star!

ORIGINAL DRAMATIC SCORE

1941

★ The Devil & Daniel Webster
Ball of Fire
Cheers for Miss Bishop
Citizen Kane
Dr. Jekyll and Mr. Hyde
How Green Was My Valley
King of the Zombies
The Little Foxes
Lydia
Sergeant York
So Ends Our Night
Sundown
Suspicion
Tanks a Million
That Uncertain Feeling

1942

★ Now, Voyager
Arabian Nights
Bambi
The Black Swan
The Corsican Brothers
Flying Tigers
I Married a Witch
Joan of Paris
The Jungle Book
The Pride of the Yankees
Random Harvest
The Shanghai Gesture
Silver Queen
Talk of the Town
To Be or Not to Be

1943

★ The Song of Bernadette
The Amazing Mrs. Holiday
Casablanca
Commandos Strike at Dawn
The Fallen Sparrow
For Whom the Bell Tolls
Hangmen Also Die
Hi Diddle Diddle
Johnny Come Lately
The Kansan
Lady of Burlesque
Madame Curie
The Moon and Sixpence
The North Star
War of the Wildcats

1944

★ Cover Girl
★ Since You Went Away
The Adventures of Mark Twain
The Bridge of San Luis Rey
Casanova Brown
Double Indemnity
Fighting Seabees
The Hairy Ape
Higher and Higher
Jack London
None But the Lonely Heart
The Princess and the Pirate
Wilson
The Woman of the Town

1945

★ Spellbound
The Bells of St. Mary's
Brewster's Millions
Captain Kidd
The Enchanted Cottage
Flame of the Barbary Coast
Guest in the House
Guest Wife
The Keys of the Kingdom
The Lost Weekend
Objective, Burma!
A Song to Remember
The Southerner
The Valley of Decision
Woman in the Window

1946

★ The Best Years of Our Lives
Anna and the King of Siam
Henry V
Humoresque
The Killers

1947

★ A Double Life
The Bishop's Wife
Captain from Castile
Forever Amber
Life with Father
The Road to Rio

1948

★ The Red Shoes
Hamlet
Joan of Arc
Johnny Belinda
The Snake Pit

1949

★ The Heiress
Beyond the Forest
Champion

1950

★ Sunset Boulevard
All About Eve
The Flame & the Arrow
Samson and Delilah

1951

★ A Place in the Sun
David and Bathsheba
Quo Vadis
A Streetcar Named Desire

1952

★ High Noon
Ivanhoe
Miracle of Our Lady of Fatima
The Thief
Viva Zapata!

1953

★ Lili
Above and Beyond
From Here to Eternity
Julius Caesar

1954

The Caine Mutiny
Genevieve
On the Waterfront
The Silver Chalice

1955

★ Love Is a Many-Splendored Thing
Battle Cry
The Man with the Golden Arm
Picnic
The Rose Tattoo

1956

★ Around the World in 80 Days
Anastasia
Between Heaven and Hell
Giant
The Rainmaker

1958

The Big Country

★ = winner

ORIGINAL DRAMATIC SCORE *cont.*

Separate Tables
The Young Lions

1959

★ Ben-Hur
The Diary of Anne Frank
The Nun's Story
On the Beach
Pillow Talk

1960

★ Exodus
The Alamo
Elmer Gantry
The Magnificent Seven
Spartacus

1961

★ Breakfast at Tiffany's
El Cid
Fanny
The Guns of Navarone
Summer and Smoke

1971

★ Summer of '42
Mary, Queen of Scots
Nicholas and Alexandra
Shaft
Straw Dogs

1972

Napoleon and Samantha
The Poseidon Adventure
Sleuth

1973

★ The Way We Were
Cinderella Liberty
The Day of the Dolphin
Papillon
A Touch of Class

1974

★ The Godfather, Part 2
Chinatown
Murder on the Orient Express
The Towering Inferno

1995

★ The Postman
Apollo 13
Braveheart
Nixon
Sense and Sensibility

1996

★ The English Patient
Hamlet
Michael Collins
Shine
Sleepers

1998

★ Life Is Beautiful
Elizabeth
Pleasantville
Saving Private Ryan

ORIGINAL MUSICAL/COMEDY SCORE

1997

★ The Full Monty
Anastasia
As Good As It Gets
Men in Black
My Best Friend's Wedding

1998

★ Shakespeare in Love
A Bug's Life
Mulan
Patch Adams
Prince of Egypt

ORIGINAL SONG SCORE AND/OR ADAPTATION

1970

★ Let It Be
The Baby Maker
Darling Lili
Scrooge

1971

★ Fiddler on the Roof
Bedknobs and Broomsticks
The Boy Friend
Tchaikovsky
Willy Wonka & the Chocolate Factory

1972

★ Cabaret
Lady Sings the Blues
Man of La Mancha

1973

★ The Sting
Jesus Christ, Superstar
Tom Sawyer

1974

★ The Great Gatsby
The Little Prince
Phantom of the Paradise

1975

★ Barry Lyndon
Funny Lady

1976

★ Bound for Glory
A Star Is Born

1977

★ A Little Night Music
Pete's Dragon

1978

★ The Buddy Holly Story
Pretty Baby
The Wiz

1979

★ All That Jazz
Breaking Away
The Muppet Movie

1982

★ Victor/Victoria
Annie
One from the Heart

1983

★ Yentl
The Sting 2
Trading Places

1984

★ Purple Rain
The Muppets Take Manhattan
Songwriter

SCORE

1934

★ One Night of Love
The Gay Divorcee
The Lost Patrol

1935

★ The Informer
Mutiny on the Bounty

1936

★ Anthony Adverse
The Charge of the Light Brigade
The Garden of Allah
The General Died at Dawn
Winterset

1937

★ 100 Men and a Girl
The Hurricane
In Old Chicago
The Life of Emile Zola
Lost Horizon
Make a Wish
Maytime
Prisoner of Zenda
Quality Street
Snow White and the Seven Dwarfs
Something to Sing About
Souls at Sea
Way Out West

1938

★ Alexander's Ragtime Band
Carefree
The Goldwyn Follies
Jezebel
Mad About Music
Sweethearts

1939

★ Stagecoach
Babes in Arms
First Love
The Hunchback of Notre Dame
Intermezzo
Mr. Smith Goes to Washington
The Private Lives of Elizabeth & Essex
They Shall Have Music
Way Down South

1940

★ Tin Pan Alley
Our Town
The Sea Hawk
Second Chorus
Strike Up the Band

1957

★ The Bridge on the River Kwai
An Affair to Remember
Raintree County

2001

A. I.: Artificial Intelligence
A Beautiful Mind
Harry Potter and the Sorcerer's Stone
Lord of the Rings 1: The Fellowship of the Rings
Monsters, Inc.

SCORING OF A MUSICAL

1941

★ Dumbo
Birth of the Blues
Buck Privates
The Chocolate Soldier
Strawberry Blonde
Sun Valley Serenade
Sunny
You'll Never Get Rich

1942

★ Yankee Doodle Dandy
For Me and My Gal
Holiday Inn
It Started with Eve
You Were Never Lovelier

1943

★ This Is the Army
The Phantom of the Opera
The Sky's the Limit
Stage Door Canteen
Star Spangled Rhythm
Thousands Cheer

1944

Hollywood Canteen
Meet Me in St. Louis
Sensations of 1945
Up in Arms

1945

★ Anchors Aweigh
Can't Help Singing
Rhapsody in Blue
State Fair
The Three Caballeros
Tonight and Every Night
Wonder Man

1946

★ The Jolson Story
Blue Skies
The Harvey Girls
Night and Day

1947

★ Mother Wore Tights

1948

★ Easter Parade
Emperor Waltz
The Pirate
Romance on the High Seas

1949

★ On the Town
Jolson Sings Again
Look for the Silver Lining

1950

★ Annie Get Your Gun
Cinderella
Three Little Words
The West Point Story

1951

★ An American in Paris
Alice in Wonderland
The Great Caruso
Show Boat

1952

Hans Christian Andersen
The Medium
Singin' in the Rain

1953

The Band Wagon
Calamity Jane
The 5000 Fingers of Dr. T
Kiss Me Kate

1954

★ Seven Brides for Seven Brothers
Carmen Jones
The Glenn Miller Story
A Star Is Born
There's No Business Like Show Business

1955

★ Oklahoma!
Daddy Long Legs
Guys and Dolls
It's Always Fair Weather
Love Me or Leave Me

1956

★ The King and I
The Eddy Duchin Story
High Society
Meet Me in Las Vegas

1958

★ Gigi
Damn Yankees
South Pacific

1959

The Five Pennies
Li'l Abner
Sleeping Beauty

1960

★ Song Without End
Bells Are Ringing
Can-Can
Let's Make Love

1961

★ West Side Story
Babes in Toyland
Flower Drum Song
Paris Blues

1968

Finian's Rainbow
Funny Girl

1969

★ Hello, Dolly!
Goodbye, Mr. Chips
Paint Your Wagon
Sweet Charity
They Shoot Horses, Don't They?

ORIGINAL SCORE

1938

★ The Adventures of Robin Hood
Breaking the Ice
The Cowboy and the Lady
Marie Antoinette
The Young in Heart

1939

★ The Wizard of Oz
Dark Victory
Eternally Yours
Golden Boy
Gone with the Wind
Gulliver's Travels
The Man in the Iron Mask
Nurse Edith Cavell
Of Mice and Men
The Rains Came
Wuthering Heights

1940

★ Pinocchio
Arizona
Dark Command
The Grapes of Wrath
The Great Dictator
The Howards of Virginia
The Letter
The Long Voyage Home
The Mark of Zorro
My Favorite Wife
One Million B.C.
Rebecca
The Thief of Bagdad
Waterloo Bridge

1959

★ **Dimitri Tiomkin**/The Old Man and the Sea

1962

★ Lawrence of Arabia
Mutiny on the Bounty
Taras Bulba
To Kill a Mockingbird

1963

★ Tom Jones
Cleopatra
55 Days at Peking
How the West Was Won
It's a Mad, Mad, Mad, Mad World

1964

★ Mary Poppins
Becket
The Fall of the Roman Empire
Hush, Hush, Sweet Charlotte
Mary Poppins
The Pink Panther

1965

★ Doctor Zhivago
The Agony and the Ecstasy
The Greatest Story Ever Told
A Patch of Blue
Umbrellas of Cherbourg

1966

★ Born Free
The Bible
Cool Hand Luke
Hawaii
The Sand Pebbles
Who's Afraid of Virginia Woolf?

1967

★ Thoroughly Modern Millie
Doctor Dolittle
Far from the Madding Crowd
In Cold Blood
Thoroughly Modern Millie

1968

★ The Lion in Winter
Planet of the Apes
The Shoes of the Fisherman
The Thomas Crown Affair

1969

★ Butch Cassidy and the Sundance Kid
Anne of the Thousand Days
The Reivers
The Wild Bunch

1970

★ Love Story
Airport
Cromwell
Patton

1975

★ Jaws
Bite the Bullet
One Flew Over the Cuckoo's Nest
Tommy
The Wind and the Lion

1976

★ The Omen
Bugsy Malone
Obsession
The Outlaw Josey Wales
Taxi Driver
Voyage of the Damned

1977

★ Star Wars
Close Encounters of the Third Kind
Julia
The Message
The Spy Who Loved Me

1978

★ Midnight Express
The Boys from Brazil
Days of Heaven
Heaven Can Wait
Superman: The Movie

1979

★ A Little Romance
The Amityville Horror
The Champ
Star Trek: The Motion Picture
10

1980

★ Fame
Altered States
The Elephant Man
The Empire Strikes Back
Tess

1981

★ Chariots of Fire
Dragonslayer
On Golden Pond
Ragtime
Raiders of the Lost Ark

1982

★ E.T.: The Extra-Terrestrial
Gandhi
An Officer and a Gentleman
Poltergeist
Sophie's Choice

1983

★ The Right Stuff
Cross Creek
Return of the Jedi
Terms of Endearment
Under Fire

1984

★ A Passage to India
Indiana Jones and the Temple of Doom
The Natural
The River
Under the Volcano

1985

★ Out of Africa
Agnes of God
The Color Purple
Silverado
Witness

1986

★ Round Midnight
Aliens
Hoosiers
The Mission
Star Trek 4: The Voyage Home

1987

★ The Last Emperor
Cry Freedom
Empire of the Sun
The Untouchables
The Witches of Eastwick

1988

★ The Milagro Beanfield War
The Accidental Tourist
Dangerous Liaisons
Gorillas in the Mist
Rain Man

1989

★ The Little Mermaid
Born on the Fourth of July
The Fabulous Baker Boys
Field of Dreams
Indiana Jones and the Last Crusade

1990

★ Dances with Wolves
Avalon
Ghost
Havana
Home Alone

1991

★ Beauty and the Beast
Bugsy
The Fisher King
JFK
The Prince of Tides

1992

★ Aladdin
Basic Instinct
Chaplin
Howard's End
A River Runs Through It

1993

★ Schindler's List
The Age of Innocence
The Firm
The Fugitive
The Remains of the Day

1994

★ The Lion King
Forrest Gump
Interview with the Vampire
Little Women
The Shawshank Redemption

1995

★ Pocahontas
The American President
Sabrina
Toy Story
Unstrung Heroes

★ = winner

1996

★ *Emma*
The First Wives Club
The Hunchback of Notre Dame
James and the Giant Peach
The Preacher's Wife

1997

★ *Titanic*
Amistad
Good Will Hunting
Kundun
L.A. Confidential

1999

★ *The Red Violin*
American Beauty
Angela's Ashes
The Cider House Rules
The Talented Mr. Ripley

2000

★ *Crouching Tiger, Hidden Dragon*
Chocolat
The Patriot

SONG

1934

★ **"The Continental"**/*The Gay Divorcee*
"Carioca"/*Flying Down to Rio*

1935

★ **"Lullaby of Broadway"**/*Gold Diggers of 1935*
"Cheek to Cheek"/*Top Hat*
"Lovely to Look At"/*Roberta*

1936

★ **"The Way You Look Tonight"**/*Swing Time*
"A Melody from the Sky"/*The Trail of the Lonesome Pine*
"Did I Remember"/*Suzy*
"I've Got You Under My Skin"/*Born to Dance*
"My Own"/*That Certain Age*

1937

★ **"Sweet Leilani"**/*Waikiki Wedding*
"That Old Feeling"/*Vogues of 1938*
"They Can't Take That Away From Me"/*Shall We Dance*

1938

★ **"Thanks for the Memories"**/*The Big Broadcast of 1938*
"Always and Always"/*Mannequin*
"Change Partners and Dance with Me"/*Carefree*
"Now It Can Be Told"/*Alexander's Ragtime Band*
"The Cowboy and the Lady"/*The Cowboy and the Lady*

1939

★ **"Over the Rainbow"**/*The Wizard of Oz*
"Faithful Forever"/*Gulliver's Travels*
"I Poured My Heart Into Song"/*Second Fiddle*
"Wishing"/*Love Affair*

1940

★ **"When You Wish Upon a Star"**/*Pinocchio*
"Down Argentine Way"/*Down Argentine Way*
"I'd Know You Anywhere"/*You'll Find Out*
"It's a Blue World"/*Music in My Heart*
"Love of My Life"/*Second Chorus*
"Only Forever"/*Rhythm on the River*
"Our Love Affair"/*Strike Up the Band*

1941

★ **"The Last Time I Saw Paris"**/*Lady Be Good*
"Baby Mine"/*Dumbo*
"Be Honest With Me"/*Ridin' on a Rainbow*
"Boogie Woogie Bugle Boy of Company B"/*Buck Privates*
"Chattanooga Choo Choo"/*Sun Valley Serenade*
"Since I Kissed My Baby Goodbye"/*You'll Never Get Rich*

1942

★ **"White Christmas"**/*Holiday Inn*
"Dearly Beloved"/*You Were Never Lovelier*
"How About You?"/*Babes on Broadway*
"I've Got a Gal in Kalamazoo"/*Orchestra Wives*
"Love Is a Song"/*Bambi*

1943

★ **"You'll Never Know"**/*Hello, Frisco, Hello*
"Happiness Is a Thing Called Joe"/*Cabin in the Sky*
"My Shining Hour"/*The Sky's the Limit*
"That Old Black Magic"/*Star Spangled Rhythm*
"They're Either Too Young or Too Old"/*Thank Your Lucky Stars*
"We Mustn't Say Goodbye"/*Stage Door Canteen*

1944

★ **"Swinging on a Star"**/*Going My Way*
"I Couldn't Sleep A Wink Last Night"/*Higher and Higher*
"I'll Walk Alone"/*Follow the Boys*
"Long Ago and Far Away"/*Cover Girl*
"Now I Know"/*Up in Arms*
"Sweet Dreams Sweetheart"/*Hollywood Canteen*
"The Trolley Song"/*Meet Me in St. Louis*

1945

★ **"It Might as Well Be Spring"**/*State Fair*
"Accentuate the Positive"/*Here Come the Waves*
"Anywhere"/*Tonight and Every Night*
"Aren't You Glad You're You"/*The Bells of St. Mary's*
"I Fall in Love Too Easily"/*Anchors Aweigh*
"More and More"/*Can't Help Singing*
"So in Love"/*Wonder Man*
"Some Sunday Morning"/*San Antonio*

1946

★ **"On the Atchison, Topeka and Santa Fe"**/*The Harvey Girls*
"I Can't Begin to Tell You"/*The Dolly Sisters*
"You Keep Coming Back Like a Song"/*Blue Skies*

1947

"I Wish I Didn't Love You So"/*The Perils of Pauline*
"Pass That Peace Pipe"/*Good News*
"You Do"/*Mother Wore Tights*

1948

★ **"Buttons and Bows"**/*The Paleface*
"For Every Man There's a Woman"/*Casbah*
"It's Magic"/*Romance on the High Seas*

1949

★ **"Baby It's Cold Outside"**/*Neptune's Daughter*
"It's a Great Feeling"/*It's a Great Feeling*
"Lavender Blue"/*So Dear to My Heart*
"Through a Long and Sleepless Night"/*Come to the Stable*

1950

"Be My Love"/*The Toast of New Orleans*
"Bibbidy-Bobbidi-Boo"/*Cinderella*

1951

★ **"In the Cool, Cool, Cool of the Evening"**/*Here Comes the Groom*
"Too Late Now"/*Royal Wedding*
"Wonder Why"/*Rich, Young and Pretty*

1952

★ **"High Noon (Do Not Forsake Me, Oh My Darlin')"**/*High Noon*
"Am I in Love"/*Son of Paleface*
"Because You're Mine"/*Because You're Mine*
"Thumbelina"/*Hans Christian Andersen*
"Zing a Little Zong"/*Just for You*

1953

★ **"Secret Love"**/*Calamity Jane*
"My Flaming Heart"/*Small Town Girl*
"Sadie Thompson's Song (Blue Pacific Blues)"/*Miss Sadie Thompson*
"That's Amore"/*The Caddy*
"The Moon is Blue"/*The Moon Is Blue*

1954

★ **"Three Coins in the Fountain"**/*Three Coins in the Fountain*
"Count Your Blessings Instead of Sheep"/*White Christmas*
"Hold My Hand"/*Susan Slept Here*
"The Man That Got Away"/*A Star Is Born*

1955

★ **"Love Is a Many-Splendored Thing"**/*Love Is a Many-Splendored Thing*
"(Love Is) The Tender Trap"/*The Tender Trap*
"I'll Never Stop Loving You"/*Love Me or Leave Me*
"Something's Gotta Give"/*Daddy Long Legs*

1956

★ **"Que Sera, Sera"**/*The Man Who Knew Too Much*
"Friendly Persuasion (Thee I Love)"/*Friendly Persuasion*
"True Love"/*High Society*
"Written on the Wind"/*Written on the Wind*

1957

"An Affair to Remember"/*An Affair to Remember*
"Tammy"/*Tammy and the Bachelor*

1958

★ **"Gigi"**/*Gigi*
"A Very Precious Love"/*Marjorie Morningstar*
"Almost in Your Arms (Love Song from Houseboat)"/*Houseboat*
"To Love and Be Loved"/*Some Came Running*

1959

★ **"High Hopes"**/*A Hole in the Head*
"Strange Are the Ways of Love"/*The Young Land*
"The Best of Everything"/*The Best of Everything*
"The Five Pennies"/*The Five Pennies*
"The Hanging Tree"/*The Hanging Tree*

1960

★ **"Never on Sunday"**/*Never on Sunday*
"The Facts of Life"/*The Facts of Life*
"The Green Leaves of Summer"/*The Alamo*

1961

★ **"Moon River"**/*Breakfast at Tiffany's*
"Bachelor in Paradise"/*Bachelor in Paradise*
"Love Theme (The Falcon and the Dove)"/*El Cid*
"Pocketful of Miracles"/*Pocketful of Miracles*
"Town without Pity"/*Town without Pity*

1962

★ **"Days of Wine and Roses"**/*Days of Wine and Roses*
"Love Song (Follow Me)"/*Mutiny on the Bounty*
"Song fromm Two for the Seesaw (Second Chance)"/*Two for the Seesaw*
"Walk on the Wild Side"/*Walk on the Wild Side*

1963

★ **"Call Me Irresponsible"**/*Papa's Delicate Condition*
"Charade"/*Charade*
"It's a Mad, Mad, Mad, Mad World"/*It's a Mad, Mad, Mad, Mad World*
"More"/*Mondo Cane*
"So Little Time"/*55 Days at Peking*

1964

★ **"Chim Chim Cher-ee"**/*Mary Poppins*
"Hush, Hush, Sweet Charlotte"/*Hush, Hush, Sweet Charlotte*
"My Kind of Town"/*Robin and the 7 Hoods*
"Where Love Has Gone"/*Where Love Has Gone*

1965

★ **"The Shadow of Your Smile"**/*The Sandpiper*
"I Will Wait for You"/*Umbrellas of Cherbourg*
"The Ballad of Cat Ballou"/*Cat Ballou*
"The Sweetheart Tree"/*The Great Race*
"What's New Pussycat?"/*What's New Pussycat?*

1966

★ **"Born Free"**/*Born Free*
"Alfie"/*Alfie*
"Georgy Girl"/*Georgy Girl*
"My Wishing Doll"/*Hawaii*

1967

★ **"Talk to the Animals"**/*Doctor Dolittle*
"The Bare Necessities"/*The Jungle Book*
"The Look of Love"/*Casino Royale*
"Thoroughly Modern Millie"/*Thoroughly Modern Millie*

1968

★ **"The Windmills of Your Mind"**/*The Thomas Crown Affair*
"Chitty Chitty Bang Bang"/*Chitty Chitty Bang Bang*
"For Love of Ivy"/*For Love of Ivy*
"Funny Girl"/*Funny Girl*
"Star!"/*Star!*

1969

★ **"Raindrops Keep Fallin' on My Head"**/*Butch Cassidy and the Sundance Kid*
"Come Saturday Morning"/*The Sterile Cuckoo*
"Jean"/*The Prime of Miss Jean Brodie*
"True Grit"/*True Grit*
"What Are You Doing the Rest of Your Life?"/*The Happy Ending*

1970

★ **"For All We Know"**/*Lovers and Other Strangers*
"Thank You Very Much"/*Scrooge*
"Till Love Touches Your Life"/*Madron*
"Whistling Away the Dark"/*Darling Lili*

1971

★ **"Theme from Shaft"**/*Shaft*
"All His Children"/*Sometimes a Great Notion*
"Bless the Beasts and the Children"/*Bless the Beasts and Children*
"Life Is What You MaKe It"/*Kotch*
"The Age of Not Believing"/*Bedknobs and Broomsticks*

1972

★ **"The Morning After"**/*The Poseidon Adventure*
"Ben"/*Ben*
"Marmalade, Molasses & Honey"/*Life & Times of Judge Roy Bean*
"Strange Are the Ways of Love"/*The Stepmother*

1973

★ **"The Way We Were"**/*The Way We Were*
"All That Love Went to Waste"/*A Touch of Class*
"Live and Let Die"/*Live and Let Die*
"Love"/*Robin Hood*
"You're So Nice to Be Around"/*Cinderella Liberty*

1974

★ **"We May Never Love Like This Again"**/*The Towering Inferno*
"Benji's Theme (I Feel Love)"/*Benji*
"Blazing Saddles"/*Blazing Saddles*
"Little Prince"/*The Little Prince*

1975

★ **"I'm Easy"**/*Nashville*
"How Lucky Can You Get"/*Funny Lady*
"Now That We're in Love"/*Whiffs*
"Richard's Window"/*The Other Side of the Mountain*
"Theme from Mahogany"/*Mahogany*

1976

★ **"Evergreen"**/*A Star Is Born*
"Ave Satani"/*The Omen*
"Come to Me"/*The Pink Panther Strikes Again*
"Gonna Fly Now"/*Rocky*

1977

★ **"You Light Up My Life"**/*You Light Up My Life*
"Candle on the Water"/*Pete's Dragon*
"Nobody Does It Better"/*The Spy Who Loved Me*
"Someone's Waiting for You"/*The Rescuers*

1978

★ **"Last Dance"**/*Thank God It's Friday*
"Hopelessly Devoted to You"/*Grease*
"Ready to Take a Chance Again"/*Foul Play*
"The Last Time I Felt Like This"/*Same Time, Next Year*
"When You're Loved"/*Magic of Lassie*

1979

★ **"It Goes Like It Goes"**/*Norma Rae*
"Song from 10 (It's Easy to Say)"/*10*
"The Rainbow Connection"/*The Muppet Movie*
"Theme from Ice Castles-Through the Eyes of Love"/*Ice Castles*
"Theme from The Promise: I'll Never Say Goodbye"/*The Promise*

1980

★ **"Fame"**/*Fame*
"Nine to Five"/*9 to 5*
"On the Road Again"/*Honeysuckle Rose*
"Out Here on My Own"/*Fame*
"People Alone"/*The Competition*

1981

★ **"Arthur's Theme"**/*Arthur*
"Endless Love"/*Endless Love*
"For Your Eyes Only"/*For Your Eyes Only*
"One More Hour"/*Ragtime*
"The First Time It Happens"/*The Great Muppet Caper*

1982

★ **"Up Where We Belong"**/*An Officer and a Gentleman*
"Eye of the Tiger"/*Rocky 3*
"How Do You Keep the Music Playing?"/*Best Friends*
"If We Were in Love"/*Yes, Giorgio*
"It Might Be You"/*Tootsie*

1983

★ **"Flashdance...What a Feeling"**/*Flashdance*
"Maniac"/*Flashdance*
"Over You"/*Tender Mercies*
"Papa, Can You Hear Me?"/*Yentl*
"The Way He Makes Me Feel"/*Yentl*

1984

★ **"I Just Called to Say I Love You"**/*The Woman in Red*
"Against All Odds (Take a Look at Me Now)"/*Against All Odds*
"Footloose"/*Footloose*
"Ghostbusters"/*Ghostbusters*
"Let's Hear It for the Boy"/*Footloose*

1985

★ **"Say You, Say Me"**/*White Nights*
"Miss Celie's Blues (Sister)"/*The Color Purple*
"Separate Lives (Love Theme from White Nights)"/*White Nights*
"Surprise, Surprise"/*A Chorus Line*
"The Power of Love"/*Back to the Future*

1986

★ **"Take My Breath Away"**/*Top Gun*
"Glory of Love"/*The Karate Kid: Part 2*

★ = winner

SONG *cont.*

"Life in a Looking Glass"/*That's Life!*
"Mean Green Mother from Outer Space"/*Little Shop of Horrors*
"Somewhere Out There"/*An American Tail*

1987
★ **"(I've Had) the Time of My Life"**/*Dirty Dancing*
"Cry Freedom"/*Cry Freedom*
"Nothing's Gonna Stop Us Now"/*Mannequin*
"Shakedown"/*Beverly Hills Cop 2*
"Storybook Love"/*The Princess Bride*

1988
★ **"Let the River Run"**/*Working Girl*
"Calling You"/*Bagdad Cafe*
"Two Hearts"/*Buster*

1989
★ **"Under the Sea"**/*The Little Mermaid*
"After All"/*Chances Are*
"I Love to See You Smile"/*Parenthood*
"Kiss the Girl"/*The Little Mermaid*
"The Girl Who Used to Be Me"/*Shirley Valentine*

1990
★ **"Sooner or Later"**/*Dick Tracy*
"Blaze of Glory"/*Young Guns 2*
"I'm Checkin' Out"/*Postcards from the Edge*
"Promise Me You'll Remember"/*The Godfather, Part 3*
"Somewhere in My Memory"/*Home Alone*

1991
★ **"Beauty and the Beast"**/*Beauty and the Beast*
"(Everything I Do) I Do It for You"/*Robin Hood: Prince of Thieves*
"Be Our Guest"/*Beauty and the Beast*
"Belle"/*Beauty and the Beast*
"When You're Alone"/*Hook*

1992
★ **"A Whole New World"**/*Aladdin*
"Beautiful Maria of My Soul"/*The Mambo Kings*
"Friend Like Me"/*Aladdin*
"I Have Nothing"/*The Bodyguard*
"Run to You"/*The Bodyguard*

1993
★ **"Streets of Philadelphia"**/*Philadelphia*
"A Wink and a Smile"/*Sleepless in Seattle*
"Again"/*Poetic Justice*
"Philadelphia"/*Philadelphia*
"The Day I Fall in Love"/*Beethoven's 2nd*

1994
★ **"Can You Feel the Love Tonight"**/*The Lion King*
"Circle of Life"/*The Lion King*
"Hakuna Matata"/*The Lion King*
"Look What Love Has Done"/*Junior*
"Make Up Your Mind"/*The Paper*

1995
★ **"Colors of the Wind"**/*Pocahontas*
"Dead Man Walking"/*Dead Man Walking*
"Have You Ever Really Loved a Woman?"/*Don Juan DeMarco*
"Moonlight"/*Sabrina*
"You've Got a Friend"/*Toy Story*

1996
★ **"You Must Love Me"**/*Evita*
"Because You Loved Me"/*Up Close and Personal*
"For the First Time"/*One Fine Day*
"I've Finally Found Someone"/*The Mirror Has Two Faces*
"That Thing You Do!"/*That Thing You Do!*

1997
★ **"My Heart Will Go On"**/*Titanic*
"Go the Distance"/*Hercules*
"How Do I Live"/*Con Air*
"Journey to the Past"/*Anastasia*
"Miss Misery"/*Good Will Hunting*

1998
★ **"When You Believe"**/*Prince of Egypt*
"A Soft Place to Fall"/*The Horse Whisperer*
"I Don't Want to Miss a Thing"/*Armageddon*
"That'll Do"/*Babe: Pig in the City*
"The Prayer"/*Quest for Camelot*

1999
★ **"You'll Be In My Heart"**/*Tarzan*
"Blame Canada"/*South Park: Bigger, Longer and Uncut*
"Music of My Heart"/*Music of the Heart*
"Save Me"/*Magnolia*
"When She Loved Me"/*Toy Story 2*

2000
★ **"Things Have Changed"**/*Wonder Boys*
"A Fool in Love"/*Meet the Parents*
"A Love Before Time"/*Crouching Tiger, Hidden Dragon*
"I've Seen It All"/*Dancer in the Dark*
"My Funny Friend and Me"/*The Emperor's New Groove*

2001
★ **"If I Didn't Have You"**/*Monsters, Inc.*
"May It Be"/*Lord of the Rings 1: The Fellowship of the Rings*
"There You'll Be"/*Pearl Harbor*
"Until"/*Kate & Leopold*
"Vanilla Sky"/*Vanilla Sky*

SOUND

1933
★ *A Farewell to Arms*
42nd Street
Gold Diggers of 1933
I Am a Fugitive from a Chain Gang

1934
★ *One Night of Love*
Cleopatra
The Gay Divorcee
Imitation of Life
Viva Villa!

1935
★ *Naughty Marietta*
The Bride of Frankenstein
Captain Blood
I Dream Too Much
The Lives of a Bengal Lancer

1936
★ *San Francisco*
The Charge of the Light Brigade
Dodsworth
General Spanky
Mr. Deeds Goes to Town
The Texas Rangers
That Girl from Paris
Three Smart Girls

1937
★ *The Hurricane*
The Girl Said No
In Old Chicago
The Life of Emile Zola
Lost Horizon
Maytime
100 Men and a Girl
Topper

1938
★ *The Cowboy and the Lady*
Four Daughters
Sweethearts
That Certain Age
Vivacious Lady
You Can't Take It with You

1939
Balalaika
Gone with the Wind
Goodbye, Mr. Chips
The Hunchback of Notre Dame
Mr. Smith Goes to Washington
Of Mice and Men
The Private Lives of Elizabeth & Essex
The Rains Came

1940
★ *Strike Up the Band*
Captain Caution
The Grapes of Wrath
The Howards of Virginia
Kitty Foyle
Our Town
The Sea Hawk

1941
★ *That Hamilton Woman*
Ball of Fire
The Chocolate Soldier
Citizen Kane
How Green Was My Valley
Sergeant York
Topper Returns

1942
★ *Yankee Doodle Dandy*
Arabian Nights
Bambi
Flying Tigers
Mrs. Miniver
Once Upon a Honeymoon
The Pride of the Yankees
The Road to Morocco
You Were Never Lovelier

1943
★ *This Land Is Mine*
Madame Curie
The North Star
The Phantom of the Opera
Sahara
So This Is Washington
The Song of Bernadette
This Is the Army
War of the Wildcats

1944
★ *Wilson*
Casanova Brown
Cover Girl
Double Indemnity
His Butler's Sister
Hollywood Canteen

1945
★ *The Bells of St. Mary's*
Flame of the Barbary Coast
Lady on a Train
Leave Her to Heaven
Rhapsody in Blue
A Song to Remember
The Southerner
They Were Expendable
The Three Caballeros
Wonder Man

1946
★ *The Jolson Story*
The Best Years of Our Lives
It's a Wonderful Life

1947
★ *The Bishop's Wife*
Green Dolphin Street
T-Men

1948
★ *The Snake Pit*
Johnny Belinda
Moonrise

1949
★ *Twelve o'Clock High*
Sands of Iwo Jima

1950
★ *All About Eve*
Cinderella
Trio

1951
★ *The Great Caruso*
A Streetcar Named Desire
Two Tickets to Broadway

1952
Hans Christian Andersen
The Promoter
The Quiet Man

1953
★ *From Here to Eternity*
Calamity Jane
Knights of the Round Table
The War of the Worlds

1954
★ *The Glenn Miller Story*
Brigadoon
The Caine Mutiny
Rear Window
Susan Slept Here

1955
★ *Oklahoma!*
Love Is a Many-Splendored Thing
Love Me or Leave Me
Mister Roberts
Not as a Stranger

1956
★ *The King and I*
The Brave One
The Eddy Duchin Story
Friendly Persuasion
The Ten Commandments

1957
★ *Sayonara*
Gunfight at the O.K. Corral
Les Girls
Pal Joey
Witness for the Prosecution

1958
★ *South Pacific*
I Want to Live!
A Time to Love & a Time to Die
Vertigo
The Young Lions

1959
★ *Ben-Hur*
Journey to the Center of the Earth
The Nun's Story

1960
★ *The Alamo*
The Apartment
Cimarron
Sunrise at Campobello

1961
★ *West Side Story*
The Children's Hour
Flower Drum Song
The Guns of Navarone
The Parent Trap

1962
★ *Lawrence of Arabia*
Bon Voyage!
The Music Man
That Touch of Mink
What Ever Happened to Baby Jane?

1963
★ *How the West Was Won*
Bye, Bye, Birdie
Captain Newman, M.D.
Cleopatra
It's a Mad, Mad, Mad, Mad World

1964
★ *My Fair Lady*
Becket
Father Goose
Mary Poppins
The Unsinkable Molly Brown

1965
★ *The Sound of Music*
The Agony and the Ecstasy
Doctor Zhivago
The Great Race
Shenandoah

1966
★ *Grand Prix*
Gambit
Hawaii
The Sand Pebbles
Who's Afraid of Virginia Woolf?

1967
★ *In the Heat of the Night*
Camelot
The Dirty Dozen
Doctor Dolittle
Thoroughly Modern Millie

1968
★ *Oliver!*
Bullitt
Finian's Rainbow
Funny Girl
Star!

1969
★ *Hello, Dolly!*
Anne of the Thousand Days
Butch Cassidy and the Sundance Kid
Marooned

1970
★ *Patton*
Airport
Ryan's Daughter
Tora! Tora! Tora!
Woodstock

1971
★ *Fiddler on the Roof*
Diamonds Are Forever
The French Connection
Kotch
Mary, Queen of Scots

1972
★ *Cabaret*
Butterflies Are Free
The Candidate
The Godfather
The Poseidon Adventure

1973
★ *The Exorcist*
The Day of the Dolphin
The Paper Chase
Paper Moon
The Sting

1974
★ *Earthquake*
Chinatown
The Conversation
The Towering Inferno
Young Frankenstein

1975
★ *Jaws*
Bite the Bullet
Funny Lady
The Hindenburg
The Wind and the Lion

1976
★ *All the President's Men*
King Kong
Rocky
Silver Streak
A Star Is Born

1977
★ *Star Wars*
Close Encounters of the Third Kind
The Deep
Sorcerer
The Turning Point

1978
★ *The Deer Hunter*
The Buddy Holly Story
Days of Heaven
Hooper
Superman: The Movie

1979
★ *Apocalypse Now*
The Electric Horseman
Meteor
1941
The Rose

1980
★ *The Empire Strikes Back*
Coal Miner's Daughter
Fame
Raging Bull

1981
★ *Raiders of the Lost Ark*
On Golden Pond
Outland
Pennies from Heaven
Reds

1982
★ *Gandhi*
Das Boot
E.T.: The Extra-Terrestrial
Tootsie
Tron

1983
★ *The Right Stuff*
Never Cry Wolf
Return of the Jedi
Terms of Endearment
WarGames

1984
★ *Amadeus*
Dune
A Passage to India
The River
2010: The Year We Make Contact

1985
★ *Out of Africa*
Back to the Future
A Chorus Line
Ladyhawke
Silverado

1986
★ *Platoon*
Aliens
Heartbreak Ridge
Star Trek 4: The Voyage Home
Top Gun

1987
★ *The Last Emperor*
Empire of the Sun
Lethal Weapon
RoboCop
The Witches of Eastwick

1988
★ *Bird*
Die Hard
Gorillas in the Mist
Mississippi Burning
Who Framed Roger Rabbit

1989
★ *Glory*
The Abyss
Black Rain
Born on the Fourth of July
Indiana Jones and the Last Crusade

1990
★ *Dances with Wolves*
Days of Thunder
Dick Tracy
The Hunt for Red October
Total Recall

1991
★ *Terminator 2: Judgment Day*
Backdraft
Beauty and the Beast
JFK
The Silence of the Lambs

1992
★ *The Last of the Mohicans*
Aladdin
A Few Good Men
Under Siege
Unforgiven

1993
★ *Jurassic Park*
Cliffhanger
The Fugitive
Geronimo: An American Legend
Schindler's List

1994
★ *Speed*
Clear and Present Danger
Forrest Gump
Legends of the Fall

★ = winner

The Shawshank Redemption

1995

★ Apollo 13
Batman Forever
Braveheart
Crimson Tide
Waterworld

1996

★ The English Patient
Evita
Independence Day
The Rock
Twister

1997

★ Titanic
Air Force One
Con Air
Contact
L.A. Confidential

1998

★ Saving Private Ryan
Armageddon
The Mask of Zorro
Shakespeare in Love
The Thin Red Line

1999

★ The Matrix
The Green Mile
The Insider
The Mummy
Star Wars: Episode 1—The Phantom Menace

2000

★ Gladiator
The Patriot
The Perfect Storm
U-571

2001

★ Black Hawk Down
Amelie
Lord of the Rings 1: The Fellowship of the Rings
Moulin Rouge
Pearl Harbor

SOUND EFFECTS EDITING

1963

★ It's a Mad, Mad, Mad, Mad World

1964

★ Goldfinger

1965

★ The Great Race

1966

★ Grand Prix

1967

★ The Dirty Dozen

1975

★ The Hindenburg

1977

★ Close Encounters of the Third Kind

1979

★ The Black Stallion

1986

★ Aliens

1990

★ The Hunt for Red October

1991

★ Terminator 2: Judgment Day

1992

★ Bram Stoker's Dracula
Aladdin
Under Siege

1993

★ Jurassic Park
Cliffhanger
The Fugitive

1996

★ The Ghost and the Darkness
Daylight
The English Patient

1997

★ Titanic
Face/Off
The Fifth Element

1998

★ Saving Private Ryan
Armageddon
The Mask of Zorro

2000

★ U-571
Space Cowboys

ADAPTED SCREENPLAY

1928

The Jazz Singer

1931

★ Cimarron
Criminal Code
Little Caesar

1932

Arrowsmith
Dr. Jekyll and Mr. Hyde

1933

★ Little Women
Lady for a Day

1934

★ It Happened One Night
The Thin Man
Viva Villa!

1956

★ Around the World in 80 Days
Baby Doll
Friendly Persuasion
Giant
Lust for Life

1957

★ The Bridge on the River Kwai
Heaven Knows, Mr. Allison
Peyton Place
Sayonara
Twelve Angry Men

1958

★ Gigi
Cat on a Hot Tin Roof
The Horse's Mouth
I Want to Live!
Separate Tables

1959

★ Room at the Top
Anatomy of a Murder
Ben-Hur
The Nun's Story
Some Like It Hot

1960

★ Elmer Gantry
Inherit the Wind
The Sundowners
Tunes of Glory

1961

★ Judgment at Nuremberg
Breakfast at Tiffany's
The Guns of Navarone
The Hustler
West Side Story

1962

★ To Kill a Mockingbird
David and Lisa
Lawrence of Arabia
Lolita
The Miracle Worker

1963

★ Tom Jones
Captain Newman, M.D.
Hud
Lilies of the Field
Sundays & Cybele

1964

★ Becket
Dr. Strangelove, or: How I Learned to Stop Worrying and Love the Bomb
Mary Poppins
My Fair Lady
Zorba the Greek

1965

★ Doctor Zhivago
Cat Ballou
The Collector
Ship of Fools
A Thousand Clowns

1966

★ A Man for All Seasons
Alfie
Cool Hand Luke
The Professionals
The Russians Are Coming, the Russians Are Coming
Who's Afraid of Virginia Woolf?

1967

★ In the Heat of the Night
The Graduate
In Cold Blood
Ulysses

1968

★ The Lion in Winter
The Odd Couple
Oliver!
Rachel, Rachel
Rosemary's Baby

1969

★ Midnight Cowboy
Anne of the Thousand Days
Goodbye Columbus
They Shoot Horses, Don't They?
Z

1970

★ M*A*S*H
Airport
I Never Sang for My Father
Lovers and Other Strangers
Women in Love

1971

★ The French Connection
A Clockwork Orange
The Conformist
The Garden of the Finzi-Continis
The Last Picture Show

1972

★ The Godfather
Cabaret
The Emigrants
Pete 'n' Tillie
Sounder

1973

★ The Exorcist
The Last Detail
The Paper Chase
Paper Moon
Serpico

1974

★ The Godfather, Part 2
The Apprenticeship of Duddy Kravitz
Lenny
Murder on the Orient Express
Young Frankenstein

1975

★ One Flew Over the Cuckoo's Nest
Barry Lyndon
The Man Who Would Be King
The Scent of a Woman
The Sunshine Boys

1976

★ All the President's Men
Bound for Glory
The Seven-Per-Cent Solution
Voyage of the Damned

1977

★ Julia
Equus
I Never Promised You a Rose Garden
Oh, God!
That Obscure Object of Desire

1978

★ Midnight Express
Bloodbrothers
California Suite
Heaven Can Wait
Same Time, Next Year

1979

★ Kramer vs. Kramer
Apocalypse Now
La Cage aux Folles
A Little Romance
Norma Rae

1980

★ Ordinary People
Breaker Morant
Coal Miner's Daughter
The Elephant Man
The Stunt Man

1981

★ On Golden Pond
The French Lieutenant's Woman
Pennies from Heaven
Prince of the City
Ragtime

1982

★ Missing
Das Boot
Sophie's Choice
The Verdict
Victor/Victoria

1983

★ Terms of Endearment
Betrayal
The Dresser
Educating Rita
Reuben, Reuben

1984

★ Amadeus
Greystoke: The Legend of Tarzan, Lord of the Apes
The Killing Fields
A Passage to India
A Soldier's Story

1985

★ Out of Africa
The Color Purple
Kiss of the Spider Woman
Prizzi's Honor
The Trip to Bountiful

1986

★ A Room with a View
Children of a Lesser God
The Color of Money
Crimes of the Heart
Stand by Me

1987

★ The Last Emperor
The Dead
Fatal Attraction
Full Metal Jacket
My Life As a Dog

1988

★ Dangerous Liaisons
The Accidental Tourist
Gorillas in the Mist
Little Dorrit, Film 1: Nobody's Fault
The Unbearable Lightness of Being

1989

★ Driving Miss Daisy
Born on the Fourth of July
Enemies, a Love Story
Field of Dreams
My Left Foot

1990

★ Dances with Wolves
Awakenings
Goodfellas
The Grifters
Reversal of Fortune

1991

★ The Silence of the Lambs
Europa, Europa
Fried Green Tomatoes
JFK
The Prince of Tides

1992

★ Howard's End
Enchanted April
The Player
A River Runs Through It
Scent of a Woman

1993

★ Schindler's List
The Age of Innocence
In the Name of the Father
The Remains of the Day
Shadowlands

1994

★ Forrest Gump
The Madness of King George
Nobody's Fool
Quiz Show
The Shawshank Redemption

1995

★ Sense and Sensibility
Apollo 13
Babe
Leaving Las Vegas
The Postman

1996

★ Sling Blade
The Crucible
The English Patient
Hamlet
Trainspotting

1997

★ L.A. Confidential
Donnie Brasco
The Sweet Hereafter
Wag the Dog
The Wings of the Dove

1998

★ Gods and Monsters
Out of Sight
Primary Colors
A Simple Plan
The Thin Red Line

1999

★ The Cider House Rules
Election
The Green Mile
The Insider
The Talented Mr. Ripley

2000

★ Traffic
Chocolat
Crouching Tiger, Hidden Dragon
O Brother Where Art Thou?
Wonder Boys

2001

★ A Beautiful Mind
Ghost World
In the Bedroom
Lord of the Rings 1: The Fellowship of the Rings
Shrek

ORIGINAL SCREENPLAY

1940

★ The Great McGinty
Angels Over Broadway
Foreign Correspondent
The Great Dictator

1941

★ Citizen Kane
The Devil & Miss Jones
Sergeant York

1942

★ Woman of the Year
One of Our Aircraft Is Missing
The Road to Morocco
Wake Island

1943

Air Force
In Which We Serve
The North Star
So Proudly We Hail

1944

★ Wilson
Hail the Conquering Hero
Miracle of Morgan's Creek
Two Girls and a Sailor
A Wing and a Prayer

1945

Dillinger

1946

★ The Seventh Veil
The Blue Dahlia
Children of Paradise
Notorious
The Road to Utopia
To Each His Own

1947

★ The Bachelor and the Bobby-Soxer
Body and Soul
A Double Life
Monsieur Verdoux
Shoeshine

1956

★ The Red Balloon
La Strada
The Ladykillers

1974

★ Chinatown
Alice Doesn't Live Here Anymore
The Conversation
Day for Night
Harry and Tonto

1975

★ Dog Day Afternoon
Amarcord
And Now My Love
Lies My Father Told Me
Shampoo

1976

★ Network
Cousin, Cousine
The Front
Rocky
Seven Beauties

1977

★ Annie Hall
The Goodbye Girl
The Late Show
Star Wars
The Turning Point

1978

★ Coming Home
Autumn Sonata
The Deer Hunter
Interiors
An Unmarried Woman

1979

★ Breaking Away
All That Jazz
And Justice for All
The China Syndrome
Manhattan

1980

★ Melvin and Howard
Brubaker
Fame
Mon Oncle d'Amerique
Private Benjamin

1981

★ Chariots of Fire
Absence of Malice
Arthur
Atlantic City
Reds

1982

★ Gandhi
Diner
E.T.: The Extra-Terrestrial
An Officer and a Gentleman
Tootsie

1983

★ Tender Mercies
The Big Chill
Fanny and Alexander
Silkwood
WarGames

1984

★ Places in the Heart
Beverly Hills Cop
Broadway Danny Rose
El Norte
Splash

1985

★ Witness
Back to the Future
Brazil
The Official Story
The Purple Rose of Cairo

1986

★ Hannah and Her Sisters
Crocodile Dundee
My Beautiful Laundrette
Platoon
Salvador

1987

★ Moonstruck
Au Revoir les Enfants
Broadcast News
Hope and Glory
Radio Days

1988

★ Rain Man
Big
Bull Durham

★ = winner

ORIGINAL SCREENPLAY *cont.*

A Fish Called Wanda
Running on Empty

1989

★ Dead Poets Society
Crimes & Misdemeanors
Do the Right Thing
sex, lies and videotape
When Harry Met Sally...

1990

★ Ghost
Alice
Avalon
Green Card
Metropolitan

1991

★ Thelma & Louise
Boyz N the Hood
Bugsy
The Fisher King
Grand Canyon

1992

★ The Crying Game
Husbands and Wives
Lorenzo's Oil
Passion Fish
Unforgiven

1993

★ The Piano
Dave
In the Line of Fire
Philadelphia
Sleepless in Seattle

1994

★ Pulp Fiction
Bullets over Broadway
Four Weddings and a Funeral
Heavenly Creatures
Trois Couleurs: Rouge

1995

★ The Usual Suspects
Braveheart
Mighty Aphrodite
Nixon
Toy Story

1996

★ Fargo
Jerry Maguire
Lone Star
Secrets and Lies
Shine

1997

★ Good Will Hunting
As Good As It Gets
Boogie Nights
Deconstructing Harry
The Full Monty

1998

★ Shakespeare in Love
Bulworth
Life Is Beautiful
Saving Private Ryan
The Truman Show

1999

★ American Beauty
Being John Malkovich
Magnolia
The Sixth Sense
Topsy Turvy

2000

★ Almost Famous
Billy Elliot
Erin Brockovich
Gladiator
Gladiator
You Can Count On Me

2001

★ Gosford Park
Amelie
Memento
Monster's Ball
The Royal Tenenbaums

SCREENPLAY

1935

★ The Informer
The Lives of a Bengal Lancer
Mutiny on the Bounty

1936

After the Thin Man
Dodsworth
Mr. Deeds Goes to Town
My Man Godfrey

1937

★ The Life of Emile Zola
The Awful Truth
Captains Courageous
Stage Door

1938

★ Pygmalion
The Citadel
Four Daughters
You Can't Take It with You

1939

★ Gone with the Wind
Goodbye, Mr. Chips
Wuthering Heights

1940

★ The Philadelphia Story
The Grapes of Wrath
Kitty Foyle
The Long Voyage Home
Rebecca

1941

★ Here Comes Mr. Jordan
How Green Was My Valley
The Little Foxes
The Maltese Falcon

1942

★ Mrs. Miniver
The Forty-Ninth Parallel
The Pride of the Yankees
Random Harvest
Talk of the Town

1943

★ Casablanca
The More the Merrier
The Song of Bernadette
Watch on the Rhine

1944

★ Going My Way
Double Indemnity
Gaslight
Laura
Meet Me in St. Louis

1945

★ The Lost Weekend
Mildred Pierce
A Tree Grows in Brooklyn

1946

★ The Best Years of Our Lives
Anna and the King of Siam
Brief Encounter
The Killers
Open City

1947

★ Miracle on 34th Street
Boomerang
Crossfire
Gentleman's Agreement
Great Expectations

1948

★ Treasure of the Sierra Madre
Johnny Belinda
The Search
The Snake Pit

1949

★ A Letter to Three Wives
All the King's Men
The Bicycle Thief
Champion
The Fallen Idol

1950

★ All About Eve
The Asphalt Jungle
Born Yesterday
Broken Arrow
Father of the Bride

1951

★ A Place in the Sun
The African Queen
Detective Story
La Ronde
A Streetcar Named Desire

1952

★ The Bad and the Beautiful
Five Fingers
High Noon
The Man in the White Suit
The Quiet Man

1953

★ From Here to Eternity
The Cruel Sea
Lili
Roman Holiday
Shane
Titanic

1954

★ Country Girl
The Caine Mutiny
Rear Window
Sabrina
Seven Brides for Seven Brothers

1955

★ Marty
Bad Day at Black Rock
Blackboard Jungle
East of Eden
Interrupted Melody
Love Me or Leave Me

STORY

1928

★ Underworld
Last Command

1931

Public Enemy

1932

★ The Champ
What Price Hollywood?

1933

The Prizefighter and the Lady
Rasputin and the Empress

1934

★ Manhattan Melodrama
Hide-Out

1935

Broadway Melody of 1936

1936

★ The Story of Louis Pasteur
Fury
The Great Ziegfeld
San Francisco
Three Smart Girls

1937

★ A Star Is Born
In Old Chicago
100 Men and a Girl

1938

★ Boys Town
Alexander's Ragtime Band
Angels with Dirty Faces
Mad About Music
Test Pilot

1939

★ Mr. Smith Goes to Washington
Bachelor Mother
Love Affair
Ninotchka
Young Mr. Lincoln

1940

Comrade X
Edison the Man
My Favorite Wife
The Westerner

1941

★ Here Comes Mr. Jordan
Ball of Fire
The Lady Eve
Meet John Doe
Tom, Dick, and Harry

1942

★ The Forty-Ninth Parallel
Holiday Inn
The Pride of the Yankees
Talk of the Town
Yankee Doodle Dandy

1943

★ The Human Comedy
Action in the North Atlantic
Destination Tokyo
The More the Merrier
Shadow of a Doubt

1944

★ Going My Way
A Guy Named Joe
Lifeboat

1945

★ House on 92nd Street
Objective, Burma!
A Song to Remember

1946

Dark Mirror
The Strange Love of Martha Ivers
The Stranger

1947

★ Miracle on 34th Street
Kiss of Death
Smash-Up: The Story of a Woman

1948

★ The Search
Louisiana Story
The Naked City
Red River
The Red Shoes

1949

★ The Stratton Story
Come to the Stable
It Happens Every Spring
Sands of Iwo Jima
White Heat

1950

★ Panic in the Streets
Bitter Rice
The Gunfighter

1951

Bullfighter & the Lady
Here Comes the Groom

1952

★ The Greatest Show on Earth
The Narrow Margin
Pride of St. Louis

1953

★ Roman Holiday
Above and Beyond
Captain's Paradise
Hondo
Titanic

1954

★ Broken Lance
Forbidden Games
There's No Business Like Show Business

1955

★ Love Me or Leave Me
The Private War of Major Benson
Rebel without a Cause
The Sheep Has Five Legs
Strategic Air Command

1956

★ The Brave One
The Eddy Duchin Story
High Society
The Proud Ones
Umberto D

STORY & SCREENPLAY

1949

★ Battleground
Jolson Sings Again
Paisan
Passport to Pimlico

1950

★ Sunset Boulevard
Adam's Rib
The Men
No Way Out

1951

★ An American in Paris
David and Bathsheba
Go for Broke!
The Well

1952

★ The Lavender Hill Mob
The Atomic City
Pat and Mike
Viva Zapata!

1953

★ Titanic
The Band Wagon
The Desert Rats
The Naked Spur

1954

★ On the Waterfront
The Barefoot Contessa
Genevieve
The Glenn Miller Story

1955

★ Interrupted Melody
The Court Martial of Billy Mitchell
It's Always Fair Weather
Mr. Hulot's Holiday
The Seven Little Foys

1957

★ Designing Woman
Funny Face
I Vitelloni
Man of a Thousand Faces
The Tin Star

1958

★ The Defiant Ones
The Goddess
Houseboat
Teacher's Pet

1959

★ Pillow Talk
The 400 Blows
North by Northwest
Operation Petticoat
Wild Strawberries

1960

★ The Apartment
The Facts of Life
Hiroshima, Mon Amour
Never on Sunday

1961

★ Splendor in the Grass
Ballad of a Soldier
La Dolce Vita
Lover Come Back

1962

★ Divorce—Italian Style
Last Year at Marienbad
That Touch of Mink
Through a Glass Darkly

1963

★ How the West Was Won
8 1/2
Love with the Proper Stranger

1964

★ Father Goose
That Man from Rio
Alun Owen/A Hard Day's Night

1965

★ Darling
Casanova '70
Those Magnificent Men in Their Flying Machines
The Train
Umbrellas of Cherbourg

1966

★ A Man and a Woman
Blow-Up
The Fortune Cookie
Khartoum
The Naked Prey

1967

★ Guess Who's Coming to Dinner
Bonnie & Clyde
Divorce American Style
Two for the Road

1968

★ The Producers
The Battle of Algiers
Faces
Hot Millions
2001: A Space Odyssey

1969

★ Butch Cassidy and the Sundance Kid
Bob & Carol & Ted & Alice
The Damned
Easy Rider
The Wild Bunch

1970

★ Patton
Five Easy Pieces
Joe
Love Story
My Night at Maud's

1971

★ The Hospital
Klute
Summer of '42
Sunday, Bloody Sunday

1972

★ The Candidate
The Discreet Charm of the Bourgeoisie
Lady Sings the Blues
Murmur of the Heart
Young Winston

1973

★ The Sting
American Graffiti
Cries and Whispers
Save the Tiger
A Touch of Class

WRITING

1929

The Leatherneck
Our Dancing Daughters

1930

All Quiet on the Western Front
Disraeli
The Divorcee

FILM—FOREIGN LANGUAGE

1948

★ Monsieur Vincent

1949

★ The Bicycle Thief

1950

★ The Walls of Malapaga

1951

★ Rashomon

1952

★ Forbidden Games

1954

★ Gate of Hell

1955

★ Samurai 1: Musashi Miyamoto

1956

★ La Strada
The Burmese Harp
Gervaise

1957

★ Nights of Cabiria

1958

★ Mon Oncle
Big Deal on Madonna Street

1959

★ Black Orpheus
The Bridge
The Great War

1960

★ The Virgin Spring
Kapo

1961

★ Through a Glass Darkly

1962

★ Sundays & Cybele

1963

★ 8 1/2
Knife in the Water

1964

★ Yesterday, Today and Tomorrow
Sallah

1965

★ The Shop on Main Street
Kwaidan
Umbrellas of Cherbourg
Woman in the Dunes

1966

★ A Man and a Woman
The Battle of Algiers
Loves of a Blonde

1967

★ Closely Watched Trains

1968

★ War and Peace
The Firemen's Ball
Stolen Kisses

 ★ = winner

1969

★ *Z*
Battle of Neretva

1970

First Love
My Night at Maud's
Tristana

1971

★ *The Garden of the Finzi-Continis*
Dodes 'ka-den
Tchaikovsky

1972

★ *The Discreet Charm of the Bourgeoisie*
I Love You Rosa

1973

★ *Day for Night*
The Deluge
The House on Chelouche Street
The Pedestrian
Turkish Delight

1974

★ *Amarcord*
Cat's Play

1975

★ *Dersu Uzala*
Land of Promise
Sandakan No. 8
The Scent of a Woman

1976

★ *Black and White in Color*
Cousin, Cousine
Jacob the Liar
Nights and Days
Seven Beauties

1977

★ *Madame Rosa*
Iphigenia
Operation Thunderbolt
A Special Day
That Obscure Object of Desire

1978

★ *Get Out Your Handkerchiefs*

1979

★ *The Tin Drum*
Maids of Wilko
Mama Turns a Hundred
A Simple Story
To Forget Venice

1980

★ *Moscow Does Not Believe in Tears*
Kagemusha
The Last Metro
The Nest

1981

★ *Mephisto*
The Boat Is Full
Man of Iron
Three Brothers

1982

Alsino and the Condor
Coup de Torchon
Flight of the Eagle
Private Life

1983

★ *Fanny and Alexander*
Carmen
Entre-Nous
Le Bal

1984

★ *Dangerous Moves*
Beyond the Walls
Camila

1985

★ *The Official Story*
Angry Harvest
Colonel Redl
Three Men and a Cradle
When Father Was Away on Business

1986

★ *The Assault*
Betty Blue
The Decline of the American Empire
My Sweet Little Village

1987

★ *Babette's Feast*
Au Revoir les Enfants
The Family
Pathfinder

1988

★ *Pelle the Conqueror*
Hanussen
The Music Teacher
Salaam Bombay!
Women on the Verge of a Nervous Breakdown

1989

★ *Cinema Paradiso*
Camille Claudel
Jesus of Montreal

1990

★ *Journey of Hope*
Cyrano de Bergerac
Ju Dou
The Nasty Girl
Open Doors

1991

★ *Mediterraneo*
The Elementary School
The Ox
Raise the Red Lantern
Sweetie

1992

★ *Indochine*
Children of Nature
Close to Eden
Daens
Schtonk

1993

★ *Belle Epoque*
Farewell My Concubine
Hedd Wyn
The Scent of Green Papaya
The Wedding Banquet

1994

★ *Burnt by the Sun*
Before the Rain
Eat Drink Man Woman
Farinelli
Strawberry and Chocolate

1995

★ *Antonia's Line*
All Things Fair
Lamerica
O Quatrilho
The Star Maker

1996

★ *Kolya*
★ *Ridicule*
A Chef in Love
The Other Side of Sunday
Prisoner of the Mountains
Ridicule

1997

★ *Character*
Beyond Silence
Four Days in September
The Thief

1998

★ *Life Is Beautiful*
Central Station
The Grandfather
Tango

1999

★ *All About My Mother*
East-West
Himalaya
Solomon and Gaenor
Under the Sun

2000

★ *Crouching Tiger, Hidden Dragon*
Amores Perros
Divided We Fall
Everybody's Famous!

2001

★ *No Man's Land*
Amelie

VISUAL EFFECTS

1963

★ *Cleopatra*

1964

★ *Mary Poppins*

1965

★ *Thunderball*

1966

★ *Fantastic Voyage*

1967

★ *Doctor Dolittle*

1968

★ *2001: A Space Odyssey*

1969

★ *Marooned*

1970

★ *Tora! Tora! Tora!*

1971

★ *Bedknobs and Broomsticks*

1972

★ *The Poseidon Adventure*

1974

★ *Earthquake*

1975

★ *The Hindenburg*

1976

★ *King Kong*
★ *Logan's Run*

1977

★ *Star Wars*

1978

★ *Superman: The Movie*

1979

★ *Alien*

1980

★ *The Empire Strikes Back*

1981

★ *Raiders of the Lost Ark*

1982

★ *E.T.: The Extra-Terrestrial*

1983

★ *Return of the Jedi*

1984

★ *Indiana Jones and the Temple of Doom*

1985

★ *Cocoon*

1986

★ *Aliens*

1987

★ *Innerspace*

1988

★ *Who Framed Roger Rabbit*

1989

★ *The Abyss*

1990

★ *Total Recall*

1991

★ *Terminator 2: Judgment Day*
Backdraft
Hook

1992

★ *Death Becomes Her*
Alien 3
Batman Returns

1993

★ *Jurassic Park*
Cliffhanger
The Nightmare before Christmas

1994

★ *Forrest Gump*
The Mask
True Lies

1995

★ *Babe*

1996

★ *Independence Day*
Dragonheart
Twister

1997

★ *Titanic*
The Lost World: Jurassic Park 2
Starship Troopers

1998

★ *What Dreams May Come*
Armageddon
Mighty Joe Young

1999

★ *The Matrix*
Star Wars: Episode 1—The Phantom Menace
Stuart Little

2000

★ *Gladiator*
The Hollow Man
The Perfect Storm

2001

A. I.: Artificial Intelligence
Lord of the Rings 1: The Fellowship of the Rings
Pearl Harbor

BRITISH ACADEMY OF FILM AND TELEVISION ARTS

ACTOR

1952

★ **Marlon Brando/***Viva Zapata!*

1953

★ **Marlon Brando/***Julius Caesar*
★ **John Gielgud/***Julius Caesar*

1954

★ **Marlon Brando/***On the Waterfront*
★ **Kenneth More/***Doctor in the House*

1955

★ **Ernest Borgnine/***Marty*
★ **Laurence Olivier/***Richard III*

1956

★ **Francois Perier/***Gervaise*

1957

★ **Henry Fonda/***Twelve Angry Men*
★ **Alec Guinness/***The Bridge on the River Kwai*

1958

★ **Trevor Howard/***The Key*
★ **Sidney Poitier/***The Defiant Ones*

1959

★ **Jack Lemmon/***Some Like It Hot*
★ **Peter Sellers/***I'm All Right Jack*

1960

★ **Jack Lemmon/***The Apartment*

1961

★ **Peter Finch/***No Love for Johnnie*
★ **Paul Newman/***The Hustler*

1962

★ **Burt Lancaster/***Birdman of Alcatraz*
★ **Peter O'Toole/***Lawrence of Arabia*

1963

★ **Dirk Bogarde/***The Servant*
★ **Marcello Mastroianni/***Divorce—Italian Style*

1964

★ **Richard Attenborough/***Seance on a Wet Afternoon*
★ **Marcello Mastroianni/***Yesterday, Today and Tomorrow*

1965

★ **Dirk Bogarde/***Darling*
★ **Lee Marvin/***Cat Ballou*

1966

★ **Richard Burton/***Who's Afraid of Virginia Woolf?*
★ **Rod Steiger/***The Pawnbroker*

1967

★ **Paul Scofield/***A Man for All Seasons*
★ **Rod Steiger/***In the Heat of the Night*

1968

★ **Spencer Tracy/***Guess Who's Coming to Dinner*

1969

★ **Dustin Hoffman/***Midnight Cowboy*

1970

★ **Robert Redford/***Butch Cassidy and the Sundance Kid*

1971

★ **Peter Finch/***Sunday, Bloody Sunday*

1972

★ **Gene Hackman/***The French Connection*

1973

★ **Walter Matthau/***Pete 'n' Tillie*

1974

★ **Jack Nicholson/***Chinatown*
★ **Jack Nicholson/***The Last Detail*

1975

★ **Al Pacino/***Dog Day Afternoon*

1976

★ **Jack Nicholson/***One Flew Over the Cuckoo's Nest*

1977

★ **Peter Finch/***Network*

1978

★ **Richard Dreyfuss/***The Goodbye Girl*

1979

★ **Jack Lemmon/***The China Syndrome*

1980

★ **John Hurt/***The Elephant Man*

1981

★ **Burt Lancaster/***Atlantic City*

1982

★ **Ben Kingsley/***Gandhi*

1983

★ **Michael Caine/***Educating Rita*
★ **Dustin Hoffman/***Tootsie*

1984

★ **Haing S. Ngor/***The Killing Fields*

1985

★ **William Hurt/***Kiss of the Spider Woman*

1986

★ **Bob Hoskins/***Mona Lisa*

1987

★ **Sean Connery/***The Name of the Rose*

1988

★ **John Cleese/***A Fish Called Wanda*

1989

★ **Daniel Day-Lewis/***My Left Foot*

1990

★ **Philippe Noiret/***Cinema Paradiso*

1991

★ **Anthony Hopkins/***The Silence of the Lambs*

1992

★ **Robert Downey, Jr./***Chaplin*

1993

★ **Anthony Hopkins/***The Remains of the Day*
Daniel Day-Lewis/*In the Name of the Father*

1994

★ **Hugh Grant/***Four Weddings and a Funeral*
Anthony Hopkins/*Shadowlands*
Liam Neeson/*Schindler's List*

1995

★ **Nigel Hawthorne/***The Madness of King George*
Nicolas Cage/*Leaving Las Vegas*
Jonathan Pryce/*Carrington*
Massimo Troisi/*The Postman*

1996

★ **Geoffrey Rush/***Shine*
Ralph Fiennes/*The English Patient*
Ian McKellen/*Richard III*
Timothy Spall/*Secrets and Lies*

1997

★ **Robert Carlyle/***The Full Monty*
Billy Connolly/*Mrs. Brown*
Kevin Spacey/*L.A. Confidential*
Ray Winstone/*Nil by Mouth*

1998

★ **Roberto Benigni/***Life Is Beautiful*
Michael Caine/*Little Voice*
Joseph Fiennes/*Shakespeare in Love*
Tom Hanks/*Saving Private Ryan*

1999

★ **Kevin Spacey/***American Beauty*
Jim Broadbent/*Topsy Turvy*
Russell Crowe/*The Insider*
Ralph Fiennes/*The End of the Affair*
Om Puri/*East Is East*

2000

★ **Jamie Bell/***Billy Elliot*

2001

★ **Russell Crowe/***A Beautiful Mind*
Jim Broadbent/*Iris*
Ian McKellen/*Lord of the Rings 1: The Fellowship of the Rings*
Kevin Spacey/*The Shipping News*
Tom Wilkinson/*In the Bedroom*

ACTOR—SUPPORTING

1971

★ **Edward Fox/***The Go-Between*

1972

★ **Ben Johnson/***The Last Picture Show*

1973

★ **Arthur Lowe/***O Lucky Man!*

1974

★ **John Gielgud/***Murder on the Orient Express*

1975

★ **Fred Astaire/***The Towering Inferno*

1976

★ **Brad Dourif/***One Flew Over the Cuckoo's Nest*

1977

★ **Edward Fox/***A Bridge Too Far*

★ = winner

ACTOR—SUPPORTING *cont.*

1978

★ **John Hurt**/*Midnight Express*

1979

★ **Robert Duvall**/*Apocalypse Now*

1981

★ **Ian Holm**/*Chariots of Fire*

1982

★ **Jack Nicholson**/*Reds*

1983

★ **Denholm Elliott**/*Trading Places*

1984

★ **Denholm Elliott**/*A Private Function*

1985

★ **Denholm Elliott**/*Defense of the Realm*

1986

★ **Ray McAnally**/*The Mission*

1987

★ **Daniel Auteuil**/*Jean de Florette*

1988

★ **Michael Palin**/*A Fish Called Wanda*

1989

★ **Ray McAnally**/*My Left Foot*

1990

★ **Salvatore Cascio**/*Cinema Paradiso*

1991

★ **Alan Rickman**/*Robin Hood: Prince of Thieves*

1992

★ **Gene Hackman**/*Unforgiven*

1993

★ **Ralph Fiennes**/*Schindler's List*
Tommy Lee Jones/*The Fugitive*
John Malkovich/*In the Line of Fire*

1994

★ **Samuel L. Jackson**/*Pulp Fiction*
Ben Kingsley/*Schindler's List*

1995

★ **Tim Roth**/*Rob Roy*
Ian Holm/*The Madness of King George*
Martin Landau/*Ed Wood*
Alan Rickman/*Sense and Sensibility*

1996

★ **Paul Scofield**/*The Crucible*
John Gielgud/*Shine*
Edward Norton/*Primal Fear*
Alan Rickman/*Michael Collins*

1997

★ **Tom Wilkinson**/*The Full Monty*
Mark Addy/*The Full Monty*
Rupert Everett/*My Best Friend's Wedding*
Burt Reynolds/*Boogie Nights*

1998

★ **Geoffrey Rush**/*Shakespeare in Love*
Ed Harris/*The Truman Show*
Geoffrey Rush/*Elizabeth*
Tom Wilkinson/*Shakespeare in Love*

1999

★ **Jude Law**/*The Talented Mr. Ripley*
Wes Bentley/*American Beauty*
Michael Caine/*The Cider House Rules*
Rhys Ifans/*Notting Hill*
Timothy Spall/*Topsy Turvy*

2000

★ **Benicio Del Toro**/*Traffic*

2001

★ **Jim Broadbent**/*Moulin Rouge*
Hugh Bonneville/*Iris*
Robbie Coltrane/*Harry Potter and the Sorcerer's Stone*
Colin Firth/*Bridget Jones's Diary*
Eddie Murphy/*Shrek*

ACTRESS

1952

★ **Vivien Leigh**/*A Streetcar Named Desire*

1953

★ **Leslie Caron**/*Lili*
★ **Audrey Hepburn**/*Roman Holiday*

1955

★ **Betsy Blair**/*Marty*
★ **Katie Johnson**/*The Ladykillers*

1956

★ **Anna Magnani**/*The Rose Tattoo*

1958

★ **Simone Signoret**/*Room at the Top*

1959

★ **Audrey Hepburn**/*The Nun's Story*
★ **Shirley MacLaine**/*Ask Any Girl*

1960

★ **Shirley MacLaine**/*The Apartment*
★ **Rachel Roberts**/*Saturday Night and Sunday Morning*

1961

★ **Sophia Loren**/*Two Women*

1962

★ **Anne Bancroft**/*The Miracle Worker*

1963

★ **Patricia Neal**/*Hud*
★ **Rachel Roberts**/*This Sporting Life*

1964

★ **Audrey Hepburn**/*Charade*

1965

★ **Julie Christie**/*Darling*
★ **Patricia Neal**/*In Harm's Way*

1966

★ **Elizabeth Taylor**/*Who's Afraid of Virginia Woolf?*

1967

★ **Anouk Aimee**/*A Man and a Woman*

1968

★ **Katharine Hepburn**/*Guess Who's Coming to Dinner*

1969

★ **Maggie Smith**/*The Prime of Miss Jean Brodie*

1970

★ **Katharine Ross**/*Butch Cassidy and the Sundance Kid*

1971

★ **Glenda Jackson**/*Sunday, Bloody Sunday*

1972

★ **Liza Minnelli**/*Cabaret*

1973

★ **Delphine Seyrig**/*The Discreet Charm of the Bourgeoisie*

1974

★ **Joanne Woodward**/*Summer Wishes, Winter Dreams*

1975

★ **Ellen Burstyn**/*Alice Doesn't Live Here Anymore*

1976

★ **Louise Fletcher**/*One Flew Over the Cuckoo's Nest*

1977

★ **Diane Keaton**/*Annie Hall*

1978

★ **Jane Fonda**/*Julia*

1979

★ **Jane Fonda**/*The China Syndrome*

1980

★ **Judy Davis**/*My Brilliant Career*

1981

★ **Meryl Streep**/*The French Lieutenant's Woman*

1982

★ **Katharine Hepburn**/*On Golden Pond*

1983

★ **Julie Walters**/*Educating Rita*

1984

★ **Maggie Smith**/*A Private Function*

1985

★ **Peggy Ashcroft**/*A Passage to India*

1986

★ **Maggie Smith**/*A Room with a View*

1987

★ **Anne Bancroft**/*84 Charing Cross Road*

1988

★ **Maggie Smith**/*The Lonely Passion of Judith Hearne*

1989

★ **Pauline Collins**/*Shirley Valentine*

1990

★ **Jessica Tandy**/*Driving Miss Daisy*

1991

★ **Jodie Foster**/*The Silence of the Lambs*

1992

★ **Emma Thompson**/*Howard's End*

1993

★ **Holly Hunter**/*The Piano*
Miranda Richardson/*Tom & Viv*

1994

★ **Susan Sarandon**/*The Client*
Emma Thompson/*The Remains of the Day*
Debra Winger/*Shadowlands*

1995

★ **Emma Thompson**/*Sense and Sensibility*
Nicole Kidman/*To Die For*
Helen Mirren/*The Madness of King George*
Elisabeth Shue/*Leaving Las Vegas*

1996

★ **Brenda Blethyn**/*Secrets and Lies*
Frances McDormand/*Fargo*
Kristin Scott Thomas/*The English Patient*
Emily Watson/*Breaking the Waves*

1997

★ **Judi Dench**/*Mrs. Brown*
Kim Basinger/*L.A. Confidential*
Helena Bonham Carter/*The Wings of the Dove*
Kathy Burke/*Nil by Mouth*

1998

★ **Cate Blanchett**/*Elizabeth*
Jane Horrocks/*Little Voice*
Gwyneth Paltrow/*Shakespeare in Love*
Emily Watson/*Hilary and Jackie*

1999

★ **Annette Bening**/*American Beauty*
Linda Bassett/*East Is East*
Julianne Moore/*The End of the Affair*
Emily Watson/*Angela's Ashes*

2000

★ **Julia Roberts**/*Erin Brockovich*

2001

★ **Judi Dench**/*Iris*
Nicole Kidman/*The Others*
Sissy Spacek/*In the Bedroom*
Audrey Tautou/*Amelie*
Renee Zellweger/*Bridget Jones's Diary*

ACTRESS—SUPPORTING

1961

★ **Dora Bryan**/*A Taste of Honey*

1969

★ **Celia Johnson**/*The Prime of Miss Jean Brodie*

1970

★ **Susannah York**/*They Shoot Horses, Don't They?*

1971

★ **Margaret Leighton**/*The Go-Between*

1972

★ **Cloris Leachman**/*The Last Picture Show*

1973

★ **Valentina Cortese**/*Day for Night*

1974

★ **Ingrid Bergman**/*Murder on the Orient Express*

1975

★ **Diane Ladd**/*Alice Doesn't Live Here Anymore*

1976

★ **Jodie Foster**/*Taxi Driver*

1977

★ **Jenny Agutter**/*Equus*

1978

★ **Geraldine Page**/*Interiors*
★ **Vanessa Redgrave**/*Julia*

1979

★ **Rachel Roberts**/*Yanks*

1982

★ **Rohini Hattangady**/*Gandhi*
★ **Maureen Stapleton**/*Reds*

1983

★ **Jamie Lee Curtis**/*Trading Places*

1984

★ **Liz Smith**/*A Private Function*

1985

★ **Rosanna Arquette**/*Desperately Seeking Susan*

1986

★ **Judi Dench**/*A Room with a View*

1987

★ **Susan Wooldridge**/*Hope and Glory*

1988

★ **Judi Dench**/*A Handful of Dust*

1989

★ **Michelle Pfeiffer**/*Dangerous Liaisons*

1990

★ **Whoopi Goldberg**/*Ghost*

1991

★ **Kate Nelligan**/*Frankie and Johnny*

1992

★ **Miranda Richardson**/*Damage*

1993

★ **Miriam Margolyes**/*The Age of Innocence*
Holly Hunter/*The Firm*
Maggie Smith/*The Secret Garden*

1994

★ **Kristin Scott Thomas**/*Four Weddings and a Funeral*
Winona Ryder/*The Age of Innocence*

1995

★ **Kate Winslet**/*Sense and Sensibility*
Joan Allen/*Nixon*
Mira Sorvino/*Mighty Aphrodite*
Elizabeth Spriggs/*Sense and Sensibility*

1996

★ **Juliette Binoche**/*The English Patient*
Lauren Bacall/*The Mirror Has Two Faces*
Marianne Jean-Baptiste/*Secrets and Lies*
Lynn Redgrave/*Shine*

1997

★ **Sigourney Weaver**/*The Ice Storm*
Jennifer Ehle/*Wilde*
Lesley Sharp/*The Full Monty*
Zoe Wanamaker/*Wilde*

1998

★ **Judi Dench**/*Shakespeare in Love*
Kathy Bates/*Primary Colors*
Brenda Blethyn/*Little Voice*
Lynn Redgrave/*Gods and Monsters*

1999

★ **Maggie Smith**/*Tea with Mussolini*
Thora Birch/*American Beauty*
Cate Blanchett/*The Talented Mr. Ripley*
Cameron Diaz/*Being John Malkovich*
Mena Suvari/*American Beauty*

2000

★ **Julie Walters**/*Billy Elliot*

2001

★ **Jennifer Connelly**/*A Beautiful Mind*
Judi Dench/*The Shipping News*
Helen Mirren/*Gosford Park*
Maggie Smith/*Gosford Park*
Kate Winslet/*Iris*

ART DIRECTION

1997

★ *William Shakespeare's Romeo and Juliet*

1999

★ *Sleepy Hollow*
American Beauty
Angela's Ashes
The End of the Affair
The Matrix

CINEMATOGRAPHY

1995

★ *Braveheart*
Apollo 13
The Madness of King George
Sense and Sensibility

1996

★ *The English Patient*

1997

★ *The Wings of the Dove*
L.A. Confidential
Titanic
William Shakespeare's Romeo and Juliet

1998

★ *Elizabeth*
Saving Private Ryan
Shakespeare in Love
The Truman Show

1999

★ *American Beauty*
Angela's Ashes
The End of the Affair
The Matrix
The Talented Mr. Ripley

2000

★ *Gladiator*

2001

Black Hawk Down
Lord of the Rings 1: The Fellowship of the Rings
Moulin Rouge

COSTUME DESIGN

1997

★ *Mrs. Brown*
L.A. Confidential
Titanic
The Wings of the Dove

1998

★ *Velvet Goldmine*
Elizabeth
The Mask of Zorro
Shakespeare in Love

1999

★ *Sleepy Hollow*
The End of the Affair
An Ideal Husband
Tea with Mussolini

2001

★ *Gosford Park*
Harry Potter and the Sorcerer's Stone
Lord of the Rings 1: The Fellowship of the Rings
Moulin Rouge
Planet of the Apes

DIRECTOR

1955

★ **Laurence Olivier**/*Richard III*

1968

★ **Mike Nichols**/*The Graduate*

1969

★ **John Schlesinger**/*Midnight Cowboy*

1970

★ **George Roy Hill**/*Butch Cassidy and the Sundance Kid*

1971

★ **John Schlesinger**/*Sunday, Bloody Sunday*

1972

★ **Bob Fosse**/*Cabaret*

1973

★ **Francois Truffaut**/*Day for Night*

1974

★ **Roman Polanski**/*Chinatown*

1975

★ **Stanley Kubrick**/*Barry Lyndon*

★ = winner

1976
★ **Milos Forman/***One Flew Over the Cuckoo's Nest*
1977
★ **Woody Allen/***Annie Hall*
1978
★ **Alan Parker/***Midnight Express*
1979
★ **Francis Ford Coppola/***Apocalypse Now*
1980
★ **Akira Kurosawa/***Kagemusha*
1981
★ **Louis Malle/***Atlantic City*
1982
★ **Richard Attenborough/***Gandhi*
1983
★ **Bill Forsyth/***Local Hero*
1984
★ **Wim Wenders/***Paris, Texas*
1986
★ **Woody Allen/***Hannah and Her Sisters*
1987
★ **Oliver Stone/***Platoon*
1988
★ **Louis Malle/***Au Revoir les Enfants*
1989
★ **Kenneth Branagh/***Henry V*
1990
★ **Martin Scorsese/***Goodfellas*
1991
★ **Alan Parker/***The Commitments*
1992
★ **Clint Eastwood/***Unforgiven*
1993
★ **Steven Spielberg/***Schindler's List*
1994
★ **Mike Newell/***Four Weddings and a Funeral*
Richard Attenborough/*Shadowlands*
Jane Campion/*The Piano*
James Ivory/*The Remains of the Day*
1995
★ **Michael Radford/***The Postman*
Mel Gibson/*Braveheart*
Nicholas Hytner/*The Madness of King George*
Ang Lee/*Sense and Sensibility*
1996
★ **Joel Coen/***Fargo*
Scott Hicks/*Shine*
Mike Leigh/*Secrets and Lies*
Anthony Minghella/*The English Patient*
1997
★ **Baz Luhrmann/***William Shakespeare's Romeo and Juliet*
James Cameron/*Titanic*
Peter Cattaneo/*The Full Monty*
Curtis Hanson/*L.A. Confidential*
1998
★ **Peter Weir/***The Truman Show*
Shekhar Kapur/*Elizabeth*
John Madden/*Shakespeare in Love*
Steven Spielberg/*Saving Private Ryan*
1999
★ **Pedro Almodovar/***All About My Mother*
Neil Jordan/*The End of the Affair*
Sam Mendes/*American Beauty*
Anthony Minghella/*The Talented Mr. Ripley*
M. Night Shyamalan/*The Sixth Sense*
2000
★ **Ang Lee/***Crouching Tiger, Hidden Dragon*
2001
★ **Peter Jackson/***Lord of the Rings 1: The Fellowship of the Rings*
Robert Altman/*Gosford Park*
Ron Howard/*A Beautiful Mind*
Jean-Pierre Jeunet/*Amelie*
Baz Luhrmann/*Moulin Rouge*

FILM

1947
★ *The Best Years of Our Lives*
★ *Odd Man Out*
1948
★ *The Fallen Idol*
★ *Hamlet*
1949
★ *The Bicycle Thief*
★ *The Third Man*
1950
★ *All About Eve*
★ *The Blue Lamp*
1951
★ *La Ronde*
★ *The Lavender Hill Mob*
1953
★ *Forbidden Games*
★ *Genevieve*
1954
★ *Hobson's Choice*
★ *Wages of Fear*
1955
★ *Richard III*
1956
★ *Gervaise*
★ *Reach for the Sky*
1957
★ *The Bridge on the River Kwai*
1958
★ *Room at the Top*
1959
★ *Ben-Hur*
★ *Sapphire*
1960
★ *The Apartment*
★ *Saturday Night and Sunday Morning*
1961
★ *Ballad of a Soldier*
★ *The Hustler*
★ *A Taste of Honey*
1962
★ *Lawrence of Arabia*
1963
★ *Tom Jones*
1964
★ *Dr. Strangelove, or: How I Learned to Stop Worrying and Love the Bomb*
★ *King and Country*
1965
★ *The Ipcress File*
★ *My Fair Lady*
1966
★ *The Spy Who Came in from the Cold*
★ *Who's Afraid of Virginia Woolf?*
1967
★ *A Man for All Seasons*
1968
★ *The Graduate*
1969
★ *Midnight Cowboy*
1970
★ *Butch Cassidy and the Sundance Kid*
1971
★ *Sunday, Bloody Sunday*
1972
★ *Cabaret*
1973
★ *Day for Night*
1975
★ *Alice Doesn't Live Here Anymore*
1976
★ *One Flew Over the Cuckoo's Nest*
1977
★ *Annie Hall*
1978
★ *Julia*
1979
★ *Manhattan*
1980
★ *The Elephant Man*
1981
★ *Chariots of Fire*
1982
★ *Gandhi*
1983
★ *Educating Rita*
1984
★ *The Killing Fields*
1985
★ *The Purple Rose of Cairo*
1986
★ *A Room with a View*
1987
★ *Hope and Glory*
★ *Jean de Florette*
1988
★ *The Last Emperor*
1989
★ *Dead Poets Society*
1990
★ *Goodfellas*
1991
★ *The Commitments*
1992
★ *Unforgiven*
1993
★ *Schindler's List*
★ *Shadowlands*
Naked
Raining Stones
Tom & Viv
1994
★ *Four Weddings and a Funeral*
The Piano
The Remains of the Day
1995
★ *Sense and Sensibility*
Babe
Carrington
Land and Freedom
The Madness of King George
Trainspotting
The Usual Suspects
1996
★ *The English Patient*
Fargo
Secrets and Lies
Shine
1997
★ *The Full Monty*
★ *Nil by Mouth*
Behind the Lines
The Borrowers
L.A. Confidential
Mrs. Brown
Titanic
24-7
1998
★ *Elizabeth*
★ *Shakespeare in Love*
Hilary and Jackie
Little Voice
Lock, Stock and 2 Smoking Barrels
My Name Is Joe
Saving Private Ryan
Sliding Doors
The Truman Show
1999
★ *American Beauty*
★ *East Is East*
The End of the Affair
Notting Hill
Onegin
Ratcatcher
The Sixth Sense
The Talented Mr. Ripley
Topsy Turvy
Wonderland
2000
★ *Billy Elliot*
★ *Gladiator*
2001
★ *Gosford Park*
★ *Lord of the Rings 1: The Fellowship of the Rings*
Amelie
A Beautiful Mind
Bridget Jones's Diary
Harry Potter and the Sorcerer's Stone
Iris
Moulin Rouge
Shrek

FILM EDITING

1997
★ *L.A. Confidential*
The Full Monty
Titanic
William Shakespeare's Romeo and Juliet
1998
★ *Shakespeare in Love*
Elizabeth
Lock, Stock and 2 Smoking Barrels
Saving Private Ryan
1999
★ *American Beauty*
Being John Malkovich
The Matrix
The Sixth Sense
2001
Amelie
Black Hawk Down
Lord of the Rings 1: The Fellowship of the Rings
Moulin Rouge

MAKEUP

1997
★ *The Wings of the Dove*
1999
★ *Topsy Turvy*
American Beauty
The End of the Affair
An Ideal Husband

SCORE

1993
Sleepless in Seattle
1994
The Piano
Schindler's List
1995
★ *The Postman*
Braveheart
The Madness of King George
Sense and Sensibility
1996
★ *The English Patient*
1997
★ *William Shakespeare's Romeo and Juliet*
The Full Monty
L.A. Confidential
Titanic
1998
★ *Elizabeth*
Hilary and Jackie
Saving Private Ryan
Shakespeare in Love
1999
★ *American Beauty*
2000
★ *Crouching Tiger, Hidden Dragon*
2001
★ *Moulin Rouge*
Amelie
Lord of the Rings 1: The Fellowship of the Rings
Mulholland Drive
Shrek

ORIGINAL SCORE

1999
The End of the Affair
The Talented Mr. Ripley

SOUND

1997
★ *L.A. Confidential*
The Full Monty
Titanic
William Shakespeare's Romeo and Juliet
1998
★ *Saving Private Ryan*
Hilary and Jackie
Little Voice
Shakespeare in Love
1999
★ *The Matrix*
American Beauty
2001
★ *Moulin Rouge*
Black Hawk Down
Harry Potter and the Sorcerer's Stone
Lord of the Rings 1: The Fellowship of the Rings
Shrek

ADAPTED SCREENPLAY

1983
★ *Heat and Dust*
1984
★ *The Killing Fields*
1985
★ *Prizzi's Honor*
1986
★ *Out of Africa*
1987
★ *Jean de Florette*
1988
★ *The Unbearable Lightness of Being*
1989
★ *Dangerous Liaisons*
1990
★ *Goodfellas*
1991
★ *The Commitments*
1992
★ *The Player*
1993
★ *Schindler's List*
In the Name of the Father
Scent of a Woman
1994
★ *Quiz Show*
The Remains of the Day
Schindler's List
Shadowlands
1995
★ *Trainspotting*
Babe
Leaving Las Vegas
The Madness of King George
The Postman
Sense and Sensibility
1996
★ *The English Patient*
The Crucible
Evita
Richard III
1997
★ *William Shakespeare's Romeo and Juliet*
The Ice Storm
L.A. Confidential
The Wings of the Dove
1998
★ *Primary Colors*
Hilary and Jackie
Little Voice
Wag the Dog
1999
★ *The End of the Affair*
East Is East
An Ideal Husband
The Talented Mr. Ripley
2000
★ *Traffic*
2001
★ *Shrek*
A Beautiful Mind
Bridget Jones's Diary
Iris
Lord of the Rings 1: The Fellowship of the Rings

ORIGINAL SCREENPLAY

1983
★ *King of Comedy*
1984
★ *Broadway Danny Rose*
1985
★ *The Purple Rose of Cairo*
1986
★ *Hannah and Her Sisters*
1987
★ *Wish You Were Here*
1988
★ *A World Apart*
1989
★ *When Harry Met Sally...*
1990
★ *Cinema Paradiso*
1991
★ *Truly, Madly, Deeply*
1992
★ *Husbands and Wives*
1993
★ *Groundhog Day*
In the Line of Fire
Sleepless in Seattle
1994
★ *Pulp Fiction*
The Piano
1995
★ *The Usual Suspects*
Bullets over Broadway
Muriel's Wedding
Seven
1996
★ *Secrets and Lies*
Brassed Off
Fargo
Lone Star
Shine
1997
★ *Nil by Mouth*
Boogie Nights
The Full Monty
Mrs. Brown
1998
★ *The Truman Show*
Elizabeth
Life Is Beautiful
Shakespeare in Love
1999
★ *Being John Malkovich*
All About My Mother
American Beauty
The Sixth Sense
Topsy Turvy

★ = *winner*

ORIGINAL SCREENPLAY *cont.*

2001
★ *Amelie*
Gosford Park
Moulin Rouge
The Others
The Royal Tenenbaums

SCREENPLAY

1955
★ *The Ladykillers*
1956
★ *The Man Who Never Was*
1957
★ *The Bridge on the River Kwai*
1959
★ *I'm All Right Jack*
1961
★ *The Day the Earth Caught Fire*
1962
★ *Lawrence of Arabia*
★ *A Taste of Honey*
1963
★ *Tom Jones*
1964
★ *The Pumpkin Eater*
1965
★ *Darling*
1966
★ *Morgan: A Suitable Case for Treatment*
1967
★ *A Man for All Seasons*
1968
★ *The Graduate*
1969
★ *Midnight Cowboy*
1970
★ *Butch Cassidy and the Sundance Kid*
1971
★ *The Go-Between*
1972
★ *The Hospital*
★ *The Last Picture Show*
1973
★ *The Discreet Charm of the Bourgeoisie*
1974
★ *Chinatown*
★ *The Last Detail*
1975
★ *Alice Doesn't Live Here Anymore*
1976
★ *Bugsy Malone*
1977
★ *Annie Hall*
1978
★ *Julia*
1979
★ *Manhattan*
1981
★ *Gregory's Girl*
1982
★ *Missing*

FILM—FOREIGN LANGUAGE

1982
★ *Christ Stopped at Eboli*
1983
★ *Danton*
1984
★ *Carmen*
1985
★ *Colonel Redl*
1986
★ *Ran*
1987
★ *The Sacrifice*
1988
★ *Babette's Feast*
1989
★ *Life and Nothing But*
1990
★ *Cinema Paradiso*
1991
★ *The Nasty Girl*
1992
★ *Raise the Red Lantern*
1993
★ *Farewell My Concubine*
Indochine
Like Water for Chocolate
Un Coeur en Hiver
1994
★ *To Live*
1995
★ *The Postman*
Burnt by the Sun
Les Miserables
Queen Margot
1996
Antonia's Line
Kolya
Nelly et Monsieur Arnaud
1997
Ma Vie en Rose
The Tango Lesson
1998
★ *Central Station*
Life Is Beautiful
Live Flesh
1999
★ *All About My Mother*
The Celebration
Run Lola Run
2000
★ *Crouching Tiger, Hidden Dragon*
2001
★ *Amores Perros*
★ *Behind the Sun*
Amelie
Monsoon Wedding

VISUAL EFFECTS

1997
★ *The Fifth Element*
1999
★ *The Matrix*
Sleepy Hollow
2001
★ *Lord of the Rings 1: The Fellowship of the Rings*
A. I.: Artificial Intelligence
Harry Potter and the Sorcerer's Stone
Moulin Rouge
Shrek

BROADCAST FILM CRITICS ASSOCIATION AWARDS

ACTOR

1995
★ **Kevin Bacon/***Murder in the First*
1996
★ **Geoffrey Rush/***Shine*
1997
★ **Jack Nicholson/***As Good As It Gets*
1998
★ **Ian McKellen/***Gods and Monsters*
1999
★ **Russell Crowe/***The Insider*
2000
★ **Russell Crowe/***Gladiator*
2001
★ **Russell Crowe/***A Beautiful Mind*
Sean Penn/*I Am Sam*
Will Smith/*Ali*

ACTOR—SUPPORTING

1995
★ **Kevin Spacey/***Seven*
★ **Kevin Spacey/***The Usual Suspects*
1996
★ **Cuba Gooding, Jr./***Jerry Maguire*
1997
★ **Anthony Hopkins/***Amistad*
1998
★ **Billy Bob Thornton/***A Simple Plan*
1999
★ **Michael Clarke Duncan/***The Green Mile*
2000
★ **Joaquin Rafael (Leaf) Phoenix/***Gladiator*
2001
Jim Broadbent/*Iris*
Jon Voight/*Ali*
2002
★ **Ben Kingsley/***Sexy Beast*

ACTRESS

1995
★ **Nicole Kidman/***To Die For*
1996
★ **Frances McDormand/***Fargo*
1997
★ **Helena Bonham Carter/***The Wings of the Dove*
1998
★ **Cate Blanchett/***Elizabeth*
1999
★ **Hilary Swank/***Boys Don't Cry*
2000
★ **Julia Roberts/***Erin Brockovich*
2001
★ **Sissy Spacek/***In the Bedroom*
Nicole Kidman/*Moulin Rouge*
Renee Zellweger/*Bridget Jones's Diary*

ACTRESS—SUPPORTING

1995
★ **Mira Sorvino/***Mighty Aphrodite*
1996
★ **Joan Allen/***The Crucible*
1997
★ **Joan Cusack/***In and Out*
1998
★ **Joan Allen/***Pleasantville*
★ **Kathy Bates/***Primary Colors*
1999
★ **Angelina Jolie/***Girl, Interrupted*
2000
★ **Frances McDormand/***Almost Famous*
2001
★ **Jennifer Connelly/***A Beautiful Mind*
Cameron Diaz/*Vanilla Sky*
Marisa Tomei/*In the Bedroom*

BREAKTHROUGH PERFORMANCE

1996
★ **Renee Zellweger/***Jerry Maguire*
1997
★ **Matt Damon/***Good Will Hunting*
1999
★ **Spike Jonze/***Three Kings*
★ **Haley Joel Osment/***The Sixth Sense*

CINEMATOGRAPHY

2000
★ *Gladiator*

DIRECTOR

1995
★ **Mel Gibson/***Braveheart*
1996
★ **Anthony Minghella/***The English Patient*
1997
★ **James Cameron/***Titanic*
1998
★ **Steven Spielberg/***Saving Private Ryan*
1999
★ **Sam Mendes/***American Beauty*
2000
★ **Steven Soderbergh/***Erin Brockovich*
★ **Steven Soderbergh/***Traffic*
2001
★ **Ron Howard/***A Beautiful Mind*
Peter Jackson/*Lord of the Rings 1: The Fellowship of the Rings*
Baz Luhrmann/*Moulin Rouge*

FILM

1995
★ *Sense and Sensibility*
1996
★ *Fargo*
1997
★ *L.A. Confidential*
1998
★ *Saving Private Ryan*
1999
★ *American Beauty*
2000
★ *Gladiator*
2001
★ *A Beautiful Mind*
Ali
In the Bedroom
Lord of the Rings 1: The Fellowship of the Rings
The Man Who Wasn't There
Memento
Moulin Rouge
Mulholland Drive
The Shipping News
Shrek

FEATURE DOCUMENTARY

1996
★ *When We Were Kings*

SCORE

1998
★ *Saving Private Ryan*
2001
★ *Lord of the Rings 1: The Fellowship of the Rings*
A. I.: Artificial Intelligence
Harry Potter and the Sorcerer's Stone
The Shipping News

SONG

1998
★ **"When You Believe"/***Prince of Egypt*
2000
★ **"My Funny Friend and Me"/***The Emperor's New Groove*
2001
★ **"May It Be"/***Lord of the Rings 1: The Fellowship of the Rings*
"There You'll Be"/*Pearl Harbor*
"Until"/*Kate & Leopold*
"Vanilla Sky"/*Vanilla Sky*

ADAPTED SCREENPLAY

1997
★ *L.A. Confidential*
1998
★ *A Simple Plan*
1999
★ *The Green Mile*
2000
★ *Traffic*

ORIGINAL SCREENPLAY

1997
★ *Good Will Hunting*
1998
★ *Shakespeare in Love*
1999
★ *American Beauty*
2000
★ *Almost Famous*

SCREENPLAY

1995
★ *Sense and Sensibility*
1996
★ *The English Patient*
2001
★ *Memento*
The Man Who Wasn't There

CAST

2001
★ *Gosford Park*
Ocean's Eleven
The Royal Tenenbaums

FILM—FOREIGN LANGUAGE

1995
★ *The Postman*
1996
★ *Ridicule*
1997
★ *Shall We Dance?*
1998
★ *Life Is Beautiful*
1999
★ *All About My Mother*
2000
★ *Crouching Tiger, Hidden Dragon*
2001
★ *Amelie*
In the Mood for Love
No Man's Land

CANADIAN GENIE

ACTOR

1980
★ **Christopher Plummer/***Murder by Decree*
1982
★ **Nick Mancuso/***Ticket to Heaven*
1983
★ **Donald Sutherland/***Threshold*
1984
★ **Eric Fryer/***The Terry Fox Story*
1986
★ **John Wildman/***My American Cousin*
1987
★ **Gordon Pinsent/***John and the Missus*
1988
★ **Roger Le Bel/***Night Zoo*
1989
★ **Jeremy Irons/***Dead Ringers*
1990
★ **Remy Girard/***Jesus of Montreal*
1993
★ **Tom McCamus/***A Man in Uniform*
1994
★ **Maury Chaykin/***Whale Music*
Martin Drainville/*King of the Airwaves*
Gary Farmer/*Henry & Verlin*
Bruce Greenwood/*Exotica*
Elias Koteas/*Exotica*
1995
★ **David La Haye/***L'Enfant d'Eau*
Lothaire Bluteau/*The Confessional*
1996
★ **William Hutt/***Long Day's Journey Into Night*
Jason Cadieux/*Lilies*
Matthew Ferguson/*Lilies*
Danny Gilmore/*Lilies*
Tom McCamus/*Long Day's Journey Into Night*
Christopher Penn/*The Boys Club*
1997
★ **Ian Holm/***The Sweet Hereafter*
Bruce Greenwood/*The Sweet Hereafter*
Peter Outerbridge/*Kissed*
1998
★ **Roshan Seth/***Such a Long Journey*
Remy Girard/*The Boys*
Tony Nardi/*La Deroute*
Jonathan Pryce/*Behind the Lines*
Samuel West/*Rupert's Land*
1999
★ **Bob Hoskins/***Felicia's Journey*
Gabriel Arcand/*Post Mortem*
Ralph Fiennes/*Sunshine*
Daniel MacIvor/*The Five Senses*

ACTOR—SUPPORTING

1981
★ **German Houde/***Les Bons Debarras*
1982
★ **Saul Rubinek/***Ticket to Heaven*
1983
★ **R.H. Thomson/***If You Could See What I Hear*
1984
★ **Michael Zelniker/***The Terry Fox Story*
1985
★ **Alan Scarfe/***The Bay Boy*
1986
★ **Alan Arkin/***Joshua Then and Now*

★ = winner

1987

★ **Gabriel Arcand/***The Decline of the American Empire*

1988

★ **German Houde/***Night Zoo*

1990

★ **Remy Girard/***Jesus of Montreal*

1993

★ **Kevin Tighe/***A Man in Uniform*

1994

★ **Don McKellar/***Exotica*

1995

★ **Kenneth Welsh/***Margaret's Museum*

1996

★ **Peter Donaldson/***Long Day's Journey Into Night*
Alexander Chapman/*Lilies*
Sean McCann/*Swann*
Ron White/*Screamers*

1997

★ **Peter MacNeill/***The Hanging Garden*

1998

★ **Callum Keith Rennie/***Last Night*
Kurush Deboo/*Such a Long Journey*
Michael Riley/*Pale Saints*
Saul Rubinek/*Pale Saints*
George Wendt/*Rupert's Land*

1999

★ **Mark McKinney/***Dog Park*
James Frain/*Sunshine*
William Hurt/*Sunshine*

2001

★ **Martin Cummins/***Love Come Down*
Julian Richings/*The Claim*

ACTRESS

1980

★ **Kate Lynch/***Meatballs*

1981

★ **Marie Tifo/***Les Bons Debarras*

1982

★ **Margot Kidder/***Heartaches*

1983

★ **Rae Dawn Chong/***Quest for Fire*

1986

★ **Margaret Langrick/***My American Cousin*

1987

★ **Martha Henry/***Dancing in the Dark*

1988

★ **Sheila McCarthy/***I've Heard the Mermaids Singing*

1989

★ **Jackie Burroughs/***A Winter Tan*

1990

★ **Rebecca Jenkins/***Bye Bye Blues*

1991

★ **Pascale Montpetit/***H*

1993

★ **Sheila McCarthy/***The Lotus Eaters*

1994

★ **Sandra Oh/***Double Happiness*
Nancy Beatty/*Henry & Verlin*
Genevieve Bujold/*Mon Amie Max*
Valerie Kaprisky/*Mouvements du Desir*

1995

★ **Helena Bonham Carter/***Margaret's Museum*

1996

★ **Martha Henry/***Long Day's Journey Into Night*
Marie Brassard/*Le Polygraphe*
Helene Clarkson/*Blood & Donuts*
Brenda Fricker/*Swann*
Louise Portal/*Sous Sol*

1997

★ **Molly Parker/***Kissed*
Isabelle Cyr/*Karmina*
Sarah Polley/*The Sweet Hereafter*
Gabrielle Rose/*The Sweet Hereafter*

1998

★ **Sandra Oh/***Last Night*
Anne-Marie Cadieux/*No*
Pascale Montpetit/*Street Heart*
Ginette Reno/*It's My Turn, Laura Cadieux*
Pierrette Robitaille/*It's My Turn, Laura Cadieux*

1999

★ **Sylvie Moreau/***Post Mortem*
Elaine Cassidy/*Felicia's Journey*
Jennifer Ehle/*Sunshine*
Rosemary Harris/*Sunshine*
Mary-Louise Parker/*The Five Senses*

ACTRESS—SUPPORTING

1980

★ **Genevieve Bujold/***Murder by Decree*

1981

★ **Kate Reid/***Atlantic City*

1983

★ **Jackie Burroughs/***The Grey Fox*

1986

★ **Linda Sorensen/***Joshua Then and Now*

1987

★ **Louise Portal/***The Decline of the American Empire*

1988

★ **Paule Baillargeon/***I've Heard the Mermaids Singing*

1989

★ **Colleen Dewhurst/***Obsessed*

1990

★ **Robyn Stevan/***Bye Bye Blues*

1992

★ **Monique Mercure/***Naked Lunch*

1995

★ **Kate Nelligan/***Margaret's Museum*

1996

★ **Martha Burns/***Long Day's Journey Into Night*
Maria De Medeiros/*Le Polygraphe*
Jose Descenes/*Le Polygraphe*

1997

★ **Seana McKenna/***The Hanging Garden*
Kerry Fox/*The Hanging Garden*
Joan Orenstein/*The Hanging Garden*

1998

★ **Monique Mercure/***Conquest*
Genevieve Bujold/*Last Night*
Rachael Crawford/*Pale Saints*
Anna Henry/*The Fishing Trip*

1999

★ **Catherine O'Hara/***The Life Before This*
Deborah Kara Unger/*Sunshine*
Rachel Weisz/*Sunshine*

2001

Mimi Kuzyk/*Lost and Delirious*
Barbara Williams/*Love Come Down*

ART DIRECTION

1992

★ *Naked Lunch*

1993

★ *Shadow of the Wolf*

1994

★ *Exotica*

1995

★ *The Confessional*

1996

★ *Lilies*
The Boys Club
Screamers
Swann

1997

★ *Karmina*

1998

★ *The Red Violin*
Behind the Lines
Cube
Last Night
Such a Long Journey

CINEMATOGRAPHY

1992

★ *Naked Lunch*

1993

★ *32 Short Films about Glenn Gould*

1994

★ *Exotica*

1995

★ *Magic in the Water*

1996

★ *Crash*
Le Polygraphe
Lilies

1997

★ *The Sweet Hereafter*

1998

★ *The Red Violin*
Behind the Lines
Last Night
Such a Long Journey

1999

★ *Felicia's Journey*
The Five Senses

2001

★ *Lost and Delirious*
Ginger Snaps

COSTUME DESIGN

1992

★ *Leolo*

1993

★ *Shadow of the Wolf*

1994

★ *Exotica*

1995

★ *Margaret's Museum*

1996

★ *Lilies*
Blood & Donuts
Kids in the Hall: Brain Candy
Swann

1997

★ *Karmina*

1998

★ *The Red Violin*
Behind the Lines
No
Pale Saints
Street Heart
Such a Long Journey

1999

★ *Grey Owl*

DIRECTOR

1980

★ **Bob (Benjamin) Clark/***Murder by Decree*

1981

★ **Francis Mankiewicz/***Les Bons Debarras*

1983

★ **Phillip Borsos/***The Grey Fox*

1984

★ **Bob (Benjamin) Clark/***A Christmas Story*
★ **David Cronenberg/***Videodrome*

1986

★ **Sandy Wilson/***My American Cousin*

1987

★ **Denys Arcand/***The Decline of the American Empire*

1988

★ **Jean-Claude Lauzon/***Night Zoo*

1989

★ **David Cronenberg/***Dead Ringers*

1990

★ **Denys Arcand/***Jesus of Montreal*

1991

★ **Bruce Beresford/***Black Robe*

1992

★ **David Cronenberg/***Naked Lunch*

1993

★ **Francois Girard/***32 Short Films about Glenn Gould*

1994

★ **Atom Egoyan/***Exotica*
Richard J. Lewis/*Whale Music*
Lea Pool/*Mouvements du Desir*
Mina Shum/*Double Happiness*

1995

★ **Robert Lepage/***The Confessional*

1996

★ **David Cronenberg/***Crash*
John Fawcett/*The Boys Club*
John Greyson/*Lilies*
Robert Lepage/*Le Polygraphe*
Bruce McDonald/*Hard Core Logo*

1997

★ **Atom Egoyan/***The Sweet Hereafter*
Thom Fitzgerald/*The Hanging Garden*
Gabriel Pelletier/*Karmina*
Lynne Stopkewich/*Kissed*

1998

★ **Francois Girard/***The Red Violin*
Sturla Gunnarsson/*Such a Long Journey*
Gilles Mackinnon/*Behind the Lines*
Don McKellar/*Last Night*
Jonathan Tammuz/*Rupert's Land*
Joel Wyner/*Pale Saints*

1999

★ **Jeremy Podeswa/***The Five Senses*
Louis Belanger/*Post Mortem*
Atom Egoyan/*Felicia's Journey*
Istvan Szabo/*Sunshine*

FILM

1980

★ *The Changeling*

1981

★ *Les Bons Debarras*

1982

★ *Ticket to Heaven*

1983

★ *The Grey Fox*

1984

★ *The Terry Fox Story*

1985

★ *The Bay Boy*

1986

★ *My American Cousin*

1987

★ *The Decline of the American Empire*

1988

★ *Night Zoo*

1989

★ *Dead Ringers*
A Winter Tan

1990

★ *Jesus of Montreal*

1991

★ *Black Robe*

1992

★ *Naked Lunch*

1993

★ *32 Short Films about Glenn Gould*

1994

★ *Exotica*
Double Happiness
King of the Airwaves
Mon Amie Max
Whale Music

1995

★ *The Confessional*

1996

★ *Lilies*
Crash
Hard Core Logo
Le Polygraphe
Long Day's Journey Into Night

1997

★ *The Sweet Hereafter*
The Hanging Garden
Karmina
Kissed

1998

★ *The Red Violin*
Behind the Lines
Last Night
Rupert's Land
Such a Long Journey

1999

★ *Sunshine*
Felicia's Journey
The Five Senses
Post Mortem

2001

Love Come Down

FILM EDITING

1992

★ *Leolo*

1993

★ *32 Short Films about Glenn Gould*

1994

★ *Double Happiness*

1995

★ *Dance Me Outside*

1996

★ *Crash*
The Boys Club
Hard Core Logo
Lilies
Long Day's Journey Into Night

1997

★ *The Sweet Hereafter*

1998

★ *Such a Long Journey*
Behind the Lines
Cube
Last Night
The Red Violin

1999

★ *eXistenZ*

2001

Ginger Snaps

SCORE

1992

★ *Being at Home with Claude*

1993

★ *Cadillac Girls*

1994

★ *Exotica*

1995

★ *Margaret's Museum*

1996

★ *Curtis's Charm*
Lilies
Screamers
Swann

1997

★ *The Sweet Hereafter*

1998

★ *The Red Violin*

1999

★ *Felicia's Journey*

2001

Love Come Down

ORIGINAL SCORE

1998

Behind the Lines
Cube
Last Night
Such a Long Journey

1999

Sunshine

SONG

1994

★ **"Claire"/***Whale Music*

1996

★ **"Swamp Baby, Who the Hell Do You Think You Are?"/***Hard Core Logo*
"Some Days It's Dark"/*Kids in the Hall: Brain Candy*

1998

★ **"River Blue"/***The Fishing Trip*
"Laura - La Belle"/*It's My Turn, Laura Cadieux*

SOUND

1992

★ *Naked Lunch*

1993

★ *Le Sexe des Etoiles*
★ *The Lotus Eaters*

1994

★ *Whale Music*

1995

★ *Magic in the Water*

1996

★ *Lilies*
Crash
Hard Core Logo
Kids in the Hall: Brain Candy
Le Polygraphe

1997

★ *The Sweet Hereafter*

2001

★ *Love Come Down*

★ = winner

ADAPTED SCREENPLAY

1992
★ *Naked Lunch*

1994
★ *Love and Human Remains*

1995
★ *Margaret's Museum*

1996
★ *Crash*
Curtis's Charm
Hard Core Logo
Le Polygraphe
Lilies

1999
★ *Felicia's Journey*

ORIGINAL SCREENPLAY

1992
★ *Leolo*

1993
★ *The Lotus Eaters*

1994
★ *Exotica*

1996
★ *Sous Sol*
Blood & Donuts
The Boys Club

SCREENPLAY

1997
★ *The Hanging Garden*
Karmina
Kissed
The Sweet Hereafter

1998
★ *The Red Violin*
Behind the Lines
No
Such a Long Journey

1999
★ *Post Mortem*
The Five Senses

2001
Lost and Delirious
Love Come Down

CANNES

ACTOR

1946
★ **Ray Milland/***The Lost Weekend*

1949
★ **Edward G. Robinson/***House of Strangers*

1951
★ **Michael Redgrave/***The Browning Version*

1952
★ **Marlon Brando/***Viva Zapata!*

1953
★ **Charles Vanel/***Wages of Fear*

1955
★ **Spencer Tracy/***Bad Day at Black Rock*

1958
★ **Paul Newman/***The Long, Hot Summer*

1961
★ **Anthony Perkins/***Goodbye Again*

1962
★ **Murray Melvin/***A Taste of Honey*

1963
★ **Richard Harris/***This Sporting Life*

1964
★ **Saro Urzi/***Seduced and Abandoned*

1965
★ **Terence Stamp/***The Collector*

1966
★ **Per Oscarsson/***Hunger*

1969
★ **Jean-Louis Trintignant/***Z*

1971
★ **Riccardo Cucciolla/***Sacco & Vanzetti*

1973
★ **Giancarlo Giannini/***Love and Anarchy*

1974
★ **Jack Nicholson/***The Last Detail*

1977
★ **Fernando Rey/***Elisa, Vida Mia*

1978
★ **Jon Voight/***Coming Home*

1979
★ **Jack Lemmon/***The China Syndrome*

1981
★ **Ugo Tognazzi/***The Tragedy of a Ridiculous Man*

1982
★ **Jack Lemmon/***Missing*

1984
★ **Alfredo Landa/***The Holy Innocents*
★ **Francesco Rabal/***The Holy Innocents*

1985
★ **William Hurt/***Kiss of the Spider Woman*

1986
★ **Michel Blanc/***Menage*
★ **Bob Hoskins/***Mona Lisa*

1987
★ **Marcello Mastroianni/***Dark Eyes*

1988
★ **Forest Whitaker/***Bird*

1989
★ **James Spader/***sex, lies and videotape*

1990
★ **Gerard Depardieu/***Cyrano de Bergerac*

1991
★ **John Turturro/***Barton Fink*

1992
★ **Tim Robbins/***The Player*

1993
★ **David Thewlis/***Naked*

1994
★ **Ge You/***To Live*

1995
★ **Jonathan Pryce/***Carrington*

1996
★ **Daniel Auteuil/***The Eighth Day*
★ **Pascal Duquenne/***The Eighth Day*

1997
★ **Sean Penn/***She's So Lovely*

1998
★ **Peter Mullan/***My Name Is Joe*

1999
★ **Emmanuel Schotte/***Humanity*

2000
★ **Tony Leung Chiu-Wai/***In the Mood for Love*

ACTRESS

1946
★ **Michele Morgan/***La Symphonie Pastorale*

1951
★ **Bette Davis/***All About Eve*

1952
★ **Lee Grant/***Detective Story*

1953
★ **Shirley Booth/***Come Back, Little Sheba*

1954
★ **Maria Schell/***The Last Bridge*

1956
★ **Susan Hayward/***I'll Cry Tomorrow*

1957
★ **Giulietta Masina/***Nights of Cabiria*

1958
★ **Bibi Andersson/***Brink of Life*
★ **Eva Dahlbeck/***Brink of Life*
★ **Ingrid Thulin/***Brink of Life*

1959
★ **Simone Signoret/***Room at the Top*

1960
★ **Melina Mercouri/***Never on Sunday*

1961
★ **Sophia Loren/***Two Women*

1962
★ **Katharine Hepburn/***Long Day's Journey into Night*
★ **Rita Tushingham/***A Taste of Honey*

1965
★ **Samantha Eggar/***The Collector*

1966
★ **Vanessa Redgrave/***Morgan: A Suitable Case for Treatment*

1967
★ **Pia Degermark/***Elvira Madigan*

1969
★ **Vanessa Redgrave/***Isadora*

1971
★ **Kitty Winn/***Panic in Needle Park*

1973
★ **Joanne Woodward/***The Effect of Gamma Rays on Man-in-the-Moon Marigolds*

1974
★ **Marie-Jose Nat/***Les Violons du Bal*

1975
★ **Valerie Perrine/***Lenny*

1976
★ **Dominique Sanda/***The Inheritance*

1978
★ **Jill Clayburgh/***An Unmarried Woman*
★ **Isabelle Huppert/***Violette*

1979
★ **Sally Field/***Norma Rae*

1981
★ **Isabelle Adjani/***Quartet*

1982
★ **Jadwiga Jankowska Cieslak/***Another Way*

1984
★ **Helen Mirren/***Cal*

1985
★ **Norma Aleandro/***The Official Story*
★ **Cher/***Mask*

1986
★ **Barbara Sukowa/***Rosa Luxemburg*

1987
★ **Barbara Hershey/***Shy People*

1988
★ **Barbara Hershey/***A World Apart*
★ **Jodhi May/***A World Apart*
★ **Linda Mvusi/***A World Apart*

1989
★ **Meryl Streep/***A Cry in the Dark*

1991
★ **Irene Jacob/***The Double Life of Veronique*

1992
★ **Pernilla August/***The Best Intentions*

1993
★ **Holly Hunter/***The Piano*

1994
★ **Virna Lisi/***Queen Margot*

1995
★ **Helen Mirren/***The Madness of King George*

1996
★ **Brenda Blethyn/***Secrets and Lies*

1997
★ **Kathy Burke/***Nil by Mouth*

1999
★ **Severine Caneele/***Humanity*
★ **Emilie Dequenne/***Rosetta*

2000
★ **Bjork/***Dancer in the Dark*

DIRECTOR

1951
★ **Luis Bunuel/***Los Olvidados*

1952
★ **Christian-Jaque/***Fanfan la Tulipe*

1955
★ **Jules Dassin/***Rififi*

1957
★ **Robert Bresson/***A Man Escaped*

1958
★ **Ingmar Bergman/***Brink of Life*

1959
★ **Francois Truffaut/***The 400 Blows*

1969
★ **Vojtech Jasny/***All My Good Countrymen*

1976
★ **Ettore Scola/***Down & Dirty*

1978
★ **Nagisa Oshima/***The Empire of Passion*

1979
★ **Terrence Malick/***Days of Heaven*

1982
★ **Werner Herzog/***Fitzcarraldo*

1983
★ **Robert Bresson/***L'Argent*

1984
★ **Bertrand Tavernier/***A Sunday in the Country*

1985
★ **Andre Techine/***Rendez-vous*

1986
★ **Martin Scorsese/***After Hours*

1989
★ **Emir Kusturica/***Time of the Gypsies*

1990
★ **Pavel (Lungin) Lounguine/***Taxi Blues*

1991
★ **Joel Coen/***Barton Fink*

1992
★ **Robert Altman/***The Player*

1993
★ **Mike Leigh/***Naked*

1994
★ **Nanni Moretti/***Caro Diario*

1995
★ **Mathieu Kassovitz/***Hate*

1996
★ **Joel Coen/***Fargo*

1997
★ **Wong Kar-Wai/***Happy Together*

1998
★ **John Boorman/***The General*

1999
★ **Pedro Almodovar/***All About My Mother*

2000
★ **Edward Yang/***Yi Yi*

FILM

1946
★ *The Lost Weekend*

1949
★ *The Third Man*

1951
★ *Los Olvidados*
★ *Miracle in Milan*
★ *Miss Julie*

1952
★ *Othello*
★ *White Mane*

1953
★ *Wages of Fear*

1954
★ *Gate of Hell*

1957
★ *Friendly Persuasion*

1958
★ *The Cranes Are Flying*

1959
★ *Black Orpheus*

1960
★ *La Dolce Vita*

1961
★ *Viridiana*

1964
★ *Umbrellas of Cherbourg*

1966
★ *A Man and a Woman*

1967
★ *Blow-Up*

1969
★ *If...*
Z

1970
★ *M*A*S*H*

1971
★ *The Go-Between*

1973
★ *Scarecrow*

1974
★ *The Conversation*

1976
★ *Taxi Driver*

1977
★ *Padre Padrone*

1978
★ *The Tree of Wooden Clogs*

1979
★ *Apocalypse Now*
★ *The Tin Drum*

1980
★ *All That Jazz*
★ *Kagemusha*

1981
★ *Man of Iron*

1982
★ *Missing*
★ *Yol*

1983
★ *The Ballad of Narayama*

1984
★ *Paris, Texas*

1985
★ *Dance with a Stranger*
★ *When Father Was Away on Business*

1986
★ *The Mission*

1987
★ *Under Satan's Sun*

1988
★ *Pelle the Conqueror*

1989
★ *sex, lies and videotape*

1990
★ *Overseas: Three Women with Man Trouble*
★ *Wild at Heart*

1991
★ *Barton Fink*

1992
★ *The Best Intentions*
★ *My New Gun*

1993
★ *Farewell My Concubine*
★ *The Piano*

1994
★ *Pulp Fiction*

1995
★ *Underground*

1996
★ *Secrets and Lies*

1997
★ *The Eel*
★ *The Taste of Cherry*

1998
★ *Eternity and a Day*

1999
★ *Rosetta*

2000
★ *Dancer in the Dark*

SCREENPLAY

2001
★ *No Man's Land*

GRAND JURY PRIZE

1951
★ *All About Eve*

1957
★ *Kanal*
★ *The Seventh Seal*

1958
★ *Mon Oncle*

1961
★ *Mother Joan of the Angels*

1964
★ *Woman in the Dunes*

1965
★ *Kwaidan*

1967
★ *Accident*
★ *Alfie*

1971
★ *Johnny Got His Gun*

1972
★ *Solaris*

★ = winner

1976

★ *Cria*

1977

The American Friend

1978

★ *The Shout*

1979

★ *Siberiade*

1980

★ *Mon Oncle d'Amerique*

1982

★ *The Night of the Shooting Stars*

1983

★ *Monty Python's The Meaning of Life*

1985

★ *Birdy*

1987

★ *Repentance*

1988

★ *A World Apart*

1989

★ *Cinema Paradiso*
★ *Too Beautiful for You*

1990

★ *Tilai*

1991

★ *La Belle Noiseuse*

1992

★ *The Stolen Children*

1993

★ *Faraway, So Close!*

1994

★ *Burnt by the Sun*
★ *To Live*

1995

★ *Ulysses' Gaze*

1996

★ *Breaking the Waves*

1997

★ *The Sweet Hereafter*

1998

★ *Life Is Beautiful*

1999

★ *Humanity*

2000

★ *Devils on the Doorstep*

SPECIAL JURY PRIZE

1954

★ *The Last Bridge*

1960

★ *L'Avventura*

1969

★ *Z*

1970

★ *The Strawberry Statement*

1972

★ *Slaughterhouse Five*

1985

★ *Colonel Redl*

1986

★ *Therese*

1989

★ *Jesus of Montreal*

1990

★ *Hidden Agenda*

1993

★ *Raining Stones*

1994

★ *Queen Margot*

1995

★ *Carrington*

1996

★ *Crash*

1997

★ *Western*

DIRECTORS GUILD OF AMERICA

DIRECTOR

1948

★ **Joseph L. Mankiewicz**/*A Letter to Three Wives*

1949

★ **Carol Reed**/*The Third Man*

1950

★ **Joseph L. Mankiewicz**/*All About Eve*

1951

★ **George Stevens**/*A Place in the Sun*

1952

★ **John Ford**/*The Quiet Man*

1953

★ **Fred Zinnemann**/*From Here to Eternity*

1954

★ **Elia Kazan**/*On the Waterfront*
★ **Billy Wilder**/*Sabrina*

1955

★ **Delbert Mann**/*Marty*

1956

★ **George Stevens**/*Giant*

1957

★ **David Lean**/*The Bridge on the River Kwai*

1958

★ **Vincente Minnelli**/*Gigi*

1959

★ **William Wyler**/*Ben-Hur*

1960

★ **Billy Wilder**/*The Apartment*

1961

★ **Jerome Robbins**/*West Side Story*
★ **Robert Wise**/*West Side Story*

1962

★ **David Lean**/*Lawrence of Arabia*

1963

★ **Tony Richardson**/*Tom Jones*

1964

★ **George Cukor**/*My Fair Lady*

1965

★ **Robert Wise**/*The Sound of Music*

1966

★ **Fred Zinnemann**/*A Man for All Seasons*

1967

★ **Mike Nichols**/*The Graduate*

1968

★ **Anthony Harvey**/*The Lion in Winter*

1969

★ **John Schlesinger**/*Midnight Cowboy*

1970

★ **Charles Jarrott**/*Anne of the Thousand Days*
★ **Franklin J. Schaffner**/*Patton*

1971

★ **William Friedkin**/*The French Connection*

1972

★ **Francis Ford Coppola**/*The Godfather*

1973

★ **George Roy Hill**/*The Sting*

1974

★ **Francis Ford Coppola**/*The Godfather, Part 2*

1975

★ **Milos Forman**/*One Flew Over the Cuckoo's Nest*

1976

★ **John G. Avildsen**/*Rocky*

1977

★ **Woody Allen**/*Annie Hall*

1978

★ **Michael Cimino**/*The Deer Hunter*

1979

★ **Robert Benton**/*Kramer vs. Kramer*

1980

★ **Robert Redford**/*Ordinary People*

1981

★ **Warren Beatty**/*Reds*

1982

★ **Richard Attenborough**/*Gandhi*

1983

★ **James L. Brooks**/*Terms of Endearment*

1984

★ **Milos Forman**/*Amadeus*

1985

★ **Steven Spielberg**/*The Color Purple*

1986

★ **Oliver Stone**/*Platoon*

1987

★ **Bernardo Bertolucci**/*The Last Emperor*

1988

★ **Barry Levinson**/*Rain Man*

1989

★ **Oliver Stone**/*Born on the Fourth of July*

1990

★ **Kevin Costner**/*Dances with Wolves*

1991

★ **Jonathan Demme**/*The Silence of the Lambs*

1992

★ **Clint Eastwood**/*Unforgiven*

1993

★ **Steven Spielberg**/*Schindler's List*
Jane Campion/*The Piano*
Andrew Davis/*The Fugitive*
James Ivory/*The Remains of the Day*
Martin Scorsese/*The Age of Innocence*

1994

★ **Robert Zemeckis**/*Forrest Gump*
Frank Darabont/*The Shawshank Redemption*
Mike Newell/*Four Weddings and a Funeral*
Robert Redford/*Quiz Show*
Quentin Tarantino/*Pulp Fiction*

1995

★ **Ron Howard**/*Apollo 13*
Mike Figgis/*Leaving Las Vegas*
Mel Gibson/*Braveheart*
Ang Lee/*Sense and Sensibility*
Michael Radford/*The Postman*

1996

★ **Anthony Minghella**/*The English Patient*
Joel Coen/*Fargo*
Cameron Crowe/*Jerry Maguire*
Scott Hicks/*Shine*
Mike Leigh/*Secrets and Lies*

1997

★ **James Cameron**/*Titanic*
James L. Brooks/*As Good As It Gets*
Curtis Hanson/*L.A. Confidential*
Steven Spielberg/*Amistad*
Gus Van Sant/*Good Will Hunting*

1998

★ **Steven Spielberg**/*Saving Private Ryan*
Roberto Benigni/*Life Is Beautiful*
John Madden/*Shakespeare in Love*
Terrence Malick/*The Thin Red Line*
Peter Weir/*The Truman Show*

1999

★ **Sam Mendes**/*American Beauty*
Frank Darabont/*The Green Mile*
Spike Jonze/*Being John Malkovich*
Michael Mann/*The Insider*
M. Night Shyamalan/*The Sixth Sense*

2000

★ **Ang Lee**/*Crouching Tiger, Hidden Dragon*
Cameron Crowe/*Almost Famous*
Ridley Scott/*Gladiator*
Steven Soderbergh/*Erin Brockovich*
Steven Soderbergh/*Traffic*

2001

★ **Ron Howard**/*A Beautiful Mind*
Peter Jackson/*Lord of the Rings 1: The Fellowship of the Rings*
Baz Luhrmann/*Moulin Rouge*
Christopher Nolan/*Memento*
Ridley Scott/*Black Hawk Down*

FEATURE DOCUMENTARY

1992

★ **Joe Berlinger**/*Brother's Keeper*
★ **Bruce Sinofsky**/*Brother's Keeper*

1995

★ **Steve James**/*Hoop Dreams*
★ **Terry Zwigoff**/*Crumb*

1996

★ **Al Pacino**/*Looking for Richard*

GOLDEN GLOBE AWARDS

ACTOR—DRAMA

1944

★ **Paul Lukas**/*Watch on the Rhine*

1945

★ **Alexander Knox**/*Wilson*

1946

★ **Ray Milland**/*The Lost Weekend*

1947

★ **Gregory Peck**/*The Yearling*

1948

★ **Ronald Colman**/*A Double Life*

1949

★ **Laurence Olivier**/*Hamlet*

1950

★ **Broderick Crawford**/*All the King's Men*

1951

★ **Jose Ferrer**/*Cyrano de Bergerac*

1953

★ **Gary Cooper**/*High Noon*

1955

★ **Marlon Brando**/*On the Waterfront*

1956

★ **Ernest Borgnine**/*Marty*

1957

★ **Kirk Douglas**/*Lust for Life*

1958

★ **Alec Guinness**/*The Bridge on the River Kwai*

1959

★ **David Niven**/*Separate Tables*

1960

★ **Anthony (Tony) Franciosa**/*Career*

1961

★ **Burt Lancaster**/*Elmer Gantry*

1962

★ **Maximilian Schell**/*Judgment at Nuremberg*

1963

★ **Gregory Peck**/*To Kill a Mockingbird*

1964

★ **Sidney Poitier**/*Lilies of the Field*

1965

★ **Peter O'Toole**/*Becket*

1966

★ **Omar Sharif**/*Doctor Zhivago*

1967

★ **Paul Scofield**/*A Man for All Seasons*

1968

★ **Rod Steiger**/*In the Heat of the Night*

1969

★ **Peter O'Toole**/*The Lion in Winter*

1970

★ **John Wayne**/*True Grit*

1971

★ **George C. Scott**/*Patton*

1972

★ **Gene Hackman**/*The French Connection*

1973

★ **Marlon Brando**/*The Godfather*

1974

★ **Al Pacino**/*Serpico*

1975

★ **Jack Nicholson**/*Chinatown*

1976

★ **Jack Nicholson**/*One Flew Over the Cuckoo's Nest*

1977

★ **Peter Finch**/*Network*

1978

★ **Richard Burton**/*Equus*

1979

★ **Jon Voight**/*Coming Home*

1980

★ **Dustin Hoffman**/*Kramer vs. Kramer*

1981

★ **Robert De Niro**/*Raging Bull*

1982

★ **Henry Fonda**/*On Golden Pond*

1983

★ **Robert Duvall**/*Tender Mercies*
★ **Ben Kingsley**/*Gandhi*

1984

★ **Tom Courtenay**/*The Dresser*

1985

★ **F. Murray Abraham**/*Amadeus*

1986

★ **Jon Voight**/*Runaway Train*

1987

★ **Bob Hoskins**/*Mona Lisa*

1988

★ **Michael Douglas**/*Wall Street*

1989

★ **Dustin Hoffman**/*Rain Man*

1990

★ **Tom Cruise**/*Born on the Fourth of July*

1991

★ **Jeremy Irons**/*Reversal of Fortune*

1992

★ **Nick Nolte**/*The Prince of Tides*

1993

★ **Al Pacino**/*Scent of a Woman*

1994

★ **Tom Hanks**/*Philadelphia*
Daniel Day-Lewis/*In the Name of the Father*
Harrison Ford/*The Fugitive*
Anthony Hopkins/*The Remains of the Day*
Liam Neeson/*Schindler's List*

1995

★ **Tom Hanks**/*Forrest Gump*
Richard Dreyfuss/*Mr. Holland's Opus*
Morgan Freeman/*The Shawshank Redemption*
Paul Newman/*Nobody's Fool*
Brad Pitt/*Legends of the Fall*
John Travolta/*Pulp Fiction*

1996

★ **Nicolas Cage**/*Leaving Las Vegas*
Anthony Hopkins/*Nixon*
Ian McKellen/*Richard III*
Sean Penn/*Dead Man Walking*

1997

★ **Geoffrey Rush**/*Shine*
Ralph Fiennes/*The English Patient*
Mel Gibson/*Ransom*
Woody Harrelson/*The People vs. Larry Flynt*
Liam Neeson/*Michael Collins*

1998

★ **Peter Fonda**/*Ulee's Gold*
Matt Damon/*Good Will Hunting*
Daniel Day-Lewis/*The Boxer*
Leonardo DiCaprio/*Titanic*
Djimon Hounsou/*Amistad*
Ian McKellen/*Gods and Monsters*

1999

★ **Jim Carrey**/*The Truman Show*
Stephen Fry/*Wilde*
Tom Hanks/*Saving Private Ryan*
Nick Nolte/*Affliction*

2000

★ **Denzel Washington**/*The Hurricane*
Russell Crowe/*The Insider*
Matt Damon/*The Talented Mr. Ripley*
Richard Farnsworth/*The Straight Story*
Kevin Spacey/*American Beauty*

★ = winner

ACTOR—DRAMA ,cont.

2002

★ **Russell Crowe**/*A Beautiful Mind*
Will Smith/*Ali*
Kevin Spacey/*The Shipping News*
Billy Bob Thornton/*The Man Who Wasn't There*
Denzel Washington/*Training Day*

ACTOR—MUSICAL/ COMEDY

1951

★ **Fred Astaire**/*Three Little Words*

1953

★ **Donald O'Connor**/*Singin' in the Rain*

1954

★ **David Niven**/*The Moon Is Blue*

1955

★ **James Mason**/*A Star Is Born*

1956

★ **Tom Ewell**/*The Seven Year Itch*

1957

★ **Cantinflas**/*Around the World in 80 Days*

1958

★ **Frank Sinatra**/*Pal Joey*

1960

★ **Jack Lemmon**/*Some Like It Hot*

1961

★ **Jack Lemmon**/*The Apartment*

1962

★ **Glenn Ford**/*Pocketful of Miracles*

1963

★ **Marcello Mastroianni**/*Divorce—Italian Style*

1965

★ **Rex Harrison**/*My Fair Lady*

1966

★ **Lee Marvin**/*Cat Ballou*

1967

★ **Alan Arkin**/*The Russians Are Coming, the Russians Are Coming*

1968

★ **Richard Harris**/*Camelot*

1969

★ **Ron Moody**/*Oliver!*

1970

★ **Peter O'Toole**/*Goodbye, Mr. Chips*

1971

★ **Albert Finney**/*Scrooge*

1972

★ **Chaim Topol**/*Fiddler on the Roof*

1974

★ **George Segal**/*A Touch of Class*

1975

★ **Art Carney**/*Harry and Tonto*

1976

★ **Walter Matthau**/*The Sunshine Boys*

1977

★ **Kris Kristofferson**/*A Star Is Born*

1978

★ **Richard Dreyfuss**/*The Goodbye Girl*

1979

★ **Warren Beatty**/*Heaven Can Wait*

1980

★ **Peter Sellers**/*Being There*

1981

★ **Ray Sharkey**/*Idolmaker*

1982

★ **Dudley Moore**/*Arthur*

1983

★ **Dustin Hoffman**/*Tootsie*

1984

★ **Michael Caine**/*Educating Rita*

1985

★ **Dudley Moore**/*Micki & Maude*

1986

★ **Jack Nicholson**/*Prizzi's Honor*

1987

★ **Paul Hogan**/*Crocodile Dundee*

1988

★ **Robin Williams**/*Good Morning, Vietnam*

1989

★ **Tom Hanks**/*Big*

1990

★ **Morgan Freeman**/*Driving Miss Daisy*

1991

★ **Gerard Depardieu**/*Green Card*

1992

★ **Robin Williams**/*The Fisher King*

1993

★ **Tim Robbins**/*The Player*

1994

★ **Robin Williams**/*Mrs. Doubtfire*
Johnny Depp/*Benny & Joon*
Tom Hanks/*Sleepless in Seattle*
Kevin Kline/*Dave*
Colm Meaney/*The Snapper*

1995

★ **Hugh Grant**/*Four Weddings and a Funeral*
Jim Carrey/*The Mask*
Johnny Depp/*Ed Wood*
Arnold Schwarzenegger/*Junior*
Terence Stamp/*The Adventures of Priscilla, Queen of the Desert*

1996

★ **John Travolta**/*Get Shorty*
Michael Douglas/*The American President*
Harrison Ford/*Sabrina*
Steve Martin/*Father of the Bride Part II*
Patrick Swayze/*To Wong Foo, Thanks for Everything, Julie Newmar*

1997

★ **Tom Cruise**/*Jerry Maguire*
Antonio Banderas/*Evita*
Kevin Costner/*Tin Cup*
Tom Cruise/*Jerry Maguire*
Nathan Lane/*The Birdcage*
Eddie Murphy/*The Nutty Professor*

1998

★ **Jack Nicholson**/*As Good As It Gets*
Antonio Banderas/*The Mask of Zorro*
Jim Carrey/*Liar Liar*
Dustin Hoffman/*Wag the Dog*
Samuel L. Jackson/*Jackie Brown*
Kevin Kline/*In and Out*

1999

★ **Michael Caine**/*Little Voice*
John Travolta/*Primary Colors*
Robin Williams/*Patch Adams*

2000

★ **Jim Carrey**/*Man on the Moon*
Robert De Niro/*Analyze This*
Rupert Everett/*An Ideal Husband*
Hugh Grant/*Notting Hill*
Sean Penn/*Sweet and Lowdown*

2001

★ **George Clooney**/*O Brother Where Art Thou?*

2002

★ *Moulin Rouge*
★ **Gene Hackman**/*The Royal Tenenbaums*
Hugh Jackman/*Kate & Leopold*
Ewan McGregor/*Moulin Rouge*
John Cameron Mitchell/*Hedwig and the Angry Inch*
Billy Bob Thornton/*Bandits*

ACTOR—SUPPORTING

1945

★ **Barry Fitzgerald**/*Going My Way*

1947

★ **Clifton Webb**/*The Razor's Edge*

1948

★ **Edmund Gwenn**/*Miracle on 34th Street*

1949

★ **Walter Huston**/*Treasure of the Sierra Madre*

1950

★ **James Whitmore**/*Battleground*

1952

★ **Peter Ustinov**/*Quo Vadis*

1954

★ **Frank Sinatra**/*From Here to Eternity*

1955

★ **Edmond O'Brien**/*The Barefoot Contessa*

1957

★ **Earl Holliman**/*The Rainmaker*

1958

★ **Red Buttons**/*Sayonara*

1959

★ **Burl Ives**/*The Big Country*

1960

★ **Stephen Boyd**/*Ben-Hur*

1961

★ **Sal Mineo**/*Exodus*

1962

★ **George Chakiris**/*West Side Story*

1963

★ **Omar Sharif**/*Lawrence of Arabia*

1964

★ **John Huston**/*The Cardinal*

1965

★ **Edmond O'Brien**/*Seven Days in May*

1966

★ **Oskar Werner**/*The Spy Who Came in from the Cold*

1967

★ **Richard Attenborough**/*The Sand Pebbles*

1968

★ **David Attenborough**/*Doctor Dolittle*

1970

★ **Gig Young**/*They Shoot Horses, Don't They?*

1971

★ **John Mills**/*Ryan's Daughter*

1972

★ **Ben Johnson**/*The Last Picture Show*

1973

★ **Joel Grey**/*Cabaret*

1974

★ **John Houseman**/*The Paper Chase*

1975

★ **Fred Astaire**/*The Towering Inferno*

1976

★ **Richard Benjamin**/*The Sunshine Boys*

1977

★ **Laurence Olivier**/*Marathon Man*

1978

★ **Peter Firth**/*Equus*

1979

★ **John Hurt**/*Midnight Express*

1980

★ **Melvyn Douglas**/*Being There*
★ **Robert Duvall**/*Apocalypse Now*

1981

★ **Timothy Hutton**/*Ordinary People*

1982

★ **John Gielgud**/*Arthur*

1983

★ **Louis Gossett, Jr.**/*An Officer and a Gentleman*

1984

★ **Jack Nicholson**/*Terms of Endearment*

1985

★ **Haing S. Ngor**/*The Killing Fields*

1986

★ **Klaus Maria Brandauer**/*Out of Africa*

1987

★ **Tom Berenger**/*Platoon*

1988

★ **Sean Connery**/*The Untouchables*

1989

★ **Martin Landau**/*Tucker: The Man and His Dream*

1990

★ **Denzel Washington**/*Glory*
Joe Pesci/*Goodfellas*

1991

★ **Bruce Davison**/*Longtime Companion*

1992

★ **Jack Palance**/*City Slickers*

1993

★ **Gene Hackman**/*Unforgiven*

1994

★ **Tommy Lee Jones**/*The Fugitive*
Leonardo DiCaprio/*What's Eating Gilbert Grape*
Ralph Fiennes/*Schindler's List*
John Malkovich/*In the Line of Fire*
Sean Penn/*Carlito's Way*

1995

★ **Martin Landau**/*Ed Wood*
Kevin Bacon/*The River Wild*
Samuel L. Jackson/*Pulp Fiction*
Gary Sinise/*Forrest Gump*
John Turturro/*Quiz Show*

1996

★ **Brad Pitt**/*12 Monkeys*
Ed Harris/*Apollo 13*
John Leguizamo/*To Wong Foo, Thanks for Everything, Julie Newmar*
Tim Roth/*Rob Roy*
Kevin Spacey/*The Usual Suspects*

1997

★ **Edward Norton**/*Primal Fear*
Cuba Gooding, Jr./*Jerry Maguire*
Samuel L. Jackson/*A Time to Kill*
Paul Scofield/*The Crucible*
James Woods/*Ghosts of Mississippi*

1998

★ **Burt Reynolds**/*Boogie Nights*
Rupert Everett/*My Best Friend's Wedding*
Anthony Hopkins/*Amistad*
Burt Reynolds/*Boogie Nights*
Jon Voight/*John Grisham's The Rainmaker*
Robin Williams/*Good Will Hunting*

1999

★ **Ed Harris**/*The Truman Show*
Robert Duvall/*A Civil Action*
Bill Murray/*Rushmore*
Geoffrey Rush/*Shakespeare in Love*
Donald Sutherland/*Without Limits*
Billy Bob Thornton/*A Simple Plan*

2000

★ **Tom Cruise**/*Magnolia*
Michael Caine/*The Cider House Rules*
Michael Clarke Duncan/*The Green Mile*
Jude Law/*The Talented Mr. Ripley*
Haley Joel Osment/*The Sixth Sense*

2001

★ **Benicio Del Toro**/*Traffic*

2002

★ **Jim Broadbent**/*Iris*
Steve Buscemi/*Ghost World*
Hayden Christensen/*Life as a House*
Ben Kingsley/*Sexy Beast*
Jude Law/*A. I.: Artificial Intelligence*
Jon Voight/*Ali*

ACTRESS—DRAMA

1944

★ **Jennifer Jones**/*The Song of Bernadette*

1945

★ **Ingrid Bergman**/*Gaslight*

1946

★ **Ingrid Bergman**/*The Bells of St. Mary's*

1947

★ **Rosalind Russell**/*Sister Kenny*

1949

★ **Jane Wyman**/*Johnny Belinda*

1950

★ **Olivia de Havilland**/*The Heiress*

1951

★ **Gloria Swanson**/*Sunset Boulevard*

1953

★ **Shirley Booth**/*Come Back, Little Sheba*

1954

★ **Audrey Hepburn**/*Roman Holiday*

1955

★ **Grace Kelly**/*Country Girl*

1956

★ **Anna Magnani**/*The Rose Tattoo*

1957

★ **Ingrid Bergman**/*Anastasia*

1958

★ **Joanne Woodward**/*The Three Faces of Eve*

1959

★ **Susan Hayward**/*I Want to Live!*

1960

★ **Elizabeth Taylor**/*Suddenly, Last Summer*

1961

★ **Greer Garson**/*Sunrise at Campobello*

1962

★ **Geraldine Page**/*Summer and Smoke*

1963

★ **Geraldine Page**/*Sweet Bird of Youth*

1966

★ **Samantha Eggar**/*The Collector*

1967

★ **Anouk Aimee**/*A Man and a Woman*

1969

★ **Joanne Woodward**/*Rachel, Rachel*

1970

★ **Genevieve Bujold**/*Anne of the Thousand Days*

1971

★ **Ali MacGraw**/*Love Story*

1972

★ **Jane Fonda**/*Klute*

1974

★ **Marsha Mason**/*Cinderella Liberty*

1975

★ **Gena Rowlands**/*A Woman under the Influence*

1976

★ **Louise Fletcher**/*One Flew Over the Cuckoo's Nest*

1977

★ **Faye Dunaway**/*Network*

1978

★ **Jane Fonda**/*Julia*

1979

★ **Jane Fonda**/*Coming Home*

1980

★ **Sally Field**/*Norma Rae*

1981

★ **Mary Tyler Moore**/*Ordinary People*

1982

★ **Meryl Streep**/*The French Lieutenant's Woman*

1983

★ **Meryl Streep**/*Sophie's Choice*

1984

★ **Shirley MacLaine**/*Terms of Endearment*

1985

★ **Sally Field**/*Places in the Heart*

1986

★ **Whoopi Goldberg**/*The Color Purple*

★ = winner

1987

★ Marlee Matlin/*Children of a Lesser God*

1988

★ Sally Kirkland/*Anna*
★ Sigourney Weaver/*Gorillas in the Mist*

1989

★ Jodie Foster/*The Accused*
★ Shirley MacLaine/*Madame Sousatzka*

1990

★ Michelle Pfeiffer/*The Fabulous Baker Boys*

1991

★ Kathy Bates/*Misery*

1992

★ Jodie Foster/*The Silence of the Lambs*

1993

★ Emma Thompson/*Howard's End*

1994

★ Holly Hunter/*The Piano*
Juliette Binoche/*Trois Couleurs: Bleu*
Michelle Pfeiffer/*The Age of Innocence*
Emma Thompson/*The Remains of the Day*
Debra Winger/*A Dangerous Woman*

1995

★ Jessica Lange/*Blue Sky*
Jodie Foster/*Nell*
Jennifer Jason Leigh/*Mrs. Parker and the Vicious Circle*
Miranda Richardson/*Tom & Viv*
Meryl Streep/*The River Wild*

1996

★ Sharon Stone/*Casino*
Susan Sarandon/*Dead Man Walking*
Elisabeth Shue/*Leaving Las Vegas*
Meryl Streep/*The Bridges of Madison County*
Emma Thompson/*Sense and Sensibility*

1997

★ Brenda Blethyn/*Secrets and Lies*
Courtney Love/*The People vs. Larry Flynt*
Kristin Scott Thomas/*The English Patient*
Meryl Streep/*Marvin's Room*
Emily Watson/*Breaking the Waves*

1998

★ Judi Dench/*Mrs. Brown*
Helena Bonham Carter/*The Wings of the Dove*
Jodie Foster/*Contact*
Jessica Lange/*A Thousand Acres*
Emily Watson/*Hilary and Jackie*
Kate Winslet/*Titanic*

1999

★ Cate Blanchett/*Elizabeth*
Fernanda Montenegro/*Central Station*
Susan Sarandon/*Stepmom*
Meryl Streep/*One True Thing*

2000

★ Hilary Swank/*Boys Don't Cry*
Annette Bening/*American Beauty*
Julianne Moore/*The End of the Affair*
Meryl Streep/*Music of the Heart*
Sigourney Weaver/*A Map of the World*

2001

★ Julia Roberts/*Erin Brockovich*

2002

★ Sissy Spacek/*In the Bedroom*
Halle Berry/*Monster's Ball*
Judi Dench/*Iris*
Nicole Kidman/*The Others*
Tilda Swinton/*The Deep End*

ACTRESS—MUSICAL/COMEDY

1951

★ Judy Holliday/*Born Yesterday*

1955

★ Judy Garland/*A Star Is Born*

1956

★ Jean Simmons/*Guys and Dolls*

1957

★ Deborah Kerr/*The King and I*

1958

★ Kay Kendall/*Les Girls*

1959

★ Rosalind Russell/*Auntie Mame*

1960

★ Marilyn Monroe/*Some Like It Hot*

1961

★ Shirley MacLaine/*The Apartment*

1963

★ Rosalind Russell/*Gypsy*

1964

★ Shirley MacLaine/*Irma La Douce*

1965

★ Julie Andrews/*Mary Poppins*

1966

★ Julie Andrews/*The Sound of Music*

1967

★ Lynn Redgrave/*Georgy Girl*

1968

★ Anne Bancroft/*The Graduate*

1969

★ Barbra Streisand/*Funny Girl*

1971

★ Carrie Snodgress/*Diary of a Mad Housewife*

1972

★ Twiggy/*The Boy Friend*

1973

★ Liza Minnelli/*Cabaret*

1974

★ Glenda Jackson/*A Touch of Class*

1975

★ Raquel Welch/*The Three Musketeers*

1976

★ Ann-Margret/*Tommy*

1977

★ Barbra Streisand/*A Star Is Born*

1978

★ Diane Keaton/*Annie Hall*
★ Marsha Mason/*The Goodbye Girl*

1979

★ Ellen Burstyn/*Same Time, Next Year*
★ Maggie Smith/*California Suite*

1980

★ Bette Midler/*The Rose*

1981

★ Sissy Spacek/*Coal Miner's Daughter*

1982

★ Bernadette Peters/*Pennies from Heaven*

1983

★ Julie Andrews/*Victor/Victoria*

1984

★ Julie Walters/*Educating Rita*

1985

★ Kathleen Turner/*Romancing the Stone*

1986

★ Kathleen Turner/*Prizzi's Honor*

1987

★ Sissy Spacek/*Crimes of the Heart*

1988

★ Cher/*Moonstruck*

1989

★ Melanie Griffith/*Working Girl*

1990

★ Jessica Tandy/*Driving Miss Daisy*

1991

★ Julia Roberts/*Pretty Woman*
Andie MacDowell/*Green Card*

1992

★ Bette Midler/*For the Boys*

1993

★ Miranda Richardson/*Enchanted April*

1994

★ Angela Bassett/*What's Love Got to Do with It?*
Stockard Channing/*Six Degrees of Separation*
Anjelica Huston/*Addams Family Values*
Diane Keaton/*Manhattan Murder Mystery*
Meg Ryan/*Sleepless in Seattle*

1995

★ Jamie Lee Curtis/*True Lies*
Geena Davis/*Speechless*
Andie MacDowell/*Four Weddings and a Funeral*
Shirley MacLaine/*Guarding Tess*
Emma Thompson/*Junior*

1996

★ Nicole Kidman/*To Die For*
Annette Bening/*The American President*
Sandra Bullock/*While You Were Sleeping*
Toni Collette/*Muriel's Wedding*
Vanessa Redgrave/*A Month by the Lake*

1997

★ Madonna/*Evita*
Glenn Close/*101 Dalmatians*
Frances McDormand/*Fargo*
Debbie Reynolds/*Mother*
Barbra Streisand/*The Mirror Has Two Faces*

1998

★ Helen Hunt/*As Good As It Gets*
Joey Lauren Adams/*Chasing Amy*
Pam Grier/*Jackie Brown*
Jennifer Lopez/*Selena*
Julia Roberts/*My Best Friend's Wedding*

1999

★ Gwyneth Paltrow/*Shakespeare in Love*
Cameron Diaz/*There's Something about Mary*
Jane Horrocks/*Little Voice*
Christina Ricci/*The Opposite of Sex*
Meg Ryan/*You've Got Mail*

2000

★ Janet McTeer/*Tumbleweeds*
Julianne Moore/*An Ideal Husband*
Julia Roberts/*Notting Hill*
Sharon Stone/*The Muse*
Reese Witherspoon/*Election*

2001

★ Renee Zellweger/*Nurse Betty*

2002

★ Nicole Kidman/*Moulin Rouge*
Thora Birch/*Ghost World*
Cate Blanchett/*Bandits*
Reese Witherspoon/*Legally Blonde*
Renee Zellweger/*Bridget Jones's Diary*

ACTRESS—SUPPORTING

1945

★ Agnes Moorehead/*Mrs. Parkington*

1946

★ Angela Lansbury/*Picture of Dorian Gray*

1947

★ Anne Baxter/*The Razor's Edge*

1948

★ Celeste Holm/*Gentleman's Agreement*

1949

★ Ellen Corby/*I Remember Mama*

1950

★ Mercedes McCambridge/*All the King's Men*

1951

★ Josephine Hull/*Harvey*

1952

★ Kim Hunter/*A Streetcar Named Desire*

1953

★ Katy Jurado/*High Noon*

1954

★ Grace Kelly/*Mogambo*

1956

★ Marisa Pavan/*The Rose Tattoo*

1957

★ Eileen Heckart/*The Bad Seed*

1958

★ Elsa Lanchester/*Witness for the Prosecution*

1959

★ Hermione Gingold/*Gigi*

1960

★ Susan Kohner/*Imitation of Life*

1961

★ Janet Leigh/*Psycho*

1962

★ Rita Moreno/*West Side Story*

1963

★ Angela Lansbury/*The Manchurian Candidate*

1964

★ Margaret Rutherford/*The V.I.P.'s*

1965

★ Agnes Moorehead/*Hush, Hush, Sweet Charlotte*

1966

★ Ruth Gordon/*Inside Daisy Clover*

1967

★ Jocelyn Lagarde/*Hawaii*

1968

★ Carol Channing/*Thoroughly Modern Millie*

1969

★ Ruth Gordon/*Rosemary's Baby*

1970

★ Goldie Hawn/*Cactus Flower*

1971

★ Karen Black/*Five Easy Pieces*
★ Maureen Stapleton/*Airport*

1972

★ Ann-Margret/*Carnal Knowledge*

1973

★ Shelley Winters/*The Poseidon Adventure*

1974

★ Linda Blair/*The Exorcist*

1975

★ Karen Black/*The Great Gatsby*

1976

★ Brenda Vaccaro/*Once Is Not Enough*

1977

★ Katharine Ross/*Voyage of the Damned*

1978

★ Vanessa Redgrave/*Julia*

1979

★ Dyan Cannon/*Heaven Can Wait*

1980

★ Meryl Streep/*Kramer vs. Kramer*

1981

★ Mary Steenburgen/*Melvin and Howard*

1982

★ Joan Hackett/*Only When I Laugh*

1983

★ Jessica Lange/*Tootsie*

1984

★ Cher/*Silkwood*

1985

★ Peggy Ashcroft/*A Passage to India*

1986

★ Meg Tilly/*Agnes of God*

1987

★ Maggie Smith/*A Room with a View*

1988

★ Olympia Dukakis/*Moonstruck*

1989

★ Sigourney Weaver/*Working Girl*

1990

★ Julia Roberts/*Steel Magnolias*
Lorraine Bracco/*Goodfellas*

1991

★ Whoopi Goldberg/*Ghost*
Nicole Kidman/*Billy Bathgate*

1992

★ Mercedes Ruehl/*The Fisher King*

1993

★ Joan Plowright/*Enchanted April*

1994

★ Winona Ryder/*The Age of Innocence*
Penelope Ann Miller/*Carlito's Way*
Anna Paquin/*The Piano*
Rosie Perez/*Fearless*
Emma Thompson/*In the Name of the Father*

1995

★ Dianne Wiest/*Bullets over Broadway*
Kirsten Dunst/*Interview with the Vampire*
Sophia Loren/*Ready to Wear*
Uma Thurman/*Pulp Fiction*
Robin Wright Penn/*Forrest Gump*

1996

★ Mira Sorvino/*Mighty Aphrodite*
Anjelica Huston/*The Crossing Guard*
Kathleen Quinlan/*Apollo 13*
Kyra Sedgwick/*Something to Talk About*
Kate Winslet/*Sense and Sensibility*

1997

★ Lauren Bacall/*The Mirror Has Two Faces*
Joan Allen/*The Crucible*
Juliette Binoche/*The English Patient*
Barbara Hershey/*Portrait of a Lady*
Marianne Jean-Baptiste/*Secrets and Lies*
Marion Ross/*The Evening Star*

1998

★ Kim Basinger/*L.A. Confidential*
Joan Cusack/*In and Out*
Julianne Moore/*Boogie Nights*
Gloria Stuart/*Titanic*
Sigourney Weaver/*The Ice Storm*

1999

★ Lynn Redgrave/*Gods and Monsters*
Kathy Bates/*Primary Colors*
Brenda Blethyn/*Little Voice*
Judi Dench/*Shakespeare in Love*
Sharon Stone/*The Mighty*

2000

★ Angelina Jolie/*Girl, Interrupted*
Cameron Diaz/*Being John Malkovich*
Catherine Keener/*Being John Malkovich*
Samantha Morton/*Sweet and Lowdown*
Natalie Portman/*Anywhere But Here*
Chloe Sevigny/*Boys Don't Cry*

2001

★ Kate Hudson/*Almost Famous*

2002

★ Jennifer Connelly/*A Beautiful Mind*
Cameron Diaz/*Vanilla Sky*
Helen Mirren/*Gosford Park*
Maggie Smith/*Gosford Park*
Marisa Tomei/*In the Bedroom*
Kate Winslet/*Iris*

BEST FILM—DRAMA

1944

★ *The Song of Bernadette*

1945

★ *Going My Way*

1946

★ *The Lost Weekend*

1947

★ *The Best Years of Our Lives*

1948

★ *Gentleman's Agreement*

★ = winner

BEST FILM—DRAMA cont.

1949
★ *Johnny Belinda*
★ *Treasure of the Sierra Madre*

1950
★ *All the King's Men*

1951
★ *Sunset Boulevard*

1952
★ *A Place in the Sun*

1953
★ *The Greatest Show on Earth*

1954
★ *The Robe*

1955
★ *On the Waterfront*

1956
★ *East of Eden*

1957
★ *Around the World in 80 Days*

1958
★ *The Bridge on the River Kwai*

1959
★ *The Defiant Ones*

1960
★ *Ben-Hur*

1961
★ *Spartacus*

1962
★ *The Guns of Navarone*

1963
★ *Lawrence of Arabia*

1964
★ *The Cardinal*

1965
★ *Becket*

1966
★ *Doctor Zhivago*

1967
★ *A Man for All Seasons*

1968
★ *In the Heat of the Night*

1969
★ *The Lion in Winter*

1970
★ *Anne of the Thousand Days*

1971
★ *Love Story*

1972
★ *The French Connection*

1973
★ *The Godfather*

1974
★ *The Exorcist*

1975
★ *Chinatown*

1976
★ *One Flew Over the Cuckoo's Nest*

1977
★ *Rocky*

1978
★ *The Turning Point*

1979
★ *Midnight Express*

1980
★ *Kramer vs. Kramer*

1981
★ *Ordinary People*

1982
★ *On Golden Pond*

1983
★ *E.T.: The Extra-Terrestrial*

1984
★ *Terms of Endearment*

1985
★ *Amadeus*

1986
★ *Out of Africa*

1987
★ *Platoon*

1988
★ *The Last Emperor*

1989
★ *Rain Man*

1990
★ *Born on the Fourth of July*
Goodfellas

1991
★ *Dances with Wolves*

1992
★ *Bugsy*

1993
★ *Scent of a Woman*

1994
★ *Schindler's List*
The Age of Innocence
In the Name of the Father
The Piano
The Remains of the Day

1995
★ *Forrest Gump*
Legends of the Fall
Nell
Pulp Fiction
Quiz Show

1996
★ *Sense and Sensibility*
Apollo 13
Braveheart
The Bridges of Madison County
Leaving Las Vegas

1997
★ *The English Patient*
Breaking the Waves
The People vs. Larry Flynt
Secrets and Lies
Shine

1998
★ *Titanic*
Amistad
The Boxer
Good Will Hunting
The Horse Whisperer
L.A. Confidential
The Truman Show

1999
★ *Saving Private Ryan*
Elizabeth
Gods and Monsters

2000
★ *American Beauty*
The End of the Affair
The Hurricane
The Insider
The Talented Mr. Ripley

2001
★ *Gladiator*

2002
★ *A Beautiful Mind*
In the Bedroom
Lord of the Rings 1: The Fellowship of the Rings
The Man Who Wasn't There
Mulholland Drive

BEST FILM—MUSICAL/COMEDY

1952
★ *An American in Paris*

1955
★ *Carmen Jones*

1956
★ *Guys and Dolls*

1957
★ *The King and I*

1958
★ *Les Girls*

1959
★ *Gigi*

1960
★ *Some Like It Hot*

1961
★ *The Apartment*
★ *Song Without End*

1962
★ *West Side Story*

1963
★ *The Music Man*
★ *That Touch of Mink*

1964
★ *Tom Jones*

1965
★ *My Fair Lady*

1966
★ *The Sound of Music*

1967
★ *The Russians Are Coming, the Russians Are Coming*

1968
★ *The Graduate*

1969
★ *Oliver!*

1971
★ *M*A*S*H*

1972
★ *Fiddler on the Roof*

1973
★ *Cabaret*

1974
★ *American Graffiti*

1975
★ *The Longest Yard*

1976
★ *The Sunshine Boys*

1977
★ *A Star Is Born*

1978
★ *The Goodbye Girl*

1979
★ *Heaven Can Wait*

1980
★ *Breaking Away*

1981
★ *Coal Miner's Daughter*

1982
★ *Arthur*

1983
★ *Tootsie*

1984
★ *Yentl*

1985
★ *Romancing the Stone*

1986
★ *Prizzi's Honor*

1987
★ *Hannah and Her Sisters*

1988
★ *Hope and Glory*

1989
★ *Working Girl*

1990
★ *Driving Miss Daisy*

1991
★ *Green Card*

1992
★ *Beauty and the Beast*

1993
★ *The Player*

1994
★ *Mrs. Doubtfire*
Dave
Much Ado about Nothing
Sleepless in Seattle
Strictly Ballroom

1995
★ *The Lion King*
The Adventures of Priscilla, Queen of the Desert
Ed Wood
Four Weddings and a Funeral
Ready to Wear

1996
★ *Babe*
The American President
Get Shorty
Sabrina
Toy Story

1997
★ *Evita*
The Birdcage
Everyone Says I Love You
Fargo
Jerry Maguire

1998
★ *As Good As It Gets*
The Full Monty
The Mask of Zorro
Men in Black
My Best Friend's Wedding
Wag the Dog

1999
★ *Shakespeare in Love*
Bulworth
Patch Adams
Still Crazy
There's Something about Mary
Warren Beatty/*Bulworth*

2000
★ *Toy Story 2*
Analyze This
Being John Malkovich
Man on the Moon
Notting Hill

2001
★ *Almost Famous*

2002
Bridget Jones's Diary
Gosford Park
Legally Blonde
Shrek

DIRECTOR

1944
★ **Henry King/***The Song of Bernadette*

1945
★ **Leo McCarey/***Going My Way*

1946
★ **Billy Wilder/***The Lost Weekend*

1947
★ **Frank Capra/***It's a Wonderful Life*

1948
★ **Elia Kazan/***Gentleman's Agreement*

1949
★ **John Huston/***Treasure of the Sierra Madre*

1950
★ **Robert Rossen/***All the King's Men*

1951
★ **Billy Wilder/***Sunset Boulevard*

1953
★ **Cecil B. DeMille/***The Greatest Show on Earth*

1954
Fred Zinnemann/*From Here to Eternity*

1955
★ **Elia Kazan/***On the Waterfront*

1956
★ **Joshua Logan/***Picnic*

1957
★ **Elia Kazan/***Baby Doll*

1958
★ **David Lean/***The Bridge on the River Kwai*

1959
★ **Vincente Minnelli/***Gigi*

1960
★ **William Wyler/***Ben-Hur*

1962
★ **Stanley Kramer/***Judgment at Nuremberg*

1963
★ **David Lean/***Lawrence of Arabia*

1965
★ **George Cukor/***My Fair Lady*

1966
★ **David Lean/***Doctor Zhivago*

1967
★ **Fred Zinnemann/***A Man for All Seasons*

1968
★ **Mike Nichols/***The Graduate*

1969
★ **Paul Newman/***Rachel, Rachel*

1970
★ **Charles Jarrott/***Anne of the Thousand Days*

1971
★ **Arthur Hiller/***Love Story*

1972
★ **William Friedkin/***The French Connection*

1973
★ **Francis Ford Coppola/***The Godfather*

1974
★ **William Friedkin/***The Exorcist*

1975
★ **Roman Polanski/***Chinatown*

1976
★ **Milos Forman/***One Flew Over the Cuckoo's Nest*

1977
★ **Sidney Lumet/***Network*

1978
★ **Herbert Ross/***The Turning Point*

1979
★ **Michael Cimino/***The Deer Hunter*

1980
★ **Francis Ford Coppola/***Apocalypse Now*

1981
★ **Robert Redford/***Ordinary People*

1982
★ **Warren Beatty/***Reds*

1983
★ **Richard Attenborough/***Gandhi*

1984
★ **Barbra Streisand/***Yentl*

1985
★ **Milos Forman/***Amadeus*

1986
★ **John Huston/***Prizzi's Honor*

1987
★ **Oliver Stone/***Platoon*

1988
★ **Bernardo Bertolucci/***The Last Emperor*

1989
★ **Clint Eastwood/***Bird*

1990
★ **Oliver Stone/***Born on the Fourth of July*
Martin Scorsese/*Goodfellas*

1991
★ **Kevin Costner/***Dances with Wolves*

1992
★ **Oliver Stone/***JFK*

1993
★ **Clint Eastwood/***Unforgiven*

1994
★ **Steven Spielberg/***Schindler's List*
Jane Campion/*The Piano*
Andrew Davis/*The Fugitive*
James Ivory/*The Remains of the Day*
Martin Scorsese/*The Age of Innocence*

1995
★ **Robert Zemeckis/***Forrest Gump*
Robert Redford/*Quiz Show*
Oliver Stone/*Natural Born Killers*
Quentin Tarantino/*Pulp Fiction*
Edward Zwick/*Legends of the Fall*

1996
★ **Mel Gibson/***Braveheart*
Mike Figgis/*Leaving Las Vegas*
Ron Howard/*Apollo 13*
Ang Lee/*Sense and Sensibility*
Rob Reiner/*The American President*
Martin Scorsese/*Casino*

1997
★ **Milos Forman/***The People vs. Larry Flynt*
Joel Coen/*Fargo*
Scott Hicks/*Shine*
Anthony Minghella/*The English Patient*
Alan Parker/*Evita*

1998
★ **James Cameron/***Titanic*
James L. Brooks/*As Good As It Gets*
Curtis Hanson/*L.A. Confidential*
Jim Sheridan/*The Boxer*
Steven Spielberg/*Amistad*

1999
★ **Steven Spielberg/***Saving Private Ryan*
Shekhar Kapur/*Elizabeth*
John Madden/*Shakespeare in Love*
Robert Redford/*The Horse Whisperer*
Peter Weir/*The Truman Show*

2000
★ **Sam Mendes/***American Beauty*
Norman Jewison/*The Hurricane*
Neil Jordan/*The End of the Affair*
Michael Mann/*The Insider*
Anthony Minghella/*The Talented Mr. Ripley*

2001
★ **Ang Lee/***Crouching Tiger, Hidden Dragon*

2002
★ **Robert Altman/***Gosford Park*
Ron Howard/*A Beautiful Mind*
Peter Jackson/*Lord of the Rings 1: The Fellowship of the Rings*
Baz Luhrmann/*Moulin Rouge*
David Lynch/*Mulholland Drive*
David Spielberg/*A. I.: Artificial Intelligence*

★ = winner

SCORE

1948
★ *Life with Father*
1949
★ *The Red Shoes*
1950
★ *The Inspector General*
1951
★ *Sunset Boulevard*
1952
★ *September Affair*
1953
★ *High Noon*
1960
★ *On the Beach*
1961
★ *The Alamo*
1962
★ *The Guns of Navarone*
1963
★ *To Kill a Mockingbird*
1965
★ *The Fall of the Roman Empire*
1966
★ *Doctor Zhivago*
1967
★ *Hawaii*
1968
★ *Camelot*
1969
★ *The Shoes of the Fisherman*
1970
★ *Butch Cassidy and the Sundance Kid*
1971
★ *Love Story*
1972
★ *Shaft*
1973
★ *The Godfather*
1974
★ *Jonathan Livingston Seagull*
1975
★ *The Little Prince*
1976
★ *Jaws*
1977
★ *A Star Is Born*
1978
★ *Star Wars*
1979
★ *Midnight Express*
1980
★ *Apocalypse Now*
1981
★ *The Stunt Man*
1983
★ *E.T.: The Extra-Terrestrial*
1984
★ *Flashdance*
1985
★ *A Passage to India*
1986
★ *Out of Africa*
1987
★ *The Mission*
1988
★ *The Last Emperor*
1989
★ *Gorillas in the Mist*
1990
★ *The Little Mermaid*
1991
★ *The Sheltering Sky*
1993
★ *Aladdin*
1994
★ *Heaven and Earth*
The Nightmare before Christmas
The Piano
Schindler's List
Trois Couleurs: Bleu
1995
★ *The Lion King*
Forrest Gump
Interview with the Vampire
Legends of the Fall
Nell
1996
★ *A Walk in the Clouds*
Braveheart
Don Juan DeMarco
Pocahontas
Sense and Sensibility
1997
★ *The English Patient*
The Hunchback of Notre Dame
Michael Collins
The Mirror Has Two Faces
Shine
1998
★ *Titanic*
Gattaca
Kundun
L.A. Confidential
Seven Years in Tibet
1999
★ *The Truman Show*
A Bug's Life
Mulan
Prince of Egypt
Saving Private Ryan
2000
★ *The Legend of 1900*
2001
★ *Gladiator*
2002
★ *Moulin Rouge*
A. I.: Artificial Intelligence
Ali
A Beautiful Mind
Lord of the Rings 1: The Fellowship of the Rings
Mulholland Drive
Pearl Harbor
The Shipping News

ORIGINAL SCORE

2000
American Beauty
Angela's Ashes
Anna and the King
The End of the Affair
Eyes Wide Shut
The Insider
The Straight Story
The Talented Mr. Ripley

SONG

1961
★ **"Town without Pity"**/*Town without Pity*
1965
★ **"Circus World"**/*Circus World*
1968
★ **"If Ever I Should Leave You"**/*Camelot*
1969
★ **"The Windmills of Your Mind"**/*The Thomas Crown Affair*
1970
★ **"Jean"**/*The Prime of Miss Jean Brodie*
1971
★ **"Whistling Away the Dark"**/*Darling Lili*
1972
★ **"Life Is What You Make It"**/*Kotch*
1973
★ **"Ben"**/*Ben*
1974
★ **"The Way We Were"**/*The Way We Were*
1975
★ **"I Feel Love"**/*Benji*
1976
★ **"I'm Easy"**/*Nashville*
1977
★ **"Evergreen"**/*A Star Is Born*
1978
★ **"You Light Up My Life"**/*You Light Up My Life*
1980
★ **"The Rose"**/*The Rose*
1981
★ **"Fame"**/*Fame*
1982
★ **"Arthur's Theme"**/*Arthur*
1983
★ **"Up Where We Belong"**/*An Officer and a Gentleman*
1984
★ **"Flashdance...What a Feeling"**/*Flashdance*
1985
★ **"I Just Called to Say I Love You"**/*The Woman in Red*
1986
★ **"Say You, Say Me"**/*White Nights*
1987
★ **"Take My Breath Away"**/*Top Gun*
1988
★ **"(I've Had) the Time of My Life"**/*Dirty Dancing*
1989
★ **"Let the River Run"**/*Working Girl*
1990
★ **"Under the Sea"**/*The Little Mermaid*
1991
★ **"Blaze of Glory"**/*Young Guns 2*
1993
★ **"A Whole New World"**/*Aladdin*
1994
★ **"Streets of Philadelphia"**/*Philadelphia*
"(You Made Me the) Thief of Your Heart"/*In the Name of the Father*
"Again"/*Poetic Justice*
"Stay"/*Faraway, So Close!*
"The Day I Fall in Love"/*Beethoven's 2nd*
1995
★ **"Can You Feel the Love Tonight?"**/*The Lion King*
"Circle of Life"/*The Lion King*
"Far Longer than Forever"/*The Swan Princess*
"I'll Remember"/*With Honors*
"Look What Love Has Done"/*Junior*
"The Color of the Night"/*Color of Night*
1996
★ **"Colors of the Wind"**/*Pocahontas*
"Have You Ever Really Loved a Woman?"/*Don Juan DeMarco*
"Hold Me, Thrill Me, Kiss Me, Kill Me"/*Batman Forever*
"Moonlight"/*Sabrina*
"You Got a Friend in Me"/*Toy Story*
1997
★ **"You Must Love Me"**/*Evita*
"Because You Loved Me"/*Up Close and Personal*
"For the First Time"/*One Fine Day*
"I've Finally Found Someone"/*The Mirror Has Two Faces*
"That Thing You Do!"/*That Thing You Do!*
1998
★ **"My Heart Will Go On"**/*Titanic*
"Go the Distance"/*Hercules*
"Journey to the Past"/*Anastasia*
"Once Upon a December"/*Anastasia*
"Tomorrow Never Dies"/*Tomorrow Never Dies*
1999
★ **"The Prayer"**/*Quest for Camelot*
"Reflection"/*Mulan*
"The Flame Still Burns"/*Still Crazy*
"The Magic Sword"/*Quest for Camelot*
"The Mighty"/*The Mighty*
"Uninvited"/*City of Angels*
"When You Believe"/*Prince of Egypt*
2000
★ **"You'll Be In My Heart"**/*Tarzan*
"Beautiful Stranger"/*Austin Powers 2: The Spy Who Shagged Me*
"How Can I Not Love You"/*Anna and the King*
"Save Me"/*Magnolia*
"When She Loved Me"/*Toy Story 2*
2001
★ **"Things Have Changed"**/*Wonder Boys*
2002
★ **"Until"**/*Kate & Leopold*
"Come What May"/*Moulin Rouge*
"May It Be"/*Lord of the Rings 1: The Fellowship of the Rings*
"There You'll Be"/*Pearl Harbor*
"Vanilla Sky"/*Vanilla Sky*

SCREENPLAY

1948
★ *Miracle on 34th Street*
1949
★ *The Search*
1950
★ *Battleground*
1951
★ *All About Eve*
1953
★ *Five Fingers*
1954
★ *Lili*
1955
★ *Sabrina*
1966
★ *Doctor Zhivago*
1967
★ *A Man for All Seasons*
1968
★ *In the Heat of the Night*
1969
★ *Charly*
1970
★ *Anne of the Thousand Days*
1971
★ *Love Story*
1972
★ *The Hospital*
1973
★ *The Godfather*
1974
★ *The Exorcist*
1975
★ *Chinatown*
1976
★ *One Flew Over the Cuckoo's Nest*
1977
★ *Network*
1978
★ *The Goodbye Girl*
1979
★ *Midnight Express*
1980
★ *Kramer vs. Kramer*
1981
★ *The Ninth Configuration*
1982
★ *On Golden Pond*
1983
★ *Gandhi*
1984
★ *Terms of Endearment*
1985
★ *Amadeus*
1986
★ *The Purple Rose of Cairo*
1987
★ *The Mission*
1988
★ *The Last Emperor*
1989
★ *Running on Empty*
1990
★ *Born on the Fourth of July*
Goodfellas
1991
★ *Dances with Wolves*
1993
★ *Scent of a Woman*
1994
★ *Schindler's List*
Philadelphia
The Piano
The Remains of the Day
Short Cuts
1995
★ *Pulp Fiction*
Forrest Gump
Four Weddings and a Funeral
Mr. Holland's Opus
Quiz Show
The Shawshank Redemption
1996
★ *Sense and Sensibility*
The American President
Braveheart
Dead Man Walking
Get Shorty
1997
★ *The People vs. Larry Flynt*
The English Patient
Fargo
Lone Star
Shine
1998
★ *Good Will Hunting*
As Good As It Gets
L.A. Confidential
Titanic
Wag the Dog
1999
★ *Shakespeare in Love*
Bulworth
Happiness
Saving Private Ryan
The Truman Show
2000
★ *American Beauty*
Being John Malkovich
The Cider House Rules
The Insider
The Sixth Sense
2001
★ *Traffic*
2002
★ *A Beautiful Mind*
Gosford Park
The Man Who Wasn't There
Memento
Mulholland Drive

FILM—FOREIGN LANGUAGE

1950
★ *The Bicycle Thief*
1955
★ *Genevieve*
1956
★ *Ordet*
1957
★ *Richard III*
★ *War and Peace*
1959
★ *A Night to Remember*
1960
★ *Black Orpheus*
★ *Odd Obsession*
★ *Wild Strawberries*
1961
★ *The Virgin Spring*
1962
★ *Two Women*
1963
★ *Divorce—Italian Style*
1964
★ *Tom Jones*
1965
★ *Marriage Italian Style*
★ *Sallah*
1966
★ *Darling*
1967
★ *Alfie*
★ *A Man and a Woman*
1969
★ *Romeo and Juliet*
★ *War and Peace*
1970
★ *Z*
1971
★ *Rider on the Rain*
★ *Women in Love*
1972
★ *Sunday, Bloody Sunday*
1973
★ *Young Winston*
1974
★ *The Pedestrian*
1975
★ *Scenes from a Marriage*
1976
★ *Lies My Father Told Me*
1977
★ *Face to Face*
1978
★ *A Special Day*
1979
★ *Autumn Sonata*
1980
★ *La Cage aux Folles*
1981
★ *Tess*
1982
★ *Chariots of Fire*
1983
★ *Gandhi*
1984
★ *Fanny and Alexander*
1985
★ *A Passage to India*

★ = *winner*

FILM—FOREIGN LANGUAGE *cont.*

1986

★ *The Official Story*

1987

★ *The Assault*

1988

★ *My Life As a Dog*

1989

★ *Pelle the Conqueror*

1990

★ *Cinema Paradiso*

1991

★ *Cyrano de Bergerac*

1992

★ *Europa, Europa*

1993

★ *Indochine*

1994

★ *Farewell My Concubine*
Flight of the Innocent
Trois Couleurs: Bleu
The Wedding Banquet

1995

★ *Farinelli*
Eat Drink Man Woman
Queen Margot
To Live
Trois Couleurs: Rouge

1996

★ *Les Miserables*
Brother of Sleep
French Twist
Shanghai Triad

1997

★ *Kolya*
The Eighth Day
Luna e L'Altra
Prisoner of the Mountains
Ridicule

1998

★ *Ma Vie en Rose*
Artemisia
The Best Man
Lea
The Thief

1999

★ *Central Station*
The Celebration
Hombres Armados

2000

★ *All About My Mother*
The Red Violin

2001

★ *Crouching Tiger, Hidden Dragon*
Amores Perros
The Widow of Saint-Pierre

2002

Amelie
Monsoon Wedding

INDEPENDENT SPIRIT AWARDS

ACTOR

1986

★ **M. Emmet Walsh**/*Blood Simple*

1987

★ **James Woods**/*Salvador*

1988

★ **Dennis Quaid**/*The Big Easy*

1989

★ **Edward James Olmos**/*Stand and Deliver*

1990

★ **Matt Dillon**/*Drugstore Cowboy*

1991

★ **Danny Glover**/*To Sleep with Anger*

1992

★ **River Phoenix**/*My Own Private Idaho*

1993

★ **Harvey Keitel**/*Bad Lieutenant*

1994

★ **Jeff Bridges**/*American Heart*
Vincent D'Onofrio/*Household Saints*
Mitchell Lichtenstein/*The Wedding Banquet*
Matthew Modine/*Equinox*
Tyrin Turner/*Menace II Society*

1995

★ **Samuel L. Jackson**/*Pulp Fiction*
Sihung Lung/*Eat Drink Man Woman*
William H. Macy/*Oleanna*
Campbell Scott/*Mrs. Parker and the Vicious Circle*
Jon Seda/*I Like It Like That*

1996

★ **Sean Penn**/*Dead Man Walking*
Nicolas Cage/*Leaving Las Vegas*
Tim Roth/*Little Odessa*
Jimmy Smits/*My Family*
Kevin Spacey/*Swimming with Sharks*

1997

★ **William H. Macy**/*Fargo*
Chris Cooper/*Lone Star*
Christopher Penn/*The Funeral*

1998

★ **Robert Duvall**/*The Apostle*
Peter Fonda/*Ulee's Gold*
Christopher Guest/*Waiting for Guffman*
Philip Baker Hall/*Hard Eight*
John Turturro/*Box of Moonlight*

1999

★ **Ian McKellen**/*Gods and Monsters*
Dylan Baker/*Happiness*
Nick Nolte/*Affliction*
Sean Penn/*Hurlyburly*
Courtney B. Vance/*Blind Faith*

2000

★ **Richard Farnsworth**/*The Straight Story*
John Cusack/*Being John Malkovich*
Terence Stamp/*The Limey*
David Strathairn/*Limbo*

2001

★ **Javier Bardem**/*Before Night Falls*
Adrien Brody/*Restaurant*
Billy Crudup/*Jesus' Son*
Mark Ruffalo/*You Can Count On Me*

2002

★ **Tom Wilkinson**/*In the Bedroom*
Brian Cox/*L.I.E.*
Jake Gyllenhaal/*Donnie Darko*
John Cameron Mitchell/*Hedwig and the Angry Inch*

ACTOR—SUPPORTING

1988

★ **Morgan Freeman**/*Street Smart*

1989

★ **Lou Diamond Phillips**/*Stand and Deliver*

1990

★ **Max Perlich**/*Drugstore Cowboy*

1991

★ **Bruce Davison**/*Longtime Companion*

1992

★ **David Strathairn**/*City of Hope*

1993

★ **Steve Buscemi**/*Reservoir Dogs*

1994

★ **Christopher Lloyd**/*Twenty Bucks*
David Chung/*Combination Platter*
Tate Donovan/*Inside Monkey Zetterland*
Todd Field/*Ruby in Paradise*
Edward Furlong/*American Heart*

1995

★ **Chazz Palminteri**/*Bullets over Broadway*
Giancarlo Esposito/*Fresh*
Larry Pine/*Vanya on 42nd Street*
Eric Stoltz/*Pulp Fiction*
Nicholas Turturro/*Federal Hill*

1996

★ **Benicio Del Toro**/*The Usual Suspects*
James LeGros/*Living in Oblivion*
David Morse/*The Crossing Guard*
Max Perlich/*Georgia*
Harold Perrineau, Jr./*Smoke*

1997

★ **Benicio Del Toro**/*Basquiat*
★ **Jason Lee**/*Chasing Amy*
Kevin Corrigan/*Walking and Talking*
Matthew Faber/*Welcome to the Dollhouse*
Gary Farmer/*Dead Man*
Richard Jenkins/*Flirting with Disaster*

1998

Efrain Figueroa/*Star Maps*
Samuel L. Jackson/*Hard Eight*
Ajay Naidu/*subUrbia*
Roy Scheider/*The Myth of Fingerprints*

1999

★ **Bill Murray**/*Rushmore*
James Coburn/*Affliction*
Charles S. Dutton/*Blind Faith*
Gary Farmer/*Smoke Signals*
Philip Seymour Hoffman/*Happiness*

2000

★ **Steve Zahn**/*Happy, Texas*
Charles S. Dutton/*Cookie's Fortune*
Clark Gregg/*The Adventures of Sebastian Cole*
Luis Guzman/*The Limey*
Terrence DaShon Howard/*The Best Man*

2001

Cole Hauser/*Tigerland*
Gary Oldman/*The Contender*
Giovanni Ribisi/*The Gift*

2002

★ **Steve Buscemi**/*Ghost World*
Billy Kay/*L.I.E.*
Garrett Morris/*Jackpot*
John C. Reilly/*The Anniversary Party*

ACTRESS

1986

★ **Geraldine Page**/*The Trip to Bountiful*

1987

★ **Isabella Rossellini**/*Blue Velvet*

1988

★ **Sally Kirkland**/*Anna*

1989

★ **Jodie Foster**/*Five Corners*

1990

★ **Andie MacDowell**/*sex, lies and videotape*

1991

★ **Anjelica Huston**/*The Grifters*

1992

★ **Judy Davis**/*Impromptu*

1993

★ **Fairuza Balk**/*Gas Food Lodging*

1994

★ **Ashley Judd**/*Ruby in Paradise*
Suzy Amis/*The Ballad of Little Jo*
May Chin/*The Wedding Banquet*
Ariyan Johnson/*Just Another Girl on the I.R.T.*
Emma Thompson/*Much Ado about Nothing*

1995

★ **Linda Fiorentino**/*The Last Seduction*
Jennifer Jason Leigh/*Mrs. Parker and the Vicious Circle*
Karen Sillas/*What Happened Was...*
Lauren Velez/*I Like It Like That*
Chien-Lien Wu/*Eat Drink Man Woman*

1996

★ **Elisabeth Shue**/*Leaving Las Vegas*
Jennifer Jason Leigh/*Georgia*
Elina Lowensohn/*Nadja*
Julianne Moore/*Safe*
Lili Taylor/*The Addiction*

1997

★ **Frances McDormand**/*Fargo*
Maria Conchita Alonso/*Caught*
Scarlett Johansson/*Manny & Lo*
Catherine Keener/*Walking and Talking*
Renee Zellweger/*The Whole Wide World*

1998

★ **Julie Christie**/*Afterglow*
Stacy Edwards/*In the Company of Men*
Alison Folland/*All Over Me*
Lisa Harrow/*Sunday*
Robin Wright Penn/*Loved*

1999

★ **Ally Sheedy**/*High Art*
Katrin Cartlidge/*Claire Dolan*
Christina Ricci/*The Opposite of Sex*
Robin Tunney/*Niagara, Niagara*
Alfre Woodard/*Down in the Delta*

2000

★ **Hilary Swank**/*Boys Don't Cry*
Diane Lane/*A Walk on the Moon*
Janet McTeer/*Tumbleweeds*
Reese Witherspoon/*Election*

2001

★ **Ellen Burstyn**/*Requiem for a Dream*
Joan Allen/*The Contender*
Sanaa Lathan/*Love and Basketball*
Laura Linney/*You Can Count On Me*
Kelly Macdonald/*Two Family House*

2002

★ **Sissy Spacek**/*In the Bedroom*
Molly Parker/*The Center of the World*
Tilda Swinton/*The Deep End*

ACTRESS—SUPPORTING

1988

★ **Anjelica Huston**/*The Dead*

1989

★ **Rosana De Soto**/*Stand and Deliver*

1990

★ **Laura San Giacomo**/*sex, lies and videotape*

1991

★ **Sheryl Lee Ralph**/*To Sleep with Anger*

1992

★ **Diane Ladd**/*Rambling Rose*

1993

★ **Alfre Woodard**/*Passion Fish*

1994

★ **Lili Taylor**/*Household Saints*
Lara Flynn Boyle/*Equinox*
Ah-Leh Gua/*The Wedding Banquet*
Lucinda Jenney/*American Heart*
Julianne Moore/*Short Cuts*

1995

★ **Dianne Wiest**/*Bullets over Broadway*
V.S. Brodie/*Go Fish*
Carla Gallo/*Spanking the Monkey*
Kelly Lynch/*Forbidden Choices*
Brooke Smith/*Vanya on 42nd Street*

1996

★ **Mare Winningham**/*Georgia*
Jennifer Lopez/*My Family*
Vanessa Redgrave/*Little Odessa*
Chloe Sevigny/*Kids*
Celia Weston/*Dead Man Walking*

1997

★ **Elizabeth Pena**/*Lone Star*
Mary Kay Place/*Manny & Lo*
Queen Latifah/*Set It Off*
Lili Taylor/*Girls Town*
Lily Tomlin/*Flirting with Disaster*

1998

★ **Debbi (Deborah) Morgan**/*Eve's Bayou*
Farrah Fawcett/*The Apostle*
Amy Madigan/*Loved*
Miranda Richardson/*The Apostle*
Patricia Richardson/*Ulee's Gold*

1999

★ **Lynn Redgrave**/*Gods and Monsters*
Stockard Channing/*The Baby Dance*
Patricia Clarkson/*High Art*
Lisa Kudrow/*The Opposite of Sex*
Joely Richardson/*In the Shadows*

2000

★ **Chloe Sevigny**/*Boys Don't Cry*
Barbara Barrie/*Judy Berlin*
Vanessa Martinez/*Limbo*
Sarah Polley/*Go*
Jean Smart/*Guinevere*

2001

★ **Zhang Ziyi**/*Crouching Tiger, Hidden Dragon*
Pat Carroll/*Songcatcher*
Jennifer Connelly/*Requiem for a Dream*
Marcia Gay Harden/*Pollock*
Lupe Ontiveros/*Chuck & Buck*

2002

★ **Carrie-Anne Moss**/*Memento*
Uma Thurman/*Tape*
Tamara Tunie/*The Caveman's Valentine*

CINEMATOGRAPHY

1986

★ *Trouble in Mind*

1987

★ *Platoon*

1988

★ *Matewan*

1989

★ *The Unbearable Lightness of Being*

1990

★ *Drugstore Cowboy*

1991

★ *Wild at Heart*

1992

★ *Kafka*

1993

★ *Night on Earth*

1994

★ *Menace II Society*
American Heart
Chain of Desire
Equinox
Ruby in Paradise

1995

★ *Barcelona*
Eat Drink Man Woman
Forbidden Choices
I Like It Like That
Suture

1996

★ *Leaving Las Vegas*
Little Odessa
Nadja
The Underneath
The Usual Suspects

1997

★ *Fargo*
Bound
Color of a Brisk and Leaping Day
Dead Man
The Funeral

1998

★ *Kama Sutra: A Tale of Love*
The Bible and Gun Club
Habit
Hard Eight
Sunday

1999

★ *Velvet Goldmine*
Affliction
Belly
High Art

2000

★ *Three Seasons*
Judy Berlin
Julien Donkey-boy
Twin Falls Idaho

2001

★ *Requiem for a Dream*
Before Night Falls
Hamlet
Shadow of the Vampire

2002

★ *Mulholland Drive*
The Deep End
Hedwig and the Angry Inch
Memento

DIRECTOR

1986

★ **Joel Coen**/*Blood Simple*
★ **Martin Scorsese**/*After Hours*

1987

★ **Oliver Stone**/*Platoon*

★ = *winner*

1988

★ **John Huston/***The Dead*

1989

★ **Ramon Menendez/***Stand and Deliver*

1990

★ **Steven Soderbergh/***sex, lies and videotape*

1991

★ **Charles Burnett/***To Sleep with Anger*

1992

★ **Martha Coolidge/***Rambling Rose*

1993

★ **Carl Franklin/***One False Move*

1994

★ **Robert Altman/***Short Cuts*
Ang Lee/*The Wedding Banquet*
Victor Nunez/*Ruby in Paradise*
Robert Rodriguez/*El Mariachi*
John Turturro/*Mac*

1995

★ **Quentin Tarantino/***Pulp Fiction*
John Dahl/*Red Rock West*
Ang Lee/*Eat Drink Man Woman*
Roman Polanski/*Death and the Maiden*
Alan Rudolph/*Mrs. Parker and the Vicious Circle*

1996

★ **Mike Figgis/***Leaving Las Vegas*
Michael Almereyda/*Nadja*
Ulu Grosbard/*Georgia*
Todd Haynes/*Safe*
John Sayles/*The Secret of Roan Inish*

1997

★ **Joel Coen/***Fargo*
Abel Ferrara/*The Funeral*
David O. Russell/*Flirting with Disaster*
Todd Solondz/*Welcome to the Dollhouse*
Robert M. Young/*Caught*

1998

★ **Robert Duvall/***The Apostle*
Larry Fessenden/*Habit*
Victor Nunez/*Ulee's Gold*
Paul Schrader/*Touch*
Wim Wenders/*The End of Violence*

1999

★ **54938/***Rushmore*
Todd Haynes/*Velvet Goldmine*
Lodge Kerrigan/*Claire Dolan*
Paul Schrader/*Affliction*
Todd Solondz/*Happiness*

2000

★ **Alexander Payne/***Election*
Harmony Korine/*Julien Donkey-boy*
Doug Liman/*Go*
David Lynch/*The Straight Story*
Steven Soderbergh/*The Limey*

2001

★ **Ang Lee/***Crouching Tiger, Hidden Dragon*
★ **Christopher Nolan/***Memento*
Darren Aronofsky/*Requiem for a Dream*
Miguel Arteta/*Chuck & Buck*
Christopher Guest/*Best in Show*
Julian Schnabel/*Before Night Falls*

2002

Michael Cuesta/*L.I.E.*
Richard Linklater/*Waking Life*
John Cameron Mitchell/*Hedwig and the Angry Inch*

FILM

1986

★ *After Hours*

1987

★ *Platoon*

1988

★ *River's Edge*

1989

★ *Stand and Deliver*

1990

★ *sex, lies and videotape*

1991

★ *The Grifters*

1992

★ *Rambling Rose*

1993

★ *The Player*

1994

★ *Short Cuts*
Equinox
Much Ado about Nothing
Ruby in Paradise
The Wedding Banquet

1995

★ *Pulp Fiction*
Bullets over Broadway
Eat Drink Man Woman
Mrs. Parker and the Vicious Circle
Wes Craven's New Nightmare

1996

★ *Leaving Las Vegas*
The Addiction
Living in Oblivion
Safe
The Secret of Roan Inish

1997

★ *Fargo*
Dead Man
The Funeral
Lone Star
Welcome to the Dollhouse

1998

★ *The Apostle*
Chasing Amy
Loved
Ulee's Gold
Waiting for Guffman

1999

★ *Gods and Monsters*
Affliction
Claire Dolan
A Soldier's Daughter Never Cries
Velvet Goldmine

2000

★ *Election*
Cookie's Fortune
The Limey
The Straight Story
Sugar Town

2001

★ *Crouching Tiger, Hidden Dragon*
Before Night Falls
Ghost Dog: The Way of the Samurai
Requiem for a Dream

2002

★ *Memento*
Hedwig and the Angry Inch
L.I.E.
Waking Life

FIRST FEATURE

1987

★ *She's Gotta Have It*

1988

★ *Dirty Dancing*

1989

★ *Mystic Pizza*

1990

★ *Heathers*

1991

★ *Metropolitan*

1992

★ *Straight out of Brooklyn*

1993

★ *The Waterdance*

1994

★ *El Mariachi*
American Heart
Combination Platter
Mac
Menace II Society

1995

★ *Spanking the Monkey*
Clean, Shaven
Clerks
I Like It Like That
Suture

1996

★ *The Brothers McMullen*
Kids
Little Odessa
Picture Bride
River of Grass

1997

★ *Sling Blade*
Big Night
I Shot Andy Warhol
Manny & Lo
Tree's Lounge
Tony Shalhoub/*Big Night*
Stanley Tucci/*Big Night*

1998

★ *Eve's Bayou*
The Bible and Gun Club
Hard Eight
In the Company of Men
Star Maps

1999

★ *The Opposite of Sex*
Buffalo 66
High Art
Pi
Slums of Beverly Hills

2000

★ *Being John Malkovich*
The Blair Witch Project
Boys Don't Cry
Judy Berlin
Three Seasons
Twin Falls Idaho
Xiu Xiu: The Sent Down Girl

2001

★ *You Can Count On Me*
Boiler Room
Girlfight
Love and Basketball

2002

★ *In the Bedroom*
The Anniversary Party
Donnie Darko
Ghost World

SCREENPLAY

1986

★ *The Trip to Bountiful*

1987

★ *Platoon*

1988

★ *River's Edge*

1989

★ *Stand and Deliver*

1990

★ *Drugstore Cowboy*

1991

★ *To Sleep with Anger*

1992

★ *My Own Private Idaho*

1993

★ *The Waterdance*

1994

★ *Short Cuts*
Combination Platter
Household Saints
Ruby in Paradise
The Wedding Banquet

1995

★ *Pulp Fiction*
Bullets over Broadway
Eat Drink Man Woman
Mrs. Parker and the Vicious Circle
Red Rock West

1996

★ *The Usual Suspects*
Leaving Las Vegas
Living in Oblivion
Safe
The Secret of Roan Inish

1997

★ *Chasing Amy*
★ *Fargo*
Dead Man
Flirting with Disaster
The Funeral
Lone Star

1998

The Apostle
Touch
Ulee's Gold
Waiting for Guffman

1999

★ *The Opposite of Sex*
Affliction
Blind Faith
Gods and Monsters
The Spanish Prisoner

2000

★ *Election*
Dogma
Guinevere
The Limey
SLC Punk!

2001

★ *Memento*
★ *You Can Count On Me*
Chuck & Buck
Love & Sex
Two Family House
Waking the Dead

2002

In the Bedroom
Monster's Ball
Waking Life

DEBUT PERFORMANCE

1995

★ **Sean Nelson/***Fresh*
Jeff Anderson/*Clerks*
Jeremy Davies/*Spanking the Monkey*
Alicia Witt/*Fun*
Renee Zellweger/*Love and a .45*

1996

★ **Justin Pierce/***Kids*
Jason Andrews/*Rhythm Thief*
Lisa Bowman/*River of Grass*
Gabriel Casseus/*New Jersey Drive*
Rose McGowan/*The Doom Generation*

1997

★ **Heather Matarazzo/***Welcome to the Dollhouse*
Jena Malone/*Bastard out of Carolina*
Brendan Sexton, III/*Welcome to the Dollhouse*
Arie Verveen/*Caught*
Jeffrey Wright/*Basquiat*

1998

★ **Aaron Eckhart/***In the Company of Men*
Tyrone Burton/*Squeeze*
Eddie Cutanda/*Squeeze*
Phuong Duong/*Squeeze*
Lysa Flores/*Star Maps*
Darling Narita/*Bang*
Douglas Spain/*Star Maps*

1999

★ **Evan Adams/***Smoke Signals*
Anthony Roth Costanzo/*A Soldier's Daughter Never Cries*
Sonja Sohn/*Slam*
Saul Williams/*Slam*

2000

★ **Kimberly J. Brown/***Tumbleweeds*
Jessica Campbell/*Election*
Chris Stafford/*Edge of Seventeen*

2001

★ **Michelle Rodriguez/***Girlfight*
Rory Culkin/*You Can Count On Me*
Emmy Rossum/*Songcatcher*
Mike White/*Chuck & Buck*

2002

★ **Paul Franklin Dano/***L.I.E.*

FIRST SCREENPLAY

1995

★ *Spanking the Monkey*
Blessing
Clerks
Fun
What Happened Was...

1996

Kids
Little Odessa
Postcards from America
River of Grass
Smoke

1997

★ *Big Night*
Girl 6
Manny & Lo
Tree's Lounge
The Whole Wide World

1998

The Bible and Gun Club
Critical Care
Hard Eight
Star Maps

1999

★ *In the Company of Men*
★ *Pi*
High Art
Niagara, Niagara
Slums of Beverly Hills
Smoke Signals

2000

★ *Being John Malkovich*
The Adventures of Sebastian Cole
Boys Don't Cry
Cookie's Fortune
The Straight Story

FILM—FOREIGN LANGUAGE

1986

★ *Kiss of the Spider Woman*

1987

★ *A Room with a View*

1988

★ *My Life As a Dog*

1989

★ *Wings of Desire*

1990

★ *My Left Foot*

1992

★ *An Angel at My Table*

1993

★ *The Crying Game*

1994

★ *The Piano*
Like Water for Chocolate
Naked
Orlando
The Story of Qiu Ju

1995

★ *Trois Couleurs: Rouge*
The Blue Kite
The Boys of St. Vincent
Ladybird, Ladybird
32 Short Films about Glenn Gould

1996

★ *Before the Rain*
The City of Lost Children
Exotica
I Am Cuba
Through the Olive Trees

1997

Breaking the Waves
Chungking Express
Lamerica
Secrets and Lies
Trainspotting

1998

★ *The Sweet Hereafter*
Happy Together
Mouth to Mouth
Nenette and Boni
Underground

1999

★ *The Celebration*
Central Station
The Eel
Fireworks
The General

2000

★ *Run Lola Run*
All About My Mother
My Son the Fanatic
Rosetta
Topsy Turvy

2001

★ *Dancer in the Dark*
In the Mood for Love
The Terrorist
The War Zone

2002

Amelie
Amores Perros
Sexy Beast

NATIONAL FILM REGISTRY

1989

★ *The Best Years of Our Lives*
★ *Casablanca*
★ *Citizen Kane*
★ *The Crowd*
★ *Dr. Strangelove, or: How I Learned to Stop Worrying and Love the Bomb*
★ *The General*
★ *Gone with the Wind*
★ *The Grapes of Wrath*
★ *High Noon*
★ *Intolerance*
★ *The Learning Tree*
★ *The Maltese Falcon*
★ *Mr. Smith Goes to Washington*
★ *Modern Times*
★ *On the Waterfront*
★ *The Searchers*
★ *Singin' in the Rain*
★ *Snow White and the Seven Dwarfs*
★ *Some Like It Hot*
★ *Star Wars*
★ *Sunrise*
★ *Sunset Boulevard*
★ *Vertigo*
★ *The Wizard of Oz*

1990

★ *All About Eve*
★ *All Quiet on the Western Front*
★ *Bringing Up Baby*
★ *Dodsworth*
★ *Duck Soup*
★ *Fantasia*
★ *The Freshman*
★ *The Godfather*
★ *Harlan County, U.S.A.*
★ *How Green Was My Valley*
★ *It's a Wonderful Life*
★ *Ninotchka*
★ *Raging Bull*
★ *Rebel without a Cause*
★ *Red River*
★ *Sullivan's Travels*
★ *Top Hat*
★ *Treasure of the Sierra Madre*
★ *A Woman under the Influence*

1991

★ *Blood of Jesus*
★ *Chinatown*
★ *City Lights*
★ *David Holzman's Diary*
★ *Frankenstein*
★ *Gigi*
★ *Greed*

★ = winner

NATIONAL FILM REGISTRY *cont.*

- ★ *I Am a Fugitive from a Chain Gang*
- ★ *The Italian*
- ★ *King Kong*
- ★ *Lawrence of Arabia*
- ★ *The Magnificent Ambersons*
- ★ *My Darling Clementine*
- ★ *Out of the Past*
- ★ *A Place in the Sun*
- ★ *A Poor Little Rich Girl*
- ★ *Prisoner of Zenda*
- ★ *Shadow of a Doubt*
- ★ *Tevye*
- ★ *2001: A Space Odyssey*

1992

- ★ *Adam's Rib*
- ★ *Annie Hall*
- ★ *The Bank Dick*
- ★ *The Big Parade*
- ★ *The Birth of a Nation*
- ★ *Bonnie & Clyde*
- ★ *Carmen Jones*
- ★ *Detour*
- ★ *Dog Star Man*
- ★ *Double Indemnity*
- ★ *Footlight Parade*
- ★ *The Gold Rush*
- ★ *Letter from an Unknown Woman*
- ★ *Morocco*
- ★ *Nashville*
- ★ *The Night of the Hunter*
- ★ *Paths of Glory*
- ★ *Psycho*
- ★ *Ride the High Country*
- ★ *Salt of the Earth*

1993

- ★ *An American in Paris*
- ★ *Badlands*
- ★ *The Black Pirate*
- ★ *Blade Runner*
- ★ *Cat People*
- ★ *The Cheat*
- ★ *The Godfather, Part 2*
- ★ *His Girl Friday*
- ★ *It Happened One Night*
- ★ *Lassie, Come Home*
- ★ *A Night at the Opera*
- ★ *Nothing but a Man*
- ★ *One Flew Over the Cuckoo's Nest*
- ★ *Shadows*
- ★ *Shane*
- ★ *Sweet Smell of Success*
- ★ *Touch of Evil*
- ★ *The Wind*
- ★ *Yankee Doodle Dandy*

1994

- ★ *The African Queen*
- ★ *The Apartment*
- ★ *The Cool World*
- ★ *E.T.: The Extra-Terrestrial*
- ★ *Force of Evil*
- ★ *Freaks*
- ★ *Hell's Hinges*
- ★ *Invasion of the Body Snatchers*
- ★ *The Lady Eve*
- ★ *Louisiana Story*
- ★ *The Manchurian Candidate*
- ★ *Marty*
- ★ *Meet Me in St. Louis*
- ★ *Midnight Cowboy*
- ★ *Pinocchio*
- ★ *Safety Last*
- ★ *Scarface*
- ★ *Tabu: A Story of the South Seas*
- ★ *Taxi Driver*

1995

- ★ *The Adventures of Robin Hood*
- ★ *All That Heaven Allows*
- ★ *American Graffiti*
- ★ *The Band Wagon*
- ★ *Cabaret*
- ★ *Chan Is Missing*
- ★ *The Conversation*
- ★ *The Day the Earth Stood Still*
- ★ *El Norte*
- ★ *The Four Horsemen of the Apocalypse*
- ★ *Fury*
- ★ *The Hospital*
- ★ *The Last of the Mohicans*
- ★ *North by Northwest*
- ★ *The Philadelphia Story*
- ★ *Stagecoach*
- ★ *To Kill a Mockingbird*

1996

- ★ *The Awful Truth*
- ★ *Broken Blossoms*
- ★ *The Deer Hunter*
- ★ *Destry Rides Again*
- ★ *The Graduate*
- ★ *The Heiress*
- ★ *The Jazz Singer*
- ★ *M*A*S*H*
- ★ *Mildred Pierce*
- ★ *The Outlaw Josey Wales*
- ★ *The Producers*
- ★ *The Road to Morocco*
- ★ *She Done Him Wrong*
- ★ *Shock Corridor*
- ★ *Show Boat*
- ★ *The Thief of Baghdad*
- ★ *To Be or Not to Be*
- ★ *Woodstock*

1997

- ★ *Ben-Hur*
- ★ *The Big Sleep*
- ★ *The Bridge on the River Kwai*
- ★ *The Great Dictator*
- ★ *Harold and Maude*
- ★ *How the West Was Won*
- ★ *The Hustler*
- ★ *Knute Rockne: All American*
- ★ *Little Fugitive*
- ★ *Mean Streets*
- ★ *The Naked Spur*
- ★ *Rear Window*
- ★ *Return of the Secaucus 7*
- ★ *The Thin Man*
- ★ *West Side Story*
- ★ *Wings*

1998

- ★ *The Bride of Frankenstein*
- ★ *Easy Rider*
- ★ *42nd Street*
- ★ *From the Manger to the Cross*
- ★ *Gun Crazy*
- ★ *The Hitch-Hiker*
- ★ *The Immigrant*
- ★ *The Last Picture Show*
- ★ *Little Miss Marker*
- ★ *The Lost World*
- ★ *The Ox-Bow Incident*
- ★ *The Phantom of the Opera*
- ★ *Public Enemy*
- ★ *Sky High*
- ★ *Tootsie*
- ★ *Twelve o'Clock High*

1999

- ★ *Civilization*
- ★ *Do the Right Thing*
- ★ *Docks of New York*
- ★ *Emperor Jones*
- ★ *Gunga Din*
- ★ *Kiss Me Deadly*
- ★ *Laura*
- ★ *My Man Godfrey*
- ★ *Night of the Living Dead*
- ★ *Raiders of the Lost Ark*
- ★ *Roman Holiday*
- ★ *The Shop Around the Corner*
- ★ *A Streetcar Named Desire*
- ★ *The Ten Commandments*
- ★ *The Wild Bunch*
- ★ *Woman of the Year*

2000

- ★ *Apocalypse Now*
- ★ *Dracula*
- ★ *Five Easy Pieces*
- ★ *Goodfellas*
- ★ *Koyaanisqatsi*
- ★ *La Chute de la Maison Usher*
- ★ *The Life of Emile Zola*
- ★ *Little Caesar*
- ★ *Love Finds Andy Hardy*
- ★ *Network*
- ★ *Peter Pan*
- ★ *Regeneration*
- ★ *Salome*
- ★ *Shaft*
- ★ *Sherman's March: An Improbable Search for Love*
- ★ *A Star Is Born*
- ★ *The Tall T*
- ★ *Will Success Spoil Rock Hunter?*

2001

- ★ *Abbott and Costello Meet Frankenstein*
- ★ *All That Jazz*
- ★ *All the King's Men*
- ★ *Hoosiers*
- ★ *It*
- ★ *Jaws*
- ★ *Manhattan*
- ★ *Miracle of Morgan's Creek*
- ★ *National Lampoon's Animal House*
- ★ *Planet of the Apes*
- ★ *The Sound of Music*
- ★ *Stormy Weather*
- ★ *The Thin Blue Line*
- ★ *The Thing*

SCREEN ACTORS GUILD AWARDS

ACTOR

1994

- ★ **Tom Hanks/***Forrest Gump*
- **Morgan Freeman/***The Shawshank Redemption*
- **Paul Newman/***Nobody's Fool*
- **Tim Robbins/***The Shawshank Redemption*
- **John Travolta/***Pulp Fiction*

1995

- ★ **Nicolas Cage/***Leaving Las Vegas*
- **Anthony Hopkins/***Nixon*
- **James Earl Jones/***Cry, the Beloved Country*
- **Sean Penn/***Dead Man Walking*
- **Massimo Troisi/***The Postman*

1996

- ★ **Geoffrey Rush/***Shine*
- **Tom Cruise/***Jerry Maguire*
- **Ralph Fiennes/***The English Patient*
- **Woody Harrelson/***The People vs. Larry Flynt*
- **Billy Bob Thornton/***Sling Blade*

1997

- ★ **Jack Nicholson/***As Good As It Gets*
- **Matt Damon/***Good Will Hunting*
- **Robert Duvall/***The Apostle*
- **Peter Fonda/***Ulee's Gold*
- **Dustin Hoffman/***Wag the Dog*

1998

- ★ **Roberto Benigni/***Life Is Beautiful*
- **Joseph Fiennes/***Shakespeare in Love*
- **Tom Hanks/***Saving Private Ryan*
- **Ian McKellen/***Gods and Monsters*
- **Nick Nolte/***Affliction*

1999

- ★ **Kevin Spacey/***American Beauty*
- **Jim Carrey/***Man on the Moon*
- **Russell Crowe/***The Insider*
- **Philip Seymour Hoffman/***Flawless*
- **Denzel Washington/***The Hurricane*

2000

- ★ **Benicio Del Toro/***Traffic*
- **Jamie Bell/***Billy Elliot*
- **Russell Crowe/***Gladiator*
- **Geoffrey Rush/***Quills*

2001

- ★ **Russell Crowe/***A Beautiful Mind*
- **Kevin Kline/***Life as a House*
- **Sean Penn/***I Am Sam*
- **Denzel Washington/***Training Day*
- **Tom Wilkinson/***In the Bedroom*

ACTOR—SUPPORTING

1994

- ★ **Martin Landau/***Ed Wood*
- **Gary Sinise/***Forrest Gump*

1995

- ★ **Ed Harris/***Apollo 13*
- **Kevin Bacon/***Murder in the First*
- **Kenneth Branagh/***Othello*
- **Don Cheadle/***Devil in a Blue Dress*
- **Kevin Spacey/***The Usual Suspects*

1996

- ★ **Cuba Gooding, Jr./***Jerry Maguire*
- **Hank Azaria/***The Birdcage*
- **Nathan Lane/***The Birdcage*
- **William H. Macy/***Fargo*
- **Noah Taylor/***Shine*

1997

- ★ **Robin Williams/***Good Will Hunting*
- **Billy Connolly/***Mrs. Brown*
- **Anthony Hopkins/***Amistad*
- **Greg Kinnear/***As Good As It Gets*
- **Burt Reynolds/***Boogie Nights*

1998

- ★ **Robert Duvall/***A Civil Action*
- **James Coburn/***Affliction*
- **David Kelly/***Waking Ned Devine*
- **Geoffrey Rush/***Shakespeare in Love*
- **Billy Bob Thornton/***A Simple Plan*

1999

- ★ **Michael Caine/***The Cider House Rules*
- **Chris Cooper/***American Beauty*
- **Tom Cruise/***Magnolia*
- **Michael Clarke Duncan/***The Green Mile*
- **Haley Joel Osment/***The Sixth Sense*

2000

- ★ **Albert Finney/***Erin Brockovich*
- **Jeff Bridges/***The Contender*
- **Willem Dafoe/***Shadow of the Vampire*
- **Gary Oldman/***The Contender*
- **Joaquin Rafael (Leaf) Phoenix/***Gladiator*

2001

- ★ **Ian McKellen/***Lord of the Rings 1: The Fellowship of the Rings*
- **Jim Broadbent/***Iris*
- **Hayden Christensen/***Life as a House*
- **Ethan Hawke/***Training Day*
- **Ben Kingsley/***Sexy Beast*

ACTRESS

1994

- ★ **Jodie Foster/***Nell*
- **Jessica Lange/***Blue Sky*
- **Meg Ryan/***When a Man Loves a Woman*
- **Susan Sarandon/***The Client*
- **Meryl Streep/***The River Wild*

1995

- ★ **Susan Sarandon/***Dead Man Walking*
- **Joan Allen/***Nixon*
- **Elisabeth Shue/***Leaving Las Vegas*
- **Meryl Streep/***The Bridges of Madison County*
- **Emma Thompson/***Sense and Sensibility*

1996

- ★ **Frances McDormand/***Fargo*
- **Brenda Blethyn/***Secrets and Lies*
- **Diane Keaton/***Marvin's Room*
- **Gena Rowlands/***Unhook the Stars*
- **Kristin Scott Thomas/***The English Patient*

1997

- ★ **Helen Hunt/***As Good As It Gets*
- **Helena Bonham Carter/***The Wings of the Dove*
- **Judi Dench/***Mrs. Brown*
- **Pam Grier/***Jackie Brown*
- **Kate Winslet/***Titanic*
- **Robin Wright Penn/***She's So Lovely*

1998

- ★ **Gwyneth Paltrow/***Shakespeare in Love*
- **Cate Blanchett/***Elizabeth*
- **Jane Horrocks/***Little Voice*
- **Meryl Streep/***One True Thing*
- **Emily Watson/***Hilary and Jackie*

1999

- ★ **Annette Bening/***American Beauty*
- **Janet McTeer/***Tumbleweeds*
- **Julianne Moore/***The End of the Affair*
- **Meryl Streep/***Music of the Heart*
- **Hilary Swank/***Boys Don't Cry*

2000

- ★ **Julia Roberts/***Erin Brockovich*
- **Joan Allen/***The Contender*
- **Juliette Binoche/***Chocolat*
- **Ellen Burstyn/***Requiem for a Dream*
- **Laura Linney/***You Can Count On Me*

2001

- ★ **Halle Berry/***Monster's Ball*
- **Jennifer Connelly/***A Beautiful Mind*
- **Judi Dench/***Iris*
- **Sissy Spacek/***In the Bedroom*
- **Renee Zellweger/***Bridget Jones's Diary*

ACTRESS—SUPPORTING

1994

- ★ **Dianne Wiest/***Bullets over Broadway*
- **Sally Field/***Forrest Gump*
- **Robin Wright Penn/***Forrest Gump*

1995

- ★ **Kate Winslet/***Sense and Sensibility*
- **Stockard Channing/***Smoke*
- **Anjelica Huston/***The Crossing Guard*
- **Mira Sorvino/***Mighty Aphrodite*
- **Mare Winningham/***Georgia*

1996

- ★ **Lauren Bacall/***The Mirror Has Two Faces*
- **Juliette Binoche/***The English Patient*
- **Marisa Tomei/***Unhook the Stars*
- **Gwen Verdon/***Marvin's Room*
- **Renee Zellweger/***Jerry Maguire*

1997

- ★ **Kim Basinger/***L.A. Confidential*
- ★ **Gloria Stuart/***Titanic*
- **Minnie Driver/***Good Will Hunting*
- **Alison Elliott/***The Wings of the Dove*
- **Julianne Moore/***Boogie Nights*

1998

- ★ **Kathy Bates/***Primary Colors*
- **Brenda Blethyn/***Little Voice*
- **Judi Dench/***Shakespeare in Love*
- **Rachel Griffiths/***Hilary and Jackie*
- **Lynn Redgrave/***Gods and Monsters*

1999

- ★ **Angelina Jolie/***Girl, Interrupted*
- **Cameron Diaz/***Being John Malkovich*
- **Angelina Jolie/***Girl, Interrupted*
- **Catherine Keener/***Being John Malkovich*
- **Julianne Moore/***Magnolia*
- **Chloe Sevigny/***Boys Don't Cry*

2000

- ★ **Judi Dench/***Chocolat*
- **Kate Hudson/***Almost Famous*
- **Frances McDormand/***Almost Famous*
- **Julie Walters/***Billy Elliot*
- **Kate Winslet/***Quills*

2001

- ★ **Helen Mirren/***Gosford Park*
- **Cate Blanchett/***Bandits*
- **Judi Dench/***The Shipping News*
- **Cameron Diaz/***Vanilla Sky*
- **Dakota Fanning/***I Am Sam*

CAST

1995

- ★ *Apollo 13*
- *Get Shorty*
- *How to Make an American Quilt*
- *Nixon*
- *Sense and Sensibility*

1996

- ★ *The Birdcage*
- *The English Patient*
- *Marvin's Room*
- *Shine*
- *Sling Blade*

1997

- ★ *The Full Monty*
- *Boogie Nights*
- *Good Will Hunting*
- *L.A. Confidential*
- *Titanic*

1998

- ★ *Shakespeare in Love*
- *Life Is Beautiful*
- *Little Voice*
- *Saving Private Ryan*
- *Waking Ned Devine*

1999

- ★ *American Beauty*
- *Being John Malkovich*
- *The Cider House Rules*
- *The Green Mile*
- *Magnolia*

2000

- ★ *Traffic*
- *Almost Famous*
- *Billy Elliot*
- *Chocolat*
- *Gladiator*

2001

- *A Beautiful Mind*
- *In the Bedroom*
- *Lord of the Rings 1: The Fellowship of the Rings*
- *Moulin Rouge*

2003

- ★ *Gosford Park*

WRITERS GUILD OF AMERICA

ADAPTED SCREENPLAY

1968

- ★ *Goodbye Columbus*

1969

- ★ *Butch Cassidy and the Sundance Kid*
- ★ *Midnight Cowboy*

★ = winner

1970

★ *I Never Sang for My Father*
★ *M*A*S*H*

1971

★ *The French Connection*
★ *Kotch*

1972

★ *Cabaret*
★ *The Godfather*

1973

★ *Paper Moon*
★ *Serpico*

1974

★ *The Apprenticeship of Duddy Kravitz*
★ *The Godfather, Part 2*

1975

★ *One Flew Over the Cuckoo's Nest*
★ *The Sunshine Boys*

1976

★ *All the President's Men*
★ *The Pink Panther Strikes Again*

1977

★ *Julia*
★ *Oh, God!*

1978

★ *Heaven Can Wait*
★ *Midnight Express*

1979

★ *Being There*
★ *Kramer vs. Kramer*

1980

★ *Airplane!*
★ *Ordinary People*

1981

★ *On Golden Pond*
★ *Rich and Famous*

1982

★ *Missing*
★ *Victor/Victoria*

1983

★ *Reuben, Reuben*
★ *Terms of Endearment*

1984

★ *The Killing Fields*

1985

★ *Prizzi's Honor*

1986

★ *A Room with a View*

1987

★ *Roxanne*

1988

★ *Dangerous Liaisons*

1989

★ *Driving Miss Daisy*

1990

★ *Dances with Wolves*

1991

★ *The Silence of the Lambs*

1992

★ *The Player*

1993

★ *Schindler's List*
The Fugitive
In the Name of the Father
The Joy Luck Club
The Remains of the Day

1994

★ *Forrest Gump*
Little Women
The Madness of King George
Quiz Show
The Shawshank Redemption

1995

★ *Sense and Sensibility*
Apollo 13
Babe
Get Shorty
Leaving Las Vegas

1996

★ *Sling Blade*
The Birdcage
Emma
The English Patient
Trainspotting

1997

★ *L.A. Confidential*
Donnie Brasco
The Ice Storm
Wag the Dog
The Wings of the Dove

1998

★ *Out of Sight*
A Civil Action
Gods and Monsters
Primary Colors
A Simple Plan

1999

★ *Election*
The Cider House Rules
The Insider
October Sky
The Talented Mr. Ripley

2000

★ *Traffic*
Chocolat
Crouching Tiger, Hidden Dragon
High Fidelity
Wonder Boys

2001

★ *A Beautiful Mind*
Black Hawk Down
Bridget Jones's Diary
Ghost World
Lord of the Rings 1: The Fellowship of the Rings

ORIGINAL SCREENPLAY

1967

★ *Bonnie & Clyde*

1968

★ *The Producers*

1969

★ *Bob & Carol & Ted & Alice*

1970

★ *The Out-of-Towners*
★ *Patton*

1971

★ *The Hospital*
★ *Sunday, Bloody Sunday*

1972

★ *The Candidate*
★ *What's Up, Doc?*

1973

★ *Save the Tiger*
★ *A Touch of Class*

1974

★ *Blazing Saddles*
★ *Chinatown*

1975

★ *Dog Day Afternoon*
★ *Shampoo*

1976

★ *The Bad News Bears*
★ *Network*

1977

★ *Annie Hall*
★ *The Turning Point*

1978

★ *Coming Home*
★ *Movie, Movie*

1979

★ *Breaking Away*
★ *The China Syndrome*

1980

★ *Melvin and Howard*
★ *Private Benjamin*

1981

★ *Arthur*
★ *Reds*

1982

★ *E.T.: The Extra-Terrestrial*
★ *Tootsie*

1983

★ *The Big Chill*
★ *Tender Mercies*

1984

★ *Broadway Danny Rose*

1985

★ *Witness*

1986

★ *Hannah and Her Sisters*

1987

★ *Moonstruck*

1988

★ *Bull Durham*

1989

★ *Crimes & Misdemeanors*

1990

★ *Avalon*

1991

★ *Thelma & Louise*

1992

★ *The Crying Game*

1993

★ *The Piano*
Dave
In the Line of Fire
Philadelphia
Sleepless in Seattle

1994

★ *Four Weddings and a Funeral*
The Adventures of Priscilla, Queen of the Desert
Bullets over Broadway
Ed Wood
Heavenly Creatures

1995

★ *Braveheart*
The American President
Clueless
Mighty Aphrodite
Muriel's Wedding

1996

★ *Fargo*
Jerry Maguire
Lone Star
Secrets and Lies
Shine

1997

★ *As Good As It Gets*
Boogie Nights
The Full Monty
Good Will Hunting
Titanic

1998

★ *Shakespeare in Love*

1999

★ *American Beauty*
Being John Malkovich
Magnolia
The Sixth Sense
Three Kings

2000

★ *You Can Count On Me*
Almost Famous
Best in Show
Billy Elliot
Erin Brockovich

2001

★ *Gosford Park*
The Man Who Wasn't There
Monster's Ball
Moulin Rouge
The Royal Tenenbaums

SCREENPLAY

1998

Bulworth
The Opposite of Sex
Saving Private Ryan
The Truman Show

GOLDEN RASPBERRY AWARDS

WORST PICTURE

1980

★ *Can't Stop the Music*

1981

★ *Mommie Dearest*

1983

★ *The Lonely Lady*

1984

★ *Bolero*

1985

★ *Rambo: First Blood, Part 2*

1986

★ *Howard the Duck*
★ *Under the Cherry Moon*

1987

★ *Leonard Part 6*

1988

★ *Cocktail*

1989

★ *Star Trek 5: The Final Frontier*

1990

★ *The Adventures of Ford Fairlane*
★ *Ghosts Can't Do It*

1991

★ *Hudson Hawk*

1992

★ *Shining Through*

1993

★ *Indecent Proposal*

1994

★ *Color of Night*
North
On Deadly Ground
The Specialist
Wyatt Earp

1995

★ *Showgirls*
Congo
It's Pat: The Movie
Waterworld

1996

★ *Striptease*
Barb Wire
Ed
The Island of Dr. Moreau
The Stupids

1997

★ *The Postman*
Anaconda
Batman and Robin
Fire Down Below
Speed 2: Cruise Control

1998

★ *An Alan Smithee Film: Burn, Hollywood, Burn*
Armageddon
The Avengers
Godzilla
Spice World: The Movie

1999

★ *Wild Wild West*
Big Daddy
The Blair Witch Project
The Haunting
Star Wars: Episode 1—The Phantom Menace

2000

★ *Battlefield Earth*
Book of Shadows: Blair Witch 2
The Flintstones in Viva Rock Vegas
Little Nicky
The Next Best Thing

2001

★ *Freddy Got Fingered*

WORST REMAKE/ SEQUEL

1994

★ *Wyatt Earp*
The Flintstones

1995

★ *The Scarlet Letter*

1997

★ *Speed 2: Cruise Control*
Batman and Robin
Home Alone 3
The Lost World: Jurassic Park 2
McHale's Navy

1998

★ *The Avengers*
★ *Godzilla*
★ *Psycho*
Godzilla
Lost in Space
Meet Joe Black
Psycho

2000

★ *Book of Shadows: Blair Witch 2*
Dr. Seuss' How the Grinch Stole Christmas
The Flintstones in Viva Rock Vegas
Get Carter
Mission: Impossible 2

2001

★ *Planet of the Apes*

WORST ACTOR

1980

★ **Neil Diamond/***The Jazz Singer*

1981

★ **Klinton Spilsbury/***Legend of the Lone Ranger*

1983

★ **Christopher Atkins/***A Night in Heaven*

1984

★ **Sylvester Stallone/***Rhinestone*

1985

★ **Sylvester Stallone/***Rambo: First Blood, Part 2*
★ **Sylvester Stallone/***Rocky 4*

1986

★ **Prince/***Under the Cherry Moon*

1987

★ **Bill Cosby/***Leonard Part 6*

1988

★ **Sylvester Stallone/***Rambo 3*

1989

★ **William Shatner/***Star Trek 5: The Final Frontier*

1990

★ **Andrew (Dice Clay) Silverstein/***The Adventures of Ford Fairlane*

1991

★ **Kevin Costner/***Robin Hood: Prince of Thieves*

1992

★ **Sylvester Stallone/***Stop! or My Mom Will Shoot*

1993

★ **Burt Reynolds/***Cop and a Half*

1994

★ **Kevin Costner/***Wyatt Earp*
Macaulay Culkin/*Getting Even with Dad*
Macaulay Culkin/*The Pagemaster*
Macaulay Culkin/*Richie Rich*
Bruce Willis/*Color of Night*
Bruce Willis/*North*

1995

★ **Pauly Shore/***Jury Duty*
Kevin Costner/*Waterworld*
Kyle MacLachlan/*Showgirls*
Sylvester Stallone/*Assassins*
Sylvester Stallone/*Judge Dredd*

1996

★ **Tom Arnold/***Big Bully*
★ **Tom Arnold/***Carpool*
★ **Tom Arnold/***The Stupids*
★ **Pauly Shore/***Bio-Dome*
Keanu Reeves/*Chain Reaction*
Adam Sandler/*Bulletproof*
Adam Sandler/*Happy Gilmore*
Sylvester Stallone/*Daylight*

1997

★ **Kevin Costner/***The Postman*
Val Kilmer/*The Saint*
Shaquille O'Neal/*Steel*
Steven Seagal/*Fire Down Below*
Jon Voight/*Anaconda*

1998

★ **Bruce Willis/***Armageddon*
★ **Bruce Willis/***Mercury Rising*
★ **Bruce Willis/***The Siege*
Ralph Fiennes/*The Avengers*
Ryan O'Neal/*An Alan Smithee Film: Burn, Hollywood, Burn*
Ryan Phillippe/*54*
Adam Sandler/*The Waterboy*

1999

★ **Adam Sandler/***Big Daddy*
Kevin Costner/*For Love of the Game*
Kevin Costner/*Message in a Bottle*
Kevin Kline/*Wild Wild West*
Arnold Schwarzenegger/*End of Days*
Robin Williams/*Bicentennial Man*
Robin Williams/*Jakob the Liar*

2000

★ **John Travolta/***Battlefield Earth*
Leonardo DiCaprio/*The Beach*
Adam Sandler/*Little Nicky*
Arnold Schwarzenegger/*The 6th Day*
Sylvester Stallone/*Get Carter*

2001

★ **Tom Green/***Freddy Got Fingered*

WORST ACTRESS

1980

★ **Brooke Shields/***The Blue Lagoon*

1981

★ **Bo Derek/***Tarzan, the Ape Man*
★ **Faye Dunaway/***Mommie Dearest*

1982

★ **Pia Zadora/***Butterfly*

1983

★ **Pia Zadora/***The Lonely Lady*

1984

★ **Bo Derek/***Bolero*

1985

★ **Linda Blair/***Night Patrol*
★ **Linda Blair/***Savage Island*
★ **Linda Blair/***Savage Streets*

1986

★ **Madonna/***Shanghai Surprise*

1987

★ **Madonna/***Who's That Girl?*
★ **Liza Minnelli/***Arthur 2: On the Rocks*

1988

★ **Liza Minnelli/***Rent-A-Cop*

1990

★ **Bo Derek/***Ghosts Can't Do It*

1991

★ **Sean Young/***A Kiss Before Dying*

1992

★ **Melanie Griffith/***Shining Through*
★ **Melanie Griffith/***A Stranger Among Us*

★ = *winner*

WORST ACTRESS, *cont.*

1993

★ **Madonna/***Body of Evidence*

1994

★ **Sharon Stone/***Intersection*
★ **Sharon Stone/***The Specialist*
Uma Thurman/*Even Cowgirls Get the Blues*

1995

★ **Elizabeth Berkley/***Showgirls*

1996

★ **Demi Moore/***Striptease*
Whoopi Goldberg/*Bogus*
Whoopi Goldberg/*Eddie*
Whoopi Goldberg/*Theodore Rex*
Melanie Griffith/*Two Much*
Demi Moore/*The Juror*
Julia Roberts/*Mary Reilly*

1997

★ **Demi Moore/***G.I. Jane*
Sandra Bullock/*Speed 2: Cruise Control*
Fran Drescher/*The Beautician and the Beast*
Lauren Holly/*A Smile Like Yours*
Lauren Holly/*Turbulence*
Alicia Silverstone/*Excess Baggage*

1998

★ **The Spice Girls/***Spice World: The Movie*
Yasmine Bleeth/*BASEketball*
Anne Heche/*Psycho*
Jessica Lange/*Hush*
Uma Thurman/*The Avengers*

1999

★ **Heather Donahue/***The Blair Witch Project*
Melanie Griffith/*Crazy in Alabama*
Milla Jovovich/*The Messenger: The Story of Joan of Arc*
Sharon Stone/*Gloria*
Catherine Zeta-Jones/*Entrapment*
Catherine Zeta-Jones/*The Haunting*

2000

★ **Madonna/***The Next Best Thing*
Kim Basinger/*Bless the Child*
Kim Basinger/*I Dreamed of Africa*
Melanie Griffith/*Cecil B. Demented*
Bette Midler/*Isn't She Great*
Demi Moore/*Passion of Mind*

2001

★ **Mariah Carey/***Glitter*

WORST SUPPORTING ACTOR

1980

★ **John Adams/***Gloria*
★ **Laurence Olivier/***The Jazz Singer*

1981

★ **Steve Forrest/***Mommie Dearest*

1982

★ **Ed McMahon/***Butterfly*

1983

★ **Jim Nabors/***Stroker Ace*

1985

★ **Rob Lowe/***St. Elmo's Fire*

1986

★ **Jerome Benton/***Under the Cherry Moon*

1987

★ **David Mendenhall/***Over the Top*

1988

★ **Dan Aykroyd/***Caddyshack 2*

1989

★ **Christopher Atkins/***Listen to Me*

1991

★ **Dan Aykroyd/***Nothing But Trouble*

1992

★ **Tom Selleck/***Christopher Columbus: The Discovery*

1993

★ **Woody Harrelson/***Indecent Proposal*

1994

★ **O.J. Simpson/***Naked Gun 33 1/3: The Final Insult*

1995

★ **Dennis Hopper/***Waterworld*
Robert Davi/*Showgirls*

1996

Marlon Brando/*The Island of Dr. Moreau*
Val Kilmer/*The Ghost and the Darkness*
Val Kilmer/*The Island of Dr. Moreau*
Burt Reynolds/*Striptease*
Steven Seagal/*Executive Decision*
Quentin Tarantino/*From Dusk Till Dawn*

1997

★ **Dennis Rodman/***Double Team*
Willem Dafoe/*Speed 2: Cruise Control*
Chris O'Donnell/*Batman and Robin*
Arnold Schwarzenegger/*Batman and Robin*
Jon Voight/*Most Wanted*
Jon Voight/*U-Turn*

1998

★ **Joe Eszterhas/***An Alan Smithee Film: Burn, Hollywood, Burn*
Sean Connery/*The Avengers*
Joe Pesci/*Lethal Weapon 4*
Sylvester Stallone/*An Alan Smithee Film: Burn, Hollywood, Burn*

1999

Kenneth Branagh/*Wild Wild West*
Gabriel Byrne/*End of Days*
Gabriel Byrne/*Stigmata*
Jake Lloyd/*Star Wars: Episode 1—The Phantom Menace*
Rob Schneider/*Big Daddy*

2000

★ **Barry Pepper/***Battlefield Earth*
Stephen Baldwin/*The Flintstones in Viva Rock Vegas*
Keanu Reeves/*The Watcher*
Forest Whitaker/*Battlefield Earth*

2001

★ **Charlton Heston/***Planet of the Apes*

WORST SUPPORTING ACTRESS

1980

★ **Amy Irving/***Honeysuckle Rose*

1981

★ **Diana Scarwid/***Mommie Dearest*

1982

★ **Aileen Quinn/***Annie*

1983

★ **Sybil Danning/***Chained Heat*
★ **Sybil Danning/***Hercules*

1984

★ **Lynn-Holly Johnson/***Where the Boys Are '84*

1985

★ **Brigitte Nielsen/***Rocky 4*

1987

★ **Daryl Hannah/***Wall Street*

1988

★ **Kristy McNichol/***Two Moon Junction*

1989

★ **Brooke Shields/***Speed Zone*

1990

★ **Sofia Coppola/***The Godfather, Part 3*

1991

★ **Sean Young/***A Kiss Before Dying*

1992

★ **Estelle Getty/***Stop! or My Mom Will Shoot*

1993

★ **Faye Dunaway/***The Temp*

1994

★ **Rosie O'Donnell/***Car 54, Where Are You?*
★ **Rosie O'Donnell/***Exit to Eden*
★ **Rosie O'Donnell/***The Flintstones*
Elizabeth Taylor/*The Flintstones*

1995

★ **Madonna/***Four Rooms*
Gina Gershon/*Showgirls*

1996

★ **Melanie Griffith/***Mulholland Falls*
Faye Dunaway/*The Chamber*
Faye Dunaway/*Dunston Checks In*
Jami Gertz/*Twister*
Daryl Hannah/*Two Much*
Teri Hatcher/*Heaven's Prisoners*
Teri Hatcher/*Two Days in the Valley*

1997

★ **Alicia Silverstone/***Batman and Robin*
Faye Dunaway/*Albino Alligator*
Milla Jovovich/*The Fifth Element*
Julia Louis-Dreyfus/*Father's Day*
Demi Moore/*G.I. Jane*
Uma Thurman/*Batman and Robin*

1998

★ **Maria Pitillo/***Godzilla*
Ellen A. Dow/*54*
Jenny McCarthy/*BASEketball*
Roger Moore/*Spice World: The Movie*
Liv Tyler/*Armageddon*
Raquel Welch/*Chairman of the Board*

1999

★ **Denise Richards/***The World Is Not Enough*
Sofia Coppola/*Star Wars: Episode 1—The Phantom Menace*
Salma Hayek/*Dogma*
Salma Hayek/*Wild Wild West*
Juliette Lewis/*The Other Sister*

2000

★ **Kelly Preston/***Battlefield Earth*
Patricia Arquette/*Little Nicky*
Joan Collins/*The Flintstones in Viva Rock Vegas*
Thandie Newton/*Mission: Impossible 2*
Rene Russo/*The Adventures of Rocky & Bullwinkle*

2001

★ **Estella Warren/***Planet of the Apes*

WORST DIRECTOR

1980

★ **Robert Greenwald/***Xanadu*

1981

★ **Michael Cimino/***Heaven's Gate*

1982

★ **Ken Annakin/***Pirate Movie*

1983

★ **Peter Sasdy/***The Lonely Lady*

1984

★ **John Derek/***Bolero*

1985

★ **Sylvester Stallone/***Rocky 4*

1986

★ **Prince/***Under the Cherry Moon*

1987

★ **Norman Mailer/***Tough Guys Don't Dance*
★ **Elaine May/***Ishtar*

1988

★ **Blake Edwards/***Sunset*
★ **Stewart Raffill/***Mac and Me*

1989

★ **William Shatner/***Star Trek 5: The Final Frontier*

1990

★ **John Derek/***Ghosts Can't Do It*

1991

★ **Michael Lehmann/***Hudson Hawk*

1992

★ **David Seltzer/***Shining Through*

1993

★ **Jennifer Lynch/***Boxing Helena*

1994

★ **Steven Seagal/***On Deadly Ground*

1995

★ **Paul Verhoeven/***Showgirls*

1996

★ **Andrew Bergman/***Striptease*
John Frankenheimer/*The Island of Dr. Moreau*
Stephen Frears/*Mary Reilly*
John Landis/*The Stupids*
Brian Levant/*Jingle All the Way*

1997

★ **Kevin Costner/***The Postman*
Jan De Bont/*Speed 2: Cruise Control*
Luis Llosa/*Anaconda*
Joel Schumacher/*Batman and Robin*
Oliver Stone/*U-Turn*

1998

★ **Gus Van Sant/***Psycho*
Michael Bay/*Armageddon*
Jeremiah S. Chechik/*The Avengers*
Roland Emmerich/*Godzilla*
Arthur Hiller/*An Alan Smithee Film: Burn, Hollywood, Burn*

1999

★ **Barry Sonnenfeld/***Wild Wild West*
Jan De Bont/*The Haunting*
Dennis Dugan/*Big Daddy*
Peter Hyams/*End of Days*
George Lucas/*Star Wars: Episode 1—The Phantom Menace*

2000

★ **Roger Christian/***Battlefield Earth*
Brian DePalma/*Mission to Mars*
John Schlesinger/*The Next Best Thing*

2001

★ **Tom Green/***Freddy Got Fingered*

WORST SCREENPLAY

1980

★ *Can't Stop the Music*

1981

★ *Mommie Dearest*

1983

★ *The Lonely Lady*

1984

★ *Bolero*

1985

★ *Rambo: First Blood, Part 2*
★ *Rocky 4*

1986

★ *Howard the Duck*

1987

★ *Leonard Part 6*

1988

★ *Cocktail*

1989

★ *Harlem Nights*

1990

★ *The Adventures of Ford Fairlane*

1991

★ *Hudson Hawk*

1992

★ *Stop! or My Mom Will Shoot*

1993

★ *Indecent Proposal*

1994

★ *The Flintstones*

1995

★ *Showgirls*

1996

★ *Striptease*
Barb Wire
Ed
The Island of Dr. Moreau
The Stupids

1997

★ *The Postman*
Anaconda
Batman and Robin
The Lost World: Jurassic Park 2
Speed 2: Cruise Control

1998

★ *An Alan Smithee Film: Burn, Hollywood, Burn*
Armageddon
The Avengers
Godzilla
Spice World: The Movie

1999

★ *Wild Wild West*
Big Daddy
The Haunting
The Mod Squad
Star Wars: Episode 1—The Phantom Menace

2000

★ *Battlefield Earth*
Book of Shadows: Blair Witch 2
Dr. Seuss' How the Grinch Stole Christmas
Little Nicky
The Next Best Thing

2001

★ *Freddy Got Fingered*

WORST SONG

1980

★ **"The Man with Bogart's Face"/***The Man with Bogart's Face*

1981

★ **"Baby Talk"/***Paternity*

1982

★ **"Pumpin' and Blowin'"/***Pirate Movie*

1983

★ **"The Way You Do It"/***The Lonely Lady*

1984

★ **"Drinkenstein"/***Rhinestone*

1985

★ **"Peace In Our Life"/***Rambo: First Blood, Part 2*

1986

★ **"Love or Money"/***Under the Cherry Moon*

1987

★ **"I Want Your Sex"/***Beverly Hills Cop 2*

1988

★ **"Jack Fresh"/***Caddyshack 2*

1989

★ **"Bring Your Daughter to the Slaughter"/***A Nightmare on Elm Street 5: Dream Child*

1990

★ **"He's Comin' Back (The Devil!)"/***Repossessed*

1991

★ **"Addams Groove"/***The Addams Family*

1992

★ **"High Times, Hard Times"/***Newsies*

1993

★ **"WHOOMP! There It Is"/***Addams Family Values*

1994

★ **"Marry the Mole"/***Thumbelina*

1995

★ **"Walk into the Wind"/***Showgirls*

1996

★ **"Pussy, Pussy, Pussy (Whose Kitty Cat Are You?)"/***Striptease*
"Welcome to Planet Boom!"/*Barb Wire*
"Whenever There Is Love"/*Daylight*

1997

★ **Entire Song Score/***The Postman*
"Fire Down Below"/*Fire Down Below*
"How Do I Live"/*Con Air*
"My Dream"/*Speed 2: Cruise Control*
"The End is The Beginning is The End"/*Batman and Robin*

1998

★ **"I Wanna Be Mike Ovitz!"/***An Alan Smithee Film: Burn, Hollywood, Burn*
"Barney, The Song"/*Barney's Great Adventure*
"I Don't Want to Miss a Thing"/*Armageddon*
"Storm"/*The Avengers*
"Too Much"/*Spice World: The Movie*

1999

★ **"Wild Wild West"/***Wild Wild West*

★ = *winner*

WORST NEW STAR

1981

★ **Klinton Spilsbury/***Legend of the Lone Ranger*

1982

★ **Pia Zadora/***Butterfly*

1983

★ **Lou Ferrigno/***Hercules*

1984

★ **Olivia D'Abo/***Bolero*
★ **Olivia D'Abo/***Conan the Destroyer*

1985

★ **Brigitte Nielsen/***Red Sonja*
★ **Brigitte Nielsen/***Rocky 4*

1987

★ **David Mendenhall/***Over the Top*

1990

★ **Sofia Coppola/***The Godfather, Part 3*

1991

★ **Vanilla Ice/***Cool As Ice*

1992

★ **Pauly Shore/***Encino Man*

1993

★ **Janet Jackson/***Poetic Justice*

1994

★ **Anna Nicole Smith/***Naked Gun 33 1/3: The Final Insult*

1995

★ **Elizabeth Berkley/***Showgirls*
David Caruso/*Kiss of Death*
Cindy Crawford/*Fair Game*
Julia Sweeney/*It's Pat: The Movie*

1996

★ **Pamela Anderson/***Barb Wire*
Ellen DeGeneres/*Mr. Wrong*

1997

★ **Dennis Rodman/***Double Team*
Tori Spelling/*The House of Yes*
Howard Stern/*Private Parts*
Chris Tucker/*The Fifth Element*
Chris Tucker/*Money Talks*

1998

★ **Joe Eszterhas/***An Alan Smithee Film: Burn, Hollywood, Burn*
★ **Jerry Springer/***Ringmaster*
Barney/*Barney's Great Adventure*
The Spice Girls/*Spice World: The Movie*
Carrot Top/*Chairman of the Board*

★ = *winner*

Cast Index

The **Cast Index** provides a complete videography for cast members with more than one appearance on video. The listings for the actor names follow an alphabetical sort by last name (although the names appear in a first name last name format). The videographies are listed chronologically, from most recent film to earliest appearance, making it easier to trace the development of your favorite actor's career. When a cast member appears in more than one film in the same year, these movies are listed alphabetically within the year. A (V) beside a movie title indicates voice-only work.

Beverly Aadland
Assault of the Rebel Girls *'59*
Raiders of Sunset Pass *'43*

Lee Aaker (1943-)
Courage of Rin Tin Tin *'83*
Rin Tin Tin, Hero of the West *'55*
Hondo *'53*
The Atomic City *'52*

Aaliyah (1979-2001)
Queen of the Damned *'02*
Romeo Must Die *'00*

Angela Aames (1956-88)
Basic Training *'86*
Bachelor Party *'84*
The Lost Empire *'83*

Willie Aames (1960-)
Cut and Run *'85*
Paradise *'82*
Zapped! *'82*
Scavenger Hunt *'79*
Frankenstein *'73*

Caroline Aaron (1952-)
Joe Dirt *'01*
Running Mates *'00*
What Planet Are You From? *'00*
Anywhere But Here *'99*
Tuesdays with Morrie *'99*
Primary Colors *'98*
Deconstructing Harry *'97*
Weapons of Mass Distraction *'97*
House Arrest *'96*
A Modern Affair *'94*
Alice *'90*
Edward Scissorhands *'90*
Crimes & Misdemeanors *'89*
Heartburn *'86*

Judith Abarbanel
American Matchmaker *'40*
The Cantor's Son *'37*
Uncle Moses *'32*

Diego Abatantuono (1955-)
The Best Man *'97*
Mediterraneo *'91*

Sean Abbananto
Bikini Med School *'98*
Bikini House Calls *'96*

Bruce Abbott (1954-)
Melanie Darrow *'97*
The Prophecy 2: Ashtown *'97*
The Demolitionist *'95*
Dillinger *'91*
Bride of Re-Animator *'89*
Trapped *'89*
Bad Dreams *'88*
Interzone *'88*
Summer Heat *'87*
Re-Animator *'84*

Bud Abbott (1895-1974)
Dance with Me, Henry *'56*
Abbott and Costello Meet the Mummy *'55*
Abbott and Costello Meet the Keystone Kops *'54*
Abbott and Costello Go to Mars *'53*
Abbott and Costello Meet Captain Kidd *'52*
Abbott and Costello Meet Dr. Jekyll and Mr. Hyde *'52*
Jack & the Beanstalk *'52*
Lost in Alaska *'52*
Abbott and Costello Meet the Invisible Man *'51*
Comin' Round the Mountain *'51*
Abbott and Costello in the Foreign Legion *'50*
Abbott and Costello Meet the Killer, Boris Karloff *'49*
Africa Screams *'49*
Abbott and Costello Meet Frankenstein *'48*
Mexican Hayride *'48*
The Noose Hangs High *'48*
Buck Privates Come Home *'47*
The Wistful Widow of Wagon Gap *'47*
Little Giant *'46*
The Time of Their Lives *'46*
Abbott and Costello in Hollywood *'45*
Here Come the Co-Eds *'45*
The Naughty Nineties *'45*
In Society *'44*
Lost in a Harem *'44*
Hit the Ice *'43*
It Ain't Hay *'43*
Pardon My Sarong *'42*
Ride 'Em Cowboy *'42*
Rio Rita *'42*
Who Done It? *'42*
Buck Privates *'41*
Hold That Ghost *'41*
In the Navy *'41*
Keep 'Em Flying *'41*
One Night in the Tropics *'40*

Diahnne Abbott (1945-)
Jo Jo Dancer, Your Life Is Calling *'86*
Love Streams *'84*
King of Comedy *'82*
New York, New York *'77*

John Abbott (1905-96)
The Merry Widow *'52*
Adventure Island *'47*
Anna and the King of Siam *'46*
Deception *'46*
Humoresque *'46*
Pursuit to Algiers *'45*
The Vampire's Ghost *'45*
Cry of the Werewolf *'44*
The Falcon in Hollywood *'44*
U-Boat Prisoner *'44*
Mrs. Miniver *'42*

Philip Abbott (1923-98)
The Fantastic World of D.C. Collins *'84*
Hangar 18 *'80*
The Invisible Boy *'57*

Kareem Abdul-Jabbar (1947-)
BASEketball *'98*
Rebound: The Legend of Earl "The Goat" Manigault *'96*
Slam Dunk Ernest *'95*
D2: The Mighty Ducks *'94*
Stephen King's The Stand *'94*
Purple People Eater *'88*
Chuck Berry: Hail! Hail! Rock 'n' Roll *'87*
Fletch *'85*
Airplane! *'80*
The Fish that Saved Pittsburgh *'79*
Game of Death *'79*

Hiroshi Abe
Tokyo Raiders *'00*
Godzilla 2000 *'99*

Alfred Abel (1879-1937)
Metropolis *'26*
Dr. Mabuse, The Gambler *'22*

Walter Abel (1898-1987)
Grace Quigley *'84*
The Man Without a Country *'73*
Silent Night, Bloody Night *'73*
Quick, Let's Get Married *'71*
Mirage *'66*
Raintree County *'57*
The Indian Fighter *'55*
Curley *'47*
Fabulous Joe *'47*
Kid from Brooklyn *'46*
13 Rue Madeleine *'46*
Mr. Skeffington *'44*
So Proudly We Hail *'43*
Holiday Inn *'42*
Wake Island *'42*
Dance, Girl, Dance *'40*
Law of the Underworld *'38*
Fury *'36*
The Three Musketeers *'35*

Jim Abele
Model Behavior *'00*
Student Affairs *'88*
Wimps *'87*

Tim Abell
Dead Simple *'01*
The Substitute 4: Failure is Not an Option *'00*
The Base *'99*
Rapid Assault *'99*
Death and Desire *'97*
Hybrid *'97*
Night Shade *'97*
Soldier of Fortune Inc. *'97*
Steel Sharks *'97*
Sexual Roulette *'96*
Attack of the 60-Foot Centerfold *'95*
Masseuse *'95*
Over the Wire *'95*

Ian Abercrombie
Rattled *'96*
Test Tube Teens from the Year 2000 *'93*
Army of Darkness *'92*
Zandalee *'91*
Curse 4: The Ultimate Sacrifice *'90*
Puppet Master 3: Toulon's Revenge *'90*
Catacombs *'89*
Kicks *'85*

Keith Aberdein (1943-)
Smash Palace *'82*
Wild Horses *'82*

Sivi Aberg
Dr. Death, Seeker of Souls *'73*
The Killing of Sister George *'69*

Abigail
Breaking Loose *'90*
Adventures of Eliza Fraser *'76*

F. Murray Abraham (1939-)
13 Ghosts *'01*
Finding Forrester *'00*
Excellent Cadavers *'99*
Muppets from Space *'99*
Noah's Ark *'99*
All New Adventures of Laurel and Hardy: For Love or Mummy *'98*
Esther *'98*
Star Trek: Insurrection *'98*
Baby Face Nelson *'97*
Color of Justice *'97*
Mimic *'97*
Larry McMurtry's Dead Man's Walk *'96*
Looking for Richard *'96*
Children of the Revolution *'95*
Dillinger and Capone *'95*
Mighty Aphrodite *'95*
Surviving the Game *'94*
By the Sword *'93*
Last Action Hero *'93*
National Lampoon's Loaded Weapon 1 *'93*
Nostradamus *'93*
Sweet Killing *'93*
Mobsters *'91*
The Bonfire of the Vanities *'90*
Beyond the Stars *'89*
An Innocent Man *'89*
Intimate Power *'89*
Slipstream *'89*
Third Solution *'89*
The Name of the Rose *'86*
Amadeus *'84*
Scarface *'83*
Madman *'79*
The Big Fix *'78*

All the President's Men '76
The Ritz '76
The Sunshine Boys '75
Prisoner of Second Avenue '74
Serpico '73
They Might Be Giants '71

Ken Abraham
Marked for Murder '89
Deadly Embrace '88
Vice Academy '88
Creepozoids '87

Jim Abrahams (1944-)
Airplane! '80
Kentucky Fried Movie '77

Jon Abrahams (1977-)
Texas Rangers '01
Boiler Room '00
Meet the Parents '00
Scary Movie '00
Bringing Out the Dead '99
Outside Providence '99
The Faculty '98
Masterminds '96
Dead Man Walking '95
Kids '95

Michele Abrams
Buffy the Vampire Slayer '92
Cool World '92

Andrei Abrikosov
Sword & the Dragon '56
Alexander Nevsky '38

Victoria Abril (1959-)
French Twist '95
Jimmy Hollywood '94
Kika '94
Intruso '93
High Heels '91
Lovers: A True Story '90
Tie Me Up! Tie Me Down! '90
Baton Rouge '88
Max, Mon Amour '86
After Darkness '85
L'Addition '85
Padre Nuestro '85
Moon in the Gutter '83
On the Line '83
I Married a Dead Man '82

Yussef Abu-Warda
Kadosh '99
The Milky Way '97

Kirk Acevedo
Band of Brothers '01
Bait '00
Boiler Room '00
The Thin Red Line '98
Witness to the Mob '98

James Acheson
The Garden of Redemption '97
Kazaam '96
Body Language '92

Sharon Acker (1935-)
Happy Birthday to Me '81
Off Your Rocker '80
The Hanged Man '74
The Stranger '73
Lucky Jim '58

Forrest J Ackerman (1916-)
Attack of the 60-Foot Centerfold '95
Dead Alive '93
Innocent Blood '92
Hard to Die '90
The Wizard of Speed and Time '88
Amazon Women on the Moon '87
Curse of the Queerwolf '87
Evil Spawn '87
Aftermath '85
The Howling '81
Kentucky Fried Movie '77
Schlock '73
Dracula vs. Frankenstein '71
Planet of Blood '66

Leslie Ackerman (1956-)
Blame It on the Night '84
Shattered Vows '84
Skag '79
Young Love, First Love '79
Joy Ride to Nowhere '78
The First Nudie Musical '75
Law and Disorder '74

Joss Ackland (1928-)
K-19: The Widowmaker '02
Passion of Mind '00
Heat of the Sun '99
Firelight '97
Swept from the Sea '97
Deadly Voyage '96
D3: The Mighty Ducks '96
Surviving Picasso '96
Citizen X '95
A Kid in King Arthur's Court '95
Jacob '94
Miracle on 34th Street '94
Mother's Boys '94
Shameless '94
Nowhere to Run '93
The Mighty Ducks '92
Once Upon a Crime '92
Project: Shadowchaser '92
Bill & Ted's Bogus Journey '91
Codename Kyril '91
The Object of Beauty '91
The Palermo Connection '91
A Woman Named Jackie '91
The Hunt for Red October '90
Jekyll and Hyde '90
A Murder of Quality '90
Spymaker: The Secret Life of Ian Fleming '90
Lethal Weapon 2 '89
To Kill a Priest '89
It Couldn't Happen Here '88
White Mischief '88
A Zed & Two Noughts '88
Queenie '87
The Sicilian '87
Lady Jane '85
Shadowlands '85
The Apple '80
Rough Cut '80
Saint Jack '79
Silver Bears '78
Watership Down '78 (V)
Who Is Killing the Great Chefs of Europe? '78
Royal Flash '75
The Little Prince '74
S*P*Y*S '74
Mind Snatchers '72
Cry of the Penguins '71
The House that Dripped Blood '71

David Ackroyd (1940-)
Raven '97
Against the Wall '94
Dead On '93
Love, Cheat & Steal '93
The Fear Inside '92
Memories of Me '88
Windmills of the Gods '88
Poor Little Rich Girl: The Barbara Hutton Story '87
The Children of Times Square '86
A Smoky Mountain Christmas '86
Cocaine: One Man's Seduction '83
When Your Lover Leaves '83
A Gun in the House '81
And I Alone Survived '78
The Dark Secret of Harvest Home '78

Rodolfo Acosta (1920-74)
Savage Run '70
Flaming Star '60
Let No Man Write My Epitaph '60
Drum Beat '54
Hondo '53
Pancho Villa Returns '50

Jay Acovone (1955-)
Crash Dive '96
Opposite Corners '96
Showdown '94
Born to Run '93
Quicksand: No Escape '91
Doctor Mordrid: Master of the Unknown '90

Acquanetta (1921-)
Grizzly Adams: The Legend Continues '90
The Lost Continent '51
Dead Man's Eyes/Pillow of Death '44
Jungle Woman '44
Captive Wild Woman '43

Eddie Acuff (1908-56)
G-Men Never Forget '48
It Happened Tomorrow '44
Guadalcanal Diary '43
They Died with Their Boots On '41
Law of the Underworld '38
The Black Legion '37

Deborah Adair (1952-)
Endless Descent '90
Gore Vidal's Lincoln '88

Dick Adair
Pay or Die '83
Blind Rage '78

Robert Adair (1900-54)
Norman Conquest '53
The Face at the Window '39

Ronald Adam
Tomb of Ligeia '64
The Obsessed '51

Amy Adams
Psycho Beach Party '00
Cruel Intentions 2 '99
Drop Dead Gorgeous '99

Beverly Adams (1945-)
The Ambushers '67
Devil's Angels '67
Torture Garden '67
Murderers' Row '66
How to Stuff a Wild Bikini '65
Roustabout '64

Brandon Adams (1979-)
Ghost in the Machine '93
The Sandlot '93
The People under the Stairs '91

Brooke Adams (1949-)
The Baby-Sitters' Club '95
The Last Hit '93
The Sandlot '93
Gas Food Lodging '92
Sometimes They Come Back '91
The Unborn '91
The Lion of Africa '87
Man on Fire '87
Almost You '85
Key Exchange '85
The Stuff '85
The Innocents Abroad '84
Dead Zone '83
Utilities '83
Tell Me a Riddle '80
Cuba '79
A Man, a Woman, and a Bank '79
Days of Heaven '78
Invasion of the Body Snatchers '78
Shock Waves '77
James Dean '76

Catlin Adams (1950-)
The Jazz Singer '80
The Jerk '79
Panic in Echo Park '77

Claire Adams (1898-1978)
The Big Parade '25
Heart's Haven '22
The Penalty '20

Don Adams (1926-)
Inspector Gadget '99 (V)
Get Smart, Again! '89
Back to the Beach '87
Jimmy the Kid '82
The Nude Bomb '80

Dorothy Adams (1915-88)
The Prodigal '55
Streets of Sin '49
The Best Years of Our Lives '46
Laura '44
So Proudly We Hail '43

Edie Adams (1931-)
Armistead Maupin's Tales of the City '93
Adventures Beyond Belief '87
Shooting Stars '85
Ernie Kovacs: Between the Laughter '84
Haunting of Harrington House '82
Cheech and Chong's Up in Smoke '79
Racquet '79
The Seekers '79
Evil Roy Slade '71
The Honey Pot '67
The Oscar '66
The Best Man '64
Call Me Bwana '63
It's a Mad, Mad, Mad, Mad World '63
Love with the Proper Stranger '63
Under the Yum-Yum Tree '63
Lover Come Back '61
The Apartment '60

Ernie Adams (1885-1946)
Sagebrush Law '43
Wings over the Pacific '43
Arizona Gunfighter '37
Gun Lords of Stirrup Basin '37
Lightning Bill Crandall '37
Ridin' the Lone Trail '37
The Gun Ranger '34
Breed of the Border '33
Galloping Romeo '33
Beyond the Rockies '32
The Tip-Off '31
The Fighting Legion '30
Nevada '27

Jane Adams (1921-)
The Brute Man '46
House of Dracula '45
Lost City of the Jungle '45

Jane Adams (1965-)
Orange County '02
The Anniversary Party '01
Wonder Boys '00
Mumford '99
Songcatcher '99
A Texas Funeral '99
Day at the Beach '98
Happiness '98
Music from Another Room '97
Father of the Bride Part II '95
Kansas City '95
Rising Son '90
Vital Signs '90

Joey Lauren Adams (1971-)
Dr. Dolittle 2 '01 (V)
In the Shadows '01
Jay and Silent Bob Strike Back '01
Beautiful '00
Big Daddy '99
The Dress Code '99
A Cool, Dry Place '98
Chasing Amy '97
Bio-Dome '96
Mallrats '95
S.F.W. '94
Sleep with Me '94
Dazed and Confused '93
The Program '93

Julie Adams (1928-)
Backtrack '89
Black Roses '88
The Killer Inside Me '76
The McCullochs '75
Psychic Killer '75
McQ '74
The Last Movie '71
The Trackers '71
Tickle Me '65
Away All Boats '56
The Private War of Major Benson '55
Creature from the Black Lagoon '54
Francis Joins the WACs '54
Man from the Alamo '53
Horizons West '52
The Lawless Breed '52
Blazing Guns '50
Sudden Death '50

Lynne Adams
Requiem for Murder '99
Time at the Top '99
Psychopath '97
Silent Hunter '94
The Carpenter '89
Blood Relations '87
Night Zoo '87

Mason Adams (1919-)
From the Earth to the Moon '98
The Lesser Evil '97
Touch '96
Houseguest '94
Son-in-Law '93
F/X '86
Rage of Angels: The Story Continues '86
Half Slave, Half Free '85
Adam '83
The Kid with the Broken Halo '82
Omen 3: The Final Conflict '81
Revenge of the Stepford Wives '80
A Shining Season '79

Maud Adams (1945-)
Silent Night, Deadly Night 4: Initiation '90
Intimate Power '89
The Kill Reflex '89
Angel 3: The Final Chapter '88
Deadly Intent '88
A Man of Passion '88
Nairobi Affair '88
Hell Hunters '87
Jane & the Lost City '87
Women's Club '87
Target Eagle '84
Octopussy '83
Tattoo '81
The Hostage Tower '80
Playing for Time '80
Killer Force '75
Rollerball '75
The Girl in Blue '74
The Man with the Golden Gun '74

Nick Adams (1931-68)
Godzilla vs. Monster Zero '68
Mission Mars '67
Mosby's Marauders '66
Die, Monster, Die! '65
Hell Is for Heroes '62
The Interns '62
The FBI Story '59
Pillow Talk '59
No Time for Sergeants '58
Teacher's Pet '58
Our Miss Brooks '56
Mister Roberts '55
Picnic '55
Rebel without a Cause '55

Polly Adams
Element of Doubt '96
A Dark Adapted Eye '93

Stanley Adams (1915-77)
The Passing of Evil '70
Lilies of the Field '63
Requiem for a Heavyweight '62
Hell Ship Mutiny '57

Ted Adams (1890-1973)
Outlaw Country '49
Billy the Kid '41
Pinto Canyon '40
Outlaw's Paradise '39
Lightnin' Carson Rides Again '38
Pals of the Saddle '38
Arizona Gunfighter '37
Border Caballero '36
Desert Phantom '36
The Lion Man '36
Undercover Man '36
Toll of the Desert '35
Ghost Valley '32
The Savage Girl '32

Tom Adams (1938-)
License to Kill '89
Fast Kill '73
The House that Dripped Blood '71
Subterfuge '68
Fathom '67
The Fighting Prince of Donegal '66
Where the Bullets Fly '66
Second Best Secret Agent in the Whole Wide World '65
The Great Escape '63

Chris(topher) Adamson
Dead of Night '99
Razor Blade Smile '98
Shameless '94

George Adamson
Christian the Lion '76
An Elephant Called Slowly '69

Meat Loaf Aday (1948-)
The Salton Sea '02
Focus '01
Crazy in Alabama '99
Fight Club '99
Black Dog '98
Everything That Rises '98
Gunshy '98
The Mighty '98
Outside Ozona '98
Spice World: The Movie '97
To Catch a Yeti '95
Leap of Faith '92
Wayne's World '92
Motorama '91
The Squeeze '87
Feel the Motion '86
Roadie '80
Americathon '79
The Rocky Horror Picture Show '75

Anthony Addabbo (1960-)
A Place Called Truth '98
Red Shoe Diaries 5: Weekend Pass '95
The Gunfighters '87

Dawn Addams (1930-85)
Vault of Horror '73
The Vampire Lovers '70
Zeta One '69
Ballad in Blue '66
Where the Bullets Fly '66
The Liars '64
The Thousand Eyes of Dr. Mabuse '60
The Two Faces of Dr. Jekyll '60
The Silent Enemy '58
A King in New York '57
The Robe '53

Robert Addie
Captain Jack '98
A Knight in Camelot '98
Another Country '84
Excalibur '81

Nancy Addison (1948-)
Somewhere Tomorrow '85
The Dain Curse '78

Mark Addy (1963-)
The Time Machine '02
Down to Earth '01
A Knight's Tale '01
The Flintstones in Viva Rock Vegas '00
Jack Frost '98
The Full Monty '96

Wesley Addy (1913-96)
Hiroshima '95
A Modern Affair '94
The Bostonians '84

The Verdict '82
The Europeans '79
Network '76
The Grissom Gang '71
Tora! Tora! Tora! '70
Seconds '66
The Big Knife '55
Kiss Me Deadly '55

Isabelle Adjani (1958-)
Diabolique '96
Queen Margot '94
Camille Claudel '89
Ishtar '87
Subway '85
Next Year If All Goes Well '83
One Deadly Summer '83
Possession '81
Quartet '81
Nosferatu the Vampyre '79
The Driver '78
Barocco '76
The Slap '76
The Tenant '76
The Story of Adele H. '75

Seth Adkins
Gepetto '00
Stir '98
First Do No Harm '97

Bill Adler
Van Nuys Blvd. '79
Blue Sunshine '78
Pom Pom Girls '76
Switchblade Sisters '75

Jay Adler (1896-1978)
Grave of the Vampire '72
Curse of the Undead '59
Crime of Passion '57
The Killing '56

Jerry Adler (1929-)
Six Ways to Sunday '99
Manhattan Murder Mystery '93
The Public Eye '92

Luther Adler (1903-84)
Absence of Malice '81
Voyage of the Damned '76
The Man in the Glass Booth '75
Mean Johnny Barrows '75
Murph the Surf '75
The Brotherhood '68
The Three Sisters '65
The Last Angry Man '59
Crashout '55
Hoodlum Empire '52
The Desert Fox '51
Kiss Tomorrow Goodbye '50
D.O.A. '49
House of Strangers '49
Wake of the Red Witch '49
The Loves of Carmen '48
Cornered '45

Matt Adler (1966-)
Diving In '90
Doin' Time on Planet Earth '88
North Shore '87
White Water Summer '87
Flight of the Navigator '86

Edvin Adolphson (1893-1979)
Boy of Two Worlds '70
Only One Night '42
Dollar '38
The Count of the Old Town '34

Frank Adonis
Suicide Ride '97
True Romance '93

Renee Adoree (1898-1933)
The Michigan Kid '28
The Big Parade '25

Mario Adorf (1930-)
Smilla's Sense of Snow '96
The Holcroft Covenant '85
Invitation au Voyage '82
Paralyzed '70s
The Tin Drum '79
The Lost Honor of Katharina Blum '75
Hired to Kill '73
Hit Men '73
Manhunt '73
The Bird with the Crystal Plumage '70
Brainwashed '60

Iris Adrian (1912-94)
Blue Hawaii '62
Carnival Rock '57
The Fast and the Furious '54
G.I. Jane '51
Stop That Cab '51
The Lovable Cheat '49
The Paleface '48
Infamous Crimes '47
The Stork Club '45
I'm from Arkansas '44
Million Dollar Kid '44
Shake Hands with Murder '44
Action in the North Atlantic '43
I Killed That Man '42
The Road to Zanzibar '41

Max Adrian (1903-73)
The Boy Friend '71
The Devils '71
The Music Lovers '71
Dr. Terror's House of Horrors '65
Henry V '44

Patricia Adriani (1958-)
I'm the One You're Looking For '88
The Nest '80

Ljubica Adzovic
Black Cat, White Cat '98
Time of the Gypsies '90

Ben Affleck (1972-)
Changing Lanes '02
The Sum of All Fears '02
Jay and Silent Bob Strike Back '01
Pearl Harbor '01
Boiler Room '00
Bounce '00
Reindeer Games '00
Dogma '99
Forces of Nature '99
Armageddon '98
Shakespeare in Love '98
200 Cigarettes '98
Chasing Amy '97
Going All the Way '97
Good Will Hunting '97
Phantoms '97
Glory Daze '96
Mallrats '95
Dazed and Confused '93
School Ties '92

Casey Affleck (1975-)
American Pie 2 '01
Ocean's Eleven '01
Soul Survivors '01
Drowning Mona '00
Hamlet '00
Attention Shoppers '99
Committed '99
Desert Blue '98
200 Cigarettes '98
Good Will Hunting '97
Race the Sun '96
To Die For '95

John Agar (1921-2002)
Body Bags '93
Invasion of Privacy '92
The Perfect Bride '91
Fear '90
Miracle Mile '89
Perfect Victims '87
King Kong '76
Big Jake '71
Chisum '70
The Undefeated '69
Hell Raiders '68
The St. Valentine's Day Massacre '67
Curse of the Swamp Creature '66
Johnny Reno '66
Women of the Prehistoric Planet '66
Zontar, the Thing from Venus '66
Cavalry Command '63
Invisible Invaders '59
Attack of the Puppet People '58
The Brain from Planet Arous '57
The Daughter of Dr. Jekyll '57
Flesh and the Spur '57
The Mole People '56
Revenge of the Creature '55
Tarantula '55
Along the Great Divide '51
Sands of Iwo Jima '49
She Wore a Yellow Ribbon '49
Fort Apache '48

Tetchie Agbayani
Deathfight '93
Rikky and Pete '88
Mission Manila '87
Gymkata '85
The Dolls '83

Pierre Agostino
Las Vegas Serial Killer '86
The Hollywood Strangler Meets the Skid Row Slasher '79

Janet Agren (1949-)
Magdalene '88
Night of the Sharks '87
Aladdin '86
Hands of Steel '86
Panic '83
Emerald Jungle '80
Gates of Hell '80
Perfect Crime '78
The Uranium Conspiracy '78

George Aguilar
Lunatics: A Love Story '92
The Trial of Billy Jack '74

Kris Aguilar
Fist of Steel '93
Bloodfist 2 '90
Bloodfist '89

Jenny Agutter (1952-)
The Railway Children '00
The Buccaneers '95
Freddie the Frog '92 (V)
Child's Play 2 '90
Darkman '90
Dark Tower '87
Secret Places '85
Silas Marner '85
An American Werewolf in London '81
Amy '81
Survivor '80
Dominique Is Dead '79
Mayflower: The Pilgrims' Adventure '79
The Riddle of the Sands '79
Sweet William '79
Gunfire '78
The Eagle Has Landed '77
Equus '77
The Man in the Iron Mask '77
Logan's Run '76
Walkabout '71
The Railway Children '70
Star! '68

Brian Aherne (1902-86)
Sword of Lancelot '63
Waltz King '63
The Best of Everything '59
The Swan '56
A Bullet Is Waiting '54
Prince Valiant '54
I Confess '53
Titanic '53
Forever and a Day '43
A Night to Remember '42
Smilin' Through '41
The Lady in Question '40
My Son, My Son '40
Beloved Enemy '36
I Live My Life '35
Sylvia Scarlett '35
The Song of Songs '33

Borje Ahlstedt (1939-)
Sunday's Children '94
Emma's Shadow '88
I Am Curious (Yellow) '67

Philip Ahn (1911-78)
Paradise, Hawaiian Style '66
Shock Corridor '63
Battle Hymn '57
Battle Circus '53
His Majesty O'Keefe '53
Impact '49
Back to Bataan '45
They Were Expendable '45
Betrayal from the East '44
China Sky '44
The Story of Dr. Wassell '44
China '43
Across the Pacific '42
Hawaii Calls '38
The General Died at Dawn '36

Charles Aidman (1925-93)
Prime Suspect '82
Zoot Suit '81
House of the Dead '80
Zone of the Dead '78
The Barbary Coast '74
The Invasion of Carol Enders '74
Picture of Dorian Gray '74
Adam at 6 a.m. '70
Menace on the Mountain '70
Countdown '68
Hour of the Gun '67
Pork Chop Hill '59

Danny Aiello (1933-)
Mambo Cafe '00
Prince of Central Park '00
Hitman's Journal '99
Dead Silence '98
The Last Don 2 '98
A Brooklyn State of Mind '97
The Last Don '97
Mojave Moon '96
Two Days in the Valley '96
Two Much '96
City Hall '95
The Road Home '95
Power of Attorney '94
The Professional '94
Ready to Wear '94
The Cemetery Club '93
Me and the Kid '93
The Pickle '93
Ruby '92
The Closer '91
Hudson Hawk '91
Mistress '91
Once Around '91
29th Street '91
Jacob's Ladder '90
Do the Right Thing '89
Harlem Nights '89
The January Man '89
The Preppie Murder '89
Third Solution '89
White Hot '88
Alone in the Neon Jungle '87
Man on Fire '87
Moonstruck '87
The Pick-Up Artist '87
Radio Days '87
Key Exchange '85
Protector '85
The Purple Rose of Cairo '85
The Stuff '85
Old Enough '84
Once Upon a Time in America '84
Chu Chu & the Philly Flash '81
Fort Apache, the Bronx '81
Hide in Plain Sight '80
Question of Honor '80
Defiance '79
Bloodbrothers '78
Fingers '78
The Front '76
Hooch '76
The Godfather, Part 2 '74
Bang the Drum Slowly '73
Deathmask '69

Rick Aiello (1958-)
Hollywood Confidential '97
Endangered '94
Uncivilized '94
The Closer '91
29th Street '91

Elaine Aiken (1927-98)
Caddyshack '80
Lonely Man '57

Liam Aiken
Sweet November '01
I Dreamed of Africa '00
Stepmom '98

Anouk Aimee (1934-)
Solomon '98
Ready to Wear '94
Dr. Bethune '90
A Man and a Woman: 20 Years Later '86
Success Is the Best Revenge '84
The Tragedy of a Ridiculous Man '81
Justine '69
A Man and a Woman '66
8 1/2 '63
Sodom and Gomorrah '62
Lola '61
La Dolce Vita '60
Modigliani '58
Paris Express '53
The Golden Salamander '51

Richard Ainley (1910-67)
Above Suspicion '43
I Dood It '43
White Cargo '42

Holly Aird (1969-)
Dreaming of Joseph Lees '99
The Theory of Flight '98
Fever Pitch '96
Intimate Relations '95
Over Indulgence '87
The Flame Trees of Thika '81

Andrew Airlie
Common Ground '00
Hard Evidence '94

Maria Aitken (1945-)
Grave Indiscretions '96
A Fish Called Wanda '88

Spottiswoode Aitken (1868-1933)
The Americano '17
The Birth of a Nation '15

Michael Aitkens
Moving Targets '87
The Highest Honor '84

Franklin Ajaye (1949-)
American Yakuza '94
The Wrong Guys '88
Fraternity Vacation '85
Get Crazy '83
The Jazz Singer '80
Convoy '78
Car Wash '76

Chantal Akerman (1950-)
News from Home '76 (N)
Je Tu Il Elle '74

Andra Akers
Desert Hearts '86
E. Nick: A Legend in His Own Mind '84

Karen Akers (1945-)
Heartburn '86
The Purple Rose of Cairo '85

Adewale Akinnuoye-Agbaje
The Mummy Returns '01
Lip Service '00
Legionnaire '98

Claude Akins (1926-94)
The Gambler Returns: The Luck of the Draw '93
Falling from Grace '92
The Curse '87
Manhunt for Claude Dallas '86
Monster in the Closet '86
Pecos Bill '86
The Concrete Cowboys '79
Killer on Board '77
Tarantulas: The Deadly Cargo '77
Tentacles '77
The Big Push '75
Eric '75
Battle for the Planet of the Apes '73
The Death Squad '73
A Man Called Sledge '71
The Night Stalker '71
The Devil's Brigade '68
Waterhole #3 '67
Return of the Magnificent Seven '66
The Killers '64
Merrill's Marauders '62
Comanche Station '60
Inherit the Wind '60
Rio Bravo '59
The Kettles on Old MacDonald's Farm '57
Sea Chase '55
The Caine Mutiny '54
From Here to Eternity '53

Carl Alacchi
Taken '99
The Pianist '91

Marc Alaimo
The Fence '94
Quicksand: No Escape '91
Arena '89
Tango and Cash '89
Archer: The Fugitive from the Empire '81

Steve Alaimo (1939-)
Alligator Alley '72
Wild Rebels '71
The Hooked Generation '69

Craig Alan
Endangered '94
Sex Crimes '92

Nelly Alard
Venice, Venice '92
Eating '90

Joe Alaskey
The Rugrats Movie '98 (V)
Casper '95 (V)
Bank Robber '93
Lucky Stiff '88

Jessica Alba (1981-)
Idle Hands '99
Never Been Kissed '99

Maria Alba (1910-99)
Chandu on the Magic Island '34
Return of Chandu '34
Mr. Robinson Crusoe '32

Captain Lou Albano (1933-)
Complex World '92
Body Slam '87
Wise Guys '86

Josh Albee
The Runaways '75
The Adventures of Tom Sawyer '73

Kevin Alber (1963-)
Alien Terminator '95
Burial of the Rats '95
The Showgirl Murders '95

Anna Maria Alberghetti (1936-)
Cinderfella '60
The Last Command '55
Here Comes the Groom '51
The Medium '51

Luis Alberni (1887-1962)
Harvest Melody '43
The Great Man Votes '38
Hats Off '37
Dancing Pirate '36
Goodbye Love '34
One Night of Love '34
Man from Monterey '33
The Sphinx '33
The Big Stampede '32

Hans Albers (1892-1960)
Die Grosse Freiheit Nr. 7 '45
Baron Munchausen '43
F.P. 1 Doesn't Answer '33
The Blue Angel '30

Eddie Albert (1908-)
The Big Picture '89

Out of Sight, Out of Her Mind '89
The Victory '88
Turnaround '87
Brenda Starr '86
Dress Gray '86
Head Office '86
Stitches '85
Burning Rage '84
Dreamscape '84
The Act '82
Yes, Giorgio '82
Goliath Awaits '81
Peter and Paul '81
Take This Job & Shove It '81
Beulah Land '80
Foolin' Around '80
How to Beat the High Cost of Living '80
The Concorde: Airport '79 '79
The Birch Interval '78
The Crash of Flight 401 '78
The Word '78
Moving Violation '76
Devil's Rain '75
Escape to Witch Mountain '75
Whiffs '75
The Longest Yard '74
McQ '74
Fireball Forward '72
The Heartbreak Kid '72
Captain Newman, M.D. '63
The Miracle of the White Stallions '63
Who's Got the Action? '63
The Longest Day '62
Beloved Infidel '59
Attack! '56
The Teahouse of the August Moon '56
I'll Cry Tomorrow '55
Oklahoma! '55
Roman Holiday '53
Actors and Sin '52
Carrie '52
The Fuller Brush Girl '50
You Gotta Stay Happy '48
Smash-Up: The Story of a Woman '47
The Perfect Marriage '46
Bombardier '43
The Wagons Roll at Night '41

Edward Albert (1951-)
Extreme Honor '01
Mimic 2 '01
Ablaze '00
The Man in the Iron Mask '97
The Secret Agent Club '96
Space Marines '96
Guarding Tess '94
Hard Drive '94
Red Sun Rising '94
Sorceress '94
Broken Trust '93
The Ice Runner '93
Sexual Malice '93
Shootfighter: Fight to the Death '93
Body Language '92
Exiled in America '90
Accidents '89
Mind Games '89
Wild Zone '89
Fist Fighter '88
The Rescue '88
The Underachievers '88
Distortions '87
Terminal Entry '87
Getting Even '86
Ellie '84
Time to Die '83
Butterfly '82
House Where Evil Dwells '82
Galaxy of Terror '81
The Squeeze '80
When Time Ran Out '80
Silent Victory: The Kitty O'Neil Story '79
The Greek Tycoon '78
The Rip Off '78
The Squeeze '78
The Domino Principle '77
The Purple Taxi '77
Death Cruise '74
Forty Carats '73
Butterflies Are Free '72
The Fool Killer '65

Laura Albert
Blood Games '90
Dr. Caligari '89
Death by Dialogue '88
The Unnamable '88

Giorgio Albertazzi
Eva '62
Last Year at Marienbad '61

Guido Alberti (1909-96)
Ten Days Wonder '72
Casanova '70 '65

Giampiero Albertini (1927-91)
Zorro '74
Commandos '73
Burn! '70

Frank Albertson (1909-64)
Psycho '60
Nightfall '56
Killer Dill '47
It's a Wonderful Life '46
Underground Agent '42
Wake Island '42
Louisiana Purchase '41
Man Made Monster '41
Room Service '38
Navy Blue and Gold '37
Fury '36
Ah, Wilderness! '35
Alice Adams '35
Hollywood Mystery '34
Rainbow over Broadway '33
Way Back Home '32
Big Business Girl '31
A Connecticut Yankee '31

Jack Albertson (1907-81)
Charlie and the Great Balloon Chase '82
Dead and Buried '81
The Fox and the Hound '81 (V)
Marriage Is Alive and Well '80
The Poseidon Adventure '72
Where the Eagle Flies '72
Willy Wonka & the Chocolate Factory '71
Changes '69
Justine '69
The Subject Was Roses '68
Flim-Flam Man '67
How to Murder Your Wife '64
Kissin' Cousins '64
The Patsy '64
Roustabout '64
Who's Got the Action? '63
Days of Wine and Roses '62
Period of Adjustment '62
Lover Come Back '61
Teacher's Pet '58
Miracle on 34th Street '47

Karl Otto Alberty
Battle of the Bulge '65
The Great Escape '63

Ariauna Albright
Mom's Outta Sight '01
Ancient Evil: Scream of the Mummy '00
Witchouse '99

Dan Albright
I Know What You Did Last Summer '97
To Dance with the White Dog '93

Hardie Albright (1903-75)
Mom & Dad '47
The Jade Mask '45
Sunset in El Dorado '45
Bambi '42 (V)
Champagne for Breakfast '35
Red Salute '35
Sing Sing Nights '35
The Scarlet Letter '34
The Song of Songs '33
The Purchase Price '32

Lola Albright (1924-)
The Impossible Years '68
Where Were You When the Lights Went Out? '68
The Way West '67
Joy House '64
Kid Galahad '62
The Monolith Monsters '57
The Tender Trap '55
Champion '49

Chris Alcaide
Rock All Night '57
Jupiter's Darling '55

Victor Alcocer (-1984)
Pistoleros Asesinos '87
It Happened at Nightmare Inn '70

Alan Alda (1936-)
What Women Want '00
The Object of My Affection '98
Mad City '97
Murder at 1600 '97
Everyone Says I Love You '96
Flirting with Disaster '95
Canadian Bacon '94
White Mile '94
And the Band Played On '93
Manhattan Murder Mystery '93
Whispers in the Dark '92
Betsy's Wedding '90
Crimes & Misdemeanors '89
A New Life '88
Sweet Liberty '86
M*A*S*H: Goodbye, Farewell & Amen '83
The Four Seasons '81
The Seduction of Joe Tynan '79
California Suite '78
Same Time, Next Year '78
The Glass House '72
Playmates '72
To Kill a Clown '72
The Mephisto Waltz '71
Jenny '70
Paper Lion '68
Gone Are the Days '63
Purlie Victorious '63

Antony Alda
The Killing Device '92
Homeboy '88
Movie Maker '86

Robert Alda (1914-86)
The Squeeze '80
Express to Terror '79
Every Girl Should Have One '78
The Rip Off '78
The Squeeze '78
Bittersweet Love '76
I Will, I Will for Now '76
Love by Appointment '76
Lisa and the Devil '75
Night Flight from Moscow '73
Revenge of the Barbarians '64
The Devil's Hand '61
Force of Impulse '60
The Beast with Five Fingers '46
Cloak and Dagger '46
The Man I Love '46
Rhapsody in Blue '45

Rutanya Alda (1945-)
The Souler Opposite '97
The Ref '93
Article 99 '92
Leaving Normal '92
The Dark Half '91
Prancer '89
Black Widow '87
Racing with the Moon '84
Girls Night Out '83
Vigilante '83
Amityville 2: The Possession '82
Mommie Dearest '81
Christmas Evil '80
When a Stranger Calls '79
The Deer Hunter '78
The Fury '78

Mary Alden (1883-1946)
Strange Interlude '32
April Fool '26
The Plastic Age '25
The Birth of a Nation '15

Norman Alden (1924-)
Ben '72
Tora! Tora! Tora! '70
The Devil's Brigade '68
Good Times '67
The Patsy '64
The Nutty Professor '63
The Sword in the Stone '63 (V)

Priscilla Alden
Death Nurse '87
Crazy Fat Ethel II '85
Criminally Insane '75

John Alderman (1933-87)
The Alpha Incident '76
Little Miss Innocence '73

Erville Alderson (1882-1957)
Objective, Burma! '45
Sergeant York '41
Sally of the Sawdust '25
America '24

John Alderton (1940-)
Speedy Death '99
Zardoz '73
The Girl Getters '66

Mari Aldon (1927-)
Race for Life '55
Summertime '55
Distant Drums '51

Tom Aldredge (1928-)
Message in a Bottle '98
Rounders '98
A Stranger in the Kingdom '98
Commandments '96
Lawn Dogs '96
Andersonville '95
Harvest of Fire '95
The Adventures of Huck Finn '93
O Pioneers! '91
Other People's Money '91
What about Bob? '91
Gentleman Bandit '81
The Rain People '69

Rhonda Aldrich
Jailbird Rock '88
Saturday the 14th Strikes Back '88

Kay Aldridge (1917-95)
The Phantom of 42nd Street '45
Haunted Harbor '44
Nyoka and the Tigermen '42

Kitty Aldridge
The Ice House '97
To Play the King '93
An African Dream '90
Slipstream '89
American Roulette '88

Michael Aldridge (1920-94)
Footlight Frenzy '84
Bullshot '83
Love for Lydia '79

Norma Aleandro (1936-)
Autumn Sun '98
One Man's War '90
Vital Signs '90
Cousins '89
Gaby: A True Story '87
The Official Story '85

Julio Aleman (1933-)
The Green Wall '70
Neutron vs. the Death Robots '62
Neutron and the Black Mask '61
Neutron vs. the Amazing Dr. Caronte '61

Aki Aleong
Lewis and Clark and George '97
The Quest '96
Farewell to the King '89
Braddock: Missing in Action 3 '88
Hanoi Hilton '87

John Ales
Uprising '01
Nutty Professor 2: The Klumps '00
Ride with the Devil '99

Barbara Lee (Niven) Alexander
Psycho Cop 2 '94
Illegal Entry: Formula for Fear '93
Hired to Kill '91

Ben Alexander (1911-69)
Man in the Shadow '57
Dragnet '54
Criminals Within '41
Legion of Missing Men '37
Western Gold '37
Red Lights Ahead '36
All Quiet on the Western Front '30
Hearts of the World '18
Little Orphan Annie '18
The Little American '17

Elizabeth Alexander
Alien Cargo '99
Scalp Merchant '77

Jace Alexander
Love and a .45 '94
City of Hope '91
Mistress '91
Crocodile Dundee 2 '88
Eight Men Out '88
Matewan '87

Jane Alexander (1939-)
The Cider House Rules '99
In Love and War '91
Glory '89
A Friendship in Vienna '88
Square Dance '87
Sweet Country '87
The Rumor Mill '86
City Heat '84
Testament '83
Calamity Jane '82
In the Custody of Strangers '82
Lovey: A Circle of Children 2 '82
Night Crossing '81
Brubaker '80
Playing for Time '80
Kramer vs. Kramer '79
The Betsy '78
A Question of Love '78
All the President's Men '76
Eleanor & Franklin '76
Death Be Not Proud '75
The New Centurions '72
A Gunfight '71
The Great White Hope '70

Jason Alexander (1959-)
Shallow Hal '01
The Trumpet of the Swan '01 (V)
The Adventures of Rocky & Bullwinkle '00
Love and Action in Chicago '99
Something About Sex '98
Cinderella '97
The Hunchback of Notre Dame '96 (V)
The Last Supper '96
Love! Valour! Compassion! '96
Bye Bye Birdie '95
Dunston Checks In '95
For Better or Worse '95
Blankman '94
North '94
The Paper '94
Coneheads '93
I Don't Buy Kisses Anymore '92
Jacob's Ladder '90
Pretty Woman '90
White Palace '90
Brighton Beach Memoirs '86
The Mosquito Coast '86
Rockabye '86
The Burning '82

Jeff Alexander (1910-89)
Twisted Brain '74
Curse of the Swamp Creature '66

John Alexander (1897-1982)
The Marrying Kind '52
Fancy Pants '50
Where There's Life '47
The Jolson Story '46
The Horn Blows at Midnight '45
A Tree Grows in Brooklyn '45
Arsenic and Old Lace '44
Mr. Skeffington '44

Katherine Alexander (1898-1981)
Dance, Girl, Dance '40
The Great Man Votes '38
That Certain Woman '37
Splendor '35
The Barretts of Wimpole Street '34
Death Takes a Holiday '34

Khandi Alexander
Thick as Thieves '99
There's Something about Mary '98
Greedy '94
Sugar Hill '94
CB4: The Movie '93
What's Love Got to Do with It? '93

Richard Alexander (1902-89)
The Kansas Terrors '39
Renfrew on the Great White Trail '38
Daring Danger '32
Scarlet Dawn '32
Texas Bad Man '32
All Quiet on the Western Front '30
The Mysterious Lady '28

Tad Alexander
Rasputin and the Empress '33
Ambassador Bill '31

Terence Alexander (1923-)
Waterloo '71
The Runaway Bus '54

Terry Alexander
Conspiracy Theory '97
Hurricane Streets '96
Amateur '94
The Horror Show '89
Day of the Dead '85
Flashpoint '84

Tiana Alexandra
Catch the Heat '87
Pearl '78

Lidia Alfonsi (1928-)
Life Is Beautiful '98
Open Doors '89
Black Sabbath '64
The Trojan Horse '62

Kristian Alfonso (1964-)
Army of One '94
Blindfold: Acts of Obsession '94

Chuck Alford
The Hollywood Strangler Meets the Skid Row Slasher '79
Commando Squad '76

Phillip Alford (1948-)
Shenandoah '65
To Kill a Mockingbird '62

Mark Alfred
Rhythm Thief '94
Spare Me '92

Hans Alfredson (1931-)
The Adventures of Picasso '80
The New Land '73

The Shame '68

Muhammad Ali (1942-)
Doin' Time '85
Body & Soul '81
Freedom Road '79
The Greatest '77
Requiem for a Heavyweight '62

Mary Alice (1941-)
Catfish in Black Bean Sauce '00
Down in the Delta '98
Laurel Avenue '93
To Sleep with Anger '90
The Women of Brewster Place '89
Charlotte Forten's Mission: Experiment in Freedom '85
Killing Floor '85
He Who Walks Alone '78
Sparkle '76

Ana Alicia (1956-)
Romero '89
Coward of the County '81

Lisa Aliff
Playroom '90
Damned River '89
Trained to Kill '88

Jeff Alin
A Matter of Love '78
American Tickler '76

Elizabeth Allan (1908-90)
The Haunted Strangler '58
No Highway in the Sky '51
Camille '36
The Shadow '36
A Tale of Two Cities '36
A Woman Rebels '36
Java Head '35
Mark of the Vampire '35
Phantom Fiend '35
Ace of Aces '33

Jed Allan (1937-)
Suspect Device '95
Lassie: Adventures of Neeka '68

Louise Allbritton (1920-79)
The Doolins of Oklahoma '49
Egg and I '47
Son of Dracula '43
Pittsburgh '42
Who Done It? '42

Michael Alldredge
Robot Jox '90
About Last Night... '86

Catherine Allegret
Paul and Michelle '74
Last Tango in Paris '73

Bambi Allen
Outlaw Riders '72
Satan's Sadists '69

Barbara Jo Allen
The Sword in the Stone '63 (V)
Sleeping Beauty '59 (V)

Bill Allen (1962-)
Sioux City '94
Born on the Fourth of July '89
Rad '86
Streamers '83
Maniac '77

Chad Allen (1974-)
Praying Mantis '93
Murder in New Hampshire: The Pamela Smart Story '91
Camp Cucamonga: How I Spent My Summer Vacation '90
Straight Up '90
The Bad Seed '85

Corey Allen (1934-)
Darby's Rangers '58
Party Girl '58
The Night of the Hunter '55
Rebel without a Cause '55

Debbie Allen (1950-)
The Old Settler '01
Jo Jo Dancer, Your Life Is Calling '86
Ragtime '81
The Fish that Saved Pittsburgh '79
Roots: The Next Generation '79

Elizabeth Allen (1934-)
Star Spangled Girl '71
Donovan's Reef '63

Fred Allen (1894-1956)
We're Not Married '52
It's in the Bag '45

Ginger Lynn Allen (1962-)
Bound and Gagged: A Love Story '93
Mind, Body & Soul '92
Vice Academy 3 '91
Leather Jackets '90
Vice Academy 2 '90
Young Guns 2 '90
Buried Alive '89
Cleo/Leo '89
Hollywood Boulevard 2 '89
Wild Man '89
Vice Academy '88

Gracie Allen (1902-64)
Two Girls and a Sailor '44
Honolulu '39
College Swing '38
A Damsel in Distress '37
Here Comes Cookie '35
Love in Bloom '35
Six of a Kind '34
We're Not Dressing '34
International House '33

India Allen (1965-)
Seduce Me: Pamela Principle 2 '94
Wild Cactus '92

Jeffrey Allen
This Stuff'll Kill Ya! '71
Something Weird '68
Moonshine Mountain '64
2000 Maniacs '64

Jo Harvey Allen
Checking Out '89
Tapeheads '89
True Stories '86

Joan Allen (1956-)
Mists of Avalon '01
The Contender '00
It's the Rage '99
When the Sky Falls '99
Pleasantville '98
Face/Off '97
The Ice Storm '97
The Crucible '96
Mad Love '95
Nixon '95
Josh and S.A.M. '93
Searching for Bobby Fischer '93
Ethan Frome '92
Without Warning: The James Brady Story '91
In Country '89
Tucker: The Man and His Dream '88
All My Sons '86
Fat Guy Goes Nutzoid '86
Manhunter '86
Peggy Sue Got Married '86

John Allen
The Odd Angry Shot '79
Roses Bloom Twice '77

Jonelle Allen (1944-)
Grave Secrets: The Legacy of Hilltop Drive '92
The Midnight Hour '86
Penalty Phase '86
The River Niger '76

Judith Allen (1911-96)
Train to Tombstone '50
Tough Kid '39
The Port of Missing Girls '38
Boots & Saddles '37
Git Along Little Dogies '37
Healer '36
Bright Eyes '34
Buffalo Stampede '33
Dancing Man '33

Karen Allen (1951-)
In the Bedroom '01
World Traveler '01
The Perfect Storm '00
The Basket '99
Wind River '98
Til There Was You '96
Ghost in the Machine '93
King of the Hill '93
The Sandlot '93
Voyage '93
Malcolm X '92
The Turning '92
Sweet Talker '91
Secret Weapon '90
Animal Behavior '89
Backfire '88
Scrooged '88
The Glass Menagerie '87
Starman '84
Until September '84
Lovey: A Circle of Children 2 '82
Shoot the Moon '82
Split Image '82
Raiders of the Lost Ark '81
Cruising '80
East of Eden '80
A Small Circle of Friends '80
Manhattan '79
Wanderers '79
National Lampoon's Animal House '78

Keith Allen (1953-)
Rancid Aluminium '00
Prince of Poisoners: The Life and Crimes of William Palmer '98
Loch Ness '95
Captives '94
Second Best '94
Shallow Grave '94
Nightscare '93
The Young Americans '93
Kafka '91
Small Time '91
Chicago Joe & the Showgirl '90
A Very British Coup '88

Krista Allen (1972-)
The Haunted Sea '97
Raven '97

Marty Allen (1922-)
Whale of a Tale '76
Harrad Summer '74

Mike Allen
Death Driver '78
Hooch '76

Nancy Allen (1950-)
Kiss Toledo Goodbye '00
Children of the Corn 666: Isaac's Return '99
Against the Law '98
Highway Hitcher '98
Out of Sight '98
Secre of the Andes '98
The Last Assassins '96
Acting on Impulse '93
RoboCop 3 '91
Memories of Murder '90
RoboCop 2 '90
Limit Up '89
Poltergeist 3 '88
RoboCop '87
Sweet Revenge '87
The Gladiator '86
Not for Publication '84
The Philadelphia Experiment '84
The Buddy System '83
Strange Invaders '83
Blow Out '81
Dressed to Kill '80
Home Movies '79
1941 '79
I Wanna Hold Your Hand '78
Carrie '76
Forced Entry '75
The Last Detail '73

Patrick Allen (1927-)
Bullet to Beijing '95
Body & Soul '93
Full Metal Ninja '89
Thirteenth Day of Christmas '85
Puppet on a Chain '72
When Dinosaurs Ruled the Earth '70
Invasion of the Body Stealers '69
Island of the Burning Doomed '67
Flight from Singapore '62
The Long Haul '57

Penelope Allen
The Thin Red Line '98
Looking for Richard '96

Rex Allen (1921-99)
Me, Myself, and Irene '00 (V)
The Secret of Navajo Cave '76 (N)
Charlie, the Lonesome Cougar '67 (N)
Legend of Lobo '62 (N)
Phantom Stallion '54
Iron Mountain Trail '53
Shadows of Tombstone '53
Border Saddlemates '52
Colorado Sundown '52
I Dream of Jeannie '52
Rodeo King and the Senorita '51
Silver City Bonanza '51
Thunder in God's Country '51
Hills of Oklahoma '50
Redwood Forest Trail '50
Trail of Robin Hood '50
Arizona Cowboy '49

Robert "Tex" Allen (1906-98)
The Awful Truth '37
The Rangers Step In '37
The Unknown Ranger '36
The Black Room '35
Crime and Punishment '35
Fighting Shadows '35
The Revenge Rider '35
The Perils of Pauline '34

Ronald Allen (1930-91)
Eat the Rich '87
Supergrass '87

Rosalind Allen
Pinocchio's Revenge '96
Ticks '93
Children of the Corn 2: The Final Sacrifice '92
To Die For 2: Son of Darkness '91

Sheila Allen (1932-)
Pascali's Island '88
Bouquet of Barbed Wire '76
The Alphabet Murders '65
Children of the Damned '63

Sian Barbara Allen (1946-)
Eric '75
Billy Two Hats '74
You'll Like My Mother '72

Steve Allen (1921-2000)
Casino '95
The St. Tammany Miracle '94
The Player '92
Great Balls of Fire '89
Amazon Women on the Moon '87
Ratings Game '84
Heart Beat '80
Where Were You When the Lights Went Out? '68
The Benny Goodman Story '55

Tanya Allen
Lone Hero '02
Tail Lights Fade '99
White Lies '98
Behind the Lines '97
Spenser: Ceremony '93

Tim Allen (1953-)
Big Trouble '02
Joe Somebody '01
Galaxy Quest '99
Toy Story 2 '99 (V)
For Richer or Poorer '97
Jungle 2 Jungle '96
Toy Story '95 (V)
The Santa Clause '94

Todd Allen (1960-)
The Apostle '97
The Postman '97
Pinocchio's Revenge '96
Tall, Dark and Deadly '95
Wyatt Earp '94
Storm and Sorrow '90
Brothers in Arms '88
Witchboard '87

Tom Allen
Clash of the Ninja '86
Shadows '60

Woody Allen (1935-)
Hollywood Ending '02
The Curse of the Jade Scorpion '01
Company Man '00
Small Time Crooks '00
Picking Up the Pieces '99
Sweet and Lowdown '99
Antz '98 (V)
The Imposters '98
Deconstructing Harry '97
Everyone Says I Love You '96
Mighty Aphrodite '95
Manhattan Murder Mystery '93
Husbands and Wives '92
Shadows and Fog '92
Scenes from a Mall '91
Crimes & Misdemeanors '89
New York Stories '89
King Lear '87
Radio Days '87 (N)
Hannah and Her Sisters '86
Broadway Danny Rose '84
Zelig '83
A Midsummer Night's Sex Comedy '82
Stardust Memories '80
Manhattan '79
Annie Hall '77
The Front '76
Love and Death '75
Sleeper '73
Everything You Always Wanted to Know about Sex (But Were Afraid to Ask) '72
Play It Again, Sam '72
Bananas '71
Take the Money and Run '69
Casino Royale '67
What's Up, Tiger Lily? '66 (N)
What's New Pussycat? '65

Fernando Allende (1954-)
Naked Lies '98
Heartbreaker '83

Kirstie Alley (1951-)
Drop Dead Gorgeous '99
The Last Don 2 '98
Deconstructing Harry '97
For Richer or Poorer '97
The Last Don '97
Nevada '97
Toothless '97
Sticks and Stones '96
It Takes Two '95
Village of the Damned '95
Look Who's Talking Now '93
Look Who's Talking, Too '90
Madhouse '90
One More Chance '90
Sibling Rivalry '90
Look Who's Talking '89
Loverboy '89
Shoot to Kill '88
Prince of Bel Air '87
Summer School '87
North and South Book 2 '86
A Bunny's Tale '85
North and South Book 1 '85
Blind Date '84
Champions '84
Runaway '84
Star Trek 2: The Wrath of Khan '82

Sara Allgood (1883-1950)
Cheaper by the Dozen '50
Challenge to Lassie '49
The Accused '48
The Fabulous Dorseys '47
Mother Wore Tights '47
The Spiral Staircase '46
The Strange Affair of Uncle Harry '45
Jane Eyre '44
The Keys of the Kingdom '44
City Without Men '43
Roxie Hart '42
Dr. Jekyll and Mr. Hyde '41
How Green Was My Valley '41
That Hamilton Woman '41
Storm in a Teacup '37
Juno and the Paycock '30
Blackmail '29

Dorothy Allison (1949-)
Rikky and Pete '88
See No Evil '71
The Third Key '57

Claud Allister (1888-1970)
Bulldog Drummond at Bay '37
The Private Life of Henry VIII '33
Bulldog Drummond '29

Gregg Allman (1947-)
Rush '91
Rush Week '88

Christopher Allport
Jack Frost 2: Revenge of the Mutant Killer Snowman '00
Jack Frost '97
News at Eleven '86
Circle of Power '83
Special Bulletin '83
Savage Weekend '80

Corbin Allred (1979-)
Diamonds '99
Address Unknown '96
Josh Kirby...Time Warrior: Chapter 5, Journey to the Magic Cavern '96
Josh Kirby...Time Warrior: Chapter 6, Last Battle for the Universe '96
Josh Kirby...Time Warrior: Chapter 1, Planet of the Dino-Knights '95
Josh Kirby...Time Warrior: Chapter 2, The Human Pets '95
Josh Kirby...Time Warrior: Chapter 3, Trapped on Toyworld '95
Josh Kirby...Time Warrior: Chapter 4, Eggs from 70 Million B.C. '95
Quest of the Delta Knights '93

Astrid Allwyn (1905-78)
Love Affair '39
International Crime '37
It Could Happen to You '37
Stowaway '36
Charlie Chan's Secret '35
Hands Across the Table '35
Beggars in Ermine '34
Monte Carlo Nights '34
Mystery Liner '34

June Allyson (1917-)
The Kid with the Broken Halo '82
Blackout '78
Vegas '78
Curse of the Black Widow '77
They Only Kill Their Masters '72
My Man Godfrey '57
The Opposite Sex '56
The McConnell Story '55
Strategic Air Command '55
Executive Suite '54
The Glenn Miller Story '54
A Woman's World '54
Battle Circus '53
Little Women '49
The Stratton Story '49
The Three Musketeers '48
Words and Music '48
Good News '47
Till the Clouds Roll By '46

Two Girls and a Sailor *'44*
Best Foot Forward *'43*
Girl Crazy *'43*
Thousands Cheer *'43*

Gila Almagor (1939-)
Under the Domim Tree *'95*
The Summer of Aviya *'88*
Every Time We Say Goodbye *'86*
Hide and Seek *'80*
The House on Chelouche Street *'73*
Sallah *'63*

Susan Almgren
Deadly Surveillance *'91*
Twin Sisters *'91*

Chelo Alonso
Girl Under the Sheet *'60s*
The Good, the Bad and the Ugly *'67*
Son of Samson *'62*
Atlas in the Land of the Cyclops *'61*

Ernesto Alonso
The Criminal Life of Archibaldo de la Cruz *'55*
Wuthering Heights *'53*

Maria Conchita Alonso (1957-)
Blind Heat *'00*
Chain of Command *'00*
High Noon *'00*
Blackheart *'98*
Catherine's Grove *'98*
Footsteps *'98*
For Which He Stands *'98*
My Husband's Secret Life *'98*
Caught *'96*
Roosters *'95*
Texas *'94*
The House of the Spirits *'93*
Teamster Boss: The Jackie Presser Story *'92*
McBain *'91*
Predator 2 *'90*
Colors *'88*
Vampire's Kiss *'88*
Blood Ties *'87*
Extreme Prejudice *'87*
The Running Man *'87*
A Fine Mess *'86*
Touch and Go *'86*
Fear City *'85*
Moscow on the Hudson *'84*

Corinne Alphen (1953-)
New York Nights *'84*
C.O.D. *'83*
Spring Break *'83*
Hot T-Shirts *'79*

Catherine Alric
The Associate *'79*
Dear Detective *'77*

Carol Alt (1960-)
Revelation *'00*
Deadly Game *'98*
Storm Trooper *'98*
Crackerjack 2 *'97*
Body Armor *'96*
Private Parts *'96*
Deadly Past *'95*
Ring of Steel *'94*
Thunder in Paradise 2 *'94*
Thunder in Paradise *'93*
Beyond Justice *'92*
A Family Matter *'91*
Millions *'90*
My Wonderful Life *'90*
Bye Bye Baby *'88*
Portfolio *'88*

John Altamura
Bikini Bistro *'94*
The Toxic Avenger, Part 2 *'89*
The Toxic Avenger, Part 3: The Last Temptation of Toxie *'89*
New York's Finest *'87*

Hector Alterio (1929-)
Wild Horses *'95*
I, the Worst of All *'90*
The Official Story *'85*
Camila *'84*
Basileus Quartet *'82*
Fridays of Eternity *'81*
The Nest *'80*

Bruce Altman
L.I.E. *'01*
To Gillian on Her 37th Birthday *'96*
Vibrations *'94*
White Mile *'94*
Mr. Jones *'93*
Mr. Wonderful *'93*
The Favor, the Watch, & the Very Big Fish *'92*
Glengarry Glen Ross *'92*
My New Gun *'92*

Jeff Altman (1951-)
Russian Roulette *'93*
Doin' Time *'85*
In Love with an Older Woman *'82*

Walter George Alton
Heavenly Bodies *'84*
The Puma Man *'80*

Angela Alvarado
Boss of Bosses *'99*
Hollywood Confidential *'97*

Crox Alvarado (1911-84)
The Curse of the Aztec Mummy *'59*
The Robot vs. the Aztec Mummy *'59*

Don Alvarado (1904-67)
Demon for Trouble *'34*
Battle of the Sexes *'28*

Magali Alvarado
Mi Vida Loca *'94*
Salsa *'88*

Trini Alvarado (1967-)
Paulie *'98*
The Frighteners *'96*
Little Women *'94*
The Perez Family *'94*
The Babe *'92*
American Friends *'91*
American Blue Note *'89*
Stella *'89*
Nitti: The Enforcer *'88*
Satisfaction *'88*
The Chair *'87*
Sweet Lorraine *'87*
Mrs. Soffel *'84*
Private Contentment *'83*
Times Square *'80*
A Movie Star's Daughter *'79*
Rich Kids *'79*

Enrique Garcia Alvarez
The Exterminating Angel *'62*
Invasion of the Vampires *'61*

John Alvin (1917-)
Objective, Burma! *'45*
The Fighting Sullivans *'42*

Anicee Alvina
Paul and Michelle *'74*
Friends *'71*

Kirk Alyn (1910-99)
Atom Man vs. Superman *'50*
Federal Agents vs. Underworld, Inc. *'49*
Radar Patrol vs. Spy King *'49*
Daughter of Don Q *'46*

Lyle Alzado (1949-92)
Comrades in Arms *'91*
Neon City *'91*
Club Fed *'90*
Tapeheads *'89*
Who's Harry Crumb? *'89*
Zapped Again *'89*
Destroyer *'88*
Ernest Goes to Camp *'87*
Oceans of Fire *'86*

Shigeru Amachi (1931-85)
Zatoichi: The Blind Swordsman's Vengeance *'66*
Zatoichi: The Life and Opinion of Masseur Ichi *'62*
The Ghost of Yatsuya *'58*

Mathieu Amalric (1965-)
Late August, Early September *'98*
My Sex Life...Or How I Got into an Argument *'96*
Diary of a Seducer *'95*

Eisei Amamoto (1926-)
Godzilla's Revenge *'69*
What's Up, Tiger Lily? *'66*
Attack of the Mushroom People *'63*

Tom Amandes
When Good Ghouls Go Bad *'01*
Brokedown Palace *'99*
Billboard Dad *'98*
From the Earth to the Moon *'98*
Second Chances *'98*
The Long Kiss Goodnight *'96*

Betty Amann (1906-90)
Nancy Drew, Reporter *'39*
Rich and Strange *'32*

Andriana Ambesi
Stranger in Paso Bravo *'73*
Fangs of the Living Dead *'68*
Secret Agent Super Dragon *'66*

Lauren Ambrose
Psycho Beach Party *'00*
Can't Hardly Wait *'98*
In and Out *'97*

Tangie Ambrose
Jackie's Back *'99*
Ringmaster *'98*

Don Ameche (1908-93)
Corrina, Corrina *'94*
Homeward Bound: The Incredible Journey *'93 (V)*
Folks! *'92*
Sunstroke *'92*
Oddball Hall *'91*
Oscar *'91*
Cocoon: The Return *'88*
Coming to America *'88*
Things Change *'88*
Harry and the Hendersons *'87*
Pals *'87*
Cocoon *'85*
Trading Places *'83*
The Boatniks *'70*
Suppose They Gave a War and Nobody Came? *'70*
Picture Mommy Dead *'66*
Guest Wife *'45*
It's in the Bag *'45*
A Wing and a Prayer *'44*
Heaven Can Wait *'43*
The Magnificent Dope *'42*
Moon over Miami *'41*
Down Argentine Way *'40*
Midnight *'39*
The Story of Alexander Graham Bell *'39*
The Three Musketeers *'39*
Alexander's Ragtime Band *'38*
Happy Landing *'38*
In Old Chicago *'37*
One in a Million *'36*

Claudio Amendola (1963-)
Jesus *'00*
Nostromo *'96*
The Horseman on the Roof *'95*
La Scorta *'94*
Queen Margot *'94*

Tony Amendola
The Mask of Zorro *'98*
Three of Hearts *'93*

George American Horse
Son of the Morning Star *'91*
Kenny Rogers as the Gambler, Part 3: The Legend Continues *'87*

Adrienne Ames (1907-47)
Panama Patrol *'39*
Harmony Lane *'35*
The Death Kiss *'33*

Heather Ames
How to Make a Monster *'58*
Blood of Dracula *'57*

Leon Ames (1902-93)
Peggy Sue Got Married *'86*
Deadly Encounter *'78*
Claws *'77*
The Big Push *'75*
The Meal *'75*
Tora! Tora! Tora! *'70*
Monkey's Uncle *'65*
The Misadventures of Merlin Jones *'63*
Son of Flubber *'63*
The Absent-Minded Professor *'61*
From the Terrace *'60*
Peyton Place *'57*
By the Light of the Silvery Moon *'53*
On Moonlight Bay *'51*
The Big Hangover *'50*
Watch the Birdie *'50*
Battleground *'49*
A Date with Judy *'48*
On an Island with You *'48*
Velvet Touch *'48*
Merton of the Movies *'47*
Song of the Thin Man *'47*
Lady in the Lake *'46*
The Postman Always Rings Twice *'46*
The Show-Off *'46*
Anchors Aweigh *'45*
Son of Lassie *'45*
They Were Expendable *'45*
Weekend at the Waldorf *'45*
Yolanda and the Thief *'45*
Thirty Seconds Over Tokyo *'44*
The Iron Major *'43*
East Side Kids *'40*
Panama Patrol *'39*
Get That Man *'35*
Murders in the Rue Morgue *'32*
Uptown New York *'32*

Ramsay Ames (1919-98)
G-Men Never Forget *'48*
The Mummy's Ghost *'44*
Calling Dr. Death/Strange Confession *'43*

Robert Ames (1889-1931)
Behind Office Doors *'31*
Millie *'31*

Madchen Amick (1970-)
Hangman *'00*
The List *'99*
Mr. Rock 'n' Roll: The Alan Freed Story *'99*
The Hunted *'98*
Bombshell *'97*
French Exit *'97*
Psychopath *'97*
Wounded *'97*
The Courtyard *'95*
The Great American Sex Scandal *'94*
Trapped in Paradise *'94*
Dream Lover *'93*
Love, Cheat & Steal *'93*
Sleepwalkers *'92*
Twin Peaks: Fire Walk with Me *'92*
Don't Tell Her It's Me *'90*
I'm Dangerous Tonight *'90*

Soudad Amidou (1959-)
Petit Con *'84*
Sorcerer *'77*

Suzy Amis (1962-)
Judgment Day *'99*
The Beneficiary *'97*
Firestorm *'97*
Titanic *'97*
Cadillac Ranch *'96*
The Ex *'96*
Last Stand at Saber River *'96*
Nadja *'95*
One Good Turn *'95*
The Usual Suspects *'95*
Blown Away *'94*
The Ballad of Little Jo *'93*
Rich in Love *'93*
Two Small Bodies *'93*
Watch It *'93*
Where the Heart Is *'90*
Twister *'89*
Plain Clothes *'88*
Rocket Gibraltar *'88*
Big Town *'87*
Fandango *'85*

Renee Ammann
Death Match *'94*
Number One Fan *'94*

Luigi Amodeo
Art House *'98*
B.A.P.'s *'97*
Red Shoe Diaries 6: How I Met My Husband *'95*

Christine Amor
Bloodmoon *'90*
Now and Forever *'82*

David Amos
Flipping *'96*
The Takeover *'94*

John Amos (1941-)
Disappearing Acts *'00*
The Players Club *'98*
For Better or Worse *'95*
Hologram Man *'95*
Mac *'93*
Mardi Gras for the Devil *'93*
Ricochet *'91*
Die Hard 2: Die Harder *'90*
Two Evil Eyes *'90*
Lock Up *'89*
Coming to America *'88*
American Flyers *'85*
Beastmaster *'82*
Touched by Love *'80*
Willa *'79*
Roots *'77*
Future Cop *'76*
Let's Do It Again *'75*
The World's Greatest Athlete *'73*
Sweet Sweetback's Baadasssss Song *'71*

John Amplas
Creepshow *'82*
Midnight *'81*
Martin *'77*

Morey Amsterdam (1908-96)
Sooner or Later *'78*
Muscle Beach Party *'64*
Beach Party *'63*
Machine Gun Kelly *'58*

Richard Anconina (1953-)
Police *'85*
Tchao Pantin *'84*

Avalon Anders
The Portrait *'99*
Wish Me Luck *'95*
Great Bikini Off-Road Adventure *'94*
Bikini Summer 2 *'92*
Sorority House Party *'92*

Glenn Anders (1889-1981)
Nancy Goes to Rio *'50*
The Lady from Shanghai *'48*

Luana Anders (1940-96)
Limit Up *'89*
Border Radio *'88*
Movers and Shakers *'85*
Irreconcilable Differences *'84*
Goin' South *'78*
The Killing Kind *'73*
Greaser's Palace *'72*
Manipulator *'71*
Easy Rider *'69*
Games *'67*
The Trip *'67*
Sex and the College Girl *'64*
Dementia 13 *'63*
Night Tide *'63*
The Pit and the Pendulum *'61*
Reform School Girl *'57*

Merry Anders (1932-)
Blood Legacy *'73*
Women of the Prehistoric Planet *'66*
The Time Travelers *'64*
Phffft! *'54*

Rudolph Anders (1895-1987)
36 Hours *'64*
She Demons *'58*
Phantom from Space *'53*
Actors and Sin *'52*
Under Nevada Skies *'46*

Bridgette Andersen (1975-)
Between Two Women *'86*
Fever Pitch *'85*
A Summer to Remember *'84*
Hansel and Gretel *'82*
Savannah Smiles *'82*

Elga Andersen (1939-94)
Night Flight from Moscow *'73*
Le Mans *'71*
Your Turn Darling *'63*
The Twilight Girls *'57*

Susy Andersen
Gangster's Law *'86*
Black Sabbath *'64*
Thor and the Amazon Women *'60*

Anthony Anderson (1970-)
Exit Wounds *'01*
Kingdom Come *'01*
See Spot Run *'01*
Two Can Play That Game *'01*
Big Momma's House *'00*
Me, Myself, and Irene *'00*
Romeo Must Die *'00*
Urban Legends 2: Final Cut *'00*
Liberty Heights *'99*
Life *'99*

Cheryl Anderson
Writer's Block *'91*
Acorn People *'82*
Rosie: The Rosemary Clooney Story *'82*

Donna Anderson (1925-)
Inherit the Wind *'60*
On the Beach *'59*

Eddie Anderson (1905-77)
It's a Mad, Mad, Mad, Mad World *'63*
The Show-Off *'46*
Brewster's Millions *'45*
Broadway Rhythm *'44*
Cabin in the Sky *'43*
Star Spangled Rhythm *'42*
Tales of Manhattan *'42*
Birth of the Blues *'41*
Topper Returns *'41*
Gone with the Wind *'39*
Honolulu *'39*
You Can't Cheat an Honest Man *'39*
Jezebel *'38*
Thanks for the Memory *'38*
You Can't Take It with You *'38*
Green Pastures *'36*
False Faces *'32*

Erich Anderson
Love Kills *'91*
Bat 21 *'88*
Friday the 13th, Part 4: The Final Chapter *'84*

Erika Anderson (1965-)
Red Shoe Diaries 8: Night of Abandon *'97*
Object of Obsession *'95*
Quake *'92*
Zandalee *'91*
A Nightmare on Elm Street 5: Dream Child *'89*

Gillian Anderson (1968-)
House of Mirth *'00*
Chicago Cab *'98*
The Mighty *'98*
Playing by Heart *'98*
Princess Mononoke *'98 (V)*
The X-Files *'98*
The Turning *'92*

Harry Anderson (1952-)
Spies, Lies and Naked Thighs *'91*
Mother Goose Rock 'n' Rhyme *'90*
Stephen King's It *'90*

Herbert Anderson (1917-94)
I Bury the Living *'58*
Battleground *'49*
Dive Bomber *'41*
The Fighting 69th *'40*

James Anderson (1872-1953)
Sergeant York *'41*
The Freshman *'25*

James Anderson (1921-69)
Take the Money and Run *'69*
The Connection *'61*

Jean Anderson (1907-2001)
Prince Brat and the Whipping Boy *'95*
Back Home *'90*
Screamtime *'83*
Lucky Jim *'58*

Jeff Anderson
Dogma *'99*
Clerks *'94*

Jo Anderson (1958-)
From the Earth to the Moon *'98*
Daylight *'96*
Season of Change *'94*
Decoration Day *'90*
Suspicion *'87*

John Anderson (1922-92)
The Desperados *'80s*
Eight Men Out *'88*
Firehouse *'87*
Donner Pass: The Road to Survival *'84*
Ashes and Embers *'82*
Zoot Suit *'81*
Smokey and the Bandit 2 *'80*
The Deerslayer *'78*
The Specialist *'75*
Smile, Jenny, You're Dead *'74*
Executive Action *'73*
The Stepmother *'71*
Cotton Comes to Harlem *'70*
Five Card Stud *'68*
Namu, the Killer Whale *'66*
Geronimo *'62*
Ride the High Country *'62*
Psycho *'60*

Judith Anderson (1898-1992)
Star Trek 3: The Search for Spock *'84*
Inn of the Damned *'74*
A Man Called Horse *'70*
Elizabeth, the Queen *'68*
Cinderfella *'60*
Cat on a Hot Tin Roof *'58*
The Ten Commandments *'56*
Salome *'53*
Pursued *'47*
The Red House *'47*
Tycoon *'47*
Diary of a Chambermaid *'46*
Spectre of the Rose *'46*
The Strange Love of Martha Ivers *'46*
And Then There Were None *'45*
Laura *'44*
Edge of Darkness *'43*
Stage Door Canteen *'43*
All Through the Night *'42*
Kings Row *'41*
Lady Scarface *'41*
Rebecca *'40*

Kevin Anderson (1960-)
Eye of God *'97*
Firelight *'97*
A Thousand Acres *'97*
The Night We Never Met *'93*
Rising Sun *'93*
The Wrong Man *'93*
Hoffa *'92*
Liebestraum *'91*
Orpheus Descending *'91*
Sleeping with the Enemy *'91*
In Country *'89*
Miles from Home *'88*
Orphans *'87*
Pink Nights *'87*
Risky Business *'83*

Lindsay Anderson (1923-94)
Blame It on the Bellboy *'92*
Prisoner of Honor *'91*
Chariots of Fire *'81*
Look Back in Anger *'80*

Lisa Anderson
Having Our Say: The Delany Sisters' First 100 Years *'99*
L.A. Crackdown 2 *'88*

Loni Anderson (1945-)
A Night at the Roxbury *'98*
3 Ninjas: High Noon at Mega Mountain *'97*
Munchie *'92*
White Hot: The Mysterious Murder of Thelma Todd *'91*
Blown Away *'90*
All Dogs Go to Heaven *'89 (V)*
Sorry, Wrong Number *'89*
My Mother's Secret Life *'84*
Stroker Ace *'83*
Sizzle *'81*
The Jayne Mansfield Story *'80*

Louie Anderson (1953-)
Coming to America *'88*
The Wrong Guys *'88*
Ferris Bueller's Day Off *'86*
Quicksilver *'86*

Mary Anderson (1921-)
The Underworld Story *'50*
Whispering City *'47*
To Each His Own *'46*
Lifeboat *'44*
Wilson *'44*
Gone with the Wind *'39*

Melissa Sue Anderson (1962-)
Chattanooga Choo Choo *'84*
First Affair *'83*
Happy Birthday to Me *'81*
On the Edge: The Survival of Dana *'79*
The Loneliest Runner *'76*
Little House on the Prairie *'74*

Melody Anderson (1955-)
Marilyn & Bobby: Her Final Affair *'94*
Landslide *'92*
Hitler's Daughter *'90*
Final Notice *'89*
Speed Zone *'88*
Beverly Hills Madam *'86*
Firewalker *'86*
Ernie Kovacs: Between the Laughter *'84*
Policewoman Centerfold *'83*
Dead and Buried *'81*
Flash Gordon *'80*

Michael Anderson, Jr. (1943-)
Sunset Grill *'92*
The Great Land of Small *'86*
A Legacy for Leonette *'85*
Sons of Katie Elder *'65*
In Search of the Castaways *'62*
The Sundowners *'60*
Tiger Bay *'59*

Michael J. Anderson
Snow White: The Fairest of Them All *'02*
Mulholland Drive *'01*
Club Vampire *'98*

Miles Anderson
A Certain Justice *'99*
Into the Blue *'97*
The Rector's Wife *'94*
A Far Off Place *'93*

Mitchell Anderson (1961-)
If These Walls Could Talk 2 *'00*
Relax... It's Just Sex! *'98*
Is There Life Out There? *'94*
Back to Hannibal: The Return of Tom Sawyer and Huckleberry Finn *'90*
Deadly Dreams *'88*
Goodbye, Miss 4th of July *'88*

Pamela Anderson (1967-)
Barb Wire *'96*
Baywatch the Movie: Forbidden Paradise *'95*
Naked Souls *'95*
Raw Justice *'93*
Snapdragon *'93*

Pat Anderson
Cover Girl Models *'75*
Summer School Teachers *'75*

Richard Anderson (1926-)
The Glass Shield *'95*
Gettysburg *'93*
The Player *'92*
Perry Mason Returns *'85*
Retrievers *'82*
Murder by Natural Causes *'79*
Pearl *'78*
The Bionic Woman *'75*
The Night Strangler *'72*
Tora! Tora! Tora! *'70*
Seconds *'66*
Kitten with a Whip *'64*
Seven Days in May *'64*
Compulsion *'59*
The Long, Hot Summer *'58*
Paths of Glory *'57*
Forbidden Planet *'56*
The Search for Bridey Murphy *'56*
Hit the Deck *'55*
Escape from Fort Bravo *'53*
Give a Girl a Break *'53*
I Love Melvin *'53*
Scaramouche *'52*
Rich, Young and Pretty *'51*
The Magnificent Yankee *'50*
The Vanishing Westerner *'50*

Richard Dean Anderson (1950-)
Past the Bleachers *'95*
Through the Eyes of a Killer *'92*
Ordinary Heroes *'85*

Stanley Anderson
40 Days and 40 Nights *'02*
Spider-Man *'02*
Proof of Life *'00*
Trial by Media *'00*
Arlington Road *'99*
Primal Fear *'96*
The Shadow Conspiracy *'96*
He Said, She Said *'91*
Son of the Morning Star *'91*

Warner Anderson (1911-76)
Armored Command *'61*
Blackboard Jungle *'55*
A Lawless Street *'55*
The Caine Mutiny *'54*
Drum Beat *'54*
A Lion Is in the Streets *'53*
Detective Story *'51*
Go for Broke! *'51*
Santa Fe *'51*
Destination Moon *'50*
Command Decision *'48*
Song of the Thin Man *'47*
Abbott and Costello in Hollywood *'45*
Objective, Burma! *'45*
Weekend at the Waldorf *'45*
Destination Tokyo *'43*

Bibi Andersson (1935-)
Babette's Feast *'87*
Law of Desire *'86*
Exposed *'83*
The Concorde: Airport '79 *'79*
Quintet *'79*
Twice a Woman *'79*
I Never Promised You a Rose Garden *'77*
Germicide *'74*
Scenes from a Marriage *'73*
The Touch *'71*
The Passion of Anna *'70*
Duel at Diablo *'66*
Persona *'66*
The Devil's Eye *'60*
The Magician *'58*
Brink of Life *'57*
Wild Strawberries *'57*
The Seventh Seal *'56*

Harriet Andersson (1932-)
Fanny and Alexander *'83*
Cries and Whispers *'72*
Through a Glass Darkly *'61*
Dreams *'55*
Smiles of a Summer Night *'55*
Lesson in Love *'54*
Sawdust & Tinsel *'53*
Monika *'52*

Keith Andes (1920-)
The Ultimate Imposter *'79*
Tora! Tora! Tora! *'70*
Away All Boats *'56*
Back from Eternity *'56*
Blackbeard the Pirate *'52*

Eiko Ando
Paper Tiger *'74*
Barbarian and the Geisha *'58*

Paul Andor
Union City *'81*
Enemy of Women *'44*

Peter Andorai
My Twentieth Century *'90*
Mephisto *'81*

Gaby Andre (1920-)
Goliath and the Dragon *'61*
The Cosmic Monsters *'58*
East of Kilimanjaro *'57*
Verdi *'53*
The Green Glove *'52*

Lona Andre (1915-92)
Slaves in Bondage *'37*
Custer's Last Stand *'36*
Lucky Terror *'36*
The Mysterious Rider *'33*

Marcel Andre (1885-1974)
The Storm Within *'48*
Beauty and the Beast *'46*
Maniac *'34*

Andre the Giant (1946-93)
The Princess Bride *'87*
Micki & Maude *'84*

Starr Andreeff
Club Vampire *'98*
Amityville Dollhouse *'96*
Vampire Journals *'96*
Syngenor *'90*
Dance of the Damned *'88*
Out of the Dark *'88*
The Terror Within *'88*

Natasha Andreichenko (1956-)
Modern Vampires *'98*
Operation Intercept *'95*
Little Odessa *'94*

Ursula Andress (1936-)
The Chinatown Murders: Man against the Mob *'92*
Peter the Great *'86*
Clash of the Titans *'81*
Tigers in Lipstick *'80*
The Fifth Musketeer *'79*
Mountain of the Cannibal God *'79*
Loves & Times of Scaramouche *'76*
The Sensuous Nurse *'76*
Loaded Guns *'75*
Stateline Motel *'75*
Red Sun *'71*
Casino Royale *'67*
The Blue Max *'66*
Once Before I Die *'65*
10th Victim *'65*
What's New Pussycat? *'65*
Four for Texas *'63*
Fun in Acapulco *'63*
Dr. No *'62*

Simon Andreu (1941-)
Hidden Assassin *'94*
Sharpe's Rifles *'93*
The Blood Spattered Bride *'72*

Simon Andrew
Blue Jeans and Dynamite *'80s*
Blood and Sand *'89*
Fist Fighter *'88*
Surprise Attack *'70s*
The Barcelona Kill *'77*
Night of the Sorcerers *'70*

Anthony Andrews (1948-)
Haunted *'95*
Hands of a Murderer *'90*
Strange Case of Dr. Jekyll & Mr. Hyde *'89*
Hanna's War *'88*
The Woman He Loved *'88*
The Lighthorsemen *'87*
Second Victory *'87*
Suspicion *'87*
A.D. *'85*
The Holcroft Covenant *'85*
Under the Volcano *'84*
Ivanhoe *'82*
The Scarlet Pimpernel *'82*
Brideshead Revisited *'81*
Danger UXB *'81*

Barry Andrews
The Blood on Satan's Claw *'71*
Dracula Has Risen from the Grave *'68*

Dana Andrews (1909-92)
Prince Jack *'83*
Danger in the Skies *'79*
Ike *'79*
Born Again *'78*
The Last Tycoon *'76*
Airport '75 *'75*
The Cobra *'68*
The Devil's Brigade *'68*
Johnny Reno *'66*
Battle of the Bulge *'65*
In Harm's Way *'65*
The Loved One *'65*
Enchanted Island *'58*
Curse of the Demon *'57*
Beyond a Reasonable Doubt *'56*
While the City Sleeps *'56*
Elephant Walk *'54*
I Want You *'51*
Boomerang *'47*
The Best Years of Our Lives *'46*
Canyon Passage *'46*
A Walk in the Sun *'46*
State Fair *'45*
Laura *'44*
The Purple Heart *'44*
Up in Arms *'44*
A Wing and a Prayer *'44*
Crash Dive *'43*
The North Star *'43*
The Ox-Bow Incident *'43*
Ball of Fire *'41*
Kit Carson *'40*
Lucky Cisco Kid *'40*
The Westerner *'40*

David Andrews (1952-)
Hannibal *'01*
From the Earth to the Moon *'98*
Under Pressure *'98*
Apollo 13 *'95*
Deconstructing Sarah *'94*
Wyatt Earp *'94*
Graveyard Shift *'90*
Cherry 2000 *'88*
Wild Horses *'84*

Edward Andrews (1914-85)
Sixteen Candles *'84*
Avanti! *'72*
How to Frame a Figg *'71*
Tora! Tora! Tora! *'70*
Over the Hill Gang *'69*
The Trouble with Girls (and How to Get into It) *'69*
The Glass Bottom Boat *'66*
Kisses for My President *'64*
A Tiger Walks *'64*
The Brass Bottle *'63*
The Thrill of It All! *'63*
Advise and Consent *'62*
40 Pounds of Trouble *'62*
The Absent-Minded Professor *'61*
Elmer Gantry *'60*
Tea and Sympathy *'56*

Giuseppe Andrews (1979-)
Detroit Rock City *'99*
American History X *'98*
Independence Day *'96*

Harry Andrews (1911-89)
Cause Celebre *'87*
Mesmerized *'84*
Hawk the Slayer *'81*
The Curse of King Tut's Tomb *'80*
S.O.S. Titanic *'79*
The Big Sleep *'78*
Death on the Nile *'78*
The Four Feathers *'78*
The Medusa Touch *'78*
Watership Down *'78 (V)*
Equus *'77*
Sky Riders *'76*
The Passover Plot *'75*
The Story of Jacob & Joseph *'74*
The Final Programme *'73*
Internecine Project *'73*
Mackintosh Man *'73*
Theatre of Blood *'73*
I Want What I Want *'72*
Man of La Mancha *'72*
The Nightcomers *'72*
The Ruling Class *'72*
Horrors of Burke & Hare *'71*
Nicholas and Alexandra *'71*
Entertaining Mr. Sloane *'70*
Too Late the Hero *'70*
Wuthering Heights *'70*
Battle of Britain *'69*
Nice Girl Like Me *'69*
The Charge of the Light Brigade *'68*
Dandy in Aspic *'68*
The Girl Getters *'66*
Modesty Blaise *'66*
The Agony and the Ecstasy *'65*
633 Squadron *'64*
The Devil's Disciple *'59*
Saint Joan *'57*
Helen of Troy *'56*
Moby Dick *'56*
Alexander the Great *'55*

Jason Andrews
Federal Hill *'94*
Rhythm Thief *'94*

Julie Andrews (1935-)
The Princess Diaries *'01*
Relative Values *'99*
A Fine Romance *'92*
Our Sons *'91*

Duet for One '86
That's Life! '86
The Man Who Loved Women '83
Victor/Victoria '82
S.O.B. '81
Little Miss Marker '80
10 '79
The Tamarind Seed '74
Darling Lili '70
Star! '68
Thoroughly Modern Millie '67
Hawaii '66
Torn Curtain '66
The Sound of Music '65
The Americanization of Emily '64
Mary Poppins '64

Naveen Andrews (1971-)
Rollerball '02
My Own Country '98
The English Patient '96
Kama Sutra: A Tale of Love '96
Wild West '93
The Buddha of Suburbia '92

Real Andrews (1963-)
Family of Cops 2: Breach of Faith '97
Soldier of Fortune Inc. '97
Red Scorpion 2 '94
Showdown '94

Slim Andrews (1906-92)
The Driftin' Kid '41
Riding the Sunset Trail '41

Stanley Andrews (1891-1969)
The Adventures of Frank and Jesse James '48
Crash Dive '43
In Old Colorado '41
Beau Geste '39
Blondie '38
Shine on, Harvest Moon '38

Tod Andrews (1914-72)
In Harm's Way '65
She Demons '58
Dive Bomber '41
They Died with Their Boots On '41

The Andrews Sisters
Melody Time '48 (V)
The Road to Rio '47
Private Buckaroo '42
Buck Privates '41
Hold That Ghost '41
In the Navy '41

James Andronica (1945-)
First Degree '98
Mirage '94
The November Men '93

Anemone (1950-)
Son of Gascogne '95
Pas Tres Catholique '93
Twisted Obsession '90
Le Grand Chemin '87

Julie Ange
Teenage Mother '67
Girl on a Chain Gang '65

Heather Angel (1909-86)
Premature Burial '62
Peter Pan '53 (V)
Lifeboat '44
The Undying Monster '42
Shadows on the Stairs '41
Suspicion '41
Half a Soldier '40
Bulldog Drummond's Bride '39
Bulldog Drummond's Secret Police '39
Arrest Bulldog Drummond '38
Bulldog Drummond Escapes '37
Western Gold '37
The Bold Caballero '36
The Last of the Mohicans '36
Headline Woman '35
The Informer '35
The Mystery of Edwin Drood '35
The Three Musketeers '35
Daniel Boone '34

Mikel Angel
Evil Spirits '91
Grotesque '87
The Black Six '74

Vanessa Angel (1963-)
Firetrap '01
Camouflage '00
Made Men '99
Partners '99
Kissing a Fool '98
Kingpin '96
The Cover Girl Murders '93
Homicidal Impulse '92

Pier Angeli (1932-71)
Octaman '71
One Step to Hell '68
Battle of the Bulge '65
Sodom and Gomorrah '62
S.O.S. Pacific '60
Somebody Up There Likes Me '56
The Silver Chalice '54

Luciana Angelillo
The Trojan Horse '62
The Girl with a Suitcase '60

Maya Angelou
The Runaway '00
How to Make an American Quilt '95
Roots '77

Muriel Angelus (1909-)
The Great McGinty '40
Night Birds '31

Angelyne
The Malibu Beach Vampires '91
Earth Girls Are Easy '89

Jean-Hugues Anglade (1955-)
Innocents '00
Elective Affinities '96
Maximum Risk '96
Nelly et Monsieur Arnaud '95
Killing Zoe '94
Queen Margot '94
La Femme Nikita '91
Betty Blue '86
Subway '85
L'Homme Blesse '83

Philip Anglim (1953-)
Deadly Currents '93
Haunted Summer '88

Sally Anglim
Thundering Trail '51
Yes, Sir, Mr. Bones '51

Alex Angulo
Live Flesh '97
The Day of the Beast '95

Christien Anholt (1971-)
The Waiting Time '99
Appetite '98
Class of '61 '92
One Against the Wind '91
Reunion '88

Jennifer Aniston (1969-)
The Good Girl '02
Rock Star '01
Iron Giant '99 (V)
The Object of My Affection '98
Office Space '98
Dream for an Insomniac '96
Picture Perfect '96
She's the One '96
Til There Was You '96
Leprechaun '93

Paul Anka (1941-)
Shake, Rattle & Rock! '94
Ordinary Magic '93
The Return of Spinal Tap '92
The Longest Day '62
Girls' Town '59

Evelyn Ankers (1918-85)
Parole, Inc. '49
The Last of the Redmen '47
Black Beauty '46
Flight to Nowhere '46
His Butler's Sister '44
The Invisible Man's Revenge '44
Jungle Woman '44
The Pearl of Death '44
Weird Woman/Frozen Ghost '44
Captive Wild Woman '43
The Mad Ghoul '43
Son of Dracula '43
The Ghost of Frankenstein '42
Sherlock Holmes: The Voice of Terror '42
Hold That Ghost '41
The Wolf Man '41

Morris Ankrum (1904-64)
X: The Man with X-Ray Eyes '63
Giant from the Unknown '58
Half Human '58
How to Make a Monster '58
Beginning of the End '57
The Giant Claw '57
Earth vs. the Flying Saucers '56
Crashout '55
Invaders from Mars '53
Borderline '50
Border Vigilantes '41
Doomed Caravan '41
In Old Colorado '41
The Light of Western Stars '40
The Showdown '40
Hopalong Cassidy Returns '36

Ann-Margret (1941-)
The 10th Kingdom '00
Any Given Sunday '99
The Happy Face Murders '99
Grumpier Old Men '95
Scarlett '94
Grumpy Old Men '93
Queen '93
Newsies '92
Our Sons '91
A New Life '88
A Tiger's Tale '87
52 Pick-Up '86
Twice in a Lifetime '85
A Streetcar Named Desire '84
I Ought to Be in Pictures '82
Lookin' to Get Out '82
Return of the Soldier '82
Middle Age Crazy '80
The Villain '79
The Cheap Detective '78
Magic '78
Joseph Andrews '77
The Last Remake of Beau Geste '77
Twist '76
Tommy '75
The Outside Man '73
Train Robbers '73
Carnal Knowledge '71
C.C. & Company '70
R.P.M.* (*Revolutions Per Minute) '70
Tiger and the Pussycat '67
Murderers' Row '66
The Cincinnati Kid '65
Kitten with a Whip '64
Bye, Bye, Birdie '63
Viva Las Vegas '63
State Fair '62
Pocketful of Miracles '61

Annabella (1909-96)
13 Rue Madeleine '46
Dinner at the Ritz '37
Wings of the Morning '37
Under the Red Robe '36
Le Million '31
Napoleon '27

Amina Annabi
The Advocate '93
The Sheltering Sky '90

Frank Annese (1950-)
Another Chance '88
House of the Rising Sun '87

Francesca Annis (1944-)
Wives and Daughters '01
Onegin '99
Reckless: The Sequel '98
Reckless '97
Doomsday Gun '94
Onassis '88
Under the Cherry Moon '86
The Maze '85
The Crackler '84
Dune '84
Krull '83
The Unbreakable Alibi '83
Coming Out of the Ice '82
Lillie '79
Edward the King '75
Macbeth '71
Flipper's New Adventure '64

Michael Ansara (1927-)
Border Shootout '90
Assassination '87
Bayou Romance '86
The KGB: The Secret War '86
Knights of the City '85
Access Code '84
The Fantastic World of D.C. Collins '84
The Guns and the Fury '83
Mission to Glory '80
Centennial '78
The Manitou '78
Day of the Animals '77
The Message '77
The Barbary Coast '74
The Bears & I '74
It's Alive '74
The Doll Squad '73
Dear Dead Delilah '72
Quick, Let's Get Married '71
Powder Keg '70
Guns of the Magnificent Seven '69
Daring Game '68
The Pink Jungle '68
And Now Miguel '66
Texas across the River '66
Harum Scarum '65
Voyage to the Bottom of the Sea '61
Abbott and Costello Meet the Mummy '55
Diane '55
Jupiter's Darling '55
The Lawless Breed '52
Hill Number One '51
Action in Arabia '44

Zachary Ansley
The Spring '00
This Boy's Life '93
Princes in Exile '90
Christmas Comes to Willow Creek '87

Susan Anspach (1939-)
Back to Back '90
The Rutanga Tapes '90
Blood Red '88
Into the Fire '88
Blue Monkey '87
Gone Are the Days '84
Misunderstood '84
The Devil & Max Devlin '81
Gas '81
Montenegro '81
The Big Fix '78
Mad Bull '77
Blume in Love '73
Deadly Encounter '72
Play It Again, Sam '72
Five Easy Pieces '70

Adam Ant (1954-)
Face Down '97
Lover's Knot '96
Desert Winds '95
Cyber Bandits '94
Acting on Impulse '93
Last Action Hero '93
Sunset Heat '92
Spellcaster '91
Trust Me '89
World Gone Wild '88
Cold Steel '87
Slamdance '87
Nomads '86

Carl Anthony
The Sinister Urge '60
Plan 9 from Outer Space '56

Gerald Anthony (1951-)
To Die Standing '91
Secret of the Ice Cave '89

Lysette Anthony (1963-)
Russell Mulcahy's Tale of the Mummy '99
Misbegotten '98
Dead Cold '96
The Fiance '96
Trilogy of Terror 2 '96
Dr. Jekyll and Ms. Hyde '95
Dracula: Dead and Loving It '95
The Hard Truth '94
The Advocate '93
A Brilliant Disguise '93
Look Who's Talking Now '93
Save Me '93
Face the Music '92
Husbands and Wives '92
The Lady and the Highwayman '89
The Bretts '88
Without a Clue '88
Krull '83
Ivanhoe '82
Oliver Twist '82

Marc Anthony (1969-)
In the Time of the Butterflies '01
Bringing Out the Dead '99
The Substitute '96
Big Night '95

Ray Anthony (1922-)
Girls' Town '59
High School Confidential '58
The Girl Can't Help It '56

Tony Anthony (1937-)
Treasure of the Four Crowns '82
Force of Impulse '60

Steve Antin (1956-)
Inside Monkey Zetterland '93
Survival Quest '89
The Accused '88
Penitentiary 3 '87
Last American Virgin '82

Susan Anton (1950-)
Lena's Holiday '90
Options '88
Making Mr. Right '86
The Boy Who Loved Trolls '84
Cannonball Run 2 '84
Spring Fever '81
Goldengirl '79

Laura Antonelli (1941-)
Collector's Item '89
Swashbuckler '84
Passion of Love '82
Tigers in Lipstick '80
Wifemistress '79
How Funny Can Sex Be? '76
The Innocent '76
Malicious '74
Till Marriage Do Us Part '74
High Heels '72
Divine Nymph '71
A Man Called Sledge '71

Omero Antonutti (1935-)
Farinelli '94
The Fencing Master '92
Good Morning, Babylon '87
Kaos '85
Basileus Quartet '82
The Night of the Shooting Stars '82
Padre Padrone '77

Scott Antony
The Freakmaker '73
Savage Messiah '72

Cas Anvar
Seducing Maarya '99
Psychopath '97

Gabrielle Anwar (1971-)
If You Only Knew '00
The Guilty '99
My Little Assassin '99
Nevada '97
The Ripper '97
Sub Down '97
The Grave '95
In Pursuit of Honor '95
Innocent Lies '95
Things to Do in Denver When You're Dead '95
Body Snatchers '93
Fallen Angels 2 '93
For Love or Money '93
The Three Musketeers '93
Scent of a Woman '92
If Looks Could Kill '91
Wild Hearts Can't Be Broken '91
A Night of Love '87

Perry Anzilotti
Air Bud 2: Golden Receiver '98
Kiss of Fire '98

Rocky Aoki
That's Adequate '90
For Us, the Living '88

Oscar Apfel (1878-1939)
Bulldog Edition '36
Rainbow's End '35

Apollonia (1961-)
Black Magic Woman '91
Back to Back '90
Ministry of Vengeance '89
Tricks of the Trade '88
Purple Rain '84
Heartbreaker '83

Peter Appel
Tadpole '02
Six Ways to Sunday '99
Extreme Measures '96
Man of the House '95

Noel Appleby
My Grandpa Is a Vampire '92
The Navigator '88

Shiri Appleby
Deal of a Lifetime '99
Perfect Family '92

Christina Applegate (1971-)
The Sweetest Thing '02
Just Visiting '01
The Brutal Truth '99
Out in Fifty '99
The Big Hit '98
Kiss of Fire '98
Mafia! '98
Nowhere '96
Wild Bill '95
Across the Moon '94
Vibrations '94
It's a Bundyful Life '92
Don't Tell Mom the Babysitter's Dead '91
Streets '90
Jaws of Satan '81

Royce D. Applegate
The Rookie '02
O Brother Where Art Thou? '00
Gettysburg '93
Outside Chance '78

John Aprea (1941-)
To the Limit '95
Cyber-Tracker '93
Direct Hit '93
Picasso Trigger '89
Savage Beach '89
Idolmaker '80
Caged Heat '74
The Godfather, Part 2 '74
The Arousers '70

Annabelle Apsion
From Hell '01
My Uncle Silas '01
The War Zone '98
Framed '93
Amy Aquino
Alan & Naomi '92
Descending Angel '90
Art Aragon
To Hell and Back '55
The Ring '52
Julian (Sonny) Arahanga
The Matrix '99
Broken English '96
Once Were Warriors '94
Tomas Arana (1959-)
Pearl Harbor '01
Gladiator '00
Wildflowers '99
The Church '98
The Bodyguard '92
The Devil's Daughter '91
Domino '88
The Last Temptation of Christ '88
Manuel Aranguiz
Eclipse '94
A Paper Wedding '89
Ray Aranha
The Kid '97
City of Hope '91
Yoshisaburo Arashi
47 Ronin, Part 1 '42
47 Ronin, Part 2 '42
Julie Araskog
Seven '95
In a Moment of Passion '93
Michiyo Aratama (1930-2001)
Kwaidan '64
The Human Condition: A Soldier's Prayer '61
The Gambling Samurai '60
The Human Condition: Road to Eternity '59
Saga of the Vagabond '59
The Human Condition: No Greater Love '58
Alfonso Arau (1932-)
Committed '99
Picking Up the Pieces '99
Dynamite and Gold '88
Three Amigos '86
Romancing the Stone '84
Posse '75
Scandalous John '71
Fatty Arbuckle (1887-1933)
Leap Year '21
Mabel & Fatty '16
Allan Arbus (1918-)
M*A*S*H: Goodbye, Farewell & Amen '83
Americathon '79
Damien: Omen 2 '78
Coffy '73
The Young Nurses '73
Greaser's Palace '72
Gabriel Arcand
Post Mortem '99
Blood of the Hunter '94
Nathaniel Arcand
American Outlaws '01
Grey Owl '99
Bernard Archard (1922-)
The Horror of Frankenstein '70
Village of the Damned '60
Anne Archer (1949-)
The Art of War '00
Innocents '00
Rules of Engagement '00
Whispers: An Elephant's Tale '00 (V)
My Husband's Secret Life '98
Mojave Moon '96
Clear and Present Danger '94
The Man in the Attic '94
Question of Faith '93
Short Cuts '93
Body of Evidence '92
The Last of His Tribe '92
Nails '92
Patriot Games '92
Eminent Domain '91
Family Prayers '91
Narrow Margin '90
Love at Large '89
Fatal Attraction '87
Check Is in the Mail '85
Too Scared to Scream '85
The Naked Face '84
Waltz across Texas '83
Green Ice '81
Hero at Large '80
Raise the Titanic '80
Good Guys Wear Black '78
Paradise Alley '78
Lifeguard '76
Cancel My Reservation '72
John Archer (1915-99)
Blue Hawaii '62
Santa Fe '51
Best of the Badmen '50
High Lonesome '50
White Heat '49
Crash Dive '43
Guadalcanal Diary '43
Hello, Frisco, Hello '43
Sherlock Holmes in Washington '43
Gangs, Inc. '41
King of the Zombies '41
Overland Stage Raiders '38
Fanny Ardant (1949-)
Balzac: A Life of Passion '99
Elizabeth '98
Pedale Douce '96
Ridicule '96
Beyond the Clouds '95
Sabrina '95
Colonel Chabert '94
Afraid of the Dark '92
The Family '87
Conseil de Famille '86
Next Summer '84
Swann in Love '84
Confidentially Yours '83
The Woman Next Door '81
Eve Arden (1907-90)
Cinderella '84
Grease 2 '82
Pandemonium '82
Under the Rainbow '81
Grease '78
A Guide for the Married Woman '78
Anatomy of a Murder '59
Our Miss Brooks '56
Phone Call from a Stranger '52
We're Not Married '52
Tea for Two '50
Three Husbands '50
My Dream Is Yours '49
One Touch of Venus '48
Song of Scheherazade '47
Kid from Brooklyn '46
Night and Day '46
Mildred Pierce '45
Cover Girl '44
That Uncertain Feeling '41
Whistling in the Dark '41
Ziegfeld Girl '41
Comrade X '40
No, No Nanette '40
Slightly Honorable '40
At the Circus '39
Eternally Yours '39
Having Wonderful Time '38
Letter of Introduction '38
Stage Door '37
Dancing Lady '33
Pierre Arditti (1944-)
The Count of Monte Cristo '99
Same Old Song '97
The Horseman on the Roof '95
Smoking/No Smoking '94
Rosita (Rosa) Arenas (1933-)
Neutron vs. the Death Robots '62
The Curse of the Crying Woman '61
Neutron and the Black Mask '61
Neutron vs. the Amazing Dr. Caronte '61
The Witch's Mirror '60
The Curse of the Aztec Mummy '59
The Robot vs. the Aztec Mummy '59
El Bruto '52
Lee Arenberg
Dungeons and Dragons '00
Brain Dead '89
Tapeheads '89
Eddi Arent (1925-)
Circus of Fear '67
The Mysterious Magician '65
The Squeaker '65
Door with the Seven Locks '62
Dead Eyes of London '61
Forger of London '61
Joey Arresco
Circle of Fear '89
Primary Target '89
Niels Arestrup (1949-)
Meeting Venus '91
Sincerely Charlotte '86
Lumiere '76
Je Tu Il Elle '74
Robert Arevalo
The Siege of Firebase Gloria '89
The Ravagers '65
Asia Argento (1975-)
XXX '02
The Church '98
New Rose Hotel '98
The Phantom of the Opera '98
B. Monkey '97
The Stendahl Syndrome '95
Queen Margot '94
Dario Argento's Trauma '93
Demons 2 '87
Dario Argento (1940-)
Innocent Blood '92
The Bird with the Crystal Plumage '70
Fiore Argento
Demons '86
Creepers '85
Carmen Argenziano
Andersonville '95
The Burning Season '94
Unlawful Entry '92
Red Scorpion '89
The Accused '88
When a Stranger Calls '79
Death Force '78
Allison Argo
A Cry from the Mountain '85
Return of Frank Cannon '80
Victor Argo (1934-)
Angel Eyes '01
Don't Say a Word '01
Blue Moon '00
The Yards '00
Ghost Dog: The Way of the Samurai '99
Lulu on the Bridge '98
Next Stop, Wonderland '98
Blue in the Face '95
Smoke '95
Household Saints '93
True Romance '93
Bad Lieutenant '92
King of New York '90
Quick Change '90
After Hours '85
Boxcar Bertha '72
David Argue
Napoleon '96 (V)
Backlash '86
Razorback '84
BMX Bandits '83
Snow: The Movie '83
Gallipoli '81
Imanol Arias (1956-)
The Flower of My Secret '95
Intruso '93
Camila '84
Demons in the Garden '82
Labyrinth of Passion '82
Anna Aries
Invasion of the Bee Girls '73
Omega Man '71
Ineko Arima
Equinox Flower '58
The Human Condition: No Greater Love '58
Ben Aris (1937-)
Tommy '75
If... '69
The Charge of the Light Brigade '68
Yareli Arizmendi
Bloody Proof '99
The Big Green '95
Like Water for Chocolate '93
Adam Arkin (1956-)
Hanging Up '99
A Slight Case of Murder '99
Halloween: H20 '98
With Friends Like These '98
Not in This Town '97
The Doctor '91
Heat Wave '90
Necessary Parties '88
Fourth Wise Man '85
Pearl '78
Alan Arkin (1934-)
Varian's War '01
Blood Money '99
Jakob the Liar '99
Slums of Beverly Hills '98
Four Days in September '97
Gattaca '97
Grosse Pointe Blank '97
Mother Night '96
Heck's Way Home '95
The Jerky Boys '95
Steal Big, Steal Little '95
Doomsday Gun '94
North '94
Cooperstown '93
Indian Summer '93
So I Married an Axe Murderer '93
Taking the Heat '93
Glengarry Glen Ross '92
The Rocketeer '91
Coupe de Ville '90
Edward Scissorhands '90
Havana '90
Necessary Parties '88
Escape from Sobibor '87
Big Trouble '86
Deadly Business '86
Bad Medicine '85
Fourth Wise Man '85
Joshua Then and Now '85
The Emperor's New Clothes '84
A Matter of Principle '83
Return of Captain Invincible '83
Improper Channels '82
The Last Unicorn '82 (V)
Chu Chu & the Philly Flash '81
Simon '80
The In-Laws '79
The Magician of Lublin '79
The Seven-Per-Cent Solution '76
Hearts of the West '75
Rafferty & the Gold Dust Twins '75
Freebie & the Bean '74
Last of the Red Hot Lovers '72
Little Murders '71
Catch-22 '70
Popi '69
The Heart Is a Lonely Hunter '68
Wait until Dark '67
Woman Times Seven '67
The Russians Are Coming, the Russians Are Coming '66
David Arkin (1941-90)
All the President's Men '76
Nashville '75
The Long Goodbye '73
M*A*S*H '70
Allen Arkus
A Matter of Honor '95
Brutal Fury '92
Elizabeth Arlen
In the Company of Spies '99
Separate Lives '94
The First Power '89
Lucky Stiff '88
Richard Arlen (1898-1976)
Hostile Guns '67
Road to Nashville '67
Apache Uprising '66
Johnny Reno '66
The Human Duplicators '64
Sex and the College Girl '64
Cavalry Command '63
The Crawling Hand '63
Warlock '59
Blonde Blackmailer '58
Hidden Guns '56
The Mountain '56
Return of Wildfire '48
Buffalo Bill Rides Again '47
Accomplice '46
Identity Unknown '45
Timber Queen '44
Wildcat '42
Flying Blind '41
Let 'Em Have It '35
Island of Lost Souls '32
The Light of Western Stars '30
The Virginian '29
Feel My Pulse '28
Wings '27
Behind the Front '26
Arletty (1898-1992)
The Longest Day '62
Portrait of an Assassin '49
Children of Paradise '44
Les Visiteurs du Soir '42
Le Jour Se Leve '39
Circonstances Attenuantes '36
Dimitra Arliss (1932-)
Eleni '85
Ski Bum '75
George Arliss (1868-1946)
Dr. Syn '37
Transatlantic Tunnel '35
The Iron Duke '34
Disraeli '30
Pedro Armendariz, Sr. (1912-63)
Captain Sinbad '63
From Russia with Love '63
Flor Silvestre '58
The Conqueror '56
Diane '55
The Littlest Outlaw '54
El Bruto '52
The Torch '50
Tulsa '49
Fort Apache '48
The Fugitive '48
The Pearl '48
Three Godfathers '48
Maria Candelaria '46
Pedro Armendariz, Jr. (1930-)
Original Sin '01
Esmeralda Comes by Night '98
The Mask of Zorro '98
Tombstone '93
Old Gringo '89
La Chevre '81
The Deadly Trackers '73
Don't Be Afraid of the Dark '73
Henry Armetta (1888-1945)
Big Store '41
Fisherman's Wharf '39
Let's Sing Again '36
The Black Cat '34
The Cat and the Fiddle '34
The Merry Widow '34
What! No Beer? '33
Speak Easily '32
Armida (1911-89)
Jungle Goddess '49
Bad Men of the Border '45
Border Romance '30
Russell Arms (1922-)
By the Light of the Silvery Moon '53
Stage to Mesa City '48
Fighting Vigilantes '47
Captains of the Clouds '42
Alun Armstrong (1946-)
Harrison's Flowers '02
The Mummy Returns '01
Proof of Life '00
The Aristocrats '99
David Copperfield '99
Onegin '99
Sleepy Hollow '99
The Saint '97
Braveheart '95
An Awfully Big Adventure '94
Black Beauty '94
Split Second '92
White Hunter, Black Heart '90
Get Carter '71
Bess Armstrong (1953-)
Forever Love '98
Pecker '98
The Perfect Daughter '96
That Darn Cat '96
Dream Lover '93
The Skateboard Kid '93
Second Sight '89
Nothing in Common '86
High Road to China '83
Jaws 3 '83
Jekyll & Hyde...Together Again '82
The Four Seasons '81
Walking Through the Fire '80
How to Pick Up Girls '78
Curtis Armstrong (1953-)
National Lampoon's Van Wilder '02
Gale Force '01
Elvis Meets Nixon '98
Safety Patrol '98
Big Bully '95
Revenge of the Nerds 4: Nerds in Love '94
The Adventures of Huck Finn '93
Revenge of the Nerds 3: The Next Generation '92
Revenge of the Nerds 2: Nerds in Paradise '87
One Crazy Summer '86
Bad Medicine '85
Better Off Dead '85
Revenge of the Nerds '84
Risky Business '83
Jack Armstrong
Eden 2 '93
Eden 3 '93
Eden 4 '93
Eden '92
Katherine Armstrong
Ambition '91
Street Soldiers '91
Kerry Armstrong
Lantana '01
Amy '98
The Hunting '92
Lee Armstrong
Leprechaun 3 '95
Magic Island '95
Louis Armstrong (1900-71)
Hello, Dolly! '69
A Man Called Adam '66
Paris Blues '61
The Five Pennies '59
High Society '56
The Glenn Miller Story '54
Here Comes the Groom '51
New Orleans '47
Cabin in the Sky '43
Melinda Armstrong
Bikini Summer 2 '92
Bikini Summer '91

R.G. Armstrong (1917-)
Invasion of Privacy '96
Payback '94
Warlock: The Armageddon '93
Dick Tracy '90
Ghetto Blaster '89
Bulletproof '88
Predator '87
Angels Die Hard '84
Children of the Corn '84
The Beast Within '82
Evilspeak '82
The Shadow Riders '82
Steel '80
Where the Buffalo Roam '80
Dear Detective '78
The Car '77
The Pack '77
Texas Detour '77
Dixie Dynamite '76
Race with the Devil '75
Boss '74
My Name Is Nobody '74
Reflections of Murder '74
Final Comedown '72
The Great Northfield Minnesota Raid '72
The Great White Hope '70
El Dorado '67
Ride the High Country '62
The Fugitive Kind '60
No Name on the Bullet '59

R.L. Armstrong
Slumber Party '57 '76
The Hard Ride '71

Robert Armstrong (1896-1973)
Mighty Joe Young '49
The Fugitive '48
The Paleface '48
Criminal Court '46
Blood on the Sun '45
Action in Arabia '44
Mr. Winkle Goes to War '44
The Mad Ghoul '43
Wings over the Pacific '43
Baby Face Morgan '42
Dive Bomber '41
Gangbusters '38
The Girl Said No '37
Three Legionnaires '37
Ex-Mrs. Bradford '36
"G" Men '35
The Mystery Man '35
Palooka '34
King Kong '33
Son of Kong '33
The Most Dangerous Game '32
The Tip-Off '31
Be Yourself '30
Danger Lights '30
Big News '29
The Racketeer '29

Todd Armstrong (1939-93)
Dead Heat on a Merry-Go-Round '66
King Rat '65
Jason and the Argonauts '63

John Arnatt (1917-99)
Crucible of Terror '72
A Challenge for Robin Hood '68
Second Best Secret Agent in the Whole Wide World '65

Desi Arnaz, Sr. (1917-86)
The Escape Artist '82
Forever Darling '56
The Long, Long Trailer '54
Holiday in Havana '49
Bataan '43
The Navy Comes Through '42
Four Jacks and a Jill '41
Too Many Girls '40

Desi Arnaz, Jr. (1953-)
The Mambo Kings '92
Fake Out '82
House of the Long Shadows '82
Great American Traffic Jam '80
How to Pick Up Girls '78
A Wedding '78
Joyride '77
Billy Two Hats '74
Marco '73
The Voyage of the Yes '72

Lucie Arnaz (1951-)
Down to You '00
Second Thoughts '83
Mating Season '81
Washington Mistress '81
The Jazz Singer '80
Death Scream '75
Who Is the Black Dahlia? '75

Adelheid Arndt
Rosa Luxemburg '86
Chinese Boxes '84

Denis Arndt
The Beast '96
Metro '96
Amelia Earhart: The Final Flight '94
Basic Instinct '92

Peter Arne (1920-83)
Victor/Victoria '82
Straw Dogs '72
The Oblong Box '69
Battle Beneath the Earth '68
The Hellfire Club '61
The Moonraker '58
The Atomic Man '56

James Arness (1923-)
The Alamo: Thirteen Days to Glory '87
Gunsmoke: Return to Dodge '87
Alias Jesse James '59
Flame of the Islands '55
Sea Chase '55
Them! '54
Hondo '53
Big Jim McLain '52
Horizons West '52
The Thing '51
Stars in My Crown '50
Two Lost Worlds '50
Wagon Master '50
Battleground '49
The Farmer's Daughter '47

Will Arnett
Series 7: The Contenders '01 (N)
The Waiting Game '99

Jeanetta Arnette
The Shipping News '01
The '70s '00
Boys Don't Cry '99
Ladybugs '92
The Shadow Riders '82
Class Reunion Massacre '77
The Redeemer '76

Stefan Arngrim (1955-)
Misbegotten '98
Class of 1984 '82
Fear No Evil '80

Alice Arno (1946-)
Female Vampire '73
The Perverse Countess '73

Edward Arnold (1890-1956)
The Ambassador's Daughter '56
City That Never Sleeps '53
Annie Get Your Gun '50
The Yellow Cab Man '50
Dear Wife '49
Take Me Out to the Ball Game '49
Three Daring Daughters '48
The Hucksters '47
Ziegfeld Follies '46
Weekend at the Waldorf '45
Mrs. Parkington '44
Johnny Eager '42
The Devil & Daniel Webster '41
Meet John Doe '41
Johnny Apollo '40
Slightly Honorable '40
Idiot's Delight '39
Let Freedom Ring '39
Mr. Smith Goes to Washington '39
You Can't Take It with You '38
Easy Living '37
Toast of New York '37
Come and Get It '36
Crime and Punishment '35
Hide-Out '34
Sadie McKee '34
I'm No Angel '33
Rasputin and the Empress '33
Roman Scandals '33

Jack Arnold (1916-92)
Into the Night '85
Law of the Underworld '38

Mal Arnold
Blood Feast '63
Scum of the Earth '63

Mark Arnold (1957-)
Threesome '94
Trancers 5: Sudden Deth '94
Trancers 4: Jack of Swords '93

Tom Arnold (1959-)
Exit Wounds '01
Ablaze '00
Animal Factory '00
Lloyd '00
Shriek If You Know What I Did Last Friday the 13th '00
Blue Ridge Fall '99
Jackie's Back '99
National Lampoon's Golf Punks '99
Austin Powers: International Man of Mystery '97
McHale's Navy '97
Sink or Swim '97
Carpool '96
Touch '96
Big Bully '95
Nine Months '95
The Stupids '95
True Lies '94
Undercover Blues '93
The Woman Who Loved Elvis '93
Hero '92
Backfield in Motion '91
Freddy's Dead: The Final Nightmare '91

Victor Arnold
The Yards '00
Shaft '71
The Incident '67

Mark Arnott (1950-)
Not Quite Human 2 '89
Return of the Secaucus 7 '80

Francoise Arnoul (1931-)
After Sex '97
The Little Theatre of Jean Renoir '71
French Can-Can '55
Forbidden Fruit '52

Charles Arnt (1908-90)
Big Town '47
That Brennan Girl '46
Strange Illusion '45
Gambler's Choice '44
The Great Gildersleeve '43
Twin Beds '42

Michael J. Aronin
Getting Even '92
Miami Cops '89
The Lone Runner '88

Judie Aronson
Desert Kickboxer '92
The Sleeping Car '90
After Midnight '89
American Ninja '85
Friday the 13th, Part 4: The Final Chapter '84

Alexis Arquette (1969-)
Cleopatra's Second Husband '00
Bride of Chucky '98
Children of the Corn 5: Fields of Terror '98
Love Kills '98
I Think I Do '97
The Wedding Singer '97
Never Met Picasso '96
Sometimes They Come Back ... Again '96
Dead Weekend '95
Frisk '95
Wigstock: The Movie '95
Don't Do It '94
Frank and Jesse '94
Grief '94
Jack Be Nimble '94
Pulp Fiction '94
Threesome '94
Jumpin' at the Boneyard '92
Miracle Beach '92
Terminal Bliss '91
Down and Out in Beverly Hills '86

David Arquette (1971-)
Eight Legged Freaks '02
See Spot Run '01
3000 Miles to Graceland '01
Ready to Rumble '00
Scream 3 '00
Free Money '99
Muppets from Space '99
Never Been Kissed '99
Ravenous '99
The Alarmist '98
Dream with the Fishes '97
R.P.M. '97
Scream 2 '97
Beautiful Girls '96
johns '96
Larry McMurtry's Dead Man's Walk '96
Scream '96
Wild Bill '95
At Home with the Webbers '94
Fall Time '94
Roadracers '94
Buffy the Vampire Slayer '92
Where the Day Takes You '92

Lewis Arquette (1935-2001)
Little Nicky '00
Ready to Rumble '00
Almost Heroes '97
Scream 2 '97
Waiting for Guffman '96
Sleep with Me '94
Attack of the 50 Ft. Woman '93
The Linguini Incident '92
Book of Love '91
Rock 'n' Roll High School Forever '91
Syngenor '90
Nobody's Fool '86

Patricia Arquette (1968-)
Human Nature '02
Little Nicky '00
Bringing Out the Dead '99
Goodbye, Lover '99
Stigmata '99
The Hi-Lo Country '98
Infinity '96
Lost Highway '96
Nightwatch '96
The Secret Agent '96
Beyond Rangoon '95
Flirting with Disaster '95
Ed Wood '94
Holy Matrimony '94
Inside Monkey Zetterland '93
True Romance '93
Ethan Frome '92
Trouble Bound '92
Dillinger '91
The Indian Runner '91
Prayer of the Rollerboys '91
Wildflower '91
Far North '88
A Nightmare on Elm Street 3: Dream Warriors '87
Pretty Smart '87

Richmond Arquette (1964-)
Spent '00
Kiss & Tell '99
Sugar Town '99
Love to Kill '97
Girls in Prison '94

Rosanna Arquette (1959-)
Good Advice '01
The Whole Nine Yards '00
The '60s '99
Sugar Town '99
Voodoo Dawn '99
Hope Floats '98
I'm Losing You '98
Buffalo 66 '97
Deceiver '97
Gone Fishin' '97
Hell's Kitchen NYC '97
Trading Favors '97
Crash '95
Pulp Fiction '94
Search and Destroy '94
Nowhere to Run '93
The Wrong Man '93
Fathers and Sons '92
The Linguini Incident '92
Black Rainbow '91
In the Deep Woods '91
Son of the Morning Star '91
...Almost '90
Don't Hang Up '90
Flight of the Intruder '90
Sweet Revenge '90
New York Stories '89
The Big Blue '88
Promised a Miracle '88
Amazon Women on the Moon '87
Nobody's Fool '86
After Hours '85
The Aviator '85
Desperately Seeking Susan '85
8 Million Ways to Die '85
Silverado '85
One Cooks, the Other Doesn't '83
Baby It's You '82
The Executioner's Song '82
Johnny Belinda '82
Off the Wall '82
A Long Way Home '81
S.O.B. '81
Gorp '80
More American Graffiti '79
The Dark Secret of Harvest Home '78

Rod Arrants (1944-)
Vamping '84
A*P*E* '76

Jeri Arredondo
Color of a Brisk and Leaping Day '95
Tecumseh: The Last Warrior '95
Silent Tongue '92
Spirit of the Eagle '90

Lisa Arrindell Anderson
Disappearing Acts '00
A Lesson Before Dying '99
Livin' Large '91

Carlos Arruza
The Alamo '60
Torero '56

Antonin Artaud (1896-1948)
Passion of Joan of Arc '28
Napoleon '27

Beatrice Arthur (1923-)
For Better or Worse '95
History of the World: Part 1 '81
Mame '74
Lovers and Other Strangers '70
How to Commit Marriage '69

Jean Arthur (1905-91)
Shane '53
A Foreign Affair '48
Lady Takes a Chance '43
The More the Merrier '43
Talk of the Town '42
The Devil & Miss Jones '41
Arizona '40
Mr. Smith Goes to Washington '39
Only Angels Have Wings '39
You Can't Take It with You '38
Easy Living '37
History Is Made at Night '37
The Plainsman '37
Ex-Mrs. Bradford '36
Mr. Deeds Goes to Town '36
The Whole Town's Talking '35
Danger Lights '30
The Silver Horde '30

Johnny Arthur (1883-1951)
The Masked Marvel '43
The Road to Singapore '40
Danger on the Air '38
The Ghost Walks '34
The Monster '25

Maureen Arthur
The Love Machine '71
The Love God? '70
How to Succeed in Business without Really Trying '67

Robert Arthur (1925-)
Naked Youth '59
Hellcats of the Navy '57
Just for You '52
The Ring '52
September Affair '50
Twelve o'Clock High '49
Mother Wore Tights '47

Douglas Arthurs
Act of War '96
Dead Ahead '96

Michael Artura
Apt Pupil '97
Money Train '95
Killer Looks '94
Kiss of Death '94
Amongst Friends '93

Ariane Ascaride
The Adventures of Felix '99
Marius and Jeannette '97

Oscar Asche (1871-1936)
Don Quixote '35
The Private Secretary '35
Scrooge '35

Leslie Ash (1960-)
Shadey '87
Murder: Ultimate Grounds for Divorce '85
Curse of the Pink Panther '83
Quadrophenia '79

William Ash
Mad About Mambo '00
All the King's Men '99

Jayne Ashbourne
Prince of Poisoners: The Life and Crimes of William Palmer '98
Sharpe's Gold '94

Lorraine Ashbourne
Fever Pitch '96
Distant Voices, Still Lives '88

Dana Ashbrook (1967-)
Angels Don't Sleep Here '00
Kisses in the Dark '97
Twin Peaks: Fire Walk with Me '92
Ghost Dad '90
Girlfriend from Hell '89
Return of the Living Dead 2 '88
Waxwork '88

Daphne Ashbrook
The Love Letter '98
Doctor Who '96
Automatic '94
Murder So Sweet '93
Intruders '92
Sunset Heat '92
Quiet Cool '86

Linden Ashby (1960-)
Facing the Enemy *'00*
Where the Truth Lies *'99*
Murder She Purred: A Mrs. Murphy Mystery *'98*
Shelter *'98*
The Beneficiary *'97*
Blast *'96*
Cadillac Ranch *'96*
Wyatt Earp *'94*
The Perfect Bride *'91*

Peggy Ashcroft (1907-91)
The Heat of the Day *'91*
Madame Sousatzka *'88*
When the Wind Blows *'86* (V)
The Jewel in the Crown *'84*
A Passage to India *'84*
Hullabaloo over Georgie & Bonnie's Pictures *'78*
The Pedestrian *'73*
Secret Ceremony *'69*
The Nun's Story *'59*
Rhodes *'36*
The 39 Steps *'35*

Jane Asher (1946-)
A Voyage 'Round My Father *'89*
Dreamchild *'85*
Success Is the Best Revenge *'84*
Deep End *'70*
Alfie *'66*
Masque of the Red Death *'65*
The Prince and the Pauper *'62*

Renee Asherson (1920-)
The Others *'01*
Grey Owl *'99*
Harnessing Peacocks *'92*
Edwin *'84*
Rasputin the Mad Monk *'66*
Henry V *'44*
Immortal Battalion *'44*

Ron Asheton
Mosquito *'95*
Frostbiter: Wrath of the Wendigo *'94*

Kate Ashfield
The Low Down *'00*
The War Zone *'98*

Edward Ashley (1904-2000)
Beyond the Next Mountain *'87*
Dick Tracy Meets Gruesome *'47*
Nocturne *'46*
The Black Swan *'42*
Bitter Sweet *'40*

Elizabeth Ashley (1939-)
Happiness *'98*
Just the Ticket *'98*
The Buccaneers *'95*
Dangerous Curves *'88*
A Man of Passion *'88*
Vampire's Kiss *'88*
Dragnet *'87*
Stagecoach *'86*
Svengali *'83*
Paternity *'81*
Windows *'80*
Coma *'78*
Great Scout & Cathouse Thursday *'76*
One of My Wives Is Missing *'76*
War Between the Tates *'76*
Rancho Deluxe *'75*
Paperback Hero *'73*
Shattered Silence *'71*
Ship of Fools *'65*
The Carpetbaggers *'64*

Jennifer Ashley
Inseminoid *'80*
Tintorera...Tiger Shark *'78*
Pom Pom Girls *'76*
Barn of the Naked Dead *'73*
Hell on Wheels *'67*

John Ashley (1934-97)
Revenge of Doctor X *'80s*
Smoke in the Wind *'75*
Beyond Atlantis *'73*
Twilight People *'72*
Woman Hunt *'72*
Beast of the Yellow Night *'70*
Mad Doctor of Blood Island *'69*
Brides of the Beast *'68*
Hell on Wheels *'67*
Beach Blanket Bingo *'65*
The Eye Creatures *'65*
How to Stuff a Wild Bikini *'65*
Bikini Beach *'64*
Muscle Beach Party *'64*
Beach Party *'63*
Hud *'63*
Frankenstein's Daughter *'58*
How to Make a Monster *'58*
Dragstrip Girl *'57*
Motorcycle Gang *'57*
High School Caesar *'56*

Aaron Ashmore
The Skulls 2 *'02*
My Husband's Double Life *'01*

Shawn Ashmore (1979-)
X-Men *'00*
Melanie Darrow *'97*
Guitarman *'95*

John Ashton (1948-)
Avalanche *'99*
Instinct *'99*
For Which He Stands *'98*
Meet the Deedles *'98*
Fast Money *'96*
Hidden Assassin *'94*
Little Big League *'94*
Trapped in Paradise *'94*
Stephen King's The Tommyknockers *'93*
Dirty Work *'92*
Love, Lies and Murder *'91*
L.A. Gangs Rising *'89*
Midnight Run *'88*
She's Having a Baby *'88*
Beverly Hills Cop 2 *'87*
Some Kind of Wonderful *'87*
The Deliberate Stranger *'86*
King Kong Lives *'86*
Beverly Hills Cop *'84*

Joseph Ashton (1986-)
The Education of Little Tree *'97*
Slappy and the Stinkers *'97*

Roger Ashton-Griffiths
Princess of Thieves *'01*
Vanity Fair *'99*
Haunted Honeymoon *'86*

Tom Ashworth
Killer Tomatoes Eat France *'91*
Killer Tomatoes Strike Back *'90*

Luke Askew (1937-)
Frailty *'02*
Traveller *'96*
Dune Warriors *'91*
Back to Back *'90*
Kung Fu: The Movie *'86*
The Warrior & the Sorceress *'84*
Wanda Nevada *'79*
The Longest Drive *'76*
Posse *'75*
The Great Northfield Minnesota Raid *'72*
Angel Unchained *'70*
Easy Rider *'69*
The Devil's Brigade *'68*
The Green Berets *'68*
Cool Hand Luke *'67*

Leon Askin (1907-)
Savage Island *'85*
Dr. Death, Seeker of Souls *'73*
Sherlock Holmes and the Deadly Necklace *'62*
Valley of the Kings *'54*

Robin Askwith (1950-)
Flesh and Blood Show *'73*
Horror Hospital *'73*
Hans Brinker *'69*

Gregoire Aslan (1908-82)
Golden Voyage of Sinbad *'73*
Moment to Moment *'66*
Paris When It Sizzles *'64*
The Red Inn *'51*

Ed Asner (1929-)
The Animal *'01*
Above Suspicion *'00*
Common Ground *'00*
Perfect Game *'00*
The Bachelor *'99*
Love and Action in Chicago *'99*
Armistead Maupin's More Tales of the City *'97*
Hard Rain *'97*
Gargoyles, The Movie: The Heroes Awaken *'94* (V)
Gypsy *'93*
Happily Ever After *'93* (V)
Heads *'93*
JFK *'91*
Silent Motive *'91*
Switched at Birth *'91*
A Friendship in Vienna *'88*
Moon over Parador *'88*
A Case of Libel *'83*
Daniel *'83*
O'Hara's Wife *'82*
Fort Apache, the Bronx *'81*
A Small Killing *'81*
The Family Man *'79*
The Gathering *'77*
Roots *'77*
Gus *'76*
The Life and Assassination of the Kingfish *'76*
Rich Man, Poor Man *'76*
Death Scream *'75*
The Wrestler *'73*
Haunts of the Very Rich *'72*
Skin Game *'71*
The Todd Killings *'71*
They Call Me Mr. Tibbs! *'70*
Change of Habit *'69*
El Dorado *'67*
The Doomsday Flight *'66*
Kid Galahad *'62*

Fred Asparagus
Just the Ticket *'98*
Colors *'88*

Armand Assante (1949-)
Federal Protection *'02*
After the Storm *'01*
On the Beach *'00*
The Road to El Dorado *'00* (V)
The Hunley *'99*
Looking for an Echo *'99*
The Odyssey *'97*
Gotti *'96*
Striptease *'96*
Judge Dredd *'95*
Kidnapped *'95*
Blind Justice *'94*
Trial by Jury *'94*
Fatal Instinct *'93*
1492: Conquest of Paradise *'92*
Hoffa *'92*
The Mambo Kings *'92*
Fever *'91*
The Marrying Man *'91*
Eternity *'90*
Q & A *'90*
Animal Behavior *'89*
Passion in Paradise *'89*
Jack the Ripper *'88*
The Penitent *'88*
Hands of a Stranger *'87*
Belizaire the Cajun *'86*
Deadly Business *'86*
Unfaithfully Yours *'84*
Rage of Angels *'83*
I, the Jury *'82*
Little Darlings *'80*
Private Benjamin *'80*
Sophia Loren: Her Own Story *'80*
Prophecy *'79*
Lady of the House *'78*
Paradise Alley *'78*
The Lords of Flatbush *'74*

Pat Ast (1942-2001)
Reform School Girls *'86*
Heat *'72*

Fred Astaire (1899-1987)
That's Dancing! *'85*
Ghost Story *'81*
The Man in the Santa Claus Suit *'79*
Family Upside Down *'78*
The Purple Taxi *'77*
The Amazing Dobermans *'76*
That's Entertainment, Part 2 *'76*
That's Entertainment *'74*
The Towering Inferno *'74*
Finian's Rainbow *'68*
Paris When It Sizzles *'64*
On the Beach *'59*
Funny Face *'57*
Silk Stockings *'57*
Daddy Long Legs *'55*
The Band Wagon *'53*
The Belle of New York *'52*
Royal Wedding *'51*
Let's Dance *'50*
Three Little Words *'50*
The Barkleys of Broadway *'49*
Easter Parade *'48*
Blue Skies *'46*
Ziegfeld Follies *'46*
Yolanda and the Thief *'45*
The Sky's the Limit *'43*
Holiday Inn *'42*
You Were Never Lovelier *'42*
You'll Never Get Rich *'41*
Broadway Melody of 1940 *'40*
Second Chorus *'40*
The Story of Vernon and Irene Castle *'39*
Carefree *'38*
A Damsel in Distress *'37*
Shall We Dance *'37*
Follow the Fleet *'36*
Swing Time *'36*
Roberta *'35*
Top Hat *'35*
The Gay Divorcee *'34*
Dancing Lady *'33*
Flying Down to Rio *'33*

Nils Asther (1897-1981)
Son of Lassie *'45*
Bluebeard *'44*
Night Monster *'42*
Make-Up *'37*
The Bitter Tea of General Yen *'33*
The Single Standard *'29*
Our Dancing Daughters *'28*
Wild Orchids *'28*

Adriana Asti (1933-)
Caligula *'80*
Phantom of Liberty *'74*
Zorro *'74*
Before the Revolution *'65*
Accatone! *'61*

John Astin (1930-)
The Frighteners *'96*
Huck and the King of Hearts *'93*
Silence of the Hams *'93*
Stepmonster *'92*
Killer Tomatoes Eat France *'91*
Gremlins 2: The New Batch *'90*
Killer Tomatoes Strike Back *'90*
Night Life *'90*
Return of the Killer Tomatoes! *'88*
Adventures Beyond Belief *'87*
Body Slam *'87*
Teen Wolf Too *'87*
National Lampoon's European Vacation *'85*
Halloween with the Addams Family *'79*
The Barcelona Kill *'77*
Freaky Friday *'76*
Only with Married Men *'74*
Brothers O'Toole *'73*
Pepper and His Wacky Taxi *'72*
Evil Roy Slade *'71*
Viva Max *'69*
Candy *'68*
The Wheeler Dealers *'63*
That Touch of Mink *'62*

MacKenzie Astin (1973-)
The Mating Habits of the Earthbound Human *'99*
Stranger than Fiction *'99*
The Last Days of Disco *'98*
Dream for an Insomniac *'96*
The Evening Star *'96*
In Love and War *'96*
Widow's Kiss *'94*
Wyatt Earp *'94*
Iron Will *'93*
The Garbage Pail Kids Movie *'87*

Sean Astin (1971-)
The Final Hit *'02*
Lord of the Rings 1: The Fellowship of the Rings *'01*
Deterrence *'00*
Bulworth *'98*
Dish Dogs *'98*
Courage Under Fire *'96*
Kurt Vonnegut's Harrison Bergeron *'95*
The Low Life *'95*
Safe Passage *'94*
Rudy *'93*
Encino Man *'92*
Where the Day Takes You *'92*
Toy Soldiers *'91*
Memphis Belle *'90*
The Willies *'90*
Staying Together *'89*
The War of the Roses *'89*
Like Father, Like Son *'87*
White Water Summer *'87*
The Goonies *'85*

Gertrude Astor (1887-1977)
After Midnight *'33*
Carnival Lady *'33*
Be Yourself *'30*
Dames Ahoy *'30*
The Cat and the Canary *'27*
The Cheerful Fraud *'27*
Strong Man *'26*

Mary Astor (1906-87)
Hush, Hush, Sweet Charlotte *'65*
Return to Peyton Place *'61*
This Happy Feeling *'58*
Any Number Can Play *'49*
Little Women *'49*
Cass Timberlane *'47*
Meet Me in St. Louis *'44*
Thousands Cheer *'43*
Across the Pacific *'42*
The Palm Beach Story *'42*
The Great Lie *'41*
The Maltese Falcon *'41*
Brigham Young: Frontiersman *'40*
Midnight *'39*
Listen, Darling *'38*
The Hurricane *'37*
Prisoner of Zenda *'37*
Dodsworth *'36*
Lady from Nowhere *'36*
The Kennel Murder Case *'33*
Red Dust *'32*
Behind Office Doors *'31*
The Royal Bed *'31*
Don Juan *'26*
Don Q., Son of Zorro *'25*
Beau Brummel *'24*
The Fighting American *'24*
Mark of Zorro *'20*

Patti Astor
Assault of the Killer Bimbos *'88*
Underground U.S.A. *'84*
The Foreigner *'78*

Nancy Moore Atchison
The Yearling *'94*
Midnight Edition *'93*

Hooper Atchley (1887-1943)
Prescott Kid *'36*
I Can't Escape *'34*
Midnight Warning *'32*
Spirit of the West *'32*
Arizona Terror *'31*
Clearing the Range *'31*

Roscoe Ates (1892-1962)
Hills of Oklahoma *'50*
Thunder in the Pines *'49*
Black Hills *'48*
Check Your Guns *'48*
The Hawk of Powder River *'48*
The Tioga Kid *'48*
West to Glory *'47*
Wild Country *'47*
Colorado Serenade *'46*
Driftin' River *'46*
Wild West *'46*
Reg'lar Fellers *'41*
Robin Hood of the Pecos *'41*
Three Texas Steers *'39*
Woman in the Shadows *'34*
Cheyenne Kid *'33*
What! No Beer? *'33*
The Champ *'32*
Come on Danger! *'32*
Freaks *'32*
Cimarron *'31*

William Atherton (1947-)
The Crow: Salvation *'00*
Introducing Dorothy Dandridge *'99*
Mad City *'97*
Bio-Dome *'96*
Hoodlum *'96*
Broken Trust *'95*
Ravenhawk *'95*
Saints and Sinners *'95*
Frank and Jesse *'94*
The Pelican Brief *'93*
Chrome Soldiers *'92*
Buried Alive *'90*
Die Hard 2: Die Harder *'90*
A Fight for Jenny *'90*
Intrigue *'90*
Grim Prairie Tales *'89*
Die Hard *'88*
No Mercy *'86*
Real Genius *'85*
Ghostbusters *'84*
Tomorrow's Child *'82*
Centennial *'78*
Looking for Mr. Goodbar *'77*
The Day of the Locust *'75*
The Hindenburg *'75*
The Sugarland Express *'74*
Class of '44 *'73*

Harvey Atkin
Critical Care *'97*
SnakeEater 2: The Drug Buster *'89*
Meatballs *'79*
War Between the Tates *'76*

Feodor Atkine (1948-)
Vatel *'00*
Spy Games *'99*
Ronin *'98*
Doctor Chance *'97*
Sharpe's Revenge *'97*
Sharpe's Siege *'96*
Three Lives and Only One Death *'96*
High Heels *'91*
Sorceress *'88*
Pauline at the Beach *'83*
Le Beau Mariage *'82*

Christopher Atkins (1961-)
Red Shoe Diaries: Four on the Floor *'96*
It's My Party *'95*
Project Shadowchaser 3000 *'95*
Die Watching *'93*
Dracula Rising *'93*
Fatal Charm *'92*
Shoot *'92*
Wet and Wild Summer *'92*
King's Ransom *'91*
Mortuary Academy *'91*

Listen to Me *'89*
Shakma *'89*
Beaks: The Movie *'87*
Secret Weapons *'85*
A Night in Heaven *'83*
Pirate Movie *'82*
Child Bride of Short Creek *'81*
The Blue Lagoon *'80*

Dave Atkins
The Last Seduction 2 *'98*
Plunkett & Macleane *'98*
The Advocate *'93*
London Kills Me *'91*
Hellraiser *'87*
Personal Services *'87*
Prick Up Your Ears *'87*
Britannia Hospital *'82*
Bury Me an Angel *'71*

Eileen Atkins (1934-)
Gosford Park *'01*
Wit *'01*
The Avengers *'98*
Jack and Sarah *'95*
Cold Comfort Farm *'94*
Wolf *'94*
The Lost Language of Cranes *'92*
Let Him Have It *'91*
The Vision *'87*
The Dresser *'83*
Oliver Twist *'82*
I Don't Want to Be Born *'75*

Essence Atkins
How High *'01*
Love Song *'00*

Tom Atkins (1938-)
Bruiser *'00*
Two Evil Eyes *'90*
Dead Man Out *'89*
Maniac Cop *'88*
Lethal Weapon *'87*
Blind Justice *'86*
Night of the Creeps *'86*
Desperate Lives *'82*
Halloween 3: Season of the Witch *'82*
Skeezer *'82*
Escape from New York *'81*
The Fog *'78*
Tarantulas: The Deadly Cargo *'77*
Special Delivery *'76*

Beverly Hope Atkinson (1935-2001)
Uforia *'81*
Heavy Traffic *'73*

Frank Atkinson (1893-1963)
Pygmalion *'38*
Young and Innocent *'37*

Jayne Atkinson (1959-)
Free Willy 2: The Adventure Home *'95*
Free Willy *'93*
Capone *'89*

Rowan Atkinson (1955-)
Scooby-Doo *'02*
Rat Race *'01*
Bernard and the Genie *'90s*
Maybe Baby *'99*
Bean *'97*
Four Weddings and a Funeral *'94*
The Lion King *'94 (V)*
Hot Shots! Part Deux *'93*
The Witches *'90*
The Tall Guy *'89*
Never Say Never Again *'83*

Yvan Attal (1965-)
Love, etc. *'96*
Portraits Chinois *'96*

Richard Attenborough (1923-)
Jack and the Beanstalk: The Real Story *'01*
Joseph and the Amazing Technicolor Dreamcoat *'00*
The Railway Children *'00*
Elizabeth *'98*
The Lost World: Jurassic Park 2 *'97*
Hamlet *'96*
Wavelength *'96*
Miracle on 34th Street *'94*
Jurassic Park *'93*
The Human Factor *'79*
Brannigan *'75*
Conduct Unbecoming *'75*
Rosebud *'75*
Ten Little Indians *'75*
10 Rillington Place *'71*
David Copperfield *'70*
Loot ... Give Me Money, Honey! *'70*
The Magic Christian *'69*
The Bliss of Mrs. Blossom *'68*
Doctor Dolittle *'67*
The Sand Pebbles *'66*
The Flight of the Phoenix *'65*
Guns at Batasi *'64*
Seance on a Wet Afternoon *'64*
The Great Escape *'63*
Only Two Can Play *'62*
Trial & Error *'62*
The League of Gentlemen *'60*
S.O.S. Pacific *'60*
Sea of Sand *'58*
Brothers in Law *'57*
The Baby and the Battleship *'56*
The Gift Horse *'52*
The Guinea Pig *'48*
Brighton Rock *'47*
Stairway to Heaven *'46*
In Which We Serve *'43*

Malcolm Atterbury (1907-92)
Emperor of the North Pole *'73*
How to Make a Monster *'58*
Blood of Dracula *'57*
Crime of Passion *'57*
I Was a Teenage Werewolf *'57*

Edward Atterton
Mists of Avalon *'01*
Britannic *'99*
Relative Values *'99*
The Man in the Iron Mask *'98*
Catherine Cookson's The Wingless Bird *'97*
The Hunchback *'97*
Far Harbor *'96*
The Vacillations of Poppy Carew *'94*

Mike Attwell
Poldark *'96*
Joseph *'95*

Barry Atwater (1918-78)
The Night Stalker *'71*
Night Gallery *'69*
Pork Chop Hill *'59*

Edith Atwater (1911-86)
Family Plot *'76*
Die Sister, Die! *'74*
Our Time *'74*
The Love Machine *'71*
True Grit *'69*
Strait-Jacket *'64*
It Happened at the World's Fair *'63*
The Body Snatcher *'45*

Lionel Atwill (1885-1946)
Fog Island *'45*
House of Dracula *'45*
Lost City of the Jungle *'45*
Captain America *'44*
House of Frankenstein *'44*
Lady in the Death House *'44*
Raiders of Ghost City *'44*
Cairo *'42*
Frankenstein Meets the Wolfman *'42*
The Ghost of Frankenstein *'42*
Night Monster *'42*
Pardon My Sarong *'42*
Sherlock Holmes and the Secret Weapon *'42*
To Be or Not to Be *'42*
Man Made Monster *'41*
Boom Town *'40*
Johnny Apollo *'40*
Balalaika *'39*
The Gorilla *'39*
The Hound of the Baskervilles *'39*
Son of Frankenstein *'39*
The Three Musketeers *'39*
The Great Waltz *'38*
Three Comrades *'38*
High Command *'37*
The Wrong Road *'37*
Captain Blood *'35*
The Devil Is a Woman *'35*
Mark of the Vampire *'35*
Beggars in Ermine *'34*
Murders in the Zoo *'33*
Mystery of the Wax Museum *'33*
The Song of Songs *'33*
The Sphinx *'33*
Doctor X *'32*
The Vampire Bat *'32*

Anat Atzmon
Double Edge *'92*
Every Time We Say Goodbye *'86*
Dead End Street *'83*
Shell Shock *'63*

Robert Atzorn (1945-)
The Wannsee Conference *'84*
From the Life of the Marionettes *'80*

Brigitte Auber (1928-)
To Catch a Thief *'55*
Rendez-vous de Juillet *'49*

Rene Auberjonois (1940-)
Gepetto *'00*
The Patriot *'00*
Sally Hemings: An American Scandal *'00*
Inspector Gadget *'99*
Cats Don't Dance *'97 (V)*
Los Locos Posse *'97*
Batman Forever *'95*
The Ballad of Little Jo *'93*
Lone Justice *'93*
Little Nemo: Adventures in Slumberland *'92 (V)*
The Lost Language of Cranes *'92*
The Player *'92*
Wildcard *'92*
The Feud *'90*
Once Upon a Midnight Scary *'90*
A Connecticut Yankee in King Arthur's Court *'89*
Gore Vidal's Billy the Kid *'89*
The Little Mermaid *'89 (V)*
My Best Friend Is a Vampire *'88*
Police Academy 5: Assignment Miami Beach *'88*
Walker *'87*
A Smoky Mountain Christmas *'86*
3:15—The Moment of Truth *'86*
Where the Buffalo Roam *'80*
Wild, Wild West Revisited *'79*
The Dark Secret of Harvest Home *'78*
Eyes of Laura Mars *'78*
The Big Bus *'76*
King Kong *'76*
Pete 'n' Tillie *'72*
McCabe & Mrs. Miller *'71*
Brewster McCloud *'70*
M*A*S*H *'70*
Petulia *'68*

Lenore Aubert (1913-93)
Abbott and Costello Meet the Killer, Boris Karloff *'49*
Abbott and Costello Meet Frankenstein *'48*
Having Wonderful Crime *'45*
Action in Arabia *'44*

James Aubrey (1947-)
Buddy's Song *'91*
Riders of the Storm *'88*
Forever Young *'85*
Home Before Midnight *'84*
The Hunger *'83*
The Terror *'79*
Bouquet of Barbed Wire *'76*
Lord of the Flies *'63*

Jimmy Aubrey (1887-1983)
Legion of Missing Men *'37*
Aces and Eights *'36*
Courage of the North *'35*
Go-Get-'Em-Haines *'35*

Juliet Aubrey
Iris *'01*
Extremely Dangerous *'99*
Still Crazy *'98*
The Unknown Soldier *'98*
Welcome to Sarajevo *'97*
Catherine Cookson's The Moth *'96*
Go Now *'96*
Jacob *'94*
Middlemarch *'93*

Danielle Aubry
Operation C.I.A. *'65*
Bikini Beach *'64*

Jacques Aubuchon (1924-91)
Thunder Road *'58*
Gun Glory *'57*

Michel Auclair (1922-)
Swashbuckler *'84*
The Story of a Love Story *'73*
Murder at 45 R.P.M. *'65*
Manon *'50*
Beauty and the Beast *'46*

Maxine Audley (1923-92)
Frankenstein Must Be Destroyed *'69*
Peeping Tom *'60*
The Trials of Oscar Wilde *'60*
A King in New York *'57*

Stephane Audran (1932-)
Madeline *'98*
Maximum Risk *'96*
Son of Gascogne *'95*
Betty *'92*
The Turn of the Screw *'92*
Babette's Feast *'87*
Poor Little Rich Girl: The Barbara Hutton Story *'87*
La Cage aux Folles 3: The Wedding *'86*
The Blood of Others *'84*
Brideshead Revisited *'81*
Coup de Torchon *'81*
The Big Red One *'80*
Eagle's Wing *'79*
Silver Bears *'78*
Violette *'78*
Blood Relatives *'77*
Twist *'76*
Vincent, Francois, Paul and the Others *'76*
Black Bird *'75*
Ten Little Indians *'75*
Wedding in Blood *'74*
The Discreet Charm of the Bourgeoisie *'72*
La Rupture *'70*
Le Boucher *'69*
Les Biches *'68*
Six in Paris *'68*
Les Bonnes Femmes *'60*

Mischa Auer (1905-67)
Arrivederci, Baby! *'66*
The Christmas That Almost Wasn't *'66*
Sputnik *'61*
Mr. Arkadin *'55*
And Then There Were None *'45*
Brewster's Millions *'45*
Around the World *'43*
Twin Beds *'42*
The Flame of New Orleans *'41*
Hold That Ghost *'41*
Seven Sinners *'40*
Destry Rides Again *'39*
The Rage of Paris *'38*
Sweethearts *'38*
You Can't Take It with You *'38*
100 Men and a Girl *'37*
Pick a Star *'37*
Vogues of 1938 *'37*
The Gay Desperado *'36*
My Man Godfrey *'36*
The Princess Comes Across *'36*
That Girl from Paris *'36*
Three Smart Girls *'36*
Condemned to Live *'35*
The Crusades *'35*
I Dream Too Much *'35*
The Lives of a Bengal Lancer *'35*
Sucker Money *'34*
Flaming Signal *'33*
Woman Condemned *'33*
The Monster Walks *'32*
Drums of Jeopardy *'31*
Inside the Lines *'30*

Claudine Auger (1942-)
Secret Places *'85*
Lobster for Breakfast *'82*
The Associate *'79*
Ricco *'74*
Head of the Family *'71*
Twitch of the Death Nerve *'71*
The Killing Game *'67*
Triple Cross *'67*
Thunderball *'65*
The Road to Lebanon *'60*

Lance August (1961-)
Stripteaser *'95*
Terror Eyes *'87*

Pernilla August (1958-)
Star Wars: Episode 2—Attack of the Clones *'02*
Mary, Mother of Jesus *'99*
Star Wars: Episode 1—The Phantom Menace *'99*
Private Confessions *'98*
Jerusalem *'96*
The Best Intentions *'92*

Robert August
The Endless Summer 2 *'94*
The Endless Summer *'66*

Sherman Augustus
ZigZag *'02*
Virus *'98*
Colors *'88*

Ewa Aulin (1950-)
The Legend of Blood Castle *'72*
Start the Revolution without Me *'70*
Candy *'68*

Jean-Pierre Aumont (1913-2001)
The Proprietor *'96*
Jefferson in Paris *'94*
Becoming Colette *'92*
A Tale of Two Cities *'91*
Windmills of the Gods *'88*
Sweet Country *'87*
The Blood of Others *'84*
Nana *'82*
Don't Look in the Attic *'81*
A Time for Miracles *'80*
Something Short of Paradise *'79*
Blackout *'78*
Cat and Mouse *'78*
Catherine & Co. *'76*
The Happy Hooker *'75*
Mahogany *'75*
Day for Night *'73*
Cauldron of Blood *'67*
The Horse Without a Head *'63*
The Devil at 4 O'Clock *'61*
John Paul Jones *'59*
Napoleon *'55*
Lili *'53*
Song of Scheherazade *'47*
Heartbeat *'46*
Bizarre Bizarre *'39*
Maria Chapdelaine *'34*

Michel Aumont (1936-)
The Closet *'00*
Alberto Express *'92*
One Woman or Two *'85*
Grain of Sand *'84*
A Sunday in the Country *'84*
Les Comperes *'83*
La Vie Continue *'82*
Hothead *'78*
Spoiled Children *'77*

Tina Aumont (1946-)
A Matter of Time *'76*
Lifespan *'75*
The Messiah *'75*
La Grande Bourgeoise *'74*
Malicious *'74*
Torso *'73*
Man of Legend *'71*
Partner *'68*
Texas across the River *'66*

Marcus Aurelius
Suspect Device *'95*
A.P.E.X. *'94*

Albert Austin (1881-1953)
Three Charlies and One Phoney! *'18*
The Cure *'17*
The Vagabond *'16*

Charlotte Austin
The Bride & the Beast *'58*
Daddy Long Legs *'55*

Julie Austin
Fatal Exposure *'90*
Elves *'89*

Karen Austin
When a Stranger Calls Back *'93*
When the Time Comes *'91*
A Girl to Kill For *'90*
Far from Home *'89*
Assassin *'86*
The Ladies Club *'86*
The Jagged Edge *'85*
Summer Rental *'85*

Pam Austin
Evil Roy Slade *'71*
Kissin' Cousins *'64*

Terri Austin (1959-)
False Witness *'89*
The Vindicator *'85*

William Austin (1884-1975)
The Private Life of Henry VIII *'33*
It *'27*
Suds *'20*

Shaun Austin-Olsen
Battlefield Earth *'00*
Extreme Measures *'96*

Daniel Auteuil (1950-)
The Closet *'00*
The Widow of Saint-Pierre *'00*
The Girl on the Bridge *'98*
La Separation *'98*
The Lost Son *'98*
Lucie Aubrac *'98*
Les Voleurs *'96*
The Eighth Day *'95*
Queen Margot *'94*
The Separation *'94*
Ma Saison Preferee *'93*
Un Coeur en Hiver *'93*
The Elegant Criminal *'92*
Mama, There's a Man in Your Bed *'89*
Jean de Florette *'87*
Manon of the Spring *'87*
Le Sex Shop *'73*

Alan Autry (1952-)
Proud Men *'87*
At Close Range *'86*
Blue De Ville *'86*

Gene Autry (1907-98)
Alias Jesse James *'59*
Last of the Pony Riders *'53*
On Top of Old Smoky *'53*
Winning of the West *'53*
Blue Canadian Rockies *'52*
Night Stage to Galveston *'52*
Hills of Utah *'51*
Valley of Fire *'51*

Cow Town '50
The Big Sombrero '49
Riders of the Whistling Pines '49
Rim of the Canyon '49
Loaded Pistols '48
Robin Hood of Texas '47
Trail to San Antone '47
Sioux City Sue '46
Bells of Capistrano '42
Call of the Canyon '42
Heart of the Rio Grande '42
Back in the Saddle '41
Down Mexico Way '41
Ridin' on a Rainbow '41
Twilight on the Rio Grande '41
Gaucho Serenade '40
Melody Ranch '40
South of the Border '39
The Man from Music Mountain '38
Oh Susannah '38
Old Barn Dance '38
Prairie Moon '38
Rootin' Tootin' Rhythm '38
Big Show '37
Boots & Saddles '37
Git Along Little Dogies '37
Manhattan Merry-Go-Round '37
Public Cowboy No. 1 '37
Round-Up Time in Texas '37
Springtime in the Rockies '37
Yodelin' Kid from Pine Ridge '37
Old Corral '36
Red River Valley '36
Ride, Ranger, Ride '36
Melody Trail '35
The Phantom Empire '35
In Old Santa Fe '34
Mystery Mountain '34

Frankie Avalon (1940-)
Casino '95
Back to the Beach '87
Blood Song '82
Grease '78
Dr. Goldfoot and the Bikini Machine '66
Beach Blanket Bingo '65
How to Stuff a Wild Bikini '65
I'll Take Sweden '65
Bikini Beach '64
Muscle Beach Party '64
Pajama Party '64
Beach Party '63
The Castilian '63
Panic in the Year Zero! '62
Voyage to the Bottom of the Sea '61
The Alamo '60

Phillip Avalon
The Cursed Mountain Mystery '93
Summer City '77

Luis Avalos (1946-)
Noriega: God's Favorite '00
Jungle 2 Jungle '96
Lone Justice 3: Showdown at Plum Creek '96
Lone Justice '93
Lone Justice 2 '93
Ghost Fever '87

Erik Avari
Planet of the Apes '01
The Mummy '99
Stargate '94
The Beast '88

Loren Avedon
Virtual Combat '95
Operation Golden Phoenix '94
The King of the Kickboxers '91
No Retreat, No Surrender 3: Blood Brothers '91
No Retreat, No Surrender 2 '89

Joe Mari Avellana
Deathfight '93
Bloodfist 2 '90
Bloodfist '89

Brian Avery
Forced to Kill '93
The Graduate '67

James Avery (1948-)
Dancing in September '00
The Colony '98
Prince of Egypt '98 (V)
Spirit Lost '96
Beastmaster 2: Through the Portal of Time '91
Fletch '85
Kicks '85

Linda Avery
Hitchhikers '72
Noon Sunday '71

Margaret Avery
White Man's Burden '95
Mardi Gras for the Devil '93
The Jacksons: An American Dream '92
Heat Wave '90
Return of Superfly '90
Riverbend '89
Blueberry Hill '88
For Us, the Living '88
The Color Purple '85
The Lathe of Heaven '80
The Fish that Saved Pittsburgh '79
Which Way Is Up? '77
Hell Up in Harlem '73
Terror at Red Wolf Inn '72

Val Avery (1924-)
Courage '86
The Pope of Greenwich Village '84
Choices '81
The Chosen '81
Continental Divide '81
The Amityville Horror '79
Wanderers '79
Black Caesar '73
Firehouse '72
The Anderson Tapes '71
Minnie and Moskowitz '71
A Dream of Kings '69
Faces '68
Nevada Smith '66

Angel Aviles
Scorpion Spring '96
Mi Vida Loca '94
Somebody to Love '94
Chain of Desire '93

Rick Aviles (1953-95)
Stephen King's The Stand '94
The Saint of Fort Washington '93
Ghost '90
Mystery Train '89
Spike of Bensonhurst '88

Mili Avital (1972-)
After the Storm '01
Uprising '01
Arabian Nights '00
Bad Seed '00
Kissing a Fool '98
Polish Wedding '97
Invasion of Privacy '96
Dead Man '95
Stargate '94

Chikage Awashima
The Human Condition: No Greater Love '58
Early Summer '51

Eddie Axberg (1947-)
The New Land '73
The Emigrants '72

Nina Axelrod
Cross Country '83
Time Walker '82
Motel Hell '80

Hannelore Axman
Five Fingers '52
The Red Menace '49

Hoyt Axton (1938-99)
King Cobra '98
Kingfish: A Story of Huey P. Long '95
Number One Fan '94
Season of Change '94
Buried Alive '90
The Rousters '90
Disorganized Crime '89
We're No Angels '89
Dixie Lanes '88
Retribution '88
Christmas Comes to Willow Creek '87
Guilty of Innocence '87
Act of Vengeance '86
Gremlins '84
Deadline Auto Theft '83
Goldilocks & the Three Bears '83
Heart Like a Wheel '83
Endangered Species '82
The Junkman '82
The Black Stallion '79

Charlotte Ayanna
Training Day '01
Dancing at the Blue Iguana '00
The Rage: Carrie 2 '99

Dan Aykroyd (1952-)
Crossroads '02
The Curse of the Jade Scorpion '01
Earth vs. the Spider '01
Evolution '01
Pearl Harbor '01
House of Mirth '00
Loser '00
Stardom '00
Diamonds '99
Antz '98 (V)
Blues Brothers 2000 '98
Dying to Get Rich '98
Grosse Pointe Blank '97
Celtic Pride '96
Feeling Minnesota '96
Getting Away With Murder '96
My Fellow Americans '96
Casper '95
Sgt. Bilko '95
Tommy Boy '95
Canadian Bacon '94
Exit to Eden '94
My Girl 2 '94
North '94
Coneheads '93
Chaplin '92
Sneakers '92
This Is My Life '92
My Girl '91
Nothing But Trouble '91
Loose Cannons '90
The Masters of Menace '90
Driving Miss Daisy '89
Ghostbusters 2 '89
Caddyshack 2 '88
The Great Outdoors '88
My Stepmother Is an Alien '88
The Couch Trip '87
Dragnet '87
Into the Night '85
Spies Like Us '85
Ghostbusters '84
Doctor Detroit '83
Trading Places '83
Twilight Zone: The Movie '83
Neighbors '81
The Blues Brothers '80
Mr. Mike's Mondo Video '79
1941 '79
All You Need Is Cash '78
Love at First Sight '76

Peter Aykroyd
Kids of the Round Table '96
The Funny Farm '82
Gas '81

Arthur Aylesworth (1883-1946)
Beau Geste '39
Sandflow '37

Felix Aylmer (1889-1979)
School for Scandal '65
The Chalk Garden '64
Victoria Regina '61
Exodus '60
From the Terrace '60
The Hands of Orlac '60
The Mummy '59
Separate Tables '58
Saint Joan '57
Anastasia '56
Knights of the Round Table '53
The Master of Ballantrae '53
Paris Express '53
Ivanhoe '52
Quo Vadis '51
Alice in Wonderland '50
Trio '50
Eye Witness '49
Hamlet '48
The October Man '48
Ghosts of Berkeley Square '47
The Magic Bow '47
A Man About the House '47
The Wicked Lady '45
Henry V '44
Mr. Emmanuel '44
The Demi-Paradise '43
Thursday's Child '43
Spellbound '41
Night Train to Munich '40
The Case of the Frightened Lady '39
Action for Slander '38
Dreaming Lips '37
As You Like It '36
Nine Days a Queen '36
The Shadow '36
The Evil Mind '34
The Iron Duke '34

John Aylward
Just Visiting '01
Instinct '99
From the Earth to the Moon '98

Agnes Ayres (1898-1940)
Son of the Sheik '26
Affairs of Anatol '21
The Sheik '21

Leah Ayres (1957-)
Bloodsport '88
Eddie Macon's Run '83
The Burning '82

Lew Ayres (1908-96)
Cast the First Stone '89
Of Mice and Men '81
Salem's Lot '79
Damien: Omen 2 '78
End of the World '76
Francis Gary Powers: The True Story of the U-2 Spy '76
Battle for the Planet of the Apes '73
The Stranger '73
The Carpetbaggers '64
Advise and Consent '62
Donovan's Brain '53
The Capture '50
Johnny Belinda '48
Dark Mirror '46
Dr. Kildare's Strange Case '40
Broadway Serenade '39
Holiday '38
All Quiet on the Western Front '30
Big News '29
The Kiss '29

Robert Ayres (1914-68)
Battle Beneath the Earth '68
Cat Girl '57
Time Lock '57
River Beat '54

Rosalind Ayres (1946-)
Beautiful People '99
Gods and Monsters '98
The Slipper and the Rose '76
That'll Be the Day '73

Hank Azaria (1964-)
America's Sweethearts '01
Uprising '01
The Cradle Will Rock '99
Mystery, Alaska '99
Mystery Men '99
Tuesdays with Morrie '99
Celebrity '98
Godzilla '98
Anastasia '97 (V)
Great Expectations '97
Grosse Pointe Blank '97
Homegrown '97
The Birdcage '95
Heat '95
Quiz Show '94
Cool Blue '88

Sabine Azema (1955-)
La Buche '00
Same Old Song '97
Le Bonheur Est Dans le Pre '95
Smoking/No Smoking '94
Life and Nothing But '89
A Sunday in the Country '84

Ayu Azhari
Without Mercy '95
Diamond Run '90

Tony Azito (1949-95)
Bloodhounds of Broadway '89
Chattanooga Choo Choo '84
Private Resort '84
Union City '81

Shabana Azmi (1948-)
Fire '96
In Custody '94
Son of the Pink Panther '93
City of Joy '92
Madame Sousatzka '88

Charles Aznavour (1924-)
Edith & Marcel '83
The Tin Drum '79
Sky Riders '76
Twist '76
Ten Little Indians '75
Blockhouse '73
The Adventurers '70
Carbon Copy '69
Candy '68
Shoot the Piano Player '62
The Testament of Orpheus '59

Candice Azzara (1945-)
Doin' Time on Planet Earth '88
Easy Money '83
Fatso '80
House Calls '78

Karin Baal (1940-)
Berlin Alexanderplatz '80
Dead Eyes of London '61
Teenage Wolfpack '57

Obba Babatunde
John Q '02
How High '01
The Visit '00
Introducing Dorothy Dandridge '99
Life '99
Apartment Complex '98
The Temptations '98
Miss Evers' Boys '97
Multiplicity '96
Soul of the Game '96
That Thing You Do! '96
A Reason to Believe '95
Philadelphia '93
Undercover Blues '93
Miami Blues '90
God Bless the Child '88

Barbara Babcock (1937-)
Space Cowboys '00
Far and Away '92
Happy Together '89
The Heart of Dixie '89
News at Eleven '86
Quarterback Princess '85
That Was Then...This Is Now '85
The Lords of Discipline '83
The Black Marble '79
On the Edge: The Survival of Dana '79
The Christmas Coal Mine Miracle '77

Fabienne Babe
Les Voleurs '96
Singing the Blues in Red '87

Lauren Bacall (1924-)
Diamonds '99
The Mirror Has Two Faces '96
My Fellow Americans '96
From the Mixed-Up Files of Mrs. Basil E. Frankweiler '95
Ready to Wear '94
A Foreign Field '93
The Portrait '93
All I Want for Christmas '91
Innocent Victim '90
Misery '90
Dinner at Eight '89
Appointment with Death '88
Mr. North '88
The Fan '81
The Shootist '76
Murder on the Orient Express '74
Harper '66
Sex and the Single Girl '64
Flame Over India '60
Designing Woman '57
Written on the Wind '56
Blood Alley '55
The Cobweb '55
A Woman's World '54
How to Marry a Millionaire '53
Young Man with a Horn '50
Key Largo '48
Dark Passage '47
The Big Sleep '46
To Have & Have Not '44

Michael Bacall
Urban Legends 2: Final Cut '00
Wait until Spring, Bandini '90

Salvatore Baccaloni
Rock-A-Bye Baby '57
Full of Life '56

Barbara Bach (1947-)
Give My Regards to Broad Street '84
Princess Daisy '83
Caveman '81
The Great Alligator '81
Screamers '80
The Unseen '80
Up the Academy '80
Jaguar Lives '79
Street Law '79
Force 10 from Navarone '78
The Spy Who Loved Me '77
The Legend of Sea Wolf '75
Stateline Motel '75

Catherine Bach (1954-)
The Nutt House '95
Rage and Honor '92
The Masters of Menace '90
Street Justice '89
Criminal Act '88
Driving Force '88
Cannonball Run 2 '84
Strange New World '75
Nicole '72

John Bach
The Sound and the Silence '93
The Lost Tribe '89
Georgia '87
Wild Horses '82

Dian Bachar (1971-)
The Adventures of Rocky & Bullwinkle '00
BASEketball '98
Orgazmo '98

Hans Bachman
Invader '91
Star Quest '89

Steve Bacic (1965-)
The 6th Day '00
Bounty Hunters 2: Hardball '97

Brian Backer (1956-)
Moving Violations '85
The Burning '82
Fast Times at Ridgemont High '82
Talk to Me '82

Jim Backus (1913-89)
Slapstick of Another Kind '84
Angel's Brigade '79
C.H.O.M.P.S. '79

The Rebels '79
Rescue from Gilligan's Island '78
Pete's Dragon '77
Crazy Mama '75
Now You See Him, Now You Don't '72
Myra Breckinridge '70
Where Were You When the Lights Went Out? '68
Billie '65
It's a Mad, Mad, Mad, Mad World '63
The Wheeler Dealers '63
The Horizontal Lieutenant '62
The Wonderful World of the Brothers Grimm '62
Zotz! '62
Ice Palace '60
Ask Any Girl '59
1001 Arabian Nights '59 (V)
Man of a Thousand Faces '57
The Pied Piper of Hamelin '57
Meet Me in Las Vegas '56
Naked Hills '56
Francis in the Navy '55
Rebel without a Cause '55
Above and Beyond '53
I Love Melvin '53
Don't Bother to Knock '52
Here Come the Nelsons '52
Pat and Mike '52
His Kind of Woman '51
I Want You '51
I'll See You in My Dreams '51
Father Was a Fullback '49
The Great Lover '49

Olga Baclanova (1899-1974)
Freaks '32
Docks of New York '28
The Man Who Laughs '27

Irving Bacon (1893-1965)
Ma and Pa Kettle at Home '54
Cause for Alarm '51
Dynamite '49
Monsieur Verdoux '47
Footlight Glamour '43
It's a Great Life '43
The Bashful Bachelor '42
Blondie for Victory '42
Blondie Goes Latin '42
Blondie's Blessed Event '42
Caught in the Draft '41
Western Union '41
Blondie Has Trouble '40
Blondie On a Budget '40
Blondie Plays Cupid '40
Dreaming Out Loud '40
The Howards of Virginia '40
Blondie Brings Up Baby '39
Blondie Meets the Boss '39
Blondie Takes a Vacation '39
Internes Can't Take Money '37
Branded Men '31

Kevin Bacon (1958-)
Novocaine '01
The Hollow Man '00
My Dog Skip '99
Stir of Echoes '99
Digging to China '98
Wild Things '98
Picture Perfect '96
Sleepers '96
Telling Lies in America '96
Apollo 13 '95
Balto '95 (V)
Murder in the First '95
The Air Up There '94
The River Wild '94
A Few Good Men '92
He Said, She Said '91
JFK '91
Pyrates '91
Queens Logic '91
Flatliners '90
The Big Picture '89
Criminal Law '89
Tremors '89
End of the Line '88
She's Having a Baby '88
Planes, Trains & Automobiles '87
White Water Summer '87
Quicksilver '86
Footloose '84
Enormous Changes '83
Trumps '83
Diner '82
Only When I Laugh '81
Friday the 13th '80
Hero at Large '80
Starting Over '79
National Lampoon's Animal House '78

Lloyd Bacon (1890-1955)
Wagon Tracks '19
Charlie Chaplin ... Our Hero! '15

Jean-Pierre Bacri (1951-)
Place Vendome '98
Same Old Song '97
Un Air de Famille '96
Entre-Nous '83

Michael Badalucco (1954-)
The Man Who Wasn't There '01
O Brother Where Art Thou? '00
Summer of Sam '99
You've Got Mail '98
Love Walked In '97
The Search for One-Eyed Jimmy '96
Two If by Sea '95
The Professional '94
Mac '93

Hermione Baddeley (1906-86)
The Aristocats '70 (V)
Mary Poppins '64
The Unsinkable Molly Brown '64
Cosh Boy '61
Room at the Top '59
The Pickwick Papers '54
The Belles of St. Trinian's '53
A Christmas Carol '51
The Woman in Question '50
Passport to Pimlico '49
Brighton Rock '47

Alan Badel (1923-82)
Nijinsky '80
The Riddle of the Sands '79
The Medusa Touch '78
Luther '74
The Day of the Jackal '73
The Adventurers '70
Arabesque '66
Children of the Damned '63
This Sporting Life '63
Three Cases of Murder '55

Sarah Badel (1943-)
Just Visiting '01
Cotton Mary '99
Mrs. Dalloway '97
Not Without My Daughter '90
Cold Comfort Farm '71

Diedrich Bader (1966-)
Ice Age '02 (V)
Jay and Silent Bob Strike Back '01
Office Space '98
The Assassination File '96
Teresa's Tattoo '94
The Beverly Hillbillies '93

Rupert Baderman
Shadowlands '85
1984 '84

Russ Badger
Shanghai Noon '00
The Gore-Gore Girls '72

Mary Badham (1952-)
This Property Is Condemned '66
To Kill a Mockingbird '62

Mina (Badiyi) Badie
The Anniversary Party '01
Georgia '95
Mrs. Parker and the Vicious Circle '94
War Between the Tates '76

Annette Badland
Little Voice '98
Angels and Insects '95
Hollow Reed '95
Captives '94
Pictures '80s
Jabberwocky '77

Jane Badler (1953-)
Under the Gun '95
Black Snow '93
Easy Kill '89
Fine Gold '88
V '83

Erykah Badu (1971-)
The Cider House Rules '99
Blues Brothers 2000 '98
Deep Red: Hatchet Murders '75

Buddy Baer (1915-86)
Giant from the Unknown '58
The Big Sky '52
Jack & the Beanstalk '52
Flame of Araby '51
Quo Vadis '51

Harry Baer
Big Boss '77
Mr. Scarface '77
Fox and His Friends '75
Rulers of the City '71
Whity '70

John Baer (1925-)
Night of the Blood Beast '58
We're No Angels '55
Above and Beyond '53
Indian Uprising '51

Max Baer, Sr. (1909-59)
The Harder They Fall '56
Riding High '50
Africa Screams '49
Buckskin Frontier '43
The Navy Comes Through '42
The Prizefighter and the Lady '33

Max Baer, Jr. (1937-)
The McCullochs '75
Macon County Line '74

Meridith Baer
The Chicken Chronicles '77
The Sister-in-Law '74

Parley Baer (1914-)
Dave '93
Time Trackers '88
Rodeo Girl '80
The Amazing Dobermans '76
Sixteen '72
The Ugly Dachshund '65
The Brass Bottle '63
Gypsy '62
The Adventures of Huckleberry Finn '60
Cash McCall '60
The Young Lions '58

Rafael Baez
Shanghai Noon '00
Went to Coney Island on a Mission from God...Be Back by Five '98

Paloma Baeza
The Way We Live Now '02
Anna Karenina '00
A Knight in Camelot '98
Far from the Madding Crowd '97
The Odyssey '97
A Kid in King Arthur's Court '95

Regina Baff
Below the Belt '80
Road Movie '72

William Bagdad (1920-75)
Blood Orgy of the She-Devils '74
The Doll Squad '73
The Astro-Zombies '67

Carol Bagdasarian
The Aurora Encounter '85
Charge of the Model T's '76

Lorri Bagley
Ice Age '02 (V)
Trick '99

Vernel Bagneris
Down by Law '86
Pennies from Heaven '81

Marcus Bagwell
Terror Tract '00
Day of the Warrior '96

Blake Bahner
Cyberstalker '96
Wizards of the Demon Sword '94
Blackbelt 2: Fatal Force '93
Fatal Exposure '90
Deadly Breed '89
Thrilled to Death '88
Sensations '87

Maxine Bahns (1971-)
Cutaway '00
She's the One '96
The Brothers McMullen '94

Wu Bai
Time and Tide '00
The Personals '98

Charles "Chuck" Bail
L.A. Bad '85
The Stunt Man '80

Bill Bailey
Heat and Sunlight '87
On the Edge '86

Blake Bailey
Head of the Family '96
Lurking Fear '94

Bunty Bailey
Spellcaster '91
Dolls '87

Eion Bailey
Band of Brothers '01
Almost Famous '00
Center Stage '00
Fight Club '99

Fred Bailey
Nam Angels '88
Silk '86

G.W. Bailey (1945-)
Jesus '00
Police Academy 7: Mission to Moscow '94
An American Story '92
Double-Crossed '91
Held Hostage '91
Write to Kill '91
Police Academy 6: City under Siege '89
Burglar '87
Mannequin '87
A Winner Never Quits '86
Rustler's Rhapsody '85
The Capture of Grizzly Adams '82

Jim Bailey
Penitentiary 3 '87
Vultures '84

Mark Bailey
Simple Men '92
The Unbelievable Truth '90

Pearl Bailey (1918-90)
Peter Gunn '89
The Member of the Wedding '83
The Fox and the Hound '81 (V)
Norman, Is That You? '76
Carmen Jones '54

Raymond Bailey (1904-80)
The Gallant Hours '60
Vertigo '58
The Incredible Shrinking Man '57
Picnic '55

Richard Bailey
Forever Amber '47
Manhunt of Mystery Island '45

Robert Bailey, Jr.
Dragonfly '02
Little John '02

Robin Bailey (1919-99)
Screamtime '83
See No Evil '71

Kirk Baily (1952-)
The Sixth Man '97
3 Ninjas: High Noon at Mega Mountain '97
Voodoo Dawn '89

Barbara Bain (1931-)
Panic '00
Spirit of '76 '91
Trust Me '89
Skinheads: The Second Coming of Hate '88
Destination Moonbase Alpha '75
Murder Once Removed '71

Conrad Bain (1923-)
Postcards from the Edge '90
Child Bride of Short Creek '81
C.H.O.M.P.S. '79
A Pleasure Doing Business '79
The Anderson Tapes '71
Bananas '71
Who Killed Mary What's 'Er Name? '71

Cynthia Bain
Hometown Boy Makes Good '93
Danielle Steel's Changes '91
Spontaneous Combustion '89
Pumpkinhead '88

Sherry Bain (1947-)
Wild & Wooly '78
Pipe Dreams '76
The Hard Ride '71
Wild Riders '71

Fay Bainter (1892-1968)
The Children's Hour '61
June Bride '48
The Secret Life of Walter Mitty '47
Kid from Brooklyn '46
The Virginian '46
State Fair '45
Dark Waters '44
The Human Comedy '43
Presenting Lily Mars '43
Journey for Margaret '42
Woman of the Year '42
Babes on Broadway '41
Our Town '40
Young Tom Edison '40
Jezebel '38
The Shining Hour '38
Quality Street '37

Jimmy Baio (1962-)
Kiss and Be Killed '91
Playing for Keeps '86
Brass '85
The Bad News Bears in Breaking Training '77

Scott Baio (1961-)
I Love N.Y. '87
Zapped! '82
Senior Trip '81
Foxes '80
Bugsy Malone '76

Harry Baird
The Oblong Box '69
The Story of a Three Day Pass '68
Tor '64

Jimmy Baird (1948-)
Black Orchid '59
Return of Dracula '58

Scott Bairstow (1970-)
New Best Friend '02
Dead in the Water '01
Delivered '98
Black Circle Boys '97
Killing Mr. Griffin '97
The Postman '97
Two for Texas '97
Wild America '97
White Fang 2: The Myth of the White Wolf '94

Mitsuko Baisho
The Eel '96
Akira Kurosawa's Dreams '90
Vengeance Is Mine '79

Jon Robin Baitz (1961-)
Last Summer In the Hamptons '96
One Fine Day '96

Sidiki Bakaba
Faces of Women '85
Le Professionnel '81

Richard Bakalyan (1931-)
The Fox and the Hound '81 (V)
The Computer Wore Tennis Shoes '69
The St. Valentine's Day Massacre '67
Von Ryan's Express '65
Panic in the Year Zero! '62
Up Periscope '59

Art Baker (1898-1966)
The Underworld Story '50
Impact '49
Task Force '49
Homecoming '48
A Southern Yankee '48

Blanche Baker (1956-)
Dead Funny '94
Livin' Large '91
The Handmaid's Tale '90
Shakedown '88
Embassy '85
Cold Feet '84
Sixteen Candles '84
Awakening of Candra '81
French Postcards '79
Mary and Joseph: A Story of Faith '79

Bob Baker (1910-75)
Riders of Pasco Basin '40
Ghost Town Riders '38
Outlaw Express '38
Western Trails '38

Carroll Baker (1931-)
Private Lessons
The Game '97
North Shore Fish '97
Just Your Luck '96
Dalva '95
Kindergarten Cop '90
Ironweed '87
Native Son '86
The Secret Diary of Sigmund Freud '84
Star 80 '83
The Watcher in the Woods '81
The World Is Full of Married Men '80
Andy Warhol's Bad '77
You've Got to Have Heart '77
Bloodbath '76
Next Victim '74
Captain Apache '71
Kiss Me, Kill Me '69
Paranoia '69
The Greatest Story Ever Told '65
Harlow '65
The Carpetbaggers '64
Cheyenne Autumn '64
How the West Was Won '63
But Not for Me '59
The Big Country '58
Baby Doll '56
Giant '56
Easy to Love '53

Colin Baker
The Waiting Time '99
War and Peace '73

David Aaron Baker (1963-)
Kate & Leopold '01
The Tao of Steve '00

Diane Baker (1938-)
Harrison's Flowers '02
Murder at 1600 '97
The Cable Guy '96
The Net '95
Imaginary Crimes '94
The Joy Luck Club '93
Twenty Bucks '93
The Closer '91
The Silence of the Lambs '91

A Woman of Substance '84
Danger in the Skies '79
Baker's Hawk '76
The Horse in the Gray Flannel Suit '68
Mirage '66
Marnie '64
Strait-Jacket '64
The Prize '63
Stolen Hours '63
The Best of Everything '59
The Diary of Anne Frank '59
Journey to the Center of the Earth '59

Dylan Baker (1958-)
Changing Lanes '02
Along Came a Spider '01
The Cell '00
Thirteen Days '00
Oxygen '99
Random Hearts '99
Simply Irresistible '99
Celebrity '98
From the Earth to the Moon '98
Happiness '98
Disclosure '94
The Last of the Mohicans '92
Love Potion #9 '92
Delirious '91
The Long Walk Home '89
The Wizard of Loneliness '88
Planes, Trains & Automobiles '87

Frank Baker (1892-1980)
Tarzan and the Green Goddess '38
The New Adventures of Tarzan '35

George Baker (1931-)
Little Lord Fauntleroy '95
The Charmer '87
Robin Hood...The Legend: Herne's Son '85
A Woman of Substance '84
Goodbye, Mr. Chips '69
Sword of Lancelot '63
Dangerous Youth '58
The Moonraker '58

Jay Baker
Naked Lies '98
Storm and Sorrow '90
April Fool's Day '86

Jill Baker
Catherine Cookson's The Girl '96
Hope and Glory '87

Joe Don Baker (1936-)
George Wallace '97
Tomorrow Never Dies '97
Mars Attacks! '96
Congo '95
Felony '95
Goldeneye '95
The Grass Harp '95
Panther '95
The Underneath '95
Reality Bites '94
Ring of Steel '94
Citizen Cohn '92
The Distinguished Gentleman '92
Cape Fear '91
The Children '90
Criminal Law '89
The Abduction of Kari Swenson '87
The Killing Time '87
Leonard Part 6 '87
The Living Daylights '87
Edge of Darkness '86
Getting Even '86
Fletch '85
Final Justice '84
The Natural '84
Joy Sticks '83
Wacko '83
Speedtrap '78
The Pack '77
Shadow of Chikara '77
Framed '75
Mitchell '75
Charley Varrick '73
Walking Tall '73
Junior Bonner '72
Wild Rovers '71
Adam at 6 a.m. '70
Guns of the Magnificent Seven '69
Cool Hand Luke '67

Jolyon Baker
Attila '01
Duel of Hearts '92
Final Analysis '92

Josephine Baker (1906-75)
The French Way '40
Princess Tam Tam '35
Zou Zou '34

Kai Baker
American Eagle '90
Stormquest '87

Kathy Baker (1950-)
The Glass House '01
Things You Can Tell Just by Looking at Her '00
The Cider House Rules '99
Ratz '99
A Season for Miracles '99
Inventing the Abbotts '97
Not in This Town '97
Weapons of Mass Distraction '97
To Gillian on Her 37th Birthday '96
Lush Life '94
Mad Dog and Glory '93
Article 99 '92
Jennifer 8 '92
Edward Scissorhands '90
Dad '89
The Image '89
Jacknife '89
Mr. Frost '89
Clean and Sober '88
Permanent Record '88
Street Smart '87
A Killing Affair '85
The Right Stuff '83

Kenny Baker (1934-)
Star Wars: Episode 2—Attack of the Clones '02
Sleeping Beauty '89
Amadeus '84
Return of the Jedi '83
Time Bandits '81
The Elephant Man '80
The Empire Strikes Back '80
Star Wars '77

Kenny L. Baker (1912-85)
The Harvey Girls '46
At the Circus '39

Kirsten Baker (1962-)
Friday the 13th, Part 2 '81
Gas Pump Girls '79
Girls Next Door '79

Ray Baker (1928-)
Anywhere But Here '99
The Final Cut '96
Camp Nowhere '94
The Hard Truth '94
Speechless '94
Heart Condition '90
Everybody's All American '88
Rockabye '86
Places in the Heart '84

Rick Baker
Kentucky Fried Movie '77
King Kong '76
The Thing with Two Heads '72

Scott Thompson Baker (1961-)
Cleo/Leo '89
New York's Finest '87
Rest in Pieces '87

Sharon Baker
Metallica '85
Captive Planet '78

Simon Baker (1969-)
The Affair of the Necklace '01
Red Planet '00
Ride with the Devil '99
Judas Kiss '98
Restaurant '98
Smoke Signals '98
L.A. Confidential '97
Most Wanted '97

Stanley Baker (1928-76)
Queen of Diamonds '80s
Zorro '74
Butterfly Affair '71
Accident '67
Robbery '67
Dingaka '65
Zulu '64
Eva '62
Sodom and Gomorrah '62
The Guns of Navarone '61
Helen of Troy '56
Richard III '55
The Cruel Sea '53
Knights of the Round Table '53
The Hidden Room '49

Timothy Baker
Out for Blood '93
Bloodfist 2 '90

Tom Baker (1934-)
Dungeons and Dragons '00
The Chronicles of Narnia '89
Angels Die Hard '84
The Zany Adventures of Robin Hood '84
Fyre '78
Candy Stripe Nurses '74
The Freakmaker '73
Golden Voyage of Sinbad '73
Vault of Horror '73
Nicholas and Alexandra '71

William "Billy" Bakewell (1908-93)
Davy Crockett, King of the Wild Frontier '55
Lucky Me '54
Radar Men from the Moon '52
The Capture '50
Romance on the High Seas '48
You Gotta Stay Happy '48
Dawn Express '42
Gone with the Wind '39
The Duke of West Point '38
Exiled to Shanghai '37
Roaring Speedboats '37
Sons of Steel '35
Dance Fools Dance '31
All Quiet on the Western Front '30
The Iron Mask '29
Annapolis '28
Battle of the Sexes '28

Brenda Bakke (1963-)
Shelter '98
The Fixer '97
Trucks '97
Lone Justice 3: Showdown at Plum Creek '96
Under Siege 2: Dark Territory '95
Star Quest '94
Tales from the Crypt Presents Demon Knight '94
Twogether '94
Fast Gun '93
Hot Shots! Part Deux '93
Lone Justice 2 '93
Fist Fighter '88
Dangerous Love '87
Death Spa '87
Scavengers '87
Hardbodies 2 '86

Brigitte Bako
Paranoia '98
Double Take '97
The Escape '95
Strange Days '95
Replikator: Cloned to Kill '94
Dark Tide '93
A Man in Uniform '93
Red Shoe Diaries '92

Muhamad Bakri
The Milky Way '97
Double Edge '92
Beyond the Walls '84
Hanna K. '83

Scott Bakula (1955-)
A Girl Thing '01
Life as a House '01
Above Suspicion '00
American Beauty '99
Luminarias '99
Mean Streak '99
Major League 3: Back to the Minors '98
Tom Clancy's Netforce '98
Cats Don't Dance '97 (V)
The Invaders '95
Lord of Illusions '95
Color of Night '94
My Family '94
A Passion to Kill '94
Mercy Mission '93
Necessary Roughness '91
Sibling Rivalry '90
The Last Fling '86

Bob Balaban (1945-)
Ghost World '01
Gosford Park '01
The Majestic '01
The Mexican '01
Best in Show '00
The Cradle Will Rock '99
Jakob the Liar '99
Three to Tango '99
Clockwatchers '97
Deconstructing Harry '97
The Late Shift '96
Waiting for Guffman '96
Pie in the Sky '95
Greedy '94
Amos and Andrew '93
For Love or Money '93
Unnatural Pursuits '91
Alice '90
Dead Bang '89
End of the Line '88
2010: The Year We Make Contact '84
Absence of Malice '81
Whose Life Is It Anyway? '81
Altered States '80
Girlfriends '78
Close Encounters of the Third Kind '77
Bank Shot '74
Catch-22 '70
The Strawberry Statement '70
Midnight Cowboy '69

Liane Balaban
World Traveler '01
New Waterford Girl '99

Belinda Balaski (1947-)
Gremlins 2: The New Batch '90
Proud Men '87
The Howling '81
Cannonball '76

Josiane Balasko (1952-)
French Twist '95
Grosse Fatigue '94
Too Beautiful for You '88
French Fried Vacation '79
This Sweet Sickness '77

Nick Baldasare
They Bite '95
Beyond Dream's Door '88

Renato Baldini (1921-)
Four Ways Out '57
Submarine Attack '54
The Wayward Wife '52

A. Michael Baldwin
Phantasm 4: Oblivion '98
Vice Girls '96
Phantasm 3: Lord of the Dead '94

Adam Baldwin (1962-)
Jackpot '01
The Patriot '00
The Right Temptation '00
Dr. Jekyll & Mr. Hyde '99
From the Earth to the Moon '98
Gargantua '98
Indiscreet '98
Independence Day '96
Lover's Knot '96
Sawbones '95
Trade Off '95
Blind Justice '94
Digital Man '94
Wyatt Earp '94
Bitter Harvest '93
Cold Sweat '93
800 Leagues Down the Amazon '93
Deadbolt '92
Radio Flyer '92
Where the Day Takes You '92
Guilty by Suspicion '91
Predator 2 '90
Next of Kin '89
The Chocolate War '88
Cohen and Tate '88
Full Metal Jacket '87
Bad Guys '86
3:15—The Moment of Truth '86
D.C. Cab '84
Hadley's Rebellion '84
Reckless '84
My Bodyguard '80
Ordinary People '80

Alec Baldwin (1958-)
Cats & Dogs '01 (V)
Final Fantasy: The Spirits Within '01 (V)
Pearl Harbor '01
The Royal Tenenbaums '01 (N)
Nuremberg '00
State and Main '00
Thomas and the Magic Railroad '00
Outside Providence '99
Thick as Thieves '99
The Confession '98
Mercury Rising '98
The Edge '97
Ghosts of Mississippi '96
The Juror '96
Looking for Richard '96
Two Bits '96 (V)
Heaven's Prisoners '95
A Streetcar Named Desire '95
The Shadow '94
The Getaway '93
Malice '93
Glengarry Glen Ross '92
Prelude to a Kiss '92
The Marrying Man '91
Alice '90
The Hunt for Red October '90
Miami Blues '90
Great Balls of Fire '89
Beetlejuice '88
Married to the Mob '88
She's Having a Baby '88
Talk Radio '88
Working Girl '88
The Alamo: Thirteen Days to Glory '87
Forever, Lulu '87
Dress Gray '86
Love on the Run '85
Code of Honor '84

Daniel Baldwin (1960-)
Homicide: The Movie '00
In Pursuit '00
Active Stealth '99
Desert Thunder '99
Silicon Towers '99
Wild Grizzly '99
Love Kills '98
On the Border '98
Phoenix '98
John Carpenter's Vampires '97
The Invader '96
Tree's Lounge '96
Yesterday's Target '96
Bodily Harm '95
Family of Cops '95
Mulholland Falls '95
Car 54, Where Are You? '94
Dead on Sight '94
Attack of the 50 Ft. Woman '93
Knight Moves '93
Lone Justice '93
Harley Davidson and the Marlboro Man '91
The Heroes of Desert Storm '91
Born on the Fourth of July '89

Janit Baldwin
Humongous '82
Ruby '77
Born Innocent '74
Gator Bait '73

Robert Baldwin (1904-96)
Courageous Dr. Christian '40
Meet Dr. Christian '39

Stephen Baldwin (1966-)
Slap Shot 2: Breaking the Ice '02
Zebra Lounge '01
Cutaway '00
The Flintstones in Viva Rock Vegas '00
Mercy '00
Xchange '00
Absence of the Good '99
Friends & Lovers '99
Dean Koontz's Mr. Murder '98
One Tough Cop '98
Scarred City '98
Half-Baked '97
Sub Down '97
Bio-Dome '96
Crimetime '96
Fled '96
Dead Weekend '95
Under the Hula Moon '95
The Usual Suspects '95
8 Seconds '94
Fall Time '94
The Great American Sex Scandal '94
New Eden '94
A Simple Twist of Fate '94
Threesome '94
Bitter Harvest '93
Posse '93
Crossing the Bridge '92
Last Exit to Brooklyn '90
Born on the Fourth of July '89
The Beast '88
The Lawrenceville Stories '88

Walter Baldwin (1889-1977)
Interrupted Melody '55
I Want You '51
Winter Meeting '48
The Best Years of Our Lives '46
Mr. Winkle Goes to War '44

William Baldwin (1963-)
Brotherhood of Murder '99
Relative Values '99
Shattered Image '98
Virus '98
Curdled '95
Fair Game '95
A Pyromaniac's Love Story '95
Sliver '93
Three of Hearts '93
Backdraft '91
Flatliners '90
Internal Affairs '90
Born on the Fourth of July '89
The Preppie Murder '89

Christian Bale (1974-)
Reign of Fire '02
Captain Corelli's Mandolin '01
Shaft '00
American Psycho '99
Mary, Mother of Jesus '99
William Shakespeare's A Midsummer Night's Dream '99
All the Little Animals '98
Velvet Goldmine '98
Metroland '97
Portrait of a Lady '96

The Secret Agent '96
Pocahontas '95 (V)
Little Women '94
Royal Deceit '94
Swing Kids '93
Newsies '92
A Murder of Quality '90
Henry V '89
Treasure Island '89
Empire of the Sun '87
The Land of Faraway '87

Carla Balenda
Phantom Stallion '54
Outlaw Women '52

Betty Balfour (1903-78)
Evergreen '34
Champagne '28

Michael Balfour (1918-97)
The Canterbury Tales '71
The Private Life of Sherlock Holmes '70
The Flesh and the Fiends '60
Fiend without a Face '58
Quatermass 2 '57
Murder on Approval '56
Genevieve '53
Moulin Rouge '52

Jennifer Balgobin
Roadside Prophets '92
Dr. Caligari '89
City Limits '85
Repo Man '83

Jeanne Balibar
Va Savoir '01
Late August, Early September '98
My Sex Life...Or How I Got into an Argument '96

Ina Balin (1937-90)
Vasectomy: A Delicate Matter '86
The Children of An Lac '80
Galyon '77
Panic on the 5:22 '74
The Don Is Dead '73
The Projectionist '71
Charro! '69
The Patsy '64
The Comancheros '61
From the Terrace '60
Black Orchid '59

Andras Balint (1943-)
Citizen X '95
Stalin '92
Colonel Redl '84
A Happy New Year! '79
25 Fireman's Street '73
Love Film '70
Father '67

Eszter Balint (1966-)
Tree's Lounge '96
The Linguini Incident '92
Bail Jumper '89
Stranger than Paradise '84

Fairuza Balk (1974-)
Deuces Wild '02
Almost Famous '00
Life in the Fast Lane '00
Red Letters '00
American History X '98
The Maker '98
The Waterboy '98
The Craft '96
The Island of Dr. Moreau '96
Danger of Love '95
Things to Do in Denver When You're Dead '95
Imaginary Crimes '94
Tollbooth '94
Gas Food Lodging '92
Shame '92
Valmont '89
Outside Chance of Maximillian Glick '88
The Worst Witch '86
Return to Oz '85

Angeline Ball
The General '98
The Gambler '97
Trojan Eddie '96
Brothers in Trouble '95
The Commitments '91

Frank Ball
Feud Maker '38
Boothill Brigade '37
Gun Lords of Stirrup Basin '37
Galloping Romeo '33
When a Man Rides Alone '33
The Forty-Niners '32

Lucille Ball (1911-89)
Mame '74
Yours, Mine & Ours '68
A Guide for the Married Man '67
The Facts of Life '60
Forever Darling '56
The Long, Long Trailer '54
Fancy Pants '50
The Fuller Brush Girl '50
A Woman of Distinction '50
Easy Living '49
Miss Grant Takes Richmond '49
Sorrowful Jones '49
Her Husband's Affairs '47
Lured '47
Dark Corner '46
Ziegfeld Follies '46
Without Love '45
Best Foot Forward '43
DuBarry Was a Lady '43
Thousands Cheer '43
Big Street '42
Seven Days' Leave '42
Valley of the Sun '42
A Girl, a Guy and a Gob '41
Look Who's Laughing '41
Dance, Girl, Dance '40
Too Many Girls '40
You Can't Fool Your Wife '40
Beauty for the Asking '39
Five Came Back '39
Panama Lady '39
The Affairs of Annabel '38
Having Wonderful Time '38
Joy of Living '38
Next Time I Marry '38
Room Service '38
Stage Door '37
Follow the Fleet '36
That Girl from Paris '36
I Dream Too Much '35
Roberta '35
Top Hat '35
Roman Scandals '33

Nicholas Ball (1946-)
Croupier '97
Claudia '85
Lifeforce '85
The House that Bled to Death '81

Samuel Ball
The Last Castle '01
Urbania '00

Vincent Ball (1924-)
Sirens '94
Breaker Morant '80
Demolition '77
Not Tonight Darling '72
Where Eagles Dare '68
A Matter of WHO '62
Dead Lucky '60
Blonde Blackmailer '58
Blood of the Vampire '58
Sea of Sand '58
John and Julie '55
Terror Ship '54

Carl Ballantine (1922-)
Dying to Get Rich '98
Mr. Saturday Night '92
Hollywood Chaos '89
World's Greatest Lover '77
Revenge of the Cheerleaders '76
Speedway '68

Kaye Ballard (1926-)
Ava's Magical Adventure '94
Eternity '90
Fate '90
Modern Love '90
Tiger Warsaw '87
Freaky Friday '76
The Ritz '76
The Girl Most Likely '57

Edoardo Ballerini
Romeo Must Die '00
Looking for an Echo '99
I Shot Andy Warhol '96
The Pest '96

Smith Ballew (1902-84)
Gun Cargo '49
Hawaiian Buckaroo '38
Panamint's Bad Man '38
Rawhide '38
Roll Along Cowboy '37
Western Gold '37

Jean-Francois Balmer (1946-)
The Swindle '97
Beaumarchais the Scoundrel '96
Madame Bovary '91
Window Shopping '86

Martin Balsam (1919-96)
Silence of the Hams '93
Cape Fear '91
Two Evil Eyes '90
Innocent Prey '88
P.I. Private Investigations '87
Queenie '87
Delta Force '86
Grown Ups '86
Death Wish 3 '85
Murder in Space '85
St. Elmo's Fire '85
Little Gloria... Happy at Last '84
The Goodbye People '83
The Salamander '82
The People vs. Jean Harris '81
The Warning '80
The House on Garibaldi Street '79
Silver Bears '78
Death Rage '77
Raid on Entebbe '77
All the President's Men '76
The Lindbergh Kidnapping Case '76
Two Minute Warning '76
Mitchell '75
Miles to Go Before I Sleep '74
Murder on the Orient Express '74
The Taking of Pelham One Two Three '74
The Stone Killer '73
Summer Wishes, Winter Dreams '73
Brand New Life '72
Confessions of a Police Captain '72
Eyes Behind the Stars '72
The Anderson Tapes '71
Season for Assassins '71
Catch-22 '70
Hard Frame '70
Little Big Man '70
Tora! Tora! Tora! '70
The Good Guys and the Bad Guys '69
Spaghetti Western '69
Hombre '67
After the Fox '66
Bedford Incident '65
Harlow '65
A Thousand Clowns '65
The Carpetbaggers '64
Seven Days in May '64
Breakfast at Tiffany's '61
Cape Fear '61
Psycho '60
Al Capone '59
Marjorie Morningstar '58
Twelve Angry Men '57

Talia Balsam (1960-)
Coldblooded '94
The Companion '94
Trust Me '89
In the Mood '87
The Kindred '87
Private Investigations '87
Crawlspace '86
Consenting Adult '85
Mass Appeal '84
Nadia '84

Calamity Jane '82
Kent State '81
On the Edge: The Survival of Dana '79
Sunnyside '79

Humbert Balsan (1954-)
I Married a Dead Man '82
Lancelot of the Lake '74

Kirk Baltz
Bloodhounds '96
Kingfish: A Story of Huey P. Long '95
Probable Cause '95
Skin Art '93
Reservoir Dogs '92

Alexander Baluyev
Deep Impact '98
The Peacemaker '97

David Bamber
The Railway Children '00
Pride and Prejudice '95
The Buddha of Suburbia '92
High Hopes '88

Jamie Bamber
Band of Brothers '01
Horatio Hornblower: The Adventure Continues '01
Lady Audley's Secret '00

Judy Bamber
The Atomic Brain '64
A Bucket of Blood '59

Gerry Bamman (1941-)
Home Alone 2: Lost in New York '92
Lorenzo's Oil '92
The Chase '91
The Ten Million Dollar Getaway '91

Eric Bana (1968-)
Black Hawk Down '01
Chopper '00
The Castle '97

Anne Bancroft (1931-)
Heartbreakers '01
Keeping the Faith '00
Up at the Villa '00
Antz '98 (V)
Critical Care '97
G.I. Jane '97
Great Expectations '97
Homecoming '96
Sunchaser '96
Dracula: Dead and Loving It '95
Home for the Holidays '95
How to Make an American Quilt '95
Oldest Confederate Widow Tells All '95
Malice '93
Mr. Jones '93
Point of No Return '93
Broadway Bound '92
Honeymoon in Vegas '92
Love Potion #9 '92
Bert Rigby, You're a Fool '89
Torch Song Trilogy '88
84 Charing Cross Road '86
'night, Mother '86
Agnes of God '85
Garbo Talks '84
To Be or Not to Be '83
The Elephant Man '80
Fatso '80
The Bell Jar '79
Jesus of Nazareth '77
The Turning Point '77
Lipstick '76
Silent Movie '76
The Hindenburg '75
Prisoner of Second Avenue '74
Young Winston '72
The Graduate '67
The Slender Thread '65
The Pumpkin Eater '64
The Miracle Worker '62
The Restless Breed '58
Girl in Black Stockings '57
Nightfall '56
Walk the Proud Land '56
Savage Wilderness '55

Demetrius and the Gladiators '54
Treasure of the Golden Condor '53
Don't Bother to Knock '52

Bradford Bancroft
A Time to Die '91
Damned River '89
Bachelor Party '84

Cameron Bancroft (1967-)
MVP2: Most Vertical Primate '01
Anything for Love '93
Just One of the Girls '93
Love and Human Remains '93

George Bancroft (1882-1956)
Whistling in Dixie '42
Texas '41
Little Men '40
Young Tom Edison '40
Each Dawn I Die '39
Stagecoach '39
Angels with Dirty Faces '38
Hell-Ship Morgan '36
Mr. Deeds Goes to Town '36
Docks of New York '28
White Gold '28
Underworld '27
Old Ironsides '26
The Pony Express '25

Antonio Banderas (1960-)
Spy Kids 2: The Island of Lost Dreams '02
The Body '01
Original Sin '01
Spy Kids '01
Play It to the Bone '99
The 13th Warrior '99
White River '99
The Mask of Zorro '98
Evita '96
Two Much '96
Assassins '95
Desperado '95
Four Rooms '95
Miami Rhapsody '95
Never Talk to Strangers '95
Interview with the Vampire '94
Of Love and Shadows '94
The House of the Spirits '93
Outrage '93
Philadelphia '93
The Mambo Kings '92
Terranova '91
Against the Wind '90
Tie Me Up! Tie Me Down! '90
Baton Rouge '88
Women on the Verge of a Nervous Breakdown '88
Law of Desire '86
Matador '86
Labyrinth of Passion '82

Kanu Banerjee
Aparajito '58
Pather Panchali '54

Karuna Banerjee
Aparajito '58
Pather Panchali '54

Victor Banerjee (1946-)
Bitter Moon '92
Foreign Body '86
The Home and the World '84
A Passage to India '84
Hullabaloo over Georgie & Bonnie's Pictures '78

Lisa Banes (1955-)
Dragonfly '02
Last Exit to Earth '96
Cocktail '88
Marie '85
The Hotel New Hampshire '84
Look Back in Anger '80

Joy Bang (1947-)
Messiah of Evil '74
Night of the Cobra Woman '72
Play It Again, Sam '72

Tallulah Bankhead (1902-68)
Die! Die! My Darling! '65
Main Street to Broadway '53
Lifeboat '44
Stage Door Canteen '43

Aaron Banks
Fist of Fear, Touch of Death '80
The Bodyguard '76

Dennis Banks
The Last of the Mohicans '92
Thunderheart '92

Ernie Banks
Finding Buck McHenry '00
Red Shoe Diaries: Luscious Lola '00
Pastime '91
King '78

Jonathan Banks (1947-)
Crocodile Dundee in Los Angeles '01
Foolish '99
Let the Devil Wear Black '99
Melanie Darrow '97
Dark Breed '96
Flipper '96
Last Man Standing '95
Marilyn & Bobby: Her Final Affair '94
Body Shot '93
Boiling Point '93
Freejack '92
There Goes the Neighborhood '92
Nightmare '91
Cold Steel '87
Armed and Dangerous '86
Assassin '86
Beverly Hills Cop '84
Nadia '84

Leslie Banks (1890-1952)
Madeleine '50
Eye Witness '49
Henry V '44
Cottage to Let '41
Chamber of Horrors '40
The Arsenal Stadium Mystery '39
Jamaica Inn '39
Fire Over England '37
21 Days '37
Wings of the Morning '37
Sanders of the River '35
Transatlantic Tunnel '35
The Man Who Knew Too Much '34
The Most Dangerous Game '32

Tyra Banks (1973-)
Halloween: Resurrection '02
Coyote Ugly '00
Life-Size '00
Love Stinks '99
Higher Learning '94

Vilma Banky (1903-91)
Son of the Sheik '26
The Eagle '25

Ian Bannen (1928-99)
To Walk with Lions '99
Waking Ned Devine '98
Braveheart '95
The Sound and the Silence '93
Blue Ice '92
Damage '92
The Big Man: Crossing the Line '91
George's Island '91
Catherine Cookson's The Fifteen Streets '90
Ghost Dad '90
The Courier '88
Hope and Glory '87
Defense of the Realm '85
Lamb '85
The Prodigal '83
Eye of the Needle '81
The Watcher in the Woods '81

Bite the Bullet '75
The Gathering Storm '74
Driver's Seat '73
From Beyond the Grave '73
Mackintosh Man '73
The Offence '73
Doomwatch '72
Fright '71
Ride to Glory '71
Too Late the Hero '70
The Flight of the Phoenix '65
Carlton Browne of the F.O. '59
A Tale of Two Cities '58
The Third Key '57

Jill Banner (1946-82)
Hard Frame '70
The President's Analyst '67
Spider Baby '64

John Banner (1910-73)
Togetherness '70
36 Hours '64
Guilty of Treason '50
The Fallen Sparrow '43
Immortal Sergeant '43

Reggie Bannister (1945-)
Phantasm 4: Oblivion '98
Phantasm 3: Lord of the Dead '94
Silent Night, Deadly Night 4: Initiation '90
Survival Quest '89
Phantasm 2 '88
Phantasm '79

Jack Bannon (1940-)
DaVinci's War '92
Miracle of the Heart: A Boys Town Story '86
Take Your Best Shot '82

Jim Bannon (1911-86)
Unknown World '51
The Fighting Redhead '50
Man from Colorado '49

Ildiko Bansagi (1947-)
Meeting Venus '91
Mephisto '81

Li Bao-Tian
Shanghai Triad '95
Ju Dou '90

Nina Bara (1920-90)
Missile to the Moon '59
Black Hills '48

Theda Bara (1890-1955)
The Love Goddesses '65
The Unchastened Woman '25
A Fool There Was '14

John Baragrey (1918-75)
Gamera, the Invincible '66
Pardners '56

Christine Baranski (1952-)
Dr. Seuss' How the Grinch Stole Christmas '00
Bowfinger '99
Bulworth '98
Cruel Intentions '98
Neil Simon's The Odd Couple 2 '98
The Birdcage '95
Jeffrey '95
New Jersey Drive '95
The War '94
Addams Family Values '93
The Night We Never Met '93
The Ref '93
To Dance with the White Dog '93
Reversal of Fortune '90
9 1/2 Weeks '86
Crackers '84

Olivia Barash (1965-)
Grave Secrets '89
Dr. Alien '88
Tuff Turf '85
Repo Man '83
Child of Glass '78

Richie Barathy
Body Trouble '92
Caged Fury '90

Luca Barbareschi (1956-)
Private Affairs '89
Bye Bye Baby '88

Adrienne Barbeau (1945-)
Across the Line '00
The Convent '00
Jack Frost 2: Revenge of the Mutant Killer Snowman '00
Burial of the Rats '95
Jailbreakers '94
Silk Degrees '94
Scott Turow's The Burden of Proof '92
Double-Crossed '91
Two Evil Eyes '90
Cannibal Women in the Avocado Jungle of Death '89
Back to School '86
Open House '86
Seduced '85
Terror at London Bridge '85
Next One '84
Charlie and the Great Balloon Chase '82
Creepshow '82
Swamp Thing '82
Cannonball Run '81
Escape from New York '81
Magic on Love Island '80
The Crash of Flight 401 '78
The Fog '78
Red Alert '77
Return to Fantasy Island '77

Ellen Barber
Blood Bride
Born Beautiful '82
The Premonition '75

Frances Barber (1958-)
Still Crazy '98
The Ice House '97
Photographing Fairies '97
Rhodes '97
A Royal Scandal '96
We Think the World of You '88
A Zed & Two Noughts '88
Castaway '87
Prick Up Your Ears '87
Sammy & Rosie Get Laid '87
Home Sweet Home '82

Gillian Barber
Double Jeopardy '99
In Cold Blood '96
Maternal Instincts '96

Glynis Barber (1955-)
Deja Vu '98
Edge of Sanity '89
The Wicked Lady '83
The Terror '79
Yesterday's Hero '79

Paul Barber
The Full Monty '96
The Long Good Friday '80

Katie Barberi
Not Quite Human 2 '89
The Garbage Pail Kids Movie '87

Urbano Barberini (1962-)
Torrents of Spring '90
Gor '88
Opera '88
Outlaw of Gor '87
Demons '86

Vincent Barbi
Lady Godiva Rides '68
The Astro-Zombies '67
The Blob '58

George Barbier (1864-1945)
The Man Who Came to Dinner '41
Week-End in Havana '41
The Adventures of Marco Polo '38
Little Miss Broadway '38
My Lucky Star '38
On the Avenue '37
Waikiki Wedding '37
The Princess Comes Across '36
Wife Versus Secretary '36
The Crusades '35
Here Comes Cookie '35
The Merry Widow '34

Paula Barbieri (1966-)
The Dangerous '95
Night Eyes 4: Fatal Passion '95
Red Shoe Diaries 5: Weekend Pass '95

Richard Barboza
Tales of Erotica '93
Small Time '91

Lisa B(arbuscia) (1971-)
Almost Heroes '97
Serpent's Lair '95

Artur Barcis
The Decalogue '88
No End '84

Caroline Barclay
Within the Rock '96
American Gothic '88

Don Barclay (1892-1975)
Outlaw Express '38
Thunder in the Desert '38
Border Phantom '37
Sweetheart of the Navy '37

Joan Barclay (1920-)
The Shanghai Cobra '45
Sagebrush Law '43
The Black Dragons '42
The Corpse Vanishes '42
Flying Wild '41
Texas Trouble '41
Outlaw's Paradise '39
Lightnin' Carson Rides Again '38
Whirlwind Horseman '38
Blake of Scotland Yard '36
The Glory Trail '36
Phantom Patrol '36
Prison Shadows '36
Shadow of Chinatown '36
West of Nevada '36
Feud of the West '35
Finishing School '33

Roy Barcroft (1902-69)
Billy the Kid Versus Dracula '66
The Kettles on Old MacDonald's Farm '57
The Last Hunt '56
Iron Mountain Trail '53
Marshal of Cedar Rock '53
Shadows of Tombstone '53
Border Saddlemates '52
Hoodlum Empire '52
Radar Men from the Moon '52
Don Daredevil Rides Again '51
Rodeo King and the Senorita '51
North of the Great Divide '50
The Vanishing Westerner '50
Arizona Cowboy '49
Down Dakota Way '49
Federal Agents vs. Underworld, Inc. '49
Outcasts of the Trail '49
Eyes of Texas '48
G-Men Never Forget '48
Jesse James Rides Again '47
Son of Zorro '47
Alias Billy the Kid '46
Stagecoach to Denver '46
Vigilantes of Boom Town '46
Bells of Rosarita '45
D-Day on Mars '45
Manhunt of Mystery Island '45
The Purple Monster Strikes '45
Sunset in El Dorado '45
The Topeka Terror '45
Haunted Harbor '44
Bordertown Gunfighters '43
Calling Wild Bill Elliott '43
Hoppy Serves a Writ '43
Raiders of Sunset Pass '43
Sagebrush Law '43
Six Gun Gospel '43
Below the Border '42
Dawn on the Great Divide '42
Sunset on the Desert '42
The Showdown '40
Yukon Flight '40
Hopalong Cassidy: Renegade Trail '39
Renegade Trail '39
The Frontiersmen '38

Javier Bardem (1969-)
Before Night Falls '00
Dance with the Devil '97
Live Flesh '97
Mouth to Mouth '95
Running Out of Time '94
Jamon, Jamon '93

Pilar Bardem
Live Flesh '97
Vacas '91

Trevor Bardette (1902-77)
Thunder Road '58
The Monolith Monsters '57
Hills of Oklahoma '50
Gun Crazy '49
Omoo Omoo, the Shark God '49
The Secret Code '42
Doomed Caravan '41
Red River Valley '41

Aleksander Bardini (1913-95)
The Silent Touch '94
Trois Couleurs: Blanc '94
The Double Life of Veronique '91
The Decalogue '88
No End '84

Brigitte Bardot (1934-)
Don Juan (Or If Don Juan Were a Woman) '73
Legend of Frenchie King '71
The Women '69
Shalako '68
Spirits of the Dead '68
A Coeur Joie '67
Head Over Heels '67
Dear Brigitte '65
Viva Maria! '65
Contempt '64
Ravishing Idiot '64
Le Repos du Guerrier '62
A Very Private Affair '62
Please Not Now! '61
Voulez-Vous Danser avec Moi? '59
The Bride Is Much Too Beautiful '58
Mam'zelle Pigalle '58
That Naughty Girl '58
Une Parisienne '58
And God Created Woman '57
The Night Heaven Fell '57
Doctor at Sea '56
Helen of Troy '56
Plucking the Daisy '56
Les Grandes Manoeuvres '55
Crazy for Love '52

Edda Barends
Broken Mirrors '85
Question of Silence '83

Lynn Bari (1913-89)
Trauma '62
Abbott and Costello Meet the Keystone Kops '54
Francis Joins the WACs '54
I Dream of Jeannie '52
I'd Climb the Highest Mountain '51
The Amazing Mr. X '48
Nocturne '46
Shock! '46
The Bridge of San Luis Rey '44
Hello, Frisco, Hello '43
The Magnificent Dope '42
Orchestra Wives '42
Sun Valley Serenade '41
Kit Carson '40

Natalie Barish
Lost and Found '99
Round Numbers '91

Sophie Barjae
Alice '86
Holiday Hotel '77

Yehuda Barkan
The Big Gag '87
Lupo '70

Clive Barker (1952-)
Quicksilver Highway '98
Sleepwalkers '92

Jess Barker (1912-2000)
Kentucky Rifle '55
Shack Out on 101 '55
Dragonfly Squadron '54

Lex Barker (1919-73)
The Torture Chamber of Dr. Sadism '69
Woman Times Seven '67
A Place Called Glory '66
Apache's Last Battle '64
Executioner of Venice '63
The Invisible Dr. Mabuse '62
Pirates of the Coast '61
The Return of Dr. Mabuse '61
La Dolce Vita '60
Mission in Morocco '59
Strange Awakening '58
Girl in Black Stockings '57
Away All Boats '56
The Black Devils of Kali '55
Mr. Blandings Builds His Dream House '48
Velvet Touch '48
The Farmer's Daughter '47

Ronnie Barker (1929-)
Porridge '91
Open All Hours '83
Robin and Marian '76
The Man Outside '68

Steve Barkett
Bikini Drive-In '94
Dark Universe '93
Dinosaur Island '93
Aftermath '85

Ellen Barkin (1955-)
Someone Like You '01
Crime and Punishment in Suburbia '00
Mercy '00
Drop Dead Gorgeous '99
White River '99
Fear and Loathing in Las Vegas '98
The Fan '96
Trigger Happy '96
Wild Bill '95
Bad Company '94
Mac '93
This Boy's Life '93
Into the West '92
Man Trouble '92
Switch '91
Johnny Handsome '89
Sea of Love '89
Blood Money: The Story of Clinton and Nadine '88
The Big Easy '87
Made in Heaven '87
Siesta '87
Act of Vengeance '86
Desert Bloom '86
Down by Law '86
Terminal Choice '85
The Adventures of Buckaroo Banzai Across the Eighth Dimension '84
Harry & Son '84
The Princess Who Never Laughed '84
Daniel '83
Eddie and the Cruisers '83
Enormous Changes '83
Tender Mercies '83
Trumps '83
Diner '82
Kent State '81

Marcie Barkin
Fade to Black '80
Chesty Anderson USN '76

Peter Barkworth (1929-)
Champions '84
The Littlest Horse Thieves '76
Where Eagles Dare '68

Ivor Barnard (1887-1953)
Beat the Devil '53
Madeleine '50

Binnie Barnes (1903-98)
Forty Carats '73
Where Angels Go, Trouble Follows '68
The Trouble with Angels '66
Decameron Nights '53
The Time of Their Lives '46
It's in the Bag '45
The Spanish Main '45
Call Out the Marines '42
I Married an Angel '42
In Old California '42
Melody Master '41
The Three Musketeers '39
The Adventures of Marco Polo '38
The Divorce of Lady X '38
Holiday '38
Broadway Melody of 1938 '37
The Last of the Mohicans '36
Three Smart Girls '36
Private Life of Don Juan '34
The Private Life of Henry VIII '33

Chris Barnes
The Ebb-Tide '97
The Bad News Bears in Breaking Training '77
The Bad News Bears '76

Christopher Barnes
Angel of Fury '93
Battle of the Bullies '85
Tut & Tuttle '82

Christopher Daniel Barnes (1972-)
A Very Brady Sequel '96
The Brady Bunch Movie '95
Murder Without Motive '92
The Little Mermaid '89 (V)

Joanna Barnes (1934-)
Kill My Wife...Please!
The Parent Trap '98
I Wonder Who's Killing Her Now? '76
The War Wagon '67
Goodbye Charlie '64
The Parent Trap '61
Spartacus '60

Priscilla Barnes (1955-)
Alone with a Stranger '99
Final Payback '99
Catherine's Grove '98
Implicated '98
The Killing Grounds '97
Mallrats '95
Ava's Magical Adventure '94
The Crossing Guard '94
Erotique '94
National Lampoon's Attack of the 5 Ft. 2 Women '94
Body Trouble '92
Stepfather 3: Father's Day '92
Talons of the Eagle '92
License to Kill '89
Lords of the Deep '89
Traxx '87
The Last Married Couple in America '80
The Seniors '78
Time Machine '78
Beyond Reason '77
Delta Fox '77
Texas Detour '77

Susan Barnes
Nurse Betty '00
Where the Money Is '00
Lover Girl '97
One Night Stand '97
Nothing to Lose '96

Serving in Silence: The Margarethe Cammermeyer Story '95
The Applegates '89
Charlie Barnett (1954-)
They Bite '95
My Man Adam '86
Nobody's Fool '86
D.C. Cab '84
Chester Barnett (1885-1947)
Trilby '17
The Wishing Ring '14
Vince Barnett (1902-77)
Charade '53
Red Planet Mars '52
Thunder in the Pines '49
Shoot to Kill '47
Captive Wild Woman '43
Baby Face Morgan '42
The Corpse Vanishes '42
I Killed That Man '42
X Marks the Spot '42
Gangs, Inc. '41
Ride 'Em Cowgirl '41
The Singing Cowgirl '39
Boots of Destiny '37
We're in the Legion Now '37
Yellow Cargo '36
I Live My Life '35
Crimson Romance '34
The Death Kiss '33
The Prizefighter and the Lady '33
Jean Marie Barnwell
Blue River '95
Born to Be Wild '95
From the Mixed-Up Files of Mrs. Basil E. Frankweiler '95
Bruce Baron
Ninja Champion '80s
Ninja Hunt '80s
Ninja Destroyer '70s
Fireback '78
Joannne Baron
Hard Luck '01
Perfume '01
St. Patrick's Day '99
Pet Shop '94
Crazy in Love '92
Lynda Baron
Open All Hours '83
Hot Millions '68
Sandy Baron (1937-2001)
Leprechaun 2 '94
Motorama '91
Vamp '86
Birdy '84
Broadway Danny Rose '84
The Out-of-Towners '70
If It's Tuesday, This Must Be Belgium '69
Sweet November '68
Targets '68
Elizabeth Barondes
Love to Kill '97
Adrenalin: Fear the Rush '96
Not of This Earth '96
Full Body Massage '95
Night of the Scarecrow '95
Byron Barr (1917-66)
Down Dakota Way '49
Pitfall '48
Big Town '47
Love Letters '45
Double Indemnity '44
Douglas Barr (1949-)
Spaced Invaders '90
Deadly Blessing '81
Jean-Marc Barr (1960-)
Dancer in the Dark '99
Don't Let Me Die on a Sunday '98
Robert Louis Stevenson's St. Ives '98
The Scarlet Tunic '97
Breaking the Waves '95
The Favorite Son '94
The Plague '92
Zentropa '92
The Big Blue '88
Hope and Glory '87
Patrick Barr (1908-85)
The Godsend '79
House of Whipcord '75
Flesh and Blood Show '73
The Satanic Rites of Dracula '73
The Case of the Frightened Lady '39
Sailing Along '38
Sharon Barr
The Reluctant Agent '95
Spittin' Image '83
Archer: The Fugitive from the Empire '81
Gianfranco Barra
Screw Loose '99
Avanti! '72
Maria Barranco (1961-)
Mouth to Mouth '95
Zafarinas '94
The Red Squirrel '93
Don Juan, My Love '90
Tie Me Up! Tie Me Down! '90
Women on the Verge of a Nervous Breakdown '88
Robert Barrat (1889-1970)
Distant Drums '51
Magnificent Doll '46
The Road to Utopia '46
Strangler of the Swamp '46
They Were Expendable '45
The Adventures of Mark Twain '44
Captain Caution '40
Go West '40
Northwest Passage '40
Bad Lands '39
Union Pacific '39
Shadows over Shanghai '38
The Texans '38
The Black Legion '37
The Charge of the Light Brigade '36
Mary of Scotland '36
The Trail of the Lonesome Pine '36
Devil Dogs of the Air '35
Heroes for Sale '33
Jean-Louis Barrault (1910-94)
La Nuit de Varennes '82
The Longest Day '62
The Testament of Dr. Cordelier '59
La Ronde '51
Children of Paradise '44
Beethoven '36
Marie-Christine Barrault (1944-)
Jesus of Montreal '89
Le Jupon Rouge '87
Swann in Love '84
Table for Five '83
Stardust Memories '80
L'Etat Sauvage '78
The Medusa Touch '78
Perceval '78
Cousin, Cousine '76
The Daydreamer '75
Chloe in the Afternoon '72
My Night at Maud's '69
Edith Barrett (1907-77)
Jane Eyre '44
I Walked with a Zombie '43
Lady for a Night '42
Jane Barrett (1923-69)
The Sword & the Rose '53
Eureka Stockade '49
John Barrett
To the Death '93
American Kickboxer 1 '91
Lights! Camera! Murder! '89
Judith Barrett (1914-)
The Road to Singapore '40
Yellowstone '36
Majel Barrett (1939-)
Mommy '95
Star Trek: Generations '94 (V)
Teresa's Tattoo '94
Star Trek 4: The Voyage Home '86
Star Trek: The Motion Picture '80
Westworld '73
Nancy Barrett (1941-)
Belizaire the Cajun '86
Night of Dark Shadows '71
House of Dark Shadows '70
Nitchie Barrett
A Time to Die '91
Preppies '82
Ray Barrett (1927-)
In the Winter Dark '98
Heaven's Burning '97
Brilliant Lies '96
Hotel de Love '96
Sorrento Beach '95
Rebel '85
Where the Green Ants Dream '84
Waterfront '83
Don's Party '76
Revenge '71
The Reptile '66
Sean Barrett
Sink the Bismarck '60
War and Peace '56
Tony Barrett
Impact '49
Dick Tracy Meets Gruesome '47
Barbara Barrie (1931-)
Spent '00
Judy Berlin '99
Hercules '97 (V)
Scarlett '94
End of the Line '88
Real Men '87
The Execution '85
Two of a Kind '82
Private Benjamin '80
To Race the Wind '80
The Bell Jar '79
Breaking Away '79
Child of Glass '78
Judith Barrie
Hidden Gold '33
Party Girls '29
Mona Barrie (1909-64)
Cass Timberlane '47
Dawn on the Great Divide '42
Today I Hang '42
One Night of Love '34
Wendy Barrie (1912-78)
The Saint Strikes Back: Criminal Court '46
Follies Girl '43
The Saint Takes Over '40
Five Came Back '39
The Hound of the Baskervilles '39
The Saint Strikes Back '39
I Am the Law '38
Dead End '37
Vengeance '37
If I Were Rich '33
The Private Life of Henry VIII '33
Wedding Rehearsal '32
Edgar Barrier (1907-64)
The Giant Claw '57
Cobra Woman '44
The Phantom of the Opera '43
Arabian Nights '42
Pat (Barringer) Barrington
Mantis in Lace '68
The Acid Eaters '67
Agony of Love '66
Orgy of the Dead '65
Phyllis Barrington
Sucker Money '34
The Drifter '32
Desmond Barrit
A Christmas Carol '99
A Midsummer Night's Dream '96
Bob Barron
Ballad of a Gunfighter '64
Tank Commando '59
Sea Hound '47
The Caravan Trail '46
Song of Old Wyoming '45
Guns of the Law '44
Dana Barron
The Perfect Nanny '00
The Man in the Iron Mask '97
National Lampoon's Vacation '83
Keith Barron (1936-)
Madame Bovary '00
Catherine Cookson's The Round Tower '98
Con Man '92
At the Earth's Core '76
Nothing But the Night '72
Baby Love '69
Robert V. Barron (1932-2000)
Bill & Ted's Excellent Adventure '89
Daddy's Boys '87
George Barrows
Hillbillies in a Haunted House '67
Robot Monster '53
Barta Barry
Dr. Jekyll and the Wolfman '71
Gladiators 7 '62
Bruce Barry (1934-)
The Good Wife '86
Plunge Into Darkness '77
Donald (Don "Red") Barry (1912-80)
Blazing Stewardesses '75
Texas Layover '75
Johnny Got His Gun '71
Hard Frame '70
The Shakiest Gun in the West '68
Hostile Guns '67
Iron Angel '64
Born Reckless '59
Square Dance Jubilee '51
Border Rangers '50
Gunfire '50
I Shot Billy the Kid '50
Red Desert '50
Train to Tombstone '50
Outlaw Gang '49
Ringside '49
Tough Assignment '49
Trail of the Mounties '47
The Purple Heart '44
California Joe '43
Sundown Kid '43
The Sombrero Kid '42
Sundown Fury '42
Adventures of Red Ryder '40
Frontier Vengeance '40
Days of Jesse James '39
Panama Patrol '39
Saga of Death Valley '39
Wyoming Outlaw '39
The Duke of West Point '38
Sinners in Paradise '38
Gene Barry (1922-)
These Old Broads '01
The Gambler Returns: The Luck of the Draw '93
Perry Mason: The Case of the Lost Love '87
The Adventures of Nellie Bly '81
A Cry for Love '80
Second Coming of Suzanne '80
Suzanne '80
Subterfuge '68
Columbo: Prescription Murder '67
Maroc 7 '67
Thunder Road '58
China Gate '57
The 27th Day '57
Back from Eternity '56
Soldier of Fortune '55
Red Garters '54
The War of the Worlds '53
The Atomic City '52
Jason Barry (1975-)
When the Sky Falls '99
Monument Ave. '98
The Last of the High Kings '96
Neill Barry (1965-)
Friends & Lovers '99
O.C. and Stiggs '87
Joey '85
Old Enough '84
Patricia Barry (1930-)
Twilight Zone: The Movie '83
Bogie: The Last Hero '80
Kitten with a Whip '64
Sammy, the Way-Out Seal '62
Riders of the Whistling Pines '49
Cry Wolf '47
Phyllis Barry (1909-)
Goodbye Love '34
What! No Beer? '33
Raymond J. Barry (1939-)
The Deep End '01
Training Day '01
Best Men '98
Flubber '97
The Chamber '96
Headless Body in Topless Bar '96
Dead Man Walking '95
Sudden Death '95
Cool Runnings '93
Falling Down '93
The Ref '93
K2: The Ultimate High '92
Rapid Fire '92
The Turning '92
Born on the Fourth of July '89
Cop '88
Daddy's Boys '87
Year of the Dragon '85
Christmas Evil '80
Thom Barry
The Fast and the Furious '01
Major League 3: Back to the Minors '98
Steel '97
Toni Barry
Proteus '95
A House in the Hills '93
Tony Barry
Paperback Hero '99
Doing Time for Patsy Cline '97
Road to Nhill '97
Shame '87
The Quest '86
We of the Never Never '82
Goodbye Pork Pie '81
Hard Knocks '80
The Odd Angry Shot '79
Little Boy Lost '78
Wendy Barry
Evil Lives '92
Knights of the City '85
Wesley Barry (1907-94)
Sunny Skies '30
Battling Bunyon '24
The Country Kid '23
Drew Barrymore (1975-)
Donnie Darko '01
Riding in Cars with Boys '01
Charlie's Angels '00
Skipped Parts '00
Titan A.E. '00 (V)
Never Been Kissed '99
Best Men '98
Ever After: A Cinderella Story '98
Home Fries '98
The Wedding Singer '97
Everyone Says I Love You '96
Scream '96
Wishful Thinking '96
Batman Forever '95
Mad Love '95
Bad Girls '94
Boys on the Side '94
The Amy Fisher Story '93
No Place to Hide '93
Wayne's World 2 '93
Guncrazy '92
Poison Ivy '92
Sketch Artist '92
Motorama '91
Waxwork 2: Lost in Time '91
Doppelganger: The Evil Within '90
Far from Home '89
See You in the Morning '89
A Conspiracy of Love '87
Babes in Toyland '86
Cat's Eye '85
Firestarter '84
Irreconcilable Differences '84
E.T.: The Extra-Terrestrial '82
Altered States '80
Ethel Barrymore (1879-1959)
Young at Heart '54
Main Street to Broadway '53
Just for You '52
Pinky '49
That Midnight Kiss '49
Moonrise '48
Portrait of Jennie '48
The Farmer's Daughter '47
The Paradine Case '47
The Spiral Staircase '46
None But the Lonely Heart '44
Rasputin and the Empress '33
John Barrymore (1882-1942)
Playmates '41
The Invisible Woman '40
Midnight '39
Bulldog Drummond's Peril '38
The Great Man Votes '38
Marie Antoinette '38
Spawn of the North '38
Bulldog Drummond Comes Back '37
Bulldog Drummond's Revenge '37
Maytime '37
Romeo and Juliet '36
Twentieth Century '34
Dinner at Eight '33
Rasputin and the Empress '33
Topaze '33
A Bill of Divorcement '32
Grand Hotel '32
State's Attorney '31
Svengali '31
The Tempest '28
The Beloved Rogue '27
Don Juan '26
Beau Brummel '24
Dr. Jekyll and Mr. Hyde '20
John Blythe Barrymore, Jr. (1932-)
Americana '81
Smokey Bites the Dust '81
The Trojan Horse '62
High School Confidential '58
Never Love a Stranger '58
High Lonesome '50
Lionel Barrymore (1878-1954)
Main Street to Broadway '53
Lone Star '52
Malaya '49
Key Largo '48
Duel in the Sun '46
It's a Wonderful Life '46
The Valley of Decision '45
A Guy Named Joe '44
Since You Went Away '44
Thousands Cheer '43
Lady Be Good '41
Dr. Kildare's Strange Case '40
Let Freedom Ring '39

On Borrowed Time '39
Test Pilot '38
You Can't Take It with You '38
Captains Courageous '37
Navy Blue and Gold '37
Saratoga '37
Camille '36
Devil Doll '36
The Gorgeous Hussy '36
Ah, Wilderness! '35
David Copperfield '35
The Little Colonel '35
Mark of the Vampire '35
The Return of Peter Grimm '35
The Girl from Missouri '34
Treasure Island '34
Dinner at Eight '33
Rasputin and the Empress '33
Grand Hotel '32
Mata Hari '32
A Free Soul '31
Free and Easy '30
Sadie Thompson '28
West of Zanzibar '28
The Bells '26
America '24

Judith Barsi (1977-88)
All Dogs Go to Heaven '89 (V)
The Land Before Time '88 (V)
Jaws: The Revenge '87

Paul Bartel (1938-2000)
Hamlet '00
Billy's Hollywood Screen Kiss '98
Armistead Maupin's More Tales of the City '97
Lewis and Clark and George '97
Basquiat '96
Skeletons '96
The Death Artist '95
The Jerky Boys '95
The Usual Suspects '95
Grief '94
Number One Fan '94
Acting on Impulse '93
Armistead Maupin's Tales of the City '93
Posse '93
Desire and Hell at Sunset Motel '92
Evil Lives '92
Liquid Dreams '92
Mortuary Academy '91
The Pope Must Diet '91
Gremlins 2: The New Batch '90
Far Out Man '89
Pucker Up and Bark Like a Dog '89
Scenes from the Class Struggle in Beverly Hills '89
Out of the Dark '88
Amazon Women on the Moon '87
Munchies '87
Chopping Mall '86
Killer Party '86
Into the Night '85
Frankenweenie '84
Get Crazy '83
Eating Raoul '82
Trick or Treats '82
Heartbeeps '81
Rock 'n' Roll High School '79
Piranha '78
Grand Theft Auto '77
Cannonball '76
Eat My Dust '76
Hollywood Boulevard '76

Eddie Barth (1931-)
Mr. Write '92
Twenty Dollar Star '91
Thunder and Lightning '77

Richard Barthelmess (1895-1963)
The Spoilers '42
Only Angels Have Wings '39
Spy of Napoleon '36
Heroes for Sale '33
The Cabin in the Cotton '32
The Dropkick '27
Just Suppose '26
Ranson's Folly '26
Shore Leave '25
Soul-Fire '25
Tol'able David '21
The Idol Dancer '20
The Love Flower '20
Way Down East '20
Broken Blossoms '19

Freddie Bartholomew (1924-92)
St. Benny the Dip '51
Sepia Cinderella '47
Tom Brown's School Days '40
Listen, Darling '38
Captains Courageous '37
Little Lord Fauntleroy '36
Lloyds of London '36
Anna Karenina '35
David Copperfield '35

Lynsey Bartilson
A Rat's Tale '98 (V)
Mrs. Santa Claus '96

Bennie Bartlett (1927-)
Bowery Boys Meet the Monsters '54
Clipped Wings '53
Master Minds '49

Bonnie Bartlett (1929-)
Shiloh 2: Shiloh Season '99
Tuesdays with Morrie '99
Primary Colors '98
Shiloh '97
Dave '93
Dead to Rights '93
Twins '88
The Deliberate Stranger '86
Dempsey '83
Love Letters '83
A Long Way Home '81
Rape and Marriage: The Rideout Case '80

Robin Bartlett (1951-)
City of Angels '98
Honey, We Shrunk Ourselves '97
Dangerous Minds '95
Fallen Angels 1 '93
Deceived '91
If Looks Could Kill '91
Regarding Henry '91
Alice '90
Postcards from the Edge '90
Lean on Me '89
Baby Boom '87

Eva Bartok (1926-98)
Blood and Black Lace '64
Operation Amsterdam '60
S.O.S. Pacific '60
Naked in the Night '58
The Gamma People '56
Norman Conquest '53
Spaceways '53
Crimson Pirate '52

Luciano Bartoli
Bizarre '87
Henry IV '85

Buzz Barton (1913-90)
The Riding Avenger '36
Feud of the West '35
Powdersmoke Range '35
The Tonto Kid '35
The Lone Defender '32
Mystery Trooper '32
Apache Kid's Escape '30

Charles T. Barton (1902-81)
Beau Geste '39
The Fighting Westerner '35

Diana Barton
Body of Influence '93
Sexual Malice '93

Gregg Barton
Silver City Bonanza '51
West to Glory '47

James Barton (1890-1962)
The Misfits '61
Naked Hills '56
Here Comes the Groom '51
The Time of Your Life '48
The Shepherd of the Hills '41

Mischa Barton (1986-)
Lost and Delirious '01
Tart '01
Skipped Parts '00
Pups '99
The Sixth Sense '99
Lawn Dogs '96

Peter Barton (1956-)
Friday the 13th, Part 4: The Final Chapter '84
Hell Night '81

Skye McCole Bartusiak
Firestarter 2: Rekindled '02
Don't Say a Word '01
Riding in Cars with Boys '01

Billy Barty (1924-2000)
Wishful Thinking '92
Digging Up Business '91
Life Stinks '91
Lobster Man from Mars '89
Snow White '89
UHF '89
Willow '88
Body Slam '87
Masters of the Universe '87
Legend '86
Rumpelstiltskin '86
Tough Guys '86
Night Patrol '85
Under the Rainbow '81
Foul Play '78
The Amazing Dobermans '76
The Day of the Locust '75
Pufnstuf '70
Harum Scarum '65
Roustabout '64
The Undead '57
Mickey the Great '39
The Bride of Frankenstein '35
A Midsummer Night's Dream '35

Leon Bary (1880-1954)
King of the Wild Horses '24
The Three Musketeers '21

Mikhail Baryshnikov (1948-)
Company Business '91
Dancers '87
That's Dancing! '85
White Nights '85
The Turning Point '77

Gary Basaraba (1959-)
Unfaithful '02
Dead Silence '96
A Horse for Danny '95
The War '94
Fried Green Tomatoes '91
Midnight Murders '91
One Magic Christmas '85
Sweet Dreams '85

Dante Basco (1975-)
Extremedays '01
Riot in the Streets '96
Hook '91

Richard Basehart (1914-84)
Marilyn: The Untold Story '80
Being There '79
The Rebels '79
Great Bank Hoax '78
The Island of Dr. Moreau '77
Flood! '76
The Bounty Man '72
Rage '72
Chato's Land '71
The Andersonville Trial '70
Hans Brinker '69
Hitler '62
Portrait in Black '60
The Brothers Karamazov '58
Moby Dick '56
Il Bidone '55
La Strada '54
Titanic '53
Reign of Terror '49
He Walked by Night '48
Cry Wolf '47

Count Basie (1904-84)
Blazing Saddles '74
Sex and the Single Girl '64
Cinderfella '60
Stage Door Canteen '43

Toni Basil (1948-)
Eating '90
Rockula '90
Angel 3: The Final Chapter '88
Slaughterhouse Rock '88
Mother, Jugs and Speed '76
Easy Rider '69
Pajama Party '64

Kim Basinger (1953-)
Bless the Child '00
I Dreamed of Africa '00
L.A. Confidential '97
Ready to Wear '94
The Getaway '93
The Real McCoy '93
Wayne's World 2 '93
Cool World '92
Final Analysis '92
The Marrying Man '91
Batman '89
My Stepmother Is an Alien '88
Blind Date '87
Nadine '87
Fool for Love '86
9 1/2 Weeks '86
No Mercy '86
The Natural '84
The Man Who Loved Women '83
Never Say Never Again '83
Mother Lode '82
Hard Country '81
Killjoy '81
From Here to Eternity '79

Elya Baskin (1951-)
Thirteen Days '00
Air Force One '97
Spy Trap '92
Deepstar Six '89
Enemies, a Love Story '89
The Name of the Rose '86
Moscow on the Hudson '84

Antoine Basler
Irma Vep '96
Rendezvous in Paris '95

Marianne Basler
Va Savoir '01
A Soldier's Tale '91
Overseas: Three Women with Man Trouble '90

Lena Basquette (1907-94)
Heroes of the Heart '94
Paradise Park '91
A Night for Crime '42
Rose of Rio Grande '38
Hello Trouble '32
Arizona Terror '31
Hard Hombre '31
Pleasure '31

Alfie Bass (1921-87)
The Fearless Vampire Killers '67
Alfie '66
Help! '65
The Lavender Hill Mob '51
Man on the Run '49

Bobby Bass (1936-2001)
The Squeeze '87
Blood Beach '81

Tamara La Seon Bass
Baby Boy '01
Bellyfruit '99

Albert Bassermann (1862-1952)
The Red Shoes '48
The Private Affairs of Bel Ami '47
Rhapsody in Blue '45
Since You Went Away '44
Madame Curie '43
The Moon and Sixpence '43
Invisible Agent '42
Reunion in France '42
The Shanghai Gesture '42
Melody Master '41
A Woman's Face '41
Foreign Correspondent '40

Angela Bassett (1958-)
Sunshine State '02
The Score '01
Boesman & Lena '00
Whispers: An Elephant's Tale '00 (V)
Music of the Heart '99
Supernova '99
How Stella Got Her Groove Back '98
Contact '97
Strange Days '95
Vampire in Brooklyn '95
Waiting to Exhale '95
What's Love Got to Do with It? '93
Innocent Blood '92
The Jacksons: An American Dream '92
Malcolm X '92
Passion Fish '92
Boyz N the Hood '91
City of Hope '91
Critters 4 '91
The Heroes of Desert Storm '91
F/X '86

Linda Bassett
Beautiful People '99
East Is East '99
Oscar and Lucinda '97
Mary Reilly '95
Waiting for the Moon '87

Steve Bassett
The Jackal '97
Spring Break '83

Alexandra Bastedo (1946-)
Draw! '81
Find the Lady '75
The Ghoul '75
The Blood Spattered Bride '72
Kashmiri Run '69

Billy Bastiani
Blood & Concrete: A Love Story '90
Salvation! '87

Steve Bastoni
Rodgers & Hammerstein's South Pacific '01
Dr. Jekyll & Mr. Hyde '99

Othon Bastos (1933-)
Behind the Sun '01
Central Station '98
Antonio Das Mortes '68
Black God, White Devil '64

Michal Bat-Adam
The Impossible Spy '87
Atalia '85
Madame Rosa '77
Rachel's Man '75
The House on Chelouche Street '73
I Love You Rosa '72

Sylvia Bataille (1908-93)
A Day in the Country '46
The Crime of Monsieur Lange '36

Alexei Batalov (1928-)
Moscow Does Not Believe in Tears '80
The Lady with the Dog '59
The Cranes Are Flying '57

Nikolai Batalov (1899-1937)
The Road to Life '31
Bed and Sofa '27
Mother '26
Aelita: Queen of Mars '24

Pierre Batcheff (1901-32)
Un Chien Andalou '28
Napoleon '27

Anthony Bate
Philby, Burgess and MacLean: Spy Scandal of the Century '84
Madhouse Mansion '74

Jason Bateman (1969-)
The Sweetest Thing '02
Love Stinks '99
Breaking the Rules '92
A Taste for Killing '92
Necessary Roughness '91
Teen Wolf Too '87
Can You Feel Me Dancing? '85

Justine Bateman (1966-)
Kiss & Tell '99
The Night We Never Met '93
Deadbolt '92
Primary Motive '92
The Closer '91
The Fatal Image '90
Satisfaction '88
Can You Feel Me Dancing? '85

Alan Bates (1934-)
The Mothman Prophecies '02
The Sum of All Fears '02
Gosford Park '01
The Prince and the Pauper '01
Arabian Nights '00
St. Patrick: The Irish Legend '00
Grave Indiscretions '96
Silent Tongue '92
Unnatural Pursuits '91
Hamlet '90
Club Extinction '89
Mr. Frost '89
A Voyage 'Round My Father '89
We Think the World of You '88
Prayer for the Dying '87
Duet for One '86
Trespasser '85
An Englishman Abroad '83
Separate Tables '83
The Wicked Lady '83
Britannia Hospital '82
Return of the Soldier '82
Quartet '81
Nijinsky '80
The Rose '79
The Shout '78
An Unmarried Woman '78
In Celebration '75
Royal Flash '75
The Story of Jacob & Joseph '74 (N)
The Story of a Love Story '73
A Day in the Death of Joe Egg '71
The Go-Between '71
Women in Love '70
The Fixer '68
Far from the Madding Crowd '67
Georgy Girl '66
The King of Hearts '66
Zorba the Greek '64
A Kind of Loving '62
Whistle down the Wind '61
The Entertainer '60

Barbara Bates (1925-69)
Rhapsody '54
The Caddy '53
I'd Climb the Highest Mountain '51
Let's Make It Legal '51
Cheaper by the Dozen '50
The Inspector General '49
June Bride '48

Florence Bates (1888-1954)
Lullaby of Broadway '51
The Judge Steps Out '49

A Letter to Three Wives *'49*
My Dear Secretary *'49*
I Remember Mama *'48*
Portrait of Jennie *'48*
Winter Meeting *'48*
The Secret Life of Walter Mitty *'47*
Diary of a Chambermaid *'46*
San Antonio *'45*
Saratoga Trunk *'45*
His Butler's Sister *'44*
The Mask of Dimitrios *'44*
Since You Went Away *'44*
Heaven Can Wait *'43*
Mr. Lucky *'43*
The Moon and Sixpence *'43*
Mexican Spitfire at Sea *'42*
The Tuttles of Tahiti *'42*
The Chocolate Soldier *'41*
Love Crazy *'41*
Road Show *'41*
Rebecca *'40*
The Son of Monte Cristo *'40*

Granville Bates (1882-1940)
My Favorite Wife *'40*
The Great Man Votes *'38*
Next Time I Marry *'38*
Waikiki Wedding *'37*

Jeanne Bates (1918-)
Mom *'89*
Eraserhead *'78*
The Strangler *'64*
Sabaka *'55*
The Mask of Diijon *'46*

Kathy Bates (1948-)
Dragonfly *'02*
My Sister's Keeper *'02*
American Outlaws *'01*
Annie *'99*
The Dress Code *'99*
Primary Colors *'98*
The Waterboy *'98*
Swept from the Sea *'97*
Titanic *'97*
Diabolique *'96*
The Late Shift *'96*
The War at Home *'96*
Angus *'95*
Curse of the Starving Class *'94*
Dolores Claiborne *'94*
North *'94*
Stephen King's The Stand *'94*
A Home of Our Own *'93*
Hostages *'93*
Prelude to a Kiss *'92*
Shadows and Fog *'92*
Used People *'92*
At Play in the Fields of the Lord *'91*
Fried Green Tomatoes *'91*
Dick Tracy *'90*
Misery *'90*
White Palace *'90*
High Stakes *'89*
Men Don't Leave *'89*
Roe vs. Wade *'89*
Signs of Life *'89*
My Best Friend Is a Vampire *'88*
Murder Ordained *'87*
Summer Heat *'87*
The Morning After *'86*
Come Back to the Five & Dime Jimmy Dean, Jimmy Dean *'82*
Straight Time *'78*

Michael Bates (1920-78)
No Sex Please—We're British *'73*
Frenzy *'72*
A Clockwork Orange *'71*
Patton *'70*
Bedazzled *'68*

Paul Bates
Instinct *'99*
The Preacher's Wife *'96*
Mr. Wonderful *'93*
True Romance *'93*
Crazy People *'90*
Coming to America *'88*

Ralph Bates (1940-91)
Letters to an Unknown Lover *'84*
Second Chance *'80*
I Don't Want to Be Born *'75*
Poldark *'75*
Poldark 2 *'75*
The Graveyard *'74*
Murder Motel *'74*
Dynasty of Fear *'72*
Dr. Jekyll and Sister Hyde *'71*
Lust for a Vampire *'71*
The Horror of Frankenstein *'70*
Taste the Blood of Dracula *'70*

R.C. Bates
Werewolf *'95*
...And God Spoke *'94*

Timothy Bateson (1926-)
The 10th Kingdom *'00*
Joseph *'95*
Heart of Darkness *'93*
The Mouse That Roared *'59*
The Guinea Pig *'48*

Randall Batinkoff (1968-)
The Last Marshal *'99*
Let the Devil Wear Black *'99*
Heartwood *'98*
As Good As It Gets *'97*
The Curve *'97*
The Peacemaker *'97*
Walking and Talking *'96*
Christy *'94*
Buffy the Vampire Slayer *'92*
The Player *'92*
School Ties *'92*
For Keeps *'88*
Streetwalkin' *'85*

Stiv Bators
Tapeheads *'89*
Polyester *'81*

Susan Batson
Bamboozled *'00*
Girl 6 *'96*

Matt Battaglia
Universal Soldier 2: Brothers in Arms *'98*
Universal Soldier 3: Unfinished Business *'98*
Raven *'97*

Rick Battaglia (1930-)
'Tis a Pity She's a Whore *'73*
Cold Steel for Tortuga *'65*
Apache's Last Battle *'64*
Roland the Mighty *'58*

Cyia Batten
At Any Cost *'00*
Red Shoe Diaries: Swimming Naked *'00*
Sins of the Mind *'97*

Hinton Battle
Child Star: The Shirley Temple Story *'01*
Foreign Student *'94*

Patrick Bauchau (1938-)
Panic Room *'02*
Secretary *'02*
Jackpot *'01 (V)*
The Cell *'00*
Twin Falls Idaho *'99*
Serpent's Lair *'95*
Lisbon Story *'94*
The New Age *'94*
Acting on Impulse *'93*
And the Band Played On *'93*
Chain of Desire *'93*
Every Breath *'93*
Blood Ties *'92*
The Rapture *'91*
Terranova *'91*
Double Identity *'89*
The Music Teacher *'88*
Creepers *'85*
Choose Me *'84*
Emmanuelle 4 *'84*
Entre-Nous *'83*
State of Things *'82*
La Collectionneuse *'67*

Vanessa Bauche
Amores Perros *'00*
Highway Patrolman *'91*

Belinda Bauer (1951-)
Poison Ivy 2: Lily *'95*
A Case for Murder *'93*
H.P. Lovecraft's Necronomicon: Book of the Dead *'93*
Servants of Twilight *'91*
The Game of Love *'90*
RoboCop 2 *'90*
Act of Piracy *'89*
The Rosary Murders *'87*
Samson and Delilah *'84*
Flashdance *'83*
Timerider *'83*
The Sins of Dorian Gray *'82*
Archer: The Fugitive from the Empire *'81*
Winter Kills *'79*

Chris Bauer
61* *'01*
Flawless *'99*
The Hunley *'99*
8mm *'98*

Michelle (McClellan) Bauer (1958-)
Assault of the Party Nerds 2: Heavy Petting Detective *'95*
Attack of the 60-Foot Centerfold *'95*
Vampire Vixens from Venus *'94*
Dinosaur Island *'93*
Evil Toons *'90*
Assault of the Party Nerds *'89*
Lady Avenger *'89*
Wild Man *'89*
Beverly Hills Vamp *'88*
Deadly Embrace *'88*
Death Row Diner *'88*
Hollywood Chainsaw Hookers *'88*
Night of the Living Babes *'87*
Nightmare Sisters *'87*
Phantom Empire *'87*
Sorority Babes in the Slimeball Bowl-A-Rama *'87*
Tomb *'86*
Roller Blade *'85*
Screen Test *'85*

Steven Bauer (1956-)
The Learning Curve *'01*
Along for the Ride *'00*
For Love or Country: The Arturo Sandoval Story *'00*
Traffic *'00*
Bloody Proof *'99*
Boss of Bosses *'99*
Naked Lies *'98*
Navajo Blues *'97*
Star Portal *'97*
Plato's Run *'96*
Primal Fear *'96*
Body Count *'95*
Wild Side *'95*
Improper Conduct *'94*
Star Quest *'94*
Stranger by Night *'94*
Snapdragon *'93*
Woman of Desire *'93*
False Arrest *'92*
Raising Cain *'92*
Red Shoe Diaries 2: Double Dare *'92*
A Climate for Killing *'91*
Sweet Poison *'91*
Gleaming the Cube *'89*
The Beast *'88*
Wildfire *'88*
Running Scared *'86*
Sword of Gideon *'86*
Thief of Hearts *'84*
Scarface *'83*

Ricardo Bauleo
Lost Diamond *'74*
The Curious Dr. Humpp *'70*

Kathrine Baumann (1948-)
Slashed Dreams *'74*
The Thing with Two Heads *'72*
Chrome and Hot Leather *'71*

Harry Baur (1880-1943)
Volpone *'39*
Beethoven *'36*
Crime and Punishment *'35*
Poil de Carotte *'31*

Frances Bavier (1902-89)
It Started with a Kiss *'59*
Horizons West *'52*
The Day the Earth Stood Still *'51*
The Lady Says No *'51*
The Stooge *'51*

Barbara Baxley (1923-90)
A Shock to the System *'90*
Come Along with Me *'84*
Nashville *'75*
Countdown *'68*
All Fall Down *'62*

David Baxt
Cloud Waltzing *'87*
The Shining *'80*

George L. Baxt
Which Way to the Front? *'70*
Black Eyes *'39*
Housemaster *'38*
Last Days of Pompeii *'35*

Alan Baxter (1908-76)
Judgment at Nuremberg *'61*
The Set-Up *'49*
She Shoulda Said No *'49*
Behind Prison Walls *'43*
Saboteur *'42*
Shadow of the Thin Man *'41*
Abe Lincoln in Illinois *'40*
Each Dawn I Die *'39*
Wide Open Faces *'38*
It Could Happen to You *'37*

Amy Lynn Baxter
Broadcast Bombshells *'95*
Bikini Bistro *'94*

Anne Baxter (1923-85)
Masks of Death *'86*
East of Eden *'80*
Jane Austen in Manhattan *'80*
Walk on the Wild Side *'62*
Cimarron *'60*
Three Violent People *'57*
The Ten Commandments *'56*
Carnival Story *'54*
I Confess *'53*
All About Eve *'50*
Ticket to Tomahawk *'50*
Homecoming *'48*
Angel on My Shoulder *'46*
The Razor's Edge *'46*
Guest in the House *'44*
Crash Dive *'43*
Five Graves to Cairo *'43*
The North Star *'43*
The Fighting Sullivans *'42*
The Magnificent Ambersons *'42*

Keith Baxter (1933-)
Berlin Blues *'89*
Ash Wednesday *'73*
Chimes at Midnight *'67*

Lynsey Baxter
Cold Light of Day *'95*
The Girl in a Swing *'89*
To the Lighthouse *'83*
The French Lieutenant's Woman *'81*

Meredith Baxter (1947-)
Crash Course *'00*
Till Murder Do Us Part *'92*
Jezebel's Kiss *'90*
The Kissing Place *'90*
Broken Badge *'85*
Take Your Best Shot *'82*
Beulah Land *'80*
The Family Man *'79*
Little Women *'78*
All the President's Men *'76*
Bittersweet Love *'76*
The Invasion of Carol Enders *'74*
The Stranger Who Looks Like Me *'74*
Ben *'72*

Warner Baxter (1891-1951)
Adam Had Four Sons *'41*
Vogues of 1938 *'37*
Broadway Bill *'34*
Stand Up and Cheer *'34*
42nd Street *'33*
Penthouse *'33*
Linda *'29*
West of Zanzibar *'28*

Frances Bay
The Operator *'01*
Goodbye, Lover *'99*
Inspector Gadget *'99*
Changing Habits *'96*
Happy Gilmore *'96*
In the Mouth of Madness *'95*
Inside Monkey Zetterland *'93*
The Neighbor *'93*
Single White Female *'92*
Critters 3 *'91*
The Pit & the Pendulum *'91*
The Attic *'80*

Nathalie Baye (1948-)
An Affair of Love *'99*
Venus Beauty Institute *'98*
The Machine *'96*
And the Band Played On *'93*
Every Other Weekend *'91*
The Man Inside *'90*
Beethoven's Nephew *'88*
Honeymoon *'87*
Detective *'85*
The Return of Martin Guerre *'83*
I Married a Dead Man *'82*
La Balance *'82*
Beau Pere *'81*
The Green Room *'78*
The Man Who Loved Women *'77*
Day for Night *'73*

Gary Bayer
Promised a Miracle *'88*
Not My Kid *'85*
Will: G. Gordon Liddy *'82*

Geoffrey Bayldon (1924-)
Porridge *'91*
Madame Sousatzka *'88*
Cause Celebre *'87*
Asylum *'72*
The Bushbaby *'70*
King Rat *'65*

Hal Baylor (1918-98)
A Boy and His Dog *'75*
Emperor of the North Pole *'73*
The Young Lions *'58*
Sands of Iwo Jima *'49*

Jordan Bayne
A Stranger in the Kingdom *'98*
Poltergeist: The Legacy *'96*

Lawrence Bayne
Getting Gotti *'94*
Lakota Woman: Siege at Wounded Knee *'94*
Black Robe *'91*
A Whisper to a Scream *'88*

Adam Beach (1972-)
Windtalkers *'02*
Joe Dirt *'01*
The Last Stop *'99*
Smoke Signals *'98*
A Boy Called Hate *'95*
Dance Me Outside *'95*
Squanto: A Warrior's Tale *'94*
Cadillac Girls *'93*
Spirit Rider *'93*

Michael Beach
Asunder *'99*
Made Men *'99*
Ruby Bridges *'98*
Casualties *'97*
Ms. Scrooge *'97*
Soul Food *'97*
A Family Thing *'96*
Rebound: The Legend of Earl "The Goat" Manigault *'96*
Waiting to Exhale *'95*
Bad Company *'94*
Sketch Artist 2: Hands That See *'94*
Final Appeal *'93*
True Romance *'93*
One False Move *'91*
Internal Affairs *'90*
Cadence *'89*
Lean on Me *'89*
In a Shallow Grave *'88*
Weekend War *'88*

Stephanie Beacham (1947-)
Wedding Bell Blues *'96*
Foreign Affairs *'93*
The Dying Truth *'91*
Super Bitch *'89*
Troop Beverly Hills *'89*
Riders *'88*
Inseminoid *'80*
Schizo *'77*
The Confessional *'75*
And Now the Screaming Starts *'73*
Dracula A.D. 1972 *'72*
The Nightcomers *'72*

John Beal (1909-97)
The Firm *'93*
The Kid Who Loved Christmas *'90*
Amityville 3: The Demon *'83*
Ten Who Dared *'60*
Edge of Darkness *'43*
The Great Commandment *'41*
I Am the Law *'38*
Double Wedding *'37*
Madame X *'37*
Break of Hearts *'35*
Les Miserables *'35*
Little Minister *'34*

Simon Russell Beale
Hamlet *'96*
Persuasion *'95*

Jennifer Beals (1963-)
The Anniversary Party *'01*
A House Divided *'00*
Militia *'99*
Something More *'99*
Turbulence 2: Fear of Flying *'99*
Body and Soul *'98*
The Last Days of Disco *'98*
The Prophecy 2: Ashtown *'97*
The Twilight of the Golds *'97*
The Spree *'96*
The Thief and the Cobbler *'96 (V)*
Wishful Thinking *'96*
Devil in a Blue Dress *'95*
Four Rooms *'95*
Dead on Sight *'94*
Mrs. Parker and the Vicious Circle *'94*
Day of Atonement *'93*
Terror Stalks the Class Reunion *'93*
In the Soup *'92*
Indecency *'92*
Blood & Concrete: A Love Story *'90*
Club Extinction *'89*
The Gamble *'88*
Split Decisions *'88*
Vampire's Kiss *'88*
The Bride *'85*
That's Dancing! *'85*
Cinderella *'84*
Flashdance *'83*
My Bodyguard *'80*

Lee Ann Beaman
Starved *'97*
Improper Conduct *'94*
Tropical Heat *'93*
The Other Woman *'92*

Orson Bean (1928-)
Being John Malkovich *'99*
Final Judgment *'92*
Instant Karma *'90*

Innerspace '87
Movie Maker '86
The Return of the King '80 (V)
The Hobbit '78 (V)
Lola '69
Anatomy of a Murder '59

Robert Bean
Creature from the Haunted Sea '60
The Wild Ride '60

Sean Bean (1959-)
Don't Say a Word '01
Lord of the Rings 1: The Fellowship of the Rings '01
Essex Boys '99
Extremely Dangerous '99
Airborne '98
Ronin '98
Sharpe's Justice '97
Sharpe's Legend '97
Sharpe's Revenge '97
Sharpe's Waterloo '97
Leo Tolstoy's Anna Karenina '96
Sharpe's Mission '96
Sharpe's Regiment '96
Sharpe's Siege '96
Goldeneye '95
When Saturday Comes '95
Black Beauty '94
Jacob '94
Scarlett '94
Sharpe's Battle '94
Sharpe's Company '94
Sharpe's Enemy '94
Sharpe's Gold '94
Sharpe's Honour '94
Sharpe's Sword '94
Sharpe's Eagle '93
Sharpe's Rifles '93
Shopping '93
A Woman's Guide to Adultery '93
Lady Chatterley '92
Patriot Games '92
Catherine Cookson's The Fifteen Streets '90
The Field '90
Lorna Doone '90
Stormy Monday '88
Troubles '88
Caravaggio '86

Matthew "Stymie" Beard (1925-81)
East of Eden '80
Broken Strings '40
Two-Gun Man from Harlem '38

Amanda Bearse (1958-)
It's a Bundyful Life '92
Fraternity Vacation '85
Fright Night '85
Protocol '84

Emmanuelle Beart (1965-)
La Buche '00
Mission: Impossible '96
Nelly et Monsieur Arnaud '95
L'Enfer '93
Un Coeur en Hiver '93
La Belle Noiseuse '90
Date with an Angel '87
Manon of the Spring '87

Allyce Beasley (1954-)
Dream with the Fishes '97
Entertaining Angels: The Dorothy Day Story '96
Rumpelstiltskin '96
National Lampoon's Loaded Weapon 1 '93
Stephen King's The Tommyknockers '93
Motorama '91
Silent Night, Deadly Night 4: Initiation '90
Moonlighting '85

John Beasley
The Sum of All Fears '02
Freedom Song '00
The Gift '00
Lost Souls '00
Crazy in Alabama '99
The General's Daughter '99
The Apostle '97

Norman Beaton (1934-94)
The Mighty Quinn '89
Playing Away '87
Growing Pains '82

Stephanie Beaton
Witchcraft 10: Mistress of the Craft '98
Witchcraft 9: Bitter Flesh '96

Clyde Beatty (1903-65)
Africa Screams '49
Darkest Africa '36
The Lost Jungle '34

Debra Beatty
Caged Heat 3000 '95
Hollywood Dreams '94

Nancy Beatty
Eye '96
Henry & Verlin '94

Ned Beatty (1937-)
Homicide: The Movie '00
Konrad '90s
Cookie's Fortune '99
Life '99
He Got Game '98
Crazy Horse '96
The Curse of Inferno '96
The Affair '95
Gulliver's Travels '95
Larry McMurtry's Streets of Laredo '95
Black Water '94
Just Cause '94
Radioland Murders '94
Replikator: Cloned to Kill '94
Ed and His Dead Mother '93
Rudy '93
Angel Square '92
Prelude to a Kiss '92
Blind Vision '91
Going Under '91
Hear My Song '91
Illusions '91
Tragedy of Flight 103: The Inside Story '91
Back to Hannibal: The Return of Tom Sawyer and Huckleberry Finn '90
Big Bad John '90
A Cry in the Wild '90
Repossessed '90
Robert Kennedy and His Times '90
Captain America '89
Chattahoochee '89
Ministry of Vengeance '89
Physical Evidence '89
Spy '89
Purple People Eater '88
Shadows in the Storm '88
Switching Channels '88
Time Trackers '88
The Unholy '88
The Big Easy '87
The Fourth Protocol '87
Midnight Crossing '87
Rolling Vengeance '87
The Trouble with Spies '87
Back to School '86
Charlotte Forten's Mission: Experiment in Freedom '85
Stroker Ace '83
Pray TV '82
Rumpelstiltskin '82
Touched '82
The Toy '82
A Woman Called Golda '82
The Incredible Shrinking Woman '81
All God's Children '80
The Guyana Tragedy: The Story of Jim Jones '80
Hopscotch '80
Superman 2 '80
Friendly Fire '79
1941 '79
Promises in the Dark '79
Wise Blood '79
Great Bank Hoax '78
A Question of Love '78
Superman: The Movie '78
The Exorcist 2: The Heretic '77
Gray Lady Down '77
Our Town '77
All the President's Men '76
The Big Bus '76
Mikey & Nicky '76
Network '76
Silver Streak '76
Nashville '75
Sniper '75
The Execution of Private Slovik '74
Dying Room Only '73
The Last American Hero '73
The Thief Who Came to Dinner '73
White Lightning '73
Deliverance '72

Robert Beatty (1909-92)
2001: A Space Odyssey '68
Where Eagles Dare '68
Time Lock '57
Postmark for Danger '56
The Love of Three Queens '54
Wings of Danger '52
Captain Horatio Hornblower '51
Against the Wind '48
Counterblast '48
San Demetrio, London '47
Appointment with Crime '45

Warren Beatty (1937-)
Town and Country '01
Bulworth '98
Love Affair '94
Bugsy '91
Dick Tracy '90
Ishtar '87
Reds '81
Heaven Can Wait '78
Shampoo '75
The Parallax View '74
Dollars '71
McCabe & Mrs. Miller '71
Bonnie & Clyde '67
Promise Her Anything '66
Mickey One '65
Lilith '64
All Fall Down '62
Roman Spring of Mrs. Stone '61
Splendor in the Grass '61

Michelle Beaudoin
Escape Velocity '99
Sabrina the Teenage Witch '96
Live Bait '95

Hugh Beaumont (1909-82)
The Human Duplicators '64
The Mole People '56
Phone Call from a Stranger '52
Cavalry Charge '51
Danger Zone '51
The Lost Continent '51
Pier 23 '51
Roaring City '51
Money Madness '47
Railroaded '47
The Blue Dahlia '46
The Lady Confesses '45
Objective, Burma! '45
Mr. Winkle Goes to War '44
The Fallen Sparrow '43
The Seventh Victim '43
To the Shores of Tripoli '42
Wake Island '42
Panama Menace '41

Kathryn Beaumont
Peter Pan '53 (V)
Alice in Wonderland '51 (V)

Lucy Beaumont (1873-1937)
Condemned to Live '35
A Free Soul '31
The Crowd '28

Garcelle Beauvais (1966-)
Bad Company '02
Double Take '01
Wild Wild West '99

Nicolas Beauvy (1958-)
Take Down '79
The Toolbox Murders '78
The Cowboys '72
Rage '72
Shoot Out '71

Jim Beaver (1950-)
Twogether '94
In Country '89

Terry Beaver
To Dance with the White Dog '93
Impure Thoughts '86

Louise Beavers (1902-62)
Tammy and the Bachelor '57
Goodbye, My Lady '56
The Jackie Robinson Story '50
Tell It to the Judge '49
Mr. Blandings Builds His Dream House '48
Delightfully Dangerous '45
Dixie Jamboree '44
DuBarry Was a Lady '43
Big Street '42
Reap the Wild Wind '42
Bullets or Ballots '38
General Spanky '36
Imitation of Life '34
In the Money '34
She Done Him Wrong '33
Coquette '29

Jennifer Beck
Gypsy '93
Troll '86
Tightrope '84

John Beck (1943-)
Extreme Limits '01
Agent of Death '99
Militia '99
Black Day Blue Night '95
Suspect Device '95
Honor Thy Father and Mother: The True Story of the Menendez Brothers '94
Last Time Out '94
A Climate for Killing '91
Fire and Rain '89
In the Cold of the Night '89
Deadly Illusion '87
Great American Traffic Jam '80
Time Machine '78
Audrey Rose '77
The Other Side of Midnight '77
The Big Bus '76
Sky Riders '76
Rollerball '75
Paperback Hero '73
Sleeper '73
Lawman '71
Three in the Attic '68

Julian Beck (1925-85)
Poltergeist 2: The Other Side '86
Oedipus Rex '67

Kimberly Beck (1956-)
In the Deep Woods '91
Private War '90
Nightmare at Noon '87
Friday the 13th, Part 4: The Final Chapter '84
Roller Boogie '79
Massacre at Central High '76

Michael Beck (1949-)
Fade to Black '93
Deadly Game '91
Blackout '85
Celebrity '85
The Golden Seal '83
Megaforce '82
Warlords of the 21st Century '82
Xanadu '80
Madman '79
Mayflower: The Pilgrims' Adventure '79
The Warriors '79
Holocaust '78

Thomas Beck (1909-95)
Charlie Chan at the Opera '36
Charlie Chan in Paris '35

Graham Beckel (1955-)
Hardball '01
Pearl Harbor '01
The '70s '00
Blue Streak '99
True Crime '99
Black Dog '98
Bulworth '98
Lost in the Bermuda Triangle '98
L.A. Confidential '97
Jennifer 8 '92
O Pioneers! '91
Separate but Equal '91
Rising Son '90
Lost Angels '89
Hazel's People '75
The Money '75
The Paper Chase '73

Ben Becker (1964-)
The Harmonists '99
Samson and Delilah '96
Brother of Sleep '95

Gerry Becker
Spider-Man '02
Mickey Blue Eyes '99
Donnie Brasco '96
Eraser '96
Legacy of Lies '92
The Public Eye '92

Gretchen Becker
Huck and the King of Hearts '93
Maniac Cop 3: Badge of Silence '93
Firehead '90

Hartmut Becker (1948-)
The Waiting Time '99
Escape from Sobibor '87
Jenny's War '85

Jacques Becker (1906-60)
Grand Illusion '37
Boudu Saved from Drowning '32

Josh Becker (1958-)
Army of Darkness '92
Evil Dead 2: Dead by Dawn '87

Meret Becker (1969-)
The Harmonists '99
The Wicked, Wicked West '97
The Promise '94

Randy Becker
Love! Valour! Compassion! '96
Lie Down with Dogs '95

Tony Becker
Agent Red '00
Cody '67

Scotty Beckett (1929-68)
The Oklahoman '56
Nancy Goes to Rio '50
Battleground '49
The Jolson Story '46
The Climax '44
Ali Baba and the Forty Thieves '43
Heaven Can Wait '43
Kings Row '41
My Favorite Wife '40
My Son, My Son '40
Love Affair '39
Devil's Party '38
Listen, Darling '38
Marie Antoinette '38
Conquest '37
The Charge of the Light Brigade '36
I Dream Too Much '35
Stand Up and Cheer '34

Kate Beckinsale (1974-)
Pearl Harbor '01
Serendipity '01
The Golden Bowl '00
Brokedown Palace '99
The Last Days of Disco '98
Shooting Fish '98
Emma '97
Haunted '95
Cold Comfort Farm '94
Royal Deceit '94
Much Ado about Nothing '93
One Against the Wind '91

Tony Beckley (1927-80)
When a Stranger Calls '79
The Fiend '71
Get Carter '71
Assault '70
The Italian Job '69

William Beckley
Too Late the Hero '70
The Killing of Sister George '69

Henry Beckman (1925-)
The Man Upstairs '93
Family Reunion '88
Marnie '64

Reginald Beckwith (1908-65)
Burn Witch, Burn! '62
Lucky Jim '58
Curse of the Demon '57
Men of Sherwood Forest '57
The Runaway Bus '54
Genevieve '53
Another Man's Poison '52
Mister Drake's Duck '50

William Beckwith
Escape from Safehaven '88
Prime Evil '88

Irene Bedard (1967-)
The Lost Child '00
Wildflowers '99
Smoke Signals '98
Navajo Blues '97
True Women '97
Two for Texas '97
Crazy Horse '96
Pocahontas '95 (V)
Lakota Woman: Siege at Wounded Knee '94
Squanto: A Warrior's Tale '94

Don Beddoe (1891-1991)
Nickel Mountain '85
Jack the Giant Killer '62
The Night of the Hunter '55
The Narrow Margin '52
The Enforcer '51
Gun Crazy '49
Buck Privates Come Home '47
Welcome Stranger '47
The Best Years of Our Lives '46
O.S.S. '46
Before I Hang '40
Blondie On a Budget '40
Blondie Meets the Boss '39
Golden Boy '39

Bonnie Bedelia (1950-)
Anywhere But Here '99
Locked in Silence '99
Bad Manners '98
Gloria '98
Homecoming '96
Judicial Consent '94
Speechless '94
Fallen Angels 2 '93
The Fire Next Time '93
Needful Things '93
Switched at Birth '91
When the Time Comes '91
Die Hard 2: Die Harder '90
Presumed Innocent '90
Somebody Has to Shoot the Picture '90
Fat Man and Little Boy '89
Die Hard '88
Prince of Pennsylvania '88
The Stranger '87
The Boy Who Could Fly '86
Death of an Angel '86
Violets Are Blue '86
Lady from Yesterday '85
Heart Like a Wheel '83

Memorial Day '83
Walking Through the Fire '80
Salem's Lot '79
The Big Fix '78
A Question of Love '78
Lovers and Other Strangers '70
They Shoot Horses, Don't They? '69

Rodney Bedell
Just for the Hell of It '68
Gruesome Twosome '67

Barbara Bedford (1903-81)
Found Alive '34
The Broken Mask '28
Mockery '27
The Notorious Lady '27
The Mad Whirl '25
Tumbleweeds '25
The Last of the Mohicans '20

Brian Bedford (1935-)
Armistead Maupin's More Tales of the City '97
Nixon '95
Scarlett '94
The Last Best Year '90
Robin Hood '73 (V)
Grand Prix '66

Kabir Bedi (1945-)
The Lost Empire '01
Lie Down with Lions '94
Beyond Justice '92
The Beast '88
Terminal Entry '87
Octopussy '83
Demon Rage '82
Archer: The Fugitive from the Empire '81

Guy Bedos
Pardon Mon Affaire, Too! '77
Pardon Mon Affaire '76

Alfonso Bedoya (1904-57)
The Stranger Wore a Gun '53
Treasure of the Sierra Madre '48

Janet Beecher (1884-1955)
The Mark of Zorro '40
I'd Give My Life '36

David Beecroft (1956-)
Octopus '00
Kidnapped in Paradise '98
The Rain Killer '90
Shadowzone '89

Daniel Beer
The Last Best Sunday '98
Talking about Sex '94
Point Break '91
Creepshow 2 '87

Noah Beery, Sr. (1884-1945)
Adventures of Red Ryder '40
Panamint's Bad Man '38
Zorro Rides Again '37
King of the Damned '36
Kentucky Kernels '34
Mystery Liner '34
Trail Beyond '34
Buffalo Stampede '33
Fighting with Kit Carson '33
Flaming Signal '33
Man of the Forest '33
She Done Him Wrong '33
To the Last Man '33
The Big Stampede '32
Cornered '32
Devil Horse '32
The Drifter '32
Kid from Spain '32
Linda '29
The Coming of Amos '25
The Vanishing American '25
Soul of the Beast '23
Mark of Zorro '20
A Mormon Maid '17

Noah Beery, Jr. (1913-94)
The Capture of Grizzly Adams '82
Mysterious Two '82
Great American Traffic Jam '80
The Bastard '78
Francis Gary Powers: The True Story of the U-2 Spy '76
Savages '75
Walking Tall: Part 2 '75
Walking Tall '73
Richard Petty Story '72
7 Faces of Dr. Lao '63
Inherit the Wind '60
Fastest Gun Alive '56
Jubal '56
War Arrow '53
Cavalry Charge '51
The Texas Rangers '51
Rocketship X-M '50
The Doolins of Oklahoma '49
Red River '48
Million Dollar Kid '44
The Avenging Hand '43
Gung Ho! '43
'Neath Brooklyn Bridge '42
Sergeant York '41
Tanks a Million '41
Carson City Kid '40
Bad Lands '39
Of Mice and Men '39
Only Angels Have Wings '39
Ace Drummond '36
Tailspin Tommy '34
Trail Beyond '34
Fighting with Kit Carson '33
Rustler's Roundup '33
Savage Fury '33
Mark of Zorro '20

Wallace Beery (1885-1949)
A Date with Judy '48
Ah, Wilderness! '35
China Seas '35
Treasure Island '34
Viva Villa! '34
Dinner at Eight '33
The Champ '32
Grand Hotel '32
The Big House '30
Min & Bill '30
We're in the Navy Now '27
Behind the Front '26
Old Ironsides '26
The Lost World '25
The Night Club '25
The Pony Express '25
Three Ages '23
White Tiger '23
Robin Hood '22
The Four Horsemen of the Apocalypse '21
The Last of the Mohicans '20
The Mollycoddle '20
Teddy at the Throttle '16

Max Beesley (1971-)
Glitter '01
Kill Me Later '01
The Match '99
Tom Jones '98

Chris Beetem
Black Hawk Down '01
Grace & Glorie '98

Jason Beghe
Baby Monitor: Sound of Fear '97
G.I. Jane '97
The Chinatown Murders: Man against the Mob '92
Monkey Shines '88

Ed Begley, Sr. (1901-70)
The Dunwich Horror '70
Firecreek '68
Road to Salina '68
Wild in the Streets '68
Hang 'Em High '67
The Oscar '66
The Unsinkable Molly Brown '64
Sweet Bird of Youth '62
Odds Against Tomorrow '59
Twelve Angry Men '57
Patterns '56
Boots Malone '52
Lone Star '52
On Dangerous Ground '51
Stars in My Crown '50
The Great Gatsby '49
It Happens Every Spring '49
Tulsa '49
Sorry, Wrong Number '48
The Street with No Name '48
Boomerang '47

Ed Begley, Jr. (1949-)
Get Over It! '01
Best in Show '00
I'm Losing You '98
Joey '98
Murder She Purred: A Mrs. Murphy Mystery '98
Horton Foote's Alone '97
Ms. Bear '97
Not in This Town '97
The Student Affair '97
The Late Shift '96
Santa with Muscles '96
Batman Forever '95
Hourglass '95
Rave Review '95
Children of Fury '94
The Crazysitter '94
Even Cowgirls Get the Blues '94
Greedy '94
Incident at Deception Ridge '94
The Pagemaster '94
Renaissance Man '94
Sensation '94
World War II: When Lions Roared '94
Cooperstown '93
The Story Lady '93
Dark Horse '92
Running Mates '92
The Great Los Angeles Earthquake '91
Spies, Lies and Naked Thighs '91
The Applegates '89
Scenes from the Class Struggle in Beverly Hills '89
She-Devil '89
The Accidental Tourist '88
Amazon Women on the Moon '87
The Legend of Sleepy Hollow '86
Transylvania 6-5000 '85
Protocol '84
Streets of Fire '84
This Is Spinal Tap '84
Get Crazy '83
Cat People '82
Eating Raoul '82
Elvis: The Movie '79
The In-Laws '79
A Shining Season '79
Blue Collar '78
Goin' South '78
Citizens Band '77
Dead of Night '77
Cockfighter '74
Showdown '73

Brionny Behets
Cassandra '87
Alvin Rides Again '74

Dani Behr
Rancid Aluminium '00
Like It Is '98

Jason Behr (1973-)
The Shipping News '01
Rites of Passage '99

Melissa Behr
Me & Will '99
Perfect Tenant '99
The Landlady '98
Dollman vs Demonic Toys '93

Bernard Behrens
Invasion! '99
Mother Night '96
The Man with Two Brains '83
Galaxy of Terror '81

Sam Behrens (1950-)
Alive '93
And You Thought Your Parents Were Weird! '91
American Blue Note '89
Murder by Numbers '89

Yerye Beirut
The Fear Chamber '68
The Sinister Invasion '68

Richard Bekins
George Washington: The Forging of a Nation '86
Model Behavior '82

Barbara Bel Geddes (1922-)
Summertree '71
The Todd Killings '71
The Five Pennies '59
Vertigo '58
Panic in the Streets '50
Caught '49
Blood on the Moon '48
I Remember Mama '48
The Long Night '47

Doris Belack
Doug's 1st Movie '99 (V)
Krippendorf's Tribe '98
Neil Simon's The Odd Couple 2 '98
What about Bob? '91
Opportunity Knocks '90

Harry Belafonte (1927-)
Kansas City '95
White Man's Burden '95
Ready to Wear '94
The Player '92
Grambling's White Tiger '81
Uptown Saturday Night '74
Buck and the Preacher '72
The Angel Levine '70
Odds Against Tomorrow '59
Island in the Sun '57
Carmen Jones '54

Shari Belafonte (1954-)
Mars '96
The Heidi Chronicles '95
French Silk '94
The Player '92
Fire, Ice and Dynamite '91
Murder by Numbers '89
Speed Zone '88
The Midnight Hour '86
Overnight Sensation '83
If You Could See What I Hear '82

Leon Belasco (1902-88)
Can-Can '60
Abbott and Costello in the Foreign Legion '50
Infamous Crimes '47
It's a Date '40
Fisherman's Wharf '39

Ana Belen
Love Can Seriously Damage Your Health '96
The Perfect Husband '92
Demons in the Garden '82

Christine Belford (1949-)
Christine '84
Kenny Rogers as the Gambler '80
The Groundstar Conspiracy '72
Pocket Money '72

Ann Bell (1940-)
When Saturday Comes '95
Christabel '89
Champions '84
The Statue '71
Fahrenheit 451 '66
The Witches '66
Dr. Terror's House of Horrors '65

Christopher Bell (1983-)
Sarah, Plain and Tall: Winter's End '99
Sarah, Plain and Tall: Skylark '93
Sarah, Plain and Tall '91
Without Warning: The James Brady Story '91

Dan Bell
The Shot '96
Terror Eyes '87

Darryl M. Bell
Mr. Write '92
School Daze '88

Drake Bell
The Jack Bull '99
The Neon Bible '95

Edward Bell
Image of Passion '86
The Premonition '75

E.E. Bell (1955-)
Grizzly Mountain '97
800 Leagues Down the Amazon '93

Hank Bell (1892-1950)
Valley of the Sun '42
Border Vengeance '35
The Fiddlin' Buckaroo '33
Beyond the Rockies '32
The Big Stampede '32
South of Santa Fe '32
Whistlin' Dan '32

James Bell (1891-1973)
Tribute to a Bad Man '56
A Lawless Street '55
Teenage Crime Wave '55
Flying Leathernecks '51
The Leopard Man '43
My Friend Flicka '43
So Proudly We Hail '43

Jeannie Bell (1944-)
Fass Black '77
The Muthers '76
TNT Jackson '75
Policewomen '73

Marie Bell (1900-85)
Phedre '68
Hotel Paradiso '66
Sandra of a Thousand Delights '65

Marshall Bell
Mercy '00
Sand '00
Black & White '99
Virus '98
The End of Violence '97
Starship Troopers '97
Too Fast, Too Young '96
Things to Do in Denver When You're Dead '95
Payback '94
The Vagrant '92
The Heroes of Desert Storm '91
Air America '90
Leather Jackets '90
Total Recall '90
Johnny Be Good '88
Tucker: The Man and His Dream '88
Twins '88
Wildfire '88
No Way Out '87
A Nightmare on Elm Street 2: Freddy's Revenge '85

Michael Bell
Rugrats in Paris: The Movie '00 (V)
The Rugrats Movie '98 (V)

Nicholas Bell
Dead Letter Office '98
Sorrento Beach '95

Rex Bell (1905-62)
Law of the Sea '38
Stormy Trails '36
West of Nevada '36
The Tonto Kid '35
Diamond Trail '33
Fighting Texans '33
Rainbow Ranch '33
Broadway to Cheyenne '32
Battling with Buffalo Bill '31

Tobin Bell
The 4th Floor '99
Best of the Best: Without Warning '98
Brown's Requiem '98
Overnight Delivery '96
Serial Killer '95
New Eden '94
The Firm '93
Ruby '92
False Identity '90

Tom Bell (1932-)
Swing '98
The Boxer '97
Swept from the Sea '97
Feast of July '95
Catherine Cookson's The Cinder Path '94
Prime Suspect '92
Let Him Have It '91
Prospero's Books '91
The Krays '90
Wish You Were Here '87
Royal Flash '75
Dressed for Death '74
Quest for Love '71
Ballad in Blue '66
The L-Shaped Room '62

Rachael Bella
The Blood Oranges '97
Household Saints '93
When Pigs Fly '93

Bill Bellamy (1965-)
The Brothers '01
Any Given Sunday '99
Love Stinks '99
Def Jam's How to Be a Player '97
Love Jones '96
Who's the Man? '93

Diana Bellamy (1944-2001)
Amelia Earhart: The Final Flight '94
The Nest '88
Stripped to Kill '87

Madge Bellamy (1899-1990)
Northwest Trail '46
The Ivory Handled Gun '35
Law for Tombstone '35
Stone of Silver Creek '35
The White Zombie '32
The White Sin '24
Soul of the Beast '23
Lorna Doone '22

Ned Bellamy
Angel's Dance '99
Ed Wood '94
Carnosaur '93
Writer's Block '91

Ralph Bellamy (1904-91)
Pretty Woman '90
War & Remembrance: The Final Chapter '89
The Good Mother '88
War & Remembrance '88
Amazon Women on the Moon '87
Disorderlies '87
Fourth Wise Man '85
Love Leads the Way '84
Trading Places '83
The Winds of War '83
Oh, God! '77
The Boy in the Plastic Bubble '76
Nightmare in Badham County '76
Return to Earth '76
Murder on Flight 502 '75
Search for the Gods '75
Missiles of October '74
Cancel My Reservation '72
Doctors' Wives '70
Rosemary's Baby '68
The Professionals '66
Sunrise at Campobello '60
The Court Martial of Billy Mitchell '55
Delightfully Dangerous '45
Lady on a Train '45
Guest in the House '44
The Ghost of Frankenstein '42
Dive Bomber '41
Footsteps in the Dark '41
The Wolf Man '41
Brother Orchid '40
Dance, Girl, Dance '40
His Girl Friday '40
Boy Meets Girl '38

I Want What I Want '72
The Charge of the Light Brigade '68
The Nanny '65
The Skull '65
Lust for Life '56
Moulin Rouge '52

Joan Bennett (1910-90)
Suspiria '77
House of Dark Shadows '70
We're No Angels '55
Father's Little Dividend '51
Father of the Bride '50
Reckless Moment '49
The Scar '48
Secret Beyond the Door '48
Colonel Effingham's Raid '45
Scarlet Street '45
Woman in the Window '44
Twin Beds '42
House Across the Bay '40
The Son of Monte Cristo '40
The Man in the Iron Mask '39
The Texans '38
Vogues of 1938 '37
Little Women '33
Disraeli '30
Bulldog Drummond '29
Power '28

John Bennett (1928-)
Priest '94
Antonia and Jane '91
Eye of the Needle '81
The House that Dripped Blood '71
Victim '61
It Takes a Thief '59

Marjorie Bennett (1896-1982)
Stacey '73
The Love God? '70
Games '67
36 Hours '64
Kiss Me Deadly '55
Abbott and Costello Meet Dr. Jekyll and Mr. Hyde '52

Nigel Bennett (1949-)
Anne of Green Gables: The Continuing Story '99
Invasion! '99
Naked City: A Killer Christmas '98
Rescuers: Stories of Courage—Two Couples '98
Gotti '96
Darkman 3: Die Darkman Die '95
Kurt Vonnegut's Harrison Bergeron '95
Madonna: Innocence Lost '95
Where's the Money, Noreen? '95
Back in Action '94
Soft Deceit '94

Ray Bennett (1895-1957)
Thundering Trail '51
Border Badmen '45
Death Rides the Plains '44

Tony Bennett (1926-)
The Scout '94
The Oscar '66

Zachary Bennett (1980-)
Bonanno: A Godfather's Story '99
By Way of the Stars '92
Looking for Miracles '90

Jack Benny (1894-1974)
A Guide for the Married Man '67
It's a Mad, Mad, Mad, Mad World '63
The Great Lover '49
Without Reservations '46
The Horn Blows at Midnight '45
It's in the Bag '45
Hollywood Canteen '44
George Washington Slept Here '42
To Be or Not to Be '42
Broadway Melody of 1936 '35
Transatlantic Merry-Go-Round '34
Medicine Man '30

Martin Benrath (1926-2000)
The White Rose '83
From the Life of the Marionettes '80

Abraham Benrubi (1969-)
George of the Jungle '97
U-Turn '97
Under Oath '97
Twister '96
Magic Island '95
The Program '93

Amber Benson (1977-)
Bye Bye, Love '94
The Crush '93
King of the Hill '93

Deborah Benson
Danger of Love '95
Mutant on the Bounty '89
Just Before Dawn '80
September 30, 1955 '77

George Benson (1911-83)
The Creeping Flesh '72
Convoy '40

Jodi Benson (1961-)
Toy Story 2 '99 (V)
Thumbelina '94 (V)
The Little Mermaid '89 (V)

Lucille Benson (1914-84)
1941 '79
Huckleberry Finn '74
Reflections of Murder '74
Cactus in the Snow '72
Private Parts '72
Duel '71

Martin Benson (1918-)
The Omen '76
Tiffany Jones '75
A Matter of WHO '62
Exodus '60
The Cosmic Monsters '58
Istanbul '57
The King and I '56

Robby Benson (1956-)
Dragonheart: A New Beginning '00 (V)
At Home with the Webbers '94
Deadly Exposure '93
Homewrecker '92
Invasion of Privacy '92
Beauty and the Beast '91 (V)
Modern Love '90
Rent-A-Cop '88
White Hot '88
City Limits '85
Harry & Son '84
Running Brave '83
Two of a Kind '82
The Chosen '81
National Lampoon Goes to the Movies '81
Die Laughing '80
Tribute '80
Ice Castles '79
The End '78
One on One '77
Our Town '77
The Death of Richie '76
The Last of Mrs. Lincoln '76
Ode to Billy Joe '76
The Virginia Hill Story '76
Death Be Not Proud '75
All the Kind Strangers '74
Jory '72

Wendy Benson
Luck of the Draw '00
Wishmaster '97

Timothy Bentinck (1953-)
Sharpe's Rifles '93
Year of the Comet '92

Michael Bentine (1922-96)
Rentadick '72
Down Among the Z Men '52

Fabrizio Bentivoglio (1957-)
The Real Thing '97
Elective Affinities '96
Apartment Zero '88

Dana Bentley
Karate Cop '93
Sorority House Massacre 2: Nighty Nightmare '92
Bad Girls from Mars '90

John Bentley (1916-)
Submarine Seahawk '59
Flight from Vienna '58
Istanbul '57
White Huntress '57
The Way Out '56
Profile '54
River Beat '54
Scarlet Spear '54
The Happiest Days of Your Life '50
Calling Paul Temple '48

Lamont Bentley (1973-)
The Wash '01
Tales from the Hood '95

Wes Bentley (1978-)
Soul Survivors '01
The Claim '00
American Beauty '99
White River '99

Barbi Benton (1950-)
Deathstalker '83
Hospital Massacre '81
For the Love of It '80

Eddie Benton
Prom Night '80
Dr. Strange '78

Jerome Benton
Graffiti Bridge '90
Under the Cherry Moon '86

Mark Benton
Topsy Turvy '99
Career Girls '97
Catherine Cookson's The Girl '96

Susanne Benton (1948-)
A Boy and His Dog '75
Catch-22 '70
That Cold Day in the Park '69

Femi Benussi (1948-)
Hatchet for the Honeymoon '70
The Hawks & the Sparrows '67

Julie Benz
The Brothers '01
Shriek If You Know What I Did Last Friday the 13th '00
Darkdrive '98
Jawbreaker '98

Daniel Benzali (1950-)
Screwed '00
Boss of Bosses '99
All the Little Animals '98
The End of Violence '97
Murder at 1600 '97
A Day in October '92
The Last of His Tribe '92
Messenger of Death '88

John Beradino (1917-96)
Don't Look Back: The Story of Leroy "Satchel" Paige '81
Moon of the Wolf '72

George Beranger (1893-1973)
Flirting with Fate '16
The Birth of a Nation '15

Iris Berben
Tea for Three '84
Companeros '70

Ady Berber (1913-66)
Door with the Seven Locks '62
Dead Eyes of London '61

Marcel Berbert
The Green Room '78
Mississippi Mermaid '69

Luca Bercovici
Hard Luck '01
The Big Squeeze '96
Drop Zone '94
Scanner Cop '94
Inside Monkey Zetterland '93
Mirror Images 2 '93
K2: The Ultimate High '92
Mission of Justice '92
Mortal Passions '90
Pacific Heights '90
Clean and Sober '88
American Flyers '85
Parasite '82
Frightmare '81

Blaze Berdahl
We're Back! A Dinosaur's Story '93 (V)
Pet Sematary '89

Tom Berenger (1950-)
Cruel and Unusual '01
Training Day '01
True Blue '01
Cutaway '00
Diplomatic Siege '99
In the Company of Spies '99
A Murder of Crows '99
Turbulence 2: Fear of Flying '99
One Man's Hero '98
Shadow of Doubt '98
The Gingerbread Man '97
Rough Riders '97
An Occasional Hell '96
The Substitute '96
The Avenging Angel '95
Body Language '95
The Last of the Dogmen '95
Chasers '94
Major League 2 '94
Gettysburg '93
Sliver '93
Sniper '92
At Play in the Fields of the Lord '91
Shattered '91
The Field '90
Born on the Fourth of July '89
Love at Large '89
Major League '89
Betrayed '88
Last Rites '88
Shoot to Kill '88
Someone to Watch Over Me '87
Platoon '86
Fear City '85
Rustler's Rhapsody '85
The Big Chill '83
Eddie and the Cruisers '83
Beyond Obsession '82
The Dogs of War '81
Butch and Sundance: The Early Days '79
In Praise of Older Women '78
Johnny We Hardly Knew Ye '77
Looking for Mr. Goodbar '77
Rush It '77
The Sentinel '76

Marisa Berenson (1948-)
Trade Secrets '90s
Women '97
Night of the Cyclone '90
White Hunter, Black Heart '90
The Secret Diary of Sigmund Freud '84
S.O.B. '81
Killer Fish '79
Sex on the Run '78
Barry Lyndon '75
Cabaret '72
Death in Venice '71

Harry Beresford (1864-1944)
Klondike Annie '36
Murders in the Zoo '33
The Sign of the Cross '33

Justin Berfield
Max Keeble's Big Move '01
The Kid with the X-Ray Eyes '99
Mom, Can I Keep Her? '98

Peter Berg (1964-)
Corky Romano '01
Cop Land '97
Girl 6 '96
The Great White Hype '96
Across the Moon '94
The Last Ride '94
The Last Seduction '94
Aspen Extreme '93
A Case for Murder '93
Fire in the Sky '93
A Midnight Clear '92
Crooked Hearts '91
Late for Dinner '91
Genuine Risk '89
Going Overboard '89
Race for Glory '89
Shocker '89
Tale of Two Sisters '89
Never on Tuesday '88

Judith-Marie Bergan
Never Pick Up a Stranger '79
Abduction '75

Francine Berge (1940-)
The Nun '66
Circle of Love '64
Judex '64

Candice Bergen (1946-)
Miss Congeniality '00
Mayflower Madam '87
Merlin and the Sword '85
My Sweet Victim '85
Stick '85
2010: The Year We Make Contact '84 (V)
Gandhi '82
Rich and Famous '81
Starting Over '79
A Night Full of Rain '78
Oliver's Story '78
The Domino Principle '77
Bite the Bullet '75
The Wind and the Lion '75
11 Harrowhouse '74
Carnal Knowledge '71
The Adventurers '70
Getting Straight '70
Soldier Blue '70
The Group '66
The Sand Pebbles '66

Edgar Bergen (1903-78)
The Muppet Movie '79
Homecoming: A Christmas Story '71
I Remember Mama '48
Fun & Fancy Free '47 (N)
Stage Door Canteen '43
Here We Go Again! '42
Look Who's Laughing '41
You Can't Cheat an Honest Man '39
The Goldwyn Follies '38
Letter of Introduction '38

Frances Bergen
Eating '90
The Morning After '86

Polly Bergen (1930-)
Dr. Jekyll and Ms. Hyde '95
Once Upon a Time ... When We Were Colored '95
The Lightning Incident '91
Cry-Baby '90
Haunting of Sarah Hardy '89
My Brother's Wife '89
War & Remembrance: The Final Chapter '89
War & Remembrance '88
Making Mr. Right '86
The Winds of War '83
Born Beautiful '82
How to Pick Up Girls '78
Murder on Flight 502 '75
Anatomy of Terror '74
Death Cruise '74
A Guide for the Married Man '67
Kisses for My President '64
Cape Fear '61
Escape from Fort Bravo '53
The Stooge '51
At War with the Army '50

Tushka Bergen (1969-)
Journey to the Center of the Earth '99
Lovelife '97
Voices from a Locked Room '95
Barcelona '94
Swing Kids '93
Wrangler '88

Deborah Berger
Rosebud '75
La Merveilleuse Visite '74

Helmut Berger (1944-)
The Godfather, Part 3 '90
Fatal Fix '80s
Code Name: Emerald '85
Mad Dog '84
Deadly Game '83
Battleforce '78
Conversation Piece '75
Romantic Englishwoman '75
Ash Wednesday '73
Order to Kill '73
Ludwig '72
The Garden of the Finzi-Continis '71
Dorian Gray '70
The Damned '69

Katya Berger (1914-)
Tales of Ordinary Madness '83
Nana '82

Michael Berger
Sarah's Child '96
Allonsanfan '73

Nicole Berger (1935-67)
The Story of a Three Day Pass '68
Shoot the Piano Player '62

Sarah Berger
Element of Doubt '96
The Green Man '91

Senta Berger (1947-)
Blitz '85
Swiss Conspiracy '77
The Boss Is Served '76
Cross of Iron '76
Smugglers '75
When Women Lost Their Tails '75
The Scarlet Letter '73
Cobra '71
When Women Had Tails '70
Mother Doesn't Always Know Best '60s
The Ambushers '67
Diabolically Yours '67
Cast a Giant Shadow '66
The Quiller Memorandum '66
Full Hearts & Empty Pockets '63
Waltz King '63
Secret of the Black Trunk '62
Sherlock Holmes and the Deadly Necklace '62
Testament of Dr. Mabuse '62

William Berger (1928-93)
I'm Dangerous Tonight '90
Dial Help '88
Django Strikes Again '87
Hell Hunters '87
Hercules 2 '85
Day of the Cobra '84
Hercules '83
Oil '78
Slaughterday '77
Superfly T.N.T. '73

Today We Kill, Tomorrow We Die '71
Five Dolls for an August Moon '70
What a Way to Die '70

Thommy Berggren (1937-)
Sunday's Children '94
The Adventurers '70
Elvira Madigan '67

Herbert Berghof (1909-90)
Master Mind '73
Five Fingers '52
Red Planet Mars '52

Patrick Bergin (1954-)
The Devil's Prey '01
Deadline '00
Invisible Circus '00
St. Patrick: The Irish Legend '00
Durango '99
Escape Velocity '99
Eye of the Beholder '99
Treasure Island '99
When the Sky Falls '99
One Man's Hero '98
Sir Arthur Conan Doyle's The Lost World '98
The Apocalypse Watch '97
The Ripper '97
The Proposition '96
Suspicious Minds '96
Lawnmower Man 2: Beyond Cyberspace '95
Triplecross '95
Double Cross '94
Soft Deceit '94
Frankenstein '93
Map of the Human Heart '93
They Watch '93
Highway to Hell '92
Love Crimes '92
Patriot Games '92
The Real Charlotte '91
Robin Hood '91
Sleeping with the Enemy '91
Mountains of the Moon '90
The Courier '88
Taffin '88

Emily Bergl (1975-)
Happy Campers '01
Chasing Sleep '00
The Rage: Carrie 2 '99

Erik "Bullen" Berglund (1887-1946)
Only One Night '42
Walpurgis Night '41
Intermezzo '36

Henry Bergman (1868-1946)
Modern Times '36
City Lights '31

Ingrid Bergman (1913-82)
A Woman Called Golda '82
Autumn Sonata '78
A Matter of Time '76
Murder on the Orient Express '74
The Hideaways '73
Walk in the Spring Rain '70
Cactus Flower '69
Goodbye Again '61
24 Hours in a Woman's Life '61
Indiscreet '58
The Inn of the Sixth Happiness '58
Anastasia '56
Elena and Her Men '56
Voyage in Italy '53
Europa '51 '52
Stromboli '50
Under Capricorn '49
Arch of Triumph '48
Joan of Arc '48
Notorious '46
The Bells of St. Mary's '45
Saratoga Trunk '45
Spellbound '45
Gaslight '44
For Whom the Bell Tolls '43
Casablanca '42
Only One Night '42
Adam Had Four Sons '41
Dr. Jekyll and Mr. Hyde '41
Walpurgis Night '41
June Night '40
Intermezzo '39
Dollar '38
A Woman's Face '38
Intermezzo '36
Swedenhielms '35
The Count of the Old Town '34

Peter Bergman (1953-)
Phantom of the Ritz '88
J-Men Forever! '79

Sandahl Bergman (1951-)
The P.A.C.K. '96
Ice Cream Man '95
Inner Sanctum 2 '94
Body of Influence '93
Lipstick Camera '93
Possessed by the Night '93
Raw Nerve '91
Hell Comes to Frogtown '88
Kandyland '87
Programmed to Kill '86
Stewardess School '86
Red Sonja '85
Getting Physical '84
She '83
Airplane 2: The Sequel '82
Conan the Barbarian '82
Xanadu '80

Elisabeth Bergner (1900-86)
The Pedestrian '73
Cry of the Banshee '70
Dreaming Lips '37
As You Like It '36
Catherine the Great '34

Helena Bergstrom (1964-)
Still Crazy '98
Under the Sun '98
The Last Dance '93
House of Angels '92
The Women on the Roof '89

Luis Beristain (1918-62)
The Exterminating Angel '62
El '52

Busby Berkeley (1895-1976)
Million Dollar Mermaid '52
Babes on Broadway '41
Dames '34
Fashions of 1934 '34
42nd Street '33
Roman Scandals '33

Xander Berkeley
Shanghai Noon '00
Time Code '00
Universal Soldier: The Return '99
Phoenix '98
Winchell '98
Air Force One '97
One Night Stand '97
Barb Wire '96
Bulletproof '96
If These Walls Could Talk '96
The Killing Jar '96
Persons Unknown '96
Within the Rock '96
Poison Ivy 2: Lily '95
Safe '95
Roswell: The U.F.O. Cover-Up '94
Attack of the 50 Ft. Woman '93
Dead to Rights '93
Candyman '92
A Few Good Men '92
The Gun in Betty Lou's Handbag '92
Internal Affairs '90
Short Time '90
Assassin '89
Tapeheads '89
Deadly Dreams '88
The Lawless Land '88
Straight to Hell '87
Sid & Nancy '86

Elizabeth Berkley (1972-)
The Curse of the Jade Scorpion '01
Any Given Sunday '99
Tail Lights Fade '99
Random Encounter '98
The Taxman '98
The Real Blonde '97
The First Wives Club '96
Showgirls '95
White Wolves 2: Legend of the Wild '94

Steven Berkoff (1937-)
Attila '01
Rancid Aluminium '00
Legionnaire '98
Another 9 1/2 Weeks '96
Flynn '96
Fair Game '95
Intruders '92
The Krays '90
Prisoner of Rio '89
War & Remembrance: The Final Chapter '89
War & Remembrance '88
Rambo: First Blood, Part 2 '85
Revolution '85
Transmutations '85
Beverly Hills Cop '84
Octopussy '83
Outland '81
The Passenger '75
A Clockwork Orange '71

Terri Berland
The Strangeness '85
Pink Motel '82

Milton Berle (1908-2002)
Storybook '95
Driving Me Crazy '91
Side by Side '88
Broadway Danny Rose '84
Cracking Up '83
Off Your Rocker '80
The Muppet Movie '79
Legend of Valentino '75
Lepke '75
Evil Roy Slade '71
Journey Back to Oz '71 (V)
Where Angels Go, Trouble Follows '68
Who's Minding the Mint? '67
The Oscar '66
The Loved One '65
It's a Mad, Mad, Mad, Mad World '63
The Bellboy '60
Let's Make Love '60
Sun Valley Serenade '41
Mark of Zorro '20

Francois Berleand
Romance '99
Place Vendome '98
Seventh Heaven '98
Capitaine Conan '96
May Fools '90
Au Revoir les Enfants '87

Jeannie Berlin (1932-)
In the Spirit '90
The Heartbreak Kid '72
Housewife '72
Portnoy's Complaint '72
The Baby Maker '70
Getting Straight '70
The Strawberry Statement '70

Charles Berling (1958-)
The Bridge '00
A Matter of Taste '00
Stardom '00
L'Ennui '98
Those Who Love Me Can Take the Train '98
Dry Cleaning '97
Love, etc. '96
Ridicule '96
Nelly et Monsieur Arnaud '95

Peter Berling (1934-)
Francesco '93
Cobra Verde '88
Aguirre, the Wrath of God '72

Warren Berlinger (1937-)
Backlash '99
Hero '92
Take Two '87
Sex and the Single Parent '82
The World According to Garp '82
Four Deuces '75
The Long Goodbye '73
Spinout '66
Billie '65
Platinum High School '60

Shelley Berman (1926-)
Motorama '91
Rented Lips '88
Beware! The Blob '72
Think Dirty '70
Divorce American Style '67
The Best Man '64
The Wheeler Dealers '63

Susan Berman
Curtain Call '97
Smithereens '82

Gael Garcia Bernal
Fidel '02
Y Tu Mama Tambien '01
Amores Perros '00

Crystal Bernard (1961-)
Jackpot '01
A Face to Kill For '99
As Good as Dead '95
Siringo '94
Slumber Party Massacre 2 '87

Ed Bernard (1939-)
Reflections of Murder '74
Across 110th Street '72

Jason Bernard (1938-96)
Liar Liar '96
Down, Out and Dangerous '95
While You Were Sleeping '95
Cosmic Slop '94
Paint It Black '89
No Way Out '87
All of Me '84

Paul Bernard (1898-1958)
Pattes Blanches '49
The Ladies of the Bois de Bologne '44

Susan Bernard
Teenager '74
Faster, Pussycat! Kill! Kill! '65

Herschel Bernardi (1923-86)
Actor: The Paul Muni Story '78
The Front '76
The Story of Jacob & Joseph '74
No Place to Run '72
Irma La Douce '63
Love with the Proper Stranger '63
1001 Arabian Nights '59 (V)
Green Fields '37

Michael Bernardo
Shootfighter 2: Kill or Be Killed! '96
Virtual Combat '95
Shootfighter: Fight to the Death '93

Lynn Bernay
The Pit and the Pendulum '61
I Bury the Living '58

Sandra Bernhard (1955-)
Playing Mona Lisa '00
Footsteps '98
Wrongfully Accused '98
An Alan Smithee Film: Burn, Hollywood, Burn '97
Lover Girl '97
Plump Fiction '97
Somewhere in the City '97
The Apocalypse '96
The Late Shift '96
Inside Monkey Zetterland '93
Hudson Hawk '91
Heavy Petting '89
Track 29 '88
Sesame Street Presents: Follow That Bird '85
King of Comedy '82

Daniel Bernhardt
G2: Mortal Conquest '99
Perfect Target '98
True Vengeance '97
Bloodsport 2: The Next Kumite '95
Bloodsport 3 '95

Kevin Bernhardt
The Immortals '95
Beauty School '93
Hellraiser 3: Hell on Earth '92
Midnight Warrior '89
Counterforce '87

Mara Berni (1934-)
The Fury of Hercules '61
Samson '61

Corbin Bernsen (1954-)
The Tomorrow Man '01
Rangers '00
An American Affair '99
Final Payback '99
The Dentist 2: Brace Yourself '98
Major League 3: Back to the Minors '98
Spacejacked '98
Bloodhounds '96
Bloodhounds 2 '96
Circuit Breaker '96
The Dentist '96
The Great White Hype '96
Kounterfeit '96
Menno's Mind '96
Baja '95
Cover Me '95
Operation Intercept '95
Someone to Die For '95
Tails You Live, Heads You're Dead '95
Tales from the Hood '95
Temptress '95
Major League 2 '94
The New Age '94
Radioland Murders '94
Savage Land '94
The Soft Kill '94
A Brilliant Disguise '93
Final Mission '93
The Ghost Brigade '93
Ring of the Musketeers '93
Frozen Assets '92
Dead on the Money '91
Shattered '91
Bert Rigby, You're a Fool '89
Disorganized Crime '89
Major League '89
Dead Aim '87
Hello Again '87
L.A. Law '86
Eat My Dust '76
King Kong '76

Olinka (Schoberova) Berova (1943-)
Togetherness '70
The Vengeance of She '68

Claude Berri (1934-)
Va Savoir '01
Le Sex Shop '73
Marry Me, Marry Me '69
Please Not Now! '61

Elizabeth Berridge (1962-)
When the Party's Over '91
Montana '90
Five Corners '88
Amadeus '84
The Funhouse '81

Rev. Daniel Berrigan (1921-)
The Mission '86
In the King of Prussia '83

Chuck Berry (1926-)
Chuck Berry: Hail! Hail! Rock 'n' Roll '87
Go, Johnny Go! '59
Rock, Rock, Rock '56

Halle Berry (1968-)
Monster's Ball '01
Swordfish '01
X-Men '00
Introducing Dorothy Dandridge '99
Bulworth '98
Why Do Fools Fall in Love? '98
B.A.P.'s '97
Executive Decision '96
Girl 6 '96
Race the Sun '96
The Rich Man's Wife '96
The Flintstones '94
Losing Isaiah '94
Father Hood '93
The Program '93
Queen '93
Boomerang '92
Jungle Fever '91
The Last Boy Scout '91
Strictly Business '91

Jules Berry (1883-1951)
Les Visiteurs du Soir '42
Le Jour Se Leve '39
The Crime of Monsieur Lange '36

Ken Berry (1933-)
The Cat from Outer Space '78
Mountain Man '77
Herbie Rides Again '74

Michael Berry
Beyond the Law '92
The Touch of Satan '70

Richard Berry (1950-)
Pedale Douce '96
L'Appat '94
Day of Atonement '93
Honeymoon '87
A Man and a Woman: 20 Years Later '86
L'Addition '85
Special Police '85

Vincent Berry
Baby '00
Sugar Town '99
The Fury Within '98
Free Willy 3: The Rescue '97
Amnesia '96

Dorothee Berryman (1948-)
Taken '99
The Pianist '91
Scanners 2: The New Order '91
A Paper Wedding '89
The Decline of the American Empire '86

Michael Berryman (1948-)
Wizards of the Demon Sword '94
Teenage Exorcist '93
Auntie Lee's Meat Pies '92
Beastmaster 2: Through the Portal of Time '91
Evil Spirits '91
The Guyver '91
Haunting Fear '91
The Secret of the Golden Eagle '91
Aftershock '88
Saturday the 14th Strikes Back '88
The Barbarians '87
Voyage of the Rock Aliens '87
Star Trek 4: The Voyage Home '86
Cut and Run '85
The Hills Have Eyes, Part 2 '84
Deadly Blessing '81
The Hills Have Eyes '77
One Flew Over the Cuckoo's Nest '75
Gator King '70

Julien Bertheau
That Obscure Object of Desire '77
Phantom of Liberty '74
Anders W. Berthelsen
Italian for Beginners '01
Mifune '99
Dehl Berti (1921-91)
Bullies '86
Wolfen '81
Sweet Hostage '75
Marina Berti
A Face in the Rain '63
Quo Vadis '51
Roland Bertin
Pas Tres Catholique '93
The Hairdresser's Husband '92
Cyrano de Bergerac '90
L'Homme Blesse '83
Diva '82
Valerie Bertinelli (1960-)
Taken Away '89
Pancho Barnes '88
Number One with a Bullet '87
Rockabye '86
Ordinary Heroes '85
Silent Witness '85
Aladdin and His Wonderful Lamp '84
Shattered Vows '84
C.H.O.M.P.S. '79
Young Love, First Love '79
Suzanne Bertish (1953-)
The Scarlet Pimpernel 3: The Kidnapped King '99
Venice, Venice '92
The Hunger '83
To the Lighthouse '83
Juliet Berto (1947-90)
Mr. Klein '76
Celine and Julie Go Boating '74
Le Sex Shop '73
The Joy of Knowledge '65
Paul Bertoya
Angels from Hell '68
Cop-Out '67
Bibi Besch (1940-96)
Rattled '96
Crazy from the Heart '91
Betsy's Wedding '90
Kill Me Again '89
Tremors '89
Date with an Angel '87
The Lonely Lady '83
The Beast Within '82
Star Trek 2: The Wrath of Khan '82
Death of a Centerfold '81
Peter Lundy and the Medicine Hat Stallion '77
Dominique Besnehard
Beaumarchais the Scoundrel '96
A Nos Amours '84
Ted Bessell (1935-96)
Acorn People '82
Breaking Up Is Hard to Do '79
Don't Drink the Water '69
Billie '65
McHale's Navy Joins the Air Force '65
Joe Besser (1907-88)
Savage Intruder '68
Africa Screams '49
Eugenie Besserer (1868-1934)
The Flesh and the Devil '27
The Jazz Singer '27
Anna Christie '23
What Happened to Rosa? '21
The Greatest Question '19
Little Orphan Annie '18
Ahmed Best
Star Wars: Episode 2—Attack of the Clones '02 (V)
Star Wars: Episode 1—The Phantom Menace '99 (V)
Edna Best (1900-74)
The Ghost and Mrs. Muir '47
Intermezzo '39
South Riding '37
The Man Who Knew Too Much '34
James Best (1926-)
Death Mask '98
Ode to Billy Joe '76
The Runaway Barge '75
Mind Warp '72
Sounder '72
Savage Run '70
Shenandoah '65
Shock Corridor '63
The Killer Shrews '59
Ride Lonesome '59
Verboten! '59
The Naked and the Dead '58
Ma and Pa Kettle at the Fair '52
Willie Best (1913-62)
The Ghost Breakers '40
The Bride Walks Out '36
The Littlest Rebel '35
Kentucky Kernels '34
The Monster Walks '32
Martine Beswick (1941-)
Night of the Scarecrow '95
Wide Sargasso Sea '92
Evil Spirits '91
Miami Blues '90
Trancers 2: The Return of Jack Deth '90
Cyclone '87
The Offspring '87
Balboa '82
The Happy Hooker Goes Hollywood '80
Strange New World '75
Seizure '74
Dr. Jekyll and Sister Hyde '71
A Bullet for the General '68
Prehistoric Women '67
One Million Years B.C. '66
Thunderball '65
From Russia with Love '63
Anne Betancourt
Bless the Child '00
Fools Rush In '97
Seedpeople '92
Sabine Bethmann (1931-)
Dr. Mabuse vs. Scotland Yard '64
The Indian Tomb '59
Journey to the Lost City '58
Zena Bethune
Who's That Knocking at My Door? '68
Sunrise at Campobello '60
Paul Bettany (1971-)
A Beautiful Mind '01
A Knight's Tale '01
Robert Louis Stevenson's The Game of Death '99
Coming Home '98
The Land Girls '98
Bent '97
Sharpe's Waterloo '97
Lyle Bettger (1915-)
Johnny Reno '66
Nevada Smith '66
Lone Ranger '56
Sea Chase '55
Carnival Story '54
All I Desire '53
Union Station '50
Laura Betti (1934-)
Courage Mountain '89
Lovers and Liars '81
1900 '76
Allonsanfan '73
Sonny and Jed '73
The Canterbury Tales '71
Twitch of the Death Nerve '71
Hatchet for the Honeymoon '70
Teorema '68
Val Bettin
The Return of Jafar '94 (V)
The Great Mouse Detective '86 (V)
Angela Bettis
The Flamingo Rising '01
Perfume '01
The Ponder Heart '01
Bless the Child '00
The Last Best Sunday '98
Robert Bettles (1962-)
Fourth Wish '75
Ride a Wild Pony '75
Franca Bettoya
Marauder '65
The Last Man on Earth '64
Daniel Betts
Heat of the Sun '99
The Magical Legend of the Leprechauns '99
The Canterville Ghost '96
Jack Betts
Spider-Man '02
Gods and Monsters '98
Dead Men Don't Die '91
The Bloody Brood '59
Carl Betz (1921-78)
Deadly Encounter '78
The Meal '75
Spinout '66
Matthew Betz (1881-1938)
Tarzan the Fearless '33
Broadway to Cheyenne '32
The Fighting Marshal '32
The Wedding March '28
The Unholy Three '25
Billy Bevan (1887-1957)
The Woman in Green '45
Mrs. Miniver '42
Dr. Jekyll and Mr. Hyde '41
Girl of the Golden West '38
The Wrong Road '37
The Lost Patrol '34
Cavalcade '33
Vanity Fair '32
High Voltage '29
The White Sin '24
Clem Bevans (1879-1963)
Gold Raiders '51
Silver City Bonanza '51
Rim of the Canyon '49
Highway 13 '48
Sergeant York '41
Abe Lincoln in Illinois '40
Helen Beverly
Meeting at Midnight '44
Overture to Glory '40
The Light Ahead '39
Green Fields '37
Leslie Bevis
The November Men '93
Alien Nation '88
Nathan Bexton (1977-)
The In Crowd '00
Psycho Beach Party '00
Go '99
Nowhere '96
Turhan Bey (1920-)
Virtual Combat '95
Parole, Inc. '49
The Amazing Mr. X '48
Out of the Blue '47
The Climax '44
Dragon Seed '44
Ali Baba and the Forty Thieves '43
Background to Danger '43
The Mad Ghoul '43
Arabian Nights '42
The Mummy's Tomb '42
Footsteps in the Dark '41
Shadows on the Stairs '41
Brad Beyer
Sorority Boys '02
Crazy in Alabama '99
The General's Daughter '99
Trick '99
Troy Beyer (1965-)
John Q '02
Let's Talk About Sex '98
B.A.P.'s '97
The Little Death '95
Weekend at Bernie's 2 '93
Rooftops '89
Richard Beymer (1939-)
Elvis Meets Nixon '98
Foxfire '96
The Disappearance of Kevin Johnson '95
The Little Death '95
Under Investigation '93
Black Belt '92
Silent Night, Deadly Night 3: Better Watch Out! '89
Cross Country '83
Free Grass '69
The Stripper '63
The Longest Day '62
West Side Story '61
The Diary of Anne Frank '59
Johnny Tremain & the Sons of Liberty '58
Indiscretion of an American Wife '54
Didier Bezace
The Chambermaid on the Titanic '97
Les Voleurs '96
Between Heaven and Earth '93
L.627 '92
The Little Thief '89
Dante "Mos Def" Beze
Showtime '02
Monster's Ball '01
Bhasker
Wild West '93
Drachenfutter '87
I Drink Your Blood '71
Daniela Bianchi (1942-)
Dirty Heroes '71
Secret Agent 00 '67
From Russia with Love '63
The Sword of El Cid '62
Yuen Biao (1957-)
Once Upon a Time in China '91
Miracles '89
Dragons Forever '88
Eastern Condors '87
The Millionaire's Express '86
Project A '83
Zu: Warriors from the Magic Mountain '83
The Prodigal Son '82
Leslie Bibb (1974-)
See Spot Run '01
The Skulls '00
Charles K. Bibby
Order of the Black Eagle '87
Unmasking the Idol '86
Abner Biberman (1909-77)
Elephant Walk '54
Betrayal from the East '44
The Keys of the Kingdom '44
The Leopard Man '43
His Girl Friday '40
Gunga Din '39
Panama Patrol '39
The Rains Came '39
Robert Bice (1914-68)
Invasion U.S.A. '52
Bandit King of Texas '49
Bruno Bichir
Midaq Alley '95
Highway Patrolman '91
Stewart Bick
Danger Beneath the Sea '02
Life with Judy Garland—Me and My Shadows '01
Mercy '00
Sex & Mrs. X '00
Captive '97
Charles Bickford (1889-1967)
A Big Hand for the Little Lady '66
Fatal Confinement '64
Days of Wine and Roses '62
The Unforgiven '60
The Big Country '58
The Court Martial of Billy Mitchell '55
Not as a Stranger '55
A Star Is Born '54
Jim Thorpe: All American '51
Branded '50
Guilty of Treason '50
Riding High '50
Babe Ruth Story '48
Command Decision '48
Four Faces West '48
Johnny Belinda '48
The Farmer's Daughter '47
Duel in the Sun '46
A Wing and a Prayer '44
Mr. Lucky '43
The Song of Bernadette '43
Reap the Wild Wind '42
Tarzan's New York Adventure '42
Mutiny in the Big House '39
Of Mice and Men '39
The Plainsman '37
Thunder Pass '37
Thunder Trail '37
The Farmer Takes a Wife '35
Little Miss Marker '34
East of Borneo '31
Anna Christie '30
Andrew Bicknell
A Dog of Flanders '99
Buffalo Girls '95
Prince Brat and the Whipping Boy '95
Heidi '93
Jean-Luc Bideau (1940-)
The Red Violin '98
Revenge of the Musketeers '94
Rendez-Moi Ma Peau '81
Jonah Who Will Be 25 in the Year 2000 '76
La Salamandre '71
Michael Biehn (1956-)
Clockstoppers '02
The Art of War '00
Chain of Command '00
Cherry Falls '00
Dying to Get Rich '98
The Magnificent Seven '98
Asteroid '97
Dead Men Can't Dance '97
Double Edge '97
Mojave Moon '96
The Rock '96
Breach of Trust '95
Frame by Frame '95
Jade '95
Blood of the Hunter '94
Deep Red '94
In the Kingdom of the Blind the Man with One Eye Is King '94
Deadfall '93
Strapped '93
Tombstone '93
K2: The Ultimate High '92
A Taste for Killing '92
Timebomb '91
Navy SEALS '90
The Abyss '89
In a Shallow Grave '88
The Seventh Sign '88
Rampage '87
Aliens '86
The Terminator '84
The Lords of Discipline '83
The Fan '81
Hog Wild '80
Coach '78
Grease '78
Dick Biel
Slime City '89
Splatter University '84
Jessica Biel (1982-)
Summer Catch '01
I'll Be Home for Christmas '98
Ulee's Gold '97
Josef Bierbichler
Winter Sleepers '97
Woyzeck '78
Heart of Glass '74
Ramon Bieri (1929-2001)
Love, Lies and Murder '91
Grandview U.S.A. '84
A Matter of Life and Death '81
A Christmas Without Snow '80
The Frisco Kid '79
Love Affair: The Eleanor & Lou Gehrig Story '77
Panic in Echo Park '77
Sorcerer '77
Badlands '74
It's Good to Be Alive '74
Nicole '72
The Andromeda Strain '71
The Passing of Evil '70
Craig Bierko (1965-)
The Suburbans '99
The Thirteenth Floor '99
Fear and Loathing in Las Vegas '98
Sour Grapes '98
The Long Kiss Goodnight '96
Til There Was You '96
Danielle Steel's Star '93
Victimless Crimes '90
Adam Biesk
Leprechaun 2 '94
The Applegates '89
Claudio Bigagli (1955-)
Fiorile '93
Mille Bolle Blu '93
Mediterraneo '91
Kaos '85
The Night of the Shooting Stars '82
Scott "Bam Bam" Bigelow (1961-)
Major Payne '95
SnakeEater 3: His Law '92
Dan Biggers
Flash '98
Basket Case 3: The Progeny '92
Sean Biggerstaff
Harry Potter and the Sorcerer's Stone '01
The Winter Guest '97
Jason Biggs (1978-)
American Pie 2 '01
Jay and Silent Bob Strike Back '01
Saving Silverman '01
Boys and Girls '00
Loser '00
American Pie '99
Richard Biggs
Ablaze '00
Forever Love '98
Roxann Biggs-Dawson (1964-)
Darkman 3: Die Darkman Die '95
Midnight's Child '93
Dirty Work '92
Guilty by Suspicion '91
Broken Angel '88
Theodore Bikel (1924-)
Second Chances '98
The Shadow Conspiracy '96
Benefit of the Doubt '93
My Family Treasure '93
The Assassination Game '92
Shattered '91
The Final Days '89
See You in the Morning '89
Dark Tower '87
Very Close Quarters '84
The Return of the King '80 (V)
Murder on Flight 502 '75
200 Motels '71
Darker than Amber '70
My Side of the Mountain '69

Sweet November '68
The Russians Are Coming, the Russians Are Coming '66
My Fair Lady '64
A Dog of Flanders '59
The Defiant Ones '58
Flight from Vienna '58
I Bury the Living '58
I Want to Live! '58
Enemy Below '57
The Pride and the Passion '57
Above Us the Waves '56
Never Let Me Go '53
Moulin Rouge '52
The African Queen '51

Fernando Bilbao
The Screaming Dead '72
Fangs of the Living Dead '68

Nicole Bilderback
Bring It On '00
Paper Bullets '99

Tony Bill (1940-)
Naked City: Justice with a Bullet '98
Barb Wire '96
The Killing Mind '90
Pee-wee's Big Adventure '85
Washington Mistress '81
Heart Beat '80
Little Dragons '80
Are You in the House Alone? '78
Initiation of Sarah '78
Shampoo '75
Haunts of the Very Rich '72
Ice Station Zebra '68
Never a Dull Moment '68
You're a Big Boy Now '66
None But the Brave '65
Come Blow Your Horn '63
Soldier in the Rain '63

Raoul Billerey
Revenge of the Musketeers '94
The Little Thief '89
Sorceress '88
Le Grand Chemin '87

Don Billett
Gloria '98
Prince of the City '81

Roy Billing
Siam Sunset '99
Doing Time for Patsy Cline '97

Dawn Ann Billings
Human Desires '97
Warlock: The Armageddon '93
Trancers 3: Deth Lives '92

Earl Billings
One False Move '91
Stakeout '87

Beau Billingslea
Silent Predators '99
Indecent Behavior 3 '95
Final Justice '94

Barbara Billingsley (1922-)
Leave It to Beaver '97
Back to the Beach '87
Eye of the Demon '87
Airplane! '80

Jennifer Billingsley
Hollywood Man '76
The Thirsty Dead '74
White Lightning '73
C.C. & Company '70
Lady in a Cage '64

Peter Billingsley (1971-)
Arcade '93
Beverly Hills Brats '89
Russkies '87
Dirt Bike Kid '86
A Christmas Story '83
Death Valley '81

Stephen Billington
Resident Evil '02
The Man Who Made Husbands Jealous '98
Braveheart '95

Sybilla Binder (1898-1962)
The Golden Salamander '51
Blanche Fury '48
Counterblast '48

Herman Bing (1889-1947)
Dumbo '41 (V)
Bitter Sweet '40
Bluebeard's Eighth Wife '38
Every Day's a Holiday '38
The Great Waltz '38
Maytime '37
Tango '36
That Girl from Paris '36
Crimson Romance '34
The Merry Widow '34
The Guardsman '31

Barbara Bingham
Beyond Darkness '92
Soldier's Fortune '91
Friday the 13th, Part 8: Jason Takes Manhattan '89

Geoffrey Binney
Raw Force '81
Hot Potato '76

Edward Binns (1916-90)
Return to Eden '89
The Verdict '82
Danger in the Skies '79
Oliver's Story '78
Night Moves '75
Hunter '73
Patton '70
The Americanization of Emily '64
A Public Affair '62
Judgment at Nuremberg '61
Compulsion '59
Curse of the Undead '59
Twelve Angry Men '57
Beyond a Reasonable Doubt '56
Without Warning '52

Juliette Binoche (1964-)
Chocolat '00
The Widow of Saint-Pierre '00
Alice et Martin '98
The English Patient '96
A Couch in New York '95
The Horseman on the Roof '95
Trois Couleurs: Blanc '94
Trois Couleurs: Rouge '94
Trois Couleurs: Bleu '93
Damage '92
Emily Bronte's Wuthering Heights '92
The Lovers on the Bridge '91
Women & Men: In Love There Are No Rules '91
The Unbearable Lightness of Being '88
Mauvais Sang '86
Hail Mary '85
Rendez-vous '85

Thelma Biral
Fridays of Eternity '81
El Muerto '75

Maurice Biraud (1922-82)
The Last Train '74
Any Number Can Win '63

Paul Birch (1913-69)
The Man Who Shot Liberty Valance '62
Queen of Outer Space '58
Apache Woman '55
Day the World Ended '55
Ride Clear of Diablo '54

Thora Birch (1982-)
Ghost World '01
Dungeons and Dragons '00
The Smokers '00
American Beauty '99
Night Ride Home '99
Alaska '96
Now and Then '95
Clear and Present Danger '94
Monkey Trouble '94
Hocus Pocus '93
Patriot Games '92
All I Want for Christmas '91
Paradise '91

Billie Bird (1908-)
Dennis the Menace '93
The End of Innocence '90
Home Alone '90
Ernest Saves Christmas '88
Sixteen Candles '84

Larry Bird
Celtic Pride '96
Blue Chips '94

Norman Bird (1919-)
The Slipper and the Rose '76
Hands of the Ripper '71
Burn Witch, Burn! '62
Victim '61
Whistle down the Wind '61

Jesse Birdsall (1963-)
Nightscare '93
Getting It Right '89
Wish You Were Here '87

Tala Birell (1907-58)
The Purple Heart '44
The White Legion '36
Crime and Punishment '35

Jane Birkin (1946-)
French Intrigue
The Last September '99
A Soldier's Daughter Never Cries '98
Same Old Song '97
Daddy Nostalgia '90
La Belle Noiseuse '90
Beethoven's Nephew '88
Le Petit Amour '87
Dust '85
Evil under the Sun '82
Make Room for Tomorrow '81
Death on the Nile '78
Catherine & Co. '76
Don Juan (Or If Don Juan Were a Woman) '73
Seven Deaths in the Cat's Eye '72
Too Pretty to Be Honest '72
Romance of a Horsethief '71
Swimming Pool '70
Wonderwall: The Movie '69
Blow-Up '66

Len Birman (1932-)
Web of Deceit '90
Undergrads '85
Captain America '79
Captain America 2: Death Too Soon '79
Lies My Father Told Me '75

Matt Birman
Family of Cops 2: Breach of Faith '97
Back in Action '94

Serafina Birman (1890-1976)
Ivan the Terrible, Part 2 '46
Ivan the Terrible, Part 1 '44
The Girl with the Hat Box '27

David Birney (1940-)
Nightfall '88
Prettykill '87
The Five of Me '81
Mom, the Wolfman and Me '80
Oh, God! Book 2 '80
Choice of Weapons '76
Caravan to Vaccares '74
Murder or Mercy '74
Only with Married Men '74

Reed Birney (1954-)
From the Earth to the Moon '98
Crimewave '85
Four Friends '81

Christopher Birt
A Soldier's Sweetheart '98
The Bodyguard '92

Debbie Bishop
Sid & Nancy '86
Scrubbers '82

Ed Bishop (1932-)
Saturn 3 '80
S.O.S. Titanic '79
Brass Target '78
The Devil's Web '74
Journey to the Far Side of the Sun '69

Jennifer Bishop
House of Terror '87
Jaws of Death '76
Jessi's Girls '75
Impulse '74
Horror of the Blood Monsters '70
The Female Bunch '69

Joey Bishop (1918-)
Trigger Happy '96
Betsy's Wedding '90
Delta Force '86
Valley of the Dolls '67
Who's Minding the Mint? '67
Texas across the River '66
Ocean's 11 '60
Deep Six '58
The Naked and the Dead '58

Julie (Jacqueline Wells) Bishop (1914-2001)
Westward the Women '51
Sands of Iwo Jima '49
The Last of the Redmen '47
Rhapsody in Blue '45
Action in the North Atlantic '43
Northern Pursuit '43
Her First Romance '40
Young Bill Hickok '40
The Kansas Terrors '39
Torture Ship '39
Bohemian Girl '36
The Black Cat '34
Tarzan the Fearless '33

Kelly Bishop (1944-)
Private Parts '96
Miami Rhapsody '95
Queens Logic '91
Dirty Dancing '87

Larry Bishop
Trigger Happy '96
Underworld '96
Soul Hustler '76
How Come Nobody's On Our Side? '73
Angel Unchained '70
The Savage Seven '68

Pat Bishop
Women of Valor '86
Don's Party '76

Stephen Bishop (1951-)
Someone to Love '87
Twilight Zone: The Movie '83
The Blues Brothers '80
National Lampoon's Animal House '78

Wes Bishop (1933-93)
Dixie Dynamite '76
Black Gestapo '75
Chain Gang Women '72
The Thing with Two Heads '72
Chrome and Hot Leather '71

William Bishop (1918-59)
Breakdown '53
The Redhead from Wyoming '53
Harriet Craig '50

Claudio Bisio
The Truce '96
Mediterraneo '91

Steve Bisley
Fast Talking '86
The Highest Honor '84
Chain Reaction '80
Mad Max '80

Whit Bissell (1919-96)
Soylent Green '73
Seven Days in May '64
Spencer's Mountain '63
The Manchurian Candidate '62
The Time Machine '60
No Name on the Bullet '59
Teenage Frankenstein '58
I Was a Teenage Werewolf '57
Invasion of the Body Snatchers '56
Shack Out on 101 '55
The Atomic Kid '54
The Caine Mutiny '54
Creature from the Black Lagoon '54
Devil's Canyon '53
Boots Malone '52
The Lost Continent '51
He Walked by Night '48
Raw Deal '48

Jacqueline Bisset (1944-)
Jesus '00
Sex & Mrs. X '00
Britannic '99
Joan of Arc '99
Let the Devil Wear Black '99
Dangerous Beauty '98
End of Summer '97
La Ceremonie '95
Crime Broker '94
The Maid '90
Wild Orchid '90
Scenes from the Class Struggle in Beverly Hills '89
High Season '88
Choices '86
Anna Karenina '85
Forbidden '85
Under the Volcano '84
Class '83
Rich and Famous '81
When Time Ran Out '80
Together? '79
The Greek Tycoon '78
Who Is Killing the Great Chefs of Europe? '78
The Deep '77
Le Magnifique '76
St. Ives '76
Spiral Staircase '75
Murder on the Orient Express '74
Day for Night '73
The Thief Who Came to Dinner '73
Life & Times of Judge Roy Bean '72
The Mephisto Waltz '71
Secrets '71
Airport '70
The Passing of Evil '70
The First Time '69
Bullitt '68
The Detective '68
Casino Royale '67
Two for the Road '67
Cul de Sac '66

Josie Bissett (1970-)
Baby Monitor: Sound of Fear '97
Mikey '92
All-American Murder '91
Book of Love '91

Chhabi Biswas (1900-62)
Devi '60
Jalsaghar '58

Bill Bixby (1934-93)
Death of the Incredible Hulk '90
The Trial of the Incredible Hulk '89
The Incredible Hulk Returns '88
The Incredible Hulk '77
Kentucky Fried Movie '77
Fantasy Island '76
Rich Man, Poor Man '76
The Apple Dumpling Gang '75
The Barbary Coast '74
Speedway '68
Clambake '67
Under the Yum-Yum Tree '63

Denise Bixler
The Assassination Game '92
Evil Dead 2: Dead by Dawn '87

Dragan Bjelogric (1963-)
The Wounds '98
Pretty Village, Pretty Flame '96
Hey, Babu Riba '88

Bjork
Dancer in the Dark '99
The Juniper Tree '87

Anita Bjork (1923-)
Secrets of Women '52
Miss Julie '50

Halvar Bjork (1928-)
Autumn Sonata '78
The New Land '73

Anna Bjorn
Sword & the Sorcerer '82
More American Graffiti '79

Gunnar Bjornstrand (1909-86)
Autumn Sonata '78
Face to Face '76
The Rite '69
The Shame '68
Persona '66
The Winter Light '62
Through a Glass Darkly '61
The Magician '58
Wild Strawberries '57
The Seventh Seal '56
Dreams '55
Smiles of a Summer Night '55
Lesson in Love '54
Torment '44

Claudia Black
Queen of the Damned '02
Pitch Black '00

Gerry Black
The Majestic '01
Re-Animator '84

Isobel Black
10 Rillington Place '71
Kiss of the Vampire '62

Jack Black (1969-)
Ice Age '02 (V)
Orange County '02
Saving Silverman '01
Shallow Hal '01
High Fidelity '00
Jesus' Son '99
Bongwater '98
Enemy of the State '98
The Jackal '97
Johnny Skidmarks '97
The Cable Guy '96
The NeverEnding Story 3: Escape from Fantasia '94

James Black
The Substitute 3: Winner Takes All '99
The First 9 1/2 Weeks '98
The Man with the Perfect Swing '95

Johanna Black
Hide and Seek '00
The Contract '98

Karen Black (1942-)
Hard Luck '01
Red Dirt '99
First Degree '98
Stir '98
Angel Blue '97
Conceiving Ada '97
Cries of Silence '97
Dogtown '97
Invisible Dad '97
Men '97
Children of the Corn 4: The Gathering '96
Crimetime '96
Dinosaur Valley Girls '96
Movies Money Murder '96
Plan 10 from Outer Space '95
Armistead Maupin's Tales of the City '93
Bound and Gagged: A Love Story '93
Auntie Lee's Meat Pies '92

Caged Fear '92
Children of the Night '92
The Double O Kid '92
Final Judgment '92
Hitz '92
The Player '92
Rubin & Ed '92
Evil Spirits '91
Haunting Fear '91
Quiet Fire '91
The Children '90
Club Fed '90
The Killer's Edge '90
Mirror, Mirror '90
Night Angel '90
Overexposed '90
Love Under Pressure '80s
Homer and Eddie '89
Twisted Justice '89
Zapped Again '89
Dixie Lanes '88
The Invisible Kid '88
Out of the Dark '88
Eternal Evil '87
Hostage '87
It's Alive 3: Island of the Alive '87
Invaders from Mars '86
Cut and Run '85
Martin's Day '85
Bad Manners '84
Killing Heat '84
Savage Dawn '84
Can She Bake a Cherry Pie? '83
Come Back to the Five & Dime Jimmy Dean, Jimmy Dean '82
Separate Ways '82
Chanel Solitaire '81
Miss Right '81
The Last Word '80
The Squeeze '80
Killer Fish '79
Mr. Horn '79
Capricorn One '78
In Praise of Older Women '78
The Rip Off '78
The Squeeze '78
Burnt Offerings '76
Family Plot '76
Airport '75 '75
Crime & Passion '75
The Day of the Locust '75
Nashville '75
Trilogy of Terror '75
The Great Gatsby '74
Law and Disorder '74
Little Laura & Big John '73
The Pyx '73
Portnoy's Complaint '72
Born to Win '71
A Gunfight '71
Five Easy Pieces '70
Easy Rider '69
You're a Big Boy Now '66
The Prime Time '60

Lucas Black (1982-)
All the Pretty Horses '00
The Miracle Worker '00
Crazy in Alabama '99
Flash '98
The X-Files '98
Ghosts of Mississippi '96
Sling Blade '96

Maurice Black (1891-1938)
Sixteen Fathoms Deep '34
Marked Money '28

Michael Ian Black
Wet Hot American Summer '01
The Bogus Witch Project '00

Ryan Black
Dance Me Outside '95
Geronimo '93

Shane Black
An Alan Smithee Film: Burn, Hollywood, Burn '97
As Good As It Gets '97
Predator '87

Richard Blackburn
Eating Raoul '82
Lemora, Lady Dracula '73

Richard Blackburn
Stephen King's The Storm of the Century '99
Down in the Delta '98
Murder at 1600 '97
In Love and War '96
Sugartime '95
A Man in Uniform '93

Honor Blackman (1926-)
Russell Mulcahy's Tale of the Mummy '99
To Walk with Lions '99
The First Olympics: Athens 1896 '84
The Cat and the Canary '79
To the Devil, a Daughter '76
Fright '71
The Virgin and the Gypsy '70
Lola '69
Shalako '68
Moment to Moment '66
Goldfinger '64
Jason and the Argonauts '63
A Matter of WHO '62
A Night to Remember '58
Suspended Alibi '56
Glass Tomb '55
Green Grow the Rushes '51
Conspirator '49

Joan Blackman (1938-)
Macon County Line '74
Daring Game '68
Blue Hawaii '62
Kid Galahad '62
Career '59
Good Day for a Hanging '58

Sidney Blackmer (1895-1973)
Rosemary's Baby '68
How to Murder Your Wife '64
Tammy and the Bachelor '57
Beyond a Reasonable Doubt '56
High Society '56
People Will Talk '51
Buffalo Bill '44
Wilson '44
War of the Wildcats '43
The Panther's Claw '42
Love Crazy '41
Law of the Pampas '39
Heidi '37
The House of Secrets '37
In Old Chicago '37
The President's Mystery '36
The Little Colonel '35
The Count of Monte Cristo '34
Goodbye Love '34
Transatlantic Merry-Go-Round '34
Deluge '33
Little Caesar '30

David Blackwell
The Rookie '02
China O'Brien '88

Taurean Blacque (1941-)
Deepstar Six '89
Oliver & Company '88 (V)
The $5.20 an Hour Dream '80

Ruben Blades (1948-)
All the Pretty Horses '00
The Cradle Will Rock '99
Chinese Box '97
The Devil's Own '96
Scorpion Spring '96
Color of Night '94
A Million to Juan '94
Life with Mikey '93
Crazy from the Heart '91
The Super '91
The Josephine Baker Story '90
The Lemon Sisters '90
Mo' Better Blues '90
One Man's War '90
Predator 2 '90
The Two Jakes '90
Dead Man Out '89
Disorganized Crime '89
Homeboy '88
The Milagro Beanfield War '88
Fatal Beauty '87
Critical Condition '86
Crossover Dreams '85
The Last Fight '82

Estella Blain (1936-81)
The Diabolical Dr. Z '65
Pirates of the Coast '61
The Twilight Girls '57

Gerard Blain (1930-2000)
The American Friend '77
Hatari! '62
The Cousins '59
Le Beau Serge '58

Vivian Blaine (1921-95)
Parasite '82
The Cracker Factory '79
The Dark '79
Guys and Dolls '55
Skirts Ahoy! '52
Doll Face '46
State Fair '45

Betsy Blair (1923-)
Scarlett '94
Suspicion '87
Il Grido '57
Marty '55

Isla Blair (1944-)
The Match '99
The Final Cut '95
Taste the Blood of Dracula '70

Janet Blair (1921-)
The One and Only, Genuine, Original Family Band '68
Boys' Night Out '62
Burn Witch, Burn! '62
Black Arrow '48
The Fuller Brush Man '48
The Fabulous Dorseys '47
Tonight and Every Night '45
Blondie Goes to College '42

Linda Blair (1959-)
Gang Boys '97
Scream '96
Sorceress '94
Dead Sleep '91
Fatal Bond '91
Bail Out '90
Repossessed '90
Bedroom Eyes 2 '89
The Chilling '89
Moving Target '89
Up Your Alley '89
Zapped Again '89
Silent Assassins '88
Witchery '88
A Woman Obsessed '88
Grotesque '87
Nightforce '86
Night Patrol '85
Red Heat '85
Savage Island '85
Chained Heat '83
Savage Streets '83
Hell Night '81
Ruckus '81
Roller Boogie '79
Wild Horse Hank '79
Summer of Fear '78
The Exorcist 2: The Heretic '77
Airport '75 '75
Sweet Hostage '75
Born Innocent '74
The Exorcist '73
The Sporting Club '72

Nicky Blair (1926-98)
The Crossing Guard '94
Viva Las Vegas '63

Selma Blair (1972-)
A Guy Thing '02
The Sweetest Thing '02
Highway '01
Kill Me Later '01
Legally Blonde '01
Storytelling '01
Down to You '00
Brown's Requiem '98
Cruel Intentions '98
Girl '98
No Laughing Matter '97

Tom Blair
The Bed You Sleep In '93
Sure Fire '90
The Game '89

Deborah (Tracey Adams) Blaisdell (1959-)
Wildest Dreams '90
Student Affairs '88
Wimps '87

Nesbitt Blaisdell (1928-)
The Mothman Prophecies '02
Addicted to Love '96

Paul Blaisdell
It Conquered the World '56
Day the World Ended '55

Amanda Blake (1929-89)
The Boost '88
B.O.R.N. '88
Gunsmoke: Return to Dodge '87
Betrayal '74
The Glass Slipper '55
Sabre Jet '53
The Duchess of Idaho '50
Stars in My Crown '50

Andre B. Blake
The Other Brother '02
Just the Ticket '98
Philadelphia '93
Who's the Man? '93

Geoffrey Blake (1962-)
Life Without Dick '01
Cast Away '00
Contact '97
Entertaining Angels: The Dorothy Day Story '96
The War at Home '96
Dominion '94
Marilyn & Bobby: Her Final Affair '94
Philadelphia Experiment 2 '93
Fatal Exposure '91
The Abduction of Kari Swenson '87

Jon Blake
The Lighthorsemen '87
Anzacs: The War Down Under '85
Early Frost '84
Freedom '81

Julia Blake
Passion '99
Hotel de Love '96
Father '90
Georgia '87
Travelling North '87
Man of Flowers '84
Lonely Hearts '82
Under Capricorn '82
My Brilliant Career '79

Larry J. Blake (-1982)
Demon Seed '77
Beginning of the End '57
Holiday Affair '49

Madge Blake (1899-1969)
Batman '66
Singin' in the Rain '52
Prowler '51

Marie Blake (1896-1978)
Sensations of 1945 '44
Love Finds Andy Hardy '38

Noah Blake (1964-)
The Base '99
Class of Fear '91
Trapper County War '89

Oliver Blake (1905-92)
Ma and Pa Kettle at Waikiki '55
Casablanca '42

Pamela Blake (1918-)
Border Rangers '50
Gunfire '50
Sky Liner '49
Highway 13 '48
Rolling Home '48
Son of God's Country '48
Hat Box Mystery '47
Sea Hound '47
Kid Dynamite '43

Robert (Bobby) Blake (1933-)
Lost Highway '96
Money Train '95
Heart of a Champion: The Ray Mancini Story '85
Of Mice and Men '81
Coast to Coast '80
Busting '74
Electra Glide in Blue '73
Counter Punch '71
Tell Them Willie Boy Is Here '69
In Cold Blood '67
This Property Is Condemned '66
PT 109 '63
Town without Pity '61
Pork Chop Hill '59
Treasure of the Golden Condor '53
Treasure of the Sierra Madre '48
Homesteaders of Paradise Valley '47
Humoresque '46
Santa Fe Uprising '46
Stagecoach to Denver '46
Vigilantes of Boom Town '46
Woman in the Window '44
Andy Hardy's Double Life '42

Colin Blakely (1930-87)
Operation Julie '85
Loophole '83
Evil under the Sun '82
The Dogs of War '81
Little Lord Fauntleroy '80
Nijinsky '80
The Big Sleep '78
Equus '77
The Pink Panther Strikes Again '76
Love Among the Ruins '75
Murder on the Orient Express '74
Shattered '72
The Private Life of Sherlock Holmes '70
The Vengeance of She '68
This Sporting Life '63

Donald Blakely
In the Shadow of Kilimanjaro '86
Vigilante '83
Short Eyes '79
Strike Force '75

Susan Blakely (1950-)
Extreme Limits '01
The Perfect Nanny '00
Honor Thy Father and Mother: The True Story of the Menendez Brothers '94
Russian Roulette '93
Intruders '92
Blackmail '91
Wildflower '91
Dead Reckoning '89
The Incident '89
My Mom's a Werewolf '89
Out of Sight, Out of Her Mind '89
Broken Angel '88
Hiroshima Maiden '88
Ladykillers '88
The Survivalist '87
Over the Top '86
A Cry for Love '80
Make Me an Offer '80
The Concorde: Airport '79 '79
Dreamer '79
Secrets '77
Rich Man, Poor Man '76
The Lords of Flatbush '74
Report to the Commissioner '74
The Towering Inferno '74
Savages '72

Olive Blakeney (1903-59)
Billy the Kid '41
Gangway '37

Ronee Blakley (1946-)
Murder by Numbers '89
Return to Salem's Lot '87
Someone to Love '87
Student Confidential '87
A Nightmare on Elm Street '84
The Baltimore Bullet '80
Desperate Women '78
The Driver '78
The Private Files of J. Edgar Hoover '77
She Came to the Valley '77
Nashville '75

Dominique Blanc (1962-)
A Soldier's Daughter Never Cries '98
Those Who Love Me Can Take the Train '98
Total Eclipse '95
Queen Margot '94
Indochine '92
May Fools '90

Erika Blanc (1942-)
Sweet Spirits '80s
The Boss Is Served '76
Mark of the Devil 2 '72
The Devil's Nightmare '71
The Night Evelyn Came Out of the Grave '71
Sartana's Here...Trade Your Pistol for a Coffin '70
Special Forces '68
Kill, Baby, Kill '66

Mel Blanc (1908-89)
Jetsons: The Movie '90 (V)
Who Framed Roger Rabbit '88 (V)
Strange Brew '83 (V)
Looney Looney Looney Bugs Bunny Movie '81 (V)
Buck Rogers in the 25th Century '79 (V)
Phantom Tollbooth '69 (V)
Hey There, It's Yogi Bear '64 (V)
Kiss Me, Stupid! '64
Gay Purr-ee '62 (V)
Neptune's Daughter '49

Michel Blanc (1952-)
The Monster '96
Grosse Fatigue '94
Ready to Wear '94
The Favor, the Watch, & the Very Big Fish '92
Prospero's Books '91
Uranus '91
Monsieur Hire '89
Menage '86
French Fried Vacation '79
The Tenant '76

Pierre Blanchar (1892-1963)
La Symphonie Pastorale '46
Man from Nowhere '37
Crime and Punishment '35

Jarred Blanchard
The Boys Club '96
The Yearling '94

Mari Blanchard (1927-70)
Son of Sinbad '55
Abbott and Costello Go to Mars '53

Rachel Blanchard (1976-)
Chasing Holden '01
Sugar & Spice '01
Road Trip '00
The Rage: Carrie 2 '99
Iron Eagle 4 '95
Young Ivanhoe '95

Susan Blanchard
Prince of Darkness '87
She's in the Army Now '81
President's Mistress '78

Tammy Blanchard (1976-)
Life with Judy Garland—Me and My Shadows *'01*

Cate Blanchett (1969-)
Bandits *'01*
Charlotte Gray *'01*
Lord of the Rings 1: The Fellowship of the Rings *'01*
The Shipping News *'01*
The Gift *'00*
The Man Who Cried *'00*
An Ideal Husband *'99*
Pushing Tin *'99*
The Talented Mr. Ripley *'99*
Elizabeth *'98*
Oscar and Lucinda *'97*
Paradise Road *'97*
The Wedding Party *'97*

Dorothee Blanck
Umbrellas of Cherbourg *'64*
Cleo from 5 to 7 *'61*

Sandrine Blancke
The Son of the Shark *'93*
Toto le Heros *'91*

Peter Bland
Tearaway *'87*
Dangerous Orphans *'86*
Came a Hot Friday *'85*

Clara Blandick (1880-1962)
Infamous Crimes *'47*
Dead Man's Eyes/Pillow of Death *'44*
It Started with Eve *'41*
Dreaming Out Loud *'40*
The Wizard of Oz *'39*
Small Town Boy *'37*
The Girl from Missouri *'34*
The Bitter Tea of General Yen *'33*
Murder at Midnight *'31*
Romance *'30*

Sally Blane (1910-97)
Fighting Mad *'39*
The Story of Alexander Graham Bell *'39*
Way Down South *'39*
Law of the Sea *'38*
The Silver Streak *'34*
Heritage of the Desert *'33*
Night of Terror *'33*
Cross Examination *'32*
Phantom Express *'32*
Probation *'32*
When the West Was Young *'32*
Vagabond Lover *'29*

Mark Blankfield (1950-)
The Great American Sex Scandal *'94*
Robin Hood: Men in Tights *'93*
Angel 3: The Final Chapter *'88*
Frankenstein General Hospital *'88*
The Midnight Hour *'86*
Jack & the Beanstalk *'83*
Jekyll & Hyde...Together Again *'82*

Billy Blanks (1956-)
Shadow Warriors *'97*
Balance of Power *'96*
Expect No Mercy *'95*
Back in Action *'94*
Tough and Deadly *'94*
Showdown *'93*
TC 2000 *'93*
Talons of the Eagle *'92*
The King of the Kickboxers *'91*
The Last Boy Scout *'91*
Timebomb *'91*
Bloodfist *'89*

Arell Blanton
Assault of the Killer Bimbos *'88*
House of Terror *'87*
Wild Riders *'71*

Charles Blavette
The Horror Chamber of Dr. Faustus *'59*
Toni *'34*

Hans-Christian Blech (1915-93)
Colonel Redl *'84*
The Wrong Move *'78*
Dirty Hands *'76*
Innocents with Dirty Hands *'75*
The Scarlet Letter *'73*
Battle of the Bulge *'65*
The Blum Affair *'48*

Jonah Blechman
Treasure Island *'99*
Fall Time *'94*
This Boy's Life *'93*

Debra Blee (1961-)
Malibu Bikini Shop *'86*
Sloane *'84*
Savage Streets *'83*
Beach Girls *'82*

Yasmine Bleeth (1968-)
Coming Soon *'99*
Undercover Angel *'99*
BASEketball *'98*
Heaven or Vegas *'98*
It Came from the Sky *'98*
Baywatch the Movie: Forbidden Paradise *'95*

Moritz Bleibtreu
Invisible Circus *'00*
Run Lola Run *'98*

Brian Blessed (1937-)
Star Wars: Episode 1—The Phantom Menace *'99*
Tarzan *'99 (V)*
Tom Jones *'98*
The Bruce *'96*
Hamlet *'96*
Catherine the Great *'95*
Kidnapped *'95*
Chasing the Deer *'94*
Much Ado about Nothing *'93*
Back in the USSR *'92*
Freddie the Frog *'92 (V)*
Prisoner of Honor *'91*
Robin Hood: Prince of Thieves *'91*
Henry V *'89*
High Road to China *'83*
The Hound of the Baskervilles *'83*
Flash Gordon *'80*
King Arthur, the Young Warlord *'75*
Young Warlord *'75*
Man of La Mancha *'72*
Cold Comfort Farm *'71*
Trojan Women *'71*

Jack Blessing
Above Suspicion *'00*
The Last of His Tribe *'92*
Galaxy of Terror *'81*

Billy Bletcher (1894-1979)
Boss of Rawhide *'44*
God's Country and the Man *'37*
Hollywood Party *'34 (V)*
Boiling Point *'32*
Branded Men *'31*

Brenda Blethyn (1946-)
Lovely & Amazing *'02*
Saving Grace *'00*
RKO 281 *'99*
In the Winter Dark *'98*
Little Voice *'98*
Girls' Night *'97*
Music from Another Room *'97*
Secrets and Lies *'95*
The Buddha of Suburbia *'92*
A River Runs Through It *'92*
The Witches *'90*
Grown Ups *'80*

Jason Blicker
Naked City: A Killer Christmas *'98*
African Journey *'89*
American Boyfriends *'89*

Bernard Blier (1916-89)
The Possessed *'88*
Buffet Froid *'79*
The Daydreamer *'75*
The Tall Blond Man with One Black Shoe *'72*
Catch Me a Spy *'71*
Casanova '70 *'65*
The Organizer *'64*
Les Miserables *'57*
The Man in the Raincoat *'57*
Dedee d'Anvers *'49*
Passion for Life *'48*
Jenny Lamour *'47*

Hunt Block
The Dirty Dozen: The Fatal Mission *'88*
Secret Weapons *'85*

Larry Block (1943-)
Dead Man Out *'89*
High Stakes *'89*
After Hours *'85*

Dan Blocker (1928-72)
Lady in Cement *'68*
Ride the Wind *'66*
The Errand Boy *'61*

Dirk Blocker (1957-)
Night of the Scarecrow *'95*
Bonanza: The Return *'93*
Prince of Darkness *'87*
Trouble in Mind *'86*

Michael Blodgett (1940-)
The Ultimate Thrill *'74*
The Velvet Vampire *'71*
Beyond the Valley of the Dolls *'70*
The Trip *'67*

Joan Blondell (1909-79)
The Baron *'88*
The Woman Inside *'83*
The Champ *'79*
The Rebels *'79*
The Glove *'78*
Grease *'78*
Opening Night *'77*
The Dead Don't Die *'75*
Death at Love House *'75*
Support Your Local Gunfighter *'71*
Stay Away, Joe *'68*
Waterhole #3 *'67*
The Cincinnati Kid *'65*
Angel Baby *'61*
Desk Set *'57*
This Could Be the Night *'57*
Will Success Spoil Rock Hunter? *'57*
The Opposite Sex *'56*
Adventure *'45*
A Tree Grows in Brooklyn *'45*
Lady for a Night *'42*
Topper Returns *'41*
Bullets or Ballots *'38*
Stand-In *'37*
Three Men on a Horse *'36*
Dames *'34*
Footlight Parade *'33*
Gold Diggers of 1933 *'33*
Three Broadway Girls *'32*
Three on a Match *'32*
Big Business Girl *'31*
Blonde Crazy *'31*
Illicit *'31*
Millie *'31*
Night Nurse *'31*
Public Enemy *'31*

Simone Blondell
Dr. Frankenstein's Castle of Freaks *'74*
Jungle Master *'56*

Anne Bloom
That's Adequate *'90*
Dirt Bike Kid *'86*

Brian Bloom (1970-)
Across the Line *'00*
Blood Money *'99*
Knocking on Death's Door *'99*
Extramarital *'98*
The Sender *'98*
Escape from Atlantis *'97*
Melanie Darrow *'97*
Vampirella *'96*
At Home with the Webbers *'94*
Confessions of Sorority Girls *'94*
Voyage of Terror: The Achille Lauro Affair *'90*
Walls of Glass *'85*

Claire Bloom (1931-)
The Lady in Question *'99*
What the Deaf Man Heard *'98*
Daylight *'96*
Mighty Aphrodite *'95*
A Village Affair *'95*
The Princess and the Goblin *'94 (V)*
Shameless *'94*
Crimes & Misdemeanors *'89*
A Doll's House *'89*
Shadow on the Sun *'88*
Intimate Contact *'87*
Queenie *'87*
Sammy & Rosie Get Laid *'87*
Anastasia: The Mystery of Anna *'86*
Hold the Dream *'86*
Shadowlands *'85*
This Lightning Always Strikes Twice *'85*
Deja Vu *'84*
Ghostwriter *'84*
Separate Tables *'83*
Brideshead Revisited *'81*
Clash of the Titans *'81*
Islands in the Stream *'77*
The Illustrated Man *'69*
Charly *'68*
Soldier in Love *'67*
The Spy Who Came in from the Cold *'65*
The Haunting *'63*
The Wonderful World of the Brothers Grimm *'62*
Brainwashed *'60*
The Brothers Karamazov *'58*
The Buccaneer *'58*
Look Back in Anger *'58*
Alexander the Great *'55*
Richard III *'55*
Innocents in Paris *'53*
Limelight *'52*

John Bloom (1945-99)
Frozen Assets *'92*
The Great Outdoors *'88*
Harry and the Hendersons *'87*
Runaway Train *'85*
Bachelor Party *'84*
The Hills Have Eyes, Part 2 *'84*
The Dark *'79*
Brain of Blood *'71*
Dracula vs. Frankenstein *'71*
The Incredible Two-Headed Transplant *'71*

John (Joe Bob Briggs) Bloom (1953-)
Casino *'95*
Stephen King's The Stand *'94*
The Texas Chainsaw Massacre 2 *'86*

Lindsay Bloom (1952-)
French Quarter *'78*
Hughes & Harlow: Angels in Hell *'77*
Texas Detour *'77*
Cover Girl Models *'75*

Orlando Bloom (1977-)
Black Hawk Down *'01*
Lord of the Rings 1: The Fellowship of the Rings *'01*

Verna Bloom (1939-)
The Last Temptation of Christ *'88*
After Hours *'85*
The Journey of Natty Gann *'85*
Honkytonk Man *'82*
Playing for Time *'80*
National Lampoon's Animal House *'78*
The Blue Knight *'75*
Where Have All the People Gone? *'74*
Badge 373 *'73*
High Plains Drifter *'73*
Hired Hand *'71*
Medium Cool *'69*

Eric Blore (1887-1959)
Fancy Pants *'50*
Love Happy *'50*
The Adventures of Ichabod and Mr. Toad *'49 (V)*
Romance on the High Seas *'48*
The Moon and Sixpence *'43*
The Shanghai Gesture *'42*
The Lady Eve *'41*
Lady Scarface *'41*
The Road to Zanzibar *'41*
Sullivan's Travels *'41*
Music in My Heart *'40*
Joy of Living *'38*
Swiss Miss *'38*
Quality Street *'37*
Shall We Dance *'37*
Ex-Mrs. Bradford *'36*
Swing Time *'36*
I Dream Too Much *'35*
I Live My Life *'35*
Top Hat *'35*
The Gay Divorcee *'34*
Flying Down to Rio *'33*

Roberts Blossom (1924-)
Balloon Farm *'97*
The Quick and the Dead *'94*
Doc Hollywood *'91*
Home Alone *'90*
Always *'89*
The Last Temptation of Christ *'88*
Candy Mountain *'87*
Vision Quest *'85*
Christine *'84*
Flashpoint *'84*
Reuben, Reuben *'83*
Johnny Belinda *'82*
Resurrection *'80*
Escape from Alcatraz *'79*
Citizens Band *'77*
Deranged *'74*
Slaughterhouse Five *'72*
The Hospital *'71*

Lisa Blount (1957-)
Box of Moonlight *'96*
Judicial Consent *'94*
Stalked *'94*
An American Story *'92*
Blind Fury *'90*
Femme Fatale *'90*
Great Balls of Fire *'89*
Nightflyers *'87*
Prince of Darkness *'87*
South of Reno *'87*
Radioactive Dreams *'86*
Cease Fire *'85*
Cut and Run *'85*
What Waits Below *'83*
An Officer and a Gentleman *'82*
Dead and Buried *'81*
September 30, 1955 *'77*

Kurtis Blow
The Show *'95*
Krush Groove *'85*

Marc Blucas (1972-)
Sunshine State *'02*
We Were Soldiers *'02*
Summer Catch *'01*

Ben Blue (1901-75)
Where Were You When the Lights Went Out? *'68*
The Russians Are Coming, the Russians Are Coming *'66*
Broadway Rhythm *'44*
Two Girls and a Sailor *'44*
For Me and My Gal *'42*
Panama Hattie *'42*
The Big Broadcast of 1938 *'38*
College Swing *'38*

Monte Blue (1890-1963)
Silver River *'48*
The Mask of Dimitrios *'44*
Across the Pacific *'42*
Casablanca *'42*
Bad Man of Deadwood *'41*
Young Bill Hickok *'40*
Helltown *'38*
Rootin' Tootin' Rhythm *'38*
A Million to One *'37*
Thunder Pass *'37*
Thunder Trail *'37*
Desert Gold *'36*
Prison Shadows *'36*
Ride, Ranger, Ride *'36*
Song of the Gringo *'36*
Undersea Kingdom *'36*
The Lives of a Bengal Lancer *'35*
Wagon Wheels *'34*
White Shadows in the South Seas *'29*
So This Is Paris *'26*
The Marriage Circle *'24*
Affairs of Anatol *'21*
Orphans of the Storm *'21*
The Man from Painted Post *'17*

Brady Bluhm
Alone in the Woods *'95*
The Crazysitter *'94*

Ina Blum
Virgin Machine *'88*
Anita, Dances of Vice *'87*

Jack Blum
SnakeEater 2: The Drug Buster *'89*
Happy Birthday to Me *'81*

Mark Blum (1950-)
Indictment: The McMartin Trial *'95*
Worth Winning *'89*
The Presidio *'88*
Blind Date *'87*
Crocodile Dundee *'86*
Desperately Seeking Susan *'85*

Alan Blumenfeld
Black Belt *'92*
Problem Child 2 *'91*
Dark Side of the Moon *'90*
Instant Karma *'90*
Night Life *'90*
Worth Winning *'89*

Graeme Blundell (1945-)
Idiot Box *'97*
The Year My Voice Broke *'87*
Doctors and Nurses *'82*
The Odd Angry Shot *'79*
Weekend of Shadows *'77*
Don's Party *'76*
Alvin Rides Again *'74*
Alvin Purple *'73*

Erin Blunt
The Bad News Bears Go to Japan *'78*
The Bad News Bears in Breaking Training *'77*
The Bad News Bears *'76*

Lothaire Bluteau (1957-)
Urbania *'00*
Restless Spirits *'99*
Conquest *'98*
Shot Through the Heart *'98*
Bent *'97*
I Shot Andy Warhol *'96*
Nostromo *'96*
The Confessional *'95*
Other Voices, Other Rooms *'95*
The Silent Touch *'94*
Mrs. 'Arris Goes to Paris *'92*
Orlando *'92*
Black Robe *'91*
Jesus of Montreal *'89*

John Bluthal (1929-)
Dark City *'97*
The Fifth Element *'97*
Leapin' Leprechauns *'95*
Help! *'65*

Margaret Blye
Silhouette *'91*

Mischief '85
Little Darlings '80
Melvin Purvis: G-Man '74
Ash Wednesday '73
The Sporting Club '72
The Italian Job '69
Waterhole #3 '67

Stanley Blystone (1894-1956)
Fighting Parson '35
Man of Action '33
The Fighting Legion '30

Ann Blyth (1928-)
The King's Thief '55
Kismet '55
Rose Marie '54
The Student Prince '54
All the Brothers Were Valiant '53
One Minute to Zero '52
The World in His Arms '52
The Great Caruso '51
Our Very Own '50
Mr. Peabody & the Mermaid '48
Mildred Pierce '45

Benedick Blythe
The Apocalypse Watch '97
One Against the Wind '91

Betty Blythe (1893-1972)
They Were Expendable '45
Girls in Chains '43
Dawn on the Great Divide '42
House of Errors '42
Miracle Kid '42
Honky Tonk '41
Misbehaving Husbands '41
The Scarlet Letter '34
She '21
Nomads of the North '20

Domini Blythe
Afterglow '97
Vampire Circus '71

Janus Blythe
Soldier's Fortune '91
The Hills Have Eyes, Part 2 '84
The Hills Have Eyes '77
Eaten Alive '76

John Blythe
This Happy Breed '47
Alfred Hitchcock's Bon Voyage '44

Peter Blythe
The Luzhin Defence '00
Carrington '95
A Challenge for Robin Hood '68
Frankenstein Created Woman '66

Bruce Boa
The Neighbor '93
White Light '90
Murder Story '89
Full Metal Jacket '87

Eleanor Boardman
She Goes to War '29
The Crowd '28

Virginia True Boardman
Brand of the Outlaws '36
Test of Donald Norton '26

Michael Boatman (1964-)
The Peacemaker '97
The Glass Shield '95
Urban Crossfire '94
China Beach '88
Hamburger Hill '87

Anne Bobby (1967-)
What the Deaf Man Heard '98
Beautiful Girls '96
Scott Turow's The Burden of Proof '92
Baby of the Bride '91
Nightbreed '90

Delia Boccardo (1948-)
Nostalghia '83
Tentacles '77
A Woman at Her Window '77

Hart Bochner (1956-)
Urban Legends 2: Final Cut '00
Anywhere But Here '99
The Break Up '98
A Good Day to Die '95
Batman: Mask of the Phantasm '93 (V)
The Innocent '93
Mad at the Moon '92
Mr. Destiny '90
Fellow Traveler '89
War & Remembrance: The Final Chapter '89
Apartment Zero '88
Die Hard '88
War & Remembrance '88
Making Mr. Right '86
Supergirl '84
The Wild Life '84
Having It All '82
Rich and Famous '81
East of Eden '80
Terror Train '80

Lloyd Bochner (1924-)
Bram Stoker's The Mummy '97
Morning Glory '93
Landslide '92
Naked Gun 2 1/2: The Smell of Fear '91
Millennium '89
Fine Gold '88
Crystal Heart '87
Louisiana '87
The Lonely Lady '83
Mazes and Monsters '82
Mary and Joseph: A Story of Faith '79
Terraces '77
Satan's School for Girls '73
Ulzana's Raid '72
The Dunwich Horror '70
The Horse in the Gray Flannel Suit '68
Point Blank '67
Tony Rome '67
The Night Walker '64

Robert Bockstael
Snap Decision '01
The Golden Spiders: A Nero Wolfe Mystery '00
Invasion! '99
All I Wanna Do '98

Jose Bodalo
Garringo '69
Django '68

Martin Boddey
Black Glove '54
Valley of the Eagles '51

Wolfgang Bodison (1966-)
Most Wanted '97
The Expert '95
Freeway '95
Little Big League '94
A Few Good Men '92

Erika Bodnar
Almanac of Fall
A Happy New Year! '79

Jenna Bodnar
The Portrait '99
Friend of the Family 2 '96

Sergei Bodrov, Jr. (1971-)
East-West '99
Brother '97
Prisoner of the Mountains '96

Karl-Heinz Boehm (1927-)
Mother Kusters Goes to Heaven '76
Fox and His Friends '75
The Wonderful World of the Brothers Grimm '62
Peeping Tom '60
Unnatural '52

Earl Boen (1945-)
Nutty Professor 2: The Klumps '00
Within the Rock '96
Norma Jean and Marilyn '95
Terminator 2: Judgment Day '91
The Terminator '84

Beatrice Boepple
A Nightmare on Elm Street 5: Dream Child '89
Quarantine '89

Dirk Bogarde (1920-99)
Daddy Nostalgia '90
The Vision '87
Despair '78
A Bridge Too Far '77
Providence '77
Permission To Kill '75
The Night Porter '74
Night Flight from Moscow '73
Death in Venice '71
The Damned '69
Justine '69
The Fixer '68
Sebastian '68
Accident '67
Modesty Blaise '66
Darling '65
King and Country '64
Doctor in Distress '63
I Could Go on Singing '63
The Servant '63
Damn the Defiant '62
Victim '61
Song Without End '60
A Tale of Two Cities '58
Doctor at Large '57
Night Ambush '57
The Spanish Gardener '57
Doctor at Sea '56
Cast a Dark Shadow '55
The Sea Shall Not Have Them '55
Simba '55
The Sleeping Tiger '54
Doctor in the House '53
The Woman in Question '50
The Blue Lamp '49

Humphrey Bogart (1899-1957)
The Harder They Fall '56
Desperate Hours '55
The Left Hand of God '55
We're No Angels '55
The Barefoot Contessa '54
The Caine Mutiny '54
Sabrina '54
Battle Circus '53
Beat the Devil '53
The African Queen '51
The Enforcer '51
Sirocco '51
Chain Lightning '50
In a Lonely Place '50
Knock on Any Door '49
Tokyo Joe '49
Key Largo '48
Treasure of the Sierra Madre '48
Dark Passage '47
Dead Reckoning '47
The Two Mrs. Carrolls '47
The Big Sleep '46
Conflict '45
Passage to Marseilles '44
To Have & Have Not '44
Action in the North Atlantic '43
Sahara '43
Thank Your Lucky Stars '43
Across the Pacific '42
All Through the Night '42
Casablanca '42
High Sierra '41
The Maltese Falcon '41
The Wagons Roll at Night '41
Brother Orchid '40
They Drive by Night '40
Virginia City '40
Dark Victory '39
Oklahoma Kid '39
The Roaring Twenties '39
Amazing Dr. Clitterhouse '38
Angels with Dirty Faces '38
Bullets or Ballots '38
The Black Legion '37
Dead End '37
Kid Galahad '37
Marked Woman '37
Stand-In '37
Petrified Forest '36
Midnight '34
Three on a Match '32

Peter Bogdanovich (1939-)
Rated X '00
Coming Soon '99
Mr. Jealousy '98
Bella Mafia '97
Saint Jack '79
Targets '68
Voyage to the Planet of Prehistoric Women '68 (N)
The Trip '67
The Wild Angels '66

Eric Bogosian (1953-)
Shot in the Heart '01
Gossip '99
A Bright Shining Lie '98
Deconstructing Harry '97
Office Killer '97
Beavis and Butt-Head Do America '96 (V)
The Thief and the Cobbler '96 (V)
Under Siege 2: Dark Territory '95
Witch Hunt '94
Naked in New York '93
Sex, Drugs, Rock & Roll: Eric Bogosian '91
Last Flight Out: A True Story '90
Suffering Bastards '90
The Caine Mutiny Court Martial '88
Talk Radio '88
Special Effects '85

Ian Bohen
Young Hercules '97
Frankenstein Sings...The Movie '95
Wyatt Earp '94

Hark Bohm
Underground '95
The Promise '94

Marita Bohme
Minna von Barnhelm or The Soldier's Fortune '62
On the Sunny Side '62

Roman Bohnen (1894-1949)
Open Secret '48
The Best Years of Our Lives '46
The Hairy Ape '44

Corinne Bohrer (1959-)
Big Eden '00
Kisses in the Dark '97
Star Kid '97
Revenge of the Nerds 4: Nerds in Love '94
Dead Solid Perfect '88
Vice Versa '88
Stewardess School '86

Richard Bohringer (1942-)
The Accompanist '93
Barjo '93
The Cook, the Thief, His Wife & Her Lover '90
Le Grand Chemin '87
L'Addition '85
Peril '85
Subway '85
Diva '82
I Married a Dead Man '82

Romane Bohringer (1974-)
The Chambermaid on the Titanic '97
Portraits Chinois '96
Total Eclipse '95
The Accompanist '93
Mina Tannenbaum '93
Les Nuits Fauves '92

Curt Bois (1901-91)
Wings of Desire '88
The Boat Is Full '81
Caught '49
Casablanca '42
The Tuttles of Tahiti '42
Bitter Sweet '40
Boom Town '40
The Lady in Question '40
The Hunchback of Notre Dame '39
Amazing Dr. Clitterhouse '38
The Great Waltz '38

Christine Boisson (1957-)
Pas Tres Catholique '93
Sorceress '88
Unsettled Land '88
Identification of a Woman '82

James Bolam (1938-)
Stella Does Tricks '96
The Maze '85
In Celebration '75
Dressed for Death '74
Crucible of Terror '72
A Kind of Loving '62
The Loneliness of the Long Distance Runner '62

Eamon Boland
All the King's Men '99
Business As Usual '88

Mary Boland (1880-1965)
Julia Misbehaves '48
Nothing But Trouble '44
New Moon '40
One Night in the Tropics '40
Pride and Prejudice '40
The Women '39
Ruggles of Red Gap '35
Six of a Kind '34

John Boles (1895-1969)
Thousands Cheer '43
Sinners in Paradise '38
Stella Dallas '37
Craig's Wife '36
Curly Top '35
The Littlest Rebel '35
Stand Up and Cheer '34
Frankenstein '31
King of Jazz '30

John Bolger
Just Looking '99
Parting Glances '86

Ray Bolger (1904-87)
That's Dancing! '85
For Heaven's Sake '79
The Runner Stumbles '79
Babes in Toyland '61
April in Paris '52
Look for the Silver Lining '49
The Harvey Girls '46
Stage Door Canteen '43
Four Jacks and a Jill '41
Sunny '41
The Wizard of Oz '39
Rosalie '38
Sweethearts '38
The Great Ziegfeld '36

Florinda Bolkan (1941-)
Black Lemons '80s
Collector's Item '89
Some Girls '88
Acqua e Sapone '83
The Day That Shook the World '78
The Word '78
Royal Flash '75
Master Touch '74
Don't Torture a Duckling '72
Ring of Death '72
The Last Valley '71

Tiffany Bolling (1947-)
Ecstasy '84
Kingdom of the Spiders '77
The Centerfold Girls '74
Wild Party '74
Bonnie's Kids '73

Ryan Bollman
The NeverEnding Story 3: Escape from Fantasia '94
Children of the Corn 2: The Final Sacrifice '92

Joseph Bologna (1938-)
Big Daddy '99
National Lampoon's The Don's Analyst '97
Heaven Before I Die '96
Love Is All There Is '96
Danger of Love '95
Revenge of the Nerds 4: Nerds in Love '94
Citizen Cohn '92
Deadly Rivals '92
Jersey Girl '92
Alligator 2: The Mutation '90
Coupe de Ville '90
Not Quite Human '87
Rags to Riches '87
Transylvania 6-5000 '85
Blame It on Rio '84
The Woman in Red '84
One Cooks, the Other Doesn't '83
My Favorite Year '82
Chapter Two '79
Torn Between Two Lovers '79
The Big Bus '76
Cops and Robbers '73
Honor Thy Father '73

Christopher Bolton
City Boy '93
Ordeal in the Arctic '93

Jon Bon Jovi (1962-)
Pay It Forward '00
U-571 '00
No Looking Back '98
Row Your Boat '98
Homegrown '97
Little City '97
The Leading Man '96
Moonlight and Valentino '95
Young Guns 2 '90

Paolo Bonacelli (1939-)
The Stendahl Syndrome '95
Francesco '93
Mille Bolle Blu '93
Johnny Stecchino '92
Night on Earth '91
Henry IV '85
Caligula '80
Christ Stopped at Eboli '79
Salo, or the 120 Days of Sodom '75

Danny Bonaduce (1959-)
America's Deadliest Home Video '91
H.O.T.S. '79
Baker's Hawk '76
Charlotte's Web '73 (V)

Louie Bonanno
Student Affairs '88
Night of the Living Babes '87
Wimps '87

Fortunio Bonanova (1895-1969)
An Affair to Remember '57
Double Indemnity '44
Ali Baba and the Forty Thieves '43
Five Graves to Cairo '43
For Whom the Bell Tolls '43
The Black Swan '42

Ivan Bonar
The Haunting Passion '83
MacArthur '77

Derek Bond (1919-)
The Hand '60
Black Tide '58
Rogue's Yarn '56
Svengali '55
The Stranger from Venus '54
Tony Draws a Horse '51
The Weaker Sex '49
Scott of the Antarctic '48
Inheritance '47
Nicholas Nickleby '46

Gary Bond (1940-95)
Growing Pains '82

Zulu '64

James Bond, III
Def by Temptation '90
School Daze '88
Go Tell It on the Mountain '84
The Fish that Saved Pittsburgh '79

Lillian Bond
The Westerner '40
The Old Dark House '32

Renee Bond
Class Reunion '87
Please Don't Eat My Mother '72

Samantha Bond
The World Is Not Enough '99
Emma '97
Tomorrow Never Dies '97
Goldeneye '95

Steve Bond (1953-)
Spacejacked '98
Tryst '94
To Die For 2: Son of Darkness '91
L.A. Gangs Rising '89
Picasso Trigger '89
To Die For '89
Magdalene '88
The Prey '80
Gas Pump Girls '79
H.O.T.S. '79
Massacre at Central High '76

Sudie Bond (1928-84)
I Am the Cheese '83
Trumps '83
Come Back to the Five & Dime Jimmy Dean, Jimmy Dean '82
Where the Lilies Bloom '74
Tomorrow '72

Ward Bond (1903-60)
Alias Jesse James '59
Rio Bravo '59
Wings of Eagles '57
Dakota Incident '56
The Searchers '56
The Long Gray Line '55
A Man Alone '55
Mister Roberts '55
Blowing Wild '54
Gypsy Colt '54
Hondo '53
Johnny Guitar '53
The Quiet Man '52
Great Missouri Raid '51
On Dangerous Ground '51
Kiss Tomorrow Goodbye '50
Only the Valiant '50
Riding High '50
Wagon Master '50
Fort Apache '48
The Fugitive '48
Three Godfathers '48
The Time of Your Life '48
Unconquered '47
Canyon Passage '46
It's a Wonderful Life '46
My Darling Clementine '46
Dakota '45
They Were Expendable '45
A Guy Named Joe '44
Tall in the Saddle '44
Hello, Frisco, Hello '43
Hitler: Dead or Alive '43
The Fighting Sullivans '42
Gentleman Jim '42
The Maltese Falcon '41
Sergeant York '41
The Shepherd of the Hills '41
Wheel of Fortune '41
Kit Carson '40
Drums Along the Mohawk '39
Gone with the Wind '39
Oklahoma Kid '39
Waterfront '39
Young Mr. Lincoln '39
Amazing Dr. Clitterhouse '38
Born to Be Wild '38
Bringing Up Baby '38
Hawaii Calls '38
Prison Break '38
Park Avenue Logger '37
You Only Live Once '37
The Crimson Trail '35
Devil Dogs of the Air '35
Fighting Shadows '35
It Happened One Night '34
Heroes for Sale '33
Hello Trouble '32
White Eagle '32
Big Trail '30

Sergei Bondarchuk (1920-94)
Battle of Neretva '69
War and Peace '68
A Summer to Remember '61

Beulah Bondi (1892-1981)
The Wonderful World of the Brothers Grimm '62
A Summer Place '59
Unholy Wife '57
Latin Lovers '53
Lone Star '52
Baron of Arizona '51
So Dear to My Heart '49
The Snake Pit '48
Breakfast in Hollywood '46
It's a Wonderful Life '46
Sister Kenny '46
Back to Bataan '45
The Southerner '45
Watch on the Rhine '43
Penny Serenade '41
The Shepherd of the Hills '41
Our Town '40
Remember the Night '40
Mr. Smith Goes to Washington '39
On Borrowed Time '39
Of Human Hearts '38
The Sisters '38
Vivacious Lady '38
The Invisible Ray '36
The Moon's Our Home '36
The Trail of the Lonesome Pine '36
Finishing School '33
Rain '32
Street Scene '31

De'Aundre Bonds
Three Strikes '00
The Wood '99
Get On the Bus '96
Sunset Park '96
Tales from the Hood '95

Christopher Bondy
The Jesse Ventura Story '99
The Dark '94
Deadly Surveillance '91

Peter Bonerz (1938-)
Man on the Moon '99
Your Place or Mine '83
Serial '80
How to Break Up a Happy Divorce '76
Catch-22 '70
Medium Cool '69
The Committee '68

Ken Bones
Bellman and True '88
Jack the Ripper '88

Charles Bonet
Way of the Black Dragon '81
Death Promise '78

Lisa Bonet (1967-)
High Fidelity '00
Enemy of the State '98
Dead Connection '94
New Eden '94
Bank Robber '93
Angel Heart '87

Nai Bonet
Gangsters '79
Nocturna '79
Fairy Tales '76
Soul Hustler '76
Devil's Angels '67

Massimo Bonetti
The Story of Boys & Girls '91
Terranova '91
Night Sun '90
Kaos '85
The Night of the Shooting Stars '82

Crispin Bonham Carter
Wuthering Heights '98
Catherine Cookson's The Rag Nymph '96
Pride and Prejudice '95

Helena Bonham Carter (1966-)
Novocaine '01
Planet of the Apes '01
Fight Club '99
Merlin '98
Sweet Revenge '98
The Theory of Flight '98
A Merry War '97
The Wings of the Dove '97
Portraits Chinois '96
Twelfth Night '96
Margaret's Museum '95
Mighty Aphrodite '95
Mary Shelley's Frankenstein '94
A Dark Adapted Eye '93
Francesco '93
Howard's End '92
Where Angels Fear to Tread '91
Hamlet '90
Getting It Right '89
Maurice '87
The Vision '87
A Room with a View '86
Lady Jane '85

Gabrielle Boni
Time at the Top '99
Little Men '98
Daddy's Girl '96

Evan Bonifant (1985-)
Blues Brothers 2000 '98
Breakout '98
3 Ninjas Kick Back '94

Jacques Bonnaffe
Va Savoir '01
Jeanne and the Perfect Guy '98
Venus Beauty Institute '98

Sandrine Bonnaire (1967-)
East-West '99
Circle of Passion '97
La Ceremonie '95
Jeanne la Pucelle '94
The Plague '92
Monsieur Hire '89
Under Satan's Sun '87
La Puritaine '86
Police '85
Vagabond '85
A Nos Amours '84

Lee Bonnell
The Navy Comes Through '42
Look Who's Laughing '41

Vivian Bonnell
Christmas in Connecticut '92
The Josephine Baker Story '90

Beverly Bonner
Basket Case 2 '90
Frankenhooker '90
Brain Damage '88
Basket Case '82

Bill Bonner
Outlaw Riders '72
Satan's Sadists '69

Frank Bonner (1942-)
The Colony '95
You Can't Hurry Love '88
Equinox '71

Priscilla Bonner (1898-1996)
Long Pants '27
Charley's Aunt '25

Tony Bonner (1943-)
Hurricane Smith '92
Dead Sleep '91
Quigley Down Under '90
The Lighthorsemen '87
Money Movers '78
Alternative '76
Inn of the Damned '74
Creatures the World Forgot '70
Eye Witness '70

Maria Bonnevie (1973-)
Insomnia '97
Jerusalem '96
The Polar Bear King '94

Hugh Bonneville
Iris '01
Blow Dry '00
Madame Bovary '00
Heat of the Sun '99
Mansfield Park '99
Notting Hill '99
The Man Who Made Husbands Jealous '98
Mosley '98

Sonny Bono (1935-98)
Under the Boardwalk '89
Hairspray '88
Dirty Laundry '87
Troll '86
The Vals '85
Airplane 2: The Sequel '82
Balboa '82
Escape to Athena '79
Murder on Flight 502 '75
Good Times '67

Brian Bonsall (1981-)
Father and Scout '94
Lily in Winter '94
Blank Check '93
Father Hood '93
Desperate Motives '92
Mikey '92

Sorrell Booke (1930-94)
Rock-a-Doodle '92 (V)
The Other Side of Midnight '77
Special Delivery '76
Bank Shot '74
Devil Times Five '74
Up the Down Staircase '67
Joy House '64
Gone Are the Days '63

Mark Boone, Jr. (1955-)
Animal Factory '00
Memento '00
The General's Daughter '99
John Carpenter's Vampires '97
Rosewood '96
Tree's Lounge '96
Landlord Blues '87

Pat Boone (1934-)
Roger & Me '89
The Cross & the Switchblade '72
The Greatest Story Ever Told '65
Goodbye Charlie '64
State Fair '62
Journey to the Center of the Earth '59

Richard Boone (1916-81)
The Bushido Blade '80
Winter Kills '79
The Big Sleep '78
The Hobbit '78 (V)
The Shootist '76
Against a Crooked Sky '75
God's Gun '75
Big Jake '71
Madron '70
The Arrangement '69
The Night of the Following Day '69
Hombre '67
The War Lord '65
Rio Conchos '64
The Alamo '60
I Bury the Living '58
The Tall T '57
Away All Boats '56
Dragnet '54
Ten Wanted Men '54
Beneath the 12-Mile Reef '53
The Robe '53
The Halls of Montezuma '50

Mika Boorem (1987-)
Blue Crush '02
Along Came a Spider '01
Hearts in Atlantis '01
Riding in Cars with Boys '01

Charley Boorman (1966-)
The Serpent's Kiss '97
Picture Windows '95
Hope and Glory '87
The Emerald Forest '85
Excalibur '81
Deliverance '72

Katrine Boorman (1958-)
Camille Claudel '89
Hope and Glory '87

Elayne Boosler
Mother Goose Rock 'n' Rhyme '90
Meatballs 2 '84

Adrian (Lorna Gray) Booth (1918-)
Son of God's Country '48
Under Colorado Skies '47
Daughter of Don Q '46
Captain America '44
Ridin' Down the Canyon '42
The Man They Could Not Hang '39

Connie Booth (1941-)
The Buccaneers '95
Leon the Pig Farmer '93
The Strange Case of the End of Civilization As We Know It '93
American Friends '91
Hawks '89
Nairobi Affair '88
Little Lord Fauntleroy '80
Monty Python and the Holy Grail '75
Romance with a Double Bass '74
And Now for Something Completely Different '72
John Cleese on How to Irritate People '68

Edwina Booth
The Last of the Mohicans '32
Trader Horn '31

James Booth (1930-)
American Ninja 4: The Annihilation '91
Bad Guys '86
Programmed to Kill '86
Pray for Death '85
Hotline '82
Zorro, the Gay Blade '81
Brannigan '75
That'll Be the Day '73
Rentadick '72
Revenge '71
Darker than Amber '70
Man Who Had Power Over Women '70
The Bliss of Mrs. Blossom '68
Robbery '67
Zulu '64
The Trials of Oscar Wilde '60

Karin Booth
Beloved Infidel '59
Tobor the Great '54

Lindy Booth
American Psycho 2: All American Girl '02
The Skulls 2 '02

Shirley Booth (1907-92)
Hot Spell '58
The Matchmaker '58
Main Street to Broadway '53
Come Back, Little Sheba '52

Powers Boothe (1949-)
Frailty '02
Attila '01
Men of Honor '00
Joan of Arc '99
True Women '97
U-Turn '97
The Spree '96
Dalva '95
Mutant Species '95
Nixon '95
Sudden Death '95
Tombstone '93
Rapid Fire '92
Wildcard '92
Blue Sky '91
By Dawn's Early Light '89
Extreme Prejudice '87
Into the Homeland '87
The Emerald Forest '85
A Breed Apart '84
Red Dawn '84
Plutonium Incident '82
Southern Comfort '81
Cruising '80
A Cry for Love '80
The Guyana Tragedy: The Story of Jim Jones '80
Skag '79

Caterina Boratto
Salo, or the 120 Days of Sodom '75
Juliet of the Spirits '65
8 1/2 '63

Cornell Borchers
Istanbul '57
The Big Lift '50

Ernst Borchert
The Murderers Are Among Us '46
The Murderers are Among Us '46

Lynn Borden (1939-)
Hellhole '85
This Is a Hijack '75
Frogs '72

Carla Borelli
Charlotte Forten's Mission: Experiment in Freedom '85
Asylum of Satan '72

Veda Ann Borg (1915-73)
The Alamo '60
Wings of Eagles '57
Guys and Dolls '55
I'll Cry Tomorrow '55
Love Me or Leave Me '55
Big Jim McLain '52
Rider from Tucson '50
Julia Misbehaves '48
The Bachelor and the Bobby-Soxer '47
Big Town '47
Blonde Savage '47
Accomplice '46
Fog Island '45
Treasure of Fear '45
The Falcon in Hollywood '44
Marked Trails '44
Isle of Forgotten Sins '43
Revenge of the Zombies '43
The Corsican Brothers '42
I Married an Angel '42
Honky Tonk '41
Dr. Christian Meets the Women '40
I Take This Oath '40
Melody Ranch '40
Kid Galahad '37
False Faces '32

Rikke Borge
Amityville 3: The Demon '83
Tattoo '81

Nelly Borgeaud (1931-)
The Accompanist '93
The Man Who Loved Women '77
Mississippi Mermaid '69

Alexandre Borges
Bossa Nova '99
Foreign Land '95

Sal Borgese
Flight of the Innocent '93
Thundersquad '85

Ernest Borgnine (1917-)
BASEketball '98
Small Soldiers '98 (V)
Gattaca '97

McHale's Navy *'97*
All Dogs Go to Heaven 2 *'95 (V)*
Mistress *'91*
Any Man's Death *'90*
Laser Mission *'90*
Moving Target *'89*
The Opponent *'89*
Skeleton Coast *'89*
The Dirty Dozen: The Fatal Mission *'88*
Spike of Bensonhurst *'88*
The Dirty Dozen: The Deadly Mission *'87*
The Manhunt *'86*
The Dirty Dozen: The Next Mission *'85*
Shoot *'85*
Codename: Wildgeese *'84*
Love Leads the Way *'84*
Vengeance Is Mine *'84*
Young Warriors *'83*
Deadly Blessing *'81*
Escape from New York *'81*
High Risk *'81*
Super Fuzz *'81*
When Time Ran Out *'80*
All Quiet on the Western Front *'79*
The Black Hole *'79*
The Double McGuffin *'79*
Convoy *'78*
The Prince and the Pauper *'78*
Fire *'77*
The Greatest *'77*
Jesus of Nazareth *'77*
Future Cop *'76*
Love by Appointment *'76*
Devil's Rain *'75*
Law and Disorder *'74*
Emperor of the North Pole *'73*
Neptune Factor *'73*
Hannie Caulder *'72*
The Poseidon Adventure *'72*
Counter Punch *'71*
The Trackers *'71*
Willard *'71*
The Adventurers *'70*
Bullet for Sandoval *'70*
Suppose They Gave a War and Nobody Came? *'70*
The Wild Bunch *'69*
Ice Station Zebra *'68*
Chuka *'67*
The Dirty Dozen *'67*
The Oscar *'66*
The Flight of the Phoenix *'65*
McHale's Navy *'64*
Barabbas *'62*
The Badlanders *'58*
Torpedo Run *'58*
The Vikings *'58*
The Catered Affair *'56*
Jubal *'56*
The Last Command *'55*
Marty *'55*
Bad Day at Black Rock *'54*
Demetrius and the Gladiators *'54*
From Here to Eternity *'53*
Johnny Guitar *'53*
The Stranger Wore a Gun *'53*
Vera Cruz *'53*

Bobby Boriello
A Walk on the Moon *'99*
Enemy of the State *'98*

Angel Boris
Interceptor Force *'99*
Warlock 3: The End of Innocence *'98*

Nicoletta Boris
Desperate Crimes *'93*
Mille Bolle Blu *'93*

Carroll Borland
Bio Hazard *'85*
Mark of the Vampire *'35*

Matt Borlenghi (1967-)
Blood Surf *'00*
The Crew *'00*
Kate's Addiction *'99*
The American Scream *'80s*

Roscoe Born
Haunting of Sarah Hardy *'89*
Lady Mobster *'88*

Katherine Borowitz
The Man Who Wasn't There *'01*
Illuminata *'98*
Mac *'93*
Men of Respect *'91*
Fellow Traveler *'89*

Jesse Borrego (1962-)
The Maker *'98*
Con Air *'97*
Retroactive *'97*
Tecumseh: The Last Warrior *'95*
I Like It Like That *'94*
Mi Vida Loca *'94*
Blood In ... Blood Out: Bound by Honor *'93*

Dieter Borsche (1909-82)
The Mad Executioners *'65*
The Phantom of Soho *'64*
The Black Abbot *'63*
Dead Eyes of London *'61*
A Time to Love & a Time to Die *'58*
Ali Baba and the 40 Thieves *'54*

Jason Bortz
Take It to the Limit *'00*
Slaves to the Underground *'96*

Jean-Mark Bory (1934-2001)
Le Repos du Guerrier *'62*
RoGoPaG *'62*
The Lovers *'59*

John Yong Bosch
Turbo: A Power Rangers Movie *'96*
Mighty Morphin Power Rangers: The Movie *'95*

Philip Bosco (1930-)
Kate & Leopold *'01*
Cupid & Cate *'00*
Shaft *'00*
Wonder Boys *'00*
Bonanno: A Godfather's Story *'99*
Moon over Broadway *'98*
Critical Care *'97*
Deconstructing Harry *'97*
My Best Friend's Wedding *'97*
The First Wives Club *'96*
It Takes Two *'95*
Against the Wall *'94*
Angie *'94*
Milk Money *'94*
Nobody's Fool *'94*
Safe Passage *'94*
Shadows and Fog *'92*
Straight Talk *'92*
F/X 2: The Deadly Art of Illusion *'91*
The Return of Eliot Ness *'91*
True Colors *'91*
Blue Steel *'90*
Quick Change *'90*
The Dream Team *'89*
Another Woman *'88*
Working Girl *'88*
Suspect *'87*
Three Men and a Baby *'87*
Children of a Lesser God *'86*
The Money Pit *'86*
Heaven Help Us *'85*
Walls of Glass *'85*
The Pope of Greenwich Village *'84*

Lucia Bose (1931-)
Lumiere *'76*
The Legend of Blood Castle *'72*

Miguel Bose
Queen Margot *'94*
High Heels *'91*

Andrea Bosic
Hornet's Nest *'70*
Pirates of the Seven Seas *'62*

Maciste in Hell *'60*

Tom Bosley (1927-)
Fire and Rain *'89*
Wicked Stepmother *'89*
Million Dollar Mystery *'87*
The Jesse Owens Story *'84*
O'Hara's Wife *'82*
For the Love of It *'80*
The Rebels *'79*
The Triangle Factory Fire Scandal *'79*
The Bastard *'78*
Gus *'76*
Death Cruise *'74*
The Streets of San Francisco *'72*
Night Gallery *'69*
The Secret War of Harry Frigg *'68*
Yours, Mine & Ours *'68*
Bang Bang Kid *'67*
Divorce American Style *'67*
The World of Henry Orient *'64*
Love with the Proper Stranger *'63*

Simon Bossell
Cut *'00*
Aberration *'97*
Hotel de Love *'96*

Barbara Bosson (1939-)
The Great American Sex Scandal *'94*
Little Sweetheart *'90*
The Last Starfighter *'84*
The Committee *'68*

Barry Bostwick (1945-)
Tales from a Parallel Universe: I Worship His Shadow *'97*
The Secret Agent Club *'96*
Spy Hard *'96*
In the Heat of Passion 2: Unfaithful *'94*
Project Metalbeast: DNA Overload *'94*
The Secretary *'94*
800 Leagues Down the Amazon *'93*
Praying Mantis *'93*
Russian Roulette *'93*
Weekend at Bernie's 2 *'93*
War & Remembrance *'88*
George Washington: The Forging of a Nation *'86*
Jailbait: Betrayed By Innocence *'86*
George Washington *'84*
A Woman of Substance *'84*
Megaforce *'82*
Red Flag: The Ultimate Game *'81*
Scruples *'80*
Murder by Natural Causes *'79*
Movie, Movie *'78*
The Rocky Horror Picture Show *'75*
Fantastic Planet *'73 (V)*
Road Movie *'72*

Jackson Bostwick
A Matter of Honor *'95*
Escape from DS-3 *'80s*

Charles Boswell
Dangerous Passion *'95*
Kiss Me a Killer *'91*

Brian Bosworth (1965-)
Mach 2 *'00*
Back in Business *'96*
Black Out *'96*
Virus *'96*
One Man's Justice *'95*
Stone Cold *'91*

Hobart Bosworth (1867-1943)
King of the Sierras *'38*
The Dark Hour *'36*
The Crusades *'35*
The Last of the Mohicans *'32*
Phantom Express *'32*
Abraham Lincoln *'30*
Dubarry *'30*
Annapolis *'28*

A Woman of Affairs *'28*
My Best Girl *'27*
The Nervous Wreck *'26*
Spangles *'26*
The Big Parade *'25*
Little Church Around the Corner *'23*
Sea Lion *'21*
The Little American *'17*
A Mormon Maid *'17*

Kate (Catherine) Bosworth (1983-)
Blue Crush *'02*
Remember the Titans *'00*
The Horse Whisperer *'97*

Wade Boteler (1888-1943)
The Green Hornet *'39*
The Mandarin Mystery *'37*
You Only Live Once *'37*
Come on Danger! *'32*
Big News *'29*
Let 'er Go Gallegher *'28*

Sara Botsford
Jumpin' Jack Flash *'86*
The Gunrunner *'84*
By Design *'82*
Deadly Eyes *'82*
Murder by Phone *'82*
Still of the Night *'82*

Benjamin Bottoms
A Shining Season *'79*
Stalk the Wild Child *'76*

Joseph Bottoms (1954-)
Liar's Edge *'92*
Treacherous Crossing *'92*
Inner Sanctum *'91*
Born to Race *'88*
Open House *'86*
Celebrity *'85*
Blind Date *'84*
Surfacing *'84*
The Sins of Dorian Gray *'82*
Intruder Within *'81*
King of the Mountain *'81*
Cloud Dancer *'80*
The Black Hole *'79*
Holocaust *'78*
Return Engagement *'78*
High Rolling in a Hot Corvette *'77*
Stalk the Wild Child *'76*
Crime & Passion *'75*
The Dove *'74*

Sam Bottoms (1955-)
Angel Blue *'97*
Mercenary 2: Thick and Thin *'97*
Project Shadowchaser 3000 *'95*
The Witching of Ben Wagner *'95*
Dolly Dearest *'92*
Hearts of Darkness: A Filmmaker's Apocalypse *'91*
Ragin' Cajun *'90*
Return to Eden *'89*
Gardens of Stone *'87*
Hunter's Blood *'87*
In 'n Out *'86*
Prime Risk *'84*
Desperate Lives *'82*
Bronco Billy *'80*
East of Eden *'80*
Apocalypse Now *'79*
Up from the Depths *'79*
The Outlaw Josey Wales *'76*
Savages *'75*
Zandy's Bride *'74*
Class of '44 *'73*
The Last Picture Show *'71*

Timothy Bottoms (1950-)
Diamondbacks *'99*
The Prince and the Surfer *'99*
The Man in the Iron Mask *'97*
Mortal Challenge *'97*
Uncle Sam *'96*
Hourglass *'95*
The Prince *'95*
Top Dog *'95*

Ava's Magical Adventure *'94*
Digger *'94*
The Gift of Love *'90*
Istanbul *'90*
Texasville *'90*
The Fantasist *'89*
The Drifter *'88*
The Land of Faraway *'87*
Husbands, Wives, Money, and Murder *'86*
In the Shadow of Kilimanjaro *'86*
Invaders from Mars *'86*
The Sea Serpent *'85*
Hambone & Hillie *'84*
Love Leads the Way *'84*
Tin Man *'83*
What Waits Below *'83*
High Country *'81*
East of Eden *'80*
Hurricane *'79*
A Shining Season *'79*
The Other Side of the Mountain, Part 2 *'78*
Rollercoaster *'77*
A Small Town in Texas *'76*
The Story of David *'76*
The White Dawn *'75*
The Paper Chase *'73*
Johnny Got His Gun *'71*
The Last Picture Show *'71*

Sami Bouajila
The Adventures of Felix *'99*
The Siege *'98*
Bye-Bye *'96*

Savannah Smith Boucher
Last Summer In the Hamptons *'96*
The Applegates *'89*

Barbara Bouchet (1943-)
Rogue *'76*
Surabaya Conspiracy *'75*
Mean Machine *'73*
Cry of a Prostitute: Love Kills *'72*
Don't Torture a Duckling *'72*
Amuck! *'71*
In Harm's Way *'65*

Willis Bouchey (1907-77)
The Man Who Shot Liberty Valance *'62*
Panic in the Year Zero! *'62*
The Horse Soldiers *'59*
Battle Cry *'55*
The Bridges at Toko-Ri *'55*
Suddenly *'54*

Elodie Bouchez (1973-)
Don't Let Me Die on a Sunday *'98*
The Dreamlife of Angels *'98*
Full Speed *'96*
Wild Reeds *'94*

Chili Bouchier (1909-99)
Old Mother Riley's New Venture *'49*
The Ghost Goes West *'36*

Patrick Bouchitey
Life Is a Long Quiet River *'88*
The Best Way *'76*

Jacques Boudet
Marius and Jeannette *'97*
Farinelli *'94*
Waiting for the Moon *'87*

Jean Bouise (1929-89)
La Femme Nikita *'91*
Le Dernier Combat *'84*
Hothead *'78*
Old Gun *'76*
I Am Cuba *'64*

Michel Boujenah
Les Miserables *'95*
Three Men and a Cradle *'85*

Daniel Boulanger (1922-)
Bed and Board *'70*
The Bride Wore Black *'68*
The King of Hearts *'66*

Breathless *'59*

Sam Bould
The End of the Affair *'99*
Hollow Reed *'95*

Ingrid Boulting
Deadly Passion *'85*
The Last Tycoon *'76*

Matthew Boulton
Night Must Fall *'37*
Sabotage *'36*

Carole Bouquet (1957-)
The Bridge *'00*
Lucie Aubrac *'98*
Grosse Fatigue *'94*
A Business Affair *'93*
Dagger Eyes *'80s*
New York Stories *'89*
Too Beautiful for You *'88*
Special Police *'85*
For Your Eyes Only *'81*
Buffet Froid *'79*
That Obscure Object of Desire *'77*

Michel Bouquet (1926-)
Tous les Matins du Monde *'92*
Toto le Heros *'91*
Le Complot *'73*
Borsalino *'70*
La Rupture *'70*
Mississippi Mermaid *'69*
The Bride Wore Black *'68*
This Special Friendship *'67*
Pattes Blanches *'49*
Monsieur Vincent *'47*

John Bourgeois
Ginger Snaps *'01*
Ms. Scrooge *'97*
Dead Silence *'96*

Bourvil (1917-70)
The Brain *'69*
La Grande Vadrouille *'66*
Jailbird's Vacation *'65*
The Sucker *'65*
Les Miserables *'57*
Four Bags Full *'56*
Crazy for Love *'52*
Mr. Peek-A-Boo *'50*

Joy Boushel
The Fly *'86*
Humongous *'82*

Nathalie Boutefeu
Irma Vep *'96*
Barjo *'93*

Dennis Boutsikaris (1952-)
Taken *'99*
In Dreams *'98*
The Three Lives of Karen *'97*
The Yarn Princess *'94*
The Dream Team *'89*
*batteries not included *'87*

Brunella Bova
The White Sheik *'52*
Miracle in Milan *'51*

Julie Bovasso (1930-91)
Article 99 *'92*
Betsy's Wedding *'90*
Moonstruck *'87*
Wise Guys *'86*
The Verdict *'82*
Gentleman Bandit *'81*
Willie & Phil *'80*

Clara Bow (1905-65)
Hoopla *'33*
Hula *'28*
It *'27*
Wings *'27*
Dancing Mothers *'26*
Mantrap *'26*
Free to Love *'25*
My Lady of Whims *'25*
Parisian Love *'25*
The Plastic Age *'25*
Down to the Sea in Ships *'22*

Simmy Bow
Zoltan...Hound of Dracula *'78*
The Doberman Gang *'72*

Dorris Bowdon
The Grapes of Wrath *'40*

Drums Along the Mohawk '39

David Bowe
UHF '89
Back to the Beach '87

John Bowe (1950-)
Cleopatra '99
Poldark '96
Body & Soul '93
Prime Suspect '92

Christopher Bowen
Cold Comfort Farm '94
The Shell Seekers '89

Dennis Bowen
Gas Pump Girls '79
Van Nuys Blvd. '79

Julie Bowen (1970-)
Joe Somebody '01
An American Werewolf in Paris '97
Happy Gilmore '96
Multiplicity '96

Michael Bowen
Magnolia '99
Jackie Brown '97
Cupid '96
Excess Baggage '96
True Crime '95
New Eden '94
Casualties of Love: The "Long Island Lolita" Story '93
The Player '92
The Taking of Beverly Hills '91
Mortal Passions '90
Season of Fear '89
The Abduction of Kari Swenson '87
Echo Park '86
Iron Eagle '86
Night of the Comet '84
Valley Girl '83
Forbidden World '82

Roger Bowen (1932-96)
What about Bob? '91
Zapped! '82
M*A*S*H '70

Malick Bowens
Ali '01
Bopha! '93
The Believers '87
Out of Africa '85

Antoinette Bower (1932-)
The Evil That Men Do '84
Blood Song '82
Prom Night '80
Die Sister, Die! '74

Tom Bower
High Crimes '02
Hearts in Atlantis '01
The Million Dollar Hotel '99
Malevolence '98
Buffalo Soldiers '97
The Killing Jar '96
The Last Time I Committed Suicide '96
The Avenging Angel '95
White Man's Burden '95
Against the Wall '94
Far from Home: The Adventures of Yellow Dog '94
Relentless 3 '93
Raising Cain '92
Love, Lies and Murder '91
True Believer '89
Promised a Miracle '88
Family Sins '87
River's Edge '87
The Lightship '86
Massive Retaliation '85
Wildrose '85
Ballad of Gregorio Cortez '83

John Bowers (1899-1936)
The White Sin '24
Lorna Doone '22
The Sky Pilot '21

David Bowie (1947-)
Mr. Rice's Secret '00
B.U.S.T.E.D. '99
Basquiat '96
The Linguini Incident '92
Twin Peaks: Fire Walk with Me '92
The Last Temptation of Christ '88
Absolute Beginners '86
Labyrinth '86
Into the Night '85
The Hunger '83
Merry Christmas, Mr. Lawrence '83
Yellowbeard '83
Christiane F. '82
Just a Gigolo '79
The Man Who Fell to Earth '76

Judi Bowker (1954-)
Anna Karenina '85
The Shooting Party '85
Clash of the Titans '81
East of Elephant Rock '76
In This House of Brede '75
Brother Sun, Sister Moon '73

Paul Bowles (1910-99)
Halfmoon '95 (N)
The Sheltering Sky '90

Peter Bowles (1936-)
In Love and War '01
The Legend of Hell House '73
The Offence '73
A Day in the Death of Joe Egg '71
Endless Night '71
The Charge of the Light Brigade '68
Blow-Up '66

Jessica Bowman
Joy Ride '01
Secrets '94
Remote '93

Laura Bowman
Son of Ingagi '40
Drums O'Voodoo '34

Lee Bowman (1914-79)
My Dream Is Yours '49
Smash-Up: The Story of a Woman '47
Tonight and Every Night '45
Cover Girl '44
Bataan '43
Buck Privates '41
Love Affair '39
Next Time I Marry '38
Internes Can't Take Money '37

John Boxer (1909-82)
The Bridge on the River Kwai '57
Mister Drake's Duck '50
The Woman in Question '50

Bruce Boxleitner (1950-)
The Perfect Nanny '00
Wyatt Earp: Return to Tombstone '94
The Secret '93
The Babe '92
Double Jeopardy '92
Kuffs '92
Perfect Family '92
Diplomatic Immunity '91
Murderous Vision '91
From the Dead of Night '89
Kenny Rogers as the Gambler, Part 3: The Legend Continues '87
Passion Flower '86
Kenny Rogers as the Gambler, Part 2: The Adventure Continues '83
Tron '82
The Baltimore Bullet '80
East of Eden '80
Kenny Rogers as the Gambler '80

Alan Boyce
Nowhere '96
Totally F***ed Up '94
Permanent Record '88

Todd Boyce
Spy Game '01
Jefferson in Paris '94
Great Expectations: The Untold Story '87

Beverly Boyd
Ghost Rider '43
Jive Junction '43

Blake Boyd
First Kid '96
Raiders of the Sun '92
Dune Warriors '91

Cameron Boyd (1984-)
Manny & Lo '96
Bye Bye, Love '94
King of the Hill '93

Guy Boyd
Cries of Silence '97
Retroactive '97
Past Midnight '92
Kiss Me a Killer '91
The Last of the Finest '90
Murder Ordained '87
The Jagged Edge '85
Body Double '84
Eyes of Fire '84
The Eyes of the Amaryllis '82
Keeping On '81
Ticket to Heaven '81

Stephen Boyd (1928-77)
The Squeeze '77
The Treasure of Jamaica Reef '74
Hannie Caulder '72
Imperial Venus '71
Black Brigade '69
Shalako '68
Caper of the Golden Bulls '67
The Bible '66
Fantastic Voyage '66
The Oscar '66
The Fall of the Roman Empire '64
Billy Rose's Jumbo '62
Ben-Hur '59
The Best of Everything '59
The Bravados '58
Abandon Ship '57
The Night Heaven Fell '57
The Man Who Never Was '55

Tanya Boyd
Roots '77
Black Shampoo '76
Ilsa, Harem Keeper of the Oil Sheiks '76

William Boyd (1898-1972)
Hopalong Cassidy: Borrowed Trouble '48
Hopalong Cassidy: Dangerous Venture '48
Hopalong Cassidy: False Paradise '48
Hopalong Cassidy: Silent Conflict '48
Hopalong Cassidy: Sinister Journey '48
Hopalong Cassidy: The Dead Don't Dream '48
Hopalong Cassidy: Hoppy's Holiday '47
Hopalong Cassidy: The Marauders '47
Hopalong Cassidy: Unexpected Guest '47
Hopalong Cassidy: The Devil's Playground '46
Mystery Man '44
Texas Masquerade '44
Border Patrol '43
Colt Comrades '43
False Colors '43
Hopalong Cassidy: Riders of the Deadline '43
Hoppy Serves a Writ '43
Leather Burners '43
Lost Canyon '43
Along the Sundown Trail '42
Prairie Pals '42
Tumbleweed Trail '42
Border Vigilantes '41
Doomed Caravan '41
In Old Colorado '41
Outlaws of the Desert '41
Riders of the Timberline '41
Twilight on the Trail '41
Santa Fe Marshal '40
The Showdown '40
Hopalong Cassidy: Renegade Trail '39
Law of the Pampas '39
Renegade Trail '39
The Frontiersmen '38
Rustler's Valley '37
Federal Agent '36
Hopalong Cassidy Returns '36
Go-Get-'Em-Haines '35
Hopalong Cassidy '35
Racing Luck '35
Midnight Warning '32
Painted Desert '31
The Flying Fool '29
High Voltage '29
His First Command '29
The Leatherneck '28
Power '28
King of Kings '27
Yankee Clipper '27
The Road to Yesterday '25

William "Stage" Boyd (1889-1935)
The Lost City '34
Laughing at Life '33
Oliver Twist '33
State's Attorney '31

Sally Boyden
Little Dragons '80
Barnaby and Me '77

Charles Boyer (1897-1978)
A Matter of Time '76
Stavisky '74
The Hot Line '69
The Madwoman of Chaillot '69
Barefoot in the Park '67
Casino Royale '67
How to Steal a Million '66
Is Paris Burning? '66
Adorable Julia '62
The Four Horsemen of the Apocalypse '62
Fanny '61
The Buccaneer '58
Une Parisienne '58
Around the World in 80 Days '56
What a Woman! '56
The Cobweb '55
Nana '55
The Earrings of Madame De... '54
First Legion '51
Arch of Triumph '48
Gaslight '44
Heart of a Nation '43 (N)
Tales of Manhattan '42
All This and Heaven Too '40
Love Affair '39
Algiers '38
Conquest '37
History Is Made at Night '37
The Garden of Allah '36
Mayerling '36
Break of Hearts '35
Liliom '35
Red Headed Woman '32

Christopher Boyer
Levitation '97
Uninvited '93

Katy Boyer
White Dwarf '95
Tapeheads '89
Trapped '89
Long Gone '87

Miriam Boyer
Un Coeur en Hiver '93
Tous les Matins du Monde '92
Window Shopping '86
Jonah Who Will Be 25 in the Year 2000 '76

Sully Boyer
The Manhattan Project '86
Car Wash '76

William Boyett
Girls in Prison '94
The Hidden '87

Lara Flynn Boyle (1971-)
Men in Black 2 '02
Dying to Get Rich '98
Happiness '98
Afterglow '97
Cafe Society '97
Since You've Been Gone '97
The Big Squeeze '96
Farmer & Chase '96
Baby's Day Out '94
Jacob '94
Past Tense '94
The Road to Wellville '94
Threesome '94
Equinox '93
Red Rock West '93
The Temp '93
Wayne's World '92
Where the Day Takes You '92
The Dark Backward '91
Eye of the Storm '91
Mobsters '91
May Wine '90
The Rookie '90
Dead Poets Society '89
How I Got into College '89
The Preppie Murder '89
Poltergeist 3 '88

Lisa Boyle (1968-)
The Last Marshal '99
Intimate Deception '96
Lost Highway '96
Friend of the Family '95
I Like to Play Games '95

Peter Boyle (1933-)
The Adventures of Pluto Nash '02
Monster's Ball '01
Dr. Dolittle '98
That Darn Cat '96
Born to Be Wild '95
Bulletproof Heart '95
Sweet Evil '95
While You Were Sleeping '95
The Shadow '94
The Surgeon '94
Urban Crossfire '94
Nervous Ticks '93
Royce '93
Taking the Heat '93
Honeymoon in Vegas '92
Malcolm X '92
Solar Crisis '92
Men of Respect '91
Tragedy of Flight 103: The Inside Story '91
Kickboxer 2: The Road Back '90
The Dream Team '89
Disaster at Silo 7 '88
Red Heat '88
Speed Zone '88
Conspiracy: The Trial of the Chicago Eight '87
Echoes in the Darkness '87
Surrender '87
Walker '87
Turk 182! '85
Johnny Dangerously '84
Yellowbeard '83
Hammett '82
Outland '81
In God We Trust '80
Where the Buffalo Roam '80
Beyond the Poseidon Adventure '79
From Here to Eternity '79
Hardcore '79
Brink's Job '78
F.I.S.T. '78
Swashbuckler '76
Taxi Driver '76
Ghost in the Noonday Sun '74
Young Frankenstein '74
Slither '73
Steelyard Blues '73
The Candidate '72
Joe '70
Medium Cool '69

Max Bozyk (1899-1970)
The Jolly Paupers '38
Mamele '38
Yidl Mitn Fidl '36

Marcel Bozzuffi (1929-88)
La Cage aux Folles 2 '81
The French Connection '71
Carbon Copy '69
Z '69

Teda Bracci
The Big Bird Cage '72
C.C. & Company '70

Elizabeth Bracco
Analyze This '98
The Imposters '98
Tree's Lounge '96
Money for Nothing '93
In the Soup '92
Mystery Train '89

Lorraine Bracco (1954-)
Riding in Cars with Boys '01
Hackers '95
The Basketball Diaries '94
Being Human '94
Even Cowgirls Get the Blues '94
Getting Gotti '94
Scam '93
Medicine Man '92
Radio Flyer '92
Traces of Red '92
Switch '91
Talent for the Game '91
Goodfellas '90
The Dream Team '89
Sing '89
The Pick-Up Artist '87
Someone to Watch Over Me '87
Camorra: The Naples Connection '85

Eddie Bracken (1920-)
Home Alone 2: Lost in New York '92
National Lampoon's Vacation '83
Shinbone Alley '70 (V)
We're Not Married '52
Summer Stock '50
Hail the Conquering Hero '44
Miracle of Morgan's Creek '44
Star Spangled Rhythm '42
Young & Willing '42
Caught in the Draft '41
Too Many Girls '40

Sidney Bracy
Tangled Destinies '32
The Cameraman '28

Kitty Bradbury
Our Hospitality '23
The Immigrant '17

Lane Bradbury
The Ultimate Warrior '75
Maybe I'll Be Home in the Spring '70

Kim Braden
Bloodsuckers from Outer Space '83
That'll Be the Day '73

Greg Bradford
Lovelines '84
Zapped! '82

Jesse Bradford (1979-)
Clockstoppers '02
Bring It On '00
Cherry Falls '00
Speedway Junky '99
A Soldier's Daughter Never Cries '98
William Shakespeare's Romeo and Juliet '96
Hackers '95
Far from Home: The Adventures of Yellow Dog '94
King of the Hill '93

Lane Bradford (1922-73)
Gun Glory '57
Ride Clear of Diablo '54
The Fighting Redhead '50

The Invisible Monster '50
Bandit King of Texas '49
The Hawk of Powder River '48

Richard Bradford (1937-)
Just the Ticket '98
Elmore Leonard's Gold Coast '97
Hoodlum '96
Indictment: The McMartin Trial '95
The Crossing Guard '94
Arctic Blue '93
The Chinatown Murders: Man against the Mob '92
Cold Heaven '92
Ambition '91
Servants of Twilight '91
Internal Affairs '90
The Heart of Dixie '89
Little Nikita '88
The Milagro Beanfield War '88
Permanent Record '88
Sunset '88
The Untouchables '87
Badge of the Assassin '85
Legend of Billie Jean '85
Mean Season '85
The Trip to Bountiful '85
Running Hot '83
A Rumor of War '80
More American Graffiti '79
Goin' South '78

Cathleen Bradley
About Adam '00
American Women '00

Christopher Bradley
Leather Jacket Love Story '98
Killer Instinct '92

David Bradley
Total Reality '97
White Cargo '96
Exit '95
Hard Justice '95
Outside the Law '95
Cyborg Soldier '94
Blood Warriors '93
Cyborg Cop '93
American Samurai '92
American Ninja 4: The Annihilation '91
Lower Level '91
American Ninja 3: Blood Hunt '89

David Bradley
The Way We Live Now '02
Harry Potter and the Sorcerer's Stone '01
Vanity Fair '99
Our Mutual Friend '98
Reckless: The Sequel '98
Reckless '97
Catherine Cookson's The Moth '96
Martin Chuzzlewit '94
The Buddha of Suburbia '92

Doug Bradley (1954-)
Hellraiser 5: Inferno '00
Killer Tongue '96
Hellraiser 4: Bloodline '95
Proteus '95
Hellraiser 3: Hell on Earth '92
Hellbound: Hellraiser 2 '88
Hellraiser '87

John H. Bradley
Ablaze '00
Sands of Iwo Jima '49

Leslie Bradley (1907-74)
Teenage Caveman '58
The Conqueror '56
Lady Godiva '55

Carl Bradshaw
Third World Cop '99
The Lunatic '92
The Harder They Come '72

Cathryn Bradshaw
Bert Rigby, You're a Fool '89
Oranges Are Not the Only Fruit '89

Alice Brady (1892-1939)
Young Mr. Lincoln '39
Joy of Living '38
In Old Chicago '37
100 Men and a Girl '37
Go West, Young Man '36
My Man Godfrey '36
Three Smart Girls '36
Gold Diggers of 1935 '35
The Gay Divorcee '34
Her Silent Sacrifice '18

Orla Brady
The Luzhin Defence '00
The Magical Legend of the Leprechauns '99
Wuthering Heights '98

Pat Brady (1914-72)
Bells of Coronado '50
Trigger, Jr. '50
Twilight in the Sierras '50
Down Dakota Way '49
The Golden Stallion '49
Song of Texas '43
Texas Legionnaires '43
Call of the Canyon '42
Sunset on the Desert '42

Scott Brady (1924-85)
Gremlins '84
Strange Behavior '81
The China Syndrome '79
When Every Day Was the Fourth of July '78
Bonnie's Kids '73
Loners '72
Cain's Cutthroats '71
Dollars '71
Gun Riders '69
Satan's Sadists '69
Arizona Bushwackers '67
Journey to the Center of Time '67
Castle of Evil '66
The Restless Breed '58
Storm Rider '57
Mohawk '56
The Maverick Queen '55
They Were So Young '55
Party Girls for Sale '54
Johnny Guitar '53
White Fire '53
Montana Belle '52
Port of New York '49
He Walked by Night '48

Eric (Hans Gudegast) Braeden (1943-)
Meet the Deedles '98
The Ambulance '90
Happily Ever After '82
Aliens Are Coming '80
The Power Within '79
The Adultress '77
Death Scream '75
The Ultimate Thrill '74
Lady Ice '73
Escape from the Planet of the Apes '71
Colossus: The Forbin Project '70
Dayton's Devils '68

Sonia Braga (1951-)
Angel Eyes '01
Perfume '01
From Dusk Till Dawn 3: The Hangman's Daughter '99
Tieta of Agreste '96
Larry McMurtry's Streets of Laredo '95
Roosters '95
The Burning Season '94
Two Deaths '94
The Last Prostitute '91
The Rookie '90
The Milagro Beanfield War '88
Moon over Parador '88
The Man Who Broke 1,000 Chains '87
Kiss of the Spider Woman '85
Gabriela '84
I Love You '81
Dona Flor and Her Two Husbands '78
Lady on the Bus '78

Wilfrid Brambell (1912-85)
Sword of the Valiant '83
The Adventures of Picasso '80
The Conqueror Worm '68
A Hard Day's Night '64
The 39 Steps '35

Francisco (Frank) Brana
Cthulhu Mansion '91
Street Warriors '87
Crypt of the Living Dead '73
Graveyard of Horror '71

Kenneth Branagh (1960-)
Shackleton '02
Conspiracy '01
How to Kill Your Neighbor's Dog '01
Love's Labour's Lost '00
The Road to El Dorado '00 (V)
Wild Wild West '99
Celebrity '98
The Theory of Flight '98
The Gingerbread Man '97
The Proposition '97
Hamlet '96
Looking for Richard '96
Othello '95
Mary Shelley's Frankenstein '94
Much Ado about Nothing '93
Swing Kids '93
Peter's Friends '92
Dead Again '91
Henry V '89
Look Back in Anger '89
High Season '88
Fortunes of War '87
The Lady's Not for Burning '87
A Month in the Country '87
Coming Through '85
To the Lighthouse '83

Rustam Branaman
Love to Kill '97
Headless Body in Topless Bar '96
Terrified '94
Hard Ticket to Hawaii '87

Lillo Brancato
In the Shadows '01
Blue Moon '00
Enemy of the State '98
Sticks '98
Provocateur '96
Crimson Tide '95
Renaissance Man '94
A Bronx Tale '93

Jewel Branch
Against a Crooked Sky '75
Baffled '72

Christopher Brand
Dracula: The Dark Prince '01
Voyage to the Prehistoric Planet '65

Neville Brand (1921-92)
Evils of the Night '85
The Return '80
The Ninth Configuration '79
The Seekers '79
Hi-Riders '77
Eaten Alive '76
The Longest Drive '76
Psychic Killer '75
This Is a Hijack '75
The Barbary Coast '74
Death Stalk '74
Cahill: United States Marshal '73
The Deadly Trackers '73
The Mad Bomber '72
No Place to Run '72
Tora! Tora! Tora! '70
Desperados '69
That Darn Cat '65
Birdman of Alcatraz '62
Scarface Mob '62
The Adventures of Huckleberry Finn '60
Lonely Man '57
The Tin Star '57
Love Me Tender '56
Mohawk '56
The Prodigal '55
Riot in Cell Block 11 '54
Stalag 17 '53
Kansas City Confidential '52
The Halls of Montezuma '50
Only the Valiant '50
D.O.A. '49

Klaus Maria Brandauer (1944-)
Druids '01
Introducing Dorothy Dandridge '99
Jeremiah '98
Becoming Colette '92
White Fang '91
The Russia House '90
Burning Secret '89
Hanussen '88
The Lightship '86
Streets of Gold '86
Out of Africa '85
Quo Vadis '85
Colonel Redl '84
Kindergarten '84
Never Say Never Again '83
Mephisto '81
The Salzburg Connection '72

Larry Brandenburg
The Mod Squad '99
Major League 3: Back to the Minors '98
Mo' Money '92
Victimless Crimes '90

Walter Brandi (-1997)
Terror Creatures from the Grave '66
The Bloody Pit of Horror '65
The Slaughter of the Vampires '62

Jonathan Brandis (1976-)
Hart's War '02
Outside Providence '99
Ride with the Devil '99
Sidekicks '93
Ladybugs '92
NeverEnding Story 2: The Next Chapter '91
Stephen King's It '90
Stepfather 2: Make Room for Daddy '89

Thomas Brandise
The Jesse Ventura Story '99
Gravesend '97

Jocelyn Brando (1919-)
A Question of Love '78
Nightfall '56
Ten Wanted Men '54
The Big Heat '53

Luisina Brando
I Don't Want to Talk About It '94
Miss Mary '86
The Lion's Share '79

Marlon Brando (1924-)
The Score '01
Free Money '99
The Island of Dr. Moreau '96
Don Juan DeMarco '94
Christopher Columbus: The Discovery '92
The Freshman '90
A Dry White Season '89
The Godfather 1902-1959: The Complete Epic '81
The Formula '80
Apocalypse Now '79
Roots: The Next Generation '79
Superman: The Movie '78
Missouri Breaks '76
Last Tango in Paris '73
The Godfather '72
The Nightcomers '72
Burn! '70
The Night of the Following Day '69
Candy '68
A Countess from Hong Kong '67
Reflections in a Golden Eye '67
The Appaloosa '66
The Chase '66
Morituri '65
Bedtime Story '63
The Ugly American '63
Mutiny on the Bounty '62
One-Eyed Jacks '61
The Fugitive Kind '60
The Young Lions '58
Sayonara '57
The Teahouse of the August Moon '56
Guys and Dolls '55
Desiree '54
On the Waterfront '54
The Wild One '54
Julius Caesar '53
Viva Zapata! '52
A Streetcar Named Desire '51
The Men '50

Rikki Brando
The Bikini Car Wash Company 2 '92
Buford's Beach Bunnies '92
Zipperface '92

Clark Brandon
Fast Food '89
My Tutor '82

David Brandon
Beyond Darkness '92
Good Morning, Babylon '87
Stagefright '87

Henry (Kleinbach) Brandon (1912-90)
Assault on Precinct 13 '76
When the North Wind Blows '74
The Land Unknown '57
The Searchers '56
War Arrow '53
Bad Man of Deadwood '41
Drums of Fu Manchu '40
Beau Geste '39
The Black Legion '37
The Garden of Allah '36
March of the Wooden Soldiers '34

Michael Brandon (1945-)
The Contaminated Man '01
Deja Vu '98
The Disappearance of Kevin Johnson '95
Rich and Famous '81
A Change of Seasons '80
Promises in the Dark '79
Red Alert '77
James Dean '76
Heavy Traffic '73
Lovers and Other Strangers '70

Luis Brandoni
A Shadow You Soon Will Be '94
Made in Argentina '86

Carlo Brandt
Ridicule '96
Indochine '92

Carolyn Brandt
The Hollywood Strangler Meets the Skid Row Slasher '79
Rat Pfink a Boo-Boo '66
The Thrill Killers '65
Incredibly Strange Creatures Who Stopped Living and Became Mixed-Up Zombies '63
Eegah! '62
Wild Guitar '62

Brandy
Double Platinum '99
I Still Know What You Did Last Summer '98

Marjorie Bransfield
Abraxas: Guardian of the Universe '90
Easy Wheels '89

Betsy Brantley (1955-)
Deep Impact '98
From the Earth to the Moon '98
Rogue Trader '98
Schizopolis '97
Washington Square '97
Little Lord Fauntleroy '95
Final Appeal '93
Havana '90
I Come in Peace '90
Dreams Lost, Dreams Found '87
The Fourth Protocol '87
Another Country '84
Five Days One Summer '82

Albert Bras
Vampyr '31
Napoleon '27

Nicoletta Braschi (1960-)
Life Is Beautiful '98
The Monster '96
Johnny Stecchino '92
Mystery Train '89
Down by Law '86

Marie Brassard
No '98
Le Polygraphe '96

Keefe Brasselle
Skirts Ahoy! '52
Streets of Sin '49

Claude Brasseur (1936-)
Detective '85
Josepha '82
Lobster for Breakfast '82
La Boum '81
A Simple Story '79
L'Etat Sauvage '78
Pardon Mon Affaire, Too! '77
Pardon Mon Affaire '76
Act of Aggression '73
Band of Outsiders '64
The Elusive Corporal '62
Please Not Now! '61
The Horror Chamber of Dr. Faustus '59

Pierre Brasseur (1905-72)
The King of Hearts '66
Carthage in Flames '60
Il Bell'Antonio '60
The Horror Chamber of Dr. Faustus '59
Where the Hot Wind Blows '59
Portrait of an Assassin '49
Children of Paradise '44

Benjamin Bratt (1963-)
The Final Hit '02
After the Storm '01
Pinero '01
Miss Congeniality '00
The Next Best Thing '00
Red Planet '00
Traffic '00
Woman Undone '95
The River Wild '94
Texas '94
Blood In ... Blood Out: Bound by Honor '93
Demolition Man '93
Bright Angel '91
One Good Cop '91

Andre Braugher (1962-)
A Better Way to Die '00
Duets '00
Frequency '00
Homicide: The Movie '00
It's the Rage '99
Love Songs '99
Passing Glory '99
Thick as Thieves '99
City of Angels '98
Get On the Bus '96
Primal Fear '96
The Tuskegee Airmen '95
Striking Distance '93
Class of '61 '92
The Court Martial of Jackie Robinson '90
Somebody Has to Shoot the Picture '90
Glory '89

Pinkas Braun (1922-)
Samson and Delilah '96
Praying Mantis '83
The Man Outside '68
Mission Stardust '68

Asher Brauner
Living to Die '91
American Eagle '90
Merchants of War '90
Treasure of the Moon Goddess '88
B.A.D. Cats '80
Boss' Son '78
Switchblade Sisters '75

Arthur Brauss
Cross of Iron '76
The Goalie's Anxiety at the Penalty Kick '71
The Train '65

Bart Braverman (1946-)
From the Earth to the Moon '98
Hollywood Hot Tubs 2: Educating Crystal '89
Alligator '80
The Great Texas Dynamite Chase '76

Robert Bray
Never Love a Stranger '58
The Caine Mutiny '54

Thom Bray
Deepstar Six '89
The Horror Show '89

Jay Brazeau (1945-)
Head Over Heels '01
Better Than Chocolate '99
Double Jeopardy '99
Air Bud 2: Golden Receiver '98
Air Bud '97
Trucks '97
Double Play '96
Kissed '96
Slam Dunk Ernest '95

Rossano Brazzi (1916-94)
Third Solution '89
Fear City '85
Formula for a Murder '85
The Far Pavilions '84
Final Justice '84
Omen 3: The Final Conflict '81
A Time for Miracles '80
Dr. Frankenstein's Castle of Freaks '74
Mr. Kingstreet's War '71
The Adventurers '70
The Italian Job '69
One Step to Hell '68
Bobo '67
Woman Times Seven '67
The Christmas That Almost Wasn't '66
Rome Adventure '62
The Battle of Austerlitz '60
South Pacific '58
Legend of the Lost '57
The Story of Esther Costello '57
Summertime '55
The Barefoot Contessa '54
Three Coins in the Fountain '54
We the Living '42

Sebastian Breaks
The Big Switch '70
The Heroes of Telemark '65

Peter Breck (1929-)
Decoy '95
Highway 61 '91
Benji '74
The Crawling Hand '63
Shock Corridor '63
The Beatniks '60
Thunder Road '58
The Commies Are Coming, the Commies Are Coming '57

Larry Breeding
A Matter of Life and Death '81
Street Music '81

Bobby Breen (1927-)
Escape to Paradise '39
Fisherman's Wharf '39
Way Down South '39
Breaking the Ice '38
Hawaii Calls '38
Make a Wish '37
It Happened in New Orleans '36
Let's Sing Again '36

Patrick Breen
Just the Ticket '98
One True Thing '98
Fallen Angels 2 '93
For Love or Money '93
Passed Away '92
Nobody's Perfect '90

Paulette Breen
The Wizard of Speed and Time '88
The Clonus Horror '79

Thomas E. Breen
The River '51
Battleground '49

Edmund Breese
Defenders of the Law '31
All Quiet on the Western Front '30

Mario Brega
The Good, the Bad and the Ugly '67
An Angel for Satan '66

Tracy Bregman
Sex & Mrs. X '00
The Concrete Jungle '82
Happy Birthday to Me '81

Marie Breillat
Dracula & Son '76
Dracula Father and Son '76

Hana Brejchova (1940-)
Loves of a Blonde '65
Fabulous Adventures of Baron Munchausen '61
The Original Fabulous Adventures of Baron Munchausen '61

Jacques Brel (1929-78)
Pain in the A— '77
Franz '72
Les Assassins de L'Ordre '71

Lucille Bremer (1917-96)
Behind Locked Doors '48
Human Gorilla '48
Till the Clouds Roll By '46
Ziegfeld Follies '46
Yolanda and the Thief '45
Meet Me in St. Louis '44

Richard Bremmer
Just Visiting '01
Dostoevsky's Crime and Punishment '99
The 13th Warrior '99

Ewen Bremner
Black Hawk Down '01
Pearl Harbor '01
Snatch '00
Julien Donkey-boy '99
The Acid House '98
Trainspotting '95
Naked '93

El Brendel (1890-1964)
The Beautiful Blonde from Bashful Bend '49
I'm from Arkansas '44
Happy Landing '38
Big Trail '30
Wings '27

Julia Brendler
Deeply '99
Moondance '95

Brid Brennan
Felicia's Journey '99
Dancing at Lughnasa '98
Trojan Eddie '96
Cracker: Brotherly Love '95
Saint-Ex: The Story of the Storyteller '95
Four Days in July '85

Eileen Brennan (1935-)
Jeepers Creepers '01
Changing Habits '96
If These Walls Could Talk '96
Reckless '95
Murder So Sweet '93
I Don't Buy Kisses Anymore '92
Texasville '90
White Palace '90
Stella '89
The New Adventures of Pippi Longstocking '88
Rented Lips '88
Sticky Fingers '88
Blood Vows: The Story of a Mafia Wife '87
Babes in Toyland '86
Clue '85
Fourth Wise Man '85
The Funny Farm '82
Pandemonium '82
Private Benjamin '80
My Old Man '79
The Cheap Detective '78
FM '78
The Death of Richie '76
Great Smokey Roadblock '76
Murder by Death '76
My Father's House '75
Daisy Miller '74
Scarecrow '73
The Sting '73
Playmates '72
The Last Picture Show '71
Divorce American Style '67

Michael Brennan
Fright '71
No Trace '50

Stephen Brennan
St. Patrick: The Irish Legend '00
Eat the Peach '86

Walter Brennan (1894-1974)
Smoke in the Wind '75
Home for the Holidays '72
Over the Hill Gang '69
Support Your Local Sheriff '69
The One and Only, Genuine, Original Family Band '68
The Gnome-Mobile '67
Who's Minding the Mint? '67
The Oscar '66
Those Calloways '65
How the West Was Won '63
Rio Bravo '59
Tammy and the Bachelor '57
Glory '56
Goodbye, My Lady '56
At Gunpoint '55
Far Country '55
Bad Day at Black Rock '54
Along the Great Divide '51
Best of the Badmen '50
The Showdown '50
Ticket to Tomahawk '50
The Green Promise '49
Task Force '49
Blood on the Moon '48
Red River '48
My Darling Clementine '46
A Stolen Life '46
Dakota '45
The Princess and the Pirate '44
To Have & Have Not '44
The North Star '43
Hangmen Also Die '42
The Pride of the Yankees '42
Meet John Doe '41
Nice Girl? '41
Sergeant York '41
Northwest Passage '40
The Westerner '40
Stanley and Livingstone '39
The Story of Vernon and Irene Castle '39
They Shall Have Music '39
The Adventures of Tom Sawyer '38
The Cowboy and the Lady '38
The Texans '38
Come and Get It '36
Fury '36
The Moon's Our Home '36
Prescott Kid '36
These Three '36
Barbary Coast '35
The Bride of Frankenstein '35
The Invisible Man '33
Man of Action '33
Phantom of the Air '33
Texas Cyclone '32
Two-Fisted Law '32

Amy Brenneman (1964-)
Things You Can Tell Just by Looking at Her '00
The Suburbans '99
Your Friends & Neighbors '98
Nevada '97
Daylight '96
Fear '96
Casper '95
Heat '95
Bye Bye, Love '94

Dori Brenner (1946-2000)
Infinity '96
Silent Victim '92
For the Boys '91
Baby Boom '87
Sex and the Single Parent '82
Altered States '80
Summer Wishes, Winter Dreams '73

Eve Brenner
The Great Mouse Detective '86 (V)
Torment '85

Eve Brent
The Green Mile '99
Tarzan and the Trappers '58

Evelyn Brent (1899-1975)
The Payoff '43
The Seventh Victim '43
Holt of the Secret Service '42
Robot Pilot '41
Daughter of the Tong '39
Panama Lady '39
Law West of Tombstone '38
Hopalong Cassidy Returns '36
The President's Mystery '36
Song of the Trail '36
The Silver Horde '30
Last Command '28
Underworld '27
Love 'Em and Leave 'Em '26
Trapped by the Mormons '22

George Brent (1904-79)
Born Again '78
FBI Girl '52
Man Bait '52
Montana Belle '52
Out of the Blue '47
The Spiral Staircase '46
Tomorrow Is Forever '46
Experiment Perilous '45
In This Our Life '42
Silver Queen '42
Twin Beds '42
The Great Lie '41
International Lady '41
The Fighting 69th '40
Dark Victory '39
The Old Maid '39
The Rains Came '39
Jezebel '38
In Person '35
The Painted Veil '34
Baby Face '33
Female '33
42nd Street '33
The Purchase Price '32
They Call It Sin '32
Lightning Warrior '31

Linda Brent
Death Valley Rangers '44
Below the Border '42

Romney Brent (1902-76)
The Sign of Zorro '60
The Virgin Queen '55
Adventures of Don Juan '49
Dreaming Lips '37
Under the Red Robe '36

Edmund Breon (1882-1951)
Forever Amber '47
Dressed to Kill '46
Casanova Brown '44
Gaslight '44
The White Cliffs of Dover '44
Woman in the Window '44
The Scarlet Pimpernel '34

Bobbie Bresee (1950-)
Pre-Madonnas: Rebels Without a Clue '95
Evil Spawn '87
Surf Nazis Must Die '87
Ghoulies '84
Mausoleum '83

Jimmy Breslin
Pogo for President: "I Go Pogo" '84 (V)
If Ever I See You Again '78

Spencer Breslin
Return to Never Land '02 (V)
Disney's The Kid '00

Felix Bressart (1895-1949)
Portrait of Jennie '48
A Song Is Born '48
Without Love '45
The Seventh Cross '44
Iceland '42
To Be or Not to Be '42
Blossoms in the Dust '41
Ziegfeld Girl '41
Bitter Sweet '40
Comrade X '40
Edison the Man '40
The Shop Around the Corner '40
Ninotchka '39

Bernard Bresslaw (1934-93)
Carry On Camping '71
Carry On Cowboy '66
Morgan: A Suitable Case for Treatment '66

Martin Brest (1951-)
Spies Like Us '85
Fast Times at Ridgemont High '82

Jean Bretonniere
Mam'zelle Pigalle '58
That Naughty Girl '58
The Green Glove '52

Danielle Brett
Jill the Ripper '00
Rated X '00

Jeremy Brett (1935-95)
Moll Flanders '96
Shameless '94
The Medusa Touch '78
Haunted: The Ferryman '74
One Deadly Owner '74
The Merchant of Venice '73
My Fair Lady '64
The Very Edge '63
War and Peace '56

Jim Breuer (1967-)
Titan A.E. '00 (V)
Dick '99
Half-Baked '97

Marita Breuer
The Princess and the Warrior '00
Heimat 1 '84

Juliette Brewer
Balto '95 (V)
The Little Rascals '94

Diane Brewster (1931-91)
Torpedo Run '58
Courage of Black Beauty '57
The Invisible Boy '57

Jordana Brewster (1980-)
The Fast and the Furious '01
Invisible Circus '00
The '60s '99
The Faculty '98

Paget Brewster
The Adventures of Rocky & Bullwinkle '00
The Specials '00
Let's Talk About Sex '98

Maia Brewton
Adventures in Babysitting '87
Back to the Future '85

Kevin Breznahan
SLC Punk! '99
Alive '93

Tom Breznahan
Terrified '94
Ski School '91
The Brain '88
Twice Dead '88

Jean-Claude Brialy (1933-)
The Count of Monte Cristo '99
Beaumarchais the Scoundrel '96
The Monster '96
Portraits Chinois '96
Son of Gascogne '95
Queen Margot '94
No Fear, No Die '90
La Nuit de Varennes '82
L'Anne Sainte '78
Robert et Robert '78
Barocco '76
Catherine & Co. '76
The Judge and the Assassin '75
Phantom of Liberty '74
Claire's Knee '71
The Bride Wore Black '68
The King of Hearts '66
Tonio Kroger '65
Circle of Love '64
The Burning Court '62
Cleo from 5 to 7 '61
Paris Belongs to Us '60
A Woman Is a Woman '60
The Cousins '59
The 400 Blows '59
Le Beau Serge '58

David Brian (1914-93)
Confessions of Tom Harris '72
Castle of Evil '66
Pocketful of Miracles '61
Ambush at Tomahawk Gap '53
Million Dollar Mermaid '52
Springfield Rifle '52
Beyond the Forest '49
Flamingo Road '49
Intruder in the Dust '49

Mary Brian (1908-)
Amazing Adventure '37
Charlie Chan in Paris '35
Monte Carlo Nights '34
Blessed Event '32
The Light of Western Stars '30
Running Wild '27
Behind the Front '26
Peter Pan '24

Shane Briant (1946-)
Twisted '96
Tunnel Vision '95
Till There Was You '91
Darlings of the Gods '90
Wrangler '88
Cassandra '87
The Lighthorsemen '87
Moving Targets '87
True Colors '87
Lady Chatterley's Lover '81
The Flame Is Love '79
Captain Kronos: Vampire Hunter '74
Dressed for Death '74
Frankenstein and the Monster from Hell '74
Picture of Dorian Gray '74
Demons of the Mind '72

Fanny Brice (1891-1951)
Ziegfeld Follies *'46*
Everybody Sing *'38*
The Great Ziegfeld *'36*
Be Yourself *'30*
Pierre Brice (1929-)
A Place Called Glory *'66*
Apache's Last Battle *'64*
The Bacchantes *'63*
Sweet Ecstasy *'62*
Mill of the Stone Women *'60*
Ron Brice
Ripe *'97*
Tar *'97*
A Horse for Danny *'95*
Fresh *'94*
Little Odessa *'94*
Fly by Night *'93*
Beth Brickell
Seducers *'77*
The Only Way Home *'72*
Alan Bridge (1891-1957)
Miracle of Morgan's Creek *'44*
Sullivan's Travels *'41*
Outlaw Rule *'36*
Cheyenne Kid *'33*
Cowboy Counselor *'33*
When a Man Rides Alone *'33*
Broadway to Cheyenne *'32*
The Forty-Niners *'32*
Man's Land *'32*
Beau Bridges (1941-)
Common Ground *'00*
Inherit the Wind *'99*
P.T. Barnum *'99*
White River *'99*
The Defenders: Taking the First *'98*
Meeting Daddy *'98*
The Defenders: Payback *'97*
RocketMan *'97*
The Second Civil War *'97*
Hidden in America *'96*
Kissinger and Nixon *'96*
Losing Chase *'96*
Nightjohn *'96*
The Outer Limits: Sandkings *'95*
Married to It *'93*
The Positively True Adventures of the Alleged Texas Cheerleader-Murdering Mom *'93*
Sidekicks *'93*
Wildflower *'91*
Without Warning: The James Brady Story *'91*
Daddy's Dyin'...Who's Got the Will? *'90*
Women & Men: Stories of Seduction *'90*
The Fabulous Baker Boys *'89*
The Iron Triangle *'89*
Signs of Life *'89*
The Wizard *'89*
Seven Hours to Judgment *'88*
The Killing Time *'87*
The Wild Pair *'87*
Outrage! *'86*
The Hotel New Hampshire *'84*
The Red Light Sting *'84*
Heart Like a Wheel *'83*
Silver Dream Racer *'83*
Love Child *'82*
Honky Tonk Freeway *'81*
Night Crossing *'81*
The Fifth Musketeer *'79*
Norma Rae *'79*
The Runner Stumbles *'79*
The Four Feathers *'78*
President's Mistress *'78*
Greased Lightning *'77*
Mutual Respect *'77*
One Summer Love *'76*
Swashbuckler *'76*
Two Minute Warning *'76*
The Other Side of the Mountain *'75*
The Stranger Who Looks Like Me *'74*
The Man Without a Country *'73*
Hammersmith Is Out *'72*
For Love of Ivy *'68*
The Incident *'67*
Village of the Giants *'65*
The Red Pony *'49*
Jeff Bridges (1949-)
K-PAX *'01*
The Contender *'00*
Arlington Road *'99*
The Muse *'99*
Simpatico *'99*
The Big Lebowski *'97*
Hidden in America *'96*
The Mirror Has Two Faces *'96*
White Squall *'96*
Wild Bill *'95*
Blown Away *'94*
Fearless *'93*
The Vanishing *'93*
American Heart *'92*
The Fisher King *'91*
Texasville *'90*
Cold Feet *'89*
The Fabulous Baker Boys *'89*
See You in the Morning *'89*
Tucker: The Man and His Dream *'88*
Nadine *'87*
The Morning After *'86*
8 Million Ways to Die *'85*
The Jagged Edge *'85*
Against All Odds *'84*
Starman *'84*
Kiss Me Goodbye *'82*
The Last Unicorn *'82 (V)*
Rapunzel *'82*
Tron *'82*
Cutter's Way *'81*
Heaven's Gate *'81*
Winter Kills *'79*
King Kong *'76*
Stay Hungry *'76*
Hearts of the West *'75*
Rancho Deluxe *'75*
Thunderbolt & Lightfoot *'74*
The Last American Hero *'73*
Bad Company *'72*
Fat City *'72*
The Last Picture Show *'71*
Yin & Yang of Mr. Go *'71*
Silent Night, Lonely Night *'69*
Jordan Bridges
Happy Campers *'01*
Frequency *'00*
P.T. Barnum *'99*
Lloyd Bridges (1913-98)
Mafia! *'98*
Meeting Daddy *'98*
The Outer Limits: Sandkings *'95*
Blown Away *'94*
Hot Shots! Part Deux *'93*
Devlin *'92*
Honey, I Blew Up the Kid *'92*
Hot Shots! *'91*
Joe Versus the Volcano *'90*
The Queen of Mean *'90*
Cousins *'89*
Winter People *'89*
Tucker: The Man and His Dream *'88*
The Wild Pair *'87*
Dress Gray *'86*
North and South Book 2 *'86*
Weekend Warriors *'86*
George Washington *'84*
Loving *'84*
The Grace Kelly Story *'83*
Airplane 2: The Sequel *'82*
The Blue and the Gray *'82*
Airplane! *'80*
Bear Island *'80*
East of Eden *'80*
Mission Galactica: The Cylon Attack *'79*
The Great Wallendas *'78*
Force of Evil *'77*
Mutual Respect *'77*
Roots *'77*
Running Wild *'73*
Haunts of the Very Rich *'72*
The Tattered Web *'71*
The Happy Ending *'69*
Silent Night, Lonely Night *'69*
Daring Game *'68*
Around the World Under the Sea *'65*
The Goddess *'58*
The Rainmaker *'56*
Wetbacks *'56*
Apache Woman *'55*
Big Deadly Game *'54*
The Limping Man *'53*
Tall Texan *'53*
High Noon *'52*
Last of the Comanches *'52*
Little Big Horn *'51*
Rocketship X-M *'50*
Try and Get Me *'50*
The White Tower *'50*
Home of the Brave *'49*
Trapped *'49*
Moonrise *'48*
Ramrod *'47*
Abilene Town *'46*
Canyon Passage *'46*
A Walk in the Sun *'46*
Strange Confession *'45*
Master Race *'44*
Calling Dr. Death/Strange Confession *'43*
The Heat's On *'43*
Sahara *'43*
Blondie Goes to College *'42*
Harmon of Michigan *'41*
Todd Bridges (1965-)
Inhumanity *'00*
Homeboys *'92*
Twice Dead *'88*
Roots *'77*
Richard Briers (1934-)
Love's Labour's Lost *'00*
Spice World: The Movie *'97*
Hamlet *'96*
A Midwinter's Tale *'95*
Mary Shelley's Frankenstein *'94*
Much Ado about Nothing *'93*
Peter's Friends *'92*
A Chorus of Disapproval *'89*
Henry V *'89*
The Norman Conquests, Part 1: Table Manners *'80*
The Norman Conquests, Part 2: Living Together *'80*
The Norman Conquests, Part 3: Round and Round the Garden *'80*
Watership Down *'78 (V)*
Rentadick *'72*
Fathom *'67*
A Matter of WHO *'62*
Julie Briggs
Brotherhood 2: The Young Warlocks *'01*
Bowery Buckaroos *'47*
Richard Bright (1937-98)
Beautiful Girls *'96*
The Ref *'93*
Who's the Man? *'93*
The Ambulance *'90*
The Godfather, Part 3 *'90*
Red Heat *'88*
Vigilante *'83*
Idolmaker *'80*
Panic in Needle Park *'75*
Rancho Deluxe *'75*
Odds Against Tomorrow *'59*
Susie Bright
Bound *'96*
Virgin Machine *'88*
Charlie Brill
Bail Out *'90*
Bloodstone *'88*
Fran Brill (1946-)
What about Bob? *'91*
Old Enough *'84*
Look Back in Anger *'80*
Patti Brill
Hard-Boiled Mahoney *'47*
Girl Rush *'44*
Steven Brill
The Mighty Ducks *'92*
sex, lies and videotape *'89*
Nick Brimble
Seven Days to Live *'01*
Fortress 2: Re-Entry *'99*
Gone Fishin' *'97*
Ivanhoe *'97*
The Final Cut *'95*
Loch Ness *'95*
Robin Hood: Prince of Thieves *'91*
Frankenstein Unbound *'90*
S.O.S. Titanic *'79*
Cynthia Brimhall (1964-)
Fit to Kill *'93*
Hard Hunted *'92*
Hard Ticket to Hawaii *'87*
Wilford Brimley (1934-)
Brigham City *'01*
Crossfire Trail *'01*
Progeny *'98*
Summer of the Monkeys *'98*
In and Out *'97*
My Fellow Americans *'96*
The Good Old Boys *'95*
The Last of the Dogmen *'95 (N)*
Mutant Species *'95*
The Firm *'93*
Hard Target *'93*
Where the Red Fern Grows: Part 2 *'92*
Eternity *'90*
Thompson's Last Run *'90*
Gore Vidal's Billy the Kid *'89*
Cocoon: The Return *'88*
End of the Line *'88*
Act of Vengeance *'86*
American Justice *'86*
Cocoon *'85*
The Ewoks: Battle for Endor *'85*
Murder in Space *'85*
Remo Williams: The Adventure Begins *'85*
Country *'84*
Harry & Son *'84*
The Hotel New Hampshire *'84*
The Natural *'84*
The Stone Boy *'84*
High Road to China *'83*
Ten to Midnight *'83*
Tender Mercies *'83*
Tough Enough *'83*
The Thing *'82*
Absence of Malice *'81*
Death Valley *'81*
Borderline *'80*
Rodeo Girl *'80*
Roughnecks *'80*
The China Syndrome *'79*
The Electric Horseman *'79*
True Grit *'69*
Michele Brin
Sexual Intent *'94*
Secret Games *'92*
Adrian Brine
Lily Was Here *'89*
Waterloo *'71*
Paul Brinegar (1918-95)
Wyatt Earp: Return to Tombstone *'94*
Charro! *'69*
How to Make a Monster *'58*
Mark Bringleson
Soldier *'98*
Dead Man *'95*
The Lawnmower Man *'92*
Christie Brinkley (1954-)
Vegas Vacation *'96*
National Lampoon's Vacation *'83*
John Brinkley
A Bucket of Blood *'59*
T-Bird Gang *'59*
Teenage Doll *'57*
Ritch Brinkley
Breakdown *'96*
Cabin Boy *'94*
Silhouette *'91*
Bo Brinkman
Gettysburg *'93*
Ice House *'89*
Charles Brinley
The Crimson Trail *'35*
Moran of the Lady Letty *'22*
Bill Brinsfield
Warbirds *'88*
Slaughterhouse *'87*
Vera Briole
A Single Girl *'96*
Pigalle *'95*
Syd Brisbane
Dead Letter Office *'98*
Alien Visitor *'95*
David Brisbin
Goodbye, Lover *'99*
From the Earth to the Moon *'98*
Leaving Las Vegas *'95*
Kiss Daddy Goodnight *'87*
Brent Briscoe (1961-)
Double Take *'01*
Driven *'01*
The Majestic *'01*
Mulholland Drive *'01*
Say It Isn't So *'01*
Beautiful *'00*
Another Day in Paradise *'98*
A Simple Plan *'98*
Sling Blade *'96*
Danielle Brisebois (1969-)
As Good As It Gets *'97*
Killcrazy *'89*
Big Bad Mama 2 *'87*
Mom, the Wolfman and Me *'80*
The Premonition *'75*
Virginia Brissac (1894-1979)
Phantom Lady *'44*
Black Friday *'40*
Carl Brisson (1893-1958)
Murder at the Vanities *'34*
The Manxman *'29*
The Ring *'27*
May Britt (1936-)
Haunts *'77*
The Unfaithfuls *'60*
The Hunters *'58*
The Young Lions *'58*
War and Peace *'56*
There Goes Barder *'54*
Morgan Brittany (1951-)
Body Armor *'96*
Sundown *'91*
LBJ: The Early Years *'88*
The Prodigal *'83*
Initiation of Sarah *'78*
Yours, Mine & Ours *'68*
The Birds *'63*
Aileen Britton
Now and Forever *'82*
My Brilliant Career *'79*
Barbara Britton (1919-80)
Dragonfly Squadron *'54*
Ride the Man Down *'53*
Bandit Queen *'51*
Champagne for Caesar *'50*
I Shot Jesse James *'49*
Loaded Pistols *'48*
The Virginian *'46*
Captain Kidd *'45*
The Story of Dr. Wassell *'44*
So Proudly We Hail *'43*
Mrs. Wiggs of the Cabbage Patch *'42*
Reap the Wild Wind *'42*
Wake Island *'42*
Young & Willing *'42*
Louisiana Purchase *'41*
Connie Britton (1968-)
Child Star: The Shirley Temple Story *'01*
No Looking Back *'98*
Escape Clause *'96*
The Brothers McMullen *'94*
Pamela Britton (1923-74)
If It's Tuesday, This Must Be Belgium *'69*
D.O.A. *'49*
Anchors Aweigh *'45*
Tony Britton (1924-)
Agatha *'79*
The Day of the Jackal *'73*
Cry of the Penguins *'71*
Dr. Syn, Alias the Scarecrow *'64*
Horsemasters *'61*
Operation Amsterdam *'60*
Jim Broadbent (1949-)
Bridget Jones's Diary *'01*
Iris *'01*
Moulin Rouge *'01*
Topsy Turvy *'99*
The Avengers *'98*
Little Voice *'98*
The Borrowers *'97*
The Secret Agent *'96*
Smilla's Sense of Snow *'96*
Richard III *'95*
Rough Magic *'95*
Bullets over Broadway *'94*
Princess Caraboo *'94*
Widow's Peak *'94*
The Wedding Gift *'93*
The Crying Game *'92*
Enchanted April *'92*
Life Is Sweet *'90*
Erik the Viking *'89*
The Good Father *'87*
Kent Broadhurst (1940-)
A Couch in New York *'95*
The Dark Half *'91*
Silver Bullet *'85*
Peter Brocco (1903-92)
One Flew Over the Cuckoo's Nest *'75*
Homebodies *'74*
Johnny Got His Gun *'71*
The Balcony *'63*
Ma and Pa Kettle on Vacation *'53*
Anne Brochet (1966-)
Barjo *'93*
Tous les Matins du Monde *'92*
Cyrano de Bergerac *'90*
Phil Brock
Mercy *'96*
Dollman vs Demonic Toys *'93*
A Climate for Killing *'91*
Stan Brock (1931-91)
Return to Africa *'89*
UHF *'89*
Tin Men *'87*
Galyon *'77*
Roy Brocksmith (1945-2001)
Kull the Conqueror *'97*
The Road to Wellville *'94*
Nickel & Dime *'92*
Bill & Ted's Bogus Journey *'91*
Arachnophobia *'90*
Total Recall *'90*
Big Business *'88*
Tales of Ordinary Madness *'83*
Killer Fish *'79*
King of the Gypsies *'78*
Gladys Brockwell (1894-1929)
The Drake Case *'29*
Spangles *'26*
Oliver Twist *'22*
Beth Broderick (1959-)
Psycho Beach Party *'00*
French Exit *'97*

Maternal Instincts '96
Are You Lonesome Tonight '92
Thousand Pieces of Gold '91

Erin Broderick
The Flamingo Rising '01
Black Dog '98

Helen Broderick (1891-1959)
Because of Him '45
Nice Girl? '41
The Rage of Paris '38
The Bride Walks Out '36
Swing Time '36
Top Hat '35

James Broderick (1927-82)
Keeping On '81
The Shadow Box '80
Dog Day Afternoon '75
The Taking of Pelham One Two Three '74
Alice's Restaurant '69
The Group '66

Matthew Broderick (1962-)
Election '99
Inspector Gadget '99
You Can Count On Me '99
Godzilla '98
The Lion King: Simba's Pride '98 (V)
Addicted to Love '96
The Cable Guy '96
Infinity '96
The Thief and the Cobbler '96 (V)
The Lion King '94 (V)
Mrs. Parker and the Vicious Circle '94
The Road to Wellville '94
A Life in the Theater '93
The Night We Never Met '93
Out on a Limb '92
The Freshman '90
Family Business '89
Glory '89
Biloxi Blues '88
Torch Song Trilogy '88
Project X '87
Ferris Bueller's Day Off '86
On Valentine's Day '86
Ladyhawke '85
1918 '85
Cinderella '84
Master Harold and the Boys '84
Max Dugan Returns '83
WarGames '83

Don Brodie (1899-2001)
Eat My Dust '76
Detour '46
Pinocchio '40 (V)

Helen Brodie
Tales of the Kama Sutra 2: Monsoon '98
Monsoon '97

Steve Brodie (1919-92)
The Wizard of Speed and Time '88
The Giant Spider Invasion '75
The Wild World of Batwoman '66
Roustabout '64
Blue Hawaii '62
The Caine Mutiny '54
The Beast from 20,000 Fathoms '53
Donovan's Brain '53
Three for Bedroom C '52
The Steel Helmet '51
The Admiral Was a Lady '50
Armored Car Robbery '50
Kiss Tomorrow Goodbye '50
Treasure of Monte Cristo '50
Home of the Brave '49
Tough Assignment '49
Desperate '47
Out of the Past '47
Badman's Territory '46
Criminal Court '46
The Saint Strikes Back: Criminal Court '46
A Walk in the Sun '46
Thirty Seconds Over Tokyo '44

Adrien Brody (1976-)
Harrison's Flowers '02
The Affair of the Necklace '01
Bread and Roses '00
Liberty Heights '99
Oxygen '99
Six Ways to Sunday '99
Summer of Sam '99
Restaurant '98
Ten Benny '98
The Thin Red Line '98
The Undertaker's Wedding '97
The Last Time I Committed Suicide '96
Solo '96
Bullet '94
Jailbreakers '94
King of the Hill '93
Home at Last '88

Harry Brogan
Broth of a Boy '59
Shake Hands with the Devil '59

Giulio Brogi
St. Michael Had a Rooster '72
The Spider's Stratagem '70

James Brolin (1940-)
A Guy Thing '02
Master of Disguise '02
Traffic '00
The Haunted Sea '97
Lewis and Clark and George '97
My Brother's War '97
Terminal Virus '96
The Expert '95
The Fighter '95
Relative Fear '95
Tracks of a Killer '95
Final Justice '94
Indecent Behavior 2 '94
Parallel Lives '94
Cheatin' Hearts '93
City Boy '93
Ted & Venus '93
Gas Food Lodging '92
Twin Sisters '91
Backstab '90
Nightmare on the 13th Floor '90
Bad Jim '89
Finish Line '89
Hold the Dream '86
Pee-wee's Big Adventure '85
Mae West '84
The Ambush Murders '82
High Risk '81
Night of the Juggler '80
The Amityville Horror '79
Capricorn One '78
Steel Cowboy '78
The Car '77
Class of '63 '73
Westworld '73
The Boston Strangler '68
Fantastic Voyage '66
Our Man Flint '66
Von Ryan's Express '65

Josh Brolin (1968-)
The Hollow Man '00
Slow Burn '00
Best Laid Plans '99
It's the Rage '99
The Mod Squad '99
Mimic '97
My Brother's War '97
Gang in Blue '96
Nightwatch '96
Bed of Roses '95
Flirting with Disaster '95
Prison for Children '93
Finish Line '89
Thrashin' '86
The Goonies '85

J. Edward Bromberg (1903-51)
A Song Is Born '48
Queen of the Amazons '47
Cloak and Dagger '46
The Missing Corpse '45
Dead Man's Eyes/Pillow of Death '44
The Phantom of the Opera '43
Son of Dracula '43
Invisible Agent '42
Reunion in France '42
The Mark of Zorro '40
Return of Frank James '40
Strange Cargo '40

John Bromfield (1922-)
Manfish '56
Big Bluff '55
Revenge of the Creature '55
Easy to Love '53
Flat Top '52

Valri Bromfield
Nothing But Trouble '91
Who's Harry Crumb? '89
Home Is Where the Hart Is '88
Mr. Mom '83

Sydney Bromley (1909-87)
Crystalstone '88
The NeverEnding Story '84
Frankenstein and the Monster from Hell '74

Eleanor Bron (1940-)
Iris '01
House of Mirth '00
Vanity Fair '99
A Little Princess '95
Saint-Ex: The Story of the Storyteller '95
Black Beauty '94
Intrigue '90
The Attic: The Hiding of Anne Frank '88
Little Dorrit, Film 1: Nobody's Fault '88
Little Dorrit, Film 2: Little Dorrit's Story '88
Turtle Diary '86
Women in Love '70
Bedazzled '68
Two for the Road '67
Alfie '66
Help! '65

William Bronder
Return to Me '00
Flush '81

Brick Bronsky
Class of Nuke 'Em High 3: The Good, the Bad and the Subhumanoid '94
Sgt. Kabukiman N.Y.P.D. '94
Class of Nuke 'Em High 2: Subhumanoid Meltdown '91

Betty Bronson (1906-71)
Naked Kiss '64
Yodelin' Kid from Pine Ridge '37
Medicine Man '30
Ben-Hur '26
Are Parents People? '25
Peter Pan '24

Charles Bronson (1921-)
Family of Cops 3 '98
Family of Cops 2: Breach of Faith '97
Family of Cops '95
Death Wish 5: The Face of Death '94
Dead to Rights '93
The Sea Wolf '93
The Indian Runner '91
Bull of the West '89
Kinjite: Forbidden Subjects '89
Messenger of Death '88
Assassination '87
Death Wish 4: The Crackdown '87
Act of Vengeance '86
Murphy's Law '86
Death Wish 3 '85
The Evil That Men Do '84
Ten to Midnight '83
Death Wish 2 '82
Cabo Blanco '81
Death Hunt '81
Borderline '80
Love and Bullets '79
Raid on Entebbe '77
Telefon '77
The White Buffalo '77
Breakheart Pass '76
From Noon Till Three '76
The Meanest Men in the West '76
St. Ives '76
Breakout '75
Chino '75
Hard Times '75
Death Wish '74
Mr. Majestyk '74
The Family '73
The Stone Killer '73
The Mechanic '72
Chato's Land '71
Cold Sweat '71
Red Sun '71
Someone Behind the Door '71
Rider on the Rain '70
Lola '69
Honor Among Thieves '68
Once Upon a Time in the West '68
Villa Rides '68
The Dirty Dozen '67
This Property Is Condemned '66
Battle of the Bulge '65
The Sandpiper '65
Guns of Diablo '64
Four for Texas '63
The Great Escape '63
Kid Galahad '62
Master of the World '61
The Magnificent Seven '60
Never So Few '59
Machine Gun Kelly '58
Showdown at Boot Hill '58
When Hell Broke Loose '58
Jubal '56
Run of the Arrow '56
Apache '54
Drum Beat '54
House of Wax '53
Miss Sadie Thompson '53
Vera Cruz '53
Pat and Mike '52

Lillian Bronson (1903-95)
Spencer's Mountain '63
The Next Voice You Hear '50

Claudio Brook (1929-95)
Cronos '94
The Bees '78
Devil's Rain '75
Dr. Tarr's Torture Dungeon '75
Sisters of Satan '75
The Peking Blond '68
Simon of the Desert '66
Viva Maria! '65
Samson in the Wax Museum '63
The Exterminating Angel '62
Neutron and the Black Mask '61
The Young One '61
Daniel Boone: Trail Blazer '56

Clive Brook (1887-1974)
On Approval '44
Convoy '40
Action for Slander '38
Cavalcade '33
Shanghai Express '32
Hula '28
Underworld '27

Faith Brook (1922-)
Eye of the Needle '81
After Julius '78
Bloodbath '76
War and Peace '73
To Sir, with Love '67
Uneasy Terms '48

Irina Brook (1962-)
Captive '87
The Girl in the Picture '86
Transmutations '85

Isabel Brook
About a Boy '02
Faust: Love of the Damned '00

Jayne Brook (1962-)
Gattaca '97
Ed '96
Last Dance '96
Bye Bye, Love '94
Clean Slate '94
Kindergarten Cop '90

Lyndon Brook (1926-)
Invasion '65
The Spanish Gardener '57
Above Us the Waves '56

Elwyn Brook-Jones (1911-62)
Rogue's Yarn '56
The Gilded Cage '54
Bonnie Prince Charlie '48

Bunny Brooke (1920-2000)
Dawn! '83
Alison's Birthday '79

Hillary Brooke (1914-99)
The Man Who Knew Too Much '56
Heat Wave '54
Invaders from Mars '53
Abbott and Costello Meet Captain Kidd '52
Never Wave at a WAC '52
The Lost Continent '51
Africa Screams '49
Big Town '47
Big Town After Dark '47
Underworld Scandal '47
The Road to Utopia '46
Strange Impersonation '46
The Strange Woman '46
The Enchanted Cottage '45
The Woman in Green '45
Jane Eyre '44
Ministry of Fear '44
Sherlock Holmes Faces Death '43
Sherlock Holmes: The Voice of Terror '42
To the Shores of Tripoli '42
Wake Island '42
Rangeland Racket '41
The Philadelphia Story '40

Paul Brooke
The Affair of the Necklace '01
Dead of Night '99
The Lair of the White Worm '88

Sandy Brooke
Crazed Cop '88
Miami Vendetta '87
Star Slammer '87
Terror on Alcatraz '86

Walter Brooke (1914-86)
The Return of Count Yorga '71
Tora! Tora! Tora! '70
Conquest of Space '55

Richard Brooker
Friday the 13th, Part 4: The Final Chapter '84
Deathstalker '83
Friday the 13th, Part 3 '82

Jacqueline Brookes (1930-)
Naked Gun 2 1/2: The Smell of Fear '91
Silent Witness '85
Hardhat & Legs '80
Rodeo Girl '80
The Gambler '74

Aimee Brooks
Critters 3 '91
Say Anything '89

Albert Brooks (1947-)
My First Mister '01
The Muse '99
Dr. Dolittle '98 (V)
Out of Sight '98
Critical Care '97
Mother '96
The Scout '94
I'll Do Anything '93
Defending Your Life '91
Broadcast News '87
Lost in America '85
Unfaithfully Yours '84
Twilight Zone: The Movie '83
Modern Romance '81
Private Benjamin '80
Real Life '79
Taxi Driver '76

Avery Brooks (1948-)
15 Minutes '01
American History X '98
The Big Hit '98
Spenser: Pale Kings & Princes '94
The Ernest Green Story '93
Spenser: Ceremony '93
Roots: The Gift '88
Uncle Tom's Cabin '87
Half Slave, Half Free '85

Carroll Brooks
Mauvais Sang '86
Boy Meets Girl '84

Clarence Brooks
Bronze Buckaroo '39
Harlem Rides the Range '39

Conrad Brooks (1931-)
The Alien Agenda: Under the Skin '97
Bikini Drive-In '94
Ed Wood '94
Test Tube Teens from the Year 2000 '93
Curse of the Queerwolf '87
The Beast of Yucca Flats '61
The Sinister Urge '60
Plan 9 from Outer Space '56
Bride of the Monster '55
Jail Bait '54
Glen or Glenda? '53

David Brooks
Magic in the Mirror: Fowl Play '96
Scream for Help '86

David Allan Brooks (1947-)
Cast Away '00
Jack Frost 2: Revenge of the Mutant Killer Snowman '00
The Kindred '87

Elisabeth Brooks (1951-97)
The Forgotten One '89
The Howling '81

Foster Brooks (1912-2001)
Oddballs '84
Cracking Up '83
The Villain '79
Super Seal '77

Geraldine Brooks (1925-77)
Bull of the West '89
Johnny Tiger '66
The Green Glove '52
Challenge to Lassie '49
Reckless Moment '49
Cry Wolf '47
The Possessed '47

Hildy Brooks
Forbidden Love '82
The Chosen '81

Jean Brooks (1916-)
Boss of Big Town '43
The Leopard Man '43
The Seventh Victim '43
Boot Hill Bandits '42

Joel Brooks
The Man Who Captured Eichmann '96
Indecent Proposal '93
Are You Lonesome Tonight '92

Leslie Brooks (1922-)
The Cobra Strikes '48
Romance on the High Seas '48
The Scar '48
Tonight and Every Night '45
City Without Men '43
Underground Agent '42
You Were Never Lovelier '42

Louise Brooks (1906-85)
Overland Stage Raiders '38
Prix de Beaute '30
Diary of a Lost Girl '29
Pandora's Box '28
It's the Old Army Game '26
Love 'Em and Leave 'Em '26
The Show Off '26

Mel Brooks (1926-)
Screw Loose '99
Dracula: Dead and Loving It '95
Robin Hood: Men in Tights '93
Silence of the Hams '93
Life Stinks '91
Look Who's Talking, Too '90 (V)
Spaceballs '87
To Be or Not to Be '83
History of the World: Part 1 '81
The Muppet Movie '79
High Anxiety '77
Silent Movie '76
Blazing Saddles '74
The Twelve Chairs '70
Putney Swope '69
The Producers '68

Phyllis Brooks (1915-95)
Dangerous Passage '44
Silver Spurs '43
The Shanghai Gesture '42
Slightly Honorable '40
Little Miss Broadway '38
Rebecca of Sunnybrook Farm '38
In Old Chicago '37

Rand Brooks (1918-)
Comanche Station '60
To Hell and Back '55
The Vanishing Westerner '50
Ladies of the Chorus '49
Hopalong Cassidy: Borrowed Trouble '48
Hopalong Cassidy: Dangerous Venture '48
Hopalong Cassidy: False Paradise '48
Hopalong Cassidy: Silent Conflict '48
Hopalong Cassidy: Sinister Journey '48
Hopalong Cassidy: The Dead Don't Dream '48
Hopalong Cassidy: Hoppy's Holiday '47
Hopalong Cassidy: The Marauders '47
Hopalong Cassidy: Unexpected Guest '47
Hopalong Cassidy: The Devil's Playground '46
The Sombrero Kid '42
Gone with the Wind '39

Randi Brooks (1956-)
Colors '88
Cop '88
Hamburger...The Motion Picture '86
Tightrope '84
The Man with Two Brains '83
Forbidden Love '82

Randy Brooks
Black Snow '93
Reservoir Dogs '92

Ray Brooks (1939-)
Office Romances '86
House of Whipcord '75
Tiffany Jones '75
Flesh and Blood Show '73
Daleks—Invasion Earth 2150 A.D. '66
The Knack '65

Richard Brooks
The Crow 2: City of Angels '96
The Substitute '96
Wolverine '96
Chameleon '95
Machine Gun Blues '95
Memphis '91
To Sleep with Anger '90
84 Charlie MoPic '89
Shocker '89
Shakedown '88
Short Fuse '88
The Hidden '87

Van Brooks
Trespasses '86
Blood Simple '85

Anthony Brophy
The Informant '97
The Run of the Country '95

Brian Brophy
Brain Dead '89
Skinheads: The Second Coming of Hate '88

Edward Brophy (1895-1960)
Last Hurrah '58
Roaring City '51
Renegade Girl '46
Swing Parade of 1946 '46
Cover Girl '44
It Happened Tomorrow '44
The Thin Man Goes Home '44
Air Force '43
Destroyer '43
Dumbo '41 (V)
Dance, Girl, Dance '40
The Invisible Woman '40
Great Guy '36
Kelly the Second '36
Mad Love '35
Show Them No Mercy '35
Evelyn Prentice '34
Hide-Out '34
What! No Beer? '33
The Champ '32
Speak Easily '32
Doughboys '30
The Cameraman '28

Kevin Brophy (1953-)
Delos Adventure '86
The Seduction '82
Time Walker '82
Hell Night '81

Pierce Brosnan (1953-)
The Tailor of Panama '00
Grey Owl '99
The Match '99
The Thomas Crown Affair '99
The World Is Not Enough '99
Quest for Camelot '98 (V)
Dante's Peak '97
The Nephew '97
Tomorrow Never Dies '97
Mars Attacks! '96
The Mirror Has Two Faces '96
Detonator 2: Night Watch '95
The Disappearance of Kevin Johnson '95
Goldeneye '95
Don't Talk to Strangers '94
Love Affair '94
The Broken Chain '93
Detonator '93
Entangled '93
Mrs. Doubtfire '93
The Lawnmower Man '92
Live Wire '92
Mister Johnson '91
Murder 101 '91
Victim of Love '91
Around the World in 80 Days '89
The Heist '89
The Deceivers '88
Noble House '88
Taffin '88
The Fourth Protocol '87
Nomads '86
The Carpathian Eagle '81
The Manions of America '81
The Long Good Friday '80
The Mirror Crack'd '80

Collette Brosset
Belle Americaine '61
Femmes de Paris '53

Dr. Joyce Brothers (1928-)
National Lampoon's Loaded Weapon 1 '93
Age Isn't Everything '91
The Naked Gun: From the Files of Police Squad '88
Love at Stake '87
The Lonely Guy '84
Desperate Lives '82
Embryo '76

Liliane Brousse
Maniac '63
Paranoiac '62

Ben Browder
Boogie Boy '98
A Kiss Before Dying '91

Jordan Brower
Night Ride Home '99
Speedway Junky '99

Amelda Brown
Little Dorrit, Film 1: Nobody's Fault '88
Little Dorrit, Film 2: Little Dorrit's Story '88
Hope and Glory '87

Barbara Brown (1902-75)
My Sister Eileen '55
Ma and Pa Kettle on Vacation '53
Jack & the Beanstalk '52
Home Town Story '51
Ma and Pa Kettle Back On the Farm '51
Born Yesterday '50
Ma and Pa Kettle Go to Town '50
Hollywood Canteen '44
The Fighting Sullivans '42

Barry Brown
He Who Walks Alone '78
The Disappearance of Aimee '76
The Ultimate Thrill '74
Bad Company '72
Flesh '68

Bille Brown
The Dish '00
Oscar and Lucinda '97
Fierce Creatures '96

Blair Brown (1948-)
Follow the Stars Home '01
Hamlet '01
In His Life: The John Lennon Story '00
Space Cowboys '00
The Astronaut's Wife '99
The Day My Parents Ran Away '93
Passed Away '92
Strapless '90
Stealing Home '88
Hands of a Stranger '87
The Bad Seed '85
A Flash of Green '85
Kennedy '83
Continental Divide '81
Altered States '80
One Trick Pony '80
And I Alone Survived '78
The Choirboys '77

Bobby Brown
Two Can Play That Game '01
A Thin Line Between Love and Hate '96
Mother Goose Rock 'n' Rhyme '90

Bruce Brown
The Endless Summer 2 '94 (N)
Zipperface '92
Eddie and the Cruisers '83
The Endless Summer '66 (N)

Bryan Brown (1950-)
On the Beach '00
Risk '00
Styx '00
Grizzly Falls '99
Journey to the Center of the Earth '99
On the Border '98
Tracked '98
Two Hands '98
Dead Heart '96
Twisted '96 (N)
Full Body Massage '95
The Last Hit '93
Blame It on the Bellboy '92
Devlin '92
Dead in the Water '91
F/X 2: The Deadly Art of Illusion '91
Prisoners of the Sun '91
Sweet Talker '91
Cocktail '88
Gorillas in the Mist '88
F/X '86
The Good Wife '86
Tai-Pan '86
The Empty Beach '85
Far East '85
Rebel '85
A Town Like Alice '85
Give My Regards to Broad Street '84
Kim '84
Parker '84
The Thorn Birds '83
The Winter of Our Dreams '82
Blood Money '80
Breaker Morant '80
The Odd Angry Shot '79
Palm Beach '79
The Irishman '78
Money Movers '78
Newsfront '78

Charles D. Brown (1887-1949)
Follow Me Quietly '49
Merton of the Movies '47
International Lady '41
Brother Orchid '40
Old Swimmin' Hole '40
The Duke of West Point '38
Shopworn Angel '38
Dance of Life '29

Clancy Brown (1959-)
Snow White: The Fairest of Them All '02
Boss of Bosses '99
The Hurricane '99
In the Company of Spies '99
Vendetta '99
Flubber '97
Starship Troopers '97
Female Perversions '96
Donor Unknown '95
The Shawshank Redemption '94
Last Light '93
Past Midnight '92
Pet Sematary 2 '92
Ambition '91
Cast a Deadly Spell '91
Love, Lies and Murder '91
Blue Steel '90
Season of Fear '89
Shoot to Kill '88
Extreme Prejudice '87
Highlander '86
The Bride '85
The Adventures of Buckaroo Banzai Across the Eighth Dimension '84
Bad Boys '83

David G. Brown
Chasing Dreams '81
Deadly Harvest '72

Drew "Bundini" Brown
Shaft's Big Score '72
Shaft '71

D.W. Brown
Mischief '85
Weekend Pass '84

Dwier Brown (1959-)
Same River Twice '97
Intimate Betrayal '96
Deconstructing Sarah '94
Lily in Winter '94
Gettysburg '93
The Cutting Edge '92
Galaxies Are Colliding '92
Mom and Dad Save the World '92
The Guardian '90
Field of Dreams '89

Eric Brown (1964-)
Video Murders '87
They're Playing with Fire '84
Private Lessons '81

Gary Brown
Invasion of the Space Preachers '90
The Glory Boys '84

Gaye Brown
Mata Hari '85
Masque of the Red Death '65

Georg Stanford Brown (1943-)
Tyson '95
Ava's Magical Adventure '94
Murder Without Motive '92
House Party 2: The Pajama Jam '91
Alone in the Neon Jungle '87
North and South Book 1 '85
The Jesse Owens Story '84
The Kid with the Broken Halo '82
The Night the City Screamed '80
Roots: The Next Generation '79
Roots '77
Colossus: The Forbin Project '70
Dayton's Devils '68

Georgia Brown (1933-92)
Victim of Love '91
Love at Stake '87
Actor: The Paul Muni Story '78
Tales That Witness Madness '73
Nothing But the Night '72
Long Ago Tomorrow '71
The Fixer '68

Henry Brown
Uncaged '91
Stepfather 2: Make Room for Daddy '89
The Man in the Glass Booth '75

James Brown (1920-93)
Courage of Rin Tin Tin '83
Adios Amigo '75
Targets '68
Space Monster '64
Rin Tin Tin, Hero of the West '55
Sands of Iwo Jima '49
Objective, Burma! '45
Air Force '43
Wake Island '42

James Brown (1933-)
Undercover Brother '02
Blues Brothers 2000 '98
Doctor Detroit '83
The Blues Brothers '80

Jim Brown (1935-)
Any Given Sunday '99
He Got Game '98
Small Soldiers '98 (V)
Mars Attacks! '96
Original Gangstas '96
The Divine Enforcer '91
Crack House '89
L.A. Vice '89
Twisted Justice '89
I'm Gonna Git You Sucka '88
L.A. Heat '88
The Running Man '87
Pacific Inferno '85
One Down, Two to Go! '82
Fingers '78
Kid Vengeance '75
Take a Hard Ride '75
Three the Hard Way '74
Slaughter's Big Ripoff '73
Slaughter '72
El Condor '70
The Passing of Evil '70
100 Rifles '69
Riot '69
Dark of the Sun '68
Ice Station Zebra '68
The Dirty Dozen '67
Rio Conchos '64

Joe E. Brown (1892-1973)
The Comedy of Terrors '64
It's a Mad, Mad, Mad, Mad World '63
Some Like It Hot '59
Around the World in 80 Days '56
Show Boat '51
The Tender Years '47
Pin-Up Girl '44
The Gladiator '38
Wide Open Faces '38
Fit for a King '37
Riding on Air '37
When's Your Birthday? '37
Earthworm Tractors '36
A Midsummer Night's Dream '35
Lottery Bride '30

Johnny Mack Brown (1904-74)
Apache Uprising '66
Border Bandits '46
Gentleman from Texas '46
The Stranger from Pecos '45
Lawmen '44
Partners of the Trail '44
Raiders of the Border '44
Range Law '44
Ghost Rider '43
Six Gun Gospel '43
Texas Kid '43
Ride 'Em Cowboy '42
Boss of Bullion City '41
Bury Me Not on the Lone Prairie '41
Man from Montana '41
The Masked Rider '41
Pony Post '40
Riders of Pasco Basin '40
Oregon Trail '39
Flaming Frontiers '38
Helltown '38
Boothill Brigade '37
The Gambling Terror '37
Guns in the Dark '37
A Lawman Is Born '37
Crooked Trail '36
Desert Phantom '36
Rogue of the Range '36
Undercover Man '36
Valley of the Lawless '36
Between Men '35
Branded a Coward '35
Courageous Avenger '35
Every Man's Law '35
Rustlers of Red Dog '35
Belle of the Nineties '34
Female '33
Fighting with Kit Carson '33
Fire Alarm '32
Coquette '29
The Single Standard '29
Annapolis '28
Our Dancing Daughters '28
A Woman of Affairs '28

Juanita Brown
Black Starlet '74
Caged Heat '74
Foxy Brown '74

Judy Brown
The Manhandlers '73
The Big Doll House '71

Julie Brown (1958-)
Plump Fiction '97
Clueless '95
Fist of the North Star '95
Out There '95
National Lampoon's Attack of the 5 Ft. 2 Women '94
Nervous Ticks '93
The Opposite Sex and How to Live With Them '93
Raining Stones '93

Shakes the Clown '92
Spirit of '76 '91
Earth Girls Are Easy '89
Bloody Birthday '80

Downtown Julie Brown
Bug Buster '99
Ride '98

Kimberly J. Brown
My Sister's Keeper '02
Stephen King's Rose Red '02
Tumbleweeds '98

Lou Brown
Death Games '82
Alison's Birthday '79
The Irishman '78

Murray Brown
Vampyres '74
Dracula '73

Pamela Brown (1917-75)
In This House of Brede '75
Dracula '73
Wuthering Heights '70
Secret Ceremony '69
Cleopatra '63
Victoria Regina '61
Lust for Life '56
Alice in Wonderland '50
I Know Where I'm Going '45
One of Our Aircraft Is Missing '41

Paul Brown
Butterfly Kiss '94
Anne of Green Gables '85
Morons from Outer Space '85
Transmutations '85

Peter Brown (1935-)
Asylum '97
The Aurora Encounter '85
The Concrete Jungle '82
Act of Vengeance '74
Eagles Attack at Dawn '74
Foxy Brown '74
Memory of Us '74
Slashed Dreams '74
Chrome and Hot Leather '71
Hard Frame '70
Kitten with a Whip '64
Ride the Wild Surf '64
A Tiger Walks '64
Merrill's Marauders '62
Red Nightmare '62
Darby's Rangers '58
The Commies Are Coming, the Commies Are Coming '57

Phil Brown (1916-)
Tropic of Cancer '70
Operation Cross Eagles '69
The Hidden Room '49
Without Reservations '46
Jungle Captive '45

Philip Brown (1958-)
Wild Zone '89
Eye of the Needle '81
Special Olympics '78

Ralph Brown (1913-90)
Star Wars: Episode 1—The Phantom Menace '99
Ivanhoe '97
Wayne's World 2 '93
Alien 3 '92
The Crying Game '92
Impromptu '90
Christabel '89
Buster '88
Withnail and I '87

Ralph Brown (1960-)
Mean Machine '01
Extremely Dangerous '99

Reb Brown (1948-)
Last Flight to Hell
Cage 2: The Arena of Death '94
The Firing Line '91
Street Hunter '90
The Cage '89
Mercenary Fighters '88
Space Mutiny '88
White Ghost '88
Strike Commando '87
Death of a Soldier '85
Howling 2: Your Sister Is a Werewolf '85
Uncommon Valor '83
Yor, the Hunter from the Future '83
Captain America '79
Captain America 2: Death Too Soon '79

Ritza Brown
The McGuffin '85
Ator the Fighting Eagle '83

Robert Brown (1918-)
The Living Daylights '87
Pilgrim, Farewell '82
One Million Years B.C. '66
Tower of London '62
It Takes a Thief '59
Shake Hands with the Devil '59
The Abominable Snowman '57

Roger Aaron Brown
Miracle in Lane Two '00
Tall Tale: The Unbelievable Adventures of Pecos Bill '95
Undesirable '92
Don't Cry, It's Only Thunder '82

Ron Brown
The Legend of Black Thunder Mountain '79
Charlie, the Lonesome Cougar '67

Sara Suzanne Brown
Killer Looks '94
Secret Games 2: The Escort '93
Test Tube Teens from the Year 2000 '93

Stanley Brown
Blondie's Blessed Event '42
Blondie Meets the Boss '39

Stephen Brown (1917-98)
Beyond Darkness '92
Metamorphosis '90

Thomas Wilson Brown (1972-)
Skeletons '96
Diggstown '92
Honey, I Shrunk the Kids '89
Welcome Home '89

Tim Brown
Pacific Inferno '85
Code Name: Zebra '84
A Place Called Today '72

Timothy Brown
The Dynamite Brothers '74
Girls Are for Loving '73
Sweet Sugar '72
M*A*S*H '70

Tom Brown (1913-90)
Operation Haylift '50
Ringside '49
Buck Privates Come Home '47
Adventures of Smilin' Jack '43
The Payoff '43
The Duke of West Point '38
In Old Chicago '37
Maytime '37
Navy Blue and Gold '37
I'd Give My Life '36
Anne of Green Gables '34

Vanessa Brown (1928-99)
Witch Who Came from the Sea '76
The Fighter '52
Three Husbands '50
The Heiress '49
The Ghost and Mrs. Muir '47
Mother Wore Tights '47

W. Earl Brown (1963-)
Dancing at the Blue Iguana '00
Lost Souls '00
Meat Loaf: To Hell and Back '00
There's Something about Mary '98
Scream '96
Dead Air '94
Excessive Force '93

Wally Brown (1904-61)
The Absent-Minded Professor '61
Girl Rush '44
Zombies on Broadway '44

Woody Brown (1956-)
Animal Instincts 2 '94
Dominion '94
Secret Games 3 '94
Alligator 2: The Mutation '90
The Rain Killer '90
The Accused '88
Killer Party '86

Charles A. Browne
Federal Agent '36
Tailspin Tommy '34

Coral Browne (1913-91)
Dreamchild '85
American Dreamer '84
An Englishman Abroad '83
Eleanor: First Lady of the World '82
Theatre of Blood '73
The Ruling Class '72
The Killing of Sister George '69
Auntie Mame '58
The Courtney Affair '47

Leslie Browne (1958-)
Dancers '87
Nijinsky '80
The Turning Point '77

Lucille Browne (1907-76)
Cheyenne Rides Again '38
Crooked Trail '36
Texas Terror '35
Western Frontier '35
Brand of Hate '34
Law of the Wild '34
The Devil's Brother '33
Mystery Squadron '33
Battling with Buffalo Bill '31

Roscoe Lee Browne (1925-)
Hamlet '01
Babe: Pig in the City '98 (N)
Dear God '96
Last Summer In the Hamptons '96
Babe '95 (N)
Forest Warrior '95
The Pompatus of Love '95
Naked in New York '93
The Mambo Kings '92
Moon 44 '90
For Us, the Living '88
Oliver & Company '88 (V)
Jumpin' Jack Flash '86
Legal Eagles '86
Haunting of Harrington House '82
Nothing Personal '80
Unknown Powers '80
King '78
Twilight's Last Gleaming '77
Logan's Run '76
Superfly T.N.T. '73
The World's Greatest Athlete '73
The Cowboys '72
The Liberation of L.B. Jones '70
Black Like Me '64
The Connection '61

Suzanne Browne
The Bikini Car Wash Company 2 '92
The Bikini Car Wash Company '90

Zachary Browne
Shiloh 2: Shiloh Season '99
Man of the House '95

Ricou Browning (1930-)
Flipper's New Adventure '64
The Creature Walks among Us '56
Creature from the Black Lagoon '54

Ryan Browning
Extremedays '01
The Smokers '00

Brenda Bruce (1919-96)
Splitting Heirs '93
Antonia and Jane '91
December Bride '91
Back Home '90
The Tenth Man '88
That'll Be the Day '73
Nightmare '63
Peeping Tom '60

Cheryl Lynn Bruce
Daughters of the Dust '91
Victimless Crimes '90
Music Box '89

Colin Bruce
Chicago Joe & the Showgirl '90
Crusoe '89
Gotham '88

David Bruce (1916-76)
Jungle Hell '55
Pier 23 '51
Can't Help Singing '45
Lady on a Train '45
Salome, Where She Danced '45
Calling Dr. Death/Strange Confession '43
The Mad Ghoul '43
The Sea Wolf '41
Sergeant York '41

Kate Bruce (1858-1946)
Struggle '31
The Idol Dancer '20
Way Down East '20
Judith of Bethulia '14

Lenny Bruce
Dynamite Chicken '70
Dance Hall Racket '58

Nigel Bruce (1895-1953)
Limelight '52
Julia Misbehaves '48
The Two Mrs. Carrolls '47
Dressed to Kill '46
Terror by Night '46
The Corn Is Green '45
House of Fear '45
Pursuit to Algiers '45
Son of Lassie '45
The Woman in Green '45
Frenchman's Creek '44
The Pearl of Death '44
Scarlet Claw '44
Spider Woman '44
Lassie, Come Home '43
Sherlock Holmes Faces Death '43
Sherlock Holmes in Washington '43
Journey for Margaret '42
Roxie Hart '42
Sherlock Holmes and the Secret Weapon '42
Sherlock Holmes: The Voice of Terror '42
The Chocolate Soldier '41
Suspicion '41
The Blue Bird '40
Rebecca '40
Susan and God '40
The Adventures of Sherlock Holmes '39
The Hound of the Baskervilles '39
The Rains Came '39
The Last of Mrs. Cheyney '37
Thunder in the City '37
The Charge of the Light Brigade '36
The Trail of the Lonesome Pine '36
Becky Sharp '35
She '35
The Scarlet Pimpernel '34
Stand Up and Cheer '34
Treasure Island '34

Virginia Bruce (1910-82)
Strangers When We Meet '60
State Department File 649 '49
Action in Arabia '44
Pardon My Sarong '42
The Invisible Woman '40
Let Freedom Ring '39
Born to Dance '36
The Great Ziegfeld '36
Let 'Em Have It '35
Jane Eyre '34

Patrick Bruel (1959-)
Lost and Found '99
Sabrina '95
Secret Obsession '88
Bandits '86

Eddie Brugman
Broken Mirrors '85
Katie Tippel '75

Beau Brummel
Three Bullets for a Long Gun '73
Village of the Giants '65

John Brumpton
Dance Me to My Song '98
Life '95

Bo Brundin (1937-)
Headless Eyes '83
Shoot the Sun Down '81
Russian Roulette '75

Valeria Bruni-Tedeschi
Those Who Love Me Can Take the Train '98
Mon Homme '96
Nenette and Boni '96

Dylan Bruno (1972-)
The One '01
Where the Heart Is '00
The Rage: Carrie 2 '99
When Trumpets Fade '98

Nando (Fernando) Bruno (1895-)
Time Out for Love '61
Two Nights with Cleopatra '54
Open City '45

Philip Bruns (1931-)
The Opposite Sex and How to Live With Them '93
Dead Men Don't Die '91
Return of the Living Dead 2 '88
The Stunt Man '80

Eric Bruskotter
Major League 3: Back to the Minors '98
Starship Troopers '97
Major League 2 '94
Can't Buy Me Love '87

Dora Bryan (1924-)
Apartment Zero '88
Screamtime '83
Hands of the Ripper '71
The Great St. Trinian's Train Robbery '66
A Taste of Honey '61
Small Hotel '57
My Son, the Vampire '52
No Trace '50
The Fallen Idol '49

Jane Bryan (1918-)
Each Dawn I Die '39
The Old Maid '39
The Sisters '38
Kid Galahad '37
Marked Woman '37

Zachery Ty Bryan (1981-)
The Rage: Carrie 2 '99
The Principal Takes a Holiday '98
True Heart '97
First Kid '96
Magic Island '95
Bigfoot: The Unforgettable Encounter '94

John Bryant (1916-89)
Run Silent, Run Deep '58
Courage of Black Beauty '57
From Here to Eternity '53

Joyce Bryant
East Side Kids '40
Across the Plains '39

Lee Bryant
Alien Nation: Dark Horizon '94
Half Slave, Half Free '85

Michael Bryant (1928-2002)
The Miracle Maker: The Story of Jesus '00 (V)
King Lear '98
Hamlet '96
Sakharov '84
The Ruling Class '72
Girly '70
Goodbye, Mr. Chips '69

Nana Bryant (1888-1955)
The Private War of Major Benson '55
Harvey '50
Ladies of the Chorus '49
Eyes of Texas '48
Inner Sanctum '48
Big Town '47
The Possessed '47
Give Me a Sailor '38
Sinners in Paradise '38

Pamela Bryant
Tigershark '87
Lunch Wagon '81

Virginia Bryant
The Barbarians '87
Demons 2 '87

William Bryant
Mountain Family Robinson '79
Corvette Summer '78

Claudia Bryar
Psycho 2 '83
Green Eyes '76

Scott Bryce
Up Close and Personal '96
Stalking Laura '93

Larry Bryggman
Spy Game '01
Die Hard: With a Vengeance '95

Andrew Bryniarski
Cyborg 3: The Recycler '95
The Program '93
Batman Returns '92

Yul Brynner (1915-85)
Death Rage '77
Futureworld '76
The Ultimate Warrior '75
Night Flight from Moscow '73
Westworld '73
Fuzz '72
Catlow '71
Light at the Edge of the World '71
Romance of a Horsethief '71
Battle of Neretva '69
The Madwoman of Chaillot '69
The Magic Christian '69
Villa Rides '68
Triple Cross '67
Cast a Giant Shadow '66
The Poppy Is Also a Flower '66
Return of the Magnificent Seven '66
Morituri '65
Invitation to a Gunfighter '64
Taras Bulba '62
The Magnificent Seven '60
Solomon and Sheba '59
The Testament of Orpheus '59
The Brothers Karamazov '58
The Buccaneer '58
Anastasia '56
The King and I '56
The Ten Commandments '56
Port of New York '49

Reine Brynolfsson (1953-)
Les Miserables '97

The Last Dance '93
House of Angels '92

Colin Buchanan
Catherine Cookson's The Secret '00
Moll Flanders '96

Edgar Buchanan (1903-79)
Yuma '70
Over the Hill Gang '69
Man from Button Willow '65 (V)
The Rounders '65
McLintock! '63
Ride the High Country '62
It Started with a Kiss '59
The Devil's Partner '58
Rage at Dawn '55
Silver Star '55
Human Desire '54
Make Haste to Live '54
Shane '53
Big Trees '52
She Couldn't Say No '52
The Big Hangover '50
Cheaper by the Dozen '50
Rawhide '50
Lust for Gold '49
Man from Colorado '49
Black Arrow '48
Coroner Creek '48
Abilene Town '46
Buffalo Bill '44
City Without Men '43
The Desperadoes '43
Destroyer '43
Talk of the Town '42
Penny Serenade '41
Texas '41
Arizona '40

Ian Buchanan (1957-)
Panic Room '02
Ivory Tower '97
Marilyn & Bobby: Her Final Affair '94
Blue Flame '93
Double Exposure '93
The Cool Surface '92

Jack Buchanan (1891-1957)
The Band Wagon '53
When Knights Were Bold '36

Robert Buchanan
That Sinking Feeling '79
The Girl Who Knew Too Much '63

Sherry Buchanan
Emmanuelle & Joanna '86
Doctor Butcher M.D. '80
Eyes Behind the Stars '72

Simone Buchanan
Shame '87
Run, Rebecca, Run '81

Christopher Buchholz
Covert Assassin '94
No Fear, No Die '90

Horst Buchholz (1932-)
The Enemy '01
Life Is Beautiful '98
Faraway, So Close! '93
Aces: Iron Eagle 3 '92
Code Name: Emerald '85
Sahara '83
Berlin Tunnel 21 '81
Avalanche Express '79
From Hell to Victory '79
Raid on Entebbe '77
Return to Fantasy Island '77
The Savage Bees '76
The Catamount Killing '74
Empty Canvas '64
Fanny '61
One, Two, Three '61
The Magnificent Seven '60
Tiger Bay '59
Teenage Wolfpack '57

Buck
Robinson Crusoe of Clipper Island '36
Robinson Crusoe of Mystery Island '36

Samantha Buck
Wirey Spindell '99
The Sticky Fingers of Time '97

John Buckler
Tarzan Escapes '36
The Black Room '35

Betty Buckley (1947-)
Simply Irresistible '99
Critical Choices '97
Last Time Out '94
Wyatt Earp '94
Rain Without Thunder '93
Babycakes '89
Another Woman '88
Frantic '88
Wild Thing '87
Tender Mercies '83
Carrie '76

Keith Buckley
Half Moon Street '86
Excalibur '81
The Virgin Witch '70

Susan Buckner
Deadly Blessing '81
Grease '78

Robert Budaska
Grizzly Mountain '97
Ice Pawn '92

Helen Buday (1963-)
Dingo '90
For Love Alone '86
Mad Max: Beyond Thunderdome '85

Jack Buetel (1915-89)
The Half-Breed '51
Best of the Badmen '50
The Outlaw '43

Marilyn Buferd
Queen of Outer Space '58
Machine to Kill Bad People '48

Buffalo Bill, Jr. (1896-1961)
Lightning Bill '35
Powdersmoke Range '35
Riding Speed '35
Rawhide Romance '34
Deadwood Pass '33
Fighting Cowboy '33
Terror Trail '33

Jimmy Buffett
From the Earth to the Moon '98
FM '78
Rancho Deluxe '75

Monica Bugajski
Shadrach '98
The Three Lives of Karen '97

Niall Buggy
The Playboys '92
Zardoz '73

Joe Bugner
The Cursed Mountain Mystery '93
Fatal Bond '91

Valerie Buhagiar
Highway 61 '91
Roadkill '89

Gerard Buhr
The Night of the Following Day '69
Bob le Flambeur '55

Genevieve Bujold (1942-)
Eye of the Beholder '99
Last Night '98
The House of Yes '97
Eye '96
Mon Amie Max '94
The Dance Goes On '92
Oh, What a Night '92
False Identity '90
A Paper Wedding '89
Dead Ringers '88
The Moderns '88
Trouble in Mind '86
Choose Me '84
Tightrope '84
Monsignor '82
Final Assignment '80
The Last Flight of Noah's Ark '80
Murder by Decree '79
Coma '78
Another Man, Another Chance '77
Journey '77
Obsession '76
Swashbuckler '76
Earthquake '74
Trojan Women '71
Anne of the Thousand Days '69
The King of Hearts '66
La Guerre Est Finie '66

Donald Buka (1921-)
Stolen Identity '53
The Street with No Name '48
Watch on the Rhine '43

Raymond Buktenica (1943-)
My Girl '91
Wait Till Your Mother Gets Home '83
The Adventures of Nellie Bly '81
The Jayne Mansfield Story '80

Peter Bull (1912-84)
Doctor Dolittle '67
Second Best Secret Agent in the Whole Wide World '65
Dr. Strangelove, or: How I Learned to Stop Worrying and Love the Bomb '64
Tom Jones '63
The African Queen '51
A Christmas Carol '51
Marie Antoinette '38
Sabotage '36

Richard Bull
Different Story '78
Lawman '71

Amelia Bullmore
Catherine Cookson's Tilly Trotter '99
Mrs. Dalloway '97

Jeremy Bulloch
Return of the Jedi '83
The Empire Strikes Back '80

Sandra Bullock (1964-)
Divine Secrets of the Ya-Ya Sisterhood '02
Murder by Numbers '02
Lisa Picard Is Famous '01
Gun Shy '00
Miss Congeniality '00
28 Days '00
Forces of Nature '99
Hope Floats '98
Practical Magic '98
Prince of Egypt '98 (V)
Speed 2: Cruise Control '97
In Love and War '96
A Time to Kill '96
The Net '95
Two If by Sea '95
While You Were Sleeping '95
Me and the Mob '94
Speed '94
Demolition Man '93
Fire on the Amazon '93
The Thing Called Love '93
The Vanishing '93
Wrestling Ernest Hemingway '93
Love Potion #9 '92
Who Shot Pat? '92
When the Party's Over '91
A Fool and His Money '88
Hangmen '87

William Bumiller
The Heroes of Desert Storm '91
Death Spa '87

Rodger Bumpass
National Lampoon's Class of '86 '86
Heavy Metal '81 (V)

Stuart Bunce
All the King's Men '99
Behind the Lines '97

Brooke Bundy (1944-)
Beverly Hills Bodysnatchers '89
A Nightmare on Elm Street 4: Dream Master '88
Twice Dead '88
A Nightmare on Elm Street 3: Dream Warriors '87
Explorers '85
Two Fathers' Justice '85
The Crash of Flight 401 '78
Francis Gary Powers: The True Story of the U-2 Spy '76
The Gay Deceivers '69

Edward (Eddie) Bunker
Animal Factory '00
Shadrach '98
Somebody to Love '94
Best of the Best 2 '93
Desperate Motives '92
Reservoir Dogs '92
Best of the Best '89
Miracle Mile '89
Relentless '89
Tango and Cash '89
Fear '88
The Running Man '87
Shy People '87
Runaway Train '85
Straight Time '78

Avis Bunnage (1923-90)
The Krays '90
No Surrender '86
Forbidden '85
The L-Shaped Room '62
The Loneliness of the Long Distance Runner '62

Luis Bunuel (1900-83)
The Discreet Charm of the Bourgeoisie '72
Un Chien Andalou '28

Cara Buono (1974-)
Happy Accidents '00
Two Ninas '00
Attention Shoppers '99
Chutney Popcorn '99
In a Class of His Own '99
Man of the Century '99
Next Stop, Wonderland '98
River Red '98
Kicking and Screaming '95
Killer: A Journal of Murder '95
The Cowboy Way '94
Gladiator '92
Waterland '92

Victor Buono (1938-82)
Flight of Dragons '82 (V)
The Man with Bogart's Face '80
More Wild, Wild West '80
Better Late Than Never '79
The Evil '78
The Man from Atlantis '77
Arnold '73
The Mad Butcher '72
Northeast of Seoul '72
Beneath the Planet of the Apes '70
Boot Hill '69
The Silencers '66
Hush, Hush, Sweet Charlotte '65
Robin and the 7 Hoods '64
The Strangler '64
Four for Texas '63
What Ever Happened to Baby Jane? '62

Sonny Bupp (1928-)
Citizen Kane '41
Three Faces West '40
Hopalong Cassidy: Renegade Trail '39
Renegade Trail '39

Hugh Burden (1913-85)
Blood from the Mummy's Tomb '71
Funeral in Berlin '66
Ghost Ship '53
Fame Is the Spur '47
Immortal Battalion '44

Suzanne Burden
A Mind to Murder '96
Strapless '90
Office Romances '86
Sharma & Beyond '84

Kim Burfield
Treasure Island '72
The Hero '71

Christopher Burgard
Full Body Massage '95
84 Charlie MoPic '89
Twice Dead '88

Gregg Burge
School Daze '88
A Chorus Line '85

Dorothy Burgess (1907-61)
Girls in Chains '43
Hold Your Man '33
Ladies They Talk About '33

John Burgess
Rosencrantz & Guildenstern Are Dead '90
Christabel '89

Gary Burghoff (1943-)
Small Kill '93
Casino '80
The Man in the Santa Claus Suit '79
M*A*S*H '70

Alfred Burke (1918-)
The House on Garibaldi Street '79
The Brontes of Haworth '73
One Day in the Life of Ivan Denisovich '71
Night Caller from Outer Space '66
The Nanny '65
Children of the Damned '63
Dead Lucky '60

Billie Burke (1885-1970)
Sergeant Rutledge '60
The Young Philadelphians '59
Small Town Girl '53
Father's Little Dividend '51
Father of the Bride '50
The Barkleys of Broadway '49
Breakfast in Hollywood '46
In This Our Life '42
They All Kissed the Bride '42
The Man Who Came to Dinner '41
Topper Returns '41
Eternally Yours '39
Topper Takes a Trip '39
The Wizard of Oz '39
Everybody Sing '38
The Young in Heart '38
The Bride Wore Red '37
Navy Blue and Gold '37
Topper '37
Craig's Wife '36
Becky Sharp '35
Doubting Thomas '35
Forsaking All Others '35
Splendor '35
Christopher Strong '33
Dinner at Eight '33
Finishing School '33
A Bill of Divorcement '32

Billy Burke
Along Came a Spider '01
Komodo '99
Mafia! '98
Without Limits '97
To Cross the Rubicon '91

Brandon Burke
Best Enemies '86
The Odd Angry Shot '79

David Burke
King Lear '98
Vibrations '94

Delta Burke (1956-)
What Women Want '00
Melanie Darrow '97
Maternal Instincts '96
Dynamite and Gold '88
A Bunny's Tale '85
First & Ten '85
First & Ten: The Team Scores Again '85
The Seekers '79

J. Frank Burke (1867-1918)
The Bargain '15
The Italian '15

James Burke (1886-1968)
Lucky Me '54
Cavalry Charge '51
Down to Earth '47
At the Circus '39
Beau Geste '39
Dawn Patrol '38
Dead End '37
The Mystery Man '35
Ruggles of Red Gap '35
Lady by Choice '34

Kathleen Burke (1913-80)
The Lives of a Bengal Lancer '35
Murders in the Zoo '33
Island of Lost Souls '32

Kathy Burke (1964-)
Kevin & Perry Go Large '00
Love, Honour & Obey '00
Dancing at Lughnasa '98
Elizabeth '98
Nil by Mouth '96

Paul Burke (1926-)
The Red Light Sting '84
Wild & Wooly '78
Psychic Killer '75
Anatomy of Terror '74
Daddy's Gone A-Hunting '69
Valley of the Dolls '67
Fatal Confinement '64
Francis in the Navy '55
Francis Goes to West Point '52

Robert John Burke (1961-)
No Such Thing '01
A Bright Shining Lie '98
First Love, Last Rites '98
From the Earth to the Moon '98
Somewhere in the City '97
Fled '96
Stephen King's Thinner '96
Killer: A Journal of Murder '95
Dust Devil '93
A Far Off Place '93
Tombstone '93
Simple Men '92
Rambling Rose '91
RoboCop 3 '91
The Unbelievable Truth '90

Robert Karl Burke
The Basket '99
Big and Hairy '98

Simon Burke (1961-)
Rodgers & Hammerstein's South Pacific '01
Pitch Black '00
Passion '99
Slate, Wyn & Me '87
The Irishman '78
The Devil's Playground '76

Laura Burkett
Daddy's Boys '87
Overkill '86

Scott Burkholder
Sketch Artist 2: Hands That See '94
Class of '61 '92
House 4: Home Deadly Home '91

Dennis Burkley
The First 9 1/2 Weeks '98
Father's Day '96
Tin Cup '96
Son-in-Law '93
Stop! or My Mom Will Shoot '92
The Doors '91
Lambada '89
Pass the Ammo '88
Murphy's Romance '85
Bummer '73

Tom Burlinson (1957-)
Landslide '92
Showdown at Williams Creek '91

Piece of Cake '90
Return to Snowy River '88
The Time Guardian '87
Windrider '86
Flesh and Blood '85
Phar Lap '84
The Man from Snowy River '82

Leo Burmester (1944-)
Limbo '99
Eye of the Storm '98
River Red '98
Switchback '97
William Faulkner's Old Man '97
Mistrial '96
The Great Elephant Escape '95
The Neon Bible '95
Truman '95
Fly by Night '93
A Perfect World '93
Passion Fish '92
The Abyss '89

Caesar Burner
Green Inferno '80s
Tombs of the Blind Dead '72

Carol Burnett (1933-)
The Trumpet of the Swan '01 (V)
Moon over Broadway '98
Noises Off '92
Follies in Concert '85
Between Friends '83
Annie '82
Chu Chu & the Philly Flash '81
The Four Seasons '81
Friendly Fire '79
Tenth Month '79
The Grass Is Always Greener Over the Septic Tank '78
A Wedding '78
The Front Page '74
Pete 'n' Tillie '72

Smiley Burnette (1911-67)
Last of the Pony Riders '53
On Top of Old Smoky '53
Winning of the West '53
Bonanza Town '51
Blazing Across the Pecos '48
Under Western Stars '45
Call of the Rockies '44
Idaho '43
King of the Cowboys '43
Raiders of Sunset Pass '43
Silver Spurs '43
Bells of Capistrano '42
Call of the Canyon '42
Heart of the Golden West '42
Heart of the Rio Grande '42
Back in the Saddle '41
Down Mexico Way '41
Ridin' on a Rainbow '41
Gaucho Serenade '40
South of the Border '39
Billy the Kid Returns '38
Hollywood Stadium Mystery '38
The Man from Music Mountain '38
Oh Susannah '38
Old Barn Dance '38
Prairie Moon '38
Rootin' Tootin' Rhythm '38
Big Show '37
Boots & Saddles '37
Dick Tracy '37
Git Along Little Dogies '37
Round-Up Time in Texas '37
Springtime in the Rockies '37
Yodelin' Kid from Pine Ridge '37
Old Corral '36
Red River Valley '36
Ride, Ranger, Ride '36
Undersea Kingdom '36
Harmony Lane '35
Melody Trail '35
The Phantom Empire '35
Dude Ranger '34
In Old Santa Fe '34
Mystery Mountain '34

Bob Burns
Waikiki Wedding '37
Rhythm on the Range '36

Carol Burns
Bad Blood '87
Dusty '85

Edmund Burns (1892-1989)
Reform School Girl '57
Sea Devils '31
Sunny Side Up '28
Made for Love '26

Edward Burns (1968-)
Life or Something Like It '02
15 Minutes '01
Sidewalks of New York '01
No Looking Back '98
Saving Private Ryan '98
She's the One '96
The Brothers McMullen '94

George Burns (1896-1996)
Radioland Murders '94
18 Again! '88
Oh, God! You Devil '84
Two of a Kind '82
Oh, God! Book 2 '80
Going in Style '79
Sgt. Pepper's Lonely Hearts Club Band '78
Oh, God! '77
The Sunshine Boys '75
Solid Gold Cadillac '56 (N)
Honolulu '39
College Swing '38
A Damsel in Distress '37
Here Comes Cookie '35
Love in Bloom '35
Six of a Kind '34
We're Not Dressing '34
International House '33

Heather Burns
Miss Congeniality '00
You Are Here * '00
You've Got Mail '98

Helen Burns
Utilities '83
Zorro, the Gay Blade '81

Jennifer Burns
Isaac Asimov's Nightfall '00
Josh Kirby...Time Warrior: Chapter 5, Journey to the Magic Cavern '96
Josh Kirby...Time Warrior: Chapter 6, Last Battle for the Universe '96
Josh Kirby...Time Warrior: Chapter 1, Planet of the Dino-Knights '95
Josh Kirby...Time Warrior: Chapter 2, The Human Pets '95
Josh Kirby...Time Warrior: Chapter 3, Trapped on Toyworld '95
Josh Kirby...Time Warrior: Chapter 4, Eggs from 70 Million B.C. '95
Haunted Symphony '94
The Liar's Club '93

Jere Burns (1954-)
Crocodile Dundee in Los Angeles '01
Life-Size '00
Santa Fe '97
Greedy '94
The Gambler Returns: The Luck of the Draw '93
Wired '89

Marilyn Burns (1956-)
The Texas Chainsaw Massacre 4: The Next Generation '95
Future Kill '85
Kiss Daddy Goodbye '81
Eaten Alive '76
Helter Skelter '76
The Texas Chainsaw Massacre '74

Marion Burns
Dawn Rider '35
Paradise Canyon '35

Mark Burns (1936-)
Bullseye! '90
House of the Living Dead '73
Death in Venice '71
The Virgin and the Gypsy '70
The Charge of the Light Brigade '68

Martha Burns
The Life Before This '99
Long Day's Journey Into Night '96

Michael Burns (1947-)
Santee '73
Thumb Tripping '72
That Cold Day in the Park '69

Robert Burns
Confessions of a Serial Killer '87
Terror in the Jungle '68

Robert Burns (1884-1957)
Western Trails '38
Gun Law '33
When a Man Rides Alone '33
South of Santa Fe '32

Raymond Burr (1917-93)
Delirious '91
Showdown at Williams Creek '91
Survival of Spaceship Earth '90 (N)
Perry Mason: The Case of the Lost Love '87
Godzilla 1985 '85
Perry Mason Returns '85
Airplane 2: The Sequel '82
Peter and Paul '81
The Curse of King Tut's Tomb '80
The Night the City Screamed '80
Out of the Blue '80
The Return '80
Love's Savage Fury '79
The Bastard '78 (N)
Centennial '78
Tomorrow Never Comes '77
Crime of Passion '57
Godzilla, King of the Monsters '56
Great Day in the Morning '56
A Man Alone '55
They Were So Young '55
Casanova's Big Night '54
Party Girls for Sale '54
Passion '54
Rear Window '54
Thunder Pass '54
FBI Girl '52
Horizons West '52
Meet Danny Wilson '52
Bride of the Gorilla '51
His Kind of Woman '51
A Place in the Sun '51
Borderline '50
Key to the City '50
Love Happy '50
Adventures of Don Juan '49
Black Magic '49
Pitfall '48
Raw Deal '48
Station West '48
Desperate '47

Robert Burr (1926-2000)
Netherworld '90
The Possession of Joel Delaney '72

Maryedith Burrell
Camp Nowhere '94
The Little Match Girl '87

Ty Burrell (1967-)
Black Hawk Down '01
Evolution '01

Hedy Burress
Valentine '01
Cabin by the Lake '00
Foxfire '96

Bonnie Burroughs
One Small Hero '99
Hard to Kill '89

Jackie Burroughs (1938-)
Lost and Delirious '01
Elvis Meets Nixon '98
Last Night '98
Armistead Maupin's More Tales of the City '97
Bleeders '97
Careful '92
Final Notice '89
A Winter Tan '88
John and the Missus '87
The Housekeeper '86
Anne of Green Gables '85
Undergrads '85
The Grey Fox '83
125 Rooms of Comfort '83
Heavy Metal '81 (V)

William S. Burroughs (1914-97)
Wax, or the Discovery of Television among the Bees '93
Bloodhounds of Broadway '89
Drugstore Cowboy '89
Twister '89
Haxan: Witchcraft through the Ages '22 (N)

Darren E. Burrows (1966-)
The Hi-Lo Country '98
Class of 1999 '90
Cry-Baby '90

Saffron Burrows (1973-)
Enigma '01
The Seventh Stream '01
Time Code '00
Deep Blue Sea '99
Miss Julie '99
Wing Commander '99
The Loss of Sexual Innocence '98
Lovelife '97
The Matchmaker '97
Nevada '97
Hotel de Love '96
Welcome II the Terrordome '95
Circle of Friends '94

Ellen Burstyn (1932-)
Divine Secrets of the Ya-Ya Sisterhood '02
Mermaid '00
Requiem for a Dream '00
The Yards '00
Night Ride Home '99
Flash '98
Playing by Heart '98
Deceiver '97
The Baby-Sitters' Club '95
The Color of Evening '95
Follow the River '95
How to Make an American Quilt '95
Roommates '95
The Spitfire Grill '95
Getting Gotti '94
Getting Out '94
Primal Secrets '94
When a Man Loves a Woman '94
The Cemetery Club '93
Grand Isle '92
Dying Young '91
Hanna's War '88
Act of Vengeance '86
Something in Common '86
Into Thin Air '85
Twice in a Lifetime '85
The Ambassador '84
The People vs. Jean Harris '81
Silence of the North '81
Resurrection '80
A Dream of Passion '78
Same Time, Next Year '78
Providence '77
Alice Doesn't Live Here Anymore '74
Harry and Tonto '74
Thursday's Game '74
The Exorcist '73
The King of Marvin Gardens '72
The Last Picture Show '71
Alex in Wonderland '70
Tropic of Cancer '70
Pit Stop '67
Goodbye Charlie '64

Benny Burt
Hawaiian Buckaroo '38
Sea Racketeers '37

Corey Burton
Return to Never Land '02 (V)
Atlantis: The Lost Empire '01 (V)
Dudley Do-Right '99 (N)

Harry Burton
Devices and Desires '91
Fortunes of War '87

Jennifer Burton
Death and Desire '97
Watch Me '96
Play Time '94
Truck Stop Women '74

John Burton
Mrs. Miniver '42
Lloyds of London '36

Julian Burton
Masque of the Red Death '65
A Bucket of Blood '59

Kate Burton (1957-)
Unfaithful '02
Celebrity '98
Ellen Foster '97
The Ice Storm '97
Mistrial '96
August '95
Love Matters '93
Uncle Tom's Cabin '87
Big Trouble in Little China '86

LeVar Burton (1957-)
Ali '01
Dancing in September '00
Star Trek: Insurrection '98
Star Trek: First Contact '96
Yesterday's Target '96
Parallel Lives '94
Star Trek: Generations '94
Firestorm: 72 Hours in Oakland '93
Roots: The Gift '88
The Midnight Hour '86
The Supernaturals '86
The Jesse Owens Story '84
Acorn People '82
Grambling's White Tiger '81
The Guyana Tragedy: The Story of Jim Jones '80
The Hunter '80
One in a Million: The Ron LeFlore Story '78
Billy: Portrait of a Street Kid '77
Roots '77

Norman Burton (1935-)
Bloodsport '88
Bad Guys '86
Crimes of Passion '84
Mausoleum '83
Fade to Black '80
The Terminal Man '74
Save the Tiger '73
Diamonds Are Forever '71
Jud '71
Simon, King of the Witches '71
Attack of the Mayan Mummy '63
Fright '56

Richard Burton (1925-84)
Wagner: The Complete Epic '85
1984 '84
Absolution '81
Circle of Two '80
Lovespell '79
Breakthrough '78
The Medusa Touch '78
Wild Geese '78
Equus '77
The Exorcist 2: The Heretic '77
The Gathering Storm '74
The Klansman '74
Massacre in Rome '73
Under Milk Wood '73
Assassination of Trotsky '72
Bluebeard '72
Divorce His, Divorce Hers '72
Hammersmith Is Out '72
Raid on Rommel '71
Anne of the Thousand Days '69
Boom! '68
Candy '68
Doctor Faustus '68
Where Eagles Dare '68
The Comedians '67
The Taming of the Shrew '67
Who's Afraid of Virginia Woolf? '66
The Sandpiper '65
The Spy Who Came in from the Cold '65
Becket '64
The Night of the Iguana '64
Zulu '64 (N)
Cleopatra '63
The Tempest '63
The V.I.P.'s '63
The Longest Day '62
The Bramble Bush '60
Ice Palace '60
Look Back in Anger '58
Alexander the Great '55
The Desert Rats '53
The Robe '53
Green Grow the Rushes '51
The Last Days of Dolwyn '49

Robert Burton
Trilogy of Terror '75
A Reason to Live, a Reason to Die '73

Robert Burton (1895-1962)
The Slime People '63
Invasion of the Animal People '62
The Gallant Hours '60
Compulsion '59
Teenage Frankenstein '58
The Tall T '57
A Man Called Peter '55
Above and Beyond '53
All the Brothers Were Valiant '53
The Girl Who Had Everything '53

Steve (Stephen) Burton (1970-)
The Last Castle '01
Cyber-Tracker 2 '95

Tony Burton
The Magnificent Seven '98
Flipping '96
Mission of Justice '92
House Party 2: The Pajama Jam '91
Armed and Dangerous '86
Oceans of Fire '86
The Shining '80
Blackjack '78
Assault on Precinct 13 '76

Warren Burton (1944-)
Bloodfist 8: Hard Way Out '96
Humanoids from the Deep '96
Gettysburg '93

Wendell Burton (1947-)
East of Eden '80
Fortune and Men's Eyes '71
The Sterile Cuckoo '69

Sean Bury (1954-)
Paul and Michelle '74
The Abominable Dr. Phibes '71
Friends '71
If... '69

Steve Buscemi (1957-)
The Laramie Project '02
Mr. Deeds '02

Spy Kids 2: The Island of Lost Dreams *'02*
Domestic Disturbance *'01*
Final Fantasy: The Spirits Within *'01 (V)*
Ghost World *'01*
Monsters, Inc. *'01 (V)*
Animal Factory *'00*
28 Days *'00*
Big Daddy *'99*
Armageddon *'98*
The Imposters *'98*
The Big Lebowski *'97*
Con Air *'97*
The Real Blonde *'97*
The Wedding Singer *'97*
Escape from L.A. *'96*
Fargo *'96*
The Search for One-Eyed Jimmy *'96*
Tree's Lounge *'96*
Desperado *'95*
Kansas City *'95*
Things to Do in Denver When You're Dead *'95*
Airheads *'94*
Billy Madison *'94*
Floundering *'94*
Living in Oblivion *'94*
Me and the Mob *'94*
Pulp Fiction *'94*
Somebody to Love *'94*
Ed and His Dead Mother *'93*
The Hudsucker Proxy *'93*
The Last Outlaw *'93*
Twenty Bucks *'93*
Crisscross *'92*
In the Soup *'92*
Reservoir Dogs *'92*
Trusting Beatrice *'92*
Barton Fink *'91*
Billy Bathgate *'91*
King of New York *'90*
Tales from the Darkside: The Movie *'90*
Mystery Train *'89*
New York Stories *'89*
Heart *'87*
Parting Glances *'86*

Ernst Busch
Kameradschaft *'31*
The Threepenny Opera *'31*

Mae Busch (1897-1946)
The Mad Monster *'42*
Ziegfeld Girl *'41*
Marie Antoinette *'38*
Bohemian Girl *'36*
The Clutching Hand *'36*
Sucker Money *'34*
Sons of the Desert *'33*
Doctor X *'32*
Without Honors *'32*
Defenders of the Law *'31*
Alibi *'29*
The Unholy Three *'25*
Foolish Wives *'22*

Gary Busey (1944-)
Slap Shot 2: Breaking the Ice *'02*
A Crack in the Floor *'00*
Tribulation *'00*
Detour *'99*
Jacob Two Two Meets the Hooded Fang *'99*
No Tomorrow *'99*
Fear and Loathing in Las Vegas *'98*
The Girl Next Door *'98*
Soldier *'98*
Two Shades of Blue *'98*
Universal Soldier 2: Brothers in Arms *'98*
Diary of a Serial Killer *'97*
The Real Thing *'97*
Rough Riders *'97*
Steel Sharks *'97*
Black Sheep *'96*
Lethal Tender *'96*
Lost Highway *'96*
Plato's Run *'96*
The Rage *'96*
Sticks and Stones *'96*
Suspicious Minds *'96*
Carried Away *'95*
Man with a Gun *'95*
Breaking Point *'94*
Chasers *'94*
Drop Zone *'94*
Surviving the Game *'94*
Warriors *'94*
Fallen Angels 1 *'93*
The Firm *'93*
Rookie of the Year *'93*
Canvas: The Fine Art of Crime *'92*
Chrome Soldiers *'92*
The Player *'92*
South Beach *'92*
Under Siege *'92*
My Heroes Have Always Been Cowboys *'91*
Point Break *'91*
Hider in the House *'90*
Predator 2 *'90*
Act of Piracy *'89*
Dangerous Life *'89*
The Neon Empire *'89*
Bulletproof *'88*
Lethal Weapon *'87*
Let's Get Harry *'87*
Eye of the Tiger *'86*
Half a Lifetime *'86*
Insignificance *'85*
Silver Bullet *'85*
D.C. Cab *'84*
Didn't You Hear? *'83*
Barbarosa *'82*
Carny *'80*
Foolin' Around *'80*
Big Wednesday *'78*
The Buddy Holly Story *'78*
Straight Time *'78*
Gumball Rally *'76*
A Star Is Born *'76*
The Execution of Private Slovik *'74*
Thunderbolt & Lightfoot *'74*
The Last American Hero *'73*
The Shrieking *'73*
Angels Hard As They Come *'71*

Jake Busey (1972-)
Fast Sofa *'01*
Tomcats *'01*
Held Up *'00*
Tail Lights Fade *'99*
Black Cat Run *'98*
Enemy of the State *'98*
Home Fries *'98*
Contact *'97*
Starship Troopers *'97*
The Frighteners *'96*
Twister *'96*
P.C.U. *'94*
S.F.W. *'94*
Windrunner *'94*

Timothy Busfield (1960-)
Time at the Top *'99*
Dream House *'98*
Wanted *'98*
Buffalo Soldiers *'97*
Shadow of a Scream *'97*
The Souler Opposite *'97*
Trucks *'97*
First Kid *'96*
Little Big League *'94*
Fade to Black *'93*
The Skateboard Kid *'93*
Striking Distance *'93*
Sneakers *'92*
Strays *'91*
Field of Dreams *'89*
Revenge of the Nerds 2: Nerds in Paradise *'87*
Revenge of the Nerds *'84*

Billy Green Bush (1935-)
Jason Goes to Hell: The Final Friday *'93*
Conagher *'91*
Elvis and Me *'88*
Critters *'86*
The Deliberate Stranger *'86*
The Hitcher *'86*
The River *'84*
Tom Horn *'80*
Alice Doesn't Live Here Anymore *'74*
Electra Glide in Blue *'73*
Culpepper Cattle Co. *'72*
Five Easy Pieces *'70*

Grand Bush
Extreme Honor *'01*
Freejack *'92*
Blind Vengeance *'90*
Colors *'88*
Streets of Fire *'84*

James Bush (1907-87)
King of the Cowboys *'43*
The Glory Trail *'36*
The Return of Peter Grimm *'35*
A Shot in the Dark *'35*
Beggars in Ermine *'34*
Crimson Romance *'34*

Jovita Bush
Foxstyle *'73*
The Cheerleaders *'72*

Anthony Bushell (1904-97)
A Night to Remember *'58*
Angel with the Trumpet *'50*
The Miniver Story *'50*
The Small Back Room *'49*
The Arsenal Stadium Mystery *'39*
Dark Journey *'37*
The Ghoul *'34*
The Scarlet Pimpernel *'34*
Vanity Fair *'32*
The Royal Bed *'31*
Disraeli *'30*

Francis X. Bushman (1883-1966)
The Phantom Planet *'61*
Sabrina *'54*
David and Bathsheba *'51*
Honky Tonk *'41*
When Lightning Strikes *'34*
Last Frontier *'32*
Ben-Hur *'26*
Eyes Right! *'26*
Midnight Faces *'26*

Akosua Busia (1968-)
Larry McMurtry's Dead Man's Walk *'96*
Rosewood *'96*
The Seventh Sign *'88*
Hard Lessons *'86*
Native Son *'86*
The Color Purple *'85*
The Final Terror *'83*

Marion Busia
Deadline Auto Theft *'83*
Gone in 60 Seconds *'74*

Pascale Bussieres (1968-)
Xchange *'00*
The Five Senses *'99*
Set Me Free *'99*
Jack Higgins' Thunder Point *'97*
The Twilight of the Ice Nymphs *'97*
When Night Is Falling *'95*

Raymond Bussieres (1907-82)
Jonah Who Will Be 25 in the Year 2000 *'76*
Paris When It Sizzles *'64*
Beauties of the Night *'52*
Casque d'Or *'52*

Budd Buster (1891-1965)
Outlaw of the Plains *'46*
Border Badmen *'45*
Frontier Outlaws *'44*
Cowboy Commandos *'43*
Raiders of Sunset Pass *'43*
The Lone Rider in Ghost Town *'41*
Trigger Men *'41*
Covered Wagon Trails *'40*
Pinto Canyon *'40*
Feud Maker *'38*
Songs and Bullets *'38*
Thunder in the Desert *'38*
Gun Grit *'36*
Texas Jack *'35*
The Gun Ranger *'34*

Mitchell Butel
Strange Fits of Passion *'99*
Dark City *'97*

Dick Butkus (1942-)
Spontaneous Combustion *'89*
Hamburger...The Motion Picture *'86*
Johnny Dangerously *'84*
Cracking Up *'83*
Deadly Games *'80*
The Legend of Sleepy Hollow *'79*
Mother, Jugs and Speed *'76*

Brett Butler
The Dress Code *'99*
Militia *'99*

Calvin Butler
July Group *'70s*
Drying Up the Streets *'76*

Cindy Butler
Boggy Creek II *'83*
Grayeagle *'77*

Daniel Butler
Enemy of the State *'98*
The Assassination File *'96*
Ernest Goes to Camp *'87*

David Butler
Rhodes *'97*
Prey for the Hunter *'92*
Crucible of Horror *'69*

David Butler (1895-1979)
The Man on the Box *'25*
The Sky Pilot *'21*
County Fair *'20*

Daws Butler
The Good, the Bad, and Huckleberry Hound *'88 (V)*
Hey There, It's Yogi Bear *'64 (V)*

Dean Butler (1956-)
The Final Goal *'94*
Desert Hearts *'86*
The Kid with the 200 I.Q. *'83*
Forever *'78*

Frank Butler (1890-1967)
Made for Love *'26*
King of the Wild Horses *'24*

Gerard Butler (1969-)
Harrison's Flowers *'02*
Reign of Fire *'02*
Attila *'01*
Dracula 2000 *'00*
Mrs. Brown *'97*

Lois Butler
High Lonesome *'50*
Mickey *'48*

Patrick Butler
Frostbiter: Wrath of the Wendigo *'94*
The Carrier *'87*

Paul Butler
Romeo Is Bleeding *'93*
Zebrahead *'92*
To Sleep with Anger *'90*

Tom Butler
Josie and the Pussycats *'01*
Deadlocked *'00*
Life-Size *'00*
Every Mother's Worst Fear *'98*
Ronnie and Julie *'97*
Dead Ahead *'96*
Maternal Instincts *'96*
Ernest Rides Again *'93*
Scanners 2: The New Order *'91*
Tales of the Klondike: The Scorn of Women *'87*
Confidential *'86*

William Butler
Inner Sanctum *'91*
Night of the Living Dead *'90*
Leatherface: The Texas Chainsaw Massacre 3 *'89*

Yancy Butler (1970-)
The Witness Files *'00*
Ravager *'97*
The Ex *'96*
Fast Money *'96*
Drop Zone *'94*
Hard Target *'93*
The Hit List *'93*

Merritt Butrick (1959-89)
From the Dead of Night *'89*
Death Spa *'87*
Shy People *'87*
When the Bough Breaks *'86*
Wired to Kill *'86*
Code of Honor *'84*
Star Trek 3: The Search for Spock *'84*
Star Trek 2: The Wrath of Khan *'82*
Zapped! *'82*

Johnny Butt
Blackmail *'29*
Q Ships *'28*

Lawson Butt
Lady of the Lake *'28*
Dante's Inferno *'24*

Charles Butterworth (1896-1946)
Dixie Jamboree *'44*
Follow the Boys *'44*
Road Show *'41*
Second Chorus *'40*
Let Freedom Ring *'39*
Every Day's a Holiday *'38*
Thanks for the Memory *'38*
Swing High, Swing Low *'37*
The Moon's Our Home *'36*
Forsaking All Others *'35*
The Cat and the Fiddle *'34*
Hollywood Party *'34*
Penthouse *'33*
Illicit *'31*

Donna Butterworth
Paradise, Hawaiian Style *'66*
Family Jewels *'65*

Red Buttons (1919-)
The Story of Us *'99*
It Could Happen to You *'94*
The Ambulance *'90*
18 Again! *'88*
Side Show *'84*
Leave 'Em Laughing *'81*
Off Your Rocker *'80*
When Time Ran Out *'80*
C.H.O.M.P.S. *'79*
Movie, Movie *'78*
Users *'78*
Pete's Dragon *'77*
Viva Knievel *'77*
The Poseidon Adventure *'72*
Who Killed Mary What's 'Er Name? *'71*
They Shoot Horses, Don't They? *'69*
Harlow *'65*
Five Weeks in a Balloon *'62*
Gay Purr-ee *'62 (V)*
Hatari! *'62*
The Longest Day *'62*
Sayonara *'57*
13 Rue Madeleine *'46*

Pat Buttram (1917-94)
Back to the Future, Part 3 *'90*
The Fox and the Hound *'81 (V)*
The Rescuers *'77 (V)*
Robin Hood *'73 (V)*
The Gatling Gun *'72*
Evil Roy Slade *'71 (N)*
The Aristocats *'70 (V)*
Roustabout *'64*
Blue Canadian Rockies *'52*
Night Stage to Galveston *'52*
Hills of Utah *'51*
Valley of Fire *'51*

Sarah Buxton (1972-)
The Climb *'97*
Listen *'96*
Fast Getaway 2 *'94*
Rock 'n' Roll High School Forever *'91*
Primal Rage *'90*

Margherita Buy
The Favorite Son *'94*
The Station *'92*

Ruth Buzzi (1939-)
Boys Will Be Boys *'97*
Troublemakers *'94*
Wishful Thinking *'92*
Digging Up Business *'91*
My Mom's a Werewolf *'89*
Up Your Alley *'89*
Dixie Lanes *'88*
Pound Puppies and the Legend of Big Paw *'88 (V)*
Bad Guys *'86*
Pogo for President: "I Go Pogo" *'84 (V)*
Surf 2 *'84*
The Being *'83*
Chu Chu & the Philly Flash *'81*
The North Avenue Irregulars *'79*
Scavenger Hunt *'79*
The Villain *'79*
Once Upon a Brothers Grimm *'77*
Freaky Friday *'76*

Dave Buzzotta
The Prophecy 3: The Ascent *'99*
Children of the Corn 5: Fields of Terror *'98*
Gang Boys *'97*
The Real Thing *'97*

Bobbie Byers
Wild Rebels *'71*
Savages from Hell *'68*

Kate Byers
The Man Who Made Husbands Jealous *'98*
Career Girls *'97*

Spring Byington (1893-1971)
Please Don't Eat the Daisies *'60*
Because You're Mine *'52*
Angels in the Outfield *'51*
Walk Softly, Stranger *'50*
The Big Wheel *'49*
In the Good Old Summertime *'49*
Singapore *'47*
The Enchanted Cottage *'45*
Thrill of a Romance *'45*
Heaven Can Wait *'43*
Roxie Hart *'42*
The Devil & Miss Jones *'41*
Meet John Doe *'41*
When Ladies Meet *'41*
The Blue Bird *'40*
Lucky Partners *'40*
The Story of Alexander Graham Bell *'39*
Jezebel *'38*
You Can't Take It with You *'38*
The Charge of the Light Brigade *'36*
Theodora Goes Wild *'36*
Ah, Wilderness! *'35*
Mutiny on the Bounty *'35*
Werewolf of London *'35*
Little Women *'33*

Rolan Bykov (1929-98)
Ivan and Abraham *'94*
Commissar *'68*
The Overcoat *'59*

John Byner (1938-)
My 5 Wives *'00*
The Black Cauldron *'85 (V)*
Transylvania 6-5000 *'85*
The Man in the Santa Claus Suit *'79*
A Pleasure Doing Business *'79*
Great Smokey Roadblock *'76*

David Byrd (1933-2001)
Thick as Thieves *'99*
The Proposition *'97*

Ralph Byrd (1909-52)
Radar Secret Service *'50*
Jungle Goddess *'49*
Thunder in the Pines *'49*
Dick Tracy Meets Gruesome *'47*
Dick Tracy's Dilemma *'47*
Guadalcanal Diary *'43*
The Jungle Book *'42*
Desperate Cargo *'41*

Dick Tracy vs. Crime Inc. '41
Life Begins for Andy Hardy '41
Misbehaving Husbands '41
The Howards of Virginia '40
The Son of Monte Cristo '40
Born to Be Wild '38
Dick Tracy Returns '38
Dick Tracy '37
S.O.S. Coast Guard '37
The Trigger Trio '37
Blake of Scotland Yard '36
Border Caballero '36
Hell-Ship Morgan '36

Thomas Jefferson Byrd (1960-)
Bamboozled '00
He Got Game '98
Get On the Bus '96
Girls of the White Orchid '85

Tom Byrd
Set It Off '96
Wet Gold '84

Miriam Byrd-Nethery
Civil War Diary '90
Leatherface: The Texas Chainsaw Massacre 3 '89

Bill Byrge
Ernest Goes to School '94
Ernest Goes to Jail '90

Anne Byrne
Manhattan '79
A Night Full of Rain '78

Antoine Byrne
I Went Down '97
Oliver Twist '97

Antony Byrne
Touching Evil '97
Catherine Cookson's The Cinder Path '94

Barbara Byrne
Sunday in the Park with George '86
Svengali '83
Mystery at Fire Island '81

Catherine Byrne
Eat the Peach '86
S.O.S. Titanic '79

David Byrne (1952-)
Heavy Petting '89
True Stories '86

Eddie Byrne (1911-81)
The Mummy '59
Dangerous Youth '58
Abandon Ship '57

Gabriel Byrne (1950-)
End of Days '99
Stigmata '99
Enemy of the State '98
The Man in the Iron Mask '98
Quest for Camelot '98 (V)
The End of Violence '97
Polish Wedding '97
Weapons of Mass Distraction '97
The Brylcreem Boys '96
The Last of the High Kings '96
Smilla's Sense of Snow '96
Somebody Is Waiting '96
This Is the Sea '96
Trigger Happy '96
Buffalo Girls '95
Dead Man '95
Frankie Starlight '95
The Usual Suspects '95
Little Women '94
Royal Deceit '94
A Simple Twist of Fate '94
Trial by Jury '94
A Dangerous Woman '93
Point of No Return '93
Cool World '92
Into the West '92
A Soldier's Tale '91
Dark Obsession '90
Miller's Crossing '90
Shipwrecked '90
The Courier '88
Gothic '87
Hello Again '87
Julia and Julia '87
Lionheart '87
Siesta '87
Christopher Columbus '85
Defense of the Realm '85
Hanna K. '83
The Keep '83
Excalibur '81

Martha Byrne
Anna to the Infinite Power '84
The Eyes of the Amaryllis '82

Michael Byrne
The Sum of All Fears '02
Mists of Avalon '01
The Musketeer '01
Battlefield Earth '00
Heat of the Sun '99
Gunshy '98
Apt Pupil '97
The Saint '97
Agatha Christie's The Pale Horse '96
The Infiltrator '95
Sharpe's Enemy '94
Sharpe's Honour '94
Indiana Jones and the Last Crusade '89
The Good Father '87
Over Indulgence '87
Vampyres '74

Rose Byrne
Star Wars: Episode 2—Attack of the Clones '02
Two Hands '98

David Byrnes
Witchcraft 9: Bitter Flesh '96
Witchcraft 7: Judgement Hour '95

Edd Byrnes (1933-)
Troop Beverly Hills '89
Back to the Beach '87
Mankillers '87
Erotic Images '85
Twirl '81
Grease '78
Go Kill and Come Back '68
Any Gun Can Play '67
Darby's Rangers '58

Jim Byrnes (1948-)
Highlander: Endgame '00
Starlight '97
Bloodhounds 2 '96
Suspicious Agenda '94
Dirty Work '92

Josephine Byrnes
Oscar and Lucinda '97
Frauds '93
Brides of Christ '91

Annie Byron
Doing Time for Patsy Cline '97
Fran '85

Arthur Byron (1872-1943)
The Whole Town's Talking '35
Gabriel Over the White House '33
The Mummy '32

David Byron
Fade to Black '93
My Brother's Wife '89

Jeffrey Byron (1955-)
Dungeonmaster '83
Metalstorm: The Destruction of Jared Syn '83
The Seniors '78

Kathleen Byron (1922-)
From a Far Country: Pope John Paul II '81
The Golden Bowl '72
Twins of Evil '71
Burn Witch, Burn! '62
Profile '54
Young Bess '53
The Gambler & the Lady '52
The Small Back Room '49
Black Narcissus '47
Stairway to Heaven '46

Marion Byron
Breed of the Border '33
Steamboat Bill, Jr. '28

Walter Byron (1899-1972)
Mr. Boggs Steps Out '38
The Savage Girl '32
Vanity Fair '32
Queen Kelly '29

Susan Byun
Deadly Target '94
Sgt. Kabukiman N.Y.P.D. '94
Crime Lords '91

James Caan (1939-)
Dead Simple '01
A Glimpse of Hell '01
In the Shadows '01
Warden of Red Rock '01
Luckytown '00
Way of the Gun '00
The Yards '00
Mickey Blue Eyes '99
This Is My Father '99
Bulletproof '96
Eraser '96
North Star '96
Bottle Rocket '95
A Boy Called Hate '95
Flesh and Bone '93
The Program '93
Honeymoon in Vegas '92
The Dark Backward '91
For the Boys '91
Dick Tracy '90
Misery '90
Alien Nation '88
Gardens of Stone '87
Bolero '82
Kiss Me Goodbye '82
The Godfather 1902-1959: The Complete Epic '81
Thief '81
Hide in Plain Sight '80
Chapter Two '79
Comes a Horseman '78
Little Moon & Jud McGraw '78
Another Man, Another Chance '77
A Bridge Too Far '77
Harry & Walter Go to New York '76
Silent Movie '76
Funny Lady '75
The Killer Elite '75
Rollerball '75
Freebie & the Bean '74
The Gambler '74
The Godfather, Part 2 '74
Cinderella Liberty '73
Slither '73
The Godfather '72
Gone with the West '72
Brian's Song '71
The Rain People '69
Countdown '68
El Dorado '67
Games '67
Red Line 7000 '65
Lady in a Cage '64

Scott Caan (1976-)
American Outlaws '01
Novocaine '01
Ocean's Eleven '01
Boiler Room '00
Gone in 60 Seconds '00
Ready to Rumble '00
Black and White '99
Bongwater '98
Enemy of the State '98
Varsity Blues '98
Nowhere '96
A Boy Called Hate '95

Katia Caballero
Madeline '98
Sharpe's Eagle '93
Beyond Innocence '87

Bruce Cabot (1904-72)
Diamonds Are Forever '71
Chisum '70
The Undefeated '69
The Green Berets '68
Hellfighters '68
The War Wagon '67
In Harm's Way '65
McLintock! '63
Hatari! '62
The Comancheros '61
Goliath and the Dragon '61
Goliath and the Barbarians '60
John Paul Jones '59
Kid Monk Baroni '52
Lost in Alaska '52
Best of the Badmen '50
Fancy Pants '50
Sorrowful Jones '49
Angel and the Badman '47
Silver Queen '42
The Flame of New Orleans '41
Sundown '41
Captain Caution '40
Susan and God '40
Dodge City '39
Sinners in Paradise '38
Fury '36
The Last of the Mohicans '36
Let 'Em Have It '35
Show Them No Mercy '35
Ann Vickers '33
Finishing School '33
King Kong '33

Sebastian Cabot (1918-77)
The Jungle Book '67 (V)
Family Jewels '65
The Sword in the Stone '63 (V)
Twice-Told Tales '63
The Time Machine '60
Johnny Tremain & the Sons of Liberty '58
Terror in a Texas Town '58
Omar Khayyam '57
Westward Ho, the Wagons! '56
Romeo and Juliet '54
Captain's Paradise '53
Old Mother Riley's Jungle Treasure '51
Old Mother Riley's New Venture '49
Dick Barton Strikes Back '48
Dual Alibi '47

Susan Cabot (1927-86)
The Wasp Woman '59
Machine Gun Kelly '58
Carnival Rock '57
Sorority Girl '57
Ride Clear of Diablo '54
Gunsmoke '53
Duel at Silver Creek '52
Son of Ali Baba '52
Flame of Araby '51

Jean Cadell (1884-1967)
The Obsessed '51
Madeleine '50
Pygmalion '38
Love from a Stranger '37

Simon Cadell (1950-96)
Cold Light of Day '95
Hi-Di-Hi '88

Anne-Marie Cadieux
Four Days '99
No '98
Street Heart '98
The Confessional '95

Jason Cadieux
Lilies '96
Iron Eagle 4 '95

Michael Cadman
Poldark 2 '75
If... '69

Frank Cady
Zandy's Bride '74
The Bad Seed '56

Adolph Caesar (1933-)
Club Paradise '86
Fortune Dane '86
The Color Purple '85
A Soldier's Story '84
Fist of Fear, Touch of Death '80
The Hitter '79

Harry Caesar
Ghetto Blaster '89
The Offspring '87
The Longest Yard '74
Emperor of the North Pole '73

Sid Caesar (1922-)
The Wonderful Ice Cream Suit '98
Vegas Vacation '96
Side by Side '88
Stoogemania '85
Cannonball Run 2 '84
Over the Brooklyn Bridge '83
Grease 2 '82
History of the World: Part 1 '81
The Munsters' Revenge '81
The Fiendish Plot of Dr. Fu Manchu '80
The Cheap Detective '78
Grease '78
Barnaby and Me '77
Curse of the Black Widow '77
Silent Movie '76
Airport '75 '75
A Guide for the Married Man '67
It's a Mad, Mad, Mad, Mad World '63

Cheri Caffaro (1945-)
Too Hot to Handle '76
Girls Are for Loving '73
The Abductors '72
Ginger '72
A Place Called Today '72

Peter Caffrey
I Went Down '97
Danny Boy '82

Stephen Caffrey (1961-)
Blowback '99
Buried Alive 2 '97
The Babe '92
Longtime Companion '90
Tour of Duty '87

Andrea Cagan
Teenager '74
Hot Box '72

Nicolas Cage (1964-)
Windtalkers '02
Captain Corelli's Mandolin '01
Family Man '00
Gone in 60 Seconds '00
Bringing Out the Dead '99
City of Angels '98
8mm '98
Snake Eyes '98
Con Air '97
Face/Off '97
The Rock '96
Leaving Las Vegas '95
Guarding Tess '94
It Could Happen to You '94
Kiss of Death '94
Trapped in Paradise '94
Amos and Andrew '93
Deadfall '93
Red Rock West '93
Honeymoon in Vegas '92
Zandalee '91
Fire Birds '90
Wild at Heart '90
Time to Kill '89
Vampire's Kiss '88
Moonstruck '87
Raising Arizona '87
Boy in Blue '86
Peggy Sue Got Married '86
Birdy '84
The Cotton Club '84
Racing with the Moon '84
Rumble Fish '83
Valley Girl '83
Fast Times at Ridgemont High '82

James Cagney (1899-1986)
Ragtime '81
One, Two, Three '61
The Gallant Hours '60
Never Steal Anything Small '59
Shake Hands with the Devil '59
Man of a Thousand Faces '57
Tribute to a Bad Man '56
Love Me or Leave Me '55
Mister Roberts '55
The Seven Little Foys '55
A Lion Is in the Streets '53
What Price Glory? '52
Kiss Tomorrow Goodbye '50
The West Point Story '50
White Heat '49
The Time of Your Life '48
13 Rue Madeleine '46
Blood on the Sun '45
Johnny Come Lately '43
Captains of the Clouds '42
Yankee Doodle Dandy '42
The Bride Came C.O.D. '41
Strawberry Blonde '41
City for Conquest '40
The Fighting 69th '40
Each Dawn I Die '39
Oklahoma Kid '39
The Roaring Twenties '39
Angels with Dirty Faces '38
Boy Meets Girl '38
Great Guy '36
Something to Sing About '36
Ceiling Zero '35
Devil Dogs of the Air '35
"G" Men '35
A Midsummer Night's Dream '35
Footlight Parade '33
Lady Killer '33
Blonde Crazy '31
Public Enemy '31

Jeanne Cagney (1908-84)
Kentucky Rifle '55
A Lion Is in the Streets '53
Don't Bother to Knock '52
Quicksand '50
The Time of Your Life '48
Yankee Doodle Dandy '42

William Cagney
Palooka '34
Ace of Aces '33

Stan Cahill
Goldrush: A Real Life Alaskan Adventure '98
JFK: Reckless Youth '93

Dean Cain (1966-)
Firetrap '01
Rat Race '01
The Broken Hearts Club '00
No Alibi '00
The Runaway '00
Militia '99
Best Men '98
Futuresport '98
Tracked '98

Howard Caine (1926-93)
Watermelon Man '70
Pressure Point '62

Michael Caine (1933-)
Austin Powers In Goldmember '02
Get Carter '00
Miss Congeniality '00
Quills '00
The Cider House Rules '99
Little Voice '98
Curtain Call '97
Mandela and de Klerk '97
Midnight in Saint Petersburg '97
Blood & Wine '96
Bullet to Beijing '95
On Deadly Ground '94
World War II: When Lions Roared '94
Blue Ice '92
Death Becomes Her '92
The Muppet Christmas Carol '92
Noises Off '92
Bullseye! '90
Jekyll and Hyde '90
Mr. Destiny '90
A Shock to the System '90
Dirty Rotten Scoundrels '88

Jack the Ripper *'88*
Without a Clue *'88*
The Fourth Protocol *'87*
Jaws: The Revenge *'87*
Surrender *'87*
The Whistle Blower *'87*
Half Moon Street *'86*
Hannah and Her Sisters *'86*
Mona Lisa *'86*
Sweet Liberty *'86*
The Holcroft Covenant *'85*
Water *'85*
Blame It on Rio *'84*
The Jigsaw Man *'84*
Beyond the Limit *'83*
Educating Rita *'83*
Deathtrap *'82*
The Hand *'81*
Victory *'81*
Dressed to Kill *'80*
The Island *'80*
Ashanti, Land of No Mercy *'79*
Beyond the Poseidon Adventure *'79*
California Suite *'78*
Silver Bears *'78*
The Swarm *'78*
A Bridge Too Far *'77*
The Eagle Has Landed *'77*
Harry & Walter Go to New York *'76*
The Man Who Would Be King *'75*
Romantic Englishwoman *'75*
The Wilby Conspiracy *'75*
The Black Windmill *'74*
The Destructors *'74*
Pulp *'72*
Sleuth *'72*
X, Y & Zee *'72*
Get Carter *'71*
The Last Valley *'71*
Too Late the Hero *'70*
Battle of Britain *'69*
The Italian Job *'69*
Woman Times Seven *'67*
Alfie *'66*
Funeral in Berlin *'66*
Gambit *'66*
The Wrong Box *'66*
The Ipcress File *'65*
Zulu *'64*
Room 43 *'58*

John Cairney
The Flesh and the Fiends *'60*
A Night to Remember *'58*

Jonathan Cake (1968-)
Noah's Ark *'99*
Mosley *'98*
Rebecca *'97*
Catherine Cookson's The Girl *'96*
The Tenant of Wildfell Hall *'96*

Clara Calamai (1915-98)
Deep Red: Hatchet Murders *'75*
White Nights *'57*
Ossessione *'42*

David Calder
The Murder of Stephen Lawrence *'01*
The World Is Not Enough *'99*
Cracker: Brotherly Love *'95*
A Question of Attribution *'91*

Anna Calder-Marshall
The Two Faces of Evil *'82*
Wuthering Heights *'70*

Paul Calderon
The Last Castle *'01*
3 A.M. *'01*
Once in the Life *'00*
Girlfight *'99*
Sweet Nothing *'96*
The Addiction *'95*
Condition Red *'95*
Four Rooms *'95*
Lotto Land *'95*
Pulp Fiction *'94*
Bad Lieutenant *'92*
Crisscross *'92*
Q & A *'90*
The Chair *'87*

Sergio Calderon (1945-)
Men in Black *'97*
Border Shootout *'90*
Old Gringo *'89*
Erendira *'83*

L. Scott Caldwell
Twilight Man *'96*
Down Came a Blackbird *'94*
God Bless the Child *'88*

Zoe Caldwell
Lantern Hill *'90*
The Purple Rose of Cairo *'85*

Paula Cale (1070-)
Brian's Song *'01*
Milo *'98*

Don Calfa
Terrified *'94*
H.P. Lovecraft's Necronomicon: Book of the Dead *'93*
Me, Myself & I *'92*
Chopper Chicks in Zombietown *'91*
Weekend at Bernie's *'89*
Blue Movies *'88*
Treasure of the Moon Goddess *'88*
Return of the Living Dead *'85*
E. Nick: A Legend in His Own Mind *'84*
The Rainbow Gang *'73*

Louis Calhern (1895-1956)
Forever Darling *'56*
High Society *'56*
Blackboard Jungle *'55*
The Prodigal *'55*
Athena *'54*
Betrayed *'54*
Executive Suite *'54*
Men of the Fighting Lady *'54*
Rhapsody *'54*
The Student Prince *'54*
Julius Caesar *'53*
Latin Lovers *'53*
Prisoner of Zenda *'52*
We're Not Married *'52*
Annie Get Your Gun *'50*
The Asphalt Jungle *'50*
A Life of Her Own *'50*
The Magnificent Yankee *'50*
Nancy Goes to Rio *'50*
Two Weeks with Love *'50*
The Red Pony *'49*
Arch of Triumph *'48*
Notorious *'46*
The Bridge of San Luis Rey *'44*
Up in Arms *'44*
Heaven Can Wait *'43*
The Gorgeous Hussy *'36*
Last Days of Pompeii *'35*
Sweet Adeline *'35*
The Count of Monte Cristo *'34*
Duck Soup *'33*
The World Gone Mad *'33*
Night After Night *'32*
They Call It Sin *'32*
Blonde Crazy *'31*
The Blot *'21*
Too Wise Wives *'21*

Alice Calhoun
Tentacles of the North *'26*
The Man on the Box *'25*

Monica Calhoun
The Best Man *'99*
The Players Club *'98*
Rebound: The Legend of Earl "The Goat" Manigault *'96*
Bagdad Cafe *'88*

Rory Calhoun (1922-99)
Pure Country *'92*
Roller Blade Warriors: Taken By Force *'90*
Bad Jim *'89*
Hell Comes to Frogtown *'88*
Avenging Angel *'85*
Angel *'84*
Mission to Glory *'80*
Motel Hell *'80*
Flatbed Annie and Sweetiepie: Lady Truckers *'79*
The Rebels *'79*
Midnight Auto Supply *'78*
Operation Cross Eagles *'69*
Dayton's Devils *'68*
Emerald of Artama *'67*
Apache Uprising *'66*
Finger on the Trigger *'65*
A Face in the Rain *'63*
Hard Drivin' *'60*
Treasure of Pancho Villa *'55*
A Bullet Is Waiting *'54*
River of No Return *'54*
I'd Climb the Highest Mountain *'51*
Ticket to Tomahawk *'50*
Adventure Island *'47*
The Red House *'47*

Joseph Cali (1950-)
The Lonely Lady *'83*
The Competition *'80*
Saturday Night Fever *'77*

Brandon Call (1976-)
For the Boys *'91*
The Adventures of Ford Fairlane *'90*
Blind Fury *'90*

R.D. Call
Murder by Numbers *'02*
Last Man Standing *'96*
Waterworld *'95*
Other People's Money *'91*
Stephen King's Golden Years *'91*
Young Guns 2 *'90*
Colors *'88*

James Callahan (1930-)
Blood for Blood *'95*
Prison for Children *'93*
Outlaw Blues *'77*
Lady Sings the Blues *'72*
Tropic of Cancer *'70*

K. Callan (1942-)
Saved by the Light *'95*
Frankie and Johnny *'91*
The Unborn *'91*
American Gigolo *'79*
A Touch of Class *'73*

Michael Callan (1938-)
Leprechaun 3 *'95*
Freeway *'88*
Donner Pass: The Road to Survival *'84*
Double Exposure *'82*
The Cat and the Canary *'79*
Lepke *'75*
Photographer *'75*
Frasier the Sensuous Lion *'73*
Cat Ballou *'65*
Bon Voyage! *'62*
The Interns *'62*
Gidget Goes Hawaiian *'61*
Mysterious Island *'61*

Rebecca Callard
The Miracle Maker: The Story of Jesus *'00 (V)*
The Return of the Borrowers *'96*
The Borrowers *'93*

Charlie Callas (1924-)
Vampire Vixens from Venus *'94*
Amazon Women on the Moon *'87*
History of the World: Part 1 *'81*
Pete's Dragon *'77 (V)*
Big Mouth *'67*

Joseph Calleia (1897-1975)
The Alamo *'60*
The Light in the Forest *'58*
Touch of Evil *'58*
The Littlest Outlaw *'54*
The Caddy *'53*
Branded *'50*
The Noose Hangs High *'48*
Lured *'47*
Deadline at Dawn *'46*
Gilda *'46*
For Whom the Bell Tolls *'43*
The Glass Key *'42*
The Jungle Book *'42*
The Monster and the Girl *'41*
Sundown *'41*
My Little Chickadee *'40*
Five Came Back *'39*
Golden Boy *'39*
Algiers *'38*
Marie Antoinette *'38*
After the Thin Man *'36*
Riff Raff *'35*

Dayton Callie
Executive Target *'97*
The Last Days of Frankie the Fly *'96*

James Callis
Bridget Jones's Diary *'01*
Heat of the Sun *'99*
The Scarlet Pimpernel 2: Mademoiselle Guillotine *'99*

Simon Callow (1949-)
No Man's Land *'01*
Bedrooms and Hallways *'98*
Shakespeare in Love *'98*
The Scarlet Tunic *'97*
The Woman in White *'97*
James and the Giant Peach *'96 (V)*
Ace Ventura: When Nature Calls *'95*
Four Weddings and a Funeral *'94*
Street Fighter *'94*
Howard's End *'92*
The Crucifer of Blood *'91*
Mr. & Mrs. Bridge *'90*
The Good Father *'87*
Maurice *'87*
A Room with a View *'86*
Amadeus *'84*

Cab Calloway (1907-94)
The Blues Brothers *'80*
The Littlest Angel *'69*
The Cincinnati Kid *'65*
Sensations of 1945 *'44*
Stormy Weather *'43*
Manhattan Merry-Go-Round *'37*
Hi-De-Ho *'35*
International House *'33*

Kirk Calloway
Cinderella Liberty *'73*
Summertree *'71*

Vanessa Bell Calloway (1957-)
Love Song *'00*
The Temptations *'98*
Daylight *'96*
America's Dream *'95*
Crimson Tide *'95*
What's Love Got to Do with It? *'93*
Bebe's Kids *'92 (V)*
Memphis *'91*
Coming to America *'88*
Number One with a Bullet *'87*

Michael Caloz (1985-)
Escape from Wildcat Canyon *'99*
Little Men *'98*
Screamers *'96*

Donald Calthrop (1888-1940)
The Phantom Light *'35*
Scrooge *'35*
No. 17 *'32*
Blackmail *'29*

Bill Calvert
Body Waves *'92*
C.H.U.D. 2: Bud the Chud *'89*
Terror Squad *'87*

Phyllis Calvert (1915-)
The Woman He Loved *'88*
Indiscreet *'58*
The Young and the Guilty *'58*
Mandy *'53*
Man of Evil *'48*
The Magic Bow *'47*
Men of Two Worlds *'46*
The Man in Grey *'45*
Kipps *'41*

Corinne Calvet (1925-2001)
Dr. Heckyl and Mr. Hype *'80*
Too Hot to Handle *'76*
Apache Uprising *'66*
Far Country *'55*
What Price Glory? *'52*

Henry Calvin
The Sign of Zorro *'60*
Toby Tyler *'59*

John Calvin
Dragonworld *'94*
The Magic Bubble *'93*
Primary Target *'89*
The Siege of Firebase Gloria *'89*
Back to the Beach *'87*
Ghostwarrior *'86*
California Dreaming *'79*

Armando Calvo
Satanik *'69*
The Witch's Mirror *'60*

Pablito Calvo
The Man Who Wagged His Tail *'57*
The Miracle of Marcelino *'55*

Mark Camacho
Nowhere in Sight *'01*
Stiletto Dance *'01*
Dead Silent *'99*
Stalker *'98*
The Kid *'97*

Godfrey Cambridge (1933-76)
Friday Foster *'75*
Whiffs *'75*
Beware! The Blob *'72*
Cotton Comes to Harlem *'70*
Watermelon Man *'70*
The President's Analyst *'67*
Gone Are the Days *'63*
Purlie Victorious *'63*

Juan Jose Camero
Veronico Cruz *'87*
El Muerto *'75*
Far Away and Long Ago *'74*

Candace Cameron (1976-)
Frankenstein Sings...The Movie *'95*
Sharon's Secret *'95*

Dean Cameron (1962-)
Ski School 2 *'94*
Sleep with Me *'94*
Miracle Beach *'92*
Ski School *'91*
Rockula *'90*
Bad Dreams *'88*
Summer School *'87*

James Cameron (1954-)
The Muse *'99*
Last Action Hero *'93*

Jane Cameron
The Unborn *'91*
Pair of Aces *'90*

Kirk Cameron (1970-)
Left Behind: The Movie *'00*
Listen to Me *'89*
Like Father, Like Son *'87*
The Best of Times *'86*

Rod Cameron (1910-83)
Midnight Auto Supply *'78*
Psychic Killer *'75*
Evel Knievel *'72*
The Last Movie *'71*
The Electronic Monster *'57*
Manhunt in the African Jungle *'54*
Ride the Man Down *'53*
Jungle *'52*
Salome, Where She Danced *'45*
G-Men vs. the Black Dragon *'43*
Wake Island *'42*
The Monster and the Girl *'41*

Trent Cameron
The Wood *'99*
The Kid Who Loved Christmas *'90*

Jesse Cameron-Glickenhaus
Timemaster *'95*
Slaughter of the Innocents *'93*

Terry Camillieri
Bill & Ted's Excellent Adventure *'89*
The Cars That Ate Paris *'74*

Colleen Camp (1953-)
Loser *'00*
Election *'99*
Plump Fiction *'97*
Speed 2: Cruise Control *'97*
Die Hard: With a Vengeance *'95*
Greedy *'94*
The Magic Bubble *'93*
Sliver *'93*
Wayne's World *'92*
Backfield in Motion *'91*
Wicked Stepmother *'89*
Track 29 *'88*
Illegally Yours *'87*
Police Academy 4: Citizens on Patrol *'87*
Walk Like a Man *'87*
Screwball Academy *'86*
Clue *'85*
D.A.R.Y.L. *'85*
Doin' Time *'85*
Police Academy 2: Their First Assignment *'85*
Rosebud Beach Hotel *'85*
Joy of Sex *'84*
Smokey and the Bandit, Part 3 *'83*
Valley Girl *'83*
The Seduction *'82*
They All Laughed *'81*
Cloud Dancer *'80*
Deadly Games *'80*
Apocalypse Now *'79*
Game of Death *'79*
Lady of the House *'78*
Midnight Auto Supply *'78*
Seducers *'77*
She Devils in Chains *'76*
Smile *'75*
The Last Porno Flick *'74*
The Swinging Cheerleaders *'74*
Cat in the Cage *'68*

Hamilton Camp (1934-)
Almost Heroes *'97*
All Dogs Go to Heaven 2 *'95 (V)*
Attack of the 50 Ft. Woman *'93*
Arena *'89*
Casey at the Bat *'85*
Lots of Luck *'85*
Rosebud Beach Hotel *'85*
Meatballs 2 *'84*
Under Fire *'83*
Eating Raoul *'82*

Frank Campanella
Blood Red *'88*
Chesty Anderson USN *'76*
The Producers *'68*

Joseph Campanella (1927-)
James Dean: Live Fast, Die Young *'97*
The Glass Cage *'96*
Magic Kid *'92*
No Retreat, No Surrender 3: Blood Brothers *'91*
Original Intent *'91*
Body Chemistry *'90*
Club Fed *'90*
Last Call *'90*
Down the Drain *'89*
Steele Justice *'87*
Comic Book Kids *'82*
Plutonium Incident *'82*
Hangar 18 *'80*

Meteor '79
Pearl '78 (N)
Return to Fantasy Island '77
Sky Hei$t '75
Terror on the 40th Floor '74
Ben '72
Murder Once Removed '71
The President's Plane Is Missing '71
The St. Valentine's Day Massacre '67

Beatrice Campbell (1922-79)
The Master of Ballantrae '53
Last Holiday '50

Billy Campbell (1959-)
Enough '02
Armistead Maupin's More Tales of the City '97
Rudyard Kipling's the Second Jungle Book: Mowgli and Baloo '97
The Brylcreem Boys '96
Lover's Knot '96
Menno's Mind '96
Out There '95
Under the Hula Moon '95
Armistead Maupin's Tales of the City '93
Gettysburg '93
The Night We Never Met '93
Bram Stoker's Dracula '92
The Rocketeer '91

Bruce Campbell (1958-)
Serving Sara '02
Spider-Man '02
The Majestic '01
The Ice Rink '99
From Dusk Till Dawn 2: Texas Blood Money '98
Goldrush: A Real Life Alaskan Adventure '98
The Love Bug '97
McHale's Navy '97
Escape from L.A. '96
Menno's Mind '96
Tornado! '96
The Hudsucker Proxy '93
Army of Darkness '92
Lunatics: A Love Story '92
Mindwarp '91
Sundown '91
Waxwork 2: Lost in Time '91
Darkman '90
Maniac Cop 2 '90
Moontrap '89
Maniac Cop '88
Evil Dead 2: Dead by Dawn '87
Thou Shalt Not Kill...Except '87
Crimewave '85
Evil Dead '83
Going Back '83

Cheryl Campbell (1949-)
The Way We Live Now '02
The Mill on the Floss '97
The Shooting Party '85
Greystoke: The Legend of Tarzan, Lord of the Apes '84
Chariots of Fire '81
McVicar '80
Lillie '79
Testament of Youth '79

Christian Campbell (1972-)
Trick '99
I've Been Waiting for You '98
Too Smooth '98
Born to Run '93
City Boy '93

David James Campbell
Killer Workout '86
Killzone '85

Elizabeth Campbell
Doctor of Doom '62
Wrestling Women vs. the Aztec Mummy '59

Eric Campbell (1879-1917)
The Cure '17
The Immigrant '17
The Fireman '16
The Vagabond '16

Glen Campbell (1936-)
Rock-a-Doodle '92 (V)
Uphill All the Way '85
True Grit '69

J. Kenneth Campbell
U.S. Seals '98
Operation Delta Force 2: Mayday '97
Ulee's Gold '97

Judy Campbell (1916-)
Dust to Dust '85
Cry of the Penguins '71
Bonnie Prince Charlie '48
The World Owes Me a Living '47
Convoy '40

Julia Campbell (1963-)
Stephen King's Rose Red '02
Bounce '00
Diary of a Serial Killer '97
Romy and Michele's High School Reunion '97
Lone Justice '93
Livin' Large '91
Opportunity Knocks '90

Kate Campbell
Monte Carlo Nights '34
Come on Tarzan '32
Ghost Valley '32

Ken Campbell
Breakfast of Champions '98
Down Periscope '96
Smart Money '88
Letter to Brezhnev '86
Joshua Then and Now '85
The Big Red One '80

Louise Campbell (1911-97)
Bulldog Drummond's Peril '38
Bulldog Drummond Comes Back '37
Bulldog Drummond's Revenge '37

Maia Campbell
Trippin' '99
Parental Guidance '98

Naomi Campbell (1970-)
Prisoner of Love '99
Girl 6 '96
Invasion of Privacy '96
Miami Rhapsody '95
Cool As Ice '91

Nell Campbell (1953-)
Great Expectations '97
Pink Floyd: The Wall '82
Shock Treatment '81
Lisztomania '75

Neve Campbell (1973-)
Drowning Mona '00
Panic '00
Scream 3 '00
Three to Tango '99
54 '98
The Lion King: Simba's Pride '98 (V)
Too Smooth '98
Wild Things '98
Scream 2 '97
The Canterville Ghost '96
The Craft '96
Scream '96
Northern Passage '95
The Dark '94

Nicholas (Nick) Campbell (1952-)
Full Disclosure '00
The Happy Face Murders '99
New Waterford Girl '99
The Boys Club '96
Guitarman '95
No Contest '94
Naked Lunch '91
The Big Slice '90
The Victory '88
Rampage '87
Going Home '86
Certain Fury '85
Knights of the City '85
July Group '70s
Fast Company '78
A Bridge Too Far '77

Paul Campbell
Third World Cop '99
The Lunatic '92

Peggy Campbell (1912-)
Big Calibre '35
Stone of Silver Creek '35
When a Man Sees Red '34

Rob Campbell
Hedwig and the Angry Inch '00
Boys Don't Cry '99
Hostile Waters '97
The Crucible '96
Lone Justice 2 '93
Unforgiven '92

Scott Michael Campbell
Hart's War '02
Radioland Murders '94

Tisha Campbell (1968-)
The Sweetest Gift '98
Sprung '96
House Party 3 '94
Boomerang '92
House Party 2: The Pajama Jam '91
House Party '90
Rooftops '89
School Daze '88
Rags to Riches '87
Little Shop of Horrors '86

Torquil Campbell
Heaven on Earth '89
The Golden Seal '83

William Campbell (1926-)
Portrait in Terror '66
Track of the Vampire '66
Dementia 13 '63
Night of Evil '62
Love Me Tender '56
Battle Cry '55
Man Without a Star '55
Battle Circus '53
Escape from Fort Bravo '53

Frank Campeau (1864-1943)
Abraham Lincoln '30
Battling Bunyon '24
His Majesty, the American '19
When the Clouds Roll By '19
The Man from Painted Post '17

Cris Campion
Field of Honor '87
Pirates '86

Tom Campitelli
Gates of Hell 2: Dead Awakening '96
Brutal Fury '92

Wally Campo
The Beast from Haunted Cave '60
Tank Commando '59
Hell Squad '58
Machine Gun Kelly '58

Bruno Campos (1974-)
Mimic 2 '01
O Quatrilho '95

Rafael Campos (1936-85)
The Return of Josey Wales '86
A Streetcar Named Desire '84
V '83
Where the Buffalo Roam '80
Centennial '78
Slumber Party '57 '76
The Hanged Man '74
The Doll Squad '73
The Astro-Zombies '67
Lady in a Cage '64
This Could Be the Night '57

Ron Canada
Dean Koontz's Black River '01
Apartment Complex '98
Lost in the Bermuda Triangle '98
Pinocchio's Revenge '96
Lone Star '95
Man of the House '95

Gianna Maria Canale (1927-)
Marauder '65
Colossus and the Amazon Queen '64
Tiger of the Seven Seas '62
Hercules '58
Evil's Commandment '56
I Vampiri '56
Man from Cairo '54
Sins of Rome '54
Go for Broke! '51

Lee Canalito
The Glass Jungle '88
Paradise Alley '78

David Canary (1938-)
Johnny Firecloud '75
Posse '75
Sharks' Treasure '75
Melvin Purvis: G-Man '74

John Henry Canavan
Torso '01
The Crossing '00

Stelio Candelli
A Man Called Rage '84
Planet of the Vampires '65

Candy Candido (1913-99)
The Great Mouse Detective '86 (V)
Peter Pan '53 (V)
Rhythm Parade '43

John Candy (1950-94)
Canadian Bacon '94
Hostage for a Day '94
Wagons East '94
Cool Runnings '93
Boris and Natasha: The Movie '92
Once Upon a Crime '92
Career Opportunities '91
Delirious '91
JFK '91
Nothing But Trouble '91
Only the Lonely '91
Home Alone '90
The Masters of Menace '90
The Rescuers Down Under '90 (V)
Uncle Buck '89
Who's Harry Crumb? '89
The Great Outdoors '88
Hot to Trot! '88 (V)
Speed Zone '88
Planes, Trains & Automobiles '87
Spaceballs '87
Tales of the Klondike: The Unexpected '87
Armed and Dangerous '86
Little Shop of Horrors '86
Really Weird Tales '86
Brewster's Millions '85
Sesame Street Presents: Follow That Bird '85
Summer Rental '85
Volunteers '85
The Last Polka '84
Splash '84
Clown Murders '83
Going Berserk '83
National Lampoon's Vacation '83
Heavy Metal '81 (V)
Stripes '81
The Blues Brothers '80
The Double Negative '80
Lost and Found '79
1941 '79
The Silent Partner '78
Tunnelvision '76
Find the Lady '75
Class of '44 '73

Charles Cane (1899-1973)
Revenge of the Creature '55
Lucky Me '54
Native Son '51
Dead Reckoning '47

Natalie Canerday
October Sky '99
Gunshy '98
Sling Blade '96
One False Move '91

Bobby Cannavale (1971-)
3 A.M. '01
The Bone Collector '99

Dyan Cannon (1939-)
The Sender '98
Beverly Hills Family Robinson '97
Out to Sea '97
8 Heads in a Duffel Bag '96
That Darn Cat '96
Based on an Untrue Story '93
The Pickle '93
Christmas in Connecticut '92
The End of Innocence '90
Caddyshack 2 '88
Jenny's War '85
Merlin and the Sword '85
Author! Author! '82
Deathtrap '82
Having It All '82
Coast to Coast '80
Honeysuckle Rose '80
Heaven Can Wait '78
Lady of the House '78
Revenge of the Pink Panther '78
The Virginia Hill Story '76
The Last of Sheila '73
Shamus '73
The Anderson Tapes '71
The Love Machine '71
Doctors' Wives '70
Bob & Carol & Ted & Alice '69

Esma Cannon
Crow Hollow '52
I Met a Murderer '39

J.D. Cannon (1922-)
Street Justice '89
Death Wish 2 '82
The Adventures of Nellie Bly '81
Pleasure Palace '80
Raise the Titanic '80
Walking Through the Fire '80
Killing Stone '78
Scorpio '73
Lawman '71
Cotton Comes to Harlem '70
Cool Hand Luke '67

Katherine (Kathy) Cannon (1953-)
Matters of the Heart '90
The Red Fury '84
Will: G. Gordon Liddy '82
High Noon: Part 2 '80
Private Duty Nurses '71

Wanda Cannon
The 6th Day '00
For the Moment '94
The Last Winter '89

Diana Canova
Night Partners '83
The First Nudie Musical '75

Judy Canova (1913-83)
Cannonball '76
The Adventures of Huckleberry Finn '60
Oklahoma Annie '51

Anne Canovos
Ready to Wear '94
High Frequency '88
Zeder '83

Antonio Cantafora (1943-)
Intervista '87
Gabriela '84
Torture Chamber of Baron Blood '72
And God Said to Cain '69

Toni Canto
All About My Mother '99
I'm the One You're Looking For '88

Eddie Cantor (1892-1964)
If You Knew Susie '48
Hollywood Canteen '44
Show Business '44
Thank Your Lucky Stars '43
Strike Me Pink '36
Kid Millions '34
Roman Scandals '33
Kid from Spain '32
Palmy Days '31
Glorifying the American Girl '30
Whoopee! '30

Yakima Canutt (1895-1986)
The Showdown '50
Calling Wild Bill Elliott '43
For Whom the Bell Tolls '43
Gone with the Wind '39
The Kansas Terrors '39
Wyoming Outlaw '39
Overland Stage Raiders '38
Santa Fe Stampede '38
Heart of the Rockies '37
Hit the Saddle '37
The Painted Stallion '37
Riders of the Rockies '37
Riders of the Whistling Skull '37
Trouble in Texas '37
Circle of Death '36
King of the Pecos '36
Outlaw Rule '36
Winds of the Wasteland '36
Branded a Coward '35
Cyclone of the Saddle '35
Dawn Rider '35
Paradise Canyon '35
Lucky Texan '34
The Man from Hell '34
Man from Utah '34
The Star Packer '34
Sagebrush Trail '33
Telegraph Trail '33
West of the Divide '33
Last Frontier '32
Battling with Buffalo Bill '31
The Fighting Stallion '26
Wild Horse Canyon '25
Branded a Bandit '24

Peter Capaldi
Shooting Fish '98
Bean '97
Smilla's Sense of Snow '96
Captives '94
Dangerous Liaisons '88
The Lair of the White Worm '88
John & Yoko: A Love Story '85
Local Hero '83

Jad Capelja
Freedom '81
Puberty Blues '81

Peter Capell
For the First Time '59
Paths of Glory '57

Virginia Capers (1925-)
Ferris Bueller's Day Off '86
Jo Jo Dancer, Your Life Is Calling '86
White Mama '80
The North Avenue Irregulars '79

Carmine Capobianco
Galactic Gigolo '87
Psychos in Love '87

John Capodice
Enemy of the State '98
Ringmaster '98
True Friends '98
Independence Day '96
Wedding Bell Blues '96
Trial by Jury '94
Honeymoon in Vegas '92
The Hard Way '91
Internal Affairs '90

Lino Capolicchio
Fiorile '93
The Garden of the Finzi-Continis '71
Nadia Capone
First Degree '95
Skull: A Night of Terror '88
A Whisper to a Scream '88
Truman Capote
Murder by Death '76
ABC Stage 67: Truman Capote's A Christmas Memory '66 (N)
Carl Capotorto
Mac '93
American Blue Note '89
Joolia Cappleman
Who's Who '78
Bleak Moments '71
Pier Paola Capponi
Man of Legend '71
The King of Hearts '66
Francis Capra
A Simple Wish '97
Kazaam '96
A Bronx Tale '93
Jordanna Capra
Watch It '93
Hired to Kill '91
Tony Caprari
Armageddon: The Final Challenge '94
River of Diamonds '90
Ahna Capri
The Specialist '75
Enter the Dragon '73
Payday '72
The Brotherhood of Satan '71
Darker than Amber '70
Jessica Capshaw
Valentine '01
The Locusts '97
Kate Capshaw (1953-)
A Girl Thing '01
The Love Letter '99
The Alarmist '98
The Locusts '97
How to Make an American Quilt '95
Just Cause '94
Love Affair '94
Next Door '94
My Heroes Have Always Been Cowboys '91
Black Rain '89
Love at Large '89
Private Affairs '89
Code Name: Dancer '87
The Quick and the Dead '87
Power '86
SpaceCamp '86
Best Defense '84
Dreamscape '84
Indiana Jones and the Temple of Doom '84
Windy City '84
A Little Sex '82
Capucine (1933-90)
The Switch '89
Scandalous '88
Curse of the Pink Panther '83
Trail of the Pink Panther '82
The Con Artists '80
From Hell to Victory '79
Jaguar Lives '79
Fellini Satyricon '69
The Honey Pot '67
What's New Pussycat? '65
The Pink Panther '64
The Seventh Dawn '64
Walk on the Wild Side '62
North to Alaska '60
Song Without End '60
Irene Cara (1959-)
Happily Ever After '93 (V)
The Magic Voyage '93 (V)
Caged in Paradiso '89
For Us, the Living '88
Busted Up '86
Certain Fury '85
Killing 'Em Softly '85
City Heat '84
D.C. Cab '84
Fame '80
Roots: The Next Generation '79
Sparkle '76
Aaron Loves Angela '75
Flora Carabella (1926-99)
A Night Full of Rain '78
The Messiah '75
Paul Carafotes
Journey to the Center of the Earth '88
All the Right Moves '83
Choices '81
Ion Caramitru
Citizen X '95
Two Deaths '94
Joseph Carberry
The Ten Million Dollar Getaway '91
Vigilante '83
Antony Carbone (1927-)
Skateboard '77
The Last Porno Flick '74
Sex Through a Window '72
The Last Woman on Earth '61
The Pit and the Pendulum '61
Creature from the Haunted Sea '60
A Bucket of Blood '59
Nestor Carbonell
The Laramie Project '02
Noriega: God's Favorite '00
Attention Shoppers '99
Linda Cardellini
Scooby-Doo '02
Legally Blonde '01
The Prince and the Surfer '99
Dee Snider's Strangeland '98
Stephen Antonio Cardenas
Turbo: A Power Rangers Movie '96
Mighty Morphin Power Rangers: The Movie '95
Pat Cardi
Twisted Brain '74
And Now Miguel '66
Bill "Chilly Billy" Cardille
Night of the Living Dead '90
Night of the Living Dead '68
Ben Cardinal
By Dawn's Early Light '00
The Wolves '95
Tantoo Cardinal (1951-)
The Lost Child '00
Big Bear '98
Smoke Signals '98
The Education of Little Tree '97
Tecumseh: The Last Warrior '95
Lakota Woman: Siege at Wounded Knee '94
Legends of the Fall '94
Where the Rivers Flow North '94
Spirit Rider '93
By Way of the Stars '92
Silent Tongue '92
Black Robe '91
The Lightning Incident '91
Dances with Wolves '90
Loyalties '86
Claudia Cardinale (1939-)
Nostromo '96
Son of the Pink Panther '93
Queen of Diamonds '80s
A Man in Love '87
The Sniper '87
Henry IV '85
Next Summer '84
Princess Daisy '83
Fitzcarraldo '82
The Gift '82
The Salamander '82
Immortal Bachelor '80
Corleone '79
Escape to Athena '79
Blonde in Black Leather '77
Jesus of Nazareth '77
Conversation Piece '75
Blood Brothers '74
Scoumoune '74
One Russian Summer '73
Butterfly Affair '71
Legend of Frenchie King '71
L'Udienza '71
Red Tent '69
Once Upon a Time in the West '68
The Lost Command '66
The Professionals '66
Sandra of a Thousand Delights '65
Circus World '64
The Pink Panther '64
Time of Indifference '64
8 1/2 '63
Cartouche '62
The Battle of Austerlitz '60
The Girl with a Suitcase '60
Il Bell'Antonio '60
Rocco and His Brothers '60
Big Deal on Madonna Street '58
Nathalie Cardone
L'Enfer '93
The Little Thief '89
John Cardos
Blood of Dracula's Castle '69
Satan's Sadists '69
Pedro Cardoso
Bossa Nova '99
Four Days in September '97
Anthony Cardoza
The Beast of Yucca Flats '61
Night of the Ghouls '59
James B. Cardwell (1920-54)
Down Dakota Way '49
The Devil on Wheels '47
Fear '46
A Walk in the Sun '46
The Shanghai Cobra '45
The Fighting Sullivans '42
Roger Carel
Soldat Duroc...Ca Va Etre Ta Fete! '75
The Two of Us '68
Annette Carell
Vulture '67
The Tell-Tale Heart '62
Julien Carette (1897-1966)
The Red Inn '51
The Rules of the Game '39
La Bete Humaine '38
Grand Illusion '37
James Carew
Non-Stop New York '37
Midnight at the Wax Museum '36
Arthur Edmund Carewe (1884-1937)
Doctor X '32
The Cat and the Canary '27
The Phantom of the Opera '25
Amie Carey
Dog Park '98
subUrbia '96
Harry Carey, Sr. (1878-1947)
So Dear to My Heart '49
Red River '48
Angel and the Badman '47
Duel in the Sun '46
The Great Moment '44
Air Force '43
The Spoilers '42
The Shepherd of the Hills '41
Sundown '41
Beyond Tomorrow '40
They Knew What They Wanted '40
Mr. Smith Goes to Washington '39
Law West of Tombstone '38
The Port of Missing Girls '38
You and Me '38
Aces Wild '37
Ghost Town '37
Kid Galahad '37
Souls at Sea '37
Last Outlaw '36
Last of the Clintons '35
Powdersmoke Range '35
Rustler's Paradise '35
Wagon Trail '35
Wild Mustang '35
Buffalo Stampede '33
Man of the Forest '33
Border Devils '32
Devil Horse '32
The Last of the Mohicans '32
Night Rider '32
Without Honors '32
Cavalier of the West '31
Trader Horn '31
Vanishing Legion '31
The Prairie Pirate '25
Straight Shootin' '17
Judith of Bethulia '14
Harry Carey, Jr. (1921-)
Last Stand at Saber River '96
Sunchaser '96
Wyatt Earp: Return to Tombstone '94
Tombstone '93
Back to the Future, Part 3 '90
Bad Jim '89
Breaking In '89
The Whales of August '87
Challenge to White Fang '86
Crossroads '86
Mask '85
Endangered Species '82
Uforia '81
The Long Riders '80
Trinity Is Still My Name '75
Cahill: United States Marshal '73
The Undefeated '69
Bandolero! '68
The Devil's Brigade '68
Alvarez Kelly '66
Billy the Kid Versus Dracula '66
Shenandoah '65
A Public Affair '62
Rio Bravo '59
The Searchers '56
Seventh Cavalry '56
Mister Roberts '55
Copper Canyon '50
Rio Grande '50
Wagon Master '50
She Wore a Yellow Ribbon '49
Moonrise '48
Red River '48
Three Godfathers '48
Pursued '47
Joyce Carey (1898-1993)
Cry, the Beloved Country '51
The October Man '48
Brief Encounter '46
Blithe Spirit '45
MacDonald Carey (1913-94)
It's Alive 3: Island of the Alive '87
Access Code '84
The Rebels '79
Summer of Fear '78
Roots '77
End of the World '76
Who Is the Black Dahlia? '75
Tammy and the Doctor '63
John Paul Jones '59
Man or Gun '58
Great Missouri Raid '51
Let's Make It Legal '51
Comanche Territory '50
Copper Canyon '50
The Great Gatsby '49
Shadow of a Doubt '43
Wake Island '42
Mariah Carey
Glitter '01
The Bachelor '99
Michele Carey (1943-)
The Desperados '80s
In the Shadow of Kilimanjaro '86
Scandalous John '71
Changes '69
Live a Little, Love a Little '68
El Dorado '67
Olive Carey (1896-1988)
Billy the Kid Versus Dracula '66
The Alamo '60
The Searchers '56
Trader Horn '31
Phil Carey (1925-)
Monster '78
Fighting Mad '76
Scream of the Wolf '74
The Time Travelers '64
Tonka '58
The Long Gray Line '55
Mister Roberts '55
Gun Fury '53
Springfield Rifle '52
Roland Carey
Revolt of the Barbarians '64
The Sword of El Cid '62
The Giants of Thessaly '60
Ron Carey (1935-)
Lucky Luke '94
Troublemakers '94
History of the World: Part 1 '81
Fatso '80
High Anxiety '77
Who Killed Mary What's 'Er Name? '71
Sandy Carey
Mysterious Jane '80s
Wham-Bam, Thank You Spaceman '75
Timothy Carey (1925-94)
Echo Park '86
Fast Walking '82
Speedtrap '78
The Killing of a Chinese Bookie '76
Minnie and Moskowitz '71
Head '68
Beach Blanket Bingo '65
Bikini Beach '64
The Mermaids of Tiburon '62
One-Eyed Jacks '61
Paths of Glory '57
Poor White Trash '57
The Killing '56
The Finger Man '55
Patrick Cargill (1918-96)
A Countess from Hong Kong '67
Help! '65
Timothy Carhart (1953-)
Black Sheep '96
America's Dream '95
Beverly Hills Cop 3 '94
Candyman 2: Farewell to the Flesh '94
Red Rock West '93
Quicksand: No Escape '91
Thelma & Louise '91
Pink Cadillac '89
Ghostbusters '84
Party Animal '83
Gia Carides (1964-)
My Big Fat Greek Wedding '02
Maze '01
Austin Powers 2: The Spy Who Shagged Me '99
The Extreme Adventures of Super Dave '98
Letters from a Killer '98
Primary Colors '98
Brilliant Lies '96
Last Breath '96
Paperback Romance '96
Bad Company '94
Strictly Ballroom '92
Backlash '86
Midnite Spares '85
Zoe Carides (1962-)
Brilliant Lies '96
Death in Brunswick '90
Stones of Death '88
Carmine Caridi (1933-)
Top Dog '95
Life Stinks '91
Split Decisions '88
KISS Meets the Phantom of the Park '78
Len Cariou (1939-)
Nuremberg '00
Thirteen Days '00
In the Company of Spies '99
Executive Decision '96
The Summer of Ben Tyler '96
Never Talk to Strangers '95
The Man in the Attic '94
Witness to the Execution '94
Class of '61 '92
The Lady in White '88
Louisiana '87
Who'll Save Our Children? '82
The Four Seasons '81
A Little Night Music '77
Drying Up the Streets '76
Richard Carle (1871-1941)
Mistaken Identity '36
Love in Bloom '35
The Ghost Walks '34
Sin Takes a Holiday '30
Claire Carleton
The Devil's Partner '58
The Fighter '52
George Carlin (1937-)
Jay and Silent Bob Strike Back '01
Dogma '99
Larry McMurtry's Streets of Laredo '95
Bill & Ted's Bogus Journey '91
The Prince of Tides '91
Bill & Ted's Excellent Adventure '89
Outrageous Fortune '87
Americathon '79 (N)
Car Wash '76
Gloria Carlin
Varian's War '01
Color of Justice '97
Hanoi Hilton '87
Goldenrod '77
Lynn Carlin (1930-)
Forbidden Love '82
Superstition '82
Deathdream '72
Wild Rovers '71
Silent Night, Lonely Night '69
Faces '68
Anne Carlisle
Perfect Strangers '84
Liquid Sky '83
Mary Carlisle (1912-)
Dead Men Walk '43
Baby Face Morgan '42
Dance, Girl, Dance '40
Champagne for Breakfast '35
One Frightened Night '35
Kentucky Kernels '34
Held for Murder '32
Kitty Carlisle Hart (1914-)
Six Degrees of Separation '93
Radio Days '87
A Night at the Opera '35
Murder at the Vanities '34
Ismael Carlo
Y2K '99
One Man Out '89

Johann Carlo
Fair Game '95
Quiz Show '94
Nadia '84
Margit Carlquist
Smiles of a Summer Night '55
To Joy '50
Jeff Carlson
Slap Shot 2: Breaking the Ice '02
Slap Shot '77
June Carlson (1924-96)
The Hawk of Powder River '48
Mom & Dad '47
Delinquent Daughters '44
Karen Carlson (1945-)
A Horse for Danny '95
Teen Vamp '88
On Wings of Eagles '86
Brotherly Love '85
Fleshburn '84
Wild Horses '84
In Love with an Older Woman '82
American Dream '81
Octagon '80
Black Oak Conspiracy '77
The Candidate '72
The Student Nurses '70
Leslie (Les) Carlson (1933-)
A Christmas Story '83
Deranged '74
Richard Carlson (1912-77)
Change of Habit '69
The Valley of Gwangi '69
The Doomsday Flight '66
Tormented '60
The Last Command '55
Creature from the Black Lagoon '54
All I Desire '53
It Came from Outer Space '53
Flat Top '52
Retreat, Hell! '52
King Solomon's Mines '50
Try and Get Me '50
The Amazing Mr. X '48
Behind Locked Doors '48
Human Gorilla '48
Presenting Lily Mars '43
White Cargo '42
Hold That Ghost '41
The Little Foxes '41
Beyond Tomorrow '40
The Ghost Breakers '40
The Howards of Virginia '40
No, No Nanette '40
Too Many Girls '40
The Duke of West Point '38
The Young in Heart '38
Steve Carlson (1955-)
Slap Shot 2: Breaking the Ice '02
Slap Shot '77
Veronica Carlson (1945-)
Freakshow '95
The Horror of Frankenstein '70
Frankenstein Must Be Destroyed '69
Dracula Has Risen from the Grave '68
Karin Carlsson
Walpurgis Night '41
A Woman's Face '38
Hope Marie Carlton (1966-)
Bloodmatch '91
Round Numbers '91
Slumber Party Massacre 3 '90
Picasso Trigger '89
Savage Beach '89
Terminal Exposure '89
Slaughterhouse Rock '88
Hard Ticket to Hawaii '87
Robert Carlyle (1961-)
The Beach '00
Angela's Ashes '99
Ravenous '99
The World Is Not Enough '99
Plunkett & Macleane '98
Carla's Song '97
Face '97
The Full Monty '96
Go Now '96
Trainspotting '95
Cracker: To Be a Somebody '94
Priest '94
Riff Raff '92
Roger C. Carmel (1932-86)
Hardly Working '81
Thunder and Lightning '77
Skullduggery '70
My Dog, the Thief '69
Alvarez Kelly '66
Gambit '66
The Silencers '66
Goodbye Charlie '64
Jeanne Carmen
The Monster of Piedras Blancas '57
In Old Montana '39
Jewel Carmen (1897-1984)
The Bat '26
American Aristocracy '17
Flirting with Fate '16
Julie Carmen (1960-)
King of the Jungle '01
Gargantua '98
True Women '97
In the Mouth of Madness '95
Seduced by Evil '94
Deadly Currents '93
Drug Wars 2: The Cocaine Cartel '92
The Hunt for the Night Stalker '91
Kiss Me a Killer '91
Gore Vidal's Billy the Kid '89
The Neon Empire '89
Paint It Black '89
Fright Night 2 '88
The Milagro Beanfield War '88
The Penitent '88
Blue City '86
Last Plane Out '83
She's in the Army Now '81
Gloria '80
Night of the Juggler '80
Can You Hear the Laughter? The Story of Freddie Prinze '79
Jean Carmet (1920-94)
Germinal '93
Secret Obsession '88
Sorceress '88
Buffet Froid '79
Violette '78
Black and White in Color '76
Dupont Lajoie '74
Return of the Tall Blond Man with One Black Shoe '74
The Tall Blond Man with One Black Shoe '72
The Little Theatre of Jean Renoir '71
La Rupture '70
Any Number Can Win '63
There Goes Barder '54
Monsieur Vincent '47
Hoagy Carmichael (1899-1981)
The Las Vegas Story '52
Young Man with a Horn '50
The Best Years of Our Lives '46
Canyon Passage '46
Johnny Angel '45
To Have & Have Not '44
Topper '37
Ian Carmichael (1920-)
Wives and Daughters '01
Dark Obsession '90
Smashing Time '67
Heavens Above '63
I'm All Right Jack '59
Lucky Jim '58
Brothers in Law '57
The Colditz Story '55
Betrayed '54
Tullio Carminati (1894-1971)
War and Peace '56
Roman Holiday '53
London Melody '37
One Night of Love '34
Michael Carmine (1959-89)
Leviathan '89
*batteries not included '87
Band of the Hand '86
Primo Carnera
Hercules Unchained '59
The Prizefighter and the Lady '33
Alan Carney (-1973)
Girl Rush '44
Zombies on Broadway '44
Art Carney (1918-)
Last Action Hero '93
Night Friend '87
The Night They Saved Christmas '87
The Blue Yonder '86
Miracle of the Heart: A Boys Town Story '86
Izzy & Moe '85
Undergrads '85
The Emperor's New Clothes '84
Firestarter '84
The Muppets Take Manhattan '84
The Naked Face '84
Better Late Than Never '83
St. Helen's, Killer Volcano '82
Bitter Harvest '81
Take This Job & Shove It '81
Roadie '80
Steel '80
Defiance '79
Going in Style '79
Sunburn '79
House Calls '78
Movie, Movie '78
The Late Show '77
Death Scream '75
Katherine '75
Harry and Tonto '74
Pot o' Gold '41
George Carney (1887-1942)
Brighton Rock '47
I Know Where I'm Going '45
In Which We Serve '43
Love on the Dole '41
Morris Carnovsky (1897-1992)
Joe's Bed-Stuy Barbershop: We Cut Heads '83
Cyrano de Bergerac '50
Gun Crazy '49
Dead Reckoning '47
Our Vines Have Tender Grapes '45
Rhapsody in Blue '45
Cindy Carol
Dear Brigitte '65
Gidget Goes to Rome '63
Linda Carol (1970-)
Carnal Crimes '91
Future Hunters '88
Reform School Girls '86
Martine Carol (1920-67)
The Battle of Austerlitz '60
Around the World in 80 Days '56
Lola Montes '55
Nana '55
Beauties of the Night '52
Voyage Suprise '46
Sheila Carol
The Beast from Haunted Cave '60
Ski Troop Attack '60
Sue Carol (1907-82)
The Lone Star Ranger '30
Walking Back '26
Captain Swagger '25
Adam Carolla
Art House '98
Too Smooth '98
Leslie Caron (1931-)
Chocolat '00
The Last of the Blonde Bombshells '00
Funny Bones '94
Damage '92
Courage Mountain '89
Dangerous Moves '84
The Unapproachable '82
Contract '80
Goldengirl '79
The Man Who Loved Women '77
Valentino '77
QB VII '74
Nicole '72
Head of the Family '71
Madron '70
Is Paris Burning? '66
Promise Her Anything '66
Father Goose '64
The L-Shaped Room '62
Fanny '61
Gigi '58
Daddy Long Legs '55
The Glass Slipper '55
Lili '53
An American in Paris '51
Carleton Carpenter (1926-)
Up Periscope '59
Summer Stock '50
Two Weeks with Love '50
Lost Boundaries '49
David Carpenter
Spiders '00
Amelia Earhart: The Final Flight '94
Gettysburg '93
Warlock '91
Fred Carpenter
Murdered Innocence '94
Small Kill '93
John Carpenter
Night of the Ghouls '59
Song of Old Wyoming '45
John Carpenter (1948-)
The Cradle Will Rock '99
Body Bags '93
Silence of the Hams '93
Paul Carpenter (1921-64)
Call Me Bwana '63
Fire Maidens from Outer Space '56
Black Glove '54
Heat Wave '54
Paid to Kill '54
Unholy Four '54
Uneasy Terms '48
Peter Carpenter
Point of Terror '71
Blood Mania '70
Camilla Carr
Making Love '82
Keep My Grave Open '80
Logan's Run '76
Poor White Trash 2 '75
Don't Look in the Basement '73
Carole Carr
Scream Dream '89
Down Among the Z Men '52
Darlene Carr
Piranha '95
The Jungle Book '67 (V)
Mary Carr (1874-1973)
The World Accuses '35
Gun Law '33
The Fighting Marshal '32
Kept Husbands '31
The Night Patrol '26
Red Kimono '25
Paul Carr
Sisters of Death '76
Sniper '75
The Bat People '74
Truck Stop Women '74
The Severed Arm '73
Ben '72
Dirt Gang '71
David Carradine (1936-)
Warden of Red Rock '01
By Dawn's Early Light '00
Codename: Jaguar '00
Isaac Asimov's Nightfall '00
Cybercity '99
Knocking on Death's Door '99
Children of the Corn 5: Fields of Terror '98
Capital Punishment '96
Last Stand at Saber River '96
The Rage '96
The Gambler Returns: The Luck of the Draw '93
Karate Cop '93
Animal Instincts '92
Distant Justice '92
Field of Fire '92
Night Rhythms '92
Roadside Prophets '92
Deadly Surveillance '91
Double Trouble '91
Dune Warriors '91
The Dying Truth '91
Project: Eliminator '91
Sundown '91
Waxwork 2: Lost in Time '91
Bird on a Wire '90
Evil Toons '90
Future Zone '90
Martial Law '90
Midnight Fear '90
Think Big '90
Future Force '89
Night Children '89
Wizards of the Lost Kingdom 2 '89
Crime Zone '88
Nowhere to Run '88
Tropical Snow '88
Warlords '88
The Misfit Brigade '87
Sonny Boy '87
Armed Response '86
Kung Fu: The Movie '86
Oceans of Fire '86
The P.O.W. Escape '86
The Bad Seed '85
North and South Book 1 '85
Jealousy '84
The Warrior & the Sorceress '84
Lone Wolf McQuade '83
On the Line '83
Q (The Winged Serpent) '82
Safari 3000 '82
Trick or Treats '82
Americana '81
Cloud Dancer '80
High Noon: Part 2 '80
The Long Riders '80
Mr. Horn '79
Circle of Iron '78
Death Sport '78
The Serpent's Egg '78
Gray Lady Down '77
Thunder and Lightning '77
Bound for Glory '76
Cannonball '76
Death Race 2000 '75
The Long Goodbye '73
Mean Streets '73
Boxcar Bertha '72
Kung Fu '72
Macho Callahan '70
Maybe I'll Be Home in the Spring '70
The McMasters '70
The Good Guys and the Bad Guys '69
Violent Ones '68
John Carradine (1906-88)
Jack-O '95
Buried Alive '89
Evil Spawn '87
Star Slammer '87
Monster in the Closet '86
Peggy Sue Got Married '86
Revenge '86
Tomb '86
Evils of the Night '85
The Monster Club '85
The Vals '85
Ice Pirates '84
Boogey Man 2 '83
Demon Rage '82
House of the Long Shadows '82
The Secret of NIMH '82 (V)
Frankenstein Island '81
Goliath Awaits '81
The Howling '81
The Boogey Man '80
The Nesting '80
Nocturna '79
The Seekers '79
The Bees '78
Monster '78
The Vampire Hookers '78
The Christmas Coal Mine Miracle '77
Golden Rendezvous '77
Satan's Cheerleaders '77
Shock Waves '77
The White Buffalo '77
The Killer Inside Me '76
The Last Tycoon '76
Mary, Mary, Bloody Mary '76
The Sentinel '76
The Shootist '76
Death at Love House '75
Bad Charleston Charlie '73
Blood Legacy '73
The House of Seven Corpses '73
The Shrieking '73
Silent Night, Bloody Night '73
Terror in the Wax Museum '73
Big Foot '72
Blood of Ghastly Horror '72
Boxcar Bertha '72
Everything You Always Wanted to Know about Sex (But Were Afraid to Ask) '72
The Gatling Gun '72
The Night Strangler '72
Cain's Cutthroats '71
Horror of the Blood Monsters '70
The McMasters '70
Myra Breckinridge '70
Shinbone Alley '70 (V)
Blood of Dracula's Castle '69
The Good Guys and the Bad Guys '69
Gun Riders '69
The Trouble with Girls (and How to Get into It) '69
Alien Massacre '67
The Astro-Zombies '67
Autopsy of a Ghost '67
Hillbillies in a Haunted House '67
The Hostage '67
Mummy & Curse of the Jackal '67
Billy the Kid Versus Dracula '66
Munster, Go Home! '66
House of the Black Death '65
Cheyenne Autumn '64
Curse of the Stone Hand '64
Horrors of the Red Planet '64
The Patsy '64
Invasion of the Animal People '62
The Man Who Shot Liberty Valance '62
The Adventures of Huckleberry Finn '60
The Cosmic Man '59
Invisible Invaders '59
Half Human '58
The Incredible Petrified World '58
Last Hurrah '58
Showdown at Boot Hill '58
Hell Ship Mutiny '57

The Unearthly '57
Around the World in 80 Days '56
Court Jester '56
The Female Jungle '56
Hidden Guns '56
The Ten Commandments '56
The Kentuckian '55
Casanova's Big Night '54
The Egyptian '54
Thunder Pass '54
Johnny Guitar '53
The C-Man '49
The Private Affairs of Bel Ami '47
Captain Kidd '45
House of Dracula '45
The Adventures of Mark Twain '44
Bluebeard '44
House of Frankenstein '44
The Invisible Man's Revenge '44
The Mummy's Ghost '44
Return of the Ape Man '44
Waterfront '44
Captive Wild Woman '43
Isle of Forgotten Sins '43
Revenge of the Zombies '43
Silver Spurs '43
Reunion in France '42
Son of Fury '42
Blood and Sand '41
Western Union '41
Brigham Young: Frontiersman '40
The Grapes of Wrath '40
Return of Frank James '40
Drums Along the Mohawk '39
Five Came Back '39
The Hound of the Baskervilles '39
Jesse James '39
Mr. Moto's Last Warning '39
Stagecoach '39
The Three Musketeers '39
Alexander's Ragtime Band '38
Of Human Hearts '38
Captains Courageous '37
The Hurricane '37
Dimples '36
The Garden of Allah '36
Mary of Scotland '36
Winterset '36
The Bride of Frankenstein '35
Les Miserables '35
The Black Cat '34
Daniel Boone '34
The Invisible Man '33
To the Last Man '33

Keith Carradine (1951-)
The Diamond of Jeru '01
Baby '00
Hostage Hotel '00
Night Ride Home '99
Out of the Cold '99
Sirens '99
Hunter's Moon '97
Standoff '97
A Thousand Acres '97
Larry McMurtry's Dead Man's Walk '96
Last Stand at Saber River '96
Two Days in the Valley '96
The Tie That Binds '95
Wild Bill '95
Andre '94
Is There Life Out There? '94
The Bachelor '93
Crisscross '92
The Ballad of the Sad Cafe '91
Eye on the Sparrow '91
Payoff '91
Daddy's Dyin'...Who's Got the Will? '90
Judgment '90
Capone '89
Cold Feet '89
The Forgotten '89
Backfire '88
The Moderns '88
The Inquiry '87
Murder Ordained '87
Half a Lifetime '86
Trouble in Mind '86
A Winner Never Quits '86
Blackout '85
Choose Me '84
Maria's Lovers '84
Chiefs '83
Southern Comfort '81
The Long Riders '80
A Rumor of War '80
An Almost Perfect Affair '79
Old Boyfriends '79
Pretty Baby '78
The Duellists '77
Welcome to L.A. '77
Lumiere '76
Nashville '75
Thieves Like Us '74
Emperor of the North Pole '73
Idaho Transfer '73
The Shrieking '73
Kung Fu '72
A Gunfight '71
Man on a String '71
McCabe & Mrs. Miller '71

Robert Carradine (1954-)
Max Keeble's Big Move '01
The Kid with the X-Ray Eyes '99
Shepherd '99
Breakout '98
Gunfighter '98
Stray Bullet '98
Humanoids from the Deep '96
Bird of Prey '95
Revenge of the Nerds 4: Nerds in Love '94
Body Bags '93
The Disappearance of Christina '93
Stephen King's The Tommyknockers '93
The Player '92
Revenge of the Nerds 3: The Next Generation '92
Clarence '91
Double-Crossed '91
Illusions '91
Somebody Has to Shoot the Picture '90
All's Fair '89
Buy & Cell '89
The Incident '89
Rude Awakening '89
Conspiracy: The Trial of the Chicago Eight '87
Number One with a Bullet '87
Revenge of the Nerds 2: Nerds in Paradise '87
Tales of the Klondike: In a Far Country '87
Monte Carlo '86
As Is '85
Aladdin and His Wonderful Lamp '84
Just the Way You Are '84
Revenge of the Nerds '84
Wavelength '83
Heartaches '82
Tag: The Assassination Game '82
The Big Red One '80
The Long Riders '80
On the Edge: The Survival of Dana '79
Blackout '78
Coming Home '78
Joyride '77
Orca '77
Cannonball '76
Jackson County Jail '76
Massacre at Central High '76
Pom Pom Girls '76
Aloha, Bobby and Rose '74
Mean Streets '73
The Cowboys '72

Carlos Carrasco
Double Take '01
One Man's Hero '98
Speed '94

Danny Carrel
The Hands of Orlac '60
Mill of the Stone Women '60

Barbara Carrera (1945-)
Love Is All There Is '96
Sawbones '95
Tryst '94
Point of Impact '93
Loverboy '89
Wicked Stepmother '89
The Underachievers '88
Love at Stake '87
Wild Geese 2 '85
Lone Wolf McQuade '83
Never Say Never Again '83
I, the Jury '82
Condorman '81
Masada '81
When Time Ran Out '80
Centennial '78
The Island of Dr. Moreau '77
Embryo '76

Tia Carrere (1967-)
Lilo & Stitch '02 (V)
Scarred City '98
Tracked '98
Kull the Conqueror '97
Top of the World '97
High School High '96
Natural Enemy '96
Hollow Point '95
The Immortals '95
Jury Duty '95
My Teacher's Wife '95
Hostile Intentions '94
True Lies '94
Quick '93
Rising Sun '93
Wayne's World 2 '93
Wayne's World '92
Showdown in Little Tokyo '91
Fatal Mission '89
Aloha Summer '88
Noble House '88
Zombie Nightmare '86

Jim Carrey (1962-)
The Majestic '01
Dr. Seuss' How the Grinch Stole Christmas '00
Me, Myself, and Irene '00
Man on the Moon '99
Simon Birch '98 (N)
The Truman Show '98
The Cable Guy '96
Liar Liar '96
Ace Ventura: When Nature Calls '95
Batman Forever '95
Dumb & Dumber '94
The Mask '94
Ace Ventura: Pet Detective '93
High Strung '91
Earth Girls Are Easy '89
Pink Cadillac '89
The Dead Pool '88
Peggy Sue Got Married '86
Once Bitten '85
Finders Keepers '84
Club Med '83
Rubberface '81

Corey Carrier (1980-)
Savage Land '94
After Dark, My Sweet '90
Men Don't Leave '89

Matthieu Carriere (1950-)
Christopher Columbus: The Discovery '92
Naked Massacre '80s
The Bay Boy '85
A Woman in Flames '84
La Passante '83
The Aviator's Wife '80
The Associate '79
Coup de Grace '78
Don Juan (Or If Don Juan Were a Woman) '73

Elpidia Carrillo
Bread and Roses '00
Dangerous Passion '95
My Family '94
The Lightning Incident '91
Assassin '89
Let's Get Harry '87
Predator '87
Salvador '86
Beyond the Limit '83
The Border '82

Leo Carrillo (1880-1961)
Pancho Villa Returns '50
The Fugitive '48
The Phantom of the Opera '43
American Empire '42
Riders of Death Valley '41
One Night in the Tropics '40
Fisherman's Wharf '39
Girl of the Golden West '38
Too Hot to Handle '38
Fit for a King '37
History Is Made at Night '37
The Gay Desperado '36
Manhattan Melodrama '34
Viva Villa! '34
Before Morning '33

Debbie Lee Carrington
Club Fed '90
Spaced Invaders '90

Regina Carrol (1943-92)
Blazing Stewardesses '75
Jessi's Girls '75
Texas Layover '75
Angels' Wild Women '72
Blood of Ghastly Horror '72
Brain of Blood '71
Dracula vs. Frankenstein '71
The Female Bunch '69
Satan's Sadists '69

Barbara Carroll
Goliath Against the Giants '63
The Last Days of Pompeii '60

Beeson Carroll
Coming Home '78
Werewolf of Washington '73

Diahann Carroll (1935-)
Livin' for Love: The Natalie Cole Story '00
Sally Hemings: An American Scandal '00
Having Our Say: The Delany Sisters' First 100 Years '99
The Sweetest Gift '98
Eve's Bayou '97
The Five Heartbeats '91
From the Dead of Night '89
I Know Why the Caged Bird Sings '79
Death Scream '75
Goodbye Again '61
Paris Blues '61
Carmen Jones '54

Helen Carroll
The Man Upstairs '93
The Dead '87

James Carroll
Police Academy 4: Citizens on Patrol '87
Girls Night Out '83
Senior Trip '81
He Knows You're Alone '80

James Dennis (Jim) Carroll (1950-)
The Basketball Diaries '94
The Unholy '88

Janet Carroll (1940-)
Forces of Nature '99
The Omega Code '99
Family Business '89
Memories of Me '88
Bluffing It '87
Risky Business '83

Joan Carroll
Tomorrow the World '44
Primrose Path '40

John Carroll (1905-79)
Rock, Baby, Rock It '57
The Farmer Takes a Wife '53
Flying Tigers '42
Rio Rita '42
Lady Be Good '41
Sunny '41
Go West '40
Susan and God '40
Only Angels Have Wings '39
Wolf Call '39
Rose of Rio Grande '38
Zorro Rides Again '37

Justin Carroll
Dark Secrets '95
Stormswept '95

Leo G. Carroll (1892-1972)
The Prize '63
One Plus One '61
The Parent Trap '61
North by Northwest '59
Tarantula '55
We're No Angels '55
Treasure of the Golden Condor '53
The Bad and the Beautiful '52
The Snows of Kilimanjaro '52
First Legion '51
Strangers on a Train '51
Father of the Bride '50
Forever Amber '47
The Paradine Case '47
House on 92nd Street '45
Spellbound '45
Bahama Passage '42
Suspicion '41
Rebecca '40
Bulldog Drummond's Secret Police '39
The Private Lives of Elizabeth & Essex '39
The Tower of London '39
Wuthering Heights '39
A Christmas Carol '38

Madeleine Carroll (1906-87)
Bahama Passage '42
My Favorite Blonde '42
My Son, My Son '40
My Love For Yours '39
On the Avenue '37
Prisoner of Zenda '37
The General Died at Dawn '36
Lloyds of London '36
The Secret Agent '36
The 39 Steps '35

Nancy Carroll (1904-65)
That Certain Age '38
Transatlantic Merry-Go-Round '34
Scarlet Dawn '32
Dance of Life '29

Pat Carroll (1927-)
Songcatcher '99
The Little Mermaid '89 (V)
Brothers O'Toole '73
With Six You Get Eggroll '68

Peter Carroll
Who Killed Baby Azaria? '83
Cass '78
The Last Wave '77

Rocky Carroll
Best Laid Plans '99
The Great White Hype '96
Crimson Tide '95

Carrot Top
Dennis the Menace Strikes Again '98
Chairman of the Board '97

Ben Carruthers
Riot '69
Shadows '60

Julius J. Carry, III
The New Guy '02
The Last Dragon '85

Charles Carson (1886-1977)
Beau Brummel '54
Cry, the Beloved Country '51
The Courageous Mr. Penn '41
Dreaming Lips '37
The Secret Agent '36
Broken Melody '34

Crystal Carson (1967-)
Kiss and Be Killed '91
Cartel '90
Killer Tomatoes Strike Back '90

Glen Carson
Ninja Death Squad '87
Ninja Phantom Heroes '87

Hunter Carson (1975-)
Mr. North '88
Invaders from Mars '86
Paris, Texas '83

Jack Carson (1910-63)
The King of the Roaring '20s: The Story of Arnold Rothstein '61
The Bramble Bush '60
Cat on a Hot Tin Roof '58
Tarnished Angels '57
Phffft! '54
Red Garters '54
A Star Is Born '54
Dangerous When Wet '53
It's a Great Feeling '49
My Dream Is Yours '49
Romance on the High Seas '48
Mildred Pierce '45
Arsenic and Old Lace '44
Hollywood Canteen '44
Thank Your Lucky Stars '43
Gentleman Jim '42
The Bride Came C.O.D. '41
Love Crazy '41
Mr. & Mrs. Smith '41
Strawberry Blonde '41
Lucky Partners '40
Destry Rides Again '39
Mr. Smith Goes to Washington '39
Carefree '38
The Saint in New York '38
Vivacious Lady '38
Stage Door '37
Stand-In '37

John Carson (1927-)
An African Dream '90
After Julius '78
Captain Kronos: Vampire Hunter '74
Emma '72
Taste the Blood of Dracula '70
Plague of the Zombies '66

John David Carson (1952-)
Empire of the Ants '77
Charge of the Model T's '76
Creature from Black Lake '76
Savage Is Loose '74

Lisa Nicole Carson (1969-)
Aftershock: Earthquake in New York '99
Life '99
Eve's Bayou '97
Love Jones '96
Devil in a Blue Dress '95

L.M. Kit Carson (1947-)
Hurricane Streets '96
Running on Empty '88
David Holzman's Diary '67

Shawn Carson
Something Wicked This Way Comes '83
The Funhouse '81

Sunset Carson (1922-)
Battling Marshal '48
Alias Billy the Kid '46
Rio Grande Raiders '46
Bells of Rosarita '45
Rough Riders of Cheyenne '45

Call of the Rockies '44
Stage Door Canteen '43

Terrence "T.C." Carson
U-571 '00
Relax... It's Just Sex! '98
Gang Related '96
Livin' Large '91

Peter Carsten (1929-)
Black Lemons '80s
Zeppelin '71
Web of the Spider '70
And God Said to Cain '69
Dark of the Sun '68
Secret of the Black Trunk '62

Margit Carstensen
Terror 2000 '92
Chinese Roulette '86
Angry Harvest '85
Possession '81
Mother Kusters Goes to Heaven '76
Satan's Brew '76
Tenderness of the Wolves '73
The Bitter Tears of Petra von Kant '72

Alex Carter
Hitched '01
The Man in the Attic '94

Alice Carter
Dangerous Heart '93
Gross Anatomy '89

Ann Carter (1936-)
The Two Mrs. Carrolls '47
Curse of the Cat People '44
I Married a Witch '42

Ben Carter (1907-)
Crash Dive '43
Kentucky Blue Streak '35

Bill Carter
Flatbed Annie and Sweetiepie: Lady Truckers '79
Battle of the Worlds '61

Dixie Carter
The Big Day '99
Going Berserk '83
Killing of Randy Webster '81

Finn Carter
Missing Pieces '00
Sweet Justice '92
How I Got into College '89
Tremors '89

Gary Carter
Late Bloomers '95
Ninja Strike Force '88

Georgianna Carter
The Wild Ride '60
Night of the Blood Beast '58

Helena Carter (1923-2000)
Invaders from Mars '53
Bugles in the Afternoon '52
Kiss Tomorrow Goodbye '50
Something in the Wind '47

Jack Carter (1923-)
Play It to the Bone '99
In the Heat of Passion '91
Satan's Princess '90
Arena '89
Robo-Chic '89
Deadly Embrace '88
Sexpot '88
Death Blow '87
Red Nights '87
Ecstasy '84
Hambone & Hillie '84
History of the World: Part 1 '81
Alligator '80
Octagon '80
The Glove '78
Rainbow '78
The Happy Hooker Goes to Washington '77
The Amazing Dobermans '76
Resurrection of Zachary Wheeler '71
Viva Las Vegas '63
The Horizontal Lieutenant '62

Janis Carter (1913-94)
Flying Leathernecks '51
The Half-Breed '51
Santa Fe '51
Miss Grant Takes Richmond '49
Lady of Burlesque '43
I Married an Angel '42

Jim Carter
Dinotopia '02
The Way We Live Now '02
The Little Vampire '00
102 Dalmatians '00
Legionnaire '98
Shakespeare in Love '98
A Merry War '97
Brassed Off '96
Grave Indiscretions '96
Black Beauty '94
Cracker: The Big Crunch '94
The Madness of King George '94
The Advocate '93
Stalin '92
A Very British Coup '88
A Month in the Country '87
Haunted Honeymoon '86

Joelle Carter
High Fidelity '00
Just One Time '00

Karen Carter
The Legend of the Wolf Woman '77
The Big Bust Out '73

Lynda Carter (1951-)
A Prayer in the Dark '97
Danielle Steel's Daddy '91
I Posed for Playboy '91
Rita Hayworth: The Love Goddess '83
Hotline '82
Last Song '80
Bobbie Jo and the Outlaw '76

Nell Carter (1948-)
The Proprietor '96
The Grass Harp '95
The Crazysitter '94
Bebe's Kids '92 (V)
Final Shot: The Hank Gathers Story '92
Modern Problems '81
Hair '79

Terry Carter (1929-)
Battlestar Galactica '78
Black Force 2 '78
Foxy Brown '74
Man on the Run '74

Thomas Carter (1953-)
Whose Life Is It Anyway? '81
Monkey Hustle '77

T.K. Carter (1956-)
Yesterday's Target '96
A Rage in Harlem '91
Ski Patrol '89
Amazon Women on the Moon '87
He's My Girl '87
Runaway Train '85
Doctor Detroit '83
The Thing '82
Southern Comfort '81
The Hollywood Knights '80
Seems Like Old Times '80

Anna Carteret
The Heat of the Day '91
The Shell Seekers '89

Katrin Cartlidge (1961-)
From Hell '01
No Man's Land '01
Hi-Life '98
The Lost Son '98
Career Girls '97
Claire Dolan '97
Breaking the Waves '95
Saint-Ex: The Story of the Storyteller '95
Before the Rain '94
Naked '93

Angela Cartwright (1952-)
Lost in Space '98
High School USA '84
Scout's Honor '80
The Sound of Music '65

Lynn Cartwright
The Wasp Woman '59
Queen of Outer Space '58

Nancy Cartwright (1959-)
The Little Mermaid '89 (V)
Pound Puppies and the Legend of Big Paw '88 (V)
Not My Kid '85
Twilight Zone: The Movie '83

Veronica Cartwright (1950-)
Scary Movie 2 '01
Sparkler '99
Quicksilver Highway '98
Money Talks '97
Candyman 2: Farewell to the Flesh '94
Dead Air '94
Mirror, Mirror 2: Raven Dance '94
Man Trouble '92
Dead in the Water '91
False Identity '90
Hitler's Daughter '90
Robert Kennedy and His Times '90
Valentino Returns '88
Wisdom '87
The Witches of Eastwick '87
Flight of the Navigator '86
My Man Adam '86
Nightmares '83
The Right Stuff '83
Prime Suspect '82
Alien '79
Goin' South '78
Invasion of the Body Snatchers '78
Kid from Not-So-Big '78
Inserts '76
The Birds '63
One Man's Way '63
Spencer's Mountain '63
The Children's Hour '61

Anthony Caruso (1913-)
Claws '77
Zebra Force '76
Legend of Earl Durand '74
When Gangland Strikes '56
Cattle Queen of Montana '54
Drum Beat '54
The Asphalt Jungle '50
Objective, Burma! '45
Watch on the Rhine '43

David Caruso (1956-)
Session 9 '01
Deadlocked '00
Proof of Life '00
Body Count '97
Cold Around the Heart '97
Elmore Leonard's Gold Coast '97
Jade '95
Kiss of Death '94
Mad Dog and Glory '93
King of New York '90
Rainbow Drive '90
China Girl '87
Blue City '86
First Blood '82
An Officer and a Gentleman '82

Betty Carvalho
Best of the Best 2 '93
Halloween 5: The Revenge of Michael Myers '89

Brent Carver (1952-)
Deeply '99
Lilies '96
Millennium '89
Crossbar '79
One Night Stand '77

Lynne Carver (1909-55)
Bataan '43
Sunset on the Desert '42
The Adventures of Huckleberry Finn '39
A Christmas Carol '38
Everybody Sing '38
The Bride Wore Red '37
Madame X '37
Maytime '37

Dana Carvey (1955-)
Master of Disguise '02
Little Nicky '00
The Shot '96
Clean Slate '94
The Road to Wellville '94
Trapped in Paradise '94
Wayne's World 2 '93
Wayne's World '92
Opportunity Knocks '90
Moving '88
Tough Guys '86
Racing with the Moon '84
This Is Spinal Tap '84

Maria Casares (1922-96)
Someone Else's America '96
La Lectrice '88
Sand and Blood '87
The Testament of Orpheus '59
Orpheus '49
La Chartreuse de Parme '48
Children of Paradise '44
The Ladies of the Bois de Bologne '44

Antonio Casas (1911-82)
Blood at Sundown '88
Tristana '70
The Texican '66

Salvatore Cascio (1979-)
The Pope Must Diet '91
Everybody's Fine '90
Cinema Paradiso '88

Kathleen Case
Human Desire '54
Last of the Pony Riders '53

Max Casella (1967-)
Dinosaur '00 (V)
Analyze This '98
Trial and Error '96
Sgt. Bilko '95
Ed Wood '94
Windrunner '94
Newsies '92

Chiara Caselli (1967-)
Sleepless '01
Forgotten City '98
Beyond the Clouds '95
Fiorile '93
My Own Private Idaho '91

Bernie Casey (1939-)
Tomcats '01
In the Mouth of Madness '95
The Cemetery Club '93
Street Knight '93
Chains of Gold '92
Another 48 Hrs. '90
Bill & Ted's Excellent Adventure '89
Backfire '88
I'm Gonna Git You Sucka '88
Rent-A-Cop '88
Steele Justice '87
Spies Like Us '85
The Fantastic World of D.C. Collins '84
Revenge of the Nerds '84
Never Say Never Again '83
Sharky's Machine '81
Sophisticated Gents '81
The Martian Chronicles: Part 1 '79
The Martian Chronicles: Part 2 '79
The Martian Chronicles: Part 3 '79
Ants '77
Dr. Black, Mr. Hyde '76
The Man Who Fell to Earth '76
Cornbread, Earl & Me '75
Panic on the 5:22 '74
Big Mo '73
Cleopatra Jones '73
Boxcar Bertha '72
Brian's Song '71
Guns of the Magnificent Seven '69

Lawrence Casey
The Hunted Lady '77
The Student Nurses '70
The Gay Deceivers '69

Johnny Cash (1932-)
Last Days of Frank & Jesse James '86
Stagecoach '86
North and South Book 1 '85
The Baron and the Kid '84
Murder in Coweta County '83
Pride of Jesse Hallum '81
A Gunfight '71
Road to Nashville '67
Door to Door Maniac '61

June Carter Cash (1929-)
The Apostle '97
Last Days of Frank & Jesse James '86
The Baron and the Kid '84
Murder in Coweta County '83

Rosalind Cash (1938-95)
Tales from the Hood '95
The Mighty Pawns '87
The Offspring '87
The Adventures of Buckaroo Banzai Across the Eighth Dimension '84
Go Tell It on the Mountain '84
Death Drug '83
Wrong Is Right '82
Keeping On '81
Sophisticated Gents '81
The Class of Miss MacMichael '78
Monkey Hustle '77
Dr. Black, Mr. Hyde '76
Cornbread, Earl & Me '75
Amazing Grace '74
Omega Man '71

Isadore Cashier (1887-1948)
The Light Ahead '39
The Cantor's Son '37
His Wife's Lover '31

Graciela Casillas
American Streetfighter 2: The Full Impact '97
Fire in the Night '85

Stefania Casini
Suspiria '77
Andy Warhol's Dracula '74

Philip Casnoff (1955-)
Kiss Tomorrow Goodbye '00
Chameleon '98
The Defenders: Taking the First '98
Temptation '94
Sinatra '92
Red Wind '91
Ironclads '90
Hands of a Stranger '87
North and South Book 2 '86
Gorp '80

John Cason (1918-61)
From Here to Eternity '53
Jungle Drums of Africa '53
Last Bullet '50
Rangeland Empire '50
Outlaw of the Plains '46

Katrina Caspary
My Mom's a Werewolf '89
Mac and Me '88
Can't Buy Me Love '87

Maurice Cass (1884-1954)
Rocky Jones, Space Ranger: Renegade Satellite '54
Spook Busters '48
Thin Ice '37

Peggy Cass (1924-99)
Cheaters '84
Paddy '70
If It's Tuesday, This Must Be Belgium '69
Gidget Goes Hawaiian '61
Auntie Mame '58
The Marrying Kind '52

John Cassavetes (1929-89)
Love Streams '84
Marvin & Tige '84
Incubus '82
The Tempest '82
Whose Life Is It Anyway? '81
Brass Target '78
The Fury '78
Opening Night '77
Mikey & Nicky '76
Two Minute Warning '76
Minnie and Moskowitz '71
Husbands '70
Rosemary's Baby '68
Devil's Angels '67
The Dirty Dozen '67
The Killers '64

Nick Cassavetes (1959-)
The Astronaut's Wife '99
Life '99
Face/Off '97
Machine Gun Blues '95
Mrs. Parker and the Vicious Circle '94
Twogether '94
Body of Influence '93
Broken Trust '93
Class of 1999 2: The Substitute '93
Sins of the Night '93
Sins of Desire '92
Delta Force 3: The Killing Game '91
Backstreet Dreams '90
Blind Fury '90
Assault of the Killer Bimbos '88
The Wraith '87

Jean-Pierre Cassel (1932-)
The Crimson Rivers '01
The Ice Rink '99
La Ceremonie '95
Ready to Wear '94
Between Heaven and Earth '93
The Favor, the Watch, & the Very Big Fish '92
The Fatal Image '90
The Maid '90
The Phantom of the Opera '90
Mr. Frost '89
The Return of the Musketeers '89
Alice '86
La Truite '83
Nudo di Donna '83
La Vie Continue '82
From Hell to Victory '79
Les Rendez-vous D'Anna '78
Who Is Killing the Great Chefs of Europe? '78
The Killing of a Chinese Bookie '76
Twist '76
The Four Musketeers '75
That Lucky Touch '75
Murder on the Orient Express '74
The Three Musketeers '74
The Discreet Charm of the Bourgeoisie '72
La Rupture '70
The Killing Game '67
Is Paris Burning? '66
Those Magnificent Men in Their Flying Machines '65
The Elusive Corporal '62

Seymour Cassel (1937-)
The Royal Tenenbaums '01
61* '01
Animal Factory '00
The Crew '00
Just One Night '00
Me & Will '99

Motel Blue '98
Relax... It's Just Sex! '98
Rushmore '98
This World, Then the Fireworks '97
Cannes Man '96
Dream for an Insomniac '96
Tree's Lounge '96
Bad Love '95
Chasers '94
Dark Side of Genius '94
Imaginary Crimes '94
It Could Happen to You '94
Tollbooth '94
Boiling Point '93
Chain of Desire '93
Hand Gun '93
Indecent Proposal '93
When Pigs Fly '93
Adventures in Spying '92
Honeymoon in Vegas '92
In the Soup '92
There Goes My Baby '92
Trouble Bound '92
Diary of a Hitman '91
White Fang '91
Dick Tracy '90
Sweet Bird of Youth '89
Wicked Stepmother '89
Colors '88
Johnny Be Good '88
Plain Clothes '88
Track 29 '88
Best Seller '87
Survival Game '87
Tin Men '87
Eye of the Tiger '86
Love Streams '84
Double Exposure '82
The Mountain Men '80
California Dreaming '79
Black Oak Conspiracy '77
Seducers '77
Valentino '77
Minnie and Moskowitz '71
Faces '68
The Killers '64

Vincent Cassel (1967-)
Birthday Girl '02
Brotherhood of the Wolf '01
The Crimson Rivers '01
Shrek '01 (V)
The Messenger: The Story of Joan of Arc '99
Elizabeth '98
Hate '95
L'Eleve '95
Cafe au Lait '94

Alan Cassell
Squizzy Taylor '84
The Club '81
Breaker Morant '80
Money Movers '78

Wally Cassell (1915-92)
Until They Sail '57
Breakdown '53
Sands of Iwo Jima '49
White Heat '49
The Story of G.I. Joe '45

Andrew Cassese
Revenge of the Nerds 2: Nerds in Paradise '87
Revenge of the Nerds '84

Gabriel Casseus
Black Hawk Down '01
Bedazzled '00
Black Dog '98
Modern Vampires '98
Buffalo Soldiers '97
Don King: Only in America '97
Fallen '97
Get On the Bus '96
Nightjohn '96
Lone Star '95
New Jersey Drive '95

David Cassidy (1950-)
Spirit of '76 '91
Instant Karma '90
The Night the City Screamed '80

Edward Cassidy (1893-1968)
Buffalo Bill Rides Again '47
Son of Zorro '47
Boss of Rawhide '44
Devil Riders '44
Frontier Outlaws '44
Rustler's Hideout '44
Wild Horse Phantom '44
Sagebrush Law '43
Aces Wild '37
Boothill Brigade '37
Boots of Destiny '37
Roaring Six Guns '37
Santa Fe Bound '37
A Face in the Fog '36
Feud of the West '35
Toll of the Desert '35

Elaine Cassidy
The Others '01
Felicia's Journey '99

Jack Cassidy (1927-76)
The Eiger Sanction '75
Columbo: Murder by the Book '71
The Andersonville Trial '70

Joanna Cassidy (1944-)
John Carpenter's Ghosts of Mars '01
Dangerous Beauty '98
Loved '97
The Second Civil War '97
Chain Reaction '96
Barbarians at the Gate '93
Stephen King's The Tommyknockers '93
Landslide '92
Live! From Death Row '92
Perfect Family '92
All-American Murder '91
Don't Tell Mom the Babysitter's Dead '91
Lonely Hearts '91
Nightmare at Bittercreek '91
A Girl of the Limberlost '90
May Wine '90
Wheels of Terror '90
Where the Heart Is '90
1969 '89
The Package '89
A Father's Revenge '88
Who Framed Roger Rabbit '88
The Fourth Protocol '87
The Children of Times Square '86
Club Paradise '86
Codename: Foxfire '85
Invitation to Hell '84
Under Fire '83
Blade Runner '82
Night Games '80
The Glove '78
The Late Show '77
Stunts '77
Bank Shot '74

Patrick Cassidy (1961-)
The Fiance '96
How the West Was Fun '95
Hitler's Daughter '90
Longtime Companion '90
Love at Stake '87
Dress Gray '86
Something in Common '86
Fever Pitch '85
Nickel Mountain '85
Just the Way You Are '84
Off the Wall '82

Shaun Cassidy (1958-)
Texas Guns '90
Roots: The Gift '88

Ted Cassidy (1932-79)
Halloween with the Addams Family '79
Sunshine Run '79
Goin' Coconuts '78
Planet Earth '74
Thunder County '74
Women's Prison Escape '74
Poor Pretty Eddie '73
Butch Cassidy and the Sundance Kid '69
MacKenna's Gold '69

Claudio Cassinelli (1938-85)
Hands of Steel '86
Hercules 2 '85
The New Gladiators '83
The Great Alligator '81
Mountain of the Cannibal God '79
Allonsanfan '73

John Cassini
Get Carter '00
The Spree '96

Nadia Cassini
Star Crash '78
Pulp '72

John Cassisi
Man's Best Friend '93
Bugsy Malone '76

Carla Cassola
The Devil's Daughter '91
Demonia '90

Jean-Pierre Castaldi
The Musketeer '01
A Fine Romance '92
La Merveilleuse Visite '74

Lou Castel (1943-)
Irma Vep '96
Three Lives and Only One Death '96
Rorret '87
The Eyes, the Mouth '83
The American Friend '77
The Scarlet Letter '73
Beware of a Holy Whore '70
Paranoia '69
A Bullet for the General '68

Dan Castellaneta (1958-)
The Settlement '99
Plump Fiction '97
The Return of Jafar '94 (V)
The War of the Roses '89
Nothing in Common '86

Richard S. Castellano (1933-88)
The Godfather 1902-1959: The Complete Epic '81
Night of the Juggler '80
Honor Thy Father '73
The Godfather '72
Lovers and Other Strangers '70

Vincent Castellanos
Mulholland Drive '01
K-911 '99
The Last Marshal '99
Anaconda '96
The Crow 2: City of Angels '96

Sergio Castellitto (1953-)
Va Savoir '01
For Sale '98
Pronto '97
Portraits Chinois '96
The Star Maker '95
Alberto Express '92
The Big Blue '88

Willy Castello (1910-53)
Confessions of a Vice Baron '42
Mad Youth '40
Cocaine Fiends '36

Nino Castelnuovo (1936-)
The English Patient '96
Camille 2000 '69
Umbrellas of Cherbourg '64

Jacques Castelot
Dishonorable Discharge '57
Forbidden Fruit '52

Christopher Castile
Beethoven's 2nd '93
Beethoven '92

Enrique Castillo
The Hi-Lo Country '98
The End of Violence '97
My Family '94
Blood In ... Blood Out: Bound by Honor '93

Gloria Castillo (1933-)
Invasion of the Saucer Men '57
Reform School Girl '57
Teenage Monster '57
The Night of the Hunter '55

Don Castle (1917-66)
Motor Patrol '50
Who Killed Doc Robbin? '48
Wake Island '42

John Castle (1940-)
The Crucifer of Blood '91
RoboCop 3 '91
The Bretts '88
Lillie '79
Antony and Cleopatra '73
Man of La Mancha '72
The Lion in Winter '68
Blow-Up '66

Mary Castle
Gunsmoke '53
White Fire '53

Nick Castle (1947-)
Halloween '78
Artists and Models '55

Peggy Castle (1927-73)
The Seven Hills of Rome '58
Beginning of the End '57
The Finger Man '55
The White Orchid '54
Invasion U.S.A. '52

Roy Castle (1932-94)
Legend of the Werewolf '75
Alice Through the Looking Glass '66
Dr. Terror's House of Horrors '65

William Castle (1914-77)
Bug '75
Shampoo '75
Rosemary's Baby '68

Patrick Catalifo
Don't Let Me Die on a Sunday '98
Sand and Blood '87

Antonio Catania
Bread and Tulips '01
Mediterraneo '91

John Cater
The Duchess of Duke Street '78
Captain Kronos: Vampire Hunter '74

Georgina Cates (1975-)
Big City Blues '99
Clay Pigeons '98
Illuminata '98
A Soldier's Sweetheart '98
Stiff Upper Lips '96
Frankie Starlight '95
An Awfully Big Adventure '94

Helen Cates
The Whole Wide World '96
The Underneath '95
A Taste for Killing '92

Phoebe Cates (1964-)
The Anniversary Party '01
My Life's in Turnaround '94
Princess Caraboo '94
Bodies, Rest & Motion '93
Drop Dead Fred '91
Gremlins 2: The New Batch '90
I Love You to Death '90
The Heart of Dixie '89
Shag: The Movie '89
Bright Lights, Big City '88
Date with an Angel '87
Gremlins '84
Private School '83
Fast Times at Ridgemont High '82
Paradise '82

Reg E. Cathey
Boycott '02
Pootie Tang '01
Seven '95
Tank Girl '94
Quick Change '90

Brigitte Catillon
Artemisia '97
Un Coeur en Hiver '93
La Lectrice '88

Mary Jo Catlett (1938-)
Ablaze '00
Bram Stoker's The Mummy '97
Trading Favors '97
Serial Mom '94
Battling for Baby '92
Blood Beach '81

Walter Catlett (1889-1960)
The Inspector General '49
I'll Be Yours '47
His Butler's Sister '44
They Got Me Covered '43
Yankee Doodle Dandy '42
It Started with Eve '41
Pinocchio '40 (V)
Pop Always Pays '40
Remedy for Riches '40
Bringing Up Baby '38
Every Day's a Holiday '38
On the Avenue '37
Mr. Deeds Goes to Town '36
A Tale of Two Cities '36
Rain '32
The Front Page '31
Maker of Men '31

Victoria Catlin
Howling 5: The Rebirth '89
Mutant on the Bounty '89

Juliette Caton
Lady Audley's Secret '00
Courage Mountain '89
The Last Temptation of Christ '88

Michael Caton
The Animal '01
The Echo of Thunder '98
The Interview '98
The Castle '97

Christine Cattall
Bedroom Eyes '86
Screwball Academy '86

Kim Cattrall (1956-)
Crossroads '02
15 Minutes '01
36 Hours to Die '99
Baby Geniuses '98
Modern Vampires '98
Unforgettable '96
Where Truth Lies '96
Above Suspicion '95
The Heidi Chronicles '95
Live Nude Girls '95
Breaking Point '94
Running Delilah '93
Wild Palms '93
Double Vision '92
Split Second '92
Miracle in the Wilderness '91
Star Trek 6: The Undiscovered Country '91
The Bonfire of the Vanities '90
Honeymoon Academy '90
Smokescreen '90
Goodnight, Michelangelo '89
The Return of the Musketeers '89
Masquerade '88
Palais Royale '88
Mannequin '87
Midnight Crossing '87
Big Trouble in Little China '86
City Limits '85
Turk 182! '85
Police Academy '84
Porky's '82
Ticket to Heaven '81
Scruples '80
Tribute '80
The Rebels '79
The Bastard '78
Rosebud '75
Deadly Harvest '72

Philippe Caubere
My Father's Glory '91
My Mother's Castle '91

Daniel Cauchy
Bob le Flambeur '55
Grisbi '53

Lane Caudell
Archer: The Fugitive from the Empire '81
Hanging on a Star '78

Jessica Cauffiel
Legally Blonde '01
Valentine '01
Urban Legends 2: Final Cut '00

Joan Caulfield (1922-91)
Pony Express Rider '76
Daring Dobermans '73
Buckskin '68
The Lady Says No '51
Dear Wife '49
Welcome Stranger '47
Blue Skies '46
Monsieur Beaucaire '46

Maxwell Caulfield (1959-)
Facing the Enemy '00
Missing Pieces '00
Submerged '00
Perfect Tenant '99
The Real Blonde '97
Backlash: Oblivion 2 '95
Empire Records '95
Alien Intruder '93
Gettysburg '93
In a Moment of Passion '93
Midnight Witness '93
No Escape, No Return '93
Animal Instincts '92
Dance with Death '91
Sundown '91
Exiled in America '90
Mind Games '89
Project: Alien '89
The Supernaturals '86
The Boys Next Door '85
Electric Dreams '84
Grease 2 '82

Gary Cavagnaro
The Bad News Bears '76
Drive-In '76

Valeria Cavalli
Double Team '97
Joseph '95
Everybody's Fine '90
A Blade in the Dark '83

Victor Cavallo
Dial Help '88
The Tragedy of a Ridiculous Man '81

Megan Cavanagh
Jimmy Neutron: Boy Genius '01 (V)
Meet the Deedles '98
For Richer or Poorer '97
Robin Hood: Men in Tights '93
A League of Their Own '92

Paul Cavanagh (1895-1959)
Francis in the Haunted House '56
The Prodigal '55
Charade '53
House of Wax '53
Bride of the Gorilla '51
The Strange Door '51
Hi-Jacked '50
Black Arrow '48
Humoresque '46
House of Fear '45
The Woman in Green '45
Captains of the Clouds '42
Shadows on the Stairs '41
Goin' to Town '35
Splendor '35
Tarzan and His Mate '34
A Bill of Divorcement '32

Tom Cavanagh
Something More '99
Bloodhounds 2 '96
A Vow to Kill '94

Christine Cavanaugh
Rugrats in Paris: The Movie '00 (V)
The Rugrats Movie '98 (V)
Babe '95 (V)
Down, Out and Dangerous '95

Hobart Cavanaugh (1886-1950)
Up in Central Park '48
Black Angel '46
The Magnificent Dope '42
Rose of Washington Square '39
Wife Versus Secretary '36
I Cover the Waterfront '33

Michael Cavanaugh
Dancing in September '00
Black Thunder '98
Full Fathom Five '90

Elise Cavanna (1902-63)
The Barber Shop '33
The Dentist '32
Pharmacist '32

Lumi Cavazos (1969-)
In the Time of the Butterflies '01
Bless the Child '00
Sugar Town '99
Last Stand at Saber River '96
Bottle Rocket '95
Manhattan Merenque! '95
Like Water for Chocolate '93

Ingrid Caven (1943-)
Malou '83
In a Year of 13 Moons '78
Mother Kusters Goes to Heaven '76
Satan's Brew '76
Shadow of Angels '76
Tenderness of the Wolves '73
The American Soldier '70
Beware of a Holy Whore '70

Dick Cavett (1936-)
The Marx Brothers in a Nutshell '90
Beetlejuice '88
Moon over Parador '88
A Nightmare on Elm Street 3: Dream Warriors '87
Annie Hall '77

James Caviezel (1968-)
The Count of Monte Cristo '02
High Crimes '02
Angel Eyes '01
Frequency '00
Pay It Forward '00
Ride with the Devil '99
The Thin Red Line '98
G.I. Jane '97
Ed '96
Wyatt Earp '94

Joseph Cawthorn (1869-1949)
Harmony Lane '35
Sweet Adeline '35
The Cat and the Fiddle '34
They Call It Sin '32
The White Zombie '32
The Taming of the Shrew '29

Elizabeth (Kaitan) Cayton
Necromancer: Satan's Servant '88
Silent Night, Deadly Night 2 '87
Slave Girls from Beyond Infinity '87

John Cazale (1936-78)
The Godfather 1902-1959: The Complete Epic '81
The Deer Hunter '78
Dog Day Afternoon '75
The Conversation '74
The Godfather, Part 2 '74
The Godfather '72

Christopher Cazenove (1945-)
A Knight's Tale '01
The Proprietor '96
Aces: Iron Eagle 3 '92
Three Men and a Little Lady '90
The Fantasist '89
The Man Who Guards the Greenhouse '88
Souvenir '88
Tears in the Rain '88
Windmills of the Gods '88
Jenny's War '85
Mata Hari '85
Children of the Full Moon '84
Until September '84
Heat and Dust '82
Eye of the Needle '81
From a Far Country: Pope John Paul II '81
The Duchess of Duke Street '78
East of Elephant Rock '76
Royal Flash '75

Daniel Ceccaldi (1927-)
Twisted Obsession '90
Charles et Lucie '79
Holiday Hotel '77
Chloe in the Afternoon '72
Bed and Board '70
The Soft Skin '64

Carlo Cecchi (1939-)
The Red Violin '98
Stealing Beauty '96
Steam: A Turkish Bath '96
La Scorta '94

Edward Cecil
Desert of the Lost '27
Wild Horse Canyon '25

Jon Cedar
Kiss Daddy Goodbye '81
The Manitou '78
Day of the Animals '77

Larry Cedar
Boris and Natasha: The Movie '92
C.H.U.D. 2: Bud the Chud '89
Feds '88

Giuseppe Cederna
For Roseanna '96
Mediterraneo '91

Cedric the Entertainer
Ice Age '02 (V)
Serving Sara '02
Kingdom Come '01
Big Momma's House '00
Ride '98

Violeta Cela
El Barbaro '84
Conquest '83

Clementine Celarie (1957-)
Les Miserables '95
Sand and Blood '87
Betty Blue '86

Henry Cele (1949-)
The Ghost and the Darkness '96
Curse 3: Blood Sacrifice '90
The Last Samurai '90
The Rutanga Tapes '90
Rage to Kill '88
Shaka Zulu '83

Maria Celedonio
Freeway 2: Confessions of a Trickbaby '99
How to Make an American Quilt '95

Adriano Celentano
The Switch '89
The Con Artists '80

Adolfo Celi (1922-)
Cafe Express '83
Intruder '77
The Arab Conspiracy '76
Ten Little Indians '75
Phantom of Liberty '74
Hired to Kill '73
Hit Men '73
Hitler: The Last Ten Days '73
1931: Once Upon a Time in New York '72
Ring of Death '72
Dirty Heroes '71
Murders in the Rue Morgue '71
Danger: Diabolik '68
Bobo '67
The Honey Pot '67
Secret Agent 00 '67
The King of Hearts '66
Target for Killing '66
The Agony and the Ecstasy '65
Thunderball '65
Von Ryan's Express '65

Teco Celio
The Truce '96
Trois Couleurs: Rouge '94

Teresa Celli
The Asphalt Jungle '50
The Black Hand '50

Antoinette Cellier
River of Unrest '37
Late Extra '35

Caroline Cellier (1945-)
L'Eleve '95
Farinelli '94
Petit Con '84
Pain in the A— '77
This Man Must Die '70

Frank Cellier (1884-1948)
The Magic Bow '47
Cottage to Let '41
Non-Stop New York '37
O.H.M.S. '37
The Man Who Lived Again '36
Nine Days a Queen '36
The Passing of the Third Floor Back '36
Rhodes '36
The 39 Steps '35

Peter Cellier
Fergie & Andrew: Behind Palace Doors '93
One Against the Wind '91
And the Ship Sails On '83
Sister Dora '77
Man Friday '75
Luther '74

Nicholas Celozzi
Hidden Obsession '92
Slaughterhouse Rock '88

Petr Cepek
The Elementary School '91
My Sweet Little Village '86

Daniel Cerney
Children of the Corn 3: Urban Harvest '95
Demonic Toys '90

Mike Cerrone
Me, Myself, and Irene '00
Outside Providence '99
Kingpin '96

Claude Cerval
Any Number Can Win '63
The Cousins '59

Carlos Cervantes
Fugitive Champion '99
Wheels of Terror '90

Gino Cervi (1901-74)
Full Hearts & Empty Pockets '63
Mistress of the World '59
The Naked Maja '59
Les Miserables '52
Little World of Don Camillo '51
The Forbidden Christ '50
Fabiola '48

Valentina Cervi
James Dean '01
Artemisia '97

Renzo Cesana (1907-70)
For the First Time '59
The Naked Maja '59
Stromboli '50

Michael Ceveris
The Mexican '01
A Woman, Her Men and Her Futon '92
Rock 'n' Roll High School Forever '91

Lacey Chabert
Not Another Teen Movie '01
Tart '01
Lost in Space '98

Amadee Chabot
Autopsy of a Ghost '67
Muscle Beach Party '64

Tom Chadbon (1946-)
Devices and Desires '91
Dance with a Stranger '85
The Beast Must Die '75

June Chadwick (1950-)
The Return of Spinal Tap '92
Rebel Storm '90
Headhunter '89
The Evil Below '87
Quiet Thunder '87
This Is Spinal Tap '84
Forbidden World '82
Golden Lady '79

Sarah Chadwick (1960-)
Journey to the Center of the Earth '99
The Adventures of Priscilla, Queen of the Desert '94
Gross Misconduct '93

Suzy Chaffee
Fire and Ice '87
Snowblind '78

George Chakiris (1933-)
Pale Blood '91
Return to Fantasy Island '77
The Hot Line '69
The Young Girls of Rochefort '68
Is Paris Burning? '66
633 Squadron '64
Diamond Head '62
West Side Story '61

Kathleen Chalfant (1945-)
A Death in the Family '02
David Searching '97
A Price above Rubies '97
Jumpin' at the Boneyard '92

Feodor Chaliapin, Jr. (1907-92)
The Church '98
The Inner Circle '91
The King's Whore '90
Stanley and Iris '90
Moonstruck '87
The Name of the Rose '86

Garry Chalk
Lone Hero '02
My Husband's Secret Life '98
The Spree '96

Sarah Chalke (1977-)
Y2K '99
I've Been Waiting for You '98
Our Mother's Murder '97
Dead Ahead '96
Robin of Locksley '95
City Boy '93

William Challee (1904-89)
Zachariah '70
Billy the Kid Versus Dracula '66
Desperate '47

Georges Chamarat (1901-82)
Fernandel the Dressmaker '57
Diabolique '55
The French Touch '54

Howland Chamberlain (1911-)
Francis the Talking Mule '49
The Best Years of Our Lives '46

Richard Chamberlain (1935-)
Bird of Prey '95
Ordeal in the Arctic '93
The Return of the Musketeers '89
The Bourne Identity '88
Casanova '87
Allan Quatermain and the Lost City of Gold '86
King Solomon's Mines '85
The Thorn Birds '83
Murder by Phone '82
Shogun '80
Centennial '78
The Swarm '78
The Last Wave '77
The Man in the Iron Mask '77
The Slipper and the Rose '76
The Four Musketeers '75
The Count of Monte Cristo '74
The Three Musketeers '74
The Towering Inferno '74
Lady Caroline Lamb '73
The Music Lovers '71
Julius Caesar '70
The Madwoman of Chaillot '69
Petulia '68
Portrait of a Lady '67

Carrie Chambers
Karate Cop '93
The Divine Enforcer '91

Justin Chambers (1970-)
The Musketeer '01
The Wedding Planner '01
Liberty Heights '99

Marilyn Chambers (1952-)
Bikini Bistro '94
Party Incorporated '89
Cassie '87
My Therapist '84
Angel of H.E.A.T. '82
Rabid '77

Michael "Boogaloo Shrimp" Chambers
Breakin' '84
Breakin' 2: Electric Boogaloo '84

Wheaton Chambers
Big Chase '54
Prowler '51

Jo Champa (1969-)
Direct Hit '93
The Family '87
Salome '85

Gower Champion (1921-80)
Jupiter's Darling '55
Three for the Show '55
Give a Girl a Break '53
Lovely to Look At '52
Show Boat '51
Mr. Music '50

Marge Champion (1921-)
The Party '68
The Swimmer '68
Jupiter's Darling '55
Three for the Show '55
Give a Girl a Break '53
Lovely to Look At '52
Mr. Music '50

Michael Champion
Dead Cold '96
Operation Intercept '95
Private Wars '93
The Swordsman '92
The Heroes of Desert Storm '91
One Man Out '89

Dennis Chan
Kickboxer 3: The Art of War '92
Kickboxer '89

Jackie Chan (1954-)
Rush Hour 2 '01
Shanghai Noon '00
Gen-X Cops '99
Gorgeous '99
Jackie Chan's Who Am I '98
Mr. Nice Guy '98
Rush Hour '98
An Alan Smithee Film: Burn, Hollywood, Burn '97
Jackie Chan's First Strike '96
Rumble in the Bronx '96
The Legend of Drunken Master '94
Crime Story '93
Supercop 2 '93
Supercop '92
Twin Dragons '92
Operation Condor '91
The Prisoner '90
Miracles '89
Dragons Forever '88
Project A: Part 2 '87
Operation Condor 2: The Armour of the Gods '86
Half a Loaf of Kung Fu '85
Heart of Dragon '85
Police Story '85
Protector '85
Cannonball Run 2 '84
Eagle's Shadow '84
Fantasy Mission Force '84
Project A '83
Dragon Lord '82
The Big Brawl '80
Young Master '80
Young Tiger '80
New Fist of Fury '76
Enter the Dragon '73
Master with Cracked Fingers '71

Kim Chan
The Corruptor '99
Who's the Man? '93
American Shaolin: King of the Kickboxers 2 '92

Michael Paul Chan
Spy Game '01
Once in the Life '00
The Insider '99
Molly '99
U.S. Marshals '98
Falling Down '93
The Joy Luck Club '93
Rapid Fire '92
Thousand Pieces of Gold '91

Philip Chan
Hard-Boiled '92
Twin Dragons '92

Naomi Chance (1930-)
Terror Ship '54
Three Stops to Murder '53
The Gambler & the Lady '52
Wings of Danger '52

Anna Chancellor
Crush '02
Longitude '00
Heart '99
The Man Who Knew Too Little '97
Pride and Prejudice '95

Norman Chancer
Local Hero '83
Victor/Victoria '82

Chick Chandler (1905-88)
The Lost Continent '51
Seven Doors to Death '44
Action in the North Atlantic '43
Rhythm Parade '43
Baby Face Morgan '42
Blondie in Society '41
Mistaken Identity '36
Tango '36
Circumstantial Evidence '35
Melody Cruise '32

George Chandler (1898-1985)
Westward the Women '51
The Next Voice You Hear '50
Behind the Mask '46
Strange Impersonation '46
Roxie Hart '42
Arizona '40
Beau Geste '39
Lady Killer '33
The Light of Western Stars '30

Helen Chandler (1906-65)
Mr. Boggs Steps Out '38
Christopher Strong '33
Dracula '31

Janet Chandler
Million Dollar Haul *'35*
Rough Riding Rangers *'35*
Jeff Chandler (1918-61)
Merrill's Marauders *'62*
Return to Peyton Place *'61*
The Jayhawkers *'59*
Man in the Shadow *'57*
Away All Boats *'56*
War Arrow *'53*
Because of You *'52*
Red Ball Express *'52*
Flame of Araby *'51*
Broken Arrow *'50*
John Chandler
Jaws of Death *'76*
Ride the High Country *'62*
John Davis Chandler
The Ultimate Thrill *'74*
Alligator Alley *'72*
Shoot Out *'71*
Karen Mayo Chandler
Death Feud *'89*
Stripped to Kill II: Live Girls *'89*
Kyle Chandler (1965-)
Angel's Dance *'99*
Convict Cowboy *'95*
Pure Country *'92*
Lane Chandler (1899-1972)
Money Madness *'47*
Laura *'44*
Rustler's Hideout *'44*
Wild Horse Phantom *'44*
Sergeant York *'41*
Pony Post *'40*
Heroes of the Alamo *'37*
Sea Racketeers *'37*
The Lawless Nineties *'36*
Winds of the Wasteland *'36*
Deluge *'33*
Lone Bandit *'33*
The Outlaw Tamer *'33*
Trouble Busters *'33*
The Single Standard *'29*
Simon Chandler
Incognito *'97*
The Man Who Knew Too Little *'97*
Middlemarch *'93*
Who's Who *'78*
Tanis Chandler
Spook Busters *'48*
Lured *'47*
Helene Chanel (1941-)
Place in Hell *'65*
Samson and the 7 Miracles of the World *'62*
Maciste in Hell *'60*
Lon Chaney, Sr. (1883-1930)
The Bushwackers *'52*
The Unholy Three *'30*
Where East Is East *'29*
West of Zanzibar *'28*
Mockery *'27*
The Unknown *'27*
The Monster *'25*
The Phantom of the Opera *'25*
The Unholy Three *'25*
He Who Gets Slapped *'24*
The Hunchback of Notre Dame *'23*
The Shock *'23*
Flesh and Blood *'22*
The Light of Faith *'22*
Oliver Twist *'22*
Shadows *'22*
The Trap *'22*
Outside the Law *'21*
Nomads of the North *'20*
The Penalty *'20*
False Faces *'18*
The Scarlet Car *'17*
Oubliette *'14*
Lon Chaney, Jr. (1906-73)
Dracula vs. Frankenstein *'71*
The Female Bunch *'69*
Buckskin *'68*
Alien Massacre *'67*
Hillbillies in a Haunted House *'67*
Apache Uprising *'66*
Johnny Reno *'66*
House of the Black Death *'65*
Spider Baby *'64*
The Haunted Palace *'63*
Face of the Screaming Werewolf *'59*
The Defiant Ones *'58*
Cyclops *'56*
Daniel Boone: Trail Blazer *'56*
The Indestructible Man *'56*
Manfish *'56*
Pardners *'56*
I Died a Thousand Times *'55*
The Indian Fighter *'55*
Not as a Stranger *'55*
Big Chase *'54*
Passion *'54*
A Lion Is in the Streets *'53*
Behave Yourself! *'52*
The Black Castle *'52*
High Noon *'52*
Springfield Rifle *'52*
Bride of the Gorilla *'51*
Flame of Araby *'51*
Only the Valiant *'50*
Abbott and Costello Meet Frankenstein *'48*
My Favorite Brunette *'47*
Here Come the Co-Eds *'45*
House of Dracula *'45*
Strange Confession *'45*
Cobra Woman *'44*
Dead Man's Eyes/Pillow of Death *'44*
House of Frankenstein *'44*
The Mummy's Curse *'44*
The Mummy's Ghost *'44*
Weird Woman/Frozen Ghost *'44*
Calling Dr. Death/Strange Confession *'43*
Son of Dracula *'43*
Frankenstein Meets the Wolfman *'42*
The Ghost of Frankenstein *'42*
The Mummy's Tomb *'42*
Billy the Kid *'41*
Man Made Monster *'41*
Overland Mail *'41*
Riders of Death Valley *'41*
The Wolf Man *'41*
One Million B.C. *'40*
Of Mice and Men *'39*
Cheyenne Rides Again *'38*
Undersea Kingdom *'36*
Sixteen Fathoms Deep *'34*
The Three Musketeers *'33*
Bird of Paradise *'32*
Last Frontier *'32*
Sylvia Chang (1953-)
The Red Violin *'98*
Eat Drink Man Woman *'94*
Twin Dragons *'92*
Mad Mission 3 *'84*
Carol Channing (1921-)
Thumbelina *'94 (V)*
Happily Ever After *'93 (V)*
Shinbone Alley *'70 (V)*
Thoroughly Modern Millie *'67*
Stockard Channing (1944-)
Life or Something Like It *'02*
The Business of Strangers *'01*
A Girl Thing *'01*
Isn't She Great *'00*
The Truth About Jane *'00*
Where the Heart Is *'00*
The Baby Dance *'98*
Practical Magic *'98*
Twilight *'98*
An Unexpected Life *'97*
The First Wives Club *'96*
Lily Dale *'96*
Moll Flanders *'96*
An Unexpected Family *'96*
Up Close and Personal *'96*
Edie & Pen *'95*
Smoke *'95*
To Wong Foo, Thanks for Everything, Julie Newmar *'95*
Married to It *'93*
Six Degrees of Separation *'93*
Bitter Moon *'92*
The Applegates *'89*
Perfect Witness *'89*
Staying Together *'89*
Tidy Endings *'88*
A Time of Destiny *'88*
Echoes in the Darkness *'87*
Heartburn *'86*
The Men's Club *'86*
Not My Kid *'85*
Table Settings *'84*
Without a Trace *'83*
Safari 3000 *'82*
The Fish that Saved Pittsburgh *'79*
Silent Victory: The Kitty O'Neil Story *'79*
The Cheap Detective *'78*
Grease *'78*
The Big Bus *'76*
The Hospital *'71*
Rosalind Chao (1949-)
What Dreams May Come *'98*
The End of Violence *'97*
The Joy Luck Club *'93*
Memoirs of an Invisible Man *'92*
Thousand Pieces of Gold *'91*
White Ghost *'88*
The Terry Fox Story *'83*
Twirl *'81*
The Big Brawl *'80*
Chinese Web *'78*
Winston Chao
Eat Drink Man Woman *'94*
The Wedding Banquet *'93*
Damian Chapa (1963-)
Hell's Gate *'01*
Cypress Edge *'99*
Hitman's Run *'99*
Sometimes They Come Back ... For More *'99*
Footsteps *'98*
Midnight Blue *'96*
Saints and Sinners *'95*
Street Fighter *'94*
Blood In ... Blood Out: Bound by Honor *'93*
Billy Chapin
The Night of the Hunter *'55*
Tobor the Great *'54*
Jonathan Chapin
Prison for Children *'93*
Twice Dead *'88*
Miles Chapin (1954-)
The People vs. Larry Flynt *'96*
Get Crazy *'83*
The Funny Farm *'82*
Pandemonium *'82*
The Funhouse *'81*
French Postcards *'79*
Bless the Beasts and Children *'71*
Robert Chapin
Dragon Fury 2 *'96*
Dragon Fury *'95*
Ring of Steel *'94*
Ben Chaplin (1970-)
Birthday Girl *'02*
Murder by Numbers *'02*
Lost Souls *'00*
The Thin Red Line *'98*
Washington Square *'97*
The Return of the Borrowers *'96*
The Truth about Cats and Dogs *'96*
Feast of July *'95*
A Fatal Inversion *'92*
Carmen Chaplin
All About the Benjamins *'02*
The Serpent's Kiss *'97*
Ma Saison Preferee *'93*
Charles Chaplin, Jr. (1925-68)
Girls' Town *'59*
High School Confidential *'58*
Fangs of the Wild *'54*
Charlie Chaplin (1889-1977)
Man in the Silk Hat *'83*
Days of Thrills and Laughter *'61*
The Chaplin Revue *'58*
A King in New York *'57*
Limelight *'52*
Monsieur Verdoux *'47*
The Great Dictator *'40*
Modern Times *'36*
City Lights *'31*
The Gold Rush *'25*
The Kid *'21*
The Circus *'19*
Three Charlies and One Phoney! *'18*
The Adventurer *'17*
The Cure *'17*
The Floorwalker *'17*
The Immigrant *'17*
Burlesque on Carmen *'16*
The Count *'16*
Easy Street *'16*
The Fireman *'16*
One A.M. *'16*
Pawnshop *'16*
The Rink *'16*
The Vagabond *'16*
Charlie Chaplin: Night at the Show *'15*
Charlie Chaplin ... Our Hero! *'15*
Tramp & a Woman *'15*
Tillie's Punctured Romance *'14*
Geraldine Chaplin (1944-)
Mary, Mother of Jesus *'99*
To Walk with Lions *'99*
Cousin Bette *'97*
Mother Teresa: In the Name of God's Poor *'97*
The Odyssey *'97*
Crimetime *'96*
Jane Eyre *'96*
Gulliver's Travels *'95*
Home for the Holidays *'95*
The Age of Innocence *'93*
A Foreign Field *'93*
Chaplin *'92*
Duel of Hearts *'92*
The Children *'90*
The Return of the Musketeers *'89*
The Moderns *'88*
White Mischief *'88*
Bolero *'82*
Voyage en Douce *'81*
The Mirror Crack'd *'80*
Mama Turns a Hundred *'79*
A Wedding *'78*
The Word *'78*
Elisa, Vida Mia *'77*
Roseland *'77*
Welcome to L.A. *'77*
Buffalo Bill & the Indians *'76*
Cria *'76*
In Memoriam *'76*
The Four Musketeers *'75*
Nashville *'75*
The Three Musketeers *'74*
Zero Population Growth *'72*
Cop-Out *'67*
I Killed Rasputin *'67*
Doctor Zhivago *'65*
Josephine Chaplin (1949-)
Jack the Ripper *'76*
Shadow Man *'75*
Escape to the Sun *'72*
The Canterbury Tales *'71*
L'Odeur des Fauves *'66*
Sydney Chaplin (1885-1965)
The Chaplin Revue *'58*
Charley's Aunt *'25*
The Man on the Box *'25*
Three Charlies and One Phoney! *'18*
Sydney Chaplin (1926-)
Satan's Cheerleaders *'77*
The Sibling *'72*
The Woman Hunter *'72*
A Countess from Hong Kong *'67*
Abdulla the Great *'56*
Land of the Pharaohs *'55*
Limelight *'52*
Alexander Chapman
Lilies *'96*
Princes in Exile *'90*
Constance Chapman
My Friend Walter *'93*
In Celebration *'75*
Daniel Chapman (1952-94)
Philadelphia *'93*
Death Collector *'89*
Exquisite Corpses *'88*
Edward Chapman (1901-77)
The Young and the Guilty *'58*
Bhowani Junction *'56*
X The Unknown *'56*
Madeleine *'50*
Man on the Run *'49*
The October Man *'48*
Convoy *'40*
Juno and the Paycock *'30*
Graham Chapman (1941-89)
Monty Python's The Meaning of Life *'83*
Yellowbeard *'83*
The Secret Policeman's Other Ball *'82*
Secret Policeman's Private Parts *'81*
Monty Python's Life of Brian *'79*
The Odd Job *'78*
Monty Python and the Holy Grail *'75*
And Now for Something Completely Different *'72*
The Magic Christian *'69*
John Cleese on How to Irritate People *'68*
Helen Chapman
Hopalong Cassidy: Borrowed Trouble *'48*
Outlaw Roundup *'44*
Judith Chapman
Fire on the Amazon *'93*
Dead Space *'90*
And God Created Woman *'88*
Scalpel *'76*
Lonny (Loni) Chapman (1921-)
Nightwatch *'96*
The China Lake Murders *'90*
52 Pick-Up *'86*
He Who Walks Alone *'78*
Alexander: The Other Side of Dawn *'77*
Moving Violation *'76*
Witch Who Came from the Sea *'76*
Where the Red Fern Grows *'74*
Take the Money and Run *'69*
The Birds *'63*
Marguerite Chapman (1918-99)
The Amazing Transparent Man *'60*
Flight to Mars *'52*
Man Bait *'52*
The Green Promise *'49*
Coroner Creek *'48*
Destroyer *'43*
Spy Smasher *'42*
Spy Smasher Returns *'42*
Charlie Chan at the Wax Museum *'40*
Mark Lindsay Chapman
Bram Stoker's The Mummy *'97*
Stephen King's The Langoliers *'95*
Separate Lives *'94*
American Gothic *'88*
Sean Chapman
Hellbound: Hellraiser 2 *'88*
Hellraiser *'87*
Dave Chappelle (1973-)
Undercover Brother *'02*
Screwed *'00*
Blue Streak *'99*
200 Cigarettes *'98*
You've Got Mail *'98*
Con Air *'97*
Half-Baked *'97*
Woo *'97*
The Nutty Professor *'96*
Getting In *'94*
Robin Hood: Men in Tights *'93*
Patricia Charbonneau (1959-)
Kiss the Sky *'98*
Portraits of a Killer *'95*
K2: The Ultimate High *'92*
RoboCop 2 *'90*
Brain Dead *'89*
Call Me *'88*
Disaster at Silo 7 *'88*
Shakedown *'88*
Desert Hearts *'86*
Stalking Danger *'86*
Tara Charendoff
Rugrats in Paris: The Movie *'00 (V)*
The Rugrats Movie *'98 (V)*
Family Pictures *'93*
Cyd Charisse (1921-)
Swimsuit *'89*
That's Dancing! *'85*
Maroc 7 *'67*
The Silencers *'66*
Two Weeks in Another Town *'62*
Black Tights *'60*
Party Girl *'58*
Silk Stockings *'57*
Meet Me in Las Vegas *'56*
It's Always Fair Weather *'55*
Brigadoon *'54*
Deep in My Heart *'54*
The Band Wagon *'53*
Singin' in the Rain *'52*
On an Island with You *'48*
Words and Music *'48*
The Harvey Girls *'46*
Josh Charles (1971-)
Muppets from Space *'99*
Meeting Daddy *'98*
Little City *'97*
Crosswords *'96*
The Grave *'95*
Norma Jean and Marilyn *'95*
Pie in the Sky *'95*
Things to Do in Denver When You're Dead *'95*
Coldblooded *'94*
Threesome *'94*
Cooperstown *'93*
Crossing the Bridge *'92*
Don't Tell Mom the Babysitter's Dead *'91*
Dead Poets Society *'89*
Ray Charles (1930-)
Limit Up *'89*
The Blues Brothers *'80*
Ballad in Blue *'66*
RuPaul Charles (1960-)
The Truth About Jane *'00*
But I'm a Cheerleader *'99*
EDtv *'99*
An Unexpected Life *'97*
The Brady Bunch Movie *'95*
A Mother's Prayer *'95*
Wigstock: The Movie *'95*
Ian Charleson (1949-90)
Codename Kyril *'91*
Opera *'88*
Troubles *'88*
Louisiana *'87*
Car Trouble *'86*

Greystoke: The Legend of Tarzan, Lord of the Apes *'84*
Gandhi *'82*
Chariots of Fire *'81*
Charo (1942-)
Thumbelina *'94 (V)*
Moon over Parador *'88*
The Concorde: Airport '79 *'79*
Charpin (1887-1944)
Well-Digger's Daughter *'46*
Le Schpountz *'38*
Cesar *'36*
The Baker's Wife *'33*
Fanny *'32*
Marius *'31*
Henri Charriere
Queen of Diamonds *'80s*
Butterfly Affair *'71*
Spencer Charters (1875-1943)
Mr. Boggs Steps Out *'38*
Three Comrades *'38*
Lady from Nowhere *'36*
The Ghost Walks *'34*
Palmy Days *'31*
The Bat Whispers *'30*
Melanie Chartoff (1955-)
Rugrats in Paris: The Movie *'00 (V)*
The Rugrats Movie *'98 (V)*
Kenny Rogers as the Gambler, Part 3: The Legend Continues *'87*
Doin' Time *'85*
Stoogemania *'85*
Having It All *'82*
Alden Chase (1902-82)
Buried Alive *'39*
Prescott Kid *'36*
Cowboy Millionaire *'35*
Annazette Chase
Fist *'79*
Truck Turner *'74*
Charley Chase (1893-1940)
Block-heads *'38*
Kelly the Second *'36*
Sons of the Desert *'33*
King of the Wild Horses *'24*
Three Charlies and One Phoney! *'18*
Chevy Chase (1943-)
Orange County *'02*
Snow Day *'00*
Dirty Work *'97*
Vegas Vacation *'96*
Man of the House *'95*
Cops and Robbersons *'94*
Last Action Hero *'93*
Hero *'92*
Memoirs of an Invisible Man *'92*
Nothing But Trouble *'91*
Fletch Lives *'89*
National Lampoon's Christmas Vacation *'89*
Caddyshack 2 *'88*
Funny Farm *'88*
Three Amigos *'86*
Fletch *'85*
National Lampoon's European Vacation *'85*
Sesame Street Presents: Follow That Bird *'85*
Spies Like Us *'85*
Deal of the Century *'83*
National Lampoon's Vacation *'83*
Modern Problems *'81*
Under the Rainbow *'81*
Caddyshack *'80*
Oh, Heavenly Dog! *'80*
Seems Like Old Times *'80*
Foul Play *'78*
Tunnelvision *'76*
The Groove Tube *'72*
Frank Chase
Attack of the 50 Foot Woman *'58*
The Creature Walks among Us *'56*
Ilka Chase
The Big Knife *'55*
The Animal Kingdom *'32*
Jeffrey Chase
In the Shadows *'01*
Scream of the Demon Lover *'71*
Jennifer Chase
Death Screams *'83*
Balboa *'82*
House of Death *'82*
Stephan Chase
The Dying Truth *'91*
The Black Arrow *'84*
Macbeth *'71*
Steve Chase (1902-82)
Eden 2 *'93*
Eden 3 *'93*
Eden 4 *'93*
Eden *'92*
The Blob *'58*
Anil Chatterjee
The Big City *'63*
Two Daughters *'61*
Soumitra Chatterjee (1934-)
The Home and the World *'84*
Distant Thunder *'73*
Days and Nights in the Forest *'70*
Charulata *'64*
Two Daughters *'61*
Devi *'60*
The World of Apu *'59*
Ruth Chatterton
Dodsworth *'36*
Female *'33*
Daniel Chatto
Little Dorrit, Film 1: Nobody's Fault *'88*
Little Dorrit, Film 2: Little Dorrit's Story *'88*
Charlotte Chatton
Stand-Ins *'97*
Hellraiser 4: Bloodline *'95*
Francois Chau (1959-)
Beverly Hills Ninja *'96*
Teenage Mutant Ninja Turtles 2: The Secret of the Ooze *'91*
Emmanuelle Chaulet
All the Vermeers in New York *'91*
Boyfriends & Girlfriends *'88*
Lilyan Chauvin
Tyson *'95*
Silent Night, Deadly Night *'84*
Bloodlust *'59*
Lost, Lonely, and Vicious *'59*
Richard Chaves
Night Eyes 2 *'91*
Predator *'87*
Maury Chaykin (1949-)
The Doorbell Rang: A Nero Wolfe Mystery *'01*
Varian's War *'01*
The Art of War *'00*
The Golden Spiders: A Nero Wolfe Mystery *'00*
What's Cooking? *'00*
Entrapment *'99*
Jacob Two Two Meets the Hooded Fang *'99*
Joan of Arc *'99*
Let the Devil Wear Black *'99*
Mystery, Alaska *'99*
Jerry and Tom *'98*
The Mask of Zorro *'98*
A Life Less Ordinary *'97*
Love and Death on Long Island *'97*
Mouse Hunt *'97*
Pale Saints *'97*
Strip Search *'97*
The Sweet Hereafter *'96*
Cutthroat Island *'95*
Devil in a Blue Dress *'95*
Sugartime *'95*
Unstrung Heroes *'95*
Camilla *'94*
Whale Music *'94*
Money for Nothing *'93*
Northern Extremes *'93*
Sommersby *'93*
Hero *'92*
Leaving Normal *'92*
The Adjuster *'91*
George's Island *'91*
The Pianist *'91*
Cold Comfort *'90*
Dances with Wolves *'90*
Mr. Destiny *'90*
Breaking In *'89*
Millennium *'89*
Higher Education *'88*
Iron Eagle 2 *'88*
Stars and Bars *'88*
Wild Thing *'87*
Canada's Sweetheart: The Saga of Hal C. Banks *'85*
Def-Con 4 *'85*
Mrs. Soffel *'84*
July Group *'70s*
Mariann (Marie-Anne) Chazel (1951-)
The Visitors *'95*
Next Year If All Goes Well *'83*
French Fried Vacation *'79*
Don Cheadle (1964-)
Ocean's Eleven *'01*
Rush Hour 2 *'01*
Swordfish *'01*
Family Man *'00*
Mission to Mars *'00*
Traffic *'00*
A Lesson Before Dying *'99*
Bulworth *'98*
Out of Sight *'98*
The Rat Pack *'98*
Boogie Nights *'97*
Volcano *'97*
Rebound: The Legend of Earl "The Goat" Manigault *'96*
Rosewood *'96*
Devil in a Blue Dress *'95*
Things to Do in Denver When You're Dead *'95*
Lush Life *'94*
Colors *'88*
Hamburger Hill *'87*
Andrea Checchi (1916-74)
Waterloo *'71*
Black Sunday *'60*
The Walls of Malapaga *'49*
Chubby Checker
Calendar Girl *'93*
Purple People Eater *'88*
Molly Cheek
American Pie 2 *'01*
Smoke Signals *'98*
Derk Cheetwood (1973-)
Frailty *'02*
U-571 *'00*
Micheline Cheirel
Cornered *'45*
Carnival in Flanders *'35*
Michael Chekhov (1891-1955)
Rhapsody *'54*
Spectre of the Rose *'46*
Spellbound *'45*
Tsilla Chelton
Tatie Danielle *'91*
Peppermint Soda *'77*
Chang Chen
Crouching Tiger, Hidden Dragon *'00*
Happy Together *'96*
Joan Chen (1961-)
What's Cooking? *'00*
In a Class of His Own *'99*
Precious Find *'96*
Judge Dredd *'95*
Wild Side *'95*
The Hunted *'94*
On Deadly Ground *'94*
Temptation of a Monk *'94*
Golden Gate *'93*
Heaven and Earth *'93*
The Killing Beach *'92*
Deadlock *'91*
Strangers *'91*
The Blood of Heroes *'89*
The Last Emperor *'87*
Night Stalker *'87*
Tai-Pan *'86*
Dim Sum: A Little Bit of Heart *'85*
Terry Chen
Almost Famous *'00*
Crash & Byrnes *'99*
Tina Chen
Lady from Yesterday *'85*
Paper Man *'71*
Alice's Restaurant *'69*
Adam Cheng
Painted Skin *'93*
Fantasy Mission Force *'84*
Zu: Warriors from the Magic Mountain *'83*
Kent Cheng
The Bodyguard from Beijing *'94*
Crime Story *'93*
Sex and Zen *'93*
Once Upon a Time in China *'91*
Cher (1946-)
Tea with Mussolini *'99*
If These Walls Could Talk *'96*
Faithful *'95*
Ready to Wear *'94*
The Player *'92*
Mermaids *'90*
Moonstruck *'87*
Suspect *'87*
The Witches of Eastwick *'87*
Mask *'85*
Silkwood *'83*
Come Back to the Five & Dime Jimmy Dean, Jimmy Dean *'82*
Good Times *'67*
Patrice Chereau (1944-)
Lucie Aubrac *'98*
The Last of the Mohicans *'92*
Danton *'82*
Nikolai Cherkasov (1903-66)
Don Quixote *'57*
Ivan the Terrible, Part 2 *'46*
Ivan the Terrible, Part 1 *'44*
Alexander Nevsky *'38*
Baltic Deputy *'37*
Virginia Cherrill (1908-96)
Late Extra *'35*
City Lights *'31*
George Chesebro (1888-1959)
Check Your Guns *'48*
Stage to Mesa City *'48*
Cheyenne Takes Over *'47*
Fighting Vigilantes *'47*
Return of the Lash *'47*
Boss of Rawhide *'44*
Devil Riders *'44*
Holt of the Secret Service *'42*
Trigger Men *'41*
Red River Valley *'36*
Roamin' Wild *'36*
Laramie Kid *'35*
The Miracle Rider *'35*
Wild Mustang *'35*
In Old Santa Fe *'34*
The Silver Bullet *'34*
Fighting Champ *'33*
Wolf Blood *'25*
Patrick Chesnais
After Sex *'97*
La Lectrice *'88*
Craig Chester (1965-)
Kiss Me, Guido *'97*
I Shot Andy Warhol *'96*
Frisk *'95*
Grief *'94*
Swoon *'91*
Vanessa Lee Chester (1984-)
The Lost World: Jurassic Park 2 *'97*
Harriet the Spy *'96*
A Little Princess *'95*
Morris Chestnut (1969-)
Like Mike *'02*
The Brothers *'01*
Two Can Play That Game *'01*
The Best Man *'99*
G.I. Jane *'97*
Under Siege 2: Dark Territory *'95*
The Ernest Green Story *'93*
Boyz N the Hood *'91*
The Last Boy Scout *'91*
Daphne Cheung
Jack Higgins' Midnight Man *'96*
Jack Higgins' On Dangerous Ground *'95*
Jacky Cheung
Meltdown *'95*
Wicked City *'92*
Once Upon a Time in China *'91*
A Bullet in the Head *'90*
Leslie Cheung (1956-)
Happy Together *'96*
Temptress Moon *'96*
The Phantom Lover *'95*
The Bride with White Hair *'93*
The Bride with White Hair 2 *'93*
Farewell My Concubine *'93*
A Better Tomorrow, Part 2 *'88*
A Better Tomorrow, Part 1 *'86*
Maggie Cheung (1964-)
In the Mood for Love *'00*
Chinese Box *'97*
Irma Vep *'96*
The Executioners *'93*
Green Snake *'93*
The Heroic Trio *'93*
Supercop *'92*
Twin Dragons *'92*
Song of the Exile *'90*
Paper Marriage *'88*
Project A: Part 2 *'87*
Police Story *'85*
Roy Cheung
The Mission *'99*
Organized Crime & Triad Bureau *'93*
Wicked City *'92*
Kevin Timothy Chevalia
Homeward Bound 2: Lost in San Francisco *'96*
Homeward Bound: The Incredible Journey *'93*
Folks! *'92*
Maurice Chevalier (1888-1972)
The Sorrow and the Pity *'71*
Monkeys, Go Home! *'66*
A New Kind of Love *'63*
In Search of the Castaways *'62*
Panic Button *'62*
Fanny *'61*
Black Tights *'60 (N)*
Breath of Scandal *'60*
Can-Can *'60*
Gigi *'58*
Love in the Afternoon *'57*
The Merry Widow *'34*
Richard Chevolleau
True Blue *'01*
No Alibi *'00*
The Wall *'99*
Tracked *'98*
Blood Brothers *'97*
Rude *'96*
Indian Summer *'93*
Arno Chevrier
Agnes Browne *'99*
The Red Dwarf *'99*
Laureen Chew
Dim Sum: A Little Bit of Heart *'85*
Chan Is Missing *'82*
Minoru Chiaki (1917-99)
Face of Another *'66*
Godzilla Raids Again *'59*
The Human Condition: Road to Eternity *'59*
The Hidden Fortress *'58*
Throne of Blood *'57*
Seven Samurai *'54*
Rashomon *'51*
Dominic Chianese (1931-)
Unfaithful *'02*
Once in the Life *'00*
The Cradle Will Rock *'99*
Went to Coney Island on a Mission from God...Be Back by Five *'98*
Gotti *'96*
Looking for Richard *'96*
Love Is All There Is *'96*
Night Falls on Manhattan *'96*
If Lucy Fell *'95*
The Night We Never Met *'93*
The Public Eye *'92*
Out for Justice *'91*
The Lost Capone *'90*
Q & A *'90*
Second Sight *'89*
And Justice for All *'79*
Firepower *'79*
On the Yard *'79*
All the President's Men *'76*
Dog Day Afternoon *'75*
The Godfather, Part 2 *'74*
Roy Chiao (1927-99)
Summer Snow *'94*
Bloodsport *'88*
Walter Chiari (1924-91)
Girl Under the Sheet *'60s*
Husband Hunting *'60s*
Bonjour Tristesse *'57*
Bellissima *'51*
Sofiko Chiaureli
Ashik Kerib *'88*
The Color of Pomegranates *'69*
Sonny Chiba (1939-)
Body Count *'95*
Immortal Combat *'94*
Aces: Iron Eagle 3 *'92*
Shogun's Ninja *'83*
Virus *'82*
Hunter in the Dark *'80*
The Bodyguard *'76*
Sister Street Fighter *'76*
Return of the Street Fighter *'74*
The Street Fighter *'74*
The Street Fighter's Last Revenge *'74*
Terror Beneath the Sea *'66*
Etienne Chicot
36 Fillete *'88*
Osa *'85*
Michael Chiklis (1963-)
Silent Witness *'99*
Body and Soul *'98*
Soldier *'98*
The Taxman *'98*
Wired *'89*
Jeremy Child (1944-)
Frenchman's Creek *'98*
Mosley *'98*
Behind the Lines *'97*
Sharpe's Enemy *'94*
Patricia Childress
Larry McMurtry's Dead Man's Walk *'96*
Shake, Rattle & Rock! *'94*
Linden Chiles (1933-)
Deadline Assault *'90*
To Heal a Nation *'88*
Forbidden World *'82*
Red Flag: The Ultimate Game *'81*
Death Be Not Proud *'75*
Who Is the Black Dahlia? *'75*
Texas across the River *'66*
Lois Chiles (1947-)
Speed 2: Cruise Control *'97*

Bliss '96
The Babysitter '95
Curdled '95
Lush Life '94
Diary of a Hitman '91
Twister '89
Broadcast News '87
Creepshow 2 '87
Raw Courage '84
Moonraker '79
Coma '78
Death on the Nile '78

Simon Chilvers
Ground Zero '88
The Big Hurt '87
Windrider '86
The Dunera Boys '85

Andre Chimene
Computer Beach Party '88
The Outing '87

Joey Chin
King of New York '90
China Girl '87

Tsai Chin (1938-)
Red Corner '97
The Joy Luck Club '93
Rentadick '72
The Virgin Soldiers '69
The Castle of Fu Manchu '68
Kiss and Kill '68
You Only Live Twice '67
Invasion '65

William Ching (1913-89)
Terror in the Haunted House '58
Give a Girl a Break '53
Never Wave at a WAC '52
Pat and Mike '52
D.O.A. '49
The Wistful Widow of Wagon Gap '47

Kieu Chinh (1939-)
Catfish in Black Bean Sauce '00
Riot in the Streets '96
The Joy Luck Club '93
Hamburger Hill '87
The Girl Who Spelled Freedom '86
The Children of An Lac '80
Operation C.I.A. '65

Nicholas Chinlund (1961-)
Training Day '01
Chutney Popcorn '99
Frogs for Snakes '98
A Brother's Kiss '97
Con Air '97
Mr. Magoo '97
Rough Riders '97
Eraser '96
Letter to My Killer '95
Unveiled '94
Red Shoe Diaries 4: Auto Erotica '93
The Ambulance '90

Erik Chitty
Doctor Zhivago '65
First Men in the Moon '64

Anna Chlumsky (1980-)
Gold Diggers: The Secret of Bear Mountain '95
My Girl 2 '94
Trading Mom '94
My Girl '91

John Cho
Earth vs. the Spider '01
Pavilion of Women '01
Yellow '98

Margaret Cho (1969-)
Spent '00
The Tavern '00
Ground Control '98
Face/Off '97
Sweethearts '97
The Doom Generation '95
It's My Party '95

Tim Choate (1954-)
Pearl Harbor '01
Live Nude Girls '95
Blind Witness '89
The Discovery Program '89
Spy '89
Def-Con 4 '85
First Time '82

Jun Chong
Street Soldiers '91
Silent Assassins '88

Marcus Chong
The Matrix '99
Panther '95

Rae Dawn Chong (1962-)
The Visit '00
Smalltime '99
Mask of Death '97
Protector '97
Starlight '97
The Break '95
Boca '94
Boulevard '94
Hideaway '94
Power of Attorney '94
Dangerous Relations '93
Time Runner '92
Common Bonds '91
Denial: The Dark Side of Passion '91
Prison Stories: Women on the Inside '91
When the Party's Over '91
Amazon '90
Curiosity Kills '90
Tales from the Darkside: The Movie '90
The Borrower '89
Far Out Man '89
The Principal '87
The Squeeze '87
Running out of Luck '86
Soul Man '86
American Flyers '85
Badge of the Assassin '85
City Limits '85
The Color Purple '85
Commando '85
Fear City '85
Beat Street '84
Cheech and Chong's The Corsican Brothers '84
Choose Me '84
Quest for Fire '82

Thomas Chong (1938-)
The Wash '01
Half-Baked '97
McHale's Navy '97
National Lampoon's Senior Trip '95
Ferngully: The Last Rain Forest '92 (V)
Spirit of '76 '91
Far Out Man '89
Tripwire '89
After Hours '85
Cheech and Chong's The Corsican Brothers '84
Cheech and Chong: Still Smokin' '83
Yellowbeard '83
Cheech and Chong: Things Are Tough All Over '82
Cheech and Chong's Nice Dreams '81
Cheech and Chong's Next Movie '80
Cheech and Chong's Up in Smoke '79

Sarita Choudhury (1966-)
3 A.M. '01
A Perfect Murder '98
Subway Stories '97
Kama Sutra: A Tale of Love '96
Down Came a Blackbird '94
The House of the Spirits '93
Wild West '93
Mississippi Masala '92

Etchika Choureau
Darby's Rangers '58
Lafayette Escadrille '58

China Chow (1974-)
Head Over Heels '01
The Big Hit '98

Valerie Chow
Chungking Express '95
Meltdown '95

Navin Chowdhry
The Seventh Coin '92
Madame Sousatzka '88

Ranjit (Chaudry) Chowdhry
Fire '96
Bleeding Hearts '94
The Night We Never Met '93
Mississippi Masala '92
Lonely in America '90

Joseph Chrest
The Underneath '95
King of the Hill '93

Emmanuelle Chriqui
A. I.: Artificial Intelligence '01
On the Line '01
100 Girls '00
Snow Day '00

Marilyn Chris
Joe Torre: Curveballs Along the Way '97
Honeymoon Killers '70

Chad Christ
Jawbreaker '98
No Laughing Matter '97

David Christensen
Turn of the Blade '97
Over the Wire '95

Erika Christensen (1982-)
Can of Worms '00
Traffic '00

Hayden Christensen (1981-)
Star Wars: Episode 2—Attack of the Clones '02
Life as a House '01

Jesper Christensen
Uprising '01
The White Lioness '96
Sofie '92

Claudia Christian (1965-)
Atlantis: The Lost Empire '01 (V)
Final Voyage '99
The Haunting of Hell House '99
The Substitute 3: Winner Takes All '99
Mercenary 2: Thick and Thin '97
The Adventures of a Gnome Named Gnorm '93
Hexed '93
The Dark Backward '91
Strays '91
Mad About You '90
Maniac Cop 2 '90
Arena '89
Mom '89
Tale of Two Sisters '89
Clean and Sober '88
Never on Tuesday '88
The Hidden '87

John Christian (1957-)
Airboss '00
The Outfit '93
Comrades in Arms '91
Covert Action '88
Mob War '88

Linda Christian (1924-)
Full Hearts & Empty Pockets '63
The V.I.P.'s '63
The Devil's Hand '61
Athena '54

Michael Christian
Hard Knocks
Private Obsession '94
Mid Knight Rider '84
The Legend of Frank Woods '77
Poor Pretty Eddie '73

Mady Christians (1900-51)
All My Sons '48
Letter from an Unknown Woman '48
Tender Comrade '43

Benjamin Christiansen (1879-1959)
The Only Way '70
Haxan: Witchcraft through the Ages '22

Audrey Christie (1912-89)
Harper Valley P.T.A. '78
Frankie and Johnny '65
Splendor in the Grass '61
Keeper of the Flame '42

Julie Christie (1941-)
No Such Thing '01
The Miracle Maker: The Story of Jesus '00 (V)
Afterglow '97
Dragonheart '96
Hamlet '96
The Railway Station Man '92
Fools of Fortune '90
Secret Obsession '88
Miss Mary '86
Power '86
Separate Tables '83
Heat and Dust '82
Return of the Soldier '82
Heaven Can Wait '78
Demon Seed '77
Nashville '75
Shampoo '75
Don't Look Now '73
The Go-Between '71
McCabe & Mrs. Miller '71
Petulia '68
Far from the Madding Crowd '67
Fahrenheit 451 '66
Darling '65
Doctor Zhivago '65
Billy Liar '63

Katia Christine
Cosmos: War of the Planets '80
Spirits of the Dead '68

Virginia Christine (1920-96)
Billy the Kid Versus Dracula '66
One Man's Way '63
The Cobweb '55
The Inner Circle '46
The Killers '46
The Mummy's Curse '44

Eric Christmas (1916-2000)
Air Bud '97
Mouse Hunt '97
The Challengers '93
Child of Darkness, Child of Light '91
Home Is Where the Hart Is '88
Porky's Revenge '85
All of Me '84
The Philadelphia Experiment '84
Porky's 2: The Next Day '83
Porky's '82
Middle Age Crazy '80
Attack of the Killer Tomatoes '77
Harold and Maude '71
Johnny Got His Gun '71

Debra Christofferson
Mouse Hunt '97
Round Numbers '91

Francoise Christophe (1925-)
Borsalino '70
The King of Hearts '66
Walk into Hell '57

Bojesse Christopher
Out in Fifty '99
Meatballs 4 '92
Point Break '91

Dennis Christopher (1955-)
It's My Party '95
Operation Intercept '95
The Silencers '95
Boys Life '94
Plughead Rewired: Circuitry Man 2 '94
H.P. Lovecraft's Necronomicon: Book of the Dead '93
False Arrest '92
Circuitry Man '90
Doppelganger: The Evil Within '90
Stephen King's It '90
A Sinful Life '89
Jake Speed '86
Didn't You Hear? '83
Jack & the Beanstalk '83
Don't Cry, It's Only Thunder '82
Chariots of Fire '81
Alien Predators '80
Fade to Black '80
The Last Word '80
Breaking Away '79
California Dreaming '79
Elvis: The Movie '79
A Wedding '78
September 30, 1955 '77
The Young Graduates '71

Thom Christopher
Jackie, Ethel, Joan: The Kennedy Women '01
Peril '00
Deathstalker 3 '89
Wizards of the Lost Kingdom '85

William (Bill) Christopher (1932-)
M*A*S*H: Goodbye, Farewell & Amen '83
For the Love of It '80
With Six You Get Eggroll '68

Kathy Christopherson
Executive Target '97
Guyver 2: Dark Hero '94

Dorothy Christy (1906-)
Sons of the Desert '33
Convicted '32
Big Business Girl '31
Night Life in Reno '31

Emily Chu
A Better Tomorrow, Part 1 '86
Heart of Dragon '85

Paul Chubb
Road to Nhill '97
The Well '97
Cosi '95
Sweet Talker '91

Christy Chung
The Bodyguard from Beijing '94
The Bride with White Hair 2 '93

David Chung
Color of a Brisk and Leaping Day '95
The Ballad of Little Jo '93
Combination Platter '93

Mok Siu Chung
Once Upon a Time in China III '93
Once Upon a Time in China II '92

Thomas Haden Church (1960-)
3000 Miles to Graceland '01
The Specials '00
Free Money '99
Dean Koontz's Mr. Murder '98
Dying to Get Rich '98
George of the Jungle '97
One Night Stand '97
Tales from the Crypt Presents Demon Knight '94
Tombstone '93

Berton Churchill (1876-1940)
Stagecoach '39
Danger on the Air '38
Wide Open Faces '38
In Old Chicago '37
The Dark Hour '36
Dimples '36
Mistaken Identity '36
Sing Sing Nights '35
Bachelor Bait '34
The Mysterious Rider '33
The Big Stampede '32
False Faces '32

Donald Churchill
The Hound of the Baskervilles '83
Victim '61

Marguerite Churchill (1909-2000)
Dracula's Daughter '36
Ambassador Bill '31
Big Trail '30

Julien Ciamaca
My Father's Glory '91
My Mother's Castle '91

Eduardo Ciannelli (1889-1969)
MacKenna's Gold '69
Houseboat '58
Monster from Green Hell '58
Mambo '55
The Creeper '48
Heartbeat '46
The Mask of Dimitrios '44
Passage to Marseilles '44
They Got Me Covered '43
Cairo '42
They Met in Bombay '41
Doctor Satan's Robot '40
Foreign Correspondent '40
Kitty Foyle '40
The Mummy's Hand '40
Mysterious Doctor Satan '40
Strange Cargo '40
Bulldog Drummond's Bride '39
Gunga Din '39
Law of the Underworld '38
Marked Woman '37

Eddie Cibrian
Say It Isn't So '01
But I'm a Cheerleader '99

Robert Cicchini
The Watcher '00
Age Isn't Everything '91

Jude Ciccolella
High Crimes '02
Beloved '98
Mad Love '95
Glengarry Glen Ross '92
Shakedown '88

Phyllis Cicero
America's Dream '95
Steele's Law '91

Anna Ciepielewska
Passenger '61
Mother Joan of the Angels '60

Jennifer Ciesar
Red Shoe Diaries 7: Burning Up '96
Red Shoe Diaries: Strip Poker '96
Inner Sanctum 2 '94
Lovers' Lovers '94

Diane Cilento (1933-)
Winner Takes All '86
The Wicker Man '75
Zero Population Growth '72
Negatives '68
Hombre '67
The Agony and the Ecstasy '65
Rattle of a Simple Man '64
Tom Jones '63
The Naked Edge '61
The Admirable Crichton '57

Leonardo Cimino
Trusting Beatrice '92
Penn and Teller Get Killed '90

Kelly Cinnante
Christmas in Connecticut '92
True Love '89

Luis Miguel Cintra
The Convent '95
Abraham's Valley '93

Charles Cioffi (1935-)
The Shadow Conspiracy '96
Newsies '92
Used People '92
Peter Gunn '89
Remo Williams: The Adventure Begins '85
All the Right Moves '83
Missing '82
Time After Time '79
The Arab Conspiracy '76
Return to Earth '76
The Don Is Dead '73
The Thief Who Came to Dinner '73
Klute '71
Shaft '71

Augusta Ciolli
Love with the Proper Stranger '63
Marty '55

Roberto Citran
Nora '00
The Truce '96

Franco Citti (1935-)
Arabian Nights '74
The Decameron '70
Porcile '69
Oedipus Rex '67
Mamma Roma '62
Accatone! '61

Jany Clair (1938-)
Hercules against the Moon Men '64
Conquest of Mycene '63
Planets Against Us '61

Cyrielle Claire (1955-)
The Worker and the Hairdresser '96
Control '87
Code Name: Emerald '85
Sword of the Valiant '83
Le Professionnel '81

Ina Claire (1892-1985)
Ninotchka '39
Three Broadway Girls '32

Rony Clanton
Def by Temptation '90
The Education of Sonny Carson '74

Gordon Clapp (1948-)
Skeletons in the Closet '00
The Rage: Carrie 2 '99
Stand Off '93
Small Sacrifices '89
Termini Station '89
Eight Men Out '88
Matewan '87
Return of the Secaucus 7 '80

Eric Clapton
Chuck Berry: Hail! Hail! Rock 'n' Roll '87
Water '85
Tommy '75

Diane Clare
Vulture '67
Beast of Morocco '66
Plague of the Zombies '66
The Haunting '63
Whistle down the Wind '61
The Reluctant Debutante '58
Murder on the Campus '52

Mary Clare (1894-1970)
Mambo '55
Moulin Rouge '52
The Three Weird Sisters '48
The Night Has Eyes '42
The Challenge '38
The Mill on the Floss '37
Young and Innocent '37
Lorna Doone '34
Power '34

O.B. Clarence (1870-1955)
Great Expectations '46
On Approval '44
The Courageous Mr. Penn '41
Pygmalion '38
The Scarlet Pimpernel '34
A Shot in the Dark '33

Aime Clariond (1894-1960)
Monsieur Vincent '47
De Mayerling a Sarajevo '40
La Marseillaise '37

Angela Clark (1912-)
The Seven Little Foys '55
Houdini '53
Miracle of Our Lady of Fatima '52

Anthony Clark (1964-)
Murder She Purred: A Mrs. Murphy Mystery '98 (V)
Hourglass '95
Teresa's Tattoo '94
The Thing Called Love '93
Dogfight '91

Blake Clark
Little Nicky '00
The Waterboy '98
Grave Secrets: The Legacy of Hilltop Drive '92
Ladybugs '92
Shakes the Clown '92
Johnny Handsome '89

Bobby Clark (1888-1960)
The Goldwyn Follies '38
Clark & McCullough '33

Brett (Baxter) Clark
Stormy Nights '97
Deathstalker 4: Match of Titans '92
Inner Sanctum '91
Eye of the Eagle '87
Alien Warrior '85

Brian Patrick Clark
Private Wars '93
Sleepaway Camp 2: Unhappy Campers '88

Buddy Clark
Melody Time '48 (V)
Seven Days' Leave '42

Candy Clark (1947-)
Cherry Falls '00
Buffy the Vampire Slayer '92
Cool As Ice '91
Original Intent '91
The Blob '88
At Close Range '86
Cat's Eye '85
Hambone & Hillie '84
Amityville 3: The Demon '83
Blue Thunder '83
Johnny Belinda '82
Q (The Winged Serpent) '82
National Lampoon Goes to the Movies '81
Rodeo Girl '80
More American Graffiti '79
The Big Sleep '78
Citizens Band '77
James Dean '76
The Man Who Fell to Earth '76
American Graffiti '73
Fat City '72

Cliff Clark (1889-1953)
Home of the Brave '49
The Wagons Roll at Night '41

Dane Clark (1913-98)
Last Rites '88
Blood Song '82
James Dean '76
Murder on Flight 502 '75
Say Goodbye, Maggie Cole '72
The McMasters '70
Blackout '54
Paid to Kill '54
Thunder Pass '54
The Gambler & the Lady '52
Moonrise '48
A Stolen Life '46
Hollywood Canteen '44
Action in the North Atlantic '43
Destination Tokyo '43
The Glass Key '42

Daniel Clark
Model Behavior '00
Grizzly Falls '99

Davison Clark
Rogue's Gallery '44
Dishonored '31

Dick Clark
Deadman's Curve '78
Wild in the Streets '68

Ed Clark
Bog '84
Bedtime for Bonzo '51

Eugene C. Clark
Turn It Up '00
TekWar '94
Trial and Error '92

Frank Clark
Roaring Ranch '30
The Spoilers '14

Fred Clark (1914-68)
The Horse in the Gray Flannel Suit '68
Dr. Goldfoot and the Bikini Machine '66
Zotz! '62
Bells Are Ringing '60
Joyful Laughter '60
Passionate Thief '60
It Started with a Kiss '59
The Mating Game '59
Don't Go Near the Water '57
Solid Gold Cadillac '56
The Court Martial of Billy Mitchell '55
Daddy Long Legs '55
Abbott and Costello Meet the Keystone Kops '54
The Caddy '53
Here Come the Girls '53
Three for Bedroom C '52
The Lemon Drop Kid '51
The Jackpot '50
Sunset Boulevard '50
Flamingo Road '49

Greydon Clark (1943-)
Bad Bunch '76
Satan's Sadists '69

Harvey Clark (1885-1938)
Law for Tombstone '35
Peck's Bad Boy '34
Shriek in the Night '33
Red Headed Woman '32

Judy Clark
Kid Sister '45
South of Santa Fe '42

Kenneth (Ken) Clark (1932-)
Tarzana, the Wild Girl '72
Desert Commandos '67
Attack of the Giant Leeches '59
Between Heaven and Hell '56

Liddy Clark
Deadly Possession '88
Kitty and the Bagman '82

Marlene Clark
The Baron '88
The Beast Must Die '75
Switchblade Sisters '75
Ganja and Hess '73
Night of the Cobra Woman '72
Slaughter '72

Matt Clark (1936-)
Kiss of Fire '98
Homegrown '97
Trilogy of Terror 2 '96
Barbarians at the Gate '93
Frozen Assets '92
The Harvest '92
Class Action '91
Back to the Future, Part 3 '90
Blind Witness '89
The Horror Show '89
Kenny Rogers as the Gambler, Part 3: The Legend Continues '87
Let's Get Harry '87
The Quick and the Dead '87
Out of the Darkness '85
Return to Oz '85
Tuff Turf '85
The Adventures of Buckaroo Banzai Across the Eighth Dimension '84
Country '84
Love Letters '83
In the Custody of Strangers '82
Chasing Dreams '81
An Eye for an Eye '81
Legend of the Lone Ranger '81
Ruckus '81
Brubaker '80
The Driver '78
The Outlaw Josey Wales '76
The Execution of Private Slovik '74
Melvin Purvis: G-Man '74
Emperor of the North Pole '73
The Great Northfield Minnesota Raid '72

Mystro Clark
Storm Catcher '99
Chairman of the Board '97

Oliver Clark (1939-)
Nightlife '90
Ernest Saves Christmas '88
One Cooks, the Other Doesn't '83
Mikey & Nicky '76
A Star Is Born '76

Petula Clark (1932-)
Goodbye, Mr. Chips '69
Finian's Rainbow '68
The Runaway Bus '54
Made in Heaven '52
The Promoter '52

Roger Clark (1909-78)
Monster '78
Girls in Chains '43
The Lady Is Willing '42

Spencer (Treat) Clark (1987-)
Gladiator '00
Unbreakable '00
Arlington Road '99
Double Jeopardy '99

Steve Clark (1891-1954)
Range Renegades '48
Fighting Vigilantes '47
Border Bandits '46
The Stranger from Pecos '45
Range Law '44
Pinto Canyon '40
Boothill Brigade '37
Gun Lords of Stirrup Basin '37
West of Nevada '36

Susan Clark (1940-)
Snowbound: The Jim and Jennifer Stolpa Story '94
Porky's '82
The Choice '81
The Double Negative '80
Murder by Decree '79
Nobody's Perfekt '79
The North Avenue Irregulars '79
Promises in the Dark '79
City on Fire '78
Airport '75 '75
The Apple Dumpling Gang '75
Babe! '75
Night Moves '75
Showdown '73
Skin Game '71
Valdez Is Coming '71
Colossus: The Forbin Project '70
Skullduggery '70
Tell Them Willie Boy Is Here '69
Coogan's Bluff '68
Madigan '68

Wallis (Clarke) Clark (1886-1961)
Penny Serenade '41
Star Reporter '39
Postal Inspector '36

Andrew Clarke
Les Patterson Saves the World '90
Anzacs: The War Down Under '85

Angela Clarke (1969-)
Land and Freedom '95
Letter to Brezhnev '86
House of Wax '53
Mrs. Mike '49

Caitlin Clarke
Penn and Teller Get Killed '90
Dragonslayer '81

Gary Clarke (1936-)
Bull of the West '89
Confessions of Tom Harris '72
Date Bait '60
Missile to the Moon '59
How to Make a Monster '58

Graham Clarke
Armageddon: The Final Challenge '94
Laser Mission '90

Hope Clarke
Seventeen Again '00
Piece of the Action '77

Lenny Clarke (1953-)
What's the Worst That Could Happen? '01
Me, Myself, and Irene '00
Rounders '98
There's Something about Mary '98
Two If by Sea '95

Mae Clarke (1907-92)
Because of You '52
Pat and Mike '52
King of the Rocketmen '49
Lost Planet Airmen '49
Here Come the Waves '45
Flying Tigers '42
Hats Off '37
Great Guy '36
Lady Killer '33
Penthouse '33
Frankenstein '31
The Front Page '31
Public Enemy '31

Melinda (Mindy) Clarke
Soldier of Fortune Inc. '97
Spawn '97
Killer Tongue '96
Return of the Living Dead 3 '93
Return to Two Moon Junction '93
Hot Under the Collar '91

Richard Clarke
Identity Crisis '90
A Night to Remember '58

Robert Clarke (1920-)
Alienator '89
Attack from Mars '88
Secret File of Hollywood '62
Terror of the Bloodhunters '62
Beyond the Time Barrier '60
Hideous Sun Demon '59
The Astounding She-Monster '58
Sword of Venus '53
Tales of Robin Hood '52
The Man from Planet X '51
Bedlam '45
The Enchanted Cottage '45

Robin Clarke
White Wolves 3: Cry of the White Wolf '98
Cyberzone '95
Inseminoid '80

Warren Clarke (1947-)
Blow Dry '00
Greenfingers '00
A Respectable Trade '98
Joseph '95
Hands of a Murderer '90
Mandela '87
Gulag '85
Cold Room '84
Lassiter '84
Enigma '82
Firefox '82
From a Far Country: Pope John Paul II '81
The Great Riviera Bank Robbery '79
S.O.S. Titanic '79
Antony and Cleopatra '73
O Lucky Man! '73
A Clockwork Orange '71

D. A. Clarke-Smith
The Ghoul '34
The Man Who Knew Too Much '34

Lana Clarkson (1962-)
Vice Girls '96
The Haunting of Morella '91
Barbarian Queen 2: The Empress Strikes Back '89
Wizards of the Lost Kingdom 2 '89
Barbarian Queen '85
Blind Date '84
Deathstalker '83

Patricia Clarkson (1960-)
Joe Gould's Secret '00
The Pledge '00
The Green Mile '99
Simply Irresistible '99
High Art '98
Playing by Heart '98
Pharoah's Army '95
Caught in the Act '93
Four Eyes and Six Guns '93
An American Story '92
Legacy of Lies '92
Blind Man's Bluff '91
The Old Man and the Sea '90
Tune in Tomorrow '90
The Dead Pool '88
Rocket Gibraltar '88

Robert Clary (1926-)
Holocaust Survivors...Remembrance of Love '83
New Faces of 1952 '54

Christian Clavier
Just Visiting '01
The Visitors '95
This Sweet Sickness '77

Nicholas Clay (1946-2000)
Merlin '98
The Odyssey '97
Sleeping Beauty '89
Lionheart '87
The Hound of the Baskervilles '83
Evil under the Sun '82
Excalibur '81
Lady Chatterley's Lover '81
Lovespell '79

Jill Clayburgh (1944-)
My Little Assassin '99
Fools Rush In '97
Going All the Way '97
Sins of the Mind '97
Honor Thy Father and Mother: The True Story of the Menendez Brothers '94
Day of Atonement '93
Firestorm: 72 Hours in Oakland '93
Naked in New York '93
Rich in Love '93
Whispers in the Dark '92
Shy People '87
Miles to Go '86
Where Are the Children? '85
Hanna K. '83
I'm Dancing as Fast as I Can '82
First Monday in October '81
It's My Turn '80
Starting Over '79
An Unmarried Woman '78
Semi-Tough '77
Griffin and Phoenix: A Love Story '76
Silver Streak '76
The Art of Crime '75

Hustling '75
The Terminal Man '74
The Thief Who Came to Dinner '73
Portnoy's Complaint '72
The Wedding Party '69

John Clayton
Out of the Body '88
High Tide '87
Warm Nights on a Slow-Moving Train '87
Freedom '81

June Clayworth (-1993)
At Sword's Point '51
Dick Tracy Meets Gruesome '47
Criminal Court '46

John Cleese (1939-)
The Adventures of Pluto Nash '02
Harry Potter and the Sorcerer's Stone '01
Rat Race '01
Isn't She Great '00
The Out-of-Towners '99
The World Is Not Enough '99
George of the Jungle '97 (V)
Fierce Creatures '96
Mr. Toad's Wild Ride '96
Mary Shelley's Frankenstein '94
Rudyard Kipling's The Jungle Book '94
The Swan Princess '94 (V)
Splitting Heirs '93
The Strange Case of the End of Civilization As We Know It '93
An American Tail: Fievel Goes West '91 (V)
Bullseye! '90
The Big Picture '89
Erik the Viking '89
A Fish Called Wanda '88
Clockwise '86
Silverado '85
Privates on Parade '84
Monty Python's The Meaning of Life '83
Whoops Apocalypse '83
Yellowbeard '83
The Secret Policeman's Other Ball '82
The Great Muppet Caper '81
Secret Policeman's Private Parts '81
Time Bandits '81
Monty Python's Life of Brian '79
Monty Python and the Holy Grail '75
Romance with a Double Bass '74
And Now for Something Completely Different '72
The Statue '71
The Magic Christian '69
The Bliss of Mrs. Blossom '68
John Cleese on How to Irritate People '68

Ellen Cleghorne
Coyote Ugly '00
Little Nicky '00
Mr. Wrong '95

Jimmy Clem
Town That Dreaded Sundown '76
Winterhawk '76

Paul Clemens
They're Playing with Fire '84
The Beast Within '82
The Family Man '79
Promises in the Dark '79

Christian Clemenson (1959-)
Lost and Found '99
And the Band Played On '93
Hero '92
Bad Influence '90

Aurore Clement
For Sale '98
The Eighties '83
Paris, Texas '83
Invitation au Voyage '82
Toute Une Nuit '82
Les Rendez-vous D'Anna '78
Le Crabe Tambour '77

Suzanne Clement
2 Seconds '98
The Confessional '95

Pierre Clementi (1942-99)
Hideous Kinky '99
Sweet Movie '75
Steppenwolf '74
The Conformist '71
Porcile '69
Partner '68
Belle de Jour '67

John Clements (1910-88)
The Silent Enemy '58
Train of Events '49
This England '42
Convoy '40
The Four Feathers '39
South Riding '37

Stanley Clements
Johnny Holiday '49
Underworld Scandal '47

Clarence Clemons (1941-)
Swing '98
Fatal Instinct '93

David Clennon (1943-)
The Visit '00
From the Earth to the Moon '98
Tecumseh: The Last Warrior '95
And the Band Played On '93
Light Sleeper '92
Man Trouble '92
Matinee '92
The Trouble with Dick '88
Conspiracy: The Trial of the Chicago Eight '87
The Couch Trip '87
Legal Eagles '86
Sweet Dreams '85
Falling in Love '84
Hanna K. '83
The Right Stuff '83
Star 80 '83
Missing '82
The Thing '82
Go Tell the Spartans '78

Corinne Clery (1950-)
Fatal Fix '80s
The Switch '89
Dangerous Obsession '88
Yor, the Hunter from the Future '83
Insanity '82
The Con Artists '80
Moonraker '79
Love by Appointment '76
The Story of O '75

Carol Cleveland (1943-)
Monty Python's The Meaning of Life '83
Monty Python's Life of Brian '79
Monty Python and the Holy Grail '75
And Now for Something Completely Different '72

George Cleveland (1886-1957)
Trigger, Jr. '50
Miss Grant Takes Richmond '49
The Wistful Widow of Wagon Gap '47
Little Giant '46
The Show-Off '46
Abroad with Two Yanks '44
Dead Man's Eyes/Pillow of Death '44
It Happened Tomorrow '44
Texas Legionnaires '43

Valley of the Sun '42
Playmates '41
Two-Faced Woman '41
Drums of Fu Manchu '40
Hidden Enemy '40
Midnight Limited '40
The Abe Lincoln of Ninth Avenue '39
Mutiny in the Big House '39
Ghost Town Riders '38
I Conquer the Sea '36
Revolt of the Zombies '36
Monte Carlo Nights '34

Philippe Clevenot
Place Vendome '98
The Hairdresser's Husband '92
Celine and Julie Go Boating '74

Jimmy Cliff
Club Paradise '86
The Harder They Come '72

John Cliff
The Three Stooges Meet Hercules '61
Teenage Frankenstein '58

Jack Clifford (1880-1956)
King of the Pecos '36
The Man from Gun Town '36
The Revenge Rider '35
South of Santa Fe '32
Sunrise Trail '31
Sweet Adeline '26

Richard Clifford
Carrington '95
Much Ado about Nothing '93
Henry V '89

Faith Clift
Savage Journey '83
Cataclysm '81

Montgomery Clift (1920-66)
Judgment at Nuremberg '61
The Misfits '61
Suddenly, Last Summer '59
Lonelyhearts '58
The Young Lions '58
Raintree County '57
Indiscretion of an American Wife '54
From Here to Eternity '53
I Confess '53
A Place in the Sun '51
The Big Lift '50
The Heiress '49
Red River '48
The Search '48

Elmer Clifton (1892-1949)
Intolerance '16
The Birth of a Nation '15

Brett Climo
Blackwater Trail '95
Archer's Adventure '85

Renee Cline
Fatal Exposure '90
Invasion Force '90

George Clinton (1941-)
Good Burger '97
P.C.U. '94
Graffiti Bridge '90

Colin Clive (1898-1937)
History Is Made at Night '37
The Bride of Frankenstein '35
Mad Love '35
Jane Eyre '34
Christopher Strong '33
Frankenstein '31

E.E. Clive (1879-1940)
The Adventures of Sherlock Holmes '39
Bulldog Drummond's Bride '39
Bulldog Drummond's Secret Police '39
The Hound of the Baskervilles '39
The Little Princess '39

Arrest Bulldog Drummond '38
Bulldog Drummond's Peril '38
Bulldog Drummond Escapes '37
Personal Property '37
The Charge of the Light Brigade '36
The Dark Hour '36
Libeled Lady '36
The Bride of Frankenstein '35
The Mystery of Edwin Drood '35
The Invisible Man '33

John Clive
A Clockwork Orange '71
Yellow Submarine '68 (V)

Teagan Clive
Vice Academy 2 '90
Alienator '89
Sinbad of the Seven Seas '89

Al Cliver (1951-)
Demonia '90
2020 Texas Gladiators '85
The Beyond '82
Forever Emmanuelle '82
Alien Contamination '81
The Black Cat '81
Zombie '80
Big Boss '77
Mr. Scarface '77
Rulers of the City '71

Kristen (Kristin) Cloke (1970-)
Final Destination '00
The Rage '96
Caged Fear '92

George Clooney (1961-)
Ocean's Eleven '01
Spy Kids '01
O Brother Where Art Thou? '00
The Perfect Storm '00
South Park: Bigger, Longer and Uncut '99 (V)
Three Kings '99
Out of Sight '98
The Thin Red Line '98
Batman and Robin '97
The Peacemaker '97
One Fine Day '96
From Dusk Till Dawn '95
The Magic Bubble '93
Red Surf '90
Return of the Killer Tomatoes! '88
Return to Horror High '87
Combat Academy '86

Rosemary Clooney (1928-)
Deep in My Heart '54
Red Garters '54
White Christmas '54
Here Come the Girls '53

Del Close (1935-99)
Mommy 2: Mommy's Day '96
Opportunity Knocks '90
The Blob '88
Big Town '87
Ferris Bueller's Day Off '86

Eric Close
Follow the Stars Home '01
The Magnificent Seven '98

Glenn Close (1947-)
Rodgers & Hammerstein's South Pacific '01
Baby '00 (N)
102 Dalmatians '00
Things You Can Tell Just by Looking at Her '00
Cookie's Fortune '99
Sarah, Plain and Tall: Winter's End '99
Tarzan '99 (V)
Air Force One '97
In the Gloaming '97
Paradise Road '97
Mars Attacks! '96
101 Dalmatians '96
Mary Reilly '95

Serving in Silence: The Margarethe Cammermeyer Story '95
The Paper '94
The House of the Spirits '93
Sarah, Plain and Tall: Skylark '93
Hook '91
Meeting Venus '91
Sarah, Plain and Tall '91
Hamlet '90
Reversal of Fortune '90
Immediate Family '89
Dangerous Liaisons '88
Light Years '88 (V)
Fatal Attraction '87
The Jagged Edge '85
Maxie '85
The Natural '84
The Stone Boy '84
The Big Chill '83
The World According to Garp '82
Orphan Train '79
Too Far to Go '79

John Close
The Slime People '63
Beginning of the End '57
Above and Beyond '53

John Scott Clough
Phantoms '97
What Ever Happened To... '93
Gross Anatomy '89
Fast Forward '84

Raymond Cloutier
Karmina '96
Riel '79

Vera Clouzot
Diabolique '55
Wages of Fear '55

David Clover
Zipperface '92
Ten Speed '76

Jennifer Cluff
Kiss or Kill '97
Death Games '82

Martin Clunes
Lorna Doone '01
Saving Grace '00
The Acid House '98
Shakespeare in Love '98
Sweet Revenge '98

George Clutesi
Nightwing '79
Prophecy '79

Francois Cluzet (1955-)
Late August, Early September '98
The Swindle '97
French Kiss '95
The Horseman on the Roof '95
Ready to Wear '94
L'Enfer '93
Olivier, Olivier '92
Chocolat '88
The Story of Women '88
Too Beautiful for You '88
Round Midnight '86
The Horse of Pride '80

Andy Clyde (1892-1967)
Hopalong Cassidy: Borrowed Trouble '48
Hopalong Cassidy: Dangerous Venture '48
Hopalong Cassidy: False Paradise '48
Hopalong Cassidy: Silent Conflict '48
Hopalong Cassidy: Sinister Journey '48
Hopalong Cassidy: The Dead Don't Dream '48
Sundown Riders '48
Hopalong Cassidy: Hoppy's Holiday '47
Hopalong Cassidy: The Marauders '47
Hopalong Cassidy: Unexpected Guest '47
Hopalong Cassidy: The Devil's Playground '46
Mystery Man '44
Texas Masquerade '44

Border Patrol '43
Colt Comrades '43
False Colors '43
Hopalong Cassidy: Riders of the Deadline '43
Hoppy Serves a Writ '43
Leather Burners '43
Lost Canyon '43
Border Vigilantes '41
Doomed Caravan '41
In Old Colorado '41
Outlaws of the Desert '41
Riders of the Timberline '41
Twilight on the Trail '41
Bad Lands '39
Red Lights Ahead '36
Yellow Dust '36
Annie Oakley '35
Ships in the Night '28

Jeremy Clyde
The Musketeer '01
Kaspar Hauser '93
Splitting Heirs '93

June Clyde (1909-87)
Behind the Mask '46
Seven Doors to Death '44
Wayne Murder Case '38
Make-Up '37
She Shall Have Music '36
Hollywood Mystery '34
A Study in Scarlet '33
Branded Men '31
Morals for Women '31

Kim Coates
Black Hawk Down '01
Pearl Harbor '01
Battlefield Earth '00
Beyond Suspicion '00
Full Disclosure '00
Xchange '00
Carpool '96
Dead Silence '96
Lethal Tender '96
Unforgettable '96
Breach of Trust '95
The Outer Limits: Sandkings '95
Black Fox: Good Men and Bad '94
The Club '94
The Spider and the Fly '94
Innocent Blood '92
The Last Boy Scout '91
The Amityville Curse '90
Red Blooded American Girl '90
Smokescreen '90
Blind Fear '89
Cold Front '89

Phyllis Coates (1927-)
The Incredible Petrified World '58
Teenage Frankenstein '58
El Paso Stampede '53
Jungle Drums of Africa '53
Marshal of Cedar Rock '53
Invasion U.S.A. '52
Superman & the Mole Men '51
Blues Busters '50

Edmund Cobb (1892-1974)
Tales of Terror '62
Buffalo Bill Rides Again '47
Sunset in El Dorado '45
Texas Kid '43
Tonto Basin Outlaws '41
Danger Trails '35
Rustler's Paradise '35
Gunners & Guns '34
Gun Law '33
Wild Horse '31
Riders of the Range '24

Lee J. Cobb (1911-76)
Bull of the West '89
The Meanest Men in the West '76
That Lucky Touch '75
The Exorcist '73
Man Who Loved Cat Dancing '73
Lawman '71
The Liberation of L.B. Jones '70
Macho Callahan '70
MacKenna's Gold '69
Coogan's Bluff '68

In Like Flint '67
Our Man Flint '66
Come Blow Your Horn '63
How the West Was Won '63
The Four Horsemen of the Apocalypse '62
Exodus '60
But Not for Me '59
Green Mansions '59
The Trap '59
The Brothers Karamazov '58
Man of the West '58
Party Girl '58
The Three Faces of Eve '57
Twelve Angry Men '57
The Man in the Gray Flannel Suit '56
The Left Hand of God '55
The Racers '55
Day of Triumph '54
On the Waterfront '54
Tall Texan '53
The Fighter '52
Sirocco '51
The Dark Past '49
Call Northside 777 '48
The Miracle of the Bells '48
Boomerang '47
Captain from Castile '47
Anna and the King of Siam '46
Buckskin Frontier '43
The Song of Bernadette '43
Men of Boys Town '41
Golden Boy '39
Danger on the Air '38
Rustler's Valley '37

Randall "Tex" Cobb (1950-)
Liar Liar '96
Diggstown '92
Raw Nerve '91
Blind Fury '90
Ernest Goes to Jail '90
Buy & Cell '89
Fletch Lives '89
Raising Arizona '87
The Golden Child '86
Uncommon Valor '83

Bill Cobbs (1935-)
Enough '02
Random Hearts '99
Always Outnumbered Always Outgunned '98
Hope Floats '98
I Still Know What You Did Last Summer '98
Paulie '98
Air Bud '97
Ed '96
First Kid '96
Ghosts of Mississippi '96
Nightjohn '96
That Thing You Do! '96
Fluke '95
Kingfish: A Story of Huey P. Long '95
Man with a Gun '95
Out There '95
Pocahontas '95 (V)
Things to Do in Denver When You're Dead '95
The Hudsucker Proxy '93
The Bodyguard '92
Carolina Skeletons '92
Decoration Day '90
Dominick & Eugene '88
Trading Places '83

Roberto Cobo (1930-)
Santitos '99
Esmeralda Comes by Night '98
Cabeza de Vaca '90
Los Olvidados '50

Charles Coburn (1877-1961)
John Paul Jones '59
Around the World in 80 Days '56
Gentlemen Prefer Blondes '53
Trouble along the Way '53
Monkey Business '52
Mr. Music '50
Impact '49
Lured '47
The Paradine Case '47
Colonel Effingham's Raid '45
Rhapsody in Blue '45
Wilson '44
Heaven Can Wait '43
The More the Merrier '43
George Washington Slept Here '42
In This Our Life '42
The Devil & Miss Jones '41
Kings Row '41
The Lady Eve '41
Edison the Man '40
The Road to Singapore '40
Three Faces West '40
Bachelor Mother '39
Idiot's Delight '39
In Name Only '39
Made for Each Other '39
Stanley and Livingstone '39
The Story of Alexander Graham Bell '39
Of Human Hearts '38
Vivacious Lady '38

James Coburn (1928-)
Snow Dogs '02
Monsters, Inc. '01 (V)
Walter and Henry '01
Missing Pieces '00
Proximity '00
Noah's Ark '99
Dean Koontz's Mr. Murder '98
Payback '98
Affliction '97
The Second Civil War '97
The Cherokee Kid '96
Eraser '96
Keys to Tulsa '96
The Nutty Professor '96
Skeletons '96
The Avenging Angel '95
The Disappearance of Kevin Johnson '95
The Set Up '95
Maverick '94
A Thousand Heroes '94
A Christmas Reunion '93
Deadfall '93
The Hit List '93
Sister Act 2: Back in the Habit '93
Hugh Hefner: Once Upon a Time '92 (N)
The Player '92
Hudson Hawk '91
Young Guns 2 '90
Death of a Soldier '85
Martin's Day '85
Pinocchio '83
Crossover '82
Draw! '81
High Risk '81
Looker '81
The Baltimore Bullet '80
Loving Couples '80
Firepower '79
Goldengirl '79
The Muppet Movie '79
The Dain Curse '78
Cross of Iron '76
Midway '76
Sky Riders '76
Bite the Bullet '75
Hard Times '75
Internecine Project '73
The Last of Sheila '73
Pat Garrett & Billy the Kid '73
A Reason to Live, a Reason to Die '73
A Fistful of Dynamite '72
Candy '68
In Like Flint '67
The President's Analyst '67
Waterhole #3 '67
Dead Heat on a Merry-Go-Round '66
Our Man Flint '66
What Did You Do in the War, Daddy? '66
The Loved One '65
Major Dundee '65
The Americanization of Emily '64
Charade '63
The Great Escape '63
Hell Is for Heroes '62
The Magnificent Seven '60
Ride Lonesome '59

Michael Coby
The Bitch '78
Supersonic Man '78

Imogene Coca (1908-2001)
National Lampoon's Vacation '83
Rabbit Test '78
Under the Yum-Yum Tree '63

Richard Coca
The Truth about Cats and Dogs '96
Street Knight '93

Eddie Cochran
Go, Johnny Go! '59
The Girl Can't Help It '56

Robert Cochran
I Stand Condemned '36
Sanders of the River '35
Scrooge '35

Steve Cochran (1917-65)
Deadly Companions '61
I, Mobster '58
Il Grido '57
Carnival Story '54
Private Hell 36 '54
The Desert Song '53
Shark River '53
Jim Thorpe: All American '51
White Heat '49
A Song Is Born '48
Copacabana '47
The Best Years of Our Lives '46
The Chase '46
Wonder Man '45

Michael Cochrane
Incognito '97
Sharpe's Regiment '96
Sharpe's Eagle '93

Rory Cochrane (1972-)
Hart's War '02
The Prime Gig '00
Black & White '99
Flawless '99
Dogtown '97
The Last Don '97
Empire Records '95
The Low Life '95
Love and a .45 '94
Dazed and Confused '93
Fathers and Sons '92

Arlene Cockburn
The Acid House '98
The Governess '98
The Winter Guest '97

Gary Cockrell
Lolita '62
War Lover '62

James Coco (1929-)
That's Adequate '90
The Chair '87
Hunk '87
The Muppets Take Manhattan '84
You Can't Take It with You '84
Only When I Laugh '81
Wholly Moses! '80
Scavenger Hunt '79
The Cheap Detective '78
Murder by Death '76
Wild Party '74
Man of La Mancha '72
A New Leaf '71
End of the Road '70
The Strawberry Statement '70
Generation '69
Ensign Pulver '64

Jean Cocteau (1889-1963)
The Testament of Orpheus '59
The Storm Within '48 (N)

Camille Coduri
King Ralph '91
Nuns on the Run '90
Strapless '90
Hawks '89

Bill Cody (1891-1948)
Outlaws of the Range '36
Frontier Days '34
Ghost City '32
Mason of the Mounted '32
Texas Pioneers '32

Iron Eyes Cody (1904-99)
Spirit of '76 '91
Ernest Goes to Camp '87
Grayeagle '77
The Longest Drive '76
El Condor '70
Son of Paleface '52
Bowery Buckaroos '47
Under Nevada Skies '46
King of the Stallions '42
Whistlin' Dan '32
The Road to Yesterday '25

Kathleen (Kathy) Cody (1953-)
Charley and the Angel '73
Girls on the Road '73
Superdad '73

Lew Cody
Dishonored '31
Mickey '17

Barry Coe (1934-)
The Oval Portrait '88
Dr. Death, Seeker of Souls '73
The Cat '66
Fantastic Voyage '66
But Not for Me '59
The Bravados '58
Peyton Place '57
Love Me Tender '56

David Allen Coe
Lady Grey '82
Take This Job & Shove It '81

George Coe
Big Eden '00
The Omega Code '99
Nick and Jane '96
The End of Innocence '90
The Hollywood Detective '89
Best Seller '87
Blind Date '87
Uncle Tom's Cabin '87
A Flash of Green '85
Remo Williams: The Adventure Begins '85
Rage of Angels '83
Sessions '83
Bustin' Loose '81
Red Flag: The Ultimate Game '81

Peter Coe (1929-87)
Sands of Iwo Jima '49
House of Frankenstein '44
The Mummy's Curse '44

Paul Coeur
White Fang 2: The Myth of the White Wolf '94
Cool Runnings '93

Colleen T. Coffey
Indecent Behavior 3 '95
The Mosaic Project '95
Relentless 4 '94

Denise Coffey
Start the Revolution without Me '70
Georgy Girl '66

Elizabeth Coffey
Female Trouble '74
Pink Flamingos '72

Scott Coffey (1967-)
Mulholland Drive '01
Route 9 '98
Lost Highway '96
Breaking Free '95
Tank Girl '94
Dream Lover '93
The Temp '93
Shout '91
Montana '90
Shag: The Movie '89
Satisfaction '88
Zombie High '87

Peter Coffield
Times Square '80
The Man Without a Country '73

Frederick Coffin (1943-)
The Base '99
Andersonville '95
A Streetcar Named Desire '95
There Goes My Baby '92
Hard to Kill '89
Shoot to Kill '88
The Bedroom Window '87
Manhunt for Claude Dallas '86
One Summer Love '76

Tristram Coffin (1909-90)
Ma Barker's Killer Brood '60
Queen for a Day '51
Rodeo King and the Senorita '51
Pirates of the High Seas '50
King of the Rocketmen '49
Lost Planet Airmen '49
Jesse James Rides Again '47
Land of the Lawless '47
Where the North Begins '47
Under Nevada Skies '46
The Corpse Vanishes '42
Holt of the Secret Service '42
Meet the Mob '42
Spy Smasher '42
Spy Smasher Returns '42
Tonto Basin Outlaws '41
Up in the Air '40

Nikki Coghill
Dark Age '88
The Time Guardian '87

Frank "Junior" Coghlan (1917-)
The Adventures of Captain Marvel '41
The Fighting 69th '40
Little Red Schoolhouse '36
Red Lights Ahead '36
Kentucky Blue Streak '35
In the Money '34
Drum Taps '33
Hell's House '32
The Last of the Mohicans '32
Square Shoulders '29
Let 'er Go Gallegher '28
Marked Money '28
Yankee Clipper '27

Emma Cohen (1946-)
Bronson's Revenge '79
Horror Rises from the Tomb '72
Cannibal Man '71

J.J. (Jeffrey Jay) Cohen
Back to the Future, Part 3 '90
Back to the Future, Part 2 '89
976-EVIL '88
The Principal '87
Back to the Future '85

Kaipo Cohen
Under the Domim Tree '95
The Summer of Aviya '88

Lynn Cohen
Hurricane Streets '96
I Shot Andy Warhol '96
Walking and Talking '96
Vanya on 42nd Street '94
Manhattan Murder Mystery '93

Sammy Cohen
The Fighting 69th '40
The Phantom of the Range '38

Scott Cohen (1964-)
The 10th Kingdom '00
Gia '98
Sweet Evil '95
The Wharf Rat '95
Vibrations '94

Enrico Colantoni (1963-)
A. I.: Artificial Intelligence '01
James Dean '01
Galaxy Quest '99
Stigmata '99
The Member of the Wedding '97
Money Train '95

Nicholas Colasanto (1924-85)
Raging Bull '80
Mad Bull '77
Family Plot '76
Fat City '72

Catero Colbert
Up Against the Wall '91
Sweet Perfection '90

Claudette Colbert (1905-96)
The Love Goddesses '65
Parrish '61
Texas Lady '56
Let's Make It Legal '51
Three Came Home '50
Egg and I '47
Tomorrow Is Forever '46
Without Reservations '46
Guest Wife '45
Since You Went Away '44
So Proudly We Hail '43
The Palm Beach Story '42
Boom Town '40
Drums Along the Mohawk '39
Midnight '39
Bluebeard's Eighth Wife '38
Cleopatra '34
Imitation of Life '34
It Happened One Night '34
I Cover the Waterfront '33
The Sign of the Cross '33

Tim Colceri
Leprechaun 4: In Space '96
Full Metal Jacket '87

Ben Cole
Edge of Sanity '89
Howling 5: The Rebirth '89

Dennis Cole (1940-)
Dead End City '88
Death House '88
Pretty Smart '87
Amateur Night '85
The Barbary Coast '74
The Connection '73
Powder Keg '70

Eric Michael Cole
New Best Friend '02
White Squall '96

Gary Cole (1957-)
One Hour Photo '02
The Gift '00
From the Earth to the Moon '98
I'll Be Home for Christmas '98
Kiss the Sky '98
Office Space '98
A Simple Plan '98
Santa Fe '97
Gang Related '96
A Very Brady Sequel '96
The Brady Bunch Movie '95
Fall from Grace '94
In the Line of Fire '93
Son of the Morning Star '91
The Old Man and the Sea '90
Echoes in the Darkness '87
Fatal Vision '84

George Cole (1925-)
Mary Reilly '95
Deadline Auto Theft '83
Gone in 60 Seconds '74
Fright '71
The Vampire Lovers '70
Dr. Syn, Alias the Scarecrow '64
The Pure Hell of St. Trinian's '61
Too Many Crooks '59
Blue Murder at St. Trinian's '56
The Adventures of Sadie '55

The Belles of St. Trinian's '53
A Christmas Carol '51
Cottage to Let '41

Jacquelin Cole
Satan's Cheerleaders '77
Bad Bunch '76

Kevin Anthony Cole
Asylum '97
Undercover Cop '94

Michael Cole (1945-)
The Apostate '98
Stephen King's It '90
Nickel Mountain '85
Chuka '67

Nat King Cole (1919-65)
Cat Ballou '65
China Gate '57
Istanbul '57
Small Town Girl '53
Killer Diller '48

Natalie Cole (1950-)
Livin' for Love: The Natalie Cole Story '00
Always Outnumbered Always Outgunned '98
Cats Don't Dance '97 (V)
Lily in Winter '94

Olivia Cole (1942-)
The Women of Brewster Place '89
The Fig Tree '87
North and South Book 1 '85
Go Tell It on the Mountain '84
Some Kind of Hero '82
Coming Home '78
Roots '77

Stephenie Cole
Grey Owl '99
Open All Hours '83

Robert Coleby
The Phantom '96
In Pursuit of Honor '95
Great Expectations: The Untold Story '87
The Blue Lightning '86
Now and Forever '82
Plumber '79

Charles Coleman (1885-1951)
Grand Canyon Trail '48
Twin Beds '42
It Started with Eve '41
First Love '39
That Certain Age '38
Bachelor Apartment '31

Charlotte Coleman (1968-2001)
Beautiful People '99
Bodywork '99
Sweet Revenge '98
Twice upon a Yesterday '98
Different for Girls '96
Four Weddings and a Funeral '94
The Vacillations of Poppy Carew '94
The Young Poisoner's Handbook '94
Oranges Are Not the Only Fruit '89

Dabney Coleman (1932-)
Inspector Gadget '99
Must Be Santa '99
Stuart Little '99
Taken '99
My Date with the President's Daughter '98
You've Got Mail '98
Judicial Consent '94
Amos and Andrew '93
The Beverly Hillbillies '93
Clifford '92
There Goes the Neighborhood '92
Never Forget '91
Short Time '90
Where the Heart Is '90
Homeboy '80s
The Applegates '89
Hot to Trot! '88
Dragnet '87
Guilty of Innocence '87
Murrow '86
The Man with One Red Shoe '85
Cloak & Dagger '84
The Muppets Take Manhattan '84
WarGames '83
Tootsie '82
Young Doctors in Love '82
Callie and Son '81
Modern Problems '81
On Golden Pond '81
How to Beat the High Cost of Living '80
Melvin and Howard '80
9 to 5 '80
Nothing Personal '80
Pray TV '80
Fist '79
North Dallas Forty '79
Viva Knievel '77
Bite the Bullet '75
The Other Side of the Mountain '75
Bad Ronald '74
The Dove '74
Cinderella Liberty '73
Dying Room Only '73
The President's Plane Is Missing '71
Downhill Racer '69
The Trouble with Girls (and How to Get into It) '69
The Scalphunters '68

Gary Coleman (1968-)
Dirty Work '97
The Fantastic World of D.C. Collins '84
The Kid with the 200 I.Q. '83
Jimmy the Kid '82
The Kid with the Broken Halo '82
On the Right Track '81
Scout's Honor '80
The Kid from Left Field '79

Jack Coleman (1958-)
The Landlady '98
Foreign Student '94
Trapped in Space '94
Rubdown '93
The Return of Eliot Ness '91
Daughter of Darkness '89

Jimmy Coleman
Priest '94
Riff Raff '92

Nancy Coleman (1917-)
Edge of Darkness '43
Desperate Journey '42
Kings Row '41

Renee Coleman
Pentathlon '94
A League of Their Own '92
Return to Eden '89
Who's Harry Crumb? '89

Rosalyn Coleman
Our Song '01
Mixing Nia '98
The Piano Lesson '94

Signy Coleman
H.P. Lovecraft's Necronomicon: Book of the Dead '93
Relentless 3 '93

Michael Coles
The Satanic Rites of Dracula '73
Dracula A.D. 1972 '72

Mildred Coles
Oklahoma Badlands '48
Lady Scarface '41

Eileen Colgan
The Secret of Roan Inish '94
Quackser Fortune Has a Cousin in the Bronx '70

John Colicos (1928-2000)
Jack Higgins' The Windsor Protocol '97
Jack Higgins' Thunder Point '97
The Last Don '97
Love and Hate: A Marriage Made in Hell '90
Shadow Dancing '88
The Postman Always Rings Twice '81
The Changeling '80
Battlestar Galactica '78
Scorpio '73
Raid on Rommel '71
Doctors' Wives '70
Anne of the Thousand Days '69
Murder on Approval '56

David Colin, Jr.
Shock '79
Beyond the Door '75

Gregoire Colin (1975-)
The Dreamlife of Angels '98
Nenette and Boni '96
Fiesta '95
Son of Gascogne '95
Before the Rain '94
Pas Tres Catholique '93
Olivier, Olivier '92

Ian Colin
Never Too Late to Mend '37
Late Extra '35

Margaret Colin (1957-)
Unfaithful '02
My Husband's Double Life '01
The Adventures of Sebastian Cole '99
The Devil's Own '96
Independence Day '96
Amos and Andrew '93
The Butcher's Wife '91
Martians Go Home! '90
Traveling Man '89
True Believer '89
Like Father, Like Son '87
Three Men and a Baby '87
Pretty in Pink '86
Something Wild '86

Christopher Collet (1968-)
Stephen King's The Langoliers '95
Prayer of the Rollerboys '91
The Manhattan Project '86
First Born '84
Sleepaway Camp '83

Toni Collette (1972-)
About a Boy '02
Changing Lanes '02
Dinner with Friends '01
Shaft '00
8 1/2 Women '99
The Sixth Sense '99
The Boys '98
Velvet Goldmine '98
Clockwatchers '97
Emma '96
The Thief and the Cobbler '96 (V)
Cosi '95
Lilian's Story '95
The Pallbearer '95
Muriel's Wedding '94
The Efficiency Expert '92

Kenneth Colley (1937-)
Prisoner of Honor '91
The Rainbow '89
A Summer Story '88
Casanova '87
And Nothing But the Truth '82
Firefox '82
Monty Python's Life of Brian '79
Lisztomania '75
The Music Lovers '71

Mark Collie
The Kid with the X-Ray Eyes '99
Fire Down Below '97

Constance Collier (1878-1955)
Rope '48
The Perils of Pauline '47
Dark Corner '46
Monsieur Beaucaire '46
Thunder in the City '37
Wee Willie Winkie '37

Lois Collier (1919-)
A Night in Casablanca '46
The Naughty Nineties '45
Cobra Woman '44
Jungle Woman '44
Weird Woman/Frozen Ghost '44

William "Buster" Collier, Jr. (1902-87)
Phantom Express '32
Cimarron '31
Street Scene '31

John Collin
Tess '80
Star! '68
The Witches '66

Patricia Collinge
Casanova Brown '44
Tender Comrade '43

Anne Collings
Return to Africa '89
The Mask '61

Peter Collingwood
The Wacky World of Wills & Burke '85
Morgan: A Suitable Case for Treatment '66

Alan Collins (1927-)
Tiger Joe '85
Exterminators in the Year 3000 '83
Tornado '83
Ark of the Sun God '82
Hunters of the Golden Cobra '82
The Last Hunter '80

Clifton (Gonzalez) Collins, Jr.
The Last Castle '01
Price of Glory '00
Tigerland '00
Traffic '00
Light It Up '99
The Replacement Killers '98
The Wonderful Ice Cream Suit '98
187 '97

Cora Sue Collins (1927-)
The World Accuses '35
Evelyn Prentice '34
The Scarlet Letter '34

Eddie Collins (1884-1940)
The Blue Bird '40
Drums Along the Mohawk '39
Young Mr. Lincoln '39

G. Pat Collins
Above and Beyond '53
Be Yourself '30

Gary Collins (1938-)
Beautiful '00
Watchers Reborn '98
Hangar 18 '80
Airport '70

Greg Collins
Operation Delta Force 3: Clear Target '98
U.S. Seals '98

Joan Collins (1933-)
These Old Broads '01
The Flintstones in Viva Rock Vegas '00
Joseph and the Amazing Technicolor Dreamcoat '00
Annie: A Royal Adventure '95
A Midwinter's Tale '95
Game for Vultures '86
Monte Carlo '86
Sins '85
Cartier Affair '84
Nutcracker Sweet '84
Her Life as a Man '83
Hansel and Gretel '82
Homework '82
Sunburn '79
The Big Sleep '78
The Bitch '78
Fearless '78
The Stud '78
Zero to Sixty '78
Empire of the Ants '77
The Bawdy Adventures of Tom Jones '76
Great Adventure '75
I Don't Want to Be Born '75
Oh, Alfie '75
Dark Places '73
Tales That Witness Madness '73
Dynasty of Fear '72
Tales from the Crypt '72
Quest for Love '71
Revenge '71
The Executioner '70
Three in the Cellar '70
Subterfuge '68
The Road to Hong Kong '62
Cosh Boy '61
Esther and the King '60
Seven Thieves '60
The Bravados '58
Stopover Tokyo '57
The Opposite Sex '56
The Adventures of Sadie '55
Land of the Pharaohs '55
The Virgin Queen '55
Decameron Nights '53
Tough Guy '53

Judy Collins
A Town Has Turned to Dust '98
Junior '94

Kevin Collins
Edward II '92
The Garden '90

Lewis Collins (1946-)
Jack the Ripper '88
Codename: Wildgeese '84
The Final Option '82

Pat Collins
Plan 10 from Outer Space '95
All Quiet on the Western Front '30

Patricia Collins
Speaking Parts '89
Pin... '88

Patrick Collins
Dirt Bike Kid '86
The Juggler of Notre Dame '84

Pauline Collins (1940-)
Paradise Road '97
My Mother's Courage '95
City of Joy '92
Shirley Valentine '89

Phil Collins (1951-)
Balto '95 (V)
And the Band Played On '93
Frauds '93
Hook '91
Buster '88
Secret Policeman's Private Parts '81

Ray Collins (1889-1965)
Touch of Evil '58
Solid Gold Cadillac '56
Desperate Hours '55
The Go-Getter '54
The Desert Song '53
Ma and Pa Kettle on Vacation '53
I Want You '51
Ma and Pa Kettle Back On the Farm '51
The Racket '51
Ma and Pa Kettle Go to Town '50
Summer Stock '50
The Fountainhead '49
Francis the Talking Mule '49
The Heiress '49
It Happens Every Spring '49
Man from Colorado '49
Command Decision '48
For the Love of Mary '48
Good Sam '48
Homecoming '48
The Bachelor and the Bobby-Soxer '47
A Double Life '47
The Best Years of Our Lives '46
Crack-Up '46
Can't Help Singing '45
Leave Her to Heaven '45
The Seventh Cross '44
Commandos Strike at Dawn '43
The Human Comedy '43
Whistling in Brooklyn '43
The Magnificent Ambersons '42
The Navy Comes Through '42
Citizen Kane '41

Rick Collins
The Toxic Avenger, Part 2 '89
The Toxic Avenger, Part 3: The Last Temptation of Toxie '89

Roberta Collins
Hardbodies '84
Whiskey Mountain '77
Eaten Alive '76
Death Race 2000 '75
Caged Heat '74
The Deadly and the Beautiful '73
Unholy Rollers '72
The Big Doll House '71
The Arousers '70

Russell Collins (1897-1965)
The Matchmaker '58
Enemy Below '57
Savage Wilderness '55
Soldier of Fortune '55

Ruth (Coreen) Collins
Dead Boyz Can't Fly '93
Wildest Dreams '90
Cemetery High '89
Death Collector '89
Doom Asylum '88
Exquisite Corpses '88
Sexpot '88
Galactic Gigolo '87
New York's Finest '87

Stephen Collins (1947-)
Drive Me Crazy '99
An Unexpected Life '97
The First Wives Club '96
An Unexpected Family '96
Scarlett '94
High Stakes '93
My New Gun '92
Till Murder Do Us Part '92
A Woman Named Jackie '91
The Big Picture '89
Stella '89
Weekend War '88
Choke Canyon '86
Hold the Dream '86
Jumpin' Jack Flash '86
Brewster's Millions '85
Chiefs '83
Inside the Third Reich '82
Summer Solstice '81
The Henderson Monster '80
Loving Couples '80
Star Trek: The Motion Picture '80
The Promise '79
Between the Lines '77
All the President's Men '76

Madeleine Collinson
The Love Machine '71
Twins of Evil '71

Mary Collinson
The Love Machine '71
Twins of Evil '71

Frank Collison
O Brother Where Art Thou? '00
Dollman '90
Wired to Kill '86

Roy Collodi
She-Devils on Wheels '68
The Girl, the Body and the Pill '67

Mark Collver
Bix '90

There's Nothing out There '90

June Collyer (1907-68)
A Face in the Fog '36
The Ghost Walks '34
Drums of Jeopardy '31

Pamela Collyer
The Kiss '88
Evil Judgment '85

Ronald Colman (1891-1958)
Around the World in 80 Days '56
Champagne for Caesar '50
A Double Life '47
Random Harvest '42
Talk of the Town '42
Lucky Partners '40
If I Were King '38
Lost Horizon '37
Prisoner of Zenda '37
A Tale of Two Cities '36
Arrowsmith '32
Raffles '30
Bulldog Drummond '29
Lady Windermere's Fan '26
Romola '25
The White Sister '23

Scott Colomby (1952-)
Porky's Revenge '85
Porky's 2: The Next Day '83
Porky's '82
Caddyshack '80
Are You in the House Alone? '78

Alex Colon (1941-95)
Death of an Angel '86
Invasion U.S.A. '85

Miriam Colon (1945-)
All the Pretty Horses '00
Lone Star '95
Sabrina '95
The House of the Spirits '93
A Life of Sin '92

Jerry Colonna (1904-86)
Meet Me in Las Vegas '56
Alice in Wonderland '51 (V)
Kentucky Jubilee '51
Strictly G.I. '44
The Road to Singapore '40
Rosalie '38

Clara Colosimo
Orchestra Rehearsal '78
Alfredo, Alfredo '72

Vince Colosimo
Lantana '01
Chopper '00
Street Hero '84
Moving Out '83

Louisa Colpeyn
Marry Me, Marry Me '69
Band of Outsiders '64

Marshall Colt (1948-)
To Heal a Nation '88
Guilty of Innocence '87
Beverly Hills Madam '86
The Jagged Edge '85

Jacque Lynn Colton
Heartbreak Hotel '88
Big Bad Mama 2 '87

Robbie Coltrane (1950-)
From Hell '01
Harry Potter and the Sorcerer's Stone '01
Alice in Wonderland '99
The World Is Not Enough '99
Frogs for Snakes '98
Message in a Bottle '98
Buddy '97
The Ebb-Tide '97
Montana '97
Cracker: Brotherly Love '95
Goldeneye '95
Cracker: Men Should Weep '94
Cracker: The Big Crunch '94
Cracker: To Be a Somebody '94
The Adventures of Huck Finn '93
Oh, What a Night '92
Perfectly Normal '91
The Pope Must Diet '91
Nuns on the Run '90
Bert Rigby, You're a Fool '89
Henry V '89
Let It Ride '89
Slipstream '89
Wonderland '88
Loose Connections '87
Caravaggio '86
Mona Lisa '86
Defense of the Realm '85
Chinese Boxes '84

Coluche
My Best Friend's Girl '84
Tchao Pantin '84

Franco (Columbo) Columbu
Desperate Crimes '93
Beretta's Island '92
Last Man Standing '87

Peter Colvey
Dead Silent '99
Silent Hunter '94

Pinto Colvig
Sleeping Beauty '59 (V)
Snow White and the Seven Dwarfs '37 (V)

Jack Colvin
Child's Play '88
The Incredible Hulk Returns '88
The Incredible Hulk '77

Michael Colyar
House Party 3 '94
Hot Shots! Part Deux '93

Richard Comar
Ebenezer '97
Kickboxer 3: The Art of War '92

Muriel Combeau
Near Misses '91
Mama, There's a Man in Your Bed '89

Holly Marie Combs (1973-)
Ocean's Eleven '01
Our Mother's Murder '97
Chain of Desire '93
Dr. Giggles '92
Simple Men '92
Born on the Fourth of July '89
Sweet Hearts Dance '88

Jeffrey Combs (1954-)
Faust: Love of the Damned '00
House on Haunted Hill '99
Caught Up '98
I Still Know What You Did Last Summer '98
Time Tracers '97
Cyberstalker '96
The Frighteners '96
Castle Freak '95
Love and a .45 '94
Lurking Fear '94
H.P. Lovecraft's Necronomicon: Book of the Dead '93
The Guyver '91
The Pit & the Pendulum '91
Doctor Mordrid: Master of the Unknown '90
Trancers 2: The Return of Jack Deth '90
Bride of Re-Animator '89
Dead Man Walking '88
Cellar Dweller '87
Cyclone '87
Phantom Empire '87
From Beyond '86
Re-Animator '84

Sean (Puffy, Puff Daddy, P. Diddy) Combs (1969-)
Made '01
Monster's Ball '01

Anjanette Comer (1942-)
Larry McMurtry's Streets of Laredo '95
The Underneath '95
Netherworld '90
Dead of Night '77
Death Stalk '74
Terror on the 40th Floor '74
The Baby '72
Night of a Thousand Cats '72
The Appaloosa '66
The Loved One '65

Dorothy Comingore (1913-71)
The Hairy Ape '44
Citizen Kane '41
Prison Train '38

Perry Como (1912-2001)
Words and Music '48
Doll Face '46

Betty Compson (1897-1974)
Hard-Boiled Mahoney '47
The Invisible Ghost '41
Mad Youth '40
Mystic Circle Murder '39
The Port of Missing Girls '38
God's Country and the Man '37
Bulldog Edition '36
The Lady Refuses '31
Inside the Lines '30
These Girls Won't Talk '20s
The Great Gabbo '29
Docks of New York '28
Paths to Paradise '25
The Pony Express '25

Fay Compton (1894-1978)
Cold Comfort Farm '71
The Haunting '63
The Story of Esther Costello '57
Othello '52
The Mill on the Floss '37

Joyce Compton (1907-97)
A Southern Yankee '48
Scared to Death '46
Christmas in Connecticut '45
Silver Spurs '43
I Take This Oath '40
Balalaika '39
Escape to Paradise '39
Rose of Washington Square '39
The Awful Truth '37
Sea Racketeers '37
Small Town Boy '37
Country Gentlemen '36
Let 'Em Have It '35
Rustlers of Red Dog '35
King Kelly of the U.S.A. '34
False Faces '32

O'Neal Compton (1951-)
Kill Me Later '01
Big Eden '00
Life '99
Deep Impact '98
Roadracers '94
Attack of the 50 Ft. Woman '93

Oliver Conant
Class of '44 '73
Summer of '42 '71

Cristi Conaway
The Colony '98
My Brother's War '97
Intimate Betrayal '96
Nina Takes a Lover '94
Attack of the 50 Ft. Woman '93
Batman Returns '92

Jeff Conaway (1950-)
Jawbreaker '98
Bounty Hunter 2002 '94
In a Moment of Passion '93
Bikini Summer 2 '92
L.A. Goddess '92
Almost Pregnant '91
Mirror Images '91
Sunset Strip '91
A Time to Die '91
Total Exposure '91
The Sleeping Car '90
The Banker '89
Ghost Writer '89
Tale of Two Sisters '89
The Dirty Dozen: The Fatal Mission '88
Elvira, Mistress of the Dark '88
The Patriot '86
Covergirl '83
For the Love of It '80
Breaking Up Is Hard to Do '79
Grease '78
I Never Promised You a Rose Garden '77
Pete's Dragon '77

James Congdon
Summerdog '78
The 300 Year Weekend '71
The 4D Man '59

Chester Conklin (1888-1971)
Miracle of Morgan's Creek '44
Harmon of Michigan '41
Sullivan's Travels '41
The Great Dictator '40
Forlorn River '37
Modern Times '36
Hallelujah, I'm a Bum '33
The Virginian '29
Behind the Front '26
The Nervous Wreck '26
Battling Bunyon '24
Greed '24
Anna Christie '23
Charlie Chaplin ... Our Hero! '15
Tillie's Punctured Romance '14

Jack Conley
Brown's Requiem '98
Payback '98

Joe Conley (1928-)
A Day for Thanks on Walton's Mountain '82
The Waltons: The Christmas Carol '80
Crime of Passion '57

Brigid Conley Walsh
Life Without Dick '01
The Day My Parents Ran Away '93
Quest of the Delta Knights '93

Jimmy Conlin (1884-1962)
Dick Tracy's Dilemma '47
Miracle of Morgan's Creek '44
Sullivan's Travels '41

Didi Conn (1951-)
Thomas and the Magic Railroad '00
Grease 2 '82
Grease '78
You Light Up My Life '77

Maureen Connell (1931-)
Black Tide '58
Lucky Jim '58
The Abominable Snowman '57

Christopher Connelly (1941-88)
Django Strikes Again '87
The Messenger '87
Mines of Kilimanjaro '87
Night of the Sharks '87
Strike Commando '87
Foxtrap '85
Jungle Raiders '85
Operation 'Nam '85
1990: The Bronx Warriors '83
Raiders of Atlantis '83
Fantastic Seven '82
Liar's Moon '82
Manhattan Baby '82
Return of the Rebels '81
The Martian Chronicles: Part 3 '79
The Crash of Flight 401 '78
Norseman '78
The Incredible Rocky Mountain Race '77
Hawmps! '76
Benji '74
The Invasion of Carol Enders '74
They Only Kill Their Masters '72

Edward Connelly
The Mysterious Lady '28
The Saphead '21

Jennifer Connelly (1970-)
A Beautiful Mind '01
Pollock '00
Requiem for a Dream '00
Waking the Dead '00
Dark City '97
Inventing the Abbotts '97
Far Harbor '96
Mulholland Falls '95
Higher Learning '94
Of Love and Shadows '94
Career Opportunities '91
The Rocketeer '91
The Hot Spot '90
Some Girls '88
Labyrinth '86
Seven Minutes in Heaven '86
Creepers '85
Once Upon a Time in America '84

Marc Connelly
Tall Story '60
Spirit of St. Louis '57

Jason Connery (1962-)
Wishmaster 3: Beyond the Gates of Hell '01
Shanghai Noon '00
Midnight in Saint Petersburg '97
Bullet to Beijing '95
Double Cross '92
Spymaker: The Secret Life of Ian Fleming '90
Casablanca Express '89
Bye Bye Baby '88
Winner Takes All '86
Robin Hood...The Legend: Herne's Son '85
Robin Hood...The Legend: The Time of the Wolf '85
The First Olympics: Athens 1896 '84

Sean Connery (1930-)
Finding Forrester '00
Entrapment '99
The Avengers '98
Playing by Heart '98
Dragonheart '96 (V)
The Rock '96
First Knight '95
A Good Man in Africa '94
Just Cause '94
Rising Sun '93
Medicine Man '92
Highlander 2: The Quickening '91
Robin Hood: Prince of Thieves '91
The Hunt for Red October '90
The Russia House '90
Family Business '89
Indiana Jones and the Last Crusade '89
Memories of Me '88
The Presidio '88
The Untouchables '87
Highlander '86
The Name of the Rose '86
Never Say Never Again '83
Sword of the Valiant '83
Five Days One Summer '82
Wrong Is Right '82
Outland '81
Time Bandits '81
Cuba '79
The Great Train Robbery '79
Meteor '79
A Bridge Too Far '77
The Arab Conspiracy '76
Robin and Marian '76
The Man Who Would Be King '75
The Wind and the Lion '75
Murder on the Orient Express '74
The Terrorists '74
The Offence '73
Zardoz '73
The Anderson Tapes '71
Diamonds Are Forever '71
Molly Maguires '70
Red Tent '69
Shalako '68
You Only Live Twice '67
A Fine Madness '66
Thunderball '65
Goldfinger '64
Marnie '64
From Russia with Love '63
Dr. No '62
The Longest Day '62
The Frightened City '61
On the Fiddle '61
Darby O'Gill & the Little People '59
Another Time, Another Place '58
Time Lock '57

Harry Connick, Jr. (1967-)
Life Without Dick '01
Rodgers & Hammerstein's South Pacific '01
Iron Giant '99 (V)
My Dog Skip '99 (N)
Hope Floats '98
Excess Baggage '96
Independence Day '96
Copycat '95
Little Man Tate '91
Memphis Belle '90

Billy Connolly (1942-)
Beautiful Joe '00
An Everlasting Piece '00
Boondock Saints '99
Deacon Brodie '98
The Imposters '98
Still Crazy '98
Mrs. Brown '97
Muppet Treasure Island '96
Pocahontas '95 (V)
Indecent Proposal '93
The Big Man: Crossing the Line '91
The Return of the Musketeers '89
Blue Money '84
The Secret Policeman's Other Ball '82
Absolution '81

Kevin Connolly
John Q '02
The Beverly Hillbillies '93
Alan & Naomi '92

Walter Connolly (1887-1940)
The Adventures of Huckleberry Finn '39
Fifth Avenue Girl '39
Too Hot to Handle '38
The Good Earth '37
Nothing Sacred '37
Libeled Lady '36
Broadway Bill '34
It Happened One Night '34
Lady by Choice '34
Twentieth Century '34
The Bitter Tea of General Yen '33
Lady for a Day '33

Kenneth Connor (1915-92)
Carry On England '76
Carry On Henry VIII '71
Carry On Cleo '65
What a Carve-Up! '62
Dentist In the Chair '60
Carry On Nurse '59
The Ladykillers '55

Chuck Connors (1921-92)
Last Flight to Hell
The Gambler Returns: The Luck of the Draw '93
Salmonberries '91
Three Days to a Kill '91

High Desert Kill '90
Texas Guns '90
One Last Run '89
Skinheads: The Second Coming of Hate '88
Trained to Kill '88
Terror Squad '87
Summer Camp Nightmare '86
The Vals '85
Target Eagle '84
Airplane 2: The Sequel '82
Balboa '82
The Capture of Grizzly Adams '82
Virus '82
Day of the Assassin '81
Bordello '79
Tourist Trap '79
Roots '77
Nightmare in Badham County '76
The Legend of Sea Wolf '75
99 & 44/100 Dead '74
Soylent Green '73
Embassy '72
The Mad Bomber '72
Pancho Villa '72
The Proud and the Damned '72
Ride to Glory '71
Flipper '63
Geronimo '62
The Big Country '58
Designing Woman '57
Old Yeller '57
Hot Rod Girl '56
Pat and Mike '52

Mike Connors (1925-)
James Dean: Live Fast, Die Young '97
Fist Fighter '88
Too Scared to Scream '85
Casino '80
Nightkill '80
Avalanche Express '79
Long Journey Back '78
Harlow '65
Good Neighbor Sam '64
Panic Button '62
Flesh and the Spur '57
Shake, Rattle and Rock '57
Voodoo Woman '57
Day the World Ended '55
Swamp Women '55
Sudden Fear '52

David Conrad
Men of Honor '00
The Weekend '00
A Season for Miracles '99
Return to Paradise '98
The Wizard of Speed and Time '88

Michael Conrad (1925-83)
Bordello '79
The Longest Yard '74
Scream Blacula Scream '73
Gone with the West '72
Thumb Tripping '72
They Shoot Horses, Don't They? '69
The War Lord '65

Mikel Conrad (1919-82)
The Flying Saucer '50
Abbott and Costello Meet the Killer, Boris Karloff '49
Check Your Guns '48

Robert Conrad (1935-)
Jingle All the Way '96
Samurai Cowboy '93
Assassin '86
Two Fathers' Justice '85
Hard Knox '83
Will: G. Gordon Liddy '82
Wrong Is Right '82
More Wild, Wild West '80
Breaking Up Is Hard to Do '79
Lady in Red '79
Wild, Wild West Revisited '79
Centennial '78
Sudden Death '77
Murph the Surf '75
Bandits '73
Crossfire '67
Palm Springs Weekend '63
The Commies Are Coming, the Commies Are Coming '57

William Conrad (1920-94)
Vengeance '89
Blitz '85
Return of Frank Cannon '80
The Return of the King '80 (V)
The Rebels '79 (N)
Night Cries '78
Moonshine County Express '77
The Ride Back '57
The Conqueror '56
Naked Jungle '54
The Desert Song '53
Cry Danger '51
The Racket '51
Body and Soul '47
The Killers '46

Hans Conried (1917-82)
Tut & Tuttle '82
Oh, God! Book 2 '80
Scruffy '80 (V)
Brothers O'Toole '73
Phantom Tollbooth '69 (V)
The Patsy '64
Robin and the 7 Hoods '64
1001 Arabian Nights '59 (V)
Jet Pilot '57
The Monster That Challenged the World '57
Rock-A-Bye Baby '57
Birds & the Bees '56
Bus Stop '56
Davy Crockett, King of the Wild Frontier '55
The Affairs of Dobie Gillis '53
The 5000 Fingers of Dr. T '53
Peter Pan '53 (V)
Behave Yourself! '52
Three for Bedroom C '52
The World in His Arms '52
Rich, Young and Pretty '51
Nancy Goes to Rio '50
Summer Stock '50
My Friend Irma '49
The Senator Was Indiscreet '47
His Butler's Sister '44
Hitler's Children '43
Blondie's Blessed Event '42
Underground Agent '42

Frances Conroy (1953-)
Murder in a Small Town '99
The Crucible '96
The Neon Bible '95
The Adventures of Huck Finn '93
Scent of a Woman '92
Another Woman '88
Rocket Gibraltar '88

Frank Conroy (1890-1964)
The Bramble Bush '60
The Day the Earth Stood Still '51
All My Sons '48
Crash Dive '43
The Ox-Bow Incident '43
I Live My Life '35
The Cat and the Fiddle '34
Manhattan Melodrama '34
Ace of Aces '33

Kevin Conroy (1955-)
Batman: Mask of the Phantasm '93 (V)
Chain of Desire '93
The Secret Passion of Robert Clayton '92

Ruaidhri Conroy (1979-)
When the Sky Falls '99
Moondance '95
Nothing Personal '95
The Van '95
Into the West '92

John Considine (1938-)
Gia '98
Tinseltown '97
Breathing Lessons '94
Opposing Force '87
Trouble in Mind '86
Dixie: Changing Habits '85
Choose Me '84
Circle of Power '83
Rita Hayworth: The Love Goddess '83
Endangered Species '82
Forbidden Love '82
The Shadow Box '80
See How She Runs '78
A Wedding '78
The Late Show '77
Welcome to L.A. '77
The Thirsty Dead '74
Dr. Death, Seeker of Souls '73
Reunion in France '42

Tim Considine (1940-)
Daring Dobermans '73
Patton '70
Sunrise at Campobello '60
The Shaggy Dog '59
The Private War of Major Benson '55
Clown '53

Michel Constantin (1924-)
Beyond Fear '75
A Very Curious Girl '69
Le Trou '59

Eddie Constantine (1917-93)
Zentropa '92
The Long Good Friday '80
It's Alive 2: It Lives Again '78
Beware of a Holy Whore '70
Attack of the Robots '66
Alphaville '65
License to Kill '64
As If It Were Raining '63
It Means That to Me '63
Your Turn Darling '63
Cleo from 5 to 7 '61
Keep Talking Baby '61
S.O.S. Pacific '60
Room 43 '58
Dishonorable Discharge '57
There Goes Barder '54

Michael Constantine (1927-)
My Big Fat Greek Wedding '02
Killing in the Sun
The Juror '96
Stephen King's Thinner '96
My Life '93
Question of Faith '93
Prancer '89
In the Mood '87
Forty Days of Musa Dagh '85
Silent Rebellion '82
Fear in the City '81
The North Avenue Irregulars '79
Billy: Portrait of a Street Kid '77
Voyage of the Damned '76
Conspiracy of Terror '75
Death Cruise '74
Say Goodbye, Maggie Cole '72
Dirty Heroes '71
Don't Drink the Water '69
If It's Tuesday, This Must Be Belgium '69
Justine '69
The Reivers '69
The Hustler '61

John Conte
Trauma '62
The Man with the Golden Arm '55
Lost in a Harem '44

Richard Conte (1914-75)
The Godfather 1902-1959: The Complete Epic '81
Violent Professionals '73
The Godfather '72
1931: Once Upon a Time in New York '72
Explosion '69
Operation Cross Eagles '69
Lady in Cement '68
Hotel '67
Tony Rome '67
Assault on a Queen '66
Circus World '64
Ocean's 11 '60
They Came to Cordura '59
Full of Life '56
Big Combo '55
I'll Cry Tomorrow '55
Race for Life '55
The Fighter '52
House of Strangers '49
Call Northside 777 '48
13 Rue Madeleine '46
A Walk in the Sun '46
The Purple Heart '44
Guadalcanal Diary '43

Steve Conte (1920-97)
The Wild World of Batwoman '66
Attack of the Mayan Mummy '63
Terror of the Bloodhunters '62

Tom Conti (1941-)
The Enemy '01
Sub Down '97
Someone Else's America '96
That Summer of White Roses '90
Shirley Valentine '89
Deep Cover '88
Dumb Waiter '87
The Gospel According to Vic '87
The Quick and the Dead '87
Beyond Therapy '86
Miracles '86
Saving Grace '86
American Dreamer '84
Merry Christmas, Mr. Lawrence '83
The Princess and the Pea '83
Reuben, Reuben '83
The Norman Conquests, Part 1: Table Manners '80
The Norman Conquests, Part 2: Living Together '80
The Norman Conquests, Part 3: Round and Round the Garden '80
The Duellists '77
Full Circle '77

Chantal Contouri (1949-)
Goodbye, Miss 4th of July '88
Thirst '87
The Night After Halloween '83
Alvin Rides Again '74

Patricio Contreras
Of Love and Shadows '94
Old Gringo '89
The Official Story '85

Frank Converse (1938-)
Brother Future '91
Tales of the Unexpected '91
Everybody Wins '90
Home at Last '88
Alone in the Neon Jungle '87
Anne of Avonlea '87
Uncle Tom's Cabin '87
Mystery at Fire Island '81
The Bushido Blade '80
Marilyn: The Untold Story '80
Danger in the Skies '79
A Movie Star's Daughter '79
Cruise into Terror '78
Sergeant Matlovich vs. the U.S. Air Force '78
Killer on Board '77
The Tattered Web '71

William Converse-Roberts
Bandits '01
Crazy in Alabama '99
Drive Me Crazy '99
Kiss the Girls '97
Serving in Silence: The Margarethe Cammermeyer Story '95
Courtship '87
The Fig Tree '87
On Valentine's Day '86
1918 '85

Bert Convy (1933-91)
Help Wanted: Male '82
Cannonball Run '81
Hero at Large '80
The Man in the Santa Claus Suit '79
Racquet '79
Jennifer '78
Semi-Tough '77
The Love Bug '68
A Bucket of Blood '59
Gunman's Walk '58

Dan Conway
Things Change '88
Blast-Off Girls '67

Gary Conway (1936-)
Liberty & Bash '90
American Ninja 2: The Confrontation '87
How to Make a Monster '58
Teenage Frankenstein '58

Kevin Conway (1942-)
Black Knight '01
Thirteen Days '00
Two Family House '99
The Confession '98
Mercury Rising '98
Calm at Sunset '96
Looking for Richard '96
Larry McMurtry's Streets of Laredo '95
Lawnmower Man 2: Beyond Cyberspace '95
Prince Brat and the Whipping Boy '95
The Quick and the Dead '94
Gettysburg '93
Jennifer 8 '92
One Good Cop '91
Rambling Rose '91
Homeboy '88
Rage of Angels '83
The Funhouse '81
The Lathe of Heaven '80
The Scarlet Letter '79
F.I.S.T. '78
Paradise Alley '78
Johnny We Hardly Knew Ye '77

Morgan Conway (1903-81)
Dick Tracy vs. Cueball '46
Dick Tracy, Detective '45
The Saint Takes Over '40
Sinners in Paradise '38

Pat Conway (1931-81)
Brighty of the Grand Canyon '67
Geronimo '62
The Deadly Mantis '57
The Annapolis Story '55

Russ Conway (1913-78)
The Screaming Skull '58
Love Me Tender '56
Twelve o'Clock High '49

Tim Conway (1933-)
Air Bud 2: Golden Receiver '98
Speed 2: Cruise Control '97
Dear God '96
The Longshot '86
Cannonball Run 2 '84
The Private Eyes '80
The Apple Dumpling Gang Rides Again '79
Prize Fighter '79
The Billion Dollar Hobo '78
They Went That-a-Way & That-a-Way '78
Gus '76
The Shaggy D.A. '76
The Apple Dumpling Gang '75
The World's Greatest Athlete '73
McHale's Navy Joins the Air Force '65
McHale's Navy '64

Tom Conway (1904-67)
Atomic Submarine '59
Voodoo Woman '57
Murder on Approval '56
Norman Conquest '53
Peter Pan '53 (N)
Three Stops to Murder '53
Bride of the Gorilla '51
One Touch of Venus '48
Criminal Court '46
The Saint Strikes Back: Criminal Court '46
The Falcon in Hollywood '44
The Falcon in Mexico '44
I Walked with a Zombie '43
The Seventh Victim '43
Cat People '42
The Falcon's Brother '42
Mrs. Miniver '42
Rio Rita '42
Lady Be Good '41
Tarzan's Secret Treasure '41

Angell Conwell (1982-)
Baby Boy '01
The Wash '01

Jackie Coogan (1914-84)
The Escape Artist '82
Dr. Heckyl and Mr. Hype '80
The Prey '80
Halloween with the Addams Family '79
Human Experiments '79
The Shakiest Gun in the West '68
Girl Happy '65
High School Confidential '58
Lonelyhearts '58
Mesa of Lost Women '52
Outlaw Women '52
College Swing '38
Free and Easy '30
Tom Sawyer '30
Oliver Twist '22
The Kid '21
My Boy '21
Peck's Bad Boy '21

Keith Coogan (1970-)
Ivory Tower '97
Downhill Willie '96
Life 101 '95
The Power Within '95
Forever: A Ghost of a Love Story '92
Book of Love '91
Don't Tell Mom the Babysitter's Dead '91
Toy Soldiers '91
Cheetah '89
Cousins '89
Under the Boardwalk '89
Adventures in Babysitting '87
Hiding Out '87

Steve Coogan
Sweet Revenge '98
Mr. Toad's Wild Ride '96

A.J. Cook
Out Cold '01
Ripper: Letter from Hell '01
Wishmaster 3: Beyond the Gates of Hell '01
The Virgin Suicides '99

Ben Cook
Restless Spirits '99
Little Men '98

Carole Cook
Lost and Found '99

Fast Money '96
Sixteen Candles '84
The Incredible Mr. Limpet '64

Christopher Cook
Spare Me '92
A Christmas Carol '54

Clyde Cook (1891-1984)
The White Cliffs of Dover '44
White Cargo '42
Through the Breakers '28
White Gold '28

Dale "Apollo" Cook
Fist of Glory '95
Raw Target '95
American Kickboxer 2: To the Death '93
Blood Ring '93
Fist of Steel '93
Triple Impact '92

Donald Cook (1901-61)
Our Very Own '50
Here Come the Co-Eds '45
Show Boat '36
Confidential '35
Viva Villa! '34
Baby Face '33
Public Enemy '31

Elisha Cook, Jr. (1906-95)
Hammett '82
Leave 'Em Laughing '81
Carny '80
The Champ '79
1941 '79
Salem's Lot '79
St. Ives '76
Winterhawk '76
Black Bird '75
Messiah of Evil '74
Electra Glide in Blue '73
Emperor of the North Pole '73
Blacula '72
The Great Northfield Minnesota Raid '72
El Condor '70
Rosemary's Baby '68
The Haunted Palace '63
Papa's Delicate Condition '63
One-Eyed Jacks '61
Platinum High School '60
House on Haunted Hill '58
Plunder Road '57
The Killing '56
The Indian Fighter '55
Drum Beat '54
Shane '53
Behave Yourself! '52
Don't Bother to Knock '52
The Great Gatsby '49
Born to Kill '47
The Long Night '47
The Big Sleep '46
Dillinger '45
Dark Mountain '44
Dark Waters '44
Phantom Lady '44
Wildcat '42
The Maltese Falcon '41
Sergeant York '41
Stranger on the Third Floor '40
Tin Pan Alley '40
They Won't Forget '37
Pigskin Parade '36

Peter Cook (1938-95)
Black Beauty '94
Getting It Right '89
Great Balls of Fire '89
Without a Clue '88
The Princess Bride '87
Yellowbeard '83
Secret Policeman's Private Parts '81
The Hound of the Baskervilles '77
Find the Lady '75
Those Daring Young Men in Their Jaunty Jalopies '69
Bedazzled '68
Dandy in Aspic '68
The Wrong Box '66

Rachael Leigh Cook (1979-)
Josie and the Pussycats '01
Texas Rangers '01
Antitrust '00
Blow Dry '00
Get Carter '00
She's All That '99
All I Wanna Do '98
The Bumblebee Flies Anyway '98
The Naked Man '98
The Defenders: Payback '97
The Eighteenth Angel '97
The House of Yes '97
True Women '97
Carpool '96
The Baby-Sitters' Club '95
Tom and Huck '95

Roderick Cook
9 1/2 Weeks '86
Our Time '74

Ron Cook
Charlotte Gray '01
102 Dalmatians '00
Topsy Turvy '99
The Odyssey '97
Secrets and Lies '95
Sharpe's Honour '94

Tommy Cook (1930-)
Missile to the Moon '59
Battle Cry '55
Teenage Crime Wave '55

Christopher Cooke
Rhythm Thief '94
The Unbelievable Truth '90

Jennifer Cooke
Friday the 13th, Part 6: Jason Lives '86
Gimme an F '85

Keith Cooke
Heatseeker '95
The King of the Kickboxers '91
China O'Brien 2 '89
China O'Brien '88

Peter Cookson
Black Tower '50
Fear '46

Spade Cooley (1910-69)
Everybody's Dancin' '50
Kid from Gower Gulch '47
Silver Bandit '47

Jennifer Coolidge
American Pie 2 '01
Down to Earth '01
Legally Blonde '01
Pootie Tang '01
Best in Show '00
American Pie '99
Slappy and the Stinkers '97
Trial and Error '96

Philip Coolidge
Inherit the Wind '60
The Tingler '59

Coolio (1963-)
Get Over It! '01
Perfume '01
The Convent '00
Dope Case Pending '00
In Pursuit '00
Shriek If You Know What I Did Last Friday the 13th '00
Submerged '00
Judgment Day '99
An Alan Smithee Film: Burn, Hollywood, Burn '97
Phat Beach '96

Kevin Cooney (1945-)
Clockwatchers '97
If These Walls Could Talk '96
Full Moon in Blue Water '88

Alice Cooper (1948-)
Wayne's World '92
Freddy's Dead: The Final Nightmare '91
Decline of Western Civilization 2: The Metal Years '88
Prince of Darkness '87
Monster Dog '82
Roadie '80
Sextette '78

Ben Cooper
The Rose Tattoo '55
Johnny Guitar '53

Camille (Cami) Cooper
Lawnmower Man 2: Beyond Cyberspace '95
The Applegates '89
Shocker '89

Chris Cooper (1951-)
The Bourne Identity '02
Me, Myself, and Irene '00
The Patriot '00
American Beauty '99
October Sky '99
Breast Men '97
Great Expectations '97
The Horse Whisperer '97
Horton Foote's Alone '97
A Time to Kill '96
Lone Star '95
Money Train '95
Pharoah's Army '95
Lone Justice '93
Return to Lonesome Dove '93
This Boy's Life '93
City of Hope '91
Guilty by Suspicion '91
Thousand Pieces of Gold '91
Matewan '87

Clancy Cooper (1906-75)
Naked Youth '59
A Time to Love & a Time to Die '58
Girls in Chains '43
The Secret Code '42

Garry Cooper
My Beautiful Laundrette '85
Quadrophenia '79

Gary Cooper
Naked Gun 33 1/3: The Final Insult '94
Dark Before Dawn '89

Gary Cooper (1901-61)
The Naked Edge '61
Alias Jesse James '59
The Hanging Tree '59
They Came to Cordura '59
The Wreck of the Mary Deare '59
Man of the West '58
Ten North Frederick '58
Love in the Afternoon '57
Friendly Persuasion '56
The Court Martial of Billy Mitchell '55
Blowing Wild '54
Return to Paradise '53
Vera Cruz '53
High Noon '52
Springfield Rifle '52
Distant Drums '51
The Fountainhead '49
It's a Great Feeling '49
Task Force '49
Good Sam '48
Unconquered '47
Cloak and Dagger '46
Along Came Jones '45
Saratoga Trunk '45
Casanova Brown '44
The Story of Dr. Wassell '44
For Whom the Bell Tolls '43
The Pride of the Yankees '42
Ball of Fire '41
Meet John Doe '41
Sergeant York '41
The Westerner '40
Beau Geste '39
The Real Glory '39
The Adventures of Marco Polo '38
Bluebeard's Eighth Wife '38
The Cowboy and the Lady '38
The Plainsman '37
Souls at Sea '37
Desire '36
The General Died at Dawn '36
Mr. Deeds Goes to Town '36
The Lives of a Bengal Lancer '35
Now and Forever '34
Today We Live '33
A Farewell to Arms '32
Fighting Caravans '31
Morocco '30
The Virginian '29
Doomsday '28
It '27
The Last Outlaw '27
Nevada '27
Wings '27

George Cooper (1892-1943)
Federal Agent '36
Uptown New York '32
Smouldering Fires '25
Little Church Around the Corner '23

Gladys Cooper (1888-1971)
Nice Girl Like Me '69
My Fair Lady '64
Separate Tables '58
At Sword's Point '51
Madame Bovary '49
The Secret Garden '49
Homecoming '48
The Pirate '48
The Bishop's Wife '47
Beware of Pity '46
Love Letters '45
The Valley of Decision '45
Mrs. Parkington '44
The White Cliffs of Dover '44
Mr. Lucky '43
The Song of Bernadette '43
Now, Voyager '42
The Black Cat '41
That Hamilton Woman '41
Kitty Foyle '40
Rebecca '40
The Iron Duke '34

Inez Cooper
'Neath Canadian Skies '46
North of the Border '46
Wings over the Pacific '43
I Married an Angel '42

Jackie Cooper (1921-)
Surrender '87
Superman 3 '83
Superman 2 '80
Superman: The Movie '78
The Love Machine '71
Maybe I'll Be Home in the Spring '70
The Navy Comes Through '42
Ziegfeld Girl '41
Return of Frank James '40
The Abe Lincoln of Ninth Avenue '39
That Certain Age '38
Peck's Bad Boy '34
Treasure Island '34
The Champ '32

Jeanne Cooper (1928-)
Sweet Hostage '75
Red Nightmare '62
Shame '61
Let No Man Write My Epitaph '60
The Commies Are Coming, the Commies Are Coming '57
Plunder Road '57
The Redhead from Wyoming '53
Shadows of Tombstone '53

Jeff Cooper
Fantastic Balloon Voyage '80s
Circle of Iron '78
The Impossible Years '68
Born Losers '67

Justin Cooper
Dennis the Menace Strikes Again '98
Liar Liar '96

Maggie Cooper
Death Ray 2000 '81
An Eye for an Eye '81
And Baby Makes Six '79

Melville Cooper (1896-1973)
Around the World in 80 Days '56
The King's Thief '55
Let's Dance '50
The Underworld Story '50
Heartbeat '46
13 Rue Madeleine '46
Immortal Sergeant '43
The Lady Eve '41
Murder over New York '40
Rebecca '40
The Adventures of Robin Hood '38
Dawn Patrol '38
Thin Ice '37
Private Life of Don Juan '34
The Scarlet Pimpernel '34

Miriam Cooper (1894-1976)
Is Money Everything? '23
The Birth of a Nation '15

Ralph Cooper (-1992)
Gang War '40
The Duke Is Tops '38

Ray Cooper
The Adventures of Baron Munchausen '89
The Lives of a Bengal Lancer '35

Stan Cooper
Great Treasure Hunt '70s
The Hanging Woman '72
Hell Commandos '69

Ted Cooper
The Caine Mutiny '54
Phantom from Space '53

Terence Cooper (1928-97)
Hell's Belles '95
Heart of the Stag '84

Trevor Cooper
Ivanhoe '97
Framed '93

Robert Coote (1909-82)
Theatre of Blood '73
Alice Through the Looking Glass '66
My Fair Lady '64
The Horse's Mouth '58
The Merry Widow '52
Othello '52
Scaramouche '52
The Elusive Pimpernel '50
Macbeth '48
The Three Musketeers '48
Forever Amber '47
The Ghost and Mrs. Muir '47
Lured '47
Stairway to Heaven '46
Commandos Strike at Dawn '43
You Can't Fool Your Wife '40
Bad Lands '39
Gunga Din '39
Mr. Moto's Last Warning '39
Nurse Edith Cavell '39

Kenneth Cope
Rentadick '72
Carry On at Your Convenience '71

Joan Copeland (1922-)
The Adventures of Sebastian Cole '99
The Peacemaker '97
The Laserman '90
Her Alibi '88
Happy New Year '87
Roseland '77

Zane R. (Lil' Zane) Copeland, Jr. (1982-)
Dr. Dolittle 2 '01
Finding Forrester '00

Michael Copeman
Focus '01
His Bodyguard '98

Geoffrey Copleston
The Belly of an Architect '91
The Black Cat '81

Peter Copley (1915-)
A Dangerous Man: Lawrence after Arabia '91
Help! '65
King and Country '64
The Golden Salamander '51

Teri Copley (1961-)
Brain Donors '92
Frozen Assets '92
Down the Drain '89
Transylvania Twist '89
In the Line of Duty: The FBI Murders '88
I Married a Centerfold '84

Alicia Coppola
Double Down '01
Blood Money '99
Velocity Trap '99

Francis Ford Coppola (1939-)
Hearts of Darkness: A Filmmaker's Apocalypse '91
Apocalypse Now '79

Sofia Coppola (1971-)
Star Wars: Episode 1—The Phantom Menace '99
Inside Monkey Zetterland '93
The Godfather, Part 3 '90
Peggy Sue Got Married '86
The Godfather '72

Ben (Benny) Corbett
Outlaw's Paradise '39
Circle of Death '36
Coyote Trails '35

Glenn Corbett (1934-93)
Shadow Force '92
Ride in a Pink Car '74
The Stranger '73
Dead Pigeon on Beethoven Street '72
Chisum '70
Shenandoah '65
Homicidal '61
All the Young Men '60
The Mountain Road '60
The Violent Years '56

Gretchen Corbett (1947-)
Change of Heart '98
Jaws of Satan '81
PSI Factor '80
Secrets of Three Hungry Wives '78
The Savage Bees '76
Let's Scare Jessica to Death '71

Harry H. Corbett (1925-82)
Silver Dream Racer '83
Jabberwocky '77
Carry On Screaming '66
Rattle of a Simple Man '64
Ladies Who Do '63
The Unstoppable Man '59

John Corbett (1962-)
My Big Fat Greek Wedding '02
Prancer Returns '01
Serendipity '01
Volcano '97
Don't Look Back '96
Wedding Bell Blues '96
Tombstone '93

Ronnie Corbett (1930-)
Fierce Creatures '96
No Sex Please—We're British '73

Barry Corbin (1940-)
Crossfire Trail '01
Held Up '00
A Face to Kill For '99
Solo '96
Curdled '95
Career Opportunities '91
The Chase '91
Conagher '91

The Hot Spot '90
Short Time '90
Who's Harry Crumb? '89
Critters 2: The Main Course '88
It Takes Two '88
LBJ: The Early Years '88
Permanent Record '88
Undercover '87
Nothing in Common '86
Hard Traveling '85
My Science Project '85
What Comes Around '85
Ballad of Gregorio Cortez '83
Prime Suspect '82
Six Pack '82
Bitter Harvest '81
Dead and Buried '81
Any Which Way You Can '80
Urban Cowboy '80

Ellen Corby (1913-99)
A Day for Thanks on Walton's Mountain '82
Homecoming: A Christmas Story '71
Support Your Local Gunfighter '71
The Glass Bottom Boat '66
The Strangler '64
Vertigo '58
All Mine to Give '56
Illegal '55
Angels in the Outfield '51
On Moonlight Bay '51
Harriet Craig '50
Ma and Pa Kettle Go to Town '50
I Remember Mama '48
Forever Amber '47
It's a Wonderful Life '46
Bedlam '45

Donna Corcoran (1942-)
Gypsy Colt '54
Don't Bother to Knock '52
Angels in the Outfield '51

Kevin Corcoran (1949-)
A Tiger Walks '64
Johnny Shiloh '63
Savage Sam '63
Mooncussers '62
Pollyanna '60
The Shaggy Dog '59
Toby Tyler '59
Old Yeller '57

Alex Cord (1931-)
Air Rage '01
To Be the Best '93
C.I.A.: Code Name Alexa '92
Roots of Evil '91
A Girl to Kill For '90
Street Asylum '90
The Dirty Dozen: The Fatal Mission '88
The Uninvited '88
Jungle Warriors '84
Goliath Awaits '81
Fire '77
Grayeagle '77
Sidewinder One '77
Inn of the Damned '74
Dead Are Alive '72
Stiletto '69
The Brotherhood '68
A Minute to Pray, a Second to Die '67

Mara Corday (1932-)
The Black Scorpion '57
The Giant Claw '57
Tarantula '55
Francis Joins the WACs '54

Rita (Paula) Corday (1920-92)
Because You're Mine '52
The Black Castle '52
Sword of Monte Cristo '51
Dick Tracy vs. Cueball '46
The Body Snatcher '45
West of the Pecos '45
The Falcon in Hollywood '44
The Leopard Man '43

Allan Corduner
The Way We Live Now '02
Joe Gould's Secret '00
Topsy Turvy '99
The Imposters '98
Voices from a Locked Room '95
Heart of Darkness '93
Mandela '87
Yentl '83

Annie Cordy
Le Chat '75
La Rupture '70

Raymond Cordy (1898-1956)
Beauties of the Night '52
Beauty and the Devil '50
A Nous la Liberte '31

Nick(y) Corello
Lansky '99
The Last Don '97
Devil in a Blue Dress '95
Blankman '94
Casualties of Love: The "Long Island Lolita" Story '93
Colors '88

Brigitte Corey
The Fury of Hercules '61
Samson '61

Prof. Irwin Corey (1912-)
The Curse of the Jade Scorpion '01
Stuck on You '84
Fairy Tales '76
How to Commit Marriage '69

Isabel Corey
The Invincible Gladiator '63
Bob le Flambeur '55

Jeff Corey (1914-)
Color of Night '94
Surviving the Game '94
Deception '92
Secret Ingredient '92
Sinatra '92
Payoff '91
Messenger of Death '88
Creator '85
Conan the Destroyer '84
Sword & the Sorcerer '82
Battle Beyond the Stars '80
Butch and Sundance: The Early Days '79
Up River '79
Jennifer '78
Wild Geese '78
Curse of the Black Widow '77
Moonshine County Express '77
Oh, God! '77
The Premonition '75
Catlow '71
Shoot Out '71
Beneath the Planet of the Apes '70
Getting Straight '70
Little Big Man '70
They Call Me Mr. Tibbs! '70
Butch Cassidy and the Sundance Kid '69
True Grit '69
The Boston Strangler '68
Seconds '66
Mickey One '65
Lady in a Cage '64
The Balcony '63
Superman & the Mole Men '51
The Nevadan '50
The Next Voice You Hear '50
Rawhide '50
Bagdad '49
Follow Me Quietly '49
Home of the Brave '49
A Southern Yankee '48
Hopalong Cassidy: Hoppy's Holiday '47
My Friend Flicka '43

Wendell Corey (1914-68)
Buckskin '68
The Astro-Zombies '67
Women of the Prehistoric Planet '66
Alias Jesse James '59
The Light in the Forest '58
Loving You '57
The Rainmaker '56
The Big Knife '55
Rear Window '54
Great Missouri Raid '51
Rich, Young and Pretty '51
Harriet Craig '50
Any Number Can Play '49
Holiday Affair '49
The Accused '48
The Search '48
Sorry, Wrong Number '48

Danny Corkill
Between Two Women '86
D.A.R.Y.L. '85
Mrs. Soffel '84

Al Corley (1956-)
A Kiss Goodnight '94
Incident at Channel Q '86
Torchlight '85
Squeeze Play '79

Annie Corley
Along for the Ride '00
Here on Earth '00
The '60s '99
Free Willy 3: The Rescue '97
Box of Moonlight '96
The Bridges of Madison County '95

Pat Corley (1930-)
Mr. Destiny '90
Poker Alice '87
Silent Witness '85
Night Shift '82
Of Mice and Men '81
Nightwing '79
The Two Worlds of Jenny Logan '79
Coming Home '78

Sharron Corley
The Substitute '96
New Jersey Drive '95

Maddie Corman (1969-)
Mickey Blue Eyes '99
I Think I Do '97
My New Gun '92
The Adventures of Ford Fairlane '90
Seven Minutes in Heaven '86

Roger Corman (1926-)
Scream 3 '00
Body Bags '93
Philadelphia '93
The Silence of the Lambs '91
Lords of the Deep '89
Swing Shift '84
State of Things '82
The Godfather 1902-1959: The Complete Epic '81
The Howling '81
Cannonball '76
The Godfather, Part 2 '74
Atlas '60
Creature from the Haunted Sea '60

Michael Cornelison
Mommy 2: Mommy's Day '96
Mommy '95

Don Cornelius
Tapeheads '89
No Way Back '74

Ellie Cornell
Chips, the War Dog '90
Halloween 5: The Revenge of Michael Myers '89
Halloween 4: The Return of Michael Myers '88

Robert Cornthwaite (1917-)
Matinee '92
Time Trackers '88
The War of the Worlds '53
The Thing '51

Anne Cornwall
Laurel & Hardy: Men O'War '29
College '27

Charlotte Cornwell
The Saint '97
The Krays '90
White Hunter, Black Heart '90

Judy Cornwell (1942-)
Prince of Poisoners: The Life and Crimes of William Palmer '98
Persuasion '95
Santa Claus: The Movie '85
Think Dirty '70
Wuthering Heights '70
Two for the Road '67

Jose Coronado
Goya in Bordeaux '99
The Disappearance of Garcia Lorca '96

Georges Corraface (1953-)
Only Love '98
Escape from L.A. '96
Red Shoe Diaries: Four on the Floor '96
Christopher Columbus: The Discovery '92
Impromptu '90
Not Without My Daughter '90

Mady Correll
Monsieur Verdoux '47
Texas Masquerade '44

Adrienne Corri (1930-)
Rosebud '75
Madhouse '74
A Clockwork Orange '71
Vampire Circus '71
Africa Texas Style '67
The Viking Queen '67
Doctor Zhivago '65
The Tell-Tale Heart '62
The Hellfire Club '61
Corridors of Blood '58
Make Me an Offer '55
Devil Girl from Mars '54
The River '51

Nick Corri
Candyman 3: Day of the Dead '98
Red Shoe Diaries: Four on the Floor '96
In the Heat of Passion '91
Slaves of New York '89
The Lawless Land '88
Tropical Snow '88
Gotcha! '85
A Nightmare on Elm Street '84

Sergio Corrieri
Memories of Underdevelopment '68
I Am Cuba '64

Kevin Corrigan (1969-)
Scotland, PA '02
Chelsea Walls '01
Steal This Movie! '00
Brown's Requiem '98
Henry Fool '98
Lulu on the Bridge '98
Slums of Beverly Hills '98
Buffalo 66 '97
Kicked in the Head '97
The Assassination File '96
Illtown '96
Tree's Lounge '96
Walking and Talking '96
Bandwagon '95
Kiss of Death '94
Living in Oblivion '94
Rhythm Thief '94
True Romance '93
Zebrahead '92

Lloyd Corrigan (1900-69)
The Manchurian Candidate '62
Bowery Boys Meet the Monsters '54
Cavalry Charge '51
Ghost Chasers '51
Blondie Hits the Jackpot '49
The Chase '46
She Wolf of London '46
Gambler's Choice '44
Since You Went Away '44
The Thin Man Goes Home '44
Captive Wild Woman '43
Hitler's Children '43
A Girl, a Guy and a Gob '41
The Lady in Question '40
Young Tom Edison '40

Ray Corrigan (1907-76)
It! The Terror from Beyond Space '58
Trail of Robin Hood '50
White Gorilla '47
Renegade Girl '46
Black Market Rustlers '43
Cowboy Commandos '43
Land of Hunted Men '43
Arizona Stagecoach '42
Boot Hill Bandits '42
Rock River Renegades '42
Thunder River Feud '42
Fugitive Valley '41
Kid's Last Ride '41
Saddle Mountain Round-Up '41
Tonto Basin Outlaws '41
Trail of the Silver Spurs '41
Tumbledown Ranch in Arizona '41
Underground Rustlers '41
Range Busters '40
Trailing Double Trouble '40
West of Pinto Basin '40
Frontier Horizon '39
Three Texas Steers '39
Wyoming Outlaw '39
Heroes of the Hills '38
Outlaws of Sonora '38
Overland Stage Raiders '38
Pals of the Saddle '38
Purple Vigilantes '38
Santa Fe Stampede '38
Come on, Cowboys '37
Heart of the Rockies '37
Hit the Saddle '37
The Painted Stallion '37
Riders of the Whistling Skull '37
Roarin' Lead '37
The Trigger Trio '37
Wild Horse Rodeo '37
Country Gentlemen '36
Ghost Town Gold '36
Undersea Kingdom '36

Shirley Corrigan
The Devil's Nightmare '71
Dr. Jekyll and the Wolfman '71

Aneta Corsaut (1933-95)
Return to Mayberry '85
The Toolbox Murders '78
The Blob '58

Silvana Corsini
Mamma Roma '62
Accatone! '61

Bud Cort (1950-)
Coyote Ugly '00
Pollock '00
South of Heaven, West of Hell '00
But I'm a Cheerleader '99
Dogma '99
The Million Dollar Hotel '99
Sweet Jane '98
Heat '95
Girl in the Cadillac '94
Ted & Venus '93
Going Under '91
Brain Dead '89
The Chocolate War '88
Out of the Dark '88
Love at Stake '87
Invaders from Mars '86
Electric Dreams '84
Maria's Lovers '84
The Secret Diary of Sigmund Freud '84
Hysterical '83
Love Letters '83
The Nightingale '83
Rumpelstiltskin '82
Die Laughing '80
Why Shoot the Teacher '79
Harold and Maude '71
Brewster McCloud '70
Gas-s-s-s! '70
M*A*S*H '70
The Strawberry Statement '70
Sweet Charity '69

Rowena Cortes
To Live and Die in Hong Kong '89
Heroes Three '84

Dan Cortese (1967-)
The Triangle '01
Volcano: Fire on the Mountain '97
Public Enemies '96
A Weekend in the Country '96
At First Sight '95

Joe Cortese (1949-)
American History X '98
Malevolence '98
Born to Run '93
Ruby '92
To Protect and Serve '92
The Closer '91
Python Wolf '88
Assault and Matrimony '87
Deadly Illusion '87
Stalking Danger '86
Letting Go '85
Evilspeak '82
Windows '80
Family Enforcer '76

Valentina Cortese (1924-)
The Adventures of Baron Munchausen '89
When Time Ran Out '80
Widow's Nest '77
Kidnap Syndicate '76
Brother Sun, Sister Moon '73
Day for Night '73
Assassination of Trotsky '72
First Love '70
The Secret of Santa Vittoria '69
Juliet of the Spirits '65
The Girl Who Knew Too Much '63
The Barefoot Contessa '54
Les Miserables '52
Malaya '49

Bella Cortez (1944-)
Tor '64
Vulcan God of Fire '62
The Giant of Metropolis '61

Ricardo Cortez (1899-1977)
Last Hurrah '58
The Inner Circle '46
I Killed That Man '42
Murder over New York '40
Mr. Moto's Last Warning '39
The Gentleman from California '37
Behind Office Doors '31
Big Business Girl '31
Illicit '31
The Maltese Falcon '31
Lost Zeppelin '29
The Phantom in the House '29
Mockery '27
The Sorrows of Satan '26
The Pony Express '25
The Swan '25

Jesse Corti
Beauty and the Beast '91 (V)
Nightlife '90
High Stakes '89

Bill Cosby (1937-)
Jack '96
The Meteor Man '93
Ghost Dad '90
Leonard Part 6 '87
The Devil & Max Devlin '81
California Suite '78
Piece of the Action '77
Mother, Jugs and Speed '76
Let's Do It Again '75
Uptown Saturday Night '74
Man & Boy '71

To All My Friends on Shore '71
Howard Cosell (1920-95)
Casey at the Bat '85
Broadway Danny Rose '84
Sleeper '73
The World's Greatest Athlete '73
Bananas '71
Daniel Cosgrove
National Lampoon's Van Wilder '02
Valentine '01
The Object of My Affection '98
James Cosmo
The Match '99
Babe: Pig in the City '98 (V)
Ivanhoe '97
Emma '96
Braveheart '95
Stormy Monday '88
Ernest Cossart (1876-1951)
Love from a Stranger '47
Kings Row '41
Kitty Foyle '40
Three Smart Girls Grow Up '39
Desire '36
The Great Ziegfeld '36
James Cossins (1933-97)
Dynasty of Fear '72
Wuthering Heights '70
The Anniversary '68
Pierre Cosso
An American Werewolf in Paris '97
My Wonderful Life '90
James Costa
L.I.E. '01
Joe the King '99
Marina Costa
Jungle Raiders '85
The Final Executioner '83
Constantin Costa-Gavras (1933-)
The Stupids '95
Spies Like Us '85
Suzanne Costallos
Lotto Land '95
True Love '89
Paulo Costanzo
40 Days and 40 Nights '02
Josie and the Pussycats '01
Road Trip '00
Robert Costanzo
61* '01
Air Bud 2: Golden Receiver '98
For Which He Stands '98
With Friends Like These '98
Plump Fiction '97
Underworld '96
For Better or Worse '95
Storybook '95
Lady in Waiting '94
Ring of Fire 3: Lion Strike '94
The Cemetery Club '93
Man's Best Friend '93
Relentless 3 '93
Honeymoon in Vegas '92
Delusion '91
Die Hard 2: Die Harder '90
The Vegas Strip Wars '84
Honeyboy '82
Bob Costas (1951-)
Pootie Tang '01
BASEketball '98
The Scout '94
Dolores Costello (1905-79)
The Magnificent Ambersons '42
Breaking the Ice '38
Little Lord Fauntleroy '36
Don Costello (1901-45)
The Blue Dahlia '46
Mystery Man '44
Texas Masquerade '44
Whistling in the Dark '41
Elvis Costello (1954-)
Austin Powers 2: The Spy Who Shagged Me '99
200 Cigarettes '98
Spice World: The Movie '97
Straight to Hell '87
No Surrender '86
Americathon '79
Helene Costello
Don Juan '26
The Man on the Box '25
Lou Costello (1906-59)
The 30-Foot Bride of Candy Rock '59
Dance with Me, Henry '56
Abbott and Costello Meet the Mummy '55
Abbott and Costello Meet the Keystone Kops '54
Abbott and Costello Go to Mars '53
Abbott and Costello Meet Captain Kidd '52
Abbott and Costello Meet Dr. Jekyll and Mr. Hyde '52
Jack & the Beanstalk '52
Lost in Alaska '52
Abbott and Costello Meet the Invisible Man '51
Comin' Round the Mountain '51
Abbott and Costello in the Foreign Legion '50
Abbott and Costello Meet the Killer, Boris Karloff '49
Africa Screams '49
Abbott and Costello Meet Frankenstein '48
Mexican Hayride '48
The Noose Hangs High '48
Buck Privates Come Home '47
The Wistful Widow of Wagon Gap '47
Little Giant '46
The Time of Their Lives '46
Abbott and Costello in Hollywood '45
Here Come the Co-Eds '45
The Naughty Nineties '45
In Society '44
Lost in a Harem '44
Hit the Ice '43
It Ain't Hay '43
Pardon My Sarong '42
Ride 'Em Cowboy '42
Rio Rita '42
Who Done It? '42
Buck Privates '41
Hold That Ghost '41
In the Navy '41
Keep 'Em Flying '41
One Night in the Tropics '40
Mariclare Costello
Heart of a Champion: The Ray Mancini Story '85
Skeezer '82
Coward of the County '81
All God's Children '80
Conspiracy of Terror '75
The Execution of Private Slovik '74
Ward (Edward) Costello
MacArthur '77
The City '76
The Gallant Hours '60
John A. Costelloe
Kazaam '96
Me and the Mob '94
Billy Bathgate '91
Nicolas Coster (1934-)
Betsy's Wedding '90
The Solitary Man '82
Stir Crazy '80
The Electric Horseman '79
MacArthur '77
The Sporting Club '72
Nikolaj Coster-Waldau (1970-)
Black Hawk Down '01
Bent '97
George Costigan
Girls' Night '97
The Hawk '93
Rita, Sue & Bob Too '87
Kevin Costner (1955-)
Dragonfly '02
3000 Miles to Graceland '01
Thirteen Days '00
For Love of the Game '99
Message in a Bottle '98
The Postman '97
Tin Cup '96
Waterworld '95
The War '94
Wyatt Earp '94
A Perfect World '93
The Bodyguard '92
JFK '91
Robin Hood: Prince of Thieves '91
Dances with Wolves '90
Revenge '90
Field of Dreams '89
Bull Durham '88
No Way Out '87
The Untouchables '87
Amazing Stories '85
American Flyers '85
Fandango '85
Silverado '85
The Gunrunner '84
Shadows Run Black '84
Stacy's Knights '83
Table for Five '83
Testament '83
Night Shift '82
Chasing Dreams '81
Sizzle Beach U.S.A. '74
Laurence Cote
Les Voleurs '96
Up/Down/Fragile '95
Nouvelle Vague '90
Tina Cote
Mean Guns '97
Omega Doom '96
Nemesis 2: Nebula '94
Kami Cotler
A Day for Thanks on Walton's Mountain '82
The Waltons: The Christmas Carol '80
Jonathon Cott
Above and Beyond '53
Battle Circus '53
Joseph Cotten (1905-94)
Delusion '84
Churchill and the Generals '81
Heaven's Gate '81
Casino '80
The Hearse '80
Screamers '80
Survivor '80
Perfect Crime '78
Airport '77 '77
Return to Fantasy Island '77
Twilight's Last Gleaming '77
The Lindbergh Kidnapping Case '76
The Big Push '75
Soylent Green '73
Lady Frankenstein '72
Torture Chamber of Baron Blood '72
The Abominable Dr. Phibes '71
The Passing of Evil '70
Tora! Tora! Tora! '70
Petulia '68
Brighty of the Grand Canyon '67
Hellbenders '67
White Comanche '67
The Oscar '66
Tramplers '66
Hush, Hush, Sweet Charlotte '65
From the Earth to the Moon '58
Touch of Evil '58
Niagara '52
Othello '52
September Affair '50
Walk Softly, Stranger '50
Beyond the Forest '49
The Third Man '49
Under Capricorn '49
Portrait of Jennie '48
The Farmer's Daughter '47
Duel in the Sun '46
Love Letters '45
Gaslight '44
Since You Went Away '44
Shadow of a Doubt '43
Journey into Fear '42
The Magnificent Ambersons '42
Citizen Kane '41
Lydia '41
Fanny Cottencon
Window Shopping '86
Special Police '85
Catherine Cotter
Outlaws of the Range '36
Pinto Rustlers '36
Chrissie Cotterill
Nil by Mouth '96
Scrubbers '82
Ralph Cotterill (1932-)
Bad Boy Bubby '93
Howling 3: The Marsupials '87
Starship '87
Burke & Wills '85
Oliver Cotton (1944-)
Beowulf '98
Christopher Columbus: The Discovery '92
Eleni '85
Robin Hood...The Legend: Herne's Son '85
Paul Coufos
Mortal Danger '94
Dragonfight '92
Boxcar Blues '90
Thunderground '89
Food of the Gods: Part 2 '88
Busted Up '86
City of Shadows '86
The Lost Empire '83
Marisa Coughlan (1973-)
Freddy Got Fingered '01
Gossip '99
Teaching Mrs. Tingle '99
George Coulouris (1903-89)
The Long Good Friday '80
It's Not the Size That Counts '74
Murder on the Orient Express '74
The Tempter '74
Papillon '73
The Stranger '73
Tower of Evil '72
Blood from the Mummy's Tomb '71
Arabesque '66
The Skull '65
The Womaneater '59
Race for Life '55
The Runaway Bus '54
Doctor in the House '53
A Southern Yankee '48
Where There's Life '47
Lady on a Train '45
A Song to Remember '45
Master Race '44
Mr. Skeffington '44
None But the Lonely Heart '44
For Whom the Bell Tolls '43
This Land Is Mine '43
Watch on the Rhine '43
Citizen Kane '41
The Lady in Question '40
Keith Coulouris
Beastmaster 3: The Eye of Braxus '95
Dead Man's Revenge '93
Take Down '92
Bernie Coulson
Cabin by the Lake '00
The Highway Man '99
Hard Core Logo '96
Adventures in Spying '92
Eddie and the Cruisers 2: Eddie Lives! '89
The Accused '88
Raymond Coulthard
Emma '97
Rhodes '97
Barbara Couper
Vanity Fair '67
The Last Days of Dolwyn '49
Clotilde Courau (1969-)
Deep in the Woods '00
Deterrence '00
Elisa '94
The Pickle '93
Nicole Courcel (1930-)
Sundays & Cybele '62
Le Cas du Dr. Laurent '57
Rendez-vous de Juillet '49
Hazel Court (1926-)
Masque of the Red Death '65
The Raven '63
Doctor Blood's Coffin '62
Premature Burial '62
The Curse of Frankenstein '57
Hour of Decision '57
Devil Girl from Mars '54
Ghost Ship '53
Dear Murderer '47
Jason Court
A Night in the Life of Jimmy Reardon '88
Grandview U.S.A. '84
Margaret Courtenay
The Mirror Crack'd '80
Hot Millions '68
Tom Courtenay (1937-)
A Rather English Marriage '98
The Old Curiosity Shop '94
The Last Butterfly '92
Let Him Have It '91
Happy New Year '87
Leonard Part 6 '87
The Dresser '83
I Heard the Owl Call My Name '73
Catch Me a Spy '71
One Day in the Life of Ivan Denisovich '71
Dandy in Aspic '68
Night of the Generals '67
Doctor Zhivago '65
King Rat '65
Operation Crossbow '65
King and Country '64
Billy Liar '63
The Loneliness of the Long Distance Runner '62
Jerome Courtland (1926-)
Tharus Son of Attila '87
Tonka '58
Santa Fe '51
The Texas Rangers '51
Battleground '49
Man from Colorado '49
Tokyo Joe '49
Alex Courtney (1940-)
And the Band Played On '93
Fatal Pulse '88
Enter the Ninja '81
Chuck Courtney (1931-2000)
Billy the Kid Versus Dracula '66
Teenage Monster '57
Inez Courtney (1908-75)
The Thirteenth Man '37
Let's Sing Again '36
The Reckless Way '36
Suzy '36
Jeni Courtney
Nothing Personal '95
The Secret of Roan Inish '94
Brian Cousins
Soldier of Fortune Inc. '97
Invisible: The Chronicles of Benjamin Knight '93
Mandroid '93
Longtime Companion '90
Christian Cousins
Twinsitters '95
Danielle Steel's Heartbeat '93
Christopher Cousins
Earth vs. the Spider '01
Hell High '86
Allen Covert
Little Nicky '00
The Wedding Singer '97
Bulletproof '96
Happy Gilmore '96
Jerome Cowan (1897-1972)
Have Rocket Will Travel '59
The West Point Story '50
Blondie Hits the Jackpot '49
June Bride '48
Cry Wolf '47
Riff-Raff '47
Blondie Knows Best '46
The Perfect Marriage '46
Fog Island '45
Jungle Captive '45
Guest in the House '44
Silver Spurs '43
Who Done It? '42
The Great Lie '41
The Maltese Falcon '41
The Saint Strikes Back '39
You Only Live Once '37
Noel Coward (1899-1973)
The Italian Job '69
Boom! '68
Paris When It Sizzles '64
Around the World in 80 Days '56
In Which We Serve '43
Hearts of the World '18
Bruce Cowling (1919-86)
To Hell and Back '55
Cause for Alarm '51
The Painted Hills '51
Battleground '49
The Stratton Story '49
Nicola Cowper (1967-)
Devices and Desires '91
Journey to the Center of the Earth '88
Lionheart '87
Dreamchild '85
Transmutations '85
Winter Flight '84
Alan Cox (1970-)
Mrs. Dalloway '97
The Odyssey '97
An Awfully Big Adventure '94
Young Sherlock Holmes '85
Alex Cox (1954-)
Dance with the Devil '97
Dead Beat '94
Brian Cox (1946-)
The Bourne Identity '02
The Rookie '02
The Affair of the Necklace '01
L.I.E. '01
Longitude '00
Mad About Mambo '00
Nuremberg '00
The Corruptor '99
For Love of the Game '99
The Minus Man '99
Desperate Measures '98
Retribution '98
Rushmore '98
The Boxer '97
Kiss the Girls '97
Chain Reaction '96
The Glimmer Man '96
The Long Kiss Goodnight '96
Braveheart '95
Rob Roy '95
Royal Deceit '94
Sharpe's Eagle '93

Sharpe's Rifles *'93*
The Lost Language of Cranes *'92*
Murder by Moonlight *'91*
Hidden Agenda *'90*
Secret Weapon *'90*
Manhunter *'86*
Pope John Paul II *'84*
Silent Scream *'84*
In Celebration *'75*
Christina Cox
Better Than Chocolate *'99*
Street Law *'95*
Jennifer Elise Cox (1973-)
EDtv *'99*
Sometimes They Come Back ... Again *'96*
A Very Brady Sequel *'96*
A Weekend in the Country *'96*
The Brady Bunch Movie *'95*
Julie Cox
Dune *'00*
The Scarlet Pimpernel 2: Mademoiselle Guillotine *'99*
20,000 Leagues Under the Sea *'97*
Mitchell Cox
A.P.E.X. *'94*
Rule #3 *'93*
Red Snow *'91*
Strait-Jacket *'64*
Richard Cox (1948-)
American Tragedy *'00*
Snowbound: The Jim and Jennifer Stolpa Story *'94*
Street Justice *'89*
Zombie High *'87*
The Vindicator *'85*
King of the Mountain *'81*
Ronny Cox (1938-)
American Outlaws *'01*
Forces of Nature *'99*
Frog and Wombat *'98*
From the Earth to the Moon *'98*
Murder at 1600 *'97*
Todd McFarlane's Spawn *'97 (V)*
Rebound: The Legend of Earl "The Goat" Manigault *'96*
Scissors *'91*
Loose Cannons *'90*
Martians Go Home! *'90*
Total Recall *'90*
Captain America *'89*
One Man Force *'89*
In the Line of Duty: The FBI Murders *'88*
Scandal in a Small Town *'88*
The Abduction of Kari Swenson *'87*
Beverly Hills Cop 2 *'87*
RoboCop *'87*
Steele Justice *'87*
Target: Favorite Son *'87*
Hollywood Vice Sqaud *'86*
Vision Quest *'85*
Beverly Hills Cop *'84*
Kavik the Wolf Dog *'84*
Raw Courage *'84*
Reckless Disregard *'84*
Tangiers *'83*
The Beast Within *'82*
Some Kind of Hero *'82*
Two of a Kind *'82*
When Hell Was in Session *'82*
Fallen Angel *'81*
Taps *'81*
Last Song *'80*
The Onion Field *'79*
Harper Valley P.T.A. *'78*
The Car *'77*
Gray Lady Down *'77*
Lost Legacy: A Girl Called Hatter Fox *'77*
Our Town *'77*
Bound for Glory *'76*
Who Is the Black Dahlia? *'75*
The Connection *'73*
Deliverance *'72*
Mind Snatchers *'72*
Ruth Cox
The Attic *'80*
Swap Meet *'79*
Tony Cox
Me, Myself, and Irene *'00*
Spaced Invaders *'90*
Veanne Cox
Big Eden *'00*
Erin Brockovich *'00*
National Lampoon's Class of '86 *'86*
Wally Cox (1924-73)
The Night Strangler *'72*
The Barefoot Executive *'71*
The Boatniks *'70*
The One and Only, Genuine, Original Family Band *'68*
A Guide for the Married Man *'67*
Bedford Incident *'65*
Morituri *'65*
Spencer's Mountain *'63*
State Fair *'62*
Courteney Cox Arquette (1964-)
Get Well Soon *'01*
3000 Miles to Graceland *'01*
Scream 3 *'00*
The Runner *'99*
Scream 2 *'97*
Commandments *'96*
Scream *'96*
Sketch Artist 2: Hands That See *'94*
Ace Ventura: Pet Detective *'93*
The Opposite Sex and How to Live With Them *'93*
Battling for Baby *'92*
Shaking the Tree *'92*
Blue Desert *'91*
Curiosity Kills *'90*
Mr. Destiny *'90*
Down Twisted *'89*
The Prize Pulitzer *'89*
Cocoon: The Return *'88*
Masters of the Universe *'87*
Misfits of Science *'85*
Jonathan Coy
Conspiracy *'01*
The Scarlet Pimpernel *'99*
The Scarlet Pimpernel 2: Mademoiselle Guillotine *'99*
The Scarlet Pimpernel 3: The Kidnapped King *'99*
The Rector's Wife *'94*
Brendan Coyle
Conspiracy *'01*
Catherine Cookson's The Glass Virgin *'95*
Richard Coyle
Lorna Doone *'01*
Othello *'01*
Prince of Poisoners: The Life and Crimes of William Palmer *'98*
Peter Coyote (1942-)
A Walk to Remember *'02*
Erin Brockovich *'00*
Red Letters *'00*
The Basket *'99*
Execution of Justice *'99*
Random Hearts *'99*
Indiscreet *'98*
Patch Adams *'98*
Road Ends *'98*
Route 9 *'98*
Sphere *'97*
Top of the World *'97*
Two for Texas *'97*
Seeds of Doubt *'96*
Unforgettable *'96*
Buffalo Girls *'95*
Dalva *'95*
Moonlight and Valentino *'95*
Terminal Justice: Cybertech P.D. *'95*
Breach of Conduct *'94*
Kika *'94*
That Eye, the Sky *'94*
Bitter Moon *'92*
Keeper of the City *'92*
Crooked Hearts *'91*
Exposure *'91*
The Man Inside *'90*
Heart of Midnight *'89*
Best Kept Secrets *'88*
Out *'88*
Baja Oklahoma *'87*
Echoes in the Darkness *'87*
A Man in Love *'87*
Outrageous Fortune *'87*
Stacking *'87*
The Blue Yonder *'86*
The Jagged Edge *'85*
Legend of Billie Jean *'85*
Heartbreakers *'84*
Slayground *'84*
Cross Creek *'83*
Strangers Kiss *'83*
Timerider *'83*
Endangered Species *'82*
E.T.: The Extra-Terrestrial *'82*
The People vs. Jean Harris *'81*
Southern Comfort *'81*
Die Laughing *'80*
Tell Me a Riddle *'80*
Cylk Cozart
Play It to the Bone *'99*
Three to Tango *'99*
Conspiracy Theory *'97*
White Men Can't Jump *'92*
Buster Crabbe (1907-83)
Alien Dead *'79*
Swim Team *'79*
Arizona Raiders *'65*
Lonesome Trail *'55*
King of the Congo *'52*
Pirates of the High Seas *'50*
The Last of the Redmen *'47*
Sea Hound *'47*
Outlaw of the Plains *'46*
Prairie Badmen *'46*
Swamp Fire *'46*
Border Badmen *'45*
Gangster's Den *'45*
His Brother's Ghost *'45*
Lightning Raiders *'45*
Shadows of Death *'45*
Devil Riders *'44*
Frontier Outlaws *'44*
Nabonga *'44*
Oath of Vengeance *'44*
Rustler's Hideout *'44*
Wild Horse Phantom *'44*
Billy the Kid Trapped *'42*
Jungle Siren *'42*
Law and Order *'42*
The Mysterious Rider *'42*
Wildcat *'42*
Flash Gordon Conquers the Universe *'40*
Flash Gordon: Rocketship *'40*
Space Soldiers Conquer the Universe *'40*
Thundering Gunslingers *'40*
Buck Rogers Conquers the Universe *'39*
Destination Saturn *'39*
Flash Gordon: Mars Attacks the World *'39*
Red Barry *'38*
Forlorn River *'37*
Desert Gold *'36*
Drift Fence *'36*
Rocketship *'36*
Buffalo Stampede *'33*
Tarzan the Fearless *'33*
To the Last Man *'33*
Island of Lost Souls *'32*
Ruth Cracknell (1923-2002)
Joey *'98*
Lilian's Story *'95*
Alice to Nowhere *'86*
Island Trader *'71*
Daniel Craig (1968-)
Lara Croft: Tomb Raider *'01*
I Dreamed of Africa *'00*
Love and Rage *'99*
Elizabeth *'98*
Love Is the Devil *'98*
The Ice House *'97*
Moll Flanders *'96*
A Kid in King Arthur's Court *'95*
The Power of One *'92*
Diane Craig (1949-)
All the Rivers Run *'84*
The Mango Tree *'77*
Roses Bloom Twice *'77*
Ned Kelly *'70*
Helen Craig
They Live by Night *'49*
The Snake Pit *'48*
James Craig (1912-85)
The Tormentors *'71*
The Devil's Brigade *'68*
Man or Gun *'58*
Naked in the Sun *'57*
Cyclops *'56*
Drums in the Deep South *'51*
Our Vines Have Tender Grapes *'45*
The Human Comedy *'43*
Valley of the Sun *'42*
The Devil & Daniel Webster *'41*
Black Friday *'40*
Kitty Foyle *'40*
Winners of the West *'40*
Thunder Trail *'37*
Michael Craig (1928-)
Robin Hood...The Legend: Herne's Son *'85*
Escape 2000 *'81*
The Irishman *'78*
Night of the Assassin *'77*
Roses Bloom Twice *'77*
Ride a Wild Pony *'75*
Inn of the Damned *'74*
Vault of Horror *'73*
Lola *'69*
Star! *'68*
Modesty Blaise *'66*
Sandra of a Thousand Delights *'65*
Stolen Hours *'63*
Mysterious Island *'61*
Sapphire *'59*
Sea of Sand *'58*
The Silent Enemy *'58*
Wendy Craig (1934-)
The Nanny *'65*
The Servant *'63*
Room at the Top *'59*
Yvonne Craig (1937-)
Digging Up Business *'91*
How to Frame a Figg *'71*
Mars Needs Women *'66*
Kissin' Cousins *'64*
It Happened at the World's Fair *'63*
The Young Land *'59*
Jeanne Crain (1925-)
The Night God Screamed *'80s*
Nefertiti, Queen of the Nile *'64*
Fastest Gun Alive *'56*
Man Without a Star *'55*
People Will Talk *'51*
Cheaper by the Dozen *'50*
A Letter to Three Wives *'49*
Pinky *'49*
Leave Her to Heaven *'45*
State Fair *'45*
Grant Cramer
Leapin' Leprechauns *'95*
Killer Klowns from Outer Space *'88*
Hardbodies *'84*
Joey Cramer (1974-)
Stone Fox *'87*
Flight of the Navigator *'86*
Marc Cramer
First Yank into Tokyo *'45*
Isle of the Dead *'45*
Richard Cramer (1889-1960)
Saps at Sea *'40*
Santa Fe Bound *'37*
Slaves in Bondage *'37*
Speed Reporter *'36*
Frontier Justice *'35*
Barbara Crampton (1962-)
Cold Harvest *'98*
The Godson *'98*
Space Truckers *'97*
Castle Freak *'95*
Robot Wars *'93*
Trancers 2: The Return of Jack Deth *'90*
Puppet Master *'89*
Kidnapped *'87*
Chopping Mall *'86*
From Beyond *'86*
Fraternity Vacation *'85*
Body Double *'84*
Re-Animator *'84*
Bob Crane (1928-78)
Gus *'76*
Superdad *'73*
Return to Peyton Place *'61*
Norma Crane (1928-73)
Fiddler on the Roof *'71*
They Call Me Mr. Tibbs! *'70*
Night Gallery *'69*
Tea and Sympathy *'56*
Richard Crane (1918-69)
The Devil's Partner *'58*
Guns Don't Argue *'57*
Rocky Jones, Space Ranger: Renegade Satellite *'54*
Winning of the West *'53*
Cavalry Charge *'51*
Dynamite *'49*
Tony Crane (1972-)
Wishmaster *'97*
An American Summer *'90*
In the Line of Duty: A Cop for the Killing *'90*
The War of the Roses *'89*
Kenneth Cranham (1944-)
The Murder of Stephen Lawrence *'01*
Born Romantic *'00*
Lady Audley's Secret *'00*
Deep in the Heart (of Texas) *'98*
Our Mutual Friend *'98*
The Boxer *'97*
Jack Higgins' Midnight Man *'96*
The Tenant of Wildfell Hall *'96*
Jack Higgins' On Dangerous Ground *'95*
Tale of a Vampire *'92*
Under Suspicion *'92*
Prospero's Books *'91*
Monkey Boy *'90*
Oranges Are Not the Only Fruit *'89*
Chocolat *'88*
Hellbound: Hellraiser 2 *'88*
Stealing Heaven *'88*
Danger UXB *'81*
Brother Sun, Sister Moon *'73*
Lorcan Cranitch (1959-)
Shackleton *'02*
Dancing at Lughnasa *'98*
Deacon Brodie *'98*
Cracker: Brotherly Love *'95*
Cracker: Men Should Weep *'94*
Cracker: To Be a Somebody *'94*
Devin Crannell
Island of the Dead *'00*
Wildflowers *'99*
Patrick Cranshaw
Bubble Boy *'01*
Best in Show *'00*
Broken Vessels *'98*
Nothing to Lose *'96*
The Amazing Transparent Man *'60*
Bryan Cranston (1956-)
Terror Tract *'00*
From the Earth to the Moon *'98*
Saving Private Ryan *'98*
That Thing You Do! *'96*
The Companion *'94*
Erotique *'94*
High Stakes *'93*
Dead Space *'90*
Nick Cravat (1911-94)
The Island of Dr. Moreau *'77*
The Scalphunters *'68*
Run Silent, Run Deep *'58*
Crimson Pirate *'52*
The Flame & the Arrow *'50*
Noel Cravat (1910-60)
The 5000 Fingers of Dr. T *'53*
Pirate Ship *'49*
The Razor's Edge *'46*
G-Men vs. the Black Dragon *'43*
Frank Craven (1875-1945)
Jack London *'44*
Son of Dracula *'43*
In This Our Life *'42*
Keeper of the Flame *'42*
Pittsburgh *'42*
City for Conquest *'40*
Dreaming Out Loud *'40*
Our Town *'40*
James Craven
D-Day on Mars *'45*
Immortal Sergeant *'43*
Sherlock Holmes and the Secret Weapon *'42*
Today I Hang *'42*
Green Archer *'40*
Matt Craven (1956-)
Dragonfly *'02*
Varian's War *'01*
Nuremberg *'00*
Things You Can Tell Just by Looking at Her *'00*
From the Earth to the Moon *'98*
Paulie *'98*
The Final Cut *'96*
The Juror *'96*
Masterminds *'96*
Breach of Trust *'95*
Bulletproof Heart *'95*
Crimson Tide *'95*
Kingfish: A Story of Huey P. Long *'95*
White Tiger *'95*
Double Cross *'94*
Indian Summer *'93*
A Few Good Men *'92*
K2: The Ultimate High *'92*
Jacob's Ladder *'90*
Smokescreen *'90*
Chattahoochee *'89*
Palais Royale *'88*
Agent on Ice *'86*
Happy Birthday to Me *'81*
Till Death Do Us Part *'72*
Mimi (Meyer) Craven
Dogwatch *'97*
Daddy's Girl *'96*
Midnight Heat *'95*
The Last Gasp *'94*
Open Fire *'94*
Mikey *'92*
Wes Craven (1939-)
Jay and Silent Bob Strike Back *'01*
Scream *'96*
ShadowZone: The Undead Express *'96*
The Fear *'94*
Wes Craven's New Nightmare *'94*
Body Bags *'93*
Andrew Crawford
The Gay Lady *'49*
Dear Murderer *'47*
Anne Crawford (1920-56)
Knights of the Round Table *'53*
Tony Draws a Horse *'51*
Night Beat *'48*
Broderick Crawford (1911-86)
Ransom Money *'88*
Upper Crust *'88*
Proof of the Man *'84*
Dark Forces *'83*
Express to Terror *'79*
A Little Romance *'79*
Hunter *'77*

Bing Crosby (1904-77)
That's Entertainment '74
Cancel My Reservation '72
Robin and the 7 Hoods '64
The Road to Hong Kong '62
Let's Make Love '60
The Road to Lebanon '60
Alias Jesse James '59
High Society '56
Country Girl '54
White Christmas '54
The Road to Bali '53
Scared Stiff '53
Just for You '52
Here Comes the Groom '51
Mr. Music '50
Riding High '50
The Adventures of Ichabod and Mr. Toad '49 (V)
A Connecticut Yankee in King Arthur's Court '49
The Legend of Sleepy Hollow '49 (N)
Emperor Waltz '48
My Favorite Brunette '47
The Road to Rio '47
Welcome Stranger '47
Blue Skies '46
The Road to Utopia '46
The Bells of St. Mary's '45
Here Come the Waves '45
Going My Way '44
The Princess and the Pirate '44
Strictly G.I. '44
They Got Me Covered '43 (V)
Holiday Inn '42
My Favorite Blonde '42
The Road to Morocco '42
Star Spangled Rhythm '42
Birth of the Blues '41
The Road to Zanzibar '41
Rhythm on the River '40
The Road to Singapore '40
Waikiki Wedding '37
Rhythm on the Range '36
We're Not Dressing '34
Going Hollywood '33
Reaching for the Moon '31
King of Jazz '30

Cathy Lee Crosby (1944-)
Ablaze '00
The Big Tease '99
The Real Howard Spitz '98
The Player '92
World War III '86
Roughnecks '80
The Dark '79
Coach '78

David Crosby (1941-)
Thunderheart '92
Backdraft '91
Hook '91
Gimme Shelter '70

Denise Crosby (1957-)
Deep Impact '98
Red Shoe Diaries: Four on the Floor '96
Mutant Species '95
Relative Fear '95
Black Water '94
Desperate Crimes '93
Dolly Dearest '92
Red Shoe Diaries 2: Double Dare '92
Miracle Mile '89
Pet Sematary '89
Skin Deep '89
Arizona Heat '87
Desert Hearts '86
The Eliminators '86
Curse of the Pink Panther '83
48 Hrs. '82

Gary Crosby (1933-95)
Chill Factor '90
Night Stalker '87
Music Shoppe '82
Justin Morgan Had a Horse '81
Girl Happy '65

Lucinda Crosby
Blue Movies '88
Naked Cage '86

Mary Crosby (1959-)
The Night Caller '97
Cupid '96
Desperate Motives '92
The Berlin Conspiracy '91
Body Chemistry '90
Corporate Affairs '90
Eating '90
Tapeheads '89
Deadly Innocence '88
Quicker Than the Eye '88
Stagecoach '86
Ice Pirates '84
Last Plane Out '83
Pearl '78

Henrietta Crosman
Personal Property '37
Charlie Chan's Secret '35

Ben Cross (1947-)
Solomon '98
The Corporate Ladder '97
20,000 Leagues Under the Sea '97
The Invader '96
Turbulence '96
First Knight '95
Temptress '95
The Ascent '94
Haunted Symphony '94
Cold Sweat '93
The Criminal Mind '93
Diamond Fleece '92
Live Wire '92
The Jeweller's Shop '90
Nightlife '90
Paperhouse '89
Steal the Sky '88
The Unholy '88
The Assisi Underground '84
The Far Pavilions '84
Coming Out of the Ice '82
Chariots of Fire '81
The Flame Trees of Thika '81

David Cross (1964-)
Scary Movie 2 '01
Small Soldiers '98
The Cable Guy '96

Dennis Cross
How to Make a Monster '58
Crime of Passion '57

Harley Cross (1978-)
Shriek If You Know What I Did Last Friday the 13th '00
Dance with the Devil '97
To Dance with the White Dog '93
Stanley and Iris '90
The Fly 2 '89
Cohen and Tate '88
The Believers '87
Where Are the Children? '85

Joseph Cross
The Spring '00
Desperate Measures '98
Jack Frost '98
Wide Awake '97

Larry Cross
The Wind and the Lion '75
Time Lock '57

Paul Cross
The Return of the Borrowers '96
The Borrowers '93
Ice Pawn '92

Rebecca Cross
The Bachelor '99
The Last Warrior '99
Leprechaun 4: In Space '96
Wet and Wild Summer '92

TJ Cross
Showtime '02
Gone in 60 Seconds '00

Rupert Crosse
The Reivers '69
Ride in the Whirlwind '66
Shadows '60

Syd Crossley (1885-1960)
Young and Innocent '37
The Deputy Drummer '35
That Certain Thing '28

Scatman Crothers (1910-86)
The Journey of Natty Gann '85
Twilight Zone: The Movie '83
Two of a Kind '83
Deadly Eyes '82
Zapped! '82
Bronco Billy '80
The Shining '80
Scavenger Hunt '79
Mean Dog Blues '78
Chesty Anderson USN '76
The Shootist '76
Silver Streak '76
Stay Hungry '76
One Flew Over the Cuckoo's Nest '75
Streetfight '75
Black Belt Jones '74
Truck Turner '74
Detroit 9000 '73
The King of Marvin Gardens '72
Bloody Mama '70
The Great White Hope '70
Lady in a Cage '64
The Patsy '64
Between Heaven and Hell '56
Yes, Sir, Mr. Bones '51

Lindsay Crouse (1948-)
Cherish '02
Imposter '01
The Insider '99
Progeny '98
The Arrival '96
If These Walls Could Talk '96
The Juror '96
Prefontaine '96
The Indian in the Cupboard '95
Norma Jean and Marilyn '95
Being Human '94
Bye Bye, Love '94
Parallel Lives '94
Chantilly Lace '93
Final Appeal '93
Desperate Hours '90
Communion '89
House of Games '87
Iceman '84
Places in the Heart '84
Daniel '83
The Verdict '82
Prince of the City '81
Summer Solstice '81
Between the Lines '77
Slap Shot '77
All the President's Men '76
Eleanor & Franklin '76

Roger Crouzet
Blue Country '77
Letters from My Windmill '54

Ashley Crow
Little Big League '94
Final Appeal '93

Emilia Crow
Grand Tour: Disaster in Time '92
Hitz '92

Graham Crowden (1922-)
I Want You '98
The Innocent Sleep '95
Monsignor Quixote '91
Code Name: Emerald '85
The Company of Wolves '85
Out of Africa '85
Britannia Hospital '82
The Little Prince '74
Romance with a Double Bass '74
Naughty Knights '71
If... '69
Morgan: A Suitable Case for Treatment '66

Russell Crowe (1964-)
A Beautiful Mind '01
Gladiator '00
Proof of Life '00
The Insider '99
Mystery, Alaska '99
Breaking Up '97
Heaven's Burning '97
L.A. Confidential '97
No Way Back '96
Rough Magic '95
Virtuosity '95
For the Moment '94
The Quick and the Dead '94
The Sum of Us '94
The Silver Stallion: King of the Wild Brumbies '93
The Crossing '92
The Efficiency Expert '92
Romper Stomper '92
Hammers over the Anvil '91
Proof '91

Josephine Crowell (1849-1932)
The Man Who Laughs '27
The Greatest Question '19
Hearts of the World '18
The Birth of a Nation '15

Dermot Crowley
Falling for a Dancer '98
The Sculptress '97
Echoes '88

Jeananne Crowley
The Real Charlotte '91
Reilly: Ace of Spies '87

Kathleen Crowley (1931-)
Curse of the Undead '59
The Rebel Set '59
The Female Jungle '56
Westward Ho, the Wagons! '56

Pat Crowley
61* '01
Wild Women of Wongo '59

Pat(ricia) Crowley (1933-)
Force of Evil '77
Return to Fantasy Island '77
Menace on the Mountain '70
Hollywood or Bust '56
Walk the Proud Land '56
Red Garters '54
Forever Female '53

Suzan Crowley
Devices and Desires '91
Christabel '89

Billy Crudup (1968-)
Charlotte Gray '01
World Traveler '01
Almost Famous '00
Waking the Dead '00
Jesus' Son '99
The Hi-Lo Country '98
Monument Ave. '98
Princess Mononoke '98 (V)
Inventing the Abbotts '97
Without Limits '97
Grind '96
Sleepers '96

Tom Cruise (1962-)
Minority Report '02
Vanilla Sky '01
Mission: Impossible 2 '00
Eyes Wide Shut '99
Magnolia '99
Jerry Maguire '96
Mission: Impossible '96
Interview with the Vampire '94
The Firm '93
Far and Away '92
A Few Good Men '92
Days of Thunder '90
Born on the Fourth of July '89
Cocktail '88
Rain Man '88
The Color of Money '86
Legend '86
Top Gun '86
All the Right Moves '83
The Outsiders '83
Risky Business '83
Losin' It '82
Endless Love '81
Taps '81

Rosalie Crutchley (1920-97)
The Franchise Affair
A Village Affair '95
Four Weddings and a Funeral '94
Monsignor Quixote '91
Eleni '85
The Hunchback of Notre Dame '82
Testament of Youth '79
Night of the Laughing Dead '75
And Now the Screaming Starts '73
Elizabeth R '72
Cold Comfort Farm '71
Six Wives of Henry VIII '71
Creatures the World Forgot '70
Wuthering Heights '70
The Haunting '63
Make Me an Offer '55

Abigail Cruttenden (1969-)
Charlotte Gray '01
Hideous Kinky '99
Into the Blue '97
Jane Eyre '97
Sharpe's Justice '97
Sharpe's Revenge '97
Sharpe's Mission '96
Sharpe's Regiment '96
Sharpe's Siege '96
Intimate Contact '87
Kipperbang '82

Greg Cruttwell
George of the Jungle '97
Two Days in the Valley '96
Naked '93

Alexis Cruz (1974-)
Why Do Fools Fall in Love? '98
Hostage High '97
Riot in the Streets '96
Larry McMurtry's Streets of Laredo '95
Stargate '94
The Old Man and the Sea '90
Gryphon '88

Brandon Cruz
Safe '95
The Bad News Bears '76

Celia Cruz
The Perez Family '94
The Mambo Kings '92

Ernesto Cruz
Midaq Alley '95
El Norte '83
Erendira '83

Penelope Cruz (1974-)
Blow '01
Captain Corelli's Mandolin '01
Vanilla Sky '01
All the Pretty Horses '00
Woman on Top '00
All About My Mother '99
The Hi-Lo Country '98
Twice upon a Yesterday '98
Live Flesh '97
Open Your Eyes '97
Love Can Seriously Damage Your Health '96
Talk of Angels '96
Framed '93
Jamon, Jamon '93
Belle Epoque '92

Raymond Cruz
Training Day '01
The Last Marshal '99
From Dusk Till Dawn 2: Texas Blood Money '98
Alien: Resurrection '97
The Substitute '96
Up Close and Personal '96
Clear and Present Danger '94
Dragstrip Girl '94

Vladimir Cruz
A Paradise Under the Stars '99
Strawberry and Chocolate '93

Wilson Cruz (1973-)
Supernova '99
Joyride '97
All Over Me '96
johns '96

Jon Cryer (1965-)
Holy Man '98
Went to Coney Island on a Mission from God...Be Back by Five '98
Glam '97
Plan B '97
The Pompatus of Love '95
Heads '93
Hot Shots! '91
Dudes '87
Hiding Out '87
Morgan Stewart's Coming Home '87
O.C. and Stiggs '87
Superman 4: The Quest for Peace '87
Pretty in Pink '86
No Small Affair '84
Noon Wine '84

Suzanne Cryer
Friends & Lovers '99
Dead Silence '98
Wag the Dog '97
Some Folks Call It a Sling Blade '94

Billy Crystal (1947-)
America's Sweethearts '01
Monsters, Inc. '01 (V)
The Adventures of Rocky & Bullwinkle '00
Analyze This '98
My Giant '98
Deconstructing Harry '97
Father's Day '96
Hamlet '96
Forget Paris '95
City Slickers 2: The Legend of Curly's Gold '94
Mr. Saturday Night '92
City Slickers '91
When Harry Met Sally... '89
Memories of Me '88
The Princess Bride '87
Throw Momma from the Train '87
Running Scared '86
This Is Spinal Tap '84
The Three Little Pigs '84
Enola Gay: The Men, the Mission, the Atomic Bomb '80
Breaking Up Is Hard to Do '79
Rabbit Test '78

Gyorgy Cserhalmi
Mephisto '81
Hungarian Rhapsody '78

Marton Csokas
XXX '02
Lord of the Rings 1: The Fellowship of the Rings '01
Broken English '96

David Cubitt (1965-)
Ali '01
I Shot a Man in Vegas '96
Swann '96

Maria Grazia Cucinotta (1969-)
Just One Night '00
Picking Up the Pieces '99
The World Is Not Enough '99
Solomon '98
A Brooklyn State of Mind '97
The Day of the Beast '95
The Postman '94

Michael Cudlitz
Band of Brothers '01
Grosse Pointe Blank '97
D3: The Mighty Ducks '96
Last Exit to Earth '96
The Liar's Club '93

Xavier Cugat (1900-90)
Neptune's Daughter '49
A Date with Judy '48
Holiday in Mexico '46
Two Girls and a Sailor '44
Stage Door Canteen '43
You Were Never Lovelier '42

Vladimir Cuk
The Sixth Man '97
Celtic Pride '96

Melinda Culea
Down, Out and Dangerous '95
Through the Eyes of a Killer '92

Kieran Culkin (1982-)
The Dangerous Lives of Altar Boys '02
Igby Goes Down '02
The Cider House Rules '99
The Magical Legend of the Leprechauns '99
Music of the Heart '99
She's All That '99
The Mighty '98
Father of the Bride Part II '95
My Summer Story '94
Nowhere to Run '93
Home Alone 2: Lost in New York '92
Father of the Bride '91
Home Alone '90

Macaulay Culkin (1980-)
Getting Even with Dad '94
The Pagemaster '94
Richie Rich '94
George Balanchine's The Nutcracker '93
The Good Son '93
Home Alone 2: Lost in New York '92
My Girl '91
Only the Lonely '91
Home Alone '90
Jacob's Ladder '90
See You in the Morning '89
Uncle Buck '89
Rocket Gibraltar '88

Michael Culkin
Dangerous Beauty '98
Into the Blue '97
Candyman '92

Rory Culkin (1989-)
Signs '02
You Can Count On Me '99

Brett Cullen (1956-)
The Replacements '00
From the Earth to the Moon '98
Levitation '97
The Killing Jar '96
Apollo 13 '95
Something to Talk About '95
A Kiss Goodnight '94
Prehysteria '93
In a Stranger's Hand '92
Leaving Normal '92
Dead Solid Perfect '88

Max Cullen (1940-)
Kings in Grass Castles '97
Kiss or Kill '97
Billy's Holiday '95
Lightning Jack '94
Hard Knocks '80
The Odd Angry Shot '79

Frederick Culley
The Four Feathers '39
The Private Life of Henry VIII '33

John Cullum (1930-)
Held Up '00
Inherit the Wind '99
Undesirable '92
Sweet Country '87
Marie '85
The Day After '83
The Prodigal '83
The Man Without a Country '73

John David (J.D.) Cullum (1966-)
Forever Young '92
Roadside Prophets '92
Ambition '91
Reversal of Fortune '90
Glory '89
Morgan Stewart's Coming Home '87

Joseph Culp
Innocents '00
The Arrival '90
Iguana '89
Dream Lover '85

Robert Culp (1930-)
Innocents '00
Newsbreak '00
Running Mates '00
Wanted '98
Most Wanted '97
Mercenary '96
Xtro 3: Watch the Skies '95
The Pelican Brief '93
Murderous Vision '91
Timebomb '91
Voyage of Terror: The Achille Lauro Affair '90
Pucker Up and Bark Like a Dog '89
Silent Night, Deadly Night 3: Better Watch Out! '89
Big Bad Mama 2 '87
The Blue Lightning '86
The Gladiator '86
The Key to Rebecca '85
Turk 182! '85
Calendar Girl Murders '84
Her Life as a Man '83
Killjoy '81
The Night the City Screamed '80
Goldengirl '79
Hot Rod '79
Flood! '76
Great Scout & Cathouse Thursday '76
Sky Riders '76
Inside Out '75
The Castaway Cowboy '74
Hannie Caulder '72
A Name for Evil '70
Bob & Carol & Ted & Alice '69
Demon with a Glass Hand '64
PT 109 '63
Sammy, the Way-Out Seal '62

Steven Culp
How to Make a Monster '01
Nurse Betty '00
Thirteen Days '00
Norma Jean and Marilyn '95
Jason Goes to Hell: The Final Friday '93

Calvin Culver
Ginger '72
Score '72

Jeffrey Culver
Bad Girls from Mars '90
Hobgoblins '87

Michael Culver (1938-)
The Green Man '91
Alamut Ambush '86
Deadly Recruits '86
Philby, Burgess and MacLean: Spy Scandal of the Century '84
Conduct Unbecoming '75
The Devil's Web '74
Fast Kill '73

Roland Culver (1900-84)
The Legend of Hell House '73
Betrayed '54
Encore '52
The Obsessed '51
The Great Lover '49
Emperor Waltz '48
Down to Earth '47
Singapore '47
To Each His Own '46
Dead of Night '45
On Approval '44
The Day Will Dawn '42
Secret Mission '42
Spitfire '42
Night Train to Munich '40

Ji-Tu Cumbuka (1942-)
Midnight Edition '93
Glitch! '88
Mandingo '75

Alan Cumming (1965-)
The Anniversary Party '01
Josie and the Pussycats '01
Spy Kids '01
Company Man '00
The Flintstones in Viva Rock Vegas '00
Get Carter '00
Urbania '00
Bernard and the Genie '90s
Annie '99
Eyes Wide Shut '99
Titus '99
Plunkett & Macleane '98
Buddy '97
Romy and Michele's High School Reunion '97
Spice World: The Movie '97
Emma '96
Goldeneye '95
Circle of Friends '94
Second Best '94

Dorothy (Dorothy G. Cummings) Cumming (1899-1983)
Applause '29
The Wind '28
King of Kings '27

Constance Cummings (1910-)
The Battle of the Sexes '60
John and Julie '55
Blithe Spirit '45
The Foreman Went to France '42
This England '42
American Madness '32
Night After Night '32
Criminal Code '31

Irving Cummings (1888-1959)
The Saphead '21
Sex '20
Uncle Tom's Cabin '14

James (Jimmy) Cummings
Southie '98
Ed's Next Move '96

Jim (Jonah) Cummings (1953-)
Balto '95 (V)
A Goofy Movie '94 (V)
The Lion King '94 (V)

Quinn Cummings (1967-)
The Babysitter '80
The Goodbye Girl '77
Intimate Strangers '77
Night Terror '76

Robert Cummings (1908-90)
Five Golden Dragons '67
Promise Her Anything '66
The Carpetbaggers '64
Beach Party '63
My Geisha '62
Dial "M" for Murder '54
Lucky Me '54
Reign of Terror '49
Tell It to the Judge '49
The Accused '48
Lost Moment '47
The Chase '46
Forever and a Day '43
Saboteur '42
The Devil & Miss Jones '41
It Started with Eve '41
Kings Row '41
Moon over Miami '41
One Night in the Tropics '40
Everything Happens at Night '39
Three Smart Girls Grow Up '39
The Texans '38
You and Me '38
Souls at Sea '37
Arizona Mahoney '36
Desert Gold '36

Susan Cummings
Verboten! '59
Swamp Women '55

Eli Cummins
Harley '90
Dakota '88

Gregory Scott Cummins
Gang Related '96
The Last of the Dogmen '95
Watchers 3 '94
Lone Justice 2 '93
Action U.S.A. '89
Dead End City '88

Juliette Cummins
Deadly Dreams '88
Slumber Party Massacre 2 '87
Friday the 13th, Part 5: A New Beginning '85
Running Hot '83

Martin Cummins (1969-)
Love Come Down '00
Poltergeist: The Legacy '96
Born to Run '93
Friday the 13th, Part 8: Jason Takes Manhattan '89

Peggy Cummins (1925-)
The Captain's Table '60
Dentist In the Chair '60
Carry On Admiral '57
Curse of the Demon '57
Gun Crazy '49
Salute John Citizen '42

Peter Cummins
Ground Zero '88
Blue Fire Lady '78

Pamela Cundell
24-7 '97
The Return of the Borrowers '96

Rusty Cundieff (1965-)
Sprung '96
Tales from the Hood '95
Fear of a Black Hat '94

Liam Cundill
Reason to Die '90
Return of the Family Man '89

Emma Cunniffe
Plain Jane '01
All the King's Men '99
Great Expectations '99

Cecil Cunningham (1888-1959)
Above Suspicion '43
Twin Beds '42
The Awful Truth '37

John Cunningham (1932-)
The Jackal '97
Twisted '86
Lost and Found '79

Liam Cunningham (1961-)
Attila '01
RKO 281 '99
Shooting the Past '99
When the Sky Falls '99
Falling for a Dancer '98
Jude '96
First Knight '95
A Little Princess '95
War of the Buttons '95

Peter "Sugarfoot" Cunningham
Bloodfist 3: Forced to Fight '92
Bloodmatch '91

Alain Cuny (1908-94)
Camille Claudel '89
Detective '85
Basileus Quartet '82
Christ Stopped at Eboli '79
Emmanuelle '74
Fellini Satyricon '69
The Milky Way '68
La Dolce Vita '60
The Lovers '59
The Hunchback of Notre Dame '57
The Forbidden Christ '50
Les Visiteurs du Soir '42

Tran Manh Cuong
The Vertical Ray of the Sun '00
Three Seasons '98

Barbara Cupisti
The Church '98
Opera '88
Stagefright '87

Lynette Curran (1945-)
The Boys '98
Road to Nhill '97
The Year My Voice Broke '87
Bliss '85

Paul Curran (-1986)
Merlin '98
Poldark '75

Tony Curran
Blade II '02
Pearl Harbor '01
The 13th Warrior '99

Cherie Currie (1959-)
Rosebud Beach Hotel '85
Twilight Zone: The Movie '83
Wavelength '83
Parasite '82
Foxes '80

Finlay Currie (1878-1968)
Billy Liar '63
The Adventures of Huckleberry Finn '60
Ben-Hur '59
Corridors of Blood '58
Abandon Ship '57
The King's Rhapsody '55
Make Me an Offer '55
Big Deadly Game '54
Ivanhoe '52
Stars and Stripes Forever '52
People Will Talk '51
Quo Vadis '51
Treasure Island '50
Trio '50
Bonnie Prince Charlie '48
Great Expectations '46
I Know Where I'm Going '45
Sleeping Car to Trieste '45
The Day Will Dawn '42
The Forty-Ninth Parallel '41
Edge of the World '37

Gordon Currie
Left Behind: The Movie '00
The Fear: Halloween Night '99
Laserhawk '99
Dog Park '98
Ripe '97
Listen '96
Blood & Donuts '95
Puppet Master 5: The Final Chapter '94
Puppet Master 4 '93

Louise Currie (1921-)
Wild West '46
Million Dollar Kid '44
The Ape Man '43
The Masked Marvel '43
The Bashful Bachelor '42
The Adventures of Captain Marvel '41

Michael Currie
The Dead Pool '88
Halloween 3: Season of the Witch '82
Pray TV '82

Sondra Currie
Runaways '84
The Concrete Jungle '82
Jessi's Girls '75
Mama's Dirty Girls '74
Policewomen '73

Christopher Curry
Home Alone 3 '97
C.H.U.D. '84

Stephen Curry
Cut '00
The Castle '97

Tim Curry (1946-)
Attila '01
Scary Movie 2 '01
Charlie's Angels '00
Four Dogs Playing Poker '00
Jackie's Back '99
Doom Runners '97
McHale's Navy '97
Tales from a Parallel Universe: Super Nova '97
Lover's Knot '96
Muppet Treasure Island '96
Titanic '96
Congo '95
The Pebble and the Penguin '94 (V)
The Shadow '94
National Lampoon's Loaded Weapon 1 '93
The Three Musketeers '93
Ferngully: The Last Rain Forest '92 (V)
Home Alone 2: Lost in New York '92
Passed Away '92
Oscar '91
The Hunt for Red October '90
Stephen King's It '90
Pass the Ammo '88
Legend '86
The Worst Witch '86
Clue '85
Blue Money '84
The Ploughman's Lunch '83
Annie '82
Oliver Twist '82
Times Square '80
The Shout '78
The Rocky Horror Picture Show '75

Jane Curtin (1947-)
Antz '98 (V)
Coneheads '93
O.C. and Stiggs '87
Suspicion '87
How to Beat the High Cost of Living '80
Mr. Mike's Mondo Video '79

Valerie Curtin
Big Trouble '86
Down and Out in Beverly Hills '86
Maxie '85
A Christmas Without Snow '80
Different Story '78

Alan Curtis (1909-53)
Apache Chief '50
Flight to Nowhere '46
Renegade Girl '46
The Naughty Nineties '45
The Invisible Man's Revenge '44
Phantom Lady '44
Gung Ho! '43
Buck Privates '41
Melody Master '41
The Duke of West Point '38
Shopworn Angel '38
Mannequin '37
Last Outlaw '36

Billy Curtis (1909-88)
Eating Raoul '82
The Incredible Shrinking Man '57
Terror of Tiny Town '38

Clifford Curtis (1968-)
Collateral Damage '02
Blow '01
The Majestic '01
Training Day '01
Bringing Out the Dead '99
Three Kings '99
Virus '98
Desperate Remedies '93

Dick Curtis
What Waits Below '83
Motel Hell '80

Dick Curtis (1902-52)
Government Agents vs. Phantom Legion *'51*
Billy the Kid *'41*
Valley of Terror *'38*
Boothill Brigade *'37*
A Lawman Is Born *'37*
Racing Luck *'35*

Donald Curtis (1915-97)
Earth vs. the Flying Saucers *'56*
Seventh Cavalry *'56*
It Came from Beneath the Sea *'55*
The Amazing Mr. X *'48*
Son of Lassie *'45*
They Were Expendable *'45*
Thirty Seconds Over Tokyo *'44*
Bataan *'43*
Criminals Within *'41*

Jack Curtis
Lawless Range *'35*
Until They Get Me *'18*

Jackie Curtis
WR: Mysteries of the Organism *'71*
Flesh *'68*

Jamie Lee Curtis (1958-)
Halloween: Resurrection *'02*
Drowning Mona *'00*
The Tailor of Panama *'00*
Halloween: H20 *'98*
Virus *'98*
Homegrown *'97*
Fierce Creatures *'96*
House Arrest *'96*
The Heidi Chronicles *'95*
Mother's Boys *'94*
My Girl 2 *'94*
True Lies *'94*
Forever Young *'92*
The Return of Spinal Tap *'92*
My Girl *'91*
Queens Logic *'91*
Blue Steel *'90*
Dominick & Eugene *'88*
A Fish Called Wanda *'88*
Amazing Grace & Chuck *'87*
A Man in Love *'87*
As Summers Die *'86*
Perfect *'85*
The Adventures of Buckaroo Banzai Across the Eighth Dimension *'84*
Grandview U.S.A. *'84*
Love Letters *'83*
Trading Places *'83*
Death of a Centerfold *'81*
Escape from New York *'81 (V)*
Halloween 2: The Nightmare Isn't Over! *'81*
Road Games *'81*
She's in the Army Now *'81*
Prom Night *'80*
Terror Train *'80*
The Fog *'78*
Halloween *'78*

Keene Curtis (1925-)
Mother Teresa: In the Name of God's Poor *'97*
Sliver *'93*
The Buddy System *'83*
Strange New World *'75*

Ken Curtis (1916-91)
Conagher *'91*
Texas Guns *'90*
Lost *'83*
California Gold Rush *'81*
Pony Express Rider *'76*
Robin Hood *'73 (V)*
The Alamo *'60*
The Horse Soldiers *'59*
The Killer Shrews *'59*
The Young Land *'59*
Wings of Eagles *'57*
Mister Roberts *'55*
The Quiet Man *'52*
Don Daredevil Rides Again *'51*
Call of the Forest *'49*

Liane (Alexandra) Curtis
Wild Orchid 2: Two Shades of Blue *'92*
Rock 'n' Roll High School Forever *'91*
Girlfriend from Hell *'89*
Critters 2: The Main Course *'88*
Hard Choices *'84*
Sixteen Candles *'84*

Robin Curtis (1956-)
Dark Breed *'96*
Santa with Muscles *'96*
The Unborn 2 *'94*
Star Trek 3: The Search for Spock *'84*

Sonia Curtis
Evil Lives *'92*
Terminal Bliss *'91*

Tony Curtis (1925-)
Bounty Hunters 2: Hardball *'97*
The Immortals *'95*
Last Action Hero *'93*
Naked in New York *'93*
Center of the Web *'92*
Christmas in Connecticut *'92*
Prime Target *'91*
Lobster Man from Mars *'89*
Midnight *'89*
The Last of Philip Banter *'87*
Club Life *'86*
Mafia Princess *'86*
Insignificance *'85*
Balboa *'82*
Brainwaves *'82*
Portrait of a Showgirl *'82*
Title Shot *'81*
Little Miss Marker *'80*
The Mirror Crack'd *'80*
The Bad News Bears Go to Japan *'78*
It Rained All Night the Day I Left *'78*
The Manitou *'78*
Sex on the Run *'78*
Sextette *'78*
Users *'78*
Vegas *'78*
The Last Tycoon *'76*
Lepke *'75*
Overture *'75*
The Count of Monte Cristo *'74*
Suppose They Gave a War and Nobody Came? *'70*
Those Daring Young Men in Their Jaunty Jalopies *'69*
The Boston Strangler *'68*
Rosemary's Baby *'68 (V)*
Arrivederci, Baby! *'66*
Boeing Boeing *'65*
The Great Race *'65*
Goodbye Charlie *'64*
Paris When It Sizzles *'64*
Sex and the Single Girl *'64*
Captain Newman, M.D. *'63*
40 Pounds of Trouble *'62*
Taras Bulba *'62*
The Great Impostor *'61*
The Rat Race *'60*
Spartacus *'60*
Operation Petticoat *'59*
The Perfect Furlough *'59*
Some Like It Hot *'59*
The Defiant Ones *'58*
Kings Go Forth *'58*
The Vikings *'58*
Sweet Smell of Success *'57*
Trapeze *'56*
The Black Shield of Falworth *'54*
Houdini *'53*
Son of Ali Baba *'52*
Winchester '73 *'50*
Francis the Talking Mule *'49*
Criss Cross *'48*

Vondie Curtis-Hall (1956-)
Freedom Song *'00*
Turn It Up *'00*
Sirens *'99*
Don King: Only in America *'97*
Eve's Bayou *'97*
Gridlock'd *'96*
William Shakespeare's Romeo and Juliet *'96*
Heaven's Prisoners *'95*
Zooman *'95*
Crooklyn *'94*
DROP Squad *'94*
Sugar Hill *'94*
Fallen Angels 2 *'93*
Falling Down *'93*
In a Stranger's Hand *'92*
The Mambo Kings *'92*
Passion Fish *'92*
Die Hard 2: Die Harder *'90*
Mystery Train *'89*
Coming to America *'88*

Pierre Curzi (1946-)
Stand Off *'93*
Pouvoir Intime *'87*
Maria Chapdelaine *'84*

George Curzon (1898-1976)
Clouds over Europe *'39*
Sexton Blake and the Hooded Terror *'38*
Young and Innocent *'37*
The Living Dead *'36*
Java Head *'35*
The Man Who Knew Too Much *'34*

Ann Cusack (1961-)
Dean Koontz's Black River *'01*
What Planet Are You From? *'00*
Stigmata *'99*
From the Earth to the Moon *'98*
Grosse Pointe Blank *'97*
Multiplicity *'96*
Tank Girl *'94*
A League of Their Own *'92*

Cyril Cusack (1910-93)
Far and Away *'92*
My Left Foot *'89*
Little Dorrit, Film 1: Nobody's Fault *'88*
Little Dorrit, Film 2: Little Dorrit's Story *'88*
The Tenth Man *'88*
Two by Forsyth *'86*
No Comebacks *'85*
1984 *'84*
True Confessions *'81*
Cry of the Innocent *'80*
Street War *'70s*
Lovespell *'79*
Les Miserables *'78*
Children of Rage *'75*
All the Way, Boys *'73*
The Day of the Jackal *'73*
The Golden Bowl *'72*
Harold and Maude *'71*
King Lear *'71*
Sacco & Vanzetti *'71*
David Copperfield *'70*
The Taming of the Shrew *'67*
Fahrenheit 451 *'66*
The Spy Who Came in from the Cold *'65*
Waltz of the Toreadors *'62*
Johnny Nobody *'61*
Night Ambush *'57*
The Spanish Gardener *'57*
The Elusive Pimpernel *'50*
The Small Back Room *'49*
Odd Man Out *'47*
Late Extra *'35*

Dick Cusack
Evil Has a Face *'96*
Crazy People *'90*

Joan Cusack (1962-)
High Fidelity *'00*
Where the Heart Is *'00*
Arlington Road *'99*
The Cradle Will Rock *'99*
Runaway Bride *'99*
Toy Story 2 *'99 (V)*
Grosse Pointe Blank *'97*
In and Out *'97*
A Smile Like Yours *'96*
Two Much *'96*
Mr. Wrong *'95*
Nine Months *'95*
Addams Family Values *'93*
Hero *'92*
Toys *'92*
My Blue Heaven *'90*
Men Don't Leave *'89*
Say Anything *'89*
Married to the Mob *'88*
Stars and Bars *'88*
Working Girl *'88*
The Allnighter *'87*
Broadcast News *'87*
Grandview U.S.A. *'84*
Sixteen Candles *'84*
My Bodyguard *'80*

John Cusack (1966-)
America's Sweethearts *'01*
Serendipity *'01*
High Fidelity *'00*
Being John Malkovich *'99*
The Cradle Will Rock *'99*
The Jack Bull *'99*
Pushing Tin *'99*
This Is My Father *'99*
Chicago Cab *'98*
The Thin Red Line *'98*
Anastasia *'97 (V)*
Con Air *'97*
Grosse Pointe Blank *'97*
Midnight in the Garden of Good and Evil *'97*
City Hall *'95*
Bullets over Broadway *'94*
Floundering *'94*
The Road to Wellville *'94*
Map of the Human Heart *'93*
Money for Nothing *'93*
Bob Roberts *'92*
The Player *'92*
Roadside Prophets *'92*
Shadows and Fog *'92*
True Colors *'91*
The Grifters *'90*
Fat Man and Little Boy *'89*
Say Anything *'89*
Tapeheads *'89*
Eight Men Out *'88*
Stars and Bars *'88*
Broadcast News *'87*
Hot Pursuit *'87*
One Crazy Summer *'86*
Stand by Me *'86*
Better Off Dead *'85*
The Journey of Natty Gann *'85*
The Sure Thing *'85*
Grandview U.S.A. *'84*
Sixteen Candles *'84*
Class *'83*

Niamh Cusack (1959-)
American Women *'00*
Catherine Cookson's Colour Blind *'98*
The Playboys *'92*

Sinead Cusack (1948-)
Passion of Mind *'00*
The Nephew *'97*
Stealing Beauty *'96*
The Cement Garden *'93*
Bad Behavior *'92*
Waterland *'92*
Rocket Gibraltar *'88*
Cyrano de Bergerac *'85*
Revenge *'71*

Peter Cushing (1913-94)
Masks of Death *'86*
Biggles *'85*
Silent Scream *'84*
Top Secret! *'84*
Sword of the Valiant *'83*
House of the Long Shadows *'82*
A Tale of Two Cities *'80*
The Uncanny *'78*
Land of the Minotaur *'77*
Shock Waves *'77*
Star Wars *'77*
At the Earth's Core *'76*
Choice of Weapons *'76*
The Beast Must Die *'75*
The Devil's Undead *'75*
The Ghoul *'75*
Legend of the Werewolf *'75*
Call Him Mr. Shatter *'74*
Frankenstein and the Monster from Hell *'74*
Madhouse *'74*
And Now the Screaming Starts *'73*
From Beyond the Grave *'73*
The Legend of the 7 Golden Vampires *'73*
The Satanic Rites of Dracula *'73*
Asylum *'72*
The Creeping Flesh *'72*
Doctor Phibes Rises Again *'72*
Dracula A.D. 1972 *'72*
Dynasty of Fear *'72*
Horror Express *'72*
Nothing But the Night *'72*
Tales from the Crypt *'72*
The House that Dripped Blood *'71*
I, Monster *'71*
Twins of Evil *'71*
The Bloodsuckers *'70*
Scream and Scream Again *'70*
The Vampire Lovers *'70*
Frankenstein Must Be Destroyed *'69*
Blood Beast Terror *'67*
Island of the Burning Doomed *'67*
Torture Garden *'67*
Daleks—Invasion Earth 2150 A.D. *'66*
Frankenstein Created Woman *'66*
Island of Terror *'66*
Dr. Terror's House of Horrors *'65*
The Skull *'65*
The Evil of Frankenstein *'64*
The Gorgon *'64*
The Hellfire Club *'61*
The Naked Edge *'61*
The Brides of Dracula *'60*
The Flesh and the Fiends *'60*
Sword of Sherwood Forest *'60*
The Hound of the Baskervilles *'59*
John Paul Jones *'59*
The Mummy *'59*
The Horror of Dracula *'58*
The Revenge of Frankenstein *'58*
The Abominable Snowman *'57*
The Curse of Frankenstein *'57*
Time Without Pity *'57*
Alexander the Great *'55*
End of the Affair *'55*
Moulin Rouge *'52*
Hamlet *'48*
A Chump at Oxford *'40*

Bob Custer (-1974)
Law of the Wild *'34*
Mark of the Spur *'32*

Lou (Cutel) Cutell
Neil Simon's The Odd Couple 2 *'98*
Glam *'97*
Frankenstein General Hospital *'88*
Frankenstein Meets the Space Monster *'65*

Elisha Cuthbert
Believe *'99*
Time at the Top *'99*

Jon Cuthbert
Virtual Assassin *'95*
Deadlock 2 *'94*

Allan Cuthbertson (1920-88)
Performance *'70*
The Seventh Dawn *'64*
The Guns of Navarone *'61*
Room at the Top *'59*

Iain Cuthbertson (1930-)
The Painted Lady *'97*
Chasing the Deer *'94*
Gorillas in the Mist *'88*
Danger UXB *'81*
The Railway Children *'70*

Allen (Culter) Cutler
Amityville Dollhouse *'96*
The Halfback of Notre Dame *'96*
Crosscut *'95*

Victor Cutler
The Best Years of Our Lives *'46*
A Walk in the Sun *'46*

Lise Cutter
Fleshtone *'94*
Nickel & Dime *'92*
Shadow Force *'92*
Havana *'90*
Buy & Cell *'89*

Zbigniew Cybulski (1927-67)
The Saragossa Manuscript *'65*
Innocent Sorcerers *'60*
Ashes and Diamonds *'58*
A Generation *'54*

Jon Cypher (1932-)
The Invaders *'95*
Kid and the Killers *'80s*
Accidents *'89*
Spontaneous Combustion *'89*
Elvis and Me *'88*
Off the Mark *'87*
Food of the Gods *'76*
Memory of Us *'74*
Valdez Is Coming *'71*

Charles Cyphers (1939-)
Major League *'89*
Big Bad Mama 2 *'87*
Escape from New York *'81*
Halloween 2: The Nightmare Isn't Over! *'81*
Coming Home *'78*
Halloween *'78*
Assault on Precinct 13 *'76*

Isabelle Cyr
P.T. Barnum *'99*
Karmina *'96*

Myriam Cyr
Kill by Inches *'99*
Species 2 *'98*
Frankenstein and Me *'96*
I Shot Andy Warhol *'96*
Savage Hearts *'95*
Gothic *'87*

Billy Ray Cyrus
Mulholland Drive *'01*
Wish You Were Dead *'00*

Henry Czerny (1959-)
Possessed *'00*
Range of Motion *'00*
Cement *'99*
Eye of the Killer *'99*
P.T. Barnum *'99*
The Girl Next Door *'98*
Glory & Honor *'98*
The Ice Storm *'97*
Mission: Impossible *'96*
Notes from Underground *'95*
When Night Is Falling *'95*
Clear and Present Danger *'94*
The Boys of St. Vincent *'93*
Northern Extremes *'93*

Zsuzsi Czinkoczi
An American Rhapsody *'01*
Nobody's Daughter *'76*

Chris D
Border Radio *'88*
No Way Out *'87*

Eric (DaRe) Da Re
Number One Fan *'94*
The Takeover *'94*
Twin Peaks: Fire Walk with Me *'92*
Silent Night, Deadly Night 3: Better Watch Out! *'89*

Erick Da Silva
Delta of Venus *'95*
The Son of the Shark *'93*

Howard da Silva (1909-86)
Garbo Talks *'84*
Mommie Dearest *'81*

The Great Gatsby '74
Missiles of October '74
Smile, Jenny, You're Dead '74
1776 '72
Nevada Smith '66
David and Lisa '62
Three Husbands '50
The Underworld Story '50
The Great Gatsby '49
They Live by Night '49
Unconquered '47
The Blue Dahlia '46
Two Years before the Mast '46
The Lost Weekend '45
Keeper of the Flame '42
Reunion in France '42
The Sea Wolf '41
Sergeant York '41
Abe Lincoln in Illinois '40

Augusta Dabney (1918-)
The Portrait '93
Running on Empty '88
Violets Are Blue '86

Maryam D'Abo (1960-)
An American Affair '99
Timelock '99
Savage Hearts '95
The Browning Version '94
Solitaire for 2 '94
Stalked '94
Double Obsession '93
Leon the Pig Farmer '93
Red Shoe Diaries 3: Another Woman's Lipstick '93
Shootfighter: Fight to the Death '93
Tomcat: Dangerous Desires '93
Tropical Heat '93
Immortal Sins '91
Nightlife '90
The Living Daylights '87
Xtro '83

Olivia D'Abo (1967-)
The Enemy '01
The Triangle '01
Seven Girlfriends '00
A Texas Funeral '99
Soccer Dog: The Movie '98
The Velocity of Gary '98
National Lampoon's Dad's Week Off '97
Sink or Swim '97
The Big Green '95
Kicking and Screaming '95
Live Nude Girls '95
Clean Slate '94
Greedy '94
The Last Good Time '94
Bank Robber '93
Midnight's Child '93
Point of No Return '93
Wayne's World 2 '93
Spirit of '76 '91
Beyond the Stars '89
Into the Fire '88
Bullies '86
Really Weird Tales '86
Dream to Believe '85
Mission to Kill '85
Bolero '84
Conan the Destroyer '84

Mark Dacascos (1964-)
Brotherhood of the Wolf '01
The Base '99
Boogie Boy '98
No Code of Conduct '98
Sanctuary '98
DNA '97
Redline '97
Drive '96
Deadly Past '95
Redemption: Kickboxer 5 '95
Double Dragon '94
Dragstrip Girl '94
Only the Strong '93
American Samurai '92

Andrew Daddo
Body Melt '93
A Kink in the Picasso '90

Cameron Daddo
Zebra Lounge '01
Anne of Green Gables: The Continuing Story '99

Frances Dade
Dracula '31
Raffles '30

Willem Dafoe (1955-)
Spider-Man '02
Pavilion of Women '01
Animal Factory '00
Shadow of the Vampire '00
American Psycho '99
Boondock Saints '99
eXistenZ '99
Lulu on the Bridge '98
New Rose Hotel '98
Affliction '97
Speed 2: Cruise Control '97
Basquiat '96
The English Patient '96
Clear and Present Danger '94
The Night and the Moment '94
Tom & Viv '94
Faraway, So Close! '93
Body of Evidence '92
Light Sleeper '92
White Sands '92
Cry-Baby '90
Flight of the Intruder '90
Wild at Heart '90
Born on the Fourth of July '89
Triumph of the Spirit '89
The Last Temptation of Christ '88
Mississippi Burning '88
Off Limits '87
Platoon '86
To Live & Die in L.A. '85
New York Nights '84
Roadhouse 66 '84
Streets of Fire '84
The Hunger '83
Loveless '83

Jensen Daggett
Major League 3: Back to the Minors '98
Asteroid '97
Friday the 13th, Part 8: Jason Takes Manhattan '89

Jean-Michel Dagory
Clowning Around 2 '93
Clowning Around '92

Lil Dagover (1897-1980)
The Pedestrian '73
The Strange Countess '61
Dr. Mabuse, The Gambler '22
Destiny '21
The Cabinet of Dr. Caligari '19
Spiders '18

Arlene Dahl (1924-)
Night of the Warrior '91
Land Raiders '69
Kisses for My President '64
Journey to the Center of the Earth '59
Slightly Scarlet '56
A Woman's World '54
Here Come the Girls '53
Three Little Words '50
Watch the Birdie '50
Reign of Terror '49
A Southern Yankee '48

Eva Dahlbeck (1920-)
The Counterfeit Traitor '62
Brink of Life '57
Dreams '55
Smiles of a Summer Night '55
Lesson in Love '54
Secrets of Women '52

Paul Dahlke
The Head '59
The Third Sex '57

Dan Dailey (1914-78)
The Private Files of J. Edgar Hoover '77
Wings of Eagles '57
Meet Me in Las Vegas '56
It's Always Fair Weather '55
There's No Business Like Show Business '54
Pride of St. Louis '52
What Price Glory? '52
Mother Wore Tights '47
Panama Hattie '42
Lady Be Good '41
Ziegfeld Girl '41

Bill Daily
Alligator 2: The Mutation '90
Magic on Love Island '80

Elizabeth (E.G. Dailey) Daily
Rugrats in Paris: The Movie '00 (V)
Babe: Pig in the City '98 (V)
The Rugrats Movie '98 (V)
Lorenzo's Oil '92
Dogfight '91
Dutch '91
Loverboy '89
Bad Dreams '88
Better Off Dead '85
Fandango '85
Pee-wee's Big Adventure '85
No Small Affair '84
Streets of Fire '84
Valley Girl '83
The Escape Artist '82
Funny Money '82
One Dark Night '82
Street Music '81

Nadia Dajani
Sidewalks of New York '01
Happy Accidents '00

Robert Dalban
Diabolique '55
The Walls of Malapaga '49

Cynthia Dale (1961-)
P.T. Barnum '99
Heavenly Bodies '84
My Bloody Valentine '81

Dick Dale (1937-)
Back to the Beach '87
Muscle Beach Party '64
Beach Party '63

Esther Dale (1885-1961)
Ma and Pa Kettle at the Fair '52
On Moonlight Bay '51
Ma and Pa Kettle Go to Town '50
Holiday Affair '49
Ma and Pa Kettle '49
A Stolen Life '46
Blondie Has Trouble '40
The Awful Truth '37
Curly Top '35

Grover Dale
The Young Girls of Rochefort '68
Half a Sixpence '67

Janet Dale
The Tenant of Wildfell Hall '96
The Buddha of Suburbia '92
Prick Up Your Ears '87

Jennifer Dale (1955-)
Love Come Down '00
The Life Before This '99
Dream House '98
Trail of a Serial Killer '98
Once a Thief '96
Whale Music '94
Cadillac Girls '93
The Adjuster '91
Separate Vacations '86
Of Unknown Origin '83
When Angels Fly '82
Ticket to Heaven '81

Jim Dale (1935-)
The Hunchback '97
The Adventures of Huckleberry Finn '85
Scandalous '84
Unidentified Flying Oddball '79
Hot Lead & Cold Feet '78
Joseph Andrews '77
Pete's Dragon '77
Digby, the Biggest Dog in the World '73
Carry On Doctor '68
Follow That Camel '67
Carry On Cowboy '66
Carry On Screaming '66
Carry On Cleo '65

Virginia Dale (1917-94)
Danger Zone '51
Holiday Inn '42

Fabienne Dali
Mayerling '68
Kill, Baby, Kill '66
Erotic Touch of Hot Skin '65

Tracy Dali
American Streetfighter '96
Virgin High '90

David DaLie
Mighty Jungle '64
Virgin Sacrifice '59

Marcel Dalio (1900-83)
How Sweet It Is! '68
How to Steal a Million '66
Lady L '65
The Monocle '64
Can-Can '60
The Perfect Furlough '59
Lafayette Escadrille '58
China Gate '57
Lucky Me '54
Sabrina '54
Lovely to Look At '52
The Merry Widow '52
The Snows of Kilimanjaro '52
Captain Blackjack '51
Rich, Young and Pretty '51
Dedee d'Anvers '49
To Have & Have Not '44
Casablanca '42
The Rules of the Game '39
Grand Illusion '37
Beethoven '36

Ewa Dalkowska (1947-)
Korczak '90
Provincial Actors '79
Without Anesthesia '78

John Dall (1918-71)
Atlantis, the Lost Continent '61
Gun Crazy '49
Rope '48
Something in the Wind '47
The Corn Is Green '45

Charlene Dallas
Criminal Act '88
Rancho Deluxe '75

Beatrice Dalle (1964-)
The Blackout '97
I Can't Sleep '93
Night on Earth '91
La Vengeance d'une Femme '89
Betty Blue '86

Joe Dallesandro (1948-)
The Limey '99
Bad Love '95
Sugar Hill '94
Guncrazy '92
Wild Orchid 2: Two Shades of Blue '92
Cry-Baby '90
Private War '90
Double Revenge '89
The Hollywood Detective '89
Sunset '88
The Cotton Club '84
Seeds of Evil '76
Andy Warhol's Dracula '74
Andy Warhol's Frankenstein '74
Heat '72
Season for Assassins '71
Trash '70
Flesh '68

Maurice Dallimore
Johnny Got His Gun '71
The Collector '65

Francesca D'Aloja
Steam: A Turkish Bath '96
Apartment Zero '88

Abby Dalton (1935-)
Buck and the Magic Bracelet '97
Cyber-Tracker '93
Roller Blade Warriors: Taken By Force '90
Whale of a Tale '76
Rock All Night '57

Audrey Dalton (1934-)
Kitten with a Whip '64
Mr. Sardonicus '61
Separate Tables '58
The Monster That Challenged the World '57
The Prodigal '55
Casanova's Big Night '54
Titanic '53

Darren Dalton (1965-)
The Wolves '95
Montana '90
Brotherhood of Justice '86

Dorothy Dalton (1894-1972)
Moran of the Lady Letty '22
The Three Musketeers '16
The Disciple '15

Timothy Dalton (1944-)
American Outlaws '01
Possessed '00
Cleopatra '99
Made Men '99
The Beautician and the Beast '97
The Informant '97
Lie Down with Lions '94
Scarlett '94
Framed '93
Last Action Hero '93
Naked in New York '93
The Rocketeer '91
The King's Whore '90
Hawks '89
License to Kill '89
The Living Daylights '87
Brenda Starr '86
The Doctor and the Devils '85
Sins '85
The Emperor's New Clothes '84 (N)
Mistral's Daughter '84
Jane Eyre '83
Chanel Solitaire '81
Flash Gordon '80
Agatha '79
The Flame Is Love '79
Centennial '78
Sextette '78
Permission To Kill '75
Mary, Queen of Scots '71
Cromwell '70
Wuthering Heights '70
The Lion in Winter '68

Roger Daltrey (1945-)
Dracula: The Dark Prince '01
Chasing Destiny '00
The Magical Legend of the Leprechauns '99
Like It Is '98
Vampirella '96
Lightning Jack '94
Buddy's Song '91
If Looks Could Kill '91
Forgotten Prisoners '90
Cold Justice '89
Mack the Knife '89
Murder: Ultimate Grounds for Divorce '85
McVicar '80
The Kids Are Alright '79
The Legacy '79
Lisztomania '75
Tommy '75

Candice Daly
Where Truth Lies '96
Liquid Dreams '92
Hell Hunters '87

James Daly (1918-78)
Resurrection of Zachary Wheeler '71
Planet of the Apes '68
The Court Martial of Billy Mitchell '55
Tender Is the Night '55

Mark Daly
Lassie from Lancashire '38
The Ghost Goes West '36

Timothy Daly (1956-)
A House Divided '00
Seven Girlfriends '00
Execution of Justice '99
Stephen King's The Storm of the Century '99
From the Earth to the Moon '98
The Object of My Affection '98
The Associate '96
Denise Calls Up '95
Dr. Jekyll and Ms. Hyde '95
Witness to the Execution '94
Caroline at Midnight '93
Dangerous Heart '93
In the Line of Duty: Ambush in Waco '93
Queen '93
Year of the Comet '92
For Love or Money '88
Love or Money? '88
The Spellbinder '88
Made in Heaven '87
The Rise & Rise of Daniel Rocket '86
Mirrors '85
I Married a Centerfold '84
Just the Way You Are '84
Diner '82

Tyne Daly (1947-)
Absence of the Good '99
Execution of Justice '99
Money Kings '98
The Student Affair '97
Tricks '97
Bye Bye Birdie '95
Christy '94
On the Town '91
The Aviator '85
Movers and Shakers '85
Your Place or Mine '83
A Matter of Life and Death '81
Zoot Suit '81
Better Late Than Never '79
Speedtrap '78
The Adultress '77
Intimate Strangers '77
Telefon '77
The Enforcer '76
Larry '74
Angel Unchained '70

Jacqueline Dalya
Miss Melody Jones '73
Behind Prison Walls '43

Bertilla Damas
True Friends '98
Mi Vida Loca '94

Paul D'Amato
The Deer Hunter '78
Slap Shot '77

Charlotte d'Amboise
Lost in the Bermuda Triangle '98
American Blue Note '89

William Dame
Stuff Stephanie in the Incinerator '89
In Deadly Heat '87

Leo Damian
Hard Drive '94
Ghosts Can't Do It '90

Marcus D'Amico
Armistead Maupin's Tales of the City '93
Full Metal Jacket '87

Cathryn Damon (1933-87)
She's Having a Baby '88
First Time '82
How to Beat the High Cost of Living '80

Gabriel Damon (1976-)
Social Misfits '00
Journey to Spirit Island '92
Little Nemo: Adventures in Slumberland '92 (V)
Iron Maze '91
RoboCop 2 '90

The Land Before Time '88 (V)
Call to Glory '84

Mark Damon (1933-)
Great Treasure Hunt '70s
The Scalawag Bunch '75
Crypt of the Living Dead '73
Devil's Wedding Night '73
Anzio '68
Black Sabbath '64
The Fall of the House of Usher '60
Between Heaven and Hell '56

Matt Damon (1970-)
The Bourne Identity '02
Spirit: Stallion of the Cimarron '02 (V)
Jay and Silent Bob Strike Back '01
Ocean's Eleven '01
All the Pretty Horses '00
The Legend of Bagger Vance '00
Titan A.E. '00 (V)
Dogma '99
The Talented Mr. Ripley '99
Rounders '98
Saving Private Ryan '98
Chasing Amy '97
Good Will Hunting '97
John Grisham's The Rainmaker '97
Courage Under Fire '96
Glory Daze '96
The Good Old Boys '95
Geronimo: An American Legend '93
School Ties '92
Rising Son '90
The Good Mother '88
Mystic Pizza '88

Vic Damone (1928-)
Hell to Eternity '60
Meet Me in Las Vegas '56
Hit the Deck '55
Kismet '55
Athena '54
Rich, Young and Pretty '51

JoJo D'Amore
Zoltan...Hound of Dracula '78
The Doberman Gang '72

Barbara Dana
Necessary Parties '88
A Matter of Principle '83

Bill Dana (1924-)
Kill My Wife...Please!
Lena's Holiday '90
I Wonder Who's Killing Her Now? '76
Harrad Summer '74

Leora Dana (1923-83)
Amityville 3: The Demon '83
Baby It's You '82
Tora! Tora! Tora! '70
Change of Habit '69
Kings Go Forth '58

Viola Dana
That Certain Thing '28
The Ice Flood '26

Malcolm Danare (1962-)
Godzilla '98
Popcorn '89
The Curse '87
Heaven Help Us '85

Charles Dance (1946-)
Dark Blue World '01
Gosford Park '01
Hilary and Jackie '98
The Stranger: Kabloonak '98
The Blood Oranges '97
In the Presence of Mine Enemies '97
Rebecca '97
Space Truckers '97
Michael Collins '96
Undertow '95
Century '94
The Surgeon '94
Last Action Hero '93
Alien 3 '92
China Moon '91
Tales of the Unexpected '91
The Phantom of the Opera '90
Goldeneye: The Secret Life of Ian Fleming '89
Out of the Shadows '88
Pascali's Island '88
White Mischief '88
Good Morning, Babylon '87
Hidden City '87
Out on a Limb '87
The Golden Child '86
The McGuffin '85
Plenty '85
This Lightning Always Strikes Twice '85
The Jewel in the Crown '84
For Your Eyes Only '81

Hugh Dancy
Black Hawk Down '01
Madame Bovary '00

Evan Dando
Heavy '94
Reality Bites '94

Tom D'Andrea (1909-98)
The Next Voice You Hear '50
Silver River '48
Dark Passage '47
Humoresque '46
Never Say Goodbye '46

Dorothy Dandridge (1922-65)
Tamango '59
Island in the Sun '57
Carmen Jones '54
Since You Went Away '44
Lady from Louisiana '42
Sun Valley Serenade '41
Sundown '41

Karl (Daen) Dane (1886-1934)
The Big House '30
Son of the Sheik '26
The Big Parade '25

Lawrence Dane (1937-)
Waking the Dead '00
Thrill Seekers '99
Bride of Chucky '98
It Takes Two '95
National Lampoon's Senior Trip '95
The Good Fight '92
Lethal Lolita—Amy Fisher: My Story '92
Rolling Vengeance '87
Clown Murders '83
Of Unknown Origin '83
Happy Birthday to Me '81
Scanners '81
Fatal Attraction '80
Rituals '79
Find the Lady '75

Patricia Dane (1918-95)
I Dood It '43
Johnny Eager '42
Rio Rita '42
Somewhere I'll Find You '42

Paul Daneman (1925-2001)
Tears in the Rain '88
Zulu '64
Time Without Pity '57

Claire Danes (1979-)
Igby Goes Down '02
Brokedown Palace '99
The Mod Squad '99
Princess Mononoke '98 (V)
I Love You, I Love You Not '97
John Grisham's The Rainmaker '97
Les Miserables '97
Polish Wedding '97
U-Turn '97
To Gillian on Her 37th Birthday '96
William Shakespeare's Romeo and Juliet '96
Home for the Holidays '95
How to Make an American Quilt '95
Little Women '94

Jean Danet (1924-2001)
The Hunchback of Notre Dame '57
There Goes Barder '54

Beverly D'Angelo (1953-)
Lansky '99
Sugar Town '99
American History X '98
Illuminata '98
A Rat's Tale '98
With Friends Like These '98
Pterodactyl Woman from Beverly Hills '97
Nowhere '96
Vegas Vacation '96
Edie & Pen '95
An Eye for an Eye '95
The Crazysitter '94
Lightning Jack '94
Widow's Kiss '94
Man Trouble '92
Lonely Hearts '91
The Miracle '91
The Pope Must Diet '91
Daddy's Dyin'...Who's Got the Will? '90
Pacific Heights '90
Cold Front '89
National Lampoon's Christmas Vacation '89
Aria '88
High Spirits '88
Hands of a Stranger '87
In the Mood '87
Maid to Order '87
Trading Hearts '87
Big Trouble '86
The Legend of Sleepy Hollow '86
Slow Burn '86
National Lampoon's European Vacation '85
Finders Keepers '84
A Streetcar Named Desire '84
National Lampoon's Vacation '83
Sleeping Beauty '83
Honky Tonk Freeway '81
Paternity '81
Coal Miner's Daughter '80
Highpoint '80
Hair '79
Every Which Way But Loose '78
Annie Hall '77
First Love '77
The Sentinel '76

Carlo D'Angelo
Secret Agent Super Dragon '66
I Vampiri '56

Mirella D'Angelo
Apartment Zero '88
Unsane '82

Rodney Dangerfield (1921-)
Little Nicky '00
My 5 Wives '00
The Godson '98
Meet Wally Sparks '97
Casper '95
Natural Born Killers '94
Ladybugs '92
Rover Dangerfield '91 (V)
Moving '88
Back to School '86
Easy Money '83
Caddyshack '80
The Projectionist '71

Jennifer Daniel
The Reptile '66
Kiss of the Vampire '62

Isa Danieli
Ciao, Professore! '94
Macaroni '85

Henry Daniell (1894-1963)
Les Girls '57
Witness for the Prosecution '57
Lust for Life '56
The Man in the Gray Flannel Suit '56
Diane '55
The Prodigal '55
The Egyptian '54
Wake of the Red Witch '49
The Body Snatcher '45
The Woman in Green '45
Jane Eyre '44
Sherlock Holmes in Washington '43
Watch on the Rhine '43
Castle in the Desert '42
Reunion in France '42
A Woman's Face '41
All This and Heaven Too '40
The Great Dictator '40
The Philadelphia Story '40
The Sea Hawk '40
The Firefly '37
Madame X '37
Camille '36

Suzanne Danielle (1957-)
The Carpathian Eagle '81
Golden Lady '79
Carry On Emmanuelle '78

Alex Daniels
Star Kid '97
Meridian: Kiss of the Beast '90
Cyborg '89

Anthony Daniels (1946-)
Star Wars: Episode 2—Attack of the Clones '02
Return of the Jedi '83
The Empire Strikes Back '80
Star Wars '77

Bebe Daniels (1901-71)
42nd Street '33
The Maltese Falcon '31
Reaching for the Moon '31
Dixiana '30
Feel My Pulse '28
Monsieur Beaucaire '24
Affairs of Anatol '21
Why Change Your Wife? '20
Male and Female '19

Ben Daniels
Conspiracy '01
The Aristocrats '99
Britannic '99
I Want You '98
Madeline '98
David '97
Passion in the Desert '97
Beautiful Thing '95

Gary Daniels
No Tomorrow '99
Cold Harvest '98
American Streetfighter 2: The Full Impact '97
Bloodmoon '97
Recoil '97
American Streetfighter '96
Capital Punishment '96
Hawk's Vengeance '96
Riot '96
Fist of the North Star '95
Heatseeker '95
Rage '95
White Tiger '95
Deadly Target '94
Firepower '93
Knights '93

J.D. Daniels (1980-)
Beanstalk '94
Roswell: The U.F.O. Cover-Up '94
Man's Best Friend '93

Jeff Daniels (1955-)
Blood Work '02
Escanaba in da Moonlight '01
Chasing Sleep '00
Cheaters '00
The Crossing '00
It's the Rage '99
My Favorite Martian '98
Pleasantville '98
Fly Away Home '96
101 Dalmatians '96
Trial and Error '96
Two Days in the Valley '96
Redwood Curtain '95
Dumb & Dumber '94
Speed '94
Gettysburg '93
Rain Without Thunder '93
Grand Tour: Disaster in Time '92
Teamster Boss: The Jackie Presser Story '92
There Goes the Neighborhood '92
The Butcher's Wife '91
Love Hurts '91
Arachnophobia '90
Welcome Home, Roxy Carmichael '90
Checking Out '89
The Caine Mutiny Court Martial '88
The House on Carroll Street '88
Love Notes '88
Sweet Hearts Dance '88
Radio Days '87
Heartburn '86
Something Wild '86
Marie '85
The Purple Rose of Cairo '85
Terms of Endearment '83
Ragtime '81
A Rumor of War '80

John Daniels
Getting Over '81
Bare Knuckles '77
Black Shampoo '76
Candy Tangerine Man '75

Mickey Daniels (1914-70)
The Great Ziegfeld '36
The Adventurous Knights '35

Phil Daniels (1958-)
Chicken Run '00 (V)
Still Crazy '98
Bad Behavior '92
The Bride '85
Meantime '81
Breaking Glass '80
Quadrophenia '79
Scum '79

William Daniels (1927-)
Skin '89
Her Alibi '88
Blind Date '87
The Little Match Girl '87
Rehearsal for Murder '82
All Night Long '81
Reds '81
The Blue Lagoon '80
City in Fear '80
Damien: The Leper Priest '80
The Rebels '79
Sunburn '79
The Bastard '78
The One and Only '78
Sergeant Matlovich vs. the U.S. Air Force '78
Black Sunday '77
Killer on Board '77
Oh, God! '77
The Parallax View '74
1776 '72
Marlowe '69
The Graduate '67
The President's Analyst '67
Two for the Road '67
A Thousand Clowns '65

Lynn Danielson
Nickel & Dime '92
Mortuary Academy '91
Out of the Dark '88

Eli Danker
Impulse '90
The Flight '89
The Taking of Flight 847: The Uli Derickson Story '88

Rick Danko (1943-99)
Man Outside '88
The Kids Are Alright '79

Roger Dann
Two for the Road '67
I Confess '53

Blythe Danner (1944-)
Invisible Circus '00
Meet the Parents '00
Forces of Nature '99
The Love Letter '99
Eye of the Storm '98
From the Earth to the Moon '98
Murder She Purred: A Mrs. Murphy Mystery '98 (V)
No Looking Back '98
Saint Maybe '98
The X-Files '98
A Call to Remember '97
Mad City '97
The Myth of Fingerprints '97
The Proposition '97
Homage '95
Oldest Confederate Widow Tells All '95
To Wong Foo, Thanks for Everything, Julie Newmar '95
Getting Up and Going Home '92
Husbands and Wives '92
Never Forget '91
The Prince of Tides '91
Alice '90
Judgment '90
Mr. & Mrs. Bridge '90
Another Woman '88
Brighton Beach Memoirs '86
Man, Woman & Child '83
Inside the Third Reich '82
The Great Santini '80
Too Far to Go '79
Are You in the House Alone? '78
Love Affair: The Eleanor & Lou Gehrig Story '77
Futureworld '76
Hearts of the West '75
1776 '72
To Kill a Clown '72

Sybil Danning (1952-)
L.A. Bounty '89
Amazon Women on the Moon '87
Phantom Empire '87
Warrior Queen '87
Reform School Girls '86
Tomb '86
Howling 2: Your Sister Is a Werewolf '85
Malibu Express '85
Private Passions '85
Young Lady Chatterly 2 '85
Day of the Cobra '84
Jungle Warriors '84
Panther Squad '84
Seven Magnificent Gladiators '84
They're Playing with Fire '84
Chained Heat '83
Hercules '83
Daughter of Death '82
The Salamander '82
Separate Ways '82
Battle Beyond the Stars '80
Kill Castro '80
The Man with Bogart's Face '80
The Mercenaries '80
Nightkill '80
The Concorde: Airport '79 '79
The Prince and the Pauper '78
Albino '76
God's Gun '75
Bluebeard '72
Cat in the Cage '68

Royal Dano (1922-94)
The Dark Half '91
Spaced Invaders '90
Texas Guns '90
Killer Klowns from Outer Space '88
Ghoulies 2 '87
House 2: The Second Story '87
Cocaine Wars '86
Teachers '84

The Right Stuff *'83*
Something Wicked This Way Comes *'83*
Bad Georgia Road *'77*
Hughes & Harlow: Angels in Hell *'77*
The Killer Inside Me *'76*
The Outlaw Josey Wales *'76*
Huckleberry Finn *'75*
Big Bad Mama *'74*
Messiah of Evil *'74*
Wild Party *'74*
Electra Glide in Blue *'73*
Moon of the Wolf *'72*
7 Faces of Dr. Lao *'63*
The Adventures of Huckleberry Finn *'60*
Man of the West *'58*
Crime of Passion *'57*
Man in the Shadow *'57*
All Mine to Give *'56*
Tribute to a Bad Man *'56*
The Trouble with Harry *'55*
Johnny Guitar *'53*
Bend of the River *'52*
Flame of Araby *'51*
The Red Badge of Courage *'51*

Leslie Danon
Hail Caesar *'94*
The Whispering *'94*

Cesare Danova (1926-92)
St. Helen's, Killer Volcano *'82*
National Lampoon's Animal House *'78*
Tentacles *'77*
Scorchy *'76*
Mean Streets *'73*
Boy, Did I Get a Wrong Number! *'66*
Gidget Goes to Rome *'63*
Viva Las Vegas *'63*

Ted Danson (1947-)
Mumford *'99*
Jerry and Tom *'98*
Saving Private Ryan *'98*
Homegrown *'97*
Gulliver's Travels *'95*
Loch Ness *'95*
Getting Even with Dad *'94*
Pontiac Moon *'94*
Made in America *'93*
Three Men and a Little Lady *'90*
Cousins *'89*
Dad *'89*
Three Men and a Baby *'87*
We Are the Children *'87*
A Fine Mess *'86*
Just Between Friends *'86*
When the Bough Breaks *'86*
Little Treasure *'85*
Creepshow *'82*
Body Heat *'81*
Our Family Business *'81*
The Onion Field *'79*
Chinese Web *'78*

Joe Dante (1946-)
Silence of the Hams *'93*
Sleepwalkers *'92*
Code Name: Zebra *'84*
Cannonball *'76*

Michael Dante (1931-)
Crazy Horse and Custer: "The Untold Story" *'90*
The Cage *'89*
Big Score *'83*
Beyond Evil *'80*
Cruise Missile *'78*
Winterhawk *'76*
Willard *'71*
Naked Kiss *'64*

Helmut Dantine (1917-82)
The Fifth Musketeer *'79*
The Killer Elite *'75*
The Wilby Conspiracy *'75*
Bring Me the Head of Alfredo Garcia *'74*
Operation Crossbow *'65*
War and Peace *'56*
Alexander the Great *'55*
The Stranger from Venus *'54*
Whispering City *'47*
Hollywood Canteen *'44*
Passage to Marseilles *'44*
Edge of Darkness *'43*
Northern Pursuit *'43*
Watch on the Rhine *'43*
Casablanca *'42*
Desperate Journey *'42*
Mrs. Miniver *'42*
The Navy Comes Through *'42*
To Be or Not to Be *'42*

Ray Danton (1931-92)
Apache Blood *'75*
The Centerfold Girls *'74*
Secret Agent Super Dragon *'66*
The Conqueror & the Empress *'64*
The Longest Day *'62*
The Rise and Fall of Legs Diamond *'60*
A Majority of One *'56*
I'll Cry Tomorrow *'55*

Tony Danza (1951-)
The Garbage-Picking, Field Goal-Kicking Philadelphia Phenomenon *'98*
Noah *'98*
A Brooklyn State of Mind *'97*
Glam *'97*
Love to Kill *'97*
North Shore Fish *'97*
Twelve Angry Men *'97*
Illtown *'96*
Angels in the Outfield *'94*
Last Action Hero *'93*
She's Out of Control *'89*
Truth or Die *'86*
Single Bars, Single Women *'84*
Going Ape! *'81*
The Hollywood Knights *'80*

Maia Danzinger
The Ice Storm *'97*
Last Exit to Brooklyn *'90*
High Stakes *'89*
Dr. Heckyl and Mr. Hype *'80*

Sun Dao-Lin
The Go-Masters *'82*
Crows and Sparrows *'49*

Ingeborga Dapkounaite (1963-)
Seven Years in Tibet *'97*
Jack Higgins' On Dangerous Ground *'95*
Burnt by the Sun *'94*

Patti D'Arbanville (1951-)
Celebrity *'98*
The Fan *'96*
Father's Day *'96*
Blind Spot *'93*
Deadly Conspiracy *'91*
Snow Kill *'90*
Wired *'89*
Call Me *'88*
Fresh Horses *'88*
The Boys Next Door *'85*
Real Genius *'85*
Modern Problems *'81*
The Fifth Floor *'80*
Hog Wild *'80*
Time After Time *'79*
Big Wednesday *'78*
Bilitis *'77*
Flesh *'68*

Patrika Darbo
Speed 2: Cruise Control *'97*
Fast Money *'96*
Leaving Normal *'92*
Daddy's Dyin'...Who's Got the Will? *'90*

Kim Darby (1947-)
Newsbreak *'00*
The Last Best Sunday *'98*
Halloween 6: The Curse of Michael Myers *'95*
Teen Wolf Too *'87*
Better Off Dead *'85*
Embassy *'85*
The Capture of Grizzly Adams *'82*
Enola Gay: The Men, the Mission, the Atomic Bomb *'80*
Flatbed Annie and Sweetiepie: Lady Truckers *'79*
The One and Only *'78*
Rich Man, Poor Man *'76*
Don't Be Afraid of the Dark *'73*
The Streets of San Francisco *'72*
The Grissom Gang *'71*
The People *'71*
The Strawberry Statement *'70*
Generation *'69*
True Grit *'69*

Mireille Darc (1938-)
Intruder *'77*
Icy Breasts *'75*
Return of the Tall Blond Man with One Black Shoe *'74*
The Tall Blond Man with One Black Shoe *'72*
The Peking Blond *'68*
Weekend *'67*
Please Not Now! *'61*

Denise Darcel (1925-)
Vera Cruz *'53*
Westward the Women *'51*
Battleground *'49*
Thunder in the Pines *'49*

Alexander D'Arcy (1908-96)
Dead Pigeon on Beethoven Street *'72*
Blood of Dracula's Castle *'69*
Fanny Hill: Memoirs of a Woman of Pleasure *'64*
Horrors of Spider Island *'59*
Abdulla the Great *'56*
Soldier of Fortune *'55*
The Awful Truth *'37*
Prisoner of Zenda *'37*

Jake D'Arcy
Gregory's Girl *'80*
A Sense of Freedom *'78*

Roy D'Arcy
Legion of Missing Men *'37*
Revolt of the Zombies *'36*

Sheila (Rebecca Wassem) Darcy
Tumbledown Ranch in Arizona *'41*
Irish Luck *'39*
Zorro's Fighting Legion *'39*

Severn Darden (1929-95)
Once Upon a Midnight Scary *'90*
Back to School *'86*
Real Genius *'85*
Saturday the 14th *'81*
In God We Trust *'80*
Wanda Nevada *'79*
The Disappearance of Aimee *'76*
Jackson County Jail *'76*
Battle for the Planet of the Apes *'73*
The Day of the Dolphin *'73*
The Legend of Hillbilly John *'73*
Conquest of the Planet of the Apes *'72*
Playmates *'72*
Hired Hand *'71*
Vanishing Point *'71*
Werewolves on Wheels *'71*
The President's Analyst *'67*
Dead Heat on a Merry-Go-Round *'66*

Debra (Deborah Dutch) Dare
Hard to Die *'90*
The Killing Zone *'90*

Florence Darel
The Count of Monte Cristo *'99*
Don't Let Me Die on a Sunday *'98*
A la Mode *'94*
The Stolen Children *'92*
A Tale of Springtime *'89*

Bobby Darin (1936-73)
Run, Stranger, Run *'73*
The Happy Ending *'69*
Cop-Out *'67*
Captain Newman, M.D. *'63*
Hell Is for Heroes *'62*
Pressure Point *'62*
State Fair *'62*
Come September *'61*

Johnny Dark
Wishful Thinking *'92*
Up Your Alley *'89*
Rip-Off *'77*

Candy Darling
Silent Night, Bloody Night *'73*
Flesh *'68*

Joan Darling (1935-)
Sunnyside *'79*
The Two Worlds of Jenny Logan *'79*

Linda Darlow
The Amy Fisher Story *'93*
Immediate Family *'89*

Gerard Darmon (1948-)
Obsession: A Taste for Fear *'89*
Betty Blue *'86*
Diva *'82*

Linda Darnell (1921-65)
Dakota Incident *'56*
Second Chance *'53*
Blackbeard the Pirate *'52*
Island of Desire *'52*
No Way Out *'50*
A Letter to Three Wives *'49*
Unfaithfully Yours *'48*
Forever Amber *'47*
Anna and the King of Siam *'46*
My Darling Clementine *'46*
Buffalo Bill *'44*
It Happened Tomorrow *'44*
City Without Men *'43*
The Loves of Edgar Allen Poe *'42*
Blood and Sand *'41*
Brigham Young: Frontiersman *'40*
The Mark of Zorro *'40*

Steve Darrell
The Adventures of Frank and Jesse James *'48*
Lightning Raiders *'45*

James Darren (1936-)
Boss' Son *'78*
Venus in Furs *'70*
Hey There, It's Yogi Bear *'64 (V)*
Gidget Goes to Rome *'63*
Diamond Head *'62*
Gidget Goes Hawaiian *'61*
The Guns of Navarone *'61*
All the Young Men *'60*
Let No Man Write My Epitaph *'60*
The Gene Krupa Story *'59*
Gidget *'59*
Gunman's Walk *'58*

Danielle Darrieux (1917-)
Scene of the Crime *'87*
L'Anne Sainte *'78*
Le Cavaleur *'78*
The Young Girls of Rochefort *'68*
Murder at 45 R.P.M. *'65*
Bluebeard *'63*
The Red and the Black *'57*
Alexander the Great *'55*
Lady Chatterley's Lover *'55*
The Earrings of Madame De... *'54*
Five Fingers *'52*
Le Plaisir *'52*
La Ronde *'51*
Rich, Young and Pretty *'51*
Ruyblas *'48*
The Rage of Paris *'38*
Mayerling *'36*
Mauvaise Graine *'33*

Frankie Darro (1917-76)
Forbidden Planet *'56*
Westward the Women *'51*
Riding High *'50*
Let's Go Collegiate *'41*
The Gang's All Here *'40*
Pinocchio *'40 (V)*
Up in the Air *'40*
Boy's Reformatory *'39*
Irish Luck *'39*
Tough Kid *'39*
Anything for a Thrill *'37*
Devil Diamond *'37*
Tough to Handle *'37*
Black Gold *'36*
The Phantom Empire *'35*
Valley of Wanted Men *'35*
Broadway Bill *'34*
Wolf Dog *'33*
Devil Horse *'32*
Lightning Warrior *'31*
Vanishing Legion *'31*

Jean-Pierre Darroussin
La Buche *'00*
Marius and Jeannette *'97*
Un Air de Famille *'96*

Henry Darrow (1933-)
Tequila Body Shots *'99*
Mom, Can I Keep Her? *'98*
The Last of the Finest *'90*
L.A. Bounty *'89*
In Dangerous Company *'88*
Death Blow *'87*
Computer Wizard *'77*
Where's Willie? *'77*

John Darrow (1907-80)
Monte Carlo Nights *'34*
The Lady Refuses *'31*
Ten Nights in a Bar-Room *'31*
Hell's Angels *'30*

Oliver Darrow
Bad Girls from Mars *'90*
Spirits *'90*
The Channeler *'89*

Tony Darrow
Small Time Crooks *'00*
Mickey Blue Eyes *'99*
Analyze This *'98*
Me and the Mob *'94*
Goodfellas *'90*

Lili Darvas (1906-74)
Love *'71*
24 Hours in a Woman's Life *'61*
Meet Me in Las Vegas *'56*

Bella Darvi
The Racers *'55*
The Egyptian *'54*

Jane Darwell (1879-1967)
Last Hurrah *'58*
Girls in Prison *'56*
The Bigamist *'53*
We're Not Married *'52*
The Lemon Drop Kid *'51*
Redwood Forest Trail *'50*
Three Husbands *'50*
Wagon Master *'50*
Three Godfathers *'48*
The Red Stallion *'47*
I Live in Grosvenor Square *'46*
My Darling Clementine *'46*
The Great Gildersleeve *'43*
The Ox-Bow Incident *'43*
Tender Comrade *'43*
All Through the Night *'42*
The Loves of Edgar Allen Poe *'42*
The Devil & Daniel Webster *'41*
Brigham Young: Frontiersman *'40*
The Grapes of Wrath *'40*
Gone with the Wind *'39*
Jesse James *'39*
The Rains Came *'39*
Little Miss Broadway *'38*
Captain January *'36*
Craig's Wife *'36*
The Poor Little Rich Girl *'36*
Curly Top *'35*
Bright Eyes *'34*
One Night of Love *'34*
Finishing School *'33*

Nandita Das
Earth *'98*
Fire *'96*

Stacey Dash (1966-)
Personals *'00*
Cold Around the Heart *'97*
Clueless *'95*
Illegal in Blue *'95*
Black Water *'94*
Renaissance Man *'94*
Mo' Money *'92*
Moving *'88*

Jules Dassin (1911-)
Phaedra *'61*
Never on Sunday *'60*
Rififi *'54*

Jean Daste (1904-94)
The Green Room *'78*
The Wild Child *'70*
La Guerre Est Finie *'66*
Grand Illusion *'37*
The Crime of Monsieur Lange *'36*
L'Atalante *'34*
Zero for Conduct *'33*
Boudu Saved from Drowning *'32*

Alex Datcher
The Expert *'95*
Body Bags *'93*
Passenger 57 *'92*
Rage and Honor *'92*

Kristin Dattilo-Hayward
Child of Darkness, Child of Light *'91*
Pyrates *'91*
Mirror, Mirror *'90*

James Daughton
Girlfriend from Hell *'89*
Blind Date *'84*
Swim Team *'79*
Malibu Beach *'78*

Claude Dauphin (1903-78)
Les Miserables *'78*
Madame Rosa *'77*
The Tenant *'76*
Rosebud *'75*
The Madwoman of Chaillot *'69*
Two for the Road *'67*
Is Paris Burning? *'66*
Lady L *'65*
Tiara Tahiti *'62*
April in Paris *'52*
Casque d'Or *'52*
Le Plaisir *'52*

Elyssa Davalos
A House in the Hills *'93*
Jericho Fever *'93*
Wild & Wooly *'78*

Richard (Dick) Davalos (1935-)
Something Wicked This Way Comes *'83*
Blood Legacy *'73*
Kelly's Heroes *'70*
Cool Hand Luke *'67*
Pit Stop *'67*
All the Young Men *'60*
Sea Chase *'55*
East of Eden *'54*

Harry Davenport (1866-1949)
December 7th: The Movie *'91*
Riding High *'50*
That Forsyte Woman *'50*
Tell It to the Judge *'49*
For the Love of Mary *'48*
Three Daring Daughters *'48*
The Bachelor and the Bobby-Soxer *'47*
The Farmer's Daughter *'47*
Courage of Lassie *'46*
The Enchanted Forest *'45*
Jack London *'44*
Meet Me in St. Louis *'44*
The Thin Man Goes Home *'44*
The Amazing Mrs. Holiday *'43*

The Ox-Bow Incident '43
Son of Fury '42
Kings Row '41
That Uncertain Feeling '41
All This and Heaven Too '40
Foreign Correspondent '40
Lucky Partners '40
Gone with the Wind '39
The Hunchback of Notre Dame '39
The Story of Alexander Graham Bell '39
The Cowboy and the Lady '38
Marie Antoinette '38
You Can't Take It with You '38
Fit for a King '37

Jack Davenport (1973-)
Russell Mulcahy's Tale of the Mummy '99
The Talented Mr. Ripley '99
Immortality '98
Ultraviolet '98
Catherine Cookson's The Moth '96

Mary Davenport
Home Movies '79
Sisters '73

Milla Davenport (1891-1936)
The Worldly Madonna '22
Daddy Long Legs '19

Nigel Davenport (1928-)
Death by Prescription '80s
Upper Crust '88
Without a Clue '88
Caravaggio '86
Mountbatten: The Last Viceroy '86
A Christmas Carol '84
Greystoke: The Legend of Tarzan, Lord of the Apes '84
Chariots of Fire '81
Nighthawks '81
Cry of the Innocent '80
The Ordeal of Dr. Mudd '80
Soul Patrol '80
Zulu Dawn '79
The Island of Dr. Moreau '77
Phase 4 '74
Picture of Dorian Gray '74
Dracula '73
Living Free '72
The Last Valley '71
Mary, Queen of Scots '71
The Virgin Soldiers '69
Sebastian '68
A Man for All Seasons '66
Ladies Who Do '63
Peeping Tom '60

Robert Davi (1953-)
My Little Assassin '99
The Bad Pack '98
For Which He Stands '98
The Beneficiary '97
An Occasional Hell '96
Body Count '95
The Dangerous '95
The Dogfighters '95
Showgirls '95
Blind Justice '94
Cops and Robbersons '94
No Contest '94
Maniac Cop 3: Badge of Silence '93
Mardi Gras for the Devil '93
The November Men '93
Quick '93
Son of the Pink Panther '93
Center of the Web '92
Christopher Columbus: The Discovery '92
Wild Orchid 2: Two Shades of Blue '92
Illicit Behavior '91
The Taking of Beverly Hills '91
White Hot: The Mysterious Murder of Thelma Todd '91
Amazon '90
Legal Tender '90
Maniac Cop 2 '90
Peacemaker '90
Predator 2 '90
License to Kill '89
Die Hard '88
Traxx '87
Wild Thing '87
The Goonies '85
Gangster Wars '81
The $5.20 an Hour Dream '80

Angel David
Two Girls and a Guy '98
The Substitute 2: School's Out '97
The Crow '93
Mixed Blood '84

Clifford David
Matters of the Heart '90
Agent on Ice '86
Resurrection '80

Eleanor David (1956-)
Topsy Turvy '99
Slipstream '89
84 Charing Cross Road '86
Sylvia '86
Comfort and Joy '84
Pink Floyd: The Wall '82
The Scarlet Pimpernel '82

Joanna David
The Way We Live Now '02
Cotton Mary '99
Murders at Lynch Cross '85

Keith David (1954-)
Final Fantasy: The Spirits Within '01 (V)
Novocaine '01
Innocents '00
Pitch Black '00
The Replacements '00
Requiem for a Dream '00
Where the Heart Is '00
Armageddon '98
There's Something about Mary '98
The Tiger Woods Story '98
Don King: Only in America '97
Executive Target '97
Todd McFarlane's Spawn '97 (V)
Volcano '97
Flipping '96
johns '96
Larger Than Life '96
Blue in the Face '95
Clockers '95
Dead Presidents '95
An Eye for an Eye '95
Gargoyles, The Movie: The Heroes Awaken '94 (V)
The Puppet Masters '94
The Quick and the Dead '94
The Last Outlaw '93
Article 99 '92
Final Analysis '92
Marked for Death '90
Men at Work '90
Always '89
Bird '88
They Live '88
Off Limits '87
Platoon '86
The Thing '82

Thayer David (1927-78)
The Duchess and the Dirtwater Fox '76
The Eiger Sanction '75
Save the Tiger '73
Savages '72
Night of Dark Shadows '71
House of Dark Shadows '70
The Story of Ruth '60
Journey to the Center of the Earth '59
The Legend of the Sea Wolf '58
A Time to Love & a Time to Die '58

Lolita (David) Davidovich (1961-)
Four Days '99
Mystery, Alaska '99
Play It to the Bone '99
Gods and Monsters '98
Santa Fe '97
Dead Silence '96
Jungle 2 Jungle '96
Touch '96
For Better or Worse '95
Harvest of Fire '95
Indictment: The McMartin Trial '95
Now and Then '95
Cobb '94
Younger & Younger '94
Boiling Point '93
Intersection '93
Keep the Change '92
Leap of Faith '92
Raising Cain '92
The Inner Circle '91
JFK '91
The Object of Beauty '91
Prison Stories: Women on the Inside '91
Blaze '89
Blindside '88
Adventures in Babysitting '87
Big Town '87
Recruits '86

Alan Davidson
Frailty '02
Rift '96

Ben Davidson
Conan the Barbarian '82
The Black Six '74

Davey Davidson
No Drums, No Bugles '71
When the Line Goes Through '71

Diana Davidson
Around the World in 80 Ways '86
Scared to Death '80

Eileen Davidson (1959-)
Eternity '90
Easy Wheels '89
The House on Sorority Row '83

Jack Davidson
Baby It's You '82
Shock Waves '77

Jaye Davidson
Stargate '94
The Crying Game '92

John Davidson (1886-1969)
Tailspin Tommy '34
Monsieur Beaucaire '24

John Davidson (1941-)
Edward Scissorhands '90
The Squeeze '87
The Concorde: Airport '79 '79
The Happiest Millionaire '67

Max Davidson (1875-1950)
Roamin' Wild '36
Daring Danger '32
Hotel Imperial '27

Tommy Davidson (1965-)
Bamboozled '00
Plump Fiction '97
Woo '97
Booty Call '96
Ace Ventura: When Nature Calls '95
Strictly Business '91

William B. Davidson (1888-1947)
They Were Expendable '45
I'm No Angel '33
Held for Murder '32
Vice Squad '31

Embeth Davidtz (1966-)
Bridget Jones's Diary '01
13 Ghosts '01
Bicentennial Man '99
Mansfield Park '99
Last Rites '98
Fallen '97
The Garden of Redemption '97
The Gingerbread Man '97
Matilda '96
Feast of July '95
Murder in the First '95
Schindler's List '93
Sweet Murder '93
Army of Darkness '92

Betty Ann Davies (1910-55)
Alias John Preston '56
Blackout '54
The Belles of St. Trinian's '53
The Blue Lamp '49

Gwen Ffrangcon Davies
The Devil Rides Out '68
The Witches '66

Jackson Davies
Dead Ahead: The Exxon Valdez Disaster '92
Dead Wrong '83
Jane Doe '83

James Davies
Wildest Dreams '90
Young Nurses in Love '89

Jeremy Davies (1969-)
The Laramie Project '02
Secretary '02
Up at the Villa '00
The Million Dollar Hotel '99
Ravenous '99
Saving Private Ryan '98
Going All the Way '97
The Locusts '97
Twister '96
Spanking the Monkey '94

John Davies (1953-)
Positive I.D. '87
Interface '84

John (Howard) Davies (1939-)
Tom Brown's School Days '51
The Rocking Horse Winner '49
Oliver Twist '48

Kimberly Davies
Psycho Beach Party '00
Twisted '96

Lindy Davies
Darlings of the Gods '90
Malcolm '86

Marion Davies
Going Hollywood '33
Show People '28

Oliver Ford Davies
Star Wars: Episode 2—Attack of the Clones '02
The Way We Live Now '02
Star Wars: Episode 1—The Phantom Menace '99
A Royal Scandal '96
Cause Celebre '87

Rachel Davies
Band of Gold '95
The House that Bled to Death '81

Rudi Davies
Frankie Starlight '95
Maria's Child '93
The Object of Beauty '91
The Lonely Passion of Judith Hearne '87

Rupert Davies (1916-76)
Frightmare '74
Waterloo '71
Zeppelin '71
The Conqueror Worm '68
The Crimson Cult '68
Dracula Has Risen from the Grave '68
Target for Killing '66
The Spy Who Came in from the Cold '65

Stephen Davies
Star Portal '97
Bloodfist 7: Manhunt '95
Dillinger and Capone '95
The Berlin Conspiracy '91
The Nest '88
Hanoi Hilton '87
The Long Good Friday '80

Luis Davila (1927-98)
The Scalawag Bunch '75
The Mummy's Revenge '73
Pancho Villa '72

Alex Davion (1929-)
The Bloodsuckers '70
Valley of the Dolls '67
Plague of the Zombies '66
Paranoiac '62

Ann B. Davis (1926-)
The Brady Bunch Movie '95
Naked Gun 33 1/3: The Final Insult '94
A Very Brady Christmas '88
Lover Come Back '61

Art Davis (1987-)
Along the Sundown Trail '42
Prairie Pals '42
Tumbleweed Trail '42
Phantom Gold '38

Bette Davis (1908-89)
Wicked Stepmother '89
The Whales of August '87
As Summers Die '86
Little Gloria... Happy at Last '84
Right of Way '84
A Piano for Mrs. Cimino '82
The Watcher in the Woods '81
White Mama '80
Strangers: The Story of a Mother and Daughter '79
The Dark Secret of Harvest Home '78
Death on the Nile '78
Return from Witch Mountain '78
Burnt Offerings '76
The Disappearance of Aimee '76
Madame Sin '71
The Anniversary '68
Hush, Hush, Sweet Charlotte '65
The Nanny '65
Empty Canvas '64
Where Love Has Gone '64
What Ever Happened to Baby Jane? '62
Pocketful of Miracles '61
John Paul Jones '59
The Catered Affair '56
The Virgin Queen '55
Another Man's Poison '52
Phone Call from a Stranger '52
All About Eve '50
Beyond the Forest '49
June Bride '48
Winter Meeting '48
Deception '46
A Stolen Life '46
The Corn Is Green '45
Hollywood Canteen '44
Mr. Skeffington '44
Thank Your Lucky Stars '43
Watch on the Rhine '43
In This Our Life '42
Now, Voyager '42
The Bride Came C.O.D. '41
The Great Lie '41
The Little Foxes '41
The Man Who Came to Dinner '41
All This and Heaven Too '40
The Letter '40
Dark Victory '39
Juarez '39
The Old Maid '39
The Private Lives of Elizabeth & Essex '39
Jezebel '38
The Sisters '38
Kid Galahad '37
Marked Woman '37
That Certain Woman '37
Petrified Forest '36
Satan Met a Lady '36
Dangerous '35
Fashions of 1934 '34
Of Human Bondage '34
Bureau of Missing Persons '33
Ex-Lady '33
The Cabin in the Cotton '32
Hell's House '32
Three on a Match '32
Way Back Home '32

Brad Davis (1949-91)
The Player '92
Child of Darkness, Child of Light '91
The Habitation of Dragons '91
Hangfire '91
When the Time Comes '91
Robert Kennedy and His Times '90
Rosalie Goes Shopping '89
Vengeance '89
The Caine Mutiny Court Martial '88
Blood Ties '87
Cold Steel '87
Heart '87
Chiefs '83
Querelle '83
Chariots of Fire '81
A Rumor of War '80
A Small Circle of Friends '80
Midnight Express '78
The Campus Corpse '77
Sybil '76

Bud Davis
Andersonville '95
House of the Rising Sun '87

Carole (Raphaelle) Davis
If Looks Could Kill '91
The Shrimp on the Barbie '90
Mannequin '87
Princess Academy '87
The Flamingo Kid '84
C.O.D. '83

Charles Davis
Hazel's People '75
The Big Doll House '71

Chet Davis
The Eye Creatures '65
Yes, Sir, Mr. Bones '51

Clifton Davis (1945-)
Kingdom Come '01
Max Keeble's Big Move '01
Dream Date '93
Don't Look Back: The Story of Leroy "Satchel" Paige '81
The Night the City Screamed '80
Little Ladies of the Night '77

Duane Davis
Angels in the Infield '00
Rocky Marciano '99
The Program '93
Diggstown '92
Final Shot: The Hank Gathers Story '92

Eddie Davis
Fighting Pilot '35
Gunners & Guns '34

Essie Davis
Kings in Grass Castles '97
The Ripper '97
Lilian's Story '95
River Street '95

Frank Davis
Killer Tomatoes Strike Back '90
Return of the Killer Tomatoes! '88

Gail Davis (1925-97)
Race for Your Life, Charlie Brown '77 (V)
Alias Jesse James '59
On Top of Old Smoky '53
Winning of the West '53
Blue Canadian Rockies '52
Flying Leathernecks '51
Valley of Fire '51
Cow Town '50
Brand of Fear '49

Geena Davis (1957-)
Stuart Little 2 '02
Stuart Little '99
The Long Kiss Goodnight '96
Cutthroat Island '95

Angie '94
Speechless '94
Hero '92
A League of Their Own '92
Thelma & Louise '91
Quick Change '90
Earth Girls Are Easy '89
The Accidental Tourist '88
Beetlejuice '88
The Fly '86
Fletch '85
Secret Weapons '85
Transylvania 6-5000 '85
Tootsie '82

Gene Davis
Messenger of Death '88
Night Games '80

Hope Davis (1964-)
Final '01
Hearts in Atlantis '01
Joe Gould's Secret '00
Arlington Road '99
Mumford '99
The Imposters '98
Next Stop, Wonderland '98
The Myth of Fingerprints '97
The Daytrippers '96
Kiss of Death '94

Jim Davis (1915-81)
Inferno in Paradise '88
Don't Look Back: The Story of Leroy "Satchel" Paige '81
Day Time Ended '80
Comes a Horseman '78
Killing Stone '78
The Choirboys '77
Law of the Land '76
The Runaway Barge '75
Bad Company '72
Dracula vs. Frankenstein '71
The Trackers '71
Monte Walsh '70
Gun Riders '69
El Dorado '67
Jesse James Meets Frankenstein's Daughter '65
Zebra in the Kitchen '65
Iron Angel '64
Frontier Uprising '61
Alias Jesse James '59
Monster from Green Hell '58
The Restless Breed '58
Guns Don't Argue '57
The Maverick Queen '55
Big Chase '54
The Outcast '54
The Big Sky '52
Little Big Horn '51
Hi-Jacked '50
The Showdown '50
Three Desperate Men '50
Hellfire '48

Joan Davis (1907-61)
The Outcast '54
If You Knew Susie '48
George White's Scandals '45
Show Business '44
Around the World '43
Hold That Ghost '41
Sun Valley Serenade '41
Just Around the Corner '38
My Lucky Star '38
On the Avenue '37
Thin Ice '37

Judy Davis (1956-)
Life with Judy Garland—Me and My Shadows '01
A Cooler Climate '99
Dash and Lilly '99
Celebrity '98
The Echo of Thunder '98
Absolute Power '97
Deconstructing Harry '97
Blood & Wine '96
Children of the Revolution '95
Serving in Silence: The Margarethe Cammermeyer Story '95
The New Age '94
The Ref '93
Husbands and Wives '92
On My Own '92
Barton Fink '91
Naked Lunch '91
One Against the Wind '91
Where Angels Fear to Tread '91
Alice '90
Impromptu '90
Georgia '87
High Tide '87
Kangaroo '86
Rocket to the Moon '86
A Passage to India '84
Heatwave '83
The Final Option '82
The Winter of Our Dreams '82
A Woman Called Golda '82
My Brilliant Career '79
High Rolling in a Hot Corvette '77

Kristen Davis (1965-)
Atomic Train '99
Doom Asylum '88

Lisa Davis
Edge of Sanity '89
101 Dalmatians '61 (V)
Queen of Outer Space '58

Mac Davis (1942-)
Jackpot '01
Angel's Dance '99
Blackmail '91
The Sting 2 '83
Cheaper to Keep Her '80
North Dallas Forty '79

Marvin Davis
Tomorrow the World '44
The Fighting Sullivans '42

Matthew Davis
Blue Crush '02
Legally Blonde '01
Tigerland '00
Urban Legends 2: Final Cut '00

Nancy Davis (1923-)
Hellcats of the Navy '57
Donovan's Brain '53
The Next Voice You Hear '50
East Side, West Side '49

Nathan Davis
Dunston Checks In '95
Shaking the Tree '92
Code of Silence '85

Ossie Davis (1917-)
Dinosaur '00 (V)
Finding Buck McHenry '00
Dr. Dolittle '98
Miss Evers' Boys '97
Twelve Angry Men '97
Get On the Bus '96
I'm Not Rappaport '96
The Android Affair '95
The Client '94
Stephen King's The Stand '94
The Ernest Green Story '93
Grumpy Old Men '93
Queen '93
Gladiator '92
Jungle Fever '91
Joe Versus the Volcano '90
Do the Right Thing '89
School Daze '88
Avenging Angel '85
Harry & Son '84
Don't Look Back: The Story of Leroy "Satchel" Paige '81
All God's Children '80
Hot Stuff '80
King '78
Billy: Portrait of a Street Kid '77
Roots '77
Let's Do It Again '75
Night Gallery '69
The Scalphunters '68
A Man Called Adam '66
Gone Are the Days '63
Purlie Victorious '63
No Way Out '50

Owen Davis, Jr. (1907-49)
It Could Happen to You '37
Special Investigator '36
All Quiet on the Western Front '30

Patricia Davis
Night Partners '83
For Ladies Only '81

Philip Davis (1953-)
Still Crazy '98
Face '97
Photographing Fairies '97
Howling 5: The Rebirth '89
High Hopes '88
The Bounty '84
Grown Ups '80
Quadrophenia '79
Who's Who '78

Phyllis E. Davis (1947-)
Terminal Island '73
Sweet Sugar '72
Beyond the Valley of the Dolls '70

Roger Davis (1939-)
Ruby '77
Flash & Firecat '75
House of Dark Shadows '70

Sammi Davis (1964-)
Stand-Ins '97
Four Rooms '95
Indecency '92
The Horseplayer '91
The Perfect Bride '91
Shadow of China '91
Final Warning '90
The Rainbow '89
Consuming Passions '88
The Lair of the White Worm '88
Hope and Glory '87
Prayer for the Dying '87
Mona Lisa '86

Sammy Davis, Jr. (1925-90)
The Kid Who Loved Christmas '90
Tap '89
Moon over Parador '88
That's Dancing! '85
Cannonball Run 2 '84
Cracking Up '83
Cannonball Run '81
Little Moon & Jud McGraw '78
Gone with the West '72
The Trackers '71
Sweet Charity '69
A Man Called Adam '66
Robin and the 7 Hoods '64
The Three Penny Opera '62
Ocean's 11 '60

Scott Davis
The Abomination '88
Tabloid! '88

Sonny Carl Davis
Bad Channels '92
Seedpeople '92
Pair of Aces '90
Verne Miller '88
Fast Money '83
Last Night at the Alamo '83
The Whole Shootin' Match '79

Stringer Davis (1896-1973)
The Smallest Show on Earth '57
The Runaway Bus '54

Tom Davis
One More Saturday Night '86
Trading Places '83
All You Need Is Cash '78
Tunnelvision '76

Tracy Davis
Nemesis 2: Nebula '94
Star Quest '89

Ursula Davis
An Angel for Satan '66
Battle of Valiant '63

Viveka Davis
Cast Away '00
Time Code '00
EDtv '99
Message in a Bottle '98
A Dangerous Woman '93
Stalking Laura '93
Man Trouble '92
The End of Innocence '90
Morgan Stewart's Coming Home '87
Not My Kid '85
Shoot the Moon '82

Warwick Davis (1970-)
Snow White: The Fairest of Them All '02
Harry Potter and the Sorcerer's Stone '01
The 10th Kingdom '00
Leprechaun 5: In the Hood '99
Prince Valiant '97
Leprechaun 4: In Space '96
Gulliver's Travels '95
Leprechaun 3 '95
Leprechaun 2 '94
Leprechaun '93
Willow '88
The Ewoks: Battle for Endor '85
The Ewok Adventure '84

William B. Davis
Mindstorm '01
The Proposal '00
Perpetrators of the Crime '98
The X-Files '98

Bruce Davison (1946-)
High Crimes '02
crazy/beautiful '01
Summer Catch '01
X-Men '00
Locked in Silence '99
Vendetta '99
At First Sight '98
Paulie '98
Apt Pupil '97
Color of Justice '97
Lovelife '97
The Crucible '96
Grace of My Heart '96
Hidden in America '96
The Baby-Sitters' Club '95
The Cure '95
Down, Out and Dangerous '95
Homage '95
It's My Party '95
Far from Home: The Adventures of Yellow Dog '94
The Skateboard Kid 2 '94
Widow's Kiss '94
Short Cuts '93
Six Degrees of Separation '93
Live! From Death Row '92
Longtime Companion '90
Steel and Lace '90
The Misfit Brigade '87
Poor Little Rich Girl: The Barbara Hutton Story '87
The Ladies Club '86
Spies Like Us '85
Crimes of Passion '84
Lies '83
Kiss My Grits '82
Tomorrow's Child '82
High Risk '81
The Lathe of Heaven '80
The Gathering: Part 2 '79
Short Eyes '79
Brass Target '78
Deadman's Curve '78
French Quarter '78
The Summer of My German Soldier '78
The Gathering '77
Mother, Jugs and Speed '76
Mame '74
The Affair '73
Ulzana's Raid '72
Willard '71
The Strawberry Statement '70
Last Summer '69

Peter Davison (1951-)
Wuthering Heights '98
Black Beauty '94
Harnessing Peacocks '92
Love for Lydia '79

Ninetto Davoli (1948-)
Arabian Nights '74
The Canterbury Tales '71
The Decameron '70
The Hawks & the Sparrows '67

Evelyn Daw
Panamint's Bad Man '38
Something to Sing About '36

Marjorie Daw
His Majesty, the American '19
Rebecca of Sunnybrook Farm '17

Pam Dawber (1951-)
I'll Remember April '99
Stay Tuned '92
Through Naked Eyes '87
Wild Horses '84
Holocaust Survivors...Remembrance of Love '83

Marpessa Dawn
The Womaneater '59
Black Orpheus '58

Sugar Dawn
Arizona Roundup '42
Lone Star Law Men '42
Dynamite Canyon '41
Riding the Sunset Trail '41

Anthony Dawson (1916-92)
Dr. No '62
The Curse of the Werewolf '61
Tiger Bay '59
The Haunted Strangler '58
Hour of Decision '57
Dial "M" for Murder '54
The Long Dark Hall '51
The Woman in Question '50
The Queen of Spades '49

Kamala Dawson
The Burning Season '94
Lightning Jack '94

Kim (Kimberly Dawn) Dawson
Jimmy Zip '00
Bikini Med School '98
Bikini House Calls '96
The Perfect Gift '95
The Voyeur '94

Richard Dawson (1932-)
The Running Man '87
How to Pick Up Girls '78
The Devil's Brigade '68
Munster, Go Home! '66
King Rat '65
War and Peace '56

Rosario Dawson (1979-)
The Adventures of Pluto Nash '02
Men in Black 2 '02
Chelsea Walls '01
Josie and the Pussycats '01
King of the Jungle '01
Sidewalks of New York '01
Down to You '00
Light It Up '99
He Got Game '98
Kids '95

Vicky Dawson
Carbon Copy '81
The Prowler '81

Doris Day (1920-98)
Turf Boy '42
Lady Be Good '41
Saga of Death Valley '39

Doris Day (1924-)
Where Were You When the Lights Went Out? '68
With Six You Get Eggroll '68
The Glass Bottom Boat '66
Send Me No Flowers '64
The Thrill of It All! '63
Billy Rose's Jumbo '62
That Touch of Mink '62
Lover Come Back '61
Midnight Lace '60
Please Don't Eat the Daisies '60
Pillow Talk '59
Teacher's Pet '58
The Tunnel of Love '58
The Pajama Game '57
The Man Who Knew Too Much '56
Love Me or Leave Me '55
Lucky Me '54
Young at Heart '54
By the Light of the Silvery Moon '53
Calamity Jane '53
April in Paris '52
The Winning Team '52
I'll See You in My Dreams '51
Lullaby of Broadway '51
On Moonlight Bay '51
Tea for Two '50
The West Point Story '50
Young Man with a Horn '50
It's a Great Feeling '49
My Dream Is Yours '49
Romance on the High Seas '48

They Got Me Covered '43

Gary Day
Crime Broker '94
Night Nurse '77

Josette Day (1914-78)
The Storm Within '48
Beauty and the Beast '46
Well-Digger's Daughter '46

Laraine Day (1917-)
Return to Fantasy Island '77
Murder on Flight 502 '75
My Dear Secretary '49
Tycoon '47
Those Endearing Young Charms '45
The Story of Dr. Wassell '44
Mr. Lucky '43
Journey for Margaret '42
Dr. Kildare's Strange Case '40
Foreign Correspondent '40
My Son, My Son '40
Doomed at Sundown '37

Marceline Day (1907-2000)
Fighting Parson '35
Flaming Signal '33
Telegraph Trail '33
Broadway to Cheyenne '32
Fighting Fool '32
The King Murder '32
The Pocatello Kid '31
Paradise Island '30
Sunny Skies '30
The Cameraman '28
The Beloved Rogue '27

Matt(hew) Day (1971-)
Shackleton '02
Doing Time for Patsy Cline '97
Kiss or Kill '97
Dating the Enemy '95
Love and Other Catastrophes '95
Muriel's Wedding '94

Morris Day (1957-)
The Adventures of Ford Fairlane '90
Graffiti Bridge '90
Purple Rain '84

Patrick Day
Hollywood Hot Tubs 2: Educating Crystal '89
The Adventures of Huckleberry Finn '85

Stuart Garrison Day
Covert Action '88
Search and Destroy '88

Vera Day (1939-)
The Womaneater '59
The Haunted Strangler '58
Up the Creek '58
Quatermass 2 '57

Daniel Day-Lewis (1957-)
The Boxer '97
The Crucible '96
The Age of Innocence '93

In the Name of the Father '93
The Last of the Mohicans '92
Eversmile New Jersey '89
My Left Foot '89
Stars and Bars '88
The Unbearable Lightness of Being '88
A Room with a View '86
My Beautiful Laundrette '85
The Bounty '84
Gandhi '82
How Many Miles to Babylon? '82
Sunday, Bloody Sunday '71

Assaf Dayan
The Uranium Conspiracy '78
Operation Thunderbolt '77

Gabrielle Daye
In Celebration '75
10 Rillington Place '71

Margit Dayka
Nice Neighbor '79
Cat's Play '74

Joaquim de Almeida (1957-)
Behind Enemy Lines '01
La Cucaracha '99
Vendetta '99
One Man's Hero '98
Women '97
Larry McMurtry's Dead Man's Walk '96
Nostromo '96
Desperado '95
Clear and Present Danger '94
Only You '94
The Fencing Master '92
Priceless Beauty '90
Good Morning, Babylon '87

Maria de Aragon
The Deadly and the Beautiful '73
The Cremators '72
Blood Mania '70

Jean De Baer
Broken Vows '87
84 Charing Cross Road '86

Isaach de Bankole
3 A.M. '01
Ghost Dog: The Way of the Samurai '99
A Soldier's Daughter Never Cries '98
The Keeper '96
Heart of Darkness '93
Night on Earth '91
No Fear, No Die '90
Chocolat '88

Brenda de Banzie (1915-81)
The Pink Panther '64
Come September '61
The Mark '61
The Entertainer '60
Too Many Crooks '59
The Man Who Knew Too Much '56
Hobson's Choice '53

Burr de Benning
Incredible Melting Man '77
Iron Horsemen '71
Sweet November '68

Andre de Beranger
The Bat '26
So This Is Paris '26

Antje De Boeck
A Dog of Flanders '99
Daens '92

Yvonne de Bray
The Storm Within '48
Eternal Return '43

Nigel de Brulier (1877-1948)
The Iron Mask '29
Ben-Hur '26
The Four Horsemen of the Apocalypse '21
The Three Musketeers '21

Celia de Burgh
Phar Lap '84
Sound of Love '77

Yvonne De Carlo (1922-)
Mirror, Mirror '90
American Gothic '88
Cellar Dweller '87
Vultures '84
House of Shadows '83
The Munsters' Revenge '81
Play Dead '81
Silent Scream '80
Nocturna '79
Satan's Cheerleaders '77
Blazing Stewardesses '75
Texas Layover '75
Arizona Bushwackers '67
Hostile Guns '67
Munster, Go Home! '66
A Global Affair '63
McLintock! '63
The Sword and the Cross '58
Band of Angels '57
Death of a Scoundrel '56
The Ten Commandments '56
Flame of the Islands '55
Shotgun '55
Passion '54
Captain's Paradise '53
Sea Devils '53
Tomahawk '51
Casbah '48
Criss Cross '48
Song of Scheherazade '47
Salome, Where She Danced '45
For Whom the Bell Tolls '43
Rhythm Parade '43
The Road to Morocco '42

Pedro de Cordoba (1881-1950)
Omoo Omoo, the Shark God '49
Mexican Hayride '48
Swamp Fire '46
In Old New Mexico '45
They Were Expendable '45
For Whom the Bell Tolls '43
Son of Fury '42
Before I Hang '40
The Ghost Breakers '40
Law of the Pampas '39
Condemned to Live '35
The Crusades '35

Arturo de Cordova (1908-73)
The New Invisible Man '58
El '52
New Orleans '47
Frenchman's Creek '44
For Whom the Bell Tolls '43

Ted de Corsia (1903-73)
The Outside Man '73
The Conqueror '56
Dance with Me, Henry '56
The Kettles in the Ozarks '56
The Killing '56
Slightly Scarlet '56
The Enforcer '51
It Happens Every Spring '49
Neptune's Daughter '49
The Lady from Shanghai '48
The Naked City '48

Eduardo de Filippo (1900-84)
The Gold of Naples '54
Seven Deadly Sins '53

Peppino de Filippo (1903-80)
Boccaccio '70 '62
Variety Lights '51

Helene de Fougerolles
Va Savoir '01
The Fall '98

Louis de Funes (1914-83)
Delusions of Grandeur '76
Le Gendarme de Saint-Tropez '67
La Grande Vadrouille '66
The Sucker '65
Belle Americaine '61
Four Bags Full '56
The Sheep Has Five Legs '54
Femmes de Paris '53
Seven Deadly Sins '53

Julio de Grazia (-1990)
The Stranger '87
Deadly Revenge '83
Funny, Dirty Little War '83
Time for Revenge '82
The Lion's Share '79

Gloria De Haven (1924-)
Out to Sea '97
Bog '84
Two Tickets to Broadway '51
Summer Stock '50
Three Little Words '50
The Yellow Cab Man '50
Summer Holiday '48
Broadway Rhythm '44
Step Lively '44
The Thin Man Goes Home '44
Two Girls and a Sailor '44
Best Foot Forward '43
Susan and God '40
Modern Times '36

Consuelo de Haviland
Barjo '93
The Unbearable Lightness of Being '88
Betty Blue '86

Olivia de Havilland (1916-)
The Woman He Loved '88
Anastasia: The Mystery of Anna '86
The Fifth Musketeer '79
Roots: The Next Generation '79
The Swarm '78
Airport '77 '77
The Adventurers '70
Hush, Hush, Sweet Charlotte '65
Lady in a Cage '64
Proud Rebel '58
The Ambassador's Daughter '56
Not as a Stranger '55
The Heiress '49
The Snake Pit '48
Dark Mirror '46
To Each His Own '46
Thank Your Lucky Stars '43
In This Our Life '42
Strawberry Blonde '41
They Died with Their Boots On '41
Santa Fe Trail '40
Dodge City '39
Gone with the Wind '39
The Private Lives of Elizabeth & Essex '39
The Adventures of Robin Hood '38
Anthony Adverse '36
The Charge of the Light Brigade '36
Captain Blood '35
A Midsummer Night's Dream '35

Wanda De Jesus
Blood Work '02
Flawless '99
Elmore Leonard's Gold Coast '97

Frank De Kova (1910-81)
Johnny Firecloud '75
Frasier the Sensuous Lion '73
Cat in the Cage '68
Atlantis, the Lost Continent '61
The Jayhawkers '59
Machine Gun Kelly '58
Teenage Caveman '58
Shack Out on 101 '55

Simon de la Brosse
Strike It Rich '90
The Little Thief '89
Pauline at the Beach '83

Agathe de la Fontaine
Train of Life '98
Another 9 1/2 Weeks '96
King of the Airwaves '94

Marguerite de la Motte (1902-50)
The Iron Mask '29
The Nut '21
Mark of Zorro '20

Danny De La Paz
Picking Up the Pieces '99
American Me '92
Miracle Mile '89
3:15—The Moment of Truth '86
Boulevard Nights '79

George de la Pena (1955-)
Brain Donors '92
Kuffs '92
The Cowboy & the Ballerina '84
Nijinsky '80

John de Lancie (1948-)
Woman on Top '00
Schemes '95
Deep Red '94
Evolver '94
Arcade '93
Fearless '93
The Hand that Rocks the Cradle '92
The Fisher King '91

Derek De Lint (1950-)
The Man Who Made Husbands Jealous '98
Poltergeist: The Legacy '96
The Endless Game '89
Diary of a Mad Old Man '88
Stealing Heaven '88
The Unbearable Lightness of Being '88
Mascara '87
Three Men and a Baby '87
The Assault '86
Soldier of Orange '78

Michael De Lorenzo
My Family '94
Somebody to Love '94
Platoon Leader '87

Terence de Marney (1909-71)
Beast of Morocco '66
Die, Monster, Die! '65
Dual Alibi '47

Drea De Matteo
Deuces Wild '02
Made '01
Swordfish '01

Maria De Medeiros (1965-)
Le Polygraphe '96
Pulp Fiction '94
Meeting Venus '91
Henry & June '90

Carlo de Mejo
Alien Contamination '81
Gates of Hell '80

Alberto De Mendoza
Bossa Nova '99
Horror Express '72
Blade of the Ripper '70

Carlo De Meyo
Other Hell '85
The Outside Man '73

Laurence De Monaghan
The Story of a Love Story '73
Claire's Knee '71

Robert De Niro (1943-)
Showtime '02
15 Minutes '01
The Score '01
The Adventures of Rocky & Bullwinkle '00
Meet the Parents '00
Men of Honor '00
Flawless '99
Analyze This '98
Ronin '98
Cop Land '97
Great Expectations '97
Jackie Brown '97
Wag the Dog '97
The Fan '96
Marvin's Room '96
Sleepers '96
Casino '95
Heat '95
Mary Shelley's Frankenstein '94
A Bronx Tale '93
Mad Dog and Glory '93
This Boy's Life '93
Night and the City '92
Backdraft '91
Cape Fear '91
Guilty by Suspicion '91
Mistress '91
Awakenings '90
Goodfellas '90
Stanley and Iris '90
Jacknife '89
We're No Angels '89
Midnight Run '88
Angel Heart '87
The Untouchables '87
The Mission '86
Brazil '85
Falling in Love '84
Once Upon a Time in America '84
King of Comedy '82
The Godfather 1902-1959: The Complete Epic '81
True Confessions '81
Raging Bull '80
The Deer Hunter '78
New York, New York '77
America at the Movies '76
The Last Tycoon '76
1900 '76
Taxi Driver '76
The Godfather, Part 2 '74
Bang the Drum Slowly '73
Mean Streets '73
Born to Win '71
The Swap '71
Bloody Mama '70
Hi, Mom! '70
The Wedding Party '69
Greetings '68

Rossy de Palma (1965-)
Talk of Angels '96
The Flower of My Secret '95
Kika '94
Ready to Wear '94
Don Juan, My Love '90
Tie Me Up! Tie Me Down! '90
Women on the Verge of a Nervous Breakdown '88

Josse De Pauw
Everybody's Famous! '00
Hombres Complicados '97
The Pointsman '86

Miranda de Pencier
Anne of Green Gables: The Continuing Story '99
Kurt Vonnegut's Harrison Bergeron '95
Anne of Green Gables '85

Lya de Putti (1897-1931)
The Informer '29
The Sorrows of Satan '26
Variety '25
Othello '22
The Indian Tomb '21

Chris De Rose
Breakaway '95
Aftershock '88

Portia de Rossi (1973-)
Stigmata '99
Girl '98
Scream 2 '97
Sirens '94

Anthony De Sando
Double Parked '00
Cement '99
Kiss Me, Guido '97
Federal Hill '94
Party Girl '94
Grand Isle '92
The Return of Eliot Ness '91

Joe De Santis (1909-89)
It's Good to Be Alive '74
Blue '68
And Now Miguel '66
Al Capone '59

Lorraine (De Sette) De Selle
The Wild Beasts '85
Women's Prison Massacre '85
Caged Women '84
House on the Edge of the Park '84

Christian de Sica (1951-)
Men Men Men '95
Detective School Dropouts '85
An Almost Perfect Affair '79

Vittorio De Sica (1902-74)
We All Loved Each Other So Much '77
Andy Warhol's Dracula '74
12 Plus 1 '70
The Shoes of the Fisherman '68
L'Odeur des Fauves '66
The Amorous Adventures of Moll Flanders '65
The Wonders of Aladdin '61
The Battle of Austerlitz '60
Generale Della Rovere '60
It Started in Naples '60
The Millionairess '60
Angel in a Taxi '59
The Earrings of Madame De... '54
The Gold of Naples '54
Pardon My Trunk '52
Peddlin' in Society '47
Teresa Venerdi '41

Guiliana de Sio
Private Affairs '89
Pool Hustlers '83

Rosana De Soto
Star Trek 6: The Undiscovered Country '91
Family Business '89
Stand and Deliver '88
La Bamba '87
Ballad of Gregorio Cortez '83
The In-Laws '79

Melissa De Sousa
Miss Congeniality '00
Ride '98

Edward De Souza (1933-)
A Question of Attribution '91
Kiss of the Vampire '62
The Phantom of the Opera '62

Jose-Luis De Villalonga (1920-)
Blood and Sand '89
Darling '65
Any Number Can Win '63
The Lovers '59

Brandon de Wilde (1942-72)
In Harm's Way '65
Those Calloways '65
Hud '63
All Fall Down '62
Missouri Traveler '58
Goodbye, My Lady '56
Shane '53
The Member of the Wedding '52

Francis De Wolff (1913-84)
Devil Doll '64
The Two Faces of Dr. Jekyll '60
The Smallest Show on Earth '57

Marie Dea
Orpheus '49
Les Visiteurs du Soir '42

Brian Deacon (1949-)
A Zed & Two Noughts '88
Jesus '79

Triple Echo '77
Vampyres '74
Richard Deacon (1921-84)
Bad Manners '84
Piranha '78
The One and Only, Genuine, Original Family Band '68
Blackbeard's Ghost '67
The Gnome-Mobile '67
Billie '65
The Patsy '64
Carousel '56
Francis in the Haunted House '56
Invasion of the Body Snatchers '56
The Kettles in the Ozarks '56
Abbott and Costello Meet the Mummy '55
Blackboard Jungle '55
Them! '54
Lucy Deakins (1971-)
There Goes My Baby '92
Cheetah '89
The Great Outdoors '88
Little Nikita '88
The Boy Who Could Fly '86
Allison Dean
Where's Marlowe? '98
Ruby in Paradise '93
Coming to America '88
Eddie Dean (1907-99)
Black Hills '48
Check Your Guns '48
The Hawk of Powder River '48
The Tioga Kid '48
West to Glory '47
Wild Country '47
The Caravan Trail '46
Colorado Serenade '46
Driftin' River '46
Wild West '46
Song of Old Wyoming '45
Wildfire '45
Knights of the Range '40
Santa Fe Marshal '40
Law of the Pampas '39
Renegade Trail '39
Felicity Dean
The Last of the Blonde Bombshells '00
Persuasion '95
The Whistle Blower '87
James Dean (1931-55)
America at the Movies '76
Giant '56
Rebel without a Cause '55
East of Eden '54
Hill Number One '51
Jeanne Dean
Clipped Wings '53
Radar Patrol vs. Spy King '49
Jimmy Dean (1928-)
Big Bad John '90
The City '76
Diamonds Are Forever '71
The Ballad of Andy Crocker '69
Loren Dean (1969-)
Space Cowboys '00
Mumford '99
Enemy of the State '98
The End of Violence '97
Gattaca '97
Mrs. Winterbourne '96
Rosewood '96
How to Make an American Quilt '95
The Passion of Darkly Noon '95
JFK: Reckless Youth '93
1492: Conquest of Paradise '92
Billy Bathgate '91
Say Anything '89
Margia Dean
The Quatermass Experiment '56
Fangs of the Wild '54
Rimfire '49
Priscilla Dean (1896-1987)
Law of the Sea '38
White Tiger '23
Outside the Law '21
Rick Dean
Carnosaur 3: Primal Species '96
Max Is Missing '95
Stripteaser '95
Cheyenne Warrior '94
Peephole '93
Bloodfist 3: Forced to Fight '92
Raiders of the Sun '92
Saturday Night Special '92
Naked Obsession '91
Heroes Stand Alone '89
Nam Angels '88
Ron Dean
The Client '94
Rudy '93
Legacy of Lies '92
Cold Justice '89
Above the Law '88
Cocktail '88
Big Score '83
Lezlie (Dean) Deane
To Protect and Serve '92
Freddy's Dead: The Final Nightmare '91
Girlfriend from Hell '89
976-EVIL '88
Justin Deas
Montana '90
Dream Lover '85
Kristine DeBell (1954-)
Cheerleaders' Wild Weekend '85
Rooster: Spurs of Death! '83
Tag: The Assassination Game '82
Lifepod '80
Willie & Phil '80
James DeBello
Crime and Punishment in Suburbia '00
100 Girls '00
John DeBello
Killer Tomatoes Eat France '91
Killer Tomatoes Strike Back '90
Out of the Dark '88
Attack of the Killer Tomatoes '77
David Deblinger
Intern '00
Frogs for Snakes '98
Nikki DeBoer
Rated X '00
Cube '98
Family of Cops 3 '98
Prom Night 4: Deliver Us from Evil '91
Lee DeBroux
Death Benefit '96
Mars '96
Open Fire '94
Hangfire '91
Sweet Hostage '75
Jean Debucourt (1894-1958)
The Crucible '57
The Earrings of Madame De... '54
Seven Deadly Sins '53
Monsieur Vincent '47
La Chute de la Maison Usher '28
Amanda DeCadenet
Fall '97
Four Rooms '95
Rosemary DeCamp (1910-2001)
Saturday the 14th '81
13 Ghosts '60
By the Light of the Silvery Moon '53
Main Street to Broadway '53
On Moonlight Bay '51
Look for the Silver Lining '49
The Story of Seabiscuit '49
Rhapsody in Blue '45
Commandos Strike at Dawn '43
The Jungle Book '42
Yankee Doodle Dandy '42
Cheers for Miss Bishop '41
Eugene Deckers (1917-77)
Lady L '65
Flame Over India '60
The Golden Salamander '51
Madeleine '50
Edward "Blue" Deckert
The Rookie '02
Home Fries '98
The Curse of Inferno '96
A Taste for Killing '92
Jan Decleir (1946-)
Molokai: The Story of Father Damien '99
Character '97
Antonia's Line '95
Daens '92
Xavier DeClie
Gangster World '98
The Survivor '98
Adrenalin: Fear the Rush '96
Nemesis 3: Time Lapse '96
Guy Decomble (1910-64)
The 400 Blows '59
Bob le Flambeur '55
Jour de Fete '48
Catherine Dee
Stuff Stephanie in the Incinerator '89
In Deadly Heat '87
Frances Dee (1907-)
Gypsy Colt '54
Because of You '52
Four Faces West '48
The Private Affairs of Bel Ami '47
I Walked with a Zombie '43
So Ends Our Night '41
Wheel of Fortune '41
If I Were King '38
Souls at Sea '37
Becky Sharp '35
Of Human Bondage '34
Finishing School '33
Little Women '33
Ruby Dee (1924-)
Finding Buck McHenry '00
Having Our Say: The Delany Sisters' First 100 Years '99
Passing Glory '99
The Wall '99
Baby Geniuses '98
A Simple Wish '97
Mr. & Mrs. Loving '96
Just Cause '94
Stephen King's The Stand '94
Cop and a Half '93
The Ernest Green Story '93
Jungle Fever '91
The Court Martial of Jackie Robinson '90
Decoration Day '90
Zora Is My Name! '90
Do the Right Thing '89
Love at Large '89
Gore Vidal's Lincoln '88
Windmills of the Gods '88
Go Tell It on the Mountain '84
Cat People '82
All God's Children '80
I Know Why the Caged Bird Sings '79
Roots: The Next Generation '79
It's Good to Be Alive '74
Buck and the Preacher '72
The Incident '67
The Balcony '63
Gone Are the Days '63
Purlie Victorious '63
A Raisin in the Sun '61
The Jackie Robinson Story '50
No Way Out '50
Sandra Dee (1942-)
Lost '83
Fantasy Island '76
The Dunwich Horror '70
Tammy and the Doctor '63
Come September '61
Portrait in Black '60
Gidget '59
Imitation of Life '59
A Summer Place '59
The Reluctant Debutante '58
Until They Sail '57
Rick Dees
Jetsons: The Movie '90 (V)
La Bamba '87
Eddie Deezen
Teenage Exorcist '93
Rock-a-Doodle '92 (V)
Mob Boss '90
Hollywood Boulevard 2 '89
Assault of the Killer Bimbos '88
Beverly Hills Vamp '88
Million Dollar Mystery '87
Desperate Moves '86
Mugsy's Girls '85
Rosebud Beach Hotel '85
Surf 2 '84
Midnight Madness '80
A Polish Vampire in Burbank '80
1941 '79
Grease '78
I Wanna Hold Your Hand '78
Mos Def
Bamboozled '00
Island of the Dead '00
Where's Marlowe? '98
Don DeFore (1917-93)
A Rare Breed '81
The Facts of Life '60
A Time to Love & a Time to Die '58
Battle Hymn '57
A Girl in Every Port '52
Jumping Jacks '52
My Friend Irma '49
Too Late for Tears '49
Romance on the High Seas '48
Ramrod '47
Without Reservations '46
The Stork Club '45
Thirty Seconds Over Tokyo '44
Calvert Deforest (1921-)
Mr. Write '92
Leader of the Band '87
Heaven Help Us '85
Ellen DeGeneres (1958-)
If These Walls Could Talk 2 '00
EDtv '99
Goodbye, Lover '99
The Love Letter '99
Mr. Wrong '95
Pia Degermark (1949-)
The Vampire Happening '71
The Looking Glass War '69
Elvira Madigan '67
Sam DeGrasse
Robin Hood '22
The Scarlet Car '17
John Dehner (1915-92)
Creator '85
The Jagged Edge '85
Airplane 2: The Sequel '82
California Gold Rush '81
Nothing Personal '80
Mountain Man '77
The Killer Inside Me '76
The Day of the Dolphin '73
Support Your Local Gunfighter '71
The Hallelujah Trail '65 (N)
The Left-Handed Gun '58
Man of the West '58
Girl in Black Stockings '57
Fastest Gun Alive '56
The King's Thief '55
The Prodigal '55
Apache '54
Hot Lead '51
Vigilantes of Boom Town '46
Khigh (Kaie Deei) Deigh (1910-91)
Noble House '88
Seconds '66
The Manchurian Candidate '62
David DeKeyser
Leon the Pig Farmer '93
Yentl '83
Valentino '77
Albert Dekker (1904-68)
The Wild Bunch '69
Gamera, the Invincible '66
Suddenly, Last Summer '59
Illegal '55
Kiss Me Deadly '55
East of Eden '54
As Young As You Feel '51
Cass Timberlane '47
Gentleman's Agreement '47
The Killers '46
Two Years before the Mast '46
Experiment Perilous '45
The Woman of the Town '44
Buckskin Frontier '43
The Kansan '43
War of the Wildcats '43
In Old California '42
Once Upon a Honeymoon '42
Wake Island '42
The Great Commandment '41
Honky Tonk '41
Dr. Cyclops '40
Seven Sinners '40
Strange Cargo '40
Beau Geste '39
Marie Antoinette '38
Louis Del Grande
Sugartime '95
Northern Extremes '93
Of Unknown Origin '83
Maria Del Mar (1964-)
Price of Glory '00
Moonshine Highway '96
Tails You Live, Heads You're Dead '95
Eclipse '94
Angel Del Pozo
Horror Express '72
Pancho Villa '72
Dulio Del Prete (1938-98)
Voices from Beyond '90
How Funny Can Sex Be? '76
The Sensuous Nurse '76
Redneck '73
Alfredo, Alfredo '72
Dolores Del Rio (1905-83)
Children of Sanchez '79
Cheyenne Autumn '64
Flaming Star '60
Flor Silvestre '58
Torero '56
The Fugitive '48
Maria Candelaria '46
Journey into Fear '42
Accused '36
Flying Down to Rio '33
Bird of Paradise '32
Evangeline '29
Laura Del Sol (1961-)
The Crew '95
El Amor Brujo '86
The Hit '85
The Stilts '84
Carmen '83
Benicio Del Toro (1967-)
The Pledge '00
Snatch '00
Traffic '00
Way of the Gun '00
Fear and Loathing in Las Vegas '98
Joyride '97
Basquiat '96
Excess Baggage '96
The Fan '96
The Funeral '96
The Usual Suspects '95
Swimming with Sharks '94
Fearless '93
Money for Nothing '93
Christopher Columbus: The Discovery '92
China Moon '91
The Indian Runner '91
License to Kill '89
Michel Delahaye
Simone Barbes '80
Alphaville '65
Suzy Delair (1916-)
Is Paris Burning? '66
Fernandel the Dressmaker '57
Gervaise '56
Utopia '51
Pattes Blanches '49
Jenny Lamour '47
Lisa (Lise) Delamare (1913-)
Baxter '89
Monsieur Vincent '47
La Marseillaise '37
Cassandra Delaney (1961-)
Hurricane Smith '92
Fair Game '85
One Night Stand '84
Charles Delaney
Captured in Chinatown '35
Hearts of Humanity '32
Joan Delaney
Don't Drink the Water '69
The President's Analyst '67
Kim Delaney (1961-)
Mission to Mars '00
Closer and Closer '96
Serial Killer '95
Tall, Dark and Deadly '95
Temptress '95
Darkman 2: The Return of Durant '94
The Force '94
Project Metalbeast: DNA Overload '94
The Disappearance of Christina '93
Body Parts '91
Hangfire '91
The Drifter '88
Campus Man '87
Christmas Comes to Willow Creek '87
Hunter's Blood '87
Delta Force '86
That Was Then...This Is Now '85
Pat Delaney
Iron Horsemen '71
Creature of Destruction '67
Zontar, the Thing from Venus '66
Michael Delano (1940-)
Out for Blood '93
Private Wars '93
Ring of Fire 2: Blood and Steel '92
Ring of Fire '91
Not of This Earth '88
Catlow '71
Dana Delany (1956-)
The Right Temptation '00
Sirens '99
Rescuers: Stories of Courage—Two Couples '98
The Curve '97
True Women '97
Wide Awake '97
Fly Away Home '96
Live Nude Girls '95
The Enemy Within '94
Exit to Eden '94
Batman: Mask of the Phantasm '93 (V)
Dead to Rights '93
Tombstone '93

Wild Palms '93
Housesitter '92
Light Sleeper '92
China Beach '88
Masquerade '88
Moon over Parador '88
Patty Hearst '88
A Winner Never Quits '86
Almost You '85

Cyril Delevanti (1887-1995)
The Killing of Sister George '69
I Bury the Living '58
Red Barry '38

Majandra Delfino (1981-)
The Learning Curve '01
Shriek If You Know What I Did Last Friday the 13th '00
The Secret Life of Girls '99
Zeus and Roxanne '96

George DelHoyo
Dead Letter Office '98
The Crying Child '96

Debra Deliso
Iced '88
Slumber Party Massacre '82

Claudia Dell (1910-77)
Boots of Destiny '37
Yellow Cargo '36
The Lost City '34
Woman Condemned '33
Hearts of Humanity '32
Midnight Warning '32
Bachelor Apartment '31

Gabriel Dell (1919-88)
Mars '96
The Escape Artist '82
Framed '75
The 300 Year Weekend '71
Blues Busters '50
Master Minds '49
Smugglers' Cove '48
Spook Busters '48
Bowery Buckaroos '47
Hard-Boiled Mahoney '47
Follow the Leader '44
Million Dollar Kid '44
Kid Dynamite '43
Let's Get Tough '42
'Neath Brooklyn Bridge '42
Smart Alecks '42
Pride of the Bowery '41
They Made Me a Criminal '39
Angels with Dirty Faces '38
Little Tough Guys '38
Dead End '37

Myrna Dell (1924-)
Ma Barker's Killer Brood '60
Naked Hills '56
The Bushwackers '52
The Judge Steps Out '49
Fighting Father Dunne '48
Nocturne '46

Michael DellaFemina
Bloodlust: Subspecies 3 '93
Invisible: The Chronicles of Benjamin Knight '93
Italian Movie '93
Mandroid '93

Erik Todd Dellums (1964-)
Boycott '02
Blackmale '99
She's Gotta Have It '86

Edouard Delmont (1893-1955)
The Sheep Has Five Legs '54
Passion for Life '48
Harvest '37
Angele '34
Toni '34

Nikki Deloach
Gunfighter's Moon '96
Traveller '96

Genevieve Deloir
The Screaming Dead '72
The Red Half-Breed '70

Alain Delon (1935-)
Nouvelle Vague '90
Swann in Love '84
The Concorde: Airport '79 '79
Les Aventuriers '77
Boomerang '76
Mr. Klein '76
Gypsy '75
Icy Breasts '75
Widow Couderc '74
Zorro '74
Scorpio '73
Assassination of Trotsky '72
Godson '72
Red Sun '71
Borsalino '70
Swimming Pool '70
The Girl on a Motorcycle '68
Honor Among Thieves '68
Spirits of the Dead '68
Diabolically Yours '67
Le Samourai '67
The Eclipse '66
Is Paris Burning? '66
The Lost Command '66
Texas across the River '66
Joy House '64
Any Number Can Win '63
Purple Noon '60
Rocco and His Brothers '60
Sois Belle et Tais-Toi '58

Nathalie Delon (1941-)
Game of Seduction '86
Le Sex Shop '73
Bluebeard '72
Eyes Behind the Stars '72
Godson '72
Le Samourai '67

Jennifer Delora (1962-)
Bedroom Eyes 2 '89
Deranged '87
New York's Finest '87
Robot Holocaust '87
Sensations '87

Michael Delorenzo
Gun Shy '00
The Wall '99

Daniele Delorme
November Moon '85
Pardon Mon Affaire '76
Les Miserables '57

Julie Delpy (1969-)
Waking Life '01
Sand '00
But I'm a Cheerleader '99
Dostoevsky's Crime and Punishment '99
The Passion of Ayn Rand '99
An American Werewolf in Paris '97
Before Sunrise '94
Killing Zoe '94
Trois Couleurs: Blanc '94
Trois Couleurs: Rouge '94
Younger & Younger '94
The Three Musketeers '93
Europa, Europa '91
Voyager '91
Beatrice '88
Mauvais Sang '86

Rene Deltgen (1909-79)
Journey to the Lost City '58
Tromba, the Tiger Man '52
The Mozart Story '48

Rudy DeLuca
Life Stinks '91
The Return of Count Yorga '71

David DeLuise
Terror Tract '00
Too Smooth '98

Dom DeLuise (1933-)
Baby Geniuses '98
The Godson '98
Boys Will Be Boys '97
Red Line '96
All Dogs Go to Heaven 2 '95 (V)
The Tin Soldier '95
A Troll in Central Park '94 (V)
Happily Ever After '93 (V)
The Magic Voyage '93 (V)
Silence of the Hams '93
The Skateboard Kid '93 (V)
Munchie '92 (V)
Almost Pregnant '91
An American Tail: Fievel Goes West '91 (V)
Driving Me Crazy '91
Loose Cannons '90
All Dogs Go to Heaven '89 (V)
Going Bananas '88
Oliver & Company '88 (V)
My African Adventure '87
Spaceballs '87
An American Tail '86 (V)
Haunted Honeymoon '86
Cannonball Run 2 '84
Johnny Dangerously '84
The Best Little Whorehouse in Texas '82
The Secret of NIMH '82 (V)
Cannonball Run '81
History of the World: Part 1 '81
Fatso '80
Hot Stuff '80
The Last Married Couple in America '80
Smokey and the Bandit 2 '80
Wholly Moses! '80
Diary of a Young Comic '79
The Muppet Movie '79
The Adventures of Sherlock Holmes' Smarter Brother '78
The Cheap Detective '78
The End '78
Sextette '78
World's Greatest Lover '77
Silent Movie '76
Blazing Saddles '74
Evil Roy Slade '71
The Twelve Chairs '70
The Glass Bottom Boat '66
Fail-Safe '64

Michael DeLuise (1970-)
Boys Will Be Boys '97
The Shot '96
Midnight Edition '93
Encino Man '92

Peter DeLuise (1966-)
National Lampoon's Attack of the 5 Ft. 2 Women '94
Rescue Me '93
Children of the Night '92
Free Ride '86
The Midnight Hour '86

Gordon DeMain (1886-1954)
The Mad Monster '42
International Lady '41
Fighting Texans '33
High Gear '33
Rainbow Ranch '33

William Demarest (1892-1983)
The McCullochs '75
Don't Be Afraid of the Dark '73
It's a Mad, Mad, Mad, Mad World '63
Viva Las Vegas '63
The Mountain '56
Sincerely Yours '56
Hell on Frisco Bay '55
Jupiter's Darling '55
The Private War of Major Benson '55
Dangerous When Wet '53
Escape from Fort Bravo '53
Here Come the Girls '53
Behave Yourself! '52
What Price Glory? '52
First Legion '51
Never a Dull Moment '50
Riding High '50
Jolson Sings Again '49
Sorrowful Jones '49
On Our Merry Way '48
The Perils of Pauline '47
The Jolson Story '46
Along Came Jones '45
The Great Moment '44
Hail the Conquering Hero '44
Miracle of Morgan's Creek '44
All Through the Night '42
The Palm Beach Story '42
Pardon My Sarong '42
The Devil & Miss Jones '41
The Lady Eve '41
Sullivan's Travels '41
Christmas in July '40
The Great McGinty '40
The Great Man Votes '38
Rebecca of Sunnybrook Farm '38
Charlie Chan at the Opera '36
The Great Ziegfeld '36
Love on the Run '36
Hands Across the Table '35
The Jazz Singer '27

Derrick DeMarney (1906-78)
Inheritance '47
Frenzy '46
Dangerous Moonlight '41
Young and Innocent '37
Things to Come '36

Orane Demazis (1904-91)
Le Schpountz '38
Harvest '37
Cesar '36
Angele '34
Fanny '32
Marius '31

Alla Demidova
The Seagull '71
Tchaikovsky '71

Cecil B. DeMille (1881-1959)
Sunset Boulevard '50
Star Spangled Rhythm '42
Free and Easy '30

Katherine DeMille (1911-95)
The Judge '49
Unconquered '47
The Gentleman from California '37
Drift Fence '36
The Black Room '35
The Crusades '35
Belle of the Nineties '34
Viva Villa! '34

Jonathan Demme (1944-)
That Thing You Do! '96
Married to the Mob '88
Into the Night '85
Incredible Melting Man '77

Mylene Demongeot (1936-)
12 Plus 1 '70
Uncle Tom's Cabin '69
The Rape of the Sabines '61
The Giant of Marathon '60
Just Another Pretty Face '58
Sois Belle et Tais-Toi '58
Bonjour Tristesse '57
The Crucible '57

Rebecca DeMornay (1962-)
A Girl Thing '01
Range of Motion '00
The Right Temptation '00
Night Ride Home '99
Thick as Thieves '99
Wicked Ways '99
The Con '98
The Winner '96
Never Talk to Strangers '95
Getting Out '94
Blind Side '93
Guilty as Sin '93
The Three Musketeers '93
The Hand that Rocks the Cradle '92
Backdraft '91
An Inconvenient Woman '91
By Dawn's Early Light '89
Dealers '89
And God Created Woman '88
Feds '88
The Murders in the Rue Morgue '86
Pecos Bill '86
Runaway Train '85
The Slugger's Wife '85
The Trip to Bountiful '85
Risky Business '83
Testament '83
One from the Heart '82

Darcy Demoss (1964-)
Forbidden Zone: Alien Abduction '96
The Death Artist '95
Eden 2 '93
Eden 3 '93
Eden 4 '93
Eden '92
Living to Die '91
Pale Blood '91
Can't Buy Me Love '87
Friday the 13th, Part 6: Jason Lives '86

Brendan F. Dempsey
About Adam '00
Waking Ned Devine '98

Patrick Dempsey (1966-)
Life in the Fast Lane '00
Scream 3 '00
Dostoevsky's Crime and Punishment '99
Me & Will '99
Jeremiah '98
Something About Sex '98
Hugo Pool '97
Bloodknot '95
The Escape '95
The Right to Remain Silent '95
Ava's Magical Adventure '94
With Honors '94
Bank Robber '93
JFK: Reckless Youth '93
Face the Music '92
For Better and for Worse '92
Mobsters '91
Run '91
Coupe de Ville '90
Happy Together '89
Loverboy '89
In a Shallow Grave '88
Some Girls '88
Can't Buy Me Love '87
In the Mood '87
Meatballs 3 '87
Heaven Help Us '85

Richard Dempsey
The Aristocrats '99
Catherine Cookson's Tilly Trotter '99
The Chronicles of Narnia '89

Tanya Dempsey
Witchouse 3: Demon Fire '01
Shrieker '97

Carol Dempster (1901-91)
The Sorrows of Satan '26
Sally of the Sawdust '25
America '24
Isn't Life Wonderful '24
The White Rose '23
Dream Street '21
The Love Flower '20

Jeffrey DeMunn (1947-)
The Majestic '01
Noriega: God's Favorite '00
The Green Mile '99
Harvest '99
Stephen King's The Storm of the Century '99
The X-Files '98
RocketMan '97
Turbulence '96
Citizen X '95
Hiroshima '95
Down Came a Blackbird '94
Barbarians at the Gate '93
Treacherous Crossing '92
Eyes of an Angel '91
Blaze '89
Betrayed '88
The Blob '88
Gore Vidal's Lincoln '88
Windmills of the Gods '88
The Hitcher '86
A Time to Live '85
Windy City '84
Sessions '83
Trumps '83
Frances '82
Christmas Evil '80

Mathieu Demy
Jeanne and the Perfect Guy '98
One Hundred and One Nights '95
Le Petit Amour '87

Judi Dench (1934-)
The Importance of Being Earnest '02
Iris '01
The Shipping News '01
Chocolat '00
The Last of the Blonde Bombshells '00
Tea with Mussolini '99
The World Is Not Enough '99
Shakespeare in Love '98
Mrs. Brown '97
Tomorrow Never Dies '97
Hamlet '96
Goldeneye '95
Jack and Sarah '95
Henry V '89
A Handful of Dust '88
Saigon: Year of the Cat '87
84 Charing Cross Road '86
A Room with a View '86
Wetherby '85
Luther '74
A Midsummer Night's Dream '68
A Study in Terror '66

Catherine Deneuve (1943-)
The Musketeer '01
Dancer in the Dark '99
East-West '99
Pola X '99
Place Vendome '98
Genealogies of a Crime '97
Les Voleurs '96
The Convent '95
Ma Saison Preferee '93
Indochine '92
Scene of the Crime '87
Love Songs '85
Fort Saganne '84
Choice of Arms '83
The Hunger '83
I Love All of You '83
The Last Metro '80
A Slightly Pregnant Man '79
March or Die '77
The Hustle '75
Lovers Like Us '75
La Grande Bourgeoise '74
Act of Aggression '73
Peau D'Ane '71
Donkey Skin '70
Tristana '70
April Fools '69
Mississippi Mermaid '69
Mayerling '68
The Young Girls of Rochefort '68
Belle de Jour '67
Repulsion '65
Umbrellas of Cherbourg '64

Jake Dengel (1933-94)
Prayer of the Rollerboys '91
Bloodsucking Pharoahs of Pittsburgh '90
Ironweed '87

Maurice Denham (1909-)
Monsignor Quixote '91
84 Charing Cross Road '86
Mr. Love '86
From a Far Country: Pope John Paul II '81
Luther '74
Negatives '68
Night Caller from Outer Space '66
The Alphabet Murders '65

The Nanny '65
Hysteria '64
The Seventh Dawn '64
The Very Edge '63
Damn the Defiant '62
Paranoiac '62
The Mark '61
Sink the Bismarck '60
Curse of the Demon '57
Animal Farm '55 (V)
Blanche Fury '48
Captain Boycott '47

Marianne (Cuau) Denicourt (1966-)
The Lost Son '98
My Sex Life...Or How I Got into an Argument '96
Up/Down/Fragile '95
Doomsday Gun '94
La Sentinelle '92
La Belle Noiseuse '90

Lydie Denier (1964-)
White Cargo '96
Guardian Angel '94
Mardi Gras for the Devil '93
Red Shoe Diaries 3: Another Woman's Lipstick '93
Under Investigation '93
Invasion of Privacy '92
Midnight Cabaret '90
Satan's Princess '90
Blood Relations '87

Jacques Denis (1943-)
This Sweet Sickness '77
Jonah Who Will Be 25 in the Year 2000 '76
The Clockmaker '73
La Salamandre '71

Alexis Denisof (1966-)
Noah's Ark '99
Sharpe's Justice '97
Sharpe's Revenge '97
Sharpe's Waterloo '97

Anthony John (Tony) Denison (1950-)
Looking for an Echo '99
For Which He Stands '98
The Corporate Ladder '97
Opposite Corners '96
Getting Gotti '94
Men of War '94
The Amy Fisher Story '93
A Brilliant Disguise '93
Full Eclipse '93
Sex, Love and Cold Hard Cash '93
The Harvest '92
Child of Darkness, Child of Light '91
City of Hope '91
Little Vegas '90
Full Exposure: The Sex Tape Scandals '89
The Great Escape 2: The Untold Story '88

Leslie Denison (1905-92)
The Snow Creature '54
O.S.S. '46
Five Graves to Cairo '43
Sherlock Holmes and the Secret Weapon '42
To Be or Not to Be '42

Michael Denison (1915-98)
Shadowlands '93
Angels One Five '54
The Franchise Affair '52
The Importance of Being Earnest '52

Tony Denman
Sorority Boys '02
Poor White Trash '00

Marie Denn
Bury Me an Angel '71
Wild Guitar '62

Brian Dennehy (1939-)
Summer Catch '01
Warden of Red Rock '01
Out of the Cold '99
Silicon Towers '99
Sirens '99
Dish Dogs '98
Tom Clancy's Netforce '98
Larry McMurtry's Dead Man's Walk '96
Nostromo '96
William Shakespeare's Romeo and Juliet '96
Tommy Boy '95
The Stars Fell on Henrietta '94
Final Appeal '93
Foreign Affairs '93
Diamond Fleece '92
Gladiator '92
Scott Turow's The Burden of Proof '92
Teamster Boss: The Jackie Presser Story '92
To Catch a Killer '92
The Belly of an Architect '91
F/X 2: The Deadly Art of Illusion '91
Indio '90
A Killing in a Small Town '90
The Last of the Finest '90
Presumed Innocent '90
Rising Son '90
Day One '89
Perfect Witness '89
Cocoon: The Return '88
A Father's Revenge '88
Miles from Home '88
Return to Snowy River '88
Best Seller '87
The Lion of Africa '87
Acceptable Risks '86
F/X '86
Legal Eagles '86
Check Is in the Mail '85
Cocoon '85
Silverado '85
Twice in a Lifetime '85
Finders Keepers '84
The River Rat '84
Gorky Park '83
Never Cry Wolf '83
First Blood '82
Split Image '82
Little Miss Marker '80
A Rumor of War '80
To Love Again '80
Butch and Sundance: The Early Days '79
The Jericho Mile '79
North Dallas Forty '79
Silent Victory: The Kitty O'Neil Story '79
10 '79
F.I.S.T. '78
Foul Play '78
Pearl '78
A Real American Hero '78
Ants '77
Johnny We Hardly Knew Ye '77
Semi-Tough '77

Barry Dennen
Liquid Dreams '92
Jesus Christ, Superstar '73
Paul Bartel's The Secret Cinema '69

Charles Denner (1926-95)
Window Shopping '86
Robert et Robert '78
The Man Who Loved Women '77
Mado '76
The Holes '72
Les Assassins de L'Ordre '71
Z '69
The Bride Wore Black '68
The Two of Us '68
Life Upside Down '64
Bluebeard '63

Richard Denning (1914-98)
Alice Through the Looking Glass '66
Twice-Told Tales '63
An Affair to Remember '57
The Black Scorpion '57
Girls in Prison '56
Day the World Ended '55
Creature from the Black Lagoon '54
Hangman's Knot '52
Double Deal '50
Unknown Island '48
Black Beauty '46
The Glass Key '42
Adam Had Four Sons '41

John Dennis
Tomb of the Undead '72
From Here to Eternity '53

Sandy Dennis (1937-92)
The Indian Runner '91
Parents '89
Another Woman '88
976-EVIL '88
The Execution '85
Come Back to the Five & Dime Jimmy Dean, Jimmy Dean '82
The Four Seasons '81
Nasty Habits '77
God Told Me To '76
Mr. Sycamore '74
The Out-of-Towners '70
That Cold Day in the Park '69
Sweet November '68
Up the Down Staircase '67
Who's Afraid of Virginia Woolf? '66
The Three Sisters '65
Splendor in the Grass '61

Reginald Denny (1891-1967)
Assault on a Queen '66
Batman '66
Cat Ballou '65
Around the World in 80 Days '56
Escape to Burma '55
Sabaka '55
Abbott and Costello Meet Dr. Jekyll and Mr. Hyde '52
Mr. Blandings Builds His Dream House '48
Escape Me Never '47
My Favorite Brunette '47
Love Letters '45
Captains of the Clouds '42
Sherlock Holmes: The Voice of Terror '42
Rebecca '40
Bulldog Drummond's Bride '39
Bulldog Drummond's Secret Police '39
Arrest Bulldog Drummond '38
Bulldog Drummond's Peril '38
Bulldog Drummond Comes Back '37
Bulldog Drummond Escapes '37
Bulldog Drummond's Revenge '37
We're in the Legion Now '37
Anna Karenina '35
The Midnight Phantom '35
The Lost Patrol '34
Of Human Bondage '34
Dancing Man '33
Parlor, Bedroom and Bath '31
Private Lives '31
Madam Satan '30
The Cheerful Fraud '27
Skinner's Dress Suit '26
California Straight Ahead '25

Catherine Dent
The Majestic '01
Replicant '01
Someone Like You '01
Venomous '01

Vernon Dent (1895-1963)
Texas Cyclone '32
The Cameraman '28
His First Flame '26
Extra Girl '23

Christa Denton
Scandal in a Small Town '88
Convicted: A Mother's Story '87
The Gate '87
The Bad Seed '85

Donna Denton
Slaughterhouse Rock '88
Death Blow '87
Glory Years '87
Outlaw of Gor '87

Graham Denton
The Young One '61
The Great St. Louis Bank Robbery '59

Bob Denver (1935-)
Back to the Beach '87
High School USA '84
Rescue from Gilligan's Island '78
Wackiest Wagon Train in the West '77
Who's Minding the Mint? '67

John Denver (1943-97)
Walking Thunder '94
Fire and Ice '87 (N)
Foxfire '87
Oh, God! '77

Elisabeth Depardieu
Jean de Florette '87
Manon of the Spring '87
Tartuffe '84

Gerard Depardieu (1948-)
The Bridge '00
The Closet '00
102 Dalmatians '00
Vatel '00
Balzac: A Life of Passion '99
The Count of Monte Cristo '99
The Man in the Iron Mask '98
Bogus '96
Hamlet '96
The Machine '96
The Secret Agent '96
Unhook the Stars '96
The Horseman on the Roof '95
Colonel Chabert '94
Elisa '94
Helas pour Moi '94
A Pure Formality '94
Germinal '93
My Father the Hero '93
1492: Conquest of Paradise '92
Tous les Matins du Monde '92
Uranus '91
Cyrano de Bergerac '90
Green Card '90
Camille Claudel '89
Too Beautiful for You '88
Jean de Florette '87
Under Satan's Sun '87
Menage '86
One Woman or Two '85
Police '85
Fort Saganne '84
Tartuffe '84
Choice of Arms '83
I Love All of You '83
Les Comperes '83
Moon in the Gutter '83
The Return of Martin Guerre '83
Danton '82
La Chevre '81
The Woman Next Door '81
The Last Metro '80
Loulou '80
Mon Oncle d'Amerique '80
Buffet Froid '79
Get Out Your Handkerchiefs '78
This Sweet Sickness '77
Barocco '76
Maitresse '76
1900 '76
Vincent, Francois, Paul and the Others '76
Going Places '74
Stavisky '74
The Holes '72

Guillaume Depardieu
The Count of Monte Cristo '99
Pola X '99
Tous les Matins du Monde '92

Johnny Depp (1963-)
Blow '01
From Hell '01
Before Night Falls '00
Chocolat '00
The Man Who Cried '00
The Astronaut's Wife '99
The Ninth Gate '99
Sleepy Hollow '99
Fear and Loathing in Las Vegas '98
Donnie Brasco '96
Dead Man '95
Nick of Time '95
Arizona Dream '94
Don Juan DeMarco '94
Ed Wood '94
Benny & Joon '93
What's Eating Gilbert Grape '93
Freddy's Dead: The Final Nightmare '91
Cry-Baby '90
Edward Scissorhands '90
Platoon '86
A Nightmare on Elm Street '84
Private Resort '84

Bo Derek (1956-)
Tommy Boy '95
Shattered Image '93
Woman of Desire '93
Hot Chocolate '92
Ghosts Can't Do It '90
Bolero '84
Tarzan, the Ape Man '81
A Change of Seasons '80
10 '79
Orca '77
Fantasies '73

John Derek (1926-98)
Once Before I Die '65
Exodus '60
Omar Khayyam '57
The Ten Commandments '56
The Annapolis Story '55
The Outcast '54
Ambush at Tomahawk Gap '53
All the King's Men '49
Knock on Any Door '49

Joe DeRita (1909-93)
The Outlaws Is Coming! '65
Around the World in a Daze '63
Four for Texas '63
It's a Mad, Mad, Mad, Mad World '63
Three Stooges in Orbit '62
Snow White and the Three Stooges '61
The Three Stooges Meet Hercules '61
Have Rocket Will Travel '59

Edouard Dermithe (1915-95)
The Testament of Orpheus '59
Les Enfants Terrible '50
Orpheus '49

Bruce Dern (1936-)
The Glass House '01
All the Pretty Horses '00
The Haunting '99
Small Soldiers '98 (V)
Down Periscope '96
Last Man Standing '96
Mrs. Munck '95
A Mother's Prayer '95
Mulholland Falls '95
Wild Bill '95
Amelia Earhart: The Final Flight '94
Dead Man's Revenge '93
Carolina Skeletons '92
Diggstown '92
Into the Badlands '92
After Dark, My Sweet '90
The Court Martial of Jackie Robinson '90
The 'Burbs '89
1969 '89
World Gone Wild '88
Big Town '87
Uncle Tom's Cabin '87
On the Edge '86
Toughlove '85
Harry Tracy '83
That Championship Season '82
Tattoo '81
Middle Age Crazy '80
Coming Home '78
The Driver '78
Black Sunday '77
Family Plot '76
Twist '76
Posse '75
Smile '75
The Great Gatsby '74
The Laughing Policeman '74
The Cowboys '72
The King of Marvin Gardens '72
Thumb Tripping '72
The Incredible Two-Headed Transplant '71
Silent Running '71
Bloody Mama '70
Rebel Rousers '69
Support Your Local Sheriff '69
They Shoot Horses, Don't They? '69
Psych-Out '68
The St. Valentine's Day Massacre '67
The Trip '67
The War Wagon '67
Waterhole #3 '67
Will Penny '67
The Wild Angels '66
Hush, Hush, Sweet Charlotte '65
Marnie '64

Laura Dern (1966-)
Focus '01
I Am Sam '01
Jurassic Park 3 '01
Novocaine '01
Dr. T & the Women '00
October Sky '99
A Season for Miracles '99
The Baby Dance '98
Citizen Ruth '96
Down Came a Blackbird '94
Fallen Angels 1 '93
Jurassic Park '93
A Perfect World '93
Afterburn '92
Rambling Rose '91
Wild at Heart '90
Fat Man and Little Boy '89
Strange Case of Dr. Jekyll & Mr. Hyde '89
Haunted Summer '88
Blue Velvet '86
Mask '85
Smooth Talk '85
Teachers '84
Foxes '80

Barbara DeRossi (1960-)
Blood Ties '87
Mussolini & I '85
Quo Vadis '85

Richard Derr (1918-92)
Adam at 6 a.m. '70
Terror Is a Man '59
The Invisible Avenger '58
When Worlds Collide '51
Guilty of Treason '50
Castle in the Desert '42

Cleavant Derricks (1953-)
World Traveler '01
Bluffing It '87
Off Beat '86
The Slugger's Wife '85
Moscow on the Hudson '84

Debi Derryberry
Jimmy Neutron: Boy Genius *'01 (V)*
Whispers: An Elephant's Tale *'00 (V)*

Janos Derzsi
Almanac of Fall
Bad Guys *'79*

Michael Des Barres (1948-)
Mulholland Drive *'01*
Sugar Town *'99*
Poison Ivy 3: The New Seduction *'97*
Silk Degrees *'94*
A Simple Twist of Fate *'94*
Widow's Kiss *'94*
The High Crusade *'92*
Waxwork 2: Lost in Time *'91*
Midnight Cabaret *'90*
Pink Cadillac *'89*
Nightflyers *'87*
I, Monster *'71*

Jean Desailly (1920-)
Le Professionnel *'81*
Assassination of Trotsky *'72*
The Soft Skin *'64*
Les Grandes Manoeuvres *'55*
La Symphonie Pastorale *'46*

Anne DeSalvo (1949-)
Hi-Life *'98*
National Lampoon's Attack of the 5 Ft. 2 Women *'94*
Casualties of Love: The "Long Island Lolita" Story *'93*
Dead in the Water *'91*
Taking Care of Business *'90*
Spike of Bensonhurst *'88*
Burglar *'87*
Compromising Positions *'85*
Perfect *'85*
Bad Manners *'84*
D.C. Cab *'84*
My Favorite Year *'82*

Stanley DeSantis (1954-)
Head Over Heels *'01*
I Am Sam *'01*
Lansky *'99*
Heartwood *'98*
Clockwatchers *'97*
Fools Rush In *'97*
The Truth about Cats and Dogs *'96*
Broken Trust *'95*
National Lampoon's Attack of the 5 Ft. 2 Women *'94*
Armistead Maupin's Tales of the City *'93*
Candyman *'92*

Gerard Desarthe
Daens *'92*
Uranus *'91*

Alex Descas
Late August, Early September *'98*
Irma Vep *'96*
Nenette and Boni *'96*
I Can't Sleep *'93*
No Fear, No Die *'90*

Jerome Deschamps
La Separation *'98*
The Separation *'94*

Mary Jo Deschanel
2010: The Year We Make Contact *'84*
The Right Stuff *'83*

Zooey Deschanel (1980-)
Big Trouble *'02*
The Good Girl *'02*
The New Guy *'02*
Almost Famous *'00*
Mumford *'99*

Sandy Descher (1948-)
The Cobweb *'55*
The Prodigal *'55*
Them! *'54*

Alex Desert
Swingers *'96*
P.C.U. *'94*

Robert Desiderio (1951-)
No Laughing Matter *'97*
Gross Anatomy *'89*
Maximum Security *'87*
Oh, God! You Devil *'84*

Florence Desmond (-1993)
Three Came Home *'50*
Accused *'36*

William Desmond (1878-1949)
Courage of the North *'35*
Cowboy & the Bandit *'35*
Cyclone of the Saddle *'35*
Powdersmoke Range *'35*
Rustlers of Red Dog *'35*
Way of the West *'35*
Tailspin Tommy *'34*
Phantom of the Air *'33*
Rustler's Roundup *'33*
Battling with Buffalo Bill *'31*
Phantom of the West *'31*
Blood and Steel *'25*

Ivan Desny (1928-2002)
Les Voleurs *'96*
The Disenchanted *'90*
Quicker Than the Eye *'88*
Escape from the KGB *'87*
Berlin Alexanderplatz *'80*
The Marriage of Maria Braun *'79*
Touch Me Not *'74*
Little Mother *'71*
Mayerling *'68*
The Snake Hunter Strangler *'66*
End of Desire *'62*
Escapade in Florence *'62*
Sherlock Holmes and the Deadly Necklace *'62*
Daniella by Night *'61*
Song Without End *'60*
Anastasia *'56*
Lola Montes *'55*
The Respectful Prostitute *'52*
Madeleine *'50*

Rosana Desoto
Mambo Cafe *'00*
The 24 Hour Woman *'99*

Nada Despotovich
Series 7: The Contenders *'01*
Babycakes *'89*
Taken Away *'89*

Natalie Desselle
B.A.P.'s *'97*
Def Jam's How to Be a Player *'97*

Amanda Detmer (1971-)
Big Fat Liar *'02*
The Majestic *'01*
Saving Silverman *'01*
Boys and Girls *'00*
Final Destination *'00*
Drop Dead Gorgeous *'99*

Maruschka Detmers (1962-)
Hidden Assassin *'94*
The Mambo Kings *'92*
Hanna's War *'88*
Devil in the Flesh *'87*
First Name: Carmen *'83*

Tamara DeTreaux
Ghoulies *'84*
Don't Be Afraid of the Dark *'73*

Geoffrey Deuel
Amateur Night *'85*
Chisum *'70*

Ernst Deutsch
The Third Man *'49*
The Golem *'20*

Patti Deutsch
The Emperor's New Groove *'00 (V)*
Jetsons: The Movie *'90 (V)*

William Devane (1939-)
The Hollow Man *'00*
Poor White Trash *'00*
Space Cowboys *'00*
Payback *'98*
Detonator 2: Night Watch *'95*
Lady in Waiting *'94*
Rubdown *'93*
A Woman Named Jackie *'91*
Chips, the War Dog *'90*
Vital Signs *'90*
The Preppie Murder *'89*
Timestalkers *'87*
Hadley's Rebellion *'84*
Urge to Kill *'84*
Jane Doe *'83*
Testament *'83*
Honky Tonk Freeway *'81*
Red Flag: The Ultimate Game *'81*
The Dark *'79*
From Here to Eternity *'79*
Yanks *'79*
The Bad News Bears in Breaking Training *'77*
Red Alert *'77*
Rolling Thunder *'77*
Family Plot *'76*
Marathon Man *'76*
Missiles of October *'74*
McCabe & Mrs. Miller *'71*
My Old Man's Place *'71*
The 300 Year Weekend *'71*

Devin Devasquez (1963-)
Society *'92*
Can't Buy Me Love *'87*
House 2: The Second Story *'87*

Alan Deveau
Recruits *'86*
Loose Screws *'85*

Nathaniel DeVeaux
In a Class of His Own *'99*
The Spree *'96*
The Escape *'95*
Hard Evidence *'94*
Bad Attitude *'93*

Ed Devereaux (1925-)
Goldeneye: The Secret Life of Ian Fleming *'89*
We'll Meet Again *'82*
Money Movers *'78*

Marie Devereux
Naked Kiss *'64*
The Mark *'61*

Kamala Devi
The Brass Bottle *'63*
Geronimo *'62*

Renee Devillers (1903-)
The French Touch *'54*
Heart of a Nation *'43*
J'Accuse *'37*

Aidan Devine
Brian's Song *'01*
Life with Judy Garland—Me and My Shadows *'01*

Andy Devine (1905-77)
Mouse and His Child *'77 (V)*
Whale of a Tale *'76*
Robin Hood *'73 (V)*
Myra Breckinridge *'70*
Smoke *'70*
Over the Hill Gang *'69*
Zebra in the Kitchen *'65*
How the West Was Won *'63*
The Man Who Shot Liberty Valance *'62*
Two Rode Together *'61*
The Adventures of Huckleberry Finn *'60*
Around the World in 80 Days *'56*
Thunder Pass *'54*
Montana Belle *'52*
The Red Badge of Courage *'51*
Slaughter Trail *'51*
Never a Dull Moment *'50*
Eyes of Texas *'48*
Far Frontier *'48*
Grand Canyon Trail *'48*
Night Time in Nevada *'48*
Under California Stars *'48*
On the Old Spanish Trail *'47*
Springtime in the Sierras *'47*
Canyon Passage *'46*
Ali Baba and the Forty Thieves *'43*
The Gay Ranchero *'42*
The Flame of New Orleans *'41*
Never Say Die *'39*
Stagecoach *'39*
In Old Chicago *'37*
A Star Is Born *'37*
Yellowstone *'36*

George Devine (1910-66)
Tom Jones *'63*
Look Back in Anger *'58*
Time Without Pity *'57*

Loretta Devine
I Am Sam *'01*
Kingdom Come *'01*
Freedom Song *'00*
Urban Legends 2: Final Cut *'00*
What Women Want *'00*
The Breaks *'99*
Introducing Dorothy Dandridge *'99*
Down in the Delta *'98*
Love Kills *'98*
Urban Legend *'98*
Don King: Only in America *'97*
Lover Girl *'97*
Hoodlum *'96*
The Preacher's Wife *'96*
Rebound: The Legend of Earl "The Goat" Manigault *'96*
Waiting to Exhale *'95*
Caged Fear *'92*
Stanley and Iris *'90*

Sean Devine
Dead Silent *'99*
Perpetrators of the Crime *'98*

Danny DeVito (1944-)
Death to Smoochy *'02*
Heist *'01*
What's the Worst That Could Happen? *'01*
The Big Kahuna *'00*
Drowning Mona *'00*
Screwed *'00*
Man on the Moon *'99*
The Virgin Suicides *'99*
Living Out Loud *'98*
Hercules *'97 (V)*
John Grisham's The Rainmaker *'97*
L.A. Confidential *'97*
Mars Attacks! *'96*
Matilda *'96*
Space Jam *'96 (V)*
Get Shorty *'95*
Junior *'94*
Renaissance Man *'94*
Jack the Bear *'93*
Look Who's Talking Now *'93 (V)*
Batman Returns *'92*
Hoffa *'92*
Other People's Money *'91*
The War of the Roses *'89*
Twins *'88*
Throw Momma from the Train *'87*
Tin Men *'87*
Head Office *'86*
Ruthless People *'86*
Wise Guys *'86*
Amazing Stories *'85*
The Jewel of the Nile *'85*
Johnny Dangerously *'84*
Ratings Game *'84*
Romancing the Stone *'84*
Terms of Endearment *'83*
Going Ape! *'81*
Goin' South *'78*
The Van *'77*
The Money *'75*
One Flew Over the Cuckoo's Nest *'75*
Hurry Up or I'll Be Thirty *'73*

Matthew Devitt
Waking Ned Devine *'98*
Funnyman *'94*

Alan Devlin
The Playboys *'92*
The Lonely Passion of Judith Hearne *'87*
Danny Boy *'82*

Don Devlin (1930-2000)
Operation Dames *'59*
Blood of Dracula *'57*

J.G. Devlin
The Miracle *'91*
The Raggedy Rawney *'90*

Gordon Devol
Killings at Outpost Zeta *'80*
Harold and Maude *'71*

Laura Devon
Red Line 7000 *'65*
Goodbye Charlie *'64*

Richard Devon (1931-)
The Battle of Blood Island *'60*
Machine Gun Kelly *'58*
Blood of Dracula *'57*
Teenage Doll *'57*
The Undead *'57*
The Prodigal *'55*

Felicity Devonshire
Lisztomania *'75*
Whose Child Am I? *'75*

Jon (John) DeVries
Sarah, Plain and Tall: Skylark *'93*
Grand Isle *'92*
Sarah, Plain and Tall *'91*
Rachel River *'87*
Truth or Die *'86*
Act of Passion: The Lost Honor of Kathryn Beck *'83*
Lianna *'83*
The 4th Man *'79*

Elaine Devry (1935-)
The Cheyenne Social Club *'70*
A Guide for the Married Man *'67*
Diary of a Madman *'63*

Eddie Dew (1909-72)
Pagan Island *'60*
Raiders of Sunset Pass *'43*
Six Gun Gospel *'43*
The Fighting 69th *'40*

Patrick Dewaere (1947-82)
Heat of Desire *'84*
Beau Pere *'81*
Get Out Your Handkerchiefs *'78*
Hothead *'78*
The Best Way *'76*
Catherine & Co. *'76*
The French Detective *'75*
Going Places *'74*

Colleen Dewhurst (1924-93)
Bed & Breakfast *'92*
Dying Young *'91*
Danielle Steel's Kaleidoscope *'90*
Lantern Hill *'90*
Termini Station *'89*
Obsessed *'88*
Anne of Avonlea *'87*
Between Two Women *'86*
The Boy Who Could Fly *'86*
Sword of Gideon *'86*
A.D. *'85*
Anne of Green Gables *'85*
The Glitter Dome *'84*
You Can't Take It with You *'84*
Dead Zone *'83*
The Blue and the Gray *'82*
Final Assignment *'80*
The Guyana Tragedy: The Story of Jim Jones *'80*
And Baby Makes Six *'79*
Ice Castles *'79*
Mary and Joseph: A Story of Faith *'79*
Silent Victory: The Kitty O'Neil Story *'79*
Third Walker *'79*
When a Stranger Calls *'79*
Annie Hall *'77*
McQ *'74*
The Story of Jacob & Joseph *'74*
The Cowboys *'72*
A Fine Madness *'66*
The Nun's Story *'59*

William Dewhurst
Non-Stop New York *'37*
Sabotage *'36*

Billy DeWolfe (1907-74)
Billie *'65*
Lullaby of Broadway *'51*
Tea for Two *'50*
Dear Wife *'49*
The Perils of Pauline *'47*
Blue Skies *'46*

Anthony Dexter (1913-2001)
Married Too Young *'62*
Fire Maidens from Outer Space *'56*

Brad Dexter (1917-)
Secret Ingredient *'92*
Winter Kills *'79*
None But the Brave *'65*
Von Ryan's Express *'65*
The Magnificent Seven *'60*
Last Train from Gun Hill *'59*
Run Silent, Run Deep *'58*
Between Heaven and Hell *'56*
The Oklahoman *'56*
The Las Vegas Story *'52*

Susan Dey (1952-)
Blue River *'95*
That's Adequate *'90*
The Trouble with Dick *'88*
Echo Park *'86*
L.A. Law *'86*
Love Leads the Way *'84*
Sunset Limousine *'83*
Looker *'81*
Comeback Kid *'80*
Little Women *'78*
First Love *'77*

Cliff DeYoung (1945-)
Deliberate Intent *'01*
Gale Force *'01*
The Runaway *'00*
George Wallace *'97*
The Last Don *'97*
Suicide Kings *'97*
The Craft *'96*
The Substitute *'96*
Andersonville *'95*
JAG *'95*
Carnosaur 2 *'94*
Star Quest *'94*
Revenge of the Red Baron *'93*
Stephen King's The Tommyknockers *'93*
Dr. Giggles *'92*
Nails *'92*
Immortal Sins *'91*
To Die Standing *'91*
Fourth Story *'90*
Robert Kennedy and His Times *'90*
Flashback *'89*
Forbidden Sun *'89*
Glory *'89*
Rude Awakening *'89*
Bulldance *'88*
Fear *'88*
In Dangerous Company *'88*
Pulse *'88*
Code Name: Dancer *'87*
The Survivalist *'87*
F/X *'86*
Flight of the Navigator *'86*
Secret Admirer *'85*
Protocol *'84*
Reckless *'84*
The Hunger *'83*
Independence Day *'83*
Awakening of Candra *'81*
Shock Treatment *'81*
Blue Collar *'78*
Centennial *'78*
King *'78*
The Lindbergh Kidnapping Case *'76*

Ayesha Dharker
The Terrorist '98
City of Joy '92
Bernard Dheran
Ridicule '96
Bernadette '90
Robert Dhery
Belle Americaine '61
Femmes de Paris '53
Dalia di Lazzaro
Creepers '85
Andy Warhol's Frankenstein '74
Andrea Di Stefano
Before Night Falls '00
The Phantom of the Opera '98
Rick Dial
The General's Daughter '99
The Apostle '97
Sling Blade '96
Don Diamond
The Old Man and the Sea '58
Borderline '50
Harold Diamond
Picasso Trigger '89
Trained to Kill '88
Hard Ticket to Hawaii '87
Neil Diamond
Saving Silverman '01
The Jazz Singer '80
Reed Edward Diamond (1964-)
High Noon '00
Homicide: The Movie '00
Secrets '94
Blind Spot '93
O Pioneers! '91
Ironclads '90
Memphis Belle '90
Selma Diamond (1920-85)
All of Me '84
Twilight Zone: The Movie '83
Bang the Drum Slowly '73
John DiAquino
Pumpkinhead '88
Slipping into Darkness '88
Cameron Diaz (1972-)
Slackers '02
The Sweetest Thing '02
Shrek '01 (V)
Vanilla Sky '01
Charlie's Angels '00
Invisible Circus '00
Things You Can Tell Just by Looking at Her '00
Any Given Sunday '99
Being John Malkovich '99
Fear and Loathing in Las Vegas '98
There's Something about Mary '98
Very Bad Things '98
A Life Less Ordinary '97
My Best Friend's Wedding '97
Feeling Minnesota '96
Head Above Water '96
Keys to Tulsa '96
The Last Supper '96
She's the One '96
The Mask '94
Guillermo Diaz
Fidel '02
Just One Time '00
200 Cigarettes '98
Half-Baked '97
I Think I Do '97
I'm Not Rappaport '96
Nowhere '96
Girls Town '95
Stonewall '95
Party Girl '94
Maria Diaz
Extramarital '98
The Heroes of Desert Storm '91
Vic Diaz (-1995)
Caged Heat 2: Stripped of Freedom '94
The Children of An Lac '80
Too Hot to Handle '76
Deathhead Virgin '74
The Deadly and the Beautiful '73
Savage! '73
The Big Bird Cage '72
Night of the Cobra Woman '72
Beast of the Yellow Night '70
Flight to Fury '66
Blood Thirst '65
Tony DiBenedetto
Gloria '98
Dangerous Passion '95
Someone to Watch Over Me '87
The Pope of Greenwich Village '84
Exterminator '80
Luigi Diberti (1939-)
For Roseanna '96
The Stendahl Syndrome '95
All Screwed Up '74
Leonardo DiCaprio (1974-)
The Beach '00
Celebrity '98
The Man in the Iron Mask '98
Titanic '97
Marvin's Room '96
William Shakespeare's Romeo and Juliet '96
Total Eclipse '95
The Basketball Diaries '94
The Quick and the Dead '94
This Boy's Life '93
What's Eating Gilbert Grape '93
Critters 3 '91
George DiCenzo
Down, Out and Dangerous '95
Exorcist 3: Legion '90
Sing '89
18 Again! '88
The New Adventures of Pippi Longstocking '88
Omega Syndrome '87
Walk Like a Man '87
About Last Night... '86
Back to the Future '85
The Night the City Screamed '80
The Frisco Kid '79
The Ninth Configuration '79
Helter Skelter '76
Bobby DiCicco (1955-)
All Dogs Go to Heaven 2 '95 (V)
Killing Obsession '94
Ghoulies 4 '93
Maniac Cop 3: Badge of Silence '93
The Baby Doll Murders '92
Frame Up '91
The Last Hour '91
A Man Called Sarge '90
Double Revenge '89
She's Back '88
Number One with a Bullet '87
Tiger Warsaw '87
The Supernaturals '86
The Philadelphia Experiment '84
Splash '84
Wavelength '83
Night Shift '82
National Lampoon Goes to the Movies '81
The Big Red One '80
1941 '79
I Wanna Hold Your Hand '78
Andy Dick (1965-)
Scotland, PA '02
Dr. Dolittle 2 '01 (V)
Loser '00
Road Trip '00
Inspector Gadget '99
Picking Up the Pieces '99
Best Men '98
Bongwater '98
The Lion King: Simba's Pride '98 (V)
The Cable Guy '96
...And God Spoke '94
In the Army Now '94
Douglas Dick (1920-)
Flaming Star '60
The Oklahoman '56
The Red Badge of Courage '51
Home of the Brave '49
The Accused '48
Casbah '48
Kim Dickens
The Gift '00
The Hollow Man '00
Committed '99
White River '99
Mercury Rising '98
Great Expectations '97
Truth or Consequences, N.M. '97
Zero Effect '97
Palookaville '95
Bonnie Dickenson
Bellyfruit '99
Little Shots of Happiness '97
Beach Dickerson (1924-)
The Dunwich Horror '70
The Trip '67
Creature from the Haunted Sea '60
T-Bird Gang '59
Teenage Caveman '58
Rock All Night '57
George Dickerson
After Dark, My Sweet '90
Death Warrant '90
Blue Velvet '86
Cutter's Way '81
Lucinda Dickey
Cheerleader Camp '88
Breakin' '84
Breakin' 2: Electric Boogaloo '84
Ninja 3: The Domination '84
Angie Dickinson (1931-)
Ocean's Eleven '01
Duets '00
Pay It Forward '00
National Lampoon's The Don's Analyst '97
The Maddening '95
Sabrina '95
Even Cowgirls Get the Blues '94
Wild Palms '93
Treacherous Crossing '92
Texas Guns '90
Fire and Rain '89
Big Bad Mama 2 '87
Jealousy '84
One Shoe Makes It Murder '82
Charlie Chan and the Curse of the Dragon Queen '81
Death Hunt '81
Dressed to Kill '80
Klondike Fever '79
Pearl '78
Big Bad Mama '74
Pray for the Wildcats '74
The Outside Man '73
Resurrection of Zachary Wheeler '71
Thief '71
Point Blank '67
Cast a Giant Shadow '66
The Chase '66
The Poppy Is Also a Flower '66
The Killers '64
Captain Newman, M.D. '63
Rome Adventure '62
The Bramble Bush '60
Ocean's 11 '60
Rio Bravo '59
China Gate '57
Hidden Guns '56
Lucky Me '54
Neil Dickson
It Couldn't Happen Here '88
The Murders in the Rue Morgue '86
Biggles '85
Bo Diddley (1928-)
Rockula '90
Eddie and the Cruisers 2: Eddie Lives! '89
Chuck Berry: Hail! Hail! Rock 'n' Roll '87
Hell's Angels Forever '83
Evelyne Didi
Celestial Clockwork '94
La Vie de Boheme '93
Gabino Diego
Love Can Seriously Damage Your Health '96
Belle Epoque '92
Ay, Carmela! '90
Juan Diego
Jamon, Jamon '93
Cabeza de Vaca '90
John Diehl (1958-)
Jurassic Park 3 '01
Pearl Harbor '01
Lost Souls '00
Anywhere But Here '99
The Hi-Lo Country '98
Monument Ave. '98
Casualties '97
The End of Violence '97
Managua '97
The Destiny of Marty Fine '96
Foxfire '96
The Lazarus Man '96
A Time to Kill '96
Buffalo Girls '95
Color of a Brisk and Leaping Day '95
The Grave '95
Three Wishes '95
Wes Craven Presents Mind Ripper '95
Almost Dead '94
Stargate '94
Falling Down '93
Gettysburg '93
Remote '93
Mikey '92
Mo' Money '92
A Climate for Killing '91
Motorama '91
Dark Side of the Moon '90
Kickboxer 2: The Road Back '90
Madhouse '90
Cool Blue '88
Glitz '88
Angel '84
Miami Vice '84
National Lampoon's Vacation '83
John Dierkes (1905-75)
Omega Man '71
The Haunted Palace '63
Premature Burial '62
The Alamo '60
The Daughter of Dr. Jekyll '57
Abbott and Costello Meet Dr. Jekyll and Mr. Hyde '52
The Red Badge of Courage '51
The Thing '51
Charles Dierkop (1936-)
Invisible Dad '97
Roots of Evil '91
Banzai Runner '86
The Fix '84
Angels Hard As They Come '71
Vin Diesel (1967-)
XXX '02
The Fast and the Furious '01
Boiler Room '00
Pitch Black '00
Iron Giant '99 (V)
Saving Private Ryan '98
Gustav Diesl (1899-1948)
Crimes of Dr. Mabuse '32
Westfront 1918 '30
Pandora's Box '28
William Dieterle (1893-1972)
Waxworks '24
Backstairs '21
Daniel Dietrich
Crossfire '89
Dawn of the Dead '78
Marlene Dietrich (1901-92)
Just a Gigolo '79
The Love Goddesses '65
Paris When It Sizzles '64
Judgment at Nuremberg '61
Touch of Evil '58
Witness for the Prosecution '57
Around the World in 80 Days '56
Rancho Notorious '52
No Highway in the Sky '51
Stage Fright '50
Jigsaw '49
A Foreign Affair '48
Golden Earrings '47
The Lady Is Willing '42
Pittsburgh '42
The Spoilers '42
The Flame of New Orleans '41
Seven Sinners '40
Destry Rides Again '39
Angel '37
Knight Without Armour '37
Desire '36
The Garden of Allah '36
The Devil Is a Woman '35
Scarlet Empress '34
The Song of Songs '33
Blonde Venus '32
Shanghai Express '32
Dishonored '31
The Blue Angel '30
Morocco '30
Frank Dietz
The Jitters '88
Zombie Nightmare '86
Rock 'n' Roll Nightmare '85
Anton Diffring (1918-89)
The Winds of War '83
Valentino '77
The Beast Must Die '75
Call Him Mr. Shatter '74
Dead Pigeon on Beethoven Street '72
Mark of the Devil 2 '72
Seven Deaths in the Cat's Eye '72
Little Mother '71
Zeppelin '71
Where Eagles Dare '68
The Blue Max '66
Fahrenheit 451 '66
The Heroes of Telemark '65
Circus of Horrors '60
The Colditz Story '55
Uschi Digart (1948-)
Kentucky Fried Movie '77
Black Gestapo '75
Supervixens '75
Ilsa, She-Wolf of the SS '74
Superchick '71
All the Lovin' Kinfolk '70
Dudley Digges (1879-1947)
Son of Fury '42
The General Died at Dawn '36
China Seas '35
Mutiny on the Bounty '35
Emperor Jones '33
The Invisible Man '33
Devotion '31
The Maltese Falcon '31
Taye Diggs (1972-)
New Best Friend '02
Way of the Gun '00
The Best Man '99
Go '99
House on Haunted Hill '99
The Wood '99
How Stella Got Her Groove Back '98
Arthur Dignam (1939-)
Gods and Monsters '98
The Nostradamus Kid '92
The Everlasting Secret Family '88
The Right Hand Man '87
The Wild Duck '84
Grendel, Grendel, Grendel '82 (V)
We of the Never Never '82
Strange Behavior '81
The Devil's Playground '76
Between Wars '74
Mark Dignam (1909-89)
Disraeli '79
The Charge of the Light Brigade '68
Sink the Bismarck '60
Irasema Dilian (1925-96)
Wuthering Heights '53
Teresa Venerdi '41
Stephen (Dillon) Dillane
Spy Game '01
Anna Karenina '00
Love and Rage '99
Deja Vu '98
Firelight '97
Kings in Grass Castles '97
Welcome to Sarajevo '97
Two If by Sea '95
The Rector's Wife '94
An Affair in Mind '89
Christabel '89
Victoria Dillard
Ali '01
The Best Man '99
Out of Sync '95
Deep Cover '92
Ricochet '91
Phyllis Diller (1917-)
A Bug's Life '98 (V)
Heartstrings '95
Happily Ever After '93 (V)
Silence of the Hams '93
The Nutcracker Prince '91 (V)
The Bone Yard '90
Pink Motel '82
A Pleasure Doing Business '79
Mad Monster Party '68 (V)
Private Navy of Sgt. O'Farrell '68
Eight on the Lam '67
Boy, Did I Get a Wrong Number! '66
Splendor in the Grass '61
Bradford Dillman (1930-)
Heroes Stand Alone '89
Lords of the Deep '89
Man Outside '88
The Treasure of the Amazon '84
Sudden Impact '83
Legend of Walks Far Woman '82
One Away '80
Love and Bullets '79
Running Scared '79
The Amsterdam Kill '78
Piranha '78
The Swarm '78
The Enforcer '76
The Widow '76
Bug '75
Force Five '75
Death in Deep Water '74
Murder or Mercy '74
99 & 44/100 Dead '74
Master Mind '73
The Way We Were '73
Moon of the Wolf '72
Escape from the Planet of the Apes '71
The Mephisto Waltz '71
Resurrection of Zachary Wheeler '71
Brother John '70
Suppose They Gave a War and Nobody Came? '70
Black Water Gold '69
The Bridge at Remagen '69

Sergeant Ryker '68
Compulsion '59
Brendan Dillon, Jr.
Lords of Magick '88
Bug '75
Premature Burial '62
Kevin Dillon (1965-)
Hidden Agenda '99
Misbegotten '98
Stag '97
Criminal Hearts '95
True Crime '95
No Escape '94
The Pathfinder '94
A Midnight Clear '92
The Doors '91
Immediate Family '89
War Party '89
When He's Not a Stranger '89
The Blob '88
Remote Control '88
The Rescue '88
Platoon '86
Heaven Help Us '85
No Big Deal '83
Matt Dillon (1964-)
Deuces Wild '02
One Night at McCool's '01
There's Something about Mary '98
Wild Things '98
In and Out '97
Albino Alligator '96
Beautiful Girls '96
Grace of My Heart '96
Frankie Starlight '95
To Die For '95
Golden Gate '93
Mr. Wonderful '93
The Saint of Fort Washington '93
Singles '92
A Kiss Before Dying '91
Women & Men: In Love There Are No Rules '91
Bloodhounds of Broadway '89
Drugstore Cowboy '89
Kansas '88
Big Town '87
Native Son '86
Rebel '85
Target '85
The Flamingo Kid '84
The Outsiders '83
Rumble Fish '83
Liar's Moon '82
Tex '82
Little Darlings '80
My Bodyguard '80
Over the Edge '79
Melinda Dillon (1939-)
Magnolia '99
Entertaining Angels: The Dorothy Day Story '96
How to Make an American Quilt '95
To Wong Foo, Thanks for Everything, Julie Newmar '95
Sioux City '94
The Prince of Tides '91
Shattered Spirits '91
Captain America '89
Nightbreaker '89
Spontaneous Combustion '89
Staying Together '89
Harry and the Hendersons '87
The Juggler of Notre Dame '84
Right of Way '84
Songwriter '84
A Christmas Story '83
Absence of Malice '81
Fallen Angel '81
Marriage Is Alive and Well '80
The Shadow Box '80
F.I.S.T. '78
Close Encounters of the Third Kind '77
Slap Shot '77
Bound for Glory '76
April Fools '69
Paul Dillon
Chicago Cab '98
Austin Powers: International Man of Mystery '97
Blink '93
The Beat '88
Kiss Daddy Goodnight '87
Tom Dillon
Night Tide '63
Dressed to Kill '46
Victor Dimattia
Danielle Steel's Heartbeat '93
Dennis the Menace: Dinosaur Hunter '93
Alan Dinehart (1889-1944)
The Heat's On '43
It's a Great Life '43
Sweet Rosie O'Grady '43
Everything Happens at Night '39
Second Fiddle '39
Baby, Take a Bow '34
After Midnight '33
A Study in Scarlet '33
Supernatural '33
Yi Ding
Pavilion of Women '01
The Amazing Panda Adventure '95
Charles Dingle (1887-1956)
The Court Martial of Billy Mitchell '55
If You Knew Susie '48
A Southern Yankee '48
The Beast with Five Fingers '46
Guest Wife '45
Here Come the Co-Eds '45
Johnny Eager '42
Somewhere I'll Find You '42
The Little Foxes '41
Ernie Dingo (1956-)
The Echo of Thunder '98
Kings in Grass Castles '97
Dead Heart '96
Clowning Around 2 '93
Clowning Around '92
Until the End of the World '91
Crocodile Dundee 2 '88
A Waltz Through the Hills '88
The Fringe Dwellers '86
Kelly Dingwall
The Custodian '94
Around the World in 80 Ways '86
Peter Dinklage
Human Nature '02
Living in Oblivion '94
Reece Dinsdale (1959-)
Hamlet '96
Young Catherine '91
Threads '85
Winter Flight '84
Bruce Dinsmore
Deadline '00
Psychopath '97
Stranger in the House '97
Madame Rose (Dion) Dione (1875-1936)
Freaks '32
Salome '22
Suds '20
Stefano Dionisi (1966-)
Sleepless '01
Kiss of Fire '98
The Loss of Sexual Innocence '98
The Truce '96
Joseph '95
Farinelli '94
Mille Bolle Blu '93
Silvia Dionisio
The Scalawag Bunch '75
Andy Warhol's Dracula '74
Dante DiPaolo
Blood and Black Lace '64
Venus Against the Son of Hercules '62
John DiResta
15 Minutes '01
Miss Congeniality '00
John Disanti
Man of the House '95
Eyes of a Stranger '81
Bob (Robert) Dishy
Kill My Wife...Please!
Judy Berlin '99
Jungle 2 Jungle '96
Don Juan DeMarco '94
My Boyfriend's Back '93
Used People '92
Brighton Beach Memoirs '86
The Big Bus '76
I Wonder Who's Killing Her Now? '76
Lovers and Other Strangers '70
Walt Disney (1901-66)
Fun & Fancy Free '47 (V)
Fantasia '40 (V)
Hollywood Party '34 (V)
Harry Ditson
Tragedy of Flight 103: The Inside Story '91
The Sender '82
Barbara Dittus
Anton, the Magician '78
The Third '72
Divine (1945-88)
Divine '90
Hairspray '88
Out of the Dark '88
Trouble in Mind '86
I Wanna Be a Beauty Queen '85
Lust in the Dust '85
Polyester '81
Female Trouble '74
Pink Flamingos '72
Multiple Maniacs '70
Mondo Trasho '69
Andrew Divoff
Faust: Love of the Damned '00
Captured '99
Stealth Fighter '99
Wishmaster 2: Evil Never Dies '98
Nemesis 4: Cry of Angels '97
Wishmaster '97
Blast '96
Deadly Voyage '96
Backlash: Oblivion 2 '95
Magic Island '95
The Stranger '95
Xtro 3: Watch the Skies '95
A Low Down Dirty Shame '94
Oblivion '94
Running Cool '93
Back in the USSR '92
Interceptor '92
Toy Soldiers '91
Richard Dix (1894-1949)
Buckskin Frontier '43
The Kansan '43
American Empire '42
Special Investigator '36
Yellow Dust '36
Transatlantic Tunnel '35
Ace of Aces '33
Lost Squadron '32
Cimarron '31
Seven Keys to Baldpate '29
Lucky Devil '25
The Vanishing American '25
The Ten Commandments '23
Robert Dix (1934-)
Killers '88
Wild Wheels '75
Cain's Cutthroats '71
Horror of the Blood Monsters '70
Blood of Dracula's Castle '69
Satan's Sadists '69
Deadwood '65
Forbidden Planet '56
Donna Dixon (1957-)
Wayne's World '92
Lucky Stiff '88
Speed Zone '88
The Couch Trip '87
Beverly Hills Madam '86
Spies Like Us '85
Doctor Detroit '83
Margin for Murder '81
Ivan Dixon (1931-)
Car Wash '76
Fer-De-Lance '74
Suppose They Gave a War and Nobody Came? '70
A Patch of Blue '65
Nothing but a Man '64
A Raisin in the Sun '61
James Dixon
The Ambulance '90
Maniac Cop 2 '90
Wicked Stepmother '89
It's Alive 3: Island of the Alive '87
Return to Salem's Lot '87
The Stuff '85
Q (The Winged Serpent) '82
It's Alive 2: It Lives Again '78
It's Alive '74
Black Caesar '73
Jean Dixon
Joy of Living '38
You Only Live Once '37
Joan Dixon
Gunplay '51
Hot Lead '51
MacIntyre Dixon (1931-)
Gettysburg '93
Funny Farm '88
Ghostwriter '84
Pamela Dixon
C.I.A. 2: Target Alexa '94
C.I.A.: Code Name Alexa '92
Magic Kid '92
Chance '89
L.A. Crackdown 2 '88
Hollywood in Trouble '87
L.A. Crackdown '87
Mayhem '87
Steve Dixon
Mosquito '95
The Carrier '87
Badja (Medu) Djola
Deterrence '00
Gunshy '98
Rosewood '96
Heaven's Prisoners '95
Who's the Man? '93
A Rage in Harlem '91
An Innocent Man '89
Mississippi Burning '88
The Serpent and the Rainbow '87
Penitentiary '79
Shae D'Lyn
Vegas Vacation '96
Secrets '94
DMX
Exit Wounds '01
Romeo Must Die '00
Belly '98
Peter J. D'Noto (1947-)
Chain Reaction '96
Keeper of the City '92
Killing Floor '85
Monsters Crash the Pajama Party '65
Mauricio Do Valle
Amazon Jail '85
Antonio Das Mortes '68
Valeria (Valerie Dobson) D'Obici (1952-)
The Best Man '97
Escape from the Bronx '85
Passion of Love '82
Alan Dobie (1932-)
White Mischief '88
War and Peace '73
The Charge of the Light Brigade '68
Lawrence (Larry) Dobkin (1919-)
Patton '70
Geronimo '62
Above and Beyond '53
Twelve o'Clock High '49
Gosia Dobrowolska (1958-)
Lust and Revenge '95
The Custodian '94
Careful '92
A Woman's Tale '92
Around the World in 80 Ways '86
Silver City '84
James Dobson
Impulse '74
Flying Leathernecks '51
Kevin Dobson (1943-)
Mom, Can I Keep Her? '98
Dirty Work '92
Code of Honor '84
All Night Long '81
Margin for Murder '81
Hardhat & Legs '80
Orphan Train '79
Midway '76
Peter Dobson (1964-)
Double Down '01
Drowning Mona '00
Wicked Ways '99
Nowhere Land '98
Quiet Days in Hollywood '97
The Big Squeeze '96
Dead Cold '96
The Frighteners '96
Riot in the Streets '96
Norma Jean and Marilyn '95
Where the Day Takes You '92
The Marrying Man '91
Sing '89
Tamara Dobson (1947-)
The Amazons '84
Chained Heat '83
Norman, Is That You? '76
Cleopatra Jones & the Casino of Gold '75
Cleopatra Jones '73
Vernon Dobtcheff (1934-)
The Body '01
Deja Vu '98
Hilary and Jackie '98
M. Butterfly '93
Pascali's Island '88
Nijinsky '80
The Messiah '75
Murder on the Orient Express '74
Darling Lili '70
The Assassination Bureau '69
Claire Dodd
The Black Cat '41
Ex-Lady '33
Jimmie Dodd
Too Late for Tears '49
Snuffy Smith, Yard Bird '42
K.K. Dodds
Soldier '98
A Life Less Ordinary '97
Megan Dodds
Bait '00
Urbania '00
Ever After: A Cinderella Story '98
The Rat Pack '98
Jack Dodson (1931-94)
A Climate for Killing '91
Return to Mayberry '85
The Getaway '72
John Doe (1954-)
Brokedown Palace '99
Forces of Nature '99
Knocking on Death's Door '99
The Rage: Carrie 2 '99
Sugar Town '99
Highway Hitcher '98
Black Circle Boys '97
Boogie Nights '97
Scorpion Spring '96
Touch '96
Georgia '95
Shake, Rattle & Rock! '94
Wyatt Earp '94
Liquid Dreams '92
Pure Country '92
Roadside Prophets '92
A Matter of Degrees '90
Great Balls of Fire '89
Slamdance '87
Tatiana Dogileva
East-West '99
A Forgotten Tune for the Flute '88
Matt Doherty (1977-)
D3: The Mighty Ducks '96
So I Married an Axe Murderer '93
The Mighty Ducks '92
Shannen Doherty (1971-)
Jay and Silent Bob Strike Back '01
The Ticket '97
Nowhere '96
Mallrats '95
Almost Dead '94
Blindfold: Acts of Obsession '94
Jailbreakers '94
Freeze Frame '92
Heathers '89
Girls Just Want to Have Fun '85
Night Shift '82
Lexa Doig
Jason X '01
No Alibi '00
Michael Dolan (1965-)
The Hunley '99
The Turning '92
Biloxi Blues '88
Hamburger Hill '87
Light of Day '87
Thomas Dolby
Rockula '90
Howard the Duck '86
Guy Doleman (1924-96)
Funeral in Berlin '66
The Ipcress File '65
Thunderball '65
Ami Dolenz (1969-)
Virtual Seduction '96
Life 101 '95
Mortal Danger '94
Pumpkinhead 2: Blood Wings '94
Rescue Me '93
Ticks '93
Witchboard 2: The Devil's Doorway '93
Children of the Night '92
Faith '92
Miracle Beach '92
Stepmonster '92
Can't Buy Me Love '87
Mickey Dolenz (1945-)
The Love Bug '97
The Brady Bunch Movie '95
Night of the Strangler '73
Head '68
Dora Doll (1922-)
Black and White in Color '76
Boomerang '76
The Young Lions '58
Patrick Dollaghan
The Bad Pack '98
Circle of Fear '89
Kill Slade '89
Murphy's Fault '88
Larry Domasin
Island of the Blue Dolphins '64
Fun in Acapulco '63
Arielle Dombasle (1955-)
Vatel '00
Trade Secrets '90s
L'Ennui '98
Three Lives and Only One Death '96
Little Indian, Big City '95

Raging Angels '95
Celestial Clockwork '94
Twisted Obsession '90
Around the World in 80 Days '89
The Boss' Wife '86
Pauline at the Beach '83
Le Beau Mariage '82
Perceval '78

Faith Domergue (1925-99)
Blood Legacy '73
The House of Seven Corpses '73
The Sibling '72
Voyage to the Prehistoric Planet '65
The Atomic Man '56
Cult of the Cobra '55
It Came from Beneath the Sea '55
This Island Earth '55
Duel at Silver Creek '52

Dagmara Dominczyk
The Count of Monte Cristo '02
Rock Star '01

Wade Dominguez (1966-98)
Shadow of Doubt '98
The Taxman '98
City of Industry '96

Arturo Dominici
The Trojan Horse '62
Black Sunday '60
Hercules '58

Fats Domino
The Girl Can't Help It '56
Rock, Rock, Rock '56

Solveig Dommartin (1961-)
Faraway, So Close! '93
Until the End of the World '91
No Fear, No Die '90
Wings of Desire '88

Angelica Domrose (1941-)
The Scorpion Woman '89
Girls Riot '88
The Legend of Paul and Paula '73
Under the Pear Tree '73

Linda Dona
Delta Heat '92
Final Embrace '92
Futurekick '91

Elinor Donahue (1937-)
The Invaders '95
Freddy's Dead: The Final Nightmare '91
Pretty Woman '90
High School USA '84
Going Berserk '83
Girls' Town '59
Love Is Better Than Ever '52
Three Daring Daughters '48

Heather Donahue
Boys and Girls '00
The Blair Witch Project '99

Troy Donahue (1936-2001)
South Seas Massacre
Showdown '93
Deadly Diamonds '91
The Pamela Principle '91
Sounds of Silence '91
Cry-Baby '90
Nudity Required '90
Omega Cop '90
Shock 'Em Dead '90
Assault of the Party Nerds '89
The Chilling '89
Deadly Spygames '89
Dr. Alien '88
Hawkeye '88
Sexpot '88
Terminal Force '88
A Woman Obsessed '88
Cyclone '87
Deadly Prey '87
Hollywood Cop '87
Grandview U.S.A. '84
Tin Man '83
The Godfather 1902-1959: The Complete Epic '81
The Legend of Frank Woods '77
Cockfighter '74
The Godfather, Part 2 '74
Seizure '74
Love Thrill Murders '71
Those Fantastic Flying Fools '67
Palm Springs Weekend '63
Rome Adventure '62
Parrish '61
Imitation of Life '59
Monster on the Campus '59
A Summer Place '59
Tarnished Angels '57

James Donald (1917-93)
The Big Sleep '78
Cast a Giant Shadow '66
King Rat '65
The Great Escape '63
Victoria Regina '61
Third Man on the Mountain '59
The Vikings '58
The Bridge on the River Kwai '57
Lust for Life '56
Beau Brummel '54
The Pickwick Papers '54
The Gay Lady '49
Immortal Battalion '44
In Which We Serve '43

Arthur Donaldson
The Broadway Drifter '27
America '24

Lesleh Donaldson
Funeral Home '82
Happy Birthday to Me '81

Norma Donaldson (1928-94)
Poetic Justice '93
The Five Heartbeats '91
Staying Alive '83
9 to 5 '80

Peter Donaldson
Invasion! '99
Escape Clause '96
Long Day's Journey Into Night '96
The Sweet Hereafter '96

Ted Donaldson (1933-)
Rusty's Birthday '49
The Red Stallion '47
Son of Rusty '47
The Adventures of Rusty '45
A Tree Grows in Brooklyn '45
Mr. Winkle Goes to War '44

Peter Donat (1928-)
The Deep End '01
The Game '97
Red Corner '97
The Babe '92
School Ties '92
The War of the Roses '89
Tucker: The Man and His Dream '88
Honeymoon '87
The Bay Boy '85
Massive Retaliation '85
Mazes and Monsters '82
The China Syndrome '79
Different Story '78
F.I.S.T. '78
Mirrors '78
Return Engagement '78
The Godfather, Part 2 '74

Robert Donat (1905-58)
The Inn of the Sixth Happiness '58
The Winslow Boy '48
Captain Boycott '47
The Adventures of Tartu '43
Goodbye, Mr. Chips '39
The Citadel '38
Knight Without Armour '37
The Ghost Goes West '36
The 39 Steps '35
The Count of Monte Cristo '34
If I Were Rich '33
The Private Life of Henry VIII '33

Ludwig Donath (1900-67)
The Lovable Cheat '49
The Jolson Story '46
The Secret Code '42

Len Doncheff
Nuremberg '00
Moving Target '96

Manuel Donde
Swamp of the Lost Monster '65
Savage Wilderness '55

Chad E. Donella
Final Destination '00
Disturbing Behavior '98

Yolande Donlan (1920-)
The Adventurers '70
Expresso Bongo '59
Mister Drake's Duck '50
The Devil Bat '41

Brian Donlevy (1899-1972)
Arizona Bushwackers '67
Five Golden Dragons '67
Hostile Guns '67
Pit Stop '67
Gamera, the Invincible '66
How to Stuff a Wild Bikini '65
The Errand Boy '61
Cowboy '58
Quatermass 2 '57
The Quatermass Experiment '56
Big Combo '55
Ride the Man Down '53
Hoodlum Empire '52
Slaughter Trail '51
Impact '49
Command Decision '48
A Southern Yankee '48
Kiss of Death '47
Song of Scheherazade '47
Canyon Passage '46
Two Years before the Mast '46
The Virginian '46
Miracle of Morgan's Creek '44
A Gentleman After Dark '42
The Glass Key '42
The Great Man's Lady '42
Hangmen Also Die '42
Wake Island '42
Billy the Kid '41
Birth of the Blues '41
Brigham Young: Frontiersman '40
The Great McGinty '40
Allegheny Uprising '39
Beau Geste '39
Destry Rides Again '39
Jesse James '39
Union Pacific '39
In Old Chicago '37
Strike Me Pink '36
Barbary Coast '35

Steve Donmyer
Terminal Exposure '89
Glitch! '88

Barnard Pierre Donnadieu (1949-)
Druids '01
Beatrice '88
The Vanishing '88
The Return of Martin Guerre '83

Jeff Donnell (1921-88)
Gidget Goes to Rome '63
My Man Godfrey '57
Because You're Mine '52
Three Guys Named Mike '51
The Fuller Brush Girl '50
In a Lonely Place '50
Redwood Forest Trail '50
Walk Softly, Stranger '50
Outcasts of the Trail '49

Donal Donnelly (1931-)
Love and Rage '99
This Is My Father '99
Mesmer '94
Squanto: A Warrior's Tale '94
The Godfather, Part 3 '90
The Dead '87
Waterloo '71
The Knack '65

Ruth Donnelly (1896-1982)
A Lawless Street '55
I'd Climb the Highest Mountain '51
My Little Chickadee '40
The Affairs of Annabel '38
Holiday '38
Mr. Deeds Goes to Town '36
Hands Across the Table '35
Red Salute '35
Bureau of Missing Persons '33
Female '33
Footlight Parade '33
Ladies They Talk About '33
Blessed Event '32

Tim Donnelly
The Clonus Horror '79
The Toolbox Murders '78

Robert Donner (1931-)
Undesirable '92
Lassie: Well of Love '90
Under the Rainbow '81
The Young Pioneers '76
Man Who Loved Cat Dancing '73
Vanishing Point '71
Cool Hand Luke '67

Joseph D'Onofrio
A Bronx Tale '93
Goodfellas '90

Vincent D'Onofrio (1959-)
The Dangerous Lives of Altar Boys '02
The Salton Sea '02
Chelsea Walls '01
Imposter '01
The Cell '00
Happy Accidents '00
Steal This Movie! '00
Spanish Judges '99
That Championship Season '99
The Thirteenth Floor '99
The Velocity of Gary '98
Claire Dolan '97
Men in Black '97
The Newton Boys '97
Feeling Minnesota '96
Good Luck '96
The Whole Wide World '96
The Winner '96
Strange Days '95
Being Human '94
Ed Wood '94
Imaginary Crimes '94
Stuart Saves His Family '94
Desire '93
Household Saints '93
Mr. Wonderful '93
The Player '92
Crooked Hearts '91
Dying Young '91
Fires Within '91
JFK '91
Naked Tango '91
The Blood of Heroes '89
Signs of Life '89
Mystic Pizza '88
Adventures in Babysitting '87
Full Metal Jacket '87
First Turn On '83

Amanda Donohoe (1962-)
Circus '00
I'm Losing You '98
A Knight in Camelot '98
The Real Howard Spitz '98
One Night Stand '97
Liar Liar '96
The Madness of King George '94
The Substitute '93
A Woman's Guide to Adultery '93
Double Cross '92
Shame '92
Paper Mask '91
Dark Obsession '90
An Affair in Mind '89
The Rainbow '89
The Lair of the White Worm '88
Castaway '87
Foreign Body '86

Donovan
Secret Policeman's Private Parts '81
Aliens from Spaceship Earth '77

Elisa Donovan
Loving Jezebel '99
A Night at the Roxbury '98
Clueless '95

Jeffrey Donovan
Bait '00
Book of Shadows: Blair Witch 2 '00
Catherine's Grove '98
When Trumpets Fade '98

King Donovan (1918-87)
The Hanging Tree '59
The Perfect Furlough '59
Cowboy '58
Invasion of the Body Snatchers '56
Private Hell 36 '54
Easy to Love '53
Forever Female '53
The Merry Widow '52
Singin' in the Rain '52
The Enforcer '51

Martin Donovan (1957-)
Insomnia '02
The Great Gatsby '01
Heaven '99
In a Savage Land '99
Onegin '99
Living Out Loud '98
The Opposite of Sex '98
Rescuers: Stories of Courage—Two Couples '98
When Trumpets Fade '98
Portrait of a Lady '96
Flirt '95
Hollow Reed '95
Nadja '95
Amateur '94
Quick '93
Simple Men '92
Surviving Desire '91
Trust '91

Robert Donovan
Curse of the Puppet Master: The Human Experiment '98
Shadow Dancer '96

Tate Donovan (1963-)
Get Well Soon '01
Hercules '97 (V)
Murder at 1600 '97
The Only Thrill '97
America's Dream '95
Holy Matrimony '94
Equinox '93
Inside Monkey Zetterland '93
Ethan Frome '92
Love Potion #9 '92
Little Noises '91
Memphis Belle '90
Dead Bang '89
Clean and Sober '88
Dangerous Curves '88
SpaceCamp '86
Into Thin Air '85
Not My Kid '85

Terence Donovan (1942-)
The Winds of Jarrah '83
The Man from Snowy River '82
Breaker Morant '80
Money Movers '78

Alison Doody (1966-)
Major League 2 '94
Temptation '94
Ring of the Musketeers '93
Duel of Hearts '92
Indiana Jones and the Last Crusade '89
Echoes '88
Taffin '88
Prayer for the Dying '87

James Doohan (1920-)
Bug Buster '99
The Duke '99
Storybook '95
Star Trek: Generations '94
Amore! '93
National Lampoon's Loaded Weapon 1 '93
Double Trouble '91
Star Trek 6: The Undiscovered Country '91
Star Trek 5: The Final Frontier '89
Star Trek 4: The Voyage Home '86
Star Trek 3: The Search for Spock '84
Star Trek 2: The Wrath of Khan '82
Star Trek: The Motion Picture '80
Man in the Wilderness '71
36 Hours '64

Paul Dooley (1928-)
Insomnia '02
Guinevere '99
Happy, Texas '99
I'll Remember April '99
Runaway Bride '99
Angels in the Endzone '98
Clockwatchers '97
Loved '97
Telling Lies in America '96
Waiting for Guffman '96
Out There '95
The Underneath '95
Evolver '94
State of Emergency '94
Cooperstown '93
A Dangerous Woman '93
My Boyfriend's Back '93
Shakes the Clown '92
White Hot: The Mysterious Murder of Thelma Todd '91
The Court Martial of Jackie Robinson '90
Flashback '89
When He's Not a Stranger '89
Last Rites '88
Lip Service '88
The Murder of Mary Phagan '87
O.C. and Stiggs '87
Big Trouble '86
Monster in the Closet '86
Sixteen Candles '84
Going Berserk '83
Strange Brew '83
Endangered Species '82
Hansel and Gretel '82
Kiss Me Goodbye '82
Rumpelstiltskin '82
Paternity '81
Popeye '80
Breaking Away '79
Rich Kids '79
A Wedding '78
Slap Shot '77

Lucinda Dooling
Lovely ... But Deadly '82
The Alchemist '81
Miracle on Ice '81

Patric Doonan (1927-58)
John and Julie '55
Blackout '50
The Blue Lamp '49
Train of Events '49

Robert DoQui (1934-)
Glam '97
Original Intent '91
Miracle Mile '89
Short Fuse '88

RoboCop '87
Nashville '75
Coffy '73
A Dream for Christmas '73
Karin Dor (1936-)
Prisoner in the Middle '74
Die Screaming, Marianne '73
Dracula vs. Frankenstein '69
Topaz '69
The Torture Chamber of Dr. Sadism '69
You Only Live Twice '67
The Last Tomahawk '65
Carpet of Horror '64
Strangler of Blackmoor Castle '63
The Bellboy and the Playgirls '62
The Invisible Dr. Mabuse '62
Forger of London '61
Ann Doran (1911-2000)
Kitten with a Whip '64
The Brass Bottle '63
It! The Terror from Beyond Space '58
Rebel without a Cause '55
Love Is Better Than Ever '52
The Painted Hills '51
Tomahawk '51
Never a Dull Moment '50
Holiday in Havana '49
Rusty's Birthday '49
The Accused '48
Pitfall '48
Fear in the Night '47
Here Come the Waves '45
Air Force '43
The More the Merrier '43
So Proudly We Hail '43
Mr. Wise Guy '42
Criminals Within '41
Dive Bomber '41
Meet John Doe '41
Penny Serenade '41
Blondie '38
Little Red Schoolhouse '36
Jesse Doran
Street Asylum '90
Heart '87
Mary Doran (1907-95)
Sing Sing Nights '35
The Strange Love of Molly Louvain '32
Criminal Code '31
The Divorcee '30
Broadway Melody '29
Richard Doran
Hollywood Boulevard '76
Harrad Summer '74
Edna Dore
Nil by Mouth '96
High Hopes '88
Johnny Dorelli (1937-)
The Odd Squad '86
Bread and Chocolate '73
How to Kill 400 Duponts '65
Stephen Dorff (1973-)
Deuces Wild '02
Cecil B. Demented '00
Earthly Possessions '99
Entropy '99
Blade '98
Space Truckers '97
Blood & Wine '96
City of Industry '96
I Shot Andy Warhol '96
Innocent Lies '95
Reckless '95
Backbeat '94
S.F.W. '94
Judgment Night '93
Rescue Me '93
The Power of One '92
The Gate '87
David Dorfman
Bounce '00
Panic '00
Diogo Doria
Voyage to the Beginning of the World '96
Abraham's Valley '93
Pierre Doris
Overseas: Three Women with Man Trouble '90
The Story of a Three Day Pass '68
Francoise Dorleac (1942-67)
The Young Girls of Rochefort '68
Cul de Sac '66
The Soft Skin '64
That Man from Rio '64
Dolores Dorn (1935-)
Truck Stop Women '74
Underworld, U.S.A. '60
Lucky Me '54
Michael Dorn (1952-)
Ali '01
Mach 2 '00
The Prophet's Game '99
Star Trek: Insurrection '98
Menno's Mind '96
Star Trek: First Contact '96
Amanda and the Alien '95
Timemaster '95
Star Trek: Generations '94
Star Trek 6: The Undiscovered Country '91
The Jagged Edge '85
Philip Dorn (1901-75)
The Fighting Kentuckian '49
I've Always Loved You '46
Random Harvest '42
Reunion in France '42
Tarzan's Secret Treasure '41
Underground '41
Ziegfeld Girl '41
Robert Dornan
Hell on Wheels '67
The Starfighters '63
Sandra Dorne (1925-92)
Eat the Rich '87
Devil Doll '64
The House in Marsh Road '60
Alias John Preston '56
Roadhouse Girl '53
Lester Dorr (1893-1980)
Meet the Mob '42
Panama Menace '41
Red Salute '35
Diana Dors (1931-84)
Steaming '86
Children of the Full Moon '84
Unicorn '83
Adventures of a Taxi Driver '76
Craze '74
The Devil's Web '74
From Beyond the Grave '73
A Man with a Maid '73
Theatre of Blood '73
Amazing Mr. Blunden '72
Hannie Caulder '72
Nothing But the Night '72
Deep End '70
There's a Girl in My Soup '70
Baby Love '69
Berserk! '67
The King of the Roaring '20s: The Story of Arnold Rothstein '61
Room 43 '58
The Long Haul '57
Unholy Wife '57
I Married a Woman '56
Man Bait '52
Oliver Twist '48
Fifi d'Orsay (1904-83)
The Gangster '47
Delinquent Daughters '44
Nabonga '44
Three Legionnaires '37
Going Hollywood '33
Girl from Calgary '32
Jimmy Dorsey
The Fabulous Dorseys '47
Hollywood Canteen '44
Tommy Dorsey
The Fabulous Dorseys '47
Presenting Lily Mars '43
Gabrielle Dorziat (1880-1979)
The Storm Within '48
Monsieur Vincent '47
De Mayerling a Sarajevo '40
Susana Dosamantes (1948-)
Counterforce '87
Target Eagle '84
Remolino de Pasiones '68
John Dossett
Nick and Jane '96
That Night '93
Longtime Companion '90
Karen Dotrice (1955-)
The Thirty-Nine Steps '79
The Gnome-Mobile '67
Mary Poppins '64
The Three Lives of Thomasina '63
Michele Dotrice (1947-)
Vanity Fair '99
The Blood on Satan's Claw '71
And Soon the Darkness '70
The Witches '66
Roy Dotrice (1925-)
The Scarlet Letter '95
The Cutting Edge '92
Suburban Commando '91
Carmilla '89
The Eliminators '86
Amadeus '84
Cheech and Chong's The Corsican Brothers '84
The Dancing Princesses '84
The Heroes of Telemark '65
Catherine Doucet
It Started with Eve '41
These Three '36
John Doucette (1921-94)
Fighting Mad '76
Patton '70
True Grit '69
Nevada Smith '66
Paradise, Hawaiian Style '66
The Hunters '58
Seven Cities of Gold '55
Doug E. Doug (1970-)
Eight Legged Freaks '02
That Darn Cat '96
Operation Dumbo Drop '95
Cool Runnings '93
Class Act '91
Hangin' with the Homeboys '91
Suzi Dougherty
Chameleon 3: Dark Angel '00
Love and Other Catastrophes '95
Angela Douglas (1940-)
Digby, the Biggest Dog in the World '73
Carry On Cowboy '66
Carry On Screaming '66
Brandon Douglas (1968-)
Journey to Spirit Island '92
Chips, the War Dog '90
The Children of Times Square '86
Burt Douglas
Hush Little Baby, Don't You Cry '86
High School Confidential '58
The Law and Jake Wade '58
Damon Douglas
From Noon Till Three '76
Massacre at Central High '76
Don Douglas (1905-45)
Club Havana '46
Behind the Rising Sun '43
Whistling in the Dark '41
Law of the Texan '38
Tomorrow's Children '34
The Great Gabbo '29
Donald Douglas (1905-45)
A Mind to Murder '96
Diana: Her True Story '93
Action in the North Atlantic '43
Sergeant York '41
Donna Douglas
Frankie and Johnny '65
Career '59
Eric Douglas (1958-)
Delta Force 3: The Killing Game '91
Student Confidential '87
Tomboy '85
Illeana Douglas (1965-)
The New Guy '02
Ghost World '01
The Next Best Thing '00
Happy, Texas '99
Lansky '99
Stir of Echoes '99
Message in a Bottle '98
Bella Mafia '97
Flypaper '97
Rough Riders '97
Sink or Swim '97
Weapons of Mass Distraction '97
Grace of My Heart '96
Picture Perfect '96
Wedding Bell Blues '96
To Die For '95
Grief '94
Search and Destroy '94
Alive '93
Household Saints '93
Cape Fear '91
Goodfellas '90
The Last Temptation of Christ '88
James B. Douglas
The Changeling '80
The Dawson Patrol '78
John Douglas
Violent Zone '89
Hell's Brigade: The Final Assault '80
Kirk Douglas (1916-)
Diamonds '99
Greedy '94
The Secret '93
Oscar '91
Queenie '87
Tough Guys '86
Amos '85
Eddie Macon's Run '83
Holocaust Survivors...Remembrance of Love '83
The Man from Snowy River '82
Draw! '81
The Final Countdown '80
Saturn 3 '80
Home Movies '79
The Villain '79
The Fury '78
The Chosen '77
Once Is Not Enough '75
Posse '75
Master Touch '74
Dr. Jekyll and Mr. Hyde '73
Catch Me a Spy '71
A Gunfight '71
Light at the Edge of the World '71
There Was a Crooked Man '70
The Arrangement '69
The Brotherhood '68
The War Wagon '67
The Way West '67
Cast a Giant Shadow '66
Is Paris Burning? '66
The Heroes of Telemark '65
In Harm's Way '65
Seven Days in May '64
For Love or Money '63
The List of Adrian Messenger '63
Lonely Are the Brave '62
Two Weeks in Another Town '62
Town without Pity '61
Spartacus '60
Strangers When We Meet '60
The Devil's Disciple '59
Last Train from Gun Hill '59
The Vikings '58
Gunfight at the O.K. Corral '57
Paths of Glory '57
Lust for Life '56
The Indian Fighter '55
Man Without a Star '55
The Racers '55
Ulysses '55
20,000 Leagues under the Sea '54
The Bad and the Beautiful '52
The Big Sky '52
Big Trees '52
Along the Great Divide '51
Detective Story '51
Young Man with a Horn '50
Champion '49
A Letter to Three Wives '49
My Dear Secretary '49
Out of the Past '47
The Strange Love of Martha Ivers '46
Mark Douglas
Moonshine Mountain '64
2000 Maniacs '64
Melvyn Douglas (1901-81)
Hot Touch '80s
Ghost Story '81
The Changeling '80
Tell Me a Riddle '80
Being There '79
The Seduction of Joe Tynan '79
Intimate Strangers '77
Twilight's Last Gleaming '77
The Tenant '76
Murder or Mercy '74
The Death Squad '73
The Candidate '72
Hard Frame '70
I Never Sang for My Father '70
Hotel '67
Lamp at Midnight '66
The Americanization of Emily '64
Hud '63
Billy Budd '62
My Forbidden Past '51
A Woman's Secret '49
Mr. Blandings Builds His Dream House '48
They All Kissed the Bride '42
That Uncertain Feeling '41
Two-Faced Woman '41
A Woman's Face '41
Ninotchka '39
The Shining Hour '38
That Certain Age '38
Angel '37
Captains Courageous '37
The Gorgeous Hussy '36
Theodora Goes Wild '36
Annie Oakley '35
Woman in the Shadows '34
As You Desire Me '32
The Old Dark House '32
The Vampire Bat '32
Tonight or Never '31
Michael Douglas (1944-)
Don't Say a Word '01
One Night at McCool's '01
Traffic '00
Wonder Boys '00
A Perfect Murder '98
The Game '97
The Ghost and the Darkness '96
The American President '95
Disclosure '94
Falling Down '93
Basic Instinct '92
Shining Through '92
Black Rain '89
The War of the Roses '89
Fatal Attraction '87
Wall Street '87
A Chorus Line '85
The Jewel of the Nile '85
Romancing the Stone '84
The Star Chamber '83
It's My Turn '80
The China Syndrome '79
Coma '78
Napoleon and Samantha '72
The Streets of San Francisco '72
Shattered Silence '71
Summertree '71
Adam at 6 a.m. '70
Hail, Hero! '69
Mike Douglas
Nasty Habits '77
Gator '76
Paul Douglas (1907-59)
The Mating Game '59
This Could Be the Night '57
The Gamma People '56
Solid Gold Cadillac '56
Green Fire '55
Executive Suite '54
Forever Female '53
Clash by Night '52
Never Wave at a WAC '52
We're Not Married '52
Angels in the Outfield '51
The Big Lift '50
Panic in the Streets '50
It Happens Every Spring '49
A Letter to Three Wives '49
Robert Douglas (1909-99)
Helen of Troy '56
King Richard and the Crusaders '54
The Desert Rats '53
At Sword's Point '51
The Flame & the Arrow '50
Adventures of Don Juan '49
The Challenge '38
London Melody '37
Sarah Douglas (1952-)
Chained Heat 3: Hell Mountain '98
Asylum '97
The Demolitionist '95
Voodoo '95
Spitfire '94
Meatballs 4 '92
Beastmaster 2: Through the Portal of Time '91
The Art of Dying '90
Puppet Master 3: Toulon's Revenge '90
Tagget '90
The Return of Swamp Thing '89
Nightfall '88
Steele Justice '87
Solarbabies '86
Conan the Destroyer '84
Superman 2 '80
Superman: The Movie '78
The People That Time Forgot '77
Dracula '73
The Final Programme '73
Shirley Douglas
A House Divided '00
Barney's Great Adventure '98
Johnny's Girl '95
Dead Ringers '88
Shadow Dancing '88
Lolita '62
Susan Douglas
Lost Boundaries '49
The Private Affairs of Bel Ami '47
Warren Douglas (1911-97)
The Inner Circle '46
The Man I Love '46

Robyn Douglass (1953-)
Freeze Frame '92
The Lonely Guy '84
Her Life as a Man '83
Partners '82

Suzzanne Douglass (1957-)
How Stella Got Her Groove Back '98
Jason's Lyric '94
Chain of Desire '93
Tap '89

Gary Dourdan
Imposter '01
Scarred City '98
Playing God '96

Brad Dourif (1950-)
Cypress Edge '99
Interceptor Force '99
The Prophecy 3: The Ascent '99
Silicon Towers '99
Best Men '98
Bride of Chucky '98 (V)
Brown's Requiem '98
Progeny '98
Senseless '98
Urban Legend '98
Alien: Resurrection '97
Sworn to Justice '97
Black Out '96
Nightwatch '96
Death Machine '95
Murder in the First '95
Phoenix '95
Color of Night '94
Amos and Andrew '93
Dario Argento's Trauma '93
Wild Palms '93
Dead Certain '92
Final Judgment '92
Body Parts '91
Child's Play 3 '91 (V)
Common Bonds '91
Critters 4 '91
The Horseplayer '91
Jungle Fever '91
London Kills Me '91
Child's Play 2 '90 (V)
Exorcist 3: Legion '90
Graveyard Shift '90
Hidden Agenda '90
Grim Prairie Tales '89
Spontaneous Combustion '89
Vengeance '89
Child's Play '88
Mississippi Burning '88
Fatal Beauty '87
Sonny Boy '87
Blue Velvet '86
Impure Thoughts '86
Rage of Angels: The Story Continues '86
Istanbul '85
Dune '84
Heaven's Gate '81
Ragtime '81
The Guyana Tragedy: The Story of Jim Jones '80
Wise Blood '79
Eyes of Laura Mars '78
Sergeant Matlovich vs. the U.S. Air Force '78
One Flew Over the Cuckoo's Nest '75

Billie Dove (1900-97)
All the Brothers Were Valiant '53
The Black Pirate '26

Ellen A. Dow
54 '98
The Wedding Singer '97

Peggy Dow
I Want You '51
Harvey '50

Tony Dow (1945-)
Back to the Beach '87
High School USA '84
Kentucky Fried Movie '77
Death Scream '75

Ann Dowd
Baby '00
Shiloh 2: Shiloh Season '99
Apt Pupil '97
Shiloh '97
All Over Me '96
Bushwhacked '95
Kingfish: A Story of Huey P. Long '95
It Could Happen to You '94
Philadelphia '93

Ned Dowd (1950-)
Bottle Rocket '95
Places in the Heart '84
48 Hrs. '82
Southern Comfort '81
Popeye '80
Slap Shot '77

Don Dowe
Test Tube Teens from the Year 2000 '93
Evil Toons '90

Raye Dowell
Landlord Blues '87
She's Gotta Have It '86

Garrick Dowhen
Appointment with Fear '85
Land of Doom '84

Freda Dowie
Oranges Are Not the Only Fruit '89
Distant Voices, Still Lives '88

Constance Dowling
Black Angel '46
Up in Arms '44

Doris Dowling (1923-)
Othello '52
Bitter Rice '49
The Blue Dahlia '46
The Lost Weekend '45

Joan Dowling
Train of Events '49
Hue and Cry '47

Lesley-Anne Down (1954-)
The King's Guard '01
The Perfect Wife '00
The Secret Agent Club '96
Beastmaster 3: The Eye of Braxus '95
Family of Cops '95
Death Wish 5: The Face of Death '94
In the Heat of Passion 2: Unfaithful '94
Mardi Gras for the Devil '93
Indiscreet '88
Ladykillers '88
Scenes from the Goldmine '87
Nomads '86
North and South Book 2 '86
Arch of Triumph '85
North and South Book 1 '85
The Hunchback of Notre Dame '82
Sphinx '81
Rough Cut '80
The Great Train Robbery '79
Hanover Street '79
The Betsy '78
A Little Night Music '77
The Pink Panther Strikes Again '76
Brannigan '75
From Beyond the Grave '73
Assault '70

Brian Downey (1044-)
Tales from a Parallel Universe: Eating Pattern '97
Tales from a Parallel Universe: Giga Shadow '97
Tales from a Parallel Universe: I Worship His Shadow '97
Tales from a Parallel Universe: Super Nova '97
George's Island '91

Morton Downey, Jr. (1933-2001)
Revenge of the Nerds 3: The Next Generation '92
The Silencer '92
Body Chemistry 2: Voice of a Stranger '91
Driving Me Crazy '91
Legal Tender '90
Predator 2 '90

Robert Downey (1936-)
Boogie Nights '97
That's Adequate '90
To Live & Die in L.A. '85

Robert Downey, Jr. (1965-)
Wonder Boys '00
Black and White '99
Bowfinger '99
Friends & Lovers '99
In Dreams '98
Two Girls and a Guy '98
U.S. Marshals '98
The Gingerbread Man '97
Hugo Pool '97
One Night Stand '97
Danger Zone '95
Home for the Holidays '95
Richard III '95
Hail Caesar '94
Natural Born Killers '94
Only You '94
Restoration '94
Heart and Souls '93
Short Cuts '93
Chaplin '92
Soapdish '91
Air America '90
Too Much Sun '90
Chances Are '89
1969 '89
True Believer '89
Johnny Be Good '88
Rented Lips '88
Less Than Zero '87
The Pick-Up Artist '87
America '86
Back to School '86
Tuff Turf '85
Weird Science '85
First Born '84
Baby It's You '82

Roma Downey (1960-)
Hercules the Legendary Journeys, Vol. 1: And the Amazon Women '94
Devlin '92
Getting Up and Going Home '92
A Woman Named Jackie '91

Penny Downie (1954-)
A Certain Justice '99
Dostoevsky's Crime and Punishment '99
Lost for Words '99
The Ice House '97

J. Downing
Robot Wars '93
Ghoulies 2 '87

Cathy Downs (1924-76)
Missile to the Moon '59
The Amazing Colossal Man '57
The Curfew Breakers '57
The Phantom from 10,000 Leagues '56
Kentucky Rifle '55
The Flaming Urge '53
The Noose Hangs High '48
Dark Corner '46
My Darling Clementine '46

Johnny Downs (1913-94)
Rhapsody in Blue '45
Harvest Melody '43
The Mad Monster '42
Adam Had Four Sons '41
Bad Boy '39
Pigskin Parade '36
March of the Wooden Soldiers '34

Denise Dowse
Killing Mr. Griffin '97
Bio-Dome '96

David Doyle (1925-97)
Archie: Return to Riverdale '90
Ghost Writer '89
Love or Money? '88
Wait Till Your Mother Gets Home '83
The Line '80
My Boys Are Good Boys '78
Wild & Wooly '78
The Comeback '77
Who Killed Mary What's 'Er Name? '71
Paper Lion '68

John (Roy Slaven) Doyle
Rock & Roll Cowboys '92
The Wicked '89
Contagion '87

Maxine Doyle (1915-73)
Come on, Cowboys '37
S.O.S. Coast Guard '37
Condemned to Live '35
The Mystery Man '35

Shawn Doyle
Don't Say a Word '01
The Majestic '01
Stiletto Dance '01
Frequency '00

Tony Doyle (1941-2000)
I Went Down '97
Adventures in Dinosaur City '92
Eat the Peach '86
The Final Option '82

Maria Doyle Kennedy
Miss Julie '99
The General '98
The Break '97
The Matchmaker '97
Nothing Personal '95
The Commitments '91

Brian Doyle-Murray (1945-)
Snow Dogs '02
Bedazzled '00
Stuart Little '99
Dennis the Menace Strikes Again '98
As Good As It Gets '97
Multiplicity '96
Waiting for Guffman '96
Jury Duty '95
Cabin Boy '94
Groundhog Day '93
Bob Roberts '92
Wayne's World '92
JFK '91
Shame of the Jungle '90 (V)
The Experts '89
Ghostbusters 2 '89
How I Got into College '89
National Lampoon's Christmas Vacation '89
Scrooged '88
Club Paradise '86
The Razor's Edge '84
Sixteen Candles '84
National Lampoon's Vacation '83
Modern Problems '81
Caddyshack '80

Heinz Drache (1923-2002)
Circus of Fear '67
The Mysterious Magician '65
The Squeaker '65
The Indian Scarf '63
Door with the Seven Locks '62
The Avenger '60

Billy Drago
Shadow Warriors '97
Deadly Heroes '96
Mirror, Mirror 3: The Voyeur '96
Sci-Fighters '96
Phoenix '95
Never Say Die '94
Solar Force '94
The Takeover '94
Cyborg 2 '93
Death Ring '93
In Self Defense '93
Lady Dragon 2 '93
The Outfit '93
Guncrazy '92
Secret Games '92
China White '91
Diplomatic Immunity '91
Martial Law 2: Undercover '91
Delta Force 2: Operation Stranglehold '90
Dark Before Dawn '89
Freeway '88
Hero and the Terror '88
Prime Suspect '88
The Untouchables '87
Vamp '86
Invasion U.S.A. '85

Betsy Drake (1923-)
Clarence, the Cross-eyed Lion '65
Will Success Spoil Rock Hunter? '57
The Second Woman '51
Every Girl Should Be Married '48

Charles Drake (1914-94)
Hail, Hero! '69
Valley of the Dolls '67
No Name on the Bullet '59
Until They Sail '57
Walk the Proud Land '56
To Hell and Back '55
Tobor the Great '54
Gunsmoke '53
It Came from Outer Space '53
Red Ball Express '52
Comanche Territory '50
Harvey '50
Winchester '73 '50
The Tender Years '47
A Night in Casablanca '46
Conflict '45
Air Force '43
Dive Bomber '41

Claudia Drake
Detour '46
Gentleman from Texas '46
The Lady Confesses '45
Enemy of Women '44
Border Patrol '43

David Drake
David Searching '97
Philadelphia '93

Dona Drake (1914-89)
The Road to Morocco '42
Louisiana Purchase '41

Frances Drake (1908-2000)
I'd Give My Life '36
The Invisible Ray '36
Forsaking All Others '35
Les Miserables '35
Mad Love '35

Larry Drake (1950-)
Dark Asylum '01
Desert Heat '99
Paranoia '98
Bean '97
The Beast '96
Overnight Delivery '96
Power 98 '96
The Journey of August King '95
Darkman 2: The Return of Durant '94
Dr. Giggles '92
Murder in New Hampshire: The Pamela Smart Story '91
Darkman '90
Tales from the Crypt '89
Dark Night of the Scarecrow '81
This Stuff'll Kill Ya! '71

Tom Drake (1918-82)
Savage Abduction '73
The Spectre of Edgar Allen Poe '73
Cycle Psycho '72
Johnny Reno '66
The Singing Nun '66
House of the Black Death '65
Warkill '65
The Bramble Bush '60
Cyclops '56
FBI Girl '52
The Great Rupert '50
The Hills of Home '48
Words and Music '48
Cass Timberlane '47
I'll Be Yours '47
Courage of Lassie '46
Meet Me in St. Louis '44
Two Girls and a Sailor '44
The White Cliffs of Dover '44
The Howards of Virginia '40

Polly Draper (1957-)
Hitman's Journal '99
The Tic Code '99
Gold Diggers: The Secret of Bear Mountain '95
Schemes '95
A Million to Juan '94
Danielle Steel's Heartbeat '93
The Pick-Up Artist '87
Making Mr. Right '86

Thomas Draper
Bikini Med School '98
Bikini House Calls '96

Milena Dravic
WR: Mysteries of the Organism '71
Man Is Not a Bird '65

Alfred Drayton
Things Happen at Night '48
Nicholas Nickleby '46
First a Girl '35

Dr. Dre (1965-)
Training Day '01
The Wash '01
The Show '95
Gunmen '93

Alex Dreier
Lady Cocoa '75
Loners '72

Fran Drescher (1957-)
Picking Up the Pieces '99
The Beautician and the Beast '97
Jack '96
Car 54, Where Are You? '94
We're Talkin' Serious Money '92
Cadillac Man '90
UHF '89
Wedding Band '89
Rosebud Beach Hotel '85
This Is Spinal Tap '84
Doctor Detroit '83
The Hollywood Knights '80
Summer of Fear '78
Saturday Night Fever '77

Sonia Dresdel (1909-76)
The Clouded Yellow '51
The Fallen Idol '49
While I Live '47

Curly Dresden
Fighting Valley '43
Trigger Men '41
Wyoming Outlaw '39
Pals of the Saddle '38
Santa Fe Stampede '38
Rough Ridin' Rhythm '37

John Dresden
No Dead Heroes '87
Final Mission '84
Raw Force '81

Louise Dresser (1878-1965)
Scarlet Empress '34
Dracula/Garden of Eden '28
The Garden of Eden '28
The Eagle '25

Lieux Dressler
Truck Stop Women '74
Grave of the Vampire '72

Marie Dressler (1869-1934)
Dinner at Eight '33
Anna Christie '30
Min & Bill '30
Vagabond Lover '29
Tillie Wakes Up '17
Tillie's Punctured Romance '14

Ellen Drew (1915-)
Baron of Arizona '51
Great Missouri Raid '51
Man in the Saddle '51
Stars in My Crown '50

Man from Colorado *'49*
Isle of the Dead *'45*
China Sky *'44*
Dark Mountain *'44*
The Monster and the Girl *'41*
Christmas in July *'40*
The Texas Rangers Ride Again *'40*
If I Were King *'38*

Gene Drew
Truck Stop Women *'74*
Steel Arena *'72*

Griffin (Griffen) Drew
The Kid with the X-Ray Eyes *'99*
Dinosaur Valley Girls *'96*
Friend of the Family *'95*
Masseuse *'95*
Dinosaur Island *'93*

Roland (Walter Goss) Drew (1900-88)
Across the Pacific *'42*
The Invisible Killer *'40*
Evangeline *'29*

Nancy Drexel (1910-89)
Man from Hell's Edges *'32*
Mason of the Mounted *'32*
Texas Buddies *'32*

James Dreyfus
Notting Hill *'99*
Boyfriends *'96*

Jean Claude Dreyfus
The City of Lost Children *'95*
Son of Gascogne *'95*
Delicatessen *'92*

Lorin Dreyfuss (1944-)
Dutch Treat *'86*
Detective School Dropouts *'85*

Richard Dreyfuss (1947-)
The Crew *'00*
Lansky *'99*
Krippendorf's Tribe *'98*
Jack London's The Call of the Wild *'97 (N)*
Oliver Twist *'97*
James and the Giant Peach *'96 (V)*
Night Falls on Manhattan *'96*
Trigger Happy *'96*
The American President *'95*
The Last Word *'95*
Mr. Holland's Opus *'95*
Silent Fall *'94*
Another Stakeout *'93*
Lost in Yonkers *'93*
Once Around *'91*
Prisoner of Honor *'91*
What about Bob? *'91*
Postcards from the Edge *'90*
Rosencrantz & Guildenstern Are Dead *'90*
Always *'89*
Let It Ride *'89*
Moon over Parador *'88*
Nuts *'87*
Stakeout *'87*
Tin Men *'87*
Down and Out in Beverly Hills *'86*
Stand by Me *'86*
The Buddy System *'83*
Whose Life Is It Anyway? *'81*
The Competition *'80*
Second Coming of Suzanne *'80*
Suzanne *'80*
The Big Fix *'78*
Close Encounters of the Third Kind *'77*
The Goodbye Girl *'77*
Inserts *'76*
Jaws *'75*
The Apprenticeship of Duddy Kravitz *'74*
American Graffiti *'73*
Dillinger *'73*
The Graduate *'67*
Valley of the Dolls *'67*

Moosie Drier (1964-)
Charlie and the Great Balloon Chase *'82*
The Hollywood Knights *'80*
Homeward Bound *'80*
Ants *'77*

Deborah Driggs
Night Rhythms *'92*
Total Exposure *'91*

Brian Drillinger
I Shot a Man in Vegas *'96*
Brighton Beach Memoirs *'86*

Carol Drinkwater
An Awfully Big Adventure *'94*
Father *'90*

Bobby Driscoll (1937-68)
Peter Pan *'53 (V)*
Treasure Island *'50*
So Dear to My Heart *'49*
The Window *'49*
O.S.S. *'46*
Identity Unknown *'45*
The Fighting Sullivans *'42*

Robert Drivas (1938-86)
God Told Me To *'76*
Road Movie *'72*
The Illustrated Man *'69*
Cool Hand Luke *'67*

Minnie Driver (1971-)
High Heels and Low Lifes *'01*
Beautiful *'00*
Return to Me *'00*
Slow Burn *'00*
An Ideal Husband *'99*
South Park: Bigger, Longer and Uncut *'99 (V)*
Tarzan *'99 (V)*
The Governess *'98*
Princess Mononoke *'98 (V)*
Uncorked *'98*
Good Will Hunting *'97*
Grosse Pointe Blank *'97*
Hard Rain *'97*
Sleepers *'96*
Big Night *'95*
Goldeneye *'95*
Circle of Friends *'94*

Jean-Claude Drouot
La Rupture *'70*
Le Bonheur *'65*

Joanne Dru (1923-96)
Super Fuzz *'81*
The Light in the Forest *'58*
Sincerely Yours *'56*
Hell on Frisco Bay *'55*
The Warriors *'55*
Thunder Bay *'53*
Pride of St. Louis *'52*
Vengeance Valley *'51*
Wagon Master *'50*
All the King's Men *'49*
She Wore a Yellow Ribbon *'49*
Red River *'48*

Alice Drummond (1929-)
Joe Gould's Secret *'00*
The Love Letter *'99*
Office Killer *'97*
Commandments *'96*
Til There Was You *'96*
Daybreak *'93*

James Drury (1934-)
The Gambler Returns: The Luck of the Draw *'93*
Walker: Texas Ranger: One Riot, One Ranger *'93*
Bull of the West *'89*
The Meanest Men in the West *'76*
Ride the High Country *'62*
Ten Who Dared *'60*
Good Day for a Hanging *'58*
Love Me Tender *'56*
The Tender Trap *'55*

Fred (John F.) Dryer (1946-)
Shakedown *'02*
Wild Grizzly *'99*
Stray Bullet *'98*
Death Before Dishonor *'87*
The Fantastic World of D.C. Collins *'84*

Robert Dryer
Fast Gun *'93*
Heartbreaker *'83*
Savage Streets *'83*

Jeanie Drynan
Paperback Hero *'99*
Soft Fruit *'99*
Muriel's Wedding *'94*
Fantasy Man *'84*
Don's Party *'76*

Gerald du Maurier
The Living Dead *'36*
Power *'34*

Carmen (De Sautoy) Du Sautoy (1952-)
It Couldn't Happen Here *'88*
Deadly Recruits *'86*
Praying Mantis *'83*

Michael Duane
The Prince of Thieves *'48*
City Without Men *'43*

Frances Dubay
Wild Women *'53*
The Body Vanished *'39*

Don Dubbins (1928-91)
Savage Run *'70*
The Illustrated Man *'69*
From the Earth to the Moon *'58*
D.I. *'57*
Tribute to a Bad Man *'56*

Ellen Dubin
Tales from a Parallel Universe: I Worship His Shadow *'97*
Tales from a Parallel Universe: Super Nova *'97*

Jessica Dublin
The Toxic Avenger, Part 3: The Last Temptation of Toxie *'89*
The Rejuvenator *'88*
Troma's War *'88*

Danielle Dublino
Emmanuelle & Joanna *'86*
St. Michael Had a Rooster *'72*

Ja'net DuBois
Waterproof *'99*
Magic Island *'95*
Heart Condition *'90*
I'm Gonna Git You Sucka *'88*
Piece of the Action *'77*

Marie DuBois (1937-)
La Petite Sirene *'80*
Mon Oncle d'Amerique *'80*
Vincent, Francois, Paul and the Others *'76*
Night Flight from Moscow *'73*
Jailbird's Vacation *'65*
Circle of Love *'64*
Jules and Jim *'62*
Shoot the Piano Player *'62*
A Woman Is a Woman *'60*

Marta DuBois
Luminarias *'99*
Black Out *'96*
Dead Badge *'94*
Fear *'90*
The Trial of the Incredible Hulk *'89*
The Grace Kelly Story *'83*
Boulevard Nights *'79*

Paulette Dubost (1911-)
May Fools *'90*
The Last Metro *'80*
Viva Maria! *'65*
The Sheep Has Five Legs *'54*
The Rules of the Game *'39*

Paul Dubov (1918-79)
Shock Corridor *'63*
Ma Barker's Killer Brood *'60*
Underworld, U.S.A. *'60*
Atomic Submarine *'59*
Verboten! *'59*
China Gate *'57*
Apache Woman *'55*
Day the World Ended *'55*

Kristie Ducati
The Bikini Car Wash Company 2 *'92*
The Bikini Car Wash Company *'90*

Michael Duchaussoy (1938-)
The Widow of Saint-Pierre *'00*
Road to Ruin *'91*
May Fools *'90*
Fort Saganne *'84*
Return of the Tall Blond Man with One Black Shoe *'74*
This Man Must Die *'70*
The Killing Game *'67*

David Duchovny (1960-)
Full Frontal *'02*
Evolution *'01*
Zoolander *'01*
Red Shoe Diaries: Luscious Lola *'00*
Red Shoe Diaries: Swimming Naked *'00*
Return to Me *'00*
The X-Files *'98*
Red Shoe Diaries 8: Night of Abandon *'97*
Playing God *'96*
Red Shoe Diaries 7: Burning Up *'96*
Red Shoe Diaries: Four on the Floor *'96*
Red Shoe Diaries: Strip Poker *'96*
Red Shoe Diaries 6: How I Met My Husband *'95*
Kalifornia *'93*
Red Shoe Diaries 3: Another Woman's Lipstick *'93*
Red Shoe Diaries 4: Auto Erotica *'93*
Beethoven *'92*
Chaplin *'92*
Red Shoe Diaries *'92*
Red Shoe Diaries 2: Double Dare *'92*
Ruby *'92*
Venice, Venice *'92*
Julia Has Two Lovers *'91*
The Rapture *'91*
New Year's Day *'89*

Ric(k) Ducommun (1949-)
MVP (Most Valuable Primate) *'00*
Final Voyage *'99*
Blank Check *'93*
Ghost in the Machine *'93*
Encino Man *'92*
Class Act *'91*
The 'Burbs *'89*
Little Monsters *'89*
Die Hard *'88*
No Small Affair *'84*

Louis Ducreux (1901-92)
The Double Life of Veronique *'91*
The Story of Women *'88*
A Sunday in the Country *'84*

Neil Dudgeon
Breathtaking *'00*
Speedy Death *'99*
Different for Girls *'96*
Piece of Cake *'90*

Michael Dudikoff (1954-)
Gale Force *'01*
Ablaze *'00*
Fugitive Mind *'99*
The Silencer *'99*
Black Thunder *'98*
Freedom Strike *'98*
Ringmaster *'98*
Bounty Hunters 2: Hardball *'97*
The Shooter *'97*
Bounty Hunters *'96*
Crash Dive *'96*
Moving Target *'96*
Chain of Command *'95*
Soldier Boyz *'95*
Virtual Assassin *'95*
Rescue Me *'93*
The Human Shield *'92*
Midnight Ride *'92*
American Ninja 4: The Annihilation *'91*
River of Death *'90*
American Ninja 2: The Confrontation *'87*
Platoon Leader *'87*
Avenging Force *'86*
Radioactive Dreams *'86*
American Ninja *'85*
Bachelor Party *'84*
I Ought to Be in Pictures *'82*
Making Love *'82*
Bloody Birthday *'80*
The Black Marble *'79*

William Duell
Elvira, Mistress of the Dark *'88*
Grace Quigley *'84*

Denice Duff
Bloodstorm: Subspecies 4 *'98*
Bloodfist 5: Human Target *'93*
Bloodlust: Subspecies 3 *'93*
Bloodstone: Subspecies 2 *'92*
Return to Frogtown *'92*

Howard Duff (1917-90)
No Way Out *'87*
Monster in the Closet *'86*
Love on the Run *'85*
The Double Negative *'80*
East of Eden *'80*
Magic on Love Island *'80*
Oh, God! Book 2 *'80*
Kramer vs. Kramer *'79*
Snowblind *'78*
A Wedding *'78*
Snatched *'72*
Boys' Night Out *'62*
While the City Sleeps *'56*
Flame of the Islands *'55*
Private Hell 36 *'54*
Spaceways *'53*
All My Sons *'48*
The Naked City *'48*

Kevin Duffis
The Expendables *'89*
Nam Angels *'88*

Julia Duffy (1951-)
Children in the Crossfire *'84*
Night Warning *'82*

Karen Duffy (1962-)
The 24 Hour Woman *'99*
Synapse *'95*
Dumb & Dumber *'94*
Reality Bites *'94*
Blank Check *'93*

Patrick Duffy (1949-)
Perfect Game *'00*
Texas *'94*
Danielle Steel's Daddy *'91*
Vamping *'84*
Enola Gay: The Men, the Mission, the Atomic Bomb *'80*
The Man from Atlantis *'77*
The Last of Mrs. Lincoln *'76*

Thomas F. Duffy
Varsity Blues *'98*
The Lost World: Jurassic Park 2 *'97*
Wagons East *'94*
Eye of the Stranger *'93*

Jacques Dufilho (1914-)
The Horse of Pride *'80*
Le Crabe Tambour *'77*
Black and White in Color *'76*

Dennis Dugan (1946-)
Happy Gilmore *'96*
Parenthood *'89*
The New Adventures of Pippi Longstocking *'88*
She's Having a Baby *'88*
Can't Buy Me Love *'87*
The Howling *'81*
Unidentified Flying Oddball *'79*
Norman, Is That You? *'76*
Night Moves *'75*
Night Call Nurses *'72*

John Dugan
The Texas Chainsaw Massacre 4: The Next Generation *'95*
The Texas Chainsaw Massacre *'74*

Michael Dugan
Gun Glory *'57*
She Wore a Yellow Ribbon *'49*

Tom Dugan (1889-1955)
I've Been Waiting for You *'98*
Galgameth *'96*
Nightwish *'89*
Take Me Out to the Ball Game *'49*
Accomplice *'46*
Gambler's Choice *'44*
Bataan *'43*
To Be or Not to Be *'42*
Pick a Star *'37*
Blessed Event *'32*
The Galloping Ghost *'31*
Medicine Man *'30*

Andrew Duggan (1923-88)
J. Edgar Hoover *'87*
Return to Salem's Lot *'87*
Doctor Detroit *'83*
The Winds of War *'83*
Frankenstein Island *'81*
The Long Days of Summer *'80*
It's Alive 2: It Lives Again *'78*
Time Machine *'78*
The Hunted Lady *'77*
The Bears & I *'74*
It's Alive *'74*
Pueblo Affair *'73*
Firehouse *'72*
Housewife *'72*
The Streets of San Francisco *'72*
Jigsaw *'71*
Skin Game *'71*
The Secret War of Harry Frigg *'68*
In Like Flint *'67*
The Incredible Mr. Limpet *'64*
Seven Days in May *'64*
Palm Springs Weekend *'63*
Merrill's Marauders *'62*
The Commies Are Coming, the Commies Are Coming *'57*

Davor Dujmovic
Underground *'95*
Time of the Gypsies *'90*

Olympia Dukakis (1931-)
The Last of the Blonde Bombshells *'00*
Joan of Arc *'99*
Mafia! *'98*
The Pentagon Wars *'98*
Armistead Maupin's More Tales of the City *'97*
Jerusalem *'96*
Picture Perfect *'96*
Jeffrey *'95*
Mighty Aphrodite *'95*
Mr. Holland's Opus *'95*
Dead Badge *'94*
Digger *'94*
Mother *'94*
Armistead Maupin's Tales of the City *'93*
The Cemetery Club *'93*
Look Who's Talking Now *'93*
Over the Hill *'93*
Sinatra *'92*
In the Spirit *'90*

Look Who's Talking, Too '90
Dad '89
Look Who's Talking '89
Steel Magnolias '89
Working Girl '88
Moonstruck '87
Walls of Glass '85
Idolmaker '80
Rich Kids '79
Wanderers '79
Death Wish '74

Bill Duke (1943-)
Exit Wounds '01
Fever '99
Foolish '99
Dying to Get Rich '98
Payback '98
Menace II Society '93
Bird on a Wire '90
Predator '87
Commando '85
American Gigolo '79

Patty Duke (1946-)
Little John '02
A Season for Miracles '99
Harvest of Fire '95
Grave Secrets: The Legacy of Hilltop Drive '92
Prelude to a Kiss '92
Amityville 4: The Evil Escapes '89
Best Kept Secrets '88
George Washington: The Forging of a Nation '86
Something Special '86
George Washington '84
September Gun '83
By Design '82
The Babysitter '80
Mom, the Wolfman and Me '80
The Miracle Worker '79
Family Upside Down '78
The Swarm '78
Curse of the Black Widow '77
Fire '77
Killer on Board '77
You'll Like My Mother '72
She Waits '71
My Sweet Charlie '70
Valley of the Dolls '67
Billie '65
The Miracle Worker '62
The 4D Man '59
The Goddess '58

Robin Duke (1954-)
Hostage for a Day '94
Motorama '91
Club Paradise '86
The Last Polka '84

David Dukes (1945-2000)
Stephen King's Rose Red '02
Supreme Sanction '99
Gods and Monsters '98
The Love Letter '98
Tinseltown '97
Last Stand at Saber River '96
Norma Jean and Marilyn '95
And the Band Played On '93
Me and the Kid '93
Held Hostage '91
The Josephine Baker Story '90
The Rutanga Tapes '90
Snow Kill '90
Strange Interlude '90
See You in the Morning '89
War & Remembrance: The Final Chapter '89
War & Remembrance '88
Catch the Heat '87
Date with an Angel '87
Rawhead Rex '87
The Men's Club '86
Cat on a Hot Tin Roof '84
George Washington '84
The Winds of War '83
Without a Trace '83
Miss All-American Beauty '82
Portrait of a Rebel: Margaret Sanger '82
Only When I Laugh '81
The First Deadly Sin '80
Mayflower: The Pilgrims' Adventure '79
The Triangle Factory Fire Scandal '79
Wild Party '74
The Strawberry Statement '70

Caitlin Dulany
Class of 1999 2: The Substitute '93
Maniac Cop 3: Badge of Silence '93

Keir Dullea (1936-)
The Audrey Hepburn Story '00
Oh, What a Night '92
Love Under Pressure '80s
Blind Date '84
Next One '84
2010: The Year We Make Contact '84
Brainwaves '82
No Place to Hide '81
The Hostage Tower '80
Leopard in the Snow '78
Full Circle '77
Welcome to Blood City '77
Black Christmas '75
Paul and Michelle '74
Paperback Hero '73
Black Water Gold '69
2001: A Space Odyssey '68
Madame X '66
The Thin Red Line '64
David and Lisa '62
The Hoodlum Priest '61

Douglass Dumbrille (1890-1974)
Shake, Rattle and Rock '57
The Ten Commandments '56
Jupiter's Darling '55
Son of Paleface '52
Abbott and Costello in the Foreign Legion '50
Riding High '50
Spook Busters '48
Blonde Savage '47
The Road to Utopia '46
Under Nevada Skies '46
Jungle Woman '44
Lost in a Harem '44
Uncertain Glory '44
Weird Woman/Frozen Ghost '44
Castle in the Desert '42
A Gentleman After Dark '42
I Married an Angel '42
Ride 'Em Cowboy '42
Big Store '41
Virginia City '40
The Three Musketeers '39
The Mysterious Rider '38
A Day at the Races '37
The Firefly '37
Mr. Deeds Goes to Town '36
The Princess Comes Across '36
Crime and Punishment '35
The Lives of a Bengal Lancer '35
Naughty Marietta '35
Treasure Island '34
Baby Face '33
Heroes for Sale '33
Rustler's Roundup '33

Denise Dumont
Heart of Midnight '89
Kiss of the Spider Woman '85

Jose Dumont
Behind the Sun '01
At Play in the Fields of the Lord '91

Margaret Dumont (1889-1965)
Zotz! '62
Shake, Rattle and Rock '57
Three for Bedroom C '52
The Horn Blows at Midnight '45
Up in Arms '44
Rhythm Parade '43
Sing Your Worries Away '42
Tales of Manhattan '42
Big Store '41
Never Give a Sucker an Even Break '41
At the Circus '39
The Women '39
A Day at the Races '37
A Night at the Opera '35
Duck Soup '33
Animal Crackers '30
The Cocoanuts '29

Ulises Dumont
Time for Revenge '82
The Lion's Share '79

Dennis Dun
Thousand Pieces of Gold '91
The Last Emperor '87
Prince of Darkness '87
Big Trouble in Little China '86

Steffi Duna (1910-92)
Law of the Pampas '39
Way Down South '39
Dancing Pirate '36
I Conquer the Sea '36

Donnie Dunagan
Bambi '42 (V)
Son of Frankenstein '39

Faye Dunaway (1941-)
Running Mates '00
The Yards '00
The Messenger: The Story of Joan of Arc '99
The Thomas Crown Affair '99
Gia '98
Rebecca '97
The Twilight of the Golds '97
Albino Alligator '96
The Chamber '96
Drunks '96
Dunston Checks In '95
Arizona Dream '94
Don Juan DeMarco '94
The Temp '93
Double Edge '92
Scorchers '92
Silhouette '91
The Handmaid's Tale '90
Wait until Spring, Bandini '90
Burning Secret '89
Cold Sassy Tree '89
The Gamble '88
Barfly '87
Casanova '87
Midnight Crossing '87
Beverly Hills Madam '86
Christopher Columbus '85
Ordeal by Innocence '84
Supergirl '84
The Wicked Lady '83
Country Girl '82
Mommie Dearest '81
The First Deadly Sin '80
The Champ '79
Eyes of Laura Mars '78
The Disappearance of Aimee '76
Network '76
Voyage of the Damned '76
The Four Musketeers '75
Three Days of the Condor '75
Chinatown '74
The Three Musketeers '74
The Towering Inferno '74
Oklahoma Crude '73
The Deadly Trap '71
Little Big Man '70
The Arrangement '69
The Thomas Crown Affair '68
Bonnie & Clyde '67

Adrian Dunbar (1958-)
The General '98
Innocent Lies '95
Widow's Peak '94
A Woman's Guide to Adultery '93
The Crying Game '92
The Playboys '92
Hear My Song '91
My Left Foot '89

Andrew Duncan
Shame of the Jungle '90 (V)
Morgan Stewart's Coming Home '87
The Gig '85
Slap Shot '77
The Rain People '69

Angus Duncan
How to Seduce a Woman '74
Hard Frame '70

Arletta Duncan (1914-95)
Roaring Speedboats '37
Fighting Champ '33
The Gallant Fool '33
Frankenstein '31

Bob Duncan
Border Feud '47
Colorado Serenade '46

Bud Duncan
Hillbilly Blitzkrieg '42
Snuffy Smith, Yard Bird '42

Carmen Duncan
Moving Targets '87
Dark Forces '83
Now and Forever '82

Julie Duncan
Haunted Ranch '43
Along the Sundown Trail '42
Fugitive Valley '41

Kenne Duncan (1903-72)
Revenge of the Virgins '62 (N)
The Sinister Urge '60
Night of the Ghouls '59
The Astounding She-Monster '58
Flesh and the Spur '57
Cyclotrode "X" '46
Manhunt of Mystery Island '45
Raiders of Sunset Pass '43
Dynamite Canyon '41
Riding the Sunset Trail '41
Pinto Canyon '40
Make-Up '37

Lindsay Duncan (1950-)
Oliver Twist '00
An Ideal Husband '99
Mansfield Park '99
Shooting the Past '99
A Midsummer Night's Dream '96
City Hall '95
The Rector's Wife '94
Body Parts '91
The Reflecting Skin '91
Traffik '90
A Year in Provence '89
Loose Connections '87
Prick Up Your Ears '87
Grown Ups '80

Mary Duncan
Morning Glory '33
City Girl '30

Michael Clarke Duncan (1957-)
The Scorpion King '02
Cats & Dogs '01 (V)
Planet of the Apes '01
See Spot Run '01
They Call Me Sirr '00
The Whole Nine Yards '00
The Green Mile '99
Armageddon '98

Neil Duncan
Sleeping with Strangers '94
Split Second '92
Murder on Line One '90

Peter Duncan (1954-)
The Lifetaker '89
The Old Curiosity Shop '75

Rachel Duncan (1985-)
Amityville Dollhouse '96
Last Stand at Saber River '96
The Crazysitter '94

Sandy Duncan (1946-)
The Swan Princess '94 (V)
Rock-a-Doodle '92 (V)
The Fox and the Hound '81 (V)
The Cat from Outer Space '78
Roots '77
Million Dollar Duck '71
Star Spangled Girl '71

Jennifer (Jennie) Dundas Lowe
Changing Lanes '02
The First Wives Club '96
Legal Eagles '86
Heaven Help Us '85
The Hotel New Hampshire '84
Mrs. Soffel '84
The Beniker Gang '83

Claude Duneton
Trois Couleurs: Bleu '93
The Double Life of Veronique '91

Katherine Dunham
Mambo '55
Casbah '48

Robert Dunham
Godzilla vs. Megalon '76
The Green Slime '68
Face of Another '66

Rosemary Dunham
The Wolves of Kromer '98
Mistress Pamela '74

Dawn Dunlap (1962-)
Barbarian Queen '85
Heartbreaker '83
Forbidden World '82

Lesley Dunlop (1956-)
Tess of the D'Urbervilles '98
The Dying Truth '91
Haunted: The Ferryman '74

Vic Dunlop
Wishful Thinking '92
Martians Go Home! '90
Jud '71

Carolyn Dunn
Hitler's Daughter '90
Breaking All the Rules '85

Conrad Dunn
The Last Don 2 '98
Mask of Death '97

Eddie Dunn (1896-1951)
Call Northside 777 '48
Mexican Spitfire at Sea '42
Billy the Kid '41
South of Santa Fe '32
Sunrise Trail '31

Emma Dunn (1875-1966)
I Married a Witch '42
Talk of the Town '42
The Great Dictator '40
You Can't Fool Your Wife '40
Son of Frankenstein '39
The Duke of West Point '38
Madame X '37
Blessed Event '32
Hell's House '32
Morals for Women '31

Harvey B. Dunn (1894-1968)
The Sinister Urge '60
Teenagers from Outer Space '59
Bride of the Monster '55

James Dunn (1905-67)
The Oscar '66
The Bramble Bush '60
That Brennan Girl '46
A Tree Grows in Brooklyn '45
The Ghost and the Guest '43
Shadows over Shanghai '38
Baby, Take a Bow '34
Bright Eyes '34
Stand Up and Cheer '34

Josephine Dunn
Between Fighting Men '32
Our Modern Maidens '29

Kevin Dunn (1956-)
Stir of Echoes '99
Godzilla '98
Small Soldiers '98
Snake Eyes '98
Almost Heroes '97
The Second Civil War '97
The Sixth Man '97
Chain Reaction '96
Picture Perfect '96
JAG '95
Mad Love '95
Nixon '95
Little Big League '94
Dave '93
Chaplin '92
Hot Shots! '91
Only the Lonely '91
Taken Away '89
Mississippi Burning '88

Liam Dunn
Blazing Saddles '74
Young Frankenstein '74
Emperor of the North Pole '73

Michael Dunn (1934-73)
Dr. Frankenstein's Castle of Freaks '74
The Freakmaker '73
Werewolf of Washington '73
House of the Damned '71
Murders in the Rue Morgue '71
Boom! '68
Madigan '68
You're a Big Boy Now '66
Ship of Fools '65

Nora Dunn (1952-)
Cherish '02
Heartbreakers '01
Max Keeble's Big Move '01
What's the Worst That Could Happen? '01
What Planet Are You From? '00
Drop Dead Gorgeous '99
Three Kings '99
Air Bud 2: Golden Receiver '98
Bulworth '98
The Last Supper '96
Shake, Rattle & Rock! '94
Born Yesterday '93
Passion Fish '92
Stepping Out '91
Miami Blues '90
How I Got into College '89
Working Girl '88

John Dunn-Hill
Varian's War '01
La Deroute '98
Bleeders '97

Dominick Dunne
An Alan Smithee Film: Burn, Hollywood, Burn '97
Addicted to Love '96

Dominique Dunne (1959-82)
Haunting of Harrington House '82
Poltergeist '82
The Shadow Riders '82
Magic on Love Island '80

Griffin Dunne (1955-)
40 Days and 40 Nights '02
Lisa Picard Is Famous '01
The Android Affair '95
I Like It Like That '94
Quiz Show '94
Search and Destroy '94
Hotel Room '93
Love Matters '93
The Pickle '93
Big Girls Don't Cry...They Get Even '92
Straight Talk '92
My Girl '91
Once Around '91
Secret Weapon '90
White Palace '90
Me and Him '89

The Big Blue '88
Lip Service '88
Amazon Women on the Moon '87
Who's That Girl? '87
After Hours '85
Almost You '85
From Here to Maternity '85
Cold Feet '84
Johnny Dangerously '84
An American Werewolf in London '81
The Fan '81
Chilly Scenes of Winter '79
The Other Side of the Mountain '75

Irene Dunne (1898-1990)
Never a Dull Moment '50
I Remember Mama '48
Life with Father '47
Anna and the King of Siam '46
A Guy Named Joe '44
The White Cliffs of Dover '44
Penny Serenade '41
My Favorite Wife '40
Love Affair '39
Joy of Living '38
The Awful Truth '37
Show Boat '36
Theodora Goes Wild '36
Roberta '35
Sweet Adeline '35
Ann Vickers '33
Bachelor Apartment '31
Cimarron '31
Consolation Marriage '31

Murphy Dunne (1942-)
Blues Brothers 2000 '98
Bad Manners '84
Going Berserk '83
The Blues Brothers '80
The Big Bus '76

Robin Dunne
American Psycho 2: All American Girl '02
The Skulls 2 '02
Cruel Intentions 2 '99

Steve (Stephen) Dunne (1918-77)
Above and Beyond '53
The Underworld Story '50
The Big Sombrero '49

Mildred Dunnock (1901-91)
The Pick-Up Artist '87
And Baby Makes Six '79
One Summer Love '76
Spiral Staircase '75
Murder or Mercy '74
Brand New Life '72
Whatever Happened to Aunt Alice? '69
Behold a Pale Horse '64
Sweet Bird of Youth '62
Butterfield 8 '60
The Nun's Story '59
Peyton Place '57
Baby Doll '56
Love Me Tender '56
The Trouble with Harry '55
Viva Zapata! '52
I Want You '51
The Corn Is Green '45

Rosemary Dunsmore
Breaking the Surface: The Greg Louganis Story '96
Personals '90
Blades of Courage '88
After the Promise '87
Anne of Avonlea '87
Dancing in the Dark '86

Kirsten Dunst (1982-)
Spider-Man '02
The Cat's Meow '01
crazy/beautiful '01
Get Over It! '01
Bring It On '00
The Crow: Salvation '00
Luckytown '00
Deeply '99
The Devil's Arthmetic '99
Dick '99
Drop Dead Gorgeous '99
Lover's Prayer '99
The Virgin Suicides '99
All I Wanna Do '98
Small Soldiers '98
Anastasia '97 (V)
Tower of Terror '97
True Heart '97
Wag the Dog '97
Mother Night '96
Jumanji '95
Interview with the Vampire '94
Little Women '94

Wilson Dunster
Yankee Zulu '95
The Rutanga Tapes '90
Swift Justice '88

Don Duong
We Were Soldiers '02
Three Seasons '98

Anny (Annie Legras) Duperey (1947-)
Charlemagne '95
Germinal '93
Les Comperes '83
From Hell to Victory '79
Bobby Deerfield '77
Pardon Mon Affaire '76
No Problem '75
Stavisky '74
The Women '69
Two or Three Things I Know about Her '66

Daphnee Lynn Duplaix
Foolish '99
Lost and Found '99

Starletta DuPois
Big Momma's House '00
Three Strikes '00
The Road to Galveston '96
A Raisin in the Sun '89
Hollywood Shuffle '87

June Duprez (1918-84)
That Brennan Girl '46
And Then There Were None '45
Brighton Strangler '45
None But the Lonely Heart '44
Tiger Fangs '43
The Lion Has Wings '40
The Thief of Bagdad '40
The Four Feathers '39
Spy in Black '39

Roy Dupuis (1963-)
Bleeders '97
Entangled '93
Being at Home with Claude '92

David Durand (1920-98)
Boy's Reformatory '39
Viva Villa! '34

Christopher Durang (1949-)
Simply Irresistible '99
Housesitter '92
The Butcher's Wife '91
In the Spirit '90
Mr. North '88
Heaven Help Us '85

Jimmy Durante (1893-1980)
Alice Through the Looking Glass '66
It's a Mad, Mad, Mad, Mad World '63
Billy Rose's Jumbo '62
The Great Rupert '50
On an Island with You '48
It Happened in Brooklyn '47
Ziegfeld Follies '46
Two Girls and a Sailor '44
The Man Who Came to Dinner '41
Melody Ranch '40
Little Miss Broadway '38
Hollywood Party '34
Palooka '34
The Lost Stooges '33
What! No Beer? '33
Speak Easily '32

Deanna Durbin (1921-)
For the Love of Mary '48
Up in Central Park '48
I'll Be Yours '47
Something in the Wind '47
Because of Him '45
Can't Help Singing '45
Lady on a Train '45
His Butler's Sister '44
The Amazing Mrs. Holiday '43
It Started with Eve '41
Nice Girl? '41
It's a Date '40
First Love '39
Three Smart Girls Grow Up '39
Mad About Music '38
That Certain Age '38
100 Men and a Girl '37
Three Smart Girls '36

John Durbin
King of the Hill '93
Ain't No Way Back '89
Dr. Caligari '89
Tapeheads '89

Minta Durfee (1889-1975)
Savage Intruder '68
Miracle Kid '42
Mickey '17

Anna Marie Duringer
Veronika Voss '82
The Lacemaker '77

Romain Duris
The Crazy Stranger '98
When the Cat's Away '96

Charles Durning (1933-)
Hostage Hotel '00
O Brother Where Art Thou? '00
State and Main '00
Backlash '99
Hi-Life '98
Jerry and Tom '98
Shelter '98
The Last Supper '96
Mrs. Santa Claus '96
One Fine Day '96
Spy Hard '96
The Grass Harp '95
Home for the Holidays '95
The Kennedys of Massachusetts '95
The Hudsucker Proxy '93
The Music of Chance '93
The Story Lady '93
When a Stranger Calls Back '93
The Water Engine '92
The Return of Eliot Ness '91
V.I. Warshawski '91
Cat Chaser '90
Dick Tracy '90
Dinner at Eight '89
Project: Alien '89
Cop '88
Far North '88
Happy New Year '87
Kenny Rogers as the Gambler, Part 3: The Legend Continues '87
The Man Who Broke 1,000 Chains '87
The Rosary Murders '87
A Tiger's Tale '87
Big Trouble '86
Brenda Starr '86
Death of a Salesman '86
The Legend of Sleepy Hollow '86
Solarbabies '86
Tough Guys '86
Where the River Runs Black '86
The Man with One Red Shoe '85
Stand Alone '85
Stick '85
Hadley's Rebellion '84
Mass Appeal '84
To Be or Not to Be '83
Two of a Kind '83
The Best Little Whorehouse in Texas '82
Tootsie '82
The Best Little Girl in the World '81
Dark Night of the Scarecrow '81
Sharky's Machine '81
True Confessions '81
Attica '80
Crisis at Central High '80
Die Laughing '80
The Final Countdown '80
The Muppet Movie '79
North Dallas Forty '79
When a Stranger Calls '79
The Fury '78
Special Olympics '78
Tilt '78
The Choirboys '77
Twilight's Last Gleaming '77
Breakheart Pass '76
Harry & Walter Go to New York '76
Dog Day Afternoon '75
The Hindenburg '75
Queen of the Stardust Ballroom '75
The Front Page '74
The Connection '73
Sisters '73
The Sting '73

Dick Durock
The Return of Swamp Thing '89
Swamp Thing '82

Jason Durr (1968-)
Killer Tongue '96
Sharpe's Battle '94
A Dark Adapted Eye '93

Michael Durrell (1943-)
Illegal in Blue '95
Family Sins '87
V '83

Ian Dury (1942-2000)
The Crow 2: City of Angels '96
Split Second '92
The Raggedy Rawney '90

Dan Duryea (1907-68)
The Bamboo Saucer '68
Five Golden Dragons '67
The Flight of the Phoenix '65
Platinum High School '60
Battle Hymn '57
Ride Clear of Diablo '54
Silver Lode '54
Terror Street '54
Thunder Bay '53
The Underworld Story '50
Winchester '73 '50
Too Late for Tears '49
Criss Cross '48
Black Angel '46
Along Came Jones '45
Great Flamarion '45
Lady on a Train '45
Scarlet Street '45
The Valley of Decision '45
Ministry of Fear '44
None But the Lonely Heart '44
Woman in the Window '44
Sahara '43
The Pride of the Yankees '42
Ball of Fire '41
The Little Foxes '41

Marj Dusay (1936-)
Love Walked In '97
Made in Heaven '87
Pendulum '69
Sweet November '68

Ann Dusenberry (1953-)
Basic Training '86
Long Time Gone '86
The Men's Club '86
Lies '83
Cutter's Way '81
Killjoy '81
Heart Beat '80
Desperate Women '78
Little Women '78
The Possessed '77

Eliza Dushku (1980-)
The New Guy '02
Jay and Silent Bob Strike Back '01
Soul Survivors '01
Bring It On '00
Race the Sun '96
Journey '95
Bye Bye, Love '94
True Lies '94
That Night '93
This Boy's Life '93

Nancy Dussault
The Nurse '97
The In-Laws '79

Andre Dussollier (1946-)
Amelie '01 (N)
Same Old Song '97
Colonel Chabert '94
Un Coeur en Hiver '93
Sand and Blood '87
Three Men and a Cradle '85
Le Beau Mariage '82
Perceval '78
And Now My Love '74

Jacques Dutronc (1943-)
Place Vendome '98
Van Gogh '92
Tricheurs '84
L'Etat Sauvage '78

Charles S. Dutton (1951-)
Deadlocked '00
For Love or Country: The Arturo Sandoval Story '00
Aftershock: Earthquake in New York '99
Cookie's Fortune '99
Random Hearts '99
The '60s '99
Black Dog '98
Blind Faith '98
Mimic '97
True Women '97
Get On the Bus '96
A Time to Kill '96
Cry, the Beloved Country '95
Nick of Time '95
Zooman '95
Foreign Student '94
A Low Down Dirty Shame '94
The Piano Lesson '94
Surviving the Game '94
Menace II Society '93
Rudy '93
Alien 3 '92
The Distinguished Gentleman '92
Mississippi Masala '92
Q & A '90
Jacknife '89
An Unremarkable Life '89
Crocodile Dundee 2 '88
The Murder of Mary Phagan '87
Cat's Eye '85

Tim Dutton
Oliver Twist '00
Darkness Falls '98
Frenchman's Creek '98
Robert Louis Stevenson's St. Ives '98
Rhodes '97
Tom & Viv '94

James Duval (1973-)
Donnie Darko '01
Gone in 60 Seconds '00
The Weekend '00
Go '99
SLC Punk! '99
Independence Day '96
Nowhere '96
The Doom Generation '95
Totally F***ed Up '94

Josey Duval
New York's Finest '87
Sex, Drugs, and Rock-n-Roll '84

Maria Duval
Samson vs. the Vampire Women '61
The Living Coffin '58

Clea DuVall (1977-)
How to Make a Monster '01
John Carpenter's Ghosts of Mars '01
The Astronaut's Wife '99
But I'm a Cheerleader '99
Committed '99
Girl, Interrupted '99
Wildflowers '99
The Faculty '98
The Defenders: Payback '97

Robert Duvall (1931-)
John Q '02
Gone in 60 Seconds '00
The 6th Day '00
A Civil Action '98
Deep Impact '98
The Apostle '97
The Gingerbread Man '97
A Family Thing '96
The Man Who Captured Eichmann '96
Phenomenon '96
Sling Blade '96
The Scarlet Letter '95
Something to Talk About '95
The Paper '94
The Stars Fell on Henrietta '94
Falling Down '93
Geronimo: An American Legend '93
Wrestling Ernest Hemingway '93
Newsies '92
The Plague '92
Stalin '92
Hearts of Darkness: A Filmmaker's Apocalypse '91
Rambling Rose '91
Days of Thunder '90
The Handmaid's Tale '90
A Show of Force '90
Lonesome Dove '89
Colors '88
Hotel Colonial '88
Let's Get Harry '87
Belizaire the Cajun '86
The Lightship '86
The Natural '84
The Stone Boy '84
Tender Mercies '83
The Terry Fox Story '83
The Godfather 1902-1959: The Complete Epic '81
The Pursuit of D.B. Cooper '81
True Confessions '81
The Great Santini '80
Apocalypse Now '79
Ike '79
The Betsy '78
Invasion of the Body Snatchers '78
The Eagle Has Landed '77
The Greatest '77
Network '76
The Seven-Per-Cent Solution '76
Breakout '75
The Killer Elite '75
The Conversation '74
The Godfather, Part 2 '74
Badge 373 '73
Lady Ice '73
The Godfather '72
The Great Northfield Minnesota Raid '72
Joe Kidd '72
Tomorrow '72
Lawman '71
THX 1138 '71
M*A*S*H '70
The Rain People '69
True Grit '69
Bullitt '68
Countdown '68
The Detective '68
The Chase '66
Captain Newman, M.D. '63
To Kill a Mockingbird '62

Shelley Duvall (1949-)
The 4th Floor '99
Russell Mulcahy's Tale of the Mummy '99
Boltneck '98
Home Fries '98
Horton Foote's Alone '97
The Twilight of the Ice Nymphs '97
Changing Habits '96
Portrait of a Lady '96
The Underneath '95
Suburban Commando '91
Mother Goose Rock 'n' Rhyme '90
Roxanne '87
Frankenweenie '84
Rapunzel '82
Rumpelstiltskin '82
Time Bandits '81
Popeye '80
The Shining '80
Annie Hall '77
Nashville '75
Thieves Like Us '74
McCabe & Mrs. Miller '71
Brewster McCloud '70

Wayne Duvall
A Better Way to Die '00
O Brother Where Art Thou? '00
Hard Rain '97
Warlords 3000 '93
Final Approach '91

Janine Duvitsky
Grown Ups '80
Dracula '79

Pierre Dux (1908-90)
La Lectrice '88
La Vie Continue '82
The Day and the Hour '63
Les Grandes Manoeuvres '55
Monsieur Vincent '47

Ann Dvorak (1912-79)
A Life of Her Own '50
Our Very Own '50
Return of Jesse James '50
The Long Night '47
Out of the Blue '47
The Private Affairs of Bel Ami '47
Abilene Town '46
Flame of the Barbary Coast '45
Manhattan Merry-Go-Round '37
"G" Men '35
The Strange Love of Molly Louvain '32
Three on a Match '32
The Guardsman '31
Scarface '31

Peter Dvorsky
Mesmer '94
The Kiss '88
Videodrome '83

Dorothy Dwan (1906-81)
The Fighting Legion '30
The Peacock Fan '29
Great K & A Train Robbery '26
The Wizard of Oz '25

Earl Dwire (1883-1940)
Lightning Bill Crandall '37
Riding On '37
Trouble in Texas '37
Cavalcade of the West '36
Assassin of Youth '35
Between Men '35
Big Calibre '35
Lawless Frontier '35
Lawless Range '35
Toll of the Desert '35
The Star Packer '34

Bill Dwyer
Little Shots of Happiness '97
Ski School 2 '94

Hilary Dwyer
Cry of the Banshee '70
Wuthering Heights '70
The Oblong Box '69
The Conqueror Worm '68

Leslie Dwyer (1906-86)
Hi-Di-Hi '88
Die, Monster, Die! '65
Black Tide '58
Roadhouse Girl '53
Immortal Battalion '44

Franklin Dyall
The Private Life of Henry VIII '33
Easy Virtue '27

Valentine Dyall (1908-85)
The Haunting '63
Horror Hotel '60
Suspended Alibi '56
The Golden Salamander '51
Room to Let '49
The Ghost of Rashmon Hall '47
Brief Encounter '46
Frenzy '46
Pink String and Sealing Wax '45
Henry V '44
Hotel Reserve '44

Cameron Dye
The Tavern '00
The Apocalypse '96
Out of the Dark '88
Heated Vengeance '87
Scenes from the Goldmine '87
Stranded '87
Fraternity Vacation '85
Body Rock '84
Joy of Sex '84
The Last Starfighter '84
Valley Girl '83

Dale Dye (1944-)
Band of Brothers '01
Rules of Engagement '00
Saving Private Ryan '98
Operation Delta Force 2: Mayday '97
Rough Riders '97
Starship Troopers '97
Mission: Impossible '96
Trial and Error '96
Within the Rock '96
Sgt. Bilko '95
Under Siege 2: Dark Territory '95
Endangered '94
Guarding Tess '94
Natural Born Killers '94
Outbreak '94
The Puppet Masters '94
Heaven and Earth '93
Sniper '92
Under Siege '92
Blue Sky '91
JFK '91
Relentless 2: Dead On '91
Servants of Twilight '91
The Court Martial of Jackie Robinson '90
Fire Birds '90
The Fourth War '90
Kid '90
Always '89
Born on the Fourth of July '89
Casualties of War '89
Spontaneous Combustion '89
Billionaire Boys Club '87
Invaders from Mars '86
Platoon '86

John Dye
Best of the Best '89
Campus Man '87

Danny Dyer
High Heels and Low Lifes '01
Mean Machine '01
Greenfingers '00
Human Traffic '99

Karen Dyer
Corrupt '99
Urban Menace '99

Matthew Dyktynski
Heaven's Burning '97
Road to Nhill '97
Love and Other Catastrophes '95

Bob Dylan (1941-)
Backtrack '89
Hearts of Fire '87
Pat Garrett & Billy the Kid '73

Peter Dyneley (1921-77)
Soul Patrol '80
The Manster '59
Strange Awakening '58
Beau Brummel '54

Richard Dysart (1929-)
Hard Rain '97
Todd McFarlane's Spawn '97 (V)
Panther '95
Truman '95
Marilyn & Bobby: Her Final Affair '94
Back to the Future, Part 3 '90
Day One '89
Wall Street '87
L.A. Law '86
The Last Days of Patton '86
The Rumor Mill '86
The Falcon and the Snowman '85
Mask '85
Pale Rider '85
Warning Sign '85
The Thing '82
Bitter Harvest '81
Churchill and the Generals '81
The People vs. Jean Harris '81
Bogie: The Last Hero '80
The Ordeal of Dr. Mudd '80
Being There '79
Meteor '79
Prophecy '79
Riding with Death '76
The Day of the Locust '75
The Hindenburg '75
The Autobiography of Miss Jane Pittman '74
The Terminal Man '74
The Hospital '71
The Lost Man '69
Petulia '68

Dick Dyszel
Night Beast '83
The Alien Factor '78

George Dzundza (1945-)
Above Suspicion '00
Instinct '99
Species 2 '98
Trading Favors '97
The Limbic Region '96
That Darn Cat '96
Crimson Tide '95
Dangerous Minds '95
The Enemy Within '94
Basic Instinct '92
The Butcher's Wife '91
Impulse '90
White Hunter, Black Heart '90
The Beast '88
Glory Years '87
No Way Out '87
No Mercy '86
Broken Badge '85
Brotherly Love '85
Best Defense '84
Act of Passion: The Lost Honor of Kathryn Beck '83
Streamers '83
A Long Way Home '81
The Deer Hunter '78

Sheila E (1957-)
The Adventures of Ford Fairlane '90
Krush Groove '85

Nicholas Eadie
Celia: Child of Terror '89
Return to Snowy River '88

Angela Eads
Things 2 '97
Dead Girls '90

Edward Earle (1882-1972)
Command Decision '48
I Accuse My Parents '45
Bordertown Gunfighters '43
California Joe '43
The Duke of West Point '38
The Revenge Rider '35
Spite Marriage '29
The Wind '28

Harry Earles (1902-85)
Freaks '32
The Unholy Three '30
The Unholy Three '25

Bo Eason
Tornado! '96
Miami Rhapsody '95

Carlos East (1942-94)
Fearmaker '89
The Fear Chamber '68
The Snake People '68

Jeff East (1957-)
Another Chance '88
Pumpkinhead '88
Deadly Blessing '81
Mary and Joseph: A Story of Faith '79
Summer of Fear '78
The Campus Corpse '77
Flight of the Grey Wolf '76
Huckleberry Finn '74
Tom Sawyer '73

Leslie Easterbrook (1951-)
Police Academy 7: Mission to Moscow '94
Police Academy 6: City under Siege '89
Police Academy 5: Assignment Miami Beach '88
The Taking of Flight 847: The Uli Derickson Story '88
Police Academy 3: Back in Training '86
Police Academy '84
Private Resort '84

Steve Eastin
Agent Red '00
Peril '00
Stealth Fighter '99
Last Man Standing '95

Todd Eastland
Mommy 2: Mommy's Day '96
Pledge Night '90

George Eastman (1854-1932)
Hands of Steel '86
After the Fall of New York '85
Blastfighter '85
Detective School Dropouts '85
Ironmaster '83
Grim Reaper '81
Bloody Avenger '80
Belle Starr '79
Call of the Wild '72
Kiss Me, Kill Me '69

Rodney Eastman
The Caveman's Valentine '01
Sand '00
Blue Ridge Fall '99
Beverly Hills Bodysnatchers '89
Deadly Weapon '88
A Nightmare on Elm Street 4: Dream Master '88
A Nightmare on Elm Street 3: Dream Warriors '87

Michael Easton
The '70s '00
Total Recall 2070: Machine Dreams '99

Richard Easton (1933-)
Dead Again '91
Henry V '89
The Red Badge of Courage '51

Robert Easton (1930-)
Just One Night '00
Working Girl '88
The Giant Spider Invasion '75
Heavy Traffic '73
Johnny Got His Gun '71
When Hell Broke Loose '58

Sheena Easton (1959-)
All Dogs Go to Heaven 2 '95 (V)
Body Bags '93
Indecent Proposal '93

Alison Eastwood (1972-)
If You Only Knew '00
The Spring '00
Black & White '99
Friends & Lovers '99
Just a Little Harmless Sex '99
Breakfast of Champions '98
Midnight in the Garden of Good and Evil '97
Tightrope '84

Clint Eastwood (1930-)
Blood Work '02
Space Cowboys '00
True Crime '99
Absolute Power '97
The Bridges of Madison County '95
Casper '95
In the Line of Fire '93
A Perfect World '93
Unforgiven '92
The Rookie '90
White Hunter, Black Heart '90
Pink Cadillac '89
The Dead Pool '88
Heartbreak Ridge '86
Pale Rider '85
City Heat '84
Tightrope '84
Sudden Impact '83
Firefox '82
Honkytonk Man '82
Any Which Way You Can '80
Bronco Billy '80
Escape from Alcatraz '79
Every Which Way But Loose '78
The Gauntlet '77
The Enforcer '76
The Outlaw Josey Wales '76
The Eiger Sanction '75
Thunderbolt & Lightfoot '74
High Plains Drifter '73
Magnum Force '73
Joe Kidd '72
Dirty Harry '71
Play Misty for Me '71
The Beguiled '70
Kelly's Heroes '70
Two Mules for Sister Sara '70
Paint Your Wagon '69
Coogan's Bluff '68
Where Eagles Dare '68
The Good, the Bad and the Ugly '67
Hang 'Em High '67
For a Few Dollars More '65
A Fistful of Dollars '64
Lafayette Escadrille '58
Escapade in Japan '57
Away All Boats '56
Francis in the Navy '55
Revenge of the Creature '55
Tarantula '55

Jayne (Jane) Eastwood
Life with Judy Garland—Me and My Shadows '01
That Old Feeling '96
Hostile Takeover '88
Kidnapping of Baby John Doe '88
Night Friend '87
My Pleasure Is My Business '74

Kyle Eastwood
Honkytonk Man '82
The Outlaw Josey Wales '76

Marjorie Eaton (1901-86)
Street Music '81
The Attic '80
The Atomic Brain '64
Night Tide '63

Mary Eaton
Glorifying the American Girl '30
The Cocoanuts '29

Roberta Eaton
The Crude Oasis '95
Split Second '92

Shirley Eaton (1936-)
Kiss and Kill '68
Eight on the Lam '67
Around the World Under the Sea '65
Goldfinger '64
Girl Hunters '63
What a Carve-Up! '62
Carry On Nurse '59
The Naked Truth '58
Doctor at Large '57
Doctor in the House '53

Wallace Eaton
Plunge Into Darkness '77
Isadora '68

John Eaves
Skier's Dream '88
Fire and Ice '87

Christine Ebersole (1953-)
Double Platinum '99
True Crime '99
My Favorite Martian '98
An Unexpected Life '97
Black Sheep '96
Til There Was You '96
An Unexpected Family '96
Pie in the Sky '95
My Girl 2 '94
Richie Rich '94
Gypsy '93
Folks! '92
Dead Again '91
Ghost Dad '90
Mac and Me '88
Acceptable Risks '86
Amadeus '84
Thief of Hearts '84
Tootsie '82

Buddy Ebsen (1908-)
The Beverly Hillbillies '93
Stone Fox '87
The Bastard '78
The Adventures of Tom Sawyer '73
The President's Plane Is Missing '71
The Andersonville Trial '70
The One and Only, Genuine, Original Family Band '68
The Interns '62
Breakfast at Tiffany's '61
Attack! '56
Between Heaven and Hell '56
Davy Crockett and the River Pirates '56
Davy Crockett, King of the Wild Frontier '55
Red Garters '54
Rodeo King and the Senorita '51
Silver City Bonanza '51
Sing Your Worries Away '42
Girl of the Golden West '38
My Lucky Star '38
Broadway Melody of 1938 '37
Born to Dance '36
Captain January '36
Broadway Melody of 1936 '35

Maude Eburne (1875-1960)
The Border Legion '40
Courageous Dr. Christian '40
Doughnuts & Society '36
Ruggles of Red Gap '35
Ladies They Talk About '33
The Vampire Bat '32
The Guardsman '31

Aimee (Amy) Eccles
Humanoid Defender *'85*
Lovelines *'84*
The Concrete Jungle *'82*
Group Marriage *'72*
Little Big Man *'70*
Christopher Eccleston (1964-)
Othello *'01*
The Others *'01*
Gone in 60 Seconds *'00*
Invisible Circus *'00*
eXistenZ *'99*
Heart *'99*
Elizabeth *'98*
A Price above Rubies *'97*
Jude *'96*
Cracker: To Be a Somebody *'94*
Shallow Grave *'94*
Let Him Have It *'91*
Guy Ecker
Night Terror *'89*
Devil Wears White *'86*
Aaron Eckhart (1968-)
Possession *'02*
Erin Brockovich *'00*
Nurse Betty *'00*
The Pledge *'00*
Any Given Sunday *'99*
Molly *'99*
Thursday *'98*
Your Friends & Neighbors *'98*
In the Company of Men *'96*
James Eckhouse (1955-)
One True Thing *'98*
Junior *'94*
Leaving Normal *'92*
The Christmas Wife *'88*
Blue Heaven *'84*
Billy Eckstine
Jo Jo Dancer, Your Life Is Calling *'86*
Skirts Ahoy! *'52*
Jean-Philippe Ecoffey (1959-)
Ma Vie en Rose *'97*
Portraits Chinois *'96*
Fiesta *'95*
Mina Tannenbaum *'93*
The Possessed *'88*
Helen Jerome Eddy (1897-1990)
Klondike Annie *'36*
A Shot in the Dark *'35*
The Country Kid *'23*
County Fair *'20*
The Tong Man *'19*
Rebecca of Sunnybrook Farm *'17*
Nelson Eddy (1901-67)
Northwest Outpost *'47*
The Phantom of the Opera *'43*
I Married an Angel *'42*
The Chocolate Soldier *'41*
Bitter Sweet *'40*
New Moon *'40*
Balalaika *'39*
Let Freedom Ring *'39*
Girl of the Golden West *'38*
Rosalie *'38*
Sweethearts *'38*
Maytime *'37*
Rose Marie *'36*
Naughty Marietta *'35*
Dancing Lady *'33*
Alfred Edel
Terror 2000 *'92*
My Father Is Coming *'91*
Herb Edelman (1930-96)
Cracking Up *'83*
On the Right Track *'81*
Strike Force *'81*
A Cry for Love *'80*
Marathon *'80*
Goin' Coconuts *'78*
Special Olympics *'78*
Charge of the Model T's *'76*
The Yakuza *'75*
A Strange and Deadly Occurrence *'74*
The Way We Were *'73*
The Odd Couple *'68*
Lisa Edelstein
Dean Koontz's Black River *'01*
Keeping the Faith *'00*
What Women Want *'00*
Barbara Eden (1934-)
Lethal Charm *'90*
Chattanooga Choo Choo *'84*
Return of the Rebels *'81*
Harper Valley P.T.A. *'78*
The Amazing Dobermans *'76*
How to Break Up a Happy Divorce *'76*
The Stranger Within *'74*
The Woman Hunter *'72*
Quick, Let's Get Married *'71*
Ride the Wild Surf *'64*
The Brass Bottle *'63*
7 Faces of Dr. Lao *'63*
Five Weeks in a Balloon *'62*
The Wonderful World of the Brothers Grimm *'62*
Voyage to the Bottom of the Sea *'61*
Flaming Star *'60*
From the Terrace *'60*
Jerome (Jerry Stallion) Eden
The Defilers *'65*
Color Me Blood Red *'64*
2000 Maniacs *'64*
Blood Feast *'63*
Mark Eden (1928-)
The Crimson Cult *'68*
Doctor Zhivago *'65*
Seance on a Wet Afternoon *'64*
The L-Shaped Room *'62*
Richard Eden (1956-)
Undercover Angel *'99*
Public Enemies *'96*
Liberty & Bash *'90*
Robert Edeson
Walking Back *'26*
On the Night Stage *'15*
George Edgely
Common Law Wife *'63*
Free, White, and 21 *'62*
Valerie Edmond
Saving Grace *'00*
Love and Rage *'99*
Dartanyan Edmonds
Rangers *'00*
Ride *'98*
Elizabeth Edmonds
Experience Preferred... But Not Essential *'83*
Scrubbers *'82*
Louis Edmonds
Next Year in Jerusalem *'98*
House of Dark Shadows *'70*
Beatie Edney
Highlander: Endgame *'00*
The Tenant of Wildfell Hall *'96*
The Affair *'95*
In the Name of the Father *'93*
The Dark Angel *'91*
Mister Johnson *'91*
Diary of a Mad Old Man *'88*
Highlander *'86*
Richard Edson (1954-)
Time Code *'00*
The Million Dollar Hotel *'99*
Thick as Thieves *'99*
Lulu on the Bridge *'98*
This World, Then the Fireworks *'97*
Intimate Betrayal *'96*
An Occasional Hell *'96*
Scorpion Spring *'96*
Wedding Bell Blues *'96*
The Winner *'96*
Bad Love *'95*
Destiny Turns on the Radio *'95*
Jury Duty *'95*
Strange Days *'95*
Attack of the 50 Ft. Woman *'93*
Joey Breaker *'93*
Love, Cheat & Steal *'93*
Posse *'93*
Super Mario Bros. *'93*
Jungle Fever *'91*
Do the Right Thing *'89*
Let It Ride *'89*
Eight Men Out *'88*
Tougher Than Leather *'88*
Good Morning, Vietnam *'87*
Ferris Bueller's Day Off *'86*
Platoon *'86*
Desperately Seeking Susan *'85*
Stranger than Paradise *'84*
Allan Edwall (1924-97)
The Sacrifice *'86*
Fanny and Alexander *'83*
Brothers Lionheart *'77*
The New Land *'73*
The Emigrants *'72*
Anthony Edwards (1962-)
Jackpot *'01*
Playing by Heart *'98*
In Cold Blood *'96*
Charlie's Ghost: The Secret of Coronado *'94*
The Client *'94*
Hometown Boy Makes Good *'93*
Delta Heat *'92*
Landslide *'92*
Pet Sematary 2 *'92*
El Diablo *'90*
Downtown *'89*
Hawks *'89*
How I Got into College *'89*
Miracle Mile *'89*
Mr. North *'88*
Revenge of the Nerds 2: Nerds in Paradise *'87*
Summer Heat *'87*
Top Gun *'86*
Going for the Gold: The Bill Johnson Story *'85*
Gotcha! *'85*
The Sure Thing *'85*
Revenge of the Nerds *'84*
Heart Like a Wheel *'83*
Fast Times at Ridgemont High *'82*
Barbara (Lee) Edwards (1960-)
House Party 3 *'94*
Another Chance *'88*
Malibu Express *'85*
Bill Edwards (1918-99)
War Lover *'62*
First Man into Space *'59*
Ladies of the Chorus *'49*
Bruce Edwards
Federal Agents vs. Underworld, Inc. *'49*
The Black Widow *'47*
The Fallen Sparrow *'43*
Hitler: Dead or Alive *'43*
The Iron Major *'43*
Cliff Edwards (1895-1971)
Fun & Fancy Free *'47 (V)*
Sagebrush Law *'43*
Dumbo *'41 (V)*
His Girl Friday *'40*
Pinocchio *'40 (V)*
Gone with the Wind *'39*
Girl of the Golden West *'38*
Saratoga *'37*
Red Salute *'35*
Dance Fools Dance *'31*
Laughing Sinners *'31*
Parlor, Bedroom and Bath *'31*
Sidewalks of New York *'31*
The Sin of Madelon Claudet *'31*
Doughboys *'30*
Gail Edwards
A Perfect Little Murder *'90*
Get Crazy *'83*
Glynn Edwards
Get Carter *'71*
Zulu *'64*
Henry Edwards (1882-1952)
The Golden Salamander *'51*
Madeleine *'50*
Hilton Edwards
Victim *'61*
Othello *'52*
James Edwards (1918-70)
Patton *'70*
The Manchurian Candidate *'62*
Pork Chop Hill *'59*
Men in War *'57*
The Killing *'56*
The Member of the Wedding *'52*
The Steel Helmet *'51*
Home of the Brave *'49*
The Set-Up *'49*
Jennifer Edwards (1959-)
Overexposed *'90*
All's Fair *'89*
Peter Gunn *'89*
Perfect Match *'88*
Sunset *'88*
That's Life! *'86*
The Man Who Loved Women *'83*
S.O.B. *'81*
Heidi *'67*
Lance Edwards
A Woman, Her Men and Her Futon *'92*
Peacemaker *'90*
Luke Edwards (1980-)
Cheaters *'00*
Little Big League *'94*
Mother's Boys *'94*
Newsies *'92*
Guilty by Suspicion *'91*
The Wizard *'89*
Mark Edwards
Tower of Evil *'72*
Blood from the Mummy's Tomb *'71*
The Boldest Job in the West *'71*
Meredith Edwards (1917-99)
A Christmas Reunion *'93*
The Electronic Monster *'57*
Penny Edwards (1928-98)
Heart of the Rockies *'51*
North of the Great Divide *'50*
Sunset in the West *'50*
Trail of Robin Hood *'50*
Ronnie Clair Edwards
8 Seconds *'94*
A Day for Thanks on Walton's Mountain *'82*
Future Cop *'76*
Sam Edwards
The Beatniks *'60*
Gang Busters *'55*
Twelve o'Clock High *'49*
Bambi *'42 (V)*
Snitz Edwards (1862-1937)
April Fool *'26*
Battling Butler *'26*
The Phantom of the Opera *'25*
Seven Chances *'25*
The Thief of Baghdad *'24*
Stacy Edwards (1965-)
Driven *'01*
Prancer Returns *'01*
Four Dogs Playing Poker *'00*
Mexico City *'00*
The Next Best Thing *'00*
The Bachelor *'99*
Black and White *'99*
Houdini *'99*
Primary Colors *'98*
In the Company of Men *'96*
Vince Edwards (1926-96)
The Fear *'94*
Jailbreakers *'94*
Dillinger *'91*
Motorama *'91*
Original Intent *'91*
To Die For 2: Son of Darkness *'91*
Andy and the Airwave Rangers *'89*
The Gumshoe Kid *'89*
Cellar Dweller *'87*
The Dirty Dozen: The Deadly Mission *'87*
Return to Horror High *'87*
Sno-Line *'85*
The Fix *'84*
Space Raiders *'83*
The Seduction *'82*
Death Stalk *'74*
Firehouse *'72*
The Mad Bomber *'72*
Desperados *'69*
The Devil's Brigade *'68*
The Three Faces of Eve *'57*
The Killing *'56*
Marshall Efron
First Time *'82*
Is There Sex After Death? *'71*
Aeryk Egan
The Secret Life of Girls *'99*
Shrunken Heads *'94*
Keeper of the City *'92*
Book of Love *'91*
Flatliners *'90*
Eddie Egan (1930-95)
Out of the Darkness *'85*
Badge 373 *'73*
The French Connection *'71*
Peter Egan (1946-)
2001: A Space Travesty *'00*
Bean *'97*
A Perfect Spy *'88*
A Woman of Substance *'84*
Lillie *'79*
Hennessy *'75*
Cold Comfort Farm *'71*
One Brief Summer *'70*
Richard Egan (1921-87)
Sweet Creek County War *'82*
Mission to Glory *'80*
The Amsterdam Kill *'78*
Esther and the King *'60*
Pollyanna *'60*
A Summer Place *'59*
The Hunters *'58*
Love Me Tender *'56*
Tension at Table Rock *'56*
Seven Cities of Gold *'55*
Underwater! *'55*
Demetrius and the Gladiators *'54*
Split Second *'53*
Blackbeard the Pirate *'52*
One Minute to Zero *'52*
Flame of Araby *'51*
Susan Egan
Man of the Century *'99*
Hercules *'97 (V)*
Will Egan
Ninja Academy *'90*
Glitch! *'88*
Julie Ege (1943-)
Craze *'74*
It's Not the Size That Counts *'74*
The Freakmaker *'73*
The Legend of the 7 Golden Vampires *'73*
Rentadick *'72*
Creatures the World Forgot *'70*
On Her Majesty's Secret Service *'69*
Samantha Eggar (1939-)
The Astronaut's Wife *'99*
Hercules *'97 (V)*
The Phantom *'96*
The Magic Voyage *'93 (V)*
Dark Horse *'92*
Round Numbers *'91*
Tales of the Unexpected *'91*
Ragin' Cajun *'90*
Hot Touch *'80s*
Curtains *'83*
Demonoid, Messenger of Death *'81*
Exterminator *'80*
Unknown Powers *'80*
The Brood *'79*
Why Shoot the Teacher *'79*
Battleforce *'78*
The Uncanny *'78*
Welcome to Blood City *'77*
The Seven-Per-Cent Solution *'76*
All the Kind Strangers *'74*
Man of Destiny *'73*
Dead Are Alive *'72*
Light at the Edge of the World *'71*
Molly Maguires *'70*
A Name for Evil *'70*
Doctor Dolittle *'67*
Walk, Don't Run *'66*
The Collector *'65*
Doctor in Distress *'63*
Nicole Eggert (1972-)
Submerged *'00*
Amanda and the Alien *'95*
The Demolitionist *'95*
Anything for Love *'93*
Blown Away *'93*
Just One of the Girls *'93*
The Double O Kid *'92*
The Haunting of Morella *'91*
Martha Eggerth
For Me and My Gal *'42*
Charm of La Boheme *'36*
Stan(ford) Egi
Paradise Road *'97*
Escape Clause *'96*
Golden Gate *'93*
Rising Sun *'93*
Come See the Paradise *'90*
Hiroshima: Out of the Ashes *'90*
Atom Egoyan (1960-)
The Stupids *'95*
Calendar *'93*
Jennifer Ehle (1969-)
Possession *'02*
Sunshine *'99*
Bedrooms and Hallways *'98*
Paradise Road *'97*
Wilde *'97*
Pride and Prejudice *'95*
Backbeat *'94*
Beth Ehlers
The Hunger *'83*
Mystery at Fire Island *'81*
Jerome Ehlers
Darlings of the Gods *'90*
Quigley Down Under *'90*
Lisa Eichhorn (1952-)
Boys and Girls *'00*
Goodbye, Lover *'99*
The Talented Mr. Ripley *'99*
Judas Kiss *'98*
Angel Blue *'97*
First Kid *'96*
A Modern Affair *'94*
King of the Hill *'93*
The Vanishing *'93*
Moon 44 *'90*
Grim Prairie Tales *'89*
Opposing Force *'87*
Blind Justice *'86*
Wildrose *'85*
Weather in the Streets *'84*
Cutter's Way *'81*
The Europeans *'79*
Yanks *'79*
Gard B. Eidsvold
Zero Degrees Kelvin *'95*
The Last Lieutenant *'94*
Christopher Eigeman
The Last Days of Disco *'98*
Mr. Jealousy *'98*
Kicking and Screaming *'95*
Barcelona *'94*
Metropolitan *'90*
David Eigenberg
The Mothman Prophecies *'02*
Daybreak *'93*
Jill Eikenberry (1946-)
My Very Best Friend *'96*

Parallel Lives '94
Chantilly Lace '93
An Inconvenient Woman '91
Cast the First Stone '89
Assault and Matrimony '87
Family Sins '87
L.A. Law '86
The Manhattan Project '86
Grace Quigley '84
Sessions '83
Arthur '81
Hide in Plain Sight '80
Butch and Sundance: The Early Days '79
Orphan Train '79
Rich Kids '79
Between the Lines '77
Rush It '77

Lisa Eilbacher (1957-)
Live Wire '92
Blind Man's Bluff '91
The Hunt for the Night Stalker '91
The Last Samurai '90
Never Say Die '90
Leviathan '89
Deadly Intent '88
Monte Carlo '86
Beverly Hills Cop '84
Ten to Midnight '83
An Officer and a Gentleman '82
On the Right Track '81
To Race the Wind '80
Run for the Roses '78
The Amazing Spider-Man '77

Sally Eilers (1908-78)
Coroner Creek '48
Strange Illusion '45
Strike Me Pink '36
Clearing the Range '31
Doughboys '30
Roaring Ranch '30
Trigger Tricks '30

Bob Einstein
The Extreme Adventures of Super Dave '98
Modern Romance '81

Aron Eisenberg (1969-)
Pterodactyl Woman from Beverly Hills '97
Playroom '90
The Horror Show '89

Hallie Kate Eisenberg (1992-)
Beautiful '00
The Miracle Worker '00
Bicentennial Man '99
The Insider '99
Paulie '98

Ned Eisenberg
Dash and Lilly '99
Path to Paradise '97
Last Man Standing '96
The Burning '82

Ike Eisenmann (1962-)
Return from Witch Mountain '78
Escape to Witch Mountain '75

Debra Eisenstadt
The Heidi Chronicles '95
Oleanna '94

Andre Eisermann
Brother of Sleep '95
Kaspar Hauser '93

Anthony Eisley (1925-)
Killer Commandos
Monster '78
Secrets '77
The Doll Squad '73
Dracula vs. Frankenstein '71
The Tormentors '71
The Witchmaker '69
Star! '68
Journey to the Center of Time '67
Lightning Bolt '67
Mummy & Curse of the Jackal '67
Navy vs. the Night Monsters '66
Frankie and Johnny '65
Naked Kiss '64
The Wasp Woman '59

David Eisner
Family Reunion '88
Happy Birthday to Me '81

Carmen Ejogo (1975-)
Boycott '02
What's the Worst That Could Happen? '01
Love's Labour's Lost '00
Sally Hemings: An American Scandal '00
The Avengers '98
Catherine Cookson's Colour Blind '98
I Want You '98
Metro '96

Anita Ekberg (1931-)
The Red Dwarf '99
Intervista '87
Gold of the Amazon Women '79
S*H*E '79
We All Loved Each Other So Much '77
Northeast of Seoul '72
How I Learned to Love Women '60s
The Cobra '68
Fangs of the Living Dead '68
Woman Times Seven '67
The Alphabet Murders '65
Call Me Bwana '63
Four for Texas '63
Boccaccio '70 '62
La Dolce Vita '60
The Mongols '60
Paris Holiday '57
Back from Eternity '56
Hollywood or Bust '56
War and Peace '56
Artists and Models '55
Blood Alley '55
Abbott and Costello Go to Mars '53

Britt Ekland (1942-)
The Children '90
Cold Heat '90
Scandal '89
Beverly Hills Vamp '88
Moon in Scorpio '86
Erotic Images '85
Fraternity Vacation '85
Marbella '85
The Monster Club '85
Ecstasy '84
Dead Wrong '83
Demon Rage '82
The Hostage Tower '80
The Great Wallendas '78
Sex on the Run '78
Slavers '77
High Velocity '76
King Solomon's Treasure '76
Royal Flash '75
The Wicker Man '75
The Man with the Golden Gun '74
The Ultimate Thrill '74
Asylum '72
What the Peeper Saw '72
Endless Night '71
Get Carter '71
The Night They Raided Minsky's '69
Stiletto '69
Bobo '67
After the Fox '66

Gosta Ekman (1890-1938)
Intermezzo '36
Swedenhielms '35
Faust '26

Gosta Ekman, Jr. (1939-)
The Inside Man '84
The Adventures of Picasso '80

Hasse (Hans) Ekman (1915-)
Devil's Wanton '49
Intermezzo '36

Nour (el-Sherif) el-Cherif
Destiny '97
An Egyptian Story '82

Jack Elam (1916-)
Bonanza: The Return '93
Uninvited '93
Shadow Force '92
Suburban Commando '91
Big Bad John '90
Dynamite and Gold '88
Hawken's Breed '87
The Aurora Encounter '85
Cannonball Run 2 '84
Lost '83
Sacred Ground '83
Cannonball Run '81
The Apple Dumpling Gang Rides Again '79
The Sacketts '79
The Villain '79
Norseman '78
Grayeagle '77
Creature from Black Lake '76
Pony Express Rider '76
The Red Pony '76
Huckleberry Finn '75
Hannie Caulder '72
Support Your Local Gunfighter '71
Rio Lobo '70
Over the Hill Gang '69
Support Your Local Sheriff '69
Firecreek '68
Never a Dull Moment '68
Once Upon a Time in the West '68
The Way West '67
The Rare Breed '66
Four for Texas '63
Pocketful of Miracles '61
The Girl in Lover's Lane '60
Pardners '56
Artists and Models '55
Kiss Me Deadly '55
The Man from Laramie '55
Cattle Queen of Montana '54
Ride Clear of Diablo '54
Vera Cruz '53
The Bushwackers '52
Kansas City Confidential '52
Rancho Notorious '52
The Ring '52
High Lonesome '50
Rawhide '50
She Shoulda Said No '49

Dana Elcar (1927-)
Inside Out '91
Toughlove '85
All of Me '84
Code of Honor '84
Blue Skies Again '83
Forbidden Love '82
Help Wanted: Male '82
Condorman '81
The Nude Bomb '80
Dying Room Only '73
Fireball Forward '72
A Gunfight '71
Adam at 6 a.m. '70
Soldier Blue '70
The Learning Tree '69
The Fool Killer '65

Ron Eldard (1965-)
Black Hawk Down '01
Mystery, Alaska '99
The Runner '99
Deep Impact '98
Delivered '98
When Trumpets Fade '98
Bastard out of Carolina '96
The Last Supper '96
Sleepers '96
Sex and the Other Man '95
Scent of a Woman '92
Drop Dead Fred '91
True Love '89

George Eldredge (1914-92)
Mom & Dad '47
Sonora Stagecoach '44
Sherlock Holmes and the Secret Weapon '42
Buzzy Rides the Range '40
Take Me Back to Oklahoma '40

Florence Eldridge (1901-88)
Inherit the Wind '60
Christopher Columbus '49
Mary of Scotland '36
Les Miserables '35

John Eldridge (1917-)
I Married a Monster from Outer Space '58
Square Dance Jubilee '51
Bad Men of the Border '45
The Black Cat '41
Dangerous '35

Carmen Electra (1972-)
Get Over It! '01
Perfume '01
Scary Movie '00
The Mating Habits of the Earthbound Human '99
The Chosen One: Legend of the Raven '98
American Vampire '97

Karra Elejalde
Tierra '95
Running Out of Time '94

Erika Eleniak (1969-)
Shakedown '02
The Opponent '01
Aftershock: Earthquake in New York '99
Final Voyage '99
Stealth Fighter '99
First Degree '98
Captive '97
Tales from the Crypt Presents Bordello of Blood '96
A Pyromaniac's Love Story '95
Chasers '94
Girl in the Cadillac '94
The Beverly Hillbillies '93
Under Siege '92
Broken Angel '88
E.T.: The Extra-Terrestrial '82

Sandor Eles
And Soon the Darkness '70
The Evil of Frankenstein '64

Bodhi (Pine) Elfman
Gone in 60 Seconds '00
Keeping the Faith '00
Sand '00
The Mod Squad '99
The Pirates of Silicon Valley '99
Enemy of the State '98

Jenna Elfman (1971-)
Town and Country '01
Keeping the Faith '00
EDtv '99
Can't Hardly Wait '98
Krippendorf's Tribe '98

Taina Elg (1930-)
Hercules in New York '70
The Bacchantes '63
Les Girls '57
Diane '55
The Prodigal '55

Alix Elias
Munchies '87
True Stories '86
Rock 'n' Roll High School '79
Citizens Band '77

Christine Elise (1965-)
Nowhere to Land '00
Escape from Mars '99
Boiling Point '93
Child's Play 2 '90

Kimberly Elise (1971-)
John Q '02
Bojangles '01
Bait '00
The Loretta Claiborne Story '00
Beloved '98
Set It Off '96

Shannon Elizabeth (1973-)
American Pie 2 '01
Jay and Silent Bob Strike Back '01
13 Ghosts '01
Tomcats '01
Scary Movie '00
American Pie '99
Dish Dogs '98

Hector Elizondo (1936-)
How High '01
The Princess Diaries '01
Tortilla Soup '01
Entropy '99
Runaway Bride '99
Safe House '99
The Other Sister '98
Dear God '96
Turbulence '96
Being Human '94
Beverly Hills Cop 3 '94
Exit to Eden '94
Getting Even with Dad '94
Perfect Alibi '94
Backstreet Justice '93
Chains of Gold '92
Samantha '92
Scott Turow's The Burden of Proof '92
There Goes the Neighborhood '92
Final Approach '91
Frankie and Johnny '91
Necessary Roughness '91
Forgotten Prisoners '90
Pretty Woman '90
Taking Care of Business '90
Diary of the Dead '80s
Leviathan '89
Courage '86
Nothing in Common '86
Out of the Darkness '85
The Flamingo Kid '84
Private Resort '84
Young Doctors in Love '82
The Fan '81
American Gigolo '79
Cuba '79
The Dain Curse '78
Report to the Commissioner '74
The Taking of Pelham One Two Three '74
Pocket Money '72
Born to Win '71
Valdez Is Coming '71

Duke Ellington (1899-1974)
Anatomy of a Murder '59
Cabin in the Sky '43
Murder at the Vanities '34
Check & Double Check '30

Biff (Elliott) Elliot (1923-)
The Dark '79
The Hard Ride '71
Pork Chop Hill '59

Jane Elliot
Zertigo Diamond Caper '82
Change of Habit '69

Ramblin' Jack Elliot
Roadie '80
Honkytonk Nights '70s

Shawn Elliot
Teenage Caveman '01
Caught '96
Hurricane Streets '96

Alison Elliott (1970-)
The Song of the Lark '01
The Miracle Worker '00
The Eternal '99
The External '99
The Wings of the Dove '97
The Buccaneers '95
Indictment: The McMartin Trial '95
The Spitfire Grill '95
The Underneath '95
Wyatt Earp '94
Home Before Midnight '84

Bob Elliott (1923-)
Cabin Boy '94
Quick Change '90
Vengeance '80

Chris Elliott (1960-)
Osmosis Jones '01
Scary Movie 2 '01
Nutty Professor 2: The Klumps '00
Snow Day '00
There's Something about Mary '98
Kingpin '96
Cabin Boy '94
CB4: The Movie '93
Groundhog Day '93
The Abyss '89
New York Stories '89

David Elliott
Ali '01
Pearl '78
The Possession of Joel Delaney '72

David James Elliott (1960-)
Clockwatchers '97
Holiday Affair '96
JAG '95

Denholm Elliott (1922-92)
Noises Off '92
Scorchers '92
Codename Kyril '91
One Against the Wind '91
Toy Soldiers '91
A Murder of Quality '90
A Doll's House '89
Indiana Jones and the Last Crusade '89
The Bourne Identity '88
Deep Cover '88
Hanna's War '88
September '88
Stealing Heaven '88
Maurice '87
Over Indulgence '87
Hotel du Lac '86
A Room with a View '86
Bleak House '85
Defense of the Realm '85
Transmutations '85
A Private Function '84
The Razor's Edge '84
The Hound of the Baskervilles '83
Trading Places '83
The Wicked Lady '83
Brimstone & Treacle '82
The Missionary '82
The Two Faces of Evil '82
Raiders of the Lost Ark '81
Rude Awakening '81
Cuba '79
Saint Jack '79
Zulu Dawn '79
The Boys from Brazil '78
Watership Down '78 (V)
A Bridge Too Far '77
The Hound of the Baskervilles '77
Robin and Marian '76
To the Devil, a Daughter '76
Voyage of the Damned '76
Russian Roulette '75
The Apprenticeship of Duddy Kravitz '74
It's Not the Size That Counts '74
Vault of Horror '73
The House that Dripped Blood '71
Quest for Love '71
Too Late the Hero '70
The Night They Raided Minsky's '69
Dr. Jekyll and Mr. Hyde '68
Strange Case of Dr. Jekyll & Mr. Hyde '68
Alfie '66
Holy Terror '65
King Rat '65
The Leather Boys '63
The Cruel Sea '53

John Elliott (1876-1956)
The Wizard of Gore '70
Death Rides the Range '40
The Phantom of the Range '38
Riding On '37

A Face in the Fog *'36*
Rogue's Tavern *'36*
Big Calibre *'35*
Bulldog Courage *'35*
Danger Trails *'35*
Toll of the Desert *'35*
The Gallant Fool *'33*
Mother and Son *'31*

Peter Elliott
Missing Link *'88*
Curse of the Demon *'57*

Robert Elliott (1879-1951)
The Return of Casey Jones *'34*
White Eagle *'32*
The Maltese Falcon *'31*
Murder at Midnight *'31*

Ross Elliott (1917-99)
Paper Man *'71*
The Indestructible Man *'56*
Tarantula *'55*
Ma and Pa Kettle at Home *'54*
Hot Lead *'51*

Sam Elliott (1944-)
We Were Soldiers *'02*
The Contender *'00*
You Know My Name *'99*
The Hi-Lo Country *'98*
The Big Lebowski *'97*
Dogwatch *'97*
Rough Riders *'97*
The Final Cut *'96*
Blue River *'95*
Buffalo Girls *'95*
Hole in the Sky *'95*
Woman Undone *'95*
The Desperate Trail *'94*
Gettysburg *'93*
Tombstone *'93*
Conagher *'91*
Rush *'91*
Sibling Rivalry *'90*
Prancer *'89*
Road House *'89*
Shakedown *'88*
Fatal Beauty *'87*
The Quick and the Dead *'87*
The Blue Lightning *'86*
Mask *'85*
The Shadow Riders *'82*
Murder in Texas *'81*
The Legacy *'79*
The Sacketts *'79*
Wild Times *'79*
Lifeguard *'76*
I Will Fight No More Forever *'75*
Frogs *'72*
Molly & Lawless John *'72*
Butch Cassidy and the Sundance Kid *'69*

Scott Elliott
The French Line *'54*
King of the Forest Rangers *'46*

Shawn Elliott
Double Take *'01*
Bloodsucking Pharoahs of Pittsburgh *'90*
Impulse *'90*
Crossover Dreams *'85*
Short Eyes *'79*

Stephen Elliott (1945-)
Taking Care of Business *'90*
Arthur 2: On the Rocks *'88*
Assassination *'87*
Perry Mason: The Case of the Lost Love *'87*
Beverly Hills Cop *'84*
Days of Hell *'84*
Roadhouse 66 *'84*
Beauty and the Beast *'83*
Arthur *'81*
Cutter's Way *'81*
Jacqueline Bouvier Kennedy *'81*
Can You Hear the Laughter? The Story of Freddie Prinze *'79*
Mrs. R's Daughter *'79*
Betrayal *'78*
Sergeant Matlovich vs. the U.S. Air Force *'78*
Report to the Commissioner *'74*
The Hospital *'71*

Wild Bill Elliott (1904-65)
The Showdown *'50*
Bordertown Gunfighters *'43*
Calling Wild Bill Elliott *'43*
Death Valley Manhunt *'43*
Man from Thunder River *'43*

William Elliott
Coffy *'73*
Hellfire *'48*

Aunjanue Ellis
Undercover Brother *'02*
The Caveman's Valentine *'01*
The Opponent *'01*
Disappearing Acts *'00*
Men of Honor *'00*
Girls Town *'95*

Chris Ellis
The Watcher *'00*
October Sky *'99*
Home Fries *'98*

Desmond Walter Ellis
The Great St. Trinian's Train Robbery *'66*
The Hellfire Club *'61*

Edward Ellis (1870-1952)
Wheel of Fortune *'41*
Fury *'36*
The Texas Rangers *'36*
The Return of Peter Grimm *'35*
The Thin Man *'34*
I Am a Fugitive from a Chain Gang *'32*

Frank Ellis (1897-1969)
Wildfire *'45*
The Big Stampede *'32*
Whistlin' Dan *'32*

James Ellis (1931-)
Resurrection Man *'97*
Spellbreaker: Secret of the Leprechauns *'96*
Leapin' Leprechauns *'95*
Priest *'94*
No Surrender *'86*

Patricia Ellis (1916-70)
Back Door to Heaven *'39*
Block-heads *'38*
Postal Inspector *'36*
The Case of the Lucky Legs *'35*
Three on a Match *'32*

Robert Ellis (1892-1974)
Captured in Chinatown *'35*
American Madness *'32*
Broadway to Cheyenne *'32*
Come on Danger! *'32*
Daring Danger *'32*
Fighting Fool *'32*
White Eagle *'32*
The Fighting Sheriff *'31*

Robin Ellis
A Dark Adapted Eye *'93*
The Curse of King Tut's Tomb *'80*
The Europeans *'79*
Poldark *'75*
Poldark 2 *'75*
Elizabeth R *'72*

Tracey Ellis
The Crow 2: City of Angels *'96*
The NeverEnding Story 3: Escape from Fantasia *'94*
This Boy's Life *'93*
The Last of the Mohicans *'92*

James Ellison (1910-93)
Kentucky Jubilee *'51*
Blazing Guns *'50*
Guns of Justice *'50*
Last Bullet *'50*
Marshal of Heldorado *'50*
Outlaw Fury *'50*
Rangeland Empire *'50*
Sudden Death *'50*
Last of the Wild Horses *'49*
I Walked with a Zombie *'43*
The Undying Monster *'42*
You Can't Fool Your Wife *'40*
Fifth Avenue Girl *'39*
Next Time I Marry *'38*
Vivacious Lady *'38*
23 1/2 Hours Leave *'37*
Hopalong Cassidy *'35*

Rebekah Elmaloglou (1974-)
Back of Beyond *'95*
The Sum of Us *'94*
In Too Deep *'90*

Nicoletta Elmi
Demons *'86*
Deep Red: Hatchet Murders *'75*
Andy Warhol's Frankenstein *'74*

Michael Elphick (1946-)
Buddy's Song *'91*
Let Him Have It *'91*
Little Dorrit, Film 1: Nobody's Fault *'88*
Little Dorrit, Film 2: Little Dorrit's Story *'88*
Withnail and I *'87*
Arthur's Hallowed Ground *'84*
The Element of Crime *'84*
Ordeal by Innocence *'84*
The Elephant Man *'80*
Cry of the Banshee *'70*

Isobel Elsom (1893-1981)
Love Is a Many-Splendored Thing *'55*
Escape Me Never *'47*
The Ghost and Mrs. Muir *'47*
Love from a Stranger *'47*
Monsieur Verdoux *'47*
Casanova Brown *'44*
The White Cliffs of Dover *'44*

Cary Elwes (1962-)
The Cat's Meow *'01*
Uprising *'01*
Race Against Time *'00*
Shadow of the Vampire *'00*
Wish You Were Dead *'00*
The Cradle Will Rock *'99*
From the Earth to the Moon *'98*
The Pentagon Wars *'98*
Quest for Camelot *'98 (V)*
The Informant *'97*
Kiss the Girls *'97*
Liar Liar *'96*
Twister *'96*
Rudyard Kipling's The Jungle Book *'94*
The Crush *'93*
Robin Hood: Men in Tights *'93*
Bram Stoker's Dracula *'92*
Hot Shots! *'91*
Days of Thunder *'90*
Leather Jackets *'90*
Glory *'89*
The Princess Bride *'87*
The Bride *'85*
Lady Jane *'85*
Another Country *'84*
Oxford Blues *'84*

Ron Ely (1938-)
Slavers *'77*
Doc Savage *'75*
Once Before I Die *'65*

Sallee Elyse
Demented *'80*
Home Sweet Home *'80*

Ethan (Randall) Embry (1978-)
Can't Hardly Wait *'98*
Dancer, Texas—Pop. 81 *'98*
Disturbing Behavior *'98*
Montana *'97*
That Thing You Do! *'96*
Vegas Vacation *'96*
White Squall *'96*
Empire Records *'95*
Evolver *'94*
Season of Change *'94*
A Far Off Place *'93*
All I Want for Christmas *'91*
Dutch *'91*

Faye Emerson (1917-83)
The Mask of Dimitrios *'44*
Uncertain Glory *'44*
Air Force *'43*
Destination Tokyo *'43*

Hope Emerson (1891-1960)
All Mine to Give *'56*
Westward the Women *'51*
Adam's Rib *'50*

Karrie Emerson
Chopping Mall *'86*
Evils of the Night *'85*

Roy Emerton (1892-1944)
Henry V *'44*
Nine Days a Queen *'36*
Lorna Doone *'34*

Dick Emery
Yellow Submarine *'68 (V)*
The Case of the Mukkinese Battle Horn *'56*

Gilbert Emery (1875-1945)
Return of the Vampire *'43*
Wife Versus Secretary *'36*
Goin' to Town *'35*
Now and Forever *'34*
The Lady Refuses *'31*
The Royal Bed *'31*

John Emery (1905-64)
Kronos *'57*
Forever Darling *'56*
The Girl Can't Help It *'56*
A Lawless Street *'55*
Rocketship X-M *'50*
The Spanish Main *'45*
Mademoiselle Fifi *'44*
Ship Ahoy *'42*
Here Comes Mr. Jordan *'41*

Katherine Emery
The Private Affairs of Bel Ami *'47*
Isle of the Dead *'45*

David Emge
Hellmaster *'92*
Dawn of the Dead *'78*

Robert Emhardt (1914-94)
Die Sister, Die! *'74*
Change of Habit *'69*
Shame *'61*
Underworld, U.S.A. *'60*

Michael Emil
Adventures in Spying *'92*
In the Spirit *'90*
New Year's Day *'89*
Someone to Love *'87*
Always *'85*
Insignificance *'85*
Can She Bake a Cherry Pie? *'83*
Sitting Ducks *'80*
Tracks *'76*

Daniel Emilfork (1924-)
The City of Lost Children *'95*
The Devil's Nightmare *'71*
Lady L *'65*

Alphonsia Emmanuel
Peter's Friends *'92*
Under Suspicion *'92*

Takis Emmanuel
Kostas *'79*
Caddie *'76*

Noah Emmerich
Windtalkers *'02*
Frequency *'00*
Love & Sex *'00*
Crazy in Alabama *'99*
Life *'99*
Monument Ave. *'98*
The Truman Show *'98*
Tumbleweeds *'98*
Cop Land *'97*
Beautiful Girls *'96*

Michael Emmet
Attack of the Giant Leeches *'59*
Night of the Blood Beast *'58*

Fern Emmett (1896-1946)
Dead Men Walk *'43*
Assassin of Youth *'35*
The Forty-Niners *'32*

Cliff Emmich
Jackson County Jail *'76*
Invasion of the Bee Girls *'73*

Akira (Tsukamoto) Emoto (1948-)
Dr. Akagi *'98*
The Eel *'96*
Shall We Dance? *'96*

Lena Endre (1955-)
Jerusalem *'96*
Sunday's Children *'94*
The Best Intentions *'92*
The Visitors *'89*

Georgia Engel (1948-)
Signs of Life *'89*
The Day the Women Got Even *'80*
The Outside Man *'73*

Tina Engel
The Promise *'94*
The Boat Is Full *'81*
The Second Awakening of Christa Klages *'78*

Constanze Engelbrecht (1955-2000)
The Count of Monte Cristo *'99*
Fiorile *'93*

Wera Engels
Hong Kong Nights *'35*
Fugitive Road *'34*

Audie England (1971-)
Free Enterprise *'98*
Legion *'98*
A Place Called Truth *'98*
Shame, Shame, Shame *'98*
Red Shoe Diaries 8: Night of Abandon *'97*
Delta of Venus *'95*
Miami Hustle *'95*
Venus Rising *'95*

Bradford English
Halloween 6: The Curse of Michael Myers *'95*
Capone *'89*

Marla English
Flesh and the Spur *'57*
Voodoo Woman *'57*

Robert Englund (1947-)
Python *'00*
Wish You Were Dead *'00*
The Prince and the Surfer *'99*
Dee Snider's Strangeland *'98*
Meet the Deedles *'98*
Perfect Target *'98*
Urban Legend *'98*
Wishmaster *'97*
Killer Tongue *'96*
The Paper Brigade *'96*
The Mangler *'94*
Wes Craven's New Nightmare *'94*
Dance Macabre *'91*
Freddy's Dead: The Final Nightmare *'91*
The Adventures of Ford Fairlane *'90*
A Nightmare on Elm Street 5: Dream Child *'89*
The Phantom of the Opera *'89*
A Nightmare on Elm Street 4: Dream Master *'88*
A Nightmare on Elm Street 3: Dream Warriors *'87*
A Nightmare on Elm Street 2: Freddy's Revenge *'85*
A Nightmare on Elm Street *'84*
V: The Final Battle *'84*
V *'83*
Mysterious Two *'82*
Dead and Buried *'81*
Galaxy of Terror *'81*
Eaten Alive *'76*
A Star Is Born *'76*
Stay Hungry *'76*
Buster and Billie *'74*
Slashed Dreams *'74*

John Enos
Brigham City *'01*
Dead Sexy *'01*
Red Shoe Diaries: Luscious Lola *'00*
Stealth Fighter *'99*
Miami Hustle *'95*
Ravenhawk *'95*
Red Shoe Diaries 6: How I Met My Husband *'95*
Bullet *'94*
Till the End of the Night *'94*

Rene Enriquez (1933-90)
Bulletproof *'88*
The Evil That Men Do *'84*
Ants *'77*

Michael Ensign
Born Yesterday *'93*
Life Stinks *'91*
House *'86*

John Entwhistle
The Kids Are Alright *'79*
Tommy *'75*

Brenda Epperson
Storybook *'95*
Amore! *'93*

Dieter Eppler (1927-)
The Sprinter *'84*
The Torture Chamber of Dr. Sadism *'69*
The Slaughter of the Vampires *'62*

Mike Epps
All About the Benjamins *'02*
Dr. Dolittle 2 *'01 (V)*
How High *'01*
Bait *'00*
Next Friday *'00*

Omar Epps (1973-)
Big Trouble *'02*
Perfume *'01*
Brother *'00*
Dracula 2000 *'00*
Love and Basketball *'00*
In Too Deep *'99*
The Mod Squad *'99*
The Wood *'99*
Breakfast of Champions *'98*
First Time Felon *'97*
Scream 2 *'97*
Deadly Voyage *'96*
Higher Learning *'94*
Major League 2 *'94*
Daybreak *'93*
The Program *'93*
Juice *'92*

Kathryn Erbe (1966-)
The Runaway *'00*
Stir of Echoes *'99*
Naked City: Justice with a Bullet *'98*
Dream with the Fishes *'97*
The Addiction *'95*
Breathing Lessons *'94*
D2: The Mighty Ducks *'94*
Kiss of Death *'94*
Rich in Love *'93*
What about Bob? *'91*

Richard Erdman (1925-)
The Learning Curve *'01*
Tomboy *'85*
Namu, the Killer Whale *'66*
Stalag 17 *'53*
Cry Danger *'51*
The Stooge *'51*
Objective, Burma! *'45*

Ethan Erickson
Fear Runs Silent *'99*
Jawbreaker *'98*

Leif Erickson (1911-86)
D.C. Cab *'84*
Penitentiary 2 *'82*
Rocky 3 *'82*

Twilight's Last Gleaming '77
Winterhawk '76
Abduction '75
Force Five '75
The Carpetbaggers '64
Roustabout '64
Strait-Jacket '64
A Gathering of Eagles '63
Istanbul '57
Fastest Gun Alive '56
Tea and Sympathy '56
On the Waterfront '54
Invaders from Mars '53
Trouble along the Way '53
Abbott and Costello Meet Captain Kidd '52
Never Wave at a WAC '52
Hill Number One '51
The Showdown '50
Three Secrets '50
Joan of Arc '48
The Snake Pit '48
Blonde Savage '47
Arabian Nights '42
Night Monster '42
Pardon My Sarong '42
One Third of a Nation '39
The Big Broadcast of 1938 '38
Conquest '37
Waikiki Wedding '37
Desert Gold '36

Devon Ericson
Can You Hear the Laughter? The Story of Freddie Prinze '79
The Runaway Barge '75

John Ericson (1927-)
Primary Target '89
House of the Dead '80
Zone of the Dead '78
Hustler Squad '76
The Bounty Man '72
The Bamboo Saucer '68
7 Faces of Dr. Lao '63
Green Fire '55
Bad Day at Black Rock '54
Rhapsody '54
The Student Prince '54

Kaj-Erik Eriksen
Captains Courageous '95
Short Time '90

R. Lee Ermey (1944-)
The Salton Sea '02
Saving Silverman '01
Chaos Factor '00
Skipped Parts '00
Avalanche '99
Life '99
Toy Story 2 '99 (V)
You Know My Name '99
Apartment Complex '98
Gunshy '98
The Sender '98
Dead Men Can't Dance '97
Rough Riders '97
Switchback '97
Weapons of Mass Distraction '97
The Frighteners '96
Prefontaine '96
Soul of the Game '96
Chain of Command '95
Dead Man Walking '95
The Fighter '95
Leaving Las Vegas '95
Murder in the First '95
Seven '95
Toy Story '95 (V)
Under the Hula Moon '95
French Silk '94
Love Is a Gun '94
On Deadly Ground '94
Body Snatchers '93
Hexed '93
Sommersby '93
The Terror Within 2 '91
Endless Descent '90
I'm Dangerous Tonight '90
Kid '90
The Take '90
Demonstone '89
Fletch Lives '89
The Siege of Firebase Gloria '89
Mississippi Burning '88
Full Metal Jacket '87
Apocalypse Now '79
The Boys in Company C '77

Krista Errickson
Martial Outlaw '93
Killer Image '92
Mortal Passions '90
First Time '82
Jekyll & Hyde...Together Again '82

Melissa Errico
Life or Something Like It '02
Frequency '00

Leon Errol (1881-1951)
Joe's Bed-Stuy Barbershop: We Cut Heads '83
The Noose Hangs High '48
Higher and Higher '44
The Invisible Man's Revenge '44
Mexican Spitfire at Sea '42
Hurry, Charlie, Hurry '41
Never Give a Sucker an Even Break '41
Pop Always Pays '40
Make a Wish '37
The Great Ziegfeld '36
We're Not Dressing '34

Patrick Ersgard
Backlash '99
Living in Peril '97
Dreaming of Rita '94
Mandroid '93
The Visitors '89

Eileen Erskine
This Happy Breed '47
Great Expectations '46

Marilyn Erskine
Above and Beyond '53
Westward the Women '51

Victor Ertmanis
Holiday Affair '96
Brainscan '94
Paris, France '94

Bill Erwin (1914-)
Chairman of the Board '97
Fallen Angels 1 '93
Hard Knox '83
Huckleberry Finn '75

Stuart Erwin (1902-67)
The Misadventures of Merlin Jones '63
Heading for Heaven '47
Killer Dill '47
The Great Mike '44
Blondie for Victory '42
The Bride Came C.O.D. '41
Back Door to Heaven '39
It Could Happen to You '39
Mr. Boggs Steps Out '38
Small Town Boy '37
Pigskin Parade '36
Ceiling Zero '35
Bachelor Bait '34
Chained '34
Palooka '34
Viva Villa! '34
Going Hollywood '33
Hold Your Man '33

Jaime Escobedo
The Bad News Bears in Breaking Training '77
The Bad News Bears '76

Carl Esmond (1908-)
The World in His Arms '52
Without Love '45
Ministry of Fear '44
The Story of Dr. Wassell '44
The Navy Comes Through '42
Panama Hattie '42
Dawn Patrol '38

Jill Esmond (1908-90)
A Man Called Peter '55
Casanova Brown '44
The White Cliffs of Dover '44
Journey for Margaret '42
F.P. 1 '33
Skin Game '31
State's Attorney '31

Bella Esperance
Lady Dragon 2 '93
Lady Dragon '92

Giancarlo Esposito (1958-)
Ali '01
Monkeybone '01
Pinero '01
Homicide: The Movie '00
Big City Blues '99
Naked City: Justice with a Bullet '98
Phoenix '98
Twilight '98
The Keeper '96
Nothing to Lose '96
Blue in the Face '95
Reckless '95
Smoke '95
The Usual Suspects '95
Fresh '94
Amos and Andrew '93
Bob Roberts '92
Malcolm X '92
Night on Earth '91
King of New York '90
Mo' Better Blues '90
Do the Right Thing '89
School Daze '88
Sweet Lorraine '87
Trading Places '83

Gianni Esposito
Paris Belongs to Us '60
Les Miserables '57

Jennifer Esposito (1973-)
Master of Disguise '02
Backflash '01
Don't Say a Word '01
Dracula 2000 '00
Just One Time '00
The Proposal '00
The Bachelor '99
Summer of Sam '99
I Still Know What You Did Last Summer '98

Paul Esser (1913-88)
Daughters of Darkness '71
The Kaiser's Lackey '51
The Merry Wives of Windsor '50

David Essex (1947-)
Journey of Honor '91
Silver Dream Racer '83
That'll Be the Day '73
Octaman '71

Christine Estabrook
Presumed Innocent '90
Second Sight '89
Almost You '85

Gloria Estefan
For Love or Country: The Arturo Sandoval Story '00
Music of the Heart '99

Robert Estes (1963-)
Aces: Iron Eagle 3 '92
Phantom of the Mall: Eric's Revenge '89
Trapper County War '89

Will Estes
Mimic 2 '01
My Husband's Double Life '01
Terror Tract '00
U-571 '00
Blue Ridge Fall '99
The Road Home '95

Emilio Estevez (1962-)
Rated X '00
Sand '00
Late Last Night '99
D3: The Mighty Ducks '96
Mission: Impossible '96
The War at Home '96
D2: The Mighty Ducks '94
Another Stakeout '93
Judgment Night '93
National Lampoon's Loaded Weapon 1 '93
Freejack '92
The Mighty Ducks '92
Men at Work '90
Young Guns 2 '90
Nightbreaker '89
Never on Tuesday '88
Young Guns '88
Stakeout '87
Wisdom '87
Maximum Overdrive '86
The Breakfast Club '85
St. Elmo's Fire '85
That Was Then...This Is Now '85
Nightmares '83
The Outsiders '83
Repo Man '83
In the Custody of Strangers '82
Tex '82

Ines Estevez
Life According to Muriel '97
Killing Grandpa '91

Joe Estevez
Fatal Justice '90s
The Catcher '98
No Code of Conduct '98
Lethal Seduction '97
Breakaway '95
Dillinger and Capone '95
The Mosaic Project '95
Werewolf '95
The Deadly Secret '94
Money to Burn '94
Beach Babes from Beyond Infinity '93
Dark Universe '93
Expert Weapon '93
Eye of the Stranger '93
In a Moment of Passion '93
Armed for Action '92
L.A. Goddess '92
Murder-in-Law '92
Dark Rider '91
Lockdown '90
Soultaker '90
Gator King '70

Ramon Estevez
Blood on the Badge '92
Cadence '89

Renee Estevez
Storm Tracker '99
Good Girls Don't '95
Endangered '94
Single White Female '92
Forbidden Sun '89
Heathers '89
Marked for Murder '89
Bulldance '88
Intruder '88
Sleepaway Camp 2: Unhappy Campers '88

Erik Estrada (1949-)
National Lampoon's Van Wilder '02
Panic in the Skies '96
The Final Goal '94
Gang Justice '94
National Lampoon's Loaded Weapon 1 '93
The Divine Enforcer '91
Do or Die '91
Caged Fury '90
Guns '90
The Last Riders '90
Night of the Wilding '90
A Show of Force '90
Spirits '90
Alien Seed '89
Andy and the Airwave Rangers '89
Twisted Justice '89
The Dirty Dozen: The Fatal Mission '88
Hour of the Assassin '86
Lightblast '85
Honeyboy '82
The Line '80
The Cross & the Switchblade '72
Jailbreakin' '72
The New Centurions '72

Pat Estrin
Dennis the Menace: Dinosaur Hunter '93
Act of Vengeance '74
America First '70

Pierre Etaix
Max, Mon Amour '86
Pickpocket '59

Treva Etienne
Black Hawk Down '01
Eyes Wide Shut '99

Ruth Etting
Hips, Hips, Hooray '34
Roman Scandals '33

Cynthia Ettinger
Frailty '02
Down, Out and Dangerous '95

Shari Eubank
Chesty Anderson USN '76
Supervixens '75

Bob Eubanks
Roger & Me '89
Johnny Dangerously '84

Corey Michael Eubanks
Forced to Kill '93
Payback '90

Wesley Eure
C.H.O.M.P.S. '79
Jennifer '78
The Toolbox Murders '78

Art Evans
Metro '96
Tales from the Hood '95
CB4: The Movie '93
The Finishing Touch '92
Trespass '92
Die Hard 2: Die Harder '90
The Mighty Quinn '89
Mom '89
School Daze '88
White of the Eye '88
Jo Jo Dancer, Your Life Is Calling '86
Native Son '86
Fright Night '85
A Soldier's Story '84
The In-Laws '79
King '78

Clifford Evans (1912-85)
One Brief Summer '70
Kiss of the Vampire '62
The Curse of the Werewolf '61
The Gilded Cage '54
I'll Get You '53
While I Live '47
The Foreman Went to France '42
The Courageous Mr. Penn '41
Love on the Dole '41
The Mutiny of the Elsinore '39

Dale Evans (1912-2001)
Bells of Coronado '50
Trigger, Jr. '50
Twilight in the Sierras '50
Down Dakota Way '49
The Golden Stallion '49
Susanna Pass '49
Apache Rose '47
Bells of San Angelo '47
Home in Oklahoma '47
Lights of Old Santa Fe '47
Helldorado '46
My Pal Trigger '46
Rainbow over Texas '46
Roll on Texas Moon '46
Song of Arizona '46
Under Nevada Skies '46
Along the Navaho Trail '45
Bells of Rosarita '45
Don't Fence Me In '45
Sunset in El Dorado '45
Utah '45
Cowboy & the Senorita '44
San Fernando Valley '44
Song of Nevada '44
The Yellow Rose of Texas '44

Douglas Evans (1904-68)
Actors and Sin '52
Sky High '51
North of the Great Divide '50
The Golden Stallion '49
The Green Hornet '39

Edith Evans (1888-1976)
A Doll's House '89
Nasty Habits '77
The Slipper and the Rose '76
Craze '74
David Copperfield '70
Scrooge '70
Crooks & Coronets '69
The Madwoman of Chaillot '69
The Chalk Garden '64
Tom Jones '63
The Nun's Story '59
Look Back in Anger '58
The Importance of Being Earnest '52
The Last Days of Dolwyn '49
The Queen of Spades '49

Evans Evans (1936-)
Dead Bang '89
The Story of a Love Story '73
Bonnie & Clyde '67

Gene Evans (1922-98)
The Shadow Riders '82
The Concrete Cowboys '79
Devil Times Five '74
Gentle Savage '73
Walking Tall '73
The Bounty Man '72
Apache Uprising '66
Nevada Smith '66
Shock Corridor '63
Operation Petticoat '59
The Sad Sack '57
Crashout '55
Cattle Queen of Montana '54
Donovan's Brain '53
Mutiny '52
The Steel Helmet '51
It Happens Every Spring '49

Joan Evans (1934-)
No Name on the Bullet '59
Skirts Ahoy! '52
Our Very Own '50

John Evans (1934-)
Escape Clause '96
Long Road Home '91
I've Heard the Mermaids Singing '87

Josh Evans (1971-)
The Doors '91
Ricochet '91
Born on the Fourth of July '89

Josh Ryan Evans
Dr. Seuss' How the Grinch Stole Christmas '00
P.T. Barnum '99

Lee Evans (1965-)
Dinotopia '02 (V)
The Ladies Man '00
There's Something about Mary '98
The Fifth Element '97
Mouse Hunt '97
Funny Bones '94

Linda Evans (1942-)
The Stepsister '97
The Gambler Returns: The Luck of the Draw '93
Kenny Rogers as the Gambler, Part 2: The Adventure Continues '83
Tom Horn '80
Avalanche Express '79
Standing Tall '78
Hunter '77
Mitchell '75
The Klansman '74
Confessions of Tom Harris '72
Beach Blanket Bingo '65
Those Calloways '65

Madge Evans (1909-81)
Sinners in Paradise '38
David Copperfield '35
Transatlantic Tunnel '35
Stand Up and Cheer '34
Dinner at Eight '33
Hallelujah, I'm a Bum '33
Three Broadway Girls '32

Maurice Evans (1901-89)
The Jerk '79

Terror in the Wax Museum '73
Beneath the Planet of the Apes '70
Invasion of the Body Stealers '69
Planet of the Apes '68
Rosemary's Baby '68
The War Lord '65
The Tempest '63
Androcles and the Lion '52
Scrooge '35
Wedding Rehearsal '32

Mike Evans
The House on Skull Mountain '74
The Voyage of the Yes '72

Monica Evans
Robin Hood '73 (V)
The Odd Couple '68

Muriel Evans (1910-2000)
The House of Secrets '37
King of the Pecos '36
Law for Tombstone '35
The New Frontier '35
The Throwback '35
Manhattan Melodrama '34
The Prizefighter and the Lady '33

Rex Evans
The Matchmaker '58
The Wrong Road '37

Robert Evans (1930-)
An Alan Smithee Film: Burn, Hollywood, Burn '97
The Best of Everything '59
Man of a Thousand Faces '57

Robin Evans
Rage of Honor '87
One Dark Night '82

Terry Evans
Mongrel '83
Cody '67

Troy Evans
Alien Fury: Countdown to Invasion '00
I'll Remember April '99
The Frighteners '96
Bodily Harm '95
Father and Scout '94
My Summer Story '94
Ace Ventura: Pet Detective '93
Article 99 '92
Kuffs '92
The Lawnmower Man '92

Edith Evanson (1900-80)
The Day the Earth Stood Still '51
The Magnificent Yankee '50
Forever Amber '47
The Jade Mask '45

Trevor Eve
David Copperfield '99
Heat of the Sun '99
Appetite '98
Dracula '79

Judith Evelyn (1913-67)
The Tingler '59
The Egyptian '54
Rear Window '54

Kimberly Evenson (1932-)
Kandyland '87
The Big Bet '85
Porky's Revenge '85

Barbara Everest (1890-1968)
Tony Draws a Horse '51
Madeleine '50
The Valley of Decision '45
Gaslight '44
Jane Eyre '44
Phantom Fiend '35

Chad Everett (1936-)
Mulholland Drive '01
Psycho '98
When Time Expires '97
Official Denial '93
The Rousters '90
Heroes Stand Alone '89
Jigsaw Murders '89
Fever Pitch '85
Airplane 2: The Sequel '82
Intruder Within '81
Centennial '78
The Impossible Years '68
Johnny Tiger '66
The Singing Nun '66
Rome Adventure '62

Francine Everett (1920-99)
Dirty Gertie from Harlem U.S.A. '46
Tall, Tan and Terrific '46

Rupert Everett (1959-)
The Importance of Being Earnest '02
The Next Best Thing '00
An Ideal Husband '99
Inspector Gadget '99
William Shakespeare's A Midsummer Night's Dream '99
Shakespeare in Love '98
B. Monkey '97
My Best Friend's Wedding '97
Cemetery Man '95
Dunston Checks In '95
The Madness of King George '94
Ready to Wear '94
Inside Monkey Zetterland '93
The Comfort of Strangers '91
Hearts of Fire '87
The Right Hand Man '87
Dance with a Stranger '85
Another Country '84
The Far Pavilions '84

Todd Everett
Blood on the Badge '92
The Capture of Grizzly Adams '82

Tom Everett
Air Force One '97
My Fellow Americans '96
Best of the Best '89
Leatherface: The Texas Chainsaw Massacre 3 '89
Prison '88
Friday the 13th, Part 4: The Final Chapter '84

Nancy Everhard (1959-)
The China Lake Murders '90
This Gun for Hire '90
Deepstar Six '89
Demonstone '89
Double Revenge '89
The Trial of the Incredible Hulk '89

Angie Everhart (1969-)
The Stray '00
The Substitute 4: Failure is Not an Option '00
D.R.E.A.M. Team '99
Bitter Sweet '98
Executive Target '97
Another 9 1/2 Weeks '96
Tales from the Crypt Presents Bordello of Blood '96
Trigger Happy '96
Jade '95

Rex Everhart (1920-2000)
Beauty and the Beast '91 (V)
Family Business '89

Jason Evers (1922-)
Basket Case 2 '90
Barracuda '78
Claws '77
Fer-De-Lance '74
Escape from the Planet of the Apes '71
The Green Berets '68

Cory Everson
Felony '95
Double Impact '91

Greg Evigan (1953-)
One of Her Own '97
Spectre '96
TekWar '94
Lies Before Kisses '92
Deepstar Six '89
Private Road: No Trespassing '87
Stripped to Kill '87

Pat Evison (1924-)
What the Moon Saw '90
Starstruck '82
Tim '79

John Ewart (1928-94)
Which Way Home '90
The Quest '86
Prince and the Great Race '83
Blue Fire Lady '78
Newsfront '78
Island Trader '71

Dwight Ewell
Intern '00
Man of the Century '99
Chasing Amy '97
Flirt '95

Tom Ewell (1909-94)
Easy Money '83
They Only Kill Their Masters '72
State Fair '62
The Girl Can't Help It '56
The Seven Year Itch '55
Lost in Alaska '52
Adam's Rib '50
A Life of Her Own '50
Mr. Music '50

Barbara Ewing
Guardian of the Abyss '82
Dracula Has Risen from the Grave '68

Richard Eyer (1945-)
The Seventh Voyage of Sinbad '58
The Invisible Boy '57
The Kettles in the Ozarks '56
Desperate Hours '55

Peter Eyre (1942-)
The Affair of the Necklace '01
Don Quixote '00
The Golden Bowl '00
Dangerous Beauty '98
The Tango Lesson '97
Surviving Picasso '96
Joseph '95
Princess Caraboo '94
Scarlett '94
Sharpe's Gold '94
Orlando '92
Diamond's Edge '88
Hedda '75

William Eythe (1918-57)
Colonel Effingham's Raid '45
House on 92nd Street '45
Wilson '44
A Wing and a Prayer '44
The Ox-Bow Incident '43

Maynard Eziashi
Ace Ventura: When Nature Calls '95
Bopha! '93
Mister Johnson '91
Twenty-One '91

Shelley Fabares (1944-)
The Canterville Ghost '91
Love or Money? '88
Hot Pursuit '87
Memorial Day '83
Great American Traffic Jam '80
Sky Hei$t '75
Brian's Song '71
Clambake '67
Spinout '66
Girl Happy '65
Ride the Wild Surf '64

Matthew Faber
Hard Luck '01
Ride with the Devil '99
Welcome to the Dollhouse '95

Fabian (1942-)
Mr. Rock 'n' Roll: The Alan Freed Story '99
Get Crazy '83
Kiss Daddy Goodbye '81
Soul Hustler '76
Little Laura & Big John '73
Dear Brigitte '65
Ride the Wild Surf '64
Five Weeks in a Balloon '62
The Longest Day '62
Mr. Hobbs Takes a Vacation '62
North to Alaska '60

Ava Fabian (1962-)
Capital Punishment '96
Last Man Standing '95
Auntie Lee's Meat Pies '92
Ski School '91
Welcome Home, Roxy Carmichael '90
To Die For '89

Francoise Fabian (1935-)
La Buche '00
Reunion '88
The French Woman '79
Love by Appointment '76
Salut l'Artiste '74
Happy New Year '73
My Night at Maud's '69
Belle de Jour '67
Mam'zelle Pigalle '58
That Naughty Girl '58
Fernandel the Dressmaker '57
Dressmaker '56

Joel Fabiani
Snake Eyes '98
Reuben, Reuben '83
President's Mistress '78

Fabio (1961-)
Bubble Boy '01
Exorcist 3: Legion '90

Nanette Fabray (1920-)
Teresa's Tattoo '94
Personal Exemptions '88
Amy '81
The Man in the Santa Claus Suit '79
Harper Valley P.T.A. '78
The Happy Ending '69
Alice Through the Looking Glass '66
The Band Wagon '53
The Private Lives of Elizabeth & Essex '39

Pierre Fabre
Bed and Board '70
The 317th Platoon '65

Aldo Fabrizi (1905-90)
The Flowers of St. Francis '50
Open City '45

Franco Fabrizi (1916-95)
Ginger & Fred '86
Aurora '84
Act of Aggression '73
A Woman of Rome '56
Il Bidone '55
I Vitelloni '53

Valeria Fabrizi
Women in Cell Block 7 '77
Beauty on the Beach '60s

Peter Facinelli (1973-)
The Scorpion King '02
Riding in Cars with Boys '01
The Big Kahuna '00
Blue Ridge Fall '99
Supernova '99
Can't Hardly Wait '98
Dancer, Texas—Pop. 81 '98
Telling You '98
Calm at Sunset '96
Foxfire '96

Robert Factor
Bad Channels '92
Ninja Academy '90
Fear '88

Bill Fagerbakke
The Reluctant Agent '95
Gargoyles, The Movie: The Heroes Awaken '94 (V)
Stephen King's The Stand '94

Jeff Fahey (1954-)
Inferno '01
Blind Heat '00
Revelation '00
Detour '99
Johnny 2.0 '99
No Tomorrow '99
Smalltime '99
Time Served '99
Catherine's Grove '98
Extramarital '98
When Justice Fails '98
Operation: Delta Force '97
The Underground '97
Lethal Tender '96
Virtual Seduction '96
Darkman 3: Die Darkman Die '95
Eye of the Wolf '95
Northern Passage '95
Serpent's Lair '95
The Sweeper '95
Firefall '94
Sketch Artist 2: Hands That See '94
Temptation '94
Wyatt Earp '94
Blindsided '93
The Hit List '93
Quick '93
Woman of Desire '93
The Lawnmower Man '92
Sketch Artist '92
Body Parts '91
Iran: Days of Crisis '91
Iron Maze '91
Curiosity Kills '90
Impulse '90
The Last of the Finest '90
White Hunter, Black Heart '90
True Blood '89
Backfire '88
Split Decisions '88
Wrangler '88
Psycho 3 '86
Execution of Raymond Graham '85
Silverado '85

Mary-Anne Fahey
Celia: Child of Terror '89
Mutant Hunt '87
The Dunera Boys '85

Elinor Fair (1903-57)
Let 'er Go Gallegher '28
Yankee Clipper '27
Big Stakes '22
Kismet '20

Jody Fair
The Brain Eaters '58
High School Confidential '58

Bruce Fairbairn (1947-99)
Cyclone '87
Nightstick '87
The Vampire Hookers '78

Christopher Fairbank
The Scarlet Pimpernel '99
The Scarlet Pimpernel 2: Mademoiselle Guillotine '99
The Scarlet Pimpernel 3: The Kidnapped King '99
How Many Miles to Babylon? '82

Douglas Fairbanks, Sr. (1883-1939)
Days of Thrills and Laughter '61
Private Life of Don Juan '34
Mr. Robinson Crusoe '32
Reaching for the Moon '31
The Iron Mask '29
The Taming of the Shrew '29
The Gaucho '27
A Kiss for Mary Pickford '27
The Black Pirate '26
Don Q., Son of Zorro '25
The Thief of Baghdad '24
Robin Hood '22
The Nut '21
The Three Musketeers '21
Mark of Zorro '20
The Mollycoddle '20
His Majesty, the American '19
When the Clouds Roll By '19
American Aristocracy '17
The Americano '17
Down to Earth '17
The Man from Painted Post '17
Reaching for the Moon '17
Flirting with Fate '16
His Picture in the Papers '16
Matrimaniac '16
Reggie Mixes In '16
The Lamb '15

Douglas Fairbanks, Jr. (1909-2000)
Ghost Story '81
The Hostage Tower '80
Mister Drake's Duck '50
Sinbad, the Sailor '47
The Corsican Brothers '42
Angels Over Broadway '40
Gunga Din '39
Having Wonderful Time '38
Joy of Living '38
The Rage of Paris '38
The Young in Heart '38
Prisoner of Zenda '37
When Thief Meets Thief '37
Accused '36
Mimi '35
Catherine the Great '34
Morning Glory '33
Scarlet Dawn '32
Little Caesar '30
Our Modern Maidens '29
Party Girls '29
A Woman of Affairs '28

Craig Fairbrass (1964-)
Killing Time '97
Galaxis '95
Proteus '95
Cliffhanger '93
Nightscare '93

Morgan Fairchild (1950-)
Peril '00
Nice Guys Sleep Alone '99
Holy Man '98
Criminal Hearts '95
Venus Rising '95
Gospa '94
Based on an Untrue Story '93
Body Chemistry 3: Point of Seduction '93
Freaked '93
Test Tube Teens from the Year 2000 '93
Writer's Block '91
Even Angels Fall '90
Mob Boss '90
Haunting of Sarah Hardy '89
Phantom of the Mall: Eric's Revenge '89
Sleeping Beauty '89
Midnight Cop '88
Campus Man '87
Deadly Illusion '87
Red Headed Stranger '87
North and South Book 2 '86
Pee-wee's Big Adventure '85
The Zany Adventures of Robin Hood '84
Honeyboy '82
The Seduction '82
The Concrete Cowboys '79
Initiation of Sarah '78

Virginia Brown Faire
Peter Pan '24
Cricket on the Hearth '23

Heather Fairfield
No Secrets '91
A Girl of the Limberlost '90
The War of the Roses '89

Michael Fairman (1934-)
Thirteen Days '00

Forces of Nature '99
The Nurse '97
The Banker '89

Donald Adeosun Faison (1974-)
Big Fat Liar '02
Josie and the Pussycats '01
Remember the Titans '00
Supreme Sanction '99
Trippin' '99
Never 2 Big '98
Clueless '95
New Jersey Drive '95
Waiting to Exhale '95

Frankie Faison (1949-)
Showtime '02
Down to Earth '01
Hannibal '01
The Thomas Crown Affair '99
Julian Po '97
Mother Night '96
The Rich Man's Wife '96
Stephen King's The Langoliers '95
The Stupids '95
The Spider and the Fly '94
Sommersby '93
Freejack '92
City of Hope '91
Do the Right Thing '89
Coming to America '88
Mississippi Burning '88
Exterminator 2 '84

Matthew Faison
Lily in Winter '94
Taken Away '89

Adam Faith (1940-)
McVicar '80
Yesterday's Hero '79
Beat Girl '60

Dolores Faith
The Human Duplicators '64
The Phantom Planet '61

Marianne Faithfull (1946-)
Absolutely Fabulous: The Last Shout '96
Crimetime '96
Moondance '95
Shopping '93
When Pigs Fly '93
The Turn of the Screw '92
Assault on Agathon '75
Madhouse Mansion '74
Hamlet '69
The Girl on a Motorcycle '68
I'll Never Forget What's 'Isname '67

Eduardo Fajardo (1918-)
Lisa and the Devil '75
Stranger in Paso Bravo '73
Django '68

Lola Falana (1942-)
Lady Cocoa '75
The Klansman '74
The Liberation of L.B. Jones '70
A Man Called Adam '66

Edie Falco (1954-)
Sunshine State '02
Judy Berlin '99
Random Hearts '99
Cop Land '97
A Price above Rubies '97
Hurricane Streets '96
The Addiction '95
Laws of Gravity '92
Trust '91
Sweet Lorraine '87

Lisanne Falk
Shattered Image '98
The First to Go '97
Night on Earth '91
Heathers '89

Peter Falk (1927-)
Corky Romano '01
Made '01
Money Kings '98
Pronto '97
Roommates '95
Faraway, So Close! '93
The Player '92
In the Spirit '90
Tune in Tomorrow '90
Cookie '89
Vibes '88
Wings of Desire '88
Happy New Year '87
The Princess Bride '87
Big Trouble '86
...All the Marbles '81
The Great Muppet Caper '81
The In-Laws '79
Brink's Job '78
The Cheap Detective '78
Griffin and Phoenix: A Love Story '76
Mikey & Nicky '76
Murder by Death '76
A Woman under the Influence '74
Columbo: Murder by the Book '71
Husbands '70
Anzio '68
Columbo: Prescription Murder '67
Luv '67
The Great Race '65
Robin and the 7 Hoods '64
The Balcony '63
Beach Party '63
It's a Mad, Mad, Mad, Mad World '63
Pressure Point '62
Pocketful of Miracles '61
The Bloody Brood '59

Rossella Falk
Modesty Blaise '66
8 1/2 '63

Deborah Fallender
S.O.S. Titanic '79
Jabberwocky '77

Jimmy Fallon (1974-)
Band of Brothers '01
Almost Famous '00

Siobhan Fallon
What's the Worst That Could Happen? '01
Krippendorf's Tribe '98
The Negotiator '98
Men in Black '97

Mary Fanaro
Truth or Dare? '86
Demon Queen '80

Al Fann
Frankie and Johnny '91
Parasite '82

Franco Fantasia
Emerald Jungle '80
Mountain of the Cannibal God '79

Ennio Fantastichini
The Blonde '92
The Station '92
Open Doors '89

Sergio Fantoni (1930-)
The Belly of an Architect '91
Hornet's Nest '70
What Did You Do in the War, Daddy? '66
Von Ryan's Express '65
The Prize '63
Atom Age Vampire '61
Esther and the King '60
The Giant of Marathon '60

Stephanie Faracy
Safety Patrol '98
Hocus Pocus '93
The Great Outdoors '88
Blind Date '87

Daniel Faraldo
Full Fathom Five '90
Above the Law '88

Debrah Farentino (1961-)
Stephen King's The Storm of the Century '99
Dead Air '94
Son of the Pink Panther '93
Bugsy '91
Mortal Sins '90
Capone '89

James Farentino (1938-)
Termination Man '97
Bulletproof '96
Honor Thy Father and Mother: The True Story of the Menendez Brothers '94
In the Line of Duty: A Cop for the Killing '90
Naked Lie '89
Her Alibi '88
Family Sins '87
Sins '85
License to Kill '84
A Summer to Remember '84
The Cradle Will Fall '83
Dead and Buried '81
The Final Countdown '80
Silent Victory: The Kitty O'Neil Story '79
The Possessed '77
The War Lord '65
Ensign Pulver '64
Psychomania '63

Debra Fares
Killer Tomatoes Eat France '91
Killer Tomatoes Strike Back '90

Antonio Fargas (1946-)
Extreme Honor '01
Three Strikes '00
The Suburbans '99
Milo '98
Howling 6: The Freaks '90
The Borrower '89
I'm Gonna Git You Sucka '88
Shakedown '88
Florida Straits '87
Night of the Sharks '87
Crimewave '85
Streetwalkin' '85
Firestarter '84
The Ambush Murders '82
Nurse '80
Pretty Baby '78
Car Wash '76
Cornbread, Earl & Me '75
Huckleberry Finn '75
Busting '74
Foxy Brown '74
Across 110th Street '72
Shaft '71
Gator King '70
Milo Milo '60s

Betty Faria
The Story of Fausta '88
Bye Bye Brazil '79

Dennis Farina (1944-)
Big Trouble '02
Sidewalks of New York '01
Bad Seed '00
Reindeer Games '00
Snatch '00
The Mod Squad '99
Out of Sight '98
Saving Private Ryan '98
Bella Mafia '97
Eddie '96
That Old Feeling '96
Get Shorty '95
Little Big League '94
Out of Annie's Past '94
Another Stakeout '93
High Stakes '93
Mac '93
Striking Distance '93
Drug Wars 2: The Cocaine Cartel '92
Street Crimes '92
We're Talkin' Serious Money '92
Men of Respect '91
The Hillside Strangler '89
Midnight Run '88
Jo Jo Dancer, Your Life Is Calling '86
Manhunter '86
Code of Silence '85
Thief '81

Gabriella Farinon
Assignment Outer Space '61
Blood and Roses '61

Anna Faris
Scary Movie 2 '01
Scary Movie '00

Chris Farley (1964-97)
Almost Heroes '97
Dirty Work '97
Beverly Hills Ninja '96
Black Sheep '96
Tommy Boy '95
Airheads '94
Billy Madison '94
Coneheads '93
Wayne's World 2 '93

Morgan Farley
Abbott and Costello Meet the Killer, Boris Karloff '49
Open Secret '48

Sean Farley
Tainted '98
Crimewave '85

Frances Farmer (1913-70)
Son of Fury '42
South of Pago Pago '40
Toast of New York '37
Come and Get It '36
Rhythm on the Range '36

Gary Farmer (1953-)
The Score '01
Angels Don't Sleep Here '00
Smoke Signals '98
Moonshine Highway '96
Dead Man '95
Henry & Verlin '94
Sioux City '94
Tales from the Crypt Presents Demon Knight '94
Blown Away '93
Powwow Highway '89
Big Town '87

Mimsy Farmer (1945-)
Codename: Wildgeese '84
The Black Cat '81
Autopsy '74
Allonsanfan '73
More '69
Road to Salina '68
Devil's Angels '67
Spencer's Mountain '63

Suzan Farmer (1943-)
Death in Deep Water '74
The Graveyard '74
Dracula, Prince of Darkness '66
Rasputin the Mad Monk '66
Die, Monster, Die! '65

Vera Farmiga (1973-)
Snow White: The Fairest of Them All '02
15 Minutes '01
Autumn in New York '00
Return to Paradise '98

Alberto (Albert Farley) Farnese (1926-)
Scalps '83
The Conqueror & the Empress '64
Gladiator of Rome '63
The Giants of Thessaly '60

Richard Farnsworth (1920-2000)
The Straight Story '99
Lassie '94
The River Pirates '94
The Fire Next Time '93
Highway to Hell '92
Havana '90
Misery '90
The Two Jakes '90
Witchery '88
Space Rage '86
Anne of Green Gables '85
Chase '85
Into the Night '85
Sylvester '85
The Natural '84
Rhinestone '84
The Grey Fox '83
Independence Day '83
Waltz across Texas '83
Legend of the Lone Ranger '81
Ruckus '81
Resurrection '80
Tom Horn '80
Comes a Horseman '78
Strange New World '75
Texas across the River '66

Franklyn Farnum (1878-1961)
Prison Train '38
Ghost Rider '35
Hopalong Cassidy '35
Powdersmoke Range '35
The Silver Bullet '34
Mark of the Spur '32
Battling with Buffalo Bill '31
The Scarlet Car '17

William Farnum (1876-1953)
Jack & the Beanstalk '52
Lone Star '52
Trail of Robin Hood '50
Gun Cargo '49
God's Country '46
My Dog Shep '46
Wildfire '45
Today I Hang '42
Law of the Sea '38
Santa Fe Stampede '38
Git Along Little Dogies '37
Public Cowboy No. 1 '37
The Clutching Hand '36
Custer's Last Stand '36
Kid Ranger '36
Undersea Kingdom '36
The Vigilantes Are Coming '36
Between Men '35
The Crusades '35
Million Dollar Haul '35
Powdersmoke Range '35
The Silver Streak '34
Supernatural '33
The Drifter '32
Mr. Robinson Crusoe '32
A Connecticut Yankee '31
Painted Desert '31
Ten Nights in a Bar-Room '31
Dubarry '30
The Spoilers '14

Derek Farr (1912-86)
Truth about Women '58
Man on the Run '49
Spellbound '41

Felicia Farr (1932-)
Charley Varrick '73
Kotch '71
Kiss Me, Stupid! '64
3:10 to Yuma '57
Jubal '56

Jamie Farr (1936-)
Fearless Tiger '94
Curse 2: The Bite '88
Scrooged '88
Speed Zone '88
Happy Hour '87
Combat Academy '86
Cannonball Run 2 '84
For Love or Money '84
M*A*S*H: Goodbye, Farewell & Amen '83
Cannonball Run '81
Return of the Rebels '81
Arnold '73
Heavy Traffic '73
With Six You Get Eggroll '68
Who's Minding the Mint? '67
No Time for Sergeants '58
Blackboard Jungle '55

Patricia Farr
Mistaken Identity '36
Tailspin Tommy '34

David Farrar (1908-95)
Beat Girl '60
John Paul Jones '59
Let's Make Up '55
Pearl of the South Pacific '55
Sea Chase '55
The Black Shield of Falworth '54
The Obsessed '51
The Small Back Room '49
Black Narcissus '47
Frieda '47
The World Owes Me a Living '47
Echo Murders '45
Meet Sexton Blake '44

Charles Farrell (1901-90)
They Made Me a Fugitive '47
Just Around the Corner '38
Moonlight Sonata '38
Aggie Appleby, Maker of Men '33
City Girl '30
Old Ironsides '26

Colin Farrell (1976-)
Hart's War '02
Minority Report '02
American Outlaws '01
Tigerland '00
Falling for a Dancer '98
The War Zone '98

Glenda Farrell (1904-71)
Disorderly Orderly '64
Kissin' Cousins '64
Heading for Heaven '47
City Without Men '43
Johnny Eager '42
A Night for Crime '42
Talk of the Town '42
Twin Beds '42
Prison Break '38
Gold Diggers of 1935 '35
Bureau of Missing Persons '33
Lady for a Day '33
Mystery of the Wax Museum '33
I Am a Fugitive from a Chain Gang '32
Little Caesar '30

Mike Farrell (1939-)
Sins of the Mind '97
Silent Motive '91
Dark River: A Father's Revenge '90
Lockdown '90
Vanishing Act '88
M*A*S*H: Goodbye, Farewell & Amen '83
Memorial Day '83
Prime Suspect '82
Sex and the Single Parent '82
Damien: The Leper Priest '80
Targets '68
Escape from Planet Earth '67
The Graduate '67

Nicholas Farrell
Charlotte Gray '01
Beautiful People '99
Legionnaire '98
Hamlet '96
Sharpe's Regiment '96
Twelfth Night '96
A Midwinter's Tale '95
Othello '95
To Play the King '93
Hold the Dream '86

Sharon Farrell (1946-)
Beyond Desire '94
Arcade '93
One Man Force '89
Can't Buy Me Love '87
Night of the Comet '84
Rage '80
The Stunt Man '80
The Premonition '75
It's Alive '74
The Love Machine '71
Marlowe '69
The Reivers '69
40 Pounds of Trouble '62

Terry Farrell (1963-)
Deep Core '00
Legion '98
Red Sun Rising '94
Danielle Steel's Star '93
Hellraiser 3: Hell on Earth '92
Off the Mark '87
Back to School '86
Beverly Hills Madam '86

Timothy Farrell (1923-89)
Gun Girls *'56*
Jail Bait *'54*
Glen or Glenda? *'53*
The Devil's Sleep *'51*
Test Tube Babies *'48*

Tommy Farrell (1921-)
Kissin' Cousins *'64*
Meet Danny Wilson *'52*
Pirates of the High Seas *'50*

Mia Farrow (1945-)
A Girl Thing *'01*
Coming Soon *'99*
Miracle at Midnight *'98*
Miami Rhapsody *'95*
Reckless *'95*
Widow's Peak *'94*
Husbands and Wives *'92*
Shadows and Fog *'92*
Alice *'90*
Crimes & Misdemeanors *'89*
New York Stories *'89*
Another Woman *'88*
September *'88*
Radio Days *'87*
Hannah and Her Sisters *'86*
The Purple Rose of Cairo *'85*
Broadway Danny Rose *'84*
Supergirl *'84*
Zelig *'83*
The Last Unicorn *'82 (V)*
A Midsummer Night's Sex Comedy *'82*
Hurricane *'79*
Avalanche *'78*
Death on the Nile *'78*
A Wedding *'78*
Full Circle *'77*
The Great Gatsby *'74*
High Heels *'72*
See No Evil *'71*
Secret Ceremony *'69*
Dandy in Aspic *'68*
Rosemary's Baby *'68*
Guns at Batasi *'64*

Tisa Farrow (1951-)
Grim Reaper *'81*
Search and Destroy *'81*
The Last Hunter *'80*
Zombie *'80*
Manhattan *'79*
Winter Kills *'79*
Fingers *'78*
Initiation of Sarah *'78*
Strange Shadows in an Empty Room *'76*
Some Call It Loving *'73*
And Hope to Die *'72*

Rainer Werner Fassbinder (1946-82)
Kamikaze '89 *'83*
Shadow of Angels *'76*
Fox and His Friends *'75*
Tenderness of the Wolves *'73*
The American Soldier *'70*
Beware of a Holy Whore *'70*
Whity *'70*

Joey Fatone
My Big Fat Greek Wedding *'02*
On the Line *'01*

Andrew Faulds (1922-2000)
Lisztomania *'75*
The Devils *'71*

James Faulkner (1948-)
All the Little Animals *'98*
A Kid in Aladdin's Palace *'97*
Crimetime *'96*
Wavelength *'96*
Devices and Desires *'91*
The Maid *'90*
Flashpoint Africa *'84*
Albino *'76*
Conduct Unbecoming *'75*

Sally Faulkner
Alien Prey *'83*
Vampyres *'74*

Stephanie Faulkner
Virus *'82*
Death Journey *'76*
The Bus Is Coming *'72*

Rene Faure
The Judge and the Assassin *'75*
La Chartreuse de Parme *'48*

David Faustino (1974-)
Killer Bud *'00*
It's a Bundyful Life *'92*
Perfect Harmony *'91*

Jon Favreau (1966-)
Made *'01*
Love & Sex *'00*
The Replacements *'00*
Rocky Marciano *'99*
Deep Impact *'98*
Very Bad Things *'98*
Dogtown *'97*
Just Your Luck *'96*
Persons Unknown *'96*
Swingers *'96*
Batman Forever *'95*
Notes from Underground *'95*
P.C.U. *'94*
Rudy *'93*

Alan Fawcett
Blindside *'88*
A Conspiracy of Love *'87*

Farrah Fawcett (1946-)
Baby *'00*
Dr. T & the Women *'00*
The Apostle *'97*
Dalva *'95*
A Good Day to Die *'95*
Man of the House *'95*
The Substitute Wife *'94*
Double Exposure: The Story of Margaret Bourke-White *'89*
See You in the Morning *'89*
Small Sacrifices *'89*
Poor Little Rich Girl: The Barbara Hutton Story *'87*
Between Two Women *'86*
Extremities *'86*
The Burning Bed *'85*
The Red Light Sting *'84*
Cannonball Run *'81*
Murder in Texas *'81*
Saturn 3 *'80*
Sunburn *'79*
Logan's Run *'76*
Murder on Flight 502 *'75*
Myra Breckinridge *'70*

George Fawcett (1860-1939)
Drums of Jeopardy *'31*
The Wedding March *'28*
The Flesh and the Devil *'27*
Son of the Sheik *'26*
The Mad Whirl *'25*
The Greatest Question *'19*

William "Bill" Fawcett (1894-1974)
Jesse James Meets Frankenstein's Daughter *'65*
King Rat *'65*
Gun Glory *'57*
Storm Rider *'57*
Black Hills *'48*
Check Your Guns *'48*
The Tioga Kid *'48*
Wild Country *'47*
Driftin' River *'46*

Dorothy Fay
Trigger Pals *'39*
Law of the Texan *'38*

Frank Fay
Love Nest *'51*
Spotlight Scandals *'43*

Alice Faye (1915-98)
Every Girl Should Have One *'78*
Magic of Lassie *'78*
State Fair *'62*
Hello, Frisco, Hello *'43*
The Great American Broadcast *'41*
Week-End in Havana *'41*
Tin Pan Alley *'40*
Rose of Washington Square *'39*
Alexander's Ragtime Band *'38*
In Old Chicago *'37*
On the Avenue *'37*
The Poor Little Rich Girl *'36*
Stowaway *'36*

Denise Faye
American Pie 2 *'01*
The Next Step *'95*

Frank Faylen (1905-85)
Gunfight at the O.K. Corral *'57*
Seventh Cavalry *'56*
The McConnell Story *'55*
Red Garters *'54*
Riot in Cell Block 11 *'54*
Hangman's Knot *'52*
Detective Story *'51*
Copper Canyon *'50*
The Nevadan *'50*
Francis the Talking Mule *'49*
The Road to Rio *'47*
Welcome Stranger *'47*
Blue Skies *'46*
It's a Wonderful Life *'46*
The Lost Weekend *'45*
Across the Pacific *'42*
Wake Island *'42*
Sergeant York *'41*
Tanks a Million *'41*
Gone with the Wind *'39*
Waterfront *'39*

Louise Fazenda (1895-1962)
The Old Maid *'39*
Doughnuts & Society *'36*
The Bat *'26*
The Night Club *'25*

Ron Fazio
Basket Case 2 *'90*
The Toxic Avenger, Part 2 *'89*
The Toxic Avenger, Part 3: The Last Temptation of Toxie *'89*

Michael Feast
Velvet Goldmine *'98*
Touching Evil *'97*

Angela Featherstone
Federal Protection *'02*
Skipped Parts *'00*
The Guilty *'99*
Palmetto *'98*
200 Cigarettes *'98*
Con Air *'97*
Family of Cops 2: Breach of Faith *'97*
The Wedding Singer *'97*
Zero Effect *'97*
Illtown *'96*
Family of Cops *'95*
Dark Angel: The Ascent *'94*

Birgitte Federspiel
Babette's Feast *'87*
Ordet *'55*

Melinda Fee
Doin' Time *'85*
Aliens Are Coming *'80*
Fade to Black *'80*

Caroleen Feeney
Avalanche *'99*
Bad Manners *'98*
Cadillac Ranch *'96*
Denise Calls Up *'95*

Bekim Fehmiu (1936-)
Battle of the Eagles *'81*
Ride to Glory *'71*
The Adventurers *'70*

Brendan Fehr (1977-)
The Forsaken *'01*
Kill Me Later *'01*

Oded Fehr (1970-)
The Mummy Returns *'01*
Texas Rangers *'01*
Deuce Bigalow: Male Gigolo *'99*
The Mummy *'99*

Alan Feinstein (1941-)
The Hunt for the Night Stalker *'91*
Bunco *'83*
The Two Worlds of Jenny Logan *'79*
The Hunted Lady *'77*
Joe Panther *'76*

Fritz Feld (1900-93)
Get Smart, Again! *'89*
History of the World: Part 1 *'81*
Herbie Goes Bananas *'80*
World's Greatest Lover *'77*
Promises! Promises! *'63*
The Errand Boy *'61*
Kentucky Jubilee *'51*
The Lovable Cheat *'49*
Mexican Hayride *'48*
The Noose Hangs High *'48*
Iceland *'42*
Four Jacks and a Jill *'41*
At the Circus *'39*
Everything Happens at Night *'39*
The Affairs of Annabel *'38*
Bringing Up Baby *'38*
Last Command *'28*

Clarence Felder
The Hidden *'87*
Killing Floor *'85*

Andrea Feldman
Heat *'72*
Trash *'70*

Corey Feldman (1971-)
The Million Dollar Kid *'99*
Legion *'98*
Storm Trooper *'98*
Born Bad *'97*
Evil Obsession *'96*
Red Line *'96*
South Beach Academy *'96*
Tales from the Crypt Presents Bordello of Blood *'96*
Voodoo *'95*
A Dangerous Place *'94*
Dream a Little Dream 2 *'94*
National Lampoon's Last Resort *'94*
Blown Away *'93*
Lipstick Camera *'93*
The Magic Voyage *'93 (V)*
National Lampoon's Loaded Weapon 1 *'93*
Meatballs 4 *'92*
Round Trip to Heaven *'92*
Stepmonster *'92*
Edge of Honor *'91*
Rock 'n' Roll High School Forever *'91*
Teenage Mutant Ninja Turtles: The Movie *'90 (V)*
The 'Burbs *'89*
Dream a Little Dream *'89*
License to Drive *'88*
The Lost Boys *'87*
Stand by Me *'86*
Friday the 13th, Part 5: A New Beginning *'85*
The Goonies *'85*
Friday the 13th, Part 4: The Final Chapter *'84*
Gremlins *'84*
The Fox and the Hound *'81 (V)*

Marty Feldman (1933-82)
Slapstick of Another Kind *'84*
Yellowbeard *'83*
In God We Trust *'80*
The Adventures of Sherlock Holmes' Smarter Brother *'78*
The Last Remake of Beau Geste *'77*
Sex with a Smile *'76*
Silent Movie *'76*
Young Frankenstein *'74*
Think Dirty *'70*

Tibor Feldman
River Red *'98*
Fat Guy Goes Nutzoid *'86*

Barbara Feldon (1941-)
Get Smart, Again! *'89*
Children of Divorce *'80*
A Guide for the Married Woman *'78*
No Deposit, No Return *'76*
Smile *'75*
Playmates *'72*

Tovah Feldshuh (1952-)
Happy Accidents *'00*
The Corruptor *'99*
A Walk on the Moon *'99*
A Day in October *'92*
Blue Iguana *'88*
Brewster's Millions *'85*
Cheaper to Keep Her *'80*
Idolmaker *'80*
The Triangle Factory Fire Scandal *'79*
Holocaust *'78*
The Amazing Howard Hughes *'77*

Jose Feliciano
Fargo *'96*
Aaron Loves Angela *'75*

Norman Fell (1924-98)
The Destiny of Marty Fine *'96*
Hexed *'93*
For the Boys *'91*
The Bone Yard *'90*
Stripped to Kill *'87*
Transylvania 6-5000 *'85*
On the Right Track *'81*
Paternity *'81*
For the Love of It *'80*
The End *'78*
Cleopatra Jones & the Casino of Gold *'75*
Death Stalk *'74*
Charley Varrick *'73*
The Stone Killer *'73*
The Boatniks *'70*
Catch-22 *'70*
If It's Tuesday, This Must Be Belgium *'69*
Bullitt *'68*
The Graduate *'67*
The Killers *'64*
It's a Mad, Mad, Mad, Mad World *'63*
Inherit the Wind *'60*
Ocean's 11 *'60*
Pork Chop Hill *'59*

Federico Fellini (1920-93)
Intervista *'87*
We All Loved Each Other So Much *'77*
Fellini's Roma *'72 (V)*
Alex in Wonderland *'70*
Ciao Federico! Fellini Directs Satyricon *'69*
The Miracle *'48*

Julian Fellowes (1950-)
The Aristocrats *'99*
Behind the Lines *'97*
The Final Cut *'95*
Sharpe's Rifles *'93*
Damage *'92*
Goldeneye: The Secret Life of Ian Fleming *'89*
Baby ... Secret of the Lost Legend *'85*

Rockliffe Fellowes
Monkey Business *'31*
Regeneration *'15*

Edith Fellows (1923-)
In the Mood *'87*
The Grace Kelly Story *'83*
Heart of the Rio Grande *'42*
Her First Romance *'40*
Music in My Heart *'40*

Hansjorg Felmy (1931-)
The Mad Executioners *'65*
The Monster of London City *'64*
Brainwashed *'60*

Tom Felton
Harry Potter and the Sorcerer's Stone *'01*
Anna and the King *'99*
The Borrowers *'97*

Verna Felton (1890-1966)
The Jungle Book *'67 (V)*
Sleeping Beauty *'59 (V)*
The Oklahoman *'56*
Lady and the Tramp *'55 (V)*
Picnic *'55*
Cinderella *'50 (V)*
Dumbo *'41 (V)*

Freddy Fender
The Milagro Beanfield War *'88*
She Came to the Valley *'77*

Edwige Fenech (1948-)
Phantom of Death *'87*
You've Got to Have Heart *'77*
Sex with a Smile *'76*
The Next Victim *'71*
Blade of the Ripper *'70*
Five Dolls for an August Moon *'70*
The Seducers *'70*

Zhang Fengyi
The Emperor and the Assassin *'99*
Temptation of a Monk *'94*
Farewell My Concubine *'93*

Tanya Fenmore
Lisa *'90*
My Stepmother Is an Alien *'88*

Sherilyn Fenn (1965-)
Cement *'99*
Darkness Falls *'98*
Outside Ozona *'98*
Just Write *'97*
Lovelife *'97*
National Lampoon's The Don's Analyst *'97*
The Assassination File *'96*
Boxing Helena *'93*
Fatal Instinct *'93*
Three of Hearts *'93*
Desire and Hell at Sunset Motel *'92*
Of Mice and Men *'92*
Ruby *'92*
Diary of a Hitman *'91*
Dillinger *'91*
Backstreet Dreams *'90*
Meridian: Kiss of the Beast *'90*
Wild at Heart *'90*
True Blood *'89*
Crime Zone *'88*
Two Moon Junction *'88*
The Wraith *'87*
Zombie High *'87*
Just One of the Guys *'85*
The Wild Life *'84*

Tod Fennell
The Kid *'97*
Stalked *'94*

Parker Fennelly
How to Frame a Figg *'71*
The Kettles on Old MacDonald's Farm *'57*

George Fenneman (1919-97)
The Marx Brothers in a Nutshell *'90*
How to Succeed in Business without Really Trying *'67*
The Thing *'51*

Frank Fenton (1906-57)
Naked Hills *'56*
The Golden Stallion *'49*
Mexican Hayride *'48*
Isle of Forgotten Sins *'43*

Lance Fenton
Heathers *'89*
Night of the Demons *'88*

Leslie Fenton (1902-78)
The House of Secrets *'37*
Fugitive Road *'34*
Marie Galante *'34*
F.P. 1 *'33*
Lady Killer *'33*
The Strange Love of Molly Louvain *'32*
Murder at Midnight *'31*
Public Enemy *'31*

Simon Fenton
A Knight in Camelot *'98*

Arabella Field (1970-)
Blowin' Smoke *'99*
Godzilla *'98*
Dante's Peak *'97*
The Pompatus of Love *'95*
Laws of Gravity *'92*
Betty Field (1918-73)
Coogan's Bluff *'68*
Birdman of Alcatraz *'62*
Butterfield 8 *'60*
Peyton Place *'57*
Bus Stop *'56*
Picnic *'55*
The Great Gatsby *'49*
The Southerner *'45*
The Great Moment *'44*
Tomorrow the World *'44*
Kings Row *'41*
The Shepherd of the Hills *'41*
Of Mice and Men *'39*
Chelsea Field (1957-)
Tom Clancy's Netforce *'98*
Wicked *'98*
Flipper *'96*
Indictment: The McMartin Trial *'95*
The Wrong Woman *'95*
Andre *'94*
The Birds 2: Land's End *'94*
A Passion to Kill *'94*
Texas *'94*
Dust Devil *'93*
Extreme Justice *'93*
Hotel Room *'93*
Royce *'93*
Snapdragon *'93*
The Dark Half *'91*
Harley Davidson and the Marlboro Man *'91*
The Last Boy Scout *'91*
Skin Deep *'89*
Prison *'88*
Commando *'85*
David Field
Chopper *'00*
Mr. Accident *'99*
Two Hands *'98*
Blackrock *'97*
Karin (Karen) Field
The Demons *'74*
The Mad Butcher *'72*
Web of the Spider *'70*
The Alley Cats *'65*
Cave of the Living Dead *'65*
Mary Field (1896-1968)
To Hell and Back *'55*
I Married a Witch *'42*
Mrs. Miniver *'42*
Wake Island *'42*
Sally Field (1946-)
Say It Isn't So *'01*
Where the Heart Is *'00*
A Cooler Climate *'99*
Homeward Bound 2: Lost in San Francisco *'96 (V)*
An Eye for an Eye *'95*
Forrest Gump *'94*
Homeward Bound: The Incredible Journey *'93 (V)*
Mrs. Doubtfire *'93*
Soapdish *'91*
Not Without My Daughter *'90*
Steel Magnolias *'89*
Punchline *'88*
Surrender *'87*
Murphy's Romance *'85*
Places in the Heart *'84*
Kiss Me Goodbye *'82*
Absence of Malice *'81*
Back Roads *'81*
Smokey and the Bandit 2 *'80*
Beyond the Poseidon Adventure *'79*
Norma Rae *'79*
The End *'78*
Hooper *'78*
Heroes *'77*
Smokey and the Bandit *'77*
Stay Hungry *'76*
Sybil *'76*
Home for the Holidays *'72*
Maybe I'll Be Home in the Spring *'70*
The Way West *'67*
Shirley Anne Field (1936-)
Lady Chatterley *'92*
Hear My Song *'91*
Getting It Right *'89*
Shag: The Movie *'89*
Two by Forsyth *'86*
My Beautiful Laundrette *'85*
House of the Living Dead *'73*
Alfie *'66*
War Lover *'62*
Beat Girl *'60*
The Entertainer *'60*
Peeping Tom *'60*
Saturday Night and Sunday Morning *'60*
Todd Field (1964-)
Eyes Wide Shut *'99*
The Haunting *'99*
Stranger than Fiction *'99*
Broken Vessels *'98*
Farmer & Chase *'96*
Walking and Talking *'96*
Sleep with Me *'94*
Ruby in Paradise *'93*
Back to Back *'90*
Full Fathom Five *'90*
Eye of the Eagle 2 *'89*
Gross Anatomy *'89*
Virginia Field (1917-92)
A Connecticut Yankee in King Arthur's Court *'49*
Dance, Girl, Dance *'40*
Waterloo Bridge *'40*
Mr. Moto's Last Warning *'39*
Lloyds of London *'36*
Dorothy Fielding
The Preppie Murder *'89*
The Abduction of Kari Swenson *'87*
Fright Night *'85*
Emma Fielding
Pandaemonium *'00*
Speedy Death *'99*
A Respectable Trade *'98*
The Scarlet Tunic *'97*
Fenella Fielding
Arrivederci, Baby! *'66*
Carry On Screaming *'66*
Marjorie Fielding (1892-1956)
The Franchise Affair *'52*
The Lavender Hill Mob *'51*
Conspirator *'49*
The Demi-Paradise *'43*
Charlie Fields
The Beniker Gang *'83*
Fish Hawk *'79*
Christopher John Fields
Alien 3 *'92*
The Gun in Betty Lou's Handbag *'92*
Indecency *'92*
Holly Fields
Interceptor Force *'99*
Wishmaster 2: Evil Never Dies *'98*
Seedpeople *'92*
Kim Fields (1969-)
Uninvited Guest *'99*
The Kid with the Broken Halo *'82*
Robert Fields
Anna *'87*
The Sporting Club *'72*
The Incident *'67*
Stanley Fields (1884-1941)
Wide Open Faces *'38*
The Gay Desperado *'36*
Island of Lost Souls *'32*
Cimarron *'31*
Tony Fields (1958-95)
Across the Moon *'94*
Backstreet Dreams *'90*
Body Beat *'88*
Trick or Treat *'86*
W.C. Fields (1879-1946)
Sensations of 1945 *'44*
Mrs. Wiggs of the Cabbage Patch *'42*
Tales of Manhattan *'42*
Never Give a Sucker an Even Break *'41*
The Bank Dick *'40*
My Little Chickadee *'40*
You Can't Cheat an Honest Man *'39*
The Big Broadcast of 1938 *'38*
David Copperfield *'35*
It's a Gift *'34*
Six of a Kind *'34*
The Barber Shop *'33*
International House *'33*
The Dentist *'32*
Pharmacist *'32*
Running Wild *'27*
It's the Old Army Game *'26*
Sally of the Sawdust *'25*
Pool Sharks *'15*
Joseph Fiennes (1970-)
Enemy at the Gates *'00*
Rancid Aluminium *'00*
Forever Mine *'99*
Elizabeth *'98*
Shakespeare in Love *'98*
The Very Thought of You *'98*
Stealing Beauty *'96*
The Vacillations of Poppy Carew *'94*
Ralph Fiennes (1962-)
The Miracle Maker: The Story of Jesus *'00 (V)*
The End of the Affair *'99*
Onegin *'99*
Sunshine *'99*
The Avengers *'98*
Prince of Egypt *'98 (V)*
Oscar and Lucinda *'97*
The English Patient *'96*
Strange Days *'95*
Quiz Show *'94*
Schindler's List *'93*
Emily Bronte's Wuthering Heights *'92*
Prime Suspect *'92*
A Dangerous Man: Lawrence after Arabia *'91*
Harvey Fierstein (1954-)
Death to Smoochy *'02*
Common Ground *'00*
Playing Mona Lisa *'00*
Double Platinum *'99*
Mulan *'98 (V)*
Safe Men *'98*
Kull the Conqueror *'97*
Independence Day *'96*
Dr. Jekyll and Ms. Hyde *'95*
Bullets over Broadway *'94*
Mrs. Doubtfire *'93*
The Harvest *'92*
Tidy Endings *'88*
Torch Song Trilogy *'88*
Apology *'86*
Garbo Talks *'84*
Mike Figgis (1948-)
One Night Stand *'97*
Internal Affairs *'90*
George Figgs
Polyester *'81*
Female Trouble *'74*
Pink Flamingos *'72*
Multiple Maniacs *'70*
Efrain Figueroa
The Visit *'00*
Eastside *'99*
The Apostate *'98*
Desperate Measures *'98*
Star Maps *'97*
Kasia (Katarzyna) Figura (1962-)
Too Fast, Too Young *'96*
Fatal Past *'94*
Ready to Wear *'94*
Near Misses *'91*
Clyde Fillmore (1875-1946)
Laura *'44*
Watch on the Rhine *'43*
Nurse Marjorie *'20*
Dennis Fimple (1940-)
My Heroes Have Always Been Cowboys *'91*
Of Mice and Men *'81*
The $5.20 an Hour Dream *'80*
The Evictors *'79*
Creature from Black Lake *'76*
King Kong *'76*
Winterhawk *'76*
Truck Stop Women *'74*
Jon Finch (1941-)
Lurking Fear *'94*
Unexplained Laughter *'89*
Game of Seduction *'86*
Witching Time *'84*
And Nothing But the Truth *'82*
Peter and Paul *'81*
Breaking Glass *'80*
Death on the Nile *'78*
The Final Programme *'73*
Lady Caroline Lamb *'73*
Frenzy *'72*
Macbeth *'71*
Peter Finch (1916-77)
Raid on Entebbe *'77*
Network *'76*
Shattered *'72*
Sunday, Bloody Sunday *'71*
Red Tent *'69*
Far from the Madding Crowd *'67*
The Flight of the Phoenix *'65*
First Men in the Moon *'64*
Girl with Green Eyes *'64*
The Pumpkin Eater *'64*
Kidnapped *'60*
No Love for Johnnie *'60*
Operation Amsterdam *'60*
The Trials of Oscar Wilde *'60*
The Nun's Story *'59*
Pursuit of the Graf Spee *'57*
Robbery under Arms *'57*
Windom's Way *'57*
Make Me an Offer *'55*
The Warriors *'55*
The Detective *'54*
Elephant Walk *'54*
The Story of Robin Hood & His Merrie Men *'52*
Wooden Horse *'50*
Eureka Stockade *'49*
Train of Events *'49*
The Fighting Rats of Tobruk *'44*
Deborah Findlay
Wives and Daughters *'01*
Heat of the Sun *'99*
Larry Fine (1902-75)
The Outlaws Is Coming! *'65*
Around the World in a Daze *'63*
Four for Texas *'63*
It's a Mad, Mad, Mad, Mad World *'63*
Three Stooges in Orbit *'62*
Snow White and the Three Stooges *'61*
The Three Stooges Meet Hercules *'61*
Have Rocket Will Travel *'59*
Gold Raiders *'51*
Hollywood Party *'34*
Dancing Lady *'33*
The Lost Stooges *'33*
Travis Fine
Tomcats *'01*
My Antonia *'94*
Child's Play 3 *'91*
Anthony Finetti
Prime Time Murder *'92*
The Expendables *'89*
Frank Finlay (1926-)
Longitude *'00*
In the Secret State
Dreaming of Joseph Lees *'99*
The Magical Legend of the Leprechauns *'99*
A Mind to Murder *'96*
Stiff Upper Lips *'96*
Gospa *'94*
Stalin *'92*
Cthulhu Mansion *'91*
The Return of the Musketeers *'89*
Casanova *'87*
Arch of Triumph *'85*
Lifeforce *'85*
A Christmas Carol *'84*
The Death of Adolf Hitler *'84*
The Ploughman's Lunch *'83*
Enigma *'82*
Return of the Soldier *'82*
Murder by Decree *'79*
The Thief of Baghdad *'78*
Wild Geese *'78*
Bouquet of Barbed Wire *'76*
The Four Musketeers *'75*
The Three Musketeers *'74*
Shaft in Africa *'73*
Gumshoe *'72*
Assault *'70*
Cromwell *'70*
Molly Maguires *'70*
I'll Never Forget What's 'Isname *'67*
Robbery *'67*
A Study in Terror *'66*
Othello *'65*
The Loneliness of the Long Distance Runner *'62*
James Finlayson (1887-1953)
To Be or Not to Be *'42*
A Chump at Oxford *'40*
Saps at Sea *'40*
The Flying Deuces *'39*
Block-heads *'38*
All Over Town *'37*
Pick a Star *'37*
Way Out West *'37*
Bohemian Girl *'36*
Our Relations *'36*
Bonnie Scotland *'35*
Clark & McCullough *'33*
The Devil's Brother *'33*
Pack Up Your Troubles *'32*
Laurel & Hardy: Chickens Come Home *'31*
Pardon Us *'31*
No Man's Law *'27*
Jon Finlayson
A Kink in the Picasso *'90*
Lonely Hearts *'82*
Cameron Finley (1987-)
Perfect Game *'00*
Hope Floats *'98*
Leave It to Beaver *'97*
Evelyn Finley
Trail Riders *'42*
Dynamite Canyon *'41*
Margot Finley
Tourist Trap *'98*
In Cold Blood *'96*
William Finley (1944-)
The Funhouse *'81*
The Fury *'78*
Eaten Alive *'76*
Phantom of the Paradise *'74*
Sisters *'73*
The Wedding Party *'69*
John Finn
Deadlocked *'00*
Atomic Train *'99*
True Crime *'99*
Crazy Horse *'96*
Turbulence *'96*
Cover-Up *'91*
Quicksand: No Escape *'91*
Glory *'89*
John Finnegan
Finish Line *'89*
An American Tail *'86 (V)*
Warren Finnerty (1925-74)
Panic in Needle Park *'75*
Cockfighter *'74*
Easy Rider *'69*
Free Grass *'69*
Cool Hand Luke *'67*
The Brig *'64*
The Connection *'61*
Albert Finney (1936-)
My Uncle Silas *'01*
Erin Brockovich *'00*
Traffic *'00*
Simpatico *'99*
Breakfast of Champions *'98*
A Rather English Marriage *'98*
Washington Square *'97*
Nostromo *'96*
The Run of the Country *'95*
The Browning Version *'94*
A Man of No Importance *'94*
Rich in Love *'93*
The Playboys *'92*
The Green Man *'91*
Miller's Crossing *'90*
The Endless Game *'89*
The Image *'89*
Orphans *'87*
Pope John Paul II *'84*
Under the Volcano *'84*
The Dresser *'83*
Loophole *'83*
Annie *'82*
Shoot the Moon *'82*
Looker *'81*
Wolfen *'81*
The Duellists *'77*
Murder on the Orient Express *'74*
Alpha Beta *'73*
Gumshoe *'72*
Scrooge *'70*
Two for the Road *'67*
Tom Jones *'63*
The Entertainer *'60*
Saturday Night and Sunday Morning *'60*
Shirley Jo Finney
Echo Park *'86*
Wilma *'77*
Elena Fiore
Seven Beauties *'76*
Seduction of Mimi *'72*
Linda Fiorentino (1960-)
What Planet Are You From? *'00*
Where the Money Is *'00*
Dogma *'99*
Body Count *'97*
Kicked in the Head *'97*
Men in Black *'97*
Larger Than Life *'96*
Unforgettable *'96*
Bodily Harm *'95*
Jade *'95*
Charlie's Ghost: The Secret of Coronado *'94*
The Desperate Trail *'94*
The Last Seduction *'94*
Acting on Impulse *'93*
Chain of Desire *'93*
Beyond the Law *'92*
Queens Logic *'91*
Shout *'91*
Strangers *'91*
The Neon Empire *'89*
The Moderns *'88*
Wildfire *'88*
After Hours *'85*
Gotcha! *'85*
Vision Quest *'85*
Ann(e) Firbank
Flame to the Phoenix *'85*
Lillie *'79*
Asylum *'72*
Persuasion *'71*
Eddie Firestone (1920-)
Duel *'71*
Two for the Seesaw *'62*
The Law and Jake Wade *'58*
Colin Firth (1961-)
The Importance of Being Earnest *'02*
Bridget Jones's Diary *'01*
Conspiracy *'01*
Relative Values *'99*
The Turn of the Screw *'99*
My Life So Far *'98*
Shakespeare in Love *'98*
A Thousand Acres *'97*
The English Patient *'96*
Fever Pitch *'96*
Nostromo *'96*
Pride and Prejudice *'95*

Abbott and Costello Go to Mars '53
Abbott and Costello Meet the Killer, Boris Karloff '49
Blondie Hits the Jackpot '49
Cloak and Dagger '46
The Shanghai Cobra '45
Abroad with Two Yanks '44
Hollywood Canteen '44
Laura '44
Uncertain Glory '44
Air Force '43
So Proudly We Hail '43
Brand of Hate '34
King Kong '33

Flea (1962-)
Fear and Loathing in Las Vegas '98
The Big Lebowski '97
The Chase '93
Motorama '91
My Own Private Idaho '91
Back to the Future, Part 2 '89
Dudes '87

John Fleck (1951-)
Gunshy '98
The Comrades of Summer '92
Mutant on the Bounty '89
Tapeheads '89

James Fleet
Charlotte Gray '01
Kevin & Perry Go Large '00
Frenchman's Creek '98
Grave Indiscretions '96
Moll Flanders '96
Sense and Sensibility '95
Cracker: The Big Crunch '94
Four Weddings and a Funeral '94

Mick Fleetwood
Zero Tolerance '93
The Running Man '87

Susan Fleetwood (1944-95)
Persuasion '95
The Buddha of Suburbia '92
The Krays '90
White Mischief '88
The Sacrifice '86
Heat and Dust '82
Murder of a Moderate Man '70s

Charles Fleischer (1950-)
Boltneck '98
Ground Control '98
Permanent Midnight '98
Gridlock'd '96
Tales from the Crypt Presents Demon Knight '94
We're Back! A Dinosaur's Story '93 (V)
Straight Talk '92
Back to the Future, Part 2 '89
Honey, I Shrunk the Kids '89 (V)
Bad Dreams '88
Who Framed Roger Rabbit '88 (V)
A Nightmare on Elm Street '84

Noah Fleiss (1984-)
Storytelling '01
Double Parked '00
Things You Can Tell Just by Looking at Her '00
The Truth About Jane '00
Joe the King '99
An Unexpected Life '97
An Unexpected Family '96
A Mother's Prayer '95
Josh and S.A.M. '93

Eric Fleming (1925-66)
The Glass Bottom Boat '66
Curse of the Undead '59
Queen of Outer Space '58
Fright '56
Conquest of Space '55

Ian Fleming (1888-1969)
The Trials of Oscar Wilde '60
Land of Fury '55
Norman Conquest '53
Butler's Dilemma '43
Murder at the Baskervilles '37
When Thief Meets Thief '37
The Triumph of Sherlock Holmes '35

Lone Fleming (1949-)
Return of the Evil Dead '75
Tombs of the Blind Dead '72
It Happened at Nightmare Inn '70

Rhonda Fleming (1923-)
The Nude Bomb '80
Alias Jesse James '59
Bullwhip '58
Gun Glory '57
Gunfight at the O.K. Corral '57
Slightly Scarlet '56
While the City Sleeps '56
Tennessee's Partner '55
Pony Express '53
Cavalry Charge '51
Cry Danger '51
A Connecticut Yankee in King Arthur's Court '49
The Great Lover '49
Adventure Island '47
Out of the Past '47
Abilene Town '46
The Spiral Staircase '46
Spellbound '45
Since You Went Away '44

Jason Flemyng (1966-)
The Body '01
From Hell '01
Mean Machine '01
Rock Star '01
Bruiser '00
Snatch '00
Deep Rising '98
Lock, Stock and 2 Smoking Barrels '98
The Red Violin '98
Tess of the D'Urbervilles '98
Spice World: The Movie '97
Alive and Kicking '96
Stealing Beauty '96
Hollow Reed '95
Rob Roy '95
A Question of Attribution '91

Robert Flemyng (1912-95)
Kafka '91
Blood Beast Terror '67
Vanity Fair '67
The Horrible Dr. Hichcock '62
Cast a Dark Shadow '55
The Man Who Never Was '55
The Blue Lamp '49
Conspirator '49
The Guinea Pig '48

Alan Fletcher
Gross Misconduct '93
Fran '85

Bramwell Fletcher (1904-88)
Random Harvest '42
The Undying Monster '42
White Cargo '42
The Scarlet Pimpernel '34
The Mummy '32
Daughter of the Dragon '31
Raffles '30

Brendan Fletcher
Jimmy Zip '00
The Five Senses '99
Summer's End '99
Air Bud '97
Trucks '97
Contagious '96
Dead Ahead '96

Dexter Fletcher (1966-)
Lock, Stock and 2 Smoking Barrels '98
The Raggedy Rawney '90
Twisted Obsession '90
The Rachel Papers '89
Lionheart '87
The Long Good Friday '80

Diane Fletcher
The Aristocrats '99
The Final Cut '95
To Play the King '93

Dusty Fletcher
Boardinghouse Blues '48
Killer Diller '48

Louise Fletcher (1934-)
Big Eden '00
The Devil's Arithmetic '99
A Map of the World '99
Time Served '99
Cruel Intentions '98
Love Kills '98
Breast Men '97
Love to Kill '97
Sins of the Mind '97
Frankenstein and Me '96
High School High '96
Two Days in the Valley '96
Edie & Pen '95
Virtuosity '95
The Haunting of Seacliff Inn '94
Tollbooth '94
Tryst '94
Return to Two Moon Junction '93
The Player '92
Blind Vision '91
Blue Steel '90
Nightmare on the 13th Floor '90
Best of the Best '89
Final Notice '89
Shadowzone '89
Two Moon Junction '88
Flowers in the Attic '87
Islands '87
J. Edgar Hoover '87
The Boy Who Could Fly '86
Invaders from Mars '86
Nobody's Fool '86
Firestarter '84
A Summer to Remember '84
Brainstorm '83
Overnight Sensation '83
Strange Invaders '83
Talk to Me '82
Strange Behavior '81
Mama Dracula '80
Lady in Red '79
The Magician of Lublin '79
Natural Enemies '79
The Cheap Detective '78
The Exorcist 2: The Heretic '77
One Flew Over the Cuckoo's Nest '75
Russian Roulette '75
Thieves Like Us '74

Neil Fletcher
Creature of Destruction '67
Zontar, the Thing from Venus '66

Page Fletcher
Ordeal in the Arctic '93
Friends, Lovers & Lunatics '89
Humongous '82

Suzanne Fletcher
Bloodsucking Pharoahs of Pittsburgh '90
Sleepwalk '88

Sam Flint (1882-1980)
Command Decision '48
The Chinese Cat '44
Spy Smasher '42
Spy Smasher Returns '42
A Face in the Fog '36
The Lawless Nineties '36
Red Lights Ahead '36
Red River Valley '36
Evelyn Prentice '34

Jay C. Flippen (1900-71)
Firecreek '68
Hellfighters '68
The Restless Breed '58
Jet Pilot '57
The Killing '56
The King and Four Queens '56
Seventh Cavalry '56
Far Country '55
Oklahoma! '55
The Wild One '54
Devil's Canyon '53
Flying Leathernecks '51
The Lemon Drop Kid '51
Winchester '73 '50
The Yellow Cab Man '50
They Live by Night '49
A Woman's Secret '49
Marie Galante '34

Calista Flockhart (1964-)
Things You Can Tell Just by Looking at Her '00
William Shakespeare's A Midsummer Night's Dream '99
Drunks '96
Jane Doe '96
Telling Lies in America '96
The Birdcage '95

Suzanne Flon (1918-)
One Deadly Summer '83
Mr. Klein '76
The Train '65
Un Singe en Hiver '62
Moulin Rouge '52

Michael Flood
Death Nurse '87
Crazy Fat Ethel II '85
Criminally Insane '75

Sheila Florance
A Woman's Tale '92
Cactus '86

Dann Florek (1950-)
Beautiful Joe '00
From the Earth to the Moon '98
Hard Rain '97
The Flintstones '94
Angel Heart '87

Florelle
The Crime of Monsieur Lange '36
Liliom '35

Von Flores (1960-)
Tracked '98
The Assignment '97
Frame by Frame '95
Eclipse '94

Holly Floria
Private Wars '93
Bikini Island '91
Presumed Guilty '91
Netherworld '90

George "Buck" Flower (1936-)
Relentless '89
Cheerleader Camp '88
Pumpkinhead '88
They Live '88
Sorority Babes in the Slimeball Bowl-A-Rama '87
In Search of a Golden Sky '84
Escape from New York '81
The Capture of Bigfoot '79
Mountain Family Robinson '79
Further Adventures of the Wilderness Family, Part 2 '77
Across the Great Divide '76
Candy Tangerine Man '75
Devil & Leroy Basset '73

Kim Flowers
Alien: Resurrection '97
Nobody's Perfect '90

Robert Floyd
The Song of the Lark '01
Cold Hearts '99

Roger Floyd
Big City Blues '99
The Walking Dead '94

Susan Floyd
Domestic Disturbance '01
Random Hearts '99
Breathing Room '96

Darlanne Fluegel (1956-)
Darkman 3: Die Darkman Die '95
Relative Fear '95
Breaking Point '94
Scanner Cop '94
Slaughter of the Innocents '93
Pet Sematary 2 '92
Lock Up '89
Project: Alien '89
Bulletproof '88
Deadly Stranger '88
Freeway '88
Running Scared '86
Tough Guys '86
To Live & Die in L.A. '85
Concrete Beat '84
Once Upon a Time in America '84
The Last Fight '82
Battle Beyond the Stars '80
Eyes of Laura Mars '78

Joel Fluellen (1907-90)
Man Friday '75
A Dream for Christmas '73
The Great White Hope '70
Run Silent, Run Deep '58
The Jackie Robinson Story '50

Barbara Flynn (1948-)
Lorna Doone '01
Wives and Daughters '01
King Lear '98
Cracker: Brotherly Love '95
Cracker: To Be a Somebody '94

Colleen Flynn (1962-)
Serving in Silence: The Margarethe Cammermeyer Story '95
Incident at Deception Ridge '94
The Temp '93

Errol Flynn (1909-59)
Assault of the Rebel Girls '59
Istanbul '57
The King's Rhapsody '55
Let's Make Up '55
The Warriors '55
The Master of Ballantrae '53
Against All Flags '52
Adventures of Captain Fabian '51
Kim '50
That Forsyte Woman '50
Adventures of Don Juan '49
It's a Great Feeling '49
Silver River '48
Cry Wolf '47
Escape Me Never '47
Never Say Goodbye '46
Objective, Burma! '45
San Antonio '45
Uncertain Glory '44
Edge of Darkness '43
Northern Pursuit '43
Thank Your Lucky Stars '43
Desperate Journey '42
Gentleman Jim '42
Dive Bomber '41
Footsteps in the Dark '41
They Died with Their Boots On '41
Santa Fe Trail '40
The Sea Hawk '40
Virginia City '40
Dodge City '39
The Private Lives of Elizabeth & Essex '39
The Adventures of Robin Hood '38
Dawn Patrol '38
The Sisters '38
The Prince and the Pauper '37
The Charge of the Light Brigade '36
Captain Blood '35

Jerome Flynn (1963-)
A Mind to Murder '96
Edward II '92
A Summer Story '88

Joe Flynn (1924-74)
The Rescuers '77 (V)
Gentle Savage '73
Superdad '73
Now You See Him, Now You Don't '72
The Barefoot Executive '71
How to Frame a Figg '71
Million Dollar Duck '71
The Computer Wore Tennis Shoes '69
My Dog, the Thief '69
Divorce American Style '67
McHale's Navy Joins the Air Force '65
McHale's Navy '64
Lover Come Back '61

Kimberly Flynn
Boys Life '94
Rhythm Thief '94
Revolution! A Red Comedy '91

Michael Flynn (1944-)
Partners in Crime '99
Address Unknown '96
Out of Annie's Past '94

Miriam Flynn
Vegas Vacation '96
National Lampoon's Christmas Vacation '89
18 Again! '88
National Lampoon's Vacation '83

Sean Flynn
Mission to Venice '63
Son of Captain Blood '62

Steve Flynn
Scarred City '98
Ulee's Gold '97
Without Warning: The James Brady Story '91

Spiros Focas (1937-)
White Palace '90
Rambo 3 '88
The Jewel of the Nile '85
Rocco and His Brothers '60

Nina Foch (1924-)
Hush '98
Til There Was You '96
Armistead Maupin's Tales of the City '93
Morning Glory '93
Sliver '93
Skin Deep '89
Dixie Lanes '88
Child of Glass '78
Jennifer '78
Mahogany '75
Salty '73
Columbo: Prescription Murder '67
Cash McCall '60
Spartacus '60
The Ten Commandments '56
Illegal '55
Executive Suite '54
Scaramouche '52
An American in Paris '51
St. Benny the Dip '51
The Dark Past '49
A Song to Remember '45
Cry of the Werewolf '44
Return of the Vampire '43

Brenda Fogarty
Fairy Tales '76
Deadly Fieldtrip '74

Vladimar Fogel
Bed and Sofa '27
The Girl with the Hat Box '27

Freda Foh Shen
Mulan '98 (V)
The Tiger Woods Story '98

Dennis Folbigge
Howling 4: The Original Nightmare '88
Zulu '64

Dave Foley (1963-)
Monkeybone '01
On the Line '01
Dick '99

Blast from the Past '98
A Bug's Life '98 (V)
From the Earth to the Moon '98
Sink or Swim '97
Kids in the Hall: Brain Candy '96
It's Pat: The Movie '94

Ellen Foley
Married to the Mob '88
Fatal Attraction '87

Jeremy Foley
Soccer Dog: The Movie '98
Dante's Peak '97

Macka Foley
WarCat '88
Las Vegas Weekend '85

Michael Foley
Karate Cop '93
Prison Planet '92
The Divine Enforcer '91

Scott Foley (1973-)
Scream 3 '00
Forever Love '98

Alison Folland (1978-)
Boys Don't Cry '99
All Over Me '96
Before and After '95
To Die For '95

Megan Follows (1968-)
Anne of Green Gables: The Continuing Story '99
The Chase '91
The Nutcracker Prince '91 (V)
Back to Hannibal: The Return of Tom Sawyer and Huckleberry Finn '90
Termini Station '89
A Time of Destiny '88
Anne of Avonlea '87
Stacking '87
Anne of Green Gables '85
Silver Bullet '85
Hockey Night '84

Bridget Fonda (1964-)
Kiss of the Dragon '01
Monkeybone '01
South of Heaven, West of Hell '00
Lake Placid '99
The Break Up '98
Finding Graceland '98
Mr. Jealousy '98
A Simple Plan '98
In the Gloaming '97
Jackie Brown '97
Grace of My Heart '96
Touch '96
Balto '95 (V)
City Hall '95
Rough Magic '95
Camilla '94
It Could Happen to You '94
The Road to Wellville '94
Bodies, Rest & Motion '93
Little Buddha '93
Point of No Return '93
Army of Darkness '92
Single White Female '92
Singles '92
Doc Hollywood '91
Iron Maze '91
Frankenstein Unbound '90
The Godfather, Part 3 '90
Leather Jackets '90
Out of the Rain '90
Strapless '90
Scandal '89
Shag: The Movie '89
Aria '88
Jacob Have I Loved '88
Light Years '88 (V)
You Can't Hurry Love '88

Henry Fonda (1905-82)
Oldest Living Graduate '82
On Golden Pond '81
Summer Solstice '81
Gideon's Trumpet '80
Home to Stay '79
Meteor '79
Roots: The Next Generation '79
Wanda Nevada '79
Battleforce '78
City on Fire '78
The Swarm '78
Last Four Days '77
Rollercoaster '77
Tentacles '77
Great Smokey Roadblock '76
Midway '76
The Red Pony '76
My Name Is Nobody '74
Ash Wednesday '73
Night Flight from Moscow '73
Sometimes a Great Notion '71
The Cheyenne Social Club '70
There Was a Crooked Man '70
Too Late the Hero '70
The Boston Strangler '68
Firecreek '68
Madigan '68
Once Upon a Time in the West '68
Yours, Mine & Ours '68
A Big Hand for the Little Lady '66
Battle of the Bulge '65
In Harm's Way '65
The Rounders '65
The Best Man '64
Fail-Safe '64
Sex and the Single Girl '64
How the West Was Won '63
Spencer's Mountain '63
Advise and Consent '62
The Longest Day '62
Warlock '59
Stage Struck '57
The Tin Star '57
Twelve Angry Men '57
War and Peace '56
The Wrong Man '56
Mister Roberts '55
Jigsaw '49
Fort Apache '48
The Fugitive '48
On Our Merry Way '48
The Long Night '47
My Darling Clementine '46
Immortal Sergeant '43
The Ox-Bow Incident '43
Big Street '42
The Magnificent Dope '42
Tales of Manhattan '42
The Lady Eve '41
The Grapes of Wrath '40
Return of Frank James '40
Drums Along the Mohawk '39
Jesse James '39
The Story of Alexander Graham Bell '39
Young Mr. Lincoln '39
Jezebel '38
Mad Miss Manton '38
Spawn of the North '38
That Certain Woman '37
Wings of the Morning '37
You Only Live Once '37
The Moon's Our Home '36
The Trail of the Lonesome Pine '36
The Farmer Takes a Wife '35
I Dream Too Much '35

Jane Fonda (1937-)
Stanley and Iris '90
Old Gringo '89
The Morning After '86
Agnes of God '85
The Dollmaker '84
On Golden Pond '81
Rollover '81
9 to 5 '80
The China Syndrome '79
The Electric Horseman '79
California Suite '78
Comes a Horseman '78
Coming Home '78
Fun with Dick and Jane '77
Julia '77
A Doll's House '73
Steelyard Blues '73
Klute '71
They Shoot Horses, Don't They? '69
Barbarella '68
Spirits of the Dead '68
Barefoot in the Park '67
Any Wednesday '66
The Chase '66
The Game Is Over '66
Cat Ballou '65
Circle of Love '64
Joy House '64
Period of Adjustment '62
Walk on the Wild Side '62
Tall Story '60

Peter Fonda (1939-)
The Laramie Project '02
Second Skin '00
South of Heaven, West of Hell '00
Thomas and the Magic Railroad '00
The Limey '99
The Passion of Ayn Rand '99
The Tempest '99
Ulee's Gold '97
Escape from L.A. '96
Grace of My Heart '96 (V)
Nadja '95
Love and a .45 '94
Molly and Gina '94
Bodies, Rest & Motion '93
Deadfall '93
South Beach '92
Fatal Mission '89
The Rose Garden '89
Mercenary Fighters '88
Hawken's Breed '87
Certain Fury '85
Jungle Heat '84
Spasms '82
Split Image '82
Cannonball Run '81
The Hostage Tower '80
Wanda Nevada '79
High Ballin' '78
Outlaw Blues '77
Fighting Mad '76
Futureworld '76
92 in the Shade '76
Killer Force '75
Race with the Devil '75
Dirty Mary Crazy Larry '74
Hired Hand '71
The Last Movie '71
Easy Rider '69
Spirits of the Dead '68
The Trip '67
The Wild Angels '66
Lilith '64
Tammy and the Doctor '63

Phil Fondacaro (1958-)
The Creeps '97
Dollman vs Demonic Toys '93
Meridian: Kiss of the Beast '90
Ghoulies 2 '87
Troll '86

Benson Fong (1916-87)
Kung Fu: The Movie '86
Our Man Flint '66
Girls! Girls! Girls! '62
Conquest of Space '55
His Majesty O'Keefe '53
Deception '46
The Scarlet Clue '45
The Shanghai Cobra '45
Charlie Chan in the Secret Service '44
The Chinese Cat '44
The Purple Heart '44

Leo Fong (1928-)
Showdown '93
Killpoint '84
The Last Reunion '80
Blind Rage '78
Enforcer from Death Row '78

Joan Fontaine (1917-)
The Witches '66
Voyage to the Bottom of the Sea '61
Island in the Sun '57
Until They Sail '57
Beyond a Reasonable Doubt '56
Casanova's Big Night '54
The Bigamist '53
Decameron Nights '53
Ivanhoe '52
Othello '52
Born to Be Bad '50
September Affair '50
Emperor Waltz '48
Letter from an Unknown Woman '48
You Gotta Stay Happy '48
Frenchman's Creek '44
Jane Eyre '44
Suspicion '41
Rebecca '40
Gunga Din '39
The Women '39
The Duke of West Point '38
Maid's Night Out '38
A Damsel in Distress '37
A Million to One '37

Genevieve Fontanel
Grain of Sand '84
The Man Who Loved Women '77

Shawn Fonteno
The Wash '01
Three Strikes '00

Hallie Foote (1953-)
Horton Foote's Alone '97
The Habitation of Dragons '91
Courtship '87
The Little Match Girl '87
On Valentine's Day '86
1918 '85

Horton Foote, Jr.
Blood Red '88
On Valentine's Day '86
1918 '85

Dick Foran (1910-79)
Brighty of the Grand Canyon '67
Atomic Submarine '59
Deputy Marshal '50
Guest Wife '45
The Mummy's Tomb '42
Private Buckaroo '42
Ride 'Em Cowboy '42
Riders of Death Valley '41
The Fighting 69th '40
The House of the Seven Gables '40
The Mummy's Hand '40
My Little Chickadee '40
Winners of the West '40
Boy Meets Girl '38
Four Daughters '38
The Sisters '38
The Black Legion '37
Earthworm Tractors '36
Petrified Forest '36
Dangerous '35

June Foray (1919-)
The Adventures of Rocky & Bullwinkle '00 (V)
Mulan '98 (V)
Thumbelina '94 (V)
DuckTales the Movie: Treasure of the Lost Lamp '90 (V)
Who Framed Roger Rabbit '88 (V)
Looney Looney Looney Bugs Bunny Movie '81 (V)
Scruffy '80 (V)
Sabaka '55

Brenda Forbes (1909-96)
The Man Upstairs '93
The White Cliffs of Dover '44
Mrs. Miniver '42

Bryan Forbes (1926-)
December Flower
The Slipper and the Rose '76
A Shot in the Dark '64
The Guns of Navarone '61
The League of Gentlemen '60
Quatermass 2 '57
The Baby and the Battleship '56
The Colditz Story '55
Wooden Horse '50

Mary Forbes (1883-1974)
You Gotta Stay Happy '48
Tender Comrade '43
You Can't Cheat an Honest Man '39
You Can't Take It with You '38
The Awful Truth '37
Vanity Fair '32

Michelle Forbes (1967-)
Perfume '01
Homicide: The Movie '00
Escape from L.A. '96
Black Day Blue Night '95
Swimming with Sharks '94
Kalifornia '93

Ralph Forbes (1902-51)
Frenchman's Creek '44
Convicts at Large '38
Legion of Missing Men '37
Make a Wish '37
I'll Name the Murderer '36
Riptide '34
Twentieth Century '34
The Phantom Broadcast '33
Smilin' Through '33
Inside the Lines '30

Anitra Ford
The Longest Yard '74
Invasion of the Bee Girls '73
Stacey '73
The Big Bird Cage '72

Ann Ford
Logan's Run '76
The Love Machine '71

Constance Ford (1923-93)
All Fall Down '62
Rome Adventure '62
Home from the Hill '60
A Summer Place '59
The Last Hunt '56

Dorothy Ford
Jack & the Beanstalk '52
On Our Merry Way '48

Faith Ford (1960-)
Sometimes They Come Back ... For More '99
A Weekend in the Country '96
North '94
Murder So Sweet '93
You Talkin' to Me? '87

Francis Ford (1881-1953)
The Quiet Man '52
She Wore a Yellow Ribbon '49
Accomplice '46
Girls in Chains '43
Lucky Cisco Kid '40
Stagecoach '39
The Texans '38
Man from Monterey '33
Battling with Buffalo Bill '31

Glenn Ford (1916-)
Final Verdict '91
Raw Nerve '91
Border Shootout '90
Casablanca Express '89
Virus '82
Day of the Assassin '81
Happy Birthday to Me '81
The Visitor '80
The Sacketts '79
Superman: The Movie '78
Midway '76
Santee '73
Smith! '69
Is Paris Burning? '66
The Rounders '65
The Courtship of Eddie's Father '62
Experiment in Terror '62
The Four Horsemen of the Apocalypse '62
Pocketful of Miracles '61
Cimarron '60
The Gazebo '59
It Started with a Kiss '59
Cowboy '58
Torpedo Run '58
Don't Go Near the Water '57
3:10 to Yuma '57
Fastest Gun Alive '56
Jubal '56
The Teahouse of the August Moon '56
Americano '55
Blackboard Jungle '55
Interrupted Melody '55
The Violent Men '55
Human Desire '54
Appointment in Honduras '53
The Big Heat '53
Man from the Alamo '53
Affair in Trinidad '52
The Green Glove '52
The White Tower '50
Lust for Gold '49
Man from Colorado '49
The Loves of Carmen '48
Gilda '46
A Stolen Life '46
The Desperadoes '43
Destroyer '43
So Ends Our Night '41
Texas '41
Blondie Plays Cupid '40
The Lady in Question '40

Harrison Ford (1884-1957)
The Nervous Wreck '26
The Average Woman '24
Foolish Wives '22
Shadows '22
Hawthorne of the USA '19
The Primitive Lover '16

Harrison Ford (1942-)
K-19: The Widowmaker '02
What Lies Beneath '00
Random Hearts '99
Six Days, Seven Nights '98
Air Force One '97
The Devil's Own '96
Sabrina '95
Clear and Present Danger '94
The Fugitive '93
Patriot Games '92
Regarding Henry '91
Presumed Innocent '90
Indiana Jones and the Last Crusade '89
Frantic '88
Working Girl '88
The Mosquito Coast '86
Witness '85
Indiana Jones and the Temple of Doom '84
Return of the Jedi '83
Blade Runner '82
Raiders of the Lost Ark '81
The Empire Strikes Back '80
Apocalypse Now '79
The Frisco Kid '79
Hanover Street '79
More American Graffiti '79
Force 10 from Navarone '78
Heroes '77
Star Wars '77
The Conversation '74
American Graffiti '73
Getting Straight '70
Zabriskie Point '70
Dead Heat on a Merry-Go-Round '66

Maria Ford
Dark Planet '97
Future Fear '97
The Glass Cage '96
The Wasp Woman '96
Alien Terminator '95
Burial of the Rats '95
Machine Gun Blues '95
Night Hunter '95
The Showgirl Murders '95
Stripteaser '95
Angel of Destruction '94
H.P. Lovecraft's Necronomicon: Book of the Dead '93

Deathstalker 4: Match of Titans '92
Final Judgment '92
Ring of Fire 2: Blood and Steel '92
Saturday Night Special '92
The Unnamable 2: The Statement of Randolph Carter '92
Futurekick '91
The Haunting of Morella '91
Naked Obsession '91
Ring of Fire '91
The Rain Killer '90
Slumber Party Massacre 3 '90
Masque of the Red Death '89
Stripped to Kill II: Live Girls '89
Dance of the Damned '88

Mick Ford
How to Get Ahead in Advertising '89
Scum '79

Paul Ford (1901-76)
Lola '69
The Comedians '67
The Russians Are Coming, the Russians Are Coming '66
Who's Got the Action? '63
Advise and Consent '62
The Music Man '62
The Matchmaker '58
Missouri Traveler '58
The Teahouse of the August Moon '56
Lust for Gold '49

Ross Ford (1923-88)
Reform School Girl '57
Project Moon Base '53
Blue Canadian Rockies '52
Jungle Patrol '48

Ruth Ford (1915-)
The Eyes of the Amaryllis '82
Strange Impersonation '46
The Woman Who Came Back '45
The Lady Is Willing '42

Steven Ford (1956-)
Black Hawk Down '01
Against the Law '98
When Harry Met Sally... '89
Body Count '87

Wallace Ford (1898-1966)
A Patch of Blue '65
Warlock '59
Last Hurrah '58
The Matchmaker '58
The Rainmaker '56
A Lawless Street '55
The Man from Laramie '55
The Maverick Queen '55
She Couldn't Say No '52
Harvey '50
Great Jesse James Raid '49
The Set-Up '49
Coroner Creek '48
Dead Reckoning '47
T-Men '47
Black Angel '46
Crack-Up '46
Blood on the Sun '45
Spellbound '45
The Ape Man '43
Shadow of a Doubt '43
All Through the Night '42
Inside the Law '42
The Mummy's Tomb '42
Seven Days' Leave '42
Wheel of Fortune '41
The Mummy's Hand '40
Back Door to Heaven '39
Jericho '38
Exiled to Shanghai '37
Mad About Money '37
O.H.M.S. '37
Swing It, Sailor! '37
Rogue's Tavern '36
Get That Man '35
The Informer '35
Mysterious Mr. Wong '35
One Frightened Night '35
The Whole Town's Talking '35
The Lost Patrol '34
Employees' Entrance '33
Night of Terror '33
Freaks '32
Skyscraper Souls '32
Possessed '31

Ken Foree
The Dentist '96
Leatherface: The Texas Chainsaw Massacre 3 '89
Glitz '88
From Beyond '86
Dawn of the Dead '78

Deborah Foreman (1962-)
Lunatics: A Love Story '92
Sundown '91
The Experts '89
Friends, Lovers & Lunatics '89
Lobster Man from Mars '89
Destroyer '88
Waxwork '88
April Fool's Day '86
My Chauffeur '86
3:15—The Moment of Truth '86
Valley Girl '83

Jamie Foreman
Breathtaking '00
Saving Grace '00

Michelle Foreman
Sunset Strip '91
Stripped to Kill '87

Mark Forest (1933-)
Goliath and the Sins of Babylon '64
Hercules vs. the Sons of the Sun '64
The Lion of Thebes '64
Terror of Rome Against the Son of Hercules '64
Son of Samson '62
Goliath and the Dragon '61
Mole Men Against the Son of Hercules '61
Colossus of the Arena '60

Michael Forest (1929-)
Cast Away '00
Body of Evidence '92
The Message '77
Dirt Gang '71
Atlas '60
The Beast from Haunted Cave '60
Ski Troop Attack '60

Farrah Forke (1967-)
Kate's Addiction '99
Ground Control '98
National Lampoon's Favorite Deadly Sins '95

Claire Forlani (1972-)
Antitrust '00
Boys and Girls '00
Mystery Men '99
Basil '98
Meet Joe Black '98
Basquiat '96
The Last Time I Committed Suicide '96
The Rock '96
Mallrats '95

Carol Forman (1919-97)
Federal Agents vs. Underworld, Inc. '49
The Black Widow '47

Milos Forman (1932-)
Keeping the Faith '00
New Year's Day '89
Heartburn '86

Richard Foronjy (1937-)
Man of the House '95
DaVinci's War '92
The Public Eye '92
Midnight Run '88
The Morning After '86
Prince of the City '81

Veronica Forque
Kika '94
Why Do They Call It Love When They Mean Sex? '92

Christine Forrest
Monkey Shines '88
Martin '77

Frederic Forrest (1938-)
Militia '99
Sweetwater: A True Rock Story '99
Black Thunder '98
Boogie Boy '98
The First 9 1/2 Weeks '98
Implicated '98
Point Blank '98
Whatever '98
The End of Violence '97
Horton Foote's Alone '97
Crash Dive '96
Andersonville '95
One Night Stand '95
Against the Wall '94
Chasers '94
Lassie '94
Dario Argento's Trauma '93
Double Obsession '93
Falling Down '93
Hidden Fears '93
Rain Without Thunder '93
Citizen Cohn '92
The Habitation of Dragons '91
Hearts of Darkness: A Filmmaker's Apocalypse '91
Twin Sisters '91
Cat Chaser '90
The Two Jakes '90
Double Exposure: The Story of Margaret Bourke-White '89
Lonesome Dove '89
Music Box '89
Best Kept Secrets '88
Gotham '88
Return '88
Shadow on the Sun '88
Tucker: The Man and His Dream '88
Valentino Returns '88
Saigon: Year of the Cat '87
Stacking '87
The Deliberate Stranger '86
The Adventures of Huckleberry Finn '85
Quo Vadis '85
Where Are the Children? '85
The Stone Boy '84
Valley Girl '83
Calamity Jane '82
Hammett '82
One from the Heart '82
Apocalypse Now '79
The Rose '79
It's Alive 2: It Lives Again '78
Missouri Breaks '76
Permission To Kill '75
The Conversation '74
Larry '74
The Don Is Dead '73
When the Legends Die '72

Irene Forrest
Bride of Re-Animator '89
Sitting Ducks '80

Sally Forrest (1928-)
Son of Sinbad '55
The Strange Door '51
Vengeance Valley '51
Streets of Sin '49

Steve Forrest (1924-)
Killer: A Journal of Murder '95
Amazon Women on the Moon '87
Gunsmoke: Return to Dodge '87
The Last of the Mohicans '85
Spies Like Us '85
Sahara '83
Hotline '82
Mommie Dearest '81
Roughnecks '80
A Rumor of War '80
Captain America '79
North Dallas Forty '79
The Deerslayer '78
The Hatfields & the McCoys '75
The Hanged Man '74
The Wild Country '71
Flaming Star '60
Heller in Pink Tights '60
Battle Circus '53
Clown '53

William Forrest (1902-89)
Billy the Kid Versus Dracula '66
The Horse Soldiers '59
Jailhouse Rock '57
I'll See You in My Dreams '51
Fighting Seabees '44
Air Force '43
The Masked Marvel '43
Wake Island '42
Dive Bomber '41
International Lady '41

Cay Forrester
Door to Door Maniac '61
D.O.A. '49

Constance Forslund (1950-)
Village of the Damned '95
River's Edge '87
A Shining Season '79
Dear Detective '78

Kathrine (Kate) Forster (1969-)
Mulholland Drive '01
Hollywood Harry '86

Robert Forster (1941-)
Human Nature '02
Lone Hero '02
Mulholland Drive '01
Family Tree '00
Kiss Toledo Goodbye '00
Me, Myself, and Irene '00
It's the Rage '99
Supernova '99
Outside Ozona '98
Psycho '98
Rear Window '98
Hindsight '97
Jackie Brown '97
Night Vision '97
Uncle Sam '96
Scanner Cop 2: Volkin's Revenge '94
Scanners: The Showdown '94
Cover Story '93
Maniac Cop 3: Badge of Silence '93
In Between '92
Committed '91
Diplomatic Immunity '91
29th Street '91
Peacemaker '90
Satan's Princess '90
The Banker '89
Once a Hero '88
Delta Force '86
Hollywood Harry '86
Vigilante '83
Walking the Edge '83
Goliath Awaits '81
Alligator '80
The Black Hole '79
Avalanche '78
Standing Tall '78
Stunts '77
The City '76
The Death Squad '73
The Don Is Dead '73
Journey Through Rosebud '72
Medium Cool '69
The Stalking Moon '69

Rudolph Forster (1884-1968)
The Mad Executioners '65
The Return of Dr. Mabuse '61
The Threepenny Opera '31

Bruce Forsyth
Bedknobs and Broomsticks '71
Star! '68

Rosemary Forsyth (1945-)
John Carpenter's Ghosts of Mars '01
Girl '98
Daylight '96
Disclosure '94
A Friendship in Vienna '88
The Gladiator '86
Gray Lady Down '77
My Father's House '75
Columbo: Murder by the Book '71
Whatever Happened to Aunt Alice? '69
Texas across the River '66
Shenandoah '65
The War Lord '65

Drew Forsythe (1950-)
Billy's Holiday '95
Wrangler '88
Burke & Wills '85
A Test of Love '84
Doctors and Nurses '82

Henderson Forsythe (1917-)
Carolina Skeletons '92
Teamster Boss: The Jackie Presser Story '92
Midnight Murders '91
Sessions '83
Crisis at Central High '80

John Forsythe (1918-)
Charlie's Angels '00 (V)
Scrooged '88
Mysterious Two '82
Sizzle '81
A Time for Miracles '80
And Justice for All '79
Cruise into Terror '78
Users '78
Sniper '75
Cry Panic '74
Terror on the 40th Floor '74
Murder Once Removed '71
The Happy Ending '69
Topaz '69
In Cold Blood '67
Madame X '66
Kitten with a Whip '64
The Ambassador's Daughter '56
The Trouble with Harry '55
Escape from Fort Bravo '53
Destination Tokyo '43

William Forsythe (1955-)
Hard Cash '01
Camouflage '00
Luck of the Draw '00
Big City Blues '99
Blue Streak '99
Deuce Bigalow: Male Gigolo '99
Four Days '99
Hitman's Journal '99
The Last Marshal '99
For Which He Stands '98
Highway Hitcher '98
Row Your Boat '98
Firestorm '97
First Time Felon '97
Hell's Kitchen NYC '97
Gotti '96
The Rock '96
The Substitute '96
The Immortals '95
Palookaville '95
Things to Do in Denver When You're Dead '95
Virtuosity '95
Beyond Desire '94
Direct Hit '93
Relentless 3 '93
American Me '92
The Gun in Betty Lou's Handbag '92
Career Opportunities '91
Out for Justice '91
Stone Cold '91
The Waterdance '91
Dick Tracy '90
Torrents of Spring '90
Dead Bang '89
Patty Hearst '88
Extreme Prejudice '87
Raising Arizona '87
Weeds '87
The Lightship '86
The Long, Hot Summer '86
Savage Dawn '84

Josef Forte
Pals of the Saddle '38
Reefer Madness '38

Marlene Forte
Our Song '01
Mob Queen '98
The Bronx War '90

Albert Fortell (1952-)
Time Troopers '89
Scandalous '88
Nuclear Conspiracy '85

John Fortune
The Tailor of Panama '00
Bloodbath at the House of Death '85

Bob Fosse (1927-87)
The Little Prince '74
My Sister Eileen '55
The Affairs of Dobie Gillis '53
Give a Girl a Break '53
Kiss Me Kate '53

Nicole Fosse
A Chorus Line '85
All That Jazz '79

Brigitte Fossey (1946-)
The Last Butterfly '92
Enigma '82
Chanel Solitaire '81
La Boum '81
Quintet '79
Blue Country '77
The Man Who Loved Women '77
Going Places '74
Honor Among Thieves '68
The Wanderer '67
Forbidden Games '52

Barry Foster (1931-2002)
After Pilkington '88
Beyond the Next Mountain '87
Maurice '87
The Whistle Blower '87
Heat and Dust '82
Quiet Day in Belfast '74
Frenzy '72
Robbery '67
King and Country '64

Ben Foster (1980-)
Big Trouble '02
Get Over It! '01
Liberty Heights '99

Dianne Foster (1928-)
The King of the Roaring '20s: The Story of Arnold Rothstein '61
Last Hurrah '58
The Kentuckian '55
The Violent Men '55

Frances Foster (1924-97)
Crooklyn '94
Enemy Territory '87

Gloria Foster (1936-2001)
The Matrix '99
Percy & Thunder '93
City of Hope '91
The House of Dies Drear '88
Leonard Part 6 '87
Man & Boy '71
To All My Friends on Shore '71
The Angel Levine '70
Nothing but a Man '64
The Cool World '63

Helen Foster (1906-82)
Young Blood '33
Boiling Point '32
Ghost City '32
Saddle Buster '32
Linda '29
The Road to Ruin '28

Jodie Foster (1963-)
The Dangerous Lives of Altar Boys '02
Panic Room '02
Anna and the King '99
Contact '97
Maverick '94
Nell '94
Sommersby '93
Shadows and Fog '92
Little Man Tate '91
The Silence of the Lambs '91
Backtrack '89
The Accused '88
Five Corners '88
Stealing Home '88
Siesta '87
The Blood of Others '84
The Hotel New Hampshire '84
Mesmerized '84
Svengali '83
O'Hara's Wife '82
Carny '80
Foxes '80
Candleshoe '78
Bugsy Malone '76
Freaky Friday '76
The Little Girl Who Lives down the Lane '76
Taxi Driver '76
Alice Doesn't Live Here Anymore '74
Smile, Jenny, You're Dead '74
One Little Indian '73
Tom Sawyer '73
Napoleon and Samantha '72

Julia Foster (1942-)
Thirteenth Reunion '81
F. Scott Fitzgerald in Hollywood '76
Great McGonagall '75
Half a Sixpence '67
Alfie '66
The Loneliness of the Long Distance Runner '62

Kimberly Foster
Broken Trust '93
It Takes Two '88

Meg Foster (1948-)
The Man in the Iron Mask '97
Space Marines '96
Backlash: Oblivion 2 '95
Immortal Combat '94
Lady in Waiting '94
Oblivion '94
Shrunken Heads '94
Undercover '94
Best of the Best 2 '93
Hidden Fears '93
Project: Shadowchaser '92
To Catch a Killer '92
Diplomatic Immunity '91
Futurekick '91
Relentless 2: Dead On '91
Backstab '90
Blind Fury '90
Jezebel's Kiss '90
Leviathan '89
Relentless '89
Stepfather 2: Make Room for Daddy '89
Tripwire '89
They Live '88
Masters of the Universe '87
The Wind '87
The Emerald Forest '85
The Osterman Weekend '83
Ticket to Heaven '81
Carny '80
The Legend of Sleepy Hollow '79
The Scarlet Letter '79
Different Story '78
James Dean '76
Things in Their Season '74
Thumb Tripping '72
Adam at 6 a.m. '70

Norman Foster (1900-76)
Journey into Fear '42
Skyscraper Souls '32

Phil Foster (1914-85)
Bang the Drum Slowly '73
Hail '73
Conquest of Space '55

Preston Foster (1902-70)
The Time Travelers '64
The Marshal's Daughter '53
Kansas City Confidential '52
Tomahawk '51
Three Desperate Men '50
The Big Cat '49
I Shot Jesse James '49
Ramrod '47
The Harvey Girls '46
The Valley of Decision '45
Guadalcanal Diary '43
My Friend Flicka '43
American Empire '42
A Gentleman After Dark '42
Sea Devils '37
Annie Oakley '35
The Informer '35
Last Days of Pompeii '35
Hoopla '33
Ladies They Talk About '33
Doctor X '32
I Am a Fugitive from a Chain Gang '32
The Last Mile '32

Stacie Foster
Cyber-Tracker 2 '95
Steel Frontier '94

Susanna Foster (1924-)
Detour '92
The Climax '44
The Phantom of the Opera '43

Byron Foulger (1899-1968)
The Devil's Partner '58
Bells of San Fernando '47
Hoppy Serves a Writ '43
The Panther's Claw '42
Sullivan's Travels '41
Prisoner of Zenda '37

Robert Foulk
Emperor of the North Pole '73
Robin and the 7 Hoods '64

Derek Fowlds
Over the Hill '93
Frankenstein Created Woman '66
Hotel Paradiso '66

Harry Fowler (1926-)
Flight from Singapore '62
Lucky Jim '58
Fire Maidens from Outer Space '56

Douglas Fowley (1911-98)
The White Buffalo '77
From Noon Till Three '76
The Good Guys and the Bad Guys '69
Poor White Trash '57
Cat Women of the Moon '53
Singin' in the Rain '52
Rider from Tucson '50
Battleground '49
Susanna Pass '49
Behind Locked Doors '48
Desperate '47
Wild Country '47
North of the Border '46
Scared to Death '46
Along the Navaho Trail '45
Shake Hands with Murder '44
Colt Comrades '43
Lost Canyon '43
Meet the Mob '42
Mr. Wise Guy '42
Sunset on the Desert '42
Tanks a Million '41
Wagon's Westward '40
It Could Happen to You '39
On the Avenue '37

Bernard Fox (1927-)
The Mummy '99
Titanic '97
House of the Dead '80
The Private Eyes '80
Zone of the Dead '78
Arnold '73
Munster, Go Home! '66
Strange Bedfellows '65

Colin Fox
The Doorbell Rang: A Nero Wolfe Mystery '01
Angels in the Infield '00
A House Divided '00
Left Behind: The Movie '00
Daylight '96
Beautiful Dreamers '92
Canada's Sweetheart: The Saga of Hal C. Banks '85
War Between the Tates '76
My Pleasure Is My Business '74

David Fox
Grey Owl '99
Conquest '98
When Night Is Falling '95
Black Fox: Good Men and Bad '94
Ordinary Magic '93

Edward Fox (1937-)
The Importance of Being Earnest '02
Lost in Space '98
Prince Valiant '97
Gulliver's Travels '95
A Month by the Lake '95
The Crucifer of Blood '91
Robin Hood '91
Anastasia: The Mystery of Anna '86
The Shooting Party '85
Wild Geese 2 '85
The Bounty '84
The Dresser '83
Never Say Never Again '83
Shaka Zulu '83
Gandhi '82
Edward and Mrs. Simpson '80
The Mirror Crack'd '80
The Cat and the Canary '79
The Big Sleep '78
Force 10 from Navarone '78
Soldier of Orange '78
A Bridge Too Far '77
The Duellists '77
The Squeeze '77
The Day of the Jackal '73
A Doll's House '73
The Go-Between '71
Skullduggery '70
Battle of Britain '69
Portrait of a Lady '67
Morgan: A Suitable Case for Treatment '66

Emilia Fox (1974-)
David Copperfield '99
The Scarlet Pimpernel '99
Shooting the Past '99
Catherine Cookson's The Round Tower '98
Rebecca '97

Huckleberry Fox (1975-)
Konrad '90s
Pharoah's Army '95
The Blue Yonder '86
A Winner Never Quits '86
Misunderstood '84

James Fox (1939-)
The Golden Bowl '00
Sexy Beast '00
Up at the Villa '00
Catherine Cookson's The Dwelling Place '90s
Lover's Prayer '99
Mickey Blue Eyes '99
Circle of Passion '97
Kings in Grass Castles '97
Leo Tolstoy's Anna Karenina '96
Doomsday Gun '94
Fall from Grace '94
The Old Curiosity Shop '94
Heart of Darkness '93
The Remains of the Day '93
Afraid of the Dark '92
Hostage '92
Patriot Games '92
A Question of Attribution '91
The Russia House '90
Farewell to the King '89
The Mighty Quinn '89
High Season '88
Shadow on the Sun '88
The Whistle Blower '87
Absolute Beginners '86
Greystoke: The Legend of Tarzan, Lord of the Apes '84
A Passage to India '84
Performance '70
Isadora '68
Thoroughly Modern Millie '67
The Chase '66
King Rat '65
Those Magnificent Men in Their Flying Machines '65
The Servant '63

Jerry Fox
Hollywood Chainsaw Hookers '88
Evil Spawn '87

Kerry Fox (1966-)
To Walk with Lions '99
Immortality '98
The Hanging Garden '97
Welcome to Sarajevo '97
The Affair '95
Country Life '95
Friends '95
A Village Affair '95
Rainbow Warrior '94
Shallow Grave '94
The Last Days of Chez Nous '92
An Angel at My Table '89

Michael Fox (1921-96)
The Longest Yard '74
Bloody Mama '70
The Dunwich Horror '70

Michael J. Fox (1961-)
Stuart Little 2 '02 (V)
Atlantis: The Lost Empire '01 (V)
Stuart Little '99 (V)
The Frighteners '96
Homeward Bound 2: Lost in San Francisco '96 (V)
Mars Attacks! '96
The American President '95
Blue in the Face '95
Coldblooded '94
Greedy '94
Where the Rivers Flow North '94
For Love or Money '93
Homeward Bound: The Incredible Journey '93 (V)
Life with Mikey '93
Doc Hollywood '91
The Hard Way '91
Back to the Future, Part 3 '90
Back to the Future, Part 2 '89
Casualties of War '89
Bright Lights, Big City '88
Light of Day '87
The Secret of My Success '87
Back to the Future '85
Poison Ivy '85
Teen Wolf '85
High School USA '84
Class of 1984 '82
Midnight Madness '80

Peter Fox
Diamond Run '90
A Minor Miracle '83

Rick Fox
The Collectors '99
Resurrection '99

Samantha Fox (1951-)
Warrior Queen '87
Delivery Boys '84
Violated '84

Sidney (Sydney) Fox (1910-42)
Don Quixote '35
Midnight '34
Murders in the Rue Morgue '32

Vivica A. Fox (1964-)
Kingdom Come '01
Two Can Play That Game '01
Hendrix '00
Idle Hands '99
A Saintly Switch '99
Teaching Mrs. Tingle '99
Solomon '98
Why Do Fools Fall in Love? '98
Batman and Robin '97
Soul Food '97
Booty Call '96
Independence Day '96
Set It Off '96
The Tuskegee Airmen '95
Born on the Fourth of July '89

Robert Foxworth (1941-)
Beyond the Stars '89
Double Standard '88
Peter and Paul '81
The Black Marble '79
Prophecy '79
Damien: Omen 2 '78
Deathmoon '78
Ants '77
The Invisible Strangler '76
The Treasure of Matecumbe '76
Frankenstein '73

Jamie Foxx (1967-)
Ali '01
Bait '00
Held Up '00
Any Given Sunday '99
The Players Club '98
Booty Call '96
The Great White Hype '96
The Truth about Cats and Dogs '96

Redd Foxx (1922-91)
Harlem Nights '89
Norman, Is That You? '76
Cotton Comes to Harlem '70

Charles Foy
The Wagons Roll at Night '41
Mutiny in the Big House '39

Eddie Foy, Jr. (1905-83)
30 Is a Dangerous Age, Cynthia '68
Gidget Goes Hawaiian '61
Bells Are Ringing '60
The Pajama Game '57
Lucky Me '54
The Farmer Takes a Wife '53
Wilson '44
Yankee Doodle Dandy '42
Four Jacks and a Jill '41

Victoria Foyt
Deja Vu '98
Last Summer In the Hamptons '96
Babyfever '94

Carla Fracci
Life of Verdi '84
Nijinsky '80

Tracy Fraim
Best Men '98
Fear '96
Dream Machine '91

James Frain (1969-)
The Count of Monte Cristo '02
Arabian Nights '00
The Miracle Maker: The Story of Jesus '00 (V)
Reindeer Games '00
Where the Heart Is '00
Sunshine '99
Titus '99
Elizabeth '98
Hilary and Jackie '98
The Mill on the Floss '97
Rasputin: Dark Servant of Destiny '96
The Buccaneers '95
Loch Ness '95
Nothing Personal '95

Jonathon Frakes (1952-)
Star Trek: Insurrection '98
Star Trek: First Contact '96
Gargoyles, The Movie: The Heroes Awaken '94 (V)
Star Trek: Generations '94
North and South Book 1 '85

Peter Frampton
Almost Famous '00
Sgt. Pepper's Lonely Hearts Club Band '78

C.V. France (1868-1949)
Night Train to Munich '40
If I Were King '38
Skin Game '31

Richard France (1930-)
Vortex '81
Dawn of the Dead '78
The Crazies '73

Victor Francen (1888-1977)
The Beast with Five Fingers '46
San Antonio '45
The Mask of Dimitrios '44
Madame Curie '43
The Tuttles of Tahiti '42
J'Accuse '37

Anthony (Tony) Franciosa (1928-)
City Hall '95
Double Threat '92
Backstreet Dreams '90
Ghost Writer '89
Death House '88
Blood Vows: The Story of a Mafia Wife '87
Stagecoach '86
Side Show '84
La Cicada '83
Daughter of Death '82
Death Wish 2 '82
Kiss My Grits '82
Unsane '82
The World Is Full of Married Men '80
Curse of the Black Widow '77
The Drowning Pool '75
Ghost in the Noonday Sun '74
Across 110th Street '72
Web of the Spider '70
Fathom '67
Assault on a Queen '66
Rio Conchos '64
Period of Adjustment '62
Career '59
The Naked Maja '59
The Long, Hot Summer '58
A Face in the Crowd '57
This Could Be the Night '57

Alec B. Francis (1867-1934)
His Private Secretary '33
Mata Hari '32
Evangeline '29
Charley's Aunt '25
The Mad Whirl '25
Beau Brummel '24
Little Church Around the Corner '23
The Wishing Ring '14

Anne Francis (1930-)
Lover's Knot '96
The Double O Kid '92
Little Vegas '90
Return '88
Laguna Heat '87
Poor Little Rich Girl: The Barbara Hutton Story '87
Mazes and Monsters '82
The Rebels '79
Born Again '78
Cry Panic '74
Fireball Forward '72
Haunts of the Very Rich '72
Pancho Villa '72
The Love God? '70
Wild Women '70
Funny Girl '68
Don't Go Near the Water '57
Forbidden Planet '56

Battle Cry *'55*
Blackboard Jungle *'55*
Bad Day at Black Rock *'54*
Susan Slept Here *'54*
A Lion Is in the Streets *'53*
Portrait of Jennie *'48*
Summer Holiday *'48*

Arlene Francis (1908-2001)
The Thrill of It All! *'63*
One, Two, Three *'61*
All My Sons *'48*
Murders in the Rue Morgue *'32*

Clive Francis (1946-)
Longitude *'00*
Sharpe's Company *'94*
The Bretts *'88*
Poldark *'75*
Man Who Had Power Over Women *'70*

Derek Francis (1923-84)
Murder Motel *'74*
Rasputin the Mad Monk *'66*
Tomb of Ligeia *'64*

Genie Francis (1960-)
North and South Book 2 *'86*
North and South Book 1 *'85*

Ivor Francis (1911-86)
House of the Dead *'80*
Zone of the Dead *'78*
Hard Frame *'70*

Kay Francis (1899-1968)
It's a Date *'40*
Little Men *'40*
In Name Only *'39*
Vice Squad *'31*
Raffles *'30*
The Cocoanuts *'29*

Noel Francis (1906-59)
Stone of Silver Creek *'35*
Fire Alarm *'32*
My Pal, the King *'32*
Bachelor Apartment *'31*

Robert Francis
The Long Gray Line *'55*
The Caine Mutiny *'54*

Ryan Francis
Social Misfits *'00*
The River Pirates *'94*

James Franciscus (1934-91)
Secret Weapons *'85*
Butterfly *'82*
Jacqueline Bouvier Kennedy *'81*
Nightkill *'80*
Killer Fish *'79*
Good Guys Wear Black *'78*
The Greek Tycoon *'78*
Puzzle *'78*
Secrets of Three Hungry Wives *'78*
Hunter *'77*
The Amazing Dobermans *'76*
The Man Inside *'76*
One of My Wives Is Missing *'76*
Jonathan Livingston Seagull *'73*
The Cat o' Nine Tails *'71*
Beneath the Planet of the Apes *'70*
Marooned *'69*
The Valley of Gwangi *'69*
Snow Treasure *'67*

Don Francks (1932-)
Summer of the Monkeys *'98*
Bogus *'96*
Madonna: Innocence Lost *'95*
The Christmas Wife *'88*
Big Town *'87*
984: Prisoner of the Future *'84*
Rock & Rule *'83 (V)*
Heavy Metal *'81 (V)*
My Bloody Valentine *'81*
Phoenix Team *'80*
Fast Company *'78*
Drying Up the Streets *'76*
Finian's Rainbow *'68*

Rainbow Sun Francks
Love Come Down *'00*
Love Song *'00*

James Franco (1978-)
Deuces Wild *'02*
Spider-Man *'02*
James Dean *'01*
At Any Cost *'00*
Whatever It Takes *'00*

Jess (Jesus) Franco (1930-)
Ilsa, the Wicked Warden *'78*
Venus in Furs *'70*
The Diabolical Dr. Z *'65*

Margarita Franco
3 Ninjas: High Noon at Mega Mountain *'97*
3 Ninjas *'92*

Ramon Franco
Shattered Image *'93*
Kiss Me a Killer *'91*
Tour of Duty *'87*
Heartbreak Ridge *'86*

Jacques Francois
The Gift *'82*
The Barkleys of Broadway *'49*

Billy Franey
Somewhere in Sonora *'33*
Ghost Valley *'32*

Ben Frank (1934-90)
Hollywood Vice Sqaud *'86*
Hollywood Zap *'86*
Don't Answer the Phone *'80*

Billy Frank
Nudity Required *'90*
Grotesque *'87*

Charles Frank (1947-)
Danielle Steel's Changes *'91*
LBJ: The Early Years *'88*
Lucky Stiff *'88*
The Right Stuff *'83*
The Chisholms *'79*
A Guide for the Married Woman *'78*
Snowblind *'78*
Tarantulas: The Deadly Cargo *'77*

Dan Frank
Intimate Deception *'96*
Great Bikini Off-Road Adventure *'94*

Diana Frank
Club Vampire *'98*
Pale Blood *'91*
Monster High *'89*
The Glass Jungle *'88*

Gary Frank (1905-75)
Getting Up and Going Home *'92*
Take Down *'92*
Deadly Weapon *'88*
Enemy Territory *'87*
Enola Gay: The Men, the Mission, the Atomic Bomb *'80*
The Night the City Screamed *'80*

Horst Frank (1929-99)
Albino *'76*
Cold Blood *'75*
The Grand Duel *'73*
Dead Are Alive *'72*
Code Name Alpha *'67*
Desert Commandos *'67*
The Head *'59*

Jason David Frank
Turbo: A Power Rangers Movie *'96*
Mighty Morphin Power Rangers: The Movie *'95*

Jerry Frank
The Big Doll House *'71*
The Flaming Teen-Age *'56*

Joanna Frank
Say Anything *'89*
Always *'85*
The Savage Seven *'68*

Tony Frank
Rush *'91*
Riverbend *'89*

Mark Frankel (1962-96)
For Roseanna *'96*
Solitaire for 2 *'94*
Leon the Pig Farmer *'93*
Young Catherine *'91*

Al Franken (1951-)
From the Earth to the Moon *'98*
Stuart Saves His Family *'94*
One More Saturday Night *'86*
Trading Places *'83*
All You Need Is Cash *'78*
Tunnelvision *'76*

Steve Franken (1932-)
Freeway *'88*
The Fiendish Plot of Dr. Fu Manchu *'80*
Ants *'77*
Which Way to the Front? *'70*

Paul Frankeur (1905-75)
Phantom of Liberty *'74*
The Milky Way *'68*
License to Kill *'64*
Le Gentleman D'Epsom *'62*
Un Singe en Hiver *'62*

William Frankfather (1944-98)
Trading Favors *'97*
Born Yesterday *'93*
Cool World *'92*
Defense Play *'88*

Aretha Franklin
Blues Brothers 2000 *'98*
The Blues Brothers *'80*

Bonnie Franklin (1944-)
Your Place or Mine *'83*
Portrait of a Rebel: Margaret Sanger *'82*
Breaking Up Is Hard to Do *'79*

David Franklin
Rock & Roll Cowboys *'92*
Early Frost *'84*

Diane Franklin
Terrorvision *'86*
Better Off Dead *'85*
Second Time Lucky *'84*
Amityville 2: The Possession *'82*
Last American Virgin *'82*

Don Franklin
Asteroid *'97*
Fast Forward *'84*

Gloria Franklin
Without Warning *'52*
Drums of Fu Manchu *'40*

Joe Franklin
29th Street *'91*
Ghoul School *'90*

John Franklin (1967-)
Children of the Corn 666: Isaac's Return *'99*
Tammy and the T-Rex *'94*
The Addams Family *'91*
Children of the Corn *'84*

Pamela Franklin (1950-)
Eleanor & Franklin *'76*
Food of the Gods *'76*
Screamer *'74*
The Legend of Hell House *'73*
Satan's School for Girls *'73*
The Witching *'72*
And Soon the Darkness *'70*
David Copperfield *'70*
The Night of the Following Day *'69*
The Prime of Miss Jean Brodie *'69*
The Nanny *'65*
Flipper's New Adventure *'64*
A Tiger Walks *'64*
The Horse Without a Head *'63*
The Innocents *'61*

William Franklyn (1926-)
Splitting Heirs *'93*
The Satanic Rites of Dracula *'73*
Quatermass 2 *'57*

Chloe Franks
Ivanhoe *'82*
The Littlest Horse Thieves *'76*
The House that Dripped Blood *'71*

Mary Frann (1943-98)
Fatal Charm *'92*
I'm Dangerous Tonight *'90*

Arthur Franz (1920-)
Bogie: The Last Hero *'80*
Sisters of Death *'76*
Dream No Evil *'75*
The Human Factor *'75*
Atomic Submarine *'59*
Monster on the Campus *'59*
The Young Lions *'58*
Hellcats of the Navy *'57*
Beyond a Reasonable Doubt *'56*
The Caine Mutiny *'54*
Invaders from Mars *'53*
Flight to Mars *'52*
The Member of the Wedding *'52*
Abbott and Costello Meet the Invisible Man *'51*
Sands of Iwo Jima *'49*
Jungle Patrol *'48*

Dennis Franz (1944-)
City of Angels *'98*
American Buffalo *'95*
Children of Fury *'94*
The Player *'92*
Die Hard 2: Die Harder *'90*
Kiss Shot *'89*
The Package *'89*
Body Double *'84*
Psycho 2 *'83*
Blow Out *'81*
Dressed to Kill *'80*
The Fury *'78*

Eduard Franz (1902-83)
Johnny Got His Gun *'71*
The Story of Ruth *'60*
The Burning Hills *'56*
The Indian Fighter *'55*
Lady Godiva *'55*
Sins of Jezebel *'54*
Latin Lovers *'53*
One Minute to Zero *'52*
The Thing *'51*
The Magnificent Yankee *'50*
Francis the Talking Mule *'49*
Outpost in Morocco *'49*
The Scar *'48*

Elizabeth Franz (1941-)
Stephen King's Thinner *'96*
The Substance of Fire *'96*
Sabrina *'95*

Bill Fraser (1908-87)
Little Dorrit, Film 1: Nobody's Fault *'88*
Little Dorrit, Film 2: Little Dorrit's Story *'88*
Pirates *'86*
Eye of the Needle *'81*
Naughty Knights *'71*
Alias John Preston *'56*

Brendan Fraser (1968-)
Monkeybone *'01*
The Mummy Returns *'01*
Bedazzled *'00*
Dudley Do-Right *'99*
The Mummy *'99*
Blast from the Past *'98*
Gods and Monsters *'98*
George of the Jungle *'97*
Still Breathing *'97*
The Twilight of the Golds *'97*
Glory Daze *'96*
Mrs. Winterbourne *'96*
Now and Then *'95*
The Passion of Darkly Noon *'95*
Airheads *'94*
Dark Side of Genius *'94*
The Scout *'94*
With Honors *'94*
Younger & Younger *'94*
Twenty Bucks *'93*
Encino Man *'92*
School Ties *'92*
Dogfight *'91*

Brent Fraser
The Little Death *'95*
Wild Orchid 2: Two Shades of Blue *'92*

Duncan Fraser
When Danger Follows You Home *'97*
Unforgettable *'96*
Captains Courageous *'95*
Timecop *'94*
Call of the Wild *'93*
The Reflecting Skin *'91*
Watchers *'88*

Elisabeth Fraser
A Patch of Blue *'65*
Two for the Seesaw *'62*
Ask Any Girl *'59*
The Tunnel of Love *'58*
Young at Heart *'54*
Hills of Oklahoma *'50*
The Man Who Came to Dinner *'41*

Helen Fraser
Start the Revolution without Me *'70*
Repulsion *'65*

Hugh Fraser
Sharpe's Waterloo *'97*
Sharpe's Mission *'96*
Sharpe's Siege *'96*
Sharpe's Battle *'94*
Sharpe's Company *'94*
Sharpe's Enemy *'94*
Sharpe's Gold *'94*
Sharpe's Honour *'94*
The Bretts *'88*
The Draughtsman's Contract *'82*

John Fraser (1931-)
Schizo *'77*
Isadora *'68*
Repulsion *'65*
Horsemasters *'61*
The Trials of Oscar Wilde *'60*

Laura Fraser (1976-)
A Knight's Tale *'01*
Kevin & Perry Go Large *'00*
A Christmas Carol *'99*
Forgive and Forget *'99*
The Match *'99*
Titus *'99*
Virtual Sexuality *'99*
Left Luggage *'98*
Small Faces *'95*

Liz Fraser (1933-)
Chicago Joe & the Showgirl *'90*
Adventures of a Taxi Driver *'76*
The Americanization of Emily *'64*
Carry On Cruising *'62*
Two-Way Stretch *'60*

Phyllis Fraser
Tough to Handle *'37*
Winds of the Wasteland *'36*

Richard Fraser (1913-71)
The Cobra Strikes *'48*
The Private Affairs of Bel Ami *'47*
Bedlam *'45*
White Pongo *'45*

Ronald Fraser (1930-97)
The Mystery of Edwin Drood *'93*
Let Him Have It *'91*
Rentadick *'72*
Too Late the Hero *'70*
The Killing of Sister George *'69*
Fathom *'67*

Sally Fraser
Dangerous Charter *'62*
Giant from the Unknown *'58*
The War of the Colossal Beast *'58*
It Conquered the World *'56*

Stuart Fratkin (1963-)
Prehysteria *'93*
Remote *'93*
Ski School *'91*
Dr. Alien *'88*

William Frawley (1887-1966)
Rancho Notorious *'52*
Abbott and Costello Meet the Invisible Man *'51*
The Lemon Drop Kid *'51*
East Side, West Side *'49*
Babe Ruth Story *'48*
Down to Earth *'47*
Miracle on 34th Street *'47*
Monsieur Verdoux *'47*
Mother Wore Tights *'47*
The Inner Circle *'46*
The Virginian *'46*
Flame of the Barbary Coast *'45*
Lady on a Train *'45*
Fighting Seabees *'44*
Whistling in Brooklyn *'43*
Gentleman Jim *'42*
Roxie Hart *'42*
Wildcat *'42*
Blondie in Society *'41*
The Bride Came C.O.D. *'41*
Footsteps in the Dark *'41*
One Night in the Tropics *'40*
Rhythm on the River *'40*
The Adventures of Huckleberry Finn *'39*
Rose of Washington Square *'39*
Mad About Music *'38*
Desire *'36*
The General Died at Dawn *'36*
The Princess Comes Across *'36*
Something to Sing About *'36*
Strike Me Pink *'36*
Harmony Lane *'35*

Jane Frazee (1918-85)
Last of the Wild Horses *'49*
Grand Canyon Trail *'48*
Under California Stars *'48*
On the Old Spanish Trail *'47*
Springtime in the Sierras *'47*
The Gay Ranchero *'42*

Robert Frazer (1891-1944)
Partners of the Trail *'44*
Dawn Express *'42*
Renfrew on the Great White Trail *'38*
The Clutching Hand *'36*
Death from a Distance *'36*
Fighting Parson *'35*
Fighting Pilot *'35*
The Miracle Rider *'35*
Found Alive *'34*
Monte Carlo Nights *'34*
Mystery Trooper *'32*
Saddle Buster *'32*
The White Zombie *'32*
Ten Nights in a Bar-Room *'31*
The Drake Case *'29*

Rupert Frazer
Back Home *'90*
The Girl in a Swing *'89*
Empire of the Sun *'87*
Testament of Youth *'79*

Joe Frazier
Just the Ticket *'98*
Home of Angels *'94*

Sheila Frazier (1948-)
The Hitter *'79*
Three the Hard Way *'74*
Superfly T.N.T. *'73*
Firehouse *'72*
Superfly *'72*

Stan Freberg (1926-)
Pogo for President: "I Go Pogo" *'84 (V)*
It's a Mad, Mad, Mad, Mad World *'63*
Lady and the Tramp *'55 (V)*

Peter Frechette (1956-)
Paint It Black '89
The Kindred '87
The Hills Have Eyes, Part 2 '84
No Small Affair '84

Richard Frechette
No '98
The Confessional '95

Blanche Frederici (1878-1933)
Buffalo Stampede '33
A Farewell to Arms '32
Night Nurse '31
Sadie Thompson '28

Lynne Frederick (1955-94)
Prisoner of Zenda '79
Schizo '77
Voyage of the Damned '76
Phase 4 '74
Amazing Mr. Blunden '72
Vampire Circus '71

Vicki Frederick (1954-)
Chopper Chicks in Zombietown '91
A Chorus Line '85
Body Rock '84
...All the Marbles '81

Alan Freed
Go, Johnny Go! '59
Rock, Rock, Rock '56

Bert Freed (1919-94)
Evel Knievel '72
Billy Jack '71
The Gazebo '59
Paths of Glory '57
The Cobweb '55
Men of the Fighting Lady '54
Detective Story '51
The Halls of Montezuma '50

Sam Freed
Stephen King's Thinner '96
Call Me '88

Al Freeman, Jr. (1934-)
Down in the Delta '98
Once Upon a Time ... When We Were Colored '95
Assault at West Point: The Court-Martial of Johnson Whittaker '94
Malcolm X '92
Seven Hours to Judgment '88
Perry Mason Returns '85
Roots: The Next Generation '79
My Sweet Charlie '70
The Lost Man '69
The Detective '68
Finian's Rainbow '68
Ensign Pulver '64

Howard Freeman (1899-1967)
Million Dollar Mermaid '52
Scaramouche '52
Double Dynamite '51
The Long Night '47
The Blue Dahlia '46
House of Horrors '46
Mr. Winkle Goes to War '44
Air Raid Wardens '43

J.E. Freeman
Go '99
Alien: Resurrection '97
Dream with the Fishes '97
It Could Happen to You '94
Mother's Boys '94
Casualties of Love: The "Long Island Lolita" Story '93
Fallen Angels 2 '93
Aces: Iron Eagle 3 '92
There Goes My Baby '92
Memphis '91
Miller's Crossing '90
Wild at Heart '90
Hard Traveling '85

Joan Freeman (1941-)
Fastest Guitar Alive '68
The Reluctant Astronaut '67
The Rounders '65
Roustabout '64
Panic in the Year Zero! '62
Tower of London '62

K. Todd Freeman
The Cider House Rules '99
The End of Violence '97
Grosse Pointe Blank '97

Kathleen Freeman (1919-2001)
Shrek '01 (V)
Nutty Professor 2: The Klumps '00
Ready to Rumble '00
Blues Brothers 2000 '98
At First Sight '95
Naked Gun 33 1/3: The Final Insult '94
Reckless Kelly '93
The Willies '90
Hollywood Chaos '89
Dragnet '87
In the Mood '87
Innerspace '87
Malibu Bikini Shop '86
Heartbeeps '81
The Blues Brothers '80
The Rounders '65
Disorderly Orderly '64
The Nutty Professor '63
The Errand Boy '61
The Fly '58
Kid Monk Baroni '52
Love Is Better Than Ever '52

Mona Freeman (1926-)
The Way Out '56
Battle Cry '55
Jumping Jacks '52
Branded '50
Copper Canyon '50
Dear Wife '49
The Heiress '49
Mother Wore Tights '47
Black Beauty '46
That Brennan Girl '46

Morgan Freeman (1937-)
High Crimes '02
The Sum of All Fears '02
Along Came a Spider '01
Nurse Betty '00
Under Suspicion '00
Deep Impact '98
Amistad '97
Hard Rain '97
Kiss the Girls '97
Chain Reaction '96
Moll Flanders '96
Seven '95
Outbreak '94
The Shawshank Redemption '94
The Power of One '92
Unforgiven '92
Robin Hood: Prince of Thieves '91
The Bonfire of the Vanities '90
Driving Miss Daisy '89
Glory '89
Johnny Handsome '89
Lean on Me '89
Blood Money: The Story of Clinton and Nadine '88
Clean and Sober '88
Street Smart '87
Execution of Raymond Graham '85
Marie '85
That Was Then...This Is Now '85
Harry & Son '84
Teachers '84
Eyewitness '81
Brubaker '80
Roll of Thunder, Hear My Cry '78

Paul Freeman (1943-)
The Devil's Arithmetic '99
Only Love '98
Double Team '97
Samson and Delilah '96
The Final Cut '95
Just Like a Woman '95
Mighty Morphin Power Rangers: The Movie '95
Aces: Iron Eagle 3 '92
A Dangerous Man: Lawrence after Arabia '91
Eminent Domain '91
Murderers Among Us: The Simon Wiesenthal Story '89
Prisoner of Rio '89
Without a Clue '88
A World Apart '88
Shanghai Surprise '86
The Sender '82
Unsuitable Job for a Woman '82
The Dogs of War '81
Raiders of the Lost Ark '81
The Long Good Friday '80
Whose Child Am I? '75

Tony Freeman
Ocean Drive Weekend '85
Invincible Gladiators '64

Paul Frees (1920-86)
The Return of the King '80 (V)
The Milpitas Monster '75 (N)
The Point '71 (V)
The Time Machine '60
Francis in the Haunted House '56 (V)
Suddenly '54
The War of the Worlds '53

Ace Frehley
Detroit Rock City '99
KISS Meets the Phantom of the Park '78

Alice Freindlikh
Rasputin '85
Stalker '79

Stephane Freiss
Does This Mean We're Married? '90
Vagabond '85

Bruce French
Coming Home '78
Ants '77
Pipe Dreams '76

Charles French (1860-1952)
Where Trails Divide '37
Gun Play '36
The Crimson Trail '35
Trail of Terror '35
The Live Wire '34
The Man from Hell '34
When a Man Sees Red '34
Man of Action '33
King of the Rodeo '28
The Bargain '15

Dawn French
Maybe Baby '99
Supergrass '87

Leigh French
The Hollywood Knights '80
Aloha, Bobby and Rose '74

Valerie French
The 27th Day '57
Jubal '56

Victor French (1934-89)
Choices '81
The House on Skull Mountain '74
Little House on the Prairie '74
The Other '72
Chato's Land '71
Charro! '69
Spencer's Mountain '63

Pierre Fresnay (1897-1975)
Monsieur Vincent '47
Le Corbeau '43
Grand Illusion '37
Cesar '36
The Man Who Knew Too Much '34
Fanny '32
Marius '31

Bernard Fresson (1931-)
Place Vendome '98
Germinal '93
The Tenant '76
French Connection 2 '75
Honor Among Thieves '68
Please Not Now! '61
Hiroshima, Mon Amour '59

Matt Frewer (1958-)
The Sign of Four '01
The Hound of the Baskervilles '00
Jailbait! '00
Dead Fire '98
In the Doghouse '98
Quicksilver Highway '98
Breast Men '97
Hercules '97 (V)
Kissinger and Nixon '96
Lawnmower Man 2: Beyond Cyberspace '95
National Lampoon's Senior Trip '95
Stephen King's The Stand '94
The Day My Parents Ran Away '93
The Positively True Adventures of the Alleged Texas Cheerleader-Murdering Mom '93
Twenty Bucks '93
The Taking of Beverly Hills '91
Short Time '90
Far from Home '89
Honey, I Shrunk the Kids '89
Speed Zone '88
The Fourth Protocol '87
Ishtar '87
Supergirl '84
The Lords of Discipline '83
Monty Python's The Meaning of Life '83

Glenn Frey
Jerry Maguire '96
Let's Get Harry '87

Leonard Frey (1938-88)
Tattoo '81
Where the Buffalo Roam '80
Fiddler on the Roof '71
The Boys in the Band '70
The Magic Christian '69

Sami Frey (1937-)
Revenge of the Musketeers '94
My Life and Times with Antonin Artaud '93
Traps '93
War & Remembrance: The Final Chapter '89
War & Remembrance '88
Black Widow '87
Sand and Blood '87
The Little Drummer Girl '84
Nea '78
Sweet Movie '75
Cesar & Rosalie '72
Band of Outsiders '64
Cleo from 5 to 7 '61

Giovanni Frezza (1972-)
The House by the Cemetery '83
Manhattan Baby '82

Grayson Fricke
The Substitute 4: Failure is Not an Option '00
Past the Bleachers '95

Brenda Fricker (1944-)
The American '01
Torso '01
Cupid & Cate '00
Durango '99
Resurrection Man '97
The Wicked, Wicked West '97
Masterminds '96
Moll Flanders '96
Swann '96
A Time to Kill '96
Journey '95
Angels in the Outfield '94
A Man of No Importance '94
Deadly Advice '93
So I Married an Axe Murderer '93
The Sound and the Silence '93
Utz '93
Home Alone 2: Lost in New York '92
Brides of Christ '91
The Field '90
My Left Foot '89

Jonathan Frid (1924-)
Seizure '74
House of Dark Shadows '70

Tom Fridley
Navajo Blues '97
Friday the 13th, Part 6: Jason Lives '86
Summer Camp Nightmare '86

Joel Friedkin
Impact '49
Money Madness '47

Will Friedle
My Date with the President's Daughter '98
Trojan War '97

David Friedman
Sex and Buttered Popcorn '91
Blood Feast '63

Peter Friedman
Someone Like You '01
I Shot Andy Warhol '96
The Heidi Chronicles '95
Safe '95
Blink '93
Single White Female '92
The Seventh Sign '88
Christmas Evil '80

John Friedrich
The Final Terror '83
A Rumor of War '80
Wanderers '79
Forever '78
The Boy in the Plastic Bubble '76

Anna Friel (1976-)
An Everlasting Piece '00
William Shakespeare's A Midsummer Night's Dream '99
The Land Girls '98
Our Mutual Friend '98
Robert Louis Stevenson's St. Ives '98
Rogue Trader '98

Colin Friels (1952-)
Child Star: The Shirley Temple Story '01
Dark City '97
Angel Baby '95
Back of Beyond '95
Cosi '95
Mr. Reliable: A True Story '95
A Good Man in Africa '94
Class Action '91
Darkman '90
Dingo '90
Grievous Bodily Harm '89
The Gold & Glory '88
Ground Zero '88
High Tide '87
Warm Nights on a Slow-Moving Train '87
Kangaroo '86
Malcolm '86
Monkey Grip '82

Philip Friend
Vulture '67
Great Day '46

Willy Fritsch (1901-73)
The Bellboy and the Playgirls '62
Congress Dances '31
Woman in the Moon '29
Spies '28

Lou Frizzell (1920-79)
Steel Cowboy '78
The Other '72
Duel '71

Gert Frobe (1912-88)
Sidney Sheldon's Bloodline '79
The Serpent's Egg '78
Shadow Man '75
Ten Little Indians '75
Ludwig '72
Dollars '71
Those Daring Young Men in Their Jaunty Jalopies '69
Chitty Chitty Bang Bang '68
I Killed Rasputin '67
Those Fantastic Flying Fools '67
Triple Cross '67
Is Paris Burning? '66
Those Magnificent Men in Their Flying Machines '65
Tonio Kroger '65
Goldfinger '64
The Longest Day '62
Testament of Dr. Mabuse '62
The Three Penny Opera '62
The Return of Dr. Mabuse '61
The Thousand Eyes of Dr. Mabuse '60
The Eternal Waltz '54

Gustav Froehlich
Homecoming '28
Metropolis '26

Samuel Froler
Private Confessions '98
The Best Intentions '92

Ewa Froling (1952-)
The Last Dance '93
The Ox '91
Fanny and Alexander '83

Milton Frome (1908-89)
The St. Valentine's Day Massacre '67
Batman '66
The Nutty Professor '63
Pardners '56
Ride 'Em Cowgirl '41

Lee Frost
Black Gestapo '75
The Thing with Two Heads '72
Tomb of the Undead '72

Lindsay Frost (1962-)
Collateral Damage '02
Monolith '93
Danielle Steel's Palomino '91
Dead Heat '88

Sadie Frost (1967-)
Uprising '01
Love, Honour & Obey '00
Rancid Aluminium '00
Captain Jack '98
Flypaper '97
Crimetime '96
Magic Hunter '96
A Pyromaniac's Love Story '95
The Cisco Kid '94
Paper Marriage '93
Shopping '93
Splitting Heirs '93
Bram Stoker's Dracula '92
Dark Obsession '90
The Krays '90

Terry Frost (1906-93)
Black Hills '48
The Hawk of Powder River '48
The Monster Maker '44
Waterfront '44
California Joe '43

Catherine Frot (1956-)
The Dinner Game '98
The New Eve '98
Un Air de Famille '96
Sorceress '88

Stephen Fry (1957-)
Gosford Park '01
Longitude '00
Stalag Luft
Relative Values '99
Spice World: The Movie '97
Wilde '97

Lone Justice 3: Showdown at Plum Creek '96
Mr. Toad's Wild Ride '96
Cold Comfort Farm '94
I.Q. '94
Peter's Friends '92

Taylor Fry (1981-)
A Little Princess '95
Lone Justice '93
Necessary Parties '88

Brittain Frye
Slumber Party Massacre 3 '90
Hide and Go Shriek '87

Dwight Frye (1899-1943)
Dead Men Walk '43
Frankenstein Meets the Wolfman '42
The Ghost of Frankenstein '42
Drums of Fu Manchu '40
Sinners in Paradise '38
The Bride of Frankenstein '35
The Crime of Dr. Crespi '35
The Invisible Man '33
The Vampire Bat '32
Dracula '31
Frankenstein '31
The Maltese Falcon '31

Sean Frye
Deadline Assault '90
E.T.: The Extra-Terrestrial '82

Soleil Moon Frye (1976-)
I've Been Waiting for You '98
Motel Blue '98
Piranha '95
Twisted Love '95
Pumpkinhead 2: Blood Wings '94
The St. Tammany Miracle '94
The Liar's Club '93
Invitation to Hell '84

Virgil Frye
Born in America '90
Secret of the Ice Cave '89
Body Beat '88
Colors '88
Hot Moves '84
Revenge of the Ninja '83
Running Hot '83
Dr. Heckyl and Mr. Hype '80
Up from the Depths '79

Gaby Fuchs
The Werewolf vs. the Vampire Woman '70
Mark of the Devil '69

Leo Fuchs (1910-94)
Avalon '90
American Matchmaker '40

Joachim Fuchsberger (1911-)
The Last Tomahawk '65
The Mysterious Magician '65
Carpet of Horror '64
The Black Abbot '63
Curse of the Yellow Snake '63
Inn on the River '62
Dead Eyes of London '61
The Strange Countess '61

Alan Fudge (1944-)
Nightmare on the 13th Floor '90
Too Young to Die '90
The Children of An Lac '80
Bug '75

Miguel Angel Fuentes
Fitzcarraldo '82
The Puma Man '80

Athol Fugard
The Killing Fields '84
Gandhi '82

Tatsuya Fuji (1941-)
In the Realm of Passion '80
The Empire of Passion '76
In the Realm of the Senses '76

Gappa the Trifibian Monster '67

Yu Fujiki (1931-)
Yog, Monster from Space '71
Godzilla vs. Mothra '64
King Kong vs. Godzilla '63

Hiroshi Fujioka (1946-)
K2: The Ultimate High '92
Ghostwarrior '86
Tidal Wave '75

John Fujioka
Pearl Harbor '01
American Samurai '92
The Last Samurai '90
A Conspiracy of Love '87

Susumu Fujita (1912-91)
Yojimbo '61
The Human Condition: Road to Eternity '59
The Hidden Fortress '58
The Men Who Tread on the Tiger's Tail '45

Kamatari (Keita) Fujiwara (1905-85)
Yojimbo '61
The Hidden Fortress '58
Seven Samurai '54

Lucio Fulci (1927-96)
Demonia '90
Manhattan Baby '82
Gates of Hell '80
Zombie '80

Christopher Fulford
Bedrooms and Hallways '98
The Sculptress '97
Moll Flanders '96
Immortal Beloved '94
Prayer for the Dying '87

Dale Fuller (1885-1948)
The Unchastened Woman '25
Greed '24
The Marriage Circle '24

Dolores Fuller (1923-)
Bride of the Monster '55
Jail Bait '54
Glen or Glenda? '53
Mesa of Lost Women '52

Jonathan Fuller
Castle Freak '95
Last Man Standing '95
Suspect Device '95
Arcade '93
The Pit & the Pendulum '91

Kurt Fuller (1952-)
The New Guy '02
Angels in the Infield '00
Scary Movie '00
Diamonds '99
Pushing Tin '99
French Exit '97
Moonbase '97
Reflections in the Dark '94
Calendar Girl '93
Wayne's World '92
Bingo '91
Eve of Destruction '90
Miracle Mile '89
No Holds Barred '89
Elvira, Mistress of the Dark '88

Lance Fuller (1928-2001)
The Bride & the Beast '58
Voodoo Woman '57
Girls in Prison '56
Apache Woman '55
Kentucky Rifle '55
Cattle Queen of Montana '54

Nancy Belle Fuller
Hard Part Begins '80s
Sky Hei$t '75

Penny Fuller (1940-)
The Beverly Hillbillies '93
Danielle Steel's Star '93
Lies Before Kisses '92
Miss Rose White '92
Fire and Rain '89
As Summers Die '86

George Washington: The Forging of a Nation '86
Cat on a Hot Tin Roof '84
License to Kill '84
Your Place or Mine '83
Lois Gibbs and the Love Canal '82
A Piano for Mrs. Cimino '82
All the President's Men '76

Robert Fuller (1934-)
Maverick '94
Donner Pass: The Road to Survival '84
The Gatling Gun '72
The Hard Ride '71
Whatever Happened to Aunt Alice? '69
Sinai Commandos '68
Return of the Magnificent Seven '66
The Brain from Planet Arous '57

Samuel Fuller (1911-97)
The End of Violence '97
La Vie de Boheme '93
Return to Salem's Lot '87
Slapstick of Another Kind '84
State of Things '82
1941 '79
The American Friend '77
The Young Nurses '73
Pierrot le Fou '65

Fiona Fullerton (1956-)
Spymaker: The Secret Life of Ian Fleming '90
The Charmer '87
Shaka Zulu '83

Brad Fulton
The Undertaker and His Pals '67
Journey Beneath the Desert '61

Christina (Kristina) Fulton
Red Shoe Diaries: Luscious Lola '00
The Girl with the Hungry Eyes '94
Hard Drive '94
Red Shoe Diaries 3: Another Woman's Lipstick '93

Eiji Funakoshi (1923-)
Gamera vs. Guiron '69
Gamera, the Invincible '66
Being Two Isn't Easy '62
Fires on the Plain '59

Annette Funicello (1942-)
Back to the Beach '87
Lots of Luck '85
Head '68
Dr. Goldfoot and the Bikini Machine '66
Beach Blanket Bingo '65
How to Stuff a Wild Bikini '65
Monkey's Uncle '65
Bikini Beach '64
Muscle Beach Party '64
Pajama Party '64
Beach Party '63
The Misadventures of Merlin Jones '63
Babes in Toyland '61
Horsemasters '61
The Shaggy Dog '59

Joseph Fuqua
David Searching '97
Gettysburg '93

John Furey
The Wolves '95
Mutant on the Bounty '89
Friday the 13th, Part 2 '81

Edward Furlong (1977-)
Animal Factory '00
Detroit Rock City '99
American History X '98
Pecker '98
Before and After '95
The Grass Harp '95
Brainscan '94

Little Odessa '94
A Home of Our Own '93
Last Action Hero '93
American Heart '92
Pet Sematary 2 '92
Terminator 2: Judgment Day '91

Benno Furmann
Anatomy '00
The Princess and the Warrior '00

Yvonne Furneaux (1928-)
Frankenstein's Great Aunt Tillie '83
Repulsion '65
The Lion of Thebes '64
La Dolce Vita '60
The Mummy '59
The Warriors '55
The House of the Arrow '53
The Master of Ballantrae '53

Betty Furness (1916-94)
The President's Mystery '36
Swing Time '36
Here Comes Cookie '35
Beggars in Ermine '34
Aggie Appleby, Maker of Men '33

Deborra-Lee Furness
The Real Macaw '98
Angel Baby '95
Voyager '91
The Last of the Finest '90
Shame '87

Joseph Furst
The Dunera Boys '85
Diamonds Are Forever '71

Stephen Furst (1955-)
Magic Kid 2 '94
Magic Kid '92
The Dream Team '89
Up the Creek '84
Silent Rage '82
Getting Wasted '80
Midnight Madness '80
The Unseen '80
Swim Team '79
Take Down '79
National Lampoon's Animal House '78

George Furth (1932-)
Goodbye, Lover '99
Doctor Detroit '83
The Man with Two Brains '83
Norman, Is That You? '76
Butch Cassidy and the Sundance Kid '69

Ed Fury (1934-)
Dinosaur Valley Girls '96
Colossus and the Amazon Queen '64
Samson Against the Sheik '62
Ursus in the Valley of the Lions '62
Wild Women of Wongo '59

Dan Futterman (1967-)
Enough '02
Urbania '00
1999 '98
Shooting Fish '98
When Trumpets Fade '98
Breathing Room '96
Far Harbor '96
The Birdcage '95
Class of '61 '92

Herbert (Fuchs) Fux (1927-)
Jack the Ripper '76
Lady Frankenstein '72
Mark of the Devil '69

Marianne Gaba
How to Stuff a Wild Bikini '65
The Choppers '61

Richard Gabai (1964-)
Virtual Girl '00
Sexual Roulette '96
Vice Girls '96

Assault of the Party Nerds 2: Heavy Petting Detective '95
Bikini Drive-In '94
Dinosaur Island '93
Hot Under the Collar '91
Virgin High '90
Assault of the Party Nerds '89

Sasson Gabai
Escape: Human Cargo '98
Blink of an Eye '92

Martin Gabel (1912-86)
Smile, Jenny, You're Dead '74
Lady in Cement '68
Divorce American Style '67
Goodbye Charlie '64
Marnie '64
The Thief '52

Scilla Gabel
Colossus of the Arena '60
Mill of the Stone Women '60

Jean Gabin (1904-78)
L'Anne Sainte '78
Le Chat '75
Any Number Can Win '63
Duke of the Derby '62
Le Gentleman D'Epsom '62
Un Singe en Hiver '62
Le Cas du Dr. Laurent '57
Les Miserables '57
Four Bags Full '56
French Can-Can '55
Napoleon '55
Grisbi '53
Le Plaisir '52
The Walls of Malapaga '49
Stormy Waters '41
Le Jour Se Leve '39
La Bete Humaine '38
Grand Illusion '37
Pepe Le Moko '37
The Lower Depths '36
Maria Chapdelaine '34
Zou Zou '34

Christopher Gable (1940-98)
The Rainbow '89
The Lair of the White Worm '88
A Woman of Substance '84
The Slipper and the Rose '76
The Boy Friend '71
The Music Lovers '71

Clark Gable (1901-60)
The Misfits '61
It Started in Naples '60
But Not for Me '59
Run Silent, Run Deep '58
Teacher's Pet '58
Band of Angels '57
The King and Four Queens '56
Soldier of Fortune '55
The Tall Men '55
Betrayed '54
Mogambo '53
Never Let Me Go '53
Lone Star '52
Across the Wide Missouri '51
Key to the City '50
To Please a Lady '50
Any Number Can Play '49
Command Decision '48
Homecoming '48
The Hucksters '47
Adventure '45
Somewhere I'll Find You '42
Honky Tonk '41
They Met in Bombay '41
Boom Town '40
Comrade X '40
Strange Cargo '40
Gone with the Wind '39
Idiot's Delight '39
Test Pilot '38
Too Hot to Handle '38
Saratoga '37
Love on the Run '36
San Francisco '36
Wife Versus Secretary '36

China Seas '35
Forsaking All Others '35
Mutiny on the Bounty '35
Chained '34
It Happened One Night '34
Manhattan Melodrama '34
Dancing Lady '33
Hold Your Man '33
The Lost Stooges '33
No Man of Her Own '32
Red Dust '32
Strange Interlude '32
Dance Fools Dance '31
A Free Soul '31
Laughing Sinners '31
Night Nurse '31
Painted Desert '31
Possessed '31
Susan Lenox: Her Fall and Rise '31

Eva Gabor (1924-95)
Naked Gun 2 1/2: The Smell of Fear '91
The Rescuers Down Under '90 (V)
Princess Academy '87
Tales of the Klondike: The Scorn of Women '87
The Rescuers '77 (V)
The Aristocats '70 (V)
A New Kind of Love '63
It Started with a Kiss '59
Gigi '58
Truth about Women '58
Don't Go Near the Water '57
My Man Godfrey '57
Artists and Models '55
The Last Time I Saw Paris '54

Zsa Zsa Gabor (1919-)
The Beverly Hillbillies '93
Happily Ever After '93 (V)
A Nightmare on Elm Street 3: Dream Warriors '87
Movie Maker '86
Frankenstein's Great Aunt Tillie '83
Every Girl Should Have One '78
Arrivederci, Baby! '66
Picture Mommy Dead '66
Boys' Night Out '62
For the First Time '59
Queen of Outer Space '58
Touch of Evil '58
Death of a Scoundrel '56
Lili '53
Lovely to Look At '52
Moulin Rouge '52
We're Not Married '52

Ruth Gabriel
Nostromo '96
Running Out of Time '94

Monique Gabrielle (1963-)
Evil Toons '90
Silk 2 '89
Not of This Earth '88
Amazon Women on the Moon '87
Deathstalker 2: Duel of the Titans '87
Emmanuelle 5 '87
Screen Test '85
Bachelor Party '84
Hard to Hold '84
Hot Moves '84
Black Venus '83

Gabriel Gabrio
Harvest '37
Pepe Le Moko '37

John Gaden
A Little Bit of Soul '97
The Wedding Party '97

Antonio Gades (1936-)
El Amor Brujo '86
Carmen '83
Blood Wedding '81

Anna Gael
Zeta One '69
Therese & Isabelle '67

Mo Gaffney
Jailbait! '00
Drop Dead Gorgeous '99
The Shot '96

Kevin Gage
Blow '01
Dee Snider's Strangeland '98
Gunshy '98
Point Blank '98
Heat '95

Patricia Gage
The Little Kidnappers '90
Rabid '77

Holly Gagnier (1962-)
The Undertaker's Wedding '97
Alligator 2: The Mutation '90
Girls Just Want to Have Fun '85

Jenny Gago (1953-)
My Family '94
Sweet 15 '90
Old Gringo '89

Max Gail (1943-)
Facing the Enemy '00
Not in This Town '97
Good Luck '96
Forest Warrior '95
Deadly Target '94
Pontiac Moon '94
Sodbusters '94
Street Crimes '92
The Game of Love '90
Judgment in Berlin '88
Where Are the Children? '85
D.C. Cab '84
Heartbreakers '84
Aliens Are Coming '80
Pearl '78
Night Moves '75
Cardiac Arrest '74

Boyd Gaines (1953-)
The Confession '98
I'm Not Rappaport '96
Piece of Cake '90
The Discovery Program '89
Call Me '88
Heartbreak Ridge '86
The Sure Thing '85
Porky's '82

Jim Gaines
Fist of Steel '93
Codename: Terminate '90
Commando Invasion '87
Blood Debts '83

Richard Gaines (1904-75)
Humoresque '46
The Enchanted Cottage '45
Mr. Winkle Goes to War '44
The More the Merrier '43

M.C. Gainey
The New Guy '02
Happy, Texas '99
Con Air '97
Breakdown '96
Citizen Ruth '96
Leap of Faith '92
El Diablo '90

Courtney Gains (1965-)
King Cobra '98
No Code of Conduct '98
The Killing Grounds '97
Behind Enemy Lines '96
Memphis Belle '90
The 'Burbs '89
Colors '88
Can't Buy Me Love '87
Back to the Future '85
Lust in the Dust '85
Children of the Corn '84
Hardbodies '84

Charlotte Gainsbourg (1972-)
La Buche '00
Jane Eyre '96
Love, etc. '96
Grosse Fatigue '94
The Cement Garden '93
Night Sun '90
The Little Thief '89
Le Petit Amour '87

Serge Gainsbourg (1928-91)
I Love All of You '83
Too Pretty to Be Honest '72
The Fury of Hercules '61
Samson '61

Cristina Gajoni
Andy Warhol's Frankenstein '74
Ursus in the Valley of the Lions '62

Janusz Gajos (1939-)
Trois Couleurs: Blanc '94
The Decalogue '88
The Interrogation '82

Michel Galabru (1924-)
Belle Epoque '92
Uranus '91
La Cage aux Folles 3: The Wedding '86
Subway '85
La Cage aux Folles 2 '81
La Cage aux Folles '78
L'Amour en Herbe '77
The Judge and the Assassin '75
Soldat Duroc...Ca Va Etre Ta Fete! '75
Le Gendarme de Saint-Tropez '67

David Gale (1936-91)
The Guyver '91
Syngenor '90
Bride of Re-Animator '89
The Brain '88
Re-Animator '84
Savage Weekend '80

Ed Gale
O Brother Where Art Thou? '00
Chopper Chicks in Zombietown '91

Eddra Gale
Revenge of the Cheerleaders '76
8 1/2 '63

June Gale (1918-96)
It Could Happen to You '39
Rainbow's End '35

Vincent Gale
Brotherhood of Murder '99
Every Mother's Worst Fear '98
Baby Monitor: Sound of Fear '97
The Escape '95
Bye Bye Blues '89

Johnny Galecki (1975-)
Vanilla Sky '01
Bounce '00
Playing Mona Lisa '00
The Opposite of Sex '98
Bean '97
I Know What You Did Last Summer '97
Suicide Kings '97
Backfield in Motion '91
National Lampoon's Christmas Vacation '89

Michael Galeota
Clubhouse Detectives '96
Rattled '96

Juan Luis Galiardo
Tango '98
Don Juan, My Love '90

Anna Galiena (1954-)
Excellent Cadavers '99
The Leading Man '96
Moses '96
Three Lives and Only One Death '96
Being Human '94
Jamon, Jamon '93
The Hairdresser's Husband '92
Rorret '87

Kelly Galindo
The Malibu Beach Vampires '91
Angels of the City '89

Nacho Galindo (1973-)
Born Reckless '59
Wetbacks '56
Green Fire '55
Borderline '50

Annie Galipeau
Grey Owl '99
Map of the Human Heart '93

Frank Gallacher
Dark City '97
Mr. Reliable: A True Story '95
Proof '91
Waterfront '83

Bronagh Gallagher
The Wicked, Wicked West '97
Mary Reilly '95
Pulp Fiction '94
The Commitments '91

Megan Gallagher (1960-)
Breaking Free '95
Crosscut '95
Trade Off '95
The Birds 2: Land's End '94
In a Stranger's Hand '92
The Ambulance '90

Peter Gallagher (1955-)
Mr. Deeds '02
Perfume '01
Center Stage '00
Cupid & Cate '00
American Beauty '99
Brotherhood of Murder '99
House on Haunted Hill '99
Cafe Society '97
Johnny Skidmarks '97
The Man Who Knew Too Little '97
Path to Paradise '97
Last Dance '96
Titanic '96
To Gillian on Her 37th Birthday '96
The Underneath '95
While You Were Sleeping '95
Mrs. Parker and the Vicious Circle '94
Mother's Boys '94
White Mile '94
Fallen Angels 1 '93
Fallen Angels 2 '93
The Hudsucker Proxy '93
Malice '93
Short Cuts '93
Watch It '93
The Player '92
An Inconvenient Woman '91
Late for Dinner '91
Tune in Tomorrow '90
sex, lies and videotape '89
The Caine Mutiny Court Martial '88
High Spirits '88
Long Day's Journey into Night '88
The Murder of Mary Phagan '87
My Little Girl '87
Dreamchild '85
Private Contentment '83
Summer Lovers '82
Idolmaker '80
Skag '79

Richard "Skeets" Gallagher (1891-1955)
Danger on the Air '38
Hats Off '37
Bachelor Bait '34
Riptide '34
Possessed '31

Camillo Gallardo
Of Love and Shadows '94
Singles '92

Carlos Gallardo
Eastside '99
Desperado '95
El Mariachi '93

Rosa Maria Gallardo
The Brainiac '61
Creature of the Walking Dead '60

Silvania Gallardo
Prison Stories: Women on the Inside '91
Out of the Dark '88

Ely Galleani
Redneck '73
Five Dolls for an August Moon '70

Gina Gallego (1959-)
Personals '90
My Demon Lover '87
Lust in the Dust '85

Rosina Galli
Escape to Paradise '39
Fisherman's Wharf '39

Zach Galligan (1963-)
Gabriela '01
The Tomorrow Man '01
Arthur's Quest '99
Raw Nerve '99
Storm Trooper '98
The First to Go '97
Prince Valiant '97
Cupid '96
Cyborg 3: The Recycler '95
Caroline at Midnight '93
Ice '93
Warlock: The Armageddon '93
All Tied Up '92
Round Trip to Heaven '92
Psychic '91
Waxwork 2: Lost in Time '91
Zandalee '91
Gremlins 2: The New Batch '90
Mortal Passions '90
Rebel Storm '90
The Lawrenceville Stories '88
Waxwork '88
Gremlins '84

Robert Gallo
Sinners '89
Mayhem '87

Vincent Gallo (1961-)
Get Well Soon '01
Hide and Seek '00
Freeway 2: Confessions of a Trickbaby '99
Buffalo 66 '97
Truth or Consequences, N.M. '97
The Funeral '96
Nenette and Boni '96
Palookaville '95
Angela '94
Arizona Dream '94
The House of the Spirits '93

Don Galloway (1937-)
Two Moon Junction '88
Demon Rage '82
Snowblind '78
Rough Night in Jericho '67

Rita Gam (1928-)
Midnight '89
Distortions '87
Seeds of Evil '76
Klute '71
Shoot Out '71
The King of Kings '61
Mohawk '56
The Thief '52

Mason Gamble (1986-)
Arlington Road '99
Rushmore '98
Bad Moon '96
Dennis the Menace '93

Jacques Gamblin
Dr. Akagi '98
Pedale Douce '96

Michael Gambon (1940-)
Charlotte Gray '01
Gosford Park '01
High Heels and Low Lifes '01
Wives and Daughters '01
Longitude '00
The Insider '99
The Last September '99
Sleepy Hollow '99
Dancing at Lughnasa '98
Plunkett & Macleane '98
The Gambler '97
Midnight in Saint Petersburg '97
The Wings of the Dove '97
Samson and Delilah '96
Bullet to Beijing '95
The Innocent Sleep '95
Mary Reilly '95
Nothing Personal '95
The Browning Version '94
Clean Slate '94
A Man of No Importance '94
Squanto: A Warrior's Tale '94
Two Deaths '94
Toys '92
The Heat of the Day '91
Mobsters '91
The Cook, the Thief, His Wife & Her Lover '90
The Rachel Papers '89
Missing Link '88
Forbidden Passion: The Oscar Wilde Movie '87
The Singing Detective '86
Turtle Diary '86
The Beast Must Die '75

Robin Gammell
The Girl Next Door '98
His Bodyguard '98
Last Night '98
Bone Daddy '97
If These Walls Could Talk '96
Sinatra '92
Guilty by Suspicion '91
Gore Vidal's Lincoln '88
Project X '87
Missing Pieces '83
Full Circle '77
Panic in Echo Park '77

James Gammon (1940-)
Life or Something Like It '02
The Cell '00
Iron Giant '99 (V)
You Know My Name '99
The Hi-Lo Country '98
One Man's Hero '98
Point Blank '98
The Man in the Iron Mask '97
Traveller '96
Larry McMurtry's Streets of Laredo '95
Truman '95
Wild Bill '95
Cabin Boy '94
Hard Vice '94
Major League 2 '94
Wyatt Earp '94
The Adventures of Huck Finn '93
Running Cool '93
Crisscross '92
Leaving Normal '92
Coupe de Ville '90
I Love You to Death '90
Revenge '90
Major League '89
Roe vs. Wade '89
Gore Vidal's Lincoln '88
The Milagro Beanfield War '88
Ironweed '87
Hard Traveling '85
Ballad of Gregorio Cortez '83
The McCullochs '75
Deadly Encounter '72
Cool Hand Luke '67

Ken Gampu
American Ninja 4: The Annihilation '91
Enemy Unseen '91
Act of Piracy '89
Scavengers '87
Chain Gang Killings '85
Kill and Kill Again '81
Soul Patrol '80
African Rage '78
The Naked Prey '66
Dingaka '65

Yvonne Gamy
Manon of the Spring '87
Letters from My Windmill '54

Chester Gan (1908-59)
Crash Dive '43
Across the Pacific '42
Carson City Kid '40

Marguerite Gance
La Chute de la Maison Usher '28
Napoleon '27

James Gandolfini (1961-)
The Last Castle '01
The Man Who Wasn't There '01
The Mexican '01
Wildflowers '99
A Civil Action '98
8mm '98
The Mighty '98
Dance with the Devil '97
Fallen '97
She's So Lovely '97
Twelve Angry Men '97
The Juror '96
Night Falls on Manhattan '96
Crimson Tide '95
Get Shorty '95
Angie '94
Terminal Velocity '94
Italian Movie '93
Mr. Wonderful '93
Money for Nothing '93
True Romance '93
A Stranger Among Us '92

Tony Ganios (1959-)
Die Hard 2: Die Harder '90
Porky's Revenge '85
Porky's 2: The Next Day '83
Porky's '82
Continental Divide '81
Wanderers '79

Richard Ganoung
Billy's Hollywood Screen Kiss '98
Parting Glances '86

Richard Gant
Kingdom Come '01
Nutty Professor 2: The Klumps '00
Sour Grapes '98
Bean '97
Raven '97
Jason Goes to Hell: The Final Friday '93
The Freshman '90

Paul Ganus
The Silencer '92
Crash and Burn '90

Bruno Ganz (1941-)
Bread and Tulips '01
Eternity and a Day '97
Saint-Ex: The Story of the Storyteller '95
Faraway, So Close! '93
The Last Days of Chez Nous '92
Children of Nature '91
Strapless '90
Wings of Desire '88
In the White City '83
Nosferatu the Vampyre '79
Knife in the Head '78
The American Friend '77
Lumiere '76
The Marquise of O '76
Black and White As Day and Night '63

Yehoram Gaon
Dead End Street '83
Operation Thunderbolt '77

Kaz Garas (1940-)
Humanoids from the Deep '96
Puppet Master 5: The Final Chapter '94
Fast Gun '93
Naked Vengeance '85
Final Mission '84
Ben '72
The Last Safari '67

Matthew Garber (1956-77)
The Gnome-Mobile '67
Mary Poppins '64
The Three Lives of Thomasina '63

Terri Garber
North and South Book 2 '86
North and South Book 1 '85

Victor Garber (1949-)
Call Me Claus *'01*
Legally Blonde *'01*
Life with Judy Garland—Me and My Shadows *'01*
Torso *'01*
Annie *'99*
Cinderella *'97*
Titanic *'97*
The First Wives Club *'96*
Jeffrey *'95*
Exotica *'94*
Kleptomania *'94*
Life with Mikey *'93*
Queen *'93*
Sleepless in Seattle *'93*
Godspell *'73*

Greta Garbo (1905-90)
The Love Goddesses *'65*
Two-Faced Woman *'41*
Ninotchka *'39*
Conquest *'37*
Camille *'36*
Anna Karenina *'35*
The Painted Veil *'34*
Queen Christina *'33*
As You Desire Me *'32*
Grand Hotel *'32*
Mata Hari *'32*
Susan Lenox: Her Fall and Rise *'31*
Anna Christie *'30*
Romance *'30*
The Kiss *'29*
The Single Standard *'29*
The Mysterious Lady *'28*
Wild Orchids *'28*
A Woman of Affairs *'28*
The Flesh and the Devil *'27*
Joyless Street *'25*
The Atonement of Gosta Berling *'24*

Ingrid Garbo
Touch Me Not *'74*
Dracula's Great Love *'72*

Mauricio Garces
The Brainiac *'61*
The Living Head *'59*

Adam Garcia (1973-)
Riding in Cars with Boys *'01*
Bootmen *'00*
Coyote Ugly *'00*

Allan Garcia (1887-1938)
South of Santa Fe *'32*
The Circus *'19*

Andy Garcia (1956-)
Ocean's Eleven *'01*
For Love or Country: The Arturo Sandoval Story *'00*
Desperate Measures *'98*
Just the Ticket *'98*
The Disappearance of Garcia Lorca *'96*
Hoodlum *'96*
Night Falls on Manhattan *'96*
Steal Big, Steal Little *'95*
Things to Do in Denver When You're Dead *'95*
When a Man Loves a Woman *'94*
Hero *'92*
Jennifer 8 *'92*
Dead Again *'91*
The Godfather, Part 3 *'90*
Internal Affairs *'90*
A Show of Force *'90*
Black Rain *'89*
American Roulette *'88*
Blood Money: The Story of Clinton and Nadine *'88*
Stand and Deliver *'88*
The Untouchables *'87*
8 Million Ways to Die *'85*
Mean Season *'85*
Blue Skies Again *'83*
A Night in Heaven *'83*

Darnell Garcia
Blind Rage *'78*
Enforcer from Death Row *'78*

Eddie Garcia (1921-)
Relax... It's Just Sex! *'98*
Twilight People *'72*
Woman Hunt *'72*
Beast of the Yellow Night *'70*

Jerry Garcia
Hell's Angels Forever *'83*
Gimme Shelter *'70*

Jsu Garcia
We Were Soldiers *'02*
Devil in the Flesh 2 *'00*

Juan Garcia
Bounce *'00*
The Banker *'89*

Nicole Garcia (1946-)
Overseas: Three Women with Man Trouble *'90*
Peril *'85*
Corrupt *'84*
Bolero *'82*
Mon Oncle d'Amerique *'80*
Le Cavaleur *'78*

Stenio Garcia
Me You Them *'00*
At Play in the Fields of the Lord *'91*

Ginette Garcin
Charles et Lucie *'79*
Blue Country *'77*
Cousin, Cousine *'76*

Henri Garcin (1929-)
The Dress *'96*
The Eighth Day *'95*
One Hundred and One Nights *'95*
Someone Behind the Door *'71*

Vincent Gardenia (1922-92)
The Super *'91*
Tragedy of Flight 103: The Inside Story *'91*
Age Old Friends *'89*
Skin Deep *'89*
Moonstruck *'87*
Little Shop of Horrors *'86*
The Odd Squad *'86*
Brass *'85*
Movers and Shakers *'85*
Kennedy *'83*
Death Wish 2 *'82*
The Last Flight of Noah's Ark *'80*
Home Movies *'79*
Marciano *'79*
Greased Lightning *'77*
Death Wish *'74*
The Front Page *'74*
Lucky Luciano *'74*
Bang the Drum Slowly *'73*
Cold Turkey *'71*
Little Murders *'71*
Jenny *'70*
Where's Poppa? *'70*
The Hustler *'61*
Parrish *'61*

Reginald Gardiner (1903-80)
Mr. Hobbs Takes a Vacation *'62*
Rock-A-Bye Baby *'57*
Birds & the Bees *'56*
The Halls of Montezuma *'50*
The Dolly Sisters *'46*
Christmas in Connecticut *'45*
The Horn Blows at Midnight *'45*
Immortal Sergeant *'43*
Sweet Rosie O'Grady *'43*
Captains of the Clouds *'42*
The Man Who Came to Dinner *'41*
Sundown *'41*
A Yank in the R.A.F. *'41*
Doctor Takes a Wife *'40*
The Great Dictator *'40*
The Flying Deuces *'39*
Everybody Sing *'38*
Marie Antoinette *'38*
A Damsel in Distress *'37*
Born to Dance *'36*

Arthur Gardner
Mystic Circle Murder *'39*
Assassin of Youth *'35*

Ava Gardner (1922-90)
Harem *'86*
The Long, Hot Summer *'86*
A.D. *'85*
Regina *'83*
The Kidnapping of the President *'80*
City on Fire *'78*
The Cassandra Crossing *'76*
The Sentinel *'76*
Permission To Kill *'75*
Earthquake *'74*
Life & Times of Judge Roy Bean *'72*
Mayerling *'68*
The Bible *'66*
The Night of the Iguana *'64*
Seven Days in May *'64*
55 Days at Peking *'63*
The Naked Maja *'59*
On the Beach *'59*
Around the World in 80 Days *'56*
Bhowani Junction *'56*
The Barefoot Contessa *'54*
Knights of the Round Table *'53*
Mogambo *'53*
Lone Star *'52*
The Snows of Kilimanjaro *'52*
My Forbidden Past *'51*
Pandora and the Flying Dutchman *'51*
Show Boat *'51*
East Side, West Side *'49*
One Touch of Venus *'48*
The Hucksters *'47*
Singapore *'47*
The Killers *'46*
Whistle Stop *'46*
Reunion in France *'42*

Joan Gardner (1915-99)
The Challenge *'38*
Dark Journey *'37*
The Man Who Could Work Miracles *'37*
Private Life of Don Juan *'34*
The Scarlet Pimpernel *'34*
Wedding Rehearsal *'32*

Jennifer Gareis (1970-)
Luckytown *'00*
Miss Congeniality *'00*
The 6th Day *'00*

Allen (Goorwitz) Garfield (1939-)
The Majestic *'01*
Absence of the Good *'99*
Crime of the Century *'96*
Diabolique *'96*
Destiny Turns on the Radio *'95*
Jack and His Friends *'92*
Family Prayers *'91*
Club Fed *'90*
Let It Ride *'89*
Night Visitor *'89*
Beverly Hills Cop 2 *'87*
Desert Bloom *'86*
The Cotton Club *'84*
Irreconcilable Differences *'84*
Get Crazy *'83*
State of Things *'82*
Continental Divide *'81*
Leave 'Em Laughing *'81*
One Trick Pony *'80*
The Stunt Man *'80*
Brink's Job *'78*
Fyre *'78*
Sketches of a Strangler *'78*
Skateboard *'77*
Mother, Jugs and Speed *'76*
The Virginia Hill Story *'76*
Nashville *'75*
Paco *'75*
Busting *'74*
The Conversation *'74*
Slither *'73*
The Candidate *'72*
Bananas *'71*
Cry Uncle *'71*
Hi, Mom! *'70*
The Owl and the Pussycat *'70*
Greetings *'68*

John Garfield (1913-52)
Force of Evil *'49*
Jigsaw *'49*
Body and Soul *'47*
Gentleman's Agreement *'47*
Humoresque *'46*
The Postman Always Rings Twice *'46*
Hollywood Canteen *'44*
Air Force *'43*
Destination Tokyo *'43*
The Fallen Sparrow *'43*
Thank Your Lucky Stars *'43*
Tortilla Flat *'42*
The Sea Wolf *'41*
Juarez *'39*
They Made Me a Criminal *'39*
Four Daughters *'38*

John David Garfield (1943-94)
The Other Side of the Mountain *'75*
White Line Fever *'75*
Golden Voyage of Sinbad *'73*
The Stepmother *'71*
MacKenna's Gold *'69*
That Cold Day in the Park *'69*
Savage Intruder *'68*
The Swimmer *'68*

Art Garfunkel (1941-)
Boxing Helena *'93*
Mother Goose Rock 'n' Rhyme *'90*
Short Fuse *'88*
Carnal Knowledge *'71*
Catch-22 *'70*

Edward (Ed) Gargan (1902-64)
The Saint Strikes Back *'39*
Hands Across the Table *'35*
Belle of the Nineties *'34*

William Gargan (1905-79)
Dynamite *'49*
Strange Impersonation *'46*
Till the End of Time *'46*
The Canterville Ghost *'44*
Miss Annie Rooney *'42*
Who Done It? *'42*
Cheers for Miss Bishop *'41*
I Wake Up Screaming *'41*
They Knew What They Wanted *'40*
Broadway Serenade *'39*
Devil's Party *'38*
You Only Live Once *'37*
Milky Way *'36*
Aggie Appleby, Maker of Men *'33*
The Animal Kingdom *'32*
Rain *'32*

Troy Garity
Bandits *'01*
Steal This Movie! *'00*

Gianni "John" Garko (1935-)
Gunslinger *'70s*
The Psychic *'78*
Stranger's Gold *'71*
Waterloo *'71*
Saul and David *'68*
Five for Hell *'67*
The Avenger *'62*
The Mongols *'60*
Kapo *'59*

Beverly Garland (1926-)
Haunted Symphony *'94*
The World's Oldest Living Bridesmaid *'92*
Gamble on Love *'86*
It's My Turn *'80*
Roller Boogie *'79*
Where the Red Fern Grows *'74*
The Voyage of the Yes *'72*
Pretty Poison *'68*
Twice-Told Tales *'63*
The Gunslinger *'56*
It Conquered the World *'56*
Desperate Hours *'55*
Swamp Women *'55*
The Go-Getter *'54*
D.O.A. *'49*

Judy Garland (1922-69)
That's Entertainment *'74*
A Child Is Waiting *'63*
I Could Go on Singing *'63*
Gay Purr-ee *'62 (V)*
Judgment at Nuremberg *'61*
A Star Is Born *'54*
Summer Stock *'50*
In the Good Old Summertime *'49*
Easter Parade *'48*
The Pirate *'48*
Words and Music *'48*
The Harvey Girls *'46*
Till the Clouds Roll By *'46*
Ziegfeld Follies *'46*
The Clock *'45*
Meet Me in St. Louis *'44*
Strictly G.I. *'44*
Girl Crazy *'43*
Presenting Lily Mars *'43*
Thousands Cheer *'43*
For Me and My Gal *'42*
Babes on Broadway *'41*
Life Begins for Andy Hardy *'41*
Ziegfeld Girl *'41*
Andy Hardy Meets Debutante *'40*
Little Nellie Kelly *'40*
Strike Up the Band *'40*
Babes in Arms *'39*
The Wizard of Oz *'39*
Everybody Sing *'38*
Listen, Darling *'38*
Love Finds Andy Hardy *'38*
Broadway Melody of 1938 *'37*
Thoroughbreds Don't Cry *'37*
Pigskin Parade *'36*

Richard Garland
Panic in the Year Zero! *'62*
The Undead *'57*

Lee Garlington
Along for the Ride *'00*
Can of Worms *'00*
The Babysitter *'95*
Reflections in the Dark *'94*
My Life *'93*
A Killing in a Small Town *'90*
Cold Sassy Tree *'89*
The Seventh Sign *'88*
Psycho 3 *'86*

Alice Garner
Love and Other Catastrophes *'95*
Monkey Grip *'82*

James Garner (1928-)
Divine Secrets of the Ya-Ya Sisterhood *'02*
Atlantis: The Lost Empire *'01 (V)*
Space Cowboys *'00*
Legalese *'98*
Twilight *'98*
Dead Silence *'96*
My Fellow Americans *'96*
Larry McMurtry's Streets of Laredo *'95*
Breathing Lessons *'94*
Maverick *'94*
Barbarians at the Gate *'93*
Fire in the Sky *'93*
The Distinguished Gentleman *'92*
Decoration Day *'90*
Sunset *'88*
Murphy's Romance *'85*
The Glitter Dome *'84*
Tank *'83*
Victor/Victoria *'82*
The Fan *'81*
The Castaway Cowboy *'74*
One Little Indian *'73*
They Only Kill Their Masters *'72*
A Man Called Sledge *'71*
Skin Game *'71*
Support Your Local Gunfighter *'71*
Marlowe *'69*
Support Your Local Sheriff *'69*
How Sweet It Is! *'68*
The Pink Jungle *'68*
Hour of the Gun *'67*
Duel at Diablo *'66*
Grand Prix *'66*
The Americanization of Emily *'64*
36 Hours *'64*
The Great Escape *'63*
The Thrill of It All! *'63*
The Wheeler Dealers *'63*
Boys' Night Out *'62*
The Children's Hour *'61*
Cash McCall *'60*
Alias Jesse James *'59*
Up Periscope *'59*
Darby's Rangers *'58*
Sayonara *'57*

Jennifer Garner (1972-)
Pearl Harbor *'01*
Dude, Where's My Car? *'00*
Aftershock: Earthquake in New York *'99*
1999 *'98*
Mr. Magoo *'97*
Washington Square *'97*
Larry McMurtry's Dead Man's Walk *'96*

Peggy Ann Garner (1931-84)
Betrayal *'78*
A Wedding *'78*
The Cat *'66*
Eight Witnesses *'54*
The Big Cat *'49*
The Lovable Cheat *'49*
A Tree Grows in Brooklyn *'45*
Jane Eyre *'44*
The Keys of the Kingdom *'44*
Blondie Brings Up Baby *'39*

Gale Garnett (1942-)
32 Short Films about Glenn Gould *'93*
Mr. & Mrs. Bridge *'90*
The Children *'80*

Tay Garnett (1898-1977)
Challenge To Be Free *'76*
Strong Man *'26*

Janeane Garofalo (1964-)
Big Trouble *'02*
The Laramie Project *'02*
Wet Hot American Summer *'01*
The Adventures of Rocky & Bullwinkle *'00*
Steal This Movie! *'00*
Titan A.E. *'00 (V)*
What Planet Are You From? *'00*
Dogma *'99*
The Minus Man *'99*
Mystery Men *'99*
Thick as Thieves *'99*
The Bumblebee Flies Anyway *'98*
Clay Pigeons *'98*
Dog Park *'98*
Permanent Midnight *'98*
200 Cigarettes *'98*
Cop Land *'97*
Half-Baked *'97*
The Matchmaker *'97*
Romy and Michele's High School Reunion *'97*
Sweethearts *'97*
The Cable Guy *'96*
I Shot a Man in Vegas *'96*
Kids in the Hall: Brain Candy *'96*
Larger Than Life *'96*
Touch *'96*
The Truth about Cats and Dogs *'96*
Bye Bye, Love *'94*
Coldblooded *'94*
Reality Bites *'94*

Armistead Maupin's Tales of the City '93
Teri Garr (1949-)
Ghost World '01
Life Without Dick '01
Dick '99
Ronnie and Julie '97
A Simple Wish '97
Changing Habits '96
Michael '96
Dumb & Dumber '94
Perfect Alibi '94
Ready to Wear '94
Mom and Dad Save the World '92
The Player '92
Take Down '92
Mother Goose Rock 'n' Rhyme '90
A Perfect Little Murder '90
Short Time '90
Waiting for the Light '90
Let It Ride '89
Out Cold '89
Full Moon in Blue Water '88
Miracles '86
After Hours '85
First Born '84
To Catch a King '84
The Black Stallion Returns '83
Mr. Mom '83
The Sting 2 '83
The Tale of the Frog Prince '83
The Escape Artist '82
One from the Heart '82
Prime Suspect '82
Tootsie '82
Honky Tonk Freeway '81
The Black Stallion '79
Mr. Mike's Mondo Video '79
Witches' Brew '79
Close Encounters of the Third Kind '77
Oh, God! '77
Once Upon a Brothers Grimm '77
The Conversation '74
Young Frankenstein '74
Head '68
Speedway '68
Pajama Party '64
Martin Garralaga (1894-1981)
Bela Lugosi Meets a Brooklyn Gorilla '52
The Fighter '52
Susanna Pass '49
South of Monterey '47
In Old New Mexico '45
For Whom the Bell Tolls '43
Casablanca '42
Boots of Destiny '37
Ivo Garrani (1924-)
Street People '76
Waterloo '71
Atom Age Vampire '61
Black Sunday '60
The Giant of Marathon '60
The Day the Sky Exploded '57
Jean-Francoise Garreaud
Betty '92
Violette '78
Maurice Garrel
Artemisia '97
Un Coeur en Hiver '93
La Discrete '90
Betty Garrett (1919-)
My Sister Eileen '55
Neptune's Daughter '49
On the Town '49
Take Me Out to the Ball Game '49
Words and Music '48
Brad Garrett
A Bug's Life '98 (V)
Casper '95 (V)
Eliza (Simons) Garrett
Love Is a Gun '94
Terraces '77
Schlock '73
Hank Garrett
Blood Frenzy '87
The Boys Next Door '85
Rosebud Beach Hotel '85
Leif Garrett (1961-)
The Whispering '94
Spirit of '76 '91
The Banker '89
Cheerleader Camp '88
Party Line '88
Shaker Run '85
Thunder Alley '85
The Outsiders '83
Peter Lundy and the Medicine Hat Stallion '77
Skateboard '77
Walking Tall: The Final Chapter '77
Kid Vengeance '75
Patsy Garrett (1921-)
Dennis the Menace: Dinosaur Hunter '93
For the Love of Benji '77
Benji '74
Roger Garrett
Night of the Cobra Woman '72
The Passing of Evil '70
Barbara Garrick
Armistead Maupin's More Tales of the City '97
Ellen Foster '97
A Couch in New York '95
Miami Rhapsody '95
Armistead Maupin's Tales of the City '93
The Firm '93
Sleepless in Seattle '93
John Garrick (1902-66)
Broken Melody '34
Lily of Killarney '34
Lottery Bride '30
Song o' My Heart '29
David Garrison
Homeboys '92
On the Town '91
Riccardo Garrone
Terror Creatures from the Grave '66
Eva '62
Two Nights with Cleopatra '54
Greer Garson (1908-96)
Little Women '78
The Happiest Millionaire '67
The Singing Nun '66
Invincible Mr. Disraeli '63
Sunrise at Campobello '60
Julius Caesar '53
The Miniver Story '50
That Forsyte Woman '50
Julia Misbehaves '48
Adventure '45
The Valley of Decision '45
Mrs. Parkington '44
Madame Curie '43
Mrs. Miniver '42
Random Harvest '42
Blossoms in the Dust '41
When Ladies Meet '41
Pride and Prejudice '40
Goodbye, Mr. Chips '39
Willie Garson
Out Cold '01
Play It to the Bone '99
Untamed Heart '93
Jennie Garth (1972-)
Telling You '98
My Brother's War '97
Power 98 '96
Danielle Steel's Star '93
Christopher Gartin
Tremors 3: Back to Perfection '01
johns '96
Tremors 2: Aftershocks '96
Danielle Steel's Changes '91
Matters of the Heart '90
No Big Deal '83
Steve Garvey (1948-)
BASEketball '98
Ice Cream Man '95
Bloodfist 6: Ground Zero '94
The Scout '94
Elizabeth Garvie
Diana: Her True Story '93
Pride and Prejudice '85
John Garwood
A Taste of Hell '73
Hell's Angels on Wheels '67
Lorraine Gary (1937-)
Jaws: The Revenge '87
1941 '79
The Crash of Flight 401 '78
Jaws 2 '78
Jaws '75
Pray for the Wildcats '74
Vincent Gaskins
The Dark Dealer '95
The Underneath '95
Alessandro Gassman (1965-)
Samson and Delilah '96
Steam: A Turkish Bath '96
A Month by the Lake '95
Sacrilege '86
Vittorio Gassman (1922-2000)
Sleepers '96
Abraham '94
The Palermo Connection '91
The Sleazy Uncle '89
The Family '87
The Tempest '82
Sharky's Machine '81
Immortal Bachelor '80
Quintet '79
A Wedding '78
We All Loved Each Other So Much '77
The Desert of the Tartars '76
The Scent of a Woman '75
12 Plus 1 '70
Catch as Catch Can '68
Tiger and the Pussycat '67
Woman Times Seven '67
The Easy Life '63
Il Sorpasso '63
Barabbas '62
The Great War '59
Big Deal on Madonna Street '58
War and Peace '56
Mambo '55
Rhapsody '54
Anna '51
Bitter Rice '49
Lure of the Sila '49
Ana Gasteyer
What's the Worst That Could Happen? '01
Gepetto '00
What Women Want '00
Dick '99
Meet the Deedles '98
Michael Gaston
High Crimes '02
Bless the Child '00
Cora Unashamed '00
Ransom '96
The Wedding Banquet '93
Lisa Gastoni (1935-)
Tharus Son of Attila '87
Submission '77
Wild, Wild Planet '65
The Great Armored Car Swindle '64
Messalina vs. the Son of Hercules '64
RoGoPaG '62
The Baby and the Battleship '56
The Runaway Bus '54
Larry Gates (1915-96)
The Henderson Monster '80
Funny Lady '75
Death of a Gunfighter '69
The Sand Pebbles '66
Toys in the Attic '63
The Hoodlum Priest '61
Underworld, U.S.A. '60
The Strange One '57
Invasion of the Body Snatchers '56
Above and Beyond '53
Francis Covers the Big Town '53
Nancy Gates (1926-)
Comanche Station '60
Some Came Running '58
The Search for Bridey Murphy '56
Wetbacks '56
Suddenly '54
Torch Song '53
The Atomic City '52
The Member of the Wedding '52
At Sword's Point '51
Check Your Guns '48
Master Race '44
Nevada '44
The Great Gildersleeve '43
Marjorie Gateson (1891-1977)
International Lady '41
The Duke of West Point '38
Arizona Mahoney '36
Goin' to Town '35
John Gatins
Leprechaun 3 '95
Witchboard 2: The Devil's Doorway '93
Jill Gatsby
The Ambulance '90
Return to Salem's Lot '87
Jennifer Gatti
Blood Money '99
Double Exposure '93
Street Knight '93
Valerie Gaunt
The Horror of Dracula '58
The Curse of Frankenstein '57
Mikkel Gaup
Breaking the Waves '95
Pathfinder '87
Dan Gauthier (1963-)
Excessive Force 2: Force on Force '95
Illegal in Blue '95
Son-in-Law '93
Shame '92
Teen Witch '89
Dick Gautier (1937-)
Get Smart, Again! '89
Glitch! '88
Marathon '80
Divorce American Style '67
Jean-Yves Gautier
A Chef in Love '96
Three Lives and Only One Death '96
Voyage to the Beginning of the World '96
The Promise '94
Jean Gaven
The Story of O '75
The Crucible '57
Erica Gavin
Caged Heat '74
Beyond the Valley of the Dolls '70
John Gavin (1928-)
House of Shadows '83
History of the World: Part 1 '81
Sophia Loren: Her Own Story '80
Jennifer '78
Murder for Sale '70
The Madwoman of Chaillot '69
Thoroughly Modern Millie '67
Back Street '61
Breath of Scandal '60
Midnight Lace '60
Psycho '60
Spartacus '60
Imitation of Life '59
A Time to Love & a Time to Die '58
Cassandra Gaviola
The Black Room '82
Conan the Barbarian '82
William Gaxton (1890-)
Best Foot Forward '43
The Heat's On '43
It's the Old Army Game '26
Gregory Gay (-1993)
Seven Doors to Death '44
The Secret Code '42
Ramon Gay
The Curse of the Aztec Mummy '59
The Robot vs. the Aztec Mummy '59
Howard Gaye (-1955)
Dante's Inferno '24
Flirting with Fate '16
The Birth of a Nation '15
Lisa Gaye
Class of Nuke 'Em High 3: The Good, the Bad and the Subhumanoid '94
Class of Nuke 'Em High 2: Subhumanoid Meltdown '91
The Toxic Avenger, Part 2 '89
The Toxic Avenger, Part 3: The Last Temptation of Toxie '89
Lisa Gaye (1935-)
Castle of Evil '66
Night of Evil '62
The Sign of Zorro '60
Shake, Rattle and Rock '57
Marvin Gaye
Chrome and Hot Leather '71
The Ballad of Andy Crocker '69
Rebecca Gayheart (1972-)
From Dusk Till Dawn 3: The Hangman's Daughter '99
Jawbreaker '98
Too Smooth '98
Urban Legend '98
Scream 2 '97
Nothing to Lose '96
Somebody Is Waiting '96
Jackie Gayle (1929-)
Bulworth '98
Mr. Saturday Night '92
Bert Rigby, You're a Fool '89
Plain Clothes '88
Tin Men '87
Pepper and His Wacky Taxi '72
Monica Gayle
Nashville Girl '76
Switchblade Sisters '75
Anna Gaylor
The Killing Game '67
Life Upside Down '64
Mitch Gaylord (1961-)
Animal Instincts '92
American Tiger '89
American Anthem '86
George Gaynes (1917-)
The Crucible '96
Police Academy 7: Mission to Moscow '94
Vanya on 42nd Street '94
Stepmonster '92
Police Academy 6: City under Siege '89
Police Academy 5: Assignment Miami Beach '88
Police Academy 4: Citizens on Patrol '87
Police Academy 3: Back in Training '86
Police Academy 2: Their First Assignment '85
It Came Upon a Midnight Clear '84
Micki & Maude '84
Police Academy '84
Dead Men Don't Wear Plaid '82
Tootsie '82
Breaking Up Is Hard to Do '79
Trilogy of Terror '75
Janet Gaynor (1906-84)
The Young in Heart '38
A Star Is Born '37
The Farmer Takes a Wife '35
Sunrise '27
Mitzi Gaynor (1930-)
For Love or Money '63
South Pacific '58
Les Girls '57
Birds & the Bees '56
There's No Business Like Show Business '54
We're Not Married '52
Eunice Gayson (1931-)
From Russia with Love '63
Dr. No '62
The Revenge of Frankenstein '58
Carry On Admiral '57
Wendy Gazelle
The Net '95
Crooked Hearts '91
Triumph of the Spirit '89
Understudy: The Graveyard Shift 2 '88
Hot Pursuit '87
Sammy & Rosie Get Laid '87
Ben Gazzara (1930-)
Brian's Song '01
Blue Moon '00
Believe '99
The List '99
Summer of Sam '99
The Thomas Crown Affair '99
Happiness '98
Illuminata '98
The Big Lebowski '97
Buffalo 66 '97
Lady Killer '97
Protector '97
The Spanish Prisoner '97
Stag '97
Vicious Circles '97
Farmer & Chase '96
The Shadow Conspiracy '96
Convict Cowboy '95
The Dogfighters '95
Parallel Lives '94
Blindsided '93
Lies Before Kisses '92
Road House '89
Quicker Than the Eye '88
Secret Obsession '88
Control '87
An Early Frost '85
Tales of Ordinary Madness '83
They All Laughed '81
Question of Honor '80
Saint Jack '79
Sidney Sheldon's Bloodline '79
Opening Night '77
The Trial of Lee Harvey Oswald '77
The Death of Richie '76
High Velocity '76
The Killing of a Chinese Bookie '76
Voyage of the Damned '76
QB VII '74
Sicilian Connection '74
Neptune Factor '73
Fireball Forward '72
Pursuit '72
Shattered Silence '71
Husbands '70
The Bridge at Remagen '69
Joyful Laughter '60
Passionate Thief '60
Anatomy of a Murder '59
The Strange One '57
Michael V. Gazzo (1923-95)
Cookie '89
The Godfather 1902-1959: The Complete Epic '81
Alligator '80
Kill Castro '80
The Mercenaries '80
Gangsters '79
Love and Bullets '79
Fingers '78
King of the Gypsies '78
Black Sunday '77

The Godfather, Part 2 '74
Valerie Gearon
Persuasion '71
Invasion '65
Anthony Geary (1947-)
Scorchers '92
Night of the Warrior '91
High Desert Kill '90
Crack House '89
UHF '89
It Takes Two '88
Pass the Ammo '88
You Can't Hurry Love '88
Dangerous Love '87
Penitentiary 3 '87
Kicks '85
The Imposter '84
Johnny Got His Gun '71
Bud Geary (1898-1946)
D-Day on Mars '45
The Topeka Terror '45
Bataan '43
Bordertown Gunfighters '43
Immortal Sergeant '43
Cynthia Geary (1965-)
Smoke Signals '98
The Killing Grounds '97
When Time Expires '97
The Heist '96
8 Seconds '94
To Grandmother's House We Go '94
Karl Geary (1972-)
Hamlet '00
The Book of Stars '99
The Eternal '99
The External '99
Nadja '95
Gordon Gebert (1941-)
To Hell and Back '55
The Narrow Margin '52
Flying Leathernecks '51
Nicholas Gecks
Seeing Red '99
The Mill on the Floss '97
Forever Young '85
Jason Gedrick (1965-)
Summer Catch '01
The Last Don 2 '98
The Last Don '97
Power 98 '96
The Force '94
Crossing the Bridge '92
Still Life '92
Backdraft '91
Rooftops '89
Promised Land '88
Stacking '87
Iron Eagle '86
The Heavenly Kid '85
Massive Retaliation '85
The Zoo Gang '85
Prunella Gee (1950-)
Witching Time '84
Never Say Never Again '83
The Wilby Conspiracy '75
Robbie Gee
Mean Machine '01
Snatch '00
Ellen Geer (1941-)
Neil Simon's The Odd Couple 2 '98
Satan's Princess '90
Hard Traveling '85
Bloody Birthday '80
Over the Edge '79
A Shining Season '79
Babe! '75
Memory of Us '74
Silence '73
Harold and Maude '71
Kevin Geer
The Tavern '00
Sweet Bird of Youth '89
Will Geer (1902-78)
Bunco '83
Unknown Powers '80
The Billion Dollar Hobo '78
My Sister, My Love '78
A Woman Called Moses '78
Moving Violation '76
The Hanged Man '74
Hurricane '74
Memory of Us '74
Executive Action '73
Silence '73
Dear Dead Delilah '72
Jeremiah Johnson '72
Napoleon and Samantha '72
Brother John '70
The Reivers '69
Bandolero! '68
The President's Analyst '67
Seconds '66
Black Like Me '64
Salt of the Earth '54
Broken Arrow '50
Comanche Territory '50
To Please a Lady '50
Winchester '73 '50
Lust for Gold '49
Judy Geeson (1948-)
The Duke '99
Houdini '99
The Plague Dogs '82 (V)
Danger UXB '81
Inseminoid '80
Adventures of a Taxi Driver '76
Carry On England '76
Poldark '75
Poldark 2 '75
It's Not the Size That Counts '74
Murder on the Midnight Express '74
Doomwatch '72
Dynasty of Fear '72
10 Rillington Place '71
The Executioner '70
It Happened at Nightmare Inn '70
Twinsanity '70
Berserk! '67
To Sir, with Love '67
Sally Geeson (1950-)
Cry of the Banshee '70
The Oblong Box '69
What's Good for the Goose '69
Deborah Geffner
Exterminator 2 '84
All That Jazz '79
Martha Gehman
Threesome '94
Unveiled '94
Father of the Bride '91
A Kiss Before Dying '91
F/X '86
The Flamingo Kid '84
Bob Geldof (1954-)
Spice World: The Movie '97
The Return of Spinal Tap '92
Pink Floyd: The Wall '82
The Secret Policeman's Other Ball '82
Secret Policeman's Private Parts '81
Alan Gelfant (1956-)
Next Stop, Wonderland '98
The Destiny of Marty Fine '96
Forced to Kill '93
Daniel Gelin (1921-)
Iran: Days of Crisis '91
Life Is a Long Quiet River '88
Murmur of the Heart '71
Is Paris Burning? '66
The Testament of Orpheus '59
The Man Who Knew Too Much '56
Plucking the Daisy '56
A Woman of Rome '56
La Ronde '51
Rendez-vous de Juillet '49
Sarah Michelle Gellar (1977-)
Scooby-Doo '02
Simply Irresistible '99
Cruel Intentions '98
Small Soldiers '98 (V)
Beverly Hills Family Robinson '97
I Know What You Did Last Summer '97
Scream 2 '97
High Stakes '89
Larry Gelman
Chatterbox '76
Slumber Party '57 '76
Grant Gelt
Mutant Species '95
Avalon '90
Rhoda Gemignani
Rocky Marciano '99
Concrete Beat '84
Giuliano Gemma (1938-)
Blood at Sundown '88
Unsane '82
The Warning '80
Corleone '79
Battleforce '78
The Desert of the Tartars '76
Smugglers '75
Master Touch '74
Erik, the Viking '72
Goliath and the Sins of Babylon '64
Hercules vs. the Sons of the Sun '64
Ruth Gemmell
The Alchemists '99
Fever Pitch '96
Band of Gold '95
Laura Gemser (1950-)
Fury '80s
Women's Prison Massacre '85
Caged Women '84
Ator the Fighting Eagle '83
Black Cobra '83
Emmanuelle's Daughter '79
Crime Busters '78
Emmanuelle in the Country '78
Naked Paradise '78
Emmanuelle on Taboo Island '76
Emmanuelle, the Joys of a Woman '76
Love Camp '76
Emmanuelle, the Queen '75
Francois-Eric Gendron
Boyfriends & Girlfriends '88
Cloud Waltzing '87
Bryan Genesse (1967-)
Agent of Death '99
Cold Harvest '98
Operation Delta Force 3: Clear Target '98
Terminal Virus '96
Live Wire: Human Timebomb '95
Terminal Impact '95
Night Siege Project: Shadowchaser 2 '94
California Casanova '89
Loose Screws '85
Leo Genn (1905-78)
Die Screaming, Marianne '73
Mackintosh Man '73
Strange Case of Dr. Jekyll & Mr. Hyde '68
Circus of Fear '67
The Longest Day '62
Moby Dick '56
Lady Chatterley's Lover '55
The Miniver Story '50
Wooden Horse '50
The Snake Pit '48
Velvet Touch '48
Green for Danger '47
Henry V '44
Immortal Battalion '44
When Thief Meets Thief '37
Minnie Gentry (-1993)
Def by Temptation '90
Georgia, Georgia '72
Roger Gentry
Alien Massacre '67
Horrors of the Red Planet '64
Carrie Genzel
Virtual Seduction '96
Caged Hearts '95
Paul Geoffrey
Emily Bronte's Wuthering Heights '92
Flame to the Phoenix '85
Excalibur '81
Stephen Geoffreys (1964-)
Moon 44 '90
976-EVIL '88
The Chair '87
Fraternity Vacation '85
Fright Night '85
Brian George
Bubble Boy '01
Ghost World '01
Smokescreen '90
Christopher George (1929-)
Pieces '83
AngKor: Cambodia Express '81
Enter the Ninja '81
Graduation Day '81
Mortuary '81
Exterminator '80
Gates of Hell '80
Cruise into Terror '78
Day of the Animals '77
Whiskey Mountain '77
Dixie Dynamite '76
Grizzly '76
Midway '76
Train Robbers '73
Man on a String '71
Chisum '70
El Dorado '67
Chief Dan George (1899-1981)
Americathon '79
The Outlaw Josey Wales '76
The Bears & I '74
Harry and Tonto '74
Dan Candy's Law '73
Cancel My Reservation '72
Little Big Man '70
Gladys George (1900-54)
Detective Story '51
Lullaby of Broadway '51
Flamingo Road '49
The Best Years of Our Lives '46
The Maltese Falcon '41
House Across the Bay '40
The Roaring Twenties '39
Marie Antoinette '38
Madame X '37
Goetz George
Advertising Rules! '01
The Trio '97
Schtonk '92
Out of Order '84
Heinrich George (1893-1946)
Kolberg '45
Jud Suess '40
Metropolis '26
Chief Leonard George
Smoke Signals '98
Man of the House '95
Lynda Day George (1946-)
Pieces '83
Young Warriors '83
The Junkman '82
Mortuary '81
Beyond Evil '80
Casino '80
Racquet '79
Cruise into Terror '78
Aliens from Spaceship Earth '77
Ants '77
Day of the Animals '77
Roots '77
The Barbary Coast '74
Panic on the 5:22 '74
Maud(e) (Ford) George (1888-1963)
The Wedding March '28
Foolish Wives '22
Blue Blazes Rawden '18
Melissa George
Mulholland Drive '01
Sugar & Spice '01
The Limey '99
Dark City '97
Rita George
On the Run '85
Hollywood Boulevard '76
Susan George (1950-)
That Summer of White Roses '90
Jack the Ripper '88
Lightning: The White Stallion '86
The Jigsaw Man '84
Pajama Tops '83
House Where Evil Dwells '82
Kiss My Grits '82
Venom '82
Enter the Ninja '81
Tintorera...Tiger Shark '78
Tomorrow Never Comes '77
A Small Town in Texas '76
Mandingo '75
Out of Season '75
Dirty Mary Crazy Larry '74
Die Screaming, Marianne '73
Dr. Jekyll and Mr. Hyde '73
Sonny and Jed '73
Straw Dogs '72
Fright '71
Eye Witness '70
Lola '69
The Looking Glass War '69
Olga Georges-Picot (-1997)
Children of Rage '75
The Graveyard '74
The Day of the Jackal '73
The Man Who Haunted Himself '70
Honor Among Thieves '68
Tom Georgeson
The Land Girls '98
Swing '98
Devices and Desires '91
A Fish Called Wanda '88
No Surrender '86
Alika Georgouli
Landscape in the Mist '88
The Travelling Players '75
Carmelita Geraghty (1901-66)
Flaming Signal '33
Night Life in Reno '31
Rogue of the Rio Grande '30
My Best Girl '27
My Lady of Whims '25
Marita Geraghty
Past Tense '94
Groundhog Day '93
Charles Gerard
Bandits '86
Happy New Year '73
Danny Gerard (1977-)
Robot in the Family '94
Desperate Hours '90
Drop-Out Mother '88
Gil Gerard (1943-)
Air Rage '01
The Stepdaughter '00
Mom, Can I Keep Her? '98
Soldier's Fortune '91
Final Notice '89
Fury to Freedom: The Life Story of Raul Ries '85
For Love or Money '84
Help Wanted: Male '82
Buck Rogers in the 25th Century '79
Killing Stone '78
Hooch '76
Steven Geray (1904-73)
Jesse James Meets Frankenstein's Daughter '65
Tobor the Great '54
Affair in Trinidad '52
The Big Sky '52
Ladies of the Chorus '49
Blondie Knows Best '46
Gilda '46
In Society '44
The Mask of Dimitrios '44
The Seventh Cross '44
The Moon and Sixpence '43
Inspector Hornleigh '39
Joan Gerber
DuckTales the Movie: Treasure of the Lost Lamp '90 (V)
Tobor the Great '54
George Gerdes
Jailbreakers '94
Iron Will '93
Richard Gere (1949-)
The Mothman Prophecies '02
Unfaithful '02
Autumn in New York '00
Dr. T & the Women '00
Runaway Bride '99
The Jackal '97
Red Corner '97
Primal Fear '96
First Knight '95
And the Band Played On '93
Intersection '93
Mr. Jones '93
Sommersby '93
Final Analysis '92
Rhapsody in August '91
Internal Affairs '90
Pretty Woman '90
Miles from Home '88
No Mercy '86
Power '86
King David '85
The Cotton Club '84
Beyond the Limit '83
Breathless '83
An Officer and a Gentleman '82
American Gigolo '79
Yanks '79
Bloodbrothers '78
Days of Heaven '78
Looking for Mr. Goodbar '77
Strike Force '75
Report to the Commissioner '74
Georges Geret (1924-96)
A Very Curious Girl '69
Z '69
Diary of a Chambermaid '64
Peter Gerety
Hollywood Ending '02
The Curse of the Jade Scorpion '01
K-PAX '01
Homicide: The Movie '00
The Legend of Bagger Vance '00
Went to Coney Island on a Mission from God...Be Back by Five '98
Louise Germaine
Lipstick on Your Collar '94
Sharpe's Company '94
Gaia Germani
Castle of the Living Dead '64
Your Turn Darling '63
Greg Germann (1962-)
Down to Earth '01
Joe Somebody '01
Sweet November '01
Jesus' Son '99
The Night We Never Met '93
Once Around '91
Charles Gerrard
The Nervous Wreck '26
Down to Earth '17
Daniel Gerroll (1951-)
A Far Off Place '93
Drop Dead Fred '91
Big Business '88
84 Charing Cross Road '86
Savina Gersak
Midnight Ride '92
Beyond the Door 3 '91
War Bus Commando '89
Curse 2: The Bite '88

Iron Warrior '87
Sonny Boy '87
Gina Gershon (1962-)
Driven '01
Black & White '99
Guinevere '99
The Insider '99
I'm Losing You '98
Legalese '98
Lulu on the Bridge '98
One Tough Cop '98
Palmetto '98
Face/Off '97
This World, Then the Fireworks '97
Bound '96
Touch '96
Best of the Best 3: No Turning Back '95
Showgirls '95
Flinch '94
Joey Breaker '93
Love Matters '93
The Player '92
Sinatra '92
City of Hope '91
Out for Justice '91
Voodoo Dawn '89
Cocktail '88
Red Heat '88
Pretty in Pink '86
Betty Lou Gerson (1914-99)
101 Dalmatians '61 (V)
The Fly '58
The Red Menace '49
Jeanne Gerson (1905-92)
The Touch of Satan '70
The Bride & the Beast '58
She Gods of Shark Reef '56
Paul Gerson
The Bellboy '60
Cricket on the Hearth '23
Berta Gersten
A Brivele der Mamen '38
Mirele Efros '38
Frank Gerstle (1915-70)
Hell on Wheels '67
The Atomic Brain '64
Submarine Seahawk '59
The Wasp Woman '59
Gang Busters '55
Above and Beyond '53
Valeska Gert (1892-1978)
Juliet of the Spirits '65
The Threepenny Opera '31
Joyless Street '25
Jami Gertz (1965-)
Lip Service '00
Seven Girlfriends '00
Twister '96
Jersey Girl '92
Don't Tell Her It's Me '90
Sibling Rivalry '90
Silence Like Glass '90
Listen to Me '89
Renegades '89
Less Than Zero '87
The Lost Boys '87
Crossroads '86
Quicksilver '86
Solarbabies '86
Mischief '85
Alphabet City '84
Sixteen Candles '84
Endless Love '81
Erwin Geschonneck (1906-)
Anton, the Magician '78
Jacob the Liar '74
Five Cartridges '60
Zen Gesner (1970-)
The Breed '01
Shallow Hal '01
Me, Myself, and Irene '00
There's Something about Mary '98
Kingpin '96
Wish Me Luck '95
Balthazar Getty (1975-)
Deuces Wild '02
The Center of the World '01
Hard Cash '01
Four Dogs Playing Poker '00
Big City Blues '99
Out in Fifty '99
Voodoo Dawn '99
Habitat '97
Lost Highway '96
White Squall '96
Red Hot '95
Dead Beat '94
Don't Do It '94
Terrified '94
Where the Day Takes You '92
December '91
My Heroes Have Always Been Cowboys '91
The Pope Must Diet '91
Lord of the Flies '90
Young Guns 2 '90
Estelle Getty (1923-)
Stuart Little '99
Stop! or My Mom Will Shoot '92
Mannequin '87
Mask '85
Tootsie '82
John Getz (1947-)
The Late Shift '96
A Passion to Kill '94
Playmaker '94
Curly Sue '91
Don't Tell Mom the Babysitter's Dead '91
Born on the Fourth of July '89
The Fly 2 '89
The Fly '86
Blood Simple '85
Concrete Beat '84
Thief of Hearts '84
Kent State '81
Tattoo '81
Stan Getz (1927-91)
Exterminator '80
The Benny Goodman Story '55
Massimo Ghini (1954-)
Up at the Villa '00
Tea with Mussolini '99
The Truce '96
Men Men Men '95
Alice Ghostley (1926-)
Whispers: An Elephant's Tale '00 (V)
Neil Simon's The Odd Couple 2 '98
Not for Publication '84
Blue Sunshine '78
Grease '78
Gator '76
With Six You Get Eggroll '68
The Graduate '67
To Kill a Mockingbird '62
New Faces of 1952 '54
Paul Giamatti (1967-)
Big Fat Liar '02
Planet of the Apes '01
Storytelling '01
Big Momma's House '00
Duets '00
If These Walls Could Talk 2 '00
The Cradle Will Rock '99
Man on the Moon '99
The Negotiator '98
Safe Men '98
Saving Private Ryan '98
Tourist Trap '98
The Truman Show '98
Winchell '98
The Break '97
My Best Friend's Wedding '97
Private Parts '96
Louis Giambalvo
Gun Shy '00
Gia '98
Illegal in Blue '95
Dead to Rights '93
Fade to Black '93
Question of Faith '93
Weekend at Bernie's '89
The Jagged Edge '85
The Ambush Murders '82
Joseph Gian (1962-)
Mad About You '90
Blackout '88
Night Stalker '87
Rick Gianasi
Sgt. Kabukiman N.Y.P.D. '94
The Occultist '89
Posed for Murder '89
Escape from Safehaven '88
Maximum Thrust '88
Mutant Hunt '87
Robot Holocaust '87
Giancarlo Giannini (1942-)
Hannibal '01
Dune '00
Mimic '97
The Disappearance of Garcia Lorca '96
Heaven Before I Die '96
A Walk in the Clouds '95
Jacob '94
Once Upon a Crime '92
Goodnight, Michelangelo '89
New York Stories '89
The Sleazy Uncle '89
Time to Kill '89
Blood Red '88
Saving Grace '86
Fever Pitch '85
American Dreamer '84
Where's Piccone '84
Lovers and Liars '81
Immortal Bachelor '80
Blood Feud '79
Life Is Beautiful '79
A Night Full of Rain '78
How Funny Can Sex Be? '76
The Innocent '76
Seven Beauties '76
Swept Away... '75
La Grande Bourgeoise '74
The Sensual Man '74
Love and Anarchy '73
Seduction of Mimi '72
The Secret of Santa Vittoria '69
Anzio '68
Cynthia Gibb (1963-)
Life with Judy Garland—Me and My Shadows '01 (N)
Volcano: Fire on the Mountain '97
Holiday Affair '96
Sin and Redemption '94
Gypsy '93
The Woman Who Loved Elvis '93
Death Warrant '90
Short Circuit 2 '88
Jack's Back '87
Malone '87
Modern Girls '86
Salvador '86
Youngblood '86
Stardust Memories '80
Donald Gibb
Magic Kid 2 '94
Revenge of the Nerds 4: Nerds in Love '94
Bloodsport '88
Robyn Gibbes
Wild Horses '82
Gone to Ground '76
Leeza Gibbons
The Player '92
Soapdish '91
Marla Gibbs (1946-)
The Brothers '01
The Visit '00
Foolish '99
Lost and Found '99
Lily in Winter '94
The Meteor Man '93
Up Against the Wall '91
Timothy Gibbs
Witchboard 2: The Devil's Doorway '93
The Kindred '87
Rebecca Gibney (1965-)
Joey '98
Paperback Romance '96
Jigsaw '90
Among the Cinders '83
Susan Gibney
Cabin by the Lake '00
And You Thought Your Parents Were Weird! '91
Henry Gibson (1935-)
A Stranger in the Kingdom '98
Asylum '97
Bio-Dome '96
Mother Night '96 (V)
Color of a Brisk and Leaping Day '95
Tom and Jerry: The Movie '93 (V)
Gremlins 2: The New Batch '90
Tune in Tomorrow '90
Around the World in 80 Days '89
Night Visitor '89
Switching Channels '88
Innerspace '87
Long Gone '87
Brenda Starr '86
Monster in the Closet '86
The Incredible Shrinking Woman '81
Tulips '81
The Blues Brothers '80
For the Love of It '80
Kentucky Fried Movie '77
Nashville '75
Charlotte's Web '73 (V)
The Long Goodbye '73
Evil Roy Slade '71
The Outlaws Is Coming! '65
Kiss Me, Stupid! '64
The Nutty Professor '63
Hoot Gibson (1892-1962)
The Horse Soldiers '59
The Marshal's Daughter '53
Arizona Whirlwind '44
Death Valley Rangers '44
Marked Trails '44
Outlaw Trail '44
Sonora Stagecoach '44
The Law Rides Again '43
The Painted Stallion '37
Cavalcade of the West '36
Last Outlaw '36
Lucky Terror '36
The Riding Avenger '36
Swifty '36
Feud of the West '35
Fighting Parson '35
Frontier Justice '35
Powdersmoke Range '35
Rainbow's End '35
Sunset Range '35
Cowboy Counselor '33
Boiling Point '32
Dude Bandit '32
Local Badman '32
Man's Land '32
Spirit of the West '32
Clearing the Range '31
Hard Hombre '31
Wild Horse '31
The Concentratin' Kid '30
Roaring Ranch '30
Spurs '30
Trailing Trouble '30
Trigger Tricks '30
Courtin' Wildcats '29
King of the Rodeo '28
The Prairie King '27
The Phantom Bullet '26
Straight Shootin' '17
Margaret Gibson
Last Days of Frank & Jesse James '86
Never a Dull Moment '50
Mel Gibson (1956-)
Signs '02
We Were Soldiers '02
Chicken Run '00 (V)
The Patriot '00
What Women Want '00
The Million Dollar Hotel '99
Lethal Weapon 4 '98
Payback '98
Conspiracy Theory '97
FairyTale: A True Story '97
Ransom '96
Braveheart '95
Casper '95
Pocahontas '95 (V)
Maverick '94
The Man Without a Face '93
Forever Young '92
Lethal Weapon 3 '92
Air America '90
Bird on a Wire '90
Hamlet '90
Lethal Weapon 2 '89
Tequila Sunrise '88
Lethal Weapon '87
Mad Max: Beyond Thunderdome '85
Attack Force Z '84
The Bounty '84
Mrs. Soffel '84
The River '84
The Road Warrior '82
The Year of Living Dangerously '82
Gallipoli '81
Mad Max '80
Tim '79
Summer City '77
Mimi Gibson
Courage of Black Beauty '57
The Monster That Challenged the World '57
Thomas Gibson (1962-)
The Lost Empire '01
The Flintstones in Viva Rock Vegas '00
Psycho Beach Party '00
Stardom '00
Eyes Wide Shut '99
Armistead Maupin's More Tales of the City '97
Barcelona '94
Secrets '94
Sleep with Me '94
Armistead Maupin's Tales of the City '93
Love and Human Remains '93
Far and Away '92
Tyrese Gibson
Baby Boy '01
Love Song '00
Virginia Gibson (1928-)
Athena '54
Seven Brides for Seven Brothers '54
Tea for Two '50
Wynne Gibson (1899-1987)
Motorcycle Squad '37
Aggie Appleby, Maker of Men '33
Night After Night '32
Bond Gideon
Stepsisters '85
Gold of the Amazon Women '79
Storyville '74
Pamela Gidley (1966-)
The Little Vampire '00
Kiss & Tell '99
Mafia! '98
Aberration '97
Bombshell '97
Bad Love '95
The Crew '95
The Little Death '95
Firefall '94
S.F.W. '94
Cheatin' Hearts '93
Highway to Hell '92
Liebestraum '91
Disturbed '90
Blue Iguana '88
Cherry 2000 '88
Permanent Record '88
Thrashin' '86
John Gielgud (1904-2000)
Elizabeth '98
Merlin '98
Quest for Camelot '98 (V)
Dragonheart '96 (V)
Hamlet '96
The Leopard Son '96 (N)
Looking for Richard '96
Portrait of a Lady '96
First Knight '95
Gulliver's Travels '95
Haunted '95
Shine '95
Scarlett '94
The Power of One '92
Shining Through '92
Prospero's Books '91
Strike It Rich '90
Getting It Right '89
Romance on the Orient Express '89
War & Remembrance: The Final Chapter '89
Appointment with Death '88
Arthur 2: On the Rocks '88
A Man for All Seasons '88
War & Remembrance '88
The Whistle Blower '87
Plenty '85
The Shooting Party '85
Wagner: The Complete Epic '85
The Far Pavilions '84
Scandalous '84
The Scarlet & the Black '83
The Wicked Lady '83
Frankenstein '82
Gandhi '82
The Hunchback of Notre Dame '82
Inside the Third Reich '82
Arthur '81
Brideshead Revisited '81
Chariots of Fire '81
Lion of the Desert '81
Priest of Love '81
Sphinx '81
Caligula '80
The Conductor '80
The Elephant Man '80
The Formula '80
The Human Factor '79
Murder by Decree '79
Les Miserables '78
James Joyce: A Portrait of the Artist as a Young Man '77
Providence '77
Edward the King '75
11 Harrowhouse '74
Murder on the Orient Express '74
QB VII '74
Invitation to the Wedding '73
Probe '72
Julius Caesar '70
The Charge of the Light Brigade '68
Sebastian '68
The Shoes of the Fisherman '68
Chimes at Midnight '67
The Loved One '65
Becket '64
Saint Joan '57
Around the World in 80 Days '56
Richard III '55
Romeo and Juliet '54
Julius Caesar '53
Hamlet '48 (V)
The Secret Agent '36
Stefan Gierasch (1926-)
Murder in the First '95
Dave '93
Blood Beach '81
Blue Sunshine '78
Carrie '76
High Plains Drifter '73
Jeremiah Johnson '72
Alan Gifford (1905-89)
Isadora '68
Town without Pity '61
Brainwashed '60
Time Lock '57
Frances Gifford (1919-94)
Riding High '50

Our Vines Have Tender Grapes '45
Thrill of a Romance '45
American Empire '42
Border Vigilantes '41

Gloria Gifford
Vice Versa '88
D.C. Cab '84

Kathie Lee Gifford (1953-)
Model Behavior '00
Dudley Do-Right '99

Roland Gift (1963-)
The Painted Lady '97
Scandal '89
Sammy & Rosie Get Laid '87

Elaine Giftos (1945-)
Angel '84
The Wrestler '73
Gas-s-s-s! '70
The Student Nurses '70

Sandro Giglio
For the First Time '59
The War of the Worlds '53

Marie Gignac
No '98
The Confessional '95

Ariadna Gil (1969-)
Talk of Angels '96
Celestial Clockwork '94
Belle Epoque '92

Vincent (Vince Gill) Gil
Body Melt '93
Mad Max '80
Solo '77

Andrew S. Gilbert
Paperback Hero '99
Idiot Box '97
Kiss or Kill '97

Billy Gilbert (1894-1971)
Fun & Fancy Free '47 (V)
Cooking Up Trouble '44
Ghost Crazy '44
Spotlight Scandals '43
Mr. Wise Guy '42
Song of the Islands '42
Valley of the Sun '42
Melody Master '41
Week-End in Havana '41
The Great Dictator '40
His Girl Friday '40
No, No, Nanette '40
Seven Sinners '40
Tin Pan Alley '40
Destry Rides Again '39
Block-heads '38
Breaking the Ice '38
Happy Landing '38
Joy of Living '38
Maid's Night Out '38
Peck's Bad Boy with the Circus '38
The Firefly '37
100 Men and a Girl '37
Snow White and the Seven Dwarfs '37 (V)
Toast of New York '37
Kelly the Second '36

Edmund Gilbert (1932-99)
Tom and Jerry: The Movie '93 (V)
Johnny Got His Gun '71
36 Hours '64

Eugenia Gilbert
Courtin' Wildcats '29
Test of Donald Norton '26

Helen Gilbert (1915-95)
Girls in Prison '56
Death Valley '46
God's Country '46
Andy Hardy Gets Spring Fever '39

Jody Gilbert
Willard '71
Actors and Sin '52

John Gilbert (1895-1936)
Queen Christina '33
A Woman of Affairs '28
The Flesh and the Devil '27
The Big Parade '25
He Who Gets Slapped '24
The Busher '19

Marcus Gilbert
Army of Darkness '92
Riders '88

Melissa Gilbert (1964-)
Dying to Remember '93
Undesirable '92
The Lookalike '90
Ice House '89
Blood Vows: The Story of a Mafia Wife '87
Choices '86
Penalty Phase '86
Sylvester '85
Family Secrets '84
The Snow Queen '83
The Miracle Worker '79
The Christmas Coal Mine Miracle '77
Little House on the Prairie '74

Pamela Gilbert
Demonwarp '87
Evil Spawn '87

Sara Gilbert (1975-)
Riding in Cars with Boys '01
High Fidelity '00
Light It Up '99
Desert Blue '98
Dead Beat '94
Poison Ivy '92
Sudie & Simpson '90

Taylor Gilbert
Alone in the T-Shirt Zone '86
Torment '85

Connie Gilchrist (1901-)
The Misadventures of Merlin Jones '63
Long John Silver '54
Houdini '53
The Half-Breed '51
Here Comes the Groom '51
Stars in My Crown '50
Ticket to Tomahawk '50
A Letter to Three Wives '49
Nothing But Trouble '44
Tortilla Flat '42

Richard Gilden
The Black Klansman '66
Lost, Lonely, and Vicious '59

Sandra Giles
Daddy-O '59
Lost, Lonely, and Vicious '59

Gwynne Gilford
Fade to Black '80
Satan's School for Girls '73
Beware! The Blob '72

Jack Gilford (1907-90)
Arthur 2: On the Rocks '88
Cocoon: The Return '88
Cocoon '85
Caveman '81
Cheaper to Keep Her '80
Wholly Moses! '80
Max '79
Harry & Walter Go to New York '76
Save the Tiger '73
They Might Be Giants '71
Catch-22 '70
Enter Laughing '67
The Incident '67
A Funny Thing Happened on the Way to the Forum '66

Marie Gillain
Elective Affinities '96
L'Appat '94

Aidan Gillen (1968-)
Lorna Doone '01
The Low Down '00
Some Mother's Son '96
Circle of Friends '94

Dana Gillespie
Scrubbers '82
The People That Time Forgot '77

Aden (John) Gillett (1958-)
Shadow of the Vampire '00
The 10th Kingdom '00
The Winslow Boy '98
The Borrowers '97
Ivanhoe '97
The House of Eliott '92

Anita Gillette (1936-)
Larger Than Life '96
She's the One '96
Boys on the Side '94
Bob Roberts '92
Moonstruck '87
Brass '85
Marathon '80
Ants '77

David Gilliam
Gunpowder '84
Sharks' Treasure '75
Frogs '72

Seth Gilliam
Starship Troopers '97
Tar '97
Courage Under Fire '96
Assault at West Point: The Court-Martial of Johnson Whittaker '94
Jefferson in Paris '94

Terry Gilliam (1940-)
Spies Like Us '85
Monty Python's The Meaning of Life '83
Secret Policeman's Private Parts '81
Monty Python's Life of Brian '79
Monty Python and the Holy Grail '75
And Now for Something Completely Different '72

Larry Gilliard, Jr.
Cecil B. Demented '00
Simply Irresistible '99
Next Stop, Wonderland '98
A Soldier's Sweetheart '98
The Waterboy '98
The Substitute 2: School's Out '97
Lotto Land '95
Money Train '95

Lawrence Gilliard
Fly by Night '93
Straight out of Brooklyn '91

Isabel Gillies
I Shot Andy Warhol '96
One Way Out '95
Metropolitan '90

Richard Gilliland (1950-)
Dogwatch '97
Star Kid '97
A Killing in a Small Town '90
Happy Hour '87
Acceptable Risks '86
Challenge of a Lifetime '85
Embassy '85
A Day for Thanks on Walton's Mountain '82
Bug '75

Linda Gillin
Windows '80
Terror at Red Wolf Inn '72

Rebecca Gilling (1953-)
Heaven Tonight '93
The Blue Lightning '86
The Naked Country '85

Claude Gillingwater (1870-1939)
Green Eyes '34
Illicit '31
My Boy '21

Ann Gillis (1927-)
Big Town After Dark '47
In Society '44
Texas Legionnaires '43
Bambi '42 (V)
'Neath Brooklyn Bridge '42
Nice Girl? '41
The Adventures of Tom Sawyer '38
Peck's Bad Boy with the Circus '38

James Gillis (1943-)
Alien Space Avenger '91
Deranged '87
Night of the Zombies '81
Dracula Sucks '79

Caroline Gillmer
The Monkey's Mask '00
Sorrento Beach '95

Margalo Gillmore
A Woman's World '54
Cause for Alarm '51

Kenneth Gilman
Nights in White Satin '87
Scavengers '87
Bedroom Eyes '86

Art Gilmore
The Gallant Hours '60
The Narcotics Story '58 (N)

Denis Gilmore
Tomb of Ligeia '64
The Unstoppable Man '59

Lowell Gilmore (1906-)
Ma and Pa Kettle at Waikiki '55
Lone Star '52
King Solomon's Mines '50
Johnny Angel '45
Picture of Dorian Gray '45
Days of Glory '43

Virginia Gilmore (1919-86)
The Loves of Edgar Allen Poe '42
Orchestra Wives '42
Western Union '41

Ian Gilmour
Dangerous Summer '82
The Odd Angry Shot '79

Jack Gilpin
From the Earth to the Moon '98
Commandments '96
Last Breath '96
Barcelona '94
White Mile '94
Unnatural Pursuits '91
Quick Change '90
Reversal of Fortune '90
Funny Farm '88
Something Wild '86

Marc Gilpin
Computer Wizard '77
Where's Willie? '77

Jessalyn Gilsig
A Cooler Climate '99
Quest for Camelot '98 (V)

Clarence Gilyard, Jr. (1955-)
Left Behind: The Movie '00
Walker: Texas Ranger: One Riot, One Ranger '93
Off the Mark '87

Daniel Gimenez Cacho
Jealousy '99
Deep Crimson '96
Midaq Alley '95
Cabeza de Vaca '90

Erica Gimpel
Imposter '01
The Fence '94

Teresa Gimpera (1936-)
Feast for the Devil '70s
Macabre '77
Crypt of the Living Dead '73
Spirit of the Beehive '73
Black Box Affair '66

Jack Ging (1931-)
Dear Detective '78
Die Sister, Die! '74
Where the Red Fern Grows '74
High Plains Drifter '73
Sssssss '73
That Man Bolt '73
Play Misty for Me '71
Mosby's Marauders '66

Hermione Gingold (1897-1987)
Garbo Talks '84
A Little Night Music '77
Those Fantastic Flying Fools '67
Munster, Go Home! '66
Promise Her Anything '66
Gay Purr-ee '62 (V)
The Music Man '62
The Naked Edge '61
Bell, Book and Candle '58
Gigi '58
Around the World in 80 Days '56
The Adventures of Sadie '55
The Pickwick Papers '54
Tough Guy '53
Butler's Dilemma '43

Bob Ginnaven
The Day It Came to Earth '77
Hootch Country Boys '75

Allen Ginsberg (1926-97)
Superstar: The Life and Times of Andy Warhol '90
Heavy Petting '89

Robert Ginty (1948-)
The Prophet's Game '99
Lady Dragon '92
Harley Davidson and the Marlboro Man '91
Madhouse '90
Vietnam, Texas '90
Bounty Hunters '89
Loverboy '89
Out on Bail '89
Codename: Vengeance '87
Three Kinds of Heat '87
Programmed to Kill '86
Mission to Kill '85
Exterminator 2 '84
Gold Raiders '84
Warrior of the Lost World '84
White Fire '83
The Act '82
The Alchemist '81
Exterminator '80
Coming Home '78

Rocky Giordani
Cop and a Half '93
After Dark, My Sweet '90
Tapeheads '89

Daniela Giordano (1948-)
The Girl in Room 2A '76
Inquisition '76
Stranger's Gold '71
Four Times That Night '69

Domiziana Giordano (1960-)
Interview with the Vampire '94
Nouvelle Vague '90
Nostalghia '83

Florence Giorgetti
Monique '83
The Lacemaker '77

Elenora Giorgi (1953-)
Creepers '85
Nudo di Donna '83
Beyond Obsession '82
Inferno '80
To Forget Venice '79

Carmine D. Giovinazzo
Black Hawk Down '01
The Learning Curve '01
Terror Tract '00
For Love of the Game '99

Cindy Girard
Raising Cain '92
Operation Dames '59

Joseph Girard (1871-1949)
Sergeant York '41
Mystery of the Hooded Horseman '37
Aces and Eights '36
The Ivory Handled Gun '35
The Tonto Kid '35
Hurricane Express '32
Defenders of the Law '31
King of the Rodeo '28
Tentacles of the North '26
Laughing at Danger '24

Remy Girard
Varian's War '01
The Boys '97
Jesus of Montreal '89

Michele Girardon
Devil of the Desert Against the Son of Hercules '62
Death in the Garden '56

Annie Girardot (1931-)
Les Miserables '95
Mussolini & I '85
Jacko & Lise '82
La Vie Continue '82
Jupiter's Thigh '81
Le Cavaleur '78
Dear Detective '77
Gypsy '75
The Organizer '64
Love and the Frenchwoman '60
Rocco and His Brothers '60

Hippolyte Girardot (1955-)
Love After Love '94
Barjo '93
Love Without Pity '91
Manon of the Spring '87

Roland Giraud
Mr. Frost '89
Three Men and a Cradle '85

Bernard Giraudeau (1947-)
A Matter of Taste '00
Water Drops on Burning Rocks '99
Ridicule '96
The Favorite Son '94
Passion of Love '82
La Boum '81
Bilitis '77

Massimo Girotti (1918-)
The Monster '96
Quo Vadis '85
Mr. Klein '76
Last Tango in Paris '73
Torture Chamber of Baron Blood '72
Red Tent '69
Teorema '68
The Giants of Thessaly '60
Senso '54
Sins of Rome '54
Ossessione '42

Jackie Giroux
Trick or Treats '82
The Cross & the Switchblade '72

Annabeth Gish (1972-)
A Death in the Family '02
Double Jeopardy '99
SLC Punk! '99
Steel '97
True Women '97
Beautiful Girls '96
Don't Look Back '96
The Last Supper '96
Nixon '95
Scarlett '94
Wyatt Earp '94
Coupe de Ville '90
Shag: The Movie '89
When He's Not a Stranger '89
Mystic Pizza '88
Hiding Out '87
Desert Bloom '86

Dorothy Gish (1898-1968)
The Cardinal '63
Romola '25
Orphans of the Storm '21
Hearts of the World '18
Home Sweet Home '14
Judith of Bethulia '14

Lillian Gish (1896-1993)
The Whales of August '87
Sweet Liberty '86
The Adventures of Huckleberry Finn '85
Hambone & Hillie '84

Hobson's Choice *'83*
A Wedding *'78*
The Comedians *'67*
Follow Me, Boys! *'66*
The Love Goddesses *'65*
The Unforgiven *'60*
The Cobweb *'55*
The Night of the Hunter *'55*
Portrait of Jennie *'48*
Duel in the Sun *'46*
Commandos Strike at Dawn *'43*
His Double Life *'33*
The Wind *'28*
Romola *'25*
The White Sister *'23*
Orphans of the Storm *'21*
Way Down East *'20*
Broken Blossoms *'19*
The Greatest Question *'19*
True Heart Susie *'19*
Hearts of the World *'18*
Intolerance *'16*
The Birth of a Nation *'15*
Home Sweet Home *'14*
Judith of Bethulia *'14*
Battle of Elderbush Gulch *'13*

Sheila Gish
Highlander: Endgame *'00*
Mansfield Park *'99*
Highlander *'86*
A Day in the Death of Joe Egg *'71*

Robert Gist (1924-98)
Jack the Giant Killer *'62*
One Minute to Zero *'52*
Jigsaw *'49*

Neil Giuntoli
Henry: Portrait of a Serial Killer 2: Mask of Sanity *'96*
Memphis Belle *'90*
Capone *'89*

Paul(o) Giusti
L'Anne Sainte *'78*
Dirty Hands *'76*
Emmanuelle on Taboo Island *'76*
Innocents with Dirty Hands *'75*

Adele Givens
Queens of Comedy *'01*
The Players Club *'98*

Robin Givens (1964-)
Blankman *'94*
Foreign Student *'94*
Boomerang *'92*
The Penthouse *'92*
A Rage in Harlem *'91*
The Women of Brewster Place *'89*
Beverly Hills Madam *'86*

George Givot (1903-)
China Gate *'57*
Lady and the Tramp *'55 (V)*
April in Paris *'52*
DuBarry Was a Lady *'43*
Leather Burners *'43*
Thin Ice *'37*
Hollywood Party *'34*

Etienne Glaser
Speak Up! It's So Dark *'93*
The Mozart Brothers *'86*

Paul Michael Glaser (1943-)
Jealousy *'84*
Single Bars, Single Women *'84*
Wait Till Your Mother Gets Home *'83*
Phobia *'80*
Fiddler on the Roof *'71*

Ned Glass (1906-84)
Street Music *'81*
Kid Galahad *'62*
West Side Story *'61*
The Rebel Set *'59*
Fright *'56*
Requiem for a Heavyweight *'56*

Ron Glass (1945-)
Back in Business *'96*
It's My Party *'95*
Houseguest *'94*
Deep Space *'87*
The Crash of Flight 401 *'78*

Seamon Glass
Winterhawk *'76*
This Is Not a Test *'62*

Isabel Glasser
Tactical Assault *'99*
Second Chances *'98*
Mother *'96*
Circumstances Unknown *'95*
The Surgeon *'94*
Death Ring *'93*
Forever Young *'92*
Pure Country *'92*

Phillip Glasser (1978-)
Voodoo Dawn *'99*
A Troll in Central Park *'94 (V)*
An American Tail: Fievel Goes West *'91 (V)*
Satan's Princess *'90*
An American Tail *'86 (V)*

Bob Glaudini
Parasite *'82*
The Alchemist *'81*

Louise Glaum (1900-70)
The Leopard Woman *'20*
Sex *'20*
Return of Draw Egan *'16*
The Three Musketeers *'16*

Karen Glave
Blind Faith *'98*
Last Night *'98*

Matthew Glave
Corky Romano *'01*
Rock Star *'01*
Mutiny *'99*
Plump Fiction *'97*
True Women *'97*
The Wedding Singer *'97*
Baby's Day Out *'94*

Eugene Glazer
New Blood *'99*
It's My Party *'95*
Bounty Tracker *'93*
The Substitute *'93*
The Five Heartbeats *'91*
Stepping Out *'91*
Dollman *'90*
Eve of Destruction *'90*
Harlem Nights *'89*
I'm Gonna Git You Sucka *'88*
Stand and Deliver *'88*
Hollywood Shuffle *'87*
Hunter's Blood *'87*
No Way Out *'87*
Vendetta *'85*

Jackie Gleason (1916-87)
Nothing in Common *'86*
Izzy & Moe *'85*
Smokey and the Bandit, Part 3 *'83*
The Sting 2 *'83*
The Toy *'82*
Smokey and the Bandit 2 *'80*
Mr. Billion *'77*
Smokey and the Bandit *'77*
Don't Drink the Water *'69*
How to Commit Marriage *'69*
Papa's Delicate Condition *'63*
Soldier in the Rain *'63*
Requiem for a Heavyweight *'62*
The Hustler *'61*
All Through the Night *'42*
Orchestra Wives *'42*
Springtime in the Rockies *'42*

James Gleason (1886-1959)
Last Hurrah *'58*
Man or Gun *'58*
Loving You *'57*
Man in the Shadow *'57*
Rock-A-Bye Baby *'57*
The Night of the Hunter *'55*
Suddenly *'54*
Forever Female *'53*
Movie Stuntmen *'53*
We're Not Married *'52*
What Price Glory? *'52*
I'll See You in My Dreams *'51*
The Jackpot *'50*
Key to the City *'50*
Riding High *'50*
The Yellow Cab Man *'50*
Miss Grant Takes Richmond *'49*
The Bishop's Wife *'47*
Down to Earth *'47*
Tycoon *'47*
The Clock *'45*
A Tree Grows in Brooklyn *'45*
Arsenic and Old Lace *'44*
A Guy Named Joe *'44*
The Keys of the Kingdom *'44*
Crash Dive *'43*
Footlight Serenade *'42*
Tales of Manhattan *'42*
Here Comes Mr. Jordan *'41*
Meet John Doe *'41*
Tanks a Million *'41*
Ex-Mrs. Bradford *'36*
Hoopla *'33*
The Crooked Circle *'32*
A Free Soul *'31*

Joanna Gleason (1950-)
The Wedding Planner *'01*
Road Ends *'98*
Boogie Nights *'97*
If These Walls Could Talk *'96*
Edie & Pen *'95*
For Richer, for Poorer *'92*
F/X 2: The Deadly Art of Illusion *'91*
Crimes & Misdemeanors *'89*
Heartburn *'86*

Pat Gleason
Criminal Court *'46*
Detour *'46*
Rogue's Gallery *'44*
I Killed That Man *'42*
Swing It, Professor *'37*

Paul Gleason (1944-)
National Lampoon's Van Wilder *'02*
Not Another Teen Movie *'01*
Social Misfits *'00*
The Brutal Truth *'99*
No Code of Conduct *'98*
The Thin Red Line *'98*
Money Talks *'97*
The Shadow Conspiracy *'96*
Digital Man *'94*
Boiling Point *'93*
Maniac Cop 3: Badge of Silence *'93*
Running Cool *'93*
Wishman *'93*
There Goes My Baby *'92*
Wild Cactus *'92*
Rich Girl *'91*
Fourth Story *'90*
Miami Blues *'90*
Night Game *'89*
Die Hard *'88*
Ghost Chase *'88*
Johnny Be Good *'88*
She's Having a Baby *'88*
Forever, Lulu *'87*
Morgan Stewart's Coming Home *'87*
The Breakfast Club *'85*
Challenge of a Lifetime *'85*
The Ewoks: Battle for Endor *'85*
Trading Places *'83*
He Knows You're Alone *'80*
Doc Savage *'75*
Private Duty Nurses *'71*

Russell Gleason (1908-45)
Condemned to Live *'35*
I Can't Escape *'34*
All Quiet on the Western Front *'30*
The Flying Fool *'29*

Brendan Gleeson (1954-)
Harrison's Flowers *'02*
A. I.: Artificial Intelligence *'01*
Mission: Impossible 2 *'00*
The Tailor of Panama *'00*
Lake Placid *'99*
This Is My Father *'99*
The General *'98*
The Break *'97*
The Butcher Boy *'97*
I Went Down *'97*
Michael Collins *'96*
Trojan Eddie *'96*
Turbulence *'96*
Braveheart *'95*

Paul Gleeson
Komodo *'99*
Idiot Box *'97*

Iain Glen (1961-)
Lara Croft: Tomb Raider *'01*
Wives and Daughters *'01*
Beautiful Creatures *'00*
Maria *'98*
The Painted Lady *'97*
The Young Americans *'93*
Fools of Fortune *'90*
Mountains of the Moon *'90*
Rosencrantz & Guildenstern Are Dead *'90*

J. Frank Glendon
Border Romance *'30*
Mid-Channel *'20*

Philip Glenister
Horatio Hornblower: The Adventure Continues *'01*
Vanity Fair *'99*
Sharpe's Justice *'97*

Montgomery Glenn
Castle of Blood *'64*
The Horrible Dr. Hichcock *'62*

Roy Glenn
Carmen Jones *'54*
Jungle Drums of Africa *'53*

Scott Glenn (1942-)
The Seventh Stream *'01*
The Shipping News *'01*
Training Day *'01*
Vertical Limit *'00*
The Last Marshal *'99*
The Virgin Suicides *'99*
Naked City: A Killer Christmas *'98*
Naked City: Justice with a Bullet *'98*
Absolute Power *'97*
Carla's Song *'97*
Firestorm *'97*
Courage Under Fire *'96*
Edie & Pen *'95*
Reckless *'95*
Tall Tale: The Unbelievable Adventures of Pecos Bill *'95*
Night of the Running Man *'94*
Past Tense *'94*
The Spy Within *'94*
Extreme Justice *'93*
Shadowhunter *'93*
Slaughter of the Innocents *'93*
The Player *'92*
Backdraft *'91*
My Heroes Have Always Been Cowboys *'91*
The Silence of the Lambs *'91*
Women & Men: In Love There Are No Rules *'91*
The Hunt for Red October *'90*
Intrigue *'90*
Miss Firecracker *'89*
Verne Miller *'88*
Man on Fire *'87*
Off Limits *'87*
As Summers Die *'86*
Silverado *'85*
Wild Geese 2 *'85*
The River *'84*
The Keep *'83*
The Right Stuff *'83*
The Challenge *'82*
Personal Best *'82*
Urban Cowboy *'80*
Apocalypse Now *'79*
More American Graffiti *'79*
She Came to the Valley *'77*
Fighting Mad *'76*
Nashville *'75*
The Shrieking *'73*
Angels Hard As They Come *'71*
The Baby Maker *'70*

Sharon Gless (1943-)
Tales of the Unexpected *'91*
Letting Go *'85*
Hobson's Choice *'83*
The Star Chamber *'83*
Hardhat & Legs *'80*
Revenge of the Stepford Wives *'80*
Centennial *'78*
The Crash of Flight 401 *'78*

Stacey Glick
Three o'Clock High *'87*
Brighton Beach Memoirs *'86*

Brian Glover (1934-97)
Stiff Upper Lips *'96*
Royal Deceit *'94*
Leon the Pig Farmer *'93*
Alien 3 *'92*
Kafka *'91*
The Company of Wolves *'85*
The McGuffin *'85*
An American Werewolf in London *'81*

Bruce Glover (1932-)
Night of the Scarecrow *'95*
Warlock: The Armageddon *'93*
Hider in the House *'90*
Killcrazy *'89*
Ghost Town *'88*
Big Bad Mama 2 *'87*
Stunts *'77*
Diamonds Are Forever *'71*
C.C. & Company *'70*

Crispin Glover (1964-)
Like Mike *'02*
Fast Sofa *'01*
Charlie's Angels *'00*
Nurse Betty *'00*
The People vs. Larry Flynt *'96*
Dead Man *'95*
Chasers *'94*
Even Cowgirls Get the Blues *'94*
Hotel Room *'93*
What's Eating Gilbert Grape *'93*
Rubin & Ed *'92*
The Doors *'91*
Little Noises *'91*
Where the Heart Is *'90*
Wild at Heart *'90*
Back to the Future, Part 2 *'89*
Twister *'89*
River's Edge *'87*
At Close Range *'86*
Back to the Future *'85*
Friday the 13th, Part 4: The Final Chapter *'84*
Racing with the Moon *'84*
Teachers *'84*
My Tutor *'82*

Danny Glover (1947-)
The Royal Tenenbaums *'01*
3 A.M. *'01*
Boesman & Lena *'00*
Freedom Song *'00*
Antz *'98 (V)*
Beloved *'98*
Lethal Weapon 4 *'98*
Prince of Egypt *'98 (V)*
Buffalo Soldiers *'97*
Gone Fishin' *'97*
John Grisham's The Rainmaker *'97*
Switchback *'97*
America's Dream *'95*
Operation Dumbo Drop *'95*
Angels in the Outfield *'94*
Maverick *'94*
Bopha! *'93*
Queen *'93*
The Saint of Fort Washington *'93*
Lethal Weapon 3 *'92*
Grand Canyon *'91*
Pure Luck *'91*
A Rage in Harlem *'91*
Flight of the Intruder *'90*
Predator 2 *'90*
To Sleep with Anger *'90*
Dead Man Out *'89*
Lethal Weapon 2 *'89*
Lonesome Dove *'89*
A Raisin in the Sun *'89*
Bat 21 *'88*
Out *'88*
Lethal Weapon *'87*
Mandela *'87*
The Color Purple *'85*
Silverado *'85*
Stand-In *'85*
Witness *'85*
Iceman *'84*
Places in the Heart *'84*
Memorial Day *'83*
Chu Chu & the Philly Flash *'81*
Keeping On *'81*
Escape from Alcatraz *'79*

Jamie Glover
In His Life: The John Lennon Story *'00*
Joseph *'95*

John Glover (1944-)
The Tempest *'99*
Payback *'98*
Batman and Robin *'97*
Love! Valour! Compassion! *'96*
In the Mouth of Madness *'95*
Schemes *'95*
Assault at West Point: The Court-Martial of Johnson Whittaker *'94*
Automatic *'94*
Night of the Running Man *'94*
Ed and His Dead Mother *'93*
What Ever Happened To... *'93*
Drug Wars 2: The Cocaine Cartel *'92*
Dead on the Money *'91*
El Diablo *'90*
Gremlins 2: The New Batch *'90*
Meet the Hollowheads *'89*
Traveling Man *'89*
The Chocolate War *'88*
Masquerade *'88*
Rocket Gibraltar *'88*
Scrooged *'88*
Apology *'86*
52 Pick-Up *'86*
Something Special *'86*
An Early Frost *'85*
A Killing Affair *'85*
Ernie Kovacs: Between the Laughter *'84*
The Evil That Men Do *'84*
A Little Sex *'82*
The Mountain Men *'80*
Last Embrace *'79*
Annie Hall *'77*

Julian Glover (1935-)
Vatel *'00*
The Infiltrator *'95*
Indiana Jones and the Last Crusade *'89*
Treasure Island *'89*
Tusks *'89*
The Fourth Protocol *'87*
Hearts of Fire *'87*
Mandela *'87*
The Secret Garden *'87*
Kim *'84*
Heat and Dust *'82*
Ivanhoe *'82*
For Your Eyes Only *'81*
The Empire Strikes Back *'80*
Luther *'74*
The Story of Jacob & Joseph *'74*
Antony and Cleopatra *'73*
Theatre of Death *'67*

The Alphabet Murders '65
Girl with Green Eyes '64
Tom Jones '63

Kara Glover
The Beat '88
Caribe '87

Savion Glover
Bojangles '01
Bamboozled '00
The Wall '99
Tap '89

Susan Glover
Random Encounter '98
Eye '96

Vadim Glowna
Advertising Rules! '01
Cross of Iron '76

Carlin Glynn (1940-)
Judy Berlin '99
Blessing '94
Night Game '89
Blood Red '88
Gardens of Stone '87
The Trip to Bountiful '85
Sixteen Candles '84
Continental Divide '81

Mathias Gnaedinger
Journey of Hope '90
The Boat Is Full '81

Hiromi Go
Samurai Cowboy '93
MacArthur's Children '85

George Gobel (1919-91)
Ellie '84
The Fantastic World of D.C. Collins '84
Better Late Than Never '79
Rabbit Test '78
Birds & the Bees '56
I Married a Woman '56

Justin Gocke
The Witching of Ben Wagner '95
My Grandpa Is a Vampire '92

Jean-Luc Godard (1930-)
King Lear '87
First Name: Carmen '83
Contempt '64
Cleo from 5 to 7 '61
Le Petit Soldat '60

Alf Goddard
Butler's Dilemma '43
Non-Stop New York '37

John Goddard
Naked Youth '59
Storm Rider '57

Mark Goddard (1936-)
Lost in Space '98
Strange Invaders '83
Roller Boogie '79
Blue Sunshine '78
The Death Squad '73

Paul Goddard
Holy Smoke '99
The Matrix '99

Paulette Goddard (1911-90)
Time of Indifference '64
Sins of Jezebel '54
Unholy Four '54
The Torch '50
On Our Merry Way '48
Unconquered '47
Diary of a Chambermaid '46
So Proudly We Hail '43
Reap the Wild Wind '42
Star Spangled Rhythm '42
Pot o' Gold '41
The Ghost Breakers '40
The Great Dictator '40
Second Chorus '40
The Women '39
The Young in Heart '38
Modern Times '36

Trevor Goddard (1965-)
Dead Tides '97
First Encounter '97
Shadow Warriors '97
Fast Money '96
Yesterday's Target '96
Men of War '94

Arthur Godfrey (1903-83)
Angel's Brigade '79
Flatbed Annie and Sweetiepie: Lady Truckers '79
Great Bank Hoax '78
Where Angels Go, Trouble Follows '68
The Glass Bottom Boat '66
Four for Texas '63

Derek Godfrey (1924-83)
Hands of the Ripper '71
A Midsummer Night's Dream '68
The Vengeance of She '68

Patrick Godfrey
Ever After: A Cinderella Story '98
Heat and Dust '82

Jacques Godin (1930-)
Being at Home with Claude '92
Double Identity '89
The Victory '88
The Man Inside '76

Judith Godreche (1972-)
Entropy '99
The Man in the Iron Mask '98
Ridicule '96
The Disenchanted '90

Alexander Godunov (1949-95)
The Dogfighters '95
North '94
The Runestone '91
Waxwork 2: Lost in Time '91
Die Hard '88
The Money Pit '86
Witness '85

Angela Goethals (1977-)
V.I. Warshawski '91
Home Alone '90
Heartbreak Hotel '88

Dave Goetz
Muppets from Space '99 (V)
Muppet Treasure Island '96 (V)
The Muppet Christmas Carol '92 (V)
Labyrinth '86
The Dark Crystal '82 (V)
The Muppet Movie '79 (V)

Michael C. Goetz
Deadly Encounter '72
Village of the Damned '60

Peter Michael Goetz (1941-)
The Empty Mirror '99
Infinity '96
The Buccaneers '95
Father of the Bride Part II '95
The Water Engine '92
Father of the Bride '91
My Girl '91
Tagget '90
Glory '89
Jumpin' Jack Flash '86
King Kong Lives '86
Beer '85
Wolfen '81

Bernhard Goetzke
Dr. Mabuse, The Gambler '22
Destiny '21
The Indian Tomb '21

John Goff
Party Plane '90
Night Stalker '87
Getting Over '81
The Capture of Bigfoot '79
The Alpha Incident '76
Devil & Leroy Basset '73

Norris Goff
The Bashful Bachelor '42
Dreaming Out Loud '40

Walton Goggins
Shanghai Noon '00

Red Dirt '99
Major League 3: Back to the Minors '98
The Apostle '97

Joanna Going (1963-)
Cupid & Cate '00
Heaven '99
Eden '98
Tom Clancy's Netforce '98
Inventing the Abbotts '97
Little City '97
Phantoms '97
Still Breathing '97
Commandments '96
Keys to Tulsa '96
A Good Day to Die '95
How to Make an American Quilt '95
Wyatt Earp '94

Gila Golan (1940-)
The Valley of Gwangi '69
Catch as Catch Can '68
Our Man Flint '66

Tracey Gold (1969-)
Dirty Little Secret '98
Wanted '98
The Perfect Daughter '96
Shoot the Moon '82

Adam Goldberg (1970-)
The Salton Sea '02
All Over the Guy '01
A Beautiful Mind '01
Fast Sofa '01
Waking Life '01
EDtv '99
Babe: Pig in the City '98 (V)
Saving Private Ryan '98
Homeward Bound 2: Lost in San Francisco '96 (V)
Dazed and Confused '93

Whoopi Goldberg (1949-)
Call Me Claus '01
Kingdom Come '01
Monkeybone '01
Rat Race '01
The Adventures of Rocky & Bullwinkle '00
Alice in Wonderland '99
Girl, Interrupted '99
Jackie's Back '99
The Magical Legend of the Leprechauns '99
The Deep End of the Ocean '98
How Stella Got Her Groove Back '98
A Knight in Camelot '98
The Rugrats Movie '98 (V)
An Alan Smithee Film: Burn, Hollywood, Burn '97
Cinderella '97
In the Gloaming '97
The Associate '96
Bogus '96
Eddie '96
Ghosts of Mississippi '96
Moonlight and Valentino '95
Theodore Rex '95
Boys on the Side '94
Corrina, Corrina '94
The Lion King '94 (V)
The Little Rascals '94
The Pagemaster '94 (V)
Star Trek: Generations '94
Made in America '93
Naked in New York '93
Sister Act 2: Back in the Habit '93
The Player '92
Sarafina! '92
Sister Act '92
Soapdish '91
Ghost '90
Homer and Eddie '89
Kiss Shot '89
The Long Walk Home '89
Clara's Heart '88
Burglar '87
Fatal Beauty '87
The Telephone '87
Jumpin' Jack Flash '86
The Color Purple '85

Jeff Goldblum (1952-)
Igby Goes Down '02
Cats & Dogs '01
Perfume '01
Beyond Suspicion '00
Holy Man '98
Prince of Egypt '98 (V)
The Lost World: Jurassic Park 2 '97
The Great White Hype '96
Independence Day '96
Trigger Happy '96
Nine Months '95
Powder '95
Hideaway '94
Lush Life '94
Jurassic Park '93
Deep Cover '92
Fathers and Sons '92
The Favor, the Watch, & the Very Big Fish '92
The Player '92
Shooting Elizabeth '92
Framed '90
Twisted Obsession '90
Earth Girls Are Easy '89
Mr. Frost '89
The Tall Guy '89
Vibes '88
Beyond Therapy '86
The Fly '86
Into the Night '85
Silverado '85
Transylvania 6-5000 '85
The Adventures of Buckaroo Banzai Across the Eighth Dimension '84
Ernie Kovacs: Between the Laughter '84
The Three Little Pigs '84
The Big Chill '83
The Right Stuff '83
Threshold '83
Rehearsal for Murder '82
The Legend of Sleepy Hollow '79
Invasion of the Body Snatchers '78
Thank God It's Friday '78
Annie Hall '77
Between the Lines '77
The Sentinel '76
Special Delivery '76
Nashville '75
Death Wish '74

Annie Golden (1951-)
One Way Out '95
The Pebble and the Penguin '94 (V)
Baby Boom '87
Forever, Lulu '87
Love at Stake '87
National Lampoon's Class of '86 '86
Desperately Seeking Susan '85
Key Exchange '85
Streetwalkin' '85
Hair '79

Norman D. Golden, II
Moby Dick '98
America's Dream '95
Cop and a Half '93

Devin Goldenberg
Fanatic '82
Cry Uncle '71
Guess What We Learned in School Today? '70

Goldie
B.U.S.T.E.D. '99
The World Is Not Enough '99

Ricky Paull Goldin (1968-)
Pastime '91
Mirror, Mirror '90
Lambada '89
The Blob '88
Hyper-Sapien: People from Another Star '86

Danny Goldman
Where the Buffalo Roam '80
Swap Meet '79

Lelia Goldoni (1937-)
Choices '81
Bloodbrothers '78

Fatal Chase '77
The Spell '77
The Disappearance of Aimee '76
Theatre of Death '67
Shadows '60

Clio Goldsmith (1957-)
Heat of Desire '84
La Cicada '83
The Gift '82
Honey '81

Jonathan Goldsmith
Phantom of the Mall: Eric's Revenge '89
Go Tell the Spartans '78

Jenette Goldstein (1960-)
Fair Game '95
Dead to Rights '93
The Presidio '88
Near Dark '87
Aliens '86

Bob(cat) Goldthwait (1962-)
Blow '01
Hercules '97 (V)
Sweethearts '97
Back to Back '96
Destiny Turns on the Radio '95
Out There '95
Radioland Murders '94
Freaked '93 (V)
Shakes the Clown '92
Little Vegas '90
Tapeheads '89
Hot to Trot! '88
Scrooged '88
Burglar '87
Police Academy 4: Citizens on Patrol '87
One Crazy Summer '86
Police Academy 3: Back in Training '86

Tony Goldwyn (1960-)
An American Rhapsody '01
The Song of the Lark '01
Bounce '00
The 6th Day '00
Tarzan '99 (V)
From the Earth to the Moon '98
Kiss the Girls '97
The Lesser Evil '97
The Boys Next Door '96
The Substance of Fire '96
The Last Word '95
Nixon '95
Pocahontas: The Legend '95
Reckless '95
Truman '95
Doomsday Gun '94
Love Matters '93
The Pelican Brief '93
Taking the Heat '93
Kuffs '92
Traces of Red '92
Iran: Days of Crisis '91
Ghost '90
Gaby: A True Story '87

Valeria Golino (1966-)
Things You Can Tell Just by Looking at Her '00
Spanish Judges '99
Escape from L.A. '96
An Occasional Hell '96
Four Rooms '95
Leaving Las Vegas '95
Clean Slate '94
Immortal Beloved '94
Hot Shots! Part Deux '93
Hot Shots! '91
The Indian Runner '91
Year of the Gun '91
The King's Whore '90
Torrents of Spring '90
Rain Man '88
A Joke of Destiny, Lying in Wait Around the Corner Like a Bandit '84

Lisa Golm
Come Back, Little Sheba '52
The Hoodlum '51

Arlene Golonka (1939-)
The Gumshoe Kid '89
Dr. Alien '88
Trained to Kill '88
Foxtrap '85
My Tutor '82
The In-Laws '79

Marina Golovine
Olivier, Olivier '92
The Stolen Children '92

Katerina Golubeva
Pola X '99
I Can't Sleep '93

Minna Gombell (1892-1973)
I'll See You in My Dreams '51
Pagan Love Song '50
The Best Years of Our Lives '46
Doomed Caravan '41
Second Fiddle '39
The Great Waltz '38
The Merry Widow '34
The Thin Man '34
Hoopla '33

Carlos Gomez
The Negotiator '98
The Replacement Killers '98
Asteroid '97
Fools Rush In '97
The Peacemaker '97
Desperado '95
Bitter Vengeance '94
Hostile Intentions '94
Silhouette '91

Carmelo Gomez
Mararia '98
Tierra '95
Running Out of Time '94
The Red Squirrel '93
Vacas '91

Fernando Gomez
Belle Epoque '92
The Stilts '84
Mama Turns a Hundred '79
Spirit of the Beehive '73

Jaime Gomez (1965-)
Gabriela '01
Training Day '01
Solo '96

Jose Luis Gomez (1940-)
Rowing with the Wind '88
Roads to the South '78
In Memoriam '76

Panchito Gomez (1963-)
Saints and Sinners '95
Mi Vida Loca '94
Sweet 15 '90
Paco '75

Thomas Gomez (1905-71)
Beneath the Planet of the Apes '70
Stay Away, Joe '68
Summer and Smoke '61
But Not for Me '59
The Conqueror '56
Trapeze '56
The Magnificent Matador '55
The Merry Widow '52
Force of Evil '49
Sorrowful Jones '49
Casbah '48
Key Largo '48
Captain from Castile '47
Singapore '47
Can't Help Singing '45
The Climax '44
In Society '44
Phantom Lady '44
Pittsburgh '42

Milton Goncalves
Orfeu '99
Subway to the Stars '87
Kiss of the Spider Woman '85

Mascha Gonska
Tea for Three '84
The Infernal Trio '74

George Gonzales
The Bad News Bears Go to Japan '78
The Bad News Bears in Breaking Training '77
The Bad News Bears '76

Augustin Gonzalez
The Grandfather '98
Caresses '97
The Nest '80

Pedro Gonzalez-Gonzalez
Lust in the Dust '85
Rio Bravo '59
The Young Land '59

Christopher Good
Bullshot '83
A Bridge Too Far '77

Meagan Good
Three Strikes '00
The Secret Life of Girls '99
Eve's Bayou '97

Caroline Goodall (1959-)
Harrison's Flowers '02
Mists of Avalon '01
The Princess Diaries '01
Casualties '97
The Sculptress '97
White Squall '96
Sorrento Beach '95
At Home with the Webbers '94
Disclosure '94
Cliffhanger '93
Schindler's List '93
The Silver Stallion: King of the Wild Brumbies '93
Hook '91
The Moon Stallion '85

Grant Goodeve (1952-)
Take Two '87
Hot Rod '79
Last Cry for Help '79

Cuba Gooding, Jr. (1968-)
Snow Dogs '02
In the Shadows '01
Pearl Harbor '01
Rat Race '01
Men of Honor '00
Chill Factor '99
Instinct '99
A Murder of Crows '99
What Dreams May Come '98
As Good As It Gets '97
Jerry Maguire '96
The Tuskegee Airmen '95
Lightning Jack '94
Losing Isaiah '94
Outbreak '94
Daybreak '93
Judgment Night '93
A Few Good Men '92
Gladiator '92
Hitz '92
Murder Without Motive '92
Boyz N the Hood '91
Coming to America '88

Michael Goodliffe (1914-76)
To the Devil, a Daughter '76
Von Ryan's Express '65
The Gorgon '64
The Seventh Dawn '64
The Battle of the Sexes '60
Sink the Bismarck '60
A Night to Remember '58
Up the Creek '58
The Way Out '56

Benny Goodman
A Song Is Born '48
Stage Door Canteen '43

Dody Goodman (1929-)
Frozen Assets '92
Cool As Ice '91
Private Resort '84
Splash '84
Magic on Love Island '80
Grease '78
Bedtime Story '63

Hazelle Goodman
Hannibal '01
Deconstructing Harry '97

Henry Goodman
The Saint '97
Broken Glass '96
Private Parts '96
Mary Reilly '95

John Goodman (1952-)
Monsters, Inc. '01 (V)
My First Mister '01
One Night at McCool's '01
Storytelling '01
The Adventures of Rocky & Bullwinkle '00
Coyote Ugly '00
The Emperor's New Groove '00 (V)
O Brother Where Art Thou? '00
What Planet Are You From? '00
Bringing Out the Dead '99
The Jack Bull '99
The Runner '99
Blues Brothers 2000 '98
The Real Macaw '98 (V)
The Big Lebowski '97
The Borrowers '97
Dirty Work '97
Fallen '97
Mother Night '96
Kingfish: A Story of Huey P. Long '95
Pie in the Sky '95
A Streetcar Named Desire '95
The Flintstones '94
Born Yesterday '93
We're Back! A Dinosaur's Story '93 (V)
The Babe '92
Matinee '92
Barton Fink '91
King Ralph '91
Arachnophobia '90
Always '89
Sea of Love '89
Stella '89
Everybody's All American '88
Punchline '88
The Wrong Guys '88
The Big Easy '87
Burglar '87
Raising Arizona '87
True Stories '86
Sweet Dreams '85
C.H.U.D. '84
Maria's Lovers '84
Revenge of the Nerds '84
Eddie Macon's Run '83
Survivors '83

Deborah Goodrich
Remote Control '88
Survival Game '87
April Fool's Day '86

Garry Goodrow
The Hollywood Knights '80
Cardiac Arrest '74
Steelyard Blues '73
The Committee '68
The Connection '61

Liat Goodson
American Chinatown '96
Vice Girls '96
The Prince '95

Alexander Goodwin
Mimic '97
Box of Moonlight '96

Angela Goodwin
Julia and Julia '87
Autopsy '74

Bill Goodwin (1910-58)
The Atomic Kid '54
Lucky Me '54
Tea for Two '50
It's a Great Feeling '49
Jolson Sings Again '49
Mickey '48
House of Horrors '46
The Jolson Story '46
To Each His Own '46
The Stork Club '45
Bathing Beauty '44
So Proudly We Hail '43
Wake Island '42

Harold Goodwin (1902-87)
The Bridge on the River Kwai '57
Abbott and Costello Meet the Keystone Kops '54
Tanks a Million '41
All Quiet on the Western Front '30
The Cameraman '28
College '27
Suds '20

Laurel Goodwin
Papa's Delicate Condition '63
Girls! Girls! Girls! '62

Michael Goodwin
Deadline Assault '90
The Dead Pool '88
Date with an Angel '87
Sizzle '81

Michael Goorjian
Deal of a Lifetime '99
Silent Witness '99
SLC Punk! '99
Something More '99
Hard Rain '97

Alicia (Lecy) Goranson
Boys Don't Cry '99
How to Make an American Quilt '95

Bernard Gorcey (1886-1955)
Bowery Boys Meet the Monsters '54
Clipped Wings '53
Ghost Chasers '51
Blues Busters '50
Spook Busters '48
Bowery Buckaroos '47
Hard-Boiled Mahoney '47
The Great Dictator '40

David Gorcey (1921-84)
Ghost Chasers '51
Blues Busters '50
Master Minds '49
She Shoulda Said No '49
Spook Busters '48
Bowery Buckaroos '47
Hard-Boiled Mahoney '47
Mr. Wise Guy '42
Flying Wild '41
Pride of the Bowery '41

Elizabeth Gorcey
Iced '88
The Trouble with Dick '88
Kidco '83

Leo Gorcey (1915-69)
It's a Mad, Mad, Mad, Mad World '63
Bowery Boys Meet the Monsters '54
Clipped Wings '53
Here Come the Marines '52
Ghost Chasers '51
Blues Busters '50
Master Minds '49
Smugglers' Cove '48
Spook Busters '48
Bowery Buckaroos '47
Hard-Boiled Mahoney '47
Follow the Leader '44
Million Dollar Kid '44
Destroyer '43
Ghost on the Loose '43
Kid Dynamite '43
Let's Get Tough '42
Mr. Wise Guy '42
'Neath Brooklyn Bridge '42
Smart Alecks '42
Bowery Blitzkrieg '41
Flying Wild '41
Pride of the Bowery '41
Spooks Run Wild '41
Boys of the City '40
That Gang of Mine '40
They Made Me a Criminal '39
Angels with Dirty Faces '38
Little Tough Guys '38
Dead End '37
Mannequin '37

Barry J. Gordon (1948-)
Body Slam '87
Love at First Bite '79
A Thousand Clowns '65
Pressure Point '62
The Girl Can't Help It '56

Ben Gordon
Goof Balls '87
Utilities '83

C. Henry Gordon (1883-1940)
Charlie Chan at the Wax Museum '40
The Charge of the Light Brigade '36
The Crusades '35
Gabriel Over the White House '33
Penthouse '33
Rasputin and the Empress '33
The Crooked Circle '32
Mata Hari '32
The Strange Love of Molly Louvain '32

Carl Gordon
Love Songs '99
The Piano Lesson '94

Colin Gordon (1911-72)
The Body Beneath '70
Burn Witch, Burn! '62
The Key Man '57
One That Got Away '57
John and Julie '55

Don Gordon (1926-)
The Borrower '89
The Beast Within '82
Omen 3: The Final Conflict '81
The Education of Sonny Carson '74
The Mack '73
Slaughter '72
Zero Population Growth '72
Bullitt '68

Dorothy Gordon
Where the Money Is '00
The Haunted Strangler '58

Eve Gordon
I'll Be Home for Christmas '98
Honey, We Shrunk Ourselves '97
The Heidi Chronicles '95
Leaving Normal '92
The Secret Passion of Robert Clayton '92
Paradise '91
Switched at Birth '91
Avalon '90

Gale Gordon (1906-95)
The 'Burbs '89
Speedway '68
The 30-Foot Bride of Candy Rock '59
Our Miss Brooks '56
Francis Covers the Big Town '53
Here We Go Again! '42

Gavin Gordon (1901-83)
The Bat '59
The Matchmaker '58
I Killed That Man '42
Turf Boy '42
The Bride of Frankenstein '35
The Bitter Tea of General Yen '33
Female '33
American Madness '32
Romance '30
The Silver Horde '30
His First Command '29

Gerald Gordon (1934-2001)
Ants '77
Force Five '75
Hell Up in Harlem '73

James Gordon
Trailin' '21
The Last of the Mohicans '20

Julia Swayne Gordon
It '27
Wings '27

Keith Gordon (1961-)
Static '87
Back to School '86
Combat Academy '86
Legend of Billie Jean '85
Christine '84
Single Bars, Single Women '84
Silent Rebellion '82
Kent State '81
Dressed to Kill '80
All That Jazz '79
Home Movies '79
Jaws 2 '78

Leo Gordon (1922-2000)
Alienator '89
Bog '84
Devil's Angels '67
Kitten with a Whip '64
The Haunted Palace '63
Shame '61
The Jayhawkers '59
Seventh Cavalry '56
Soldier of Fortune '55
Riot in Cell Block 11 '54
Ten Wanted Men '54
Hondo '53

Mary Gordon (1882-1963)
Little Giant '46
The Woman in Green '45
Follow the Leader '44
Million Dollar Kid '44
Boss of Big Town '43
Sherlock Holmes and the Secret Weapon '42
Riot Squad '41
The Adventures of Sherlock Holmes '39
Double Wedding '37
Texas Cyclone '32

Pamela Gordon
Bloodlust: Subspecies 3 '93
Bloodstone: Subspecies 2 '92

Philip Gordon
The Bridge to Nowhere '86
Came a Hot Friday '85

Roy Gordon (1896-1978)
The Wasp Woman '59
Attack of the 50 Foot Woman '58
The Real Glory '39
The Great Man Votes '38

Ruth Gordon (1896-1985)
The Trouble with Spies '87
Voyage of the Rock Aliens '87
Maxie '85
Mugsy's Girls '85
Don't Go to Sleep '82
Jimmy the Kid '82
Any Which Way You Can '80
My Bodyguard '80
Every Which Way But Loose '78
The Prince of Central Park '77
The Big Bus '76
Harold and Maude '71
Where's Poppa? '70
Whatever Happened to Aunt Alice? '69
Rosemary's Baby '68
Inside Daisy Clover '65
Action in the North Atlantic '43
Edge of Darkness '43
Two-Faced Woman '41
Abe Lincoln in Illinois '40

Serena Gordon
The Aristocrats '99
Goldeneye '95
A Tale of Two Cities '91
Riders '88

Susan Gordon
Picture Mommy Dead '66
Tormented '60
Attack of the Puppet People '58

Joseph Gordon-Levitt (1981-)
Along for the Ride '00
Picking Up the Pieces '99
Ten Things I Hate about You '99
Halloween: H20 '98
Sweet Jane '98
The Juror '96
The Great Elephant Escape '95
Angels in the Outfield '94
Holy Matrimony '94

Charles Gordone
Angel Heart '87
Streetfight '75

Sandy Gore
Brides of Christ '91
Wrangler '88
Street Hero '84

Galyn Gorg
RoboCop 2 '90
Body Beat '88
Malibu Bikini Shop '86

Mel Gorham (1959-)
The Center of the World '01
Wishful Thinking '96
Blue in the Face '95
Curdled '95
Smoke '95

Marius Goring (1012-1998)
Charlie Boy '81
Holocaust '78
Zeppelin '71
Exodus '60
The Unstoppable Man '59
The Moonraker '58
Night Ambush '57
Paris Express '53
The Red Shoes '48
Stairway to Heaven '46
The Case of the Frightened Lady '39
Spy in Black '39

Cliff Gorman (1936-)
King of the Jungle '01
Ghost Dog: The Way of the Samurai '99
The '60s '99
Down Came a Blackbird '94
Hoffa '92
Night and the City '92
Angel '84
Night of the Juggler '80
All That Jazz '79
An Unmarried Woman '78
Rosebud '75
Strike Force '75
Class of '63 '73
Cops and Robbers '73
The Boys in the Band '70

Jonathan Gorman
Gang Justice '94
Street Soldiers '91

Robert Gorman
Leprechaun '93
Mr. Nanny '93

Karen (Lynn) Gorney (1945-)
Ripe '97
The Hard Way '91
Saturday Night Fever '77

Walt Gorney
Friday the 13th, Part 2 '81
Friday the 13th '80

Frederic Gorny
Jeanne and the Perfect Guy '98
Wild Reeds '94

Frank Gorshin (1934-)
Beethoven's 3rd '00
Luck of the Draw '00
Man of the Century '99
Bloodmoon '97
The Twilight of the Ice Nymphs '97
12 Monkeys '95
Hail Caesar '94
Amore! '93
The Meteor Man '93
Body Trouble '92
Sweet Justice '92

Beverly Hills Bodysnachers '89
Midnight '89
Upper Crust '88
Hollywood Vice Sqaud '86
Hot Resort '85
Underground Aces '80
Sky Hei$t '75
Batman '66
That Darn Cat '65
The Great Impostor '61
Studs Lonigan '60
Where the Boys Are '60
Dragstrip Girl '57
Invasion of the Saucer Men '57
Between Heaven and Hell '56

Marjoe Gortner (1944-)
Wild Bill '95
Fire, Ice and Dynamite '91
American Ninja 3: Blood Hunt '89
The Survivalist '87
Hellhole '85
Jungle Warriors '84
Mausoleum '83
Star Crash '78
Sidewinder One '77
Viva Knievel '77
Bobbie Jo and the Outlaw '76
Food of the Gods '76
Earthquake '74
Pray for the Wildcats '74
Marjoe '72

Ryan Gosling
Murder by Numbers '02
Remember the Titans '00

David Goss
Hollywood Cop '87
She '83

Luke Goss
Blade II '02
ZigZag '02

Mark Paul Gosselaar (1974-)
Dead Man on Campus '97
Specimen '97
Kounterfeit '96
Twisted Love '95
The St. Tammany Miracle '94
Necessary Parties '88

Louis Gossett, Jr. (1936-)
The Highway Man '99
Love Songs '99
Strange Justice: The Clarence Thomas and Anita Hill Story '99
Y2K '99
The Inspectors '98
Bram Stoker's The Mummy '97
In His Father's Shoes '97
Managua '97
Inside '96
Run for the Dream: The Gail Devers Story '96
Iron Eagle 4 '95
Zooman '95
Curse of the Starving Class '94
Flashfire '94
A Good Man in Africa '94
Dangerous Relations '93
Monolith '93
Return to Lonesome Dove '93
Aces: Iron Eagle 3 '92
Carolina Skeletons '92
Diggstown '92
Keeper of the City '92
Cover-Up '91
Murder on the Bayou '91
Toy Soldiers '91
El Diablo '90
The Josephine Baker Story '90
The Punisher '90
Straight Up '90
Sudie & Simpson '90
Zora Is My Name! '90
Goodbye, Miss 4th of July '88
Iron Eagle 2 '88
Roots: The Gift '88
The Father Clements Story '87
The Principal '87
Firewalker '86
Iron Eagle '86
Enemy Mine '85
Finders Keepers '84
The Guardian '84
Jaws 3 '83
Sadat '83
An Officer and a Gentleman '82
Don't Look Back: The Story of Leroy "Satchel" Paige '81
The Lazarus Syndrome '79
He Who Walks Alone '78
It Rained All Night the Day I Left '78
The Choirboys '77
The Deep '77
Little Ladies of the Night '77
J.D.'s Revenge '76
The River Niger '76
The White Dawn '75
It's Good to Be Alive '74
The Laughing Policeman '74
Travels with My Aunt '72
Skin Game '71
The Bushbaby '70
A Raisin in the Sun '61

Robert Gossett
Jimmy Zip '00
Arlington Road '99

Roland Got
G-Men vs. the Black Dragon '43
Across the Pacific '42

Walter Gotell (1925-97)
Prince Valiant '97
Puppet Master 3: Toulon's Revenge '90
Sleepaway Camp 2: Unhappy Campers '88
The Living Daylights '87
Basic Training '86
For Your Eyes Only '81
Moonraker '79
The Spy Who Loved Me '77
Lord Jim '65
From Russia with Love '63
The Guns of Navarone '61
The African Queen '51

Michael Gothard (1939-93)
Lifeforce '85
For Your Eyes Only '81
King Arthur, the Young Warlord '75
Young Warlord '75
The Valley Obscured by the Clouds '72
The Devils '71

Gilbert Gottfried (1955-)
Dr. Dolittle '98 (V)
Def Jam's How to Be a Player '97
Aladdin and the King of Thieves '96 (V)
The Return of Jafar '94 (V)
Silk Degrees '94
Thumbelina '94 (V)
Aladdin '92 (V)
Highway to Hell '92
Problem Child 2 '91
The Adventures of Ford Fairlane '90
Problem Child '90
Beverly Hills Cop 2 '87
Bad Medicine '85

Carl Gottlieb (1938-)
Cannonball '76
Jaws '75
The Committee '68

Franz Gottlieb
M*A*S*H '70
The Black Abbot '63

John Gottowt
Waxworks '24
Nosferatu '22

Ferdinand Gottschalk (1869-1944)
Sing Sing Nights '35
King Kelly of the U.S.A. '34
Ex-Lady '33
Female '33
Tonight or Never '31

Thomas Gottschalk (1950-)
Ring of the Musketeers '93
Sister Act 2: Back in the Habit '93
Driving Me Crazy '91

Jetta Goudal (1891-1985)
White Gold '28
The Coming of Amos '25
The Road to Yesterday '25

Michael Gough (1917-)
Sleepy Hollow '99
Robert Louis Stevenson's St. Ives '98
Batman and Robin '97
Batman Forever '95
A Village Affair '95
The Advocate '93
The Age of Innocence '93
Nostradamus '93
Wittgenstein '93
Batman Returns '92
Let Him Have It '91
Strapless '90
Batman '89
The Shell Seekers '89
The Fourth Protocol '87
The Serpent and the Rainbow '87
Caravaggio '86
Out of Africa '85
Oxford Blues '84
Top Secret! '84
The Dresser '83
To the Lighthouse '83
Venom '82
Horror Hospital '73
The Legend of Hell House '73
Savage Messiah '72
The Go-Between '71
Women in Love '70
Crucible of Horror '69
The Crimson Cult '68
They Came from Beyond Space '67
Dr. Terror's House of Horrors '65
The Skull '65
The Phantom of the Opera '62
What a Carve-Up! '62
The Horror of Dracula '58
The Horse's Mouth '58
Richard III '55
Rob Roy—The Highland Rogue '53
The Sword & the Rose '53
The Small Back Room '49
Anna Karenina '48
Blanche Fury '48

Elliott Gould (1938-)
Kill Shot '01
Ocean's Eleven '01
Playing Mona Lisa '00
Picking Up the Pieces '99
American History X '98
The Big Hit '98
johns '96
November Conspiracy '96
A Boy Called Hate '95
Cover Me '95
The Dangerous '95
The Glass Shield '95
Kicking and Screaming '95
Bleeding Hearts '94
Amore! '93
Beyond Justice '92
Hitz '92
The Player '92
Wet and Wild Summer '92
Bugsy '91
Dead Men Don't Die '91
Inside Out '91
The Lemon Sisters '90
My Wonderful Life '90
Night Visitor '89
Vanishing Act '88
Conspiracy: The Trial of the Chicago Eight '87
Dangerous Love '87
Lethal Obsession '87
The Telephone '87
Casey at the Bat '85
The Naked Face '84
Jack & the Beanstalk '83
Over the Brooklyn Bridge '83
The Devil & Max Devlin '81
Dirty Tricks '81
Falling in Love Again '80
The Last Flight of Noah's Ark '80
Escape to Athena '79
The Lady Vanishes '79
The Muppet Movie '79
Capricorn One '78
Matilda '78
The Silent Partner '78
A Bridge Too Far '77
Harry & Walter Go to New York '76
I Will, I Will for Now '76
Mean Johnny Barrows '75
Nashville '75
Roboman '75
Whiffs '75
Busting '74
S*P*Y*S '74
The Long Goodbye '73
Little Murders '71
Quick, Let's Get Married '71
The Touch '71
Getting Straight '70
I Love My...Wife '70
M*A*S*H '70
Bob & Carol & Ted & Alice '69
The Night They Raided Minsky's '69

Harold Gould (1923-)
Master of Disguise '02
Brown's Requiem '98
My Giant '98
Patch Adams '98
The Love Bug '97
Killer: A Journal of Murder '95
Get Smart, Again! '89
Romero '89
Playing for Keeps '86
Fourth Wise Man '85
Dream Chasers '84
The Red Light Sting '84
Kenny Rogers as the Gambler, Part 2: The Adventure Continues '83
Help Wanted: Male '82
Kenny Rogers as the Gambler '80
Seems Like Old Times '80
Better Late Than Never '79
Actor: The Paul Muni Story '78
The One and Only '78
How to Break Up a Happy Divorce '76
Love and Death '75
The Sting '73

Jason Gould (1966-)
The Prince of Tides '91
The Big Picture '89
Say Anything '89

William (Bill) Gould (1960-)
Man from Montana '41
Tanks a Million '41
Rio Rattler '35
Phantom Thunderbolt '33
The Phantom '31

Robert Goulet (1933-)
Toy Story 2 '99 (V)
Mr. Wrong '95
Based on an Untrue Story '93
Naked Gun 2 1/2: The Smell of Fear '91
Beetlejuice '88
Scrooged '88
Gay Purr-ee '62 (V)

Olivier Gourmet
Rosetta '99
La Promesse '96

Gibson Gowland (1877-1951)
Gun Cargo '49
The Secret of the Loch '34
Without Honors '32
Hell Harbor '30
The Phantom of the Opera '25
Greed '24

Patrick Goyette
Four Days '99
Le Polygraphe '96
The Confessional '95

Harry Goz
Rappin' '85
Bill: On His Own '83
Bill '81
Mommie Dearest '81

GQ
On the Line '01
What's the Worst That Could Happen? '01

Jody Graber
Edward II '92
The Garden '90

Betty Grable (1916-73)
The Love Goddesses '65
Three for the Show '55
The Farmer Takes a Wife '53
How to Marry a Millionaire '53
The Beautiful Blonde from Bashful Bend '49
Mother Wore Tights '47
The Dolly Sisters '46
Pin-Up Girl '44
Strictly G.I. '44
Sweet Rosie O'Grady '43
Footlight Serenade '42
Song of the Islands '42
Springtime in the Rockies '42
I Wake Up Screaming '41
Moon over Miami '41
A Yank in the R.A.F. '41
Down Argentine Way '40
Tin Pan Alley '40
Day the Bookies Wept '39
College Swing '38
Give Me a Sailor '38
Follow the Fleet '36
Pigskin Parade '36
The Gay Divorcee '34
Hold 'Em Jail '32
Probation '32
Whoopee! '30

Sofie Graboel
Mifune '99
The Silent Touch '94
The Wolf at the Door '87

Anna Grace
Fiona '98
Girls Town '95

April Grace
Finding Forrester '00
Waterproof '99
Headless Body in Topless Bar '96

Nickolas Grace (1949-)
Shooting Fish '98
The Final Cut '95
Tom & Viv '94
Two Deaths '94
The Green Man '91
Diamond's Edge '88
Salome's Last Dance '88
Robin Hood...The Legend: Herne's Son '85
Robin Hood...The Legend: The Time of the Wolf '85
Robin Hood...The Legend: Robin Hood and the Sorcerer '83
Robin Hood...The Legend: The Swords of Wayland '83
Heat and Dust '82

Topher Grace (1978-)
Ocean's Eleven '01
Traffic '00

Wayne Grace
The Lazarus Man '96
My Summer Story '94
Fallen Angels 2 '93
Heroes Stand Alone '89

Elizabeth (Ward) Gracen (1960-)
The Expert '95
Discretion Assured '93
Final Mission '93
Lower Level '91
Death of the Incredible Hulk '90

Sally Gracie (1920-2001)
Opportunity Knocks '90
The Rain People '69

Paulo Gracindo
Amor Bandido '79
Earth Entranced '66

Paul Graetz (1887-1937)
Heart's Desire '37
Bulldog Jack '35
Mimi '35
Power '34

David Graf (1950-2001)
Citizen Ruth '96
The Brady Bunch Movie '95
Father and Scout '94
Police Academy 7: Mission to Moscow '94
Roseanne: An Unauthorized Biography '94
Suture '93
Police Academy 6: City under Siege '89
Police Academy 5: Assignment Miami Beach '88
Police Academy 4: Citizens on Patrol '87
Police Academy 3: Back in Training '86
Police Academy 2: Their First Assignment '85

Robert Graf (1923-66)
The Great Escape '63
Forger of London '61

Ilene Graff
Rodgers & Hammerstein's South Pacific '01
The Great American Sex Scandal '94
Ladybugs '92

Todd Graff (1959-)
City of Hope '91
Framed '90
Opportunity Knocks '90
The Abyss '89
Dominick & Eugene '88
Five Corners '88
Sweet Lorraine '87

Wilton Graff (1903-69)
Bloodlust '59
Compulsion '59
The West Point Story '50
The Mozart Story '48
Dead Man's Eyes/Pillow of Death '44

Aimee Graham
Shriek If You Know What I Did Last Friday the 13th '00
Time Code '00
Brokedown Palace '99
Dance with the Devil '97
Jackie Brown '97
Amos and Andrew '93
Fallen Angels 1 '93

Bill Graham (1931-91)
Bugsy '91
The Doors '91
Gardens of Stone '87
Gimme Shelter '70

Billy Graham
Bugged! '96
The Prodigal '83

C.J. Graham
Highway to Hell '92
Friday the 13th, Part 6: Jason Lives '86

Currie Graham
Blacklight '98
Blood Money '98

Fred Graham (1918-79)
The Last Hunt '56
Trader Tom of the China Seas '54
Escape from Fort Bravo '53
Heart of the Rockies '51
The Fuller Brush Girl '50

Gary (Rand) Graham
Running Woman '98
Alien Nation: Dark Horizon '94
Robot Jox '90
The Last Warrior '89
The Dirty Dozen: The Deadly Mission '87
No Place to Hide '81
The Hollywood Knights '80

Gerrit Graham
The Love Letter '98
One True Thing '98
Stuart Saves His Family '94
Philadelphia Experiment 2 '93
This Boy's Life '93
Frozen Assets '92
Child's Play 2 '90
Martians Go Home! '90
Night of the Cyclone '90
Big Man on Campus '89
C.H.U.D. 2: Bud the Chud '89
It's Alive 3: Island of the Alive '87
Chopping Mall '86
Last Resort '86
Terrorvision '86
The Annihilators '85
The Man with One Red Shoe '85
Ratings Game '84
National Lampoon's Class Reunion '82
Soup for One '82
Spaceship '81
Used Cars '80
Home Movies '79
Pretty Baby '78
Demon Seed '77
Cannonball '76
Special Delivery '76
Tunnelvision '76
Phantom of the Paradise '74
Beware! The Blob '72
Hi, Mom! '70
Greetings '68

Heather Graham (1970-)
From Hell '01
Say It Isn't So '01
Sidewalks of New York '01
Austin Powers 2: The Spy Who Shagged Me '99
Bowfinger '99
Committed '99
Kiss & Tell '99
Lost in Space '98
Two Girls and a Guy '98
Boogie Nights '97
Scream 2 '97
Entertaining Angels: The Dorothy Day Story '96
Nowhere '96
Swingers '96
Desert Winds '95
Don't Do It '94
Terrified '94
The Ballad of Little Jo '93
Six Degrees of Separation '93
Diggstown '92
Guilty as Charged '92
Twin Peaks: Fire Walk with Me '92
O Pioneers! '91
Shout '91
I Love You to Death '90
Drugstore Cowboy '89

Lauren Graham
Sweet November '01
Chasing Destiny '00
One True Thing '98
Nightwatch '96

Marcus Graham (1963-)
Mulholland Drive '01
Animal Instincts 3: The Seductress '95

Morland Graham (1891-1949)
Bonnie Prince Charlie '48
Tower of Terror '42
Night Train to Munich '40
The Scarlet Pimpernel '34

Ronny Graham (1919-99)
The Substance of Fire '96
Ratings Game '84
Gallipoli '81
World's Greatest Lover '77
New Faces of 1952 '54

Sasha Graham
Rage of the Werewolf '99
Addicted to Murder 2: Tainted Blood '97
The Alien Agenda: Out of the Darkness '96
Addicted to Murder '95

Stuart Graham
One Man's Hero '98
The Informant '97
Michael Collins '96

Gloria Grahame (1925-81)
The Nesting '80
Autopsy '70s
The Big Scam '79
Chilly Scenes of Winter '79
Mama's Dirty Girls '74
Loners '72
The Todd Killings '71
Odds Against Tomorrow '59
The Cobweb '55
The Man Who Never Was '55
Not as a Stranger '55
Oklahoma! '55
Human Desire '54
The Big Heat '53
The Bad and the Beautiful '52
The Greatest Show on Earth '52
Macao '52
Sudden Fear '52
In a Lonely Place '50
A Woman's Secret '49
Crossfire '47
It Happened in Brooklyn '47
Merton of the Movies '47
Song of the Thin Man '47
It's a Wonderful Life '46

Margot Grahame (1911-82)
Fabulous Joe '47
The Informer '35
The Three Musketeers '35
Broken Melody '34

Gawn Grainger
Love and Death on Long Island '97
August '95

Kelsey Grammer (1954-)
15 Minutes '01
Animal Farm '99 (V)
Toy Story 2 '99 (V)
The Pentagon Wars '98
The Real Howard Spitz '98
Anastasia '97 (V)
Down Periscope '96
Galaxies Are Colliding '92

Sam Grana
The Boys of St. Vincent '93
90 Days '86

Alexander Granach (1893-1945)
The Seventh Cross '44
For Whom the Bell Tolls '43
Hangmen Also Die '42
Joan of Paris '42
Kameradschaft '31
Dracula/Garden of Eden '28
Nosferatu '22

Daisy Granados
A Paradise Under the Stars '99
A Very Old Man with Enormous Wings '88
Portrait of Teresa '79
Memories of Underdevelopment '68

Rosario Granados
A Woman Without Love '51
The Great Madcap '49

Bjorn Granath
The Ox '91
Pelle the Conqueror '88

Dario Grandinetti
The Day Silence Died '98
The Dark Side of the Heart '92

Pippa Grandison
Hotel de Love '96
Dating the Enemy '95
Over the Hill '93

Dorothy Granger (1912-95)
Killer Dill '47
The Dentist '32
Fighting Fool '32

Farley Granger (1925-)
Sweet Spirits '80s
Imagemaker '86
Very Close Quarters '84
The Prowler '81
The Widow '76
The Slasher '74
Arnold '73
Night Flight from Moscow '73
They Call Me Trinity '72
Amuck! '71
Deathmask '69
Senso '54
Small Town Girl '53
Behave Yourself! '52
Hans Christian Andersen '52
I Want You '51
Strangers on a Train '51
Our Very Own '50
They Live by Night '49
Rope '48
The Purple Heart '44
The North Star '43

Stewart Granger (1913-93)
Fine Gold '88
Hell Hunters '87
Wild Geese '78
Code Name Alpha '67
The Last Safari '67
Target for Killing '66
Sodom and Gomorrah '62
North to Alaska '60
Harry Black and the Tiger '58
Gun Glory '57
Bhowani Junction '56
The Last Hunt '56
Green Fire '55
Moonfleet '55
Beau Brummel '54
All the Brothers Were Valiant '53
Salome '53
Young Bess '53
Prisoner of Zenda '52
Scaramouche '52
King Solomon's Mines '50
Woman Hater '49
Blanche Fury '48
Man of Evil '48
Captain Boycott '47
The Magic Bow '47
Caesar and Cleopatra '46
The Man in Grey '45
Thursday's Child '43
Secret Mission '42
Convoy '40

Nils T. Granlund
Take It Big '44
Rhythm Parade '43

William Grannel
Girls Are for Loving '73
The Abductors '72
Ginger '72

Beth Grant (1949-)
The Rookie '02
Rock Star '01
Dance with Me '98
Under Oath '97
Lawn Dogs '96
Speed '94
White Sands '92
The Dark Half '91
Love Field '91
Rain Man '88

Cary Grant (1904-86)
Walk, Don't Run '66
Father Goose '64
Charade '63
That Touch of Mink '62
The Grass Is Greener '61
North by Northwest '59
Operation Petticoat '59
Houseboat '58
Indiscreet '58
An Affair to Remember '57
The Pride and the Passion '57
To Catch a Thief '55
Monkey Business '52
People Will Talk '51
I Was a Male War Bride '49
Every Girl Should Be Married '48
Mr. Blandings Builds His Dream House '48
The Bachelor and the Bobby-Soxer '47
The Bishop's Wife '47
Night and Day '46
Notorious '46
Without Reservations '46
Arsenic and Old Lace '44
None But the Lonely Heart '44
Destination Tokyo '43
Mr. Lucky '43
Once Upon a Honeymoon '42
Talk of the Town '42
Penny Serenade '41
Suspicion '41
His Girl Friday '40
The Howards of Virginia '40
My Favorite Wife '40
The Philadelphia Story '40
Gunga Din '39
In Name Only '39
Only Angels Have Wings '39
Bringing Up Baby '38
Holiday '38
Amazing Adventure '37
The Awful Truth '37
Toast of New York '37
Topper '37
Suzy '36
Sylvia Scarlett '35
The Eagle and the Hawk '33
I'm No Angel '33
She Done Him Wrong '33
Blonde Venus '32

Charles Grant
Playback '95
Lady in Waiting '94

David Marshall Grant (1955-)
Noriega: God's Favorite '00
The Chamber '96
The Lazarus Man '96
Three Wishes '95
And the Band Played On '93
Forever Young '92
Through the Eyes of a Killer '92
Air America '90
Bat 21 '88
Big Town '87
American Flyers '85
Sessions '83
End of August '82
Happy Birthday, Gemini '80

Deborah Grant
Bouquet of Barbed Wire '76
Suburban Roulette '67

Faye Grant (1957-)
Drive Me Crazy '99
Vibrations '94
Omen 4: The Awakening '91
Internal Affairs '90
V '83
Senior Trip '81

Frances Grant
Oh Susannah '38
Cavalry '36
Red River Valley '36

Hugh Grant (1960-)
About a Boy '02
Bridget Jones's Diary '01
Small Time Crooks '00
Mickey Blue Eyes '99
Notting Hill '99
Extreme Measures '96
The Englishman Who Went up a Hill But Came down a Mountain '95
Nine Months '95
Sense and Sensibility '95
An Awfully Big Adventure '94
Four Weddings and a Funeral '94
Restoration '94
Sirens '94
Night Train to Venice '93
The Remains of the Day '93
Bitter Moon '92
The Big Man: Crossing the Line '91
Our Sons '91
Impromptu '90
The Lady and the Highwayman '89
The Dawning '88
The Lair of the White Worm '88
Rowing with the Wind '88
White Mischief '88
Maurice '87

James Grant
The Innocent '93
Prick Up Your Ears '87

Kathryn Grant (1933-)
Anatomy of a Murder '59
1001 Arabian Nights '59 (V)
Gunman's Walk '58
The Seventh Voyage of Sinbad '58

Kirby Grant (1914-85)
Comin' Round the Mountain '51
Bad Men of the Border '45
The Stranger from Pecos '45
In Society '44

Lawrence Grant (1870-1952)
Son of Frankenstein '39
Werewolf of London '35
The Mask of Fu Manchu '32
Shanghai Express '32
Speak Easily '32
Bulldog Drummond '29
Doomsday '28
The Grand Duchess and the Waiter '26

Lee Grant (1927-)
Mulholland Drive '01
Dr. T & the Women '00
It's My Party '95
Citizen Cohn '92
Defending Your Life '91
A Billion for Boris '90
Big Town '87
Teachers '84
Visiting Hours '82
Charlie Chan and the Curse of the Dragon Queen '81
For Ladies Only '81
Little Miss Marker '80
Damien: Omen 2 '78
My Sister, My Love '78
The Swarm '78
Airport '77 '77
The Spell '77
Voyage of the Damned '76
Shampoo '75
Internecine Project '73
Portnoy's Complaint '72
Plaza Suite '71
There Was a Crooked Man '70
Marooned '69
Buona Sera, Mrs. Campbell '68
Divorce American Style '67
In the Heat of the Night '67
Valley of the Dolls '67
The Balcony '63
Detective Story '51

Leon Grant
Playing for Keeps '86
Beat Street '84

Micah Grant
Terminal Bliss '91
High Desert Kill '90

Richard E. Grant (1957-)
Gosford Park '01
The Little Vampire '00
The Miracle Maker: The Story of Jesus '00 (V)
A Christmas Carol '99
The Match '99
The Scarlet Pimpernel '99
The Scarlet Pimpernel 2: Mademoiselle Guillotine '99
The Scarlet Pimpernel 3: The Kidnapped King '99
Robert Louis Stevenson's St. Ives '98
A Merry War '97
The Serpent's Kiss '97
Spice World: The Movie '97
Portrait of a Lady '96
A Royal Scandal '96
Twelfth Night '96
Cold Light of Day '95
Jack and Sarah '95
Ready to Wear '94
The Age of Innocence '93
Bram Stoker's Dracula '92
The Player '92
Codename Kyril '91
Hudson Hawk '91
L.A. Story '91
Warlock '91
Henry & June '90
Mountains of the Moon '90
How to Get Ahead in Advertising '89
Withnail and I '87

Rodney A. Grant (1959-)
The Jack Bull '99
Wild Wild West '99
White Wolves 3: Cry of the White Wolf '98
The Killing Grounds '97
Two for Texas '97
The Substitute '96
The Last Ride '94
Wagons East '94
Geronimo: An American Legend '93
Son of the Morning Star '91
Dances with Wolves '90

Schuyler Grant
Anne of Green Gables: The Continuing Story '99
Anne of Avonlea '87
Anne of Green Gables '85

Shelby Grant
The Witchmaker '69
Fantastic Voyage '66
Our Man Flint '66

Allan Granville
Prey for the Hunter '92
Black Terrorist '85

Bonita Granville (1923-88)
Lone Ranger '56
Guilty of Treason '50
Breakfast in Hollywood '46
Love Laughs at Andy Hardy '46
Hitler's Children '43
The Glass Key '42
Now, Voyager '42
The Mortal Storm '40
Nancy Drew, Reporter '39
Quality Street '37
These Three '36

Charley Grapewin (1869-1956)
Follow the Boys '44
They Died with Their Boots On '41
The Grapes of Wrath '40
Johnny Apollo '40
Rhythm on the River '40
The Texas Rangers Ride Again '40
The Wizard of Oz '39
Of Human Hearts '38
Shopworn Angel '38

Three Comrades '38
Captains Courageous '37
The Good Earth '37
Libeled Lady '36
Petrified Forest '36
Ah, Wilderness! '35
Alice Adams '35
One Frightened Night '35
Anne of Green Gables '34
Heroes for Sale '33
Hell's House '32

Karen Grassle (1944-)
Wyatt Earp '94
Harry's War '84
Cocaine: One Man's Seduction '83
President's Mistress '78
Little House on the Prairie '74

Bill Gratton
Devil in the Flesh 2 '00
Syngenor '90

Ernest Graves
Hercules in New York '70
One Plus One '61

Karron Graves
The Crucible '96
The Fig Tree '87

Peter Graves (1911-94)
The Adventurers '70
The Magic Christian '69
The Admirable Crichton '57
Encore '52
Maytime in Mayfair '52

Peter Graves (1925-)
These Old Broads '01
Number One with a Bullet '87
The Guns and the Fury '83
The Winds of War '83
Airplane 2: The Sequel '82
Savannah Smiles '82
Airplane! '80
Survival Run '80
The Clonus Horror '79
The Rebels '79
Cruise Missile '78
The Slipper and the Rose '76
Scream of the Wolf '74
Where Have All the People Gone? '74
The President's Plane Is Missing '71
Sergeant Ryker '68
Texas across the River '66
The Legend of the Sea Wolf '58
Beginning of the End '57
Poor White Trash '57
It Conquered the World '56
The Court Martial of Billy Mitchell '55
Let's Make Up '55
The Night of the Hunter '55
Killers from Space '54
Beneath the 12-Mile Reef '53
Stalag 17 '53
Red Planet Mars '52

Ralph Graves (1900-77)
Three Texas Steers '39
That Certain Thing '28
Extra Girl '23
Dream Street '21
The Greatest Question '19

Rupert Graves (1963-)
Cleopatra '99
Dreaming of Joseph Lees '99
Sweet Revenge '98
Bent '97
Mrs. Dalloway '97
Different for Girls '96
The Tenant of Wildfell Hall '96
The Innocent Sleep '95
Intimate Relations '95
The Madness of King George '94
Damage '92
Where Angels Fear to Tread '91
The Children '90
A Handful of Dust '88
Fortunes of War '87
Maurice '87
A Room with a View '86

Teresa Graves
Get Christie Love! '74
That Man Bolt '73

Fernand Gravet (1904-70)
The Madwoman of Chaillot '69
How to Steal a Million '66
La Ronde '51
The Fantastic Night '42
The Great Waltz '38

Carla Gravina (1941-)
Boomerang '76
And Now My Love '74
Salut l'Artiste '74
The Tempter '74
Alfredo, Alfredo '72

Cesare Gravina (1858-1954)
The Wedding March '28
Merry-Go-Round '23
Foolish Wives '22

Billy Gray (1938-)
Werewolves on Wheels '71
Two for the Seesaw '62
By the Light of the Silvery Moon '53
The Day the Earth Stood Still '51
On Moonlight Bay '51

Bruce Gray
My Big Fat Greek Wedding '02
Dangerous Evidence: The Lori Jackson Story '99
The Happy Face Murders '99
Odd Birds '85

Charles Gray (1928-2000)
Mr. & Mrs. Loving '96
Dreams Lost, Dreams Found '87
The Jigsaw Man '84
An Englishman Abroad '83
Shock Treatment '81
The Mirror Crack'd '80
The House on Garibaldi Street '79
Silver Bears '78
The Seven-Per-Cent Solution '76
The Beast Must Die '75
The Rocky Horror Picture Show '75
Murder on the Midnight Express '74
Diamonds Are Forever '71
The Executioner '70
Nine Ages of Nakedness '69 (N)
The Devil Rides Out '68
The Man Outside '68
Night of the Generals '67
You Only Live Twice '67

Coleen Gray (1922-)
A Cry from the Mountain '85
The Phantom Planet '61
The Leech Woman '59
The Killing '56
Kansas City Confidential '52
Riding High '50
Red River '48
Kiss of Death '47

David Barry Gray
Lawn Dogs '96
Soldier Boyz '95
Cops and Robbersons '94
S.F.W. '94

Dolores Gray (1924-)
Designing Woman '57
The Opposite Sex '56
Kismet '55

Donald Gray (1914-78)
Flight from Vienna '58
Island of Desire '52
Murder on the Campus '52
The Four Feathers '39

Dorian Gray (1934-)
Colossus and the Amazon Queen '64
Il Grido '57
Nights of Cabiria '57

Dulcie Gray (1919-)
Angels One Five '54
The Franchise Affair '52
A Man About the House '47
Mine Own Executioner '47

Elspet Gray
Catherine Cookson's The Wingless Bird '97
The Girl in a Swing '89

Erin Gray (1950-)
A Dangerous Place '94
Honor Thy Father and Mother: The True Story of the Menendez Brothers '94
T-Force '94
Jason Goes to Hell: The Final Friday '93
Official Denial '93
Breaking Home Ties '87
Born Beautiful '82
Six Pack '82
Buck Rogers in the 25th Century '79
The Ultimate Imposter '79

Eve Gray
Department Store '35
Night Birds '31

Gary Gray (1936-)
The Painted Hills '51
The Next Voice You Hear '50
Two Weeks with Love '50
Rachel and the Stranger '48

Lawrence Gray (1898-1970)
A Face in the Fog '36
Love 'Em and Leave 'Em '26
Are Parents People? '25

Linda Gray (1940-)
Accidental Meeting '93
Bonanza: The Return '93
Kenny Rogers as the Gambler, Part 3: The Legend Continues '87
The Wild and the Free '80
The Two Worlds of Jenny Logan '79
The Grass Is Always Greener Over the Septic Tank '78

Marc Gray
Which Way Home '90
Flirting '89

Nadia Gray (1923-94)
Two for the Road '67
Maniac '63
The Captain's Table '60
La Dolce Vita '60
Une Parisienne '58
Valley of the Eagles '51

Pamela Gray
The Devil's Advocate '97
Commandments '96

Rebecca Gray
Tinseltown '97
A Matter of Honor '95

Sally Gray (1916-)
Keeper '84
I'll Get You '53
The Hidden Room '49
They Made Me a Fugitive '47
Dangerous Moonlight '41
Lady in Distress '39
The Saint in London '39

Sam Gray
Burnzy's Last Call '95
Heart '87
Wolfen '81
Christmas Evil '80

Spalding Gray (1941-)
How High '01
Kate & Leopold '01
Coming Soon '99
Bliss '96
Diabolique '96
Drunks '96
Glory Daze '96
Gray's Anatomy '96
Beyond Rangoon '95
Bad Company '94
The Paper '94
King of the Hill '93
The Pickle '93
Twenty Bucks '93
Monster in a Box '92
Straight Talk '92
Heavy Petting '89
The Image '89
Our Town '89
Beaches '88
Clara's Heart '88
Spalding Gray: Terrors of Pleasure '88
Stars and Bars '88
Swimming to Cambodia '87
True Stories '86
Almost You '85
Hard Choices '84
The Killing Fields '84

Vivean Gray
The Last Wave '77
Picnic at Hanging Rock '75

Willoughby Gray
Absolution '81
Waterloo '71

Jerry Grayson
Pushing Tin '99
Mob Queen '98

Kathryn Grayson (1922-)
The Desert Song '53
Kiss Me Kate '53
Lovely to Look At '52
Show Boat '51
The Toast of New Orleans '50
That Midnight Kiss '49
It Happened in Brooklyn '47
Till the Clouds Roll By '46
Anchors Aweigh '45
Thousands Cheer '43
Rio Rita '42
Andy Hardy's Private Secretary '41

Irene Grazioli
The Red Violin '98
Mediterraneo '91

Jose Greco (1918-2000)
Ship of Fools '65
Goliath and the Sins of Babylon '64

Juliette Greco (1927-)
Uncle Tom's Cabin '69
Elena and Her Men '56
The Green Glove '52
Orpheus '49

Adolph Green (1915-)
Follies in Concert '85
Lily in Love '85
My Favorite Year '82
Simon '80

Al Green
On the Line '01
Beverly Hills Cop 3 '94

Anthony Green
The Scarlet Pimpernel '99
The Scarlet Pimpernel 2: Mademoiselle Guillotine '99
The Scarlet Pimpernel 3: The Kidnapped King '99

Brian Austin Green (1973-)
Laws of Deception '97
An American Summer '90
Kid '90

Danny Green (1903-73)
The Seventh Voyage of Sinbad '58
The Ladykillers '55
Non-Stop New York '37

Harry Green
A King in New York '57
Be Yourself '30
The Light of Western Stars '30

Janet-Laine Green
Anne of Green Gables: The Continuing Story '99
When the Dark Man Calls '95
Medicine River '94
Cowboys Don't Cry '88
Kidnapping of Baby John Doe '88
Bullies '86

Kerri Green (1967-)
Blue Flame '93
Tainted Blood '93
Three for the Road '87
Lucas '86
The Goonies '85
Summer Rental '85

Marika Green
Emmanuelle '74
Pickpocket '59

Mitzie Green (1920-69)
Lost in Alaska '52
Little Orphan Annie '32
Tom Sawyer '30

Nigel Green (1924-72)
The Ruling Class '72
The Pink Jungle '68
The Wrecking Crew '68
Africa Texas Style '67
Khartoum '66
Tobruk '66
The Ipcress File '65
Masque of the Red Death '65
The Skull '65
Zulu '64
Jason and the Argonauts '63
Mysterious Island '61
Beat Girl '60
Sword of Sherwood Forest '60
Corridors of Blood '58
Reach for the Sky '56

Robson Green (1964-)
Catherine Cookson's The Gambling Man '98
Reckless: The Sequel '98
Reckless '97
Touching Evil '97

Seth Green (1974-)
Austin Powers In Goldmember '02
America's Sweethearts '01
Josie and the Pussycats '01
Rat Race '01
The Trumpet of the Swan '01 (V)
Austin Powers 2: The Spy Who Shagged Me '99
Idle Hands '99
Can't Hardly Wait '98
Enemy of the State '98
Stonebrook '98
Austin Powers: International Man of Mystery '97
Airborne '93
Arcade '93
My Stepmother Is an Alien '88
Can't Buy Me Love '87
Radio Days '87
Something Special '86
The Hotel New Hampshire '84

Tom Green (1971-)
Freddy Got Fingered '01
Charlie's Angels '00
Road Trip '00

Esther Greenberg
Lupo '70
Sallah '63

Shon Greenblatt
There Goes My Baby '92
Freddy's Dead: The Final Nightmare '91

William Greenblatt
Ms. Scrooge '97
The Abduction '96
Homecoming '96

Angela Greene (1923-78)
The Cosmic Man '59
Night of the Blood Beast '58

Daniel Greene
Me, Myself, and Irene '00
American Tiger '89
The Opponent '89
Skeleton Coast '89
Elvira, Mistress of the Dark '88
Hands of Steel '86
Weekend Warriors '86
Pulsebeat '85

Ellen Greene (1952-)
One Fine Day '96
Killer: A Journal of Murder '95
Murdered Innocence '94
The Professional '94
Wagons East '94
Fathers and Sons '92
Rock-a-Doodle '92 (V)
Stepping Out '91
Glory! Glory! '90
Pump Up the Volume '90
Dinner at Eight '89
Me and Him '89
Talk Radio '88
Little Shop of Horrors '86
Next Stop, Greenwich Village '76

Graham Greene (1952-)
Snow Dogs '02
Lost and Delirious '01
The Green Mile '99
Grey Owl '99
Shattered Image '98
The Education of Little Tree '97
Wounded '97
Eye '96
Die Hard: With a Vengeance '95
Camilla '94
Maverick '94
Medicine River '94
North '94
The Pathfinder '94
Savage Land '94
Benefit of the Doubt '93
The Broken Chain '93
Cooperstown '93
Huck and the King of Hearts '93
Rain Without Thunder '93
Spirit Rider '93
Clearcut '92
The Last of His Tribe '92
Thunderheart '92
Lost in the Barrens '91
Dances with Wolves '90
Powwow Highway '89

James Greene (1926-)
Philadelphia Experiment 2 '93
Pals '87
The Moon Stallion '85

Joe "Mean Joe" Greene (1946-)
Smokey and the Bandit 2 '80
Lady Cocoa '75
The Black Six '74
Twisted Brain '74

Jon Greene
Swift Justice '88
Alley Cat '84

Kim Morgan Greene
Grizzly Mountain '97
The Corporation '96
The Soft Kill '94
Scorned '93

Leon Greene
A Challenge for Robin Hood '68
The Devil Rides Out '68

Lorne Greene (1915-87)
The Alamo: Thirteen Days to Glory '87
Vasectomy: A Delicate Matter '86
A Time for Miracles '80
Klondike Fever '79
Mission Galactica: The Cylon Attack '79
The Bastard '78
Battlestar Galactica '78
Roots '77
The Trial of Lee Harvey Oswald '77

Tidal Wave '75
Earthquake '74
Ride the Wind '66
The Errand Boy '61
The Trap '59
The Buccaneer '58
Peyton Place '57
Autumn Leaves '56
Tight Spot '55
The Silver Chalice '54

Michael Greene (1934-)
Last Man Standing '95
Rubin & Ed '92
In the Heat of Passion '91
Nightmare on the 13th Floor '90
Johnny Be Good '88
Moon over Parador '88
The Night Before '88
White of the Eye '88
Lost in America '85
Americana '81
The Clones '73
The Naked Angels '69

Michele Greene (1962-)
Wild Grizzly '99
Stranger in the House '97
Daddy's Girl '96
How the West Was Fun '95
Stranger by Night '94
The Unborn 2 '94
Silent Victim '92
Danielle Steel's Palomino '91
I Posed for Playboy '91
Double Standard '88

Peter Greene
Ticker '01
Blue Streak '99
Out in Fifty '99
Black Cat Run '98
Permanent Midnight '98
Trading Favors '97
The Rich Man's Wife '96
Sworn Enemies '96
Bang '95
The Usual Suspects '95
The Mask '94
Pulp Fiction '94
Clean, Shaven '93
Judgment Night '93
Laws of Gravity '92

Richard Greene (1918-85)
Special Effects '85
Tales from the Crypt '72
The Castle of Fu Manchu '68
Island of the Lost '68
Kiss and Kill '68
Sword of Sherwood Forest '60
Robin Hood: The Movie '55
Captain Scarlett '53
The Black Castle '52
Forever Amber '47
The Hound of the Baskervilles '39
The Little Princess '39
Stanley and Livingstone '39
My Lucky Star '38

Shecky Greene (1926-)
Lovelines '84
Splash '84
The Love Machine '71

Kate Greenfield
Night Gallery '69
Robinson Crusoe of Clipper Island '36

Kate Greenhouse
The Miracle Worker '00
The Assistant '97

Raymond Greenleaf (1892-1963)
When Gangland Strikes '56
Pier 23 '51
Harriet Craig '50

Brad Greenquist (1959-)
Crime and Punishment in Suburbia '00
Lost Souls '00
Inherit the Wind '99
Gang Related '96
The Yearling '94
Pet Sematary '89
Mutants In Paradise '88
The Bedroom Window '87

Sydney Greenstreet (1879-1954)
Flamingo Road '49
It's a Great Feeling '49
Malaya '49
Velvet Touch '48
The Hucksters '47
Christmas in Connecticut '45
Conflict '45
Hollywood Canteen '44
The Mask of Dimitrios '44
Passage to Marseilles '44
Background to Danger '43
Across the Pacific '42
Casablanca '42
The Maltese Falcon '41
They Died with Their Boots On '41

Bruce Greenwood (1956-)
The Magnificent Ambersons '02
A Girl Thing '01
Here on Earth '00
Hide and Seek '00
Rules of Engagement '00
Thirteen Days '00
Double Jeopardy '99
Thick as Thieves '99
The Color of Courage '98
Disturbing Behavior '98
The Lost Son '98
Father's Day '96
The Sweet Hereafter '96
Bitter Vengeance '94
The Companion '94
Dream Man '94
Exotica '94
Adrift '93
Rio Diablo '93
Passenger 57 '92
Servants of Twilight '91
The Little Kidnappers '90
Wild Orchid '90
Spy '89
Another Chance '88
In the Line of Duty: The FBI Murders '88
The Climb '87
Striker's Mountain '87
Malibu Bikini Shop '86

Charlotte Greenwood (1890-1978)
Glory '56
Oklahoma! '55
Dangerous When Wet '53
Springtime in the Rockies '42
Moon over Miami '41
Down Argentine Way '40
Young People '40
Palmy Days '31
Parlor, Bedroom and Bath '31

Joan Greenwood (1921-87)
Little Dorrit, Film 1: Nobody's Fault '88
Little Dorrit, Film 2: Little Dorrit's Story '88
The Hound of the Baskervilles '77
Tom Jones '63
Mysterious Island '61
Stage Struck '57
Moonfleet '55
The Detective '54
The Importance of Being Earnest '52
The Man in the White Suit '51
Mr. Peek-A-Boo '50
Kind Hearts and Coronets '49
The October Man '48
Whiskey Galore '48
Frenzy '46
A Girl in a Million '46

Dabbs Greer (1917-)
The Green Mile '99
Two Moon Junction '88
Rage '72
Shenandoah '65
Roustabout '64
Cash McCall '60
It! The Terror from Beyond Space '58
Private Hell 36 '54
Rose Marie '54
Above and Beyond '53
Trouble along the Way '53

Jane Greer (1924-2001)
Immediate Family '89
Just Between Friends '86
Against All Odds '84
Billie '65
Where Love Has Gone '64
Man of a Thousand Faces '57
Clown '53
Prisoner of Zenda '52
Big Steal '49
Station West '48
Out of the Past '47
Sinbad, the Sailor '47
They Won't Believe Me '47
Dick Tracy, Detective '45
George White's Scandals '45

Judy Greer (1971-)
The Wedding Planner '01
The Specials '00
What Planet Are You From? '00
What Women Want '00
Three Kings '99
Jawbreaker '98
Kissing a Fool '98

Michael Greer
Messiah of Evil '74
Fortune and Men's Eyes '71

Bradley Gregg
Eye of the Storm '91
Class of 1999 '90
Madhouse '90

Clark Gregg (1964-)
We Were Soldiers '02
The Adventures of Sebastian Cole '99
Tyson '95
Lana in Love '92

Everley Gregg (1903-59)
The Woman in Question '50
Brief Encounter '46
Great Expectations '46
Pygmalion '38
The Ghost Goes West '36
The Private Life of Henry VIII '33

John Gregg
Ebbtide '94
Trouble in Paradise '88
Heatwave '83

Julie Gregg
The Seekers '79
From Hell to Borneo '64

Virginia Gregg (1916-86)
No Way Back '74
Walk in the Spring Rain '70
Columbo: Prescription Murder '67
Spencer's Mountain '63
Psycho '60 (V)
The Hanging Tree '59
Operation Petticoat '59
D.I. '57
Love Is a Many-Splendored Thing '55
The Amazing Mr. X '48

Ezio Greggio
2001: A Space Travesty '00
Screw Loose '99
Silence of the Hams '93

Pascal Greggory (1954-)
The Messenger: The Story of Joan of Arc '99
Those Who Love Me Can Take the Train '98
Queen Margot '94
Pauline at the Beach '83
Le Beau Mariage '82

Rose Gregorio (1932-)
Maze '01
Tarantella '95
City of Hope '91
Five Corners '88
The Last Innocent Man '87
Desperate Characters '71
The Swimmer '68

Andre Gregory (1934-)
Goodbye, Lover '99
Celebrity '98
Last Summer In the Hamptons '96
Vanya on 42nd Street '94
The Linguini Incident '92
The Bonfire of the Vanities '90
The Last Temptation of Christ '88
Some Girls '88
Street Smart '87
The Mosquito Coast '86
Always '85
Follies in Concert '85
Protocol '84
Author! Author! '82
My Dinner with Andre '81

Celia Gregory
Children of the Full Moon '84
Agatha '79

James Gregory (1911-)
Wait Till Your Mother Gets Home '83
Great American Traffic Jam '80
Shoot Out '71
Beneath the Planet of the Apes '70
The Love God? '70
The Ambushers '67
Clambake '67
Murderers' Row '66
The Silencers '66
Sons of Katie Elder '65
Captain Newman, M.D. '63
PT 109 '63
The Manchurian Candidate '62
Two Weeks in Another Town '62
Gun Glory '57
Nightfall '56

Mark Gregory (1965-)
War Bus Commando '89
Thunder Warrior 3 '88
Escape from the Bronx '85
Thunder Warrior '85
Thunder Warrior 2 '85

Mary Gregory
Lassie: Well of Love '90
Coming Home '78

Paul Gregory
Henry V '89
Whoopee! '30

Sebastian Gregory
Sweet Trash '70
Help Wanted Female '68

Thea Gregory
Paid to Kill '54
Profile '54

John Gregson (1919-75)
Fright '71
Hans Brinker '69
Night of the Generals '67
The Frightened City '61
The Captain's Table '60
S.O.S. Pacific '60
Sea of Sand '58
Above Us the Waves '56
Three Cases of Murder '55
Angels One Five '54
Genevieve '53
The Lavender Hill Mob '51

Stephen Greif
The Dying Truth '91
The Great Riviera Bank Robbery '79

Robert Greig (1880-1958)
Sullivan's Travels '41
The Great Ziegfeld '36
Tonight or Never '31
Animal Crackers '30

Kim Greist (1958-)
Homeward Bound 2: Lost in San Francisco '96
Last Exit to Earth '96
Houseguest '94
Roswell: The U.F.O. Cover-Up '94
Homeward Bound: The Incredible Journey '93
Duplicates '92
Payoff '91
Why Me? '90
Punchline '88
Throw Momma from the Train '87
Manhunter '86
Brazil '85
C.H.U.D. '84

Joyce Grenfell (1910-79)
The Americanization of Emily '64
The Pure Hell of St. Trinian's '61
Blue Murder at St. Trinian's '56
The Belles of St. Trinian's '53
Genevieve '53
The Happiest Days of Your Life '50

Adrian Grenier (1976-)
Hart's War '02
A. I.: Artificial Intelligence '01
Cecil B. Demented '00
The Adventures of Sebastian Cole '99
Drive Me Crazy '99

Zach Grenier
Swordfish '01
Chasing Sleep '00
Shaft '00
Ride with the Devil '99
Donnie Brasco '96
Maximum Risk '96
Twister '96

Macha Grenon
Jack Higgins' The Windsor Protocol '97
Sworn Enemies '96
The Pianist '91

Googy Gress
Bloodhounds of Broadway '89
Promised Land '88
Vibes '88
Babes in Toyland '86
First Turn On '83

Laurent Grevill
I Can't Sleep '93
Camille Claudel '89

Anne Grey
Kiss of Death '47
No. 17 '32

Denise Grey (1896-1996)
La Boum '81
Sputnik '61
Carve Her Name with Pride '58
Devil in the Flesh '46

Jennifer Grey (1960-)
Bounce '00
Since You've Been Gone '97
Lover's Knot '96
Portraits of a Killer '95
Eyes of a Witness '94
A Case for Murder '93
Wind '92
Criminal Justice '90
Stroke of Midnight '90
Bloodhounds of Broadway '89
Light Years '88 (V)
Dirty Dancing '87
Ferris Bueller's Day Off '86
American Flyers '85
The Cotton Club '84
Reckless '84
Red Dawn '84

Joel Grey (1932-)
A Christmas Carol '99
Dancer in the Dark '99
The Empty Mirror '99
The Dangerous '95
The Fantasticks '95
The Music of Chance '93
The Player '92
Kafka '91
Queenie '87
Remo Williams: The Adventure Begins '85
Buffalo Bill & the Indians '76
The Seven-Per-Cent Solution '76
Cabaret '72
Man on a String '71
Come September '61

Nan Grey (1918-93)
The House of the Seven Gables '40
The Invisible Man Returns '40
Three Smart Girls Grow Up '39
The Tower of London '39
Danger on the Air '38
Dracula's Daughter '36
Three Smart Girls '36

Shirley Grey (1910-81)
The Mystery of the Mary Celeste '37
Circumstantial Evidence '35
Green Eyes '34
Cornered '32
Drifting Souls '32
Get That Girl '32
Hurricane Express '32
The Riding Tornado '32
Texas Cyclone '32
Uptown New York '32

Virginia Grey (1917-)
Bachelor in Paradise '69
Madame X '66
Love Has Many Faces '65
Naked Kiss '64
Portrait in Black '60
Crime of Passion '57
All That Heaven Allows '55
The Last Command '55
The Rose Tattoo '55
Slaughter Trail '51
Bullfighter & the Lady '50
Three Desperate Men '50
Threat '49
Mexican Hayride '48
Unknown Island '48
Who Killed Doc Robbin? '48
Unconquered '47
House of Horrors '46
Swamp Fire '46
Idaho '43
Sweet Rosie O'Grady '43
Bells of Capistrano '42
Tarzan's New York Adventure '42
Big Store '41
Whistling in the Dark '41
Another Thin Man '39
Broadway Serenade '39
The Michigan Kid '28
Uncle Tom's Cabin '27

Zena Grey
Max Keeble's Big Move '01
Summer Catch '01

Michael Greyeyes (1967-)
ZigZag '02
The Lost Child '00
Skipped Parts '00
The Magnificent Seven '98
The Minion '98
Smoke Signals '98
Firestorm '97
True Women '97
Crazy Horse '96
Dance Me Outside '95
Geronimo '93

Clinton Greyn
The Love Machine '71
Raid on Rommel '71

Bill Gribble
Dogs of Hell '83
The Wild and the Free '80

Eddie Gribbon (1890-1965)
Rio Rattler *'35*
Dames Ahoy *'30*
Harry Gribbon (1885-1961)
Ride Him, Cowboy *'32*
The Cameraman *'28*
The Tomboy *'24*
Richard Grieco (1965-)
Harold Robbins' Body Parts *'01*
Final Payback *'99*
Against the Law *'98*
The Apostate *'98*
Blackheart *'98*
Heaven or Vegas *'98*
A Night at the Roxbury *'98*
When Time Expires *'97*
Circuit Breaker *'96*
The Demolitionist *'95*
Sin and Redemption *'94*
Suspicious Agenda *'94*
A Vow to Kill *'94*
Born to Run *'93*
Tomcat: Dangerous Desires *'93*
If Looks Could Kill *'91*
Mobsters *'91*
Helmut Griem (1932-)
Escape *'90*
La Passante *'83*
Malou *'83*
Les Rendez-vous D'Anna *'78*
The Desert of the Tartars *'76*
Voyage of the Damned *'76*
Children of Rage *'75*
Cabaret *'72*
Ludwig *'72*
McKenzie Break *'70*
The Damned *'69*
David Alan Grier (1955-)
15 Minutes *'01*
The Adventures of Rocky & Bullwinkle *'00*
Angels in the Infield *'00*
Return to Me *'00*
Three Strikes *'00*
Freeway 2: Confessions of a Trickbaby *'99*
A Saintly Switch *'99*
The '60s *'99*
Stuart Little *'99 (V)*
McHale's Navy *'97*
Top of the World *'97*
Jumanji *'95*
Tales from the Hood *'95*
Blankman *'94*
In the Army Now *'94*
Boomerang *'92*
The Player *'92*
Loose Cannons *'90*
I'm Gonna Git You Sucka *'88*
Off Limits *'87*
Beer *'85*
A Soldier's Story *'84*
Pam Grier (1949-)
The Adventures of Pluto Nash *'02*
Bones *'01*
John Carpenter's Ghosts of Mars *'01*
3 A.M. *'01*
Snow Day *'00*
Fortress 2: Re-Entry *'99*
Holy Smoke *'99*
In Too Deep *'99*
No Tomorrow *'99*
Jawbreaker *'98*
Jackie Brown *'97*
Strip Search *'97*
Woo *'97*
Escape from L.A. *'96*
Mars Attacks! *'96*
Original Gangstas *'96*
Serial Killer *'95*
Posse *'93*
Bill & Ted's Bogus Journey *'91*
Class of 1999 *'90*
The Package *'89*
Above the Law *'88*
On the Edge *'86*
Badge of the Assassin *'85*
Stand Alone *'85*
The Vindicator *'85*
Something Wicked This Way Comes *'83*
Tough Enough *'83*
Fort Apache, the Bronx *'81*
Greased Lightning *'77*
Drum *'76*
Bucktown *'75*
Friday Foster *'75*
Sheba, Baby *'75*
Foxy Brown *'74*
The Arena *'73*
Coffy *'73*
Scream Blacula Scream *'73*
The Big Bird Cage *'72*
Twilight People *'72*
The Big Doll House *'71*
Beyond the Valley of the Dolls *'70*
Roosevelt "Rosie" Grier (1932-)
Sophisticated Gents *'81*
The Seekers *'79*
The Glove *'78*
The Big Push *'75*
The Treasure of Jamaica Reef *'74*
The Thing with Two Heads *'72*
Black Brigade *'69*
Jonathan (Jon Francis) Gries
Jackpot *'01*
Twin Falls Idaho *'99*
Casualties *'97*
Kill Me Again *'89*
Pucker Up and Bark Like a Dog *'89*
Fright Night 2 *'88*
Number One with a Bullet *'87*
Real Genius *'85*
Joy Sticks *'83*
More American Graffiti *'79*
Swap Meet *'79*
Will Penny *'67*
Joe Grifasi (1944-)
61* *'01*
Looking for an Echo *'99*
The Naked Man *'98*
One Fine Day *'96*
Sunday *'96*
Two Bits *'96*
Batman Forever *'95*
Money Train *'95*
Heavy *'94*
Benny & Joon *'93*
Household Saints *'93*
City of Hope *'91*
The Feud *'90*
Presumed Innocent *'90*
Chances Are *'89*
Perfect Witness *'89*
Ironweed *'87*
Matewan *'87*
F/X *'86*
Bad Medicine *'85*
The Pope of Greenwich Village *'84*
Still of the Night *'82*
Gentleman Bandit *'81*
On the Yard *'79*
The Deer Hunter *'78*
Simone Griffeth (1955-)
The Patriot *'86*
Hot Target *'85*
Delusion *'84*
Death Race 2000 *'75*
Sixteen *'72*
Ethel Griffies
The Birds *'63*
The Mystery of Edwin Drood *'35*
Eddie Griffin (1968-)
John Q *'02*
The New Guy *'02*
Undercover Brother *'02*
Double Take *'01*
Deuce Bigalow: Male Gigolo *'99*
Foolish *'99*
The Mod Squad *'99*
Picking Up the Pieces *'99*
The Walking Dead *'94*
The Last Boy Scout *'91*
Josephine Griffin (1928-)
The Spanish Gardener *'57*
Postmark for Danger *'56*
The Man Who Never Was *'55*
Kathy Griffin
Intern *'00*
Muppets from Space *'99*
The Cable Guy *'96*
It's Pat: The Movie *'94*
Pulp Fiction *'94*
Lorie Griffin
Aloha Summer *'88*
Cheerleader Camp *'88*
Lynne Griffin
Obsessed *'88*
Strange Brew *'83*
Merv Griffin
The Lonely Guy *'84*
The Man with Two Brains *'83*
Rhonda Griffin
The Creeps *'97*
Hideous *'97*
Robert E. (Bob) Griffin (1902-60)
Monster from Green Hell *'58*
Crime of Passion *'57*
I Was a Teenage Werewolf *'57*
Tony Griffin
Robin Hood: Men in Tights *'93*
Evil Laugh *'86*
Andy Griffith (1926-)
Spy Hard *'96*
Return to Mayberry *'85*
Rustler's Rhapsody *'85*
Fatal Vision *'84*
Murder in Coweta County *'83*
Murder in Texas *'81*
From Here to Eternity *'79*
Centennial *'78*
Hearts of the West *'75*
Savages *'75*
Pray for the Wildcats *'74*
No Time for Sergeants *'58*
A Face in the Crowd *'57*
Anthony Griffith
Panther *'95*
Tales from the Hood *'95*
Charles B. Griffith
Hollywood Boulevard *'76*
Atlas *'60*
It Conquered the World *'56*
Corine Griffith
Dracula/Garden of Eden *'28*
The Garden of Eden *'28*
Eva Griffith
Ride a Wild Pony *'75*
The Turn of the Screw *'74*
Gordon Griffith
Outlaws of the Range *'36*
Little Annie Rooney *'25*
Hugh Griffith (1912-80)
The Big Scam *'79*
Legend of the Werewolf *'75*
The Passover Plot *'75*
Craze *'74*
Luther *'74*
Diary of Forbidden Dreams *'73*
The Final Programme *'73*
Doctor Phibes Rises Again *'72*
The Abominable Dr. Phibes *'71*
The Canterbury Tales *'71*
Who Slew Auntie Roo? *'71*
Cry of the Banshee *'70*
Start the Revolution without Me *'70*
Wuthering Heights *'70*
The Fixer *'68*
Oliver! *'68*
Oh Dad, Poor Dad (Momma's Hung You in the Closet & I'm Feeling So Sad) *'67*
How to Steal a Million *'66*
Tom Jones *'63*
The Counterfeit Traitor *'62*
Mutiny on the Bounty *'62*
Exodus *'60*
Ben-Hur *'59*
Lucky Jim *'58*
The Sleeping Tiger *'54*
Kind Hearts and Coronets *'49*
The Last Days of Dolwyn *'49*
James Griffith (1916-93)
The Legend of Sleepy Hollow *'79*
The Amazing Transparent Man *'60*
Bullwhip *'58*
Tribute to a Bad Man *'56*
Jeff Griffith
The 13th Mission *'91*
Nam Angels *'88*
Kenneth Griffith (1921-)
The Englishman Who Went up a Hill But Came down a Mountain *'95*
Four Weddings and a Funeral *'94*
The Final Option *'82*
Night of the Laughing Dead *'75*
Revenge *'71*
The Assassination Bureau *'69*
Koroshi *'67*
The Frightened City *'61*
Circus of Horrors *'60*
Tiger Bay *'59*
Lucky Jim *'58*
A Night to Remember *'58*
Melanie Griffith (1957-)
Stuart Little 2 *'02 (V)*
Tart *'01*
Along for the Ride *'00*
Cecil B. Demented *'00*
Crazy in Alabama *'99*
RKO 281 *'99*
Another Day in Paradise *'98*
Celebrity *'98*
Shadow of Doubt *'98*
Lolita *'97*
Two Much *'96*
Buffalo Girls *'95*
Mulholland Falls *'95*
Now and Then *'95*
Milk Money *'94*
Nobody's Fool *'94*
Born Yesterday *'93*
Shining Through *'92*
A Stranger Among Us *'92*
Paradise *'91*
The Bonfire of the Vanities *'90*
In the Spirit *'90*
Pacific Heights *'90*
Women & Men: Stories of Seduction *'90*
Cherry 2000 *'88*
The Milagro Beanfield War *'88*
Stormy Monday *'88*
Working Girl *'88*
Something Wild *'86*
Fear City *'85*
Body Double *'84*
She's in the Army Now *'81*
Underground Aces *'80*
Steel Cowboy *'78*
Joyride *'77*
One on One *'77*
The Drowning Pool *'75*
Night Moves *'75*
Smile *'75*
Harrad Experiment *'73*
Raymond Griffith (1894-1937)
All Quiet on the Western Front *'30*
Hands Up *'26*
The Night Club *'25*
Paths to Paradise *'25*
White Tiger *'23*
Thomas Ian Griffith (1962-)
Avalanche *'99*
John Carpenter's Vampires *'97*
Kull the Conqueror *'97*
Behind Enemy Lines *'96*
Hollow Point *'95*
Beyond Forgiveness *'94*
Crackerjack *'94*
Excessive Force *'93*
Ulterior Motives *'92*
The Karate Kid: Part 3 *'89*
Tom Griffith (1945-)
Hawk and Castile
Night Beast *'83*
The Alien Factor *'78*
Tracy Griffith (1965-)
Skeeter *'93*
All Tied Up *'92*
The Finest Hour *'91*
Fast Food *'89*
The First Power *'89*
Sleepaway Camp 3: Teenage Wasteland *'89*
The Good Mother *'88*
Linda Griffiths
Reno and the Doc *'84*
Lianna *'83*
Overdrawn at the Memory Bank *'83*
Michael Griffiths
Timeless *'96*
Living in Oblivion *'94*
Rachel Griffiths (1968-)
The Rookie *'02*
Blow *'01*
Blow Dry *'00*
Me Myself I *'99*
Among Giants *'98*
Amy *'98*
Hilary and Jackie *'98*
My Best Friend's Wedding *'97*
My Son the Fanatic *'97*
Welcome to Woop Woop *'97*
Jude *'96*
Children of the Revolution *'95*
Cosi *'95*
Muriel's Wedding *'94*
Richard Griffiths (1947-)
Harry Potter and the Sorcerer's Stone *'01*
Vatel *'00*
Sleepy Hollow *'99*
Guarding Tess *'94*
Blame It on the Bellboy *'92*
Naked Gun 2 1/2: The Smell of Fear *'91*
Withnail and I *'87*
Shanghai Surprise *'86*
A Private Function *'84*
Whoops Apocalypse *'83*
Jeff Griggs
Breaking Point *'94*
Eden 2 *'93*
Eden 3 *'93*
Eden 4 *'93*
Eden *'92*
Johanna Grika
Vice Academy 3 *'91*
Visitants *'87*
Frank Grimes
Catherine Cookson's The Wingless Bird *'97*
The Dive *'89*
Crystalstone *'88*
Gary Grimes (1955-)
Cahill: United States Marshal *'73*
Class of '44 *'73*
Culpepper Cattle Co. *'72*
Summer of '42 *'71*
Scott Grimes (1971-)
Band of Brothers *'01*
Mystery, Alaska *'99*
Night Life *'90*
Critters 2: The Main Course *'88*
Critters *'86*
It Came Upon a Midnight Clear *'84*
Tammy Grimes (1934-)
High Art *'98*
A Modern Affair *'94*
Backstreet Justice *'93*
Mr. North *'88*
America *'86*
The Stuff *'85*
No Big Deal *'83*
The Last Unicorn *'82 (V)*
The Runner Stumbles *'79*
Jim Grimshaw
Chill Factor *'99*
Basket Case 3: The Progeny *'92*
Herbert Grimwood (-1929)
Romola *'25*
When the Clouds Roll By *'19*
Anouk Grinberg
Mon Homme *'96*
A Self-Made Hero *'95*
Nikolai Grinko (1920-89)
Stalker *'79*
Solaris *'72*
Andrei Rublev *'66*
Stephen Grives
Inseminoid *'80*
Flambards *'78*
George Grizzard (1928-)
Small Time Crooks *'00*
Scarlett *'94*
Iran: Days of Crisis *'91*
Caroline? *'90*
False Witness *'89*
The Deliberate Stranger *'86*
Embassy *'85*
Bachelor Party *'84*
Oldest Living Graduate *'82*
Wrong Is Right *'82*
Attica *'80*
Seems Like Old Times *'80*
Comes a Horseman *'78*
The Stranger Within *'74*
Pueblo Affair *'73*
Advise and Consent *'62*
From the Terrace *'60*
Larry Groce
Heroes of the Heart *'94*
Paradise Park *'91*
Charles Grodin (1935-)
My Summer Story *'94*
Beethoven's 2nd *'93*
Dave *'93*
Heart and Souls *'93*
So I Married an Axe Murderer *'93*
Beethoven *'92*
Clifford *'92*
Taking Care of Business *'90*
Midnight Run *'88*
You Can't Hurry Love *'88*
The Couch Trip *'87*
Ishtar *'87*
Grown Ups *'86*
Last Resort *'86*
Movers and Shakers *'85*
The Lonely Guy *'84*
The Woman in Red *'84*
The Great Muppet Caper *'81*
The Incredible Shrinking Woman *'81*
It's My Turn *'80*
Seems Like Old Times *'80*
Real Life *'79*
Sunburn *'79*
The Grass Is Always Greener Over the Septic Tank *'78*
Heaven Can Wait *'78*
Just Me & You *'78*
King Kong *'76*
The Meanest Men in the West *'76*
11 Harrowhouse *'74*
The Heartbreak Kid *'72*
Catch-22 *'70*
Rosemary's Baby *'68*

Ride with the Devil '99
All I Wanna Do '98
Lassie '94
The Sandlot '93

Henri Guisol (1904-)
Murder at 45 R.P.M. '65
The Twilight Girls '57
Bizarre Bizarre '39
The Crime of Monsieur Lange '36

Tito Guizar (1908-99)
On the Old Spanish Trail '47
Blondie Goes Latin '42
The Gay Ranchero '42

Clu Gulager (1928-)
Gunfighter '98
The Killing Device '92
My Heroes Have Always Been Cowboys '91
Tapeheads '89
I'm Gonna Git You Sucka '88
Teen Vamp '88
The Uninvited '88
The Hidden '87
Hunter's Blood '87
The Offspring '87
Into the Night '85
A Nightmare on Elm Street 2: Freddy's Revenge '85
Return of the Living Dead '85
Chattanooga Choo Choo '84
The Initiation '84
Kenny Rogers as the Gambler, Part 2: The Adventure Continues '83
Lies '83
Living Proof: The Hank Williams Jr. Story '83
Kenny Rogers as the Gambler '80
Touched by Love '80
Force of One '79
Willa '79
He Who Walks Alone '78
A Question of Love '78
Snowblind '78
The Other Side of Midnight '77
Wonderland Cove '75
Hit Lady '74
McQ '74
Smile, Jenny, You're Dead '74
The Glass House '72
The Last Picture Show '71
Winning '69
And Now Miguel '66
The Killers '64

Sean Gullette
Happy Accidents '00
Requiem for a Dream '00
Pi '98

Dorothy Gulliver (1908-)
Faces '68
The Fighting Marshal '32
Outlaw Justice '32
Shadow of the Eagle '32
The Galloping Ghost '31
Under Montana Skies '30

Leo Gullotta (1946-)
Men Men Men '95
La Scorta '94
Sinbad of the Seven Seas '89

David Gulpilil (1954-)
Until the End of the World '91
Dark Age '88
Crocodile Dundee '86
The Last Wave '77
Mad Dog Morgan '76
Walkabout '71

Devon Gummersall (1978-)
Earth vs. the Spider '01
Dick '99
When Trumpets Fade '98
Lured Innocence '97
Trading Favors '97
Independence Day '96
It's My Party '95

Anna Gunn
Enemy of the State '98
Without Evidence '96

David Gunn
The Convent '00
Vampire Journals '96

Janet Gunn (1961-)
Inferno '01
The Nurse '97
Carnosaur 3: Primal Species '96
Marquis de Sade '96
The Quest '96

Moses Gunn (1929-)
Memphis '91
Perfect Harmony '91
The Women of Brewster Place '89
The House of Dies Drear '88
Heartbreak Ridge '86
Certain Fury '85
Charlotte Forten's Mission: Experiment in Freedom '85
Killing Floor '85
Firestarter '84
The NeverEnding Story '84
Amityville 2: The Possession '82
Ragtime '81
Aaron Loves Angela '75
Cornbread, Earl & Me '75
Rollerball '75
Amazing Grace '74
Haunts of the Very Rich '72
Shaft's Big Score '72
Shaft '71
Wild Rovers '71
The Great White Hope '70
The Hot Rock '70
Black Brigade '69

Sean Gunn
The Specials '00
Tromeo & Juliet '95

Dan Gunther
Lewis and Clark and George '97
Denise Calls Up '95

Bob Gunton (1945-)
61* '01
The Perfect Storm '00
Running Mates '00
Bats '99
Elvis Meets Nixon '98
Patch Adams '98
Buffalo Soldiers '97
Changing Habits '96
The Glimmer Man '96
Ace Ventura: When Nature Calls '95
Broken Arrow '95
In Pursuit of Honor '95
Kingfish: A Story of Huey P. Long '95
Roswell: The U.F.O. Cover-Up '94
The Shawshank Redemption '94
Demolition Man '93
Father Hood '93
Lone Justice '93
Wild Palms '93
Dead Ahead: The Exxon Valdez Disaster '92
Sinatra '92
Mission of the Shark '91
Judgment '90
Cookie '89
Glory '89
Matewan '87
Static '87
Lois Gibbs and the Love Canal '82
Rollover '81

Neena Gupta
Cotton Mary '99
In Custody '94

Alizia Gur
Beast of Morocco '66
From Russia with Love '63

Sigrid Gurie (1911-69)
Enemy of Women '44
Three Faces West '40
The Adventures of Marco Polo '38
Algiers '38

Jennifer Gurney
Heroes of the Heart '94
Paradise Park '91

Sharon Gurney
Cold Comfort Farm '71
Crucible of Horror '69

Eric Gurry
Something Special '86
The Zoo Gang '85
Bad Boys '83
Mystery at Fire Island '81

Annabelle Gurwitch
One Night Stand '97
The Cable Guy '96
Masterminds '96
Not Like Us '96
Pizza Man '91

Louis Guss (1918-)
The Cemetery Club '93
American Blue Note '89
Nitti: The Enforcer '88
Moonstruck '87
Willie & Phil '80

Ray Guth
A Rat's Tale '98 (V)
Emperor of the North Pole '73

Arlo Guthrie
Roadside Prophets '92
Alice's Restaurant '69

Tani Phelps Guthrie
The Thirsty Dead '74
Daughters of Satan '72

Tyrone Guthrie
Beachcomber '38
Sidewalks of London '38

Zaide Silvia Gutierrez
In the Country Where Nothing Happens '99
Highway Patrolman '91
El Norte '83

Emilio Gutierrez-Caba
Mouth to Mouth '95
The Hunt '65

Steve Guttenberg (1958-)
Airborne '98
Home Team '98
Tower of Terror '97
Zeus and Roxanne '96
The Big Green '95
Home for the Holidays '95
It Takes Two '95
Don't Tell Her It's Me '90
Three Men and a Little Lady '90
Cocoon: The Return '88
High Spirits '88
Amazon Women on the Moon '87
The Bedroom Window '87
Police Academy 4: Citizens on Patrol '87
Surrender '87
Three Men and a Baby '87
Pecos Bill '86
Police Academy 3: Back in Training '86
Short Circuit '86
Bad Medicine '85
Cocoon '85
Police Academy 2: Their First Assignment '85
Police Academy '84
The Day After '83
The Man Who Wasn't There '83
Diner '82
Miracle on Ice '81
Can't Stop the Music '80
To Race the Wind '80
The Boys from Brazil '78
The Chicken Chronicles '77

Lucy Gutteridge (1956-)
Grief '94
Tusks '89
The Woman He Loved '88
The Secret Garden '87
The Trouble with Spies '87
A Christmas Carol '84
Top Secret! '84

Ronald Guttman
Just the Ticket '98
Kisses in the Dark '97
The Beast '96
The Pillow Book '95
And the Band Played On '93
Josh and S.A.M. '93
Iran: Days of Crisis '91

DeJuan Guy
One Man's Justice '95
Candyman '92

Jasmine Guy (1964-)
Guinevere '99
Cats Don't Dance '97 (V)
Perfect Crime '97
America's Dream '95
Queen '93
Harlem Nights '89
School Daze '88

Sheila Guyse
Miracle in Harlem '48
Sepia Cinderella '47
Boy! What a Girl '45

Joe Guzaldo (1960-)
Evil Has a Face '96
Hoodlum '96
The Woman Who Loved Elvis '93
Bingo '91
Smooth Talker '90

Luis Guzman (1956-)
The Count of Monte Cristo '02
The Salton Sea '02
Luckytown '00
Traffic '00
The Bone Collector '99
The Limey '99
One Tough Cop '98
Out of Sight '98
Snake Eyes '98
Boogie Nights '97
Pronto '97
The Substitute '96
Lotto Land '95
Stonewall '95
The Burning Season '94
Carlito's Way '93
Guilty as Sin '93
Mr. Wonderful '93
Jumpin' at the Boneyard '92
The Hard Way '91
Q & A '90
Crocodile Dundee 2 '88

Teri Guzman
Escape from Cell Block 3 '78
Women Unchained '72

Jack Gwaltney
The Siege '98
One Way Out '95
Risk '94
Vital Signs '90

Edmund Gwenn (1875-1959)
It's a Dog's Life '55
The Trouble with Harry '55
The Student Prince '54
Them! '54
The Bigamist '53
A Woman of Distinction '50
Challenge to Lassie '49
The Hills of Home '48
Green Dolphin Street '47
Life with Father '47
Miracle on 34th Street '47
Undercurrent '46
The Keys of the Kingdom '44
Forever and a Day '43
Lassie, Come Home '43
Cheers for Miss Bishop '41
The Devil & Miss Jones '41
Doctor Takes a Wife '40
Foreign Correspondent '40
Pride and Prejudice '40
South Riding '37
Anthony Adverse '36
Java Head '35
Sylvia Scarlett '35
If I Were Rich '33
Skin Game '31

David Gwillim
Peter and Paul '81
The Island at the Top of the World '74

Jack (Gwyllam) Gwillim (1912-2001)
The Bushbaby '70
Jason and the Argonauts '63
Flame Over India '60
Sink the Bismarck '60
Sword of Sherwood Forest '60

Michael Gwynn (1916-76)
The Scars of Dracula '70
Jason and the Argonauts '63
Village of the Damned '60
The Revenge of Frankenstein '58

Anne Gwynne (1918-)
Adam at 6 a.m. '70
Teenage Monster '57
Breakdown '53
King of the Bullwhip '51
Black Tower '50
Dick Tracy Meets Gruesome '47
Killer Dill '47
Fear '46
House of Frankenstein '44
Weird Woman/Frozen Ghost '44
Ride 'Em Cowboy '42
The Black Cat '41
Nice Girl? '41
Black Friday '40

Fred Gwynne (1926-93)
My Cousin Vinny '92
Shadows and Fog '92
Disorganized Crime '89
Pet Sematary '89
Vanishing Act '88
Fatal Attraction '87
Ironweed '87
Murder by the Book '87
The Secret of My Success '87
The Boy Who Could Fly '86
Off Beat '86
Water '85
The Cotton Club '84
The Mysterious Stranger '82
The Munsters' Revenge '81
Simon '80
Sanctuary of Fear '79
The Littlest Angel '69
Munster, Go Home! '66

Michael C. Gwynne (1942-)
The Last of the Finest '90
Cherry 2000 '88
Seduced '85
Harry Tracy '83
The Streets of L.A. '79
Special Delivery '76
Payday '72

Peter Gwynne
Tim '79
Puzzle '78
The Dove '74

Jake Gyllenhaal (1980-)
The Good Girl '02
Lovely & Amazing '02
Bubble Boy '01
Donnie Darko '01
Highway '01
October Sky '99

Maggie Gyllenhaal (1977-)
40 Days and 40 Nights '02
Secretary '02
Donnie Darko '01
Riding in Cars with Boys '01
Cecil B. Demented '00

Kim Gyngell
Love and Other Catastrophes '95
Heaven Tonight '93
Boulevard of Broken Dreams '88
The Wacky World of Wills & Burke '85

Greta Gynt (1916-2000)
Dear Murderer '47
Mr. Emmanuel '44
The Arsenal Stadium Mystery '39
The Human Monster '39
The Hooded Terror '38
Sexton Blake and the Hooded Terror '38

Christina Haag
Lost in the Bermuda Triangle '98
Shaking the Tree '92

Dolly Haas
I Confess '53
Spy of Napoleon '36

Hugo Haas (1902-68)
King Solomon's Mines '50
The Fighting Kentuckian '49
Casbah '48
For the Love of Mary '48
My Girl Tisa '48
Merton of the Movies '47
Northwest Outpost '47
The Private Affairs of Bel Ami '47
Holiday in Mexico '46
Days of Glory '43

Lukas Haas (1976-)
Breakfast of Champions '98
Everyone Says I Love You '96
johns '96
Mars Attacks! '96
Boys '95
Warrior Spirit '94
Alan & Naomi '92
Leap of Faith '92
Rambling Rose '91
Shattered Spirits '91
Music Box '89
See You in the Morning '89
The Lady in White '88
The Wizard of Loneliness '88
Solarbabies '86
Witness '85

Alessandro Haber
Men Men Men '95
The Story of Boys & Girls '91

Eva Habermann (1976-)
Tales from a Parallel Universe: Eating Pattern '97
Tales from a Parallel Universe: Giga Shadow '97
Tales from a Parallel Universe: I Worship His Shadow '97
Tales from a Parallel Universe: Super Nova '97

Matthias Habich (1940-)
Enemy at the Gates '00
The Savage Woman '91
Straight for the Heart '88
Coup de Grace '78

Olivia Hack
A Very Brady Sequel '96
The Brady Bunch Movie '95

Shelley Hack (1952-)
The Finishing Touch '92
Me, Myself & I '92
A Casualty of War '90
Blind Fear '89
The Stepfather '87
Troll '86
Kicks '85
Single Bars, Single Women '84
King of Comedy '82
If Ever I See You Again '78

George Hackathorne (1895-1940)
Merry-Go-Round '23
The Worldly Madonna '22
The Last of the Mohicans '20

Joseph Hacker
Little Treasure '85

The Ultimate Imposter *'79*

Buddy Hackett (1924-)
Paulie *'98*
The Little Mermaid *'89 (V)*
Scrooged *'88*
Bud and Lou *'78*
Muscle Beach Party *'64*
It's a Mad, Mad, Mad, Mad World *'63*
The Music Man *'62*
The Wonderful World of the Brothers Grimm *'62*
God's Little Acre *'58*

Claire Hackett
Liam *'00*
Gallowglass *'95*

Joan Hackett (1942-83)
Flicks *'85*
The Escape Artist *'82*
Only When I Laugh *'81*
The Long Days of Summer *'80*
One Trick Pony *'80*
Dead of Night *'77*
The Possessed *'77*
The Treasure of Matecumbe *'76*
Reflections of Murder *'74*
The Terminal Man *'74*
Class of '63 *'73*
The Last of Sheila *'73*
Rivals *'72*
Support Your Local Sheriff *'69*
Will Penny *'67*
The Group *'66*

Karl Hackett (1893-1948)
Outlaw of the Plains *'46*
His Brother's Ghost *'45*
Lightning Raiders *'45*
Sonora Stagecoach *'44*
Bordertown Gunfighters *'43*
Sagebrush Law *'43*
Texas Trouble *'41*
Take Me Back to Oklahoma *'40*
Yukon Flight *'40*
Feud Maker *'38*
Phantom Ranger *'38*
Songs and Bullets *'38*
Border Phantom *'37*
Gun Lords of Stirrup Basin *'37*
The Red Rope *'37*
Cavalry *'36*

Sandy Hackett
Ex-Cop *'93*
Hamburger...The Motion Picture *'86*

Penne Hackforth-Jones (1943-)
Paradise Road *'97*
The Old Curiosity Shop *'84 (V)*
Image of Death *'77*
Alvin Purple *'73*

Gene Hackman (1930-)
Behind Enemy Lines *'01*
Heartbreakers *'01*
Heist *'01*
The Mexican *'01*
The Royal Tenenbaums *'01*
The Replacements *'00*
Under Suspicion *'00*
Antz *'98 (V)*
Enemy of the State *'98*
Twilight *'98*
Absolute Power *'97*
The Chamber *'96*
Extreme Measures *'96*
The Birdcage *'95*
Crimson Tide *'95*
Get Shorty *'95*
The Quick and the Dead *'94*
Wyatt Earp *'94*
The Firm *'93*
Geronimo: An American Legend *'93*
Unforgiven *'92*
Class Action *'91*
Company Business *'91*
Loose Cannons *'90*
Narrow Margin *'90*
Postcards from the Edge *'90*
The Package *'89*
Another Woman *'88*
Bat 21 *'88*
Full Moon in Blue Water *'88*
Mississippi Burning *'88*
Split Decisions *'88*
No Way Out *'87*
Superman 4: The Quest for Peace *'87*
Hoosiers *'86*
Power *'86*
Target *'85*
Twice in a Lifetime *'85*
Misunderstood *'84*
Uncommon Valor *'83*
Under Fire *'83*
All Night Long *'81*
Eureka! *'81*
Reds *'81*
Superman 2 *'80*
Superman: The Movie *'78*
A Bridge Too Far *'77*
The Domino Principle *'77*
March or Die *'77*
America at the Movies *'76*
Bite the Bullet *'75*
French Connection 2 *'75*
Night Moves *'75*
The Conversation *'74*
Young Frankenstein *'74*
Zandy's Bride *'74*
Scarecrow *'73*
The Poseidon Adventure *'72*
Prime Cut *'72*
The French Connection *'71*
Doctors' Wives *'70*
I Never Sang for My Father *'70*
Downhill Racer *'69*
Marooned *'69*
Riot *'69*
Bonnie & Clyde *'67*
Hawaii *'66*
Lilith *'64*

Michiko Hada
Flowers of Shanghai *'98*
Rowing Through *'96*
The Mystery of Rampo *'94*

Jonathan Hadary
A Simple Wish *'97*
Private Parts *'96*
The New Age *'94*
As Is *'85*

Suheil Haddad
The Milky Way *'97*
Cup Final *'92*

Dayle Haddon (1949-)
Fiesta *'95*
Cyborg *'89*
Bedroom Eyes *'86*
North Dallas Forty *'79*
The Cheaters *'76*
Paperback Hero *'73*
The World's Greatest Athlete *'73*

Ron Haddrick (1929-)
Quigley Down Under *'90*
Great Expectations: The Untold Story *'87*
Camel Boy *'84 (V)*
Dawn! *'83*

Sara Haden (1897-1981)
The Great Rupert *'50*
A Life of Her Own *'50*
Love Laughs at Andy Hardy *'46*
Mr. Ace *'46*
She Wolf of London *'46*
Our Vines Have Tender Grapes *'45*
Andy Hardy's Double Life *'42*
Somewhere I'll Find You *'42*
Andy Hardy Meets Debutante *'40*
The Shop Around the Corner *'40*
Andy Hardy Gets Spring Fever *'39*
The Poor Little Rich Girl *'36*
Mad Love *'35*
Anne of Green Gables *'34*
Finishing School *'33*

Reed Hadley (1911-74)
Brain of Blood *'71*
Kansas Pacific *'53*
Baron of Arizona *'51*
The Half-Breed *'51*
Little Big Horn *'51*
Return of Jesse James *'50*
I Shot Jesse James *'49*
Rimfire *'49*
A Southern Yankee *'48*
Dark Corner *'46*
Doll Face *'46*
Guadalcanal Diary *'43*
Whistling in the Dark *'41*
Ziegfeld Girl *'41*
The Bank Dick *'40*
Zorro's Fighting Legion *'39*
Hollywood Stadium Mystery *'38*

Marianne Hagan
I Think I Do *'97*
Halloween 6: The Curse of Michael Myers *'95*

Molly Hagan (1962-)
Miracle in Lane Two *'00*
Playing Mona Lisa *'00*
Election *'99*
Ringmaster *'98*
Some Kind of Wonderful *'87*
Code of Silence *'85*

Jean Hagen (1923-77)
Alexander: The Other Side of Dawn *'77*
Panic in the Year Zero! *'62*
Sunrise at Campobello *'60*
The Shaggy Dog *'59*
The Big Knife *'55*
Latin Lovers *'53*
Singin' in the Rain *'52*
Adam's Rib *'50*
The Asphalt Jungle *'50*
A Life of Her Own *'50*

Ross Hagen (1938-)
Midnight Tease 2 *'95*
Bikini Drive-In *'94*
Dinosaur Island *'93*
Blood Games *'90*
Alienator *'89*
Marked for Murder *'89*
B.O.R.N. *'88*
Warlords *'88*
Commando Squad *'87*
Phantom Empire *'87*
Star Slammer *'87*
Armed Response *'86*
Avenging Angel *'85*
Angel *'84*
Night Creature *'79*
Bad Charleston Charlie *'73*
The Deadly and the Beautiful *'73*
Angels' Wild Women *'72*
Hellcats *'68*
Speedway *'68*

Uta Hagen (1919-)
Reversal of Fortune *'90*
The Boys from Brazil *'78*
The Other *'72*

Julie Hagerty (1955-)
Freddy Got Fingered *'01*
Storytelling *'01*
Held Up *'00*
Jackie's Back *'99*
The Story of Us *'99*
Tourist Trap *'98*
Boys Will Be Boys *'97*
U-Turn *'97*
The Wife *'95*
Noises Off *'92*
What about Bob? *'91*
Reversal of Fortune *'90*
Bloodhounds of Broadway *'89*
Rude Awakening *'89*
Necessary Parties *'88*
Beyond Therapy *'86*
Bad Medicine *'85*
Goodbye, New York *'85*
Lost in America *'85*
Airplane 2: The Sequel *'82*
A Midsummer Night's Sex Comedy *'82*
Airplane! *'80*
The Day the Women Got Even *'80*

Michael G. (Mike) Hagerty (1953-)
Best Laid Plans *'99*
Inspector Gadget *'99*
Speed 2: Cruise Control *'97*

Merle Haggard
Huckleberry Finn *'75*
Hillbillies in a Haunted House *'67*

Dan Haggerty (1941-)
Grizzly Mountain *'97*
Abducted 2: The Reunion *'94*
Cheyenne Warrior *'94*
The Magic Voyage *'93 (V)*
Ice Pawn *'92*
Deadly Diamonds *'91*
Mind Trap *'91*
Soldier's Fortune *'91*
The Inheritor *'90*
Repo Jake *'90*
Spirit of the Eagle *'90*
Chance *'89*
The Channeler *'89*
The Chilling *'89*
Elves *'89*
Night Wars *'88*
Abducted *'86*
Angels Die Hard *'84*
The Capture of Grizzly Adams *'82*
California Gold Rush *'81*
King of the Mountain *'81*
Desperate Women *'78*
Terror out of the Sky *'78*
The Adventures of Frontier Fremont *'75*
Life & Times of Grizzly Adams *'74*
When the North Wind Blows *'74*
The Shrieking *'73*
Starbird and Sweet William *'73*
Bury Me an Angel *'71*
The Tender Warrior *'71*

Don Haggerty (1914-88)
The Killers *'64*
Hell Is for Heroes *'62*
Command Decision *'48*

Sean Haggerty
Rhythm Thief *'94*
Spare Me *'92*

Kenichi Hagiwara
Traffic Jam *'91*
Kagemusha *'80*

Michael Hagiwara
Josh Kirby...Time Warrior: Chapter 5, Journey to the Magic Cavern *'96*
Prehysteria 2 *'94*

Marvin Hagler
Indio 2: The Revolt *'92*
Indio *'90*

Larry Hagman (1939-)
Primary Colors *'98*
Nixon *'95*
S.O.B. *'81*
President's Mistress *'78*
The Eagle Has Landed *'77*
Intimate Strangers *'77*
The Big Bus *'76*
Mother, Jugs and Speed *'76*
Harry and Tonto *'74*
Hurricane *'74*
Antonio *'73*
Beware! The Blob *'72*
Deadly Encounter *'72*
No Place to Run *'72*
Hired Hand *'71*
Three in the Cellar *'70*
The Group *'66*
In Harm's Way *'65*
Ensign Pulver *'64*
Fail-Safe *'64*

Archie Hahn
Amazon Women on the Moon *'87*
Glory Years *'87*
Meatballs 2 *'84*
Protocol *'84*
This Is Spinal Tap *'84*
Pray TV *'80*
Cannonball *'76*
Phantom of the Paradise *'74*

Eric Hahn
Fist of Glory *'95*
Crossfire *'89*
Nam Angels *'88*

Gisela Hahn
Alien Contamination *'81*
Big Boss *'77*
Mr. Scarface *'77*

Jess Hahn (1922-98)
Mama Dracula *'80*
Mean Frank and Crazy Tony *'75*
The Grand Duel *'73*
The Night of the Following Day *'69*
Triple Cross *'67*
Secret Agent Super Dragon *'66*
Topkapi *'64*

Jessica Hahn
Bikini Summer 2 *'92*
Thunder & Mud *'89*

Charles Haid (1943-)
The Third Miracle *'99*
Broken Trust *'95*
Cooperstown *'93*
The Fire Next Time *'93*
The Chinatown Murders: Man against the Mob *'92*
Freeze Frame *'92*
Storyville *'92*
In the Line of Duty: A Cop for the Killing *'90*
Nightbreed *'90*
Capone *'89*
Fire and Rain *'89*
Cop *'88*
The Great Escape 2: The Untold Story *'88*
The Rescue *'88*
Weekend War *'88*
Children in the Crossfire *'84*
Twirl *'81*
Altered States *'80*
Deathmoon *'78*
Oliver's Story *'78*
Who'll Stop the Rain? *'78*
The Choirboys *'77*

Ion Haiduc
Bloodlust: Subspecies 3 *'93*
Bloodstone: Subspecies 2 *'92*

Stacy Haiduk (1968-)
Gabriela *'01*
Desert Thunder *'99*
The Beneficiary *'97*
Yesterday's Target *'96*
Luther the Geek *'90*
Steel and Lace *'90*

Sid Haig (1939-)
Jackie Brown *'97*
The Forbidden Dance *'90*
Wizards of the Lost Kingdom 2 *'89*
Warlords *'88*
Commando Squad *'87*
Aftermath *'85*
Galaxy of Terror *'81*
Busting *'74*
Foxy Brown *'74*
Coffy *'73*
The Deadly and the Beautiful *'73*
Emperor of the North Pole *'73*
The Big Bird Cage *'72*
The Big Doll House *'71*
C.C. & Company *'70*
Pit Stop *'67*
Track of the Vampire *'66*
Spider Baby *'64*

Kenneth Haigh (1929-)
The Bitch *'78*
Cleopatra *'63*
Teenage Bad Girl *'59*

Louisa Haigh
Shipwrecked *'90*
Murderers Among Us: The Simon Wiesenthal Story *'89*

Marian Hailey
Jenny *'70*
Lovers and Other Strangers *'70*

Corey Haim (1972-)
Snowboard Academy *'96*
Demolition High *'95*
Life 101 *'95*
Dream a Little Dream 2 *'94*
Fast Getaway 2 *'94*
National Lampoon's Last Resort *'94*
Anything for Love *'93*
Blown Away *'93*
Just One of the Girls *'93*
The Double O Kid *'92*
Oh, What a Night *'92*
Dream Machine *'91*
Fast Getaway *'91*
Prayer of the Rollerboys *'91*
Dream a Little Dream *'89*
License to Drive *'88*
Watchers *'88*
The Lost Boys *'87*
Lucas *'86*
Murphy's Romance *'85*
Secret Admirer *'85*
Silver Bullet *'85*
A Time to Live *'85*
First Born *'84*

Patricia Haines
The Virgin Witch *'70*
Night Caller from Outer Space *'66*

Richard Haines (-1990)
An African Dream *'90*
Alien from L.A. *'87*

William Haines (1900-73)
The Girl Said No *'37*
Way Out West *'37*
Free and Easy *'30*
Show People *'28*
Little Annie Rooney *'25*

Jester Hairston (1901-2000)
I'm Gonna Git You Sucka *'88*
The Alamo *'60*

Khrystyne Haje (1968-)
Cyborg 3: The Recycler *'95*
Scanner Cop 2: Volkin's Revenge *'94*
Scanners: The Showdown *'94*

Haji
Ilsa, Harem Keeper of the Oil Sheiks *'76*
Supervixens *'75*
Beyond the Valley of the Dolls *'70*
Faster, Pussycat! Kill! Kill! *'65*
Motor Psycho *'65*

Alan Hale (1892-1950)
Stars in My Crown *'50*
Adventures of Don Juan *'49*
The Inspector General *'49*
My Girl Tisa *'48*
South of St. Louis *'48*
Pursued *'47*
The Man I Love *'46*
Night and Day *'46*
The Adventures of Mark Twain *'44*
Action in the North Atlantic *'43*
Destination Tokyo *'43*
Thank Your Lucky Stars *'43*
This Is the Army *'43*
Captains of the Clouds *'42*
Desperate Journey *'42*
Gentleman Jim *'42*
Footsteps in the Dark *'41*
Strawberry Blonde *'41*
The Fighting 69th *'40*
Santa Fe Trail *'40*
The Sea Hawk *'40*
They Drive by Night *'40*
Virginia City *'40*
Dodge City *'39*
The Man in the Iron Mask *'39*
The Private Lives of Elizabeth & Essex *'39*
The Adventures of Marco Polo *'38*

The Adventures of Robin Hood '38
Algiers '38
Listen, Darling '38
The Prince and the Pauper '37
Stella Dallas '37
Thin Ice '37
When Thief Meets Thief '37
Our Relations '36
The Crusades '35
Last Days of Pompeii '35
Great Expectations '34
Imitation of Life '34
It Happened One Night '34
Little Minister '34
The Lost Patrol '34
Of Human Bondage '34
The Scarlet Letter '34
The Sin of Madelon Claudet '31
Susan Lenox: Her Fall and Rise '31
The Leatherneck '28
Power '28
Dick Turpin '25
The Covered Wagon '23
Robin Hood '22
The Trap '22
The Four Horsemen of the Apocalypse '21

Alan Hale, Jr. (1918-90)
Back to the Beach '87
Hambone & Hillie '84
Johnny Dangerously '84
The Fifth Musketeer '79
The North Avenue Irregulars '79
Rescue from Gilligan's Island '78
The Giant Spider Invasion '75
There Was a Crooked Man '70
The Crawling Hand '63
Hard Drivin' '60
Up Periscope '59
Battle Hymn '57
All Mine to Give '56
The Indian Fighter '55
Young at Heart '54
Big Trees '52
At Sword's Point '51
Home Town Story '51
The Underworld Story '50
The West Point Story '50
It Happens Every Spring '49
Rim of the Canyon '49
The Spirit of West Point '47
Watch on the Rhine '43
To the Shores of Tripoli '42
Wake Island '42
Dive Bomber '41

Barbara Hale (1921-)
Perry Mason: The Case of the Lost Love '87
Perry Mason Returns '85
Flight of the Grey Wolf '76
The Giant Spider Invasion '75
Airport '70
Buckskin '68
The Oklahoman '56
Seventh Cavalry '56
A Lion Is in the Streets '53
Last of the Comanches '52
The Jackpot '50
The Clay Pigeon '49
Jolson Sings Again '49
The Window '49
The Boy with the Green Hair '48
First Yank into Tokyo '45
West of the Pecos '45
The Falcon in Hollywood '44
Going to Town '44

Binnie Hale
Love from a Stranger '37
The Phantom Light '35

Creighton Hale (1882-1965)
Action in the North Atlantic '43
Watch on the Rhine '43
Dive Bomber '41
Sergeant York '41
Shop Angel '32
The Cat and the Canary '27
The Marriage Circle '24
Broken Hearts of Broadway '23
The Idol Dancer '20
Way Down East '20

Georgina Hale (1943-)
Castaway '87
Mahler '74
The Boy Friend '71
The Devils '71

Jean Hale
In Like Flint '67
The St. Valentine's Day Massacre '67
Psychomania '63

Jonathan Hale (1891-1966)
Men of the Fighting Lady '54
The Judge '49
Call Northside 777 '48
Silver River '48
Blondie Knows Best '46
Hollywood Canteen '44
Footlight Glamour '43
It's a Great Life '43
Blondie for Victory '42
Blondie Goes Latin '42
Blondie Goes to College '42
Blondie's Blessed Event '42
Hangmen Also Die '42
Blondie in Society '41
Blondie Has Trouble '40
Blondie Plays Cupid '40
The Saint Takes Over '40
The Saint's Double Trouble '40
Blondie Brings Up Baby '39
Blondie Meets the Boss '39
The Saint Strikes Back '39
The Story of Alexander Graham Bell '39
Blondie '38
Breaking the Ice '38
Bringing Up Baby '38
The Duke of West Point '38
Exiled to Shanghai '37
Saratoga '37
You Only Live Once '37

Louise Closser Hale (1872-1933)
Today We Live '33
Shanghai Express '32
Devotion '31
Platinum Blonde '31

Monte Hale (1921-)
Missourians '50
Trail of Robin Hood '50
The Vanishing Westerner '50
Outcasts of the Trail '49
Pioneer Marshal '49
Son of God's Country '48
Under Colorado Skies '47

Sonnie Hale (1902-59)
It's Love Again '36
First a Girl '35
Evergreen '34

Brian Haley (1963-)
Pearl Harbor '01
McHale's Navy '97
That Darn Cat '96
Baby's Day Out '94

Jack Haley (1899-1979)
People Are Funny '46
George White's Scandals '45
Treasure of Fear '45
Higher and Higher '44
One Body Too Many '44
Take It Big '44
Moon over Miami '41
The Wizard of Oz '39
Alexander's Ragtime Band '38
Rebecca of Sunnybrook Farm '38
Pick a Star '37
Pigskin Parade '36
The Poor Little Rich Girl '36

Jackie Earle Haley (1961-)
Maniac Cop 3: Badge of Silence '93
Dollman '90
The Zoo Gang '85
Losin' It '82
Breaking Away '79
The Bad News Bears Go to Japan '78
The Bad News Bears in Breaking Training '77
Damnation Alley '77
The Bad News Bears '76

H.B. Halicki (1941-89)
Deadline Auto Theft '83
The Junkman '82
Gone in 60 Seconds '74

Albert Hall (1937-)
Ali '01
Beloved '98
Get On the Bus '96
Devil in a Blue Dress '95
Major Payne '95
Malcolm X '92
Hearts of Darkness: A Filmmaker's Apocalypse '91
Separate but Equal '91
Betrayed '88
Uncle Tom's Cabin '87
The Long, Hot Summer '86
Apocalypse Now '79

Anthony Michael Hall (1968-)
All About the Benjamins '02
The Caveman's Valentine '01
Freddy Got Fingered '01
Hitched '01
61* '01
Happy Accidents '00
The Pirates of Silicon Valley '99
Exit in Red '97
The Killing Grounds '97
Trojan War '97
The Death Artist '95
The Grave '95
Hail Caesar '94
Me and the Mob '94
Texas '94
The Adventures of a Gnome Named Gnorm '93
Six Degrees of Separation '93
Into the Sun '92
Edward Scissorhands '90
Johnny Be Good '88
Out of Bounds '86
The Breakfast Club '85
Weird Science '85
Sixteen Candles '84
National Lampoon's Vacation '83
Six Pack '82

Arch Hall, Jr. (1945-)
Deadwood '65
Nasty Rabbit '64
The Sadist '63
Eegah! '62
Wild Guitar '62
The Choppers '61

Arch (Archie) Hall, Sr. (1908-78)
The Thrill Killers '65
Wild Guitar '62
Border Badmen '45
His Brother's Ghost '45

Arsenio Hall (1956-)
Harlem Nights '89
Coming to America '88
Amazon Women on the Moon '87

Brad Hall (1958-)
Bye Bye, Love '94
The Guardian '90
Limit Up '89
Worth Winning '89
Troll '86

Bug Hall (1985-)
Skipped Parts '00
Safety Patrol '98
Honey, We Shrunk Ourselves '97
The Big Green '95
The Stupids '95
The Little Rascals '94

Delores Hall
Leap of Faith '92
Lethal Weapon 3 '92

Ellen Hall (1922-99)
Raiders of the Border '44
Range Law '44

Gabriella Hall
The Seductress '00
The Portrait '99
Lolida 2000 '97
Sexual Roulette '96
Shadow Dancer '96

Grayson Hall (1927-85)
Night of Dark Shadows '71
Adam at 6 a.m. '70
House of Dark Shadows '70
The Night of the Iguana '64
Satan in High Heels '61

Hanna Hall
The Virgin Suicides '99
Homecoming '96

Harriet Hall
The Witching of Ben Wagner '95
Foxfire '87

Henry Hall (1898-1989)
Command Decision '48
Lightning Raiders '45
The Ape '40
Circle of Death '36
Rainbow Ranch '33
Midnight Warning '32

Huntz Hall (1920-99)
Auntie Lee's Meat Pies '92
Cyclone '87
The Escape Artist '82
Gas Pump Girls '79
Valentino '77
Gentle Giant '67
Bowery Boys Meet the Monsters '54
Clipped Wings '53
Here Come the Marines '52
Ghost Chasers '51
Blues Busters '50
Master Minds '49
Smugglers' Cove '48
Spook Busters '48
Bowery Buckaroos '47
Hard-Boiled Mahoney '47
A Walk in the Sun '46
Follow the Leader '44
Million Dollar Kid '44
Ghost on the Loose '43
Kid Dynamite '43
Junior G-Men of the Air '42
Let's Get Tough '42
Mr. Wise Guy '42
'Neath Brooklyn Bridge '42
Smart Alecks '42
Zis Boom Bah '42
Bowery Blitzkrieg '41
Pride of the Bowery '41
Spooks Run Wild '41
Junior G-Men '40
They Made Me a Criminal '39
Angels with Dirty Faces '38
Little Tough Guys '38
Dead End '37

Irma P. Hall (1937-)
A Lesson Before Dying '99
Beloved '98
The Love Letter '98
Patch Adams '98
Buddy '97
Midnight in the Garden of Good and Evil '97
Soul Food '97
Steel '97
A Family Thing '96
Nothing to Lose '96

James Hall (1900-40)
Millie '31
Hell's Angels '30
Hotel Imperial '27

Jerry Hall (1956-)
R.P.M. '97
Savage Hearts '95
Batman '89
Running out of Luck '86

Jon Hall (1913-79)
The Beach Girls and the Monster '65
Hell Ship Mutiny '57
Deputy Marshal '50
Pirate Ship '49
The Prince of Thieves '48
The Last of the Redmen '47
Cobra Woman '44
The Invisible Man's Revenge '44
Ali Baba and the Forty Thieves '43
Arabian Nights '42
Invisible Agent '42
The Tuttles of Tahiti '42
Kit Carson '40
South of Pago Pago '40
The Hurricane '37
The Lion Man '36

Juanita Hall (1901-68)
Flower Drum Song '61
South Pacific '58
Paradise in Harlem '40

Kevin Peter Hall (1955-91)
Highway to Hell '92
Predator 2 '90
Harry and the Hendersons '87
Predator '87
Misfits of Science '85

Landon Hall
The Escort '97
Witchcraft 9: Bitter Flesh '96
Over the Wire '95
Stolen Hearts '95

Lois Hall (1926-)
Kalifornia '93
Dead Again '91
Pirates of the High Seas '50

Michael Keys Hall
Flight of Black Angel '91
Blackout '88

Philip Baker Hall (1931-)
The Sum of All Fears '02
The Contender '00
Lost Souls '00
Rules of Engagement '00
The Cradle Will Rock '99
The Insider '99
Let the Devil Wear Black '99
Magnolia '99
The Talented Mr. Ripley '99
Enemy of the State '98
Psycho '98
Rush Hour '98
Sour Grapes '98
The Truman Show '98
Witness to the Mob '98
Air Force One '97
Boogie Nights '97
Hard Eight '96
Kiss of Death '94
Blue Desert '91
Dark River: A Father's Revenge '90
Three o'Clock High '87
Secret Honor '85
The Last Reunion '80

Porter Hall (1888-1953)
The Half-Breed '51
The Beautiful Blonde from Bashful Bend '49
Intruder in the Dust '49
Miracle on 34th Street '47
Singapore '47
Unconquered '47
Murder, He Says '45
Weekend at the Waldorf '45
Double Indemnity '44
Going My Way '44
The Great Moment '44
Miracle of Morgan's Creek '44
The Woman of the Town '44
The Desperadoes '43
Sullivan's Travels '41
Arizona '40
His Girl Friday '40
Mr. Smith Goes to Washington '39
They Shall Have Music '39
Bulldog Drummond's Peril '38
Bulldog Drummond Escapes '37
The Plainsman '37
Souls at Sea '37
The General Died at Dawn '36
Petrified Forest '36
The Princess Comes Across '36
Satan Met a Lady '36
The Story of Louis Pasteur '36
The Case of the Lucky Legs '35
The Thin Man '34

Regina Hall
The Other Brother '02
Scary Movie 2 '01
Disappearing Acts '00
Scary Movie '00

Ron Hall
Raw Target '95
Triple Impact '92

Ruth Hall (1910-9)
The Return of Casey Jones '34
Man from Monterey '33
Strawberry Roan '33
Between Fighting Men '32
Kid from Spain '32
Ride Him, Cowboy '32
Monkey Business '31

Scott H. Hall
Color Me Blood Red '64
Blood Feast '63

Shannah Hall
The Princess & the Call Girl '84
Boogey Man 2 '83

Thurston Hall (1883-1958)
The Go-Getter '54
Night Stage to Galveston '52
Rim of the Canyon '49
Up in Central Park '48
West of the Pecos '45
In Society '44
Song of Nevada '44
Crash Dive '43
Footlight Glamour '43
The Great Gildersleeve '43
I Dood It '43
Call of the Canyon '42
Twin Beds '42
The Invisible Woman '40
Each Dawn I Die '39
Jeepers Creepers '39
You Can't Cheat an Honest Man '39
Amazing Dr. Clitterhouse '38
Lady from Nowhere '36
Theodora Goes Wild '36
The Black Room '35

Zooey Hall
I Dismember Mama '74
Fortune and Men's Eyes '71

Lillian Hall-Davis (1896-1933)
The Farmer's Wife '28
The Ring '27
The Last of the Mohicans '20

Charles Hallahan (1943-97)
Dante's Peak '97
The Pest '96
The Rich Man's Wife '96
Warlock: The Armageddon '93
Wild Palms '93
Body of Evidence '92
True Believer '89
A Winner Never Quits '86
Pale Rider '85
Vision Quest '85
The Thing '82
Margin for Murder '81
Nightwing '79

John Hallam (1941-)
Lifeforce '85
Under Capricorn '82
Dragonslayer '81
The Offence '73
Jane Hallaren
A Night in the Life of Jimmy Reardon '88
Lianna '83
Body Heat '81
Gisli Halldorsson (1927-98)
Devil's Island '96
Cold Fever '95
Children of Nature '91
Tom Hallick
A Rare Breed '81
Hangar 18 '80
John Halliday (1880-1947)
The Philadelphia Story '40
That Certain Age '38
Desire '36
Finishing School '33
Consolation Marriage '31
Millie '31
Lori Hallier
Running Wild '99
Blacklight '98
Night of the Twisters '95
Blindside '88
Higher Education '88
The Gunfighters '87
My Bloody Valentine '81
William (Bill) Halligan (1883-1957)
Jive Junction '43
Turf Boy '42
Robot Pilot '41
Johnny Hallyday
Conseil de Famille '86
Detective '85
Billy Halop (1920-76)
Too Late for Tears '49
Junior G-Men of the Air '42
Pride of the Bowery '41
Junior G-Men '40
They Made Me a Criminal '39
Angels with Dirty Faces '38
Little Tough Guys '38
Dead End '37
Luke Halpin (1948-)
Flipper '96
Matinee '92
Shock Waves '77
If It's Tuesday, This Must Be Belgium '69
Island of the Lost '68
Flipper's Odyssey '66
Flipper's New Adventure '64
Flipper '63
Peter Pan '60
Brett Halsey (1933-)
First Degree '95
Beyond Justice '92
Black Cat '90
Demonia '90
Dangerous Obsession '88
The Crash of Flight 401 '78
Magnificent Adventurer '76
Four Times That Night '69
Twice-Told Tales '63
Return to Peyton Place '61
The Girl in Lover's Lane '60
Atomic Submarine '59
Jet Over the Atlantic '59
Return of the Fly '59
Submarine Seahawk '59
To Hell and Back '55
Ma and Pa Kettle at Home '54
Michael Halsey
Postmortem '98
Mean Guns '97
Dollman '90
Treasure Island '89
Under the Gun '88
Rodger Halstead
Carnosaur 3: Primal Species '96
Alien Terminator '95
Julie Halston
Joe Gould's Secret '00
David Searching '97

Charles Halton (1876-1959)
Friendly Persuasion '56
A Star Is Born '54
Carrie '52
Here Comes the Groom '51
My Dear Secretary '49
If You Knew Susie '48
The Best Years of Our Lives '46
It's a Wonderful Life '46
Sister Kenny '46
Rhapsody in Blue '45
A Tree Grows in Brooklyn '45
Enemy of Women '44
The Thin Man Goes Home '44
Up in Arms '44
Wilson '44
Heaven Can Wait '43
Across the Pacific '42
Captains of the Clouds '42
In Old California '42
The Lady Is Willing '42
Saboteur '42
The Spoilers '42
To Be or Not to Be '42
Dance Hall '41
Lady Scarface '41
Look Who's Laughing '41
Mr. & Mrs. Smith '41
Dr. Cyclops '40
Doctor Takes a Wife '40
Foreign Correspondent '40
The Shop Around the Corner '40
Stranger on the Third Floor '40
They Drive by Night '40
Virginia City '40
The Westerner '40
Dodge City '39
Golden Boy '39
Jesse James '39
Juarez '39
Nancy Drew, Reporter '39
Young Mr. Lincoln '39
I Am the Law '38
Mad Miss Manton '38
Room Service '38
The Saint in New York '38
The Young in Heart '38
Dead End '37
Pick a Star '37
Prisoner of Zenda '37
Come and Get It '36
Dodsworth '36
The Adventurer '17
Mie Hama (1943-)
You Only Live Twice '67
What's Up, Tiger Lily? '66
King Kong vs. Godzilla '63
Veronica Hamel (1945-)
Secrets '94
High Stakes '93
Taking Care of Business '90
A New Life '88
Sessions '83
The Gathering: Part 2 '79
Snowblind '78
The Gathering '77
Cannonball '76
Jayne Hamil
Vice Academy 2 '90
Vice Academy '88
Mark Hamill (1952-)
Jay and Silent Bob Strike Back '01
Laserhawk '99
Watchers Reborn '98
When Time Expires '97
Phantom 2040 Movie: The Ghost Who Walks '95 (V)
Village of the Damned '95
The Raffle '94
Silk Degrees '94
Batman: Mask of the Phantasm '93 (V)
Body Bags '93
Midnight Ride '92
Sleepwalkers '92
Time Runner '92
Black Magic Woman '91
The Guyver '91

Slipstream '89
Return of the Jedi '83
Britannia Hospital '82
The Night the Lights Went Out in Georgia '81
The Big Red One '80
The Empire Strikes Back '80
Corvette Summer '78
Star Wars '77
The City '76
Eric '75
Pete Hamill
The Insider '99
One Fine Day '96
Antony Hamilton (1953-95)
Howling 4: The Original Nightmare '88
Mirrors '85
Samson and Delilah '84
Bernie Hamilton (1929-)
Bucktown '75
Scream Blacula Scream '73
The Losers '70
The Lost Man '69
Captain Sinbad '63
The Young One '61
Carrie Hamilton (1963-2002)
Cool World '92
Shag: The Movie '89
Tokyo Pop '88
Derek Hamilton
Extremedays '01
Out Cold '01
Ripper: Letter from Hell '01
George Hamilton (1939-)
Hollywood Ending '02
P.T. Barnum '99
Rough Riders '97
8 Heads in a Duffel Bag '96
Playback '95
Amore! '93
Once Upon a Crime '92
Doc Hollywood '91
The Godfather, Part 3 '90
Poker Alice '87
Monte Carlo '86
Two Fathers' Justice '85
Zorro, the Gay Blade '81
Express to Terror '79
From Hell to Victory '79
Love at First Bite '79
The Seekers '79
Sextette '78
Users '78
The Happy Hooker Goes to Washington '77
Killer on Board '77
The Dead Don't Die '75
Once Is Not Enough '75
Medusa '74
Evel Knievel '72
Togetherness '70
Viva Maria! '65
Two Weeks in Another Town '62
Angel Baby '61
By Love Possessed '61
Home from the Hill '60
Where the Boys Are '60
Hale Hamilton (1883-1942)
The Champ '32
Murder at Midnight '31
Susan Lenox: Her Fall and Rise '31
Jane (Veronica Hart) Hamilton (1962-)
Beauty School '93
Bloodsucking Pharoahs of Pittsburgh '90
Wildest Dreams '90
Bedroom Eyes 2 '89
Cleo/Leo '89
Deranged '87
New York's Finest '87
Slammer Girls '87
John Hamilton (1886-1958)
Outcasts of the City '58
On the Waterfront '54

Bandit King of Texas '49
I Killed That Man '42
Phantom Killer '42
The Fatal Hour '40
The Saint's Double Trouble '40
Josh Hamilton (1968-)
Urbania '00
Blowin' Smoke '99
The '60s '99
The House of Yes '97
Don't Look Back '96
The Proprietor '96
Kicking and Screaming '95
With Honors '94
Alive '93
O Pioneers! '91
Judd Hamilton
Fanatic '82
Star Crash '78
Gun Crazy '69
Linda Hamilton (1956-)
A Girl Thing '01
Sex & Mrs. X '00
Skeletons in the Closet '00
The Secret Life of Girls '99
The Color of Courage '98
Rescuers: Stories of Courage—Two Couples '98
Dante's Peak '97
The Shadow Conspiracy '96
A Mother's Prayer '95
Separate Lives '94
Silent Fall '94
Terminator 2: Judgment Day '91
Mr. Destiny '90
Black Moon Rising '86
King Kong Lives '86
Secret Weapons '85
Children of the Corn '84
The Stone Boy '84
The Terminator '84
Tag: The Assassination Game '82
Rape and Marriage: The Rideout Case '80
Lisa Gay Hamilton (1964-)
Hamlet '01
A House Divided '00
True Crime '99
Beloved '98
Jackie Brown '97
Drunks '96
Last Breath '96
Nick and Jane '96
Palookaville '95
Mahlon Hamilton (1880-1960)
Peg o' My Heart '22
Daddy Long Legs '19
Margaret Hamilton (1902-85)
The Night Strangler '72
The Anderson Tapes '71
Brewster McCloud '70
13 Ghosts '60
Comin' Round the Mountain '51
People Will Talk '51
Riding High '50
The Red Pony '49
The Sin of Harold Diddlebock '47
George White's Scandals '45
Guest in the House '44
City Without Men '43
Twin Beds '42
The Invisible Woman '40
My Little Chickadee '40
The Wizard of Oz '39
The Adventures of Tom Sawyer '38
Breaking the Ice '38
Nothing Sacred '37
You Only Live Once '37
The Moon's Our Home '36
These Three '36
Broadway Bill '34

Murray Hamilton (1923-86)
The Last Days of Patton '86
Too Scared to Scream '85
Mazes and Monsters '82
Brubaker '80
The Amityville Horror '79
Last Cry for Help '79
1941 '79
Casey's Shadow '78
Jaws 2 '78
The Drowning Pool '75
Jaws '75
The Way We Were '73
The Tattered Web '71
If It's Tuesday, This Must Be Belgium '69
The Boston Strangler '68
The Brotherhood '68
No Way to Treat a Lady '68
Sergeant Ryker '68
The Graduate '67
Seconds '66
Papa's Delicate Condition '63
The Hustler '61
Anatomy of a Murder '59
The FBI Story '59
Darby's Rangers '58
Houseboat '58
No Time for Sergeants '58
Spirit of St. Louis '57
Neil Hamilton (1899-1984)
Batman '66
The Patsy '64
The Devil's Hand '61
X Marks the Spot '42
King of the Texas Rangers '41
The Saint Strikes Back '39
Hollywood Stadium Mystery '38
Tarzan and His Mate '34
The Animal Kingdom '32
Tarzan, the Ape Man '32
What Price Hollywood? '32
Laughing Sinners '31
The Sin of Madelon Claudet '31
America '24
Isn't Life Wonderful '24
The White Rose '23
Patricia Hamilton
Anne of Green Gables: The Continuing Story '99
Holiday Affair '96
The Christmas Wife '88
Anne of Avonlea '87
Anne of Green Gables '85
Richard Hamilton (1920-)
Message in a Bottle '98
Reach the Rock '98
Sommersby '93
In Country '89
Greetings '68
Suzanna Hamilton (1960-)
Duel of Hearts '92
Tale of a Vampire '92
Out of Africa '85
Wetherby '85
1984 '84
Brimstone & Treacle '82
Tony Hamilton
Fatal Instinct '92
Nocturna '79
Victoria Hamilton
Victoria & Albert '01
Mansfield Park '99
King Lear '98
Persuasion '95
Wendy Hamilton
The Dallas Connection '94
Ski School 2 '94
The Scars of Dracula '70
Harry Hamlin (1951-)
Perfume '01
Silent Predators '99
Frogs for Snakes '98
The Hunted '98
Ebbtide '94
Murder So Sweet '93
Save Me '93
Under Investigation '93
Take Down '92

Deceptions '90
Dinner at Eight '89
Laguna Heat '87
Target: Favorite Son '87
L.A. Law '86
Maxie '85
Blue Skies Again '83
Making Love '82
Clash of the Titans '81
King of the Mountain '81
Movie, Movie '78
Warren Hammack
Mars Needs Women '66
Zontar, the Thing from Venus '66
The Eye Creatures '65
Hammer (1962-)
One Man's Justice '95
Last Action Hero '93
Alvin Hammer
Command Decision '48
A Walk in the Sun '46
Ben Hammer (1925-)
Crazy People '90
Survival Quest '89
Beastmaster '82
The Execution of Private Slovik '74
Invasion of the Bee Girls '73
Johnny Got His Gun '71
John Hammil
Phantoms '97
Young Guns 2 '90
Crossover Dreams '85
Brandon Hammond
Soul Food '97
Tales from the Hood '95
Darrell Hammond
The King and I '99 (V)
Blues Brothers 2000 '98
John Hammond
The Prodigal '83
The Blue and the Gray '82
Enforcer from Death Row '78
Kay Hammond
Blithe Spirit '45
Abraham Lincoln '30
Nicholas Hammond (1950-)
Trouble in Paradise '88
The Martian Chronicles: Part 1 '79
The Martian Chronicles: Part 3 '79
Chinese Web '78
Spiderman: The Deadly Dust '78
The Amazing Spider-Man '77
The Sound of Music '65
Roger Hammond
Lady Chatterley '92
A Dangerous Man: Lawrence after Arabia '91
Olivia Hamnett
The Ripper '97
Deadly Possession '88
Earthling '80
The Last Wave '77
Plunge Into Darkness '77
Walter Hampden (1879-1955)
The Prodigal '55
Sabrina '54
Five Fingers '52
The Adventures of Mark Twain '44
Reap the Wild Wind '42
They Died with Their Boots On '41
The Hunchback of Notre Dame '39
Emily Hampshire
The Happy Face Murders '99
Eye '96
Susan Hampshire (1938-)
Coming Home '98
The Story of David '76
Cry Terror '74
Baffled '72
Living Free '72

David Copperfield '70
Those Daring Young Men in Their Jaunty Jalopies '69
Vanity Fair '67
The Fighting Prince of Donegal '66
The Three Lives of Thomasina '63

James Hampton (1936-)
Sling Blade '96
World War III '86
Teen Wolf '85
Bunco '83
Condorman '81
Hangar 18 '80
The China Syndrome '79
The Amazing Howard Hughes '77
Hawmps! '76
Force Five '75
The Longest Yard '74

Lionel Hampton
Force of Impulse '60
The Benny Goodman Story '55

Paul Hampton
Deadly Exposure '93
They Came from Within '75
Hit! '73
Lady Sings the Blues '72
Private Duty Nurses '71

Maggie Han
Open Season '95
The Last Emperor '87

Master Bong Soo Han
Force: Five '81
Kill the Golden Goose '79

Herbie Hancock
Indecent Proposal '93
Round Midnight '86

John Hancock (1939-)
Why Me? '90
Traxx '87
In the Custody of Strangers '82
Archer: The Fugitive from the Empire '81
The Black Marble '79

Lou Hancock
Miracle Mile '89
Evil Dead 2: Dead by Dawn '87

Sheila Hancock (1933-)
Love and Death on Long Island '97
The Buccaneers '95
A Business Affair '93
Three Men and a Little Lady '90
Hawks '89
Buster '88
The Anniversary '68

Irene Handl (1901-87)
Secrets and Lies '95
Adventures of a Private Eye '87
Riding High '78
The Private Life of Sherlock Holmes '70
Wonderwall: The Movie '69
Smashing Time '67
Morgan: A Suitable Case for Treatment '66
Small Hotel '57
The Belles of St. Trinian's '53
Brief Encounter '46
Night Train to Munich '40

Evan Handler (1961-)
Harvest '99
Ransom '96
Sweet Lorraine '87
Ruby's Dream '82

James Handy
15 Minutes '01
Unbreakable '00
K-911 '99
Time Served '99
Gang Related '96
Rave Review '95
The O.J. Simpson Story '94
False Arrest '92
The Rocketeer '91
Arachnophobia '90
K-9 '89
The Preppie Murder '89
Bird '88
Burglar '87
The Verdict '82

Anne Haney (1934-2001)
Psycho '98
The Lesser Evil '97
Midnight in the Garden of Good and Evil '97
Changing Habits '96
Liar Liar '96
The Bad Seed '85

Daryl Haney (1963-)
Concealed Weapon '94
Lords of the Deep '89
Daddy's Boys '87

Helen Hanft
Used People '92
Stardust Memories '80

Roger Hanin (1925-)
Day of Atonement '93
My Other Husband '85
Rocco and His Brothers '60
Sois Belle et Tais-Toi '58

Larry Hankin (1945-)
Money Talks '97
Billy Madison '94
Prehysteria 2 '94
Out on a Limb '92
Black Magic Woman '91
Armed and Dangerous '86

Colin Hanks (1977-)
Orange County '02
Band of Brothers '01
Get Over It! '01
Whatever It Takes '00
That Thing You Do! '96

Jim Hanks
Xtro 3: Watch the Skies '95
Buford's Beach Bunnies '92

Tom Hanks (1956-)
Road to Perdition '02
Cast Away '00
The Green Mile '99
Toy Story 2 '99 (V)
Saving Private Ryan '98
You've Got Mail '98
That Thing You Do! '96
Apollo 13 '95
Toy Story '95 (V)
Forrest Gump '94
Fallen Angels 2 '93
Philadelphia '93
Sleepless in Seattle '93
A League of Their Own '92
Radio Flyer '92 (N)
The Bonfire of the Vanities '90
Joe Versus the Volcano '90
The 'Burbs '89
Turner and Hooch '89
Big '88
Punchline '88
Dragnet '87
Every Time We Say Goodbye '86
The Money Pit '86
Nothing in Common '86
The Man with One Red Shoe '85
Volunteers '85
Bachelor Party '84
Splash '84
Mazes and Monsters '82
He Knows You're Alone '80

Jenny Hanley (1947-)
Flesh and Blood Show '73
The Scars of Dracula '70
On Her Majesty's Secret Service '69

Jimmy Hanley (1918-70)
The Blue Lamp '49
Room to Let '49
Captive Heart '47
Immortal Battalion '44
Salute John Citizen '42
Gaslight '40
Housemaster '38

Adam Hann-Byrd
Halloween: H20 '98
The Ice Storm '97
Diabolique '96
Jumanji '95
Digger '94
Little Man Tate '91

Daryl Hannah (1960-)
A Walk to Remember '02
Hard Cash '01
Jack and the Beanstalk: The Real Story '01
Jackpot '01
Dancing at the Blue Iguana '00
Hide and Seek '00
Diplomatic Siege '99
Speedway Junky '99
Wildflowers '99
Hi-Life '98
My Favorite Martian '98
Rear Window '98
The Gingerbread Man '97
The Last Don '97
The Real Blonde '97
The Last Days of Frankie the Fly '96
Two Much '96
Grumpier Old Men '95
The Tie That Binds '95
The Little Rascals '94
Attack of the 50 Ft. Woman '93
Grumpy Old Men '93
Memoirs of an Invisible Man '92
At Play in the Fields of the Lord '91
Crazy People '90
Crimes & Misdemeanors '89
Steel Magnolias '89
High Spirits '88
Roxanne '87
Wall Street '87
The Clan of the Cave Bear '86
Legal Eagles '86
The Pope of Greenwich Village '84
Reckless '84
Splash '84
The Final Terror '83
Blade Runner '82
Summer Lovers '82
Hard Country '81
The Fury '78

John Hannah (1962-)
The Mummy Returns '01
Circus '00
Pandaemonium '00
The Hurricane '99
The Mummy '99
The Love Bug '97
Resurrection Man '97
Sliding Doors '97
The Final Cut '96
The Innocent Sleep '95
Madagascar Skin '95
Four Weddings and a Funeral '94

Page Hannah (1964-)
Shag: The Movie '89
Creepshow 2 '87
My Man Adam '86
Racing with the Moon '84

Alyson Hannigan (1974-)
American Pie 2 '01
Boys and Girls '00
American Pie '99
Dead Man on Campus '97
My Stepmother Is an Alien '88

Donna Hanover
Series 7: The Contenders '01
Just the Ticket '98
The People vs. Larry Flynt '96

Lawrence Hanray (1874-1947)
On Approval '44
Mimi '35
The Private Life of Henry VIII '33

Gale Hansen (1969-)
Double Vision '92
Shaking the Tree '92
The Finest Hour '91
Dead Poets Society '89
The Deadly and the Beautiful '73

Gunnar Hansen (1947-)
Hellblock 13 '97
Freakshow '95
Mosquito '95
Hollywood Chainsaw Hookers '88
The Demon Lover '77
The Texas Chainsaw Massacre '74

Heidi Hansen
Superbug Super Agent '76
Fanny Hill: Memoirs of a Woman of Pleasure '64

Holger Juul Hansen
The Kingdom 2 '97
The Kingdom '95

Joachim Hansen (1931-)
Anne of Green Gables '85
Frozen Alive '64
Secret of the Black Trunk '62

Patti Hansen
Hard to Hold '84
They All Laughed '81

Paul Hansen
The Return of Count Yorga '71
Count Yorga, Vampire '70

Valda Hansen
Wham-Bam, Thank You Spaceman '75
Cain's Cutthroats '71
Night of the Ghouls '59

William Hansen
Homebodies '74
Willard '71
The Member of the Wedding '52

Dave Hanson
Slap Shot 2: Breaking the Ice '02
Slap Shot '77

Lars Hanson (1886-1965)
Walpurgis Night '41
The Informer '29
Homecoming '28
The Wind '28
The Flesh and the Devil '27
The Atonement of Gosta Berling '24

Peter Hanson
Cavalry Charge '51
When Worlds Collide '51

Setsuko Hara (1920-)
Tokyo Story '53
Early Summer '51
The Idiot '51
Late Spring '49
No Regrets for Our Youth '46

Kinako Harada
Godzilla vs. King Ghidora '91
Days of Hell '84

Meiko Harada (1958-)
Akira Kurosawa's Dreams '90
Ran '85
Nomugi Pass '79

Haya Harareet (1931-)
The Interns '62
Journey Beneath the Desert '61
Ben-Hur '59
Hill 24 Doesn't Answer '55

Clement Harari
Train of Life '98
Flight of the Eagle '82
The Fiendish Plot of Dr. Fu Manchu '80
Monkeys, Go Home! '66

Matthew Harbour
The Witness Files '00
Time at the Top '99

James Harcourt (1873-1951)
The Hidden Room '49
The Avenging Hand '43
Night Train to Munich '40
I Met a Murderer '39

Diana Hardcastle
Catherine Cookson's The Tide of Life '96
Fortunes of War '87

Ernest Harden (1952-)
White Men Can't Jump '92
The Final Terror '83
White Mama '80

Marcia Gay Harden (1959-)
Pollock '00
Space Cowboys '00
Small Vices: A Spenser Mystery '99
Desperate Measures '98
Meet Joe Black '98
Curtain Call '97
Flubber '97
Path to Paradise '97
The Daytrippers '96
Far Harbor '96
The First Wives Club '96
Spy Hard '96
Convict Cowboy '95
The Spitfire Grill '95
Safe Passage '94
Crush '93
Sinatra '92
Used People '92
Fever '91
Late for Dinner '91
Miller's Crossing '90

Crofton Hardester
Devastator '85
Android '82

Kate Hardie (1969-)
Heart '99
Croupier '97
The Krays '90
Conspiracy '89
Mona Lisa '86

Jerry Hardin (1929-)
The Firm '93
The Hot Spot '90
Blaze '89
Wanted Dead or Alive '86
Cujo '83
Wolf Lake '79

Melora Hardin (1967-)
Seven Girlfriends '00
Absolute Power '97
Chameleon '95
Reckless Kelly '93
The Rocketeer '91
Big Man on Campus '89
Dead Poets Society '89
Lambada '89
Iron Eagle '86
The North Avenue Irregulars '79

Ty Hardin (1930-)
Bad Jim '89
Rooster: Spurs of Death! '83
You're Jinxed, Friend, You've Met Sacramento '70
One Step to Hell '68
Berserk! '67
Battle of the Bulge '65
Palm Springs Weekend '63
PT 109 '63
Merrill's Marauders '62
I Married a Monster from Outer Space '58

Ann Harding (1901-81)
The Man in the Gray Flannel Suit '56
Promise to Murder '56
The Magnificent Yankee '50
Two Weeks with Love '50
Love from a Stranger '37
The Animal Kingdom '32
Devotion '31

John Harding
The Impossible Years '68
This Property Is Condemned '66

Kay Harding
The Mummy's Curse '44
Scarlet Claw '44

Lyn Harding (1876-1952)
The Mutiny of the Elsinore '39
Murder at the Baskervilles '37
The Man Who Lived Again '36
Old Spanish Custom '36
The Speckled Band '31

Kadeem Hardison (1965-)
Showtime '02
Dancing in September '00
Blind Faith '98
The Sixth Man '97
Drive '96
Panther '95
Vampire in Brooklyn '95
Renaissance Man '94
Dream Date '93
Gunmen '93
White Men Can't Jump '92
Def by Temptation '90
I'm Gonna Git You Sucka '88
School Daze '88
Beat Street '84

Derek Hardwick
Among the Cinders '83
Carry Me Back '82

Cedric Hardwicke (1883-1964)
The Pumpkin Eater '64
Five Weeks in a Balloon '62
The Magic Fountain '61
Around the World in 80 Days '56
Helen of Troy '56
The Ten Commandments '56
Diane '55
Richard III '55
Botany Bay '53
Salome '53
The War of the Worlds '53 (V)
The Green Glove '52
The Desert Fox '51
The White Tower '50
A Connecticut Yankee in King Arthur's Court '49
I Remember Mama '48
Rope '48
The Winslow Boy '48
Lured '47
Tycoon '47
Beware of Pity '46
Nicholas Nickleby '46
The Keys of the Kingdom '44
Wilson '44
A Wing and a Prayer '44
Commandos Strike at Dawn '43
The Ghost of Frankenstein '42
Invisible Agent '42
Valley of the Sun '42
Sundown '41
Suspicion '41
The Howards of Virginia '40
The Invisible Man Returns '40
Tom Brown's School Days '40
The Hunchback of Notre Dame '39
On Borrowed Time '39
Stanley and Livingstone '39
King Solomon's Mines '37
Nine Days a Queen '36
Things to Come '36
Becky Sharp '35
Les Miserables '35
The Ghoul '34
Power '34

Edward Hardwicke (1932-)
The Alchemists '99
Appetite '98
Elizabeth '98
Photographing Fairies '97
Hollow Reed '95
The Scarlet Letter '95
Shadowlands '93

Jonathan Hardy
The Wacky World of Wills & Burke '85
Lonely Hearts '82
The Devil's Playground '76

Oliver Hardy (1892-1957)
Days of Thrills and Laughter '61
Utopia '51
Riding High '50
The Fighting Kentuckian '49
Bullfighters '45
Nothing But Trouble '44
Air Raid Wardens '43
Great Guns '41
A Chump at Oxford '40
Saps at Sea '40
The Flying Deuces '39
Block-heads '38
Swiss Miss '38
Pick a Star '37
Way Out West '37
Bohemian Girl '36
Our Relations '36
Bonnie Scotland '35
Hollywood Party '34
March of the Wooden Soldiers '34
The Devil's Brother '33
Laurel & Hardy and the Family '33
Laurel & Hardy: Stan "Helps" Ollie '33
Sons of the Desert '33
Laurel & Hardy: At Work '32
Pack Up Your Troubles '32
Laurel & Hardy: Be Big '31
Laurel & Hardy: Chickens Come Home '31
Laurel & Hardy: Laughing Gravy '31
Pardon Us '31
Laurel & Hardy: Another Fine Mess '30
Laurel & Hardy: Below Zero '30
Laurel & Hardy: Blotto '30
Laurel & Hardy: Brats '30
Laurel & Hardy: Hog Wild '30
Laurel & Hardy: Night Owls '30
Laurel & Hardy On the Lam '30
Laurel & Hardy: Berth Marks '29
Laurel & Hardy: Men O'War '29
Laurel & Hardy: Perfect Day '29
No Man's Law '27
The Wizard of Oz '25
Three Ages '23

Robert Hardy (1925-)
The 10th Kingdom '00
Mrs. Dalloway '97
Gulliver's Travels '95
Sense and Sensibility '95
Mary Shelley's Frankenstein '94
Middlemarch '93
War & Remembrance: The Final Chapter '89
War & Remembrance '88
The Woman He Loved '88
Northanger Abbey '87
Jenny's War '85
The Shooting Party '85
Edward the King '75
Dark Places '73
Demons of the Mind '72
Elizabeth R '72

Sam Hardy (1883-1935)
Break of Hearts '35
Powdersmoke Range '35
King Kong '33
The Miracle Woman '31
Big News '29

Sophie Hardy
Erotic Touch of Hot Skin '65
The Mysterious Magician '65

Thomas (Tom) Hardy
Band of Brothers '01
Black Hawk Down '01

Lumsden Hare (1875-1964)
Rose Marie '54
That Forsyte Woman '50
The White Cliffs of Dover '44
Shadows on the Stairs '41
Northwest Passage '40
Gunga Din '39
The Princess Comes Across '36
The Crusades '35
The Lives of a Bengal Lancer '35

Robertson Hare (1891-1979)
The Adventures of Sadie '55
Murder on the Campus '52
Things Happen at Night '48

Mark Harelik
Jurassic Park 3 '01
Election '99
The Swan Princess '94 (V)

Dorian Harewood (1950-)
Glitter '01
The Triangle '01
Hendrix '00
Change of Heart '98
Twelve Angry Men '97
Hank Aaron: Chasing the Dream '95 (N)
Sudden Death '95
Shattered Image '93
Getting Up and Going Home '92
Pacific Heights '90
Kiss Shot '89
God Bless the Child '88
Full Metal Jacket '87
Guilty of Innocence '87
The Falcon and the Snowman '85
Against All Odds '84
The Jesse Owens Story '84
Tank '83
The Ambush Murders '82
Strike Force '81
Beulah Land '80
An American Christmas Carol '79
Roots: The Next Generation '79
Panic in Echo Park '77
Sparkle '76

Mariska Hargitay (1964-)
Perfume '01
Lake Placid '99
Leaving Las Vegas '95
Hotel Room '93
Finish Line '89
Welcome to 18 '87
Ghoulies '84

Mickey Hargitay (1927-)
Lady Frankenstein '72
The Bloody Pit of Horror '65
The Loves of Hercules '60
Will Success Spoil Rock Hunter? '57

Doris Hargrave
Last Night at the Alamo '83
The Hollywood Knights '80
The Whole Shootin' Match '79

Amy Hargreaves
Saint Maybe '98
Brainscan '94

John Hargreaves (1945-96)
Country Life '95
Lust and Revenge '95
Sorrento Beach '95
Cry Freedom '87
Sky Pirates '87
Malcolm '86
Careful, He Might Hear You '84
Great Gold Swindle '84
My First Wife '84
Killing of Angel Street '81
Beyond Reasonable Doubt '80
The Odd Angry Shot '79
Little Boy Lost '78
Deathcheaters '76
Don's Party '76

Gordon Harker (1885-1967)
Small Hotel '57
Things Happen at Night '48
Inspector Hornleigh '39
The Phantom Light '35
Champagne '28
The Farmer's Wife '28
The Ring '27

Susannah Harker (1965-)
Heat of the Sun '99
Ultraviolet '98
Pride and Prejudice '95
The Crucifer of Blood '91
House of Cards '90
A Dry White Season '89
Troubles '88
The Lady's Not for Burning '87

John Harkins (1932-99)
Crime of the Century '96
This Gun for Hire '90
Slaves of New York '89
City Killer '87
Rampage '87
Birdy '84
Amityville 3: The Demon '83
Absence of Malice '81

Kenneth Harlan (1895-1967)
Death Valley Rangers '44
Dawn Express '42
Phantom Killer '42
Santa Fe Marshal '40
The Duke of West Point '38
Law of the Texan '38
A Million to One '37
Renfrew of the Royal Mounted '37
Paradise Island '30
Under Montana Skies '30
The Ice Flood '26
Little Church Around the Corner '23
The Virginian '23
The Penalty '20
The Primitive Lover '16

Otis Harlan (1865-1940)
Mr. Boggs Steps Out '38
Outlaws of Sonora '38
Snow White and the Seven Dwarfs '37 (V)
Western Gold '37
I Can't Escape '34
King Kelly of the U.S.A. '34
Telegraph Trail '33
Ride Him, Cowboy '32
Dames Ahoy '30
Mountain Justice '30

Jean Harlow (1911-37)
The Love Goddesses '65
Personal Property '37
Saratoga '37
Libeled Lady '36
Suzy '36
Wife Versus Secretary '36
China Seas '35
Reckless '35
Riff Raff '35
The Girl from Missouri '34
Bombshell '33
Dinner at Eight '33
Hold Your Man '33
Red Dust '32
Red Headed Woman '32
City Lights '31
Platinum Blonde '31
Public Enemy '31
Hell's Angels '30

Shalom Harlow (1973-)
The Salton Sea '02
Head Over Heels '01
In and Out '97

Deborah Harmon (1951-)
Prince of Bel Air '87
Bachelor Party '84
Used Cars '80

Mark Harmon (1951-)
Crossfire Trail '01
I'll Remember April '99
Fear and Loathing in Las Vegas '98
From the Earth to the Moon '98
Casualties '97
The First to Go '97
The Last Supper '96
Magic in the Water '95
Wyatt Earp '94
Cold Heaven '92
Dillinger '91
Long Road Home '91
Till There Was You '91
Fourth Story '90
Sweet Bird of Youth '89
Worth Winning '89
The Presidio '88
Stealing Home '88
After the Promise '87
Let's Get Harry '87
Prince of Bel Air '87
Summer School '87
The Deliberate Stranger '86
Goliath Awaits '81
Beyond the Poseidon Adventure '79
Centennial '78
Comes a Horseman '78

Renee Harmon
Night of Terror '87
Lady Street Fighter '86
The Executioner, Part 2: Frozen Scream '84

Tom Harmon
The Spirit of West Point '47
Harmon of Michigan '41

Raymond Harmstorf
The Wolves '95
Thunder Warrior '85

Ricci Harnett
A Certain Justice '99
The Object of Beauty '91

Elisabeth Harnois (1979-)
My Date with the President's Daughter '98
One Magic Christmas '85
Where Are the Children? '85

Christina Harnos
Hollywood Confidential '97
Bloodhounds '96
Hellraiser 4: Bloodline '95
Denial: The Dark Side of Passion '91
The Rescue '88

Jamie Harold
The Score '01
Chain of Desire '93
Family Pictures '93

Ralf Harolde (1899-1974)
Behind Locked Doors '48
Baby Face Morgan '42
I Killed That Man '42
The Sea Wolf '41
I'm No Angel '33
Night Nurse '31
Hook, Line and Sinker '30

Frank Harper
Lock, Stock and 2 Smoking Barrels '98
24-7 '97
In the Name of the Father '93

Gerald Harper
If It's a Man, Hang Up '75
The Admirable Crichton '57

Hill Harper (1973-)
The Skulls '00
The Visit '00
In Too Deep '99
Loving Jezebel '99
Slaves of Hollywood '99
He Got Game '98
Mama Flora's Family '98
Hav Plenty '97
The Nephew '97
Steel '97
Get On the Bus '96
Zooman '95

Jessica Harper (1954-)
Safe '95
Mr. Wonderful '93
Big Man on Campus '89
Eat a Bowl of Tea '89
Blue Iguana '88
Imagemaker '86
My Favorite Year '82
Pennies from Heaven '81
Shock Treatment '81
Stardust Memories '80
The Evictors '79
Suspiria '77
Inserts '76
Phantom of the Paradise '74

Kyra Harper
Swann '96
Buffalo Jump '90

Robert Harper (1931-)
Molly '99
The Wrong Man '93
Final Analysis '92
Running Mates '92
Held Hostage '91
Not Quite Human '87

Tess Harper (1950-)
The In Crowd '00
The Jackal '97
The Road to Galveston '96
Children of Fury '94
Christy '94
My New Gun '92
The Turning '92
The Man in the Moon '91
My Heroes Have Always Been Cowboys '91
Daddy's Dyin'...Who's Got the Will? '90
Dark River: A Father's Revenge '90
Criminal Law '89
Far North '88
Her Alibi '88
Ishtar '87
Crimes of the Heart '86
Flashpoint '84
Reckless Disregard '84
A Summer to Remember '84
Amityville 3: The Demon '83
Chiefs '83
Tender Mercies '83

Valerie Harper (1940-)
Drop-Out Mother '88
The Execution '85
Blame It on Rio '84
Don't Go to Sleep '82
The Last Married Couple in America '80
The Shadow Box '80
Chapter Two '79
Night Terror '76
Freebie & the Bean '74
Thursday's Game '74

Cindy Harrel
The Final Terror '83
Model Behavior '82

Jim Harrell
A Family Thing '96
Don't Open the Door! '74

Brett Harrelson
Dee Snider's Strangeland '98
From Dusk Till Dawn 2: Texas Blood Money '98
The People vs. Larry Flynt '96

Woody Harrelson (1962-)
Austin Powers 2: The Spy Who Shagged Me '99
EDtv '99
Play It to the Bone '99
The Hi-Lo Country '98
Palmetto '98
The Thin Red Line '98
Wag the Dog '97
Welcome to Sarajevo '97
Kingpin '96
The People vs. Larry Flynt '96
Sunchaser '96
Money Train '95
The Cowboy Way '94
Natural Born Killers '94
Indecent Proposal '93
Ted & Venus '93
White Men Can't Jump '92
Doc Hollywood '91
Mother Goose Rock 'n' Rhyme '90
Cool Blue '88
Eye of the Demon '87
Wildcats '86

William Harrigan (1894-1966)
Flying Leathernecks '51
Exiled to Shanghai '37
"G" Men '35
The Invisible Man '33

Laura Harring
John Q '02
Mulholland Drive '01
Rio Diablo '93

Cheryl Francis Harrington
Legal Deceit '95
Perfume '91

Desmond Harrington (1976-)
We Were Soldiers '02
My First Mister '01
Riding in Cars with Boys '01
The Messenger: The Story of Joan of Arc '99

Laura Harrington (1958-)
Paulie '98
The Devil's Advocate '97
Dead Air '94
Linda '93
The Secret '93
What's Eating Gilbert Grape '93
Perfect Witness '89
Maximum Overdrive '86

Pat Harrington (1929-)
These Old Broads '01
Ablaze '00
The Affair '73
Easy Come, Easy Go '67
The President's Analyst '67

Barbara Harris (1937-)
Grosse Pointe Blank '97
Dirty Rotten Scoundrels '88
Nice Girls Don't Explode '87
Peggy Sue Got Married '86
The North Avenue Irregulars '79
The Seduction of Joe Tynan '79
Movie, Movie '78
Family Plot '76
Freaky Friday '76
Nashville '75
Plaza Suite '71
Oh Dad, Poor Dad (Momma's Hung You in the Closet & I'm Feeling So Sad) '67
A Thousand Clowns '65

Baxter Harris
Species 2 '98
Home Alone 3 '97
Stephen King's The Langoliers '95

Brad Harris (1933-)
Seven Magnificent Gladiators '84
Hercules '83
Jungle Inferno '70s
Rattler Kid '70s
King of Kong Island '78
The Freakmaker '73
Island of Lost Girls '73
The Mad Butcher '72
Goliath Against the Giants '63
The Fury of Hercules '61
Samson '61

Cynthia Harris
Pancho Barnes '88
Three Men and a Baby '87

Izzy & Moe '85
Reuben, Reuben '83
Edward and Mrs. Simpson '80
Isadora '68

Danielle Harris (1977-)
Killer Bud '00
Urban Legend '98
Back to Back '96
Daylight '96
Wish upon a Star '96
Roseanne: An Unauthorized Biography '94
The Woman Who Loved Elvis '93
The Last Boy Scout '91
Nightmare '91
Marked for Death '90
Halloween 5: The Revenge of Michael Myers '89
Halloween 4: The Return of Michael Myers '88

David Harris
Undercover '87
Badge of the Assassin '85
The Warriors '79
She-Devils on Wheels '68

Ed Harris (1949-)
A Beautiful Mind '01
Enemy at the Gates '00
Pollock '00
The Prime Gig '00
The Third Miracle '99
Stepmom '98
The Truman Show '98
Absolute Power '97
Riders of the Purple Sage '96
The Rock '96
Apollo 13 '95
An Eye for an Eye '95
Nixon '95
Just Cause '94
Milk Money '94
Stephen King's The Stand '94
The Firm '93
Needful Things '93
Glengarry Glen Ross '92
Running Mates '92
China Moon '91
Paris Trout '91
State of Grace '90
The Abyss '89
Jacknife '89
To Kill a Priest '89
The Last Innocent Man '87
Walker '87
Alamo Bay '85
Code Name: Emerald '85
A Flash of Green '85
Sweet Dreams '85
Places in the Heart '84
Swing Shift '84
The Right Stuff '83
Under Fire '83
Creepshow '82
Knightriders '81
Borderline '80
The Seekers '79
Coma '78

Edna Mae Harris (1910-97)
Paradise in Harlem '40
Lying Lips '39

Estelle Harris (1926-)
Good Advice '01
Playing Mona Lisa '00
What's Cooking? '00
Lost and Found '99
Toy Story 2 '99 (V)
Chairman of the Board '97
Downhill Willie '96

Fox Harris (1936-88)
Alienator '89
Dr. Caligari '89
Warlords '88
Repo Man '83

Gail Harris
Cellblock Sisters: Banished Behind Bars '95
Virtual Desire '95

George Harris
Black Hawk Down '01
Soul Survivor '95

Harriet Harris
Memento '00
Nurse Betty '00

Jared Harris (1961-)
Mr. Deeds '02
How to Kill Your Neighbor's Dog '01
Lush '01
Perfume '01
Shadow Magic '00
The Weekend '00
The Eternal '99
The External '99
Happiness '98
Lost in Space '98
B. Monkey '97
Father's Day '96
I Shot Andy Warhol '96
Sunday '96
Blue in the Face '95
Dead Man '95
Nadja '95
Smoke '95
Tall Tale: The Unbelievable Adventures of Pecos Bill '95
The Public Eye '92

Jim Harris
Waitress '81
Squeeze Play '79

Jo Ann Harris
Deadly Games '80
Act of Vengeance '74
The Beguiled '70

Jonathan Harris
Toy Story 2 '99 (V)
A Bug's Life '98 (V)

Julie Harris (1925-)
Bad Manners '98
Ellen Foster '97
Carried Away '95
One Christmas '95
Scarlett '94
Secrets '94
Housesitter '92
The Dark Half '91
The Christmas Wife '88
Gorillas in the Mist '88
The Woman He Loved '88
The Bell Jar '79
America at the Movies '76
The Last of Mrs. Lincoln '76
Voyage of the Damned '76
The Hiding Place '75
Home for the Holidays '72
The People Next Door '70
Reflections in a Golden Eye '67
Harper '66
You're a Big Boy Now '66
Holy Terror '65
The Haunting '63
Requiem for a Heavyweight '62
Victoria Regina '61
A Doll's House '59
Truth about Women '58
I Am a Camera '55
East of Eden '54
The Member of the Wedding '52

Julius W. Harris
Shrunken Heads '94
Murder on the Bayou '91
Prayer of the Rollerboys '91
Crimewave '85
Missing Pieces '83
The Taking of Pelham One Two Three '74
Black Caesar '73
Hell Up in Harlem '73
Live and Let Die '73
Shaft's Big Score '72
Superfly '72
Nothing but a Man '64

Kirk Harris
Hard Luck '01
Loser '97

Lara Harris
Habitat '97
Circuit Breaker '96
The Dogfighters '95
All Tied Up '92
The Fourth War '90
Blood Red '88
No Man's Land '87

Laura Harris (1976-)
The Highway Man '99
The Faculty '98
Just the Ticket '98
Suicide Kings '97

Leigh Anne Harris
I, the Jury '82
Sorceress '82

Lynette Harris
I, the Jury '82
Sorceress '82

Mel Harris (1957-)
Firetrap '01
Out of Time '00
Sonic Impact '99
Sharon's Secret '95
The Pagemaster '94
The Secretary '94
The Spider and the Fly '94
Suture '93
Desperate Motives '92
Raising Cain '92
Scott Turow's The Burden of Proof '92
Cameron's Closet '89
K-9 '89
My Brother's Wife '89
Wanted Dead or Alive '86

Michael (M.K.) Harris
I Love You, Don't Touch Me! '97
Mr. Stitch '95
Dead Air '94
Sleepstalker: The Sandman's Last Rites '94
The Soft Kill '94
Shattered Image '93
Suture '93
The Horseplayer '91
Satan's Princess '90
Slumber Party Massacre 3 '90
Genuine Risk '89
Shriek of the Mutilated '74

Neil Patrick Harris (1973-)
Undercover Brother '02
The Next Best Thing '00
Joan of Arc '99
The Proposition '97
Starship Troopers '97
Animal Room '95
The Man in the Attic '94
My Antonia '94
Snowbound: The Jim and Jennifer Stolpa Story '94
Cold Sassy Tree '89
Clara's Heart '88
Purple People Eater '88

Phil Harris (1906-95)
Rock-a-Doodle '92 (V)
Robin Hood '73 (V)
The Gatling Gun '72
The Aristocats '70 (V)
The Jungle Book '67 (V)
The Patsy '64
The Wheeler Dealers '63
Goodbye, My Lady '56
Here Comes the Groom '51
Dreaming Out Loud '40
Melody Cruise '32

Richard Harris (1932-)
The Count of Monte Cristo '02
Harry Potter and the Sorcerer's Stone '01
Gladiator '00
Grizzly Falls '99
To Walk with Lions '99
The Hunchback '97
Smilla's Sense of Snow '96
This Is the Sea '96
Trojan Eddie '96
Cry, the Beloved Country '95
Savage Hearts '95
Abraham '94
King of the Wind '93
Wrestling Ernest Hemingway '93
Patriot Games '92
Silent Tongue '92
Unforgiven '92
The Field '90
Mack the Knife '89
Game for Vultures '86
Martin's Day '85
Your Ticket Is No Longer Valid '84
Triumphs of a Man Called Horse '83
Tarzan, the Ape Man '81
Highpoint '80
The Last Word '80
Wild Geese '78
Golden Rendezvous '77
Gulliver's Travels '77
Orca '77
The Cassandra Crossing '76
The Return of a Man Called Horse '76
Robin and Marian '76
Juggernaut '74
99 & 44/100 Dead '74
The Deadly Trackers '73
The Hero '71
Man in the Wilderness '71
Cromwell '70
A Man Called Horse '70
Molly Maguires '70
Camelot '67
The Bible '66
Hawaii '66
The Heroes of Telemark '65
Major Dundee '65
The Red Desert '64
This Sporting Life '63
Mutiny on the Bounty '62
The Guns of Navarone '61
The Wreck of the Mary Deare '59

Ricky Harris
Bones '01
Simon Sez '99
Thick as Thieves '99

Robert Harris (1900-95)
Valley of the Dolls '67
Apache Uprising '66
How to Make a Monster '58
The Invisible Boy '57

Robin Harris (1953-90)
Sorority House Massacre 2: Nighty Nightmare '92
Hard to Die '90
House Party '90
Mo' Better Blues '90
I'm Gonna Git You Sucka '88

Rosalind Harris
Mrs. Santa Claus '96
Fiddler on the Roof '71

Rosemary Harris (1930-)
Spider-Man '02
Blow Dry '00
The Gift '00
Sunshine '99
My Life So Far '98
Hamlet '96
Tom & Viv '94
Crossing Delancey '88
Heartbreak House '86
The Ploughman's Lunch '83
To the Lighthouse '83
The Chisholms '79
Beau Brummel '54

Ross Harris
Testament '83
Scream, Baby, Scream '69

Stacy Harris (1918-73)
Bloody Mama '70
The Hunters '58
New Orleans After Dark '58
The Redhead from Wyoming '53

Steve Harris
The Skulls '00
The Mod Squad '99

Ted Harris
Uforia '81
Blacula '72

Wood Harris
Hendrix '00
Remember the Titans '00
Small Vices: A Spenser Mystery '99

Zelda Harris
He Got Game '98
The Baby-Sitters' Club '95
Crooklyn '94
The Piano Lesson '94

Cathryn Harrison (1960-)
Heat of the Sun '99
A Handful of Dust '88
Empire State '87
The Dresser '83
Blue Fire Lady '78

George Harrison (1943-2001)
Shanghai Surprise '86
Water '85
Monty Python's Life of Brian '79
All You Need Is Cash '78
Let It Be '70
Yellow Submarine '68 (V)
Magical Mystery Tour '67
Help! '65
A Hard Day's Night '64

Gregory Harrison (1952-)
First Daughter '99
Running Wild '99
Air Bud 2: Golden Receiver '98
It's My Party '95
Hard Evidence '94
Cadillac Girls '93
Caught in the Act '93
Duplicates '92
Bare Essentials '91
Body Chemistry 2: Voice of a Stranger '91
Dangerous Pursuit '89
North Shore '87
The Hasty Heart '86
Oceans of Fire '86
Seduced '85
Razorback '84
For Ladies Only '81
Enola Gay: The Men, the Mission, the Atomic Bomb '80
Centennial '78
The Gathering '77
Trilogy of Terror '75

Jenilee Harrison (1959-)
Fists of Iron '94
Prime Target '91
Curse 3: Blood Sacrifice '90
Tank '83

Kathleen Harrison (1892-1995)
A Cry from the Streets '57
Cast a Dark Shadow '55
Let's Make Up '55
The Pickwick Papers '54
A Christmas Carol '51
Trio '50
The Winslow Boy '48
The Ghost Train '41
Night Must Fall '37
The Ghoul '34

Linda Harrison (1945-)
Cocoon '85
Beneath the Planet of the Apes '70
Planet of the Apes '68

Lottie Harrison
Driftin' River '46
Lost in a Harem '44

Noel Harrison
Deja Vu '98
Tagget '90

Rex Harrison (1908-90)
Anastasia: The Mystery of Anna '86
Heartbreak House '86
Time to Die '83
Ashanti, Land of No Mercy '79
The Fifth Musketeer '79
Deadly Thief '78
The Prince and the Pauper '78
Doctor Dolittle '67
The Honey Pot '67
The Agony and the Ecstasy '65
My Fair Lady '64
Cleopatra '63
Midnight Lace '60
The Reluctant Debutante '58
King Richard and the Crusaders '54
Main Street to Broadway '53
The Long Dark Hall '51
Unfaithfully Yours '48
The Ghost and Mrs. Muir '47
Anna and the King of Siam '46
I Live in Grosvenor Square '46
Blithe Spirit '45
Major Barbara '41
Night Train to Munich '40
The Citadel '38
Sidewalks of London '38
Men Are Not Gods '37
Storm in a Teacup '37

Richard Harrison (1935-)
Ninja Powerforce '90
Ninja Showdown '90
Ninja Champion '80s
The Channeler '89
Ninja Strike Force '88
Terminal Force '88
Ninja Commandments '87
Ninja Operation: Licensed to Terminate '87
His Name Was King '85
Blood Debts '83
Fireback '78
Thirty-Six Hours of Hell '77
Between God, the Devil & a Winchester '72
Messalina vs. the Son of Hercules '64
Giants of Rome '63
Gun Fight at Red Sands '63
The Invincible Gladiator '63
Gladiators 7 '62
Medusa Against the Son of Hercules '62

Schae Harrison
Interlocked '98
Magic Island '95

David Harrod
The Thin Red Line '98
The House on Todville Road '95
The Tuskegee Airmen '95
Armed for Action '92
Blood on the Badge '92

Jamie Harrold
The Sum of All Fears '02
A Glimpse of Hell '01
I Think I Do '97
I Shot Andy Warhol '96

Kathryn Harrold (1950-)
The '70s '00
The Companion '94
Deadly Desire '91
Rainbow Drive '90
Dead Solid Perfect '88
Someone to Love '87
Raw Deal '86
Into the Night '85
Heartbreakers '84
The Sender '82
Yes, Giorgio '82
Modern Romance '81
The Pursuit of D.B. Cooper '81
Bogie: The Last Hero '80
The Hunter '80
Nightwing '79

John Harron (1903-39)
Midnight Warning '32
The White Zombie '32
The Night Cry '26
West-Bound Limited '23

Robert "Bobbie" Harron (1893-1920)
The Greatest Question '19
True Heart Susie '19
Hearts of the World '18
Hoodoo Ann '16

The Birth of a Nation '15
Home Sweet Home '14
Judith of Bethulia '14

Lisa Harrow (1943-)
Sunday '96
That Eye, the Sky '94
The Last Days of Chez Nous '92
Shaker Run '85
Under Capricorn '82
From a Far Country: Pope John Paul II '81
Omen 3: The Final Conflict '81
All Creatures Great and Small '74

Deborah Harry (1945-)
Deuces Wild '02
The Fluffer '01
Six Ways to Sunday '99
Cop Land '97
Dead Beat '94
Heavy '94
Body Bags '93
Intimate Stranger '91
Mother Goose Rock 'n' Rhyme '90
Tales from the Darkside: The Movie '90
New York Stories '89
Hairspray '88
Satisfaction '88
Forever, Lulu '87
Videodrome '83
Union City '81
Mr. Mike's Mondo Video '79
The Foreigner '78

Ray Harryhausen
Mighty Joe Young '98
Spies Like Us '85

Christina Hart
Helter Skelter '76
Games Girls Play '75
Johnny Firecloud '75
The Runaway Barge '75

Dianne Lee Hart
Pom Pom Girls '76
The Giant Spider Invasion '75

Dolores Hart (1938-)
Where the Boys Are '60
King Creole '58
Lonelyhearts '58
Loving You '57

Ian Hart (1964-)
Harry Potter and the Sorcerer's Stone '01
Aberdeen '00
American Women '00
Born Romantic '00
Liam '00
Longitude '00
The End of the Affair '99
Wonderland '99
Frogs for Snakes '98
Monument Ave. '98
B. Monkey '97
The Butcher Boy '97
Michael Collins '96
The Englishman Who Went up a Hill But Came down a Mountain '95
Hollow Reed '95
Land and Freedom '95
Nothing Personal '95
Backbeat '94
The Hours and Times '92

John Hart
Blackenstein '73
The Fighting Redhead '50

Kevin Hart
Lone Wolf '88
Mindkiller '87

Linda Hart
Crazy in Alabama '99
Tin Cup '96
Gypsy '93
A Perfect World '93

Melissa Joan Hart (1976-)
Backflash '01
Drive Me Crazy '99
Sabrina the Teenage Witch '96

Neal Hart
Trigger Tricks '30
Sands of Sacrifice '21

Pamela Hart
Pi '98
The Young Girls of Rochefort '68

Roxanne Hart (1952-)
Follow the Stars Home '01
The Runaway '00
Horton Foote's Alone '97
Our Mother's Murder '97
Once Around '91
Tagget '90
Vengeance '89
Pulse '88
The Last Innocent Man '87
Highlander '86
Samaritan: The Mitch Snyder Story '86
Oh, God! You Devil '84
Old Enough '84
The Tender Age '84
Special Bulletin '83
The Verdict '82

Susan Hart (1941-)
Dr. Goldfoot and the Bikini Machine '66
Pajama Party '64
Ride the Wild Surf '64
The Slime People '63

Teddy Hart
Mickey One '65
Ma and Pa Kettle at Waikiki '55

William S. Hart (-1946)
Show People '28
Tumbleweeds '25
Three Word Brand '21
The Toll Gate '20
Wagon Tracks '19
Blue Blazes Rawden '18
Narrow Trail '17
Hell's Hinges '16
Return of Draw Egan '16
The Bargain '15
The Disciple '15
The Fugitive: Taking of Luke McVane '15
On the Night Stage '15

Douglas Hartier
Invasion Force '90
White Fury '90

Pat Hartigan
Ranson's Folly '26
King of the Wild Horses '24

Clare Hartley
Trancers 5: Sudden Deth '94
Trancers 4: Jack of Swords '93

Mariette Hartley (1940-)
Encino Man '92
1969 '89
Passion in Paradise '89
Silence of the Heart '84
M.A.D.D.: Mothers Against Drunk Driving '83
Improper Channels '82
O'Hara's Wife '82
No Place to Hide '81
Nightmare at 43 Hillcrest '74
The Return of Count Yorga '71
Marnie '64
Ride the High Country '62

Elizabeth Hartman (1941-87)
The Secret of NIMH '82 (V)
Walking Tall '73
The Beguiled '70
The Fixer '68
The Group '66
You're a Big Boy Now '66
A Patch of Blue '65

Margot Hartman
Voyage to the Planet of Prehistoric Women '68
Curse of the Living Corpse '64

Phil Hartman (1948-98)
Small Soldiers '98
The Second Civil War '97
Jingle All the Way '96
Sgt. Bilko '95
The Crazysitter '94
Greedy '94
Houseguest '94
CB4: The Movie '93
Coneheads '93
Daybreak '93
National Lampoon's Loaded Weapon 1 '93
So I Married an Axe Murderer '93
Quick Change '90
Fletch Lives '89
How I Got into College '89
Amazon Women on the Moon '87
Blind Date '87
Jumpin' Jack Flash '86
Last Resort '86
Three Amigos '86
Pee-wee's Big Adventure '85
Weekend Pass '84
The Pee-wee Herman Show '82
Cheech and Chong's Next Movie '80

Lisa Hartman Black (1956-)
Bare Essentials '91
Red Wind '91
The Return of Eliot Ness '91
The Take '90
Full Exposure: The Sex Tape Scandals '89
The Seventeenth Bride '84
Where the Boys Are '84 '84
Deadly Blessing '81
Just Tell Me You Love Me '80
Magic on Love Island '80

William Hartnell (1908-75)
This Sporting Life '63
The Mouse That Roared '59
Brighton Rock '47
Appointment with Crime '45
Immortal Battalion '44

Josh Hartnett (1978-)
40 Days and 40 Nights '02
Black Hawk Down '01
O '01
Pearl Harbor '01
Town and Country '01
Blow Dry '00
Here on Earth '00
The Virgin Suicides '99
The Faculty '98
Halloween: H20 '98

Rainbow Harvest
Mirror, Mirror '90
Old Enough '84

Alex Harvey
Fire Down Below '97
Gettysburg '93

Don Harvey
Sparkler '99
The Con '98
The Thin Red Line '98
Crime of the Century '96
Last Dance '96
Sawbones '95
Better Off Dead '94
Men of War '94
Tank Girl '94
American Heart '92
Mission of the Shark '91
Prey of the Chameleon '91
Die Hard 2: Die Harder '90
Casualties of War '89
The Beast '88
Eight Men Out '88

Forrester Harvey (1890-1945)
Mrs. Miniver '42
The Wolf Man '41
Thoroughbreds Don't Cry '37
The Eagle and the Hawk '33

Harry Harvey (1901-85)
The Narrow Margin '52
Tea for Two '50
I'm from Arkansas '44
Ridin' the Trail '40
Code of the Fearless '39
In Old Montana '39
King of the Sierras '38
The Reckless Way '36

Harry Harvey, Jr.
King of the Sierras '38
Reefer Madness '38

Laurence Harvey (1928-73)
Escape to the Sun '72
Night Watch '72
The Magic Christian '69
Dandy in Aspic '68
Spy with a Cold Nose '66
Darling '65
Of Human Bondage '64
The Manchurian Candidate '62
Walk on the Wild Side '62
The Wonderful World of the Brothers Grimm '62
Summer and Smoke '61
The Alamo '60
Butterfield 8 '60
Expresso Bongo '59
Room at the Top '59
The Silent Enemy '58
Truth about Women '58
I Am a Camera '55
King Richard and the Crusaders '54
Romeo and Juliet '54
Innocents in Paris '53
Man on the Run '49

Paul Harvey (1882-1955)
Three for the Show '55
April in Paris '52
Riding High '50
The Yellow Cab Man '50
Call Northside 777 '48
A Southern Yankee '48
Helldorado '46
A Night in Casablanca '46
Blondie's Blessed Event '42
Arizona '40
Meet Dr. Christian '39
23 1/2 Hours Leave '37
The Whole Town's Talking '35

Rodney Harvey (1967-98)
Guncrazy '92
My Own Private Idaho '91
Five Corners '88
Salsa '88

Terence Harvey
From Hell '01
The Phantom of the Opera '89

Tom Harvey
Moving Target '96
And Then You Die '88

Verna Harvey
That'll Be the Day '73
The Nightcomers '72

Kazuo Hasegawa (1908-84)
An Actor's Revenge '63
The Crucified Lovers '54
Gate of Hell '54

David Haskell
Body Double '84
Godspell '73

Peter Haskell (1934-)
Robot Wars '93
Child's Play 3 '91
The Cracker Factory '79
Christina '74
Legend of Earl Durand '74
The Ballad of Andy Crocker '69

Susan Haskell
Smart House '00
Mrs. Winterbourne '96

Imogen Hassall
The Bloodsuckers '70
When Dinosaurs Ruled the Earth '70

O.E. Hasse (1903-78)
State of Siege '73
The Elusive Corporal '62
Above Us the Waves '56
Betrayed '54
I Confess '53
The Big Lift '50

Danny Hassel
A Nightmare on Elm Street 5: Dream Child '89
A Nightmare on Elm Street 4: Dream Master '88

David Hasselhoff (1952-)
The Big Tease '99
Baywatch the Movie: Forbidden Paradise '95
Ring of the Musketeers '93
Bail Out '90
The Final Alliance '89
Fire and Rain '89
Witchery '88
Terror at London Bridge '85
Cartier Affair '84
Star Crash '78
Revenge of the Cheerleaders '76

Marilyn Hassett (1947-)
Twenty Dollar Star '91
Messenger of Death '88
Body Count '87
The Bell Jar '79
The Other Side of the Mountain, Part 2 '78
Two Minute Warning '76
The Other Side of the Mountain '75

Signe Hasso (1910-)
A Double Life '47
Where There's Life '47
A Scandal in Paris '46
House on 92nd Street '45
Johnny Angel '45
The Seventh Cross '44
The Story of Dr. Wassell '44
Heaven Can Wait '43
Journey for Margaret '42

Bob Hastings (1925-)
Shadow Force '92
Snowballing '85
The Munsters' Revenge '81
Harper Valley P.T.A. '78
McHale's Navy Joins the Air Force '65
McHale's Navy '64

Richard Hatch (1945-)
Unseen Evil '99
Delta Force Commando 2 '90
Ghetto Blaster '89
Party Line '88
Heated Vengeance '87
Prisoners of the Lost Universe '84
Charlie Chan and the Curse of the Dragon Queen '81
Mission Galactica: The Cylon Attack '79
Battlestar Galactica '78
Deadman's Curve '78
The Hatfields & the McCoys '75

Mary Hatcher
Tales of Robin Hood '52
The Big Wheel '49
Holiday in Havana '49
Variety Girl '47

Teri Hatcher (1964-)
Spy Kids '01
Running Mates '00
Fever '99
Since You've Been Gone '97
Tomorrow Never Dies '97
Two Days in the Valley '96
Heaven's Prisoners '95
Brain Smasher...A Love Story '93
All Tied Up '92
The Cool Surface '92
Straight Talk '92
Dead in the Water '91
Soapdish '91
The Big Picture '89
Tango and Cash '89

Hurd Hatfield (1918-98)
Her Alibi '88
Crimes of the Heart '86
King David '85
The Word '78
Thief '71
The Boston Strangler '68
Lamp at Midnight '66
Mickey One '65
Invincible Mr. Disraeli '63
El Cid '61
The King of Kings '61
Diary of a Chambermaid '46
Picture of Dorian Gray '45
Dragon Seed '44

Amy Hathaway
Smiling Fish & Goat on Fire '99
Joyride '97

Anne Hathaway (1982-)
The Other Side of Heaven '02
The Princess Diaries '01

Noah Hathaway (1971-)
Mortal Danger '94
Troll '86
The NeverEnding Story '84

Shawn Hatosy (1975-)
A Guy Thing '02
John Q '02
Down to You '00
Anywhere But Here '99
Outside Providence '99
Simpatico '99
Witness Protection '99
The Thin Red Line '98
In and Out '97
The Postman '97

Raymond Hatton (1887-1971)
Flesh and the Spur '57
Invasion of the Saucer Men '57
Motorcycle Gang '57
Shake, Rattle and Rock '57
Girls in Prison '56
Day the World Ended '55
Kentucky Jubilee '51
Blazing Guns '50
Guns of Justice '50
Marshal of Heldorado '50
Sudden Death '50
Rolling Home '48
Land of the Lawless '47
Border Bandits '46
Gentleman from Texas '46
Northwest Trail '46
The Stranger from Pecos '45
Lawmen '44
Partners of the Trail '44
Raiders of the Border '44
Range Law '44
Ghost Rider '43
Six Gun Gospel '43
Texas Kid '43
Below the Border '42
Dawn on the Great Divide '42
Down Texas Way '42
Ghost Town Law '42
Reap the Wild Wind '42
Riders of the West '42
West of the Law '42
Arizona Bound '41
Forbidden Trails '41
Gunman from Bodie '41
Covered Wagon Days '40
Rocky Mountain Rangers '40
Cowboys from Texas '39
Frontier Horizon '39
The Kansas Terrors '39
Rough Riders' Roundup '39
Wyoming Outlaw '39
Come on Rangers '38
The Texans '38
Desert Gold '36
The Vigilantes Are Coming '36
Rustlers of Red Dog '35
Buffalo Stampede '33
Hidden Gold '33

Lady Killer '33
Terror Trail '33
The Three Musketeers '33
Cornered '32
The Crooked Circle '32
Drifting Souls '32
Uptown New York '32
Rogue of the Rio Grande '30
The Silver Horde '30
We're in the Navy Now '27
Behind the Front '26
The Fighting American '24
The Virginian '23
Peck's Bad Boy '21
Male and Female '19
The Little American '17

Rondo Hatton (1894-1946)
The Brute Man '46
House of Horrors '46
Jungle Captive '45
The Pearl of Death '44

Didier Haudepin
The Innocent '76
This Special Friendship '67

Rutger Hauer (1944-)
The 10th Kingdom '00
New World Disorder '99
Partners in Crime '99
Tactical Assault '99
Merlin '98
Bleeders '97
Bone Daddy '97
Hostile Waters '97
Jack London's The Call of the Wild '97
Redline '97
Tales from a Parallel Universe: Eating Pattern '97
Blast '96
Crossworlds '96
Omega Doom '96
Precious Find '96
Mr. Stitch '95
Amelia Earhart: The Final Flight '94
Beyond Forgiveness '94
Fatherland '94
Forbidden Choices '94
Surviving the Game '94
Arctic Blue '93
Blind Side '93
Nostradamus '93
Voyage '93
Beyond Justice '92
Buffy the Vampire Slayer '92
Past Midnight '92
Split Second '92
Deadlock '91
Blind Fury '90
The Blood of Heroes '89
Bloodhounds of Broadway '89
Escape from Sobibor '87
The Hitcher '86
Wanted Dead or Alive '86
Flesh and Blood '85
Ladyhawke '85
A Breed Apart '84
Mysteries '84
Fatal Error '83
The Osterman Weekend '83
Blade Runner '82
Inside the Third Reich '82
Chanel Solitaire '81
Eureka! '81
Nighthawks '81
Spetters '80
Soldier of Orange '78
Cold Blood '75
Katie Tippel '75
The Wilby Conspiracy '75
Dandelions '74
Turkish Delight '73

Angelika Hauff (1923-83)
The Life and Loves of Mozart '59
Tromba, the Tiger Man '52
The Marriage of Figaro '49

Ullrich Haupt
Morocco '30
The Iron Mask '29
Captain Swagger '25

Cole Hauser (1975-)
Hart's War '02
Pitch Black '00
Tigerland '00
The Hi-Lo Country '98
Gang Boys '97
Good Will Hunting '97
All Over Me '96
Higher Learning '94
Dazed and Confused '93
School Ties '92

Fay Hauser
Candyman 2: Farewell to the Flesh '94
Jo Jo Dancer, Your Life Is Calling '86
Christmas Lilies of the Field '84
Marvin & Tige '84
Jimmy the Kid '82

Wings Hauser (1948-)
The Insider '99
Gang Boys '97
Tales from the Hood '95
Watchers 3 '94
In Between '92
Mind, Body & Soul '92
Beastmaster 2: Through the Portal of Time '91
Deadly Conspiracy '91
Frame Up '91
Living to Die '91
Pale Blood '91
The Art of Dying '90
Coldfire '90
Exiled in America '90
The Killer's Edge '90
Reason to Die '90
Street Asylum '90
Wilding '90
Bedroom Eyes 2 '89
The Carpenter '89
L.A. Bounty '89
Marked for Murder '89
Out of Sight, Out of Her Mind '89
The Siege of Firebase Gloria '89
Dead Man Walking '88
Hostage '87
Nightmare at Noon '87
No Safe Haven '87
Tough Guys Don't Dance '87
The Wind '87
Jo Jo Dancer, Your Life Is Calling '86
The Long, Hot Summer '86
Code of Honor '84
A Soldier's Story '84
Deadly Force '83
Mutant '83
Homework '82
Vice Squad '82

Richie Havens (1941-)
Perfect Harmony '91
Street Hunter '90
Boss' Son '78

June Haver (1926-)
Love Nest '51
Look for the Silver Lining '49
The Dolly Sisters '46

Phyllis Haver
Battle of the Sexes '28
The Nervous Wreck '26

Nigel Havers (1949-)
Element of Doubt '96
Catherine Cookson's The Glass Virgin '95
The Burning Season '94
Lie Down with Lions '94
Farewell to the King '89
The Charmer '87
Empire of the Sun '87
The Little Princess '87
The Whistle Blower '87
Hold the Dream '86
Burke & Wills '85
A Passage to India '84
Chariots of Fire '81
Who Is Killing the Great Chefs of Europe? '78

Thom Haverstock
Fall from Innocence '88
Skullduggery '79

Allen Havey
Checking Out '89
Love or Money? '88

Alex Havier
They Were Expendable '45
Bataan '43

June Havoc (1916-)
Return to Salem's Lot '87
Gentleman's Agreement '47
Brewster's Millions '45
Timber Queen '44
Hello, Frisco, Hello '43
Sing Your Worries Away '42
Four Jacks and a Jill '41

Robin Hawdon (1939-)
When Dinosaurs Ruled the Earth '70
The Love Factor '69
Zeta One '69
Bedazzled '68

Keeley Hawes (1977-)
Othello '01
Wives and Daughters '01
The Last September '99
The Avengers '98
Our Mutual Friend '98
Retribution '98
The Moonstone '97

Jeremy Hawk (1918-2002)
Lucky Jim '58
Who Done It? '56

Ethan Hawke (1971-)
Tape '01
Training Day '01
Waking Life '01
Hamlet '00
Joe the King '99
Snow Falling on Cedars '99
Gattaca '97
Great Expectations '97
The Newton Boys '97
Before Sunrise '94
Floundering '94
Reality Bites '94
Search and Destroy '94
White Fang 2: The Myth of the White Wolf '94
Alive '93
Rich in Love '93
A Midnight Clear '92
Waterland '92
Mystery Date '91
White Fang '91
Dad '89
Dead Poets Society '89
Explorers '85

John Hawkes
The Perfect Storm '00
I Still Know What You Did Last Summer '98
Playing God '96
Night of the Scarecrow '95
Roadracers '94
Murder Rap '87

John Hawkes
Hardball '01
Sand '00

Terri Hawkes
The Killing Man '94
Watch It '93

Jack Hawkins (1910-73)
Tales That Witness Madness '73
Theatre of Blood '73
Escape to the Sun '72
Restless '72
Young Winston '72
Nicholas and Alexandra '71
Waterloo '71
Lola '69
Those Daring Young Men in Their Jaunty Jalopies '69
Lord Jim '65
Guns at Batasi '64
Zulu '64
Lawrence of Arabia '62
The League of Gentlemen '60
Ben-Hur '59
The Bridge on the River Kwai '57
The Third Key '57
Land of Fury '55
Land of the Pharaohs '55
The Prisoner '55
Angels One Five '54
The Cruel Sea '53
Malta Story '53
Mandy '53
The Adventurers '51
No Highway in the Sky '51
The Elusive Pimpernel '50
The Fallen Idol '49
The Small Back Room '49
Bonnie Prince Charlie '48
Phantom Fiend '35
A Shot in the Dark '33

Jimmy Hawkins
Zotz! '62
Private Hell 36 '54

Screamin' Jay Hawkins (1929-2000)
Dance with the Devil '97
A Rage in Harlem '91
Mystery Train '89
Two Moon Junction '88

Monte Hawley
Look Out Sister '48
Miracle in Harlem '48
Tall, Tan and Terrific '46
Gang War '40
Mystery in Swing '40
Double Deal '39

Richard Hawley
Jane Eyre '97
Captives '94
Paper Marriage '93

Wanda (Petit) Hawley (1895-1963)
American Pluck '25
Smouldering Fires '25
Affairs of Anatol '21

Goldie Hawn (1945-)
Town and Country '01
The Out-of-Towners '99
Everyone Says I Love You '96
The First Wives Club '96
Crisscross '92
Death Becomes Her '92
Housesitter '92
Deceived '91
Bird on a Wire '90
Overboard '87
Wildcats '86
Protocol '84
Swing Shift '84
Best Friends '82
Lovers and Liars '81
Private Benjamin '80
Seems Like Old Times '80
Foul Play '78
The Duchess and the Dirtwater Fox '76
Shampoo '75
The Girl from Petrovka '74
The Sugarland Express '74
Butterflies Are Free '72
Dollars '71
There's a Girl in My Soup '70
Cactus Flower '69
The One and Only, Genuine, Original Family Band '68

Jill Haworth (1945-)
The Freakmaker '73
Tower of Evil '72
The Ballad of Andy Crocker '69
In Harm's Way '65
Exodus '60

Nigel Hawthorne (1929-2001)
Call Me Claus '01
Victoria & Albert '01
The Big Brass Ring '99
Tarzan '99 (V)
Madeline '98
The Object of My Affection '98
Uncorked '98
The Winslow Boy '98
Amistad '97
Murder in Mind '97
Inside '96
Twelfth Night '96
Richard III '95
The Madness of King George '94
Demolition Man '93
Freddie the Frog '92 (V)
Tartuffe '90
The Black Cauldron '85 (V)
Jenny's War '85
Mapp & Lucia '85
Pope John Paul II '84
Firefox '82
S*P*Y*S '74

Charles Hawtrey (1914-88)
Carry On at Your Convenience '71
Carry On Camping '71
Carry On Henry VIII '71
Zeta One '69
The Terrornauts '67
Carry On Cowboy '66
Carry On Screaming '66
Carry On Cleo '65
Room to Let '49
A Canterbury Tale '44
Sabotage '36

Alexandra Hay (1944-93)
How Come Nobody's On Our Side? '73
The Love Machine '71

Christian Hay
Autopsy '70s
You're Jinxed, Friend, You've Met Sacramento '70

Colin Hay
Heaven's Burning '97
Cosi '95

Sessue Hayakawa (1889-1973)
Hell to Eternity '60
The Swiss Family Robinson '60
Green Mansions '59
The Geisha Boy '58
The Bridge on the River Kwai '57
Three Came Home '50
Tokyo Joe '49
Daughter of the Dragon '31
The Tong Man '19
The Cheat '15

Marc Hayashi
The Laserman '90
White of the Eye '88
Chan Is Missing '82

Harry Hayden (1884-1955)
Double Dynamite '51
Gun Crazy '49
Merton of the Movies '47
The Rains Came '39

Linda Hayden (1953-)
The Barcelona Kill '77
The House on Straw Hill '76
Madhouse '74
The Blood on Satan's Claw '71
Taste the Blood of Dracula '70
Baby Love '69

Russell Hayden (1912-81)
Apache Chief '50
Blazing Guns '50
Guns of Justice '50
Last Bullet '50
Marshal of Heldorado '50
Outlaw Fury '50
Rangeland Empire '50
Sudden Death '50
Rolling Home '48
Trail of the Mounties '47
Where the North Begins '47
'Neath Canadian Skies '46
North of the Border '46
Lost City of the Jungle '45
Gambler's Choice '44
Frontier Law '43
Border Vigilantes '41
Doomed Caravan '41
In Old Colorado '41
Knights of the Range '40
The Light of Western Stars '40
Santa Fe Marshal '40
The Showdown '40
Hopalong Cassidy: Renegade Trail '39
Law of the Pampas '39
Renegade Trail '39
The Frontiersmen '38
The Mysterious Rider '38

Sterling Hayden (1916-86)
The Blue and the Gray '82
Deadly Strangers '82
Venom '82
Gas '81
The Godfather 1902-1959: The Complete Epic '81
9 to 5 '80
Winter Kills '79
King of the Gypsies '78
1900 '76
The Final Programme '73
The Long Goodbye '73
The Godfather '72
Cobra '71
Spaghetti Western '69
Dr. Strangelove, or: How I Learned to Stop Worrying and Love the Bomb '64
Terror in a Texas Town '58
Crime of Passion '57
The Killing '56
The Last Command '55
Shotgun '55
Prince Valiant '54
Suddenly '54
Fighter Attack '53
Johnny Guitar '53
Kansas Pacific '53
Flat Top '52
The Denver & Rio Grande '51
The Asphalt Jungle '50
Bahama Passage '42

Richard Haydn (1905-85)
Young Frankenstein '74
Clarence, the Cross-eyed Lion '65
The Sound of Music '65
Mutiny on the Bounty '62
Please Don't Eat the Daisies '60
Jupiter's Darling '55
Never Let Me Go '53
The Merry Widow '52
Pride of St. Louis '52
Emperor Waltz '48
Forever Amber '47
Singapore '47
Adventure '45

Julie Haydon (1910-94)
It's Pat: The Movie '94
Come on Danger! '32

Helen Haye (1874-1957)
Man of Evil '48
The Case of the Frightened Lady '39
Spy in Black '39
Sidewalks of London '38
The 39 Steps '35
Skin Game '31

Salma Hayek (1966-)
In the Time of the Butterflies '01
Time Code '00
Traffic '00
Dogma '99
Wild Wild West '99
The Faculty '98
54 '98
The Velocity of Gary '98
Breaking Up '97
Fools Rush In '97
The Hunchback '97
Fled '96
Desperado '95
Fair Game '95
Four Rooms '95
From Dusk Till Dawn '95
Midaq Alley '95
Mi Vida Loca '94
Roadracers '94

Jeff Hayenga
The Unborn '91
Prince of Pennsylvania '88

Allan Hayes
Neon Maniacs '86
Sam's Son '84

Allison Hayes (1930-77)
The Crawling Hand '63
Attack of the 50 Foot Woman '58
The Undead '57
The Unearthly '57
Zombies of Moratau '57
The Gunslinger '56
Francis Joins the WACs '54

Bernadene Hayes (1903-87)
Santa Fe Marshal '40
Heroes in Blue '39
Sweetheart of the Navy '37

Billie Hayes
Pufnstuf '70
Li'l Abner '59

George "Gabby" Hayes (1885-1969)
The Cariboo Trail '50
Return of the Bad Men '48
Home in Oklahoma '47
Lights of Old Santa Fe '47
Trail Street '47
Badman's Territory '46
Great Expectations '46
Helldorado '46
My Pal Trigger '46
Rainbow over Texas '46
Roll on Texas Moon '46
Song of Arizona '46
Under Nevada Skies '46
Along the Navaho Trail '45
Bells of Rosarita '45
Don't Fence Me In '45
Sunset in El Dorado '45
Utah '45
Tall in the Saddle '44
Bordertown Gunfighters '43
Calling Wild Bill Elliott '43
Death Valley Manhunt '43
Man from Thunder River '43
War of the Wildcats '43
Heart of the Golden West '42
Man from Cheyenne '42
Ridin' Down the Canyon '42
Romance on the Range '42
Sons of the Pioneers '42
South of Santa Fe '42
Sunset on the Desert '42
Sunset Serenade '42
Bad Man of Deadwood '41
In Old Cheyenne '41
Jesse James at Bay '41
Red River Valley '41
Robin Hood of the Pecos '41
The Border Legion '40
Carson City Kid '40
Colorado '40
Dark Command '40
Melody Ranch '40
Ranger and the Lady '40
Wagon's Westward '40
Young Bill Hickok '40
Young Buffalo Bill '40
Arizona Kid '39
Days of Jesse James '39
Hopalong Cassidy: Renegade Trail '39
In Old Caliente '39
Renegade Trail '39
Saga of Death Valley '39
Southward Ho! '39
Billy the Kid Returns '38
Come on Rangers '38
The Frontiersmen '38
The Plainsman '37
Rustler's Valley '37
Hopalong Cassidy Returns '36
The Lawless Nineties '36
Smokey Smith '36
Song of the Trail '36
The Texas Rangers '36
Hopalong Cassidy '35
Lawless Frontier '35
Texas Terror '35
The Throwback '35
Beggars in Ermine '34
Blue Steel '34
Brand of Hate '34
House of Mystery '34
In Old Santa Fe '34
The Lost City '34
Lucky Texan '34
The Man from Hell '34
Man from Utah '34
Monte Carlo Nights '34
Mystery Liner '34
'Neath the Arizona Skies '34
Randy Rides Alone '34
The Return of Casey Jones '34
The Star Packer '34
Breed of the Border '33
Fighting Champ '33
The Gallant Fool '33
Galloping Romeo '33
The Outlaw Tamer '33
The Phantom Broadcast '33
Riders of Destiny '33
The Sphinx '33
West of the Divide '33
Boiling Point '32
Border Devils '32
Broadway to Cheyenne '32
Man from Hell's Edges '32
Night Rider '32
Texas Buddies '32
Without Honors '32
Cavalier of the West '31

Gloria Hayes
Judgment Day '88
Witchboard '87

Grace Hayes
Zis Boom Bah '42
Rainbow over Broadway '33

Helen Hayes (1900-93)
Candleshoe '78
Family Upside Down '78
One of Our Dinosaurs Is Missing '75
Herbie Rides Again '74
Airport '70
Third Man on the Mountain '59
Anastasia '56
Main Street to Broadway '53
Stage Door Canteen '43
Arrowsmith '32
A Farewell to Arms '32
The Sin of Madelon Claudet '31

Isaac Hayes (1942-)
Dr. Dolittle 2 '01 (V)
Reindeer Games '00
Shaft '00
Six Ways to Sunday '99
South Park: Bigger, Longer and Uncut '99 (V)
Woo '97
Flipper '96
Illtown '96
Uncle Sam '96
Backlash: Oblivion 2 '95
It Could Happen to You '94
Oblivion '94
Acting on Impulse '93
Deadly Exposure '93
Posse '93
Robin Hood: Men in Tights '93
Final Judgment '92
Guilty as Charged '92
Prime Target '91
I'm Gonna Git You Sucka '88
Counterforce '87
Dead Aim '87
Nightstick '87
Jailbait: Betrayed By Innocence '86
Escape from New York '81
Truck Turner '74

Linda Hayes (1922-95)
Ridin' Down the Canyon '42
South of Santa Fe '42
Danger on the Air '38

Maggie Hayes
Girls' Town '59
Good Day for a Hanging '58

Margaret Hayes (1916-)
Omar Khayyam '57
Blackboard Jungle '55
In Old Colorado '41
Sullivan's Travels '41

Patricia Hayes (1909-98)
Super Bitch '89
A Fish Called Wanda '88
Little Dorrit, Film 1: Nobody's Fault '88
Little Dorrit, Film 2: Little Dorrit's Story '88
Willow '88
The NeverEnding Story '84

Peter Lind Hayes (1915-98)
The 5000 Fingers of Dr. T '53
Seven Days' Leave '42
Zis Boom Bah '42
Playmates '41

Sean P. Hayes
Cats & Dogs '01 (V)
Billy's Hollywood Screen Kiss '98

Tony Haygarth (1945-)
Chicken Run '00 (V)
Don Quixote '00
Swept from the Sea '97
The Return of the Borrowers '96
The Infiltrator '95
Royal Deceit '94
The Borrowers '93
Devices and Desires '91
A Month in the Country '87
A Private Function '84
Dracula '79

Lisa Hayland
Fatal Passion '94
Novel Desires '92

Cyd Hayman
The Godsend '79
After Julius '78
Rogue Male '76

David Hayman (1950-)
The Tailor of Panama '00
Vertical Limit '00
The Match '99
My Name Is Joe '98
Behind the Lines '97
The Jackal '97
Rob Roy '95
Hope and Glory '87
Sid & Nancy '86
A Sense of Freedom '78

Dick Haymes (1916-80)
Betrayal '74
St. Benny the Dip '51
One Touch of Venus '48
Up in Central Park '48
State Fair '45
DuBarry Was a Lady '43

Cal Haynes
Kemek '88
Fyre '78

Linda Haynes
Human Experiments '79
Rolling Thunder '77

Loren Haynes
Eve of Destruction '90
The Expendables '89

Roberta Haynes (1929-)
The Adventurers '70
Hell Ship Mutiny '57
Return to Paradise '53
The Fighter '52

Jim Haynie
The Peacemaker '97
The Bridges of Madison County '95
Danielle Steel's Star '93
Grand Tour: Disaster in Time '92
Sleepwalkers '92
Too Much Sun '90
From Hollywood to Deadwood '89
Men Don't Leave '89
Out '88
Jack's Back '87
On the Edge '86
Hard Traveling '85
Bitter Harvest '81

Robert Hays (1947-)
Dr. T & the Women '00
The Abduction '96
Homeward Bound 2: Lost in San Francisco '96
Cyber Bandits '94
No Dessert Dad, 'Til You Mow the Lawn '94
Homeward Bound: The Incredible Journey '93
Hot Chocolate '92
Honeymoon Academy '90
Running Against Time '90
Murder by the Book '87
Cat's Eye '85
Scandalous '84
Trenchcoat '83
Utilities '83
Airplane 2: The Sequel '82
Touched '82
California Gold Rush '81
Take This Job & Shove It '81
Airplane! '80
The Fall of the House of Usher '80
Initiation of Sarah '78
The Young Pioneers '76

Dennis Haysbert (1955-)
Love and Basketball '00
What's Cooking? '00
The Minus Man '99
Random Hearts '99
The Thirteenth Floor '99
Major League 3: Back to the Minors '98
Absolute Power '97
Standoff '97
Heat '95
Waiting to Exhale '95
Major League 2 '94
Widow's Kiss '94
Return to Lonesome Dove '93
Suture '93
Mr. Baseball '92
Love Field '91
Navy SEALS '90
Major League '89

James Hayter (1907-83)
The Blood on Satan's Claw '71
A Challenge for Robin Hood '68
Cop-Out '67
Abandon Ship '57
Beau Brummel '54
The Pickwick Papers '54
Four Sided Triangle '53
Tom Brown's School Days '51
Trio '50
The Fallen Idol '49

Chad Hayward
Violent Zone '89
The Killing Game '87

David Hayward
Accidental Meeting '93
Thousand Pieces of Gold '91
Delusion '84
Who'll Save Our Children? '82

Louis Hayward (1909-85)
Terror in the Wax Museum '73
The Christmas Kid '68
Chuka '67
Promise to Murder '56
The Search for Bridey Murphy '56
Black Arrow '48
The Strange Woman '46
And Then There Were None '45
Dance, Girl, Dance '40
My Son, My Son '40
The Son of Monte Cristo '40
The Man in the Iron Mask '39
The Duke of West Point '38
The Saint in New York '38
Anthony Adverse '36

Rachel Hayward
Cruel and Unusual '01
The Fear: Halloween Night '99
Anything for Love '93
Breaking All the Rules '85

Susan Hayward (1918-75)
Say Goodbye, Maggie Cole '72
The Honey Pot '67
Valley of the Dolls '67
Where Love Has Gone '64
Stolen Hours '63
Back Street '61
I Want to Live! '58
The Conqueror '56
I'll Cry Tomorrow '55
Soldier of Fortune '55
Demetrius and the Gladiators '54
The Lusty Men '52
The Snows of Kilimanjaro '52
David and Bathsheba '51
I'd Climb the Highest Mountain '51
Rawhide '50
House of Strangers '49
Tulsa '49
Lost Moment '47
Smash-Up: The Story of a Woman '47
They Won't Believe Me '47
Canyon Passage '46
Deadline at Dawn '46
Fighting Seabees '44
The Hairy Ape '44
Jack London '44
Jack Frost '43
I Married a Witch '42
Reap the Wild Wind '42
Star Spangled Rhythm '42
Young & Willing '42
Adam Had Four Sons '41
Beau Geste '39

Chris Haywood (1949-)
Blackrock '97
Kiss or Kill '97
Lust and Revenge '95
Shine '95
Alex '92
A Woman's Tale '92
Sweet Talker '91
Quigley Down Under '90
The Navigator '88
The Tale of Ruby Rose '87
Malcolm '86
Burke & Wills '85
Attack Force Z '84
The Coca-Cola Kid '84
Man of Flowers '84
Razorback '84
Heatwave '83
Waterfront '83
Breaker Morant '80
Newsfront '78

Rita Hayworth (1918-87)
Road to Salina '68
The Rover '67
The Poppy Is Also a Flower '66
The Love Goddesses '65
Circus World '64
They Came to Cordura '59
Separate Tables '58
Fire Down Below '57
Pal Joey '57
Miss Sadie Thompson '53
Salome '53
Affair in Trinidad '52
The Lady from Shanghai '48
The Loves of Carmen '48
Down to Earth '47
Gilda '46
Tonight and Every Night '45
Cover Girl '44
Tales of Manhattan '42
You Were Never Lovelier '42
Blood and Sand '41
Strawberry Blonde '41
You'll Never Get Rich '41
Angels Over Broadway '40
Blondie On a Budget '40
The Lady in Question '40
Music in My Heart '40
Susan and God '40
Only Angels Have Wings '39
Hit the Saddle '37
Trouble in Texas '37

Jonathan Haze (1929-)
The St. Valentine's Day Massacre '67
Track of the Vampire '66
The Terror '63
X: The Man with X-Ray Eyes '63
Little Shop of Horrors '60
Teenage Caveman '58
Carnival Rock '57
Poor White Trash '57
Rock All Night '57
The Gunslinger '56
It Conquered the World '56
Apache Woman '55
Day the World Ended '55
Swamp Women '55
Monster from the Ocean Floor '54

James Hazeldine
Emma '97
My Friend Walter '93

Noni Hazlehurst (1954-)
True Colors '87
Fran '85
Waterfront '83
Monkey Grip '82

Murray Head (1946-)
Beaumarchais the Scoundrel '96
White Mischief '88
Sunday, Bloody Sunday '71

Lena Headey (1976-)
Possession '02
Aberdeen '00
Gossip '99
Onegin '99
Merlin '98
Twice upon a Yesterday '98
Face '97
Mrs. Dalloway '97
Grave Indiscretions '96
Century '94
Rudyard Kipling's The Jungle Book '94
The Summer House '94
Waterland '92

Shari Headley (1964-)
The Preacher's Wife '96
Coming to America '88

Glenne Headly (1955-)
A Girl Thing '01
What's the Worst That Could Happen? '01
The Sandy Bottom Orchestra '00
Time Code '00
Babe: Pig in the City '98 (V)
Breakfast of Champions '98
My Own Country '98
Winchell '98
The X-Files '98
Pronto '97
Bastard out of Carolina '96
Two Days in the Valley '96
Mr. Holland's Opus '95
Sgt. Bilko '95
Getting Even with Dad '94
And the Band Played On '93
Hotel Room '93
Ordinary Magic '93
Grand Isle '92
Mortal Thoughts '91
Dick Tracy '90
Paperhouse '89
Dirty Rotten Scoundrels '88
Stars and Bars '88
Nadine '87
Making Mr. Right '86

Seize the Day '86
Fandango '85
The Purple Rose of Cairo '85
Doctor Detroit '83

Anthony Heald (1944-)
Proof of Life '00
Deep Rising '98
8mm '98
A Time to Kill '96
Bushwhacked '95
The Client '94
Kiss of Death '94
The Ballad of Little Jo '93
Whispers in the Dark '92
The Silence of the Lambs '91
Postcards from the Edge '90

Myron Healey (1922-)
Pulse '88
Claws '77
Smoke in the Wind '75
Cavalry Command '63
Varan the Unbelievable '61
Guns Don't Argue '57
The Unearthly '57
Gang Busters '55
Bonanza Town '51
Down to Earth '47

David Healy (1932-95)
Unnatural Pursuits '91
Supergirl '84
The Sign of Four '83
Lust for a Vampire '71

Mary Healy (1918-)
The 5000 Fingers of Dr. T '53
Zis Boom Bah '42
Second Fiddle '39

Patricia Healy
Sweet Poison '91
Ultraviolet '91

Ted Healy (1896-1937)
Mad Love '35
Reckless '35
Hollywood Party '34
Dancing Lady '33

Darin Heames
The Fear '94
Night of the Demons 2 '94

John Heard (1946-)
O '01
Animal Factory '00
Pollock '00
The Pact '99
Desert Blue '98
Snake Eyes '98
Men '97
187 '97
My Fellow Americans '96
Before and After '95
Me & Veronica '93
The Pelican Brief '93
Dead Ahead: The Exxon Valdez Disaster '92
Gladiator '92
Home Alone 2: Lost in New York '92
Radio Flyer '92
Waterland '92
Deceived '91
Mindwalk: A Film for Passionate Thinkers '91
Rambling Rose '91
Awakenings '90
Blown Away '90
The End of Innocence '90
Home Alone '90
The Package '89
Beaches '88
Betrayed '88
Big '88
The Milagro Beanfield War '88
The Seventh Sign '88
Out on a Limb '87
The Telephone '87
After Hours '85
Heaven Help Us '85
Too Scared to Scream '85
The Trip to Bountiful '85
C.H.U.D. '84
Violated '84
Best Revenge '83
Legs '83
Cat People '82
Cutter's Way '81
Heart Beat '80
Chilly Scenes of Winter '79
On the Yard '79
The Scarlet Letter '79
Between the Lines '77
First Love '77

Ann Hearn
The War at Home '96
Lorenzo's Oil '92
Mirror, Mirror '90
The Accused '88

George Hearn (1934-)
Durango '99
Barney's Great Adventure '98
The Devil's Own '96
All Dogs Go to Heaven 2 '95 (V)
Annie: A Royal Adventure '95
The Vanishing '93
Sneakers '92
See You in the Morning '89
Sweeney Todd: The Demon Barber of Fleet Street '84
A Piano for Mrs. Cimino '82
Sanctuary of Fear '79

Patty (Patricia Campbell) Hearst (1954-)
Cecil B. Demented '00
Pecker '98
Serial Mom '94
Cry-Baby '90

Rick Hearst
Warlock 3: The End of Innocence '98
Crossing the Line '90

Darrell Heath
Woo '97
Don't Be a Menace to South Central While Drinking Your Juice in the Hood '95

Thomas Heathcote (1917-86)
Luther '74
Demons of the Mind '72
Village of the Damned '60
Above Us the Waves '56

Jean Heather
Murder, He Says '45
Double Indemnity '44

Clifford Heatherley (1888-1937)
Bitter Sweet '33
If I Were Rich '33
Champagne '28

Joey Heatherton (1944-)
Cry-Baby '90
The Happy Hooker Goes to Washington '77
Bluebeard '72
The Ballad of Andy Crocker '69
Where Love Has Gone '64

Patricia Heaton (1959-)
The New Age '94
Beethoven '92
Memoirs of an Invisible Man '92

Tom Heaton
Mermaid '00
Call of the Wild '93
April Fool's Day '86

David Heavener
The Catcher '98
Fugitive X '96
Eye of the Stranger '93
Kill or Be Killed '93
L.A. Goddess '92
Prime Target '91
Ragin' Cajun '90
Deadly Reactor '89
Killcrazy '89
Twisted Justice '89
Outlaw Force '87

Anne Heche (1969-)
John Q '02
Beyond Suspicion '00
One Kill '00
The Third Miracle '99
Psycho '98
Return to Paradise '98
Six Days, Seven Nights '98
I Know What You Did Last Summer '97
Subway Stories '97
Volcano '97
Wag the Dog '97
Donnie Brasco '96
If These Walls Could Talk '96
The Juror '96
Walking and Talking '96
Kingfish: A Story of Huey P. Long '95
Pie in the Sky '95
Wild Side '95
Against the Wall '94
Girls in Prison '94
Milk Money '94
A Simple Twist of Fate '94
The Adventures of Huck Finn '93
O Pioneers! '91

Paul Hecht (1941-)
Private Parts '96
Mary and Joseph: A Story of Faith '79
The Savage Bees '76
The Reincarnation of Peter Proud '75

Eileen Heckart (1919-2001)
The First Wives Club '96
Breathing Lessons '94
Heartbreak Ridge '86
Table Settings '84
White Mama '80
Sorrows of Gin '79
The Hiding Place '75
Zandy's Bride '74
Butterflies Are Free '72
No Way to Treat a Lady '68
Up the Down Staircase '67
Heller in Pink Tights '60
A Doll's House '59
Hot Spell '58
The Bad Seed '56
Bus Stop '56
Somebody Up There Likes Me '56

Andrew Heckler
Time Code '00
Stir '98

Dan Hedaya (1940-)
Mulholland Drive '01
The Crew '00
Shaft '00
Dick '99
The Hurricane '99
Locked in Silence '99
The Extreme Adventures of Super Dave '98
A Night at the Roxbury '98
Alien: Resurrection '97
The Garden of Redemption '97
A Life Less Ordinary '97
The Second Civil War '97
Daylight '96
The First Wives Club '96
Marvin's Room '96
Ransom '96
Clueless '95
Freeway '95
The Reluctant Agent '95
To Die For '95
The Usual Suspects '95
Maverick '94
Based on an Untrue Story '93
Benny & Joon '93
Boiling Point '93
Fallen Angels 2 '93
For Love or Money '93
Four Eyes and Six Guns '93
Mr. Wonderful '93
Rookie of the Year '93
The Addams Family '91
Joe Versus the Volcano '90
Pacific Heights '90
Tune in Tomorrow '90
Courage '86
Running Scared '86
Slow Burn '86
A Smoky Mountain Christmas '86
Wise Guys '86
Blood Simple '85
Commando '85
The Adventures of Buckaroo Banzai Across the Eighth Dimension '84
Reckless '84
Tightrope '84
The Hunger '83
Endangered Species '82
The Prince of Central Park '77

Amel Hedhili
Honey & Ashes '96
The Silences of the Palace '94

Serene Hedin
Hawken's Breed '87
Boggy Creek II '83

David Hedison (1928-)
Undeclared War '91
License to Kill '89
Kemek '88
A.D. '85
The Naked Face '84
Kenny Rogers as the Gambler, Part 2: The Adventure Continues '83
ffolkes '80
The Power Within '79
The Art of Crime '75
Live and Let Die '73
The Fly '58
Enemy Below '57

Jack Hedley (1930-)
New York Ripper '82
For Your Eyes Only '81
Goodbye, Mr. Chips '69
The Anniversary '68
The Very Edge '63

Tippi Hedren (1935-)
The Break Up '98
Footsteps '98
Citizen Ruth '96
The Birds 2: Land's End '94
Teresa's Tattoo '94
Through the Eyes of a Killer '92
Pacific Heights '90
Deadly Spygames '89
In the Cold of the Night '89
Foxfire Light '82
Harrad Experiment '73
Mr. Kingstreet's War '71
A Countess from Hong Kong '67
Satan's Harvest '65
Marnie '64
The Birds '63

Deborah Hedwall
Shadrach '98
Sessions '83

Wayne Heffley
Johnny Got His Gun '71
Submarine Seahawk '59

Kyle T. Heffner
Mutant on the Bounty '89
Flashdance '83

Marta Heflin
Come Back to the Five & Dime Jimmy Dean, Jimmy Dean '82
A Star Is Born '76

Nora Heflin
Chilly Scenes of Winter '79
Our Time '74

Van Heflin (1910-71)
Airport '70
The Ruthless Four '70
The Man Outside '68
The Greatest Story Ever Told '65
Cry of Battle '63
They Came to Cordura '59
Gunman's Walk '58
3:10 to Yuma '57
Patterns '56
Battle Cry '55
A Woman's World '54
Shane '53
Prowler '51
Tomahawk '51
East Side, West Side '49
Madame Bovary '49
The Three Musketeers '48
Green Dolphin Street '47
The Possessed '47
The Strange Love of Martha Ivers '46
Till the Clouds Roll By '46
Presenting Lily Mars '43
Johnny Eager '42
Santa Fe Trail '40
Back Door to Heaven '39
Flight from Glory '37
A Woman Rebels '36

Hugh Hefner (1926-)
Hugh Hefner: Once Upon a Time '92
Beverly Hills Cop 2 '87
History of the World: Part 1 '81

O.P. Heggie (1879-1936)
The Bride of Frankenstein '35
Anne of Green Gables '34
The Count of Monte Cristo '34
Midnight '34
Peck's Bad Boy '34
Smilin' Through '33
Devotion '31

Robert Hegyes
Just Tell Me You Love Me '80
Underground Aces '80

Peter Hehir
Sweet Talker '91
Fast Talking '86
I Live with Me Dad '86
Two Friends '86

Katherine Heigl (1978-)
Valentine '01
100 Girls '00
Bug Buster '99
The Tempest '99
Bride of Chucky '98
Prince Valiant '97
Stand-Ins '97
Wish upon a Star '96
Under Siege 2: Dark Territory '95
King of the Hill '93
My Father the Hero '93

Elayne Heilveil
The Adventures of Nellie Bly '81
Birds of Prey '72

Laurie Heineman
Lady in Red '79
Save the Tiger '73

Amelia Heinle
Earth vs. the Spider '01
The Limey '99
Black Cat Run '98
Quicksilver Highway '98
Uncorked '98

Jayne Heitmeyer
An American Affair '99
Believe '99
Beyond Redemption '99
Requiem for Murder '99
Dead End '98
Sir Arthur Conan Doyle's The Lost World '98
Face the Evil '97
Sci-Fighters '96
Suspicious Minds '96

Brit Helfer
Body Trouble '92
Alley Cat '84

Marg Helgenberger (1958-)
Erin Brockovich '00
The Happy Face Murders '99
Species 2 '98
Elmore Leonard's Gold Coast '97
Fire Down Below '97
The Last Time I Committed Suicide '96
Bad Boys '95
Frame by Frame '95
Species '95
The Cowboy Way '94
Lie Down with Lions '94
Fallen Angels 2 '93
Stephen King's The Tommyknockers '93
Death Dreams '92
Desperate Motives '92
Through the Eyes of a Killer '92
Crooked Hearts '91
Blind Vengeance '90
After Midnight '89
Always '89
China Beach '88

Erik Hell (1911-73)
The Passion of Anna '70
The Rite '69
Port of Call '48

Richard Hell (1949-)
Desperately Seeking Susan '85
Geek Maggot Bingo '83
Smithereens '82

Thomas Hellberg
Man from Mallorca '84
The Assignment '78

Randee Heller
Matter of Trust '98
Danielle Steel's Changes '91
The Karate Kid '84
Can You Hear the Laughter? The Story of Freddie Prinze '79
Fast Break '79

Anne Helm (1938-)
Nightmare in Wax '69
The Unkissed Bride '66
Follow That Dream '61

Brigitte Helm (1906-96)
The Love of Jeanne Ney '27
Metropolis '26

Fay Helm (1913-)
Phantom Lady '44
The Wolf Man '41
Blondie On a Budget '40
Blondie Brings Up Baby '39

Levon Helm (1943-)
Fire Down Below '97
Feeling Minnesota '96
End of the Line '88
Man Outside '88
Smooth Talk '85
The Dollmaker '84
Best Revenge '83
The Right Stuff '83
Coal Miner's Daughter '80

Charlotte J. Helmkamp
Frankenhooker '90
Posed for Murder '89

Katherine Helmond (1934-)
The Perfect Nanny '00
Fear and Loathing in Las Vegas '98
Ms. Scrooge '97
The Spy Within '94
Amore! '93
Inside Monkey Zetterland '93
The Lady in White '88
Overboard '87
Shadey '87
World War III '86
Brazil '85
Jack & the Beanstalk '83
Rosie: The Rosemary Clooney Story '82
Time Bandits '81
Scout's Honor '80
Pearl '78
Family Plot '76
The Autobiography of Miss Jane Pittman '74
Larry '74
The Hospital '71

Tom Helmore (1904-95)
Flipper's New Adventure '64
Vertigo '58
Designing Woman '57
This Could Be the Night '57
The Tender Trap '55
Trouble along the Way '53

Robert Helpmann (1909-86)
Patrick '78
Puzzle '78
The Mango Tree '77
The Tales of Hoffmann '51
The Red Shoes '48
Henry V '44

Sheila Helpmann
The Getting of Wisdom '77
Image of Death '77

Percy Helton
Crashout '55
Kiss Me Deadly '55

David Hemblen
Rollerball '02
Family of Cops 2: Breach of Faith '97
Booty Call '96
The Sweet Hereafter '96
Hollow Point '95
Brainscan '94
Exotica '94
Mesmer '94
A Man in Uniform '93
The Adjuster '91
Speaking Parts '89
Short Circuit 2 '88
Family Viewing '87
The Room '87

Mark Hembrow
Desperate Prey '94
Out of the Body '88
Return to Snowy River '88
High Tide '87

Margaux Hemingway (1955-96)
Bad Love '95
Inner Sanctum 2 '94
Double Obsession '93
Deadly Rivals '92
Deadly Conspiracy '91
Inner Sanctum '91
Over the Brooklyn Bridge '83
They Call Me Bruce? '82
Killer Fish '79
Lipstick '76

Mariel Hemingway (1961-)
Perfume '01
First Daughter '99
Little Men '98
Road Ends '98
Deconstructing Harry '97
Bad Moon '96
The Crying Child '96
Deceptions 2: Edge of Deception '94
Falling from Grace '92
Into the Badlands '92
Delirious '91
Steal the Sky '88
Sunset '88
Superman 4: The Quest for Peace '87
Creator '85
Mean Season '85
Star 80 '83
Personal Best '82
Manhattan '79
Lipstick '76

David Hemmings (1941-)
Mean Machine '01
Spy Game '01
Gladiator '00
A Mind to Murder '96
The Deadly Game '80s
The Rainbow '89
The Turn of the Screw '89
Thirst '87
The Key to Rebecca '85
Dark Forces '83
Man, Woman & Child '83
The Snow Queen '83
Calamity Jane '82
Disappearance '81
Power Play '81
Beyond Reasonable Doubt '80
Beyond Erotica '79
Just a Gigolo '79
Murder by Decree '79
Blood Relatives '77
Islands in the Stream '77
The Squeeze '77
Deep Red: Hatchet Murders '75
The Old Curiosity Shop '75
Juggernaut '74
The Love Machine '71
Barbarella '68
The Charge of the Light Brigade '68
Camelot '67
Blow-Up '66
The Girl Getters '66

Anouska (Anoushka) Hempel (1941-)
Tiffany Jones '75
Blacksnake! '73
The Scars of Dracula '70
On Her Majesty's Secret Service '69

John Hemphill
Hostage for a Day '94
Sodbusters '94

Sherman Hemsley (1938-)
Screwed '00
Home of Angels '94
Mr. Nanny '93
Camp Cucamonga: How I Spent My Summer Vacation '90
Club Fed '90
Ghost Fever '87
Combat Academy '86
Ghost Dance '83
Love at First Bite '79

Richard Hench
Endangered '94
Tomb '86
Bio Hazard '85

Bill Henderson (1925-)
Smiling Fish & Goat on Fire '99
Trippin' '99
City Slickers '91
Movie Maker '86
Murphy's Law '86
Clue '85
Get Crazy '83

Dell Henderson (1883-1956)
Love Affair '39
Rainbow over Broadway '33
The Crowd '28
Show People '28

Don Henderson (1931-97)
The Adventures of Baron Munchausen '89
The Island '80
The Ghoul '75

Doug(las) Henderson (1918-78)
The Manchurian Candidate '62
King Dinosaur '55
From Here to Eternity '53

Florence Henderson (1934-)
The Brady Bunch Movie '95
Shakes the Clown '92
A Very Brady Christmas '88
Song of Norway '70

Jo Henderson (1934-88)
Matewan '87
Rachel River '87
Lianna '83

Marcia Henderson
Naked Hills '56
Thunder Bay '53

Shirley Henderson (1966-)
The Way We Live Now '02
Bridget Jones's Diary '01
Topsy Turvy '99
Wonderland '99
Rob Roy '95
Trainspotting '95

Ty Henderson
Happy Hour '87
The Competition '80

Tony Hendra
Life with Mikey '93
This Is Spinal Tap '84

Benjamin Hendrickson
Spanking the Monkey '94
Manhunter '86

Elaine Hendrix (1971-)
Wish You Were Dead '00
Molly '99
Superstar '99
The Parent Trap '98
Romy and Michele's High School Reunion '97
Last Dance '91

Wanda Hendrix (1928-81)
My Outlaw Brother '51
The Admiral Was a Lady '50
Welcome Stranger '47

Gloria Hendry (1949-)
Pumpkinhead 2: Blood Wings '94
Bare Knuckles '77
Black Belt Jones '74
Black Caesar '73
Hell Up in Harlem '73
Live and Let Die '73
Slaughter's Big Ripoff '73

Ian Hendry (1931-84)
The Bitch '78
The Passenger '75
Captain Kronos: Vampire Hunter '74
Killer with Two Faces '74
Theatre of Blood '73
Tales from the Crypt '72
Get Carter '71
McKenzie Break '70
Journey to the Far Side of the Sun '69
The Saint '68
Repulsion '65
Children of the Damned '63
Room at the Top '59

Sonja Henie (1912-69)
Wintertime '43
Iceland '42
Sun Valley Serenade '41
Everything Happens at Night '39
Second Fiddle '39
Happy Landing '38
My Lucky Star '38
Thin Ice '37
One in a Million '36

Barry (Shabaka) Henley
Ali '01
Life '99
How Stella Got Her Groove Back '98

Marilu Henner (1952-)
Man on the Moon '99
Titanic '96
Chasers '94
Chains of Gold '92
Grand Larceny '92
Noises Off '92
L.A. Story '91
Ladykillers '88
Grown Ups '86
Love with a Perfect Stranger '86
Perfect '85
Rustler's Rhapsody '85
Stark '85
Cannonball Run 2 '84
Johnny Dangerously '84
The Man Who Loved Women '83
Hammett '82
Bloodbrothers '78
Between the Lines '77

Jill(ian) Hennessey (1969-)
Exit Wounds '01
Jackie, Ethel, Joan: The Kennedy Women '01
Autumn in New York '00
Nuremberg '00
Two Ninas '00
Chutney Popcorn '99
Komodo '99
Molly '99
Row Your Boat '98
Most Wanted '97
I Shot Andy Warhol '96
A Smile Like Yours '96

Eva Henning
Devil's Wanton '49
Three Strange Loves '49

Sam Hennings
Indecent Behavior 3 '95
Drop Zone '94
Seedpeople '92
Night Angel '90
Mission Manila '87

Paul Henreid (1908-92)
The Exorcist 2: The Heretic '77
The Madwoman of Chaillot '69
The Four Horsemen of the Apocalypse '62
Never So Few '59
Battle Shock '56
Deep in My Heart '54
Tall Lie '53
A Stolen Face '52
The Scar '48
Deception '46
The Spanish Main '45
Casablanca '42
Joan of Paris '42
Now, Voyager '42
Night Train to Munich '40
Goodbye, Mr. Chips '39

Lance Henriksen (1940-)
Scream 3 '00
Tarzan '99 (V)
Face the Evil '97
Gunfighter's Moon '96
The Last Assassins '96
Profile for Murder '96
Baja '95
Dead Man '95
Felony '95
Operation Intercept '95
Powder '95
Wes Craven Presents Mind Ripper '95
Boulevard '94
Color of Night '94
Nature of the Beast '94
No Escape '94
The Quick and the Dead '94
Spitfire '94
The Criminal Mind '93
Excessive Force '93
Hard Target '93
Knights '93
Man's Best Friend '93
The Outfit '93
Super Mario Bros. '93
Alien 3 '92
Delta Heat '92
Jennifer 8 '92
Comrades in Arms '91
The Pit & the Pendulum '91
Stone Cold '91
The Last Samurai '90
The Horror Show '89
Johnny Handsome '89
Survival Quest '89
Deadly Intent '88
The Hit List '88
Pumpkinhead '88
Near Dark '87
Aliens '86
Choke Canyon '86
The Jagged Edge '85
Savage Dawn '84
The Terminator '84
Nightmares '83
The Right Stuff '83
Piranha 2: The Spawning '82
Prince of the City '81
The Visitor '80
Damien: Omen 2 '78
Dog Day Afternoon '75

Anders Henrikson (1896-1965)
Miss Julie '50
A Woman's Face '38
Intermezzo '36

Buck Henry (1930-)
Town and Country '01
Breakfast of Champions '98
I'm Losing You '98
1999 '98
Curtain Call '97
The Real Blonde '97
Kurt Vonnegut's Harrison Bergeron '95
To Die For '95
Grumpy Old Men '93
Short Cuts '93
Keep the Change '92
The Linguini Incident '92
The Player '92
Defending Your Life '91
Tune in Tomorrow '90
Dark Before Dawn '89
Rude Awakening '89
Aria '88
Eating Raoul '82
Gloria '80
Old Boyfriends '79
Heaven Can Wait '78
The Man Who Fell to Earth '76
The Day of the Dolphin '73 (V)
Is There Sex After Death? '71
Catch-22 '70
The Graduate '67

Charlotte Henry (1913-80)
Bowery Blitzkrieg '41
God's Country and the Man '37
The Mandarin Mystery '37
Charlie Chan at the Opera '36
March of the Wooden Soldiers '34

Gloria Henry
Phantasm 3: Lord of the Dead '94
Miss Grant Takes Richmond '49

Gregg Henry (1952-)
The Big Brass Ring '99
Payback '98
Star Trek: Insurrection '98
Bodily Harm '95
Sharon's Secret '95
Kiss of a Killer '93
The Positively True Adventures of the Alleged Texas Cheerleader-Murdering Mom '93
Fair Game '89
The Last of Philip Banter '87
The Patriot '86
Body Double '84
Funny Money '82
Just Before Dawn '80
Hot Rod '79
Mean Dog Blues '78
Pearl '78

Hank Henry
Robin and the 7 Hoods '64
Pal Joey '57

Judith Henry
Germinal '93
La Discrete '90

Justin Henry (1971-)
Chasing Destiny '00
Andersonville '95
Sweet Hearts Dance '88
Martin's Day '85
Sixteen Candles '84
Tiger Town '83
Kramer vs. Kramer '79

Lenny Henry
Bernard and the Genie '90s
True Identity '91

Martha Henry (1938-)
Anne of Green Gables: The Continuing Story '99
Long Day's Journey Into Night '96
Glory Enough for All: The Discovery of Insulin '92
White Light '90
Dancing in the Dark '86

Mike Henry (1939-)
Smokey and the Bandit, Part 3 '83
Smokey and the Bandit 2 '80
Smokey and the Bandit '77
Adios Amigo '75
The Longest Yard '74
The Green Berets '68

Robert "Buzzy" Henry (1931-71)
Danny Boy '46
Wild West '46
The Great Mike '44
Turf Boy '42
Buzzy Rides the Range '40
The Unknown Ranger '36
Western Frontier '35

Thomas B(rowne). Henry (1907-80)
Beginning of the End '57
Blood of Dracula '57
The Brain from Planet Arous '57
20 Million Miles to Earth '57

Tim Henry
125 Rooms of Comfort '83
The Dawson Patrol '78

William Henry (1918-82)
The Alamo '60
Mister Roberts '55
Marshal of Cedar Rock '53
Movie Stuntmen '53
Trail to San Antone '47
The Adventures of Mark Twain '44
Dance Hall '41
Madame X '37
Tarzan Escapes '36

Douglas Henshall
Anna Karenina '00
Twice upon a Yesterday '98
Kull the Conqueror '97
Orphans '97
Sharpe's Justice '97
Angels and Insects '95

Lisa Hensley
Paradise Road '97
Dating the Enemy '95
Mr. Reliable: A True Story '95
Brides of Christ '91
The 13th Floor '88

Pamela Hensley (1950-)
Double Exposure '82
The Nude Bomb '80
Buck Rogers in the 25th Century '79
The Rebels '79
Doc Savage '75

Elden (Ratliff) Henson (1977-)
O '01
Idle Hands '99
She's All That '99
The Mighty '98
D3: The Mighty Ducks '96
The Mighty Ducks '92

Gladys Henson
The Leather Boys '63
Train of Events '49

Jim Henson (1936-90)
Into the Night '85
Sesame Street Presents: Follow That Bird '85 (V)
The Muppets Take Manhattan '84 (V)
The Dark Crystal '82 (V)
The Muppet Movie '79 (V)

Nicky Henson (1945-)
Number 1 of the Secret Service '77
Psychomania '73
The Conqueror Worm '68

Natasha Henstridge (1974-)
John Carpenter's Ghosts of Mars '01
A Better Way to Die '00
Bounce '00
Caracara '00
Jason and the Argonauts '00
Second Skin '00
The Whole Nine Yards '00
Dog Park '98
Species 2 '98
Standoff '97
Adrenalin: Fear the Rush '96
Maximum Risk '96

Species '95
Audrey Hepburn (1929-93)
Always '89
They All Laughed '81
Sidney Sheldon's Bloodline '79
Robin and Marian '76
Two for the Road '67
Wait until Dark '67
How to Steal a Million '66
My Fair Lady '64
Paris When It Sizzles '64
Charade '63
Breakfast at Tiffany's '61
The Children's Hour '61
The Unforgiven '60
Green Mansions '59
The Nun's Story '59
Funny Face '57
Love in the Afternoon '57
War and Peace '56
Sabrina '54
Roman Holiday '53
The Lavender Hill Mob '51
Katharine Hepburn (1907-)
One Christmas '95
Love Affair '94
The Man Upstairs '93
Grace Quigley '84
On Golden Pond '81
Olly Olly Oxen Free '78
Love Among the Ruins '75
Rooster Cogburn '75
Trojan Women '71
The Madwoman of Chaillot '69
The Lion in Winter '68
Guess Who's Coming to Dinner '67
Long Day's Journey into Night '62
Suddenly, Last Summer '59
Desk Set '57
The Rainmaker '56
Summertime '55
Pat and Mike '52
The African Queen '51
Adam's Rib '50
State of the Union '48
Undercurrent '46
Without Love '45
Dragon Seed '44
Stage Door Canteen '43
Keeper of the Flame '42
Woman of the Year '42
The Philadelphia Story '40
Bringing Up Baby '38
Holiday '38
Quality Street '37
Stage Door '37
Mary of Scotland '36
A Woman Rebels '36
Alice Adams '35
Break of Hearts '35
Sylvia Scarlett '35
Little Minister '34
Spitfire '34
Christopher Strong '33
Little Women '33
Morning Glory '33
A Bill of Divorcement '32
Bernard Hepton (1925-)
Emma '97
Eminent Domain '91
Woman in Black '89
Stealing Heaven '88
The Charmer '87
The Lady's Not for Burning '87
Shadey '87
Mansfield Park '85
Get Carter '71
Charles Herbert (1948-)
13 Ghosts '60
The Fly '58
Gun Glory '57
Holmes Herbert (1883-1956)
Command Decision '48
Invisible Agent '42
Sherlock Holmes and the Secret Weapon '42
British Intelligence '40
Bad Boy '39
Stanley and Livingstone '39
The House of Secrets '37
Sons of Steel '35
The Invisible Man '33
Mystery of the Wax Museum '33
Dr. Jekyll and Mr. Hyde '32
Shop Angel '32
Daughter of the Dragon '31
The Kiss '29
Through the Breakers '28
Hugh Herbert (1887-1952)
The Beautiful Blonde from Bashful Bend '49
On Our Merry Way '48
A Song Is Born '48
It's a Great Life '43
Sherlock Holmes and the Secret Weapon '42
The Black Cat '41
The Villain Still Pursued Her '41
Eternally Yours '39
The Great Waltz '38
One Rainy Afternoon '36
Gold Diggers of 1935 '35
A Midsummer Night's Dream '35
Sweet Adeline '35
Fashions of 1934 '34
Bureau of Missing Persons '33
Diplomaniacs '33
Hook, Line and Sinker '30
Percy Herbert (1920-92)
Blacksnake! '73
The Fiend '71
Man in the Wilderness '71
Too Late the Hero '70
Carry On Cowboy '66
One Million Years B.C. '66
Call Me Bwana '63
Mutiny on the Bounty '62
The Guns of Navarone '61
Mysterious Island '61
The Bridge on the River Kwai '57
Becky Herbst
Donor Unknown '95
Shrunken Heads '94
Carla Herd
Deathstalker 3 '89
Wild Zone '89
Richard Herd (1932-)
I Married a Monster '98
The Survivor '98
Cosmic Slop '94
The Judas Project: The Ultimate Encounter '94
V '83
Lovely ... But Deadly '82
Wolf Lake '79
Eileen Herlie
Angel with the Trumpet '50
Hamlet '48
Roberto Herlitzka
The Favorite Son '94
Summer Night with Greek Profile, Almond Eyes & Scent of Basil '87
David Herman
Dude, Where's My Car? '00
Office Space '98
Jack Herman
The Naked Witch '64
The Yesterday Machine '63
Jimmy Herman
Crazy Horse '96
Medicine River '94
Warrior Spirit '94
Geronimo '93
Dances with Wolves '90
Paul Herman
Somebody to Love '94
New York Stories '89
The Last Temptation of Christ '88
The Squeeze '87
Woody Herman
New Orleans '47
Sensations of 1945 '44
Wintertime '43
Irm Hermann (1942-)
The Last Five Days '82
Mother Kusters Goes to Heaven '76
Ali: Fear Eats the Soul '74
The Bitter Tears of Petra von Kant '72
The Merchant of Four Seasons '71
Jay Hernandez
The Rookie '02
crazy/beautiful '01
Jonathan Hernandez
A Million to Juan '94
My Family '94
Juano Hernandez (1901-70)
They Call Me Mr. Tibbs! '70
Sergeant Rutledge '60
The Mark of the Hawk '57
Something of Value '57
Stars in My Crown '50
Intruder in the Dust '49
Blake Heron
We Were Soldiers '02
Cheaters '00
Wind River '98
Shiloh '97
Trilogy of Terror 2 '96
Marcel Herrand (1897-1953)
Fanfan la Tulipe '51
Children of Paradise '44
Les Visiteurs du Soir '42
Mark Herrier
Porky's Revenge '85
Spraggue '84
Porky's 2: The Next Day '83
Tank '83
Porky's '82
Aggie Herring
That Certain Thing '28
Oliver Twist '22
Laura Herring
The Forbidden Dance '90
Silent Night, Deadly Night 3: Better Watch Out! '89
Edward Herrmann (1943-)
The Cat's Meow '01
Double Take '01
James Dean '01
Atomic Train '99
Vendetta '99
Saint Maybe '98
Critical Care '97
Soul of the Game '96
Nixon '95
Foreign Student '94
Richie Rich '94
Born Yesterday '93
A Foreign Field '93
My Boyfriend's Back '93
Sweet Poison '91
Big Business '88
The Lawrenceville Stories '88
The Lost Boys '87
Overboard '87
The Private History of a Campaign That Failed '87
Murrow '86
Compromising Positions '85
The Man with One Red Shoe '85
The Purple Rose of Cairo '85
Harry's War '84
Mrs. Soffel '84
Memorial Day '83
A Little Sex '82
Death Valley '81
Reds '81
Freedom Road '79
The North Avenue Irregulars '79
Portrait of a Stripper '79
Sorrows of Gin '79
Take Down '79
The Betsy '78
Brass Target '78
Love Affair: The Eleanor & Lou Gehrig Story '77
Eleanor & Franklin '76
The Great Waldo Pepper '75
The Great Gatsby '74
The Day of the Dolphin '73
The Paper Chase '73
Mark Herron
Girl in Gold Boots '69
8 1/2 '63
Gary Hershberger
The Siege of Firebase Gloria '89
Free Ride '86
Paradise Motel '84
Barbara Hershey (1948-)
Lantana '01
Passion '99
Breakfast of Champions '98
Frogs for Snakes '98
A Soldier's Daughter Never Cries '98
Portrait of a Lady '96
The Last of the Dogmen '95
The Pallbearer '95
Abraham '94
A Dangerous Woman '93
Falling Down '93
Return to Lonesome Dove '93
Splitting Heirs '93
Swing Kids '93
The Public Eye '92
Defenseless '91
Paris Trout '91
A Killing in a Small Town '90
Tune in Tomorrow '90
Beaches '88
The Last Temptation of Christ '88
A World Apart '88
Shy People '87
Tin Men '87
Hannah and Her Sisters '86
Hoosiers '86
Passion Flower '86
My Wicked, Wicked Ways '84
The Natural '84
The Entity '83
The Nightingale '83
The Right Stuff '83
Americana '81
Take This Job & Shove It '81
Angel on My Shoulder '80
The Stunt Man '80
From Here to Eternity '79
Choice of Weapons '76
Flood! '76
Boxcar Bertha '72
Diamonds '72
The Baby Maker '70
The Liberation of L.B. Jones '70
The Pursuit of Happiness '70
Last Summer '69
With Six You Get Eggroll '68
Jean Hersholt (1886-1956)
Melody for Three '41
They Meet Again '41
Courageous Dr. Christian '40
Dr. Christian Meets the Women '40
Remedy for Riches '40
Meet Dr. Christian '39
Alexander's Ragtime Band '38
Happy Landing '38
Heidi '37
One in a Million '36
Break of Hearts '35
Mark of the Vampire '35
The Cat and the Fiddle '34
The Painted Veil '34
Dinner at Eight '33
Grand Hotel '32
Hearts of Humanity '32
The Mask of Fu Manchu '32
Skyscraper Souls '32
Private Lives '31
The Sin of Madelon Claudet '31
Susan Lenox: Her Fall and Rise '31
Hell Harbor '30
Battle of the Sexes '28
Greed '24
Heart's Haven '22
Tess of the Storm Country '22
The Disciple '15
Gerard Herter
Hornet's Nest '70
Last Day of the War '69
Any Gun Can Play '67
Brighton Hertford
Can of Worms '00
Mystery Kids '99
Evil Has a Face '96
Irene Hervey (1910-98)
Play Misty for Me '71
Mickey '48
Mr. Peabody & the Mermaid '48
Night Monster '42
Destry Rides Again '39
Gangbusters '38
The Girl Said No '37
The Count of Monte Cristo '34
Dude Ranger '34
Jason Hervey (1972-)
Trading Favors '97
Back to School '86
Back to the Future '85
Pee-wee's Big Adventure '85
Frankenweenie '84
Werner Herzog (1942-)
Julien Donkey-boy '99
Man of Flowers '84
Burden of Dreams '82
Grant Heslov (1963-)
The Scorpion King '02
Dante's Peak '97
Black Sheep '96
Congo '95
True Lies '94
David A(lexander) Hess (1942-)
Let It Rock '86
House on the Edge of the Park '84
Avalanche Express '79
Last House on the Left '72
Joe Hess
Bloodmoon '97
Master Blaster '85
Sandra Hess
Mortal Kombat 2: Annihilation '97
Beastmaster 3: The Eye of Braxus '95
Endangered '94
Howard Hesseman (1940-)
Gridlock'd '96
Out of Sync '95
Home for Christmas '93
Rubin & Ed '92
The Diamond Trap '91
Inside Out '91
Murder in New Hampshire: The Pamela Smart Story '91
Amazon Women on the Moon '87
Heat '87
Flight of the Navigator '86
My Chauffeur '86
Clue '85
Police Academy 2: Their First Assignment '85
The Princess Who Never Laughed '84
Silence of the Heart '84
This Is Spinal Tap '84
Doctor Detroit '83
One Shoe Makes It Murder '82
Honky Tonk Freeway '81
Private Lessons '81
Great American Traffic Jam '80
Americathon '79
Tarantulas: The Deadly Cargo '77
The Big Bus '76
Jackson County Jail '76
Tunnelvision '76
Shampoo '75
The Sunshine Boys '75
Steelyard Blues '73
Billy Jack '71
The Committee '68
Catherine Hessling
Renoir Shorts '27
Charleston '26
Charlton Heston (1924-)
Cats & Dogs '01 (V)
Planet of the Apes '01
Town and Country '01
Any Given Sunday '99
Hercules '97 (N)
Alaska '96
Hamlet '96
The Avenging Angel '95
In the Mouth of Madness '95
A Thousand Heroes '94
True Lies '94
Tombstone '93
Wayne's World 2 '93
Solar Crisis '92
The Crucifer of Blood '91
Almost an Angel '90
The Little Kidnappers '90
Treasure Island '89
A Man for All Seasons '88
Nairobi Affair '88
Proud Men '87
Chiefs '83
Mother Lode '82
The Awakening '80
The Mountain Men '80
The Prince and the Pauper '78
Gray Lady Down '77
America at the Movies '76 (N)
Midway '76
Two Minute Warning '76
Airport '75 '75
The Four Musketeers '75
Earthquake '74
The Three Musketeers '74
Antony and Cleopatra '73
Soylent Green '73
Call of the Wild '72
Omega Man '71
Beneath the Planet of the Apes '70
Julius Caesar '70
Elizabeth, the Queen '68
Planet of the Apes '68
Will Penny '67
Khartoum '66
The Agony and the Ecstasy '65
The Greatest Story Ever Told '65
Major Dundee '65
The War Lord '65
55 Days at Peking '63
Diamond Head '62
El Cid '61
Ben-Hur '59
The Wreck of the Mary Deare '59
The Big Country '58
The Buccaneer '58
Touch of Evil '58
Three Violent People '57
The Ten Commandments '56
The Private War of Major Benson '55
Naked Jungle '54
Arrowhead '53
Pony Express '53
The Greatest Show on Earth '52
Ruby Gentry '52
Lori Heuring
True Blue '01
The In Crowd '00
Jennifer Love Hewitt (1979-)
Heartbreakers '01
The Audrey Hepburn Story '00
The Suburbans '99
Can't Hardly Wait '98

Troublemakers '94
Miami Supercops '85
Go for It '83
Super Fuzz '81
Crime Busters '78
Odds and Evens '78
March or Die '77
Mr. Billion '77
Trinity Is Still My Name '75
My Name Is Nobody '74
All the Way, Boys '73
They Call Me Trinity '72
Boot Hill '69
Ace High '68

Teresa Hill
Twin Falls Idaho '99
Bio-Dome '96
In the Heat of Passion 2: Unfaithful '94
Puppet Master 5: The Final Chapter '94
Puppet Master 4 '93

Thomas Hill
An Empty Bed '90
The NeverEnding Story '84

Wendy Hiller (1912-)
Anne of Avonlea '87
The Lonely Passion of Judith Hearne '87
Mountbatten: The Last Viceroy '86
Making Love '82
The Curse of King Tut's Tomb '80
The Elephant Man '80
The Cat and the Canary '79
Voyage of the Damned '76
Murder on the Orient Express '74
David Copperfield '70
A Man for All Seasons '66
Toys in the Attic '63
Separate Tables '58
Something of Value '57
I Know Where I'm Going '45
Major Barbara '41
Pygmalion '38

John Hillerman (1932-)
Hands of a Murderer '90
Around the World in 80 Days '89
Assault and Matrimony '87
Little Gloria... Happy at Last '84
Up the Creek '84
History of the World: Part 1 '81
Magnum P.I.: Don't Eat the Snow in Hawaii '80
Marathon '80
Betrayal '78
Audrey Rose '77
Blazing Saddles '74
Chinatown '74
The Outside Man '73
Paper Moon '73
The Thief Who Came to Dinner '73
The Last Picture Show '71
Lawman '71

Verna Hillie (1914-97)
House of Mystery '34
Trail Beyond '34
Man of the Forest '33

Candace Hilligoss
Curse of the Living Corpse '64
Carnival of Souls '62

Richard Hillman
Teenage Caveman '01
Bring It On '00
Men '97

Gillian Hills (1946-)
Demons of the Mind '72
Blow-Up '66
Beat Girl '60

Daisy Hilton
Chained for Life '51
Freaks '32

George Hilton (1934-)
Day of the Maniac '77
Guns for Dollars '73
The Next Victim '71
The Scorpion's Tail '71
Blade of the Ripper '70
Bullet for Sandoval '70
Dead for a Dollar '70
The Ruthless Four '70
Sartana's Here...Trade Your Pistol for a Coffin '70
The Battle of El Alamein '68
Any Gun Can Play '67

Violet Hilton
Chained for Life '51
Freaks '32

Pippa Hinchley
Fergie & Andrew: Behind Palace Doors '93
And a Nightingale Sang '91

Madeline Hinde
The Fiend '71
The Bloodsuckers '70

Art Hindle (1948-)
The World's Oldest Living Bridesmaid '92
Dixie Lanes '88
Into the Fire '88
Surrogate '88
The Gunfighters '87
J. Edgar Hoover '87
Say Yes! '86
Raw Courage '84
The Man Who Wasn't There '83
Porky's 2: The Next Day '83
Wild Pony '83
Desperate Lives '82
Porky's '82
Octagon '80
The Brood '79
The Power Within '79
Invasion of the Body Snatchers '78
Black Christmas '75

Earl Hindman (1942-)
The Ballad of the Sad Cafe '91
Murder in Coweta County '83
The Taking of Pelham One Two Three '74

Ciaran Hinds (1953-)
The Sum of All Fears '02
Jason and the Argonauts '00
The Lost Son '98
Ivanhoe '97
Jane Eyre '97
Oscar and Lucinda '97
Some Mother's Son '96
The Affair '95
Mary Reilly '95
Persuasion '95
Catherine Cookson's The Man Who Cried '93
A Dark Adapted Eye '93
Hostages '93
December Bride '91

Cindy Hinds
Deadline '82
The Brood '79

Samuel S. Hinds (1875-1948)
It's a Wonderful Life '46
Scarlet Street '45
The Strange Affair of Uncle Harry '45
Weekend at the Waldorf '45
Cobra Woman '44
Jungle Woman '44
Son of Dracula '43
Pardon My Sarong '42
Ride 'Em Cowboy '42
Blossoms in the Dust '41
Man Made Monster '41
It's a Date '40
Destry Rides Again '39
Devil's Party '38
Test Pilot '38
You Can't Take It with You '38
The Black Legion '37
Navy Blue and Gold '37
Rhythm on the Range '36
The Raven '35
Deluge '33
Gabriel Over the White House '33

Damon Hines
Once Upon a Time ... When We Were Colored '95
Lethal Weapon '87

Gregory Hines (1946-)
Bojangles '01
Echo of Murder '00
Once in the Life '00
Things You Can Tell Just by Looking at Her '00
The Tic Code '99
Color of Justice '97
Subway Stories '97
The Cherokee Kid '96
Good Luck '96
The Preacher's Wife '96
Trigger Happy '96
A Stranger in Town '95
Waiting to Exhale '95
Bleeding Hearts '94
Dead Air '94
Renaissance Man '94
T Bone N Weasel '92
A Rage in Harlem '91
White Lie '91
Eve of Destruction '90
Tap '89
Off Limits '87
Running Scared '86
White Nights '85
The Cotton Club '84
The Muppets Take Manhattan '84
Puss 'n Boots '84
Deal of the Century '83
Eubie! '82
History of the World: Part 1 '81
Wolfen '81

Johnny Hines (1895-1970)
The Speed Spook '24
A Girl's Folly '17
Tillie Wakes Up '17

Robert Hines
Devices and Desires '91
Echoes '88
Hellraiser '87

Ronald Hines
We'll Meet Again '82
Elizabeth R '72

Pat Hingle (1923-)
The Runaway '00
Shaft '00
Muppets from Space '99
Batman and Robin '97
Hunter's Moon '97
A Thousand Acres '97
Larger Than Life '96
Batman Forever '95
One Christmas '95
Truman '95
Lightning Jack '94
The Quick and the Dead '94
Batman Returns '92
Citizen Cohn '92
The Habitation of Dragons '91
The Grifters '90
Batman '89
The Land Before Time '88 (V)
LBJ: The Early Years '88
Baby Boom '87
The Private History of a Campaign That Failed '87
In 'n Out '86
Manhunt for Claude Dallas '86
Maximum Overdrive '86
Brewster's Millions '85
Broken Badge '85
The Falcon and the Snowman '85
Lady from Yesterday '85
Going Berserk '83
Running Brave '83
Sudden Impact '83
The Act '82
Of Mice and Men '81
Elvis: The Movie '79
Norma Rae '79
Running Scared '79
Wild Times '79
The Gauntlet '77
Tarantulas: The Deadly Cargo '77
Hazel's People '75
Running Wild '73
Bloody Mama '70
The Ballad of Andy Crocker '69
Hang 'Em High '67
Nevada Smith '66
Invitation to a Gunfighter '64
The Ugly American '63
The Strange One '57

Tommy Hinkley
The Little Vampire '00
The Human Shield '92
Back to the Beach '87

Skip Hinnant
Nine Lives of Fritz the Cat '74 (V)
Fritz the Cat '72 (V)

Darby Hinton (1957-)
Malibu Express '85
The Treasure of Jamaica Reef '74
Firecracker '71

Michael Hinz
Touch Me Not '74
The Bridge '59

Bill (William Heinzman) Hinzman
Revenge of the Living Zombies '88
The Majorettes '87
Night of the Living Dead '68

Paul Hipp (1963-)
Teenage Caveman '01
Cleopatra's Second Husband '00
Waking the Dead '00
Another Day in Paradise '98
Midnight in the Garden of Good and Evil '97
Vicious Circles '97
The Funeral '96
Bad Channels '92

Akihiko Hirata (1927-84)
Godzilla vs. the Cosmic Monster '74
Son of Godzilla '66
King Kong vs. Godzilla '63
Mothra '62
The Secret of the Telegian '61
H-Man '59
Godzilla, King of the Monsters '56
Samurai 2: Duel at Ichijoji Temple '55

Thora Hird (1911-)
Lost for Words '99
The Wedding Gift '93
Consuming Passions '88
The Nightcomers '72
Rattle of a Simple Man '64
A Kind of Loving '62
The Entertainer '60
Dangerous Youth '58
Conspirator '49

Daniel Hirsch
Lady Avenger '89
Zero Boys '86
Sky High '84

Emile Hirsch
The Dangerous Lives of Altar Boys '02
Gargantua '98

Judd Hirsch (1935-)
A Beautiful Mind '01
Man on the Moon '99
Out of the Cold '99
Rocky Marciano '99
Color of Justice '97
Independence Day '96
The Great Escape 2: The Untold Story '88
Running on Empty '88
Brotherly Love '85
Teachers '84
The Goodbye People '83
Without a Trace '83
Marriage Is Alive and Well '80
Ordinary People '80
King of the Gypsies '78
Sooner or Later '78
Legend of Valentino '75
Fury on Wheels '71

Robert Hirsch
The Hunchback of Notre Dame '57
Plucking the Daisy '56

Hallee Hirsh
My Sister's Keeper '02
Joe Gould's Secret '00
You've Got Mail '98

Alice Hirson
Blind Date '87
Miss All-American Beauty '82

Christianne Hirt
Firestorm '97
For the Moment '94
Tokyo Cowboy '94
Blades of Courage '88

Alfred Hitchcock (1899-1980)
Family Plot '76
The Birds '63
Psycho '60
The Lady Vanishes '38
Blackmail '29
The Lodger '26

Michael Hitchcock
Best in Show '00
Happy, Texas '99
Wishmaster '97

Patricia Hitchcock
Psycho '60
Strangers on a Train '51

Iben Hjejle
High Fidelity '00
Mifune '99

Judith Hoag (1968-)
Acting on Impulse '93
Switched at Birth '91
Danielle Steel's Fine Things '90
A Matter of Degrees '90
Teenage Mutant Ninja Turtles: The Movie '90

Florence Hoath
Back to the Secret Garden '01
The Governess '98
FairyTale: A True Story '97

Doug Hobart
The Death Curse of Tartu '66
The Professor '58

Rose Hobart (1906-2000)
Cass Timberlane '47
The Farmer's Daughter '47
Conflict '45
The Mad Ghoul '43
Susan and God '40
Dr. Jekyll and Mr. Hyde '32
East of Borneo '31

Halliwell Hobbes (1877-1962)
You Gotta Stay Happy '48
Casanova Brown '44
Gaslight '44
Sherlock Holmes Faces Death '43
Journey for Margaret '42
Son of Fury '42
To Be or Not to Be '42
The Undying Monster '42
You Can't Take It with You '38
Dr. Jekyll and Mr. Hyde '32

Peter Hobbs
In the Mood '87
Next One '84

Rebecca Hobbs
Siam Sunset '99
The Ugly '96

William Hobbs
Captain Kronos: Vampire Hunter '74
The Three Musketeers '74

Mara Hobel (1971-)
Broadway Damage '98
Mommie Dearest '81
Sorrows of Gin '79

Valerie Hobson (1917-98)
The Promoter '52
Interrupted Journey '49
Kind Hearts and Coronets '49
The Rocking Horse Winner '49
Train of Events '49
Blanche Fury '48
Great Expectations '46
The Adventures of Tartu '43
Contraband '40
Clouds over Europe '39
Spy in Black '39
Drums '38
When Thief Meets Thief '37
The Bride of Frankenstein '35
The Mystery of Edwin Drood '35
Werewolf of London '35

Danny Hoch
Black Hawk Down '01
White Boyz '99
Subway Stories '97

Kristen Hocking
The Wolves '95
Bitter Vengeance '94

Kane Hodder (1951-)
Jason X '01
Watchers Reborn '98
Wishmaster '97
Pumpkinhead 2: Blood Wings '94
Jason Goes to Hell: The Final Friday '93
Friday the 13th, Part 8: Jason Takes Manhattan '89
Friday the 13th, Part 7: The New Blood '88

Douglas Hodge (1960-)
The Way We Live Now '02
Hollow Reed '95
Middlemarch '93
A Fatal Inversion '92
Buddy's Song '91
Dark Obsession '90
Salome's Last Dance '88

Kate Hodge
Desire '95
The Hidden 2 '94
Rapid Fire '92
Love Kills '91
Leatherface: The Texas Chainsaw Massacre 3 '89

Mike Hodge
Boycott '02
Fiona '98
Office Killer '97

Patricia Hodge (1946-)
The Moonstone '97
The Leading Man '96
The Heat of the Day '91
Spymaker: The Secret Life of Ian Fleming '90
The Shell Seekers '89
Diamond's Edge '88
Sunset '88
Dust to Dust '85
Betrayal '83

Eddie Hodges (1947-)
Live a Little, Love a Little '68
Summer Magic '63
The Adventures of Huckleberry Finn '60
A Hole in the Head '59

Tom (Thomas E.) Hodges (1965-)
Since You've Been Gone '97
The Baby Doll Murders '92
Lucas '86

Earle Hodgins (1893-1964)
The Man Who Shot Liberty Valance '62
The Topeka Terror '45
Colt Comrades '43
Hoppy Serves a Writ '43

The Bashful Bachelor '42
Inside the Law '42
Boss of Bullion City '41
Santa Fe Marshal '40
Heroes of the Alamo '37
A Lawman Is Born '37
Aces and Eights '36
Law for Tombstone '35

Leyland Hodgson (1894-1949)
Bedlam '45
International Lady '41
My Son, My Son '40
The Eagle and the Hawk '33

John Hodiak (1914-55)
Dragonfly Squadron '54
Ambush at Tomahawk Gap '53
Conquest of Cochise '53
Across the Wide Missouri '51
The Miniver Story '50
Battleground '49
Malaya '49
Command Decision '48
Homecoming '48
Love from a Stranger '47
The Harvey Girls '46
Lifeboat '44

Paul Hoerbiger
The Third Man '49
The Mozart Story '48

Dennis Hoey (1893-1960)
David and Bathsheba '51
Golden Earrings '47
Where There's Life '47
Anna and the King of Siam '46
Roll on Texas Moon '46
She Wolf of London '46
Terror by Night '46
House of Fear '45
A Thousand and One Nights '45
The Pearl of Death '44
Spider Woman '44
Uncertain Glory '44
Sherlock Holmes and the Secret Weapon '42
Son of Fury '42
Power '34

Abbie Hoffman
Born on the Fourth of July '89
Heavy Petting '89

Basil Hoffman (1941-)
The Ice Runner '93
The Double O Kid '92
Communion '89
Lambada '89
Love at First Bite '79

Connie Hoffman
Blazing Stewardesses '75
Texas Layover '75

David Hoffman (1904-61)
Children in the Crossfire '84
Wolf Lake '79
A Woman's World '54

Dustin Hoffman (1937-)
The Messenger: The Story of Joan of Arc '99
Mad City '97
Sphere '97
Wag the Dog '97
Sleepers '96
American Buffalo '95
Outbreak '94
Hero '92
Billy Bathgate '91
Hook '91
Dick Tracy '90
Family Business '89
Rain Man '88
Ishtar '87
Death of a Salesman '86
Tootsie '82
Agatha '79
Kramer vs. Kramer '79
Straight Time '78
All the President's Men '76
Marathon Man '76
Lenny '74
Papillon '73
Alfredo, Alfredo '72
Straw Dogs '72
Little Big Man '70
Midnight Cowboy '69
The Graduate '67
Madigan's Millions '67

Elizabeth Hoffman
Dante's Peak '97
Fear No Evil '80

Erika Hoffman
The Final Cut '95
To Play the King '93

Gaby Hoffman (1982-)
Perfume '01
Black and White '99
Coming Soon '99
All I Wanna Do '98
200 Cigarettes '98
Volcano '97
Everyone Says I Love You '96
Now and Then '95
The Man Without a Face '93
Sleepless in Seattle '93
This Is My Life '92
Field of Dreams '89
Uncle Buck '89

Jane Hoffman (1911-)
Static '87
Senior Trip '81
Sybil '76
Up the Sandbox '72

Linda Hoffman
Captured '99
The Dentist 2: Brace Yourself '98
The Dentist '96

Philip Seymour Hoffman (1967-)
Almost Famous '00
State and Main '00
Flawless '99
Magnolia '99
The Talented Mr. Ripley '99
Happiness '98
Patch Adams '98
The Big Lebowski '97
Boogie Nights '97
Montana '97
Hard Eight '96
Twister '96
Nobody's Fool '94
When a Man Loves a Woman '94
The Yearling '94
Joey Breaker '93
Leap of Faith '92
Scent of a Woman '92

Robert Hoffman
Joe Panther '76
Eyes Behind the Stars '72
A Black Veil for Lisa '68

Thom Hoffman (1957-)
Orlando '92
Lily Was Here '89
The 4th Man '79

Jutta Hoffmann
Bandits '99
The Third '72

Charlie Hofheimer
Black Hawk Down '01
Music of the Heart '99
Father's Day '96

Isabella Hofmann (1958-)
Homicide: The Movie '00
Atomic Dog '98
The Colony '98
Tripwire '89

Marco Hofschneider
Urban Legends 2: Final Cut '00
The Island of Dr. Moreau '96
Foreign Student '94
Immortal Beloved '94
Europa, Europa '91

Bosco Hogan
In the Name of the Father '93
James Joyce: A Portrait of the Artist as a Young Man '77
Zardoz '73

Dick Hogan
Action in the North Atlantic '43
So Proudly We Hail '43

Hulk Hogan (1953-)
Shadow Warriors '97
Shadow Warriors 2: Hunt for the Death Merchant '97
3 Ninjas: High Noon at Mega Mountain '97
Santa with Muscles '96
The Secret Agent Club '96
Thunder in Paradise 2 '94
Thunder in Paradise 3 '94
Mr. Nanny '93
Thunder in Paradise '93
Suburban Commando '91
Gremlins 2: The New Batch '90
No Holds Barred '89

Michael Hogan
End of Summer '97
Clearcut '92
Smokescreen '90
Lost '86
The Peanut Butter Solution '85

Pat Hogan (1920-66)
Indian Paint '64
Seventh Cavalry '56
Davy Crockett, King of the Wild Frontier '55
Savage Wilderness '55

Paul Hogan (1939-)
Crocodile Dundee in Los Angeles '01
Flipper '96
Lightning Jack '94
Almost an Angel '90
Crocodile Dundee 2 '88
Crocodile Dundee '86
Anzacs: The War Down Under '85

Robert Hogan
Maze '01
Gone Are the Days '84
Lady in Red '79
Memory of Us '74

Susan Hogan
Rupert's Land '98
When Danger Follows You Home '97
White Fang '91
Title Shot '81
Phobia '80
The Brood '79

B.J. Hogg
Resurrection Man '97
Rudyard Kipling's the Second Jungle Book: Mowgli and Baloo '97

Ian Hogg
Rasputin: Dark Servant of Destiny '96
The Legacy '79

Arthur Hohl (1889-1964)
Mystery of the Riverboat '44
Son of Fury '42
Blondie Has Trouble '40
Devil Doll '36
The Whole Town's Talking '35
The Sign of the Cross '33
Island of Lost Souls '32

Solbjorg Hojfeldt
The Kingdom 2 '97
The Kingdom '95

David Holbrook
Creepshow 2 '87
Return to Salem's Lot '87

Hal Holbrook (1925-)
The Majestic '01
Men of Honor '00
Waking the Dead '00
The Bachelor '99
Hush '98
Judas Kiss '98
My Own Country '98
Cats Don't Dance '97 (V)
Eye of God '97
Hercules '97 (V)
Operation: Delta Force '97
Carried Away '95
The Firm '93
A Killing in a Small Town '90
Day One '89
Fletch Lives '89
Sorry, Wrong Number '89
The Unholy '88
Wall Street '87
Dress Gray '86
North and South Book 2 '86
Behind Enemy Lines '85
North and South Book 1 '85
George Washington '84
Girls Night Out '83
The Star Chamber '83
Creepshow '82
When Hell Was in Session '82
Killing of Randy Webster '81
The Kidnapping of the President '80
Murder by Natural Causes '79
Natural Enemies '79
Rituals '79
Capricorn One '78
The Fog '78
Julia '77
Our Town '77
All the President's Men '76
Midway '76
The Girl from Petrovka '74
Magnum Force '73
Pueblo Affair '73
They Only Kill Their Masters '72
The Great White Hope '70
The People Next Door '70
Wild in the Streets '68
The Group '66

Kathryn Holcomb
Skag '79
Our Time '74

Sarah Holcomb
Caddyshack '80
Happy Birthday, Gemini '80
National Lampoon's Animal House '78

Alexandra Holden
Sugar & Spice '01
Uprising '01
Dancer, Texas—Pop. 81 '98
In and Out '97

Diane Holden
Black Starlet '74
Grave of the Vampire '72

Fay Holden (1895-1973)
The Big Hangover '50
Samson and Delilah '50
Love Laughs at Andy Hardy '46
Andy Hardy's Double Life '42
Andy Hardy's Private Secretary '41
Blossoms in the Dust '41
Life Begins for Andy Hardy '41
Ziegfeld Girl '41
Andy Hardy Meets Debutante '40
Bitter Sweet '40
Andy Hardy Gets Spring Fever '39
Love Finds Andy Hardy '38

Frankie J. Holden
Ebbtide '94
High Tide '87

Gloria Holden (1908-91)
The Adventures of Rusty '45
Behind the Rising Sun '43
A Gentleman After Dark '42
Hawaii Calls '38
The Life of Emile Zola '37
Dracula's Daughter '36

Jan Holden
One Brief Summer '70
Fire Maidens from Outer Space '56

Laurie Holden (1972-)
The Majestic '01
The Magnificent Seven '98
Past Perfect '98
The Pathfinder '94

Marjean Holden
Mortal Kombat 2: Annihilation '97
Ballistic '94
Philadelphia Experiment 2 '93
Secret Agent 00-Soul '89
Stripped to Kill II: Live Girls '89

Rebecca Holden
Twenty Dollar Star '91
The Sisterhood '88

William Holden (1918-81)
S.O.B. '81
Earthling '80
When Time Ran Out '80
Ashanti, Land of No Mercy '79
Escape to Athena '79
Damien: Omen 2 '78
Network '76
21 Hours at Munich '76
The Towering Inferno '74
Wild Rovers '71
When Wolves Cry '69
The Wild Bunch '69
The Devil's Brigade '68
Casino Royale '67
Alvarez Kelly '66
Paris When It Sizzles '64
The Seventh Dawn '64
The Counterfeit Traitor '62
The World of Suzie Wong '60
The Horse Soldiers '59
The Key '58
The Bridge on the River Kwai '57
The Bridges at Toko-Ri '55
Love Is a Many-Splendored Thing '55
Picnic '55
Country Girl '54
Executive Suite '54
Sabrina '54
Escape from Fort Bravo '53
Forever Female '53
The Moon Is Blue '53
Stalag 17 '53
Boots Malone '52
Born Yesterday '50
Sunset Boulevard '50
Union Station '50
The Dark Past '49
Dear Wife '49
Man from Colorado '49
Miss Grant Takes Richmond '49
Rachel and the Stranger '48
Young & Willing '42
Texas '41
Arizona '40
Our Town '40
Golden Boy '39

Kris Holdenried
Hendrix '00
Night of the Demons 3 '97
Young Ivanhoe '95

Geoffrey Holder (1930-)
Boomerang '92
Swashbuckler '76
Live and Let Die '73
The Man Without a Country '73
Everything You Always Wanted to Know about Sex (But Were Afraid to Ask) '72
Doctor Dolittle '67

Roy Holder
The Land That Time Forgot '75
Loot ... Give Me Money, Honey! '70
Othello '65
Whistle down the Wind '61

Sacha Holder
Soft Fruit '99
Praise '98

Ticky Holgado
French Twist '95
Delicatessen '92

Hope Holiday
The Rounders '65
The Apartment '60

Eric Holland
Masquerade '88
Gardens of Stone '87

John Holland (1908-93)
They Saved Hitler's Brain '64
Girl in Black Stockings '57
House of Errors '42
Gentleman from Dixie '41
Up in the Air '40
Defenders of the Law '31
Morals for Women '31
Hell Harbor '30

Tom Hollander (1969-)
Enigma '01
Gosford Park '01
Wives and Daughters '01
Maybe Baby '99
Bedrooms and Hallways '98
The Very Thought of You '98

Judy Holliday (1922-65)
Bells Are Ringing '60
Full of Life '56
Solid Gold Cadillac '56
It Should Happen to You '54
Phffft! '54
The Marrying Kind '52
Adam's Rib '50
Born Yesterday '50

Polly Holliday (1937-)
Konrad '90s
The Parent Trap '98
Mr. Wrong '95
Moon over Parador '88
Lots of Luck '85
Gremlins '84
All the President's Men '76

Earl Holliman (1928-)
Perfect Tenant '99
Gunsmoke: Return to Dodge '87
The Solitary Man '82
Sharky's Machine '81
Alexander: The Other Side of Dawn '77
Cry Panic '74
I Love You ... Goodbye '73
Smoke '70
Tribes '70
Anzio '68
Sons of Katie Elder '65
Armored Command '61
Summer and Smoke '61
Last Train from Gun Hill '59
The Trap '59
Hot Spell '58
Don't Go Near the Water '57
Gunfight at the O.K. Corral '57
Forbidden Planet '56
Giant '56
The Rainmaker '56
Big Combo '55
The Bridges at Toko-Ri '55
I Died a Thousand Times '55
Broken Lance '54

Tommy Hollis (1954-2001)
Primary Colors '98
The Piano Lesson '94
Malcolm X '92

Bridget Hollman
Evils of the Night '85
Slumber Party '57 '76

Laurel Holloman
Lush '01
Loving Jezebel '99
Tumbleweeds '98
Boogie Nights '97
The First to Go '97
The Myth of Fingerprints '97
Prefontaine '96

The Incredibly True Adventure of Two Girls in Love '95
Julian Holloway
Porridge '91
Carry On Henry VIII '71
Stanley Holloway (1890-1982)
The Private Life of Sherlock Holmes '70
Mrs. Brown, You've Got a Lovely Daughter '68
In Harm's Way '65
My Fair Lady '64
On the Fiddle '61
No Love for Johnnie '60
The Lavender Hill Mob '51
Passport to Pimlico '49
Hamlet '48
This Happy Breed '47
Brief Encounter '46
Nicholas Nickleby '46
Immortal Battalion '44
Salute John Citizen '42
Cotton Queen '37
Lily of Killarney '34
Sterling Holloway (1905-92)
Super Seal '77
Thunder and Lightning '77
The Aristocats '70 (V)
Live a Little, Love a Little '68
The Jungle Book '67 (V)
The Adventures of Huckleberry Finn '60
Shake, Rattle and Rock '57
Kentucky Rifle '55
Alice in Wonderland '51 (V)
The Beautiful Blonde from Bashful Bend '49
Robin Hood of Texas '47
Trail to San Antone '47
Death Valley '46
Sioux City Sue '46
A Walk in the Sun '46
The Three Caballeros '45 (V)
Wildfire '45
Bambi '42 (V)
The Lady Is Willing '42
Cheers for Miss Bishop '41
Dumbo '41 (V)
Melody Master '41
Twilight on the Rio Grande '41
Remember the Night '40
Doubting Thomas '35
I Live My Life '35
The Merry Widow '34
Tomorrow's Children '34
International House '33
Ellen Holly
School Daze '88
Cops and Robbers '73
Lauren Holly (1963-)
The Final Hit '02
Jackie, Ethel, Joan: The Kennedy Women '01
What Women Want '00
Any Given Sunday '99
Entropy '99
Money Kings '98
No Looking Back '98
Beautiful Girls '96
Down Periscope '96
A Smile Like Yours '96
Turbulence '96
Sabrina '95
Dumb & Dumber '94
Dangerous Heart '93
Dragon: The Bruce Lee Story '93
Fugitive Among Us '92
The Adventures of Ford Fairlane '90
Archie: Return to Riverdale '90
Band of the Hand '86
Seven Minutes in Heaven '86
Celeste Holm (1919-)
Still Breathing '97
Murder by the Book '87
Three Men and a Baby '87
Bittersweet Love '76
Death Cruise '74
Tom Sawyer '73
Cinderella '64
High Society '56
The Tender Trap '55
All About Eve '50
Champagne for Caesar '50
Come to the Stable '49
A Letter to Three Wives '49 (V)
Road House '48
The Snake Pit '48
Gentleman's Agreement '47
Ian Holm (1931-)
From Hell '01
Lord of the Rings 1: The Fellowship of the Rings '01
Beautiful Joe '00
Bless the Child '00
Joe Gould's Secret '00
The Last of the Blonde Bombshells '00
The Miracle Maker: The Story of Jesus '00 (V)
Animal Farm '99 (V)
eXistenZ '99
The Match '99
King Lear '98
The Fifth Element '97
A Life Less Ordinary '97
Night Falls on Manhattan '96
The Return of the Borrowers '96
The Sweet Hereafter '96
Big Night '95
Loch Ness '95
The Madness of King George '94
Mary Shelley's Frankenstein '94
The Advocate '93
The Borrowers '93
Kafka '91
Naked Lunch '91
Hamlet '90
The Endless Game '89
Henry V '89
Another Woman '88
Brazil '85
Dance with a Stranger '85
Dreamchild '85
Wetherby '85
Greystoke: The Legend of Tarzan, Lord of the Apes '84
Singleton's Pluck '84
Inside the Third Reich '82
Return of the Soldier '82
Chariots of Fire '81
Time Bandits '81
Alien '79
S.O.S. Titanic '79
Holocaust '78
The Thief of Baghdad '78
The Man in the Iron Mask '77
March or Die '77
Robin and Marian '76
Shout at the Devil '76
Juggernaut '74
Young Winston '72
Mary, Queen of Scots '71
The Fixer '68
A Midsummer Night's Dream '68
Clare Holman
Tom & Viv '94
Afraid of the Dark '92
Let Him Have It '91
Catherine Cookson's The Fifteen Streets '90
Harry Holman (1874-1947)
Inside the Law '42
Mexican Spitfire at Sea '42
Fugitive Road '34
Rex Holman
Panic in the Year Zero! '62
The Choppers '61
Katie Holmes (1978-)
The Gift '00
Wonder Boys '00
Go '99
Teaching Mrs. Tingle '99
Disturbing Behavior '98
The Ice Storm '97
Luree Holmes
How to Stuff a Wild Bikini '65
Pajama Party '64
Phillips Holmes (1909-42)
Housemaster '38
General Spanky '36
Great Expectations '34
Dinner at Eight '33
Penthouse '33
Criminal Code '31
Prudence Wright Holmes
In Dreams '98
Kingpin '96
Stuart Holmes (1887-1971)
People Will Talk '51
My Pal, the King '32
Beyond the Trail '26
The Four Horsemen of the Apocalypse '21
Taylor Holmes (1872-1959)
Sleeping Beauty '59 (V)
Tobor the Great '54
Beware, My Lovely '52
Hoodlum Empire '52
Copper Canyon '50
Double Deal '50
Boomerang '47
Before Morning '33
Teck Holmes
National Lampoon's Van Wilder '02
Love Song '00
Tina Holmes
Prince of Central Park '00
Edge of Seventeen '99
Wendell Holmes
Lotto Land '95
Good Day for a Hanging '58
Lost Boundaries '49
Rosie Holotik
Encounter with the Unknown '75
Twisted Brain '74
Don't Look in the Basement '73
Charlene Holt (1939-)
El Dorado '67
Red Line 7000 '65
Man's Favorite Sport? '63
David Holt
The Adventures of Tom Sawyer '38
Last Days of Pompeii '35
Hans Holt
Almost Angels '62
The Mozart Story '48
Jack Holt (1888-1951)
Across the Wide Missouri '51
King of the Bullwhip '51
Red Desert '50
Trail of Robin Hood '50
Task Force '49
Loaded Pistols '48
Wild Frontier '48
The Chase '46
Flight to Nowhere '46
My Pal Trigger '46
Renegade Girl '46
They Were Expendable '45
Cat People '42
Holt of the Secret Service '42
San Francisco '36
The Littlest Rebel '35
Maker of Men '31
The Little American '17
Jennifer Holt (1920-97)
The Hawk of Powder River '48
Range Renegades '48
Stage to Mesa City '48
The Tioga Kid '48
Buffalo Bill Rides Again '47
Fighting Vigilantes '47
Ghost Town Renegades '47
Where the North Begins '47
Song of Old Wyoming '45
Outlaw Trail '44
Frontier Law '43
Raiders of Sunset Pass '43
Patrick Holt (1912-93)
Psychomania '73
When Dinosaurs Ruled the Earth '70
Vulture '67
Flight from Singapore '62
It Takes a Thief '59
Men of Sherwood Forest '57
Alias John Preston '56
Suspended Alibi '56
Unholy Four '54
Sandrine Holt (1971-)
Loving Jezebel '99
1999 '98
Once a Thief '96
Pocahontas: The Legend '95
Rapa Nui '93
Black Robe '91
Tim Holt (1918-73)
This Stuff'll Kill Ya! '71
The Yesterday Machine '63
The Monster That Challenged the World '57
Gunplay '51
His Kind of Woman '51
Hot Lead '51
Dynamite Pass '50
Rider from Tucson '50
Storm over Wyoming '50
Mysterious Desperado '49
Riders of the Range '49
Treasure of the Sierra Madre '48
My Darling Clementine '46
Hitler's Children '43
Sagebrush Law '43
The Magnificent Ambersons '42
Fifth Avenue Girl '39
Stagecoach '39
Law West of Tombstone '38
Stella Dallas '37
Ula Holt
Tarzan and the Green Goddess '38
The New Adventures of Tarzan '35
Mark Holton
Leprechaun '93
A League of Their Own '92
Easy Wheels '89
Pee-wee's Big Adventure '85
Stoogemania '85
Sean Holton
Presumed Guilty '91
White Fury '90
Operation Warzone '89
Maria Holvoe
The Last Warrior '89
Worth Winning '89
Arabella Holzbog
Red Shoe Diaries: Swimming Naked '00
Carnosaur 2 '94
Evil Lives '92
Stone Cold '91
The Last Samurai '90
Robert E. Homans (1874-1947)
The Scarlet Clue '45
Rogue's Gallery '44
X Marks the Spot '42
I Take This Oath '40
Man from Hell's Edges '32
The Concentratin' Kid '30
Spurs '30
Trigger Tricks '30
David Homb
Street Soldiers '91
The Channeler '89
Skip Homeier (1930-)
Starbird and Sweet William '73
The Voyage of the Yes '72
The Ghost and Mr. Chicken '66
Johnny Shiloh '63
Comanche Station '60
The Tall T '57
The Burning Hills '56
Cry Vengeance '54
Ten Wanted Men '54
The Gunfighter '50
The Halls of Montezuma '50
Tomorrow the World '44
Oscar Homolka (1898-1978)
The Executioner '70
Song of Norway '70
The Madwoman of Chaillot '69
Dr. Jekyll and Mr. Hyde '68
Strange Case of Dr. Jekyll & Mr. Hyde '68
Funeral in Berlin '66
The Long Ships '64
Boys' Night Out '62
Mooncussers '62
The Wonderful World of the Brothers Grimm '62
Mr. Sardonicus '61
The Key '58
War and Peace '56
The Seven Year Itch '55
The House of the Arrow '53
The White Tower '50
I Remember Mama '48
Ball of Fire '41
Comrade X '40
The Invisible Woman '40
Seven Sinners '40
Rhodes '36
Sabotage '36
James Hong (1929-)
The Art of War '00
Epoch '00
G2: Mortal Conquest '99
Breakout '98
Broken Vessels '98
Mulan '98 (V)
Red Corner '97
The Secret Agent Club '96
South Beach Academy '96
Bloodsport 2: The Next Kumite '95
Bloodsport 3 '95
Femme Fontaine: Killer Babe for the C.I.A. '95
Bad Company '94
Operation Golden Phoenix '94
Question of Faith '93
Wayne's World 2 '93
Body Trouble '92
Dragonfight '92
L.A. Goddess '92
Merlin '92
Talons of the Eagle '92
Crime Lords '91
Caged Fury '90
Tax Season '90
The Brotherhood of the Rose '89
Shadowzone '89
Tango and Cash '89
The Vineyard '89
The Jitters '88
Black Widow '87
Revenge of the Nerds 2: Nerds in Paradise '87
Big Trouble in Little China '86
The Golden Child '86
Yes, Giorgio '82
Airplane! '80
Go Tell the Spartans '78
Bethune '77
The Dynamite Brothers '74
The Sand Pebbles '66
China Gate '57
Kojiro Hongo (1938-)
Destroy All Planets '68
Gamera vs. Gaos '67
Gamera vs. Barugon '66
Darla Hood (1931-79)
The Bat '59
Bohemian Girl '36
Don Hood
Dean Koontz's Mr. Murder '98
Blind Vengeance '90
Marie '85
Absence of Malice '81
Brian Hooks
Nothin' 2 Lose '00
Three Strikes '00
Phat Beach '96
Jan Hooks (1957-)
Simon Birch '98
Coneheads '93
A Dangerous Woman '93
Batman Returns '92
Pee-wee's Big Adventure '85
Kevin Hooks (1958-)
Innerspace '87
Can You Hear the Laughter? The Story of Freddie Prinze '79
Take Down '79
Aaron Loves Angela '75
Sounder '72
Robert Hooks (1937-)
Seventeen Again '00
Free of Eden '98
Posse '93
Passenger 57 '92
Heat Wave '90
The Execution '85
Words by Heart '84
Fast Walking '82
A Woman Called Moses '78
Aaron Loves Angela '75
Black Brigade '69
Sweet Love, Bitter '67
Tobe Hooper (1946-)
Body Bags '93
Sleepwalkers '92
Peter Hooten
2020 Texas Gladiators '85
Deadly Mission '78
Dr. Strange '78
Slashed Dreams '74
Fantasies '73
William Hootkins (1950-)
The Magnificent Ambersons '02
The Omega Code '99
This World, Then the Fireworks '97
Death Machine '95
Dust Devil '93
Hear My Song '91
American Gothic '88
Valentino '77
Joseph Hoover
The Astro-Zombies '67
Hell Is for Heroes '62
The Man Who Shot Liberty Valance '62
Phil Hoover
Black Gestapo '75
Policewomen '73
Chain Gang Women '72
Bob Hope (1903-)
The Muppet Movie '79
Cancel My Reservation '72
Bachelor in Paradise '69
How to Commit Marriage '69
Private Navy of Sgt. O'Farrell '68
Eight on the Lam '67
Boy, Did I Get a Wrong Number! '66
The Oscar '66
I'll Take Sweden '65
Call Me Bwana '63
A Global Affair '63
The Road to Hong Kong '62
The Facts of Life '60
The Road to Lebanon '60
Alias Jesse James '59
Paris Holiday '57
The Seven Little Foys '55
Casanova's Big Night '54
Here Come the Girls '53
Off Limits '53
The Road to Bali '53
Scared Stiff '53
Son of Paleface '52
The Lemon Drop Kid '51
Fancy Pants '50
The Great Lover '49
Sorrowful Jones '49
The Paleface '48
My Favorite Brunette '47
The Road to Rio '47
Where There's Life '47
Monsieur Beaucaire '46

The Road to Utopia *'46*
The Princess and the Pirate *'44*
Strictly G.I. *'44*
They Got Me Covered *'43*
My Favorite Blonde *'42*
The Road to Morocco *'42*
Star Spangled Rhythm *'42*
Caught in the Draft *'41*
Louisiana Purchase *'41*
The Road to Zanzibar *'41*
The Ghost Breakers *'40*
The Road to Singapore *'40*
Never Say Die *'39*
Rhythm Romance *'39*
The Big Broadcast of 1938 *'38*
College Swing *'38*
Give Me a Sailor *'38*
Thanks for the Memory *'38*

Leslie Hope
Bruiser *'00*
The Life Before This *'99*
Restless Spirits *'99*
Bram Stoker's Shadowbuilder *'98*
Summer of the Monkeys *'98*
Rowing Through *'96*
First Degree *'95*
Schemes *'95*
Fun *'94*
Paris, France *'94*
Caught in the Act *'93*
Sweet Killing *'93*
The Abduction of Allison Tate *'92*
The Big Slice *'90*
Doppelganger: The Evil Within *'90*
Men at Work *'90*
It Takes Two *'88*
Kansas *'88*
Talk Radio *'88*
Sword of Gideon *'86*
Prep School *'81*

Nicholas Hope
Lust and Revenge *'95*
Bad Boy Bubby *'93*

Richard Hope
Antonia and Jane *'91*
A Casualty of War *'90*
Piece of Cake *'90*
Bellman and True *'88*
Singleton's Pluck *'84*

Tamara Hope
The Deep End *'01*
The Sandy Bottom Orchestra *'00*

Vida Hope (1918-63)
Angels One Five *'54*
Roadhouse Girl *'53*
The Woman in Question *'50*
They Made Me a Fugitive *'47*

William Hope
Hellbound: Hellraiser 2 *'88*
Aliens *'86*

Alan Hopgood
Hotel de Love *'96*
Road Games *'81*
My Brilliant Career *'79*

Anthony Hopkins (1937-)
Bad Company *'02*
Hannibal *'01*
Hearts in Atlantis *'01*
Dr. Seuss' How the Grinch Stole Christmas *'00 (N)*
Mission: Impossible 2 *'00*
Instinct *'99*
Titus *'99*
The Mask of Zorro *'98*
Meet Joe Black *'98*
Amistad *'97*
The Edge *'97*
Surviving Picasso *'96*
August *'95*
Nixon *'95*
Legends of the Fall *'94*
The Road to Wellville *'94*
The Innocent *'93*
The Remains of the Day *'93*
Shadowlands *'93*
The Trial *'93*
Bram Stoker's Dracula *'92*
Chaplin *'92*
The Efficiency Expert *'92*
Freejack *'92*
Howard's End *'92*
The Silence of the Lambs *'91*
Desperate Hours *'90*
One Man's War *'90*
A Chorus of Disapproval *'89*
A Doll's House *'89*
Great Expectations *'89*
The Dawning *'88*
The Tenth Man *'88*
The Good Father *'87*
84 Charing Cross Road *'86*
Arch of Triumph *'85*
Mussolini & I *'85*
The Bounty *'84*
A Married Man *'84*
The Hunchback of Notre Dame *'82*
Peter and Paul *'81*
A Change of Seasons *'80*
The Elephant Man *'80*
Mayflower: The Pilgrims' Adventure *'79*
International Velvet *'78*
Magic *'78*
Audrey Rose *'77*
A Bridge Too Far *'77*
The Lindbergh Kidnapping Case *'76*
All Creatures Great and Small *'74*
The Girl from Petrovka *'74*
Juggernaut *'74*
QB VII *'74*
War and Peace *'73*
Young Winston *'72*
Hamlet *'69*
The Looking Glass War *'69*
The Lion in Winter *'68*

Bo Hopkins (1942-)
Big Brother Trouble *'00*
A Crack in the Floor *'00*
Time Served *'99*
From Dusk Till Dawn 2: Texas Blood Money *'98*
U-Turn *'97*
November Conspiracy *'96*
Uncle Sam *'96*
Painted Hero *'95*
Texas Payback *'95*
Cheyenne Warrior *'94*
Wyatt Earp: Return to Tombstone *'94*
The Ballad of Little Jo *'93*
Inside Monkey Zetterland *'93*
President's Target *'93*
Blood Ties *'92*
Center of the Web *'92*
The Legend of Wolf Mountain *'92*
Big Bad John *'90*
Bounty Hunters *'89*
The Final Alliance *'89*
Trapper County War *'89*
Nightmare at Noon *'87*
A Smoky Mountain Christmas *'86*
What Comes Around *'85*
Mutant *'83*
Plutonium Incident *'82*
Sweet 16 *'81*
Casino *'80*
The Fifth Floor *'80*
Rodeo Girl *'80*
More American Graffiti *'79*
Midnight Express *'78*
Tentacles *'77*
A Small Town in Texas *'76*
The Day of the Locust *'75*
The Killer Elite *'75*
Posse *'75*
The Runaway Barge *'75*
American Graffiti *'73*
White Lightning *'73*
Culpepper Cattle Co. *'72*
The Getaway *'72*
The Only Way Home *'72*
The Wild Bunch *'69*

Harold Hopkins
Joey *'98*
Resistance *'92*
Fantasy Man *'84*
Monkey Grip *'82*
Gallipoli *'81*
Sara Dane *'81*
Demonstrator *'71*

Jermaine "Huggy" Hopkins (1973-)
Def Jam's How to Be a Player *'97*
Phat Beach *'96*
Juice *'92*

Joan Hopkins
Man on the Run *'49*
The Weaker Sex *'49*

Josh Hopkins
Love & Sex *'00*
The Perfect Storm *'00*
The Pirates of Silicon Valley *'99*

Katherine Hopkins
Legend of Big Foot *'82*
The Capture of Bigfoot *'79*

Miriam Hopkins (1902-72)
Savage Intruder *'68*
The Chase *'66*
Fanny Hill: Memoirs of a Woman of Pleasure *'64*
The Children's Hour *'61*
Carrie *'52*
The Heiress *'49*
A Gentleman After Dark *'42*
Virginia City *'40*
The Old Maid *'39*
Men Are Not Gods *'37*
These Three *'36*
Barbary Coast *'35*
Becky Sharp *'35*
Splendor *'35*
Dr. Jekyll and Mr. Hyde *'32*

Paul Hopkins
Armistead Maupin's More Tales of the City *'97*
Snowboard Academy *'96*
A Young Connecticut Yankee in King Arthur's Court *'95*

Rhonda Leigh Hopkins
Cover Girl Models *'75*
Summer School Teachers *'75*
Tidal Wave *'75*

Telma Hopkins (1948-)
Trancers 3: Deth Lives *'92*
Vital Signs *'90*
Trancers *'84*
The Kid with the Broken Halo *'82*

Rolf Hoppe (1930-)
Palmetto *'98*
Schtonk *'92*
Spring Symphony *'86*
Mephisto *'81*

Dennis Hopper (1936-)
Firestarter 2: Rekindled *'02*
Ticker *'01*
Choke *'00*
Jason and the Argonauts *'00*
Luck of the Draw *'00*
EDtv *'99*
Jesus' Son *'99*
The Prophet's Game *'99*
Straight Shooter *'99*
The Apostate *'98*
Meet the Deedles *'98*
Road Ends *'98*
Tycus *'98*
The Blackout *'97*
Lured Innocence *'97*
Space Truckers *'97*
Top of the World *'97*
Basquiat *'96*
The Last Days of Frankie the Fly *'96*
Samson and Delilah *'96*
Carried Away *'95*
Waterworld *'95*
Chasers *'94*
Search and Destroy *'94*
Speed *'94*
Witch Hunt *'94*
Boiling Point *'93*
Red Rock West *'93*
Super Mario Bros. *'93*
True Romance *'93*
Nails *'92*
Sunset Heat *'92*
Double-Crossed *'91*
Eye of the Storm *'91*
Hearts of Darkness: A Filmmaker's Apocalypse *'91*
The Indian Runner *'91*
Paris Trout *'91*
Superstar: The Life and Times of Andy Warhol *'90*
Backtrack *'89*
Chattahoochee *'89*
Flashback *'89*
Blood Red *'88*
Riders of the Storm *'88*
Black Widow *'87*
O.C. and Stiggs *'87*
The Pick-Up Artist *'87*
River's Edge *'87*
Straight to Hell *'87*
Blue Velvet *'86*
Hoosiers *'86*
Let It Rock *'86*
Running out of Luck *'86*
The Texas Chainsaw Massacre 2 *'86*
My Science Project *'85*
Stark *'85*
The Inside Man *'84*
The Osterman Weekend *'83*
Rumble Fish *'83*
King of the Mountain *'81*
Out of the Blue *'80*
Apocalypse Now *'79*
Wild Times *'79*
Reborn *'78*
The American Friend *'77*
Bloodbath *'76*
Mad Dog Morgan *'76*
Tracks *'76*
The Last Movie *'71*
Easy Rider *'69*
True Grit *'69*
Head *'68*
Cool Hand Luke *'67*
The Glory Stompers *'67*
The Trip *'67*
Planet of Blood *'66*
Sons of Katie Elder *'65*
Night Tide *'63*
The Young Land *'59*
Giant *'56*
Rebel without a Cause *'55*

Hedda Hopper (1890-1966)
Breakfast in Hollywood *'46*
Reap the Wild Wind *'42*
Midnight *'39*
Maid's Night Out *'38*
Tarzan's Revenge *'38*
Thanks for the Memory *'38*
Dangerous Holiday *'37*
Vogues of 1938 *'37*
The Dark Hour *'36*
Doughnuts & Society *'36*
Dracula's Daughter *'36*
Alice Adams *'35*
I Live My Life *'35*
One Frightened Night *'35*
As You Desire Me *'32*
Speak Easily *'32*
The Racketeer *'29*
The Dropkick *'27*
Don Juan *'26*
Skinner's Dress Suit *'26*
Seven Keys to Baldpate *'17*

Victoria Hopper
The Mill on the Floss *'37*
Lorna Doone *'34*

William Hopper (1915-70)
The Deadly Mantis *'57*
20 Million Miles to Earth *'57*
The Bad Seed *'56*
Conquest of Space *'55*
Rebel without a Cause *'55*
The Fighting 69th *'40*

Russell Hopton (1900-45)
West of the Pecos *'45*
Zombies on Broadway *'44*
Hopalong Cassidy: Renegade Trail *'39*
Renegade Trail *'39*
Death from a Distance *'36*
Last Outlaw *'36*
The World Accuses *'35*
The Girl from Missouri *'34*
I'm No Angel *'33*
The Miracle Woman *'31*

Barbara Horan
Bayou Romance *'86*
Malibu Bikini Shop *'86*

Gerard Horan
A Midwinter's Tale *'95*
Much Ado about Nothing *'93*
Look Back in Anger *'89*

James Horan
The Haunting of Seacliff Inn *'94*
Image of Passion *'86*

Roy Horan
Eagle's Shadow *'84*
Snuff-Bottle Connection *'82*

Michael Hordern (1911-95)
Middlemarch *'93*
Freddie the Frog *'92 (V)*
The Green Man *'91*
Dark Obsession *'90*
The Secret Garden *'87*
Suspicion *'87*
The Trouble with Spies *'87*
Lady Jane *'85*
Young Sherlock Holmes *'85*
Yellowbeard *'83*
Ivanhoe *'82*
The Missionary *'82*
Oliver Twist *'82*
The Medusa Touch *'78*
Watership Down *'78 (V)*
Joseph Andrews *'77*
The Slipper and the Rose *'76*
The Old Curiosity Shop *'75*
Royal Flash *'75*
Mackintosh Man *'73*
Theatre of Blood *'73*
Demons of the Mind *'72*
The Possession of Joel Delaney *'72*
Anne of the Thousand Days *'69*
Where Eagles Dare *'68*
How I Won the War *'67*
I'll Never Forget What's 'Isname *'67*
The Taming of the Shrew *'67*
A Funny Thing Happened on the Way to the Forum *'66*
Khartoum *'66*
Lamp at Midnight *'66*
The Spy Who Came in from the Cold *'65*
Dr. Syn, Alias the Scarecrow *'64*
Cleopatra *'63*
Sink the Bismarck *'60*
The Spaniard's Curse *'58*
The Spanish Gardener *'57*
The Baby and the Battleship *'56*
The Man Who Never Was *'55*
The Warriors *'55*
The Promoter *'52*
A Christmas Carol *'51*
Train of Events *'49*

David Horne (1898-1970)
Men of Two Worlds *'46*
Spitfire *'42*
Night Train to Munich *'40*
Late Extra *'35*

Geoffrey Horne
Bonjour Tristesse *'57*
The Bridge on the River Kwai *'57*

Lena Horne (1917-)
The Wiz *'78*
Death of a Gunfighter *'69*
The Duchess of Idaho *'50*
Words and Music *'48*
Till the Clouds Roll By *'46*
Ziegfeld Follies *'46*
Broadway Rhythm *'44*
Two Girls and a Sailor *'44*
Cabin in the Sky *'43*
I Dood It *'43*
Stormy Weather *'43*
Thousands Cheer *'43*
Panama Hattie *'42*
The Duke Is Tops *'38*

Victoria Horne (1911-)
Harvey *'50*
Abbott and Costello Meet the Killer, Boris Karloff *'49*

Wil Horneff (1979-)
Harvest *'99*
Born to Be Wild *'95*
Oldest Confederate Widow Tells All *'95*
The Yearling *'94*
Ghost in the Machine *'93*

Penelope Horner
Dracula *'73*
Man Who Had Power Over Women *'70*
Half a Sixpence *'67*

David Horovitch (1945-)
102 Dalmatians *'00*
Solomon and Gaenor *'98*
Ivanhoe *'97*
The Sculptress *'97*
Paper Marriage *'93*
Piece of Cake *'90*

Adam Horovitz (1966-)
Roadside Prophets *'92*
A Kiss Before Dying *'91*
Long Road Home *'91*
Lost Angels *'89*

Jane Horrocks (1964-)
Born Romantic *'00*
Chicken Run *'00 (V)*
Little Voice *'98*
Second Best *'94*
Deadly Advice *'93*
Catherine Cookson's The Fifteen Streets *'90*
Life Is Sweet *'90*
Memphis Belle *'90*
The Witches *'90*
The Dressmaker *'89*
Getting It Right *'89*

Michael Horse (1951-)
Navajo Blues *'97*
Lakota Woman: Siege at Wounded Knee *'94*
Wagons East *'94*
The Avenging *'92*
House of Cards *'92*
Passenger 57 *'92*
Border Shootout *'90*
Deadly Weapon *'88*
Buckeye and Blue *'87*
Legend of the Lone Ranger *'81*

Anna Maria Horsford (1948-)
How High *'01*
Dancing in September *'00*
Nutty Professor 2: The Klumps *'00*
Dear God *'96*
One Fine Day *'96*
Set It Off *'96*
Friday *'95*
Widow's Kiss *'94*
Murder Without Motive *'92*
Presumed Innocent *'90*
Taken Away *'89*
Street Smart *'87*
Heartburn *'86*
Charlotte Forten's Mission: Experiment in Freedom *'85*
St. Elmo's Fire *'85*
Times Square *'80*

John Horsley (1920-)
Sink the Bismarck *'60*
Black Tide *'58*
The Runaway Bus *'54*

Lee Horsley (1955-)
French Silk *'94*
Unlawful Passage *'94*
Danielle Steel's Palomino *'91*

Sword & the Sorcerer '82

Edward Everett Horton (1886-1970)
Cold Turkey '71
Sex and the Single Girl '64
It's a Mad, Mad, Mad, Mad World '63
Pocketful of Miracles '61
Down to Earth '47
Her Husband's Affairs '47
Lady on a Train '45
Arsenic and Old Lace '44
Forever and a Day '43
Thank Your Lucky Stars '43
I Married an Angel '42
The Magnificent Dope '42
Springtime in the Rockies '42
Here Comes Mr. Jordan '41
Sunny '41
Ziegfeld Girl '41
Bluebeard's Eighth Wife '38
College Swing '38
Holiday '38
Angel '37
Lost Horizon '37
Shall We Dance '37
The Devil Is a Woman '35
The Private Secretary '35
Top Hat '35
The Gay Divorcee '34
The Merry Widow '34
The Front Page '31
Lonely Wives '31
Reaching for the Moon '31

Peter Horton (1953-)
From the Earth to the Moon '98
The End of Violence '97
Into Thin Air: Death on Everest '97
Crazy Horse '96
Death Benefit '96
Two Days in the Valley '96
The Baby-Sitters' Club '95
Singles '92
Side Out '90
Amazon Women on the Moon '87
Where the River Runs Black '86
Children of the Corn '84

Robert Horton
The Green Slime '68
Men of the Fighting Lady '54

Bobby Hosea
61* '01
Gargantua '98
Independence Day '96
French Silk '94
The O.J. Simpson Story '94

Shizuko Hoshi
M. Butterfly '93
Come See the Paradise '90

Yuriko Hoshi (1943-)
Last War '68
Ghidrah the Three Headed Monster '65
Godzilla vs. Mothra '64

Bob Hoskins (1942-)
Don Quixote '00
Enemy at the Gates '00
Noriega: God's Favorite '00
David Copperfield '99
Felicia's Journey '99
White River '99
American Virgin '98
Captain Jack '98
Cousin Bette '97
Spice World: The Movie '97
24-7 '97
Michael '96
The Secret Agent '96
Balto '95 (V)
Nixon '95
World War II: When Lions Roared '94
Super Mario Bros. '93
Blue Ice '92
The Favor, the Watch, & the Very Big Fish '92
Passed Away '92
Hook '91
The Inner Circle '91
Shattered '91
Heart Condition '90
Mermaids '90
The Raggedy Rawney '90
Who Framed Roger Rabbit '88
The Lonely Passion of Judith Hearne '87
Prayer for the Dying '87
Mona Lisa '86
Sweet Liberty '86
Brazil '85
The Dunera Boys '85
Mussolini & I '85
The Cotton Club '84
Lassiter '84
Beyond the Limit '83
Pink Floyd: The Wall '82
The Long Good Friday '80
Zulu Dawn '79
Inserts '76
Royal Flash '75
Cry Terror '74

Allison Hossack
Escape from Mars '99
White Light '90

Robert Hossein (1927-)
Venus Beauty Institute '98
Wax Mask '97
Bolero '82
Le Professionnel '81
Don Juan (Or If Don Juan Were a Woman) '73
Carbon Copy '69
The Battle of El Alamein '68
Le Repos du Guerrier '62
Double Agents '59

Yukihiro Hotaru
Zeram 2 '94
Zeram '91

Donald Hotton
The Freeway Maniac '88
The Hearse '80

German Houde
Night Zoo '87
Les Bons Debarras '81

James Houghton
Superstition '82
More American Graffiti '79

Katharine Houghton (1945-)
The Night We Never Met '93
Ethan Frome '92
Billy Bathgate '91
Mr. North '88
The Eyes of the Amaryllis '82
Seeds of Evil '76
Guess Who's Coming to Dinner '67

Djimon Hounsou (1964-)
Gladiator '00
Deep Rising '98
Amistad '97

Ned Hourani
Fist of Steel '93
Raiders of the Sun '92
Triple Impact '92

Billy House (1890-1961)
Joe's Bed-Stuy Barbershop: We Cut Heads '83
People Will Talk '51
Santa Fe '51
Egg and I '47
Bedlam '45

Ron House
Stoogemania '85
Footlight Frenzy '84
Bullshot '83

Arthur Houseman
The Bat '26
Manhandled '24

John Houseman (1902-88)
Another Woman '88
Bright Lights, Big City '88
Gore Vidal's Lincoln '88
The Naked Gun: From the Files of Police Squad '88
A.D. '85
The Winds of War '83
Murder by Phone '82
Ghost Story '81
The Babysitter '80
A Christmas Without Snow '80
Gideon's Trumpet '80
My Bodyguard '80
Wholly Moses! '80
Old Boyfriends '79
The Cheap Detective '78
The Fog '78
Our Town '77
St. Ives '76
Rollerball '75
Three Days of the Condor '75
The Paper Chase '73
Seven Days in May '64

Jerry Houser (1952-)
A Very Brady Christmas '88
Magic '78
Slap Shot '77
Class of '44 '73
Summer of '42 '71

Donald Houston (1923-)
Tales That Witness Madness '73
The Bushbaby '70
Where Eagles Dare '68
The Viking Queen '67
A Study in Terror '66
Maniac '63
The Prince and the Pauper '62
The Mark '61
Room at the Top '59
Doctor in the House '53
Crow Hollow '52

George Houston (1898-1944)
The Lone Rider in Cheyenne '42
Texas Justice '42
Border Roundup '41
The Lone Rider in Ghost Town '41
Rangeland Racket '41
Frontier Scout '38
The Great Waltz '38
Wallaby Jim of the Islands '37
Let's Sing Again '36

Glyn Houston
Conspiracy '89
River Beat '54

Joff Houston
Ninja: American Warrior '90
Ninja Death Squad '87

Renee Houston (1902-)
Legend of the Werewolf '75
Repulsion '65
The Flesh and the Fiends '60
The Horse's Mouth '58
Time Without Pity '57
The Belles of St. Trinian's '53

Whitney Houston (1963-)
Cinderella '97
The Preacher's Wife '96
Waiting to Exhale '95
The Bodyguard '92

Anders (Tofting) Hove (1956-)
Mifune '99
Bloodstorm: Subspecies 4 '98
Bloodlust: Subspecies 3 '93
Bloodstone: Subspecies 2 '92
Subspecies '90

Adrian Hoven (1922-81)
Fox and His Friends '75
Mark of the Devil '69
Castle of the Creeping Flesh '68
Cave of the Living Dead '65
Tromba, the Tiger Man '52

Natasha Hovey
Demons '86
Acqua e Sapone '83

Adam Coleman Howard
No Secrets '91
Slaves of New York '89
Quiet Cool '86

Alan Howard (1937-)
The Secret Rapture '94
A Casualty of War '90
The Cook, the Thief, His Wife & Her Lover '90
Strapless '90
The Heroes of Telemark '65

Anne Howard
Prince of Darkness '87
The Ghost of Rashmon Hall '47

Arliss Howard (1955-)
The Song of the Lark '01
A Map of the World '99
You Know My Name '99
The Lesser Evil '97
The Lost World: Jurassic Park 2 '97
William Faulkner's Old Man '97
Beyond the Call '96
johns '96
The Man Who Captured Eichmann '96
The Infiltrator '95
To Wong Foo, Thanks for Everything, Julie Newmar '95
Natural Born Killers '94
The Sandlot '93 (V)
Tales of Erotica '93
Wilder Napalm '93
Crisscross '92
Ruby '92
Till Death Do Us Part '92
For the Boys '91
Iran: Days of Crisis '91
Somebody Has to Shoot the Picture '90
Men Don't Leave '89
Plain Clothes '88
Tequila Sunrise '88
Full Metal Jacket '87
Hands of a Stranger '87
The Lightship '86
Door to Door '84
The Prodigal '83

Arthur Howard (1910-95)
Another Country '84
Paradisio '61
The Belles of St. Trinian's '53
The Happiest Days of Your Life '50
The Reckless Way '36

Barbara Howard
Where's Marlowe? '98
Lucky Stiff '88
Running Mates '86

Bob Howard
Murder with Music '45
Junction 88 '40

Boothe Howard (1887-1936)
Oh Susannah '38
Red River Valley '36
Mystery Liner '34

Brie Howard
The Runnin' Kind '89
Android '82

Clint Howard (1959-)
Dr. Seuss' How the Grinch Stole Christmas '00
Little Nicky '00
Arthur's Quest '99
Austin Powers 2: The Spy Who Shagged Me '99
EDtv '99
The Million Dollar Kid '99
From the Earth to the Moon '98
The Waterboy '98
Under Oath '97
Barb Wire '96
Body Armor '96
Humanoids from the Deep '96
Rattled '96
Santa with Muscles '96
That Thing You Do! '96
Dillinger and Capone '95
Ice Cream Man '95
Bigfoot: The Unforgettable Encounter '94
Cheyenne Warrior '94
Leprechaun 2 '94
Carnosaur '93
Forced to Kill '93
Far and Away '92
Backdraft '91
Disturbed '90
Silent Night, Deadly Night 4: Initiation '90
B.O.R.N. '88
End of the Line '88
Freeway '88
The Wraith '87
Cocoon '85
Gung Ho '85
Get Crazy '83
Cotton Candy '82
Evilspeak '82
Night Shift '82
Rock 'n' Roll High School '79
Grand Theft Auto '77
The Death of Richie '76
Eat My Dust '76
The Red Pony '76
Huckleberry Finn '75
Salty '73
The Wild Country '71
Gentle Giant '67

Curly Howard (1903-52)
Hollywood Party '34
Dancing Lady '33
The Lost Stooges '33

Esther Howard (1892-1965)
Detour '46
Klondike Annie '36
Vice Squad '31

Frank Howard
That Was Then...This Is Now '85
Hard Knox '83

Jeffrey Howard
The Wedding Banquet '93
Simple Men '92

John Howard (1913-95)
Make Haste to Live '54
Radar Secret Service '50
The Fighting Kentuckian '49
Love from a Stranger '47
The Undying Monster '42
The Invisible Woman '40
The Philadelphia Story '40
The Texas Rangers Ride Again '40
Bulldog Drummond's Bride '39
Bulldog Drummond's Secret Police '39
Arrest Bulldog Drummond '38
Bulldog Drummond's Peril '38
Bulldog Drummond Comes Back '37
Bulldog Drummond's Revenge '37
Lost Horizon '37

John Howard (1952-)
The Road from Coorain '02
Dating the Enemy '95
Young Einstein '89
The Highest Honor '84
Prince and the Great Race '83
The Club '81

Joyce Howard
Appointment with Crime '45
The Night Has Eyes '42

Kathleen Howard (1879-1956)
Crash Dive '43
Blossoms in the Dust '41
Young People '40
First Love '39
It's a Gift '34

Ken Howard (1944-)
Tactical Assault '99
At First Sight '98
The Net '95
Ulterior Motives '92
Murder in New Hampshire: The Pamela Smart Story '91
Oscar '91
Strange Interlude '90
Pudd'nhead Wilson '87
Rage of Angels: The Story Continues '86
Rage of Angels '83
Second Thoughts '83
The Thorn Birds '83
Country Girl '82
Damien: The Leper Priest '80
Manhunter '74
1776 '72

Kevyn Major Howard
Alien Nation '88
Full Metal Jacket '87

Kyle Howard (1978-)
Orange County '02
Baby Geniuses '98
Address Unknown '96
House Arrest '96
The Paper Brigade '96
Skeletons '96

Leslie Howard (1893-1943)
Pimpernel Smith '42
Spitfire '42
The Forty-Ninth Parallel '41
Gone with the Wind '39
Intermezzo '39
Pygmalion '38
Stand-In '37
Petrified Forest '36
Romeo and Juliet '36
Of Human Bondage '34
The Scarlet Pimpernel '34
Smilin' Through '33
The Animal Kingdom '32
Devotion '31
A Free Soul '31

Lisa Howard (1963-)
Bounty Hunters 2: Hardball '97
Bounty Hunters '96
Rolling Vengeance '87
Sabaka '55

Mary Howard (1912-89)
The Loves of Edgar Allen Poe '42
Billy the Kid '41
Abe Lincoln in Illinois '40
All Over Town '37

Moe Howard (1897-1975)
Dr. Death, Seeker of Souls '73
The Outlaws Is Coming! '65
Around the World in a Daze '63
Four for Texas '63
It's a Mad, Mad, Mad, Mad World '63
Three Stooges in Orbit '62
Snow White and the Three Stooges '61
The Three Stooges Meet Hercules '61
Have Rocket Will Travel '59
Gold Raiders '51
Swing Parade of 1946 '46
Hollywood Party '34
Dancing Lady '33
The Lost Stooges '33

Rance Howard (1929-)
A Crack in the Floor '00
Psycho '98
The Student Affair '97
Bigfoot: The Unforgettable Encounter '94
Ed Wood '94
Forced to Kill '93
Far and Away '92
Dark Before Dawn '89
B.O.R.N. '88
Grand Theft Auto '77
Eat My Dust '76
Huckleberry Finn '75
Where the Lilies Bloom '74
Bloody Trail '72
The Wild Country '71
Cool Hand Luke '67

Ron Howard (1954-)
Osmosis Jones *'01 (V)*
Return to Mayberry *'85*
Bitter Harvest *'81*
More American Graffiti *'79*
Grand Theft Auto *'77*
Eat My Dust *'76*
The Shootist *'76*
The First Nudie Musical *'75*
Huckleberry Finn *'75*
The Migrants *'74*
American Graffiti *'73*
Run, Stranger, Run *'73*
The Wild Country *'71*
Smoke *'70*
Village of the Giants *'65*
The Courtship of Eddie's Father *'62*
The Music Man *'62*
Door to Door Maniac *'61*

Ronald Howard (1918-96)
Pattern for Plunder *'62*
The Naked Edge *'61*
The Queen of Spades *'49*
Night Beat *'48*

Shawn Michael Howard
Boycott *'02*
Sunset Park *'96*

Shemp Howard (1895-1955)
Gold Raiders *'51*
Africa Screams *'49*
Blondie Knows Best *'46*
Cooking Up Trouble *'44*
Ghost Crazy *'44*
It Ain't Hay *'43*
Pittsburgh *'42*
Private Buckaroo *'42*
Buck Privates *'41*
Hold That Ghost *'41*
The Bank Dick *'40*
The Invisible Woman *'40*

Susan Howard (1944-)
The Power Within *'79*
Moonshine County Express *'77*
Sidewinder One *'77*

Terrence DaShon Howard
Boycott *'02*
Hart's War *'02*
Angel Eyes *'01*
Glitter *'01*
Big Momma's House *'00*
The Best Man *'99*
Never 2 Big *'98*
johns *'96*
Sunset Park *'96*
The Jacksons: An American Dream *'92*

Traylor Howard
Me, Myself, and Irene *'00*
Dirty Work *'97*

Trevor Howard (1916-88)
The Dawning *'88*
The Unholy *'88*
White Mischief *'88*
Foreign Body *'86*
Dust *'85*
This Lightning Always Strikes Twice *'85*
Flashpoint Africa *'84*
George Washington *'84*
Shaka Zulu *'83*
Sword of the Valiant *'83*
Deadly Game *'82*
Gandhi *'82*
Inside the Third Reich *'82*
The Missionary *'82*
Sea Wolves *'81*
Windwalker *'81*
Staying On *'80*
Hurricane *'79*
Meteor *'79*
Stevie *'78*
Superman: The Movie *'78*
Slavers *'77*
Adventures of Eliza Fraser *'76*
Albino *'76*
The Bawdy Adventures of Tom Jones *'76*
Conduct Unbecoming *'75*
Hennessy *'75*
Roboman *'75*
The Count of Monte Cristo *'74*
Craze *'74*
11 Harrowhouse *'74*
The Graveyard *'74*
Catholics *'73*
A Doll's House *'73*
The Offence *'73*
Ludwig *'72*
Catch Me a Spy *'71*
Mary, Queen of Scots *'71*
The Night Visitor *'70*
Ryan's Daughter *'70*
Battle of Britain *'69*
Lola *'69*
The Charge of the Light Brigade *'68*
Triple Cross *'67*
The Poppy Is Also a Flower *'66*
Morituri *'65*
Operation Crossbow *'65*
Von Ryan's Express *'65*
Father Goose *'64*
Invincible Mr. Disraeli *'63*
Mutiny on the Bounty *'62*
The Key *'58*
Around the World in 80 Days *'56*
The Gift Horse *'52*
The Clouded Yellow *'51*
The Golden Salamander *'51*
The Third Man *'49*
Green for Danger *'47*
They Made Me a Fugitive *'47*
Brief Encounter *'46*
I See a Dark Stranger *'46*

Vanessa Howard
Picture of Dorian Gray *'74*
Girly *'70*
Blood Beast Terror *'67*

Clark Howat
Billy Jack *'71*
The Giant Claw *'57*

C. Thomas Howell (1966-)
Avalanche *'99*
The Crimson Code *'99*
Cybercity *'99*
The Million Dollar Kid *'99*
The Prince and the Surfer *'99*
Shepherd *'99*
Dead Fire *'98*
First Degree *'98*
Last Lives *'98*
Matter of Trust *'98*
Stalker *'98*
Baby Face Nelson *'97*
Dilemma *'97*
Laws of Deception *'97*
The Big Fall *'96*
Pure Danger *'96*
Hourglass *'95*
Suspect Device *'95*
The Sweeper *'95*
Dangerous Indiscretion *'94*
Payback *'94*
Shameless *'94*
Teresa's Tattoo *'94*
Acting on Impulse *'93*
Gettysburg *'93*
Jailbait *'93*
That Night *'93*
Breaking the Rules *'92*
Nickel & Dime *'92*
Tattle Tale *'92*
To Protect and Serve *'92*
Curiosity Kills *'90*
Eyes of the Panther *'90*
Kid *'90*
Side Out *'90*
Far Out Man *'89*
The Return of the Musketeers *'89*
Into the Homeland *'87*
A Tiger's Tale *'87*
The Hitcher *'86*
Soul Man *'86*
Secret Admirer *'85*
Grandview U.S.A. *'84*
Red Dawn *'84*
The Outsiders *'83*
Tank *'83*
E.T.: The Extra-Terrestrial *'82*

Hoke Howell (1930-97)
Vice Girls *'96*
Alienator *'89*
B.O.R.N. *'88*
Humanoids from the Deep *'80*

Jean Howell
Crime of Passion *'57*
The Fast and the Furious *'54*

Ursula Howells
Girly *'70*
The Gilded Cage *'54*

Frankie Howerd (1922-92)
Night of the Laughing Dead *'75*
Naughty Knights *'71*
Carry On Doctor *'68*
The Great St. Trinian's Train Robbery *'66*
Cool Mikado *'63*
The Runaway Bus *'54*

Reed Howes (1900-64)
The Sinister Urge *'60*
Dead or Alive *'44*
Fugitive Valley *'41*
Covered Wagon Days *'40*
A Million to One *'37*
The Clutching Hand *'36*
Custer's Last Stand *'36*
Confidential *'35*
Feud of the West *'35*
Million Dollar Haul *'35*
Queen of the Jungle *'35*
Cyclone Cavalier *'25*

Sally Ann Howes (1930-)
Death Ship *'80*
Chitty Chitty Bang Bang *'68*
The Admirable Crichton *'57*
Anna Karenina *'48*
Nicholas Nickleby *'46*
Dead of Night *'45*
Pink String and Sealing Wax *'45*
Thursday's Child *'43*

Chris Howland
The Mad Executioners *'65*
Fanny Hill: Memoirs of a Woman of Pleasure *'64*

Jobyna Howland
Topaze *'33*
Hook, Line and Sinker *'30*

Olin Howlin (1886-1959)
The Blob *'58*
Storm Rider *'57*
Apache Rose *'47*
The Wistful Widow of Wagon Gap *'47*
Nancy Drew, Reporter *'39*
Girl of the Golden West *'38*
Earthworm Tractors *'36*
Satan Met a Lady *'36*

Jack Hoxie (1885-1965)
Gun Law *'33*
Law and Lawless *'33*
Trouble Busters *'33*
Outlaw Justice *'32*
Backfire *'22*
Blue Blazes Rawden *'18*

Cristina Hoyos
El Amor Brujo *'86*
Carmen *'83*
Blood Wedding *'81*

Arthur Hoyt (1874-1953)
The Great McGinty *'40*
In the Money *'34*
His Private Secretary *'33*
American Madness *'32*

Carol Hoyt
Midnight Confessions *'95*
Illegal Entry: Formula for Fear *'93*

John Hoyt (1905-91)
Flesh Gordon *'72*
The Time Travelers *'64*
X: The Man with X-Ray Eyes *'63*
Merrill's Marauders *'62*
Curse of the Undead *'59*
Attack of the Puppet People *'58*
The Conqueror *'56*
Forever Darling *'56*
Wetbacks *'56*
Blackboard Jungle *'55*
Sins of Jezebel *'54*
Julius Caesar *'53*
The Black Castle *'52*
Loan Shark *'52*
The Lost Continent *'51*
Trapped *'49*
Winter Meeting *'48*
O.S.S. *'46*

Rudolf Hrusinsky (1921-94)
The Elementary School *'91*
My Sweet Little Village *'86*
Larks on a String *'68*
Murder Czech Style *'66*

Brigitte Lin Ching Hsia
The Bride with White Hair *'93*
The Bride with White Hair 2 *'93*

Chen Hsing
Duel of Fists *'89*
Rage of Wind *'82*

Kelly Hu (1967-)
The Scorpion King *'02*
No Way Back *'96*
Strange Days *'95*
Surf Ninjas *'93*
The Doors *'91*
Harley Davidson and the Marlboro Man *'91*
Friday the 13th, Part 8: Jason Takes Manhattan *'89*

John Hubbard (1914-88)
Mexican Hayride *'48*
Cowboy & the Senorita *'44*
The Mummy's Tomb *'42*
Road Show *'41*

Cork Hubbert
The Ballad of the Sad Cafe *'91*
Caveman *'81*

Harold Huber (1904-59)
A Gentleman After Dark *'42*
Charlie Chan in Rio *'41*
Dance, Girl, Dance *'40*
Beau Geste *'39*
The Gay Desperado *'36*
Kelly the Second *'36*
Klondike Annie *'36*
Ladies They Talk About *'33*

Season Hubley (1951-)
Kiss the Sky *'98*
Stepfather 3: Father's Day *'92*
Total Exposure *'91*
Child in the Night *'90*
Prettykill *'87*
The Key to Rebecca *'85*
Vice Squad *'82*
Escape from New York *'81*
Elvis: The Movie *'79*
Hardcore *'79*
Mrs. R's Daughter *'79*

Whip Hubley (1957-)
Armistead Maupin's More Tales of the City *'97*
Black Scorpion 2: Ground Zero *'96*
Daddy's Girl *'96*
Executive Decision *'96*
Unveiled *'94*
Desire and Hell at Sunset Motel *'92*
A Connecticut Yankee in King Arthur's Court *'89*
Russkies *'87*
Top Gun *'86*

Paul (Christian) Hubschmid (1917-2001)
Funeral in Berlin *'66*
The Indian Tomb *'59*
Journey to the Lost City *'58*
The Day the Sky Exploded *'57*
The Beast from 20,000 Fathoms *'53*
Bagdad *'49*

Cooper Huckabee
Gettysburg *'93*
Love Field *'91*
Night Eyes *'90*
Cohen and Tate *'88*
The Curse *'87*
The Funhouse *'81*
Getting Wasted *'80*
Joni *'79*

Walter Hudd (1897-1963)
The Prince and the Pauper *'62*
Sink the Bismarck *'60*
Cast a Dark Shadow *'55*
I Know Where I'm Going *'45*
Black Limelight *'38*
Housemaster *'38*
Elephant Boy *'37*
Rembrandt *'36*

David Huddleston (1930-)
The Big Lebowski *'97*
Life with Mikey *'93*
Double Exposure: The Story of Margaret Bourke-White *'89*
Frantic *'88*
The Tracker *'88*
When the Bough Breaks *'86*
On the Run *'85*
Santa Claus: The Movie *'85*
Finnegan Begin Again *'84*
Go for It *'83*
Smokey and the Bandit 2 *'80*
Crime Busters *'78*
Billy Two Hats *'74*
Blazing Saddles *'74*
McQ *'74*
Rio Lobo *'70*

Michael Huddleston
Wyatt Earp *'94*
Bad Channels *'92*
Bombs Away! *'86*
Four Friends *'81*
World's Greatest Lover *'77*

Reginald (Reggie) Hudlin (1961-)
Joe's Apartment *'96 (V)*
Posse *'93*
She's Gotta Have It *'86*

Bill Hudson (1949-)
Hysterical *'83*
KISS Meets the Phantom of the Park *'78*

Ernie Hudson (1945-)
Miss Congeniality *'00*
Nowhere to Land *'00*
Red Letters *'00*
The Watcher *'00*
Corrupt *'99*
Interceptor Force *'99*
Paper Bullets *'99*
Shark Attack *'99*
Stealth Fighter *'99*
Urban Menace *'99*
Best of the Best: Without Warning *'98*
For Which He Stands *'98*
Never 2 Big *'98*
A Stranger in the Kingdom *'98*
Levitation *'97*
Mr. Magoo *'97*
Operation: Delta Force *'97*
The Cherokee Kid *'96*
Just Your Luck *'96*
The Substitute *'96*
Tornado! *'96*
Congo *'95*
Airheads *'94*
The Basketball Diaries *'94*
The Cowboy Way *'94*
In the Army Now *'94*
No Escape *'94*
Speechless *'94*
Sugar Hill *'94*
The Crow *'93*
Wild Palms *'93*
The Hand that Rocks the Cradle *'92*
Ghostbusters 2 *'89*
Leviathan *'89*
Trapper County War *'89*
The Wrong Guys *'88*
Weeds *'87*
Ghostbusters *'84*
Joy of Sex *'84*
Going Berserk *'83*
Spacehunter: Adventures in the Forbidden Zone *'83*
Penitentiary 2 *'82*
The $5.20 an Hour Dream *'80*
The Jazz Singer *'80*
Dolemite 2: Human Tornado *'76*

Gary Hudson
Extreme Limits *'01*
My Husband's Double Life *'01*
The Stepdaughter *'00*
Bridge of Dragons *'99*
Eye of the Killer *'99*
Black Thunder *'98*
Serial Killer *'95*
Texas Payback *'95*
The Force *'94*
Scanner Cop *'94*
Sexual Intent *'94*
Indecent Behavior *'93*
Martial Outlaw *'93*
Mind Twister *'93*
Wild Cactus *'92*
Night Angel *'90*

John Hudson
When Gangland Strikes *'56*
Return to Paradise *'53*

Kate Hudson (1979-)
About Adam *'00*
Almost Famous *'00*
Dr. T & the Women *'00*
Gossip *'99*
Desert Blue *'98*
200 Cigarettes *'98*

Larry Hudson
Tank Commando *'59*
The Creature Walks among Us *'56*

Oliver Hudson (1976-)
The Smokers *'00*
The Out-of-Towners *'99*

Rochelle Hudson (1914-72)
Alien Massacre *'67*
The Night Walker *'64*
Strait-Jacket *'64*
Rebel without a Cause *'55*
The Devil's Cargo *'48*
Bush Pilot *'47*
Curly Top *'35*
Les Miserables *'35*
Show Them No Mercy *'35*
Bachelor Bait *'34*
Imitation of Life *'34*
Mr. Skitch *'33*
Beyond the Rockies *'32*
The Savage Girl *'32*

Rock Hudson (1925-85)
World War III *'86*
The Ambassador *'84*
The Vegas Strip Wars *'84*
The Mirror Crack'd *'80*
The Martian Chronicles: Part 1 *'79*
The Martian Chronicles: Part 2 *'79*
The Martian Chronicles: Part 3 *'79*
Avalanche *'78*
Embryo *'76*
Showdown *'73*
Darling Lili *'70*
Hornet's Nest *'70*
The Undefeated *'69*
Ice Station Zebra *'68*
Seconds *'66*
Tobruk *'66*
Strange Bedfellows *'65*
Send Me No Flowers *'64*
A Gathering of Eagles *'63*
Man's Favorite Sport? *'63*
Come September *'61*
Lover Come Back *'61*

Pillow Talk '59
Battle Hymn '57
Something of Value '57
Tarnished Angels '57
Giant '56
Written on the Wind '56
All That Heaven Allows '55
Magnificent Obsession '54
Gun Fury '53
Sea Devils '53
Bend of the River '52
Here Come the Nelsons '52
Horizons West '52
The Lawless Breed '52
Tomahawk '51
Winchester '73 '50

Toni Hudson
The Uninvited '88
Just One of the Guys '85
Prime Risk '84

William (Bill) Hudson (1925-74)
Attack of the 50 Foot Woman '58
The Screaming Skull '58
The Amazing Colossal Man '57
Objective, Burma! '45

Matthias Hues
Suicide Ride '97
Alone in the Woods '95
Cyberzone '95
Death Match '94
Digital Man '94
Fists of Iron '94
Bounty Tracker '93
TC 2000 '93
Black Belt '92
Mission of Justice '92
Talons of the Eagle '92
Fist Fighter '88

Brent Huff (1961-)
Submerged '00
The Bad Pack '98
Final Justice '94
Falling from Grace '92
Stormquest '87
Armed Response '86
Deadly Passion '85
Nine Deaths of the Ninja '85
The Perils of Gwendoline '84

David Huffman (1945-85)
Last Plane Out '83
Firefox '82
St. Helen's, Killer Volcano '82
Blood Beach '81
Ice Castles '79
F.I.S.T. '78
The Winds of Kitty Hawk '78

Felicity Huffman
Snap Decision '01
A Slight Case of Murder '99
The Spanish Prisoner '97
Hackers '95
Quicksand: No Escape '91
Stephen King's Golden Years '91

Billy Hufsey
Magic Kid '92
Off the Wall '82

Daniel Hugh-Kelly (1954-)
Jackie, Ethel, Joan: The Kennedy Women '01
Chill Factor '99
Passing Glory '99
Atomic Dog '98
From the Earth to the Moon '98
Star Trek: Insurrection '98
The Tuskegee Airmen '95
Bad Company '94
The Good Son '93
Nowhere to Hide '87
Cujo '83

Andrew Hughes
Destroy All Monsters '68
Terror Beneath the Sea '66

Barnard Hughes (1915-)
The Cradle Will Rock '99
Neil Simon's The Odd Couple 2 '98
The Fantasticks '95
Past the Bleachers '95
Primal Secrets '94
Sister Act 2: Back in the Habit '93
Doc Hollywood '91
Day One '89
The Incident '89
Da '88
Hobo's Christmas '87
The Lost Boys '87
The Adventures of Huckleberry Finn '85
Maxie '85
Under the Biltmore Clock '85
Where Are the Children? '85
Little Gloria... Happy at Last '84
Best Friends '82
Tron '82
First Monday in October '81
Homeward Bound '80
Sanctuary of Fear '79
Oh, God! '77
Sisters '73
Rage '72
Cold Turkey '71
The Hospital '71
Where's Poppa? '70
Midnight Cowboy '69

Brendan Hughes
Howling 6: The Freaks '90
To Die For '89
Return to Horror High '87

Carol Hughes (1915-)
Home in Oklahoma '47
Miracle Kid '42
Desperate Cargo '41
Robot Pilot '41
Silver Stallion '41
The Border Legion '40
Flash Gordon Conquers the Universe '40
Space Soldiers Conquer the Universe '40
Love Affair '39
The Man from Music Mountain '38
Renfrew of the Royal Mounted '37
Earthworm Tractors '36
Three Men on a Horse '36

Charles Hughes
Call of the Forest '49
The Frontiersmen '38

Finola Hughes (1960-)
Tycus '98
Prison of Secrets '97
The Crying Child '96
Dark Side of Genius '94
Aspen Extreme '93
Soapdish '91
Nutcracker Sweet '84
Staying Alive '83

Frank John Hughes
Band of Brothers '01
Angel's Dance '99

Heather Hughes
Blood Freak '72
Flesh Feast '69

Helen Hughes
Night of the Twisters '95
The Amityville Curse '90
Kidnapping of Baby John Doe '88
The Peanut Butter Solution '85
Incubus '82
Off Your Rocker '80
Outrageous! '77

Kathleen Hughes
Cult of the Cobra '55
It Came from Outer Space '53

Kay Hughes (1914-98)
The Mandarin Mystery '37
Ride, Ranger, Ride '36
The Vigilantes Are Coming '36

Lloyd Hughes (1897-1958)
Blake of Scotland Yard '36
A Face in the Fog '36
Kelly of the Secret Service '36
Drums of Jeopardy '31
Where East Is East '29
Ella Cinders '26
The Lost World '25
Tess of the Storm Country '22
Beau Revel '21
Dangerous Hours '19

Mary Beth Hughes (1919-95)
Square Dance Jubilee '51
Holiday Rhythm '50
Last of the Wild Horses '49
Rimfire '49
Inner Sanctum '48
Return of Wildfire '48
Great Flamarion '45
I Accuse My Parents '45
The Lady Confesses '45
Take It Big '44
Timber Queen '44
The Ox-Bow Incident '43
Orchestra Wives '42
Charlie Chan in Rio '41
The Great American Broadcast '41
Lucky Cisco Kid '40

Miko Hughes (1986-)
Fly Boy '99
Mercury Rising '98
Spawn '97
Zeus and Roxanne '96
Apollo 13 '95
Cops and Robbersons '94
Wes Craven's New Nightmare '94
Jack the Bear '93
Pet Sematary '89

Roddy Hughes
Old Mother Riley's Jungle Treasure '51
The Last Days of Dolwyn '49

Sharon Hughes
Grotesque '87
Chained Heat '83

Tresa Hughes
Sarah, Plain and Tall: Skylark '93
Coming Home '78

Wendy Hughes (1952-)
Paradise Road '97
Lust and Revenge '95
Princess Caraboo '94
Wild Orchid 2: Two Shades of Blue '92
A Woman Named Jackie '91
The Heist '89
Happy New Year '87
Warm Nights on a Slow-Moving Train '87
Echoes of Paradise '86
An Indecent Obsession '85
Remember Me '85
Careful, He Might Hear You '84
My First Wife '84
Dangerous Summer '82
Lonely Hearts '82
Touch & Go '80
Kostas '79
My Brilliant Career '79
Newsfront '78
Puzzle '78
High Rolling in a Hot Corvette '77
Alternative '76
Jock Petersen '74

D.L. Hughley (1964-)
The Brothers '01
Inspector Gadget '99 (V)

Claude Hulbert
The Dummy Talks '43
Bulldog Jack '35

Tom Hulce (1953-)
The Hunchback of Notre Dame '96 (V)
The Heidi Chronicles '95
Mary Shelley's Frankenstein '94
Fearless '93
Black Rainbow '91
The Inner Circle '91
Parenthood '89
Dominick & Eugene '88
Slamdance '87
Echo Park '86
The Rise & Rise of Daniel Rocket '86
Amadeus '84
Those Lips, Those Eyes '80
National Lampoon's Animal House '78
September 30, 1955 '77

Dianne Hull (1948-)
The New Adventures of Pippi Longstocking '88
Christmas Evil '80
The Fifth Floor '80
Aloha, Bobby and Rose '74
Girls on the Road '73

Henry Hull (1890-1977)
The Fool Killer '65
Master of the World '61
The Buccaneer '58
Return of Jesse James '50
The Fountainhead '49
The Great Gatsby '49
Rimfire '49
Portrait of Jennie '48
Objective, Burma! '45
Lifeboat '44
The Woman of the Town '44
High Sierra '41
My Son, My Son '40
Return of Frank James '40
Jesse James '39
Stanley and Livingstone '39
Boys Town '38
Three Comrades '38
Werewolf of London '35
Great Expectations '34
Midnight '34

Josephine Hull (1884-1957)
Harvey '50
Arsenic and Old Lace '44

Warren Hull (1903-74)
Bowery Blitzkrieg '41
Hidden Enemy '40
Yukon Flight '40
Star Reporter '39
Hawaii Calls '38

George Humbert
Music in My Heart '40
Hearts of Humanity '32

Benita Hume (1906-67)
It Happened in New Orleans '36
Suzy '36
Tarzan Escapes '36
Power '34
Private Life of Don Juan '34
Lady of the Lake '28

Renee Humphrey
Hard Luck '01
Jay and Silent Bob Strike Back '01
Lover Girl '97
Cadillac Ranch '96
The Cure '95
Devil in a Blue Dress '95
French Kiss '95
Mallrats '95
Fun '94
Jailbait '93

Cecil Humphreys
The Razor's Edge '46
Accused '36

William Humphreys
The Unholy Three '25
Beau Brummel '24

Barry Humphries (1934-)
Spice World: The Movie '97
Welcome to Woop Woop '97
The Leading Man '96
Immortal Beloved '94
Les Patterson Saves the World '90
Shock Treatment '81
The Getting of Wisdom '77
Barry McKenzie Holds His Own '74
Bedazzled '68

Tessa Humphries
Paradise Road '97
Out of the Body '88
Cassandra '87

Robert Hundar
Bronson's Revenge '79
Fighting Fists of Shanghai Joe '65

Sammo Hung (1952-)
Mr. Nice Guy '98
Painted Skin '93
The Prisoner '90
Dragons Forever '88
Paper Marriage '88
Eastern Condors '87
The Millionaire's Express '86
Heart of Dragon '85
Project A '83
Zu: Warriors from the Magic Mountain '83
The Prodigal Son '82
Spooky Encounters '80

Arthur Hunnicutt (1911-79)
Winterhawk '76
Harry and Tonto '74
The Bounty Man '72
Shoot Out '71
El Dorado '67
Apache Uprising '66
Born Reckless '59
The Tall T '57
The Kettles in the Ozarks '56
The French Line '54
Devil's Canyon '53
The Big Sky '52
The Lusty Men '52
She Couldn't Say No '52
Distant Drums '51
The Red Badge of Courage '51
Broken Arrow '50
Stars in My Crown '50
Ticket to Tomahawk '50
Abroad with Two Yanks '44
Wildcat '42

Gayle Hunnicutt (1943-)
Con Man '92
Turnaround '87
Dream Lover '85
No Comebacks '85
Target '85
Flashpoint Africa '84
A Woman of Substance '84
Return of the Man from U.N.C.L.E. '83
The Martian Chronicles: Part 2 '79
The Martian Chronicles: Part 3 '79
Once in Paris... '79
Sell Out '76
Strange Shadows in an Empty Room '76
Shadow Man '75
Spiral Staircase '75
The Legend of Hell House '73
Scorpio '73
The Golden Bowl '72
The Love Machine '71
Marlowe '69
The Wild Angels '66

Bonnie Hunt (1964-)
Monsters, Inc. '01 (V)
Return to Me '00
The Green Mile '99
Random Hearts '99
A Bug's Life '98 (V)
Kissing a Fool '98
Subway Stories '97
Getting Away With Murder '96
Jerry Maguire '96
Jumanji '95
Now and Then '95
Only You '94
Beethoven's 2nd '93
Dave '93
Beethoven '92
Rain Man '88

Brad Hunt
Dream with the Fishes '97
Fire Down Below '97

Christopher Hunt
Idle Hands '99
Addams Family Values '93
The Addams Family '91
Lady Terminator '89

David Hunt
The Dead Pool '88
Date with an Angel '87

Eleanor Hunt (-1981)
Yellow Cargo '36
Go-Get-'Em-Haines '35
Whoopee! '30

Gareth Hunt (1943-)
A Chorus of Disapproval '89
It Couldn't Happen Here '88
Bloodbath at the House of Death '85
Funny Money '82
The World Is Full of Married Men '80

Helen Hunt (1963-)
The Curse of the Jade Scorpion '01
Cast Away '00
Dr. T & the Women '00
Pay It Forward '00
What Women Want '00
As Good As It Gets '97
Twister '96
Kiss of Death '94
Into the Badlands '92
Mr. Saturday Night '92
Only You '92
Trancers 3: Deth Lives '92
Murder in New Hampshire: The Pamela Smart Story '91
The Waterdance '91
Dark River: A Father's Revenge '90
Trancers 2: The Return of Jack Deth '90
Next of Kin '89
Miles from Home '88
Stealing Home '88
Project X '87
Peggy Sue Got Married '86
Girls Just Want to Have Fun '85
Quarterback Princess '85
Code of Honor '84
Trancers '84
Bill: On His Own '83
Desperate Lives '82
The Best Little Girl in the World '81
Child Bride of Short Creek '81
The Spell '77
Death Scream '75
Pioneer Woman '73

Jimmy Hunt (1939-)
Invaders from Mars '53
The Capture '50
Rusty's Birthday '49
Pitfall '48

Linda Hunt (1945-)
Dragonfly '02
Eat Your Heart Out '96
The Relic '96
Pocahontas '95 (V)
Ready to Wear '94
Younger & Younger '94
Rain Without Thunder '93
Twenty Bucks '93
If Looks Could Kill '91
Kindergarten Cop '90
She-Devil '89
The Room '87
Waiting for the Moon '87
Eleni '85
Silverado '85
The Bostonians '84
Dune '84
The Year of Living Dangerously '82
Popeye '80

Marsha Hunt (1917-)
Johnny Got His Gun '71
Actors and Sin '52
Raw Deal '48
Carnegie Hall '47
Smash-Up: The Story of a Woman '47
The Valley of Decision '45
Blossoms in the Dust '41

Star Reporter '39
Helltown '38
Thunder Pass '37
Thunder Trail '37
Desert Gold '36
Marsha A. Hunt (1947-)
Howling 2: Your Sister Is a Werewolf '85
Britannia Hospital '82
The Sender '82
Dracula A.D. 1972 '72
Martita Hunt (1900-69)
The Unsinkable Molly Brown '64
The Wonderful World of the Brothers Grimm '62
The Brides of Dracula '60
Song Without End '60
Me and the Colonel '58
The Admirable Crichton '57
Anastasia '56
The King's Rhapsody '55
The Story of Robin Hood & His Merrie Men '52
Anna Karenina '48
Little Ballerina '47
Great Expectations '46
Nine Days a Queen '36
Sabotage '36
When Knights Were Bold '36
First a Girl '35
William Dennis Hunt
Peephole '93
Flesh Gordon 2: Flesh Gordon Meets the Cosmic Cheerleaders '90
Bill Hunter (1940-)
The Echo of Thunder '98
Moby Dick '98
Road to Nhill '97
Race the Sun '96
River Street '95
The Adventures of Priscilla, Queen of the Desert '94
The Custodian '94
Muriel's Wedding '94
The Last Days of Chez Nous '92
Strictly Ballroom '92
Fever '88
Rikky and Pete '88
The Hit '85
An Indecent Obsession '85
Rebel '85
Heatwave '83
Return of Captain Invincible '83
Hard Knocks '80
In Search of Anna '79
Newsfront '78
Holly Hunter (1958-)
Harlan County War '00
O Brother Where Art Thou? '00
Things You Can Tell Just by Looking at Her '00
Time Code '00
Jesus' Son '99
Living Out Loud '98
Woman Wanted '98
A Life Less Ordinary '97
Copycat '95
Crash '95
Home for the Holidays '95
The Firm '93
The Piano '93
The Positively True Adventures of the Alleged Texas Cheerleader-Murdering Mom '93
Crazy in Love '92
Murder on the Bayou '91
Once Around '91
Always '89
Animal Behavior '89
Miss Firecracker '89
Roe vs. Wade '89
End of the Line '88
Broadcast News '87
Raising Arizona '87
Blood Simple '85
Swing Shift '84
Urge to Kill '84
Svengali '83
The Burning '82
Ian Hunter
Order of the Black Eagle '87
Unmasking the Idol '86
Ian Hunter (1900-75)
Doctor Blood's Coffin '62
Flame Over India '60
Pursuit of the Graf Spee '57
Andy Hardy's Private Secretary '41
Billy the Kid '41
Dr. Jekyll and Mr. Hyde '41
Smilin' Through '41
Ziegfeld Girl '41
Bitter Sweet '40
Broadway Melody of 1940 '40
The Long Voyage Home '40
Strange Cargo '40
Broadway Serenade '39
The Little Princess '39
Tarzan Finds a Son '39
The Tower of London '39
The Adventures of Robin Hood '38
The Sisters '38
That Certain Woman '37
A Midsummer Night's Dream '35
The Phantom Light '35
Easy Virtue '27
The Ring '27
Jeffrey Hunter (1925-69)
The Christmas Kid '68
Private Navy of Sgt. O'Farrell '68
A Witch Without a Broom '68
A Guide for the Married Man '67
The Longest Day '62
No Man Is an Island '62
The King of Kings '61
Hell to Eternity '60
Sergeant Rutledge '60
Last Hurrah '58
The Great Locomotive Chase '56
The Searchers '56
Seven Cities of Gold '55
Kaki Hunter (1955-)
Porky's Revenge '85
Just the Way You Are '84
Porky's 2: The Next Day '83
Porky's '82
Whose Life Is It Anyway? '81
Roadie '80
Willie & Phil '80
Kim Hunter (1922-)
Out of the Cold '99
Midnight in the Garden of Good and Evil '97
A Price above Rubies '97
Two Evil Eyes '90
Drop-Out Mother '88
The Kindred '87
Dark August '76
Bad Ronald '74
Born Innocent '74
Escape from the Planet of the Apes '71
Beneath the Planet of the Apes '70
Planet of the Apes '68
The Swimmer '68
Lamp at Midnight '66
Lilith '64
Requiem for a Heavyweight '56
A Streetcar Named Desire '51
Stairway to Heaven '46
The Seventh Victim '43
Tender Comrade '43
Rachel Hunter
Rock Star '01
TripFall '00
Just a Little Harmless Sex '99
Two Shades of Blue '98
Ronald Hunter
Jakarta '88
Adventure of the Action Hunters '87
Rage of Angels '83
Tab Hunter (1931-)
Cameron's Closet '89
Out of the Dark '88
Grotesque '87
Lust in the Dust '85
Grease 2 '82
Pandemonium '82
Polyester '81
The Kid from Left Field '79
The Big Push '75
The Arousers '70
One Step to Hell '68
Hostile Guns '67
The Loved One '65
Ride the Wild Surf '64
They Came to Cordura '59
Damn Yankees '58
Gunman's Walk '58
Lafayette Escadrille '58
The Burning Hills '56
Battle Cry '55
Sea Chase '55
Island of Desire '52
Thomas Hunter
Escape from the KGB '87
Battle of the Commandos '71
The Vampire Happening '71
Web of Deception '71
Sam Huntington
Not Another Teen Movie '01
Detroit Rock City '99
Jungle 2 Jungle '96
G.P. (Tim) Huntley, Jr. (1904-71)
Journey for Margaret '42
They Died with Their Boots On '41
Beau Geste '39
The Charge of the Light Brigade '36
Raymond Huntley (1904-90)
Hot Millions '68
The Mummy '59
Room at the Top '59
The Prisoner '55
The Long Dark Hall '51
I See a Dark Stranger '46
Immortal Battalion '44
Night Train to Munich '40
Isabelle Huppert (1955-)
La Separation '98
The Swindle '97
Elective Affinities '96
La Ceremonie '95
Amateur '94
Love After Love '94
The Separation '94
Madame Bovary '91
La Vengeance d'une Femme '89
The Possessed '88
The Story of Women '88
The Bedroom Window '87
Cactus '86
Sincerely Charlotte '86
My Best Friend's Girl '84
Entre-Nous '83
La Truite '83
Passion '82
Coup de Torchon '81
Heaven's Gate '81
Loulou '80
Violette '78
The Lacemaker '77
The Judge and the Assassin '75
Rosebud '75
Going Places '74
Elizabeth Hurley (1965-)
Serving Sara '02
Bedazzled '00
Austin Powers 2: The Spy Who Shagged Me '99
EDtv '99
My Favorite Martian '98
Permanent Midnight '98
Austin Powers: International Man of Mystery '97
Dangerous Ground '96
Samson and Delilah '96
Shameless '94
Sharpe's Enemy '94
Nightscare '93
Passenger 57 '92
Kill Cruise '90
Christabel '89
Rowing with the Wind '88
Brandon Hurst (1866-1947)
Stanley and Livingstone '39
House of Mystery '34
The Lost Patrol '34
Murders in the Rue Morgue '32
The White Zombie '32
Murder at Midnight '31
The Man Who Laughs '27
Made for Love '26
The Thief of Baghdad '24
The Hunchback of Notre Dame '23
Dr. Jekyll and Mr. Hyde '20
David Hurst
Kelly's Heroes '70
Tony Draws a Horse '51
Michael Hurst (1957-)
Hercules the Legendary Journeys, Vol. 1: And the Amazon Women '94
Hercules the Legendary Journeys, Vol. 2: The Lost Kingdom '94
Hercules the Legendary Journeys, Vol. 3: The Circle of Fire '94
Hercules the Legendary Journeys, Vol. 4: In the Underworld '94
Desperate Remedies '93
Death Warmed Up '85
Paul Hurst (1888-1953)
Missourians '50
The Vanishing Westerner '50
Outcasts of the Trail '49
Pioneer Marshal '49
Under Colorado Skies '47
Girl Rush '44
Caught in the Draft '41
Bad Lands '39
Gone with the Wind '39
It Could Happen to You '39
Alexander's Ragtime Band '38
Legion of Missing Men '37
Hold Your Man '33
The Sphinx '33
The Big Stampede '32
My Pal, the King '32
13th Guest '32
Mountain Justice '30
Paradise Island '30
Battling Bunyon '24
Ryan Hurst
We Were Soldiers '02
Remember the Titans '00
Veronica Hurst (1931-)
Second Best Secret Agent in the Whole Wide World '65
Peeping Tom '60
Angels One Five '54
The Gilded Cage '54
John Hurt (1940-)
Captain Corelli's Mandolin '01
Harry Potter and the Sorcerer's Stone '01
Lost Souls '00
New Blood '99
All the Little Animals '98
The Climb '97
Contact '97
Love and Death on Long Island '97
Dead Man '95
Rob Roy '95
Wild Bill '95
Even Cowgirls Get the Blues '94
Second Best '94
Thumbelina '94 (V)
Monolith '93
Shades of Fear '93
King Ralph '91
The Field '90
Frankenstein Unbound '90
Little Sweetheart '90
Scandal '89
Aria '88
White Mischief '88
Spaceballs '87
Vincent: The Life and Death of Vincent van Gogh '87 (V)
From the Hip '86
Jake Speed '86
After Darkness '85
The Black Cauldron '85 (V)
The Hit '85
Champions '84
1984 '84
Success Is the Best Revenge '84
The Osterman Weekend '83
Partners '82
The Plague Dogs '82 (V)
Disappearance '81
Heaven's Gate '81
History of the World: Part 1 '81
Night Crossing '81
The Elephant Man '80
Alien '79
The Lord of the Rings '78 (V)
Midnight Express '78
The Shout '78
Watership Down '78 (V)
East of Elephant Rock '76
The Ghoul '75
The Naked Civil Servant '75
Cry of the Penguins '71
10 Rillington Place '71
A Man for All Seasons '66
Mary Beth Hurt (1948-)
Bringing Out the Dead '99
Affliction '97
From the Journals of Jean Seberg '95
The Age of Innocence '93
My Boyfriend's Back '93
Six Degrees of Separation '93
Light Sleeper '92
Defenseless '91
Parents '89
Slaves of New York '89
Baby Girl Scott '87
Compromising Positions '85
D.A.R.Y.L. '85
The World According to Garp '82
A Change of Seasons '80
Chilly Scenes of Winter '79
Interiors '78
William Hurt (1950-)
Changing Lanes '02
A. I.: Artificial Intelligence '01
The Contaminated Man '01
The Flamingo Rising '01
Rare Birds '01
Varian's War '01
Dune '00
The Miracle Maker: The Story of Jesus '00 (V)
The Big Brass Ring '99
The 4th Floor '99
Silent Witness '99
Sunshine '99
Lost in Space '98
One True Thing '98
Dark City '97
Loved '97
The Proposition '97
Jane Eyre '96
Michael '96
A Couch in New York '95
Smoke '95
Second Best '94
Trial by Jury '94
Mr. Wonderful '93
The Plague '92
The Doctor '91
Until the End of the World '91
Alice '90
I Love You to Death '90
The Accidental Tourist '88
A Time of Destiny '88
Broadcast News '87
Children of a Lesser God '86
Kiss of the Spider Woman '85
The Big Chill '83
Gorky Park '83
Body Heat '81
Eyewitness '81
Altered States '80
Ferlin Husky (1927-)
Hillbillies in a Haunted House '67
Las Vegas Hillbillys '66
Toby Huss
Human Nature '02
Dear God '96
Dogs: The Rise and Fall of an All-Girl Bookie Joint '96
Down Periscope '96
Olivia Hussey (1951-)
Bloody Proof '99
Shame, Shame, Shame '98
Ice Cream Man '95
Quest of the Delta Knights '93
Save Me '93
Undeclared War '91
The Jeweller's Shop '90
Psycho 4: The Beginning '90
Stephen King's It '90
Distortions '87
Ivanhoe '82
Virus '82
Escape 2000 '81
The Man with Bogart's Face '80
The Cat and the Canary '79
The Bastard '78
Death on the Nile '78
Black Christmas '75
Ricco '74
H-Bomb '71
Romeo and Juliet '68
Ruth Hussey (1914-)
The Facts of Life '60
Stars and Stripes Forever '52
Hill Number One '51
Mr. Music '50
The Great Gatsby '49
The Uninvited '44
Marine Raiders '43
Tender Comrade '43
Northwest Passage '40
The Philadelphia Story '40
Susan and God '40
Another Thin Man '39
The Women '39
Madame X '37
Francis Huster (1947-)
The Dinner Game '98
I Married a Dead Man '82
Another Man, Another Chance '77
Lumiere '76
Anjelica Huston (1951-)
Blood Work '02
Mists of Avalon '01
The Royal Tenenbaums '01
The Golden Bowl '00
Agnes Browne '99
Ever After: A Cinderella Story '98
Phoenix '98
Buffalo 66 '97
Buffalo Girls '95
The Crossing Guard '94
The Perez Family '94
Addams Family Values '93
And the Band Played On '93
Family Pictures '93
Manhattan Murder Mystery '93
The Player '92

The Addams Family '91
The Grifters '90
The Witches '90
Crimes & Misdemeanors '89
Enemies, a Love Story '89
Lonesome Dove '89
A Handful of Dust '88
Mr. North '88
The Dead '87
Gardens of Stone '87
Prizzi's Honor '85
The Cowboy & the Ballerina '84
Ice Pirates '84
This Is Spinal Tap '84
Beauty and the Beast '83
The Postman Always Rings Twice '81
The Last Tycoon '76
Hamlet '69

Danny Huston (1962-)
Time Code '00
Leo Tolstoy's Anna Karenina '96

John Huston (1906-87)
Mr. Corbett's Ghost '90
The Black Cauldron '85 (N)
Lovesick '83
A Minor Miracle '83
Cannery Row '82 (N)
Fatal Attraction '80
The Return of the King '80 (V)
The Visitor '80
Jaguar Lives '79
Winter Kills '79
Wise Blood '79
Battleforce '78
The Hobbit '78 (V)
The Word '78
Angela '77
Tentacles '77
Breakout '75
The Wind and the Lion '75
Chinatown '74
Battle for the Planet of the Apes '73
Man in the Wilderness '71
Ride to Glory '71
Myra Breckinridge '70
Candy '68
Casino Royale '67
The Bible '66 (N)
The Cardinal '63

Virginia Huston (1925-81)
Flight to Mars '52
Night Stage to Galveston '52
Sudden Fear '52
The Doolins of Oklahoma '49
Flamingo Road '49
Out of the Past '47
Nocturne '46

Walter Huston (1884-1950)
December 7th: The Movie '91
Summer Holiday '48
Treasure of the Sierra Madre '48
Duel in the Sun '46
And Then There Were None '45
Dragon Seed '44
Edge of Darkness '43
The North Star '43
The Outlaw '43
In This Our Life '42
The Shanghai Gesture '42
Yankee Doodle Dandy '42
The Devil & Daniel Webster '41
The Maltese Falcon '41
Of Human Hearts '38
Dodsworth '36
Rhodes '36
Transatlantic Tunnel '35
Ann Vickers '33
Gabriel Over the White House '33
The Prizefighter and the Lady '33
American Madness '32
Rain '32
Criminal Code '31
Abraham Lincoln '30
The Virginian '29

Michael Hutchence (1960-97)
Frankenstein Unbound '90
Dogs in Space '87

David Hutcheson (1905-76)
The Abominable Dr. Phibes '71
Murder in the Footlights '51
No Highway in the Sky '51

Geoffrey Hutchings
Heart of Darkness '93
Wish You Were Here '87

Will Hutchins (1932-)
Maverick '94
Slumber Party '57 '76
Clambake '67
The Shooting '66
Spinout '66
Merrill's Marauders '62
Lafayette Escadrille '58
No Time for Sergeants '58

Fiona Hutchinson
Rage '95
American Gothic '88

Josephine Hutchinson (1904-98)
The Adventures of Huckleberry Finn '60
North by Northwest '59
Love Is Better Than Ever '52
Cass Timberlane '47
The Tender Years '47
My Son, My Son '40
Son of Frankenstein '39
The Story of Louis Pasteur '36

Doug Hutchison
The Salton Sea '02
I Am Sam '01
Bait '00
The Green Mile '99

Ken Hutchison
Ladyhawke '85
Deadly Strangers '82

William Hutt
Long Day's Journey Into Night '96
The Fixer '68

Betty Hutton (1921-)
The Greatest Show on Earth '52
Annie Get Your Gun '50
Let's Dance '50
The Perils of Pauline '47
Here Come the Waves '45
The Stork Club '45
Miracle of Morgan's Creek '44
Star Spangled Rhythm '42

Brian Hutton
Last Train from Gun Hill '59
Carnival Rock '57

Jim Hutton (1933-79)
Psychic Killer '75
Nightmare at 43 Hillcrest '74
Don't Be Afraid of the Dark '73
Bachelor in Paradise '69
The Green Berets '68
Hellfighters '68
Who's Minding the Mint? '67
Walk, Don't Run '66
The Hallelujah Trail '65
Major Dundee '65
The Horizontal Lieutenant '62
Period of Adjustment '62
The Honeymoon Machine '61
Where the Boys Are '60

Lauren Hutton (1943-)
Caracara '00
Trade Secrets '90s
Just a Little Harmless Sex '99
54 '98
A Rat's Tale '98
My Father the Hero '93
Guilty as Charged '92
Missing Pieces '91
Fear '90
Millions '90
Forbidden Sun '89
Bulldance '88
Scandalous '88
Malone '87
Timestalkers '87
Monte Carlo '86
From Here to Maternity '85
Once Bitten '85
Lassiter '84
The Cradle Will Fall '83
The Snow Queen '83
Starflight One '83
Paternity '81
Zorro, the Gay Blade '81
American Gigolo '79
A Wedding '78
Viva Knievel '77
Welcome to L.A. '77
Gator '76
Nashville '75
The Gambler '74
Paper Lion '68

Marion Hutton
Love Happy '50
In Society '44

Robert Hutton (1920-94)
Cry of the Banshee '70
They Came from Beyond Space '67
Vulture '67
The Slime People '63
Cinderfella '60
Invisible Invaders '59
Naked Youth '59
Outcasts of the City '58
Showdown at Boot Hill '58
Big Bluff '55
Slaughter Trail '51
The Steel Helmet '51
Hollywood Canteen '44
Destination Tokyo '43

Timothy Hutton (1960-)
Sunshine State '02
Deliberate Intent '01
The Doorbell Rang: A Nero Wolfe Mystery '01
Deterrence '00
The Golden Spiders: A Nero Wolfe Mystery '00
Just One Night '00
The General's Daughter '99
Aldrich Ames: Traitor Within '98
Money Kings '98
Beautiful Girls '96
City of Industry '96
Mr. & Mrs. Loving '96
Playing God '96
The Substance of Fire '96
French Kiss '95
The Last Word '95
The Temp '93
The Dark Half '91
Strangers '91
Q & A '90
Torrents of Spring '90
Everybody's All American '88
A Time of Destiny '88
Made in Heaven '87
The Falcon and the Snowman '85
Turk 182! '85
Iceman '84
Daniel '83
Oldest Living Graduate '82
A Long Way Home '81
Taps '81
Father Figure '80
Ordinary People '80
And Baby Makes Six '79
Friendly Fire '79
Young Love, First Love '79

Richard Huw
A Certain Justice '99
The Buccaneers '95
The Four Minute Mile '92
Getting It Right '89

Leila Hyams (1905-77)
Yellow Dust '36
Ruggles of Red Gap '35
Freaks '32
Island of Lost Souls '32
Red Headed Woman '32
The Big House '30
Spite Marriage '29

Jacquelyn Hyde
House of Terror '87
Take the Money and Run '69

Jonathan Hyde
Attila '01
The Prince and the Pauper '01
Princess of Thieves '01
Joan of Arc '99
The Mummy '99
Titanic '97
Anaconda '96
Jumanji '95
Richie Rich '94
Fellow Traveler '89
An Indecent Obsession '85

Alex Hyde-White (1958-)
Mars '96
Unknown Origin '95
Wyatt Earp: Return to Tombstone '94
Silent Victim '92
Ironclads '90
Pretty Woman '90
Indiana Jones and the Last Crusade '89
The Phantom of the Opera '89
Time Trackers '88
Echoes in the Darkness '87
Biggles '85
The First Olympics: Athens 1896 '84
The Seekers '79

Wilfrid Hyde-White (1903-91)
Heartburn '86
Fanny Hill '83
The Toy '82
Tarzan, the Ape Man '81
Damien: The Leper Priest '80
In God We Trust '80
Oh, God! Book 2 '80
Scout's Honor '80
The Cat and the Canary '79
The Rebels '79
King Solomon's Treasure '76
Brand New Life '72
Skullduggery '70
The Magic Christian '69
My Fair Lady '64
In Search of the Castaways '62
On the Fiddle '61
Flame Over India '60
Two-Way Stretch '60
Carry On Nurse '59
Teenage Bad Girl '59
Truth about Women '58
Up the Creek '58
The Vicious Circle '57
John and Julie '55
Betrayed '54
The Browning Version '51
The Golden Salamander '51
Angel with the Trumpet '50
Last Holiday '50
Mister Drake's Duck '50
The Third Man '49
Ghosts of Berkeley Square '47
The Man Who Knew Too Much '34

Martha Hyer (1924-)
Catch as Catch Can '68
The House of 1000 Dolls '67
The Chase '66
Night of the Grizzly '66
Picture Mommy Dead '66
Sons of Katie Elder '65
Bikini Beach '64
The Carpetbaggers '64
First Men in the Moon '64
Ice Palace '60
The Best of Everything '59
Mistress of the World '59
Houseboat '58
Some Came Running '58
Battle Hymn '57
My Man Godfrey '57
Paris Holiday '57
The Delicate Delinquent '56
Francis in the Navy '55
Cry Vengeance '54
Lucky Me '54
Sabrina '54
Scarlet Spear '54
Abbott and Costello Go to Mars '53
Geisha Girl '52

Diana Hyland (1936-77)
The Boy in the Plastic Bubble '76
Hercules and the Princess of Troy '65
One Man's Way '63

Frances Hyland (1927-)
When the Dark Man Calls '95
The Lotus Eaters '93
Happy Birthday to Me '81
Home to Stay '79

Scott Hylands (1943-)
36 Hours to Die '99
The Halfback of Notre Dame '96
Titanic '96
Decoy '95
Ordeal in the Arctic '93
Tales of the Klondike: In a Far Country '87
Coming Out Alive '84
Savage Hunger '84
The Winds of Kitty Hawk '78
The Boys in Company C '77
Earthquake '74
Fools '70
Daddy's Gone A-Hunting '69

Jane Hylton (1926-79)
Circus of Horrors '60
The Manster '59
Dear Murderer '47

Richard Hylton
The Halls of Montezuma '50
Lost Boundaries '49

Phyllis Hyman
The Kill Reflex '89
School Daze '88

Warren Hymer (1906-48)
Hitler: Dead or Alive '43
Baby Face Morgan '42
Lure of the Islands '42
Meet the Mob '42
Mr. Wise Guy '42
Phantom Killer '42
Birth of the Blues '41
Joy of Living '38
You and Me '38
Sea Racketeers '37
You Only Live Once '37
Rhythm on the Range '36
Tango '36
Confidential '35
Hong Kong Nights '35
Show Them No Mercy '35
In the Money '34
The Mysterious Rider '33
The Lone Star Ranger '30

Joyce Hyser (1956-)
Wedding Band '89
Just One of the Guys '85
The Hollywood Knights '80

Steve Hytner
Air Rage '01
Forces of Nature '99
Love Stinks '99
The Prophecy 3: The Ascent '99
The Prophecy 2: Ashtown '97
Down, Out and Dangerous '95

Chaing I
Return of the Tiger '78
They Shoot Horses, Don't They? '69

Mirta Ibarra
Mararia '98
Guantanamera '95
Strawberry and Chocolate '93
Up to a Certain Point '83

Ice Cube (1969-)
All About the Benjamins '02
John Carpenter's Ghosts of Mars '01
Next Friday '00
Three Kings '99
I Got the Hook-Up '98
The Players Club '98
Anaconda '96
Dangerous Ground '96
Friday '95
The Glass Shield '95
Higher Learning '94
Trespass '92
Boyz N the Hood '91

Ice-T (1958-)
Air Rage '01
Guardian '01
Kept '01
3000 Miles to Graceland '01
Ticker '01
Ablaze '00
The Guardian '00
Luck of the Draw '00
Agent of Death '99
Corrupt '99
Final Voyage '99
Jacob Two Two Meets the Hooded Fang '99
Judgment Day '99
Leprechaun 5: In the Hood '99
Sonic Impact '99
Stealth Fighter '99
Urban Menace '99
The Wrecking Crew '99
Crazy Six '98
Body Count '97
The Deli '97
Mean Guns '97
Johnny Mnemonic '95
Surviving the Game '94
Tank Girl '94
Who's the Man? '93
Trespass '92
New Jack City '91
Ricochet '91

Etsuko Ichihara
The Eel '96
Black Rain '88
Snow Country '57

Raizo Ichikawa (1931-69)
Sleepy Eyes of Death: The Chinese Jade '63
Enjo '58
Shin Heike Monogatari '55

Utaemon Ichikawa
47 Ronin, Part 1 '42
47 Ronin, Part 2 '42

Eric Idle (1943-)
102 Dalmatians '00 (V)
Dudley Do-Right '99
South Park: Bigger, Longer and Uncut '99 (V)
Quest for Camelot '98 (V)
An Alan Smithee Film: Burn, Hollywood, Burn '97
Mr. Toad's Wild Ride '96
Casper '95
Splitting Heirs '93
Mom and Dad Save the World '92
Missing Pieces '91
Nuns on the Run '90
Too Much Sun '90
The Adventures of Baron Munchausen '89
Around the World in 80 Days '89
Transformers: The Movie '86 (V)
The Pied Piper of Hamelin '84
Monty Python's The Meaning of Life '83
Yellowbeard '83
Secret Policeman's Private Parts '81

Jason Isaacs (1963-)
Black Hawk Down '01
Sweet November '01
The Patriot '00
The End of the Affair '99
Armageddon '98
The Last Don 2 '98
Robert Louis Stevenson's St. Ives '98
Soldier '98
Event Horizon '97
Dragonheart '96
Solitaire for 2 '94

Chris Isaak (1956-)
Blue Ridge Fall '99
From the Earth to the Moon '98
Grace of My Heart '96
That Thing You Do! '96
Little Buddha '93
Twin Peaks: Fire Walk with Me '92
The Silence of the Lambs '91
Married to the Mob '88

Katharine Isabelle
Insomnia '02
Bones '01
Ginger Snaps '01

Tom Isbell
A Case of Deadly Force '86
Behind Enemy Lines '85

Ryo Ishibashi
Back to Back '96
American Yakuza '94
Blue Tiger '94
The Crossing Guard '94

Takaaki Ishibashi
Major League 3: Back to the Minors '98
Major League 2 '94

Kevin Isola
24 Nights '99
The Summer of Ben Tyler '96

Ravil Issyanov
Doomsdayer '99
Back in the USSR '92

Juzo Itami (1933-97)
MacArthur's Children '85
The Family Game '83

Emi Ito (1946-)
Ghidrah the Three Headed Monster '65
Godzilla vs. Mothra '64
Mothra '62

Hisaya Ito
Destroy All Monsters '68
Ghidrah the Three Headed Monster '65

Robert Ito (1931-)
The Omega Code '99
Once a Thief '96
Pray for Death '85
The Adventures of Buckaroo Banzai Across the Eighth Dimension '84
Women of the Prehistoric Planet '66

Toshiya Ito
Ran '85
Space Riders '83

Yumi Ito (1946-)
Ghidrah the Three Headed Monster '65
Godzilla vs. Mothra '64
Mothra '62

Yunosuke Ito
The Burmese Harp '56
Ikiru '52

Jose Iturbi (1895-1980)
That Midnight Kiss '49
Three Daring Daughters '48
Holiday in Mexico '46
Anchors Aweigh '45
Two Girls and a Sailor '44

Gregory Itzin
Life or Something Like It '02
Evolution '01
Original Sin '01
Fly Boy '99

Marcel Iures
Hart's War '02
The Peacemaker '97

Rosalind Ivan (1884-1959)
The Corn Is Green '45
Pursuit to Algiers '45
Dead Man's Eyes/Pillow of Death '44

Zeljko Ivanek (1957-)
Unfaithful '02
Black Hawk Down '01
Hannibal '01
Homicide: The Movie '00
Dancer in the Dark '99
Dash and Lilly '99
A Civil Action '98
From the Earth to the Moon '98
The Rat Pack '98
Ellen Foster '97
Julian Po '97
Courage Under Fire '96
Donnie Brasco '96
Infinity '96
White Squall '96
Truman '95
School Ties '92
Our Sons '91
Echoes in the Darkness '87
Rachel River '87
Mass Appeal '84
The Sender '82

Stan Ivar
High Stakes '93
Creature '85

Terri Ivens
Trancers 5: Sudden Deth '94
Trancers 4: Jack of Swords '93

Daniel Ivernel (1920-99)
High Heels '72
Diary of a Chambermaid '64
Manon '50

Robert Ivers
G.I. Blues '60
The Delicate Delinquent '56

Burl Ives (1909-95)
Two Moon Junction '88
Poor Little Rich Girl: The Barbara Hutton Story '87
Uphill All the Way '85
The Ewok Adventure '84 (N)
Roots '77
Baker's Hawk '76
Hugo the Hippo '76 (V)
The McMasters '70
Those Fantastic Flying Fools '67
Ensign Pulver '64
The Brass Bottle '63
Summer Magic '63
Let No Man Write My Epitaph '60
The Big Country '58
Cat on a Hot Tin Roof '58
Desire Under the Elms '58
East of Eden '54
So Dear to My Heart '49
Station West '48

Dana Ivey (1942-)
Orange County '02
Disney's The Kid '00
Mumford '99
The Imposters '98
Simon Birch '98
Sabrina '95
The Scarlet Letter '95
Addams Family Values '93
The Adventures of Huck Finn '93
Guilty as Sin '93
Class of '61 '92
Home Alone 2: Lost in New York '92
The Addams Family '91
Postcards from the Edge '90
Dirty Rotten Scoundrels '88
Explorers '85

Judith Ivey (1951-)
Stephen King's Rose Red '02
Mystery, Alaska '99
What the Deaf Man Heard '98
The Devil's Advocate '97
A Life Less Ordinary '97
Washington Square '97
Without Limits '97
The Summer of Ben Tyler '96 (N)
There Goes the Neighborhood '92
Love Hurts '91
Decoration Day '90
Everybody Wins '90
In Country '89
Miles from Home '88
Hello Again '87
Sister, Sister '87
We Are the Children '87
Brighton Beach Memoirs '86
The Long, Hot Summer '86
Compromising Positions '85
Dixie: Changing Habits '85
Harry & Son '84
The Lonely Guy '84
The Woman in Red '84

Shima Iwashita (1941-)
Gonza the Spearman '86
MacArthur's Children '85
Double Suicide '69
Red Lion '69
An Autumn Afternoon '62

Victor Izay
Blood Orgy of the She-Devils '74
The Trial of Billy Jack '74
Billy Jack '71
Premonition '71
The Astro-Zombies '67

Eddie Izzard (1962-)
The Cat's Meow '01
Circus '00
Shadow of the Vampire '00
Mystery Men '99
The Avengers '98
Velvet Goldmine '98

Ja Rule
The Fast and the Furious '01
Turn It Up '00

Michael Jace (1965-)
Planet of the Apes '01
The Replacements '00
Thick as Thieves '99
Bombshell '97
Boogie Nights '97
The Great White Hype '96
Strange Days '95

Jackee (1956-)
The Reluctant Agent '95
Ladybugs '92
The Women of Brewster Place '89

Ian Jacklin
American Streetfighter '96
Capital Punishment '96
Warrior of Justice '96
Death Match '94
Expert Weapon '93
Kickboxer 3: The Art of War '92

Hugh Jackman (1968-)
Kate & Leopold '01
Someone Like You '01
Swordfish '01
X-Men '00
Erskinville Kings '99
Paperback Hero '99

Andrew Jackson
Bram Stoker's Shadowbuilder '98
The Last Don 2 '98
Twists of Terror '98
Family of Cops 2: Breach of Faith '97
Specimen '97

Anne Jackson (1926-)
Rescuers: Stories of Courage "Two Women" '97
Folks! '92
Funny About Love '90
Out on a Limb '87
Sam's Son '84
Blood Debts '83
Blinded by the Light '82
A Woman Called Golda '82
Leave 'Em Laughing '81
The Shining '80
The Bell Jar '79
The Family Man '79
Nasty Habits '77
The Angel Levine '70
Lovers and Other Strangers '70
Secret Life of an American Wife '68
Tall Story '60

David Jackson
The Vernonia Incident '89
Music Shoppe '82

Eugene Jackson (1916-2001)
Shenandoah '65
Red River Valley '36

Freda Jackson (1909-90)
The Valley of Gwangi '69
Die, Monster, Die! '65
The Brides of Dracula '60
Bhowani Junction '56
Beware of Pity '46
Great Expectations '46
Henry V '44

Glenda Jackson (1936-)
King of the Wind '93
A Murder of Quality '90
Strange Interlude '90
The Rainbow '89
Business As Usual '88
Salome's Last Dance '88
Beyond Therapy '86
Turtle Diary '86
Sakharov '84
And Nothing But the Truth '82
Return of the Soldier '82
Hopscotch '80
Lost and Found '79
The Class of Miss MacMichael '78
House Calls '78
Stevie '78
Nasty Habits '77
Triple Echo '77
The Incredible Sarah '76
Hedda '75
Romantic Englishwoman '75
A Touch of Class '73
Elizabeth R '72
Mary, Queen of Scots '71
The Music Lovers '71
Sunday, Bloody Sunday '71
Women in Love '70
Negatives '68

Gordon Jackson (1923-90)
Noble House '88
The Whistle Blower '87
My Brother Tom '86
A Town Like Alice '85
Gunpowder '84
Bergonzi Hand '70
Hamlet '69
The Prime of Miss Jean Brodie '69
The Fighting Prince of Donegal '66
The Ipcress File '65
Those Magnificent Men in Their Flying Machines '65
The Great Escape '63
Abandon Ship '57
The Baby and the Battleship '56
Death Goes to School '53
Against the Wind '48
Whiskey Galore '48
Pink String and Sealing Wax '45

Howard Jackson
Full Contact '93
Out for Blood '93
Dolemite 2: Human Tornado '76

Janet Jackson (1966-)
Nutty Professor 2: The Klumps '00
Poetic Justice '93

Jennie Jackson
Lady Godiva Rides '68
Ride the High Country '62

John M. Jackson
The Spitfire Grill '95
Roswell: The U.F.O. Cover-Up '94
An American Story '92
Career Opportunities '91
Love, Lies and Murder '91
Switched at Birth '91
Eve of Destruction '90
Sudie & Simpson '90
Cold Sassy Tree '89
Ginger Ale Afternoon '89
The Hitcher '86

Jonathan Jackson (1982-)
Insomnia '02
On the Edge '00
Skeletons in the Closet '00
The Deep End of the Ocean '98
Double Play '96
Camp Nowhere '94

Joshua Jackson (1978-)
Ocean's Eleven '01
The Skulls '00
Gossip '99
Cruel Intentions '98
Urban Legend '98
Apt Pupil '97
Ronnie and Julie '97
D3: The Mighty Ducks '96
Magic in the Water '95
Robin of Locksley '95
Andre '94
Digger '94
The Mighty Ducks '92

Kate Jackson (1949-)
Panic in the Skies '96
Adrift '93
Homewrecker '92 (V)
Loverboy '89
Listen to Your Heart '83
Making Love '82
Dirty Tricks '81
Thunder and Lightning '77
Death at Love House '75
Death Scream '75
Death Cruise '74
Satan's School for Girls '73
Night of Dark Shadows '71

Lamont Jackson
Class Act '91
Assault with a Deadly Weapon '82

Leonard Jackson
Basket Case 2 '90
Ganja and Hess '73

Linda Jackson
Black Bikers from Hell '70
The Outlaw Bikers—Gang Wars '70

Mary Jackson (1910-)
A Family Thing '96
Skinned Alive '89
Terror at Red Wolf Inn '72
Targets '68

Mel Jackson
Uninvited Guest '99
Soul Food '97

Peter Jackson (1961-)
Dead Alive '93
Bad Taste '88

Philip Jackson (1948-)
Little Voice '98
Girls' Night '97
Brassed Off '96
Bad Behavior '92
High Hopes '88

Reggie Jackson (1946-)
BASEketball '98
Richie Rich '94
The Naked Gun: From the Files of Police Squad '88

Sam Jackson
Return of Superfly '90
Dead Man Out '89

Sammy Jackson (1937-95)
Shame, Shame on the Bixby Boys '82
Fastest Guitar Alive '68
None But the Brave '65

Samuel L. Jackson (1948-)
Changing Lanes '02
Star Wars: Episode 2—Attack of the Clones '02
XXX '02
The Caveman's Valentine '01
Rules of Engagement '00
Shaft '00
Unbreakable '00
Deep Blue Sea '99
Star Wars: Episode 1—The Phantom Menace '99
The Negotiator '98
Out of Sight '98
The Red Violin '98
Eve's Bayou '97
Jackie Brown '97
187 '97
Sphere '97
The Great White Hype '96
Hard Eight '96
The Long Kiss Goodnight '96
The Search for One-Eyed Jimmy '96
A Time to Kill '96
Tree's Lounge '96
Die Hard: With a Vengeance '95
Fluke '95 (V)
Against the Wall '94
Assault at West Point: The Court-Martial of Johnson Whittaker '94
Fresh '94
Hail Caesar '94
Kiss of Death '94
Losing Isaiah '94
The New Age '94
Pulp Fiction '94
Amos and Andrew '93
Jurassic Park '93
Menace II Society '93
National Lampoon's Loaded Weapon 1 '93
True Romance '93
Fathers and Sons '92
Johnny Suede '92
Juice '92
Jumpin' at the Boneyard '92
Patriot Games '92
White Sands '92
Jungle Fever '91
Def by Temptation '90
Goodfellas '90
Mo' Better Blues '90
Coming to America '88
School Daze '88

Selmer Jackson (1888-1971)
The Gallant Hours '60
Pitfall '48
Guadalcanal Diary '43
The Fighting Sullivans '42
International Lady '41
Sergeant York '41
They Died with Their Boots On '41
The Thirteenth Man '37

Sherry Jackson (1942-)
Daughters of the Dust '91
Stingray '78
Bare Knuckles '77
Cotter '72
The Adventures of Huckleberry Finn '60
Trouble along the Way '53
Miracle of Our Lady of Fatima '52

Stoney Jackson
Trippin' '99
Black Scorpion 2: Ground Zero '96
The Disappearance of Kevin Johnson '95
Up Against the Wall '91

Sweet Perfection '90
Knights of the City '85
Streets of Fire '84
Roller Boogie '79

Tom Jackson
Grizzly Falls '99
Medicine River '94
Spirit Rider '93

Victoria Jackson (1959-)
Wedding Bell Blues '96
Based on an Untrue Story '93
I Love You to Death '90
Dream a Little Dream '89
Family Business '89
UHF '89
Casual Sex? '88
Baby Boom '87
The Pick-Up Artist '87
Stoogemania '85

Catherine Jacob
The Green House '96
Tatie Danielle '91

Irene Jacob (1966-)
The Big Brass Ring '99
Spy Games '99
My Life So Far '98
U.S. Marshals '98
Incognito '97
Beyond the Clouds '95
Othello '95
Trois Couleurs: Rouge '94
Trusting Beatrice '92
The Double Life of Veronique '91
Au Revoir les Enfants '87

Derek Jacobi (1938-)
The Body '01
Gladiator '00
Jason and the Argonauts '00
Up at the Villa '00
Molokai: The Story of Father Damien '99
Basil '98
Love Is the Devil '98
Hamlet '96
Breaking the Code '95
Circle of Deceit '94
Dead Again '91
Henry V '89
Little Dorrit, Film 1: Nobody's Fault '88
Little Dorrit, Film 2: Little Dorrit's Story '88
The Tenth Man '88
The Secret Garden '87
Cyrano de Bergerac '85
Philby, Burgess and MacLean: Spy Scandal of the Century '84
Enigma '82
The Hunchback of Notre Dame '82
Inside the Third Reich '82
The Secret of NIMH '82 (V)
The Human Factor '79
The Medusa Touch '78
The Odessa File '74
Blue Blood '73
The Day of the Jackal '73
The Strauss Family '73
Othello '65

Ernst Jacobi
Hamsun '96
Germany, Pale Mother '80

Lou Jacobi (1913-)
I.Q. '94
I Don't Buy Kisses Anymore '92
Avalon '90
Amazon Women on the Moon '87
The Boss' Wife '86
My Favorite Year '82
Arthur '81
Chu Chu & the Philly Flash '81
Off Your Rocker '80
Better Late Than Never '79
The Magician of Lublin '79
Roseland '77
Next Stop, Greenwich Village '76

Everything You Always Wanted to Know about Sex (But Were Afraid to Ask) '72
Little Murders '71
Cotton Comes to Harlem '70
Song Without End '60
The Diary of Anne Frank '59

Andre Jacobs
Curse of the Crystal Eye '93
Prey for the Hunter '92
Pursuit '90
Emissary '89

Lawrence-Hilton Jacobs (1953-)
Indecent Behavior '93
The Jacksons: An American Dream '92
Quiet Fire '91
Angels of the City '89
Chance '89
East L.A. Warriors '89
Killcrazy '89
L.A. Vice '89
L.A. Heat '88
Paramedics '88
The Annihilators '85
For the Love of It '80
Cooley High '75

Manny Jacobs
The Seventh Sign '88
Battle of the Bullies '85

Mark Evan Jacobs
Bleeding Hearts '94
Trusting Beatrice '92

Steve Jacobs (1967-)
Father '90
Alice to Nowhere '86
Echoes of Paradise '86

Ulla Jacobsson (1929-82)
Fox and His Friends '75
The Heroes of Telemark '65
Zulu '64
Smiles of a Summer Night '55

Billy Jacoby (1969-)
Dr. Alien '88
Party Camp '87
Just One of the Guys '85
Cujo '83
Beastmaster '82
Bloody Birthday '80

Bobby Jacoby (1973-)
Fear Runs Silent '99
Night of the Demons 2 '94
The Day My Parents Ran Away '93
The Applegates '89
Tremors '89
Wizards of the Lost Kingdom 2 '89
Iron Eagle '86

Dale Jacoby
Guardian Angel '94
Ring of Fire 2: Blood and Steel '92
Bloodmatch '91
Ring of Fire '91

Scott Jacoby (1956-)
To Die For 2: Son of Darkness '91
To Die For '89
Return to Horror High '87
Midnight Auto Supply '78
The Little Girl Who Lives down the Lane '76
Bad Ronald '74
Rivals '72

Carlos Jacott
Bats '99
Mr. Jealousy '98
Kicking and Screaming '95

Hattie Jacques (1924-80)
Carry On at Your Convenience '71
Make Mine Mink '60
Carry On Nurse '59
A Christmas Carol '51

Claude Jade
Love on the Run '78

Bed and Board '70
Stolen Kisses '68

Scott Jaeck
Killing Mr. Griffin '97
Washington Square '97
JAG '95

Richard Jaeckel (1926-97)
Martial Outlaw '93
The King of the Kickboxers '91
Delta Force 2: Operation Stranglehold '90
Ghetto Blaster '89
Black Moon Rising '86
The Dirty Dozen: The Next Mission '85
Pacific Inferno '85
The Fix '84
Starman '84
Airplane 2: The Sequel '82
Blood Song '82
...All the Marbles '81
Awakening of Candra '81
Cold River '81
The $5.20 an Hour Dream '80
Herbie Goes Bananas '80
The Dark '79
Speedtrap '78
Day of the Animals '77
Twilight's Last Gleaming '77
Grizzly '76
Jaws of Death '76
The Drowning Pool '75
Surabaya Conspiracy '75
Walking Tall: Part 2 '75
Born Innocent '74
The Kill '73
Pat Garrett & Billy the Kid '73
Firehouse '72
Ulzana's Raid '72
Sometimes a Great Notion '71
Chisum '70
The Devil's Brigade '68
The Green Slime '68
The Dirty Dozen '67
Once Before I Die '65
Town without Pity '61
Flaming Star '60
The Gallant Hours '60
Platinum High School '60
Cowboy '58
When Hell Broke Loose '58
3:10 to Yuma '57
Attack! '56
Come Back, Little Sheba '52
Hoodlum Empire '52
Battleground '49
Sands of Iwo Jima '49
Jungle Patrol '48
A Wing and a Prayer '44
Guadalcanal Diary '43

Frederick Jaeger
Nijinsky '80
Slaughterday '77

Hannes Jaenicke (1960-)
Extreme Limits '01
Mom's Outta Sight '01
Venomous '01
Active Stealth '99
Bandits '99
Restraining Order '99
The Hunted '98
The Heist '96
Jack Higgins' Midnight Man '96
Catherine the Great '95
Out of Order '84

Chapelle Jaffe
Sin and Redemption '94
Confidential '86
One Night Stand '77

Sam Jaffe (1891-1984)
On the Line '83
Battle Beyond the Stars '80
Gideon's Trumpet '80
Bedknobs and Broomsticks '71
The Dunwich Horror '70
Night Gallery '69

A Guide for the Married Man '67
Ben-Hur '59
Barbarian and the Geisha '58
The Day the Earth Stood Still '51
The Asphalt Jungle '50
The Accused '48
13 Rue Madeleine '46
Gunga Din '39
Lost Horizon '37
Scarlet Empress '34

Seth Jaffe
Scorned 2 '96
Beverly Hills Bodysnatchers '89
Stark '85

Madhur Jaffrey (1933-)
Chutney Popcorn '99
Cotton Mary '99
Vanya on 42nd Street '94
Heat and Dust '82
Autobiography of a Princess '75
Shakespeare Wallah '65

Saeed Jaffrey (1929-)
Masala '91
The Deceivers '88
The Courtesans of Bombay '85
My Beautiful Laundrette '85
The Razor's Edge '84
Gandhi '82
Hullabaloo over Georgie & Bonnie's Pictures '78
The Man Who Would Be King '75
The Wilby Conspiracy '75

Sakina Jaffrey
Chutney Popcorn '99
Cotton Mary '99
Masala '91

Bianca Jagger
C.H.U.D. 2: Bud the Chud '89
All You Need Is Cash '78

Dean Jagger (1903-91)
Evil Town '87
Alligator '80
Gideon's Trumpet '80
Game of Death '79
End of the World '76
The Lindbergh Kidnapping Case '76
Hootch Country Boys '75
The Hanged Man '74
I Heard the Owl Call My Name '73
The Stranger '73
Visions of Evil '73
The Glass House '72
Vanishing Point '71
Firecreek '68
Billy Rose's Jumbo '62
The Honeymoon Machine '61
Parrish '61
Cash McCall '60
Elmer Gantry '60
The Nun's Story '59
King Creole '58
Proud Rebel '58
X The Unknown '56
It's a Dog's Life '55
Bad Day at Black Rock '54
Executive Suite '54
Private Hell 36 '54
White Christmas '54
The Robe '53
The Denver & Rio Grande '51
Rawhide '50
The C-Man '49
Twelve o'Clock High '49
Pursued '47
I Live in Grosvenor Square '46
Sister Kenny '46
The North Star '43
Valley of the Sun '42
Western Union '41
Brigham Young: Frontiersman '40
Exiled to Shanghai '37

Revolt of the Zombies '36

Mick Jagger (1943-)
Bent '97
Freejack '92
Running out of Luck '86
The Nightingale '83
Burden of Dreams '82
All You Need Is Cash '78
Gimme Shelter '70
Ned Kelly '70
Performance '70
Sympathy for the Devil '70

Henry Jaglom (1943-)
Last Summer In the Hamptons '96
Venice, Venice '92
New Year's Day '89
Someone to Love '87
Always '85
Sitting Ducks '80
Psych-Out '68

Lisa Jakub (1978-)
Dream House '98
The Beautician and the Beast '97
The Wicked, Wicked West '97
The Story Lady '93
Matinee '92
Rambling Rose '91
The Phone Call '89

Anthony James (1942-)
Unforgiven '92
Slow Burn '90
The Teacher '74
Columbo: Prescription Murder '67
The Last Days of Dolwyn '49

Brion James (1945-99)
The Operator '01
Arthur's Quest '99
Brown's Requiem '98
In God's Hands '98
A Place Called Truth '98
Bombshell '97
The Fifth Element '97
Hunter's Moon '97
Pterodactyl Woman from Beverly Hills '97
American Strays '96
Back in Business '96
Evil Obsession '96
The Killing Jar '96
The Lazarus Man '96
Precious Find '96
Virtual Assassin '95
Cabin Boy '94
The Companion '94
The Dark '94
Dominion '94
Hong Kong '97 '94
The Last Ride '94
Nature of the Beast '94
Radioland Murders '94
Savage Land '94
Scanner Cop '94
Sketch Artist 2: Hands That See '94
The Soft Kill '94
Steel Frontier '94
Future Shock '93
Rio Diablo '93
Striking Distance '93
Wishman '93
Black Magic '92
The Player '92
Time Runner '92
Ultimate Desires '91
Another 48 Hrs. '90
Beyond the Silhouette '90
Mutator '90
Street Asylum '90
The Horror Show '89
Mom '89
Red Scorpion '89
Tango and Cash '89
Dead Man Walking '88
Nightmare at Noon '87
Steel Dawn '87
Armed and Dangerous '86
Crimewave '85
Enemy Mine '85
Flesh and Blood '85
A Breed Apart '84

Ballad of Gregorio Cortez '83
Blade Runner '82
48 Hrs. '82
Southern Comfort '81
Blue Sunshine '78
KISS Meets the Phantom of the Park '78

Clifton James (1923-)
The Summer of Ben Tyler '96
Lone Star '95
Carolina Skeletons '92
The Bonfire of the Vanities '90
Eight Men Out '88
Where Are the Children? '85
Talk to Me '82
The Bad News Bears in Breaking Training '77
Rancho Deluxe '75
Sniper '75
Bank Shot '74
Buster and Billie '74
The Man with the Golden Gun '74
The Last Detail '73
Live and Let Die '73
Werewolf of Washington '73
Cool Hand Luke '67
Will Penny '67
Black Like Me '64
David and Lisa '62
The Strange One '57

Dalton James
My Father the Hero '93
The Substitute '93

Etta James
Tap '89
Chuck Berry: Hail! Hail! Rock 'n' Roll '87

Gennie James (1977-)
The River Pirates '94
Broadcast News '87
The Secret Garden '87
A Smoky Mountain Christmas '86

Gerald James
Tess of the D'Urbervilles '98
Hope and Glory '87

Geraldine James (1950-)
The Luzhin Defence '00
Lover's Prayer '99
The Man Who Knew Too Little '97
Rebecca '97
Moll Flanders '96
Band of Gold '95
If Looks Could Kill '91
The Tall Guy '89
Echoes '88
The Jewel in the Crown '84

Gladden James (1892-1948)
Paradise Island '30
The Peacock Fan '29
The Social Secretary '16

Godfrey James
Magic in the Mirror: Fowl Play '96
Spellbreaker: Secret of the Leprechauns '96
Leapin' Leprechauns '95
At the Earth's Core '76
The Land That Time Forgot '75

Harry James (1916-83)
The Benny Goodman Story '55
Strictly G.I. '44
Two Girls and a Sailor '44
Best Foot Forward '43
Private Buckaroo '42

Hawthorne James
Heaven's Prisoners '95
Speed '94
The Five Heartbeats '91

Ida James
The Devil's Daughter '39
Hi-De-Ho '35

Jesse James
Blow *'01*
A Dog of Flanders *'99*
Hanging Up *'99*
Jesse James, Jr. (1876-1951)
Message in a Bottle *'98*
The Gingerbread Man *'97*
Jesse James Under the Black Flag *'21*
Jessica James
Immediate Family *'89*
Diner *'82*
I, the Jury *'82*
John James (-1960)
Peril *'00*
Secret Passions *'78*
Lonesome Trail *'55*
Range Renegades *'48*
The Devil Bat's Daughter *'46*
Man from Thunder River *'43*
Julie James
Terror Beach *'80s*
Night of the Death Cult *'75*
Ken James (1948-)
The Third Miracle *'99*
Tracked *'98*
Landslide *'92*
Switching Channels *'88*
Lee James
The Taking of Beverly Hills *'91*
Cassandra *'87*
Lennie James
Snatch *'00*
Among Giants *'98*
Lost in Space *'98*
Michael James
Commando Invasion *'87*
Warriors of the Apocalypse *'85*
Richard James
Mr. Toad's Wild Ride *'96*
Sebastiane *'79*
Ron James
Ernest Rides Again *'93*
The Boogey Man *'80*
Sidney James (1913-76)
Carry On Behind *'75*
Carry On Dick *'75*
Carry On at Your Convenience *'71*
Carry On Camping *'71*
Carry On Henry VIII *'71*
Carry On Cowboy *'66*
Carry On Cleo *'65*
Carry On Cruising *'62*
What a Carve-Up! *'62*
The Silent Enemy *'58*
Quatermass 2 *'57*
The Smallest Show on Earth *'57*
Glass Tomb *'55*
John and Julie *'55*
Heat Wave *'54*
The Belles of St. Trinian's *'53*
Norman Conquest *'53*
The Lavender Hill Mob *'51*
Sonny James
Hillbillies in a Haunted House *'67*
Las Vegas Hillbillys *'66*
Steve James (1955-93)
Bloodfist 5: Human Target *'93*
Weekend at Bernie's 2 *'93*
The Player *'92*
McBain *'91*
Street Hunter *'90*
American Ninja 3: Blood Hunt *'89*
Riverbend *'89*
Hero and the Terror *'88*
I'm Gonna Git You Sucka *'88*
Johnny Be Good *'88*
Python Wolf *'88*
American Ninja 2: The Confrontation *'87*
Avenging Force *'86*
The P.O.W. Escape *'86*
Stalking Danger *'86*
American Ninja *'85*
The Brother from Another Planet *'84*
Exterminator *'80*
The Land That Time Forgot *'75*
Walter James (1882-1946)
The Kid Brother *'27*
Battling Butler *'26*
Little Annie Rooney *'25*
The Monster *'25*
The Idol Dancer *'20*
Joyce Jameson (1932-87)
Hardbodies *'84*
Pray TV *'80*
Savage Run *'70*
The Comedy of Terrors *'64*
Good Neighbor Sam *'64*
The Balcony *'63*
Tales of Terror *'62*
Malcom Jamieson
Meridian: Kiss of the Beast *'90*
Pictures *'80s*
Krystyna Janda (1955-)
The Decalogue *'88*
The Interrogation *'82*
Man of Iron *'81*
Mephisto *'81*
The Conductor *'80*
Without Anesthesia *'78*
Man of Marble *'76*
Thomas Jane (1969-)
The Sweetest Thing *'02*
Original Sin *'01*
61* *'01*
Under Suspicion *'00*
Deep Blue Sea *'99*
Molly *'99*
The Thin Red Line *'98*
Thursday *'98*
The Velocity of Gary *'98*
Boogie Nights *'97*
Hollywood Confidential *'97*
The Crow 2: City of Angels *'96*
The Last Time I Committed Suicide *'96*
Conrad Janis (1928-)
The Cable Guy *'96*
November Conspiracy *'96*
Mr. Saturday Night *'92*
Sonny Boy *'87*
Oh, God! Book 2 *'80*
The Buddy Holly Story *'78*
The Duchess and the Dirtwater Fox *'76*
Oleg (Yankovsky) Jankowsky (1944-)
Mute Witness *'95*
My Twentieth Century *'90*
Nostalghia *'83*
The Shooting Party *'77*
The Mirror *'75*
Allison Janney (1960-)
A Girl Thing *'01*
Nurse Betty *'00*
American Beauty *'99*
Drop Dead Gorgeous *'99*
Ten Things I Hate about You *'99*
Celebrity *'98*
The Imposters *'98*
The Object of My Affection *'98*
Primary Colors *'98*
Six Days, Seven Nights *'98*
First Do No Harm *'97*
The Ice Storm *'97*
Julian Po *'97*
Private Parts *'96*
Big Night *'95*
Leon Janney
Charly *'68*
Police Court *'37*
William Janney (1908-92)
Hopalong Cassidy Returns *'36*
Coquette *'29*
Emil Jannings (1884-1950)
The Blue Angel *'30*
Last Command *'28*
Faust *'26*
Variety *'25*
The Last Laugh *'24*
Waxworks *'24*
Othello *'22*
Fortune's Fool *'21*
Passion *'19*
Walter Janovitz
The Hollywood Knights *'80*
Billy the Kid Versus Dracula *'66*
Thom Jansen
The Gambler *'97*
Suite 16 *'94*
Horst Janson
To Catch a King *'84*
Captain Kronos: Vampire Hunter *'74*
McKenzie Break *'70*
David Janssen (1930-80)
City in Fear *'80*
High Ice *'80*
S.O.S. Titanic *'79*
Centennial *'78*
The Word *'78*
Golden Rendezvous *'77*
Swiss Conspiracy *'77*
Stalk the Wild Child *'76*
Two Minute Warning *'76*
Once Is Not Enough *'75*
Fer-De-Lance *'74*
Prisoner in the Middle *'74*
Smile, Jenny, You're Dead *'74*
Pioneer Woman *'73*
Birds of Prey *'72*
Moon of the Wolf *'72*
Macho Callahan *'70*
Generation *'69*
Marooned *'69*
The Green Berets *'68*
The Shoes of the Fisherman *'68*
The King of the Roaring '20s: The Story of Arnold Rothstein *'61*
Hell to Eternity *'60*
Darby's Rangers *'58*
Lafayette Escadrille *'58*
Francis in the Haunted House *'56*
Francis in the Navy *'55*
To Hell and Back *'55*
Francis Goes to West Point *'52*
Swamp Fire *'46*
Eilene Janssen
On Our Merry Way *'48*
Curley *'47*
Famke Janssen (1964-)
Don't Say a Word *'01*
Made *'01*
Circus *'00*
Love & Sex *'00*
X-Men *'00*
House on Haunted Hill *'99*
Celebrity *'98*
Deep Rising *'98*
The Faculty *'98*
Monument Ave. *'98*
Rounders *'98*
The Gingerbread Man *'97*
R.P.M. *'97*
City of Industry *'96*
Goldeneye *'95*
Lord of Illusions *'95*
Model by Day *'94*
Relentless 4 *'94*
Fathers and Sons *'92*
Walther Jansson
The Mozart Story *'48*
Destiny *'21*
Lois January (1912-)
Lightning Bill Crandall *'37*
The Red Rope *'37*
The Roamin' Cowboy *'37*
Border Caballero *'36*
Cocaine Fiends *'36*
Bulldog Courage *'35*
Agnes Jaoui (1964-)
Same Old Song *'97*
Un Air de Famille *'96*
Claude Jarman, Jr. (1934-)
Hangman's Knot *'52*
Rio Grande *'50*
Intruder in the Dust *'49*
The Sun Comes Up *'49*
The Yearling *'46*
Jim Jarmusch (1953-)
Sling Blade *'96*
Blue in the Face *'95*
In the Soup *'92*
Leningrad Cowboys Go America *'89*
Straight to Hell *'87*
American Autobahn *'84*
Ernst Hugo Jarogard
The Kingdom 2 *'97*
The Kingdom *'95*
John Jarratt (1952-)
Dead Heart *'96*
Talk *'94*
Dark Age *'88*
Next of Kin *'82*
The Odd Angry Shot *'79*
Sound of Love *'77*
Summer City *'77*
Stig Jarrel
The Devil's Eye *'60*
Torment *'44*
Catherine Jarrett
A Fine Romance *'92*
Quicker Than the Eye *'88*
S.A.S. San Salvador *'84*
Graham Jarvis (1930-)
Misery *'90*
Parents *'89*
Vanishing Act *'88*
Doin' Time *'85*
Mischief *'85*
Draw! *'81*
Middle Age Crazy *'80*
Cold Turkey *'71*
Alice's Restaurant *'69*
Martin Jarvis
Lorna Doone *'01*
Buster *'88*
Taste the Blood of Dracula *'70*
David Jason
All the King's Men *'99*
Open All Hours *'83*
Donna Jason
Abducted 2: The Reunion *'94*
Undefeatable *'94*
Honor and Glory *'92*
Harvey Jason (1940-)
The Lost World: Jurassic Park 2 *'97*
Oklahoma Crude *'73*
The Witching *'72*
Too Late the Hero *'70*
Star! *'68*
Peter Jason
The Demolitionist *'95*
In the Mouth of Madness *'95*
Rage *'95*
Village of the Damned *'95*
Deconstructing Sarah *'94*
Arachnophobia *'90*
Alien Nation *'88*
They Live *'88*
Heartbreak Ridge *'86*
Hyper-Sapien: People from Another Star *'86*
Trick or Treats *'82*
Texas Lightning *'81*
Rick Jason (1926-2000)
Partners *'82*
Witch Who Came from the Sea *'76*
Eagles Attack at Dawn *'74*
Color Me Dead *'69*
Sybil Jason
The Blue Bird *'40*
The Little Princess *'39*
Star Jasper
Jersey Girl *'92*
True Love *'89*
Mark Jax
Merlin *'98*
Stealing Heaven *'88*
Ricky Jay (1948-)
Heartbreakers *'01*
Heist *'01*
Mystery Men *'99*
Boogie Nights *'97*
Sink or Swim *'97*
The Spanish Prisoner *'97*
Tomorrow Never Dies *'97*
Hole in the Sky *'95*
Things Change *'88*
House of Games *'87*
Michael Jayston (1936-)
20,000 Leagues Under the Sea *'97*
Element of Doubt *'96*
Macbeth *'90*
Dust to Dust *'85*
From a Far Country: Pope John Paul II *'81 (N)*
Craze *'74*
Nicholas and Alexandra *'71*
A Midsummer Night's Dream *'68*
Gregory Jbara
William Shakespeare's A Midsummer Night's Dream *'99*
In and Out *'97*
Gloria Jean (1927-)
The Ladies' Man *'61*
Copacabana *'47*
Never Give a Sucker an Even Break *'41*
Jasmine Jean
Vampire Centerfolds *'98*
Vampire Conspiracy *'96*
Marianne Jean-Baptiste (1967-)
The Murder of Stephen Lawrence *'01*
Spy Game *'01*
The Cell *'00*
28 Days *'00*
A Murder of Crows *'99*
The 24 Hour Woman *'99*
Mr. Jealousy *'98*
Secrets and Lies *'95*
Zizi Jeanmarie
Black Tights *'60*
Hans Christian Andersen *'52*
Marcel Jeannin
The Sign of Four *'01*
The Audrey Hepburn Story *'00*
Isabel Jeans (1891-1985)
The Magic Christian *'69*
Heavens Above *'63*
Gigi *'58*
Elizabeth of Ladymead *'48*
Great Day *'46*
Easy Virtue *'27*
Ursula Jeans (1906-73)
Flame Over India *'60*
Dam Busters *'55*
The Weaker Sex *'49*
The Life and Death of Colonel Blimp *'43*
Dark Journey *'37*
Cavalcade *'33*
Colin Jeavons
To Play the King *'93*
Bartleby *'70*
Allan Jeayes (1885-1963)
The Hidden Room *'49*
The Four Feathers *'39*
The Scarlet Pimpernel *'34*
Herbert Jefferson, Jr.
World War III *'86*
Detroit 9000 *'73*
Private Duty Nurses *'71*
Doug Jeffery
Tales of the Kama Sutra 2: Monsoon *'98*
Monsoon *'97*
Indecent Behavior 3 *'95*
Irresistible Impulse *'95*
Married People, Single Sex 2: For Better or Worse *'94*
Barbara Jefford (1930-)
The Ninth Gate *'99*
A Village Affair *'95*
Where Angels Fear to Tread *'91*
When the Whales Came *'89*
Reunion *'88*
Murders at Lynch Cross *'85*
And the Ship Sails On *'83*
Lust for a Vampire *'71*
A Midsummer Night's Dream *'68*
Ulysses *'67*
Myles Jeffrey
Tart *'01*
Babe: Pig in the City *'98 (V)*
Peter Jeffrey (1929-99)
The Scarlet Pimpernel 2: Mademoiselle Guillotine *'99*
Rasputin: Dark Servant of Destiny *'96*
Middlemarch *'93*
Hands of a Murderer *'90*
The Adventures of Baron Munchausen *'89*
The Odessa File *'74*
Doctor Phibes Rises Again *'72*
Elizabeth R *'72*
The Abominable Dr. Phibes *'71*
The Horsemen *'70*
Twinsanity *'70*
If... *'69*
Ring of Bright Water *'69*
The Fixer *'68*
Anne Jeffreys (1923-)
Return of the Bad Men *'48*
Riff-Raff *'47*
Trail Street *'47*
Dick Tracy vs. Cueball *'46*
Dick Tracy, Detective *'45*
Dillinger *'45*
Those Endearing Young Charms *'45*
Nevada *'44*
Step Lively *'44*
Zombies on Broadway *'44*
Bordertown Gunfighters *'43*
Calling Wild Bill Elliott *'43*
Death Valley Manhunt *'43*
Man from Thunder River *'43*
Billy the Kid Trapped *'42*
I Married an Angel *'42*
X Marks the Spot *'42*
Chuck Jeffreys
Bloodmoon *'97*
Deathfight *'93*
Honor and Glory *'92*
Aftershock *'88*
Hawkeye *'88*
Fran Jeffries
Harum Scarum *'65*
Sex and the Single Girl *'64*
Herbert Jeffries (1911-)
Chrome and Hot Leather *'71*
Bronze Buckaroo *'39*
Harlem Rides the Range *'39*
Harlem on the Prairie *'38*
Two-Gun Man from Harlem *'38*
Lang Jeffries
Mission Stardust *'68*
Alone Against Rome *'62*
Lionel Jeffries (1926-)
Jekyll and Hyde *'90*
A Chorus of Disapproval *'89*
Letting the Birds Go Free *'86*
Prisoner of Zenda *'79*
Bananas Boat *'78*
Royal Flash *'75*
Who Slew Auntie Roo? *'71*
Eye Witness *'70*
Lola *'69*
Chitty Chitty Bang Bang *'68*
Camelot *'67*

The Forty-Ninth Parallel '41
South Riding '37

Mervyn Johns (1899-1992)
Day of the Triffids '63
No Love for Johnnie '60
Romeo and Juliet '54
The Master of Ballantrae '53
A Christmas Carol '51
Tony Draws a Horse '51
Counterblast '48
Captain Boycott '47
Captive Heart '47
San Demetrio, London '47
Dead of Night '45
Pink String and Sealing Wax '45

Stratford Johns (1925-2002)
Splitting Heirs '93
The Strange Case of the End of Civilization As We Know It '93
A Demon in My View '92
The Lair of the White Worm '88
Salome's Last Dance '88
Dance with a Stranger '85
Great Expectations '81
The Fiendish Plot of Dr. Fu Manchu '80
Who Done It? '56

Tracy C. Johns (1963-)
New Jack City '91
Mo' Better Blues '90
She's Gotta Have It '86

A.J. (Anthony) Johnson
O '01
I Got the Hook-Up '98
The Players Club '98
B.A.P.'s '97
Def Jam's How to Be a Player '97
Double Trouble '91
House Party '90

Amy Jo Johnson (1970-)
Cold Hearts '99
Sweetwater: A True Rock Story '99
Killing Mr. Griffin '97
Turbo: A Power Rangers Movie '96
Mighty Morphin Power Rangers: The Movie '95

Anne-Marie Johnson (1960-)
Down in the Delta '98
Asteroid '97
Dream Date '93
True Identity '91
Robot Jox '90
I'm Gonna Git You Sucka '88
Hollywood Shuffle '87

Ariyan Johnson
Bulworth '98
Just Another Girl on the I.R.T. '93

Arnold Johnson (1922-2000)
My Demon Lover '87
Putney Swope '69

Arte Johnson (1934-)
Assault of the Party Nerds 2: Heavy Petting Detective '95
Munchie '92
Evil Spirits '91
Evil Toons '90
The Red Raven Kiss-Off '90
Tax Season '90
What Comes Around '85
Bunco '83
If Things Were Different '79
Love at First Bite '79
Bud and Lou '78
Charge of the Model T's '76
The President's Analyst '67

Ashley Johnson
What Women Want '00
Dancer, Texas—Pop. 81 '98
Annie: A Royal Adventure '95

Ben Johnson (1920-96)
The Evening Star '96
Ruby Jean and Joe '96
Angels in the Outfield '94
Bonanza: The Return '93
Radio Flyer '92
The Chase '91
My Heroes Have Always Been Cowboys '91
Back to Back '90
Bull of the West '89
Dark Before Dawn '89
Cherry 2000 '88
Let's Get Harry '87
Trespasses '86
Champions '84
Red Dawn '84
Soggy Bottom U.S.A. '84
Wild Horses '84
The Shadow Riders '82
Tex '82
Ruckus '81
Terror Train '80
The Sacketts '79
Wild Times '79
The Swarm '78
Grayeagle '77
Breakheart Pass '76
The Red Pony '76
The Savage Bees '76
Town That Dreaded Sundown '76
Bite the Bullet '75
The Sugarland Express '74
Dillinger '73
Train Robbers '73
The Getaway '72
Junior Bonner '72
The Last Picture Show '71
Chisum '70
The Undefeated '69
The Wild Bunch '69
Will Penny '67
The Rare Breed '66
Major Dundee '65
One-Eyed Jacks '61
Tomboy & the Champ '58
Shane '53
Rio Grande '50
Wagon Master '50
Mighty Joe Young '49
She Wore a Yellow Ribbon '49
Three Godfathers '48

Beverly Johnson (1952-)
Crossroads '02
Def Jam's How to Be a Player '97
True Vengeance '97
The Cover Girl Murders '93
Ashanti, Land of No Mercy '79

Brad Johnson (1959-)
Crossfire Trail '01
Across the Line '00
Left Behind: The Movie '00
Rough Riders '97
Soldier of Fortune Inc. '97
Lone Justice 3: Showdown at Plum Creek '96
The Birds 2: Land's End '94
Dominion '94
Siringo '94
Lone Justice 2 '93
Philadelphia Experiment 2 '93
An American Story '92
Flight of the Intruder '90
Always '89
Nam Angels '88

C. David Johnson
Aldrich Ames: Traitor Within '98
The Legend of Gator Face '96

Candy Johnson
Bikini Beach '64
Muscle Beach Party '64
Pajama Party '64
Beach Party '63

Celia Johnson (1908-82)
Unicorn '83
The Hostage Tower '80
Staying On '80
Les Miserables '78
The Prime of Miss Jean Brodie '69
Captain's Paradise '53
This Happy Breed '47
Brief Encounter '46
In Which We Serve '43

Chic Johnson (1891-1962)
All Over Town '37
Country Gentlemen '36

Clark Johnson (1954-)
Boycott '02
Deliberate Intent '01
Disappearing Acts '00
Homicide: The Movie '00
Love Come Down '00
Blood Brothers '97
Junior's Groove '97
Rude '96
Soul Survivor '95
Final Round '93
The Finishing Touch '92
Personals '90
Colors '88

Don Johnson (1950-)
Goodbye, Lover '99
Tin Cup '96
In Pursuit of Honor '95
Born Yesterday '93
Guilty as Sin '93
Harley Davidson and the Marlboro Man '91
Paradise '91
Tales of the Unexpected '91
The Hot Spot '90
Dead Bang '89
Sweet Hearts Dance '88
The Long, Hot Summer '86
Cease Fire '85
Miami Vice '84
Soggy Bottom U.S.A. '84
Melanie '82
Beulah Land '80
Revenge of the Stepford Wives '80
The Rebels '79
Snowblind '78
The City '76
Law of the Land '76
A Boy and His Dog '75
Return to Macon County '75
Harrad Experiment '73
Zachariah '70

Dots Johnson
Paisan '46
Tall, Tan and Terrific '46

Dwayne "The Rock" Johnson (1972-)
The Scorpion King '02
The Mummy Returns '01

Georgann Johnson
Twilight Man '96
Murphy's Romance '85

Helen Johnson (1954-)
Vice Squad '31
The Divorcee '30
Sin Takes a Holiday '30

Joey Johnson
Courier of Death '84
Grad Night '81

Julie Johnson
Barney's Great Adventure '98 (V)
The Islander '88

Karl Johnson (-1993)
Love Is the Devil '98
Saint-Ex: The Story of the Storyteller '95
Wittgenstein '93

Katie Johnson
John and Julie '55
The Ladykillers '55

Kay Johnson (1904-75)
Son of Fury '42
The Real Glory '39
American Madness '32
Madam Satan '30

Kelly Johnson
Utu '83
Carry Me Back '82
Goodbye Pork Pie '81

Kurt Johnson
Sole Survivor '84
Jane Austen in Manhattan '80

Kyle Johnson
Man on the Run '74
The Learning Tree '69

Laura Johnson (1957-)
Judge & Jury '96
Cheatin' Hearts '93
Dario Argento's Trauma '93
Deadly Exposure '93
Fatal Instinct '92
Red Shoe Diaries 2: Double Dare '92
Murderous Vision '91
Nick Knight '89
Beyond Reason '77
Opening Night '77

Lynn-Holly Johnson (1958-)
Fugitive X '96
The Criminal Mind '93
Digging Up Business '91
Hyper Space '89
The Sisterhood '88
Where the Boys Are '84 '84
For Your Eyes Only '81
The Watcher in the Woods '81
Alien Predators '80
Ice Castles '79

Mae Johnson
The Defilers '65
Keep Punching '39

Mel Johnson, Jr.
Hideous '97
Total Recall '90
Eubie! '82

Melody Johnson
Jason X '01
Jailbait! '00

Michael Johnson
Bride of Chucky '98
Lust for a Vampire '71

Michelle Johnson (1965-)
Specimen '97
The Glimmer Man '96
Moving Target '96
When the Bullet Hits the Bone '96
The Donor '94
Incident at Deception Ridge '94
Body Shot '93
Blood Ties '92
Death Becomes Her '92
Far and Away '92
Till Murder Do Us Part '92
Wishful Thinking '92
Driving Me Crazy '91
Genuine Risk '89
Jigsaw Murders '89
Slipping into Darkness '88
Waxwork '88
Beaks: The Movie '87
A Chorus Line '85
Gung Ho '85
Blame It on Rio '84

Noble Johnson (1881-1978)
North of the Great Divide '50
She Wore a Yellow Ribbon '49
The Ghost Breakers '40
The Lives of a Bengal Lancer '35
King Kong '33
The Most Dangerous Game '32
The Mummy '32
Murders in the Rue Morgue '32
The Navigator '24

Penny Johnson
Deliberate Intent '01
The Road to Galveston '96
What's Love Got to Do with It? '93

Rebekah Johnson
Liberty Heights '99
Ruby Jean and Joe '96

Reggie Johnson
Seven Hours to Judgment '88
Platoon '86

Richard Johnson (1927-)
Lara Croft: Tomb Raider '01
Breaking the Code '95
Duel of Hearts '92
The Crucifer of Blood '91
Diving In '90
Spymaker: The Secret Life of Ian Fleming '90
Treasure Island '89
A Man for All Seasons '88
Turtle Diary '86
Lady Jane '85
The Great Alligator '81
Screamers '80
Zombie '80
The Big Scam '79
The Four Feathers '78
The Comeback '77
Beyond the Door '75
Hennessy '75
Fifth Day of Peace '72
Restless '72
The Rover '67
Khartoum '66
The Witch '66
The Amorous Adventures of Moll Flanders '65
Operation Crossbow '65
The Pumpkin Eater '64
Tomb of Ligeia '64
The Haunting '63
Never So Few '59

Rita Johnson (1913-65)
All Mine to Give '56
The Big Clock '48
They Won't Believe Me '47
The Perfect Marriage '46
The Naughty Nineties '45
My Friend Flicka '43
The Major and the Minor '42
Here Comes Mr. Jordan '41
Edison the Man '40
Broadway Serenade '39
Honolulu '39

Robin Johnson
Splitz '84
Times Square '80

Ron Johnson
Shadow Dancer '96
Zebrahead '92

Russell Johnson (1924-)
Undesirable '92
Blue Movies '88
The Great Skycopter Rescue '82
Rescue from Gilligan's Island '78
Fatal Chase '77
Rock All Night '57
Ma and Pa Kettle at Waikiki '55
This Island Earth '55
Ride Clear of Diablo '54
It Came from Outer Space '53

Stacii Jae Johnson
Da Hip Hop Witch '00
Parental Guidance '98

Steve Johnson
Angel of H.E.A.T. '82
Lemora, Lady Dracula '73

Sunny Johnson (1953-84)
The Red Light Sting '84
Flashdance '83
Dr. Heckyl and Mr. Hype '80

Tor Johnson (1903-71)
The Beast of Yucca Flats '61
Night of the Ghouls '59
The Unearthly '57
Carousel '56
Plan 9 from Outer Space '56
Bride of the Monster '55
Houdini '53
Abbott and Costello in the Foreign Legion '50
Behind Locked Doors '48
Human Gorilla '48

Van Johnson (1916-)
Three Days to a Kill '91
Delta Force Commando 2 '90
The Purple Rose of Cairo '85
Scorpion with Two Tails '82
The Kidnapping of the President '80
Where Angels Go, Trouble Follows '68
Yours, Mine & Ours '68
Divorce American Style '67
The Doomsday Flight '66
The Pied Piper of Hamelin '57
End of the Affair '55
Brigadoon '54
The Caine Mutiny '54
The Last Time I Saw Paris '54
Men of the Fighting Lady '54
Easy to Love '53
Go for Broke! '51
Three Guys Named Mike '51
The Big Hangover '50
The Duchess of Idaho '50
Battleground '49
In the Good Old Summertime '49
Command Decision '48
State of the Union '48
Thrill of a Romance '45
Weekend at the Waldorf '45
A Guy Named Joe '44
Thirty Seconds Over Tokyo '44
Two Girls and a Sailor '44
The White Cliffs of Dover '44
The Human Comedy '43
Madame Curie '43
Too Many Girls '40

Victoria (Vicki) Johnson
Starship Invasions '77
Grizzly '76

Grace Johnston
One Good Cop '91
God Bless the Child '88

J.J. Johnston
K-911 '99
The Fixer '97
Stranger by Night '94
Mad Dog and Glory '93
Things Change '88
Fatal Attraction '87

John Dennis Johnston
Firestarter 2: Rekindled '02
Mercenary 2: Thick and Thin '97
In Pursuit of Honor '95
Wyatt Earp '94
Miracle in the Wilderness '91
Big Bad John '90
Pink Cadillac '89
Into Thin Air '85
A Breed Apart '84
Streets of Fire '84
The Beast Within '82
Dear Detective '78
KISS Meets the Phantom of the Park '78

Kristen Johnston
The Flintstones in Viva Rock Vegas '00
Austin Powers 2: The Spy Who Shagged Me '99

Margaret Johnston (1917-)
Sebastian '68
Burn Witch, Burn! '62
A Man About the House '47

The Edge '97
In Cold Blood '96
Tornado! '96
Casino '95
Lightning Jack '94
Grizzly Adams: The Legend Continues '90
River of Death '90
Bulletproof '88
Lone Wolf McQuade '83
Sacred Ground '83
Timerider '83
The Beast Within '82
Standing Tall '78
Mother, Jugs and Speed '76
Winterhawk '76
A Boy and His Dog '75
White Line Fever '75
Manhunter '74
A Strange and Deadly Occurrence '74
Fireball Forward '72
Richard Petty Story '72
The Brotherhood of Satan '71
Ballad of Cable Hogue '70
The McMasters '70
The Wild Bunch '69
Stay Away, Joe '68
Iron Angel '64
Hell Is for Heroes '62
Ride the High Country '62
Flaming Star '60
Torpedo Run '58
The Young Lions '58
Men in War '57
Love Me Tender '56
The Annapolis Story '55
Battle Cry '55

Marcia Mae Jones (1924-)
Lady in the Death House '44
Let's Go Collegiate '41
The Gang's All Here '40
Old Swimmin' Hole '40
Tomboy '40
The Little Princess '39
The Adventures of Tom Sawyer '38
Mad About Music '38
Heidi '37
These Three '36
The Champ '32

Mark Lewis Jones
Mists of Avalon '01
Solomon and Gaenor '98

Mickey Jones (1941-)
Sling Blade '96
Tin Cup '96
It Came from Outer Space 2 '95
Drop Zone '94
Forced to Kill '93
National Lampoon's Vacation '83

Morgan Jones
The Bus Is Coming '72
The Giant Claw '57
Apache Woman '55

Nicholas Jones (1946-)
Horatio Hornblower: The Adventure Continues '01
Black Beauty '94
A Dangerous Man: Lawrence after Arabia '91
Crucible of Horror '69

O-lan Jones
American Virgin '98
Miracle Mile '89

Orlando Jones (1968-)
The Time Machine '02
Double Take '01
Evolution '01
Say It Isn't So '01
Bedazzled '00
The Replacements '00
Liberty Heights '99
Waterproof '99
Office Space '98

Peter Jones (1920-2000)
Whoops Apocalypse '83
Hot Millions '68
John and Julie '55
Man of Evil '48

Richard Jones (1946-)
Where the Heart Is '00
The Newton Boys '97
Two for Texas '97
The Good Old Boys '95
Lone Star '95
Under Siege '92
Another Pair of Aces: Three of a Kind '91
Blue Sky '91

Richard T. Jones (1972-)
Beyond Suspicion '00
The Wood '99
Event Horizon '97
Hollywood Confidential '97
Kiss the Girls '97
The Trigger Effect '96
Renaissance Man '94

Robert Earl Jones
Rain Without Thunder '93
Cockfighter '74

Rosie Jones
Ganjasaurus Rex '87
Alice to Nowhere '86

Sam Jones (1954-)
Dead Sexy '01
T.N.T. '98
American Strays '96
Where Truth Lies '96
Texas Payback '95
Ballistic '94
Fists of Iron '94
Hard Vice '94
Expert Weapon '93
Lady Dragon 2 '93
Thunder in Paradise '93
DaVinci's War '92
Fist of Honor '92
Maximum Force '92
Night Rhythms '92
The Other Woman '92
In Gold We Trust '91
One Man Force '89
Driving Force '88
Silent Assassins '88
Under the Gun '88
WhiteForce '88
Jane & the Lost City '87
My Chauffeur '86
Flash Gordon '80

Sharon Lee Jones
Josh Kirby...Time Warrior: Chapter 3, Trapped on Toyworld '95
Leapin' Leprechauns '95

Shirley Jones (1934-)
Shriek If You Know What I Did Last Friday the 13th '00
Black Devil Doll from Hell '84
Tank '83
Who'll Save Our Children? '82
The Children of An Lac '80
Beyond the Poseidon Adventure '79
Last Cry for Help '79
The Girls of Huntington House '73
The Cheyenne Social Club '70
The Happy Ending '69
Silent Night, Lonely Night '69
Bedtime Story '63
The Courtship of Eddie's Father '62
The Music Man '62
Two Rode Together '61
Elmer Gantry '60
Never Steal Anything Small '59
Carousel '56
Oklahoma! '55

Simon Jones (1950-)
Operation Delta Force 2: Mayday '97
The Devil's Own '96
Miracle on 34th Street '94
Green Card '90
Club Paradise '86
Privates on Parade '84
Monty Python's The Meaning of Life '83
The Hitchhiker's Guide to the Galaxy '81

Tamala Jones (1974-)
The Brothers '01
On the Line '01
Two Can Play That Game '01
The Ladies Man '00
Next Friday '00
Turn It Up '00
Blue Streak '99
The Wood '99
Booty Call '96

Terry Jones (1942-)
Mr. Toad's Wild Ride '96
Erik the Viking '89
Monty Python's The Meaning of Life '83
The Secret Policeman's Other Ball '82
Secret Policeman's Private Parts '81
Monty Python's Life of Brian '79
Jabberwocky '77
Monty Python and the Holy Grail '75
And Now for Something Completely Different '72

Tom Jones (1940-)
Agnes Browne '99
Mars Attacks! '96
The Jerky Boys '95
The Last Days of Dolwyn '49

Tommy Lee Jones (1946-)
Men in Black 2 '02
Rules of Engagement '00
Space Cowboys '00
Double Jeopardy '99
Small Soldiers '98 (V)
U.S. Marshals '98
Men in Black '97
Volcano '97
Batman Forever '95
The Good Old Boys '95
Blown Away '94
The Client '94
Cobb '94
Natural Born Killers '94
The Fugitive '93
Heaven and Earth '93
House of Cards '92
Under Siege '92
Blue Sky '91
JFK '91
Fire Birds '90
Lonesome Dove '89
The Package '89
Gotham '88
Stormy Monday '88
Big Town '87
Broken Vows '87
Black Moon Rising '86
Yuri Nosenko, KGB '86
The Park Is Mine '85
Cat on a Hot Tin Roof '84
The River Rat '84
Nate and Hayes '83
The Executioner's Song '82
Back Roads '81
Coal Miner's Daughter '80
The Betsy '78
Eyes of Laura Mars '78
The Amazing Howard Hughes '77
Rolling Thunder '77
Jackson County Jail '76
Eliza's Horoscope '70
Love Story '70

Vinnie Jones (1965-)
Mean Machine '01
Swordfish '01
Gone in 60 Seconds '00
Snatch '00
Lock, Stock and 2 Smoking Barrels '98

Betsy Jones-Moreland
The Last Woman on Earth '61
Creature from the Haunted Sea '60

Richard Jordahl
To the Shores of Hell '65
The Starfighters '63

Bobby Jordan (1923-65)
Spook Busters '48
Bowery Buckaroos '47
Hard-Boiled Mahoney '47
Kid Dynamite '43
Let's Get Tough '42
'Neath Brooklyn Bridge '42
Bowery Blitzkrieg '41
Flying Wild '41
Pride of the Bowery '41
Spooks Run Wild '41
Boys of the City '40
That Gang of Mine '40
Young Tom Edison '40
They Made Me a Criminal '39
Angels with Dirty Faces '38
Dead End '37

Dorothy Jordan (1906-88)
The Searchers '56
The Cabin in the Cotton '32
Min & Bill '30

James Carroll Jordan
Tales of the Unexpected '91
Slashdance '89

Jeremy Jordan
Never Been Kissed '99
Nowhere '96

Jim Jordan (1896-1988)
The Rescuers '77 (V)
Here We Go Again! '42
Look Who's Laughing '41

Joanne Moore Jordan
I Dismember Mama '74
Faces '68

Leslie Jordan
Jason Goes to Hell: The Final Friday '93
Ski Patrol '89
Frankenstein General Hospital '88

Louis Jordan (1908-75)
Look Out Sister '48
Reet, Petite and Gone '47
Beware '46

Marian Jordan
Here We Go Again! '42
Look Who's Laughing '41

Marsha Jordan
Class Reunion '87
Sweet Georgia '72
Count Yorga, Vampire '70
Lady Godiva Rides '68

Nick Jordan
Reactor '85
Five for Hell '67

Patrick Jordan
Too Late the Hero '70
The Heroes of Telemark '65

Richard Jordan (1938-93)
Gettysburg '93
Posse '93
Primary Motive '92
Heaven Is a Playground '91
The Hunt for the Night Stalker '91
Shout '91
Timebomb '91
The Hunt for Red October '90
Romero '89
The Murder of Mary Phagan '87
The Secret of My Success '87
The Men's Club '86
Solarbabies '86
A Flash of Green '85
Mean Season '85
Dune '84
Washington Mistress '81
Raise the Titanic '80
The Big Scam '79
Old Boyfriends '79
Interiors '78
Les Miserables '78
Logan's Run '76
Rooster Cogburn '75
The Yakuza '75
Trial of the Catonsville Nine '72
Chato's Land '71
Lawman '71
Valdez Is Coming '71

William Jordan
Kingpin '96
The Doors '91
The Red Fury '84
The Buddy Holly Story '78
I Wanna Hold Your Hand '78
King '78

Daniel Jordano
Playing for Keeps '86
Alphabet City '84

Victor Jory (1902-82)
The Mountain Men '80
Devil Dog: The Hound of Hell '78
Frasier the Sensuous Lion '73
Papillon '73
Cheyenne Autumn '64
The Miracle Worker '62
The Fugitive Kind '60
Death of a Scoundrel '56
Manfish '56
Sabaka '55
Valley of the Kings '54
Cat Women of the Moon '53
Man from the Alamo '53
Son of Ali Baba '52
The Capture '50
The Cariboo Trail '50
A Woman's Secret '49
The Loves of Carmen '48
South of St. Louis '48
Buckskin Frontier '43
Colt Comrades '43
Hoppy Serves a Writ '43
The Kansan '43
Leather Burners '43
Border Vigilantes '41
Charlie Chan in Rio '41
Riders of the Timberline '41
Green Archer '40
Knights of the Range '40
The Light of Western Stars '40
Dodge City '39
Each Dawn I Die '39
Gone with the Wind '39
Susannah of the Mounties '39
The Adventures of Tom Sawyer '38
Bulldog Drummond at Bay '37
Hell-Ship Morgan '36
A Midsummer Night's Dream '35

Jackie Joseph (1934-)
Gremlins 2: The New Batch '90
Gremlins '84
Get Crazy '83
Little Shop of Horrors '60

Paterson Joseph
The Beach '00
Greenfingers '00
In the Name of the Father '93

Erland Josephson (1923-)
Ulysses' Gaze '95
Good Evening, Mr. Wallenberg '93
Sofie '92
Meeting Venus '91
The Ox '91
Prospero's Books '91
Hanussen '88
The Unbearable Lightness of Being '88
Control '87
The Sacrifice '86
Saving Grace '86
After the Rehearsal '84
Fanny and Alexander '83
Nostalghia '83
Montenegro '81
To Forget Venice '79
Autumn Sonata '78
Face to Face '76
Scenes from a Marriage '73
Cries and Whispers '72
The Passion of Anna '70
Hour of the Wolf '68
Brink of Life '57

Larry Joshua
Spider-Man '02
Sugar Hill '94
Romeo Is Bleeding '93
A Midnight Clear '92
Svengali '83
The Burning '82

Allyn Joslyn (1901-81)
Fastest Gun Alive '56
I Love Melvin '53
As Young As You Feel '51
Harriet Craig '50
If You Knew Susie '48
Moonrise '48
The Horn Blows at Midnight '45
Heaven Can Wait '43
Immortal Sergeant '43
I Wake Up Screaming '41
Only Angels Have Wings '39
The Shining Hour '38
They Won't Forget '37

Darwin Joston (1937-98)
Eraserhead '78
Assault on Precinct 13 '76
Cain's Cutthroats '71

Jennifer Jostyn
Milo '98
Telling You '98
The First to Go '97
Midnight Blue '96
The Brothers McMullen '94
Omega Cop '90

Jacques Jouanneau
Bed and Board '70
Judex '64

Louis Jourdan (1919-)
Grand Larceny '92
Year of the Comet '92
The Return of Swamp Thing '89
Counterforce '87
Beverly Hills Madam '86
For the Love of Angela '86
Double Deal '84
The First Olympics: Athens 1896 '84
Octopussy '83
Escape to Love '82
Swamp Thing '82
Silver Bears '78
The Man in the Iron Mask '77
The Count of Monte Cristo '74
The V.I.P.'s '63
Can-Can '60
The Best of Everything '59
The Bride Is Much Too Beautiful '58
Gigi '58
The Swan '56
Three Coins in the Fountain '54
Decameron Nights '53
Madame Bovary '49
Letter from an Unknown Woman '48
The Paradine Case '47

Louis Jouvet (1887-1951)
Jenny Lamour '47
Heart of a Nation '43
Bizarre Bizarre '39
Volpone '39
La Marseillaise '37
The Lower Depths '36
Carnival in Flanders '35
Topaze '33

Milla Jovovich (1975-)
Resident Evil '02
Zoolander '01
The Claim '00
The Messenger: The Story of Joan of Arc '99

The Million Dollar Hotel '99
He Got Game '98
The Fifth Element '97
Dazed and Confused '93
Chaplin '92
Kuffs '92
Return to the Blue Lagoon '91
The Night Train to Kathmandu '88

Leatrice Joy (1893-)
Old Swimmin' Hole '40
First Love '39
Made for Love '26

Mark Joy
Pecker '98
The Perfect Daughter '96
Black Rainbow '91

Nicholas Joy (1894-1964)
Native Son '51
Abbott and Costello Meet the Killer, Boris Karloff '49
Gentleman's Agreement '47

Robert Joy (1951-)
Joe Somebody '01
Perfume '01
The Shipping News '01
61* '01
Sweet November '01
The '70s '00
Resurrection '99
Fallen '97
Harriet the Spy '96
Waterworld '95
Henry & Verlin '94
A Modern Affair '94
Shadows and Fog '92
The Dark Half '91
Longtime Companion '90
Millennium '89
The Lawrenceville Stories '88
She's Back '88
Big Shots '87
Miracle at Moreaux '86
Sword of Gideon '86
Desperately Seeking Susan '85
Joshua Then and Now '85
Amityville 3: The Demon '83
Atlantic City '81

Alice Joyce (1890-1955)
Song o' My Heart '29
Dancing Mothers '26

Brenda Joyce (1917-)
Little Giant '46
The Enchanted Forest '45
Strange Confession '45
Dead Man's Eyes/Pillow of Death '44
Calling Dr. Death/Strange Confession '43
The Rains Came '39

Elaine Joyce (1945-)
Honor Thy Father and Mother: The True Story of the Menendez Brothers '94
Trick or Treat '86
Motel Hell '80
How to Frame a Figg '71

William Joyce
The Young Nurses '73
I Eat Your Skin '64

Yootha Joyce
Horrors of Burke & Hare '71
Die! Die! My Darling! '65

Odette Joyeux (1917-2000)
La Ronde '51
Sylvia and the Phantom '45

Mario Joyner
Pootie Tang '01
Hangin' with the Homeboys '91

Michelle Joyner
Painted Hero '95
Cliffhanger '93
Traces of Red '92

Ashley Judd (1968-)
Divine Secrets of the Ya-Ya Sisterhood '02
High Crimes '02
Someone Like You '01
Where the Heart Is '00
Double Jeopardy '99
Eye of the Beholder '99
Simon Birch '98
Kiss the Girls '97
The Locusts '97
Normal Life '96
A Time to Kill '96
Heat '95
Norma Jean and Marilyn '95
The Passion of Darkly Noon '95
Smoke '95
Natural Born Killers '94
Ruby in Paradise '93

Carolyn Judd
Escape from Cell Block 3 '78
Women Unchained '72

Edward Judd (1932-)
The Kitchen Toto '87
Flambards '78
Whose Child Am I? '75
Murder Motel '74
The Vengeance of She '68
Island of Terror '66
Invasion '65
Strange Bedfellows '65
First Men in the Moon '64
The Long Ships '64
Stolen Hours '63
The Day the Earth Caught Fire '61

Naomi Judd (1946-)
Family Tree '00
Rio Diablo '93
Living Proof: The Hank Williams Jr. Story '83
More American Graffiti '79

Robert Judd
Crossroads '86
Fight for Your Life '79

Charles (Judel, Judells) Judels (1882-1969)
Baby Face Morgan '42
Pinocchio '40 (V)
Love on the Run '36

Arline Judge (1912-74)
The Crawling Hand '63
Take It Big '44
Girls in Chains '43
Song of Texas '43
The Lady Is Willing '42
Law of the Jungle '42
Wildcat '42
One in a Million '36
Pigskin Parade '36
Mysterious Mr. Wong '35

Mike Judge (1962-)
Spy Kids 2: The Island of Lost Dreams '02
South Park: Bigger, Longer and Uncut '99 (V)
Office Space '98
Beavis and Butt-Head Do America '96 (V)

Arno Juerging
Andy Warhol's Dracula '74
Andy Warhol's Frankenstein '74

Raul Julia (1940-94)
The Burning Season '94
Down Came a Blackbird '94
Street Fighter '94
Addams Family Values '93
A Life of Sin '92
The Plague '92
The Addams Family '91
Frankenstein Unbound '90
Havana '90
Presumed Innocent '90
The Rookie '90
Mack the Knife '89
Romero '89
Moon over Parador '88
Onassis '88
The Penitent '88
Tango Bar '88
Tequila Sunrise '88

The Alamo: Thirteen Days to Glory '87
Florida Straits '87
Trading Hearts '87
The Morning After '86
Compromising Positions '85
Kiss of the Spider Woman '85
Strong Medicine '84
Overdrawn at the Memory Bank '83
The Escape Artist '82
One from the Heart '82
The Tempest '82
Eyes of Laura Mars '78
Gumball Rally '76
Death Scream '75
Panic in Needle Park '75
The Organization '71
Stiletto '69

Janet (Johnson) Julian (1959-)
King of New York '90
Ghostwarrior '86
Humongous '82
Smokey Bites the Dust '81

Max Julien
Def Jam's How to Be a Player '97
The Mack '73
Getting Straight '70

Julissa
Dance of Death '68
The Fear Chamber '68
The Snake People '68

Gordon Jump (1932-)
Bitter Vengeance '94
Ransom Money '88
Making the Grade '84
Dirkham Detective Agency '83
Conquest of the Planet of the Apes '72

Tito Junco (1915-83)
The Exterminating Angel '62
Invasion of the Vampires '61
Death in the Garden '56
A Woman Without Love '51

Calvin Jung
American Ninja 3: Blood Hunt '89
In the Shadow of Kilimanjaro '86

John Junkin
A Handful of Dust '88
A Hard Day's Night '64

Katy Jurado (1927-)
The Hi-Lo Country '98
Fearmaker '89
Under the Volcano '84
Children of Sanchez '79
Once Upon a Scoundrel '73
Pat Garrett & Billy the Kid '73
Stay Away, Joe '68
Barabbas '62
One-Eyed Jacks '61
The Badlanders '58
Trapeze '56
Broken Lance '54
Arrowhead '53
El Bruto '52
High Noon '52
Bullfighter & the Lady '50

Peter Jurasik (1950-)
The Late Shift '96
Problem Child '90
Full Exposure: The Sex Tape Scandals '89
Peter Gunn '89
Tron '82

Curt Jurgens (1912-82)
French Intrigue
Goldengirl '79
Just a Gigolo '79
Sleep of Death '79
Breakthrough '78
Cruise Missile '78
The Spy Who Loved Me '77
Twist '76
Vault of Horror '73
Battle of the Commandos '71

Dirty Heroes '71
The Mephisto Waltz '71
Nicholas and Alexandra '71
Murder for Sale '70
The Assassination Bureau '69
Battle of Britain '69
Battle of Neretva '69
The Invincible Six '68
Target for Killing '66
Lord Jim '65
The Miracle of the White Stallions '63
The Longest Day '62
The Three Penny Opera '62
Brainwashed '60
Ferry to Hong Kong '59
Tamango '59
The Inn of the Sixth Happiness '58
Me and the Colonel '58
This Happy Feeling '58
And God Created Woman '57
Enemy Below '57
The Devil in Silk '56
The Mozart Story '48

Deana Jurgens
Code Name: Zebra '84
Tin Man '83

James Robertson Justice (1905-75)
The Love Factor '69
Zeta One '69
Mayerling '68
Spirits of the Dead '68
Doctor in Distress '63
Le Repos du Guerrier '62
Murder She Said '62
The Guns of Navarone '61
Doctor at Large '57
Above Us the Waves '56
Doctor at Sea '56
Land of the Pharaohs '55
Doctor in the House '53
Rob Roy—The Highland Rogue '53
The Sword & the Rose '53
David and Bathsheba '51
The Lady Says No '51
Whiskey Galore '48

Katherine Justice
Captain America 2: Death Too Soon '79
Frasier the Sensuous Lion '73
The Stepmother '71
Five Card Stud '68
Columbo: Prescription Murder '67

John Justin
Lisztomania '75
The Thief of Bagdad '40

William Justine
Trauma '62
The Bride & the Beast '58

Jeff Kaake
D.R.E.A.M. Team '99
Border Shootout '90

Suzanne Kaaren (1912-)
The Devil Bat '41
Phantom Ranger '38
Undercover Man '36

Jane Kaczmarek (1955-)
Pleasantville '98
All's Fair '89
D.O.A. '88
Vice Versa '88
The Heavenly Kid '85
Door to Door '84
Falling in Love '84

Karen Kadler
The Beatniks '60
It Conquered the World '56

Piotr Kadochnikev
Ivan the Terrible, Part 2 '46
Ivan the Terrible, Part 1 '44

Charlotte Kady
Revenge of the Musketeers '94
L.627 '92

Diane Kagan
Mr. & Mrs. Bridge '90

The Life and Assassination of the Kingfish '76

Elaine Kagan
Sharon's Secret '95
Babyfever '94

Kyoko Kagawa (1931-)
Mothra '62
The Lower Depths '57
The Crucified Lovers '54
Sansho the Bailiff '54
Mother '52

David Kagen
Body Chemistry '90
Conspiracy: The Trial of the Chicago Eight '87
Friday the 13th, Part 6: Jason Lives '86

Steve Kahan
Lethal Weapon 4 '98
Warlock: The Armageddon '93
Lethal Weapon 3 '92
Predator 2 '90
Lethal Weapon 2 '89
Lethal Weapon '87

Wolf Kahler
One Against the Wind '91
Raiders of the Lost Ark '81

Madeline Kahn (1942-99)
Judy Berlin '99
A Bug's Life '98 (V)
Nixon '95
Mixed Nuts '94
For Richer, for Poorer '92
Betsy's Wedding '90
Wanted: The Perfect Guy '90
An American Tail '86 (V)
Clue '85
City Heat '84
Slapstick of Another Kind '84
Yellowbeard '83
History of the World: Part 1 '81
First Family '80
Happy Birthday, Gemini '80
Simon '80
Wholly Moses! '80
The Muppet Movie '79
The Adventures of Sherlock Holmes' Smarter Brother '78
The Cheap Detective '78
High Anxiety '77
Blazing Saddles '74
Young Frankenstein '74
The Hideaways '73
Paper Moon '73
What's Up, Doc? '72

Alexander Kaidanovsky (1946-95)
Magic Hunter '96
Stalker '79

Khalil Kain
Bones '01
Execution of Justice '99
Passing Glory '99
The Tiger Woods Story '98
Love Jones '96
Zooman '95
Renaissance Man '94
Juice '92

Joel Kaiser
Dead Certain '92
Home for Christmas '90

Suki Kaiser
Bloodhounds 2 '96
Virtual Assassin '95

Elizabeth Kaitan
South Beach Academy '96
Virtual Encounters '96
Desperate Crimes '93
Vice Academy 3 '91
Roller Blade Warriors: Taken By Force '90
Nightwish '89
Aftershock '88
Assault of the Killer Bimbos '88
Friday the 13th, Part 7: The New Blood '88

Bonita Kalem
Escape from Cell Block 3 '78
Women Unchained '72

Toni Kalem
American Strays '96
Billy Galvin '86
Silent Rage '82
Wanderers '79

Patricia Kalember (1957-)
A Far Off Place '93
Big Girls Don't Cry...They Get Even '92
Jacob's Ladder '90
Fletch Lives '89

Jean-Pierre Kalfon (1938-)
The Cry of the Owl '87
Condorman '81
The Valley Obscured by the Clouds '72
Weekend '67

Helena Kallianiotes
Backtrack '89
Five Easy Pieces '70

Alexander Kalyagin
A Slave of Love '78
An Unfinished Piece for a Player Piano '77

Danny Kamekona (1926-96)
Robot Wars '93
Robot Jox '90
The Karate Kid: Part 2 '86

Stanley Kamel
Escape under Pressure '00
Stonebrook '98
Honor Thy Father and Mother: The True Story of the Menendez Brothers '94
Murder by Numbers '89

Dan Kamin
The Rookie '02
America's Dream '95
Another Pair of Aces: Three of a Kind '91

Ida Kaminska
The Angel Levine '70
The Shop on Main Street '65

Kris Kamm
Andersonville '95
Wyatt Earp '94
Born to Ride '91

Fritz Kampers
Kameradschaft '31
Westfront 1918 '30

Melina Kanakaredes (1967-)
15 Minutes '01
Rounders '98
Saint Maybe '98
The Long Kiss Goodnight '96

Anna Kanakis
After the Fall of New York '85
Warriors of the Wasteland '83

Steve Kanaly (1946-)
Midnight Blue '96
Pumpkinhead 2: Blood Wings '94
Double Trouble '91
Driving Me Crazy '91
Eye of the Eagle 3 '91
Headhunter '89
Fleshburn '84
Balboa '82
The Wind and the Lion '75

Sean Kanan
Chasing Holden '01
Chaos Factor '00
Rich Girl '91
The Karate Kid: Part 3 '89

Big Daddy Kane
Gunmen '93
Posse '93

Carol Kane (1952-)
My First Mister '01
Noah's Ark '99
The Tic Code '99
Jawbreaker '98

Gone Fishin' '97
Office Killer '97
American Strays '96
Sunset Park '96
Tree's Lounge '96
Big Bully '95
The Pallbearer '95
The Crazysitter '94
Addams Family Values '93
Ted & Venus '93
When a Stranger Calls Back '93
Baby on Board '92
In the Soup '92
The Lemon Sisters '90
My Blue Heaven '90
Flashback '89
Drop-Out Mother '88
License to Drive '88
Scrooged '88
Sticky Fingers '88
Ishtar '87
The Princess Bride '87
Jumpin' Jack Flash '86
Casey at the Bat '85
Transylvania 6-5000 '85
Burning Rage '84
Racing with the Moon '84
The Secret Diary of Sigmund Freud '84
Strong Medicine '84
Over the Brooklyn Bridge '83
Norman Loves Rose '82
Pandemonium '82
Keeping On '81
The Muppet Movie '79
When a Stranger Calls '79
My Sister, My Love '78
Annie Hall '77
Valentino '77
World's Greatest Lover '77
Harry & Walter Go to New York '76
Dog Day Afternoon '75
Hester Street '75
The Last Detail '73
Wedding in White '72
Carnal Knowledge '71
Desperate Characters '71

Christian Kane (1974-)
Life or Something Like It '02
Crossfire Trail '01
Summer Catch '01
Love Song '00

Ivan Kane
Bound '96
Gettysburg '93
Platoon '86

Marjorie "Babe" Kane (1909-92)
The Dentist '32
Pharmacist '32
Be Yourself '30
Border Romance '30
Sunny Skies '30
The Great Gabbo '29

Nobuo Kaneko
The Human Condition: A Soldier's Prayer '61
Ikiru '52

Takeshi Kaneshiro
Chungking Express '95
Fallen Angels '95

John Kani
The Ghost and the Darkness '96
Sarafina! '92
An African Dream '90
Options '88
Killing Heat '84

Alexis Kanner (1942-)
Nightfall '88
Kings and Desperate Men '83
Twinsanity '70

China Kantner
The Evening Star '96
The Stoned Age '94

Ivar Kants
Gallagher's Travels '87
The Naked Country '85
Silver City '84
Plumber '79

Jack Kao
Flowers of Shanghai '98
Goodbye South, Goodbye '96

John Kapelos (1956-)
Cold Blooded '00
The Deep End of the Ocean '98
The Late Shift '96
Man Trouble '92
Internal Affairs '90
All's Fair '89
The Boost '88
Roxanne '87
Nothing in Common '86
The Breakfast Club '85

Gabe Kaplan (1945-)
Tulips '81
Fast Break '79
Nobody's Perfekt '79

Jonathan Kaplan (1947-)
Cannonball '76
Hollywood Boulevard '76

Mady Kaplan
The Falcon and the Snowman '85
The Deer Hunter '78

Marvin Kaplan (1924-)
Witchboard 2: The Devil's Doorway '93
Fangs '75
The Severed Arm '73
Angels in the Outfield '51
Adam's Rib '50

Shashi Kapoor (1938-)
Gulliver's Travels '95
In Custody '94
The Deceivers '88
Sammy & Rosie Get Laid '87
Heat and Dust '82
Bombay Talkie '70
Shakespeare Wallah '65
The Householder '63

Valerie Kaprisky (1963-)
Glam '97
Mouvements du Desir '94
Iran: Days of Crisis '91
L'Annee des Meduses '86
Breathless '83

Mitzi Kapture (1964-)
His Bodyguard '98
Perfect Crime '97
Liberty & Bash '90
Angel 3: The Final Chapter '88
Private Road: No Trespassing '87

Ron Karabatsos
Rich Girl '91
29th Street '91
Hollywood Heartbreak '89
Flashdance '83
Missing Pieces '83

Mirjana Karanovic
Underground '95
When Father Was Away on Business '85

James Karen (1923-)
Mulholland Drive '01
Thirteen Days '00
Fly Boy '99
Girl '98
Joyride '97
Up Close and Personal '96
Piranha '95
A Kiss Goodnight '94
Lies Before Kisses '92
The Closer '91
The Unborn '91
Vital Signs '90
The Willies '90
Girlfriend from Hell '89
Return of the Living Dead 2 '88
Billionaire Boys Club '87
Wall Street '87
Hardbodies 2 '86
The Jagged Edge '85
Latino '85
Return of the Living Dead '85
Sam's Son '84

Poltergeist '82
Time Walker '82
The China Syndrome '79
All the President's Men '76
Hercules in New York '70
Frankenstein Meets the Space Monster '65

Manfred Karge
Under the Pear Tree '73
The Adventures of Werner Holt '65

Anna Karin
The Fear '94
Body of Influence '93
Wild Cactus '92

Rita Karin (1919-93)
Age Isn't Everything '91
He Said, She Said '91
Enemies, a Love Story '89
Sophie's Choice '82

Anna Karina (1940-)
Up/Down/Fragile '95
Chinese Roulette '86
Regina '83
Ski Bum '75
Bread and Chocolate '73
The Salzburg Connection '72
The Nun '66
Alphaville '65
Pierrot le Fou '65
Band of Outsiders '64
Les Carabiniers '63
My Life to Live '62
Cleo from 5 to 7 '61
Le Petit Soldat '60
A Woman Is a Woman '60

Vassilli Karis
Animal Called Man '87
SS Girls '78

Richard Karlan
Star! '68
Abbott and Costello Meet the Mummy '55

Olga Karlatos
Purple Rain '84
Zombie '80

John Karlen (1933-)
Roseanne: An Unauthorized Biography '94
Surf Ninjas '93
Nightmare on the 13th Floor '90
Babycakes '89
Native Son '86
Gimme an F '85
Impulse '84
Racing with the Moon '84
Rosie: The Rosemary Clooney Story '82
American Dream '81
Trilogy of Terror '75
Melvin Purvis: G-Man '74
Daughters of Darkness '71
Night of Dark Shadows '71
House of Dark Shadows '70

Miriam Karlin (1925-)
The Attic: The Hiding of Anne Frank '88
A Clockwork Orange '71
Ladies Who Do '63
Room at the Top '59

Boris Karloff (1887-1969)
The Crimson Cult '68
Dance of Death '68
The Fear Chamber '68
Mad Monster Party '68 (V)
The Sinister Invasion '68
The Snake People '68
Targets '68
Cauldron of Blood '67
Die, Monster, Die! '65
Bikini Beach '64
Black Sabbath '64
The Comedy of Terrors '64
Mondo Balordo '64 (N)
The Raven '63
The Terror '63
Corridors of Blood '58
The Haunted Strangler '58
Sabaka '55
Island Monster '53

Abbott and Costello Meet Dr. Jekyll and Mr. Hyde '52
The Black Castle '52
The Strange Door '51
Abbott and Costello Meet the Killer, Boris Karloff '49
Dick Tracy Meets Gruesome '47
Lured '47
The Secret Life of Walter Mitty '47
Unconquered '47
Bedlam '45
The Body Snatcher '45
Isle of the Dead '45
The Climax '44
House of Frankenstein '44
The Ape '40
Before I Hang '40
Black Friday '40
British Intelligence '40
Doomed to Die '40
The Fatal Hour '40
You'll Find Out '40
The Man They Could Not Hang '39
Mr. Wong in Chinatown '39
Mystery of Mr. Wong '39
Son of Frankenstein '39
The Tower of London '39
Mr. Wong, Detective '38
Juggernaut '37
Charlie Chan at the Opera '36
The Invisible Ray '36
The Man Who Lived Again '36
The Black Room '35
The Bride of Frankenstein '35
The Raven '35
The Black Cat '34
The Ghoul '34
The Lost Patrol '34
The Mask of Fu Manchu '32
The Mummy '32
The Old Dark House '32
Criminal Code '31
Frankenstein '31
Scarface '31
Tonight or Never '31
King of the Kongo '29
The Bells '26
Old Ironsides '26
Dynamite Dan '24
The Last of the Mohicans '20

John Karlsen
Waterfront '83
Maciste in Hell '60

Oscar Karlweis
Meet Me in Las Vegas '56
Five Fingers '52

Richard Karn
Air Bud 4: Seventh Inning Fetch '02
MVP2: Most Vertical Primate '01
Bram Stoker's The Mummy '97

Roscoe Karns (1893-1970)
The Devil's Cargo '48
Vigilantes of Boom Town '46
His Butler's Sister '44
Woman of the Year '42
Footsteps in the Dark '41
Frolics on Ice '40
His Girl Friday '40
They Drive by Night '40
You and Me '38
It Happened One Night '34
Twentieth Century '34
Today We Live '33
The Crooked Circle '32
Night After Night '32
Laughing Sinners '31
Pleasure '31
Wings '27

Sarah Rose Karr
Beethoven's 2nd '93
Beethoven '92
Homewrecker '92

Alex Karras (1935-)
Against All Odds '84
Goldilocks & the Three Bears '83
Porky's '82
Victor/Victoria '82
Nobody's Perfekt '79
Centennial '78
FM '78
Mad Bull '77
Babe! '75
Hootch Country Boys '75
Blazing Saddles '74
Win, Place, or Steal '72
Paper Lion '68

Sabine Karsenti
Battlefield Earth '00
Silent Hunter '94

Buck Kartalian (1922-)
Josh Kirby...Time Warrior: Chapter 3, Trapped on Toyworld '95
Please Don't Eat My Mother '72
The Acid Eaters '67
Cool Hand Luke '67

Vincent Kartheiser (1979-)
Bad Seed '00
Crime and Punishment in Suburbia '00
Luckytown '00
All I Wanna Do '98
Another Day in Paradise '98
Alaska '96
Masterminds '96

Claudia Karvan (1973-)
Risk '00
Paperback Hero '99
Passion '99
Flynn '96
Dating the Enemy '95
Lust and Revenge '95
Desperate Prey '94
High Tide '87

Tcheky Karyo (1953-)
Kiss of the Dragon '01
Arabian Nights '00
The Patriot '00
Saving Grace '00
The Messenger: The Story of Joan of Arc '99
Wing Commander '99
From the Earth to the Moon '98
My Life So Far '98
Habitat '97
Addicted to Love '96
Bad Boys '95
Foreign Land '95
Goldeneye '95
And the Band Played On '93
Nostradamus '93
Red Shoe Diaries 3: Another Woman's Lipstick '93
1492: Conquest of Paradise '92
Sketch Artist '92
Exposure '91
Husbands and Lovers '91
La Femme Nikita '91
The Bear '89
Sorceress '88
Full Moon in Paris '84
Toute Une Nuit '82

Alex Karzis
Stalked '94
A Man in Uniform '93

Lawrence Kasdan (1949-)
As Good As It Gets '97
Into the Night '85

Casey Kasem (1933-)
Undercover Angel '99
James Dean: Live Fast, Die Young '97
The Return of the King '80 (V)
The Dark '79
Soul Hustler '76
Wild Wheels '75

The Incredible Two-Headed Transplant '71
Free Grass '69
Escape from Planet Earth '67
The Glory Stompers '67

Daniel Kash
Life with Judy Garland—Me and My Shadows '01
Bone Daddy '97
Wounded '97

Linda Kash
Ernest Goes to Africa '97
Ernest Goes to School '94
Ernest Rides Again '93

Anna Kashfi
Cowboy '58
Battle Hymn '57

Harold Kasket (1926-2002)
The Seventh Voyage of Sinbad '58
Moulin Rouge '52

Gary Kasper (1958-)
Final Equinox '95
Josh Kirby...Time Warrior: Chapter 4, Eggs from 70 Million B.C. '95
Ring of Steel '94
Humanoid Defender '85

John Kassir
Pocahontas '95 (V)
Tales from the Crypt Presents Demon Knight '94 (V)

Mathieu Kassovitz (1967-)
Birthday Girl '02
Amelie '01
Jakob the Liar '99
The Fifth Element '97
Mon Homme '96
A Self-Made Hero '95
Cafe au Lait '94

Daphna Kastner (1961-)
Time Code '00
Lana in Love '92
Venice, Venice '92
Julia Has Two Lovers '91
Eating '90

Peter Kastner (1944-)
Unfinished Business '89
Frightmare '81
You're a Big Boy Now '66

Kurt Kasznar (1913-79)
The Ambushers '67
For the First Time '59
Legend of the Lost '57
Flame of the Islands '55
My Sister Eileen '55
Valley of the Kings '54
All the Brothers Were Valiant '53
Give a Girl a Break '53
Lili '53
Lovely to Look At '52

Anna (Katerina) Katarina
The Game '97
Omega Doom '96
The Blood of Heroes '89
Slaves of New York '89

Kurt Katch (1896-1958)
Abbott and Costello Meet the Mummy '55
The Mask of Dimitrios '44
The Mummy's Curse '44
The Seventh Cross '44
Ali Baba and the Forty Thieves '43
Background to Danger '43
Watch on the Rhine '43

Bernard Kates
The Babe '92
Seedpeople '92

Kimberley Kates
Highway '01
First Degree '98
Bad Blood '94
Chained Heat 2 '92

Branka Katic
Black Cat, White Cat '98
The Wounds '98

Daisuke Kato
Yojimbo '61
Snow Country '57
Samurai 2: Duel at Ichijoji Temple '55
Seven Samurai '54
Rashomon '51

Kazuo Kato
Hiroshima '95
Ran '85
Body Snatcher from Hell '69

Masaya Kato (1963-)
Brother '00
Nobody '99
Drive '96
Crime Broker '94
The Seventh Floor '93

Takeshi Kato
Ran '85
None But the Brave '65

Rosanne Katon (1954-)
Bachelor Party '84
Zapped! '82
Lunch Wagon '81
Motel Hell '80
Chesty Anderson USN '76
The Muthers '76
She Devils in Chains '76
The Swinging Cheerleaders '74

Shintaro Katsu (1932-97)
The Razor: Sword of Justice '72
Zatoichi vs. Yojimbo '70
Zatoichi: The Blind Swordsman and the Fugitives '68
Zatoichi: The Blind Swordsman's Vengeance '66
Zatoichi: The Blind Swordsman and the Chess Expert '65
Zatoichi: Master Ichi and a Chest of Gold '64
Zatoichi: Zatoichi's Flashing Sword '64
Zatoichi: The Life and Opinion of Masseur Ichi '62

Andreas Katsulas
Path to Paradise '97
The Fugitive '93
Blame It on the Bellboy '92
Communion '89
Next of Kin '89
Someone to Watch Over Me '87

Nicky Katt (1970-)
Full Frontal '02
Insomnia '02
Waking Life '01
Boiler Room '00
Way of the Gun '00
The Limey '99
Delivered '98
One True Thing '98
Phantoms '97
johns '96
subUrbia '96
The Babysitter '95

William Katt (1950-)
Circuit '02
Twin Falls Idaho '99
Deadly Game '98
Jawbreaker '98
Mother Teresa: In the Name of God's Poor '97
Rough Riders '97
Daddy's Girl '96
Rattled '96
Piranha '95
American Cop '94
The Paperboy '94
Stranger by Night '94
Tollbooth '94
Desperate Motives '92
House 4: Home Deadly Home '91
Naked Obsession '91
Last Call '90
Swimsuit '89
Wedding Band '89
White Ghost '88
Perry Mason: The Case of the Lost Love '87
House '86
Baby ... Secret of the Lost Legend '85
Perry Mason Returns '85
Thumbelina '82
Pippin '81
Butch and Sundance: The Early Days '79
Big Wednesday '78
First Love '77
Carrie '76

Chris Kattan (1970-)
Undercover Brother '02
Corky Romano '01
Monkeybone '01
House on Haunted Hill '99
A Night at the Roxbury '98

Omri Katz (1976-)
Hocus Pocus '93
Adventures in Dinosaur City '92
Matinee '92

Yftach Katzur
Young Love—Lemon Popsicle 7 '87
Atalia '85
Baby Love '83
Hot Bubblegum '81

Andy Kaufman (1949-84)
Heartbeeps '81
In God We Trust '80
God Told Me To '76

David Kaufman
Invisible: The Chronicles of Benjamin Knight '93
The Last Prostitute '91

Gunther Kaufman
Kamikaze '89 '83
In a Year of 13 Moons '78
Whity '70

Christine Kaufmann (1944-)
Bagdad Cafe '88
Welcome to 18 '87
Murders in the Rue Morgue '71
Taras Bulba '62
Town without Pity '61
The Last Days of Pompeii '60

Joseph Kaufmann
Heavy Traffic '73
Johnny Got His Gun '71
Jud '71
Private Duty Nurses '71

Maurice Kaufmann (1928-97)
Next Victim '74
The Abominable Dr. Phibes '71
Fright '71
The Hero '71
Die! Die! My Darling! '65

Caroline Kava
Born on the Fourth of July '89
Little Nikita '88

Christine Kavanagh
In His Life: The John Lennon Story '00
Catherine Cookson's The Glass Virgin '95
Monkey Boy '90

John Kavanagh
The Informant '97
Sharpe's Sword '94
Widow's Peak '94
Bellman and True '88
Cal '84

Julie Kavner (1951-)
Judy Berlin '99
Dr. Dolittle '98 (V)
Deconstructing Harry '97
Forget Paris '95
I'll Do Anything '93
Shadows and Fog '92
This Is My Life '92
Alice '90
Awakenings '90
New York Stories '89
Radio Days '87
Surrender '87
Hannah and Her Sisters '86
Bad Medicine '85
Revenge of the Stepford Wives '80
Katherine '75

Tamio Kawachi
Tokyo Drifter '66
Story of a Prostitute '65

Chojuro Kawarazaki
47 Ronin, Part 1 '42
47 Ronin, Part 2 '42

Kunitaro Kawarazaki
47 Ronin, Part 1 '42
47 Ronin, Part 2 '42

Hiroyuki Kawase
Godzilla vs. Megalon '76
Godzilla vs. the Smog Monster '72

Seizaburo Kawazu
Yojimbo '61
A Geisha '53

Yusuke Kawazu
Fighting Elegy '66
The Human Condition: A Soldier's Prayer '61
The Cruel Story of Youth '60
The Human Condition: Road to Eternity '59

Barnaby Kay
Conspiracy '01
Oscar and Lucinda '97

Bernard Kay
The Conqueror Worm '68
Doctor Zhivago '65

Charles Kay
Beautiful People '99
Henry V '89
Fortunes of War '87

Dianne Kay (1955-)
Andy and the Airwave Rangers '89
Portrait of a Showgirl '82
1941 '79

Jody Kay
Death Screams '83
House of Death '82
One Armed Executioner '80

Mary Ellen Kay
Thunder Pass '54
Border Saddlemates '52
Colorado Sundown '52
Government Agents vs. Phantom Legion '51
Rodeo King and the Senorita '51
Silver City Bonanza '51
Thunder in God's Country '51

Melody Kay
Camp Nowhere '94
The NeverEnding Story 3: Escape from Fantasia '94

Yuzo Kayama (1937-)
Zero '84
Red Beard '65
Sanjuro '62

Caren Kaye (1951-)
Pumpkinhead 2: Blood Wings '94
Satan's Princess '90
Poison Ivy '85
Help Wanted: Male '82
My Tutor '82
Kill Castro '80
The Mercenaries '80

Celia Kaye
Final Comedown '72
Island of the Blue Dolphins '64

Danny Kaye (1913-87)
The Madwoman of Chaillot '69
The Five Pennies '59
Me and the Colonel '58
Court Jester '56
White Christmas '54
Hans Christian Andersen '52
The Inspector General '49
It's a Great Feeling '49
A Song Is Born '48
The Secret Life of Walter Mitty '47
Kid from Brooklyn '46
Wonder Man '45
Up in Arms '44

David Kaye
3000 Miles to Graceland '01
Mermaid '00

Lila Kaye (1929-)
Dragonworld '94
Mrs. 'Arris Goes to Paris '92
Antonia and Jane '91
Nuns on the Run '90
An American Werewolf in London '81

Norman Kaye
Heaven's Burning '97
Lust and Revenge '95
Bad Boy Bubby '93
The Killing Beach '92
A Woman's Tale '92
Frenchman's Farm '87
Warm Nights on a Slow-Moving Train '87
Cactus '86
Man of Flowers '84
Where the Green Ants Dream '84
Lonely Hearts '82

Stubby Kaye (1918-97)
Who Framed Roger Rabbit '88
The Big Push '75
The Way West '67
Cat Ballou '65
Cool Mikado '63
40 Pounds of Trouble '62
Li'l Abner '59
Guys and Dolls '55

Lainie Kazan (1942-)
My Big Fat Greek Wedding '02
The Crew '00
If You Only Knew '00
What's Cooking? '00
The Big Hit '98
Safety Patrol '98
Love Is All There Is '96
Movies Money Murder '96
The Cemetery Club '93
I Don't Buy Kisses Anymore '92
29th Street '91
Eternity '90
Beaches '88
Out of the Dark '88
Harry and the Hendersons '87
Delta Force '86
The Journey of Natty Gann '85
Lust in the Dust '85
Obsessive Love '84
Pinocchio '83
Sunset Limousine '83
My Favorite Year '82
One from the Heart '82
A Cry for Love '80
Love Affair: The Eleanor & Lou Gehrig Story '77
Romance of a Horsethief '71
Dayton's Devils '68
Lady in Cement '68

Tim Kazurinsky (1950-)
Poor White Trash '00
Shakes the Clown '92
A Billion for Boris '90
Dinner at Eight '89
Wedding Band '89
Hot to Trot! '88
Police Academy 4: Citizens on Patrol '87
Police Academy 3: Back in Training '86
The Princess and the Pea '83
Continental Divide '81
My Bodyguard '80

James Keach (1948-)
The Dance Goes On '92
The Experts '89
Options '88
Evil Town '87
Wildcats '86
Moving Violations '85
Stand Alone '85
The Razor's Edge '84
Love Letters '83
National Lampoon's Vacation '83
The Long Riders '80
Hurricane '79
Smokey & the Hotwire Gang '79
Slashed Dreams '74
Till Death Do Us Part '72

Stacy Keach (1941-)
Children of the Corn 666: Isaac's Return '99
Fear Runs Silent '99
Militia '99
American History X '98
Future Fear '97
Legend of the Lost Tomb '97
Escape from L.A. '96
Amanda and the Alien '95
Young Ivanhoe '95
New Crime City: Los Angeles 2020 '94
The Pathfinder '94
Texas '94
Batman: Mask of the Phantasm '93 (V)
Body Bags '93
Raw Justice '93
Rio Diablo '93
Sunset Grill '92
Mission of the Shark '91
Class of 1999 '90
False Identity '90
The Forgotten '89
Mistral's Daughter '84
Princess Daisy '83
The Blue and the Gray '82
Butterfly '82
Dynasty '82
That Championship Season '82
Cheech and Chong's Nice Dreams '81
Road Games '81
Saturday the 14th '81
The Long Riders '80
A Rumor of War '80
Cheech and Chong's Up in Smoke '79
Diary of a Young Comic '79
Mountain of the Cannibal God '79
The Ninth Configuration '79
Battleforce '78
Gray Lady Down '77
The Squeeze '77
The Killer Inside Me '76
Street People '76
Conduct Unbecoming '75
All the Kind Strangers '74
Luther '74
Man of Destiny '73
Watched '73
Fat City '72
Life & Times of Judge Roy Bean '72
The New Centurions '72
Brewster McCloud '70
End of the Road '70
The Heart Is a Lonely Hunter '68

Stacy Keach, Sr.
Mission of the Shark '91
Ants '77

Marie Kean (1922-94)
The Dead '87
The Lonely Passion of Judith Hearne '87
Girl with Green Eyes '64

Staci Keanan (1975-)
Downhill Willie '96
Lisa '90

Edward (Ed Kean, Keene) Keane (1884-1959)
Rogue's Gallery '44
Midnight Limited '40
Heroes in Blue '39
A Night at the Opera '35

James Keane
Cannery Row '82
Apocalypse Now '79

Kerrie Keane
Steel '97
Malarek '89
Distant Thunder '88
Obsessed '88
Nightstick '87
Kung Fu: The Movie '86
Hot Pursuit '84
Incubus '82
Spasms '82

Robert Emmett Keane (1883-1981)
Hills of Oklahoma '50
Susanna Pass '49
Fear in the Night '47
Born to Be Wild '38

Gillian Kearney
In His Life: The John Lennon Story '00
Catherine Cookson's The Tide of Life '96

Stephen Kearney
The Nutt House '95
Rikky and Pete '88

Billy Kearns
Bed and Board '70
The Day and the Hour '63
Purple Noon '60

Charles Keating (1941-)
The Thomas Crown Affair '99
The Bodyguard '92
Brideshead Revisited '81

Fred Keating (1897-1961)
My 5 Wives '00
Tin Pan Alley '40
Prison Train '38
I Live My Life '35

Larry Keating (1896-1963)
The Incredible Mr. Limpet '64
Daddy Long Legs '55
Gypsy Colt '54
Above and Beyond '53
Give a Girl a Break '53
A Lion Is in the Streets '53
Monkey Business '52
Francis Goes to the Races '51
When Worlds Collide '51

Buster Keaton (1895-1966)
Man in the Silk Hat '83
A Funny Thing Happened on the Way to the Forum '66
Beach Blanket Bingo '65
How to Stuff a Wild Bikini '65
Railrodder '65
Pajama Party '64
It's a Mad, Mad, Mad, Mad World '63
Days of Thrills and Laughter '61
The Adventures of Huckleberry Finn '60
Around the World in 80 Days '56
Limelight '52
Sunset Boulevard '50
In the Good Old Summertime '49
Boom in the Moon '46
God's Country '46
Two Girls and a Sailor '44
Forever and a Day '43
The Villain Still Pursued Her '41
Li'l Abner '40
New Moon '40
Old Spanish Custom '36
What! No Beer? '33
Speak Easily '32
Parlor, Bedroom and Bath '31
Sidewalks of New York '31
Doughboys '30
Free and Easy '30
Spite Marriage '29
The Cameraman '28
Steamboat Bill, Jr. '28
College '27
Battling Butler '26
The General '26
Seven Chances '25
The Navigator '24

Our Hospitality *'23*
Three Ages *'23*
The Saphead *'21*

Diane Keaton (1946-)
Town and Country *'01*
Hanging Up *'99*
The Other Sister *'98*
The Only Thrill *'97*
The First Wives Club *'96*
Marvin's Room *'96*
Father of the Bride Part II *'95*
Amelia Earhart: The Final Flight *'94*
Look Who's Talking Now *'93 (V)*
Manhattan Murder Mystery *'93*
Running Mates *'92*
Father of the Bride *'91*
The Godfather, Part 3 *'90*
The Lemon Sisters *'90*
The Good Mother *'88*
Baby Boom *'87*
Radio Days *'87*
Crimes of the Heart *'86*
The Little Drummer Girl *'84*
Mrs. Soffel *'84*
Shoot the Moon *'82*
The Godfather 1902-1959: The Complete Epic *'81*
Reds *'81*
Manhattan *'79*
Interiors *'78*
Annie Hall *'77*
Looking for Mr. Goodbar *'77*
Harry & Walter Go to New York *'76*
I Will, I Will for Now *'76*
Love and Death *'75*
The Godfather, Part 2 *'74*
Sleeper *'73*
The Godfather *'72*
Play It Again, Sam *'72*
Lovers and Other Strangers *'70*

Joe Keaton
The General *'26*
Our Hospitality *'23*

Michael Keaton (1951-)
Desperate Measures *'98*
Jack Frost *'98*
Out of Sight *'98*
Jackie Brown *'97*
Multiplicity *'96*
The Paper *'94*
Speechless *'94*
Much Ado about Nothing *'93*
My Life *'93*
Batman Returns *'92*
One Good Cop *'91*
Pacific Heights *'90*
Batman *'89*
The Dream Team *'89*
Beetlejuice *'88*
Clean and Sober *'88*
The Squeeze *'87*
Touch and Go *'86*
Gung Ho *'85*
Johnny Dangerously *'84*
Mr. Mom *'83*
Night Shift *'82*

Ele Keats (1973-)
White Dwarf *'95*
Mother *'94*
White Wolves 2: Legend of the Wild *'94*
Lipstick Camera *'93*

Steven Keats (1946-94)
Eternity *'90*
The Spring *'89*
In Dangerous Company *'88*
Badge of the Assassin *'85*
The Executioner's Song *'82*
Silent Rage *'82*
For Ladies Only *'81*
Mysterious Island of Beautiful Women *'79*
Black Sunday *'77*
Hester Street *'75*

Hugh Keays-Byrne
Journey to the Center of the Earth *'99*
Moby Dick *'98*
Resistance *'92*
Kangaroo *'86*
Mad Max *'80*
Death Train *'79*

Lila Kedrova (1918-2000)
Some Girls *'88*
Sword of the Valiant *'83*
Tell Me a Riddle *'80*
Le Cavaleur *'78*
Widow's Nest *'77*
The Tenant *'76*
Escape to the Sun *'72*
Torn Curtain *'66*
Zorba the Greek *'64*
Modigliani *'58*

James Kee
Double Standard *'88*
Shadow Dancing *'88*

Cornelius Keefe (1900-72)
The Trigger Trio *'37*
Death from a Distance *'36*
Hong Kong Nights *'35*
Mystery Liner *'34*
The Adorable Cheat *'28*
Man from Headquarters *'28*

Don Keefer
Candy Stripe Nurses *'74*
The Young Nurses *'73*

Andrew Keegan (1979-)
O *'01*
Teenage Caveman *'01*
The Broken Hearts Club *'00*
Ten Things I Hate about You *'99*
Camp Nowhere *'94*

Howard Keel (1917-)
Arizona Bushwackers *'67*
The War Wagon *'67*
Man from Button Willow *'65 (V)*
Day of the Triffids *'63*
Armored Command *'61*
Jupiter's Darling *'55*
Kismet *'55*
Deep in My Heart *'54*
Rose Marie *'54*
Seven Brides for Seven Brothers *'54*
Calamity Jane *'53*
I Love Melvin *'53*
Kiss Me Kate *'53*
Lovely to Look At *'52*
Across the Wide Missouri *'51 (N)*
Show Boat *'51*
Texas Carnival *'51*
Three Guys Named Mike *'51*
Annie Get Your Gun *'50*
Pagan Love Song *'50*

Ruby Keeler (1909-93)
That's Dancing! *'85*
Dames *'34*
Flirtation Walk *'34*
Footlight Parade *'33*
42nd Street *'33*
Gold Diggers of 1933 *'33*

Diane Keen
Jekyll and Hyde *'90*
Silver Dream Racer *'83*

Geoffrey Keen (1918-)
The Living Daylights *'87*
Amin: The Rise and Fall *'82*
For Your Eyes Only *'81*
Moonraker *'79*
Number 1 of the Secret Service *'77*
The Spy Who Loved Me *'77*
Sacco & Vanzetti *'71*
Taste the Blood of Dracula *'70*
Doctor Zhivago *'65*
Dr. Syn, Alias the Scarecrow *'64*
A Matter of WHO *'62*
Sink the Bismarck *'60*
The Third Key *'57*
Postmark for Danger *'56*
The Man Who Never Was *'55*
Angels One Five *'54*
Black Glove *'54*
Doctor in the House *'53*
Genevieve *'53*
The Clouded Yellow *'51*
Cry, the Beloved Country *'51*
The Fallen Idol *'49*
The Third Man *'49*

Malcolm Keen
The Manxman *'29*
The Lodger *'26*

Pat Keen
Without a Clue *'88*
A Kind of Loving *'62*

Monica Keena (1979-)
Crime and Punishment in Suburbia *'00*
First Daughter *'99*
All I Wanna Do *'98*
Ripe *'97*
Snow White: A Tale of Terror *'97*
While You Were Sleeping *'95*

Caroline Keenan
Killer Bud *'00*
Vice Girls *'96*

Will Keenan
Waiting *'00*
Tromeo & Juliet *'95*

Tom (George Duryea) Keene (1898-1963)
Plan 9 from Outer Space *'56*
Trail of Robin Hood *'50*
Arizona Roundup *'42*
Lone Star Law Men *'42*
Western Mail *'42*
Where Trails End *'42*
The Driftin' Kid *'41*
Dynamite Canyon *'41*
Riding the Sunset Trail *'41*
God's Country and the Man *'37*
Where Trails Divide *'37*
Desert Gold *'36*
Drift Fence *'36*
The Glory Trail *'36*
Hong Kong Nights *'35*
Our Daily Bread *'34*
Cheyenne Kid *'33*
Beyond the Rockies *'32*
Come on Danger! *'32*
Ghost Valley *'32*
Saddle Buster *'32*
Pardon My Gun *'30*
Marked Money *'28*

Catherine Keener (1961-)
Death to Smoochy *'02*
Full Frontal *'02*
Lovely & Amazing *'02*
Simone *'02*
Being John Malkovich *'99*
Simpatico *'99*
8mm *'98*
Out of Sight *'98*
Your Friends & Neighbors *'98*
The Real Blonde *'97*
Box of Moonlight *'96*
The Destiny of Marty Fine *'96*
If These Walls Could Talk *'96*
Walking and Talking *'96*
Living in Oblivion *'94*
Johnny Suede *'92*
Survival Quest *'89*

Eliott Keener (1949-99)
Running Wild *'94*
Hard Target *'93*
Angel Heart *'87*

Matt Keeslar (1972-)
Stephen King's Rose Red *'02*
Texas Rangers *'01*
Dune *'00*
Psycho Beach Party *'00*
Scream 3 *'00*
Urbania *'00*
Durango *'99*
Splendor *'99*
The Last Days of Disco *'98*
Sour Grapes *'98*
The Deli *'97*
Mr. Magoo *'97*
Waiting for Guffman *'96*
The Run of the Country *'95*
The Stupids *'95*
Safe Passage *'94*

Jack Kehler
Big Trouble *'02*
Austin Powers 2: The Spy Who Shagged Me *'99*
Dudley Do-Right *'99*
The Lesser Evil *'97*
187 *'97*
Lost Highway *'96*
My Fellow Americans *'96*
The Shot *'96*
Desert Winds *'95*
The Invaders *'95*
Wyatt Earp *'94*
Blindsided *'93*
Casualties of Love: The "Long Island Lolita" Story *'93*
Bloodstone *'88*

Jack Kehoe (1938-)
Falling Down *'93*
Servants of Twilight *'91*
Young Guns 2 *'90*
The Untouchables *'87*
A Winner Never Quits *'86*
The Pope of Greenwich Village *'84*
On the Nickel *'80*
The Fish that Saved Pittsburgh *'79*
Law and Disorder *'74*
Serpico *'73*

Andrew Keir (1926-97)
Rob Roy *'95*
Dragonworld *'94*
Absolution *'81*
The Thirty-Nine Steps *'79*
Blood from the Mummy's Tomb *'71*
Zeppelin *'71*
The Night Visitor *'70*
The Viking Queen *'67*
Daleks—Invasion Earth 2150 A.D. *'66*
Dracula, Prince of Darkness *'66*
The Fighting Prince of Donegal *'66*
Lord Jim *'65*
Cleopatra *'63*
Suspended Alibi *'56*

Harvey Keitel (1947-)
Little Nicky *'00*
Prince of Central Park *'00*
U-571 *'00*
Holy Smoke *'99*
Finding Graceland *'98*
Lulu on the Bridge *'98*
Shadrach *'98*
Three Seasons *'98*
Cop Land *'97*
FairyTale: A True Story *'97*
City of Industry *'96*
Head Above Water *'96*
Blue in the Face *'95*
Clockers *'95*
From Dusk Till Dawn *'95*
Get Shorty *'95*
Smoke *'95*
Ulysses' Gaze *'95*
Imaginary Crimes *'94*
Monkey Trouble *'94*
Pulp Fiction *'94*
Somebody to Love *'94*
Dangerous Game *'93*
The Piano *'93*
Point of No Return *'93*
Rising Sun *'93*
The Young Americans *'93*
Bad Lieutenant *'92*
Reservoir Dogs *'92*
Sister Act *'92*
Bugsy *'91*
Mortal Thoughts *'91*
Thelma & Louise *'91*
Two Evil Eyes *'90*
The Two Jakes *'90*
The January Man *'89*
Blindside *'88*
The Last Temptation of Christ *'88*
The Inquiry *'87*
The Pick-Up Artist *'87*
The Men's Club *'86*
Off Beat *'86*
Camorra: The Naples Connection *'85*
Star Knight *'85*
Corrupt *'84*
Falling in Love *'84*
Exposed *'83*
The Border *'82*
La Nuit de Varennes *'82*
Death Watch *'80*
Saturn 3 *'80*
Eagle's Wing *'79*
Blue Collar *'78*
Fingers *'78*
The Duellists *'77*
Welcome to L.A. *'77*
Buffalo Bill & the Indians *'76*
Mother, Jugs and Speed *'76*
Taxi Driver *'76*
The Virginia Hill Story *'76*
Shining Star *'75*
Alice Doesn't Live Here Anymore *'74*
Mean Streets *'73*
Who's That Knocking at My Door? *'68*

Brian Keith (1921-97)
Rough Riders *'97*
Entertaining Angels: The Dorothy Day Story *'96*
National Lampoon's Favorite Deadly Sins *'95*
Picture Windows *'95*
Walking Thunder *'94 (N)*
The Gambler Returns: The Luck of the Draw *'93*
Escape *'90*
Bull of the West *'89*
Welcome Home *'89*
Young Guns *'88*
The Alamo: Thirteen Days to Glory *'87*
Death Before Dishonor *'87*
World War III *'86*
Charlie Chan and the Curse of the Dragon Queen *'81*
Sharky's Machine *'81*
The Mountain Men *'80*
The Chisholms *'79*
Meteor *'79*
The Seekers *'79*
Centennial *'78*
Hooper *'78*
Joe Panther *'76*
The Loneliest Runner *'76*
The Longest Drive *'76*
The Wind and the Lion *'75*
The Yakuza *'75*
Scandalous John *'71*
McKenzie Break *'70*
Suppose They Gave a War and Nobody Came? *'70*
With Six You Get Eggroll *'68*
Reflections in a Golden Eye *'67*
Nevada Smith *'66*
The Rare Breed *'66*
The Russians Are Coming, the Russians Are Coming *'66*
The Hallelujah Trail *'65*
Those Calloways *'65*
A Tiger Walks *'64*
Johnny Shiloh *'63*
Savage Sam *'63*
Moon Pilot *'62*
Deadly Companions *'61*
The Parent Trap *'61*
Ten Who Dared *'60*
The Young Philadelphians *'59*
Dino *'57*
Nightfall *'56*
Run of the Arrow *'56*
Tight Spot *'55*
The Violent Men *'55*
Arrowhead *'53*

David Keith (1954-)
Behind Enemy Lines *'01*
World Traveler *'01*
Epoch *'00*
Men of Honor *'00*
U-571 *'00*
Hot Blooded *'98*
Secre of the Andes *'98*
Invasion of Privacy *'96*
Judge & Jury *'96*
Born Wild *'95*
Deadly Sins *'95*
Gold Diggers: The Secret of Bear Mountain *'95*
The Indian in the Cupboard *'95*
Major League 2 *'94*
Temptation *'94*
Texas *'94*
Till the End of the Night *'94*
Raw Justice *'93*
Caged Fear *'92*
Desperate Motives *'92*
Liar's Edge *'92*
Off and Running *'90*
The Two Jakes *'90*
The Further Adventures of Tennessee Buck *'88*
Heartbreak Hotel *'88*
White of the Eye *'88*
The Curse *'87*
Gulag *'85*
Firestarter *'84*
Independence Day *'83*
The Lords of Discipline *'83*
An Officer and a Gentleman *'82*
Back Roads *'81*
Take This Job & Shove It *'81*
Brubaker *'80*
The Great Santini *'80*
The Rose *'79*

Donald Keith (1903-69)
Outlaw Justice *'32*
Branded Men *'31*
Bare Knees *'28*
Dancing Mothers *'26*
Free to Love *'25*
My Lady of Whims *'25*
Parisian Love *'25*
The Plastic Age *'25*

Ian Keith (1899-1960)
It Came from Beneath the Sea *'55*
The Black Shield of Falworth *'54*
Dick Tracy's Dilemma *'47*
Dick Tracy vs. Cueball *'46*
Song of Old Wyoming *'45*
The Chinese Cat *'44*
Bordertown Gunfighters *'43*
Corregidor *'43*
Five Graves to Cairo *'43*
Man from Thunder River *'43*
The Payoff *'43*
Mary of Scotland *'36*
The White Legion *'36*
The Crusades *'35*
The Three Musketeers *'35*
Queen Christina *'33*
The Sign of the Cross *'33*
Abraham Lincoln *'30*
Manhandled *'24*

Penelope Keith (1940-)
Coming Home *'98*
The Norman Conquests, Part 1: Table Manners *'80*
The Norman Conquests, Part 2: Living Together *'80*
The Norman Conquests, Part 3: Round and Round the Garden *'80*
Madhouse Mansion *'74*

Robert Keith (1898-1966)
Cimarron *'60*
Men in War *'57*
My Man Godfrey *'57*
Between Heaven and Hell *'56*
Written on the Wind *'56*
Love Me or Leave Me *'55*
Drum Beat *'54*
The Wild One *'54*
Young at Heart *'54*
Battle Circus *'53*
Devil's Canyon *'53*
Small Town Girl *'53*
Here Comes the Groom *'51*

I Want You '51
Boomerang '47

Rosalind Keith
Bad Boy '39
Theodora Goes Wild '36

Sheila Keith
House of the Long Shadows '82
The Comeback '77
The Confessional '75
Frightmare '74

Peter Keleghan
Ginger Snaps '01
Angels in the Infield '00
Escape from Wildcat Canyon '99
Screwballs '83

Joseph Kell
White Lies '98
Bone Daddy '97
Cupid '96

Robert Kellard
Gentleman from Dixie '41
Drums of Fu Manchu '40

Cecil Kellaway (1893-1973)
Quick, Let's Get Married '71
Getting Straight '70
Guess Who's Coming to Dinner '67
Spinout '66
Hush, Hush, Sweet Charlotte '65
The Cardinal '63
Zotz! '62
Interrupted Melody '55
The Prodigal '55
The Beast from 20,000 Fathoms '53
Young Bess '53
Francis Goes to the Races '51
Harvey '50
Kim '50
Portrait of Jennie '48
Unconquered '47
Monsieur Beaucaire '46
The Postman Always Rings Twice '46
Love Letters '45
Frenchman's Creek '44
It Ain't Hay '43
I Married a Witch '42
Birth of the Blues '41
Brother Orchid '40
The House of the Seven Gables '40
The Letter '40
The Mummy's Hand '40
Gunga Din '39
Wuthering Heights '39
Maid's Night Out '38

Tina Kellegher
Scarlett '94
The Snapper '93

Tim Kelleher
Thirteen Days '00
Understudy: The Graveyard Shift 2 '88

Hiram Keller
Countryman '83
Lifespan '75
A Real Young Girl '75
Ciao Federico! Fellini Directs Satyricon '69
Fellini Satyricon '69

Joel S. Keller
Brotherhood of Murder '99
The Life Before This '99
The Hanging Garden '97

Marthe Keller (1945-)
Women '97
Mon Amie Max '94
Young Catherine '91
The Nightmare Years '89
Dark Eyes '87
Red Kiss '85
The Amateur '82
The Formula '80
Black Sunday '77
Bobby Deerfield '77
Marathon Man '76
And Now My Love '74

Mary Page Keller (1961-)
Venomous '01
Dirty Little Secret '98
Any Place But Home '97
The Colony '95
Ulterior Motives '92
Scared Stiff '87

Barbara Kellerman
The Chronicles of Narnia '89
Quatermass Conclusion '79

Sally Kellerman (1938-)
Kill Shot '01
American Virgin '98
The Student Affair '97
Mirror, Mirror 2: Raven Dance '94
Ready to Wear '94
Younger & Younger '94
Happily Ever After '93 (V)
Boris and Natasha: The Movie '92
The Player '92
Victim of Beauty '91
Doppelganger: The Evil Within '90
All's Fair '89
Limit Up '89
Secret of the Ice Cave '89
You Can't Hurry Love '88
Meatballs 3 '87
Someone to Love '87
Three for the Road '87
Back to School '86
The KGB: The Secret War '86
That's Life! '86
Moving Violations '85
Secret Weapons '85
Dempsey '83
Dirkham Detective Agency '83
September Gun '83
Fatal Attraction '80
Foxes '80
Loving Couples '80
Serial '80
A Little Romance '79
Centennial '78
It Rained All Night the Day I Left '78
Magee and the Lady '78
Welcome to L.A. '77
The Big Bus '76
Rafferty & the Gold Dust Twins '75
Slither '73
Last of the Red Hot Lovers '72
A Reflection of Fear '72
Brewster McCloud '70
M*A*S*H '70
April Fools '69
The Boston Strangler '68
Hands of a Stranger '62
Reform School Girl '57

Susan Kellerman
Elvira, Mistress of the Dark '88
Oh, Heavenly Dog! '80
Where the Buffalo Roam '80

Barry Kelley (1908-91)
Jack the Giant Killer '62
The Manchurian Candidate '62
Carrie '52
Francis Goes to the Races '51
The Well '51
The Asphalt Jungle '50
Ma and Pa Kettle '49
Too Late for Tears '49

DeForest Kelley (1920-99)
Star Trek 6: The Undiscovered Country '91
Bull of the West '89
Star Trek 5: The Final Frontier '89
Star Trek 4: The Voyage Home '86
Star Trek 3: The Search for Spock '84
Star Trek 2: The Wrath of Khan '82
Star Trek: The Motion Picture '80
Apache Uprising '66
Warlock '59
The Law and Jake Wade '58
Gunfight at the O.K. Corral '57
The Man in the Gray Flannel Suit '56
Illegal '55
Fear in the Night '47
Variety Girl '47

Kimberly Kelley
Midnight Tease 2 '95
Hard Bounty '94

Sheila Kelley (1964-)
Dancing at the Blue Iguana '00
Nurse Betty '00
Santa Fe '97
One Fine Day '96
Deconstructing Sarah '94
The Secretary '94
Passion Fish '92
Singles '92
The Chase '91
Pure Luck '91
Soapdish '91
Mortal Passions '90
Breaking In '89

Walter Kelley
Men in War '57
Marty '55
Come Back, Little Sheba '52

Mike Kellin (1922-83)
Sleepaway Camp '83
On the Yard '79
Girlfriends '78
God Told Me To '76
Next Stop, Greenwich Village '76
Freebie & the Bean '74
The Last Porno Flick '74
Riot '69
The Boston Strangler '68
The Incident '67
Invitation to a Gunfighter '64
Hell Is for Heroes '62
The Great Impostor '61
Wackiest Ship in the Army '61
The Mountain Road '60
Lonelyhearts '58
At War with the Army '50

Catherine Kellner
Pearl Harbor '01
Shaft '00
Day at the Beach '98
Restaurant '98
200 Cigarettes '98
No Way Home '96
Rosewood '96
Six Degrees of Separation '93

Bruce Kellogg
Unknown World '51
They Were Expendable '45

John Kellogg (1916-2000)
Jacob Have I Loved '88
Violets Are Blue '86
The Enforcer '51
Twelve o'Clock High '49
Hopalong Cassidy: Borrowed Trouble '48
To Be or Not to Be '42

Brian Kelly (1932-)
Flipper's Odyssey '66
Around the World Under the Sea '65
Flipper's New Adventure '64

Claire Kelly (1934-)
Dressed for Death '74
And Soon the Darkness '70
A Guide for the Married Man '67
Georgy Girl '66
Ask Any Girl '59
The Badlanders '58
Party Girl '58

Craig Kelly
When Saturday Comes '95
Nightscare '93
The Young Americans '93
Silence '73

David Kelly (1929-)
Mean Machine '01
Greenfingers '00
Waking Ned Devine '98
The Run of the Country '95
A Man of No Importance '94
Into the West '92

David Patrick Kelly
K-PAX '01
In Too Deep '99
Songcatcher '99
Cafe Society '97
Trojan War '97
Last Man Standing '96
Flirting with Disaster '95
Crooklyn '94
The Crow '93
Malcolm X '92
Cheap Shots '91
The Adventures of Ford Fairlane '90
Penn and Teller Get Killed '90
The Misfit Brigade '87
Pirates '86
Commando '85
Dreamscape '84
The Jigsaw Man '84
48 Hrs. '82
The Warriors '79

Gene Kelly (1912-96)
The Marx Brothers in a Nutshell '90 (N)
North and South Book 1 '85
Sins '85
That's Dancing! '85
Xanadu '80
Viva Knievel '77
That's Entertainment, Part 2 '76
That's Entertainment '74
Forty Carats '73
The Young Girls of Rochefort '68
Inherit the Wind '60
Let's Make Love '60
Marjorie Morningstar '58
Les Girls '57
Invitation to the Dance '56
It's Always Fair Weather '55
Brigadoon '54
Deep in My Heart '54
Love Is Better Than Ever '52
Singin' in the Rain '52
An American in Paris '51
The Black Hand '50
Summer Stock '50
On the Town '49
Take Me Out to the Ball Game '49
The Pirate '48
The Three Musketeers '48
Words and Music '48
Ziegfeld Follies '46
Anchors Aweigh '45
Cover Girl '44
DuBarry Was a Lady '43
Thousands Cheer '43
For Me and My Gal '42

Grace Kelly (1928-82)
The Children of Theatre Street '77 (N)
High Society '56
The Swan '56
The Bridges at Toko-Ri '55
Green Fire '55
To Catch a Thief '55
Country Girl '54
Dial "M" for Murder '54
Rear Window '54
Mogambo '53
High Noon '52

Jack Kelly (1927-92)
The Gambler Returns: The Luck of the Draw '93
Commandos '73
Red Nightmare '62

The Commies Are Coming, the Commies Are Coming '57
Forbidden Planet '56
Cult of the Cobra '55
To Hell and Back '55
Gunsmoke '53
The Redhead from Wyoming '53
Red Ball Express '52

James F. Kelly
Marilyn & Bobby: Her Final Affair '94
Sinatra '92

Jean (Louisa) Kelly (1972-)
A Stranger in the Kingdom '98
The Fantasticks '95
Harvest of Fire '95
Mr. Holland's Opus '95
Breathing Lessons '94
Uncle Buck '89

Jim Kelly (1946-)
One Down, Two to Go! '82
Black Eliminator '78
Kill Factor '78
Black Samurai '77
Hot Potato '76
Take a Hard Ride '75
Black Belt Jones '74
Three the Hard Way '74
Enter the Dragon '73

Judy Kelly (1913-)
Dead of Night '45
Butler's Dilemma '43
House of Mystery '41
Make-Up '37
The Private Life of Henry VIII '33

Kathleen Kelly (1912-)
The Avenging Hand '43
The Mutiny of the Elsinore '39
Heart's Desire '37
The Deputy Drummer '35

Kevin Kelly
An Empty Bed '90
The Amazing Transparent Man '60

Lew Kelly (1879-1944)
Forlorn River '37
Death from a Distance '36
Mistaken Identity '36

Lisa Robin Kelly
Late Last Night '99
Amityville Dollhouse '96

Mike Kelly
To Live and Die in Hong Kong '89
Heroes Three '84

Moira Kelly (1968-)
Dangerous Beauty '98
Hi-Life '98
Love Walked In '97
Changing Habits '96
Entertaining Angels: The Dorothy Day Story '96
Unhook the Stars '96
The Tie That Binds '95
The Lion King '94 (V)
Little Odessa '94
With Honors '94
Daybreak '93
Chaplin '92
The Cutting Edge '92
Twin Peaks: Fire Walk with Me '92
Billy Bathgate '91
Love, Lies and Murder '91

Nancy Kelly (1921-95)
The Bad Seed '56
The Woman Who Came Back '45
Betrayal from the East '44
Gambler's Choice '44
To the Shores of Tripoli '42
One Night in the Tropics '40
Stanley and Livingstone '39

Patsy Kelly (1910-81)
The North Avenue Irregulars '79
Freaky Friday '76
Rosemary's Baby '68
Naked Kiss '64
Please Don't Eat the Daisies '60
In Old California '42
Sing Your Worries Away '42
Broadway Limited '41
Playmates '41
Road Show '41
The Gorilla '39
The Cowboy and the Lady '38
Swiss Miss '38
Pick a Star '37
Kelly the Second '36
Pigskin Parade '36
The Girl from Missouri '34
Going Hollywood '33

Paul Kelly (1899-1956)
Bail Out at 43,000 '57
The Curfew Breakers '57
Gunsmoke '53
Split Second '53
Springfield Rifle '52
The Painted Hills '51
Guilty of Treason '50
Adventure Island '47
Crossfire '47
Fear in the Night '47
San Antonio '45
Dead Man's Eyes/Pillow of Death '44
The Story of Dr. Wassell '44
Texas Legionnaires '43
Call Out the Marines '42
Flying Tigers '42
The Secret Code '42
Tarzan's New York Adventure '42
Ziegfeld Girl '41
The Howards of Virginia '40
The Roaring Twenties '39
Devil's Party '38
Fit for a King '37
Navy Blue and Gold '37
Star of Midnight '35
Girl from Calgary '32

Paula Kelly (1943-)
Once Upon a Time ... When We Were Colored '95
The Women of Brewster Place '89
Uncle Tom's Cabin '87
Jo Jo Dancer, Your Life Is Calling '86
Soylent Green '73
The Spook Who Sat by the Door '73
Top of the Heap '72
The Andromeda Strain '71
Sweet Charity '69

Rae'ven (Alyia Larrymore) Kelly (1985-)
Freedom Song '00
Milo '98
Ms. Scrooge '97
A Time to Kill '96
America's Dream '95
Lily in Winter '94
What's Love Got to Do with It? '93

Roz Kelly (1943-)
American Pop '81 (V)
New Year's Evil '78
Curse of the Black Widow '77

Sharon Kelly
Ilsa, Harem Keeper of the Oil Sheiks '76
Supervixens '75
Ilsa, She-Wolf of the SS '74

Sheila Kelly
A Passion to Kill '94
Some Girls '88

Terence Kelly
The Silencer '99
Accident '83

Tommy Kelly
The Adventures of Tom Sawyer '38
Peck's Bad Boy with the Circus '38

Fred Kelsey (1884-1961)
People's Choice '46
Paths to Paradise '25
Linda Kelsey (1946-)
Baby Girl Scott '87
Eleanor & Franklin '76
Picture of Dorian Gray '74
Pert Kelton (1907-68)
The Comic '69
The Music Man '62
Kelly the Second '36
Annie Oakley '35
Bachelor Bait '34
Richard Kelton
The Ultimate Warrior '75
Silence '73
Edward Kemmer
Earth vs. the Spider '58
Giant from the Unknown '58
Warren Kemmerling
The Dark '79
Eat My Dust '76
Family Plot '76
The Execution of Private Slovik '74
Hit! '73
Trauma '62
Brandis Kemp (1951-)
South of Reno '87
Surf 2 '84
Goldilocks & the Three Bears '83
Elizabeth Kemp
Eating '90
Killing Hour '84
He Knows You're Alone '80
Gary Kemp (1960-)
Magic Hunter '96
Killing Zoe '94
Paper Marriage '93
The Bodyguard '92
The Krays '90
Jeremy Kemp (1935-)
Angels and Insects '95
Four Weddings and a Funeral '94
Duel of Hearts '92
Prisoner of Honor '91
War & Remembrance: The Final Chapter '89
When the Whales Came '89
War & Remembrance '88
Top Secret! '84
Sadat '83
The Winds of War '83
Prisoner of Zenda '79
The Treasure Seekers '79
East of Elephant Rock '76
The Seven-Per-Cent Solution '76
The Belstone Fox '73
Blockhouse '73
Darling Lili '70
The Blue Max '66
Operation Crossbow '65
Lindsay Kemp
Sebastiane '79
The Wicker Man '75
Savage Messiah '72
Martin Kemp (1961-)
Sugar Town '99
Desire '95
Embrace of the Vampire '95
Boca '94
Cyber Bandits '94
Fleshtone '94
Aspen Extreme '93
Waxwork 2: Lost in Time '91
The Krays '90
Matty Kemp (1907-)
Law of the Texan '38
Red Lights Ahead '36
Tango '36
Paul Kemp
Charm of La Boheme '36
M '31
Will Kempe
Hit the Dutchman '92
Metropolitan '90
Pledge Night '90

Charles Kemper (1900-50)
On Dangerous Ground '51
Mr. Music '50
The Nevadan '50
Stars in My Crown '50
Ticket to Tomahawk '50
The Doolins of Oklahoma '49
Fighting Father Dunne '48
Gerhard Kempinski
Beware of Pity '46
Thursday's Child '43
Rachel Kempson (1910-)
Deja Vu '98
Stealing Heaven '88
Out of Africa '85
Little Lord Fauntleroy '80
Love for Lydia '79
The Virgin Soldiers '69
The Charge of the Light Brigade '68
Georgy Girl '66
Captive Heart '47
Felicity Kendal (1946-)
We're Back! A Dinosaur's Story '93 (V)
Valentino '77
Shakespeare Wallah '65
Jennifer Kendal
Heat and Dust '82
Bombay Talkie '70
Cy Kendall (1898-1953)
Girl Rush '44
Outlaw Trail '44
Johnny Eager '42
Tarzan's New York Adventure '42
Billy the Kid '41
The Saint Takes Over '40
The Green Hornet '39
Bulldog Edition '36
King of the Pecos '36
Henry Kendall (1897-1962)
Butler's Dilemma '43
Amazing Adventure '37
The Shadow '36
The Ghost Camera '33
Rich and Strange '32
Katherine Kendall
Devil in the Flesh 2 '00
Eye of the Storm '98
Swingers '96
Kay Kendall (1926-59)
The Reluctant Debutante '58
Les Girls '57
Abdulla the Great '56
Doctor in the House '53
Genevieve '53
The Shadow Man '53
Wings of Danger '52
Suzy Kendall (1944-)
Adventures of a Private Eye '87
Craze '74
Tales That Witness Madness '73
Torso '73
Assault '70
The Bird with the Crystal Plumage '70
Darker than Amber '70
30 Is a Dangerous Age, Cynthia '68
Circus of Fear '67
To Sir, with Love '67
Tony Kendall (1936-)
Oil '78
People Who Own the Dark '75
Return of the Evil Dead '75
Island of Lost Girls '73
When the Screaming Stops '73
The Whip and the Body '63
Alexa Kenin (1962-85)
Pretty in Pink '86
Honkytonk Man '82
A Piano for Mrs. Cimino '82

Arthur Kennedy (1914-90)
Signs of Life '89
Emmanuelle on Taboo Island '76
The Sentinel '76
Let Sleeping Corpses Lie '74
The Tempter '74
Mean Machine '73
My Old Man's Place '71
The President's Plane Is Missing '71
Hail, Hero! '69
Anzio '68
Shark! '68
A Minute to Pray, a Second to Die '67
Fantastic Voyage '66
Nevada Smith '66
Cheyenne Autumn '64
Barabbas '62
Lawrence of Arabia '62
Murder She Said '62
Elmer Gantry '60
A Summer Place '59
Some Came Running '58
Peyton Place '57
Crashout '55
Desperate Hours '55
Impulse '55
The Man from Laramie '55
Bend of the River '52
The Lusty Men '52
Rancho Notorious '52
Champion '49
Too Late for Tears '49
The Window '49
Boomerang '47
Air Force '43
Desperate Journey '42
High Sierra '41
They Died with Their Boots On '41
City for Conquest '40
Beth Kennedy
The Tomorrow Man '01
Jerome '98
Bill Kennedy (1909-97)
Silver City Bonanza '51
Two Lost Worlds '50
Deborah Kennedy
Idiot Box '97
The Wedding Party '97
The Sum of Us '94
Douglas Kennedy (1915-73)
The Amazing Transparent Man '60
The Land Unknown '57
Big Chase '54
South of St. Louis '48
Edgar Kennedy (1890-1948)
My Dream Is Yours '49
Unfaithfully Yours '48
The Sin of Harold Diddlebock '47
It Happened Tomorrow '44
Air Raid Wardens '43
Hillbilly Blitzkrieg '42
Snuffy Smith, Yard Bird '42
Blondie in Society '41
Dr. Christian Meets the Women '40
Frolics on Ice '40
Remedy for Riches '40
Peck's Bad Boy with the Circus '38
Double Wedding '37
When's Your Birthday? '37
Cowboy Millionaire '35
King Kelly of the U.S.A. '34
The Silver Streak '34
Twentieth Century '34
Duck Soup '33
Hold 'Em Jail '32
Little Orphan Annie '32
Laurel & Hardy: Night Owls '30
Laurel & Hardy: Perfect Day '29
George Kennedy (1925-)
Dennis the Menace Strikes Again '98

Small Soldiers '98 (V)
Cats Don't Dance '97 (V)
Naked Gun 33 1/3: The Final Insult '94
Distant Justice '92
Final Shot: The Hank Gathers Story '92
Driving Me Crazy '91
Hangfire '91
Hired to Kill '91
Naked Gun 2 1/2: The Smell of Fear '91
Brain Dead '89
Bull of the West '89
Ministry of Vengeance '89
Born to Race '88
The Naked Gun: From the Files of Police Squad '88
The Terror Within '88
The Uninvited '88
Counterforce '87
Creepshow 2 '87
Demonwarp '87
The Gunfighters '87
Kenny Rogers as the Gambler, Part 3: The Legend Continues '87
Nightmare at Noon '87
Private Road: No Trespassing '87
Delta Force '86
Radioactive Dreams '86
Bolero '84
Chattanooga Choo Choo '84
The Jesse Owens Story '84
Proof of the Man '84
Savage Dawn '84
Wacko '83
Virus '82
Archer: The Fugitive from the Empire '81
Modern Romance '81
A Rare Breed '81
Search and Destroy '81
Death Ship '80
Just Before Dawn '80
Steel '80
Hot Wire '70s
The Concorde: Airport '79 '79
The Double McGuffin '79
Brass Target '78
Death on the Nile '78
Mean Dog Blues '78
Airport '77 '77
Airport '75 '75
The Blue Knight '75
The Eiger Sanction '75
The Human Factor '75
Earthquake '74
Thunderbolt & Lightfoot '74
Cahill: United States Marshal '73
Airport '70
The Good Guys and the Bad Guys '69
Guns of the Magnificent Seven '69
Bandolero! '68
The Boston Strangler '68
The Pink Jungle '68
Cool Hand Luke '67
The Dirty Dozen '67
Mirage '66
The Flight of the Phoenix '65
In Harm's Way '65
Shenandoah '65
Sons of Katie Elder '65
Island of the Blue Dolphins '64
McHale's Navy '64
Strait-Jacket '64
Charade '63
Lonely Are the Brave '62
Gerald Kennedy
Puzzle '78
The Mango Tree '77
Gerard Kennedy
Body Melt '93
The Lighthorsemen '87
Panic Station '82
Newsfront '78
Graham Kennedy (1934-)
Return of Captain Invincible '83

The Club '81
The Odd Angry Shot '79
Don's Party '76
Jamie Kennedy (1970-)
Max Keeble's Big Move '01
Bait '00
Boiler Room '00
Scream 3 '00
The Specials '00
Bowfinger '99
Sparkler '99
Three Kings '99
Bongwater '98
Enemy of the State '98
Highway Hitcher '98
Clockwatchers '97
Scream 2 '97
Scream '96
Jayne Kennedy (1951-)
Body & Soul '81
Mysterious Island of Beautiful Women '79
Death Force '78
Fighting Mad '77
The Muthers '76
Group Marriage '72
Leon Isaac Kennedy (1949-)
Skeleton Coast '89
Penitentiary 3 '87
Hollywood Vice Sqaud '86
Too Scared to Scream '85
Lone Wolf McQuade '83
Penitentiary 2 '82
Body & Soul '81
Penitentiary '79
Death Force '78
Fighting Mad '77
Marklen Kennedy
Magenta '96
Witchcraft 5: Dance with the Devil '92
Merle Kennedy
Switchback '97
Night of the Demons 2 '94
Nemesis '93
Merna Kennedy (1908-44)
Come on Tarzan '32
Ghost Valley '32
The Circus '19
Mimi Kennedy (1949-)
Death Becomes Her '92
Pump Up the Volume '90
Immediate Family '89
Patricia Kennedy
Road to Nhill '97
Country Life '95
My Brilliant Career '79
The Getting of Wisdom '77
Rigg Kennedy
Hostile Intentions '94
Perfect Alibi '94
Dangerous Relations '93
Maid to Order '87
Jessi's Girls '75
Girls on the Road '73
R.P.M.* (* Revolutions Per Minute) '70
Dayton's Devils '68
Sarah Kennedy
Jack Be Nimble '94
Working Girls '75
Sheila Kennedy
Dead Boyz Can't Fly '93
Ellie '84
First Turn On '83
Tom Kennedy (1885-1965)
Invasion U.S.A. '52
Pirate Ship '49
The Devil's Cargo '48
Day the Bookies Wept '39
Hollywood Party '34
Monkey Business '31
Big News '29
Marked Money '28
Mantrap '26
Donald Kenney
Clayton County Line '80s
The Bellboy and the Playgirls '62
Doug Kenney
Heavy Metal '81 (V)

National Lampoon's Animal House '78
James Kenney
Above Us the Waves '56
Tough Guy '53
June Kenney
Bloodlust '59
Attack of the Puppet People '58
Earth vs. the Spider '58
Sorority Girl '57
Teenage Doll '57
Sean Kenney
Savage Abduction '73
The Corpse Grinders '71
Tom Kenny
Dead Weekend '95
Shakes the Clown '92
Patsy Kensit (1968-)
Hell's Gate '01
Speedway Junky '99
The Last Don 2 '98
Human Bomb '97
Grace of My Heart '96
Angels and Insects '95
Tunnel Vision '95
Dream Man '94
Fall from Grace '94
Kleptomania '94
Bitter Harvest '93
Full Eclipse '93
Blame It on the Bellboy '92
The Turn of the Screw '92
Timebomb '91
Twenty-One '91
Blue Tornado '90
Bullseye! '90
Chicago Joe & the Showgirl '90
Does This Mean We're Married? '90
Kill Cruise '90
A Chorus of Disapproval '89
Lethal Weapon 2 '89
Absolute Beginners '86
Silas Marner '85
Monty Python and the Holy Grail '75
The Great Gatsby '74
Anne Kent
Catherine Cookson's The Gambling Man '98
Widow's Peak '94
Barbara Kent (1906-)
Oliver Twist '33
Vanity Fair '32
Chinatown After Dark '31
Indiscreet '31
Feet First '30
The Dropkick '27
The Flesh and the Devil '27
No Man's Law '27
Crauford Kent (1881-1953)
Tea for Two '50
Seven Keys to Baldpate '29
Virtue's Revolt '24
Dorothea Kent
Behind the Mask '46
Danger Ahead '40
Elizabeth Kent
Trapped Alive '93
Mindwarp '91
Gary Kent
Satan's Sadists '69
The Thrill Killers '65
Jean Kent (1921-)
The Haunted Strangler '58
Bonjour Tristesse '57
The Browning Version '51
The Woman in Question '50
The Gay Lady '49
Man of Evil '48
The Magic Bow '47
Sleeping Car to Trieste '45
Julie Kent
Center Stage '00
Dancers '87
Kenneth Kent (1892-1963)
Dangerous Moonlight '41
House of Mystery '41
Night Train to Munich '40

Marjorie Kent
Blondie Hits the Jackpot '49
Blondie Knows Best '46
Robert Kent (1908-)
The Phantom Rider '46
The Phantom Creeps '39
Gang Bullets '38
The Gladiator '38
Dimples '36
Dambisa Kente
Cry, the Beloved Country '95
Friends '95
Doris Kenyon (1897-1979)
Burning Daylight '28
Monsieur Beaucaire '24
A Girl's Folly '17
Gwen Kenyon (1916-99)
In Old New Mexico '45
Charlie Chan in the Secret Service '44
The Great Mike '44
Meet the Mob '42
Sandy Kenyon
The Loch Ness Horror '82
The Arousers '70
Danny Keogh
Operation Delta Force 3: Clear Target '98
Kill Slade '89
Playing with Fire '70s
Evelyne Ker
A Nos Amours '84
Love Play '60
Ken Kercheval (1935-)
Beretta's Island '92
Corporate Affairs '90
California Casanova '89
Calamity Jane '82
Too Far to Go '79
Judge Horton and the Scottsboro Boys '76
Roger Kern
Delos Adventure '86
The Young Pioneers '76
Joanna (Joanna DeVarona) Kerns (1954-)
All Over the Guy '01
No Dessert Dad, 'Til You Mow the Lawn '94
The Nightman '93
The Great Los Angeles Earthquake '91
An American Summer '90
The Preppie Murder '89
Street Justice '89
Cross My Heart '88
Broken Badge '85
A Bunny's Tale '85
A*P*E* '76
Bill Kerr (1924-)
Sweet Talker '91
The Lighthorsemen '87
Miracle Down Under '87
Dusty '85
The Coca-Cola Kid '84
Razorback '84
Vigil '84
Pirate Movie '82
The Year of Living Dangerously '82
Deadline '81
Gallipoli '81
Deborah Kerr (1921-)
Hold the Dream '86
A Woman of Substance '84
America at the Movies '76
The Arrangement '69
Casino Royale '67
The Chalk Garden '64
The Night of the Iguana '64
The Grass Is Greener '61
The Innocents '61
The Naked Edge '61
The Sundowners '60
Beloved Infidel '59
Separate Tables '58
An Affair to Remember '57
Bonjour Tristesse '57
Heaven Knows, Mr. Allison '57
The King and I '56
Tea and Sympathy '56
End of the Affair '55
From Here to Eternity '53
Julius Caesar '53
Young Bess '53
Prisoner of Zenda '52
Quo Vadis '51
King Solomon's Mines '50
Black Narcissus '47
The Hucksters '47
I See a Dark Stranger '46
The Life and Death of Colonel Blimp '43
The Day Will Dawn '42
The Courageous Mr. Penn '41
Love on the Dole '41
Major Barbara '41
E. Katherine Kerr (1937-)
Songcatcher '99
The Siege '98
The Buccaneers '95
Suspect '87
Children of a Lesser God '86
Power '86
Reuben, Reuben '83
Edward Kerr (1966-)
Legalese '98
Above Suspicion '95
Magic Island '95
John Kerr (1931-)
The Pit and the Pendulum '61
South Pacific '58
Tea and Sympathy '56
The Cobweb '55
Linda Kerridge (1959-)
Down Twisted '89
Alien from L.A. '87
Mixed Blood '84
Surf 2 '84
Strangers Kiss '83
Fade to Black '80
J.M. Kerrigan (1884-1964)
Fastest Gun Alive '56
Mrs. Mike '49
Fighting Seabees '44
Action in the North Atlantic '43
The Great Man Votes '38
The Informer '35
The Lost Patrol '34
Song o' My Heart '29
John Kerry
Memorial Valley Massacre '88
Bad Georgia Road '77
Norman Kerry (1889-1956)
Tanks a Million '41
Bachelor Apartment '31
The Claw '27
The Unknown '27
The Phantom of the Opera '25
The Hunchback of Notre Dame '23
Is Money Everything? '23
Merry-Go-Round '23
Amarilly of Clothesline Alley '18
Doug Kershaw
Music Shoppe '82
Zachariah '70
Brian Kerwin (1949-)
Common Ground '00
Flash '98
Mr. Jealousy '98
Critical Choices '97
The Myth of Fingerprints '97
Unlikely Angel '97
Volcano: Fire on the Mountain '97
Getting Away With Murder '96
Jack '96
Gold Diggers: The Secret of Bear Mountain '95
It Came from Outer Space 2 '95
Hard Promises '92
Love Field '91
Switched at Birth '91
Code Name: Chaos '90
Torch Song Trilogy '88
King Kong Lives '86
Murphy's Romance '85
Nickel Mountain '85
Wet Gold '84
Miss All-American Beauty '82
Getting Wasted '80
Hometown U.S.A. '79
A Real American Hero '78
Lance Kerwin (1960-)
Enemy Mine '85
Fourth Wise Man '85
Side Show '84
The Snow Queen '83
The Mysterious Stranger '82
Shooting '82
Children of Divorce '80
Salem's Lot '79
The Loneliest Runner '76
Reflections of Murder '74
Maureen Kerwin
Reunion '88
The Destructors '74
Jillian Kesner (1950-)
Roots of Evil '91
Beverly Hills Vamp '88
Trick or Treats '82
Starhops '78
Firecracker '71
Quin Kessler
Wishman '93
She '83
Sara Kestelman (1944-)
Lady Jane '85
Lisztomania '75
Zardoz '73
Boyd Kestner (1964-)
Black Hawk Down '01
Cleopatra's Second Husband '00
The Art of Murder '99
The General's Daughter '99
Entertaining Angels: The Dorothy Day Story '96
Lethal Lolita—Amy Fisher: My Story '92
Bryan Kestner
In Dark Places '97
Fire Birds '90
Janet Key
And Now the Screaming Starts '73
Dracula A.D. 1972 '72
Evelyn Keyes (1919-)
Wicked Stepmother '89
Return to Salem's Lot '87
Around the World in 80 Days '56
The Seven Year Itch '55
Prowler '51
Mrs. Mike '49
The Jolson Story '46
A Thousand and One Nights '45
The Desperadoes '43
Here Comes Mr. Jordan '41
Before I Hang '40
The Lady in Question '40
Slightly Honorable '40
Gone with the Wind '39
Union Pacific '39
Irwin Keyes (1952-)
Backlash: Oblivion 2 '95
The Flintstones '94
Frankenstein General Hospital '88
Mark Keyloun (1960-)
Separate Vacations '86
Gimme an F '85
Mike's Murder '84
Persis Khambatta (1950-98)
Deadly Intent '88
Phoenix the Warrior '88
First Strike '85
Warrior of the Lost World '84
Megaforce '82
Nighthawks '81
Star Trek: The Motion Picture '80
Conduct Unbecoming '75
The Wilby Conspiracy '75
Arsinee Khanjian
Felicia's Journey '99
Late August, Early September '98
Ms. Scrooge '97
Irma Vep '96
The Sweet Hereafter '96
Exotica '94
Calendar '93
The Adjuster '91
Speaking Parts '89
Family Viewing '87
Nozha Khouadra
The New Eve '98
Bye-Bye '96
Honey & Ashes '96
Makram Khoury
The Body '01
The Milky Way '97
Leleti Khumalo
Cry, the Beloved Country '95
Sarafina! '92
Guy Kibbee (1882-1956)
Fort Apache '48
Three Godfathers '48
The Horn Blows at Midnight '45
Dixie Jamboree '44
Miss Annie Rooney '42
Whistling in Dixie '42
It Started with Eve '41
Our Town '40
Babes in Arms '39
Let Freedom Ring '39
Mr. Smith Goes to Washington '39
Joy of Living '38
Of Human Hearts '38
Three Comrades '38
Captain January '36
Earthworm Tractors '36
Little Lord Fauntleroy '36
Three Men on a Horse '36
Captain Blood '35
Dames '34
Footlight Parade '33
42nd Street '33
Gold Diggers of 1933 '33
Lady for a Day '33
Rain '32
Scarlet Dawn '32
The Strange Love of Molly Louvain '32
Laughing Sinners '31
Sandrine Kiberlain
For Sale '98
Beaumarchais the Scoundrel '96
Michael Kidd (1919-)
Smile '75
It's Always Fair Weather '55
Margot Kidder (1948-)
Common Ground '00
Tribulation '00
Junior's Groove '97
Never Met Picasso '96
Bloodknot '95
Phantom 2040 Movie: The Ghost Who Walks '95 (V)
Young Ivanhoe '95
Beanstalk '94
Henry & Verlin '94
Windrunner '94
To Catch a Killer '92
Mob Story '90
Vanishing Act '88
Louisiana '87
Superman 4: The Quest for Peace '87
Keeping Track '86
Little Treasure '85
The Glitter Dome '84
Superman 3 '83
Trenchcoat '83
Heartaches '82
Some Kind of Hero '82
Miss Right '81
Shoot the Sun Down '81
Superman 2 '80
Willie & Phil '80
The Amityville Horror '79
Mr. Mike's Mondo Video '79
Superman: The Movie '78
92 in the Shade '76
Black Christmas '75
The Great Waldo Pepper '75
The Reincarnation of Peter Proud '75
Quiet Day in Belfast '74
Sisters '73
The Bounty Man '72
Quackser Fortune Has a Cousin in the Bronx '70
Nicole Kidman (1966-)
Birthday Girl '02
Moulin Rouge '01
The Others '01
Eyes Wide Shut '99
Practical Magic '98
The Peacemaker '97
The Leading Man '96
Portrait of a Lady '96
Batman Forever '95
To Die For '95
Malice '93
My Life '93
Far and Away '92
Billy Bathgate '91
Days of Thunder '90
Dead Calm '89
Flirting '89
Night Master '87
Windrider '86
Archer's Adventure '85
BMX Bandits '83
Prince and the Great Race '83
James Kidnie
Resurrection '99
Rescuers: Stories of Courage—Two Couples '98
Hostile Intent '97
Gate 2 '92
Body Parts '91
Richard Kiel (1939-)
Happy Gilmore '96
Think Big '90
Pale Rider '85
Mad Mission 3 '84
Hysterical '83
So Fine '81
War of the Wizards '81
Moonraker '79
Force 10 from Navarone '78
They Went That-a-Way & That-a-Way '78
The Spy Who Loved Me '77
Silver Streak '76
Flash & Firecat '75
The Longest Yard '74
The Human Duplicators '64
Roustabout '64
Eegah! '62
The Phantom Planet '61
Sue Kiel
Survivor '87
Red Heat '85
Wolfgang Kieling
Out of Order '84
The Oppermann Family '82
Udo Kier (1944-)
Just One Night '00
Life in the Fast Lane '00
Red Letters '00
Shadow of the Vampire '00
Dancer in the Dark '99
Doomsdayer '99
End of Days '99
Spy Games '99
Blade '98
Modern Vampires '98
The End of Violence '97
The Kingdom 2 '97
Prince Valiant '97
The Adventures of Pinocchio '96
Barb Wire '96
Red Shoe Diaries 7: Burning Up '96
Breaking the Waves '95
Johnny Mnemonic '95
The Kingdom '95
Ace Ventura: Pet Detective '93
For Love or Money '93
Terror 2000 '92
Zentropa '92
My Own Private Idaho '91
Seduction: The Cruel Woman '89
The Stationmaster's Wife '77
Suspiria '77
The House on Straw Hill '76
The Story of O '75
Andy Warhol's Dracula '74
Andy Warhol's Frankenstein '74
Mark of the Devil '69
Robbie Kiger (1973-)
Welcome Home, Roxy Carmichael '90
Children of the Corn '84
Table for Five '83
Susan Kiger (1953-)
Death Screams '83
House of Death '82
The Return '80
H.O.T.S. '79
Seven '79
Rya Kihlstedt (1970-)
She Creature '01
Deep Impact '98
Home Alone 3 '97
Jaded '96
The Buccaneers '95
Jorgen Kiil
Webmaster '98
Parallel Corpse '83
Nicholas Kilbertus
Rescuers: Stories of Courage—Two Couples '98
The Defenders: Payback '97
The Kiss '88
Percy Kilbride (1888-1964)
Ma and Pa Kettle at Waikiki '55
Ma and Pa Kettle at Home '54
Ma and Pa Kettle on Vacation '53
Ma and Pa Kettle at the Fair '52
Ma and Pa Kettle Back On the Farm '51
Ma and Pa Kettle Go to Town '50
Riding High '50
Ma and Pa Kettle '49
You Gotta Stay Happy '48
Egg and I '47
Riff-Raff '47
Welcome Stranger '47
The Southerner '45
State Fair '45
The Adventures of Mark Twain '44
Guest in the House '44
The Woman of the Town '44
George Washington Slept Here '42
Keeper of the Flame '42
Terence (Terry) Kilburn (1926-)
Lolita '62
Fiend without a Face '58
National Velvet '44
Goodbye, Mr. Chips '39
They Shall Have Music '39
A Christmas Carol '38
Richard Kiley (1922-99)
Patch Adams '98
Phenomenon '96
Secrets '94
Jurassic Park '93 (V)
The Canterville Ghost '91
Separate but Equal '91
The Final Days '89
A.D. '85
The Adventures of Huckleberry Finn '85
The Bad Seed '85
George Washington '84
The Thorn Birds '83
Pray TV '82
Endless Love '81

Angel on My Shoulder '80
Looking for Mr. Goodbar '77
The Little Prince '74
Jigsaw '71
Murder Once Removed '71
Night Gallery '69
Pendulum '69
Blackboard Jungle '55
Pickup on South Street '53

Victor Kilian (1891-1979)
One Too Many '51
Unknown World '51
Rimfire '49
Dangerous Passage '44
Dr. Cyclops '40
Young Tom Edison '40
The Adventures of Tom Sawyer '38
Lady from Nowhere '36
Riff Raff '35

Val Kilmer (1959-)
The Salton Sea '02
Hard Cash '01
Pollock '00
Red Planet '00
Joe the King '99
At First Sight '98
Prince of Egypt '98 (V)
The Saint '97
The Ghost and the Darkness '96
The Island of Dr. Moreau '96
Batman Forever '95
Heat '95
The Real McCoy '93
Tombstone '93
True Romance '93
Thunderheart '92
The Doors '91
Gore Vidal's Billy the Kid '89
Kill Me Again '89
Willow '88
The Man Who Broke 1,000 Chains '87
The Murders in the Rue Morgue '86
Top Gun '86
Real Genius '85
Top Secret! '84

Kevin Kilner (1958-)
Smart House '00
Home Alone 3 '97
Music from Another Room '97
Danielle Steel's Heartbeat '93

Lincoln Kilpatrick (1933-)
Piranha '95
Fortress '93
Prison '88
Deadly Force '83
Omega Man '71

Patrick Kilpatrick
The Substitute 4: Failure is Not an Option '00
Free Willy 3: The Rescue '97
Last Stand at Saber River '96
Riot '96
Beastmaster 3: The Eye of Braxus '95
3 Ninjas Knuckle Up '95
Open Fire '94
Scanner Cop 2: Volkin's Revenge '94
Scanners: The Showdown '94
Showdown '93
The Cellar '90
Class of 1999 '90
Death Warrant '90
Roanoak '86
Remo Williams: The Adventure Begins '85

Bobby Kim
Kill Line '91
Manchurian Avenger '84

Evan C. Kim
The Dead Pool '88
Go Tell the Spartans '78

Jacqueline Kim
The Operator '01
Brokedown Palace '99
Volcano '97

Joon Kim
Gang Justice '94
Street Soldiers '91

Sandrine Kimberlain
Seventh Heaven '98
A Self-Made Hero '95

Charles Kimbrough (1936-)
The Wedding Planner '01
The Hunchback of Notre Dame '96 (V)
The Good Mother '88
Switching Channels '88
Sunday in the Park with George '86

Clinton Kimbrough (1933-96)
Night Call Nurses '72
Bloody Mama '70

Bruce Kimmel (1947-)
Spaceship '81
The First Nudie Musical '75

Dana Kimmell
Friday the 13th, Part 3 '82
Sweet 16 '81

Kenneth Kimmins
My Best Friend Is a Vampire '88
Eleanor: First Lady of the World '82

Isao Kimura
Black Lizard '68
Stray Dog '49

Aron Kincaid
The Proud and the Damned '72
Creature of Destruction '67

Richard Kind (1956-)
A Bug's Life '98 (V)
Sink or Swim '97
Tom and Jerry: The Movie '93 (V)
All-American Murder '91

Kevin Kindlin
Heartstopper '92
Revenge of the Living Zombies '88
The Majorettes '87

Adrienne King
Friday the 13th, Part 2 '81
Friday the 13th '80

Alan King (1927-)
Rush Hour 2 '01
Casino '95
The Infiltrator '95
Night and the City '92
The Bonfire of the Vanities '90
Enemies, a Love Story '89
Memories of Me '88
Cat's Eye '85
Author! Author! '82
I, the Jury '82
Just Tell Me What You Want '80
Pleasure Palace '80
How to Pick Up Girls '78
The Anderson Tapes '71

Andrea King (1919-)
The Linguini Incident '92
Blackenstein '73
House of the Black Death '65
Band of Angels '57
Red Planet Mars '52
The World in His Arms '52
The Lemon Drop Kid '51
Mr. Peabody & the Mermaid '48
The Beast with Five Fingers '46
The Man I Love '46

Atlas King
The Thrill Killers '65
Incredibly Strange Creatures Who Stopped Living and Became Mixed-Up Zombies '63

B.B. King
Blues Brothers 2000 '98
Amazon Women on the Moon '87

Brad King
Outlaws of the Desert '41
Riders of the Timberline '41
Twilight on the Trail '41

Brett King
Flying Leathernecks '51
Battleground '49

Cammie King
Bambi '42 (V)
Gone with the Wind '39

Charles King (1889-1944)
The Silver Bullet '34
Broadway Melody '29

Charles "Blackie" King (1895-1957)
Ambush Trail '46
The Caravan Trail '46
Colorado Serenade '46
Outlaw of the Plains '46
Border Badmen '45
Flaming Bullets '45
Gangster's Den '45
His Brother's Ghost '45
Three in the Saddle '45
Boss of Rawhide '44
Dead or Alive '44
Devil Riders '44
Frontier Outlaws '44
Oath of Vengeance '44
Rustler's Hideout '44
Wild Horse Phantom '44
California Joe '43
Texas Kid '43
Along the Sundown Trail '42
Arizona Stagecoach '42
Below the Border '42
Prairie Pals '42
Trail Riders '42
Where Trails End '42
Trigger Men '41
Death Rides the Range '40
Down the Wyoming Trail '39
Mesquite Buckaroo '39
Trigger Pals '39
Wild Horse Canyon '39
Gun Packer '38
The Phantom of the Range '38
Songs and Bullets '38
Thunder in the Desert '38
The Gambling Terror '37
God's Country and the Man '37
Hittin' the Trail '37
A Lawman Is Born '37
Lightning Bill Crandall '37
Mystery of the Hooded Horseman '37
The Red Rope '37
Riders of the Rockies '37
Ridin' the Lone Trail '37
Santa Fe Bound '37
Desert Phantom '36
Headin' for the Rio Grande '36
Last of the Warrens '36
The Lawless Nineties '36
Lucky Terror '36
Red River Valley '36
Rip Roarin' Buckaroo '36
Fighting Parson '35
Trail of Terror '35
Fighting Champ '33
Young Blood '33
Outlaw Justice '32
Branded Men '31
The Pocatello Kid '31
Range Law '31
Two Gun Man '31
Oklahoma Cyclone '30

Charmion King
Jackie, Ethel, Joan: The Kennedy Women '01
Anne of Green Gables '85
Who Has Seen the Wind? '77

Damu King (1917-91)
Blackjack '78
Black Godfather '74
Black Starlet '74

Dave King (1929-2002)
Revolution '85
The Long Good Friday '80
Naughty Knights '71

Erik King
Atomic Train '99
True Crime '99
Joey Breaker '93
Casualties of War '89

James King (1979-)
Slackers '02
Blow '01
Happy Campers '01
Pearl Harbor '01

Joe King
Alexander's Ragtime Band '38
Woman in the Shadows '34
Shifting Sands '18
Until They Get Me '18

John King, III
Psycho from Texas '83
Black Bikers from Hell '70
The Outlaw Bikers—Gang Wars '70

John "Dusty" King (1909-87)
Haunted Ranch '43
Two-Fisted Justice '43
Arizona Stagecoach '42
Boot Hill Bandits '42
Law of the Jungle '42
Rock River Renegades '42
Texas to Bataan '42
Thunder River Feud '42
Trail Riders '42
Fugitive Valley '41
Kid's Last Ride '41
Saddle Mountain Round-Up '41
Tonto Basin Outlaws '41
Trail of the Silver Spurs '41
Tumbledown Ranch in Arizona '41
Underground Rustlers '41
Half a Soldier '40
Midnight Limited '40
Trailing Double Trouble '40
West of Pinto Basin '40
Ace Drummond '36

Kenneth King
Jade '95
Polyester '81

Larry King (1933-)
America's Sweethearts '01
An Alan Smithee Film: Burn, Hollywood, Burn '97
Dave '93
Eddie and the Cruisers 2: Eddie Lives! '89
Pink Nights '87

Leslie King
Cotton Candy '82
Gas Pump Girls '79

Mabel King (1932-99)
Dead Men Don't Die '91
The Jerk '79
The Wiz '78
Ganja and Hess '73

Meegan King
Money to Burn '83
Humanoids from the Deep '80
Sweater Girls '78

Morgana King (1930-)
A Brooklyn State of Mind '97
A Time to Remember '90
The Godfather, Part 2 '74
The Godfather '72

Perry King (1948-)
The Perfect Wife '00
A Cry in the Night '93
Jericho Fever '93
Switch '91
Danielle Steel's Kaleidoscope '90
The Prize Pulitzer '89
Disaster at Silo 7 '88
The Hasty Heart '86
Killing Hour '84
Class of 1984 '82
Search and Destroy '81
City in Fear '80
The Cracker Factory '79
Love's Savage Fury '79
Different Story '78
Andy Warhol's Bad '77
The Choirboys '77
Lipstick '76
Mandingo '75
The Lords of Flatbush '74
Wild Party '74
The Possession of Joel Delaney '72
Slaughterhouse Five '72

Regina King (1971-)
Down to Earth '01
If These Walls Could Talk 2 '00
Love and Action in Chicago '99
Where the Truth Lies '99
Enemy of the State '98
How Stella Got Her Groove Back '98
Mighty Joe Young '98
Jerry Maguire '96
A Thin Line Between Love and Hate '96
Friday '95
Higher Learning '94
Poetic Justice '93

Rowena King
Framed '93
To Play the King '93
Wide Sargasso Sea '92

Stephen King (1947-)
Stephen King's Thinner '96
Stephen King's The Langoliers '95
Stephen King's The Stand '94
Sleepwalkers '92
Stephen King's Golden Years '91
Pet Sematary '89
Creepshow 2 '87
Maximum Overdrive '86
Creepshow '82

Tony King
Cannibal Apocalypse '80
The Last Hunter '80
Sparkle '76
Report to the Commissioner '74
Gordon's War '73

Walter Woolf King (1899-1984)
Smart Alecks '42
Today I Hang '42
Yank in Libya '42
Go West '40
Swiss Miss '38
A Night at the Opera '35

Wright King (1923-)
Invasion of the Bee Girls '73
King Rat '65
Dangerous Charter '62

Yolanda King (1955-)
Selma, Lord, Selma '99
Ghosts of Mississippi '96
America's Dream '95

Zalman King (1941-)
Galaxy of Terror '81
Blue Sunshine '78
The Passover Plot '75
Ski Bum '75
Deadly Fieldtrip '74
Smile, Jenny, You're Dead '74
Some Call It Loving '73

Walter Kingsford (1881-1958)
Velvet Touch '48
My Favorite Blonde '42
The Man in the Iron Mask '39
It Could Happen to You '37
The Invisible Ray '36
The Story of Louis Pasteur '36

Ben Kingsley (1943-)
A. I.: Artificial Intelligence '01 (N)
The Triumph of Love '01
Rules of Engagement '00
Sexy Beast '00
What Planet Are You From? '00
Alice in Wonderland '99
Dostoevsky's Crime and Punishment '99
The Confession '98
The Assignment '97
Photographing Fairies '97
Weapons of Mass Distraction '97
Moses '96
Twelfth Night '96
Joseph '95
Species '95
Death and the Maiden '94
Dave '93
Schindler's List '93
Searching for Bobby Fischer '93
Freddie the Frog '92 (V)
Sneakers '92
Bugsy '91
The Children '90
The Fifth Monkey '90
Murderers Among Us: The Simon Wiesenthal Story '89
Slipstream '89
Pascali's Island '88
Without a Clue '88
Maurice '87
Turtle Diary '86
Harem '85
Silas Marner '85
Betrayal '83
Gandhi '82
Hard Labour '73

Danitza Kingsley
Jack's Back '87
South of Reno '87
Amazons '86

Susan Kingsley
The Dollmaker '84
Old Enough '84

Alex Kingston (1963-)
Essex Boys '99
Croupier '97
Moll Flanders '96
Carrington '95
The Infiltrator '95

Natalie Kingston (1905-91)
His Private Secretary '33
Tarzan the Tiger '29
His First Flame '26

Sam Kinison (1953-92)
It's a Bundyful Life '92
Back to School '86

Amelia Kinkade
Night of the Demons 3 '97
Night of the Demons 2 '94

Kathleen Kinmont (1965-)
The Corporate Ladder '97
That Thing You Do! '96
Stormswept '95
Texas Payback '95
C.I.A. 2: Target Alexa '94
Final Round '93
C.I.A.: Code Name Alexa '92
Sweet Justice '92
Final Impact '91
Night of the Warrior '91
The Art of Dying '90
Roller Blade Warriors: Taken By Force '90
Bride of Re-Animator '89
SnakeEater 2: The Drug Buster '89
Halloween 4: The Return of Michael Myers '88
Phoenix the Warrior '88
Rush Week '88
Fraternity Vacation '85
Hardbodies '84

Greg Kinnear (1963-)
We Were Soldiers '02
Dinner with Friends '01
Someone Like You '01
The Gift '00
Loser '00
Nurse Betty '00
What Planet Are You From? '00
Mystery Men '99
You've Got Mail '98
As Good As It Gets '97
Dear God '96
A Smile Like Yours '96
Sabrina '95

Roy Kinnear (1934-88)
The Return of the Musketeers '89

A Man for All Seasons '88
Pirates '86
The Zany Adventures of Robin Hood '84
Hawk the Slayer '81
The Adventures of Sherlock Holmes' Smarter Brother '78
Herbie Goes to Monte Carlo '77
The Hound of the Baskervilles '77
The Four Musketeers '75
Juggernaut '74
Melody '71
Willy Wonka & the Chocolate Factory '71
Taste the Blood of Dracula '70
How I Won the War '67
Help! '65

Kathy Kinney
This Boy's Life '93
Parting Glances '86

Terry Kinney (1954-)
The Laramie Project '02
Save the Last Dance '01
House of Mirth '00
Luminous Motion '00
Oxygen '99
That Championship Season '99
Critical Choices '97
George Wallace '97
Fly Away Home '96
Sleepers '96
Devil in a Blue Dress '95
The Good Old Boys '95
Body Snatchers '93
The Firm '93
JFK: Reckless Youth '93
The Last of the Mohicans '92
Talent for the Game '91
Murder Ordained '87

Leonid Kinskey (1903-98)
Can't Help Singing '45
Fighting Seabees '44
Casablanca '42
I Married an Angel '42
Lady for a Night '42
Somewhere I'll Find You '42
Broadway Limited '41
Down Argentine Way '40
Everything Happens at Night '39
The Great Waltz '38
Les Miserables '35
The Lives of a Bengal Lancer '35
Duck Soup '33

Klaus Kinski (1926-91)
Cobra Verde '88
Rough Justice '87
Timestalkers '87
Crawlspace '86
Gangster's Law '86
Creature '85
His Name Was King '85
Star Knight '85
Codename: Wildgeese '84
The Little Drummer Girl '84
The Secret Diary of Sigmund Freud '84
Beauty and the Beast '83
Android '82
Burden of Dreams '82
Fitzcarraldo '82
The Soldier '82
Venom '82
Buddy Buddy '81
Schizoid '80
The French Woman '79
Nosferatu the Vampyre '79
Woyzeck '78
Liberators '77
Night of the Assassin '77
Operation Thunderbolt '77
Jack the Ripper '76
Lifespan '75
Primal Impulse '74
Shoot the Living, Pray for the Dead '73
Aguirre, the Wrath of God '72
Count Dracula '71
Slaughter Hotel '71
Creature with the Blue Hand '70
Double Face '70
The Ruthless Four '70
Venus in Furs '70
Web of the Spider '70
And God Said to Cain '69
Twice a Judas '69
A Bullet for the General '68
Deadly Sanctuary '68
Psychopath '68
Circus of Fear '67
Fistful of Death '67
Five for Hell '67
Five Golden Dragons '67
Heroes in Hell '67
Target for Killing '66
Doctor Zhivago '65
Fighting Fists of Shanghai Joe '65
For a Few Dollars More '65
The Squeaker '65
The Indian Scarf '63
Door with the Seven Locks '62
Inn on the River '62
Dead Eyes of London '61
The Avenger '60
A Time to Love & a Time to Die '58

Nastassia Kinski (1959-)
An American Rhapsody '01
Town and Country '01
The Claim '00
Red Letters '00
Dying to Get Rich '98
The Lost Son '98
Playing by Heart '98
Savior '98
Your Friends & Neighbors '98
Bella Mafia '97
Little Boy Blue '97
One Night Stand '97
Father's Day '96
Somebody Is Waiting '96
Crackerjack '94
Terminal Velocity '94
Faraway, So Close! '93
The Blonde '92
Torrents of Spring '90
Magdalene '88
Spring Symphony '86
Harem '85
Revolution '85
The Hotel New Hampshire '84
Maria's Lovers '84
Unfaithfully Yours '84
Boarding School '83
Exposed '83
Moon in the Gutter '83
Paris, Texas '83
Cat People '82
One from the Heart '82
Tess '80
For Your Love Only '79
Stay As You Are '78
The Wrong Move '78
To the Devil, a Daughter '76

Bruce Kirby (1928-)
Blood Money '99
Interlocked '98
Rave Review '95
Mr. Wonderful '93
Getting Up and Going Home '92
Throw Momma from the Train '87
Armed and Dangerous '86
Fyre '78
Cinderella Liberty '73
The Young Graduates '71

Bruno Kirby (1949-)
American Tragedy '00
Spy Games '99
Stuart Little '99 (V)
Donnie Brasco '96
Sleepers '96
The Basketball Diaries '94
Fallen Angels 2 '93
Golden Gate '93
City Slickers '91
The Freshman '90
Bert Rigby, You're a Fool '89
We're No Angels '89
When Harry Met Sally... '89
Nitti: The Enforcer '88
Good Morning, Vietnam '87
Tin Men '87
Flesh and Blood '85
Birdy '84
This Is Spinal Tap '84
Kiss My Grits '82
The Godfather 1902-1959: The Complete Epic '81
Modern Romance '81
Borderline '80
Where the Buffalo Roam '80
Between the Lines '77
The Godfather, Part 2 '74
Harrad Experiment '73

George Kirby (1924-95)
Trouble in Mind '86
Oh Dad, Poor Dad (Momma's Hung You in the Closet & I'm Feeling So Sad) '67

Jay Kirby (1920-64)
Sundown Riders '48
Border Patrol '43
Colt Comrades '43
Hoppy Serves a Writ '43
Leather Burners '43
Lost Canyon '43

Michael Kirby (1925-97)
Shadows and Fog '92
Swoon '91
Another Woman '88
The Girl in Blue '74

Joe (Joseph) Kirk (1903-75)
Abbott and Costello Go to Mars '53
Impact '49
The Noose Hangs High '48
The Naughty Nineties '45
Smart Alecks '42

Phyllis Kirk (1926-)
The Sad Sack '57
Back from Eternity '56
River Beat '54
House of Wax '53
Three Guys Named Mike '51
A Life of Her Own '50
Our Very Own '50
Two Weeks with Love '50

Tommy Kirk (1941-)
Attack of the 60-Foot Centerfold '95
Blood of Ghastly Horror '72
It's Alive! '68
Mars Needs Women '66
The Unkissed Bride '66
Monkey's Uncle '65
Village of the Giants '65
Pajama Party '64
The Misadventures of Merlin Jones '63
Savage Sam '63
Son of Flubber '63
Bon Voyage! '62
Escapade in Florence '62
Moon Pilot '62
The Absent-Minded Professor '61
Babes in Toyland '61
Horsemasters '61
The Swiss Family Robinson '60
The Shaggy Dog '59
Old Yeller '57

Donald Kirke (1901-71)
A Night for Crime '42
Oh Susannah '38
Country Gentlemen '36

Sally Kirkland (1944-)
Another Woman's Husband '00
Wish You Were Dead '00
EDtv '99
Starry Night '99
Dead Silence '98
Paranoia '98
Amnesia '96
Excess Baggage '96
Cheatin' Hearts '93
Eye of the Stranger '93
Gunmen '93
The Woman Who Loved Elvis '93
Double Jeopardy '92
Double Threat '92
Forever: A Ghost of a Love Story '92
Hit the Dutchman '92
The Player '92
Primary Motive '92
Prime Time Murder '92
In the Heat of Passion '91
JFK '91
Bullseye! '90
Heat Wave '90
Revenge '90
Superstar: The Life and Times of Andy Warhol '90
Two Evil Eyes '90
Best of the Best '89
Cold Feet '89
High Stakes '89
Paint It Black '89
White Hot '88
Anna '87
Talking Walls '85
Fatal Games '84
Love Letters '83
Private Benjamin '80
Hometown U.S.A. '79
Breakheart Pass '76
Pipe Dreams '76
A Star Is Born '76
Bite the Bullet '75
Crazy Mama '75
Death Scream '75
Big Bad Mama '74
Candy Stripe Nurses '74
Cinderella Liberty '73
The Way We Were '73
The Young Nurses '73
Coming Apart '69
Futz '69
Blue '68

Gene Kirkwood
The Crossing Guard '94
Night and the City '92

Jack Kirkwood
Fancy Pants '50
Never a Dull Moment '50

Mia Kirshner (1976-)
New Best Friend '02
Not Another Teen Movie '01
Innocents '00
Out of the Cold '99
Mad City '97
The Crow 2: City of Angels '96
Leo Tolstoy's Anna Karenina '96
The Grass Harp '95
Johnny's Girl '95
Murder in the First '95
Exotica '94
Cadillac Girls '93
Love and Human Remains '93

Terry Kiser
Forest Warrior '95
Pet Shop '94
Tammy and the T-Rex '94
Weekend at Bernie's 2 '93
Into the Sun '92
Mannequin 2: On the Move '91
Weekend at Bernie's '89
Friday the 13th, Part 7: The New Blood '88
The Offspring '87
Surf 2 '84
Starflight One '83
Making Love '82
Steel '80

Keiko Kishi (1932-)
The Makioka Sisters '83
Master Mind '73
Kwaidan '64
Qui Etes Vous, Mr. Sorge? '61
Snow Country '57

Kyoko Kishida (1930-)
Face of Another '66
Woman in the Dunes '64
The Human Condition: A Soldier's Prayer '61

Charles Kissinger (1925-91)
Grizzly '76
Sheba, Baby '75
Asylum of Satan '72
Three on a Meathook '72

Tawny Kitaen (1961-)
Dead Tides '97
Playback '95
Hercules the Legendary Journeys, Vol. 3: The Circle of Fire '94
Hercules the Legendary Journeys, Vol. 4: In the Underworld '94
White Hot '88
Crystal Heart '87
Glory Years '87
Happy Hour '87
Witchboard '87
Instant Justice '86
Bachelor Party '84
The Perils of Gwendoline '84

Kazuo Kitamura
Black Rain '88
Tora! Tora! Tora! '70

Takeshi "Beat" Kitano (1948-)
Brother '00
Kikujiro '99
Fireworks '97
Sonatine '96
Johnny Mnemonic '95
Boiling Point '90
Violent Cop '89
Merry Christmas, Mr. Lawrence '83

Michael Kitchen (1948-)
Lorna Doone '01
Oliver Twist '00
Proof of Life '00
The Railway Children '00
The World Is Not Enough '99
Reckless: The Sequel '98
Mrs. Dalloway '97
Reckless '97
A Royal Scandal '96
Wilderness '96
The Buccaneers '95
Goldeneye '95
Kidnapped '95
Doomsday Gun '94
Fatherland '94
To Play the King '93
Enchanted April '92
Fools of Fortune '90
The Russia House '90
The Dive '89
Out of Africa '85
The Brontes of Haworth '73

Eartha Kitt (1928-)
The Emperor's New Groove '00 (V)
Harriet the Spy '96
Boomerang '92
Ernest Scared Stupid '91
Erik the Viking '89
Master of Dragonard Hill '89
Dragonard '88
The Pink Chiquitas '86
Naughty Knights '71
The Mark of the Hawk '57
New Faces of 1952 '54

John Kitzmiller (1913-)
Uncle Tom's Cabin '69
Cave of the Living Dead '65
Dr. No '62
Jungle Master '56

Barry Kivel
Bound '96
One Fine Day '96

Alf Kjellin (1920-88)
Summer Interlude '50
Torment '44

Bjorn Kjellman
All Things Fair '95
The Best Intentions '92

Uri Klauzner
Kippur '00
Kadosh '99

Chris Klein (1979-)
Rollerball '02
We Were Soldiers '02
American Pie 2 '01
Say It Isn't So '01
Here on Earth '00
American Pie '99
Election '99

Erik S. Klein
Anton, the Magician '78
Under the Pear Tree '73

Gerard Klein
Frantic '88
La Passante '83

Nita Klein
Dr. Petiot '90
Muriel '63

Robert Klein (1942-)
Labor Pains '99
Next Stop, Wonderland '98
Primary Colors '98
One Fine Day '96
Mixed Nuts '94
Radioland Murders '94
The Marx Brothers in a Nutshell '90
Tales from the Darkside: The Movie '90
Dangerous Curves '88
A Secret Space '88
Poison Ivy '85
Table Settings '84
Pajama Tops '83
Your Place or Mine '83
The Last Unicorn '82 (V)
The Bell Jar '79
Nobody's Perfekt '79
Hooper '78
Rivals '72
The Owl and the Pussycat '70
The Pursuit of Happiness '70

Rudolf Klein-Rogge (1888-1955)
Crimes of Dr. Mabuse '32
Spies '28
Metropolis '26
Kriemhilde's Revenge '24
Dr. Mabuse, The Gambler '22
Destiny '21
The Cabinet of Dr. Caligari '19

Werner Klemperer (1920-2000)
Judgment at Nuremberg '61
Istanbul '57

Kevin Kline (1947-)
Orange County '02
The Anniversary Party '01
Life as a House '01
The Road to El Dorado '00 (V)
Wild Wild West '99
William Shakespeare's A Midsummer Night's Dream '99
The Ice Storm '97
In and Out '97
Fierce Creatures '96
The Hunchback of Notre Dame '96 (V)
Looking for Richard '96
French Kiss '95
Princess Caraboo '94
Dave '93
George Balanchine's The Nutcracker '93 (N)
Chaplin '92
Consenting Adults '92
Grand Canyon '91
Soapdish '91
I Love You to Death '90
The January Man '89
A Fish Called Wanda '88
Cry Freedom '87
Violets Are Blue '86
Silverado '85
The Big Chill '83

The Pirates of Penzance '83
Sophie's Choice '82
Richard Kline
Liberty Heights '99
Treehouse Hostage '99
Heidi Kling
D3: The Mighty Ducks '96
The Mighty Ducks '92
Out on a Limb '92
Evan J. Klisser
Prey for the Hunter '92
Hellgate '89
Jack Klugman (1922-)
The Twilight of the Golds '97
Dear God '96
Parallel Lives '94
Around the World in 80 Days '89
One of My Wives Is Missing '76
Two Minute Warning '76
Goodbye Columbus '69
The Detective '68
I Could Go on Singing '63
Days of Wine and Roses '62
Twelve Angry Men '57
Justice '55
Vincent Klyn
Urban Menace '99
Nemesis '93
Bloodmatch '91
Point Break '91
Dollman '90
Cyborg '89
Skelton Knaggs (1911-55)
Dick Tracy Meets Gruesome '47
Forever Amber '47
Dick Tracy vs. Cueball '46
Bedlam '45
Isle of the Dead '45
Evalyn Knapp (1908-)
Hawaiian Buckaroo '38
Rawhide '38
Bulldog Edition '36
Mistaken Identity '36
Confidential '35
In Old Santa Fe '34
The Perils of Pauline '34
His Private Secretary '33
The Strange Love of Molly Louvain '32
Herbert Knaup
Nuremberg '00
Run Lola Run '98
Hildegarde Knef (1925-2002)
Witchery '88
The Murderers Are Among Us '46
The Murderers are Among Us '46
David Knell
Chopper Chicks in Zombietown '91
Spring Break '83
Bitter Harvest '81
Rob Knepper
Jackie, Ethel, Joan: The Kennedy Women '01
Love & Sex '00
Absence of the Good '99
Kidnapped in Paradise '98
Getting Out '94
Gas Food Lodging '92
Where the Day Takes You '92
Young Guns 2 '90
Renegades '89
Wild Thing '87
That's Life! '86
Christopher Knight
The Brady Bunch Movie '95
The Doom Generation '95
Good Girls Don't '95
A Very Brady Christmas '88
Studs Lonigan '60
Damien Knight
Class Reunion Massacre '77
The Redeemer '76
David Knight (1927-)
Nightmare '63
Across the Bridge '57
David Edwin Knight (1972-)
Who Shot Pat? '92
Demons 2 '87
Esmond Knight (1906-87)
The Element of Crime '84
Peeping Tom '60
Sink the Bismarck '60
The River '51
Hamlet '48
The Red Shoes '48
Black Narcissus '47
A Canterbury Tale '44
Henry V '44
Contraband '40
The Arsenal Stadium Mystery '39
Fuzzy Knight (1901-76)
Hostile Guns '67
Naked Hills '56
Oklahoma Annie '51
Apache Chief '50
Blazing Guns '50
Hills of Oklahoma '50
Marshal of Heldorado '50
Rimfire '49
The Adventures of Gallant Bess '48
Bad Men of the Border '45
Take It Big '44
Frontier Law '43
Boss of Bullion City '41
Bury Me Not on the Lone Prairie '41
Man from Montana '41
The Masked Rider '41
The Shepherd of the Hills '41
My Little Chickadee '40
Pony Post '40
Riders of Pasco Basin '40
Oregon Trail '39
The Cowboy and the Lady '38
Spawn of the North '38
Kelly of the Secret Service '36
Song of the Gringo '36
Song of the Trail '36
The Trail of the Lonesome Pine '36
To the Last Man '33
Gladys Knight
Twenty Bucks '93
Pipe Dreams '76
Harlan E. Knight
Whistlin' Dan '32
The Fighting Sheriff '31
Lily Knight
An Unremarkable Life '89
Static '87
Michael E. Knight
Hexed '93
Date with an Angel '87
Sandra Knight
Track of the Vampire '66
The Terror '63
Tower of London '62
Frankenstein's Daughter '58
Thunder Road '58
Shirley Knight (1937-)
Divine Secrets of the Ya-Ya Sisterhood '02
My Louisiana Sky '02
The Salton Sea '02
Angel Eyes '01
As Good As It Gets '97
Little Boy Blue '97
Diabolique '96
If These Walls Could Talk '96
Somebody Is Waiting '96
A Good Day to Die '95
Indictment: The McMartin Trial '95
Color of Night '94
Stuart Saves His Family '94
The Sender '82
Endless Love '81
Beyond the Poseidon Adventure '79
Return to Earth '76
21 Hours at Munich '76
Juggernaut '74
Secrets '71
The Rain People '69
Petulia '68
The Group '66
Sweet Bird of Youth '62
Ice Palace '60
Ted (Edward) Knight (1923-86)
Caddyshack '80
Countdown '68
Psycho '60
Trenton Knight (1982-)
Invisible Mom '96
The Tin Soldier '95
Charlie's Ghost: The Secret of Coronado '94
The Skateboard Kid 2 '94
Tuesday Knight
Cover Story '93
A Nightmare on Elm Street 4: Dream Master '88
Wayne Knight (1955-)
Rat Race '01
Tarzan '99 (V)
Toy Story 2 '99 (V)
For Richer or Poorer '97
Space Jam '96
Chameleon '95
To Die For '95
Fallen Angels 2 '93
Jurassic Park '93
Basic Instinct '92
Dead Again '91
JFK '91
William Knight
Action U.S.A. '89
The Lost Platoon '89
Wyatt Knight (1955-)
Porky's Revenge '85
Porky's 2: The Next Day '83
Porky's '82
Keira Knightley
Princess of Thieves '01
Oliver Twist '00
Sascha Knopf
What's the Worst That Could Happen? '01
Blackmale '99
Andrew Knott
Black Beauty '94
The Secret Garden '93
Don Knotts (1924-)
Pleasantville '98
Cats Don't Dance '97 (V)
Big Bully '95
Return to Mayberry '85
Cannonball Run 2 '84
The Private Eyes '80
The Apple Dumpling Gang Rides Again '79
Prize Fighter '79
Hot Lead & Cold Feet '78
Herbie Goes to Monte Carlo '77
No Deposit, No Return '76
The Apple Dumpling Gang '75
How to Frame a Figg '71
The Love God? '70
The Shakiest Gun in the West '68
The Reluctant Astronaut '67
The Ghost and Mr. Chicken '66
The Incredible Mr. Limpet '64
It's a Mad, Mad, Mad, Mad World '63
No Time for Sergeants '58
Elizabeth Knowles
Wild Riders '71
Lady Godiva Rides '68
Patric Knowles (1911-95)
Arnold '73
Chisum '70
The Devil's Brigade '68
Auntie Mame '58
Band of Angels '57
Mutiny '52
Three Came Home '50
Big Steal '49
Monsieur Beaucaire '46
O.S.S. '46
Hit the Ice '43
Frankenstein Meets the Wolfman '42
Who Done It? '42
How Green Was My Valley '41
The Wolf Man '41
Beauty for the Asking '39
Five Came Back '39
The Adventures of Robin Hood '38
The Sisters '38
The Charge of the Light Brigade '36
Alexander Knox (1907-95)
Joshua Then and Now '85
Cry of the Innocent '80
The Chosen '77
Puppet on a Chain '72
Nicholas and Alexandra '71
Shalako '68
Accident '67
Khartoum '66
Modesty Blaise '66
The Longest Day '62
Operation Amsterdam '60
The Wreck of the Mary Deare '59
The Vikings '58
Alias John Preston '56
Reach for the Sky '56
The Sleeping Tiger '54
Europa '51 '52
I'd Climb the Highest Mountain '51
Man in the Saddle '51
The Judge Steps Out '49
Tokyo Joe '49
Sister Kenny '46
Wilson '44
Commandos Strike at Dawn '43
The Sea Wolf '41
The Four Feathers '39
Elyse Knox (1917-)
Joe's Bed-Stuy Barbershop: We Cut Heads '83
Don Winslow of the Coast Guard '43
Hit the Ice '43
The Mummy's Tomb '42
Tanks a Million '41
Mickey Knox (1922-)
Cemetery Man '95
Frankenstein Unbound '90
Western Pacific Agent '51
Patricia Knox
Flaming Bullets '45
I Accuse My Parents '45
Terence Knox (1946-)
The Invaders '95
The Spy Within '94
Murder So Sweet '93
Children of the Corn 2: The Final Sacrifice '92
Forever: A Ghost of a Love Story '92
Snow Kill '90
Tripwire '89
City Killer '87
Distortions '87
The Mighty Pawns '87
Murder Ordained '87
Tour of Duty '87
Humanoid Defender '85
Rebel Love '85
Circle of Power '83
Johnny Knoxville (1971-)
Big Trouble '02
Deuces Wild '02
Men in Black 2 '02
Life Without Dick '01
Peggy Knudsen (1923-80)
Istanbul '57
Copper Canyon '50
The Big Sleep '46
Humoresque '46
Never Say Goodbye '46
A Stolen Life '46
Gustav Knuth
Heidi '65
Tromba, the Tiger Man '52
Keiju Kobayashi (1923-)
Godzilla 1985 '85
Tidal Wave '75
Sanjuro '62
Shoji Kobayashi
Godzilla vs. King Ghidora '91
Youth of the Beast '63
Yukiko Kobayashi
Yog, Monster from Space '71
Destroy All Monsters '68
Jeff Kober
American Tragedy '00
Militia '99
The Colony '98
The Maker '98
Elmore Leonard's Gold Coast '97
The Big Fall '96
Demolition High '95
One Man's Justice '95
Automatic '94
Tank Girl '94
Lone Justice '93
The Baby Doll Murders '92
Keep the Change '92
The First Power '89
Alien Nation '88
China Beach '88
Lucky Stiff '88
Out of Bounds '86
Edward I. Koch
Somewhere in the City '97
New York Stories '89
Marianne Koch (1931-)
A Place Called Glory '66
A Fistful of Dollars '64
Frozen Alive '64
The Monster of London City '64
Pete Koch
Adventures in Dinosaur City '92
Heartbreak Ridge '86
Walter Koenig (1936-)
Star Trek: Generations '94
Star Trek 6: The Undiscovered Country '91
Moontrap '89
Star Trek 5: The Final Frontier '89
Star Trek 4: The Voyage Home '86
Star Trek 3: The Search for Spock '84
Star Trek 2: The Wrath of Khan '82
Star Trek: The Motion Picture '80
Michiyo Kogure
Street of Shame '56
Shin Heike Monogatari '55
A Geisha '53
Fred Kohler, Sr. (1889-1938)
The Texas Rangers '36
Honor of the Range '34
Deluge '33
The Fiddlin' Buckaroo '33
Texas Bad Man '32
Fighting Caravans '31
Underworld '27
Riders of the Purple Sage '25
Anna Christie '23
Fred Kohler, Jr. (1912-93)
Daniel Boone: Trail Blazer '56
Calling Wild Bill Elliott '43
Western Mail '42
Pigskin Parade '36
Pecos Kid '35
Toll of the Desert '35
The Man from Hell '34
Lee Kohlmar
Death from a Distance '36
Love in Bloom '35
Susan Kohner (1936-)
The Gene Krupa Story '59
Imitation of Life '59
Dino '57
To Hell and Back '55
Hiroshi Koizumi (1926-)
Dagora, the Space Monster '65
Ghidrah the Three Headed Monster '65
Godzilla vs. Mothra '64
Attack of the Mushroom People '63
Mothra '62
Clarence (C. William) Kolb (1874-1964)
Impact '49
Caught in the Draft '41
His Girl Friday '40
Honolulu '39
Give Me a Sailor '38
Henry Kolker (1870-1947)
The Real Glory '39
Union Pacific '39
The Cowboy and the Lady '38
Charlie Chan in Paris '35
Mad Love '35
The Mystery Man '35
The Ghost Walks '34
Baby Face '33
Rasputin and the Empress '33
Coquette '29
Amos Kollek
Whore 2 '94
Double Edge '92
Goodbye, New York '85
Tetsu Komai (1893-1970)
The Real Glory '39
The Princess Comes Across '36
Hong Kong Nights '35
Bulldog Drummond '29
Hosei Komatsu
A Taxing Woman's Return '88
Double Suicide '69
Rich Komenich
Henry: Portrait of a Serial Killer 2: Mask of Sanity '96
Two Wrongs Make a Right '89
Liliana Komorowska
The Art of War '00
The Assignment '97
Martial Outlaw '93
Scanners 3: The Takeover '92
Maja Komorowska (1937-)
The Decalogue '88
Year of the Quiet Sun '84
Contract '80
Maids of Wilko '79
Family Life '71
Queen Kong
Slashdance '89
Deathstalker 2: Duel of the Titans '87
Magda Konopka
When Dinosaurs Ruled the Earth '70
Satanik '69
Phyllis Konstam
Skin Game '31
Murder '30
Guich Koock (1944-)
Picasso Trigger '89
Square Dance '87
American Ninja '85
Seven '79
Kool Moe Dee
Crossroads '02
Storm Trooper '98
Milos Kopecky
Lemonade Joe '64
Fabulous Adventures of Baron Munchausen '61
The Original Fabulous Adventures of Baron Munchausen '61

Bernie Kopell (1933-)
Bug Buster '99
Get Smart, Again! '89
Combat Academy '86
The Loved One '65

Kim Kopf
Stormswept '95
Witchcraft 8: Salem's Ghost '95

Karen Kopins
Lady in Waiting '94
Archie: Return to Riverdale '90
Jake Speed '86
Creator '85
Once Bitten '85

Mia Korf
Blood Brothers '97
Color of Justice '97

Arnold Korff
Doughboys '30
The Haunted Castle '21

Jon Korkes
Syngenor '90
Jaws of Satan '81
The Day of the Dolphin '73
Little Murders '71
Catch-22 '70

Baltasar Kormakur
No Such Thing '01
Devil's Island '96

Harvey Korman (1927-)
The Flintstones in Viva Rock Vegas '00
Jingle All the Way '96
Dracula: Dead and Loving It '95
The Flintstones '94 (V)
Radioland Murders '94
Based on an Untrue Story '93
Betrayal of the Dove '92
Munchies '87
The Longshot '86
Gone Are the Days '84
Curse of the Pink Panther '83
History of the World: Part 1 '81
Herbie Goes Bananas '80
Americathon '79
Bud and Lou '78
High Anxiety '77
Blazing Saddles '74
Huckleberry Finn '74
April Fools '69

Mary Kornman (1915-73)
Swing It, Professor '37
The Adventurous Knights '35
Desert Trail '35
Queen of the Jungle '35

Alix Koromzay
Mimic 2 '01
Children of the Corn 666: Isaac's Return '99
The Haunting '99
Nightwatch '96

Charlie Korsmo (1978-)
Can't Hardly Wait '98
The Doctor '91
Hook '91
What about Bob? '91
Dick Tracy '90
Heat Wave '90
Men Don't Leave '89

Robert F. (Bob) Kortman (1887-1967)
Guns of the Law '44
Fugitive Valley '41
Hopalong Cassidy: Renegade Trail '39
Law of the Texan '38
The Rangers Step In '37
Sandflow '37
Robinson Crusoe of Clipper Island '36
The Crimson Trail '35
Feud of the West '35
Wild Mustang '35
When a Man Sees Red '34
The Fiddlin' Buckaroo '33
Phantom Thunderbolt '33
Rainbow Ranch '33
Terror Trail '33
Come on Tarzan '32
Island of Lost Souls '32
The Lone Defender '32

Fritz Kortner (1892-1970)
Woman in Brown '48
Pandora's Box '28
The Hands of Orlac '25
Warning Shadows '23
Backstairs '21

Charles Korvin (1907-98)
Ship of Fools '65
Berlin Express '48

Sylva Koscina (1933-94)
Lisa and the Devil '75
The Slasher '74
Hornet's Nest '70
Deadly Sanctuary '68
The Secret War of Harry Frigg '68
Juliet of the Spirits '65
Hercules Unchained '59
Uncle Was a Vampire '59
Hercules '58

Martin Kosleck (1907-94)
The Flesh Eaters '64
36 Hours '64
House of Horrors '46
She Wolf of London '46
Pursuit to Algiers '45
The Mummy's Curse '44
Weird Woman/Frozen Ghost '44
All Through the Night '42
International Lady '41
Underground '41
Foreign Correspondent '40

Paul Koslo (1944-)
Downdraft '96
Judge & Jury '96
Chained Heat 2 '92
Project: Shadowchaser '92
Xtro 2: The Second Encounter '91
Robot Jox '90
A Night in the Life of Jimmy Reardon '88
The Annihilators '85
Roots: The Next Generation '79
Maniac '77
Rooster Cogburn '75
Joe Kidd '72
Omega Man '71
Vanishing Point '71

David Kossoff (1919-)
Unicorn '83
The Two Faces of Dr. Jekyll '60
The Mouse That Roared '59
Who Done It? '56
Svengali '55

Maria Kosti
Night of the Death Cult '75
Exorcism '74

Nick Kostopoulos
Addicted to Murder 3: Bloodlust '99
The Alien Agenda: Under the Skin '97

Kane (Takeshi) Kosugi (1973-)
Journey of Honor '91
Nine Deaths of the Ninja '85
Pray for Death '85
Revenge of the Ninja '83

Sho Kosugi (1948-)
Journey of Honor '91
Blind Fury '90
Kingfisher the Killer '80s
Aloha Summer '88
Black Eagle '88
Rage of Honor '87
Nine Deaths of the Ninja '85
Pray for Death '85
Ninja 3: The Domination '84
Revenge of the Ninja '83
Enter the Ninja '81

Yoshio Kosugi (1903-68)
The Human Condition: No Greater Love '58
Seven Samurai '54
The Men Who Tread on the Tiger's Tail '45

Eva Kotamanidou
Landscape in the Mist '88
The Travelling Players '75

Elias Koteas (1961-)
Collateral Damage '02
Harrison's Flowers '02
Novocaine '01
Shot in the Heart '01
Dancing at the Blue Iguana '00
Lost Souls '00
Living Out Loud '98
The Thin Red Line '98
Apt Pupil '97
Fallen '97
Gattaca '97
Crash '95
The Prophecy '95
Sugartime '95
Camilla '94
Exotica '94
Power of Attorney '94
Chain of Desire '93
Cyborg 2 '93
Teenage Mutant Ninja Turtles 3 '93
The Adjuster '91
Almost an Angel '90
Desperate Hours '90
Look Who's Talking, Too '90
Teenage Mutant Ninja Turtles: The Movie '90
Friends, Lovers & Lunatics '89
Malarek '89
Blood Red '88
Full Moon in Blue Water '88
Tucker: The Man and His Dream '88
Gardens of Stone '87
Some Kind of Wonderful '87

Oded Kotler
Hanna K. '83
My Michael '75

Yaphet Kotto (1937-)
Stiletto Dance '01
Homicide: The Movie '00
The Defenders: Payback '97
Out of Sync '95
Two If by Sea '95
Dead Badge '94
The Puppet Masters '94
Almost Blue '93
Extreme Justice '93
In Self Defense '93
Chrome Soldiers '92
Freddy's Dead: The Final Nightmare '91
Hangfire '91
After the Shock '90
Jigsaw Murders '89
Ministry of Vengeance '89
Tripwire '89
Midnight Run '88
A Whisper to a Scream '88
Prettykill '87
The Running Man '87
Terminal Entry '87
Eye of the Tiger '86
Harem '86
Badge of the Assassin '85
The Park Is Mine '85
Warning Sign '85
The Star Chamber '83
Fighting Back '82
Brubaker '80
Rage '80
Alien '79
Blue Collar '78
Monkey Hustle '77
Raid on Entebbe '77
Drum '76
Friday Foster '75
Sharks' Treasure '75
Report to the Commissioner '74
Truck Turner '74
Live and Let Die '73
Across 110th Street '72
Housewife '72
Man & Boy '71
Five Card Stud '68
The Thomas Crown Affair '68
Nothing but a Man '64

Adam Kotz
All the King's Men '99
Shot Through the Heart '98
Touching Evil '97
Max and Helen '90

Hubert Kounde
Hate '95
Cafe au Lait '94

Nancy Kovack (1935-)
The Silencers '66
Frankie and Johnny '65
The Outlaws Is Coming! '65
Diary of a Madman '63
Jason and the Argonauts '63

Ernie Kovacs (1919-62)
North to Alaska '60
Strangers When We Meet '60
Bell, Book and Candle '58

Geza Kovacs
Return to the Lost World '93
Baby on Board '92

Lajos Kovacs
Woyzeck '94
Maria's Day '84

Martin Kove (1946-)
Extreme Honor '01
Final Payback '99
Timelock '99
Nowhere Land '98
Baby Face Nelson '97
Grizzly Mountain '97
Shadow Warriors '97
Shadow Warriors 2: Hunt for the Death Merchant '97
Top of the World '97
Judge & Jury '96
Mercenary '96
Final Equinox '95
Without Mercy '95
Death Match '94
Endangered '94
Uncivilized '94
Wyatt Earp '94
Wyatt Earp: Return to Tombstone '94
Future Shock '93
The Outfit '93
President's Target '93
Shootfighter: Fight to the Death '93
To Be the Best '93
Firehawk '92
Project: Shadowchaser '92
White Light '90
The Karate Kid: Part 3 '89
Steele Justice '87
The Karate Kid: Part 2 '86
Rambo: First Blood, Part 2 '85
The Karate Kid '84
Seven '79
Death Race 2000 '75
Last House on the Left '72

Jeff Kovski
Zone 39 '96
Life '95

Andras Kozak
The Red and the White '68
The Round Up '66

Harley Jane Kozak (1957-)
Dark Planet '97
Titanic '96
The Android Affair '95
Magic in the Water '95
The Amy Fisher Story '93
The Favor '92
All I Want for Christmas '91
Necessary Roughness '91
The Taking of Beverly Hills '91
Arachnophobia '90
Side Out '90
Parenthood '89
When Harry Met Sally... '89

Linda Kozlowski (1958-)
Crocodile Dundee in Los Angeles '01
Village of the Damned '95
Backstreet Justice '93
The Neighbor '93
Almost an Angel '90
Crocodile Dundee 2 '88
Pass the Ammo '88
Target: Favorite Son '87
Crocodile Dundee '86

Jeroen Krabbe (1944-)
Jesus '00
An Ideal Husband '99
Dangerous Beauty '98
Ever After: A Cinderella Story '98
Left Luggage '98
Only Love '98
The Odyssey '97
Business for Pleasure '96
The Disappearance of Garcia Lorca '96
Farinelli '94
Immortal Beloved '94
For a Lost Soldier '93
The Fugitive '93
King of the Hill '93
Stalin '92
Kafka '91
The Prince of Tides '91
Robin Hood '91
Till There Was You '91
The Punisher '90
Secret Weapon '90
Scandal '89
Crossing Delancey '88
A World Apart '88
Code Name: Dancer '87
The Living Daylights '87
Jumpin' Jack Flash '86
No Mercy '86
Turtle Diary '86
A Flight of Rainbirds '81
The 4th Man '79
Soldier of Orange '78

Jane Krakowski (1966-)
Ice Age '02 (V)
The Flintstones in Viva Rock Vegas '00
Go '99
Dance with Me '98
Stepping Out '91
National Lampoon's Vacation '83
No Big Deal '83

Eric Allen Kramer
The Colony '98
Robin Hood: Men in Tights '93
The Comrades of Summer '92
Quest for the Mighty Sword '90

Grant Kramer
Addicted to Murder 3: Bloodlust '99
New Year's Evil '78

Jeffrey Kramer (1952-)
Halloween 2: The Nightmare Isn't Over! '81
Jaws 2 '78
Hollywood Boulevard '76

Stephanie Kramer
Twin Sisters '91
Terror at London Bridge '85
The Man with Two Brains '83

Robert Krantz
Winners Take All '87
Paradise Motel '84

Brian Krause (1972-)
Return to Cabin by the Lake '01
Within the Rock '96
Breaking Free '95
Naked Souls '95
The Liar's Club '93
Sleepwalkers '92
December '91
Return to the Blue Lagoon '91
An American Summer '90

Werner Krauss (1884-1959)
Jud Suess '40
Joyless Street '25
Secrets of a Soul '25
Variety '25
Waxworks '24
Othello '22
Shattered '21
The Cabinet of Dr. Caligari '19

Hans Kremer
Mendel '98
The Promise '94

Connie Kreski
Black Bird '75
The Trackers '71

Thomas Kretschmann (1962-)
Blade II '02
U-571 '00
Esther '98
Prince Valiant '97
Total Reality '97
The Stendahl Syndrome '95
Stalingrad '94

Kurt Kreuger (1917-)
Unfaithfully Yours '48
Dark Corner '46
Mademoiselle Fifi '44
Sahara '43

Elisabeth (Lisa) Kreuzer (1945-)
Birgitt Haas Must Be Killed '83
A Man Like Eva '83
Basileus Quartet '82
The American Friend '77
Kings of the Road—In the Course of Time '76
Alice in the Cities '74

David Kriegel
Speed '94
Alive '93
Quest of the Delta Knights '93

Anneline Kriel
Reason to Die '90
Kill and Kill Again '81

Alice Krige (1955-)
Dinotopia '02
Attila '01
The Little Vampire '00
In the Company of Spies '99
Molokai: The Story of Father Damien '99
Habitat '97
The Twilight of the Ice Nymphs '97
Hidden in America '96
Star Trek: First Contact '96
Donor Unknown '95
Institue Benjamenta or This Dream People Call Human Life '95
Joseph '95
Sharpe's Honour '94
Ladykiller '92
Sleepwalkers '92
Iran: Days of Crisis '91
Code Name: Chaos '90
Max and Helen '90
See You in the Morning '89
Haunted Summer '88
Barfly '87
King David '85
Chariots of Fire '81
Ghost Story '81
A Tale of Two Cities '80

Sylvia Kristel (1952-)
Beauty School '93
Hot Blood '89
Dracula's Widow '88
Casanova '87
Game of Seduction '86
The Big Bet '85
Mata Hari '85
Red Heat '85
Emmanuelle 4 '84
Mysteries '84
Private School '83
Lady Chatterley's Lover '81
Private Lessons '81
The Nude Bomb '80
Tigers in Lipstick '80

The Concorde: Airport '79 '79
The Fifth Musketeer '79
Goodbye Emmanuelle '79
Emmanuelle, the Joys of a Woman '76
Because of the Cats '74
Emmanuelle '74

Marta Kristen (1945-)
Lost in Space '98
Body Count '97
Gemini Affair '80s
Battle Beyond the Stars '80
Terminal Island '73
Beach Blanket Bingo '65
Savage Sam '63

Jason Kristofer
The Crossing Guard '94
Spy Trap '92

Romano Kristoff
Slash '87
Warbus '85

Kris Kristofferson (1936-)
Blade II '02
Chelsea Walls '01
Planet of the Apes '01
Limbo '99
Molokai: The Story of Father Damien '99
Blade '98
Dance with Me '98
Outlaw Justice '98
Payback '98
A Soldier's Daughter Never Cries '98
Tom Clancy's Netforce '98
Fire Down Below '97
Girls' Night '97
Two for Texas '97
Lone Star '95
Pharoah's Army '95
The Road Home '95
Sodbusters '94
Cheatin' Hearts '93
Knights '93
No Place to Hide '93
Christmas in Connecticut '92
Another Pair of Aces: Three of a Kind '91
Miracle in the Wilderness '91
Original Intent '91
Night of the Cyclone '90
Pair of Aces '90
Millennium '89
Welcome Home '89
Big Top Pee-wee '88
The Tracker '88
Last Days of Frank & Jesse James '86
Stagecoach '86
Trouble in Mind '86
Flashpoint '84
Songwriter '84
Act of Passion: The Lost Honor of Kathryn Beck '83
Heaven's Gate '81
Rollover '81
Freedom Road '79
Convoy '78
Semi-Tough '77
The Sailor Who Fell from Grace with the Sea '76
A Star Is Born '76
Alice Doesn't Live Here Anymore '74
Bring Me the Head of Alfredo Garcia '74
Blume in Love '73
Pat Garrett & Billy the Kid '73
The Last Movie '71

Berry Kroeger (1912-91)
Demon Seed '77
The Incredible Two-Headed Transplant '71
Blood Alley '55
Yellowneck '55
Guilty of Treason '50
Gun Crazy '49

Gary Kroeger (1957-)
Secret Ingredient '92
Archie: Return to Riverdale '90
A Man Called Sarge '90

Joachim Krol
The Princess and the Warrior '00
Run Lola Run '98
Maybe ... Maybe Not '94

Josef Kroner (1924-98)
Another Way '82
The Shop on Main Street '65

Margareta Krook (1925-2001)
Pay Off '89
The Adventures of Picasso '80
Persona '66

Chad Krowchuk
Poltergeist: The Legacy '96
Heck's Way Home '95

Manfred Krug (1937-)
Trace of Stones '66
Minna von Barnhelm or The Soldier's Fortune '62
On the Sunny Side '62
Five Cartridges '60

Alma Kruger (1868-1960)
Forever Amber '47
A Scandal in Paris '46
The Great Waltz '38
100 Men and a Girl '37
Craig's Wife '36
These Three '36

Christiane Kruger
Le Dernier Combat '84
Little Mother '71

Hardy Kruger (1928-)
The Inside Man '84
Wrong Is Right '82
Blue Fin '78
Wild Geese '78
A Bridge Too Far '77
Barry Lyndon '75
Paper Tiger '74
What the Peeper Saw '72
Battle of Neretva '69
Red Tent '69
The Secret of Santa Vittoria '69
The Flight of the Phoenix '65
Hatari! '62
Sundays & Cybele '62
Bachelor of Hearts '58
One That Got Away '57
Liana, Jungle Goddess '56

Otto Kruger (1885-1974)
The Wonderful World of the Brothers Grimm '62
Cash McCall '60
The Young Philadelphians '59
High Noon '52
Jungle Captive '45
The Woman Who Came Back '45
Wonder Man '45
Cover Girl '44
Murder, My Sweet '44
Corregidor '43
Hitler's Children '43
Saboteur '42
Another Thin Man '39
Black Eyes '39
Housemaster '38
I Am the Law '38
Thanks for the Memory '38
They Won't Forget '37
Dracula's Daughter '36
Chained '34
Treasure Island '34
The Prizefighter and the Lady '33

David Krumholtz (1978-)
The Mexican '01
Sidewalks of New York '01
Liberty Heights '99
Ten Things I Hate about You '99
Slums of Beverly Hills '98
The Ice Storm '97
The Santa Clause '94
Addams Family Values '93
Life with Mikey '93

Gene Krupa (1909-73)
The Benny Goodman Story '55
The Glenn Miller Story '54
Ball of Fire '41
Rhythm Romance '39

Olek Krupa
Behind Enemy Lines '01
Thirteen Days '00
Blue Streak '99
Home Alone 3 '97
Kicked in the Head '97
Mac '93
Ivory Hunters '90

Jack Kruschen (1922-2002)
Cheaters '84
Money to Burn '83
Mountain Man '77
Satan's Cheerleaders '77
Freebie & the Bean '74
Dear Brigitte '65
McLintock! '63
Cape Fear '61
Follow That Dream '61
The Ladies' Man '61
Lover Come Back '61
The Apartment '60
The Last Voyage '60
Where the Boys Are '60
The Angry Red Planet '59
Reform School Girl '57
Soldier of Fortune '55
Abbott and Costello Go to Mars '53
The War of the Worlds '53
Meet Danny Wilson '52

Boris Krutonog
Thirteen Days '00
My Antonia '94

Khalid Ksouri
Halfmoon '95
Man of Ashes '86

Alex Kubik
Trapped Alive '93
Carnal Crimes '91

Akira Kubo (1926-)
Yog, Monster from Space '71
Destroy All Monsters '68
Godzilla vs. Monster Zero '68
Son of Godzilla '66
Attack of the Mushroom People '63
Snow Country '57
Throne of Blood '57

Youki Kudoh (1971-)
Snow Falling on Cedars '99
Heaven's Burning '97
Picture Bride '94
Mystery Train '89

Lisa Kudrow (1963-)
All Over the Guy '01
Dr. Dolittle 2 '01 (V)
Lucky Numbers '00
Hanging Up '99
Analyze This '98
The Opposite of Sex '98
Clockwatchers '97
Romy and Michele's High School Reunion '97
Mother '96

Yoshiko Kuga
The Cruel Story of Youth '60
Shin Heike Monogatari '55
The Idiot '51

Vladimir Kulich
The 13th Warrior '99
Firestorm '97

Jarl Kulle (1927-97)
Babette's Feast '87
Fanny and Alexander '83
The Devil's Eye '60
Smiles of a Summer Night '55
Secrets of Women '52

Nancy Kulp (1921-91)
The Aristocats '70 (V)
Strange Bedfellows '65
The Patsy '64
Who's Minding the Store? '63
The Three Faces of Eve '57
Forever Darling '56

William J. Kulzer
Lust for Freedom '87
Shadows Run Black '84

Pravesh Kumar
Tales of the Kama Sutra: The Perfumed Garden '98
Brothers in Trouble '95

Magda Kun
Dead of Night '45
Meet Sexton Blake '44

Mila Kunis
American Psycho 2: All American Girl '02
Get Over It! '01

William Kunstler
Malcolm X '92
The Doors '91

Simon Kunz
The Affair of the Necklace '01
The Parent Trap '98

Yasuka Kurata
Fist of Legend '94
Rage of Wind '82

Alwyn Kurts (1915-2000)
Road to Nhill '97
The Efficiency Expert '92
Earthling '80
Tim '79

Swoosie Kurtz (1944-)
Bubble Boy '01
Get Over It! '01
White River '99
Cruel Intentions '98
My Own Country '98
Outside Ozona '98
Armistead Maupin's More Tales of the City '97
Citizen Ruth '96
Liar Liar '96
One Christmas '95
Storybook '95
Reality Bites '94
And the Band Played On '93
The Positively True Adventures of the Alleged Texas Cheerleader-Murdering Mom '93
A Shock to the System '90
Stanley and Iris '90
The Image '89
Bright Lights, Big City '88
Dangerous Liaisons '88
Vice Versa '88
Baja Oklahoma '87
True Stories '86
Wildcats '86
A Time to Live '85
Against All Odds '84
The World According to Garp '82
Marriage Is Alive and Well '80
Walking Through the Fire '80
Slap Shot '77

Katy Kurtzman (1965-)
Child of Glass '78
Long Journey Back '78
When Every Day Was the Fourth of July '78

Clyde Kusatsu (1948-)
American Tragedy '00
Paradise Road '97
Top Dog '95
Dream Lover '93
Made in America '93
Dr. Strange '78
Go Tell the Spartans '78
The Choirboys '77

Richard Kuss
Warlock '91
The Deer Hunter '78

Dylan Kussman
Way of the Gun '00
Journey of Honor '91
Wild Hearts Can't Be Broken '91
Dead Poets Society '89

Emir Kusturica (1954-)
The Widow of Saint-Pierre '00
Underground '95

Ashton Kutcher (1978-)
Texas Rangers '01
Down to You '00
Dude, Where's My Car? '00

Miyuki Kuwano
The Cruel Story of Youth '60
Equinox Flower '58

Alexander Kuznitsov
Agent Red '00
The Ice Runner '93

Mimi Kuzyk
Lost and Delirious '01
The Golden Spiders: A Nero Wolfe Mystery '00
Thrill Seekers '99
The Defenders: Payback '97
Family of Cops 2: Breach of Faith '97
Dead Silence '96
Malicious '95
The Kiss '88
Family Sins '87
Striker's Mountain '87
Blind Justice '86
Miles to Go '86

Nancy Kwan (1939-)
Dragon: The Bruce Lee Story '93
Night Children '89
Stickfighter '89
Blade in Hong Kong '85
Fowl Play '83
Walking the Edge '83
Night Creature '79
Project: Kill! '77
The Deadly and the Beautiful '73
The McMasters '70
The Wrecking Crew '68
The Corrupt Ones '67
Arrivederci, Baby! '66
Lt. Robin Crusoe, U.S.N. '66
Flower Drum Song '61
The World of Suzie Wong '60

Rosamund Kwan
Once Upon a Time in China III '93
Once Upon a Time in China II '92
Once Upon a Time in China '91
Operation Condor 2: The Armour of the Gods '86

Philip Kwok
The Phantom Lover '95
Hard-Boiled '92

Burt Kwouk (1930-)
Kiss of the Dragon '01
Bullet to Beijing '95
Son of the Pink Panther '93
Empire of the Sun '87
Plenty '85
Trail of the Pink Panther '82
Revenge of the Pink Panther '78
The Pink Panther Strikes Again '76

Sam Kydd (1917-82)
Eye of the Needle '81
Too Late the Hero '70
Island of Terror '66
The House in Marsh Road '60

David Kyle (1951-)
L.A. Gangs Rising '89
Halloween '78
Cruisin' High '75

Machiko Kyo (1924-)
Face of Another '66
Odd Obsession '60
Drifting Weeds '59
Street of Shame '56
The Teahouse of the August Moon '56
Princess Yang Kwei Fei '55
Gate of Hell '54
Ugetsu '53
Rashomon '51

Kay Kyser (1897-1995)
Around the World '43
Stage Door Canteen '43
Thousands Cheer '43
Playmates '41
You'll Find Out '40

Jake La Motta (1921-)
Mob War '88
Hangmen '87
The Hustler '61

Alison La Placa (1959-)
Madhouse '90
Voyage of the Rock Aliens '87
Fletch '85

Rosemary La Planche (1923-79)
Federal Agents vs. Underworld, Inc. '49
The Devil Bat's Daughter '46
Strangler of the Swamp '46

Laura La Plante (1904-96)
Hold Your Man '33
Lonely Wives '31
The Cat and the Canary '27
Skinner's Dress Suit '26
Smouldering Fires '25

Rod La Rocque (1898-1969)
Meet John Doe '41
Beyond Tomorrow '40
Dr. Christian Meets the Women '40
The Hunchback of Notre Dame '39
International Crime '37
The Shadow Strikes '37
Our Modern Maidens '29
Show People '28
Stand and Deliver '28
Braveheart '25
Captain Swagger '25
The Coming of Amos '25
The Ten Commandments '23

Rita La Roy (-1993)
The Mandarin Mystery '37
Sin Takes a Holiday '30

Eriq La Salle (1962-)
One Hour Photo '02
Rebound: The Legend of Earl "The Goat" Manigault '96
Color of Night '94
DROP Squad '94
Jacob's Ladder '90
Coming to America '88
Cut and Run '85

Barbara Laage
Bed and Board '70
Therese & Isabelle '67
The Respectful Prostitute '52

Samuel Labarthe
The Green House '96
The Accompanist '93

Patti LaBelle (1944-)
Fire and Rain '89
Sing '89
Unnatural Causes '86
A Soldier's Story '84

Halina Labonarska
A Woman and a Woman '80
Provincial Actors '79

Matthew Laborteaux (1966-)
Shattered Spirits '91
Deadly Friend '86
Aliens Are Coming '80
A Woman under the Influence '74

Patrick Laborteaux (1965-)
JAG '95
3 Ninjas '92

Heathers '89
Prince of Bel Air '87

Elina Labourdette
Lola '61
The Ladies of the Bois de Bologne '44

Dominique Labourier
Jonah Who Will Be 25 in the Year 2000 '76
Celine and Julie Go Boating '74

Catherine Lacey (1904-79)
The Private Life of Sherlock Holmes '70
The Servant '63
Pink String and Sealing Wax '45
Cottage to Let '41
The Lady Vanishes '38

Ingrid Lacey
In Love and War '96
Funnyman '94
A Woman's Guide to Adultery '93

Margaret Lacey
Diamonds Are Forever '71
Seance on a Wet Afternoon '64

Ronald Lacey (1935-91)
Landslide '92
Jailbird Rock '88
The Lone Runner '88
Into the Darkness '86
Flesh and Blood '85
The Adventures of Buckaroo Banzai Across the Eighth Dimension '84
Making the Grade '84
The Hound of the Baskervilles '83
Sahara '83
Firefox '82
Raiders of the Lost Ark '81
Nijinsky '80
Next Victim '74
Crucible of Terror '72
Disciple of Death '72
The Fearless Vampire Killers '67

Stephen Lack
All the Vermeers in New York '91
Dead Ringers '88
Perfect Strangers '84
Scanners '81
Fatal Attraction '80

Frank Lackteen (1894-1968)
The Sea Wolf '41
Red Barry '38
Rustler's Roundup '33
The Pony Express '25

Andre Lacombe
Dr. Petiot '90
The Bear '89

Ghalia Lacroix
For Ever Mozart '96
The Silences of the Palace '94

Alan Ladd (1913-64)
The Carpetbaggers '64
Duel of Champions '61
All the Young Men '60
The Badlanders '58
Deep Six '58
Proud Rebel '58
Hell on Frisco Bay '55
The McConnell Story '55
Drum Beat '54
Botany Bay '53
Shane '53
Branded '50
The Great Gatsby '49
My Favorite Brunette '47
The Blue Dahlia '46
O.S.S. '46
Two Years before the Mast '46
China '43
The Glass Key '42
Joan of Paris '42
Star Spangled Rhythm '42
This Gun for Hire '42
The Black Cat '41
Citizen Kane '41
Gangs, Inc. '41
They Met in Bombay '41
Captain Caution '40
Her First Romance '40
The Howards of Virginia '40
Island of Lost Souls '32

Cheryl Ladd (1951-)
A Dog of Flanders '99
Every Mother's Worst Fear '98
Permanent Midnight '98
Dancing with Danger '93
Poison Ivy '92
Danielle Steel's Changes '91
Jekyll and Hyde '90
Lisa '90
Fulfillment '89
Millennium '89
Romance on the Orient Express '89
The Hasty Heart '86
Purple Hearts '84
The Grace Kelly Story '83
Now and Forever '82
The Treasure of Jamaica Reef '74
Satan's School for Girls '73

David Ladd (1947-)
The Treasure of Jamaica Reef '74
Catlow '71
Misty '61
A Dog of Flanders '59

Diane Ladd (1939-)
Forever Together '00
28 Days '00
Primary Colors '98
Family of Cops 2: Breach of Faith '97
James Dean: Live Fast, Die Young '97
Citizen Ruth '96
Mrs. Munck '95
Raging Angels '95
Mother '94
Carnosaur '93
The Cemetery Club '93
Father Hood '93
Hold Me, Thrill Me, Kiss Me '93
Forever: A Ghost of a Love Story '92
A Kiss Before Dying '91
Rambling Rose '91
Code Name: Chaos '90
The Lookalike '90
Wild at Heart '90
National Lampoon's Christmas Vacation '89
Plain Clothes '88
Black Widow '87
I Married a Centerfold '84
The Grace Kelly Story '83
Something Wicked This Way Comes '83
Desperate Lives '82
All Night Long '81
Willa '79
Embryo '76
Alice Doesn't Live Here Anymore '74
Chinatown '74
Rebel Rousers '69
The Wild Angels '66

Jordan Ladd (1975-)
The Specials '00
Never Been Kissed '99
Every Mother's Worst Fear '98
Stand-Ins '97
Nowhere '96
Embrace of the Vampire '95

John Lafayette
White Sands '92
Full Fathom Five '90

Pat Laffan
American Women '00
The Snapper '93

Patricia Laffan
Devil Girl from Mars '54
Quo Vadis '51

Art LaFleur (1944-)
The Replacements '00
The Garbage-Picking, Field Goal-Kicking Philadelphia Phenomenon '98
Hijacking Hollywood '97
Lewis and Clark and George '97
First Kid '96
Man of the House '95
Jack the Bear '93
The Sandlot '93
Forever Young '92
Live! From Death Row '92
Oscar '91
Rampage '87
Trancers '84
Zone Troopers '84
The Hollywood Knights '80

Bernadette LaFont (1938-)
Genealogies of a Crime '97
Son of Gascogne '95
Dingo '90
Waiting for the Moon '87
The Perils of Gwendoline '84
Violette '78
The Mother and the Whore '73
Too Pretty to Be Honest '72
Catch Me a Spy '71
A Very Curious Girl '69
Les Bonnes Femmes '60
Le Beau Serge '58

Roc Lafortune
The List '99
The Minion '98
The Boys '97

Marika Lagercrantz
All Things Fair '95
Dreaming of Rita '94

Caroline Lagerfelt
Glam '97
Home at Last '88
Iron Eagle '86

Valerie Lagrange (1942-)
Cat and Mouse '78
Weekend '67
A Man and a Woman '66
Morgan the Pirate '60

Bert Lahr (1895-1967)
The Night They Raided Minsky's '69
Rose Marie '54
Ship Ahoy '42
Sing Your Worries Away '42
The Wizard of Oz '39
Just Around the Corner '38

Christine Lahti (1950-)
Trial by Media '00
Hope '97
Subway Stories '97
A Weekend in the Country '96
Pie in the Sky '95
Hideaway '94
The Fear Inside '92
The Good Fight '92
Leaving Normal '92
Crazy from the Heart '91
The Doctor '91
Funny About Love '90
Gross Anatomy '89
Miss Firecracker '89
Running on Empty '88
Housekeeping '87
Stacking '87
Just Between Friends '86
Single Bars, Single Women '84
Swing Shift '84
The Executioner's Song '82
Whose Life Is It Anyway? '81
The Henderson Monster '80
And Justice for All '79

Leon Lai
Fallen Angels '95
Wicked City '92

Leah Lail (1966-)
Late Last Night '99
Something About Sex '98
Body Waves '92

Cleo Laine
The Last of the Blonde Bombshells '00
On the Town '91

Jenny Laird (1917-2001)
Village of the Damned '60
Black Narcissus '47
Beware of Pity '46

Alan Lake
Con Man '92
Don't Open Till Christmas '84

Alice Lake
Broken Hearts of Broadway '23
Playing Dead '15

Arthur Lake (1905-87)
Blondie Hits the Jackpot '49
Blondie Knows Best '46
Footlight Glamour '43
It's a Great Life '43
Blondie for Victory '42
Blondie Goes Latin '42
Blondie Goes to College '42
Blondie's Blessed Event '42
Blondie in Society '41
Blondie Has Trouble '40
Blondie On a Budget '40
Blondie Plays Cupid '40
Blondie Brings Up Baby '39
Blondie Meets the Boss '39
Blondie Takes a Vacation '39
Blondie '38
Exiled to Shanghai '37
23 1/2 Hours Leave '37
The Silver Streak '34
Skinner's Dress Suit '26

Don Lake
Best in Show '00
Hostage for a Day '94
Sodbusters '94
Big Town '87

Florence Lake (1904-80)
Savage Intruder '68
Going to Town '44
Crash Dive '43
Next Time I Marry '38
Quality Street '37
Romance '30

Ricki Lake (1968-)
Cecil B. Demented '00
Murder She Purred: A Mrs. Murphy Mystery '98
Mrs. Winterbourne '96
Cabin Boy '94
Serial Mom '94
Based on an Untrue Story '93
Inside Monkey Zetterland '93
Skinner '93
Where the Day Takes You '92
The Chase '91
Cry-Baby '90
Last Exit to Brooklyn '90
Babycakes '89
Cookie '89
Hairspray '88
Working Girl '88

Veronica Lake (1919-73)
Flesh Feast '69
Ramrod '47
The Blue Dahlia '46
So Proudly We Hail '43
The Glass Key '42
I Married a Witch '42
Star Spangled Rhythm '42
This Gun for Hire '42
Sullivan's Travels '41

Christine Lakin
Mystery Kids '99
Boltneck '98

Lorena Lalazquez (1937-)
Doctor of Doom '62
Samson vs. the Vampire Women '61
Wrestling Women vs. the Aztec Mummy '59

James Lally
Critical Care '97
Working Girl '88

Michael Lally
The Secret of Roan Inish '94
Cool World '92
The Nesting '80

Hedy Lamarr (1913-2000)
The Love of Three Queens '54
Copper Canyon '50
Samson and Delilah '50
Dishonored Lady '47
The Strange Woman '46
Experiment Perilous '45
Tortilla Flat '42
White Cargo '42
Ziegfeld Girl '41
Boom Town '40
Comrade X '40
Algiers '38
Ecstasy '33

Phil LaMarr
Free Enterprise '98
Pulp Fiction '94

Jean LaMarre
Deadly Voyage '96
Fresh '94
Malcolm X '92

Fernando Lamas (1915-82)
The Cheap Detective '78
Murder on Flight 502 '75
Powder Keg '70
100 Rifles '69
Violent Ones '68
Rose Marie '54
Dangerous When Wet '53
The Girl Who Had Everything '53
The Merry Widow '52
Rich, Young and Pretty '51

Lorenzo Lamas (1958-)
The Muse '99
Undercurrent '99
The Debt '98
Mask of Death '97
The Rage '96
Blood for Blood '95
Gladiator Cop: The Swordsman 2 '95
Terminal Justice: Cybertech P.D. '95
Bad Blood '94
C.I.A. 2: Target Alexa '94
Bounty Tracker '93
Final Round '93
C.I.A.: Code Name Alexa '92
SnakeEater 3: His Law '92
The Swordsman '92
Final Impact '91
Killing Streets '91
Night of the Warrior '91
SnakeEater '89
SnakeEater 2: The Drug Buster '89
Body Rock '84
Take Down '79
Grease '78

Debra Lamb (1963-)
Evil Spirits '91
The Invisible Maniac '90
Rock & the Money-Hungry Party Girls '89
Stripped to Kill II: Live Girls '89
Beverly Hills Vamp '88
B.O.R.N. '88

Larry Lamb
Essex Boys '99
Buster '88
Shadey '87
Transmutations '85

Anne Louise Lambert (1956-)
Napoleon '96 (V)
Lilian's Story '95
Great Expectations: The Untold Story '87
The Draughtsman's Contract '82
Picnic at Hanging Rock '75

Christopher Lambert (1959-)
Druids '01
Highlander: Endgame '00
Fortress 2: Re-Entry '99
Resurrection '99
Beowulf '98
Mean Guns '97
Adrenalin: Fear the Rush '96
North Star '96
Mortal Kombat 1: The Movie '95
The Road Killers '95
Highlander: The Final Dimension '94
The Hunted '94
Fortress '93
Gunmen '93
Knight Moves '93
Highlander: The Gathering '92
Highlander 2: The Quickening '91
Priceless Beauty '90
Why Me? '90
To Kill a Priest '89
The Sicilian '87
Highlander '86
Love Songs '85
Subway '85
Greystoke: The Legend of Tarzan, Lord of the Apes '84

Jack Lambert (1899-1976)
Three Cases of Murder '55
Hue and Cry '47
The Ghost Goes West '36

Jack Lambert (1920-)
Machine Gun Kelly '58
Kiss Me Deadly '55
Montana Belle '52
North of the Great Divide '50
Stars in My Crown '50
Dick Tracy's Dilemma '47

Jane Lambert
Crazy Fat Ethel II '85
The Fury '78

Mark Lambert
Durango '99
Cracker: Brotherly Love '95

Heath Lamberts
Tom and Huck '95
Ordinary Magic '93
To Kill a Clown '72

Ellie Lambetti
A Matter of Dignity '57
Girl in Black '56

Vassili Lambrinos
Last Rites '88
That Man Bolt '73

Anne Lambton
American History X '98
Love Is the Devil '98

Karen Lamm
Ants '77
The Hatfields & the McCoys '75

Duncan Lamont (1918-78)
The Creeping Flesh '72
Frankenstein Created Woman '66
The Evil of Frankenstein '64
Murder at the Gallop '63
The Golden Coach '52

Marten Lamont
Redwood Forest Trail '50
Federal Operator 99 '45
Son of Fury '42
International Lady '41

Molly Lamont (1910-2001)
The Devil Bat's Daughter '46
Somewhere I'll Find You '42
The Awful Truth '37

Pascal Lamorisse
Voyage en Balloon '59
The Red Balloon '56

John Lamotta
Showdown '94

We're Talkin' Serious Money '92
One More Chance '90
Revenge of the Ninja '83

Dorothy Lamour (1914-96)
Creepshow 2 '87
The Love Goddesses '65
Pajama Party '64
Donovan's Reef '63
The Road to Hong Kong '62
The Road to Bali '53
The Greatest Show on Earth '52
Here Comes the Groom '51
On Our Merry Way '48
My Favorite Brunette '47
The Road to Rio '47
The Road to Utopia '46
They Got Me Covered '43
The Road to Morocco '42
Star Spangled Rhythm '42
Caught in the Draft '41
The Road to Zanzibar '41
Johnny Apollo '40
The Road to Singapore '40
The Big Broadcast of 1938 '38
Spawn of the North '38
The Hurricane '37
Swing High, Swing Low '37
Dixiana '30

Jutta Lampe
The Possessed '88
Marianne and Juliane '82
Sisters, Or the Balance of Happiness '79

Zohra Lampert (1937-)
Alan & Naomi '92
Stanley and Iris '90
American Blue Note '89
Isle of Secret Passion '85
Izzy & Moe '85
Alphabet City '84
Teachers '84
Opening Night '77
The Connection '73
Let's Scare Jessica to Death '71
Splendor in the Grass '61

Chus (Maria Jesus) Lampreave (1930-)
The Flower of My Secret '95
I'm the One You're Looking For '88
Matador '86
What Have I Done to Deserve This? '85

Gunter Lamprecht
Red Kiss '85
Berlin Alexanderplatz '80

Ann Lancaster
The Railway Children '70
Hot Millions '68

Burt Lancaster (1913-94)
Separate but Equal '91
The Jeweller's Shop '90
The Phantom of the Opera '90
Voyage of Terror: The Achille Lauro Affair '90
Field of Dreams '89
Rocket Gibraltar '88
Control '87
Barnum '86
On Wings of Eagles '86
Tough Guys '86
Little Treasure '85
Local Hero '83
The Osterman Weekend '83
Atlantic City '81
Zulu Dawn '79
Go Tell the Spartans '78
The Island of Dr. Moreau '77
Twilight's Last Gleaming '77
America at the Movies '76
Buffalo Bill & the Indians '76
The Cassandra Crossing '76
Moses '76
1900 '76
Conversation Piece '75
Executive Action '73
Scorpio '73
Ulzana's Raid '72
Lawman '71
Valdez Is Coming '71
Airport '70
The Scalphunters '68
The Swimmer '68
The Professionals '66
The Hallelujah Trail '65
The Train '65
Seven Days in May '64
A Child Is Waiting '63
The List of Adrian Messenger '63
Birdman of Alcatraz '62
Judgment at Nuremberg '61
Elmer Gantry '60
The Unforgiven '60
The Devil's Disciple '59
Run Silent, Run Deep '58
Separate Tables '58
Gunfight at the O.K. Corral '57
Sweet Smell of Success '57
The Rainmaker '56
Trapeze '56
The Kentuckian '55
The Rose Tattoo '55
Apache '54
From Here to Eternity '53
His Majesty O'Keefe '53
Vera Cruz '53
Come Back, Little Sheba '52
Crimson Pirate '52
Jim Thorpe: All American '51
Vengeance Valley '51
The Flame & the Arrow '50
All My Sons '48
Criss Cross '48
Sorry, Wrong Number '48
The Killers '46

James Lancaster
Leprechaun 2 '94
Gettysburg '93

Stuart Lancaster (1920-2000)
Beneath the Valley of the Ultra-Vixens '79
Mistress of the Apes '79
Mantis in Lace '68
Born Losers '67
Faster, Pussycat! Kill! Kill! '65

Karl Lanchbury
Vampyres '74
The House that Vanished '73

Elsa Lanchester (1902-86)
Die Laughing '80
Murder by Death '76
Arnold '73
Terror in the Wax Museum '73
Willard '71
My Dog, the Thief '69
Blackbeard's Ghost '67
Easy Come, Easy Go '67
That Darn Cat '65
Pajama Party '64
Bell, Book and Candle '58
Witness for the Prosecution '57
The Glass Slipper '55
Androcles and the Lion '52
Come to the Stable '49
The Inspector General '49
The Secret Garden '49
The Big Clock '48
The Bishop's Wife '47
Northwest Outpost '47
The Razor's Edge '46
The Spiral Staircase '46
Forever and a Day '43
Lassie, Come Home '43
Son of Fury '42
Tales of Manhattan '42
Beachcomber '38
The Ghost Goes West '36
Rembrandt '36
The Bride of Frankenstein '35
David Copperfield '35
Naughty Marietta '35
The Private Life of Henry VIII '33

Micheline Lanctot
Blood Relatives '77
The Apprenticeship of Duddy Kravitz '74

Geoffrey Land
Hospital of Terror '78
Against a Crooked Sky '75
The Female Bunch '69

Paul Land
Spring Break '83
Idolmaker '80

Rodolfo Landa
Neutron vs. the Amazing Dr. Caronte '61
The Criminal Life of Archibaldo de la Cruz '55

David Landau (1878-1935)
Gabriel Over the White House '33
False Faces '32
Horse Feathers '32
The Purchase Price '32
Street Scene '31

Juliet Landau (1965-)
Ravager '97
Theodore Rex '95
Ed Wood '94
Direct Hit '93
Neon City '91

Martin Landau (1931-)
The Majestic '01
Ready to Rumble '00
Bonanno: A Godfather's Story '99
EDtv '99
Sleepy Hollow '99
Rounders '98
The X-Files '98
B.A.P.'s '97
The Adventures of Pinocchio '96
City Hall '95
The Color of Evening '95
Joseph '95
Ed Wood '94
Eye of the Stranger '93
Intersection '93
No Place to Hide '93
Sliver '93
12:01 '93
Legacy of Lies '92
Mistress '91
Firehead '90
Max and Helen '90
Real Bullets '90
By Dawn's Early Light '89
Crimes & Misdemeanors '89
The Neon Empire '89
Paint It Black '89
Tucker: The Man and His Dream '88
Cyclone '87
Death Blow '87
Empire State '87
Run If You Can '87
Sweet Revenge '87
Kung Fu: The Movie '86
Access Code '84
The Being '83
Alone in the Dark '82
The Fall of the House of Usher '80
The Last Word '80
The Return '80
Meteor '79
Strange Shadows in an Empty Room '76
Destination Moonbase Alpha '75
A Town Called Hell '72
They Call Me Mr. Tibbs! '70
The Hallelujah Trail '65
Cleopatra '63
The Gazebo '59
North by Northwest '59
Pork Chop Hill '59

Dinsdale Landen (1931-)
Catherine Cookson's The Wingless Bird '97
Morons from Outer Space '85
Anatomy of Terror '74
Digby, the Biggest Dog in the World '73

David Lander (1947-)
Scary Movie '00
Ava's Magical Adventure '94
Tom and Jerry: The Movie '93 (V)
Betrayal of the Dove '92
A League of Their Own '92
Steel and Lace '90
Funland '89
The Man with One Red Shoe '85
Used Cars '80
1941 '79
The Tell-Tale Heart '62

Audrey Landers (1959-)
California Casanova '89
Ghost Writer '89
Getting Even '86
A Chorus Line '85
Deadly Twins '85
Underground Aces '80
1941 '79
Tennessee Stallion '78

Harry Landers (1921-)
The Gallant Hours '60
The Indian Fighter '55
Phantom from Space '53
The C-Man '49

Judy Landers (1961-)
Expert Weapon '93
The Divine Enforcer '91
Club Fed '90
Ghost Writer '89
Dr. Alien '88
Armed and Dangerous '86
Stewardess School '86
Deadly Twins '85
Doin' Time '85
Hellhole '85
The Black Marble '79
Tennessee Stallion '78
The Yum-Yum Girls '78

Michael Landes (1972-)
Rescuers: Stories of Courage "Two Women" '97
Dream for an Insomniac '96
An American Summer '90

Steve Landesberg (1945-)
The Souler Opposite '97
The Crazysitter '94
Sodbusters '94
Mission of the Shark '91
Final Notice '89
Leader of the Band '87
Blade '72

Clayton Landey
Assault of the Killer Bimbos '88
First & Ten: The Team Scores Again '85

Janet Landgard
Land Raiders '69
The Swimmer '68

Gudrun Landgrebe (1950-)
Advertising Rules! '01
The Berlin Affair '85
Colonel Redl '84
A Woman in Flames '84

Karl Landgren
The Black Cobra '87
Urban Warriors '75

Sonny Landham (1941-)
Best of the Best 2 '93
Taxi Dancers '93
Three Days to a Kill '91
Lock Up '89
Predator '87
The Dirty Dozen: The Next Mission '85
Fleshburn '84
48 Hrs. '82

Elissa Landi (1904-48)
Corregidor '43
After the Thin Man '36
The Count of Monte Cristo '34
The Sign of the Cross '33

Marla Landi
First Man into Space '59
Across the Bridge '57

Sal Landi
Xtro 3: Watch the Skies '95
Back to Back '90
Savage Streets '83

D.W. Landingham
Karate Cop '93
Omega Cop '90

Carole Landis (1919-48)
Out of the Blue '47
A Scandal in Paris '46
Having Wonderful Crime '45
Wintertime '43
Orchestra Wives '42
Dance Hall '41
I Wake Up Screaming '41
Moon over Miami '41
Road Show '41
Topper Returns '41
One Million B.C. '40
Cowboys from Texas '39
Three Texas Steers '39
Daredevils of the Red Circle '38

Cullen Landis (1895-1975)
The Broken Mask '28
Soul of the Beast '23

Jessie Royce Landis (1904-72)
Airport '70
Gidget Goes to Rome '63
Bon Voyage! '62
Boys' Night Out '62
Goodbye Again '61
North by Northwest '59
My Man Godfrey '57
The Swan '56
To Catch a Thief '55
It Happens Every Spring '49

John Landis (1950-)
Diamonds '99
Freeway 2: Confessions of a Trickbaby '99
Laws of Deception '97
Silence of the Hams '93
Sleepwalkers '92
Venice, Venice '92
Body Chemistry 2: Voice of a Stranger '91
Darkman '90
Spontaneous Combustion '89
The Muppets Take Manhattan '84
The Blues Brothers '80
1941 '79
Death Race 2000 '75
Battle for the Planet of the Apes '73
Schlock '73

Margaret Landis
The Confession '20
Amarilly of Clothesline Alley '18

Monte Landis
Yellowbeard '83
Candy Stripe Nurses '74
Young Frankenstein '74
Targets '68
The Mouse That Roared '59

Nina Landis
Komodo '99
Rikky and Pete '88

Joe Lando
No Code of Conduct '98
Any Place But Home '97
Seeds of Doubt '96

Avice Landon
The Blood on Satan's Claw '71
The Leather Boys '63

Hal Landon, Jr.
Bill & Ted's Bogus Journey '91
Eraserhead '78

Laurene Landon (1958-)
The Ambulance '90
Maniac Cop 2 '90
Wicked Stepmother '89
Maniac Cop '88
It's Alive 3: Island of the Alive '87
America 3000 '86
Hundra '85
Yellow Hair & the Fortress of Gold '84
I, the Jury '82

Michael Landon (1936-91)
Sam's Son '84
The Loneliest Runner '76
Little House on the Prairie '74
Ride the Wind '66
The Errand Boy '61
Legend of Tom Dooley '59
God's Little Acre '58
High School Confidential '58
Fight for the Title '57
I Was a Teenage Werewolf '57

Karen Landry
Roadracers '94
Heartbreak Hotel '88
Patti Rocks '88
The Personals '83

Tamara Landry
Bikini Med School '98
Bikini House Calls '96
Beach Babes from Beyond Infinity '93

David Landsberg
Dutch Treat '86
Detective School Dropouts '85

Valerie Landsburg
The Triangle Factory Fire Scandal '79
Thank God It's Friday '78

Abbe Lane (1932-)
Twilight Zone: The Movie '83
Americano '55
Ride Clear of Diablo '54

Allan "Rocky" Lane (1904-73)
El Paso Stampede '53
Marshal of Cedar Rock '53
Night Riders of Montana '50
Trail of Robin Hood '50
Bandit King of Texas '49
Oklahoma Badlands '48
Wild Frontier '48
Homesteaders of Paradise Valley '47
Santa Fe Uprising '46
Stagecoach to Denver '46
Vigilantes of Boom Town '46
Silver City Kid '45
The Topeka Terror '45
Perils of the Darkest Jungle '44
Maid's Night Out '38
Night Nurse '31

Charles Lane (1869-1945)
Sadie Thompson '28
Romola '25
The White Sister '23
Dr. Jekyll and Mr. Hyde '20

Charles Lane (1905-)
Acting on Impulse '93
War & Remembrance '88
Date with an Angel '87
Murphy's Romance '85
Strange Invaders '83
Sunset Limousine '83
The Winds of War '83
Strange Behavior '81
Little Dragons '80
Billie '65
But Not for Me '59
The Mating Game '59

Teacher's Pet '58
The Affairs of Dobie Gillis '53
Borderline '50
Riding High '50
Call Northside 777 '48
The Invisible Woman '40
It's a Date '40
Rhythm on the River '40
Mr. Smith Goes to Washington '39
Twentieth Century '34

Charles Lane (1953-)
Posse '93
True Identity '91

Colin Lane
The Blood Oranges '97
Broken Harvest '94

Diane Lane (1965-)
Unfaithful '02
The Glass House '01
Hardball '01
The Perfect Storm '00
My Dog Skip '99
The Virginian '99
A Walk on the Moon '99
Grace & Glorie '98
Gunshy '98
Murder at 1600 '97
The Only Thrill '97
Jack '96
Trigger Happy '96
Judge Dredd '95
Oldest Confederate Widow Tells All '95
A Streetcar Named Desire '95
Wild Bill '95
Fallen Angels 1 '93
Indian Summer '93
Knight Moves '93
Chaplin '92
My New Gun '92
Descending Angel '90
Priceless Beauty '90
Vital Signs '90
Lonesome Dove '89
Big Town '87
Lady Beware '87
The Cotton Club '84
Streets of Fire '84
The Outsiders '83
Rumble Fish '83
Miss All-American Beauty '82
Six Pack '82
Child Bride of Short Creek '81
National Lampoon Goes to the Movies '81
Touched by Love '80
A Little Romance '79

Jackie Lane
Venus Against the Son of Hercules '62
Dangerous Youth '58

Kent Lane
Defiant '70
Changes '69

Lola Lane (1909-81)
Deadline at Dawn '46
Buckskin Frontier '43
Lost Canyon '43
Four Daughters '38
Marked Woman '37
Death from a Distance '36
Woman Condemned '33

Lupino Lane (1892-1959)
The Deputy Drummer '35
Isn't Life Wonderful '24

Mike Lane (1931-)
Curse of the Crystal Eye '93
Code Name: Zebra '84
Zebra Force '76
A Name for Evil '70
The Harder They Fall '56

Nathan Lane (1956-)
Stuart Little 2 '02 (V)
Isn't She Great '00
Love's Labour's Lost '00
Titan A.E. '00 (V)
Trixie '00
Stuart Little '99 (V)
At First Sight '98
The Lion King: Simba's Pride '98 (V)
Mouse Hunt '97
The Boys Next Door '96
The Birdcage '95
Jeffrey '95
The Lion King '94 (V)
Life with Mikey '93
Frankie and Johnny '91
He Said, She Said '91
Ironweed '87

Nora Lane
The Outlaw Deputy '35
Western Frontier '35

Priscilla Lane (1917-95)
Arsenic and Old Lace '44
Saboteur '42
Silver Queen '42
The Roaring Twenties '39
Four Daughters '38

Richard Lane (1900-82)
The Jackie Robinson Story '50
Take Me Out to the Ball Game '49
Bullfighters '45
Mr. Winkle Goes to War '44
Air Force '43
Arabian Nights '42
Ride 'Em Cowboy '42
Sunny '41
Day the Bookies Wept '39
It Could Happen to You '39

Rosemary Lane (1914-74)
Harvest Melody '43
Oklahoma Kid '39
Four Daughters '38

Eric Laneuville (1952-)
Love at First Bite '79
Omega Man '71

Judith Lang
Count Yorga, Vampire '70
The Trip '67

June Lang (1915-)
Wee Willie Winkie '37
Captain January '36
Bonnie Scotland '35

Katherine Kelly Lang
The Corporation '96
Till the End of the Night '94

k.d. lang (1961-)
Eye of the Beholder '99
The Last Don '97
Teresa's Tattoo '94
Salmonberries '91

Perry Lang (1959-)
Mortuary Academy '91
Little Vegas '90
Eight Men Out '88
Jailbird Rock '88
Jocks '87
Sahara '83
Spring Break '83
O'Hara's Wife '82
Tag: The Assassination Game '82
Body & Soul '81
Alligator '80
The Big Red One '80
A Rumor of War '80
Girls Next Door '79
1941 '79
Great Ride '78
Greedy Terror '78

Stephen Lang (1952-)
After the Storm '01
The Proposal '00
Trixie '00
Escape: Human Cargo '98
A Town Has Turned to Dust '98
Fire Down Below '97
Niagara, Niagara '97
Gang in Blue '96
An Occasional Hell '96
The Shadow Conspiracy '96
The Amazing Panda Adventure '95
Tall Tale: The Unbelievable Adventures of Pecos Bill '95
Gettysburg '93
Guilty as Sin '93
Tombstone '93
Another You '91
The Hard Way '91
Last Exit to Brooklyn '90
Finish Line '89
Project X '87
Band of the Hand '86
Death of a Salesman '86
Manhunter '86

Glenn Langan (1917-91)
The Amazing Colossal Man '57
Big Chase '54
Hangman's Knot '52
Treasure of Monte Cristo '50
The Snake Pit '48

Harry Langdon (1884-1944)
House of Errors '42
Double Trouble '41
Misbehaving Husbands '41
Mad About Money '37
Long Pants '27
Ella Cinders '26
His First Flame '26
Strong Man '26

Lillian Langdon (1884-1944)
Daddy Long Legs '19
His Majesty, the American '19
Shifting Sands '18
The Americano '17
Flirting with Fate '16
The Lamb '15

Sue Ane Langdon (1936-)
Zapped! '82
The Evictors '79
The Cheyenne Social Club '70
A Guide for the Married Man '67
Frankie and Johnny '65
The Rounders '65
Roustabout '64

Artie Lange
The Bachelor '99
The 4th Floor '99
Lost and Found '99
Dirty Work '97

Carl Lange (1909-99)
Creature with the Blue Hand '70
The Torture Chamber of Dr. Sadism '69
Carpet of Horror '64

Hope Lange (1931-)
Cooperstown '93
Tune in Tomorrow '90
Ford: The Man & the Machine '87
Blue Velvet '86
A Nightmare on Elm Street 2: Freddy's Revenge '85
I Am the Cheese '83
The Prodigal '83
Beulah Land '80
Pleasure Palace '80
Death Wish '74
Fer-De-Lance '74
I Love You ... Goodbye '73
The Love Bug '68
Pocketful of Miracles '61
Wild in the Country '61
The Best of Everything '59
The Young Lions '58
Peyton Place '57
Bus Stop '56

Jessica Lange (1949-)
Titus '99
Hush '98
Cousin Bette '97
A Thousand Acres '97
Rob Roy '95
A Streetcar Named Desire '95
Losing Isaiah '94
Night and the City '92
Blue Sky '91
Cape Fear '91
O Pioneers! '91
Men Don't Leave '89
Music Box '89
Everybody's All American '88
Far North '88
Crimes of the Heart '86
Sweet Dreams '85
Cat on a Hot Tin Roof '84
Country '84
Frances '82
Tootsie '82
The Postman Always Rings Twice '81
How to Beat the High Cost of Living '80
All That Jazz '79
King Kong '76

Ted Lange (1947-)
Perfume '91
Terminal Exposure '89
Glitch! '88

Jack Langedijk
Codename: Jaguar '00
Left Behind: The Movie '00
The Pact '99
Dead End '98
A Young Connecticut Yankee in King Arthur's Court '95
Blind Fear '89
Evil Judgment '85

Frank Langella (1940-)
Sweet November '01
Innocents '00
Jason and the Argonauts '00
Stardom '00
Kurt Vonnegut's Monkey House '90s
The Ninth Gate '99
I'm Losing You '98
Small Soldiers '98 (V)
Lolita '97
Eddie '96
Moses '96
Cutthroat Island '95
Bad Company '94
Brainscan '94
Doomsday Gun '94
Junior '94
Dave '93
Body of Evidence '92
1492: Conquest of Paradise '92
True Identity '91
And God Created Woman '88
Masters of the Universe '87
The Men's Club '86
Sphinx '81
Those Lips, Those Eyes '80
Dracula '79
The Deadly Trap '71
Diary of a Mad Housewife '70
The Twelve Chairs '70

Sarah Langenfeld
Bloodlink '86
Gold Raiders '84
The Act '82

Heather Langenkamp (1964-)
Fugitive Mind '99
The Demolitionist '95
Wes Craven's New Nightmare '94
Shocker '89
A Nightmare on Elm Street 3: Dream Warriors '87
Nickel Mountain '85
A Nightmare on Elm Street '84

A.J. (Allison Joy) Langer (1974-)
Meet the Deedles '98
Escape from L.A. '96
The People under the Stairs '91

Frances Langford (1914-)
Deputy Marshal '50
Melody Time '48 (V)
Dixie Jamboree '44
Girl Rush '44
Yankee Doodle Dandy '42
Dreaming Out Loud '40
Too Many Girls '40
Born to Dance '36

Wallace (Wally) Langham (1965-)
The Chocolate War '88
The Invisible Kid '88
Thunder Run '86

Amanda Langlet
A Summer's Tale '96
Pauline at the Beach '83

Lisa Langlois (1959-)
Mindfield '89
The Nest '88
Transformations '88
Truth or Die '86
Joy of Sex '84
The Man Who Wasn't There '83
Class of 1984 '82
Deadly Eyes '82
Blood Relatives '77

Margaret Langrick (1971-)
Boxcar Blues '90
Cold Comfort '90
American Boyfriends '89
Thunderground '89
Harry and the Hendersons '87
My American Cousin '85

Caroline Langrishe (1958-)
Cleopatra '99
Mosley '98
Rogue Trader '98
Sharpe's Justice '97
Sharpe's Regiment '96
Eagle's Wing '79

Murray Langston
Wishful Thinking '92
Digging Up Business '91
Up Your Alley '89
Night Patrol '85

Brooke Langton (1970-)
Playing Mona Lisa '00
The Replacements '00
Reach the Rock '98
Listen '96
Swingers '96

David Langton (1912-94)
The Whistle Blower '87
Quintet '79
Abandon Ship '57

Jeff Langton
Maximum Force '92
Final Impact '91

Paul Langton (1913-80)
The Cosmic Man '59
It! The Terror from Beyond Space '58
The Incredible Shrinking Man '57
The Big Knife '55
To Hell and Back '55
The Snow Creature '54
They Were Expendable '45
Thirty Seconds Over Tokyo '44

Kim Lankford (1962-)
Street Corner Justice '96
Cameron's Closet '89
Octagon '80
Malibu Beach '78

Frank Lanning (1872-1945)
The Lone Defender '32
Stand and Deliver '28
The Unknown '27

Les Lannom
Centennial '78
Stingray '78

Victor Lanoux (1936-)
Louisiana '87
Scene of the Crime '87
National Lampoon's European Vacation '85
Dog Day '83
Make Room for Tomorrow '81
Investigation '79
One Wild Moment '78
A Woman at Her Window '77
Cousin, Cousine '76
Pardon Mon Affaire '76
The French Detective '75

Angela Lansbury (1925-)
Anastasia '97 (V)
Mrs. Santa Claus '96
Mrs. 'Arris Goes to Paris '92
Beauty and the Beast '91 (V)
The Shell Seekers '89
Rage of Angels: The Story Continues '86
The Company of Wolves '85
The First Olympics: Athens 1896 '84
Little Gloria... Happy at Last '84
Sweeney Todd: The Demon Barber of Fleet Street '84
The Pirates of Penzance '83
The Last Unicorn '82 (V)
The Mirror Crack'd '80
The Lady Vanishes '79
Death on the Nile '78
Bedknobs and Broomsticks '71
Something for Everyone '70
The Amorous Adventures of Moll Flanders '65
The Greatest Story Ever Told '65
Harlow '65
The World of Henry Orient '64
All Fall Down '62
Blue Hawaii '62
The Manchurian Candidate '62
Breath of Scandal '60
The Long, Hot Summer '58
The Reluctant Debutante '58
Court Jester '56
A Lawless Street '55
Mutiny '52
Samson and Delilah '50
State of the Union '48
The Three Musketeers '48
The Private Affairs of Bel Ami '47
The Harvey Girls '46
Picture of Dorian Gray '45
Gaslight '44
National Velvet '44

David Lansbury (1961-)
Cupid & Cate '00
A Stranger in the Kingdom '98
Truman '95
Parallel Lives '94
Gas Food Lodging '92

John Lansing
More American Graffiti '79
Sunnyside '79

Joi Lansing (1928-72)
Big Foot '72
Hillbillies in a Haunted House '67
Atomic Submarine '59
A Hole in the Head '59
Touch of Evil '58
The Brave One '56
Son of Sinbad '55
The French Line '54
The Merry Widow '52
Singin' in the Rain '52
Pier 23 '51
Two Tickets to Broadway '51
Neptune's Daughter '49
Easter Parade '48
Julia Misbehaves '48

Robert Lansing (1929-94)
The Nest '88
Island Claw '80
S*H*E '79
Empire of the Ants '77
Bittersweet Love '76
Scalpel '76
The Widow '76

The Grissom Gang '71
Namu, the Killer Whale '66
Talion '66
Under the Yum-Yum Tree '63
The 4D Man '59

Virginia Lantry
The Ghost of Fletcher Ridge '80s
Ain't No Way Back '89

Gerard Lanvin
Mon Homme '96
The Favorite Son '94

Mario Lanza (1921-59)
For the First Time '59
The Seven Hills of Rome '58
Because You're Mine '52
The Great Caruso '51
The Toast of New Orleans '50
That Midnight Kiss '49

Fabio Lanzoni
Death Becomes Her '92
Scenes from a Mall '91

Anthony LaPaglia (1959-)
The Salton Sea '02
Lantana '01
Autumn in New York '00
Company Man '00
House of Mirth '00
Lansky '99
Summer of Sam '99
Sweet and Lowdown '99
Phoenix '98
The Garden of Redemption '97
Brilliant Lies '96
Commandments '96
Paperback Romance '96
Tree's Lounge '96
Bulletproof Heart '95
Chameleon '95
Empire Records '95
The Client '94
The Custodian '94
Mixed Nuts '94
Past Tense '94
So I Married an Axe Murderer '93
Black Magic '92
Innocent Blood '92
Keeper of the City '92
Whispers in the Dark '92
He Said, She Said '91
One Good Cop '91
29th Street '91
Betsy's Wedding '90
Criminal Justice '90
Mortal Sins '90
Nitti: The Enforcer '88

Daniel Lapaine
The 10th Kingdom '00
Brokedown Palace '99
Dangerous Beauty '98
1999 '98
Polish Wedding '97
Muriel's Wedding '94

Francine Lapensee
Bounty Hunter 2002 '94
Demon Wind '90
Born Killer '89
Hollywood's New Blood '88

Peter Lapis
Undeclared War '91
Death Blow '87

Victor Laplace
Letters from the Park '88
Under the Earth '86

Jane Lapotaire (1944-)
Shooting Fish '98
Surviving Picasso '96
The Dark Angel '91
Murder by Moonlight '91
Eureka! '81
Piaf '81
The Asphyx '72

Joe Lara (1962-)
Doomsdayer '99
Operation: Delta Force '97
Warhead '96
Final Equinox '95
Hologram Man '95
Live Wire: Human Timebomb '95
American Cyborg: Steel Warrior '94
Steel Frontier '94

John Larch (1922-)
The Amityville Horror '79
Future Cop '76
Bad Ronald '74
Santee '73
Dirty Harry '71
Play Misty for Me '71
Hail, Hero! '69
The Wrecking Crew '68
Man in the Shadow '57

Vincent Laresca
Hard Cash '01
Just One Time '00
Forever Mine '99
Music from Another Room '97
Ripe '97
Money Train '95
Juice '92

Veronica Lario
Sotto, Sotto '85
Unsane '82

Bryan Larkin
Born on the Fourth of July '89
She-Devil '89

Chris Larkin
Shackleton '02
The Flamingo Rising '01
Angels and Insects '95

Linda Larkin (1970-)
Aladdin and the King of Thieves '96 (V)
The Return of Jafar '94 (V)
Aladdin '92 (V)

Mary Laroche
Psychomania '73
Gidget '59
Run Silent, Run Deep '58

Michele Laroque (1960-)
The Closet '00
Ma Vie en Rose '97
Pedale Douce '96
Nelly et Monsieur Arnaud '95

Pierre Larquey
Topaze '51
Le Corbeau '43

Tito Larriva
Just a Little Harmless Sex '99
True Stories '86
The Pee-wee Herman Show '82

John Larroquette (1947-)
Walter and Henry '01
Isn't She Great '00
The 10th Kingdom '00
The Defenders: Payback '97
Richie Rich '94
Madhouse '90
Tune in Tomorrow '90
Second Sight '89
Blind Date '87
Convicted '86
Summer Rental '85
Choose Me '84
Meatballs 2 '84
Star Trek 3: The Search for Spock '84
Twilight Zone: The Movie '83
Cat People '82
Green Ice '81
Stripes '81
Altered States '80
Heart Beat '80
The Texas Chainsaw Massacre '74 (N)

Erik Larsen
Young & Free '78
Trap on Cougar Mountain '72

Ham Larsen
Mountain Family Robinson '79
Further Adventures of the Wilderness Family, Part 2 '77

Keith Larsen (1926-)
Whitewater Sam '78
Trap on Cougar Mountain '72
Mission Batangas '69
Flat Top '52

Bobby Larson
Leather Burners '43
The Underdog '43

Darrell Larson (1951-)
Shadrach '98
Stepmom '98
Stuart Saves His Family '94
Hero '92
The Last Innocent Man '87
Murder Ordained '87
City Limits '85
Mike's Murder '84
Red, White & Busted '75
The Girls of Huntington House '73
The Student Nurses '70

Eric Larson (1905-88)
Demon Wind '90
The Uninvited '88
'68 '87

Wolf Larson (1959-)
Shakedown '02
Crash & Byrnes '99
Storm Chasers: Revenge of the Twister '98
The Heist '96
Tracks of a Killer '95

Ali Larter (1976-)
American Outlaws '01
Jay and Silent Bob Strike Back '01
Legally Blonde '01
Final Destination '00
Drive Me Crazy '99
House on Haunted Hill '99
Varsity Blues '98

Eva LaRue
Crash and Burn '90
The Barbarians '87

Frank LaRue (1878-1960)
Range Renegades '48
Border Bandits '46
Devil Riders '44
Riders of Pasco Basin '40
Mesquite Buckaroo '39
Trigger Pals '39
Overland Stage Raiders '38
Songs and Bullets '38
Boothill Brigade '37
Gun Lords of Stirrup Basin '37
A Lawman Is Born '37
Lightning Bill Crandall '37
Red River Valley '36
The Throwback '35
Sidewalks of New York '31

Jack LaRue (1902-84)
The Young Nurses '73
Robin and the 7 Hoods '64
Ride the Man Down '53
The Road to Utopia '46
Dangerous Passage '44
Follow the Leader '44
The Law Rides Again '43
The Payoff '43
X Marks the Spot '42
Footsteps in the Dark '41
Gentleman from Dixie '41
Captains Courageous '37
Dangerous Holiday '37
Dancing Pirate '36
Strike Me Pink '36
Yellow Cargo '36
Headline Woman '35
The Fighting Rookie '34
The Kennel Murder Case '33
To the Last Man '33
A Farewell to Arms '32

Lash LaRue (1917-96)
Pair of Aces '90
The Dark Power '85
The Black Lash '52
King of the Bullwhip '51
Thundering Trail '51
Outlaw Country '49
Stage to Mesa City '48
Border Feud '47
Cheyenne Takes Over '47
Fighting Vigilantes '47
Ghost Town Renegades '47
Law of the Lash '47
Return of the Lash '47
The Caravan Trail '46
Wild West '46
Song of Old Wyoming '45
Master Key '44
Gangs, Inc. '41

Robert LaSardo
Running Woman '98
The Real Thing '97
Under Oath '97
Gang Related '96
Tiger Heart '96

David Lascher
A Call to Remember '97
White Squall '96

Dieter Laser
The Man Inside '90
The Lost Honor of Katharina Blum '75

Michael Laskin
Bounce '00
Limbo '99
The Disappearance of Kevin Johnson '95
Passion Fish '92
Eight Men Out '88
The Personals '83

Kathleen Lasky
Getting Gotti '94
Lethal Lolita—Amy Fisher: My Story '92
Love & Murder '91

Tommy Lasorda (1927-)
Homeward Bound 2: Lost in San Francisco '96 (V)
Ladybugs '92
Americathon '79

Dagmar Lassander (1943-)
S.A.S. San Salvador '84
The Black Cat '81
Flatfoot '78
Dandelions '74
The Frightened Woman '71
Hatchet for the Honeymoon '70

Louise Lasser (1939-)
Requiem for a Dream '00
Mystery Men '99
Happiness '98
Sudden Manhattan '96
The Night We Never Met '93
Frankenhooker '90
Modern Love '90
Rude Awakening '89
Sing '89
Blood Rage '87
Surrender '87
Crimewave '85
For Ladies Only '81
In God We Trust '80
Just Me & You '78
Slither '73
Everything You Always Wanted to Know about Sex (But Were Afraid to Ask) '72
Bananas '71
Take the Money and Run '69

Sarah Lassez
In Pursuit '00
The Blackout '97
Nowhere '96
Malicious '95
Roosters '95

Rolf Lassgard
Under the Sun '98
The White Lioness '96

Sydney Lassick (1922-)
American Vampire '97
Money to Burn '94
Deep Cover '92
Shakes the Clown '92
Committed '91
Cool As Ice '91
The Art of Dying '90
Smooth Talker '90
Out on Bail '89
Tale of Two Sisters '89
Curse 2: The Bite '88
Sonny Boy '87
Night Patrol '85
Silent Madness '84
Monaco Forever '83
Alligator '80
The Unseen '80
The Billion Dollar Hobo '78
Carrie '76

Lyle Latell (1905-67)
Dick Tracy Meets Gruesome '47
Dick Tracy's Dilemma '47
Dick Tracy vs. Cueball '46
Dick Tracy, Detective '45

Dick Latessa
Stigmata '99
Rockabye '86
Izzy & Moe '85

Anne Latham
Thieves Like Us '74
Mind Warp '72

Louise Latham
In Cold Blood '96
Crazy from the Heart '91
Love Field '91
Paradise '91
Toughlove '85
Mass Appeal '84
Lois Gibbs and the Love Canal '82
Pray TV '82
Dying Room Only '73
White Lightning '73
Adam at 6 a.m. '70
Marnie '64

Philip Latham
The Two Faces of Evil '82
Dracula, Prince of Darkness '66

Sanaa Lathan (1971-)
Catfish in Black Bean Sauce '00
Disappearing Acts '00
Love and Basketball '00
The Best Man '99
The Wood '99
Blade '98

Hugh Latimer (1913-)
The Cosmic Monsters '58
Rogue's Yarn '56
Someone at the Door '50

Michael Latimer
Man of Violence '71
Prehistoric Women '67

Frank Latimore (1925-)
Patton '70
The Dolly Sisters '46
The Razor's Edge '46
Shock! '46
13 Rue Madeleine '46

Ney Latorraca (1944-)
The Fable of the Beautiful Pigeon Fancier '88
The Dolphin '87
Opera do Malandro '87

Matt Lattanzi (1959-)
Diving In '90
Catch Me ... If You Can '89
Roxanne '87
My Tutor '82
Rich and Famous '81

Andy Lau (1961-)
Running out of Time '99
The Legend of Drunken Master '94

Damian Lau
Jet Li's The Enforcer '95
The Heroic Trio '93
Last Hurrah for Chivalry '78

Chester Lauck
The Bashful Bachelor '42
Dreaming Out Loud '40

Philippe Laudenbach
Four Adventures of Reinette and Mirabelle '89
Confidentially Yours '83

Andrew Lauer (1965-)
Gun Shy '00
I'll Be Home for Christmas '98
Screamers '96
Never on Tuesday '88

Jack Laufer
The Learning Curve '01
The Man Who Captured Eichmann '96
And the Band Played On '93
Lost in Yonkers '93

John Laughlin
Storm Trooper '98
Back to Back '96
Improper Conduct '94
Night Fire '94
Sexual Malice '93
The Lawnmower Man '92
Memphis '91
Motorama '91
Midnight Crossing '87
Space Rage '86
Crimes of Passion '84
Footloose '84
The Hills Have Eyes, Part 2 '84

Tom Laughlin (1939-)
The Trial of Billy Jack '74
Billy Jack '71
Born Losers '67
Tall Story '60
South Pacific '58

Charles Laughton (1899-1962)
Advise and Consent '62
Spartacus '60
Witness for the Prosecution '57
Hobson's Choice '53
Salome '53
Young Bess '53
Abbott and Costello Meet Captain Kidd '52
The Strange Door '51
Arch of Triumph '48
The Big Clock '48
Man on the Eiffel Tower '48
The Paradine Case '47
Because of Him '45
Captain Kidd '45
The Canterville Ghost '44
Forever and a Day '43
This Land Is Mine '43
Tales of Manhattan '42
The Tuttles of Tahiti '42
It Started with Eve '41
They Knew What They Wanted '40
The Hunchback of Notre Dame '39
Jamaica Inn '39
Beachcomber '38
Sidewalks of London '38
Rembrandt '36
Les Miserables '35
Mutiny on the Bounty '35
Ruggles of Red Gap '35
The Barretts of Wimpole Street '34
The Private Life of Henry VIII '33
The Sign of the Cross '33
Island of Lost Souls '32
The Old Dark House '32

S. John Launer
Crime of Passion '57
I Was a Teenage Werewolf '57

Cyndi Lauper (1953-)
Life with Mikey '93
Mother Goose Rock 'n' Rhyme '90
Off and Running '90
Vibes '88

Matthew Laurance (1950-)
Eddie and the Cruisers 2: Eddie Lives! '89
Eddie and the Cruisers '83

Mitchell Laurance (1950-)
The Portrait '93
The Hand that Rocks the Cradle '92
Syngenor '90
Stepfather 2: Make Room for Daddy '89
A Conspiracy of Love '87

Carole Laure (1951-)
Surrogate '88
Sweet Country '87

Heartbreakers '84
Maria Chapdelaine '84
Victory '81
Get Out Your Handkerchiefs '78
Strange Shadows in an Empty Room '76
Sweet Movie '75

Stan Laurel (1890-1965)
Days of Thrills and Laughter '61
Utopia '51
Bullfighters '45
Nothing But Trouble '44
Air Raid Wardens '43
Great Guns '41
A Chump at Oxford '40
Saps at Sea '40
The Flying Deuces '39
Block-heads '38
Swiss Miss '38
Pick a Star '37
Way Out West '37
Bohemian Girl '36
Our Relations '36
Bonnie Scotland '35
Hollywood Party '34
March of the Wooden Soldiers '34
The Devil's Brother '33
Laurel & Hardy and the Family '33
Laurel & Hardy: Stan "Helps" Ollie '33
Sons of the Desert '33
Laurel & Hardy: At Work '32
Pack Up Your Troubles '32
Laurel & Hardy: Be Big '31
Laurel & Hardy: Chickens Come Home '31
Laurel & Hardy: Laughing Gravy '31
Pardon Us '31
Laurel & Hardy: Another Fine Mess '30
Laurel & Hardy: Below Zero '30
Laurel & Hardy: Blotto '30
Laurel & Hardy: Brats '30
Laurel & Hardy: Hog Wild '30
Laurel & Hardy: Night Owls '30
Laurel & Hardy On the Lam '30
Laurel & Hardy: Berth Marks '29
Laurel & Hardy: Men O'War '29
Laurel & Hardy: Perfect Day '29

Greg Lauren
The Prophet's Game '99
Boys Life '94

Rod Lauren
Once Before I Die '65
The Crawling Hand '63

Tammy Lauren
Wishmaster '97
The Last Flight of Noah's Ark '80

Veronica Lauren
Homeward Bound 2: Lost in San Francisco '96
Homeward Bound: The Incredible Journey '93

Ashley Laurence
Cypress Edge '99
Warlock 3: The End of Innocence '98
The Real Thing '97
Cupid '96
Felony '95
The Fighter '95
Outside the Law '95
Triplecross '95
American Cop '94
Hellraiser 3: Hell on Earth '92
Mikey '92
One Last Run '89
Hellbound: Hellraiser 2 '88
Hellraiser '87

James Laurenson (1935-)
The Cat's Meow '01
Sharpe's Mission '96
Sharpe's Regiment '96
Sharpe's Siege '96
Cold Light of Day '95
A House in the Hills '93
Codename Kyril '91
Rainbow Drive '90
Heartbreakers '84
Pink Floyd: The Wall '82
Rude Awakening '81
Assault '70

Agnes Laurent
Girl in His Pocket '57
The Twilight Girls '57

Remy Laurent
The Gift '82
La Cage aux Folles '78

Dan Lauria (1947-)
Common Ground '00
Full Disclosure '00
Hangman '00
Fear Runs Silent '99
Dean Koontz's Mr. Murder '98
From the Earth to the Moon '98
True Friends '98
Dogwatch '97
Prison of Secrets '97
Wide Awake '97
Independence Day '96
In the Line of Duty: Ambush in Waco '93
In the Line of Duty: A Cop for the Killing '90
Skin '89
Stakeout '87

Carol Laurie
Naked Massacre '80s
Dirty Dishes '82

Hugh Laurie (1959-)
Stuart Little 2 '02
Life with Judy Garland—Me and My Shadows '01
Maybe Baby '99
Stuart Little '99
The Man in the Iron Mask '98
The Borrowers '97
Cousin Bette '97
Spice World: The Movie '97
101 Dalmatians '96
Sense and Sensibility '95
Peter's Friends '92
Strapless '90

John Laurie (1897-1980)
The Reptile '66
Devil Girl from Mars '54
Encore '52
Madeleine '50
No Trace '50
Trio '50
Bonnie Prince Charlie '48
Hamlet '48
Man of Evil '48
Mine Own Executioner '47
The World Owes Me a Living '47
Henry V '44
Immortal Battalion '44
Dangerous Moonlight '41
Clouds over Europe '39
The Four Feathers '39
Edge of the World '37
Nine Days a Queen '36
The 39 Steps '35
Juno and the Paycock '30

Piper Laurie (1932-)
Possessed '00
Inherit the Wind '99
St. Patrick's Day '99
The Faculty '98
Horton Foote's Alone '97
The Road to Galveston '96
The Grass Harp '95
The Crossing Guard '94
Dario Argento's Trauma '93
Rich in Love '93
Wrestling Ernest Hemingway '93
Storyville '92
Other People's Money '91
Rising Son '90
Dream a Little Dream '89
Appointment with Death '88
Distortions '87
Tiger Warsaw '87
Children of a Lesser God '86
Return to Oz '85
Toughlove '85
Mae West '84
The Thorn Birds '83
Skag '79
Tim '79
Boss' Son '78
Ruby '77
Carrie '76
The Hustler '61
Days of Wine and Roses '58
Until They Sail '57
Dangerous Mission '54
Son of Ali Baba '52
Francis Goes to the Races '51

Charlotte Laurier
2 Seconds '98
Les Bons Debarras '81

Lucie Laurier
Stiletto Dance '01
Strip Search '97

Ed Lauter (1940-)
Not Another Teen Movie '01
Thirteen Days '00
A Bright Shining Lie '98
For Which He Stands '98
Mercenary '96
Rattled '96
Breach of Trust '95
Leaving Las Vegas '95
Mulholland Falls '95
Ravenhawk '95
The Sweeper '95
Black Water '94
Digital Man '94
Girl in the Cadillac '94
Trial by Jury '94
Extreme Justice '93
Murder So Sweet '93
True Romance '93
Under Investigation '93
School Ties '92
The Rocketeer '91
Stephen King's Golden Years '91
Goodbye, Miss 4th of July '88
Revenge of the Nerds 2: Nerds in Paradise '87
The Last Days of Patton '86
Youngblood '86
Yuri Nosenko, KGB '86
Death Wish 3 '85
Girls Just Want to Have Fun '85
Nickel Mountain '85
Cartier Affair '84
Finders Keepers '84
Lassiter '84
Big Score '83
Cujo '83
Timerider '83
The Amateur '82
In the Custody of Strangers '82
Death Hunt '81
Eureka! '81
Love's Savage Fury '79
Magic '78
The Chicken Chronicles '77
Breakheart Pass '76
Family Plot '76
King Kong '76
The Longest Yard '74
The Migrants '74
Class of '63 '73
Rage '72

Harry Lauter (1920-90)
Escape from the Planet of the Apes '71
Trader Tom of the China Seas '54
Bandit King of Texas '49

Kathrin Lautner
Two Bits & Pepper '95
Final Impact '91
The Last Riders '90
Night of the Wilding '90
Spirits '90

Dominque Lavanant
The Monster '96
Three Men and a Cradle '85

Denis Lavant
The Lovers on the Bridge '91
Mauvais Sang '86
Boy Meets Girl '84

Lucille LaVerne (1872-1945)
Snow White and the Seven Dwarfs '37 (V)
Kentucky Kernels '34
Hearts of Humanity '32
The White Rose '23

Daliah Lavi (1940-)
Those Fantastic Flying Fools '67
The Silencers '66
Spy with a Cold Nose '66
Lord Jim '65
Apache's Last Battle '64
The Whip and the Body '63
Two Weeks in Another Town '62
The Return of Dr. Mabuse '61

Gabriele Lavia
Revenge of the Dead '84
Zeder '83
Deep Red: Hatchet Murders '75

Linda Lavin (1937-)
Collected Stories '02
See You in the Morning '89
Maricela '88
The Muppets Take Manhattan '84
A Matter of Life and Death '81
The $5.20 an Hour Dream '80

Marc Lavoine
Fiesta '95
L'Enfer '93

Adam LaVorgna
Outside Providence '99
I'll Be Home for Christmas '98

John Phillip Law (1937-)
Hindsight '97
My Magic Dog '97
Cold Heat '90
Alienator '89
Space Mutiny '88
Thunder Warrior 3 '88
Moon in Scorpio '86
L.A. Bad '85
American Commandos '84
Attack Force Z '84
Night Train to Terror '84
Overthrow '82
Tarzan, the Ape Man '81
African Rage '78
No Time to Die '78
The Cassandra Crossing '76
Spiral Staircase '75
Golden Voyage of Sinbad '73
The Last Movie '71
The Love Machine '71
Barbarella '68
Danger: Diabolik '68
The Russians Are Coming, the Russians Are Coming '66

Jude Law (1972-)
Road to Perdition '02
A. I.: Artificial Intelligence '01
Enemy at the Gates '00
Love, Honour & Obey '00
eXistenZ '99
The Talented Mr. Ripley '99
Immortality '98
Bent '97
Gattaca '97
I Love You, I Love You Not '97
Midnight in the Garden of Good and Evil '97
Music from Another Room '97
Wilde '97
Shopping '93

Phyllida Law (1932-)
The Time Machine '02
The Magical Legend of the Leprechauns '99
I Want You '98
The Winter Guest '97
Emma '96
Leo Tolstoy's Anna Karenina '96
Before the Rain '94
Much Ado about Nothing '93
Peter's Friends '92
Hitler: The Last Ten Days '73

Christopher Lawford (1955-)
The 6th Day '00
Thirteen Days '00
Mary, Mother of Jesus '99
The Confession '98
Kiss Me, Guido '97
The Abduction '96
The Russia House '90
Mr. North '88

Peter Lawford (1923-84)
War in the Sky '82 (N)
Body & Soul '81
Angel's Brigade '79
Mysterious Island of Beautiful Women '79
Fantasy Island '76
Rosebud '75
They Only Kill Their Masters '72
Togetherness '70
April Fools '69
Buona Sera, Mrs. Campbell '68
A Man Called Adam '66
The Oscar '66
Harlow '65
Advise and Consent '62
The Longest Day '62
Exodus '60
Ocean's 11 '60
Never So Few '59
It Should Happen to You '54
Royal Wedding '51
Little Women '49
Easter Parade '48
Julia Misbehaves '48
On an Island with You '48
Good News '47
It Happened in Brooklyn '47
Picture of Dorian Gray '45
Son of Lassie '45
The Canterville Ghost '44
The White Cliffs of Dover '44
Immortal Sergeant '43
Sahara '43
Mrs. Miniver '42

Lucy Lawless
Spider-Man '02
Hercules the Legendary Journeys, Vol. 1: And the Amazon Women '94

Yvonne Lawley
Death in Brunswick '90
Among the Cinders '83

Stephanie Lawlor
Hot T-Shirts '79
Cherry Hill High '76

Barbara Lawrence (1928-)
Kronos '57
Man in the Shadow '57
Oklahoma! '55
Here Come the Nelsons '52
A Letter to Three Wives '49
The Street with No Name '48

Bruno Lawrence (1941-95)
Jack Be Nimble '94
Rainbow Warrior '94
The Efficiency Expert '92
Grievous Bodily Harm '89
Rikky and Pete '88
The Bridge to Nowhere '86
An Indecent Obsession '85
The Quiet Earth '85
Heart of the Stag '84
Treasure of the Yankee Zephyr '83
Utu '83
Smash Palace '82

Carol Lawrence (1934-)
Shattered Image '93
Summer of Fear '78
New Faces of 1952 '54

Cary Lawrence
Canvas: The Fine Art of Crime '92
The Dance Goes On '92

Delphi Lawrence (1926-)
Frozen Alive '64
Murder on Approval '56
Three Stops to Murder '53

Elizabeth Lawrence (1922-2000)
Unbreakable '00
The Crucible '96
Sleeping with the Enemy '91

Gertrude Lawrence (1898-1952)
Stage Door Canteen '43
Men Are Not Gods '37
Rembrandt '36
Mimi '35

Joey Lawrence (1976-)
Tequila Body Shots '99
Radioland Murders '94
Chains of Gold '92
Oliver & Company '88 (V)
Pulse '88
Wait Till Your Mother Gets Home '83

John Lawrence (1931-92)
They Live '88
The Asphyx '72
The Manchurian Candidate '62

Marc Lawrence (1910-)
Gotti '96
Ruby '92
The Big Easy '87
Night Train to Terror '84
Cataclysm '81
Goin' Coconuts '78
King of Kong Island '78
Dream No Evil '75
The Man with the Golden Gun '74
Frasier the Sensuous Lion '73
Pigs '73
Abbott and Costello in the Foreign Legion '50
The Asphalt Jungle '50
The Black Hand '50
Jigsaw '49
Cloak and Dagger '46
'Neath Brooklyn Bridge '42
The Monster and the Girl '41
Charlie Chan at the Wax Museum '40
I Am the Law '38
Vengeance '37

Mark Christopher Lawrence
That Darn Cat '96
Fear of a Black Hat '94

Martin Lawrence (1965-)
Black Knight '01
What's the Worst That Could Happen? '01
Big Momma's House '00
Blue Streak '99
Life '99
Nothing to Lose '96
A Thin Line Between Love and Hate '96
Bad Boys '95
You So Crazy '94
Boomerang '92
House Party 2: The Pajama Jam '91

Talkin' Dirty after Dark '91
House Party '90
Matthew Lawrence (1980-)
Family Tree '00
All I Wanna Do '98
Angels in the Endzone '98
Boltneck '98
Undesirable '92
Tales from the Darkside: The Movie '90
Michael Lawrence
Othello '52
Elizabeth of Ladymead '48
Peter Lee Lawrence (1943-73)
Garringo '69
They Paid with Bullets: Chicago 1929 '69
Special Forces '68
Rosina Lawrence (1913-97)
Pick a Star '37
Way Out West '37
General Spanky '36
Charlie Chan's Secret '35
Scott Lawrence
Timecop '94
Laurel Avenue '93
God's Bloody Acre '75
Sharon Lawrence (1963-)
Aftershock: Earthquake in New York '99
Gossip '99
The Only Thrill '97
The Heidi Chronicles '95
Sheldon Lawrence
Sweet Beat '62
Black Tide '58
Stephanie Lawrence (1949-2000)
The Phantom of the Opera '89
Buster '88
Steve Lawrence (1935-)
Ocean's Eleven '01
The Yards '00
Blues Brothers 2000 '98
The Lonely Guy '84
The Blues Brothers '80
Express to Terror '79
Bianca Lawson
Bones '01
Save the Last Dance '01
Boltneck '98
Denis Lawson (1947-)
Horatio Hornblower '99
Catherine Cookson's The Round Tower '98
A Royal Scandal '96
Local Hero '83
Return of the Jedi '83
Leigh Lawson (1945-)
Back to the Secret Garden '01
Battling for Baby '92
O Pioneers! '91
Madame Sousatzka '88
Tears in the Rain '88
Sword of the Valiant '83
Fire and Sword '82
Charlie Boy '81
Tess '80
Disraeli '79
Love Among the Ruins '75
It's Not the Size That Counts '74
Madhouse Mansion '74
Brother Sun, Sister Moon '73
Louise Lawson
Creeping Terror '64
The Bellboy and the Playgirls '62
Priscilla Lawson (1914-58)
Flash Gordon: Rocketship '40
Girl of the Golden West '38
Richard Lawson (1947-)
How Stella Got Her Groove Back '98
The Reluctant Agent '95
The Forgotten '89
Johnnie Gibson F.B.I. '87
Streets of Fire '84
Poltergeist '82
Fist '79
Coming Home '78
Foxstyle '73
Scream Blacula Scream '73
Sarah Lawson
The Devil Rides Out '68
Island of the Burning Doomed '67
Shannon Lawson
Possessed '00
Anne of Green Gables: The Continuing Story '99
Heck's Way Home '95
Wilfred Lawson (1900-66)
Room at the Top '59
War and Peace '56
The Prisoner '55
Man of Evil '48
Thursday's Child '43
The Night Has Eyes '42
Tower of Terror '42
Pygmalion '38
The Terror '38
Frank Lawton (1904-69)
A Night to Remember '58
The Winslow Boy '48
The Secret Four '40
The Mill on the Floss '37
Devil Doll '36
The Invisible Ray '36
David Copperfield '35
Cavalcade '33
Skin Game '31
Me Me Lay
Emerald Jungle '80
Crucible of Terror '72
Evelyn Laye (1900-96)
Say Hello to Yesterday '71
Theatre of Death '67
John Lazar
Attack of the 60-Foot Centerfold '95
Night of the Scarecrow '95
Over the Wire '95
Deathstalker 2: Duel of the Titans '87
Every Girl Should Have One '78
Beyond the Valley of the Dolls '70
Paul Lazar
Mickey Blue Eyes '99
Los Locos Posse '97
Buffalo Girls '95
Trapped in Paradise '94
Philadelphia '93
Justin Lazard (1967-)
The Brutal Truth '99
Universal Soldier: The Return '99
Species 2 '98
The Big Fall '96
Dead Center '94
Eugene Lazarev
The Saint '97
The Ice Runner '93
Eusebio Lazaro
Twice upon a Yesterday '98
The Return of the Musketeers '89
George Lazenby (1939-)
Four Dogs Playing Poker '00
Fatally Yours '95
Twinsitters '95
Gettysburg '93
Eyes of the Beholder '92
Hell Hunters '87
Never Too Young to Die '86
Saint Jack '79
Black Eliminator '78
Kill Factor '78
Kentucky Fried Movie '77
On Her Majesty's Secret Service '69
Bruce Le
Clones of Bruce Lee '80
Bruce Lee Fights Back from the Grave '76
Becky Le Beau
The Malibu Beach Vampires '91
Not of This Earth '88
Maiwenn Le Besco
The Fifth Element '97
The Elegant Criminal '92
Samuel Le Bihan
Brotherhood of the Wolf '01
For Sale '98
Venus Beauty Institute '98
Capitaine Conan '96
Trois Couleurs: Rouge '94
Gene Le Brock
Beyond Darkness '92
Metamorphosis '90
Fortress of Amerikka '89
Kelly Le Brock (1960-)
Wrongfully Accused '98
Tracks of a Killer '95
Hard Bounty '94
Betrayal of the Dove '92
Hard to Kill '89
Weird Science '85
The Woman in Red '84
Michael Le Clair
Leave 'Em Laughing '81
Anatomy of a Seduction '79
Bernard Le Coq
Capitaine Conan '96
Van Gogh '92
Steve Le Marquand
Rodgers & Hammerstein's South Pacific '01
Vertical Limit '00
John Le Mesurier (1912-83)
A Married Man '84
Brideshead Revisited '81
The Fiendish Plot of Dr. Fu Manchu '80
The Adventures of Sherlock Holmes' Smarter Brother '78
Jabberwocky '77
Dead Lucky '60
Jack the Ripper '60
Brothers in Law '57
The Baby and the Battleship '56
Nicholas Le Prevost
A Fatal Inversion '92
The Girl in a Swing '89
Sylvestria Le Touzel
Catherine Cookson's The Gambling Man '98
Mansfield Park '85
Nicholas Lea (1962-)
Kiss Tomorrow Goodbye '00
Vertical Limit '00
Once a Thief '96
The Raffle '94
Xtro 2: The Second Encounter '91
Ron Lea
Sea People '00
A Map of the World '99
The Neighbor '93
Clearcut '92
The Phone Call '89
Rosemary Leach (1925-)
Catherine Cookson's Tilly Trotter '99
Berkeley Square '98
The Buccaneers '95
The Hawk '93
The Mystery of Edwin Drood '93
The Children '90
The Charmer '87
A Room with a View '86
Turtle Diary '86
D.P. '85
The Seventeenth Bride '84
Disraeli '79
Ghost in the Noonday Sun '74
That'll Be the Day '73
Cloris Leachman (1930-)
Hanging Up '99
Iron Giant '99 (V)
Music of the Heart '99
Beavis and Butt-Head Do America '96 (V)
Now and Then '95
Double Double Toil and Trouble '94
A Troll in Central Park '94 (V)
The Beverly Hillbillies '93
Fade to Black '93
My Boyfriend's Back '93
Danielle Steel's Fine Things '90
Texasville '90
Prancer '89
The Victory '88
Walk Like a Man '87
Shadow Play '86
Dixie: Changing Habits '85
Ernie Kovacs: Between the Laughter '84
The Woman Who Willed a Miracle '83
Acorn People '82
Miss All-American Beauty '82
Oldest Living Graduate '82
History of the World: Part 1 '81
Foolin' Around '80
Herbie Goes Bananas '80
Mrs. R's Daughter '79
The Muppet Movie '79
The North Avenue Irregulars '79
Scavenger Hunt '79
S.O.S. Titanic '79
Willa '79
Long Journey Back '78
High Anxiety '77
Mouse and His Child '77 (V)
Crazy Mama '75
Death Scream '75
Someone I Touched '75
Daisy Miller '74
Death Sentence '74
The Migrants '74
Thursday's Game '74
Young Frankenstein '74
Charley and the Angel '73
Dillinger '73
Dying Room Only '73
Run, Stranger, Run '73
Brand New Life '72
Haunts of the Very Rich '72
The Last Picture Show '71
The Steagle '71
Lovers and Other Strangers '70
The People Next Door '70
Butch Cassidy and the Sundance Kid '69
Silent Night, Lonely Night '69
Kiss Me Deadly '55
Damien Leake
Killing Floor '85
Apocalypse Now '79
Michael Learned (1939-)
Dragon: The Bruce Lee Story '93
Murder in New Hampshire: The Pamela Smart Story '91
Roots: The Gift '88
All My Sons '86
Deadly Business '86
Power '86
A Christmas Without Snow '80
Nurse '80
The Widow '76
Denis Leary (1957-)
Ice Age '02 (V)
Final '01
Company Man '00
Sand '00
Jesus' Son '99
Silent Witness '99
The Thomas Crown Affair '99
True Crime '99
A Bug's Life '98 (V)
Monument Ave. '98
Small Soldiers '98
Love Walked In '97
The Matchmaker '97
The Real Blonde '97
The Second Civil War '97
Subway Stories '97
Suicide Kings '97
Wag the Dog '97
Wide Awake '97
Underworld '96
National Lampoon's Favorite Deadly Sins '95
The Neon Bible '95
Operation Dumbo Drop '95
Two If by Sea '95
Natural Born Killers '94
Demolition Man '93
Gunmen '93
Judgment Night '93
National Lampoon's Loaded Weapon 1 '93
The Ref '93
The Sandlot '93
Who's the Man? '93
Timothy Leary (1920-96)
Conceiving Ada '97
Hold Me, Thrill Me, Kiss Me '93
Ted & Venus '93
Roadside Prophets '92
Fatal Skies '90
Shocker '89
Rex Lease (1901-66)
Lost in Alaska '52
Gun Cargo '49
People's Choice '46
Fast Bullets '44
Haunted Ranch '43
Texas Trouble '41
Heroes of the Alamo '37
Riding On '37
Aces and Eights '36
Cavalcade of the West '36
The Clutching Hand '36
Custer's Last Stand '36
The Man from Gun Town '36
Roaring Guns '36
Cowboy & the Bandit '35
Cyclone of the Saddle '35
Fighting Caballero '35
Ghost Rider '35
Pals of the Range '35
Rough Riding Rangers '35
Inside Information '34
The Monster Walks '32
Chinatown After Dark '31
Sunny Skies '30
Jean-Pierre Leaud (1944-)
A Matter of Taste '00
Irma Vep '96
Mon Homme '96
Diary of a Seducer '95
La Vie de Boheme '93
36 Fillete '88
Detective '85
Love on the Run '78
Day for Night '73
Last Tango in Paris '73
The Mother and the Whore '73
Two English Girls '72
Bed and Board '70
Porcile '69
Stolen Kisses '68
Weekend '67
Masculine Feminine '66
Alphaville '65
The Joy of Knowledge '65
Pierrot le Fou '65
The 400 Blows '59
The Testament of Orpheus '59
Madeleine LeBeau (1921-)
8 1/2 '63
Une Parisienne '58
Casablanca '42
Ivan Lebedeff (1899-1953)
Love on the Run '36
Goin' to Town '35
Walking Back '26
Matt LeBlanc (1967-)
Charlie's Angels '00
Lost in Space '98
Ed '96
Showdown '94
Red Shoe Diaries 3: Another Woman's Lipstick '93
Brian Leckner
Joy Ride '01
Sgt. Bilko '95
Bonanza: The Return '93
Ginette LeClerc (1912-92)
Le Corbeau '43
Man from Nowhere '37
The Baker's Wife '33
Jean LeClerc
Blown Away '93
Whispers '89
Friedrich Ledebur
The 27th Day '57
Moby Dick '56
Paul Leder (1926-96)
How to Succeed with Girls '64
Five Minutes to Love '63
Francis Lederer (1899-2000)
Terror Is a Man '59
Return of Dracula '58
The Ambassador's Daughter '56
Lisbon '56
Stolen Identity '53
A Woman of Distinction '50
Diary of a Chambermaid '46
The Bridge of San Luis Rey '44
Midnight '39
One Rainy Afternoon '36
Romance in Manhattan '34
Pandora's Box '28
Suzanne Lederer
Women of Valor '86
Judge Horton and the Scottsboro Boys '76
Heath Ledger (1979-)
A Knight's Tale '01
Monster's Ball '01
The Patriot '00
Ten Things I Hate about You '99
Two Hands '98
Fernand Ledoux (1897-1993)
Pattes Blanches '49
Les Visiteurs du Soir '42
Volpone '39
La Bete Humaine '38
Virginie Ledoyen (1976-)
The Beach '00
Jeanne and the Perfect Guy '98
Late August, Early September '98
A Soldier's Daughter Never Cries '98
A Single Girl '96
La Ceremonie '95
Anna Lee (1913-)
Eleanor & Franklin '76
In Like Flint '67
The Sound of Music '65
Jack the Giant Killer '62
What Ever Happened to Baby Jane? '62
The Horse Soldiers '59
Fort Apache '48
The Ghost and Mrs. Muir '47
Bedlam '45
Commandos Strike at Dawn '43
Flying Tigers '42
Hangmen Also Die '42
How Green Was My Valley '41
The Secret Four '40
King Solomon's Mines '37
Non-Stop New York '37
O.H.M.S. '37
The Man Who Lived Again '36
The Passing of the Third Floor Back '36
First a Girl '35

Belinda Lee (1935-61)
That Long Night in '43 *'60*
Who Done It? *'56*
Blackout *'54*
The Runaway Bus *'54*
The Belles of St. Trinian's *'53*
Bernard Lee (1908-81)
Moonraker *'79*
The Spy Who Loved Me *'77*
Frankenstein and the Monster from Hell *'74*
It's Not the Size That Counts *'74*
The Man with the Golden Gun *'74*
Live and Let Die *'73*
Diamonds Are Forever *'71*
Long Ago Tomorrow *'71*
10 Rillington Place *'71*
On Her Majesty's Secret Service *'69*
You Only Live Twice *'67*
Thunderball *'65*
Goldfinger *'64*
From Russia with Love *'63*
The Brain *'62*
Dr. No *'62*
The L-Shaped Room *'62*
Whistle down the Wind *'61*
Across the Bridge *'57*
The Spanish Gardener *'57*
The Detective *'54*
Beat the Devil *'53*
The Gift Horse *'52*
The Adventurers *'51*
Last Holiday *'50*
The Blue Lamp *'49*
The Fallen Idol *'49*
The Third Man *'49*
Elizabeth of Ladymead *'48*
The Courtney Affair *'47*
The Terror *'38*
Rhodes *'36*
Billy Lee
Reg'lar Fellers *'41*
Wagon Wheels *'34*
Brandon Lee (1965-93)
The Crow *'93*
Rapid Fire *'92*
Showdown in Little Tokyo *'91*
Laser Mission *'90*
Kung Fu: The Movie *'86*
Legacy of Rage *'86*
Britton Lee
Ironheart *'92*
The Power of the Ninjitsu *'88*
Bruce Lee (1940-73)
The Three Avengers *'80*
Game of Death *'79*
Chinese Connection *'73*
Enter the Dragon *'73*
Fists of Fury *'73*
Return of the Dragon *'73*
Marlowe *'69*
Canada Lee (1907-52)
Cry, the Beloved Country *'51*
Lost Boundaries *'49*
Body and Soul *'47*
Lifeboat *'44*
Keep Punching *'39*
Carl Lee (1926-86)
Keeping On *'81*
Gordon's War *'73*
Superfly *'72*
The Cool World *'63*
The Connection *'61*
China Lee
Good Times *'67*
What's Up, Tiger Lily? *'66*
Christopher Lee (1922-)
Star Wars: Episode 2—Attack of the Clones *'02*
Lord of the Rings 1: The Fellowship of the Rings *'01*
Russell Mulcahy's Tale of the Mummy *'99*
Sleepy Hollow *'99*
Ivanhoe *'97*
The Odyssey *'97*
Moses *'96*
The Stupids *'95*
Funnyman *'94*
Police Academy 7: Mission to Moscow *'94*
Detonator *'93*
Double Vision *'92*
Journey of Honor *'91*
Sherlock Holmes and the Incident at Victoria Falls *'91*
Curse 3: Blood Sacrifice *'90*
Gremlins 2: The New Batch *'90*
Around the World in 80 Days *'89*
Murder Story *'89*
The Return of the Musketeers *'89*
Treasure Island *'89*
Jocks *'87*
The Land of Faraway *'87*
Desperate Moves *'86*
The Girl *'86*
Many Faces of Sherlock Holmes *'86*
Howling 2: Your Sister Is a Werewolf *'85*
Rosebud Beach Hotel *'85*
The Far Pavilions *'84*
Keeper *'84*
Return of Captain Invincible *'83*
Shaka Zulu *'83*
House of the Long Shadows *'82*
The Last Unicorn *'82 (V)*
Safari 3000 *'82*
The Salamander *'82*
The Boy Who Left Home to Find Out About the Shivers *'81*
An Eye for an Eye *'81*
Goliath Awaits *'81*
Bear Island *'80*
Serial *'80*
Captain America 2: Death Too Soon *'79*
Jaguar Lives *'79*
1941 *'79*
Circle of Iron *'78*
Return from Witch Mountain *'78*
Airport '77 *'77*
Starship Invasions *'77*
Albino *'76*
Dracula & Son *'76*
Dracula Father and Son *'76*
End of the World *'76*
To the Devil, a Daughter *'76*
The Devil's Undead *'75*
The Four Musketeers *'75*
The Wicker Man *'75*
The Man with the Golden Gun *'74*
The Three Musketeers *'74*
Dark Places *'73*
The Satanic Rites of Dracula *'73*
The Creeping Flesh *'72*
Dracula A.D. 1972 *'72*
Hannie Caulder *'72*
Horror Express *'72*
Nothing But the Night *'72*
Count Dracula *'71*
The House that Dripped Blood *'71*
I, Monster *'71*
The Private Life of Sherlock Holmes *'70*
The Scars of Dracula *'70*
Scream and Scream Again *'70*
Taste the Blood of Dracula *'70*
The Magic Christian *'69*
The Oblong Box *'69*
The Torture Chamber of Dr. Sadism *'69*
The Castle of Fu Manchu *'68*
The Crimson Cult *'68*
The Devil Rides Out *'68*
Dracula Has Risen from the Grave *'68*
Kiss and Kill *'68*
Circus of Fear *'67*
Five Golden Dragons *'67*
Island of the Burning Doomed *'67*
Theatre of Death *'67*
Dracula, Prince of Darkness *'66*
Rasputin the Mad Monk *'66*
Dr. Terror's House of Horrors *'65*
The Skull *'65*
The Virgin of Nuremberg *'65*
Castle of the Living Dead *'64*
The Gorgon *'64*
Hercules in the Haunted World *'64*
The Whip and the Body *'63*
The Longest Day *'62*
Sherlock Holmes and the Deadly Necklace *'62*
Scream of Fear *'61*
Beat Girl *'60*
The Hands of Orlac *'60*
Horror Hotel *'60*
The Two Faces of Dr. Jekyll *'60*
The Hound of the Baskervilles *'59*
The Mummy *'59*
Uncle Was a Vampire *'59*
Corridors of Blood *'58*
The Horror of Dracula *'58*
A Tale of Two Cities *'58*
The Curse of Frankenstein *'57*
Night Ambush *'57*
Alias John Preston *'56*
Crimson Pirate *'52*
Moulin Rouge *'52*
Captain Horatio Hornblower *'51*
Valley of the Eagles *'51*
Hamlet *'48*
Scott of the Antarctic *'48*
Conan Lee
The Eliminators *'86*
Gymkata *'85*
Cosette Lee
The Fly *'86*
Deranged *'74*
Danny Lee
Organized Crime & Triad Bureau *'93*
The Untold Story *'93*
The Killer *'90*
The Mighty Peking Man *'77*
DeWitt Lee
The Legend of Jedediah Carver *'70s*
Apache Blood *'75*
Dorothy Lee (1911-99)
Cockeyed Cavaliers *'34*
Hips, Hips, Hooray *'34*
Half-Shot at Sunrise *'30*
Hook, Line and Sinker *'30*
Elizabeth Lee
Organized Crime & Triad Bureau *'93*
Something Weird *'68*
Eric Lee
Out for Blood *'93*
Ring of Fire *'91*
Etta Lee
The Thief of Baghdad *'24*
The Untamable *'23*
Gypsy Rose Lee (1914-70)
Over the Hill Gang *'69*
The Trouble with Angels *'66*
The Stripper *'63*
My Lucky Star *'38*
Jason Lee (1970-)
Big Trouble *'02*
A Guy Thing *'02*
Heartbreakers *'01*
Jay and Silent Bob Strike Back *'01*
Vanilla Sky *'01*
Almost Famous *'00*
Dogma *'99*
Mumford *'99*
Enemy of the State *'98*
Kissing a Fool *'98*
Chasing Amy *'97*
Weapons of Mass Distraction *'97*
Mallrats *'95*
Jason Scott Lee (1966-)
Lilo & Stitch *'02 (V)*
Arabian Nights *'00*
Russell Mulcahy's Tale of the Mummy *'99*
Soldier *'98*
Murder in Mind *'97*
Rudyard Kipling's The Jungle Book *'94*
Dragon: The Bruce Lee Story *'93*
Map of the Human Heart *'93*
Rapa Nui *'93*
The Lookalike *'90*
Back to the Future, Part 2 *'89*
Jesse Lee (1984-)
A Very Brady Sequel *'96*
The Brady Bunch Movie *'95*
From the Mixed-Up Files of Mrs. Basil E. Frankweiler *'95*
Matinee *'92*
Joanna Lee
Making the Grade *'84*
Sam's Son *'84*
The Brain Eaters *'58*
Plan 9 from Outer Space *'56*
Joie Lee (1962-)
Crooklyn *'94*
Fathers and Sons *'92*
Mo' Better Blues *'90*
Bail Jumper *'89*
School Daze *'88*
She's Gotta Have It *'86*
Jon Kit Lee
Romeo Must Die *'00*
The Corruptor *'99*
Kaiulani Lee
Hush *'98*
Before and After *'95*
Zelly & Me *'88*
Cujo *'83*
Karen Lee
Eye on the Sparrow *'91*
Roadhouse 66 *'84*
Lila Lee (1901-73)
A Nation Aflame *'37*
Country Gentlemen *'36*
Champagne for Breakfast *'35*
I Can't Escape *'34*
Stand Up and Cheer *'34*
False Faces *'32*
The Unholy Three *'30*
The Adorable Cheat *'28*
Midnight Girl *'25*
Blood and Sand *'22*
Hawthorne of the USA *'19*
Male and Female *'19*
Margaret Lee (1943-)
Rogue *'76*
Slaughter Hotel *'71*
Dorian Gray *'70*
Murder for Sale *'70*
Venus in Furs *'70*
Circus of Fear *'67*
Five for Hell *'67*
Five Golden Dragons *'67*
Secret Agent Super Dragon *'66*
Casanova '70 *'65*
How to Kill 400 Duponts *'65*
Mark Lee (1958-)
Nowhere to Land *'00*
Chameleon 2: Death Match *'99*
Blackwater Trail *'95*
The Everlasting Secret Family *'88*
The City's Edge *'83*
Gallipoli *'81*
Mary Lee (1925-96)
Back in the Saddle *'41*
Ridin' on a Rainbow *'41*
Gaucho Serenade *'40*
Nancy Drew, Reporter *'39*
Michele Lee (1942-)
Broadway Bound *'92*
The Fatal Image *'90*
Bud and Lou *'78*
The Comic *'69*
The Love Bug *'68*
How to Succeed in Business without Really Trying *'67*
Moon Lee
Mr. Vampire *'86*
Zu: Warriors from the Magic Mountain *'83*
Peggy Lee (1920-2002)
Lady and the Tramp *'55 (V)*
Pete Kelly's Blues *'55*
Mr. Music *'50*
Stage Door Canteen *'43*
Robbie Lee
Switchblade Sisters *'75*
Big Bad Mama *'74*
RonReaco Lee
How I Spent My Summer Vacation *'97*
Glory *'89*
Ruta Lee (1936-)
Funny Bones *'94*
Sweet Bird of Youth *'89*
First & Ten *'85*
First & Ten: The Team Scores Again *'85*
Rooster: Spurs of Death! *'83*
Escape from Planet Earth *'67*
Sam Lee
Gen-X Cops *'99*
Biozombie *'98*
Shannon Lee
Epoch *'00*
High Voltage *'98*
Sheryl Lee (1967-)
Hitched *'01*
Angel's Dance *'99*
Kiss the Sky *'98*
The Blood Oranges *'97*
David *'97*
John Carpenter's Vampires *'97*
This World, Then the Fireworks *'97*
Bliss *'96*
Mother Night *'96*
Follow the River *'95*
Homage *'95*
Notes from Underground *'95*
Backbeat *'94*
Don't Do It *'94*
Fall Time *'94*
Red Shoe Diaries 4: Auto Erotica *'93*
Jersey Girl *'92*
Twin Peaks: Fire Walk with Me *'92*
Love, Lies and Murder *'91*
Wild at Heart *'90*
Sophie Lee (1968-)
Bootmen *'00*
Holy Smoke *'99*
The Castle *'97*
Muriel's Wedding *'94*
Spike Lee (1957-)
Lisa Picard Is Famous *'01*
Summer of Sam *'99*
Girl 6 *'96*
Crooklyn *'94*
DROP Squad *'94*
Malcolm X *'92*
Jungle Fever *'91*
Mo' Better Blues *'90*
Do the Right Thing *'89*
School Daze *'88*
She's Gotta Have It *'86*
Stan Lee
Mallrats *'95*
The Ambulance *'90*
Stephen Lee (1951-)
Me and the Mob *'94*
Prehysteria *'93*
The Pit & the Pendulum *'91*
Dolls *'87*
Purple Hearts *'84*
Tommy Lee
The New Guy *'02*
The Sand Pebbles *'66*
Waise Lee
Running out of Time *'99*
Wing Chun *'94*
Fatal Chase *'92*
A Bullet in the Head *'90*
A Better Tomorrow, Part 1 *'86*
Richard Leech
The Moonraker *'58*
The Third Key *'57*
Stephen Leeder
Resistance *'92*
Fatal Bond *'91*
Andrea Leeds (1914-74)
The Real Glory *'39*
They Shall Have Music *'39*
The Goldwyn Follies *'38*
Letter of Introduction *'38*
It Could Happen to You *'37*
Stage Door *'37*
Come and Get It *'36*
Song of the Trail *'36*
Lila Leeds
She Shoulda Said No *'49*
The Show-Off *'46*
Phil Leeds (1916-98)
Lost and Found *'99*
Frankie and Johnny *'91*
He Said, She Said *'91*
Ghost *'90*
Enemies, a Love Story *'89*
Saturday the 14th Strikes Back *'88*
Haunting of Harrington House *'82*
Jane Leeves (1962-)
James and the Giant Peach *'96 (V)*
Miracle on 34th Street *'94*
Mr. Write *'92*
Jean (Lefevre) Lefebvre (1922-)
No Problem *'75*
Le Gendarme de Saint-Tropez *'67*
Adam LeFevre
Tadpole *'02*
Hearts in Atlantis *'01*
L.I.E. *'01*
The Ref *'93*
Return of the Secaucus 7 *'80*
Rene Lefevre
The Crime of Monsieur Lange *'36*
Le Million *'31*
Eva LeGallienne
Resurrection *'80*
The Devil's Disciple *'59*
Lance LeGault (1935-)
Roadracers *'94*
Shadow Force *'92*
Kidnapped *'87*
Stripes *'81*
Kenny Rogers as the Gambler *'80*
French Quarter *'78*
Phoebe Legere
The Toxic Avenger, Part 2 *'89*
The Toxic Avenger, Part 3: The Last Temptation of Toxie *'89*
Alison Leggatt
Day of the Triffids *'63*
This Happy Breed *'47*
James LeGros (1962-)
Scotland, PA *'02*
World Traveler *'01*
Common Ground *'00*
If You Only Knew *'00*
Enemy of the State *'98*
Highway Hitcher *'98*
Psycho *'98*
Thursday *'98*
The Myth of Fingerprints *'97*
Pronto *'97*
The Destiny of Marty Fine *'96*
Infinity *'96*
Marshal Law *'96*
Serial Bomber *'96*
Wishful Thinking *'96*
Destiny Turns on the Radio *'95*
The Low Life *'95*

Safe '95
Bad Girls '94
Don't Do It '94
Floundering '94
Living in Oblivion '94
Nervous Ticks '93
Guncrazy '92
My New Gun '92
Singles '92
Where the Day Takes You '92
Point Break '91
Blood & Concrete: A Love Story '90
Leather Jackets '90
Drugstore Cowboy '89
Hollywood Heartbreak '89
Phantasm 2 '88

John Leguizamo (1964-)
Collateral Damage '02
Ice Age '02 *(V)*
ZigZag '02
King of the Jungle '01
Moulin Rouge '01
What's the Worst That Could Happen? '01
Arabian Nights '00
Titan A.E. '00 *(V)*
Joe the King '99
Summer of Sam '99
Dr. Dolittle '98 *(V)*
Frogs for Snakes '98
Body Count '97
A Brother's Kiss '97
Spawn '97
Executive Decision '96
The Fan '96
The Pest '96
William Shakespeare's Romeo and Juliet '96
A Pyromaniac's Love Story '95
To Wong Foo, Thanks for Everything, Julie Newmar '95
Carlito's Way '93
Super Mario Bros. '93
Whispers in the Dark '92
Hangin' with the Homeboys '91
Out for Justice '91
Regarding Henry '91
Die Hard 2: Die Harder '90
Street Hunter '90
Casualties of War '89

Kristen Lehman
Way of the Gun '00
Dog Park '98
Bleeders '97

Carla Lehmann (1917-90)
Fame Is the Spur '47
Secret Mission '42
Cottage to Let '41

Beatrix Lehmann
The Cat and the Canary '79
Love for Lydia '79

Frederic Lehne
Balloon Farm '97
Dream Lover '93
Man's Best Friend '93
This Gun for Hire '90
Amityville 4: The Evil Escapes '89
Billionaire Boys Club '87
Coward of the County '81
Ordinary People '80

John Lehne
A Long Way Home '81
The Disappearance of Aimee '76
Griffin and Phoenix: A Love Story '76
Roboman '75

Fritz Leiber (1883-1949)
Equinox '71
Bagdad '49
Cry of the Werewolf '44
The Story of Louis Pasteur '36

Ron Leibman (1937-)
Just the Ticket '98
Don King: Only in America '97
Night Falls on Manhattan '96
Seven Hours to Judgment '88
Door to Door '84
Phar Lap '84
Rhinestone '84
Romantic Comedy '83
Zorro, the Gay Blade '81
Up the Academy '80
Norma Rae '79
A Question of Guilt '78
The Art of Crime '75
Slaughterhouse Five '72
The Hot Rock '70
Where's Poppa? '70

Don Leifert
Deadly Neighbor '91
Galaxy Invader '85
Fiend '83
The Alien Factor '78

Barbara Leigh (1946-)
Mistress of the Apes '79
Seven '79
Boss '74
Smile, Jenny, You're Dead '74
Junior Bonner '72
The Student Nurses '70

Cassandra Leigh
Alien Terminator '95
Caged Heat 3000 '95
Midnight Tease '94

Frank Leigh (1876-1948)
Below the Deadline '29
American Pluck '25
Nurse Marjorie '20

Janet Leigh (1926-)
Halloween: H20 '98
The Fog '78
Harper '66
Bye, Bye, Birdie '63
The Manchurian Candidate '62
Psycho '60
The Perfect Furlough '59
Touch of Evil '58
The Vikings '58
Jet Pilot '57
My Sister Eileen '55
Pete Kelly's Blues '55
The Black Shield of Falworth '54
Prince Valiant '54
Houdini '53
The Naked Spur '53
Scaramouche '52
Angels in the Outfield '51
Two Tickets to Broadway '51
That Forsyte Woman '50
Holiday Affair '49
Little Women '49
The Hills of Home '48
Words and Music '48

Jennifer Jason Leigh (1963-)
Road to Perdition '02
The Anniversary Party '01
Skipped Parts '00
eXistenZ '99
The Love Letter '98
A Thousand Acres '97
Washington Square '97
Bastard out of Carolina '96
Georgia '95
Kansas City '95
Dolores Claiborne '94
Mrs. Parker and the Vicious Circle '94
The Hudsucker Proxy '93
Short Cuts '93
Single White Female '92
Backdraft '91
Crooked Hearts '91
Rush '91
Buried Alive '90
Last Exit to Brooklyn '90
Miami Blues '90
The Big Picture '89
Heart of Midnight '89
Sister, Sister '87
Undercover '87
The Hitcher '86
The Men's Club '86
Flesh and Blood '85
Girls of the White Orchid '85
Grandview U.S.A. '84
Easy Money '83
Fast Times at Ridgemont High '82
Wrong Is Right '82
The Best Little Girl in the World '81
Eyes of a Stranger '81
Killing of Randy Webster '81
Angel City '80

Nelson Leigh (1905-85)
The Gallant Hours '60
Ma Barker's Killer Brood '60
Texas Masquerade '44

Spencer Leigh
Smart Money '88
The Last of England '87
Caravaggio '86

Steven Leigh
Sword of Honor '94
To Be the Best '93
China White '91
Deadly Bet '91

Suzanna Leigh (1945-)
The Fiend '71
Lust for a Vampire '71
Paradise, Hawaiian Style '66
Boeing Boeing '65

Vivien Leigh (1913-67)
Ship of Fools '65
Roman Spring of Mrs. Stone '61
A Streetcar Named Desire '51
Anna Karenina '48
Caesar and Cleopatra '46
That Hamilton Woman '41
Waterloo Bridge '40
Gone with the Wind '39
Sidewalks of London '38
Dark Journey '37
Fire Over England '37
Storm in a Teacup '37
21 Days '37

Barbara Leigh-Hunt (1935-)
Wives and Daughters '01
Longitude '00
A Merry War '97
Pride and Prejudice '95
Paper Mask '91
The Plague Dogs '82 *(V)*
Frenzy '72

Laura Leighton
Seven Girlfriends '00
Naked City: A Killer Christmas '98

Lillian (Lillianne, Lyllian) Leighton (1874-1956)
Man from Monterey '33
Parisian Love '25
Peck's Bad Boy '21
The Jack Knife Man '20

Margaret Leighton (1922-76)
Choice of Weapons '76
From Beyond the Grave '73
X, Y & Zee '72
The Go-Between '71
The Madwoman of Chaillot '69
The Loved One '65
The Best Man '64
Waltz of the Toreadors '62
Carrington, V.C. '54
The Elusive Pimpernel '50
Under Capricorn '49
Bonnie Prince Charlie '48
The Winslow Boy '48

Roberta Leighton
Covergirl '83
Barracuda '78

Harald Leipnitz (1926-2000)
Fight for Gold '86
Hell Hounds of Alaska '73
River of Evil '64

Frederick Leister (1885-)
Green Grow the Rushes '51
Spellbound '41
O.H.M.S. '37

David Leisure (1950-)
Three Strikes '00
Ten Things I Hate about You '99
Gangster World '98
Hollywood Safari '96
Nowhere '96
You Can't Hurry Love '88

Donovan Leitch (1968-)
Big City Blues '99
The '60s '99
Love Kills '98
One Night Stand '97
I Shot Andy Warhol '96
Dark Horse '92
Gas Food Lodging '92
Cutting Class '89
Glory '89
And God Created Woman '88
The Blob '88
The In Crowd '88

Tyron Leitso
Dinotopia '02
Snow White: The Fairest of Them All '02

Paul LeMat (1952-)
American History X '98
Children of Fury '94
Sensation '94
Wishman '93
Woman with a Past '92
Blind Witness '89
Easy Wheels '89
Grave Secrets '89
Puppet Master '89
Hanoi Hilton '87
Into the Homeland '87
The Night They Saved Christmas '87
Private Investigations '87
Long Time Gone '86
On Wings of Eagles '86
The Burning Bed '85
P.K. and the Kid '85
Rock & Rule '83 *(V)*
Strange Invaders '83
Jimmy the Kid '82
Death Valley '81
Melvin and Howard '80
More American Graffiti '79
Citizens Band '77
Aloha, Bobby and Rose '74
American Graffiti '73
Firehouse '72

Harvey Lembeck (1923-82)
Beach Blanket Bingo '65
How to Stuff a Wild Bikini '65
Bikini Beach '64
Pajama Party '64
Beach Party '63
Love with the Proper Stranger '63
Between Heaven and Hell '56
Stalag 17 '53

Michael Lembeck (1948-)
Danielle Steel's Heartbeat '93
Conspiracy: The Trial of the Chicago Eight '87
On the Right Track '81
Gorp '80
The In-Laws '79
The Boys in Company C '77

Rachel Lemieux
Mommy 2: Mommy's Day '96
Mommy '95

Tutte Lemkow
The Guns of Navarone '61
Moulin Rouge '52

Chris Lemmon (1954-)
Best of the Best: Without Warning '98
Just the Ticket '98
Land of the Free '98
Wishmaster '97
Thunder in Paradise 2 '94
Thunder in Paradise '93
Corporate Affairs '90
Firehead '90
Lena's Holiday '90
Dad '89
Going Undercover '88
That's Life! '86
Weekend Warriors '86
Swing Shift '84
C.O.D. '83
The Happy Hooker Goes Hollywood '80
Just Before Dawn '80

Jack Lemmon (1925-2001)
The Legend of Bagger Vance '00
Inherit the Wind '99
Tuesdays with Morrie '99
Neil Simon's The Odd Couple 2 '98
Out to Sea '97
Twelve Angry Men '97
Getting Away With Murder '96
Hamlet '96
My Fellow Americans '96
A Weekend in the Country '96
The Grass Harp '95
Grumpier Old Men '95
Grumpy Old Men '93
A Life in the Theater '93
Short Cuts '93
For Richer, for Poorer '92
Glengarry Glen Ross '92
The Player '92
JFK '91
Dad '89
Long Day's Journey into Night '88
The Murder of Mary Phagan '87
That's Life! '86
Macaroni '85
Mass Appeal '84
Missing '82
Buddy Buddy '81
Tribute '80
The China Syndrome '79
Airport '77 '77
The Front Page '74
Prisoner of Second Avenue '74
Save the Tiger '73
Avanti! '72
The Out-of-Towners '70
April Fools '69
The Odd Couple '68
Luv '67
The Fortune Cookie '66
The Great Race '65
Good Neighbor Sam '64
How to Murder Your Wife '64
Irma La Douce '63
Under the Yum-Yum Tree '63
Days of Wine and Roses '62
Wackiest Ship in the Army '61
The Apartment '60
Some Like It Hot '59
Voyage en Balloon '59 *(N)*
Bell, Book and Candle '58
Cowboy '58
Fire Down Below '57
Mister Roberts '55
My Sister Eileen '55
Three for the Show '55
It Should Happen to You '54
Phffft! '54

Kasi Lemmons (1961-)
Til There Was You '96
DROP Squad '94
Fear of a Black Hat '94
Hard Target '93
Candyman '92
School Daze '88
Vampire's Kiss '88

Michel Lemoine
The Sensuous Teenager '70
Conquest of Mycene '63
Planets Against Us '61

Genevieve Lemon
Soft Fruit '99
Billy's Holiday '95
The Piano '93
Sweetie '89

Ute Lemper
Appetite '98
Bogus '96
Moscow Parade '92

Mark Lenard (1928-96)
Star Trek 6: The Undiscovered Country '91
Star Trek 4: The Voyage Home '86
Star Trek 3: The Search for Spock '84
Star Trek: The Motion Picture '80
Noon Sunday '71

Harry J. Lennix
Collateral Damage '02
Love and Basketball '00
Titus '99
Get On the Bus '96
Bob Roberts '92
Mo' Money '92
The Five Heartbeats '91

Jarrett Lennon (1982-)
Amityville Dollhouse '96
Short Cuts '93
Servants of Twilight '91

John Lennon (1940-80)
Chuck Berry: Hail! Hail! Rock 'n' Roll '87
Let It Be '70
The Magic Christian '69
Yellow Submarine '68 *(V)*
How I Won the War '67
Magical Mystery Tour '67
Help! '65
A Hard Day's Night '64

Julian Lennon (1963-)
Leaving Las Vegas '95
The Linguini Incident '92
Chuck Berry: Hail! Hail! Rock 'n' Roll '87

Annie Lennox (1954-)
Edward II '92
The Room '87
Revolution '85

Jay Leno (1950-)
The Flintstones '94
Dave '93
We're Back! A Dinosaur's Story '93 *(V)*
Collision Course '89
Americathon '79
Silver Bears '78

Jack Lenoir
Breakfast in Paris '81
Once in Paris... '79

Lotte Lenya (1899-1981)
Semi-Tough '77
From Russia with Love '63
Roman Spring of Mrs. Stone '61
The Threepenny Opera '31

Kay Lenz (1953-)
A Gun, a Car, a Blonde '97
Gunfighter's Moon '96
Trapped in Space '94
Falling from Grace '92
Hitler's Daughter '90
Headhunter '89
Murder by Night '89
Physical Evidence '89
Fear '88
Death Wish 4: The Crackdown '87
Stripped to Kill '87
House '86
Prisoners of the Lost Universe '84
Fast Walking '82
Sanctuary of Fear '79
Initiation of Sarah '78

Mean Dog Blues '78
Great Scout & Cathouse Thursday '76
Moving Violation '76
Rich Man, Poor Man '76
White Line Fever '75

Rick Lenz (1939-)
Little Dragons '80
Scandalous John '71
Cactus Flower '69

Melissa Leo (1960-)
Homicide: The Movie '00
The 24 Hour Woman '99
Last Summer In the Hamptons '96
Scarlett '94
Carolina Skeletons '92
Venice, Venice '92
A Time of Destiny '88
Deadtime Stories '86
Always '85
Silent Witness '85
Streetwalkin' '85

Leon (1962-)
Bats '99
Friends & Lovers '99
Mean Streak '99
Mr. Rock 'n' Roll: The Alan Freed Story '99
The Temptations '98
Pure Danger '96
Spirit Lost '96
Once Upon a Time ... When We Were Colored '95
Waiting to Exhale '95
Above the Rim '94
Bad Attitude '93
Cliffhanger '93
Cool Runnings '93
The Five Heartbeats '91
Colors '88

Loles Leon
Don Juan, My Love '90
Tie Me Up! Tie Me Down! '90

Valerie Leon (1945-)
Never Say Never Again '83
The Spy Who Loved Me '77
Blood from the Mummy's Tomb '71
Zeta One '69

Joshua Leonard
Men of Honor '00
Sacrifice '00
The Blair Witch Project '99

Lu Leonard (1945-)
A Climate for Killing '91
Circuitry Man '90
Shadowzone '89
Princess Academy '87

Robert Sean Leonard (1969-)
Chelsea Walls '01
Driven '01
A Glimpse of Hell '01
Tape '01
Ground Control '98
The Last Days of Disco '98
I Love You, I Love You Not '97
In the Gloaming '97
Standoff '97
The Boys Next Door '96
Killer: A Journal of Murder '95
Safe Passage '94
The Age of Innocence '93
Married to It '93
Much Ado about Nothing '93
Swing Kids '93
Mr. & Mrs. Bridge '90
Dead Poets Society '89
My Best Friend Is a Vampire '88
Bluffing It '87

Sheldon Leonard (1907-97)
Brink's Job '78
The Road to Lebanon '60
Guys and Dolls '55
Breakdown '53
Here Come the Nelsons '52
Abbott and Costello Meet the Invisible Man '51
Chained for Life '51
Force of Evil '49
Shep Comes Home '49
Open Secret '48
Sinbad, the Sailor '47
It's a Wonderful Life '46
Rainbow over Texas '46
Captain Kidd '45
The Falcon in Hollywood '44
Gambler's Choice '44
Timber Queen '44
To Have & Have Not '44
Uncertain Glory '44
Zombies on Broadway '44
City Without Men '43
Harvest Melody '43
Tortilla Flat '42
Week-End in Havana '41

Marco Leonardi (1971-)
Texas Rangers '01
The Five Senses '99
From Dusk Till Dawn 3: The Hangman's Daughter '99
David '97
Manhattan Merenque! '95
The Stendahl Syndrome '95
Like Water for Chocolate '93
Cinema Paradiso '88

Al Leong
Hard Hunted '92
Bill & Ted's Excellent Adventure '89
Lethal Weapon '87

Tea Leoni (1966-)
Hollywood Ending '02
Jurassic Park 3 '01
Family Man '00
Life in the Fast Lane '00
Deep Impact '98
Bad Boys '95
Flirting with Disaster '95
Wyatt Earp '94
A League of Their Own '92

Chauncey Leopardi (1981-)
ShadowZone: The Undead Express '96
Sticks and Stones '96
The Big Green '95
Houseguest '94
Huck and the King of Hearts '93
The Sandlot '93

Philippe Leotard (1940-2001)
Les Miserables '95
La Balance '82
La Petite Sirene '80
Cat and Mouse '78
Two English Girls '72

Robert Lepage (1957-)
Stardom '00
Jesus of Montreal '89

Ted Leplat
American Kickboxer 1 '91
Emissary '89
Swift Justice '88
The Kirlian Witness '78

Ken Lerner
Senseless '98
Mother's Boys '94
Relentless 4 '94
Fallen Angels 1 '93
Unlawful Entry '92
Fast Getaway '91
Relentless '89

Michael Lerner (1941-)
Attention Shoppers '99
The Mod Squad '99
Russell Mulcahy's Tale of the Mummy '99
Celebrity '98
Godzilla '98
My Favorite Martian '98
Safe Men '98
The Beautician and the Beast '97
For Richer or Poorer '97
No Way Back '96
A Pyromaniac's Love Story '95
Girl in the Cadillac '94
No Escape '94
Radioland Murders '94
The Road to Wellville '94
Amos and Andrew '93
Blank Check '93
The Comrades of Summer '92
Newsies '92
Barton Fink '91
The Closer '91
Omen 4: The Awakening '91
Any Man's Death '90
Maniac Cop 2 '90
Harlem Nights '89
Anguish '88
Eight Men Out '88
Hands of a Stranger '87
The Execution '85
Rita Hayworth: The Love Goddess '83
Strange Invaders '83
National Lampoon's Class Reunion '82
The Postman Always Rings Twice '81
Coast to Coast '80
Outlaw Blues '77
F. Scott Fitzgerald in Hollywood '76
Busting '74
Reflections of Murder '74
The Candidate '72
Firehouse '72

Maxime LeRoux
The Son of the Shark '93
Mama, There's a Man in Your Bed '89

Phillippe LeRoy (1930-)
Vatel '00
Quo Vadis '85
Three Men and a Cradle '85
The Night Porter '74
The Frightened Woman '71
A Married Woman '65
Castle of the Living Dead '64
Alone Against Rome '62
Le Trou '59

Ed LeSaint
Texas Bad Man '32
Range Feud '31

Bethel Leslie (1929-99)
Message in a Bottle '98
Saint Maybe '98
In Cold Blood '96
Long Day's Journey into Night '88
Ironweed '87

Joan Leslie (1925-)
Jubilee Trail '54
Man in the Saddle '51
Born to Be Bad '50
Rhapsody in Blue '45
Hollywood Canteen '44
The Sky's the Limit '43
Thank Your Lucky Stars '43
This Is the Army '43
Yankee Doodle Dandy '42
High Sierra '41
Sergeant York '41
The Wagons Roll at Night '41
Love Affair '39

John Leslie
It's Called Murder, Baby '82
Dracula Sucks '79

Nan Leslie (1926-2000)
The Bamboo Saucer '68
Iron Mountain Trail '53
Rim of the Canyon '49
Desperate '47
The Devil Thumbs a Ride '47

Mimi Lesseos
Beyond Fear '93
Pushed to the Limit '92
Final Impact '91
The American Angels: Baptism of Blood '89

Anton Lesser
Charlotte Gray '01
Lorna Doone '01
Vanity Fair '99
Moses '96

Len Lesser (1922-)
The Ghost of Fletcher Ridge '80s
Ain't No Way Back '89
Grandma's House '88
Dubeat-E-O '84
Joy Ride to Nowhere '78
Kelly's Heroes '70
How to Stuff a Wild Bikini '65
Shack Out on 101 '55

Ben Lessy
Pajama Party '64
The Jackie Robinson Story '50

Adrian Lester
Born Romantic '00
Jason and the Argonauts '00
Love's Labour's Lost '00
Maybe Baby '99
Primary Colors '98

Bruce Lester (1912-)
Charade '53
Golden Earrings '47
Shadows on the Stairs '41
British Intelligence '40
The Letter '40
Boy Meets Girl '38

Buddy Lester (1917-)
Cracking Up '83
Big Mouth '67
The Patsy '64
The Nutty Professor '63
Ocean's 11 '60

Jeff Lester
In the Cold of the Night '89
Once a Hero '88

Kate Lester
The Hunchback of Notre Dame '23
The Social Secretary '16

Mark Lester (1958-)
The Prince and the Pauper '78
Redneck '73
What the Peeper Saw '72
Black Beauty '71
Melody '71
Who Slew Auntie Roo? '71
Eye Witness '70
Oliver! '68
Fahrenheit 451 '66

Ron Lester
Not Another Teen Movie '01
Varsity Blues '98
Good Burger '97

David Letch
Dark of the Night '85
Death Warmed Up '85

Shelli Lether
The Sender '98
Born to Run '93

Lori Lethin
Return to Horror High '87
Brotherly Love '85
Bloody Birthday '80
The Prey '80

Ken Letner
The Big Sweat '90
Strangers in Paradise '84

Jared Leto (1971-)
Panic Room '02
Highway '01
Requiem for a Dream '00
American Psycho '99
Black and White '99
Fight Club '99
Girl, Interrupted '99
Basil '98
The Thin Red Line '98
Urban Legend '98
Switchback '97
The Last of the High Kings '96
Prefontaine '96
How to Make an American Quilt '95

Matt Letscher
Jackie, Ethel, Joan: The Kennedy Women '01
The Mask of Zorro '98
Lovelife '97

Dan Lett
The Life Before This '99
Blind Faith '98
Frame by Frame '95
Paris, France '94

Al Lettieri (1928-75)
The Godfather 1902-1959: The Complete Epic '81
McQ '74
Mr. Majestyk '74
The Deadly Trackers '73
The Don Is Dead '73
The Getaway '72
The Godfather '72
Pulp '72

Tony Leung Chiu-Wai (1962-)
In the Mood for Love '00
Tokyo Raiders '00
Gorgeous '99
Flowers of Shanghai '98
Happy Together '96
Chungking Express '95
Cyclo '95
Hard-Boiled '92
A Bullet in the Head '90

Tony Leung Ka-Fai (1958-)
The Lover '92
The Laserman '90
The Prisoner '90
A Better Tomorrow, Part 3 '89
Prison on Fire '87

Clinton Leupp
Trick '99
Nick and Jane '96

Lynn Levand
Kill or Be Killed '93
Hellbent '90

Oscar Levant (1906-72)
The Cobweb '55
The Band Wagon '53
An American in Paris '51
The Barkleys of Broadway '49
Romance on the High Seas '48
Humoresque '46
Rhythm on the River '40
Dance of Life '29

Calvin Levels (1954-)
Within the Rock '96
Hellbound '94
Point of No Return '93
Johnny Suede '92
Live! From Death Row '92
Adventures in Babysitting '87
A Christmas Without Snow '80

Sam Levene (1905-80)
God Told Me To '76
A Dream of Kings '69
Designing Woman '57
Sweet Smell of Success '57
Babe Ruth Story '48
Boomerang '47
The Killers '46
The Purple Heart '44
Action in the North Atlantic '43
I Dood It '43
Whistling in Brooklyn '43
Shadow of the Thin Man '41
Golden Boy '39
Mad Miss Manton '38
Shopworn Angel '38
Three Men on a Horse '36

Marcel Levesque
The Fantastic Night '42
Les Vampires '15

John Levin
Bounce '00
Zoltan...Hound of Dracula '78

Rachel Levin
White Palace '90
Gaby: A True Story '87

Floyd Levine
Watchers Reborn '98
Ice '93

Jean Levine
Hollywood in Trouble '87
The Newlydeads '87

Jerry Levine (1957-)
Born on the Fourth of July '89
Casual Sex? '88
Iron Eagle '86

Ted Levine (1958-)
Ali '01
Evolution '01
The Fast and the Furious '01
Joy Ride '01 (V)
Harlan County War '00
Wild Wild West '99
From the Earth to the Moon '98
Moby Dick '98
Ellen Foster '97
Flubber '97
Mad City '97
Switchback '97
Georgia '95
Heat '95
Bullet '94
The Mangler '94
Detonator '93
The Last Outlaw '93
Nowhere to Run '93
The Silence of the Lambs '91
Fulfillment '89
Love at Large '89
Ironweed '87

Barry Levinson (1942-)
Jimmy Hollywood '94
Quiz Show '94
History of the World: Part 1 '81

Emile Levisetti
Alien Terminator '95
Sexual Response '92
Bix '90

Steve Levitt
Blue Movies '88
The Incredible Hulk Returns '88
Hunk '87
Last Resort '86

Uta Levka (1942-)
Scream and Scream Again '70
Carmen, Baby '66
The Alley Cats '65

Eugene Levy (1946-)
Like Mike '02
American Pie 2 '01
Down to Earth '01
Serendipity '01
Best in Show '00
The Ladies Man '00
American Pie '99
The Secret Life of Girls '99
Almost Heroes '97
Multiplicity '96
Waiting for Guffman '96
Father of the Bride Part II '95
Kurt Vonnegut's Harrison Bergeron '95
Stay Tuned '92
Father of the Bride '91
Speed Zone '88
Armed and Dangerous '86
Club Paradise '86
The Last Polka '84
Splash '84
Going Berserk '83
National Lampoon's Vacation '83
Heavy Metal '81 (V)

James Lew (1952-)
Deep Core '00
Boogie Boy '98
High Voltage '98
Balance of Power '96
Robo Warriors '96
Blood for Blood '95
Red Sun Rising '94
Private Wars '93

Jose Lewgoy (1920-)
Cobra Verde '88
Kiss of the Spider Woman '85
Fitzcarraldo '82

Earth Entranced '66
Al Lewis (1910-)
South Beach Academy '96
Car 54, Where Are You? '94
My Grandpa Is a Vampire '92
Fright House '89
Married to the Mob '88
Comic Cabby '87
The Munsters' Revenge '81
Used Cars '80
Way He Was '76
The Night Strangler '72
They Shoot Horses, Don't They? '69
Munster, Go Home! '66
Brittney Lewis
Rubin & Ed '92
Dream Machine '91
Charlotte Lewis (1968-)
Navajo Blues '97
The Glass Cage '96
Decoy '95
Embrace of the Vampire '95
Red Shoe Diaries 6: How I Met My Husband '95
Men of War '94
Excessive Force '93
Sketch Artist '92
Storyville '92
Bare Essentials '91
Tripwire '89
Dial Help '88
The Golden Child '86
Pirates '86
David Lewis (1916-2000)
Lake Placid '99
The Apartment '60
Dawnn Lewis (1961-)
The 10th Kingdom '00
Race to Freedom: The Story of the Underground Railroad '94
I'm Gonna Git You Sucka '88
Diana Lewis (1919-97)
Somewhere I'll Find You '42
Whistling in Dixie '42
Andy Hardy Meets Debutante '40
Go West '40
Fiona Lewis (1946-)
Innerspace '87
Strange Invaders '83
Strange Behavior '81
Wanda Nevada '79
Tintorera...Tiger Shark '78
Stunts '77
Drum '76
Lisztomania '75
Blue Blood '73
Dracula '73
Doctor Phibes Rises Again '72
The Fearless Vampire Killers '67
Forrest Lewis
The Monster of Piedras Blancas '57
Escape from Fort Bravo '53
Gary Lewis
Billy Elliot '00
My Name Is Joe '98
Postmortem '98
Carla's Song '97
Orphans '97
Hardly Working '81
Geoffrey Lewis (1935-)
The New Guy '02
Way of the Gun '00
The Prophet's Game '99
Midnight in the Garden of Good and Evil '97
Rough Riders '97
An Occasional Hell '96
Trilogy of Terror 2 '96
When the Dark Man Calls '95
Army of One '94
Maverick '94
National Lampoon's Last Resort '94
White Fang 2: The Myth of the White Wolf '94
The Man Without a Face '93
Only the Strong '93
Point of No Return '93
Wishman '93
The Lawnmower Man '92
Double Impact '91
Disturbed '90
Matters of the Heart '90
Catch Me ... If You Can '89
Fletch Lives '89
Pink Cadillac '89
Out of the Dark '88
Pancho Barnes '88
Maximum Security '87
Lust in the Dust '85
Stitches '85
Night of the Comet '84
Return of the Man from U.N.C.L.E. '83
September Gun '83
I, the Jury '82
Heaven's Gate '81
Shoot the Sun Down '81
Any Which Way You Can '80
Bronco Billy '80
Every Which Way But Loose '78
Tilt '78
When Every Day Was the Fourth of July '78
The Return of a Man Called Horse '76
The Great Waldo Pepper '75
Smile '75
The Wind and the Lion '75
Macon County Line '74
Thunderbolt & Lightfoot '74
Culpepper Cattle Co. '72
Moon of the Wolf '72
George Lewis (1903-95)
Indian Paint '64
The Sign of Zorro '60
King of the Bullwhip '51
The Big Sombrero '49
Federal Operator 99 '45
Perils of the Darkest Jungle '44
Zorro's Black Whip '44
Outlaws of the Desert '41
Gilbert Lewis
Candyman '92
The Kid Who Loved Christmas '90
Touched '82
Greg Lewis
Prehysteria 2 '94
Frankie and Johnny '91
Huey Lewis (1950-)
Duets '00
Shadow of Doubt '98
Short Cuts '93
Back to the Future '85
Jenifer Lewis (1957-)
The Brothers '01
Cast Away '00
Dancing in September '00
Jackie's Back '99
Partners '99
The Mighty '98
Girl 6 '96
The Preacher's Wife '96
Corrina, Corrina '94
Deconstructing Sarah '94
Renaissance Man '94
What's Love Got to Do with It? '93
Jenny Lewis (1977-)
Little Boy Blue '97
Foxfire '96
Runaway Father '91
Troop Beverly Hills '89
The Wizard '89
A Friendship in Vienna '88
Trading Hearts '87
Jerry Lewis (1926-)
Arizona Dream '94
Funny Bones '94
Mr. Saturday Night '92
Cookie '89
Slapstick of Another Kind '84
Cracking Up '83
King of Comedy '82
Hardly Working '81
Rascal Dazzle '81 (N)
Which Way to the Front? '70
Don't Raise the Bridge, Lower the River '68
Big Mouth '67
Boeing Boeing '65
Family Jewels '65
Disorderly Orderly '64
The Patsy '64
It's a Mad, Mad, Mad, Mad World '63
The Nutty Professor '63
Who's Minding the Store? '63
The Errand Boy '61
The Ladies' Man '61
The Bellboy '60
Cinderfella '60
The Geisha Boy '58
Rock-A-Bye Baby '57
The Sad Sack '57
The Delicate Delinquent '56
Hollywood or Bust '56
Pardners '56
Artists and Models '55
The Caddy '53
The Road to Bali '53
Scared Stiff '53
Jumping Jacks '52
The Stooge '51
At War with the Army '50
My Friend Irma '49
Jerry Lee Lewis
Chuck Berry: Hail! Hail! Rock 'n' Roll '87
High School Confidential '58
Joe Lewis
Force: Five '81
Jaguar Lives '79
Joe E. Lewis
Lady in Cement '68
Private Buckaroo '42
Juliette Lewis (1973-)
Enough '02
My Louisiana Sky '02
Way of the Gun '00
The 4th Floor '99
The Other Sister '98
The Evening Star '96
From Dusk Till Dawn '95
Strange Days '95
The Basketball Diaries '94
Mixed Nuts '94
Natural Born Killers '94
Kalifornia '93
Romeo Is Bleeding '93
That Night '93
What's Eating Gilbert Grape '93
Husbands and Wives '92
Cape Fear '91
Crooked Hearts '91
Too Young to Die '90
Meet the Hollowheads '89
National Lampoon's Christmas Vacation '89
My Stepmother Is an Alien '88
Leigh Lewis
Revelation '00
Tribulation '00
Louise Lewis
Blood of Dracula '57
I Was a Teenage Werewolf '57
Matthew Lewis
Harry Potter and the Sorcerer's Stone '01
The Legend of Wolf Mountain '92
Michael Lewis (1939-)
Signs of Life '89
Gruesome Twosome '67
Mitchell Lewis (1880-1956)
Cairo '42
Billy the Kid '41
The Wizard of Oz '39
Linda '29
Salome '22
Phill Lewis (1968-)
Spent '00
Once Upon a Time ... When We Were Colored '95 (N)
Brother Future '91
City Slickers '91
Ralph Lewis (1872-1937)
Sucker Money '34
Somewhere in Sonora '33
Dante's Inferno '24
Outside the Law '21
When the Clouds Roll By '19
The Birth of a Nation '15
Richard Lewis (1947-)
Hugo Pool '97
Drunks '96
A Weekend in the Country '96
Danger of Love '95
Leaving Las Vegas '95
Wagons East '94
Robin Hood: Men in Tights '93
Once Upon a Crime '92
The Return of Spinal Tap '92
That's Adequate '90
The Wrong Guys '88
Diary of a Young Comic '79
Robert Lewis (1909-97)
Misbegotten '98
My Very Best Friend '96
Hello Again '87
Monsieur Verdoux '47
Son of Lassie '45
Ronald Lewis (1928-82)
Paul and Michelle '74
Friends '71
Billy Budd '62
Mr. Sardonicus '61
Scream of Fear '61
Conspiracy of Hearts '60
Bachelor of Hearts '58
Robbery under Arms '57
Helen of Troy '56
Sheldon Lewis (1869-1958)
Tombstone Canyon '35
The Phantom '31
Beyond the Trail '26
With Kit Carson over the Great Divide '25
Vera Lewis
Ella Cinders '26
Nurse Marjorie '20
Vicki Lewis (1960-)
Pushing Tin '99
Breakfast of Champions '98
Godzilla '98
Mouse Hunt '97
John Ley
Out of the Body '88
BMX Bandits '83
Leo Leyden
Quiet Day in Belfast '74
The Mask '61
Jacob Leygraf
Sunday's Children '94
The Slingshot '93
Johan Leysen (1950-)
The Gambler '97
Trahir '93
Daens '92
Egg '88
The Music Teacher '88
Hail Mary '85
John Leyton (1939-)
Schizo '77
Seaside Swingers '65
Von Ryan's Express '65
Guns at Batasi '64
The Great Escape '63
Thierry Lhermitte (1957-)
The Closet '00
The Dinner Game '98
An American Werewolf in Paris '97
Augustin '95
Little Indian, Big City '95
Grosse Fatigue '94
My Best Friend's Girl '84
My New Partner '84
Until September '84
Next Year If All Goes Well '83
Bruce Li
Chinese Connection 2 '84
Counter Attack '84
Fists of Fury 2 '80
The Young Bruce Lee '80
Return of the Tiger '78
Gong Li (1965-)
The Emperor and the Assassin '99
Chinese Box '97
Temptress Moon '96
Shanghai Triad '95
To Live '94
Farewell My Concubine '93
Raise the Red Lantern '91
The Story of Qiu Ju '91
Ju Dou '90
Red Sorghum '87
Jet Li (1963-)
Kiss of the Dragon '01
The One '01
Romeo Must Die '00
Lethal Weapon 4 '98
Black Mask '96
Jet Li's The Enforcer '95
Meltdown '95
The Bodyguard from Beijing '94
Fist of Legend '94
Once Upon a Time in China III '93
Twin Warriors '93
Once Upon a Time in China II '92
Once Upon a Time in China '91
Peter Paul Liapis
Fast Getaway 2 '94
Ghoulies 4 '93
Starhops '78
Brian Libby
Platoon Leader '87
Silent Rage '82
Liberace
The Loved One '65
Sincerely Yours '56
Anne Libert
The Demons '74
Virgin among the Living Dead '71
Richard Libertini (1933-)
Telling You '98
Nell '94
And You Thought Your Parents Were Weird! '91 (V)
The Bonfire of the Vanities '90
DuckTales the Movie: Treasure of the Lost Lamp '90 (V)
Animal Behavior '89
Fletch Lives '89
Big Trouble '86
Fletch '85
Fourth Wise Man '85
All of Me '84
Unfaithfully Yours '84
Deal of the Century '83
Going Berserk '83
Soup for One '82
Sharky's Machine '81
Popeye '80
The In-Laws '79
Richard Liberty
Day of the Dead '85
The Crazies '73
Jeremy Licht (1971-)
Next One '84
Twilight Zone: The Movie '83
Lois Gibbs and the Love Canal '82
Father Figure '80
The Seekers '79
Mitchell Lichtenstein
The Wedding Banquet '93
Streamers '83
Gabriella Licudi
The Last Safari '67
The Unearthly Stranger '64
G. Gordon Liddy (1930-)
Adventures in Spying '92
Camp Cucamonga: How I Spent My Summer Vacation '90
Street Asylum '90
Super Force '90
When Nature Calls '85
Anki Liden
Expectations '97
My Life As a Dog '85
Mimi Lieber
Wilder Napalm '93
Last Resort '86
Leon Liebgold (-1993)
The Dybbuk '37
Yidl Mitn Fidl '36
Michael Liebman
2 by 4 '98
The Painted Lady '97
Lo Lieh
Sex and Zen '93
The Stranger and the Gunfighter '76
Jennifer Lien
SLC Punk! '99
American History X '98
Albert Lieven (1906-71)
Brainwashed '60
Frieda '47
Beware of Pity '46
The Seventh Veil '46
Sleeping Car to Trieste '45
The Life and Death of Colonel Blimp '43
Night Train to Munich '40
Tina Lifford
The Loretta Claiborne Story '00
The '70s '00
Letters from a Killer '98
The Temptations '98
Mandela and de Klerk '97
America's Dream '95
The Ernest Green Story '93
Grand Canyon '91
Paris Trout '91
Colors '88
Marilyn Lightstone
Grand Tour: Disaster in Time '92
Abraxas: Guardian of the Universe '90
Surrogate '88
Anne of Green Gables '85
Wild Pony '83
Spasms '82
Lies My Father Told Me '75
Tom Ligon
Judge Horton and the Scottsboro Boys '76
Fury on Wheels '71
Lil' Bow Wow (1987-)
All About the Benjamins '02
Like Mike '02
Dennis (Denis) Lill (1942-)
Element of Doubt '96
Bad Blood '87
Lillie '79
Matthew Lillard (1970-)
Scooby-Doo '02
Summer Catch '01
13 Ghosts '01
Love's Labour's Lost '00
She's All That '99
SLC Punk! '99
Spanish Judges '99
Wing Commander '99
Dish Dogs '98
Senseless '98
Telling You '98
The Curve '97
Without Limits '97
Animal Room '95
Hackers '95
Tarantella '95
Serial Mom '94

Beatrice Lillie (1898-1989)
Thoroughly Modern Millie '67
Around the World in 80 Days '56
On Approval '44
Brigitte (Lin Chinag-hsia) Lin (1954-)
Chungking Express '95
Dream Lovers '86
Police Story '85
Fantasy Mission Force '84
Zu: Warriors from the Magic Mountain '83
Aida Linares
U-Turn '97
Clueless '95
Peter Linari
The Curse of the Jade Scorpion '01
Fat Guy Goes Nutzoid '86
Abbey Lincoln (1930-)
Mo' Better Blues '90
For Love of Ivy '68
Nothing but a Man '64
The Girl Can't Help It '56
Andrew Lincoln
The Woman in White '97
Boston Kickout '95
Elmo Lincoln (1889-1952)
Tarzan's New York Adventure '42
Wyoming Outlaw '39
The Adventures of Tarzan '21
Tarzan of the Apes '17
Lar Park Lincoln
Friday the 13th, Part 7: The New Blood '88
House 2: The Second Story '87
Princess Academy '87
Pamela Lincoln
Anatomy of a Psycho '61
The Tingler '59
Gillian Lind
And Now the Screaming Starts '73
Dynasty of Fear '72
Traci Lind (1966-)
The End of Violence '97
Wolverine '96
The Road to Wellville '94
My Boyfriend's Back '93
No Secrets '91
Voyager '91
Class of 1999 '90
The Handmaid's Tale '90
Survival Quest '89
Fright Night 2 '88
A Tiger's Tale '87
Boguslaw Linda (1952-)
The Decalogue '88
Danton '82
Chad Lindberg
The Rookie '02
The Fast and the Furious '01
October Sky '99
Black Circle Boys '97
Gunnel Lindblom (1935-)
Hunger '66
The Virgin Spring '59
The Seventh Seal '56
Doris Linden
Hillbilly Blitzkrieg '42
Snuffy Smith, Yard Bird '42
Eric Linden (1909-94)
Criminals Within '41
Gone with the Wind '39
Sweetheart of the Navy '37
Ah, Wilderness! '35
Let 'Em Have It '35
Hal Linden (1931-)
Out to Sea '97
The Colony '95
A New Life '88
I Do! I Do! '84
My Wicked, Wicked Ways '84
Starflight One '83
Father Figure '80
How to Break Up a Happy Divorce '76
Mr. Inside, Mr. Outside '74
Jennie Linden (1939-)
Hedda '75
Women in Love '70
Nightmare '63
Cec Linder (1921-92)
Heavenly Bodies '84
Deadly Eyes '82
The Devil's Web '74
A Touch of Class '73
Goldfinger '64
Lolita '62
Quatermass and the Pit '58
Max Linder (1883-1925)
Man in the Silk Hat '83
Pop Goes the Cork '22
Seven Years Bad Luck '20
Man in the Silk Hat '15
Viveca Lindfors (1920-95)
Last Summer In the Hamptons '96
Stargate '94
Backstreet Justice '93
The Linguini Incident '92
Child of Darkness, Child of Light '91
Zandalee '91
Exiled in America '90
Exorcist 3: Legion '90
The Ann Jillian Story '88
Lady Beware '87
Rachel River '87
Secret Weapons '85
The Sure Thing '85
Silent Madness '84
Creepshow '82
Inside the Third Reich '82
The Best Little Girl in the World '81
For Ladies Only '81
The Hand '81
Marilyn: The Untold Story '80
Mom, the Wolfman and Me '80
Natural Enemies '79
Girlfriends '78
A Question of Guilt '78
A Wedding '78
Welcome to L.A. '77
Bell from Hell '74
The Way We Were '73
Coming Apart '69
Cauldron of Blood '67
The King of Kings '61
The Story of Ruth '60
Moonfleet '55
Four in a Jeep '51
Adventures of Don Juan '49
Peter Lindgren
The New Land '73
I Am Curious (Yellow) '67
Audra Lindley (1918-97)
Sudden Death '95
The New Age '94
Troop Beverly Hills '89
The Spellbinder '88
Stamp of a Killer '87
Desert Hearts '86
Best Friends '82
Cannery Row '82
Revenge of the Stepford Wives '80
The Heartbreak Kid '72
Carl Michael Lindner
The Extreme Adventures of Super Dave '98
Slappy and the Stinkers '97
Delroy Lindo (1952-)
Heist '01
The Last Castle '01
The One '01
Gone in 60 Seconds '00
Romeo Must Die '00
The Book of Stars '99
The Cider House Rules '99
Strange Justice: The Clarence Thomas and Anita Hill Story '99
Glory & Honor '98
The Devil's Advocate '97
First Time Felon '97
A Life Less Ordinary '97
Feeling Minnesota '96
Ransom '96
Soul of the Game '96
The Winner '96
Broken Arrow '95
Clockers '95
Get Shorty '95
Crooklyn '94
Blood In ... Blood Out: Bound by Honor '93
Mr. Jones '93
Malcolm X '92
Bright Angel '91
Mountains of the Moon '90
More American Graffiti '79
Olga Lindo
The Hidden Room '49
Things Happen at Night '48
Vincent Lindon (1959-)
Seventh Heaven '98
A Man in Love '87
Betty Blue '86
Margaret Lindsay (1910-81)
Please Don't Eat the Daisies '60
Cass Timberlane '47
Club Havana '46
The Adventures of Rusty '45
The Spoilers '42
British Intelligence '40
The House of the Seven Gables '40
Jezebel '38
Dangerous '35
Devil Dogs of the Air '35
"G" Men '35
Baby Face '33
Cavalcade '33
Lady Killer '33
Robert Lindsay (1949-)
Horatio Hornblower: The Adventure Continues '01
Oliver Twist '00
Horatio Hornblower '99
Fierce Creatures '96
Genghis Cohn '93
Strike It Rich '90
Bert Rigby, You're a Fool '89
That'll Be the Day '73
Stuart Lindsell
Profile '54
Man of Evil '48
George Lindsey
Return to Mayberry '85
Robin Hood '73 (V)
Joseph Lindsey
Caught Up '98
Public Enemies '96
Amongst Friends '93
Blake Lindsley
Trial by Media '00
Starship Troopers '97
Swingers '96
Pierre Lindstedt
The New Land '73
The Emigrants '72
Helga Line (1932-)
Pulsebeat '85
Black Venus '83
The Mummy's Revenge '73
When the Screaming Stops '73
Horror Express '72
Horror Rises from the Tomb '72
The Saga of the Draculas '72
Nightmare Castle '65
Richard Lineback
Ready to Rumble '00
Dangerous Evidence: The Lori Jackson Story '99
The Baby Dance '98
Meet the Deedles '98
Varsity Blues '98
The Jackal '97
Tin Cup '96
Speed '94
Woman with a Past '92
Beyond the Next Mountain '87
Stephi Lineburg
Breathing Lessons '94
Richie Rich '94
Rosaleen Linehan (1937-)
About Adam '00
Mad About Mambo '00
The Hi-Lo Country '98
The Matchmaker '97
Sharpe's Gold '94
Bai Ling (1972-)
The Breed '01
The Lost Empire '01
Anna and the King '99
Wild Wild West '99
Row Your Boat '98
Red Corner '97
Somewhere in the City '97
Dead Weekend '95
The Crow '93
Wendy Lingham
Demonstrator '71
Zeta One '69
Paul (Link) Linke (1948-)
The Fear Inside '92
Parenthood '89
Motel Hell '80
Richard Linklater (1961-)
Waking Life '01
Beavis and Butt-Head Do America '96 (V)
The Underneath '95
Slacker '91
Art Linkletter
Champagne for Caesar '50
People Are Funny '46
Rex Linn
Crossfire Trail '01
Neil Simon's The Odd Couple 2 '98
Rush Hour '98
The Postman '97
Breakdown '96
Tin Cup '96
Children of Fury '94
Drop Zone '94
Wyatt Earp '94
Cliffhanger '93
Mark Linn-Baker (1954-)
Noises Off '92
Bare Essentials '91
Me and Him '89 (V)
Ghostwriter '84
My Favorite Year '82
Manhattan '79
Laura Linney (1964-)
The Laramie Project '02
The Mothman Prophecies '02
Lush '01
Maze '01
House of Mirth '00
Running Mates '00
You Can Count On Me '99
The Truman Show '98
Absolute Power '97
Armistead Maupin's More Tales of the City '97
Primal Fear '96
Congo '95
A Simple Twist of Fate '94
Armistead Maupin's Tales of the City '93
Blind Spot '93
Dave '93
Class of '61 '92
Joanne Linville (1928-)
James Dean '01
From the Dead of Night '89
Secrets '77
Scorpio '73
Larry Linville (1939-2000)
No Dessert Dad, 'Til You Mow the Lawn '94
Body Waves '92
Rock 'n' Roll High School Forever '91
Earth Girls Are Easy '89
Blue Movies '88
School Spirit '85
Night Partners '83
The Night Stalker '71
The Stepmother '71
Alex D. Linz (1989-)
Max Keeble's Big Move '01
Bounce '00
Titan A.E. '00 (V)
The Dress Code '99
Tarzan '99 (V)
Home Alone 3 '97
The Cable Guy '96
One Fine Day '96
Lio (1962-)
Love After Love '94
Window Shopping '86
The Eighties '83
Leon M. Lion
Amazing Adventure '37
No. 17 '32
Alberto Lionello
Till Marriage Do Us Part '74
Porcile '69
Therese Liotard
My Father's Glory '91
My Mother's Castle '91
The Disenchanted '90
Cloud Waltzing '87
One Sings, the Other Doesn't '77
Ray Liotta (1955-)
John Q '02
Blow '01
Hannibal '01
Heartbreakers '01
A Rumor of Angels '00
Forever Mine '99
Inferno '99
Muppets from Space '99
Phoenix '98
The Rat Pack '98
Cop Land '97
Turbulence '96
Unforgettable '96
Operation Dumbo Drop '95
Corrina, Corrina '94
No Escape '94
Article 99 '92
Unlawful Entry '92
Women & Men: In Love There Are No Rules '91
Goodfellas '90
Field of Dreams '89
Dominick & Eugene '88
Something Wild '86
The Lonely Lady '83
Lu Liping
Shadow Magic '00
The Blue Kite '93
Eugene Lipinski
Bless the Child '00
Restless Spirits '99
Small Vices: A Spenser Mystery '99
Aldrich Ames: Traitor Within '98
Perfectly Normal '91
Riders of the Storm '88
Going Home '86
Moonlighting '82
Maureen Lipman (1946-)
Captain Jack '98
Solomon and Gaenor '98
The Little Princess '87
Educating Rita '83
Jonathan Lipnicki (1990-)
Like Mike '02
Stuart Little 2 '02
The Little Vampire '00
Stuart Little '99
Jerry Maguire '96
Jonathon Lippe
Blood Voyage '77
Green Eyes '76
David Lipper
Federal Protection '02
Bug Buster '99
Sarah K. Lippmann
Addicted to Murder 3: Bloodlust '99
Addicted to Murder 2: Tainted Blood '97
Dennis Lipscomb
Automatic '94
Retribution '88
Guilty of Innocence '87
Sister, Sister '87
Slow Burn '86
Eyes of Fire '84
Union City '81
Peggy Lipton (1947-)
Jackpot '01
Intern '00
The '70s '00
Skipped Parts '00
The Postman '97
The Spider and the Fly '94
Fatal Charm '92
Twin Peaks: Fire Walk with Me '92
Kinjite: Forbidden Subjects '89
I'm Gonna Git You Sucka '88
Purple People Eater '88
Mosby's Marauders '66
(Lisa Ray MacCoy) LisaRaye (1967-)
The Wood '99
The Players Club '98
Joe Lisi
Traces of Red '92
Come See the Paradise '90
Virna Lisi (1937-)
Balzac: A Life of Passion '99
Queen Margot '94
I Love N.Y. '87
Christopher Columbus '85
La Cicada '83
Miss Right '81
Night Flight from Moscow '73
Bluebeard '72
The Statue '71
Carbon Copy '69
The Secret of Santa Vittoria '69
When Wolves Cry '69
Assault on a Queen '66
Casanova '70 '65
How to Murder Your Wife '64
Eva '62
Leon Lissek
Bloodmoon '90
The Unbearable Lightness of Being '88
Adventures of Eliza Fraser '76
Blockhouse '73
Moira Lister (1923-)
The 10th Kingdom '00
Cop-Out '67
Abandon Ship '57
John and Julie '55
The Limping Man '53
Trouble in Store '53
Uneasy Terms '48
Tommy (Tiny) Lister
The Wash '01
Circus '00
Little Nicky '00
Next Friday '00
Judgment Day '99
Supreme Sanction '99
I Got the Hook-Up '98
Never 2 Big '98
The Players Club '98
Wishmaster 2: Evil Never Dies '98
Body Count '97
The Fifth Element '97
Jackie Brown '97
Phat Beach '96
White Cargo '96
Friday '95
Hologram Man '95
Things to Do in Denver When You're Dead '95
Immortal Combat '94
Men of War '94
Posse '93
9 1/2 Ninjas '90
No Holds Barred '89
Secret Agent 00-Soul '89
Prison '88
Beverly Hills Cop 2 '87
Extreme Prejudice '87

Giorgio Listuzzi
White Nights '57
The Roof '56
Litefoot
Kull the Conqueror '97
Mortal Kombat 2: Annihilation '97
The Indian in the Cupboard '95
John Litel (1892-1972)
Montana Belle '52
The Fuller Brush Girl '50
Outpost in Morocco '49
Rusty's Birthday '49
Pitfall '48
Cass Timberlane '47
Northwest Trail '46
San Antonio '45
Boss of Big Town '43
So Proudly We Hail '43
Invisible Agent '42
They Died with Their Boots On '41
The Fighting 69th '40
Nancy Drew, Reporter '39
Amazing Dr. Clitterhouse '38
The Black Legion '37
John Lithgow (1945-)
Orange County '02
Shrek '01 (V)
Don Quixote '00
Rugrats in Paris: The Movie '00 (V)
A Civil Action '98
Homegrown '97
Johnny Skidmarks '97
Hollow Point '95
Redwood Curtain '95
The Tuskegee Airmen '95
A Good Man in Africa '94
Princess Caraboo '94
Silent Fall '94
World War II: When Lions Roared '94
Cliffhanger '93
Love, Cheat & Steal '93
The Pelican Brief '93
The Wrong Man '93
Raising Cain '92
At Play in the Fields of the Lord '91
Ricochet '91
Ivory Hunters '90
Memphis Belle '90
Out Cold '89
Traveling Man '89
Distant Thunder '88
Baby Girl Scott '87
Harry and the Hendersons '87
The Manhattan Project '86
Santa Claus: The Movie '85
The Adventures of Buckaroo Banzai Across the Eighth Dimension '84
Footloose '84
The Glitter Dome '84
Mesmerized '84
2010: The Year We Make Contact '84
The Day After '83
Goldilocks & the Three Bears '83
Terms of Endearment '83
Twilight Zone: The Movie '83
I'm Dancing as Fast as I Can '82
Oldest Living Graduate '82
The World According to Garp '82
Blow Out '81
Mom, the Wolfman and Me '80
All That Jazz '79
Rich Kids '79
The Big Fix '78
Obsession '76
Cleavon Little (1939-92)
Perfect Harmony '91
Separate but Equal '91
Fletch Lives '89
Murder by Numbers '89
Gore Vidal's Lincoln '88
The Gig '85
Once Bitten '85
E. Nick: A Legend in His Own Mind '84
Surf 2 '84
Toy Soldiers '84
Double Exposure '82
Jimmy the Kid '82
The Salamander '82
Don't Look Back: The Story of Leroy "Satchel" Paige '81
High Risk '81
Scavenger Hunt '79
FM '78
Greased Lightning '77
Once Upon a Brothers Grimm '77
Blazing Saddles '74
Homecoming: A Christmas Story '71
Vanishing Point '71
Cotton Comes to Harlem '70
Kim Little
Social Intercourse '01
Sorority House Party '92
Mark Little
The Wacky World of Wills & Burke '85
Waterfront '83
Michelle Little
Apollo 13 '95
Heartstrings '95
Blood Clan '91
Bluffing It '87
My Demon Lover '87
Radioactive Dreams '86
Appointment with Fear '85
Natasha Little
Greenfingers '00
Vanity Fair '99
Rich Little (1938-)
The Late Shift '96
Happy Hour '87
Dirty Tricks '81
Sacheen Little Feather
Shoot the Sun Down '81
Johnny Firecloud '75
The Trial of Billy Jack '74
Little Nell
I Wanna Be a Beauty Queen '85
The Rocky Horror Picture Show '75
Little Richard (1932-)
Mystery, Alaska '99
Why Do Fools Fall in Love? '98
Last Action Hero '93
The Pickle '93
Mother Goose Rock 'n' Rhyme '90
Scenes from the Class Struggle in Beverly Hills '89
Purple People Eater '88
Down and Out in Beverly Hills '86
The Girl Can't Help It '56
Eddie Little Sky
Journey Through Rosebud '72
Savage Run '70
Lucien Littlefield (1895-1960)
Susanna Pass '49
Zorro's Black Whip '44
Bells of Capistrano '42
Hillbilly Blitzkrieg '42
Jeepers Creepers '39
The Gladiator '38
Hollywood Stadium Mystery '38
Wide Open Faces '38
Bulldog Drummond's Revenge '37
Let's Sing Again '36
The Bitter Tea of General Yen '33
Rainbow over Broadway '33
Strangers of the Evening '32
Tom Sawyer '30
Seven Keys to Baldpate '29
The Cat and the Canary '27
My Best Girl '27
Charley's Aunt '25
Tumbleweeds '25
The Sheik '21
Gary Littlejohn
Badlands '74
Angels Hard As They Come '71
Bury Me an Angel '71
Harrison Liu
Black Robe '91
Dr. Bethune '90
Lucy Alexis Liu (1968-)
Charlie's Angels '00
Shanghai Noon '00
The Mating Habits of the Earthbound Human '99
Molly '99
Play It to the Bone '99
Payback '98
Flypaper '97
Eric Lively
Uprising '01
Crash Course '00
Ernie Lively
Senseless '98
Accidental Meeting '93
Jason Lively
Maximum Force '92
Rock 'n' Roll High School Forever '91
Ghost Chase '88
Night of the Creeps '86
National Lampoon's European Vacation '85
Robin (Robyn) Lively (1972-)
Crazy from the Heart '91
The Karate Kid: Part 3 '89
Not Quite Human 2 '89
Teen Witch '89
Buckeye and Blue '87
Not Quite Human '87
Jack Livesey
The World Owes Me a Living '47
Never Too Late to Mend '37
Roger Livesey (1906-76)
Of Human Bondage '64
The Entertainer '60
The League of Gentlemen '60
The Master of Ballantrae '53
Green Grow the Rushes '51
Stairway to Heaven '46
I Know Where I'm Going '45
The Life and Death of Colonel Blimp '43
Drums '38
Lorna Doone '34
Barry Livingston (1953-)
Steel Sharks '97
Invisible Mom '96
Easy Wheels '89
John Livingston
Where's Marlowe? '98
Dogtown '97
Mr. Wrong '95
Margaret Livingston (1895-1984)
The Lady Refuses '31
Seven Keys to Baldpate '29
Through the Breakers '28
Sunrise '27
The Busher '19
Robert "Bob" Livingston (1904-88)
Blazing Stewardesses '75
Texas Layover '75
I Spit on Your Corpse '74
Grand Canyon Trail '48
Don't Fence Me In '45
Law of the Saddle '45
Death Rides the Plains '44
Raiders of Red Gap '43
Covered Wagon Days '40
Rocky Mountain Rangers '40
Cowboys from Texas '39
The Kansas Terrors '39
Heroes of the Hills '38
Outlaws of Sonora '38
Purple Vigilantes '38
Come on, Cowboys '37
Heart of the Rockies '37
Hit the Saddle '37
Riders of the Whistling Skull '37
Roarin' Lead '37
The Bold Caballero '36
Ghost Town Gold '36
The Vigilantes Are Coming '36
Ron Livingston
Band of Brothers '01
A Rumor of Angels '00
Two Ninas '00
The Big Brass Ring '99
Body Shots '99
Office Space '98
Swingers '96
Shelby Livingston
2000 Maniacs '64
Nude on the Moon '61
Stanley Livingston (1950-)
Attack of the 60-Foot Centerfold '95
Smokey & the Hotwire Gang '79
Private Parts '72
Kari Lizer
Private School '83
Smokey Bites the Dust '81
L.L. Cool J. (1968-)
Rollerball '02
Kingdom Come '01
Charlie's Angels '00
Any Given Sunday '99
Deep Blue Sea '99
In Too Deep '99
Caught Up '98
Halloween: H20 '98
Woo '97
Out of Sync '95
The Right to Remain Silent '95
Toys '92
The Hard Way '91
Desmond Llewelyn (1914-99)
The World Is Not Enough '99
Tomorrow Never Dies '97
Goldeneye '95
Merlin '92
License to Kill '89
The Living Daylights '87
A View to a Kill '85
For Your Eyes Only '81
Moonraker '79
The Spy Who Loved Me '77
The Man with the Golden Gun '74
Diamonds Are Forever '71
On Her Majesty's Secret Service '69
You Only Live Twice '67
Thunderball '65
Goldfinger '64
From Russia with Love '63
Christopher Lloyd (1938-)
When Good Ghouls Go Bad '01
Wit '01
Chasing Destiny '00
Wish You Were Dead '00
Alice in Wonderland '99
Angels in the Endzone '98
Baby Geniuses '98
It Came from the Sky '98
My Favorite Martian '98
Premonition '98
Quicksilver Highway '98
Anastasia '97 (V)
The Real Blonde '97
Cadillac Ranch '96
Changing Habits '96
Rent-A-Kid '95
The Right to Remain Silent '95
Things to Do in Denver When You're Dead '95
Angels in the Outfield '94
Camp Nowhere '94
The Pagemaster '94 (V)
Radioland Murders '94
Addams Family Values '93
Dennis the Menace '93
Twenty Bucks '93
Dead Ahead: The Exxon Valdez Disaster '92
T Bone N Weasel '92
The Addams Family '91
Suburban Commando '91
Back to the Future, Part 3 '90
DuckTales the Movie: Treasure of the Lost Lamp '90 (V)
Why Me? '90
Back to the Future, Part 2 '89
The Dream Team '89
Eight Men Out '88
Track 29 '88
Who Framed Roger Rabbit '88
Walk Like a Man '87
Miracles '86
Back to the Future '85
Clue '85
The Adventures of Buckaroo Banzai Across the Eighth Dimension '84
The Cowboy & the Ballerina '84
Joy of Sex '84
Star Trek 3: The Search for Spock '84
Street Hawk '84
Mr. Mom '83
September Gun '83
To Be or Not to Be '83
Pilgrim, Farewell '82
Legend of the Lone Ranger '81
National Lampoon Goes to the Movies '81
The Postman Always Rings Twice '81
The Black Marble '79
Lady in Red '79
Goin' South '78
Three Warriors '77
One Flew Over the Cuckoo's Nest '75
Danny Lloyd
Will: G. Gordon Liddy '82
The Shining '80
Doris Lloyd (1896-1968)
The Time Machine '60
The Invisible Man's Revenge '44
Journey for Margaret '42
A Shot in the Dark '35
Disraeli '30
The Drake Case '29
Emily Lloyd (1971-)
Boogie Boy '98
The Real Thing '97
Welcome to Sarajevo '97
Under the Hula Moon '95
When Saturday Comes '95
A River Runs Through It '92
Scorchers '92
Chicago Joe & the Showgirl '90
Cookie '89
In Country '89
Wish You Were Here '87
Emily Ann Lloyd
Annie: A Royal Adventure '95
Apollo 13 '95
Eric Lloyd (1986-)
Luminous Motion '00
Chameleon '98
Deconstructing Harry '97
Dunston Checks In '95
The Santa Clause '94
George Lloyd (1897-1967)
I Accuse My Parents '45
White Pongo '45
Harold Lloyd (1893-1971)
Days of Thrills and Laughter '61
The Sin of Harold Diddlebock '47
Milky Way '36
Feet First '30
Speedy '28
The Kid Brother '27
For Heaven's Sake '26
The Freshman '25
Girl Shy '24
Safety Last '23
Harold Lloyd, Jr. (1931-71)
Married Too Young '62
Platinum High School '60
Girls' Town '59
The Flaming Urge '53
Hugh Lloyd
Cider with Rosie '99
August '95
Jake Lloyd (1989-)
Star Wars: Episode 1—The Phantom Menace '99
Jingle All the Way '96
Unhook the Stars '96
Jimmy Lloyd (1918-88)
G.I. Jane '51
Miss Grant Takes Richmond '49
Riders of the Whistling Pines '49
Sea Hound '47
The Jolson Story '46
The Story of G.I. Joe '45
John Bedford Lloyd
Fair Game '95
Killer: A Journal of Murder '95
Philadelphia '93
Waiting for the Light '90
The Abyss '89
Crossing Delancey '88
Sweet Lorraine '87
Tough Guys Don't Dance '87
Kathleen Lloyd (1949-)
Fly Boy '99
Call to Glory '84
Gangster Wars '81
The Jayne Mansfield Story '80
Take Down '79
It's Alive 2: It Lives Again '78
The Car '77
Skateboard '77
Missouri Breaks '76
Norman Lloyd (1914-)
The Song of the Lark '01
The Adventures of Rocky & Bullwinkle '00
Journey of Honor '91
Amityville 4: The Evil Escapes '89
Jaws of Satan '81
The Nude Bomb '80
Audrey Rose '77
A Walk in the Sun '46
The Southerner '45
Saboteur '42
Rollo Lloyd
The Lives of a Bengal Lancer '35
Carnival Lady '33
Sue Lloyd (1939-)
Bullet to Beijing '95
The Bitch '78
Number 1 of the Secret Service '77
Ned Kelly '70
The Ipcress File '65
Hysteria '64
Chi Muoi Lo
Catfish in Black Bean Sauce '00
The Relic '96
Enrico Lo Verso (1964-)
Hannibal '01
Moses '96
Lamerica '95
Farinelli '94
La Scorta '94
The Stolen Children '92
Tony LoBianco (1935-)
Rocky Marciano '99
Mafia! '98

Sworn to Justice '97
The Juror '96
Nixon '95
Tyson '95
The Ascent '94
Boiling Point '93
Teamster Boss: The Jackie Presser Story '92
City of Hope '91
The Ten Million Dollar Getaway '91
The Ann Jillian Story '88
Blood Ties '87
City Heat '84
Separate Ways '82
Last Cry for Help '79
Marciano '79
Bloodbrothers '78
F.I.S.T. '78
Magee and the Lady '78
Goldenrod '77
God Told Me To '76
Mean Frank and Crazy Tony '75
Mr. Inside, Mr. Outside '74
The Story of Jacob & Joseph '74
The Seven-Ups '73
The French Connection '71
Honeymoon Killers '70

Jane Lobre
The Green Room '78
A Gentle Woman '69

Amy Locane (1972-)
Hell's Gate '01
Bongwater '98
Implicated '98
Route 9 '98
Bram Stoker's The Mummy '97
Ebenezer '97
End of Summer '97
Going All the Way '97
Love to Kill '97
Prefontaine '96
Carried Away '95
Criminal Hearts '95
Airheads '94
School Ties '92
Blue Sky '91
No Secrets '91
Cry-Baby '90
Lost Angels '89

David Lochary (1944-77)
Female Trouble '74
Pink Flamingos '72
Multiple Maniacs '70
Mondo Trasho '69

Katherine Locke (1910-95)
People Will Talk '51
Try and Get Me '50
The Seventh Cross '44

Philip Locke (1928-)
Othello '95
Tom & Viv '94
And the Ship Sails On '83

Sondra Locke (1947-)
The Prophet's Game '99
Tales of the Unexpected '91
Ratboy '86
Sudden Impact '83
Rosie: The Rosemary Clooney Story '82
Any Which Way You Can '80
Bronco Billy '80
Second Coming of Suzanne '80
Suzanne '80
Every Which Way But Loose '78
The Gauntlet '77
Seducers '77
Shadow of Chikara '77
The Outlaw Josey Wales '76
A Reflection of Fear '72
Willard '71
The Heart Is a Lonely Hunter '68

Anne Lockhart (1953-)
Bug Buster '99
Big Bad John '90
Dark Tower '87
Troll '86
Hambone & Hillie '84
Savage Hunger '84
Joyride '77
Slashed Dreams '74

Calvin Lockhart (1934-)
Predator 2 '90
The Baron '88
Coming to America '88
Three Days in Beirut '83
The Beast Must Die '75
Let's Do It Again '75
Honeybaby '74
Uptown Saturday Night '74
Cotton Comes to Harlem '70
Dark of the Sun '68

Gene Lockhart (1891-1957)
Carousel '56
The Man in the Gray Flannel Suit '56
Francis Covers the Big Town '53
Face to Face '52
A Girl in Every Port '52
Hoodlum Empire '52
I'd Climb the Highest Mountain '51
The Big Hangover '50
Riding High '50
The Inspector General '49
Madame Bovary '49
Her Husband's Affairs '47
Miracle on 34th Street '47
A Scandal in Paris '46
The Strange Woman '46
House on 92nd Street '45
Leave Her to Heaven '45
Action in Arabia '44
Going My Way '44
Northern Pursuit '43
Hangmen Also Die '42
Billy the Kid '41
The Devil & Daniel Webster '41
International Lady '41
Meet John Doe '41
The Sea Wolf '41
They Died with Their Boots On '41
Abe Lincoln in Illinois '40
Edison the Man '40
His Girl Friday '40
South of Pago Pago '40
The Story of Alexander Graham Bell '39
Algiers '38
Blondie '38
A Christmas Carol '38
Of Human Hearts '38
Sinners in Paradise '38
Earthworm Tractors '36
Something to Sing About '36
Crime and Punishment '35

June Lockhart (1925-)
Lost in Space '98
The Colony '95
Out There '95
Sleep with Me '94
Dead Women in Lingerie '90
The Gift of Love '90
The Big Picture '89
Rented Lips '88
Troll '86
Strange Invaders '83
Butterfly '82
The Capture of Grizzly Adams '82
Deadly Games '80
Just Tell Me You Love Me '80
Walking Through the Fire '80
Curse of the Black Widow '77
Lassie's Great Adventure '62
T-Men '47
She Wolf of London '46
The Yearling '46
Son of Lassie '45
Meet Me in St. Louis '44
The White Cliffs of Dover '44
Miss Annie Rooney '42
Adam Had Four Sons '41
Sergeant York '41
All This and Heaven Too '40

Heather Locklear (1962-)
Money Talks '97
The First Wives Club '96
The Great American Sex Scandal '94
Fade to Black '93
Body Language '92
Illusions '91
The Big Slice '90
Lethal Charm '90
The Return of Swamp Thing '89
City Killer '87
Firestarter '84
Twirl '81

Loryn Locklin
Fortress '93
Taking Care of Business '90
Catch Me ... If You Can '89

Gary Lockwood (1937-)
Night of the Scarecrow '95
Terror in Paradise '90
The Wild Pair '87
Survival Zone '84
The Incredible Journey of Dr. Meg Laurel '79
Bad Georgia Road '77
Project: Kill! '77
Manhunter '74
R.P.M.* (* Revolutions Per Minute) '70
Firecreek '68
2001: A Space Odyssey '68
It Happened at the World's Fair '63
The Magic Sword '62
Wild in the Country '61

Margaret Lockwood (1911-90)
The Slipper and the Rose '76
Cast a Dark Shadow '55
Trouble in the Glen '54
The Man in Grey '45
The Wicked Lady '45
Night Train to Munich '40
The Stars Look Down '39
Susannah of the Mounties '39
The Lady Vanishes '38
Dr. Syn '37
Lorna Doone '34

Thomas Lockyer
Jesus '00
Ultraviolet '98
Incognito '97
The Scarlet Tunic '97
Teenagers from Outer Space '59

Barbara Loden
Iron Cowboy '68
Splendor in the Grass '61

Anne Marie Loder
Life-Size '00
Blacklight '98

John Loder (1898-1988)
Small Hotel '57
The Story of Esther Costello '57
Dishonored Lady '47
Brighton Strangler '45
The Woman Who Came Back '45
Abroad with Two Yanks '44
The Hairy Ape '44
Passage to Marseilles '44
How Green Was My Valley '41
Tin Pan Alley '40
Dr. Syn '37
King Solomon's Mines '37
Non-Stop New York '37
River of Unrest '37
The Man Who Lived Again '36
Sabotage '36
Java Head '35
The Silent Passenger '35
Lorna Doone '34
My Song Goes Round the World '34
The Private Life of Henry VIII '33
Wedding Rehearsal '32

Kathryn Loder
Foxy Brown '74
The Big Doll House '71

David Lodge (1921-)
Edge of Sanity '89
Killer with Two Faces '74
The Railway Children '70
Trial & Error '62
The Hellfire Club '61
Two-Way Stretch '60

Jean Lodge
Terror Ship '54
Dick Barton Strikes Back '48

John Lodge (1903-85)
The Witchmaker '69
De Mayerling a Sarajevo '40
Bulldog Drummond at Bay '37
River of Unrest '37
The Little Colonel '35
Scarlet Empress '34
Murders in the Zoo '33

Fiona Loewi
Invasion! '99
Blackheart '98
Love and Death on Long Island '97

Jeanette Loff (1906-42)
Fighting Thru '30
King of Jazz '30
Party Girls '29
Annapolis '28

Marianne Lofgren
Only One Night '42
June Night '40

Arthur Loft (1897-1947)
Charlie Chan in the Secret Service '44
Woman in the Window '44
Carson City Kid '40
Riders of Pasco Basin '40
Gang Bullets '38
I Am the Law '38

Lenny Y. Loftin
From Dusk Till Dawn 3: The Hangman's Daughter '99
Underground Terror '88

Jacqueline Logan (1901-83)
King of the Kongo '29
Ships in the Night '28
King of Kings '27

Phyllis Logan (1956-)
All the King's Men '99
Invasion: Earth '98
Secrets and Lies '95
Freddie the Frog '92 (V)
And a Nightingale Sang '91
Goldeneye: The Secret Life of Ian Fleming '89
The Inquiry '87
The Kitchen Toto '87
The Doctor and the Devils '85
The McGuffin '85
Another Time, Another Place '83

Ricky Dean Logan
Freddy's Dead: The Final Nightmare '91
Back to the Future, Part 3 '90
Back to the Future, Part 2 '89

Robert F. Logan (1941-)
Man Outside '88
Death Ray 2000 '81
Mountain Family Robinson '79
Sea Gypsies '78
Further Adventures of the Wilderness Family, Part 2 '77
Snowbeast '77
Across the Great Divide '76
The Adventures of the Wilderness Family '76

Stanley Logan
That Forsyte Woman '50
My Son, My Son '40

Susan Logan
Deadly Encounter '78
The Meal '75

Robert Loggia (1930-)
Return to Me '00
Bonanno: A Godfather's Story '99
Joan of Arc '99
The Suburbans '99
American Virgin '98
Holy Man '98
Flypaper '97
Joe Torre: Curveballs Along the Way '97
National Lampoon's The Don's Analyst '97
The Proposition '97
Wide Awake '97
Independence Day '96
Lost Highway '96
Mistrial '96
Smilla's Sense of Snow '96
Man with a Gun '95
Picture Windows '95
The Right to Remain Silent '95
Bad Girls '94
Coldblooded '94
I Love Trouble '94
White Mile '94
Lifepod '93
Mercy Mission '93
Wild Palms '93
Afterburn '92
Gladiator '92
Innocent Blood '92
The Marrying Man '91
Necessary Roughness '91
Code Name: Chaos '90
Intrigue '90
Opportunity Knocks '90
Relentless '89
Running Away '89
Triumph of the Spirit '89
Big '88
Oliver & Company '88 (V)
The Believers '87
Conspiracy: The Trial of the Chicago Eight '87
Echoes in the Darkness '87
Gaby: A True Story '87
Hot Pursuit '87
Target: Favorite Son '87
Armed and Dangerous '86
Over the Top '86
That's Life! '86
The Jagged Edge '85
Prizzi's Honor '85
Curse of the Pink Panther '83
Overnight Sensation '83
Psycho 2 '83
Scarface '83
An Officer and a Gentleman '82
Trail of the Pink Panther '82
A Woman Called Golda '82
S.O.B. '81
The Ninth Configuration '79
Revenge of the Pink Panther '78
Speedtrap '78
First Love '77
The Greatest Story Ever Told '65
The Three Sisters '65
The Lost Missile '58
The Nine Lives of Elfego Baca '58
Somebody Up There Likes Me '56

Donal Logue (1966-)
The Patriot '00
Reindeer Games '00
Steal This Movie! '00
The Tao of Steve '00
The Big Tease '99
The Million Dollar Hotel '99
Runaway Bride '99
Blade '98
A Bright Shining Lie '98
The Thin Red Line '98
Glam '97
Dear God '96
Metro '96
Baja '95
The Crew '95
The Grave '95
And the Band Played On '93
Gettysburg '93

Lindsay Lohan
Life-Size '00
The Parent Trap '98

Marie Lohr (1890-1975)
Abandon Ship '57
Small Hotel '57
Escapade '55
Counterblast '48
The Magic Bow '47
Pygmalion '38
South Riding '37

Gina Lollobrigida (1927-)
Bad Man's River '72
King, Queen, Knave '72
Imperial Venus '71
Buona Sera, Mrs. Campbell '68
Private Navy of Sgt. O'Farrell '68
Hotel Paradiso '66
Strange Bedfellows '65
Come September '61
The Unfaithfuls '60
Never So Few '59
Solomon and Sheba '59
Where the Hot Wind Blows '59
Four Ways Out '57
The Hunchback of Notre Dame '57
Trapeze '56
A Woman of Rome '56
Beat the Devil '53
Beauties of the Night '52
The Wayward Wife '52
Fanfan la Tulipe '51
Young Caruso '51

Herbert Lom (1917-)
Son of the Pink Panther '93
The Devil's Daughter '91
The Pope Must Diet '91
Masque of the Red Death '90
River of Death '90
Skeleton Coast '89
Ten Little Indians '89
Going Bananas '88
King Solomon's Mines '85
Curse of the Pink Panther '83
Dead Zone '83
Whoops Apocalypse '83
Trail of the Pink Panther '82
Peter and Paul '81
Hopscotch '80
The Man with Bogart's Face '80
The Lady Vanishes '79
Revenge of the Pink Panther '78
The Pink Panther Strikes Again '76
Ten Little Indians '75
Return of the Pink Panther '74
And Now the Screaming Starts '73
Asylum '72
Count Dracula '71
Murders in the Rue Morgue '71
Dorian Gray '70
Journey to the Far Side of the Sun '69
Mark of the Devil '69
99 Women '69
Uncle Tom's Cabin '69
Villa Rides '68
Gambit '66
A Shot in the Dark '64
The Horse Without a Head '63

The Phantom of the Opera '62
Tiara Tahiti '62
The Frightened City '61
Mysterious Island '61
Flame Over India '60
Spartacus '60
Third Man on the Mountain '59
Room 43 '58
Fire Down Below '57
War and Peace '56
The Ladykillers '55
Paris Express '53
The Golden Salamander '51
Night and the City '50
Dual Alibi '47
The Seventh Veil '46
Appointment with Crime '45
Hotel Reserve '44
Secret Mission '42

Carole Lombard (1908-42)
To Be or Not to Be '42
Mr. & Mrs. Smith '41
They Knew What They Wanted '40
In Name Only '39
Made for Each Other '39
Nothing Sacred '37
Swing High, Swing Low '37
My Man Godfrey '36
The Princess Comes Across '36
Hands Across the Table '35
Lady by Choice '34
Now and Forever '34
Twentieth Century '34
We're Not Dressing '34
The Eagle and the Hawk '33
Supernatural '33
No Man of Her Own '32
These Girls Won't Talk '20s
Big News '29
High Voltage '29
The Racketeer '29
Mack & Carole '28
Power '28

Karina Lombard (1969-)
Footsteps '98
Kull the Conqueror '97
Last Man Standing '96
Legends of the Fall '94
The Firm '93
Wide Sargasso Sea '92

Louise Lombard
Russell Mulcahy's Tale of the Mummy '99
Esther '98
The House of Eliott '92

Louis Lombardi
Deuces Wild '02
The Animal '01
3000 Miles to Graceland '01
The Crew '00
Suicide Kings '97
Father's Day '96
The Immortals '95
The Usual Suspects '95
Beverly Hills Cop 3 '94
Natural Born Killers '94
Amongst Friends '93

Ulli Lommel (1944-)
Chinese Roulette '86
Strangers in Paradise '84
Boogey Man 2 '83
Effi Briest '74
The American Soldier '70
Beware of a Holy Whore '70
Whity '70
Fanny Hill: Memoirs of a Woman of Pleasure '64

Tadeusz Lomnicki (1927-92)
Contract '80
Man of Marble '76
Innocent Sorcerers '60
A Generation '54

Beba Loncar
Don't Look in the Attic '81
The Long Ships '64

Alexandra London
Le Bonheur Est Dans le Pre '95
Van Gogh '92

Daniel London
Four Dogs Playing Poker '00
Patch Adams '98
A Soldier's Sweetheart '98

Jason London (1972-)
Out Cold '01
The Hound of the Baskervilles '00
Jason and the Argonauts '00
Poor White Trash '00
Spent '00
Alien Cargo '99
The Rage: Carrie 2 '99
Broken Vessels '98
If These Walls Could Talk '96
Serial Bomber '96
My Teacher's Wife '95
To Wong Foo, Thanks for Everything, Julie Newmar '95
Fall Time '94
Safe Passage '94
Dazed and Confused '93
Blood Ties '92
December '91
The Man in the Moon '91

Jeremy London (1972-)
Journey to the Center of the Earth '99
The Defenders: Taking the First '98
Levitation '97
The Babysitter '95
Breaking Free '95
Mallrats '95
White Wolves 2: Legend of the Wild '94

Julie London (1926-2000)
Man of the West '58
The Girl Can't Help It '56
Task Force '49
The Red House '47
Nabonga '44

Lisa London
Savage Beach '89
H.O.T.S. '79

Tom London (1893-1963)
Tribute to a Bad Man '56
Blue Canadian Rockies '52
Red Desert '50
Brand of Fear '49
Under Colorado Skies '47
Alias Billy the Kid '46
Sunset in El Dorado '45
Fighting Seabees '44
Zorro's Black Whip '44
Fugitive Valley '41
Flaming Lead '39
Western Gold '37
Courage of the North '35
The Miracle Rider '35
Rio Rattler '35
Toll of the Desert '35
Beyond the Rockies '32
Outlaw Justice '32
Arizona Terror '31
Two Gun Man '31

John Lone (1952-)
Rush Hour 2 '01
The Hunted '94
The Shadow '94
M. Butterfly '93
Shadow of China '91
The Moderns '88
The Last Emperor '87
Echoes of Paradise '86
Year of the Dragon '85
Iceman '84
Americathon '79

Audrey Long (1924-)
Indian Uprising '51
The Adventures of Gallant Bess '48
Desperate '47

Howie Long (1960-)
3000 Miles to Graceland '01

Firestorm '97
Broken Arrow '95

Jodi Long
Amos and Andrew '93
Patty Hearst '88

Justin Long
Crossroads '02
Happy Campers '01
Jeepers Creepers '01

Kathy Long (1965-)
The Stranger '95
Under the Gun '95
Knights '93

Lotus Long
Phantom of Chinatown '40
Mr. Wong in Chinatown '39
Mystery of Mr. Wong '39
Mysterious Mr. Wong '35

Melissa Long
Reactor '85
War of the Robots '78

Nia Long (1970-)
Big Momma's House '00
Boiler Room '00
The Broken Hearts Club '00
Held Up '00
If These Walls Could Talk 2 '00
The Best Man '99
In Too Deep '99
Stigmata '99
Never 2 Big '98
Soul Food '97
Love Jones '96
Friday '95
Made in America '93
Boyz N the Hood '91

Richard Long (1927-74)
Death Cruise '74
House on Haunted Hill '58
Cult of the Cobra '55
Ma and Pa Kettle Back On the Farm '51
Ma and Pa Kettle Go to Town '50
Ma and Pa Kettle '49
Criss Cross '48
Egg and I '47
The Stranger '46
Tomorrow Is Forever '46

Shelley Long (1949-)
Dr. T & the Women '00
A Very Brady Sequel '96
The Brady Bunch Movie '95
Frozen Assets '92
Don't Tell Her It's Me '90
Troop Beverly Hills '89
Hello Again '87
Outrageous Fortune '87
The Money Pit '86
Irreconcilable Differences '84
Losin' It '82
Night Shift '82
Caveman '81
A Small Circle of Friends '80
The Cracker Factory '79

Tom Long
The Dish '00
Risk '00
Two Hands '98
Doing Time for Patsy Cline '97

Walter Long (1879-1952)
Silver Stallion '41
Flaming Lead '39
Man's Country '38
Six Shootin' Sheriff '38
The Glory Trail '36
Cornered '32
Sea Devils '31
Yankee Clipper '27
Soul-Fire '25
Little Church Around the Corner '23
Blood and Sand '22
Moran of the Lady Letty '22
The Sheik '21
The Little American '17
The Birth of a Nation '15

John Longden (1900-71)
Quatermass 2 '57

Alias John Preston '56
Tower of Terror '42
Clouds over Europe '39
Young and Innocent '37
Juno and the Paycock '30
Blackmail '29

Terence Longdon
Another Time, Another Place '58
Murder on the Campus '52

Victoria Longley
Talk '94
Celia: Child of Terror '89

Tony Longo (1962-)
Hard Luck '01
Houseguest '94
Prehysteria '93
Remote '93
Rapid Fire '92
The Last Boy Scout '91
Suburban Commando '91
Bloodhounds of Broadway '89
Worth Winning '89
Fletch '85

Emily Longstreth
Confessions of a Hit Man '94
Rising Son '90
Too Young to Die '90
The Big Picture '89
Wired to Kill '86
Private Resort '84

Ray Lonnen
Belfast Assassin '84
Guardian of the Abyss '82

Michael (Michel) Lonsdale (1931-)
Ronin '98
Nelly et Monsieur Arnaud '95
The Remains of the Day '93
Souvenir '88
The Name of the Rose '86
The Holcroft Covenant '85
Erendira '83
Enigma '82
Moonraker '79
Mr. Klein '76
Phantom of Liberty '74
Les Assassins de L'Ordre '71
Murmur of the Heart '71
The Bride Wore Black '68
Stolen Kisses '68
Is Paris Burning? '66

Leon Lontoc
The Gallant Hours '60
The Hunters '58

Richard Loo (1903-83)
The Man with the Golden Gun '74
The Sand Pebbles '66
Battle Hymn '57
Love Is a Many-Splendored Thing '55
Five Fingers '52
The Steel Helmet '51
The Clay Pigeon '49
Malaya '49
Back to Bataan '45
First Yank into Tokyo '45
Betrayal from the East '44
China Sky '44
The Purple Heart '44
China '43
Across the Pacific '42
Mr. Wong in Chinatown '39
The Bitter Tea of General Yen '33

Michael (Mike) Lookinland (1960-)
The Brady Bunch Movie '95
Stephen King's The Stand '94
A Very Brady Christmas '88

Nancy Loomis
Halloween '78
Assault on Precinct 13 '76

Rod Loomis
Bill & Ted's Excellent Adventure '89
Jack's Back '87

Theodore Loos (1883-1954)
M '31
Metropolis '26
Kriemhilde's Revenge '24

Tanya Lopert
Tales of Ordinary Madness '83
Navajo Joe '67

Carmen Lopez
Our Song '01
Curdled '95

Jennifer Lopez (1970-)
Enough '02
Angel Eyes '01
The Wedding Planner '01
The Cell '00
Antz '98 (V)
Out of Sight '98
U-Turn '97
Anaconda '96
Blood & Wine '96
Jack '96
Selena '96
Money Train '95
My Family '94

Kamala Lopez
Erotique '94
Crazy from the Heart '91
Dollman '90
Exiled in America '90
Born in East L.A. '87

Mario Lopez (1973-)
The Street King '02
Outta Time '01
Big Brother Trouble '00
A Crack in the Floor '00
Eastside '99
Depraved '98
Killing Mr. Griffin '97
Breaking the Surface: The Greg Louganis Story '96

Perry Lopez (1931-)
Chinatown '74
Kelly's Heroes '70
McLintock! '63
Taras Bulba '62
Battle Cry '55
Mister Roberts '55

Priscilla Lopez
Center Stage '00
Chutney Popcorn '99
Jesse '88

Sal Lopez
Price of Glory '00
Luminarias '99
Selena '96
The Fire Next Time '93
American Me '92
Full Metal Jacket '87

Seidy Lopez
Gabriela '01
The Stray '00
Depraved '98
Solo '96
Mi Vida Loca '94

Sergei Lopez
With a Friend Like Harry '00
An Affair of Love '99
Lisboa '99
The New Eve '98
Caresses '97
Western '96

Trini Lopez (1937-)
Antonio '73
The Dirty Dozen '67
The Poppy Is Also a Flower '66

Sophie Lorain
The Sign of Four '01
Home Team '98

Isabel Lorca
She's Having a Baby '88
Lightning: The White Stallion '86

Theodore Lorch (1880-1947)
The Man on the Box '25
The Last of the Mohicans '20

Jack Lord (1920-98)
The Doomsday Flight '66
Dr. No '62
God's Little Acre '58

Man of the West '58
The Court Martial of Billy Mitchell '55

Justine Lord
Skeezer '82
He Kills Night After Night After Night '70

Marjorie Lord (1922-)
Boy, Did I Get a Wrong Number! '66
Riding High '50
Johnny Come Lately '43
Sherlock Holmes in Washington '43

Traci Lords (1968-)
D.R.E.A.M. Team '99
Me & Will '99
Blade '98
Boogie Boy '98
Extramarital '98
Stir '98
Nowhere '96
As Good as Dead '95
The Nutt House '95
Dragstrip Girl '94
Plughead Rewired: Circuitry Man 2 '94
Serial Mom '94
Desperate Crimes '93
Ice '93
Skinner '93
Stephen King's The Tommyknockers '93
Laser Moon '92
Raw Nerve '91
A Time to Die '91
Cry-Baby '90
Shock 'Em Dead '90
Fast Food '89
Not of This Earth '88

Tony Lorea
Smokey & the Hotwire Gang '79
The Deadly and the Beautiful '73

Donna Loren (1947-)
Bikini Beach '64
Muscle Beach Party '64
Pajama Party '64

Sophia Loren (1934-)
Grumpier Old Men '95
Ready to Wear '94
Running Away '89
Courage '86
Aurora '84
Sophia Loren: Her Own Story '80
Blood Feud '79
Firepower '79
Lady of the Evening '79
Brass Target '78
Angela '77
A Special Day '77
The Cassandra Crossing '76
Get Rita '75
Man of La Mancha '72
A Countess from Hong Kong '67
Arabesque '66
Lady L '65
The Love Goddesses '65
Operation Crossbow '65
The Fall of the Roman Empire '64
Marriage Italian Style '64
Yesterday, Today and Tomorrow '64
Boccaccio '70 '62
El Cid '61
Two Women '61
Breath of Scandal '60
Heller in Pink Tights '60
It Started in Naples '60
The Millionairess '60
Black Orchid '59
Desire Under the Elms '58
Houseboat '58
The Key '58
Legend of the Lost '57
The Pride and the Passion '57
What a Woman! '56
The Gold of Naples '54
Two Nights with Cleopatra '54
Quo Vadis '51

Tray Loren
The American Angels: Baptism of Blood '89
Gator Bait 2: Cajun Justice '88
Rocktober Blood '85
Livio Lorenzon (1923-71)
The Good, the Bad and the Ugly '67
The Invincible Gladiator '63
Gladiators 7 '62
Pirates of the Coast '61
Susanne Loret
Atom Age Vampire '61
Uncle Was a Vampire '59
Teala Loring
Hard-Boiled Mahoney '47
Delinquent Daughters '44
James Lorinz
The Jerky Boys '95
Me and the Mob '94
Frankenhooker '90
Punch the Clock '90
Street Trash '87
Jean-Pierre Lorit
A Matter of Taste '00
Jeanne la Pucelle '94
Trois Couleurs: Rouge '94
Marion Lorne
The Graduate '67
Strangers on a Train '51
George Loros
Shakedown '88
Apology '86
Louise Lorraine
Near the Rainbow's End '30
The Adventures of Tarzan '21
Peter Lorre (1904-64)
The Comedy of Terrors '64
Muscle Beach Party '64
The Patsy '64
The Raven '63
Five Weeks in a Balloon '62
Tales of Terror '62
Voyage to the Bottom of the Sea '61
Hell Ship Mutiny '57
The Sad Sack '57
Silk Stockings '57
Around the World in 80 Days '56
Meet Me in Las Vegas '56
Promise to Murder '56
20,000 Leagues under the Sea '54
Beat the Devil '53
The Lost One '51
Quicksand '50
Casbah '48
My Favorite Brunette '47
The Beast with Five Fingers '46
Black Angel '46
The Chase '46
Arsenic and Old Lace '44
Hollywood Canteen '44
The Mask of Dimitrios '44
Passage to Marseilles '44
Background to Danger '43
All Through the Night '42
Casablanca '42
Invisible Agent '42
The Maltese Falcon '41
They Met in Bombay '41
Strange Cargo '40
Stranger on the Third Floor '40
You'll Find Out '40
Mr. Moto's Last Warning '39
The Secret Agent '36
Crime and Punishment '35
Mad Love '35
The Man Who Knew Too Much '34
F.P. 1 Doesn't Answer '33
M '31
Joan Lorring (1926-)
Good Sam '48
The Gangster '47
The Corn Is Green '45
Diana Lorys (1940-)
House of Psychotic Women '73
Fangs of the Living Dead '68
Lightning Bolt '67
The Texican '66
The Awful Dr. Orloff '62
Eb Lottimer
Diamondbacks '99
Termination Man '97
Bloodfist 7: Manhunt '95
Dead Center '94
Beyond the Call of Duty '92
Quake '92
The Finest Hour '91
Futurekick '91
Streets '90
Lords of the Deep '89
Stripped to Kill II: Live Girls '89
Quicker Than the Eye '88
Alexander Lou
Ninja the Battalion '90
Ninja in the U.S.A. '88
Ninja Condors '87
Mafia vs. Ninja '84
Louanne (1970-)
A Night in the Life of Jimmy Reardon '88
Missing Pieces '83
The Long Days of Summer '80
Oh, God! Book 2 '80
Lance Loud (1950-2001)
Armistead Maupin's Tales of the City '93
Inside Monkey Zetterland '93
Dorothy Loudon
Midnight in the Garden of Good and Evil '97
Garbo Talks '84
Jackie Loughery
D.I. '57
Pardners '56
Abbott and Costello Go to Mars '53
Lori Loughlin (1965-)
One of Her Own '97
To Grandmother's House We Go '94
The Night Before '88
Back to the Beach '87
Rad '86
The New Kids '85
Secret Admirer '85
Amityville 3: The Demon '83
Bill Louie
Fist of Fear, Touch of Death '80
The Bodyguard '76
Joe Louis
This Is the Army '43
The Spirit of Youth '37
Justin Louis
Stiletto Dance '01
Everything Put Together '00
National Lampoon's Dad's Week Off '97
Blood & Donuts '95
The Big Slice '90
Hello Mary Lou: Prom Night 2 '87
Willard Louis (1886-1926)
Don Juan '26
Beau Brummel '24
Robin Hood '22
Julia Louis-Dreyfus (1961-)
Gepetto '00
Animal Farm '99 (V)
A Bug's Life '98 (V)
Deconstructing Harry '97
Father's Day '96
North '94
Jack the Bear '93
National Lampoon's Christmas Vacation '89
Troll '86
Anita Louise (1915-70)
Retreat, Hell! '52
Love Letters '45
Casanova Brown '44
Harmon of Michigan '41
The Villain Still Pursued Her '41
Wagon's Westward '40
The Gorilla '39
The Little Princess '39
Marie Antoinette '38
The Sisters '38
That Certain Woman '37
Anthony Adverse '36
The Story of Louis Pasteur '36
Judge Priest '34
Millie '31
Square Shoulders '29
Tina Louise (1934-)
Johnny Suede '92
Dixie Lanes '88
O.C. and Stiggs '87
Evils of the Night '85
Hellriders '84
The Day the Women Got Even '80
Mean Dog Blues '78
Nightmare in Badham County '76
Death Scream '75
The Stepford Wives '75
The Good Guys and the Bad Guys '69
The Happy Ending '69
How to Commit Marriage '69
The Wrecking Crew '68
Armored Command '61
The Trap '59
God's Little Acre '58
Todd Louiso (1970-)
High Fidelity '00
8 Heads in a Duffel Bag '96
Jerry Maguire '96
Tim Lounibos
Steel Sharks '97
Erotique '94
Alan Love
The Apple '80
That Sinking Feeling '79
Bessie Love (1898-1986)
Vampyres '74
Catlow '71
Isadora '68
The Poppy Is Also a Flower '66
Roman Spring of Mrs. Stone '61
Morals for Women '31
Broadway Melody '29
The King on Main Street '25
The Lost World '25
Soul-Fire '25
Intolerance '16
Reggie Mixes In '16
Courtney Love (1964-)
Man on the Moon '99
200 Cigarettes '98
Basquiat '96
Feeling Minnesota '96
The People vs. Larry Flynt '96
Tapeheads '89
Straight to Hell '87
Sid & Nancy '86
Darlene Love (1938-)
Lethal Weapon 4 '98
Lethal Weapon 3 '92
Lethal Weapon 2 '89
Lethal Weapon '87
Faizon Love
Blue Crush '02
Made '01
Inhumanity '00
The Replacements '00
Three Strikes '00
The Players Club '98
Bebe's Kids '92 (V)
Lucretia Love
Dr. Heckyl and Mr. Hype '80
Phenomenal and the Treasure of Tutankamen '70s
The Arena '73
The She-Beast '65
Montagu Love (1877-1943)
Wings over the Pacific '43
Lady for a Night '42
Sherlock Holmes: The Voice of Terror '42
All This and Heaven Too '40
The Mark of Zorro '40
The Son of Monte Cristo '40
Gunga Din '39
The Adventures of Robin Hood '38
A Damsel in Distress '37
The Prince and the Pauper '37
Prisoner of Zenda '37
Lloyds of London '36
One in a Million '36
The Crusades '35
His Double Life '33
The Riding Tornado '32
Vanity Fair '32
Inside the Lines '30
Bulldog Drummond '29
The Wind '28
Don Juan '26
Hands Up '26
Son of the Sheik '26
Mother Love
Twinsitters '95
The Surgeon '94
Armistead Maupin's Tales of the City '93
Mr. Nanny '93
Suzanna Love
Boogey Man 2 '83
Devonsville Terror '83
Olivia '83
Brainwaves '82
The Boogey Man '80
Cocaine Cowboys '79
Victor Love (1957-)
A Gun, a Car, a Blonde '97
The Assassination File '96
Gang Related '96
Final Shot: The Hank Gathers Story '92
Heaven Is a Playground '91
Guilty of Innocence '87
Native Son '86
Alec Lovejoy
Murder on Lenox Avenue '41
Moon over Harlem '39
Frank Lovejoy (1914-62)
Americano '55
The Finger Man '55
Shack Out on 101 '55
Strategic Air Command '55
Men of the Fighting Lady '54
The Hitch-Hiker '53
House of Wax '53
Retreat, Hell! '52
The Winning Team '52
I'll See You in My Dreams '51
In a Lonely Place '50
Three Secrets '50
Try and Get Me '50
Home of the Brave '49
Jacqueline Lovell (1974-)
A Place Called Truth '98
Erotic House of Wax '97
Hideous '97
Lolida 2000 '97
Femalien '96
Head of the Family '96
Raymond Lovell (1900-53)
Appointment with Crime '45
Hotel Reserve '44
Immortal Battalion '44
Contraband '40
King of the Damned '36
Ray Lovelock (1950-)
From Hell to Victory '79
You've Got to Have Heart '77
Autopsy '74
Let Sleeping Corpses Lie '74
One Russian Summer '73
Fiddler on the Roof '71
Ed Lover
Gunmen '93
Who's the Man? '93
Dorothy Lovett (1915-98)
Call Out the Marines '42
They Meet Again '41
Courageous Dr. Christian '40
Dr. Christian Meets the Women '40
Remedy for Riches '40
Lyle Lovett (1959-)
The New Age '94
Cookie's Fortune '99
Fear and Loathing in Las Vegas '98
The Opposite of Sex '98
Bastard out of Carolina '96
Ready to Wear '94
Short Cuts '93
The Player '92
David Lovgren
Something More '99
Live Bait '95
Jon Lovitz (1957-)
Cats & Dogs '01 (V)
Good Advice '01
Rat Race '01
3000 Miles to Graceland '01
Little Nicky '00
Sand '00
Small Time Crooks '00
Lost and Found '99
Happiness '98
The Wedding Singer '97
The Great White Hype '96
High School High '96
City Slickers 2: The Legend of Curly's Gold '94
North '94
Trapped in Paradise '94
National Lampoon's Loaded Weapon 1 '93
A League of Their Own '92
Mom and Dad Save the World '92
An American Tail: Fievel Goes West '91 (V)
Mr. Destiny '90
Big '88
My Stepmother Is an Alien '88
Jumpin' Jack Flash '86
Last Resort '86
Three Amigos '86
Celia Lovsky
36 Hours '64
I, Mobster '58
Rhapsody '54
Victor Low
Everybody's Famous! '00
Character '97
Alex Lowe
Haunted '95
Peter's Friends '92
Arthur Lowe (1915-82)
The Strange Case of the End of Civilization As We Know It '93
Sweet William '79
The Bawdy Adventures of Tom Jones '76
No Sex Please—We're British '73
O Lucky Man! '73
Theatre of Blood '73
The Ruling Class '72
If... '69
This Sporting Life '63
Black Tide '58
Kind Hearts and Coronets '49
Chad Lowe (1968-)
Unfaithful '02
Apartment Complex '98
Floating '97
In the Presence of Mine Enemies '97
Quiet Days in Hollywood '97
Trading Favors '97
Siringo '94
Highway to Hell '92
An Inconvenient Woman '91
Nobody's Perfect '90
True Blood '89
Apprentice to Murder '88
Silence of the Heart '84
Edmund Lowe (1890-1971)
Heller in Pink Tights '60
Wings of Eagles '57
Good Sam '48
Dillinger '45
The Enchanted Forest '45
Call Out the Marines '42
I Love You Again '40
Every Day's a Holiday '38
The Squeaker '37
Dinner at Eight '33
Chandu the Magician '32
The Eyes of Youth '19
Harrison Lowe
Buffalo Soldiers '97
Geronimo '93
Patrick Lowe
Primal Rage '90
Slumber Party Massacre 2 '87
Rob Lowe (1964-)
Escape under Pressure '00
Proximity '00
The Specials '00
Atomic Train '99
Austin Powers 2: The Spy Who Shagged Me '99
Dead Silent '99
Crazy Six '98
For Hire '98
Contact '97
Hostile Intent '97
Living in Peril '97
Jack Higgins' Midnight Man '96
First Degree '95
Jack Higgins' On Dangerous Ground '95
Mulholland Falls '95
Tommy Boy '95
Frank and Jesse '94
Stephen King's The Stand '94
Wayne's World '92
The Dark Backward '91
The Finest Hour '91
Bad Influence '90
Stroke of Midnight '90
Masquerade '88
Illegally Yours '87
Square Dance '87
About Last Night... '86
Youngblood '86
St. Elmo's Fire '85
The Hotel New Hampshire '84
Oxford Blues '84
Class '83
The Outsiders '83
Susan Lowe
Serial Mom '94
Hairspray '88
Polyester '81
Desperate Living '77
Female Trouble '74
Multiple Maniacs '70
Carey Lowell (1961-)
Fierce Creatures '96
Leaving Las Vegas '95
Sleepless in Seattle '93
Road to Ruin '91
The Guardian '90
Down Twisted '89
License to Kill '89
Me and Him '89
Club Paradise '86
Dangerously Close '86
Tom Lowell
The Carpetbaggers '64
The Manchurian Candidate '62
Curt Lowens
Operation Intercept '95
Invisible: The Chronicles of Benjamin Knight '93
Mandroid '93
A Midnight Clear '92
Werewolf in a Girl's Dormitory '61

Elina Lowensohn (1967-)
Get Well Soon '01
Six Ways to Sunday '99
Immortality '98
In the Presence of Mine Enemies '97
Basquiat '96
I'm Not Rappaport '96
Jane Doe '96
Nadja '95
Amateur '94
My Antonia '94
Simple Men '92

Andrew Lowery
Color of Night '94
JFK: Reckless Youth '93
My Boyfriend's Back '93
School Ties '92

Carolyn Lowery
Octopus '00
Vicious Circles '97

Robert Lowery (1914-71)
The Undertaker and His Pals '67
Johnny Reno '66
The Rise and Fall of Legs Diamond '60
Western Pacific Agent '51
Border Rangers '50
Gunfire '50
I Shot Billy the Kid '50
Train to Tombstone '50
Call of the Forest '49
Outlaw Gang '49
Shep Comes Home '49
Highway 13 '48
Big Town '47
Queen of the Amazons '47
Trail of the Mounties '47
Death Valley '46
God's Country '46
House of Horrors '46
Dangerous Passage '44
Dark Mountain '44
The Mummy's Ghost '44
Mystery of the Riverboat '44
Navy Way '44
Revenge of the Zombies '43
Rhythm Parade '43
Dawn on the Great Divide '42
Lure of the Islands '42
Murder over New York '40
Drums Along the Mohawk '39

William E. (W.E., William A., W.A.) Lowery (1885-1941)
Robin Hood '22
The Nut '21
Reggie Mixes In '16
The Lamb '15

Klaus Lowitsch (1936-)
The Marriage of Maria Braun '79
Despair '78
Cross of Iron '76
Shadow of Angels '76
The Odessa File '74

Lynn Lowry
Sugar Cookies '77
Fighting Mad '76
They Came from Within '75
The Crazies '73
Score '72

Morton Lowry
Immortal Sergeant '43
Dawn Patrol '38

T.J. Lowther
Mad Love '95
One Christmas '95
A Perfect World '93

Myrna Loy (1905-93)
Summer Solstice '81
Just Tell Me What You Want '80
The End '78
Ants '77
Airport '75 '75
From the Terrace '60
Midnight Lace '60
Lonelyhearts '58
The Ambassador's Daughter '56
Cheaper by the Dozen '50
The Red Pony '49
Mr. Blandings Builds His Dream House '48
The Bachelor and the Bobby-Soxer '47
Song of the Thin Man '47
The Best Years of Our Lives '46
The Thin Man Goes Home '44
Love Crazy '41
Shadow of the Thin Man '41
I Love You Again '40
Another Thin Man '39
The Rains Came '39
Test Pilot '38
Too Hot to Handle '38
Double Wedding '37
After the Thin Man '36
The Great Ziegfeld '36
Libeled Lady '36
Wife Versus Secretary '36
Broadway Bill '34
Evelyn Prentice '34
Manhattan Melodrama '34
The Thin Man '34
Penthouse '33
The Prizefighter and the Lady '33
Topaze '33
The Animal Kingdom '32
Arrowsmith '32
The Mask of Fu Manchu '32
Vanity Fair '32
A Connecticut Yankee '31
Consolation Marriage '31
Rogue of the Rio Grande '30
The Jazz Singer '27
Don Juan '26
So This Is Paris '26

Margarita Lozano (1931-)
Night Sun '90
Jean de Florette '87
Manon of the Spring '87
Half of Heaven '86
Kaos '85
The Night of the Shooting Stars '82
Viridiana '61
Lazarillo '59

Lisa Lu
The Joy Luck Club '93
Demon Seed '77

Arthur Lucan (1887-1954)
My Son, the Vampire '52
Old Mother Riley's Jungle Treasure '51
Old Mother Riley, Headmistress '50
Old Mother Riley's New Venture '49
Old Mother Riley's Ghosts '41

Joshua Lucas
A Beautiful Mind '01
The Deep End '01
Session 9 '01
American Psycho '99
Class of '61 '92

Laurent Lucas
With a Friend Like Harry '00
Pola X '99

Lisa Lucas (1961-)
Hadley's Rebellion '84
Forbidden Love '82
The Migrants '74
A House without a Christmas Tree '72

Wilfrid Lucas (1871-1940)
A Chump at Oxford '40
Roaring Speedboats '37
Dishonored '31
The Phantom '31

William Lucas
The Very Edge '63
X The Unknown '56

Susan Lucci (1945-)
French Silk '94
Hit Woman: The Double Edge '93
Lady Mobster '88
Anastasia: The Mystery of Anna '86
Mafia Princess '86
Invitation to Hell '84
Secret Passions '78

Angela Luce
'Tis a Pity She's a Whore '73
The Decameron '70

Enrique Lucero (1920-89)
The Evil That Men Do '84
Mr. Horn '79
The Woman Hunter '72

Fabrice Luchini (1951-)
Beaumarchais the Scoundrel '96
Colonel Chabert '94
Uranus '91
La Discrete '90
Full Moon in Paris '84
Perceval '78

Chip Lucio
Primary Target '89
Hospital Massacre '81

Laurence Luckinbill (1934-)
Dash and Lilly '99
Star Trek 5: The Final Frontier '89
Cocktail '88
Messenger of Death '88
To Heal a Nation '88
Not for Publication '84
Mating Season '81
Ike '79
The Promise '79
The Lindbergh Kidnapping Case '76
The Money '75
Death Sentence '74
Panic on the 5:22 '74
The Boys in the Band '70

William Lucking
K-PAX '01
The Last Best Sunday '98
The Trigger Effect '96
Rescue Me '93
Duplicates '92
Naked Lie '89
Kung Fu: The Movie '86
Humanoid Defender '85
Coast to Coast '80
Doc Savage '75
Hell's Belles '69

Barbara Luddy
Sleeping Beauty '59 (V)
Lady and the Tramp '55 (V)

Jack Luden
Phantom Gold '38
The Last Outlaw '27

Charles Ludlam
The Big Easy '87
Imposters '84

Patrick Ludlow (1903-96)
Gangway '37
Evergreen '34

Pamela Ludwig
Pale Blood '91
Race for Glory '89
Dead Man Walking '88
Rush Week '88
Death of an Angel '86
Over the Edge '79

Laurette Luez (1928-99)
Ballad of a Gunfighter '64
Prehistoric Women '50
D.O.A. '49

Lorna Luft
Life with Judy Garland—Me and My Shadows '01
Where the Boys Are '84 '84
Grease 2 '82

Bela Lugosi (1882-1956)
Plan 9 from Outer Space '56
Bride of the Monster '55
Glen or Glenda? '53
Bela Lugosi Meets a Brooklyn Gorilla '52
My Son, the Vampire '52
Abbott and Costello Meet Frankenstein '48
Scared to Death '46
The Body Snatcher '45
One Body Too Many '44
Return of the Ape Man '44
Zombies on Broadway '44
The Ape Man '43
Ghost on the Loose '43
Return of the Vampire '43
The Black Dragons '42
Bowery at Midnight '42
The Corpse Vanishes '42
Frankenstein Meets the Wolfman '42
The Ghost of Frankenstein '42
Night Monster '42
The Black Cat '41
The Devil Bat '41
The Invisible Ghost '41
Spooks Run Wild '41
The Wolf Man '41
Black Friday '40
The Saint's Double Trouble '40
You'll Find Out '40
The Gorilla '39
The Human Monster '39
Ninotchka '39
The Phantom Creeps '39
Son of Frankenstein '39
The Mystery of the Mary Celeste '37
S.O.S. Coast Guard '37
The Invisible Ray '36
Postal Inspector '36
Shadow of Chinatown '36
Mark of the Vampire '35
Murder by Television '35
Mysterious Mr. Wong '35
The Raven '35
The Black Cat '34
Chandu on the Magic Island '34
Return of Chandu '34
The Death Kiss '33
International House '33
Night of Terror '33
Whispering Shadow '33
Chandu the Magician '32
Island of Lost Souls '32
Murders in the Rue Morgue '32
The White Zombie '32
Dracula '31
Midnight Girl '25

James Luisi (1928-)
Feds '88
Murphy's Law '86
The Dark Ride '84
Fade to Black '80
One in a Million: The Ron LeFlore Story '78
Stunts '77

Paul Lukas (1887-1971)
Lord Jim '65
55 Days at Peking '63
Fun in Acapulco '63
20,000 Leagues under the Sea '54
Kim '50
Berlin Express '48
Whispering City '47
Deadline at Dawn '46
Experiment Perilous '45
Uncertain Glory '44
Watch on the Rhine '43
The Monster and the Girl '41
The Ghost Breakers '40
Strange Cargo '40
Lady in Distress '39
The Mutiny of the Elsinore '39
The Lady Vanishes '38
Dinner at the Ritz '37
Dodsworth '36
The Three Musketeers '35
Little Women '33
Vice Squad '31

Paul Lukather
Hands of a Stranger '62
Dinosaurus! '60

Benny Luke
La Cage aux Folles 3: The Wedding '86
La Cage aux Folles 2 '81
La Cage aux Folles '78

Jorge Luke
Salvador '86
The Evil That Men Do '84
Shark Hunter '84
Foxtrot '76
Ulzana's Raid '72

Keye Luke (1904-91)
Alice '90
Gremlins 2: The New Batch '90
The Mighty Quinn '89
Dead Heat '88
Kung Fu: The Movie '86
Blade in Hong Kong '85
Gremlins '84
The Amsterdam Kill '78
Kung Fu '72
Noon Sunday '71
Battle Hell '56
Across the Pacific '42
The Falcon's Brother '42
Bowery Blitzkrieg '41
Let's Go Collegiate '41
The Gang's All Here '40
No, No Nanette '40
Phantom of Chinatown '40
The Green Hornet '39
The Good Earth '37
Charlie Chan at the Opera '36
Charlie Chan in Paris '35
Mad Love '35

Wolfgang Lukschy
Frozen Alive '64
Dead Eyes of London '61

Folco Lulli (1912-70)
Lightning Bolt '67
The Organizer '64
The Great War '59
Wages of Fear '55
Submarine Attack '54
Variety Lights '51

Pierro Lulli (1923-91)
The Triumph of Hercules '66
Samson Against the Sheik '62

Lum & Abner
So This Is Washington '43
Two Weeks to Live '43

Carl Lumbly (1952-)
Men of Honor '00
Buffalo Soldiers '97
Nightjohn '96
America's Dream '95
Eyes of a Witness '94
South Central '92
Brother Future '91
Pacific Heights '90
To Sleep with Anger '90
Everybody's All American '88
Judgment in Berlin '88
The Bedroom Window '87
The Adventures of Buckaroo Banzai Across the Eighth Dimension '84

Jenny Lumet
Q & A '90
Tougher Than Leather '88

Sidney Lumet (1924-)
Running on Empty '88
One Third of a Nation '39

Joanna Lumley (1946-)
The Cat's Meow '01
Whispers: An Elephant's Tale '00 (V)
Maybe Baby '99
Coming Home '98
A Rather English Marriage '98
Prince Valiant '97
Absolutely Fabulous: The Last Shout '96
James and the Giant Peach '96 (V)
Innocent Lies '95
Cold Comfort Farm '94
Shirley Valentine '89
Weather in the Streets '84
Curse of the Pink Panther '83
The Satanic Rites of Dracula '73
On Her Majesty's Secret Service '69

Barbara Luna (1939-)
The Concrete Jungle '82
The Hanged Man '74
Gentle Savage '73
The Gatling Gun '72
Firecreek '68

Art Lund (1915-90)
Bucktown '75
Black Caesar '73
The Last American Hero '73

Deanna Lund (1937-)
Red Wind '91
Elves '89
Hardly Working '81
Dr. Goldfoot and the Bikini Machine '66

John Lund (1913-92)
Wackiest Ship in the Army '61
Dakota Incident '56
Latin Lovers '53
The Duchess of Idaho '50
My Friend Irma '49
A Foreign Affair '48
The Perils of Pauline '47
To Each His Own '46

Lucille Lund (1913-2002)
Prison Shadows '36
The Black Cat '34

Nicole Lund
Grizzly Mountain '97
The Legend of Wolf Mountain '92

Christine Lunde
Masque of the Red Death '90
Hardcase and Fist '89
Dead End City '88

Dolph Lundgren (1959-)
Hidden Agenda '01
Agent Red '00
Jill the Ripper '00
Bridge of Dragons '99
The Last Warrior '99
Storm Catcher '99
Sweepers '99
The Minion '98
The Peacekeeper '98
Blackjack '97
Silent Trigger '97
Johnny Mnemonic '95
Army of One '94
Hidden Assassin '94
Men of War '94
Pentathlon '94
Universal Soldier '92
Cover-Up '91
Showdown in Little Tokyo '91
I Come in Peace '90
The Punisher '90
Red Scorpion '89
Masters of the Universe '87
Rocky 4 '85
A View to a Kill '85

William Lundigan (1914-75)
Terror Ship '54
The White Orchid '54
I'd Climb the Highest Mountain '51
Love Nest '51
Follow Me Quietly '49
Pinky '49
State Department File 649 '49
Dishonored Lady '47
Andy Hardy's Double Life '42
The Fighting 69th '40
Three Smart Girls Grow Up '39
Danger on the Air '38
Wives under Suspicion '38

Vic Lundin
Robinson Crusoe on Mars '64
Two for the Seesaw '62

Ma Barker's Killer Brood '60

Steve Lundquist
Killer Tomatoes Eat France '91
Killer Tomatoes Strike Back '90
Return of the Killer Tomatoes! '88

Jessica Lundy
Just a Little Harmless Sex '99
RocketMan '97
The Stupids '95
Madhouse '90
Caddyshack 2 '88

Jamie Luner
Sacrifice '00
Confessions of Sorority Girls '94
The St. Tammany Miracle '94

Sihung Lung
Eat Drink Man Woman '94
The Wedding Banquet '93
Pushing Hands '92

Ti Lung
The Legend of Drunken Master '94
Duel of Fists '89
A Better Tomorrow, Part 1 '86

Cherie Lunghi (1953-)
Back to the Secret Garden '01
Horatio Hornblower '99
An Alan Smithee Film: Burn, Hollywood, Burn '97
The Canterville Ghost '96
The Buccaneers '95
Jack and Sarah '95
Mary Shelley's Frankenstein '94
Intrigue '90
To Kill a Priest '89
The Lady's Not for Burning '87
Tales of the Klondike: The Unexpected '87
Harem '86
The Mission '86
King David '85
Letters to an Unknown Lover '84
Praying Mantis '83
The Sign of Four '83
Oliver Twist '82
Excalibur '81

Roldano Lupi
The Giant of Metropolis '61
The Mongols '60

Ida Lupino (1914-95)
My Boys Are Good Boys '78
Food of the Gods '76
Devil's Rain '75
Junior Bonner '72
While the City Sleeps '56
The Big Knife '55
Private Hell 36 '54
The Bigamist '53
Beware, My Lovely '52
On Dangerous Ground '51
Lust for Gold '49
Road House '48
Escape Me Never '47
The Man I Love '46
Hollywood Canteen '44
Forever and a Day '43
Thank Your Lucky Stars '43
High Sierra '41
The Sea Wolf '41
They Drive by Night '40
The Adventures of Sherlock Holmes '39
Sea Devils '37
The Gay Desperado '36
One Rainy Afternoon '36
The Ghost Camera '33

Alberto Lupo (1924-84)
Django Shoots First '74
The Agony and the Ecstasy '65
Coriolanus, Man without a Country '64

The Bacchantes '63
Atom Age Vampire '61
The Giant of Marathon '60
Herod the Great '60

Patti LuPone (1949-)
Heist '01
Cold Blooded '00
State and Main '00
Bonanno: A Godfather's Story '99
Just Looking '99
Summer of Sam '99
The 24 Hour Woman '99
Song Spinner '95
The Water Engine '92
Family Prayers '91
Driving Miss Daisy '89
LBJ: The Early Years '88
Wise Guys '86
Witness '85
Fighting Back '82
1941 '79

Robert LuPone
American Tragedy '00
Palookaville '95
High Stakes '89

Federico Luppi (1934-)
The Devil's Backbone '01
Lisboa '99
Autumn Sun '98
Hombres Armados '97
Cronos '94
A Place in the World '92
Killing Grandpa '91
Mayalunta '86
Funny, Dirty Little War '83
Time for Revenge '82

John Lupton (1926-93)
Private Parts '72
Jesse James Meets Frankenstein's Daughter '65
The Rebel Set '59
Battle Cry '55
Diane '55
All the Brothers Were Valiant '53
Escape from Fort Bravo '53

Peter Lupus (1932-)
Acting on Impulse '93
Think Big '90
Pulsebeat '85
Escapist '83
Muscle Beach Party '64

Evan Lurie
Mortal Challenge '97
Hologram Man '95
Shadow Warriors '95
T-Force '94
American Kickboxer 2: To the Death '93
Martial Law 2: Undercover '91

John Lurie (1952-)
New Rose Hotel '98
The Last Temptation of Christ '88
Down by Law '86
Permanent Vacation '84
Stranger than Paradise '84

Jaques Lussier
Norman's Awesome Experience '88
Pouvoir Intime '87

Aaron Lustig
Tuesdays with Morrie '99
Pinocchio's Revenge '96
Stuart Saves His Family '94
Bad Channels '92

William Lustig (1955-)
Army of Darkness '92
Darkman '90
Maniac '80

Eric Lutes
Bram Stoker's The Mummy '97
Distant Justice '92

Alfred Lutter
The Bad News Bears in Breaking Training '77
The Bad News Bears '76

Franc Luz
Ghost Town '88
The Nest '88

Ecstasy '84

Christine Lydon
Vampires of Sorority Row: Kickboxers From Hell '99
Amazon Warrior '97

Gary Lydon
The Last September '99
Nothing Personal '95

Jimmy Lydon (1923-)
The Magnificent Yankee '50
Life with Father '47
Strange Illusion '45
Little Men '40
Tom Brown's School Days '40
Back Door to Heaven '39

John (Johnny Rotten) Lydon
The Filth and the Fury '99
Corrupt '84

Reg Lye (1912-88)
Freedom '81
King Rat '65
Walk into Hell '57

Leslie Lyles
Coming Soon '99
My Teacher's Wife '95

Dorothy Lyman (1947-)
Ruby in Paradise '93
Camp Cucamonga: How I Spent My Summer Vacation '90
Ollie Hopnoodle's Haven of Bliss '88
Summer Fantasy '84
The 300 Year Weekend '71

Will Lyman
The Siege '98
Floating '97

Alfred Lynch (1933-)
The Krays '90
Blockhouse '73
On the Fiddle '61

David Lynch (1946-)
Nadja '95
Twin Peaks: Fire Walk with Me '92
Zelly & Me '88

Helen Lynch
Smouldering Fires '25
The Return of Grey Wolf '22

Jimmy Lynch
Avenging Disco Godfather '76
Dolemite 2: Human Tornado '76

John Lynch (1961-)
The Seventh Stream '01
The Quarry '98
Sliding Doors '97
Moll Flanders '96
Some Mother's Son '96
This Is the Sea '96
Angel Baby '95
Nothing Personal '95
Princess Caraboo '94
The Secret of Roan Inish '94
In the Name of the Father '93
The Secret Garden '93
Edward II '92
The Railway Station Man '92
Hardware '90
Monkey Boy '90
Cal '84

John Carroll Lynch
Bubble Boy '01
Tuesdays with Morrie '99
From the Earth to the Moon '98
Restaurant '98
Face/Off '97
A Thousand Acres '97
Volcano '97
Fargo '96

Kate Lynch
Lethal Lolita—Amy Fisher: My Story '92
Def-Con 4 '85
Reckless Disregard '84
Summer's Children '84

Meatballs '79

Kelly Lynch (1959-)
Joe Somebody '01
Charlie's Angels '00
Brotherhood of Murder '99
Cold Around the Heart '97
Homegrown '97
Mr. Magoo '97
Persons Unknown '96
Heaven's Prisoners '95
Virtuosity '95
White Man's Burden '95
Forbidden Choices '94
Imaginary Crimes '94
Three of Hearts '93
For Better and for Worse '92
Curly Sue '91
Desperate Hours '90
Drugstore Cowboy '89
Road House '89
Warm Summer Rain '89
Cocktail '88
Osa '85

Ken Lynch (1910-90)
My Pleasure Is My Business '74
Legend of Tom Dooley '59
Pork Chop Hill '59
I Married a Monster from Outer Space '58
Run Silent, Run Deep '58

Pauline Lynch
Attila '01
Trainspotting '95

Richard Lynch
Under Oath '97
The Proposition '96

Richard Lynch (1936-)
Eastside '99
Terminal Virus '96
Warrior of Justice '96
Cyborg 3: The Recycler '95
Destination Vegas '95
Dragon Fury '95
Midnight Confessions '95
Werewolf '95
Scanner Cop '94
Terrified '94
H.P. Lovecraft's Necronomicon: Book of the Dead '93
Showdown '93
Double Threat '92
Inside Edge '92
Maximum Force '92
Merlin '92
Alligator 2: The Mutation '90
The Forbidden Dance '90
Invasion Force '90
Lockdown '90
Puppet Master 3: Toulon's Revenge '90
Trancers 2: The Return of Jack Deth '90
High Stakes '89
One Man Force '89
Aftershock '88
Bad Dreams '88
The Baron '88
Little Nikita '88
The Barbarians '87
Nightforce '86
Cut and Run '85
Invasion U.S.A. '85
Savage Dawn '84
Sword & the Sorcerer '82
Sizzle '81
The Formula '80
Steel '80
Death Sport '78
Delta Fox '77
God Told Me To '76
The Premonition '75
Scarecrow '73

Susan Lynch (1971-)
From Hell '01
Beautiful Creatures '00
Nora '00
Waking Ned Devine '98
Ivanhoe '97
Kings in Grass Castles '97
A Royal Scandal '96
The Secret of Roan Inish '94

Northern Lights '79

Helen Lynd
So Proudly We Hail '43
Hats Off '37

Paul Lynde (1926-82)
The Villain '79
Rabbit Test '78
Hugo the Hippo '76 (V)
Charlotte's Web '73 (V)
Journey Back to Oz '71 (V)
How Sweet It Is! '68
The Glass Bottom Boat '66
Beach Blanket Bingo '65
Send Me No Flowers '64
Bye, Bye, Birdie '63
Son of Flubber '63
Under the Yum-Yum Tree '63
New Faces of 1952 '54

Nicholas Lyndhurst
Stalag Luft
David Copperfield '99
Gulliver's Travels '95

Amy Lyndon
Big City Blues '99
Slaves of Hollywood '99

Simon Lyndon
Chopper '00
Blackrock '97

Carol Lynley (1942-)
Howling 6: The Freaks '90
Spirits '90
Blackout '88
Dark Tower '87
Vigilante '83
Balboa '82
The Cat and the Canary '79
Bad Georgia Road '77
Washington Affair '77
Fantasy Island '76
Flood! '76
Four Deuces '75
If It's a Man, Hang Up '75
Death Stalk '74
Beware! The Blob '72
Cotter '72
The Poseidon Adventure '72
The Night Stalker '71
Blood Island '68
The Cardinal '63
The Stripper '63
Under the Yum-Yum Tree '63
Return to Peyton Place '61
The Light in the Forest '58

Ann Lynn
Estate of Insanity '70
Baby Love '69

Betty Lynn (1926-)
Return to Mayberry '85
Texas John Slaughter: Geronimo's Revenge '60
Meet Me in Las Vegas '56
Cheaper by the Dozen '50
Father Was a Fullback '49
June Bride '48

Cheryl Lynn
Fate '90
Emanon '86
Thunder Run '86

Diana Lynn (1924-71)
The Annapolis Story '55
The Kentuckian '55
Bedtime for Bonzo '51
My Friend Irma '49
Every Girl Should Be Married '48
Miracle of Morgan's Creek '44
The Major and the Minor '42

Emmett Lynn (1897-1958)
The Fighting Redhead '50
The Caravan Trail '46
Song of Old Wyoming '45
Frontier Outlaws '44

Fonda Lynn
Ninja Brothers of Blood '89
Deadly Darling '85

George Lynn
Teenage Frankenstein '58
To Be or Not to Be '42

Jeffrey Lynn (1909-95)
Tony Rome '67
Home Town Story '51
A Letter to Three Wives '49
For the Love of Mary '48
Underground '41
All This and Heaven Too '40
The Fighting 69th '40
The Roaring Twenties '39
Four Daughters '38

Jonathan Lynn (1943-)
Greedy '94
Three Men and a Little Lady '90

Mara Lynn (1927-88)
G.I. Jane '51
Leave It to the Marines '51
Sky High '51
Prehistoric Women '50

Meredith Scott Lynn
Legally Blonde '01
Forces of Nature '99
Billy's Hollywood Screen Kiss '98
I Love You, Don't Touch Me! '97

Peter George Lynn (1906-67)
Mr. Wong in Chinatown '39
Mystery Plane '39
Wolf Call '39

Rebecca Lynn
Thrilled to Death '88
Sensations '87

Theresa Lynn
Psycho Sisters '98
Private Parts '96

Melanie Lynskey (1977-)
Stephen King's Rose Red '02
Coyote Ugly '00
Ever After: A Cinderella Story '98
Heavenly Creatures '94

Ben Lyon (1901-79)
Mad About Money '37
Crimson Romance '34
I Cover the Waterfront '33
The Crooked Circle '32
Indiscreet '31
Night Nurse '31
Hell's Angels '30

Richard Lyon
The Tender Years '47
Anna and the King of Siam '46

Sue Lyon (1946-)
Alligator '80
End of the World '76
The Invisible Strangler '76
Evel Knievel '72
Four Rode Out '69
Flim-Flam Man '67
Tony Rome '67
The Night of the Iguana '64
Lolita '62

Wendy Lyon
Hello Mary Lou: Prom Night 2 '87
Anne of Green Gables '85

Natasha Lyonne (1979-)
ZigZag '02
American Pie 2 '01
Fast Sofa '01
Kate & Leopold '01
Scary Movie 2 '01
If These Walls Could Talk 2 '00
American Pie '99
But I'm a Cheerleader '99
Detroit Rock City '99
Freeway 2: Confessions of a Trickbaby '99
Krippendorf's Tribe '98
Modern Vampires '98
Slums of Beverly Hills '98
Everyone Says I Love You '96

Bruce Lyons
The Navigator '88
Model Behavior '82

Cliff Lyons
The Horse Soldiers '59
She Wore a Yellow Ribbon '49

James Lyons
I Shot Andy Warhol '96
Frisk '95
Postcards from America '95
Poison '91

Jennifer Lyons
Tequila Body Shots '99
Tiger Heart '96

Phyllis Lyons
The Rat Pack '98
Casualties of Love: The "Long Island Lolita" Story '93

Robert F. Lyons (1940-)
The Omega Code '99
American Eagle '90
Platoon Leader '87
Murphy's Law '86
Cease Fire '85
Black Oak Conspiracy '77
Shoot Out '71
The Todd Killings '71
Getting Straight '70

Susan Lyons (1957-)
Napoleon '96 (V)
Ebbtide '94
The Winds of Jarrah '83

Stanislav Lyubshin
To See Paris and Die '93
The Theme '79

Tzi Ma
Catfish in Black Bean Sauce '00
Rush Hour '98
Dante's Peak '97
Red Corner '97
Chain Reaction '96
Golden Gate '93
Rapid Fire '92

Hidde Maas
The Delivery '99
Amsterdamned '88

Byron Mabe
The Doberman Gang '72
The Defilers '65

Ricky Mabe
Believe '99
Little Men '98

Kate Maberly
Gulliver's Travels '95
Stephen King's The Langoliers '95
The Secret Garden '93

Eric Mabius (1971-)
Resident Evil '02
The Crow: Salvation '00
The Minus Man '99
Splendor '99
Wirey Spindell '99
Around the Fire '98
Cruel Intentions '98
Black Circle Boys '97
I Shot Andy Warhol '96
Lawn Dogs '96
Welcome to the Dollhouse '95

Moms (Jackie) Mabley (1894-1975)
Amazing Grace '74
Boardinghouse Blues '48
Killer Diller '48

Bernie Mac (1958-)
Ocean's Eleven '01
What's the Worst That Could Happen? '01
Life '99
The Players Club '98
Def Jam's How to Be a Player '97
Don King: Only in America '97
Booty Call '96
Get On the Bus '96
Friday '95
Above the Rim '94
House Party 3 '94

Anne MacAdams
Don't Look in the Basement '73
Common Law Wife '63

James MacArthur (1937-)
Storm Chasers: Revenge of the Twister '98
Hang 'Em High '67
Mosby's Marauders '66
Battle of the Bulge '65
Bedford Incident '65
Cry of Battle '63
Spencer's Mountain '63
The Interns '62
Kidnapped '60
The Swiss Family Robinson '60
Third Man on the Mountain '59
The Light in the Forest '58

Charles Macaulay (1927-99)
The Big Red One '80
Blacula '72

Marc Macaulay
Holy Man '98
Wild Things '98
Cop and a Half '93
Hidden Fears '93

Donald MacBride (1889-1957)
Meet Danny Wilson '52
Holiday Rhythm '50
Buck Privates Come Home '47
Egg and I '47
A Night to Remember '42
The Invisible Woman '40
Murder over New York '40
The Saint's Double Trouble '40
Blondie Takes a Vacation '39
The Great Man Votes '38
Room Service '38

Ralph Macchio (1961-)
Forever Together '00
Naked in New York '93
My Cousin Vinny '92
Too Much Sun '90
The Karate Kid: Part 3 '89
Distant Thunder '88
Crossroads '86
The Karate Kid: Part 2 '86
The Karate Kid '84
Teachers '84
The Outsiders '83
Up the Academy '80

Aldo Maccione (1935-)
The Chambermaid on the Titanic '97
Loose in New York '80s
Too Shy to Try '82
Loves & Times of Scaramouche '76

Katherine (Katriona) MacColl (1954-)
The House by the Cemetery '83
The Beyond '82
Gates of Hell '80

Simon MacCorkindale (1952-)
The Girl Next Door '98
Family of Cops '95
Obsessive Love '84
Jaws 3 '83
Robbers of the Sacred Mountain '83
Sword & the Sorcerer '82
Cabo Blanco '81
The Manions of America '81
Visitor from the Grave '81
Quatermass Conclusion '79
The Riddle of the Sands '79
Death on the Nile '78

Ann-Marie MacDonald
Better Than Chocolate '99
I've Heard the Mermaids Singing '87

Bill MacDonald
Mercy '00
One Kill '00
The Corruptor '99

Edmund MacDonald (1908-51)
Shoot to Kill '47
Detour '46
The Lady Confesses '45

J. Farrell MacDonald (1875-1952)
Texas Masquerade '44
Phantom Killer '42
Snuffy Smith, Yard Bird '42
Riders of the Timberline '41
I Take This Oath '40
Knights of the Range '40
Susannah of the Mounties '39
Come on Rangers '38
Gang Bullets '38
Riff Raff '35
Romance in Manhattan '34
Hearts of Humanity '32
Phantom Express '32
Probation '32
13th Guest '32
Sunrise '27
Sky High '22

James MacDonald
Sour Grapes '98
Cinderella '50 (V)

Jeanette MacDonald (1901-65)
The Sun Comes Up '49
Three Daring Daughters '48
Cairo '42
I Married an Angel '42
Smilin' Through '41
Bitter Sweet '40
New Moon '40
Broadway Serenade '39
Girl of the Golden West '38
Sweethearts '38
The Firefly '37
Maytime '37
Rose Marie '36
San Francisco '36
Naughty Marietta '35
The Cat and the Fiddle '34
The Merry Widow '34
Lottery Bride '30

Jennifer MacDonald
Alien Chaser '96
Headless Body in Topless Bar '96
Dead Weekend '95
Clean, Shaven '93

Kelly Macdonald (1977-)
Gosford Park '01
Entropy '99
Splendor '99
Two Family House '99
The Loss of Sexual Innocence '98
My Life So Far '98
Cousin Bette '97
Stella Does Tricks '96
Trainspotting '95

Kenneth MacDonald (1950-2001)
Touching Evil '97
U-Boat Prisoner '44
Six Gun Gospel '43
Border Vengeance '35

Michael MacDonald
The Nutcracker Prince '91 (V)
Mystery of the Million Dollar Hockey Puck '80s
Mr. Nice Guy '86

Norm MacDonald (1963-)
Dr. Dolittle 2 '01 (V)
Screwed '00
Dr. Dolittle '98 (V)
Dirty Work '97
The People vs. Larry Flynt '96
Billy Madison '94

Wallace MacDonald (1891-1978)
Between Fighting Men '32
Daring Danger '32
Hello Trouble '32
The Riding Tornado '32
Texas Cyclone '32
Two-Fisted Law '32
Range Feud '31
Red Signals '27

Wendy MacDonald
Broken Trust '93
Dark Side of the Moon '90
Blood Frenzy '87
Heat Street '87
Mayhem '87

Andie MacDowell (1958-)
Crush '02
Harrison's Flowers '02
Dinner with Friends '01
Town and Country '01
Muppets from Space '99
The Muse '99
Just the Ticket '98
Shadrach '98
The End of Violence '97
Michael '96
Multiplicity '96
Unstrung Heroes '95
Bad Girls '94
Four Weddings and a Funeral '94
Groundhog Day '93
Short Cuts '93
Deception '92
The Player '92
Hudson Hawk '91
The Object of Beauty '91
Women & Men: In Love There Are No Rules '91
Green Card '90
sex, lies and videotape '89
St. Elmo's Fire '85
Greystoke: The Legend of Tarzan, Lord of the Apes '84

Rita Macedo (1928-93)
The Curse of the Crying Woman '61
Nazarin '58
The Criminal Life of Archibaldo de la Cruz '55

Sterling Macer
Double Take '01
The Beast '96
Dragon: The Bruce Lee Story '93

Angus Macfadyen (1964-)
Divine Secrets of the Ya-Ya Sisterhood '02
Jason and the Argonauts '00
Second Skin '00
Styx '00
The Cradle Will Rock '99
Titus '99
Facade '98
The Rat Pack '98
Nevada '97
Still Breathing '97
Warriors of Virtue '97
The Brylcreem Boys '96
Braveheart '95
The Lost Language of Cranes '92

Matthew MacFadyen
The Way We Live Now '02
Enigma '01

Moyna MacGill (1895-1975)
Three Daring Daughters '48
The Strange Affair of Uncle Harry '45
Frenchman's Creek '44
Gaslight '40

Niall MacGinnis (1913-78)
The Viking Queen '67
Island of Terror '66
The War Lord '65
A Face in the Rain '63
Jason and the Argonauts '63
Sword of Sherwood Forest '60
Curse of the Demon '57
Helen of Troy '56
Lust for Life '56
Betrayed '54
Martin Luther '53
No Highway in the Sky '51
Anna Karenina '48
Captain Boycott '47
Henry V '44
The Day Will Dawn '42
Edge of the World '37

Jack MacGowran (1975-)
The Exorcist '73
King Lear '71
Start the Revolution without Me '70
Wonderwall: The Movie '69
The Fearless Vampire Killers '67
Cul de Sac '66
Doctor Zhivago '65
Lord Jim '65
The Brain '62
The Quiet Man '52

Tara MacGowran (1964-)
The Dawning '88
Las Vegas Serial Killer '86
Secret Places '85

Ali MacGraw (1938-)
Glam '97
Natural Causes '94
Murder Elite '86
The Winds of War '83
Just Tell Me What You Want '80
Players '79
Convoy '78
The Getaway '72
Love Story '70
Goodbye Columbus '69

Ignacy Machowski
Contract '80
First Spaceship on Venus '60

Gabriel Macht (1972-)
American Outlaws '01
Behind Enemy Lines '01
The Audrey Hepburn Story '00

Stephen Macht (1942-)
Watchers Reborn '98
Galgameth '96
Siringo '94
Trancers 5: Sudden Deth '94
Trancers 4: Jack of Swords '93
Amityville 1992: It's About Time '92
Trancers 3: Deth Lives '92
Graveyard Shift '90
Blind Witness '89
A Friendship in Vienna '88
The Monster Squad '87
American Dream '81
Killjoy '81
Enola Gay: The Men, the Mission, the Atomic Bomb '80
Galaxina '80
Nightwing '79
The Choirboys '77

Angus MacInnes
Strange Brew '83
The Sender '82
Outland '81

Keegan Macintosh
The Road Home '95
Henry & Verlin '94

Daniel MacIvor
Beefcake '99
The Five Senses '99
Eclipse '94

Betty Mack (1901-80)
Rough Ridin' Rhythm '37
Outlaw Rule '36
Toll of the Desert '35
Fighting Texans '33
The Forty-Niners '32

Charles Mack
America '24
Dream Street '21

Helen Mack (1913-86)
His Girl Friday '40
Fit for a King '37
The Wrong Road '37
Milky Way '36
The Return of Peter Grimm '35
She '35
Son of Kong '33
Fargo Express '32
Melody Cruise '32
Struggle '31

Kerry Mack (1957-)
Fantasy Man '84
Savage Attraction '83
Fair Game '82

Wayne Mack (1924-93)
Mardi Gras Massacre '78
Crypt of Dark Secrets '76
Storyville '74

Dorothy Mackaill (1903-90)
Bulldog Drummond at Bay '37
No Man of Her Own '32
Kept Husbands '31
Ranson's Folly '26
Shore Leave '25

Barry Mackay (1906-)
Sailing Along '38
Gangway '37
The Private Secretary '35
Evergreen '34

Fulton Mackay (1922-87)
Porridge '91
Defense of the Realm '85
Local Hero '83
A Sense of Freedom '78
Nothing But the Night '72

John MacKay
Niagara, Niagara '97
Simple Men '92
Trust '91
Alligator Eyes '90
The Rejuvenator '88
I Was a Teenage TV Terrorist '87
Fat Guy Goes Nutzoid '86

Matthew Mackay
Mouvements du Desir '94
The Peanut Butter Solution '85

Helen MacKellar
Bad Boy '39
Delinquent Parents '38

Kenneth MacKenna
Judgment at Nuremberg '61
Sin Takes a Holiday '30

Evan Mackenzie
Children of the Night '92
Ghoulies 3: Ghoulies Go to College '91

Giselle MacKenzie
The Oval Portrait '88
Music Shoppe '82

Jan MacKenzie
The American Angels: Baptism of Blood '89
Gator Bait 2: Cajun Justice '88

Patch MacKenzie
Defense Play '88
Isle of Secret Passion '85
Graduation Day '81
Black Eliminator '78
Goodbye, Norma Jean '75

Peter M. MacKenzie
Major League 3: Back to the Minors '98
Tom and Huck '95

Allison Mackie
Original Sin '01
Rear Window '98
The Souler Opposite '97
Schemes '95
Lurking Fear '94

Steven Mackintosh (1967-)
Lady Audley's Secret '00
The Land Girls '98
Lock, Stock and 2 Smoking Barrels '98
Our Mutual Friend '98
The Ebb-Tide '97
Different for Girls '96
Grave Indiscretions '96
Twelfth Night '96
Blue Juice '95
The Return of the Native '94
A Dark Adapted Eye '93

The Buddha of Suburbia '92
London Kills Me '91
Jim MacKrell
Cannibal Women in the Avocado Jungle of Death '89
Just Between Friends '86
Love at the Top '86
Andrew MacLachlan
The Adventures of Baron Munchausen '89
Erik the Viking '89
A Fish Called Wanda '88
Monty Python's The Meaning of Life '83
Monty Python's Life of Brian '79
Janet MacLachlan
For Us, the Living '88
Murphy's Law '86
She's in the Army Now '81
Roll of Thunder, Hear My Cry '78
Big Mo '73
Sounder '72
Darker than Amber '70
Kyle MacLachlan (1959-)
Perfume '01
Hamlet '00
The Spring '00
Time Code '00
Xchange '00
Route 9 '98
Jack Higgins' The Windsor Protocol '97
Jack Higgins' Thunder Point '97
One Night Stand '97
Moonshine Highway '96
The Trigger Effect '96
Trigger Happy '96
Showgirls '95
Against the Wall '94
The Flintstones '94
Roswell: The U.F.O. Cover-Up '94
Rich in Love '93
The Trial '93
Twin Peaks: Fire Walk with Me '92
Where the Day Takes You '92
The Doors '91
Don't Tell Her It's Me '90
The Hidden '87
Blue Velvet '86
Dune '84
Shirley MacLaine (1934-)
These Old Broads '01
The Dress Code '99
Joan of Arc '99
The Evening Star '96
Mrs. Winterbourne '96
A Smile Like Yours '96
Guarding Tess '94
Wrestling Ernest Hemingway '93
Used People '92
Postcards from the Edge '90
Waiting for the Light '90
Steel Magnolias '89
Madame Sousatzka '88
Out on a Limb '87
That's Dancing! '85
Cannonball Run 2 '84
Terms of Endearment '83
A Change of Seasons '80
Loving Couples '80
Being There '79
The Turning Point '77
The Possession of Joel Delaney '72
Desperate Characters '71
Two Mules for Sister Sara '70
Sweet Charity '69
The Bliss of Mrs. Blossom '68
Woman Times Seven '67
Gambit '66
Irma La Douce '63
My Geisha '62
Two for the Seesaw '62
All in a Night's Work '61
The Children's Hour '61
The Apartment '60
Can-Can '60
Ocean's 11 '60
Ask Any Girl '59
Career '59
Hot Spell '58
The Matchmaker '58
Some Came Running '58
Around the World in 80 Days '56
Artists and Models '55
The Trouble with Harry '55
Barton MacLane (1902-69)
Buckskin '68
Arizona Bushwackers '67
The Geisha Boy '58
Naked in the Sun '57
Three Violent People '57
Wetbacks '56
Kansas Pacific '53
Bugles in the Afternoon '52
Drums in the Deep South '51
The Half-Breed '51
Let's Dance '50
Silver River '48
Treasure of the Sierra Madre '48
Unknown Island '48
The Spanish Main '45
Treasure of Fear '45
Cry of the Werewolf '44
The Mummy's Ghost '44
Nabonga '44
Bombardier '43
Marine Raiders '43
Song of Texas '43
The Underdog '43
All Through the Night '42
Big Street '42
Dr. Jekyll and Mr. Hyde '41
The Maltese Falcon '41
Western Union '41
Melody Ranch '40
Mutiny in the Big House '39
Bullets or Ballots '38
Prison Break '38
You and Me '38
The Prince and the Pauper '37
You Only Live Once '37
Black Fury '35
The Case of the Lucky Legs '35
Ceiling Zero '35
"G" Men '35
Man of the Forest '33
To the Last Man '33
Mary MacLaren (1896-1985)
The Duke of West Point '38
A Lawman Is Born '37
The New Frontier '35
The Three Musketeers '21
Gavin MacLeod (1930-)
Scruples '80
Only with Married Men '74
Kelly's Heroes '70
The Party '68
The Sand Pebbles '66
McHale's Navy Joins the Air Force '65
McHale's Navy '64
Compulsion '59
Pork Chop Hill '59
Mary MacLeod
I Want You '98
If.... '69
Michael MacLiammoir
What's the Matter with Helen? '71
Othello '52
Ellie MacLure (1985-)
Air Hawk '84
Heat of the Flame '82
Alvin Purple '73
Aline MacMahon (1899-1991)
I Could Go on Singing '63
The Man from Laramie '55
The Flame & the Arrow '50
The Search '48
Dragon Seed '44
Guest in the House '44
The Lady Is Willing '42
Back Door to Heaven '39
Ah, Wilderness! '35
I Live My Life '35
Gold Diggers of 1933 '33
Heroes for Sale '33
Fred MacMurray (1908-91)
The Swarm '78
Beyond the Bermuda Triangle '75
Charley and the Angel '73
The Happiest Millionaire '67
Follow Me, Boys! '66
Kisses for My President '64
Son of Flubber '63
Bon Voyage! '62
The Absent-Minded Professor '61
The Apartment '60
The Shaggy Dog '59
Good Day for a Hanging '58
At Gunpoint '55
The Caine Mutiny '54
A Woman's World '54
Borderline '50
Never a Dull Moment '50
Father Was a Fullback '49
The Miracle of the Bells '48
On Our Merry Way '48
Egg and I '47
Singapore '47
Murder, He Says '45
Double Indemnity '44
Above Suspicion '43
The Lady Is Willing '42
Dive Bomber '41
Remember the Night '40
My Love For Yours '39
Swing High, Swing Low '37
The Princess Comes Across '36
The Texas Rangers '36
The Trail of the Lonesome Pine '36
Alice Adams '35
Hands Across the Table '35
Alan MacNaughton
The Dark Angel '91
A Very British Coup '88
Robert MacNaughton
I Am the Cheese '83
E.T.: The Extra-Terrestrial '82
Patrick Macnee (1922-)
The Avengers '98
Thunder in Paradise 2 '94
The Gambler Returns: The Luck of the Draw '93
The Hound of London '93
Thunder in Paradise '93
Sherlock Holmes and the Incident at Victoria Falls '91
Waxwork 2: Lost in Time '91
Chill Factor '90
Super Force '90
Around the World in 80 Days '89
Lobster Man from Mars '89
Masque of the Red Death '89
Sorry, Wrong Number '89
Transformations '88
Waxwork '88
Shadey '87
Down Under '86
A View to a Kill '85
This Is Spinal Tap '84
Return of the Man from U.N.C.L.E. '83
Rehearsal for Murder '82
Young Doctors in Love '82
The Howling '81
Sea Wolves '81
Spaceship '81
Sweet 16 '81
Battlestar Galactica '78
Dead of Night '77
King Solomon's Treasure '76
The Bloodsuckers '70
Les Girls '57
A Christmas Carol '51
The Elusive Pimpernel '50
Peter MacNeill
Angel Eyes '01
Sex & Mrs. X '00
Dangerous Evidence: The Lori Jackson Story '99
The Hanging Garden '97
Closer and Closer '96
Crash '95
A Vow to Kill '94
Peter MacNicol (1954-)
The Ponder Heart '01
Baby Geniuses '98
Bean '97
Dracula: Dead and Loving It '95
Radioland Murders '94
Roswell: The U.F.O. Cover-Up '94
Addams Family Values '93
Hard Promises '92
Housesitter '92
American Blue Note '89
Ghostbusters 2 '89
Heat '87
Sophie's Choice '82
The Boy Who Left Home to Find Out About the Shivers '81
Dragonslayer '81
Elle Macpherson (1964-)
A Girl Thing '01
With Friends Like These '98
Batman and Robin '97
The Edge '97
Jane Eyre '96
The Mirror Has Two Faces '96
If Lucy Fell '95
Sirens '94
Alice '90
George MacQuarrie
The Idol Dancer '20
The Love Flower '20
Gordon MacRae (1921-86)
Danger in the Skies '79
Carousel '56
Oklahoma! '55
By the Light of the Silvery Moon '53
The Desert Song '53
On Moonlight Bay '51
Tea for Two '50
The West Point Story '50
Look for the Silver Lining '49
Heather MacRae
Secrets of Three Hungry Wives '78
Bang the Drum Slowly '73
The Connection '73
Meredith MacRae (1944-2000)
Husbands, Wives, Money, and Murder '86
Vultures '84
Sketches of a Strangler '78
Bikini Beach '64
Michael MacRae (1949-)
Masterminds '96
Madhouse '87
Isle of Secret Passion '85
Dear Detective '78
Great Ride '78
Greedy Terror '78
George Macready (1908-73)
The Return of Count Yorga '71
Tora! Tora! Tora! '70
Night Gallery '69
The Great Race '65
The Human Duplicators '64
Seven Days in May '64
Where Love Has Gone '64
Taras Bulba '62
Two Weeks in Another Town '62
Paths of Glory '57
I Beheld His Glory '53
Julius Caesar '53
The Stranger Wore a Gun '53
Vera Cruz '53
The Green Glove '52
Detective Story '51
The Nevadan '50
The Doolins of Oklahoma '49
Knock on Any Door '49
The Big Clock '48
Black Arrow '48
Coroner Creek '48
Down to Earth '47
Gilda '46
The Seventh Cross '44
Bruce MacVittie
Where the Money Is '00
Hi-Life '98
Stonewall '95
Bill Macy (1922-)
Analyze This '98
Me, Myself & I '92
The Doctor '91
Sibling Rivalry '90
Bad Medicine '85
Casey at the Bat '85
Movers and Shakers '85
My Favorite Year '82
Serial '80
Diary of a Young Comic '79
The Jerk '79
The Late Show '77
Oh! Calcutta! '72
William H. Macy (1950-)
Focus '01
Jurassic Park 3 '01
Panic '00
State and Main '00
Happy, Texas '99
Magnolia '99
Mystery Men '99
A Slight Case of Murder '99
A Civil Action '98
The Con '98
Jerry and Tom '98
Pleasantville '98
Psycho '98
Air Force One '97
Boogie Nights '97
Wag the Dog '97
Down Periscope '96
Fargo '96
Ghosts of Mississippi '96
Andersonville '95
Mr. Holland's Opus '95
Murder in the First '95
Being Human '94
Children of Fury '94
The Client '94
Dead on Sight '94
Evolver '94 (V)
Oleanna '94
Benny & Joon '93
Searching for Bobby Fischer '93
Twenty Bucks '93
A Private Matter '92
The Water Engine '92
Homicide '91
Things Change '88
Ciaran Madden (1945-)
Ivanhoe '97
Fortunes of War '87
A Married Man '84
The Beast Must Die '75
John Madden (1949-)
The Replacements '00
Little Giants '94
P.K. and the Kid '85
Peter Madden (1905-76)
Frankenstein Created Woman '66
Doctor Zhivago '65
Kiss of the Vampire '62
The Loneliness of the Long Distance Runner '62
Victor Maddern (1926-93)
I'm All Right Jack '59
Blood of the Vampire '58
Abandon Ship '57
Amy Madigan (1957-)
The Laramie Project '02
Shot in the Heart '01
Pollock '00
A Bright Shining Lie '98
With Friends Like These '98
Loved '97
Female Perversions '96
Riders of the Purple Sage '96
The Dark Half '91
Field of Dreams '89
Roe vs. Wade '89
Uncle Buck '89
Prince of Pennsylvania '88
Nowhere to Hide '87
Alamo Bay '85
Twice in a Lifetime '85
Places in the Heart '84
Streets of Fire '84
Love Letters '83
The Ambush Murders '82
Love Child '82
James Madio
Band of Brothers '01
The Basketball Diaries '94
Hero '92
Guy Madison (1922-96)
Computer Wizard '77
Where's Willie? '77
Hell Commandos '69
Special Forces '68
Bang Bang Kid '67
Superargo '67
Five Giants from Texas '66
The Snake Hunter Strangler '66
Cold Steel for Tortuga '65
Place in Hell '65
Apache's Last Battle '64
The Conqueror & the Empress '64
Executioner of Venice '63
Jet Over the Atlantic '59
Bullwhip '58
Savage Wilderness '55
Drums in the Deep South '51
Till the End of Time '46
Since You Went Away '44
Noel Madison (1897-1975)
Footsteps in the Dark '41
Sailing Along '38
Gangway '37
The House of Secrets '37
A Nation Aflame '37
Cocaine Fiends '36
Rock Madison
Creature of the Walking Dead '60
Man Beast '55
Philip Madoc (1934-)
A Mind to Kill '95
A Very British Coup '88
Ruth Madoc
Agatha Christie's The Pale Horse '96
Hi-Di-Hi '88
Madonna (1959-)
The Next Best Thing '00
Evita '96
Girl 6 '96
Blue in the Face '95
Four Rooms '95
Dangerous Game '93
Body of Evidence '92
A League of Their Own '92
Shadows and Fog '92
Truth or Dare '91
Dick Tracy '90
Bloodhounds of Broadway '89
Who's That Girl? '87
Shanghai Surprise '86
Desperately Seeking Susan '85
Certain Sacrifice '80
Michael Madsen (1959-)
Extreme Honor '01
Choke '00
High Noon '00

Luck of the Draw '00
Sacrifice '00
The Stray '00
Agent of Death '99
Detour '99
Supreme Sanction '99
Voodoo Dawn '99
Catherine's Grove '98
The Florentine '98
The Maker '98
The Sender '98
Species 2 '98
Surface to Air '98
Trail of a Serial Killer '98
Diary of a Serial Killer '97
Executive Target '97
Love to Kill '97
Donnie Brasco '96
The Last Days of Frankie the Fly '96
Red Line '96
The Winner '96
Free Willy 2: The Adventure Home '95
Man with a Gun '95
Mulholland Falls '95
Species '95
Dead Connection '94
Season of Change '94
Wyatt Earp '94
Almost Blue '93
Free Willy '93
The Getaway '93
A House in the Hills '93
Money for Nothing '93
Beyond the Law '92
Fatal Instinct '92
Inside Edge '92
Reservoir Dogs '92
Straight Talk '92
Trouble Bound '92
The Doors '91
Thelma & Louise '91
The End of Innocence '90
Iguana '89
Kill Me Again '89
Shadows in the Storm '88
The Natural '84
Racing with the Moon '84
One for the Road '82

Virginia Madsen (1963-)
Crossfire Trail '01
Full Disclosure '00
The Haunting '99
The Florentine '98
The Apocalypse Watch '97
John Grisham's The Rainmaker '97
Ghosts of Mississippi '96
Just Your Luck '96
The Prophecy '95
Bitter Vengeance '94
Blue Tiger '94
Caroline at Midnight '93
Linda '93
Becoming Colette '92
Candyman '92
Highlander 2: The Quickening '91
Love Kills '91
Victim of Love '91
The Hot Spot '90
Ironclads '90
The Heart of Dixie '89
Third Degree Burn '89
Gotham '88
Hot to Trot! '88
Mr. North '88
Long Gone '87
Slamdance '87
Zombie High '87
Fire with Fire '86
Modern Girls '86
Creator '85
The Hearst and Davies Affair '85
Dune '84
Electric Dreams '84

Beverly Maeda
Face of Another '66
Son of Godzilla '66

Mia Maestro
In the Time of the Butterflies '01
For Love or Country: The Arturo Sandoval Story '00
Time Code '00
Tango '98

Roma Maffia
Things You Can Tell Just by Looking at Her '00
Double Jeopardy '99
Route 9 '98
The Defenders: Payback '97
Kiss the Girls '97
Mistrial '96
The Heidi Chronicles '95
Nick of Time '95
Disclosure '94

Dominic Mafham (1968-)
The Scarlet Pimpernel '99
Our Mutual Friend '98
Shooting Fish '98

Cass Magda
Blade Boxer '97
Hawk's Vengeance '96

Patrick Magee (1922-82)
The Monster Club '85
The Black Cat '81
Chariots of Fire '81
Rough Cut '80
Sleep of Death '79
Telefon '77
Barry Lyndon '75
A Killer in Every Corner '74
Luther '74
And Now the Screaming Starts '73
The Final Programme '73
Asylum '72
Demons of the Mind '72
Young Winston '72
A Clockwork Orange '71
The Fiend '71
King Lear '71
Trojan Women '71
Cromwell '70
Anzio '68
Portrait in Terror '66
Die, Monster, Die! '65
Masque of the Red Death '65
The Skull '65
Seance on a Wet Afternoon '64
Zulu '64
Dementia 13 '63
The Very Edge '63

Jad Mager
Big City Blues '99
Blue Flame '93

Brandon Maggart
Running Mates '92
The World According to Garp '82
Christmas Evil '80
Dressed to Kill '80

Benoit Magimel (1974-)
Les Voleurs '96
A Single Girl '96
Life Is a Long Quiet River '88

Anna Magnani (1907-73)
Fellini's Roma '72
The Secret of Santa Vittoria '69
Mamma Roma '62
The Fugitive Kind '60
Joyful Laughter '60
Passionate Thief '60
The Rose Tattoo '55
The Golden Coach '52
Bellissima '51
Amore '48
The Miracle '48
Peddlin' in Society '47
Open City '45
Teresa Venerdi '41

Donna Magnani
Epoch '00
29th Street '91

Ann Magnuson (1956-)
Panic Room '02
The Caveman's Valentine '01
Glitter '01
Love & Sex '00
From the Earth to the Moon '98
Small Soldiers '98
Levitation '97
Still Breathing '97
Before and After '95
Cabin Boy '94
Tank Girl '94
Checking Out '89
Heavy Petting '89
Love at Large '89
A Night in the Life of Jimmy Reardon '88
Sleepwalk '88
Tequila Sunrise '88
Making Mr. Right '86
Desperately Seeking Susan '85
Perfect Strangers '84
The Hunger '83
Vortex '81

Pierre Maguelon
Alice et Martin '98
Cyrano de Bergerac '90
Bed and Board '70

Tobey Maguire (1975-)
Spider-Man '02
Cats & Dogs '01 (V)
Wonder Boys '00
The Cider House Rules '99
Ride with the Devil '99
Fear and Loathing in Las Vegas '98
Pleasantville '98
Deconstructing Harry '97
The Ice Storm '97
Joyride '97
Revenge of the Red Baron '93

Valerie Mahaffey
Jungle 2 Jungle '96
National Lampoon's Senior Trip '95
Witch Hunt '94
They Watch '93
Code Name: Dancer '87
The Rise & Rise of Daniel Rocket '86
Women of Valor '86

George Maharis (1928-)
Sword & the Sorcerer '82
The Crash of Flight 401 '78
Return to Fantasy Island '77
Murder on Flight 502 '75
Desperados '69
Land Raiders '69
Last Day of the War '69
Exodus '60

Bill Maher (1956-)
Pizza Man '91
Cannibal Women in the Avocado Jungle of Death '89
House 2: The Second Story '87

Joseph Maher (1934-98)
Surviving Picasso '96
Bulletproof Heart '95
I.Q. '94
Sister Act '92
Funny Farm '88
My Stepmother Is an Alien '88
The Evil That Men Do '84
Frankenweenie '84
Under the Rainbow '81

Grace Mahlaba
Being Human '94
Bopha! '93

Bruce Mahler
Funland '89
Police Academy 6: City under Siege '89

Shiek Mahmud-Bey
Small Vices: A Spenser Mystery '99
Path to Paradise '97
Joe's Apartment '96
Night Falls on Manhattan '96

Michael Mahonen (1964-)
Giant Steps
Captured '99
By Way of the Stars '92

Brian Mahoney
Boondock Saints '99
Red Snow '91

Jock Mahoney (1919-89)
Bad Bunch '76
The Glory Stompers '67
The Walls of Hell '64
A Time to Love & a Time to Die '58
Battle Hymn '57
The Land Unknown '57
Cow Town '50
The Nevadan '50
Rim of the Canyon '49

John Mahoney (1940-)
Atlantis: The Lost Empire '01 (V)
The Broken Hearts Club '00
Iron Giant '99 (V)
Antz '98 (V)
Primal Fear '96
She's the One '96
The American President '95
Reality Bites '94
The Hudsucker Proxy '93
In the Line of Fire '93
Striking Distance '93
Article 99 '92
The Secret Passion of Robert Clayton '92
The Water Engine '92
Barton Fink '91
Love Hurts '91
The Ten Million Dollar Getaway '91
Unnatural Pursuits '91
The Russia House '90
Dinner at Eight '89
The Image '89
Say Anything '89
Betrayed '88
Eight Men Out '88
Frantic '88
Moonstruck '87
Suspect '87
Tin Men '87
The Manhattan Project '86
Trapped in Silence '86

Tim Maier
Turnaround '87
Raw Courage '84

Steven Mailer
Ride with the Devil '99
24 Nights '99
Quiet Days in Hollywood '97
Getting In '94

Laurie Main
Tarzan, the Ape Man '81
Private Parts '72

Marjorie Main (1890-1975)
The Kettles on Old MacDonald's Farm '57
Friendly Persuasion '56
The Kettles in the Ozarks '56
Ma and Pa Kettle at Waikiki '55
The Long, Long Trailer '54
Ma and Pa Kettle at Home '54
Rose Marie '54
Ma and Pa Kettle on Vacation '53
The Belle of New York '52
Ma and Pa Kettle at the Fair '52
Ma and Pa Kettle Back On the Farm '51
Ma and Pa Kettle Go to Town '50
Summer Stock '50
Ma and Pa Kettle '49
Egg and I '47
The Wistful Widow of Wagon Gap '47
The Harvey Girls '46
The Show-Off '46
Undercurrent '46
Murder, He Says '45
Heaven Can Wait '43
Johnny Come Lately '43
Honky Tonk '41
The Shepherd of the Hills '41
A Woman's Face '41
Dark Command '40
Susan and God '40
They Shall Have Music '39
The Women '39
Little Tough Guys '38
Dead End '37
Stella Dallas '37
The Wrong Road '37

Valerie Mairesse (1955-)
The Sacrifice '86
Investigation '79
One Sings, the Other Doesn't '77

Marne Maitland (1916-91)
Fellini's Roma '72
The Bushbaby '70
The Reptile '66
Bhowani Junction '56

Tina Majorino (1985-)
Alice in Wonderland '99
Santa Fe '97
True Women '97
Waterworld '95
Andre '94
Corrina, Corrina '94
When a Man Loves a Woman '94

Lee Majors (1940-)
Big Fat Liar '02
Out Cold '01
Trojan War '97
The Cover Girl Murders '93
Chinatown Connection '90
Keaton's Cop '90
Scrooged '88
A Smoky Mountain Christmas '86
The Cowboy & the Ballerina '84
Starflight One '83
The Agency '81
Last Chase '81
High Noon: Part 2 '80
Steel '80
Killer Fish '79
Norseman '78
Francis Gary Powers: The True Story of the U-2 Spy '76
The Bionic Woman '75
The Ballad of Andy Crocker '69
Will Penny '67
Strait-Jacket '64

Chris Makepeace (1964-)
Synapse '95
Aloha Summer '88
Captive Hearts '87
Vamp '86
Undergrads '85
Savage Hunger '84
The Terry Fox Story '83
Mazes and Monsters '82
The Mysterious Stranger '82
Last Chase '81
My Bodyguard '80

Wendy Makkena
Air Bud '97
Finding North '97
Death Benefit '96
Serving in Silence: The Margarethe Cammermeyer Story '95
Camp Nowhere '94
Sister Act 2: Back in the Habit '93
Sister Act '92

Mako (1933-)
Pearl Harbor '01
Rugrats in Paris: The Movie '00 (V)
Seven Years in Tibet '97
Sworn to Justice '97
Balance of Power '96
Riot in the Streets '96
Blood for Blood '95
A Dangerous Place '94
Highlander: The Final Dimension '94
Red Sun Rising '94
Rising Sun '93
Sidekicks '93
My Samurai '92
Hiroshima: Out of the Ashes '90
Pacific Heights '90
Taking Care of Business '90
Fatal Mission '89
An Unremarkable Life '89
Tucker: The Man and His Dream '88
The Wash '88
Armed Response '86
Kung Fu: The Movie '86
The P.O.W. Escape '86
Girls of the White Orchid '85
Conan the Destroyer '84
The Nightingale '83
Conan the Barbarian '82
An Eye for an Eye '81
Under the Rainbow '81
The Big Brawl '80
The Killer Elite '75
The Island at the Top of the World '74
The Streets of San Francisco '72
Private Navy of Sgt. O'Farrell '68
The Sand Pebbles '66

Dragan Maksimovic
Pretty Village, Pretty Flame '96
Meetings with Remarkable Men '79

Mala (1906-52)
The Tuttles of Tahiti '42
Hawk of the Wilderness '38
Robinson Crusoe of Clipper Island '36
Robinson Crusoe of Mystery Island '36

Patrick Malahide (1945-)
Captain Corelli's Mandolin '01
Victoria & Albert '01
The Franchise Affair
All the King's Men '99
Fortress 2: Re-Entry '99
Heaven '99
Deacon Brodie '98
Miracle at Midnight '98
The Beautician and the Beast '97
The Long Kiss Goodnight '96
Til There Was You '96
Cutthroat Island '95
Kidnapped '95
A Man of No Importance '94
Two Deaths '94
Middlemarch '93
December Bride '91
A Month in the Country '87
The Singing Detective '86
Comfort and Joy '84

Christophe MaLavoy (1952-)
Madame Bovary '91
The Cry of the Owl '87
Peril '85

Paolo Malco
The House by the Cemetery '83
New York Ripper '82

Christopher Malcolm
We'll Meet Again '82
The Great Riviera Bank Robbery '79

Karl Malden (1914-)
Nuts '87
Billy Galvin '86
Fatal Vision '84
Urge to Kill '84
The Sting 2 '83
Miracle on Ice '81

Beyond the Poseidon Adventure '79
Meteor '79
Skag '79
Ricco '74
The Streets of San Francisco '72
The Cat o' Nine Tails '71
Wild Rovers '71
Patton '70
Blue '68
Hot Millions '68
Hotel '67
The Adventures of Bullwhip Griffin '66
Murderers' Row '66
Nevada Smith '66
The Cincinnati Kid '65
Cheyenne Autumn '64
How the West Was Won '63
All Fall Down '62
Birdman of Alcatraz '62
Gypsy '62
The Great Impostor '61
One-Eyed Jacks '61
Parrish '61
Pollyanna '60
The Hanging Tree '59
Fear Strikes Out '57
Baby Doll '56
On the Waterfront '54
I Confess '53
Diplomatic Courier '52
Ruby Gentry '52
A Streetcar Named Desire '51
The Gunfighter '50
The Halls of Montezuma '50
Boomerang '47
Kiss of Death '47
13 Rue Madeleine '46
They Knew What They Wanted '40

Ruth Maleczech
The Ballad of Little Jo '93
In the Soup '92
Anna '87

Arthur Malet
A Little Princess '95
Beastmaster 2: Through the Portal of Time '91
Hook '91
The Black Cauldron '85 (V)
Halloween '78
Munster, Go Home! '66
King Rat '65

Laurent Malet (1955-)
The Possessed '88
Sword of Gideon '86
Querelle '83
Invitation au Voyage '82
Jacko & Lise '82
Roads to the South '78
Blood Relatives '77

Wendie Malick (1950-)
The Emperor's New Groove '00 (V)
Dead Husbands '98
Jerome '98
North Shore Fish '97
Trojan War '97
The American President '95
Madonna: Innocence Lost '95

Keram Malicki-Sanchez
Happy Campers '01
Cherry Falls '00
Skin Deep '94

Art Malik (1952-)
Cleopatra '99
Catherine Cookson's Colour Blind '98
Path to Paradise '97
Booty Call '96
A Kid in King Arthur's Court '95
True Lies '94
City of Joy '92
The Killing Beach '92
Year of the Comet '92
The Living Daylights '87
Harem '86

Transmutations '85
The Jewel in the Crown '84

Joshua Malina
Bulworth '98
From the Earth to the Moon '98

Judith Malina (1926-)
Let It Snow '99
The Deli '97
Music from Another Room '97
Household Saints '93
The Addams Family '91
Enemies, a Love Story '89

Ross Malinger (1984-)
Club Vampire '98
Frog and Wombat '98
Toothless '97
Little Bigfoot '96
Sudden Death '95
Bye Bye, Love '94
Sleepless in Seattle '93
Late for Dinner '91
Eve of Destruction '90

Sam Malkin
Blood Relations '87
Caribe '87

John Malkovich (1953-)
Shadow of the Vampire '00
Being John Malkovich '99
The Messenger: The Story of Joan of Arc '99
RKO 281 '99
The Man in the Iron Mask '98
Rounders '98
Con Air '97
The Ogre '96
Portrait of a Lady '96
Beyond the Clouds '95
The Convent '95
Mary Reilly '95
Mulholland Falls '95
Alive '93 (N)
Heart of Darkness '93
In the Line of Fire '93
Jennifer 8 '92
Of Mice and Men '92
Shadows and Fog '92
The Object of Beauty '91
Queens Logic '91
The Sheltering Sky '90
Dangerous Liaisons '88
Miles from Home '88
Empire of the Sun '87
The Glass Menagerie '87
Death of a Salesman '86
Making Mr. Right '86
Rocket to the Moon '86
True West '86
Eleni '85
The Killing Fields '84
Places in the Heart '84
American Dream '81

Miles Malleson (1888-1969)
The Brides of Dracula '60
Peeping Tom '60
The Horror of Dracula '58
Brothers in Law '57
The King's Rhapsody '55
Captain's Paradise '53
A Christmas Carol '51
The Golden Salamander '51
Kind Hearts and Coronets '49
Train of Events '49
Dead of Night '45
The Thief of Bagdad '40
Nine Days a Queen '36

Perry Mallette
Thou Shalt Not Kill...Except '87
Going Back '83

Patricia "Boots" Mallory (1913-58)
Powdersmoke Range '35
Sing Sing Nights '35
Carnival Lady '33
Wolf Dog '33

Matt Malloy
Changing Lanes '02
The Great Gatsby '01
Dr. T & the Women '00

Everything Put Together '00
Running Mates '00
Cookie's Fortune '99
Drop Dead Gorgeous '99
Election '99
In the Company of Men '96
Surviving Desire '91

Jan Malmsjo
Fanny and Alexander '83
Scenes from a Marriage '73

Birger Malmsten (1920-91)
The Silence '63
Summer Interlude '50
To Joy '50
Three Strange Loves '49
Night Is My Future '47

Bonz Malone
White Boyz '99
Slam '98

Dorothy Malone (1925-)
Basic Instinct '92
Rest in Pieces '87
Day Time Ended '80
Off Your Rocker '80
Winter Kills '79
Abduction '75
The Man Who Would Not Die '75
Beach Party '63
The Last Voyage '60
Warlock '59
Man of a Thousand Faces '57
Tarnished Angels '57
Sincerely Yours '56
Tension at Table Rock '56
Written on the Wind '56
Artists and Models '55
At Gunpoint '55
Battle Cry '55
The Fast and the Furious '54
Private Hell 36 '54
Young at Heart '54
Scared Stiff '53
Torpedo Alley '53
The Bushwackers '52
The Nevadan '50
South of St. Louis '48
The Big Sleep '46
Night and Day '46

Jena Malone (1984-)
The Dangerous Lives of Altar Boys '02
Donnie Darko '01
Life as a House '01
Cheaters '00
The Book of Stars '99
For Love of the Game '99
Stepmom '98
Contact '97
Ellen Foster '97
Hope '97
Bastard out of Carolina '96
Hidden in America '96

Mollie Malone
Battling Bunyon '24
Straight Shootin' '17

Patrick Malone
Hostage High '97
Grand Canyon '91
Rock 'n' Roll High School Forever '91

Michael Maloney (1957-)
The Painted Lady '97
Hamlet '96
A Midwinter's Tale '95
Othello '95
Truly, Madly, Deeply '91
Henry V '89
Sharma & Beyond '84

Peter Maloney
Washington Square '97
Robot in the Family '94

H.F. Maltby
Pygmalion '38
Young and Innocent '37

Leonard Maltin (1950-)
Forgotten Silver '96
Gremlins 2: The New Batch '90

The Lost Stooges '33 (N)

Eily Malyon (1879-1961)
She Wolf of London '46
The Seventh Cross '44
I Married a Witch '42

David Mamet (1947-)
The Water Engine '92
Black Widow '87

Robert Mammone
Heaven's Burning '97
The Crossing '92

Biff Manard
Trancers 2: The Return of Jack Deth '90
Zone Troopers '84

Michael Manasseri
When Danger Follows You Home '97
License to Drive '88

Melissa Manchester
For the Boys '91
The Great Mouse Detective '86 (V)

Al Mancini
The Ticket '97
My Summer Story '94
Mission Manila '87
The Dirty Dozen '67

Ray "Boom Boom" Mancini (1961-)
Body and Soul '98
The Search for One-Eyed Jimmy '96
Wishful Thinking '92
Timebomb '91
Backstreet Dreams '90
The Dirty Dozen: The Fatal Mission '88
Oceans of Fire '86

Nick Mancuso (1948-)
Revelation '00
Tribulation '00
Captured '99
The Pact '99
Total Recall 2070: Machine Dreams '99
Against the Law '98
Matter of Trust '98
Misbegotten '98
Past Perfect '98
Twists of Terror '98
Laws of Deception '97
The Ex '96
The Invader '96
Marquis de Sade '96
Provocateur '96
Under Siege 2: Dark Territory '95
A Young Connecticut Yankee in King Arthur's Court '95
Young Ivanhoe '95
Flinch '94
Suspicious Agenda '94
The Takeover '94
Wild Palms '93
Lies Before Kisses '92
Rapid Fire '92
Fatal Exposure '91
Lena's Holiday '90
Double Identity '89
Death of an Angel '86
Half a Lifetime '86
Embassy '85
Blame It on the Night '84
Heartbreakers '84
Maria Chapdelaine '84
Tell Me That You Love Me '84
Legend of Walks Far Woman '82
Mother Lode '82
Ticket to Heaven '81
Death Ship '80
The House on Garibaldi Street '79
Nightwing '79

Elena Mandalis
Head On '98
Only the Brave '94

Robert Mandan (1932-)
The Nutt House '95
National Lampoon's Last Resort '94

Perry Mason: The Case of the Lost Love '87
In Love with an Older Woman '82
Zapped! '82
Return of the Rebels '81

Howie Mandel (1955-)
Tribulation '00
Kurt Vonnegut's Harrison Bergeron '95
Shake, Rattle & Rock! '94
Gremlins 2: The New Batch '90 (V)
Mother Goose Rock 'n' Rhyme '90
Little Monsters '89
Walk Like a Man '87
A Fine Mess '86
Gremlins '84 (V)
The Princess Who Never Laughed '84
Gas '81

Miles Mander (1888-1946)
Brighton Strangler '45
Picture of Dorian Gray '45
Murder, My Sweet '44
The Pearl of Death '44
Scarlet Claw '44
The White Cliffs of Dover '44
Five Graves to Cairo '43
Guadalcanal Diary '43
Return of the Vampire '43
To Be or Not to Be '42
Shadows on the Stairs '41
Primrose Path '40
The Little Princess '39
Stanley and Livingstone '39
The Three Musketeers '39
The Tower of London '39
Wuthering Heights '39
Mad Miss Manton '38
Don Quixote '35
The Three Musketeers '35
The Private Life of Henry VIII '33
Murder '30

Barbara Mandrell
Burning Rage '84
The Concrete Cowboys '79

Neil Mandt
Arthur's Quest '99
Hijacking Hollywood '97

Costas Mandylor (1965-)
The Pledge '00
Bonanno: A Godfather's Story '99
Stealth Fighter '99
The Fury Within '98
Shame, Shame, Shame '98
Shelter '98
Double Take '97
Just Write '97
Stand-Ins '97
Last Exit to Earth '96
Crosscut '95
Delta of Venus '95
Fist of the North Star '95
Portraits of a Killer '95
Venus Rising '95
Virtuosity '95
Almost Dead '94
Fatal Past '94
The Doors '91
Mobsters '91
Soapdish '91
Triumph of the Spirit '89

Louis Mandylor (1966-)
My Big Fat Greek Wedding '02
Price of Glory '00
Rogue Force '99
The Quest '96

Tyler Mane
How to Make a Monster '01
X-Men '00

Larry Manetti (1947-)
The Corporation '96
Body Chemistry 4: Full Exposure '95
Exit '95
C.I.A. 2: Target Alexa '94
The Take '90

Magnum P.I.: Don't Eat the Snow in Hawaii '80

Nino Manfredi (1921-)
Alberto Express '92
In the Name of the Pope-King '85
Cafe Express '83
Nudo di Donna '83
Spaghetti House '82
We All Loved Each Other So Much '77
Down & Dirty '76
Bread and Chocolate '73
Head of the Family '71

Anthony Mangano
All Saint's Day '98
8 Heads in a Duffel Bag '96

Silvana Mangano (1930-89)
Dark Eyes '87
Dune '84
Conversation Piece '75
Ludwig '72
Death in Venice '71
The Decameron '70
Teorema '68
Oedipus Rex '67
Barabbas '62
The Great War '59
Mambo '55
Ulysses '55
The Gold of Naples '54
Anna '51
Bitter Rice '49
Lure of the Sila '49

Alec Mango
The Cosmic Monsters '58
The Seventh Voyage of Sinbad '58

Camryn Manheim (1961-)
A Girl Thing '01
The Loretta Claiborne Story '00
The 10th Kingdom '00
What Planet Are You From? '00
The Tic Code '99
Happiness '98
David Searching '97
Romy and Michele's High School Reunion '97
Wide Awake '97

Karin Mani
Avenging Angel '85
Alley Cat '84

Cindy Manion
The Toxic Avenger '86
Preppies '82

Blu Mankuma
Mermaid '00
Atomic Train '99
Premonition '98
A Call to Remember '97
Bliss '96
Dead Silence '96
Watchers '88

Dudley Manlove
The Creation of the Humanoids '62
Plan 9 from Outer Space '56

Byron Mann
The Corruptor '99
Double Edge '97
Red Corner '97
Street Fighter '94

Danny Mann
Babe: Pig in the City '98 (V)
Babe '95 (V)
Balto '95 (V)
Pocahontas '95 (V)

Gabriel Mann
The Bourne Identity '02
Josie and the Pussycats '01
Summer Catch '01
Cherry Falls '00
Outside Providence '99
American Virgin '98
High Art '98
Kiss of Fire '98

Hank Mann (1887-1971)
City Lights '31
Spite Marriage '29

Leonard Mann
Cut and Run '85
Corrupt '84
Night School '81
Leslie Mann (1972-)
Orange County '02
Perfume '01
Time Code '00
Big Daddy '99
George of the Jungle '97
The Cable Guy '96
Last Man Standing '96
She's the One '96
Terrence Mann (1951-)
True Women '97
Mrs. Santa Claus '96
Critters 4 '91
The Ten Million Dollar Getaway '91
Critters 2: The Main Course '88
Light Years '88 (V)
Critters '86
A Chorus Line '85
Tracey Mann
Fast Talking '86
Hard Knocks '80
Yanka (Doris Keating) Mann
Flesh Feast '69
Pagan Island '60
Guido Mannari
Cop in Blue Jeans '78
Driver's Seat '73
David Manners (1901-98)
The Mystery of Edwin Drood '35
The Black Cat '34
The Death Kiss '33
A Bill of Divorcement '32
The Mummy '32
They Call It Sin '32
Three Broadway Girls '32
Dracula '31
The Miracle Woman '31
Lucie Mannheim (1899-1979)
Hotel Reserve '44
High Command '37
The 39 Steps '35
Ettore Manni (1927-79)
City of Women '81
Street People '76
The Battle of El Alamein '68
Heroes in Hell '67
Mademoiselle '66
Giants of Rome '63
Hercules and the Captive Women '63
The Battle of Austerlitz '60
Angel in a Taxi '59
Two Nights with Cleopatra '54
Vic Manni
Trapped in Paradise '94
29th Street '91
Marilyn Manning
The Sadist '63
What's Up Front '63
Eegah! '62
Taryn Manning (1978-)
Crossroads '02
crazy/beautiful '01
Sheila (Manors) Mannors (1911-)
Nancy Drew, Reporter '39
Torture Ship '39
Waterfront '39
Cocaine Fiends '36
Desert Phantom '36
Kelly of the Secret Service '36
Prescott Kid '36
Lawless Range '35
Westward Ho '35
Cowboy Counselor '33
Dinah Manoff (1958-)
The Lost Child '00
Welcome Home, Roxy Carmichael '90
Bloodhounds of Broadway '89
Backfire '88
Child's Play '88
Table Settings '84
I Ought to Be in Pictures '82
For Ladies Only '81
Ordinary People '80
Grease '78
The Possessed '77
Miki (Predrag) Manojlovic (1950-)
Set Me Free '99
Cabaret Balkan '98
Artemisia '97
Portraits Chinois '96
Someone Else's America '96
Underground '95
Every Other Weekend '91
When Father Was Away on Business '85
Predrag Manojlovic
Black Cat, White Cat '98
Tito and Me '92
Jayne Mansfield (1932-67)
Single Room Furnished '68
A Guide for the Married Man '67
Las Vegas Hillbillys '66
Dog Eat Dog '64
Promises! Promises! '63
Panic Button '62
The Loves of Hercules '60
It Takes a Thief '59
Will Success Spoil Rock Hunter? '57
The Female Jungle '56
The Girl Can't Help It '56
Hell on Frisco Bay '55
Illegal '55
Pete Kelly's Blues '55
Underwater! '55
Martha Mansfield (1899-1927)
Is Money Everything? '23
Dr. Jekyll and Mr. Hyde '20
Leonor Manso
Made in Argentina '86
House of Shadows '83
Far Away and Long Ago '74
Alan Manson (1918-2002)
Whiffs '75
Let's Scare Jessica to Death '71
The Rain People '69
Paul Mantee (1931-)
Memorial Day '98
Lurking Fear '94
The Manitou '78
Robinson Crusoe on Mars '64
Joe Mantegna (1947-)
The Trumpet of the Swan '01 (V)
Liberty Heights '99
My Little Assassin '99
The Runner '99
Small Vices: A Spenser Mystery '99
Body and Soul '98
Celebrity '98
For Hire '98
Hoods '98
Jerry and Tom '98
The Last Don 2 '98
The Rat Pack '98
The Wonderful Ice Cream Suit '98
A Call to Remember '97
Face Down '97
The Last Don '97
Albino Alligator '96
Persons Unknown '96
Stephen King's Thinner '96
Underworld '96
Up Close and Personal '96
Above Suspicion '95
Captain Nuke and the Bomber Boys '95
An Eye for an Eye '95
For Better or Worse '95
Forget Paris '95
National Lampoon's Favorite Deadly Sins '95
Airheads '94
Baby's Day Out '94
State of Emergency '94
Fallen Angels 2 '93
Searching for Bobby Fischer '93
Body of Evidence '92
The Comrades of Summer '92
The Water Engine '92
Bugsy '91
Family Prayers '91
Homicide '91
Queens Logic '91
Alice '90
The Godfather, Part 3 '90
Wait until Spring, Bandini '90
Things Change '88
House of Games '87
Suspect '87
Weeds '87
Critical Condition '86
The Money Pit '86
Off Beat '86
Three Amigos '86
Compromising Positions '85
Second Thoughts '83
Elvis: The Movie '79
Henriette Mantel
A Very Brady Sequel '96
The Brady Bunch Movie '95
Joe Mantell (1920-)
Chinatown '74
The Birds '63
Marty '55
Michael Mantell
Chain of Command '00
Gun Shy '00
Sins of the Mind '97
Dead Funny '94
The Night We Never Met '93
City of Hope '91
Eight Men Out '88
Fernando Soto Mantequilla (1911-80)
Invasion of the Vampires '61
The Illusion Travels by Streetcar '53
Boom in the Moon '46
Randolph Mantooth
Agent Red '00
Terror at London Bridge '85
The Seekers '79
Leslie Manville
Plain Jane '01
Topsy Turvy '99
The Painted Lady '97
Secrets and Lies '95
High Hopes '88
High Season '88
Dance with a Stranger '85
Grown Ups '80
Linda Manz (1961-)
Gummo '97
The Snow Queen '83
Out of the Blue '80
Orphan Train '79
Wanderers '79
Days of Heaven '78
Angela (Mao Ying) Mao (1950-)
When Taekwondo Strikes '83
Return of the Tiger '78
Enter the Dragon '73
Marla Maples
Black and White '99
Happiness '98
Adele Mara (1923-)
Sands of Iwo Jima '49
Night Time in Nevada '48
Robin Hood of Texas '47
The Inner Circle '46
Bells of Rosarita '45
Twilight on the Rio Grande '41
Mary Mara
K-PAX '01
Lloyd '00
Bound '96
Love Potion #9 '92
Mr. Saturday Night '92
Steve Marachuk
Hot Target '85
Piranha 2: The Spawning '82
The Spawning '82
Waikiki '80
Jean Marais (1913-98)
Stealing Beauty '96
Peau D'Ane '71
Donkey Skin '70
The Rape of the Sabines '61
The Battle of Austerlitz '60
The Testament of Orpheus '59
Girl in His Pocket '57
White Nights '57
Elena and Her Men '56
Orpheus '49
The Eagle Has Two Heads '48
Ruyblas '48
The Storm Within '48
Beauty and the Beast '46
Eternal Return '43
Cindy Maranne
Provoked '89
Slashdance '89
Dominique Marcas
La Vie de Boheme '93
Dr. Petiot '90
Marcel Marceau
Silent Movie '76
Barbarella '68
Sophie Marceau (1966-)
Lost and Found '99
William Shakespeare's A Midsummer Night's Dream '99
The World Is Not Enough '99
Firelight '97
Leo Tolstoy's Anna Karenina '96
Beyond the Clouds '95
Braveheart '95
Revenge of the Musketeers '94
Police '85
Fort Saganne '84
La Boum '81
Elspeth March (1911-99)
The Magician of Lublin '79
Goodbye, Mr. Chips '69
Woman Times Seven '67
The Three Lives of Thomasina '63 (V)
Roman Spring of Mrs. Stone '61
Midnight Lace '60
Quo Vadis '51
Fredric March (1897-1975)
Hombre '67
Seven Days in May '64
Inherit the Wind '60
The Man in the Gray Flannel Suit '56
Alexander the Great '55
The Bridges at Toko-Ri '55
Desperate Hours '55
A Christmas Carol '54
Executive Suite '54
Christopher Columbus '49
The Best Years of Our Lives '46
The Adventures of Mark Twain '44
Tomorrow the World '44
I Married a Witch '42
So Ends Our Night '41
Susan and God '40
Nothing Sacred '37
A Star Is Born '37
Anthony Adverse '36
Mary of Scotland '36
Anna Karenina '35
Les Miserables '35
The Barretts of Wimpole Street '34
Death Takes a Holiday '34
The Eagle and the Hawk '33
The Sign of the Cross '33
Smilin' Through '33
Dr. Jekyll and Mr. Hyde '32
Jane March
Dracula: The Dark Prince '01
Tarzan and the Lost City '98
Circle of Passion '97
Provocateur '96
Color of Night '94
The Lover '92
Georges Marchal (1920-97)
Belle de Jour '67
Death in the Garden '56
The French Way '40
Corinne Marchand (1937-)
Bandits '86
Borsalino '70
Cleo from 5 to 7 '61
Guy Marchand (1937-)
May Wine '90
Conseil de Famille '86
Heat of Desire '84
Petit Con '84
Entre-Nous '83
Coup de Torchon '81
Loulou '80
Dear Detective '77
Cousin, Cousine '76
Nancy Marchand (1928-2000)
Dear God '96
Sabrina '95
Brain Donors '92
Regarding Henry '91
The Naked Gun: From the Files of Police Squad '88
North and South Book 2 '86
The Bostonians '84
Killjoy '81
The Hospital '71
Josh Marchette
Tequila Body Shots '99
Floating '97
Ron Marchini
Karate Cop '93
Return Fire '91
Omega Cop '90
Forgotten Warrior '86
Wolf '86
Death Machines '76
David Marciano (1960-)
The Last Don 2 '98
The Last Don '97
Hellbent '90
Kiss Shot '89
Vanessa Marcil
Nice Guys Sleep Alone '99
The Rock '96
Paul Marco
Night of the Ghouls '59
Plan 9 from Outer Space '56
Bride of the Monster '55
Andre Marcon
Up/Down/Fragile '95
Jeanne la Pucelle '94
Ted Marcoux
Andersonville '95
Ghost in the Machine '93
The Nightman '93
Andrea Marcovicci (1948-)
Jack the Bear '93
The Water Engine '92
Someone to Love '87
The Stuff '85
Spraggue '84
Kings and Desperate Men '83
Packin' It In '83
Spacehunter: Adventures in the Forbidden Zone '83
The Hand '81
The Concorde: Airport '79 '79
The Front '76
The Devil's Web '74
James Marcus
A Clockwork Orange '71
Oliver Twist '22
James A. Marcus (1867-1937)
The Lone Avenger '33
The Broken Mask '28
Sadie Thompson '28
The Eagle '25
Jeff Marcus
Legal Deceit '95
Alien Nation: Dark Horizon '94
Richard Marcus
Cannibal Campout '88
Deadly Friend '86
Enemy Mine '85
Stephen Marcus
Lock, Stock and 2 Smoking Barrels '98
My Beautiful Laundrette '85
Jordan Marder
American History X '98
Lord of Illusions '95
Walking on Air '87
Tom Mardirosian
The Dark Half '91
Presumed Innocent '90
Arthur Margetson (1887-1951)
Sherlock Holmes Faces Death '43
Juggernaut '37
The Mystery of the Mary Celeste '37
Margo (1917-85)
Who's Got the Action? '63
I'll Cry Tomorrow '55
Viva Zapata! '52
Behind the Rising Sun '43
The Leopard Man '43
Lost Horizon '37
Winterset '36
Janet Margolin (1943-93)
The Game of Love '90
Ghostbusters 2 '89
Distant Thunder '88
Plutonium Incident '82
Last Embrace '79
The Triangle Factory Fire Scandal '79
Annie Hall '77
Planet Earth '74
Pray for the Wildcats '74
Take the Money and Run '69
Buona Sera, Mrs. Campbell '68
Enter Laughing '67
Nevada Smith '66
Morituri '65
David and Lisa '62
Stuart Margolin (1940-)
The Student Affair '97
To Grandmother's House We Go '94
Guilty by Suspicion '91
Bye Bye Blues '89
Iron Eagle 2 '88
A Fine Mess '86
The Glitter Dome '84
Class '83
Running Hot '83
S.O.B. '81
Days of Heaven '78
The Big Bus '76
Futureworld '76
Death Wish '74
Kelly's Heroes '70
Women of the Prehistoric Planet '66
Mark Margolis (1939-)
Hardball '01
The Tailor of Panama '00
Jakob the Liar '99
The Thomas Crown Affair '99
Pi '98
Where the Rivers Flow North '94
Descending Angel '90
Miriam Margolyes (1941-)
Cats & Dogs '01
Dreaming of Joseph Lees '99
End of Days '99

Sunshine *'99*
Vanity Fair *'99*
Mulan *'98 (V)*
Different for Girls *'96*
James and the Giant Peach *'96 (V)*
William Shakespeare's Romeo and Juliet *'96*
Babe *'95 (V)*
Balto *'95 (V)*
Cold Comfort Farm *'94*
Immortal Beloved *'94*
The Age of Innocence *'93*
Ed and His Dead Mother *'93*
Stalin *'92*
The Butcher's Wife *'91*
Orpheus Descending *'91*
I Love You to Death *'90*
Pacific Heights *'90*
Little Dorrit, Film 1: Nobody's Fault *'88*
Little Dorrit, Film 2: Little Dorrit's Story *'88*

Michael Margotta
Can She Bake a Cherry Pie? *'83*
The Blue Knight *'75*

David Margulies (1937-)
Looking for an Echo *'99*
Last Breath *'96*
Out on a Limb *'92*
Family Prayers *'91*
Funny About Love *'90*
Ghostbusters 2 *'89*
Running on Empty *'88*
9 1/2 Weeks *'86*
Ghostbusters *'84*
Dressed to Kill *'80*
All That Jazz *'79*

Julianna Margulies (1966-)
Mists of Avalon *'01*
Dinosaur *'00 (V)*
What's Cooking? *'00*
The Big Day *'99*
The Newton Boys *'97*
Paradise Road *'97*
A Price above Rubies *'97*
Traveller *'96*
Out for Justice *'91*

Constance Marie
Tortilla Soup *'01*
The Last Marshal *'99*
Selena *'96*
My Family *'94*

Jeanne Marie
Young Nurses in Love *'89*
If Looks Could Kill *'86*

Lisa Marie
Sleepy Hollow *'99*
Tail Lights Fade *'99*
Frogs for Snakes *'98*
Breast Men *'97*
Mars Attacks! *'96*
Ed Wood *'94*
Roller Blade *'85*
Dead and Buried *'81*

Jean-Pierre Marielle (1932-)
L'Eleve *'95*
Tous les Matins du Monde *'92*
Uranus *'91*
Menage *'86*
Coup de Torchon *'81*
One Wild Moment *'78*
The Women *'69*

Eli Marienthal (1986-)
American Pie 2 *'01*
Iron Giant *'99 (V)*
First Love, Last Rites *'98*
Jack Frost *'98*
Slums of Beverly Hills *'98*

Marietto
It Started in Naples *'60*
Angel in a Taxi *'59*

Jacques Marin (1919-)
The Island at the Top of the World *'74*
Shaft in Africa *'73*
Darling Lili *'70*
The Night of the Following Day *'69*
How to Steal a Million *'66*
The Train *'65*
Forbidden Games *'52*

Richard "Cheech" Marin (1946-)
Spy Kids *'01*
Luminarias *'99*
Picking Up the Pieces *'99*
Paulie *'98*
The Great White Hype *'96*
Tin Cup *'96*
The Courtyard *'95*
Desperado *'95*
From Dusk Till Dawn *'95*
Charlie's Ghost: The Secret of Coronado *'94*
The Cisco Kid *'94*
The Lion King *'94 (V)*
A Million to Juan *'94*
Ring of the Musketeers *'93*
Ferngully: The Last Rain Forest *'92 (V)*
Mother Goose Rock 'n' Rhyme *'90*
The Shrimp on the Barbie *'90*
Far Out Man *'89*
Ghostbusters 2 *'89*
Rude Awakening *'89*
Oliver & Company *'88 (V)*
Born in East L.A. *'87*
Fatal Beauty *'87*
Echo Park *'86*
After Hours *'85*
Cheech and Chong's The Corsican Brothers *'84*
Cheech and Chong: Still Smokin' *'83*
Yellowbeard *'83*
Cheech and Chong: Things Are Tough All Over *'82*
Cheech and Chong's Nice Dreams *'81*
Cheech and Chong's Next Movie *'80*
Cheech and Chong's Up in Smoke *'79*

Rikki Marin
Cheech and Chong's The Corsican Brothers *'84*
Cheech and Chong: Things Are Tough All Over *'82*

Ed Marinaro (1950-)
Deadly Game *'98*
Panic in the Skies *'96*
Dancing with Danger *'93*
Lethal Lolita—Amy Fisher: My Story *'92*
The Diamond Trap *'91*
Queens Logic *'91*
The Game of Love *'90*
Dead Aim *'87*
Policewoman Centerfold *'83*
Born Beautiful *'82*

Dan Marino
Little Nicky *'00*
Ace Ventura: Pet Detective *'93*

Ken Marino
Joe Somebody *'01*
Wet Hot American Summer *'01*
Alphabet City *'84*
Prince of the City *'81*

Beth Marion (1912-)
Phantom Gold *'38*
The Phantom of the Range *'38*
Rip Roarin' Buckaroo *'36*
Between Men *'35*
Trail of Terror *'35*

George F. Marion, Sr. (1860-1945)
Death from a Distance *'36*
Anna Christie *'30*
The Big House *'30*
Hook, Line and Sinker *'30*
Evangeline *'29*
Anna Christie *'23*

Howard Marion-Crawford (1914-69)
The Castle of Fu Manchu *'68*
The Charge of the Light Brigade *'68*
Kiss and Kill *'68*
Mister Drake's Duck *'50*
Man on the Run *'49*

Mona Maris (1903-91)
Heartbeat *'46*
The Falcon in Mexico *'44*
I Married an Angel *'42*
Underground *'41*
Love on the Run *'36*

Sari Maritza (1910-87)
Crimson Romance *'34*
International House *'33*
Greek Street *'30*

Robert Marius
Fist of Glory *'95*
Triple Impact *'92*
The 13th Mission *'91*

Heidi Mark
Rock Star *'01*
Red Shoe Diaries: Luscious Lola *'00*

Jane (Jeanne) Marken (1895-1976)
Crazy for Love *'52*
Dedee d'Anvers *'49*
A Day in the Country *'46*
Children of Paradise *'44*
Eternal Return *'43*

Enid Markey (1896-1981)
Tarzan of the Apes *'17*
Civilization *'16*
The Fugitive: Taking of Luke McVane *'15*

Kika Markham
Wonderland *'99*
Deep Cover *'88*
Miss A & Miss M *'86*
Outland *'81*
Two English Girls *'72*

Monte Markham (1935-)
At First Sight *'95*
Piranha *'95*
Counter Measures *'80s*
Defense Play *'88*
Judgment Day *'88*
Hot Pursuit *'87*
Hotline *'82*
Off the Wall *'82*
Shame, Shame on the Bixby Boys *'82*
Airport '77 *'77*
Hustling *'75*
Ginger in the Morning *'73*
Guns of the Magnificent Seven *'69*

Brian Markinson
The Curse of the Jade Scorpion *'01*
Sweet and Lowdown *'99*

Ted Markland
American Kickboxer 2: To the Death *'93*
Merlin *'92*
Fatal Mission *'89*
Wanda Nevada *'79*
Angels from Hell *'68*

Stephen Markle
984: Prisoner of the Future *'84*
Perfect Timing *'84*

Margaret Markov
The Arena *'73*
Hot Box *'72*
Run, Angel, Run! *'69*

Olivera Markovic
Tito and Me *'92*
Siberian Lady Macbeth *'61*

Alfred Marks (1921-96)
Antonia and Jane *'91*
Valentino *'77*
Scream and Scream Again *'70*
The Frightened City *'61*

Jennifer Marks
Naked Wishes *'00*
The Strangers *'98*

Winnie Markus (1922-2002)
The Devil in Silk *'56*
The Mozart Story *'48*

Arnold Marle
The Snake Woman *'61*
Men of Two Worlds *'46*

Ben Marley
From the Earth to the Moon *'98*
The Mosaic Project *'95*

John Marley (1907-84)
On the Edge *'86*
The Glitter Dome *'84*
Robbers of the Sacred Mountain *'83*
Threshold *'83*
Utilities *'83*
The Godfather 1902-1959: The Complete Epic *'81*
Hooper *'78*
It's Alive 2: It Lives Again *'78*
The Car *'77*
The Greatest *'77*
Framed *'75*
Kid Vengeance *'75*
Dead Are Alive *'72*
Deathdream *'72*
The Godfather *'72*
Jory *'72*
A Man Called Sledge *'71*
Love Story *'70*
Faces *'68*

Carla Marlier
Spirits of the Dead *'68*
Any Number Can Win *'63*
The Avenger *'62*
Zazie dans le Metro *'61*

Lucy Marlow
My Sister Eileen *'55*
Queen Bee *'55*

Hugh Marlowe (1911-82)
Castle of Evil *'66*
Seven Days in May *'64*
Birdman of Alcatraz *'62*
Elmer Gantry *'60*
Earth vs. the Flying Saucers *'56*
Illegal *'55*
Casanova's Big Night *'54*
Bugles in the Afternoon *'52*
Monkey Business *'52*
The Day the Earth Stood Still *'51*
All About Eve *'50*
Night and the City *'50*
Rawhide *'50*
Come to the Stable *'49*
Twelve o'Clock High *'49*

June Marlowe (1903-84)
The Lone Defender *'32*
Pardon Us *'31*
Don Juan *'26*
The Night Cry *'26*

Linda Marlowe
The Green Man *'91*
Mr. Love *'86*
Night Slasher *'84*
Big Zapper *'73*
He Kills Night After Night After Night *'70*

Florence Marly (1919-78)
Dr. Death, Seeker of Souls *'73*
Games *'67*
Planet of Blood *'66*
Tokyo Joe *'49*

Percy Marmont (1883-1977)
Lisbon *'56*
Four Sided Triangle *'53*
Young and Innocent *'37*
The Secret Agent *'36*
Rich and Strange *'32*
Lady of the Lake *'28*
Mantrap *'26*

Kelli Maroney (1964-)
Face Down *'97*
Servants of Twilight *'91*
Chopping Mall *'86*
Zero Boys *'86*
Night of the Comet *'84*
Slayground *'84*
Fast Times at Ridgemont High *'82*

Michael Maronna
40 Days and 40 Nights *'02*
Slackers *'02*

Carl Marotte (1959-)
One Kill *'00*
Prisoner of Love *'99*
Twists of Terror *'98*
When Justice Fails *'98*
Breaking All the Rules *'85*
Pick-Up Summer *'79*

Christian Marquand (1927-2000)
The Corrupt Ones *'67*
End of Desire *'62*
Love Play *'60*
And God Created Woman *'57*

Serge Marquand (1930-)
The Big Red One *'80*
Barbarella *'68*
Blood and Roses *'61*
Please Not Now! *'61*

Maria Elena Marques (1926-)
Ambush at Tomahawk Gap *'53*
Across the Wide Missouri *'51*
The Pearl *'48*

Ron Marquette (-1995)
Red Shoe Diaries 7: Burning Up *'96*
Deadly Past *'95*
Red Shoe Diaries 5: Weekend Pass *'95*
Public Access *'93*

Margaret Marquis
Brand of the Outlaws *'36*
Last of the Warrens *'36*

Eddie Marr
I Was a Teenage Werewolf *'57*
Hollywood Canteen *'44*

David Marriott
Monster High *'89*
Operation Warzone *'89*

Moore Marriott (1885-1949)
Oh, Mr. Porter *'37*
The Flying Scotsman *'29*

Sylvia Marriott
The Story of Adele H. *'75*
Two English Girls *'72*
Beast of Morocco *'66*
Crimes at the Dark House *'39*

Kenneth Mars (1936-)
Citizen Ruth *'96*
Thumbelina *'94 (V)*
We're Back! A Dinosaur's Story *'93 (V)*
Shadows and Fog *'92*
Get Smart, Again! *'89*
The Little Mermaid *'89 (V)*
For Keeps *'88*
Rented Lips *'88*
Illegally Yours *'87*
Radio Days *'87*
Beer *'85*
Fletch *'85*
Misfits of Science *'85*
Protocol *'84*
Yellowbeard *'83*
The Apple Dumpling Gang Rides Again *'79*
Goin' Coconuts *'78*
Night Moves *'75*
The Parallax View *'74*
Young Frankenstein *'74*
What's Up, Doc? *'72*
Desperate Characters *'71*
April Fools *'69*
Butch Cassidy and the Sundance Kid *'69*
The Producers *'68*

Maurice Marsac (1920-)
The Big Red One *'80*
Clarence, the Cross-eyed Lion *'65*
Werewolf in a Girl's Dormitory *'61*
Tarzan and the Trappers *'58*
China Gate *'57*

Branford Marsalis
School Daze *'88*
Throw Momma from the Train *'87*

Eddie Marsan
Dostoevsky's Crime and Punishment *'99*
Second Sight *'99*

James Marsden (1973-)
Sugar & Spice *'01*
X-Men *'00*
Gossip *'99*
Disturbing Behavior *'98*
Bella Mafia *'97*
Public Enemies *'96*

Jason Marsden
How to Make a Monster *'01*
The Lion King: Simba's Pride *'98 (V)*
White Squall *'96*
A Goofy Movie *'94 (V)*

Roy Marsden (1941-)
A Certain Justice *'99*
A Mind to Murder *'96*
Devices and Desires *'91*
Vanity Fair *'67*

Carol Marsh (1929-)
The Horror of Dracula *'58*
A Christmas Carol *'51*
Alice in Wonderland *'50*
Brighton Rock *'47*

Garry Marsh (1902-81)
Who Done It? *'56*
Old Mother Riley's Jungle Treasure *'51*
Someone at the Door *'50*
Just William's Luck *'47*
A Girl in a Million *'46*
Dead of Night *'45*
Pink String and Sealing Wax *'45*
Department Store *'35*

Jamie Marsh
Beethoven's 3rd *'00*
Best Laid Plans *'99*
Brainscan *'94*

Jean Marsh (1934-)
Agatha Christie's The Pale Horse *'96*
Fatherland *'94*
A Connecticut Yankee in King Arthur's Court *'89*
Willow *'88*
Return to Oz *'85*
Goliath Awaits *'81*
The Changeling *'80*
Frenzy *'72*
The Unearthly Stranger *'64*
Horsemasters *'61*

Joan Marsh (1914-2000)
Manhunt in the African Jungle *'54*
Follow the Leader *'44*
Champagne for Breakfast *'35*
High Gear *'33*
Rainbow over Broadway *'33*
Maker of Men *'31*

Mae Marsh (1895-1968)
From the Terrace *'60*
Sergeant Rutledge *'60*
While the City Sleeps *'56*
The Tall Men *'55*
The Quiet Man *'52*
The Gunfighter *'50*
Impact *'49*
Fort Apache *'48*
Three Godfathers *'48*
The Fighting Sullivans *'42*
How Green Was My Valley *'41*
The White Rose *'23*
Hoodoo Ann *'16*
Intolerance *'16*
The Birth of a Nation *'15*
Home Sweet Home *'14*
Judith of Bethulia *'14*

Marian Marsh (1913-)
House of Errors *'42*
Gentleman from Dixie *'41*
When's Your Birthday? *'37*
Youth on Parole *'37*
The Black Room *'35*
Crime and Punishment *'35*

Svengali '31
Matthew Marsh
Spy Game '01
In the Secret State
A Certain Justice '99
An Affair in Mind '89
Michele Marsh
Evil Town '87
Deadly Alliance '78
Fiddler on the Roof '71
Alan Marshal (1909-61)
House on Haunted Hill '58
The White Cliffs of Dover '44
Lydia '41
Tom, Dick, and Harry '41
The Howards of Virginia '40
The Hunchback of Notre Dame '39
Conquest '37
Night Must Fall '37
After the Thin Man '36
The Garden of Allah '36
Brenda Marshall (1915-92)
Strange Impersonation '46
Background to Danger '43
Captains of the Clouds '42
Footsteps in the Dark '41
The Sea Hawk '40
Bryan Marshall (1938-)
Return to Snowy River '88
The Long Good Friday '80
Because of the Cats '74
Vanity Fair '67
David Anthony Marshall
The Demolitionist '95
Another 48 Hrs. '90
Dodie Marshall
Easy Come, Easy Go '67
Spinout '66
Don Marshall
Terminal Island '73
The Thing with Two Heads '72
E.G. Marshall (1910-98)
Absolute Power '97
The Defenders: Payback '97
Miss Evers' Boys '97
Nixon '95
Oldest Confederate Widow Tells All '95
Russian Roulette '93
Stephen King's The Tommyknockers '93
Consenting Adults '92
Ironclads '90
Two Evil Eyes '90
National Lampoon's Christmas Vacation '89
Saigon: Year of the Cat '87
My Chauffeur '86
Power '86
Kennedy '83
Creepshow '82
Eleanor: First Lady of the World '82
Superman 2 '80
The Lazarus Syndrome '79
Interiors '78
Abduction of St. Anne '75
Pursuit '72
The Pursuit of Happiness '70
Tora! Tora! Tora! '70
The Bridge at Remagen '69
The Littlest Angel '69
The Chase '66
Is Paris Burning? '66
The Poppy Is Also a Flower '66
Town without Pity '61
Cash McCall '60
Compulsion '59
The Buccaneer '58
Twelve Angry Men '57
The Mountain '56
The Left Hand of God '55
Broken Lance '54
The Caine Mutiny '54
The Silver Chalice '54
Call Northside 777 '48
13 Rue Madeleine '46
Garry Marshall (1934-)
Orange County '02
Forever Together '00
Never Been Kissed '99
With Friends Like These '98
The Twilight of the Golds '97
Dear God '96
Hocus Pocus '93
A League of Their Own '92
Soapdish '91
Jumpin' Jack Flash '86
Lost in America '85
Herbert Marshall (1890-1966)
The Fly '58
Stage Struck '57
The Virgin Queen '55
The Black Shield of Falworth '54
Captain Blackjack '51
The Underworld Story '50
The Secret Garden '49
Crack-Up '46
Duel in the Sun '46
The Razor's Edge '46
The Enchanted Cottage '45
Forever and a Day '43
The Moon and Sixpence '43
The Little Foxes '41
When Ladies Meet '41
Foreign Correspondent '40
The Letter '40
Mad About Music '38
Angel '37
A Woman Rebels '36
The Painted Veil '34
Riptide '34
Blonde Venus '32
Murder '30
James Marshall (1967-)
Luck of the Draw '00
Soccer Dog: The Movie '98
The Ticket '97
Don't Do It '94
Vibrations '94
A Few Good Men '92
Gladiator '92
Twin Peaks: Fire Walk with Me '92
Ken Marshall (1953-)
Double Exposure: The Story of Margaret Bourke-White '89
Feds '88
Krull '83
Tilt '78
Marion Marshall
The Stooge '51
I Was a Male War Bride '49
Paula Marshall (1964-)
Thursday '98
A Gun, a Car, a Blonde '97
A Family Thing '96
That Old Feeling '96
The New Age '94
Warlock: The Armageddon '93
Hellraiser 3: Hell on Earth '92
Penny Marshall (1947-)
Get Shorty '95
Hocus Pocus '93
The Hard Way '91
Challenge of a Lifetime '85
Movers and Shakers '85
1941 '79
How Come Nobody's On Our Side? '73
Evil Roy Slade '71
Peter Marshall
Americathon '79
A Guide for the Married Woman '78
Return of Jesse James '50
Sarah Marshall
French Silk '94
The People vs. Jean Harris '81
Sean Marshall
Pete's Dragon '77
Wonderland Cove '75
Trudy Marshall (1922-)
Joe's Bed-Stuy Barbershop: We Cut Heads '83
Married Too Young '62
Crash Dive '43
The Fighting Sullivans '42
Tully Marshall (1864-1943)
Behind Prison Walls '43
Mr. Boggs Steps Out '38
Night of Terror '33
The Cabin in the Cotton '32
Red Dust '32
Strangers of the Evening '32
Two-Fisted Law '32
Fighting Caravans '31
Big Trail '30
Tom Sawyer '30
Queen Kelly '29
The Cat and the Canary '27
Smouldering Fires '25
He Who Gets Slapped '24
Broken Hearts of Broadway '23
Let's Go! '23
What Happened to Rosa? '21
Hawthorne of the USA '19
William Marshall (1917-)
That Brennan Girl '46
State Fair '45
William Marshall (1924-)
Vasectomy: A Delicate Matter '86
The Great Skycopter Rescue '82
Twilight's Last Gleaming '77
Scream Blacula Scream '73
Blacula '72
The Boston Strangler '68
Demetrius and the Gladiators '54
Zena Marshall
The Terrornauts '67
Dr. No '62
Christina Marsillach
Opera '88
Every Time We Say Goodbye '86
Tony Marsina
Last Mercenary '84
Tornado '83
Lynn(e) Marta (1946-)
Blood Beach '81
Joe Kidd '72
Richard Petty Story '72
Arlene Martel
Angels from Hell '68
Demon with a Glass Hand '64
June Martel (1909-78)
Santa Fe Stampede '38
Forlorn River '37
Arizona Mahoney '36
K.C. Martel
White Water Summer '87
E.T.: The Extra-Terrestrial '82
The Munsters' Revenge '81
The Amityville Horror '79
Chris Martell
Flesh Feast '69
Scream, Baby, Scream '69
Gruesome Twosome '67
Donna (Dona Martel) Martell (1927-)
Ten Wanted Men '54
Give a Girl a Break '53
Project Moon Base '53
Abbott and Costello Meet the Killer, Boris Karloff '49
Gillian Martell
Cause Celebre '87
Oliver Twist '85
Peter Martell
Mission Phantom '79
Planet on the Prowl '65
Cynthia Martells
The Wood '99
Broken Trust '95
Zooman '95
A Modern Affair '94
Blind Spot '93
Frank Marth
Showdown '93
Fright '56
Andrea Martin (1947-)
My Big Fat Greek Wedding '02
All Over the Guy '01
Jimmy Neutron: Boy Genius '01 (V)
Hedwig and the Angry Inch '00
Loser '00
Believe '99
Wag the Dog '97
Bogus '96
Guitarman '95
Kurt Vonnegut's Harrison Bergeron '95
Gypsy '93
Ted & Venus '93
Boris and Natasha: The Movie '92
All I Want for Christmas '91
Stepping Out '91
Too Much Sun '90
Rude Awakening '89
Worth Winning '89
Club Paradise '86
Soup for One '82
Black Christmas '75
Barney Martin
Arthur 2: On the Rocks '88
Arthur '81
Charles Martin
Fighting Black Kings '76
You've Ruined Me, Eddie '58
Chris-Pin (Ethier Crispin Martini) Martin (1893-1953)
Lucky Cisco Kid '40
Stagecoach '39
The Texans '38
South of Santa Fe '32
Christopher Martin (1963-)
House Party 3 '94
Class Act '91
House Party 2: The Pajama Jam '91
House Party '90
Damon Martin
Amityville 1992: It's About Time '92
Ghoulies 2 '87
Dan Martin
Sleepwalkers '92
The Last Tomahawk '65
Dean Martin (1917-95)
That's Dancing! '85
Cannonball Run 2 '84
Cannonball Run '81
Showdown '73
Airport '70
Bandolero! '68
Five Card Stud '68
The Wrecking Crew '68
The Ambushers '67
Rough Night in Jericho '67
Murderers' Row '66
The Silencers '66
Texas across the River '66
Sons of Katie Elder '65
Kiss Me, Stupid! '64
Robin and the 7 Hoods '64
Four for Texas '63
Toys in the Attic '63
Who's Got the Action? '63
All in a Night's Work '61
Bells Are Ringing '60
Ocean's 11 '60
Career '59
Rio Bravo '59
Some Came Running '58
The Young Lions '58
Hollywood or Bust '56
Pardners '56
Artists and Models '55
The Caddy '53
The Road to Bali '53
Scared Stiff '53
Jumping Jacks '52
The Stooge '51
At War with the Army '50
My Friend Irma '49
Dean Paul (Dino Martin Jr.) Martin (1951-87)
Backfire '88
Misfits of Science '85
Players '79
Dewey Martin (1923-)
Seven Alone '75
Flight to Fury '66
Savage Sam '63
Desperate Hours '55
Land of the Pharaohs '55
Men of the Fighting Lady '54
The Big Sky '52
The Thing '51
Diana Martin
Minnesota Clay '65
Hyena of London '62
Dick Martin (1922-)
Air Bud 2: Golden Receiver '98
Carbon Copy '81
The Glass Bottom Boat '66
Duane Martin
Mutiny '99
Scream 2 '97
Woo '97
Down Periscope '96
Above the Rim '94
D'Urville Martin (1938-84)
Big Score '83
Blind Rage '78
Death Journey '76
Dolemite '75
Sheba, Baby '75
Boss '74
Final Comedown '72
Watermelon Man '70
Edie Martin
The Ladykillers '55
Genevieve '53
George Martin
Drunks '96
One Fine Day '96
Blood at Sundown '88
Crossing Delancey '88
Falling in Love '84
Psychopath '68
Gilbert Martin
Beautiful People '99
Rob Roy '95
Helen Martin (1909-2000)
I Got the Hook-Up '98
Don't Be a Menace to South Central While Drinking Your Juice in the Hood '95
Doc Hollywood '91
House Party 2: The Pajama Jam '91
Night Angel '90
Hollywood Shuffle '87
A Hero Ain't Nothin' but a Sandwich '78
Jared Martin (1943-)
Twinsitters '95
Karate Warrior '88
Quiet Cool '86
The Sea Serpent '85
The Lonely Lady '83
The New Gladiators '83
Second Coming of Suzanne '80
Jean Martin
Lucie Aubrac '98
The Messiah '75
The Battle of Algiers '66
John Martin
The Underneath '95
Dark Before Dawn '89
Black Roses '88
Fire in the Night '85
The Tell-Tale Heart '62
Kellie Martin (1975-)
Christy '94
A Goofy Movie '94 (V)
Matinee '92
Troop Beverly Hills '89
Kiel Martin (1944-90)
Convicted: A Mother's Story '87
Child Bride of Short Creek '81
Panic in Needle Park '75
Lewis Martin
Men of the Fighting Lady '54
The War of the Worlds '53
Lock Martin
Invaders from Mars '53
The Day the Earth Stood Still '51
Marion Martin (1918-85)
The Great Mike '44
Mexican Spitfire at Sea '42
Big Store '41
The Man in the Iron Mask '39
Sinners in Paradise '38
Mary Martin (1913-90)
Peter Pan '60
Main Street to Broadway '53
Night and Day '46
Star Spangled Rhythm '42
Birth of the Blues '41
Rhythm on the River '40
Mel Martin
Poldark '96
Darlings of the Gods '90
White Hunter, Black Heart '90
Love for Lydia '79
Millicent Martin (1934-)
Alfie '66
Those Magnificent Men in Their Flying Machines '65
Horsemasters '61
Nan Martin (1927-)
Shallow Hal '01
The Song of the Lark '01
Big Eden '00
Cast Away '00
Matters of the Heart '90
A Nightmare on Elm Street 3: Dream Warriors '87
Proud Men '87
The Young Nurses '73
Goodbye Columbus '69
For Love of Ivy '68
Toys in the Attic '63
Pamela Sue Martin (1953-)
A Cry in the Wild '90
Eye of the Demon '87
Flicks '85
Torchlight '85
Lady in Red '79
Buster and Billie '74
Our Time '74
The Girls of Huntington House '73
Pepper Martin
Evil Altar '89
Scream '83
The Longest Yard '74
Angels from Hell '68
Remi Martin
The Possessed '88
Conseil de Famille '86
Richard Martin (1919-94)
Gunplay '51
Dynamite Pass '50
Rider from Tucson '50
Storm over Wyoming '50
Mysterious Desperado '49
Riders of the Range '49
West of the Pecos '45
Nevada '44
Tender Comrade '43
Ross Martin (1920-81)
More Wild, Wild West '80
The Seekers '79
Wild, Wild West Revisited '79
Wild & Wooly '78
Dying Room Only '73
Experiment in Terror '62

Geronimo '62
Conquest of Space '55

Rudolf Martin
Dracula: The Dark Prince '01
Swordfish '01
Bedazzled '00
Fall '97

Sandy Martin (1950-)
Sparkler '99
Vendetta '85
Scalpel '76

Sharlene Martin
Possession: Until Death Do You Part '90
Friday the 13th, Part 8: Jason Takes Manhattan '89

Skip Martin
Horror Hospital '73
Masque of the Red Death '65

Steve Martin (1945-)
Novocaine '01
Joe Gould's Secret '00
Bowfinger '99
The Out-of-Towners '99
Prince of Egypt '98 (V)
The Spanish Prisoner '97
Father of the Bride Part II '95
Sgt. Bilko '95
Mixed Nuts '94
A Simple Twist of Fate '94
And the Band Played On '93
Housesitter '92
Leap of Faith '92
Father of the Bride '91
Grand Canyon '91
L.A. Story '91
My Blue Heaven '90
Parenthood '89
Dirty Rotten Scoundrels '88
Planes, Trains & Automobiles '87
Roxanne '87
Little Shop of Horrors '86
Three Amigos '86
Movers and Shakers '85
All of Me '84
The Lonely Guy '84
The Man with Two Brains '83
Dead Men Don't Wear Plaid '82
Pennies from Heaven '81
The Jerk '79
The Kids Are Alright '79
The Muppet Movie '79
Sgt. Pepper's Lonely Hearts Club Band '78

Strother Martin (1919-80)
Hot Wire '70s
Better Late Than Never '79
The Champ '79
Cheech and Chong's Up in Smoke '79
Love and Bullets '79
Nightwing '79
The Villain '79
Steel Cowboy '78
Slap Shot '77
Hard Times '75
Rooster Cogburn '75
Sssssss '73
Hannie Caulder '72
Pocket Money '72
The Brotherhood of Satan '71
Ballad of Cable Hogue '70
Butch Cassidy and the Sundance Kid '69
True Grit '69
The Wild Bunch '69
Cool Hand Luke '67
Shenandoah '65
Invitation to a Gunfighter '64
McLintock! '63
The Man Who Shot Liberty Valance '62
The Horse Soldiers '59
Attack! '56
Kiss Me Deadly '55

Tina Martin
Spellbreaker: Secret of the Leprechauns '96
Leapin' Leprechauns '95

Tony Martin
The Interview '98
A Cry in the Dark '88

Tony Martin (1913-)
Meet Me in Las Vegas '56
Hit the Deck '55
Easy to Love '53
Here Come the Girls '53
Two Tickets to Broadway '51
Casbah '48
Till the Clouds Roll By '46
Big Store '41
Ziegfeld Girl '41
Music in My Heart '40
Pigskin Parade '36

Vera Martin
Loyalties '86
The Noose Hangs High '48

Vince Martin
Breaking Loose '90
Night Master '87

Vivian Martin
The Belles of St. Trinian's '53
The Wishing Ring '14

W.T. Martin
High Stakes '89
Hardhat & Legs '80

Margo Martindale
Proof of Life '00
28 Days '00
Earthly Possessions '99
Ride with the Devil '99
In Dreams '98
Twilight '98
Critical Care '97
Eye of God '97
Marvin's Room '96
Dead Man Walking '95
Nobody's Fool '94
Lorenzo's Oil '92

Elsa Martinelli (1932-)
Once Upon a Crime '92
Belle Starr '79
Candy '68
Madigan's Millions '67
Maroc 7 '67
Oldest Profession '67
Woman Times Seven '67
10th Victim '65
The Trial '63
The V.I.P.'s '63
Hatari! '62
Blood and Roses '61
The Indian Fighter '55

A. Martinez (1948-)
What's Cooking? '00
Last Rites '98
Wind River '98
The Cherokee Kid '96
One Night Stand '95
Where's the Money, Noreen? '95
Deconstructing Sarah '94
The Hunt for the Night Stalker '91
Powwow Highway '89
She-Devil '89
Born in East L.A. '87
Centennial '78
Joe Panther '76
Once Upon a Scoundrel '73
Starbird and Sweet William '73
The Cowboys '72

Fele Martinez (1976-)
Lovers of the Arctic Circle '98
Open Your Eyes '97
Thesis '96

Joaquin Martinez
The Cowboy Way '94
Jeremiah Johnson '72

Nacho Martinez
Law of Desire '86
Matador '86

Olivier Martinez (1966-)
Unfaithful '02
Before Night Falls '00

The Chambermaid on the Titanic '97
Mon Homme '96
The Horseman on the Roof '95

Steven Martini
Smiling Fish & Goat on Fire '99
Major Payne '95

Al Martino
The Godfather, Part 3 '90
The Godfather '72

Orlando Martins (1899-1985)
Call Me Bwana '63
Simba '55
Men of Two Worlds '46

Lee Marvin (1924-87)
Delta Force '86
The Dirty Dozen: The Next Mission '85
Dog Day '83
Gorky Park '83
Death Hunt '81
The Big Red One '80
Avalanche Express '79
Great Scout & Cathouse Thursday '76
The Meanest Men in the West '76
Shout at the Devil '76
The Klansman '74
Emperor of the North Pole '73
Pocket Money '72
Prime Cut '72
Monte Walsh '70
Hell in the Pacific '69
Paint Your Wagon '69
Sergeant Ryker '68
The Dirty Dozen '67
Point Blank '67
The Professionals '66
Cat Ballou '65
Ship of Fools '65
The Killers '64
Donovan's Reef '63
The Man Who Shot Liberty Valance '62
The Comancheros '61
Missouri Traveler '58
Raintree County '57
Attack! '56
I Died a Thousand Times '55
Pete Kelly's Blues '55
Shack Out on 101 '55
Bad Day at Black Rock '54
The Caine Mutiny '54
The Wild One '54
The Big Heat '53
Gun Fury '53
The Stranger Wore a Gun '53
Duel at Silver Creek '52
Hangman's Knot '52
Union Station '50

Brett Marx
The Bad News Bears Go to Japan '78
The Bad News Bears in Breaking Training '77
The Bad News Bears '76

Chico Marx (1886-1961)
The Marx Brothers in a Nutshell '90
Love Happy '50
A Night in Casablanca '46
Big Store '41
Go West '40
At the Circus '39
Room Service '38
A Day at the Races '37
A Night at the Opera '35
Duck Soup '33
Horse Feathers '32
Monkey Business '31
Animal Crackers '30
The Cocoanuts '29

Groucho Marx (1890-1977)
The Marx Brothers in a Nutshell '90
Will Success Spoil Rock Hunter? '57
A Girl in Every Port '52

Double Dynamite '51
Love Happy '50
Mr. Music '50
Copacabana '47
A Night in Casablanca '46
Big Store '41
Go West '40
At the Circus '39
Room Service '38
A Day at the Races '37
A Night at the Opera '35
Duck Soup '33
Horse Feathers '32
Monkey Business '31
Animal Crackers '30
The Cocoanuts '29

Harpo Marx (1888-1964)
The Marx Brothers in a Nutshell '90
Love Happy '50
A Night in Casablanca '46
Strictly G.I. '44
Stage Door Canteen '43
Big Store '41
Go West '40
At the Circus '39
Room Service '38
A Day at the Races '37
A Night at the Opera '35
Duck Soup '33
Horse Feathers '32
Monkey Business '31
Animal Crackers '30
The Cocoanuts '29

Zeppo Marx (1901-79)
The Marx Brothers in a Nutshell '90
Duck Soup '33
Horse Feathers '32
Monkey Business '31
Animal Crackers '30
The Cocoanuts '29

Franca Marzi (1926-89)
Nights of Cabiria '57
Island Monster '53

Ron Masak
Harper Valley P.T.A. '78
Tora! Tora! Tora! '70

Marino (Martin) Mase (1939-)
The Belly of an Architect '91
Zorro '74
Les Carabiniers '63

Vladimir Mashkov
Behind Enemy Lines '01
Dancing at the Blue Iguana '00
The Thief '97

Giulietta Masina (1921-94)
Ginger & Fred '86
The Madwoman of Chaillot '69
Juliet of the Spirits '65
Nights of Cabiria '57
Il Bidone '55
La Strada '54
Europa '51 '52
The White Sheik '52
Variety Lights '51

Ace Mask
Transylvania Twist '89
Not of This Earth '88

Connie Mason
2000 Maniacs '64
Blood Feast '63

Elliot Mason
On Approval '44
The Ghost Goes West '36

Eric Mason
Kiss of the Tarantula '75
Black Starlet '74

Hilary Mason (1917-)
Meridian: Kiss of the Beast '90
Robot Jox '90
Dolls '87
Don't Look Now '73

Jackie Mason (1934-)
Caddyshack 2 '88
History of the World: Part 1 '81
The Jerk '79

James Mason (1890-1954)
The Plainsman '37
Hopalong Cassidy '35
Border Law '31
The Concentratin' Kid '30
For Heaven's Sake '26

James Mason (1909-84)
A.D. '85
The Shooting Party '85
The Assisi Underground '84
George Washington '84
Yellowbeard '83
Dangerous Summer '82
Evil under the Sun '82
Ivanhoe '82
The Verdict '82
ffolkes '80
Street War '70s
Murder by Decree '79
Salem's Lot '79
Sidney Sheldon's Bloodline '79
Water Babies '79
The Boys from Brazil '78
Heaven Can Wait '78
Jesus of Nazareth '77
Cross of Iron '76
Kidnap Syndicate '76
Voyage of the Damned '76
Autobiography of a Princess '75
Inside Out '75
Mandingo '75
The Destructors '74
11 Harrowhouse '74
The Last of Sheila '73
Mackintosh Man '73
Bad Man's River '72
Cold Sweat '71
Yin & Yang of Mr. Go '71
Mayerling '68
Cop-Out '67
The Blue Max '66
Georgy Girl '66
Lord Jim '65
The Fall of the Roman Empire '64
The Pumpkin Eater '64
Lolita '62
Tiara Tahiti '62
The Trials of Oscar Wilde '60
Journey to the Center of the Earth '59
North by Northwest '59
Island in the Sun '57
Forever Darling '56
Prince Valiant '54
A Star Is Born '54
20,000 Leagues under the Sea '54
Botany Bay '53
Charade '53
The Desert Rats '53
Julius Caesar '53
Face to Face '52
Five Fingers '52
Prisoner of Zenda '52
The Desert Fox '51
Pandora and the Flying Dutchman '51
Caught '49
East Side, West Side '49
Madame Bovary '49
Reckless Moment '49
Man of Evil '48
Odd Man Out '47
The Seventh Veil '46
The Man in Grey '45
The Wicked Lady '45
Hotel Reserve '44
The Night Has Eyes '42
Secret Mission '42
I Met a Murderer '39
Fire Over England '37
High Command '37
The Mill on the Floss '37
Late Extra '35

Laurence Mason
Ali '01
Hackers '95
Parallel Sons '95
The Crow '93

Leroy Mason (1903-47)
Daughter of Don Q '46
The Phantom Rider '46
Vigilantes of Boom Town '46 (N)
California Joe '43
Western Mail '42
Silver Stallion '41
Rocky Mountain Rangers '40
Wyoming Outlaw '39
Outlaw Express '38
Santa Fe Stampede '38
The Painted Stallion '37
Western Gold '37
Black Gold '36
Go-Get-'Em-Haines '35
The Mystery Man '35
When a Man Sees Red '34
Phantom of the Air '33

Madison Mason
Thirteen Days '00
Glitz '88

Marsha Mason (1942-)
Life with Judy Garland—Me and My Shadows '01
Restless Spirits '99
Two Days in the Valley '96
Broken Trust '95
Nick of Time '95
Drop Dead Fred '91
Dinner at Eight '89
The Image '89
Stella '89
Heartbreak Ridge '86
Trapped in Silence '86
Max Dugan Returns '83
Lois Gibbs and the Love Canal '82
Only When I Laugh '81
Chapter Two '79
Promises in the Dark '79
The Cheap Detective '78
Audrey Rose '77
The Goodbye Girl '77
Blume in Love '73
Cinderella Liberty '73

Pamela Mason (1922-96)
Navy vs. the Night Monsters '66
Door to Door Maniac '61
Charade '53

Tom Mason
Looking for an Echo '99
Runaway Bride '99
Maternal Instincts '96
My Very Best Friend '96
The Amy Fisher Story '93
Final Appeal '93
Men Don't Leave '89
Mississippi Burning '88
Kicks '85
Aliens Are Coming '80
Walking Through the Fire '80
Apocalypse Now '79
Night of the Ghouls '59
Plan 9 from Outer Space '56

Lea Massari (1930-)
Vengeance '86
Christ Stopped at Eboli '79
Les Rendez-vous D'Anna '78
Allonsanfan '73
The Story of a Love Story '73
And Hope to Die '72
Murmur of the Heart '71
The Things of Life '70
L'Avventura '60

Michael Massee
The Last Don '97
Lost Highway '96
One Fine Day '96
Playing God '96
Tales from the Hood '95
The Crow '93
My Father Is Coming '91

Osa Massen (1916-)
Outcasts of the City '58
Rocketship X-M '50
Cry of the Werewolf '44
Master Race '44

Background to Danger '43
Iceland '42
A Woman's Face '41

Andrew Masset
From the Earth to the Moon '98
Perfect Crime '97

Anna Massey (1937-)
The Importance of Being Earnest '02
Dark Blue World '01
Captain Jack '98
Deja Vu '98
A Respectable Trade '98
Grave Indiscretions '96
Angels and Insects '95
Haunted '95
A Tale of Two Cities '91
Impromptu '90
Mountains of the Moon '90
A Doll's House '89
The Man from the Pru '89
The Tall Guy '89
Foreign Body '86
Hotel du Lac '86
Anna Karenina '85
Mansfield Park '85
The McGuffin '85
Another Country '84
The Little Drummer Girl '84
Sweet William '79
Vault of Horror '73
Frenzy '72
Peeping Tom '60

Athena Massey (1971-)
Harold Robbins' Body Parts '01
Shadow of a Scream '97
Star Portal '97
Termination Man '97
Red Shoe Diaries: Strip Poker '96
Virtual Combat '95
Undercover '94

Daniel Massey (1933-98)
The Miracle Maker: The Story of Jesus '00 (V)
Samson and Delilah '96
The Vacillations of Poppy Carew '94
Catherine Cookson's The Man Who Cried '93
In the Name of the Father '93
Stalin '92
Scandal '89
Intimate Contact '87
Love with a Perfect Stranger '86
Dance with a Stranger '85
Victory '81
The Cat and the Canary '79
The Incredible Sarah '76
Vault of Horror '73
The Golden Bowl '72
Mary, Queen of Scots '71
Star! '68
The Entertainer '60

Edith Massey (1918-84)
Polyester '81
Desperate Living '77
Female Trouble '74
Pink Flamingos '72
Multiple Maniacs '70

Ilona Massey (1910-74)
Love Happy '50
Northwest Outpost '47
Holiday in Mexico '46
Frankenstein Meets the Wolfman '42
Invisible Agent '42
International Lady '41
Melody Master '41
Balalaika '39
Rosalie '38

Raymond Massey (1896-1983)
The President's Plane Is Missing '71
MacKenna's Gold '69
How the West Was Won '63
The Great Impostor '61
The Naked and the Dead '58
Omar Khayyam '57
Battle Cry '55
East of Eden '54
The Desert Song '53
David and Bathsheba '51
Chain Lightning '50
The Fountainhead '49
The Possessed '47
Stairway to Heaven '46
Arsenic and Old Lace '44
Woman in the Window '44
Action in the North Atlantic '43
Desperate Journey '42
Reap the Wild Wind '42
The Forty-Ninth Parallel '41
Abe Lincoln in Illinois '40
Santa Fe Trail '40
Black Limelight '38
Drums '38
Dreaming Lips '37
Fire Over England '37
The Hurricane '37
Prisoner of Zenda '37
Things to Come '36
Under the Red Robe '36
The Scarlet Pimpernel '34
The Old Dark House '32
The Speckled Band '31

Paul Massie
The Two Faces of Dr. Jekyll '60
Sapphire '59

Ben Masters (1947-)
Running Mates '92
Noble House '88
The Deliberate Stranger '86
Making Mr. Right '86
Celebrity '85
Dream Lover '85
Key Exchange '85
The Shadow Box '80
Mandingo '75

Chase Masterson (1963-)
Sometimes They Come Back ... For More '99
In a Moment of Passion '93
Married People, Single Sex '93

Christopher K. Masterson
Scary Movie 2 '01
Dragonheart: A New Beginning '00
Girl '98

Danny Masterson (1976-)
Dracula 2000 '00
Star Kid '97
Bye Bye, Love '94

Fay Masterson
Eyes Wide Shut '99
Apartment Complex '98
Cops and Robbersons '94
The Man Without a Face '93
The Power of One '92

Mary Stuart Masterson (1966-)
The Book of Stars '99
Digging to China '98
The Florentine '98
Dogtown '97
Lily Dale '96
Bed of Roses '95
Heaven's Prisoners '95
Bad Girls '94
Radioland Murders '94
Benny & Joon '93
Married to It '93
Mad at the Moon '92
Fried Green Tomatoes '91
Funny About Love '90
Chances Are '89
Immediate Family '89
Mr. North '88
Gardens of Stone '87
My Little Girl '87
Some Kind of Wonderful '87
At Close Range '86
Heaven Help Us '85
The Stepford Wives '75

Peter Masterson (1934-)
Gardens of Stone '87
A Question of Guilt '78
The Stepford Wives '75
The Exorcist '73

Mary Elizabeth Mastrantonio (1958-)
The Perfect Storm '00
Limbo '99
Witness Protection '99
My Life So Far '98
Two Bits '96
Three Wishes '95
Consenting Adults '92
White Sands '92
Class Action '91
Robin Hood: Prince of Thieves '91
Fools of Fortune '90
The Abyss '89
The January Man '89
Slamdance '87
The Color of Money '86
Scarface '83

Gina Mastrogiacomo (1962-2001)
Bloodhounds '96
Tall, Dark and Deadly '95
Alien Space Avenger '91

Chiara Mastroianni (1972-)
For Sale '98
Nowhere '96
Three Lives and Only One Death '96
Diary of a Seducer '95
Ma Saison Preferee '93

Marcello Mastroianni (1923-96)
Three Lives and Only One Death '96
Voyage to the Beginning of the World '96
Beyond the Clouds '95
One Hundred and One Nights '95
I Don't Want to Talk About It '94
Ready to Wear '94
A Fine Romance '92
Used People '92
Everybody's Fine '90
Dark Eyes '87
Intervista '87
Ginger & Fred '86
Henry IV '85
Macaroni '85
Gabriela '84
Beyond Obsession '82
La Nuit de Varennes '82
City of Women '81
Blood Feud '79
Lady of the Evening '79
A Slightly Pregnant Man '79
Wifemistress '79
Stay As You Are '78
A Special Day '77
We All Loved Each Other So Much '77
Lunatics & Lovers '76
Get Rita '75
Salut l'Artiste '74
Allonsanfan '73
Diary of Forbidden Dreams '73
La Grande Bouffe '73
Massacre in Rome '73
Fellini's Roma '72
Divine Nymph '71
The Poppy Is Also a Flower '66
Shoot Loud, Louder, I Don't Understand! '66
Casanova '70 '65
10th Victim '65
Marriage Italian Style '64
The Organizer '64
Yesterday, Today and Tomorrow '64
8 1/2 '63
Divorce—Italian Style '62
A Very Private Affair '62
Il Bell'Antonio '60
La Dolce Vita '60
Where the Hot Wind Blows '59
Big Deal on Madonna Street '58
White Nights '57
What a Woman! '56

Richard Masur (1948-)
61* '01
Noriega: God's Favorite '00
Play It to the Bone '99
Fire Down Below '97
Multiplicity '96
Forget Paris '95
Hiroshima '95
My Girl 2 '94
And the Band Played On '93
The Man Without a Face '93
Six Degrees of Separation '93
Encino Man '92
My Girl '91
Stephen King's It '90
Cast the First Stone '89
Far from Home '89
Flashback '89
Third Degree Burn '89
Hiroshima Maiden '88
License to Drive '88
Rent-A-Cop '88
Shoot to Kill '88
The Believers '87
Walker '87
Hard Lessons '86
Heartburn '86
When the Bough Breaks '86
The Burning Bed '85
Embassy '85
Mean Season '85
My Science Project '85
Wild Horses '84
Adam '83
Nightmares '83
Risky Business '83
Timerider '83
Under Fire '83
The Thing '82
Fallen Angel '81
Heaven's Gate '81
East of Eden '80
Walking Through the Fire '80
Betrayal '78
Who'll Stop the Rain? '78
Semi-Tough '77

Clelia Matania
Don't Look Now '73
The Seven Hills of Rome '58

Heather Matarazzo (1982-)
Sorority Boys '02
The Princess Diaries '01
Blue Moon '00
Company Man '00
Scream 3 '00
All I Wanna Do '98
54 '98
The Deli '97
The Devil's Advocate '97
Hurricane Streets '96
Welcome to the Dollhouse '95

Julian Mateos (1938-96)
Four Rode Out '69
Kashmiri Run '69
Hellbenders '67
Return of the Magnificent Seven '66

Aubrey Mather (1885-1958)
That Forsyte Woman '50
Adventures of Don Juan '49
House of Fear '45
Jane Eyre '44
Hello, Frisco, Hello '43
Mrs. Miniver '42
The Undying Monster '42
Sabotage '36
The Silent Passenger '35

Marie Matheron
Come Undone '00
Western '96

Jerry Mathers (1948-)
Down the Drain '89
Back to the Beach '87
The Trouble with Harry '55
Men of the Fighting Lady '54

Marissa Mathes
Track of the Vampire '66
How to Succeed with Girls '64

Hans Matheson (1975-)
Mists of Avalon '01
Bodywork '99
Still Crazy '98
Les Miserables '97
Poldark '96

Judy Matheson
Flesh and Blood Show '73
The House that Vanished '73
Crucible of Terror '72
Twins of Evil '71

Michelle Matheson
Threesome '94
Test Tube Teens from the Year 2000 '93
Howling 6: The Freaks '90

Tim Matheson (1947-)
National Lampoon's Van Wilder '02
The Story of Us '99
Deadly Game '98
Forever Love '98
Buried Alive 2 '97
Black Sheep '96
Twilight Man '96
A Very Brady Sequel '96
Midnight Heat '95
Tails You Live, Heads You're Dead '95
Fallen Angels 1 '93
Solar Crisis '92
Trial and Error '92
Drop Dead Fred '91
Quicksand: No Escape '91
Sometimes They Come Back '91
Buried Alive '90
Little White Lies '89
Speed Zone '88
Eye of the Demon '87
Blind Justice '86
Fletch '85
Impulse '84
Up the Creek '84
Listen to Your Heart '83
To Be or Not to Be '83
A Little Sex '82
The Apple Dumpling Gang Rides Again '79
Dreamer '79
1941 '79
National Lampoon's Animal House '78
Mary White '77
The Captive: The Longest Drive 2 '76
The Longest Drive '76
The Runaway Barge '75
Magnum Force '73
How to Commit Marriage '69
Yours, Mine & Ours '68

Carole Mathews (1925-)
Strange Awakening '58
Swamp Women '55
Shark River '53

George Mathews
The Man with the Golden Arm '55
Last of the Comanches '52

Kerwin Mathews (1926-)
Killer Likes Candy '78
Nightmare in Blood '75
Octaman '71
Battle Beneath the Earth '68
Maniac '63
Waltz King '63
Jack the Giant Killer '62
The Devil at 4 O'Clock '61
The Three Worlds of Gulliver '59
The Seventh Voyage of Sinbad '58

Thom Mathews (1965-)
Heatseeker '95
Bloodmatch '91
Midnight Cabaret '90
Down Twisted '89
Return of the Living Dead 2 '88
Alien from L.A. '87
Friday the 13th, Part 6: Jason Lives '86

Marion Mathie
Dracula Has Risen from the Grave '68
Lolita '62

Samantha Mathis (1970-)
Collected Stories '02
Mists of Avalon '01
Mermaid '00
American Psycho '99
Sweet Jane '98
The American President '95
Broken Arrow '95
How to Make an American Quilt '95
Jack and Sarah '95
Little Women '94
The Music of Chance '93
Super Mario Bros. '93
The Thing Called Love '93
Ferngully: The Last Rain Forest '92 (V)
This Is My Life '92
Pump Up the Volume '90

Jacques Mathou
Ridicule '96
The Hairdresser's Husband '92
Year of the Comet '92
Betty Blue '86

Marlee Matlin (1965-)
Where the Truth Lies '99
Two Shades of Blue '98
When Justice Fails '98
Dead Silence '96
It's My Party '95
Hear No Evil '93
The Linguini Incident '92
The Player '92
Bridge to Silence '89
Walker '87
Children of a Lesser God '86

Daniel Matmor
Buffalo Heart: The Pain of Death '96
The Mangler '94

John Matshikiza
Yankee Zulu '95
Dust Devil '93
Mandela '87
Dust '85

Chieko Matsubara
Black Tight Killers '66
Tokyo Drifter '66

Eiko Matsuda
Sweet Evil '95
In the Realm of the Senses '76

Yusaku Matsuda (1950-89)
Black Rain '89
The Family Game '83
Murder in the Doll House '79

Kayo Matsuo
Shogun Assassin '80
Gate of Flesh '64

Eva Mattes (1954-)
Enemy at the Gates '00
Jew-boy Levi '98
The Promise '94
A Man Like Eva '83
Celeste '81
Germany, Pale Mother '80
David '79
In a Year of 13 Moons '78
Woyzeck '78
Stroszek '77
The Bitter Tears of Petra von Kant '72

Pam Matteson
Prehysteria 3 '95
Punchline '88
Walter Matthau (1920-2000)
Hanging Up '99
Neil Simon's The Odd Couple 2 '98
Out to Sea '97
I'm Not Rappaport '96
The Grass Harp '95
Grumpier Old Men '95
I.Q. '94
Dennis the Menace '93
Grumpy Old Men '93
JFK '91
The Incident '89
The Couch Trip '87
Pirates '86
Movers and Shakers '85
Survivors '83
I Ought to Be in Pictures '82
Buddy Buddy '81
First Monday in October '81
Hopscotch '80
Little Miss Marker '80
California Suite '78
Casey's Shadow '78
House Calls '78
The Bad News Bears '76
The Sunshine Boys '75
Earthquake '74
The Front Page '74
The Laughing Policeman '74
The Taking of Pelham One Two Three '74
Charley Varrick '73
Pete 'n' Tillie '72
Kotch '71
A New Leaf '71
Plaza Suite '71
Cactus Flower '69
Hello, Dolly! '69
Candy '68
The Odd Couple '68
Secret Life of an American Wife '68
A Guide for the Married Man '67
The Fortune Cookie '66
Mirage '66
Ensign Pulver '64
Fail-Safe '64
Goodbye Charlie '64
Charade '63
Who's Got the Action? '63
Lonely Are the Brave '62
Strangers When We Meet '60
King Creole '58
A Face in the Crowd '57
The Indian Fighter '55
The Kentuckian '55
Atomic Attack '50
A.E. Matthews (1869-1960)
Carry On Admiral '57
Made in Heaven '52
Mister Drake's Duck '50
Immortal Battalion '44
The Iron Duke '34
Al Matthews
American Roulette '88
Aliens '86
The Sender '82
Brian Matthews
Red Nights '87
The Burning '82
Dakin Matthews
Thirteen Days '00
The Muse '99
From the Earth to the Moon '98
The Siege '98
Bean '97
Rough Riders '97
The Swan Princess '94 (V)
White Mile '94
And the Band Played On '93
The Temp '93
In a Stranger's Hand '92
Revolver '92
Child's Play 3 '91
My Brother's Wife '89
Naked Lie '89
Permanent Record '88
Nuts '87
DeLane Matthews
From the Earth to the Moon '98
The Invaders '95
Francis Matthews (1927-)
The McGuffin '85
Dracula, Prince of Darkness '66
Rasputin the Mad Monk '66
Murder Ahoy '64
The Hellfire Club '61
Corridors of Blood '58
The Revenge of Frankenstein '58
Small Hotel '57
Bhowani Junction '56
Fritz Matthews
Born Killer '89
Hell on the Battleground '88
Deadly Prey '87
Jessie Matthews (1907-81)
The Hound of the Baskervilles '77
Candles at Nine '44
Forever and a Day '43
Sailing Along '38
Gangway '37
It's Love Again '36
First a Girl '35
Evergreen '34
John Matthews
A Secret Space '88
Sleuth '72
Lester Matthews (1900-75)
King Richard and the Crusaders '54
Objective, Burma! '45
The Invisible Man's Revenge '44
Across the Pacific '42
The Raven '35
Werewolf of London '35
Liesl Matthews
Air Force One '97
A Little Princess '95
Terumi Matthews
The Sticky Fingers of Time '97
Madonna: Innocence Lost '95
Robin Mattson (1956-)
In Between '92
Take Two '87
Captain America '79
Hot Rod '79
Wolf Lake '79
Return to Macon County '75
Candy Stripe Nurses '74
Bonnie's Kids '73
Island of the Lost '68
Namu, the Killer Whale '66
Victor Mature (1915-99)
Samson and Delilah '84
Head '68
After the Fox '66
The Long Haul '57
Savage Wilderness '55
Betrayed '54
Dangerous Mission '54
Demetrius and the Gladiators '54
The Egyptian '54
The Robe '53
Androcles and the Lion '52
The Las Vegas Story '52
Million Dollar Mermaid '52
Samson and Delilah '50
Easy Living '49
Kiss of Death '47
My Darling Clementine '46
Footlight Serenade '42
Seven Days' Leave '42
The Shanghai Gesture '42
Song of the Islands '42
I Wake Up Screaming '41
Captain Caution '40
No, No Nanette '40
One Million B.C. '40
John Matuszak (1950-89)
Down the Drain '89
Ghost Writer '89
One Man Force '89
The Goonies '85
Ice Pirates '84
Caveman '81
North Dallas Forty '79
Semi-Tough '77
Johanna (Hannerl) Matz (1932-)
The Life and Loves of Mozart '59
They Were So Young '55
Party Girls for Sale '54
Joan Maude (1908-98)
The Temptress '49
Power '34
Monica Maughan (1938-)
Road to Nhill '97
A Woman's Tale '92
Cactus '86
Wayne Maunder
Crazy Horse and Custer: "The Untold Story" '90
Porky's '82
Sarah Maur-Thorp
River of Death '90
Edge of Sanity '89
Ten Little Indians '89
Carmen Maura (1945-)
Lisboa '99
Alice et Martin '98
Women '97
Le Bonheur Est Dans le Pre '95
Between Heaven and Earth '93
How to Be a Woman and Not Die in the Attempt '91
Ay, Carmela! '90
Baton Rouge '88
Women on the Verge of a Nervous Breakdown '88
Law of Desire '86
Matador '86
Extramuros '85
What Have I Done to Deserve This? '85
Dark Habits '84
Pepi, Luci, Bom and Other Girls on the Heap '80
Joshua Maurer
Taken Away '89
Tour of Duty '87
Nicole Maurey (1925-)
Day of the Triffids '63
The Jayhawkers '59
Me and the Colonel '58
Rogue's Yarn '56
Diary of a Country Priest '50
Claire Maurier (1929-)
Amelie '01
Un Air de Famille '96
La Cage aux Folles '78
A Very Curious Girl '69
Sweet Ecstasy '62
The 400 Blows '59
Back to the Wall '56
Gerda Maurus
Woman in the Moon '29
Spies '28
Gary Mavers
The Unknown Soldier '98
Body & Soul '93
Dawn Maxey
Ringmaster '98
Normal Life '96
That Thing You Do! '96
Edwin Maxwell (1886-1948)
Woman in Brown '48
Swamp Fire '46
Waterfront '44
Behind Prison Walls '43
Way Down South '39
Mystery Liner '34
Night of Terror '33
The Taming of the Shrew '29
Frank Maxwell (1916-)
The Haunted Palace '63
Shame '61
Lonelyhearts '58
John Maxwell
Prowler '51
Boss of Big Town '43
The Payoff '43
Honky Tonk '41
Larry Maxwell (1953-96)
Public Access '93
Poison '91
Lois Maxwell (1927-)
Eternal Evil '87
A View to a Kill '85
For Your Eyes Only '81
Moonraker '79
The Spy Who Loved Me '77
The Man with the Golden Gun '74
Live and Let Die '73
Diamonds Are Forever '71
On Her Majesty's Secret Service '69
You Only Live Twice '67
Thunderball '65
Goldfinger '64
From Russia with Love '63
The Haunting '63
Dr. No '62
Lolita '62
The Unstoppable Man '59
Time Without Pity '57
Submarine Attack '54
Marilyn Maxwell (1922-72)
Wild Women '70
Arizona Bushwackers '67
Rock-A-Bye Baby '57
Off Limits '53
The Lemon Drop Kid '51
Key to the City '50
Champion '49
Summer Holiday '48
The Show-Off '46
Lost in a Harem '44
Paul Maxwell
Cloud Waltzing '87
Going Home '86
Roberta Maxwell (1944-)
Full Disclosure '00
Last Night '98
The Postman '97
Mistrial '96
Dead Man Walking '95
Philadelphia '93
Psycho 3 '86
Lois Gibbs and the Love Canal '82
The Changeling '80
Deborah May
Caged Fear '92
Johnny Be Good '88
Rage of Angels '83
Donald May
Bogie: The Last Hero '80
Kisses for My President '64
Elaine May (1932-)
Small Time Crooks '00
In the Spirit '90
California Suite '78
A New Leaf '71
Enter Laughing '67
Luv '67
Jack May (1922-97)
Night Slasher '84
He Kills Night After Night After Night '70
Jodhi May (1975-)
House of Mirth '00
The Aristocrats '99
The Turn of the Screw '99
The Gambler '97
Sister My Sister '94
The Last of the Mohicans '92
Eminent Domain '91
Max and Helen '90
A World Apart '88
Mathilda May (1965-)
Only Love '98
The Jackal '97
Prince Brat and the Whipping Boy '95
Grosse Fatigue '94
Becoming Colette '92
Naked Tango '91
The Cry of the Owl '87
Lifeforce '85
Letters to an Unknown Lover '84
Herschel Mayall
Kismet '20
The Bargain '15
Rik Mayall (1958-)
Jesus Christ Superstar '00
Drop Dead Fred '91
Little Noises '91
Whoops Apocalypse '83
An American Werewolf in London '81
Eye of the Needle '81
Shock Treatment '81
Anthony (Jose, J. Antonio, J.A.) Mayans (1939-)
Heat of the Flame '82
Revenge in the House of Usher '82
Zombie Lake '80
Sex Is Crazy '79
Eddie Mayehoff (1914-92)
How to Murder Your Wife '64
Artists and Models '55
The Stooge '51
Chip Mayer
Fugitive Champion '99
Liar Liar '96
Survivor '87
Our Family Business '81
Ray Mayer
Swing It, Sailor! '37
Special Investigator '36
Peter Mayhew (1944-)
Return of the Jedi '83
The Empire Strikes Back '80
Star Wars '77
John Maynard
Biohazard: The Alien Force '95
Dark Universe '93
Ken Maynard (1895-1973)
Arizona Whirlwind '44
Death Valley Rangers '44
The Law Rides Again '43
Death Rides the Range '40
Lightning Strikes West '40
Flaming Lead '39
Phantom Rancher '39
Six Shootin' Sheriff '38
Whirlwind Horseman '38
Boots of Destiny '37
Tombstone Canyon '35
Trail Drive '35
Western Frontier '35
Honor of the Range '34
In Old Santa Fe '34
Mystery Mountain '34
Drum Taps '33
The Fiddlin' Buckaroo '33
The Lone Avenger '33
Phantom Thunderbolt '33
Strawberry Roan '33
Between Fighting Men '32
Come on Tarzan '32
Dynamite Ranch '32
False Faces '32
Fargo Express '32
Hell Fire Austin '32
Sunset Trail '32
Texas Gunfighter '32
Whistlin' Dan '32
Arizona Terror '31
Branded Men '31
The Pocatello Kid '31
Range Law '31
Two Gun Man '31
Fightin' Ranch '30
The Fighting Legion '30
Fighting Thru '30
Mountain Justice '30
$50,000 Reward '25
Kermit Maynard (1897-1971)
The Black Lash '52
Trail of Robin Hood '50
Ambush Trail '46
'Neath Canadian Skies '46
Gangster's Den '45
The Stranger from Pecos '45
Devil Riders '44
Frontier Outlaws '44
Texas Kid '43
Along the Sundown Trail '42
Arizona Stagecoach '42
The Mysterious Rider '42
Prairie Pals '42
Billy the Kid '41
Bury Me Not on the Lone Prairie '41
Man from Montana '41
Pony Post '40
Riders of Pasco Basin '40
The Showdown '40
Valley of Terror '38
Galloping Dynamite '37
Roaring Six Guns '37
Rough Ridin' Rhythm '37
Phantom Patrol '36
Song of the Trail '36
Whistling Bullets '36
His Fighting Blood '35
The Fighting Trooper '34
Drum Taps '33
Outlaw Justice '32
Mimi Maynard
Adventures in Dinosaur City '92
False Identity '90
Ferdinand "Ferdy" Mayne (1916-98)
Benefit of the Doubt '93
River of Diamonds '90
A Friendship in Vienna '88
Magdalene '88
Howling 2: Your Sister Is a Werewolf '85
Night Train to Terror '84
The Secret Diary of Sigmund Freud '84
Yellowbeard '83
Frightmare '81
Hawk the Slayer '81
The Vampire Happening '71
The Adventurers '70
The Vampire Lovers '70
The Magic Christian '69
Where Eagles Dare '68
The Fearless Vampire Killers '67
Masters of Venus '59
Abandon Ship '57
Captain's Paradise '53
Roadhouse Girl '53
White Fire '53
The Temptress '49
Juliette Mayniel (1936-)
The Trojan Horse '62
The Cousins '59
The Horror Chamber of Dr. Faustus '59
Alfredo Mayo
Bell from Hell '74
The Hunt '65
Frank Mayo (1886-1963)
Across the Pacific '42
The Fighting 69th '40
Tim Tyler's Luck '37
Hell's Headquarters '32
Doughboys '30
Virginia Mayo (1920-)
Midnight Witness '93
Evil Spirits '91
The Haunted '79
French Quarter '78
Castle of Evil '66
Jet Over the Atlantic '59
Great Day in the Morning '56
Pearl of the South Pacific '55
King Richard and the Crusaders '54
The Silver Chalice '54
Devil's Canyon '53
Along the Great Divide '51
Captain Horatio Hornblower '51

The Flame & the Arrow *'50*
The West Point Story *'50*
White Heat *'49*
A Song Is Born *'48*
Out of the Blue *'47*
The Secret Life of Walter Mitty *'47*
The Best Years of Our Lives *'46*
Kid from Brooklyn *'46*
Wonder Man *'45*
Jack London *'44*
The Princess and the Pirate *'44*

Whitman Mayo (1930-2001)
Boycott *'02*
Waterproof *'99*
Boyz N the Hood *'91*
Of Mice and Men *'81*

Gale Mayron
Almost Blue *'93*
The Feud *'90*
Heart of Midnight *'89*

Melanie Mayron (1952-)
Range of Motion *'00*
Toothless *'97*
Ordeal in the Arctic *'93*
My Blue Heaven *'90*
Wanted: The Perfect Guy *'90*
Checking Out *'89*
Sticky Fingers *'88*
The Boss' Wife *'86*
Missing *'82*
The Best Little Girl in the World *'81*
Heartbeeps *'81*
Playing for Time *'80*
Girlfriends *'78*
You Light Up My Life *'77*
Car Wash *'76*

Jefferson Mays
The Big Brass Ring *'99*
Some Folks Call It a Sling Blade *'94*

Bob Maza (1939-2000)
Back of Beyond *'95*
Reckless Kelly *'93*
Ground Zero *'88*
The Fringe Dwellers *'86*

Debi Mazar (1964-)
Life in the Fast Lane *'00*
The Insider *'99*
Frogs for Snakes *'98*
Hush *'98*
Witness to the Mob *'98*
Meet Wally Sparks *'97*
She's So Lovely *'97*
Space Truckers *'97*
Girl 6 *'96*
Nowhere *'96*
Tree's Lounge *'96*
Bad Love *'95*
Batman Forever *'95*
Empire Records *'95*
Witch Hunt *'94*
Beethoven's 2nd *'93*
Inside Monkey Zetterland *'93*
Money for Nothing *'93*
In the Soup *'92*
Little Man Tate *'91*
Goodfellas *'90*

Monet Mazur
40 Days and 40 Nights *'02*
Angel Eyes *'01*
The Learning Curve *'01*
Raging Angels *'95*

Mike Mazurki (1907-90)
Doin' Time *'85*
The Adventures of Huckleberry Finn *'78*
The Incredible Rocky Mountain Race *'77*
Challenge To Be Free *'76*
The McCullochs *'75*
Cheyenne Autumn *'64*
Donovan's Reef *'63*
The Errand Boy *'61*
Some Like It Hot *'59*
Hell Ship Mutiny *'57*
Blood Alley *'55*
Night and the City *'50*
Come to the Stable *'49*
Neptune's Daughter *'49*
The Noose Hangs High *'48*
Killer Dill *'47*
Sinbad, the Sailor *'47*
Unconquered *'47*
Abbott and Costello in Hollywood *'45*
Dick Tracy, Detective *'45*
The Canterville Ghost *'44*
Murder, My Sweet *'44*
Behind the Rising Sun *'43*
The Shanghai Gesture *'42*

Paul Mazursky (1930-)
Crazy in Alabama *'99*
Antz *'98 (V)*
Why Do Fools Fall in Love? *'98*
Weapons of Mass Distraction *'97*
Touch *'96*
Two Days in the Valley *'96*
Faithful *'95*
Miami Rhapsody *'95*
Love Affair *'94*
Man Trouble *'92*
Enemies, a Love Story *'89*
Scenes from the Class Struggle in Beverly Hills *'89*
Moon over Parador *'88*
Punchline *'88*
Into the Night *'85*
History of the World: Part 1 *'81*
A Man, a Woman, and a Bank *'79*
A Star Is Born *'76*
Alex in Wonderland *'70*
Blackboard Jungle *'55*

Joseph Mazzello (1983-)
Simon Birch *'98*
The Lost World: Jurassic Park 2 *'97*
Star Kid *'97*
The Cure *'95*
Three Wishes *'95*
The River Wild *'94*
Jurassic Park *'93*
Shadowlands *'93*
Jersey Girl *'92*
Radio Flyer *'92*

M.C. Lyte
An Alan Smithee Film: Burn, Hollywood, Burn *'97*
Fly by Night *'93*

Andi McAfee
Land Before Time 7: The Stone of Cold Fire *'00 (V)*
Conagher *'91*

Des McAleer
When the Sky Falls *'99*
I Want You *'98*
Kings in Grass Castles *'97*
This Is the Sea *'96*
Butterfly Kiss *'94*
Hidden Agenda *'90*
Four Days in July *'85*

Ray McAnally (1926-89)
My Left Foot *'89*
We're No Angels *'89*
A Perfect Spy *'88*
Taffin *'88*
A Very British Coup *'88*
Empire State *'87*
The Fourth Protocol *'87*
The Mission *'86*
No Surrender *'86*
Cal *'84*
Danny Boy *'82*
Sea of Sand *'58*

Marianne McAndrew
The Bat People *'74*
Hello, Dolly! *'69*

Andrea McArdle
Annie *'99*
Rainbow *'78*

Alex McArthur (1957-)
Route 666 *'01*
Devil in the Flesh *'98*
Kiss the Girls *'97*
Lady Killer *'97*
Sharon's Secret *'95*
Drug Wars 2: The Cocaine Cartel *'92*
Race for Glory *'89*
Rampage *'87*
Silent Witness *'85*
Urge to Kill *'84*

Hugh McArthur
Panama Patrol *'39*
Marihuana *'36*

May McAvoy (1899-1994)
Gun Glory *'57*
The Jazz Singer *'27*
Ben-Hur *'26*
Lady Windermere's Fan *'26*

Diane McBain (1941-)
Puppet Master 5: The Final Chapter *'94*
Flying from the Hawk *'86*
Donner Pass: The Road to Survival *'84*
Monster *'78*
Deathhead Virgin *'74*
Spinout *'66*
Parrish *'61*

Daron McBee
Mortal Kombat 2: Annihilation *'97*
T-Force *'94*
The Killing Zone *'90*

Chi McBride (1961-)
Undercover Brother *'02*
Dancing in September *'00*
Disney's The Kid *'00*
Gone in 60 Seconds *'00*
Mercury Rising *'98*
The Frighteners *'96*
Hoodlum *'96*
Cosmic Slop *'94*
What's Love Got to Do with It? *'93*

Jon McBride
Blades *'89*
Woodchipper Massacre *'89*
Cannibal Campout *'88*

Michelle McBride
Masque of the Red Death *'90*
Subspecies *'90*

Simon McBurney
Mesmer *'94*
Kafka *'91*

Richard McCabe
Heat of the Sun *'99*
Notting Hill *'99*

Ruth McCabe
American Women *'00*
An Everlasting Piece *'00*
Talk of Angels *'96*
The Snapper *'93*
My Left Foot *'89*

Tony McCabe
Something Weird *'68*
Suburban Roulette *'67*

Frankie McCafferty
The Informant *'97*
Fools of Fortune *'90*

John McCafferty
The Perfect Gift *'95*
Deathrow Gameshow *'88*

James McCaffrey
The Tic Code *'99*
Nick and Jane *'96*
Burnzy's Last Call *'95*
Schemes *'95*

Frances Lee McCain
Patch Adams *'98*
Question of Faith *'93*
The Lookalike *'90*
Broken Badge *'85*
Gremlins *'84*
Tex *'82*
Two of a Kind *'82*
Real Life *'79*

William (Bill, Billy) McCall (1870-1938)
Outlaws of the Range *'36*
Trailing Trouble *'30*
Rounding Up the Law *'22*

Irish McCalla (1929-2002)
Hands of a Stranger *'62*
She Demons *'58*

Holt McCallany (1964-)
Kiss Tomorrow Goodbye *'00*
Men of Honor *'00*
Three Kings *'99*
The Peacemaker *'97*
Rough Riders *'97*
The Search for One-Eyed Jimmy *'96*
Tecumseh: The Last Warrior *'95*
Tyson *'95*
Alien 3 *'92*
Creepshow 2 *'87*

Lon (Bud) McCallister (1923-)
The Big Cat *'49*
The Story of Seabiscuit *'49*
The Red House *'47*
Stage Door Canteen *'43*

David McCallum (1933-)
Coming Home *'98*
Mortal Challenge *'97*
Shattered Image *'93*
The Haunting of Morella *'91*
Hear My Song *'91*
The Wind *'87*
Behind Enemy Lines *'85*
Terminal Choice *'85*
Return of the Man from U.N.C.L.E. *'83*
The Watcher in the Woods *'81*
King Solomon's Treasure *'76*
Kingfisher Caper *'76*
She Waits *'71*
Around the World Under the Sea *'65*
The Great Escape *'63*
Billy Budd *'62*
A Night to Remember *'58*
Robbery under Arms *'57*

Joanna McCallum
The Franchise Affair
Tom & Viv *'94*
Testament of Youth *'79*

John McCallum (1917-)
Devil on Horseback *'54*
Valley of the Eagles *'51*
The Woman in Question *'50*

Macon McCalman
Doc Hollywood *'91*
Fleshburn *'84*
The Ultimate Imposter *'79*

Mercedes McCambridge (1918-)
Echoes *'83*
The Concorde: Airport '79 *'79*
The Sacketts *'79*
The Exorcist *'73 (V)*
The Girls of Huntington House *'73*
Sixteen *'72*
The President's Plane Is Missing *'71*
99 Women *'69*
Deadly Sanctuary *'68*
Angel Baby *'61*
Cimarron *'60*
Suddenly, Last Summer *'59*
Touch of Evil *'58*
Giant *'56*
Tender Is the Night *'55*
Johnny Guitar *'53*
All the King's Men *'49*

Tom McCamus
The Passion of Ayn Rand *'99*
Long Day's Journey Into Night *'96*
The Sweet Hereafter *'96*
First Degree *'95*
A Man in Uniform *'93*
Norman's Awesome Experience *'88*

Chuck McCann (1936-)
Storyville *'92*
DuckTales the Movie: Treasure of the Lost Lamp *'90 (V)*
That's Adequate *'90*
Cameron's Closet *'89*
Thrashin' *'86*
Rosebud Beach Hotel *'85*
C.H.O.M.P.S. *'79*
If Things Were Different *'79*
Foul Play *'78*
They Went That-a-Way & That-a-Way *'78*
The Projectionist *'71*
The Heart Is a Lonely Hunter *'68*

Donal McCann (1943-99)
Illuminata *'98*
The Nephew *'97*
The Serpent's Kiss *'97*
Stealing Beauty *'96*
December Bride *'91*
The Miracle *'91*
The Dead *'87*
Rawhead Rex *'87*
Out of Africa *'85*
Cal *'84*
Hard Way *'80*
Screamer *'74*

Sean McCann
A House Divided *'00*
Tracked *'98*
Affliction *'97*
Gang in Blue *'96*
Swann *'96*
Iron Eagle 4 *'95*
The Air Up There *'94*
Trapped in Paradise *'94*
Guilty as Sin *'93*
Trial and Error *'92*
Run *'91*
Mindfield *'89*
Unnatural Causes *'86*
Canada's Sweetheart: The Saga of Hal C. Banks *'85*
Quiet Day in Belfast *'74*

Brian McCardie (1965-)
200 Cigarettes *'98*
Speed 2: Cruise Control *'97*
The Ghost and the Darkness *'96*
Kidnapped *'95*
Rob Roy *'95*

Fred McCarren (1952-)
Red Flag: The Ultimate Game *'81*
Marriage Is Alive and Well *'80*
How to Pick Up Girls *'78*

Andrew McCarthy (1963-)
Nowhere in Sight *'01*
Beyond Redemption *'99*
New Waterford Girl *'99*
New World Disorder *'99*
I'm Losing You *'98*
Stag *'97*
Escape Clause *'96*
The Heist *'96*
The Courtyard *'95*
Mulholland Falls *'95*
Dead Funny *'94*
Dream Man *'94*
Getting In *'94*
Mrs. Parker and the Vicious Circle *'94*
Night of the Running Man *'94*
The Joy Luck Club *'93*
Weekend at Bernie's 2 *'93*
Only You *'92*
Year of the Gun *'91*
Club Extinction *'89*
Weekend at Bernie's *'89*
Fresh Horses *'88*
Kansas *'88*
Less Than Zero *'87*
Mannequin *'87*
Waiting for the Moon *'87*
Pretty in Pink *'86*
Heaven Help Us *'85*
St. Elmo's Fire *'85*
The Beniker Gang *'83*
Class *'83*

Frank McCarthy (-1986)
A Case of Deadly Force *'86*
The Man with Two Brains *'83*
Dead Men Don't Wear Plaid *'82*

Jenny McCarthy (1972-)
Python *'00*
Scream 3 *'00*
Diamonds *'99*
BASEketball *'98*
Things to Do in Denver When You're Dead *'95*

Kevin McCarthy (1914-)
The Sister-in-Law *'95*
Just Cause *'94*
The Distinguished Gentleman *'92*
Duplicates *'92*
Matinee *'92*
Dead on the Money *'91*
Final Approach *'91*
Ghoulies 3: Ghoulies Go to College *'91*
The Rose and the Jackal *'90*
The Sleeping Car *'90*
Texas Guns *'90*
Fast Food *'89*
UHF *'89*
For Love or Money *'88*
LBJ: The Early Years *'88*
Love or Money? *'88*
Dark Tower *'87*
Hostage *'87*
Innerspace *'87*
Poor Little Rich Girl: The Barbara Hutton Story *'87*
The Midnight Hour *'86*
Invitation to Hell *'84*
Ratings Game *'84*
Twilight Zone: The Movie *'83*
My Tutor *'82*
Rosie: The Rosemary Clooney Story *'82*
The Howling *'81*
Hero at Large *'80*
Those Lips, Those Eyes *'80*
Invasion of the Body Snatchers *'78*
Piranha *'78*
Buffalo Bill & the Indians *'76*
Dan Candy's Law *'73*
Order to Kill *'73*
Ace High *'68*
Dead Right *'68*
Hotel *'67*
A Big Hand for the Little Lady *'66*
Mirage *'66*
The Three Sisters *'65*
The Best Man *'64*
A Gathering of Eagles *'63*
40 Pounds of Trouble *'62*
Invasion of the Body Snatchers *'56*
The Annapolis Story *'55*

Lin McCarthy
D.I. *'57*
Yellowneck *'55*

Molly McCarthy
The Flamingo Kid *'84*
The Great St. Louis Bank Robbery *'59*

Neil McCarthy
Where Eagles Dare *'68*
Zulu *'64*

Nobu McCarthy (1934-2002)
Pacific Heights *'90*
The Wash *'88*
The Karate Kid: Part 2 *'86*
The Geisha Boy *'58*

Sheila McCarthy (1956-)
Rare Birds *'01*
You Know My Name *'99*
Armistead Maupin's More Tales of the City *'97*
House Arrest *'96*
The Lotus Eaters *'93*
Beautiful Dreamers *'92*
Beethoven Lives Upstairs *'92*
A Private Matter *'92*

Bright Angel '91
George's Island '91
Paradise '91
Stepping Out '91
Die Hard 2: Die Harder '90
Pacific Heights '90
Friends, Lovers & Lunatics '89
I've Heard the Mermaids Singing '87
Really Weird Tales '86

Steven McCarthy
The Crossing '00
Locked in Silence '99

Linda McCartney (1941-98)
Eat the Rich '87
Give My Regards to Broad Street '84

Paul McCartney (1942-)
Eat the Rich '87
Give My Regards to Broad Street '84
Let It Be '70
Yellow Submarine '68 (V)
Magical Mystery Tour '67
Help! '65
A Hard Day's Night '64

Patti McCarty (1920-85)
Outlaw of the Plains '46
Devil Riders '44
Fighting Valley '43

Rod McCary
Night of the Demons 2 '94
A Girl to Kill For '90
Rebel Storm '90
No Drums, No Bugles '71

Constance McCashin (1947-)
Nightmare at Bittercreek '91
Love on the Run '85
Obsessive Love '84
The Two Worlds of Jenny Logan '79
Special Olympics '78

Charles McCaughan
Impulse '90
Slaves of New York '89
Heat and Dust '82

Saundra McClain
The Sixth Man '97
Mr. & Mrs. Bridge '90

Rue McClanahan (1935-)
A Saintly Switch '99
Out to Sea '97
Starship Troopers '97
This World, Then the Fireworks '97
Dear God '96
Baby of the Bride '91
After the Shock '90
Modern Love '90
Survival of Spaceship Earth '90
The Little Match Girl '87
Sergeant Matlovich vs. the U.S. Air Force '78
Hollywood after Dark '65
How to Succeed with Girls '64
Five Minutes to Love '63

Gary McCleery
The Chair '87
Hard Choices '84

Michael (Mick) McCleery
Addicted to Murder 3: Bloodlust '99
Rage of the Werewolf '99
If I Die Before I Wake '98
Addicted to Murder 2: Tainted Blood '97
The Alien Agenda: Out of the Darkness '96
Addicted to Murder '95

Catherine McClements
Desperate Prey '94
My Brother Tom '86

Sean McClory (1924-)
Fools of Fortune '90
My Chauffeur '86
Roller Boogie '79
Diane '55
The King's Thief '55
Them! '54
Charade '53
The Quiet Man '52

Leigh McCloskey (1955-)
Accidental Meeting '93
Cameron's Closet '89
Double Revenge '89
Dirty Laundry '87
Hamburger...The Motion Picture '86
Fraternity Vacation '85
Just One of the Guys '85
Hearts & Armour '83
Inferno '80
Alexander: The Other Side of Dawn '77

Doug McClure (1934-95)
Maverick '94
The Gambler Returns: The Luck of the Draw '93
Battling for Baby '92
Bull of the West '89
Dark Before Dawn '89
Tapeheads '89
Prime Suspect '88
Omega Syndrome '87
52 Pick-Up '86
Fight for Gold '86
House Where Evil Dwells '82
Firebird 2015 A.D. '81
Humanoids from the Deep '80
The Rebels '79
Bananas Boat '78
Wild & Wooly '78
The People That Time Forgot '77
At the Earth's Core '76
The Land That Time Forgot '75
Hell Hounds of Alaska '73
Playmates '72
Shenandoah '65
The Unforgiven '60
Enemy Below '57

Marc McClure (1957-)
That Thing You Do! '96
Back to the Future, Part 3 '90
After Midnight '89
Grim Prairie Tales '89
Perfect Match '88
Superman 4: The Quest for Peace '87
Back to the Future '85
Supergirl '84
Superman 3 '83
Pandemonium '82
Strange Behavior '81
Superman 2 '80
I Wanna Hold Your Hand '78
Superman: The Movie '78

Molly McClure
Finding North '97
Pure Country '92
Daddy's Dyin'...Who's Got the Will? '90

Tane McClure (1959-)
Death and Desire '97
Night Shade '97
Scorned 2 '96
Sexual Roulette '96
Caged Hearts '95
Lap Dancing '95
Midnight Tease 2 '95
Stripshow '95
Hot Under the Collar '91

Edie McClurg (1950-)
Master of Disguise '02
A Bug's Life '98 (V)
Murder She Purred: A Mrs. Murphy Mystery '98
Flubber '97
Circuit Breaker '96
The Prince '95
Under the Hula Moon '95
Airborne '93
A River Runs Through It '92
The Little Mermaid '89 (V)
Elvira, Mistress of the Dark '88
She's Having a Baby '88
Planes, Trains & Automobiles '87
Back to School '86
Ferris Bueller's Day Off '86
Cheech and Chong's The Corsican Brothers '84
Mr. Mom '83
Eating Raoul '82
Pandemonium '82
The Pee-wee Herman Show '82
The Secret of NIMH '82 (V)
Cheech and Chong's Next Movie '80
Carrie '76

Stephen McCole
The Acid House '98
Postmortem '98
Rushmore '98
Orphans '97

Warren McCollum
The Great Commandment '41
Boy's Reformatory '39
Reefer Madness '38

Matt McColm
Body Armor '96
Red Scorpion 2 '94

Lorissa McComas
Lap Dancing '95
Stormswept '95

Heather McComb (1977-)
If These Walls Could Talk 2 '00
Blowin' Smoke '99
Apt Pupil '97
Stay Tuned '92
New York Stories '89

Matthew McConaughey (1969-)
Frailty '02
Reign of Fire '02
The Wedding Planner '01
U-571 '00
EDtv '99
Amistad '97
Contact '97
The Newton Boys '97
Glory Daze '96
Larger Than Life '96
Scorpion Spring '96
A Time to Kill '96
Lone Star '95
The Texas Chainsaw Massacre 4: The Next Generation '95
Boys on the Side '94
Dazed and Confused '93

John McConnell
King of the Hill '93
Delta Heat '92

Keith McConnell
Border Saddlemates '52
Five Fingers '52

Marilyn McCoo
My Mom's a Werewolf '89
The Fantastic World of D.C. Collins '84

John McCook
Scorned 2 '96
Codename: Foxfire '85

Kent McCord (1942-)
Accidental Meeting '93
Return of the Living Dead 3 '93
Illicit Behavior '91
Predator 2 '90
Nashville Beat '89
Airplane 2: The Sequel '82
For Heaven's Sake '79

Catherine McCormack (1972-)
Spy Game '01
Born Romantic '00
A Rumor of Angels '00
Shadow of the Vampire '00
The Tailor of Panama '00
Dancing at Lughnasa '98
Dangerous Beauty '98
Deacon Brodie '98
The Land Girls '98
North Star '96
Braveheart '95
Loaded '94

Eric McCormack (1963-)
The Audrey Hepburn Story '00
Free Enterprise '98
Holy Man '98
Call of the Wild '93

Mary McCormack (1969-)
Full Frontal '02
High Heels and Low Lifes '01
K-PAX '01
World Traveler '01
The Broken Hearts Club '00
Gun Shy '00
The Big Tease '99
Harvest '99
Mystery, Alaska '99
True Crime '99
The Alarmist '98
Deep Impact '98
Private Parts '96

Patty McCormack (1945-)
Silent Predators '99
Mommy 2: Mommy's Day '96
Mommy '95
Saturday the 14th Strikes Back '88
Invitation to Hell '84
Bug '75
The Adventures of Huckleberry Finn '60
All Mine to Give '56
The Bad Seed '56

Carolyn McCormick
You Know My Name '99
Rain Without Thunder '93
Enemy Mine '85

Gilmer McCormick
Silent Night, Deadly Night '84
Godspell '73

Maureen McCormick (1956-)
The Million Dollar Kid '99
Dogtown '97
Panic in the Skies '96
A Very Brady Christmas '88
Return to Horror High '87
Texas Lightning '81
Idolmaker '80
Take Down '79
Moonshine County Express '77
Pony Express Rider '76

Merrill McCormick (1892-1953)
Cowboy Counselor '33
Robin Hood '22

Michelle McCormick
Showdown '93
Fatal Pulse '88

Myron McCormick (1908-62)
A Public Affair '62
The Hustler '61
No Time for Sergeants '58
Not as a Stranger '55
Three for the Show '55
Jigsaw '49
One Third of a Nation '39

Pat McCormick (1934-)
Chinatown Connection '90
Rented Lips '88
Bombs Away! '86
Doin' Time '85
E. Nick: A Legend in His Own Mind '84
The Princess and the Pea '83
Smokey and the Bandit, Part 3 '83
Under the Rainbow '81
Smokey and the Bandit 2 '80
A Wedding '78
If You Don't Stop It...You'll Go Blind '77
Smokey and the Bandit '77

Grayson McCouch
Armageddon '98
Sins of the Mind '97

Emer McCourt
Boston Kickout '95
Riff Raff '92
London Kills Me '91

Malachy McCourt
JFK: Reckless Youth '93
Q (The Winged Serpent) '82
Manny's Orphans '78

Alec McCowen (1925-)
Longitude '00
The Age of Innocence '93
Maria's Child '93
Henry V '89
Cry Freedom '87
Personal Services '87
A Dedicated Man '86
Forever Young '85
Hanover Street '79
Stevie '78
Frenzy '72
Travels with My Aunt '72
The Witches '66
A Night to Remember '58
The Silent Enemy '58
Time Without Pity '57

Larry McCoy
The Players Club '98
Bulletproof '96

Matt McCoy (1958-)
Forever Together '00
Rangers '00
Tales of the Kama Sutra 2: Monsoon '98
Buck and the Magic Bracelet '97
L.A. Confidential '97
Monsoon '97
The Apocalypse '96
Fast Money '96
Little Bigfoot '96
Rent-A-Kid '95
Synapse '95
Bigfoot: The Unforgettable Encounter '94
Hard Bounty '94
Hard Drive '94
The Soft Kill '94
Dead On '93
Samurai Cowboy '93
The Cool Surface '92
Eyes of the Beholder '92
The Hand that Rocks the Cradle '92
Archie: Return to Riverdale '90
Deepstar Six '89
Police Academy 6: City under Siege '89
Police Academy 5: Assignment Miami Beach '88
Fraternity Vacation '85

Sylvester McCoy (1943-)
Doctor Who '96
Spellbreaker: Secret of the Leprechauns '96
Leapin' Leprechauns '95

Tim McCoy (1891-1978)
Run of the Arrow '56
Below the Border '42
Dawn on the Great Divide '42
Down Texas Way '42
Ghost Town Law '42
Riders of the West '42
West of the Law '42
Arizona Bound '41
Forbidden Trails '41
Gunman from Bodie '41
Arizona Gangbusters '40
Gun Code '40
Fighting Renegade '39
Outlaw's Paradise '39
Texas Wildcats '39
Lightnin' Carson Rides Again '38
Phantom Ranger '38
Aces and Eights '36
Border Caballero '36
Ghost Patrol '36
Lion's Den '36
The Man from Gun Town '36
Prescott Kid '36
Roaring Guns '36
The Traitor '36
Bulldog Courage '35
Fighting Shadows '35
The Outlaw Deputy '35
The Revenge Rider '35
Man of Action '33
Cornered '32
Daring Danger '32
Fighting Fool '32
The Fighting Marshal '32
The Riding Tornado '32
Texas Cyclone '32
Two-Fisted Law '32

Mark McCracken
Pumpkinhead 2: Blood Wings '94
Matinee '92

Paul McCrane (1961-)
From the Earth to the Moon '98
The Portrait '93
RoboCop '87
Purple Hearts '84
Fame '80

Darius McCrary
15 Minutes '01
Kingdom Come '01
Don King: Only in America '97
Big Shots '87

Jody McCrea (1934-)
The Glory Stompers '67
Beach Blanket Bingo '65
How to Stuff a Wild Bikini '65
Bikini Beach '64
Muscle Beach Party '64
Pajama Party '64
Beach Party '63
Force of Impulse '60

Joel McCrea (1905-90)
Ride the High Country '62
Lafayette Escadrille '58
The Oklahoman '56
Stars in My Crown '50
Four Faces West '48
South of St. Louis '48
Ramrod '47
The Virginian '46
Buffalo Bill '44
The Great Moment '44
The More the Merrier '43
The Great Man's Lady '42
The Palm Beach Story '42
Sullivan's Travels '41
Foreign Correspondent '40
Primrose Path '40
They Shall Have Music '39
Union Pacific '39
Dead End '37
Internes Can't Take Money '37
Come and Get It '36
These Three '36
Barbary Coast '35
Our Little Girl '35
Splendor '35
Bird of Paradise '32
The Most Dangerous Game '32
Kept Husbands '31
The Silver Horde '30

Helen McCrory
Charlotte Gray '01
Anna Karenina '00
Dad Savage '97

Bruce McCulloch (1961-)
Dick '99
Dog Park '98
Kids in the Hall: Brain Candy '96

Ian McCulloch (1939-)
Witching Time '84
Alien Contamination '81
Doctor Butcher M.D. '80
Zombie '80

Kyle McCulloch
Careful '92
Tales from the Gimli Hospital '88

Julie McCullough (1965-)
The St. Tammany Miracle '94
Round Trip to Heaven '92
Big Bad Mama 2 '87

Philo (Philip, P.H., P.M.) McCullough
Captured in Chinatown '35
Ridin' Thru '35
Inside Information '34
Tarzan the Fearless '33

Natalie McCurry
Glass '90
Stones of Death '88
Dead End Drive-In '86

Bill McCutcheon (1924-2002)
Mr. Destiny '90
Tune in Tomorrow '90
Family Business '89
Steel Magnolias '89
Santa Claus Conquers the Martians '64

Hattie McDaniel (1895-1952)
Mickey '48
Never Say Goodbye '46
Since You Went Away '44
Johnny Come Lately '43
George Washington Slept Here '42
In This Our Life '42
The Great Lie '41
They Died with Their Boots On '41
Gone with the Wind '39
Carefree '38
Mad Miss Manton '38
Shopworn Angel '38
Saratoga '37
The Bride Walks Out '36
Libeled Lady '36
Show Boat '36
Alice Adams '35
Harmony Lane '35
The Little Colonel '35
I'm No Angel '33
Blonde Venus '32

James McDaniel (1958-)
Sunshine State '02
Deliberate Intent '01
Livin' for Love: The Natalie Cole Story '00
Out of Time '00
The Road to Galveston '96
Malcolm X '92

Dean McDermott (1966-)
Brian's Song '01
The Wall '99

Dylan McDermott (1962-)
Texas Rangers '01
Three to Tango '99
Til There Was You '96
Destiny Turns on the Radio '95
Home for the Holidays '95
The Cowboy Way '94
Miracle on 34th Street '94
In the Line of Fire '93
The Fear Inside '92
Into the Badlands '92
Jersey Girl '92
Where Sleeping Dogs Lie '91
Hardware '90
The Neon Empire '89
Steel Magnolias '89
Twister '89
Blue Iguana '88
Hamburger Hill '87

Hugh McDermott
Devil Girl from Mars '54
The Seventh Veil '46

Ruth McDevitt (1895-1976)
Homebodies '74
Change of Habit '69
The Shakiest Gun in the West '68
The Birds '63
The Parent Trap '61

Ian McDiarmid (1947-)
Star Wars: Episode 2—Attack of the Clones '02
All the King's Men '99
Sleepy Hollow '99
Star Wars: Episode 1—The Phantom Menace '99
Touching Evil '97
Rasputin: Dark Servant of Destiny '96
Annie: A Royal Adventure '95
The Awakening '80

Audra McDonald
Wit '01
Annie '99
Having Our Say: The Delany Sisters' First 100 Years '99

Christopher McDonald (1955-)
61* '01
The Perfect Storm '00
Requiem for a Dream '00
The Skulls '00
Iron Giant '99 (V)
SLC Punk! '99
The Faculty '98
Dirty Work '97
The Eighteenth Angel '97
Flubber '97
Into Thin Air: Death on Everest '97
Leave It to Beaver '97
Celtic Pride '96
Happy Gilmore '96
House Arrest '96
Jaded '96
Lawn Dogs '96
The Rich Man's Wife '96
A Smile Like Yours '96
Unforgettable '96
Best of the Best 3: No Turning Back '95
Fair Game '95
My Teacher's Wife '95
The Tuskegee Airmen '95
Monkey Trouble '94
Quiz Show '94
Terminal Velocity '94
Benefit of the Doubt '93
Bums '93
Cover Story '93
Fatal Instinct '93
Grumpy Old Men '93
Conflict of Interest '92
Wild Orchid 2: Two Shades of Blue '92
Fatal Exposure '91
Red Wind '91
Thelma & Louise '91
Playroom '90
Chances Are '89
Paramedics '88
The Boys Next Door '85
Breakin' '84
Chattanooga Choo Choo '84
Grease 2 '82

Country Joe McDonald
Armistead Maupin's Tales of the City '93
Zachariah '70

Francis McDonald (1891-1968)
Bad Men of the Border '45
Mystery Man '44
Mystery of the Riverboat '44
Texas Masquerade '44
Zorro's Black Whip '44
The Sea Wolf '41
Carson City Kid '40
Terror Trail '33
Hidden Valley '32
Texas Buddies '32
Morocco '30
The Notorious Lady '27
Battling Butler '26
The Confession '20

Garry McDonald (1948-)
Moulin Rouge '01
Ghosts Can Do It '90
The Wacky World of Wills & Burke '85
Pirate Movie '82

Grace McDonald (1918-99)
Follow the Boys '44
Gung Ho! '43
It Ain't Hay '43

Jeff McDonald
Sugar Town '99
Spirit of '76 '91

Kenneth McDonald
The Coast Patrol '25
Dynamite Dan '24

Kevin McDonald (1961-)
The Godson '98
Kids in the Hall: Brain Candy '96
National Lampoon's Senior Trip '95

Marie McDonald (1923-65)
Promises! Promises! '63
The Geisha Boy '58
Tell It to the Judge '49
Guest in the House '44

Mary Ann McDonald
Far Cry from Home '70s
Love at First Sight '76

Peter McDonald (1972-)
Blow Dry '00
Nora '00
When Brendan Met Trudy '00
Felicia's Journey '99
Captain Jack '98
I Went Down '97

Mary McDonnell (1952-)
Donnie Darko '01
Mumford '99
Evidence of Blood '97
Twelve Angry Men '97
Independence Day '96
Woman Undone '95
Blue Chips '94
Passion Fish '92
Sneakers '92
Grand Canyon '91
Dances with Wolves '90
Matewan '87
Tiger Warsaw '87

Mary (Elizabeth) McDonough (1961-)
Mom '89
Snowballing '85
A Day for Thanks on Walton's Mountain '82
The Waltons: The Christmas Carol '80

Neal McDonough (1966-)
Minority Report '02
Band of Brothers '01
Ravenous '99
Grace & Glorie '98
Balloon Farm '97
Star Trek: First Contact '96
Blue River '95
White Dwarf '95

Frances McDormand (1958-)
The Man Who Wasn't There '01
Almost Famous '00
Wonder Boys '00
Madeline '98
Johnny Skidmarks '97
Paradise Road '97
Fargo '96
Hidden in America '96
Primal Fear '96
Talk of Angels '96
Beyond Rangoon '95
The Good Old Boys '95
Lone Star '95
Palookaville '95
Short Cuts '93
Crazy in Love '92
Passed Away '92
The Butcher's Wife '91
Darkman '90
Hidden Agenda '90
Chattahoochee '89
Mississippi Burning '88
Raising Arizona '87
Blood Simple '85
Crimewave '85

Betty McDowall
Ballad in Blue '66
Dead Lucky '60
Jack the Ripper '60
Time Lock '57

Roddy McDowall (1928-98)
Behind the Planet of the Apes '98 (N)
A Bug's Life '98 (V)
Rudyard Kipling's the Second Jungle Book: Mowgli and Baloo '97
Unlikely Angel '97
Last Summer In the Hamptons '96
Fatally Yours '95
The Grass Harp '95
It's My Party '95
Star Hunter '95
Unknown Origin '95
Mirror, Mirror 2: Raven Dance '94
Heads '93
Deadly Game '91
Double Trouble '91
An Inconvenient Woman '91
Around the World in 80 Days '89
The Big Picture '89
Carmilla '89
Cutting Class '89
Shakma '89
Doin' Time on Planet Earth '88
Fright Night 2 '88
Dead of Winter '87
Overboard '87
Fright Night '85
Mae West '84
The Zany Adventures of Robin Hood '84
Class of 1984 '82
Evil under the Sun '82
Charlie Chan and the Curse of the Dragon Queen '81
The Return of the King '80 (V)
The Martian Chronicles: Part 2 '79
The Martian Chronicles: Part 3 '79
Scavenger Hunt '79
The Cat from Outer Space '78
Circle of Iron '78
Laserblast '78
Rabbit Test '78
The Thief of Baghdad '78
Embryo '76
Flood! '76
Funny Lady '75
Mean Johnny Barrows '75
Dirty Mary Crazy Larry '74
Arnold '73
Battle for the Planet of the Apes '73
The Legend of Hell House '73
Conquest of the Planet of the Apes '72
Life & Times of Judge Roy Bean '72
The Poseidon Adventure '72
Bedknobs and Broomsticks '71
Escape from the Planet of the Apes '71
Night Gallery '69
Five Card Stud '68
Planet of the Apes '68
The Adventures of Bullwhip Griffin '66
The Greatest Story Ever Told '65
Inside Daisy Clover '65
The Loved One '65
That Darn Cat '65
Cleopatra '63
The Tempest '63
The Longest Day '62
Midnight Lace '60
Hill Number One '51
Everybody's Dancin' '50
Macbeth '48
Holiday in Mexico '46
The Keys of the Kingdom '44
The White Cliffs of Dover '44
Lassie, Come Home '43
My Friend Flicka '43
Son of Fury '42
How Green Was My Valley '41

Claire McDowell (1877-1966)
Ben-Hur '26
The Show Off '26
The Big Parade '25
West-Bound Limited '23

Malcolm McDowell (1943-)
Firestarter 2: Rekindled '02
Just Visiting '01
Princess of Thieves '01
The Void '01
Can of Worms '00
Island of the Dead '00
St. Patrick: The Irish Legend '00
Y2K '99
The First 9 1/2 Weeks '98
My Life So Far '98
Asylum '97
Hugo Pool '97
Mr. Magoo '97
Tales from a Parallel Universe: Giga Shadow '97
Kids of the Round Table '96
Where Truth Lies '96
Yesterday's Target '96
Cyborg 3: The Recycler '95
Fist of the North Star '95
Dangerous Indiscretion '94
Milk Money '94
Star Trek: Generations '94
The Surgeon '94
Tank Girl '94
Bopha! '93
Chain of Desire '93
Night Train to Venice '93
The Player '92
The Light in the Jungle '91
Class of 1999 '90
Disturbed '90
Jezebel's Kiss '90
Moon 44 '90
Buy & Cell '89
Sunset '88
The Caller '87
Monte Carlo '86
Gulag '85
Merlin and the Sword '85
Blue Thunder '83
Cross Creek '83
Get Crazy '83
Little Red Riding Hood '83
Britannia Hospital '82
Cat People '82
Caligula '80
Look Back in Anger '80
Time After Time '79
Voyage of the Damned '76
Royal Flash '75
O Lucky Man! '73
A Clockwork Orange '71
Long Ago Tomorrow '71
If... '69

Nelson McDowell (1870-1947)
Desert Phantom '36
Feud of the West '35
Texas Jack '35
Rustler's Roundup '33
Come on Tarzan '32
Mason of the Mounted '32
Oliver Twist '22
The Last of the Mohicans '20

Trevyn McDowell
Mary Shelley's Frankenstein '94
Middlemarch '93

James McEachin (1930-)
Double Exposure '93
Honeyboy '82
He Who Walks Alone '78
The Dead Don't Die '75
The Groundstar Conspiracy '72

Ellen McElduff
Working Girls '87
Imposters '84

Ian McElhinney
Hamlet '96
Small Faces '95
A Woman's Guide to Adultery '93
The Playboys '92

Natascha (Natasha) McElhone (1971-)
The Contaminated Man '01
Love's Labour's Lost '00
Ronin '98
The Truman Show '98
Mrs. Dalloway '97
The Devil's Own '96
Surviving Picasso '96

John McEnery (1945-)
Merlin '98
Tess of the D'Urbervilles '98
When Saturday Comes '95
Black Beauty '94
The Buddha of Suburbia '92
Codename Kyril '91
The Krays '90
A.D. '85
Gulag '85
Pope John Paul II '84
Schizo '77
The Land That Time Forgot '75
One Russian Summer '73
Bartleby '70

Peter McEnery (1940-)
Pictures '80s
The Cat and the Canary '79
Tales That Witness Madness '73
Entertaining Mr. Sloane '70
Negatives '68
I Killed Rasputin '67
The Fighting Prince of Donegal '66
The Game Is Over '66
The Moon-Spinners '64
Victim '61

Annie McEnroe
Cop '88
True Stories '86
Howling 2: Your Sister Is a Werewolf '85
Purple Hearts '84
Warlords of the 21st Century '82
The Hand '81
Running Scared '79

Reba McEntire (1955-)
One Night at McCool's '01
Forever Love '98
Buffalo Girls '95
Is There Life Out There? '94
North '94
The Gambler Returns: The Luck of the Draw '93
The Man from Left Field '93
Tremors '89

Barry McEvoy
An Everlasting Piece '00
Gloria '98

Geraldine McEwan (1932-)
Love's Labour's Lost '00
The Love Letter '99
Titus '99
Moses '96
Robin Hood: Prince of Thieves '91
Henry V '89
Oranges Are Not the Only Fruit '89
Foreign Body '86
Mapp & Lucia '85

Gates (Cheryl) McFadden (1949-)
Star Trek: Insurrection '98
Star Trek: First Contact '96
Star Trek: Generations '94

Taking Care of Business '90

Joseph McFadden
Dad Savage '97
Small Faces '95

George "Spanky" McFarland (1928-93)
The Aurora Encounter '85
Peck's Bad Boy with the Circus '38
General Spanky '36
The Trail of the Lonesome Pine '36
Kentucky Kernels '34

Douglas McFerran
Antitrust '00
Sliding Doors '97

William F. McGaha
Iron Horsemen '71
The Speed Lovers '68

Mark McGann (1961-)
Shackleton '02
Samson and Delilah '96
Catherine the Great '95
Let Him Have It '91
John & Yoko: A Love Story '85

Paul McGann (1959-)
Queen of the Damned '02
Horatio Hornblower: The Adventure Continues '01
Our Mutual Friend '98
FairyTale: A True Story '97
Doctor Who '96
Catherine the Great '95
Afraid of the Dark '92
Alien 3 '92
Paper Mask '91
Innocent Victim '90
Dealers '89
The Rainbow '89
Withnail and I '87

Darren McGavin (1922-)
Smalltime '99
Billy Madison '94
Perfect Harmony '91
Blood & Concrete: A Love Story '90
Child in the Night '90
Around the World in 80 Days '89
By Dawn's Early Light '89
Captain America '89
Dead Heat '88
Sunset '88
Raw Deal '86
Turk 182! '85
The Baron and the Kid '84
My Wicked, Wicked Ways '84
The Natural '84
A Christmas Story '83
Power, Passion & Murder '83
Firebird 2015 A.D. '81
Hangar 18 '80
Waikiki '80
Ike '79
The Martian Chronicles: Part 1 '79
The Martian Chronicles: Part 2 '79
The Martian Chronicles: Part 3 '79
Zero to Sixty '78
Airport '77 '77
No Deposit, No Return '76
The Night Strangler '72
Richard Petty Story '72
Say Goodbye, Maggie Cole '72
The Night Stalker '71
Tribes '70
Mission Mars '67
The Delicate Delinquent '56
The Court Martial of Billy Mitchell '55
The Man with the Golden Arm '55
Summertime '55
Queen for a Day '51

Patrick McGaw
Dream with the Fishes '97
Scorpion Spring '96
Malicious '95
The Basketball Diaries '94
Forbidden Choices '94
Amongst Friends '93

Jack McGee
Bread and Roses '00
Chairman of the Board '97
The Last Days of Frankie the Fly '96
The Quest '96
Crash and Burn '90

Vic McGee
Alien Massacre '67
Monsters Crash the Pajama Party '65
Horrors of the Red Planet '64

Vonetta McGee (1948-)
You Must Remember This '92
Brother Future '91
To Sleep with Anger '90
Repo Man '83
The Eiger Sanction '75
The Big Bust Out '73
Shaft in Africa '73
Blacula '72

Johnny Rae McGhee
Love Field '91
Project X '87

William Bill McGhee
1918 '85
Don't Look in the Basement '73

Bruce McGill (1950-)
The Sum of All Fears '02
Ali '01
Exit Wounds '01
Shallow Hal '01
61* '01
Deep Core '00
The Legend of Bagger Vance '00
Running Mates '00
A Dog of Flanders '99
The Insider '99
Everything That Rises '98
Ground Control '98
Letters from a Killer '98
Murder She Purred: A Mrs. Murphy Mystery '98
Black Sheep '96
Lawn Dogs '96
Rosewood '96
The Good Old Boys '95
Timecop '94
My Cousin Vinny '92
The Last Boy Scout '91
Little Vegas '90
Out Cold '89
End of the Line '88
The Last Innocent Man '87
Waiting for the Moon '87
No Mercy '86
Wildcats '86
Charlotte Forten's Mission: Experiment in Freedom '85
Into the Night '85
Ballad of Gregorio Cortez '83
Silkwood '83
Tough Enough '83
The Hand '81
Whale for the Killing '81
National Lampoon's Animal House '78
Citizens Band '77

Everett McGill (1945-)
My Fellow Americans '96
Under Siege 2: Dark Territory '95
The People under the Stairs '91
Jezebel's Kiss '90
Iguana '89
License to Kill '89
Field of Honor '86
Heartbreak Ridge '86
Silver Bullet '85
Dune '84
Quest for Fire '82
Union City '81
Brubaker '80

Kelly McGillis (1957-)
The Monkey's Mask '00
The Settlement '99
At First Sight '98
Ground Control '98
Storm Chasers: Revenge of the Twister '98
The Wicked, Wicked West '97
North '94
The Babe '92
Grand Isle '92
Cat Chaser '90
Winter People '89
The Accused '88
The House on Carroll Street '88
Unsettled Land '88
Made in Heaven '87
Top Gun '86
Witness '85
Code of Honor '84
Reuben, Reuben '83

John C. McGinley (1959-)
The Animal '01
Highway '01
Get Carter '00
Any Given Sunday '99
The Jack Bull '99
Three to Tango '99
Office Space '98
The Pentagon Wars '98
Flypaper '97
Truth or Consequences, N.M. '97
Mother '96
Nothing to Lose '96
The Rock '96
Set It Off '96
Born to Be Wild '95
Seven '95
Car 54, Where Are You? '94
Mother's Boys '94
On Deadly Ground '94
Surviving the Game '94
Wagons East '94
Hear No Evil '93
The Last Outlaw '93
Watch It '93
Article 99 '92
A Midnight Clear '92
Highlander 2: The Quickening '91
Little Noises '91
Point Break '91
Suffering Bastards '90
Fat Man and Little Boy '89
Lost Angels '89
Prisoners of Inertia '89
Talk Radio '88
Wall Street '87
Platoon '86

Sean McGinley
American Women '00
The Claim '00
The General '98
The Break '97
The Butcher Boy '97
The Informant '97
Resurrection Man '97
Michael Collins '96
Trojan Eddie '96
Braveheart '95
The Field '90

Ted McGinley (1958-)
Daybreak '01
Pearl Harbor '01
Dick '99
Every Mother's Worst Fear '98
Major League 3: Back to the Minors '98
Tails You Live, Heads You're Dead '95
Covert Assassin '94
Revenge of the Nerds 4: Nerds in Love '94
Linda '93
It's a Bundyful Life '92
Revenge of the Nerds 3: The Next Generation '92
Blue Tornado '90
Physical Evidence '89
Revenge of the Nerds '84

Scott McGinnis (1958-)
You Can't Hurry Love '88
Odd Jobs '85
Making the Grade '84
Joy Sticks '83

John McGiver (1912-75)
The Adventures of Tom Sawyer '73
Arnold '73
Lawman '71
Bachelor in Paradise '69
Midnight Cowboy '69
The Glass Bottom Boat '66
A Global Affair '63
Man's Favorite Sport? '63
Who's Got the Action? '63
Who's Minding the Store? '63
The Manchurian Candidate '62
Mr. Hobbs Takes a Vacation '62
Period of Adjustment '62
Breakfast at Tiffany's '61
The Gazebo '59
Love in the Afternoon '57
The Man in the Raincoat '57

Mike McGlone
Hardball '01
The Bone Collector '99
One Tough Cop '98
Subway Stories '97
Ed '96
She's the One '96
The Brothers McMullen '94

Frank McGlynn (1866-1951)
Rogue's Gallery '44
Western Gold '37
Custer's Last Stand '36
These Three '36
Hopalong Cassidy '35
America '24

Patrick McGoohan (1928-)
The Phantom '96
A Time to Kill '96
Braveheart '95
Baby ... Secret of the Lost Legend '85
Three Sovereigns for Sarah '85
Kings and Desperate Men '83
Jamaica Inn '82
Scanners '81
Hard Way '80
Escape from Alcatraz '79
Brass Target '78
The Man in the Iron Mask '77
Silver Streak '76
Mary, Queen of Scots '71
Ice Station Zebra '68
Koroshi '67
Dr. Syn, Alias the Scarecrow '64
The Three Lives of Thomasina '63
I Am a Camera '55

Barry McGovern
Miracle at Midnight '98
Braveheart '95
Joe Versus the Volcano '90
Riders to the Sea '88

Elizabeth McGovern (1961-)
The Flamingo Rising '01
House of Mirth '00
The Scarlet Pimpernel '99
The Scarlet Pimpernel 2: Mademoiselle Guillotine '99
The Scarlet Pimpernel 3: The Kidnapped King '99
Twice upon a Yesterday '98
The Wings of the Dove '97
Broken Glass '96
The Summer of Ben Tyler '96
Broken Trust '95
King of the Hill '93
Me & Veronica '93
The Favor '92
The Handmaid's Tale '90
A Shock to the System '90
Tune in Tomorrow '90
Women & Men: Stories of Seduction '90
Johnny Handsome '89
She's Having a Baby '88
The Bedroom Window '87
Native Son '86
Once Upon a Time in America '84
Racing with the Moon '84
Lovesick '83
Snow White and the Seven Dwarfs '83
Ragtime '81
Ordinary People '80

Terence McGovern
DuckTales the Movie: Treasure of the Lost Lamp '90 (V)
Americathon '79

J(ohn) P(aterson) McGowan (1880-1952)
Heart of the Rockies '37
Hit the Saddle '37
The Outlaw Tamer '33
Somewhere in Sonora '33
Red Signals '27

Rose McGowan (1975-)
Monkeybone '01
Ready to Rumble '00
The Last Stop '99
Devil in the Flesh '98
Jawbreaker '98
Southie '98
Going All the Way '97
Lewis and Clark and George '97
Phantoms '97
Scream '96
The Doom Generation '95

Tom McGowan
As Good As It Gets '97
Bean '97
The Birdcage '95
Mrs. Parker and the Vicious Circle '94

Michael McGrady
The Deep End of the Ocean '98
Malevolence '98
Operation Delta Force 2: Mayday '97
White Dwarf '95
The Babe '92

Walter McGrail (1888-1970)
Code of the Fearless '39
The Green Hornet '39
Night Nurse '31
The Lone Star Ranger '30

Alethea McGrath
Alien Visitor '95
That Eye, the Sky '94

Derek McGrath
Stuart Bliss '98
Chameleon '95
Freaked '93

Douglas McGrath
Company Man '00
Pale Rider '85
Porky's '82

Matt McGrath (1969-)
The Broken Hearts Club '00
Boys Don't Cry '99
The Imposters '98
1999 '98
The Member of the Wedding '97
Last Breath '96
Desperate Hours '90

Charles McGraw (1914-80)
Twilight's Last Gleaming '77
The Killer Inside Me '76
A Boy and His Dog '75
Johnny Got His Gun '71
Pendulum '69
Tell Them Willie Boy Is Here '69
The Birds '63
The Horizontal Lieutenant '62
Cimarron '60
Spartacus '60
The Defiant Ones '58
The Bridges at Toko-Ri '55
The Narrow Margin '52
One Minute to Zero '52
His Kind of Woman '51
Armored Car Robbery '50
Ma and Pa Kettle Go to Town '50
Threat '49
T-Men '47
The Killers '46
The Mad Ghoul '43

Melinda McGraw
Nutty Professor 2: The Klumps '00
Wrongfully Accused '98

Angela Punch McGregor (1953-)
The Efficiency Expert '92
Double Deal '84
A Test of Love '84
We of the Never Never '82
The Island '80
Survivor '80
Newsfront '78

Charles McGregor
The Baron '88
Superfly '72

Ewan McGregor (1971-)
Star Wars: Episode 2—Attack of the Clones '02
Black Hawk Down '01
Moulin Rouge '01
Nora '00
Eye of the Beholder '99
Star Wars: Episode 1—The Phantom Menace '99
Little Voice '98
Rogue Trader '98
Velvet Goldmine '98
A Life Less Ordinary '97
The Serpent's Kiss '97
Brassed Off '96
Emma '96
Nightwatch '96
Blue Juice '95
The Pillow Book '95
Trainspotting '95
Lipstick on Your Collar '94
Shallow Grave '94

Kenneth John McGregor
The Ten Million Dollar Getaway '91
Primal Scream '87

Malcolm McGregor (1892-1945)
The Reckless Way '36
Smouldering Fires '25
The Untamable '23

Kate McGregor-Stewart
Pavilion of Women '01
The Maker '98
In and Out '97

Aislin McGuckin
The Unknown Soldier '98
The Nephew '97
Trojan Eddie '96

Barry McGuire
Werewolves on Wheels '71
The President's Analyst '67

Biff McGuire (1926-)
Deadline Assault '90
Child of Glass '78
Werewolf of Washington '73
Justice '55

Don McGuire (1919-99)
Double Dynamite '51
The Fuller Brush Man '48
The Man I Love '46

Dorothy McGuire (1918-2001)
Caroline? '90
The Last Best Year '90
Amos '85
The Incredible Journey of Dr. Meg Laurel '79
Little Women '78
Rich Man, Poor Man '76
The Runaways '75
She Waits '71
The Greatest Story Ever Told '65
Summer Magic '63
The Swiss Family Robinson '60

A Summer Place '59
Old Yeller '57
Friendly Persuasion '56
Make Haste to Live '54
Three Coins in the Fountain '54
I Want You '51
Gentleman's Agreement '47
The Spiral Staircase '46
Till the End of Time '46
The Enchanted Cottage '45
A Tree Grows in Brooklyn '45

John McGuire (1910-80)
Sands of Iwo Jima '49
The Invisible Ghost '41
Stranger on the Third Floor '40
Outlaw Rule '36

Kathryn McGuire (1903-78)
Lost Zeppelin '29
Midnight Faces '26
The Navigator '24

Kim McGuire
Acting on Impulse '93
Cry-Baby '90

Marcy McGuire
Around the World '43
Seven Days' Leave '42

Michael McGuire
Bird '88
Blinded by the Light '82
The Long Days of Summer '80
The Ordeal of Dr. Mudd '80
Home to Stay '79
Sanctuary of Fear '79
Larry '74
Report to the Commissioner '74

Stephen McHattie
The Highway Man '99
The Climb '97
Convict Cowboy '95
Beverly Hills Cop 3 '94
The Dark '94
Deadlock 2 '94
Geronimo: An American Legend '93
Erik '90
Bloodhounds of Broadway '89
One Man Out '89
Call Me '88
Sticky Fingers '88
Caribe '87
Salvation! '87
Belizaire the Cajun '86
Death Valley '81
Roughnecks '80
Mary and Joseph: A Story of Faith '79
Centennial '78
Tomorrow Never Comes '77
James Dean '76
Moving Violation '76
Search for the Gods '75
The People Next Door '70

Frank McHugh (1898-1981)
Easy Come, Easy Go '67
A Tiger Walks '64
Last Hurrah '58
There's No Business Like Show Business '54
A Lion Is in the Streets '53
Mighty Joe Young '49
Miss Grant Takes Richmond '49
Velvet Touch '48
Carnegie Hall '47
State Fair '45
Going My Way '44
Marine Raiders '43
All Through the Night '42
City for Conquest '40
The Fighting 69th '40
I Love You Again '40
Virginia City '40
Dodge City '39
The Roaring Twenties '39
Boy Meets Girl '38
Bullets or Ballots '38
Three Men on a Horse '36
Devil Dogs of the Air '35
Gold Diggers of 1935 '35
Fashions of 1934 '34
Ex-Lady '33
Mystery of the Wax Museum '33
Telegraph Trail '33
Tomorrow at Seven '33
The Strange Love of Molly Louvain '32
Corsair '31
Millie '31

Julia McIlvaine
The Lost Child '00
The Summer of Ben Tyler '96

David McIlwraith
Caracara '00
Cruel Intentions 2 '99
The Happy Face Murders '99
In the Company of Spies '99
Gunfighter's Moon '96
On My Own '92
Millennium '89
Really Weird Tales '86
The Vindicator '85
Happy Birthday, Gemini '80
Outrageous! '77

Tim (McInnerny) McInnery (1956-)
Longitude '00
102 Dalmatians '00
Notting Hill '99
Rogue Trader '98
FairyTale: A True Story '97
A Very British Coup '88
Wetherby '85

John McIntire (1907-91)
Heroes of the Heart '94
As Summers Die '86
Cloak & Dagger '84
Honkytonk Man '82
American Dream '81
The Fox and the Hound '81 (V)
Mrs. R's Daughter '79
Rooster Cogburn '75
Herbie Rides Again '74
Rough Night in Jericho '67
Summer and Smoke '61
Two Rode Together '61
Elmer Gantry '60
Flaming Star '60
Psycho '60
The Light in the Forest '58
The Mark of the Hawk '57
The Tin Star '57
Far Country '55
The Kentuckian '55
Apache '54
A Lion Is in the Streets '53
War Arrow '53
Horizons West '52
The Lawless Breed '52
The World in His Arms '52
Westward the Women '51
The Asphalt Jungle '50
Walk Softly, Stranger '50
Winchester '73 '50
Francis the Talking Mule '49
Call Northside 777 '48

Tim McIntire (1943-86)
Sacred Ground '83
Fast Walking '82
The Choirboys '77
Gumball Rally '76
A Boy and His Dog '75 (V)
Aloha, Bobby and Rose '74
The Sterile Cuckoo '69
Shenandoah '65

Burr McIntosh (1862-1942)
The Adorable Cheat '28
That Certain Thing '28
The Average Woman '24
Way Down East '20

Christine McIntyre (1911-84)
Land of the Lawless '47
Gentleman from Texas '46
The Stranger from Pecos '45
Partners of the Trail '44

Marvin J. McIntyre
Born to Be Wild '95
Wilder Napalm '93
Fandango '85

Susan McIver
Smokey and the Bandit '77
I Spit on Your Corpse '74

David McKay
My Name Is Joe '98
The Girl in the Picture '86

John McKay
Assault of the Rebel Girls '59
Rocket Attack U.S.A. '58

Scott McKay (1922-87)
Christmas Evil '80
Creature of Destruction '67
Guest in the House '44
Thirty Seconds Over Tokyo '44

Wanda McKay (1916-96)
Jungle Goddess '49
There Goes Kelly '45
The Monster Maker '44
Raiders of Ghost City '44
The Black Raven '43
Corregidor '43
Bowery at Midnight '42
Texas Justice '42
Twilight on the Trail '41

Michael McKean (1947-)
My First Mister '01
Beautiful '00
Best in Show '00
Little Nicky '00
Teaching Mrs. Tingle '99
True Crime '99
Final Justice '98
Highway Hitcher '98
Small Soldiers '98 (V)
With Friends Like These '98
Jack '96
Nothing to Lose '96
That Darn Cat '96
The Brady Bunch Movie '95
Edie & Pen '95
Across the Moon '94
Airheads '94
Radioland Murders '94
Coneheads '93
Man Trouble '92
Memoirs of an Invisible Man '92
The Return of Spinal Tap '92
Book of Love '91
Hider in the House '90
The Big Picture '89
Earth Girls Are Easy '89
Flashback '89
Portrait of a White Marriage '88
Short Circuit 2 '88
Light of Day '87
Planes, Trains & Automobiles '87
Jumpin' Jack Flash '86
Clue '85
D.A.R.Y.L. '85
This Is Spinal Tap '84
Young Doctors in Love '82
Used Cars '80
1941 '79

Donna McKechnie (1940-)
Breakin' Through '84
Twirl '81
The Little Prince '74

Gina McKee (1964-)
Divine Secrets of the Ya-Ya Sisterhood '02
Notting Hill '99
Wonderland '99
Croupier '97
Element of Doubt '96
Naked '93

John McKee
The Gallant Hours '60
Above and Beyond '53

Lafe (Lafayette) McKee (1872-1959)
Inside the Law '42
Covered Wagon Trails '40
Riders of Pasco Basin '40
Brothers of the West '37
Melody of the Plains '37
Mystery of the Hooded Horseman '37
The Rangers Step In '37
Santa Fe Bound '37
Last of the Warrens '36
Boss Cowboy '35
Ghost Rider '35
The Miracle Rider '35
The Revenge Rider '35
Ridin' Thru '35
Rustlers of Red Dog '35
Law of the Wild '34
Man from Utah '34
Rawhide Romance '34
The Silver Bullet '34
Deadwood Pass '33
Fighting Champ '33
Jaws of Justice '33
Lightning Range '33
Man from Monterey '33
Telegraph Trail '33
Terror Trail '33
The Big Stampede '32
Boiling Point '32
The Riding Tornado '32
The Pocatello Kid '31
Range Law '31
Two Gun Man '31
Near the Rainbow's End '30
Under Montana Skies '30
Little Orphan Annie '18

Lonette McKee (1954-)
Men of Honor '00
Having Our Say: The Delany Sisters' First 100 Years '99
Blind Faith '98
He Got Game '98
Dangerous Passion '95
Queen '93
Malcolm X '92
Jungle Fever '91
The Women of Brewster Place '89
Gardens of Stone '87
Round Midnight '86
Brewster's Millions '85
The Cotton Club '84
Cuba '79
Which Way Is Up? '77
Sparkle '76
Detroit 9000 '73

Raymond (Ray) McKee (1892-1984)
Campus Knights '29
Free to Love '25
Down to the Sea in Ships '22

Todd McKee
Devil in the Flesh 2 '00
Blade Boxer '97

Michael McKeever
Around the Fire '98
Junior '86
The Three Stooges Meet Hercules '61

Danica McKellar (1976-)
Sidekicks '93
Camp Cucamonga: How I Spent My Summer Vacation '90

Don McKellar (1963-)
Sea People '00
eXistenZ '99
The Passion of Ayn Rand '99
Last Night '98
The Red Violin '98
In the Presence of Mine Enemies '97
Never Met Picasso '96
When Night Is Falling '95
Exotica '94
The Adjuster '91
Highway 61 '91
Roadkill '89

Ian McKellen (1939-)
Lord of the Rings 1: The Fellowship of the Rings '01
X-Men '00
David Copperfield '99
Gods and Monsters '98
Apt Pupil '97
Bent '97
Swept from the Sea '97
Rasputin: Dark Servant of Destiny '96
Jack and Sarah '95
Richard III '95
Cold Comfort Farm '94
Heaven's a Drag '94 (N)
Restoration '94
The Shadow '94
And the Band Played On '93
Armistead Maupin's Tales of the City '93
The Ballad of Little Jo '93
Six Degrees of Separation '93
Scandal '89
Windmills of the Gods '88
Plenty '85
The Keep '83
The Scarlet Pimpernel '82
Priest of Love '81

Alex McKenna
Joey '98
Safety Patrol '98
The Stupids '95

Siobhan McKenna (1923-86)
Doctor Zhivago '65
Of Human Bondage '64
Playboy of the Western World '62
The King of Kings '61
The Adventurers '51

T.P. McKenna (1929-)
Red Scorpion '89
Valmont '89
Bleak House '85
The Doctor and the Devils '85
To the Lighthouse '83
James Joyce: A Portrait of the Artist as a Young Man '77
All Creatures Great and Small '74
Next Victim '74
Straw Dogs '72
Beast in the Cellar '70
The Charge of the Light Brigade '68
Ulysses '67
Girl with Green Eyes '64

Virginia McKenna (1931-)
Sliding Doors '97
Duel of Hearts '92
The First Olympics: Athens 1896 '84
Disappearance '81
The Chosen '77
Christian the Lion '76
The Gathering Storm '74
Waterloo '71
An Elephant Called Slowly '69
Ring of Bright Water '69
Born Free '66
The Wreck of the Mary Deare '59
Carve Her Name with Pride '58
The Smallest Show on Earth '57
Simba '55
The Cruel Sea '53

Dallas McKennon
Mystery Mansion '83
Lady and the Tramp '55 (V)

Fay McKenzie (1918-)
Heart of the Rio Grande '42
Down Mexico Way '41
Death Rides the Range '40
Ghost Town Riders '38
Boss Cowboy '35

Jacqueline McKenzie (1967-)
Divine Secrets of the Ya-Ya Sisterhood '02
On the Beach '00
Deep Blue Sea '99
Angel Baby '95
Mr. Reliable: A True Story '95
Talk '94
Traps '93
Romper Stomper '92

Julia McKenzie
The Old Curiosity Shop '94
Shirley Valentine '89

Richard McKenzie
In Love and War '91
Corvette Summer '78

Tim McKenzie
The 13th Floor '88
The Lighthorsemen '87
Gallipoli '81

Doug McKeon (1966-)
The Empty Mirror '99
From the Earth to the Moon '98
Sub Down '97
Where the Red Fern Grows: Part 2 '92
Breaking Home Ties '87
Turnaround '87
Heart of a Champion: The Ray Mancini Story '85
Mischief '85
Desperate Lives '82
Night Crossing '81
On Golden Pond '81
Centennial '78

Nancy McKeon (1966-)
Just Write '97
The Wrong Woman '95
Teresa's Tattoo '94
Where the Day Takes You '92
The Lightning Incident '91
Poison Ivy '85
High School USA '84
Scruffy '80 (V)

Philip McKeon
Red Surf '90
Return to Horror High '87

Charles McKeown
The Adventures of Baron Munchausen '89
Erik the Viking '89

Leo McKern (1920-)
Molokai: The Story of Father Damien '99
A Foreign Field '93
Monsignor Quixote '91
Travelling North '87
Ladyhawke '85
The French Lieutenant's Woman '81
The Blue Lagoon '80
The House on Garibaldi Street '79
The Adventures of Sherlock Holmes' Smarter Brother '78
Candleshoe '78
The Omen '76
Massacre in Rome '73
Ryan's Daughter '70
The Shoes of the Fisherman '68
The Amorous Adventures of Moll Flanders '65
Help! '65
King and Country '64
Doctor in Distress '63
The Horse Without a Head '63
The Day the Earth Caught Fire '61
The Mouse That Roared '59
Time Without Pity '57
X The Unknown '56

Kevin McKidd (1973-)
Anna Karenina '00
Topsy Turvy '99
The Acid House '98
Bedrooms and Hallways '98
Behind the Lines '97

Dad Savage '97
Small Faces '95
Trainspotting '95

Robert McKim (1886-1927)
The Bat '26
Heart's Haven '22
Wagon Tracks '19
Blue Blazes Rawden '18
Hell's Hinges '16
The Disciple '15

Bill McKinney
It Came from Outer Space 2 '95
City Slickers 2: The Legend of Curly's Gold '94
Lone Justice 2 '93
The China Lake Murders '90
Against All Odds '84
Heart Like a Wheel '83
St. Helen's, Killer Volcano '82
Tex '82
Bronco Billy '80
The Gauntlet '77
Cannonball '76
The Outlaw Josey Wales '76
The Shootist '76
The Parallax View '74
Deliverance '72
Angel Unchained '70
She-Freak '67

Gregory McKinney (1957-98)
Recoil '97
Star Quest '94
A Brilliant Disguise '93

Kurt McKinney
Cupid & Cate '00
Sworn to Justice '97
No Retreat, No Surrender '86

Mark McKinney (1959-)
Jacob Two Two Meets the Hooded Fang '99
The Out-of-Towners '99
Superstar '99
Dog Park '98
A Night at the Roxbury '98
Spice World: The Movie '97
Kids in the Hall: Brain Candy '96

Mira McKinney
Heart of the Rockies '51
Double Trouble '41

Nina Mae McKinney (1912-67)
Pinky '49
The Devil's Daughter '39
Hallelujah! '29

Mona McKinnon
Plan 9 from Outer Space '56
Jail Bait '54

Ray McKinnon
O Brother Where Art Thou? '00
Goodbye, Lover '99
Larry McMurtry's Dead Man's Walk '96
The Net '95
A Perfect World '93
Indecency '92
Paris Trout '91

Victor McLaglen (1886-1959)
Around the World in 80 Days '56
Lady Godiva '55
Prince Valiant '54
Trouble in the Glen '54
The Quiet Man '52
Rio Grande '50
She Wore a Yellow Ribbon '49
Fort Apache '48
Whistle Stop '46
The Princess and the Pirate '44
Forever and a Day '43
Call Out the Marines '42
Broadway Limited '41
South of Pago Pago '40
Gunga Din '39
Let Freedom Ring '39
Devil's Party '38
Sea Devils '37
Wee Willie Winkie '37
Klondike Annie '36
The Informer '35
The Lost Patrol '34
Murder at the Vanities '34
Laughing at Life '33
Dishonored '31
The Unholy Three '25

Hollis McLaren
Vengeance Is Mine '84
Atlantic City '81
Lost and Found '79
Outrageous! '77

Ron McLarty
Mean Streak '99
The Postman '97
Two Bits '96
The Feud '90
Enormous Changes '83
Tiger Town '83
Trumps '83

Bill McLaughlin
Comic Cabby '87
Silk '86
Naked Vengeance '85

Duane McLaughlin
Finding Buck McHenry '00
The Runaway '00

Ellen McLaughlin
Everything Relative '96
The Bed You Sleep In '93

Gibb McLaughlin (1884-1960)
Inspector Hornleigh '39
Mr. Reeder in Room 13 '38
Bulldog Jack '35
The Old Curiosity Shop '35
Power '34
The Scarlet Pimpernel '34
The Private Life of Henry VIII '33

Maya McLaughlin
Milo '98
Children of the Night '92

David McLean (1922-95)
Death Sport '78
Hughes & Harlow: Angels in Hell '77
The Strangler '64

B.J. McLellan
Little Men '98
Summer of the Monkeys '98

Zoe McLellan
Dungeons and Dragons '00
Stonebrook '98

Catherine McLeod (1921-97)
Sword of Venus '53
I've Always Loved You '46

Duncan McLeod
Tomb of the Undead '72
Beyond the Valley of the Dolls '70

Gordon McLeod
Meet Sexton Blake '44
Clouds over Europe '39

Kenneth McLeod
Virtual Combat '95
Deadly Target '94
Guardian Angel '94
Out for Blood '93
Showdown '93
Judgment Day '88

Allyn Ann McLerie (1926-)
Living Proof: The Hank Williams Jr. Story '83
And Baby Makes Six '79
A Shining Season '79
Death Scream '75
Someone I Touched '75
Jeremiah Johnson '72
They Shoot Horses, Don't They? '69
Calamity Jane '53
The Desert Song '53

John McLiam (1918-94)
Split Decisions '88
The Ambush Murders '82
The Five of Me '81
Freedom Road '79
Showdown '73
Cool Hand Luke '67

Rachel McLish
Ravenhawk '95
Aces: Iron Eagle 3 '92

Marshall McLuhan
Third Walker '79
Annie Hall '77

Pauline McLynn
An Everlasting Piece '00
When Brendan Met Trudy '00
Angela's Ashes '99

Ed McMahon (1923-)
For Which He Stands '98
Safety Patrol '98
Just Write '97
Butterfly '82
Great American Traffic Jam '80
The Kid from Left Field '79
Fun with Dick and Jane '77
Slaughter's Big Ripoff '73
The Incident '67
Daughter of Horror '55 (N)

Horace McMahon (1906-71)
The Delicate Delinquent '56
My Sister Eileen '55
Abbott and Costello Go to Mars '53
Detective Story '51
Birth of the Blues '41
Melody Ranch '40
The Wrong Road '37

Julian McMahon
Chasing Sleep '00
Magenta '96
Wet and Wild Summer '92

Cody McMains
Not Another Teen Movie '01
Bring It On '00

Don McManus
The 6th Day '00
True Colors '91

James McManus
La Cucaracha '99
The Big Empty '98

Michael McManus
Tales from a Parallel Universe: Eating Pattern '97
Tales from a Parallel Universe: Giga Shadow '97
Tales from a Parallel Universe: I Worship His Shadow '97
Tales from a Parallel Universe: Super Nova '97
Funland '89
Speaking Parts '89
Poltergeist '82
Captain America '79

John McMartin
The Dish '00
Separate but Equal '91
Little Sweetheart '90
A Shock to the System '90
Day One '89
Gore Vidal's Lincoln '88
Roots: The Gift '88
Legal Eagles '86
Murrow '86
Native Son '86
Dream Lover '85
Private Contentment '83
Sweet Charity '69

Niles McMaster
Alice Sweet Alice '76
Bloodsucking Freaks '75

Kenneth McMillan (1932-)
Three Fugitives '89
Malone '87
Acceptable Risks '86
Armed and Dangerous '86
Cat's Eye '85
Dixie: Changing Habits '85
Runaway Train '85
Concrete Beat '84
Dune '84
Killing Hour '84
The Pope of Greenwich Village '84
Protocol '84
Reckless '84
Blue Skies Again '83
In the Custody of Strangers '82
Partners '82
Eyewitness '81
Heartbeeps '81
Ragtime '81
True Confessions '81
Whose Life Is It Anyway? '81
Borderline '80
Carny '80
Hide in Plain Sight '80
Chilly Scenes of Winter '79
Salem's Lot '79
Bloodbrothers '78
Girlfriends '78
Johnny We Hardly Knew Ye '77
The Taking of Pelham One Two Three '74

Richard McMillan
The Sandy Bottom Orchestra '00
Bram Stoker's Shadowbuilder '98
Naked City: A Killer Christmas '98
M. Butterfly '93
Ordeal in the Arctic '93

W.G. McMillan
The Sister-in-Law '74
The Crazies '73

James McMullan
Sex Through a Window '72
Shenandoah '65

Sam McMurray
Lucky Numbers '00
Drop Dead Gorgeous '99
The Mod Squad '99
Slappy and the Stinkers '97
Savage '96
Getting Even with Dad '94
National Lampoon's Attack of the 5 Ft. 2 Women '94
L.A. Story '91
Stone Cold '91
Raising Arizona '87
C.H.U.D. '84
Union City '81

Pamela McMyler
Blood Beach '81
The $5.20 an Hour Dream '80
The Stick-Up '77

Mercedes McNab (1981-)
White Wolves 3: Cry of the White Wolf '98
Escape from Atlantis '97
Savage Land '94
Addams Family Values '93

Barbara McNair (1939-)
The Organization '71
They Call Me Mr. Tibbs! '70
Venus in Furs '70
Change of Habit '69
Stiletto '69
Dead Right '68

Kevin McNally
Shackleton '02
Conspiracy '01
High Heels and Low Lifes '01
When the Sky Falls '99
Abraham '94
Jekyll and Hyde '90
Cry Freedom '87
The Berlin Affair '85
Poldark 2 '75

Stephen McNally (1913-94)
Dear Detective '78
Hi-Riders '77
Tribute to a Bad Man '56
A Bullet Is Waiting '54
Make Haste to Live '54
Devil's Canyon '53
Split Second '53
The Black Castle '52
Diplomatic Courier '52
Duel at Silver Creek '52
No Way Out '50
Winchester '73 '50
Criss Cross '48
Magnificent Doll '46
Thirty Seconds Over Tokyo '44
Air Raid Wardens '43
For Me and My Gal '42
Keeper of the Flame '42

Brian McNamara
The Ghost of Spoon River '00
Where the Truth Lies '99
Mystery Date '91
When the Party's Over '91
Arachnophobia '90
Billionaire Boys Club '87
Short Circuit '86
Detective Sadie & Son '84

Julianne McNamara
Class of Fear '91
Saturday the 14th Strikes Back '88

Maggie McNamara (1928-78)
The Cardinal '63
Three Coins in the Fountain '54
The Moon Is Blue '53

Pat McNamara
Commandments '96
The Daytrippers '96
Trusting Beatrice '92

William McNamara (1965-)
Time Lapse '01
Paper Bullets '99
Implicated '98
Ringmaster '98
Sweet Jane '98
Glam '97
Stag '97
The Brylcreem Boys '96
Natural Enemy '96
Copycat '95
Storybook '95
Black Water '94
Chasers '94
Girl in the Cadillac '94
Radio Inside '94
Surviving the Game '94
Wildflower '91
Texasville '90
Dream a Little Dream '89
The Beat '88
Opera '88
Stealing Home '88

Alan McNaughton
Frankenstein Created Woman '66
Victim '61

Gus McNaughton (1881-1969)
Clouds over Europe '39
Sidewalks of London '38
The 39 Steps '35

Julia McNeal
The Refrigerator '91
The Unbelievable Truth '90

Howard McNear (1905-69)
Kiss Me, Stupid! '64
Fun in Acapulco '63
The Errand Boy '61
Follow That Dream '61
Escape from Fort Bravo '53

Ian McNeice (1950-)
The Body '01
Conspiracy '01
Dune '00
A Certain Justice '99
David Copperfield '99
The Beautician and the Beast '97
A Life Less Ordinary '97
Ace Ventura: When Nature Calls '95
The Englishman Who Went up a Hill But Came down a Mountain '95
Funny Bones '94
No Escape '94
Year of the Comet '92
The Russia House '90
Valmont '89
The Lonely Passion of Judith Hearne '87

Claudia McNeil (1916-93)
Roll of Thunder, Hear My Cry '78
Cry Panic '74
The Migrants '74
A Raisin in the Sun '61

Kate McNeil
One Kill '00
Escape Clause '96
Shadow Dancer '96
Sudden Death '95
Monkey Shines '88
The House on Sorority Row '83

Jimmy (James Vincent) McNichol (1961-)
Escape from El Diablo '83
Blinded by the Light '82
Night Warning '82
Smokey Bites the Dust '81

Kristy McNichol (1962-)
Baby of the Bride '91
The Forgotten One '89
Two Moon Junction '88
You Can't Hurry Love '88
Women of Valor '86
Dream Lover '85
Just the Way You Are '84
Blinded by the Light '82
Pirate Movie '82
The Night the Lights Went Out in Georgia '81
Only When I Laugh '81
Little Darlings '80
My Old Man '79
The End '78
The Summer of My German Soldier '78

Kevin McNulty
A Call to Remember '97
Tricks '97
Maternal Instincts '96
Titanic '96
Live Bait '95
The NeverEnding Story 3: Escape from Fantasia '94
Timecop '94
Anything for Love '93

Sandy McPeak (1935-97)
Eye on the Sparrow '91
Inside Out '91
The Flight '89
The Taking of Flight 847: The Uli Derickson Story '88
My Mother's Secret Life '84
Tarantulas: The Deadly Cargo '77
Ode to Billy Joe '76

Kris McQuade (1952-)
Billy's Holiday '95
Resistance '92
Strictly Ballroom '92
Two Friends '86
The Coca-Cola Kid '84

Murdock McQuarrie (1878-1942)
Man from Montana '41
Ghost Town Riders '38
Laramie Kid '35
The New Frontier '35
The Tonto Kid '35
Daring Danger '32

Butterfly McQueen (1911-95)
The Mosquito Coast '86
The Adventures of Huckleberry Finn '85
Amazing Grace '74
Killer Diller '48
Duel in the Sun '46
I Dood It '43
Gone with the Wind '39

Chad McQueen (1960-)
Surface to Air '98
Trail of a Serial Killer '98
Red Line '96
Indecent Behavior 2 '94

Money to Burn '94
New York Cop '94
Number One Fan '94
Death Ring '93
Firepower '93
Possessed by the Night '93
Sexual Malice '93
Where the Red Fern Grows: Part 2 '92
Martial Law '90
Nightforce '86
Fever Pitch '85
The Karate Kid '84
Skateboard '77

Steve McQueen (1930-80)
The Hunter '80
Tom Horn '80
The Towering Inferno '74
Papillon '73
The Getaway '72
Junior Bonner '72
Le Mans '71
The Reivers '69
Bullitt '68
The Thomas Crown Affair '68
Nevada Smith '66
The Sand Pebbles '66
The Cincinnati Kid '65
Baby, the Rain Must Fall '64
The Great Escape '63
Love with the Proper Stranger '63
Soldier in the Rain '63
Hell Is for Heroes '62
War Lover '62
The Honeymoon Machine '61
The Magnificent Seven '60
The Great St. Louis Bank Robbery '59
Never So Few '59
The Blob '58
Never Love a Stranger '58
Somebody Up There Likes Me '56

Alan McRae
3 Ninjas: High Noon at Mega Mountain '97
3 Ninjas '92

Elizabeth McRae
The Conversation '74
The Incredible Mr. Limpet '64

Frank McRae (1952-)
Lightning Jack '94
Last Action Hero '93
Sketch Artist '92
Farewell to the King '89
License to Kill '89
Lock Up '89
*batteries not included '87
National Lampoon's Vacation '83
Cannery Row '82
1941 '79

Hilton McRae
Voices from a Locked Room '95
The Secret Rapture '94

Leslie McRae
Blood Orgy of the She-Devils '74
Girl in Gold Boots '69

Gerald McRaney (1948-)
Danger Beneath the Sea '02
Murder by Moonlight '91
Blind Vengeance '90
Dynamite and Gold '88
City Killer '87
Hobo's Christmas '87
American Justice '86
The NeverEnding Story '84
The Haunting Passion '83
Night of Bloody Horror '76
Mind Warp '72

Peter McRobbie
Kill by Inches '99
The Neon Bible '95
And the Band Played On '93
Johnny Suede '92

Ian McShane (1942-)
Sexy Beast '00
D.R.E.A.M. Team '99
Con Man '92
Grand Larceny '92
War & Remembrance: The Final Chapter '89
The Great Escape 2: The Untold Story '88
War & Remembrance '88
Young Charlie Chaplin '88
The Murders in the Rue Morgue '86
A.D. '85
Too Scared to Scream '85
Torchlight '85
Ordeal by Innocence '84
Exposed '83
The Grace Kelly Story '83
Disraeli '79
The Fifth Musketeer '79
The Great Riviera Bank Robbery '79
Yesterday's Hero '79
Code Name: Diamond Head '77
Journey into Fear '74
The Terrorists '74
The Last of Sheila '73
Battle of Britain '69
If It's Tuesday, This Must Be Belgium '69

Jenny McShane
The Watcher '00
Shark Attack '99
Tales of the Kama Sutra 2: Monsoon '98
Monsoon '97
Stag '97

Kitty McShane (1898-1964)
Old Mother Riley's Jungle Treasure '51
Old Mother Riley, Headmistress '50
Old Mother Riley's New Venture '49
Old Mother Riley's Ghosts '41

Michael McShane (1957-)
Drop Dead Gorgeous '99
A Bug's Life '98 (V)
Office Space '98
Tom and Huck '95
Richie Rich '94
Robin Hood: Prince of Thieves '91

Gerard McSorley
Felicia's Journey '99
The Boxer '97
Michael Collins '96
Some Mother's Son '96
Moondance '95
Nothing Personal '95
An Awfully Big Adventure '94
Widow's Peak '94
In the Name of the Father '93

Bud McTaggart
Billy the Kid Trapped '42
Meet the Mob '42

Janet McTeer (1962-)
Waking the Dead '00
Songcatcher '99
Tumbleweeds '98
Carrington '95
Saint-Ex: The Story of the Storyteller '95
Catherine Cookson's The Black Velvet Gown '92
Emily Brontë's Wuthering Heights '92
Hawks '89

Patrick McVey
Top of the Heap '72
Desperate Characters '71

Paul McVey
Phantom of Chinatown '40
Buried Alive '39

Tyler McVey (1912-)
The Gallant Hours '60
Attack of the Giant Leeches '59
Night of the Blood Beast '58

From Here to Eternity '53

Daniel McVicar (1958-)
Alone in the Woods '95
Guardian Angel '94
Scorned '93

Margaret McWade (1872-1956)
Mr. Deeds Goes to Town '36
Theodora Goes Wild '36
The Confession '20

Robert McWade (1872-1938)
Healer '36
Kept Husbands '31
Feet First '30

Jillian McWhirter
The Dentist 2: Brace Yourself '98
Progeny '98
Bloodfist 7: Manhunt '95
Last Man Standing '95
Manhunt '95
Rage '95
Stranglehold '94
Beyond the Call of Duty '92
Dune Warriors '91
After Midnight '89

Caroline McWilliams (1945-)
Switched at Birth '91
Mermaids '90
Into Thin Air '85
Shattered Vows '84
Rage '80

Courtland Mead (1987-)
Tom and Huck '95
Dragonworld '94
The Little Rascals '94

Taylor Mead
Frogs for Snakes '98
Superstar: The Life and Times of Andy Warhol '90

Jayne Meadows (1920-)
The Story of Us '99
Casino '95
The Player '92
City Slickers '91
Murder by Numbers '89
Ratings Game '84
Miss All-American Beauty '82
James Dean '76
Norman, Is That You? '76
David and Bathsheba '51
Song of the Thin Man '47
Lady in the Lake '46

Joyce Meadows
Zebra in the Kitchen '65
The Girl in Lover's Lane '60
The Brain from Planet Arous '57
Flesh and the Spur '57

Stanley Meadows
Performance '70
The Terrornauts '67

Stephen Meadows
Sunstroke '92
Ultraviolet '91
A Cry in the Wild '90
The End of Innocence '90

Tim Meadows
The Ladies Man '00
It's Pat: The Movie '94

Karen Meagher
Threads '85
Experience Preferred... But Not Essential '83

Ray Meagher (1944-)
Bootleg '89
Dark Age '88
Breaker Morant '80
The Odd Angry Shot '79

Colm Meaney (1953-)
Four Days '99
The Magical Legend of the Leprechauns '99
Mystery, Alaska '99
This Is My Father '99
Monument Ave. '98
Claire Dolan '97
Con Air '97

The Last of the High Kings '96
The Englishman Who Went up a Hill But Came down a Mountain '95
The Van '95
War of the Buttons '95
The Road to Wellville '94
Scarlett '94
The Snapper '93
Far and Away '92
Into the West '92
The Last of the Mohicans '92
The Commitments '91
Die Hard 2: Die Harder '90

Russell Means (1939-)
Black Cat Run '98
Wind River '98
Buffalo Girls '95
Natural Born Killers '94
The Pathfinder '94
Wagons East '94
Windrunner '94
The Last of the Mohicans '92

Anne Meara (1929-)
Get Well Soon '01
Judy Berlin '99
Southie '98
The Daytrippers '96
The Search for One-Eyed Jimmy '96
Heavyweights '94
Kiss of Death '94
Reality Bites '94
Awakenings '90
That's Adequate '90
My Little Girl '87
The Longshot '86
Fame '80
Nasty Habits '77
Lovers and Other Strangers '70
The Out-of-Towners '70

Michael Mears
Sharpe's Legend '97
The Old Curiosity Shop '94
Sharpe's Rifles '93

Julio Mechoso
Heartbreakers '01
Jurassic Park 3 '01
All the Pretty Horses '00
Missing Pieces '00
Krippendorf's Tribe '98
Virus '98
Switchback '97
White Squall '96
Bad Boys '95

Karen Medak
Galaxies Are Colliding '92
Treacherous Crossing '92
A Girl to Kill For '90

Kay Medford (1920-80)
Windows '80
Lola '69
Funny Girl '68
Butterfield 8 '60
The Rat Race '60

Harriet Medin
Blood Beach '81
Blood and Black Lace '64
The Ghost '63
The Whip and the Body '63
The Horrible Dr. Hichcock '62

Patricia Medina (1920-)
The Big Push '75
The Killing of Sister George '69
Snow White and the Three Stooges '61
Mr. Arkadin '55
Botany Bay '53
Abbott and Costello in the Foreign Legion '50
The Jackpot '50
Francis the Talking Mule '49
The Three Musketeers '48
Hotel Reserve '44
The Day Will Dawn '42
Spitfire '42
Dinner at the Ritz '37

Frank Medrano
The Apostate '98
Kissing a Fool '98
The Replacement Killers '98
Telling You '98
Winchell '98
Sleepers '96

Heather Medway
Serpent's Lair '95
The Fear '94

Michael Medwin (1923-)
The Jigsaw Man '84
A Countess from Hong Kong '67
Rattle of a Simple Man '64
Above Us the Waves '56
Genevieve '53
Four in a Jeep '51
Someone at the Door '50
The Gay Lady '49
The Courtney Affair '47

Lew Meehan (1890-1951)
Feud Maker '38
Thunder in the Desert '38
Melody of the Plains '37
Ridin' the Lone Trail '37
Feud of the West '35
Ridin' Thru '35
Texas Jack '35
The Silver Bullet '34
Whistlin' Dan '32
Backfire '22

Donald Meek (1880-1946)
Fabulous Joe '47
Magic Town '47
Because of Him '45
Colonel Effingham's Raid '45
State Fair '45
Bathing Beauty '44
The Thin Man Goes Home '44
Two Girls and a Sailor '44
Air Raid Wardens '43
DuBarry Was a Lady '43
They Got Me Covered '43
Keeper of the Flame '42
Mrs. Wiggs of the Cabbage Patch '42
Tortilla Flat '42
A Woman's Face '41
My Little Chickadee '40
Return of Frank James '40
Blondie Takes a Vacation '39
Jesse James '39
Stagecoach '39
Young Mr. Lincoln '39
The Adventures of Tom Sawyer '38
Little Miss Broadway '38
You Can't Take It with You '38
Three Legionnaires '37
Toast of New York '37
One Rainy Afternoon '36
Barbary Coast '35
The Informer '35
Mark of the Vampire '35
The Return of Peter Grimm '35
The Whole Town's Talking '35
The Merry Widow '34

Jeffrey Meek (1959-)
Timelock '99
Breaking the Surface: The Greg Louganis Story '96
The St. Tammany Miracle '94
Heart Condition '90
Night of the Cyclone '90
Winter People '89

George Meeker (1889-1958)
The Invisible Monster '50
Twilight in the Sierras '50
Omoo Omoo, the Shark God '49
Apache Rose '47
People's Choice '46
I Accuse My Parents '45

Dead Man's Eyes/Pillow of Death '44
Seven Doors to Death '44
Dive Bomber '41
Danger on the Air '38
Tango '36
Murder by Television '35
Night of Terror '33

Ralph Meeker (1920-88)
Winter Kills '79
My Boys Are Good Boys '78
Hi-Riders '77
The Alpha Incident '76
Food of the Gods '76
Brannigan '75
The Dead Don't Die '75
Johnny Firecloud '75
Cry Panic '74
Birds of Prey '72
Mind Snatchers '72
The Anderson Tapes '71
The Night Stalker '71
The Detective '68
The Dirty Dozen '67
Gentle Giant '67
The St. Valentine's Day Massacre '67
Paths of Glory '57
Battle Shock '56
Run of the Arrow '56
Kiss Me Deadly '55
Four in a Jeep '51

Armand Meffre
Jean de Florette '87
Manon of the Spring '87
Here Comes Santa Claus '84
Blue Country '77

John Megna (1953-95)
Go Tell the Spartans '78
To Kill a Mockingbird '62

Don Megowan (1922-81)
The Devil's Brigade '68
The Creation of the Humanoids '62
The Jayhawkers '59
The Creature Walks among Us '56
A Lawless Street '55

Blanche Mehaffey (1907-68)
Devil Monster '46
Silent Code '35
Sunrise Trail '31
Battling Orioles '24

Tobias Mehler
Wishmaster 3: Beyond the Gates of Hell '01
Sabrina the Teenage Witch '96

Thomas Meighan (1879-1936)
Peck's Bad Boy '34
Peck's Bad Boy '21
Why Change Your Wife? '20
Male and Female '19
The Forbidden City '18

John Meillon (1934-89)
Crocodile Dundee 2 '88
Frenchman's Farm '87
The Blue Lightning '86
Crocodile Dundee '86
The Dunera Boys '85
Camel Boy '84 (V)
Fourth Wish '75
Ride a Wild Pony '75
The Cars That Ate Paris '74
Inn of the Damned '74
Walkabout '71
Billy Budd '62

Kurt Meisel (1912-94)
The Odessa File '74
A Time to Love & a Time to Die '58
Wozzeck '47

Kathryn Meisle
Rosewood '96
Basket Case 2 '90

Gunter Meisner (1928-94)
Magdalene '88

In a Glass Cage '86
Between Wars '74
Willy Wonka & the Chocolate Factory '71

Gerardo Mejia (1965-)
A Million to Juan '94
Somebody to Love '94
Colors '88
Can't Buy Me Love '87
Winners Take All '87

Isabelle Mejias
Scanners 2: The New Order '91
Unfinished Business '89
Fall from Innocence '88
Higher Education '88
Meatballs 3 '87
The Bay Boy '85
Daughter of Death '82

Mariangela Melato (1941-)
Dancers '87
Summer Night with Greek Profile, Almond Eyes & Scent of Basil '87
So Fine '81
To Forget Venice '79
Swept Away... '75
By the Blood of Others '73
Love and Anarchy '73
Seduction of Mimi '72

Wendel Meldrum
Melanie Darrow '97
National Lampoon's Dad's Week Off '97
Sodbusters '94
City Boy '93
Beautiful Dreamers '92

Nicholas Mele
Impulse '90
Capone '89
A Nightmare on Elm Street 5: Dream Child '89

George Melford (1877-1961)
A Woman's World '54
Call Northside 777 '48

Jack Melford (1899-1972)
The Ladykillers '55
When Thief Meets Thief '37
Department Store '35

Jill Melford
Edge of Sanity '89
Abandon Ship '57

Joseph Mell
36 Hours '64
I Was a Teenage Werewolf '57

Marisa Mell (1939-92)
Mad Dog '84
Hostages '79
Danger: Diabolik '68
Secret Agent Super Dragon '66

Randle Mell
Cookie's Fortune '99
Wyatt Earp '94

Andree Melly
The Brides of Dracula '60
The Belles of St. Trinian's '53

Christopher Meloni
Wet Hot American Summer '01
Runaway Bride '99
The Souler Opposite '97
Bound '96

Frank Melton (1907-51)
Tanks a Million '41
The Glory Trail '36
Stand Up and Cheer '34

Sid Melton (1920-)
Hit! '73
Lady Sings the Blues '72
Leave It to the Marines '51
The Lost Continent '51
Sky High '51
The Steel Helmet '51
Stop That Cab '51
Girls in Chains '43

Sam Melville
Twice Dead '88
Roughnecks '80

Murray Melvin (1932-)
Let Him Have It '91
The Krays '90
The Bawdy Adventures of Tom Jones '76
Lisztomania '75
Madhouse Mansion '74
The Devils '71
Start the Revolution without Me '70
The Fixer '68
Alfie '66
A Taste of Honey '61

George Memmoli (1938-85)
Hot Potato '76
Phantom of the Paradise '74
Mean Streets '73

Stephen Mendel
Midnight Heat '95
Scanner Cop 2: Volkin's Revenge '94
Scanners: The Showdown '94

Ben Mendelsohn (1969-)
Vertical Limit '00
Amy '98
Idiot Box '97
Cosi '95
Sirens '94
The Efficiency Expert '92
Quigley Down Under '90
The Year My Voice Broke '87

David Mendenhall (1971-)
Streets '90
Secret of the Ice Cave '89
Going Bananas '88
Over the Top '86
Witchfire '86
Space Raiders '83

Eva Mendez
Exit Wounds '01
Training Day '01
Urban Legends 2: Final Cut '00
Children of the Corn 5: Fields of Terror '98

Stephen Mendillo
Ethan Frome '92
Slap Shot '77

Mauro Mendonca
Love Strange Love '82
Dona Flor and Her Two Husbands '78

Natalie Mendoza
Moulin Rouge '01
Rodgers & Hammerstein's South Pacific '01

Victor Manuel Mendoza (1913-95)
Cowboy '58
The Proud Ones '53
Susana '51

Alex Meneses
The Flintstones in Viva Rock Vegas '00
Living in Peril '97
Amanda and the Alien '95
Payback '89

Bernard Menez (1944-)
Dracula & Son '76
Dracula Father and Son '76
No Problem '75

John Mengatti
Knights of the City '85
Meatballs 2 '84

Alex Menglet
Zone 39 '96
A Woman's Tale '92

Adolphe Menjou (1890-1963)
Pollyanna '60
Paths of Glory '57
The Ambassador's Daughter '56
Bundle of Joy '56
I Married a Woman '56
Across the Wide Missouri '51
To Please a Lady '50
My Dream Is Yours '49
State of the Union '48
The Hucksters '47
I'll Be Yours '47
Heartbeat '46
Step Lively '44
Hi Diddle Diddle '43
Sweet Rosie O'Grady '43
Roxie Hart '42
You Were Never Lovelier '42
Road Show '41
Golden Boy '39
The Goldwyn Follies '38
Letter of Introduction '38
100 Men and a Girl '37
Stage Door '37
A Star Is Born '37
Milky Way '36
One in a Million '36
Gold Diggers of 1935 '35
Little Miss Marker '34
Morning Glory '33
A Farewell to Arms '32
The Front Page '31
Morocco '30
The Grand Duchess and the Waiter '26
The Sorrows of Satan '26
Are Parents People? '25
The King on Main Street '25
The Swan '25
The Marriage Circle '24
The Sheik '21

Oleg Menshikov (1960-)
East-West '99
Prisoner of the Mountains '96
Burnt by the Sun '94

Vladimir Mensik
All My Good Countrymen '68
Murder Czech Style '66

Heather Menzies (1949-)
Captain America '79
Piranha '78
Red, White & Busted '75
Sssssss '73
The Sound of Music '65

Christian Meoli
The Song of the Lark '01
The Low Life '95
Alive '93

Julino Mer
The Last Warrior '99
Under the Domim Tree '95

Doro Merande (1892-1975)
The Russians Are Coming, the Russians Are Coming '66
Kiss Me, Stupid! '64
The Gazebo '59
The Man with the Golden Arm '55
The Seven Year Itch '55

Hector Mercado
Leather Jacket Love Story '98
Nomads '86

Beryl Mercer (1862-1939)
Jane Eyre '34
Cavalcade '33
Smilin' Through '33
Supernatural '33
The Miracle Woman '31
Public Enemy '31
All Quiet on the Western Front '30

Mae Mercer
Pretty Baby '78
The Swinging Cheerleaders '74
Frogs '72

Vivien Merchant (1929-83)
The Offence '73
Under Milk Wood '73
Frenzy '72
Accident '67
Alfie '66

Denis Mercier
Bogus '96
Le Sexe des Etoiles '93

Michele Mercier (1939-)
Call of the Wild '72
Web of the Spider '70
Oldest Profession '67
Casanova '70 '65
Black Sabbath '64
A Global Affair '63
Shoot the Piano Player '62

Melina Mercouri (1925-94)
A Dream of Passion '78
Nasty Habits '77
Once Is Not Enough '75
Topkapi '64
Phaedra '61
Never on Sunday '60
Where the Hot Wind Blows '59
Stella '55

Monique Mercure (1930-)
Set Me Free '99
Conquest '98
The Red Violin '98
When Justice Fails '98
Naked Lunch '91
Tramp at the Door '87
The Odyssey of the Pacific '82
Third Walker '79

Micole Mercurio
Bandits '01
While You Were Sleeping '95
Colors '88

Paul Mercurio (1963-)
The First 9 1/2 Weeks '98
Dark Planet '97
Back of Beyond '95
Cosi '95
Joseph '95
Exit to Eden '94
Strictly Ballroom '92

Burgess Meredith (1908-97)
Grumpier Old Men '95
Across the Moon '94
Grumpy Old Men '93
Oddball Hall '91
Mr. Corbett's Ghost '90
Rocky 5 '90
State of Grace '90
Full Moon in Blue Water '88
King Lear '87
Outrage! '86
Santa Claus: The Movie '85
Wet Gold '84
Twilight Zone: The Movie '83
Rocky 3 '82
Thumbelina '82
Clash of the Titans '81
Last Chase '81
True Confessions '81
Final Assignment '80
When Time Ran Out '80
Rocky 2 '79
Foul Play '78
Great Bank Hoax '78
Magic '78
The Manitou '78
Golden Rendezvous '77
Johnny We Hardly Knew Ye '77
Burnt Offerings '76
92 in the Shade '76
Rocky '76
The Sentinel '76
The Day of the Locust '75
The Hindenburg '75
Beware! The Blob '72
Probe '72
Yin & Yang of Mr. Go '71
There Was a Crooked Man '70
MacKenna's Gold '69
Stay Away, Joe '68
Torture Garden '67
Batman '66
A Big Hand for the Little Lady '66
Madame X '66
In Harm's Way '65
The Cardinal '63
Advise and Consent '62
Jigsaw '49
Man on the Eiffel Tower '48
On Our Merry Way '48
Mine Own Executioner '47
Diary of a Chambermaid '46
Magnificent Doll '46
The Story of G.I. Joe '45
That Uncertain Feeling '41
Tom, Dick, and Harry '41
Second Chorus '40
Idiot's Delight '39
Of Mice and Men '39
Winterset '36

Don Meredith (1938-)
Wyatt Earp: Return to Tombstone '94
The Night the City Screamed '80
Express to Terror '79
Sky Hei$t '75
Terror on the 40th Floor '74

Ifan Meredith
Metroland '97
The Mill on the Floss '97

Iris Meredith (1915-80)
Green Archer '40
A Lawman Is Born '37
Mystery of the Hooded Horseman '37

Judi Meredith
Planet of Blood '66
Jack the Giant Killer '62

Lee Meredith
The Sunshine Boys '75
The Producers '68

Luc Merenda (1942-)
Could It Happen Here? '80s
The Cheaters '76
Violent Professionals '73
Le Mans '71

Stanislas Merhar
The Count of Monte Cristo '99
Dry Cleaning '97

Jalal Merhi
Expect No Mercy '95
Fearless Tiger '94
Operation Golden Phoenix '94
TC 2000 '93
Talons of the Eagle '92
Tiger Claws '91

Macha Meril (1940-)
Meeting Venus '91
Chinese Roulette '86
Vagabond '85
Beau Pere '81
Robert et Robert '78
Deep Red: Hatchet Murders '75
A Married Woman '65

Eda Reiss Merin
For Better or Worse '95
The Reluctant Agent '95
Don't Tell Mom the Babysitter's Dead '91

Philip Merivale (1886-1946)
Sister Kenny '46
Nothing But Trouble '44
Lady for a Night '42

Lee Meriwether (1935-)
Brothers O'Toole '73
The Undefeated '69
Batman '66
Namu, the Killer Whale '66
The 4D Man '59

Una Merkel (1903-86)
Spinout '66
A Tiger Walks '64
Summer Magic '63
The Parent Trap '61
Summer and Smoke '61
The Mating Game '59
The Girl Most Likely '57
The Kettles in the Ozarks '56
The Kentuckian '55
I Love Melvin '53
The Merry Widow '52
Rich, Young and Pretty '51
It's a Joke, Son! '47
Twin Beds '42
The Road to Zanzibar '41
The Bank Dick '40
Destry Rides Again '39
On Borrowed Time '39
Rhythm Romance '39
Saratoga '37
Born to Dance '36
Broadway Melody of 1936 '35
Riff Raff '35
Evelyn Prentice '34
The Merry Widow '34
Bombshell '33
42nd Street '33
Red Headed Woman '32
They Call It Sin '32
The Maltese Falcon '31
Private Lives '31
Abraham Lincoln '30
The Bat Whispers '30

S. Epatha Merkerson (1952-)
A Mother's Prayer '95
A Place for Annie '94
She's Gotta Have It '86

Jan Merlin (1925-)
Silk 2 '89
Twilight People '72
Take the Money and Run '69

Joanna Merlin (1931-)
City of Angels '98
Two Bits '96
Class Action '91
Mystic Pizza '88
Baby It's You '82
Fame '80

Ethel Merman (1909-84)
Airplane! '80
Journey Back to Oz '71 (V)
It's a Mad, Mad, Mad, Mad World '63
There's No Business Like Show Business '54
Stage Door Canteen '43
Alexander's Ragtime Band '38
Happy Landing '38
Strike Me Pink '36
Kid Millions '34
We're Not Dressing '34

Mary Merrall (1890-1976)
The Belles of St. Trinian's '53
The Obsessed '51
They Made Me a Fugitive '47
Nicholas Nickleby '46
Dead of Night '45
Pink String and Sealing Wax '45

Charlotte Merriam
Night Nurse '31
One-Punch O'Day '26

Lynn Merrick (1919-)
Down to Earth '47
California Joe '43
The Sombrero Kid '42

Dina Merrill (1925-)
Open Season '95
Suture '93
The Player '92
True Colors '91
Fear '90
Caddyshack 2 '88
Twisted '86
Anna to the Infinite Power '84
Hot Pursuit '84
Tenth Month '79
Deadly Encounter '78
A Wedding '78
The Greatest '77
The Meal '75
Running Wild '73
I'll Take Sweden '65
The Courtship of Eddie's Father '62
Butterfield 8 '60
The Sundowners '60
Operation Petticoat '59
Desk Set '57

Frank Merrill
Tarzan the Tiger '29

The Adventures of Tarzan '21

Gary Merrill (1915-90)
The Seekers '79
Huckleberry Finn '74
Pueblo Affair '73
Clambake '67
The Incident '67
Around the World Under the Sea '65
The Great Impostor '61
Mysterious Island '61
Missouri Traveler '58
Another Man's Poison '52
Phone Call from a Stranger '52
All About Eve '50
Twelve o'Clock High '49

Ryan Merriman (1983-)
Smart House '00
Just Looking '99
Lansky '99
The Deep End of the Ocean '98
Everything That Rises '98

Clive Merrison (1945-)
Photographing Fairies '97
The English Patient '96
An Awfully Big Adventure '94
Heavenly Creatures '94

George Merritt
I, Monster '71
Clouds over Europe '39
Young and Innocent '37

Theresa Merritt (1922-98)
Billy Madison '94
Voodoo Dawn '89
The Serpent and the Rainbow '87

Jane Merrow (1941-)
The Appointment '82
Hands of the Ripper '71
The Lion in Winter '68
Island of the Burning Doomed '67
The Girl Getters '66

John Merton (1901-59)
Border Bandits '46
Devil Riders '44
Rustler's Hideout '44
Wild Horse Phantom '44
Cowboy Commandos '43
Fighting Valley '43
Boot Hill Bandits '42
The Mysterious Rider '42
Prairie Pals '42
Billy the Kid in Texas '40
Covered Wagon Days '40
Code of the Fearless '39
Hopalong Cassidy: Renegade Trail '39
In Old Montana '39
Gang Bullets '38
Phantom Ranger '38
Valley of Terror '38
The Rangers Step In '37
Roaring Six Guns '37
Slaves in Bondage '37
Two-Gun Troubador '37
Aces and Eights '36
Crooked Trail '36
The Gun Ranger '34

William Mervyn (1912-76)
The Ruling Class '72
The Railway Children '70
Murder Ahoy '64
The Battle of the Sexes '60

John Mese
Red Dirt '99
Excessive Force 2: Force on Force '95
Night of the Scarecrow '95

Donald E. Messick (1926-97)
Jetsons: The Movie '90 (V)
Flight of Dragons '82 (V)

Debra Messing (1968-)
Hollywood Ending '02
The Mothman Prophecies '02
Jesus '00
McHale's Navy '97
A Walk in the Clouds '95

Gertrude Messinger (1911-95)
Miracle Kid '42
Aces Wild '37
The Adventurous Knights '35
Fighting Pilot '35
Roaring Roads '35
Rustler's Paradise '35
Social Error '35
Hidden Valley '32

George Metaxa
The Mask of Dimitrios '44
Doctor Takes a Wife '40

Laurie Metcalf (1955-)
Runaway Bride '99
Toy Story 2 '99 (V)
Always Outnumbered Always Outgunned '98
Bulworth '98
Chicago Cab '98
Balloon Farm '97
Scream 2 '97
U-Turn '97
Dear God '96
Leaving Las Vegas '95
Toy Story '95 (V)
Blink '93
A Dangerous Woman '93
JFK '91
Mistress '91
Internal Affairs '90
Pacific Heights '90
Uncle Buck '89
Miles from Home '88
Stars and Bars '88
Candy Mountain '87
Making Mr. Right '86
Desperately Seeking Susan '85
Execution of Raymond Graham '85

Mark Metcalf (1946-)
Drive Me Crazy '99
Hijacking Hollywood '97
Rage '95
The Stupids '95
Dead Ahead: The Exxon Valdez Disaster '92
Mr. North '88
One Crazy Summer '86
The Final Terror '83
National Lampoon's Animal House '78

Earl Metcalfe
The Notorious Lady '27
With Kit Carson over the Great Divide '25

Ken Metcalfe
Nam Angels '88
Warriors of the Apocalypse '85

Aaron Michael Metchik
The Baby-Sitters' Club '95
Trading Mom '94

Asher Metchik
Milo '98
Trading Mom '94

Saul Meth
Double Agent 73 '80
Deadly Weapons '70

Method Man
How High '01
Belly '98

Mayo Methot (1904-51)
Marked Woman '37
Goodbye Love '34
Corsair '31

Art Metrano (1937-)
Beverly Hills Bodysnatchers '89
Police Academy 3: Back in Training '86
Malibu Express '85
Police Academy 2: Their First Assignment '85
Breathless '83
Going Ape! '81
How to Beat the High Cost of Living '80
Seven '79
Prisoner in the Middle '74
Slaughter's Big Ripoff '73
The Heartbreak Kid '72
They Only Kill Their Masters '72
Rocket Attack U.S.A. '58

Nancy Mette
Meet the Hollowheads '89
Matewan '87
Key Exchange '85

Jim Metzler (1955-)
St. Patrick's Day '99
A Gun, a Car, a Blonde '97
Cadillac Ranch '96
Children of the Corn 3: Urban Harvest '95
French Silk '94
Plughead Rewired: Circuitry Man 2 '94
Delusion '91
Love Kills '91
One False Move '91
Circuitry Man '90
Murder by Night '89
Old Gringo '89
Hot to Trot! '88
976-EVIL '88
The Little Match Girl '87
River's Edge '87
On Wings of Eagles '86
Tex '82
Four Friends '81
Squeeze Play '79

Paul Meurisse (1912-79)
Gypsy '75
The Monocle '64
Picnic on the Grass '59
Diabolique '55

Anne-Laure Meury
Boyfriends & Girlfriends '88
The Aviator's Wife '80

Jason Mewes (1974-)
Jay and Silent Bob Strike Back '01
Scream 3 '00
Dogma '99
Chasing Amy '97
Mallrats '95
Clerks '94

Bess Meyer
H.P. Lovecraft's Necronomicon: Book of the Dead '93
The Inner Circle '91

Breckin Meyer (1974-)
Josie and the Pussycats '01
Kate & Leopold '01
Rat Race '01
Road Trip '00
Go '99
Tail Lights Fade '99
Dancer, Texas—Pop. 81 '98
54 '98
Prefontaine '96
Touch '96
Clueless '95

Dina Meyer (1968-)
Federal Protection '02
Time Lapse '01
Bats '99
Stranger than Fiction '99
Nowhere Land '98
Starship Troopers '97
Dragonheart '96
Johnny Mnemonic '95

Emile Meyer (1910-87)
Good Day for a Hanging '58
Blackboard Jungle '55
Riot in Cell Block 11 '54
Shane '53

Hans Meyer
Brotherhood of the Wolf '01
Mauvais Sang '86
Le Magnifique '76

Michael Meyer
Virtual Desire '95
Crossfire '89

Russ Meyer (1922-)
Amazon Women on the Moon '87
Motor Psycho '65

Torben Meyer (1884-)
Judgment at Nuremberg '61
The Matchmaker '58
Sullivan's Travels '41
Thin Ice '37

Ari Meyers (1969-)
Dark Horse '92
Think Big '90
Shakma '89
License to Kill '84

Gerard Meylan
Marius and Jeannette '97
Nenette and Boni '96

Michelle Meyrink (1962-)
Permanent Record '88
Nice Girls Don't Explode '87
One Magic Christmas '85
Real Genius '85
Joy of Sex '84
Revenge of the Nerds '84
Valley Girl '83

Myriam Meziere
Mouth to Mouth '95
Jonah Who Will Be 25 in the Year 2000 '76

Vittorio Mezzogiorno (1942-94)
Car Crash
Cafe Express '83
L'Homme Blesse '83
Moon in the Gutter '83
Three Brothers '80

Robert Miano (1942-)
Dungeons and Dragons '00
Loser '00
Luckytown '00
Thick as Thieves '99
Matter of Trust '98
Smoke Signals '98
Laws of Deception '97
Donnie Brasco '96
Opposite Corners '96
Taxi Dancers '93
Chained Heat '83

Cora Miao
Eat a Bowl of Tea '89
Dim Sum: A Little Bit of Heart '85

Gertrude Michael (1911-64)
Flamingo Road '49
Behind Prison Walls '43
Cleopatra '34
I'm No Angel '33

Ralph Michael (1907-94)
Diary of a Mad Old Man '88
The Heroes of Telemark '65
Murder Most Foul '65
Children of the Damned '63
A Night to Remember '58
Abandon Ship '57
San Demetrio, London '47
Johnny Frenchman '46
Dead of Night '45

Genia Michaela
Is There Life Out There? '94
Fallen Angels 2 '93

Dario Michaelis
The Day the Sky Exploded '57
I Vampiri '56

Al Michaels
BASEketball '98
Homeward Bound 2: Lost in San Francisco '96 (V)

Bret Michaels
In God's Hands '98
No Code of Conduct '98

Corinne Michaels
Consenting Adult '85
Laboratory '80

Julie Michaels
Jason Goes to Hell: The Final Friday '93
Witchboard 2: The Devil's Doorway '93
Road House '89

Jeff Michalski
Star Maps '97
Pet Shop '94

Dominique Michel
King of the Airwaves '94
The Decline of the American Empire '86

Marc Michel
Umbrellas of Cherbourg '64
Lola '61
Le Trou '59

Marcella Michelangeli
Could It Happen Here? '80s
Padre Padrone '77
And God Said to Cain '69

Michael Michele (1966-)
Ali '01
Homicide: The Movie '00
The Sixth Man '97
The Substitute 2: School's Out '97
New Jack City '91

Helena Michell
Devices and Desires '91
Piece of Cake '90

Keith Michell (1928-)
The Deceivers '88
My Brother Tom '86
Grendel, Grendel, Grendel '82 (V)
Ruddigore '70s
Tenth Month '79
The Story of David '76
The Story of Jacob & Joseph '74
Six Wives of Henry VIII '71
The Executioner '70
Soldier in Love '67
The Hellfire Club '61

Anne Michelle
The Haunted '79
French Quarter '78
House of Whipcord '75
Mistress Pamela '74
The Virgin Witch '70

Janee Michelle
The House on Skull Mountain '74
Scream Blacula Scream '73

Shelley Michelle
Married People, Single Sex '93
Bikini Summer '91
Sunset Strip '91

Maria Michi (1921-80)
Last Tango in Paris '73
Redneck '73
Paisan '46
Open City '45

Frank Middlemass (1919-)
One Against the Wind '91
The Bretts '88
Oliver Twist '85
The Island '80

Charles Middleton (1879-1949)
Spook Busters '48
Northwest Trail '46
Strangler of the Swamp '46
Western Union '41
Flash Gordon Conquers the Universe '40
Flash Gordon: Rocketship '40
Space Soldiers Conquer the Universe '40
Flash Gordon: Mars Attacks the World '39
Oklahoma Kid '39
Wyoming Outlaw '39
Dick Tracy Returns '38
Yodelin' Kid from Pine Ridge '37
Rocketship '36
Hopalong Cassidy '35
The Miracle Rider '35
Mystery Ranch '34
Duck Soup '33
The Strange Love of Molly Louvain '32
The Miracle Woman '31
Palmy Days '31

Guy Middleton (1907-73)
The Belles of St. Trinian's '53
The Happiest Days of Your Life '50
A Man About the House '47
The Demi-Paradise '43
Dangerous Moonlight '41

Noelle Middleton (1926-)
The Vicious Circle '57
John and Julie '55
Carrington, V.C. '54

Ray Middleton (1907-84)
A Christmas Carol '54
Jubilee Trail '54
I Dream of Jeannie '52
Lady for a Night '42
Lady from Louisiana '42

Robert Middleton (1911-77)
Harrad Experiment '73
Career '59
The Law and Jake Wade '58
Tarnished Angels '57
Court Jester '56
Love Me Tender '56
Desperate Hours '55

Dale Midkiff (1959-)
Route 666 '01
Air Bud 3: World Pup '00
Alien Fury: Countdown to Invasion '00
Another Woman's Husband '00
The Crow: Salvation '00
The Magnificent Seven '98
Any Place But Home '97
Toothless '97
Love Potion #9 '92
Blackmail '91
Pet Sematary '89
Elvis and Me '88
Nightmare Weekend '86
Streetwalkin' '85

Bette Midler (1945-)
Drowning Mona '00
Isn't She Great '00
What Women Want '00
The First Wives Club '96
That Old Feeling '96
Get Shorty '95
Gypsy '93
Hocus Pocus '93
For the Boys '91
Scenes from a Mall '91
Stella '89
Beaches '88
Big Business '88
Oliver & Company '88 (V)
Outrageous Fortune '87
Down and Out in Beverly Hills '86
Ruthless People '86
Jinxed '82
The Rose '79
The Thorn '73
Hawaii '66

Anne-Marie Mieville (1945-)
Here and Elsewhere '70s
Comment Ca Va? '76

Toshiro Mifune (1920-97)
Picture Bride '94
Shadow of the Wolf '92
Journey of Honor '91
Proof of the Man '84
The Challenge '82
Shogun '80
1941 '79
Winter Kills '79
Love and Faith '78
Midway '76
Paper Tiger '74
Red Sun '71
The Battle of the Japan Sea '70
Zatoichi vs. Yojimbo '70
Hell in the Pacific '69

Red Lion '69
Samurai Rebellion '67
Sword of Doom '67
Grand Prix '66
Red Beard '65
Attack Squadron '63
High & Low '62
Sanjuro '62
Yojimbo '61
The Bad Sleep Well '60
The Gambling Samurai '60
I Bombed Pearl Harbor '60
Saga of the Vagabond '59
The Hidden Fortress '58
Rikisha-Man '58
The Lower Depths '57
Throne of Blood '57
Samurai 3: Duel at Ganryu Island '56
I Live in Fear '55
Samurai 1: Musashi Miyamoto '55
Samurai 2: Duel at Ichijoji Temple '55
Seven Samurai '54
Life of Oharu '52
The Idiot '51
Rashomon '51
Scandal '50
A Quiet Duel '49
Stray Dog '49
Drunken Angel '48

Julia Migenes-Johnson
The Krays '90
Berlin Blues '89
Mack the Knife '89

R.A. Mihailoff
Pumpkinhead 2: Blood Wings '94
Leatherface: The Texas Chainsaw Massacre 3 '89

Tatsuya Mihashi (1923-)
Tora! Tora! Tora! '70
What's Up, Tiger Lily? '66
None But the Brave '65
High & Low '62
The Burmese Harp '56

Dash Mihok (1974-)
The Perfect Storm '00
White Boyz '99
Telling You '98
The Thin Red Line '98

Nikita Mikhalkov (1945-)
Burnt by the Sun '94
Close to Eden '90
Siberiade '79
An Unfinished Piece for a Player Piano '77

Norihei Miki (-1999)
Black Rain '88
Himatsuri '85

Izabella Miko (1981-)
The Forsaken '01
Coyote Ugly '00

Rentaro Mikuni (1923-)
Rikyu '90
A Taxing Woman's Return '88
The Go-Masters '82
Nomugi Pass '79
Vengeance Is Mine '79
Swords of Death '71
Kwaidan '64
The Burmese Harp '56
Samurai 1: Musashi Miyamoto '55

Lita Milan
I, Mobster '58
The Left-Handed Gun '58
Never Love a Stranger '58
Naked in the Sun '57
Poor White Trash '57
The Ride Back '57

Alyssa Milano (1972-)
Goldrush: A Real Life Alaskan Adventure '98
Body Count '97
Hugo Pool '97
Fear '96
Glory Daze '96
Public Enemies '96
Deadly Sins '95
Embrace of the Vampire '95
Poison Ivy 2: Lily '95
Confessions of Sorority Girls '94
Double Dragon '94
Casualties of Love: The "Long Island Lolita" Story '93
Conflict of Interest '92
Little Sister '92
Where the Day Takes You '92
Commando '85
Old Enough '84

Adolph Milar (1886-1950)
The Savage Girl '32
Bulldog Drummond '29
The Michigan Kid '28

Oliver Milburn
Tess of the D'Urbervilles '98
Loaded '94

Bernard Miles (1907-91)
Sapphire '59
The Smallest Show on Earth '57
The Man Who Knew Too Much '56
Never Let Me Go '53
The Guinea Pig '48
Fame Is the Spur '47
Great Expectations '46
Nicholas Nickleby '46
In Which We Serve '43

Betty Miles
Sonora Stagecoach '44
The Law Rides Again '43
Lone Star Law Men '42
The Driftin' Kid '41
Riding the Sunset Trail '41

Joanna Miles (1940-)
Crossfire Trail '01
Horton Foote's Alone '97
The Avenging Angel '95
Cooperstown '93
The Water Engine '92
Rosencrantz & Guildenstern Are Dead '90
Blackout '88
Sound of Murder '82
The Orphan '79
The Dark Secret of Harvest Home '78
Bug '75
The Ultimate Warrior '75
Born Innocent '74

Kevin Miles
Endplay '75
The Cars That Ate Paris '74

Lillian Miles
Reefer Madness '38
Get That Man '35

Maria Miles
Catherine Cookson's The Cinder Path '94
Cold Comfort Farm '94

Peter Miles
Trigger, Jr. '50
The Red Pony '49

Rosalind Miles
The Black Six '74
I Spit on Your Corpse '74
The Manhandlers '73
Shaft's Big Score '72

Sarah Miles (1941-)
The Silent Touch '94
White Mischief '88
Hope and Glory '87
Queenie '87
Harem '86
Steaming '86
Ordeal by Innocence '84
Dynasty '82
Venom '82
The Big Sleep '78
The Sailor Who Fell from Grace with the Sea '76
Lady Caroline Lamb '73
Man Who Loved Cat Dancing '73
Ryan's Daughter '70
Blow-Up '66
Those Magnificent Men in Their Flying Machines '65
The Servant '63

Sherry Miles
The Todd Killings '71
The Velvet Vampire '71

Sylvia Miles (1932-)
Denise Calls Up '95
Superstar: The Life and Times of Andy Warhol '90
She-Devil '89
Sleeping Beauty '89
Crossing Delancey '88
Spike of Bensonhurst '88
No Big Deal '83
Evil under the Sun '82
The Funhouse '81
Deadly Thief '78
Zero to Sixty '78
The Sentinel '76
Farewell, My Lovely '75
Heat '72
The Last Movie '71
Who Killed Mary What's 'Er Name? '71
Midnight Cowboy '69
Psychomania '63
Parrish '61

Vera Miles (1929-)
Separate Lives '94
Into the Night '85
The Initiation '84
Psycho 2 '83
Brainwaves '82
Mazes and Monsters '82
Our Family Business '81
Roughnecks '80
And I Alone Survived '78
Run for the Roses '78
Fire '77
Twilight's Last Gleaming '77
Judge Horton and the Scottsboro Boys '76
The Castaway Cowboy '74
A Strange and Deadly Occurrence '74
One Little Indian '73
Baffled '72
Molly & Lawless John '72
Jigsaw '71
Mission Batangas '69
Hellfighters '68
Sergeant Ryker '68
Gentle Giant '67
Follow Me, Boys! '66
Those Calloways '65
A Tiger Walks '64
The Man Who Shot Liberty Valance '62
Back Street '61
Psycho '60
The FBI Story '59
Autumn Leaves '56
The Searchers '56
The Wrong Man '56

Vicki (Allison Louise Downe) Miles
Scum of the Earth '63
Nature's Playmates '62

Kim Milford
Corvette Summer '78
Laserblast '78

Penelope Milford (1948-)
Henry: Portrait of a Serial Killer 2: Mask of Sanity '96
Normal Life '96
Cold Justice '89
Heathers '89
Bloodlink '86
The Burning Bed '85
The Golden Seal '83
Oldest Living Graduate '82
Rosie: The Rosemary Clooney Story '82
Seizure: The Story of Kathy Morris '82
Take This Job & Shove It '81
The Last Word '80
Coming Home '78

Tomas Milian (1937-)
For Love or Country: The Arturo Sandoval Story '00
Traffic '00
The Yards '00
Amistad '97
Fools Rush In '97
The Burning Season '94
The Cowboy Way '94
Nails '92
JFK '91
Cat Chaser '90
Havana '90
Revenge '90
Salome '85
Identification of a Woman '82
Almost Human '79
Blood and Guns '79
Cop in Blue Jeans '78
Sonny and Jed '73
Don't Torture a Duckling '72
Counter Punch '71
Companeros '70
Time of Indifference '64
Boccaccio '70 '62
Il Bell'Antonio '60

Frank Military
The Last Castle '01
Everybody Wins '90
Dead Bang '89

John Miljan (1892-1960)
Mrs. Mike '49
Queen of the Amazons '47
I Accuse My Parents '45
Wildfire '45
Boss of Big Town '43
The Fallen Sparrow '43
Riot Squad '41
Young Bill Hickok '40
Arizona Mahoney '36
Charlie Chan in Paris '35
Belle of the Nineties '34
The Ghost Walks '34
What! No Beer? '33
Kid from Spain '32
Possessed '31
Susan Lenox: Her Fall and Rise '31
The Unholy Three '30
Yankee Clipper '27
The Unchastened Woman '25

Hugh Millais
The Dogs of War '81
McCabe & Mrs. Miller '71

Robyn Millan
Murph the Surf '75
Murder Motel '74
The Witchmaker '69

Victor Millan
Boulevard Nights '79
Terror in a Texas Town '58
Touch of Evil '58

Ray Milland (1905-86)
Game for Vultures '86
Masks of Death '86
The Sea Serpent '85
Starflight One '83
Our Family Business '81
The Attic '80
Survival Run '80
Blackout '78
Cruise into Terror '78
Oil '78
Oliver's Story '78
The Uncanny '78
Slavers '77
Swiss Conspiracy '77
The Last Tycoon '76
Rich Man, Poor Man '76
The Dead Don't Die '75
Escape to Witch Mountain '75
Night of the Laughing Dead '75
Terror in the Wax Museum '73
Embassy '72
Frogs '72
The Thing with Two Heads '72
Quick, Let's Get Married '71
Love Story '70
X: The Man with X-Ray Eyes '63
Panic in the Year Zero! '62
Premature Burial '62
Lisbon '56
A Man Alone '55
Dial "M" for Murder '54
Bugles in the Afternoon '52
The Thief '52
Copper Canyon '50
A Life of Her Own '50
A Woman of Distinction '50
It Happens Every Spring '49
The Big Clock '48
Golden Earrings '47
The Lost Weekend '45
Ministry of Fear '44
The Uninvited '44
Forever and a Day '43
The Major and the Minor '42
Reap the Wild Wind '42
Star Spangled Rhythm '42
Doctor Takes a Wife '40
Beau Geste '39
Everything Happens at Night '39
Bulldog Drummond Escapes '37
Easy Living '37
Three Smart Girls '36
We're Not Dressing '34
Ambassador Bill '31
Blonde Crazy '31
The Flying Scotsman '29

Gregory Millar
Lethal Weapon 3 '92
Uncaged '91

Allan Miller
Warlock '91
Obsessive Love '84
Pearl '78

Andrew Miller
Cube '98
The Last of the Dogmen '95

Ann Miller (1919-)
Mulholland Drive '01
The Opposite Sex '56
Hit the Deck '55
Deep in My Heart '54
Kiss Me Kate '53
Small Town Girl '53
Lovely to Look At '52
Texas Carnival '51
Watch the Birdie '50
On the Town '49
Easter Parade '48
Melody Ranch '40
Too Many Girls '40
Room Service '38
You Can't Take It with You '38

Aubree Miller
The Ewoks: Battle for Endor '85
The Ewok Adventure '84

Barry Miller (1958-)
Flawless '99
Love Affair '94
The Pickle '93
Love at Large '89
The Last Temptation of Christ '88
Peggy Sue Got Married '86
Roommate '84
The Chosen '81
Fame '80
Saturday Night Fever '77

Bodil Miller
Reptilicus '62
Ma and Pa Kettle on Vacation '53

Charles Miller
Being Human '94
The Little Kidnappers '90

Charles F. Miller (-1955)
Call Northside 777 '48
Phantom of Chinatown '40

Cheryl Miller
Mountain Man '77
Dr. Death, Seeker of Souls '73
Clarence, the Cross-eyed Lion '65

Christa Miller
The Operator '01
Smiling Fish & Goat on Fire '99

C.T. Miller
Friend of the Family '95
Lap Dancing '95

David Keith Miller
Turn of the Blade '97
Playing Dangerous '95

Dax Miller
Blood Surf '00
The Convent '00

Dennis Miller (1953-)
Joe Dirt '01
Murder at 1600 '97
Tales from the Crypt Presents Bordello of Blood '96
The Net '95
Never Talk to Strangers '95
Disclosure '94
Madhouse '90
The Everlasting Secret Family '88
The Quest '86

Denny Miller
Buck and the Preacher '72
The Party '68

Dick Miller (1928-)
Small Soldiers '98
National Lampoon's Attack of the 5 Ft. 2 Women '94
Pulp Fiction '94
Shake, Rattle & Rock! '94
Tales from the Crypt Presents Demon Knight '94
Batman: Mask of the Phantasm '93 *(V)*
Fallen Angels 1 '93
Fallen Angels 2 '93
Amityville 1992: It's About Time '92
Body Waves '92
Matinee '92
Quake '92
Unlawful Entry '92
Motorama '91
Evil Toons '90
Gremlins 2: The New Batch '90
Far from Home '89
Under the Boardwalk '89
Amazon Women on the Moon '87
Innerspace '87
Project X '87
Chopping Mall '86
Night of the Creeps '86
After Hours '85
Explorers '85
Gremlins '84
The Terminator '84
All the Right Moves '83
Get Crazy '83
Heart Like a Wheel '83
Lies '83
Twilight Zone: The Movie '83
Heartbeeps '81
The Howling '81
Dr. Heckyl and Mr. Hype '80
Used Cars '80
Lady in Red '79
Rock 'n' Roll High School '79
Piranha '78
Starhops '78
New York, New York '77
Cannonball '76
Hollywood Boulevard '76
Crazy Mama '75
Big Bad Mama '74
Candy Stripe Nurses '74
Truck Turner '74
The Young Nurses '73
Night Call Nurses '72
The St. Valentine's Day Massacre '67
The Trip '67
The Wild Angels '66
The Terror '63
X: The Man with X-Ray Eyes '63
Premature Burial '62

Atlas '60
Little Shop of Horrors '60
A Bucket of Blood '59
Carnival Rock '57
Rock All Night '57
Sorority Girl '57
The Undead '57
The Gunslinger '56
It Conquered the World '56
Eve Miller (1923-73)
Kansas Pacific '53
April in Paris '52
Big Trees '52
The Winning Team '52
F.E. (Flourney) Miller (1887-1971)
Yes, Sir, Mr. Bones '51
Mystery in Swing '40
Bronze Buckaroo '39
Harlem Rides the Range '39
Harlem on the Prairie '38
Gabrielle Miller
The Silencer '99
Rupert's Land '98
Geri Miller
Trash '70
Flesh '68
Glenn Miller
Orchestra Wives '42
Sun Valley Serenade '41
Jason Miller (1939-2001)
Mommy '95
Murdered Innocence '94
Rudy '93
Small Kill '93
Exorcist 3: Legion '90
Light of Day '87
Vengeance '86
Toy Soldiers '84
Monsignor '82
That Championship Season '82
The Best Little Girl in the World '81
The Henderson Monster '80
Marilyn: The Untold Story '80
The Ninth Configuration '79
The Dain Curse '78
F. Scott Fitzgerald in Hollywood '76
A Home of Our Own '75
The Exorcist '73
Jean Miller
Speak of the Devil '90
Silent Night, Deadly Night 2 '87
Jennifer Miller
Terminal Impact '95
Never Say Die '94
Jeremy Miller (1976-)
The Willies '90
Emanon '86
John Miller
Hero Bunker '71
The Brave Bunch '70
Jonny Lee Miller (1974-)
Dracula 2000 '00
Love, Honour & Obey '00
Mansfield Park '99
Plunkett & Macleane '98
Retribution '98
Afterglow '97
Behind the Lines '97
Larry McMurtry's Dead Man's Walk '96
Hackers '95
Trainspotting '95
Joshua John Miller
And You Thought Your Parents Were Weird! '91
Class of 1999 '90
Teen Witch '89
Near Dark '87
River's Edge '87
Stoogemania '85
Kathleen Miller
Coming Home '78
Fighting Mad '76
Strange New World '75
Kelly Miller
Newsbreak '00

George of the Jungle '97
Kenny Miller
Bloodstalkers '76
Surf Party '64
Kristine Miller
High Lonesome '50
Too Late for Tears '49
Jungle Patrol '48
Larry Miller (1953-)
Max Keeble's Big Move '01
The Princess Diaries '01
What's the Worst That Could Happen? '01
Best in Show '00
Nutty Professor 2: The Klumps '00
The Big Tease '99
The Minus Man '99
Ten Things I Hate about You '99
Chairman of the Board '97
For Richer or Poorer '97
Dear God '96
Waiting for Guffman '96
Corrina, Corrina '94
Radioland Murders '94
Dream Lover '93
Undercover Blues '93
The Favor '92
Frozen Assets '92
Suburban Commando '91
Pretty Woman '90
Linda Miller (1942-)
Elvis and Me '88
Alice Sweet Alice '76
One Summer Love '76
Lorraine Miller (1922-78)
Lonesome Trail '55
White Gorilla '47
Ambush Trail '46
Border Badmen '45
Frontier Fugitives '45
Mark Miller (1953-)
Love Field '91
Savannah Smiles '82
Ginger in the Morning '73
Mark Thomas Miller
Mom '89
Blue De Ville '86
Misfits of Science '85
Martin Miller (1899-1969)
Bergonzi Hand '70
Children of the Damned '63
The Phantom of the Opera '62
Peeping Tom '60
Man on the Run '49
Frenzy '46
Hotel Reserve '44
Marvin Miller (1913-85)
Kiss Daddy Goodbye '81
The Day the Earth Froze '59 (N)
Sleeping Beauty '59 (V)
Forbidden Planet '56 (V)
Off Limits '53
Red Planet Mars '52
Dead Reckoning '47
Mary Louise Miller
The Night Cry '26
Sparrows '26
Mirta Miller (1948-)
Icebox Murders '80s
Dracula's Great Love '72
Dr. Jekyll and the Wolfman '71
Patsy Ruth Miller (1905-95)
Lonely Wives '31
So This Is Paris '26
Head Winds '25
The Hunchback of Notre Dame '23
The Sheik '21
Penelope Ann Miller (1964-)
Along Came a Spider '01
Along for the Ride '00
Full Disclosure '00
Rocky Marciano '99
The Break Up '98
Outside Ozona '98
Ruby Bridges '98

The Last Don '97
Little City '97
The Relic '96
The Shadow '94
Witch Hunt '94
Carlito's Way '93
Chaplin '92
The Gun in Betty Lou's Handbag '92
Year of the Comet '92
Other People's Money '91
Awakenings '90
The Freshman '90
Kindergarten Cop '90
Dead Bang '89
Downtown '89
Our Town '89
Big Top Pee-wee '88
Biloxi Blues '88
Miles from Home '88
Adventures in Babysitting '87
Percy (Master P) Miller (1970-)
Gone in 60 Seconds '00
Foolish '99
No Tomorrow '99
I Got the Hook-Up '98
Rebecca Miller
Mrs. Parker and the Vicious Circle '94
The Pickle '93
Consenting Adults '92
Wind '92
The Murder of Mary Phagan '87
Roger Miller (1936-92)
Lucky Luke '94 (V)
Robin Hood '73 (V)
Sarah Jane Miller
Mommy 2: Mommy's Day '96
Mommy '95
Sherry Miller
Tribulation '00
Sabrina the Teenage Witch '96
Rent-A-Kid '95
Sidney Miller (1916-)
There Goes Kelly '45
Men of Boys Town '41
Boys Town '38
Stephen E. Miller
Air Bud '97
Home Is Where the Hart Is '88
The Stepfather '87
Jane Doe '83
Ty Miller
Trancers 5: Sudden Deth '94
Trancers 4: Jack of Swords '93
Walter Miller (1892-1940)
Ghost Patrol '36
The Ivory Handled Gun '35
Law for Tombstone '35
Rustlers of Red Dog '35
Stone of Silver Creek '35
Tailspin Tommy '34
Blessed Event '32
The Lone Defender '32
Shadow of the Eagle '32
The Galloping Ghost '31
Andra Millian
Nightfall '88
Stacy's Knights '83
James Millican (1910-55)
The Winning Team '52
Man from Colorado '49
Rimfire '49
The Adventures of Gallant Bess '48
Spike Milligan (1918-2002)
Monty Python's Life of Brian '79
The Hound of the Baskervilles '77
Great McGonagall '75
Ghost in the Noonday Sun '74
Digby, the Biggest Dog in the World '73

Rentadick '72
The Magic Christian '69
The Case of the Mukkinese Battle Horn '56
Goon Movie '53
Down Among the Z Men '52
Angie Milliken
Paperback Hero '99
Dead Heart '96
Talk '94
Alley Mills (1951-)
Tainted Blood '93
Going Berserk '83
Rape and Marriage: The Rideout Case '80
Brooke Mills
Dream No Evil '75
The Student Teachers '73
The Big Doll House '71
Donna Mills (1942-)
False Arrest '92
The World's Oldest Living Bridesmaid '92
Runaway Father '91
Bunco '83
Waikiki '80
Curse of the Black Widow '77
Fire '77
The Hunted Lady '77
Beyond the Bermuda Triangle '75
Murph the Surf '75
Killer with Two Faces '74
One Deadly Owner '74
Haunts of the Very Rich '72
Play Misty for Me '71
The Incident '67
Eddie Mills
At Any Cost '00
The Tempest '99
Dancer, Texas—Pop. 81 '98
Heartwood '98
Grace Mills
Night of the Howling Beast '75
Exorcism '74
Hayley Mills (1946-)
A Troll in Central Park '94 (V)
Back Home '90
Appointment with Death '88
Deadly Strangers '82
The Flame Trees of Thika '81
Bananas Boat '78
Kingfisher Caper '76
Cry of the Penguins '71
Endless Night '71
Africa Texas Style '67
The Trouble with Angels '66
That Darn Cat '65
The Chalk Garden '64
The Moon-Spinners '64
Summer Magic '63
In Search of the Castaways '62
The Parent Trap '61
Whistle down the Wind '61
Pollyanna '60
Tiger Bay '59
John Mills (1908-)
Hamlet '96
Martin Chuzzlewit '94
Frankenstein '93
A Tale of Two Cities '91
Around the World in 80 Days '89
The Lady and the Highwayman '89
Who's That Girl? '87
Hold the Dream '86
Masks of Death '86
When the Wind Blows '86 (V)
A Woman of Substance '84
Sahara '83
Gandhi '82
Quatermass Conclusion '79
The Thirty-Nine Steps '79
Zulu Dawn '79
The Big Sleep '78
Dr. Strange '78
Choice of Weapons '76

The Human Factor '75
Lady Caroline Lamb '73
Oklahoma Crude '73
Young Winston '72
Ryan's Daughter '70
A Black Veil for Lisa '68
Africa Texas Style '67
Chuka '67
The Wrong Box '66
King Rat '65
Operation Crossbow '65
The Chalk Garden '64
Tiara Tahiti '62
The Swiss Family Robinson '60
Tunes of Glory '60
Tiger Bay '59
The Vicious Circle '57
Above Us the Waves '56
Around the World in 80 Days '56
The Baby and the Battleship '56
War and Peace '56
The Colditz Story '55
End of the Affair '55
Escapade '55
Hobson's Choice '53
The October Man '48
Scott of the Antarctic '48
This Happy Breed '47
Great Expectations '46
In Which We Serve '43
We Dive at Dawn '43
Cottage to Let '41
Goodbye, Mr. Chips '39
O.H.M.S. '37
Nine Days a Queen '36
The Ghost Camera '33
Judson Mills (1969-)
Chill Factor '99
Major League 3: Back to the Minors '98
Joyride '97
Juliet Mills (1941-)
The Other Sister '98
Waxwork 2: Lost in Time '91
The Cracker Factory '79
Alexander: The Other Side of Dawn '77
Barnaby and Me '77
Beyond the Door '75
QB VII '74
Jonathan Livingston Seagull '73
Avanti! '72
The Rare Breed '66
The October Man '48
Martin Milner (1927-)
Nashville Beat '89
The Seekers '79
Flood! '76
Hurricane '74
Columbo: Murder by the Book '71
Valley of the Dolls '67
Zebra in the Kitchen '65
13 Ghosts '60
Compulsion '59
Sweet Smell of Success '57
Francis in the Navy '55
Mister Roberts '55
Pete Kelly's Blues '55
I Want You '51
The Halls of Montezuma '50
Our Very Own '50
Sands of Iwo Jima '49
Life with Father '47
Jean-Roger Milo
Lucie Aubrac '98
L.627 '92
Sandra Milo (1935-)
Dead for a Dollar '70
Bang Bang Kid '67
Juliet of the Spirits '65
8 1/2 '63
Vanina Vanini '61
Generale Della Rovere '60
Herod the Great '60
Ernest Milton
Alice in Wonderland '50
The Scarlet Pimpernel '34
Mantoyo Mimasu
47 Ronin, Part 1 '42
47 Ronin, Part 2 '42

Yvette Mimieux (1939-)
Obsessive Love '84
Circle of Power '83
Night Partners '83
Forbidden Love '82
The Black Hole '79
Devil Dog: The Hound of Hell '78
Outside Chance '78
Snowbeast '77
Jackson County Jail '76
Legend of Valentino '75
Hit Lady '74
Journey into Fear '74
Neptune Factor '73
Dark of the Sun '68
Three in the Attic '68
Caper of the Golden Bulls '67
Monkeys, Go Home! '66
Toys in the Attic '63
Diamond Head '62
The Four Horsemen of the Apocalypse '62
The Wonderful World of the Brothers Grimm '62
Platinum High School '60
The Time Machine '60
Where the Boys Are '60
Christiane Minazolli
Betty '92
The Story of O '75
Esther Minciotti
Full of Life '56
Marty '55
Sal Mineo (1939-76)
Escape from the Planet of the Apes '71
Cheyenne Autumn '64
The Longest Day '62
Exodus '60
The Gene Krupa Story '59
Tonka '58
Dino '57
Giant '56
Rock, Pretty Baby '56
Somebody Up There Likes Me '56
The Private War of Major Benson '55
Rebel without a Cause '55
Jan Miner (1917-)
Mermaids '90
Willie & Phil '80
Lenny '74
Ming Na (1968-)
Final Fantasy: The Spirits Within '01 (V)
Mulan '98 (V)
One Night Stand '97
Hong Kong '97 '94
Star Quest '94
Street Fighter '94
The Joy Luck Club '93
Claudette Mink
Children of the Corn: Revelation '01
Deadly Heroes '96
Liza Minnelli (1946-)
Jackie's Back '99
Parallel Lives '94
Stepping Out '91
Arthur 2: On the Rocks '88
Rent-A-Cop '88
That's Dancing! '85
A Time to Live '85
The Muppets Take Manhattan '84
The Princess and the Pea '83
King of Comedy '82
Arthur '81
New York, New York '77
A Matter of Time '76
Silent Movie '76
Cabaret '72
Journey Back to Oz '71 (V)
The Sterile Cuckoo '69
In the Good Old Summertime '49
Kylie Minogue
Moulin Rouge '01
Cut '00
Bio-Dome '96
Street Fighter '94

The Enforcer '76
The Outlaw Josey Wales '76
Big Foot '72
Bloody Trail '72
The Devil's Sleep '51

Robert Mitchum (1917-97)
James Dean: Live Fast, Die Young '97
Dead Man '95
Backfire! '94
Tombstone '93 (N)
Woman of Desire '93
Midnight Ride '92
Cape Fear '91
Thompson's Last Run '90
The Brotherhood of the Rose '89
War & Remembrance: The Final Chapter '89
Mr. North '88
Scrooged '88
War & Remembrance '88
The Hearst and Davies Affair '85
North and South Book 1 '85
The Ambassador '84
Maria's Lovers '84
The Winds of War '83
One Shoe Makes It Murder '82
That Championship Season '82
The Agency '81
Nightkill '80
The Amsterdam Kill '78
The Big Sleep '78
Breakthrough '78
Matilda '78
The Last Tycoon '76
Midway '76
Farewell, My Lovely '75
The Yakuza '75
Ryan's Daughter '70
The Good Guys and the Bad Guys '69
Secret Ceremony '69
Anzio '68
Five Card Stud '68
Villa Rides '68
El Dorado '67
The Way West '67
The List of Adrian Messenger '63
The Longest Day '62
Two for the Seesaw '62
Cape Fear '61
The Grass Is Greener '61
Home from the Hill '60
The Sundowners '60
The Hunters '58
Thunder Road '58
Enemy Below '57
Fire Down Below '57
Heaven Knows, Mr. Allison '57
The Night of the Hunter '55
Not as a Stranger '55
River of No Return '54
Second Chance '53
The Lusty Men '52
Macao '52
One Minute to Zero '52
She Couldn't Say No '52
His Kind of Woman '51
My Forbidden Past '51
The Racket '51
Big Steal '49
Holiday Affair '49
The Red Pony '49
Blood on the Moon '48
Rachel and the Stranger '48
Crossfire '47
Out of the Past '47
Pursued '47
Till the End of Time '46
Undercurrent '46
The Story of G.I. Joe '45
West of the Pecos '45
Girl Rush '44
Nevada '44
Thirty Seconds Over Tokyo '44
Colt Comrades '43
False Colors '43
Gung Ho! '43
Hopalong Cassidy: Riders of the Deadline '43
Hoppy Serves a Writ '43
The Human Comedy '43
Leather Burners '43

Labina Mitevska
I Want You '98
Before the Rain '94

Rhona Mitra
Get Carter '00
Beowulf '98
A Kid in Aladdin's Palace '97

Koji Mitsui
Woman in the Dunes '64
The Hidden Fortress '58

Art Mix (1895-1972)
Yodelin' Kid from Pine Ridge '37
Powdersmoke Range '35
Rustlers of Red Dog '35
Way of the West '35
Border Devils '32
Mason of the Mounted '32

Ruth Mix (1912-77)
Custer's Last Stand '36
The Riding Avenger '36
The Tonto Kid '35

Tom Mix (1880-1940)
Justice Rides Again '30s
The Miracle Rider '35
Hidden Gold '33
Rustler's Roundup '33
Terror Trail '33
My Pal, the King '32
Texas Bad Man '32
Great K & A Train Robbery '26
Dick Turpin '25
Riders of the Purple Sage '25
Sky High '22
Trailin' '21
Child of the Prairie '18
Heart of Texas Ryan '16
In the Days of the Thundering Herd & the Law & the Outlaw '14

Jerod Mixon (1981-)
The New Guy '02
Me, Myself, and Irene '00

Seiji Miyaguchi (1913-85)
The Human Condition: No Greater Love '58
Seven Samurai '54
Early Summer '51

Kuniko Miyake
Good Morning '59
Early Summer '51

Nobuko Miyamoto (1945-)
Minbo—Or the Gentle Art of Japanese Extortion '92
A Taxing Woman's Return '88
A Taxing Woman '87
Tampopo '86
The Funeral '84

Eric Miyeni
Dangerous Ground '96
Cry, the Beloved Country '95

Kim Miyori
Metro '96
Body Shot '93
Hiroshima: Out of the Ashes '90
The Punisher '90
The Big Picture '89
When the Bough Breaks '86
John & Yoko: A Love Story '85

Eiko Miyoshi
The Hidden Fortress '58
Snow Country '57
I Live in Fear '55
Samurai 1: Musashi Miyamoto '55

Isaac Mizrahi
Hollywood Ending '02
Celebrity '98
For Love or Money '93

Kumi Mizuno (1937-)
War of the Gargantuas '70
Godzilla vs. Monster Zero '68
What's Up, Tiger Lily? '66
Attack of the Mushroom People '63

Genevieve Mnich
Beau Pere '81
The Mother and the Whore '73

Mary Ann Mobley (1939-)
Crazy Horse and Custer: "The Untold Story" '90
My Dog, the Thief '69
Girl Happy '65
Harum Scarum '65

Roger Mobley
Emil and the Detectives '64
Jack the Giant Killer '62

Tony Mockus, Sr.
Charming Billy '98
Backdraft '91

Jayne Modean
Street Hawk '84
Spring Break '83

Matthew Modine (1959-)
The American '01
In the Shadows '01
Jack and the Beanstalk: The Real Story '01
Any Given Sunday '99
The Maker '98
What the Deaf Man Heard '98
The Blackout '97
The Real Blonde '97
Cutthroat Island '95
Fluke '95
The Browning Version '94
Bye Bye, Love '94
Jacob '94
And the Band Played On '93
Equinox '93
Short Cuts '93
Wind '92
Memphis Belle '90
Pacific Heights '90
Gross Anatomy '89
The Gamble '88
Married to the Mob '88
Full Metal Jacket '87
Orphans '87
Vision Quest '85
Birdy '84
The Hotel New Hampshire '84
Mrs. Soffel '84
Private School '83
Streamers '83
Baby It's You '82

Gaston Modot (1887-1970)
Casque d'Or '52
Beauty and the Devil '50
Children of Paradise '44
The Rules of the Game '39
Grand Illusion '37
L'Age D'Or '30
Under the Roofs of Paris '29

Enrica Maria Modugno
The Story of Boys & Girls '91
Kaos '85

Ralph (Ralf) Moeller (1959-)
The Scorpion King '02
Gladiator '00
The Bad Pack '98
The Viking Sagas '95
Best of the Best 2 '93

Donald Moffat (1930-)
61* '01
Cookie's Fortune '99
The Evening Star '96
A Smile Like Yours '96
Clear and Present Danger '94
Is There Life Out There? '94
Trapped in Paradise '94
Armistead Maupin's Tales of the City '93
Love, Cheat & Steal '93
Housesitter '92
Teamster Boss: The Jackie Presser Story '92
Class Action '91
Regarding Henry '91
When the Time Comes '91
The Bonfire of the Vanities '90
Danielle Steel's Kaleidoscope '90
Music Box '89
The Bourne Identity '88
Far North '88
Necessary Parties '88
The Unbearable Lightness of Being '88
The Best of Times '86
Alamo Bay '85
License to Kill '84
The Right Stuff '83
The Thing '82
Jacqueline Bouvier Kennedy '81
The Long Days of Summer '80
On the Nickel '80
Mrs. R's Daughter '79
Promises in the Dark '79
Strangers: The Story of a Mother and Daughter '79
Winter Kills '79
Mary White '77
Showdown '73
The Great Northfield Minnesota Raid '72
Rachel, Rachel '68

D.W. Moffett (1954-)
Kill Me Later '01
Traffic '00
Molly '99
Stealing Beauty '96
The Little Death '95
Rough Magic '95
Falling Down '93
In the Deep Woods '91
Danielle Steel's Fine Things '90
Lisa '90
Black Widow '87
The Misfit Brigade '87
An Early Frost '85

Gregory Moffett
Robot Monster '53
Let's Dance '50

Michelle Moffett
Indecent Behavior '93
Deathstalker 4: Match of Titans '92
Wild Cactus '92
Hired to Kill '91

Sharyn Moffett
The Judge Steps Out '49
The Body Snatcher '45

Carl Mohner (1921-)
A Woman at Her Window '77
Wanted: Babysitter '75
Cave of the Living Dead '65
Sink the Bismarck '60
It Takes a Thief '59
The Last Bridge '54
Rififi '54

Gerald Mohr (1914-68)
The Angry Red Planet '59
Terror in the Haunted House '58
Duel at Silver Creek '52
Invasion U.S.A. '52
The Ring '52
Son of Ali Baba '52
Detective Story '51
Sirocco '51
Hunt the Man Down '50
The Monster and the Girl '41
Love Affair '39

Jay Mohr (1970-)
The Adventures of Pluto Nash '02
Simone '02
Dean Koontz's Black River '01
Cherry Falls '00
Pay It Forward '00
Go '99
From the Earth to the Moon '98
Mafia! '98
Paulie '98 (V)
Playing by Heart '98
Small Soldiers '98
200 Cigarettes '98
Suicide Kings '97
Jerry Maguire '96
Picture Perfect '96
For Better or Worse '95

Zia Mohyeddin
We Are the Children '87
Bombay Talkie '70

Richard Moir (1950-)
Welcome to Woop Woop '97
Wrangler '88
An Indecent Obsession '85
Remember Me '85
Heatwave '83
Panic Station '82
In Search of Anna '79
The Odd Angry Shot '79

Jose Mojica Marins (1929-)
Hallucinations of a Deranged Mind '70
Awakenings of the Beast '68
Strange World of Coffin Joe '68
At Midnight, I'll Take Your Soul '63

Karen Mok
Black Mask '96
Fallen Angels '95

Zakes Mokae (1935-)
Krippendorf's Tribe '98
Vampire in Brooklyn '95
Dust Devil '93
Percy & Thunder '93
Body Parts '91
A Rage in Harlem '91
Dad '89
A Dry White Season '89
Gross Anatomy '89
Cry Freedom '87
The Serpent and the Rainbow '87
The Comedians '67
A World of Strangers '62

Gretchen Mol (1973-)
The Magnificent Ambersons '02
Get Carter '00
The Cradle Will Rock '99
Forever Mine '99
Just Looking '99
Sweet and Lowdown '99
The Thirteenth Floor '99
Celebrity '98
Finding Graceland '98
New Rose Hotel '98
Rounders '98
Music from Another Room '97
Calm at Sunset '96
The Funeral '96
The Last Time I Committed Suicide '96

Karin Molander
Thomas Graal's First Child '18
Thomas Graal's Best Film '17

Jeff Moldovan
Trancers 5: Sudden Deth '94
Master Blaster '85

Alfred Molina (1953-)
Texas Rangers '01
Chocolat '00
The Miracle Maker: The Story of Jesus '00 (V)
Dudley Do-Right '99
The Imposters '98
Rescuers: Stories of Courage—Two Couples '98
Boogie Nights '97
The Man Who Knew Too Little '97
Leo Tolstoy's Anna Karenina '96
Mojave Moon '96
Scorpion Spring '96
Before and After '95
Dead Man '95
Species '95
Maverick '94
The Perez Family '94
White Fang 2: The Myth of the White Wolf '94
The Trial '93
When Pigs Fly '93
Enchanted April '92
American Friends '91
Not Without My Daughter '90
A Night of Love '87
Prick Up Your Ears '87
Letter to Brezhnev '86
Ladyhawke '85
Meantime '81
Raiders of the Lost Ark '81

Angela Molina (1955-)
Live Flesh '97
1492: Conquest of Paradise '92
Half of Heaven '86
Camorra: The Naples Connection '85
The Eyes, the Mouth '83
Demons in the Garden '82
That Obscure Object of Desire '77

Antonio Molina
Curse of the Devil '73
For Whom the Bell Tolls '43

Jacinto (Jack) Molina (1934-)
The Craving '80
Human Beasts '80
Inquisition '76
Night of the Howling Beast '75
People Who Own the Dark '75
The Devil's Possessed '74
Exorcism '74
Curse of the Devil '73
House of Psychotic Women '73
The Mummy's Revenge '73
The Rue Morgue Massacres '73
Dracula's Great Love '72
The Hanging Woman '72
Horror Rises from the Tomb '72
Vengeance of the Zombies '72
Dr. Jekyll and the Wolfman '71
The Fury of the Wolfman '70
The Werewolf vs. the Vampire Woman '70
Dracula vs. Frankenstein '69

Rolando Molina
crazy/beautiful '01
Next Friday '00

Charles Moll
Combat Academy '86
Night Train to Terror '84
Cataclysm '81

Georgia Moll
What a Way to Die '70
Contempt '64
Thief of Baghdad '61

Richard Moll (1943-)
Evolution '01
Scary Movie 2 '01
Boltneck '98
Dish Dogs '98
The Survivor '98
Living in Peril '97
The Glass Cage '96
The Secret Agent Club '96
Galaxis '95
Storybook '95
Beanstalk '94
The Flintstones '94
No Dessert Dad, 'Til You Mow the Lawn '94
Dream Date '93
National Lampoon's Loaded Weapon 1 '93
Sidekicks '93
Highlander: The Gathering '92
Driving Me Crazy '91

Blonde Venus '32
Dorothy Moore
Death Kiss '77
Blondie Meets the Boss '39
Dudley Moore (1935-2002)
A Weekend in the Country '96
The Disappearance of Kevin Johnson '95
Parallel Lives '94
The Pickle '93
Blame It on the Bellboy '92
Crazy People '90
The Adventures of Milo & Otis '89 (N)
Arthur 2: On the Rocks '88
Like Father, Like Son '87
Santa Claus: The Movie '85
Best Defense '84
Micki & Maude '84
Unfaithfully Yours '84
Lovesick '83
Romantic Comedy '83
Six Weeks '82
Arthur '81
Wholly Moses! '80
10 '79
Foul Play '78
The Hound of the Baskervilles '77
Those Daring Young Men in Their Jaunty Jalopies '69
Bedazzled '68
30 Is a Dangerous Age, Cynthia '68
The Wrong Box '66
Duke Moore (1913-76)
The Sinister Urge '60
Night of the Ghouls '59
Plan 9 from Outer Space '56
Frank Moore
Blood & Donuts '95
Hostage for a Day '94
Kings and Desperate Men '83
Rabid '77
Patchwork Girl of Oz '14
Gar Moore (1920-85)
The Underworld Story '50
Abbott and Costello Meet the Killer, Boris Karloff '49
Paisan '46
Ida Moore
Rock-A-Bye Baby '57
Money Madness '47
Jeanie Moore
Dream Trap '90
The Final Alliance '89
Vampire at Midnight '88
Joanna Moore (1934-97)
Scout's Honor '80
Iron Horsemen '71
The Dunwich Horror '70
Countdown '68
Never a Dull Moment '68
Son of Flubber '63
Follow That Dream '61
Monster on the Campus '59
Touch of Evil '58
Juanita Moore (1922-)
A Dream for Christmas '73
Foxstyle '73
The Singing Nun '66
Imitation of Life '59
The Girl Can't Help It '56
Julianne Moore (1961-)
Evolution '01
Hannibal '01
The Shipping News '01
World Traveler '01
The Ladies Man '00
Cookie's Fortune '99
The End of the Affair '99
An Ideal Husband '99
Magnolia '99
A Map of the World '99
Chicago Cab '98
Psycho '98
The Big Lebowski '97
Boogie Nights '97
The Lost World: Jurassic Park 2 '97
The Myth of Fingerprints '97
Surviving Picasso '96
Assassins '95
Nine Months '95
Roommates '95
Safe '95
Vanya on 42nd Street '94
Benny & Joon '93
The Fugitive '93
Short Cuts '93
Body of Evidence '92
The Gun in Betty Lou's Handbag '92
The Hand that Rocks the Cradle '92
Cast a Deadly Spell '91
Tales from the Darkside: The Movie '90
Kieron Moore (1925-)
Arabesque '66
The Thin Red Line '64
Day of the Triffids '63
Doctor Blood's Coffin '62
Darby O'Gill & the Little People '59
The Key '58
David and Bathsheba '51
Anna Karenina '48
A Man About the House '47
Mine Own Executioner '47
Mandy Moore (1984-)
A Walk to Remember '02
The Princess Diaries '01
Mary Moore
Murder at 1600 '97
D-Day on Mars '45
Mary Tyler Moore (1937-)
Labor Pains '99
Keys to Tulsa '96
Flirting with Disaster '95
The Last Best Year '90
Gore Vidal's Lincoln '88
Just Between Friends '86
Finnegan Begin Again '84
Six Weeks '82
Ordinary People '80
Change of Habit '69
Thoroughly Modern Millie '67
Matt Moore (1888-1960)
I Bury the Living '58
An Affair to Remember '57
That Forsyte Woman '50
Deluge '33
Consolation Marriage '31
Coquette '29
The Unholy Three '25
White Tiger '23
Pride of the Clan '18
20,000 Leagues under the Sea '16
Traffic in Souls '13
Melba Moore
All Dogs Go to Heaven '89 (V)
Charlotte Forten's Mission: Experiment in Freedom '85
Melissa Moore
Stormswept '95
Evil Lives '92
Sorority House Massacre 2: Nighty Nightmare '92
Hard to Die '90
The Invisible Maniac '90
The Killing Zone '90
Vampire Cop '90
Scream Dream '89
Michael Moore (1954-)
Lucky Numbers '00
The Insider '99
The Big One '98 (N)
Canadian Bacon '94
Roger & Me '89
Norma Moore
Poor White Trash 2 '75
Fear Strikes Out '57
Owen Moore (1886-1939)
She Done Him Wrong '33
As You Desire Me '32
Married? '26
Pauline Moore (1914-2001)
Carson City Kid '40
Young Buffalo Bill '40
Days of Jesse James '39
The Three Musketeers '39
Richard Moore
Human Bomb '97
Band of Gold '95
R.J. Moore
Fit to Kill '93
Hard Hunted '92
Roger Moore (1928-)
The Enemy '01
D.R.E.A.M. Team '99
Spice World: The Movie '97
The Quest '96
Bed & Breakfast '92
Fire, Ice and Dynamite '91
Bullseye! '90
A View to a Kill '85
The Naked Face '84
Octopussy '83
Cannonball Run '81
For Your Eyes Only '81
Sea Wolves '81
ffolkes '80
Escape to Athena '79
Moonraker '79
Wild Geese '78
The Spy Who Loved Me '77
Shout at the Devil '76
Street People '76
Overture '75
That Lucky Touch '75
The Man with the Golden Gun '74
Live and Let Die '73
The Man Who Haunted Himself '70
The Saint '68
Vendetta for the Saint '68
Fiction Makers '67
The Rape of the Sabines '61
Diane '55
Interrupted Melody '55
The King's Thief '55
The Last Time I Saw Paris '54
Rudy Ray Moore
Devil's Son-in-Law '77
Monkey Hustle '77
Avenging Disco Godfather '76
Dolemite 2: Human Tornado '76
Dolemite '75
Shemar Moore
The Brothers '01
Mama Flora's Family '98
Never 2 Big '98
Shiela Moore
The Reflecting Skin '91
Bye Bye Blues '89
Stephen Moore (1937-)
Prince of Poisoners: The Life and Crimes of William Palmer '98
Under Suspicion '92
Clockwise '86
Terry Moore (1929-)
Second Chances '98
Beverly Hills Brats '89
Death Blow '87
Hellhole '85
Kill Factor '78
Platinum High School '60
Peyton Place '57
Between Heaven and Hell '56
Postmark for Danger '56
Daddy Long Legs '55
Shack Out on 101 '55
Beneath the 12-Mile Reef '53
Come Back, Little Sheba '52
The Great Rupert '50
Mighty Joe Young '49
Gaslight '44
Since You Went Away '44
Victor Moore (1876-1962)
The Seven Year Itch '55
We're Not Married '52
On Our Merry Way '48
Ziegfeld Follies '46
The Heat's On '43
Star Spangled Rhythm '42
Louisiana Purchase '41
Swing Time '36
Agnes Moorehead (1906-74)
Charlotte's Web '73 (V)
Dear Dead Delilah '72
What's the Matter with Helen? '71
Bachelor in Paradise '69
The Ballad of Andy Crocker '69
Alice Through the Looking Glass '66
The Singing Nun '66
Hush, Hush, Sweet Charlotte '65
How the West Was Won '63
Who's Minding the Store? '63
Pollyanna '60
The Bat '59
Raintree County '57
The Conqueror '56
Meet Me in Las Vegas '56
The Opposite Sex '56
Pardners '56
All That Heaven Allows '55
The Left Hand of God '55
Magnificent Obsession '54
Main Street to Broadway '53
Adventures of Captain Fabian '51
Captain Blackjack '51
Show Boat '51
The Stratton Story '49
Johnny Belinda '48
Station West '48
Summer Holiday '48
Dark Passage '47
Lost Moment '47
Our Vines Have Tender Grapes '45
Dragon Seed '44
Jane Eyre '44
Mrs. Parkington '44
The Seventh Cross '44
Since You Went Away '44
Tomorrow the World '44
Big Street '42
Journey into Fear '42
The Magnificent Ambersons '42
Citizen Kane '41
Natalie Moorhead (1901-92)
The Thin Man '34
Dancing Man '33
The King Murder '32
Murder on the High Seas '32
Illicit '31
Morals for Women '31
Hook, Line and Sinker '30
Esai Morales (1962-)
Atomic Train '99
The Wonderful Ice Cream Suit '98
Dogwatch '97
The Real Thing '97
The Disappearance of Garcia Lorca '96
Scorpion Spring '96
The Burning Season '94
Deadlock 2 '94
Don't Do It '94
In the Army Now '94
My Family '94
Rapa Nui '93
Freejack '92
Naked Tango '91
Ultraviolet '91
Bloodhounds of Broadway '89
La Bamba '87
The Principal '87
On Wings of Eagles '86
L.A. Bad '85
Great Love Experiment '84
Bad Boys '83
Ines Morales
Curse of the Devil '73
House of Psychotic Women '73
Santos Morales
Hot to Trot! '88
The Boys in Company C '77
Dolores Moran (1924-82)
The Man I Love '46
The Horn Blows at Midnight '45
To Have & Have Not '44
Erin Moran (1960-)
Galaxy of Terror '81
Twirl '81
Watermelon Man '70
How Sweet It Is! '68
Frank Moran
Return of the Ape Man '44
Ships in the Night '28
Jackie Moran (1923-90)
There Goes Kelly '45
Since You Went Away '44
Let's Go Collegiate '41
The Gang's All Here '40
Old Swimmin' Hole '40
Tomboy '40
Buck Rogers Conquers the Universe '39
The Adventures of Tom Sawyer '38
Mad About Music '38
Lee Moran (1888-1961)
High Gear '33
Pardon My Gun '30
My Lady of Whims '25
The Tomboy '24
Nick Moran
The Musketeer '01
The Proposal '00
Rancid Aluminium '00
New Blood '99
Lock, Stock and 2 Smoking Barrels '98
Pat Moran
Desperate Living '77
Female Trouble '74
Pink Flamingos '72
Multiple Maniacs '70
Patrick Moran
Biohazard: The Alien Force '95
Dark Universe '93
Peggy Moran
The Mummy's Hand '40
One Night in the Tropics '40
Polly Moran
Adam's Rib '50
Hollywood Party '34
Rob Moran
Shallow Hal '01
Me, Myself, and Irene '00
There's Something about Mary '98
Kingpin '96
Dumb & Dumber '94
Rick Moranis (1954-)
Honey, We Shrunk Ourselves '97
Big Bully '95
The Flintstones '94
Little Giants '94
Splitting Heirs '93
Honey, I Blew Up the Kid '92
My Blue Heaven '90
Ghostbusters 2 '89
Honey, I Shrunk the Kids '89
Parenthood '89
Spaceballs '87
Club Paradise '86
Head Office '86
Little Shop of Horrors '86
Brewster's Millions '85
Ghostbusters '84
Hockey Night '84
The Last Polka '84
Streets of Fire '84
The Wild Life '84
Strange Brew '83
Richard Morant (1945-)
Scandal '89
John & Yoko: A Love Story '85
Poldark '75
Mahler '74
Milburn (Milt) Morante (1884-1964)
Ghost Rider '43
Between Men '35
Sherlock's Rivals & Where's My Wife '27
Wolf Blood '25
Kenneth More (1914-82)
A Tale of Two Cities '80
Unidentified Flying Oddball '79
Leopard in the Snow '78
Where Time Began '77
The Slipper and the Rose '76
Scrooge '70
Battle of Britain '69
Dark of the Sun '68
The Longest Day '62
Flame Over India '60
Sink the Bismarck '60
A Night to Remember '58
The Admirable Crichton '57
Reach for the Sky '56
The Adventures of Sadie '55
Doctor in the House '53
Genevieve '53
Never Let Me Go '53
The Clouded Yellow '51
No Highway in the Sky '51
Man on the Run '49
Scott of the Antarctic '48
Jeanne Moreau (1928-)
Balzac: A Life of Passion '99
Ever After: A Cinderella Story '98
I Love You, I Love You Not '97
The Proprietor '96
Beyond the Clouds '95
Catherine the Great '95
The Summer House '94
A Foreign Field '93
Map of the Human Heart '93
Alberto Express '92
The Lover '92 (N)
La Femme Nikita '91
The Old Lady Who Walked in the Sea '91
Until the End of the World '91
Heat of Desire '84
Your Ticket Is No Longer Valid '84
La Truite '83
Querelle '83
The Last Tycoon '76
Lumiere '76
Mr. Klein '76
Going Places '74
The Little Theatre of Jean Renoir '71
Alex in Wonderland '70
Monte Walsh '70
The Bride Wore Black '68
Chimes at Midnight '67
Oldest Profession '67
Mademoiselle '66
The Train '65
Viva Maria! '65
Diary of a Chambermaid '64
The Fire Within '64
The Trial '63
Eva '62
Jules and Jim '62
Dangerous Liaisons '60
The 400 Blows '59
The Lovers '59
Frantic '58
Back to the Wall '56
Grisbi '53
Marguerite Moreau
Firestarter 2: Rekindled '02
Queen of the Damned '02

Wet Hot American Summer '01
Marsha Moreau
The Last Winter '89
Miracle at Moreaux '86
Nathaniel Moreau
George's Island '91
The Last Winter '89
Sylvie Moreau
The Widow of Saint-Pierre '00
Post Mortem '99
Yolanda Moreau
Amelie '01
Vagabond '85
Elizabeth Morehead
Sand Trap '97
Interceptor '92
Mantan Moreland (1902-73)
The Young Nurses '73
Spider Baby '64
Juke Joint '47
Tall, Tan and Terrific '46
The Jade Mask '45
The Scarlet Clue '45
The Shanghai Cobra '45
Charlie Chan in the Secret Service '44
The Chinese Cat '44
Meeting at Midnight '44
Pin-Up Girl '44
Revenge of the Zombies '43
Footlight Serenade '42
Law of the Jungle '42
Phantom Killer '42
King of the Zombies '41
Let's Go Collegiate '41
The Gang's All Here '40
Up in the Air '40
Frontier Scout '38
Harlem on the Prairie '38
Next Time I Marry '38
Two-Gun Man from Harlem '38
The Spirit of Youth '37
Andre Morell (1909-78)
10 Rillington Place '71
Dark of the Sun '68
Plague of the Zombies '66
The Hound of the Baskervilles '59
Quatermass and the Pit '58
The Bridge on the River Kwai '57
The Baby and the Battleship '56
The Man Who Never Was '55
A Stolen Face '52
The Clouded Yellow '51
Madeleine '50
Antonio Moreno (1887-1967)
The Searchers '56
Creature from the Black Lagoon '54
Captain from Castile '47
Valley of the Sun '42
Rose of Rio Grande '38
It '27
Jose Elias Moreno
Night of the Bloody Apes '68
Santa Claus '59
Lea Moreno
Doom Runners '97
Jungle Boy '96
Rene L. Moreno
Band of Brothers '01
Tequila Body Shots '99
Rita Moreno (1931-)
Pinero '01
Blue Moon '00
Slums of Beverly Hills '98
The Spree '96
Angus '95
The Wharf Rat '95
I Like It Like That '94
Italian Movie '93
Age Isn't Everything '91
Portrait of a Showgirl '82
The Four Seasons '81
Happy Birthday, Gemini '80
Anatomy of a Seduction '79
Boss' Son '78
The Ritz '76
Carnal Knowledge '71
Marlowe '69
The Night of the Following Day '69
Popi '69
Cry of Battle '63
Summer and Smoke '61
West Side Story '61
The King and I '56
Seven Cities of Gold '55
The Ring '52
Singin' in the Rain '52
Pagan Love Song '50
The Toast of New Orleans '50
George Morfogen
Twenty Bucks '93
Deadly Business '86
Yuri Nosenko, KGB '86
Chesty Morgan
Double Agent 73 '80
Deadly Weapons '70
Cindy Morgan
Tron '82
Caddyshack '80
Clive Morgan
Gunga Din '39
The Lives of a Bengal Lancer '35
Debbi (Deborah) Morgan (1956-)
Love and Basketball '00
The Runaway '00
Asunder '99
The Hurricane '99
Eve's Bayou '97
Guilty of Innocence '87
The Jesse Owens Story '84
Monkey Hustle '77
Dennis Morgan (1910-94)
Pearl of the South Pacific '55
It's a Great Feeling '49
Christmas in Connecticut '45
Thank Your Lucky Stars '43
Captains of the Clouds '42
In This Our Life '42
The Fighting 69th '40
Kitty Foyle '40
Waterfront '39
The Great Ziegfeld '36
I Conquer the Sea '36
Frank Morgan (1890-1949)
Key to the City '50
Any Number Can Play '49
The Stratton Story '49
Summer Holiday '48
The Three Musketeers '48
Courage of Lassie '46
Casanova Brown '44
The White Cliffs of Dover '44
The Human Comedy '43
Thousands Cheer '43
Tortilla Flat '42
White Cargo '42
Honky Tonk '41
Boom Town '40
Broadway Melody of 1940 '40
The Mortal Storm '40
The Shop Around the Corner '40
Balalaika '39
Broadway Serenade '39
The Wizard of Oz '39
Rosalie '38
Sweethearts '38
The Last of Mrs. Cheyney '37
Saratoga '37
Dancing Pirate '36
Dimples '36
The Great Ziegfeld '36
I Live My Life '35
Naughty Marietta '35
The Cat and the Fiddle '34
Hallelujah, I'm a Bum '33
Manhandled '24
Gary Morgan
The Power Within '95
Storybook '95
Harry (Henry) Morgan (1915-)
The Incident '89
Dragnet '87
M*A*S*H: Goodbye, Farewell & Amen '83
Roughnecks '80
Scout's Honor '80
The Apple Dumpling Gang Rides Again '79
Better Late Than Never '79
Roots: The Next Generation '79
Wild, Wild West Revisited '79
The Bastard '78
The Cat from Outer Space '78
The Shootist '76
The Apple Dumpling Gang '75
Charley and the Angel '73
Snowball Express '72
The Barefoot Executive '71
Scandalous John '71
Support Your Local Gunfighter '71
Support Your Local Sheriff '69
Flim-Flam Man '67
What Did You Do in the War, Daddy? '66
Frankie and Johnny '65
How the West Was Won '63
Inherit the Wind '60
The Mountain Road '60
It Started with a Kiss '59
The Teahouse of the August Moon '56
Far Country '55
The Glenn Miller Story '54
Torch Song '53
Bend of the River '52
Boots Malone '52
High Noon '52
The Well '51
The Showdown '50
Holiday Affair '49
All My Sons '48
The Big Clock '48
Moonrise '48
The Gangster '47
State Fair '45
A Wing and a Prayer '44
Crash Dive '43
The Ox-Bow Incident '43
Orchestra Wives '42
To the Shores of Tripoli '42
Helen Morgan (1900-41)
Frankie and Johnny '36
Show Boat '36
Marie Galante '34
Applause '29
Jeffrey Dean Morgan (1966-)
Legal Deceit '95
Undercover '94
Uncaged '91
Melissa Morgan
Deadwood '65
Nasty Rabbit '64
Michele Morgan (1920-)
The Other Brother '02
Bulworth '98
Everybody's Fine '90
Cat and Mouse '78
The Lost Command '66
Bluebeard '63
Les Grandes Manoeuvres '55
The Proud Ones '53
The Fallen Idol '49
Fabiola '48
The Chase '46
La Symphonie Pastorale '46
Higher and Higher '44
Passage to Marseilles '44
Heart of a Nation '43
Joan of Paris '42
Stormy Waters '41
Nancy Morgan (1949-)
Lucky Luke '94
Danielle Steel's Heartbeat '93
The Nest '88
Pray TV '80
Americathon '79
Grand Theft Auto '77
Ralph Morgan (1882-1956)
Heart of the Rockies '51
The Creeper '48
Song of the Thin Man '47
Enemy of Women '44
The Monster Maker '44
Weird Woman/Frozen Ghost '44
Night Monster '42
Dick Tracy vs. Crime Inc. '41
Way Down South '39
Shadows over Shanghai '38
Mannequin '37
General Spanky '36
Yellowstone '36
Condemned to Live '35
Transatlantic Merry-Go-Round '34
The Kennel Murder Case '33
Rasputin and the Empress '33
Strange Interlude '32
Red Morgan
The Adventures of Buckaroo Banzai Across the Eighth Dimension '84
The Amazing Transparent Man '60
Richard Morgan
The Wicked '89
Innocent Prey '88
Shelley Taylor Morgan
Malibu Express '85
My Tutor '82
Stafford Morgan
Legend of Big Foot '82
The Capture of Bigfoot '79
The Alpha Incident '76
Terence Morgan (1921-)
The Lifetaker '89
Svengali '55
The Love of Three Queens '54
Tracy Morgan (1968-)
Half-Baked '97
A Thin Line Between Love and Hate '96
Trevor Morgan (1986-)
The Rookie '02
The Glass House '01
Jurassic Park 3 '01
A Rumor of Angels '00
I'll Remember April '99
The Sixth Sense '99
Barney's Great Adventure '98
In the Doghouse '98
Wendy Morgan
Pictures '80s
The Mirror Crack'd '80
Maia Morgenstern (1962-)
Ulysses' Gaze '95
The Oak '93
Trahir '93
Stephanie Morgenstern
P.T. Barnum '99
The Sweet Hereafter '96
John Morghen
Deadly Impact '84
Cannibal Apocalypse '80
Masayuki Mori (1911-73)
The Bad Sleep Well '60
When a Woman Ascends the Stairs '60
Princess Yang Kwei Fei '55
Ugetsu '53
The Idiot '51
Rashomon '51
The Men Who Tread on the Tiger's Tail '45
Toschia Mori
The Bitter Tea of General Yen '33
The Secrets of Wu Sin '32
Pat Moriarity
Kings Row '41
Mutiny in the Big House '39
Cathy Moriarty (1961-)
Prince of Central Park '00
But I'm a Cheerleader '99
Crazy in Alabama '99
The Crimson Code '99
New Waterford Girl '99
Digging to China '98
Gloria '98
P.U.N.K.S. '98
A Brother's Kiss '97
Cop Land '97
Dream with the Fishes '97
Hugo Pool '97
Foxfire '96
Opposite Corners '96
Casper '95
Forget Paris '95
Pontiac Moon '94
Another Stakeout '93
Me and the Kid '93
The Gun in Betty Lou's Handbag '92
The Mambo Kings '92
Matinee '92
Soapdish '91
Kindergarten Cop '90
Burndown '89
White of the Eye '88
Neighbors '81
Raging Bull '80
James Moriarty
Ten Benny '94
Someone to Watch Over Me '87
Michael Moriarty (1941-)
Along Came a Spider '01
James Dean '01
Mindstorm '01
Cold Blooded '00
The Art of Murder '99
Shiloh 2: Shiloh Season '99
Woman Wanted '98
Managua '97
Shiloh '97
Calm at Sunset '96
Courage Under Fire '96
Crime of the Century '96
A Good Day to Die '95
Full Fathom Five '90
Secret of the Ice Cave '89
Tailspin: Behind the Korean Airline Tragedy '89
Nitti: The Enforcer '88
Windmills of the Gods '88
Dark Tower '87
Hanoi Hilton '87
It's Alive 3: Island of the Alive '87
Return to Salem's Lot '87
Bloodlink '86
Troll '86
Odd Birds '85
Pale Rider '85
The Stuff '85
Q (The Winged Serpent) '82
Sound of Murder '82
Too Far to Go '79
Holocaust '78
Reborn '78
Who'll Stop the Rain? '78
The Winds of Kitty Hawk '78
Report to the Commissioner '74
Shoot It Black, Shoot It Blue '74
Bang the Drum Slowly '73
The Last Detail '73
My Old Man's Place '71
P. H. Moriarty
Dune '00
Lock, Stock and 2 Smoking Barrels '98
The Long Good Friday '80
Tara Morice
Sorrento Beach '95
Strictly Ballroom '92
Philippe Morier-Genoud
Trois Couleurs: Blanc '94
Cyrano de Bergerac '90
Au Revoir les Enfants '87
Confidentially Yours '83
Johnny Morina
Home Team '98
Kids of the Round Table '96
The Boys of St. Vincent '93
Patricia Morison (1914-)
Song Without End '60
The Prince of Thieves '48
Return of Wildfire '48
Queen of the Amazons '47
Song of the Thin Man '47
Dressed to Kill '46
Without Love '45
Calling Dr. Death/Strange Confession '43
The Fallen Sparrow '43
Alanis Morissette
Jay and Silent Bob Strike Back '01
Dogma '99
Noriyuki "Pat" Morita (1932-)
Desert Heat '99
I'll Remember April '99
King Cobra '98
Mulan '98 (V)
Bloodsport 2: The Next Kumite '95
Bloodsport 3 '95
Timemaster '95
Even Cowgirls Get the Blues '94
The Next Karate Kid '94
North '94
Auntie Lee's Meat Pies '92
Honeymoon in Vegas '92
Miracle Beach '92
Do or Die '91
Hiroshima: Out of the Ashes '90
Lena's Holiday '90
Collision Course '89
The Karate Kid: Part 3 '89
Captive Hearts '87
Babes in Toyland '86
The Karate Kid: Part 2 '86
Amos '85
Night Patrol '85
The Karate Kid '84
Slapstick of Another Kind '84
The Vegas Strip Wars '84
For the Love of It '80
When Time Ran Out '80
Cancel My Reservation '72
Evil Roy Slade '71
The Shakiest Gun in the West '68
Thoroughly Modern Millie '67
Louisa Moritz (1946-)
Chained Heat '83
Last American Virgin '82
True Confessions '81
New Year's Evil '78
Death Race 2000 '75
One Flew Over the Cuckoo's Nest '75
Henning Moritzen (1928-)
The Celebration '98
Sofie '92
Memories of a Marriage '90
Cries and Whispers '72
Yuko Moriyama
Zeram 2 '94
Zeram '91
Karen Morley (1905-)
Beloved Enemy '36
Healer '36
The Littlest Rebel '35
Our Daily Bread '34
Dinner at Eight '33
Gabriel Over the White House '33
The Mask of Fu Manchu '32
Mata Hari '32

Scarface '31
The Sin of Madelon Claudet '31

Robert Morley (1908-92)

A Troll in Central Park '94 (V)
Istanbul '90
Around the World in 80 Days '89
The Lady and the Highwayman '89
War & Remembrance: The Final Chapter '89
Little Dorrit, Film 1: Nobody's Fault '88
Little Dorrit, Film 2: Little Dorrit's Story '88
War & Remembrance '88
The Trouble with Spies '87
The Wind '87
Second Time Lucky '84
High Road to China '83
Loophole '83
Deadly Game '82
The Great Muppet Caper '81
Oh, Heavenly Dog! '80
The Human Factor '79
Scavenger Hunt '79
Who Is Killing the Great Chefs of Europe? '78
Hugo the Hippo '76 (V)
Theatre of Blood '73
Cromwell '70
Song of Norway '70
Lola '69
Hot Millions '68
Woman Times Seven '67
A Study in Terror '66
The Alphabet Murders '65
The Loved One '65
Those Magnificent Men in Their Flying Machines '65
Of Human Bondage '64
Topkapi '64
Ladies Who Do '63
Murder at the Gallop '63
The Battle of the Sexes '60
Around the World in 80 Days '56
Beau Brummel '54
Beat the Devil '53
Curtain Up '53
The African Queen '51
The Small Back Room '49
Ghosts of Berkeley Square '47
I Live in Grosvenor Square '46
The Foreman Went to France '42
Major Barbara '41
Marie Antoinette '38

Alicia Moro

Hot Blood '89
Slugs '87
Exterminators in the Year 3000 '83

Mike Moroff

The Crew '00
My Little Assassin '99
The Wonderful Ice Cream Suit '98
Angel Town '89
The Cage '89

Priscilla Morrill (1927-94)

Right of Way '84
The People vs. Jean Harris '81

Adrian Morris

Angels with Dirty Faces '38
Radio Patrol '37

Anita Morris (1944-94)

Radioland Murders '94
Home for Christmas '93
Me and the Kid '93
Martians Go Home! '90
Off and Running '90
Bloodhounds of Broadway '89
A Sinful Life '89
Aria '88
18 Again! '88
Absolute Beginners '86
Blue City '86
Ruthless People '86
A Smoky Mountain Christmas '86
The Hotel New Hampshire '84
Maria's Lovers '84

Aubrey Morris

She Creature '01
Lifeforce '85
Lisztomania '75
A Clockwork Orange '71
Night Caller from Outer Space '66

Barboura Morris (1975-)

The Dunwich Horror '70
The St. Valentine's Day Massacre '67
The Trip '67
The Haunted Palace '63
X: The Man with X-Ray Eyes '63
Atlas '60
A Bucket of Blood '59
The Wasp Woman '59
Machine Gun Kelly '58
Sorority Girl '57
Teenage Doll '57

Beth Morris

That'll Be the Day '73
Crucible of Terror '72

Chester Morris (1901-70)

The Great White Hope '70
Gambler's Choice '44
Wagon's Westward '40
Five Came Back '39
Law of the Underworld '38
Flight from Glory '37
Frankie and Johnny '36
Tomorrow at Seven '33
Red Headed Woman '32
Corsair '31
The Bat Whispers '30
The Big House '30
The Divorcee '30
Alibi '29

Colleen Morris

Prehysteria '93
Crossing the Line '90

Dorothy Morris (1922-)

Club Havana '46
Thirty Seconds Over Tokyo '44
Bataan '43

Garrett Morris (1944-)

Jackpot '01
Twin Falls Idaho '99
Black Scorpion 2: Ground Zero '96
Santa with Muscles '96
Black Scorpion '95
Machine Gun Blues '95
Almost Blue '93
Children of the Night '92
Severed Ties '92
Motorama '91
The Underachievers '88
Husbands, Wives, Money, and Murder '86
The Stuff '85
Cooley High '75
The Anderson Tapes '71
Where's Poppa? '70

Greg Morris (1934-96)

Vegas '78
The Doomsday Flight '66

Haviland (Haylie) Morris (1959-)

Home Alone 3 '97
Larry McMurtry's Dead Man's Walk '96
Gremlins 2: The New Batch '90
For Love or Money '88
Love or Money? '88
Who's That Girl? '87
Sixteen Candles '84

Howard Morris (1919-)

The Wonderful Ice Cream Suit '98
It Came from Outer Space 2 '95
Tom and Jerry: The Movie '93 (V)
Life Stinks '91
End of the Line '88
Splash '84
Portrait of a Showgirl '82
History of the World: Part 1 '81
The Munsters' Revenge '81
High Anxiety '77
The Nutty Professor '63
40 Pounds of Trouble '62

Jane Morris

Pet Shop '94
Frankie and Johnny '91
Pretty Woman '90
Nothing in Common '86

Jeff Morris

The Crossing Guard '94
Payday '72
Kelly's Heroes '70

John Morris

Toy Story 2 '99 (V)
Toy Story '95 (V)
Beyond Innocence '87

Jonathan Morris

Bloodstorm: Subspecies 4 '98
Vampire Journals '96
The Fantasticks '95

Judy Morris (1947-)

Best Enemies '86
Phar Lap '84
Razorback '84
In Search of Anna '79
Plumber '79
Cass '78
Between Wars '74

Kathryn Morris

Inherit the Wind '99
Sleepstalker: The Sandman's Last Rites '94

Kirk Morris

Terror of the Steppes '64
Devil of the Desert Against the Son of Hercules '62
Maciste in Hell '60

Lana Morris (1930-98)

The Woman in Question '50
The Gay Lady '49
The Weaker Sex '49

Mary Morris (1915-88)

Train of Events '49
Pimpernel Smith '42
The Thief of Bagdad '40

Phil Morris (1958-)

Atlantis: The Lost Empire '01 (V)
Clay Pigeons '98
Devil in the Flesh '98
Legal Deceit '95

Robert Morris

One Deadly Owner '74
Frankenstein Created Woman '66

Wayne Morris (1914-59)

Paths of Glory '57
Plunder Road '57
The Bushwackers '52
Task Force '49
Kid Galahad '37

Jenny Morrison

Urban Legends 2: Final Cut '00
Stir of Echoes '99
Intersection '93

Joe Morrison

The Checkered Flag '63
Love in Bloom '35

Kenny Morrison

NeverEnding Story 2: The Next Chapter '91
The Quick and the Dead '87

Peter Morrison

Trailing Trouble '30
Trigger Tricks '30

Sammy (Earnest) Morrison (1912-89)

Follow the Leader '44
Let's Get Tough '42
'Neath Brooklyn Bridge '42
Flying Wild '41
Spooks Run Wild '41

Shelly Morrison

Devil Times Five '74
Castle of Evil '66

Temuera Morrison (1961-)

Star Wars: Episode 2—Attack of the Clones '02
Vertical Limit '00
From Dusk Till Dawn 3: The Hangman's Daughter '99
Six Days, Seven Nights '98
Speed 2: Cruise Control '97
Barb Wire '96
The Island of Dr. Moreau '96
Once Were Warriors '94

David Morrissey (1963-)

Captain Corelli's Mandolin '01
Born Romantic '00
Robert Louis Stevenson's The Game of Death '99
Hilary and Jackie '98
Our Mutual Friend '98
Framed '93
Cause Celebre '87

Eamon Morrissey

The Seventh Stream '01
Eat the Peach '86

Neil Morrissey

The Match '99
A Woman's Guide to Adultery '93

Jeff Morrow (1913-93)

Blood Legacy '73
Octaman '71
The Story of Ruth '60
The Giant Claw '57
Hour of Decision '57
Kronos '57
The Creature Walks among Us '56
Pardners '56
This Island Earth '55
The Robe '53

Jo Morrow (1940-)

Dr. Death, Seeker of Souls '73
13 Ghosts '60
Legend of Tom Dooley '59
The Three Worlds of Gulliver '59

Mari Morrow

Uninvited Guest '99
Dead Man on Campus '97
Def Jam's How to Be a Player '97
Children of the Corn 3: Urban Harvest '95

Neyle Morrow

China Gate '57
The Steel Helmet '51

Patricia Morrow

Surf Party '64
The Kettles on Old MacDonald's Farm '57

Rob Morrow (1962-)

Maze '01
Labor Pains '99
Only Love '98
Last Dance '96
Mother '96
Quiz Show '94
Private Resort '84

Susan Morrow

Battle Cry '55
Cat Women of the Moon '53

Vic Morrow (1932-82)

1990: The Bronx Warriors '83
Twilight Zone: The Movie '83
B.A.D. Cats '80
Humanoids from the Deep '80
The Evictors '79
Express to Terror '79
The Seekers '79
Wild & Wooly '78
Curse of the Black Widow '77
Funeral for an Assassin '77
The Bad News Bears '76
The Treasure of Matecumbe '76
Wanted: Babysitter '75
Death Stalk '74
Dirty Mary Crazy Larry '74
The Adventures of Tom Sawyer '73
The Glass House '72
Cimarron '60
God's Little Acre '58
King Creole '58
Men in War '57
Tribute to a Bad Man '56
Blackboard Jungle '55

Barry Morse (1918-)

Anne of Green Gables: The Continuing Story '99
Glory! Glory! '90
Sadat '83
Whoops Apocalypse '83
Power Play '81
The Changeling '80
A Tale of Two Cities '80
The Martian Chronicles: Part 2 '79
The Martian Chronicles: Part 3 '79
Welcome to Blood City '77
Love at First Sight '76
Destination Moonbase Alpha '75
Asylum '72
The Golden Bowl '72
No Trace '50

David Morse (1953-)

Hearts in Atlantis '01
Bait '00
Proof of Life '00
Crazy in Alabama '99
Dancer in the Dark '99
The Green Mile '99
The Negotiator '98
Contact '97
The Long Kiss Goodnight '96
The Rock '96
Stephen King's The Langoliers '95
Tecumseh: The Last Warrior '95
12 Monkeys '95
The Crossing Guard '94
The Getaway '93
The Good Son '93
Dead Ahead: The Exxon Valdez Disaster '92
The Indian Runner '91
Desperate Hours '90
The Brotherhood of the Rose '89
Shattered Vows '84
Prototype '83
Inside Moves '80

Helen Morse (1946-)

Iris '89
Far East '85
A Town Like Alice '85
Agatha '79
Caddie '76
Picnic at Hanging Rock '75

Laila Morse

Love, Honour & Obey '00
Great Expectations '99
Nil by Mouth '96

Robert Morse (1931-)

Wild Palms '93
The Boatniks '70
Where Were You When the Lights Went Out? '68
A Guide for the Married Man '67
How to Succeed in Business without Really Trying '67
Oh Dad, Poor Dad (Momma's Hung You in the Closet & I'm Feeling So Sad) '67
The Loved One '65
The Matchmaker '58

Robin Morse

Rock All Night '57
Marty '55

Glenn Morshower (1959-)

Black Hawk Down '01
Pearl Harbor '01
The Jack Bull '99
My Little Assassin '99
Dominion '94
84 Charlie MoPic '89
Drive-In '76

Viggo Mortensen (1958-)

Lord of the Rings 1: The Fellowship of the Rings '01
28 Days '00
A Walk on the Moon '99
A Perfect Murder '98
Psycho '98
G.I. Jane '97
Albino Alligator '96
Daylight '96
Portrait of a Lady '96
The Crew '95
Crimson Tide '95
The Passion of Darkly Noon '95
The Prophecy '95
American Yakuza '94
Boiling Point '93
Carlito's Way '93
The Young Americans '93
Deception '92
The Indian Runner '91
The Reflecting Skin '91
Young Guns 2 '90
Leatherface: The Texas Chainsaw Massacre 3 '89
Fresh Horses '88
Prison '88
Salvation! '87
Witness '85

Janne Mortil

Johnny's Girl '95
Tokyo Cowboy '94
Nightmare at Bittercreek '91

Emily Mortimer (1971-)

Lovely & Amazing '02
Disney's The Kid '00
Love's Labour's Lost '00
Scream 3 '00
Cider with Rosie '99
Noah's Ark '99
Coming Home '98
Elizabeth '98
The Saint '97
The Ghost and the Darkness '96
The Last of the High Kings '96
Catherine Cookson's The Glass Virgin '95
Sharpe's Sword '94

Clive Morton (1904-75)

Cop-Out '67
A Matter of WHO '62
Lucky Jim '58
The Moonraker '58
Kind Hearts and Coronets '49

Joe Morton (1947-)

Dragonfly '02
Ali '01
Bounce '00
What Lies Beneath '00
The Astronaut's Wife '99
Mutiny '99
Blues Brothers 2000 '98
Apt Pupil '97
Miss Evers' Boys '97
Speed 2: Cruise Control '97
Executive Decision '96
The Pest '96
Lone Star '95
The Inkwell '94
Speed '94
The Walking Dead '94
Forever Young '92
Legacy of Lies '92
Of Mice and Men '92
City of Hope '91
Terminator 2: Judgment Day '91
Skin '89
Tap '89
The Good Mother '88
Zelly & Me '88

Alone in the Neon Jungle '87
Crossroads '86
Trouble in Mind '86
The Brother from Another Planet '84

Samantha Morton (1977-)
Minority Report '02
Pandaemonium '00
Dreaming of Joseph Lees '99
Jesus' Son '99
Sweet and Lowdown '99
Tom Jones '98
Emma '97
Jane Eyre '97
Under the Skin '97
This Is the Sea '96
Band of Gold '95
Cracker: The Big Crunch '94

Gastone Moschin (1929-)
A Joke of Destiny, Lying in Wait Around the Corner Like a Bandit '84
A Woman at Her Window '77
Mr. Superinvisible '73
The Conformist '71

Maurice (Moscovitch) Moscovich (1871-1940)
The Great Commandment '41
The Great Dictator '40
Everything Happens at Night '39
Love Affair '39

David Moscow (1974-)
Riding in Cars with Boys '01
Loving Jezebel '99
Restaurant '98
River Red '98
Newsies '92
Big '88

Bill Moseley (1957-)
The Convent '00
Crash and Burn '90
Night of the Living Dead '90
Fair Game '89
Silent Night, Deadly Night 3: Better Watch Out! '89
The Texas Chainsaw Massacre 2 '86
Osa '85

David Moses (1962-)
Storm Tracker '99
Scared to Death '80
Daring Dobermans '73

Harry Moses
Sweater Girls '78
The Van '77

Marian Moses
Buona Sera, Mrs. Campbell '68
Dead Heat on a Merry-Go-Round '66

Mark Moses
One Man's Hero '98
Rough Riders '97
A Kiss Goodnight '94
Gettysburg '93
Dead Men Don't Die '91
Hollywood Heartbreak '89
The Tracker '88
Platoon '86

William R. Moses (1959-)
Chain of Command '00
Missing Pieces '00
The Perfect Wife '00
Alone with a Stranger '99
Wicked '98
The Nurse '97
Evil Has a Face '96
The Fiance '96
Circumstances Unknown '95
Almost Dead '94
Fun '94
The Haunting of Seacliff Inn '94
Double Exposure '93
Mystic Pizza '88
Alien from L.A. '87

Roger E. Mosley (1944-)
Letters from a Killer '98
A Thin Line Between Love and Hate '96
Pentathlon '94
Unlawful Entry '92
Heart Condition '90
Attica '80
Magnum P.I.: Don't Eat the Snow in Hawaii '80
Pray TV '80
Steel '80
I Know Why the Caged Bird Sings '79
The Jericho Mile '79
The Greatest '77
The River Niger '76
Darktown Strutters '74
The Mack '73

Arnold Moss (1910-89)
The Fool Killer '65
The 27th Day '57
Viva Zapata! '52
Reign of Terror '49
The Loves of Carmen '48

Bertha Moss
The Exterminating Angel '62
Invasion of the Vampires '61

Carrie-Anne Moss (1970-)
Chocolat '00
The Crew '00
Memento '00
Red Planet '00
The Matrix '99
New Blood '99
Lethal Tender '96
The Soft Kill '94

Elissabeth (Elisabeth, Elizabeth, Liz) Moss (1983-)
Earthly Possessions '99
Girl, Interrupted '99
Mumford '99
A Thousand Acres '97
Imaginary Crimes '94
Separate Lives '94
Midnight's Child '93

Ron Moss
Hard Ticket to Hawaii '87
Hearts & Armour '83

Stewart Moss (1938-)
The Bat People '74
Dr. Death, Seeker of Souls '73
In Harm's Way '65

Donny Most (1953-)
EDtv '99
Acting on Impulse '93
Crazy Mama '75
Huckleberry Finn '75

Josh Mostel (1946-)
Big Daddy '99
Rounders '98
Great Expectations '97
The Maddening '95
The Basketball Diaries '94
Billy Madison '94
City Slickers 2: The Legend of Curly's Gold '94
The Chase '93
City of Hope '91
City Slickers '91
Little Man Tate '91
Animal Behavior '89
Heavy Petting '89
Matewan '87
Radio Days '87
Wall Street '87
The Money Pit '86
Almost You '85
Compromising Positions '85
Stoogemania '85
Windy City '84
Star 80 '83
Sophie's Choice '82
Deadly Hero '75
Harry and Tonto '74
Jesus Christ, Superstar '73
The King of Marvin Gardens '72

Zero Mostel (1915-77)
Watership Down '78 (V)
The Front '76
Foreplay '75
Journey into Fear '74
Marco '73
Master Mind '73
Once Upon a Scoundrel '73
The Angel Levine '70
The Hot Rock '70
The Producers '68
A Funny Thing Happened on the Way to the Forum '66
The Enforcer '51
Sirocco '51
Panic in the Streets '50
DuBarry Was a Lady '43

Zeze Motta (1944-)
Orfeu '99
Tieta of Agreste '96
Quilombo '84
Xica '76

Greg Mottola
Hollywood Ending '02
Celebrity '98

John Moulder-Brown (1953-)
Rumpelstiltskin '86
Killing Heat '84
King, Queen, Knave '72
Vampire Circus '71
Deep End '70
First Love '70

Anson Mount
Crossroads '02
Urban Legends 2: Final Cut '00

Moustache
Beyond Fear '75
Zorro '74

Movita (1916-)
Panic in Echo Park '77
Tower of Terror '42
Wolf Call '39
Rose of Rio Grande '38
Mutiny on the Bounty '35

Alan Mowbray (1896-1969)
The King and I '56
A Majority of One '56
The Man Who Knew Too Much '56
The King's Thief '55
Ma and Pa Kettle at Home '54
Abbott and Costello Meet the Killer, Boris Karloff '49
The Lovable Cheat '49
My Dear Secretary '49
The Prince of Thieves '48
Captain from Castile '47
Lured '47
Merton of the Movies '47
My Darling Clementine '46
Terror by Night '46
The Phantom of 42nd Street '45
His Butler's Sister '44
So This Is Washington '43
Panama Hattie '42
I Wake Up Screaming '41
That Hamilton Woman '41
That Uncertain Feeling '41
The Villain Still Pursued Her '41
Music in My Heart '40
Never Say Die '39
Topper Takes a Trip '39
Way Down South '39
On the Avenue '37
Stand-In '37
Vogues of 1938 '37
Desire '36
It Happened in New Orleans '36
Mary of Scotland '36
My Man Godfrey '36
In Person '35
The Girl from Missouri '34
A Study in Scarlet '33

Jack Mower (1890-1965)
The Fiddlin' Buckaroo '33
Mystery Squadron '33
Ships in the Night '28

Patrick Mower (1940-)
Carry On England '76
Catch Me a Spy '71
The Bloodsuckers '70
Cry of the Banshee '70
The Devil Rides Out '68

Stephen Moyer
Princess of Thieves '01
Uprising '01
Catherine Cookson's The Secret '00
Comic Act '98
Ultraviolet '98
Prince Valiant '97

Bridget Moynahan (1972-)
The Sum of All Fears '02
Serendipity '01
Coyote Ugly '00

David Mucci
Unforgiven '92
Prom Night '80

Leonard Mudie
British Intelligence '40
The Mummy '32

Cookie Mueller (1949-89)
Polyester '81
Desperate Living '77
Female Trouble '74
Pink Flamingos '72
Multiple Maniacs '70

Maureen Mueller
Larger Than Life '96
Oldest Confederate Widow Tells All '95
The New Age '94
In a Shallow Grave '88

Armin Mueller-Stahl (1930-)
Jesus '00
Inferno '99
Jakob the Liar '99
The Third Miracle '99
The Thirteenth Floor '99
The X-Files '98
The Assistant '97
The Game '97
In the Presence of Mine Enemies '97
The Peacemaker '97
Twelve Angry Men '97
The Ogre '96
A Pyromaniac's Love Story '95
Red Hot '95
Shine '95
Theodore Rex '95
Holy Matrimony '94
The Last Good Time '94
The House of the Spirits '93
Utz '93
The Power of One '92
Kafka '91
Night on Earth '91
Avalon '90
Music Box '89
Midnight Cop '88
Lethal Obsession '87
Angry Harvest '85
Forget Mozart '85
Colonel Redl '84
A Love in Germany '84
Jacob the Liar '74
The Third '72
Five Cartridges '60

Marianne Muellerleile
Return to Me '00
A Smile Like Yours '96
Curse 2: The Bite '88
The Trouble with Dick '88

Amanda Muggleton
Idiot Box '97
Queen of the Road '84

Ulrich Muhe
Straight Shooter '99
Funny Games '97

Anita (Yim-Fong) Mui (1963-)
Rumble in the Bronx '96
Jet Li's The Enforcer '95
The Legend of Drunken Master '94
The Executioners '93
The Heroic Trio '93
A Better Tomorrow, Part 3 '89
Miracles '89

Esther Muir (1903-95)
Misbehaving Husbands '41
A Day at the Races '37
Racing Luck '35

Gavin Muir (1900-72)
Night Tide '63
Abbott and Costello Meet the Invisible Man '51
O.S.S. '46
House of Fear '45
Sherlock Holmes Faces Death '43
Mary of Scotland '36

Oliver Muirhead
MVP (Most Valuable Primate) '00
The Duke '99

Majhabi Mukherjee
Charulata '64
The Big City '63

Diana Muldaur (1938-)
Return of Frank Cannon '80
Beyond Reason '77
McQ '74
Planet Earth '74
The Other '72

Patrick Muldoon (1969-)
Hell's Gate '01
Chain of Command '00
The Crimson Code '99
Stigmata '99
The Arrival 2 '98
Black Cat Run '98
Wicked '98
Starship Troopers '97
Rage and Honor 2: Hostile Takeover '93

Nancy Mulford
Act of Piracy '89
Skeleton Coast '89

Kate Mulgrew (1955-)
Captain Nuke and the Bomber Boys '95
Camp Nowhere '94
Danielle Steel's Daddy '91
Round Numbers '91
Roots: The Gift '88
Throw Momma from the Train '87
Remo Williams: The Adventure Begins '85
A Stranger Is Watching '82
The Manions of America '81
A Time for Miracles '80
Lovespell '79
The Word '78

Jack Mulhall (1887-1979)
'Neath Canadian Skies '46
North of the Border '46
Dawn Express '42
I Killed That Man '42
Mr. Wise Guy '42
Desperate Cargo '41
International Lady '41
Outlaws of Sonora '38
100 Men and a Girl '37
Radio Patrol '37
Tim Tyler's Luck '37
The Clutching Hand '36
Custer's Last Stand '36
A Face in the Fog '36
Kelly of the Secret Service '36
Rogue's Tavern '36
Skull & Crown '35
Mystery Squadron '33
Hell's Headquarters '32
Murder on the High Seas '32

Edward Mulhare (1923-97)
Out to Sea '97
Megaforce '82
Our Man Flint '66
Von Ryan's Express '65
Hill 24 Doesn't Answer '55

Michael Mulheren
The Curse of the Jade Scorpion '01
Johnny Suede '92

Matt Mulhern (1960-)
Sunchaser '96
Biloxi Blues '88
Extreme Prejudice '87

Chris Mulkey
Jimmy Zip '00
Requiem for Murder '99
Sugar Town '99
Psychopath '97
Sub Down '97
Weapons of Mass Distraction '97
Behind Enemy Lines '96
Dead Cold '96
Bound and Gagged: A Love Story '93
Ghost in the Machine '93
Deadbolt '92
Gas Food Lodging '92
The Silencer '92
Runaway Father '91
Write to Kill '91
Rainbow Drive '90
K-9000 '89
Roe vs. Wade '89
Heartbreak Hotel '88
In Dangerous Company '88
Patti Rocks '88
Tricks of the Trade '88
The Hidden '87
Jack's Back '87

Martin Mull (1943-)
Attention Shoppers '99
Zack & Reba '98
Beverly Hills Family Robinson '97
Jingle All the Way '96
Movies Money Murder '96
Edie & Pen '95
How the West Was Fun '95
The Day My Parents Ran Away '93
Ted & Venus '93
Miracle Beach '92
Mr. Write '92
The Player '92
Dance with Death '91
Think Big '90
Cutting Class '89
Far Out Man '89
Ski Patrol '89
Home Is Where the Hart Is '88
Portrait of a White Marriage '88
Rented Lips '88
O.C. and Stiggs '87
The Boss' Wife '86
Pecos Bill '86
Clue '85
Flicks '85
Lots of Luck '85
Bad Manners '84
Mr. Mom '83
Take This Job & Shove It '81
My Bodyguard '80
Serial '80
FM '78

Megan Mullally (1958-)
Monkeybone '01
Everything Put Together '00
Winchell '98
Last Resort '86

Peter Mullan
Session 9 '01
The Claim '00
Miss Julie '99
My Name Is Joe '98

Jack Mullaney (1932-82)
George! '70
Spinout '66
Tickle Me '65
The Honeymoon Machine '61

Greg Mullavey (1939-)
Deadly Conspiracy '91
Not Quite Human 2 '89
Body Count '87

Husbands, Wives, Money, and Murder '86
I Dismember Mama '74
The Love Machine '71
C.C. & Company '70
Barbara Mullen
The Very Edge '63
It Takes a Thief '59
Marie Mullen
When Brendan Met Trudy '00
Dancing at Lughnasa '98
Patty Mullen
Frankenhooker '90
Doom Asylum '88
Harrison Muller
Miami Cops '89
2020 Texas Gladiators '85
The Final Executioner '83
She '83
Violent Breed '83
Paul Muller (1923-)
The Arena '73
Lady Frankenstein '72
Virgin among the Living Dead '71
Fangs of the Living Dead '68
Nightmare Castle '65
Goliath and the Sins of Babylon '64
Four Ways Out '57
I Vampiri '56
The Black Devils of Kali '55
Two Nights with Cleopatra '54
Richard Mulligan (1932-2000)
Gore Vidal's Lincoln '88
Oliver & Company '88 (V)
Poker Alice '87
Babes in Toyland '86
A Fine Mess '86
Doin' Time '85
The Heavenly Kid '85
Meatballs 2 '84
Micki & Maude '84
Teachers '84
S.O.B. '81
Scavenger Hunt '79
The Big Bus '76
The Hideaways '73
Pueblo Affair '73
Little Big Man '70
The Group '66
Terry David Mulligan
Can of Worms '00
Sweetwater: A True Rock Story '99
Deadly Sins '95
Rod Mullinar (1942-)
Dead Calm '89
Echoes of Paradise '86
Breakfast in Paris '81
Breaker Morant '80
Patrick '78
Dermot Mulroney (1963-)
Lovely & Amazing '02
Trixie '00
Where the Money Is '00
Goodbye, Lover '99
My Best Friend's Wedding '97
Bastard out of Carolina '96
Box of Moonlight '96
The Trigger Effect '96
Copycat '95
How to Make an American Quilt '95
Kansas City '95
Angels in the Outfield '94
Bad Girls '94
Living in Oblivion '94
Family Pictures '93
The Last Outlaw '93
Point of No Return '93
The Thing Called Love '93
Samantha '92
Silent Tongue '92
There Goes My Baby '92
Where the Day Takes You '92
Bright Angel '91
Career Opportunities '91
Longtime Companion '90
Staying Together '89
Survival Quest '89
Sunset '88
Young Guns '88
Long Gone '87
Kieran Mulroney (1965-)
From the Earth to the Moon '98
The Immortals '95
The Spitfire Grill '95
Sensation '94
Gettysburg '93
Career Opportunities '91
Nowhere to Run '88
Kelsey Mulrooney
Second Chances '98
She's So Lovely '97
The Christmas Box '95
Danny Mummert (1934-)
Blondie Hits the Jackpot '49
Blondie Knows Best '46
Footlight Glamour '43
It's a Great Life '43
Blondie for Victory '42
Blondie Goes Latin '42
Blondie Goes to College '42
Blondie's Blessed Event '42
Blondie in Society '41
Blondie Has Trouble '40
Blondie On a Budget '40
Blondie Plays Cupid '40
Blondie Brings Up Baby '39
Blondie Meets the Boss '39
Blondie Takes a Vacation '39
Billy Mumy (1954-)
Twilight Zone: The Movie '83
Bless the Beasts and Children '71
Dear Brigitte '65
Sammy, the Way-Out Seal '62
Herbert Mundin (1898-1939)
The Adventures of Robin Hood '38
Mutiny on the Bounty '35
Cavalcade '33
Hoopla '33
Kevin Mundy
Jailbait! '00
Better Than Chocolate '99
Ian Mune
Dangerous Orphans '86
Sleeping Dogs '77
Paul Muni (1895-1967)
The Last Angry Man '59
Angel on My Shoulder '46
A Song to Remember '45
Commandos Strike at Dawn '43
Stage Door Canteen '43
Juarez '39
The Good Earth '37
The Life of Emile Zola '37
The Story of Louis Pasteur '36
Black Fury '35
I Am a Fugitive from a Chain Gang '32
Scarface '31
Frankie Muniz (1985-)
Big Fat Liar '02
Deuces Wild '02
Miracle in Lane Two '00
My Dog Skip '99
What the Deaf Man Heard '98
Pep Munne
Barcelona '94
Where Time Began '77
Caroline Munro (1950-)
Black Cat '90
Slaughter High '86
Don't Open Till Christmas '84
Fanatic '82
Maniac '80
Star Crash '78
The Spy Who Loved Me '77
At the Earth's Core '76
I Don't Want to Be Born '75
Captain Kronos: Vampire Hunter '74
Golden Voyage of Sinbad '73
Doctor Phibes Rises Again '72
Dracula A.D. 1972 '72
The Abominable Dr. Phibes '71
Gun Crazy '69
Janet Munro (1934-72)
The Day the Earth Caught Fire '61
Horsemasters '61
The Swiss Family Robinson '60
Darby O'Gill & the Little People '59
Third Man on the Mountain '59
The Crawling Eye '58
The Young and the Guilty '58
Small Hotel '57
Lochlyn Munro
Kill Me Later '01
Camouflage '00
Dracula 2000 '00
Scary Movie '00
A Night at the Roxbury '98
Dead Man on Campus '97
Trancers 5: Sudden Deth '94
Wagons East '94
Anything for Love '93
Neil Munro
Beethoven Lives Upstairs '92
Gate 2 '92
Confidential '86
Dancing in the Dark '86
Jules Munshin (1915-70)
Take Me Out to the Ball Game '49
That Midnight Kiss '49
Easter Parade '48
Ona Munson (1906-56)
The Red House '47
Dakota '45
Idaho '43
Lady from Louisiana '42
The Shanghai Gesture '42
Wagon's Westward '40
Gone with the Wind '39
Fuyuki Murakami
Godzilla vs. Monster Zero '68
Godzilla, King of the Monsters '56
Jean Murat (1888-1968)
Dishonorable Discharge '57
Rich, Young and Pretty '51
Eternal Return '43
Carnival in Flanders '35
Takehiro Murata
Godzilla 2000 '99
Okoge '93
Minbo—Or the Gentle Art of Japanese Extortion '92
George Murcell (1925-98)
Cutthroat Island '95
Year of the Gun '91
Enrique Murciano (1973-)
Black Hawk Down '01
Traffic '00
Speed 2: Cruise Control '97
Vince Murdocco
L.A. Wars '94
Ring of Fire 2: Blood and Steel '92
Ring of Fire '91
Flesh Gordon 2: Flesh Gordon Meets the Cosmic Cheerleaders '90
George Murdock
Orange County '02
Crosscut '95
Firepower '93
Grand Tour: Disaster in Time '92
Strange Case of Dr. Jekyll & Mr. Hyde '89
In Love with an Older Woman '82
Breaker! Breaker! '77
Jack Murdock
Rain Man '88
Altered States '80
Tim Murdock
They Were Expendable '45
Thirty Seconds Over Tokyo '44
Christopher Murney
Barton Fink '91
The Ten Million Dollar Getaway '91
Murder by the Book '87
Maximum Overdrive '86
The Last Dragon '85
Peter Murnik
Hard Rain '97
Rowing Through '96
Andersonville '95
Golden Gate '93
Body Parts '91
Audie Murphy (1924-71)
The Texican '66
Arizona Raiders '65
The Unforgiven '60
No Name on the Bullet '59
Walk the Proud Land '56
To Hell and Back '55
Ride Clear of Diablo '54
Gunsmoke '53
Duel at Silver Creek '52
The Red Badge of Courage '51
Barri Murphy
Armed for Action '92
Action U.S.A. '89
Ben Murphy (1942-)
The Cradle Will Fall '83
The Winds of War '83
Time Walker '82
The Chisholms '79
Riding with Death '76
Brittany Murphy (1977-)
Don't Say a Word '01
Riding in Cars with Boys '01
Sidewalks of New York '01
Summer Catch '01
Cherry Falls '00
Common Ground '00
Trixie '00
The Devil's Arithmetic '99
Drop Dead Gorgeous '99
Girl, Interrupted '99
Bongwater '98
Phoenix '98
Zack & Reba '98
The Prophecy 2: Ashtown '97
Drive '96
Clueless '95
Freeway '95
Cillian Murphy
The Way We Live Now '02
On the Edge '00
Donald Murphy
Frankenstein's Daughter '58
Shack Out on 101 '55
Donna Murphy (1958-)
Center Stage '00
The Astronaut's Wife '99
Star Trek: Insurrection '98
Eddie Murphy (1961-)
The Adventures of Pluto Nash '02
Showtime '02
Dr. Dolittle 2 '01
Shrek '01 (V)
Nutty Professor 2: The Klumps '00
Bowfinger '99
Life '99
Dr. Dolittle '98
Holy Man '98
Mulan '98 (V)
Metro '96
The Nutty Professor '96
Vampire in Brooklyn '95
Beverly Hills Cop 3 '94
Boomerang '92
The Distinguished Gentleman '92
Another 48 Hrs. '90
Harlem Nights '89
Coming to America '88
Beverly Hills Cop 2 '87
The Golden Child '86
Best Defense '84
Beverly Hills Cop '84
Trading Places '83
48 Hrs. '82
George Murphy (1902-92)
Battleground '49
Having Wonderful Crime '45
Broadway Rhythm '44
Show Business '44
Step Lively '44
Bataan '43
This Is the Army '43
For Me and My Gal '42
The Navy Comes Through '42
A Girl, a Guy and a Gob '41
Tom, Dick, and Harry '41
Broadway Melody of 1940 '40
Little Nellie Kelly '40
Letter of Introduction '38
Little Miss Broadway '38
Broadway Melody of 1938 '37
Kid Millions '34
Horace Murphy (1880-1975)
Bad Man of Deadwood '41
Down the Wyoming Trail '39
Wide Open Faces '38
Boothill Brigade '37
Border Phantom '37
Come on, Cowboys '37
Last of the Warrens '36
Undercover Man '36
Jimmy Murphy
Platinum High School '60
Curse of the Undead '59
Johnny Murphy
War of the Buttons '95
The Commitments '91
Kim Murphy
The In Crowd '00
Houseguest '94
Mary Murphy (1931-)
40 Pounds of Trouble '62
The Electronic Monster '57
Desperate Hours '55
A Man Alone '55
The Maverick Queen '55
The Wild One '54
Houdini '53
Main Street to Broadway '53
Carrie '52
Maurice Murphy (1913-78)
Abe Lincoln in Illinois '40
Delinquent Parents '38
Found Alive '34
Tailspin Tommy '34
Megan Murphy
Money Buys Happiness '99
Shredder Orpheus '89
Michael Murphy (1938-)
Breaking the Surface: The Greg Louganis Story '96
Private Parts '96
Kansas City '95
Clean Slate '94
Batman Returns '92
Dead Ahead: The Exxon Valdez Disaster '92
Folks! '92
Shocker '89
Tailspin: Behind the Korean Airline Tragedy '89
The Caine Mutiny Court Martial '88
Tanner '88 '88
Salvador '86
Cloak & Dagger '84
Mesmerized '84
Talk to Me '82
The Year of Living Dangerously '82
Strange Behavior '81
Hot Money '79
Manhattan '79
The Class of Miss MacMichael '78
Great Bank Hoax '78
An Unmarried Woman '78
The Front '76
Nashville '75
The Autobiography of Miss Jane Pittman '74
Phase 4 '74
The Thief Who Came to Dinner '73
McCabe & Mrs. Miller '71
Brewster McCloud '70
Count Yorga, Vampire '70
M*A*S*H '70
That Cold Day in the Park '69
Countdown '68
Double Trouble '67
M.R. Murphy
Stuff Stephanie in the Incinerator '89
In Deadly Heat '87
Rosemary Murphy (1927-)
Message in a Bottle '98
The Tuskegee Airmen '95
For the Boys '91
A Woman Named Jackie '91
The Attic '80
Julia '77
Eleanor & Franklin '76
Walking Tall '73
Ben '72
You'll Like My Mother '72
Any Wednesday '66
To Kill a Mockingbird '62
Timothy Patrick Murphy (1959-88)
Doin' Time on Planet Earth '88
Sam's Son '84
The Seekers '79
William Murphy
Sands of Iwo Jima '49
The Story of G.I. Joe '45
Barbara Murray (1929-)
The Bretts '88
A Cry from the Streets '57
Death Goes to School '53
Another Man's Poison '52
Tony Draws a Horse '51
Beverly Murray
The Carpenter '89
Cathy's Curse '77
Bill Murray (1950-)
Osmosis Jones '01
The Royal Tenenbaums '01
Charlie's Angels '00
Hamlet '00
The Cradle Will Rock '99
Rushmore '98
Wild Things '98
With Friends Like These '98
The Man Who Knew Too Little '97
Kingpin '96
Larger Than Life '96
Space Jam '96
Ed Wood '94
Groundhog Day '93
Mad Dog and Glory '93
What about Bob? '91
Quick Change '90
Shame of the Jungle '90 (V)
Ghostbusters 2 '89
Scrooged '88
Little Shop of Horrors '86
Ghostbusters '84
The Razor's Edge '84
Tootsie '82
Stripes '81
Caddyshack '80
Where the Buffalo Roam '80
Meatballs '79

Mr. Mike's Mondo Video '79
All You Need Is Cash '78
Don Murray (1929-)
Kickboxer the Champion '91
Ghosts Can't Do It '90
Made in Heaven '87
Mistress '87
Peggy Sue Got Married '86
Radioactive Dreams '86
Scorpion '86
Something in Common '86
Quarterback Princess '85
License to Kill '84
I Am the Cheese '83
Endless Love '81
Justin Morgan Had a Horse '81
Return of the Rebels '81
If Things Were Different '79
Rainbow '78
Deadly Hero '75
Confessions of Tom Harris '72
Conquest of the Planet of the Apes '72
Cotter '72
Sweet Love, Bitter '67
The Viking Queen '67
Baby, the Rain Must Fall '64
One Man's Way '63
Advise and Consent '62
The Hoodlum Priest '61
Shake Hands with the Devil '59
Bus Stop '56
James Murray (1901-36)
All the King's Men '99
Skull & Crown '35
Baby Face '33
High Gear '33
The Crowd '28
Joel Murray
The Cable Guy '96
One Crazy Summer '86
Ken Murray (1903-88)
Follow Me, Boys! '66
The Man Who Shot Liberty Valance '62
The Marshal's Daughter '53
Stephen Murray (1912-83)
Elizabeth R '72
Four Sided Triangle '53
Alice in Wonderland '50
Pygmalion '38
Kate Murtagh
Doctor Detroit '83
Switchblade Sisters '75
James Murtaugh
River Red '98
Private Parts '96
The Rosary Murders '87
Lionel Murton
Carry On Admiral '57
Meet the Navy '46
Tony Musante (1936-)
The Yards '00
Collector's Item '89
The Pope of Greenwich Village '84
High Ice '80
Breaking Up Is Hard to Do '79
Fatal Chase '77
The Grissom Gang '71
The Bird with the Crystal Plumage '70
The Detective '68
The Incident '67
Clarence Muse (1889-1979)
The Black Stallion '79
A Dream for Christmas '73
Watch on the Rhine '43
Gentleman from Dixie '41
The Invisible Ghost '41
Broken Strings '40
That Gang of Mine '40
Way Down South '39
Prison Train '38
The White Zombie '32
Louis Mustillo
Dudley Do-Right '99
Just the Ticket '98
Marjorie Ann Mutchie
Footlight Glamour '43
It's a Great Life '43
Ellen Muth
Cora Unashamed '00
The Truth About Jane '00
Ornella Muti (1955-)
The Count of Monte Cristo '99
Esther '98
Somewhere in the City '97
Once Upon a Crime '92
Oscar '91
Wait until Spring, Bandini '90
Casanova '87
Swann in Love '84
Tales of Ordinary Madness '83
Flash Gordon '80
Life Is Beautiful '79
Summer Affair '79
Leonor '75
Roger Mutton
The Charge of the Light Brigade '68
The Girl on a Motorcycle '68
Bruce Myers
The Mahabharata '89
The Unbearable Lightness of Being '88
The Awakening '80
Carmel Myers (1899-1980)
Chinatown After Dark '31
Pleasure '31
Ben-Hur '26
Beau Brummel '24
Harry C. (Henry) Myers (1882-1938)
Rainbow over Broadway '33
Convicted '32
The Savage Girl '32
City Lights '31
The Marriage Circle '24
Kim Myers (1966-)
Letters from a Killer '98
Hellraiser 4: Bloodline '95
White Palace '90
A Nightmare on Elm Street 2: Freddy's Revenge '85
Lou Myers
Tin Cup '96
The Piano Lesson '94
Mike Myers (1963-)
Austin Powers In Goldmember '02
Shrek '01 (V)
Austin Powers 2: The Spy Who Shagged Me '99
Mystery, Alaska '99
54 '98
Austin Powers: International Man of Mystery '97
So I Married an Axe Murderer '93
Wayne's World 2 '93
Wayne's World '92
Susan Myers
Desperate Women '78
The Spell '77
Peter Mygind
The Kingdom 2 '97
The Kingdom '95
Bruce Myles (1940-)
A Woman's Tale '92
Sweet Talker '91
A Cry in the Dark '88
John (Jack) Mylong (1892-1975)
The Mermaids of Tiburon '62
Robot Monster '53
For Whom the Bell Tolls '43
Jim Nabors (1933-)
Return to Mayberry '85
Cannonball Run 2 '84
Stroker Ace '83
The Best Little Whorehouse in Texas '82
Mikola Nademsy
Earth '30
Zvenigora '28
George Nader (1921-2002)
Beyond Atlantis '73
The House of 1000 Dolls '67
The Human Duplicators '64
Away All Boats '56
Lady Godiva '55
Carnival Story '54
Sins of Jezebel '54
Robot Monster '53
Michael Nader (1945-)
The Finishing Touch '92
The Flash '90
Nick Knight '89
The Great Escape 2: The Untold Story '88
Lady Mobster '88
The Trip '67
Lycia Naff
Chopper Chicks in Zombietown '91
Lethal Weapon '87
Masatoshi Nagase (1966-)
Cold Fever '95
Autumn Moon '92
Mystery Train '89
Anne Nagel (1912-66)
The Spirit of West Point '47
Don Winslow of the Navy '43
Dawn Express '42
The Mad Monster '42
The Secret Code '42
Man Made Monster '41
Black Friday '40
Winners of the West '40
The Green Hornet '39
Gang Bullets '38
Three Legionnaires '37
Conrad Nagel (1897-1970)
All That Heaven Allows '55
Woman in Brown '48
The Adventures of Rusty '45
Yellow Cargo '36
Ann Vickers '33
The Divorcee '30
Dubarry '30
The Kiss '29
The Michigan Kid '28
The Mysterious Lady '28
Alan Naggar
Cleo/Leo '89
New York's Finest '87
Ajay Naidu
K-PAX '01
You Are Here * '00
Chutney Popcorn '99
Office Space '98
Pi '98
subUrbia '96
Touch and Go '86
Where the River Runs Black '86
Jimmy Nail (1954-)
The 10th Kingdom '00
Still Crazy '98
Evita '96
Crusoe '89
Dream Demon '88
Howling 2: Your Sister Is a Werewolf '85
Morons from Outer Space '85
Joanne Nail
The Visitor '80
Switchblade Sisters '75
J. Carrol Naish (1900-73)
Dracula vs. Frankenstein '71
Force of Impulse '60
This Could Be the Night '57
Hit the Deck '55
The Last Command '55
Rage at Dawn '55
Beneath the 12-Mile Reef '53
Fighter Attack '53
Clash by Night '52
Across the Wide Missouri '51
The Denver & Rio Grande '51
Annie Get Your Gun '50
The Black Hand '50
Rio Grande '50
The Toast of New Orleans '50
That Midnight Kiss '49
The Fugitive '48
The Beast with Five Fingers '46
Humoresque '46
The Southerner '45
Strange Confession '45
Dragon Seed '44
House of Frankenstein '44
Jungle Woman '44
The Monster Maker '44
Waterfront '44
Behind the Rising Sun '43
Calling Dr. Death/Strange Confession '43
Sahara '43
The Corsican Brothers '42
Tales of Manhattan '42
Birth of the Blues '41
Blood and Sand '41
Down Argentine Way '40
Beau Geste '39
Sea Racketeers '37
Thunder Trail '37
The Charge of the Light Brigade '36
Special Investigator '36
Black Fury '35
Captain Blood '35
Confidential '35
The Lives of a Bengal Lancer '35
Mystery Squadron '33
The World Gone Mad '33
Kid from Spain '32
The Royal Bed '31
Laurence Naismith (1908-92)
Amazing Mr. Blunden '72
Diamonds Are Forever '71
Quest for Love '71
The Bushbaby '70
The Valley of Gwangi '69
Jason and the Argonauts '63
The Prince and the Pauper '62
Greyfriars Bobby '61
Sink the Bismarck '60
The Trials of Oscar Wilde '60
Village of the Damned '60
The World of Suzie Wong '60
Third Man on the Mountain '59
A Night to Remember '58
Abandon Ship '57
Robbery under Arms '57
The Man Who Never Was '55
Carrington, V.C. '54
Room to Let '49
Train of Events '49
Takashi Naito
After Life '98
Maborosi '95
Merry Christmas, Mr. Lawrence '83
Taketoshi Naito
After Life '98
The Human Condition: A Soldier's Prayer '61
Kathy Najimy (1957-)
Rat Race '01
The Wedding Planner '01
If These Walls Could Talk 2 '00
Attention Shoppers '99
Bride of Chucky '98
Hope Floats '98
Zack & Reba '98
Cats Don't Dance '97 (V)
Nevada '97
Jeffrey '95
It's Pat: The Movie '94
Hocus Pocus '93
Sister Act 2: Back in the Habit '93
Sister Act '92
The Fisher King '91
Soapdish '91
Tatsuya Nakadai (1932-)
Wicked City '92
Ran '85
The Wolves '82
Hunter in the Dark '80
Kagemusha '80
Phoenix '78
Today We Kill, Tomorrow We Die '71
Kojiro '67
Samurai Rebellion '67
Sword of Doom '67
Face of Another '66
Kwaidan '64
High & Low '62
Sanjuro '62
The Human Condition: A Soldier's Prayer '61
Yojimbo '61
When a Woman Ascends the Stairs '60
The Human Condition: Road to Eternity '59
Enjo '58
The Human Condition: No Greater Love '58
Haruo Nakajima
War of the Gargantuas '70
King Kong vs. Godzilla '63
Ganjiro Nakamura (1902-83)
An Actor's Revenge '63
Odd Obsession '60
Drifting Weeds '59
Enjo '58
The Lower Depths '57
Satoshi Nakamura
That Man Bolt '73
The Manster '59
Tadao Nakamura
What's Up, Tiger Lily? '66
The Secret of the Telegian '61
Tamao Nakamura
Sleepy Eyes of Death: The Chinese Jade '63
The Human Condition: A Soldier's Prayer '61
Toru Nakamura (1965-)
Tokyo Raiders '00
Gen-X Cops '99
Blue Tiger '94
New York Cop '94
Reggie Nalder (1911-91)
Dracula Sucks '79
Salem's Lot '79
Zoltan...Hound of Dracula '78
Mark of the Devil 2 '72
The Bird with the Crystal Plumage '70
Mark of the Devil '69
The Day and the Hour '63
Nita Naldi (1897-1961)
You Can't Fool Your Wife '40
Cobra '25
The Ten Commandments '23
Blood and Sand '22
The Man from Beyond '22
Dr. Jekyll and Mr. Hyde '20
Joe Namath (1943-)
Chattanooga Choo Choo '84
Marriage Is Alive and Well '80
Avalanche Express '79
C.C. & Company '70
Jack Nance (1943-96)
Little Witches '96
Lost Highway '96
The Secret Agent Club '96
The Demolitionist '95
Voodoo '95
Across the Moon '94
Meatballs 4 '92
Motorama '91
The Hot Spot '90
Wild at Heart '90
Colors '88
Barfly '87
Blue Velvet '86
Dune '84
Ghoulies '84
Eraserhead '78
Breaker! Breaker! '77
Chieko Naniwa
Snow Country '57
A Geisha '53
Erica Nann
Mind Twister '93
Legion of Iron '90
Isabelle Nanty
Amelie '01
Tatie Danielle '91
Neriah Napaul (1972-)
The Bikini Car Wash Company 2 '92
The Bikini Car Wash Company '90
Alan Napier (1903-88)
Batman '66
The Loved One '65
Marnie '64
36 Hours '64
The Sword in the Stone '63 (V)
Premature Burial '62
Wild in the Country '61
Journey to the Center of the Earth '59
Until They Sail '57
The Mole People '56
Across the Wide Missouri '51
The Strange Door '51
Challenge to Lassie '49
Master Minds '49
Adventure Island '47
Forever Amber '47
Lured '47
House of Horrors '46
A Scandal in Paris '46
Isle of the Dead '45
Action in Arabia '44
The Hairy Ape '44
Mademoiselle Fifi '44
Ministry of Fear '44
Thirty Seconds Over Tokyo '44
The Uninvited '44
Cat People '42
The House of the Seven Gables '40
The Secret Four '40
Charles Napier (1936-)
Extreme Honor '01
Nutty Professor 2: The Klumps '00
Austin Powers 2: The Spy Who Shagged Me '99
The Big Tease '99
Cypress Edge '99
Austin Powers: International Man of Mystery '97
Hunter's Moon '97
Steel '97
The Cable Guy '96
Riot '96
Felony '95
Hard Justice '95
Jury Duty '95
Max Is Missing '95
3 Ninjas Knuckle Up '95
Tyson '95
Ballistic '94
Mortal Danger '94
Silk Degrees '94
Body Shot '93
Raw Justice '93
Skeeter '93
Center of the Web '92
Dragonfight '92
Eyes of the Beholder '92
Indio 2: The Revolt '92
Return to Frogtown '92
Treacherous Crossing '92
The Silence of the Lambs '91
Soldier's Fortune '91
Ernest Goes to Jail '90
Future Zone '90
The Grifters '90
Miami Blues '90

One Man Force '89
The Hit List '88
The Incredible Hulk Returns '88
Married to the Mob '88
Deep Space '87
Kidnapped '87
Night Stalker '87
Instant Justice '86
Something Wild '86
Rambo: First Blood, Part 2 '85
In Search of a Golden Sky '84
The Blues Brothers '80
Last Embrace '79
Citizens Band '77
Supervixens '75
Beyond the Valley of the Dolls '70

Jessica Napier
Cut '00
Love Serenade '96

Marshall Napier
Starlight Hotel '90
The Navigator '88

Russell Napier
The Mark '61
Unholy Four '54

Toni Naples
Dinosaur Island '93
Deathstalker 2: Duel of the Titans '87

Tony Nardi (1958-)
Bonanno: A Godfather's Story '99
La Deroute '98
Speaking Parts '89

Tom Nardini
Self-Defense '88
Africa Texas Style '67

Kathrine Narducci
Two Family House '99
A Bronx Tale '93

Darling Narita
Pups '99
Bang '95

Nas
Ticker '01
Belly '98

Arthur J. Nascarelli
Bringing Out the Dead '99
Cop Land '97

Paul (Jacinto Molina) Naschy (1934-)
The Craving '80
Human Beasts '80
Inquisition '76
Night of the Howling Beast '75
People Who Own the Dark '75
The Devil's Possessed '74
Exorcism '74
Curse of the Devil '73
House of Psychotic Women '73
The Mummy's Revenge '73
The Rue Morgue Massacres '73
Dracula's Great Love '72
The Hanging Woman '72
Horror Rises from the Tomb '72
Vengeance of the Zombies '72
Dr. Jekyll and the Wolfman '71
The Fury of the Wolfman '70
The Werewolf vs. the Vampire Woman '70
Dracula vs. Frankenstein '69

Chris Nash
Mischief '85
Silent Witness '85

Graham Nash
Elvis Meets Nixon '98
Gimme Shelter '70

Marilyn Nash (1924-)
Unknown World '51
Monsieur Verdoux '47
The Rains Came '39

Mary Nash (1885-1976)
Cobra Woman '44
The Philadelphia Story '40
Easy Living '37
Heidi '37

Noreen Nash (1924-)
Phantom from Space '53
The Devil on Wheels '47
The Red Stallion '47
The Tender Years '47

Deborah Ann Nassar
Dance of the Damned '88
Stripped to Kill '87

Marie-Jose Nat (1940-)
Les Violons du Bal '74
Embassy '72
Love and the Frenchwoman '60

Anthony Natale
His Bodyguard '98
Mr. Holland's Opus '95

Adam Nathan
I Was a Teenage TV Terrorist '87
Parting Glances '86

Stephen Nathan
You Light Up My Life '77
The First Nudie Musical '75
1776 '72

Zoe Nathenson
One Night Stand '97
The Raggedy Rawney '90
Mona Lisa '86
Those Glory, Glory Days '83

Francesca "Kitten" Natividad (1948-)
Tomb '86
Doin' Time '85
The Wild Life '84
My Tutor '82
Beneath the Valley of the Ultra-Vixens '79

Mari Natsuki
Remembering the Cosmos Flower '99
The Hunted '94

Yosuke Natsuki
Dagora, the Space Monster '65
Ghidrah the Three Headed Monster '65

Masako Natsume (1958-85)
The Imperial Japanese Empire '85
MacArthur's Children '85
Antarctica '84

Mildred Natwick (1905-94)
Dangerous Liaisons '88
Kiss Me Goodbye '82
Daisy Miller '74
A House without a Christmas Tree '72
If It's Tuesday, This Must Be Belgium '69
Barefoot in the Park '67
Tammy and the Bachelor '57
Court Jester '56
The Trouble with Harry '55
Against All Flags '52
The Quiet Man '52
Cheaper by the Dozen '50
She Wore a Yellow Ribbon '49
Three Godfathers '48
The Enchanted Cottage '45
Yolanda and the Thief '45
The Long Voyage Home '40

David Naughton (1951-)
A Crack in the Floor '00
Mirror, Mirror 3: The Voyeur '96
Ice Cream Man '95
Beanstalk '94
Desert Steel '94
Amityville: A New Generation '93
Body Bags '93
Wild Cactus '92
Overexposed '90
The Sleeping Car '90
Steel and Lace '90
Private Affairs '89
Kidnapped '87
Boy in Blue '86
Separate Vacations '86
Getting Physical '84
Not for Publication '84
Hot Dog ... The Movie! '83
Separate Ways '82
An American Werewolf in London '81
Midnight Madness '80

James Naughton (1945-)
The Truth About Jane '00
Oxygen '99
First Kid '96
The First Wives Club '96
The Birds 2: Land's End '94
Blown Away '90
Second Wind '90
The Good Mother '88
The Glass Menagerie '87
Cat's Eye '85
A Stranger Is Watching '82
The Paper Chase '73

Demetrius Navarro
The Wash '01
187 '97
Soldier Boyz '95

Cliff Nazarro (1904-61)
'Neath Canadian Skies '46
Rhythm Parade '43
Hillbilly Blitzkrieg '42
Dive Bomber '41
In Old Colorado '41
Singing Buckaroo '37

Alla Nazimova (1879-1945)
The Bridge of San Luis Rey '44
Since You Went Away '44
Blood and Sand '41
Salome '22
Camille '21

Amedeo Nazzari (1907-79)
Nefertiti, Queen of the Nile '64
Journey Beneath the Desert '61
The Naked Maja '59
Nights of Cabiria '57
Lure of the Sila '49

Anna Neagle (1904-86)
Teenage Bad Girl '59
The King's Rhapsody '55
Let's Make Up '55
Maytime in Mayfair '52
Elizabeth of Ladymead '48
The Courtney Affair '47
I Live in Grosvenor Square '46
Forever and a Day '43
Sunny '41
No, No Nanette '40
Nurse Edith Cavell '39
London Melody '37
Bitter Sweet '33

Billie Neal (1955-99)
Sweet Nothing '96
Consenting Adults '92
Mortal Thoughts '91
Down by Law '86

Dylan Neal
40 Days and 40 Nights '02
Prom Night 3: The Last Kiss '89

Edwin Neal (1945-)
Neurotic Cabaret '90
Future Kill '85
The Texas Chainsaw Massacre '74

Elise Neal (1970-)
Brian's Song '01
Mission to Mars '00
Restaurant '98
Def Jam's How to Be a Player '97
Money Talks '97
Scream 2 '97
Rosewood '96

Ella Neal
Doctor Satan's Robot '40
Mysterious Doctor Satan '40

Patricia Neal (1926-)
Cookie's Fortune '99
Heidi '93
Caroline? '90
An Unremarkable Life '89
Love Leads the Way '84
Shattered Vows '84
Ghost Story '81
All Quiet on the Western Front '79
The Bastard '78
Love Affair: The Eleanor & Lou Gehrig Story '77
Widow's Nest '77
Eric '75
Things in Their Season '74
Run, Stranger, Run '73
Homecoming: A Christmas Story '71
The Subject Was Roses '68
In Harm's Way '65
Hud '63
Breakfast at Tiffany's '61
A Face in the Crowd '57
The Stranger from Venus '54
Diplomatic Courier '52
The Day the Earth Stood Still '51
Three Secrets '50
The Fountainhead '49

Peggy Neal
X from Outer Space '67
Terror Beneath the Sea '66

Rome Neal
Pinero '01
Hamlet '00

Tom Neal (1914-72)
Danger Zone '51
Fingerprints Don't Lie '51
G.I. Jane '51
King of the Bullwhip '51
Stop That Cab '51
Apache Chief '50
I Shot Billy the Kid '50
Radar Secret Service '50
Red Desert '50
Train to Tombstone '50
Great Jesse James Raid '49
Hat Box Mystery '47
Trail of the Mounties '47
The Brute Man '46
Club Havana '46
Detour '46
My Dog Shep '46
First Yank into Tokyo '45
Behind the Rising Sun '43
Bowery at Midnight '42
Miracle Kid '42
Andy Hardy Meets Debutante '40
Courageous Dr. Christian '40

Kevin Nealon (1953-)
Little Nicky '00
The Principal Takes a Holiday '98
The Wedding Singer '97
Happy Gilmore '96
All I Want for Christmas '91
Roxanne '87

Christopher Neame (1947-)
The Apocalypse Watch '97
Project Shadowchaser 3000 '95
Hellbound '94
Street Knight '93
Boris and Natasha: The Movie '92
Still Not Quite Human '92
Edge of Honor '91
Suburban Commando '91
Bloodstone '88
D.O.A. '88
Transformations '88
Steel Dawn '87
Dracula A.D. 1972 '72

Holly Near
Dogfight '91
Minnie and Moskowitz '71

Claire Nebout
Venus Beauty Institute '98
Beaumarchais the Scoundrel '96
Ponette '95
Scene of the Crime '87

Vaclav Neckar
Larks on a String '68
Closely Watched Trains '66

Raisa Nedashkovskaya
Commissar '68
The Tsar's Bride '66

Tracey Needham (1967-)
Backlash '99
Buried Alive 2 '97
Last Stand at Saber River '96
Sensation '94

Nique Needles
Beverly Hills Family Robinson '97
The Four Minute Mile '92
Dogs in Space '87

Ted Neeley (1943-)
Hard Country '81
Of Mice and Men '81
Shadow of Chikara '77
Jesus Christ, Superstar '73

Cam Neely
Me, Myself, and Irene '00
Dumb & Dumber '94

Mark Neely
The Siege of Firebase Gloria '89
Off the Mark '87

Liam Neeson (1952-)
K-19: The Widowmaker '02
Gun Shy '00
The Haunting '99
Star Wars: Episode 1—The Phantom Menace '99
Les Miserables '97
Michael Collins '96
Before and After '95
Rob Roy '95
Nell '94
Schindler's List '93
Deception '92
Ethan Frome '92
Husbands and Wives '92
Leap of Faith '92
Shining Through '92
Under Suspicion '92
The Big Man: Crossing the Line '91
Darkman '90
Next of Kin '89
The Dead Pool '88
The Good Mother '88
High Spirits '88
Satisfaction '88
Prayer for the Dying '87
Suspect '87
Duet for One '86
Hold the Dream '86
The Mission '86
Lamb '85
The Bounty '84
A Woman of Substance '84
Krull '83
Excalibur '81

Hildegarde Neff (1925-)
Bluebeard '63
The Three Penny Opera '62
Svengali '55
Diplomatic Courier '52
The Snows of Kilimanjaro '52
Unnatural '52

Natalia (Natalya) Negoda (1964-)
Back in the USSR '92
The Comrades of Summer '92
Little Vera '88

Francois Negret
Night and Day '91
Au Revoir les Enfants '87

Pola Negri (1894-1987)
The Moon-Spinners '64
Hi Diddle Diddle '43
Hotel Imperial '27
One Arabian Night '21
Passion '19
Gypsy Blood '18

Mary Joan Negro
No Big Deal '83
The Family Man '79

Taylor Negron (1958-)
Call Me Claus '01
The Fluffer '01
Lloyd '00
Loser '00
A Kid in Aladdin's Palace '97
Mr. Stitch '95
The Last Boy Scout '91
Nothing But Trouble '91
Punchline '88
Bad Medicine '85
Better Off Dead '85
Easy Money '83

David Neidorf
Empire of the Sun '87
Undercover '87
Hoosiers '86
Platoon '86

Hildegard(e) Neil (1939-)
Antony and Cleopatra '73
A Touch of Class '73
The Man Who Haunted Himself '70

Richard Neil
Blondes Have More Guns '95
The Disappearance of Kevin Johnson '95

Noel Neill (1920-)
Invasion U.S.A. '52
Atom Man vs. Superman '50
The Adventures of Frank and Jesse James '48
Here Come the Waves '45
The Stork Club '45

Sam Neill (1948-)
Jurassic Park 3 '01
The Dish '00
Sally Hemings: An American Scandal '00
Bicentennial Man '99
Molokai: The Story of Father Damien '99
Merlin '98
Sweet Revenge '98
Event Horizon '97
The Horse Whisperer '97
Snow White: A Tale of Terror '97
Forgotten Silver '96
In Cold Blood '96
Children of the Revolution '95
Country Life '95
In the Mouth of Madness '95
Rainbow Warrior '94
Restoration '94
Rudyard Kipling's The Jungle Book '94
Sirens '94
Family Pictures '93
Jurassic Park '93
The Piano '93
Question of Faith '93
Hostage '92
Memoirs of an Invisible Man '92
Fever '91
One Against the Wind '91
Until the End of the World '91
Death in Brunswick '90
The Hunt for Red October '90
Dead Calm '89
A Cry in the Dark '88
Reilly: Ace of Spies '87
For Love Alone '86
The Good Wife '86
Plenty '85
Attack Force Z '84
The Blood of Others '84
Enigma '82
Ivanhoe '82
From a Far Country: Pope John Paul II '81

Omen 3: The Final Conflict '81
Possession '81
My Brilliant Career '79
Sleeping Dogs '77

Don Nakaya Neilsen
Blood Ring '93
Fist of Steel '93

John Neilson
Terror at Red Wolf Inn '72
Honky '71

George Neise (1916-96)
The Three Stooges Meet Hercules '61
Outcasts of the City '58

Stacey Nelkin
Everything Relative '96
Halloween 3: Season of the Witch '82
Children of Divorce '80
Up the Academy '80
The Triangle Factory Fire Scandal '79

Nathalie Nell
Echoes '83
Rape of Love '79

Kate Nelligan (1951-)
Walter and Henry '01
The Cider House Rules '99
U.S. Marshals '98
Calm at Sunset '96
Up Close and Personal '96
How to Make an American Quilt '95
Margaret's Museum '95
A Mother's Prayer '95
Wolf '94
Fatal Instinct '93
Terror Stalks the Class Reunion '93
Diamond Fleece '92
Shadows and Fog '92
Frankie and Johnny '91
The Prince of Tides '91
Love and Hate: A Marriage Made in Hell '90
Control '87
Eleni '85
Without a Trace '83
Crossover '82
Eye of the Needle '81
Dracula '79
Bethune '77
Romantic Englishwoman '75
The Count of Monte Cristo '74

Adam Nelson
Phantoms '97
The Abyss '89

Ann Nelson
My Girl '91
Ghosts That Still Walk '77

Barry Nelson (1920-)
Island Claw '80
The Shining '80
Pete 'n' Tillie '72
Airport '70
Bataan '43
The Human Comedy '43
Johnny Eager '42
Shadow of the Thin Man '41

Bob Nelson
Brain Donors '92
Miracles '86
Ryder P.I. '86
Sorceress '82

Bobby Nelson (1923-)
Boothill Brigade '37
The Red Rope '37
Cowboy & the Bandit '35
Cyclone of the Saddle '35
Ghost Rider '35
Way of the West '35
Cowboy Counselor '33
Roaring Ranch '30

Byron Nelson
The Caddy '53
The Fighting 69th '40

Craig Richard Nelson (1947-)
My Bodyguard '80
The Grass Is Always Greener Over the Septic Tank '78
The Paper Chase '73

Craig T. Nelson (1946-)
Dirty Pictures '00
The Skulls '00
The Devil's Advocate '97
Ghosts of Mississippi '96
If These Walls Could Talk '96
I'm Not Rappaport '96
Probable Cause '95
The Fire Next Time '93
The Josephine Baker Story '90
Me and Him '89
Murderers Among Us: The Simon Wiesenthal Story '89
Troop Beverly Hills '89
Turner and Hooch '89
Action Jackson '88
Red Riding Hood '88
Rachel River '87
Poltergeist 2: The Other Side '86
Call to Glory '84
The Killing Fields '84
All the Right Moves '83
Man, Woman & Child '83
The Osterman Weekend '83
Silkwood '83
Poltergeist '82
Murder in Texas '81
Private Benjamin '80
Rage '80
Stir Crazy '80
Where the Buffalo Roam '80
And Justice for All '79
Flesh Gordon '72 (V)
The Return of Count Yorga '71

Danny Nelson
A Good Baby '99
Blood Salvage '90

David Nelson (1936-)
Cry-Baby '90
High School USA '84
Peyton Place '57
Here Come the Nelsons '52

Ed Nelson (1928-)
Jackie Chan's Who Am I '98
Cries of Silence '97
The Bone Yard '90
Deadly Weapon '88
Brenda Starr '86
Enola Gay: The Men, the Mission, the Atomic Bomb '80
Return of Frank Cannon '80
Anatomy of a Seduction '79
For the Love of Benji '77
Airport '75 '75
Shining Star '75
Soldier in the Rain '63
A Bucket of Blood '59
T-Bird Gang '59
The Devil's Partner '58
Night of the Blood Beast '58
Carnival Rock '57
Invasion of the Saucer Men '57
Teenage Doll '57
Swamp Women '55

Gene Nelson (1920-96)
The Atomic Man '56
The Way Out '56
Oklahoma! '55
Lullaby of Broadway '51
Tea for Two '50
The West Point Story '50

Harriet Hilliard Nelson (1909-94)
The Kid with the 200 I.Q. '83
Here Come the Nelsons '52
Take It Big '44
Follow the Fleet '36

Herbert Nelson
Future Cop '76
When the North Wind Blows '74

Jerry Nelson
The Muppet Christmas Carol '92 (V)
The Muppet Movie '79 (V)

John Allen Nelson (1959-)
Shelter '98
Deathstalker 3 '89
Killer Klowns from Outer Space '88
Saigon Commandos '88
Hunk '87

Judd Nelson (1959-)
Dark Asylum '01
Jay and Silent Bob Strike Back '01
Return to Cabin by the Lake '01
Cabin by the Lake '00
Light It Up '99
Mr. Rock 'n' Roll: The Alan Freed Story '99
Steel '97
Blackwater Trail '95
Circumstances Unknown '95
Airheads '94
Blindfold: Acts of Obsession '94
Flinch '94
Hail Caesar '94
Caroline at Midnight '93
Entangled '93
Every Breath '93
Conflict of Interest '92
Primary Motive '92
The Dark Backward '91
New Jack City '91
Hiroshima: Out of the Ashes '90
Far Out Man '89
Relentless '89
Billionaire Boys Club '87
Blue City '86
From the Hip '86
Transformers: The Movie '86 (V)
The Breakfast Club '85
Fandango '85
St. Elmo's Fire '85
Making the Grade '84

Lloyd Nelson
The Wild World of Batwoman '66
Curse of the Stone Hand '64
The Incredible Petrified World '58
Man Beast '55

Lori Nelson (1933-)
The Pied Piper of Hamelin '57
Hot Rod Girl '56
Mohawk '56
Pardners '56
Day the World Ended '55
I Died a Thousand Times '55
Ma and Pa Kettle at Waikiki '55
Revenge of the Creature '55
Francis Goes to West Point '52
Ma and Pa Kettle at the Fair '52

Margaret Nelson
Scalp Merchant '77
Picnic at Hanging Rock '75

Novella Nelson (1939-)
A Perfect Murder '98
Manny & Lo '96
Mercy '96

Ozzie Nelson (1906-75)
The Impossible Years '68
Here Come the Nelsons '52
People Are Funny '46
Take It Big '44
Big Street '42

Peter Nelson
Eye of the Eagle 3 '91
Sounds of Silence '91
The Expendables '89
Silk 2 '89
Crime Zone '88
V '83

Portia Nelson (1921-2001)
The Other '72
The Sound of Music '65

Ricky Nelson (1940-85)
Over the Hill Gang '69
Wackiest Ship in the Army '61
Rio Bravo '59
Here Come the Nelsons '52

Ruth Nelson (1905-92)
The Haunting Passion '83
A Christmas Without Snow '80
Humoresque '46
Wilson '44

Sandra Nelson
Life as a House '01
The Halfback of Notre Dame '96
Maternal Instincts '96

Sean Nelson
The Wood '99
A Stranger in the Kingdom '98
American Buffalo '95
Fresh '94

Steven Nelson
Men Cry Bullets '00
Little Ninjas '92

Tim Blake Nelson (1965-)
Cherish '02
The Good Girl '02
O Brother Where Art Thou? '00
The Thin Red Line '98

Tracy Nelson (1963-)
Perfect Game '00
The Perfect Nanny '00
Perfect Tenant '99
The Night Caller '97
The Game of Love '90
Down and Out in Beverly Hills '86
Maria's Lovers '84
Yours, Mine & Ours '68

Willie Nelson (1933-)
Austin Powers 2: The Spy Who Shagged Me '99
Outlaw Justice '98
Gone Fishin' '97
Half-Baked '97
Starlight '97
Wag the Dog '97
Another Pair of Aces: Three of a Kind '91
Pair of Aces '90
Texas Guns '90
Dynamite and Gold '88
Baja Oklahoma '87
Red Headed Stranger '87
Amazons '86
Last Days of Frank & Jesse James '86
Stagecoach '86
Songwriter '84
Hell's Angels Forever '83
Barbarosa '82
Coming Out of the Ice '82
Thief '81
Honeysuckle Rose '80
The Electric Horseman '79

Corin "Corky" Nemec (1971-)
Killer Bud '00
The First to Go '97
The War at Home '96
Operation Dumbo Drop '95
Drop Zone '94
Stephen King's The Stand '94
White Wolves 2: Legend of the Wild '94
Solar Crisis '92
Tucker: The Man and His Dream '88

Francesca Neri (1964-)
Collateral Damage '02
Hannibal '01
Live Flesh '97
Flight of the Innocent '93
Outrage '93

Rosalba (Sara Bay) Neri (1940-)
The Arena '73
Devil's Wedding Night '73
Lady Frankenstein '72
Amuck! '71
Slaughter Hotel '71
The Seducers '70
The Castle of Fu Manchu '68
Conquest of Mycene '63

David Nerman
The Witness Files '00
The Minion '98
Sir Arthur Conan Doyle's The Lost World '98
Witchboard 3: The Possession '95
The Scorpio Factor '90

Franco Nero (1942-)
David '97
The Painted Lady '97
Talk of Angels '96
The Innocent Sleep '95
Young Catherine '91
Die Hard 2: Die Harder '90
Magdalene '88
Windmills of the Gods '88
Django Strikes Again '87
Sweet Country '87
Challenge to White Fang '86
The Girl '86
Wagner: The Complete Epic '85
Day of the Cobra '84
Shark Hunter '84
Querelle '83
The Salamander '82
Enter the Ninja '81
The Man with Bogart's Face '80
Street Law '79
Force 10 from Navarone '78
Last Four Days '77
Submission '77
21 Hours at Munich '76
Legend of Valentino '75
Sardinia Kidnapped '75
Blood Brothers '74
Falcon '74
High Crime '73
Redneck '73
Confessions of a Police Captain '72
Fifth Day of Peace '72
Ring of Death '72
Devil's Crude '71
Companeros '70
Tristana '70
The Virgin and the Gypsy '70
Battle of Neretva '69
Spaghetti Western '69
Django '68
Camelot '67
The Bible '66
Wild, Wild Planet '65

Toni Nero
No Dead Heroes '87
Silent Night, Deadly Night '84

Cathleen Nesbitt (1888-1982)
Family Plot '76
Promise Her Anything '66
The Parent Trap '61
Separate Tables '58
An Affair to Remember '57
Desiree '54
Man of Evil '48
Men of Two Worlds '46
Nicholas Nickleby '46
Pygmalion '38
The Passing of the Third Floor Back '36

Derren Nesbitt (1935-)
Funny Money '82
Horrors of Burke & Hare '71
Where Eagles Dare '68
The Blue Max '66
Victim '61

James Nesbitt (1966-)
Waking Ned Devine '98
Resurrection Man '97
Welcome to Sarajevo '97
Go Now '96

Michael Nesmith (1942-)
Tapeheads '89
Head '68

Loni Nest
Joyless Street '25
The Golem '20

Lois Nettleton (1929-)
Mirror, Mirror 2: Raven Dance '94
Bull of the West '89
Manhunt for Claude Dallas '86
Brass '85
Soggy Bottom U.S.A. '84
The Best Little Whorehouse in Texas '82
Butterfly '82
Deadly Blessing '81
Centennial '78
The Man in the Glass Booth '75
The Good Guys and the Bad Guys '69
The Bamboo Saucer '68
Period of Adjustment '62

Martin Neufeld
Relative Fear '95
H '90

Dorothy Neumann (1914-94)
Private Parts '72
The Terror '63
The Undead '57

Jenny Neumann
Delos Adventure '86
Stage Fright '83
Hell Night '81
Mistress of the Apes '79
Swim Team '79

Bebe Neuwirth (1958-)
Tadpole '02
Cupid & Cate '00
Dash and Lilly '99
Liberty Heights '99
Summer of Sam '99
Celebrity '98
The Faculty '98
The Adventures of Pinocchio '96
The Associate '96
All Dogs Go to Heaven 2 '95 (V)
Jumanji '95
Malice '93
The Paint Job '93
Wild Palms '93
Bugsy '91
Green Card '90
Say Anything '89

Aaron Neville (1941-)
The Last Ride '94
Posse '93
Zandalee '91

John Neville (1925-)
The Duke '99
Goodbye, Lover '99
Sunshine '99
Urban Legend '98
The X-Files '98
Behind the Lines '97
The Fifth Element '97
Swann '96
Dangerous Minds '95
Song Spinner '95
Baby's Day Out '94
Little Women '94
The Road to Wellville '94
The Adventures of Baron Munchausen '89
A Study in Terror '66
The Unearthly Stranger '64
Billy Budd '62

Robyn Nevin (1942-)
Angel Baby '95
Resistance '92
Careful, He Might Hear You '84
The Irishman '78
Fourth Wish '75

Claudette Nevins
Child of Darkness, Child of Light '91
Sleeping with the Enemy '91
Take Your Best Shot '82
The Possessed '77
The Mask '61

Derek Newark (1933-98)
Bellman and True '88
The Offence '73
The Blue Max '66

George Newbern
If These Walls Could Talk 2 '00
Friends & Lovers '99
The Simple Life of Noah Dearborn '99
The Evening Star '96
Far Harbor '96
Father of the Bride Part II '95
Witness to the Execution '94
Father of the Bride '91
Doppelganger: The Evil Within '90
It Takes Two '88
Paramedics '88
Switching Channels '88
Adventures in Babysitting '87
My Little Girl '87

Anthony Newcastle
Metallica '85
Captive Planet '78

William "Billy" Newell (1894-1967)
Escape from Fort Bravo '53
Doctor Satan's Robot '40
The Invisible Killer '40
The Mandarin Mystery '37
Bulldog Edition '36

Bob Newhart (1929-)
In and Out '97
The Rescuers Down Under '90 (V)
First Family '80
Little Miss Marker '80
Marathon '80
The Rescuers '77 (V)
Thursday's Game '74
Cold Turkey '71
Catch-22 '70
On a Clear Day You Can See Forever '70
Hot Millions '68
Hell Is for Heroes '62

James Newill (1911-75)
Boss of Rawhide '44
Guns of the Law '44
Outlaw Roundup '44
Fighting Valley '43
Rangers Take Over '43
The Great American Broadcast '41
Danger Ahead '40
Murder on the Yukon '40
Sky Bandits '40
Yukon Flight '40
Fighting Mad '39
Renfrew on the Great White Trail '38
Renfrew of the Royal Mounted '37

Anthony Newlands
Scream and Scream Again '70
Circus of Fear '67

Anthony Newley (1931-99)
Boris and Natasha: The Movie '92
The Garbage Pail Kids Movie '87
Outrage! '86
Stagecoach '86
Blade in Hong Kong '85
The Old Curiosity Shop '75
Sweet November '68
Doctor Dolittle '67
Let's Get Married '63
Fire Down Below '57
Above Us the Waves '56
X The Unknown '56
Oliver Twist '48
Little Ballerina '47

Alec Newman
Dune '00
Catherine Cookson's The Rag Nymph '96

Barry Newman (1938-)
40 Days and 40 Nights '02
Good Advice '01
True Blue '01
Bowfinger '99
Goodbye, Lover '99
The Limey '99
Brown's Requiem '98
Daylight '96
Fatal Vision '84
Having It All '82
Amy '81
Deadline '81
City on Fire '78
The Salzburg Connection '72
Vanishing Point '71

Danny Newman
The Return of the Borrowers '96
Shopping '93

Laraine Newman (1952-)
Jingle All the Way '96
Alone in the Woods '95
The Flintstones '94
Coneheads '93
Revenge of the Red Baron '93
Witchboard 2: The Devil's Doorway '93
Problem Child 2 '91
Invaders from Mars '86
Perfect '85
Her Life as a Man '83
Wholly Moses! '80
Mr. Mike's Mondo Video '79
Tunnelvision '76

Nanette Newman (1934-)
The Mystery of Edwin Drood '93
The Stepford Wives '75
Long Ago Tomorrow '71
The Madwoman of Chaillot '69
The Wrong Arm of the Law '63

Paul Newman (1925-)
Road to Perdition '02
Where the Money Is '00
Message in a Bottle '98
Twilight '98
Nobody's Fool '94
The Hudsucker Proxy '93
Mr. & Mrs. Bridge '90
Blaze '89
Fat Man and Little Boy '89
The Color of Money '86
Harry & Son '84
The Verdict '82
Absence of Malice '81
Fort Apache, the Bronx '81
When Time Ran Out '80
Quintet '79
Slap Shot '77
Buffalo Bill & the Indians '76
Silent Movie '76
The Drowning Pool '75
The Towering Inferno '74
Mackintosh Man '73
The Sting '73
Life & Times of Judge Roy Bean '72
Pocket Money '72
Sometimes a Great Notion '71
Butch Cassidy and the Sundance Kid '69
Winning '69
The Secret War of Harry Frigg '68
Cool Hand Luke '67
Hombre '67
Harper '66
Torn Curtain '66
Lady L '65
Hud '63
A New Kind of Love '63
The Prize '63
Sweet Bird of Youth '62
The Hustler '61
Paris Blues '61
Exodus '60
From the Terrace '60
The Young Philadelphians '59
Cat on a Hot Tin Roof '58
The Left-Handed Gun '58
The Long, Hot Summer '58
Until They Sail '57
Bang the Drum Slowly '56
Somebody Up There Likes Me '56
The Silver Chalice '54

Phyllis Newman (1933-)
The Beautician and the Beast '97
A Price above Rubies '97
A Secret Space '88
Follies in Concert '85
Picnic '55

Stephen D. Newman
Yuri Nosenko, KGB '86
Sophie's Choice '82

Julie Newmar (1935-)
Backlash: Oblivion 2 '95
To Wong Foo, Thanks for Everything, Julie Newmar '95
Oblivion '94
Nudity Required '90
Body Beat '88
Deep Space '87
Evils of the Night '85
Streetwalkin' '85
Ecstasy '84
Hysterical '83
Terraces '77
MacKenna's Gold '69
For Love or Money '63
Li'l Abner '59
Seven Brides for Seven Brothers '54

Lisa Marie Newmyer
The House on Todville Road '95
The Texas Chainsaw Massacre 4: The Next Generation '95

John Haymes Newton
Operation Sandman: Warriors in Hell '00
Alive '93
Desert Kickboxer '92

Margit Evelyn Newton
Hell of the Living Dead '83
The Last Hunter '80

Robert Newton (1905-56)
Around the World in 80 Days '56
Long John Silver '54
The Desert Rats '53
Androcles and the Lion '52
Blackbeard the Pirate '52
Tom Brown's School Days '51
Treasure Island '50
The Hidden Room '49
Oliver Twist '48
Odd Man Out '47
This Happy Breed '47
Henry V '44
Gaslight '40
Jamaica Inn '39
Beachcomber '38
21 Days '37

Thandie Newton (1972-)
Mission: Impossible 2 '00
Beloved '98
Besieged '98
Gridlock'd '96
The Leading Man '96
The Journey of August King '95
Jefferson in Paris '94
Loaded '94
The Young Americans '93
Flirting '89

Theodore Newton
Ace of Aces '33
The Sphinx '33

Wayne Newton (1942-)
Ocean's Eleven '01
Elvis Meets Nixon '98
Vegas Vacation '96
Best of the Best 2 '93
The Dark Backward '91
The Adventures of Ford Fairlane '90
License to Kill '89

Olivia Newton-John (1948-)
It's My Party '95
Two of a Kind '83
Xanadu '80
Grease '78

Richard Ney (1915-)
Premature Burial '62
The Lovable Cheat '49
Mrs. Miniver '42

Marina Neyelova
Autumn Marathon '79
The Errors of Youth '78

Anne Neyland
Jailhouse Rock '57
Motorcycle Gang '57

Jinpachi Nezu
Nobody '99
Ran '85

Carrie Ng
Sex and Zen '93
Naked Killer '92

Frances Ng
The Mission '99
The Bride with White Hair '93

Lawrence Ng
Sex and Zen '93
Lethal Panther '90

Haing S. Ngor (1940-96)
Fortunes of War '94
Heaven and Earth '93
My Life '93
Ambition '91
In Love and War '91
Last Flight Out: A True Story '90
Vietnam, Texas '90
The Iron Triangle '89
Eastern Condors '87
The Killing Fields '84

Dustin Nguyen (1962-)
3 Ninjas Kick Back '94
Heaven and Earth '93
No Escape, No Return '93
Rapid Fire '92

Michelle Nicastro (1960-)
The Swan Princess 2: Escape from Castle Mountain '97 (V)
The Swan Princess '94 (V)
When Harry Met Sally... '89
Bad Guys '86
Body Rock '84

Maurizio Nichetti (1948-)
Luna e L'Altra '96
Stephano Quantestorie '93
Volere Volare '92
The Icicle Thief '89
Allegro Non Troppo '76

Angela Nicholas
Alien Space Avenger '91
Galactic Gigolo '87

Anna Nicholas
Bloodstone '88
Mutants In Paradise '88

Denise Nicholas (1944-)
Ghost Dad '90
Sophisticated Gents '81
Piece of the Action '77
Let's Do It Again '75
Blacula '72

Harold Nicholas (1921-2000)
The Five Heartbeats '91
Tap '89
Fass Black '77

Paul Nicholas (1945-)
Alice '86
Nutcracker Sweet '84
The World Is Full of Married Men '80
Yesterday's Hero '79
Lisztomania '75
Tommy '75
Invitation to the Wedding '73

Thomas Ian Nicholas (1980-)
Halloween: Resurrection '02
American Pie 2 '01
American Pie '99
A Kid in Aladdin's Palace '97
Judge & Jury '96
A Kid in King Arthur's Court '95
Rookie of the Year '93
The Fear Inside '92

Allan Nicholls
Home Free All '84
Slap Shot '77

Anthony Nicholls (1902-77)
If... '69
Othello '65
Burn Witch, Burn! '62
Victim '61
The Franchise Affair '52

George Nicholls, Jr. (1897-1939)
Finishing School '33
White Gold '28
The Eagle '25
The Country Kid '23
The Greatest Question '19

Phoebe Nicholls (1958-)
Second Sight '99
FairyTale: A True Story '97
Gulliver's Travels '95
Persuasion '95
Heart of Darkness '93
Deep Cover '88
Maurice '87

Melanie Nicholls-King
Rude '96
Skin Deep '94

Barbara Nichols (1929-76)
The Human Duplicators '64
Scarface Mob '62
Where the Boys Are '60
Pal Joey '57
Sweet Smell of Success '57
Beyond a Reasonable Doubt '56
The King and Four Queens '56
Manfish '56

Britt Nichols
The Demons '74
Virgin among the Living Dead '71

Conrad Nichols
Buck and the Magic Bracelet '97
Days of Hell '84
A Man Called Rage '84
Rush '84

Dandy Nichols (1907-86)
Georgy Girl '66
Ladies Who Do '63
The Leather Boys '63
The Fallen Idol '49

Nichelle Nichols (1933-)
Snow Dogs '02
Star Trek 6: The Undiscovered Country '91
Star Trek 5: The Final Frontier '89
Star Trek 4: The Voyage Home '86
The Supernaturals '86
Star Trek 3: The Search for Spock '84
Star Trek 2: The Wrath of Khan '82
Star Trek: The Motion Picture '80
Truck Turner '74
Say Goodbye, Maggie Cole '72

Robert Nichols
The Night They Robbed Big Bertha's '83
The Thing '51

Stephen Nichols (1951-)
The Glass Cage '96
Phoenix '95
Soapdish '91
Witchboard '87

Taylor Nichols
Jurassic Park 3 '01
Boiler Room '00
Born Bad '97
Headless Body in Topless Bar '96
The Next Step '95
Norma Jean and Marilyn '95
Serpent's Lair '95
Barcelona '94
Metropolitan '90

Jack Nicholson (1937-)
The Pledge '00
As Good As It Gets '97
Blood & Wine '96
The Evening Star '96
Mars Attacks! '96
The Crossing Guard '94
Wolf '94
A Few Good Men '92
Hoffa '92
Man Trouble '92
The Two Jakes '90
Batman '89
Broadcast News '87
Ironweed '87
The Witches of Eastwick '87
Heartburn '86
Prizzi's Honor '85
Terms of Endearment '83
The Border '82
The Postman Always Rings Twice '81
Reds '81
The Shining '80
Goin' South '78
The Last Tycoon '76
Missouri Breaks '76
One Flew Over the Cuckoo's Nest '75
The Passenger '75
Tommy '75
Chinatown '74
The Last Detail '73
The King of Marvin Gardens '72
Carnal Knowledge '71
Five Easy Pieces '70
On a Clear Day You Can See Forever '70
Easy Rider '69
Rebel Rousers '69
Psych-Out '68
Hell's Angels on Wheels '67
The St. Valentine's Day Massacre '67
Flight to Fury '66
Ride in the Whirlwind '66
The Shooting '66
Ensign Pulver '64
The Raven '63
The Terror '63
Little Shop of Horrors '60
Studs Lonigan '60
The Wild Ride '60

Nick Nicholson
Fist of Steel '93
Raiders of the Sun '92
Triple Impact '92

Denise Nickerson (1959-)
Zero to Sixty '78
Smile '75
Willy Wonka & the Chocolate Factory '71

Michael A. (M.A.) Nickles (1968-)
Baja '95
Desert Winds '95
Wayne's World 2 '93

Hamburger Hill '87

Julia Nickson-Soul (1959-)
White Tiger '95
Double Dragon '94
Amityville: A New Generation '93
Sidekicks '93
The Chinatown Murders: Man against the Mob '92
K2: The Ultimate High '92
China Cry '91
Around the World in 80 Days '89
Glitch! '88
Noble House '88
Rambo: First Blood, Part 2 '85

Alex Nicol (1919-2001)
A*P*E* '76
A Matter of WHO '62
The Screaming Skull '58
Stranger in Town '57
Great Day in the Morning '56
The Man from Laramie '55
Black Glove '54
The Gilded Cage '54
Heat Wave '54
The Redhead from Wyoming '53
Because of You '52
Meet Danny Wilson '52
Red Ball Express '52
Tomahawk '51

Daria Nicolodi (1950-)
Opera '88
Creepers '85
Macaroni '85
Unsane '82
Shock '79
Deep Red: Hatchet Murders '75

Michael Nicolosi
Persons Unknown '96
Things to Do in Denver When You're Dead '95
Dream a Little Dream 2 '94
Sketch Artist 2: Hands That See '94

Brigitte Nielsen (1963-)
Doomsdayer '99
Snowboard Academy '96
Body Count '95
Galaxis '95
Chained Heat 2 '92
The Double O Kid '92
Mission of Justice '92
Murder by Moonlight '91
Bye Bye Baby '88
Domino '88
Beverly Hills Cop 2 '87
Cobra '86
Red Sonja '85
Rocky 4 '85

Connie Nielsen (1965-)
One Hour Photo '02
Gladiator '00
Innocents '00
Mission to Mars '00
Rushmore '98
Soldier '98
The Devil's Advocate '97
Voyage '93

Hans Nielsen (1911-65)
The Monster of London City '64
Sherlock Holmes and the Deadly Necklace '62
The Third Sex '57

Leslie Nielsen (1926-)
Camouflage '00
2001: A Space Travesty '00
Safety Patrol '98
Wrongfully Accused '98
Mr. Magoo '97
Spy Hard '96
Dracula: Dead and Loving It '95
Rent-A-Kid '95
Digger '94
Naked Gun 33 1/3: The Final Insult '94
Surf Ninjas '93
All I Want for Christmas '91
Naked Gun 2 1/2: The Smell of Fear '91
Repossessed '90
Dangerous Curves '88
Home Is Where the Hart Is '88
The Naked Gun: From the Files of Police Squad '88
Nightstick '87
Nuts '87
Striker's Mountain '87
The Patriot '86
Soul Man '86
Blade in Hong Kong '85
Reckless Disregard '84
Creepshow '82
Foxfire Light '82
Wrong Is Right '82
Spaceship '81
Airplane! '80
Prom Night '80
Riel '79
The Amsterdam Kill '78
City on Fire '78
Day of the Animals '77
Project: Kill! '77
Viva Knievel '77
Snatched '72
Resurrection of Zachary Wheeler '71
Four Rode Out '69
How to Commit Marriage '69
Dayton's Devils '68
The Reluctant Astronaut '67
Harlow '65
Tammy and the Bachelor '57
Forbidden Planet '56
The Opposite Sex '56

Lisa Niemi
Super Force '90
Steel Dawn '87

Jane Nigh (1925-93)
Motor Patrol '50
Operation Haylift '50

Bill Nighy (1949-)
Blow Dry '00
Longitude '00
Still Crazy '98
FairyTale: A True Story '97
Alive and Kicking '96
Antonia and Jane '91
The Phantom of the Opera '89

Miho Nikaido
Flirt '95
Tokyo Decadence '91

Jan Niklas
The House of the Spirits '93
Club Extinction '89
The Rose Garden '89
Anastasia: The Mystery of Anna '86
Colonel Redl '84

Valery (Valeri Nikolayev) Nikolaev (1963-)
Aberration '97
The Saint '97
U-Turn '97

Anna Q. Nilsson (1888-1974)
Fighting Father Dunne '48
Riders of the Timberline '41
The Toll Gate '20
Seven Keys to Baldpate '17
Regeneration '15

Inger Nilsson (1959-)
Pippi Goes on Board '75
Pippi in the South Seas '74
Pippi Longstocking '73

Maj-Britt Nilsson (1924-)
Secrets of Women '52
Summer Interlude '50
To Joy '50

Rob Nilsson (1940-)
Heat and Sunlight '87
Northern Lights '79

Leonard Nimoy (1931-)
Atlantis: The Lost Empire '01 (V)
David '97
The Pagemaster '94 (V)
Never Forget '91
Star Trek 6: The Undiscovered Country '91
Star Trek 5: The Final Frontier '89
Star Trek 4: The Voyage Home '86
Transformers: The Movie '86 (V)
Aladdin and His Wonderful Lamp '84
Star Trek 3: The Search for Spock '84
Seizure: The Story of Kathy Morris '83
Star Trek 2: The Wrath of Khan '82
A Woman Called Golda '82
Star Trek: The Motion Picture '80
Invasion of the Body Snatchers '78
Baffled '72
Catlow '71
The Balcony '63
The Brain Eaters '58
Them! '54
Kid Monk Baroni '52
Zombies of the Stratosphere '52

Najwa Nimri
Before Night Falls '00
Open Your Eyes '97

Annibale Ninchi
Time Out for Love '61
La Dolce Vita '60

Yvette Nipar
Kept '01
Twilight Man '96
Doctor Mordrid: Master of the Unknown '90
Ski Patrol '89
Run If You Can '87

John Nishio
Overkill '86
Dim Sum: A Little Bit of Heart '85

Greta Nissen
Melody Cruise '32
Ambassador Bill '31

Ronald Nitschke
Sons of Trinity '95
The Innocent '93

Barbara Niven
Alone with a Stranger '99
Depraved '98
I Married a Monster '98

David Niven (1909-83)
Better Late Than Never '83
Curse of the Pink Panther '83
Trail of the Pink Panther '82
Sea Wolves '81
Rough Cut '80
The Big Scam '79
Escape to Athena '79
Candleshoe '78
Death on the Nile '78
Murder by Death '76
No Deposit, No Return '76
Paper Tiger '74
King, Queen, Knave '72
The Statue '71
The Brain '69
The Impossible Years '68
Casino Royale '67
Lady L '65
The Pink Panther '64
Bedtime Story '63
55 Days at Peking '63
The Guns of Navarone '61
Please Don't Eat the Daisies '60
Ask Any Girl '59
Separate Tables '58
Bonjour Tristesse '57
My Man Godfrey '57
Around the World in 80 Days '56
Birds & the Bees '56
The King's Thief '55
Carrington, V.C. '54
The Moon Is Blue '53
Happy Go Lovely '51
The Lady Says No '51
The Elusive Pimpernel '50
The Toast of New Orleans '50
Bonnie Prince Charlie '48
The Bishop's Wife '47
Magnificent Doll '46
The Perfect Marriage '46
Stairway to Heaven '46
Immortal Battalion '44
Spitfire '42
Bachelor Mother '39
Eternally Yours '39
The Real Glory '39
Wuthering Heights '39
Bluebeard's Eighth Wife '38
Dawn Patrol '38
Dinner at the Ritz '37
Prisoner of Zenda '37
Beloved Enemy '36
The Charge of the Light Brigade '36
Dodsworth '36
Rose Marie '36
Barbary Coast '35
Splendor '35

Kip Niven
New Year's Evil '78
Magnum Force '73

Alessandro Nivola (1972-)
Jurassic Park 3 '01
Love's Labour's Lost '00
Time Code '00
Best Laid Plans '99
Mansfield Park '99
I Want You '98
Reach the Rock '98
Face/Off '97

Allan Nixon (1920-95)
Mesa of Lost Women '52
Prehistoric Women '50

Cynthia Nixon (1966-)
Marvin's Room '96
Let It Ride '89
Tanner '88 '88
The Manhattan Project '86
Amadeus '84

Marion (Marian) Nixon (1904-83)
The Reckless Way '36
Tango '36
Hands Up '26
Spangles '26

Marni Nixon (1930-)
Mulan '98 (V)
I Think I Do '97
The Sound of Music '65
Daughter of Horror '55 (V)

Mojo Nixon
Super Mario Bros. '93
Rock 'n' Roll High School Forever '91

Stephanie Niznik
Epoch '00
Memorial Day '98

Chelsea Noble (1964-)
Left Behind: The Movie '00
Instant Karma '90

Christian Noble
Human Desires '97
Illegal Affairs '96

James Noble (1922-)
Chances Are '89
When the Bough Breaks '86
Dempsey '83
The Woman Who Willed a Miracle '83
One Summer Love '76
Roboman '75

Nancy Lee Noble
Just for the Hell of It '68
She-Devils on Wheels '68
The Girl, the Body and the Pill '67

Ray Noble
Here We Go Again! '42
A Damsel in Distress '37

Trisha Noble
Deadline '81
The Private Eyes '80

Bernard Noel
A Married Woman '65
The Fire Within '64

Magali Noel (1932-)
The Eighties '83
Les Rendez-vous D'Anna '78
Amarcord '74
La Dolce Vita '60
Elena and Her Men '56

Noelia Noel
Night of the Bloody Apes '68
Sputnik '61

Ulrich Noethen
The Harmonists '99
Jew-boy Levi '98

Yumiko Nogawa
Zatoichi: The Blind Swordsman and the Fugitives '68
Story of a Prostitute '65
Gate of Flesh '64

Natalija Nogulich
Confessions of Sorority Girls '94
Hoffa '92
Homicide '91
The Guardian '90
Sister, Sister '87

Philippe Noiret (1931-)
Grosse Fatigue '94
The Postman '94
Revenge of the Musketeers '94
The Palermo Connection '91
Uranus '91
Life and Nothing But '89
The Return of the Musketeers '89
Cinema Paradiso '88
The Family '87
Aurora '84
Fort Saganne '84
My New Partner '84
Next Summer '84
Birgitt Haas Must Be Killed '83
Coup de Torchon '81
Jupiter's Thigh '81
Three Brothers '80
Who Is Killing the Great Chefs of Europe? '78
Dear Detective '77
The Purple Taxi '77
A Woman at Her Window '77
The Desert of the Tartars '76
Old Gun '76
The Judge and the Assassin '75
Le Secret '74
The Clockmaker '73
La Grande Bouffe '73
Night Flight from Moscow '73
The Holes '72
Murphy's War '71
The Assassination Bureau '69
Justine '69
Topaz '69
Night of the Generals '67
Woman Times Seven '67
Lady L '65
Zazie dans le Metro '61

Bob Nolan (1908-80)
Melody Time '48 (V)
Lights of Old Santa Fe '47
Song of Arizona '46
Heart of the Golden West '42
Sunset on the Desert '42

Doris Nolan
Follies Girl '43
Holiday '38

Jeanette Nolan (1911-98)
The Horse Whisperer '97
Street Justice '89
Cloak & Dagger '84
The Fox and the Hound '81 (V)
The Manitou '78
The Rescuers '77 (V)
Babe! '75
The Reluctant Astronaut '67
The Man Who Shot Liberty Valance '62
Psycho '60 (V)
Seventh Cavalry '56
Tribute to a Bad Man '56
A Lawless Street '55
Hangman's Knot '52
Macbeth '48

John Nolan (1933-2000)
Following '99
The Terror '79
In the Steps of a Dead Man '74

Lloyd Nolan (1902-85)
Hannah and Her Sisters '86
It Came Upon a Midnight Clear '84
Prince Jack '83
My Boys Are Good Boys '78
Galyon '77
Abduction of St. Anne '75
Earthquake '74
Airport '70
Ice Station Zebra '68
Sergeant Ryker '68
Circus World '64
Girl Hunters '63
Portrait in Black '60
Abandon Ship '57
Peyton Place '57
The Last Hunt '56
The Lemon Drop Kid '51
Easy Living '49
The Sun Comes Up '49
The Street with No Name '48
Lady in the Lake '46
House on 92nd Street '45
A Tree Grows in Brooklyn '45
Bataan '43
Guadalcanal Diary '43
House Across the Bay '40
Johnny Apollo '40
Every Day's a Holiday '38
Internes Can't Take Money '37
The Texas Rangers '36
"G" Men '35

Tom Nolan
Voyage of the Rock Aliens '87
School Spirit '85

Claude Nollier
Forbidden Fruit '52
Moulin Rouge '52

Jacques Nolot
Under the Sand '00
Artemisia '97
Nenette and Boni '96

Nick Nolte (1941-)
The Golden Bowl '00
Trixie '00
Simpatico '99
Breakfast of Champions '98
The Thin Red Line '98
Affliction '97
Afterglow '97
U-Turn '97
Mother Night '96
Nightwatch '96
Mulholland Falls '95
Blue Chips '94
I Love Trouble '94
Jefferson in Paris '94
I'll Do Anything '93
Lorenzo's Oil '92
The Player '92
Cape Fear '91
The Prince of Tides '91
Another 48 Hrs. '90
Everybody Wins '90
Q & A '90
Farewell to the King '89
New York Stories '89
Three Fugitives '89
Extreme Prejudice '87
Weeds '87
Down and Out in Beverly Hills '86
Grace Quigley '84
Teachers '84
Under Fire '83

Cannery Row *'82*
48 Hrs. *'82*
Heart Beat *'80*
North Dallas Forty *'79*
Who'll Stop the Rain? *'78*
The Deep *'77*
Rich Man, Poor Man *'76*
Return to Macon County *'75*
The Runaway Barge *'75*
Death Sentence *'74*

Tom NonDorf
Rage of the Werewolf *'99*
Addicted to Murder 2: Tainted Blood *'97*

John Ford Noonan
Flirting with Disaster *'95*
Adventures in Babysitting *'87*

Tom Noonan (1951-)
The Pledge *'00*
The Astronaut's Wife *'99*
Phoenix *'98*
The Wife *'95*
What Happened Was... *'94*
Last Action Hero *'93*
RoboCop 2 *'90*
Mystery Train *'89*
The Monster Squad *'87*
Manhunter *'86*
The Man with One Red Shoe *'85*
Wolfen *'81*

Tommy Noonan (1921-68)
Three Nuts in Search of a Bolt *'64*
Promises! Promises! *'63*
The Girl Most Likely *'57*
The Ambassador's Daughter *'56*
A Star Is Born *'54*
Gentlemen Prefer Blondes *'53*
Adam's Rib *'50*
Return of Jesse James *'50*
Jungle Patrol *'48*

Kathleen Noone
Citizen Ruth *'96*
Serpent's Lair *'95*

Ghita Norby (1935-)
The Kingdom 2 *'97*
Hamsun *'96*
The Kingdom *'95*
Like It Never Was Before *'95*
The Best Intentions *'92*
Sofie *'92*
Freud Leaving Home *'91*
Memories of a Marriage *'90*
Babette's Feast *'87 (N)*
The Wolf at the Door *'87*

Christine Norden
Night Beat *'48*
Mine Own Executioner *'47*

Jeffrey Nordling (1962-)
Turbulence 2: Fear of Flying *'99*
Saint Maybe *'98*
True Women *'97*
D3: The Mighty Ducks *'96*
A Stranger in Town *'95*
Holy Matrimony *'94*
And the Band Played On *'93*
Dangerous Heart *'93*

Carsten Norgaard
Red Shoe Diaries 6: How I Met My Husband *'95*
Out of Annie's Past *'94*

Eduardo Noriega (1973-)
The Devil's Backbone *'01*
The Yellow Fountain *'99*
Open Your Eyes *'97*
Thesis *'96*

Felix Noriego
Battle Cry *'55*
To Hell and Back *'55*

Maidie Norman (1913-98)
Sixteen *'72*
What Ever Happened to Baby Jane? *'62*

Susan Norman
Safe *'95*
Poison *'91*

Zack Norman
Crosscut *'95*
Babyfever *'94*
Venice, Venice *'92*
Cadillac Man *'90*
America *'86*
Romancing the Stone *'84*
Sitting Ducks *'80*
Tracks *'76*

Mabel Normand (1894-1930)
Extra Girl *'23*
What Happened to Rosa? *'21*
Mickey *'17*
Mabel & Fatty *'16*
Charlie Chaplin ... Our Hero! *'15*
Tillie's Punctured Romance *'14*

David Norona
Mrs. Santa Claus *'96*
Twisted *'96*

Bruce Norris (1960-)
The Sixth Sense *'99*
A Civil Action *'98*
Reach the Rock *'98*

Chuck Norris (1939-)
Forest Warrior *'95*
Top Dog *'95*
Hellbound *'94*
Sidekicks *'93*
Walker: Texas Ranger: One Riot, One Ranger *'93*
The Hitman *'91*
Delta Force 2: Operation Stranglehold *'90*
Braddock: Missing in Action 3 *'88*
Hero and the Terror *'88*
Delta Force *'86*
Firewalker *'86*
Code of Silence *'85*
Invasion U.S.A. *'85*
Missing in Action 2: The Beginning *'85*
Missing in Action *'84*
Lone Wolf McQuade *'83*
Forced Vengeance *'82*
Silent Rage *'82*
An Eye for an Eye *'81*
Slaughter in San Francisco *'81*
Octagon *'80*
Force of One *'79*
Game of Death *'79*
Good Guys Wear Black *'78*
Breaker! Breaker! *'77*
Enter the Dragon *'73*
Return of the Dragon *'73*
The Student Teachers *'73*

Dean Norris
Three Strikes *'00*
My Little Assassin *'99*
Starship Troopers *'97*
Without Limits *'97*
The Lawnmower Man *'92*
Hard to Kill *'89*

Edward Norris (1910-)
Heartaches *'47*
Wings over the Pacific *'43*
The Man with Two Lives *'42*
Back in the Saddle *'41*
Road Show *'41*
The Lady in Question *'40*
They Won't Forget *'37*
Show Them No Mercy *'35*

Mike Norris (1963-)
Dragon Fury 2 *'96*
Ripper Man *'96*
Death Ring *'93*
Delta Force 3: The Killing Game *'91*
Survival Game *'87*
Born American *'86*

Simon Norrthon
Like It Never Was Before *'95*
Speak Up! It's So Dark *'93*

Alan North (1920-2000)
The Jerky Boys *'95*
Crazy People *'90*
Glory *'89*
Lean on Me *'89*
Rachel River *'87*
Billy Galvin *'86*
Highlander *'86*

Heather North
The Barefoot Executive *'71*
Git! *'65*

Jay North (1952-)
Scout's Honor *'80*
The Teacher *'74*
Maya *'66*
Zebra in the Kitchen *'65*

J.J. North
Psycho Sisters *'98*
Hellblock 13 *'97*
Attack of the 60-Foot Centerfold *'95*

Noelle North
Sweater Girls *'78*
Slumber Party '57 *'76*

Sheree North (1933-)
Dying to Get Rich *'98*
Defenseless *'91*
Maniac Cop *'88*
Legs *'83*
Only Once in a Lifetime *'83*
Marilyn: The Untold Story *'80*
Portrait of a Stripper *'79*
Telefon *'77*
Most Wanted *'76*
The Shootist *'76*
Breakout *'75*
Charley Varrick *'73*
Snatched *'72*
Lawman *'71*
The Organization *'71*
The Trouble with Girls (and How to Get into It) *'69*

Ted North
The Devil Thumbs a Ride *'47*
Charlie Chan in Rio *'41*

Jeremy Northam (1961-)
Possession *'02*
Enigma *'01*
Gosford Park *'01*
The Golden Bowl *'00*
Happy, Texas *'99*
An Ideal Husband *'99*
Gloria *'98*
The Winslow Boy *'98*
Mimic *'97*
Emma *'96*
Carrington *'95*
The Net *'95*
A Village Affair *'95*
Voices from a Locked Room *'95*
Emily Bronte's Wuthering Heights *'92*
A Fatal Inversion *'92*
Suspicion *'87*

Ryan Northcott
Ripper: Letter from Hell *'01*
Mystery, Alaska *'99*

Alex Norton
The Count of Monte Cristo *'02*
Beautiful Creatures *'00*
Orphans *'97*
Squanto: A Warrior's Tale *'94*
Hidden City *'87*
Comfort and Joy *'84*
Gregory's Girl *'80*
A Sense of Freedom *'78*

Barry Norton (1905-56)
Devil Monster *'46*
Dishonored *'31*
Dracula (Spanish Version) *'31*

Edgar Norton
Son of Frankenstein *'39*
Dr. Jekyll and Mr. Hyde *'32*

Edward Norton (1969-)
Death to Smoochy *'02*
The Score *'01*
Keeping the Faith *'00*
Fight Club *'99*
American History X *'98*
Rounders *'98*
Everyone Says I Love You *'96*
The People vs. Larry Flynt *'96*
Primal Fear *'96*

Jack Norton
The Bank Dick *'40*
Finishing School *'33*

Jim Norton (1938-)
Midnight's Child *'93*
Memoirs of an Invisible Man *'92*
Hidden Agenda *'90*

Ken Norton (1945-)
Dirty Work *'97*
Kiss and Be Killed *'91*
Oceans of Fire *'86*
Drum *'76*
Mandingo *'75*

Richard Norton (1950-)
Black Thunder *'98*
Mr. Nice Guy *'98*
Fugitive X *'96*
Under the Gun *'95*
Cyber-Tracker *'93*
Deathfight *'93*
Direct Hit *'93*
Rage and Honor 2: Hostile Takeover *'93*
Ironheart *'92*
Lady Dragon *'92*
Rage and Honor *'92*
Raiders of the Sun *'92*
The Kick Fighter *'91*
China O'Brien 2 *'89*
Crossfire *'89*
Hyper Space *'89*
China O'Brien *'88*
Equalizer 2000 *'86*
The Millionaire's Express *'86*
Gymkata *'85*

Terry Norton
American Kickboxer 1 *'91*
Emissary *'89*

Judy Norton-Taylor
A Day for Thanks on Walton's Mountain *'82*
The Waltons: The Christmas Carol *'80*

Brandy Norwood
Osmosis Jones *'01 (V)*
Cinderella *'97*

Jack Noseworthy (1969-)
Undercover Brother *'02*
Cecil B. Demented *'00*
U-571 *'00*
Idle Hands *'99*
Event Horizon *'97*
Barb Wire *'96*
Breakdown *'96*
The Brady Bunch Movie *'95*
A Place for Annie *'94*
S.F.W. *'94*
Alive *'93*

Ralph Nossek
Citizen X *'95*
Chicago Joe & the Showgirl *'90*

Christopher Noth (1956-)
The Glass House *'01*
Cast Away *'00*
A Texas Funeral *'99*
The Confession *'98*
Cold Around the Heart *'97*
Rough Riders *'97*
Burnzy's Last Call *'95*
Jakarta *'88*
Baby Boom *'87*
Apology *'86*
Off Beat *'86*
Smithereens *'82*

Michael Nouri (1945-)
61* *'01*
Finding Forrester *'00*
Overkill *'96*
Hologram Man *'95*
To the Limit *'95*
American Yakuza *'94*
Fortunes of War *'94*
The Hidden 2 *'94*
Inner Sanctum 2 *'94*
Lady in Waiting *'94*
Shattered Dreams *'94*
No Escape, No Return *'93*
Black Ice *'92*
DaVinci's War *'92*
Danielle Steel's Changes *'91*
Psychic *'91*
Total Exposure *'91*
Little Vegas *'90*
Project: Alien *'89*
Thieves of Fortune *'89*
The Hidden *'87*
Between Two Women *'86*
Imagemaker *'86*
Rage of Angels: The Story Continues *'86*
Spraggue *'84*
Flashdance *'83*
Gangster Wars *'81*

Eva Novak (1898-1988)
Red Signals *'27*
Laughing at Danger *'24*
Sky High *'22*
Trailin' *'21*

Frank Novak
Virtual Seduction *'96*
Watchers 3 *'94*

Jane Novak
Three Word Brand *'21*
Wagon Tracks *'19*

Kim Novak (1933-)
Liebestraum *'91*
The Children *'90*
The Mirror Crack'd *'80*
Just a Gigolo *'79*
The White Buffalo *'77*
Tales That Witness Madness *'73*
The Amorous Adventures of Moll Flanders *'65*
Kiss Me, Stupid! *'64*
Of Human Bondage *'64*
Boys' Night Out *'62*
Strangers When We Meet *'60*
Bell, Book and Candle *'58*
Vertigo *'58*
Pal Joey *'57*
The Eddy Duchin Story *'56*
The Man with the Golden Arm *'55*
Picnic *'55*
The French Line *'54*
Phffft! *'54*

Mel Novak
Capital Punishment *'96*
Expert Weapon *'93*
Lovely ... But Deadly *'82*
Family Reunion *'79*
Cat in the Cage *'68*

Ramon Novarro (1899-1968)
Heller in Pink Tights *'60*
Big Steal *'49*
The Cat and the Fiddle *'34*
Mata Hari *'32*
The Student Prince in Old Heidelberg *'27*
Ben-Hur *'26*

Don Novello (1943-)
Atlantis: The Lost Empire *'01 (V)*
The Adventures of Rocky & Bullwinkle *'00*
Just One Night *'00*
Just the Ticket *'98*
Jack *'96*
Casper *'95*
One Night Stand *'95*
Armistead Maupin's Tales of the City *'93*
Teenage Bonnie & Klepto Clyde *'93*
Spirit of '76 *'91*
The Godfather, Part 3 *'90*
New York Stories *'89*
Tucker: The Man and His Dream *'88*

Ivor Novello (1893-1951)
Phantom Fiend *'35*
The Lodger *'26*
The White Rose *'23*

Jay Novello (1904-82)
What Did You Do in the War, Daddy? *'66*
Harum Scarum *'65*
The Pride and the Passion *'57*
The Prodigal *'55*
Sabaka *'55*
Ma and Pa Kettle on Vacation *'53*
Miracle of Our Lady of Fatima *'52*
Bad Man of Deadwood *'41*
Robin Hood of the Pecos *'41*
The Border Legion *'40*

Tom Novembre
The Ice Rink *'99*
An American Werewolf in Paris *'97*

Nancho Novo (1958-)
Lovers of the Arctic Circle *'98*
Tierra *'95*
The Red Squirrel *'93*

Tom Nowicki
Flash *'98*
Kiss of Fire *'98*
Nightjohn *'96*

Philomena Nowlin
Ebony Dreams *'80*
Miss Melody Jones *'73*

Zachi Noy (1953-)
Young Love—Lemon Popsicle 7 *'87*
Baby Love *'83*
Private Manoeuvres *'83*
Hot Bubblegum *'81*

Joanna Noyes
Bleeders *'97*
The Reaper *'97*

Bruce Nozick
Gale Force *'01*
Tuesdays with Morrie *'99*
Hit the Dutchman *'92*
Killer Instinct *'92*

Winston Ntshona
Tarzan and the Lost City *'98*
Night of the Cyclone *'90*
A Dry White Season *'89*

Danny Nucci (1968-)
Firestarter 2: Rekindled *'02*
Codename: Jaguar *'00*
Friends & Lovers *'99*
Love Walked In *'97*
Titanic *'97*
The Big Squeeze *'96*
Eraser *'96*
The Rock *'96*
That Old Feeling *'96*
Crimson Tide *'95*
Homage *'95*
Roosters *'95*
Book of Love *'91*
The Children of Times Square *'86*

Eddie Nugent (1904-95)
Doughnuts & Society *'36*
Prison Shadows *'36*
Kentucky Blue Streak *'35*
Night Nurse *'31*

Elliott Nugent (1900-80)
Welcome Stranger *'47*
Romance *'30*
The Unholy Three *'30*

Miguel Nunez
Life *'99*
For Richer or Poorer *'97*
Return of the Living Dead *'85*

Bill Nunn (1953-)
Spider-Man *'02*
The Substitute 4: Failure is Not an Option *'00*
Foolish *'99*
Passing Glory *'99*
The Tic Code *'99*
Always Outnumbered Always Outgunned *'98*
He Got Game *'98*
The Legend of 1900 *'98*
Quicksilver Highway *'98*
Blood Brothers *'97*

Ellen Foster '97
Kiss the Girls '97
Mad City '97
Bulletproof '96
Extreme Measures '96
Mr. & Mrs. Loving '96
The Affair '95
Money Train '95
Things to Do in Denver When You're Dead '95
True Crime '95
Canadian Bacon '94
Candyman 2: Farewell to the Flesh '94
The Last Seduction '94
Save Me '93
Sister Act '92
New Jack City '91
Regarding Henry '91
White Lie '91
Def by Temptation '90
Mo' Better Blues '90
Do the Right Thing '89
School Daze '88

Teri Nunn
Follow That Car '80
Thank God It's Friday '78

Rudolf Nureyev (1938-93)
Exposed '83
Valentino '77

Loredana Nusciak
Django '68
Gladiators 7 '62

Danny Nussbaum
Beautiful People '99
24-7 '97

Mike Nussbaum
The Water Engine '92
Things Change '88
House of Games '87

Jeff Nuttal
Beaumarchais the Scoundrel '96
Captives '94
Robin Hood '91

Mayf Nutter
Hunter's Blood '87
The $5.20 an Hour Dream '80

France Nuyen (1939-)
A Smile Like Yours '96
A Passion to Kill '94
The Joy Luck Club '93
China Cry '91
Code Name: Diamond Head '77
Return to Fantasy Island '77
Black Water Gold '69
Diamond Head '62
South Pacific '58

N!xau
The Gods Must Be Crazy 2 '89
The Gods Must Be Crazy '84

Carrie Nye (1937-)
Hello Again '87
Creepshow '82
The Group '66

Carroll Nye
Gone with the Wind '39
Lottery Bride '30

Louis Nye (1922-)
O.C. and Stiggs '87
Harper Valley P.T.A. '78
Charge of the Model T's '76
A Guide for the Married Man '67
The Wheeler Dealers '63
The Facts of Life '60

Lena Nyman (1944-)
The Adventures of Picasso '80
Autumn Sonata '78
I Am Curious (Yellow) '67

Henry O
The Lost Empire '01
Dragonheart: A New Beginning '00
Romeo Must Die '00
Shanghai Noon '00

Jack Oakie (1903-78)
Lover Come Back '61
The Rat Race '60
Around the World in 80 Days '56
Tomahawk '51
It Happened Tomorrow '44
Hello, Frisco, Hello '43
Wintertime '43
Iceland '42
Song of the Islands '42
The Great American Broadcast '41
The Great Dictator '40
Little Men '40
Tin Pan Alley '40
Young People '40
The Affairs of Annabel '38
Toast of New York '37
The Texas Rangers '36
That Girl from Paris '36
Murder at the Vanities '34
The Eagle and the Hawk '33
Uptown New York '32

Simon Oakland (1922-83)
Emperor of the North Pole '73
The Night Strangler '72
Chato's Land '71
The Night Stalker '71
On a Clear Day You Can See Forever '70
Bullitt '68
Tony Rome '67
The Sand Pebbles '66
Follow That Dream '61
West Side Story '61
Psycho '60
The Rise and Fall of Legs Diamond '60
I Want to Live! '58

Wheeler Oakman (1890-1949)
Teenage '44
Meet the Mob '42
Double Trouble '41
Wolf Call '39
Slaves in Bondage '37
Aces and Eights '36
Death from a Distance '36
Ghost Patrol '36
The Man from Gun Town '36
Roaring Guns '36
Song of the Trail '36
Frontier Days '34
In Old Santa Fe '34
The Lost Jungle '34
Man of Action '33
Boiling Point '32
The Riding Tornado '32
Texas Cyclone '32
Two-Fisted Law '32
Roaring Ranch '30
The Broken Mask '28
Outside the Law '21
Peck's Bad Boy '21
The Spoilers '14

Simon Oates
Doomwatch '72
The Terrornauts '67

Warren Oates (1928-82)
Blue Thunder '83
Tough Enough '83
The Blue and the Gray '82
The Border '82
Stripes '81
East of Eden '80
Prime Time '80
And Baby Makes Six '79
My Old Man '79
1941 '79
Brink's Job '78
Gunfire '78
Sleeping Dogs '77
Dixie Dynamite '76
Drum '76
92 in the Shade '76
Race with the Devil '75
The White Dawn '75
Badlands '74
Bring Me the Head of Alfredo Garcia '74
Cockfighter '74
Dillinger '73
The Thief Who Came to Dinner '73
Tom Sawyer '73
Hired Hand '71
Two Lane Blacktop '71
There Was a Crooked Man '70
Crooks & Coronets '69
The Wild Bunch '69
In the Heat of the Night '67
Return of the Magnificent Seven '66
The Shooting '66
Shenandoah '65
Ride the High Country '62

Philip Ober (1902-82)
The Ghost and Mr. Chicken '66
The Facts of Life '60
Beloved Infidel '59
The Mating Game '59
North by Northwest '59
Escapade in Japan '57
From Here to Eternity '53
Come Back, Little Sheba '52
The Magnificent Yankee '50
Never a Dull Moment '50

Merle Oberon (1911-79)
Interval '73
Hotel '67
The Oscar '66
Deep in My Heart '54
Desiree '54
Berlin Express '48
A Song to Remember '45
Dark Waters '44
Forever and a Day '43
Stage Door Canteen '43
Lydia '41
That Uncertain Feeling '41
The Lion Has Wings '40
Wuthering Heights '39
The Cowboy and the Lady '38
The Divorce of Lady X '38
Beloved Enemy '36
These Three '36
Broken Melody '34
Private Life of Don Juan '34
The Scarlet Pimpernel '34
The Private Life of Henry VIII '33
Wedding Rehearsal '32

Jacqueline Obradors (1967-)
Atlantis: The Lost Empire '01 (V)
Tortilla Soup '01
Deuce Bigalow: Male Gigolo '99
Six Days, Seven Nights '98
Soldier Boyz '95

Anna (Ana Garcia) Obregon (1955-)
Car Crash
Bolero '84
Treasure of the Four Crowns '82

Claudio Obregon
Esmeralda Comes by Night '98
Midaq Alley '95
Reed: Insurgent Mexico '73

Rodrigo Obregon
L.A. Wars '94
Enemy Gold '93
Fit to Kill '93
Hard Hunted '92
Tides of War '90
Picasso Trigger '89
Savage Beach '89
Django Strikes Again '87
Hard Ticket to Hawaii '87

Hugh O'Brian (1925-)
Wyatt Earp: Return to Tombstone '94
The Gambler Returns: The Luck of the Draw '93
Doin' Time on Planet Earth '88
Twins '88
The Seekers '79
Cruise into Terror '78
Fantasy Island '76
The Shootist '76
Killer Force '75
Murder on Flight 502 '75
Probe '72
Wild Women '70
Africa Texas Style '67
In Harm's Way '65
Love Has Many Faces '65
Alias Jesse James '59
Broken Lance '54
There's No Business Like Show Business '54
Man from the Alamo '53
The Lawless Breed '52
Red Ball Express '52
Son of Ali Baba '52
Little Big Horn '51
Vengeance Valley '51
Return of Jesse James '50
Rocketship X-M '50

Austin O'Brien (1981-)
The Baby-Sitters' Club '95
Lawnmower Man 2: Beyond Cyberspace '95
My Girl 2 '94
Last Action Hero '93
Prehysteria '93

Clay O'Brien (1961-)
Cahill: United States Marshal '73
One Little Indian '73
The Cowboys '72

Dave O'Brien (1912-69)
Enemy of the Law '45
Flaming Bullets '45
Frontier Fugitives '45
Marked for Murder '45
The Phantom of 42nd Street '45
Three in the Saddle '45
Boss of Rawhide '44
Dead or Alive '44
Gangsters of the Frontier '44
Guns of the Law '44
Fighting Valley '43
Rangers Take Over '43
Bowery at Midnight '42
King of the Stallions '42
The Devil Bat '41
Double Trouble '41
Spooks Run Wild '41
Buzzy Rides the Range '40
Danger Ahead '40
Murder on the Yukon '40
Sky Bandits '40
That Gang of Mine '40
Yukon Flight '40
Daughter of the Tong '39
The Singing Cowgirl '39
Water Rustlers '39
Law of the Texan '38
Reefer Madness '38
Brothers of the West '37
Lightning Bill Crandall '37
Lion's Den '36

Donald O'Brien
Quest for the Mighty Sword '90
Trap Them & Kill Them '84
Doctor Butcher M.D. '80
The Train '65

Edmond O'Brien (1915-)
Dream No Evil '75
Lucky Luciano '74
99 & 44/100 Dead '74
They Only Kill Their Masters '72
Jigsaw '71
The Love God? '70
The Wild Bunch '69
The Doomsday Flight '66
Fantastic Voyage '66
Rio Conchos '64
Seven Days in May '64
Birdman of Alcatraz '62
The Longest Day '62
The Man Who Shot Liberty Valance '62
Moon Pilot '62
The Great Impostor '61
The Last Voyage '60
Up Periscope '59
Stopover Tokyo '57
D-Day, the Sixth of June '56
The Girl Can't Help It '56
Pete Kelly's Blues '55
The Barefoot Contessa '54
The Bigamist '53
The Hitch-Hiker '53
Julius Caesar '53
The Denver & Rio Grande '51
The Admiral Was a Lady '50
D.O.A. '49
White Heat '49
For the Love of Mary '48
A Double Life '47
The Killers '46
The Amazing Mrs. Holiday '43
A Girl, a Guy and a Gob '41
The Hunchback of Notre Dame '39

George O'Brien (1900-85)
Cheyenne Autumn '64
Gold Raiders '51
She Wore a Yellow Ribbon '49
Bullet Code '40
Legion of the Lawless '40
Racketeers of the Range '39
Park Avenue Logger '37
Windjammer '37
Cowboy Millionaire '35
Thunder Mountain '35
Daniel Boone '34
Dude Ranger '34
Mystery Ranch '34
Painted Desert '31
The Lone Star Ranger '30
Sunrise '27

Joan O'Brien (1936-)
It Happened at the World's Fair '63
Samar '62
The Alamo '60
Operation Petticoat '59

Kieran O'Brien (1973-)
Jason and the Argonauts '00
Virtual Sexuality '99
Cracker: Brotherly Love '95
Bellman and True '88

Margaret O'Brien (1937-)
Amy '81
Heller in Pink Tights '60
Glory '56
Little Women '49
The Secret Garden '49
Our Vines Have Tender Grapes '45
The Canterville Ghost '44
Jane Eyre '44
Meet Me in St. Louis '44
Thousands Cheer '43
Journey for Margaret '42

Maria O'Brien
In a Stranger's Hand '92
Promised a Miracle '88

Maureen O'Brien (1943-)
American Women '00
Falling for a Dancer '98
The Land Girls '98

Myles O'Brien
Scorned 2 '96
Sexual Roulette '96

Niall O'Brien
Broken Harvest '94
Class of '61 '92
Rawhead Rex '87
Excalibur '81
Lovespell '79

Pat O'Brien
Doomed Caravan '41
Hawaiian Buckaroo '38
Tim Tyler's Luck '37

Pat O'Brien (1899-1983)
Ragtime '81
Scout's Honor '80
The End '78
Some Like It Hot '59
Last Hurrah '58
Jubilee Trail '54
The Boy with the Green Hair '48
Fighting Father Dunne '48
Riff-Raff '47
Crack-Up '46
Having Wonderful Crime '45
His Butler's Sister '44
Bombardier '43
The Iron Major '43
Marine Raiders '43
The Navy Comes Through '42
The Fighting 69th '40
Knute Rockne: All American '40
Slightly Honorable '40
Angels with Dirty Faces '38
Boy Meets Girl '38
Ceiling Zero '35
Devil Dogs of the Air '35
Flirtation Walk '34
Bombshell '33
Bureau of Missing Persons '33
The World Gone Mad '33
American Madness '32
Hell's House '32
Consolation Marriage '31
The Front Page '31

Peter O'Brien (1960-)
Hotel de Love '96
Angel of Fury '93
A Kink in the Picasso '90
The Grand Duel '73

Richard O'Brien (1942-)
Dungeons and Dragons '00
Dark City '97
Spice World: The Movie '97
Robin Hood...The Legend: The Time of the Wolf '85
Shock Treatment '81
The Rocky Horror Picture Show '75

Shauna O'Brien (1970-)
The Seductress '00
The Escort '97
Body Armor '96
Friend of the Family 2 '96
Fugitive Rage '96
Friend of the Family '95
Over the Wire '95

Tom O'Brien (1965-)
The Accused '88
The Big Easy '87

Virginia O'Brien (1921-2001)
Merton of the Movies '47
The Harvey Girls '46
The Show-Off '46
Till the Clouds Roll By '46
Two Girls and a Sailor '44
DuBarry Was a Lady '43
Thousands Cheer '43
Panama Hattie '42
Ship Ahoy '42
Big Store '41
Lady Be Good '41

Erin O'Brien-Moore (1902-79)
Destination Moon '50
The Black Legion '37
Our Little Girl '35

Jeffrey Obrow
The Kindred '87
The Power '80

Pat O'Bryan
976-EVIL 2: The Astral Factor '91
Relentless '89
976-EVIL '88

Sean O'Bryan
Big Fat Liar '02
The Princess Diaries '01
Nice Guys Sleep Alone '99
I'll Be Home for Christmas '98
The Twilight of the Golds '97

Brian F. O'Byrne
Bandits '01
An Everlasting Piece '00

Ric Ocasek
Hairspray '88

Made in Heaven '87

Andrea Occhipinti (1957-)
Running Away '89
Control '87
The Family '87
Bolero '84
El Barbaro '84
A Blade in the Dark '83
Conquest '83
New York Ripper '82

Uwe Ochsenknecht (1956-)
Kaspar Hauser '93
Schtonk '92
Fire, Ice and Dynamite '91
Men... '85
Das Boot '81

Arthur O'Connell (1908-81)
The Hiding Place '75
Huckleberry Finn '74
Ben '72
They Only Kill Their Masters '72
The Last Valley '71
There Was a Crooked Man '70
The Reluctant Astronaut '67
Fantastic Voyage '66
The Silencers '66
Monkey's Uncle '65
Kissin' Cousins '64
7 Faces of Dr. Lao '63
Follow That Dream '61
The Great Impostor '61
Misty '61
Pocketful of Miracles '61
Cimarron '60
Anatomy of a Murder '59
Gidget '59
Operation Petticoat '59
Man of the West '58
Bus Stop '56
The Man in the Gray Flannel Suit '56
Solid Gold Cadillac '56
Picnic '55
Open Secret '48
Blondie's Blessed Event '42
Law of the Jungle '42
Citizen Kane '41

Charlie O'Connell
The Devil's Prey '01
Dude, Where's My Car? '00
Derby '71

Deirdre O'Connell
Hearts in Atlantis '01
Murder in a Small Town '99
Lifeform '96
Fearless '93
Cool World '92
Falling from Grace '92
Straight Talk '92
Pastime '91

Jerry O'Connell (1974-)
Tomcats '01
Mission to Mars '00
Body Shots '99
The '60s '99
Can't Hardly Wait '98
What the Deaf Man Heard '98
Scream 2 '97
Jerry Maguire '96
Joe's Apartment '96
Blue River '95
Hole in the Sky '95
Calendar Girl '93
Ollie Hopnoodle's Haven of Bliss '88
Stand by Me '86

Patrick O'Connell
We'll Meet Again '82
McKenzie Break '70

Raoul O'Connell
Lifeform '96
Frisk '95
Boys Life '94

Taaffe O'Connell
Galaxy of Terror '81
Caged Fury '80

Carroll O'Connor (1925-2001)
Return to Me '00
36 Hours to Die '99
The Father Clements Story '87
Convicted '86
Brass '85
Law and Disorder '74
Doctors' Wives '70
Kelly's Heroes '70
Death of a Gunfighter '69
Marlowe '69
The Devil's Brigade '68
For Love of Ivy '68
Point Blank '67
Waterhole #3 '67
Hawaii '66
What Did You Do in the War, Daddy? '66
In Harm's Way '65
Cleopatra '63
Lonely Are the Brave '62
Parrish '61
Johnny Frenchman '46

Derrick O'Connor
End of Days '99
Deep Rising '98
How to Make an American Quilt '95
Dealers '89
Lethal Weapon 2 '89
Hope and Glory '87

Donald O'Connor (1925-)
Out to Sea '97
Toys '92
A Time to Remember '90
Pandemonium '82
Ragtime '81
The Wonders of Aladdin '61
Francis in the Navy '55
Francis Joins the WACs '54
There's No Business Like Show Business '54
Francis Covers the Big Town '53
I Love Melvin '53
Francis Goes to West Point '52
Singin' in the Rain '52
Francis Goes to the Races '51
Francis the Talking Mule '49
Something in the Wind '47
Private Buckaroo '42
Beau Geste '39

Frances O'Connor (1969-)
The Importance of Being Earnest '02
Windtalkers '02
A. I.: Artificial Intelligence '01
About Adam '00
Bedazzled '00
Madame Bovary '00
Mansfield Park '99
Kiss or Kill '97
A Little Bit of Soul '97
The Wedding Party '97
Love and Other Catastrophes '95

Glynnis O'Connor (1956-)
New Best Friend '02
Saint Maybe '98
Ellen Foster '97
Past the Bleachers '95
To Heal a Nation '88
A Conspiracy of Love '87
The Deliberate Stranger '86
Johnny Dangerously '84
Melanie '82
Night Crossing '81
Those Lips, Those Eyes '80
California Dreaming '79
The Dark Side of Love '79
Our Town '77
The Boy in the Plastic Bubble '76
Ode to Billy Joe '76
Kid Vengeance '75
Someone I Touched '75

Kevin J. O'Connor (1964-)
Chill Factor '99
The Mummy '99
Black Cat Run '98
Deep Rising '98
Gods and Monsters '98
The Love Bug '97
Lord of Illusions '95
Virtuosity '95
Canadian Bacon '94
Color of Night '94
No Escape '94
Equinox '93
Hero '92
Love at Large '89
Signs of Life '89
Steel Magnolias '89
The Caine Mutiny Court Martial '88
The Moderns '88
Candy Mountain '87
Peggy Sue Got Married '86
Special Effects '85
Bogie: The Last Hero '80
Let's Scare Jessica to Death '71

Renee O'Connor (1971-)
Follow the River '95
Darkman 2: The Return of Durant '94
Hercules the Legendary Journeys, Vol. 2: The Lost Kingdom '94

Robert Emmett O'Connor
A Night at the Opera '35
Kid from Spain '32

Sinead O'Connor (1966-)
The Butcher Boy '97
Emily Bronte's Wuthering Heights '92

Tim O'Connor (1927-)
Naked Gun 2 1/2: The Smell of Fear '91
Manhunter '74
Sssssss '73
Across 110th Street '72
The Groundstar Conspiracy '72

Una O'Connor (1880-1959)
Witness for the Prosecution '57
Fighting Father Dunne '48
Hopalong Cassidy: Unexpected Guest '47
Christmas in Connecticut '45
The Canterville Ghost '44
This Land Is Mine '43
Strawberry Blonde '41
The Sea Hawk '40
The Adventures of Robin Hood '38
Personal Property '37
Lloyds of London '36
The Bride of Frankenstein '35
David Copperfield '35
The Informer '35
The Barretts of Wimpole Street '34
Chained '34
Cavalcade '33
The Invisible Man '33

Hugh O'Conor (1975-)
Chocolat '00
The Young Poisoner's Handbook '94
My Left Foot '89
Da '88
Lamb '85

Nell O'Day (1909-89)
Boss of Rawhide '44
Bury Me Not on the Lone Prairie '41
Man from Montana '41
The Masked Rider '41
Pony Post '40

Denis O'Dea (1905-78)
Esther and the King '60
The Story of Esther Costello '57

Captain Horatio Hornblower '51
The Long Dark Hall '51
Treasure Island '50
The Fallen Idol '49
Under Capricorn '49

Bob Odenkirk (1962-)
Sink or Swim '97
The Cable Guy '96
The Truth about Cats and Dogs '96
Waiting for Guffman '96
Clean Slate '94
Wayne's World 2 '93

Christophe Odent
Nouvelle Vague '90
First Name: Carmen '83

Odetta
The Fire Next Time '93
The Autobiography of Miss Jane Pittman '74

Cathy O'Donnell (1925-70)
Ben-Hur '59
Terror in the Haunted House '58
The Man from Laramie '55
The Love of Three Queens '54
Detective Story '51
The Miniver Story '50
They Live by Night '49
The Amazing Mr. X '48
The Best Years of Our Lives '46

Chris O'Donnell (1970-)
Vertical Limit '00
The Bachelor '99
Cookie's Fortune '99
Batman and Robin '97
The Chamber '96
In Love and War '96
Batman Forever '95
Mad Love '95
Circle of Friends '94
The Three Musketeers '93
Scent of a Woman '92
School Ties '92
Blue Sky '91
Fried Green Tomatoes '91
Men Don't Leave '89

Rosie O'Donnell (1962-)
Tarzan '99 (V)
The Twilight of the Golds '97
Wide Awake '97
Beautiful Girls '96
Harriet the Spy '96
Now and Then '95
Car 54, Where Are You? '94
Exit to Eden '94
The Flintstones '94
Another Stakeout '93
Sleepless in Seattle '93
A League of Their Own '92

"Spec" (Walter) O'Donnell (1911-86)
Hello Trouble '32
Sparrows '26
The Country Kid '23

Martha O'Driscoll (1922-98)
Carnegie Hall '47
Criminal Court '46
Here Come the Co-Eds '45
House of Dracula '45
Follow the Boys '44
The Fallen Sparrow '43
Reap the Wild Wind '42
Young & Willing '42

Bernadette O'Farrell (1924-99)
Robin Hood: The Movie '55
Scotland Yard Inspector '52
The Happiest Days of Your Life '50

Conor O'Farrell
Stir of Echoes '99
From the Earth to the Moon '98
Baby of the Bride '91

George Offerman, Jr. (1917-63)
A Walk in the Sun '46
The Fighting Sullivans '42
The Outlaw Deputy '35

Nick Offerman
Groove '00
Treasure Island '99

Damian O'Flynn (1907-82)
Daniel Boone: Trail Blazer '56
The Devil on Wheels '47
Crack-Up '46
Wake Island '42
X Marks the Spot '42

Ken Ogata (1937-)
The Pillow Book '95
Mishima: A Life in Four Chapters '85
The Ballad of Narayama '83
Virus '82
Eijanaika '81
Vengeance Is Mine '79

Mayumi Ogawa
The Go-Masters '82
Vengeance Is Mine '79
Zatoichi: The Blind Swordsman's Vengeance '66

Bulle Ogier (1939-)
Shattered Image '98
Venus Beauty Institute '98
Somewhere in the City '97
Irma Vep '96
Son of Gascogne '95
Candy Mountain '87
Tricheurs '84
Maitresse '76
Celine and Julie Go Boating '74
The Discreet Charm of the Bourgeoisie '72
The Valley Obscured by the Clouds '72
La Salamandre '71

Ian Ogilvy (1943-)
The Disappearance of Kevin Johnson '95
Puppet Master 5: The Final Chapter '94
Death Becomes Her '92
Invasion of Privacy '92
Anna Karenina '85
And Now the Screaming Starts '73
From Beyond the Grave '73
No Sex Please—We're British '73
Waterloo '71
Wuthering Heights '70
The Conqueror Worm '68
The Invincible Six '68
Cop-Out '67
The She-Beast '65

Jorgo Ognenovski
Stalked '99
Warrior of Justice '96

Dean O'Gorman (1976-)
When Love Comes '98
Young Hercules '97

Gail O'Grady (1963-)
Another Woman's Husband '00
Deuce Bigalow: Male Gigolo '99
The Three Lives of Karen '97
Celtic Pride '96
That Old Feeling '96
Spellcaster '91
Nobody's Perfect '90
Blackout '88

Sandra Oh (1971-)
Big Fat Liar '02
The Princess Diaries '01
Dancing at the Blue Iguana '00
Waking the Dead '00
Guinevere '99
Last Night '98
Bean '97
Double Happiness '94

Soon-Teck Oh
True Blue '01
Mulan '98 (V)
Yellow '98
Beverly Hills Ninja '96
Red Sun Rising '94
A Home of Our Own '93
Missing in Action 2: The Beginning '85
East of Eden '80
The Man with the Golden Gun '74

Brian O'Halloran
Jay and Silent Bob Strike Back '01
Mallrats '95
Clerks '94

Jack O'Halloran (1943-)
Hero and the Terror '88
Dragnet '87
The Baltimore Bullet '80
Superman 2 '80
Superman: The Movie '78
King Kong '76
Farewell, My Lovely '75

Natsuko Ohama
Skin Deep '94
Speed '94

Claudia Ohana (1962-)
Erotique '94
Priceless Beauty '90
The Fable of the Beautiful Pigeon Fancier '88
Luzia '88
Opera do Malandro '87
Erendira '83

George O'Hanlon
Jetsons: The Movie '90 (V)
Heading for Heaven '47

George O'Hanlon, Jr.
The Evil '78
Our Time '74
Where Have All the People Gone? '74

Brian O'Hara
Married Too Young '62
California Joe '43

Catherine O'Hara (1954-)
Orange County '02
Best in Show '00
Late Last Night '99
The Life Before This '99
Home Fries '98
Hope '97
The Last of the High Kings '96
Waiting for Guffman '96
Tall Tale: The Unbelievable Adventures of Pecos Bill '95
The Paper '94
A Simple Twist of Fate '94
Wyatt Earp '94
The Nightmare before Christmas '93 (V)
Home Alone 2: Lost in New York '92
There Goes the Neighborhood '92
Betsy's Wedding '90
Dick Tracy '90
Home Alone '90
Little Vegas '90
Beetlejuice '88
Heartburn '86
Really Weird Tales '86
After Hours '85
The Last Polka '84
Rock & Rule '83 (V)
Nothing Personal '80

David O'Hara (1965-)
Crossfire Trail '01
Made '01
Jesus '00
Fever '99
The Match '99
The Matchmaker '97
Oliver Twist '97
Some Mother's Son '96
Braveheart '95
Maria's Child '93
WarCat '88

Jenny O'Hara (1942-)
The Truth About Jane *'00*
Wishmaster *'97*
A Mother's Prayer *'95*
Angie *'94*
Career Opportunities *'91*
Last Song *'80*

Maureen O'Hara (1920-)
The Christmas Box *'95*
Only the Lonely *'91*
The Red Pony *'76*
Big Jake *'71*
The Rare Breed *'66*
McLintock! *'63*
Spencer's Mountain *'63*
Mr. Hobbs Takes a Vacation *'62*
Deadly Companions *'61*
The Parent Trap *'61*
Wings of Eagles *'57*
Lisbon *'56*
Lady Godiva *'55*
The Long Gray Line *'55*
The Magnificent Matador *'55*
The Redhead from Wyoming *'53*
War Arrow *'53*
Against All Flags *'52*
The Quiet Man *'52*
At Sword's Point *'51*
Flame of Araby *'51*
Comanche Territory *'50*
Rio Grande *'50*
Bagdad *'49*
Father Was a Fullback *'49*
A Woman's Secret *'49*
Miracle on 34th Street *'47*
Sinbad, the Sailor *'47*
The Spanish Main *'45*
Buffalo Bill *'44*
The Fallen Sparrow *'43*
Immortal Sergeant *'43*
This Land Is Mine *'43*
The Black Swan *'42*
To the Shores of Tripoli *'42*
How Green Was My Valley *'41*
Dance, Girl, Dance *'40*
The Hunchback of Notre Dame *'39*
Jamaica Inn *'39*

Denis O'Hare
The Anniversary Party *'01*
River Red *'98*
Saint Maybe *'98*

Michael O'Hare
C.H.U.D. *'84*
The Promise *'79*

Caitlin (Kathleen Heaney) O'Heaney
He Knows You're Alone *'80*
Savage Weekend *'80*

Cornelia Hayes O'Herlihy
Mother Teresa: In the Name of God's Poor *'97*
Rudyard Kipling's the Second Jungle Book: Mowgli and Baloo *'97*
The Old Curiosity Shop *'94*

Dan O'Herlihy (1919-)
The Rat Pack *'98*
Love, Cheat & Steal *'93*
RoboCop 2 *'90*
A Waltz Through the Hills *'88*
The Dead *'87*
RoboCop *'87*
Two by Forsyth *'86*
No Comebacks *'85*
The Last Starfighter *'84*
Halloween 3: Season of the Witch *'82*
Death Ray 2000 *'81*
MacArthur *'77*
The Tamarind Seed *'74*
The People *'71*
Waterloo *'71*
Fail-Safe *'64*
The King of the Roaring '20s: The Story of Arnold Rothstein *'61*
The Young Land *'59*
The Virgin Queen *'55*
The Black Shield of Falworth *'54*
Sword of Venus *'53*
Actors and Sin *'52*
Invasion U.S.A. *'52*
At Sword's Point *'51*
Macbeth *'48*
Odd Man Out *'47*

Gavan O'Herlihy (1954-)
Prince Valiant *'97*
Hidden Assassin *'94*
Tailspin: Behind the Korean Airline Tragedy *'89*
Willow *'88*
Space Riders *'83*

Carol Ohmart (1927-)
Spider Baby *'64*
One Man's Way *'63*
Born Reckless *'59*
Naked Youth *'59*
House on Haunted Hill *'58*

John O'Hurley
Firetrap *'01*
The Power Within *'95*
Mirror Images *'91*

Eiji Okada (1920-95)
Traffic Jam *'91*
X from Outer Space *'67*
Face of Another *'66*
Woman in the Dunes *'64*
She and He *'63*
The Ugly American *'63*
Hiroshima, Mon Amour *'59*
Mother *'52*

Mariko Okada (1933-)
An Autumn Afternoon *'62*
Samurai 3: Duel at Ganryu Island *'56*
Samurai 2: Duel at Ichijoji Temple *'55*

Dennis O'Keefe (1908-68)
The Naked Flame *'68*
Great Dan Patch *'49*
Raw Deal *'48*
Dishonored Lady *'47*
T-Men *'47*
Doll Face *'46*
Brewster's Millions *'45*
Abroad with Two Yanks *'44*
Fighting Seabees *'44*
Sensations of 1945 *'44*
The Story of Dr. Wassell *'44*
Hi Diddle Diddle *'43*
The Leopard Man *'43*
Hangmen Also Die *'42*
Broadway Limited *'41*
Lady Scarface *'41*
Topper Returns *'41*
Pop Always Pays *'40*
You'll Find Out *'40*
Libeled Lady *'36*
Cimarron *'31*

Doug O'Keefe
Specimen *'97*
When the Bullet Hits the Bone *'96*

Jodi Lyn O'Keefe (1978-)
The Crow: Salvation *'00*
Devil in the Flesh 2 *'00*
Whatever It Takes *'00*
She's All That *'99*
Halloween: H20 *'98*

John E. O'Keefe
Conceiving Ada *'97*
Out of the Rain *'90*

Michael O'Keefe (1955-)
The Glass House *'01*
Prancer Returns *'01*
Just One Night *'00*
The Pledge *'00*
Ghosts of Mississippi *'96*
Edie & Pen *'95*
Three Wishes *'95*
Incident at Deception Ridge *'94*
Nina Takes a Lover *'94*
Me & Veronica *'93*
Fear *'90*
Out of the Rain *'90*
Too Young to Die *'90*
Bridge to Silence *'89*
Disaster at Silo 7 *'88*
Ironweed *'87*
The Whoopee Boys *'86*
The Slugger's Wife *'85*
Finders Keepers *'84*
Nate and Hayes *'83*
Split Image *'82*
Caddyshack *'80*
The Great Santini *'80*
A Rumor of War *'80*
The Dark Secret of Harvest Home *'78*
Gray Lady Down *'77*

Miles O'Keeffe (1954-)
Diamondbacks *'99*
Dead Tides *'97*
True Vengeance *'97*
Marked Man *'96*
Pocahontas: The Legend *'95*
Silent Hunter *'94*
Acting on Impulse *'93*
Zero Tolerance *'93*
Shoot *'92*
The Colombian Connection *'91*
King's Ransom *'91*
Relentless 2: Dead On *'91*
Cartel *'90*
Liberty & Bash *'90*
The Drifter *'88*
The Lone Runner *'88*
Waxwork *'88*
Campus Man *'87*
Iron Warrior *'87*
Blade Master *'84*
S.A.S. San Salvador *'84*
Ator the Fighting Eagle *'83*
Sword of the Valiant *'83*
Tarzan, the Ape Man *'81*

Don O'Kelly
The Hostage *'67*
Frontier Uprising *'61*

Donal O'Kelly
I Went Down *'97*
The Van *'95*

Tim O'Kelly
The Passing of Evil *'70*
Targets *'68*

Denjiro Okochi
The Men Who Tread on the Tiger's Tail *'45*
Sanshiro Sugata *'43*

Sophie Okonedo
Go Now *'96*
Ace Ventura: When Nature Calls *'95*

Yuji Okumoto
I'll Remember April *'99*
Partners *'99*
Mean Guns *'97*
Hard Justice *'95*
Bloodfist 5: Human Target *'93*
Nemesis *'93*
Robot Wars *'93*
True Believer *'89*
Aloha Summer *'88*
The Karate Kid: Part 2 *'86*

Warner Oland (1880-1938)
Charlie Chan at the Opera *'36*
Charlie Chan in Paris *'35*
Charlie Chan's Secret *'35*
Werewolf of London *'35*
The Painted Veil *'34*
Shanghai Express *'32*
Daughter of the Dragon *'31*
Dishonored *'31*
Drums of Jeopardy *'31*
Stand and Deliver *'28*
The Jazz Singer *'27*
Don Juan *'26*
Riders of the Purple Sage *'25*
The Fighting American *'24*

Ken Olandt (1958-)
Interceptor Force *'99*
Velocity Trap *'99*
Darkdrive *'98*
Digital Man *'94*
Leprechaun *'93*
Super Force *'90*
April Fool's Day *'86*

Daniel Olbrychski (1945-)
Ivan and Abraham *'94*
The Decalogue *'88*
The Unbearable Lightness of Being *'88*
Rosa Luxemburg *'86*
La Truite *'83*
Maids of Wilko *'79*
The Tin Drum *'79*
Land of Promise *'74*
The Deluge *'73*
Family Life *'71*
Colonel Wolodyjowski *'69*
The Structure of Crystals *'69*

Eric Oldfield (1948-)
Stones of Death *'88*
Air Hawk *'84*
Gone to Ground *'76*
Island Trader *'71*

William Oldham
Thousand Pieces of Gold *'91*
Matewan *'87*

Gary Oldman (1958-)
Hannibal *'01*
The Contender *'00*
Jesus *'00*
Lost in Space *'98*
Quest for Camelot *'98 (V)*
Air Force One *'97*
The Fifth Element *'97*
Basquiat *'96*
Murder in the First *'95*
The Scarlet Letter *'95*
Immortal Beloved *'94*
The Professional *'94*
Fallen Angels 2 *'93*
Romeo Is Bleeding *'93*
True Romance *'93*
Bram Stoker's Dracula *'92*
JFK *'91*
Rosencrantz & Guildenstern Are Dead *'90*
State of Grace *'90*
Chattahoochee *'89*
Criminal Law *'89*
Track 29 *'88*
We Think the World of You *'88*
Prick Up Your Ears *'87*
Sid & Nancy *'86*
Meantime *'81*

Gabriel Olds
Urbania *'00*
A Town Has Turned to Dust *'98*
Without Limits *'97*
Andersonville *'95*
Animal Room *'95*
Calendar Girl *'93*

Matt O'Leary
Frailty *'02*
Domestic Disturbance *'01*

William O'Leary
Candyman 2: Farewell to the Flesh *'94*
In the Line of Duty: Ambush in Waco *'93*
Flight of Black Angel *'91*
Hot Shots! *'91*
Nice Girls Don't Explode *'87*

Larisa Oleynik (1981-)
100 Girls *'00*
Ten Things I Hate about You *'99*
The Baby-Sitters' Club *'95*

Ken Olin (1954-)
Til There Was You *'96*
Queens Logic *'91*
The Game of Love *'90*

Lena Olin (1955-)
Queen of the Damned *'02*
Chocolat *'00*
Mystery Men *'99*
The Ninth Gate *'99*
Polish Wedding *'97*
Night Falls on Manhattan *'96*
The Night and the Moment *'94*
Mr. Jones *'93*
Romeo Is Bleeding *'93*
Havana *'90*
Enemies, a Love Story *'89*
The Unbearable Lightness of Being *'88*
After the Rehearsal *'84*

Barret Oliver (1973-)
Cocoon: The Return *'88*
The Secret Garden *'87*
Cocoon *'85*
D.A.R.Y.L. *'85*
Frankenweenie *'84*
Invitation to Hell *'84*
The NeverEnding Story *'84*

Charles Oliver
The Avenging Hand *'43*
Midnight at the Wax Museum *'36*

Christian Oliver
Kept *'01*
Eat Your Heart Out *'96*

David Oliver
The Chosen One: Legend of the Raven *'98*
Defense Play *'88*
Postal Inspector *'36*

Edna May Oliver (1883-1942)
Pride and Prejudice *'40*
Drums Along the Mohawk *'39*
Nurse Edith Cavell *'39*
Second Fiddle *'39*
The Story of Vernon and Irene Castle *'39*
Little Miss Broadway *'38*
Rosalie *'38*
Romeo and Juliet *'36*
A Tale of Two Cities *'36*
David Copperfield *'35*
Ann Vickers *'33*
Little Women *'33*
Hold 'Em Jail *'32*
Cimarron *'31*
Half-Shot at Sunrise *'30*
Lucky Devil *'25*

Gordon Oliver (1911-95)
The Spiral Staircase *'46*
Follies Girl *'43*
Blondie *'38*
Youth on Parole *'37*

Michael Oliver
Problem Child 2 *'91*
Problem Child *'90*

Rochelle Oliver (1937-)
Scent of a Woman *'92*
An Unremarkable Life *'89*
Courtship *'87*
On Valentine's Day *'86*
1918 *'85*

Stephen Oliver
Savage Abduction *'73*
Cycle Psycho *'72*
Werewolves on Wheels *'71*
Angels from Hell *'68*
Motor Psycho *'65*

Susan Oliver (1937-90)
Tomorrow's Child *'82*
Hardly Working *'81*
Widow's Nest *'77*
Ginger in the Morning *'73*
Black Brigade *'69*
Disorderly Orderly *'64*
Guns of Diablo *'64*
Butterfield 8 *'60*
The Gene Krupa Story *'59*

Robert Oliveri (1978-)
Honey, I Blew Up the Kid *'92*
Edward Scissorhands *'90*
Honey, I Shrunk the Kids *'89*

Laurence Olivier (1907-89)
A Voyage 'Round My Father *'89*
Ebony Tower *'86*
Peter the Great *'86*
Wagner: The Complete Epic *'85*
Wild Geese 2 *'85*
The Bounty *'84*
The Jigsaw Man *'84*
Brideshead Revisited *'81*
Clash of the Titans *'81*
The Jazz Singer *'80*
Dracula *'79*
A Little Romance *'79*
The Betsy *'78*
The Boys from Brazil *'78*
A Bridge Too Far *'77*
Jesus of Nazareth *'77*
Marathon Man *'76*
The Seven-Per-Cent Solution *'76*
Love Among the Ruins *'75*
Lady Caroline Lamb *'73*
The Merchant of Venice *'73*
Sleuth *'72*
Nicholas and Alexandra *'71*
David Copperfield *'70*
Battle of Britain *'69*
Romeo and Juliet *'68 (N)*
The Shoes of the Fisherman *'68*
Khartoum *'66*
Othello *'65*
The Entertainer *'60*
Spartacus *'60*
The Devil's Disciple *'59*
The Prince and the Showgirl *'57*
Richard III *'55*
Carrie *'52*
Hamlet *'48*
This Happy Breed *'47 (N)*
Henry V *'44*
The Demi-Paradise *'43*
The Forty-Ninth Parallel *'41*
That Hamilton Woman *'41*
Pride and Prejudice *'40*
Rebecca *'40*
Clouds over Europe *'39*
Wuthering Heights *'39*
The Divorce of Lady X *'38*
Fire Over England *'37*
21 Days *'37*
As You Like It *'36*
I Stand Condemned *'36*

Paul Olivier
A Nous la Liberte *'31*
Le Million *'31*

Silvio Oliviero
Gotti *'96*
Understudy: The Graveyard Shift 2 *'88*
A Whisper to a Scream *'88*
Graveyard Shift *'87*
Psycho Girls *'86*

Walter Olkewicz (1948-)
Meeting Daddy *'98*
Milo *'98*
Pronto *'97*
The Good Old Boys *'95*
The Client *'94*
1941 *'79*
Can I Do It...Till I Need Glasses? *'77*

Edward James Olmos (1949-)
In the Time of the Butterflies *'01*
The Road to El Dorado *'00 (V)*
Bonanno: A Godfather's Story *'99*
Gossip *'99*
The Wall *'99*
The Wonderful Ice Cream Suit *'98*
Hollywood Confidential *'97*
Twelve Angry Men *'97*
Caught *'96*
The Disappearance of Garcia Lorca *'96*
Larry McMurtry's Dead Man's Walk *'96*
The Limbic Region *'96*
Selena *'96*
Roosters *'95*
The Burning Season *'94*
A Million to Juan *'94*
Mirage *'94*
My Family *'94 (N)*
American Me *'92*
Talent for the Game *'91*
Triumph of the Spirit *'89*
Stand and Deliver *'88*
Saving Grace *'86*
Ballad of Gregorio Cortez *'83*
Blade Runner *'82*

Virus '82
Wolfen '81
Zoot Suit '81

Gertrude (Olmstead) Olmsted (1897-1975)
The Cheerful Fraud '27
Sweet Adeline '26
California Straight Ahead '25
Cobra '25
The Monster '25

Gerald S. O'Loughlin (1921-)
Three Strikes '00
Crime of the Century '96
Quicksilver '86
Frances '82
A Matter of Life and Death '81
Pleasure Palace '80
The Crash of Flight 401 '78
Desperate Characters '71
Ensign Pulver '64

Ashley (Fuller) Olsen (1986-)
Billboard Dad '98
How the West Was Fun '95
It Takes Two '95
Double Double Toil and Trouble '94
To Grandmother's House We Go '94

Larry Olsen
Who Killed Doc Robbin? '48
Curley '47

Mary-Kate Olsen (1986-)
Billboard Dad '98
How the West Was Fun '95
It Takes Two '95
Double Double Toil and Trouble '94
To Grandmother's House We Go '94

Merlin Olsen (1940-)
The Juggler of Notre Dame '84
Mitchell '75
The Undefeated '69

Moroni Olsen (1899-1954)
Father's Little Dividend '51
Father of the Bride '50
Task Force '49
Call Northside 777 '48
The Long Night '47
The Possessed '47
Notorious '46
Buffalo Bill '44
Cobra Woman '44
Air Force '43
Ali Baba and the Forty Thieves '43
The Glass Key '42
Reunion in France '42
Dive Bomber '41
Allegheny Uprising '39
Rose of Washington Square '39
Susannah of the Mounties '39
Snow White and the Seven Dwarfs '37 (V)
Mary of Scotland '36
Yellow Dust '36
Annie Oakley '35
The Three Musketeers '35

Ole Olsen (1892-1963)
All Over Town '37
Country Gentlemen '36

Richard Olsen
Stephen King's The Night Flier '96
Wildflower '91

James Olson (1943-)
Rachel River '87
Commando '85
Amityville 2: The Possession '82
Ragtime '81
My Sister, My Love '78
The Spell '77
Someone I Touched '75
Strange New World '75
The Groundstar Conspiracy '72
The Andromeda Strain '71
Paper Man '71
Rachel, Rachel '68
The Three Sisters '65
The Strange One '57

Nancy Olson (1928-)
Making Love '82
Airport '75 '75
Snowball Express '72
Son of Flubber '63
The Absent-Minded Professor '61
Pollyanna '60
Battle Cry '55
Big Jim McLain '52
Mr. Music '50
Sunset Boulevard '50
Union Station '50

Niclas Olund
Expectations '97
The Slingshot '93

Timothy Olyphant (1968-)
Rock Star '01
Beyond Suspicion '00
The Broken Hearts Club '00
Gone in 60 Seconds '00
Go '99
When Trumpets Fade '98
Ellen Foster '97
Scream 2 '97

Daragh O'Malley (1954-)
Longitude '00
Cleopatra '99
The Magnificent Seven '98
Sharpe's Justice '97
Sharpe's Revenge '97
Sharpe's Waterloo '97
Sharpe's Mission '96
Sharpe's Regiment '96
Sharpe's Siege '96
Sharpe's Battle '94
Sharpe's Company '94
Sharpe's Enemy '94
Sharpe's Gold '94
Sharpe's Honour '94
Sharpe's Sword '94
Sharpe's Eagle '93
Sharpe's Rifles '93

J. Pat O'Malley (1901-85)
A Small Killing '81
Willard '71
Star! '68
The Jungle Book '67 (V)
Hey There, It's Yogi Bear '64 (V)
101 Dalmatians '61 (V)
Courage of Black Beauty '57
Lassie, Come Home '43

Pat O'Malley (1891-1966)
Invasion of the Body Snatchers '56
The Adventures of Ichabod and Mr. Toad '49 (V)
Stunt Pilot '39
Fighting Marines '36
The Miracle Rider '35
Evelyn Prentice '34
The Perils of Pauline '34
The Fighting Marshal '32
Spangles '26
The Fighting American '24
The Virginian '23

Rex O'Malley
Midnight '39
Camille '36

Kate O'Mara (1939-)
Nativity '78
Whose Child Am I? '75
The Horror of Frankenstein '70
The Vampire Lovers '70

Mollie O'Mara
Escape from Safehaven '88
Girls School Screamers '86

Judd Omen
Bounty Tracker '93
Dollman '90
Howling 2: Your Sister Is a Werewolf '85
Pee-wee's Big Adventure '85

Afemo Omilami
Bringing Out the Dead '99
DROP Squad '94

Pat O'Moore
The Two Mrs. Carrolls '47
Sahara '43

Anny Ondra
Blackmail '29
The Manxman '29

Anne O'Neal
Gun Crazy '49
Open Secret '48

Griffin O'Neal (1964-)
Evil Lives '92
Ghoulies 3: Ghoulies Go to College '91
Night Children '89
Assault of the Killer Bimbos '88
The Wraith '87
April Fool's Day '86
The Children of Times Square '86
Hadley's Rebellion '84
The Escape Artist '82

Patrick O'Neal (1927-94)
Under Siege '92
For the Boys '91
Alice '90
Q & A '90
New York Stories '89
Perry Mason Returns '85
The Stuff '85
Spraggue '84
Make Me an Offer '80
The Stepford Wives '75
Silent Night, Bloody Night '73
The Way We Were '73
El Condor '70
Stiletto '69
Secret Life of an American Wife '68
Where Were You When the Lights Went Out? '68
Alvarez Kelly '66
A Fine Madness '66
In Harm's Way '65
King Rat '65
From the Terrace '60
The Black Shield of Falworth '54

Ron O'Neal (1937-)
Original Gangstas '96
Up Against the Wall '91
Hyper Space '89
Hero and the Terror '88
Mercenary Fighters '88
Trained to Kill '88
As Summers Die '86
Red Dawn '84
St. Helen's, Killer Volcano '82
Sophisticated Gents '81
Freedom Road '79
The Hitter '79
When a Stranger Calls '79
Superfly T.N.T. '73
Superfly '72

Ryan O'Neal (1941-)
Epoch '00
Coming Soon '99
The List '99
An Alan Smithee Film: Burn, Hollywood, Burn '97
Sink or Swim '97
Zero Effect '97
Faithful '95
The Man Upstairs '93
Chances Are '89
Small Sacrifices '89
Tough Guys Don't Dance '87
Fever Pitch '85
Irreconcilable Differences '84
Partners '82
Green Ice '81
So Fine '81
The Main Event '79
The Driver '78
Oliver's Story '78
A Bridge Too Far '77
Barry Lyndon '75
Paper Moon '73
The Thief Who Came to Dinner '73
What's Up, Doc? '72
Wild Rovers '71
Love Story '70

Shaquille O'Neal (1972-)
Good Burger '97
Steel '97
Kazaam '96
Blue Chips '94

Tatum O'Neal (1963-)
Basquiat '96
Little Noises '91
Certain Fury '85
Goldilocks & the Three Bears '83
Circle of Two '80
Little Darlings '80
International Velvet '78
The Bad News Bears '76
Paper Moon '73

Ty O'Neal (1978-)
American Outlaws '01
Bug Buster '99
D2: The Mighty Ducks '94

Barbara O'Neil (1910-80)
Flame of the Islands '55
I Remember Mama '48
Secret Beyond the Door '48
All This and Heaven Too '40
Gone with the Wind '39
The Tower of London '39
I Am the Law '38
Stella Dallas '37

Nance O'Neil
Cimarron '31
The Royal Bed '31

Sally O'Neil (1910-68)
Sixteen Fathoms Deep '34
Battle of the Sexes '28
Battling Butler '26

Angela O'Neill
Enemy Unseen '91
River of Diamonds '90
Sorority House Massacre '86

Chris O'Neill (1945-97)
2 by 4 '98
Backbeat '94
James Joyce's Women '85

Dick O'Neill (1928-98)
My Summer Story '94
Dark Justice '91
She's Out of Control '89
The Mosquito Coast '86
Wolfen '81
The Jerk '79
The Taking of Pelham One Two Three '74
Hail '73
Pretty Poison '68
Gamera, the Invincible '66

Ed O'Neill (1946-)
Lucky Numbers '00
The 10th Kingdom '00
The Bone Collector '99
The Spanish Prisoner '97
Prefontaine '96
Blue Chips '94
Little Giants '94
Wayne's World 2 '93
It's a Bundyful Life '92
Wayne's World '92
Dutch '91
The Adventures of Ford Fairlane '90
Sibling Rivalry '90
Disorganized Crime '89
K-9 '89
When Your Lover Leaves '83
The Day the Women Got Even '80
Deliverance '72

Henry O'Neill (1891-1961)
Holiday Affair '49
The Virginian '46
Nothing But Trouble '44
Air Raid Wardens '43
Whistling in Brooklyn '43
Johnny Eager '42
White Cargo '42
Billy the Kid '41
Honky Tonk '41
Men of Boys Town '41
Shadow of the Thin Man '41
The Fighting 69th '40
Amazing Dr. Clitterhouse '38
Black Fury '35
Lady Killer '33
America '24

Jennifer O'Neill (1948-)
The Corporate Ladder '97
Bad Love '95
The Cover Girl Murders '93
Discretion Assured '93
Invasion of Privacy '92
Perfect Family '92
Committed '91
Personals '90
Full Exposure: The Sex Tape Scandals '89
I Love N.Y. '87
A.D. '85
Chase '85
Scanners '81
Cloud Dancer '80
Steel '80
Force of One '79
Love's Savage Fury '79
The Psychic '78
The Innocent '76
The Reincarnation of Peter Proud '75
Whiffs '75
Lady Ice '73
Summer of '42 '71
Rio Lobo '70

Maggie O'Neill
Invasion: Earth '98
Under Suspicion '92

Maire O'Neill (1885-1952)
Great Day '46
Sidewalks of London '38
Juno and the Paycock '30

Michael O'Neill
The Legend of Bagger Vance '00
Dancer, Texas—Pop. 81 '98
Sunchaser '96
The Gun in Betty Lou's Handbag '92
Gore-Met Zombie Chef from Hell '87

Remy O'Neill
To Die For 2: Son of Darkness '91
Hollywood Hot Tubs 2: Educating Crystal '89

Terry O'Neill
Kull the Conqueror '97
Dragonheart '96

Yoko Ono (1933-)
Let It Be '70
The Magic Christian '69

Peter Onorati (1954-)
Dancing in September '00
The Art of Murder '99
Just Looking '99
Shelter '98
True Friends '98
Tycus '98
RocketMan '97
Dead Ahead '96
Not Like Us '96
Donor Unknown '95
Camp Nowhere '94
Fire Birds '90
Goodfellas '90

Lupe Ontiveros
Gabriela '01
Storytelling '01
Chuck & Buck '00
Picking Up the Pieces '99
Candyman 3: Day of the Dead '98
As Good As It Gets '97
Selena '96
My Family '94
El Norte '83

Michael Ontkean (1950-)
Just a Little Harmless Sex '99
Summer of the Monkeys '98
Swann '96
Legacy of Lies '92
Postcards from the Edge '90
Bye Bye Blues '89
Cold Front '89
Street Justice '89
Clara's Heart '88
The Allnighter '87
Maid to Order '87
The Blood of Others '84
Just the Way You Are '84
Making Love '82
Willie & Phil '80
Slap Shot '77
Girls on the Road '73
Where the Eagle Flies '72
The Witching '72
Peacekillers '71

Amanda Ooms
Wilderness '96
The Women on the Roof '89

David Opatoshu (1918-96)
Forty Days of Musa Dagh '85
Americathon '79
Who'll Stop the Rain? '78
Conspiracy of Terror '75
Romance of a Horsethief '71
The Fixer '68
Torn Curtain '66
Exodus '60
The Light Ahead '39

Alan Oppenheimer (1930-)
Trancers 5: Sudden Deth '94
Invisible: The Chronicles of Benjamin Knight '93
Trancers 4: Jack of Swords '93
Child of Darkness, Child of Light '91
A Pleasure Doing Business '79
Helter Skelter '76
The Bionic Woman '75
The Groundstar Conspiracy '72
Star! '68

Don Opper (1949-)
Critters 3 '91
Critters 4 '91
The Forgotten '89
Critters 2: The Main Course '88
Critters '86
Android '82

Terry O'Quinn (1952-)
American Outlaws '01
Rated X '00
Murder in a Small Town '99
The X-Files '98
Breast Men '97
Primal Fear '96
The Shadow Conspiracy '96
JAG '95
Shadow Warriors '95
Don't Talk to Strangers '94
Amityville: A New Generation '93
Lipstick Camera '93
Tombstone '93
The Cutting Edge '92
The Good Fight '92
My Samurai '92
Take Down '92
Wildcard '92
Company Business '91
Prisoners of the Sun '91
The Rocketeer '91
Son of the Morning Star '91
When the Time Comes '91
Blind Fury '90
The Forgotten One '89
Roe vs. Wade '89

Tilai '90

Andre Oumansky
Spy Games '99
Othello '95
Burnt by the Sun '94
Joy House '64

Gerard Oury (1919-)
The Prize '63
Back to the Wall '56
The Love of Three Queens '54

Sverre Anker Ousdal (1944-)
Insomnia '97
Hamsun '96
Kristin Lavransdatter '95
The Last Place on Earth '94

Maria Ouspenskaya (1876-1949)
Frankenstein Meets the Wolfman '42
The Shanghai Gesture '42
Kings Row '41
The Wolf Man '41
Beyond Tomorrow '40
Dance, Girl, Dance '40
Waterloo Bridge '40
Love Affair '39
The Rains Came '39
Conquest '37
Dodsworth '36

Peter Outerbridge (1966-)
Mission to Mars '00
Better Than Chocolate '99
Escape from Mars '99
Escape Velocity '99
Thrill Seekers '99
Closer and Closer '96
Kissed '96
The Android Affair '95
For the Moment '94
Paris, France '94
Cool Runnings '93
Victim of Beauty '91

Park Overall (1957-)
Sparkler '99
The Good Old Boys '95
The Gambler Returns: The Luck of the Draw '93
Undercover Blues '93
The Vanishing '93
House of Cards '92
Kindergarten Cop '90
Lost Angels '89
Biloxi Blues '88
Mississippi Burning '88
Tainted '88

Lynne Overman (1887-1943)
Reap the Wild Wind '42
Roxie Hart '42
Caught in the Draft '41
Edison the Man '40
Union Pacific '39
Little Miss Marker '34
Midnight '34

Frank Overton
To Kill a Mockingbird '62
Desire Under the Elms '58

Rick Overton (1954-)
EDtv '99
National Lampoon's Attack of the 5 Ft. 2 Women '94
The High Crusade '92
Blind Fury '90
Earth Girls Are Easy '89
A Sinful Life '89
Million Dollar Mystery '87
Traxx '87
Odd Jobs '85
Beverly Hills Cop '84

Baard Owe
The Kingdom 2 '97
The Kingdom '95
Gertrud '64

Bill Owen (1914-99)
Singleton's Pluck '84
The Comeback '77
In Celebration '75
Georgy Girl '66
The Hellfire Club '61
The Gay Lady '49

Chris Owen (1980-)
National Lampoon's Van Wilder '02
American Pie 2 '01
Ready to Rumble '00
American Pie '99
October Sky '99
Angus '95

Clive Owen (1965-)
The Bourne Identity '02
Gosford Park '01
Greenfingers '00
Second Sight '99
Bent '97
Croupier '97
The Rich Man's Wife '96
Century '94
The Return of the Native '94
Class of '61 '92
Close My Eyes '91
Lorna Doone '90

Garry Owen
Dark Mirror '46
Hold Your Man '33

Michael Owen
Youth Aflame '59
Dick Tracy vs. Crime Inc. '41

Reginald Owen (1887-1972)
The Thrill of It All! '63
Red Garters '54
The Miniver Story '50
Challenge to Lassie '49
Julia Misbehaves '48
The Pirate '48
The Three Musketeers '48
Diary of a Chambermaid '46
Monsieur Beaucaire '46
Captain Kidd '45
The Valley of Decision '45
The Canterville Ghost '44
National Velvet '44
Above Suspicion '43
Madame Curie '43
Cairo '42
I Married an Angel '42
Mrs. Miniver '42
Random Harvest '42
Reunion in France '42
Somewhere I'll Find You '42
White Cargo '42
Woman of the Year '42
Tarzan's Secret Treasure '41
They Met in Bombay '41
A Woman's Face '41
The Real Glory '39
A Christmas Carol '38
Everybody Sing '38
Rosalie '38
The Bride Wore Red '37
Conquest '37
Madame X '37
Personal Property '37
The Great Ziegfeld '36
Love on the Run '36
Rose Marie '36
A Tale of Two Cities '36
Anna Karenina '35
Fashions of 1934 '34
Of Human Bondage '34
Queen Christina '33
A Study in Scarlet '33
Ghost City '32

Rena Owen
Dance Me to My Song '98
When Love Comes '98
Once Were Warriors '94

Seena Owen (1894-1966)
Queen Kelly '29
Intolerance '16
The Lamb '15

Ciaran Owens
Agnes Browne '99
Angela's Ashes '99

Eamon Owens (1983-)
St. Patrick: The Irish Legend '00
The General '98
The Butcher Boy '97

Gary Owens (1936-)
Digging Up Business '91
Killcrazy '89
I'm Gonna Git You Sucka '88

Patricia Owens (1925-2000)
Hell to Eternity '60
The Fly '58
The Law and Jake Wade '58
Sayonara '57
The Happiest Days of Your Life '50

Earl Owensby (1936-)
The Rutherford County Line '87
Dogs of Hell '83
Manhunter '83
The Wolfman '82
Death Driver '78
Challenge '74

Monroe Owsley
Goin' to Town '35
Ex-Lady '33

Catherine Oxenberg (1961-)
Frozen in Fear '00
The Collectors '99
The Omega Code '99
Time Served '99
Deadly Game '98
Boys Will Be Boys '97
Heaven Before I Die '96
Charles & Diana: A Palace Divided '93
Rubdown '93
Sexual Response '92
Overexposed '90
K-9000 '89
Swimsuit '89
The Lair of the White Worm '88

David Oxley
House of the Living Dead '73
Night Ambush '57

Moishe Oysher
The Singing Blacksmith '38
The Cantor's Son '37

Frank Oz (1944-)
Star Wars: Episode 2—Attack of the Clones '02 *(V)*
Monsters, Inc. '01 *(V)*
Muppets from Space '99 *(V)*
Star Wars: Episode 1—The Phantom Menace '99 *(V)*
Blues Brothers 2000 '98
Muppet Treasure Island '96 *(V)*
Innocent Blood '92
The Muppet Christmas Carol '92 *(V)*
Sesame Street Presents: Follow That Bird '85 *(V)*
Spies Like Us '85
The Muppets Take Manhattan '84 *(V)*
Return of the Jedi '83 *(V)*
The Dark Crystal '82 *(V)*
An American Werewolf in London '81
The Great Muppet Caper '81 *(V)*
The Blues Brothers '80
The Empire Strikes Back '80
The Muppet Movie '79 *(V)*

Eitaro (Sakae, Saka Ozawa) Ozawa (1909-)
Sandakan No. 8 '74
The Human Condition: No Greater Love '58
Princess Yang Kwei Fei '55
Ugetsu '53
Record of a Tenement Gentleman '47

Shoichi Ozawa
Black Rain '88
The Ballad of Narayama '83
The Pornographers '66

Madeleine Ozeray
Crime and Punishment '35
Liliom '35

Jack Paar (1918-)
Love Nest '51
Walk Softly, Stranger '50
Easy Living '49

Judy Pace (1946-)
Frogs '72
Brian's Song '71
Cotton Comes to Harlem '70
Three in the Cellar '70

Tom Pace
Blood Orgy of the She-Devils '74
Girl in Gold Boots '69
The Astro-Zombies '67

Frederico Pacifici
Fluke '95
Flight of the Innocent '93

Al Pacino (1940-)
Insomnia '02
Simone '02
Any Given Sunday '99
The Insider '99
The Devil's Advocate '97
Donnie Brasco '96
Looking for Richard '96
Two Bits '96
City Hall '95
Heat '95
Carlito's Way '93
Glengarry Glen Ross '92
Scent of a Woman '92
Frankie and Johnny '91
Dick Tracy '90
The Godfather, Part 3 '90
Sea of Love '89
Revolution '85
Scarface '83
Author! Author! '82
The Godfather 1902-1959: The Complete Epic '81
Cruising '80
And Justice for All '79
Bobby Deerfield '77
America at the Movies '76
Dog Day Afternoon '75
Panic in Needle Park '75
The Godfather, Part 2 '74
Scarecrow '73
Serpico '73
The Godfather '72

Charles Lloyd Pack (1905-)
If... '69
Bedazzled '68
The Reptile '66
Victim '61
The Horror of Dracula '58
Stranger in Town '57
River Beat '54

Roger Lloyd Pack
The Young Poisoner's Handbook '94
Fright '71

David Packer (1962-)
Silent Motive '91
The Runnin' Kind '89
Trust Me '89
You Can't Hurry Love '88

Joanna Pacula (1957-)
The Art of Murder '99
Crash & Byrnes '99
My Giant '98
Virus '98
The White Raven '98
The Haunted Sea '97
Business for Pleasure '96
Heaven Before I Die '96
Not Like Us '96
Captain Nuke and the Bomber Boys '95
Timemaster '95
Deep Red '94
The Last Gasp '94
Every Breath '93
Silence of the Hams '93
Tombstone '93
Under Investigation '93
Warlock: The Armageddon '93
Black Ice '92
Eyes of the Beholder '92
Husbands and Lovers '91
Marked for Death '90
The Kiss '88
Options '88
Sweet Lies '88
Death Before Dishonor '87
Escape from Sobibor '87
Not Quite Paradise '86
Gorky Park '83

Sarah Padden (1881-1967)
Wild West '46
Song of Old Wyoming '45
Wildfire '45
Girl Rush '44
Range Law '44
The Mad Monster '42
Riders of the West '42
Snuffy Smith, Yard Bird '42
In Old Colorado '41
Reg'lar Fellers '41
Three Comrades '38
Exiled to Shanghai '37
Tomorrow's Children '34
Cross Examination '32

Hugh Paddick (1915-2000)
Naughty Knights '71
The Killing of Sister George '69

Pilar Padilla
In the Time of the Butterflies '01
Bread and Roses '00

Robert Padilla
Twisted Nightmare '87
The Great Gundown '75

Lea Padovani
The Naked Maja '59
Modigliani '58

Anita Page (1910-)
After Midnight '33
Jungle Bride '33
Skyscraper Souls '32
Sidewalks of New York '31
Free and Easy '30
Broadway Melody '29
Our Modern Maidens '29
Our Dancing Daughters '28

Bradley Page (1901-85)
The Affairs of Annabel '38
Mistaken Identity '36
Champagne for Breakfast '35

Dorothy Page (1904-61)
Ride 'Em Cowgirl '41
The Singing Cowgirl '39
Water Rustlers '39

Gale Page (1913-83)
Knute Rockne: All American '40
They Drive by Night '40
Amazing Dr. Clitterhouse '38
Four Daughters '38

Genevieve Page (1930-)
Buffet Froid '79
The Private Life of Sherlock Holmes '70
Gun Crazy '69
Mayerling '68
Belle de Jour '67
The Day and the Hour '63
El Cid '61
Song Without End '60
Girl in His Pocket '57
Fanfan la Tulipe '51

Geraldine Page (1924-87)
Riders to the Sea '88
My Little Girl '87
Native Son '86
The Adventures of Huckleberry Finn '85
The Bride '85
The Trip to Bountiful '85
Walls of Glass '85
White Nights '85
The Dollmaker '84
Harry's War '84
Loving '84
The Pope of Greenwich Village '84
I'm Dancing as Fast as I Can '82
Honky Tonk Freeway '81
Interiors '78
Nasty Habits '77
The Rescuers '77 *(V)*
The Day of the Locust '75
Hazel's People '75
Pete 'n' Tillie '72
The Beguiled '70
Whatever Happened to Aunt Alice? '69
The Happiest Millionaire '67
ABC Stage 67: Truman Capote's A Christmas Memory '66
Barefoot in Athens '66
You're a Big Boy Now '66
The Three Sisters '65
Toys in the Attic '63
Sweet Bird of Youth '62
Summer and Smoke '61
Hondo '53

Grant Page
Road Games '81
Deathcheaters '76

Harrison Page
Carnosaur '93
Lionheart '90
Beyond the Valley of the Dolls '70

Joy Page
Conquest of Cochise '53
Fighter Attack '53
Casablanca '42

Ken Page
The Nightmare before Christmas '93 *(V)*
The Kid Who Loved Christmas '90

LaWanda Page (1920-)
Friday '95
The Meteor Man '93
Shakes the Clown '92
Mausoleum '83
Zapped! '82
B.A.D. Cats '80

Patti Page
Boys' Night Out '62
Elmer Gantry '60

Tony Page
Q (The Winged Serpent) '82
Gangsters '79

Alfred Paget (1880-1925)
Intolerance '16
The Lamb '15

Debra Paget (1933-)
The Mercenaries '65
The Haunted Palace '63
Tales of Terror '62
The Indian Tomb '59
From the Earth to the Moon '58
Journey to the Lost City '58
Omar Khayyam '57
The Last Hunt '56
Love Me Tender '56
The Ten Commandments '56
Demetrius and the Gladiators '54
Prince Valiant '54
Stars and Stripes Forever '52
Broken Arrow '50
House of Strangers '49

Nicola Pagett (1945-)
An Awfully Big Adventure '94
Privates on Parade '84
A Woman of Substance '84
Oliver's Story '78
The Viking Queen '67

Marcel Pagliero
Dedee d'Anvers '49
Open City '45

Liana Pai
Happy Accidents '00
The Siege '98

Janis Paige (1922-)
Natural Causes '94
Love at the Top '86
Angel on My Shoulder '80
Magic on Love Island '80
Bachelor in Paradise '69

Please Don't Eat the Daisies '60
Silk Stockings '57
Romance on the High Seas '48
Winter Meeting '48
Hollywood Canteen '44

Mabel Paige (1879-1954)
The Scar '48
Nocturne '46
Murder, He Says '45

Robert Paige (1910-87)
Abbott and Costello Go to Mars '53
The Green Promise '49
The Red Stallion '47
Can't Help Singing '45
Son of Dracula '43
Pardon My Sarong '42
The Monster and the Girl '41

Geraldine Pailhas
Don Juan DeMarco '94
Suite 16 '94

Didier Pain
My Father's Glory '91
My Mother's Castle '91

Cathy Paine
Image of Death '77
Helter Skelter '76

Heidi Paine
Wizards of the Demon Sword '94
Lethal Games '90
Wildest Dreams '90
Alien Seed '89
New York's Finest '87

Josh Pais
Scotland, PA '02
Music of the Heart '99

Nestor Paiva (1905-66)
Jesse James Meets Frankenstein's Daughter '65
Ballad of a Gunfighter '64
They Saved Hitler's Brain '64
Girls! Girls! Girls! '62
Frontier Uprising '61
The Nine Lives of Elfego Baca '58
Outcasts of the City '58
The Mole People '56
Revenge of the Creature '55
Tarantula '55
Creature from the Black Lagoon '54
Five Fingers '52
Double Dynamite '51
Follow Me Quietly '49
Shoot to Kill '47
Fear '46
The Road to Utopia '46
The Falcon in Mexico '44
The Purple Heart '44
Hold That Ghost '41
Beau Geste '39
Prison Train '38

Maria Pakulnis
The Decalogue '88
No End '84

Holly Palance (1950-)
Cast the First Stone '89
The Best of Times '86
Tuxedo Warrior '82
The Omen '76

Jack Palance (1919-)
Prancer Returns '01
Sarah, Plain and Tall: Winter's End '99
Treasure Island '99
Ebenezer '97
Buffalo Girls '95
City Slickers 2: The Legend of Curly's Gold '94
Cops and Robbersons '94
The Swan Princess '94 (V)
Cyborg 2 '93
Keep the Change '92
Solar Crisis '92
City Slickers '91
Batman '89
Tango and Cash '89
Bagdad Cafe '88
Gor '88
Young Guns '88
Outlaw of Gor '87
The Last Contract '86
Black Cobra '83
Alone in the Dark '82
Hawk the Slayer '81
Bloody Avenger '80
Hell's Brigade: The Final Assault '80
Unknown Powers '80
Angel's Brigade '79
Cocaine Cowboys '79
The Last Ride of the Dalton Gang '79
Cop in Blue Jeans '78
One Man Jury '78
Big Boss '77
Mr. Scarface '77
Portrait of a Hitman '77
Welcome to Blood City '77
The Sensuous Nurse '76
Sting of the West '76
Four Deuces '75
God's Gun '75
Great Adventure '75
The Hatfields & the McCoys '75
Craze '74
Dracula '73
Oklahoma Crude '73
Battle of the Commandos '71
Chato's Land '71
Rulers of the City '71
Companeros '70
The Horsemen '70
The McMasters '70
Monte Walsh '70
Desperados '69
Deadly Sanctuary '68
Dr. Jekyll and Mr. Hyde '68
Strange Case of Dr. Jekyll & Mr. Hyde '68
Torture Garden '67
Alice Through the Looking Glass '66
The Professionals '66
Contempt '64
Barabbas '62
The Battle of Austerlitz '60
The Mongols '60
Lonely Man '57
Attack! '56
Requiem for a Heavyweight '56
The Big Knife '55
I Died a Thousand Times '55
The Silver Chalice '54
Arrowhead '53
Second Chance '53
Shane '53
Sudden Fear '52
The Halls of Montezuma '50
Panic in the Streets '50

Ron Palillo (1949-)
Committed '91
Hellgate '89
SnakeEater '89
Doin' Time '85

Michael Palin (1943-)
Fierce Creatures '96
Mr. Toad's Wild Ride '96
American Friends '91
A Fish Called Wanda '88
Brazil '85
A Private Function '84
Monty Python's The Meaning of Life '83
The Missionary '82
The Secret Policeman's Other Ball '82
Secret Policeman's Private Parts '81
Time Bandits '81
Monty Python's Life of Brian '79
All You Need Is Cash '78
Jabberwocky '77
Monty Python and the Holy Grail '75
And Now for Something Completely Different '72
John Cleese on How to Irritate People '68

Anna Palk
The Nightcomers '72
Fahrenheit 451 '66

Aleksa Palladino
Storytelling '01
The Adventures of Sebastian Cole '99
Red Dirt '99
Manny & Lo '96

Erik Palladino
Life Without Dick '01
U-571 '00
Can't Hardly Wait '98

Anita Pallenberg
Performance '70
Barbarella '68
Candy '68

Eugene Pallette (1889-1954)
Pin-Up Girl '44
Sensations of 1945 '44
Heaven Can Wait '43
It Ain't Hay '43
Big Street '42
Silver Queen '42
The Bride Came C.O.D. '41
The Lady Eve '41
The Mark of Zorro '40
Young Tom Edison '40
First Love '39
Mr. Smith Goes to Washington '39
The Adventures of Robin Hood '38
100 Men and a Girl '37
Topper '37
The Ghost Goes West '36
My Man Godfrey '36
Stowaway '36
The Kennel Murder Case '33
Shanghai Express '32
Strangers of the Evening '32
The Virginian '29
Mantrap '26
The Three Musketeers '21
Intolerance '16
The Birth of a Nation '15

Joseph Pallister
Broadcast Bombshells '95
Bikini Bistro '94

Gabriella Pallotta (1938-)
Hero of Rome '63
The Mongols '60
Il Grido '57
The Roof '56

Mimmo Palmara
The Trojan Horse '62
The Last Days of Pompeii '60

Ulf Palme
Dreams '55
Miss Julie '50

Betsy Palmer (1929-)
The Fear: Halloween Night '99
Still Not Quite Human '92
Friday the 13th, Part 2 '81
Friday the 13th '80
The Last Angry Man '59
The Tin Star '57
The Long Gray Line '55
Mister Roberts '55
Queen Bee '55

Geoffrey Palmer (1927-)
Stalag Luft
Mrs. Brown '97
Tomorrow Never Dies '97
A Question of Attribution '91
Christabel '89
A Fish Called Wanda '88

Gregg (Hunter) Palmer (1927-)
The Rebel Set '59
Zombies of Moratau '57
The Creature Walks among Us '56
To Hell and Back '55
Francis Goes to West Point '52

Gretchen Palmer
I Got the Hook-Up '98
Chopper Chicks in Zombietown '91

Lilli Palmer (1914-86)
The Holcroft Covenant '85
The Boys from Brazil '78
What the Peeper Saw '72
Murders in the Rue Morgue '71
Sebastian '68
The Amorous Adventures of Moll Flanders '65
The Miracle of the White Stallions '63
Adorable Julia '62
The Counterfeit Traitor '62
Conspiracy of Hearts '60
But Not for Me '59
Modigliani '58
The Devil in Silk '56
The Long Dark Hall '51
My Girl Tisa '48
Body and Soul '47
Beware of Pity '46
Cloak and Dagger '46
Chamber of Horrors '40
The Secret Agent '36

Maria Palmer (1917-81)
Outcasts of the City '58
By the Light of the Silvery Moon '53
Days of Glory '43

Shirley Palmer
Somewhere in Sonora '33
Campus Knights '29

Chazz Palminteri (1952-)
Down to Earth '01
Boss of Bosses '99
Excellent Cadavers '99
Stuart Little '99 (V)
Analyze This '98
Hurlyburly '98
Scarred City '98
Diabolique '96
Faithful '95
Jade '95
The Last Word '95
Mulholland Falls '95
The Usual Suspects '95
Bullets over Broadway '94
The Perez Family '94
A Bronx Tale '93
Innocent Blood '92
There Goes the Neighborhood '92
Oscar '91

Carlos Palomino
Die Watching '93
Geronimo: An American Legend '93
My Samurai '92
Nasty Hero '89
Strangers Kiss '83

Gwyneth Paltrow (1973-)
Possession '02
The Anniversary Party '01
The Royal Tenenbaums '01
Shallow Hal '01
Bounce '00
Duets '00
The Talented Mr. Ripley '99
Hush '98
A Perfect Murder '98
Shakespeare in Love '98
Great Expectations '97
Sliding Doors '97
Emma '96
Hard Eight '96
Moonlight and Valentino '95
The Pallbearer '95
Seven '95
Jefferson in Paris '94
Mrs. Parker and the Vicious Circle '94
Flesh and Bone '93
Malice '93
Hook '91

Luciana Paluzzi (1931-)
The Klansman '74
Medusa '74
Manhunt '73
99 Women '69
A Black Veil for Lisa '68
The Green Slime '68
Chuka '67
One-Eyed Soldiers '67
Thunderball '65
Muscle Beach Party '64
Return to Peyton Place '61
Carlton Browne of the F.O. '59
Journey to the Lost City '58

Alessandra Panaro (1939-)
The Bacchantes '63
Conquest of Mycene '63
Executioner of Venice '63
Rocco and His Brothers '60

Richard Panebianco
Dogfight '91
China Girl '87

Hayden Panettiere
The Affair of the Necklace '01
Joe Somebody '01
Dinosaur '00 (V)
Remember the Titans '00
A Bug's Life '98 (V)

Franklin Pangborn (1889-1958)
Romance on the High Seas '48
I'll Be Yours '47
The Sin of Harold Diddlebock '47
The Great Moment '44
Hail the Conquering Hero '44
His Butler's Sister '44
Two Weeks to Live '43
Call Out the Marines '42
The Palm Beach Story '42
The Flame of New Orleans '41
A Girl, a Guy and a Gob '41
Never Give a Sucker an Even Break '41
Sullivan's Travels '41
The Bank Dick '40
Christmas in July '40
Fifth Avenue Girl '39
Topper Takes a Trip '39
Bluebeard's Eighth Wife '38
Carefree '38
Just Around the Corner '38
Vivacious Lady '38
All Over Town '37
Dangerous Holiday '37
Easy Living '37
Hats Off '37
The Mandarin Mystery '37
A Star Is Born '37
Doughnuts & Society '36
My Man Godfrey '36
Tango '36
King Kelly of the U.S.A. '34
Flying Down to Rio '33

Stuart Pankin (1946-)
Chasing Destiny '00
Honey, We Shrunk Ourselves '97
Down, Out and Dangerous '95
Beanstalk '94
Father and Scout '94
Squanto: A Warrior's Tale '94
Silence of the Hams '93
Betrayal of the Dove '92
The Vagrant '92
Life Stinks '91
Mannequin 2: On the Move '91
Arachnophobia '90
That's Adequate '90
Second Sight '89
Fatal Attraction '87
Love at Stake '87
Dirt Bike Kid '86
The Hollywood Knights '80

John Pankow (1954-)
The Object of My Affection '98
A Stranger Among Us '92
Mortal Thoughts '91
Year of the Gun '91
Johnny Be Good '88
Monkey Shines '88
Talk Radio '88
To Live & Die in L.A. '85

Joe Pantoliano (1951-)
The Adventures of Pluto Nash '02
Cats & Dogs '01 (V)
A Better Way to Die '00
Memento '00
Ready to Rumble '00
Black and White '99
The Life Before This '99
The Matrix '99
New Blood '99
Hoods '98
The Taxman '98
U.S. Marshals '98
Tinseltown '97
Top of the World '97
Bound '96
Natural Enemy '96
Bad Boys '95
The Immortals '95
The Last Word '95
Steal Big, Steal Little '95
Baby's Day Out '94
Robot in the Family '94
The Spy Within '94
Teresa's Tattoo '94
Calendar Girl '93
Dangerous Heart '93
The Fugitive '93
Me and the Kid '93
Three of Hearts '93
Through the Eyes of a Killer '92
Used People '92
Zandalee '91
El Diablo '90
The Last of the Finest '90
Short Time '90
Downtown '89
Nightbreaker '89
Tales from the Crypt '89
The In Crowd '88
Midnight Run '88
Empire of the Sun '87
La Bamba '87
Scenes from the Goldmine '87
The Squeeze '87
Running Scared '86
The Goonies '85
Mean Season '85
Eddie and the Cruisers '83
The Final Terror '83
Risky Business '83
Idolmaker '80

Cecile Paoli
Sharpe's Revenge '97
Sharpe's Waterloo '97
Riders '88

Michael (Mike) Papajohn (1964-)
Spider-Man '02
The Animal '01
Charlie's Angels '00
For Love of the Game '99
My Giant '98
Spawn '97
Eraser '96
The Indian in the Cupboard '95
Naked Souls '95
Dominion '94
Little Big League '94
The Babe '92
The Last Boy Scout '91
Predator 2 '90

Irene Papas (1926-)
Captain Corelli's Mandolin '01
The Odyssey '97
Party '96
Jacob '94
High Season '88
Sweet Country '87
Into the Night '85
The Assisi Underground '84
Erendira '83
Lion of the Desert '81
Christ Stopped at Eboli '79
Sidney Sheldon's Bloodline '79
Iphigenia '77
The Message '77
Moses '76

Don't Torture a Duckling '72
1931: Once Upon a Time in New York '72
Trojan Women '71
Anne of the Thousand Days '69
A Dream of Kings '69
Z '69
The Brotherhood '68
Zorba the Greek '64
The Guns of Navarone '61
The Unfaithfuls '60
Tribute to a Bad Man '56

Laslo Papas
Slipping into Darkness '88
Bloodshed '83
Crazed '82

Ike Pappas
The Package '89
Moon over Parador '88

Anna Paquin (1982-)
Almost Famous '00
Finding Forrester '00
X-Men '00
It's the Rage '99
She's All That '99
A Walk on the Moon '99
Hurlyburly '98
Amistad '97
The Member of the Wedding '97
Fly Away Home '96
Jane Eyre '96
The Piano '93

Vanessa Paradis
The Girl on the Bridge '98
Elisa '94

John Paragon
UHF '89
Elvira, Mistress of the Dark '88
Pee-wee's Big Adventure '85
Eating Raoul '82
The Pee-wee Herman Show '82

Kiri Paramore
Doing Time for Patsy Cline '97
The Last Days of Chez Nous '92
Flirting '89

Kip Pardue
Driven '01
Remember the Titans '00

Jessica Pare
Lost and Delirious '01
Stardom '00

Michael Pare (1958-)
Peril '00
In the Dead of Space '99
Men of Means '99
The Debt '98
Hope Floats '98
Falling Fire '97
Strip Search '97
Bad Moon '96
Carver's Gate '96
Deadly Heroes '96
Sworn Enemies '96
The Dangerous '95
Raging Angels '95
Triplecross '95
Village of the Damned '95
Solar Force '94
Warriors '94
Point of Impact '93
Blink of an Eye '92
Dragonfight '92
Into the Sun '92
Sunset Heat '92
The Closer '91
Killing Streets '91
The Last Hour '91
Moon 44 '90
Eddie and the Cruisers 2: Eddie Lives! '89
World Gone Wild '88
Women's Club '87
Instant Justice '86
Space Rage '86
The Philadelphia Experiment '84
Streets of Fire '84
Eddie and the Cruisers '83

Marisa Paredes (1946-)
The Devil's Backbone '01
All About My Mother '99
Life Is Beautiful '98
Doctor Chance '97
Deep Crimson '96
Talk of Angels '96
Three Lives and Only One Death '96
The Flower of My Secret '95
High Heels '91
In a Glass Cage '86
Dark Habits '84

Mila Parely (1917-)
Three Stops to Murder '53
Beauty and the Beast '46
The Rules of the Game '39

Monique Parent (1965-)
The Pornographer '00
The Catcher '98
James Dean: Live Fast, Die Young '97
Tender Flesh '97
Illegal Affairs '96
Mirror, Mirror 3: The Voyeur '96
Dark Secrets '95
Masseuse '95
Midnight Confessions '95
The Perfect Gift '95
Stripshow '95
Married People, Single Sex 2: For Better or Worse '94
Play Time '94
Buford's Beach Bunnies '92

Judy Parfitt (1935-)
Berkeley Square '98
Ever After: A Cinderella Story '98
Wilde '97
Element of Doubt '96
The Return of the Borrowers '96
Dolores Claiborne '94
Midnight's Child '93
Dark Obsession '90
Getting It Right '89
The Charmer '87
Maurice '87
Office Romances '86
The Jewel in the Crown '84
Hamlet '69

Woodrow Parfrey
The Outlaw Josey Wales '76
Oklahoma Crude '73

Anne Parillaud (1960-)
The Man in the Iron Mask '98
Shattered Image '98
Frankie Starlight '95
Map of the Human Heart '93
Innocent Blood '92
La Femme Nikita '91

Jerry Paris (1925-86)
Evil Roy Slade '71
D-Day, the Sixth of June '56
Marty '55
The Caine Mutiny '54
The Wild One '54

Kris Park
Drive Me Crazy '99
I Love You, I Love You Not '97

Ray Park
X-Men '00
Star Wars: Episode 1—The Phantom Menace '99

Reg Park (1928-)
Hercules in the Haunted World '64
Hercules, Prisoner of Evil '64
Hercules and the Captive Women '63

Evan Dexter Parke
Planet of the Apes '01
The Replacements '00
The Cider House Rules '99

MacDonald Parke
The Mouse That Roared '59
Summertime '55

Cecil Parker (1897-1971)
A Study in Terror '66
Lady L '65
Heavens Above '63
The Brain '62
On the Fiddle '61
The Pure Hell of St. Trinian's '61
The Wreck of the Mary Deare '59
A Tale of Two Cities '58
The Admirable Crichton '57
Court Jester '56
The Ladykillers '55
The Detective '54
Tony Draws a Horse '51
Under Capricorn '49
The Weaker Sex '49
Captain Boycott '47
The Magic Bow '47
Caesar and Cleopatra '46
Dangerous Moonlight '41
The Stars Look Down '39
Housemaster '38
The Lady Vanishes '38
Storm in a Teacup '37
The Man Who Lived Again '36

Cecilia Parker (1905-93)
Andy Hardy's Double Life '42
Andy Hardy Meets Debutante '40
Andy Hardy Gets Spring Fever '39
Love Finds Andy Hardy '38
Roll Along Cowboy '37
Sweetheart of the Navy '37
Ah, Wilderness! '35
Naughty Marietta '35
Tombstone Canyon '35
Honor of the Range '34
The Lost Jungle '34
Mystery Ranch '34
Rainbow Ranch '33
Riders of Destiny '33

Chris Parker
Red Nights '87
Permanent Vacation '84

Corey Parker (1965-)
Mr. & Mrs. Loving '96
A Mother's Prayer '95
Broadway Bound '92
The Lost Language of Cranes '92
I'm Dangerous Tonight '90
White Palace '90
Big Man on Campus '89
How I Got into College '89
Biloxi Blues '88

Ed Parker (1931-90)
Curse of the Pink Panther '83
Kill the Golden Goose '79

Eddie (Ed, Eddy, Edwin) Parker (1900-60)
The Secret Code '42
God's Country and the Man '37
Ghost Rider '35

Eleanor Parker (1922-)
Dead on the Money '91
She's Dressed to Kill '79
The Bastard '78
Fantasy Island '76
Home for the Holidays '72
Maybe I'll Be Home in the Spring '70
Hans Brinker '69
Tiger and the Pussycat '67
The Oscar '66
The Sound of Music '65
Panic Button '62
Return to Peyton Place '61
Home from the Hill '60
A Hole in the Head '59
The King and Four Queens '56
Interrupted Melody '55

The Man with the Golden Arm '55
Naked Jungle '54
Valley of the Kings '54
Above and Beyond '53
Escape from Fort Bravo '53
Scaramouche '52
Detective Story '51
Chain Lightning '50
Three Secrets '50
It's a Great Feeling '49
Escape Me Never '47
Never Say Goodbye '46
Hollywood Canteen '44

F. William Parker
Jack Frost '97
Hard Eight '96

Fess Parker (1926-)
Hell Is for Heroes '62
Alias Jesse James '59
The Jayhawkers '59
The Light in the Forest '58
Old Yeller '57
Davy Crockett and the River Pirates '56
The Great Locomotive Chase '56
Westward Ho, the Wagons! '56
Battle Cry '55
Davy Crockett, King of the Wild Frontier '55
Them! '54

Jameson Parker (1947-)
Curse of the Crystal Eye '93
Spy '89
Prince of Darkness '87
American Justice '86
Callie and Son '81
A Small Circle of Friends '80
Anatomy of a Seduction '79
The Gathering: Part 2 '79

Jean Parker (1912-)
Apache Uprising '66
A Lawless Street '55
The Gunfighter '50
Rolling Home '48
Bluebeard '44
Dead Man's Eyes/Pillow of Death '44
Lady in the Death House '44
Navy Way '44
One Body Too Many '44
Flying Blind '41
Beyond Tomorrow '40
Knights of the Range '40
The Flying Deuces '39
The Ghost Goes West '36
The Texas Rangers '36
Gabriel Over the White House '33
Lady for a Day '33
Little Women '33
Rasputin and the Empress '33

Kim Parker
Fiend without a Face '58
Fire Maidens from Outer Space '56

Lara Parker (1942-)
Foxfire Light '82
The Solitary Man '82
Race with the Devil '75
Night of Dark Shadows '71
Hi, Mom! '70

Lloyd "Sunshine" Parker (1928-99)
Spittin' Image '83
Cannery Row '82

Mary-Louise Parker (1964-)
Cupid & Cate '00
The Five Senses '99
Goodbye, Lover '99
Let the Devil Wear Black '99
The Simple Life of Noah Dearborn '99
Legalese '98
The Maker '98
Saint Maybe '98
Murder in Mind '97
Portrait of a Lady '96

Reckless '95
Sugartime '95
Boys on the Side '94
Bullets over Broadway '94
The Client '94
A Place for Annie '94
Mr. Wonderful '93
Naked in New York '93
Fried Green Tomatoes '91
Grand Canyon '91
Longtime Companion '90
Signs of Life '89

Michael Parker
Kill Line '91
My Own Private Idaho '91

Molly Parker (1971-)
The Center of the World '01
Rare Birds '01
Waking the Dead '00
The Five Senses '99
Sunshine '99
Wonderland '99
In the Shadows '98
Kissed '96
Hole in the Sky '95
Anything for Love '93

Monica Parker
Coming Out Alive '84
Improper Channels '82

Nathaniel Parker (1963-)
Lover's Prayer '99
Vanity Fair '99
David '97
Far from the Madding Crowd '97
Into Thin Air: Death on Everest '97
Beverly Hills Ninja '96
Othello '95
A Village Affair '95
Squanto: A Warrior's Tale '94
Wide Sargasso Sea '92
Hamlet '90
Piece of Cake '90

Nicole Parker
Remember the Titans '00
Blue Streak '99
200 Cigarettes '98
Boogie Nights '97
The End of Violence '97
The Incredibly True Adventure of Two Girls in Love '95

Nicole Ari Parker
Dancing in September '00
The Loretta Claiborne Story '00
Loving Jezebel '99

Noelle Parker (1969-)
Newsbreak '00
Lethal Lolita—Amy Fisher: My Story '92
Ernest Saves Christmas '88
Twisted '86

Norman Parker
Question of Faith '93
Killing Hour '84

Paula Jai Parker
The Breaks '99
Woo '97
Sprung '96
Tales from the Hood '95
Cosmic Slop '94

Sachi (MacLaine) Parker (1956-)
Welcome Home, Roxy Carmichael '90
Riders to the Sea '88
Peggy Sue Got Married '86
The Dancing Princesses '84

Sarah Jessica Parker (1965-)
Life Without Dick '01
State and Main '00
Dudley Do-Right '99
Extreme Measures '96
The First Wives Club '96
Mars Attacks! '96
The Substance of Fire '96
Til There Was You '96
If Lucy Fell '95
Miami Rhapsody '95

Ed Wood '94
Hocus Pocus '93
Striking Distance '93
Honeymoon in Vegas '92
L.A. Story '91
Flight of the Navigator '86
Girls Just Want to Have Fun '85
Going for the Gold: The Bill Johnson Story '85
Somewhere Tomorrow '85
Almost Royal Family '84
First Born '84
Footloose '84

Suzy Parker (1932-)
The Interns '62
The Best of Everything '59
Ten North Frederick '58
Funny Face '57

Trey Parker (1969-)
South Park: Bigger, Longer and Uncut '99 (V)
BASEketball '98
Orgazmo '98
Cannibal! The Musical '96

Willard Parker (1912-96)
Bandit Queen '51
Great Jesse James Raid '49
You Gotta Stay Happy '48

Gerard Parkes
A House Divided '00
Rescuers: Stories of Courage "Two Women" '97
It Takes Two '95
The Last Winter '89
Speaking Parts '89
Spasms '82

Shaun Parkes
The Mummy Returns '01
Human Traffic '99

Barbara Parkins (1942-)
Calendar Girl Murders '84
To Catch a King '84
Breakfast in Paris '81
Bear Island '80
Law of the Land '76
Shout at the Devil '76
Christina '74
Asylum '72
Puppet on a Chain '72
Snatched '72
The Deadly Trap '71
The Mephisto Waltz '71
Valley of the Dolls '67

Bert Parks (1914-92)
The Freshman '90
Shining Star '75

Catherine Parks
Body of Influence '93
Friday the 13th, Part 3 '82

James Parks
Spent '00
You Know My Name '99

Larry Parks (1914-75)
Love Is Better Than Ever '52
Jolson Sings Again '49
Down to Earth '47
Her Husband's Affairs '47
The Jolson Story '46
Destroyer '43
Blondie Goes to College '42
You Were Never Lovelier '42
Harmon of Michigan '41

Michael Parks (1938-)
From Dusk Till Dawn 3: The Hangman's Daughter '99
Wicked '98
Julian Po '97
Niagara, Niagara '97
From Dusk Till Dawn '95
Death Wish 5: The Face of Death '94
Stranger by Night '94
Storyville '92
The Hitman '91
The China Lake Murders '90
Gore Vidal's Billy the Kid '89

Welcome to Spring Break '88
Arizona Heat '87
Stamp of a Killer '87
Club Life '86
The Return of Josey Wales '86
Chase '85
French Quarter Undercover '85
Savannah Smiles '82
Hard Country '81
ffolkes '80
The Evictors '79
Breakthrough '78
Midnight Auto Supply '78
Night Cries '78
The Private Files of J. Edgar Hoover '77
Sidewinder One '77
The Savage Bees '76
The Bible '66

Tammy Parks
Attack of the 60-Foot Centerfold '95
Play Time '94

Trina Parks
The Muthers '76
Darktown Strutters '74
Diamonds Are Forever '71

Parkyakarkus (Harry Einstein) (1904-58)
Yank in Libya '42
Strike Me Pink '36

Steve Parlavecchio
The First to Go '97
Bandwagon '95
Amongst Friends '93

Dita Parlo (1906-71)
Grand Illusion '37
L'Atalante '34
Homecoming '28

Emory Parnell (1892-1979)
Man of the West '58
Pardners '56
Ma and Pa Kettle at Home '54
Shadows of Tombstone '53
Lost in Alaska '52
Ma and Pa Kettle at the Fair '52
Ma and Pa Kettle Back On the Farm '51
Trail of Robin Hood '50
The Show-Off '46
Casanova Brown '44
Miracle of Morgan's Creek '44
I Married a Witch '42
They All Kissed the Bride '42

Helen Parrish (1924-59)
Sunset Serenade '42
They All Kissed the Bride '42
X Marks the Spot '42
Overland Mail '41
You'll Find Out '40
First Love '39
Three Smart Girls Grow Up '39
Little Tough Guys '38
Mad About Music '38
Big Trail '30

Julie Parrish
The Doberman Gang '72
Paradise, Hawaiian Style '66

Leslie Parrish (1935-)
The Invisible Strangler '76
The Giant Spider Invasion '75
Sex and the Single Girl '64
For Love or Money '63
The Manchurian Candidate '62
Li'l Abner '59

Steve Parrish
Scanners 3: The Takeover '92
Midnight '89

David Parry
Auntie Lee's Meat Pies '92
Dr. Caligari '89

The Lost Platoon '89

Nastasha Parry
Haunted: The Ferryman '74
Crow Hollow '52

Tom Parsekian
Club Life '86
Hot Resort '85

Frederick Parslow
Wrangler '88
The Last Wave '77

Estelle Parsons (1927-)
The Love Letter '98
Looking for Richard '96
That Darn Cat '96
A Private Matter '92
Dick Tracy '90
Come Along with Me '84
Gentleman Bandit '81
Foreplay '75
For Pete's Sake '74
I Never Sang for My Father '70
Watermelon Man '70
Don't Drink the Water '69
Rachel, Rachel '68
Bonnie & Clyde '67

Karyn Parsons (1968-)
The Ladies Man '00
Mixing Nia '98
Gulliver's Travels '95
Major Payne '95
Class Act '91

Mike Parsons
The Ravagers '65
The Walls of Hell '64

Nancy Parsons (1942-2001)
Lakota Woman: Siege at Wounded Knee '94
Wishman '93
Ladybugs '92
Porky's Revenge '85
Porky's 2: The Next Day '83
Porky's '82
Motel Hell '80

Percy Parsons (1878-1944)
Dangerous Moonlight '41
Rhodes '36
Power '34
Blackmail '29

Dolly Parton (1946-)
Jackie's Back '99
Unlikely Angel '97
The Beverly Hillbillies '93
Straight Talk '92
Steel Magnolias '89
A Smoky Mountain Christmas '86
Rhinestone '84
The Best Little Whorehouse in Texas '82
9 to 5 '80

Julia Parton
Good Girls Don't '95
Vice Academy 3 '91

Christine Pascal (1953-96)
Le Grand Chemin '87
Sincerely Charlotte '86
Maids of Wilko '79
Spoiled Children '77
The Best Way '76
The Clockmaker '73

Mary Ann Pascal
Lethal Lolita—Amy Fisher: My Story '92
Writer's Block '91

Olivia Pascal
Bloody Moon '83
C.O.D. '83

Isabelle Pasco (1966-)
Invisible Circus '00
Sous Sol '96
Prospero's Books '91
High Frequency '88

Richard Pasco (1926-)
Mrs. Brown '97
The Watcher in the Woods '81

Rasputin the Mad Monk '66
The Gorgon '64
Sword of Sherwood Forest '60
Room at the Top '59

Adrian Pasdar (1965-)
The Big Day '99
Mutiny '99
A Brother's Kiss '97
Wounded '97
Just Like a Woman '95
The Pompatus of Love '95
The Last Good Time '94
Carlito's Way '93
The Ghost Brigade '93
Grand Isle '92
The Lost Capone '90
Vital Signs '90
Cookie '89
Torn Apart '89
Made in USA '88
Near Dark '87
Streets of Gold '86
Top Gun '86

Pier Paolo Pasolini (1922-75)
The Canterbury Tales '71
The Decameron '70
Oedipus Rex '67

Cyndi Pass
Hindsight '97
The Night Caller '97
Serial Killer '95
The Force '94
Scanner Cop '94
Bounty Tracker '93
Deadbolt '92
Desperate Motives '92
Mission of Justice '92
Bikini Island '91

Earl Pastko
Masterminds '96
The Sweet Hereafter '96
Eclipse '94
Highway 61 '91

Rosana Pastor
The Break '97
Land and Freedom '95

Vincent Pastore (1946-)
Deuces Wild '02
Serving Sara '02
Made '01
Blue Moon '00
Hitman's Journal '99
The Hurricane '99
Mickey Blue Eyes '99
Mafia! '98
Witness to the Mob '98
Gotti '96
Walking and Talking '96
West New York '96
The Jerky Boys '95
Money Train '95
The Ref '93
True Love '89

Robert Pastorelli (1954-)
Rodgers & Hammerstein's South Pacific '01
Bait '00
Modern Vampires '98
A Simple Wish '97
Eraser '96
Michael '96
The Yarn Princess '94
The Paint Job '93
Sister Act 2: Back in the Habit '93
Striking Distance '93
Folks! '92
Dances with Wolves '90
Beverly Hills Cop 2 '87

Willie Pastrano
Alligator Alley '72
Wild Rebels '71

Patachou
The Adventures of Felix '99
French Can-Can '55

Michael Pataki (1938-)
One More Chance '90
Death House '88
Halloween 4: The Return of Michael Myers '88
The Underachievers '88
American Anthem '86

Remo Williams: The Adventure Begins '85
Rocky 4 '85
Delinquent School Girls '84
Dead and Buried '81
The Last Word '80
Love at First Bite '79
On the Edge: The Survival of Dana '79
When Every Day Was the Fourth of July '78
Zoltan...Hound of Dracula '78
The Amazing Spider-Man '77
The Bat People '74
The Last Porno Flick '74
The Baby '72
Grave of the Vampire '72
Dirt Gang '71

Wally Patch (1888-1970)
Calling Paul Temple '48
Butler's Dilemma '43
Cottage to Let '41
Night Train to Munich '40
Inspector Hornleigh '39
Pygmalion '38
Don Quixote '35
The Private Life of Henry VIII '33

Michael Pate (1920-)
Howling 3: The Marsupials '87
Camel Boy '84 (V)
Return of Captain Invincible '83
The Singing Nun '66
McLintock! '63
Tower of London '62
Curse of the Undead '59
Green Mansions '59
The Oklahoman '56
Seventh Cavalry '56
A Lawless Street '55
King Richard and the Crusaders '54
Hondo '53
Houdini '53
Julius Caesar '53
Face to Face '52
Five Fingers '52
The Strange Door '51

Bill Paterson (1945-)
Crush '02
Wives and Daughters '01
Heart '99
The Match '99
Hilary and Jackie '98
Retribution '98
Spice World: The Movie '97
Chaplin '92
The Object of Beauty '91
Truly, Madly, Deeply '91
Traffik '90
The Witches '90
The Adventures of Baron Munchausen '89
The Rachel Papers '89
Coming Up Roses '87
Dutch Girls '87
Hidden City '87
Defense of the Realm '85
Comfort and Joy '84
The Killing Fields '84
A Private Function '84
The Ploughman's Lunch '83

Mandy Patinkin (1952-)
Pinero '01
Strange Justice: The Clarence Thomas and Anita Hill Story '99
Lulu on the Bridge '98
Hombres Armados '97
The Hunchback '97
Broken Glass '96
Squanto: A Warrior's Tale '94
The Music of Chance '93
The Doctor '91
True Colors '91
Dick Tracy '90
Impromptu '90
Alien Nation '88
The House on Carroll Street '88

The Princess Bride '87
Sunday in the Park with George '86
Follies in Concert '85
Maxie '85
Daniel '83
Yentl '83
Ragtime '81
Night of the Juggler '80
French Postcards '79
Last Embrace '79
The Big Fix '78

Tatjana Patitz
Restraining Order '99
Rising Sun '93

Angela Paton
The Con '98
Trapped in Paradise '94
Groundhog Day '93

Laurie Paton
The Amy Fisher Story '93
Norman's Awesome Experience '88

Jason Patric (1966-)
Your Friends & Neighbors '98
Incognito '97
Speed 2: Cruise Control '97
Sleepers '96
The Journey of August King '95
Geronimo: An American Legend '93
Denial: The Dark Side of Passion '91
Rush '91
After Dark, My Sweet '90
Frankenstein Unbound '90
The Beast '88
The Lost Boys '87
Solarbabies '86
Toughlove '85

Dennis Patrick (1918-)
The Air Up There '94
Heated Vengeance '87
Choices '81
Dear Dead Delilah '72
Joe '70
The Time Travelers '64

Dorothy Patrick (1922-87)
Men of the Fighting Lady '54
Thunder Pass '54
Torch Song '53
Follow Me Quietly '49
New Orleans '47

Gail Patrick (1911-80)
Brewster's Millions '45
Love Crazy '41
Doctor Takes a Wife '40
My Favorite Wife '40
Mad About Music '38
Wives under Suspicion '38
Stage Door '37
My Man Godfrey '36
Death Takes a Holiday '34
Wagon Wheels '34
Badmen of Nevada '33
Murders in the Zoo '33
The Mysterious Rider '33
The Phantom Broadcast '33
To the Last Man '33

Gregory Patrick
Sexpot '88
A Woman Obsessed '88

Lee Patrick (1911-82)
Black Bird '75
7 Faces of Dr. Lao '63
Summer and Smoke '61
Pillow Talk '59
Vertigo '58
The Fuller Brush Girl '50
Inner Sanctum '48
Gambler's Choice '44
Mrs. Parkington '44
In This Our Life '42
Somewhere I'll Find You '42
Footsteps in the Dark '41
The Maltese Falcon '41
Fisherman's Wharf '39
Law of the Underworld '38

Nigel Patrick (1913-81)
Mackintosh Man '73
The Executioner '70
Battle of Britain '69
The Virgin Soldiers '69
Johnny Nobody '61
The League of Gentlemen '60
The Trials of Oscar Wilde '60
Sapphire '59
Raintree County '57
The Pickwick Papers '54
Encore '52
The Browning Version '51
Pandora and the Flying Dutchman '51
Trio '50
Uneasy Terms '48

Robert Patrick (1959-)
Backflash '01
Spy Kids '01
Texas Rangers '01
All the Pretty Horses '00
Angels Don't Sleep Here '00
Mexico City '00
Rogue Force '99
Tactical Assault '99
A Texas Funeral '99
The Faculty '98
Forgotten City '98
From Dusk Till Dawn 2: Texas Blood Money '98
Asylum '97
Cop Land '97
The Only Thrill '97
Striptease '96
Decoy '95
Double Dragon '94
Hong Kong '97 '94
The Last Gasp '94
Body Shot '93
Fire in the Sky '93
Last Action Hero '93
Zero Tolerance '93
The Cool Surface '92
Terminator 2: Judgment Day '91
Die Hard 2: Die Harder '90
Future Hunters '88
Eye of the Eagle '87
Behind Enemy Lines '85

Luana Patten (1938-96)
Follow Me, Boys! '66
Johnny Tremain & the Sons of Liberty '58
Rock, Pretty Baby '56
So Dear to My Heart '49

Elizabeth Patterson (1875-1966)
Pal Joey '57
Intruder in the Dust '49
Welcome Stranger '47
Lady on a Train '45
Follow the Boys '44
The Sky's the Limit '43
I Married a Witch '42
Remember the Night '40
Bluebeard's Eighth Wife '38
Go West, Young Man '36
Hide-Out '34
Hold Your Man '33
A Bill of Divorcement '32
No Man of Her Own '32

Jay Patterson (1954-)
Excessive Force 2: Force on Force '95
Nobody's Fool '94
McBain '91
Double Exposure: The Story of Margaret Bourke-White '89
D.O.A. '88
Nadine '87
Street Smart '87
Heaven Help Us '85

John D. Patterson
Helltown '38
Forlorn River '37

Lee Patterson (1929-)
Bullseye! '90
He Lives: The Search for the Evil One '88
Chato's Land '71

Jack the Ripper *'60*
The Spaniard's Curse *'58*
The Key Man *'57*
The Story of Esther Costello *'57*
Time Lock *'57*
Above Us the Waves *'56*

Lorna Patterson
The Imposter *'84*
Airplane! *'80*

Neva Patterson (1922-)
Women of Valor *'86*
V *'83*
The Runaways *'75*
David and Lisa *'62*
An Affair to Remember *'57*
Desk Set *'57*
Solid Gold Cadillac *'56*

Pat Patterson
The Body Shop *'72*
Gas-s-s-s! *'70*
Moonshine Mountain *'64*

Rocky Patterson
Time Tracers *'97*
The Dark Dealer *'95*
Armed for Action *'92*
Blood on the Badge *'92*
Nail Gun Massacre *'86*

Sarah Patterson
Snow White *'89*
The Company of Wolves *'85*

Scott Patterson
Alien Nation: Dark Horizon *'94*
Little Big League *'94*

Shirley Patterson (1922-95)
Black Hills *'48*
Driftin' River *'46*
Texas Kid *'43*

Bill(y) (William Patten) Patton (1894-1951)
Rustlers of Red Dog *'35*
Beyond the Trail *'26*
Fangs of Fate *'25*

Mark Patton
A Nightmare on Elm Street 2: Freddy's Revenge *'85*
Anna to the Infinite Power *'84*

Will Patton (1954-)
The Mothman Prophecies *'02*
Gone in 60 Seconds *'00*
Remember the Titans *'00*
Trixie *'00*
Entrapment *'99*
Jesus' Son *'99*
Armageddon *'98*
Breakfast of Champions *'98*
Inventing the Abbotts *'97*
The Postman *'97*
This World, Then the Fireworks *'97*
Fled *'96*
Copycat *'95*
The Spitfire Grill *'95*
The Client *'94*
Judicial Consent *'94*
Natural Causes *'94*
The Puppet Masters *'94*
Tollbooth *'94*
Midnight Edition *'93*
The Paint Job *'93*
Romeo Is Bleeding *'93*
Cold Heaven *'92*
In the Soup *'92*
Deadly Desire *'91*
Dillinger *'91*
In the Deep Woods *'91*
Murder on the Bayou *'91*
The Rapture *'91*
Everybody Wins *'90*
A Shock to the System *'90*
Signs of Life *'89*
Stars and Bars *'88*
Wildfire *'88*
No Way Out *'87*
Belizaire the Cajun *'86*
After Hours *'85*
Desperately Seeking Susan *'85*
Chinese Boxes *'84*
Variety *'83*

Tina Ona Paukstelis
5 Dark Souls *'96*
The Unearthing *'93*

Aaron Paul
K-PAX *'01*
Whatever It Takes *'00*

Adrian Paul (1959-)
The Breed *'01*
The Void *'01*
Highlander: Endgame *'00*
Dying to Get Rich *'98*
Premonition *'98*
Dead Men Can't Dance *'97*
The Cover Girl Murders *'93*
Highlander: The Gathering *'92*
Masque of the Red Death *'89*

Alexandra Paul (1963-)
Facing the Enemy *'00*
Spectre *'96*
Baywatch the Movie: Forbidden Paradise *'95*
Detonator 2: Night Watch *'95*
Piranha *'95*
Cyber Bandits *'94*
The Paperboy *'94*
Detonator *'93*
In Between *'92*
Sunset Grill *'92*
Prey of the Chameleon *'91*
Millions *'90*
Out of the Shadows *'88*
Dragnet *'87*
American Flyers *'85*
8 Million Ways to Die *'85*
Christine *'84*
Getting Physical *'84*
Just the Way You Are *'84*
American Nightmare *'81*

David Paul
Twinsitters *'95*
Double Trouble *'91*
Think Big *'90*
Ghost Writer *'89*
The Barbarians *'87*

Don Michael Paul (1963-)
Robot Wars *'93*
Rich Girl *'91*
The Heart of Dixie *'89*
Aloha Summer *'88*
Alien from L.A. *'87*
Rolling Vengeance *'87*
Winners Take All *'87*
Brotherhood of Justice *'86*
Lovelines *'84*

Peter Paul
Twinsitters *'95*
Double Trouble *'91*
Think Big *'90*
Ghost Writer *'89*
The Barbarians *'87*

Richard Paul (1940-98)
The People vs. Larry Flynt *'96*
Beanstalk *'94*
Bloodfist 3: Forced to Fight *'92*
Pass the Ammo *'88*
Princess Academy *'87*
Not for Publication *'84*
Eating Raoul *'82*

Richard Joseph Paul
Wounded *'97*
Vampirella *'96*
Oblivion *'94*
Under the Boardwalk *'89*

Stuart Paul
Fate *'90*
Emanon *'86*

Scott Paulin
My Little Assassin *'99*
Deceit *'93*
Knights *'93*
Pump Up the Volume *'90*
Capone *'89*
Captain America *'89*
From Hollywood to Deadwood *'89*
Grim Prairie Tales *'89*
Turner and Hooch *'89*
To Heal a Nation *'88*
Tricks of the Trade *'88*

Weekend War *'88*
The Last of Philip Banter *'87*
Teen Wolf *'85*
A Soldier's Story *'84*
The Right Stuff *'83*
Forbidden World *'82*

Morgan Paull
Surf 2 *'84*
Fade to Black *'80*
Patton *'70*

Albert Paulsen
The Arab Conspiracy *'76*
The Manchurian Candidate *'62*

Arno Paulsen
The Murderers Are Among Us *'46*
The Murderers are Among Us *'46*

Pat Paulsen (1927-97)
Auntie Lee's Meat Pies *'92*
They Still Call Me Bruce *'86*
Night Patrol *'85*
Ellie *'84*
Harper Valley P.T.A. *'78*
Foreplay *'75*
Where Were You When the Lights Went Out? *'68*

Rob Paulsen (1956-)
Jimmy Neutron: Boy Genius *'01 (V)*
Land Before Time 7: The Stone of Cold Fire *'00 (V)*
A Goofy Movie *'94 (V)*
Perfect Match *'88*
Eyes of Fire *'84*

Sarah Paulson
Held Up *'00*
What Women Want *'00*
The Other Sister *'98*
Levitation *'97*

Marisa Pavan (1932-)
John Paul Jones *'59*
Solomon and Sheba *'59*
The Man in the Gray Flannel Suit *'56*
Diane *'55*
The Rose Tattoo *'55*
Drum Beat *'54*
What Price Glory? *'52*

Muriel Pavlow (1921-)
Murder She Said *'62*
Doctor at Large *'57*
Doctor in the House *'53*
Malta Story *'53*

Lennox Pawle
David Copperfield *'35*
Sylvia Scarlett *'35*

Adam Pawlikowski
Lotna *'64*
Ashes and Diamonds *'58*

James Pax
The Chinatown Murders: Man against the Mob *'92*
In Love and War *'91*

Katina Paxinou (1900-73)
Rocco and His Brothers *'60*
Inheritance *'47*
For Whom the Bell Tolls *'43*

Bill Paxton (1955-)
Frailty *'02*
U-571 *'00*
Vertical Limit *'00*
A Bright Shining Lie *'98*
Mighty Joe Young *'98*
A Simple Plan *'98*
Titanic *'97*
The Evening Star *'96*
The Last Supper *'96*
Traveller *'96*
Twister *'96*
Apollo 13 *'95*
Frank and Jesse *'94*
True Lies *'94*
Boxing Helena *'93*
Future Shock *'93*
Indian Summer *'93*
Monolith *'93*
Tombstone *'93*
Trespass *'92*
The Vagrant *'92*
The Dark Backward *'91*
One False Move *'91*
Back to Back *'90*

The Last of the Finest *'90*
Navy SEALS *'90*
Predator 2 *'90*
Brain Dead *'89*
Next of Kin *'89*
Slipstream *'89*
Pass the Ammo *'88*
Near Dark *'87*
Aliens *'86*
Commando *'85*
Weird Science *'85*
Impulse *'84*
Streets of Fire *'84*
The Terminator *'84*
The Lords of Discipline *'83*
Crazy Mama *'75*

Johnny Paycheck (1937-)
Heroes of the Heart *'94*
Paradise Park *'91*
Hell's Angels Forever *'83*
Sweet Country Road *'81*
Take This Job & Shove It *'81*

David Paymer (1954-)
Focus *'01*
Bait *'00*
Bounce *'00*
For Love or Country: The Arturo Sandoval Story *'00*
State and Main *'00*
Chill Factor *'99*
Dash and Lilly *'99*
The Hurricane *'99*
Mumford *'99*
Partners *'99*
Mighty Joe Young *'98*
Outside Ozona *'98*
Payback *'98*
Amistad *'97*
The Lesser Evil *'97*
The Sixth Man *'97*
Carpool *'96*
Crime of the Century *'96*
Gang Related *'96*
Unforgettable *'96*
The American President *'95*
City Hall *'95*
Get Shorty *'95*
Nixon *'95*
City Slickers 2: The Legend of Curly's Gold *'94*
Quiz Show *'94*
Heart and Souls *'93*
Searching for Bobby Fischer *'93*
Mr. Saturday Night *'92*
City Slickers *'91*
Crazy People *'90*
No Way Out *'87*

Allen Payne
The Perfect Storm *'00*
A Price above Rubies *'97*
The Tuskegee Airmen *'95*
Vampire in Brooklyn *'95*
Jason's Lyric *'94*
The Walking Dead *'94*
CB4: The Movie *'93*
New Jack City *'91*

Bruce Payne (1960-)
Ripper: Letter from Hell *'01*
Dungeons and Dragons *'00*
Highlander: Endgame *'00*
Britannic *'99*
Cleopatra *'99*
Sweepers *'99*
Warlock 3: The End of Innocence *'98*
Face the Evil *'97*
Ravager *'97*
Kounterfeit *'96*
One Man's Justice *'95*
Operation Intercept *'95*
The Cisco Kid *'94*
Full Eclipse *'93*
H.P. Lovecraft's Necronomicon: Book of the Dead *'93*
Passenger 57 *'92*
Pyrates *'91*
Switch *'91*
Howling 6: The Freaks *'90*
Wonderland *'88*

Carl Anthony Payne, II
The Breaks *'99*
Ed *'96*

Eric Payne
Gridlock'd *'96*
She's Gotta Have It *'86*

John Payne (1912-89)
Bail Out at 43,000 *'57*
Slightly Scarlet *'56*
Tennessee's Partner *'55*
Silver Lode *'54*
Kansas City Confidential *'52*
Miracle on 34th Street *'47*
The Dolly Sisters *'46*
The Razor's Edge *'46*
Hello, Frisco, Hello *'43*
Footlight Serenade *'42*
Iceland *'42*
Springtime in the Rockies *'42*
To the Shores of Tripoli *'42*
The Great American Broadcast *'41*
Sun Valley Serenade *'41*
Week-End in Havana *'41*
Tin Pan Alley *'40*
College Swing *'38*
Hats Off *'37*
Dodsworth *'36*

Laurence Payne (1919-)
One Deadly Owner *'74*
Vampire Circus *'71*
The Tell-Tale Heart *'62*
The Crawling Eye *'58*
Train of Events *'49*

Sally Payne (1914-99)
Man from Cheyenne *'42*
Romance on the Range *'42*
Bad Man of Deadwood *'41*
Jesse James at Bay *'41*
Red River Valley *'41*
Young Bill Hickok *'40*

Amanda Pays (1959-)
Ablaze *'00*
Spacejacked *'98*
Hollywood Confidential *'97*
Solitaire for 2 *'94*
Dead on the Money *'91*
Exposure *'91*
The Flash *'90*
Leviathan *'89*
The Kindred *'87*
Off Limits *'87*
A.D. *'85*
Cold Room *'84*
Oxford Blues *'84*

Barbara Payton (1927-67)
Four Sided Triangle *'53*
Bride of the Gorilla *'51*
Drums in the Deep South *'51*
Kiss Tomorrow Goodbye *'50*
Only the Valiant *'50*
Great Jesse James Raid *'49*
Trapped *'49*

Pamela Payton-Wright
In Dreams *'98*
Resurrection *'80*

Rock Peace
Killer Tomatoes Strike Back *'90*
Return of the Killer Tomatoes! *'88*
Attack of the Killer Tomatoes *'77*

Mary Peach (1934-)
Disraeli *'79*
Ballad in Blue *'66*
A Gathering of Eagles *'63*
No Love for Johnnie *'60*
Room at the Top *'59*

Trevor Peacock
Madame Bovary *'00*
A Christmas Carol *'99*
For Roseanna *'96*

E.J. Peaker
The Banker *'89*
Hello, Dolly! *'69*

Adele Pearce
Pop Always Pays *'40*
Wyoming Outlaw *'39*

Alice Pearce (1917-66)
The Glass Bottom Boat *'66*
Dear Brigitte *'65*
The Belle of New York *'52*

Craig Pearce
The Seventh Floor *'93*
Vicious *'88*

Guy Pearce (1967-)
The Count of Monte Cristo *'02*
The Time Machine *'02*
Memento *'00*
Rules of Engagement *'00*
Ravenous *'99*
L.A. Confidential *'97*
Flynn *'96*
Dating the Enemy *'95*
The Adventures of Priscilla, Queen of the Desert *'94*
Heaven Tonight *'93*
The Hunting *'92*

Jacqueline Pearce
Princess Caraboo *'94*
White Mischief *'88*
Don't Raise the Bridge, Lower the River *'68*
Plague of the Zombies *'66*
The Reptile *'66*

Joanne Pearce
Morons from Outer Space *'85*
Whoops Apocalypse *'83*

Mary Vivian Pearce
Pecker *'98*
Serial Mom *'94*
Cry-Baby *'90*
Hairspray *'88*
Polyester *'81*
Desperate Living *'77*
Female Trouble *'74*
Pink Flamingos *'72*
Multiple Maniacs *'70*
Mondo Trasho *'69*

Patricia Pearcy
Delusion *'84*
Squirm *'76*

Barry Pearl
Avenging Angel *'85*
Grease *'78*

Randy Pearlstein
Dead Man on Campus *'97*
My Teacher's Wife *'95*
Revenge of the Radioactive Reporter *'91*

Drew Pearson
The Day the Earth Stood Still *'51*
Betrayal from the East *'44*

Neil Pearson
Rhodes *'97*
Fever Pitch *'96*
The Secret Rapture *'94*

Richard Pearson (1918-)
Pirates *'86*
Thirteenth Reunion *'81*
The Woman in Question *'50*

Virginia Pearson (1886-1958)
The Taxi Mystery *'26*
The Phantom of the Opera *'25*
The Wizard of Oz *'25*

Harold (Hal) Peary (1908-85)
Clambake *'67*
Wetbacks *'56*
The Great Gildersleeve *'43*
Here We Go Again! *'42*
Seven Days' Leave *'42*
Look Who's Laughing *'41*

Patsy Pease
Improper Conduct *'94*
He Knows You're Alone *'80*

Sierra Pecheur
Kalifornia *'93*
Bronco Billy *'80*

Bob Peck (1945-99)
The Miracle Maker: The Story of Jesus *'00 (V)*

The Green Mile *'99*
Enemy of the State *'98*
Saving Private Ryan *'98*
Firestorm *'97*
Dead Silence *'96*

Marilia Pera (1943-)
Central Station *'98*
Tieta of Agreste *'96*
Mixed Blood *'84*
Pixote *'81*

Piper Perabo (1977-)
Lost and Delirious *'01*
The Adventures of Rocky & Bullwinkle *'00*
Coyote Ugly *'00*
White Boyz *'99*

Ed Peranio
Desperate Living *'77*
Female Trouble *'74*
Multiple Maniacs *'70*

Eileen (Elaine Persey) Percy (1900-73)
Let's Go! *'23*
Down to Earth *'17*
The Man from Painted Post *'17*
Reaching for the Moon *'17*

Esme Percy (1887-1957)
Dead of Night *'45*
Pygmalion *'38*
21 Days *'37*
Accused *'36*
Old Spanish Custom *'36*
Bitter Sweet *'33*

Tony Perenski
Varsity Blues *'98*
The Texas Chainsaw Massacre 4: The Next Generation *'95*
The Underneath *'95*

George Perez
Manhattan Merenque! *'95*
Bounty Tracker *'93*

Jose Perez (1940-)
Miami Blues *'90*
Courage *'86*
One Shoe Makes It Murder *'82*
Short Eyes *'79*

Rosie Perez (1964-)
Human Nature *'02*
King of the Jungle *'01*
The Road to El Dorado *'00 (V)*
The 24 Hour Woman *'99*
A Brother's Kiss *'97*
Dance with the Devil *'97*
Subway Stories *'97*
It Could Happen to You *'94*
Somebody to Love *'94*
Fearless *'93*
Untamed Heart *'93*
White Men Can't Jump *'92*
Night on Earth *'91*
Criminal Justice *'90*
Do the Right Thing *'89*

Vincent Perez (1964-)
Queen of the Damned *'02*
Bride of the Wind *'01*
I Dreamed of Africa *'00*
Shot Through the Heart *'98*
Those Who Love Me Can Take the Train *'98*
Swept from the Sea *'97*
The Crow 2: City of Angels *'96*
Talk of Angels *'96*
Beyond the Clouds *'95*
Queen Margot *'94*
Indochine *'92*
Cyrano de Bergerac *'90*

Francois Perier (1919-)
Tartuffe *'84*
Stavisky *'74*
Godson *'72*
Z *'69*
Le Samourai *'67*
The Organizer *'64*
The Testament of Orpheus *'59*
Nights of Cabiria *'57*
Gervaise *'56*
Orpheus *'49*

Sylvia and the Phantom *'45*

George Periolat
Nurse Marjorie *'20*
Eyes of Julia Deep *'18*

Anthony Perkins (1932-92)
A Demon in My View *'92*
In the Deep Woods *'91*
I'm Dangerous Tonight *'90*
Psycho 4: The Beginning *'90*
Daughter of Darkness *'89*
Edge of Sanity *'89*
Destroyer *'88*
Psycho 3 *'86*
Crimes of Passion *'84*
The Glory Boys *'84*
Psycho 2 *'83*
The Sins of Dorian Gray *'82*
The Double Negative *'80*
ffolkes *'80*
The Black Hole *'79*
Twice a Woman *'79*
Winter Kills *'79*
Les Miserables *'78*
Mahogany *'75*
Murder on the Orient Express *'74*
Life & Times of Judge Roy Bean *'72*
Ten Days Wonder *'72*
Someone Behind the Door *'71*
Catch-22 *'70*
Pretty Poison *'68*
Is Paris Burning? *'66*
The Fool Killer *'65*
Ravishing Idiot *'64*
The Trial *'63*
Goodbye Again *'61*
Phaedra *'61*
Psycho *'60*
Tall Story *'60*
Green Mansions *'59*
On the Beach *'59*
Desire Under the Elms *'58*
The Matchmaker *'58*
Fear Strikes Out *'57*
Lonely Man *'57*
The Tin Star *'57*
Friendly Persuasion *'56*

Elizabeth Perkins (1960-)
My Sister's Keeper *'02*
Cats & Dogs *'01*
If These Walls Could Talk 2 *'00*
28 Days *'00*
Crazy in Alabama *'99*
From the Earth to the Moon *'98*
I'm Losing You *'98*
Rescuers: Stories of Courage "Two Women" *'97*
Moonlight and Valentino *'95*
The Flintstones *'94*
Miracle on 34th Street *'94*
Indian Summer *'93*
The Doctor *'91*
He Said, She Said *'91*
Avalon *'90*
Enid Is Sleeping *'90*
Love at Large *'89*
Big *'88*
Sweet Hearts Dance *'88*
About Last Night... *'86*
From the Hip *'86*

Emily Perkins
Ginger Snaps *'01*
Small Sacrifices *'89*

Millie Perkins (1938-)
The Chamber *'96*
Bodily Harm *'95*
Pistol: The Birth of a Legend *'90*
Two Moon Junction *'88*
Wall Street *'87*
At Close Range *'86*
A.D. *'85*
License to Kill *'84*
Shattered Vows *'84*
The Haunting Passion *'83*
Table for Five *'83*
Witch Who Came from the Sea *'76*

Cockfighter *'74*
Wild in the Streets *'68*
Ride in the Whirlwind *'66*
The Shooting *'66*
Ensign Pulver *'64*
Wild in the Country *'61*
The Diary of Anne Frank *'59*

Osgood Perkins (1892-1937)
Scarface *'31*
Love 'Em and Leave 'Em *'26*

Osgood Perkins, II (1974-)
Legally Blonde *'01*
Wolf *'94*
Six Degrees of Separation *'93*
Psycho 2 *'83*

Orli Perl
Pick a Card *'97*
Under the Domim Tree *'95*

Max Perlich (1968-)
Deuces Wild *'02*
Blow *'01*
Homicide: The Movie *'00*
Freeway 2: Confessions of a Trickbaby *'99*
Goodbye, Lover *'99*
House on Haunted Hill *'99*
Sometimes They Come Back ... For More *'99*
Gummo *'97*
Truth or Consequences, N.M. *'97*
Beautiful Girls *'96*
The Curse of Inferno *'96*
Homeward Bound 2: Lost in San Francisco *'96*
Georgia *'95*
Dead Beat *'94*
Maverick *'94*
Shake, Rattle & Rock! *'94*
Terrified *'94*
Born Yesterday *'93*
Cliffhanger *'93*
The Butcher's Wife *'91*
Rush *'91*
Drugstore Cowboy *'89*
Can't Buy Me Love *'87*
Ferris Bueller's Day Off *'86*

Rhea Perlman (1948-)
Houdini *'99*
In the Doghouse *'98*
Carpool *'96*
Matilda *'96*
Sunset Park *'96*
Canadian Bacon *'94*
To Grandmother's House We Go *'94*
Ted & Venus *'93*
We're Back! A Dinosaur's Story *'93 (V)*
There Goes the Neighborhood *'92*
Class Act *'91*
Enid Is Sleeping *'90*
Stamp of a Killer *'87*
Amazing Stories *'85*
Ratings Game *'84*
Intimate Strangers *'77*

Ron Perlman (1950-)
Blade II *'02*
Shakedown *'02*
The King's Guard *'01*
Enemy at the Gates *'00*
Operation Sandman: Warriors in Hell *'00*
Price of Glory *'00*
Titan A.E. *'00 (V)*
Happy, Texas *'99*
Houdini *'99*
Supreme Sanction *'99*
Frogs for Snakes *'98*
The Magnificent Seven *'98*
A Town Has Turned to Dust *'98*
Alien: Resurrection *'97*
Prince Valiant *'97*
The Second Civil War *'97*
Tinseltown *'97*
Body Armor *'96*
The Island of Dr. Moreau *'96*
The Last Supper *'96*

The City of Lost Children *'95*
Fluke *'95*
Mr. Stitch *'95*
Phantom 2040 Movie: The Ghost Who Walks *'95 (V)*
Cronos *'94*
Police Academy 7: Mission to Moscow *'94*
Sensation *'94*
The Adventures of Huck Finn *'93*
Double Exposure *'93*
Romeo Is Bleeding *'93*
When the Bough Breaks *'93*
Sleepwalkers *'92*
Blind Man's Bluff *'91*
The Name of the Rose *'86*
Ice Pirates *'84*
Quest for Fire *'82*

Florence Pernel
Trois Couleurs: Blanc *'94*
Trois Couleurs: Bleu *'93*

Gigi Perreau (1941-)
Hell on Wheels *'67*
Journey to the Center of Time *'67*
Girls' Town *'59*
Dance with Me, Henry *'56*
The Man in the Gray Flannel Suit *'56*
Never a Dull Moment *'50*

Paul Perri
Without Evidence *'96*
Hellraiser 4: Bloodline *'95*
Delta Force 2: Operation Stranglehold *'90*
Hit & Run *'82*

Mireille Perrier
The Ice Rink *'99*
Trahir *'93*
Love Without Pity *'91*
Toto le Heros *'91*
Chocolat *'88*
Mauvais Sang *'86*
Boy Meets Girl *'84*

Jack Perrin (1896-1967)
Sunrise at Campobello *'60*
When Gangland Strikes *'56*
The Court Martial of Billy Mitchell *'55*
Ten Wanted Men *'54*
Them! *'54*
Bandit Queen *'51*
I Shot Billy the Kid *'50*
The North Star *'43*
New Moon *'40*
West of Pinto Basin *'40*
The Story of Vernon and Irene Castle *'39*
Gun Grit *'36*
Texas Jack *'35*
Hell Fire Austin *'32*
Apache Kid's Escape *'30*
Midnight Faces *'26*

Jacques Perrin (1941-)
Flight of the Innocent *'93*
Cinema Paradiso *'88*
Le Crabe Tambour *'77*
Black and White in Color *'76*
The Desert of the Tartars *'76*
State of Siege *'73*
Peau D'Ane *'71*
Donkey Skin *'70*
Z *'69*
The Young Girls of Rochefort *'68*
The 317th Platoon *'65*
The Girl with a Suitcase *'60*

Valerie Perrine (1944-)
What Women Want *'00*
Brown's Requiem *'98*
A Place Called Truth *'98*
Shame, Shame, Shame *'98*
Curtain Call *'97*
The Break *'95*
Girl in the Cadillac *'94*
Boiling Point *'93*
Bright Angel *'91*
Sweet Bird of Youth *'89*
Maid to Order *'87*

Water *'85*
The Three Little Pigs *'84*
When Your Lover Leaves *'83*
The Border *'82*
The Agency *'81*
Can't Stop the Music *'80*
Superman 2 *'80*
The Electric Horseman *'79*
The Magician of Lublin *'79*
Superman: The Movie *'78*
Mr. Billion *'77*
Lenny *'74*
The Last American Hero *'73*
Slaughterhouse Five *'72*

Harold Perrineau, Jr.
Woman on Top *'00*
The Best Man *'99*
The Tempest *'99*
The Edge *'97*
Blood & Wine *'96*
William Shakespeare's Romeo and Juliet *'96*
Smoke *'95*

Joe Perrino
The Bumblebee Flies Anyway *'98*
The Mighty *'98*
Sleepers *'96*

Leslie Perrins (1902-62)
Man on the Run *'49*
Nine Days a Queen *'36*
The Silent Passenger *'35*

Michel Perron
The Sign of Four *'01*
Battlefield Earth *'00*

Francois Perrot (1924-)
Life and Nothing But *'89*
Women's Prison Massacre *'85*
My Best Friend's Girl *'84*
Innocents with Dirty Hands *'75*

Felton Perry (1955-)
Buck and the Magic Bracelet *'97*
Dumb & Dumber *'94*
RoboCop 3 *'91*
RoboCop 2 *'90*
Checking Out *'89*
RoboCop *'87*
Sudden Death *'77*
Walking Tall *'73*
Night Call Nurses *'72*

Jeffery (Jeff) Perry (1955-)
Wild Things *'98*
Kingfish: A Story of Huey P. Long *'95*
Playmaker *'94*

Jeffery S. (Jeff) Perry
The Chronicles of Narnia *'89*
Oxford Blues *'84*

John Bennett Perry (1941-)
Fools Rush In *'97*
George of the Jungle *'97*
The Last Fling *'86*
A Matter of Life and Death *'81*
Only When I Laugh *'81*

Lou Perry
The Texas Chainsaw Massacre 2 *'86*
Last Night at the Alamo *'83*

Luke Perry (1966-)
The Enemy *'01*
The Triangle *'01*
Attention Shoppers *'99*
Storm Tracker *'99*
The Florentine *'98*
Indiscreet *'98*
The Fifth Element *'97*
American Strays *'96*
Last Breath *'96*
Normal Life *'96*
Riot in the Streets *'96*
8 Seconds *'94*
Buffy the Vampire Slayer *'92*
Terminal Bliss *'91*

Sweet Trash *'70*

Matthew Perry (1969-)
Serving Sara *'02*
The Whole Nine Yards *'00*
Three to Tango *'99*
Almost Heroes *'97*
Fools Rush In *'97*
A Night in the Life of Jimmy Reardon *'88*
The Whole Shootin' Match *'79*

Rod Perry
Black Gestapo *'75*
Black Godfather *'74*

Roger Perry
Roller Boogie *'79*
Conspiracy of Terror *'75*
The Thing with Two Heads *'72*
The Return of Count Yorga *'71*
Count Yorga, Vampire *'70*
The Cat *'66*

Maria Perschy (1938-)
People Who Own the Dark *'75*
Exorcism *'74*
Horror of the Zombies *'74*
House of Psychotic Women *'73*
The Rue Morgue Massacres *'73*
Last Day of the War *'69*
The Castle of Fu Manchu *'68*
A Witch Without a Broom *'68*
The Mad Executioners *'65*
633 Squadron *'64*
Man's Favorite Sport? *'63*
No Survivors, Please *'63*

Lisa Jane Persky (1955-)
An American Rhapsody *'01*
My First Mister *'01*
Meat Loaf: To Hell and Back *'00*
Female Perversions *'96*
Dead Funny *'94*
Pontiac Moon *'94*
Coneheads *'93*
The Last of the Finest *'90*
Vital Signs *'90*
Great Balls of Fire *'89*
When Harry Met Sally... *'89*
The Big Easy *'87*
Peggy Sue Got Married *'86*
The Sure Thing *'85*
The Cotton Club *'84*
Shattered Vows *'84*
Breathless *'83*
American Pop *'81 (V)*
The Great Santini *'80*
KISS Meets the Phantom of the Park *'78*

Nehemiah Persoff (1920-)
An American Tail: Fievel Goes West *'91 (V)*
The Last Temptation of Christ *'88*
Twins *'88*
An American Tail *'86 (V)*
Sadat *'83*
Yentl *'83*
The Henderson Monster *'80*
The Rebels *'79*
Killing Stone *'78*
Francis Gary Powers: The True Story of the U-2 Spy *'76*
Voyage of the Damned *'76*
Eric *'75*
The Stranger Within *'74*
Deadly Harvest *'72*
The People Next Door *'70*
A Global Affair *'63*
The Comancheros *'61*
Al Capone *'59*
Green Mansions *'59*
Some Like It Hot *'59*
The Badlanders *'58*
Men in War *'57*
The Wrong Man *'56*
On the Waterfront *'54*

Essy Persson (1941-)
Cry of the Banshee '70
Mission Stardust '68
Vibration '68
Therese & Isabelle '67
I, a Woman '66
Jon Pertwee (1919-96)
The House that Dripped Blood '71
Carry On Screaming '66
Ladies Who Do '63
Mister Drake's Duck '50
Sean Pertwee (1964-)
Seven Days to Live '01
Love, Honour & Obey '00
Cleopatra '99
Russell Mulcahy's Tale of the Mummy '99
Soldier '98
Event Horizon '97
Deadly Voyage '96
Stiff Upper Lips '96
Blue Juice '95
Shopping '93
Jorge Perugorria
Life According to Muriel '97
Guantanamera '95
Strawberry and Chocolate '93
Frank Pesce
Night Vision '97
Trapped in Paradise '94
The Pamela Principle '91
29th Street '91
Vigilante '83
Joe Pesci (1943-)
Lethal Weapon 4 '98
Gone Fishin' '97
8 Heads in a Duffel Bag '96
Casino '95
Jimmy Hollywood '94
With Honors '94
A Bronx Tale '93
Home Alone 2: Lost in New York '92
Lethal Weapon 3 '92
My Cousin Vinny '92
The Public Eye '92
JFK '91
The Super '91
Betsy's Wedding '90
Goodfellas '90
Home Alone '90
Backtrack '89
Lethal Weapon 2 '89
Man on Fire '87
Once Upon a Time in America '84
Easy Money '83
I'm Dancing as Fast as I Can '82
Ruby's Dream '82
Eureka! '81
Raging Bull '80
Family Enforcer '76
Lisa Pescia
The Dark Dancer '95
Body Chemistry 2: Voice of a Stranger '91
Body Chemistry '90
Donna Pescow (1954-)
Partners '99
Dead Husbands '98
Ivory Tower '97
Glory Years '87
Policewoman Centerfold '83
Saturday Night Fever '77
Bernadette Peters (1948-)
Let It Snow '99
What the Deaf Man Heard '98
Anastasia '97 (V)
Cinderella '97
The Odyssey '97
Alice '90
Impromptu '90
The Last Best Year '90
Pink Cadillac '89
Slaves of New York '89
Sunday in the Park with George '86
Sleeping Beauty '83
Annie '82
Heartbeeps '81
Pennies from Heaven '81
Tulips '81
The Jerk '79
The Martian Chronicles: Part 2 '79
The Martian Chronicles: Part 3 '79
Silent Movie '76
The Longest Yard '74
Brock Peters (1927-)
The Secret '93
Star Trek 6: The Undiscovered Country '91
Alligator 2: The Mutation '90
To Heal a Nation '88
Star Trek 4: The Voyage Home '86
The Adventures of Huckleberry Finn '78
Framed '75
Slaughter's Big Ripoff '73
Soylent Green '73
The McMasters '70
Ace High '68
Daring Game '68
The Incident '67
The Pawnbroker '65
The L-Shaped Room '62
To Kill a Mockingbird '62
Carmen Jones '54
Clarke Peters
A Casualty of War '90
Mona Lisa '86
Outland '81
House Peters, Sr. (1880-1967)
Head Winds '25
Human Hearts '22
House Peters, Jr. (1916-)
Red Planet Mars '52
Outlaw Country '49
Jean Peters (1926-2000)
Peter and Paul '81
A Man Called Peter '55
Apache '54
Broken Lance '54
Three Coins in the Fountain '54
Pickup on South Street '53
Niagara '52
Viva Zapata! '52
As Young As You Feel '51
It Happens Every Spring '49
Captain from Castile '47
Luan Peters
Con Man '92
Land of the Minotaur '77
Flesh and Blood Show '73
Not Tonight Darling '72
Man of Violence '71
Twins of Evil '71
Molly Peters
Target for Killing '66
Thunderball '65
Ralph Peters (1902-59)
Meeting at Midnight '44
I Married a Witch '42
Death Rides the Range '40
Man's Country '38
Rough Ridin' Rhythm '37
Rick Peters
The Happy Face Murders '99
American Virgin '98
Elvis Meets Nixon '98
The Disappearance of Kevin Johnson '95
Night of the Demons 2 '94
Scott Peters (-1994)
They Saved Hitler's Brain '64
Girl Hunters '63
Susan Peters
Andy Hardy's Double Life '42
Random Harvest '42
Werner Peters (1918-71)
The Bird with the Crystal Plumage '70
The Corrupt Ones '67
The Phantom of Soho '64
36 Hours '64
Curse of the Yellow Snake '63
The Counterfeit Traitor '62
The Kaiser's Lackey '51
Chris Petersen
Vampire Raiders—Ninja Queen '89
Ninja Masters of Death '85
Little Dragons '80
When Every Day Was the Fourth of July '78
Pat Petersen
Cold River '81
Little Dragons '80
William L. Petersen (1953-)
The Contender '00
The Skulls '00
Gunshy '98
Kiss the Sky '98
The Rat Pack '98
Twelve Angry Men '97
The Beast '96
Fear '96
The Kennedys of Massachusetts '95
Mulholland Falls '95
In the Kingdom of the Blind the Man with One Eye Is King '94
Deadly Currents '93
Return to Lonesome Dove '93
Hard Promises '92
Keep the Change '92
Passed Away '92
Young Guns 2 '90
Cousins '89
Amazing Grace & Chuck '87
Long Gone '87
Manhunter '86
To Live & Die in L.A. '85
Amanda Peterson (1971-)
Windrunner '94
Fatal Charm '92
I Posed for Playboy '91
Listen to Me '89
The Lawless Land '88
Can't Buy Me Love '87
Explorers '85
Cassandra Peterson (1951-)
Acting on Impulse '93
Ted & Venus '93
Elvira, Mistress of the Dark '88
Echo Park '86
Pee-wee's Big Adventure '85
Balboa '82
Working Girls '75
Dorothy Peterson (1900-79)
Woman in the Window '44
Air Force '43
Peck's Bad Boy '34
I'm No Angel '33
Eric Peterson
Henry & Verlin '94
Tramp at the Door '87
Kimberlee Peterson
Legend of the Lost Tomb '97
Homecoming '96
Stewart Peterson
Pony Express Rider '76
Against a Crooked Sky '75
Seven Alone '75
Where the Red Fern Grows '74
Vidal Peterson
Wizards of the Lost Kingdom '85
Something Wicked This Way Comes '83
Edward Petherbridge (1936-)
Gulliver's Travels '95
An Awfully Big Adventure '94
Strange Interlude '90
Lovers of Their Time '85
Pascale Petit
Four Times That Night '69
End of Desire '62
Victor Petit
Terror Beach '80s
Street Warriors '87
Night of the Death Cult '75
Steven Petrarca
Sparkler '99
The Lesser Evil '97
Gio Petre
The Doll '62
Gorilla '56
Hay Petrie (1895-1948)
Great Expectations '46
A Canterbury Tale '44
On Approval '44
Spellbound '41
Contraband '40
Clouds over Europe '39
Crimes at the Dark House '39
The Four Feathers '39
Spy in Black '39
21 Days '37
The Ghost Goes West '36
The Old Curiosity Shop '35
The Private Life of Henry VIII '33
Susan Petrie
Snapshot '77
They Came from Within '75
Joanna Pettet (1944-)
Terror in Paradise '90
Sweet Country '87
Double Exposure '82
Cry of the Innocent '80
Return of Frank Cannon '80
The Evil '78
A Killer in Every Corner '74
Pioneer Woman '73
Blue '68
Casino Royale '67
Night of the Generals '67
Robbery '67
The Group '66
Christopher Pettiet (1976-2000)
Carried Away '95
The Goodbye Bird '93
Fatal Exposure '91
Brian Pettifer
Conspiracy '01
If... '69
Valarie Pettiford
Glitter '01
Street Hunter '90
Frank Pettingell (1891-1966)
Trial & Error '62
Butler's Dilemma '43
Gaslight '40
Lori Petty (1964-)
Firetrap '01
Route 666 '01
Blood Money '98
Relax... It's Just Sex! '98
Serial Bomber '96
The Glass Shield '95
In the Army Now '94
Tank Girl '94
Free Willy '93
A League of Their Own '92
Point Break '91
Cadillac Man '90
Richard Petty
Richard Petty Story '72
Speedway '68
Tom Petty
The Postman '97
Made in Heaven '87
Angelique Pettyjohn (1943-92)
Revenge of Doctor X '80s
The Wizard of Speed and Time '88
Bio Hazard '85
The Lost Empire '83
Repo Man '83
Confessions of Tom Harris '72
G.I. Executioner '71
Hell's Belles '69
Mad Doctor of Blood Island '69
Clambake '67
Joseph Pevney (1920-)
The Street with No Name '48
Body and Soul '47
Nocturne '46
Penny Peyser (1951-)
Indecent Behavior '93
Messenger of Death '88
The Frisco Kid '79
The In-Laws '79
Dedee Pfeiffer (1965-)
Meat Loaf: To Hell and Back '00
Up Close and Personal '96
Deadly Past '95
Double Exposure '93
Falling Down '93
Running Cool '93
Shoot '92
A Climate for Killing '91
King's Ransom '91
Red Surf '90
The Horror Show '89
Brothers in Arms '88
The Midnight Hour '86
Vamp '86
Toughlove '85
Michelle Pfeiffer (1957-)
I Am Sam '01
What Lies Beneath '00
The Story of Us '99
William Shakespeare's A Midsummer Night's Dream '99
The Deep End of the Ocean '98
Prince of Egypt '98 (V)
A Thousand Acres '97
One Fine Day '96
To Gillian on Her 37th Birthday '96
Up Close and Personal '96
Dangerous Minds '95
Wolf '94
The Age of Innocence '93
Batman Returns '92
Frankie and Johnny '91
Love Field '91
The Russia House '90
The Fabulous Baker Boys '89
Dangerous Liaisons '88
Married to the Mob '88
Tequila Sunrise '88
Amazon Women on the Moon '87
The Witches of Eastwick '87
Sweet Liberty '86
Into the Night '85
Ladyhawke '85
Power, Passion & Murder '83
Scarface '83
Grease 2 '82
The Solitary Man '82
Callie and Son '81
Charlie Chan and the Curse of the Dragon Queen '81
B.A.D. Cats '80
Falling in Love Again '80
The Hollywood Knights '80
JoAnn Pflug (1947-)
The Day the Women Got Even '80
Scream of the Wolf '74
Catlow '71
M*A*S*H '70
Joe Phelan
Terminal Exposure '89
Fatal Pulse '88
South of Reno '87
Zero Boys '86
Shawn (Michael) Phelan (1975-98)
Breaking the Rules '92
Toy Soldiers '91
Caroline? '90
Peter Phelps (1960-)
Lantana '01
Zone 39 '96
Blackwater Trail '95
Merlin '92
Rock & Roll Cowboys '92
Breaking Loose '90
Starlight Hotel '90
The Lighthorsemen '87
Mekhi Phifer (1975-)
The Other Brother '02
Brian's Song '01
Imposter '01
O '01
Shaft '00
A Lesson Before Dying '99
Uninvited Guest '99
I Still Know What You Did Last Summer '98
Hell's Kitchen NYC '97
Soul Food '97
High School High '96
Clockers '95
John Philbin
The Crew '95
The Four Minute Mile '92
Point Break '91
Martians Go Home! '90
North Shore '87
Shy People '87
Mary Philbin (1903-93)
The Man Who Laughs '27
The Phantom of the Opera '25
Merry-Go-Round '23
Human Hearts '22
Regis Philbin
Little Nicky '00
Dudley Do-Right '99
Night and the City '92
The Bad News Bears Go to Japan '78
Sextette '78
James Philbrook (1924-82)
Last Day of the War '69
Finger on the Trigger '65
Sound of Horror '64
The Thin Red Line '64
Dominic Philie
For Hire '98
The Boys '97
Robert Philip
Adios Amigo '75
Children Shouldn't Play with Dead Things '72
Gerard Philipe (1922-59)
Dangerous Liaisons '60
Fever Mounts at El Pao '59
Modigliani '58
The Red and the Black '57
Les Grandes Manoeuvres '55
The Proud Ones '53
Beauties of the Night '52
Fanfan la Tulipe '51
La Ronde '51
Beauty and the Devil '50
La Chartreuse de Parme '48
Devil in the Flesh '46
L'Idiot '46
Gina Philips
Bella Mafia '97
Breaking Free '95
Lee Philips (1927-99)
Psychomania '63
The Hunters '58
Peyton Place '57
Mary (Phillips) Philips (1901-75)
Prince Valiant '54
Leave Her to Heaven '45
A Farewell to Arms '32
Ryan Phillippe (1974-)
Igby Goes Down '02
Gosford Park '01
Antitrust '00
Company Man '00
Way of the Gun '00
Cruel Intentions '98
54 '98
Playing by Heart '98
Homegrown '97
I Know What You Did Last Summer '97
Little Boy Blue '97
Lifeform '96

Nowhere *'96*
White Squall *'96*
Angie Phillips
Duets *'00*
Manny & Lo *'96*
Barney (Bernard) Phillips (1913-82)
Savage Run *'70*
The Sand Pebbles *'66*
I Was a Teenage Werewolf *'57*
Bijou Phillips (1980-)
Bully *'01*
Fast Sofa *'01*
Tart *'01*
Almost Famous *'00*
Black and White *'99*
Bill Phillips
The Last Hunt *'56*
Thirty Seconds Over Tokyo *'44*
Bobbie Phillips (1972-)
Chameleon 3: Dark Angel *'00*
Red Shoe Diaries: Luscious Lola *'00*
Chameleon 2: Death Match *'99*
American Virgin *'98*
Chameleon *'98*
Back in Action *'94*
Hail Caesar *'94*
Ring of Fire 3: Lion Strike *'94*
TC 2000 *'93*
Chris Phillips
Doug's 1st Movie *'99 (V)*
Felix the Cat: The Movie *'91 (V)*
Chynna Phillips (1968-)
Bye Bye Birdie *'95*
The Prize Pulitzer *'89*
Say Anything *'89*
Caddyshack 2 *'88*
Goodbye, Miss 4th of July *'88*
The Invisible Kid *'88*
Eddie (Edward) Phillips (1899-1965)
Phantom Patrol *'36*
The Throwback *'35*
Probation *'32*
The Love Light *'21*
Emo Phillips
Meet the Parents *'91*
UHF *'89*
Ethan Phillips (1955-)
From the Earth to the Moon *'98*
Green Card *'90*
Bloodhounds of Broadway *'89*
Glory *'89*
Lean on Me *'89*
Frank Phillips
Battle of the Eagles *'81*
The Runaway Bus *'54*
Grace Phillips
Alien Fury: Countdown to Invasion *'00*
Truth or Consequences, N.M. *'97*
All the Vermeers in New York *'91*
John Phillips (1915-95)
Max and Helen *'90*
The Mummy's Shroud *'67*
Village of the Damned *'60*
Black Angel *'46*
Joseph C. Phillips
Let's Talk About Sex *'98*
Strictly Business *'91*
Julianne Phillips (1960-)
Big Bully *'95*
Where's the Money, Noreen? *'95*
A Vow to Kill *'94*
Getting Up and Going Home *'92*
Fletch Lives *'89*
Skin Deep *'89*

Seven Hours to Judgment *'88*
Sweet Lies *'88*
Summer Fantasy *'84*
Leslie Phillips (1924-)
Lara Croft: Tomb Raider *'01*
Agatha Christie's The Pale Horse *'96*
The Canterville Ghost *'96*
August *'95*
Mountains of the Moon *'90*
Scandal *'89*
Empire of the Sun *'87*
Maroc 7 *'67*
The Smallest Show on Earth *'57*
The Limping Man *'53*
Train of Events *'49*
Lou Diamond Phillips (1962-)
Lone Hero *'02*
Route 666 *'01*
A Better Way to Die *'00*
Hangman *'00*
Bats *'99*
Brokedown Palace *'99*
In a Class of His Own *'99*
Picking Up the Pieces *'99*
Supernova *'99*
Another Day in Paradise *'98*
The Big Hit *'98*
Courage Under Fire *'96*
Undertow *'95*
The Wharf Rat *'95*
Boulevard *'94*
Dangerous Touch *'94*
Sioux City *'94*
Teresa's Tattoo *'94*
Extreme Justice *'93*
Shadow of the Wolf *'92*
Ambition *'91*
The Dark Wind *'91*
Harley *'90*
A Show of Force *'90*
Young Guns 2 *'90*
Disorganized Crime *'89*
The First Power *'89*
Renegades *'89*
Dakota *'88*
Stand and Deliver *'88*
Young Guns *'88*
La Bamba *'87*
Trespasses *'86*
MacKenzie Phillips (1959-)
True Friends *'98*
Love Child *'82*
More American Graffiti *'79*
Eleanor & Franklin *'76*
Rafferty & the Gold Dust Twins *'75*
Miles to Go Before I Sleep *'74*
American Graffiti *'73*
Michelle Phillips (1944-)
Sweetwater: A True Rock Story *'99*
Army of One *'94*
Rubdown *'93*
Scissors *'91*
Let It Ride *'89*
Assault and Matrimony *'87*
American Anthem *'86*
Secrets of a Married Man *'84*
Sidney Sheldon's Bloodline *'79*
Valentino *'77*
The Death Squad *'73*
Dillinger *'73*
Peg Phillips
How the West Was Fun *'95*
Dogfight *'91*
Robert Phillips
The Killing of a Chinese Bookie *'76*
The Dirty Dozen *'67*
Samantha (Sam) Phillips (1966-)
The Dallas Connection *'94*
Deceit *'93*
Sexual Malice *'93*
Phantasm 2 *'88*

Sian Phillips (1934-)
Attila *'01*
The Aristocrats *'99*
Ivanhoe *'97*
The Return of the Borrowers *'96*
The Vacillations of Poppy Carew *'94*
The Borrowers *'93*
Heidi *'93*
Valmont *'89*
The Doctor and the Devils *'85*
The Ewoks: Battle for Endor *'85*
Dune *'84*
The Carpathian Eagle *'81*
Clash of the Titans *'81*
Nijinsky *'80*
Murphy's War *'71*
Goodbye, Mr. Chips *'69*
Sydney Coale Phillips
Maximum Breakout *'91*
Cause of Death *'90*
Wendy Phillips (1952-)
Bugsy *'91*
Midnight Run *'88*
Death Be Not Proud *'75*
Max Phipps (1939-2000)
Dark Age *'88*
Sky Pirates *'87*
The Blue Lightning *'86*
Nate and Hayes *'83*
Return of Captain Invincible *'83*
The Road Warrior *'82*
Nicholas Phipps (1913-80)
Captain's Paradise *'53*
Maytime in Mayfair *'52*
Elizabeth of Ladymead *'48*
William Phipps
Cavalry Command *'63*
The War of the Worlds *'53*
Cinderella *'50 (V)*
The Vanishing Westerner *'50*
Joaquin Rafael (Leaf) Phoenix (1974-)
Signs *'02*
Gladiator *'00*
Quills *'00*
The Yards *'00*
Clay Pigeons *'98*
8mm *'98*
Return to Paradise *'98*
Inventing the Abbotts *'97*
U-Turn *'97*
To Die For *'95*
Parenthood *'89*
Russkies *'87*
SpaceCamp *'86*
Rain Phoenix (1973-)
O *'01*
Spent *'00*
Even Cowgirls Get the Blues *'94*
River Phoenix (1970-93)
The Thing Called Love *'93*
Silent Tongue *'92*
Sneakers *'92*
Dogfight *'91*
My Own Private Idaho *'91*
I Love You to Death *'90*
Indiana Jones and the Last Crusade *'89*
Little Nikita *'88*
A Night in the Life of Jimmy Reardon *'88*
Running on Empty *'88*
The Mosquito Coast *'86*
Stand by Me *'86*
Explorers *'85*
Summer Phoenix (1978-)
SLC Punk! *'99*
Girl *'98*
Maurice Pialat (1925-)
Under Satan's Sun *'87*
A Nos Amours *'84*
This Man Must Die *'70*

Jean Piat
Tower of Screaming Virgins *'68*
The Would-Be Gentleman *'58*
Ben Piazza (1934-91)
Guilty by Suspicion *'91*
Clean and Sober *'88*
Consenting Adult *'85*
Scene of the Crime *'85*
The Five of Me *'81*
The Children of An Lac *'80*
Nightwing *'79*
The Hanging Tree *'59*
A Dangerous Age *'57*
Tony Pica
House of Psychotic Women *'73*
Yesterday, Today and Tomorrow *'64*
Robert Picardo (1953-)
Small Soldiers *'98*
Menno's Mind *'96*
Star Trek: First Contact *'96*
Revenge of the Nerds 4: Nerds in Love *'94*
Wagons East *'94*
White Mile *'94*
Matinee *'92*
Frame Up *'91*
Motorama *'91*
Gremlins 2: The New Batch *'90*
China Beach *'88*
976-EVIL *'88*
Innerspace *'87*
Jack's Back *'87*
Munchies *'87*
Back to School *'86*
Explorers *'85*
The Howling *'81*
Michel Piccoli (1925-)
Genealogies of a Crime *'97*
Passion in the Desert *'97*
Beaumarchais the Scoundrel *'96*
Party *'96*
One Hundred and One Nights *'95*
Martha and I *'91*
La Belle Noiseuse *'90*
May Fools *'90*
La Puritaine *'86*
Mauvais Sang *'86*
Peril *'85*
Dangerous Moves *'84*
Prize of Peril *'84*
Success Is the Best Revenge *'84*
La Passante *'83*
Beyond Obsession *'82*
La Nuit de Varennes *'82*
Passion *'82*
Atlantic City *'81*
L'Etat Sauvage *'78*
Spoiled Children *'77*
Mado *'76*
Vincent, Francois, Paul and the Others *'76*
Leonor *'75*
The Infernal Trio *'74*
Phantom of Liberty *'74*
Wedding in Blood *'74*
La Grande Bouffe *'73*
The Discreet Charm of the Bourgeoisie *'72*
Ten Days Wonder *'72*
The Things of Life *'70*
Topaz *'69*
Danger: Diabolik *'68*
The Milky Way *'68*
The Young Girls of Rochefort *'68*
Belle de Jour *'67*
The Game Is Over *'66*
La Guerre Est Finie *'66*
Lady L *'65*
Contempt *'64*
Diary of a Chambermaid *'64*
The Day and the Hour *'63*
Le Doulos *'61*
Death in the Garden *'56*
Paul Picerni (1922-)
Fearmaker *'89*
The Scalphunters *'68*

To Hell and Back *'55*
House of Wax *'53*
Irving Pichel (1891-1954)
How Green Was My Valley *'41 (N)*
Torture Ship *'39*
Dick Tracy *'37*
Dracula's Daughter *'36*
General Spanky *'36*
Oliver Twist *'33*
Jean-Francois Pichette
Mouvements du Desir *'94*
Being at Home with Claude *'92*
Joe Pichler (1987-)
When Good Ghouls Go Bad *'01*
Beethoven's 3rd *'00*
Shiloh 2: Shiloh Season *'99*
Varsity Blues *'98*
John Pickard (-1993)
Above and Beyond *'53*
Government Agents vs. Phantom Legion *'51*
Raymond Pickard
The Borrowers *'97*
The Canterville Ghost *'96*
Sorrels Pickard
Hardbodies *'84*
Running Hot *'83*
James Pickens, Jr.
Liberty Heights *'99*
A Slight Case of Murder *'99*
RocketMan *'97*
Bloodhounds *'96*
Ghosts of Mississippi *'96*
Gridlock'd *'96*
Sharon's Secret *'95*
Lily in Winter *'94*
Sodbusters *'94*
Slim Pickens (1919-83)
Crazy Horse and Custer: "The Untold Story" *'90*
Charlie and the Great Balloon Chase *'82*
Pink Motel *'82*
Sweet Creek County War *'82*
The Howling *'81*
Story of a Cowboy Angel *'81*
Honeysuckle Rose *'80*
Tom Horn *'80*
Beyond the Poseidon Adventure *'79*
1941 *'79*
The Swarm *'78*
Mr. Billion *'77*
Shadow of Chikara *'77*
The White Buffalo *'77*
Hawmps! *'76*
Pony Express Rider *'76*
The Apple Dumpling Gang *'75*
Babe! *'75*
Rancho Deluxe *'75*
White Line Fever *'75*
Blazing Saddles *'74*
Legend of Earl Durand *'74*
Ginger in the Morning *'73*
Pat Garrett & Billy the Kid *'73*
Poor Pretty Eddie *'73*
The Cowboys *'72*
The Getaway *'72*
Iron Horsemen *'71*
Ride to Glory *'71*
Ballad of Cable Hogue *'70*
Never a Dull Moment *'68*
Flim-Flam Man *'67*
Rough Night in Jericho *'67*
Talion *'66*
In Harm's Way *'65*
Major Dundee *'65*
Dr. Strangelove, or: How I Learned to Stop Worrying and Love the Bomb *'64*
One-Eyed Jacks *'61*
Phantom Stallion *'54*
Iron Mountain Trail *'53*
Shadows of Tombstone *'53*
Border Saddlemates *'52*
Colorado Sundown *'52*

Josh Picker
Beverly Hills Family Robinson *'97*
Alex *'92*
Flirting *'89*
Sarah Pickering
Little Dorrit, Film 1: Nobody's Fault *'88*
Little Dorrit, Film 2: Little Dorrit's Story *'88*
Blake Pickett
Dark Universe *'93*
HauntedWeen *'91*
Bobby "Boris" Pickett (1940-)
Lobster Man from Mars *'89*
Frankenstein General Hospital *'88*
Hot Money *'79*
Cindy Pickett (1947-)
The Stepdaughter *'00*
Atomic Dog *'98*
Painted Hero *'95*
Evolver *'94*
The Goodbye Bird *'93*
Son-in-Law *'93*
Sleepwalkers *'92*
Wildcard *'92*
Crooked Hearts *'91*
Original Intent *'91*
Deepstar Six *'89*
Hot to Trot! *'88*
Echoes in the Darkness *'87*
Ferris Bueller's Day Off *'86*
The Men's Club *'86*
Call to Glory *'84*
Circle of Power *'83*
Hysterical *'83*
Margin for Murder *'81*
Night Games *'80*
Mary Pickford (1893-1979)
Coquette *'29*
The Taming of the Shrew *'29*
A Kiss for Mary Pickford *'27*
My Best Girl *'27*
Sparrows *'26*
Little Annie Rooney *'25*
Tess of the Storm Country *'22*
The Love Light *'21*
Pollyanna *'20*
Suds *'20*
Daddy Long Legs *'19*
Amarilly of Clothesline Alley *'18*
Pride of the Clan *'18*
Stella Maris *'18*
The Little American *'17*
A Poor Little Rich Girl *'17*
Rebecca of Sunnybrook Farm *'17*
Christina Pickles (1935-)
Angels Don't Sleep Here *'00*
Murder She Purred: A Mrs. Murphy Mystery *'98*
Weapons of Mass Distraction *'97*
The Wedding Singer *'97*
William Shakespeare's Romeo and Juliet *'96*
Revenge of the Nerds 4: Nerds in Love *'94*
Seizure *'74*
Vivian Pickles (1933-)
Suspicion *'87*
Candleshoe *'78*
Elizabeth R *'72*
Harold and Maude *'71*
Ronald Pickup (1941-)
Horatio Hornblower *'99*
Ivanhoe *'97*
The Rector's Wife *'94*
Scarlett *'94*
My Friend Walter *'93*
Journey of Honor *'91*
Dr. Bethune *'90*
Jekyll and Hyde *'90*
A Murder of Quality *'90*
The Attic: The Hiding of Anne Frank *'88*
Fortunes of War *'87*
The Mission *'86*

Eleni '85
Life of Verdi '84
Ivanhoe '82
Nijinsky '80

Molly Picon (1898-1992)
Cannonball Run 2 '84
Cannonball Run '81
Murder on Flight 502 '75
For Pete's Sake '74
Fiddler on the Roof '71
Come Blow Your Horn '63
Mamele '38
Yidl Mitn Fidl '36
East and West '24

Jim Piddock
She Creature '01
Traces of Red '92

Rebecca Pidgeon (1963-)
Heist '01
State and Main '00
The Winslow Boy '98
The Spanish Prisoner '97
Homicide '91
The Dawning '88

Walter Pidgeon (1897-1984)
Sextette '78
The Lindbergh Kidnapping Case '76
Two Minute Warning '76
Murder on Flight 502 '75
Neptune Factor '73
Funny Girl '68
Cinderella '64
Advise and Consent '62
Big Red '62
Voyage to the Bottom of the Sea '61
Forbidden Planet '56
The Glass Slipper '55 (N)
Hit the Deck '55
Deep in My Heart '54
Executive Suite '54
The Last Time I Saw Paris '54
Men of the Fighting Lady '54
The Bad and the Beautiful '52
Million Dollar Mermaid '52
Quo Vadis '51 (N)
The Miniver Story '50
That Forsyte Woman '50
Command Decision '48
Julia Misbehaves '48
Cass Timberlane '47
Holiday in Mexico '46
Weekend at the Waldorf '45
Mrs. Parkington '44
Madame Curie '43
Mrs. Miniver '42
White Cargo '42
Blossoms in the Dust '41
How Green Was My Valley '41
Dark Command '40
House Across the Bay '40
It's a Date '40
Girl of the Golden West '38
Listen, Darling '38
Shopworn Angel '38
Too Hot to Handle '38
Saratoga '37

Claude Pieplu (1923-)
This Sweet Sickness '77
The Best Way '76
Phantom of Liberty '74
Wedding in Blood '74

Adrienne Pierce
Styx '00
Warriors from Hell '90

Bradley Michael Pierce (1982-)
The Borrowers '97
Doom Runners '97
Jumanji '95
Beauty and the Beast '91 (V)

Brock Pierce
Legend of the Lost Tomb '97
First Kid '96

Charles B. Pierce
Boggy Creek II '83
Grayeagle '77
Town That Dreaded Sundown '76
Winterhawk '76

David Hyde Pierce (1959-)
Full Frontal '02
Osmosis Jones '01 (V)
Wet Hot American Summer '01
Isn't She Great '00
Jackie's Back '99
The Mating Habits of the Earthbound Human '99 (N)
A Bug's Life '98 (V)
Nixon '95
Wolf '94
The Fisher King '91
Little Man Tate '91
Crossing Delancey '88
Vampire's Kiss '88

Jill Pierce
Omega Doom '96
Cyborg Soldier '94
Darkroom '90

Justin Pierce (1975-2000)
Next Friday '00
Blackmale '99
A Brother's Kiss '97
Kids '95

Preston Pierce
Whiskey Mountain '77
I Spit on Your Corpse '74

Stack Pierce
24 Hours to Midnight '92
Enemy Unseen '91
A Rage in Harlem '91
Murphy's Fault '88
Night Call Nurses '72

Tony Pierce
Big Bully '95
Trancers 3: Deth Lives '92

Wendell Pierce
The 24 Hour Woman '99
Bulworth '98
Get On the Bus '96
Hackers '95
Waiting to Exhale '95
Bye Bye, Love '94
It Could Happen to You '94

Eric Pierpont
Little Witches '96
Where Truth Lies '96
Blood for Blood '95
The Stranger '95
Alien Nation: Dark Horizon '94

Olivier Pierre
The Lonely Lady '83
The Sender '82

Frederic Pierrot
Artemisia '97
For Ever Mozart '96
Land and Freedom '95

Sarah Pierse
Heavenly Creatures '94
The Navigator '88

Geoffrey Pierson
Venomous '01
Necessary Parties '88

Angela Pietropinto
Shaft '00
Finding North '97
Welcome to the Dollhouse '95
It Could Happen to You '94
Honeymoon in Vegas '92
Goodfellas '90

Alexandra Pigg
Bullseye! '90
Chicago Joe & the Showgirl '90
Strapless '90
Smart Money '88
Letter to Brezhnev '86

Tim Pigott-Smith (1946-)
The Remains of the Day '93
The Jewel in the Crown '84
The Hunchback of Notre Dame '82

Luciano Pigozzi
Hatchet for the Honeymoon '70
And God Said to Cain '69

Joe Pilato
Fatal Passion '94
Married People, Single Sex '93
Day of the Dead '85

Nova Pilbeam (1919-)
Counterblast '48
Young and Innocent '37
Nine Days a Queen '36
The Man Who Knew Too Much '34

Mitch Pileggi (1952-)
Gun Shy '00
The X-Files '98
Ravenhawk '95
Shocker '89

Lorraine Pilkington
Human Traffic '99
The Nephew '97
The Last of the High Kings '96
The Miracle '91

Alison Pill
Baby '00
Skipped Parts '00

Jeffrey Pillars
Bloodmoon '97
Ernest Rides Again '93

Soren Pilmark
The Kingdom 2 '97
The Kingdom '95

Daniel Pilon
Left Behind: The Movie '00
Sex & Mrs. X '00
The Collectors '99
Poltergeist: The Legacy '96
Suspicious Minds '96
Obsessed '88
Snowballin' '85
Starship Invasions '77
Brannigan '75
The Red Half-Breed '70
In Trouble '67

Donald Pilon (1941-)
It's My Turn, Laura Cadieux '98
Keeping Track '86
Left for Dead '78
The Pyx '73

Silvia Pinal (1931-)
Simon of the Desert '66
The Exterminating Angel '62
Viridiana '61

Bronson Pinchot (1959-)
Out of the Cold '99
All New Adventures of Laurel and Hardy: For Love or Mummy '98
Quest for Camelot '98 (V)
Slappy and the Stinkers '97
Courage Under Fire '96
The First Wives Club '96
It's My Party '95
Stephen King's The Langoliers '95
Beverly Hills Cop 3 '94
The Great American Sex Scandal '94
True Romance '93
Blame It on the Bellboy '92
Second Sight '89
After Hours '85
Hot Resort '85
Beverly Hills Cop '84
The Flamingo Kid '84
Risky Business '83

Larry Pine
The Shipping News '01
Let It Snow '99
A Stranger in the Kingdom '98
Sunday '96
Dead Man Walking '95
Vanya on 42nd Street '94
Plain Clothes '88
Anna '87
Hullabaloo over Georgie & Bonnie's Pictures '78

Phillip Pine (1920-)
Money to Burn '83
Pot, Parents, and Police '71
The Lost Missile '58
Men in War '57
The Phantom from 10,000 Leagues '56

Robert Pine (1941-)
Body Count '97
Sins of the Mind '97
Independence Day '96
Are You Lonesome Tonight '92
Mysterious Two '82
Enola Gay: The Men, the Mission, the Atomic Bomb '80
Empire of the Ants '77
Munster, Go Home! '66

Miguel Pinero (1946-88)
Almost You '85
Alphabet City '84
Short Eyes '79

John Pinette
My 5 Wives '00
Simon Sez '99

Jada Pinkett Smith (1971-)
Ali '01
Kingdom Come '01
Bamboozled '00
Princess Mononoke '98 (V)
Return to Paradise '98
Scream 2 '97
Woo '97
If These Walls Could Talk '96
The Nutty Professor '96
Set It Off '96
The Inkwell '94
Jason's Lyric '94
A Low Down Dirty Shame '94
Tales from the Crypt Presents Demon Knight '94
Menace II Society '93

Dominique Pinon (1955-)
Amelie '01
Alien: Resurrection '97
The City of Lost Children '95
Alberto Express '92
Delicatessen '92
Moon in the Gutter '83
Diva '82

Gordon Pinsent (1930-)
The Shipping News '01
Pale Saints '97
A Vow to Kill '94
Blood Clan '91
Babar: The Movie '88 (V)
John and the Missus '87
Newman's Law '74
Blacula '72
Colossus: The Forbin Project '70
The Thomas Crown Affair '68

Leah K. Pinsent (1968-)
Virus '96
The Little Kidnappers '90
Brutal Glory '89
Double Identity '89
April Fool's Day '86
The Bay Boy '85

Danny Pintauro (1976-)
The Great American Sex Scandal '94
The Beniker Gang '83
Cujo '83

Harold Pinter (1930-)
Wit '01
The Tailor of Panama '00
Mansfield Park '99
Breaking the Code '95
Accident '67

Frederick Piper (1902-79)
The Frightened City '61
The Blue Lamp '49
Hue and Cry '47
San Demetrio, London '47
Johnny Frenchman '46
Pink String and Sealing Wax '45
Oh, Mr. Porter '37
Sabotage '36

Kelly Piper
Rawhead Rex '87
Maniac '80

Roddy Piper (1951-)
Cybercity '99
Shepherd '99
The Bad Pack '98
Dead Tides '97
First Encounter '97
Marked Man '96
Sci-Fighters '96
Terminal Rush '96
Jungleground '95
Back in Action '94
Immortal Combat '94
No Contest '94
Tough and Deadly '94
Buy & Cell '89
Hell Comes to Frogtown '88
They Live '88
Body Slam '87

Mark Pirro (1956-)
Curse of the Queerwolf '87
A Polish Vampire in Burbank '80

Carla Pisacane
Joyful Laughter '60
Paisan '46

Joe Piscopo (1951-)
Captain Nuke and the Bomber Boys '95
Open Season '95
Two Bits & Pepper '95
Huck and the King of Hearts '93
Sidekicks '93
Dead Heat '88
Wise Guys '86
Johnny Dangerously '84
American Tickler '76
King Kong '76

Marie-France Pisier (1944-)
The Ice Rink '99
Son of Gascogne '95
Hot Touch '80s
Prize of Peril '84
Chanel Solitaire '81
Miss Right '81
French Postcards '79
We Will Not Enter the Forest '79
Love on the Run '78
The Other Side of Midnight '77
Barocco '76
Cousin, Cousine '76
Celine and Julie Go Boating '74
Nous N'Irons Plus au Bois '69

Luigi Pistilli (1930-96)
The Scorpion's Tail '71
Twitch of the Death Nerve '71
The Libertine '69
The Good, the Bad and the Ugly '67

Kimberly Pistone
WhiteForce '88
Blue De Ville '86

Mario Pisu
The Sensuous Nurse '76
Juliet of the Spirits '65

Maria Pitillo (1965-)
Godzilla '98
Dear God '96
Bye Bye, Love '94
Cooperstown '93
True Romance '93
The Lost Capone '90
Spike of Bensonhurst '88

Sacha (Sascha) Pitoeff (1920-90)
Inferno '80
Last Year at Marienbad '61
Anastasia '56

Anne Pitoniak (1922-)
A Thousand Acres '97
House of Cards '92
The Ballad of the Sad Cafe '91
Old Gringo '89
The Wizard of Loneliness '88
Best Seller '87
Sister, Sister '87
Agnes of God '85
Old Enough '84

Brad Pitt (1963-)
Full Frontal '02
The Mexican '01
Ocean's Eleven '01
Spy Game '01
Snatch '00
Fight Club '99
Meet Joe Black '98
Seven Years in Tibet '97
The Devil's Own '96
Sleepers '96
Seven '95
12 Monkeys '95
Interview with the Vampire '94
Legends of the Fall '94
Kalifornia '93
True Romance '93
Cool World '92
The Favor '92
Johnny Suede '92
A River Runs Through It '92
Thelma & Louise '91
Too Young to Die '90
Across the Tracks '89
Cutting Class '89
Happy Together '89

Charles Pitt
Moving Target '89
Monaco Forever '83

Ingrid Pitt (1937-)
Hanna's War '88
Transmutations '85
The Final Option '82
The Wicker Man '75
The House that Dripped Blood '71
The Vampire Lovers '70
Where Eagles Dare '68
Sound of Horror '64

Michael Pitt (1981-)
Murder by Numbers '02
Bully '01
Hedwig and the Angry Inch '00

Carl Pitti
Gun Glory '57
Tribute to a Bad Man '56
Billy the Kid '41

Tom Pittman
The Zodiac Killer '71
Verboten! '59

ZaSu Pitts (1898-1963)
It's a Mad, Mad, Mad, Mad World '63
The Thrill of It All! '63
This Could Be the Night '57
Francis Joins the WACs '54
The Denver & Rio Grande '51
Francis the Talking Mule '49
Life with Father '47
Breakfast in Hollywood '46
The Perfect Marriage '46
The Bashful Bachelor '42
Meet the Mob '42
Mexican Spitfire at Sea '42
Mrs. Wiggs of the Cabbage Patch '42
Broadway Limited '41
No, No Nanette '40
Eternally Yours '39
Nurse Edith Cavell '39
Way Out West '37
Ruggles of Red Gap '35
Dames '34
Aggie Appleby, Maker of Men '33
Mr. Skitch '33
The Crooked Circle '32
Strangers of the Evening '32
The Guardsman '31
Lottery Bride '30
Sin Takes a Holiday '30
Risky Business '28
Sunny Side Up '28
The Wedding March '28
Greed '24

Jeremy Piven (1965-)
Black Hawk Down '01
Highway '01
Rush Hour 2 '01
Serendipity '01
The Crew '00
Red Letters '00
Phoenix '98
Very Bad Things '98
Don King: Only in America '97
Grosse Pointe Blank '97
Just Write '97
Kiss the Girls '97
Music from Another Room '97
The Real Thing '97
Larger Than Life '96
Wavelength '96
Heat '95
Miami Rhapsody '95
Car 54, Where Are You? '94
Floundering '94
P.C.U. '94
Twogether '94
Judgment Night '93
12:01 '93
Singles '92
Body Chemistry 2: Voice of a Stranger '91
The Grifters '90
Say Anything '89

Lou Place
Apache Woman '55
Swamp Women '55

Mary Kay Place (1947-)
Human Nature '02
My First Mister '01
Being John Malkovich '99
Girl, Interrupted '99
Pecker '98
Eye of God '97
John Grisham's The Rainmaker '97
Citizen Ruth '96
Manny & Lo '96
My Very Best Friend '96
Teresa's Tattoo '94
Armistead Maupin's Tales of the City '93
Captain Ron '92
Samantha '92
Bright Angel '91
Crazy from the Heart '91
A New Life '88
Portrait of a White Marriage '88
The Girl Who Spelled Freedom '86
Explorers '85
Smooth Talk '85
For Love or Money '84
The Big Chill '83
Waltz across Texas '83
Modern Problems '81
Private Benjamin '80
More American Graffiti '79
Starting Over '79
New York, New York '77

Michele Placido (1946-)
Lamerica '95
Drug Wars 2: The Cocaine Cartel '92
Forever Mary '89
Private Affairs '89
Big Business '88
Summer Night with Greek Profile, Almond Eyes & Scent of Basil '87
The Sicilian Connection '85
Three Brothers '80
Ernesto '79
Till Marriage Do Us Part '74

Tony Plana (1953-)
Fidel '02
Noriega: God's Favorite '00
Backlash '99
My Little Assassin '99
187 '97
Santa Fe '97
Sub Down '97
Primal Fear '96
The Burning Season '94
A Million to Juan '94
JFK '91
One Good Cop '91
Havana '90
In the Line of Duty: A Cop for the Killing '90
Sweet 15 '90
Why Me? '90
The Hillside Strangler '89
Romero '89
Break of Dawn '88
Born in East L.A. '87
Salvador '86
Latino '85

Roger Planchon
The Return of Martin Guerre '83
Roads to the South '78

Nigel Planer (1955-)
Mr. Toad's Wild Ride '96
Supergrass '87

Scott Plank
Frozen in Fear '00
Moonbase '97
Marshal Law '96
Without Evidence '96
Saints and Sinners '95
Dying to Remember '93
Red Shoe Diaries 4: Auto Erotica '93
Pastime '91
The In Crowd '88

Dana Plato (1964-99)
Blade Boxer '97
High School USA '84
Return to Boggy Creek '77
Beyond the Bermuda Triangle '75

Edward Platt (1916-74)
Atlantis, the Lost Continent '61
North by Northwest '59
The Rebel Set '59
Gunman's Walk '58
Designing Woman '57
Rock, Pretty Baby '56
Written on the Wind '56
Rebel without a Cause '55

Louise Platt (1915-)
Captain Caution '40
Stagecoach '39
Spawn of the North '38

Marc Platt (1913-)
Down to Earth '47
Tonight and Every Night '45

Oliver Platt (1960-)
ZigZag '02
Don't Say a Word '01
Gun Shy '00
Ready to Rumble '00
Bicentennial Man '99
Lake Placid '99
Three to Tango '99
Bulworth '98
Dangerous Beauty '98
Dr. Dolittle '98
The Imposters '98
Simon Birch '98
Executive Decision '96
A Time to Kill '96
The Infiltrator '95
Tall Tale: The Unbelievable Adventures of Pecos Bill '95
Funny Bones '94
Benny & Joon '93
Indecent Proposal '93
The Temp '93
The Three Musketeers '93
Beethoven '92
Diggstown '92
Flatliners '90
Postcards from the Edge '90
Working Girl '88

Alice Playten (1947-)
Doug's 1st Movie '99 (V)
Felix the Cat: The Movie '91 (V)
Legend '86

Angela Pleasence
The Favor, the Watch, & the Very Big Fish '92
Stealing Heaven '88
A Christmas Carol '84
The Godsend '79
Six Wives of Henry VIII '71

Donald Pleasence (1919-95)
Halloween 6: The Curse of Michael Myers '95
The Advocate '93
Shadows and Fog '92
Millions '90
River of Death '90
American Tiger '89
Buried Alive '89
Casablanca Express '89
Halloween 5: The Revenge of Michael Myers '89
Ten Little Indians '89
Deep Cover '88
The Great Escape 2: The Untold Story '88
Ground Zero '88
Halloween 4: The Return of Michael Myers '88
Hanna's War '88
The House of Usher '88
Django Strikes Again '87
Phantom of Death '87
Prince of Darkness '87
The Room '87
Specters '87
Warrior Queen '87
Into the Darkness '86
Arch of Triumph '85
Creepers '85
Mansfield Park '85
The Monster Club '85
Nothing Underneath '85
Operation 'Nam '85
The Ambassador '84
The Black Arrow '84
A Breed Apart '84
To Kill a Stranger '84
The Treasure of the Amazon '84
Warrior of the Lost World '84
Devonsville Terror '83
Frankenstein's Great Aunt Tillie '83
Treasure of the Yankee Zephyr '83
Alone in the Dark '82
Escape from New York '81
Halloween 2: The Nightmare Isn't Over! '81
Power Play '81
The Puma Man '80
All Quiet on the Western Front '79
Better Late Than Never '79
Dracula '79
Gold of the Amazon Women '79
Jaguar Lives '79
Night Creature '79
The Bastard '78
The Dark Secret of Harvest Home '78 (N)
Halloween '78
Sgt. Pepper's Lonely Hearts Club Band '78
The Uncanny '78
Blood Relatives '77
The Eagle Has Landed '77
Goldenrod '77
Land of the Minotaur '77
Oh, God! '77
Telefon '77
Tomorrow Never Comes '77
Choice of Weapons '76
The Last Tycoon '76
Escape to Witch Mountain '75
Hearts of the West '75
I Don't Want to Be Born '75
The Passover Plot '75
Barry McKenzie Holds His Own '74
The Black Windmill '74
The Count of Monte Cristo '74
Journey into Fear '74
Dr. Jekyll and Mr. Hyde '73
The Freakmaker '73
From Beyond the Grave '73
The Rainbow Gang '73
Tales That Witness Madness '73
Wedding in White '72
House of the Damned '71
The Shaming '71
THX 1138 '71
Soldier Blue '70
The Madwoman of Chaillot '69
Night of the Generals '67
Will Penny '67
You Only Live Twice '67
Cul de Sac '66
Fantastic Voyage '66
The Greatest Story Ever Told '65
The Hallelujah Trail '65
The Great Escape '63
What a Carve-Up! '62
Horsemasters '61
The Battle of the Sexes '60
Circus of Horrors '60
The Flesh and the Fiends '60
The Hands of Orlac '60
No Love for Johnnie '60
Look Back in Anger '58
A Tale of Two Cities '58

John Pleshette (1942-)
James Dean '01
The Curse of Inferno '96
Eye of the Stranger '93
Lies of the Twins '91
Burning Rage '84
The Kid with the Broken Halo '82
The Trial of Lee Harvey Oswald '77

Suzanne Pleshette (1937-)
The Lion King: Simba's Pride '98 (V)
Battling for Baby '92
The Queen of Mean '90
Alone in the Neon Jungle '87
Dixie: Changing Habits '85
Kojak: The Belarus File '85
For Love or Money '84
One Cooks, the Other Doesn't '83
Help Wanted: Male '82
Hot Stuff '80
Oh, God! Book 2 '80
If Things Were Different '79
The Shaggy D.A. '76
Legend of Valentino '75
Support Your Local Gunfighter '71
Hard Frame '70
Suppose They Gave a War and Nobody Came? '70
If It's Tuesday, This Must Be Belgium '69
Blackbeard's Ghost '67
The Adventures of Bullwhip Griffin '66
Nevada Smith '66
The Ugly Dachshund '65
The Birds '63
40 Pounds of Trouble '62
Rome Adventure '62
The Geisha Boy '58

George Plimpton (1927-)
Just Visiting '01
Just Cause '94
Little Man Tate '91
Easy Wheels '89
A Fool and His Money '88
Volunteers '85
Reds '81
Rio Lobo '70

Martha Plimpton (1970-)
The Defenders: Taking the First '98
Pecker '98
200 Cigarettes '98
The Defenders: Payback '97
Eye of God '97
Music from Another Room '97
Beautiful Girls '96
I Shot Andy Warhol '96
I'm Not Rappaport '96
Last Summer in the Hamptons '96
Forbidden Choices '94
Mrs. Parker and the Vicious Circle '94
My Life's in Turnaround '94
A Woman at War '94
Chantilly Lace '93
Daybreak '93
Inside Monkey Zetterland '93
Josh and S.A.M. '93
Samantha '94
Silence Like Glass '90
Stanley and Iris '90
Parenthood '89
Another Woman '88
Running on Empty '88
Stars and Bars '88
Shy People '87
The Mosquito Coast '86
The Goonies '85
The River Rat '84
Rollover '81

Jack Plotnick
Say It Isn't So '01
Gods and Monsters '98
Chairman of the Board '97

Melinda Plowman
Billy the Kid Versus Dracula '66
Home Town Story '51

Hilda Plowright
36 Hours '64
Separate Tables '58

Joan Plowright (1929-)
Back to the Secret Garden '01
Dinosaur '00 (V)
Tea with Mussolini '99
Aldrich Ames: Traitor Within '98
Dance with Me '98
The Assistant '97
Jane Eyre '96
101 Dalmatians '96
Surviving Picasso '96
Mr. Wrong '95
A Pyromaniac's Love Story '95
The Scarlet Letter '95
Sorrento Beach '95
A Place for Annie '94
The Return of the Native '94
The Summer House '94
Widow's Peak '94
Dennis the Menace '93
Last Action Hero '93
Enchanted April '92
Stalin '92
And a Nightingale Sang '91
Avalon '90
I Love You to Death '90
The Dressmaker '89
Drowning by Numbers '87
A Dedicated Man '86
Revolution '85
Brimstone & Treacle '82
Britannia Hospital '82
Equus '77
The Merchant of Venice '73
School for Scandal '65
The Entertainer '60
Time Without Pity '57

Eve Plumb (1958-)
...And God Spoke '94
I'm Gonna Git You Sucka '88
A Very Brady Christmas '88
Little Women '78
Secrets of Three Hungry Wives '78
Alexander: The Other Side of Dawn '77
Force of Evil '77

Amanda Plummer (1957-)
Seven Days to Live '01
8 1/2 Women '99
The Million Dollar Hotel '99
Apartment Complex '98
Hercules '97 (V)
A Simple Wish '97
Don't Look Back '96
Drunks '96
The Final Cut '96
Freeway '95
The Prophecy '95
The Right to Remain Silent '95
Butterfly Kiss '94
Pulp Fiction '94
Last Light '93
Needful Things '93
Nostradamus '93
So I Married an Axe Murderer '93
Freejack '92
Miss Rose White '92
The Fisher King '91
Joe Versus the Volcano '90
Prisoners of Inertia '89
Gryphon '88
Riders to the Sea '88
Courtship '87
Made in Heaven '87
Static '87
The Dollmaker '84
The Hotel New Hampshire '84
Daniel '83
The World According to Garp '82

Christopher Plummer (1927-)
A Beautiful Mind '01
American Tragedy '00
Dracula 2000 '00
Full Disclosure '00
Nuremberg '00
Possessed '00
Hidden Agenda '99
The Insider '99
Blackheart '98
Winchell '98
Skeletons '96
Kurt Vonnegut's Harrison Bergeron '95
12 Monkeys '95
Crackerjack '94
Dolores Claiborne '94
Wolf '94
Liar's Edge '92
Malcolm X '92
Rock-a-Doodle '92 (V)
Star Trek 6: The Undiscovered Country '91
Young Catherine '91
Firehead '90
Red Blooded American Girl '90
Where the Heart Is '90
Mindfield '89
Light Years '88 (V)
Shadow Dancing '88
Souvenir '88
Dragnet '87
I Love N.Y. '87
An American Tail '86 (V)
The Boss' Wife '86
Boy in Blue '86
Many Faces of Sherlock Holmes '86
Lily in Love '85
Dreamscape '84
Little Gloria... Happy at Last '84
Ordeal by Innocence '84
Prototype '83
The Scarlet & the Black '83
The Thorn Birds '83
The Amateur '82
Disappearance '81
Eyewitness '81
Highpoint '80
The Shadow Box '80
Somewhere in Time '80
Hanover Street '79
Murder by Decree '79
Riel '79
The Assignment '78
The Day That Shook the World '78
International Velvet '78
The Silent Partner '78
Star Crash '78
Conduct Unbecoming '75
The Man Who Would Be King '75
Spiral Staircase '75
Return of the Pink Panther '74
The Pyx '73
Waterloo '71
Battle of Britain '69

Night of the Generals '67
Triple Cross '67
Inside Daisy Clover '65
The Sound of Music '65
The Fall of the Roman Empire '64
A Doll's House '59
Stage Struck '57

Glenn Plummer (1966-)
The Salton Sea '02
Rangers '00
Interceptor Force '99
Smalltime '99
Spy Games '99
Thursday '98
One Night Stand '97
Pronto '97
Speed 2: Cruise Control '97
The Destiny of Marty Fine '96
The Substitute '96
Up Close and Personal '96
Convict Cowboy '95
Showgirls '95
Strange Days '95
Things to Do in Denver When You're Dead '95
Speed '94
Menace II Society '93
South Central '92
Pastime '91
Colors '88

Gerard Plunkett
A Cooler Climate '99
My Husband's Secret Life '98
Baby Monitor: Sound of Fear '97

Werner Pochath (1939-93)
Laser Mission '90
Thunder Warrior 3 '88
Flatfoot '78

Rick Podell
World Gone Wild '88
Lunch Wagon '81

Rossana Podesta (1934-)
The Sensual Man '74
The Virgin of Nuremberg '65
Alone Against Rome '62
Sodom and Gomorrah '62
Helen of Troy '56
Ulysses '55

Fernando Poe, Jr.
The Ravagers '65
The Walls of Hell '64

Kathryn Pogson
Over Indulgence '87
The Company of Wolves '85

Ken Pogue
Crossfire Trail '01
Out of Time '00
The 6th Day '00
The Jack Bull '99
National Lampoon's Dad's Week Off '97
Bad Moon '96
The Amy Fisher Story '93
Still Not Quite Human '92
Blind Man's Bluff '91
The Hitman '91
Run '91
Crazy Moon '87
Dead of Winter '87
Keeping Track '86
Miracle at Moreaux '86
The Grey Fox '83

Eric Pohlmann (1913-79)
Tiffany Jones '75
Glass Tomb '55
Terror Street '54
The Belles of St. Trinian's '53
Three Stops to Murder '53
Moulin Rouge '52
Blackout '50

Larry Poindexter
Steel Sharks '97
Body Chemistry 4: Full Exposure '95
Sorceress '94
Blue Movies '88
American Ninja 2: The Confrontation '87

Priscilla Pointer (1924-)
Carried Away '95
The Magic Bubble '93
Disturbed '90
A Nightmare on Elm Street 3: Dream Warriors '87
Blue Velvet '86
Rumpelstiltskin '86
The Falcon and the Snowman '85
Mysterious Two '82
Archer: The Fugitive from the Empire '81
The Competition '80
Honeysuckle Rose '80

Jean Poiret
The Elegant Criminal '92
The Last Metro '80

Sidney Poitier (1924-)
The Simple Life of Noah Dearborn '99
Free of Eden '98
The Jackal '97
Mandela and de Klerk '97
A Good Day to Die '95
Sneakers '92
Separate but Equal '91
Little Nikita '88
Shoot to Kill '88
Piece of the Action '77
Let's Do It Again '75
The Wilby Conspiracy '75
Uptown Saturday Night '74
Buck and the Preacher '72
The Organization '71
Brother John '70
They Call Me Mr. Tibbs! '70
The Lost Man '69
For Love of Ivy '68
Guess Who's Coming to Dinner '67
In the Heat of the Night '67
To Sir, with Love '67
Duel at Diablo '66
Bedford Incident '65
The Greatest Story Ever Told '65
A Patch of Blue '65
The Slender Thread '65
The Long Ships '64
Lilies of the Field '63
Pressure Point '62
Paris Blues '61
A Raisin in the Sun '61
All the Young Men '60
The Defiant Ones '58
Band of Angels '57
The Mark of the Hawk '57
Something of Value '57
Goodbye, My Lady '56
Blackboard Jungle '55
Red Ball Express '52
Cry, the Beloved Country '51
No Way Out '50

Sydney Tamiia Poitier (1973-)
Noah's Ark '99
True Crime '99
Free of Eden '98

Simon Poland
Nemesis 4: Cry of Angels '97
Alien from L.A. '87

Roman Polanski (1933-)
Grosse Fatigue '94
A Pure Formality '94
Back in the USSR '92
The Tenant '76
Andy Warhol's Dracula '74
Chinatown '74
Diary of Forbidden Dreams '73
Ciao Federico! Fellini Directs Satyricon '69
The Magic Christian '69
The Fearless Vampire Killers '67
Innocent Sorcerers '60
A Generation '54

Victor Poletti
Meeting Venus '91
And the Ship Sails On '83

Maurice Poli
Gangster's Law '86
Five Dolls for an August Moon '70

Jon Polito (1950-)
The Man Who Wasn't There '01
Mimic 2 '01
The Adventures of Rocky & Bullwinkle '00
Homicide: The Movie '00
Angel's Dance '99
Russell Mulcahy's Tale of the Mummy '99
Apartment Complex '98
Nowhere Land '98
With Friends Like These '98
Music from Another Room '97
Homeward Bound 2: Lost in San Francisco '96 (V)
Just Your Luck '96
Bushwhacked '95
Fluke '95
The Invaders '95
Blankman '94
Girls in Prison '94
The Crow '93
Fallen Angels 2 '93
Barton Fink '91
The Freshman '90
Leather Jackets '90
Miller's Crossing '90
Deadly Business '86
Fire with Fire '86
Highlander '86

Lina Polito
All Screwed Up '74
Blood Brothers '74

Haydee Politoff
Dracula's Great Love '72
La Collectionneuse '67

Vic Polizos
Light It Up '99
Winchell '98
Kiss of a Killer '93
C.H.U.D. '84

Oscar Polk
Gone with the Wind '39
Green Pastures '36

Ben Pollack
The Benny Goodman Story '55
The Glenn Miller Story '54

Sydney Pollack (1934-)
Changing Lanes '02
Eyes Wide Shut '99
Random Hearts '99
A Civil Action '98
Death Becomes Her '92
Husbands and Wives '92
The Player '92
Tootsie '82

Cheryl Pollak (1967-)
Sin and Redemption '94
Crossing the Bridge '92
Night Life '90
Pump Up the Volume '90
Swimsuit '89
My Best Friend Is a Vampire '88

Kevin Pollak (1958-)
Dr. Dolittle 2 '01
3000 Miles to Graceland '01
The Wedding Planner '01
Deterrence '00
Steal This Movie! '00
The Whole Nine Yards '00
Deal of a Lifetime '99
End of Days '99
She's All That '99
From the Earth to the Moon '98
Hoods '98
Outside Ozona '98
Ruby Bridges '98
National Lampoon's The Don's Analyst '97
Truth or Consequences, N.M. '97
House Arrest '96
That Thing You Do! '96
Casino '95
Chameleon '95
Grumpier Old Men '95
Miami Rhapsody '95
The Usual Suspects '95
Canadian Bacon '94
Clean Slate '94
Grumpy Old Men '93
Indian Summer '93
The Opposite Sex and How to Live With Them '93
Wayne's World 2 '93
A Few Good Men '92
Another You '91
L.A. Story '91
Ricochet '91
Avalon '90
Willow '88

Tracy Pollan (1960-)
The Kennedys of Massachusetts '95
A Stranger Among Us '92
Danielle Steel's Fine Things '90
Bright Lights, Big City '88
Promised Land '88
The Abduction of Kari Swenson '87
Great Love Experiment '84
The Tender Age '84
Baby It's You '82

Daphne Pollard (1894-1978)
Our Relations '36
Bonnie Scotland '35

Michael J. Pollard (1939-)
Along for the Ride '00
Stir '98
Tumbleweeds '98
The Odyssey '97
Trigger Happy '96
Skeeter '93
Split Second '92
Motorama '91
The Arrival '90
The Art of Dying '90
Dick Tracy '90
I Come in Peace '90
Why Me? '90
Fast Food '89
Next of Kin '89
Night Visitor '89
Season of Fear '89
Sleepaway Camp 3: Teenage Wasteland '89
Tango and Cash '89
American Gothic '88
Riders of the Storm '88
Scrooged '88
Heated Vengeance '87
Roxanne '87
America '86
The Patriot '86
Vengeance Is Mine '84
Melvin and Howard '80
Between the Lines '77
Legend of Frenchie King '71
Bonnie & Clyde '67
Enter Laughing '67
The Wild Angels '66

Snub Pollard (1886-1962)
The Errand Boy '61
Arizona Days '37
A Nation Aflame '37
Riders of the Rockies '37
The White Legion '36

Sarah Polley (1979-)
No Such Thing '01
The Claim '00
Love Come Down '00
eXistenZ '99
Go '99
Guinevere '99
The Life Before This '99
Last Night '98
White Lies '98
The Hanging Garden '97
Junior's Groove '97
The Sweet Hereafter '96
Exotica '94
Lantern Hill '90
The Adventures of Baron Munchausen '89
Babar: The Movie '88 (V)
Big Town '87

David Pollock
The Bad News Bears Go to Japan '78
The Bad News Bears in Breaking Training '77
The Bad News Bears '76

Dee Pollock
Legend of Tom Dooley '59
Beware, My Lovely '52

Eileen Pollock
Far and Away '92
Four Days in July '85

Ellen Pollock (1903-97)
Horror Hospital '73
Non-Stop New York '37

Teri Polo (1969-)
Domestic Disturbance '01
Meet the Parents '00
A Prayer in the Dark '97
The Arrival '96
Aspen Extreme '93
Golden Gate '93
The House of the Spirits '93
Quick '93
Passed Away '92
Born to Ride '91
Mystery Date '91
The Phantom of the Opera '90

John Polson
Mission: Impossible 2 '00
The Boys '98
Idiot Box '97
Back of Beyond '95
Sirens '94
The Sum of Us '94
Dangerous Game '90

Max Pomeranc (1984-)
Fluke '95
Journey '95
Searching for Bobby Fischer '93

Eusebio Poncela (1947-)
A Shadow You Soon Will Be '94
Law of Desire '86
Matador '86
Cannibal Man '71

Lily Pons
That Girl from Paris '36
I Dream Too Much '35

Yvan Ponton (1945-)
The Boys '97
Scanners 2: The New Order '91
Men of Steel '88
Pouvoir Intime '87

Bray Poor
Two Ninas '00
Anima '98

Iggy Pop (1947-)
Snow Day '00
The Crow 2: City of Angels '96
Dead Man '95
Tank Girl '94
Cry-Baby '90
Hardware '90
Sid & Nancy '86

Marc Poppel
Separate Lives '94
Damned River '89

Albert "Poppy" Popwell (1926-99)
Scissors '91
Wild at Heart '90
The Siege of Firebase Gloria '89
Who's That Girl? '87
Sudden Impact '83
The Buddy Holly Story '78
The Enforcer '76
Cleopatra Jones & the Casino of Gold '75
Charley Varrick '73
Cleopatra Jones '73
Magnum Force '73
Fuzz '72
Dirty Harry '71
Coogan's Bluff '68
The Harder They Fall '56
The Joe Louis Story '53

Johnny Popwell
Manhunter '83
Challenge '74

Jorge Porcel
Carlito's Way '93
Naked Is Better '73

Marc Porel (1949-83)
The Psychic '78
The Innocent '76
Don't Torture a Duckling '72

Paulina Porizkova (1965-)
Dark Asylum '01
Intern '00
Partners in Crime '99
Thursday '98
Female Perversions '96
Wedding Bell Blues '96
Arizona Dream '94
Her Alibi '88
Portfolio '88
Anna '87

Louise Portal (1951-)
Sous Sol '96
The Decline of the American Empire '86
The Klutz '73

Robert Portal
Mrs. Dalloway '97
Stiff Upper Lips '96

Billy Porter
The Broken Hearts Club '00
Intern '00
Twisted '96

Brett Porter
Stiletto Dance '01
Firehead '90

Don Porter (1912-96)
The Christmas Coal Mine Miracle '77
The Candidate '72
Bachelor in Paradise '69
Live a Little, Love a Little '68
Our Miss Brooks '56
The Racket '51
Buck Privates Come Home '47
She Wolf of London '46
Night Monster '42
Who Done It? '42

Eric Porter (1928-95)
Oliver Twist '85
Churchill and the Generals '81
Little Lord Fauntleroy '80
The Thirty-Nine Steps '79
Macbeth '76
Hennessy '75
Antony and Cleopatra '73
The Belstone Fox '73
Hands of the Ripper '71
The Heroes of Telemark '65
The Fall of the Roman Empire '64
The Pumpkin Eater '64

Jean Porter (1925-)
G.I. Jane '51
Kentucky Jubilee '51
Abbott and Costello in Hollywood '45
Bathing Beauty '44

Robert Porter
Deadly Fieldtrip '74
The Jesus Trip '71

Susie Porter
Bootmen '00
The Monkey's Mask '00
Two Hands '98
Idiot Box '97
Paradise Road '97
Welcome to Woop Woop '97

Eric Portman (1903-69)
Bedford Incident '65
The Naked Edge '61
The Colditz Story '55
Dear Murderer '47
Great Day '46
Men of Two Worlds '46
A Canterbury Tale '44
We Dive at Dawn '43
The Forty-Ninth Parallel '41

One of Our Aircraft Is Missing '41
Moonlight Sonata '38
The Crimes of Stephen Hawke '36
Murder in the Old Red Barn '36

Natalie Portman (1981-)
Star Wars: Episode 2—Attack of the Clones '02
Where the Heart Is '00
Anywhere But Here '99
Star Wars: Episode 1—The Phantom Menace '99
Beautiful Girls '96
Everyone Says I Love You '96
Mars Attacks! '96
Heat '95
The Professional '94

Richard Portnow (1950-)
Double Down '01
The Ghost of Spoon River '00
Happy Accidents '00
Desert Thunder '99
Ghost Dog: The Way of the Samurai '99
The Substitute 3: Winner Takes All '99
Witness Protection '99
Private Parts '96
Donor Unknown '95
Man of the House '95
S.F.W. '94
Trial by Jury '94
Sister Act '92
Barton Fink '91
Kindergarten Cop '90
Meet the Hollowheads '89
Say Anything '89
In Dangerous Company '88
Good Morning, Vietnam '87

Parker Posey (1968-)
The Sweetest Thing '02
The Anniversary Party '01
Josie and the Pussycats '01
Best in Show '00
Scream 3 '00
Henry Fool '98
You've Got Mail '98
Armistead Maupin's More Tales of the City '97
Clockwatchers '97
The House of Yes '97
Basquiat '96
The Daytrippers '96
Drunks '96
subUrbia '96
Waiting for Guffman '96
The Doom Generation '95
Flirt '95
Frisk '95
Kicking and Screaming '95
Party Girl '94
Sleep with Me '94
Armistead Maupin's Tales of the City '93
Dazed and Confused '93

Markie Post (1950-)
I've Been Waiting for You '98
There's Something about Mary '98
Glitz '88
Tricks of the Trade '88
Scene of the Crime '85
TripleCross '85

Saskia Post
Dogs in Space '87
One Night Stand '84

William Post, Jr. (1901-89)
Call Northside 777 '48
House on 92nd Street '45
Sherlock Holmes and the Secret Weapon '42
Ship Ahoy '42

Pete Postlethwaite (1945-)
The Shipping News '01
Alice in Wonderland '99
Animal Farm '99
Lost for Words '99
When the Sky Falls '99
Among Giants '98
Amistad '97
The Lost World: Jurassic Park 2 '97
The Serpent's Kiss '97
Brassed Off '96
Crimetime '96
Dragonheart '96
James and the Giant Peach '96 (V)
William Shakespeare's Romeo and Juliet '96
The Usual Suspects '95
When Saturday Comes '95
Martin Chuzzlewit '94
Sharpe's Company '94
Sharpe's Enemy '94
Suite 16 '94
In the Name of the Father '93
The Last of the Mohicans '92
Split Second '92
Waterland '92
Hamlet '90
The Dressmaker '89
To Kill a Priest '89
Distant Voices, Still Lives '88
A Private Function '84

Laurens C. Postma
To Live and Die in Hong Kong '89
Heroes Three '84

Tom Poston (1921-)
The Story of Us '99
Krippendorf's Tribe '98
A Perfect Little Murder '90
Carbon Copy '81
Up the Academy '80
Cold Turkey '71
Soldier in the Rain '63
The Tempest '63
Zotz! '62

Victor Potel (1889-1947)
Miracle of Morgan's Creek '44
Thunder Over Texas '34
Border Romance '30
Doughboys '30
Paradise Island '30
Captain Swagger '25
Anna Christie '23

Franka Potente (1974-)
The Bourne Identity '02
Blow '01
Storytelling '01
Anatomy '00
The Princess and the Warrior '00
Run Lola Run '98

Madeleine Potter (1963-)
The Golden Bowl '00
Spellbreaker: Secret of the Leprechauns '96
Two Evil Eyes '90
Bloodhounds of Broadway '89
Slaves of New York '89
Hello Again '87
The Bostonians '84

Martin Potter (1944-)
Gunpowder '84
The Only Way '70
Twinsanity '70
Ciao Federico! Fellini Directs Satyricon '69
Fellini Satyricon '69

Monica Potter (1971-)
Along Came a Spider '01
Head Over Heels '01
A Cool, Dry Place '98
Patch Adams '98
The Very Thought of You '98
Con Air '97
Without Limits '97

Annie Potts (1952-)
Toy Story 2 '99 (V)
Toy Story '95 (V)
Breaking the Rules '92
Texasville '90
Ghostbusters 2 '89
Who's Harry Crumb? '89
Pass the Ammo '88
Bayou Romance '86
Jumpin' Jack Flash '86
Pretty in Pink '86
Crimes of Passion '84
Ghostbusters '84
It Came Upon a Midnight Clear '84
Heartaches '82
Flatbed Annie and Sweetiepie: Lady Truckers '79
Corvette Summer '78
King of the Gypsies '78

Cliff (Potter) Potts (1942-)
Sahara '83
The Last Ride of the Dalton Gang '79
Little Women '78
The Groundstar Conspiracy '72
Silent Running '71

Jonathan Potts
Jason X '01
Torso '01

Ely Pouget (1961-)
Total Reality '97
Death Machine '95
Lawnmower Man 2: Beyond Cyberspace '95
Red Shoe Diaries 5: Weekend Pass '95
Tall, Dark and Deadly '95
Silent Victim '92
Endless Descent '90
Cool Blue '88

Georges Poujouly
Frantic '58
Forbidden Games '52

CCH Pounder (1952-)
Boycott '02
Cora Unashamed '00
Disappearing Acts '00
End of Days '99
Final Justice '98
Tom Clancy's Netforce '98
Face/Off '97
Aladdin and the King of Thieves '96 (V)
If These Walls Could Talk '96
White Dwarf '95
Zooman '95
Tales from the Crypt Presents Demon Knight '94
Benny & Joon '93
The Disappearance of Christina '93
The Ernest Green Story '93
Lifepod '93
Question of Faith '93
Return to Lonesome Dove '93
Sliver '93
RoboCop 3 '91
Postcards from the Edge '90
Psycho 4: The Beginning '90
Bagdad Cafe '88
Prizzi's Honor '85
Union City '81

Melvil Poupaud (1973-)
Genealogies of a Crime '97
A Summer's Tale '96
Three Lives and Only One Death '96
Diary of a Seducer '95
The Lover '92

Henri Poupon
Harvest '37
Angele '34

Addison Powell
The Rosary Murders '87
The Man Without a Country '73

Brittney Powell
Dragonworld '94
Airborne '93
To Be the Best '93

Charles Powell (1963-)
Grey Owl '99
Screamers '96
Cheyenne Warrior '94

Clifton Powell
Bones '01
The Brothers '01
The Breaks '99
Selma, Lord, Selma '99
Caught Up '98
The Pentagon Wars '98
Phantoms '97
Dead Presidents '95

Dick Powell (1904-63)
Susan Slept Here '54
The Bad and the Beautiful '52
Cry Danger '51
Mrs. Mike '49
Pitfall '48
Station West '48
Cornered '45
It Happened Tomorrow '44
Murder, My Sweet '44
Star Spangled Rhythm '42
In the Navy '41
Christmas in July '40
On the Avenue '37
Gold Diggers of 1935 '35
A Midsummer Night's Dream '35
Dames '34
Flirtation Walk '34
Footlight Parade '33
42nd Street '33
Gold Diggers of 1933 '33
Blessed Event '32

Eleanor Powell (1912-82)
The Duchess of Idaho '50
Sensations of 1945 '44
I Dood It '43
Thousands Cheer '43
Ship Ahoy '42
Lady Be Good '41
Broadway Melody of 1940 '40
Honolulu '39
Rosalie '38
Broadway Melody of 1938 '37
Born to Dance '36
Broadway Melody of 1936 '35

Esteban Louis Powell
Hitman's Run '99
Powder '95

Jane Powell (1929-)
The Sandy Bottom Orchestra '00
Enchanted Island '58
The Girl Most Likely '57
Hit the Deck '55
Athena '54
Deep in My Heart '54
Seven Brides for Seven Brothers '54
Small Town Girl '53
Rich, Young and Pretty '51
Royal Wedding '51
Nancy Goes to Rio '50
Two Weeks with Love '50
A Date with Judy '48
Three Daring Daughters '48
Holiday in Mexico '46
Delightfully Dangerous '45

Lee Powell (1908-44)
Along the Sundown Trail '42
Prairie Pals '42
Tumbleweed Trail '42
Trigger Pals '39
Fighting Devil Dogs '38
The Lone Ranger '38

Marcus Powell
Kill by Inches '99
The Rejuvenator '88

Michael Powell (1905-90)
Peeping Tom '60
Edge of the World '37

Robert Powell (1944-)
The Mystery of Edwin Drood '93
The Jigsaw Man '84
Dark Forces '83
Shaka Zulu '83
What Waits Below '83
Frankenstein '82
The Hunchback of Notre Dame '82
Jane Austen in Manhattan '80
Survivor '80
The Thirty-Nine Steps '79
The Four Feathers '78
Jesus of Nazareth '77
Tommy '75
Mahler '74
The Asphyx '72
Asylum '72
Jude the Obscure '71
Secrets '71

William Powell (1892-1984)
Mister Roberts '55
The Girl Who Had Everything '53
How to Marry a Millionaire '53
Mr. Peabody & the Mermaid '48
Life with Father '47
The Senator Was Indiscreet '47
Song of the Thin Man '47
Ziegfeld Follies '46
The Thin Man Goes Home '44
Love Crazy '41
Shadow of the Thin Man '41
I Love You Again '40
Another Thin Man '39
Double Wedding '37
The Last of Mrs. Cheyney '37
After the Thin Man '36
Ex-Mrs. Bradford '36
The Great Ziegfeld '36
Libeled Lady '36
My Man Godfrey '36
Reckless '35
Star of Midnight '35
Evelyn Prentice '34
Fashions of 1934 '34
Manhattan Melodrama '34
The Thin Man '34
The Kennel Murder Case '33
Feel My Pulse '28
Last Command '28
Nevada '27
Romola '25

Power
Black and White '99
Belly '98

Chad Power
3 Ninjas Knuckle Up '95
3 Ninjas '92

Hartley Power
Dead of Night '45
Evergreen '34

Taryn Power (1953-)
Sinbad and the Eye of the Tiger '77
Tracks '76
The Count of Monte Cristo '74

Tyrone Power (1913-58)
Abandon Ship '57
Witness for the Prosecution '57
The Eddy Duchin Story '56
The Long Gray Line '55
Diplomatic Courier '52
Rawhide '50
Captain from Castile '47
The Razor's Edge '46
Crash Dive '43
The Black Swan '42
Son of Fury '42
Blood and Sand '41
A Yank in the R.A.F. '41
Brigham Young: Frontiersman '40
Johnny Apollo '40
The Mark of Zorro '40
Jesse James '39
The Rains Came '39
Rose of Washington Square '39
Second Fiddle '39
Alexander's Ragtime Band '38
Marie Antoinette '38
In Old Chicago '37
Thin Ice '37
Lloyds of London '36

Tyrone Power, Jr. (1959-)
Evil Lives '92
California Casanova '89
Shag: The Movie '89
Cocoon '85

Tyrone Power, Sr. (1869-1931)
Big Trail '30
Test of Donald Norton '26
Red Kimono '25
Dream Street '21

Alexandra Powers (1967-)
Double Down '01
Storm Tracker '99
Last Man Standing '96
The Seventh Coin '92
Cast a Deadly Spell '91
Dangerous Pursuit '89
Dead Poets Society '89
Sonny Boy '87
Mask '85

Beverly (Hills) Powers
Knights & Emeralds '87
Sixteen '72
Brides of the Beast '68
The Comedy of Terrors '64
Kissin' Cousins '64

Lucille Powers
Texas Bad Man '32
Two Gun Man '31

Mala Powers (1931-)
Daddy's Gone A-Hunting '69
Escape from Planet Earth '67
Storm Rider '57
Rage at Dawn '55
City That Never Sleeps '53
Cyrano de Bergerac '50

Stefanie Powers (1942-)
Scott Turow's The Burden of Proof '92
Shadow on the Sun '88
Family Secrets '84
Mistral's Daughter '84
Escape to Athena '79
Little Moon & Jud McGraw '78
The Invisible Strangler '76
The Man Inside '76
Return to Earth '76
Sky Hei$t '75
Herbie Rides Again '74
Manhunter '74
Gone with the West '72
No Place to Run '72
Paper Man '71
The Boatniks '70
Die! Die! My Darling! '65
Love Has Many Faces '65
McLintock! '63
Palm Springs Weekend '63
Experiment in Terror '62
The Interns '62

Tom Powers (1890-1955)
Lucky Me '54
Destination Moon '50
The Nevadan '50
Mexican Hayride '48
Station West '48
Up in Central Park '48
The Blue Dahlia '46
Double Indemnity '44

Vicki Powers
Deadly Encounter '78
The Meal '75

Leon Pownall
Dirty Pictures '00
Hiroshima '95
How the West Was Fun '95
Love and Hate: A Marriage Made in Hell '90
Bye Bye Blues '89
Termini Station '89

Clare Powney
The Girl '86
Operation Julie '85

Jose Maria Prada
The Diabolical Dr. Z '65
The Hunt '65

Bruno Pradal
Charlie Bravo '80s
November Moon '85

Lilia Prado (1929-)
The Illusion Travels by Streetcar '53
Wuthering Heights '53
Mexican Bus Ride '51

Jerome Pradon
Jesus Christ Superstar '00
Simon Sez '99

Michael Praed (1960-)
Darkness Falls '98
To Die For 2: Son of Darkness '91
Writer's Block '91
Riders '88
Nightflyers '87
Robin Hood...The Legend: Robin Hood and the Sorcerer '83
Robin Hood...The Legend: The Swords of Wayland '83

Stanley Prager (1917-72)
Gun Crazy '49
A Foreign Affair '48
You Gotta Stay Happy '48

Pras
Da Hip Hop Witch '00
Turn It Up '00

Joan Prather (1950-)
The Deerslayer '78
Devil's Rain '75
Smile '75
Big Bad Mama '74

Judson Pratt
The Horse Soldiers '59
Monster on the Campus '59

Keri Lynn Pratt
The Smokers '00
Cruel Intentions 2 '99

Kyla Pratt (1988-)
Dr. Dolittle 2 '01
Love and Basketball '00
Barney's Great Adventure '98
Dr. Dolittle '98

Susan May Pratt
Center Stage '00
Drive Me Crazy '99
Ten Things I Hate about You '99

George Pravda
The Duchess of Duke Street '78
Frankenstein Must Be Destroyed '69

Wolfgang Preiss (1910-)
Club Extinction '89
A Bridge Too Far '77
Raid on Rommel '71
Cave of the Living Dead '65
The Mad Executioners '65
The Train '65
Von Ryan's Express '65
The Invisible Dr. Mabuse '62
Testament of Dr. Mabuse '62
The Return of Dr. Mabuse '61
Mill of the Stone Women '60
The Thousand Eyes of Dr. Mabuse '60
Mistress of the World '59

June Preisser
Strike Up the Band '40
Babes in Arms '39

Albert Prejean (1893-1979)
Princess Tam Tam '35
Under the Roofs of Paris '29
Italian Straw Hat '27
The Crazy Ray '22

Otto Preminger (1906-86)
The Hobbit '78 (V)
Stalag 17 '53
They Got Me Covered '43

Luis Prendes (1913-98)
Alien Predators '80
The Christmas Kid '68
Ursus in the Valley of the Lions '62

Paula Prentiss (1939-)
Mrs. Winterbourne '96
M.A.D.D.: Mothers Against Drunk Driving '83
Packin' It In '83
Buddy Buddy '81
Saturday the 14th '81
The Black Marble '79
No Room to Run '78
The Stepford Wives '75
The Parallax View '74
Last of the Red Hot Lovers '72
Born to Win '71
Catch-22 '70
Bachelor in Paradise '69
In Harm's Way '65
What's New Pussycat? '65
The World of Henry Orient '64
Man's Favorite Sport? '63
The Horizontal Lieutenant '62
The Honeymoon Machine '61
Where the Boys Are '60

Robert Prescott
Blue De Ville '86
Real Genius '85
Bachelor Party '84

Micheline Presle (1922-)
A Chef in Love '96
Diary of a Seducer '95
Pas Tres Catholique '93
Legend of Frenchie King '71
The King of Hearts '66
The Nun '66
The Prize '63
Time Out for Love '61
Mistress of the World '59
The Bride Is Much Too Beautiful '58
Adventures of Captain Fabian '51
Devil in the Flesh '46
The Fantastic Night '42
The French Way '40

Elvis Presley (1935-77)
This Is Elvis '81
Change of Habit '69
Charro! '69
The Trouble with Girls (and How to Get into It) '69
Live a Little, Love a Little '68
Speedway '68
Stay Away, Joe '68
Clambake '67
Double Trouble '67
Easy Come, Easy Go '67
Paradise, Hawaiian Style '66
Spinout '66
Frankie and Johnny '65
Girl Happy '65
Harum Scarum '65
Tickle Me '65
Kissin' Cousins '64
Roustabout '64
Fun in Acapulco '63
It Happened at the World's Fair '63
Viva Las Vegas '63
Blue Hawaii '62
Girls! Girls! Girls! '62
Kid Galahad '62
Follow That Dream '61
Wild in the Country '61
Flaming Star '60
G.I. Blues '60
King Creole '58
Jailhouse Rock '57
Loving You '57
Love Me Tender '56

Priscilla Presley (1946-)
Naked Gun 33 1/3: The Final Insult '94
Naked Gun 2 1/2: The Smell of Fear '91
The Adventures of Ford Fairlane '90
The Naked Gun: From the Files of Police Squad '88

Harve Presnell (1933-)
Escanaba in da Moonlight '01
Jackie, Ethel, Joan: The Kennedy Women '01
The Legend of Bagger Vance '00
A Bright Shining Lie '98
Everything That Rises '98
Patch Adams '98
Saving Private Ryan '98
Face/Off '97
Julian Po '97
Fargo '96
Larger Than Life '96
The Whole Wide World '96
Paint Your Wagon '69
The Unsinkable Molly Brown '64

Jaime Pressly (1977-)
Joe Dirt '01
Not Another Teen Movie '01
Ticker '01
Tomcats '01
100 Girls '00
Poor White Trash '00
Ringmaster '98
Poison Ivy 3: The New Seduction '97

Lawrence Pressman (1939-)
American Pie '99
The Maker '98
Mighty Joe Young '98
The Late Shift '96
Sunchaser '96
Trial and Error '96
Angus '95
White Hot: The Mysterious Murder of Thelma Todd '91
Fire and Rain '89
Hanoi Hilton '87
The Deliberate Stranger '86
On Wings of Eagles '86
For Love or Money '84
The Winds of War '83
Rehearsal for Murder '82
The Gathering: Part 2 '79
The Gathering '77
The Trial of Lee Harvey Oswald '77
Rich Man, Poor Man '76
The Man in the Glass Booth '75
The Hellstrom Chronicle '71
Shaft '71

Jason Presson (1971-)
The Lady in White '88
Saturday the 14th Strikes Back '88
Explorers '85
The Stone Boy '84

Billy Preston (1946-)
Wired '89
Blame It on the Night '84
Let It Be '70

Cyndy Preston
Total Recall 2070: Machine Dreams '99
Black Fox: The Price of Peace '94
Whale Music '94
Prom Night 3: The Last Kiss '89
The Brain '88
Pin... '88
The Darkside '87

Cynthia Preston
Facing the Enemy '00
Premonition '98

J.A. Preston
Harvest of Fire '95
A Few Good Men '92
Fire Birds '90
Remo Williams: The Adventure Begins '85
Body Heat '81
The Spook Who Sat by the Door '73

Kelly Preston (1963-)
Battlefield Earth '00
For Love of the Game '99
Holy Man '98
Jack Frost '98
Addicted to Love '96
Citizen Ruth '96
Jerry Maguire '96
Nothing to Lose '96
From Dusk Till Dawn '95
Mrs. Munck '95
Cheyenne Warrior '94
Double Cross '94
Love Is a Gun '94
Only You '92
The Perfect Bride '91
Run '91
The Experts '89
The Spellbinder '88
Twins '88
Amazon Women on the Moon '87
Love at Stake '87
A Tiger's Tale '87
52 Pick-Up '86
SpaceCamp '86
Mischief '85
Secret Admirer '85
Christine '84
Metalstorm: The Destruction of Jared Syn '83

Mike (Michael) Preston (1938-)
Blade in Hong Kong '85
Hot Pursuit '84
Metalstorm: The Destruction of Jared Syn '83
The Road Warrior '82
Surabaya Conspiracy '75

Robert Preston (1918-87)
Outrage! '86
Finnegan Begin Again '84
The Last Starfighter '84
September Gun '83
Rehearsal for Murder '82
Victor/Victoria '82
S.O.B. '81
The Chisholms '79
Semi-Tough '77
My Father's House '75
Mame '74
Junior Bonner '72
How the West Was Won '63
The Music Man '62
Savage Wilderness '55
Face to Face '52
My Outlaw Brother '51
Best of the Badmen '50
Tulsa '49
Blood on the Moon '48
Reap the Wild Wind '42
This Gun for Hire '42
Wake Island '42
Beau Geste '39
Union Pacific '39

Wayde Preston
Smokey & the Judge '80
Today We Kill, Tomorrow We Die '71

Giancarlo (Timothy Brent) Prete (1942-2001)
Escape from the Bronx '85
Tornado '83
Warriors of the Wasteland '83
Sting of the West '76

Daniel Prevost
The Dinner Game '98
Uranus '91

Francoise Prevost (1930-97)
L'Amour en Herbe '77
Spirits of the Dead '68
Time Out for Love '61
Love Play '60
Paris Belongs to Us '60

Marie Prevost (1898-1937)
Tango '36
Hands Across the Table '35
The Sin of Madelon Claudet '31
The Flying Fool '29
Party Girls '29
The Marriage Circle '24
Yankee Doodle in Berlin '19

Alan Price
Oh, Alfie '75
O Lucky Man! '73

Dennis Price (1915-73)
Horror Hospital '73
Theatre of Blood '73
Pulp '72
The Screaming Dead '72
Twins of Evil '71
The Horror of Frankenstein '70
Venus in Furs '70
Murder Most Foul '65
Cool Mikado '63
The V.I.P.'s '63
The Wrong Arm of the Law '63
What a Carve-Up! '62
Victim '61
The Millionairess '60
No Love for Johnnie '60
Tunes of Glory '60
The Naked Truth '58
The Adventurers '51
Kind Hearts and Coronets '49
Dear Murderer '47
The Magic Bow '47
Echo Murders '45
A Canterbury Tale '44

Hal Price (1886-1964)
Rustler's Hideout '44
Trigger Men '41
Across the Plains '39
Man from Texas '39
Melody of the Plains '37
Where Trails Divide '37
Cavalry '36
Desert Phantom '36

Kate Price
Linda '29
Amarilly of Clothesline Alley '18

Marc Price (1968-)
Killer Tomatoes Eat France '91
The Rescue '88
Trick or Treat '86

Molly Price (1966-)
Chasing Sleep '00
Kiss Me, Guido '97
Risk '94
Jersey Girl '92

Nancy Price (1880-1970)
The Three Weird Sisters '48
Secret Mission '42
The Speckled Band '31

Richard Price (1949-)
Night and the City '92
Shocker '89
Wanderers '79

Stanley Price (1892-1955)
The Invisible Monster '50
Rangeland Empire '50
Sudden Death '50
The Driftin' Kid '41
Dynamite Canyon '41
The Singing Cowgirl '39

Sue Price
Nemesis 4: Cry of Angels '97
Nemesis 3: Time Lapse '96
Nemesis 2: Nebula '94

Vincent Price (1911-93)
The Thief and the Cobbler '96 (V)
Edward Scissorhands '90
Once Upon a Midnight Scary '90 (N)
Backtrack '89
Dead Heat '88
The Offspring '87
The Whales of August '87
Escapes '86
The Great Mouse Detective '86 (V)
Bloodbath at the House of Death '85
The Monster Club '85
Pogo for President: "I Go Pogo" '84 (V)
Snow White and the Seven Dwarfs '83
House of the Long Shadows '82
The Boy Who Left Home to Find Out About the Shivers '81 (V)
Ruddigore '70s
Scavenger Hunt '79
Butterfly Ball '76 (N)
It's Not the Size That Counts '74
Journey into Fear '74
Madhouse '74
Theatre of Blood '73
Doctor Phibes Rises Again '72
The Abominable Dr. Phibes '71
Cry of the Banshee '70
Scream and Scream Again '70
The Oblong Box '69
The Trouble with Girls (and How to Get into It) '69
The Conqueror Worm '68
Spirits of the Dead '68 (N)
The House of 1000 Dolls '67
The Jackals '67
Dr. Goldfoot and the Bikini Machine '66
Masque of the Red Death '65
The Comedy of Terrors '64
The Last Man on Earth '64
Nefertiti, Queen of the Nile '64
Pirate Warrior '64
Tomb of Ligeia '64
Beach Party '63
Diary of a Madman '63
The Haunted Palace '63
The Raven '63
Twice-Told Tales '63
Tales of Terror '62
Tower of London '62
Master of the World '61
The Pit and the Pendulum '61
The Fall of the House of Usher '60
The Bat '59
Return of the Fly '59
The Tingler '59
The Fly '58
House on Haunted Hill '58
The Ten Commandments '56
While the City Sleeps '56
Son of Sinbad '55
Casanova's Big Night '54
Dangerous Mission '54
House of Wax '53
The Las Vegas Story '52
Adventures of Captain Fabian '51
Baron of Arizona '51
His Kind of Woman '51
Champagne for Caesar '50
Bagdad '49
Abbott and Costello Meet Frankenstein '48 (V)
The Three Musketeers '48
Up in Central Park '48
The Long Night '47
Shock! '46
Leave Her to Heaven '45
The Keys of the Kingdom '44
Laura '44
Wilson '44
The Song of Bernadette '43

Brigham Young: Frontiersman *'40*
The House of the Seven Gables *'40*
The Invisible Man Returns *'40*
The Private Lives of Elizabeth & Essex *'39*
The Tower of London *'39*

Robert Prichard
Alien Space Avenger *'91*
Class of Nuke 'Em High *'86*
The Toxic Avenger *'86*

Dan Priest
Rattlers *'76*
Black Like Me *'64*

Martin Priest
Zebrahead *'92*
The Plot Against Harry *'69*
Nothing but a Man *'64*

Pat Priest (1936-)
Some Call It Loving *'73*
The Incredible Two-Headed Transplant *'71*
Easy Come, Easy Go *'67*

Jason Priestley (1969-)
Cherish *'02*
Double Down *'01*
Common Ground *'00*
Homicide: The Movie *'00*
Kiss Tomorrow Goodbye *'00*
Eye of the Beholder *'99*
The Highway Man *'99*
Love and Death on Long Island *'97*
Sink or Swim *'97*
Coldblooded *'94*
Calendar Girl *'93*
Tombstone *'93*
Nowhere to Run *'88*
The Boy Who Could Fly *'86*

Aurore Prieto
Dr. Petiot *'90*
Therese *'86*

Paco Christian Prieto
Street Law *'95*
Only the Strong *'93*

Suzy Prim
Heart of a Nation *'43*
The Lower Depths *'36*

Louis Prima
The Jungle Book *'67 (V)*
Manhattan Merry-Go-Round *'37*

Barry Primus (1938-)
James Dean *'01*
Elmore Leonard's Gold Coast *'97*
Crime of the Century *'96*
Flipping *'96*
Trade Off *'95*
Night and the City *'92*
Denial: The Dark Side of Passion *'91*
Guilty by Suspicion *'91*
Cannibal Women in the Avocado Jungle of Death *'89*
Torn Apart *'89*
Big Business *'88*
The Stranger *'87*
Down and Out in Beverly Hills *'86*
Brotherly Love *'85*
Talking Walls *'85*
Shooting *'82*
Absence of Malice *'81*
Heartland *'81*
Night Games *'80*
New York, New York *'77*
Autopsy *'74*
Boxcar Bertha *'72*

Prince (1958-)
Graffiti Bridge *'90*
Under the Cherry Moon *'86*
Purple Rain *'84*

Clayton Prince
Dark Justice *'91*
Hairspray *'88*

Faith Prince (1957-)
A Season for Miracles *'99*
Picture Perfect *'96*
Big Bully *'95*
Dave *'93*
My Father the Hero *'93*
The Last Dragon *'85*

Jonathan Prince
Private School *'83*
Pray TV *'82*

William Prince (1913-96)
The Portrait *'93*
The Taking of Beverly Hills *'91*
Second Sight *'89*
Spontaneous Combustion *'89*
Vice Versa *'88*
Nuts *'87*
Spies Like Us *'85*
The Soldier *'82*
City in Fear *'80*
The Promise *'79*
Johnny We Hardly Knew Ye *'77*
Family Plot *'76*
The Stepford Wives *'75*
Justice *'55*
Cyrano de Bergerac *'50*
Lust for Gold *'49*
Carnegie Hall *'47*
Dead Reckoning *'47*
Objective, Burma! *'45*
Destination Tokyo *'43*

Victoria Principal (1950-)
The Abduction *'96*
Scott Turow's The Burden of Proof *'92*
Nightmare *'91*
Blind Witness *'89*
Naked Lie *'89*
Mistress *'87*
Pleasure Palace *'80*
Fantasy Island *'76*
I Will, I Will for Now *'76*
Earthquake *'74*
Life & Times of Judge Roy Bean *'72*

Andrew Prine (1936-)
Without Evidence *'96*
Serial Killer *'95*
Deadly Exposure *'93*
Gettysburg *'93*
Mission of the Shark *'91*
Chill Factor *'90*
The Eliminators *'86*
The Last of the Mohicans *'85*
Donner Pass: The Road to Survival *'84*
They're Playing with Fire *'84*
V *'83*
Amityville 2: The Possession *'82*
Callie and Son *'81*
A Small Killing *'81*
The Evil *'78*
The Christmas Coal Mine Miracle *'77*
Grizzly *'76*
Riding with Death *'76*
Town That Dreaded Sundown *'76*
The Centerfold Girls *'74*
Barn of the Naked Dead *'73*
Crypt of the Living Dead *'73*
One Little Indian *'73*
Simon, King of the Witches *'71*
Generation *'69*
Bandolero! *'68*
The Devil's Brigade *'68*
Texas across the River *'66*
The Miracle Worker *'62*

Aileen Pringle (1895-1989)
Sons of Steel *'35*
Jane Eyre *'34*
Convicted *'32*
Murder at Midnight *'31*

Bryan Pringle (1935-)
Getting It Right *'89*
Haunted Honeymoon *'86*
Saturday Night and Sunday Morning *'60*

Joan Pringle
Original Sin *'01*
J.D.'s Revenge *'76*

Sandra Prinsloo
Claws *'85*
The Gods Must Be Crazy *'84*
The Outcast *'84*
African Rage *'78*

Freddie Prinze, Jr. (1976-)
Scooby-Doo *'02*
Head Over Heels *'01*
Summer Catch *'01*
Boys and Girls *'00*
Down to You *'00*
She's All That *'99*
Sparkler *'99*
Wing Commander *'99*
I Still Know What You Did Last Summer *'98*
Money Kings *'98*
Hostage High *'97*
The House of Yes *'97*
I Know What You Did Last Summer *'97*
To Gillian on Her 37th Birthday *'96*

Ted Prior
The P.A.C.K. *'96*
Mutant Species *'95*
Possessed by the Night *'93*
Center of the Web *'92*
Raw Nerve *'91*
Future Zone *'90*
Born Killer *'89*
Final Sanction *'89*
Hardcase and Fist *'89*
Jungle Assault *'89*
Hell on the Battleground *'88*
Deadly Prey *'87*
Killer Workout *'86*
Killzone *'85*
Sledgehammer *'83*

Albert Priscoe
The Prairie King *'27*
The Love Light *'21*

David Pritchard
Slashed Dreams *'74*
The Devil's Brigade *'68*

Michael Pritchard
Lightblast *'85*
Massive Retaliation *'85*

Lucien Prival (1900-94)
Panama Menace *'41*
Hell's Angels *'30*
Party Girls *'29*

Juergen Prochnow (1941-)
Dark Asylum *'01*
Ripper: Letter from Hell *'01*
Heaven's Fire *'99*
The Last Stop *'99*
Wing Commander *'99*
Esther *'98*
The Fall *'98*
The Replacement Killers *'98*
Air Force One *'97*
DNA *'97*
Human Bomb *'97*
The English Patient *'96*
In the Mouth of Madness *'95*
Jack Higgins' On Dangerous Ground *'95*
Judge Dredd *'95*
The Other Side of the Law *'95*
Lie Down with Lions *'94*
The Fire Next Time *'93*
Body of Evidence *'92*
Hurricane Smith *'92*
Interceptor *'92*
Twin Peaks: Fire Walk with Me *'92*
Robin Hood *'91*
The Fourth War *'90*
Kill Cruise *'90*
The Man Inside *'90*
A Dry White Season *'89*
The Seventh Sign *'88*
Beverly Hills Cop 2 *'87*
The Cop & the Girl *'86*
Blitz *'85*
Forbidden *'85*
My Sweet Victim *'85*
Dune *'84*
The Keep *'83*
Das Boot *'81*
The Lost Honor of Katharina Blum *'75*
Tenderness of the Wolves *'73*

Emily (Proctor) Procter (1968-)
Body Shots *'99*
Guinevere *'99*
Breast Men *'97*

Marland Proctor
Terrorists *'83*
All the Lovin' Kinfolk *'70*

Phil(ip) Proctor (1940-)
The Rugrats Movie *'98 (V)*
Lobster Man from Mars *'89*
J-Men Forever! *'79*

Luigi Proietti
Revenge of the Musketeers *'94*
The Libertine *'69*

Melissa Prophet
Invasion U.S.A. *'85*
Better Late Than Never *'83*
Van Nuys Blvd. *'79*

Robert Prosky (1930-)
Dudley Do-Right *'99*
Mad City *'97*
The Chamber *'96*
Dead Man Walking *'95*
The Scarlet Letter *'95*
Miracle on 34th Street *'94*
Hit Woman: The Double Edge *'93*
Last Action Hero *'93*
Mrs. Doubtfire *'93*
Rudy *'93*
Far and Away *'92*
Hoffa *'92*
Teamster Boss: The Jackie Presser Story *'92*
Age Isn't Everything *'91*
Funny About Love *'90*
Green Card *'90*
Gremlins 2: The New Batch *'90*
From the Dead of Night *'89*
Things Change *'88*
Big Shots *'87*
Broadcast News *'87*
The Murder of Mary Phagan *'87*
World War III *'86*
Into Thin Air *'85*
Christine *'84*
The Natural *'84*
The Keep *'83*
The Lords of Discipline *'83*
Thief *'81*

Jed Prouty (1879-1956)
Remedy for Riches *'40*
Danger on the Air *'38*
100 Men and a Girl *'37*
Small Town Boy *'37*
Broadway Melody *'29*
Ella Cinders *'26*

David Proval (1942-)
Double Down *'01*
Mob Queen *'98*
The Siege *'98*
Flipping *'96*
The Phantom *'96*
Four Rooms *'95*
To the Limit *'95*
Romeo Is Bleeding *'93*
Innocent Blood *'92*
Vice Versa *'88*
Wizards *'77 (V)*
Mean Streets *'73*

Dorothy Provine (1937-)
Never a Dull Moment *'68*
Who's Minding the Mint? *'67*
That Darn Cat *'65*
Good Neighbor Sam *'64*
It's a Mad, Mad, Mad, Mad World *'63*
The 30-Foot Bride of Candy Rock *'59*

Jon(athan) Provost (1950-)
This Property Is Condemned *'66*
Lassie's Great Adventure *'62*
Escapade in Japan *'57*
All Mine to Give *'56*

David Prowse (1935-)
Return of the Jedi *'83*
The Empire Strikes Back *'80*
Jabberwocky *'77*
Star Wars *'77*
Frankenstein and the Monster from Hell *'74*
Blacksnake! *'73*
A Clockwork Orange *'71*
Vampire Circus *'71*
The Horror of Frankenstein *'70*

Juliet Prowse (1937-96)
Dingaka *'65*
Can-Can *'60*
G.I. Blues *'60*

Anna Prucnall
City of Women *'81*
Sweet Movie *'75*

Harold P. Pruett (1969-2002)
The Perfect Daughter *'96*
Precious Find *'96*
Spellcaster *'91*
Summer Camp Nightmare *'86*

Karl Pruner
Finding Buck McHenry *'00*
Total Recall 2070: Machine Dreams *'99*
The Fixer *'97*

Jonathan Pryce (1947-)
The Affair of the Necklace *'01*
Bride of the Wind *'01*
Robert Louis Stevenson's The Game of Death *'99*
Stigmata *'99*
Ronin *'98*
Behind the Lines *'97*
David *'97*
Tomorrow Never Dies *'97*
Evita *'96*
Carrington *'95*
A Troll in Central Park *'94 (V)*
The Age of Innocence *'93*
Barbarians at the Gate *'93*
A Business Affair *'93*
Deadly Advice *'93*
Shades of Fear *'93*
Shopping *'93*
Thicker Than Water *'93*
Freddie the Frog *'92 (V)*
Glengarry Glen Ross *'92*
The Adventures of Baron Munchausen *'89*
The Man from the Pru *'89*
The Rachel Papers *'89*
Consuming Passions *'88*
Man on Fire *'87*
Haunted Honeymoon *'86*
Jumpin' Jack Flash *'86*
Brazil *'85*
The Doctor and the Devils *'85*
Loophole *'83*
The Ploughman's Lunch *'83*
Praying Mantis *'83*
Something Wicked This Way Comes *'83*
Breaking Glass *'80*
Voyage of the Damned *'76*

Nicholas Pryor (1935-)
American Tragedy *'00*
Hail Caesar *'94*
Hoffa *'92*
Pacific Heights *'90*
Brain Dead *'89*
Nightbreaker *'89*
Morgan Stewart's Coming Home *'87*
The Falcon and the Snowman *'85*
Into Thin Air *'85*
Risky Business *'83*
East of Eden *'80*
The $5.20 an Hour Dream *'80*
Last Song *'80*
The Fish that Saved Pittsburgh *'79*
Damien: Omen 2 *'78*
Gumball Rally *'76*
The Life and Assassination of the Kingfish *'76*
Night Terror *'76*
Force Five *'75*
The Happy Hooker *'75*
Smile *'75*

Richard Pryor (1940-)
Lost Highway *'96*
Trigger Happy *'96*
Another You *'91*
Harlem Nights *'89*
See No Evil, Hear No Evil *'89*
Moving *'88*
Critical Condition *'86*
Jo Jo Dancer, Your Life Is Calling *'86*
Brewster's Millions *'85*
Superman 3 *'83*
Some Kind of Hero *'82*
The Toy *'82*
Bustin' Loose *'81*
In God We Trust *'80*
Stir Crazy *'80*
Wholly Moses! *'80*
Blue Collar *'78*
California Suite *'78*
The Wiz *'78*
Greased Lightning *'77*
Which Way Is Up? *'77*
Bingo Long Traveling All-Stars & Motor Kings *'76*
Car Wash *'76*
Silver Streak *'76*
Adios Amigo *'75*
Uptown Saturday Night *'74*
Hit! *'73*
The Mack *'73*
Some Call It Loving *'73*
Lady Sings the Blues *'72*
Dynamite Chicken *'70*
Black Brigade *'69*
Wild in the Streets *'68*

Roger Pryor (1901-74)
Identity Unknown *'45*
Kid Sister *'45*
Meet the Mob *'42*
Panama Menace *'41*
The Man They Could Not Hang *'39*
Headline Woman *'35*
Belle of the Nineties *'34*
Lady by Choice *'34*

Wojciech (Wojtek Psoniak) Pszoniak (1942-)
Angry Harvest *'85*
Danton *'82*
Land of Promise *'74*

Tito Puente (1925-2000)
The Mambo Kings *'92*
Radio Days *'87*

Robert Pugh
Enigma *'01*
A Mind to Murder *'96*
Priest *'94*
Thicker Than Water *'93*
Danger UXB *'81*

Willard Pugh
Puppet Master 5: The Final Chapter *'94*
CB4: The Movie *'93*
Ambition *'91*
A Rage in Harlem *'91*
Native Son *'86*
The Color Purple *'85*

Frank Puglia (1892-1975)
Girls! Girls! Girls! *'62*
20 Million Miles to Earth *'57*
The Black Hand *'50*
Bagdad *'49*
Without Reservations *'46*
Ali Baba and the Forty Thieves *'43*
For Whom the Bell Tolls *'43*
Casablanca *'42*
Billy the Kid *'41*
The Fatal Hour *'40*

Bulldog Drummond's Revenge '37
Viva Villa! '34
Romola '25

Aldo Puglisi
Marriage Italian Style '64
Seduced and Abandoned '64

Benjamin Pullen
Intern '00
An Ideal Husband '99
Prince Valiant '97

Keisha Knight Pulliam (1979-)
A Connecticut Yankee in King Arthur's Court '89
The Little Match Girl '87

Bill Pullman (1953-)
Igby Goes Down '02
Lucky Numbers '00
Titan A.E. '00 (V)
Brokedown Palace '99
The Guilty '99
Lake Placid '99
Spy Games '99
The Virginian '99
The End of Violence '97
Zero Effect '97
Independence Day '96
Lost Highway '96
Mistrial '96
Casper '95
Mr. Wrong '95
While You Were Sleeping '95
The Last Seduction '94
Wyatt Earp '94
Malice '93
Nervous Ticks '93
Sleepless in Seattle '93
Sommersby '93
Crazy in Love '92
The Favor '92
A League of Their Own '92
Newsies '92
Singles '92
Bright Angel '91
Going Under '91
Liebestraum '91
Sibling Rivalry '90
Brain Dead '89
Cold Feet '89
The Accidental Tourist '88
Rocket Gibraltar '88
The Serpent and the Rainbow '87
Spaceballs '87
Ruthless People '86

Lilo (Liselotte) Pulver (1929-)
The Nun '66
A Global Affair '63
A Time to Love & a Time to Die '58

Bernard Punsley
Angels with Dirty Faces '38
Dead End '37

Dick Purcell (1908-44)
Captain America '44
Timber Queen '44
Phantom Killer '42
X Marks the Spot '42
King of the Zombies '41
The Abe Lincoln of Ninth Avenue '39
Heroes in Blue '39
Irish Luck '39
Tough Kid '39

James Purcell
Playroom '90
White Light '90

Lee Purcell (1957-)
Movies Money Murder '96
Long Road Home '91
The Incredible Hulk Returns '88
To Heal a Nation '88
Jailbait: Betrayed By Innocence '86
Space Rage '86
Eddie Macon's Run '83
Valley Girl '83
Homework '82
Killing at Hell's Gate '81
Kenny Rogers as the Gambler '80
Stir Crazy '80
Big Wednesday '78
Summer of Fear '78
The Amazing Howard Hughes '77
Mr. Majestyk '74
The Witching '72
Adam at 6 a.m. '70

Noel Purcell (1900-85)
Mutiny on the Bounty '62
Lust for Life '56
Land of Fury '55
Encore '52
Captain Boycott '47

Reginald Purdell (1896-1953)
Brighton Rock '47
Candles at Nine '44
Clouds over Europe '39
The Old Curiosity Shop '35

Edmund Purdom (1924-)
After the Fall of New York '85
Don't Open Till Christmas '84
Ator the Fighting Eagle '83
Big Boss '77
Mr. Scarface '77
Dr. Frankenstein's Castle of Freaks '74
Rulers of the City '71
Nefertiti, Queen of the Nile '64
Herod the Great '60
The King's Thief '55
The Prodigal '55
Athena '54
The Egyptian '54
The Student Prince '54

Carolyn Purdy-Gordon
Dolls '87
From Beyond '86
Re-Animator '84

James Purefoy (1964-)
Resident Evil '02
A Knight's Tale '01
Don Quixote '00
Dead of Night '99
Mansfield Park '99
Maybe Baby '99
Bedrooms and Hallways '98
Catherine Cookson's The Tide of Life '96
The Tenant of Wildfell Hall '96
Feast of July '95

Om Puri
East Is East '99
Such a Long Journey '98
My Son the Fanatic '97
The Ghost and the Darkness '96
Brothers in Trouble '95
In Custody '94
Wolf '94
City of Joy '92

Linda Purl (1953-)
Perfect Tenant '99
Mighty Joe Young '98
Incident at Deception Ridge '94
Natural Causes '94
Accidental Meeting '93
In Self Defense '93
Body Language '92
Spies, Lies and Naked Thighs '91
Web of Deceit '90
Viper '88
Outrage! '86
Visiting Hours '82
The Adventures of Nellie Bly '81
High Country '81
The Manions of America '81
The Night the City Screamed '80
The Flame Is Love '79
Last Cry for Help '79
Little Ladies of the Night '77
Eleanor & Franklin '76
The Young Pioneers '76
Crazy Mama '75

Edna Purviance (1894-1958)
The Chaplin Revue '58
The Kid '21
Three Charlies and One Phoney! '18
The Cure '17
The Immigrant '17
Burlesque on Carmen '16
The Fireman '16
The Vagabond '16
Charlie Chaplin: Night at the Show '15
Charlie Chaplin ... Our Hero! '15
Tramp & a Woman '15

Alexandra Purvis (1988-)
Ronnie and Julie '97
Contagious '96
Poltergeist: The Legacy '96

John Putch (1961-)
Same River Twice '97
The Souler Opposite '97
Fallen Angels 2 '93
Curfew '88
Impure Thoughts '86
Jaws 3 '83

Hy Pyke
Halloween Night '90
Lemora, Lady Dracula '73

Denver Pyle (1920-97)
Maverick '94
Legend of the Northwest '78
Mountain Man '77
Hawmps! '76
Winterhawk '76
The Adventures of Frontier Fremont '75
Life & Times of Grizzly Adams '74
Murder or Mercy '74
The Legend of Hillbilly John '73
Bonnie & Clyde '67
The Rounders '65
Shenandoah '65
Geronimo '62
The Man Who Shot Liberty Valance '62
The Alamo '60
The Horse Soldiers '59
Naked Hills '56
Seventh Cavalry '56
To Hell and Back '55
Ride Clear of Diablo '54
Johnny Guitar '53
Hills of Utah '51
Oklahoma Annie '51
Dynamite Pass '50
Rim of the Canyon '49
Too Late for Tears '49
Where the North Begins '47

Missi Pyle (1973-)
Josie and the Pussycats '01
Galaxy Quest '99
Trick '99
As Good As It Gets '97

John Pyper-Ferguson
The Tempest '99
For Richer or Poorer '97
Drive '96
Hard Core Logo '96
Space Marines '96
Killer Image '92
Showdown at Williams Creek '91

Xu Qing
The Emperor's Shadow '96
Life on a String '90

John Quade
And You Thought Your Parents Were Weird! '91
The Tracker '88
Tigershark '87
Fury to Freedom: The Life Story of Raul Ries '85
Dirkham Detective Agency '83
Peter Lundy and the Medicine Hat Stallion '77
Night Terror '76
The Outlaw Josey Wales '76

Stephen Quadros
Auntie Lee's Meat Pies '92
C.I.A.: Code Name Alexa '92
Shock 'Em Dead '90

Buddy Quaid
Psycho Beach Party '00
Ice House '89

Dennis Quaid (1954-)
The Rookie '02
Dinner with Friends '01
Frequency '00
Traffic '00
Any Given Sunday '99
Everything That Rises '98
The Parent Trap '98
Playing by Heart '98
Savior '98
Switchback '97
Dragonheart '96
Gang Related '96
Something to Talk About '95
Wyatt Earp '94
Flesh and Bone '93
Undercover Blues '93
Wilder Napalm '93
Come See the Paradise '90
Postcards from the Edge '90
Great Balls of Fire '89
D.O.A. '88
Everybody's All American '88
The Big Easy '87
Innerspace '87
Suspect '87
Enemy Mine '85
Dreamscape '84
Bill: On His Own '83
Jaws 3 '83
The Right Stuff '83
Tough Enough '83
Johnny Belinda '82
All Night Long '81
Bill '81
Caveman '81
The Night the Lights Went Out in Georgia '81
Gorp '80
The Long Riders '80
Breaking Away '79
The Seniors '78
I Never Promised You a Rose Garden '77
September 30, 1955 '77

Randy Quaid (1953-)
The Adventures of Pluto Nash '02
Not Another Teen Movie '01
The Adventures of Rocky & Bullwinkle '00
Sand '00
Bug Buster '99
The Magical Legend of the Leprechauns '99
Purgatory '99
Last Rites '98
P.U.N.K.S. '98
Hard Rain '97
Protector '97
Get On the Bus '96
Independence Day '96
Kingpin '96
Last Dance '96
Moonshine Highway '96
Vegas Vacation '96
Larry McMurtry's Streets of Laredo '95
Legends of the North '95
Woman Undone '95
Bye Bye, Love '94
Curse of the Starving Class '94
Major League 2 '94
Next Door '94
The Paper '94
Frankenstein '93
Freaked '93
Days of Thunder '90
Martians Go Home! '90
Quick Change '90
Texasville '90
Bloodhounds of Broadway '89
National Lampoon's Christmas Vacation '89
Out Cold '89
Parents '89
Caddyshack 2 '88
Dead Solid Perfect '88
LBJ: The Early Years '88
Moving '88
No Man's Land '87
Sweet Country '87
The Wraith '87
Fool for Love '86
The Slugger's Wife '85
A Streetcar Named Desire '84
The Wild Life '84
National Lampoon's Vacation '83
Inside the Third Reich '82
Heartbeeps '81
Of Mice and Men '81
Foxes '80
The Guyana Tragedy: The Story of Jim Jones '80
The Long Riders '80
To Race the Wind '80
The Last Ride of the Dalton Gang '79
Midnight Express '78
The Choirboys '77
Three Warriors '77
Bound for Glory '76
Missouri Breaks '76
Breakout '75
The Apprenticeship of Duddy Kravitz '74
The Last Detail '73
Paper Moon '73
What's Up, Doc? '72
The Last Picture Show '71
Targets '68

John Qualen (1899-1987)
I'll Take Sweden '65
A Patch of Blue '65
Those Calloways '65
Cheyenne Autumn '64
7 Faces of Dr. Lao '63
The Man Who Shot Liberty Valance '62
Terror in the Haunted House '58
The Searchers '56
At Gunpoint '55
Sea Chase '55
Passion '54
The Fugitive '48
The Scar '48
Song of Scheherazade '47
Adventure '45
Captain Kidd '45
Dark Waters '44
Casablanca '42
The Jungle Book '42
Tortilla Flat '42
The Devil & Daniel Webster '41
Angels Over Broadway '40
Blondie On a Budget '40
The Grapes of Wrath '40
His Girl Friday '40
Knute Rockne: All American '40
The Long Voyage Home '40
Black Fury '35
Charlie Chan in Paris '35
Our Daily Bread '34

DJ Qualls (1978-)
The New Guy '02
Chasing Holden '01
Road Trip '00

Tonya Qualls
Vampire Centerfolds '98
Vampire Conspiracy '96

Jonathan Ke Quan
Breathing Fire '91
The Goonies '85

Robert Quarry (1924-)
Teenage Exorcist '93
Evil Spirits '91
Spirits '90
Alienator '89
Warlords '88
Commando Squad '87
Cyclone '87
Phantom Empire '87
Madhouse '74
Doctor Phibes Rises Again '72
The Return of Count Yorga '71
Count Yorga, Vampire '70
Crime of Passion '57
Soldier of Fortune '55

Hugh Quarshie
The Murder of Stephen Lawrence '01
Star Wars: Episode 1—The Phantom Menace '99
To Walk with Lions '99
The Church '98

Philip Quast
Ultraviolet '98
Napoleon '96 (V)
Around the World in 80 Ways '86

James Quattrochi
True Friends '98
Wanted '98

Anna Quayle (1936-)
Mistress Pamela '74
Naughty Knights '71
Chitty Chitty Bang Bang '68
Smashing Time '67
Arrivederci, Baby! '66
A Hard Day's Night '64

Anthony Quayle (1913-89)
The Endless Game '89
The Bourne Identity '88
Buster '88
Magdalene '88
Misunderstood '87
The Key to Rebecca '85
Masada '81
Murder by Decree '79
The Chosen '77
The Eagle Has Landed '77
Moses '76
The Story of David '76
21 Hours at Munich '76
QB VII '74
The Tamarind Seed '74
Everything You Always Wanted to Know about Sex (But Were Afraid to Ask) '72
Anne of the Thousand Days '69
MacKenna's Gold '69
Barefoot in Athens '66
A Study in Terror '66
Operation Crossbow '65
The Fall of the Roman Empire '64
Damn the Defiant '62
Lawrence of Arabia '62
The Guns of Navarone '61
It Takes a Thief '59
Pursuit of the Graf Spee '57
The Wrong Man '56
Hamlet '48

Queen Latifah (1970-)
The Bone Collector '99
Living Out Loud '98
Mama Flora's Family '98
Sphere '97
Hoodlum '96
Set It Off '96
My Life '93
House Party 2: The Pajama Jam '91

Valerie Quennessen (1957-89)
Conan the Barbarian '82
Summer Lovers '82
French Postcards '79

John Quentin
The Stendahl Syndrome '95
Blue '93 (N)
Wittgenstein '93
The Terrorists '74
Isadora '68

Mae Questel (1908-98)
National Lampoon's Christmas Vacation '89
New York Stories '89
Who Framed Roger Rabbit '88 (V)
A Majority of One '56

Hugues Quester
Trois Couleurs: Bleu '93
A Tale of Springtime '89

Diana Quick (1946-)
Heat of the Sun *'99*
The Leading Man *'96*
Rasputin: Dark Servant of Destiny *'96*
Nostradamus *'93*
The Misadventures of Mr. Wilt *'90*
Ordeal by Innocence *'84*
Brideshead Revisited *'81*
The Duellists *'77*

Charles Quigley (1906-64)
Cyclotrode "X" *'46*
A Woman's Face *'41*
Heroes in Blue *'39*
Daredevils of the Red Circle *'38*
Lady from Nowhere *'36*
Charlie Chan's Secret *'35*
Saddle Buster *'32*

Linnea Quigley (1958-)
Kolobos *'99*
Boogie Boy *'98*
Death Mask *'98*
Assault of the Party Nerds 2: Heavy Petting Detective *'95*
Jack-O *'95*
Pumpkinhead 2: Blood Wings *'94*
Beach Babes from Beyond Infinity *'93*
Innocent Blood *'92*
Vice Academy 2 *'90*
Virgin High *'90*
Assault of the Party Nerds *'89*
WitchTrap *'89*
Deadly Embrace *'88*
Hollywood Chainsaw Hookers *'88*
Night of the Demons *'88*
Vice Academy *'88*
Creepozoids *'87*
Nightmare Sisters *'87*
Sorority Babes in the Slimeball Bowl-A-Rama *'87*
Return of the Living Dead *'85*
Savage Streets *'83*
The Black Room *'82*

Rita Quigley
Riot Squad *'41*
Susan and God *'40*

Tim Quill
Suicide Ride *'97*
Endangered *'94*
Army of Darkness *'92*
Listen to Me *'89*
Staying Together *'89*
Hamburger Hill *'87*
Hiding Out *'87*
Thou Shalt Not Kill...Except *'87*

Eddie Quillan (1907-90)
Dark Mountain *'44*
Mystery of the Riverboat *'44*
Here Comes Kelly *'43*
It Ain't Hay *'43*
The Grapes of Wrath *'40*
Young Mr. Lincoln *'39*
The Mandarin Mystery *'37*
Mutiny on the Bounty *'35*
The Tip-Off *'31*

Marie Quillen
Saddle Buster *'32*
Campus Knights *'29*

Denis Quilley (1927-)
A Dangerous Man: Lawrence after Arabia *'91*
Mister Johnson *'91*
The Shell Seekers *'89*
Foreign Body *'86*
A.D. *'85*
Privates on Parade *'84*
Murder of a Moderate Man *'70s*
In This House of Brede *'75*
Murder on the Orient Express *'74*

Veronica Quilligan
Halfmoon *'95*
Danny Boy *'82*
Lisztomania *'75*

Richard Quine (1920-89)
For Me and My Gal *'42*
Babes on Broadway *'41*

Kathleen Quinlan (1952-)
A Civil Action *'98*
My Giant *'98*
Event Horizon *'97*
Breakdown *'96*
Lawn Dogs *'96*
Zeus and Roxanne *'96*
Apollo 13 *'95*
Perfect Alibi *'94*
Trial by Jury *'94*
Last Light *'93*
An American Story *'92*
The Doors *'91*
Strays *'91*
Trapped *'89*
Clara's Heart *'88*
Man Outside *'88*
Sunset *'88*
Dreams Lost, Dreams Found *'87*
Wild Thing *'87*
Blackout *'85*
Warning Sign *'85*
The Last Winter *'84*
Independence Day *'83*
Twilight Zone: The Movie *'83*
Hanky Panky *'82*
She's in the Army Now *'81*
The Promise *'79*
The Runner Stumbles *'79*
Airport '77 *'77*
I Never Promised You a Rose Garden *'77*
Lifeguard *'76*
Where Have All the People Gone? *'74*
American Graffiti *'73*

Aidan Quinn (1959-)
The Prince and the Pauper *'01*
Music of the Heart *'99*
Songcatcher *'99*
This Is My Father *'99*
In Dreams *'98*
Practical Magic *'98*
The Assignment *'97*
Commandments *'96*
Looking for Richard *'96*
Michael Collins *'96*
Haunted *'95*
Legends of the Fall *'94*
Mary Shelley's Frankenstein *'94*
The Stars Fell on Henrietta *'94*
Benny & Joon *'93*
Blink *'93*
The Playboys *'92*
A Private Matter *'92*
At Play in the Fields of the Lord *'91*
Lies of the Twins *'91*
Avalon *'90*
The Handmaid's Tale *'90*
The Lemon Sisters *'90*
Crusoe *'89*
Perfect Witness *'89*
Stakeout *'87*
All My Sons *'86*
The Mission *'86*
Desperately Seeking Susan *'85*
An Early Frost *'85*
Reckless *'84*

Anthony Quinn (1915-2001)
Gotti *'96*
A Walk in the Clouds *'95*
Hercules the Legendary Journeys, Vol. 1: And the Amazon Women *'94*
Hercules the Legendary Journeys, Vol. 2: The Lost Kingdom *'94*
Hercules the Legendary Journeys, Vol. 3: The Circle of Fire *'94*
Hercules the Legendary Journeys, Vol. 4: In the Underworld *'94*
Somebody to Love *'94*
Last Action Hero *'93*
Jungle Fever *'91*
Mobsters *'91*
Only the Lonely *'91*
Ghosts Can't Do It *'90*
The Old Man and the Sea *'90*
Revenge *'90*
The Switch *'89*
A Man of Passion *'88*
Onassis *'88*
Regina *'83*
The Salamander *'82*
High Risk *'81*
Lion of the Desert *'81*
The Con Artists *'80*
Children of Sanchez *'79*
African Rage *'78*
The Greek Tycoon *'78*
Jesus of Nazareth *'77*
The Message *'77*
The Inheritance *'76*
The Destructors *'74*
The Don Is Dead *'73*
Across 110th Street *'72*
R.P.M.* (* Revolutions Per Minute) *'70*
Walk in the Spring Rain *'70*
A Dream of Kings *'69*
The Secret of Santa Vittoria *'69*
The Shoes of the Fisherman *'68*
The Rover *'67*
The Lost Command *'66*
Behold a Pale Horse *'64*
Zorba the Greek *'64*
Barabbas *'62*
Lawrence of Arabia *'62*
Requiem for a Heavyweight *'62*
The Guns of Navarone *'61*
Heller in Pink Tights *'60*
Portrait in Black *'60*
Black Orchid *'59*
Last Train from Gun Hill *'59*
Warlock *'59*
Hot Spell *'58*
The Hunchback of Notre Dame *'57*
The Ride Back *'57*
Lust for Life *'56*
The Magnificent Matador *'55*
Seven Cities of Gold *'55*
Ulysses *'55*
Blowing Wild *'54*
La Strada *'54*
Against All Flags *'52*
Viva Zapata! *'52*
The World in His Arms *'52*
Sinbad, the Sailor *'47*
Tycoon *'47*
Back to Bataan *'45*
Buffalo Bill *'44*
China Sky *'44*
Guadalcanal Diary *'43*
The Ox-Bow Incident *'43*
The Black Swan *'42*
The Road to Morocco *'42*
Blood and Sand *'41*
They Died with Their Boots On *'41*
City for Conquest *'40*
The Ghost Breakers *'40*
The Road to Singapore *'40*
The Texas Rangers Ride Again *'40*
Union Pacific *'39*
The Plainsman *'37*
Waikiki Wedding *'37*

Bill Quinn (1912-94)
Twilight Zone: The Movie *'83*
Bustin' Loose *'81*
Dead and Buried *'81*
Big Calibre *'35*

Colin Quinn
Who's the Man? *'93*
Crocodile Dundee 2 *'88*

Daniel Quinn
Wolverine *'96*
A Reason to Believe *'95*
American Cop *'94*
Scanner Cop *'94*
Scanner Cop 2: Volkin's Revenge *'94*
Scanners: The Showdown *'94*
Conagher *'91*

Elizabeth Quinn
Love and Death on Long Island *'97*
The Sound and the Silence *'93*

Francesco Quinn (1962-)
Nowhere Land *'98*
Rough Riders *'97*
Cannes Man *'96*
The Dark Dancer *'95*
Red Shoe Diaries 5: Weekend Pass *'95*
Top Dog *'95*
Dead Certain *'92*
Deadly Rivals *'92*
Indio *'90*
The Old Man and the Sea *'90*
Priceless Beauty *'90*
Platoon *'86*
Quo Vadis *'85*

Glenn Quinn
At Any Cost *'00*
Live Nude Girls *'95*
Dr. Giggles *'92*

James W. Quinn
WitchTrap *'89*
Witchboard *'87*

J.C. Quinn
Primary Colors *'98*
The Babe *'92*
Crisscross *'92*
All-American Murder *'91*
Megaville *'91*
Prayer of the Rollerboys *'91*
Priceless Beauty *'90*
The Abyss *'89*
Turner and Hooch *'89*
Barfly *'87*
Heartbreak Ridge *'86*
Twisted *'86*
Violated *'84*

Louis Quinn
Unholy Rollers *'72*
Superchick *'71*

Martha Quinn (1961-)
Bad Channels *'92*
The Return of Spinal Tap *'92*
Chopper Chicks in Zombietown *'91*
Motorama *'91*
Eddie and the Cruisers 2: Eddie Lives! *'89*
Tapeheads *'89*

Pat Quinn
Clean and Sober *'88*
Zachariah *'70*
Alice's Restaurant *'69*

Patricia Quinn
Witching Time *'84*
Monty Python's The Meaning of Life *'83*
Shock Treatment *'81*
The Rocky Horror Picture Show *'75*

Terry Quinn
The Witching *'72*
The Two Faces of Dr. Jekyll *'60*

Adolfo "Shabba Doo" Quinones
Deadly Dancer *'90*
Lambada *'89*
Breakin' *'84*
Breakin' 2: Electric Boogaloo *'84*

Jonathan Quint
Silicon Towers *'99*
Floating *'97*

Pauline Quirke
David Copperfield *'99*
The Sculptress *'97*

Beulah Quo
The Children of An Lac *'80*
The Seventh Dawn *'64*
Girls! Girls! Girls! *'62*

Marianne Quon
Charlie Chan in the Secret Service *'44*
China *'43*

Elie Raab
The Ref *'93*
Eyes of an Angel *'91*
The Fabulous Baker Boys *'89*

Kurt Raab (1946-88)
Angry Harvest *'85*
Mussolini & I *'85*
Parker *'84*
Tricheurs *'84*
The Stationmaster's Wife *'77*
Satan's Brew *'76*
Fox and His Friends *'75*
Tenderness of the Wolves *'73*
The American Soldier *'70*
Beware of a Holy Whore *'70*
Why Does Herr R. Run Amok? *'69*

Birgitte Raabjerg
The Kingdom 2 *'97*
The Kingdom *'95*

Francesco Rabal (1925-)
Goya in Bordeaux *'99*
Talk of Angels *'96*
Tie Me Up! Tie Me Down! *'90*
A Time of Destiny *'88*
Camorra: The Naples Connection *'85*
Padre Nuestro *'85*
Diary of a Rebel *'84*
The Holy Innocents *'84*
The Stilts *'84*
City of the Walking Dead *'83*
Reborn *'78*
Stay As You Are *'78*
Sorcerer *'77*
El Muerto *'75*
Exorcism's Daughter *'74*
Devil's Crude *'71*
Belle de Jour *'67*
The Eclipse *'66*
The Nun *'66*
Viridiana *'61*
Nazarin *'58*

Pamela Rabe (1959-)
Paradise Road *'97*
The Well *'97*
Cosi *'95*
Sirens *'94*

Francine Racette (1947-)
Au Revoir les Enfants *'87*
Lumiere *'76*
Mr. Klein *'76*

Alan Rachins (1947-)
Leave It to Beaver *'97*
Meet Wally Sparks *'97*
The Stepsister *'97*
Showgirls *'95*
Star Quest *'94*
Heart Condition *'90*
Mistress *'87*
L.A. Law *'86*
Always *'85*

Victoria Racimo
White Fang 2: The Myth of the White Wolf *'94*
Ernest Goes to Camp *'87*
Roanoak *'86*
Prophecy *'79*
Green Eyes *'76*
Search for the Gods *'75*
G.I. Executioner *'71*

Daniel Radcliffe (1989-)
Harry Potter and the Sorcerer's Stone *'01*
The Tailor of Panama *'00*
David Copperfield *'99*

Rosemary Radcliffe
Anne of Green Gables: The Continuing Story *'99*
Anne of Green Gables *'85*

Sascha Radetsky
Center Stage *'00*
Home at Last *'88*

Basil Radford (1897-1952)
Passport to Pimlico *'49*
Whiskey Galore *'48*
The Winslow Boy *'48*
Captive Heart *'47*
Dead of Night *'45*
Night Train to Munich *'40*
The Lady Vanishes *'38*
Young and Innocent *'37*

Natalie Radford
Agent Red *'00*
P.T. Barnum *'99*
The Android Affair *'95*
Tomcat: Dangerous Desires *'93*

Ken Radley
Mr. Reliable: A True Story *'95*
Sniper *'92*

Gilda Radner (1946-89)
Haunted Honeymoon *'86*
Movers and Shakers *'85*
The Woman in Red *'84*
Hanky Panky *'82*
First Family *'80*
Mr. Mike's Mondo Video *'79*
All You Need Is Cash *'78*
The Last Detail *'73*

Jerzy Radziwilowicz (1950-)
No End *'84*
Passion *'82*
Man of Iron *'81*
Man of Marble *'76*

Cassidy Rae
Extremedays *'01*
National Lampoon's Favorite Deadly Sins *'95*
Evolver *'94*

Charlotte Rae (1926-)
Another Woman's Husband *'00*
Thunder in Paradise *'93*
Tom and Jerry: The Movie *'93 (V)*
The Worst Witch *'86*
Words by Heart *'84*
The Triangle Factory Fire Scandal *'79*
Sidewinder One *'77*
Queen of the Stardust Ballroom *'75*
Bananas *'71*
The Hot Rock *'70*
Jenny *'70*

Bob Rafelson (1933-)
Always *'85*
Head *'68*

Giuliano Raffaelli
And God Said to Cain *'69*
Blood and Black Lace *'64*

Chips Rafferty (1909-71)
Skullduggery *'70*
Double Trouble *'67*
Wackiest Ship in the Army *'61*
The Sundowners *'60*
Walk into Hell *'57*
The Desert Rats *'53*
Eureka Stockade *'49*
Overlanders *'46*
The Fighting Rats of Tobruk *'44*
Forty Thousand Horsemen *'41*

Frances Rafferty (1922-)
Curley *'47*
Money Madness *'47*
Abbott and Costello in Hollywood *'45*
Mrs. Parkington *'44*

Deborah Raffin (1953-)
Morning Glory *'93*
Scanners 2: The New Order *'91*
Night of the Fox *'90*
Noble House *'88*
Claudia *'85*
Death Wish 3 *'85*
Jungle Heat *'84*
Killing at Hell's Gate *'81*

For the Love of It '80
Touched by Love '80
Willa '79
Hanging on a Star '78
How to Pick Up Girls '78
Snowblind '78
Maniac '77
God Told Me To '76
Nightmare in Badham County '76
The Sentinel '76
Once Is Not Enough '75
The Dove '74
Forty Carats '73

George Raft (1895-1980)
Sextette '78
Casino Royale '67
Five Golden Dragons '67
Ocean's 11 '60
Jet Over the Atlantic '59
Some Like It Hot '59
Around the World in 80 Days '56
Man from Cairo '54
I'll Get You '53
Loan Shark '52
Outpost in Morocco '49
Mr. Ace '46
Nocturne '46
Whistle Stop '46
Johnny Angel '45
Follow the Boys '44
Background to Danger '43
Stage Door Canteen '43
House Across the Bay '40
They Drive by Night '40
Each Dawn I Die '39
Spawn of the North '38
You and Me '38
Souls at Sea '37
Night After Night '32
Palmy Days '31
Scarface '31

Rags Ragland (1905-46)
The Canterville Ghost '44
DuBarry Was a Lady '43
Whistling in Brooklyn '43
Panama Hattie '42
Whistling in Dixie '42
Whistling in the Dark '41

Joe Ragno
Day at the Beach '98
Jane Doe '96
No Way Home '96
The Babe '92

William Ragsdale (1961-)
Just a Little Harmless Sex '99
National Lampoon's Favorite Deadly Sins '95
Mannequin 2: On the Move '91
Fright Night 2 '88
Fright Night '85
Smooth Talk '85

Umberto Raho
The Blonde '92
Aladdin '86
Amuck! '71
The Night Evelyn Came Out of the Grave '71
The Bird with the Crystal Plumage '70
Satanik '69
The Ghost '63

Steve Railsback (1948-)
Ed Gein '01
Made Men '99
Me & Will '99
Disturbing Behavior '98
Stranger in the House '97
Termination Man '97
Barb Wire '96
Street Corner Justice '96
Calendar Girl '93
Final Mission '93
Nukie '93
Private Wars '93
Save Me '93
Forever: A Ghost of a Love Story '92
Quake '92
Sunstroke '92
Scissors '91
Alligator 2: The Mutation '90
Assassin '89
The Forgotten '89
Deadly Intent '88
Blue Monkey '87
Distortions '87
Scenes from the Goldmine '87
The Survivalist '87
The Wind '87
Armed and Dangerous '86
Lifeforce '85
Torchlight '85
The Golden Seal '83
Trick or Treats '82
Escape 2000 '81
Deadly Games '80
The Stunt Man '80
From Here to Eternity '79
Angela '77
Helter Skelter '76

Sam Raimi (1959-)
Stephen King's The Stand '94
Body Bags '93
Indian Summer '93
Innocent Blood '92
Maniac Cop '88
Evil Dead 2: Dead by Dawn '87
Thou Shalt Not Kill...Except '87
Evil Dead '83

Theodore (Ted) Raimi (1965-)
Spider-Man '02
The Shot '96
Clear and Present Danger '94
Stuart Saves His Family '94
Hard Target '93
Skinner '93
Army of Darkness '92
The Finishing Touch '92
Lunatics: A Love Story '92
Patriot Games '92
Darkman '90
Shocker '89
Evil Dead 2: Dead by Dawn '87
Thou Shalt Not Kill...Except '87
Crimewave '85
Evil Dead '83

Raimu (1883-1946)
Well-Digger's Daughter '46
Heart of a Nation '43
Cesar '36
The Baker's Wife '33
Fanny '32
Marius '31

Douglas Rain
2010: The Year We Make Contact '84 (V)
2001: A Space Odyssey '68 (V)

Jeramie Rain
The Abductors '72
Last House on the Left '72

Jack Raine (1897-1979)
The Killing of Sister George '69
Above and Beyond '53
The Ghoul '34
Night Birds '31

Luise Rainer (1910-)
The Gambler '97
Tiefland '44
The Great Waltz '38
The Good Earth '37
The Great Ziegfeld '36

Christina Raines (1952-)
North Shore '87
Quo Vadis '85
Nightmares '83
Silver Dream Racer '83
Touched by Love '80
Centennial '78
The Duellists '77
The Sentinel '76
Nashville '75
Russian Roulette '75
The Shrieking '73
Stacey '73

Ella Raines (1921-88)
Ride the Man Down '53
Impact '49
The Senator Was Indiscreet '47
The Strange Affair of Uncle Harry '45
Hail the Conquering Hero '44
Phantom Lady '44
Tall in the Saddle '44

Frances Raines
Disconnected '87
The Mutilator '85

Ford Rainey (1908-)
Bed & Breakfast '92
The Cellar '90
Strangers: The Story of a Mother and Daughter '79
Mountain Man '77
Babe! '75
Strange New World '75
Sixteen '72
My Sweet Charlie '70
The Sand Pebbles '66
Flaming Star '60

Claude Rains (1889-1967)
The Greatest Story Ever Told '65
Lawrence of Arabia '62
Battle of the Worlds '61
The Pied Piper of Hamelin '57
Lisbon '56
Paris Express '53
The White Tower '50
Angel on My Shoulder '46
Caesar and Cleopatra '46
Deception '46
Notorious '46
Mr. Skeffington '44
Passage to Marseilles '44
Forever and a Day '43
The Phantom of the Opera '43
Casablanca '42
Now, Voyager '42
Here Comes Mr. Jordan '41
Kings Row '41
The Wolf Man '41
The Sea Hawk '40
Juarez '39
Mr. Smith Goes to Washington '39
They Made Me a Criminal '39
The Adventures of Robin Hood '38
Four Daughters '38
The Prince and the Pauper '37
They Won't Forget '37
Anthony Adverse '36
The Mystery of Edwin Drood '35
The Evil Mind '34
The Invisible Man '33

Pierre-Loup Rajot
The Adventures of Felix '99
The New Eve '98

Tommy (Thomas) Rall (1929-)
Dancers '87
My Sister Eileen '55
Seven Brides for Seven Brothers '54
Kiss Me Kate '53

Giovanna Ralli (1935-)
Sex with a Smile '76
Caper of the Golden Bulls '67
What Did You Do in the War, Daddy? '66

Christopher Ralph
The Skulls 2 '02
Hendrix '00

Jessie Ralph (1864-1944)
They Met in Bombay '41
The Bank Dick '40
The Blue Bird '40
Drums Along the Mohawk '39
Double Wedding '37
The Last of Mrs. Cheyney '37
After the Thin Man '36
Little Lord Fauntleroy '36
San Francisco '36
Yellow Dust '36
I Live My Life '35
Les Miserables '35
Evelyn Prentice '34
One Night of Love '34

Sheryl Lee Ralph (1956-)
Deterrence '00
Personals '00
Bogus '96
White Man's Burden '95
Witch Hunt '94
Sister Act 2: Back in the Habit '93
The Distinguished Gentleman '92
Mistress '91
To Sleep with Anger '90
The Mighty Quinn '89
Oliver & Company '88 (V)
Codename: Foxfire '85

Esther Ralston (1902-94)
Tin Pan Alley '40
Shadows of the Orient '37
We're in the Legion Now '37
To the Last Man '33
Lonely Wives '31
Old Ironsides '26
$50,000 Reward '25
Lucky Devil '25
Peter Pan '24
Oliver Twist '22

Jobyna Ralston (1900-67)
The Kid Brother '27
Wings '27
For Heaven's Sake '26
The Freshman '25
Girl Shy '24

Vera (Hruba) Ralston (1921-)
Jubilee Trail '54
Hoodlum Empire '52
The Fighting Kentuckian '49
Dakota '45

Cecil Ramage
Kind Hearts and Coronets '49
King of the Damned '36

Enrique Rambal
The Man and the Monster '65
The Exterminating Angel '62

Marjorie Rambeau (1889-1970)
Man of a Thousand Faces '57
A Man Called Peter '55
Forever Female '53
Torch Song '53
Primrose Path '40
Santa Fe Marshal '40
The Rains Came '39
Laughing Sinners '31
Min & Bill '30

Dack Rambo (1942-94)
Ultra Warrior '92
River of Diamonds '90
The Spring '89
Waikiki '80
Hit Lady '74

Henry Ramer
The Big Slice '90
Hockey Night '84
Reno and the Doc '84
Starship Invasions '77
My Pleasure Is My Business '74

Carlos Ramirez (1914-86)
Anchors Aweigh '45
Bathing Beauty '44
Two Girls and a Sailor '44

Frank Ramirez
Miracle in Rome '88
Smith! '69

Harold Ramis (1944-)
Orange County '02
As Good As It Gets '97
Love Affair '94
Ghostbusters 2 '89
Stealing Home '88
Baby Boom '87
Ghostbusters '84
Heavy Metal '81 (V)
Stripes '81

Eulalia Ramon
Goya in Bordeaux '99
Outrage '93
Letters from Alou '90

Rudy Ramos (1950-)
The Spy Within '94
Blindsided '93
Colors '88
Open House '86
Quicksilver '86

Charlotte Rampling (1945-)
My Uncle Silas '01
Spy Game '01
Aberdeen '00
Signs & Wonders '00
Under the Sand '00
Great Expectations '99
The Wings of the Dove '97
Invasion of Privacy '96
Hammers over the Anvil '91
D.O.A. '88
Angel Heart '87
Mascara '87
Max, Mon Amour '86
The Verdict '82
Stardust Memories '80
Orca '77
The Purple Taxi '77
Foxtrot '76
Farewell, My Lovely '75
Sardinia Kidnapped '75
Ski Bum '75
Caravan to Vaccares '74
The Night Porter '74
'Tis a Pity She's a Whore '73
Zardoz '73
Asylum '72
The Damned '69
Georgy Girl '66

Anne Elizabeth Ramsay (1960-)
The Final Cut '96
A League of Their Own '92

Bruce Ramsay
Island of the Dead '00
Bonanno: A Godfather's Story '99
Dead Beat '94
Killing Zoe '94
The New Age '94
Alive '93

Remak Ramsay (1937-)
Addicted to Love '96
Mr. & Mrs. Bridge '90
The Dining Room '86

Anne Ramsey (1929-88)
Perfect Alibi '94
The River Pirates '94
Meet the Hollowheads '89
Another Chance '88
Dr. Hackenstein '88
Throw Momma from the Train '87
Weeds '87
Deadly Friend '86
The Goonies '85
A Small Killing '81
Marilyn: The Untold Story '80
White Mama '80
The Black Marble '79
Goin' South '78
The Boy in the Plastic Bubble '76

Bruce Ramsey
Curdled '95
Hellraiser 4: Bloodline '95

David Ramsey
Pay It Forward '00
Mutiny '99

Logan Ramsey (1921-2000)
Dr. Hackenstein '88
Say Yes! '86
The Beast Within '82
Conspiracy of Terror '75
Confessions of Tom Harris '72
Fury on Wheels '71
Head '68
The Hoodlum Priest '61

Lois Ramsey
Road to Nhill '97
River Street '95

Marion Ramsey
Police Academy 6: City under Siege '89
Police Academy 5: Assignment Miami Beach '88
Police Academy 3: Back in Training '86

Stacey Linn Ramsower
The Baby-Sitters' Club '95
The Quick and the Dead '94
Tank Girl '94

Nick Ramus
3 Ninjas Knuckle Up '95
Geronimo '93
Journey to Spirit Island '92

Addison Randall
Chance '89
Deadly Breed '89
Hollow Gate '88

Addison "Jack" Randall (1906-45)
Covered Wagon Trails '40
Across the Plains '39
Wild Horse Canyon '39
Gun Packer '38
Gunsmoke Trail '38
Man's Country '38
Red Lights Ahead '36

Lexi (Faith) Randall (1980-)
Sarah, Plain and Tall: Winter's End '99
The Stars Fell on Henrietta '94
The War '94
Heidi '93
Sarah, Plain and Tall: Skylark '93
Sarah, Plain and Tall '91

Meg Randall (1926-)
Ma and Pa Kettle Back On the Farm '51
Ma and Pa Kettle Go to Town '50
Ma and Pa Kettle '49

Monica Randall (1942-)
Inquisition '76
Witches' Mountain '71
Commando Attack '67
Five Giants from Texas '66

Stacie Randall
Evil Obsession '96
Excessive Force 2: Force on Force '95
Dream a Little Dream 2 '94
Trancers 5: Sudden Deth '94
Trancers 4: Jack of Swords '93

Tony Randall (1920-)
Fatal Instinct '93
Gremlins 2: The New Batch '90 (V)
That's Adequate '90
King of Comedy '82
Foolin' Around '80
Scavenger Hunt '79
Everything You Always Wanted to Know about Sex (But Were Afraid to Ask) '72
The Littlest Angel '69
The Alphabet Murders '65
Robin and the 7 Hoods '64
Send Me No Flowers '64
The Brass Bottle '63
7 Faces of Dr. Lao '63
Boys' Night Out '62

Lover Come Back *'61*
The Adventures of Huckleberry Finn *'60*
Let's Make Love *'60*
The Mating Game *'59*
Pillow Talk *'59*
Will Success Spoil Rock Hunter? *'57*

Steven Randazzo
Mac *'93*
In the Soup *'92*

Ron Randell (1918-)
Girl in Black Stockings *'57*
The Story of Esther Costello *'57*
Omoo Omoo, the Shark God *'49*
The Loves of Carmen *'48*

Theresa Randle (1967-)
Livin' for Love: The Natalie Cole Story *'00*
Spawn *'97*
Girl 6 *'96*
Space Jam *'96*
Bad Boys *'95*
Beverly Hills Cop 3 *'94*
Sugar Hill *'94*
CB4: The Movie *'93*
Malcolm X *'92*

Anders Randolf (1870-1930)
The Kiss *'29*
Ranson's Folly *'26*
The Idol Dancer *'20*
The Love Flower *'20*

Donald Randolph (1906-93)
The Deadly Mantis *'57*
Gunsmoke *'53*

Jane Randolph (1919-)
Abbott and Costello Meet Frankenstein *'48*
Open Secret *'48*
Railroaded *'47*
Curse of the Cat People *'44*
Cat People *'42*
The Falcon's Brother *'42*

John Randolph (1915-)
You've Got Mail *'98*
A Price above Rubies *'97*
A Foreign Field *'93*
Iron Maze *'91*
National Lampoon's Christmas Vacation *'89*
The Wizard of Loneliness *'88*
As Summers Die *'86*
Prizzi's Honor *'85*
Frances *'82*
Lovely ... But Deadly *'82*
The Adventures of Nellie Bly *'81*
The Winds of Kitty Hawk *'78*
Secrets *'77*
King Kong *'76*
The Runaways *'75*
Serpico *'73*
Conquest of the Planet of the Apes *'72*
Escape from the Planet of the Apes *'71*
There Was a Crooked Man *'70*
Pretty Poison *'68*
Seconds *'66*

Lillian Randolph
Magic *'78*
How to Seduce a Woman *'74*

Ty Randolph
Nudity Required *'90*
Deadly Embrace *'88*

Robert Random
Danger Zone 3: Steel Horse War *'90*
Danger Zone 2 *'89*

Salvo Randone (1906-91)
Fellini Satyricon *'69*
Spirits of the Dead *'68*
10th Victim *'65*

Joe Ranft
Toy Story 2 *'99 (V)*
A Bug's Life *'98 (V)*

Dan Ranger
Cop-Out *'91*
The Last Ride *'91*

Arthur (L.) Rankin (1900-47)
Terror Trail *'33*
Fighting Fool *'32*
Below the Deadline *'29*
Walking Back *'26*

Kenny Ransom
Prison for Children *'93*
There Goes My Baby *'92*

Tim Ransom (1963-)
Courage Under Fire *'96*
Vital Signs *'90*
The Dressmaker *'89*

Prunella Ransome
Man in the Wilderness *'71*
Far from the Madding Crowd *'67*

Michael Rapaport (1970-)
Dr. Dolittle 2 *'01 (V)*
King of the Jungle *'01*
Bamboozled *'00*
Kiss Toledo Goodbye *'00*
Lucky Numbers *'00*
Men of Honor *'00*
The 6th Day *'00*
Small Time Crooks *'00*
Deep Blue Sea *'99*
The Naked Man *'98*
Palmetto *'98*
A Brother's Kiss *'97*
Cop Land *'97*
Kicked in the Head *'97*
Subway Stories *'97*
Beautiful Girls *'96*
Illtown *'96*
Metro *'96*
Mighty Aphrodite *'95*
The Pallbearer *'95*
The Basketball Diaries *'94*
Higher Learning *'94*
Kiss of Death *'94*
The Scout *'94*
Hand Gun *'93*
Money for Nothing *'93*
True Romance *'93*
Zebrahead *'92*

Anthony Rapp (1971-)
A Beautiful Mind *'01*
Road Trip *'00*
Man of the Century *'99*
David Searching *'97*
Dazed and Confused *'93*
Six Degrees of Separation *'93*
School Ties *'92*
Far from Home *'89*
Adventures in Babysitting *'87*

David Rappaport (1952-90)
Peter Gunn *'89*
The Bride *'85*
Mysteries *'84*

Eva Ras
The Love Affair, or The Case of the Missing Switchboard Operator *'67*
Man Is Not a Bird *'65*

Renato Rascel (1912-91)
The Secret of Santa Vittoria *'69*
Uncle Was a Vampire *'59*
The Seven Hills of Rome *'58*

David Rasche (1944-)
Divine Secrets of the Ya-Ya Sisterhood *'02*
Hostage Hotel *'00*
The Big Tease *'99*
Friends & Lovers *'99*
The Settlement *'99*
Tourist Trap *'98*
That Old Feeling *'96*
Dead Weekend *'95*
Out There *'95*
Bigfoot: The Unforgettable Encounter *'94*
A Million to Juan *'94*
Twenty Bucks *'93*
Bingo *'91*
Delirious *'91*
Silhouette *'91*
The Masters of Menace *'90*
An Innocent Man *'89*
Wedding Band *'89*
Wicked Stepmother *'89*
Made in Heaven *'87*
Native Son *'86*
Manhattan *'79*
Sanctuary of Fear *'79*

Phylicia Rashad (1949-)
The Old Settler *'01*
The Visit *'00*
Loving Jezebel *'99*
Free of Eden *'98*
Once Upon a Time ... When We Were Colored *'95*
False Witness *'89*
Uncle Tom's Cabin *'87*

Fritz Rasp (1891-1976)
The Threepenny Opera *'31*
Diary of a Lost Girl *'29*
Spies *'28*
The Love of Jeanne Ney *'27*
Metropolis *'26*

Julien Rassam (1968-)
Queen Margot *'94*
The Accompanist *'93*

Ivan Rassimov (1938-)
Emerald Jungle *'80*
Shock *'79*
Man from Deep River *'77*
The Next Victim *'71*
Blade of the Ripper *'70*
Planet of the Vampires *'65*

Rada Rassimov
Torture Chamber of Baron Blood *'72*
The Good, the Bad and the Ugly *'67*

Thalmus Rasulala (1939-)
Mom and Dad Save the World *'92*
New Jack City *'91*
Blind Vengeance *'90*
The Package *'89*
Above the Law *'88*
Bulletproof *'88*
Born American *'86*
Sophisticated Gents *'81*
Adios Amigo *'75*
Bucktown *'75*
Friday Foster *'75*
Blacula *'72*

Mikhail Rasumny (1890-1956)
Anna and the King of Siam *'46*
For Whom the Bell Tolls *'43*
Wake Island *'42*

Jeremy Ratchford (1965-)
Angel Eyes *'01*
The Crew *'00*
Fly Away Home *'96*
Moonshine Highway *'96*
Prom Night 3: The Last Kiss *'89*

Sandy Ratcliff
Yesterday's Hero *'79*
Family Life *'71*

Basil Rathbone (1892-1967)
Many Faces of Sherlock Holmes *'86*
Autopsy of a Ghost *'67*
Hillbillies in a Haunted House *'67*
Planet of Blood *'66*
Voyage to the Prehistoric Planet *'65*
The Comedy of Terrors *'64*
The Magic Sword *'62*
Tales of Terror *'62*
Victoria Regina *'61*
Last Hurrah *'58*
Court Jester *'56*
We're No Angels *'55*
Casanova's Big Night *'54*
A Christmas Carol *'54*
The Adventures of Ichabod and Mr. Toad *'49 (N)*
Dressed to Kill *'46*
Heartbeat *'46*
Terror by Night *'46*
House of Fear *'45*
Pursuit to Algiers *'45*
The Woman in Green *'45*
Bathing Beauty *'44*
Frenchman's Creek *'44*
The Pearl of Death *'44*
Scarlet Claw *'44*
Spider Woman *'44*
Above Suspicion *'43*
Sherlock Holmes Faces Death *'43*
Sherlock Holmes in Washington *'43*
Sherlock Holmes and the Secret Weapon *'42*
Sherlock Holmes: The Voice of Terror *'42*
The Black Cat *'41*
International Lady *'41*
The Mark of Zorro *'40*
Rhythm on the River *'40*
The Adventures of Sherlock Holmes *'39*
The Hound of the Baskervilles *'39*
Son of Frankenstein *'39*
The Tower of London *'39*
The Adventures of Marco Polo *'38*
The Adventures of Robin Hood *'38*
Dawn Patrol *'38*
If I Were King *'38*
Love from a Stranger *'37*
Make a Wish *'37*
The Garden of Allah *'36*
Romeo and Juliet *'36*
A Tale of Two Cities *'36*
Anna Karenina *'35*
Captain Blood *'35*
David Copperfield *'35*
Last Days of Pompeii *'35*
Sin Takes a Holiday *'30*

Benjamin Ratner
Firestorm *'97*
Bounty Hunters *'96*

Gregory Ratoff (1897-1960)
Exodus *'60*
Abdulla the Great *'56*
All About Eve *'50*
I'm No Angel *'33*
Skyscraper Souls *'32*

Devin Ratray
Home Alone 2: Lost in New York *'92*
Spy Trap *'92*
Home Alone *'90*

Peter Ratray
Stonewall *'95*
Will: G. Gordon Liddy *'82*

Heather Rattray (1966-)
Basket Case 2 *'90*
Mountain Family Robinson *'79*
Sea Gypsies *'78*
Further Adventures of the Wilderness Family, Part 2 *'77*
Across the Great Divide *'76*

John Ratzenberger (1947-)
Monsters, Inc. *'01 (V)*
Toy Story 2 *'99 (V)*
A Bug's Life *'98 (V)*
Under Pressure *'98*
One Night Stand *'97*
That Darn Cat *'96*
Toy Story *'95 (V)*
Camp Cucamonga: How I Spent My Summer Vacation *'90*
House 2: The Second Story *'87*
Timestalkers *'87*
Combat Academy *'86*
Outland *'81*
The Empire Strikes Back *'80*
Motel Hell *'80*
The Bitch *'78*
A Bridge Too Far *'77*
Twilight's Last Gleaming *'77*

Andrea Rau
Beyond Erotica *'79*
Daughters of Darkness *'71*

Siegfried Rauch (1932-)
Sons of Trinity *'95*
Alien Contamination *'81*
The Big Red One *'80*
Patton *'70*
Nous N'Irons Plus au Bois *'69*

Alida Rauffe
Cesar *'36*
Fanny *'32*

Mike Raven (1924-97)
Crucible of Terror *'72*
Disciple of Death *'72*
I, Monster *'71*
Lust for a Vampire *'71*

Raven-Symone (1985-)
Dr. Dolittle 2 *'01*
Dr. Dolittle *'98*
Queen *'93*

Christopher Ravenscroft
A Mind to Murder *'96*
Henry V *'89*

Gina Ravera (1968-)
The Temptations *'98*
Kiss the Girls *'97*
Soul Food *'97*
Soul of the Game *'96*
Showgirls *'95*

Adrian Rawlins
Breaking the Waves *'95*
Woman in Black *'89*

Herbert Rawlinson (1885-1953)
Jail Bait *'54*
Nabonga *'44*
Shake Hands with Murder *'44*
Colt Comrades *'43*
Lost Canyon *'43*
I Killed That Man *'42*
The Panther's Claw *'42*
Smart Alecks *'42*
Bad Man of Deadwood *'41*
Gentleman from Dixie *'41*
Riot Squad *'41*
Blind Fools *'40*
Blake of Scotland Yard *'36*
Robinson Crusoe of Clipper Island *'36*
Robinson Crusoe of Mystery Island *'36*
Confidential *'35*
Show Them No Mercy *'35*
The Tomboy *'24*

Lou Rawls (1936-)
Malevolence *'98*
Motel Blue *'98*
Watchers Reborn *'98*
Don King: Only in America *'97*
Still Breathing *'97*
The Prince *'95*
Showdown *'94*

Aldo Ray (1926-91)
Shock 'Em Dead *'90*
Shooters *'89*
Blood Red *'88*
Swift Justice *'88*
Hollywood Cop *'87*
Star Slammer *'87*
Terror on Alcatraz *'86*
Bio Hazard *'85*
Evils of the Night *'85*
Bog *'84*
The Executioner, Part 2: Frozen Scream *'84*
To Kill a Stranger *'84*
Vultures *'84*
Frankenstein's Great Aunt Tillie *'83*
Mongrel *'83*
Dark Sanity *'82*
The Great Skycopter Rescue *'82*
The Secret of NIMH *'82 (V)*
Mission to Glory *'80*
The Haunted *'79*
Human Experiments *'79*
Nightstalker *'79*
Black Eliminator *'78*
The Glove *'78*
Kill Factor *'78*
Little Moon & Jud McGraw *'78*
The Lucifer Complex *'78*
Haunts *'77*
Bad Bunch *'76*
Inside Out *'75*
The Man Who Would Not Die *'75*
Psychic Killer *'75*
Seven Alone *'75*
The Centerfold Girls *'74*
The Dynamite Brothers *'74*
And Hope to Die *'72*
Gone with the West *'72*
Angel Unchained *'70*
The Green Berets *'68*
Dead Heat on a Merry-Go-Round *'66*
What Did You Do in the War, Daddy? *'66*
Johnny Nobody *'61*
God's Little Acre *'58*
The Naked and the Dead *'58*
Men in War *'57*
Nightfall *'56*
Battle Cry *'55*
We're No Angels *'55*
Miss Sadie Thompson *'53*
The Marrying Kind *'52*
Pat and Mike *'52*

Andrew Ray (1939-)
Mission Phantom *'79*
Tarzana, the Wild Girl *'72*
The Young and the Guilty *'58*
Escapade *'55*

Anthony Ray
Shadows *'60*
Men in War *'57*

Charles Ray (1891-1943)
Dracula/Garden of Eden *'28*
The Garden of Eden *'28*
Sweet Adeline *'26*
The Busher *'19*
Clodhopper *'17*

James Ray (1932-88)
She's Having a Baby *'88*
Mass Appeal *'84*
Return Engagement *'78*

Michel Ray (1944-)
Lawrence of Arabia *'62*
The Tin Star *'57*
The Brave One *'56*

Nicholas Ray (1911-79)
Hair *'79*
The American Friend *'77*

Rene Ray (1911-93)
The Vicious Circle *'57*
They Made Me a Fugitive *'47*
Housemaster *'38*
The Passing of the Third Floor Back *'36*

Martha Raye (1916-94)
Pippin *'81*
The Concorde: Airport '79 *'79*
Pufnstuf *'70*
Billy Rose's Jumbo *'62*
Monsieur Verdoux *'47*
Pin-Up Girl *'44*
Keep 'Em Flying *'41*
Never Say Die *'39*
The Big Broadcast of 1938 *'38*
College Swing *'38*
Give Me a Sailor *'38*
Waikiki Wedding *'37*
Rhythm on the Range *'36*

Bill Raymond
A Death in the Family *'02*

A Stranger in the Kingdom '98
Where the Rivers Flow North '94
The Crow '93
The Ref '93
My New Gun '92
City of Hope '91
The Man Who Envied Women '85
Sudden Death '77
Candy (Candida) Raymond (1950-)
Monkey Grip '82
Freedom '81
Money Movers '78
Don's Party '76
Cyril Raymond (1897-1973)
Angels One Five '54
Brief Encounter '46
Men of Two Worlds '46
Spy in Black '39
The Shadow '36
Gary Raymond (1935-)
Scarlett '94
The Two Faces of Evil '82
Jason and the Argonauts '63
Playboy of the Western World '62
Look Back in Anger '58
The Moonraker '58
Gene Raymond (1908-98)
The Best Man '64
Plunder Road '57
Hit the Deck '55
Mr. & Mrs. Smith '41
Smilin' Through '41
The Bride Walks Out '36
That Girl from Paris '36
Sadie McKee '34
Transatlantic Merry-Go-Round '34
Ex-Lady '33
Flying Down to Rio '33
Red Dust '32
Jack Raymond
Shake Hands with Murder '44
Last Command '28
Lina Raymond
The Key to Rebecca '85
The Gypsy Warriors '78
Paula Raymond (1924-)
Blood of Dracula's Castle '69
King Richard and the Crusaders '54
The Beast from 20,000 Fathoms '53
City That Never Sleeps '53
Texas Carnival '51
Adam's Rib '50
The Duchess of Idaho '50
Richard Raymond
Days of Hell '84
Rats '83
Robin Raymond
High School Confidential '58
Rogue's Gallery '44
Girls in Chains '43
Usher Raymond (1978-)
Texas Rangers '01
Gepetto '00
Light It Up '99
She's All That '99
The Faculty '98
Michael Raynor
The Waiting Game '99
A Brother's Kiss '97
Federal Hill '94
Peggy Rea (1921-)
Made in America '93
Love Field '91
In Country '89
The Waltons: The Christmas Carol '80
Stephen Rea (1946-)
The Musketeer '01
On the Edge '00
The End of the Affair '99
Guinevere '99
The Life Before This '99
This Is My Father '99
In Dreams '98
Still Crazy '98
The Break '97
The Butcher Boy '97
Sink or Swim '97
Crime of the Century '96
Fever Pitch '96
The Last of the High Kings '96
Michael Collins '96
Trojan Eddie '96
Citizen X '95
Angie '94
Interview with the Vampire '94
Princess Caraboo '94
Ready to Wear '94
Bad Behavior '92
The Crying Game '92
Life Is Sweet '90
Loose Connections '87
The Company of Wolves '85
The Doctor and the Devils '85
Four Days in July '85
Danny Boy '82
Barbara Read
Behind the Mask '46
Three Smart Girls '36
James Read (1953-)
Harvest of Fire '95
When the Dark Man Calls '95
Walking Thunder '94
Love Crimes '92
Web of Deceit '90
Beaches '88
Eight Men Out '88
Poor Little Rich Girl: The Barbara Hutton Story '87
North and South Book 2 '86
North and South Book 1 '85
The Initiation '84
Rufus Read
Double Parked '00
Happiness '98
Ronald Reagan (1911-)
The Killers '64
Hellcats of the Navy '57
Tennessee's Partner '55
Cattle Queen of Montana '54
The Winning Team '52
Bedtime for Bonzo '51
Cavalry Charge '51
It's a Great Feeling '49
This Is the Army '43
Desperate Journey '42
Kings Row '41
Knute Rockne: All American '40
Santa Fe Trail '40
Dark Victory '39
Boy Meets Girl '38
Rex Reason (1912-)
Band of Angels '57
The Creature Walks among Us '56
Lady Godiva '55
This Island Earth '55
Sady Rebbot
Friends '71
My Life to Live '62
James Rebhorn (1948-)
Scotland, PA '02
The Adventures of Rocky & Bullwinkle '00
Meet the Parents '00
Snow Falling on Cedars '99
The Talented Mr. Ripley '99
A Bright Shining Lie '98
From the Earth to the Moon '98
The Game '97
Independence Day '96
Mistrial '96
My Fellow Americans '96
Up Close and Personal '96
The Buccaneers '95
If Lucy Fell '95
8 Seconds '94
I Love Trouble '94
Carlito's Way '93
JFK: Reckless Youth '93
Sarah, Plain and Tall: Skylark '93
Lorenzo's Oil '92
Scent of a Woman '92
White Sands '92
Deadly Business '86
Rockabye '86
Will: G. Gordon Liddy '82
He Knows You're Alone '80
Richard Rebrere
Heavenly Bodies '84
Happy Birthday to Me '81
Jeff Rector
Rapid Assault '99
Dinosaur Valley Girls '96
Friend of the Family 2 '96
Street Soldiers '91
Lois Red Elk
Outside Ozona '98
Three Warriors '77
Mary-Robin Redd
Mirrors '78
The Group '66
Lance Reddick
Don't Say a Word '01
I Dreamed of Africa '00
The Siege '98
Keith Reddin
Eye of the Storm '98
Lolita '97
Brian Reddy
Lost Souls '00
O Brother Where Art Thou? '00
Dante's Peak '97
Helen Reddy (1942-)
Pete's Dragon '77
Airport '75 '75
Quinn (K.) Redeker (1936-)
Coast to Coast '80
Spider Baby '64
The Three Stooges Meet Hercules '61
Dennis Redfield
The Tempest '99
Pulse '88
The Annihilators '85
The McCullochs '75
Private Duty Nurses '71
William Redfield (1927-76)
One Flew Over the Cuckoo's Nest '75
Death Wish '74
For Pete's Sake '74
A New Leaf '71
The Hot Rock '70
Fantastic Voyage '66
Morituri '65
The Connection '61
Conquest of Space '55
Robert Redford (1937-)
The Last Castle '01
Spy Game '01
The Horse Whisperer '97
Up Close and Personal '96
Indecent Proposal '93
Incident at Oglala: The Leonard Peltier Story '92 (N)
Sneakers '92
Havana '90
Legal Eagles '86
Out of Africa '85
The Natural '84
Brubaker '80
The Electric Horseman '79
A Bridge Too Far '77
All the President's Men '76
The Great Waldo Pepper '75
Three Days of the Condor '75
The Great Gatsby '74
The Sting '73
The Way We Were '73
The Candidate '72
Jeremiah Johnson '72
The Hot Rock '70
Butch Cassidy and the Sundance Kid '69
Downhill Racer '69
Tell Them Willie Boy Is Here '69
Barefoot in the Park '67
The Chase '66
This Property Is Condemned '66
Inside Daisy Clover '65
Rockets Redglare (1948-2001)
In the Soup '92
Cookie '89
Mystery Train '89
Shakedown '88
Salvation! '87
Down by Law '86
After Hours '85
Corin Redgrave (1939-)
Enigma '01
Ultraviolet '98
The Ice House '97
The Woman in White '97
Persuasion '95
Four Weddings and a Funeral '94
In the Name of the Father '93
Excalibur '81
Between Wars '74
The Charge of the Light Brigade '68
Jemma Redgrave (1965-)
The Acid House '98
Mosley '98
Diana: Her True Story '93
The Buddha of Suburbia '92
Howard's End '92
Dream Demon '88
Lynn Redgrave (1943-)
My Sister's Keeper '02
How to Kill Your Neighbor's Dog '01
Varian's War '01
The Next Best Thing '00
Deeply '99
A Season for Miracles '99
All I Wanna Do '98
Gods and Monsters '98
White Lies '98
Toothless '97
Shine '95
The Great American Sex Scandal '94
What Ever Happened To... '93
Getting It Right '89
Midnight '89
Morgan Stewart's Coming Home '87
Walking on Air '87
The Bad Seed '85
Rehearsal for Murder '82
Shooting '82
To Love Again '80
Centennial '78
Sooner or Later '78
The Big Bus '76
The Happy Hooker '75
The Turn of the Screw '74
Everything You Always Wanted to Know about Sex (But Were Afraid to Ask) '72
The Virgin Soldiers '69
Smashing Time '67
Georgy Girl '66
Girl with Green Eyes '64
Tom Jones '63
Michael Redgrave (1908-85)
Dr. Jekyll and Mr. Hyde '73
The Go-Between '71
Nicholas and Alexandra '71
Twinsanity '70
Battle of Britain '69
Goodbye, Mr. Chips '69
Heidi '67
The Heroes of Telemark '65
The Loneliness of the Long Distance Runner '62
The Innocents '61
Shake Hands with the Devil '59
The Wreck of the Mary Deare '59
Time Without Pity '57
Dam Busters '55
Mr. Arkadin '55
The Sea Shall Not Have Them '55
The Importance of Being Earnest '52
The Browning Version '51
Secret Beyond the Door '48
Captive Heart '47
Fame Is the Spur '47
Dead of Night '45
Kipps '41
Lady in Distress '39
The Stars Look Down '39
The Lady Vanishes '38
Vanessa Redgrave (1937-)
Jack and the Beanstalk: The Real Story '01
If These Walls Could Talk 2 '00
The Pledge '00
A Rumor of Angels '00
The Cradle Will Rock '99
Girl, Interrupted '99
Deep Impact '98
Deja Vu '98
Lulu on the Bridge '98
Bella Mafia '97
Mrs. Dalloway '97
Wilde '97
Looking for Richard '96
Mission: Impossible '96
Smilla's Sense of Snow '96
A Month by the Lake '95
Down Came a Blackbird '94
Little Odessa '94
Mother's Boys '94
The House of the Spirits '93
Shades of Fear '93
They Watch '93
What Ever Happened To... '93
Howard's End '92
The Ballad of the Sad Cafe '91
Orpheus Descending '91
Young Catherine '91
Consuming Passions '88
A Man for All Seasons '88
Prick Up Your Ears '87
Peter the Great '86
Steaming '86
Three Sovereigns for Sarah '85
Wagner: The Complete Epic '85
Wetherby '85
The Bostonians '84
Snow White and the Seven Dwarfs '83
Bear Island '80
Playing for Time '80
Agatha '79
Yanks '79
Julia '77
The Seven-Per-Cent Solution '76
Out of Season '75
Murder on the Orient Express '74
The Devils '71
Mary, Queen of Scots '71
Trojan Women '71
The Charge of the Light Brigade '68
Isadora '68
Camelot '67
Blow-Up '66
A Man for All Seasons '66
Morgan: A Suitable Case for Treatment '66
Juli Reding
Tormented '60
Mission in Morocco '59
Nick Reding
In Love and War '01
Croupier '97
Mister Johnson '91
Christian Redl
The Trio '97
Lea '96
Amanda Redman (1959-)
Sexy Beast '00
King Lear '98
Body & Soul '93
Richard's Things '80
Joyce Redman (1918-)
The Rector's Wife '94
Othello '65
Tom Jones '63
Liam Redmond (1913-89)
The Last Safari '67
The Ghost and Mr. Chicken '66
Curse of the Demon '57
Devil on Horseback '54
Moira Redmond
Catherine Cookson's The Wingless Bird '97
Nightmare '63
Siobhan Redmond
Beautiful People '99
Captives '94
Look Back in Anger '89
Manning Redwood
Outland '81
Shock Treatment '81
Alan Reed (1907-77)
Shinbone Alley '70 (V)
Tarnished Angels '57
Lady and the Tramp '55 (V)
A Woman's World '54
Actors and Sin '52
The Postman Always Rings Twice '46
Days of Glory '43
Alan Reed, Jr.
Peyton Place '57
Rock, Pretty Baby '56
Alyson Reed
Manhattan Merenque! '95
Skin Deep '89
A Chorus Line '85
Donald Reed
Slaves in Bondage '37
Evangeline '29
Donna Reed (1921-86)
The Benny Goodman Story '55
The Last Time I Saw Paris '54
The Caddy '53
From Here to Eternity '53
Gun Fury '53
Trouble along the Way '53
Hangman's Knot '52
Green Dolphin Street '47
It's a Wonderful Life '46
Picture of Dorian Gray '45
They Were Expendable '45
The Human Comedy '43
Thousands Cheer '43
Shadow of the Thin Man '41
George Reed
Strange Illusion '45
Green Pastures '36
Hal Reed
The Doberman Gang '72
The Zodiac Killer '71
Jerry Reed (1937-)
The Waterboy '98
Bat 21 '88
What Comes Around '85
Smokey and the Bandit, Part 3 '83
Survivors '83
Hot Stuff '80
Smokey and the Bandit 2 '80
The Concrete Cowboys '79
High Ballin' '78
Smokey and the Bandit '77
Gator '76
Lou Reed (1942-)
Blue in the Face '95
Faraway, So Close! '93
Superstar: The Life and Times of Andy Warhol '90
Get Crazy '83
One Trick Pony '80
Marshall Reed
The Hard Ride '71

They Saved Hitler's Brain '64

Maxwell Reed (1919-74)
Roadhouse Girl '53
Sea Devils '53
The Clouded Yellow '51
Flame of Araby '51
Blackout '50
Night Beat '48
Dear Murderer '47

Oliver Reed (1938-99)
Gladiator '00
Jeremiah '98
The Bruce '96
Funny Bones '94
Return to Lonesome Dove '93
Severed Ties '92
Hired to Kill '91
The Pit & the Pendulum '91
Prisoner of Honor '91
The Revenger '90
The Adventures of Baron Munchausen '89
The Lady and the Highwayman '89
Master of Dragonard Hill '89
The Return of the Musketeers '89
Skeleton Coast '89
Treasure Island '89
Captive Rage '88
Dragonard '88
Gor '88
The House of Usher '88
Rage to Kill '88
Captive '87
Castaway '87
The Misfit Brigade '87
Christopher Columbus '85
The Black Arrow '84
Fanny Hill '83
The Sting 2 '83
Two of a Kind '83
Spasms '82
Venom '82
Condorman '81
Lion of the Desert '81
Dr. Heckyl and Mr. Hype '80
The Brood '79
The Big Sleep '78
The Class of Miss MacMichael '78
The Prince and the Pauper '78
Maniac '77
Tomorrow Never Comes '77
Triple Echo '77
Burnt Offerings '76
Great Scout & Cathouse Thursday '76
Sell Out '76
The Four Musketeers '75
Lisztomania '75
Royal Flash '75
Ten Little Indians '75
Tommy '75
The Three Musketeers '74
Blue Blood '73
One Russian Summer '73
Zero Population Growth '72
The Devils '71
Women in Love '70
The Assassination Bureau '69
Dante's Inferno: Life of Dante Gabriel Rossetti '69
Blood Island '68
Oliver! '68
I'll Never Forget What's 'Isname '67
The Girl Getters '66
Trap '66
Paranoiac '62
The Curse of the Werewolf '61
Beat Girl '60
No Love for Johnnie '60
Sword of Sherwood Forest '60
The Two Faces of Dr. Jekyll '60

Pamela Reed (1949-)
Proof of Life '00
Why Do Fools Fall in Love? '98
Bean '97
Critical Choices '97
Santa Fe '97
Junior '94
Bob Roberts '92
Passed Away '92
Woman with a Past '92
Cadillac Man '90
Caroline? '90
Kindergarten Cop '90
Chattahoochee '89
Tanner '88 '88
Rachel River '87
The Best of Times '86
The Clan of the Cave Bear '86
The Goodbye People '83
The Right Stuff '83
Young Doctors in Love '82
Eyewitness '81
The Long Riders '80
Melvin and Howard '80

Penelope Reed
Hired to Kill '91
Amazons '86

Philip Reed (1908-96)
Bandit Queen '51
Unknown Island '48
Big Town '47
Big Town After Dark '47
Song of Scheherazade '47
Song of the Thin Man '47
Underworld Scandal '47
A Gentleman After Dark '42
Madame X '37
Klondike Annie '36
Female '33

Robert Reed (1932-92)
Prime Target '91
A Very Brady Christmas '88
Death of a Centerfold '81
Casino '80
Nurse '80
Love's Savage Fury '79
The Seekers '79
Bud and Lou '78
No Prince for My Cinderella '78
The Hunted Lady '77
The Boy in the Plastic Bubble '76
Nightmare in Badham County '76
Rich Man, Poor Man '76
Haunts of the Very Rich '72
Snatched '72
The Love Bug '68
Star! '68
Bloodlust '59
The Hunters '58

Shanna Reed (1956-)
The Night Caller '97
Rattled '96
The Sister-in-Law '95
Don't Talk to Strangers '94
The Banker '89
Legs '83

Suzanne Reed
Up from the Depths '79
Beyond the Bermuda Triangle '75

Tracy Reed
Piece of the Action '77
No Way Back '74
Dr. Strangelove, or: How I Learned to Stop Worrying and Love the Bomb '64

Walter Reed (1916-2001)
The Sand Pebbles '66
Macumba Love '60
The Horse Soldiers '59
How to Make a Monster '58
Government Agents vs. Phantom Legion '51
The Torch '50
Seven Days' Leave '42

Lady Reeds
Avenging Disco Godfather '76

Dolemite 2: Human Tornado '76
Dolemite '75

Norman Reedus (1969-)
Blade II '02
Deuces Wild '02
Bad Seed '00
Sand '00
Boondock Saints '99
Gossip '99
Let the Devil Wear Black '99
Six Ways to Sunday '99
Dark Harbor '98
Reach the Rock '98
Floating '97

Harry (Herbert Streicher) Reems (1947-)
R.S.V.P. '84
Deadly Weapons '70

Angharad Rees (1949-)
The Wolves of Kromer '98
Poldark '75
Poldark 2 '75
Hands of the Ripper '71

Donough Rees
Crush '93
Starship '87

Roger Rees (1944-)
Return to Never Land '02 (V)
The Scorpion King '02
The Crossing '00
Blackmale '99
Double Platinum '99
William Shakespeare's A Midsummer Night's Dream '99
The Bumblebee Flies Anyway '98
Next Stop, Wonderland '98
Sudden Manhattan '96
Titanic '96
Charles & Diana: A Palace Divided '93
Robin Hood: Men in Tights '93
Stop! or My Mom Will Shoot '92
If Looks Could Kill '91
Mountains of the Moon '90
Ebony Tower '86
A Christmas Carol '84
Star 80 '83
The Life and Adventures of Nicholas Nickleby '81

Della Reese (1932-)
Dinosaur '00 (V)
Having Our Say: The Delany Sisters' First 100 Years '99
Mama Flora's Family '98
A Thin Line Between Love and Hate '96
The Kid Who Loved Christmas '90
Harlem Nights '89
Nightmare in Badham County '76
Psychic Killer '75
The Voyage of the Yes '72

Christopher Reeve (1952-)
Rear Window '98
Above Suspicion '95
Village of the Damned '95
Black Fox: Blood Horse '94
Black Fox: Good Men and Bad '94
Black Fox: The Price of Peace '94
Speechless '94
Morning Glory '93
The Remains of the Day '93
The Sea Wolf '93
Death Dreams '92
Mortal Sins '92
Noises Off '92
The Rose and the Jackal '90
The Great Escape 2: The Untold Story '88
Switching Channels '88

Street Smart '87
Superman 4: The Quest for Peace '87
Anna Karenina '85
The Aviator '85
The Bostonians '84
Sleeping Beauty '83
Superman 3 '83
Deathtrap '82
Monsignor '82
Somewhere in Time '80
Superman 2 '80
Superman: The Movie '78
Gray Lady Down '77

George Reeves (1914-59)
Westward Ho, the Wagons! '56
Forever Female '53
From Here to Eternity '53
Bugles in the Afternoon '52
Rancho Notorious '52
Superman & the Mole Men '51
The Great Lover '49
Jungle Goddess '49
Pirate Ship '49
Thunder in the Pines '49
Border Patrol '43
Colt Comrades '43
Hoppy Serves a Writ '43
Leather Burners '43
So Proudly We Hail '43
Blood and Sand '41
Lydia '41
Strawberry Blonde '41
The Fighting 69th '40
Gone with the Wind '39

Keanu Reeves (1964-)
Hardball '01
Sweet November '01
The Gift '00
The Replacements '00
The Watcher '00
The Matrix '99
The Devil's Advocate '97
Chain Reaction '96
Feeling Minnesota '96
The Last Time I Committed Suicide '96
Johnny Mnemonic '95
A Walk in the Clouds '95
Even Cowgirls Get the Blues '94
Speed '94
Freaked '93
Little Buddha '93
Much Ado about Nothing '93
Bram Stoker's Dracula '92
Bill & Ted's Bogus Journey '91
My Own Private Idaho '91
Point Break '91
I Love You to Death '90
Tune in Tomorrow '90
Bill & Ted's Excellent Adventure '89
Parenthood '89
Dangerous Liaisons '88
The Night Before '88
Permanent Record '88
Prince of Pennsylvania '88
River's Edge '87
Act of Vengeance '86
Babes in Toyland '86
Brotherhood of Justice '86
Youngblood '86
Dream to Believe '85

Kynaston Reeves (1893-1971)
Hot Millions '68
Fiend without a Face '58
Phantom Fiend '35

Lisa Reeves
Snowblind '78
The Chicken Chronicles '77
Pom Pom Girls '76

Perrey Reeves
Red Shoe Diaries: Luscious Lola '00
Child's Play 3 '91

Saskia Reeves
Dune '00
A Christmas Carol '99
Heart '99
Different for Girls '96

Butterfly Kiss '94
Traps '93
Antonia and Jane '91
Close My Eyes '91
December Bride '91
A Woman of Substance '84

Scott Reeves
Edge of Honor '91
Friday the 13th, Part 8: Jason Takes Manhattan '89

Steve Reeves (1926-2000)
The Avenger '62
Pirates of the Seven Seas '62
The Trojan Horse '62
Thief of Baghdad '61
The Giant of Marathon '60
Goliath and the Barbarians '60
The Last Days of Pompeii '60
Morgan the Pirate '60
Hercules Unchained '59
Hercules '58
Athena '54
Jail Bait '54

Steve Reevis
Wild Grizzly '99
Crazy Horse '96
Fargo '96
The Last of the Dogmen '95

Joe Regalbuto (1949-)
Bodily Harm '95
Writer's Block '91
The Queen of Mean '90
Invitation to Hell '84
Lassiter '84
Missing '82

Jayne Regan (1909-2000)
Texas Jack '35
The Silver Bullet '34

Mary Regan
Fever '88
Midnight Dancer '87
Sylvia '86
Heart of the Stag '84

Phil Regan (1906-96)
Swing Parade of 1946 '46
Sweet Rosie O'Grady '43
Manhattan Merry-Go-Round '37

Vincent Regan
Black Knight '01
Invasion: Earth '98

George Regas (1890-1940)
Beau Geste '39
Gunga Din '39
The Rains Came '39
The Charge of the Light Brigade '36
Hell-Ship Morgan '36
The Lives of a Bengal Lancer '35
Sixteen Fathoms Deep '34
The Love Light '21

Duncan Regehr (1952-)
Air Bud 3: World Pup '00
Blood Surf '00
Timemaster '95
The Last Samurai '90
The Banker '89
Gore Vidal's Billy the Kid '89
The Monster Squad '87
My Wicked, Wicked Ways '84

Benoit Regent (1953-94)
Trois Couleurs: Rouge '94
Trois Couleurs: Bleu '93
Club Extinction '89

Serge Reggiani (1922-)
Mauvais Sang '86
Cat and Mouse '78
Vincent, Francois, Paul and the Others '76
Le Doulos '61
Les Miserables '57
Casque d'Or '52

La Ronde '51
Manon '50

Nadja Regin
Goldfinger '64
From Russia with Love '63

Paul Regina (1956-)
It's My Party '95
Sharon's Secret '95
Adam '83
A Long Way Home '81

Regine
My New Partner '84
Robert et Robert '78
The Seven-Per-Cent Solution '76
Marry Me, Marry Me '69

Meg Register
Boxing Helena '93
Demonia '90

Charles Regnier
A Man Like Eva '83
A Time to Love & a Time to Die '58

Frank Reicher (1875-1965)
Watch on the Rhine '43
To Be or Not to Be '42
Dr. Cyclops '40
King Kong '33
Scarlet Dawn '32

Wolfgang Reichmann (1932-91)
Beethoven's Nephew '88
Woyzeck '78
Signs of Life '68
The Nun '66

Anne Reid
Liam '00
Catherine Cookson's The Wingless Bird '97

Beryl Reid (1920-96)
Duel of Hearts '92
The Doctor and the Devils '85
Yellowbeard '83
Carry On Emmanuelle '78
Joseph Andrews '77
No Sex Please—We're British '73
Psychomania '73
Doctor Phibes Rises Again '72
Beast in the Cellar '70
Entertaining Mr. Sloane '70
The Assassination Bureau '69
The Killing of Sister George '69
Star! '68
Trial & Error '62
The Belles of St. Trinian's '53

Carl Benton Reid (1893-1973)
Pressure Point '62
The Bramble Bush '60
The Gallant Hours '60
The Trap '59
Battle Hymn '57
The Egyptian '54
Escape from Fort Bravo '53
Indian Uprising '51
The Fuller Brush Girl '50
In a Lonely Place '50
The Little Foxes '41

Christopher Reid
House Party 3 '94
Class Act '91
House Party 2: The Pajama Jam '91
House Party '90

Elliott Reid (1920-)
Follow Me, Boys! '66
The Thrill of It All! '63
Inherit the Wind '60
A Woman's World '54
Gentlemen Prefer Blondes '53
The Story of Dr. Wassell '44

Fiona Reid (1951-)
My Big Fat Greek Wedding '02
Bogus '96
Blood & Donuts '95

Beethoven Lives Upstairs '92
Mark Twain and Me '91
Heaven on Earth '89
Accident '83

Frances Reid
The Affair '73
Seconds '66

Kate Reid (1930-93)
Teamster Boss: The Jackie Presser Story '92
Deceived '91
The Last Best Year '90
Bye Bye Blues '89
Signs of Life '89
Control '87
Death of a Salesman '86
Fire with Fire '86
Execution of Raymond Graham '85
Heaven Help Us '85
The Blood of Others '84
Atlantic City '81
Circle of Two '80
Death Ship '80
The Double Negative '80
Highpoint '80
Crossbar '79
The Rainbow Gang '73
The Andromeda Strain '71
This Property Is Condemned '66
Holy Terror '65
Invincible Mr. Disraeli '63
One Plus One '61

Sheila Reid
The Winter Guest '97
Othello '65

Tara Reid (1975-)
National Lampoon's Van Wilder '02
American Pie 2 '01
Josie and the Pussycats '01
Just Visiting '01
Dr. T & the Women '00
American Pie '99
Body Shots '99
Around the Fire '98
Girl '98
Urban Legend '98
The Big Lebowski '97

Tim Reid (1944-)
Race to Freedom: The Story of the Underground Railroad '94
You Must Remember This '92
The Fourth War '90
Stephen King's It '90
Dead Bang '89

Wallace Reid (1891-1923)
Affairs of Anatol '21
Hawthorne of the USA '19
The Roaring Road '19
The Birth of a Nation '15

Timothy Reifsnyder
Hearts in Atlantis '01
Wide Awake '97

Charles Nelson Reilly (1931-)
Boys Will Be Boys '97
A Troll in Central Park '94 (V)
Rock-a-Doodle '92 (V)
All Dogs Go to Heaven '89 (V)
Body Slam '87
Cannonball Run 2 '84

Hugh Reilly (1916-98)
Chuka '67
Lassie's Great Adventure '62

John C. Reilly (1965-)
The Good Girl '02
The Anniversary Party '01
The Perfect Storm '00
For Love of the Game '99
Magnolia '99
Never Been Kissed '99
The Settlement '99
Chicago Cab '98
The Thin Red Line '98
Boogie Nights '97
Hard Eight '96
Nightwatch '96
Boys '95
Georgia '95
Dolores Claiborne '94
The River Wild '94
Fallen Angels 1 '93
What's Eating Gilbert Grape '93
Hoffa '92
Out on a Limb '92
Days of Thunder '90
State of Grace '90
Casualties of War '89
We're No Angels '89
Touch and Go '86
Missing Pieces '83

Luke Reilly
Zebrahead '92
Bye Bye Blues '89

Tom Reilly
Mirror Images 2 '93
Kiss and Be Killed '91

Gary Reineke
The Golden Spiders: A Nero Wolfe Mystery '00
George's Island '91

Carl Reiner (1922-)
Ocean's Eleven '01
The Adventures of Rocky & Bullwinkle '00
Slums of Beverly Hills '98
The Right to Remain Silent '95
Spirit of '76 '91
Pinocchio '83
Dead Men Don't Wear Plaid '82
The Jerk '79
The End '78
Generation '69
A Guide for the Married Man '67
The Russians Are Coming, the Russians Are Coming '66
It's a Mad, Mad, Mad, Mad World '63
The Thrill of It All! '63
Gidget Goes Hawaiian '61
The Gazebo '59

Rob Reiner (1945-)
EDtv '99
The Muse '99
The Story of Us '99
Primary Colors '98
The First Wives Club '96
Trigger Happy '96
For Better or Worse '95
Bullets over Broadway '94
Bye Bye, Love '94
Mixed Nuts '94
Sleepless in Seattle '93
The Return of Spinal Tap '92
Spirit of '76 '91
Postcards from the Edge '90
Throw Momma from the Train '87
Johnny Appleseed '86
This Is Spinal Tap '84
The Jerk '79
Thursday's Game '74
How Come Nobody's On Our Side? '73
Where's Poppa? '70
Enter Laughing '67

Tracy Reiner (1964-)
Apollo 13 '95
A League of Their Own '92
Frankie and Johnny '91
Masque of the Red Death '89
New Year's Day '89
Jumpin' Jack Flash '86
Nothing in Common '86

Judge Reinhold (1958-)
Beethoven's 3rd '00
Newsbreak '00
Boltneck '98
Last Lives '98
Tom Clancy's Netforce '98
Crackerjack 2 '97
Homegrown '97
As Good as Dead '95
The Right to Remain Silent '95
The Wharf Rat '95
Beverly Hills Cop 3 '94
The Santa Clause '94
Bank Robber '93
Four Eyes and Six Guns '93
Baby on Board '92
Black Magic '92
Near Misses '91
A Soldier's Tale '91
Zandalee '91
Daddy's Dyin'...Who's Got the Will? '90
Enid Is Sleeping '90
Rosalie Goes Shopping '89
Promised a Miracle '88
Vice Versa '88
Beverly Hills Cop 2 '87
Head Office '86
Off Beat '86
Ruthless People '86
Beverly Hills Cop '84
Gremlins '84
Roadhouse 66 '84
The Lords of Discipline '83
Fast Times at Ridgemont High '82
Pandemonium '82
Stripes '81
On the Edge: The Survival of Dana '79
Running Scared '79

Ann Reinking (1949-)
Micki & Maude '84
Annie '82
All That Jazz '79

Michelle Reis
Flowers of Shanghai '98
Fallen Angels '95

Geri Reischl
I Dismember Mama '74
The Brotherhood of Satan '71

Hans Reiser
The Great Escape '63
Secret of the Black Trunk '62

Paul Reiser (1956-)
One Night at McCool's '01
The Story of Us '99
Bye Bye, Love '94
Mr. Write '92
Family Prayers '91
The Marrying Man '91
Crazy People '90
Cross My Heart '88
Beverly Hills Cop 2 '87
Aliens '86
From Here to Maternity '85
Odd Jobs '85
Beverly Hills Cop '84
Sunset Limousine '83
Diner '82

Winston Rekert (1949-)
A Cooler Climate '99
The Last Stop '99
The World's Oldest Living Bridesmaid '92
Glory! Glory! '90
Eternal Evil '87
Toby McTeague '87
Agnes of God '85
Dead Wrong '83
Heartaches '82

Maria Therese Relin
Quo Vadis '85
Secret Places '85

James Remar (1953-)
Guardian '01
The Guardian '00
Hellraiser 5: Inferno '00
What Lies Beneath '00
Blowback '99
D.R.E.A.M. Team '99
Rites of Passage '99
Psycho '98
Born Bad '97
Mortal Kombat 2: Annihilation '97
The Phantom '96
The Quest '96
Robo Warriors '96
One Good Turn '95
Across the Moon '94
Boys on the Side '94
Confessions of a Hit Man '94
Miracle on 34th Street '94
Renaissance Man '94
The Surgeon '94
Blink '93
Fatal Instinct '93
The Tigress '93
Fatal Charm '92
Indecency '92
Deadlock '91
White Fang '91
Silence Like Glass '90
Tales from the Darkside: The Movie '90
The Dream Team '89
Drugstore Cowboy '89
Rent-A-Cop '88
The Clan of the Cave Bear '86
Quiet Cool '86
The Cotton Club '84
48 Hrs. '82
Windwalker '81
The Warriors '79

Erika Remberg (1932-)
The Lickerish Quartet '70
Cave of the Living Dead '65
Circus of Horrors '60

Lee Remick (1935-91)
Around the World in 80 Days '89
Bridge to Silence '89
Jesse '88
The Vision '87
Follies in Concert '85
Toughlove '85
I Do! I Do! '84
Mistral's Daughter '84
The Snow Queen '83
The Competition '80
Tribute '80
The Europeans '79
Ike '79
Torn Between Two Lovers '79
Breaking Up '78
The Medusa Touch '78
Telefon '77
The Omen '76
Hennessy '75
Hustling '75
QB VII '74
Touch Me Not '74
Sometimes a Great Notion '71
Loot ... Give Me Money, Honey! '70
The Detective '68
No Way to Treat a Lady '68
The Hallelujah Trail '65
Baby, the Rain Must Fall '64
The Tempest '63
The Wheeler Dealers '63
Days of Wine and Roses '62
Experiment in Terror '62
Anatomy of a Murder '59
The Long, Hot Summer '58
A Face in the Crowd '57

Bert Remsen (1925-99)
Crime of the Century '96
Humanoids from the Deep '96
Maverick '94
Evil Spirits '91
Only the Lonely '91
Daddy's Dyin'...Who's Got the Will? '90
Payback '90
Peacemaker '90
Miss Firecracker '89
Curfew '88
South of Reno '87
Eye of the Tiger '86
Tai-Pan '86
Terrorvision '86
Code of Silence '85
Burning Rage '84
I Married a Centerfold '84
Lies '83
M.A.D.D.: Mothers Against Drunk Driving '83
Policewoman Centerfold '83
Joni '79
Tarantulas: The Deadly Cargo '77
Nashville '75
Sweet Hostage '75
Thieves Like Us '74
The Death Squad '73
McCabe & Mrs. Miller '71
Pork Chop Hill '59

Kerry Remsen
Pumpkinhead '88
Ghoulies 2 '87
Appointment with Fear '85

Albert Remy (1911-67)
The Train '65
Shoot the Piano Player '62
The 400 Blows '59
Children of Paradise '44

Ronald Remy
Revenge of Doctor X '80s
Mad Doctor of Blood Island '69
The Vampire People '66
No Man Is an Island '62

Duncan Renaldo (1904-80)
Manhunt in the African Jungle '54
The Capture '50
Guns of Fury '45
In Old New Mexico '45
South of the Rio Grande '45
Fighting Seabees '44
Perils of the Darkest Jungle '44
Border Patrol '43
For Whom the Bell Tolls '43
Tiger Fangs '43
Down Mexico Way '41
Outlaws of the Desert '41
Panama Menace '41
Covered Wagon Days '40
Gaucho Serenade '40
Rocky Mountain Rangers '40
Cowboys from Texas '39
The Kansas Terrors '39
Rough Riders' Roundup '39
Rose of Rio Grande '38
Spawn of the North '38
The Painted Stallion '37
Roaring Speedboats '37
Zorro Rides Again '37
Trader Horn '31

Tito Renaldo
The Story of G.I. Joe '45
For Whom the Bell Tolls '43

Simone Renant (1911-)
Dear Detective '77
That Man from Rio '64
Dangerous Liaisons '60
Jenny Lamour '47

Francis Renaud
Perfect Love '96
Pigalle '95

Madeleine Renaud (1900-94)
Le Plaisir '52
Stormy Waters '41
Maria Chapdelaine '34

Isabelle Renauld
Eternity and a Day '97
Perfect Love '96

Georges Renavent
Whistlin' Dan '32
East of Borneo '31

Liz Renay (1926-)
Desperate Living '77
Blackenstein '73
The Thrill Killers '65

Brad Renfro (1982-)
Deuces Wild '02
Bully '01
Ghost World '01
Happy Campers '01
Tart '01
Skipped Parts '00
Apt Pupil '97
Sleepers '96
Telling Lies in America '96
The Cure '95
Tom and Huck '95
The Client '94

Jeremie Renier
Brotherhood of the Wolf '01
La Promesse '96

Patrick Renna (1979-)
P.U.N.K.S. '98
Address Unknown '96
The Big Green '95
Blue River '95
Beanstalk '94
The Sandlot '93
Son-in-Law '93

Deborah Rennard
Lionheart '90
Land of Doom '84

Callum Keith Rennie (1960-)
Slap Shot 2: Breaking the Ice '02
Torso '01
Memento '00
eXistenZ '99
The Highway Man '99
The Last Stop '99
The Life Before This '99
Last Night '98
Tricks '97
Curtis's Charm '96
Hard Core Logo '96
Masterminds '96
Double Happiness '94

Michael Rennie (1909-71)
Surabaya Conspiracy '75
Die Screaming, Marianne '73
Dracula vs. Frankenstein '69
The Battle of El Alamein '68
The Devil's Brigade '68
Commando Attack '67
Hotel '67
Third Man on the Mountain '59
Omar Khayyam '57
Mambo '55
Seven Cities of Gold '55
Soldier of Fortune '55
Demetrius and the Gladiators '54
Desiree '54
The Robe '53
Five Fingers '52
Phone Call from a Stranger '52
The Day the Earth Stood Still '51
Trio '50
Uneasy Terms '48
The Wicked Lady '45
Tower of Terror '42

Ginette Reno
It's My Turn, Laura Cadieux '98
Leolo '92

Jean Reno (1948-)
Rollerball '02
The Crimson Rivers '01
Just Visiting '01
Godzilla '98
Ronin '98
For Roseanna '96
Mission: Impossible '96
Beyond the Clouds '95
French Kiss '95
The Visitors '95
The Professional '94
La Femme Nikita '91
The Big Blue '88
Subway '85
Le Dernier Combat '84

John Reno
Bloodspell '87
Mirror of Death '87

Kelly Reno (1966-)
Brady's Escape '84
The Black Stallion Returns '83
The Black Stallion '79

Jean Renoir (1894-1979)
The Little Theatre of Jean Renoir '71
The Rules of the Game '39

Pierre Renoir (1885-1952)
Children of Paradise '44

La Marseillaise '37
Madame Bovary '34

Sophie Renoir
Boyfriends & Girlfriends '88
Le Beau Mariage '82

Eva Renzi (1944-)
Night of the Assassin '77
The Bird with the Crystal Plumage '70
The Pink Jungle '68
Funeral in Berlin '66

Maggie Renzi
Passion Fish '92
City of Hope '91
Eight Men Out '88
Matewan '87
The Brother from Another Planet '84
Return of the Secaucus 7 '80

Dan Resin
Caddyshack '80
Hail '73

Antonio Resines
How to Be a Woman and Not Die in the Attempt '91
Skyline '84

Frank Ressel
Tarzana, the Wild Girl '72
Blood and Black Lace '64

Dale Resteghini
Da Hip Hop Witch '00
Colorz of Rage '97

Tommy Rettig (1941-96)
The Cobweb '55
River of No Return '54
The 5000 Fingers of Dr. T '53

Raul Retzer
2069: A Sex Odyssey '78
The Vampire Happening '71

Gloria Reuben (1964-)
Little John '02
Cold Blooded '00
Shaft '00
Inferno '99
Indiscreet '98
Johnny's Girl '95
Nick of Time '95
Dead Air '94
Timecop '94
Percy & Thunder '93

Paul (Pee-wee Herman) Reubens (1952-)
Blow '01
South of Heaven, West of Hell '00
Mystery Men '99
Dr. Dolittle '98 (V)
Buddy '97
Matilda '96
Dunston Checks In '95
The Nightmare before Christmas '93 (V)
Batman Returns '92
Buffy the Vampire Slayer '92
Big Top Pee-wee '88
Back to the Beach '87
Flight of the Navigator '86 (V)
Pee-wee's Big Adventure '85
Meatballs 2 '84
Pinocchio '83
Pandemonium '82
The Pee-wee Herman Show '82
Cheech and Chong's Nice Dreams '81
The Blues Brothers '80
Cheech and Chong's Next Movie '80

Anne Revere (1903-90)
A Place in the Sun '51
Secret Beyond the Door '48
Body and Soul '47
Forever Amber '47
Gentleman's Agreement '47
The Keys of the Kingdom '44
National Velvet '44
The Thin Man Goes Home '44
The Song of Bernadette '43
The Howards of Virginia '40

Dorothy Revier (1904-93)
Circumstantial Evidence '35
Green Eyes '34
When a Man Sees Red '34
The King Murder '32
The Secrets of Wu Sin '32
Dance of Life '29
The Dropkick '27

Clive Revill (1930-)
The Thief and the Cobbler '96 (V)
The Sea Wolf '93
Let Him Have It '91
Mack the Knife '89
Rumpelstiltskin '86
George Washington '84
Zorro, the Gay Blade '81
The Empire Strikes Back '80
Matilda '78
One of Our Dinosaurs Is Missing '75
The Black Windmill '74
Ghost in the Noonday Sun '74
The Little Prince '74
The Legend of Hell House '73
Avanti! '72
Escape to the Sun '72
The Private Life of Sherlock Holmes '70
The Assassination Bureau '69
Fathom '67
A Fine Madness '66
Modesty Blaise '66

Rex
Robinson Crusoe of Clipper Island '36
Robinson Crusoe of Mystery Island '36
King of the Wild Horses '24

Simon Rex
The Forsaken '01
Shriek If You Know What I Did Last Friday the 13th '00

Alejandro Rey (1930-87)
Stickfighter '89
Terrorvision '86
Moscow on the Hudson '84
The Grace Kelly Story '83
Rita Hayworth: The Love Goddess '83
The Ninth Configuration '79
The Stepmother '71
Fun in Acapulco '63
Solomon and Sheba '59

Antonia Rey
Tarantella '95
Spike of Bensonhurst '88

Fernando Rey (1917-94)
1492: Conquest of Paradise '92
Naked Tango '91
The Tunnel '89
Moon over Parador '88
Angel of Death '86
Saving Grace '86
A.D. '85
The Hit '85
Padre Nuestro '85
Star Knight '85
Insanity '82
Monsignor '82
Cabo Blanco '81
Honey '81
Autopsy '70s
Quintet '79
The Assignment '78
Elisa, Vida Mia '77
That Obscure Object of Desire '77
The Desert of the Tartars '76
Seven Beauties '76
French Connection 2 '75
La Grande Bourgeoise '74
Antony and Cleopatra '73
High Crime '73
The Discreet Charm of the Bourgeoisie '72
A Town Called Hell '72
The French Connection '71
The Adventurers '70
Cold Eyes of Fear '70
Companeros '70
Tristana '70
Guns of the Magnificent Seven '69
Chimes at Midnight '67
Navajo Joe '67
Attack of the Robots '66
The Castilian '63
Goliath Against the Giants '63
Viridiana '61
Pantaloons '57
The Miracle of Marcelino '55

Mony Rey
Not Without My Daughter '90
Mademoiselle '66

Walter Reyer
The Indian Tomb '59
Journey to the Lost City '58

Ernie Reyes, Jr. (1972-)
Kill Shot '01
Rush Hour 2 '01
White Wolves 2: Legend of the Wild '94
Surf Ninjas '93
Teenage Mutant Ninja Turtles 2: The Secret of the Ooze '91

Julian Reyes
Mi Vida Loca '94
Point Break '91

Kamar Reyes
Coldfire '90
East L.A. Warriors '89

Dominique Reymond
Come Undone '00
Will It Snow for Christmas? '96

Janine Reynaud
The Scorpion's Tail '71
The Sensuous Teenager '70
Castle of the Creeping Flesh '68

Burt Reynolds (1936-)
The Final Hit '02
Driven '01
The Crew '00
Hostage Hotel '00
Big City Blues '99
Mystery, Alaska '99
Pups '99
Waterproof '99
Crazy Six '98
Universal Soldier 3: Unfinished Business '98
Bean '97
Boogie Nights '97
Hunter's Moon '97
Meet Wally Sparks '97
Raven '97
The Cherokee Kid '96
Citizen Ruth '96
Frankenstein and Me '96
Striptease '96
Trigger Happy '96
The Maddening '95
Cop and a Half '93
The Man from Left Field '93
The Player '92
Modern Love '90
All Dogs Go to Heaven '89 (V)
Breaking In '89
Physical Evidence '89
Rent-A-Cop '88
Switching Channels '88
Heat '87
Malone '87
Stick '85
Uphill All the Way '85
Cannonball Run 2 '84
City Heat '84
The Man Who Loved Women '83
Smokey and the Bandit, Part 3 '83
Stroker Ace '83
Best Friends '82
The Best Little Whorehouse in Texas '82
Cannonball Run '81
Paternity '81
Sharky's Machine '81
Rough Cut '80
Smokey and the Bandit 2 '80
Starting Over '79
The End '78
Hooper '78
Semi-Tough '77
Smokey and the Bandit '77
Gator '76
Silent Movie '76
The Hustle '75
The Longest Yard '74
Man Who Loved Cat Dancing '73
Shamus '73
White Lightning '73
Deliverance '72
Everything You Always Wanted to Know about Sex (But Were Afraid to Ask) '72
Fuzz '72
Hard Frame '70
Savage Run '70
Skullduggery '70
100 Rifles '69
Iron Cowboy '68
Shark! '68
Navajo Joe '67
Operation C.I.A. '65
Angel Baby '61
Armored Command '61

Craig Reynolds
Nevada '44
I Take This Oath '40

Debbie Reynolds (1932-)
These Old Broads '01
Rugrats in Paris: The Movie '00 (V)
Zack & Reba '98
In and Out '97
Mother '96
Wedding Bell Blues '96
Heaven and Earth '93
Battling for Baby '92
The Bodyguard '92
Detective Sadie & Son '84
Charlotte's Web '73 (V)
What's the Matter with Helen? '71
How Sweet It Is! '68
Divorce American Style '67
The Singing Nun '66
Goodbye Charlie '64
The Unsinkable Molly Brown '64
How the West Was Won '63
The Rat Race '60
The Gazebo '59
It Started with a Kiss '59
The Mating Game '59
This Happy Feeling '58
Tammy and the Bachelor '57
Bundle of Joy '56
The Catered Affair '56
Meet Me in Las Vegas '56
Hit the Deck '55
The Tender Trap '55
Athena '54
Susan Slept Here '54
The Affairs of Dobie Gillis '53
Give a Girl a Break '53
I Love Melvin '53
Singin' in the Rain '52
Skirts Ahoy! '52
Three Little Words '50
Two Weeks with Love '50

Gene Reynolds (1925-)
Country Girl '54
Jungle Patrol '48
The Tuttles of Tahiti '42
Andy Hardy's Private Secretary '41
Life Begins for Andy Hardy '41
They Shall Have Music '39
Boys Town '38
Love Finds Andy Hardy '38
In Old Chicago '37

Marjorie Reynolds (1916-97)
His Kind of Woman '51
Home Town Story '51
Monsieur Beaucaire '46
The Time of Their Lives '46
Ministry of Fear '44
Holiday Inn '42
Robin Hood of the Pecos '41
Doomed to Die '40
The Fatal Hour '40
Midnight Limited '40
Up in the Air '40
The Abe Lincoln of Ninth Avenue '39
Gone with the Wind '39
Mr. Wong in Chinatown '39
Mystery Plane '39
Racketeers of the Range '39
Stunt Pilot '39
Man's Country '38
Six Shootin' Sheriff '38
Western Trails '38

Michael J. Reynolds
Ms. Scrooge '97
War Between the Tates '76

Peter Reynolds (1926-75)
The Great Armored Car Swindle '64
The Hands of Orlac '60
It Takes a Thief '59
Devil Girl from Mars '54

Robert Reynolds
Element of Doubt '96
Tunnel Vision '95
Traps '93
Daughter of Darkness '89

Ryan Reynolds (1976-)
National Lampoon's Van Wilder '02
Coming Soon '99
Dick '99
The Alarmist '98
Boltneck '98
Sabrina the Teenage Witch '96
Ordinary Magic '93

Vera Reynolds (1900-62)
The Monster Walks '32
Tangled Destinies '32
Risky Business '28
Sunny Side Up '28
The Night Club '25
The Road to Yesterday '25

William Reynolds (1931-)
The Land Unknown '57
All That Heaven Allows '55
Cult of the Cobra '55
Gunsmoke '53
Carrie '52
Francis Goes to West Point '52
Son of Ali Baba '52

Ving Rhames (1961-)
Little John '02
Baby Boy '01
Final Fantasy: The Spirits Within '01 (V)
Sins of the Father '01
American Tragedy '00
Holiday Heart '00
Mission: Impossible 2 '00
Bringing Out the Dead '99
Entrapment '99
Out of Sight '98
Body Count '97
Con Air '97
Don King: Only in America '97
Dangerous Ground '96
Mission: Impossible '96
Rosewood '96
Striptease '96
DROP Squad '94
Kiss of Death '94
Pulp Fiction '94
Dave '93
The Saint of Fort Washington '93
Homicide '91
The People under the Stairs '91
Flight of the Intruder '90
Jacob's Ladder '90
Rising Son '90
The Long Walk Home '89
Patty Hearst '88

Pamela Rhea
How to Make a Doll '68
The Girl, the Body and the Pill '67

Phillip Rhee (1960-)
Best of the Best: Without Warning '98
Best of the Best 3: No Turning Back '95
Best of the Best 2 '93
Best of the Best '89
Silent Assassins '88

Simon Rhee
The Substitute 4: Failure is Not an Option '00
Best of the Best 2 '93
Best of the Best '89

Ashlie Rhey
Bikini Drive-In '94
Midnight Tease '94
Play Time '94

Julian Rhind-Tutt (1968-)
Lara Croft: Tomb Raider '01
Heat of the Sun '99
Reckless '97
The Madness of King George '94

Barbara Rhoades (1947-)
Sex and the Single Parent '82
The Day the Women Got Even '80
Serial '80
The Choirboys '77
The Goodbye Girl '77
Conspiracy of Terror '75
Hunter '73
Scream Blacula Scream '73
Up the Sandbox '72
The Shakiest Gun in the West '68

Bobby Rhodes (1947-)
Demons 2 '87
Endgame '85
The Last Hunter '80

Cynthia Rhodes (1957-)
Curse of the Crystal Eye '93
Dirty Dancing '87
Runaway '84
Flashdance '83
Staying Alive '83

Donnelly Rhodes (1937-)
Big and Hairy '98
Guitarman '95
Dirty Work '92
The Penthouse '92
Showdown at Williams Creek '91
Hard Part Begins '80s
After the Promise '87
Goldenrod '77

Dusty Rhodes
Heroes of the Heart '94
Paradise Park '91

Erik Rhodes (1906-90)
Special Investigator '36
Charlie Chan in Paris '35
Top Hat '35
The Gay Divorcee '34

Grandon Rhodes
Revenge of the Creature '55
Magnificent Doll '46

Hari Rhodes (1932-92)
Coma '78
A Woman Called Moses '78
Detroit 9000 '73
A Dream for Christmas '73
Conquest of the Planet of the Apes '72
Shock Corridor '63
Marjorie Rhodes (1903-79)
Hands of the Ripper '71
Decameron Nights '53
Great Day '46
Butler's Dilemma '43
Busta Rhymes (1972-)
Halloween: Resurrection '02
Finding Forrester '00
Shaft '00
The Rugrats Movie '98 (V)
Matthew Rhys
Heart '99
Titus '99
Paul Rhys (1963-)
King Lear '98
Gallowglass '95
Nina Takes a Lover '94
Becoming Colette '92
Chaplin '92
Vincent & Theo '90
John Rhys-Davies (1944-)
Lord of the Rings 1: The Fellowship of the Rings '01
Britannic '99
Secre of the Andes '98
Cats Don't Dance '97 (V)
Aladdin and the King of Thieves '96 (V)
Glory Daze '96
The Great White Hype '96
Marquis de Sade '96
Bloodsport 3 '95
Catherine the Great '95
Beyond Forgiveness '94
Robot in the Family '94
Cyborg Cop '93
Return to the Lost World '93
Ring of the Musketeers '93
Canvas: The Fine Art of Crime '92
The Double O Kid '92
The High Crusade '92
The Lost World '92
The Seventh Coin '92
Sunset Grill '92
The Unnamable 2: The Statement of Randolph Carter '92
Journey of Honor '91
Rebel Storm '90
Secret Weapon '90
Great Expectations '89
Indiana Jones and the Last Crusade '89
The Trial of the Incredible Hulk '89
Tusks '89
War & Remembrance: The Final Chapter '89
Nairobi Affair '88
Noble House '88
War & Remembrance '88
Waxwork '88
The Little Match Girl '87
The Living Daylights '87
In the Shadow of Kilimanjaro '86
King Solomon's Mines '85
Kim '84
Best Revenge '83
Sadat '83
Sahara '83
Sword of the Valiant '83
Ivanhoe '82
Victor/Victoria '82
Raiders of the Lost Ark '81
Sphinx '81
Shogun '80
Nativity '78
Griff Rhys Jones
The Misadventures of Mr. Wilt '90
Morons from Outer Space '85
Jonathan Rhys Meyers (1977-)
The Magnificent Ambersons '02
Ride with the Devil '99
Titus '99
The Governess '98
The Loss of Sexual Innocence '98
The Maker '98
Velvet Goldmine '98
B. Monkey '97
Killer Tongue '96
Michael Collins '96
Samson and Delilah '96
Telling Lies in America '96
Candice Rialson (1952-)
Moonshine County Express '77
Chatterbox '76
Hollywood Boulevard '76
Summer School Teachers '75
Candy Stripe Nurses '74
Mama's Dirty Girls '74
Alfonso Ribeiro
Ticks '93
The Mighty Pawns '87
Jacques Riberolles
The Young Girls of Rochefort '68
Please Not Now! '61
Giovanni Ribisi (1976-)
Shot in the Heart '01
Boiler Room '00
The Gift '00
Gone in 60 Seconds '00
It's the Rage '99
The Mod Squad '99
The Virgin Suicides '99 (N)
First Love, Last Rites '98
The Other Sister '98
Saving Private Ryan '98
The Postman '97
subUrbia '96
That Thing You Do! '96
Promised a Miracle '88
Marissa Ribisi (1974-)
True Crime '99
Changing Habits '96
Armistead Maupin's Tales of the City '93
Dazed and Confused '93
Christina Ricci (1980-)
The Laramie Project '02
All Over the Guy '01
Bless the Child '00
The Man Who Cried '00
Sleepy Hollow '99
Desert Blue '98
Fear and Loathing in Las Vegas '98
The Opposite of Sex '98
Pecker '98
Small Soldiers '98 (V)
200 Cigarettes '98
Buffalo 66 '97
The Ice Storm '97
Bastard out of Carolina '96
The Last of the High Kings '96
That Darn Cat '96
Casper '95
Gold Diggers: The Secret of Bear Mountain '95
Now and Then '95
Addams Family Values '93
The Cemetery Club '93
The Addams Family '91
The Hard Way '91
Mermaids '90
Bill Rice
Landlord Blues '87
Doomed Love '83
Vortex '81
Florence Rice (1911-74)
Boss of Big Town '43
The Ghost and the Guest '43
At the Circus '39
Sweethearts '38
Double Wedding '37
Navy Blue and Gold '37
Frank Rice (1892-1936)
The Gore-Gore Girls '72
The Ivory Handled Gun '35
The Fiddlin' Buckaroo '33
Phantom Thunderbolt '33
Somewhere in Sonora '33
Hello Trouble '32
Border Law '31
The Fighting Legion '30
Red Signals '27
Dynamite Dan '24
Joan Rice (1930-97)
The Horror of Frankenstein '70
His Majesty O'Keefe '53
The Story of Robin Hood & His Merrie Men '52
Mandy Rice-Davies (1944-)
Absolute Beginners '86
Black Venus '83
Kuni Lemel in Tel Aviv '77
Adam Rich
Zertigo Diamond Caper '82
The Devil & Max Devlin '81
Allan Rich (1926-)
Matters of the Heart '90
Archer: The Fugitive from the Empire '81
The Seekers '79
Charlie Rich
Weeds '87
Take This Job & Shove It '81
Christopher Rich (1953-)
The Joy Luck Club '93
Midnight Murders '91
Archie: Return to Riverdale '90
Prisoners of Inertia '89
Claude Rich (1929-)
La Buche '00
Balzac: A Life of Passion '99
Capitaine Conan '96
The Green House '96
Revenge of the Musketeers '94
Maria Chapdelaine '84
Le Crabe Tambour '77
The Bride Wore Black '68
Is Paris Burning? '66
The Burning Court '62
The Elusive Corporal '62
Eli Rich
Deadly Diamonds '91
Nudity Required '90
Murderlust '86
Irene Rich (1891-1988)
Angel and the Badman '47
The Lady in Question '40
The Mortal Storm '40
That Certain Age '38
The Champ '32
Held for Murder '32
Beau Brummel '24
The Trap '22
Emily Richard
Empire of the Sun '87
The Life and Adventures of Nicholas Nickleby '81
Jean Richard (1921-2001)
Elena and Her Men '56
Seven Deadly Sins '53
Jean-Louis Richard (1921-)
After Sex '97
Jeanne la Pucelle '94
La Sentinelle '92
Le Professionnel '81
The Last Metro '80
It Means That to Me '63
Nathalie Richard
Irma Vep '96
Up/Down/Fragile '95
Pierre Richard (1895-1983)
Suicide Patrol '70s
Johnny Frenchman '46
Pierre Richard (1934-)
A Chef in Love '96
Les Comperes '83
Too Shy to Try '82
La Chevre '81
The Daydreamer '75
Return of the Tall Blond Man with One Black Shoe '74
The Tall Blond Man with One Black Shoe '72
Robert Ri'chard
Alley Cats Strike '00
Light It Up '99
In His Father's Shoes '97
Addison Richards (1887-1964)
Call Northside 777 '48
A Southern Yankee '48
Criminal Court '46
Bells of Rosarita '45
Betrayal from the East '44
Fighting Seabees '44
Since You Went Away '44
Air Force '43
The Fighting Sullivans '42
The Man with Two Lives '42
Ridin' Down the Canyon '42
Underground Agent '42
Dive Bomber '41
Bad Lands '39
The Black Legion '37
Our Daily Bread '34
Ann Richards (1917-)
Breakdown '53
Sorry, Wrong Number '48
Lost Honeymoon '47
Love from a Stranger '47
Badman's Territory '46
Love Letters '45
Ariana Richards (1979-)
Tremors 3: Back to Perfection '01
The Lost World: Jurassic Park 2 '97
Angus '95
Jurassic Park '93
Grand Tour: Disaster in Time '92
Switched at Birth '91
Spaced Invaders '90
Prancer '89
Tremors '89
Beah Richards (1926-2000)
Beloved '98
Inside Out '91
Drugstore Cowboy '89
Acceptable Risks '86
As Summers Die '86
A Christmas Without Snow '80
Roots: The Next Generation '79
A Dream for Christmas '73
Guess Who's Coming to Dinner '67
Gone Are the Days '63
The Miracle Worker '62
Cordelia Richards
Original Sin '01
North Shore Fish '97
Denise Richards (1971-)
Undercover Brother '02
Good Advice '01
Kill Shot '01
Valentine '01
Drop Dead Gorgeous '99
Tail Lights Fade '99
The World Is Not Enough '99
Wild Things '98
Starship Troopers '97
Tammy and the T-Rex '94
Evan Richards
Mute Witness '95
Society '92
Dream Machine '91
Rock 'n' Roll High School Forever '91
Down and Out in Beverly Hills '86
Jeff Richards (1922-89)
Born Reckless '59
It's a Dog's Life '55
Seven Brides for Seven Brothers '54
Above and Beyond '53
Battle Circus '53
Angels in the Outfield '51
Keith Richards
Chuck Berry: Hail! Hail! Rock 'n' Roll '87
The Kids Are Alright '79
Gimme Shelter '70
Kim Richards (1964-)
Escape '90
Tuff Turf '85
Meatballs 2 '84
Devil Dog: The Hound of Hell '78
Return from Witch Mountain '78
Assault on Precinct 13 '76
Escape to Witch Mountain '75
Kyle Richards
Curfew '88
The Watcher in the Woods '81
Halloween '78
Eaten Alive '76
Lisa Richards
Eating '90
Return '88
The Prince of Central Park '77
Michael Richards (1948-)
Trial and Error '96
Unstrung Heroes '95
Airheads '94
Coneheads '93
So I Married an Axe Murderer '93
Problem Child '90
UHF '89
Transylvania 6-5000 '85
Michele Lamar Richards
Top Dog '95
The Bodyguard '92
Paul (E.) Richards (1924-74)
Kiss Daddy Goodnight '87
Beneath the Planet of the Apes '70
All the Young Men '60
Tom Richards (1922-)
The Cursed Mountain Mystery '93
Dawn! '83
Plunge Into Darkness '77
Ian Richardson (1934-)
From Hell '01
102 Dalmatians '00
The King and I '99 (V)
A Knight in Camelot '98
B.A.P.'s '97
Dark City '97
Incognito '97
The Woman in White '97
A Royal Scandal '96 (N)
Catherine the Great '95
The Final Cut '95
Foreign Affairs '93
M. Butterfly '93
To Play the King '93
Year of the Comet '92
Monsignor Quixote '91
House of Cards '90
The Phantom of the Opera '90
Rosencrantz & Guildenstern Are Dead '90
Burning Secret '89
Troubles '88
Cry Freedom '87
The Fourth Protocol '87
Mountbatten: The Last Viceroy '86
Brazil '85
The Hound of the Baskervilles '83
The Sign of Four '83
Whoops Apocalypse '83
A Midsummer Night's Dream '68
Jack (H.) Richardson (1883-1957)
Trigger Tricks '30
Marked Money '28
Dynamite Dan '24
The Toll Gate '20
Jay Richardson
Fugitive Rage '96
Illegal Affairs '96
Attack of the 60-Foot Centerfold '95
Killing for Love '95
Wizards of the Demon Sword '94
Teenage Exorcist '93
Mind, Body & Soul '92
Sins of Desire '92
Original Intent '91
Vice Academy 3 '91
Bad Girls from Mars '90
Vice Academy 2 '90
Alienator '89
The Channeler '89
Slashdance '89
Death Row Diner '88
Hollywood Chainsaw Hookers '88
The Newlydeads '87
Gator King '70
Joely Richardson (1965-)
The Affair of the Necklace '01
The Patriot '00
Return to Me '00
Maybe Baby '99
In the Shadows '98
Event Horizon '97
101 Dalmatians '96
Hollow Reed '95
Loch Ness '95
Sister My Sister '94
I'll Do Anything '93
Lady Chatterley '92
Shining Through '92
King Ralph '91
Drowning by Numbers '87
Wetherby '85
The Charge of the Light Brigade '68
John Richardson (1936-)
Broadcast Bombshells '95
Cosmos: War of the Planets '80
Frankenstein '80 '79
Eyeball '78
Torso '73
The Vengeance of She '68
One Million Years B.C. '66
Black Sunday '60
Kevin M. Richardson
Whispers: An Elephant's Tale '00 (V)
Bound '96
Latanya Richardson
Introducing Dorothy Dandridge '99
U.S. Marshals '98
Julian Po '97
Losing Isaiah '94
When a Man Loves a Woman '94
Lee Richardson (1926-99)
Sarah, Plain and Tall: Skylark '93
A Stranger Among Us '92
Q & A '90
The Fly 2 '89
The Believers '87
Sweet Lorraine '87
Tiger Warsaw '87
Prizzi's Honor '85
Miranda Richardson (1958-)
Snow White: The Fairest of Them All '02
Chicken Run '00 (V)
Get Carter '00
The Miracle Maker: The Story of Jesus '00 (V)
Alice in Wonderland '99
The Big Brass Ring '99
Jacob Two Two Meets the Hooded Fang '99
The King and I '99 (V)

Sleepy Hollow '99
Merlin '98
Robert Louis Stevenson's St. Ives '98
The Apostle '97
The Designated Mourner '97
The Evening Star '96
Swann '96
Kansas City '95
Saint-Ex: The Story of the Storyteller '95
Century '94
Fatherland '94
The Night and the Moment '94
Tom & Viv '94
The Bachelor '93
The Crying Game '92
Damage '92
Enchanted April '92
Twisted Obsession '90
After Pilkington '88
Eat the Rich '87
Empire of the Sun '87
Dance with a Stranger '85
Transmutations '85
A Woman of Substance '84

Natasha Richardson (1963-)
Chelsea Walls '01
Blow Dry '00
The Parent Trap '98
Nell '94
Widow's Peak '94
Hostages '93
The Favor, the Watch, & the Very Big Fish '92
Past Midnight '92
The Comfort of Strangers '91
The Handmaid's Tale '90
Fat Man and Little Boy '89
Patty Hearst '88
Gothic '87
A Month in the Country '87

Patricia Richardson (1951-)
Dead Simple '01
Ulee's Gold '97
In Country '89
Christmas Evil '80

Ralph Richardson (1902-82)
A Doll's House '89
Wagner: The Complete Epic '85
Give My Regards to Broad Street '84
Greystoke: The Legend of Tarzan, Lord of the Apes '84
Dragonslayer '81
Early Days '81
Time Bandits '81
Watership Down '78 (V)
The Man in the Iron Mask '77
Invitation to the Wedding '73
Lady Caroline Lamb '73
O Lucky Man! '73
Tales from the Crypt '72
Who Slew Auntie Roo? '71
Battle of Britain '69
The Looking Glass War '69
Chimes at Midnight '67 (N)
Khartoum '66
The Wrong Box '66
Doctor Zhivago '65
Long Day's Journey into Night '62
Exodus '60
Richard III '55
The Fallen Idol '49
The Heiress '49
Anna Karenina '48
The Day Will Dawn '42
The Lion Has Wings '40
Clouds over Europe '39
The Four Feathers '39
The Citadel '38
The Divorce of Lady X '38
Amazing Adventure '37
The Man Who Could Work Miracles '37
South Riding '37
Thunder in the City '37
Things to Come '36
Bulldog Jack '35
Java Head '35
The Ghoul '34

Regina Richardson
Nine Deaths of the Ninja '85
Tightrope '84

Russell Richardson
The Rookie '02
Ancient Evil: Scream of the Mummy '00
Tigerland '00

Salli Richardson (1967-)
Never 2 Big '98
True Women '97
The Great White Hype '96
Soul of the Game '96
Gargoyles, The Movie: The Heroes Awaken '94 (V)
Lily in Winter '94
A Low Down Dirty Shame '94
Sioux City '94
Posse '93
How U Like Me Now? '92
Up Against the Wall '91

Sy Richardson
Floundering '94
Ring of Fire 2: Blood and Steel '92
Street Asylum '90
Backtrack '89
Tapeheads '89
Bad Dreams '88
Colors '88
Dead Man Walking '88
They Live '88
Straight to Hell '87
Repo Man '83
Fairy Tales '76

Carole Richert
The Night and the Moment '94
Tous les Matins du Monde '92

William Richert
The Man in the Iron Mask '97
My Own Private Idaho '91

Julian Richings
The Claim '00
Cube '98

Peter Mark Richman (1927-)
Naked Gun 2 1/2: The Smell of Fear '91
Friday the 13th, Part 8: Jason Takes Manhattan '89
Judgment Day '88
City Killer '87
Dempsey '83
PSI Factor '80
Black Orchid '59
The Strange One '57

Anthony Richmond (1942-)
One Wish Too Many '55
Devil Girl from Mars '54

Branscombe Richmond (1955-)
The Scorpion King '02
To the Limit '95
Jericho Fever '93
Christopher Columbus: The Discovery '92
DaVinci's War '92
Inside Edge '92
The Taking of Beverly Hills '91

Deon Richmond
National Lampoon's Van Wilder '02
Not Another Teen Movie '01
Scream 3 '00
Trippin' '99

Fiona Richmond
Eat the Rich '87
The House on Straw Hill '76

Kane Richmond (1906-73)
Behind the Mask '46
Haunted Harbor '44
Action in the North Atlantic '43
Spy Smasher '42
Spy Smasher Returns '42
Anything for a Thrill '37
Devil Diamond '37
Motorcycle Squad '37
Tough to Handle '37
The Reckless Way '36
Confidential '35
Silent Code '35
The Lost City '34
Cavalier of the West '31

Warner Richmond (1886-1948)
Colorado Serenade '46
Wild West '46
Wild Horse Canyon '39
Doomed at Sundown '37
A Lawman Is Born '37
Where Trails Divide '37
Headin' for the Rio Grande '36
Song of the Gringo '36
The New Frontier '35
Rainbow's End '35
The Lost Jungle '34
Big News '29
The Speed Spook '24

Andy Richter (1966-)
Big Trouble '02
Dr. Dolittle 2 '01
Pootie Tang '01
Scary Movie 2 '01
Dr. T & the Women '00
Cabin Boy '94
The Positively True Adventures of the Alleged Texas Cheerleader-Murdering Mom '93

Deborah Richter (1961-)
The Banker '89
Cyborg '89
Promised Land '88
Square Dance '87
Hot Moves '84
Twirl '81
The Rebels '79
Swap Meet '79

Jason James Richter (1980-)
Laserhawk '99
Free Willy 3: The Rescue '97
Free Willy 2: The Adventure Home '95
Cops and Robbersons '94
The NeverEnding Story 3: Escape from Fantasia '94
Free Willy '93

Paul Richter (1887-1961)
Kriemhilde's Revenge '24
Siegfried '24
Dr. Mabuse, The Gambler '22
The Indian Tomb '21

Tony Rickards
Castaway '87
Robbery '85
Great Gold Swindle '84
Waterfront '83

Don Rickles (1926-)
Toy Story 2 '99 (V)
Dennis the Menace Strikes Again '98
Quest for Camelot '98 (V)
Dirty Work '97
Casino '95
Toy Story '95 (V)
Innocent Blood '92
Keaton's Cop '90
For the Love of It '80
Kelly's Heroes '70
Enter Laughing '67
Beach Blanket Bingo '65
Bikini Beach '64
Muscle Beach Party '64
Pajama Party '64
X: The Man with X-Ray Eyes '63
The Rat Race '60
Run Silent, Run Deep '58

Alan Rickman (1946-)
Harry Potter and the Sorcerer's Stone '01
Blow Dry '00
Dogma '99
Galaxy Quest '99
Dark Harbor '98
Judas Kiss '98
Michael Collins '96
Rasputin: Dark Servant of Destiny '96
Sense and Sensibility '95
An Awfully Big Adventure '94
Mesmer '94
Fallen Angels 1 '93
Bob Roberts '92
Close My Eyes '91
Robin Hood: Prince of Thieves '91
Truly, Madly, Deeply '91
Closet Land '90
Quigley Down Under '90
The January Man '89
Die Hard '88

Allen Rickman
I Was a Teenage Zombie '87
Shock! Shock! Shock! '87

Maria Ricossa
Bojangles '01
Dead Man Out '89

Stephane Rideau (1976-)
Come Undone '00
Sitcom '97
Full Speed '96
Wild Reeds '94

John Ridgely (1909-68)
Cavalry Charge '51
Task Force '49
Cry Wolf '47
The Possessed '47
The Big Sleep '46
The Man I Love '46
Arsenic and Old Lace '44
Air Force '43
Destination Tokyo '43

Robert Ridgely (1931-96)
Boogie Nights '97
Hard Eight '96
Philadelphia '93
The Ref '93
Beverly Hills Cop 2 '87
Rosie: The Rosemary Clooney Story '82
Who Am I This Time? '82

Stanley Ridges (1891-1951)
No Way Out '50
Task Force '49
The Possessed '47
Mr. Ace '46
Because of Him '45
Master Race '44
The Story of Dr. Wassell '44
Wilson '44
Air Force '43
The Lady Is Willing '42
To Be or Not to Be '42
The Sea Wolf '41
Sergeant York '41
They Died with Their Boots On '41
Black Friday '40
Each Dawn I Die '39
Union Pacific '39
If I Were King '38
Internes Can't Take Money '37

Leni Riefenstahl (1902-)
Tiefland '44
The Blue Light '32

Peter Riegert (1947-)
Bojangles '01
How to Kill Your Neighbor's Dog '01
Passion of Mind '00
Traffic '00
The Baby Dance '98
Hi-Life '98
Jerry and Tom '98
Face Down '97
North Shore Fish '97
Infinity '96
The Infiltrator '95
Pie in the Sky '95
Bleeding Hearts '94
Coldblooded '94
The Mask '94
Barbarians at the Gate '93
Gypsy '93
Utz '93
Passed Away '92
The Object of Beauty '91
Oscar '91
The Runestone '91
A Shock to the System '90
That's Adequate '90
Crossing Delancey '88
A Man in Love '87
The Stranger '87
News at Eleven '86
Local Hero '83
National Lampoon Goes to the Movies '81
Americathon '79
Chilly Scenes of Winter '79
National Lampoon's Animal House '78

Richard Riehle (1948-)
Bandits '01
The Fluffer '01
Say It Isn't So '01
Deuce Bigalow: Male Gigolo '99
Desperate Measures '98
Office Space '98
The Lesser Evil '97
Trading Favors '97
A Stranger in Town '95
Dominion '94
Holy Matrimony '94
Lightning Jack '94
A Dangerous Woman '93
Lone Justice 2 '93
Body of Evidence '92
Hero '92
Of Mice and Men '92
The Public Eye '92
Glory '89

Katja Riemann (1963-)
Balzac: A Life of Passion '99
Bandits '99
The Harmonists '99
Maybe ... Maybe Not '94

Adam Rifkin (1966-)
Something About Sex '98
The Dark Backward '91

Ron Rifkin (1939-)
Dragonfly '02
The Sum of All Fears '02
Deliberate Intent '01
The Majestic '01
Boiler Room '00
Keeping the Faith '00
The Negotiator '98
L.A. Confidential '97
I'm Not Rappaport '96
Last Summer In the Hamptons '96
The Substance of Fire '96
Norma Jean and Marilyn '95
Wolf '94
Manhattan Murder Mystery '93
Courage '86
The Chosen '81
Mrs. R's Daughter '79
Silent Running '71

Jorge (George) Rigaud (1905-84)
Horror Express '72
Black Box Affair '66
The Castilian '63
Quatorze Juliet '32

Cathy Rigby
Challenge of a Lifetime '85
The Great Wallendas '78

Edward Rigby (1879-1951)
The Happiest Days of Your Life '50
Convoy '40
Young and Innocent '37
Lorna Doone '34

Terence Rigby
Essex Boys '99
Plunkett & Macleane '98
The Young Americans '93
Get Carter '71

Diana Rigg (1938-)
The American '01
Victoria & Albert '01
Speedy Death '99
Rebecca '97
Moll Flanders '96
Samson and Delilah '96
A Good Man in Africa '94
Genghis Cohn '93
Running Delilah '93
Mrs. 'Arris Goes to Paris '92
Snow White '89
Unexplained Laughter '89
The Worst Witch '86
Bleak House '85
Evil under the Sun '82
The Great Muppet Caper '81
A Little Night Music '77
In This House of Brede '75
Theatre of Blood '73
The Hospital '71
Julius Caesar '70
The Assassination Bureau '69
On Her Majesty's Secret Service '69
A Midsummer Night's Dream '68

Rebecca Rigg (1967-)
Tunnel Vision '95
The Efficiency Expert '92
The Hunting '92
Fortress '85
Doctors and Nurses '82

Massimo Righi
Black Sabbath '64
Blood and Black Lace '64

Alex(andre) Rignault (1901-85)
Numero Deux '75
The Horror Chamber of Dr. Faustus '59
Eternal Return '43

Brad Rijn
Special Effects '85
Perfect Strangers '84

Robin Riker
Stepmonster '92
Body Chemistry 2: Voice of a Stranger '91
Alligator '80

Elaine Riley (1923-)
Clipped Wings '53
Rider from Tucson '50
Hopalong Cassidy: Borrowed Trouble '48
Hopalong Cassidy: The Devil's Playground '46

Jack Riley (1935-)
Rugrats in Paris: The Movie '00 (V)
The Rugrats Movie '98 (V)
Portrait of a White Marriage '88
Night Patrol '85
Attack of the Killer Tomatoes '77
McCabe & Mrs. Miller '71

Jeannine Riley (1939-)
Wackiest Wagon Train in the West '77
Electra Glide in Blue '73
The Comic '69
Big Mouth '67

Larry Riley (1953-92)
Dead Solid Perfect '88
Long Gone '87
Crackers '84
A Soldier's Story '84

Michael Riley
The Way We Live Now '02
Pale Saints '97
French Kiss '95
Heck's Way Home '95
The Prince '95
...And God Spoke '94

Race to Freedom: The Story of the Underground Railroad '94
Because Why? '93
To Catch a Killer '92
Perfectly Normal '91

Walter Rilla (1894-1980)
Frozen Alive '64
The Gamma People '56
The Golden Salamander '51
Mr. Emmanuel '44
House of Mystery '41
Black Eyes '39
The Scarlet Pimpernel '34

Shane Rimmer (1932-)
Space Truckers '97
Crusoe '89
Dreamchild '85
Out of Africa '85
The People That Time Forgot '77
S*P*Y*S '74
Dr. Strangelove, or: How I Learned to Stop Worrying and Love the Bomb '64

Molly Ringwald (1968-)
Not Another Teen Movie '01
Cut '00
The Brutal Truth '99
Requiem for Murder '99
Teaching Mrs. Tingle '99
Office Killer '97
Since You've Been Gone '97
Baja '95
Malicious '95
Some Folks Call It a Sling Blade '94
Stephen King's The Stand '94
Face the Music '92
Betsy's Wedding '90
Strike It Rich '90
Women & Men: Stories of Seduction '90
For Keeps '88
Fresh Horses '88
King Lear '87
The Pick-Up Artist '87
Johnny Appleseed '86
Pretty in Pink '86
The Breakfast Club '85
P.K. and the Kid '85
Sixteen Candles '84
Packin' It In '83
Spacehunter: Adventures in the Forbidden Zone '83
The Tempest '82

Lisa Rinna
Another Woman's Husband '00
Robot Wars '93

David Rintoul
Horatio Hornblower: The Adventure Continues '01
Pride and Prejudice '85
Legend of the Werewolf '75

Nicole Rio
Visitants '87
Sorority House Massacre '86
Zero Boys '86

Marjorie (Reardon) Riordan (1921-84)
The Hoodlum '51
South of Monterey '47
Pursuit to Algiers '45
Stage Door Canteen '43

Fay Ripley
For Roseanna '96
Mute Witness '95

Michael Ripper (1913-2000)
No Surrender '86
The Creeping Flesh '72
Girly '70
The Scars of Dracula '70
Taste the Blood of Dracula '70
Dracula Has Risen from the Grave '68
Plague of the Zombies '66
The Reptile '66
Where the Bullets Fly '66
The Curse of the Werewolf '61
The Brides of Dracula '60
Dead Lucky '60
The Mummy '59
Quatermass 2 '57
Eye Witness '49

Leon Rippy
Eight Legged Freaks '02
The Patriot '00
Stargate '94
Beyond the Law '92
Kuffs '92
Eye of the Storm '91
The Hot Spot '90
Moon 44 '90
Young Guns 2 '90
Jesse '88
Track 29 '88

Maurice Risch
Beau Pere '81
The Last Metro '80

Elisabeth Risdon (1887-1958)
Scaramouche '52
Guilty of Treason '50
Hills of Oklahoma '50
Down Dakota Way '49
The Amazing Mrs. Holiday '43
The Lady Is Willing '42
Mexican Spitfire at Sea '42
Reap the Wild Wind '42
The Great Man Votes '38
Mannequin '37
Theodora Goes Wild '36
Crime and Punishment '35

Miriam Riselle
Tevye '39
The Singing Blacksmith '38

Jacques Rispal
Le Chat '75
Act of Aggression '73
Bed and Board '70

Michael Rispoli
Death to Smoochy '02
Summer of Sam '99
The Third Miracle '99
Two Family House '99
Rounders '98
Scarred City '98
Snake Eyes '98
Volcano '97
Homeward Bound 2: Lost in San Francisco '96
While You Were Sleeping '95
Household Saints '93

Robbie (Reist) Rist (1964-)
Unseen Evil '99
Teenage Mutant Ninja Turtles: The Movie '90 (V)
Iron Eagle '86
He Is My Brother '75

Lazar Ristovski
Underground '95
Tito and Me '92

Cyril Ritchard (1897-)
Hans Brinker '69
Half a Sixpence '67
Peter Pan '60
Blackmail '29

Clint Ritchie
Peacekillers '71
The St. Valentine's Day Massacre '67

June Ritchie
A Kind of Loving '62
The Mouse on the Moon '62
The Three Penny Opera '62

Martin Ritt (1914-90)
The Slugger's Wife '85
Conrack '74

John Ritter (1948-)
Tadpole '02
Panic '00
Terror Tract '00
TripFall '00
The Million Dollar Kid '99
Bride of Chucky '98
Dead Husbands '98
It Came from the Sky '98
Shadow of Doubt '98
A Gun, a Car, a Blonde '97
Montana '97
Sink or Swim '97
Mercenary '96
Nowhere '96
Sling Blade '96
The Colony '95
North '94
Danielle Steel's Heartbeat '93
Prison for Children '93
Noises Off '92
Stay Tuned '92
Problem Child 2 '91
Problem Child '90
Stephen King's It '90
My Brother's Wife '89
Skin Deep '89
Tricks of the Trade '88
Real Men '87
The Last Fling '86
A Smoky Mountain Christmas '86
Unnatural Causes '86
Letting Go '85
Sunset Limousine '83
Flight of Dragons '82 (V)
In Love with an Older Woman '82
Pray TV '82
They All Laughed '81
Comeback Kid '80
Hero at Large '80
Wholly Moses! '80
Americathon '79
The Stone Killer '73
The Other '72
The Barefoot Executive '71
Evil Roy Slade '71
Scandalous John '71

Tex Ritter (1905-74)
The Girl from Tobacco Row '66
The Marshal's Daughter '53
Holiday Rhythm '50
Enemy of the Law '45
Flaming Bullets '45
Frontier Fugitives '45
Marked for Murder '45
Three in the Saddle '45
Dead or Alive '44
Gangsters of the Frontier '44
The Pioneers '41
Take Me Back to Oklahoma '40
Down the Wyoming Trail '39
Man from Texas '39
Roll, Wagons, Roll '39
Rollin' Plains '38
Utah Trail '38
Arizona Days '37
Hittin' the Trail '37
Mystery of the Hooded Horseman '37
Riders of the Rockies '37
Sing, Cowboy, Sing '37
Tex Rides with the Boy Scouts '37
Trouble in Texas '37
Headin' for the Rio Grande '36
Song of the Gringo '36

Thelma Ritter (1905-69)
The Incident '67
Boeing Boeing '65
For Love or Money '63
How the West Was Won '63
A New Kind of Love '63
Birdman of Alcatraz '62
The Misfits '61
A Hole in the Head '59
Pillow Talk '59
Daddy Long Legs '55
Rear Window '54
The Farmer Takes a Wife '53
Pickup on South Street '53
Titanic '53
As Young As You Feel '51
All About Eve '50
Father Was a Fullback '49
A Letter to Three Wives '49
Miracle on 34th Street '47

Al Ritz (1901-65)
The Gorilla '39
The Three Musketeers '39
The Goldwyn Follies '38
On the Avenue '37
One in a Million '36

Harry Ritz (1906-86)
Silent Movie '76
Blazing Stewardesses '75
Texas Layover '75
The Gorilla '39
The Three Musketeers '39
The Goldwyn Follies '38
On the Avenue '37
One in a Million '36

Jimmy Ritz (1903-85)
Blazing Stewardesses '75
Texas Layover '75
The Gorilla '39
The Three Musketeers '39
The Goldwyn Follies '38
On the Avenue '37
One in a Million '36

Emmanuelle Riva (1927-)
Trois Couleurs: Bleu '93
Leon Morin, Priest '61
Hiroshima, Mon Amour '59
Kapo '59

Carlos Rivas (1928-)
True Grit '69
They Saved Hitler's Brain '64
The Black Scorpion '57
The King and I '56

Chita Rivera (1933-)
Mayflower Madam '87
Pippin '81
Once Upon a Brothers Grimm '77
Sweet Charity '69

Jorge (George) Rivero (1938-)
Warrior of Justice '96
Werewolf '95
Ice '93
Fist Fighter '88
Counterforce '87
Target Eagle '84
Conquest '83
Day of the Assassin '81
Priest of Love '81
Rio Lobo '70
Soldier Blue '70
Sin of Adam & Eve '67

Julian Rivero (1890-1976)
Underground Agent '42
Arizona Gangbusters '40
Death Rides the Range '40
Heroes of the Alamo '37
Ridin' the Lone Trail '37
Phantom Patrol '36
Beyond the Rockies '32
Man from Hell's Edges '32

Joan Rivers (1933-)
Intern '00
Whispers: An Elephant's Tale '00 (V)
Napoleon '96 (V)
Serial Mom '94
Les Patterson Saves the World '90
Spaceballs '87
The Muppets Take Manhattan '84

Victor Rivers
What's Cooking? '00
Two for Texas '97
A Million to Juan '94
Blood In ... Blood Out: Bound by Honor '93
Black Magic Woman '91

George Riviere
The Virgin of Nuremberg '65
Castle of Blood '64
Journey Beneath the Desert '61

Julien Riviere
Ma Vie en Rose '97
Les Voleurs '96

Marie Riviere (1956-)
Autumn Tale '98
A Tale of Winter '92
Four Adventures of Reinette and Mirabelle '89
Summer '86
The Aviator's Wife '80

Gianni Rizzo
Mission Stardust '68
Desert Commandos '67

Bert Roach (1891-1971)
The Great Waltz '38
The Crowd '28
Smouldering Fires '25

Daryl Roach
Gang Boys '97
Watchers 3 '94

Linus Roache (1964-)
Hart's War '02
Pandaemonium '00
Siam Sunset '99
Shot Through the Heart '98
The Wings of the Dove '97
Priest '94

Adam Roarke (1938-96)
Sioux City '94
Trespasses '86
Beach Girls '82
The Stunt Man '80
Hughes & Harlow: Angels in Hell '77
Four Deuces '75
This Is a Hijack '75
Dirty Mary Crazy Larry '74
How Come Nobody's On Our Side? '73
Frogs '72
The Losers '70
Hell's Belles '69
The Savage Seven '68
Hell's Angels on Wheels '67
Women of the Prehistoric Planet '66

Jason Robards, Sr. (1892-1963)
Western Pacific Agent '51 (N)
Rimfire '49
Mr. Blandings Builds His Dream House '48
Return of the Bad Men '48
Desperate '47
Riff-Raff '47
Trail Street '47
Bedlam '45
Isle of the Dead '45
Mademoiselle Fifi '44
The Fatal Hour '40
Stunt Pilot '39
Wayne Murder Case '38
Sweetheart of the Navy '37
Fighting Marines '36
The Miracle Rider '35
Crimson Romance '34
Carnival Lady '33
White Eagle '32

Jason Robards, Jr. (1922-2000)
Magnolia '99
Beloved '98
Enemy of the State '98
Heartwood '98
The Real Macaw '98
A Thousand Acres '97
Crimson Tide '95
Journey '95
The Enemy Within '94
Little Big League '94
My Antonia '94
The Paper '94
The Adventures of Huck Finn '93
Heidi '93
Philadelphia '93
The Trial '93
Storyville '92
Black Rainbow '91
An Inconvenient Woman '91
Mark Twain and Me '91
Final Warning '90
Quick Change '90
Dream a Little Dream '89
Parenthood '89
Bright Lights, Big City '88
The Christmas Wife '88
The Good Mother '88
Reunion '88
Breaking Home Ties '87
Laguna Heat '87
Square Dance '87
The Long, Hot Summer '86
Sakharov '84
You Can't Take It with You '84
The Day After '83
Max Dugan Returns '83
Something Wicked This Way Comes '83
Burden of Dreams '82
Cabo Blanco '81
Legend of the Lone Ranger '81
Melvin and Howard '80
Raise the Titanic '80
Hurricane '79
A Christmas to Remember '78
Comes a Horseman '78
Julia '77
All the President's Men '76
A Boy and His Dog '75
Mr. Sycamore '74
A House without a Christmas Tree '72
Johnny Got His Gun '71
Murders in the Rue Morgue '71
Ballad of Cable Hogue '70
Fools '70
Julius Caesar '70
Tora! Tora! Tora! '70
The Night They Raided Minsky's '69
Isadora '68
Once Upon a Time in the West '68
Divorce American Style '67
Hour of the Gun '67
The St. Valentine's Day Massacre '67
Any Wednesday '66
A Big Hand for the Little Lady '66
A Thousand Clowns '65
Long Day's Journey into Night '62
By Love Possessed '61
A Doll's House '59

Sam Robards (1961-)
A. I.: Artificial Intelligence '01
Hamlet '01
Life as a House '01
Bounce '00
American Beauty '99
Beautiful Girls '96
The Man Who Captured Eichmann '96
Donor Unknown '95
Mrs. Parker and the Vicious Circle '94
Ready to Wear '94
The Ballad of Little Jo '93
Casualties of War '89
Pancho Barnes '88
Not Quite Paradise '86
Fandango '85
Into Thin Air '85
The Tempest '82

David Robb
Behind the Lines '97
The Flame Trees of Thika '81

Amy Robbins
All the Little Animals '98
Rudyard Kipling's the Second Jungle Book: Mowgli and Baloo '97

Brian Robbins (1964-)
DaVinci's War '92
C.H.U.D. 2: Bud the Chud '89
Cellar Dweller '87

Gale Robbins (1921-80)
Parasite '82
The Belle of New York '52
The Fuller Brush Girl '50

Three Little Words '50
The Barkleys of Broadway '49
My Girl Tisa '48

Jessie Robbins
The Fearless Vampire Killers '67
Magical Mystery Tour '67

Marty Robbins (1925-82)
Hell on Wheels '67
Road to Nashville '67
Ballad of a Gunfighter '64

Oliver Robbins
Poltergeist 2: The Other Side '86
Poltergeist '82

Skeeter Bill Robbins (1887-1933)
Fighting Parson '35
Cowboy Counselor '33
Boiling Point '32
Man's Land '32
Hard Hombre '31

Tim Robbins (1958-)
Human Nature '02
Antitrust '00
High Fidelity '00
Mission to Mars '00
Arlington Road '99
Austin Powers 2: The Spy Who Shagged Me '99
Nothing to Lose '96
I.Q. '94
Ready to Wear '94
The Shawshank Redemption '94
The Hudsucker Proxy '93
Short Cuts '93
Bob Roberts '92
The Player '92
Jungle Fever '91
Cadillac Man '90
Jacob's Ladder '90
Erik the Viking '89
Miss Firecracker '89
Tapeheads '89
Twister '89
Bull Durham '88
Five Corners '88
Howard the Duck '86
Top Gun '86
Fraternity Vacation '85
Quarterback Princess '85
The Sure Thing '85
No Small Affair '84
Toy Soldiers '84

Richard Rober (1910-52)
Jet Pilot '57
Kid Monk Baroni '52
Man in the Saddle '51
The Well '51
Task Force '49
Call Northside 777 '48

David Roberson
Steel Sharks '97
The O.J. Simpson Story '94

Yves Robert (1920-2002)
The Judge and the Assassin '75
Les Grandes Manoeuvres '55

Allene Roberts (1928-)
The Hoodlum '51
Union Station '50
The Red House '47

Arthur Roberts
The Capitol Conspiracy '99
Femme Fontaine: Killer Babe for the C.I.A. '95
Illegal Entry: Formula for Fear '93
Not of This Earth '88
Revenge of the Ninja '83
Deadly Vengeance '81

Christian Roberts
The Adventurers '70
Desperados '69
The Anniversary '68
To Sir, with Love '67

Conrad Roberts
The Scorpion King '02
The Million Dollar Hotel '99
The Serpent and the Rainbow '87
The Mosquito Coast '86

Des Roberts
Black Bikers from Hell '70
The Outlaw Bikers—Gang Wars '70

Doris Roberts (1930-)
All Over the Guy '01
My Giant '98
The Night We Never Met '93
Used People '92
National Lampoon's Christmas Vacation '89
Simple Justice '89
The Fig Tree '87
Number One with a Bullet '87
Ordinary Heroes '85
Hester Street '75
The Taking of Pelham One Two Three '74
Honeymoon Killers '70

Edith Roberts (1899-1935)
Man from Headquarters '28
The Taxi Mystery '26

Emma Roberts
Blow '01
Persuasion '95

Eric Roberts (1956-)
Fast Sofa '01
The King's Guard '01
Mindstorm '01
Stiletto Dance '01
Cecil B. Demented '00
Frozen in Fear '00
Luck of the Draw '00
No Alibi '00
Race Against Time '00
TripFall '00
Agent of Death '99
Heaven's Fire '99
Hitman's Run '99
La Cucaracha '99
Lansky '99
Purgatory '99
Restraining Order '99
Wildflowers '99
Bitter Sweet '98
Dead End '98
Facade '98
Past Perfect '98
T.N.T. '98
Two Shades of Blue '98
Most Wanted '97
The Odyssey '97
The Prophecy 2: Ashtown '97
American Strays '96
Doctor Who '96
The Glass Cage '96
In Cold Blood '96
Power 98 '96
Public Enemies '96
The Grave '95
Heaven's Prisoners '95
The Immortals '95
It's My Party '95
Saved by the Light '95
Babyfever '94
Firefall '94
The Hard Truth '94
Love Is a Gun '94
Nature of the Beast '94
Sensation '94
The Specialist '94
Best of the Best 2 '93
By the Sword '93
Love, Cheat & Steal '93
Voyage '93
Final Analysis '92
Fugitive Among Us '92
A Family Matter '91
Lonely Hearts '91
The Ambulance '90
Descending Angel '90
The Lost Capone '90
Best of the Best '89
Rude Awakening '89
Blood Red '88
Options '88
To Heal a Nation '88
Nobody's Fool '86
Slow Burn '86
Runaway Train '85
The Coca-Cola Kid '84
The Pope of Greenwich Village '84
Star 80 '83
Raggedy Man '81
King of the Gypsies '78

Ewan Roberts
Day of the Triffids '63
Curse of the Demon '57

Florence Roberts (1861-1940)
Harmony Lane '35
Sons of Steel '35
Hoopla '33
Kept Husbands '31

Francesca Roberts
Prison Stories: Women on the Inside '91
The Heart of Dixie '89

Ian Roberts
Tarzan and the Lost City '98
Mandela and de Klerk '97
Terminal Impact '95
The Power of One '92

Jay Roberts, Jr.
Warlords 3000 '93
Aftershock '88
White Phantom: Enemy of Darkness '87

Jeremy Roberts
The Thirteenth Floor '99
Jungle Boy '96

J.H. Roberts (1884-1961)
Uneasy Terms '48
Spitfire '42
The Courageous Mr. Penn '41
Young and Innocent '37
Nine Days a Queen '36

Joe Roberts
Cider with Rosie '99
Shakespeare in Love '98

Julia Roberts (1967-)
Full Frontal '02
America's Sweethearts '01
The Mexican '01
Ocean's Eleven '01
Erin Brockovich '00
Notting Hill '99
Runaway Bride '99
Stepmom '98
Conspiracy Theory '97
My Best Friend's Wedding '97
Everyone Says I Love You '96
Michael Collins '96
Mary Reilly '95
Something to Talk About '95
I Love Trouble '94
Ready to Wear '94
The Pelican Brief '93
The Player '92
Dying Young '91
Hook '91
Sleeping with the Enemy '91
Flatliners '90
Pretty Woman '90
Steel Magnolias '89
Blood Red '88
Mystic Pizza '88
Satisfaction '88
Baja Oklahoma '87
Firehouse '87

Ken Roberts
Fatal Pulse '88
The Great Land of Small '86

Kimberly Roberts
Range of Motion '00
Vice Girls '96

Leonard Roberts
The '60s '99
Love Jones '96

Lynne Roberts (1922-78)
Because of You '52
Dynamite Pass '50
Hunt the Man Down '50
Eyes of Texas '48
Robin Hood of Texas '47
Sioux City Sue '46
Frolics on Ice '40
In Old Caliente '39
Rough Riders' Roundup '39
Billy the Kid Returns '38
Come on Rangers '38
Hollywood Stadium Mystery '38
Shine on, Harvest Moon '38
Heart of the Rockies '37

Mark Roberts
Bulletproof '96
Posse '75

Michael D. Roberts
Live! From Death Row '92
Rain Man '88
Ice Pirates '84
Heartbreaker '83

Pascale Roberts (1933-)
Marius and Jeannette '97
Le Grand Chemin '87
Friends '71
The Peking Blond '68
Dishonorable Discharge '57

Pernell Roberts (1928-)
Around the World in 80 Days '89
The Night Train to Kathmandu '88
High Noon: Part 2 '80
Hot Rod '79
Magic of Lassie '78
Paco '75
Sniper '75
Four Rode Out '69
Kashmiri Run '69
The Errand Boy '61
Ride Lonesome '59

Rachel Roberts (1927-80)
Charlie Chan and the Curse of the Dragon Queen '81
The Hostage Tower '80
Sorrows of Gin '79
When a Stranger Calls '79
Yanks '79
Foul Play '78
Picnic at Hanging Rock '75
Murder on the Orient Express '74
Alpha Beta '73
The Belstone Fox '73
O Lucky Man! '73
Baffled '72
Wild Rovers '71
Doctors' Wives '70
This Sporting Life '63
Saturday Night and Sunday Morning '60

Roy Roberts (1900-75)
I'll Take Sweden '65
The King and Four Queens '56
Second Chance '53
The Enforcer '51
Santa Fe '51
Borderline '50
Force of Evil '49
He Walked by Night '48
Guadalcanal Diary '43
The Fighting Sullivans '42

Tanya Roberts (1954-)
Deep Down '94
Sins of Desire '92
Almost Pregnant '91
Inner Sanctum '91
Legal Tender '90
Night Eyes '90
Purgatory '89
Body Slam '87
A View to a Kill '85
Sheena '84
Hearts & Armour '83
Beastmaster '82
California Dreaming '79
Racquet '79
Tourist Trap '79
Fingers '78
The Yum-Yum Girls '78
Forced Entry '75

Ted Jan Roberts (1979-)
Hollywood Safari '96
Tiger Heart '96
The Power Within '95
A Dangerous Place '94
Magic Kid 2 '94
Magic Kid '92

Theodore Roberts (1861-1928)
The Ten Commandments '23
Affairs of Anatol '21
Suds '20
The Roaring Road '19

Tony Roberts (1939-)
Our Sons '91
Switch '91
Popcorn '89
18 Again! '88
Radio Days '87
Hannah and Her Sisters '86
Seize the Day '86
Key Exchange '85
Amityville 3: The Demon '83
Packin' It In '83
A Midsummer Night's Sex Comedy '82
Just Tell Me What You Want '80
Question of Honor '80
Stardust Memories '80
If Things Were Different '79
Annie Hall '77
The Lindbergh Kidnapping Case '76
Lovers Like Us '75
The Taking of Pelham One Two Three '74
Serpico '73
Play It Again, Sam '72
Million Dollar Duck '71
Star Spangled Girl '71

Tracey Roberts (1914-2002)
The Naked Flame '68
The Prodigal '55
Actors and Sin '52
Queen for a Day '51

Wink Roberts
The Day It Came to Earth '77
The First Time '69

Cliff Robertson (1925-)
Spider-Man '02
Family Tree '00
Mach 2 '00
Escape from L.A. '96
Renaissance Man '94
Wind '92
Wild Hearts Can't Be Broken '91
Dead Reckoning '89
Ford: The Man & the Machine '87
Malone '87
The Key to Rebecca '85
Shaker Run '85
Shoot '85
Brainstorm '83
Class '83
Star 80 '83
Two of a Kind '82
Danger in the Skies '79
Dominique Is Dead '79
Midway '76
Obsession '76
Return to Earth '76
My Father's House '75
Out of Season '75
Three Days of the Condor '75
The Man Without a Country '73
The Great Northfield Minnesota Raid '72
Too Late the Hero '70
Charly '68
The Devil's Brigade '68
The Honey Pot '67
Love Has Many Faces '65
The Best Man '64
633 Squadron '64
PT 109 '63
The Interns '62
All in a Night's Work '61
Underworld, U.S.A. '60
Gidget '59
Days of Wine and Roses '58
The Naked and the Dead '58
The Girl Most Likely '57
Autumn Leaves '56
Picnic '55

Dale Robertson (1923-)
The Last Ride of the Dalton Gang '79
Melvin Purvis: G-Man '74
One-Eyed Soldiers '67
Man from Button Willow '65 (V)
Dakota Incident '56
Son of Sinbad '55
Devil's Canyon '53
The Farmer Takes a Wife '53

Francoise Robertson
The Minion '98
Twists of Terror '98
Armistead Maupin's More Tales of the City '97

Iain Robertson
The Match '99
Plunkett & Macleane '98
Small Faces '95

Jenny Robertson (1963-)
The Boys Next Door '96
Danger of Love '95
The Nightman '93
Bull Durham '88
Jacob Have I Loved '88

Kathleen Robertson (1973-)
Scary Movie 2 '01
Torso '01
Beautiful '00
Psycho Beach Party '00
Splendor '99
Dog Park '98
Nowhere '96
Blown Away '93

Ken Robertson
Yellow Hair & the Fortress of Gold '84
Nighthawks '78

Kimmy Robertson
Speed 2: Cruise Control '97
Leprechaun 2 '94
Beauty and the Beast '91 (V)

Robbie Robertson
The Crossing Guard '94
Carny '80

Willard Robertson (1886-1948)
Air Force '43
Remember the Night '40
Park Avenue Logger '37
Supernatural '33

Paul Robeson (1898-1976)
Tales of Manhattan '42
Jericho '38
Big Fella '37
King Solomon's Mines '37
Show Boat '36
Song of Freedom '36
Sanders of the River '35
Emperor Jones '33
Body and Soul '24

George Robey
Henry V '44
Don Quixote '35

Kim Robillard
Ali '01
Home Fries '98
Breakdown '96
Chrome Soldiers '92
Rain Man '88

Herb Robins
The Worm Eaters '77
The Thrill Killers '65

Laila Robins (1959-)
Oxygen '99
True Crime '99
The Blood Oranges '97
Female Perversions '96
Live Nude Girls '95
Welcome Home, Roxy Carmichael '90

An Innocent Man '89
Planes, Trains & Automobiles '87

Andrew (Andy) Robinson (1942-)
Running Woman '98
Pumpkinhead 2: Blood Wings '94
Fatal Charm '92
Into the Badlands '92
There Goes My Baby '92
Trancers 3: Deth Lives '92
Child's Play 3 '91
Prime Target '91
Shoot to Kill '88
Hellraiser '87
Cobra '86
Mask '85
Not My Kid '85
Someone I Touched '75
Charley Varrick '73
Dirty Harry '71

Ann (Robin) Robinson (1935-)
Attack from Mars '88
Dragnet '54
The War of the Worlds '53

Bill Robinson (1878-1949)
Stormy Weather '43
Just Around the Corner '38
Rebecca of Sunnybrook Farm '38
The Little Colonel '35
The Littlest Rebel '35
Dixiana '30

Bruce Robinson (1946-)
Still Crazy '98
The Story of Adele H. '75

Charles Robinson (1945-)
Land of the Free '98
Set It Off '96
Fatal Chase '77
Black Gestapo '75
Daring Dobermans '73
The Brotherhood of Satan '71
Shenandoah '65

Chris Robinson (1938-)
Viper '88
Ace of Hearts '85
Savannah Smiles '82
Amy '81
Sunshine Run '79
Thunder County '74
Women's Prison Escape '74
Stanley '72
Darker than Amber '70

Claudia Robinson
Back in the USSR '92
Wide Sargasso Sea '92

Dar Robinson
Cyclone '87
Stick '85

Eartha D. Robinson
The Old Settler '01
Daughters of the Dust '91

Edward G. Robinson (1893-1973)
Soylent Green '73
Song of Norway '70
MacKenna's Gold '69
Never a Dull Moment '68
The Peking Blond '68
The Cincinnati Kid '65
Cheyenne Autumn '64
Good Neighbor Sam '64
Robin and the 7 Hoods '64
The Prize '63
My Geisha '62
Two Weeks in Another Town '62
Seven Thieves '60
A Hole in the Head '59
Hell on Frisco Bay '55
Illegal '55
Tight Spot '55
The Violent Men '55
Actors and Sin '52
House of Strangers '49
It's a Great Feeling '49
All My Sons '48
Key Largo '48
The Red House '47
The Stranger '46
Our Vines Have Tender Grapes '45
Scarlet Street '45
Double Indemnity '44
Mr. Winkle Goes to War '44
Woman in the Window '44
Destroyer '43
Tales of Manhattan '42
The Sea Wolf '41
Brother Orchid '40
Amazing Dr. Clitterhouse '38
Bullets or Ballots '38
I Am the Law '38
Kid Galahad '37
Thunder in the City '37
Barbary Coast '35
The Whole Town's Talking '35
Little Caesar '30

Frances Robinson (1916-71)
Smilin' Through '41
Riders of Pasco Basin '40
Red Barry '38
Tim Tyler's Luck '37

Jay Robinson (1930-)
Dying to Remember '93
Sinatra '92
Transylvania Twist '89
Malibu Bikini Shop '86
Partners '82
This Is a Hijack '75
Three the Hard Way '74
Everything You Always Wanted to Know about Sex (But Were Afraid to Ask) '72
My Man Godfrey '57
The Virgin Queen '55
Demetrius and the Gladiators '54
The Robe '53

Joe Robinson (1929-)
Diamonds Are Forever '71
Tor '64
Thor and the Amazon Women '60

John Robinson
Zero Patience '94
Uneasy Terms '48

Leon Robinson (1962-)
The Father Clements Story '87
Band of the Hand '86
Streetwalkin' '85
Sole Survivor '84

Madeleine Robinson (1916-)
Camille Claudel '89
I Married a Dead Man '82
Mission to Venice '63

Paul Michael Robinson
Kept '01
The Capitol Conspiracy '99
Friend of the Family 2 '96

Roger Robinson
Burnzy's Last Call '95
Newman's Law '74

Sherry Robinson
Hot Summer in Barefoot County '74
Gruesome Twosome '67

"Sugar Ray" Robinson
Candy '68
Paper Lion '68

Wendy Raquel Robinson
Two Can Play That Game '01
Miss Congeniality '00
Ringmaster '98

German Robles (1929-)
The Brainiac '61
Genie of Darkness '60
The Monster Demolisher '60
The Living Head '59
The Vampire's Coffin '58
The Vampire '57

Rudy Robles (1910-70)
Omoo Omoo, the Shark God '49
Across the Pacific '42
The Real Glory '39

Flora Robson (1902-84)
A Tale of Two Cities '80
Les Miserables '78
Restless '72
Beast in the Cellar '70
Blood Island '68
Those Magnificent Men in Their Flying Machines '65
Guns at Batasi '64
55 Days at Peking '63
Murder at the Gallop '63
Romeo and Juliet '54
Malta Story '53
Black Narcissus '47
Frieda '47
Caesar and Cleopatra '46
Great Day '46
Saratoga Trunk '45
Bahama Passage '42
The Lion Has Wings '40
The Sea Hawk '40
Wuthering Heights '39
Fire Over England '37
Catherine the Great '34

Greer Robson
Starlight Hotel '90
Smash Palace '82

May Robson (1858-1942)
Joan of Paris '42
Playmates '41
The Texas Rangers Ride Again '40
Nurse Edith Cavell '39
The Adventures of Tom Sawyer '38
Bringing Up Baby '38
Four Daughters '38
The Texans '38
A Star Is Born '37
It Happened in New Orleans '36
Wife Versus Secretary '36
Anna Karenina '35
Reckless '35
Lady by Choice '34
Dancing Lady '33
Dinner at Eight '33
Lady for a Day '33
Little Orphan Annie '32
Red Headed Woman '32
Strange Interlude '32

Wayne Robson
Harlan County War '00
Cube '98
Murder She Purred: A Mrs. Murphy Mystery '98
Affliction '97
Two If by Sea '95
Stand Off '93
Love & Murder '91
Bye Bye Blues '89
And Then You Die '88
The Grey Fox '83

Patricia Roc (1915-)
Captain Blackjack '51
Man on the Eiffel Tower '48
Canyon Passage '46
Johnny Frenchman '46
The Wicked Lady '45

Pascale Rocard
Field of Honor '87
Police '85

Daniela Rocca (1938-95)
Divorce—Italian Style '62
The Giant of Marathon '60

Stefania Rocca
Jesus '00
Love's Labour's Lost '00
The Talented Mr. Ripley '99
Solomon '98

Alex Rocco (1936-)
The Wedding Planner '01
Dudley Do-Right '99
Goodbye, Lover '99
A Bug's Life '98 (V)
Just Write '97
That Thing You Do! '96
The Spy Within '94
Boris and Natasha: The Movie '92
The Pope Must Diet '91
A Perfect Little Murder '90
Dream a Little Dream '89
Wired '89
The Lady in White '88
Return to Horror High '87
Scenes from the Goldmine '87
Badge of the Assassin '85
Gotcha! '85
P.K. and the Kid '85
The Entity '83
The Godfather 1902-1959: The Complete Epic '81
Herbie Goes Bananas '80
The Stunt Man '80
The Grass Is Always Greener Over the Septic Tank '78
A Question of Guilt '78
Rabbit Test '78
The Blue Knight '75
Hustling '75
Three the Hard Way '74
Bonnie's Kids '73
Detroit 9000 '73
Slither '73
The Godfather '72
Stanley '72
Wild Riders '71
Blood Mania '70
The St. Valentine's Day Massacre '67
Motor Psycho '65

Eugene Roche (1928-)
When a Man Loves a Woman '94
Eternity '90
Oh, God! You Devil '84
Rape and Marriage: The Rideout Case '80
Corvette Summer '78
Foul Play '78
The Winds of Kitty Hawk '78
The Late Show '77
The Possessed '77
Newman's Law '74
W '74
Slaughterhouse Five '72
They Might Be Giants '71
Cotton Comes to Harlem '70

Sebastien Roche
The Crossing '00
The Hunley '99
Merlin '98
Naked City: Justice with a Bullet '98
Household Saints '93

Suzzy Roche
Crossing Delancey '88
Almost You '85

Jean Rochefort (1930-)
The Closet '00
The Count of Monte Cristo '99
Ridicule '96
Ready to Wear '94
The Hairdresser's Husband '92
My Wonderful Life '90
Birgitt Haas Must Be Killed '83
I Sent a Letter to My Love '81
Le Cavaleur '78
Who Is Killing the Great Chefs of Europe? '78
Le Crabe Tambour '77
Pardon Mon Affaire, Too! '77
Dirty Hands '76
Pardon Mon Affaire '76
Innocents with Dirty Hands '75
Mean Frank and Crazy Tony '75
Return of the Tall Blond Man with One Black Shoe '74
Salut l'Artiste '74
Till Marriage Do Us Part '74
The Clockmaker '73
Le Complot '73
The Tall Blond Man with One Black Shoe '72

Claire Rochelle (1908-81)
Shake Hands with Murder '44
Harvest Melody '43
Texas Justice '42
Buzzy Rides the Range '40
Code of the Fearless '39
Boothill Brigade '37
Guns in the Dark '37
Ridin' the Lone Trail '37
Two-Gun Troubador '37

Debbie Rochon (1968-)
Witchouse 3: Demon Fire '01
American Nightmare '00
Rage of the Werewolf '99
The Alien Agenda: Endangered Species '97
Hellblock 13 '97
Broadcast Bombshells '95
Tromeo & Juliet '95
Abducted 2: The Reunion '94

Lela Rochon (1966-)
Any Given Sunday '99
Labor Pains '99
The Big Hit '98
Knock Off '98
Ruby Bridges '98
Why Do Fools Fall in Love? '98
The Chamber '96
Gang Related '96
Mr. & Mrs. Loving '96
Legal Deceit '95
Waiting to Exhale '95

Chris Rock (1966-)
Bad Company '02
A. I.: Artificial Intelligence '01 (V)
Down to Earth '01
Jay and Silent Bob Strike Back '01
Osmosis Jones '01 (V)
Pootie Tang '01
Nurse Betty '00
Dogma '99
Dr. Dolittle '98 (V)
Lethal Weapon 4 '98
Beverly Hills Ninja '96
The Immortals '95
CB4: The Movie '93
Coneheads '93
Boomerang '92
New Jack City '91
I'm Gonna Git You Sucka '88
Beverly Hills Cop 2 '87

Charles Rocket (1949-)
The Killing Grounds '97
Father's Day '96
Steal Big, Steal Little '95
Tom and Huck '95
Dumb & Dumber '94
It's Pat: The Movie '94
Hocus Pocus '93
Wild Palms '93
Delirious '91
Dances with Wolves '90
Down Twisted '89
Earth Girls Are Easy '89
How I Got into College '89
Miracles '86
Fraternity Vacation '85

Jack Rockwell (1949-)
Raiders of Sunset Pass '43
Tumbleweed Trail '42
Twilight on the Trail '41
Hopalong Cassidy: Renegade Trail '39
Renegade Trail '39
The Rangers Step In '37
Brand of the Outlaws '36
Outlaw Rule '36
The Tonto Kid '35
The Man from Hell '34
The Fiddlin' Buckaroo '33
Come on Tarzan '32

Rick Rockwell
Killer Tomatoes Eat France '91
Killer Tomatoes Strike Back '90

Robert Rockwell
Lassie: Adventures of Neeka '68
The Red Menace '49

Sam Rockwell (1968-)
Heist '01
Charlie's Angels '00
Galaxy Quest '99
The Green Mile '99
William Shakespeare's A Midsummer Night's Dream '99
Jerry and Tom '98
Safe Men '98
Box of Moonlight '96
Glory Daze '96
Lawn Dogs '96
Mercy '96
The Search for One-Eyed Jimmy '96
Jack and His Friends '92
Clown House '88

Jay Rodan
The Caveman's Valentine '01
Lost Battalion '01
The Triumph of Love '01

Ziva Rodann (1935-)
Samar '62
The Giants of Thessaly '60
Macumba Love '60
Last Train from Gun Hill '59
Teenage Doll '57

Marcia Rodd (1940-)
Keeping On '81
Citizens Band '77
How to Break Up a Happy Divorce '76
Little Murders '71

Ebbe Rode (1910-98)
Babette's Feast '87
Topsy Turvy '84
Gertrud '64

Karel Roden
Blade II '02
15 Minutes '01
Crackerjack 2 '97

Anton Rodgers (1933-)
Impromptu '90
Pictures '80s
Dirty Rotten Scoundrels '88
Disraeli '79
Lillie '79

Dennis Rodman
Cutaway '00
Simon Sez '99
Double Team '97

Serge Rodnunsky
Lovers' Lovers '94
Body Beat '88

Estelita Rodriguez (1928-66)
Sunset in the West '50
Twilight in the Sierras '50
The Golden Stallion '49
Susanna Pass '49
The Gay Ranchero '42

Freddy Rodriguez (1975-)
For Love or Country: The Arturo Sandoval Story '00
The Pest '96
Dead Presidents '95
A Walk in the Clouds '95

Marco Rodriguez
Angel Blue '97
Two for Texas '97
Serial Killer '95
... And the Earth Did Not Swallow Him '94
The Crow '93
Internal Affairs '90
The Rookie '90

Michelle Rodriguez (1978-)
Blue Crush '02
Resident Evil '02
The Fast and the Furious '01

3 A.M. '01
Girlfight '99

Paul Rodriguez (1955-)
Blood Work '02
Ali '01
Crocodile Dundee in Los Angeles '01
Rat Race '01
Tortilla Soup '01
Mambo Cafe '00
Price of Glory '00
Rough Magic '95
A Million to Juan '94
Made in America '93
Born in East L.A. '87
Miracles '86
Quicksilver '86
The Whoopee Boys '86

Valente Rodriguez
The Big Squeeze '96
Ed '96

Norman Rodway (1929-2001)
The Empty Mirror '99
The Bretts '88
Coming Through '85
Chimes at Midnight '67

Channon Roe
Girl '98
Marshal Law '96
Persons Unknown '96
Soldier Boyz '95

Matt Roe
Last Call '90
Puppet Master '89

Paul Roebling
Carolina Skeletons '92
End of August '82

Daniel Roebuck (1963-)
Double Take '01
A Glimpse of Hell '01
Final Destination '00
Stir '98
U.S. Marshals '98
Money Talks '97
The Late Shift '96
The Fugitive '93
The Killing Mind '90
Disorganized Crime '89
Miles from Home '88
Dudes '87
River's Edge '87
Terror Eyes '87
Cave Girl '85

William Roerick (1912-95)
A Separate Peace '73
The Love Machine '71
The Wasp Woman '59

Maurice Roeves (1937-)
Beautiful Creatures '00
Forgive and Forget '99
The Acid House '98
David '97
Moses '96
The Last of the Mohicans '92
The Big Man: Crossing the Line '91
Hidden Agenda '90
Danger UXB '81
Ulysses '67

Michael Rogan
Punch the Clock '90
Doom Asylum '88

Bill Rogers
For Love of the Game '99
The Girl, the Body and the Pill '67
Shanty Tramp '67
A Taste of Blood '67

Charles "Buddy" Rogers (1904-99)
Mexican Spitfire at Sea '42
Double Trouble '41
My Best Girl '27
Wings '27

Ginger Rogers (1911-95)
That's Dancing! '85
Quick, Let's Get Married '71
Cinderella '64
Tight Spot '55
Forever Female '53
Monkey Business '52
We're Not Married '52
The Barkleys of Broadway '49
Heartbeat '46
Magnificent Doll '46
Weekend at the Waldorf '45
Tender Comrade '43
The Major and the Minor '42
Once Upon a Honeymoon '42
Roxie Hart '42
Tales of Manhattan '42
Tom, Dick, and Harry '41
Kitty Foyle '40
Lucky Partners '40
Primrose Path '40
Bachelor Mother '39
Fifth Avenue Girl '39
The Story of Vernon and Irene Castle '39
Carefree '38
Having Wonderful Time '38
Vivacious Lady '38
Shall We Dance '37
Stage Door '37
Follow the Fleet '36
Swing Time '36
In Person '35
Roberta '35
Star of Midnight '35
Top Hat '35
The Gay Divorcee '34
Romance in Manhattan '34
Finishing School '33
Flying Down to Rio '33
42nd Street '33
Gold Diggers of 1933 '33
Shriek in the Night '33
13th Guest '32
The Tip-Off '31

Ivan Rogers (1954-)
Slow Burn '90
Ballbuster '89
Two Wrongs Make a Right '89
Crazed Cop '88

Jean Rogers (1916-91)
Whistling in Brooklyn '43
Brigham Young: Frontiersman '40
Flash Gordon: Rocketship '40
Flash Gordon: Mars Attacks the World '39
Ace Drummond '36
Rocketship '36

Jimmy Rogers (1915-97)
Mystery Man '44
Texas Masquerade '44
False Colors '43
Hopalong Cassidy: Riders of the Deadline '43

Kenny Rogers (1938-)
The Gambler Returns: The Luck of the Draw '93
Rio Diablo '93
The Return of Spinal Tap '92
Kenny Rogers as the Gambler, Part 3: The Legend Continues '87
Wild Horses '84
Kenny Rogers as the Gambler, Part 2: The Adventure Continues '83
Six Pack '82
Coward of the County '81
Kenny Rogers as the Gambler '80

Mimi Rogers (1956-)
Ginger Snaps '01
Common Ground '00
Seven Girlfriends '00
Cruel Intentions 2 '99
The Devil's Arithmetic '99
Lost in Space '98
Austin Powers: International Man of Mystery '97
Tricks '97
Weapons of Mass Distraction '97
The Mirror Has Two Faces '96
Tree's Lounge '96
Bulletproof Heart '95
Full Body Massage '95
Far from Home: The Adventures of Yellow Dog '94
Monkey Trouble '94
Reflections in the Dark '94
Dark Horse '92
Ladykiller '92
The Player '92
Shooting Elizabeth '92
White Sands '92
Deadlock '91
The Doors '91
The Palermo Connection '91
The Rapture '91
Desperate Hours '90
Fourth Story '90
Hider in the House '90
The Rousters '90
The Mighty Quinn '89
Someone to Watch Over Me '87
Street Smart '87
Embassy '85
Gung Ho '85
Blue Skies Again '83

Paul Rogers (1917-)
The Return of the Native '94
The Tenth Man '88
Edwin '84
The Looking Glass War '69
A Midsummer Night's Dream '68
Stolen Hours '63
Billy Budd '62
The Mark '61
The Trials of Oscar Wilde '60
Svengali '55
Beau Brummel '54

Reg Rogers
Attila '01
Runaway Bride '99

Roxanne Rogers
Punk Vacation '90
Slow Moves '84

Roy Rogers (1912-98)
Alias Jesse James '59
Son of Paleface '52
Heart of the Rockies '51
Bells of Coronado '50
North of the Great Divide '50
Sunset in the West '50
Trail of Robin Hood '50
Trigger, Jr. '50
Twilight in the Sierras '50
Down Dakota Way '49
The Golden Stallion '49
Susanna Pass '49
Eyes of Texas '48
Far Frontier '48
Grand Canyon Trail '48
Melody Time '48
Night Time in Nevada '48
Under California Stars '48
Apache Rose '47
Bells of San Angelo '47
Home in Oklahoma '47
Lights of Old Santa Fe '47
On the Old Spanish Trail '47
Springtime in the Sierras '47
Helldorado '46
My Pal Trigger '46
Rainbow over Texas '46
Roll on Texas Moon '46
Song of Arizona '46
Under Nevada Skies '46
Along the Navaho Trail '45
Bells of Rosarita '45
Don't Fence Me In '45
Sunset in El Dorado '45
Under Western Stars '45
Utah '45
Cowboy & the Senorita '44
San Fernando Valley '44
Song of Nevada '44
The Yellow Rose of Texas '44
Hands Across the Border '43
Idaho '43
King of the Cowboys '43
Silver Spurs '43
Song of Texas '43
Texas Legionnaires '43
The Gay Ranchero '42
Heart of the Golden West '42
Man from Cheyenne '42
Ridin' Down the Canyon '42
Romance on the Range '42
Sons of the Pioneers '42
South of Santa Fe '42
Sunset on the Desert '42
Sunset Serenade '42
Bad Man of Deadwood '41
In Old Cheyenne '41
Jesse James at Bay '41
Nevada City '41
Red River Valley '41
Robin Hood of the Pecos '41
Sheriff of Tombstone '41
The Border Legion '40
Carson City Kid '40
Colorado '40
Dark Command '40
Ranger and the Lady '40
Young Bill Hickok '40
Young Buffalo Bill '40
Arizona Kid '39
Days of Jesse James '39
Frontier Pony Express '39
In Old Caliente '39
Jeepers Creepers '39
Rough Riders' Roundup '39
Saga of Death Valley '39
Southward Ho! '39
Wall Street Cowboy '39
Billy the Kid Returns '38
Come on Rangers '38
Old Barn Dance '38
Shine on, Harvest Moon '38
Old Corral '36

Steve Rogers
Triple Impact '92
Trident Force '88

Tristan Rogers (1946-)
Night Eyes 3 '93
Evil Lives '92
The Rescuers Down Under '90 (V)
Flesh and Blood Show '73

Wayne Rogers (1933-)
Ghosts of Mississippi '96
The Goodbye Bird '93
Hot Touch '80s
Passion in Paradise '89
Drop-Out Mother '88
The Killing Time '87
The Girl Who Spelled Freedom '86
The Gig '85
Lady from Yesterday '85
Chiefs '83
Once in Paris... '79
Pocket Money '72
Cool Hand Luke '67

Will Rogers (1879-1935)
Doubting Thomas '35
Judge Priest '34
Mr. Skitch '33
Ambassador Bill '31
A Connecticut Yankee '31

Maria Rohm (1949-)
Count Dracula '71
Dorian Gray '70
Venus in Furs '70
Kiss and Kill '68
The House of 1000 Dolls '67

Clayton Rohner (1961-)
The Big Day '99
Sometimes They Come Back ... For More '99
Where's Marlowe? '98
The Relic '96
Naked Souls '95
Caroline at Midnight '93
I, Madman '89
Nightwish '89
Bat 21 '88
Private Investigations '87
April Fool's Day '86
Just One of the Guys '85

Eduardo Lopez Rojas
My Family '94
Reed: Insurgent Mexico '73

Gustavo Rojo (1926-)
The Valley of Gwangi '69
The Christmas Kid '68
A Witch Without a Broom '68
Apache's Last Battle '64
No Survivors, Please '63
It Started with a Kiss '59

Helena Rojo
Mary, Mary, Bloody Mary '76
Aguirre, the Wrath of God '72

Maria Rojo (1943-)
Esmeralda Comes by Night '98
Midaq Alley '95
Danzon '91
Break of Dawn '88
Mary, My Dearest '83
Candy Stripe Nurses '74

Ruben Rojo (1925-93)
Cauldron of Blood '67
Samson in the Wax Museum '63
The Brainiac '61

Gilbert Roland (1905-94)
Barbarosa '82
Cabo Blanco '81
The Sacketts '79
Islands in the Stream '77
Running Wild '73
Between God, the Devil & a Winchester '72
The Ruthless Four '70
Go Kill and Come Back '68
Any Gun Can Play '67
The Poppy Is Also a Flower '66
Cheyenne Autumn '64
Samar '62
Three Violent People '57
Around the World in 80 Days '56
The Racers '55
Treasure of Pancho Villa '55
Underwater! '55
The French Line '54
Beneath the 12-Mile Reef '53
Thunder Bay '53
The Bad and the Beautiful '52
Miracle of Our Lady of Fatima '52
Bullfighter & the Lady '50
The Torch '50
Malaya '49
Ridin' the California Trail '47
South of Monterey '47
Captain Kidd '45
The Sea Hawk '40
Thunder Pass '37
Thunder Trail '37
She Done Him Wrong '33
The Plastic Age '25

Gylian Roland
Deadly Sunday '82
Barn of the Naked Dead '73

Tutta Rolf
Dollar '38
Swedenhielms '35

Guy Rolfe (1915-)
Retro Puppet Master '99
Puppet Master 5: The Final Chapter '94
Puppet Master 4 '93
The Dark Angel '91
Puppet Master 3: Toulon's Revenge '90
Dolls '87
And Now the Screaming Starts '73
The Alphabet Murders '65
Mr. Sardonicus '61
Young Bess '53

Kirsten Rolffes
The Kingdom 2 '97
The Kingdom '95
Sofie '92

Esther Rolle (1920-98)
Down in the Delta '98
My Fellow Americans '96
Rosewood '96
How to Make an American Quilt '95
Scarlett '94
To Dance with the White Dog '93
House of Cards '92
The Kid Who Loved Christmas '90
Age Old Friends '89
Driving Miss Daisy '89
The Mighty Quinn '89
A Raisin in the Sun '89
P.K. and the Kid '85
I Know Why the Caged Bird Sings '79
The Summer of My German Soldier '78

Henry Rollins (1961-)
The New Guy '02
Time Lapse '01
Jack Frost '98
Lost Highway '96
Heat '95
Johnny Mnemonic '95
The Chase '93

Howard E. Rollins, Jr. (1950-96)
Drunks '96
For Us, the Living '88
The House of Dies Drear '88
Johnnie Gibson F.B.I. '87
The Children of Times Square '86
A Soldier's Story '84
The Member of the Wedding '83
Ragtime '81
King '78

Mark Rolston (1952-)
Wicked Ways '99
From the Earth to the Moon '98
Letters from a Killer '98
Rush Hour '98
George Wallace '97
Hard Rain '97
Daylight '96
Eraser '96
Humanoids from the Deep '96
Best of the Best 3: No Turning Back '95
Scanner Cop '94
The Shawshank Redemption '94
Body of Evidence '92
The Comrades of Summer '92
Prancer '89
A Sinful Life '89
Survival Quest '89
Weeds '87
Aliens '86

Yvonne Romain (1938-)
Double Trouble '67
Devil Doll '64
The Curse of the Werewolf '61
The Frightened City '61

Candice Roman
The Big Bird Cage '72
Unholy Rollers '72

Freddie Roman
Finding North '97
Sweet Lorraine '87

Leticia Roman
Fanny Hill: Memoirs of a Woman of Pleasure '64
The Girl Who Knew Too Much '63
G.I. Blues '60

Ruth Roman (1924-99)
Echoes '83
The Sacketts '79

Day of the Animals '77
Impulse '74
The Killing Kind '73
The Baby '72
Love Has Many Faces '65
Great Day in the Morning '56
Far Country '55
Blowing Wild '54
Strangers on a Train '51
Three Secrets '50
Beyond the Forest '49
Champion '49
The Window '49
Good Sam '48
Since You Went Away '44

Susan (Suzan) Roman (1957-)
Rock & Rule '83 *(V)*
Rabid '77
Weekend with the Babysitter '70

Viviane Romance (1909-91)
Any Number Can Win '63
Panique '47
Princess Tam Tam '35

Beatrice Romand (1952-)
Autumn Tale '98
Four Adventures of Reinette and Mirabelle '89
Summer '86
House of the Yellow Carpet '84
Le Beau Mariage '82
Claire's Knee '71

Carla Romanelli
The Lonely Lady '83
Fighting Fists of Shanghai Joe '65

Andy Romano (1936-)
Eraser '96
Fast Money '96
Listen '96
Two Bits '96
Chameleon '95
Under Siege 2: Dark Territory '95
Drop Zone '94
Tryst '94
Afterburn '92
Unlawful Entry '92
Pump Up the Volume '90
Over the Edge '79
Get Christie Love! '74

Renato Romano
Frankenstein '80 '79
The Bird with the Crystal Plumage '70
Dorian Gray '70

Rino Romano
Rocky Marciano '99
The Club '94

Anna Romantowska
The Interrogation '82
A Woman and a Woman '80

Richard Romanus (1943-)
Cops and Robbersons '94
Point of No Return '93
To Protect and Serve '92
Oscar '91
Hollywood Heartbreak '89
The Couch Trip '87
Murphy's Law '86
Protocol '84
Strangers Kiss '83
Heavy Metal '81 *(V)*
Sitting Ducks '80
Wizards '77 *(V)*
Night Terror '76
Mean Streets '73

Robert Romanus
The Resurrected '91
Pulse '88
Bad Medicine '85
Fast Times at Ridgemont High '82

Lina Romay (1922-)
Love Laughs at Andy Hardy '46
Adventure '45

Lina Romay (1954-)
Tender Flesh '97
Revenge in the House of Usher '82
Sex Is Crazy '79
Ilsa, the Wicked Warden '78
Jack the Ripper '76
Female Vampire '73
The Perverse Countess '73

Cindy Rome
Knock Outs '92
Swift Justice '88

Sydne Rome (1947-)
The Puma Man '80
Just a Gigolo '79
Twist '76
That Lucky Touch '75
Wanted: Babysitter '75
Diary of Forbidden Dreams '73
Order to Kill '73

Rachel Romen
Ransom Money '88
The Girl from Tobacco Row '66

Cesar Romero (1907-94)
Mortuary Academy '91
Simple Justice '89
Judgment Day '88
Lust in the Dust '85
Mission to Glory '80
The Big Push '75
The Spectre of Edgar Allen Poe '73
Now You See Him, Now You Don't '72
The Proud and the Damned '72
The Computer Wore Tennis Shoes '69
Crooks & Coronets '69
Gun Crazy '69
Hot Millions '68
Madigan's Millions '67
Batman '66
The Castilian '63
Donovan's Reef '63
Ocean's 11 '60
Around the World in 80 Days '56
Americano '55
The Racers '55
The Shadow Man '53
Vera Cruz '53
FBI Girl '52
Jungle '52
Scotland Yard Inspector '52
Happy Go Lovely '51
The Lost Continent '51
The Beautiful Blonde from Bashful Bend '49
Julia Misbehaves '48
Captain from Castile '47
Wintertime '43
Orchestra Wives '42
Springtime in the Rockies '42
Tales of Manhattan '42
Dance Hall '41
The Great American Broadcast '41
Week-End in Havana '41
Lucky Cisco Kid '40
The Little Princess '39
Happy Landing '38
My Lucky Star '38
Wee Willie Winkie '37
The Devil Is a Woman '35
Show Them No Mercy '35
The Thin Man '34

Chanda Romero
Olongape: The American Dream '89
The Last Reunion '80

George A. Romero (1940-)
Dawn of the Dead '78
Martin '77
Night of the Living Dead '68

Joanelle Romero
Miracle in the Wilderness '91
Lost Legacy: A Girl Called Hatter Fox '77

Ned Romero (1925-)
The Lost Child '00
The Magnificent Seven '98
Children of the Corn 2: The Final Sacrifice '92
House 4: Home Deadly Home '91
The Last of the Mohicans '85
The Deerslayer '78
I Will Fight No More Forever '75

Rebecca Romijn-Stamos
Rollerball '02
X-Men '00
Austin Powers 2: The Spy Who Shagged Me '99

Paul Ronan
Durango '99
The Devil's Own '96

Maurice Ronet (1927-83)
Beau Pere '81
Sphinx '81
Sidney Sheldon's Bloodline '79
Don Juan (Or If Don Juan Were a Woman) '73
The Deadly Trap '71
Swimming Pool '70
The Women '69
How Sweet It Is! '68
Scandal Man '67
L'Odeur des Fauves '66
The Lost Command '66
The Fire Within '64
Time Out for Love '61
Purple Noon '60
Carve Her Name with Pride '58
Frantic '58
Without Warning '52
Rendez-vous de Juillet '49

Linda Ronstadt
Chuck Berry: Hail! Hail! Rock 'n' Roll '87
The Pirates of Penzance '83
FM '78

Michael Rooker (1956-)
Replicant '01
Here on Earth '00
Newsbreak '00
The 6th Day '00
The Bone Collector '99
Rogue Force '99
Wicked Ways '99
Bram Stoker's Shadowbuilder '98
Brown's Requiem '98
The Replacement Killers '98
Deceiver '97
Back to Back '96
Bastard out of Carolina '96
Keys to Tulsa '96
Rosewood '96
The Trigger Effect '96
Mallrats '95
The Hard Truth '94
Cliffhanger '93
Tombstone '93
Afterburn '92
The Dark Half '91
JFK '91
Days of Thunder '90
Henry: Portrait of a Serial Killer '90
Music Box '89
Sea of Love '89
Above the Law '88
Eight Men Out '88
Mississippi Burning '88
Light of Day '87

Mickey Rooney (1920-)
Babe: Pig in the City '98
Boys Will Be Boys '97
The Road Home '95
The Gambler Returns: The Luck of the Draw '93
The Magic Voyage '93 *(V)*
Revenge of the Red Baron '93
The Legend of Wolf Mountain '92
Little Nemo: Adventures in Slumberland '92 *(V)*
Maximum Force '92
Sweet Justice '92
My Heroes Have Always Been Cowboys '91
Silent Night, Deadly Night 5: The Toymaker '91
Home for Christmas '90
Erik the Viking '89
Lightning: The White Stallion '86
Ace of Hearts '85
It Came Upon a Midnight Clear '84
Bill: On His Own '83
The Odyssey of the Pacific '82
Bill '81
The Fox and the Hound '81 *(V)*
Leave 'Em Laughing '81
Senior Trip '81
The Black Stallion '79
The Dark Side of Love '79
Magic of Lassie '78
The Domino Principle '77
Pete's Dragon '77
Find the Lady '75
Rachel's Man '75
Thunder County '74
Women's Prison Escape '74
Pulp '72
Evil Roy Slade '71
Journey Back to Oz '71 *(V)*
Manipulator '71
The Comic '69
How to Stuff a Wild Bikini '65
It's a Mad, Mad, Mad, Mad World '63
Requiem for a Heavyweight '62
Breakfast at Tiffany's '61
The King of the Roaring '20s: The Story of Arnold Rothstein '61
Platinum High School '60
Francis in the Haunted House '56
The Bridges at Toko-Ri '55
The Atomic Kid '54
Off Limits '53
My Outlaw Brother '51
Quicksand '50
The Big Wheel '49
Summer Holiday '48
Words and Music '48
Love Laughs at Andy Hardy '46
National Velvet '44
Girl Crazy '43
The Human Comedy '43
Thousands Cheer '43
Andy Hardy's Double Life '42
Andy Hardy's Private Secretary '41
Babes on Broadway '41
Life Begins for Andy Hardy '41
Men of Boys Town '41
Andy Hardy Meets Debutante '40
Strike Up the Band '40
Young Tom Edison '40
The Adventures of Huckleberry Finn '39
Andy Hardy Gets Spring Fever '39
Babes in Arms '39
Mickey the Great '39
Boys Town '38
Love Finds Andy Hardy '38
Captains Courageous '37
Thoroughbreds Don't Cry '37
Healer '36
Little Lord Fauntleroy '36
Ah, Wilderness! '35
A Midsummer Night's Dream '35
Riff Raff '35
Hide-Out '34
Manhattan Melodrama '34
My Pal, the King '32

Tim Rooney
Storyville '74
Village of the Giants '65

Camilla Overbye Roos
The Guilty '99
Facade '98
On the Border '98
Hotel Room '93

Buddy Roosevelt (1898-1973)
Tribute to a Bad Man '56
Boss Cowboy '35
Powdersmoke Range '35
Range Riders '35
Circle Canyon '33
Lightning Range '33

Amanda Root (1963-)
Anna Karenina '00
Deep in the Heart (of Texas) '98
Jane Eyre '96
Breaking the Code '95
Persuasion '95
Catherine Cookson's The Man Who Cried '93

Stephen (Steve) Root (1951-)
Ice Age '02 *(V)*
O Brother Where Art Thou? '00
Bicentennial Man '99
From the Earth to the Moon '98
Krippendorf's Tribe '98
Office Space '98
The Road to Galveston '96
Night of the Scarecrow '95
Bye Bye, Love '94
Dave '93
Extreme Justice '93
Bed & Breakfast '92
Buffy the Vampire Slayer '92
Till Murder Do Us Part '92
Guilty by Suspicion '91
RoboCop 3 '91
Stephen King's Golden Years '91
V.I. Warshawski '91
Ghost '90
Black Rain '89
Crocodile Dundee 2 '88
Monkey Shines '88

Noel Roquevert (1892-1973)
Une Parisienne '58
Fanfan la Tulipe '51
Antoine et Antoinette '47
Le Corbeau '43

Hayden Rorke (1910-87)
The Night Walker '64
Spencer's Mountain '63
Above and Beyond '53
Francis Goes to the Races '51

Tom Rosales
John Carpenter's Vampires '97
Bail Out '90

Bert Rosario
A Million to Juan '94
Cold Justice '89

Tony Rosato (1954-)
Rent-A-Kid '95
The Good Fight '92
Switching Channels '88
Busted Up '86
City of Shadows '86
Hog Wild '80

Francoise Rosay (1891-1974)
The Pedestrian '73
Me and the Colonel '58
Seven Deadly Sins '53
The Red Inn '51
September Affair '50
Johnny Frenchman '46
Bizarre Bizarre '39
Carnival in Flanders '35

Gabrielle Rose
The Five Senses '99
The Sweet Hereafter '96
Timecop '94
The Adjuster '91
Speaking Parts '89
Family Viewing '87

George Rose (1920-88)
Pound Puppies and the Legend of Big Paw '88 *(V)*
You Can't Take It with You '84
The Pirates of Penzance '83
The Hideaways '73
A New Leaf '71
The Pink Jungle '68
The Flesh and the Fiends '60
Jack the Ripper '60
The Devil's Disciple '59
A Night to Remember '58

Jamie Rose (1960-)
Chopper Chicks in Zombietown '91
To Die Standing '91
Playroom '90
Rebel Love '85
Heartbreakers '84
Tightrope '84
In Love with an Older Woman '82
Twirl '81

Laurie Rose (1948-)
Blood Voyage '77
Working Girls '75
Hot Box '72
Woman Hunt '72

Robin Pearson Rose
Lucy and Desi: Before the Laughter '91
Last Resort '86

Sherrie Rose
Me & Will '99
Devil in the Flesh '98
The Nurse '97
Black Scorpion 2: Ground Zero '96
New Crime City: Los Angeles 2020 '94
Double Threat '92
Maximum Force '92
Martial Law 2: Undercover '91

Rose Marie (1925-)
Shriek If You Know What I Did Last Friday the 13th '00
Ghetto Blaster '89
Witchboard '87
Cheaper to Keep Her '80
Memory of Us '74
Dead Heat on a Merry-Go-Round '66

Roseanne (1952-)
Blue in the Face '95
Even Cowgirls Get the Blues '94
The Woman Who Loved Elvis '93
Backfield in Motion '91
Freddy's Dead: The Final Nightmare '91
Look Who's Talking, Too '90 *(V)*
She-Devil '89

John Roselius
Con Air '97
Devil in a Blue Dress '95
JAG '95

Ed Roseman
America '24
Sands of Sacrifice '21

Michael Rosenbaum (1972-)
Sorority Boys '02
Sweet November '01
Urban Legend '98

Alan Rosenberg (1950-)
Crash Course '00
The Temptations '98
Witch Hunt '94
In a Stranger's Hand '92
Impulse '90
After Midnight '89
Capone '89
Miracle Mile '89

White of the Eye *'88*
Happy Birthday, Gemini *'80*
Wanderers *'79*

Michael Rosenberg (1900-72)
Mirele Efros *'38*
The Two Sisters *'37*
His Wife's Lover *'31*

Maxie "Slapsie" Rosenbloom (1903-76)
The Bellboy *'60*
I Married a Monster from Outer Space *'58*
Hollywood or Bust *'56*
Abbott and Costello Meet the Keystone Kops *'54*
Cooking Up Trouble *'44*
Ghost Crazy *'44*
Here Comes Kelly *'43*
To the Shores of Tripoli *'42*
Louisiana Purchase *'41*
Each Dawn I Die *'39*
Amazing Dr. Clitterhouse *'38*
Kelly the Second *'36*

Rosette (1959-)
A Tale of Winter *'92*
Summer *'86*
Pauline at the Beach *'83*

Caroline Rosi
Abraham *'94*
The Palermo Connection *'91*

Annie Ross (1930-)
Short Cuts *'93*
Basket Case 3: The Progeny *'92*
Basket Case 2 *'90*
Pump Up the Volume *'90*
Superman 3 *'83*
Funny Money *'82*
Yanks *'79*
Dressed for Death *'74*

Betsy King Ross
The Phantom Empire *'35*
Fighting with Kit Carson *'33*

Beverly Ross
Slipping into Darkness *'88*
Bloodshed *'83*
Crazed *'82*
S.O.S. Titanic *'79*

Charlotte Ross (1968-)
Kidnapped in Paradise *'98*
Foreign Student *'94*
Savage Land *'94*

Chelcie Ross (1942-)
The Majestic *'01*
Snap Decision *'01*
The Gift *'00*
Charming Billy *'98*
A Simple Plan *'98*
Chain Reaction *'96*
Evil Has a Face *'96*
Amos and Andrew *'93*
Rudy *'93*
Basic Instinct *'92*
Legacy of Lies *'92*
Bill & Ted's Bogus Journey *'91*
The Last Boy Scout *'91*
Major League *'89*
Above the Law *'88*
Keep My Grave Open *'80*

David Ross
Oliver Twist *'00*
Little Odessa *'94*

Diana Ross (1944-)
Double Platinum *'99*
The Wiz *'78*
Mahogany *'75*
Lady Sings the Blues *'72*

Gene Ross (1930-)
Lost Highway *'96*
Halloween 4: The Return of Michael Myers *'88*
Keep My Grave Open *'80*
Encounter with the Unknown *'75*
Poor White Trash 2 *'75*
Don't Open the Door! *'74*
Don't Look in the Basement *'73*

Herbert Ross (1927-2001)
Play It Again, Sam *'72*
Goodbye, Mr. Chips *'69*

Howard (Red) Ross (1934-96)
The New Gladiators *'83*
New York Ripper *'82*
The Legend of the Wolf Woman *'77*
Five Dolls for an August Moon *'70*

Katharine Ross (1942-)
Donnie Darko *'01*
A Climate for Killing *'91*
Conagher *'91*
Red Headed Stranger *'87*
The Shadow Riders *'82*
Wrong Is Right *'82*
Murder in Texas *'81*
The Final Countdown *'80*
Rodeo Girl *'80*
The Legacy *'79*
Murder by Natural Causes *'79*
The Betsy *'78*
The Swarm *'78*
Voyage of the Damned *'76*
The Stepford Wives *'75*
Pigs *'73*
They Only Kill Their Masters *'72*
Fools *'70*
Butch Cassidy and the Sundance Kid *'69*
Tell Them Willie Boy Is Here *'69*
Hellfighters *'68*
Games *'67*
The Graduate *'67*
The Singing Nun *'66*
Shenandoah *'65*

Kimberly Ross
Pumpkinhead *'88*
Nightmare at Noon *'87*
The Last Starfighter *'84*

Lee Ross
Dreaming of Joseph Lees *'99*
Metroland *'97*
Secrets and Lies *'95*
Buddy's Song *'91*

Marion Ross
The Last Best Sunday *'98*
The Evening Star *'96*
On the Edge: The Survival of Dana *'79*
Pearl *'78*
Grand Theft Auto *'77*
Teacher's Pet *'58*
Forever Female *'53*

Matt Ross
Stephen King's Rose Red *'02*
Just Visiting *'01*
American Psycho *'99*
Pushing Tin *'99*
Face/Off *'97*
Ed's Next Move *'96*

Merrie Lynn Ross
Class of 1984 *'82*
The Lucifer Complex *'78*
Way He Was *'76*

Michael Ross
The Wedding Party *'97*
Attack of the 50 Foot Woman *'58*
D.O.A. *'49*

Milton Ross
False Faces *'18*
Narrow Trail *'17*

Ricco Ross
Aliens *'86*
The Dirty Dozen: The Next Mission *'85*

Ron Ross
Battle Beyond the Stars *'80*
Joy Ride to Nowhere *'78*

Shavar Ross
The House of Dies' Drear *'88*
Friday the 13th, Part 5: A New Beginning *'85*

Shirley Ross (1913-75)
Mindkiller *'87*
Night Vision *'87*
Rhythm Romance *'39*
The Big Broadcast of 1938 *'38*
Thanks for the Memory *'38*
Waikiki Wedding *'37*

Stanley Ralph Ross (1936-2000)
Babe: Pig in the City *'98 (V)*
Candy Stripe Nurses *'74*

Ted Ross
Arthur 2: On the Rocks *'88*
Stealing Home *'88*
Arthur *'81*
The Wiz *'78*

Isabella Rossellini (1952-)
Don Quixote *'00*
The Imposters *'98*
Left Luggage *'98*
Merlin *'98*
The Odyssey *'97*
Crime of the Century *'96*
The Funeral *'96*
Big Night *'95*
Immortal Beloved *'94*
Wyatt Earp *'94*
Fallen Angels 1 *'93*
Fearless *'93*
The Innocent *'93*
The Pickle *'93*
Death Becomes Her *'92*
Lies of the Twins *'91*
Ivory Hunters *'90*
Wild at Heart *'90*
Cousins *'89*
Red Riding Hood *'88*
Zelly & Me *'88*
Siesta *'87*
Tough Guys Don't Dance *'87*
Blue Velvet *'86*
White Nights *'85*
A Matter of Time *'76*

Carol Rossen
The Fury *'78*
The Stepford Wives *'75*

Kathryn Rossetter
Whatever *'98*
Shakedown *'88*

Leo Rossi
One Night at McCool's *'01*
Crackerjack 3 *'00*
Analyze This *'98*
Sticks *'98*
True Friends *'98*
In Cold Blood *'96*
Wedding Bell Blues *'96*
Felony *'95*
Mutant Species *'95*
Rave Review *'95*
Beyond Desire *'94*
Fast Getaway 2 *'94*
Relentless 4 *'94*
Casualties of Love: The "Long Island Lolita" Story *'93*
Raw Justice *'93*
Relentless 3 *'93*
We're Talkin' Serious Money *'92*
Where the Day Takes You *'92*
Fast Getaway *'91*
Relentless 2: Dead On *'91*
Maniac Cop 2 *'90*
Relentless *'89*
The Accused *'88*
The Hit List *'88*
River's Edge *'87*
Heart Like a Wheel *'83*

Eleanora Rossi-Drago (1925-)
Dorian Gray *'70*
Camille 2000 *'69*
Uncle Tom's Cabin *'69*

Giacomo "Jack" Rossi-Stuart (1931-)
Macabre *'77*
Zorro *'74*
The Night Evelyn Came Out of the Grave *'71*
Hornet's Nest *'70*
Kill, Baby, Kill *'66*
Knives of the Avenger *'65*
Planet on the Prowl *'65*
The Last Man on Earth *'64*
Gun Fight at Red Sands *'63*
The Avenger *'62*

Paul Rossilli
Bayou Romance *'86*
The Haunting Passion *'83*

Norman Rossington (1928-99)
Let Him Have It *'91*
The Krays *'90*
Man in the Wilderness *'71*
The Charge of the Light Brigade *'68*
Negatives *'68*
A Hard Day's Night *'64*
Lawrence of Arabia *'62*
Saturday Night and Sunday Morning *'60*

Leonard Rossiter (1926-84)
Water *'85*
Britannia Hospital *'82*
The Pink Panther Strikes Again *'76*
Luther *'74*
2001: A Space Odyssey *'68*
King Rat *'65*

Angelo Rossitto (1908-91)
The Offspring *'87*
Mad Max: Beyond Thunderdome *'85*
Brain of Blood *'71*
Dracula vs. Frankenstein *'71*
Invasion of the Saucer Men *'57*
Daughter of Horror *'55*
Mesa of Lost Women *'52*
The Corpse Vanishes *'42*

Rick Rossovich (1957-)
Miracle in Lane Two *'00*
Telling You *'98*
Legend of the Lost Tomb *'97*
Truth or Consequences, N.M. *'97*
Black Scorpion *'95*
Cover Me *'95*
Fatally Yours *'95*
New Crime City: Los Angeles 2020 *'94*
The Gambler Returns: The Luck of the Draw *'93*
Tropical Heat *'93*
Secret Ingredient *'92*
Navy SEALS *'90*
Paint It Black *'89*
The Spellbinder *'88*
Let's Get Harry *'87*
Roxanne *'87*
The Morning After *'86*
Top Gun *'86*
Warning Sign *'85*
Streets of Fire *'84*
The Terminator *'84*
The Lords of Discipline *'83*

Emmy Rossum
An American Rhapsody *'01*
Songcatcher *'99*

Carlo Rota
Boondock Saints *'99*
32 Short Films about Glenn Gould *'93*

Andrea Roth
The Stepdaughter *'00*
Hidden Agenda *'99*
Crossworlds *'96*
Divided by Hate *'96*
The Club *'94*
The Good Fight *'92*
Seedpeople *'92*

Cecilia (Celia) Roth (1958-)
All About My Mother *'99*
A Place in the World *'92*
The Stranger *'87*
Labyrinth of Passion *'82*

Gene Roth (1903-76)
Attack of the Giant Leeches *'59*
Earth vs. the Spider *'58*
She Demons *'58*
Pirates of the High Seas *'50*

Joanna Roth (1965-)
Stalin *'92*
The Real Charlotte *'91*
Rosencrantz & Guildenstern Are Dead *'90*

Lillian Roth (1910-80)
Alice Sweet Alice *'76*
Ladies They Talk About *'33*
Animal Crackers *'30*
Madam Satan *'30*

Louis Roth
Ninja Connection *'90*
Clash of the Ninja *'86*

Tim Roth (1961-)
The Musketeer *'01*
Planet of the Apes *'01*
Lucky Numbers *'00*
Vatel *'00*
The Million Dollar Hotel *'99*
The Legend of 1900 *'98*
Deceiver *'97*
Everyone Says I Love You *'96*
Gridlock'd *'96*
Hoodlum *'96*
No Way Home *'96*
Four Rooms *'95*
Rob Roy *'95*
Captives *'94*
Little Odessa *'94*
Pulp Fiction *'94*
Bodies, Rest & Motion *'93*
Heart of Darkness *'93*
Jumpin' at the Boneyard *'92*
The Perfect Husband *'92*
Reservoir Dogs *'92*
The Cook, the Thief, His Wife & Her Lover *'90*
Rosencrantz & Guildenstern Are Dead *'90*
Vincent & Theo *'90*
To Kill a Priest *'89*
A World Apart *'88*
The Hit *'85*
Meantime *'81*

John Rothman (1949-)
Say It Isn't So *'01*
The Siege *'98*
Hostile Waters *'97*
Copycat *'95*
Gettysburg *'93*
The Boost *'88*

Cynthia Rothrock (1957-)
Night Vision *'97*
Sworn to Justice *'97*
Fast Getaway 2 *'94*
Guardian Angel *'94*
Undefeatable *'94*
Angel of Fury *'93*
Lady Dragon 2 *'93*
Rage and Honor 2: Hostile Takeover *'93*
Honor and Glory *'92*
Lady Dragon *'92*
Rage and Honor *'92*
24 Hours to Midnight *'92*
Fast Getaway *'91*
Martial Law 2: Undercover *'91*
Tiger Claws *'91*
Martial Law *'90*
China O'Brien 2 *'89*
No Retreat, No Surrender 2 *'89*
China O'Brien *'88*
The Millionaire's Express *'86*

Yella Rottlaender
Alice in the Cities *'74*
The Scarlet Letter *'73*

Brigitte Rouan (1965-)
After Sex *'97*
Olivier, Olivier *'92*
Overseas: Three Women with Man Trouble *'90*

Richard Roundtree (1942-)
Corky Romano *'01*
Antitrust *'00*
Shaft *'00*
Having Our Say: The Delany Sisters' First 100 Years *'99*
Any Place But Home *'97*
George of the Jungle *'97*
Steel *'97*
Original Gangstas *'96*
Once Upon a Time ... When We Were Colored *'95*
Seven *'95*
Theodore Rex *'95*
Ballistic *'94*
Gypsy Angels *'94*
Amityville: A New Generation *'93*
Body of Influence *'93*
Bonanza: The Return *'93*
Mind Twister *'93*
Bloodfist 3: Forced to Fight *'92*
Christmas in Connecticut *'92*
Deadly Rivals *'92*
Getting Even *'92*
A Time to Die *'91*
Bad Jim *'89*
The Banker *'89*
Crack House *'89*
Miami Cops *'89*
Night Visitor *'89*
Angel 3: The Final Chapter *'88*
Maniac Cop *'88*
Party Line *'88*
Jocks *'87*
Opposing Force *'87*
Game for Vultures *'86*
The Last Contract *'86*
A.D. *'85*
The Baron and the Kid *'84*
City Heat *'84*
Killpoint *'84*
Big Score *'83*
Young Warriors *'83*
One Down, Two to Go! *'82*
Q (The Winged Serpent) *'82*
Day of the Assassin *'81*
An Eye for an Eye *'81*
Escape to Athena *'79*
Portrait of a Hitman *'77*
Man Friday *'75*
Earthquake *'74*
Shaft in Africa *'73*
Diamonds *'72*
Embassy *'72*
Firehouse *'72*
Shaft's Big Score *'72*
Shaft *'71*

Robert Rounseville
Carousel *'56*
The Tales of Hoffmann *'51*

Mickey Rourke (1955-)
Animal Factory *'00*
Get Carter *'00*
The Pledge *'00*
Out in Fifty *'99*
Point Blank *'98*
Thursday *'98*
Buffalo 66 *'97*
Double Team *'97*
Exit in Red *'97*
John Grisham's The Rainmaker *'97*
Another 9 1/2 Weeks *'96*
Bullet *'94*
Fall Time *'94*
The Last Ride *'94*
Francesco *'93*
The Last Outlaw *'93*
White Sands *'92*
Harley Davidson and the Marlboro Man *'91*
Desperate Hours *'90*
Wild Orchid *'90*
Johnny Handsome *'89*
Homeboy *'88*
Angel Heart *'87*
Barfly *'87*
Prayer for the Dying *'87*
9 1/2 Weeks *'86*
Year of the Dragon *'85*
The Pope of Greenwich Village *'84*
Rumble Fish *'83*

Diner '82
Body Heat '81
Eureka! '81
Heaven's Gate '81
City in Fear '80
Fade to Black '80
Rape and Marriage: The Rideout Case '80
1941 '79

Graham Rouse (1934-)
The Odd Angry Shot '79
Weekend of Shadows '77
Ride a Wild Pony '75

Myriem Roussel (1962-)
Sacrilege '86
Hail Mary '85
First Name: Carmen '83

Nathalie Roussel
My Father's Glory '91
My Mother's Castle '91

Jean-Paul Roussillon
Same Old Song '97
Baxter '89

Alison Routledge
The Bridge to Nowhere '86
The Quiet Earth '85

Catherine Rouvel (1939-)
Va Savoir '01
Sand and Blood '87
Black and White in Color '76
Les Assassins de L'Ordre '71
Borsalino '70
La Rupture '70
Picnic on the Grass '59

Dominic Rowan
David '97
Emma '97

Kelly Rowan (1967-)
Proximity '00
The Truth About Jane '00
Three to Tango '99
187 '97
Black Fox: Good Men and Bad '94
Candyman 2: Farewell to the Flesh '94
Adrift '93
The Gate '87

Brad Rowe
The '70s '00
Body Shots '99
Billy's Hollywood Screen Kiss '98
Stonebrook '98

Douglas Rowe
Writer's Block '91
Appointment with Fear '85

Kimberly Rowe
Knocking on Death's Door '99
Rumble in the Streets '96

Misty Rowe (1950-)
Goodnight, Sweet Marilyn '89
Meatballs 2 '84
Double Exposure '82
The Man with Bogart's Face '80
A Pleasure Doing Business '79
Goodbye, Norma Jean '75
Hitchhikers '72

Nevan Rowe
Nutcase '83
Sleeping Dogs '77

Nicholas (Nick) Rowe (1966-)
Shackleton '02
Longitude '00
Sharpe's Enemy '94
The Lawrenceville Stories '88
Young Sherlock Holmes '85

Victoria Rowell (1962-)
Barb Wire '96
Dumb & Dumber '94
The Distinguished Gentleman '92

Henry Rowland
Beneath the Valley of the Ultra-Vixens '79
Supervixens '75
36 Hours '64

Oscar Rowland
Bats '99
Promised Land '88

Paige Rowland
Doomsdayer '99
Riot '96

Rodney Rowland
Dancing at the Blue Iguana '00
The 6th Day '00
Marshal Law '96

Steve Rowland
Naked Youth '59
Gun Glory '57

David Rowlands
Minnie and Moskowitz '71
Husbands '70

Gena Rowlands (1934-)
The Weekend '00
Grace & Glorie '98
Hope Floats '98
The Mighty '98
Paulie '98
Playing by Heart '98
She's So Lovely '97
Unhook the Stars '96
The Neon Bible '95
Something to Talk About '95
Parallel Lives '94
Ted & Venus '93
Crazy in Love '92
Night on Earth '91
Once Around '91
Montana '90
Another Woman '88
Light of Day '87
An Early Frost '85
Love Streams '84
Rapunzel '82
The Tempest '82
Gloria '80
Strangers: The Story of a Mother and Daughter '79
Brink's Job '78
A Question of Love '78
Opening Night '77
Two Minute Warning '76
A Woman under the Influence '74
Minnie and Moskowitz '71
Faces '68
Tony Rome '67
A Child Is Waiting '63
Lonely Are the Brave '62

Polly Rowles (1914-2001)
Power '86
Springtime in the Rockies '37

Richard Roxburgh (1962-)
The Road from Coorain '02
Moulin Rouge '01
Mission: Impossible 2 '00
The Last September '99
Passion '99
In the Winter Dark '98
Doing Time for Patsy Cline '97
Oscar and Lucinda '97
The Wedding Party '97
Billy's Holiday '95
Children of the Revolution '95
Talk '94

Deep Roy
Alien from L.A. '87
Starship '87

Maxim Roy
Federal Protection '02
Hidden Agenda '01
Stalker '98

Allan Royal
The Pirates of Silicon Valley '99
Men of Steel '88

Lionel Royce (1886-1946)
White Pongo '45
My Favorite Blonde '42
Panama Menace '41
The Road to Zanzibar '41

Roselyn Royce
Retrievers '82
Sizzle Beach U.S.A. '74

Virginia Roye
Pace That Kills '28
The Road to Ruin '28

Selena Royle (1904-83)
Robot Monster '53
The Big Hangover '50
The Heiress '49
My Dream Is Yours '49
A Date with Judy '48
Moonrise '48
Summer Holiday '48
Cass Timberlane '47
Courage of Lassie '46
The Harvey Girls '46
Mrs. Parkington '44
Thirty Seconds Over Tokyo '44
The Fighting Sullivans '42

William Royle (1887-1940)
Mr. Wong in Chinatown '39
Mutiny in the Big House '39
The Rains Came '39

Gregory Rozakis
Five Corners '88
Abduction '75

Christian Rub
Pinocchio '40 (V)
100 Men and a Girl '37

Alma Rubens (1897-1931)
She Goes to War '29
The Americano '17

Jan Rubes (1920-)
Believe '99
Rescuers: Stories of Courage—Two Couples '98
The White Raven '98
Flood: A River's Rampage '97
Music from Another Room '97
Serving in Silence: The Margarethe Cammermeyer Story '95
The Birds 2: Land's End '94
D2: The Mighty Ducks '94
Mesmer '94
By Way of the Stars '92
Class Action '91
Deceived '91
The Amityville Curse '90
Descending Angel '90
Blind Fear '89
Courage Mountain '89
The Kiss '88
Blood Relations '87
Dead of Winter '87
Charlie Grant's War '80

Andrew Rubin
From the Earth to the Moon '98
Sunnyside '79

Benny Rubin (1899-1986)
The Tender Trap '55
Torch Song '53
The Noose Hangs High '48
The Bashful Bachelor '42
Mr. Wise Guy '42
Zis Boom Bah '42
Sunny '41
Sunny Skies '30

Jennifer Rubin (1964-)
Deal of a Lifetime '99
Last Lives '98
Twists of Terror '98
Kisses in the Dark '97
Loved '97
Plump Fiction '97
Little Witches '96
Screamers '96
The Wasp Woman '96
Saints and Sinners '95
Deceptions 2: Edge of Deception '94
Playmaker '94
Red Scorpion 2 '94
Stranger by Night '94
Bitter Harvest '93
The Crush '93
The Fear Inside '92
A Woman, Her Men and Her Futon '92
Delusion '91
Victim of Beauty '91
Bad Dreams '88
Blueberry Hill '88
Permanent Record '88
A Nightmare on Elm Street 3: Dream Warriors '87

Daphne Rubin-Vega
Flawless '99
Wild Things '98

Saul Rubinek (1949-)
The Doorbell Rang: A Nero Wolfe Mystery '01
Rush Hour 2 '01
The Contender '00
The Golden Spiders: A Nero Wolfe Mystery '00
Dick '99
36 Hours to Die '99
Bad Manners '98
Past Perfect '98
Blackjack '97
Color of Justice '97
Pale Saints '97
The Android Affair '95
Hiroshima '95
Nixon '95
Open Season '95
Synapse '95
Getting Even with Dad '94
I Love Trouble '94
And the Band Played On '93
The Quarrel '93
True Romance '93
Undercover Blues '93
Man Trouble '92
Unforgiven '92
The Bonfire of the Vanities '90
Obsessed '88
Outside Chance of Maximillian Glick '88
Wall Street '87
Half a Lifetime '86
Against All Odds '84
Soup for One '82
Young Doctors in Love '82
The Agency '81
Ticket to Heaven '81
Death Ship '80
Highpoint '80

Giulia Rubini (1935-)
Stranger in Paso Bravo '73
Adios, Hombre '68
Journey Beneath the Desert '61

Sergio Rubini (1959-)
The Count of Monte Cristo '99
The Talented Mr. Ripley '99
A Pure Formality '94
The Blonde '92
Intervista '87

John Rubinstein (1946-)
Mercy '96
Norma Jean and Marilyn '95
Another Stakeout '93
Shadow on the Sun '88
Someone to Watch Over Me '87
Happily Ever After '82
Killjoy '81
She's Dressed to Kill '79
The Car '77
Defiant '70
Getting Straight '70
Zachariah '70
The Trouble with Girls (and How to Get into It) '69

Zelda Rubinstein (1936-)
Little Witches '96
Acting on Impulse '93
Teen Witch '89
Anguish '88
Poltergeist 3 '88
Poltergeist 2: The Other Side '86
Sixteen Candles '84
Poltergeist '82
Under the Rainbow '81

Richard Ruccolo
All Over the Guy '01
Luck of the Draw '00

Alan Ruck (1960-)
Everything Put Together '00
From the Earth to the Moon '98
Twister '96
Speed '94
Star Trek: Generations '94
Young Guns 2 '90
Three Fugitives '89
Three for the Road '87
Ferris Bueller's Day Off '86
Hard Knox '83

Paul Rudd (1969-)
The Great Gatsby '01
Wet Hot American Summer '01
The Cider House Rules '99
The Object of My Affection '98
200 Cigarettes '98
The Locusts '97
Overnight Delivery '96
William Shakespeare's Romeo and Juliet '96
Clueless '95
Beulah Land '80
Last Song '80
Johnny We Hardly Knew Ye '77

Michael Rudder
Buying Time '89
Blindside '88

John Ruddock (1897-)
Lawrence of Arabia '62
Martin Luther '53
The Fallen Idol '49

Herbert Rudley (1911-)
Beloved Infidel '59
The Jayhawkers '59
The Young Lions '58
Artists and Models '55
The Scar '48
A Walk in the Sun '46
Rhapsody in Blue '45
The Seventh Cross '44
Abe Lincoln in Illinois '40

Rita Rudner (1955-)
A Weekend in the Country '96
Peter's Friends '92

Lars Rudolph
The Princess and the Warrior '00
The Inheritors '98

Joshua Rudoy
Flatliners '90
Harry and the Hendersons '87

Reed Rudy
Zapped Again '89
Free Ride '86

Mercedes Ruehl (1948-)
The Lost Child '00
What's Cooking? '00
The Minus Man '99
Out of the Cold '99
Gia '98
North Shore Fish '97
Subway Stories '97
For Roseanna '96
Indictment: The McMartin Trial '95
Last Action Hero '93
Lost in Yonkers '93
Another You '91
The Fisher King '91
Crazy People '90
Slaves of New York '89
Big '88
Married to the Mob '88
Leader of the Band '87
Radio Days '87
84 Charing Cross Road '86
Heartburn '86
The Warriors '79

Heinz Ruehmann (1902-94)
Ship of Fools '65
The Captain from Koepenick '56

Mark Ruffalo (1967-)
Windtalkers '02
The Last Castle '01
Committed '99
Houdini '99
Ride with the Devil '99
You Can Count On Me '99
Safe Men '98
The Destiny of Marty Fine '96
Mirror, Mirror 3: The Voyeur '96

Gene Ruffini
Ghost Dog: The Way of the Samurai '99
Little Odessa '94

Leonora Ruffo
Hercules in the Haunted World '64
Goliath and the Dragon '61

Rufus (1942-)
Amelie '01
Train of Life '98
Metroland '97
Les Miserables '95
Erendira '83
Jonah Who Will Be 25 in the Year 2000 '76

Charlie Ruggles (1886-1970)
Follow Me, Boys! '66
The Ugly Dachshund '65
Papa's Delicate Condition '63
Son of Flubber '63
All in a Night's Work '61
The Parent Trap '61
Look for the Silver Lining '49
The Lovable Cheat '49
Ramrod '47
The Perfect Marriage '46
A Stolen Life '46
The Invisible Woman '40
Balalaika '39
Breaking the Ice '38
Bringing Up Baby '38
Ruggles of Red Gap '35
Goodbye Love '34
Six of a Kind '34
Murders in the Zoo '33
Melody Cruise '32

Vyto Ruginis
The Fast and the Furious '01
The Glass House '01
The Devil's Advocate '97
A Thousand Acres '97
Clean Slate '94
The Last Gasp '94
Descending Angel '90

Barbara Ruick (1930-74)
Carousel '56
Above and Beyond '53
The Affairs of Dobie Gillis '53

Anthony Michael Ruivivar (1970-)
Starship Troopers '97
Race the Sun '96
White Fang 2: The Myth of the White Wolf '94

Janice Rule (1931-)
American Flyers '85
L.A. Bad '85
Missing '82
The Word '78
Gumshoe '72
Doctors' Wives '70
The Swimmer '68
The Ambushers '67
Alvarez Kelly '66
The Chase '66
Invitation to a Gunfighter '64
Battle Shock '56

Sig Rumann (1884-1967)
36 Hours '64

The Errand Boy '61
Wings of Eagles '57
Houdini '53
Ma and Pa Kettle on Vacation '53
Stalag 17 '53
The World in His Arms '52
Emperor Waltz '48
The Dolly Sisters '46
A Night in Casablanca '46
House of Frankenstein '44
It Happened Tomorrow '44
Sweet Rosie O'Grady '43
To Be or Not to Be '42
Love Crazy '41
That Uncertain Feeling '41
The Wagons Roll at Night '41
Bitter Sweet '40
Comrade X '40
Never Say Die '39
Ninotchka '39
Only Angels Have Wings '39
The Great Waltz '38
A Day at the Races '37
Nothing Sacred '37
On the Avenue '37
Thin Ice '37
The Bold Caballero '36
The Princess Comes Across '36
A Night at the Opera '35
Marie Galante '34

Run DMC
The Show '95
Tougher Than Leather '88

Jenny Runacre (1943-)
Hussy '80
The Passenger '75
The Final Programme '73
The Creeping Flesh '72
The Canterbury Tales '71
Husbands '70

Joseph Runningfox
Lakota Woman: Siege at Wounded Knee '94
Geronimo '93
The Avenging '92

Tygh Runyan
Cruel and Unusual '01
Antitrust '00

Jennifer Runyon (1960-)
Carnosaur '93
A Man Called Sarge '90
18 Again! '88
The In Crowd '88
A Very Brady Christmas '88
Blue De Ville '86
The Falcon and the Snowman '85
Up the Creek '84
To All a Goodnight '80

Ying Ruocheng
Little Buddha '93
The Last Emperor '87

Al Ruscio (1924-)
Boss of Bosses '99
The Garbage-Picking, Field Goal-Kicking Philadelphia Phenomenon '98
The Cage '89
Romero '89
Deadly Force '83
The Naked Flame '68
Al Capone '59

Elizabeth Ruscio
Letters from a Killer '98
Death Benefit '96
Glory Daze '96
The Positively True Adventures of the Alleged Texas Cheerleader-Murdering Mom '93
Hider in the House '90

Barbara Rush (1927-)
Widow's Kiss '94
Web of Deceit '90
The Seekers '79
Superdad '73
Moon of the Wolf '72
Hombre '67
Robin and the 7 Hoods '64
Come Blow Your Horn '63
The Bramble Bush '60
Strangers When We Meet '60
The Young Philadelphians '59
Harry Black and the Tiger '58
The Young Lions '58
The Black Shield of Falworth '54
Magnificent Obsession '54
It Came from Outer Space '53
First Legion '51
When Worlds Collide '51

Deborah Rush
Three to Tango '99
In and Out '97
Reckless '95
Unnatural Pursuits '91
Family Business '89
Parents '89
The Purple Rose of Cairo '85

Geoffrey Rush (1951-)
Lantana '01
Quills '00
The Tailor of Panama '00
House on Haunted Hill '99
Mystery Men '99
Elizabeth '98
Shakespeare in Love '98
Les Miserables '97
A Little Bit of Soul '97
Oscar and Lucinda '97 (N)
Twisted '96
Children of the Revolution '95
Shine '95

Claire Rushbrook
Plunkett & Macleane '98
Spice World: The Movie '97
Under the Skin '97
Secrets and Lies '95

Jared Rushton (1974-)
Pet Sematary 2 '92
A Cry in the Wild '90
Honey, I Shrunk the Kids '89
Big '88
The Lady in White '88

Joseph Ruskin (1925-)
King Cobra '98
The Criminal Mind '93
Cyber-Tracker '93
Firepower '93
Saturday the 14th Strikes Back '88
Prizzi's Honor '85
Captain America '79
The Gypsy Warriors '78

Robert Rusler (1965-)
The Assassination Game '92
Final Embrace '92
Sometimes They Come Back '91
The Game of Love '90
Shag: The Movie '89
Thrashin' '86
Vamp '86
A Nightmare on Elm Street 2: Freddy's Revenge '85

Tim Russ
Bitter Vengeance '94
Night Eyes 2 '91

William Russ (1950-)
American History X '98
When Danger Follows You Home '97
Aspen Extreme '93
Traces of Red '92
Crazy from the Heart '91
Pastime '91
Disorganized Crime '89
The Unholy '88
Dead of Winter '87
The Long, Hot Summer '86
Wanted Dead or Alive '86
Beer '85
The Right Stuff '83

Andy Russell
Copacabana '47
The Stork Club '45

Betsy Russell (1964-)
The Break '95
Amore! '93
Delta Heat '92
The Prize Pulitzer '89
Trapper County War '89
Cheerleader Camp '88
Avenging Angel '85
Out of Control '85
Tomboy '85
Private School '83

Bing Russell (1928-)
Elvis: The Movie '79
Satan's School for Girls '73
Billy the Kid Versus Dracula '66
Stakeout '62
The Horse Soldiers '59
Good Day for a Hanging '58

Bryan Russell
The Adventures of Bullwhip Griffin '66
Emil and the Detectives '64

Clive Russell
Mists of Avalon '01
The Railway Children '00
Bodywork '99
Great Expectations '99
The 13th Warrior '99
Oscar and Lucinda '97
Cracker: Brotherly Love '95
Margaret's Museum '95

Elizabeth Russell (1916-)
Bedlam '45
Curse of the Cat People '44
Cat People '42
The Corpse Vanishes '42
Meet the Mob '42

Gail Russell (1925-61)
Great Dan Patch '49
Wake of the Red Witch '49
Moonrise '48
Angel and the Badman '47
The Uninvited '44

Harold Russell (1914-2002)
Dogtown '97
The Best Years of Our Lives '46

Jane Russell (1921-)
Darker than Amber '70
Born Losers '67
Johnny Reno '66
The Tall Men '55
Underwater! '55
The French Line '54
Gentlemen Prefer Blondes '53
The Road to Bali '53
The Las Vegas Story '52
Macao '52
Montana Belle '52
Son of Paleface '52
Double Dynamite '51
His Kind of Woman '51
The Paleface '48
The Outlaw '43

John Russell (1921-91)
Under the Gun '88
Pale Rider '85
Runaways '84
The Changeling '80
The Outlaw Josey Wales '76
Smoke in the Wind '75
Blood Legacy '73
Noon Sunday '71
Buckskin '68
Hostile Guns '67
Apache Uprising '66
Rio Bravo '59
Jubilee Trail '54
The Sun Shines Bright '53
Hoodlum Empire '52
Man in the Saddle '51
Oklahoma Annie '51
Forever Amber '47
The Blue Bird '40

Karen Russell
Dead Certain '92
Lethal Games '90
Shock 'Em Dead '90
Wilding '90
Easy Wheels '89
Vice Academy '88

Ken Russell (1927-)
Tales of Erotica '93
The Russia House '90

Keri Russell (1976-)
We Were Soldiers '02
Mad About Mambo '00
The Curve '97
Eight Days a Week '97
Honey, I Blew Up the Kid '92

Kimberly Russell
Prison of Secrets '97
The O.J. Simpson Story '94
Hangin' with the Homeboys '91

Kurt Russell (1951-)
3000 Miles to Graceland '01
Vanilla Sky '01
Soldier '98
Breakdown '96
Escape from L.A. '96
Executive Decision '96
Stargate '94
Tombstone '93
Captain Ron '92
Unlawful Entry '92
Backdraft '91
Tango and Cash '89
Winter People '89
Tequila Sunrise '88
Overboard '87
The Best of Times '86
Big Trouble in Little China '86
Mean Season '85
Swing Shift '84
Silkwood '83
Amber Waves '82
The Thing '82
Escape from New York '81
The Fox and the Hound '81 (V)
Used Cars '80
Elvis: The Movie '79
The Christmas Coal Mine Miracle '77
The Captive: The Longest Drive 2 '76
The Longest Drive '76
Search for the Gods '75
Sniper '75
Charley and the Angel '73
Superdad '73
Now You See Him, Now You Don't '72
The Barefoot Executive '71
The Computer Wore Tennis Shoes '69
The Horse in the Gray Flannel Suit '68
The One and Only, Genuine, Original Family Band '68
Follow Me, Boys! '66
Mosby's Marauders '66
Guns of Diablo '64
It Happened at the World's Fair '63

Monte Russell
Lily in Winter '94
Laurel Avenue '93

Nipsey Russell (1924-)
Car 54, Where Are You? '94
Posse '93
The Wiz '78

Reb Russell (1905-78)
Outlaw Rule '36
Border Vengeance '35
The Man from Hell '34

Robert Russell
Dune '00
Bedazzled '68
The Conqueror Worm '68

Rosalind Russell (1908-76)
Where Angels Go, Trouble Follows '68
Oh Dad, Poor Dad (Momma's Hung You in the Closet & I'm Feeling So Sad) '67
The Trouble with Angels '66
Gypsy '62
Auntie Mame '58
A Majority of One '56
Picnic '55
Never Wave at a WAC '52
A Woman of Distinction '50
Tell It to the Judge '49
Velvet Touch '48
Sister Kenny '46
They Met in Bombay '41
His Girl Friday '40
The Women '39
The Citadel '38
Night Must Fall '37
Craig's Wife '36
China Seas '35
Forsaking All Others '35
Reckless '35
Evelyn Prentice '34

Theresa Russell (1957-)
Earth vs. the Spider '01
Luckytown '00
Running Woman '98
Wild Things '98
Grave Indiscretions '96
The Proposition '96
Public Enemies '96
Trade Off '95
A Young Connecticut Yankee in King Arthur's Court '95
Being Human '94
The Spy Within '94
Thicker Than Water '93
A Woman's Guide to Adultery '93
Cold Heaven '92
Kafka '91
Whore '91
Impulse '90
Physical Evidence '89
Aria '88
Track 29 '88
Black Widow '87
Insignificance '85
The Razor's Edge '84
Eureka! '81
Straight Time '78
The Last Tycoon '76

Tony Russell
The Hard Ride '71
Wild, Wild Planet '65

Chelsea Russo
An Unexpected Life '97
An Unexpected Family '96

Gianni Russo
Kill Shot '01
Lepke '75
The Godfather, Part 2 '74

James Russo (1953-)
Deep Core '00
Jimmy Zip '00
Detour '99
The Ninth Gate '99
Paper Bullets '99
Sonic Impact '99
Voodoo Dawn '99
Bitter Sweet '98
First Degree '98
My Husband's Secret Life '98
Laws of Deception '97
Love to Kill '97
The Postman '97
The Real Thing '97
Under Oath '97
American Strays '96
Donnie Brasco '96
No Way Home '96
Condition Red '95
Panther '95
The Set Up '95
Bad Girls '94
The Secretary '94
Dangerous Game '93
Dario Argento's Trauma '93
Cold Heaven '92
DaVinci's War '92
Illicit Behavior '91
Intimate Stranger '91
A Kiss Before Dying '91
My Own Private Idaho '91
We're No Angels '89
Blue Iguana '88
Freeway '88
China Girl '87
Extremities '86
Beverly Hills Cop '84
Fast Times at Ridgemont High '82
Vortex '81

John A. Russo
The Majorettes '87
Night of the Living Dead '68

Michael Russo
Pure Danger '96
Demonic Toys '90
Nitti: The Enforcer '88

Rene Russo (1954-)
Big Trouble '02
Showtime '02
The Adventures of Rocky & Bullwinkle '00
The Thomas Crown Affair '99
Lethal Weapon 4 '98
Buddy '97
Ransom '96
Tin Cup '96
Get Shorty '95
Outbreak '94
In the Line of Fire '93
Freejack '92
Lethal Weapon 3 '92
One Good Cop '91
Mr. Destiny '90
Major League '89

Leon Russom (1941-)
The Big Lebowski '97
A Private Matter '92
Long Road Home '91
Silver Bullet '85

Richard Rust (1938-)
Double Revenge '89
The Great Gundown '75
The Student Nurses '70
The Naked Angels '69
Comanche Station '60
Legend of Tom Dooley '59

Babe Ruth
The Pride of the Yankees '42
Headin' Home '24

Mary Ruth
Gentleman from Dixie '41
Riot Squad '41

Ann Rutherford (1917-)
They Only Kill Their Masters '72
Operation Haylift '50
Adventures of Don Juan '49
The Secret Life of Walter Mitty '47
Whistling in Brooklyn '43
Andy Hardy's Double Life '42
Orchestra Wives '42
Whistling in Dixie '42
Andy Hardy's Private Secretary '41
Life Begins for Andy Hardy '41
Whistling in the Dark '41
Andy Hardy Meets Debutante '40
Pride and Prejudice '40
Andy Hardy Gets Spring Fever '39
Gone with the Wind '39
A Christmas Carol '38
Love Finds Andy Hardy '38
Of Human Hearts '38
Doughnuts & Society '36
Fighting Marines '36
The Lawless Nineties '36
Melody Trail '35
Ghost City '32

Kelly Rutherford (1968-)
Angels Don't Sleep Here '00
Chaos Factor '00

Margaret Rutherford (1892-1972)
Chimes at Midnight '67
A Countess from Hong Kong '67
The Alphabet Murders '65
Murder Most Foul '65
Murder Ahoy '64

Murder at the Gallop '63
The V.I.P.'s '63
The Mouse on the Moon '62
Murder She Said '62
The Smallest Show on Earth '57
The Runaway Bus '54
Curtain Up '53
Innocents in Paris '53
Trouble in Store '53
The Importance of Being Earnest '52
The Happiest Days of Your Life '50
Passport to Pimlico '49
Blithe Spirit '45
The Demi-Paradise '43

Susan Ruttan (1950-)
Love Kills '98
Funny About Love '90
A Perfect Little Murder '90
Sweet 15 '90
Chances Are '89
Fire and Rain '89
Bad Dreams '88
Eye of the Demon '87
L.A. Law '86
Bad Manners '84

Barbara Rutting (1927-)
The Squeaker '65
The Phantom of Soho '64
River of Evil '64
Town without Pity '61
A Time to Love & a Time to Die '58
The Last Bridge '54

Sif Ruud
Like It Never Was Before '95
Face to Face '76

Wolf Ruvinskis (1921-99)
Neutron vs. the Death Robots '62
Neutron vs. the Maniac '62
Neutron and the Black Mask '61
Neutron vs. the Amazing Dr. Caronte '61

Basil Ruysdael (1888-1960)
Davy Crockett, King of the Wild Frontier '55
Carrie '52
People Will Talk '51
Broken Arrow '50
High Lonesome '50
The Cocoanuts '29

David Ryall
One Against the Wind '91
Truly, Madly, Deeply '91

Amanda Ryan
Britannic '99
David Copperfield '99
Metroland '97
Poldark '96

Anne Ryan
Three o'Clock High '87
All the Lovin' Kinfolk '70

Eddie Ryan
Breakfast in Hollywood '46
The Fighting Sullivans '42

Edmon Ryan
Tora! Tora! Tora! '70
Two for the Seesaw '62

Eileen Ryan
Anywhere But Here '99
The Crossing Guard '94
Benny & Joon '93
Winter People '89
At Close Range '86

Fran Ryan (1926-2000)
Suture '93
Archie: Return to Riverdale '90
Chances Are '89
Gunsmoke: Return to Dodge '87
Quiet Cool '86
Pale Rider '85
Eyes of Fire '84
Private School '83
Johnny Belinda '82

Ger Ryan
Forgive and Forget '99
Moll Flanders '96
The Van '95

James Ryan
Redemption: Kickboxer 5 '95
The Last Samurai '90
Pursuit '90
Rage to Kill '88
Space Mutiny '88
Go for the Gold '84
Kill and Kill Again '81
Kill or Be Killed '80

Jeri Ryan (1968-)
Dracula 2000 '00
Men Cry Bullets '00

John P. Ryan (1938-)
Bound '96
American Cyborg: Steel Warrior '94
C.I.A. 2: Target Alexa '94
Hoffa '92
Star Time '92
White Sands '92
Delta Force 3: The Killing Game '91
Class of 1999 '90
Delta Force 2: Operation Stranglehold '90
Eternity '90
Best of the Best '89
Paramedics '88
Rent-A-Cop '88
Death Wish 4: The Crackdown '87
Three o'Clock High '87
Avenging Force '86
City of Shadows '86
Runaway Train '85
Breathless '83
The Right Stuff '83
The Postman Always Rings Twice '81
It's Alive 2: It Lives Again '78
Death Scream '75
It's Alive '74
Cops and Robbers '73
Shamus '73

Kathleen Ryan (1922-85)
Try and Get Me '50
Captain Boycott '47
Odd Man Out '47

Lisa Dean Ryan
The Stepdaughter '00
Twisted Love '95
Hostile Intentions '94

Marisa Ryan
Riding in Cars with Boys '01
Wet Hot American Summer '01
Cold Hearts '99
Slaves to the Underground '96

Meg Ryan (1961-)
Kate & Leopold '01
Proof of Life '00
Hanging Up '99
City of Angels '98
Hurlyburly '98
You've Got Mail '98
Anastasia '97 (V)
Addicted to Love '96
Courage Under Fire '96
French Kiss '95
I.Q. '94
Restoration '94
When a Man Loves a Woman '94
Flesh and Bone '93
Sleepless in Seattle '93
Prelude to a Kiss '92
The Doors '91
Joe Versus the Volcano '90
When Harry Met Sally... '89
D.O.A. '88
The Presidio '88
Promised Land '88
Innerspace '87
Armed and Dangerous '86
Top Gun '86
Amityville 3: The Demon '83
Rich and Famous '81

Mitchell Ryan (1928-)
Aftershock: Earthquake in New York '99
Grosse Pointe Blank '97
The Devil's Own '96
Liar Liar '96
Halloween 6: The Curse of Michael Myers '95
Speechless '94
Danielle Steel's Star '93
Hot Shots! Part Deux '93
The Opposite Sex and How to Live With Them '93
Aces: Iron Eagle 3 '92
Dirty Work '92
Blue Sky '91
Judgment '90
Double Exposure: The Story of Margaret Bourke-White '89
Winter People '89
Lethal Weapon '87
The Choice '81
Death of a Centerfold '81
The Five of Me '81
Of Mice and Men '81
Angel City '80
Sergeant Matlovich vs. the U.S. Air Force '78
The Christmas Coal Mine Miracle '77
Peter Lundy and the Medicine Hat Stallion '77
Electra Glide in Blue '73
High Plains Drifter '73
Magnum Force '73
My Old Man's Place '71
Monte Walsh '70
Thunder Road '58

Peggy Ryan
Here Come the Co-Eds '45
Miss Annie Rooney '42

Remi Ryan
Ava's Magical Adventure '94
RoboCop 3 '91

R.L. Ryan
Street Trash '87
Class of Nuke 'Em High '86
Eat and Run '86

Robert Ryan (1909-73)
Executive Action '73
The Man Without a Country '73
And Hope to Die '72
Lawman '71
The Love Machine '71
The Wild Bunch '69
Anzio '68
The Dirty Dozen '67
Hour of the Gun '67
A Minute to Pray, a Second to Die '67
The Professionals '66
Battle of the Bulge '65
Billy Budd '62
The Longest Day '62
The King of Kings '61
Ice Palace '60
Odds Against Tomorrow '59
God's Little Acre '58
Lonelyhearts '58
Men in War '57
Back from Eternity '56
Escape to Burma '55
The Tall Men '55
Bad Day at Black Rock '54
The Naked Spur '53
Beware, My Lovely '52
Clash by Night '52
Horizons West '52
Flying Leathernecks '51
On Dangerous Ground '51
The Racket '51
Best of the Badmen '50
Born to Be Bad '50
Caught '49
The Set-Up '49
Berlin Express '48
The Boy with the Green Hair '48
Return of the Bad Men '48
Crossfire '47
Trail Street '47
Behind the Rising Sun '43
Bombardier '43
The Iron Major '43
Marine Raiders '43
The Sky's the Limit '43
Tender Comrade '43

Sheila Ryan (1921-75)
On Top of Old Smoky '53
Fingerprints Don't Lie '51
Gold Raiders '51
Mask of the Dragon '51
Western Pacific Agent '51
Ringside '49
The Cobra Strikes '48
Heartaches '47
Railroaded '47
Great Guns '41

Thomas Ryan
The Relic '96
Body Count '87

Thomas Jay Ryan
The Legend of Bagger Vance '00
Henry Fool '98

Tim Ryan (1899-1956)
From Here to Eternity '53
Here Come the Marines '52
Detour '46
Harmon of Michigan '41

Tim Ryan (1958-)
The Lightning Incident '91
The Runestone '91
China Beach '88

Will Ryan
Thumbelina '94 (V)
The Land Before Time '88 (V)
An American Tail '86 (V)

Georg Rydeberg (1907-83)
Hour of the Wolf '68
Walpurgis Night '41
Dollar '38
A Woman's Face '38

Bobby Rydell (1942-)
Mr. Rock 'n' Roll: The Alan Freed Story '99
Marco Polo, Jr. '72 (V)
Bye, Bye, Birdie '63

Christopher Rydell
By the Sword '93
Dario Argento's Trauma '93
Flesh and Bone '93
For the Boys '91
In the Deep Woods '91
Side Out '90
Blood and Sand '89
How I Got into College '89
Gotcha! '85

Derek Rydell
Night Visitor '89
Phantom of the Mall: Eric's Revenge '89
Popcorn '89

Mark Rydell (1934-)
Hollywood Ending '02
James Dean '01
Havana '90
Punchline '88
The Long Goodbye '73

Alfred Ryder (1919-95)
Bogie: The Last Hero '80
Probe '72
True Grit '69
T-Men '47

Winona Ryder (1971-)
Mr. Deeds '02
Autumn in New York '00
Lost Souls '00
Girl, Interrupted '99
Celebrity '98
Alien: Resurrection '97
The Crucible '96
Looking for Richard '96
Boys '95
How to Make an American Quilt '95
Little Women '94
Reality Bites '94
The Age of Innocence '93
The House of the Spirits '93
Bram Stoker's Dracula '92
Night on Earth '91
Edward Scissorhands '90
Mermaids '90
Welcome Home, Roxy Carmichael '90
Great Balls of Fire '89
Heathers '89
1969 '89
Beetlejuice '88
Square Dance '87
Lucas '86

Patrick Ryecart (1952-)
Coming Home '98
Heart of Darkness '93
Twenty-One '91
Goldeneye: The Secret Life of Ian Fleming '89
The Bretts '88
True Colors '87
Jenny's War '85
Silas Marner '85

Mark Rylance (1960-)
Angels and Insects '95
Institue Benjamenta or This Dream People Call Human Life '95
Prospero's Books '91

Rex Ryon
The Man in the Iron Mask '97
Jack's Back '87

Chishu Ryu (1904-93)
Akira Kurosawa's Dreams '90
An Autumn Afternoon '62
The Human Condition: A Soldier's Prayer '61
Good Morning '59
Equinox Flower '58
Twenty-Four Eyes '54
Tokyo Story '53
Early Summer '51
Late Spring '49
Record of a Tenement Gentleman '47

Bruno S
Stroszek '77
Every Man for Himself & God Against All '75

Daryl Sabara (1992-)
Spy Kids 2: The Island of Lost Dreams '02
Spy Kids '01

Antonio Sabato, Jr. (1972-)
Mindstorm '01
Chaos Factor '00
Fatal Error '99
The Big Hit '98
High Voltage '98
Wolverine '96
Jailbreakers '94

Antonio (Tony) Sabato (1943-)
High Voltage '98
Black Lemons '80s
Thundersquad '85
Crimebusters '79
War of the Robots '78
This Time I'll Make You Rich '75
New Mafia Boss '72
Twice a Judas '69
Beyond the Law '68

Bo Sabato
L.A. Crackdown 2 '88
Neon Maniacs '86

Ernie Sabella
The Lion King: Simba's Pride '98 (V)
The Lion King '94 (V)

Marcel Sabourin
Lilies '96
The Hitman '91

Sabu (1924-63)
A Tiger Walks '64
Mistress of the World '59
Jungle Hell '55
The Treasure of Bengal '53
Pardon My Trunk '52
Savage Drums '51
Black Narcissus '47
Cobra Woman '44
Arabian Nights '42
The Jungle Book '42
The Thief of Bagdad '40
Drums '38
Elephant Boy '37

Robert Sacchi
Cold Heat '90
The Man with Bogart's Face '80

Orlando Sacha
To Die Standing '91
Crime Zone '88

Adrienne Sachs
In the Cold of the Night '89
Two to Tango '88

Robin Sachs
Galaxy Quest '99
Deadly Recruits '86

Salli Sachse
Devil's Angels '67
The Trip '67

Graham Sack
Dunston Checks In '95
A Pig's Tale '94

Michael Sacks (1948-)
Bunco '83
The Sugarland Express '74
Slaughterhouse Five '72

Jose Sacristan
A Place in the World '92
El Diputado '78

Keiji Sada (1926-64)
An Autumn Afternoon '62
The Human Condition: Road to Eternity '59
The Human Condition: No Greater Love '58

Nicholas Sadler
Idle Hands '99
Sawbones '95
Acting on Impulse '93

William Sadler (1950-)
The Green Mile '99
Disturbing Behavior '98
Reach the Rock '98
RocketMan '97
Poltergeist: The Legacy '96
Solo '96
Roadracers '94
The Shawshank Redemption '94
Tales from the Crypt Presents Demon Knight '94
Freaked '93
Trespass '92
Bill & Ted's Bogus Journey '91
Rush '91
Die Hard 2: Die Harder '90
The Hot Spot '90
Tagget '90
Hard to Kill '89
Tales from the Crypt '89
Project X '87

Isabelle Sadoyan
The Eighth Day '95
Trois Couleurs: Bleu '93

Marianne Saegebrecht (1945-)
Left Luggage '98
Dust Devil '93
Martha and I '91
Rosalie Goes Shopping '89
The War of the Roses '89
Bagdad Cafe '88
Moon over Parador '88
Sugarbaby '85

Libuse Safrankova
Kolya '96
The Elementary School '91

Elizabeth Sagal
Skinheads: The Second Coming of Hate '88
Howard the Duck '86
Flashdance '83

Katey Sagal
Smart House '00 (V)
Mr. Headmistress '98
It's a Bundyful Life '92
The Good Mother '88

Jonathan Sagalle (1962-)
Deadly Outbreak '96
Schindler's List '93
Drifting '82

William Sage
Double Parked '00
Urbania '00
American Psycho '99
High Art '98
Rift '96
Boys '95

Flirt '95
Two Plus One '95
Simple Men '92

Melissa Sagemiller
Sorority Boys '02
Get Over It! '01
Soul Survivors '01

Ray Sager
The Gore-Gore Girls '72
This Stuff'll Kill Ya! '71
The Wizard of Gore '70
Just for the Hell of It '68
Blast-Off Girls '67
The Girl, the Body and the Pill '67
Gruesome Twosome '67

Bob Saget (1956-)
Father and Scout '94
To Grandmother's House We Go '94

Ken Sagoes
Death by Dialogue '88
A Nightmare on Elm Street 4: Dream Master '88

Elena Sahagun
Firetrap '01
Teenage Exorcist '93
Uncaged '91

Kenji Sahara (1932-)
Yog, Monster from Space '71
War of the Gargantuas '70
Godzilla's Revenge '69
Destroy All Monsters '68
Son of Godzilla '66
Ghidrah the Three Headed Monster '65
Godzilla vs. Mothra '64
Attack of the Mushroom People '63
King Kong vs. Godzilla '63
Mothra '62
H-Man '59
The Mysterians '58
Rodan '56

He Saifei
Temptress Moon '96
Blush '95

Eva Marie Saint (1924-)
I Dreamed of Africa '00
Titanic '96
My Antonia '94
Kiss of a Killer '93
Danielle Steel's Palomino '91
Voyage of Terror: The Achille Lauro Affair '90
Breaking Home Ties '87
The Last Days of Patton '86
Nothing in Common '86
Fatal Vision '84
Love Leads the Way '84
Jane Doe '83
When Hell Was in Session '82
The Best Little Girl in the World '81
The Curse of King Tut's Tomb '80
A Christmas to Remember '78
Cancel My Reservation '72
The Stalking Moon '69
Grand Prix '66
The Russians Are Coming, the Russians Are Coming '66
The Sandpiper '65
36 Hours '64
All Fall Down '62
Exodus '60
North by Northwest '59
Raintree County '57
On the Waterfront '54

Michael St. Clair (1921-2001)
Our Man Flint '66
Von Ryan's Express '65

Lili St. Cyr (1918-99)
The Naked and the Dead '58
Son of Sinbad '55

Michael St. Gerard
Replikator: Cloned to Kill '94
Star Time '92
Great Balls of Fire '89
Hairspray '88
Senior Week '88

Raymond St. Jacques (1930-90)
Timebomb '91
Glory '89
Voodoo Dawn '89
They Live '88
The Wild Pair '87
The Evil That Men Do '84
Sophisticated Gents '81
Kill Castro '80
The Mercenaries '80
The Private Files of J. Edgar Hoover '77
Search for the Gods '75
Final Comedown '72
Cotton Comes to Harlem '70
Dead Right '68
The Green Berets '68
The Comedians '67

Susan St. James (1946-)
Don't Cry, It's Only Thunder '82
Sex and the Single Parent '82
Carbon Copy '81
How to Beat the High Cost of Living '80
Love at First Bite '79
S.O.S. Titanic '79
Desperate Women '78
Night Cries '78
Outlaw Blues '77
Where Angels Go, Trouble Follows '68

Al "Fuzzy" St. John (1892-1963)
The Black Lash '52
King of the Bullwhip '51
Thundering Trail '51
Outlaw Country '49
Stage to Mesa City '48
Border Feud '47
Cheyenne Takes Over '47
Fighting Vigilantes '47
Ghost Town Renegades '47
Law of the Lash '47
Return of the Lash '47
Outlaw of the Plains '46
Gangster's Den '45
His Brother's Ghost '45
Lightning Raiders '45
Shadows of Death '45
Death Rides the Plains '44
Devil Riders '44
Frontier Outlaws '44
Oath of Vengeance '44
Rustler's Hideout '44
Wild Horse Phantom '44
Dead Men Walk '43
Raiders of Red Gap '43
Billy the Kid Trapped '42
Law and Order '42
The Lone Rider in Cheyenne '42
The Mysterious Rider '42
Prairie Pals '42
Texas Justice '42
Border Roundup '41
The Lone Rider in Ghost Town '41
Rangeland Racket '41
Texas Trouble '41
Trigger Men '41
Billy the Kid in Texas '40
Trigger Pals '39
Gunsmoke Trail '38
Ranger's Roundup '38
Songs and Bullets '38
Melody of the Plains '37
The Roamin' Cowboy '37
A Face in the Fog '36
West of Nevada '36
His Private Secretary '33
Riders of Destiny '33
Oklahoma Cyclone '30
Dance of Life '29
She Goes to War '29
Mabel & Fatty '16

Betta St. John (1929-)
Horror Hotel '60
Corridors of Blood '58
Alias John Preston '56
The Student Prince '54
All the Brothers Were Valiant '53

Christopher St. John
Top of the Heap '72
Shaft '71

Howard St. John (1905-74)
Strange Bedfellows '65
Strait-Jacket '64
Lover Come Back '61
Li'l Abner '59
I Died a Thousand Times '55
Illegal '55
The Tender Trap '55
Born Yesterday '50

Jill St. John (1940-)
Out There '95
The Player '92
Around the World in 80 Days '89
The Act '82
The Concrete Jungle '82
Diamonds Are Forever '71
Eight on the Lam '67
Tony Rome '67
The Oscar '66
Come Blow Your Horn '63
Who's Minding the Store? '63
Roman Spring of Mrs. Stone '61

Michelle St. John
Smoke Signals '98
Pocahontas '95 (V)
Geronimo '93
Spirit Rider '93
Where the Spirit Lives '89

Trevor St. John
The King's Guard '01
Dogtown '97

Hubert Saint Macary
Lucie Aubrac '98
Genealogies of a Crime '97
Diary of a Seducer '95

Irma St. Paul
Where the Money Is '00
Fever '99

John St. Polis (1873-1946)
Rocky Mountain Rangers '40
Phantom Ranger '38
Death from a Distance '36
Terror Trail '33
Coquette '29
Party Girls '29
The Unknown '27
The Phantom of the Opera '25
The Untamable '23
The Four Horsemen of the Apocalypse '21

Lucile Saint-Simon
The Hands of Orlac '60
Les Bonnes Femmes '60

Marin Sais (1890-1971)
The Fighting Redhead '50
Lightning Raiders '45
Frontier Outlaws '44

Frankie Sakai (1929-96)
Master Mind '73
Last War '68
Mothra '62

Sachio Sakai (1929-)
Godzilla's Revenge '69
Godzilla, King of the Monsters '56
Samurai 2: Duel at Ichijoji Temple '55

S.Z. Sakall (1884-1955)
The Student Prince '54
Small Town Girl '53
Lullaby of Broadway '51
Tea for Two '50
In the Good Old Summertime '49
Look for the Silver Lining '49
My Dream Is Yours '49
Romance on the High Seas '48
The Dolly Sisters '46
Never Say Goodbye '46
Christmas in Connecticut '45
San Antonio '45
Wonder Man '45
Hollywood Canteen '44
Wintertime '43
Casablanca '42
Yankee Doodle Dandy '42
Ball of Fire '41
The Devil & Miss Jones '41
It's a Date '40

Sumiko Sakamota
The Ballad of Narayama '83
The Pornographers '66

Ryuichi Sakamoto (1952-)
New Rose Hotel '98
The Last Emperor '87
Merry Christmas, Mr. Lawrence '83

Amy Sakasitz
House Arrest '96
Mad Love '95
Dennis the Menace '93
A Home of Our Own '93

Harold Sakata (1920-82)
Black Eliminator '78
Goin' Coconuts '78
Kill Factor '78
Jaws of Death '76
Impulse '74
The Wrestler '73
Goldfinger '64

Gene Saks (1921-)
Deconstructing Harry '97
I.Q. '94
Nobody's Fool '94
A Fine Romance '92
The One and Only '78
Prisoner of Second Avenue '74
A Thousand Clowns '65

Renato Sala
Full Metal Ninja '89
Ninja of the Magnificence '89

Abel Salazar (1917-95)
The Man and the Monster '65
The Brainiac '61
The Curse of the Crying Woman '61
The Living Head '59
The Vampire's Coffin '58
The Vampire '57

Theresa Saldana (1954-)
Thrill Seekers '99
Angel Town '89
Double Revenge '89
The Night Before '88
The Evil That Men Do '84
Raging Bull '80
Defiance '79
I Wanna Hold Your Hand '78

Zoe Saldana
Crossroads '02
Get Over It! '01
Center Stage '00

Charles "Chic" Sale (1885-1936)
You Only Live Once '37
The Fighting Westerner '35
Treasure Island '34

Kario Salem
Savage '96
Killing Zoe '94
1492: Conquest of Paradise '92
Triumph of the Spirit '89
Centennial '78

Pamela Salem
After Darkness '85
Salome '85
Never Say Never Again '83

Meredith Salenger (1970-)
Bug Buster '99
Lake Placid '99
No Code of Conduct '98
Glory Daze '96
Village of the Damned '95
Dead Beat '94
Edge of Honor '91
Dream a Little Dream '89
The Kiss '88
A Night in the Life of Jimmy Reardon '88
The Journey of Natty Gann '85

Enrico Maria Salerno (1926-94)
The Cheaters '76
The Bird with the Crystal Plumage '70
That Long Night in '43 '60

John Salew (1897-1961)
Black Glove '54
Kind Hearts and Coronets '49
Beware of Pity '46

Diane Salinger
The Kid with the X-Ray Eyes '99
Last Summer In the Hamptons '96
One Night Stand '95
The Scarlet Letter '95
The Magic Bubble '93
Venice, Venice '92
The Butcher's Wife '91
The Morning After '86
Creature '85
Pee-wee's Big Adventure '85

Emmanuel Salinger
Kill by Inches '99
My Sex Life...Or How I Got into an Argument '96
One Hundred and One Nights '95
La Sentinelle '92

Matt Salinger (1960-)
Babyfever '94
Fortunes of War '94
Firehawk '92
Captain America '89
Options '88
Manhunt for Claude Dallas '86
Power '86

Jason Salkey
The Turn of the Screw '99
Sharpe's Rifles '93

Pascale Salkin
Window Shopping '86
The Eighties '83

John Salley
Eddie '96
Bad Boys '95

Peter Sallis
Taste the Blood of Dracula '70
The Curse of the Werewolf '61

Albert Salmi (1928-90)
Breaking In '89
Gore Vidal's Billy the Kid '89
Jesse '88
Born American '86
Hard to Hold '84
The Guns and the Fury '83
Love Child '82
St. Helen's, Killer Volcano '82
Superstition '82
Sweet Creek County War '82
Dragonslayer '81
Kill Castro '80
The Mercenaries '80
Steel '80
Black Oak Conspiracy '77
Empire of the Ants '77
Moonshine County Express '77
Viva Knievel '77
The Meanest Men in the West '76
Lawman '71
Menace on the Mountain '70
The Ambushers '67
Hour of the Gun '67
The Unforgiven '60
The Bravados '58
Bang the Drum Slowly '56

Colin Salmon
Dinotopia '02
Resident Evil '02
The World Is Not Enough '99
Immortality '98
Tomorrow Never Dies '97
Captives '94

Lea Salonga (1971-)
Mulan '98 (V)
Redwood Curtain '95
Aladdin '92 (V)

Frank S. Salsedo
Magic in the Water '95
Creepshow 2 '87

Jennifer Salt (1944-)
Out of the Darkness '85
Sisters '73
Play It Again, Sam '72
Hi, Mom! '70

Renato Salvatori (1933-88)
La Cicada '83
State of Siege '73
Burn! '70
The Organizer '64
RoGoPaG '62
Rocco and His Brothers '60
Big Deal on Madonna Street '58

Aldo Sambrel (1937-)
Hot Blood '89
Voodoo Black Exorcist '89
Navajo Joe '67
The Texican '66

Udo Samel
Kaspar Hauser '93
Knife in the Head '78

Emma Samms (1960-)
Humanoids from the Deep '96
Star Quest '94
Delirious '91
Illusions '91
The Shrimp on the Barbie '90
A Connecticut Yankee in King Arthur's Court '89
The Lady and the Highwayman '89
Goliath Awaits '81

Candy Samples
Beneath the Valley of the Ultra-Vixens '79
Flesh Gordon '72

Robert Sampson (1932-)
The Arrival '90
Dark Side of the Moon '90
Netherworld '90
Robot Jox '90
Re-Animator '84
Gates of Hell '80
The Grass Is Always Greener Over the Septic Tank '78
Ethan '71

Will Sampson (1935-87)
Poltergeist 2: The Other Side '86
Roanoak '86
Insignificance '85
Fish Hawk '79
From Here to Eternity '79
Standing Tall '78
Vegas '78
The Hunted Lady '77
Orca '77
The White Buffalo '77
Buffalo Bill & the Indians '76
The Outlaw Josey Wales '76
One Flew Over the Cuckoo's Nest '75

Jeffrey D. Sams
Hope '97
Just Write '97
Soul Food '97
Waiting to Exhale '95
Fly by Night '93

Joanne Samuel (1957-)
Gallagher's Travels '87
Queen of the Road '84
Mad Max '80
Alison's Birthday '79

Laura San Giacomo (1962-)
With Friends Like These '98
Suicide Kings '97
The Apocalypse '96
Eat Your Heart Out '96
The Right to Remain Silent '95
Nina Takes a Lover '94
Stephen King's The Stand '94
Stuart Saves His Family '94
Under Suspicion '92
Where the Day Takes You '92 (V)
Once Around '91
Pretty Woman '90
Quigley Down Under '90
Vital Signs '90
sex, lies and videotape '89
Miles from Home '88

Olga San Juan (1927-)
The Beautiful Blonde from Bashful Bend '49
One Touch of Venus '48
Variety Girl '47
Blue Skies '46

Henry Sanada
Royal Warriors '86
Shogun's Ninja '83

Jon Sanborne
Addicted to Murder 3: Bloodlust '99
Rage of the Werewolf '99

Jaime Sanchez
Pinero '01
The Wild Bunch '69
The Pawnbroker '65

Marisol Padilla Sanchez
Traffic '00
Fever '99
Dementia '98

Paul Sanchez
Navy SEALS '90
Platoon '86

Pedro Sanchez (1924-)
Night and the City '92
White Fang and the Hunter '85
Any Gun Can Play '67

Victoria Sanchez
Codename: Jaguar '00
P.T. Barnum '99

Aitana Sanchez-Gijon (1968-)
Jealousy '99
The Chambermaid on the Titanic '97
Love Walked In '97
Mouth to Mouth '95
A Walk in the Clouds '95
The Perfect Husband '92
Rowing with the Wind '88

Fernando (Fernand) Sancho (1916-90)
Voodoo Black Exorcist '89
Blood at Sundown '88
Return of the Evil Dead '75
Orloff and the Invisible Man '70

Jose Sancho
Arachnid '01
Live Flesh '97
Ay, Carmela! '90

Paul Sand (1935-)
Chuck & Buck '00
Frozen Assets '92
Getting Up and Going Home '92
Teen Wolf Too '87
The Last Fling '86
Can't Stop the Music '80
Second Coming of Suzanne '80
Wholly Moses! '80
The Legend of Sleepy Hollow '79
Great Bank Hoax '78
Once Upon a Brothers Grimm '77

Dominique Sanda (1948-)
The Crimson Rivers '01
Joseph '95
I, the Worst of All '90
Voyage of Terror: The Achille Lauro Affair '90
Cabo Blanco '81
Voyage en Douce '81
Damnation Alley '77
The Inheritance '76
1900 '76
Steppenwolf '74
Mackintosh Man '73
The Story of a Love Story '73
The Conformist '71
The Garden of the Finzi-Continis '71
First Love '70
A Gentle Woman '69

Walter Sande (1906-71)
I'll Take Sweden '65
The Gallant Hours '60
Rim of the Canyon '49
The Red House '47
Nocturne '46
Don Winslow of the Navy '43

Otto Sander (1941-)
The Promise '94
Faraway, So Close! '93
Wings of Desire '88
Rosa Luxemburg '86
The Marquise of O '76

John Sanderford
Leprechaun '93
The Alchemist '81

Dirk Sanders
Pierrot le Fou '65
Black Tights '60

George Sanders (1906-72)
Psychomania '73
Doomwatch '72
Endless Night '71
Invasion of the Body Stealers '69
One Step to Hell '68
Good Times '67
The Jungle Book '67 (V)
The Quiller Memorandum '66
The Amorous Adventures of Moll Flanders '65
A Shot in the Dark '64
In Search of the Castaways '62
The Last Voyage '60
Village of the Damned '60
Solomon and Sheba '59
From the Earth to the Moon '58
Outcasts of the City '58
Rock-A-Bye Baby '57
Death of a Scoundrel '56
While the City Sleeps '56
Jupiter's Darling '55
The King's Thief '55
Moonfleet '55
King Richard and the Crusaders '54
Voyage in Italy '53
Ivanhoe '52
Captain Blackjack '51
All About Eve '50
Samson and Delilah '50
Forever Amber '47
The Ghost and Mrs. Muir '47
Lured '47
The Private Affairs of Bel Ami '47
The Saint Strikes Back: Criminal Court '46
A Scandal in Paris '46
The Strange Woman '46
Picture of Dorian Gray '45
The Strange Affair of Uncle Harry '45
Action in Arabia '44
The Moon and Sixpence '43
This Land Is Mine '43
The Black Swan '42
The Falcon's Brother '42
Son of Fury '42
Tales of Manhattan '42
Sundown '41
Bitter Sweet '40
Foreign Correspondent '40
The House of the Seven Gables '40
Rebecca '40
The Saint Takes Over '40
The Saint's Double Trouble '40
The Son of Monte Cristo '40
Allegheny Uprising '39
Mr. Moto's Last Warning '39
Nurse Edith Cavell '39
The Saint in London '39
The Saint Strikes Back '39
Lloyds of London '36

Henry Sanders
Deadly Sunday '82
Boss' Son '78

Hugh Sanders (1911-66)
The Fighter '52
Pride of St. Louis '52
The Magnificent Yankee '50

Jay O. Sanders (1953-)
Along Came a Spider '01
My Husband's Double Life '01
Boss of Bosses '99
Earthly Possessions '99
The Jack Bull '99
Music of the Heart '99
The Confession '98
Neil Simon's The Odd Couple 2 '98
Tumbleweeds '98
For Richer or Poorer '97
Kiss the Girls '97
The Matchmaker '97
Daylight '96
The Big Green '95
Three Wishes '95
Angels in the Outfield '94
Down Came a Blackbird '94
Kiss of Death '94
Hostages '93
My Boyfriend's Back '93
JFK '91
Meeting Venus '91
V.I. Warshawski '91
Mr. Destiny '90
Glory '89
Assault of the Killer Bimbos '88

Richard Sanders
Forbidden Choices '94
Neon City '91

Martyn Sanderson
An Angel at My Table '89
Beyond Reasonable Doubt '80
Solo '77

William Sanderson (1948-)
Crossfire Trail '01
Nice Guys Sleep Alone '99
George Wallace '97
Last Man Standing '96
Lone Justice 3: Showdown at Plum Creek '96
Andersonville '95
Forest Warrior '95
Hologram Man '95
Phoenix '95
Mirror, Mirror 2: Raven Dance '94
Wagons East '94
Return to Lonesome Dove '93
Sometimes They Come Back '91
Mirror, Mirror '90
Circle Man '87
Last Man Standing '87
Fletch '85
City Heat '84
Ballad of Gregorio Cortez '83
Blade Runner '82
Raggedy Man '81
Savage Weekend '80
Fight for Your Life '79

Elizabeth Sandifer
Animal Instincts 2 '94
Indecent Behavior 2 '94

Adam Sandler (1966-)
Mr. Deeds '02
Little Nicky '00
Big Daddy '99
The Waterboy '98
Dirty Work '97
The Wedding Singer '97
Bulletproof '96
Happy Gilmore '96
Airheads '94
Billy Madison '94
Mixed Nuts '94
Coneheads '93
Shakes the Clown '92
Going Overboard '89

Debra Sandlund (1962-)
Victimless Crimes '90
Murder by Numbers '89
Tough Guys Don't Dance '87

Steve Sandor
Stryker '83
The Only Way Home '72

Miguel (Michael) Sandoval (1951-)
Collateral Damage '02
Human Nature '02
Blow '01
The Crew '00
Things You Can Tell Just by Looking at Her '00
Apartment Complex '98
Route 9 '98
The Fixer '97
Mrs. Winterbourne '96
Scorpion Spring '96
Up Close and Personal '96
Breach of Trust '95
Fair Game '95
Clear and Present Danger '94
Girls in Prison '94
Dancing with Danger '93
Lone Justice '93
White Sands '92
El Diablo '90
Walker '87

Stefania Sandrelli (1946-)
Stealing Beauty '96
Of Love and Shadows '94
Jamon, Jamon '93
The Sleazy Uncle '89
The Family '87
We All Loved Each Other So Much '77
1900 '76
Alfredo, Alfredo '72
The Conformist '71
Partner '68
Seduced and Abandoned '64
Divorce—Italian Style '62

Billy (Billie) Sands (1911-84)
Harrad Experiment '73
McHale's Navy Joins the Air Force '65
McHale's Navy '64

Diana Sands (1934-73)
Three Days in Beirut '83
Honeybaby '74
Georgia, Georgia '72
Doctors' Wives '70
A Raisin in the Sun '61

Julian Sands (1958-)
Stephen King's Rose Red '02
Mercy '00
Time Code '00
Vatel '00
The Million Dollar Hotel '99
The Loss of Sexual Innocence '98
The Phantom of the Opera '98
Circle of Passion '97
End of Summer '97
One Night Stand '97
The Great Elephant Escape '95
Leaving Las Vegas '95
Black Water '94
The Browning Version '94
Witch Hunt '94
Boxing Helena '93
Warlock: The Armageddon '93
Crazy in Love '92
Grand Isle '92
Tale of a Vampire '92
The Turn of the Screw '92
Husbands and Lovers '91
Murder by Moonlight '91
Naked Lunch '91
Warlock '91
Arachnophobia '90
Impromptu '90
Night Sun '90
Vibes '88
Gothic '87
The Room '87
Siesta '87
Harem '86
A Room with a View '86
After Darkness '85
The Doctor and the Devils '85
The Killing Fields '84
Oxford Blues '84
Privates on Parade '84

Tommy Sands
None But the Brave '65
Babes in Toyland '61

Gary Sandy (1945-)
Mommy 2: Mommy's Day '96
Troll '86
Hail '73

Erskine Sanford (1885-1969)
The Lady from Shanghai '48
Crack-Up '46
Ministry of Fear '44
The Magnificent Ambersons '42
Citizen Kane '41

Garwin Sanford (1955-)
Get Carter '00
Life-Size '00
Mr. Rice's Secret '00
Firestorm '97
Ronnie and Julie '97
Maternal Instincts '96
My Very Best Friend '96
Unforgettable '96
Quarantine '89

Isabel Sanford
Desperate Moves '86
Love at First Bite '79

Ralph Sanford
There Goes Kelly '45
A Night for Crime '42

Shiro Sano
Godzilla 2000 '99
Violent Cop '89

Renoly Santiago
Daylight '96
Dangerous Minds '95
Hackers '95

Saundra Santiago (1957-)
Hi-Life '98
Nick and Jane '96
Beat Street '84
Miami Vice '84

Ruben Santiago-Hudson
Domestic Disturbance '01
American Tragedy '00
Shaft '00
Rear Window '98
The Devil's Advocate '97
Which Way Home '90

Pierre Santini
Dirty Dishes '82
Innocents with Dirty Hands '75

Santo (1917-84)
Samson in the Wax Museum '63
Invasion of the Zombies '61
Samson vs. the Vampire Women '61

Espartaco (Spartaco) Santoni (1932-98)
Lisa and the Devil '75
Exorcism's Daughter '74
The Castilian '63

Reni Santoni (1939-)
28 Days '00
Dr. Dolittle '98 (V)
The Late Shift '96
Private Parts '96
The Package '89
Cobra '86
Bad Boys '83
Dead Men Don't Wear Plaid '82
Dirty Harry '71
The Student Nurses '70
Guns of the Magnificent Seven '69
Anzio '68
Enter Laughing '67

Gaston Santos
Swamp of the Lost Monster '65
The Living Coffin '58
Black Pit of Dr. M '47

Joe Santos (1931-)
Beyond Suspicion '00
The Postman '97
Tyson '95
Trial by Jury '94
Mo' Money '92
Sinatra '92
Deadly Desire '91
The Last Boy Scout '91
Revenge '90
Fear City '85
Zandy's Bride '74
Shaft's Big Score '72

Thomas Santschi (1878-1931)
Phantom of the West '31
Ten Nights in a Bar-Room '31
Paradise Island '30
Paths to Paradise '25
Little Orphan Annie '18
The Spoilers '14

Michael Sanville
Dreams Come True '84
First Turn On '83

Horatio Sanz
The New Guy '02
Tomcats '01

Jorge Sanz (1969-)
The Break '97
The Garden of Redemption '97
Zafarinas '94
Belle Epoque '92
Why Do They Call It Love When They Mean Sex? '92
Lovers: A True Story '90

Al Sapienza
Blind Heat '00
Sweet Evil '98
Animal Instincts 2 '94
The Voyeur '94

Mia Sara (1967-)
Jack and the Beanstalk: The Real Story '01
Black Day Blue Night '95
Bullet to Beijing '95
The Maddening '95
The Pompatus of Love '95
The Set Up '95
Undertow '95
Timecop '94
Blindsided '93
By the Sword '93
Call of the Wild '93
Caroline at Midnight '93
A Stranger Among Us '92
A Climate for Killing '91
Any Man's Death '90
Daughter of Darkness '89
Apprentice to Murder '88
Shadows in the Storm '88
Queenie '87
Ferris Bueller's Day Off '86
Legend '86

Richard Sarafian (1935-)
Dr. Dolittle 2 '01 (V)
Bulworth '98
Bound '96
Gotti '96
Miami Hustle '95
The Crossing Guard '94
Ruby '92
Bugsy '91

Chris Sarandon (1942-)
Perfume '01
Race Against Time '00
Let the Devil Wear Black '99
Little Men '98
Road Ends '98
The Reaper '97
Tales from the Crypt Presents Bordello of Blood '96
Edie & Pen '95
Temptress '95
Terminal Justice: Cybertech P.D. '95
When the Dark Man Calls '95
Just Cause '94
Dark Tide '93
The Nightmare before Christmas '93 (V)
The Resurrected '91
Forced March '90
Collision Course '89
Slaves of New York '89
Tailspin: Behind the Korean Airline Tragedy '89
Whispers '89
Child's Play '88
Goodbye, Miss 4th of July '88
Mayflower Madam '87
The Princess Bride '87
Fright Night '85
Protocol '84
The Osterman Weekend '83
A Tale of Two Cities '80
Cuba '79
Lipstick '76
The Sentinel '76
Dog Day Afternoon '75

Susan Sarandon (1946-)
Igby Goes Down '02
Cats & Dogs '01 (V)
Joe Gould's Secret '00
Rugrats in Paris: The Movie '00 (V)
Anywhere But Here '99
The Cradle Will Rock '99
Earthly Possessions '99
Illuminata '98
Stepmom '98
Twilight '98
James and the Giant Peach '96 (V)
Dead Man Walking '95
The Client '94
Little Women '94
Safe Passage '94
Bob Roberts '92
Light Sleeper '92
Lorenzo's Oil '92
The Player '92
Thelma & Louise '91
White Palace '90
A Dry White Season '89
The January Man '89
Bull Durham '88
Sweet Hearts Dance '88
The Witches of Eastwick '87
Women of Valor '86
A.D. '85
Compromising Positions '85
Mussolini & I '85
Beauty and the Beast '83
The Buddy System '83
The Hunger '83
The Tempest '82
Who Am I This Time? '82
Atlantic City '81
Loving Couples '80
Something Short of Paradise '79
King of the Gypsies '78
Pretty Baby '78
The Other Side of Midnight '77
Great Smokey Roadblock '76
One Summer Love '76
The Great Waldo Pepper '75
The Rocky Horror Picture Show '75
The Front Page '74
Joe '70

Martine Sarcey
One Wild Moment '78
Pardon Mon Affaire '76

Rosa Maria Sarda
Beloved/Friend '99
Caresses '97
Why Do They Call It Love When They Mean Sex? '92

Fernand Sardou
The Little Theatre of Jean Renoir '71
Picnic on the Grass '59

Dick Sargent (1933-94)
Acting on Impulse '93
Frame Up '91
Twenty Dollar Star '91
Murder by Numbers '89
Teen Witch '89
Body Count '87
Tanya's Island '81
The Clonus Horror '79
Hardcore '79
Fantasy Island '76
Melvin Purvis: G-Man '74
Live a Little, Love a Little '68
Private Navy of Sgt. O'Farrell '68
The Ghost and Mr. Chicken '66
Billie '65
For Love or Money '63
That Touch of Mink '62

Lewis Sargent
The New Adventures of Tarzan '35
Oliver Twist '22

Michael Sarne (1939-)
Head Over Heels '67
Seaside Swingers '65

Michael Sarrazin (1940-)
The Arrival 2 '98
The Peacekeeper '98
Crackerjack 2 '97
Jack Higgins' Thunder Point '97
Midnight in Saint Petersburg '97
Jack Higgins' Midnight Man '96
Bullet to Beijing '95
Lena's Holiday '90
Malarek '89
The Phone Call '89
Captive Hearts '87
Mascara '87
Keeping Track '86
Joshua Then and Now '85
The Train Killer '83
Fighting Back '82
The Seduction '82
Beulah Land '80
The Double Negative '80
Gumball Rally '76
Loves & Times of Scaramouche '76
The Reincarnation of Peter Proud '75
For Pete's Sake '74
The Groundstar Conspiracy '72
Sometimes a Great Notion '71
The Pursuit of Happiness '70
They Shoot Horses, Don't They? '69
Flim-Flam Man '67
The Doomsday Flight '66

Peter Sarsgaard
K-19: The Widowmaker '02
The Salton Sea '02
The Center of the World '01
Boys Don't Cry '99
The Man in the Iron Mask '98

Gailard Sartain (1946-)
Ali '01
The Replacements '00
The Patriot '99
The Pirates of Silicon Valley '99
All New Adventures of Laurel and Hardy: For Love or Mummy '98
Joe Torre: Curveballs Along the Way '97
Murder in Mind '97
Open Season '95
The Spitfire Grill '95
Getting Even with Dad '94
Speechless '94
Wagons East '94
Equinox '93
The Real McCoy '93
Walker: Texas Ranger: One Riot, One Ranger '93
Wishman '93
Stop! or My Mom Will Shoot '92
Fried Green Tomatoes '91
Guilty by Suspicion '91
Ernest Goes to Jail '90
The Grifters '90
Blaze '89
Mississippi Burning '88
Ernest Goes to Camp '87
Leader of the Band '87
Trouble in Mind '86
Hard Country '81
The Hollywood Knights '80
Roadie '80

Katsuhiko Sasakai
Terror of Mechagodzilla '78
Godzilla vs. Megalon '76

Jacqueline Sassard (1940-)
Les Biches '68
Accident '67
Pirates of the Seven Seas '62

Will Sasso
Drop Dead Gorgeous '99
Brown's Requiem '98

Catya (Cat) Sassoon (1968-2001)
Bloodfist 4: Die Trying '92
Dance with Death '91
Tuff Turf '85

Ines Sastre
Druids '01
The Count of Monte Cristo '99
The Best Man '97
Beyond the Clouds '95

Lina Sastri (1953-)
Goodnight, Michelangelo '89
The Inquiry '87
Where's Piccone '84

Tura Satana
The Doll Squad '73
The Astro-Zombies '67
Faster, Pussycat! Kill! Kill! '65

Kei Sato
Zatoichi: The Blind Swordsman's Vengeance '66
Onibaba '64

Paul Satterfield
Arena '89
Creepshow 2 '87

Jennifer Saunders (1958-)
Spice World: The Movie '97
Absolutely Fabulous: The Last Shout '96
Muppet Treasure Island '96
A Midwinter's Tale '95
Supergrass '87

Ann Savage (1921-)
Pier 23 '51
Detour '46
Renegade Girl '46
Treasure of Fear '45
Footlight Glamour '43
The More the Merrier '43

Ben Savage (1980-)
Wild Palms '93
Big Girls Don't Cry...They Get Even '92
Little Monsters '89

Fred Savage (1976-)
Little Monsters '89
The Wizard '89
Vice Versa '88
Convicted: A Mother's Story '87
The Princess Bride '87
The Boy Who Could Fly '86

John Savage (1949-)
The Jack Bull '99
Summer of Sam '99
The Virginian '99
Club Vampire '98
Message in a Bottle '98
The Thin Red Line '98
Hostile Intent '97
Little Boy Blue '97
Managua '97
American Strays '96
Amnesia '96
Hollywood Safari '96
Where Truth Lies '96
White Squall '96
The Dangerous '95
One Good Turn '95
Carnosaur 2 '94
C.I.A. 2: Target Alexa '94
The Crossing Guard '94
Killing Obsession '94
Red Scorpion 2 '94
The Takeover '94
Daybreak '93
Shattered Image '93
The Hunting '92
Primary Motive '92
Any Man's Death '90
The Godfather, Part 3 '90
Do the Right Thing '89
The Beat '88
Hotel Colonial '88
Nairobi Affair '88
Caribe '87
Salvador '86
Silent Witness '85
Brady's Escape '84
Maria's Lovers '84
Soldier's Revenge '84
The Tender Age '84
The Amateur '82
Coming Out of the Ice '82
Inside Moves '80
Hair '79
The Onion Field '79
The Deer Hunter '78
Eric '75
All the Kind Strangers '74
The Sister-in-Law '74
The Killing Kind '73
Steelyard Blues '73
Bad Company '72

Rick Savage (1960-)
Ex-Cop '93
Sensations '87

Dany Saval
Boeing Boeing '65
Moon Pilot '62

George Savalas (1926-)
Kojak: The Belarus File '85
Kelly's Heroes '70

Telly Savalas (1924-94)
Mind Twister '93
The Hollywood Detective '89
The Dirty Dozen: The Fatal Mission '88
The Dirty Dozen: The Deadly Mission '87
Kojak: The Belarus File '85
Cannonball Run 2 '84
Cartier Affair '84
Fake Out '82
Silent Rebellion '82
Beyond the Poseidon Adventure '79
Escape to Athena '79
The Muppet Movie '79
Capricorn One '78
Beyond Reason '77
Inside Out '75
Killer Force '75
Lisa and the Devil '75
The Family '73
A Reason to Live, a Reason to Die '73
Redneck '73
Sonny and Jed '73
Horror Express '72
New Mafia Boss '72
Pancho Villa '72
Scenes from a Murder '72
A Town Called Hell '72
Kelly's Heroes '70
The Assassination Bureau '69
Crooks & Coronets '69
Land Raiders '69
MacKenna's Gold '69
On Her Majesty's Secret Service '69
Buona Sera, Mrs. Campbell '68
The Scalphunters '68
The Dirty Dozen '67
Battle of the Bulge '65
The Greatest Story Ever Told '65
The Slender Thread '65
Birdman of Alcatraz '62
The Interns '62
Cape Fear '61

Doug Savant (1964-)
A Face to Kill For '99
First Daughter '99
Godzilla '98
Maniac Cop 3: Badge of Silence '93
Shaking the Tree '92
Red Surf '90
Paint It Black '89
Masquerade '88
Trick or Treat '86

Lyudmila Savelyeva
The Seagull '71
War and Peace '68

John Savident (1938-)
Othello '95
Middlemarch '93
Brain Donors '92
Mrs. 'Arris Goes to Paris '92
One Against the Wind '91
Impromptu '90
Mountains of the Moon '90
Waterloo '71

Tom Savini (1946-)
Demon Lust '01
The Demolitionist '95
From Dusk Till Dawn '95
Mr. Stitch '95
Heartstopper '92
Innocent Blood '92
Creepshow 2 '87
Creepshow '82
Knightriders '81
Maniac '80
Dawn of the Dead '78
Martin '77

Camille Saviola
Sunset Park '96
Stuart Saves His Family '94
Nightlife '90

Suzanne Savoy
The Man with the Perfect Swing '95
The Cellar '90

Devon Sawa (1978-)
Slackers '02
Final Destination '00
The Guilty '99
Idle Hands '99
SLC Punk! '99
Around the Fire '98
A Cool, Dry Place '98
Wild America '97
The Boys Club '96
Night of the Twisters '95
Robin of Locksley '95
Little Giants '94

Julia Sawalha (1968-)
Chicken Run '00 (V)
Mr. Toad's Wild Ride '96
A Midwinter's Tale '95
Pride and Prejudice '95
Martin Chuzzlewit '94

Nadim Sawalha (1935-)
Cleopatra '99
The Awakening '80
The Wind and the Lion '75

Ikio Sawamura (1905-75)
War of the Gargantuas '70
Godzilla's Revenge '69
Yojimbo '61

Joseph (Joe) Sawyer (1906-82)
The Kettles in the Ozarks '56
The Killing '56
Mr. Walkie Talkie '52
As You Were '51
Comin' Round the Mountain '51
Indian Uprising '51
Fighting Father Dunne '48
The Naughty Nineties '45
The Outlaw '43
Tanks a Million '41
They Died with Their Boots On '41
The Border Legion '40
Lucky Cisco Kid '40
Melody Ranch '40
The Roaring Twenties '39
The Black Legion '37
Petrified Forest '36
Special Investigator '36
The Informer '35

John Saxon (1935-)
Outta Time '01
Final Payback '99
From Dusk Till Dawn '95
Beverly Hills Cop 3 '94
Killing Obsession '94
Wes Craven's New Nightmare '94
No Escape, No Return '93
Animal Instincts '92
The Baby Doll Murders '92
Hellmaster '92
Maximum Force '92
Blackmail '91
Deadly Conspiracy '91
Payoff '91
The Arrival '90
Blood Salvage '90
Crossing the Line '90
The Last Samurai '90
The Final Alliance '89
My Mom's a Werewolf '89
Aftershock '88
Criminal Act '88
Death House '88
Welcome to Spring Break '88
A Nightmare on Elm Street 3: Dream Warriors '87
Hands of Steel '86
Fever Pitch '85
Half Slave, Half Free '85
A Nightmare on Elm Street '84
Prisoners of the Lost Universe '84
Big Score '83
Scorpion with Two Tails '82
Unsane '82
Wrong Is Right '82
Blood Beach '81
Battle Beyond the Stars '80
Beyond Evil '80
Cannibal Apocalypse '80
The Electric Horseman '79
Running Scared '79
The Bees '78
Deadly Thief '78
Fast Company '78
The Glove '78
Moonshine County Express '77
Raid on Entebbe '77
Swiss Conspiracy '77
Strange Shadows in an Empty Room '76
Black Christmas '75
Mitchell '75
Strange New World '75
Planet Earth '74
Enter the Dragon '73
Joe Kidd '72
Snatched '72
Mr. Kingstreet's War '71

Death of a Gunfighter '69
The Appaloosa '66
The Doomsday Flight '66
Night Caller from Outer Space '66
Planet of Blood '66
The Ravagers '65
The Cardinal '63
The Girl Who Knew Too Much '63
Mr. Hobbs Takes a Vacation '62
Portrait in Black '60
The Unforgiven '60
The Reluctant Debutante '58
This Happy Feeling '58
Rock, Pretty Baby '56

Diane Sayer
Kitten with a Whip '64
The Strangler '64

Philip Sayer (1947-89)
A.D. '85
Slayground '84
Green Horizon '83
Xtro '83

Alexei Sayle (1952-)
Swing '98
Deadly Currents '93
Reckless Kelly '93
Siesta '87
Whoops Apocalypse '83

John Sayles (1950-)
Girlfight '99
Gridlock'd '96
My Life's in Turnaround '94
Matinee '92
Straight Talk '92
City of Hope '91
Little Vegas '90
Eight Men Out '88
Matewan '87
Something Wild '86
Unnatural Causes '86
The Brother from Another Planet '84
Hard Choices '84
Lianna '83
Return of the Secaucus 7 '80

Syd Saylor (1895-1962)
Abbott and Costello Meet the Invisible Man '51
Ambush Trail '46
Harvest Melody '43
Helltown '38
Arizona Days '37
Forlorn River '37
Sea Racketeers '37
Headin' for the Rio Grande '36
Kelly of the Secret Service '36
Kelly the Second '36
Prison Shadows '36
The Lost Jungle '34
When a Man Sees Red '34
The Light of Western Stars '30

John Sayre
Crystal's Diary '99
Crack Up '97

Kyu Sazanka
Yojimbo '61
Fires on the Plain '59

Raphael Sbarge (1964-)
Pearl Harbor '01
Message in a Bottle '98
Quicksilver Highway '98
Independence Day '96
The Hidden 2 '94
Carnosaur '93
Prison for Children '93
Murder 101 '91
Back to Hannibal: The Return of Tom Sawyer and Huckleberry Finn '90
Billionaire Boys Club '87
My Man Adam '86
My Science Project '85
Risky Business '83
Abuse '82

Mattia Sbragia
Year of the Gun '91
Dial Help '88

Greta Scacchi (1960-)
Cotton Mary '99
Love and Rage '99
The Red Violin '98
The Odyssey '97
The Serpent's Kiss '97
Emma '96
Rasputin: Dark Servant of Destiny '96
Cosi '95
Country Life '95
The Browning Version '94
Jefferson in Paris '94
Desire '93
The Killing Beach '92
The Player '92
Fires Within '91
Shattered '91
Presumed Innocent '90
White Mischief '88
Good Morning, Babylon '87
A Man in Love '87
Ebony Tower '86
Burke & Wills '85
Defense of the Realm '85
The Coca-Cola Kid '84
Waterfront '83
Heat and Dust '82

Gia Scala (1934-72)
The Guns of Navarone '61
The Tunnel of Love '58
Don't Go Near the Water '57

Prunella Scales (1932-)
Emma '97
Stiff Upper Lips '96
Breaking the Code '95
An Awfully Big Adventure '94
The Rector's Wife '94
Second Best '94
Wolf '94
My Friend Walter '93
Howard's End '92
A Question of Attribution '91
A Chorus of Disapproval '89
Consuming Passions '88
The Lonely Passion of Judith Hearne '87
Mapp & Lucia '85
The Wicked Lady '83
Room at the Top '59

Jack Scalia (1951-)
Kill Shot '01
Silent Predators '99
Chained Heat 3: Hell Mountain '98
First Degree '98
Under Oath '97
Act of War '96
Dark Breed '96
The Silencers '95
Storybook '95
Tall, Dark and Deadly '95
T-Force '94
Amore! '93
Casualties of Love: The "Long Island Lolita" Story '93
Shattered Image '93
Undesirable '92
Deadly Desire '91
Illicit Behavior '91
Runaway Father '91
After the Shock '90
Endless Descent '90
Fear City '85
The Amazons '84

Carlo Scandiuzzi
Darkdrive '98
Killing Zoe '94
Red Snow '91
Shredder Orpheus '89

Sean Scanlan
A Mind to Murder '96
A Sense of Freedom '78

Kevin Scannell
Backfield in Motion '91
Shoot to Kill '88

Michelle Scarabelli (1955-)
The Colony '95
Alien Nation: Dark Horizon '94

Deadbolt '92
Age Old Friends '89
SnakeEater 2: The Drug Buster '89
Perfect Timing '84

Don Scardino
He Knows You're Alone '80
Squirm '76

Hal Scardino (1984-)
Marvin's Room '96
The Indian in the Cupboard '95
Searching for Bobby Fischer '93

Alan Scarfe
Sanctuary '98
Back in Business '96
Once a Thief '96
Heart of Darkness '93
Jericho Fever '93
Iron Eagle 2 '88
Python Wolf '88
Keeping Track '86
The Bay Boy '85
Joshua Then and Now '85
The Deserters '83
Cathy's Curse '77

Jonathan Scarfe (1975-)
Blood Money '99
White Lies '98
The Lesser Evil '97
Our Mother's Murder '97
Eye '96

Renato Scarpa (1939-)
For Roseanna '96
The Postman '94
Volere Volare '92
The Icicle Thief '89
St. Michael Had a Rooster '72

Carmen Scarpitta
In the Name of the Pope-King '85
La Cage aux Folles '78

Diana Scarwid (1955-)
A Guy Thing '02
Dirty Pictures '00
What Lies Beneath '00
From the Earth to the Moon '98
Ruby Bridges '98
Critical Choices '97
Bastard out of Carolina '96
If These Walls Could Talk '96
The Cure '95
Gold Diggers: The Secret of Bear Mountain '95
The Neon Bible '95
Truman '95
JFK: Reckless Youth '93
After the Promise '87
Brenda Starr '86
Extremities '86
The Ladies Club '86
Psycho 3 '86
A Bunny's Tale '85
Rumble Fish '83
Silkwood '83
Strange Invaders '83
Desperate Lives '82
Mommie Dearest '81
Inside Moves '80
Forever '78
Pretty Baby '78
The Possessed '77

Monica Scattini
Men Men Men '95
Priceless Beauty '90

Wendy Schaal (1954-)
Small Soldiers '98
Out There '95
Going Under '91
When the Time Comes '91
Innerspace '87
Munchies '87
Creature '85
Where the Boys Are '84 '84

Sam Schacht
Heart of Midnight '89
A Secret Space '88

Johnathon Schaech (1969-)
The Forsaken '01

How to Kill Your Neighbor's Dog '01
Caracara '00
If You Only Knew '00
The Brutal Truth '99
Houdini '99
Splendor '99
Finding Graceland '98
Hush '98
Welcome to Woop Woop '97
Invasion of Privacy '96
That Thing You Do! '96
The Doom Generation '95
How to Make an American Quilt '95
Poison Ivy 2: Lily '95

Joshua Schaefer
Eight Days a Week '97
johns '96
No Dessert Dad, 'Til You Mow the Lawn '94

Laura Schaefer
Curse 4: The Ultimate Sacrifice '90
Catacombs '89
Ghost Town '88

Eric Schaeffer (1962-)
One Night at McCool's '01
Wirey Spindell '99
Gunshy '98
Fall '97
If Lucy Fell '95
My Life's in Turnaround '94

Rebecca Schaeffer (1967-89)
The End of Innocence '90
Voyage of Terror: The Achille Lauro Affair '90
Scenes from the Class Struggle in Beverly Hills '89

Natalie Schafer (1900-91)
I'm Dangerous Tonight '90
Rescue from Gilligan's Island '78
Forever Darling '56
Caught '49
The Time of Your Life '48
Wonder Man '45

William Schallert (1922-)
Shake, Rattle & Rock! '94
Matinee '92
Held Hostage '91
House Party 2: The Pajama Jam '91
The Incident '89
War & Remembrance: The Final Chapter '89
War & Remembrance '88
Innerspace '87
The Grace Kelly Story '83
Twilight Zone: The Movie '83
Death Sentence '74
Trial of the Catonsville Nine '72
Man on a String '71
Colossus: The Forbin Project '70
The Computer Wore Tennis Shoes '69
Speedway '68
The Gallant Hours '60
The Incredible Shrinking Man '57
Man in the Shadow '57
Tarnished Angels '57
The Gunslinger '56
Them! '54
Sword of Venus '53
Invasion U.S.A. '52
The Man from Planet X '51

Tom Schanley
Footsteps '98
Nothing Underneath '85

Heidi Schanz
Universal Soldier: The Return '99
Mixing Nia '98
Shame, Shame, Shame '98
Body Language '95

Sabrina Scharf
Hunter '73
Easy Rider '69

Hell's Angels on Wheels '67

Roy Scheider (1934-)
Daybreak '01
Time Lapse '01
Angels Don't Sleep Here '00
Chain of Command '00
The Doorway '00
RKO 281 '99
The Peacekeeper '98
The White Raven '98
Executive Target '97
John Grisham's The Rainmaker '97
The Myth of Fingerprints '97
Plato's Run '96
The Rage '96
Covert Assassin '94
Romeo Is Bleeding '93
Naked Lunch '91
The Fourth War '90
The Russia House '90
Somebody Has to Shoot the Picture '90
Listen to Me '89
Night Game '89
Cohen and Tate '88
52 Pick-Up '86
The Men's Club '86
Mishima: A Life in Four Chapters '85 (N)
2010: The Year We Make Contact '84
Blue Thunder '83
Tiger Town '83
Still of the Night '82
All That Jazz '79
Last Embrace '79
Jaws 2 '78
Sorcerer '77
Marathon Man '76
Jaws '75
The Outside Man '73
The Seven-Ups '73
The French Connection '71
Klute '71
Stiletto '69
Paper Lion '68
Curse of the Living Corpse '64

Raynor Scheine
The Rookie '02
The War '94

Clemens Scheitz
Stroszek '77
Heart of Glass '74

Carl Schell
Quick, Let's Get Married '71
Werewolf in a Girl's Dormitory '61

Catherine Schell (1946-)
On the Third Day '83
Gulliver's Travels '77
Return of the Pink Panther '74
On Her Majesty's Secret Service '69

Maria Schell (1926-)
Christmas Lilies of the Field '84
Samson and Delilah '84
La Passante '83
Inside the Third Reich '82
Just a Gigolo '79
Twist '76
Voyage of the Damned '76
The Odessa File '74
99 Women '69
End of Desire '62
The Mark '61
Cimarron '60
The Hanging Tree '59
The Brothers Karamazov '58
White Nights '57
Gervaise '56
Napoleon '55
The Last Bridge '54
Angel with the Trumpet '50

Maximilian Schell (1930-)
The Song of the Lark '01
Joan of Arc '99

Deep Impact '98
Left Luggage '98
The Eighteenth Angel '97
John Carpenter's Vampires '97
Telling Lies in America '96
Abraham '94
Little Odessa '94
A Far Off Place '93
Miss Rose White '92
Stalin '92
Young Catherine '91
The Freshman '90
The Rose Garden '89
Peter the Great '86
The Assisi Underground '84
The Chosen '81
Avalanche Express '79
The Black Hole '79
Players '79
Together? '79
The Day That Shook the World '78
A Bridge Too Far '77
Julia '77
Cross of Iron '76
St. Ives '76
The Man in the Glass Booth '75
The Odessa File '74
The Pedestrian '73
First Love '70
Simon Bolivar '69
The Castle '68
Heidi '67
Topkapi '64
Judgment at Nuremberg '61
The Young Lions '58

Ronnie Schell
Jetsons: The Movie '90 (V)
Gus '76

August Schellenberg
High Noon '00
Out of Time '00
Free Willy 3: The Rescue '97
True Heart '97
Crazy Horse '96
Free Willy 2: The Adventure Home '95
Tecumseh: The Last Warrior '95
Getting Gotti '94
Lakota Woman: Siege at Wounded Knee '94
Free Willy '93
Geronimo '93
Iron Will '93
Black Robe '91
Striker's Mountain '87
Tramp at the Door '87
Confidential '86
Mark of Cain '84

Mary Kate Schellhardt
Apollo 13 '95
What's Eating Gilbert Grape '93

Wolfgang Schenck
Effi Briest '74
Tenderness of the Wolves '73

Robert Schenkkan
Act of Vengeance '86
The Manhattan Project '86
Sanctuary of Fear '79

Jean Schertler
Runaway Bride '99
Pecker '98

Rosanna Schiaffino (1938-)
Simon Bolivar '69
Code Name Alpha '67
The Rover '67
Arrivederci, Baby! '66
The Witch '66
The Long Ships '64
RoGoPaG '62
Two Weeks in Another Town '62
Roland the Mighty '58

Vincent Schiavelli (1948-)
Death to Smoochy '02

Snow White: The Fairest of Them All '02
Three Strikes '00
Desert Heat '99
Man on the Moon '99
The Prince and the Surfer '99
Milo '98
Tomorrow Never Dies '97
Back to Back '96
The People vs. Larry Flynt '96
Two Much '96
The Courtyard '95
Lord of Illusions '95
Prince Brat and the Whipping Boy '95
3 Ninjas Knuckle Up '95
Lurking Fear '94
Batman Returns '92
Miracle Beach '92
Ghost '90
Playroom '90
Waiting for the Light '90
Cold Feet '89
Valmont '89
Better Off Dead '85
Lots of Luck '85
The Adventures of Buckaroo Banzai Across the Eighth Dimension '84
Amadeus '84
Fast Times at Ridgemont High '82
Night Shift '82 (V)
The Return '80
One Flew Over the Cuckoo's Nest '75

Dieter Schidor
Schnelles Geld '84
Cross of Iron '76

Richard Schiff (1959-)
I Am Sam '01
What's the Worst That Could Happen? '01
Along for the Ride '00
Gun Shy '00
Lucky Numbers '00
Whatever It Takes '00
Crazy in Alabama '99
Forces of Nature '99
Heaven '99
Deep Impact '98
Dr. Dolittle '98
Living Out Loud '98
The Pentagon Wars '98
The Lost World: Jurassic Park 2 '97
The Trigger Effect '96
City Hall '95

Claudia Schiffer (1970-)
Life Without Dick '01
In Pursuit '00
Black and White '99
Friends & Lovers '99
The Blackout '97
Richie Rich '94

Joseph Schildkraut (1895-1964)
The Diary of Anne Frank '59
Monsieur Beaucaire '46
Flame of the Barbary Coast '45
The Shop Around the Corner '40
Idiot's Delight '39
The Man in the Iron Mask '39
The Rains Came '39
The Three Musketeers '39
Marie Antoinette '38
The Life of Emile Zola '37
Souls at Sea '37
The Garden of Allah '36
The Crusades '35
Cleopatra '34
Viva Villa! '34
King of Kings '27
The Road to Yesterday '25
Orphans of the Storm '21
Wandering Jew '20

Gus Schilling (1908-57)
The Lady from Shanghai '48
A Thousand and One Nights '45
Citizen Kane '41

Vivian Schilling (1968-)
Savage Land '94
Future Shock '93
In a Moment of Passion '93
The Legend of Wolf Mountain '92
Project: Eliminator '91
Soultaker '90
Terror Eyes '87

Tom Schioler
Maniac Warriors '92
Storm '87

Sharon Schlarth
Eat and Run '86
Dead As a Doorman '85

Charlie Schlatter (1966-)
Ed '96
Police Academy 7: Mission to Moscow '94
Sunset Heat '92
All-American Murder '91
Bright Lights, Big City '88
18 Again! '88
Heartbreak Hotel '88

Ariane Schluter
The Dress '96
1-900 '94

Walter Schmidinger
Hanussen '88
From the Life of the Marionettes '80

Marlene Schmidt
Scorchy '76
The Stepmother '71

Christiane Schmidtmer (1940-)
The Giant Spider Invasion '75
The Big Doll House '71
Boeing Boeing '65

Sybille Schmitz (1909-)
F.P. 1 Doesn't Answer '33
Vampyr '31
Diary of a Lost Girl '29

August Schmolzer
Bride of the Wind '01
Requiem for Dominic '91

Stefan Schnabel (1912-99)
Anna '87
Two Weeks in Another Town '62
The 27th Day '57
Houdini '53

Monika Schnarre (1971-)
Dead Fire '98
The Peacekeeper '98
Bulletproof Heart '95
Fearless Tiger '94
The Death Merchant '91
Waxwork 2: Lost in Time '91

Bonnie Schneider
Murderlust '86
Mama Dracula '80

Dan Schneider (1966-)
Good Burger '97
The Big Picture '89
Happy Together '89
Better Off Dead '85

Helmut Schneider
Fifth Day of Peace '72
Captain Sinbad '63

John Schneider (1960-)
Snow Day '00
True Women '97
Night of the Twisters '95
Texas '94
Ministry of Vengeance '89
Speed Zone '88
Christmas Comes to Willow Creek '87
The Curse '87
Cocaine Wars '86
Stagecoach '86
Eddie Macon's Run '83
Smokey and the Bandit '77

Maria Schneider (1952-)
Jane Eyre '96
Les Nuits Fauves '92
Crime of Honor '85
Mama Dracula '80
The Passenger '75
Wanted: Babysitter '75
Last Tango in Paris '73

Michael Schneider
Schindler's List '93
Double Edge '92

Rob Schneider (1963-)
The Animal '01
Little Nicky '00
Big Daddy '99
Deuce Bigalow: Male Gigolo '99
Muppets from Space '99
Dying to Get Rich '98
Knock Off '98
The Waterboy '98
The Adventures of Pinocchio '96
Down Periscope '96
Judge Dredd '95
The Beverly Hillbillies '93
Surf Ninjas '93
Home Alone 2: Lost in New York '92

Romy Schneider (1938-82)
La Passante '83
Death Watch '80
Sidney Sheldon's Bloodline '79
A Simple Story '79
A Woman at Her Window '77
Dirty Hands '76
Mado '76
Old Gun '76
Innocents with Dirty Hands '75
The Infernal Trio '74
The Last Train '74
Assassination of Trotsky '72
Cesar & Rosalie '72
Ludwig '72
The Hero '71
Swimming Pool '70
The Things of Life '70
Triple Cross '67
What's New Pussycat? '65
Good Neighbor Sam '64
The Trial '63
Boccaccio '70 '62

Andrea Schober
Chinese Roulette '86
The Merchant of Four Seasons '71

Michael Schoeffling
Wild Hearts Can't Be Broken '91
Longtime Companion '90
Mermaids '90
Let's Get Harry '87
Belizaire the Cajun '86
Sylvester '85
Vision Quest '85
Sixteen Candles '84

Jill Schoelen (1970-)
When a Stranger Calls Back '93
Adventures in Spying '92
There Goes My Baby '92
Rich Girl '91
Cutting Class '89
The Phantom of the Opera '89
Popcorn '89
Curse 2: The Bite '88
Billionaire Boys Club '87
The Stepfather '87
Babes in Toyland '86
That Was Then...This Is Now '85
Thunder Alley '85
D.C. Cab '84
Hot Moves '84

Ingrid Schoeller
They Paid with Bullets: Chicago 1929 '69
Psychopath '68

Margareta Schoen
Kriemhilde's Revenge '24
Siegfried '24

Reiner Schoene
Mortal Kombat 2: Annihilation '97
The Gunfighters '87

Ingeborg (Inge) Schoener (1935-)
Mr. Superinvisible '73
Mark of the Devil '69
Cold Steel for Tortuga '65

Dietmar Schoenherr
Journey of Hope '90
The Monster of London City '64

Andrew Schofield
Liam '00
Sid & Nancy '86

Annabel Schofield (1963-)
Exit in Red '97
Body Armor '96
Midnight Blue '96
Solar Crisis '92
Dragonard '88

David Schofield
The Musketeer '01
Gladiator '00
Leo Tolstoy's Anna Karenina '96
Band of Gold '95
Jekyll and Hyde '90
An American Werewolf in London '81

Tom Scholte
Goldrush: A Real Life Alaskan Adventure '98
Live Bait '95

Jason Schombing
Asylum '97
3 Ninjas Kick Back '94
Timecop '94

Reiner Schone
My Little Assassin '99
Crash Dive '96

Frank Schorpion
No Alibi '00
Escape from Wildcat Canyon '99
Dead End '98
Random Encounter '98

Bob Schott (1949-)
Head of the Family '96
Out for Blood '93
Future Hunters '88

Maria Schrader
Advertising Rules! '01
Aimee & Jaguar '98

Lisa Schrage
China White '91
Food of the Gods: Part 2 '88
Hello Mary Lou: Prom Night 2 '87

Bitty Schram
Cleopatra's Second Husband '00
Kissing a Fool '98
Caught '96
One Fine Day '96
My Family Treasure '93
A League of Their Own '92

Max Schreck
Dracula/Garden of Eden '28
Nosferatu '22

Avery Schreiber (1935-2002)
The Student Affair '97
Saturday the 14th Strikes Back '88
Hunk '87
Caveman '81
Galaxina '80
Silent Scream '80

Liev Schreiber (1967-)
The Sum of All Fears '02
Kate & Leopold '01
Hamlet '00
Scream 3 '00
The Hurricane '99
Jakob the Liar '99
RKO 281 '99
A Walk on the Moon '99
Twilight '98
Phantoms '97
Scream 2 '97
Since You've Been Gone '97
Sphere '97
The Daytrippers '96
Ransom '96
Scream '96
Walking and Talking '96
Buffalo Girls '95
Denise Calls Up '95
Mixed Nuts '94
Party Girl '94

Greta Schroder
Nosferatu '22
The Golem '20

Rick Schroder (1970-)
Lost Battalion '01
Ebenezer '97
Hostage High '97
Crimson Tide '95
Texas '94
Call of the Wild '93
Return to Lonesome Dove '93
There Goes My Baby '92
Across the Tracks '89
Lonesome Dove '89
Two Kinds of Love '85
Hansel and Gretel '82
Earthling '80
The Last Flight of Noah's Ark '80
Little Lord Fauntleroy '80
The Champ '79

Barbet Schroeder (1941-)
Celine and Julie Go Boating '74
Six in Paris '68

Steven Schub
The Thirteenth Floor '99
Footsteps '98
Caught '96

Karin Schubert (1944-)
Delusions of Grandeur '76
Till Marriage Do Us Part '74
Cold Eyes of Fear '70

John Schuck (1940-)
The Curse of the Jade Scorpion '01
Holy Matrimony '94
Tales from the Crypt Presents Demon Knight '94
Star Trek 6: The Undiscovered Country '91
My Mom's a Werewolf '89
Second Sight '89
The New Adventures of Pippi Longstocking '88
Star Trek 4: The Voyage Home '86
Finders Keepers '84
Butch and Sundance: The Early Days '79
Thieves Like Us '74
Blade '72
Hammersmith Is Out '72
McCabe & Mrs. Miller '71
Brewster McCloud '70
M*A*S*H '70

Rudolf Schuendler
The American Friend '77
Suspiria '77

Al Schuerman
The Bible and Gun Club '96
Presumed Guilty '91

Rebecca Schull
Analyze This '98
Neil Simon's The Odd Couple 2 '98
That Darn Cat '96
My Life '93

Albert Schultz
White Lies '98
Ebenezer '97
Beethoven Lives Upstairs '92

Dwight Schultz (1947-)
Star Trek: First Contact '96
The Temp '93
Woman with a Past '92
Fat Man and Little Boy '89
The Long Walk Home '89
When Your Lover Leaves '83
Alone in the Dark '82

Matt Schulze
Blade II '02
The Fast and the Furious '01
Dementia '98

Paul Schulze
Panic Room '02
Don't Say a Word '01
Alien Fury: Countdown to Invasion '00
Drowning Mona '00
Grind '96
Illtown '96

Paul Schulzie
Hand Gun '93
Laws of Gravity '92

Wendy Schumacher (1971-)
Fugitive Rage '96
Scorned 2 '96
Animal Instincts 3: The Seductress '95
Star Hunter '95

Hans Schumm
Spy Smasher '42
Spy Smasher Returns '42

Reinhold Schunzel (1886-1954)
Woman in Brown '48
Golden Earrings '47
Notorious '46
The Threepenny Opera '31
Fortune's Fool '21

Maurice Schutz
Vampyr '31
Napoleon '27

Maurice Schwartz (1890-1960)
Salome '53
Tevye '39
Uncle Moses '32

Scott Schwartz (1968-)
Bridge of Dragons '99
A Time to Live '85
Kidco '83
The Toy '82

Jason Schwartzman (1980-)
Simone '02
Slackers '02
Rushmore '98

Arnold Schwarzenegger (1947-)
Collateral Damage '02
The 6th Day '00
End of Days '99
Batman and Robin '97
Eraser '96
Jingle All the Way '96
Junior '94
True Lies '94
Dave '93
Last Action Hero '93
Beretta's Island '92
Terminator 2: Judgment Day '91
Kindergarten Cop '90
Total Recall '90
Red Heat '88
Twins '88
Predator '87
The Running Man '87
Raw Deal '86
Commando '85
Red Sonja '85
Conan the Destroyer '84
The Terminator '84
Conan the Barbarian '82
The Jayne Mansfield Story '80
The Villain '79
Stay Hungry '76
The Long Goodbye '73
Hercules in New York '70

Eric Schweig (1967-)
Big Eden '00

Larry McMurtry's Dead Man's Walk *'96*
Follow the River *'95*
Tom and Huck *'95*
Pontiac Moon *'94*
Squanto: A Warrior's Tale *'94*
The Broken Chain *'93*
The Last of the Mohicans *'92*

Til Schweiger (1963-)
Driven *'01*
SLC Punk! *'99*
Judas Kiss *'98*
The Replacement Killers *'98*
Maybe ... Maybe Not *'94*

Jan Schweiterman
Warlock 3: The End of Innocence *'98*
Good Burger *'97*

David Schwimmer (1966-)
Band of Brothers *'01*
Uprising *'01*
It's the Rage *'99*
Picking Up the Pieces *'99*
Kissing a Fool *'98*
Six Days, Seven Nights *'98*
Apt Pupil *'97*
Breast Men *'97*
Since You've Been Gone *'97*
The Pallbearer *'95*
Flight of the Intruder *'90*

Rusty Schwimmer
The Perfect Storm *'00*
Los Locos Posse *'97*
North Shore Fish *'97*
Prison of Secrets *'97*
Lone Justice 3: Showdown at Plum Creek *'96*
A Little Princess *'95*
Jason Goes to Hell: The Final Friday *'93*
Lone Justice 2 *'93*

Hanna Schygulla (1943-)
Lea *'96*
Dead Again *'91*
The Summer of Miss Forbes *'88*
Casanova *'87*
Forever, Lulu *'87*
Barnum *'86*
Delta Force *'86*
A Love in Germany *'84*
Sheer Madness *'84*
La Nuit de Varennes *'82*
Passion *'82*
Berlin Alexanderplatz *'80*
The Marriage of Maria Braun *'79*
The Wrong Move *'78*
Effi Briest *'74*
The Bitter Tears of Petra von Kant *'72*
The Merchant of Four Seasons *'71*
Beware of a Holy Whore *'70*
Whity *'70*
Gods of the Plague *'69*
Why Does Herr R. Run Amok? *'69*

Yvonne Scio
Sorority Boys *'02*
Redline *'97*

Annabella Sciorra (1964-)
King of the Jungle *'01*
Above Suspicion *'00*
Once in the Life *'00*
Mr. Jealousy *'98*
New Rose Hotel *'98*
What Dreams May Come *'98*
Asteroid *'97*
Cop Land *'97*
Little City *'97*
The Funeral *'96*
Underworld *'96*
The Addiction *'95*
The Cure *'95*
The Innocent Sleep *'95*
National Lampoon's Favorite Deadly Sins *'95*
Mr. Wonderful *'93*
The Night We Never Met *'93*
Romeo Is Bleeding *'93*
The Hand that Rocks the Cradle *'92*
Whispers in the Dark *'92*
The Hard Way *'91*
Jungle Fever *'91*
Prison Stories: Women on the Inside *'91*
Cadillac Man *'90*
Internal Affairs *'90*
Reversal of Fortune *'90*
True Love *'89*

Edith Scob (1937-)
Brotherhood of the Wolf *'01*
The Milky Way *'68*
The Burning Court *'62*
The Horror Chamber of Dr. Faustus *'59*

Dean Scofield
The Last Assassins *'96*
Prehysteria 2 *'94*
Eden 3 *'93*
Eden 4 *'93*

Paul Scofield (1922-)
Animal Farm *'99 (V)*
The Crucible *'96*
Martin Chuzzlewit *'94*
Quiz Show *'94*
Utz *'93*
Hamlet *'90*
Mr. Corbett's Ghost *'90*
Henry V *'89*
When the Whales Came *'89*
The Attic: The Hiding of Anne Frank *'88*
Anna Karenina *'85*
The Curse of King Tut's Tomb *'80 (N)*
Scorpio *'73*
King Lear *'71*
Bartleby *'70*
A Man for All Seasons *'66*
The Train *'65*
Carve Her Name with Pride *'58*

Tracy Scoggins (1959-)
A Crack in the Floor *'00*
The Great American Sex Scandal *'94*
Alien Intruder *'93*
Dead On *'93*
Dollman vs Demonic Toys *'93*
Play Murder for Me *'91*
Timebomb *'91*
Ultimate Desires *'91*
Beyond the Silhouette *'90*
Demonic Toys *'90*
The Red Raven Kiss-Off *'90*
Watchers 2 *'90*
The Gumshoe Kid *'89*
One Last Run *'89*
In Dangerous Company *'88*
Toy Soldiers *'84*
Twirl *'81*

Peter Scolari (1954-)
From the Earth to the Moon *'98*
That Thing You Do! *'96*
Camp Nowhere *'94*
Fallen Angels 2 *'93*
Ticks *'93*
Perfect Harmony *'91*
Corporate Affairs *'90*
Rosebud Beach Hotel *'85*

Zvee Scooler (-1985)
Trumps *'83*
Uncle Moses *'32*

Martin Scorsese (1942-)
The Muse *'99*
With Friends Like These *'98*
Quiz Show *'94*
Search and Destroy *'94*
The Age of Innocence *'93*
Guilty by Suspicion *'91*
Akira Kurosawa's Dreams *'90*
Round Midnight *'86*
After Hours *'85*
Cannonball *'76*
Taxi Driver *'76*
Boxcar Bertha *'72*

Nicolette Scorsese
Aspen Extreme *'93*
Boxing Helena *'93*

Izabela Scorupco
Reign of Fire *'02*
Vertical Limit *'00*
Goldeneye *'95*

Adam Scott
High Crimes *'02*
The Lesser Evil *'97*

Alex Scott (1929-)
Peter's Friends *'92*
Romper Stomper *'92*
Next of Kin *'82*
The Asphyx *'72*
The Abominable Dr. Phibes *'71*
Fahrenheit 451 *'66*

Andrew Scott
The American *'01*
Nora *'00*

Bainbridge Scott
Death Chase *'87*
Hell Squad *'85*

Brenda Scott
Simon, King of the Witches *'71*
Johnny Tiger *'66*

Campbell Scott (1962-)
Follow the Stars Home *'01*
Hamlet *'01*
Lush *'01*
Invasion! *'99*
Hi-Life *'98*
The Imposters *'98*
The Love Letter *'98*
The Spanish Prisoner *'97*
The Daytrippers *'96*
Big Night *'95*
The Kennedys of Massachusetts *'95*
Mrs. Parker and the Vicious Circle *'94*
The Innocent *'93*
Singles *'92*
Dead Again *'91*
Dying Young *'91*
Longtime Companion *'90*
The Sheltering Sky *'90*
The Ghost of Fletcher Ridge *'80s*
Ain't No Way Back *'89*

Carey Scott
Diving In *'90*
Making the Grade *'84*

Debralee Scott (1953-)
Police Academy *'84*
Just Tell Me You Love Me *'80*
Deathmoon *'78*
Our Time *'74*

Donovan Scott (1946-)
Sheena *'84*
Goldilocks & the Three Bears *'83*
Savannah Smiles *'82*
Zorro, the Gay Blade *'81*
1941 *'79*

Dougray Scott (1965-)
Enigma *'01*
Arabian Nights *'00*
Mission: Impossible 2 *'00*
Deep Impact *'98*
Ever After: A Cinderella Story *'98*
Behind the Lines *'97*
Twin Town *'97*
Another 9 1/2 Weeks *'96*

Eric Scott
A Day for Thanks on Walton's Mountain *'82*
The Waltons: The Christmas Carol *'80*

Fred Scott (1902-91)
The Black Six *'74*
Ridin' the Trail *'40*
Code of the Fearless *'39*
In Old Montana *'39*
Ranger's Roundup *'38*
Songs and Bullets *'38*
Melody of the Plains *'37*
The Roamin' Cowboy *'37*
Singing Buckaroo *'37*
Two-Gun Troubador *'37*

Geoffrey Scott
The Morning After *'86*
First & Ten *'85*
First & Ten: The Team Scores Again *'85*

George C. Scott (1927-99)
Inherit the Wind *'99*
Rocky Marciano *'99*
Gloria *'98*
Twelve Angry Men *'97*
Titanic *'96*
Angus *'95*
Prince Brat and the Whipping Boy *'95*
Tyson *'95*
Deadly Currents *'93*
Malice *'93*
Descending Angel *'90*
Exorcist 3: Legion *'90*
The Rescuers Down Under *'90 (V)*
Pals *'87*
Choices *'86*
The Last Days of Patton *'86*
The Murders in the Rue Morgue *'86*
A Christmas Carol *'84*
Firestarter *'84*
Oliver Twist *'82*
Taps *'81*
The Changeling *'80*
The Formula *'80*
Hardcore *'79*
Movie, Movie *'78*
The Prince and the Pauper *'78*
Islands in the Stream *'77*
The Hindenburg *'75*
Bank Shot *'74*
Savage Is Loose *'74*
The Day of the Dolphin *'73*
Oklahoma Crude *'73*
The New Centurions *'72*
Rage *'72*
The Hospital *'71*
They Might Be Giants *'71*
Patton *'70*
Petulia *'68*
Flim-Flam Man *'67*
The Bible *'66*
Dr. Strangelove, or: How I Learned to Stop Worrying and Love the Bomb *'64*
The List of Adrian Messenger *'63*
The Hustler *'61*
Anatomy of a Murder *'59*
The Hanging Tree *'59*

Gordon Scott (1927-)
Death Ray
Tramplers *'66*
Hercules and the Princess of Troy *'65*
Marauder *'65*
Coriolanus, Man without a Country *'64*
Conquest of Mycene *'63*
Gladiator of Rome *'63*
Hero of Rome *'63*
Samson and the 7 Miracles of the World *'62*
Tarzan and the Trappers *'58*

Jacqueline Scott (1935-)
Empire of the Ants *'77*
Charley Varrick *'73*
Duel *'71*

Janette Scott (1938-)
Day of the Triffids *'63*
Paranoiac *'62*
Helen of Troy *'56*

Jay Scott (1931-)
Grave of the Vampire *'72*
All the Lovin' Kinfolk *'70*
The Cut Throats *'69*

John Scott
Horror of Party Beach *'64*
The Tell-Tale Heart *'62*

Judith Scott
Murder She Purred: A Mrs. Murphy Mystery *'98*
Soul Survivor *'95*
Burn Witch, Burn! *'62*

Kathryn Leigh Scott (1933-)
The Last Days of Patton *'86*
Murrow *'86*
Visitor from the Grave *'81*
Witches' Brew *'79*
House of Dark Shadows *'70*

Keith Scott
The Adventures of Rocky & Bullwinkle *'00 (V)*
George of the Jungle *'97 (N)*

Ken Scott (1928-86)
Fantastic Voyage *'66*
Stopover Tokyo *'57*

Kenn Scott
Sworn to Justice *'97*
Shootfighter: Fight to the Death *'93*
Showdown *'93*

Kimberly Scott
K-PAX *'01*
Bellyfruit *'99*
Toothless *'97*
Batman Forever *'95*
Flatliners *'90*
The Abyss *'89*

Larry B. Scott (1961-)
The Bad Pack *'98*
Fear of a Black Hat *'94*
Revenge of the Nerds 4: Nerds in Love *'94*
Super Force *'90*
SnakeEater 2: The Drug Buster *'89*
Extreme Prejudice *'87*
Revenge of the Nerds 2: Nerds in Paradise *'87*
The Children of Times Square *'86*
Iron Eagle *'86*
My Man Adam *'86*
SpaceCamp *'86*
That Was Then...This Is Now *'85*
Revenge of the Nerds *'84*
A Hero Ain't Nothin' but a Sandwich *'78*

Lizabeth Scott (1922-)
Pulp *'72*
Loving You *'57*
Silver Lode *'54*
Scared Stiff *'53*
A Stolen Face *'52*
The Racket *'51*
Easy Living *'49*
Too Late for Tears *'49*
Pitfall *'48*
Dead Reckoning *'47*
The Strange Love of Martha Ivers *'46*

Margaretta Scott (1912-)
Calling Paul Temple *'48*
Counterblast *'48*
Man of Evil *'48*
Action for Slander *'38*
Things to Come *'36*

Martha Scott (1914-)
Adam *'83*
Father Figure *'80*
The Turning Point *'77*
Ben-Hur *'59*
Sayonara *'57*
The Ten Commandments *'56*
Desperate Hours *'55*
Hi Diddle Diddle *'43*
War of the Wildcats *'43*
Cheers for Miss Bishop *'41*
The Howards of Virginia *'40*
Our Town *'40*

Pippa Scott (1935-)
Bad Ronald *'74*
Cold Turkey *'71*
Petulia *'68*

Randolph Scott (1898-1987)
Ride the High Country *'62*
Comanche Station *'60*
Ride Lonesome *'59*
The Tall T *'57*
Seventh Cavalry *'56*
A Lawless Street *'55*
Rage at Dawn *'55*
Ten Wanted Men *'54*
The Stranger Wore a Gun *'53*
Hangman's Knot *'52*
Man in the Saddle *'51*
Santa Fe *'51*
The Cariboo Trail *'50*
The Nevadan *'50*
The Doolins of Oklahoma *'49*
Coroner Creek *'48*
Return of the Bad Men *'48*
Trail Street *'47*
Abilene Town *'46*
Badman's Territory *'46*
Captain Kidd *'45*
China Sky *'44*
Bombardier *'43*
The Desperadoes *'43*
Gung Ho! *'43*
Pittsburgh *'42*
The Spoilers *'42*
To the Shores of Tripoli *'42*
Western Union *'41*
My Favorite Wife *'40*
Virginia City *'40*
Jesse James *'39*
Susannah of the Mounties *'39*
Rebecca of Sunnybrook Farm *'38*
The Texans *'38*
Follow the Fleet *'36*
Go West, Young Man *'36*
The Last of the Mohicans *'36*
The Fighting Westerner *'35*
Roberta *'35*
She *'35*
Wagon Wheels *'34*
Buffalo Stampede *'33*
Heritage of the Desert *'33*
Man of the Forest *'33*
Murders in the Zoo *'33*
Supernatural *'33*
To the Last Man *'33*
Island of Lost Souls *'32*
When the West Was Young *'32*

Seann William Scott (1976-)
American Pie 2 *'01*
Evolution *'01*
Jay and Silent Bob Strike Back *'01*
Dude, Where's My Car? *'00*
Final Destination *'00*
Road Trip *'00*
American Pie *'99*

Susan Scott
Student Confidential *'87*
Trap Them & Kill Them *'84*
Day of the Maniac *'77*
The Slasher *'74*

Timothy Scott (1938-95)
Lone Justice *'93*
Return to Lonesome Dove *'93*
Fried Green Tomatoes *'91*
Inside Out *'91*
Love Me Deadly *'76*

Tom Everett Scott (1970-)
National Lampoon's Van Wilder *'02*
Boiler Room *'00*
Inherit the Wind *'99*
Invasion! *'99*
The Love Letter *'99*
One True Thing *'98*
River Red *'98*
An American Werewolf in Paris *'97*
Dead Man on Campus *'97*
That Thing You Do! *'96*

William Lee Scott (1973-)
Pearl Harbor *'01*
Gone in 60 Seconds *'00*
Black and White *'99*
October Sky *'99*

The Opposite of Sex '98
Zachary Scott (1914-65)
The Young One '61
Flame of the Islands '55
Shotgun '55
Appointment in Honduras '53
Wings of Danger '52
Let's Make It Legal '51
Born to Be Bad '50
Flamingo Road '49
South of St. Louis '48
Cass Timberlane '47
Mildred Pierce '45
The Southerner '45
The Mask of Dimitrios '44
Kristin Scott Thomas (1960-)
Gosford Park '01
Life as a House '01
Up at the Villa '00
Random Hearts '99
Sweet Revenge '98
The Horse Whisperer '97
The English Patient '96
Angels and Insects '95
The Confessional '95
Gulliver's Travels '95
The Pompatus of Love '95
Richard III '95
Four Weddings and a Funeral '94
An Unforgettable Summer '94
The Bachelor '93
Body & Soul '93
Weep No More My Lady '93
Bitter Moon '92
Framed '90
Spymaker: The Secret Life of Ian Fleming '90
The Endless Game '89
A Handful of Dust '88
The Tenth Man '88
Under the Cherry Moon '86
Serena Scott Thomas (1961-)
The World Is Not Enough '99
Relax... It's Just Sex! '98
Nostromo '96
Diana: Her True Story '93
Harnessing Peacocks '92
Andrea Scotti
The Legend of the Wolf Woman '77
Hercules vs. the Sons of the Sun '64
Atom Age Vampire '61
Vito Scotti (1918-96)
I Wonder Who's Killing Her Now? '76
The McCullochs '75
Caper of the Golden Bulls '67
What Did You Do in the War, Daddy? '66
Von Ryan's Express '65
Two Weeks in Another Town '62
Alexander Scourby (1913-85)
The Stuff '85
Me and the Colonel '58
The Big Heat '53
The Redhead from Wyoming '53
Affair in Trinidad '52
Because of You '52
Don Scribner
Rapid Assault '99
Wild Man '89
Slave Girls from Beyond Infinity '87
Angus Scrimm (1926-)
Phantasm 4: Oblivion '98
Vampirella '96
Phantasm 3: Lord of the Dead '94
Mindwarp '91
Subspecies '90
Transylvania Twist '89
Phantasm 2 '88
The Lost Empire '83
Phantasm '79
Sandra Seacat
Crazy in Alabama '99
The Destiny of Marty Fine '96
The New Age '94
Promised Land '88
Susan Seaforth Hayes
Dream Machine '91
Billie '65
Steven Seagal (1952-)
Exit Wounds '01
Ticker '01
The Patriot '99
My Giant '98
Fire Down Below '97
Executive Decision '96
The Glimmer Man '96
Under Siege 2: Dark Territory '95
On Deadly Ground '94
Under Siege '92
Out for Justice '91
Marked for Death '90
Hard to Kill '89
Above the Law '88
Jenny Seagrove (1958-)
Magic Moments '90s
Deadly Game '91
Sherlock Holmes and the Incident at Victoria Falls '91
Bullseye! '90
The Guardian '90
A Chorus of Disapproval '89
Appointment with Death '88
Hold the Dream '86
A Woman of Substance '84
Local Hero '83
Nate and Hayes '83
Douglas Seale (1913-99)
Aladdin '92 (V)
Mr. Destiny '90
Ernest Saves Christmas '88
Franklyn Seales
Southern Comfort '81
The Onion Field '79
Nick Searcy
Cast Away '00
From the Earth to the Moon '98
Perfect Crime '97
The War '94
Jackie Searl (1920-)
That Certain Age '38
Peck's Bad Boy '34
The Return of Casey Jones '34
High Gear '33
Topaze '33
Hearts of Humanity '32
Fred F. Sears (1913-57)
Bonanza Town '51
Down to Earth '47
Heather Sears (1935-94)
Estate of Insanity '70
The Phantom of the Opera '62
Room at the Top '59
The Story of Esther Costello '57
James Seay (1914-92)
The Amazing Colossal Man '57
Beginning of the End '57
Phantom from Space '53
Heartaches '47
Ridin' Down the Canyon '42
Turf Boy '42
In Old Colorado '41
Dorothy Sebastian (1906-57)
Rough Riders' Roundup '39
They Never Come Back '32
His First Command '29
The Single Standard '29
Spite Marriage '29
Our Dancing Daughters '28
A Woman of Affairs '28
Lobo Sebastian
Next Friday '00
Major League 3: Back to the Minors '98
187 '97
Tracy Sebastian
Running Cool '93
On the Air Live with Captain Midnight '79
Jean Seberg (1938-79)
Airport '70
Macho Callahan '70
Paint Your Wagon '69
Pendulum '69
A Fine Madness '66
Moment to Moment '66
Lilith '64
Time Out for Love '61
Let No Man Write My Epitaph '60
Love Play '60
Breathless '59
The Mouse That Roared '59
Bonjour Tristesse '57
Saint Joan '57
Harry Secombe (1921-2001)
Song of Norway '70
Goon Movie '53
Down Among the Z Men '52
Kyle Secor (1958-)
Homicide: The Movie '00
Children of Fury '94
Drop Zone '94
Untamed Heart '93
Silent Victim '92
City Slickers '91
Delusion '91
Sleeping with the Enemy '91
The Heart of Dixie '89
Jon Seda (1970-)
The Street King '02
Homicide: The Movie '00
Price of Glory '00
Dear God '96
Mistrial '96
Primal Fear '96
Selena '96
Sunchaser '96
12 Monkeys '95
I Like It Like That '94
Gladiator '92
Margaret Seddon (1872-1968)
Mr. Deeds Goes to Town '36
The Return of Casey Jones '34
Smilin' Through '33
Little Church Around the Corner '23
Kyra Sedgwick (1965-)
What's Cooking? '00
Labor Pains '99
Critical Care '97
Montana '97
Losing Chase '96
Phenomenon '96
The Low Life '95
Murder in the First '95
Something to Talk About '95
Family Pictures '93
Heart and Souls '93
Miss Rose White '92
Singles '92
Pyrates '91
Women & Men: In Love There Are No Rules '91
Mr. & Mrs. Bridge '90
Born on the Fourth of July '89
Kansas '88
Tai-Pan '86
War & Love '84
Robert Sedgwick
Tune in Tomorrow '90
Nasty Hero '89
Morgan Stewart's Coming Home '87
Miriam Seegar
Strangers of the Evening '32
Seven Keys to Baldpate '29
George Segal (1934-)
Houdini '99
The Cable Guy '96
The Mirror Has Two Faces '96
November Conspiracy '96
The Babysitter '95
Flirting with Disaster '95
It's My Party '95
To Die For '95
Army of One '94
Deep Down '94
Direct Hit '93
Look Who's Talking Now '93
Taking the Heat '93
Me, Myself & I '92
For the Boys '91
All's Fair '89
The Endless Game '89
Look Who's Talking '89
Killing 'Em Softly '85
Not My Kid '85
Stick '85
Cold Room '84
The Zany Adventures of Robin Hood '84
Deadly Game '82
Carbon Copy '81
The Last Married Couple in America '80
Lost and Found '79
Who Is Killing the Great Chefs of Europe? '78
Fun with Dick and Jane '77
Rollercoaster '77
The Duchess and the Dirtwater Fox '76
Black Bird '75
Russian Roulette '75
The Terminal Man '74
Blume in Love '73
A Touch of Class '73
Born to Win '71
The Hot Rock '70
The Owl and the Pussycat '70
Where's Poppa? '70
The Bridge at Remagen '69
No Way to Treat a Lady '68
The St. Valentine's Day Massacre '67
The Lost Command '66
The Quiller Memorandum '66
Who's Afraid of Virginia Woolf? '66
King Rat '65
Ship of Fools '65
Invitation to a Gunfighter '64
Zohra Segal (1912-)
Bhaji on the Beach '94
Masala '91
The Courtesans of Bombay '85
Jonathan Segall
Young Love—Lemon Popsicle 7 '87
Baby Love '83
Hot Bubblegum '81
Pamela Segall
Plump Fiction '97
Eat Your Heart Out '96
Bed of Roses '95
Sgt. Bilko '95
Gate 2 '92
After Midnight '89
Say Anything '89
Something Special '86
Bad Manners '84
Paolo Seganti (1966-)
Sex & Mrs. X '00
Tea with Mussolini '99
L.A. Confidential '97
Still Breathing '97
Jason Segel
Slackers '02
SLC Punk! '99
Santiago Segura
Blade II '02
Dance with the Devil '97
The Day of the Beast '95
Emmanuelle Seigner (1966-)
The Ninth Gate '99
Place Vendome '98
R.P.M. '97
Bitter Moon '92
Frantic '88
Louis Seigner (1903-95)
Mr. Klein '76
This Special Friendship '67
The Eclipse '66
The Would-Be Gentleman '58
Seven Deadly Sins '53
Mathilde Seigner
With a Friend Like Harry '00
Venus Beauty Institute '98
Dry Cleaning '97
John Seitz
Forced March '90
Out of the Rain '90
Five Corners '88
Hard Choices '84
The Prowler '81
Johnny Sekka (1939-)
The Message '77
The Bloodsuckers '70
The Last Safari '67
Khartoum '66
David Selby (1941-)
Horton Foote's Alone '97
Soldier of Fortune Inc. '97
D3: The Mighty Ducks '96
Headless Body in Topless Bar '96
White Squall '96
Intersection '93
Grave Secrets: The Legacy of Hilltop Drive '92
Dying Young '91
Rich and Famous '81
Rich Kids '79
The Girl in Blue '74
Up the Sandbox '72
Night of Dark Shadows '71
Nicholas Selby
Macbeth '71
A Midsummer Night's Dream '68
Sarah Selby (1905-80)
Huckleberry Finn '75
An Affair to Remember '57
Battle Cry '55
Men of the Fighting Lady '54
Battle Circus '53
Marian Seldes (1928-)
Hollywood Ending '02
Town and Country '01
Duets '00
If These Walls Could Talk 2 '00
The Haunting '99
Digging to China '98
Affliction '97
Home Alone 3 '97
Tom and Huck '95
Truman '95
Fingers '78
William (Bill) Self (1921-)
The Thing '51
Sands of Iwo Jima '49
The Story of G.I. Joe '45
Elizabeth Sellars (1923-)
A Voyage 'Round My Father '89
The Mummy's Shroud '67
The Chalk Garden '64
Never Let Go '60
Three Cases of Murder '55
Desiree '54
Madeleine '50
Connie Sellecca (1955-)
The Brotherhood of the Rose '89
The Last Fling '86
Captain America 2: Death Too Soon '79
She's Dressed to Kill '79
Tom Selleck (1945-)
Crossfire Trail '01
Running Mates '00
The Love Letter '99
In and Out '97
Last Stand at Saber River '96
Ruby Jean and Joe '96
Broken Trust '95
Open Season '95
Christopher Columbus: The Discovery '92
Folks! '92
Mr. Baseball '92
Quigley Down Under '90
Three Men and a Little Lady '90
An Innocent Man '89
Her Alibi '88
Three Men and a Baby '87
Lassiter '84
Runaway '84
Bunco '83
High Road to China '83
The Shadow Riders '82
Magnum P.I.: Don't Eat the Snow in Hawaii '80
The Concrete Cowboys '79
The Sacketts '79
Coma '78
The Gypsy Warriors '78
Washington Affair '77
Midway '76
Most Wanted '76
Terminal Island '73
Daughters of Satan '72
Myra Breckinridge '70
Peter Sellers (1925-80)
King Lear '87
Trail of the Pink Panther '82
The Fiendish Plot of Dr. Fu Manchu '80
Being There '79
Prisoner of Zenda '79
Revenge of the Pink Panther '78
America at the Movies '76
Murder by Death '76
The Pink Panther Strikes Again '76
Great McGonagall '75
Ghost in the Noonday Sun '74
Return of the Pink Panther '74
Blockhouse '73
There's a Girl in My Soup '70
The Magic Christian '69
I Love You, Alice B. Toklas! '68
The Party '68
Bobo '67
Casino Royale '67
Woman Times Seven '67
After the Fox '66
The Wrong Box '66
What's New Pussycat? '65
Dr. Strangelove, or: How I Learned to Stop Worrying and Love the Bomb '64
The Pink Panther '64
A Shot in the Dark '64
The World of Henry Orient '64
Heavens Above '63
The Wrong Arm of the Law '63
Lolita '62
Only Two Can Play '62
The Road to Hong Kong '62
Trial & Error '62
Waltz of the Toreadors '62
The Battle of the Sexes '60
The Millionairess '60
Never Let Go '60
Two-Way Stretch '60
Carlton Browne of the F.O. '59
I'm All Right Jack '59
The Mouse That Roared '59
The Naked Truth '58
Tom Thumb '58
Up the Creek '58
The Smallest Show on Earth '57

The Case of the Mukkinese Battle Horn '56
John and Julie '55
The Ladykillers '55
Goon Movie '53
Down Among the Z Men '52

Charles Sellon (1870-1937)
Bright Eyes '34
Ride Him, Cowboy '32
Behind Office Doors '31
Bulldog Drummond '29
The Prairie King '27
The Monster '25

Morton Selten
The Thief of Bagdad '40
The Ghost Goes West '36

David Selvas
Beloved/Friend '99
Caresses '97

Katy Selverstone
Divine Secrets of the Ya-Ya Sisterhood '02
Seven Girlfriends '00

Milton Selzer (1918-)
Miss Rose White '92
Tapeheads '89
The Triangle Factory Fire Scandal '79
The Evil '78

Harry Semels (1887-1946)
Stone of Silver Creek '35
Ghost Valley '32
Texas Buddies '32
America '24

Larry Semon (1889-1928)
Underworld '27
The Wizard of Oz '25

Aparna Sen
Hullabaloo over Georgie & Bonnie's Pictures '78
Bombay Talkie '70

Koreya Senda (1904-)
Tora! Tora! Tora! '70
Face of Another '66
H-Man '59
Gate of Hell '54

Joe Seneca (1914-96)
The Saint of Fort Washington '93
Mississippi Masala '92
Murder on the Bayou '91
Mo' Better Blues '90
The Blob '88
School Daze '88
Crossroads '86
Samaritan: The Mitch Snyder Story '86
Half Slave, Half Free '85
The Verdict '82
Wilma '77

Noriko Sengoku
Godzilla vs. Monster Zero '68
Snow Country '57

Mack Sennett (1980-60)
Man in the Silk Hat '83
Abbott and Costello Meet the Keystone Kops '54
Charlie Chaplin ... Our Hero! '15

Massimo Serato (1916-89)
Don't Look Now '73
Camille 2000 '69
10th Victim '65
Wild, Wild Planet '65
Battle of Valiant '63
Venus Against the Son of Hercules '62
The Naked Maja '59
The Love of Three Queens '54

Rade Serbedzija (1946-)
Rodgers & Hammerstein's South Pacific '01
Mission: Impossible 2 '00
Snatch '00
Space Cowboys '00
Eyes Wide Shut '99
Stigmata '99

Mighty Joe Young '98
Polish Wedding '97
The Saint '97
Broken English '96
The Truce '96
Before the Rain '94

Ivan Sergei (1972-)
Playing Mona Lisa '00
The Big Day '99
The Opposite of Sex '98
Gunfighter's Moon '96
Once a Thief '96

Yahoo Serious (1954-)
Mr. Accident '99
Reckless Kelly '93
Young Einstein '89

Andy Serkis
Lord of the Rings 1: The Fellowship of the Rings '01
Oliver Twist '00
Pandaemonium '00
Among Giants '98
Career Girls '97
Stella Does Tricks '96

Assumpta Serna (1957-)
Managua '97
The Craft '96
Hidden Assassin '94
Sharpe's Company '94
Sharpe's Enemy '94
Chain of Desire '93
Nostradamus '93
Sharpe's Eagle '93
Sharpe's Rifles '93
The Fencing Master '92
Revolver '92
I, the Worst of All '90
Wild Orchid '90
Matador '86

Pepe Serna (1944-)
A Million to Juan '94
American Me '92
The Rookie '90
Bad Jim '89
The Forgotten '89
Break of Dawn '88
Fandango '85
The Adventures of Buckaroo Banzai Across the Eighth Dimension '84
Ballad of Gregorio Cortez '83
The Jerk '79
Sniper '75
Shoot Out '71
The Student Nurses '70

Jacques Sernas (1925-)
Superfly T.N.T. '73
Hornet's Nest '70
55 Days at Peking '63
La Dolce Vita '60
Helen of Troy '56
The Golden Salamander '51

Raymond Serra (1937-)
Men of Means '99
Marilyn & Bobby: Her Final Affair '94
Sugar Hill '94
Alphabet City '84
Splitz '84
Hardhat & Legs '80
Hooch '76

Diego Serrano
The 24 Hour Woman '99
Mixing Nia '98

Julieta Serrano (1933-)
Caresses '97
Tie Me Up! Tie Me Down! '90
Women on the Verge of a Nervous Breakdown '88
Matador '86
Dark Habits '84

Nestor Serrano
Showtime '02
Bait '00
Bringing Out the Dead '99
The Insider '99
The Negotiator '98

Bad Boys '95
City Hall '95
Hangin' with the Homeboys '91
Brenda Starr '86

Michel Serrault (1928-)
Artemisia '97
The Swindle '97
Beaumarchais the Scoundrel '96
Le Bonheur Est Dans le Pre '95
Nelly et Monsieur Arnaud '95
The Old Lady Who Walked in the Sea '91
Dr. Petiot '90
La Cage aux Folles 3: The Wedding '86
La Cage aux Folles 2 '81
The Associate '79
Buffet Froid '79
La Cage aux Folles '78
The Holes '72
The King of Hearts '66
Diabolique '55

Henri Serre
The Fire Within '64
Jules and Jim '62

Jean Servais (1910-76)
The Devil's Nightmare '71
Black Jesus '68
Murder at 45 R.P.M. '65
The Liars '64
That Man from Rio '64
Fever Mounts at El Pao '59
Tamango '59
Rififi '54

Almira Sessions (1888-1974)
Oklahoma Annie '51
Diary of a Chambermaid '46
Miracle of Morgan's Creek '44
The Heat's On '43

John Sessions (1953-)
William Shakespeare's A Midsummer Night's Dream '99
Tom Jones '98
Cousin Bette '97
The Scarlet Tunic '97
A Midwinter's Tale '95
Princess Caraboo '94
Freddie the Frog '92 (V)
Sweet Revenge '90
Henry V '89

Roshan Seth (1942-)
Vertical Limit '00
Such a Long Journey '98
Solitaire for 2 '94
Street Fighter '94
The Buddha of Suburbia '92
Mississippi Masala '92
Stalin '92
London Kills Me '91
Mountains of the Moon '90
Not Without My Daughter '90
Little Dorrit, Film 1: Nobody's Fault '88
Little Dorrit, Film 2: Little Dorrit's Story '88
My Beautiful Laundrette '85
Gandhi '82

Bruce Seton (1909-69)
Gorgo '61
The Blue Lamp '49
Love from a Stranger '37
Demon Barber of Fleet Street '36

Matthew Settle (1969-)
Divine Secrets of the Ya-Ya Sisterhood '02
The In Crowd '00
U-571 '00

Gerard Sety
Van Gogh '92
Modigliani '58

Joan Severance (1958-)
The Last Seduction 2 '98
Matter of Trust '98
In Dark Places '97
Black Scorpion 2: Ground Zero '96
Profile for Murder '96
Black Scorpion '95
Dangerous Indiscretion '94
Hard Evidence '94
Payback '94
Lake Consequence '92
Red Shoe Diaries 2: Double Dare '92
Almost Pregnant '91
Another Pair of Aces: Three of a Kind '91
Illicit Behavior '91
The Runestone '91
Write to Kill '91
No Holds Barred '89
See No Evil, Hear No Evil '89
Lethal Weapon '87

William Severn
Son of Lassie '45
Journey for Margaret '42

Chloe Sevigny (1975-)
If These Walls Could Talk 2 '00
American Psycho '99
Boys Don't Cry '99
Julien Donkey-boy '99
A Map of the World '99
The Last Days of Disco '98
Palmetto '98
Gummo '97
Tree's Lounge '96
Kids '95

Carmen Sevilla
The Boldest Job in the West '71
Pantaloons '57

Billie Seward (1912-82)
The Man from Gun Town '36
Branded a Coward '35
The Revenge Rider '35

Rufus Sewell (1967-)
A Knight's Tale '01
She Creature '01
Arabian Nights '00
Bless the Child '00
In a Savage Land '99
Dangerous Beauty '98
Illuminata '98
Uncorked '98
The Very Thought of You '98
Dark City '97
Hamlet '96
Carrington '95
Cold Comfort Farm '94
A Man of No Importance '94
Middlemarch '93
Twenty-One '91

Andrzej Seweryn (1946-)
Lucie Aubrac '98
Genealogies of a Crime '97
Schindler's List '93
The Conductor '80
Without Anesthesia '78
Land of Promise '74

Brendan Sexton, III (1980-)
Black Hawk Down '01
Session 9 '01
Boys Don't Cry '99
Desert Blue '98
Pecker '98
Hurricane Streets '96
Welcome to the Dollhouse '95

Athene Seyler (1889-1990)
Curse of the Demon '57
The Franchise Affair '52
Sailing Along '38
Non-Stop New York '37
Private Life of Don Juan '34

Anne Seymour
Gemini Affair '80s
All the King's Men '49

Cara Seymour
American Psycho '99
Dancer in the Dark '99
A Good Baby '99

Carolyn Seymour (1947-)
Red Shoe Diaries: Swimming Naked '00
The Break '97
Red Shoe Diaries: Strip Poker '96
Midnight Cabaret '90
Girls of the White Orchid '85
The Assignment '78
The Bitch '78
Gumshoe '72
The Ruling Class '72

Dan Seymour (1915-93)
Return of the Fly '59
Abbott and Costello Meet the Mummy '55
Key Largo '48
Hard-Boiled Mahoney '47
A Night in Casablanca '46
To Have & Have Not '44

Jane Seymour (1951-)
Quest for Camelot '98 (V)
Heidi '93
Praying Mantis '93
Are You Lonesome Tonight '92
Sunstroke '92
Matters of the Heart '90
The Tunnel '89
War & Remembrance: The Final Chapter '89
Jack the Ripper '88
Onassis '88
War & Remembrance '88
The Woman He Loved '88
Head Office '86
Lassiter '84
The Haunting Passion '83
Jamaica Inn '82
The Scarlet Pimpernel '82
East of Eden '80
Oh, Heavenly Dog! '80
Somewhere in Time '80
Battlestar Galactica '78
The Four Feathers '78
Killer on Board '77
Sinbad and the Eye of the Tiger '77
The Story of David '76
Live and Let Die '73
The Strauss Family '73
Young Winston '72
The Only Way '70

Jeff Seymour
Wedding Bell Blues '96
Rave Review '95

Ralph Seymour
Rain Man '88
Empire of the Sun '87
Killer Party '86
Fletch '85
Meatballs 2 '84

Delphine Seyrig (1932-90)
Window Shopping '86
Grain of Sand '84
I Sent a Letter to My Love '81
The Black Windmill '74
A Doll's House '73
The Discreet Charm of the Bourgeoisie '72
Daughters of Darkness '71
Peau D'Ane '71
Donkey Skin '70
The Milky Way '68
Stolen Kisses '68
Accident '67
Muriel '63
Last Year at Marienbad '61

Serif Sezer
Steam: A Turkish Bath '96
Yol '82

Ted Shackleford (1946-)
The Spider and the Fly '94
Dying to Remember '93

Baby of the Bride '91
Sweet Revenge '87
Summer Fantasy '84

Glenn Shadix (1952-)
The Empty Mirror '99
Red Dirt '99
Chairman of the Board '97
Dunston Checks In '95
Dark Side of Genius '94
Love Affair '94
My Summer Story '94
Demolition Man '93
The Nightmare before Christmas '93 (V)
Sleepwalkers '92
Bingo '91
Nightlife '90
The Applegates '89
Heathers '89
Beetlejuice '88

Bobby Ray Shafer
Psycho Cop 2 '94
Psycho Cop '88

Paul Shaffer (1949-)
Blues Brothers 2000 '98
Hercules '97 (V)
The Return of Spinal Tap '92
Light Years '88 (V)
This Is Spinal Tap '84
Mr. Mike's Mondo Video '79

Jamal Shah
K2: The Ultimate High '92
Traffik '90

Naseeruddin Shah
Monsoon Wedding '01
Such a Long Journey '98

Tupac Shakur (1971-96)
Gang Related '96
Gridlock'd '96
Above the Rim '94
Bullet '94
Poetic Justice '93
Juice '92

Victoria Shalet
Haunted '95
The Maid '90

Tony Shalhoub (1953-)
Life or Something Like It '02
Imposter '01
The Man Who Wasn't There '01
Spy Kids '01
13 Ghosts '01
Galaxy Quest '99
That Championship Season '99
The Tic Code '99
A Civil Action '98
The Imposters '98
Paulie '98
Primary Colors '98
The Siege '98
Gattaca '97
A Life Less Ordinary '97
Men in Black '97
Big Night '95
I.Q. '94
Honeymoon in Vegas '92
Barton Fink '91
Quick Change '90

Chuck Shamata
Snap Decision '01
Princes in Exile '90
Unfinished Business '89
Night Friend '87
Mafia Princess '86
Joshua Then and Now '85
Death Weekend '76

Garry Shandling (1949-)
Town and Country '01
What Planet Are You From? '00
Dr. Dolittle '98 (V)
Hurlyburly '98
Love Affair '94
Mixed Nuts '94
The Night We Never Met '93
Mother Goose Rock 'n' Rhyme '90

Michael Shaner
Traveller '96
The Expert '95
Bloodfist '89
Crime Zone '88

Amelia Shankley
The Little Princess '87
Dreamchild '85

Don Shanks (1950-)
3 Ninjas Knuckle Up '95
The Legend of Wolf Mountain '92
Spirit of the Eagle '90
Halloween 5: The Revenge of Michael Myers '89
The Last of the Mohicans '85
Mountain Man '77
Life & Times of Grizzly Adams '74

Michael Shanks
Escape from Mars '99
Terror Train '80

Al Shannon
Out of the Rain '90
The Drifter '88

Frank Shannon
Flash Gordon Conquers the Universe '40
Flash Gordon: Rocketship '40

Harry Shannon (1890-1964)
Summer and Smoke '61
Man or Gun '58
Written on the Wind '56
Phantom Stallion '54
Cow Town '50
The Jackie Robinson Story '50
The Underworld Story '50
Fighting Father Dunne '48
The Red House '47
The Yellow Rose of Texas '44
Idaho '43
Song of Texas '43
The Lady Is Willing '42
Citizen Kane '41

Michael Shannon
High Crimes '02
Pearl Harbor '01
Vanilla Sky '01
Chicago Cab '98

Michael J. Shannon
Detonator 2: Night Watch '95
We'll Meet Again '82
Future Cop '76

Molly Shannon (1964-)
Osmosis Jones '01
Serendipity '01
Wet Hot American Summer '01
Dr. Seuss' How the Grinch Stole Christmas '00
My 5 Wives '00
Never Been Kissed '99
Superstar '99
Analyze This '98
A Night at the Roxbury '98
The Phantom of the Opera '89

Peggy Shannon (1910-41)
The Case of the Lucky Legs '35
Deluge '33
False Faces '32

Polly Shannon
The Triangle '01
The Girl Next Door '98
A Young Connecticut Yankee in King Arthur's Court '95

Vicellous Reon Shannon
Hart's War '02
Dancing in September '00
Freedom Song '00
The Hurricane '99

Omar Sharif (1932-)
The 13th Warrior '99
Heaven Before I Die '96
Catherine the Great '95
Gulliver's Travels '95
Lie Down with Lions '94
Beyond Justice '92
Grand Larceny '92
Mrs. 'Arris Goes to Paris '92
The Possessed '88
Anastasia: The Mystery of Anna '86
Harem '86
Peter the Great '86
The Far Pavilions '84
Top Secret! '84
Green Ice '81
The Baltimore Bullet '80
Oh, Heavenly Dog! '80
Pleasure Palace '80
Ashanti, Land of No Mercy '79
S*H*E '79
Sidney Sheldon's Bloodline '79
Crime & Passion '75
Funny Lady '75
Juggernaut '74
The Tamarind Seed '74
The Last Valley '71
The Horsemen '70
MacKenna's Gold '69
Funny Girl '68
Mayerling '68
Night of the Generals '67
Doctor Zhivago '65
Behold a Pale Horse '64
The Fall of the Roman Empire '64
Lawrence of Arabia '62

David Shark (1962-)
Femme Fontaine: Killer Babe for the C.I.A. '95
The Legend of Wolf Mountain '92
Dark Rider '91
Invasion Force '90
Soultaker '90

Ray Sharkey (1953-93)
Urban Crossfire '94
Cop and a Half '93
Caged Fear '92
Chrome Soldiers '92
Round Trip to Heaven '92
Zebrahead '92
Relentless 2: Dead On '91
The Rain Killer '90
The Take '90
Act of Piracy '89
Capone '89
The Neon Empire '89
Scenes from the Class Struggle in Beverly Hills '89
Wired '89
Private Investigations '87
No Mercy '86
Wise Guys '86
Behind Enemy Lines '85
Hellhole '85
Body Rock '84
Dubeat-E-O '84
Regina '83
Some Kind of Hero '82
Heart Beat '80
Idolmaker '80
Willie & Phil '80
Who'll Stop the Rain? '78

John Sharp
Misunderstood '87
The Fiendish Plot of Dr. Fu Manchu '80

Lesley Sharp
The Full Monty '96
Priest '94
Naked '93
The Rachel Papers '89
Rita, Sue & Bob Too '87

Leslie Sharp
From Hell '01
Great Expectations '99

Thom Sharp
Heartbreak Ridge '86
Stoogemania '85

Albert Sharpe
Darby O'Gill & the Little People '59
Up in Central Park '48

Cornelia Sharpe (1947-)
Venom '82
S*H*E '79
The Arab Conspiracy '76
The Reincarnation of Peter Proud '75
Busting '74
Serpico '73

David Sharpe (1911-79)
Colorado Serenade '46
Haunted Ranch '43
Two-Fisted Justice '43
Texas to Bataan '42
Trail Riders '42
Silver Stallion '41
Covered Wagon Trails '40
Doomed at Sundown '37
Melody of the Plains '37
Where Trails Divide '37
Gun Grit '36
The Adventurous Knights '35
Roaring Roads '35
Social Error '35

Melanie Shatner (1964-)
Surface to Air '98
Unknown Origin '95
Cthulhu Mansion '91
Syngenor '90
Star Trek 5: The Final Frontier '89

William Shatner (1931-)
American Psycho 2: All American Girl '02
Showtime '02
Osmosis Jones '01 (V)
Miss Congeniality '00
Free Enterprise '98
Land of the Free '98
Double Play '96
Star Trek: Generations '94
TekWar '94
National Lampoon's Loaded Weapon 1 '93
Bill & Ted's Bogus Journey '91
Star Trek 6: The Undiscovered Country '91
Star Trek 5: The Final Frontier '89
Broken Angel '88
Star Trek 4: The Voyage Home '86
Secrets of a Married Man '84
Star Trek 3: The Search for Spock '84
Airplane 2: The Sequel '82
Star Trek 2: The Wrath of Khan '82
Visiting Hours '82
The Babysitter '80
The Kidnapping of the President '80
Star Trek: The Motion Picture '80
Riel '79
Third Walker '79
The Bastard '78
The Crash of Flight 401 '78
Little Women '78
Kingdom of the Spiders '77
Whale of a Tale '76
Devil's Rain '75
The Barbary Coast '74
Big Bad Mama '74
Impulse '74
Pray for the Wildcats '74
Pioneer Woman '73
The People '71
The Andersonville Trial '70
White Comanche '67
Incubus '65
Judgment at Nuremberg '61
Shame '61
The Brothers Karamazov '58

Shari Shattuck (1960-)
Body Chemistry 3: Point of Seduction '93
Dead On '93
Out for Blood '93
Mad About You '90
Arena '89
The Spring '89
Desert Warrior '88
Tainted '88
The Uninvited '88
Hot Child in the City '87
Number One with a Bullet '87
Naked Cage '86

Grant Shaud (1960-)
The Crow: Salvation '00
From the Earth to the Moon '98
The Distinguished Gentleman '92
Wall Street '87

Mickey Shaughnessy (1920-85)
Primal Scream '87
My Dog, the Thief '69
A Global Affair '63
The King of the Roaring '20s: The Story of Arnold Rothstein '61
Pocketful of Miracles '61
The Adventures of Huckleberry Finn '60
Gunman's Walk '58
Designing Woman '57
Jailhouse Rock '57
Conquest of Space '55
From Here to Eternity '53
Last of the Comanches '52

Helen Shaver (1952-)
Tremors 3: Back to Perfection '01
Common Ground '00
The Sweetest Gift '98
The Craft '96
Poltergeist: The Legacy '96
Rowing Through '96
Tremors 2: Aftershocks '96
Born to Be Wild '95
Open Season '95
The Outer Limits: Sandkings '95
Morning Glory '93
Murder So Sweet '93
That Night '93
Trial and Error '92
Zebrahead '92
Dr. Bethune '90
Innocent Victim '90
Pair of Aces '90
The Land Before Time '88 (V)
The Believers '87
The Color of Money '86
Desert Hearts '86
Lost '86
The Park Is Mine '85
Shoot '85
The War Boy '85
Best Defense '84
Coming Out Alive '84
Harry Tracy '83
The Osterman Weekend '83
Gas '81
Off Your Rocker '80
The Amityville Horror '79
High Ballin' '78
In Praise of Older Women '78
Outrageous! '77
Starship Invasions '77
Who Has Seen the Wind? '77

Anabel Shaw (1923-)
To Hell and Back '55
Gun Crazy '49
Shock! '46

Bill Shaw
Total Reality '97
Ghostriders '87

Bobbi Shaw
Beach Blanket Bingo '65
How to Stuff a Wild Bikini '65
Pajama Party '64

C. Montague Shaw (1884-1968)
Holt of the Secret Service '42
The Rains Came '39
Square Shoulders '29

Crystal Shaw
Laser Moon '92
Hardbodies '84

Fiona Shaw (1959-)
Harry Potter and the Sorcerer's Stone '01
The Seventh Stream '01
The Triumph of Love '01
The Last September '99
RKO 281 '99
The Avengers '98
The Butcher Boy '97
Jane Eyre '96
Leo Tolstoy's Anna Karenina '96
Persuasion '95
Maria's Child '93
Super Mario Bros. '93
Undercover Blues '93
London Kills Me '91
Mountains of the Moon '90
Three Men and a Little Lady '90
My Left Foot '89

Martin Shaw (1945-)
The Scarlet Pimpernel '99
The Scarlet Pimpernel 2: Mademoiselle Guillotine '99
The Scarlet Pimpernel 3: The Kidnapped King '99
Rhodes '97
The Last Place on Earth '94
Intrigue '90
The Hound of the Baskervilles '83
Golden Voyage of Sinbad '73
Macbeth '71

Oscar Shaw (1887-1067)
Rhythm on the River '40
The Cocoanuts '29

Reta Shaw (1912-)
The Ghost and Mr. Chicken '66
The Pajama Game '57
All Mine to Give '56
Picnic '55

Robert Shaw (1927-78)
Avalanche Express '79
Force 10 from Navarone '78
Black Sunday '77
The Deep '77
Robin and Marian '76
Swashbuckler '76
Jaws '75
The Taking of Pelham One Two Three '74
The Sting '73
Diamonds '72
A Reflection of Fear '72
A Town Called Hell '72
Young Winston '72
Battle of Britain '69
A Man for All Seasons '66
Battle of the Bulge '65
From Russia with Love '63

Sandie Shaw
Eat the Rich '87
Absolute Beginners '86

Sebastian Shaw (1905-94)
High Season '88
Reilly: Ace of Spies '87
Return of the Jedi '83
A Midsummer Night's Dream '68
Spy in Black '39
The Squeaker '37
Department Store '35

Stan Shaw (1952-)
Freedom Song '00
Snake Eyes '98
Daylight '96
Cutthroat Island '95
Houseguest '94
Lifepod '93
Body of Evidence '92
Fried Green Tomatoes '91
The Court Martial of Jackie Robinson '90
Fear '90
Billionaire Boys Club '87
Busted Up '86
The Gladiator '86
Samaritan: The Mitch Snyder Story '86
D.P. '85
Runaway '84
Dirkham Detective Agency '83
Tough Enough '83
Roots: The Next Generation '79
The Boys in Company C '77
Bingo Long Traveling All-Stars & Motor Kings '76

Susan Shaw (1929-78)
Blonde Blackmailer '58
Fire Maidens from Outer Space '56
The Woman in Question '50
Train of Events '49

Susan Damante Shaw
Image of Passion '86
Mountain Family Robinson '79
Further Adventures of the Wilderness Family, Part 2 '77
The Adventures of the Wilderness Family '76
The Student Teachers '73

Victoria Shaw
Alvarez Kelly '66
The Eddy Duchin Story '56

Vinessa Shaw (1976-)
40 Days and 40 Nights '02
Corky Romano '01
The '70s '00
Eyes Wide Shut '99
Fallen Angels 2 '93
Hocus Pocus '93
Ladybugs '92

Joan Shawlee (1929-87)
The Reluctant Astronaut '67
The Apartment '60
Some Like It Hot '59
Francis Joins the WACs '54
Prehistoric Women '50
Buck Privates Come Home '47
House of Horrors '46

Dick Shawn (1929-)
Rented Lips '88
Maid to Order '87
Beer '85
Check Is in the Mail '85
Angel '84
The Emperor's New Clothes '84
The Secret Diary of Sigmund Freud '84
Young Warriors '83
Goodbye Cruel World '82
Love at First Bite '79
Evil Roy Slade '71
The Happy Ending '69
The Producers '68
What Did You Do in the War, Daddy? '66
It's a Mad, Mad, Mad, Mad World '63

Wallace Shawn (1943-)
The Curse of the Jade Scorpion '01
The Prime Gig '00
Toy Story 2 '99 (V)
My Favorite Martian '98
Noah '98
Critical Care '97
Just Write '97
House Arrest '96
Vegas Vacation '96
All Dogs Go to Heaven 2 '95 (V)
Clueless '95
Toy Story '95 (V)
The Wife '95

Canadian Bacon '94
A Goofy Movie '94 (V)
Mrs. Parker and the Vicious Circle '94
Vanya on 42nd Street '94
The Cemetery Club '93
The Magic Bubble '93
The Double O Kid '92
Mom and Dad Save the World '92
Nickel & Dime '92
Shadows and Fog '92
Scenes from the Class Struggle in Beverly Hills '89
She's Out of Control '89
We're No Angels '89
The Moderns '88
The Bedroom Window '87
Nice Girls Don't Explode '87
Prick Up Your Ears '87
The Princess Bride '87
Radio Days '87
Heaven Help Us '85
The Bostonians '84
Crackers '84
The Hotel New Hampshire '84
Micki & Maude '84
Strong Medicine '84
Deal of the Century '83
Strange Invaders '83
First Time '82
A Little Sex '82
My Dinner with Andre '81
Simon '80
Manhattan '79

Lin Shaye (1944-)
Attention Shoppers '99
Detroit Rock City '99
There's Something about Mary '98
Trading Favors '97
Kingpin '96
Dumb & Dumber '94

Konstantin Shayne (1888-1974)
The Stranger '46
The Seventh Cross '44
Five Graves to Cairo '43

Robert Shayne (1900-92)
Teenage Caveman '58
The Giant Claw '57
The Indestructible Man '56
Marshal of Cedar Rock '53
The Spirit of West Point '47
Welcome Stranger '47
Behind the Mask '46
Christmas in Connecticut '45
Rhapsody in Blue '45

Tamara Shayne
The Jolson Story '46
Somewhere I'll Find You '42

Elizabeth She
The Howling: New Moon Rising '95
Howling 5: The Rebirth '89

Gloria Shea (1913-)
Last Days of Pompeii '35
Demon for Trouble '34
The Fiddlin' Buckaroo '33
Phantom of the Air '33
Dude Bandit '32

John Shea (1948-)
Magic Moments '90s
The Adventures of Sebastian Cole '99
Southie '98
The Apocalypse Watch '97
Backstreet Justice '93
Freejack '92
Honey, I Blew Up the Kid '92
Ladykiller '92
Small Sacrifices '89
Light Years '88 (V)
A New Life '88
Stealing Home '88
Unsettled Land '88
Honeymoon '87
The Impossible Spy '87
A Case of Deadly Force '86
The Dining Room '86
Windy City '84
Kennedy '83
Missing '82
Hussy '80
Nativity '78

Katt Shea
Barbarian Queen '85
Devastator '85
Hollywood Hot Tubs '84
Preppies '82

Al Shean (1868-1949)
Ziegfeld Girl '41
The Great Waltz '38
It Could Happen to You '37
Tim Tyler's Luck '37
San Francisco '36

Harry Shearer (1943-)
Dick '99
EDtv '99
Godzilla '98
Small Soldiers '98 (V)
Almost Heroes '97 (V)
A League of Their Own '92 (V)
The Return of Spinal Tap '92
The Fisher King '91
Pure Luck '91
Blood & Concrete: A Love Story '90
Portrait of a White Marriage '88
This Is Spinal Tap '84
The Right Stuff '83
One Trick Pony '80

Moira Shearer (1926-)
Black Tights '60
Peeping Tom '60
The Tales of Hoffmann '51
The Red Shoes '48

Norma Shearer (1900-83)
Idiot's Delight '39
The Women '39
Marie Antoinette '38
Romeo and Juliet '36
The Barretts of Wimpole Street '34
Riptide '34
Smilin' Through '33
Strange Interlude '32
A Free Soul '31
Private Lives '31
The Divorcee '30
The Student Prince in Old Heidelberg '27
He Who Gets Slapped '24

Alan Shearman
Mother Teresa: In the Name of God's Poor '97
Stoogemania '85
Footlight Frenzy '84
Bullshot '83

Ally Sheedy (1962-)
Sugar Town '99
The Fury Within '98
High Art '98
Buried Alive 2 '97
Amnesia '96
One Night Stand '95
The Tin Soldier '95
The Haunting of Seacliff Inn '94
Parallel Lives '94
Chantilly Lace '93
Man's Best Friend '93
The Pickle '93
Red Shoe Diaries 4: Auto Erotica '93
Tattle Tale '92
Only the Lonely '91
Betsy's Wedding '90
Fear '90
The Lost Capone '90
The Heart of Dixie '89
Maid to Order '87
We Are the Children '87
Blue City '86
Short Circuit '86
The Breakfast Club '85
St. Elmo's Fire '85
Twice in a Lifetime '85
Oxford Blues '84
Bad Boys '83
WarGames '83
The Best Little Girl in the World '81

Gladys Sheehan
Hear My Song '91
Rawhead Rex '87

Charlie Sheen (1965-)
Good Advice '01
Lisa Picard Is Famous '01
Rated X '00
Being John Malkovich '99
Free Money '99
No Code of Conduct '98
Postmortem '98
Under Pressure '98
Money Talks '97
The Arrival '96
The Shadow Conspiracy '96
All Dogs Go to Heaven 2 '95 (V)
Major League 2 '94
Terminal Velocity '94
The Chase '93
Deadfall '93
Hot Shots! Part Deux '93
National Lampoon's Loaded Weapon 1 '93
The Three Musketeers '93
Beyond the Law '92
Hot Shots! '91
Men at Work '90
Navy SEALS '90
The Rookie '90
Backtrack '89
Cadence '89
Courage Mountain '89
Major League '89
Tale of Two Sisters '89 (N)
Eight Men Out '88
Never on Tuesday '88
Young Guns '88
No Man's Land '87
Three for the Road '87
Wall Street '87
The Wraith '87
Ferris Bueller's Day Off '86
Lucas '86
Platoon '86
The Boys Next Door '85
Red Dawn '84
Silence of the Heart '84

Martin Sheen (1940-)
O '01
D.R.E.A.M. Team '99
Lost and Found '99
Storm Tracker '99
A Texas Funeral '99
Thrill Seekers '99
Gunfighter '98
Monument Ave. '98
No Code of Conduct '98
A Stranger in the Kingdom '98
Hostile Waters '97
One of Her Own '97
Spawn '97
Truth or Consequences, N.M. '97
Entertaining Angels: The Dorothy Day Story '96
The War at Home '96
The American President '95
Born Wild '95
The Break '95
Captain Nuke and the Bomber Boys '95
Dillinger and Capone '95
Boca '94
Fortunes of War '94
Gospa '94
Roswell: The U.F.O. Cover-Up '94
Gettysburg '93
The Ghost Brigade '93
Hear No Evil '93
Hot Shots! Part Deux '93
Queen '93
When the Bough Breaks '93
Hearts of Darkness: A Filmmaker's Apocalypse '91
Original Intent '91
Shattered Spirits '91
The Maid '90
Beverly Hills Brats '89
Beyond the Stars '89
Cadence '89
Cold Front '89
Nightbreaker '89
Da '88
Judgment in Berlin '88
The Believers '87
Conspiracy: The Trial of the Chicago Eight '87
Siesta '87
Wall Street '87
News at Eleven '86
Samaritan: The Mitch Snyder Story '86
Consenting Adult '85
Fourth Wise Man '85
Out of the Darkness '85
Firestarter '84
The Guardian '84
Dead Zone '83
In the King of Prussia '83
Kennedy '83
Loophole '83
Man, Woman & Child '83
Blind Ambition '82
Enigma '82
Gandhi '82
In the Custody of Strangers '82
That Championship Season '82
The Final Countdown '80
Apocalypse Now '79
Eagle's Wing '79
The Cassandra Crossing '76
The Little Girl Who Lives down the Lane '76
Sweet Hostage '75
Badlands '74
The Execution of Private Slovik '74
Legend of Earl Durand '74
Missiles of October '74
Catholics '73
Pursuit '72
Rage '72
Where the Eagle Flies '72
No Drums, No Bugles '71
When the Line Goes Through '71
The Andersonville Trial '70
Catch-22 '70
The Subject Was Roses '68
The Incident '67

Michael Sheen (1969-)
Wilde '97
Gallowglass '95
Mary Reilly '95
Othello '95

Ruth Sheen
The Young Poisoner's Handbook '94
High Hopes '88

Chad Sheets
Lone Star Kid '88
Dirt Bike Kid '86

Craig Sheffer (1960-)
Maze '01
Deep Core '00
Hellraiser 5: Inferno '00
Turbulence 2: Fear of Flying '99
The Fall '98
Shadow of Doubt '98
Double Take '97
Flypaper '97
Miss Evers' Boys '97
Bliss '96
Head Above Water '96
Bloodknot '95
The Grave '95
In Pursuit of Honor '95
The Road Killers '95
The Desperate Trail '94
Sleep with Me '94
Fire in the Sky '93
Fire on the Amazon '93
The Program '93
A River Runs Through It '92
Blue Desert '91
Eye of the Storm '91
Instant Karma '90
Nightbreed '90
Babycakes '89
Split Decisions '88
Some Kind of Wonderful '87
Voyage of the Rock Aliens '87
Fire with Fire '86
That Was Then...This Is Now '85

John(ny) Sheffield (1931-)
Tarzan's New York Adventure '42
Tarzan's Secret Treasure '41
Tarzan Finds a Son '39

Maceo B. Sheffield (1897-1959)
Look Out Sister '48
Gang War '40
Harlem on the Prairie '38

Reginald (Reggie, Reggy) Sheffield (1901-57)
Second Chance '53
Gunga Din '39
The Lives of a Bengal Lancer '35

Gene Sheldon (1909-82)
The Sign of Zorro '60
Toby Tyler '59
The Dolly Sisters '46

Tom Shell
Dinosaur Island '93
Teenage Exorcist '93
Beverly Hills Vamp '88
Surf Nazis Must Die '87

Stephen Shellen (1957-)
Luscious '97
Rude '96
Dr. Jekyll and Ms. Hyde '95
Deceptions 2: Edge of Deception '94
Model by Day '94
Stand Off '93
A River Runs Through It '92
Still Life '92
Victim of Beauty '91
Damned River '89
Casual Sex? '88
Murder One '88
The Stepfather '87
Gimme an F '85
Talking Walls '85

Barbara Shelley (1933-)
The Dark Angel '91
Madhouse Mansion '74
Dracula, Prince of Darkness '66
Rasputin the Mad Monk '66
The Gorgon '64
Village of the Damned '60
Blood of the Vampire '58
Cat Girl '57

Carol(e) Shelley (1939-)
Hercules '97 (V)
Robin Hood '73 (V)
The Aristocats '70 (V)
The Odd Couple '68

Rachel Shelley
B.U.S.T.E.D. '99
Dead of Night '99
Photographing Fairies '97

Adrienne Shelly (1966-)
Grind '96
Sudden Manhattan '96
The Road Killers '95
Sleep with Me '94
Sleeping with Strangers '94
Teresa's Tattoo '94
Hexed '93
Hold Me, Thrill Me, Kiss Me '93
Big Girls Don't Cry...They Get Even '92
Trust '91
The Unbelievable Truth '90

Deborah Shelton (1952-)
Desire '95
Plughead Rewired: Circuitry Man 2 '94
Silk Degrees '94
Sins of the Night '93
Blind Vision '91
Hunk '87
Perfect Victims '87
Body Double '84
Mysterious Island of Beautiful Women '79

John Shelton
The Time of Their Lives '46
Ghost City '32

Joy Shelton (1922-2000)
Impulse '55
Norman Conquest '53
Uneasy Terms '48

Marla Shelton
Escape to Paradise '39
The Phantom Rider '37
Stand-In '37

Marley Shelton (1974-)
Bubble Boy '01
Sugar & Spice '01
Valentine '01
The Bachelor '99
Never Been Kissed '99
Pleasantville '98
Too Smooth '98
Lured Innocence '97
Trojan War '97
Warriors of Virtue '97
The Sandlot '93

Reid Shelton (1925-97)
First & Ten '85
First & Ten: The Team Scores Again '85
Breakin' Through '84

Parry Shen (1979-)
The New Guy '02
Shrieker '97

Paul Shenar (1936-89)
The Big Blue '88
The Bedroom Window '87
Best Seller '87
Man on Fire '87
Raw Deal '86
Brass '85
Dream Lover '85
Deadly Force '83
Scarface '83

Ben Shenkman
Chasing Sleep '00
Pi '98

Hilary Shepard
Avalanche '99
Last Exit to Earth '96
Scanner Cop '94
Peacemaker '90

Jan Shepard
Attack of the Giant Leeches '59
King Creole '58

Jewel Shepard (1962-)
Caged Heat 2: Stripped of Freedom '94
Scanners: The Showdown '94
Hollywood Hot Tubs 2: Educating Crystal '89
Scenes from the Goldmine '87
Return of the Living Dead '85
Hollywood Hot Tubs '84
My Tutor '82

Patty (Patti) Shepard (1945-)
Surprise Attack '70s
The Stranger and the Gunfighter '76
Crypt of the Living Dead '73
Curse of the Devil '73
Witches' Mountain '71
The Werewolf vs. the Vampire Woman '70
Dracula vs. Frankenstein '69

Sam Shepard (1943-)
Black Hawk Down '01
Shot in the Heart '01
Swordfish '01
All the Pretty Horses '00
Hamlet '00
One Kill '00
The Pledge '00
Dash and Lilly '99
Purgatory '99
Snow Falling on Cedars '99

Curtain Call '97
The Only Thrill '97
Lily Dale '96
The Good Old Boys '95
Larry McMurtry's Streets of Laredo '95
Safe Passage '94
The Pelican Brief '93
Thunderheart '92
Bright Angel '91
Defenseless '91
Voyager '91
Steel Magnolias '89
Baby Boom '87
Crimes of the Heart '86
Fool for Love '86
Country '84
The Right Stuff '83
Frances '82
Raggedy Man '81
Resurrection '80
Days of Heaven '78

Cybill Shepherd (1950-)
The Last Word '95
Married to It '93
Once Upon a Crime '92
Memphis '91
Alice '90
Texasville '90
Which Way Home '90
Chances Are '89
The Long, Hot Summer '86
Moonlighting '85
Seduced '85
Secrets of a Married Man '84
The Return '80
Americathon '79
The Lady Vanishes '79
A Guide for the Married Woman '78
Silver Bears '78
Special Delivery '76
Taxi Driver '76
Daisy Miller '74
The Heartbreak Kid '72
The Last Picture Show '71

Elizabeth Shepherd (1936-)
End of Summer '97
The Double Negative '80
Phoenix Team '80
Invitation to the Wedding '73
Tomb of Ligeia '64

Jack Shepherd (1940-)
Charlotte Gray '01
Lorna Doone '01
Wonderland '99
The Scarlet Tunic '97
No Escape '94
Twenty-One '91
Murderers Among Us: The Simon Wiesenthal Story '89
Escape from Sobibor '87
The Virgin Soldiers '69

John Shepherd
Banzai Runner '86
Thunder Run '86
Friday the 13th, Part 5: A New Beginning '85

Simon Shepherd (1956-)
Catherine Cookson's Tilly Trotter '99
Tales of Erotica '93
Emily Bronte's Wuthering Heights '92
Fire, Ice and Dynamite '91
Murder on Line One '90
Henry V '89

Suzanne Shepherd
Lolita '97
The Jerky Boys '95
Palookaville '95

W. Morgan Shepherd
The Escape '95
Elvira, Mistress of the Dark '88

Michael Shepley (1907-61)
Mine Own Executioner '47
Henry V '44

The Demi-Paradise '43
Housemaster '38
The Private Secretary '35
A Shot in the Dark '33

Delia Sheppard (1961-)
Dead Boyz Can't Fly '93
Animal Instincts '92
Night Rhythms '92
Secret Games '92
Sins of Desire '92
Mirror Images '91
Roots of Evil '91
Witchcraft 2: The Temptress '90

Mark Sheppard
Out of the Cold '99
Soldier of Fortune Inc. '97
In the Name of the Father '93

Paula Sheppard
Liquid Sky '83
Alice Sweet Alice '76

William Morgan Sheppard
Goldrush: A Real Life Alaskan Adventure '98
Gettysburg '93

Anthony Sher (1949-)
The Miracle Maker: The Story of Jesus '00 (V)
Horatio Hornblower '99
Shakespeare in Love '98
Mrs. Brown '97
The Moonstone '97
Alive and Kicking '96
Mr. Toad's Wild Ride '96
The Young Poisoner's Handbook '94
Genghis Cohn '93
Tartuffe '90
Erik the Viking '89
Shadey '87

Maurice Sherbanee
Mausoleum '83
Jud '71

Ann Sheridan (1915-67)
The Opposite Sex '56
Appointment in Honduras '53
I Was a Male War Bride '49
Good Sam '48
Silver River '48
Edge of Darkness '43
Thank Your Lucky Stars '43
George Washington Slept Here '42
Kings Row '41
The Man Who Came to Dinner '41
City for Conquest '40
They Drive by Night '40
Dodge City '39
They Made Me a Criminal '39
Angels with Dirty Faces '38
Letter of Introduction '38
The Black Legion '37
The Fighting Westerner '35

Dave Sheridan
Bubble Boy '01
Corky Romano '01
Ghost World '01
Scary Movie '00

Dinah Sheridan (1920-)
Thirteenth Reunion '81
The Railway Children '70
Genevieve '53
Blackout '50
No Trace '50
Calling Paul Temple '48
Salute John Citizen '42

Jamey Sheridan (1951-)
Hamlet '01
Life as a House '01
The Lost Child '00
Luminous Motion '00
The Cradle Will Rock '99
Let the Devil Wear Black '99
The Echo of Thunder '98
The Ice Storm '97
Wild America '97

Stephen King's The Stand '94
A Stranger Among Us '92
Whispers in the Dark '92
All I Want for Christmas '91
Talent for the Game '91
Quick Change '90
Stanley and Iris '90
Jumpin' Jack Flash '86

Jim Sheridan (1949-)
Moll Flanders '96
Way of the West '35

Margaret Sheridan
One Minute to Zero '52
The Thing '51

Nicolette Sheridan (1963-)
Raw Nerve '99
Dead Husbands '98
Beverly Hills Ninja '96
Spy Hard '96
Silver Strand '95
Noises Off '92
Deceptions '90
The Sure Thing '85

Bobby Sherman
Get Crazy '83
He Is My Brother '75

Lowell Sherman (1885-1934)
False Faces '32
Three Broadway Girls '32
What Price Hollywood? '32
Bachelor Apartment '31
The Royal Bed '31
The Garden of Eden '28
Monsieur Beaucaire '24
Way Down East '20

J. Barney Sherry
The White Sister '23
The Bargain '15

Anthony Sherwood
Closer and Closer '96
Eddie and the Cruisers 2: Eddie Lives! '89
Terror Train '80

David Sherwood
Curse of the Crystal Eye '93
River of Diamonds '90

Madeline Sherwood (1922-)
Broken Vows '87
Teachers '84
Pendulum '69
Sweet Bird of Youth '62
Parrish '61

Robin Sherwood
Love Butcher '82
Tourist Trap '79

Vladek Sheybal (1923-92)
The Wind and the Lion '75
S*P*Y*S '74
Scorpio '73
The Boy Friend '71
Women in Love '70
Kanal '56

Arthur Shields (1896-1970)
Enchanted Island '58
The Daughter of Dr. Jekyll '57
The King and Four Queens '56
The Quiet Man '52
The River '51
She Wore a Yellow Ribbon '49
Fighting Father Dunne '48
The Fabulous Dorseys '47
The Corn Is Green '45
The Keys of the Kingdom '44
The White Cliffs of Dover '44
Gentleman Jim '42
How Green Was My Valley '41
Drums Along the Mohawk '39

Brooke Shields (1965-)
The Weekend '00
The Bachelor '99
Black and White '99

Born Wild '95
Freeway '95
Freaked '93
The Seventh Floor '93
Stalking Laura '93
The Diamond Trap '91
Backstreet Dreams '90
Speed Zone '88
Brenda Starr '86
The Muppets Take Manhattan '84
Wet Gold '84
Sahara '83
Endless Love '81
The Blue Lagoon '80
Wanda Nevada '79
King of the Gypsies '78
Pretty Baby '78
Tilt '78
The Prince of Central Park '77
Alice Sweet Alice '76

Nicholas Shields
Liar's Edge '92
Lost in the Barrens '91
Princes in Exile '90

James Shigeta (1933-)
Brother '00
Mulan '98 (V)
Drive '96
Space Marines '96
Blood for Blood '95
China Cry '91
The Cage '89
Die Hard '88
Tomorrow's Child '82
Enola Gay: The Men, the Mission, the Atomic Bomb '80
Paradise, Hawaiian Style '66
Flower Drum Song '61

Marion Shilling (1914-)
Cavalcade of the West '36
The Clutching Hand '36
Gun Play '36
I'll Name the Murderer '36
Captured in Chinatown '35
Rio Rattler '35
A Shot in the Dark '35
Stone of Silver Creek '35
Inside Information '34
Thunder Over Texas '34
Man's Land '32
Shop Angel '32

Shmuel Shilo
Double Edge '92
Goodbye, New York '85
Noa at Seventeen '82

Joseph Shiloah
The Lion of Africa '87
Private Manoeuvres '83
Eagles Attack at Dawn '74
I Love You Rosa '72

Yoko Shimada (1953-)
The Hunted '94
My Champion '84
Shogun '80

Armin Shimerman (1949-)
Arena '89
Stoogemania '85

Misa Shimizu
The Eel '96
Okoge '93

Joanna Shimkus (1943-)
Les Aventuriers '77
The Virgin and the Gypsy '70
The Lost Man '69
Boom! '68
Six in Paris '68

Sab Shimono (1943-)
The Big Hit '98
Paradise Road '97
3 Ninjas Kick Back '94
Suture '93
Teenage Mutant Ninja Turtles 3 '93
Come See the Paradise '90
Hiroshima: Out of the Ashes '90

Presumed Innocent '90
The Wash '88
Gung Ho '85

Takashi Shimura (1905-82)
Love and Faith '78
Last Days of Planet Earth '74
Ghidrah the Three Headed Monster '65
Kwaidan '64
Mothra '62
Yojimbo '61
The Bad Sleep Well '60
The Hidden Fortress '58
The Mysterians '58
Throne of Blood '57
Godzilla, King of the Monsters '56
I Live in Fear '55
Seven Samurai '54
Ikiru '52
The Idiot '51
Rashomon '51
Scandal '50
A Quiet Duel '49
Stray Dog '49
Drunken Angel '48
The Men Who Tread on the Tiger's Tail '45
Sanshiro Sugata '43

Sofia Shinas
Dilemma '97
Hostile Intent '97
Hourglass '95
The Crow '93

Eitaro Shindo (1899-1977)
The Crucified Lovers '54
Sansho the Bailiff '54
A Geisha '53
Sisters of the Gion '36

David Shiner
Man of the House '95
Silent Tongue '92

Ronald Shiner
Butler's Dilemma '43
Thursday's Child '43

Chen Shing
The Amsterdam Connection '70s
The Two Great Cavaliers '73

Fui-On Shing
The Untold Story '93
The Killer '90

Sue Shiomi
Shogun's Ninja '83
The Bodyguard '76
Sister Street Fighter '76
The Street Fighter's Last Revenge '74

Toshi Shioya
Mr. Baseball '92
Prisoners of the Sun '91

John Wesley Shipp (1956-)
Soft Deceit '94
Baby of the Bride '91
NeverEnding Story 2: The Next Chapter '91
The Flash '90

Yumi Shirakawa (1936-)
The Secret of the Telegian '61
H-Man '59
The Mysterians '58
Rodan '56

Talia Shire (1946-)
The Visit '00
The Landlady '98
Lured Innocence '97
Chantilly Lace '93
Bed & Breakfast '92
Cold Heaven '92
For Richer, for Poorer '92
Mark Twain and Me '91
The Godfather, Part 3 '90
Rocky 5 '90
New York Stories '89
Murderer's Keep '88
Blood Vows: The Story of a Mafia Wife '87
Lionheart '87

Hyper-Sapien: People from Another Star '86
Rad '86
Rip van Winkle '85
Rocky 4 '85
Rocky 3 '82
The Godfather 1902-1959: The Complete Epic '81
Windows '80
Old Boyfriends '79
Prophecy '79
Rocky 2 '79
Rich Man, Poor Man '76
Rocky '76
The Godfather, Part 2 '74
The Godfather '72
The Dunwich Horror '70
Gas-s-s-s! '70

Bill Shirk
Ballbuster '89
Escapist '83

Anne Shirley (1918-93)
Murder, My Sweet '44
Bombardier '43
The Devil & Daniel Webster '41
Four Jacks and a Jill '41
Law of the Underworld '38
Stella Dallas '37
Anne of Green Gables '34
Rasputin and the Empress '33

Bill (William) Shirley (1921-89)
Sleeping Beauty '59 (V)
Abbott and Costello Meet Captain Kidd '52
I Dream of Jeannie '52

Cathie Shirriff
Star Trek 3: The Search for Spock '84
Covergirl '83

Joe Shishido (1933-)
Branded to Kill '67
Gate of Flesh '64
Youth of the Beast '63

Stephan Shkurat
Chapayev '34
Earth '30

Samia Shoaib
Pi '98
subUrbia '96

William Shockley
Girl in the Cadillac '94
Dream Lover '93
Howling 5: The Rebirth '89

Ann Shoemaker
Sunrise at Campobello '60
Thirty Seconds Over Tokyo '44
My Favorite Wife '40
Alice Adams '35

Craig Shoemaker
Safe House '99
Acting on Impulse '93

Dan Shor (1961-)
Red Rock West '93
Bill & Ted's Excellent Adventure '89
Daddy's Boys '87
Mesmerized '84
Mike's Murder '84
Strangers Kiss '83
Tron '82
Strange Behavior '81
A Rumor of War '80

Miriam Shor
Bedazzled '00
Hedwig and the Angry Inch '00
Let It Snow '99

Dinah Shore (1917-94)
Oh, God! '77
Fun & Fancy Free '47 (N)
Till the Clouds Roll By '46
Up in Arms '44
Thank Your Lucky Stars '43

Pauly Shore (1968-)
The Wash '01
The Bogus Witch Project '00
Bio-Dome '96
The Curse of Inferno '96
Jury Duty '95
In the Army Now '94

Dream Date '93
Son-in-Law '93
Encino Man '92
Phantom of the Mall: Eric's Revenge '89
18 Again! '88

Bobby Short
For Love or Money '93
Hardhat & Legs '80

Dorothy Short (1915-)
Trail of the Silver Spurs '41
Pony Post '40
Daughter of the Tong '39
Wild Horse Canyon '39
Reefer Madness '38
Brothers of the West '37
Assassin of Youth '35
Savage Fury '33

Florence Short
The Love Flower '20
Way Down East '20

Martin Short (1950-)
Get Over It! '01
Jimmy Neutron: Boy Genius '01 (V)
Alice in Wonderland '99
Mumford '99
Merlin '98
Prince of Egypt '98 (V)
A Simple Wish '97
Jungle 2 Jungle '96
Mars Attacks! '96
Father of the Bride Part II '95
The Pebble and the Penguin '94 (V)
We're Back! A Dinosaur's Story '93 (V)
Captain Ron '92
Clifford '92
The Return of Spinal Tap '92
Father of the Bride '91
Pure Luck '91
The Big Picture '89
Three Fugitives '89
Cross My Heart '88
Innerspace '87
Johnny Appleseed '86
Really Weird Tales '86
Three Amigos '86
Sunset Limousine '83
The Family Man '79
Lost and Found '79

Ken Shorter
Dragonheart: A New Beginning '00
Ned Kelly '70

Robin Shou (1960-)
Mortal Kombat 2: Annihilation '97
Beverly Hills Ninja '96
Fatal Chase '92
Honor and Glory '92
Interpol Connection '92

Grant Show (1962-)
The Alchemists '99
Texas '94
Treacherous Crossing '92
A Woman, Her Men and Her Futon '92

Max (Casey Adams) Showalter (1917-2000)
Racing with the Moon '84
Sixteen Candles '84
Summer and Smoke '61
The Monster That Challenged the World '57
Bus Stop '56
The Indestructible Man '56
Niagara '52
What Price Glory? '52

Michael Showalter
Signs '02
Wet Hot American Summer '01

Kathy Shower (1953-)
Hindsight '97
To the Limit '95
Improper Conduct '94
Married People, Single Sex 2: For Better or Worse '94
American Kickboxer 2: To the Death '93
Sexual Malice '93
L.A. Goddess '92
Wild Cactus '92
Bedroom Eyes 2 '89
Out on Bail '89
Robo-Chic '89
Frankenstein General Hospital '88
The Further Adventures of Tennessee Buck '88
Commando Squad '87

John Shrapnel (1942-)
The Body '01
Gladiator '00
Fatherland '94
Two Deaths '94
Tragedy of Flight 103: The Inside Story '91
How to Get Ahead in Advertising '89

Kin Shriner (1953-)
The Corporation '96
The Crying Child '96
Cyberzone '95
Escape '90
Angel 3: The Final Chapter '88
Vendetta '85
Obsessive Love '84

Sonny Shroyer (1935-)
The Runaway '00
The Gingerbread Man '97
John Grisham's The Rainmaker '97
Wild America '97
Bastard out of Carolina '96
Forrest Gump '94
The Ernest Green Story '93
Love Crimes '92
The Devil & Max Devlin '81
They Went That-a-Way & That-a-Way '78
Smokey and the Bandit '77
Gator '76
The Longest Yard '74
Payday '72

Elisabeth Shue (1963-)
The Hollow Man '00
Molly '99
Palmetto '98
Cousin Bette '97
Deconstructing Harry '97
The Saint '97
The Trigger Effect '96
Leaving Las Vegas '95
The Underneath '95
Blind Justice '94
Radio Inside '94
Heart and Souls '93
Twenty Bucks '93
The Marrying Man '91
Soapdish '91
Back to the Future, Part 3 '90
Back to the Future, Part 2 '89
Cocktail '88
Adventures in Babysitting '87
Link '86
Call to Glory '84
The Karate Kid '84

Richard B. Shull (1929-99)
Trapped in Paradise '94
Housesitter '92
Splash '84
Unfaithfully Yours '84
Heartbeeps '81
Dreamer '79
The Pack '77
The Big Bus '76
Cockfighter '74
Hail '73
Slither '73
Sssssss '73
The Anderson Tapes '71

Antonina Shuranova (1936-)
An Unfinished Piece for a Player Piano '77
Tchaikovsky '71
War and Peace '68

Sabrina Siani (1963-)
El Barbaro '84
Ator the Fighting Eagle '83
Conquest '83
Throne of Fire '82

Jane Sibbett (1961-)
The Arrival 2 '98
Noah '98
It Takes Two '95
The Resurrected '91

Alexander Siddig
Vertical Limit '00
A Dangerous Man: Lawrence after Arabia '91

Sylvia Sidney (1910-99)
Mars Attacks! '96
Used People '92
Beetlejuice '88
Pals '87
An Early Frost '85
Come Along with Me '84
Corrupt '84
Finnegan Begin Again '84
Hammett '82
Having It All '82
A Small Killing '81
The Shadow Box '80
Damien: Omen 2 '78
I Never Promised You a Rose Garden '77
Raid on Entebbe '77
Snowbeast '77
God Told Me To '76
Death at Love House '75
Summer Wishes, Winter Dreams '73
Love from a Stranger '47
Mr. Ace '46
Blood on the Sun '45
The Wagons Roll at Night '41
One Third of a Nation '39
You and Me '38
Dead End '37
You Only Live Once '37
Fury '36
Sabotage '36
The Trail of the Lonesome Pine '36
Street Scene '31

Charles Siebert (1938-)
A Cry for Love '80
Blue Sunshine '78
Tarantulas: The Deadly Cargo '77

Jim Siedow
The Texas Chainsaw Massacre 2 '86
The Texas Chainsaw Massacre '74

Donald Siegel (1912-91)
Into the Night '85
Invasion of the Body Snatchers '78
Play Misty for Me '71
Invasion of the Body Snatchers '56

George Siegmann (1882-1928)
Hotel Imperial '27
The Man Who Laughs '27
Uncle Tom's Cabin '27
Anna Christie '23
Oliver Twist '22
The Three Musketeers '21
The Birth of a Nation '15

Casey Siemaszko (1961-)
The Crew '00
Chameleon 2: Death Match '99
Limbo '99
Stephen King's The Storm of the Century '99
Bliss '96
Mistrial '96
Black Scorpion '95
Milk Money '94
My Life's in Turnaround '94
Teresa's Tattoo '94
Of Mice and Men '92
The Chase '91
Near Misses '91
The Big Slice '90
Back to the Future, Part 2 '89
Breaking In '89
Biloxi Blues '88
Young Guns '88
Gardens of Stone '87
Three o'Clock High '87
Miracle of the Heart: A Boys Town Story '86
Stand by Me '86
Amazing Stories '85
Back to the Future '85
Secret Admirer '85
Class '83

Nina Siemaszko (1970-)
Goodbye, Lover '99
Jakob the Liar '99
Armistead Maupin's More Tales of the City '97
The American President '95
Sawbones '95
Airheads '94
Power of Attorney '94
Red Shoe Diaries 3: Another Woman's Lipstick '93
The Saint of Fort Washington '93
Twenty Bucks '93
Bed & Breakfast '92
Sinatra '92
Wild Orchid 2: Two Shades of Blue '92
Tucker: The Man and His Dream '88

Gregory Sierra (1941-)
Blood Money '99
The Wonderful Ice Cream Suit '98
Hot Shots! Part Deux '93
Deep Cover '92
Honey, I Blew Up the Kid '92
Dynamite and Gold '88
Code Name: Dancer '87
Let's Get Harry '87
Miami Vice '84
Mean Dog Blues '78
The Clones '73
The Thief Who Came to Dinner '73
Pocket Money '72

Tom Signorelli (1939-)
Robot in the Family '94
Crossover Dreams '85
One Down, Two to Go! '82
Alice Sweet Alice '76
Big Bad Mama '74
The Last Porno Flick '74
Kelly's Heroes '70
The St. Valentine's Day Massacre '67
The Trip '67

Simone Signoret (1921-85)
I Sent a Letter to My Love '81
Madame Rosa '77
Le Chat '75
Widow Couderc '74
Games '67
Is Paris Burning? '66
Ship of Fools '65
The Day and the Hour '63
Le Joli Mai '62 (N)
Room at the Top '59
The Crucible '57
Death in the Garden '56
Diabolique '55
Casque d'Or '52
La Ronde '51
Dedee d'Anvers '49
Against the Wind '48

Caroline Sihol
Tous les Matins du Monde '92
Confidentially Yours '83

Cynthia Sikes (1951-)
Love Hurts '91
Oceans of Fire '86
The Man Who Loved Women '83
Goodbye Cruel World '82

James B. Sikking (1934-)
Nowhere to Land '00
Mutiny '99
In Pursuit of Honor '95
Tyson '95
Dead Badge '94
Seduced by Evil '94
The Pelican Brief '93
Final Approach '91
Narrow Margin '90
The Night God Screamed '80s
Around the World in 80 Days '89
The Brotherhood of the Rose '89
Ollie Hopnoodle's Haven of Bliss '88
Dress Gray '86
Morons from Outer Space '85
Star Trek 3: The Search for Spock '84
Up the Creek '84
The Star Chamber '83
Outland '81
The Competition '80
Ordinary People '80
The Electric Horseman '79
Black Force 2 '78
Man on the Run '74
The Terminal Man '74
Scorpio '73
The New Centurions '72
Charro! '69
Daddy's Gone A-Hunting '69
Point Blank '67
Von Ryan's Express '65
The Strangler '64

Tusse Silberg
Citizen X '95
Hidden City '87
The Company of Wolves '85

Vira (Vera) Silenti (1931-)
Son of Samson '62
Atlas in the Land of the Cyclops '61
Maciste in Hell '60

Karen Sillas (1965-)
Reach the Rock '98
Sour Grapes '98
The Beast '96
Female Perversions '96
Risk '94
What Happened Was... '94
Simple Men '92

David Silva
Sisters of Satan '75
Senora Tentacion '49

Geno Silva
Geronimo '93
Drug Wars 2: The Cocaine Cartel '92
Night Eyes 2 '91

Henry Silva (1928-)
Ocean's Eleven '01
Killing in the Sun
Backlash '99
Ghost Dog: The Way of the Samurai '99
The End of Violence '97
Trigger Happy '96
The Prince '95
Possessed by the Night '93
The Harvest '92
The Colombian Connection '91
Three Days to a Kill '91
The Desperados '80s
Above the Law '88
Bulletproof '88
Trained to Kill '88
Thirst '87
Code of Silence '85
Escape from the Bronx '85
Lust in the Dust '85
Shoot '85
Cannonball Run 2 '84
Chained Heat '83
Violent Breed '83
Deadly Sting '82
Megaforce '82
Wrong Is Right '82
Day of the Assassin '81
Sharky's Machine '81
Alligator '80
Killer '70s
Almost Human '79
Buck Rogers in the 25th Century '79
Crimebusters '79
Love and Bullets '79
Hired to Kill '73
Hit Men '73
Manhunt '73
Cry of a Prostitute: Love Kills '72
Man & Boy '71
Never a Dull Moment '68
A Gathering of Eagles '63
The Manchurian Candidate '62
Cinderfella '60
Ocean's 11 '60
Green Mansions '59
The Jayhawkers '59
The Bravados '58
The Law and Jake Wade '58
The Tall T '57

Maria Silva (1941-)
Curse of the Devil '73
The Mummy's Revenge '73
Tombs of the Blind Dead '72
The Awful Dr. Orloff '62

Simone Silva
Big Deadly Game '54
The Shadow Man '53

Trinidad Silva (1950-88)
UHF '89
Colors '88
The Night Before '88
Crackers '84
The Jerk '79

Aldo Silvani
Nights of Cabiria '57
La Strada '54
Valley of the Kings '54

Leonor Silveira
Party '96
Voyage to the Beginning of the World '96
The Convent '95
Abraham's Valley '93

Fawn Silver
Terror in the Jungle '68
Orgy of the Dead '65

Joe Silver (1922-)
Switching Channels '88
Mr. Nice Guy '86
Almost You '85
The Gig '85
Rabid '77
You Light Up My Life '77
They Came from Within '75
The Apprenticeship of Duddy Kravitz '74

Ron Silver (1946-)
Ali '01
American Tragedy '00
Cutaway '00
Black & White '99
In the Company of Spies '99
Ratz '99
The White Raven '98
The Beneficiary '97
The Arrival '96
Deadly Outbreak '96
Girl 6 '96
Kissinger and Nixon '96
ShadowZone: The Undead Express '96
Skeletons '96
Danger Zone '95
Timecop '94
Blind Side '93
Lifepod '93
Married to It '93
Live Wire '92
Mr. Saturday Night '92
Blue Steel '90
Forgotten Prisoners '90
Reversal of Fortune '90
Enemies, a Love Story '89
Fellow Traveler '89
A Father's Revenge '88
Billionaire Boys Club '87

Eat and Run '86
Trapped in Silence '86
Garbo Talks '84
Oh, God! You Devil '84
Romancing the Stone '84
The Entity '83
The Goodbye People '83
Lovesick '83
Silkwood '83
Best Friends '82
Silent Rage '82
Betrayal '78
Semi-Tough '77
Tunnelvision '76

Veronique Silver
Toute Une Nuit '82
The Woman Next Door '81
This Sweet Sickness '77

Frank Silvera (1914-)
Valdez Is Coming '71
The St. Valentine's Day Massacre '67
Toys in the Attic '63
Death Tide '58
Killer's Kiss '55
The Fighter '52
Miracle of Our Lady of Fatima '52
White Mane '52

Jay Silverheels (1919-80)
Man Who Loved Cat Dancing '73
Santee '73
True Grit '69
Indian Paint '64
Justice of the West '61
Alias Jesse James '59
Lone Ranger '56
Walk the Proud Land '56
War Arrow '53
Broken Arrow '50
Lust for Gold '49

David Michael Silverman (1966-)
Metro '96
Copycat '95

Jonathan Silverman (1966-)
These Old Broads '01
Lip Service '00
Just a Little Harmless Sex '99
The Inspectors '98
Neil Simon's The Odd Couple 2 '98
Something About Sex '98
French Exit '97
At First Sight '95
Little Big League '94
Sketch Artist 2: Hands That See '94
Teresa's Tattoo '94
12:01 '93
Weekend at Bernie's 2 '93
Breaking the Rules '92
Broadway Bound '92
Death Becomes Her '92
For Richer, for Poorer '92
Little Sister '92
Age Isn't Everything '91
Class Action '91
Traveling Man '89
Weekend at Bernie's '89
Caddyshack 2 '88
Stealing Home '88
Brighton Beach Memoirs '86
Challenge of a Lifetime '85

Robert A. Silverman
Naked Lunch '91
Scanners '81
The Brood '79

Phil Silvers (1912-85)
The Happy Hooker Goes Hollywood '80
Racquet '79
The Cheap Detective '78
The Chicken Chronicles '77
The Boatniks '70
Buona Sera, Mrs. Campbell '68
Follow That Camel '67
A Guide for the Married Man '67
A Funny Thing Happened on the Way to the Forum '66
It's a Mad, Mad, Mad, Mad World '63
40 Pounds of Trouble '62
Lucky Me '54
Summer Stock '50
A Thousand and One Nights '45
Cover Girl '44
Lady Takes a Chance '43
All Through the Night '42
Footlight Serenade '42
Roxie Hart '42
Lady Be Good '41
Tom, Dick, and Harry '41

Sid Silvers
Born to Dance '36
Broadway Melody of 1936 '35

Andrew (Dice Clay) Silverstein (1957-)
One Night at McCool's '01
My 5 Wives '00
Foolish '99
Jury Duty '95
National Lampoon's Favorite Deadly Sins '95
No Contest '94
Brain Smasher...A Love Story '93
The Adventures of Ford Fairlane '90
Casual Sex? '88
Amazon Women on the Moon '87
Pretty in Pink '86
Night Patrol '85
Making the Grade '84
Private Resort '84
Wacko '83

Alicia Silverstone (1976-)
Love's Labour's Lost '00
Blast from the Past '98
Batman and Robin '97
Excess Baggage '96
The Babysitter '95
Clueless '95
True Crime '95
Hideaway '94
The Crush '93

Ben Silverstone (1979-)
Get Real '99
Lolita '97
The Browning Version '94

Armando Silvestre (1926-)
The Killing Zone '90
The Last Riders '90
Night of the Bloody Apes '68
Doctor of Doom '62
Geronimo '62
Neutron vs. the Death Robots '62
Neutron and the Black Mask '61
Neutron vs. the Amazing Dr. Caronte '61
Wrestling Women vs. the Aztec Mummy '59
The White Orchid '54

Alastair Sim (1900-76)
The Littlest Horse Thieves '76
Rogue Male '76
Royal Flash '75
The Ruling Class '72
Cold Comfort Farm '71
The Millionairess '60
Blue Murder at St. Trinian's '56
Escapade '55
The Belles of St. Trinian's '53
Innocents in Paris '53
A Christmas Carol '51
The Happiest Days of Your Life '50
Stage Fright '50
Captain Boycott '47
Green for Danger '47
Hue and Cry '47
Cottage to Let '41
Inspector Hornleigh '39
The Terror '38
Gangway '37
Late Extra '35
The Private Secretary '35

Gerald Sim (1925-)
No Sex Please—We're British '73
Dr. Jekyll and Sister Hyde '71
Long Ago Tomorrow '71
King Rat '65

Sheila Sim (1922-)
Pandora and the Flying Dutchman '51
The Guinea Pig '48
Great Day '46
A Canterbury Tale '44

Jon Simanton
The Creeps '97
Turbo: A Power Rangers Movie '96

John Simm
Forgive and Forget '99
Human Traffic '99
Wonderland '99
Boston Kickout '95

Dick Simmons (1913-)
Men of the Fighting Lady '54
Above and Beyond '53
Battle Circus '53

Gene Simmons (1949-)
The New Guy '02
Wish You Were Dead '00
Detroit Rock City '99
Red Surf '90
Decline of Western Civilization 2: The Metal Years '88
Never Too Young to Die '86
Trick or Treat '86
Wanted Dead or Alive '86
Runaway '84
KISS Meets the Phantom of the Park '78

Jaason Simmons (1970-)
Frankenstein Reborn '98
Highway Hitcher '98
Nowhere '96

Jean Simmons (1929-)
Final Fantasy: The Spirits Within '01 (V)
December Flower
How to Make an American Quilt '95
Great Expectations '89
The Dawning '88
A Friendship in Vienna '88 (N)
Going Undercover '88
Perry Mason: The Case of the Lost Love '87
North and South Book 2 '86
North and South Book 1 '85
The Thorn Birds '83
A Small Killing '81
Dominique Is Dead '79
The Dain Curse '78
Mr. Sycamore '74
Say Hello to Yesterday '71
The Happy Ending '69
Divorce American Style '67
Heidi '67
Rough Night in Jericho '67
Soldier in Love '67
The Grass Is Greener '61
Elmer Gantry '60
Spartacus '60
The Big Country '58
This Could Be the Night '57
Until They Sail '57
Guys and Dolls '55
A Bullet Is Waiting '54
Desiree '54
The Egyptian '54
The Robe '53
Young Bess '53
Androcles and the Lion '52
She Couldn't Say No '52
The Clouded Yellow '51
Trio '50
Hamlet '48
Black Narcissus '47
Inheritance '47
Great Expectations '46
Mr. Emmanuel '44

J.K. Simmons (1955-)
Spider-Man '02
The Mexican '01
The Gift '00
The Cider House Rules '99
For Love of the Game '99
Celebrity '98
Face Down '97
The Jackal '97
Love Walked In '97
Extreme Measures '96
The Ref '93

Pat Simmons
My Science Project '85
The Giant Gila Monster '59

Peter Simmons
Sand '00
Best of the Best 3: No Turning Back '95
Renaissance Man '94

Ginny Simms (1913-94)
Night and Day '46
Broadway Rhythm '44
Hit the Ice '43
Seven Days' Leave '42
Playmates '41

Larry Simms (1934-)
Blondie Hits the Jackpot '49
Blondie Knows Best '46
Footlight Glamour '43
It's a Great Life '43
Blondie for Victory '42
Blondie Goes Latin '42
Blondie Goes to College '42
Blondie's Blessed Event '42
Blondie in Society '41
Blondie Has Trouble '40
Blondie On a Budget '40
Blondie Plays Cupid '40
Blondie Brings Up Baby '39
Blondie Meets the Boss '39
Blondie Takes a Vacation '39
Blondie '38

Francois Simon (1917-82)
Christ Stopped at Eboli '79
Lumiere '76
Charles: Dead or Alive '69

Michel Simon (1895-1975)
The Two of Us '68
The Train '65
The Head '59
Beauty and the Devil '50
Fabiola '48
Panique '47
Bizarre Bizarre '39
Circonstances Attenuantes '36
L'Atalante '34
Boudu Saved from Drowning '32
La Chienne '31
Passion of Joan of Arc '28

Paul Simon (1941-)
Mother Goose Rock 'n' Rhyme '90
One Trick Pony '80
All You Need Is Cash '78
Annie Hall '77

Robert F. Simon (1908-92)
Chinese Web '78
Spiderman: The Deadly Dust '78
The Man Who Shot Liberty Valance '62
Compulsion '59
Gunman's Walk '58
The Nine Lives of Elfego Baca '58
The Catered Affair '56
The Court Martial of Billy Mitchell '55

Simone Simon (1911-)
Le Plaisir '52
La Ronde '51
Women in Prison '49
Curse of the Cat People '44
Mademoiselle Fifi '44
Cat People '42
The Devil & Daniel Webster '41
La Bete Humaine '38

David Simonds
Amateur '94
The Refrigerator '91

Martine Simonet
The Last Metro '80
Simone Barbes '80

Jimmi Simpson
Stephen King's Rose Red '02
Loser '00

O.J. Simpson (1947-)
Naked Gun 33 1/3: The Final Insult '94
No Place to Hide '93
C.I.A.: Code Name Alexa '92
Naked Gun 2 1/2: The Smell of Fear '91
The Naked Gun: From the Files of Police Squad '88
Hambone & Hillie '84
Firepower '79
Capricorn One '78
Roots '77
The Cassandra Crossing '76
The Klansman '74
The Towering Inferno '74

Russell Simpson (1880-1959)
The Horse Soldiers '59
The Sun Shines Bright '53
Ma and Pa Kettle at the Fair '52
They Were Expendable '45
Texas Masquerade '44
Border Patrol '43
The Grapes of Wrath '40
Three Faces West '40
Sixteen Fathoms Deep '34
The Riding Tornado '32
Abraham Lincoln '30
The Lone Star Ranger '30
The Virginian '23
Human Hearts '22
Peg o' My Heart '22

Joan Sims (1930-2001)
The Last of the Blonde Bombshells '00
The Canterville Ghost '96
Carry On Behind '75
Carry On Dick '75
One of Our Dinosaurs Is Missing '75
Carry On at Your Convenience '71
Carry On Camping '71
Carry On Henry VIII '71
Carry On Cowboy '66
Carry On Screaming '66
Carry On Cleo '65
Carry On Admiral '57
The Belles of St. Trinian's '53

Mike Sims
Ghetto Revenge
The Bus Is Coming '72

Robin Sims
The Channeler '89
Shooters '89

Frank Sinatra (1915-98)
Who Framed Roger Rabbit '88 (V)
Cannonball Run 2 '84
The First Deadly Sin '80
That's Entertainment '74
The Detective '68
Lady in Cement '68
Tony Rome '67
Assault on a Queen '66
Cast a Giant Shadow '66
The Oscar '66
None But the Brave '65
Von Ryan's Express '65
Paris When It Sizzles '64
Robin and the 7 Hoods '64
Come Blow Your Horn '63
Four for Texas '63
The List of Adrian Messenger '63
The Manchurian Candidate '62
The Devil at 4 O'Clock '61
Can-Can '60
Ocean's 11 '60
A Hole in the Head '59
Never So Few '59
Kings Go Forth '58
Some Came Running '58
Pal Joey '57
The Pride and the Passion '57
Around the World in 80 Days '56
High Society '56
Meet Me in Las Vegas '56
Guys and Dolls '55
The Man with the Golden Arm '55
Not as a Stranger '55
The Tender Trap '55
Suddenly '54
Young at Heart '54
From Here to Eternity '53
Meet Danny Wilson '52
Double Dynamite '51
On the Town '49
Take Me Out to the Ball Game '49
The Miracle of the Bells '48
It Happened in Brooklyn '47
Till the Clouds Roll By '46
Anchors Aweigh '45
Higher and Higher '44
Step Lively '44
Strictly G.I. '44

Frank Sinatra, Jr. (1944-)
Cool World '92
Code Name: Zebra '84
Pepper and His Wacky Taxi '72
A Man Called Adam '66

Nancy Sinatra
Speedway '68
The Wild Angels '66

Sinbad (1956-)
Good Burger '97
The Cherokee Kid '96
First Kid '96
Homeward Bound 2: Lost in San Francisco '96 (V)
Jingle All the Way '96
Houseguest '94
Coneheads '93
The Meteor Man '93
Necessary Roughness '91

Gordon John Sinclair (1962-)
The Brylcreem Boys '96
Erik the Viking '89
Gregory's Girl '80

Hugh Sinclair (1903-62)
No Trace '50
The Gay Lady '49
The Rocking Horse Winner '49
The Secret Four '40

Madge Sinclair (1938-95)
The Lion King '94 (V)
Queen '93
The End of Innocence '90
Coming to America '88
Convoy '78
One in a Million: The Ron LeFlore Story '78
Cornbread, Earl & Me '75
Conrack '74

Donald Sinden (1923-)
The Canterville Ghost '96
The Children '90
The Island at the Top of the World '74
Rentadick '72
The Captain's Table '60
Doctor at Large '57
Above Us the Waves '56
Simba '55
Doctor in the House '53

Jeremy Sinden (1950-96)
The Innocent '93

Fortunes of War *'87*
Danger UXB *'81*
Ngai Sing
Jet Li's The Enforcer *'95*
The Bodyguard from Beijing *'94*
Campbell Singer
The Hands of Orlac *'60*
The Young and the Guilty *'58*
Linda Singer
Junior *'86*
Zombie Nightmare *'86*
Lori Singer (1962-)
The Last Ride *'94*
Equinox *'93*
Short Cuts *'93*
Sunset Grill *'92*
Warlock *'91*
Storm and Sorrow *'90*
Made in USA *'88*
Summer Heat *'87*
Trouble in Mind *'86*
The Falcon and the Snowman *'85*
The Man with One Red Shoe *'85*
Footloose *'84*
Born Beautiful *'82*
Marc Singer (1948-)
Street Corner Justice *'96*
Beastmaster 3: The Eye of Braxus *'95*
Cyberzone *'95*
The Fighter *'95*
Silk Degrees *'94*
Sweet Justice *'92*
Beastmaster 2: Through the Portal of Time *'91*
The Berlin Conspiracy *'91*
Deadly Game *'91*
Ultimate Desires *'91*
Beyond the Silhouette *'90*
Body Chemistry *'90*
Dead Space *'90*
High Desert Kill *'90*
A Man Called Sarge *'90*
The Red Raven Kiss-Off *'90*
Watchers 2 *'90*
In the Cold of the Night *'89*
Born to Race *'88*
V: The Final Battle *'84*
Her Life as a Man *'83*
V *'83*
Beastmaster *'82*
If You Could See What I Hear *'82*
For Ladies Only *'81*
Roots: The Next Generation *'79*
The Two Worlds of Jenny Logan *'79*
Go Tell the Spartans *'78*
Sergeant Matlovich vs. the U.S. Air Force *'78*
Things in Their Season *'74*
Richard Singer
American Pop *'81 (V)*
Girls Next Door *'79*
Joseph Singleton (1888-)
The Mad Whirl *'25*
The Toll Gate *'20*
Reggie Mixes In *'16*
Penny Singleton (1908-)
Jetsons: The Movie *'90 (V)*
Blondie Hits the Jackpot *'49*
Blondie Knows Best *'46*
Footlight Glamour *'43*
It's a Great Life *'43*
Blondie for Victory *'42*
Blondie Goes Latin *'42*
Blondie Goes to College *'42*
Blondie's Blessed Event *'42*
Blondie in Society *'41*
Blondie Has Trouble *'40*
Blondie On a Budget *'40*
Blondie Plays Cupid *'40*
Blondie Brings Up Baby *'39*
Blondie Meets the Boss *'39*
Blondie Takes a Vacation *'39*
Blondie *'38*
Boy Meets Girl *'38*
Vogues of 1938 *'37*
Linda Sini
Sartana's Here...Trade Your Pistol for a Coffin *'70*
Venus Against the Son of Hercules *'62*
Gary Sinise (1955-)
Imposter *'01*
Mission to Mars *'00*
Reindeer Games *'00*
The Dress Code *'99*
The Green Mile *'99*
It's the Rage *'99*
That Championship Season *'99*
Snake Eyes *'98*
George Wallace *'97*
Albino Alligator *'96*
Ransom *'96*
Apollo 13 *'95*
Truman *'95*
Forrest Gump *'94*
The Quick and the Dead *'94*
Stephen King's The Stand *'94*
Jack the Bear *'93*
A Midnight Clear *'92*
Of Mice and Men *'92*
True West *'86*
Sir Lancelot (1903-2001)
Zombies on Broadway *'44*
I Walked with a Zombie *'43*
Joseph Siravo
Walking and Talking *'96*
Carlito's Way *'93*
G. Anthony "Tony" Sirico (1942-)
Mob Queen *'98*
Backtrack *'89*
Cookie *'89*
Joseph Sirola
Seizure *'74*
Hail *'73*
Marina Sirtis (1960-)
Star Trek: Insurrection *'98*
Star Trek: First Contact *'96*
Gargoyles, The Movie: The Heroes Awaken *'94 (V)*
Star Trek: Generations *'94*
Waxwork 2: Lost in Time *'91*
Death Wish 3 *'85*
Blind Date *'84*
Sisqo
Snow Dogs *'02*
Get Over It! *'01*
Noble Sissle
Murder with Music *'45*
Junction 88 *'40*
Jeremy Sisto (1974-)
Angel Eyes *'01*
Jesus *'00*
The '60s *'99*
Bongwater *'98*
Playing by Heart *'98*
Suicide Kings *'97*
Without Limits *'97*
White Squall *'96*
Clueless *'95*
The Crew *'95*
Moonlight and Valentino *'95*
Hideaway *'94*
Grand Canyon *'91*
Rocco Sisto
Innocent Blood *'92*
Red Riding Hood *'88*
Truth or Die *'86*
After Hours *'85*
Emil Sitka (1915-98)
The Outlaws Is Coming! *'65*
Three Stooges in Orbit *'62*
Frank Sivero (1952-)
Foolish *'99*
Cop and a Half *'93*
Fist of Honor *'92*
Goodfellas *'90*
The Godfather, Part 2 *'74*
Tom Sizemore (1964-)
Big Trouble *'02*
Black Hawk Down *'01*
Pearl Harbor *'01*
Sins of the Father *'01*
Ticker *'01*
Red Planet *'00*
Bringing Out the Dead *'99*
The Match *'99*
Play It to the Bone *'99*
Witness Protection *'99*
Enemy of the State *'98*
The Florentine *'98*
Saving Private Ryan *'98*
Witness to the Mob *'98*
The Relic *'96*
Bad Love *'95*
Devil in a Blue Dress *'95*
Heat *'95*
Strange Days *'95*
Natural Born Killers *'94*
Wyatt Earp *'94*
Heart and Souls *'93*
Striking Distance *'93*
True Romance *'93*
Watch It *'93*
An American Story *'92*
Passenger 57 *'92*
Harley Davidson and the Marlboro Man *'91*
Where Sleeping Dogs Lie *'91*
Blue Steel *'90*
Flight of the Intruder *'90*
A Matter of Degrees *'90*
Born on the Fourth of July *'89*
Gunnar Sjoberg
Brink of Life *'57*
June Night *'40*
Victor Sjostrom (1879-1960)
Wild Strawberries *'57*
To Joy *'50*
Walpurgis Night *'41*
Thomas Graal's First Child *'18*
The Outlaw and His Wife *'17*
Thomas Graal's Best Film *'17*
George Skaff (1930-95)
Frogs *'72*
The Incredible Petrified World *'58*
Man Beast *'55*
Jimmie F. Skaggs
Backlash: Oblivion 2 *'95*
Tecumseh: The Last Warrior *'95*
Thousand Pieces of Gold *'91*
The Lost Capone *'90*
Puppet Master *'89*
Ghost Town *'88*
Norman Skaggs
Getting Out *'94*
Chrome Soldiers *'92*
Lilia Skala (1900-94)
House of Games *'87*
Flashdance *'83*
Heartland *'81*
Deadly Hero *'75*
Probe *'72*
Charly *'68*
Lilies of the Field *'63*
Stellan Skarsgard (1951-)
The Glass House *'01*
Aberdeen *'00*
Harlan County War *'00*
Passion of Mind *'00*
Signs & Wonders *'00*
Time Code *'00*
Deep Blue Sea *'99*
Ronin *'98*
Savior *'98*
Amistad *'97*
Good Will Hunting *'97*
Insomnia *'97*
My Son the Fanatic *'97*
Breaking the Waves *'95*
Zero Degrees Kelvin *'95*
Good Evening, Mr. Wallenberg *'93*
The Slingshot *'93*
Wind *'92*
The Ox *'91*
The Women on the Roof *'89*
The Unbearable Lightness of Being *'88*
Hip Hip Hurrah! *'87*
Noon Wine *'84*
Jackie Skarvellis
The Rats Are Coming! The Werewolves Are Here! *'72*
The Body Beneath *'70*
Brigitte Skay
Four Times That Night *'69*
Zeta One *'69*
Hal Skelly
Struggle *'31*
Dance of Life *'29*
Red Skelton (1913-97)
Those Magnificent Men in Their Flying Machines *'65*
Ocean's 11 *'60*
Around the World in 80 Days *'56*
Clown *'53*
Lovely to Look At *'52*
Texas Carnival *'51*
The Fuller Brush Girl *'50*
Three Little Words *'50*
Watch the Birdie *'50*
The Yellow Cab Man *'50*
Neptune's Daughter *'49*
The Fuller Brush Man *'48*
A Southern Yankee *'48*
Merton of the Movies *'47*
The Show-Off *'46*
Ziegfeld Follies *'46*
Bathing Beauty *'44*
DuBarry Was a Lady *'43*
I Dood It *'43*
Thousands Cheer *'43*
Whistling in Brooklyn *'43*
Panama Hattie *'42*
Ship Ahoy *'42*
Whistling in Dixie *'42*
Lady Be Good *'41*
Whistling in the Dark *'41*
Having Wonderful Time *'38*
Tom Skerritt (1933-)
Texas Rangers *'01*
High Noon *'00*
Trial by Media *'00*
Aftershock: Earthquake in New York *'99*
The Other Sister *'98*
Smoke Signals *'98*
What the Deaf Man Heard *'98*
Contact *'97*
Two for Texas *'97*
Divided by Hate *'96*
Knight Moves *'93*
Getting Up and Going Home *'92*
Poison Ivy *'92*
A River Runs Through It *'92*
Singers *'92*
Wild Orchid 2: Two Shades of Blue *'92*
Nightmare at Bittercreek *'91*
Child in the Night *'90*
The China Lake Murders *'90*
The Rookie *'90*
Big Man on Campus *'89*
The Heist *'89*
Red King, White Knight *'89*
Steel Magnolias *'89*
Poltergeist 3 *'88*
Big Town *'87*
Maid to Order *'87*
Opposing Force *'87*
Poker Alice *'87*
Wisdom *'87*
Miles to Go *'86*
SpaceCamp *'86*
Top Gun *'86*
Calendar Girl Murders *'84*
Dead Zone *'83*
Dangerous Summer *'82*
Fighting Back *'82*
Silence of the North *'81*
Alien *'79*
Cheech and Chong's Up in Smoke *'79*
Ice Castles *'79*
The Turning Point *'77*
Devil's Rain *'75*
Big Bad Mama *'74*
Thieves Like Us *'74*
Fuzz *'72*
Wild Rovers *'71*
M*A*S*H *'70*
Anita Skinner
Sole Survivor *'84*
Girlfriends *'78*
Carole Skinner
Napoleon *'96 (V)*
Adventures of Eliza Fraser *'76*
Claire Skinner (1965-)
Second Sight *'99*
Sleepy Hollow *'99*
Catherine Cookson's The Wingless Bird *'97*
The Return of the Native *'94*
Naked *'93*
Life Is Sweet *'90*
Keith Skinner
The Slipper and the Rose *'76*
Mademoiselle *'66*
Pat Skipper
Ed Gein *'01*
Chain of Command *'00*
Trade Off *'95*
Dancing with Danger *'93*
Alison Skipworth (1863-1952)
Wide Open Faces *'38*
The Princess Comes Across *'36*
Satan Met a Lady *'36*
Dangerous *'35*
The Devil Is a Woman *'35*
Doubting Thomas *'35*
Six of a Kind *'34*
The Song of Songs *'33*
Night After Night *'32*
Tonight or Never *'31*
Dubarry *'30*
Raffles *'30*
Espen Skjonberg
The Last Lieutenant *'94*
One Day in the Life of Ivan Denisovich *'71*
Jerzy Skolimowski (1938-)
Big Shots *'87*
White Nights *'85*
Innocent Sorcerers *'60*
Helgi Skulason
Pathfinder *'87*
Revenge of the Barbarians *'85*
Azura Skye
The Salton Sea *'02*
Bandits *'01*
28 Days *'00*
Dementia *'98*
Ione Skye (1971-)
Went to Coney Island on a Mission from God...Be Back by Five *'98*
One Night Stand *'97*
Dream for an Insomniac *'96*
The Color of Evening *'95*
Four Rooms *'95*
Girls in Prison *'94*
Gas Food Lodging *'92*
Guncrazy *'92*
Samantha *'92*
Mindwalk: A Film for Passionate Thinkers *'91*
Carmilla *'89*
The Rachel Papers *'89*
Say Anything *'89*
A Night in the Life of Jimmy Reardon *'88*
River's Edge *'87*
Stranded *'87*
Tristen Skylar
Book of Shadows: Blair Witch 2 *'00*
Cadillac Man *'90*
Kidco *'83*
Demian Slade
Back to the Beach *'87*
Better Off Dead *'85*
Max Elliott Slade (1980-)
Apollo 13 *'95*
3 Ninjas Knuckle Up *'95*
3 Ninjas Kick Back *'94*
3 Ninjas *'92*
Jeremy Slate (1926-)
The Lawnmower Man *'92*
Dream Machine *'91*
Dead Pit *'89*
Goodnight, Sweet Marilyn *'89*
Mr. Horn *'79*
Summer of Fear *'78*
The Centerfold Girls *'74*
Alligator Alley *'72*
Hell's Angels '69 *'69*
Hell's Belles *'69*
The Hooked Generation *'69*
True Grit *'69*
The Devil's Brigade *'68*
Born Losers *'67*
I'll Take Sweden *'65*
Girls! Girls! Girls! *'62*
G.I. Blues *'60*
Christian Slater (1969-)
Windtalkers *'02*
Hard Cash *'01*
3000 Miles to Graceland *'01*
The Contender *'00*
Basil *'98*
Very Bad Things *'98*
Hard Rain *'97*
Julian Po *'97*
Bed of Roses *'95*
Broken Arrow *'95*
Murder in the First *'95*
Interview with the Vampire *'94*
Jimmy Hollywood *'94*
True Romance *'93*
Untamed Heart *'93*
Ferngully: The Last Rain Forest *'92 (V)*
Kuffs *'92*
Where the Day Takes You *'92*
Mobsters *'91*
Robin Hood: Prince of Thieves *'91*
Star Trek 6: The Undiscovered Country *'91*
Pump Up the Volume *'90*
Tales from the Darkside: The Movie *'90*
Young Guns 2 *'90*
Beyond the Stars *'89*
Gleaming the Cube *'89*
Heathers *'89*
The Wizard *'89*
Tucker: The Man and His Dream *'88*
The Name of the Rose *'86*
Twisted *'86*
Legend of Billie Jean *'85*
Living Proof: The Hank Williams Jr. Story *'83*
Helen Slater (1963-)
Nowhere in Sight *'01*
Toothless *'97*
No Way Back *'96*
Lassie *'94*
Parallel Lives *'94*
Chantilly Lace *'93*
A House in the Hills *'93*
12:01 *'93*
Betrayal of the Dove *'92*
City Slickers *'91*
Happy Together *'89*
Sticky Fingers *'88*
The Secret of My Success *'87*
Ruthless People *'86*
Legend of Billie Jean *'85*
Supergirl *'84*
Ryan Slater
Home Team *'98*
The Amazing Panda Adventure *'95*
John Slattery
A Death in the Family *'02*
Harvest *'99*
From the Earth to the Moon *'98*
The Naked Man *'98*
Where's Marlowe? *'98*
Lily Dale *'96*
Tony Slattery
Heaven's a Drag *'94*

Peter's Friends '92

Tod Slaughter (1885-1956)
The Greed of William Hart '48
Crimes at the Dark House '39
The Face at the Window '39
The Hooded Terror '38
Sexton Blake and the Hooded Terror '38
Never Too Late to Mend '37
Ticket of Leave Man '37
The Crimes of Stephen Hawke '36
Demon Barber of Fleet Street '36
Murder in the Old Red Barn '36

Darla Slavens
Married People, Single Sex '93
Red Snow '91

Millie Slavin
One Night Stand '95
The People vs. Jean Harris '81

Bobby Slayton
Bandits '01
The Rat Pack '98

Tommy Sledge
Movie ... In Your Face '90
Lobster Man from Mars '89

Victor Slezak
The Cat's Meow '01
Lost Souls '00
One Tough Cop '98
The Siege '98
Beyond Rangoon '95
The Bridges of Madison County '95
Bed & Breakfast '92

Walter Slezak (1902-83)
Treasure Island '72
Black Beauty '71
Caper of the Golden Bulls '67
Emil and the Detectives '64
The Wonderful World of the Brothers Grimm '62
Come September '61
Bedtime for Bonzo '51
People Will Talk '51
Abbott and Costello in the Foreign Legion '50
The Yellow Cab Man '50
The Inspector General '49
The Pirate '48
Born to Kill '47
Riff-Raff '47
Sinbad, the Sailor '47
Cornered '45
Salome, Where She Danced '45
The Spanish Main '45
Lifeboat '44
The Princess and the Pirate '44
Step Lively '44
The Fallen Sparrow '43
This Land Is Mine '43
Once Upon a Honeymoon '42

Grace Slick
Jackie's Back '99
Gimme Shelter '70

Everett Sloane (1909-65)
Hercules and the Princess of Troy '65
Disorderly Orderly '64
The Patsy '64
Home from the Hill '60
Marjorie Morningstar '58
Lust for Life '56
Patterns '56
Somebody Up There Likes Me '56
The Big Knife '55
The Enforcer '51
Sirocco '51
The Men '50
The Lady from Shanghai '48
Citizen Kane '41

Joey Slotnick
The Hollow Man '00
The Pirates of Silicon Valley '99
Blast from the Past '98
Since You've Been Gone '97
Twister '96
A League of Their Own '92

Georgia Slowe
The Company of Wolves '85
The Black Arrow '84

James Sloyan (1941-)
Danielle Steel's Changes '91
Deadline Assault '90
Billionaire Boys Club '87
Code Name: Dancer '87
Amos '85
Prime Suspect '82
Callie and Son '81
The Disappearance of Aimee '76

Errol Slue
Baby on Board '92
Murder One '88

Marya Small
Zapped! '82
American Pop '81 (V)

Phillips Smalley
The Taxi Mystery '26
Charley's Aunt '25

Jimmy Smallhorne
When the Sky Falls '99
2 by 4 '98

Amy Smart (1976-)
Scotland, PA '02
Rat Race '01
Road Trip '00
The '70s '00
Outside Providence '99
Dee Snider's Strangeland '98
High Voltage '98
Varsity Blues '98

Dee Smart
Welcome to Woop Woop '97
Back of Beyond '95
Blackwater Trail '95

Jean Smart (1959-)
Disney's The Kid '00
Snow Day '00
Guinevere '99
Change of Heart '98
Neil Simon's The Odd Couple 2 '98
The Brady Bunch Movie '95
Edie & Pen '95
A Stranger in Town '95
Scarlett '94
The Yarn Princess '94
The Yearling '94
Homeward Bound: The Incredible Journey '93
Mistress '91
A Fight for Jenny '90
Maximum Security '87
Project X '87
Fire with Fire '86

Rebecca Smart
Blackrock '97
Celia: Child of Terror '89

Richard Smedley
The Abductors '72
A Place Called Today '72
Brain of Blood '71

Ron Smerczak
Jackie Chan's Who Am I '98
Return of the Family Man '89
Hunted '88

Robert Smigel
Little Nicky '00 (V)
Happy Gilmore '96

Tava Smiley
A Girl, 3 Guys and a Gun '01
Outta Time '01

Yakov Smirnoff (1951-)
Up Your Alley '89
Heartburn '86
The Adventures of Buckaroo Banzai Across the Eighth Dimension '84

Alexis Smith (1921-93)
The Age of Innocence '93
Dress Gray '86
Tough Guys '86
La Truite '83
Casey's Shadow '78
The Little Girl Who Lives down the Lane '76
Once Is Not Enough '75
The Young Philadelphians '59
This Happy Feeling '58
The Sleeping Tiger '54
Split Second '53
Here Comes the Groom '51
Any Number Can Play '49
South of St. Louis '48
The Two Mrs. Carrolls '47
Night and Day '46
Conflict '45
The Horn Blows at Midnight '45
Rhapsody in Blue '45
San Antonio '45
The Adventures of Mark Twain '44
Hollywood Canteen '44
Gentleman Jim '42
Dive Bomber '41

Allison Smith (1969-)
Terror Tract '00
At First Sight '95
A Reason to Believe '95
Jason Goes to Hell: The Final Friday '93
Wildflower '91

Amber Smith (1972-)
Def Jam's How to Be a Player '97
L.A. Confidential '97
Laws of Deception '97
Mars '96
Private Parts '96
Red Shoe Diaries 7: Burning Up '96

Anna Deavere Smith (1950-)
The American President '95
Dave '93
Philadelphia '93

Anna Nicole Smith
Skyscraper '95
To the Limit '95

Art Smith (1899-1973)
The Painted Hills '51
In a Lonely Place '50
The Next Voice You Hear '50
Caught '49
Letter from an Unknown Woman '48
Mr. Peabody & the Mermaid '48

Bill Smith
Spirit of the Eagle '90
Atlantis, the Lost Continent '61

Brandon Smith
Jeepers Creepers '01
Powder '95

Britta Smith
American Women '00
A Certain Justice '99
Moll Flanders '96
The Summer House '94
In the Name of the Father '93

Brooke Smith (1967-)
Bad Company '02
Series 7: The Contenders '01
Last Summer In the Hamptons '96
Kansas City '95
Vanya on 42nd Street '94
The Night We Never Met '93
The Silence of the Lambs '91

Bubba Smith (1945-)
Silence of the Hams '93
Fist of Honor '92
My Samurai '92
Escape from DS-3 '80s
Police Academy 6: City under Siege '89
Police Academy 5: Assignment Miami Beach '88
Police Academy 4: Citizens on Patrol '87
The Wild Pair '87
Police Academy 3: Back in Training '86
Police Academy 2: Their First Assignment '85
Police Academy '84
Stroker Ace '83

Sir C. Aubrey Smith (1863-1948)
Unconquered '47
And Then There Were None '45
The Adventures of Mark Twain '44
Sensations of 1945 '44
The White Cliffs of Dover '44
Forever and a Day '43
Madame Curie '43
Beyond Tomorrow '40
Rebecca '40
Waterloo Bridge '40
Another Thin Man '39
Balalaika '39
Eternally Yours '39
Five Came Back '39
The Four Feathers '39
The Hurricane '37
Prisoner of Zenda '37
Thoroughbreds Don't Cry '37
Wee Willie Winkie '37
The Garden of Allah '36
Little Lord Fauntleroy '36
Lloyds of London '36
China Seas '35
The Crusades '35
The Lives of a Bengal Lancer '35
Transatlantic Tunnel '35
Cleopatra '34
Scarlet Empress '34
Bombshell '33
Queen Christina '33
Trader Horn '31

Cedric Smith
Sea People '00
Jack Higgins' Thunder Point '97
Witchboard 3: The Possession '95
The Penthouse '92
Love and Hate: A Marriage Made in Hell '90
Anne of Green Gables '85

Charles Martin Smith (1953-)
P.T. Barnum '99
Apartment Complex '98
Deep Impact '98
The Beast '96
Dead Silence '96
The Final Cut '96
Wedding Bell Blues '96
Larry McMurtry's Streets of Laredo '95
The Road Home '95
Roswell: The U.F.O. Cover-Up '94
Speechless '94
And the Band Played On '93
Boris and Natasha: The Movie '92
Deep Cover '92
The Hot Spot '90
The Experts '89
The Untouchables '87
Starman '84
Never Cry Wolf '83
Cotton Candy '82
Herbie Goes Bananas '80
More American Graffiti '79
The Buddy Holly Story '78
The Campus Corpse '77
Law of the Land '76
No Deposit, No Return '76
Rafferty & the Gold Dust Twins '75
American Graffiti '73
Pat Garrett & Billy the Kid '73
Culpepper Cattle Co. '72
Fuzz '72

Cheryl "Rainbeaux" Smith (1955-)
Independence Day '83
Parasite '82
Vice Squad '82
Melvin and Howard '80
Cheech and Chong's Up in Smoke '79
Laserblast '78
Incredible Melting Man '77
Drum '76
Massacre at Central High '76
Pom Pom Girls '76
Revenge of the Cheerleaders '76
Slumber Party '57 '76
Farewell, My Lovely '75
Caged Heat '74
The Swinging Cheerleaders '74
Lemora, Lady Dracula '73

Connie Smith (1941-)
Hell on Wheels '67
Road to Nashville '67
Treasure of the Golden Condor '53
Room to Let '49

Cotter Smith (1949-)
Ride the Wild Fields '00
Lifeform '96
Midnight's Child '93
The Last Prostitute '91
Cameron's Closet '89
K-9 '89
Lady Beware '87
Broken Badge '85
A Bunny's Tale '85

Cynthia Smith
For the Love of Benji '77
Benji '74

Cyril Smith (1892-1963)
John and Julie '55
Old Mother Riley, Headmistress '50
Appointment with Crime '45
Sidewalks of London '38

David Anthony Smith
Terror in Paradise '90
Judgment Day '88

Ebbe Roe Smith
Tapeheads '89
Big Bad Mama 2 '87
The Big Easy '87

Ethel Smith
Melody Time '48 (V)
Bathing Beauty '44

Garnett Smith
Whitcomb's War '87
Laboratory '80

Geraldine Smith
Spike of Bensonhurst '88
Mixed Blood '84
Flesh '68

Gregory Smith (1983-)
American Outlaws '01
The Climb '97

Gregory Edward Smith (1983-)
Krippendorf's Tribe '98
Small Soldiers '98
Harriet the Spy '96
Spellbreaker: Secret of the Leprechauns '96
Leapin' Leprechauns '95

Hillary Bailey Smith
Last Breath '96
Love Potion #9 '92

Howard Smith (1893-)
The Brass Bottle '63
I Bury the Living '58
No Time for Sergeants '58
Call Northside 777 '48
State of the Union '48

Howard K. Smith
Dawn of the Dead '78
Nasty Habits '77

Jaclyn Smith (1947-)
My Very Best Friend '96
Lies Before Kisses '92
Danielle Steel's Kaleidoscope '90
The Bourne Identity '88
Windmills of the Gods '88
The Night They Saved Christmas '87
Rage of Angels: The Story Continues '86
Deja Vu '84
George Washington '84
Rage of Angels '83
Jacqueline Bouvier Kennedy '81
Nightkill '80
Users '78
Probe '72
The Adventurers '70
Goodbye Columbus '69

Jamie Renee Smith (1987-)
MVP (Most Valuable Primate) '00
Dante's Peak '97
Children of the Corn 4: The Gathering '96
Magic in the Mirror: Fowl Play '96

John Smith (1932-95)
The Kettles on Old MacDonald's Farm '57
We're No Angels '55

John W. Smith
Star Crystal '85
Hot Rod Girl '56

Julie K. Smith
Return to Savage Beach '97
The Dallas Connection '94

Kent Smith (1907-85)
Die Sister, Die! '74
The Affair '73
Pete 'n' Tillie '72
Probe '72
The Night Stalker '71
Games '67
The Balcony '63
Strangers When We Meet '60
The Badlanders '58
Party Girl '58
Sayonara '57
Magic Town '47
The Spiral Staircase '46
Curse of the Cat People '44
Cat People '42
Back Door to Heaven '39

Kerr Smith (1972-)
The Forsaken '01
Final Destination '00

Kevin Smith (1963-2002)
Young Hercules '97
Desperate Remedies '93

Kevin Smith (1970-)
Jay and Silent Bob Strike Back '01
Scream 3 '00
Dogma '99
Chasing Amy '97
Mallrats '95
Clerks '94

Kurtwood Smith (1943-)
A Bright Shining Lie '98
The Magnificent Seven '98
Safety Patrol '98
Shelter '98
Citizen Ruth '96
Prefontaine '96
A Time to Kill '96
The Last of the Dogmen '95
To Die For '95
Dead on Sight '94
Boxing Helena '93
The Crush '93
Fortress '93
Shadows and Fog '92
Company Business '91
Star Trek 6: The Undiscovered Country '91
Quick Change '90
Dead Poets Society '89
The Heart of Dixie '89

The Nightmare Years '89
True Believer '89
Rambo 3 '88
RoboCop '87

Lane Smith (1936-)
The Legend of Bagger Vance '00
Inherit the Wind '99
From the Earth to the Moon '98
The Hi-Lo Country '98
Why Do Fools Fall in Love? '98
The Scout '94
The Spy Within '94
Son-in-Law '93
The Distinguished Gentleman '92
Duplicates '92
False Arrest '92
The Mighty Ducks '92
My Cousin Vinny '92
Air America '90
Blind Vengeance '90
The Final Days '89
Night Game '89
Prison '88
Weeds '87
Dress Gray '86
Frances '82
Prime Suspect '82
The Solitary Man '82
A Rumor of War '80
Blue Collar '78

Lewis Smith (1958-)
Wyatt Earp '94
Diary of a Hitman '91
Fulfillment '89
North and South Book 2 '86
The Heavenly Kid '85
The Adventures of Buckaroo Banzai Across the Eighth Dimension '84
The Final Terror '83

Linda Smith
Taken '99
The Phone Call '89

Liz Smith (1925-)
A Christmas Carol '99
Sweet Revenge '98
A Merry War '97
Apartment Zero '88
We Think the World of You '88
A Private Function '84

Lois Smith (1930-)
The Pledge '00
The Eternal '99
Tumbleweeds '98
Larger Than Life '96
Twister '96
Dead Man Walking '95
How to Make an American Quilt '95
Truman '95
Holy Matrimony '94
Falling Down '93
Sarah, Plain and Tall: Skylark '93
Hard Promises '92
Keep the Change '92
Fried Green Tomatoes '91
Switched at Birth '91
Green Card '90
Black Widow '87
Twisted '86
Reckless '84
Reuben, Reuben '83
Five Easy Pieces '70

Loring Smith
Ma and Pa Kettle at Waikiki '55
Shadow of the Thin Man '41

Madeleine Smith (1949-)
Frankenstein and the Monster from Hell '74
Live and Let Die '73
The Vampire Lovers '70

Madolyn Smith (1957-)
Final Approach '91
The Super '91
The Rose and the Jackal '90
Funny Farm '88
The Caller '87
All of Me '84
Ernie Kovacs: Between the Laughter '84
2010: The Year We Make Contact '84
Sadat '83
Pray TV '82
Rehearsal for Murder '82
Urban Cowboy '80

Maggie Smith (1934-)
Divine Secrets of the Ya-Ya Sisterhood '02
Gosford Park '01
Harry Potter and the Sorcerer's Stone '01
All the King's Men '99
David Copperfield '99
The Last September '99
Tea with Mussolini '99
Curtain Call '97
Washington Square '97
The First Wives Club '96
Richard III '95
The Secret Garden '93
Sister Act 2: Back in the Habit '93
Sister Act '92
Hook '91
The Lonely Passion of Judith Hearne '87
A Room with a View '86
Lily in Love '85
Mrs. Silly '85
A Private Function '84
Better Late Than Never '83
Evil under the Sun '82
The Missionary '82
Clash of the Titans '81
Quartet '81
California Suite '78
Death on the Nile '78
Murder by Death '76
Travels with My Aunt '72
The Prime of Miss Jean Brodie '69
Hot Millions '68
The Honey Pot '67
Othello '65
The Pumpkin Eater '64
The V.I.P.'s '63

Maurice Smith
Fist of Glory '95
Bloodfist 2 '90

Mel Smith (1952-)
Twelfth Night '96
Brain Donors '92
The Misadventures of Mr. Wilt '90
The Princess Bride '87
Morons from Outer Space '85
Slayground '84

Melanie Smith (1962-)
Night Hunter '95
The Baby Doll Murders '92
Trancers 3: Deth Lives '92

Oliver Smith
Hellbound: Hellraiser 2 '88
Hellraiser '87

Patricia Smith
Save the Tiger '73
Spirit of St. Louis '57

Paul Smith
Maverick '94
Desert Kickboxer '92
Caged Fury '90
Crossing the Line '90
Gor '88
Death Chase '87
Outlaw Force '87
Sonny Boy '87
Haunted Honeymoon '86
Platypus Cove '86
Crimewave '85
The Fire in the Stone '85
Red Sonja '85
Sno-Line '85
Dune '84
Jungle Warriors '84
Pieces '83
The Salamander '82
Mortuary '81
Popeye '80
Midnight Express '78
Return of the Tiger '78
Madron '70
Men of the Fighting Lady '54

Pete Smith
The Boys '98
Once Were Warriors '94

Quinn Smith
The Bad News Bears in Breaking Training '77
The Bad News Bears '76

Rex Smith (1956-)
A Passion to Kill '94
The Trial of the Incredible Hulk '89
Transformations '88
Street Hawk '84
The Pirates of Penzance '83
Snow White and the Seven Dwarfs '83
Sooner or Later '78

Riley Smith
Eight Legged Freaks '02
Not Another Teen Movie '01
Voodoo Academy '00
Wild Grizzly '99

Robin Smith
Never Say Die '94
Bopha! '93

Roger Smith
Auntie Mame '58
Man of a Thousand Faces '57

Roger Guenveur Smith
All About the Benjamins '02
Hamlet '01
Final Destination '00
Summer of Sam '99
The Color of Courage '98
Get On the Bus '96
Tales from the Hood '95
Deep Cover '92

Savannah Smith
Everybody's All American '88
Code of Honor '84
The Long Riders '80

Sean Smith
Children of the Corn: Revelation '01
Atomic Train '99
The King and I '99 (V)

Seth Smith
The Climb '97
Home Alone 3 '97

Shawn Smith (1922-95)
It! The Terror from Beyond Space '58
The Land Unknown '57

Shawnee Smith (1970-)
Breakfast of Champions '98
Bombshell '97
Dogtown '97
The Low Life '95
Stephen King's The Stand '94
Desperate Hours '90
Who's Harry Crumb? '89
The Blob '88
Summer School '87

Shelley Smith (1952-)
The Fantastic World of D.C. Collins '84
National Lampoon's Class Reunion '82
The Night the City Screamed '80

Stuart Smith
Ninja Hunt '80s
Ninja Destroyer '70s

Sydney Smith
The Gallant Hours '60
No Time for Sergeants '58

Will Smith (1968-)
Men in Black 2 '02
Ali '01
The Legend of Bagger Vance '00
Wild Wild West '99
Enemy of the State '98
Men in Black '97
Independence Day '96
Bad Boys '95
Made in America '93
Six Degrees of Separation '93
Where the Day Takes You '92

William Smith (1934-)
Broken Vessels '98
The Shooter '97
Cartel '90
The Last Riders '90
Slow Burn '90
Terror in Beverly Hills '90
Action U.S.A. '89
Deadly Breed '89
East L.A. Warriors '89
Emperor of the Bronx '89
Evil Altar '89
Jungle Assault '89
L.A. Vice '89
B.O.R.N. '88
Hell on the Battleground '88
Maniac Cop '88
Memorial Valley Massacre '88
Commando Squad '87
Platoon Leader '87
Eye of the Tiger '86
Moon in Scorpio '86
Fever Pitch '85
Mean Season '85
Angels Die Hard '84
Red Dawn '84
Conan the Barbarian '82
Any Which Way You Can '80
The Frisco Kid '79
The Rebels '79
Seven '79
Blackjack '78
Fast Company '78
Twilight's Last Gleaming '77
Hollywood Man '76
Scorchy '76
The Ultimate Warrior '75
Boss '74
The Deadly Trackers '73
Gentle Savage '73
Invasion of the Bee Girls '73
A Taste of Hell '73
Grave of the Vampire '72
Chrome and Hot Leather '71
C.C. & Company '70
Darker than Amber '70
The Losers '70
Run, Angel, Run! '69

Yeardley Smith (1964-)
As Good As It Gets '97
Just Write '97
We're Back! A Dinosaur's Story '93 (V)
City Slickers '91
Ginger Ale Afternoon '89
Maximum Overdrive '86
Heaven Help Us '85
Legend of Billie Jean '85

J. Smith-Cameron
The Rage: Carrie 2 '99
In and Out '97
Harriet the Spy '96

Jamie Smith-Jackson
Bug '75
Satan's School for Girls '73

Jan Smithers
Mr. Nice Guy '86
Where the Lilies Bloom '74

William (Bill) Smithers (1927-)
Death Sport '78
Scorpio '73
Attack! '56

Bill Smitrovich (1947-)
The Golden Spiders: A Nero Wolfe Mystery '00
Kiss Toledo Goodbye '00
Thirteen Days '00
The '60s '99
Around the Fire '98
Dean Koontz's Mr. Murder '98
Futuresport '98
Air Force One '97
Independence Day '96
The Trigger Effect '96
Bodily Harm '95
Nick of Time '95
Crazy People '90
Renegades '89
A Killing Affair '85
Silver Bullet '85

Jimmy Smits (1956-)
Star Wars: Episode 2—Attack of the Clones '02
Bless the Child '00
Price of Glory '00
The Million Dollar Hotel '99
Murder in Mind '97
Marshal Law '96
The Last Word '95
The Cisco Kid '94
My Family '94
Gross Misconduct '93
Stephen King's The Tommyknockers '93
Fires Within '91
Switch '91
Vital Signs '90
Old Gringo '89
Glitz '88
The Believers '87
Stamp of a Killer '87
L.A. Law '86
Running Scared '86

Sonja Smits (1958-)
Life with Judy Garland—Me and My Shadows '01
That's My Baby! '88
Videodrome '83
The Pit '81
War Brides '80

Jurnee Smollett
Selma, Lord, Selma '99
Eve's Bayou '97

Dick Smothers (1939-)
Casino '95
Tales of the Unexpected '91
Speed Zone '88

Tom Smothers (1937-)
Speed Zone '88
Pandemonium '82
Serial '80
The Kids Are Alright '79
A Pleasure Doing Business '79
Silver Bears '78
Alice Through the Looking Glass '66

Victoria Smurfit (1974-)
About a Boy '02
Berkeley Square '98
Ivanhoe '97
The Run of the Country '95

Ann Smyrner
Beyond the Law '68
The House of 1000 Dolls '67
Reptilicus '62

Wesley Snipes (1962-)
Blade II '02
ZigZag '02
The Art of War '00
Disappearing Acts '00
Blade '98
Down in the Delta '98
Futuresport '98
U.S. Marshals '98
Murder at 1600 '97
One Night Stand '97
The Fan '96
America's Dream '95
Money Train '95
To Wong Foo, Thanks for Everything, Julie Newmar '95
Waiting to Exhale '95
Drop Zone '94
Sugar Hill '94
Boiling Point '93
Demolition Man '93
Rising Sun '93
Passenger 57 '92
White Men Can't Jump '92
Jungle Fever '91
New Jack City '91
The Waterdance '91
King of New York '90
Mo' Better Blues '90
Major League '89
Streets of Gold '86
Wildcats '86

Carrie Snodgress (1946-)
Ed Gein '01
The Forsaken '01
A Stranger in the Kingdom '98
Wild Things '98
Death Benefit '96
Phantom 2040 Movie: The Ghost Who Walks '95 (V)
White Man's Burden '95
8 Seconds '94
The Ballad of Little Jo '93
Woman with a Past '92
Blue Sky '91
Mission of the Shark '91
Chill Factor '90
The Rose and the Jackal '90
Across the Tracks '89
Blueberry Hill '88
Murphy's Law '86
L.A. Bad '85
Pale Rider '85
Nadia '84
A Night in Heaven '83
The Solitary Man '82
Trick or Treats '82
The Attic '80
The Fury '78
Diary of a Mad Housewife '70
Silent Night, Lonely Night '69

Snoop Dogg (1971-)
Baby Boy '01
Bones '01
Training Day '01
The Wash '01
Urban Menace '99
The Wrecking Crew '99
Caught Up '98
Ride '98
Half-Baked '97

Raven Snow
Delta of Venus '95
Red Shoe Diaries 6: How I Met My Husband '95

Victoria Snow
My Husband's Double Life '01
Buffalo Jump '90
Love and Hate: A Marriage Made in Hell '90

Arlen Dean Snyder (1933-)
Cora Unashamed '00
Mommy 2: Mommy's Day '96
Running Cool '93
Internal Affairs '90
Marked for Death '90
Wheels of Terror '90
Heartbreak Ridge '86
Deadly Force '83
Night Partners '83
No Place to Hide '81
Red Flag: The Ultimate Game '81
Yanks '79
Young Love, First Love '79
Dear Detective '78
Scalpel '76

Drew Snyder
Blindfold: Acts of Obsession '94
Separate Lives '94
Dance with Death '91
Project: Eliminator '91
Izzy & Moe '85
Firestarter '84
Night School '81

Suzanne Snyder
Killer Klowns from Outer Space '88
The Night Before '88
Retribution '88
Return of the Living Dead 2 '88
Prettykill '87

Michele (Michael) Soavi (1957-)
Demons '86
Creepers '85
A Blade in the Dark '83
Gates of Hell '80

Barry Sobel (1959-)
That Thing You Do! '96
Doc Hollywood '91
Martians Go Home! '90
Punchline '88

Leelee Sobieski (1982-)
The Glass House '01
Joy Ride '01
My First Mister '01
Uprising '01
Here on Earth '00
Eyes Wide Shut '99
Joan of Arc '99
Never Been Kissed '99
Deep Impact '98
A Soldier's Daughter Never Cries '98
Jungle 2 Jungle '96
A Horse for Danny '95

Ron Soble (1932-2002)
The Beast Within '82
True Grit '69

Maria Socas
Deathstalker 2: Duel of the Titans '87
The Warrior & the Sorceress '84

Kristina Soderbaum (1912-2001)
Night Train to Venice '93
Kolberg '45
Jud Suess '40

Steven Soderbergh (1963-)
Waking Life '01
Schizopolis '97

Camilla Soeberg (1966-)
The Empty Mirror '99
Mouse Hunt '97
Erotique '94
A Night of Love '87
Twist & Shout '84

Abraham Sofaer (1896-1988)
Demon with a Glass Hand '64
Captain Sinbad '63
Bhowani Junction '56
Elephant Walk '54
Naked Jungle '54
Quo Vadis '51
Calling Paul Temple '48
Dual Alibi '47

Rena Sofer (1968-)
Keeping the Faith '00
Traffic '00
The Stepsister '97
Twinsitters '95

Hans Sohnker (1903-81)
The Phantom of Soho '64
Sherlock Holmes and the Deadly Necklace '62
For the First Time '59
Die Grosse Freiheit Nr. 7 '45

Sojin
Seven Samurai '54
The Thief of Baghdad '24

Marilyn Sokol
Something Short of Paradise '79
The Goodbye Girl '77

Marla Sokoloff (1980-)
Sugar & Spice '01
Dude, Where's My Car? '00
Whatever It Takes '00

Vladimir Sokoloff (1889-1962)
Taras Bulba '62
Mr. Sardonicus '61
Beyond the Time Barrier '60
I Was a Teenage Werewolf '57
Baron of Arizona '51
Cloak and Dagger '46
A Scandal in Paris '46
For Whom the Bell Tolls '43
The Road to Morocco '42
Comrade X '40
The Real Glory '39
Conquest '37
The Lower Depths '36

Miguel Angel Sola (1950-)
Tango '98
A Shadow You Soon Will Be '94
Mayalunta '86
Funny, Dirty Little War '83

Silvia Solar (1940-)
The Gentleman Killer '78
Night of the Howling Beast '75
Finger on the Trigger '65
As If It Were Raining '63

Fernando Soler
Susana '51
The Great Madcap '49

Paul Soles
The Score '01
The Lotus Eaters '93
Beethoven Lives Upstairs '92
The Gunrunner '84
Ticket to Heaven '81

P.J. Soles (1955-)
Jawbreaker '98
Little Bigfoot '96
Out There '95
Soldier's Fortune '91
Alienator '89
B.O.R.N. '88
Innocent Prey '88
Saigon Commandos '88
Sweet Dreams '85
Stripes '81
Rock 'n' Roll High School '79
Halloween '78
The Possessed '77
The Boy in the Plastic Bubble '76
Carrie '76

Yulia Solntseva
Earth '30
Aelita: Queen of Mars '24

Bruce Solomon (1944-)
Night of the Creeps '86
Foul Play '78
Children Shouldn't Play with Dead Things '72

Charles Solomon
Witchcraft 4: Virgin Heart '92
Witchcraft 2: The Temptress '90
Witchcraft 3: The Kiss of Death '90
The Channeler '89

Todd Solondz (1960-)
As Good As It Gets '97
Fear, Anxiety and Depression '89

Anatoli (Otto) Solonitzin (1934-82)
Stalker '79
Solaris '72
Andrei Rublev '66

Elena Solovei (1947-)
Oblomov '81
A Slave of Love '78
An Unfinished Piece for a Player Piano '77

Yanti Somer
Reactor '85
Cosmos: War of the Planets '80

Kristi Somers
Tomboy '85
Hardbodies '84

Suzanne Somers (1946-)
Say It Isn't So '01
No Laughing Matter '97
Seduced by Evil '94
Serial Mom '94
Happily Ever After '82
Nothing Personal '80
Yesterday's Hero '79
Ants '77
Sky Hei$t '75
American Graffiti '73

Geraldine Somerville
Gosford Park '01
The Aristocrats '99
Cracker: Brotherly Love '95
Haunted '95
Cracker: Men Should Weep '94
Cracker: To Be a Somebody '94
Catherine Cookson's The Black Velvet Gown '92

Julie Sommars (1942-)
Sex and the Single Parent '82
Herbie Goes to Monte Carlo '77
I'm the Girl He Wants to Kill '74

Elke Sommer (1940-)
Severed Ties '92
Adventures Beyond Belief '87
Anastasia: The Mystery of Anna '86
Jenny's War '85
Lily in Love '85
No One Cries Forever '85
Fantastic Seven '82
Inside the Third Reich '82
One Away '80
The Big Scam '79
The Double McGuffin '79
Prisoner of Zenda '79
The Treasure Seekers '79
Left for Dead '78
Swiss Conspiracy '77
The Invisible Strangler '76
Carry On Behind '75
Lisa and the Devil '75
Ten Little Indians '75
It's Not the Size That Counts '74
Probe '72
Torture Chamber of Baron Blood '72
Zeppelin '71
The Invincible Six '68
The Wrecking Crew '68
The Corrupt Ones '67
Boy, Did I Get a Wrong Number! '66
The Oscar '66
A Shot in the Dark '64
The Prize '63
Sweet Ecstasy '62
Daniella by Night '61

Josef Sommer (1934-)
The Sum of All Fears '02
The Next Best Thing '00
Shaft '00
Patch Adams '98
The Proposition '97
Hidden in America '96
Mistrial '96
Letter to My Killer '95
Moonlight and Valentino '95
Strange Days '95
The Enemy Within '94
Nobody's Fool '94
Hostages '93
Malice '93
An American Story '92
The Mighty Ducks '92
Shadows and Fog '92
A Woman Named Jackie '91
Forced March '90
Bloodhounds of Broadway '89
Bridge to Silence '89
Chances Are '89
Dracula's Widow '88
The Rosary Murders '87
Yuri Nosenko, KGB '86
Execution of Raymond Graham '85
Target '85
Witness '85
Iceman '84
Independence Day '83
Silkwood '83
Still of the Night '82
Absence of Malice '81
Reds '81
Rollover '81
Hide in Plain Sight '80
The Scarlet Letter '79

Helga Sommerfeld
Code Name Alpha '67
The Phantom of Soho '64

Gale Sondergaard (1899-1985)
Echoes '83
The Return of a Man Called Horse '76
Savage Intruder '68
East Side, West Side '49
The Road to Rio '47
Anna and the King of Siam '46
The Time of Their Lives '46
The Climax '44
The Invisible Man's Revenge '44
Spider Woman '44
Isle of Forgotten Sins '43
My Favorite Blonde '42
A Night to Remember '42
The Black Cat '41
The Blue Bird '40
The Letter '40
The Mark of Zorro '40
Juarez '39
Never Say Die '39
The Life of Emile Zola '37
Anthony Adverse '36

Paul Sonkkila
The Interview '98
Mr. Reliable: A True Story '95

Michael Sonye
Sorority Babes in the Slimeball Bowl-A-Rama '87 (V)
Surf Nazis Must Die '87

Jack Soo (1916-79)
Return from Witch Mountain '78
The Green Berets '68
Flower Drum Song '61

Michael Sopkiw
After the Fall of New York '85
Blastfighter '85
Massacre in Dinosaur Valley '85

Agnes Soral (1960-)
Window to Paris '95
Blitz '85
Tchao Pantin '84
One Wild Moment '78

Kevin Sorbo (1958-)
Kull the Conqueror '97
Hercules the Legendary Journeys, Vol. 1: And the Amazon Women '94
Hercules the Legendary Journeys, Vol. 2: The Lost Kingdom '94
Hercules the Legendary Journeys, Vol. 3: The Circle of Fire '94
Hercules the Legendary Journeys, Vol. 4: In the Underworld '94

Alberto Sordi (1920-)
Those Magnificent Men in Their Flying Machines '65
The Great War '59
Two Nights with Cleopatra '54
I Vitelloni '53
The White Sheik '52

Guy Sorel
Mayflower: The Pilgrims' Adventure '79
Honeymoon Killers '70

Jean Sorel (1934-)
Paralyzed '70s
Belle de Jour '67
Sandra of a Thousand Delights '65

Louise Sorel (1940-)
Mazes and Monsters '82
When Every Day Was the Fourth of July '78
Get Christie Love! '74
Plaza Suite '71
The President's Plane Is Missing '71

Ted (Theodore) Sorel (1936-)
Me and the Mob '94
Basket Case 2 '90
From Beyond '86

Linda Sorensen (1942-)
Relative Fear '95
Family Reunion '88
Joshua Then and Now '85
Kavik the Wolf Dog '84
Stone Cold Dead '80

Ricky Sorenson (-1994)
The Sword in the Stone '63 (V)
Tarzan and the Trappers '58

Charo Soriano (1928-)
Orgy of the Vampires '73
Dracula's Great Love '72
The Garden of Delights '70

Arleen (Arlene) Sorkin (1956-)
It's Pat: The Movie '94
I Don't Buy Kisses Anymore '92
From Here to Maternity '85

Mira Sorvino (1967-)
The Great Gatsby '01
The Triumph of Love '01
Free Money '99
Summer of Sam '99
At First Sight '98
Lulu on the Bridge '98
The Replacement Killers '98
Mimic '97
Romy and Michele's High School Reunion '97
Beautiful Girls '96
Sweet Nothing '96
Blue in the Face '95
The Buccaneers '95
Mighty Aphrodite '95
Norma Jean and Marilyn '95
Tarantella '95
Barcelona '94
New York Cop '94
Parallel Lives '94
Quiz Show '94
Amongst Friends '93
Tales of Erotica '93

Paul Sorvino (1939-)
Perfume '01
See Spot Run '01
Cheaters '00
Houdini '99
That Championship Season '99
Bulworth '98
Knock Off '98
Dogwatch '97
Joe Torre: Curveballs Along the Way '97
Money Talks '97
Most Wanted '97
Escape Clause '96
Love Is All There Is '96
William Shakespeare's Romeo and Juliet '96
Cover Me '95
Nixon '95
Parallel Lives '94
Backstreet Justice '93
The Firm '93
Age Isn't Everything '91
Nightmare '91
The Rocketeer '91
Dick Tracy '90
Goodfellas '90
Almost Partners '87
A Fine Mess '86
Jailbait: Betrayed By Innocence '86
Vasectomy: A Delicate Matter '86
The Stuff '85
Turk 182! '85
My Mother's Secret Life '84
Very Close Quarters '84
Chiefs '83
I, the Jury '82
Melanie '82
Off the Wall '82
That Championship Season '82
Reds '81
Cruising '80
Question of Honor '80
Lost and Found '79
Bloodbrothers '78
Brink's Job '78
Oh, God! '77
I Will, I Will for Now '76
Panic in Needle Park '75
The Gambler '74
Tell Me Where It Hurts '74
The Day of the Dolphin '73
A Touch of Class '73
Cry Uncle '71
Fury on Wheels '71
Where's Poppa? '70

Roberto Sosa
Hombres Armados '97
Lolo '92
Highway Patrolman '91
Cabeza de Vaca '90

Shannyn Sossamon
40 Days and 40 Nights '02
A Knight's Tale '01

Ann Sothern (1909-2001)
The Whales of August '87
Little Dragons '80
The Manitou '78
Crazy Mama '75
The Killing Kind '73
The Best Man '64
Lady in a Cage '64
Nancy Goes to Rio '50
The Judge Steps Out '49
A Letter to Three Wives '49
Words and Music '48
Panama Hattie '42
Lady Be Good '41
Brother Orchid '40
Hell-Ship Morgan '36
Kid Millions '34

Hugo Soto
Man Facing Southeast '86
Times to Come '81

Talisa Soto (1967-)
Pinero '01
Island of the Dead '00
The Corporate Ladder '97
Flypaper '97
Mortal Kombat 2: Annihilation '97
Sunchaser '96
Vampirella '96
Mortal Kombat 1: The Movie '95
Don Juan DeMarco '94
Hostage '92
The Mambo Kings '92
Prison Stories: Women on the Inside '91
Silhouette '91
License to Kill '89
Spike of Bensonhurst '88

Kath Soucie
Return to Never Land '02 (V)
Rugrats in Paris: The Movie '00 (V)
The Rugrats Movie '98 (V)

David Soul (1943-)
Pentathlon '94
Grave Secrets: The Legacy of Hilltop Drive '92
Tides of War '90
In the Cold of the Night '89
Appointment with Death '88
In the Line of Duty: The FBI Murders '88
Hanoi Hilton '87
Through Naked Eyes '87
World War III '86
The Key to Rebecca '85
The Manions of America '81
Homeward Bound '80
Rage '80
Salem's Lot '79
Little Ladies of the Night '77
The Stick-Up '77
Dog Pound Shuffle '75

Magnum Force '73
Johnny Got His Gun '71

Renee Soutendijk (1957-)
Keeper of the City '92
Eve of Destruction '90
Forced March '90
Grave Secrets '89
Murderers Among Us: The Simon Wiesenthal Story '89
Second Victory '87
Cold Room '84
Out of Order '84
Inside the Third Reich '82
Spetters '80
The 4th Man '79

Charles Southwood
Guns for Dollars '73
Sartana's Here...Trade Your Pistol for a Coffin '70

Ben Soutten
The Mutiny of the Elsinore '39
The Crimes of Stephen Hawke '36

Catherine Spaak (1945-)
Honey '81
The Cat o' Nine Tails '71
Counter Punch '71
The Libertine '69
Hotel '67
Circle of Love '64
Empty Canvas '64
The Easy Life '63
Le Trou '59

Arthur Space (1908-83)
Terror at Red Wolf Inn '72
The Vanishing Westerner '50
Miss Grant Takes Richmond '49
A Southern Yankee '48
The Red House '47
Magnificent Doll '46
Riot Squad '41

Sissy Spacek (1949-)
In the Bedroom '01
The Straight Story '99
Blast from the Past '98
Affliction '97
Beyond the Call '96
If These Walls Could Talk '96
The Good Old Boys '95
The Grass Harp '95
Larry McMurtry's Streets of Laredo '95
A Place for Annie '94
Trading Mom '94
Hard Promises '92
A Private Matter '92
JFK '91
The Long Walk Home '89
Crimes of the Heart '86
'night, Mother '86
Violets Are Blue '86
Marie '85
The River '84
The Man with Two Brains '83 (V)
Missing '82
Raggedy Man '81
Coal Miner's Daughter '80
Heart Beat '80
Welcome to L.A. '77
Carrie '76
Katherine '75
Badlands '74
The Migrants '74
Ginger in the Morning '73
The Girls of Huntington House '73
Prime Cut '72

Kevin Spacey (1959-)
K-PAX '01
The Shipping News '01
The Big Kahuna '00
Pay It Forward '00
American Beauty '99
A Bug's Life '98 (V)
Hurlyburly '98
The Negotiator '98
L.A. Confidential '97
Midnight in the Garden of Good and Evil '97
Looking for Richard '96
A Time to Kill '96
Seven '95
The Usual Suspects '95
Doomsday Gun '94
Outbreak '94
Swimming with Sharks '94
Iron Will '93
The Ref '93
Consenting Adults '92
Glengarry Glen Ross '92
Henry & June '90
Dad '89
See No Evil, Hear No Evil '89
Long Day's Journey into Night '88
Rocket Gibraltar '88
Working Girl '88
The Murder of Mary Phagan '87

David Spade (1964-)
Joe Dirt '01
The Emperor's New Groove '00 (V)
Loser '00
Lost and Found '99
The Rugrats Movie '98 (V)
Senseless '98
Black Sheep '96
8 Heads in a Duffel Bag '96
Tommy Boy '95
P.C.U. '94
Coneheads '93

James Spader (1961-)
Secretary '02
Slow Burn '00
The Watcher '00
Supernova '99
Critical Care '97
Curtain Call '97
Keys to Tulsa '96
Two Days in the Valley '96
Crash '95
Stargate '94
Wolf '94
Dream Lover '93
The Music of Chance '93
Bob Roberts '92
Storyville '92
True Colors '91
Bad Influence '90
White Palace '90
The Rachel Papers '89
sex, lies and videotape '89
Baby Boom '87
Jack's Back '87
Less Than Zero '87
Mannequin '87
Wall Street '87
Pretty in Pink '86
The New Kids '85
Tuff Turf '85
Family Secrets '84
Endless Love '81

Douglas Spain
What's Cooking? '00
The Last Best Sunday '98
Star Maps '97
Twelve Angry Men '97
Riot in the Streets '96

Fay Spain (1932-83)
The Godfather, Part 2 '74
Flight to Fury '66
Hercules and the Captive Women '63
Al Capone '59
God's Little Acre '58
Dragstrip Girl '57
Teenage Doll '57

Timothy Spall (1957-)
Rock Star '01
Vanilla Sky '01
Chicken Run '00 (V)
Love's Labour's Lost '00
Vatel '00
Shooting the Past '99
Topsy Turvy '99
Immortality '98
Our Mutual Friend '98
Still Crazy '98
Hamlet '96
Secrets and Lies '95
Life Is Sweet '90
The Sheltering Sky '90
White Hunter, Black Heart '90
Crusoe '89
Dream Demon '88
Dutch Girls '87
Gothic '87
Home Sweet Home '82

Joe Spano (1946-)
Hart's War '02
Texas Rangers '01
From the Earth to the Moon '98
A Call to Remember '97
Primal Fear '96
Rave Review '95
Fever '91
Cast the First Stone '89
Disaster at Silo 7 '88
Brotherhood of Justice '86
The Dunera Boys '85
Terminal Choice '85
Northern Lights '79
American Graffiti '73
Warlock Moon '73

Vincent Spano (1962-)
Texas Rangers '01
The Prophecy 3: The Ascent '99
A Brooklyn State of Mind '97
Downdraft '96
The Tie That Binds '95
The Ascent '94
Alive '93
Indian Summer '93
Afterburn '92
City of Hope '91
Oscar '91
And God Created Woman '88
High Frequency '88
Blood Ties '87
Good Morning, Babylon '87
Creator '85
Alphabet City '84
Maria's Lovers '84
The Black Stallion Returns '83
Rumble Fish '83
Baby It's You '82
Senior Trip '81
The Double McGuffin '79
Over the Edge '79

Adrian Sparks
It Came from Outer Space 2 '95
My Stepmother Is an Alien '88
Roanoak '86

Ned Sparks (1883-1957)
Hawaii Calls '38
The Bride Walks Out '36
One in a Million '36
Sweet Adeline '35
Imitation of Life '34
Marie Galante '34
42nd Street '33
Going Hollywood '33
Gold Diggers of 1933 '33
Lady for a Day '33
Corsair '31
Kept Husbands '31

Camilla Sparv (1943-)
Survival Zone '84
Downhill Racer '69
Dead Heat on a Merry-Go-Round '66
Murderers' Row '66

Tracy Spaulding
Stormy Nights '97
The Deadly Secret '94
Striking Point '94

Dan Speaker
Wizards of the Demon Sword '94
Glitch! '88

Jeff Speakman (1958-)
Timelock '99
Land of the Free '98
Memorial Day '98
Escape from Atlantis '97
Deadly Outbreak '96
Plato's Run '96
The Expert '95
Street Knight '93
The Perfect Weapon '91

Bernard Spear
Yentl '83
Bedazzled '68

David Speck
Crazy in Alabama '99
Other Voices, Other Rooms '95

Carol Speed (1945-)
Avenging Disco Godfather '76
Bummer '73
The Mack '73
Savage! '73
The Big Bird Cage '72

Scott Speedman (1975-)
Duets '00
Rescuers: Stories of Courage—Two Couples '98
Dead Silence '96

Hermann Speelmanns
Baron Munchausen '43
F.P. 1 Doesn't Answer '33

Hugo Speer (1969-)
Mainline Run '98
Swing '98
The Full Monty '96

Martin Speer
The Dark Ride '84
The Hills Have Eyes '77

Richard Speight, Jr.
Band of Brothers '01
Speed 2: Cruise Control '97
Independence Day '96
Menno's Mind '96
Amanda and the Alien '95
Dead Weekend '95
Out There '95
Demonic Toys '90
Goodbye, Miss 4th of July '88
Ernest Goes to Camp '87
Love Leads the Way '84

Dona Speir (1964-)
Fit to Kill '93
Hard Hunted '92
Do or Die '91
Guns '90
Picasso Trigger '89
Savage Beach '89
Hard Ticket to Hawaii '87

George Spell (1958-)
All God's Children '80
A Dream for Christmas '73
Man & Boy '71

Tori Spelling (1973-)
Scary Movie 2 '01
Trick '99
Perpetrators of the Crime '98
The House of Yes '97
Scream 2 '97
Last Action Hero '93

Peter Spellos
Bound '96
Dinosaur Island '93

Georgina Spelvin (1936-)
Next Year in Jerusalem '98
Police Academy '84
Honkytonk Nights '70s
I Spit on Your Corpse '74

Bruce Spence (1945-)
Queen of the Damned '02
Moby Dick '98
Dark City '97
Sweet Talker '91
...Almost '90
The Shrimp on the Barbie '90
Rikky and Pete '88
The Year My Voice Broke '87
Mad Max: Beyond Thunderdome '85
Midnite Spares '85
Where the Green Ants Dream '84
The Road Warrior '82

Peter Spence
Unfinished Business '89
Crazy Moon '87

Sebastian Spence (1969-)
Family of Cops 3 '98
Family of Cops 2: Breach of Faith '97
Firestorm '97
Family of Cops '95
The Boys of St. Vincent '93

Bud Spencer (1929-)
Troublemakers '94
Aladdin '86
Miami Supercops '85
Go for It '83
Crime Busters '78
Flatfoot '78
Odds and Evens '78
Trinity Is Still My Name '75
All the Way, Boys '73
A Reason to Live, a Reason to Die '73
They Call Me Trinity '72
Today We Kill, Tomorrow We Die '71
Boot Hill '69
Ace High '68
Beyond the Law '68

Chris Spencer
The Sixth Man '97
Don't Be a Menace to South Central While Drinking Your Juice in the Hood '95

Douglas Spencer (1910-60)
River of No Return '54
Trouble along the Way '53
The Thing '51

John Spencer (1946-)
Ravenous '99
The Negotiator '98
Twilight '98
Cafe Society '97
Cold Around the Heart '97
Cop Land '97
Albino Alligator '96
The Rock '96
Forget Paris '95
Presumed Innocent '90
Black Rain '89
Simple Justice '89
Echoes '83

Volker Spengler
The Ogre '96
Chinese Roulette '86
Veronika Voss '82
Despair '78
In a Year of 13 Moons '78
The Stationmaster's Wife '77
Satan's Brew '76

Jeremy Spenser (1937-)
The Prince and the Showgirl '57
Escapade '55
Summertime '55
Devil on Horseback '54
Kind Hearts and Coronets '49

Tony Sperandeo
La Scorta '94
Acla's Descent into Floristella '87

Wendie Jo Sperber (1958-)
Mr. Write '92
Back to the Future, Part 3 '90
Stewardess School '86
Back to the Future '85
Moving Violations '85
Bachelor Party '84
First Time '82
Used Cars '80
1941 '79
I Wanna Hold Your Hand '78

Scott Spiegel (1957-)
Darkman '90
The Dead Next Door '89
Skinned Alive '89
Thou Shalt Not Kill...Except '87
Evil Dead '83

David Spielberg (1939-)
Silent Predators '99
Alice '90
The Stranger '87
Christine '84
Policewoman Centerfold '83
The Best Little Girl in the World '81
The Henderson Monster '80
Prime Time '80
Sergeant Matlovich vs. the U.S. Air Force '78
Force Five '75

Laurent Spielvogel
A Matter of Taste '00
The Monster '96
French Kiss '95

Riva Spier
Syngenor '90
Ghost Keeper '80

Jacques Spiesser (1947-)
Baxter '89
La Truite '83
Black and White in Color '76

Mickey Spillane (1918-)
Mommy 2: Mommy's Day '96
Mommy '95
Girl Hunters '63

Grazia Maria Spina
Revolt of the Barbarians '64
Tiger of the Seven Seas '62

Joe Spinell (1938-89)
Operation Warzone '89
Rapid Fire '89
The Pick-Up Artist '87
Hollywood Harry '86
Big Score '83
Vigilante '83
Walking the Edge '83
Fanatic '82
The Last Fight '82
Night Shift '82
One Down, Two to Go! '82
The Godfather 1902-1959: The Complete Epic '81
Nighthawks '81
Forbidden Zone '80
Little Dragons '80
Maniac '80
Winter Kills '79
One Man Jury '78
Star Crash '78
Taxi Driver '76
The Godfather, Part 2 '74
Cops and Robbers '73

Stephen Spinella
Bubble Boy '01
Ravenous '99
What the Deaf Man Heard '98
David Searching '97
Great Expectations '97
The Jackal '97
Love! Valour! Compassion! '96
Tarantella '95
Virtuosity '95
And the Band Played On '93

Brent Spiner (1949-)
Master of Disguise '02
A Girl Thing '01
Gepetto '00
Introducing Dorothy Dandridge '99
South Park: Bigger, Longer and Uncut '99 (V)
Star Trek: Insurrection '98
Out to Sea '97
Independence Day '96
Phenomenon '96
Star Trek: First Contact '96
Star Trek: Generations '94
Crazy from the Heart '91
Family Sins '87

Victor Spinetti (1932-)
The Krays '90
Voyage of the Damned '76
The Little Prince '74

Return of the Pink Panther '74
Start the Revolution without Me '70
Magical Mystery Tour '67
Help! '65
A Hard Day's Night '64

Kevin Blair Spirtas
Bloodlust: Subspecies 3 '93
Bloodstone: Subspecies 2 '92
Friday the 13th, Part 7: The New Blood '88
The Hills Have Eyes, Part 2 '84

Gregory Sporleder
Black Hawk Down '01
Clay Pigeons '98
Uncorked '98
The Rock '96
Twister '96
True Romance '93
A League of Their Own '92

G.D. Spradlin (1920-)
Dick '99
The Long Kiss Goodnight '96
Riders of the Purple Sage '96
Nick of Time '95
Canadian Bacon '94
Ed Wood '94
Carolina Skeletons '92
The War of the Roses '89
Call to Glory '84
The Lords of Discipline '83
Tank '83
Wrong Is Right '82
The Godfather 1902-1959: The Complete Epic '81
The Formula '80
The Jayne Mansfield Story '80
Apocalypse Now '79
North Dallas Forty '79
And I Alone Survived '78
One on One '77
The Godfather, Part 2 '74
The Only Way Home '72
Zabriskie Point '70

Charlie Spradling (1968-)
Spent '00
Johnny Skidmarks '97
Angel of Destruction '94
Bad Channels '92
To Sleep with a Vampire '92
Meridian: Kiss of the Beast '90
Mirror, Mirror '90
Puppet Master 2 '90
Wild at Heart '90

Elizabeth Spriggs (1929-)
A Christmas Carol '99
Paradise Road '97
The Secret Agent '96
Sense and Sensibility '95
Impromptu '90
Oranges Are Not the Only Fruit '89

Jerry Springer (1944-)
Austin Powers 2: The Spy Who Shagged Me '99
Ringmaster '98

Rick Springfield (1949-)
Legion '98
Silent Motive '91
Dead Reckoning '89
Nick Knight '89
Hard to Hold '84

Bruce Springsteen
High Fidelity '00
Chuck Berry: Hail! Hail! Rock 'n' Roll '87

Pamela Springsteen (1962-)
The Gumshoe Kid '89
Sleepaway Camp 3: Teenage Wasteland '89
Dixie Lanes '88
Sleepaway Camp 2: Unhappy Campers '88
My Science Project '85
Reckless '84
Fast Times at Ridgemont High '82

Dina Spybey
Julian Po '97
subUrbia '96

Ronald Squire (1886-1958)
Encore '52
No Highway in the Sky '51
Woman Hater '49
Action for Slander '38

Rebecca Staab
The Substitute 3: Winner Takes All '99
Stray Bullet '98
T.N.T. '98

Robert Stack (1919-)
Killer Bud '00
Mumford '99
BASEketball '98
Beavis and Butt-Head Do America '96 (V)
The Return of Eliot Ness '91
Joe Versus the Volcano '90
Caddyshack 2 '88
Dangerous Curves '88
Plain Clothes '88
Big Trouble '86
Transformers: The Movie '86 (V)
George Washington '84
Uncommon Valor '83
Strike Force '81
Airplane! '80
1941 '79
Most Wanted '76
Murder on Flight 502 '75
A Strange and Deadly Occurrence '74
The Corrupt Ones '67
Is Paris Burning? '66
Scarface Mob '62
The Last Voyage '60
John Paul Jones '59
Tarnished Angels '57
Great Day in the Morning '56
Written on the Wind '56
Conquest of Cochise '53
Sabre Jet '53
My Outlaw Brother '51
Bullfighter & the Lady '50
Mr. Music '50
A Date with Judy '48
To Be or Not to Be '42
Nice Girl? '41
The Mortal Storm '40
First Love '39

James Stacy (1936-)
Matters of the Heart '90
Something Wicked This Way Comes '83
Double Exposure '82
The Dark Side of Love '79
Posse '75
Paper Man '71
A Swingin' Summer '65

Lewis J. Stadlen (1947-)
The Imposters '98
In and Out '97
Windy City '84
Between the Lines '77
Savages '72

Michael Stadvec
The Chosen One: Legend of the Raven '98
The Dentist '96

Ann Stafford
Keep My Grave Open '80
Poor White Trash 2 '75

Frederick Stafford (1928-79)
The Legend of the Wolf Woman '77
Topaz '69
The Battle of El Alamein '68

Jim Stafford
Kid Colter '85
E.S.P. '83

Jon Stafford
Crossing the Line '90
Full Metal Jacket '87
Munchies '87

Carola Stagnaro
Dial Help '88
Unsane '82

Nick Stahl (1979-)
Bully '01
In the Bedroom '01
Lover's Prayer '99
Disturbing Behavior '98
The Thin Red Line '98
Eye of God '97
Blue River '95
Tall Tale: The Unbelievable Adventures of Pecos Bill '95
Safe Passage '94
The Man Without a Face '93

Richard Stahl (1932-)
Private School '83
Beware! The Blob '72
Five Easy Pieces '70
The Student Nurses '70

Brent Stait
Born to Run '93
Call of the Wild '93

Marion Stalens
Trois Couleurs: Rouge '94
The Lovers on the Bridge '91

James Staley
Robot Wars '93
Sweet Dreams '85
American Dreamer '84
Protocol '84

Joan Staley
The Ghost and Mr. Chicken '66
Roustabout '64

Frank Stallone (1950-)
Public Enemies '96
Hudson Hawk '91
Lethal Games '90
Masque of the Red Death '90
Terror in Beverly Hills '90
Death Feud '89
Easy Kill '89
Heart of Midnight '89
Order of the Eagle '89
Ten Little Indians '89
Fear '88
Midnight Cop '88
Prime Suspect '88
Barfly '87
Death Blow '87
Outlaw Force '87
Take Two '87
The Pink Chiquitas '86

Sage Stallone (1976-)
Daylight '96
Fatally Yours '95
Rocky 5 '90

Sylvester Stallone (1946-)
Driven '01
Get Carter '00
Antz '98 (V)
An Alan Smithee Film: Burn, Hollywood, Burn '97
Cop Land '97
Daylight '96
Assassins '95
Judge Dredd '95
The Specialist '94
Cliffhanger '93
Demolition Man '93
Stop! or My Mom Will Shoot '92
Oscar '91
Rocky 5 '90
Lock Up '89
Tango and Cash '89
Rambo 3 '88
Cobra '86
Over the Top '86
Rambo: First Blood, Part 2 '85
Rocky 4 '85
Rhinestone '84
First Blood '82
Rocky 3 '82
Nighthawks '81
Victory '81
Rocky 2 '79
F.I.S.T. '78
Paradise Alley '78
Cannonball '76
Rocky '76
Death Race 2000 '75
Farewell, My Lovely '75
The Lords of Flatbush '74
Prisoner of Second Avenue '74
The Italian Stallion '73
Rebel '73
Bananas '71

Anne Stallybrass (1940-)
Diana: Her True Story '93
The Strauss Family '73
Six Wives of Henry VIII '71

Lynn Stalmaster
Flying Leathernecks '51
The Steel Helmet '51

David Stambaugh
The Bad News Bears Go to Japan '78
Breaking Up '78
The Bad News Bears in Breaking Training '77
The Bad News Bears '76

John Stamos (1963-)
The Disappearance of Christina '93
Born to Ride '91
Never Too Young to Die '86

Terence Stamp (1940-)
Red Planet '00
Bowfinger '99
The Limey '99
Star Wars: Episode 1—The Phantom Menace '99
Kiss the Sky '98
Love Walked In '97
Bliss '96
The Adventures of Priscilla, Queen of the Desert '94
The Real McCoy '93
Genuine Risk '89
Alien Nation '88
Young Guns '88
The Sicilian '87
Wall Street '87
Alamut Ambush '86
Cold War Killers '86
Deadly Recruits '86
Legal Eagles '86
Link '86
The Hit '85
Insanity '82
Vatican Conspiracy '81
Superman 2 '80
Meetings with Remarkable Men '79
Together? '79
Superman: The Movie '78
The Thief of Baghdad '78
Divine Nymph '71
Blue '68
Iron Cowboy '68
Spirits of the Dead '68
Teorema '68
Far from the Madding Crowd '67
Modesty Blaise '66
The Collector '65
Billy Budd '62

Wadeck Stanczak
Scene of the Crime '87
Rendez-vous '85

Lionel Stander (1908-94)
The Last Good Time '94
Cookie '89
Wicked Stepmother '89
The Squeeze '80
1941 '79
The Squeeze '78
New York, New York '77
Black Hand '76
The Cassandra Crossing '76
Sting of the West '76
Black Bird '75
The Sensual Man '74
1931: Once Upon a Time in New York '72
Pulp '72
Treasure Island '72
Boot Hill '69
Beyond the Law '68
Dandy in Aspic '68
Once Upon a Time in the West '68
Cul de Sac '66
Promise Her Anything '66
The Loved One '65
St. Benny the Dip '51
Call Northside 777 '48
Unfaithfully Yours '48
The Sin of Harold Diddlebock '47
Spectre of the Rose '46
Guadalcanal Diary '43
A Star Is Born '37
Mr. Deeds Goes to Town '36
I Live My Life '35

Guy Standing (1873-1937)
Bulldog Drummond Comes Back '37
Bulldog Drummond Escapes '37
I'd Give My Life '36
Lloyds of London '36
The Lives of a Bengal Lancer '35
Death Takes a Holiday '34
Now and Forever '34
The Eagle and the Hawk '33

Joan Standing
Cricket on the Hearth '23
Oliver Twist '22

John Standing (1934-)
Longitude '00
8 1/2 Women '99
Rogue Trader '98
The Man Who Knew Too Little '97
Mrs. Dalloway '97
The Woman in White '97
Gulliver's Travels '95
Chaplin '92
The Endless Game '89
Riders '88
Nightflyers '87
To Catch a King '84
The Legacy '79
Rogue Male '76
Walk, Don't Run '66
King Rat '65

Arnold Stang (1925-)
Dennis the Menace '93
Ghost Dad '90
Pogo for President: "I Go Pogo" '84 (V)
Hercules in New York '70
The Wonderful World of the Brothers Grimm '62
The Man with the Golden Arm '55
Seven Days' Leave '42

Florence Stanley
Atlantis: The Lost Empire '01 (V)
Neil Simon's The Odd Couple 2 '98
A Goofy Movie '94 (V)
Trapped in Paradise '94
Trouble Bound '92
A Perfect Little Murder '90

Forrest Stanley
Outlaws of the Desert '41
Bare Knees '28

Helene Stanley
The Snows of Kilimanjaro '52
Bandit King of Texas '49

Kim Stanley (1925-2001)
Cat on a Hot Tin Roof '84
The Right Stuff '83
Frances '82
The Three Sisters '65
Seance on a Wet Afternoon '64
To Kill a Mockingbird '62 (N)
The Goddess '58

Louise Stanley (1915-82)
Pinto Canyon '40
Sky Bandits '40
Yukon Flight '40
Danger on the Air '38
Gun Packer '38
Thunder in the Desert '38
Gun Lords of Stirrup Basin '37
Riders of the Rockies '37

Paul Stanley (1952-)
Detroit Rock City '99
KISS Meets the Phantom of the Park '78
I Heard the Owl Call My Name '73

Rebecca Stanley
Body Double '84
Eyes of Fire '84

Don Stannard (1916-49)
The Temptress '49
Dick Barton, Special Agent '48
Dick Barton Strikes Back '48
Pink String and Sealing Wax '45

Claire Stansfield
Sweepers '99
Darkdrive '98
Red Shoe Diaries 5: Weekend Pass '95
Wes Craven Presents Mind Ripper '95
Drop Zone '94
Sensation '94
Best of the Best 2 '93
The Swordsman '92

Harry Dean Stanton (1926-)
The Man Who Cried '00
The Pledge '00
Sand '00
The Green Mile '99
The Straight Story '99
Fear and Loathing in Las Vegas '98
The Mighty '98
Fire Down Below '97
She's So Lovely '97
Down Periscope '96
Larry McMurtry's Dead Man's Walk '96
Midnight Blue '96
Never Talk to Strangers '95
Playback '95
Against the Wall '94
Blue Tiger '94
Hostages '93
Hotel Room '93
Man Trouble '92
Twin Peaks: Fire Walk with Me '92
Payoff '91
The Fourth War '90
Wild at Heart '90
Dream a Little Dream '89
Twister '89
The Last Temptation of Christ '88
Mr. North '88
Stars and Bars '88
Slamdance '87
Fool for Love '86
Pretty in Pink '86
One Magic Christmas '85
Rip van Winkle '85
Christine '84
Red Dawn '84
Paris, Texas '83
Repo Man '83
Oldest Living Graduate '82
One from the Heart '82
Young Doctors in Love '82
Escape from New York '81
The Godfather 1902-1959: The Complete Epic '81
Uforia '81
Death Watch '80
Private Benjamin '80
Alien '79
The Black Marble '79
Flatbed Annie and Sweetiepie: Lady Truckers '79
The Rose '79
Wise Blood '79
Straight Time '78
Missouri Breaks '76
92 in the Shade '76
Farewell, My Lovely '75

Rafferty & the Gold Dust Twins *'75*
Rancho Deluxe *'75*
Cockfighter *'74*
The Godfather, Part 2 *'74*
Where the Lilies Bloom *'74*
Zandy's Bride *'74*
Dillinger *'73*
Pat Garrett & Billy the Kid *'73*
Two Lane Blacktop *'71*
Kelly's Heroes *'70*
Rebel Rousers *'69*
Cool Hand Luke *'67*
The Hostage *'67*
Ride in the Whirlwind *'66*
The Adventures of Huckleberry Finn *'60*
Proud Rebel *'58*

John Stanton (1944-)
Day of the Panther *'88*
Rent-A-Cop *'88*
Great Expectations: The Untold Story *'87*
Tai-Pan *'86*
Dusty *'85*
The Naked Country *'85*
Bellamy *'80*

Paul Stanton (1884-1955)
Across the Pacific *'42*
Whistling in the Dark *'41*
Stanley and Livingstone *'39*

Robert Stanton
Mercury Rising *'98*
Next Stop, Wonderland *'98*
Red Corner *'97*
Washington Square *'97*
Dennis the Menace *'93*
Bob Roberts *'92*
I Eat Your Skin *'64*
Abbott and Costello in Hollywood *'45*

Barbara Stanwyck (1907-90)
The Thorn Birds *'83*
The Night Walker *'64*
Roustabout *'64*
Walk on the Wild Side *'62*
Crime of Passion *'57*
Escape to Burma *'55*
The Maverick Queen *'55*
The Violent Men *'55*
Blowing Wild *'54*
Cattle Queen of Montana *'54*
Executive Suite *'54*
All I Desire *'53*
Titanic *'53*
Clash by Night *'52*
To Please a Lady *'50*
East Side, West Side *'49*
Sorry, Wrong Number *'48*
Cry Wolf *'47*
The Two Mrs. Carrolls *'47*
The Strange Love of Martha Ivers *'46*
Christmas in Connecticut *'45*
Double Indemnity *'44*
Hollywood Canteen *'44*
Lady of Burlesque *'43*
The Great Man's Lady *'42*
Ball of Fire *'41*
The Lady Eve *'41*
Meet John Doe *'41*
Remember the Night *'40*
Golden Boy *'39*
Union Pacific *'39*
Mad Miss Manton *'38*
Internes Can't Take Money *'37*
Stella Dallas *'37*
The Bride Walks Out *'36*
Annie Oakley *'35*
Red Salute *'35*
Baby Face *'33*
The Bitter Tea of General Yen *'33*
Ladies They Talk About *'33*
The Purchase Price *'32*
Illicit *'31*
The Miracle Woman *'31*
Night Nurse *'31*

Huub Stapel (1954-)
Amsterdamned *'88*
The Attic: The Hiding of Anne Frank *'88*
The Lift *'85*

Jean Stapleton (1923-)
Baby *'00*
You've Got Mail *'98*
Lily Dale *'96*
Michael *'96*
The Habitation of Dragons *'91*
Mother Goose Rock 'n' Rhyme *'90*
Grown Ups *'86*
Cinderella *'84*
The Buddy System *'83*
Jack & the Beanstalk *'83*
Eleanor: First Lady of the World *'82*
Cold Turkey *'71*
Klute *'71*
Up the Down Staircase *'67*
Bells Are Ringing *'60*
Damn Yankees *'58*

Maureen Stapleton (1925-)
Dead Silence *'98*
Addicted to Love *'96*
The Last Good Time *'94*
Trading Mom *'94*
Miss Rose White *'92*
Passed Away *'92*
Cocoon: The Return *'88*
Doin' Time on Planet Earth *'88*
Made in Heaven *'87*
Nuts *'87*
Sweet Lorraine *'87*
Heartburn *'86*
The Money Pit *'86*
Cocoon *'85*
Family Secrets *'84*
Johnny Dangerously *'84*
Little Gloria... Happy at Last *'84*
The Fan *'81*
On the Right Track *'81*
Reds *'81*
The Gathering: Part 2 *'79*
Lost and Found *'79*
The Runner Stumbles *'79*
Interiors *'78*
The Gathering *'77*
Queen of the Stardust Ballroom *'75*
Tell Me Where It Hurts *'74*
The Cosmic Eye *'71 (V)*
Plaza Suite *'71*
Airport *'70*
Bye, Bye, Birdie *'63*
The Fugitive Kind *'60*
Lonelyhearts *'58*

Richard Stapley
D-Day, the Sixth of June *'56*
The Strange Door *'51*

Don Stark
Double Edge *'97*
Santa with Muscles *'96*
Bloodfist 5: Human Target *'93*
Evilspeak *'82*
Switchblade Sisters *'75*

Graham Stark (1922-)
Adventures Beyond Belief *'87*
Blind Date *'87*
Bloodbath at the House of Death *'85*
Alfie *'66*

Jonathan Stark (1952-)
House 2: The Second Story *'87*
Project X *'87*
Fright Night *'85*

Koo Stark (1956-)
Eat the Rich *'87*
Electric Dreams *'84*
Emily *'77*
The Rocky Horror Picture Show *'75*

Anthony Starke (1963-)
The Magnificent Seven *'98*
Repossessed *'90*
18 Again! *'88*
Return of the Killer Tomatoes! *'88*

Pauline Starke (1901-77)
Dante's Inferno *'24*
Little Church Around the Corner *'23*
Until They Get Me *'18*

Beau Starr
The Golden Spiders: A Nero Wolfe Mystery *'00*
Mercy *'00*
Mean Streak *'99*
Prisoner of Love *'99*
Hoodlum *'96*
Devil in a Blue Dress *'95*
Never Talk to Strangers *'95*
Dead Air *'94*
Trial by Jury *'94*
Goodfellas *'90*
Halloween 5: The Revenge of Michael Myers *'89*
Halloween 4: The Return of Michael Myers *'88*
Manhunt for Claude Dallas *'86*
Fletch *'85*

Fredro Starr
Save the Last Dance *'01*
Light It Up *'99*
Ride *'98*
Sunset Park *'96*
The Addiction *'95*

Mike Starr (1950-)
3 A.M. *'01*
The Lady in Question *'99*
Murder in a Small Town *'99*
Frogs for Snakes *'98*
Gloria *'98*
The Deli *'97*
Path to Paradise *'97*
Flipping *'96*
Hoodlum *'96*
Just Your Luck *'96*
Two If by Sea *'95*
Dumb & Dumber *'94*
Ed Wood *'94*
Trial by Jury *'94*
Mad Dog and Glory *'93*
Mardi Gras for the Devil *'93*
The Bodyguard *'92*
Billy Bathgate *'91*
Goodfellas *'90*
Nasty Hero *'89*

Ringo Starr (1940-)
Water *'85*
Give My Regards to Broad Street *'84*
Princess Daisy *'83*
Caveman *'81*
The Kids Are Alright *'79*
Sextette *'78*
Lisztomania *'75*
That'll Be the Day *'73*
Born to Boogie *'72*
The Point *'71 (N)*
200 Motels *'71*
Let It Be *'70*
The Magic Christian *'69*
Candy *'68*
Yellow Submarine *'68 (V)*
Magical Mystery Tour *'67*
Help! *'65*
A Hard Day's Night *'64*

Charles Starrett (1903-86)
Bonanza Town *'51*
Blazing Across the Pecos *'48*
Make a Million *'35*
A Shot in the Dark *'35*
Sons of Steel *'35*
Dangerous Appointment *'34*
Green Eyes *'34*
The Return of Casey Jones *'34*
The Silver Streak *'34*
Jungle Bride *'33*
Mr. Skitch *'33*
The Mask of Fu Manchu *'32*

Jack Starrett (1936-89)
Nightwish *'89*
Brothers in Arms *'88*
Death Chase *'87*
First Blood *'82*
Mr. Horn *'79*
Angels from Hell *'68*

Jason Statham (1972-)
John Carpenter's Ghosts of Mars *'01*
Mean Machine *'01*
The One *'01*
Snatch *'00*
Turn It Up *'00*
Lock, Stock and 2 Smoking Barrels *'98*

Liz Stauber
Almost Famous *'00*
Teaching Mrs. Tingle *'99*
Three Kings *'99*

Imelda Staunton (1956-)
Crush *'02*
Chicken Run *'00 (V)*
David Copperfield *'99*
Shakespeare in Love *'98*
Twelfth Night *'96*
Citizen X *'95*
Sense and Sensibility *'95*
Deadly Advice *'93*
Much Ado about Nothing *'93*
Peter's Friends *'92*
Antonia and Jane *'91*

Mary Stavin
The Opponent *'89*
House *'86*
Open House *'86*

Eddie Stazak
Day of the Panther *'88*
Fists of Blood *'87*

Alison Steadman (1946-)
Pride and Prejudice *'95*
Secrets and Lies *'95*
Blame It on the Bellboy *'92*
Life Is Sweet *'90*
The Misadventures of Mr. Wilt *'90*
Tartuffe *'90*
The Adventures of Baron Munchausen *'89*
Shirley Valentine *'89*
Clockwise *'86*
Coming Through *'85*
Champions *'84*
A Private Function *'84*
Kipperbang *'82*
Abigail's Party *'77*
Nuts in May *'76*
Hard Labour *'73*

John Steadman (1909-93)
Fade to Black *'80*
The Hills Have Eyes *'77*
Poco *'77*

Ken Steadman
Hindsight *'97*
I Like to Play Games *'95*

Red Steagall (1937-)
Big Bad John *'90*
Dark Before Dawn *'89*
Benji the Hunted *'87*

Michael Stearns (1940-)
Battle for the Planet of the Apes *'73*
Chain Gang Women *'72*
Chrome and Hot Leather *'71*

Ray Dennis Steckler (1939-)
Las Vegas Weekend *'85*
The Thrill Killers *'65*
Incredibly Strange Creatures Who Stopped Living and Became Mixed-Up Zombies *'63*
Eegah! *'62*
Wild Guitar *'62*

Myrtle Stedman (1889-1938)
The Mad Whirl *'25*
Sex *'20*
In the Days of the Thundering Herd & the Law & the Outlaw *'14*

Alan Steel
Hercules against the Moon Men *'64*
Samson and His Mighty Challenge *'64*
The Fury of Hercules *'61*
Samson *'61*

Amy Steel (1963-)
What Ever Happened To... *'93*
Walk Like a Man *'87*
April Fool's Day *'86*
Friday the 13th, Part 2 *'81*

Anthony Steel (1920-2001)
Perfect Crime *'78*
The Story of O *'75*
I'm the Girl He Wants to Kill *'74*
Massacre in Rome *'73*
Revenge of the Barbarians *'64*
Tiger of the Seven Seas *'62*
48 Hours to Live *'60*
Harry Black and the Tiger *'58*
Malta Story *'53*
The Master of Ballantrae *'53*
Another Man's Poison *'52*
Wooden Horse *'50*

Barbara Steele (1937-)
The Capitol Conspiracy *'99*
The Winds of War *'83*
Silent Scream *'80*
Piranha *'78*
Pretty Baby *'78*
They Came from Within *'75*
Caged Heat *'74*
The Crimson Cult *'68*
An Angel for Satan *'66*
Terror Creatures from the Grave *'66*
Nightmare Castle *'65*
The She-Beast *'65*
Castle of Blood *'64*
The Monocle *'64*
8 1/2 *'63*
The Ghost *'63*
The Horrible Dr. Hichcock *'62*
The Pit and the Pendulum *'61*
Black Sunday *'60*
La Dolce Vita *'60*

Bob Steele (1907-88)
Atomic Submarine *'59*
Pork Chop Hill *'59*
Rio Bravo *'59*
Giant from the Unknown *'58*
Pardners *'56*
The Enforcer *'51*
Battling Outlaws *'40s*
Ambush Trail *'46*
The Big Sleep *'46*
Northwest Trail *'46*
Rio Grande Raiders *'46*
Wildfire *'45*
Arizona Whirlwind *'44*
Death Valley Rangers *'44*
Marked Trails *'44*
Outlaw Trail *'44*
Sonora Stagecoach *'44*
Texas Trouble *'41*
Trigger Men *'41*
Twilight on the Rio Grande *'41*
Billy the Kid in Texas *'40*
Carson City Kid *'40*
City for Conquest *'40*
Pinto Canyon *'40*
El Diablo Rides *'39*
Mesquite Buckaroo *'39*
Of Mice and Men *'39*
Durango Valley Raiders *'38*
Feud Maker *'38*
Thunder in the Desert *'38*
Arizona Gunfighter *'37*
Border Phantom *'37*
Doomed at Sundown *'37*
Gun Lords of Stirrup Basin *'37*
Lightning Bill Crandall *'37*
Paroled to Die *'37*
The Red Rope *'37*
Ridin' the Lone Trail *'37*
Brand of the Outlaws *'36*
Cavalry *'36*
Kid Ranger *'36*
Last of the Warrens *'36*
The Law Rides *'36*
Smokey Smith *'36*
Sundown Saunders *'36*
Alias John Law *'35*
Big Calibre *'35*
Kid Courageous *'35*
No Man's Range *'35*
Powdersmoke Range *'35*
Rider of the Law *'35*
Trail of Terror *'35*
Western Justice *'35*
Brand of Hate *'34*
Demon for Trouble *'34*
The Gun Ranger *'34*
Tombstone Terror *'34*
Breed of the Border *'33*
Fighting Champ *'33*
The Gallant Fool *'33*
Galloping Romeo *'33*
Mystery Squadron *'33*
Young Blood *'33*
Hidden Valley *'32*
Man from Hell's Edges *'32*
Riders of the Desert *'32*
South of Santa Fe *'32*
Texas Buddies *'32*
Sunrise Trail *'31*
Near the Rainbow's End *'30*
Oklahoma Cyclone *'30*

Don Steele (1936-97)
Eating Raoul *'82*
Rock 'n' Roll High School *'79*
Death Race 2000 *'75*

Fred Steele
Demolition *'77*
The Story of G.I. Joe *'45*

Jadrien Steele
The Secret Garden *'87*
The Mosquito Coast *'86*

Karen Steele (1931-)
Trap on Cougar Mountain *'72*
The Rise and Fall of Legs Diamond *'60*
Ride Lonesome *'59*
Bail Out at 43,000 *'57*
Marty *'55*

Marjorie Steele
Face to Face *'52*
Tough Assignment *'49*

Pippa Steele
Lust for a Vampire *'71*
The Vampire Lovers *'70*

Tommy Steele (1936-)
Finian's Rainbow *'68*
Half a Sixpence *'67*
The Happiest Millionaire *'67*
G-Men Never Forget *'48*

Jessica Steen (1965-)
Slap Shot 2: Breaking the Ice *'02*
Smart House *'00*
Armageddon *'98*
The Principal Takes a Holiday *'98*
Dogwatch *'97*
Trial and Error *'96*
Still Life *'92*
Sing *'89*
John and the Missus *'87*
Striker's Mountain *'87*
The Housekeeper *'86*
Dream to Believe *'85*

Paprika Steen
Mifune *'99*
The Celebration *'98*

Mary Steenburgen (1952-)
Sunshine State *'02*
I Am Sam *'01*
Life as a House *'01*
The Trumpet of the Swan *'01 (V)*
Wish You Were Dead *'00*
Noah's Ark *'99*
The Grass Harp *'95*
Gulliver's Travels *'95*
Nixon *'95*
Powder *'95*

My Family *'94*
My Summer Story *'94*
Pontiac Moon *'94*
Philadelphia *'93*
What's Eating Gilbert Grape *'93*
Clifford *'92*
The Butcher's Wife *'91*
Back to the Future, Part 3 *'90*
The Long Walk Home *'89 (N)*
Miss Firecracker *'89*
Parenthood *'89*
The Attic: The Hiding of Anne Frank *'88*
End of the Line *'88*
Dead of Winter *'87*
The Whales of August *'87*
One Magic Christmas *'85*
Cross Creek *'83*
Little Red Riding Hood *'83*
Romantic Comedy *'83*
A Midsummer Night's Sex Comedy *'82*
Ragtime *'81*
Melvin and Howard *'80*
Time After Time *'79*
Goin' South *'78*

Leslie Stefanson
Jackie, Ethel, Joan: The Kennedy Women *'01*
Beautiful *'00*
Unbreakable *'00*
The General's Daughter *'99*
Delivered *'98*
An Alan Smithee Film: Burn, Hollywood, Burn *'97*

Anthony Steffen (1932-)
Escape from Hell *'89*
Savage Island *'85*
The Gentleman Killer *'78*
Stranger in Paso Bravo *'73*
The Night Evelyn Came Out of the Grave *'71*
Garringo *'69*
An Angel for Satan *'66*
The Last Tomahawk *'65*

Bernice Stegers
Little Lord Fauntleroy *'95*
A Dark Adapted Eye *'93*
To Play the King *'93*
The Girl *'86*
Xtro *'83*
City of Women *'81*
Macabre *'80*

Rod Steiger (1925-)
Frozen in Fear *'00*
Crazy in Alabama *'99*
Cypress Edge *'99*
End of Days *'99*
The Hurricane *'99*
Shiloh 2: Shiloh Season *'99*
Body and Soul *'98*
Modern Vampires *'98*
Incognito *'97*
The Kid *'97*
The Real Thing *'97*
Shiloh *'97*
Truth or Consequences, N.M. *'97*
Carpool *'96*
Mars Attacks! *'96*
Captain Nuke and the Bomber Boys *'95*
Dalva *'95*
In Pursuit of Honor *'95*
Out There *'95*
Black Water *'94*
The Specialist *'94*
Armistead Maupin's Tales of the City *'93*
The Neighbor *'93*
Guilty as Charged *'92*
The Player *'92*
Sinatra *'92*
The Ballad of the Sad Cafe *'91*
Midnight Murders *'91*
That Summer of White Roses *'90*
The January Man *'89*
Passion in Paradise *'89*
American Gothic *'88*
Catch the Heat *'87*
The Kindred *'87*
The Last Contract *'86*
Sword of Gideon *'86*
The Glory Boys *'84*
The Naked Face *'84*
The Chosen *'81*
Lion of the Desert *'81*
The Amityville Horror *'79*
Klondike Fever *'79*
Love and Bullets *'79*
Wolf Lake *'79*
Breakthrough *'78*
F.I.S.T. *'78*
Last Four Days *'77*
Portrait of a Hitman *'77*
Dirty Hands *'76*
Hennessy *'75*
Innocents with Dirty Hands *'75*
Lucky Luciano *'74*
A Fistful of Dynamite *'72*
Waterloo *'71*
The Illustrated Man *'69*
No Way to Treat a Lady *'68*
In the Heat of the Night *'67*
Doctor Zhivago *'65*
The Loved One *'65*
The Pawnbroker *'65*
Time of Indifference *'64*
The Longest Day *'62*
The Mark *'61*
Seven Thieves *'60*
Al Capone *'59*
Across the Bridge *'57*
Unholy Wife *'57*
Back from Eternity *'56*
The Harder They Fall *'56*
Jubal *'56*
Run of the Arrow *'56*
The Big Knife *'55*
The Court Martial of Billy Mitchell *'55*
Oklahoma! *'55*
On the Waterfront *'54*

Ben Stein (1944-)
Casper *'95*
Miami Rhapsody *'95*
The Mask *'94*
My Girl 2 *'94*
North *'94*
Dave *'93*
Honeymoon in Vegas *'92*
Mr. Write *'92*
Ghostbusters 2 *'89*
Planes, Trains & Automobiles *'87*
Ferris Bueller's Day Off *'86*

Margaret Sophie Stein
Sarah, Plain and Tall: Skylark *'93*
Sarah, Plain and Tall *'91*
Enemies, a Love Story *'89*

Saul Stein
Grind *'96*
Illtown *'96*
New Jersey Drive *'95*

David Steinberg (1942-)
The Marx Brothers in a Nutshell *'90*
Something Short of Paradise *'79*
The End *'78*
The Lost Man *'69*

John Steiner (1941-)
Dagger Eyes *'80s*
Sinbad of the Seven Seas *'89*
The Lone Runner *'88*
Operation 'Nam *'85*
Yor, the Hunter from the Future *'83*
Ark of the Sun God *'82*
Hunters of the Golden Cobra *'82*
Unsane *'82*
Caligula *'80*
The Last Hunter *'80*
Blood and Guns *'79*
Shock *'79*
Massacre in Rome *'73*

Sherry Steiner
Heaven Help Us *'85*
Asylum of Satan *'72*
Three on a Meathook *'72*

Jake Steinfeld
Tough Guys *'86*
Home Sweet Home *'80*

Richard Steinmetz
The One *'01*
Skyscraper *'95*
Liquid Dreams *'92*

Robert J. Steinmiller, Jr. (1978-)
Jack the Bear *'93*
The Ref *'93*
Rudy *'93*
Bingo *'91*

William (Bill) Steis (1945-95)
Raiders of the Sun *'92*
Demon of Paradise *'87*
Eye of the Eagle *'87*
Equalizer 2000 *'86*

Anna Sten (1908-93)
Soldier of Fortune *'55*
So Ends Our Night *'41*
The Girl with the Hat Box *'27*

Yutte Stensgaard (1946-)
Lust for a Vampire *'71*
Scream and Scream Again *'70*
The Love Factor *'69*
Zeta One *'69*

Karel Stepanek (1899-1981)
Second Best Secret Agent in the Whole Wide World *'65*
Devil Doll *'64*
Brainwashed *'60*
Sink the Bismarck *'60*
Never Let Me Go *'53*
The Fallen Idol *'49*
Counterblast *'48*
Secret Mission *'42*

Nicole Stephane (1928-)
Carve Her Name with Pride *'58*
Les Enfants Terrible *'50*
La Silence de la Mer *'47*

Daniel Stephen
2020 Texas Gladiators *'85*
Warbus *'85*

Susan Stephen (1931-2000)
White Huntress *'57*
Heat Wave *'54*
A Stolen Face *'52*

Harvey Stephens (1901-86)
The Lady Is Willing *'42*
Sergeant York *'41*
Abe Lincoln in Illinois *'40*
The Fighting 69th *'40*
The Texas Rangers Ride Again *'40*
Beau Geste *'39*
Oklahoma Kid *'39*
The Texans *'38*
Forlorn River *'37*
Let 'Em Have It *'35*
Evelyn Prentice *'34*

Heather Stephens
Tomcats *'01*
Blue Ridge Fall *'99*
Forever Love *'98*
The Disappearance of Kevin Johnson *'95*

James Stephens (1951-)
Pancho Barnes *'88*
Mysterious Two *'82*
First Monday in October *'81*

Martin Stephens (1949-)
The Innocents *'61*
Village of the Damned *'60*

Nancy Stephens
Halloween: H20 *'98*
Halloween *'78*

Perry Stephens
Grizzly Mountain *'97*
Norma Jean and Marilyn *'95*
Two Bits & Pepper *'95*

Robert Stephens (1931-95)
Century *'94*
The Secret Rapture *'94*
Searching for Bobby Fischer *'93*
Afraid of the Dark *'92*
Chaplin *'92*
The Bonfire of the Vanities *'90*
The Children *'90*
Henry V *'89*
American Roulette *'88*
High Season *'88*
Wonderland *'88*
Empire of the Sun *'87*
Fortunes of War *'87*
Luther *'74*
The Asphyx *'72*
Travels with My Aunt *'72*
The Private Life of Sherlock Holmes *'70*
The Prime of Miss Jean Brodie *'69*
Morgan: A Suitable Case for Treatment *'66*
A Taste of Honey *'61*

Toby Stephens (1969-)
The Great Gatsby *'01*
Onegin *'99*
Cousin Bette *'97*
Photographing Fairies *'97*
The Tenant of Wildfell Hall *'96*
Twelfth Night *'96*

Henry Stephenson (1871-1956)
Challenge to Lassie *'49*
Oliver Twist *'48*
Heartbeat *'46*
Mr. Lucky *'43*
Lady from Louisiana *'42*
Down Argentine Way *'40*
It's a Date *'40*
The Old Maid *'39*
Tarzan Finds a Son *'39*
Marie Antoinette *'38*
Conquest *'37*
The Prince and the Pauper *'37*
The Charge of the Light Brigade *'36*
Mutiny on the Bounty *'35*
Tomorrow at Seven *'33*
The Animal Kingdom *'32*
A Bill of Divorcement *'32*
Red Headed Woman *'32*

James Stephenson (1889-)
The Letter *'40*
The Sea Hawk *'40*
Beau Geste *'39*
Boy Meets Girl *'38*

Mark Kinsey Stephenson
The Unnamable 2: The Statement of Randolph Carter *'92*
The Unnamable *'88*

Michael Stephenson
Beyond Darkness *'92*
Troll 2 *'92*

Pamela Stephenson (1950-)
Ghosts Can Do It *'90*
Les Patterson Saves the World *'90*
Bloodbath at the House of Death *'85*
Finders Keepers *'84*
Scandalous *'84*
History of the World: Part 1 *'81*
The Comeback *'77*

Craig Stepp
Indecent Behavior 2 *'94*
Married People, Single Sex 2: For Better or Worse *'94*
Play Time *'94*

Ford Sterling (1883-1939)
Headline Woman *'35*
The Show Off *'26*
He Who Gets Slapped *'24*
Yankee Doodle in Berlin *'19*

Jan Sterling (1923-)
First Monday in October *'81*
The Dark Side of Love *'79*
The Incident *'67*
High School Confidential *'58*
The Harder They Fall *'56*
Pony Express *'53*
Split Second *'53*
Union Station *'50*

Mindy Sterling (1953-)
Austin Powers 2: The Spy Who Shagged Me *'99*
Drop Dead Gorgeous *'99*
Austin Powers: International Man of Mystery *'97*

Philip Sterling (1922-98)
My Giant *'98*
Death of the Incredible Hulk *'90*

Robert Sterling (1917-)
A Global Affair *'63*
Return to Peyton Place *'61*
Voyage to the Bottom of the Sea *'61*
Johnny Eager *'42*
Somewhere I'll Find You *'42*
Two-Faced Woman *'41*

Tisha Sterling (1944-)
The Whales of August *'87*
The Killer Inside Me *'76*
Betrayal *'74*
Snatched *'72*
Defiant *'70*
Powder Keg *'70*
Coogan's Bluff *'68*
Village of the Giants *'65*

Daniel Stern (1957-)
Dead Simple *'01*
Tourist Trap *'98*
Very Bad Things *'98*
Celtic Pride *'96*
Bushwhacked *'95*
City Slickers 2: The Legend of Curly's Gold *'94*
Rookie of the Year *'93*
Home Alone 2: Lost in New York *'92*
City Slickers *'91*
Coupe de Ville *'90*
The Court Martial of Jackie Robinson *'90*
Home Alone *'90*
My Blue Heaven *'90*
Friends, Lovers & Lunatics *'89*
Leviathan *'89*
Little Monsters *'89*
D.O.A. *'88*
The Milagro Beanfield War *'88*
Weekend War *'88*
Born in East L.A. *'87*
The Boss' Wife *'86*
Hannah and Her Sisters *'86*
Key Exchange *'85*
C.H.U.D. *'84*
Frankenweenie *'84*
Blue Thunder *'83*
Get Crazy *'83*
Diner *'82*
I'm Dancing as Fast as I Can *'82*
It's My Turn *'80*
One Trick Pony *'80*
Stardust Memories *'80*
Breaking Away *'79*
Starting Over *'79*

Howard Stern
Private Parts *'96*
Ryder P.I. *'86*

Tom Stern (1965-)
Freaked *'93*
Hell's Angels '69 *'69*
Angels from Hell *'68*
The Devil's Brigade *'68*

Wes Stern
Three in the Cellar *'70*
The First Time *'69*

Frances Sternhagen (1930-)
The Con *'98*
Curtain Call *'97*
Raising Cain *'92*
Doc Hollywood *'91*
Stephen King's Golden Years *'91*
Misery *'90*
Sibling Rivalry *'90*
Communion *'89*
See You in the Morning *'89*
Bright Lights, Big City *'88*
The Dining Room *'86*
Independence Day *'83*
Prototype *'83*
Romantic Comedy *'83*
Who'll Save Our Children? *'82*
Outland *'81*
Mother & Daughter: A Loving War *'80*
Starting Over *'79*

Robyn Stevan
Stepping Out *'91*
Bye Bye Blues *'89*

Jean-Francois Stevenin
Brotherhood of the Wolf *'01*
For Sale *'98*
Olivier, Olivier *'92*
Small Change *'76*

Andrew Stevens (1955-)
The Shooter *'97*
The Corporation *'96*
Scorned 2 *'96*
Body Chemistry 4: Full Exposure *'95*
Night Eyes 4: Fatal Passion *'95*
Illicit Dreams *'94*
The Skateboard Kid 2 *'94*
Body Chemistry 3: Point of Seduction *'93*
Eyewitness to Murder *'93*
Night Eyes 3 *'93*
Scorned *'93*
Deadly Rivals *'92*
Double Threat *'92*
Munchie *'92*
Night Eyes 2 *'91*
The Terror Within 2 *'91*
Night Eyes *'90*
Red Blooded American Girl *'90*
Down the Drain *'89*
Tusks *'89*
Deadly Innocence *'88*
Fine Gold *'88*
The Ranch *'88*
The Terror Within *'88*
Counterforce *'87*
Scared Stiff *'87*
Ten to Midnight *'83*
Forbidden Love *'82*
The Seduction *'82*
Death Hunt *'81*
Miracle on Ice *'81*
The Rebels *'79*
The Bastard *'78*
The Fury *'78*
The Boys in Company C *'77*
Day of the Animals *'77*
Secrets *'77*
Las Vegas Lady *'76*
Massacre at Central High *'76*

Brinke Stevens (1954-)
Demon Lust *'01*
Mom's Outta Sight *'01*
Witchouse 3: Demon Fire *'01*
American Nightmare *'00*
The Kid with the X-Ray Eyes *'99*
Hybrid *'97*
Mommy 2: Mommy's Day *'96*
Cyberzone *'95*
Jack-O *'95*
Masseuse *'95*
Mommy *'95*
Acting on Impulse *'93*
Teenage Exorcist *'93*
Haunting Fear *'91*
Bad Girls from Mars *'90*
Spirits *'90*

Phantom of the Mall: Eric's Revenge '89
Transylvania Twist '89
Grandma's House '88
Warlords '88
Nightmare Sisters '87
Slave Girls from Beyond Infinity '87
Sorority Babes in the Slimeball Bowl-A-Rama '87
Sole Survivor '84
Slumber Party Massacre '82

Charles Stevens (1893-)
Buffalo Bill Rides Again '47
Border Bandits '46
The Lives of a Bengal Lancer '35
The Three Musketeers '21
Mark of Zorro '20

Connie Stevens (1938-)
James Dean: Live Fast, Die Young '97
Love Is All There Is '96
Tapeheads '89
Back to the Beach '87
Side Show '84
Scruples '80
Love's Savage Fury '79
Scorchy '76
Playmates '72
The Grissom Gang '71
The Littlest Angel '69
Palm Springs Weekend '63
Parrish '61
Rock-A-Bye Baby '57

Craig Stevens (1918-2000)
La Truite '83
S.O.B. '81
Secrets of Three Hungry Wives '78
The Deadly Mantis '57
The French Line '54
Abbott and Costello Meet Dr. Jekyll and Mr. Hyde '52
Phone Call from a Stranger '52
Drums in the Deep South '51
Blues Busters '50
Humoresque '46
The Man I Love '46
Since You Went Away '44
Dive Bomber '41

Fisher Stevens (1963-)
The Tic Code '99
Cold Fever '95
Hackers '95
The Right to Remain Silent '95
Nina Takes a Lover '94
Only You '94
Super Mario Bros. '93
The Marrying Man '91
Mystery Date '91
When the Party's Over '91
Reversal of Fortune '90
Short Circuit 2 '88
Short Circuit '86
My Science Project '85
The Flamingo Kid '84
The Burning '82

Inger Stevens (1934-70)
Savage Run '70
A Dream of Kings '69
Firecreek '68
Five Card Stud '68
Madigan '68
A Guide for the Married Man '67
Hang 'Em High '67
The Buccaneer '58

K.T. Stevens (1919-94)
They're Playing with Fire '84
Missile to the Moon '59
Jungle Hell '55
Harriet Craig '50
Port of New York '49

Mark Stevens (1915-94)
The Fury of the Wolfman '70
Frozen Alive '64
Cry Vengeance '54
Torpedo Alley '53
Mutiny '52
The Snake Pit '48
The Street with No Name '48
Dark Corner '46
Objective, Burma! '45

Morgan Stevens
Survival Zone '84
Up River '79

Onslow Stevens (1902-77)
Tribute to a Bad Man '56
Fangs of the Wild '54
Them! '54
A Lion Is in the Streets '53
One Too Many '51
The Creeper '48
Angel on My Shoulder '46
O.S.S. '46
House of Dracula '45
Hands Across the Border '43
The Monster and the Girl '41
Flight from Glory '37
Yellow Dust '36
The Three Musketeers '35
I Can't Escape '34

Paul Stevens (1921-86)
Get Christie Love! '74
Patton '70
Hercules and the Princess of Troy '65
The Mask '61
Exodus '60

Rise Stevens
Going My Way '44
The Chocolate Soldier '41

Ronnie Stevens
The Parent Trap '98
Dentist In the Chair '60

Shadoe Stevens
The Death Artist '95
Traxx '87

Stella Stevens (1936-)
By Dawn's Early Light '00
The Corporation '96
In Cold Blood '96
Invisible Mom '96
Body Chemistry 4: Full Exposure '95
The Nutt House '95
Star Hunter '95
Virtual Combat '95
The Granny '94
Hard Drive '94
Molly and Gina '94
National Lampoon's Attack of the 5 Ft. 2 Women '94
Eye of the Stranger '93
The Terror Within 2 '91
Exiled in America '90
Last Call '90
Down the Drain '89
Mom '89
Adventures Beyond Belief '87
The Longshot '86
Monster in the Closet '86
The Amazons '84
Chained Heat '83
Power, Passion & Murder '83
Wacko '83
Twirl '81
Make Me an Offer '80
Express to Terror '79
Cruise into Terror '78
The Manitou '78
Las Vegas Lady '76
Cleopatra Jones & the Casino of Gold '75
Arnold '73
Slaughter '72
A Town Called Hell '72
Ballad of Cable Hogue '70
Where Angels Go, Trouble Follows '68
The Silencers '66
The Nutty Professor '63
The Courtship of Eddie's Father '62
Girls! Girls! Girls! '62
Li'l Abner '59

Warren Stevens (1919-)
No Name on the Bullet '59
Man or Gun '58
Forbidden Planet '56
Shark River '53

Cynthia Stevenson (1963-)
Air Bud 4: Seventh Inning Fetch '02
Air Bud 2: Golden Receiver '98
From the Earth to the Moon '98
Happiness '98
Forget Paris '95
Home for the Holidays '95
Live Nude Girls '95
The Reluctant Agent '95
Watch It '93
The Player '92

Juliet Stevenson (1956-)
The Road from Coorain '02
Cider with Rosie '99
Emma '96
The Secret Rapture '94
The Trial '93
Truly, Madly, Deeply '91
Drowning by Numbers '87

McLean Stevenson (1929-96)
Armistead Maupin's Tales of the City '93
The Cat from Outer Space '78
Win, Place, or Steal '72

Parker Stevenson (1952-)
Legion '98
Not of This Earth '96
Official Denial '93
Are You Lonesome Tonight '92
North and South Book 2 '86
Shooting Stars '85
Stitches '85
Stroker Ace '83
Lifeguard '76
Our Time '74
A Separate Peace '73

Ray Stevenson (1964-)
The Theory of Flight '98
Catherine Cookson's The Tide of Life '96
The Return of the Native '94

Robert Stevenson (1905-86)
One of Our Dinosaurs Is Missing '75
Fangs of the Wild '54

Tom Stevenson
Gaslight '44
Across the Pacific '42

Venetia Stevenson
Horror Hotel '60
Darby's Rangers '58

Joe Stewardson
City of Blood '88
Flatfoot '78
Follow That Rainbow '66

Alexandra Stewart (1939-)
Under the Sand '00
Son of Gascogne '95
Kemek '88
Sans Soleil '82 (N)
The Agency '81
Last Chase '81
In Praise of Older Women '78
Because of the Cats '74
The Destructors '74
Day for Night '73
Zeppelin '71
Mickey One '65
The Fire Within '64
RoGoPaG '62
Exodus '60

Amy Stewart
Trucks '97
Mark Twain and Me '91

Athole Stewart
Accused '36
The Speckled Band '31

Byron Stewart
How U Like Me Now? '92
Grambling's White Tiger '81

Catherine Mary Stewart (1959-)
Dead Silent '99
The Reaper '97
Number One Fan '94
Out of Annie's Past '94
Ordeal in the Arctic '93
Samurai Cowboy '93
The Sea Wolf '93
Cafe Romeo '91
Perfect Harmony '91
Psychic '91
Passion in Paradise '89
Weekend at Bernie's '89
World Gone Wild '88
Dudes '87
Murder by the Book '87
Nightflyers '87
Scenes from the Goldmine '87
Mischief '85
Sins '85
The Last Starfighter '84
Night of the Comet '84
Nighthawks '81
The Apple '80

Charlotte Stewart (1941-)
Tremors 3: Back to Perfection '01
Dark Angel: The Ascent '94
Tremors '89
Eraserhead '78

Don Stewart
Lost '83
The Doomsday Flight '66

Elaine Stewart (1929-)
The Rise and Fall of Legs Diamond '60
Meet Me in Las Vegas '56
Riders of the Timberline '41

Eleanor Stewart
Mystery Man '44
Flaming Lead '39
Arizona Days '37
The Rangers Step In '37
Where Trails Divide '37
Headin' for the Rio Grande '36
The Gun Ranger '34

Evelyn Stewart (1942-)
The Psychic '78
Django Shoots First '74
The Scorpion's Tail '71
Murder Mansion '70
Blood for a Silver Dollar '66

Ewan Stewart
Conspiracy '01
American Women '00
The Big Brass Ring '99
Stella Does Tricks '96
Rob Roy '95

Frank Stewart
Cemetery High '89
Sexpot '88
Galactic Gigolo '87
Psychos in Love '87
Sensations '87

French Stewart (1964-)
Clockstoppers '02
Love Stinks '99
McHale's Navy '97
Glory Daze '96
Magic Island '95

James Stewart (1908-97)
An American Tail: Fievel Goes West '91 (V)
North and South Book 2 '86
Right of Way '84
Green Horizon '83
War in the Sky '82 (N)
The Big Sleep '78
Magic of Lassie '78
Airport '77 '77
The Shootist '76
The Cheyenne Social Club '70
Bandolero! '68
Firecreek '68
The Rare Breed '66
Dear Brigitte '65
The Flight of the Phoenix '65
Shenandoah '65
Cheyenne Autumn '64
How the West Was Won '63
The Man Who Shot Liberty Valance '62
Mr. Hobbs Takes a Vacation '62
Two Rode Together '61
The Mountain Road '60
Anatomy of a Murder '59
The FBI Story '59
Bell, Book and Candle '58
Vertigo '58
Spirit of St. Louis '57
The Man Who Knew Too Much '56
Far Country '55
The Man from Laramie '55
Strategic Air Command '55
The Glenn Miller Story '54
Rear Window '54
The Naked Spur '53
Thunder Bay '53
Bend of the River '52
The Greatest Show on Earth '52
No Highway in the Sky '51
Broken Arrow '50
Harvey '50
The Jackpot '50
Winchester '73 '50
Malaya '49
The Stratton Story '49
Call Northside 777 '48
On Our Merry Way '48
Rope '48
You Gotta Stay Happy '48
Magic Town '47
It's a Wonderful Life '46
Pot o' Gold '41
Ziegfeld Girl '41
The Mortal Storm '40
The Philadelphia Story '40
The Shop Around the Corner '40
Destry Rides Again '39
Made for Each Other '39
Mr. Smith Goes to Washington '39
Of Human Hearts '38
Shopworn Angel '38
Vivacious Lady '38
You Can't Take It with You '38
Navy Blue and Gold '37
After the Thin Man '36
Born to Dance '36
The Gorgeous Hussy '36
Rose Marie '36
Wife Versus Secretary '36

John Stewart
Boots Malone '52
Last of the Comanches '52

Johna Stewart
Young Hercules '97
Address Unknown '96
Galgameth '96

Jon Stewart (1962-)
Death to Smoochy '02
Jay and Silent Bob Strike Back '01
Big Daddy '99
The Faculty '98
Playing by Heart '98
Half-Baked '97
Since You've Been Gone '97
Wishful Thinking '96

Kate McGregor Stewart
Father of the Bride Part II '95
Safe '95
Father of the Bride '91

Malcolm Stewart
Deadlocked '00
Screwed '00
Fatal Error '99
Titanic '96
Timecop '94

Mel Stewart (1929-2002)
Bride of Re-Animator '89
The Kid with the 200 I.Q. '83

Pamela Stewart
100 Proof '96
Amateur '94

Patrick Stewart (1940-)
Jimmy Neutron: Boy Genius '01 (V)
X-Men '00
Animal Farm '99 (V)
A Christmas Carol '99
Safe House '99
Moby Dick '98
Prince of Egypt '98 (V)
Star Trek: Insurrection '98
Conspiracy Theory '97
Dad Savage '97
The Canterville Ghost '96
Masterminds '96
Star Trek: First Contact '96
Jeffrey '95
The Pagemaster '94 (V)
Star Trek: Generations '94
Detonator '93
Gunmen '93
L.A. Story '91
Code Name: Emerald '85
The Doctor and the Devils '85
Lady Jane '85
Lifeforce '85
Dune '84
The Plague Dogs '82 (V)
Excalibur '81
Hedda '75

Paul Stewart (1908-86)
Seduced '85
The Tempest '82
Opening Night '77
Bite the Bullet '75
Murph the Surf '75
How to Commit Marriage '69
King Creole '58
The Cobweb '55
Kiss Me Deadly '55
The Joe Louis Story '53
Walk Softly, Stranger '50
Champion '49
Easy Living '49
Twelve o'Clock High '49
Mr. Lucky '43
Citizen Kane '41

Peggy Stewart (1923-)
The Black Lash '52
The Fighting Redhead '50
Son of Zorro '47
Trail to San Antone '47
Alias Billy the Kid '46
The Phantom Rider '46
Stagecoach to Denver '46
Vigilantes of Boom Town '46
Rough Riders of Cheyenne '45
The Vampire's Ghost '45
Girls in Chains '43

Penelope Stewart
Boulevard of Broken Dreams '88
Vigil '84

Richard Stewart
Watch Me When I Kill '81
Terror Ship '54

Robert Stewart (1961-)
Motel Blue '98
Annie O '95
Someone to Die For '95

Roy Stewart (1883-1933)
Rustler's Roundup '33
Come on Tarzan '32
Sparrows '26
With Kit Carson over the Great Divide '25

Sara Stewart
Drop Dead Gorgeous '99
The Winslow Boy '98
Sophie Stewart (1908-77)
Devil Girl from Mars '54
My Son, My Son '40
Murder in the Old Red Barn '36
Trish Stewart
Breaking Up Is Hard to Do '79
Wild Times '79
Dorothy Stickney (1900-98)
I Never Sang for My Father '70
The Uninvited '44
Phyllis Stickney
The Inkwell '94
What's Love Got to Do with It? '93
Talkin' Dirty after Dark '91
David Ogden Stiers (1942-)
Lilo & Stitch '02 (V)
Atlantis: The Lost Empire '01 (V)
The Curse of the Jade Scorpion '01
The Majestic '01
Tomcats '01
Krippendorf's Tribe '98
Meet Wally Sparks '97
Everyone Says I Love You '96
The Hunchback of Notre Dame '96 (V)
Jungle 2 Jungle '96
Mighty Aphrodite '95
Pocahontas '95 (V)
Steal Big, Steal Little '95
Bad Company '94
Past Tense '94
Iron Will '93
The Last of His Tribe '92
Shadows and Fog '92
Beauty and the Beast '91 (V)
Doc Hollywood '91
The Kissing Place '90
Day One '89
The Final Days '89
Final Notice '89
The Accidental Tourist '88
Another Woman '88
J. Edgar Hoover '87
Perry Mason: The Case of the Lost Love '87
The Bad Seed '85
Better Off Dead '85
Creator '85
The Man with One Red Shoe '85
North and South Book 1 '85
The First Olympics: Athens 1896 '84
Harry's War '84
The Innocents Abroad '84
M*A*S*H: Goodbye, Farewell & Amen '83
Oldest Living Graduate '82
Damien: The Leper Priest '80
Breaking Up Is Hard to Do '79
Magic '78
Sergeant Matlovich vs. the U.S. Air Force '78
Oh, God! '77
Hugo Stiglitz (1940-)
Naked Lies '98
Fantastic Balloon Voyage '80s
Counterforce '87
City of the Walking Dead '83
Night of a Thousand Cats '72
Robinson Crusoe & the Tiger '72
Julia Stiles (1981-)
The Bourne Identity '02
A Guy Thing '02
The Business of Strangers '01
O '01
Save the Last Dance '01
Down to You '00
Hamlet '00
State and Main '00
The '60s '99
Ten Things I Hate about You '99
Wicked '98
Robin Stille
American Ninja 4: The Annihilation '91
Slumber Party Massacre '82
Ben Stiller (1965-)
The Royal Tenenbaums '01
Zoolander '01
Keeping the Faith '00
Meet the Parents '00
Black and White '99
Mystery Men '99
The Suburbans '99
Permanent Midnight '98
There's Something about Mary '98
Your Friends & Neighbors '98
Zero Effect '97
The Cable Guy '96
Happy Gilmore '96
Flirting with Disaster '95
If Lucy Fell '95
Heavyweights '94
Reality Bites '94
Next of Kin '89
Stella '89
Fresh Horses '88
Empire of the Sun '87
Hot Pursuit '87
Jerry Stiller (1927-)
On the Line '01
Zoolander '01
My 5 Wives '00
The Suburbans '99
A Rat's Tale '98
Secre of the Andes '98
The Deli '97
Stag '97
Subway Stories '97
Heavyweights '94
The Pickle '93
Women & Men: In Love There Are No Rules '91
Little Vegas '90
That's Adequate '90
Hairspray '88
Hot Pursuit '87
Nadine '87
Seize the Day '86
The McGuffin '85
Those Lips, Those Eyes '80
Nasty Habits '77
The Ritz '76
The Taking of Pelham One Two Three '74
Brett Stimely
Cannibal Women in the Avocado Jungle of Death '89
Bloodstone '88
Sting (1951-)
Lock, Stock and 2 Smoking Barrels '98
Grave Indiscretions '96
The Adventures of Baron Munchausen '89
Stormy Monday '88
Julia and Julia '87
The Bride '85
Plenty '85
Dune '84
Brimstone & Treacle '82
The Secret Policeman's Other Ball '82
Quadrophenia '79
Colin Stinton
The Winslow Boy '98
In Love and War '96
Linda Stirling (1921-97)
Jesse James Rides Again '47
Cyclotrode "X" '46
Rio Grande Raiders '46
D-Day on Mars '45
Manhunt of Mystery Island '45
The Purple Monster Strikes '45
The Topeka Terror '45
Perils of the Darkest Jungle '44
Zorro's Black Whip '44
Rachael Stirling
The Triumph of Love '01
Maybe Baby '99
Retribution '98
Still Crazy '98
Brian Stirner
Poldark 2 '75
All Creatures Great and Small '74
Barbara Stock
Verne Miller '88
Long Time Gone '86
Nigel Stock (1919-86)
The Lion in Winter '68
The Great Escape '63
Victim '61
The Silent Enemy '58
Brighton Rock '47
Amy Stock-Poynton
Beanstalk '94
Bill & Ted's Bogus Journey '91
Bill & Ted's Excellent Adventure '89
Carl Stockdale (1874-1953)
Condemned to Live '35
The Crimson Trail '35
The Ivory Handled Gun '35
Law for Tombstone '35
Get That Girl '32
Oliver Twist '22
The Greatest Question '19
The Americano '17
Werner Stocker
November Moon '85
A Man Like Eva '83
The White Rose '83
Dean Stockwell (1936-)
Inferno '01
In Pursuit '00
Restraining Order '99
Rites of Passage '99
Air Force One '97
John Grisham's The Rainmaker '97
Living in Peril '97
McHale's Navy '97
Midnight Blue '96
Twilight Man '96
Madonna: Innocence Lost '95
Mr. Wrong '95
Naked Souls '95
Stephen King's The Langoliers '95
Chasers '94
Bonanza: The Return '93
The Player '92
Shame '92
Son of the Morning Star '91
Smokescreen '90
Backtrack '89
Buying Time '89
Limit Up '89
Stickfighter '89
Blue Iguana '88
Married to the Mob '88
Palais Royale '88
Tucker: The Man and His Dream '88
Beverly Hills Cop 2 '87
Gardens of Stone '87
Kenny Rogers as the Gambler, Part 3: The Legend Continues '87
The Time Guardian '87
Banzai Runner '86
Blue Velvet '86
Legend of Billie Jean '85
To Live & Die in L.A. '85
Dune '84
To Kill a Stranger '84
Paris, Texas '83
Alsino and the Condor '82
Wrong Is Right '82
One Away '80
She Came to the Valley '77
Tracks '76
Werewolf of Washington '73
Loners '72
Win, Place, or Steal '72
Paper Man '71
The Dunwich Horror '70
Psych-Out '68
Long Day's Journey into Night '62
Compulsion '59
Kim '50
Stars in My Crown '50
The Secret Garden '49
The Boy with the Green Hair '48
Gentleman's Agreement '47
Song of the Thin Man '47
Anchors Aweigh '45
Guy Stockwell (1934-2002)
Santa Sangre '90
Grotesque '87
It's Alive '74
The Gatling Gun '72
And Now Miguel '66
Tobruk '66
The War Lord '65
John Stockwell (1961-)
Breast Men '97
The Nurse '97
Stag '97
I Shot a Man in Vegas '96
Legal Deceit '95
Operation Intercept '95
Born to Ride '91
Eyes of the Panther '90
Billionaire Boys Club '87
Dangerously Close '86
Radioactive Dreams '86
Top Gun '86
City Limits '85
My Science Project '85
Quarterback Princess '85
Christine '84
Eddie and the Cruisers '83
Losin' It '82
Malcolm Stoddard (1948-)
Coming Home '98
Catherine Cookson's The Girl '96
The Assassination Run '84
The Godsend '79
Luther '74
Austin Stoker (1948-)
The Uninvited '88
Time Walker '82
Assault on Precinct 13 '76
Sheba, Baby '75
Twisted Brain '74
Battle for the Planet of the Apes '73
Barry Stokes
Alien Prey '83
Spaced Out '80
Susan Stokey
Phantom Empire '87
Tomb '86
The Power '80
Mink Stole
Cecil B. Demented '00
Shriek If You Know What I Did Last Friday the 13th '00
But I'm a Cheerleader '99
Leather Jacket Love Story '98
Pecker '98
The Death Artist '95
Serial Mom '94
Liquid Dreams '92
Cry-Baby '90
Hairspray '88
Polyester '81
Desperate Living '77
Female Trouble '74
Pink Flamingos '72
Multiple Maniacs '70
Mondo Trasho '69
Shirley Stoler (1929-99)
Malcolm X '92
Frankenhooker '90
Miami Blues '90
Shakedown '88
Sticky Fingers '88
Splitz '84
The Deer Hunter '78
Seven Beauties '76
A Real Young Girl '75
Honeymoon Killers '70
Gunther Stoll
Cold Blood '75
The Castle of Fu Manchu '68
Fred Stoller
Chairman of the Board '97
Downhill Willie '96
Dumb & Dumber '94
Eric Stoltz (1961-)
Common Ground '00
House of Mirth '00
One Kill '00
A Murder of Crows '99
The Passion of Ayn Rand '99
Hi-Life '98
Mr. Jealousy '98
Anaconda '96
Don't Look Back '96
Grace of My Heart '96
Inside '96
Jerry Maguire '96
Keys to Tulsa '96
Two Days in the Valley '96
Fluke '95
Kicking and Screaming '95
The Prophecy '95
Rob Roy '95
Killing Zoe '94
Little Women '94
Pulp Fiction '94
Sleep with Me '94
A Woman at War '94
Bodies, Rest & Motion '93
Foreign Affairs '93
Naked in New York '93
Singles '92
The Waterdance '91
Memphis Belle '90
The Discovery Program '89
The Fly 2 '89
Our Town '89
Say Anything '89
Haunted Summer '88
Lionheart '87
A Night of Love '87
Sister, Sister '87
Some Kind of Wonderful '87
Code Name: Emerald '85
Mask '85
The New Kids '85
Surf 2 '84
The Wild Life '84
Running Hot '83
Fast Times at Ridgemont High '82
The Seekers '79
The Grass Is Always Greener Over the Septic Tank '78
Lena Stolze (1956-)
The Nasty Girl '90
The White Rose '83
The Last Five Days '82
Christopher Stone (1940-95)
Dying to Remember '93
Blue Movies '88
The Annihilators '85
Cujo '83
The Junkman '82
The Howling '81
Love Me Deadly '76
Prisoner in the Middle '74
The Passing of Evil '70
Danton Stone
Series 7: The Contenders '01
McHale's Navy '97
He Said, She Said '91
Once Around '91
Crazy People '90
Fred Stone
The Westerner '40
The Trail of the Lonesome Pine '36
Alice Adams '35
George E. Stone (1903-67)
Jungle Hell '55
Timber Queen '44
Broadway Limited '41
Road Show '41
You and Me '38
Viva Villa! '34
42nd Street '33
The Last Mile '32
The Vampire Bat '32
Cimarron '31
Medicine Man '30
Harold J. Stone (1911-)
Legend of Valentino '75
The McCullochs '75
Mitchell '75
Big Mouth '67
The St. Valentine's Day Massacre '67
Girl Happy '65
X: The Man with X-Ray Eyes '63
The Invisible Boy '57
Leonard Stone
Blood Money '99
Willy Wonka & the Chocolate Factory '71
Lewis Stone (1879-1953)
All the Brothers Were Valiant '53
Prisoner of Zenda '52
Scaramouche '52
Angels in the Outfield '51
Key to the City '50
Stars in My Crown '50
Any Number Can Play '49
The Sun Comes Up '49
State of the Union '48
Love Laughs at Andy Hardy '46
Andy Hardy's Double Life '42
Andy Hardy's Private Secretary '41
Life Begins for Andy Hardy '41
Andy Hardy Meets Debutante '40
Andy Hardy Gets Spring Fever '39
Love Finds Andy Hardy '38
Suzy '36
China Seas '35
David Copperfield '35
The Girl from Missouri '34
Treasure Island '34
Bureau of Missing Persons '33
Queen Christina '33
Grand Hotel '32
The Mask of Fu Manchu '32
Mata Hari '32
Red Headed Woman '32
The Sin of Madelon Claudet '31
The Big House '30
Romance '30
Wild Orchids '28
A Woman of Affairs '28
The Notorious Lady '27
The Lost World '25
Beau Revel '21
Nomads of the North '20
Matt Stone (1971-)
South Park: Bigger, Longer and Uncut '99 (V)
BASEketball '98
Orgazmo '98
Cannibal! The Musical '96
Michael Stone
Bloody Murder '99
The Quick and the Dead '94
Milburn Stone (1904-80)
The Private War of Major Benson '55
Arrowhead '53
Pickup on South Street '53
The Sun Shines Bright '53
The Atomic City '52
Branded '50
The Judge '49
Heading for Heaven '47
Killer Dill '47
Strange Confession '45

Gail Strickland
Last Time Out '94
Three of Hearts '93
Scott Turow's The Burden of Proof '92
The Man in the Moon '91
Hyper-Sapien: People from Another Star '86
Oxford Blues '84
Protocol '84
Lies '83
Eleanor: First Lady of the World '82
A Matter of Life and Death '81
Rape and Marriage: The Rideout Case '80
The Gathering: Part 2 '79
Snowblind '78
Who'll Stop the Rain? '78
The Gathering '77
One on One '77

Anita Strindberg
Women in Cell Block 7 '77
The Tempter '74
The Scorpion's Tail '71

Sherry Stringfield
Dead Simple '01
Autumn in New York '00
54 '98
Burnzy's Last Call '95

Elaine Stritch (1925-)
Autumn in New York '00
Screwed '00
Small Time Crooks '00
Krippendorf's Tribe '98
Out to Sea '97
An Unexpected Life '97
September '88
Follies in Concert '85
Providence '77
The Perfect Furlough '59
Three Violent People '57

Woody Strode (1914-94)
Posse '93
Storyville '92
Murder on the Bayou '91
Super Brother '90
Lust in the Dust '85
Jungle Warriors '84
The Final Executioner '83
Scream '83
Vigilante '83
Violent Breed '83
Kill Castro '80
The Mercenaries '80
Jaguar Lives '79
Oil '78
Kingdom of the Spiders '77
Winterhawk '76
Loaded Guns '75
Hired to Kill '73
Hit Men '73
Manhunt '73
The Gatling Gun '72
Ride to Glory '71
Boot Hill '69
Black Jesus '68
Once Upon a Time in the West '68
Shalako '68
The Professionals '66
The Man Who Shot Liberty Valance '62
The Last Voyage '60
Sergeant Rutledge '60
Spartacus '60
Pork Chop Hill '59

Edson Stroll
Three Stooges in Orbit '62
Snow White and the Three Stooges '61

Brenda Strong
Terror Tract '00
Undercurrent '99
Black Dog '98
The Deep End of the Ocean '98

Danny Strong
Shriek If You Know What I Did Last Friday the 13th '00
Perpetrators of the Crime '98

Johnny Strong
Black Hawk Down '01
The Fast and the Furious '01
Get Carter '00
The Glimmer Man '96

Mark Strong
Anna Karenina '00
Sunshine '99
Twice upon a Yesterday '98
Emma '97
Fever Pitch '96
Sharpe's Mission '96

Michael Strong (1924-80)
Queen of the Stardust Ballroom '75
Patton '70
Point Blank '67

Rider Strong
The Pact '99
My Giant '98
Benefit of the Doubt '93

Don Stroud (1937-)
Dance with the Devil '97
The Haunted Sea '97
Wild America '97
Little Bigfoot '96
Criminal Hearts '95
Dillinger and Capone '95
Sawbones '95
Unknown Origin '95
Return to Frogtown '92
The Divine Enforcer '91
The King of the Kickboxers '91
Prime Target '91
Cartel '90
Down the Drain '89
Hyper Space '89
Twisted Justice '89
Two to Tango '88
Armed and Dangerous '86
The Night the Lights Went Out in Georgia '81
Search and Destroy '81
Sweet 16 '81
The Amityville Horror '79
Express to Terror '79
The Buddy Holly Story '78
The Choirboys '77
Sudden Death '77
Death Weekend '76
Hollywood Man '76
The Killer Inside Me '76
Murph the Surf '75
Slaughter's Big Ripoff '73
Joe Kidd '72
Angel Unchained '70
Bloody Mama '70
Explosion '69
Coogan's Bluff '68
Madigan '68
Games '67

Duke Stroud
Human Desires '97
Children of the Corn 3: Urban Harvest '95

Shepperd Strudwick (1907-83)
Cops and Robbers '73
The Man Without a Country '73
Psychomania '63
Beyond a Reasonable Doubt '56
Let's Dance '50
Three Husbands '50
All the King's Men '49
The Red Pony '49
The Loves of Edgar Allen Poe '42

Joe Strummer (1952-)
Doctor Chance '97
Mystery Train '89
Candy Mountain '87
Straight to Hell '87

Sally Struthers (1948-)
A Gun in the House '81
Intimate Strangers '77
The Getaway '72
Five Easy Pieces '70

Carel Struycken (1949-)
Men in Black '97
Backlash: Oblivion 2 '95
Out There '95
Under the Hula Moon '95
Oblivion '94
Addams Family Values '93
The Addams Family '91
Servants of Twilight '91
The Witches of Eastwick '87
The Ewoks: Battle for Endor '85

Cassie Stuart
Dolls '87
Hidden City '87

Gloria Stuart (1910-)
The Love Letter '99
The Million Dollar Hotel '99
Titanic '97
My Favorite Year '82
The Two Worlds of Jenny Logan '79
Enemy of Women '44
It Could Happen to You '39
The Three Musketeers '39
Rebecca of Sunnybrook Farm '38
The Poor Little Rich Girl '36
Gold Diggers of 1935 '35
The Invisible Man '33
Roman Scandals '33
The Old Dark House '32

James R. Stuart
Reactor '85
War of the Robots '78

John Stuart (1898-1979)
Sink the Bismarck '60
Village of the Damned '60
The Mummy '59
Alias John Preston '56
John and Julie '55
The Gilded Cage '54
Man on the Run '49
The Temptress '49
Candles at Nine '44
Old Mother Riley's Ghosts '41
No. 17 '32

Katie Stuart (1985-)
Atomic Dog '98
Frog and Wombat '98
Summer of the Monkeys '98
Masterminds '96

Maxine Stuart (1918-)
The Haunting of Seacliff Inn '94
The Rousters '90
Coast to Coast '80

Randy Stuart
The Incredible Shrinking Man '57
I Was a Male War Bride '49

Imogen Stubbs (1961-)
Twelfth Night '96
Jack and Sarah '95
Sense and Sensibility '95
True Colors '91
Erik the Viking '89
Fellow Traveler '89
A Summer Story '88

Stephen Stucker (1947-86)
Delinquent School Girls '84
Trading Places '83
Airplane 2: The Sequel '82
Airplane! '80

Wes Studi (1947-)
Mystery Men '99
Deep Rising '98
Wind River '98
Crazy Horse '96
The Killing Jar '96
Lone Justice 3: Showdown at Plum Creek '96
Heat '95
Larry McMurtry's Streets of Laredo '95
Street Fighter '94
The Broken Chain '93
Geronimo: An American Legend '93
Lone Justice 2 '93
The Last of the Mohicans '92
The Doors '91
Dances with Wolves '90

Jerzy Stuhr (1947-)
Trois Couleurs: Blanc '94
Deja Vu '89
The Decalogue '88
Camera Buff '79
Provincial Actors '79

Neil Stuke
Circus '00
Robert Louis Stevenson's The Game of Death '99
Twice upon a Yesterday '98
Century '94

Johnny Stumper
Covert Action '88
Mob War '88

Wolfgang Stumpf
Signs of Life '68
The Bridge '59

Preston Sturges (1898-1959)
Paris Holiday '57
Star Spangled Rhythm '42

Shannon Sturges
The Perfect Wife '00
Silent Predators '99
Tornado! '96
Pre-Madonnas: Rebels Without a Clue '95

Joris Stuyck
Sinatra '92
We'll Meet Again '82

Trudie Styler (1955-)
Grave Indiscretions '96
Fair Game '89
Poldark 2 '75

Krystyna Stypulkowska
Trace of Stones '66
Innocent Sorcerers '60

Emma Suarez (1964-)
Tierra '95
The Red Squirrel '93
Vacas '91
Against the Wind '90

Tara Subkoff
Teenage Caveman '01
The Cell '00
The Last Days of Disco '98
As Good As It Gets '97
Black Circle Boys '97
Lover Girl '97
All Over Me '96

Michel Subor
Please Not Now! '61
Le Petit Soldat '60

David Suchet (1946-)
The Way We Live Now '02
Victoria & Albert '01
RKO 281 '99
Wing Commander '99
A Perfect Murder '98
Solomon '98
Deadly Voyage '96
Executive Decision '96
Moses '96
Sunday '96
Don't Hang Up '90
To Kill a Priest '89
When the Whales Came '89
A World Apart '88
Cause Celebre '87
Harry and the Hendersons '87
The Last Innocent Man '87
Iron Eagle '86
Murrow '86
Crime of Honor '85
The Falcon and the Snowman '85
Gulag '85

Skipp (Robert L.) Sudduth (1956-)
Flawless '99
54 '98
Ronin '98
George Wallace '97
Money Train '95

Ichiro Sugai
Sansho the Bailiff '54
Early Summer '51

Haruko Sugimura (1905-97)
Drifting Weeds '59
Late Chrysanthemums '54
Tokyo Story '53
Early Summer '51
Late Spring '49

Barbara Sukowa (1950-)
Urbania '00
The Cradle Will Rock '99
The Lady in Question '99
The Third Miracle '99
Office Killer '97
Johnny Mnemonic '95
M. Butterfly '93
Zentropa '92
Voyager '91
The Sicilian '87
Rosa Luxemburg '86
Deadly Game '83
Marianne and Juliane '82
Berlin Alexanderplatz '80

Ania Suli
Stuart Bliss '98
Fun '94
Hold Me, Thrill Me, Kiss Me '93

Margaret Sullavan (1911-60)
So Ends Our Night '41
The Mortal Storm '40
The Shop Around the Corner '40
The Shining Hour '38
Shopworn Angel '38
Three Comrades '38
The Moon's Our Home '36

Barry Sullivan (1912-94)
Casino '80
The Bastard '78
No Room to Run '78
Oh, God! '77
Washington Affair '77
The Human Factor '75
Take a Hard Ride '75
Earthquake '74
Hurricane '74
Kung Fu '72
Yuma '70
Night Gallery '69
Tell Them Willie Boy Is Here '69
Buckskin '68
Shark! '68
Planet of the Vampires '65
A Gathering of Eagles '63
Another Time, Another Place '58
The Legend of the Sea Wolf '58
Texas Lady '56
The Maverick Queen '55
Queen Bee '55
Strategic Air Command '55
The Bad and the Beautiful '52
Skirts Ahoy! '52
Cause for Alarm '51
Three Guys Named Mike '51
A Life of Her Own '50
Nancy Goes to Rio '50
Any Number Can Play '49
The Great Gatsby '49
The Gangster '47
The Woman of the Town '44

Billy L. Sullivan
The Big Green '95
Little Big League '94

Brad Sullivan (1931-)
Bushwhacked '95
The Jerky Boys '95
Sister Act 2: Back in the Habit '93
Guilty by Suspicion '91
Orpheus Descending '91
The Prince of Tides '91
True Colors '91
Funny Farm '88
Slap Shot '77

Don Sullivan (1938-)
The Giant Gila Monster '59
The Rebel Set '59
Teenage Zombies '58
The Monster of Piedras Blancas '57

Elliott Sullivan
Vampyres '74
Action in the North Atlantic '43

Erik Per Sullivan (1991-)
Unfaithful '02
Joe Dirt '01
The Cider House Rules '99
Armageddon '98

Francis L. Sullivan (1903-56)
The Prodigal '55
Behave Yourself! '52
Night and the City '50
Christopher Columbus '49
Oliver Twist '48
Caesar and Cleopatra '46
Great Expectations '46
Butler's Dilemma '43
The Day Will Dawn '42
Pimpernel Smith '42
The Secret Four '40
Action for Slander '38
Non-Stop New York '37
21 Days '37
Spy of Napoleon '36
The Mystery of Edwin Drood '35
Great Expectations '34
Power '34

Jean Sullivan
Squirm '76
Uncertain Glory '44

Jenny Sullivan
Katherine '75
The Other '72

Matthew Sullivan
Dementia '98
Max Is Missing '95

Michael Sullivan
Great Ride '78
Greaser's Palace '72

Susan Sullivan (1942-)
My Best Friend's Wedding '97
Rage of Angels: The Story Continues '86
The Dark Ride '84
City in Fear '80
Marriage Is Alive and Well '80
The Ordeal of Dr. Mudd '80
Deadman's Curve '78
The Incredible Hulk '77

Frank Sully
The Tender Trap '55
Inside the Law '42

Cree Summer
Atlantis: The Lost Empire '01 (V)
The Rugrats Movie '98 (V)

Diane Summerfield
Blackjack '78
Black Godfather '74

Eleanor Summerfield
Black Glove '54
Man on the Run '49

Roy Summerset
Cold Heat '90
Overkill '86

Slim Summerville (1892-1946)
I'm from Arkansas '44
Western Union '41
Jesse James '39
Rebecca of Sunnybrook Farm '38
Captain January '36
The Farmer Takes a Wife '35
All Quiet on the Western Front '30
Under Montana Skies '30
King of the Rodeo '28
The Beloved Rogue '27

Bart Sumner
Video Violence '87
Video Violence Part 2...The Exploitation! '87

Donald (Don) Sumpter (1943-)
The Buddha of Suburbia '92

Rosencrantz & Guildenstern Are Dead '90
Black Panther '77

Clinton Sundberg (1906-87)
The Thief and the Cobbler '96 (V)
Main Street to Broadway '53
The Belle of New York '52
As Young As You Feel '51
Annie Get Your Gun '50
Two Weeks with Love '50
In the Good Old Summertime '49
Mr. Peabody & the Mermaid '48
Undercurrent '46

Bjorn Sundquist (1948-)
The Other Side of Sunday '96
Zero Degrees Kelvin '95
The Last Lieutenant '94
Shipwrecked '90
The Dive '89

Gerry Sundquist
Don't Open Till Christmas '84
Great Expectations '81
Alexandria...Why? '78

Ethan Suplee
John Q '02
Blow '01
Evolution '01
Remember the Titans '00
Road Trip '00
American History X '98
Desert Blue '98

Cristina Suriani
Horror Rises from the Tomb '72
The Saga of the Draculas '72

Nicolas Surovy (1944-)
All Over the Guy '01
When Danger Follows You Home '97
The Man Who Captured Eichmann '96
Breaking Free '95
12:01 '93
Forever Young '92
Anastasia: The Mystery of Anna '86
Stark '85
The Act '82

Todd Susman (1947-)
Bodily Harm '95
The Invaders '95
Only the Strong '93
Beverly Hills Cop 2 '87
Star Spangled Girl '71

Paul Sutera (1979-)
A Very Brady Sequel '96
The Brady Bunch Movie '95
Problem Child 2 '91

Donald Sutherland (1934-)
Final Fantasy: The Spirits Within '01 (V)
Uprising '01
The Art of War '00
Panic '00
Space Cowboys '00
Free Money '99
The Hunley '99
Instinct '99
Virus '98
The Assignment '97
Fallen '97
Without Limits '97
Natural Enemy '96
The Shadow Conspiracy '96
A Time to Kill '96
Citizen X '95
Hollow Point '95
Oldest Confederate Widow Tells All '95
Red Hot '95
Disclosure '94
Outbreak '94
The Puppet Masters '94
Younger & Younger '94
Benefit of the Doubt '93
Six Degrees of Separation '93
Buffy the Vampire Slayer '92
The Railway Station Man '92
Shadow of the Wolf '92
Backdraft '91
Eminent Domain '91
JFK '91
Long Road Home '91
Quicksand: No Escape '91
Dr. Bethune '90
A Dry White Season '89
Lock Up '89
Lost Angels '89
Apprentice to Murder '88
The Rosary Murders '87
The Trouble with Spies '87
The Wolf at the Door '87
Heaven Help Us '85
Revolution '85
Crackers '84
Ordeal by Innocence '84
Max Dugan Returns '83
Threshold '83
Disappearance '81
Eye of the Needle '81
Gas '81
Bear Island '80
Nothing Personal '80
Ordinary People '80
The Great Train Robbery '79
A Man, a Woman, and a Bank '79
Murder by Decree '79
Invasion of the Body Snatchers '78
National Lampoon's Animal House '78
Bethune '77
Blood Relatives '77
The Eagle Has Landed '77
Kentucky Fried Movie '77
1900 '76
The Day of the Locust '75
S*P*Y*S '74
Dan Candy's Law '73
Don't Look Now '73
Lady Ice '73
Steelyard Blues '73
Johnny Got His Gun '71
Klute '71
Little Murders '71
Alex in Wonderland '70
Kelly's Heroes '70
M*A*S*H '70
Start the Revolution without Me '70
Sebastian '68
The Dirty Dozen '67
Bedford Incident '65
Die! Die! My Darling! '65
Dr. Terror's House of Horrors '65
Castle of the Living Dead '64

Kiefer Sutherland (1967-)
The Right Temptation '00
Eye of the Killer '99
Picking Up the Pieces '99
The Break Up '98
Ground Control '98
A Soldier's Sweetheart '98
Woman Wanted '98
Dark City '97
Truth or Consequences, N.M. '97
The Last Days of Frankie the Fly '96
A Time to Kill '96
An Eye for an Eye '95
Freeway '95
The Cowboy Way '94
Teresa's Tattoo '94
Last Light '93
The Three Musketeers '93
The Vanishing '93
Article 99 '92
A Few Good Men '92
Twin Peaks: Fire Walk with Me '92
The Nutcracker Prince '91 (V)
Chicago Joe & the Showgirl '90
Flatliners '90
Young Guns 2 '90
Flashback '89
1969 '89
Renegades '89
Bright Lights, Big City '88
Promised Land '88
Young Guns '88
Crazy Moon '87
The Killing Time '87
The Lost Boys '87
At Close Range '86
Brotherhood of Justice '86
Stand by Me '86
Trapped in Silence '86
Amazing Stories '85
The Bay Boy '85
Max Dugan Returns '83

James Sutorius (1944-)
On Wings of Eagles '86
My Mother's Secret Life '84
Windy City '84
Prototype '83
A Question of Love '78

Dolores Sutton
F. Scott Fitzgerald in Hollywood '76
Where Angels Go, Trouble Follows '68

Dudley Sutton (1933-)
Edward II '92
Orlando '92
Cry of the Penguins '71
The Devils '71
The Leather Boys '63

Frank Sutton
Hurricane '74
Town without Pity '61
Marty '55

Grady Sutton (1908-95)
Paradise, Hawaiian Style '66
Going to Town '44
The More the Merrier '43
The Bashful Bachelor '42
The Bank Dick '40
Dangerous Holiday '37
Waikiki Wedding '37
Alice Adams '35
Bachelor Bait '34
Pharmacist '32

John Sutton (1908-63)
The Bat '59
Beloved Infidel '59
Return of the Fly '59
Five Fingers '52 (N)
David and Bathsheba '51
The Second Woman '51
Bagdad '49
Mickey '48
Captain from Castile '47
Jane Eyre '44
A Yank in the R.A.F. '41
The Invisible Man Returns '40
The Tower of London '39
Arrest Bulldog Drummond '38

Kay Sutton
Sergeant York '41
The Saint in New York '38

Michael Sutton
Dracula: The Dark Prince '01
Wanted '98

Mena Suvari (1979-)
American Pie 2 '01
The Musketeer '01
Sugar & Spice '01
Loser '00
American Beauty '99
American Pie '99
Atomic Train '99
The Rage: Carrie 2 '99
American Virgin '98
Nowhere '96

Janet Suzman (1939-)
Leon the Pig Farmer '93
Nuns on the Run '90
A Dry White Season '89
Mountbatten: The Last Viceroy '86
The Singing Detective '86
The Zany Adventures of Robin Hood '84
And the Ship Sails On '83
The Draughtsman's Contract '82
Priest of Love '81
Nijinsky '80
The House on Garibaldi Street '79
Macbeth '76
Voyage of the Damned '76
The Black Windmill '74
A Day in the Death of Joe Egg '71
Nicholas and Alexandra '71

Semyon Svashenko (1904-69)
Earth '30
Arsenal '29
Zvenigora '28

Bo Svenson (1941-)
Crackerjack 3 '00
Speed 2: Cruise Control '97
Private Obsession '94
Savage Land '94
Steel Frontier '94
Beyond the Door 3 '91
Steele's Law '91
Three Days to a Kill '91
Primal Rage '90
Tides of War '90
Andy and the Airwave Rangers '89
The Kill Reflex '89
Curse 2: The Bite '88
Deep Space '87
Delta Force Commando '87
The Dirty Dozen: The Deadly Mission '87
White Phantom: Enemy of Darkness '87
Choke Canyon '86
Delta Force '86
Heartbreak Ridge '86
The Last Contract '86
The Manhunt '86
Thunder Warrior '85
Thunder Warrior 2 '85
Wizards of the Lost Kingdom '85
Deadly Impact '84
Jealousy '84
Night Warning '82
Virus '82
Gold of the Amazon Women '79
North Dallas Forty '79
Deadly Mission '78
Portrait of a Hitman '77
Snowbeast '77
Walking Tall: The Final Chapter '77
Special Delivery '76
The Great Waldo Pepper '75
Walking Tall: Part 2 '75
Big Mo '73
Frankenstein '73

Zdenek Sverak
Kolya '96
The Elementary School '91

Bob Swaim (1943-)
Spies Like Us '85
La Balance '82

Dominique Swain (1980-)
New Best Friend '02
Dead in the Water '01
Happy Campers '01
Tart '01
Intern '00
The Smokers '00
Girl '98
Face/Off '97
Lolita '97

Howard Swain
Night of the Scarecrow '95
Jon Jost's Frameup '93

Mack Swain (1876-1935)
The Chaplin Revue '58
The Beloved Rogue '27
Hands Up '26
The Nervous Wreck '26
The Gold Rush '25
Three Charlies and One Phoney! '18
Tillie's Punctured Romance '14

Darwyn Swalve (1946-99)
Deadly Reactor '89
Take Two '87

Hilary Swank (1974-)
Insomnia '02
The Affair of the Necklace '01
The Gift '00
Boys Don't Cry '99
Heartwood '98
Quiet Days in Hollywood '97
Kounterfeit '96
Sometimes They Come Back ... Again '96
The Next Karate Kid '94
Buffy the Vampire Slayer '92

Brenda Swanson
Scanners: The Showdown '94
Secret Games 3 '94
Prototype X29A '92

Gary Swanson
Coldfire '90
The Guardian '90
Witchfire '86
TripleCross '85
Vice Squad '82

Gloria Swanson (1897-1983)
Airport '75 '75
The Love Goddesses '65
Three for Bedroom C '52
Sunset Boulevard '50
Indiscreet '31
Tonight or Never '31
Queen Kelly '29
Sadie Thompson '28
Manhandled '24
Affairs of Anatol '21
Why Change Your Wife? '20
Male and Female '19
Shifting Sands '18
Teddy at the Throttle '16

Jackie Swanson
Oblivion '94
Lethal Weapon '87

Kristy Swanson (1969-)
Zebra Lounge '01
Dude, Where's My Car? '00
Big Daddy '99
Supreme Sanction '99
Ground Control '98
Meeting Daddy '98
Lover Girl '97
Tinseltown '97
8 Heads in a Duffel Bag '96
Marshal Law '96
The Phantom '96
Getting In '94
Higher Learning '94
The Chase '93
The Program '93
Buffy the Vampire Slayer '92
Highway to Hell '92
Hot Shots! '91
Mannequin 2: On the Move '91
Diving In '90
Dream Trap '90
Flowers in the Attic '87
Deadly Friend '86
Ferris Bueller's Day Off '86
Pretty in Pink '86

Maureen Swanson (1932-)
Robbery under Arms '57
The Spanish Gardener '57
Moulin Rouge '52

Rochelle Swanson
On the Border '98
Deadly Outbreak '96
Cyberzone '95
Hard Bounty '94
Indecent Behavior 2 '94
Night Fire '94
Secret Games 3 '94

Rufus Swart
Dust Devil '93
The House of Usher '88

Don Swayze (1958-)
The Prophet's Game '99
Money to Burn '94
Beach Babes from Beyond Infinity '93
Body of Influence '93
Broken Trust '93
Death Ring '93
Eye of the Stranger '93
Forced to Kill '93
Sexual Malice '93
Edge of Honor '91
Payback '90
Trapper County War '89
Driving Force '88
The Tracker '88
Death Blow '87
Shy People '87

Patrick Swayze (1952-)
Donnie Darko '01
Along for the Ride '00
Black Dog '98
Letters from a Killer '98
Tall Tale: The Unbelievable Adventures of Pecos Bill '95
Three Wishes '95
To Wong Foo, Thanks for Everything, Julie Newmar '95
Father Hood '93
City of Joy '92
Point Break '91
Ghost '90
Next of Kin '89
Road House '89
Dirty Dancing '87
Steel Dawn '87
Tiger Warsaw '87
North and South Book 2 '86
Youngblood '86
North and South Book 1 '85
Grandview U.S.A. '84
Red Dawn '84
The Outsiders '83
Uncommon Valor '83
Return of the Rebels '81

Heidi Swedberg (1964-)
The Ticket '97
Father and Scout '94
Hot Shots! '91

Bob Sweeney (-1992)
Toby Tyler '59
A Christmas Carol '54

D.B. Sweeney (1961-)
Hardball '01
Dinosaur '00 (V)
The Weekend '00
The Book of Stars '99
Introducing Dorothy Dandridge '99
Spawn '97
Roommates '95
Fire in the Sky '93
Hear No Evil '93
The Cutting Edge '92
A Day in October '92
Miss Rose White '92
Blue Desert '91
Heaven Is a Playground '91
Leather Jackets '90
Memphis Belle '90
Lonesome Dove '89
Eight Men Out '88
Gardens of Stone '87
No Man's Land '87
Fire with Fire '86

Dominic Sweeney
In Too Deep '90
Jigsaw '90

Garry Sweeney
The Acid House '98
Small Faces '95

Joseph Sweeney
Twelve Angry Men '57
The Man in the Gray Flannel Suit '56

Julia Sweeney (1961-)
Clockstoppers '02
Beethoven's 3rd '00
Whatever It Takes '00
God Said "Ha!" '99
Stuart Little '99
Thick as Thieves '99
Vegas Vacation '96

It's Pat: The Movie *'94*
Pulp Fiction *'94*
Stuart Saves His Family *'94*
Coneheads *'93*
Honey, I Blew Up the Kid *'92*

Steve Sweeney
Beautiful People *'99*
Lock, Stock and 2 Smoking Barrels *'98*
Nil by Mouth *'96*

Blanche Sweet (1895-1986)
The Silver Horde *'30*
Anna Christie *'23*
Avenging Conscience *'14*
Home Sweet Home *'14*
Judith of Bethulia *'14*

Dolph Sweet (1920-85)
Acorn People *'82*
Jacqueline Bouvier Kennedy *'81*
Reds *'81*
Wanderers *'79*
Deathmoon *'78*
Go Tell the Spartans *'78*
The Bad News Bears in Breaking Training *'77*
Amazing Grace *'74*
The Migrants *'74*
Cops and Robbers *'73*
Sisters *'73*
The Lost Man *'69*
Finian's Rainbow *'68*

Gary Sweet (1957-)
Fever *'88*
The Lighthorsemen *'87*
An Indecent Obsession *'85*
Stage Fright *'83*

Vonte Sweet
Restaurant *'98*
American Strays *'96*
Marshal Law *'96*
The Walking Dead *'94*
Laurel Avenue *'93*
Menace II Society *'93*

Rod Sweitzer
The Malibu Beach Vampires *'91*
The Invisible Maniac *'90*

Inga Swenson
North and South Book 1 *'85*
The Miracle Worker *'62*

Jeep Swenson (1957-97)
Batman and Robin *'97*
Bulletproof *'96*

Karl Swenson (1908-78)
Brighty of the Grand Canyon *'67*
Seconds *'66*
The Sword in the Stone *'63 (V)*
Judgment at Nuremberg *'61*
Flaming Star *'60*
The Gallant Hours *'60*
The Hanging Tree *'59*
No Name on the Bullet *'59*

Tommy Swerdlow
Child's Play *'88*
Hamburger Hill *'87*

Josef Swickard (1866-1940)
Custer's Last Stand *'36*
The Lone Defender *'32*
The Night Patrol *'26*
The Wizard of Oz *'25*
Dante's Inferno *'24*
The Four Horsemen of the Apocalypse *'21*

Clive Swift
The Aristocrats *'99*
Frenzy *'72*

Francie Swift
The Great Gatsby *'01*
Fall *'97*
Last Breath *'96*

Jeremy Swift
Gosford Park *'01*
Vanity Fair *'99*

Paul Swift (1934-94)
Female Trouble *'74*
Pink Flamingos *'72*
Multiple Maniacs *'70*

Nora Swinburne (1902-2000)
Strange Awakening *'58*
Helen of Troy *'56*
Betrayed *'54*
Quo Vadis *'51*
The River *'51*
Man of Evil *'48*

Tilda Swinton (1961-)
The Deep End *'01*
Vanilla Sky *'01*
The Beach *'00*
Love Is the Devil *'98*
The War Zone *'98*
Conceiving Ada *'97*
Female Perversions *'96*
Blue *'93 (N)*
Wittgenstein *'93*
Edward II *'92*
Orlando *'92*
The Garden *'90*
The Last of England *'87*
Caravaggio *'86*

Loretta Swit (1937-)
Miracle at Moreaux *'86*
Beer *'85*
The Execution *'85*
First Affair *'83*
M*A*S*H: Goodbye, Farewell & Amen *'83*
S.O.B. *'81*
Race with the Devil *'75*
Freebie & the Bean *'74*

Carl "Alfalfa" Switzer (1926-59)
Motorcycle Gang *'57*
Pat and Mike *'52*
Cause for Alarm *'51*
Redwood Forest Trail *'50*
Underworld Scandal *'47*
It's a Wonderful Life *'46*
The Great Mike *'44*
Reg'lar Fellers *'41*
General Spanky *'36*

Ken Swofford (1932-)
The Taking of Beverly Hills *'91*
Black Roses *'88*
All God's Children *'80*
Sky Hei$t *'75*
Bless the Beasts and Children *'71*

Topo Swope
My Old Man's Place *'71*
The Hot Rock *'70*

Tracy Brooks Swope (1952-)
White Wolves 3: Cry of the White Wolf *'98*
Inner Sanctum 2 *'94*
The Power of One *'92*
The Big Picture *'89*

Meera Syal
Forgive and Forget *'99*
Sammy & Rosie Get Laid *'87*

Basil Sydney (1894-1968)
The Hands of Orlac *'60*
The Devil's Disciple *'59*
John Paul Jones *'59*
The Three Worlds of Gulliver *'59*
Dam Busters *'55*
Salome *'53*
Angel with the Trumpet *'50*
Treasure Island *'50*
Hamlet *'48*
The Secret Four *'40*
Accused *'36*
Rhodes *'36*

Brenda Sykes (1949-)
Mandingo *'75*
Cleopatra Jones *'73*
Honky *'71*

Eric Sykes
The Others *'01*
Those Daring Young Men in Their Jaunty Jalopies *'69*
Heavens Above *'63*

Harold Sylvester
Trippin' *'99*
The Sixth Man *'97*
The Reluctant Agent *'95*
In the Deep Woods *'91*
In the Line of Duty: A Cop for the Killing *'90*
Innerspace *'87*
Uncommon Valor *'83*
Fast Break *'79*

William Sylvester (1923-95)
2001: A Space Odyssey *'68*
Beast of Morocco *'66*
Devil Doll *'64*
Gorgo *'61*
Postmark for Danger *'56*
Unholy Four *'54*

Kary Sylway
Face to Face *'76*
Cries and Whispers *'72*

Robert Symonds (1926-)
Mandroid *'93*
Rumpelstiltskin *'86*
Ice Pirates *'84*

Sylvia Syms (1934-)
Catherine Cookson's The Glass Virgin *'95*
Shining Through *'92*
A Chorus of Disapproval *'89*
Shirley Valentine *'89*
Intimate Contact *'87*
Murders at Lynch Cross *'85*
The Tamarind Seed *'74*
Asylum *'72*
Desperados *'69*
Fiction Makers *'67*
Victim *'61*
Conspiracy of Hearts *'60*
The World of Suzie Wong *'60*
Expresso Bongo *'59*
Ferry to Hong Kong *'59*
Teenage Bad Girl *'59*
Bachelor of Hearts *'58*
The Moonraker *'58*

Del Synnott
Othello *'01*
Princess of Thieves *'01*

Clancy Syrko
Black Bikers from Hell *'70*
The Outlaw Bikers—Gang Wars *'70*

Laszlo Szabo
The Unbearable Lightness of Being *'88*
Passion *'82*
The Last Metro *'80*
Bad Guys *'79*
Nice Neighbor *'79*
Adoption *'75*
Alphaville *'65*
Le Petit Soldat *'60*

Grazyna Szapolowska
No End *'84*
Another Way *'82*

Keith Szarabajka (1952-)
Andre *'94*
A Perfect World *'93*
Stephen King's Golden Years *'91*
Unnatural Pursuits *'91*
Nightlife *'90*
The Misfit Brigade *'87*
Billy Galvin *'86*
Marie *'85*
Protocol *'84*

Magda Szubanski
The Crocodile Hunter: Collision Course *'02*
Babe: Pig in the City *'98*
Babe *'95*

Oleg Tabakov
Oblomov *'81*
An Unfinished Piece for a Player Piano *'77*

Eron Tabor
Krush Groove *'85*
I Spit on Your Grave *'77*

Kristopher Tabori (1952-)
Last Summer In the Hamptons *'96*
Marilyn & Bobby: Her Final Affair *'94*
Girlfriends *'78*
The Glass House *'72*

Hiroshi Tachikawa
Attack of the Mushroom People *'63*
Yojimbo *'61*

Sydney Tafler (1916-79)
The Adventurers *'70*
Alfie *'66*
Sink the Bismarck *'60*
Carve Her Name with Pride *'58*
Fire Maidens from Outer Space *'56*
The Way Out *'56*
Uneasy Terms *'48*

Cary-Hiroyuki Tagawa (1950-)
Planet of the Apes *'01*
The Art of War *'00*
Bridge of Dragons *'99*
Tom Clancy's Netforce *'98*
Double Edge *'97*
John Carpenter's Vampires *'97*
Top of the World *'97*
The Phantom *'96*
Provocateur *'96*
Danger Zone *'95*
Mortal Kombat 1: The Movie *'95*
Soldier Boyz *'95*
White Tiger *'95*
Natural Causes *'94*
Picture Bride *'94*
Nemesis *'93*
Rising Sun *'93*
American Me *'92*
Showdown in Little Tokyo *'91*
The Last Warrior *'89*

Rita Taggart
Limbo *'99*
At Home with the Webbers *'94*
Coupe de Ville *'90*
The Horror Show *'89*
Weeds *'87*
Torchlight *'85*
Used Cars *'80*
Coming Home *'78*

Sharon Taggart
Harrad Experiment *'73*
The Last Picture Show *'71*

Said Taghmaoui (1973-)
Hideous Kinky *'99*
Three Kings *'99*
Hate *'95*

Sharmila Tagore (1936-)
Mississippi Masala *'92*
Days and Nights in the Forest *'70*
Devi *'60*
The World of Apu *'59*

Tomoroh Taguchi (1957-)
Tetsuo 2: Body Hammer *'97*
The Eel *'96*
Tetsuo: The Iron Man *'92*

Taj Mahal (1942-)
Songcatcher *'99*
Outside Ozona *'98*
Bill & Ted's Bogus Journey *'91*
Sounder *'72*

Yoshifumi Tajima (1918-)
War of the Gargantuas *'70*
Godzilla's Revenge *'69*
Destroy All Monsters *'68*
Godzilla vs. Mothra *'64*

Miiko Taka
Walk, Don't Run *'66*
A Global Affair *'63*
Sayonara *'57*

Koji Takahashi
Hiroshima *'95*
Godzilla vs. Biollante *'89*
Professional Killers 1 *'73*

Ken Takakura (1931-)
Mr. Baseball *'92*
Black Rain *'89*
Antarctica *'84*
Station *'81*
The Yakuza *'75*
Too Late the Hero *'70*

Hideko Takamine (1924-)
When a Woman Ascends the Stairs *'60*
Twenty-Four Eyes *'54*
Mistress *'53*

Akira Takarada (1934-)
Minbo—Or the Gentle Art of Japanese Extortion *'92*
Godzilla vs. Monster Zero *'68*
Last War *'68*
Godzilla vs. Mothra *'64*
Half Human *'58*
Godzilla, King of the Monsters *'56*

Masahiro Takashima
Godzilla vs. Mechagodzilla II *'93*
Godzilla vs. Biollante *'89*

Tadao Takashima
Son of Godzilla *'66*
King Kong vs. Godzilla *'63*

George Takei (1940-)
Bug Buster *'99*
Mulan *'98 (V)*
Kissinger and Nixon *'96*
Backlash: Oblivion 2 *'95*
Oblivion *'94*
Bruce Lee: Curse of the Dragon *'93 (N)*
Prisoners of the Sun *'91*
Star Trek 6: The Undiscovered Country *'91*
Star Trek 5: The Final Frontier *'89*
Star Trek 4: The Voyage Home *'86*
Star Trek 3: The Search for Spock *'84*
Star Trek 2: The Wrath of Khan *'82*
Star Trek: The Motion Picture *'80*
The Green Berets *'68*
Red Line 7000 *'65*
Ice Palace *'60*

Naoto Takenaka
Shall We Dance? *'96*
The Mystery of Rampo *'94*

Osamu Takizawa
Zatoichi vs. Yojimbo *'70*
Fires on the Plain *'59*

Oleg Taktarov
Rollerball *'02*
15 Minutes *'01*

Gloria Talbot
The Leech Woman *'59*
Crashout *'55*

Helen Talbot
King of the Forest Rangers *'46*
Federal Operator 99 *'45*
California Joe *'43*

Lyle Talbot (1902-96)
Sunrise at Campobello *'60*
High School Confidential *'58*
Plan 9 from Outer Space *'56*
Jail Bait *'54*
Trader Tom of the China Seas *'54*
Clipped Wings *'53*
Glen or Glenda? *'53*
Mesa of Lost Women *'52*
Gold Raiders *'51*
One Too Many *'51*
Atom Man vs. Superman *'50*
Border Rangers *'50*
Parole, Inc. *'49*
Pirate Ship *'49*
She Shoulda Said No *'49*
Thunder in the Pines *'49*
The Devil's Cargo *'48*
Highway 13 *'48*
North of the Border *'46*
Song of Arizona *'46*
Strange Impersonation *'46*
Gambler's Choice *'44*
Mystery of the Riverboat *'44*
One Body Too Many *'44*
Sensations of 1945 *'44*
Up in Arms *'44*
A Night for Crime *'42*
Second Fiddle *'39*
Torture Ship *'39*
Three Legionnaires *'37*
Vengeance *'37*
Go West, Young Man *'36*
The Case of the Lucky Legs *'35*
Our Little Girl *'35*
One Night of Love *'34*
Ladies They Talk About *'33*
Shriek in the Night *'33*
The Purchase Price *'32*
13th Guest *'32*
Three on a Match *'32*

Nita Talbot (1930-)
Amityville 1992: It's About Time *'92*
Puppet Master 2 *'90*
Take Two *'87*
Fraternity Vacation *'85*
Chained Heat *'83*
The Concrete Jungle *'82*
Night Shift *'82*
Sweet Creek County War *'82*
Frightmare *'81*
Girl Happy *'65*
Who's Got the Action? *'63*
I Married a Woman *'56*

Gloria Talbott (1933-2000)
Arizona Raiders *'65*
Alias Jesse James *'59*
Girls' Town *'59*
I Married a Monster from Outer Space *'58*
The Daughter of Dr. Jekyll *'57*
The Kettles on Old MacDonald's Farm *'57*
Cyclops *'56*
The Oklahoman *'56*
All That Heaven Allows *'55*
We're No Angels *'55*

Michael Talbott
Miami Vice *'84*
Racing with the Moon *'84*

Hal Taliaferro (1895-1980)
Frontier Law *'43*
Hoppy Serves a Writ *'43*
Leather Burners *'43*
Border Vigilantes *'41*
Riders of the Timberline *'41*
Phantom Gold *'38*
The Rangers Step In *'37*
The Unknown Ranger *'36*

Michael "Bear" Taliferro
The Replacements *'00*
Life *'99*

Margaret Tallichet
It Started with Eve *'41*
Stranger on the Third Floor *'40*

Patricia Tallman
Army of Darkness *'92*
Night of the Living Dead *'90*

Constance Talmadge (1900-73)
Intolerance *'16*
Matrimaniac *'16*
The Primitive Lover *'16*

Norma Talmadge (1895-1957)
Dubarry *'30*
The Forbidden City *'18*
The Social Secretary *'16*

Richard Talmadge (1892-1981)
Speed Reporter *'36*
Fighting Pilot *'35*
The Live Wire *'34*
Get That Girl *'32*
The Night Patrol *'26*
Laughing at Danger *'24*
Let's Go! *'23*

William Talman (1917-68)
Crashout *'55*

The Hitch-Hiker '53
One Minute to Zero '52
Armored Car Robbery '50
Isao Tamagawa
Branded to Kill '67
Story of a Prostitute '65
Tetsuro Tamba (1922-)
A Taxing Woman's Return '88
Tokyo Pop '88
The Imperial Japanese Empire '85
Zero '84
Hunter in the Dark '80
Last Days of Planet Earth '74
You Only Live Twice '67
The Seventh Dawn '64
One-Eyed Swordsman '63
Carlo Tamberlani
The Trojan Horse '62
The Fury of Hercules '61
Nando Tamberlani
Hercules against the Moon Men '64
The Trojan Horse '62
Russ Tamblyn (1934-)
My Magic Dog '97
Invisible Mom '96
Attack of the 60-Foot Centerfold '95
Cabin Boy '94
Desert Steel '94
Wizards of the Demon Sword '94
Running Mates '92
Aftershock '88
Blood Screams '88
B.O.R.N. '88
Necromancer: Satan's Servant '88
Commando Squad '87
Cyclone '87
Phantom Empire '87
Dracula vs. Frankenstein '71
The Last Movie '71
War of the Gargantuas '70
The Female Bunch '69
Free Grass '69
Satan's Sadists '69
The Long Ships '64
The Haunting '63
How the West Was Won '63
The Wonderful World of the Brothers Grimm '62
West Side Story '61
Cimarron '60
High School Confidential '58
Tom Thumb '58
Don't Go Near the Water '57
Peyton Place '57
Fastest Gun Alive '56
The Last Hunt '56
Hit the Deck '55
Seven Brides for Seven Brothers '54
Retreat, Hell! '52
The Winning Team '52
Father's Little Dividend '51
Father of the Bride '50
Gun Crazy '49
Jeffrey Tambor (1944-)
Get Well Soon '01
Dr. Seuss' How the Grinch Stole Christmas '00
Pollock '00
Girl, Interrupted '99
Muppets from Space '99
Teaching Mrs. Tingle '99
Dr. Dolittle '98
Meet Joe Black '98
There's Something about Mary '98
Weapons of Mass Distraction '97
The Man Who Captured Eichmann '96
Big Bully '95
My Teacher's Wife '95
At Home with the Webbers '94
Heavyweights '94
Radioland Murders '94
A House in the Hills '93
Article 99 '92
Crossing the Bridge '92
Scott Turow's The Burden of Proof '92
City Slickers '91
Life Stinks '91
Pastime '91
Lisa '90
A Perfect Little Murder '90
Three o'Clock High '87
Brenda Starr '86
Desert Hearts '86
The Man Who Wasn't There '83
Mr. Mom '83
Sadat '83
Take Your Best Shot '82
A Gun in the House '81
Saturday the 14th '81
And Justice for All '79
Jenny Tamburi
Bloody Avenger '80
Women in Cell Block 7 '77
Zoe Tamerlis
Special Effects '85
Ms. 45 '81
Akim Tamiroff (1899-1972)
Deadly Sanctuary '68
Vulture '67
Hotel Paradiso '66
Lt. Robin Crusoe, U.S.N. '66
Alphaville '65
Lord Jim '65
Topkapi '64
The Bacchantes '63
The Trial '63
Panic Button '62
Ocean's 11 '60
Me and the Colonel '58
Touch of Evil '58
Anastasia '56
Battle Hell '56
Mr. Arkadin '55
Black Magic '49
Outpost in Morocco '49
My Girl Tisa '48
The Gangster '47
A Scandal in Paris '46
Can't Help Singing '45
The Bridge of San Luis Rey '44
Dragon Seed '44
His Butler's Sister '44
Miracle of Morgan's Creek '44
Five Graves to Cairo '43
For Whom the Bell Tolls '43
The Corsican Brothers '42
Tortilla Flat '42
The Great McGinty '40
The Texas Rangers Ride Again '40
Union Pacific '39
Spawn of the North '38
Desire '36
The General Died at Dawn '36
The Story of Louis Pasteur '36
The Lives of a Bengal Lancer '35
The Merry Widow '34
Mary Tamm (1950-)
The Assassination Run '84
The Odessa File '74
Tales That Witness Madness '73
Takahiro Tamura
The Silk Road '92
In the Realm of Passion '80
The Empire of Passion '76
Tora! Tora! Tora! '70
Haruo Tanaka
The Pornographers '66
Snow Country '57
Kinuyo Tanaka (1910-77)
Sandakan No. 8 '74
Equinox Flower '58
Sansho the Bailiff '54
Ugetsu '53
Life of Oharu '52
Mother '52
Utamaro and His Five Women '46
Sara Tanaka
Rushmore '98
Race the Sun '96
Toru Tanaka (1930-2000)
3 Ninjas '92
Tax Season '90
Yoshiko Tanaka
Godzilla vs. Biollante '89
Black Rain '88
Jessica Tandy (1909-94)
Camilla '94
Nobody's Fool '94
The Story Lady '93
To Dance with the White Dog '93
Used People '92
Fried Green Tomatoes '91
Driving Miss Daisy '89
Cocoon: The Return '88
The House on Carroll Street '88
*batteries not included '87
Foxfire '87
Cocoon '85
The Bostonians '84
Gin Game '84
Best Friends '82
Still of the Night '82
The World According to Garp '82
The Birds '63
The Light in the Forest '58
The Desert Fox '51
September Affair '50
Forever Amber '47
The Valley of Decision '45
The Seventh Cross '44
Mark Tandy (1957-)
The Buccaneers '95
The Railway Station Man '92
Maurice '87
Yoko Tani (1932-99)
Koroshi '67
Invasion '65
Samson and the 7 Miracles of the World '62
First Spaceship on Venus '60
William Tannen (-1976)
Jupiter's Darling '55
Whistling in the Dark '41
Gordon Tanner
Dr. Strangelove, or: How I Learned to Stop Worrying and Love the Bomb '64
Time Lock '57
Warhawk Tanzania
Black Force '75
Gang Wars '75
Guo Tao
So Close to Paradise '98
To Live '94
Amanda Tapping
The Void '01
Terror Train '80
Quentin Tarantino (1963-)
Little Nicky '00
Kisses in the Dark '97
Girl 6 '96
Desperado '95
Destiny Turns on the Radio '95
Four Rooms '95
From Dusk Till Dawn '95
Pulp Fiction '94
Sleep with Me '94
Somebody to Love '94
Reservoir Dogs '92
Fran Tarkenton
First & Ten '85
First & Ten: The Team Scores Again '85
Rockne Tarkington (1932-)
Trained to Kill, U.S.A. '83
Zebra Force '76
Black Starlet '74
Clarence, the Cross-eyed Lion '65
Lilyan Tashman (1899-1934)
Riptide '34
Scarlet Dawn '32
Millie '31
Bulldog Drummond '29
So This Is Paris '26
Manhandled '24
Coralina Cataldi Tassoni
Evil Clutch '89
Opera '88
Demons 2 '87
Jun Tatara
The Human Condition: Road to Eternity '59
Seven Samurai '54
Larenz Tate (1975-)
Love Come Down '00
Why Do Fools Fall in Love? '98
The Postman '97
Love Jones '96
Dead Presidents '95
The Inkwell '94
Menace II Society '93
Laura Tate
Dead Space '90
Subspecies '90
Nick (Nicholas) Tate (1942-)
A Cry in the Dark '88
The Devil's Playground '76
Destination Moonbase Alpha '75
Reginald Tate
The King's Rhapsody '55
Immortal Battalion '44
Sharon Tate (1943-69)
12 Plus 1 '70
Ciao Federico! Fellini Directs Satyricon '69
The Wrecking Crew '68
The Fearless Vampire Killers '67
Valley of the Dolls '67
Jacques Tati (1908-82)
Parade '74
Traffic '71
Playtime '67
Mon Oncle '58
Mr. Hulot's Holiday '53
Jour de Fete '48
Sylvia and the Phantom '45
Bradford Tatum
Not in This Town '97
Pronto '97
Down Periscope '96
Within the Rock '96
Powder '95
Sven-Bertil Taube (1934-)
Jerusalem '96
Codename Kyril '91
Puppet on a Chain '72
Vibration '68
Audrey Tautou (1978-)
Amelie '01
Happenstance '00
Venus Beauty Institute '98
Nils (Niels) Tavernier (1965-)
After Sex '97
Revenge of the Musketeers '94
Mina Tannenbaum '93
L.627 '92
Beatrice '88
The Story of Women '88
Arthur Taxier
Donnie Darko '01
Open Fire '94
Vic Tayback (1930-90)
The Horseplayer '91
All Dogs Go to Heaven '89 (V)
Beverly Hills Bodysnatchers '89
Criminal Act '88
Murderer's Keep '88
The Underachievers '88
Weekend Warriors '86
Mysterious Two '82
Tut & Tuttle '82
Great American Traffic Jam '80
The Night the City Screamed '80
Rage '80
Portrait of a Stripper '79
The Cheap Detective '78
The Choirboys '77
The Big Bus '76
Special Delivery '76
Lepke '75
Alice Doesn't Live Here Anymore '74
Emperor of the North Pole '73
With Six You Get Eggroll '68
Door to Door Maniac '61
Benedict Taylor (1960-)
Charles & Diana: A Palace Divided '93
Duel of Hearts '92
A Perfect Spy '88
Every Time We Say Goodbye '86
The Black Arrow '84
The Far Pavilions '84
Buck Taylor (1938-)
Tombstone '93
Conagher '91
Gunsmoke: Return to Dodge '87
Pony Express Rider '76
And Now Miguel '66
Christine Taylor (1971-)
Zoolander '01
Kiss Toledo Goodbye '00
Something About Sex '98
The Wedding Singer '97
The Craft '96
Overnight Delivery '96
A Very Brady Sequel '96
The Brady Bunch Movie '95
Breaking Free '95
Night of the Demons 2 '94
Courtney Taylor
Cover Me '95
Tracks of a Killer '95
Prom Night 3: The Last Kiss '89
Delores Taylor
The Trial of Billy Jack '74
Billy Jack '71
Don Taylor (1920-98)
Men of Sherwood Forest '57
I'll Cry Tomorrow '55
Stalag 17 '53
Father's Little Dividend '51
Flying Leathernecks '51
Father of the Bride '50
Battleground '49
For the Love of Mary '48
The Naked City '48
Song of the Thin Man '47
Dub Taylor (1908-94)
Maverick '94
Falling from Grace '92
Conagher '91
My Heroes Have Always Been Cowboys '91
Back to the Future, Part 3 '90
Texas Guns '90
On the Run '85
Soggy Bottom U.S.A. '84
1941 '79
Moonshine County Express '77
Creature from Black Lake '76
Gator '76
Pony Express Rider '76
Flash & Firecat '75
This Is a Hijack '75
Poor Pretty Eddie '73
The Getaway '72
Support Your Local Gunfighter '71
A Man Called Horse '70
The Wild Bunch '69
The Shakiest Gun in the West '68
Bonnie & Clyde '67
Spencer's Mountain '63
Parrish '61
Them! '54
Riding High '50
Brand of Fear '49
Range Renegades '48
You Can't Take It with You '38
Elayne J. Taylor
Rules of Engagement '00
The Wood '99
Elizabeth Taylor (1932-)
These Old Broads '01
The Flintstones '94
Sweet Bird of Youth '89
Poker Alice '87
The Rumor Mill '86
North and South Book 1 '85
Between Friends '83
The Mirror Crack'd '80
Winter Kills '79
Return Engagement '78
A Little Night Music '77
Ash Wednesday '73
Driver's Seat '73
Under Milk Wood '73
Divorce His, Divorce Hers '72
Hammersmith Is Out '72
Night Watch '72
X, Y & Zee '72
Secret Ceremony '69
Boom! '68
Doctor Faustus '68
The Comedians '67
Reflections in a Golden Eye '67
The Taming of the Shrew '67
Who's Afraid of Virginia Woolf? '66
The Love Goddesses '65
The Sandpiper '65
Cleopatra '63
The V.I.P.'s '63
Butterfield 8 '60
Suddenly, Last Summer '59
Cat on a Hot Tin Roof '58
Raintree County '57
Giant '56
Beau Brummel '54
Elephant Walk '54
The Last Time I Saw Paris '54
Rhapsody '54
The Girl Who Had Everything '53
Ivanhoe '52
Love Is Better Than Ever '52
Father's Little Dividend '51
A Place in the Sun '51
Quo Vadis '51
The Big Hangover '50
Father of the Bride '50
Conspirator '49
Little Women '49
A Date with Judy '48
Julia Misbehaves '48
Life with Father '47
Courage of Lassie '46
Jane Eyre '44
National Velvet '44
The White Cliffs of Dover '44
Lassie, Come Home '43
Estelle Taylor (1899-1958)
The Southerner '45
Cimarron '31
Street Scene '31
Where East Is East '29
Don Juan '26
Forrest Taylor (1883-1965)
Iron Mountain Trail '53
Border Saddlemates '52
Colorado Serenade '46
Driftin' River '46
Mystery Man '44
Shake Hands with Murder '44
Sons of the Pioneers '42
Trail Riders '42
Trigger Men '41

Arizona Gangbusters '40
Outlaw's Paradise '39
Ghost Town Riders '38
Lightnin' Carson Rides Again '38
The Phantom of the Range '38
The Red Rope '37
The Roamin' Cowboy '37
A Face in the Fog '36
Kelly of the Secret Service '36
Prison Shadows '36
Trail of Terror '35
Riders of Destiny '33

Frank Hoyt Taylor
A Lesson Before Dying '99
Matewan '87

Grant Taylor (1917-71)
Long John Silver '54
His Majesty O'Keefe '53
The Fighting Rats of Tobruk '44
Forty Thousand Horsemen '41

Holland Taylor (1943-)
Legally Blonde '01
Happy Accidents '00
Keeping the Faith '00
Next Stop, Wonderland '98
The Truman Show '98
George of the Jungle '97
Just Write '97
Last Summer In the Hamptons '96
One Fine Day '96
Steal Big, Steal Little '95
To Die For '95
Cop and a Half '93
The Favor '92
Alice '90
She's Having a Baby '88
The Jewel of the Nile '85

Jack Taylor (1936-)
The Ninth Gate '99
Icebox Murders '80s
Where Time Began '77
Horror of the Zombies '74
Female Vampire '73
The Mummy's Revenge '73
Orgy of the Vampires '73
Dr. Jekyll and the Wolfman '71
Night of the Sorcerers '70
Black Tide '58

Jana Taylor
Dreamscape '84
Hell's Angels on Wheels '67

Joan Taylor (1925-)
Omar Khayyam '57
20 Million Miles to Earth '57
Earth vs. the Flying Saucers '56
Girls in Prison '56
Apache Woman '55
Rose Marie '54

John Taylor (1960-)
Four Dogs Playing Poker '00
Sugar Town '99
The Seventh Sign '88
Foxstyle '73

Kent Taylor (1906-87)
I Spit on Your Corpse '74
Angels' Wild Women '72
Blood of Ghastly Horror '72
Brain of Blood '71
Satan's Sadists '69
Brides of the Beast '68
The Crawling Hand '63
The Phantom from 10,000 Leagues '56
Slightly Scarlet '56
Western Pacific Agent '51
Escape to Paradise '39
Five Came Back '39
Gangbusters '38
Death Takes a Holiday '34
Badmen of Nevada '33
I'm No Angel '33
The Mysterious Rider '33

Kimberly Taylor
Beauty School '93
Party Incorporated '89

Kit Taylor (1942-)
Innocent Prey '88
Cassandra '87
Long John Silver '54

Lili Taylor (1967-)
High Fidelity '00
The Haunting '99
The Imposters '98
Pecker '98
Kicked in the Head '97
Subway Stories '97
I Shot Andy Warhol '96
Illtown '96
Ransom '96
The Addiction '95
Cold Fever '95
Four Rooms '95
Girls Town '95
Arizona Dream '94
Mrs. Parker and the Vicious Circle '94
Ready to Wear '94
Household Saints '93
Rudy '93
Short Cuts '93
Watch It '93
Bright Angel '91
Dogfight '91
Say Anything '89
Mystic Pizza '88

Lindsay Taylor
Hellraiser 5: Inferno '00
Hard to Die '90

Marjorie Taylor
The Face at the Window '39
Never Too Late to Mend '37
Ticket of Leave Man '37
The Crimes of Stephen Hawke '36

Mark L. Taylor (1954-)
Color of Justice '97
Eight Days a Week '97
Arachnophobia '90

Meshach Taylor (1947-)
Virtual Seduction '96
Double Double Toil and Trouble '94
Ultra Warrior '92
Class Act '91
Inside Out '91
Mannequin 2: On the Move '91
House of Games '87
Mannequin '87
Explorers '85
The Beast Within '82
The Howling '81
Damien: Omen 2 '78

Noah Taylor (1969-)
Lara Croft: Tomb Raider '01
Vanilla Sky '01
Almost Famous '00
Life in the Fast Lane '00
Shine '95
One Crazy Night '93
The Nostradamus Kid '92
Flirting '89
The Year My Voice Broke '87

Ray Taylor (1888-1952)
Man from Montana '41
Robinson Crusoe of Mystery Island '36

Regina Taylor
Cora Unashamed '00
Strange Justice: The Clarence Thomas and Anita Hill Story '99
The Negotiator '98
Hostile Waters '97
Courage Under Fire '96
A Family Thing '96
The Keeper '96
Spirit Lost '96
A Good Day to Die '95
Lean on Me '89

Renee Taylor (1935-)
61* '01
Love Is All There Is '96
Forever: A Ghost of a Love Story '92
Delirious '91

The End of Innocence '90
That's Adequate '90
White Palace '90
Last of the Red Hot Lovers '72
The Errand Boy '61

Rip Taylor (1934-)
Private Obsession '94
Indecent Proposal '93
Silence of the Hams '93
Tom and Jerry: The Movie '93 (V)
Wayne's World 2 '93
DuckTales the Movie: Treasure of the Lost Lamp '90 (V)
Cheech and Chong: Things Are Tough All Over '82

Robert Taylor
Vertical Limit '00
The Matrix '99

Robert Taylor (1911-69)
The Hot Line '69
Where Angels Go, Trouble Follows '68
Johnny Tiger '66
The Night Walker '64
The Miracle of the White Stallions '63
The Law and Jake Wade '58
Party Girl '58
D-Day, the Sixth of June '56
The Last Hunt '56
Valley of the Kings '54
Above and Beyond '53
All the Brothers Were Valiant '53
I Love Melvin '53
Knights of the Round Table '53
Ivanhoe '52
Quo Vadis '51
Westward the Women '51
Conspirator '49
Undercurrent '46
Bataan '43
Johnny Eager '42
Billy the Kid '41
When Ladies Meet '41
Waterloo Bridge '40
Three Comrades '38
Broadway Melody of 1938 '37
Personal Property '37
Camille '36
The Gorgeous Hussy '36
Broadway Melody of 1936 '35

Rod Taylor (1929-)
Nowhere to Hide
Welcome to Woop Woop '97
Open Season '95
Danielle Steel's Palomino '91
Marbella '85
Time to Die '83
Jacqueline Bouvier Kennedy '81
Cry of the Innocent '80
The Treasure Seekers '79
Hell River '75
Germicide '74
The Deadly Trackers '73
Train Robbers '73
Darker than Amber '70
Man Who Had Power Over Women '70
Powder Keg '70
Zabriskie Point '70
Dark of the Sun '68
Chuka '67
Hotel '67
The Glass Bottom Boat '66
Colossus and the Amazon Queen '64
36 Hours '64
The Birds '63
A Gathering of Eagles '63
The V.I.P.'s '63
101 Dalmatians '61 (V)
The Time Machine '60
Ask Any Girl '59
Separate Tables '58
Raintree County '57

The Catered Affair '56
Giant '56
Long John Silver '54

Russi Taylor
Babe: Pig in the City '98 (V)
DuckTales the Movie: Treasure of the Lost Lamp '90 (V)
Jetsons: The Movie '90 (V)

Tamara Taylor
Introducing Dorothy Dandridge '99
Senseless '98

Tammy Taylor
Lovelines '84
Meatballs 2 '84

Vaughn Taylor (1910-83)
The Gallant Hours '60
Jailhouse Rock '57
Meet Danny Wilson '52
Francis Goes to the Races '51

Wally Taylor (1930-)
Hidden Fears '93
Night of the Creeps '86
Shaft's Big Score '72

Zack Taylor
The Young Nurses '73
Group Marriage '72

Leigh Taylor-Young (1944-)
Slackers '02
Bliss '96
Honeymoon Academy '90
Accidents '89
The Jagged Edge '85
Secret Admirer '85
Looker '81
Can't Stop the Music '80
Marathon '80
Soylent Green '73
The Adventurers '70
The Horsemen '70
I Love You, Alice B. Toklas! '68

Jun Tazaki (1910-85)
Ran '85
War of the Gargantuas '70
Destroy All Monsters '68
Godzilla vs. Monster Zero '68
King Kong vs. Godzilla '63
Seven Samurai '54

Ludmila Tcherina
Sins of Rome '54
The Red Shoes '48

Kiri Te Kanawa
Meeting Venus '91 (V)
The Ring '52

Phil Tead
Fangs of the Wild '54
Music in My Heart '40

Anthony Teague
The Trouble with Girls (and How to Get into It) '69
How to Succeed in Business without Really Trying '67

Marshall Teague
Across the Line '00
Crime and Punishment in Suburbia '00
The Bad Pack '98
The Colony '95
Fists of Iron '94
Guardian Angel '94
Super Force '90
Road House '89
Trained to Kill '88
The Shadow Riders '82

Ray Teal (1902-76)
Judgment at Nuremberg '61
Band of Angels '57
Lucky Me '54
Ambush at Tomahawk Gap '53
Carrie '52
Jumping Jacks '52
Montana Belle '52
Distant Drums '51
Rusty's Birthday '49
The Best Years of Our Lives '46
Hollywood Canteen '44

Owen Teale (1961-)
Conspiracy '01
Cleopatra '99
Wilderness '96
The Hawk '93
Robin Hood '91
Catherine Cookson's The Fifteen Streets '90

Conway Tearle (1878-1938)
Klondike Annie '36
Headline Woman '35
Sing Sing Nights '35
Held for Murder '32
Hurricane Express '32
The King Murder '32
Vanity Fair '32
Morals for Women '31
Pleasure '31
Lost Zeppelin '29
Dancing Mothers '26
Stella Maris '18

Godfrey Tearle
One of Our Aircraft Is Missing '41
The 39 Steps '35

Verree Teasdale (1904-87)
Milky Way '36
Goodbye Love '34
Skyscraper Souls '32

Sandor Tecsi
Fever '99
Angel Blue '97
'68 '87

Travis Tedford
Slappy and the Stinkers '97
The Little Rascals '94

Irene Tedrow (1908-95)
The Two Worlds of Jenny Logan '79
Special Olympics '78

Maureen Teefy (1954-)
Star Time '92
Supergirl '84
Legs '83
Fame '80

Joan A. Teeter
Vampire Centerfolds '98
Vampire Conspiracy '96

Blair Tefkin
Dream Lover '93
A Sinful Life '89

Aaron Teich
Darkroom '90
Bloodspell '87

Rut Tellefsen
Kristin Lavransdatter '95
The Last Lieutenant '94

Teller
Penn and Teller Get Killed '90
Light Years '88 (V)
Long Gone '87

Sybil Temchen
Lip Service '00
Body Shots '99
Nice Guys Sleep Alone '99
The Passion of Ayn Rand '99
Restaurant '98
Ten Benny '98
Floating '97

Shirley Temple (1928-)
The Story of Seabiscuit '49
Fort Apache '48
The Bachelor and the Bobby-Soxer '47
Since You Went Away '44
Miss Annie Rooney '42
The Blue Bird '40
Young People '40
The Little Princess '39
Susannah of the Mounties '39
Just Around the Corner '38
Little Miss Broadway '38
Rebecca of Sunnybrook Farm '38
Heidi '37
Wee Willie Winkie '37
Captain January '36
Dimples '36

The Poor Little Rich Girl '36
Stowaway '36
Curly Top '35
The Little Colonel '35
The Littlest Rebel '35
Our Little Girl '35
Baby, Take a Bow '34
Bright Eyes '34
Little Miss Marker '34
Now and Forever '34
Stand Up and Cheer '34
Kid 'n' Hollywood and Polly Tix in Washington '33
To the Last Man '33

John Tench
The Ticket '97
Dead Ahead '96

Victoria Tennant (1953-)
Bram Stoker's The Mummy '97
Edie & Pen '95
L.A. Story '91
The Handmaid's Tale '90
War & Remembrance: The Final Chapter '89
Whispers '89
War & Remembrance '88
Best Seller '87
Flowers in the Attic '87
The Holcroft Covenant '85
All of Me '84
Chiefs '83
Dempsey '83
Strangers Kiss '83
The Winds of War '83
The Dogs of War '81
Inseminoid '80
Little Lord Fauntleroy '80

Anne Tenney
The Castle '97
Dead Heart '96

Jon Tenney (1961-)
Entropy '99
You Can Count On Me '99
With Friends Like These '98
Fools Rush In '97
Homegrown '97
Lovelife '97
Music from Another Room '97
The Twilight of the Golds '97
The Phantom '96
Free Willy 2: The Adventure Home '95
Lassie '94
Tombstone '93
Watch It '93

Julius Tennon
Lone Justice 2 '93
Riverbend '89

William Tepper
Bachelor Party '84
Miss Right '81

Johanna Ter Steege (1961-)
Paradise Road '97
Immortal Beloved '94
Meeting Venus '91
Vincent & Theo '90
The Vanishing '88

Susumu Terajima
Brother '00
After Life '98
Fireworks '97

Akira Terao
Akira Kurosawa's Dreams '90
Ran '85

Lee Tergesen (1965-)
Shot in the Heart '01
Shaft '00

Max Terhune (1891-1973)
Black Market Rustlers '43
Cowboy Commandos '43
Haunted Ranch '43
Land of Hunted Men '43
Two-Fisted Justice '43
Arizona Stagecoach '42
Boot Hill Bandits '42
Texas to Bataan '42
Thunder River Feud '42
Trail Riders '42

Fugitive Valley '41
Kid's Last Ride '41
Saddle Mountain Round-Up '41
Tonto Basin Outlaws '41
Trail of the Silver Spurs '41
Tumbledown Ranch in Arizona '41
Underground Rustlers '41
Range Busters '40
Trailing Double Trouble '40
West of Pinto Basin '40
Three Texas Steers '39
Heroes of the Hills '38
Outlaws of Sonora '38
Overland Stage Raiders '38
Pals of the Saddle '38
Purple Vigilantes '38
Santa Fe Stampede '38
Come on, Cowboys '37
Heart of the Rockies '37
Hit the Saddle '37
Riders of the Whistling Skull '37
Roarin' Lead '37
The Trigger Trio '37
Ghost Town Gold '36
Ride, Ranger, Ride '36

Studs Terkel
Eight Men Out '88
Long Shadows '86

John Terlesky
Battling for Baby '92
Damned River '89
When He's Not a Stranger '89
The Allnighter '87
Deathstalker 2: Duel of the Titans '87
Chopping Mall '86

Leonard Termo
Midnight Cabaret '90
Year of the Dragon '85

Scott Terra
Eight Legged Freaks '02
Shadrach '98

John Canada Terrell
The Five Heartbeats '91
Def by Temptation '90
She's Gotta Have It '86

Ken Terrell (1904-66)
Attack of the 50 Foot Woman '58
The Brain from Planet Arous '57
The Indestructible Man '56

Steven Terrell
Dragstrip Girl '57
Invasion of the Saucer Men '57
Motorcycle Gang '57

Bob Terry
Danger Ahead '40
Down the Wyoming Trail '39
Outlaw's Paradise '39
Brothers of the West '37

Don Terry (1902-88)
Don Winslow of the Coast Guard '43
Don Winslow of the Navy '43
Border Romance '30

Harry Terry
The Face at the Window '39
Broken Melody '34

John Terry
Change of Heart '98
The Big Green '95
Reflections in the Dark '94
A Dangerous Woman '93
Iron Will '93
Of Mice and Men '92
The Resurrected '91
Silhouette '91
A Killing in a Small Town '90
In Country '89
Full Metal Jacket '87
Hawk the Slayer '81

Kim Terry
Rushmore '98
Slugs '87

Nigel Terry (1945-)
The Ebb-Tide '97
Far from the Madding Crowd '97
Blue '93 (N)
Christopher Columbus: The Discovery '92
Edward II '92
Caravaggio '86
Sylvia '86
Deja Vu '84
Excalibur '81
The Lion in Winter '68

Phillip Terry (1909-93)
The Leech Woman '59
To Each His Own '46
George White's Scandals '45
The Lost Weekend '45
Bataan '43
Wake Island '42
The Monster and the Girl '41

Ruth Terry (1920-)
Hands Across the Border '43
Texas Legionnaires '43
Blondie Goes Latin '42
Call of the Canyon '42
Heart of the Golden West '42
Alexander's Ragtime Band '38

Sheila Terry (1910-57)
Go-Get-'Em-Haines '35
Lawless Frontier '35
'Neath the Arizona Skies '34
The Sphinx '33
Haunted Gold '32
Scarlet Dawn '32

Terry-Thomas (1911-89)
The Bawdy Adventures of Tom Jones '76
Robin Hood '73 (V)
Vault of Horror '73
Doctor Phibes Rises Again '72
The Abominable Dr. Phibes '71
12 Plus 1 '70
Those Daring Young Men in Their Jaunty Jalopies '69
Danger: Diabolik '68
Don't Raise the Bridge, Lower the River '68
How Sweet It Is! '68
Where Were You When the Lights Went Out? '68
A Guide for the Married Man '67
Those Fantastic Flying Fools '67
La Grande Vadrouille '66
Munster, Go Home! '66
How to Kill 400 Duponts '65
Strange Bedfellows '65
Those Magnificent Men in Their Flying Machines '65
How to Murder Your Wife '64
It's a Mad, Mad, Mad, Mad World '63
A Matter of WHO '62
The Mouse on the Moon '62
The Wonderful World of the Brothers Grimm '62
Make Mine Mink '60
Carlton Browne of the F.O. '59
I'm All Right Jack '59
Too Many Crooks '59
Lucky Jim '58
The Naked Truth '58
Tom Thumb '58
Brothers in Law '57
Blue Murder at St. Trinian's '56

Laurent Terzieff (1935-)
Fiesta '95
Germinal '93
Detective '85
Red Kiss '85
Medea '70
The Milky Way '68
A Coeur Joie '67
Head Over Heels '67
Vanina Vanini '61
Kapo '59

Robert Tessier (1934-2000)
Future Force '89
Nightwish '89
No Safe Haven '87
Avenging Angel '85
The Last of the Mohicans '85
The Fix '84
The Lost Empire '83
Sword & the Sorcerer '82
The Villain '79
Star Crash '78
The Longest Yard '74
The Velvet Vampire '71
Cry Blood, Apache '70
Born Losers '67
The Glory Stompers '67

Desmond Tester (1919-)
Non-Stop New York '37
Nine Days a Queen '36
Sabotage '36

Fabio Testi (1941-)
Contraband '86
Mussolini & I '85
The Ambassador '84
Gunfire '78
The Uranium Conspiracy '78
The Inheritance '76
Stateline Motel '75
'Tis a Pity She's a Whore '73
The Garden of the Finzi-Continis '71

Lauren Tewes (1954-)
The Doom Generation '95
It Came from Outer Space 2 '95
National Lampoon's Attack of the 5 Ft. 2 Women '94
Magic Kid '92
Camp Cucamonga: How I Spent My Summer Vacation '90
The China Lake Murders '90
Eyes of a Stranger '81

Tia Texada
Glitter '01
Bait '00
Paulie '98

Gilda Texter
Angels Hard As They Come '71
Vanishing Point '71

Eric Thal
Prisoner of Love '99
Snow Falling on Cedars '99
Mixing Nia '98
Samson and Delilah '96
Wishful Thinking '96
The Puppet Masters '94
Six Degrees of Separation '93
The Gun in Betty Lou's Handbag '92
A Stranger Among Us '92

Katharina Thalbach (1954-)
Good Evening, Mr. Wallenberg '93
Kaspar Hauser '93
The Tin Drum '79
The Second Awakening of Christa Klages '78

Byron Thames
84 Charlie MoPic '89
Seven Minutes in Heaven '86
Blame It on the Night '84

Heather Thatcher (1896-1987)
The Moon and Sixpence '43
Son of Fury '42
The Undying Monster '42
Beau Geste '39
If I Were King '38

Torin Thatcher (1905-81)
Dr. Jekyll and Mr. Hyde '68
Holy Terror '65
From Hell to Borneo '64
Jack the Giant Killer '62
Darby's Rangers '58
The Seventh Voyage of Sinbad '58
Band of Angels '57
Istanbul '57
Helen of Troy '56
Diane '55
Lady Godiva '55
Love Is a Many-Splendored Thing '55
The Black Shield of Falworth '54
The Desert Rats '53
Houdini '53
The Robe '53
Affair in Trinidad '52
Crimson Pirate '52
The Snows of Kilimanjaro '52
Great Expectations '46
Young and Innocent '37
Sabotage '36

John Thaw (1942-2002)
Goodnight, Mr. Tom '99
The Waiting Time '99
Into the Blue '97
Chaplin '92
A Year in Provence '89
Business As Usual '88
Cry Freedom '87
Killing Heat '84

Phyllis Thaxter (1921-)
Three Sovereigns for Sarah '85
Superman: The Movie '78
The World of Henry Orient '64
Springfield Rifle '52
Jim Thorpe: All American '51
Weekend at the Waldorf '45
Thirty Seconds Over Tokyo '44

Brynn Thayer (1949-)
The Game of Love '90
Hero and the Terror '88
The Tracker '88

Max Thayer
No Retreat, No Surrender 2 '89
No Dead Heroes '87
The Dolls '83
Retrievers '82

Michael Thayer
Planet of the Dinosaurs '80
Ilsa, Harem Keeper of the Oil Sheiks '76

Tina Thayer
Jive Junction '43
The Payoff '43

Marcello Thedford
Freedom Song '00
An Alan Smithee Film: Burn, Hollywood, Burn '97

Ulrich Thein
Anton, the Magician '78
Five Cartridges '60

Brother Theodore (1906-2001)
That's Adequate '90
The 'Burbs '89
The Invisible Kid '88

Charlize Theron (1975-)
The Curse of the Jade Scorpion '01
15 Minutes '01
Sweet November '01
The Legend of Bagger Vance '00
Men of Honor '00
Reindeer Games '00
The Yards '00
The Astronaut's Wife '99
The Cider House Rules '99
Celebrity '98
Mighty Joe Young '98
The Devil's Advocate '97
Hollywood Confidential '97
That Thing You Do! '96
Trial and Error '96
Two Days in the Valley '96

Justin Theroux
Mulholland Drive '01
The Broken Hearts Club '00
American Psycho '99
Sirens '99
Frogs for Snakes '98
Body Count '97

Ernest Thesiger (1879-1961)
The Battle of the Sexes '60
Who Done It? '56
The Robe '53
A Christmas Carol '51
Beware of Pity '46
Henry V '44
The Bride of Frankenstein '35
The Ghoul '34
The Old Dark House '32

Reggie Theus
Like Mike '02
Sweet Perfection '90

David Thewlis (1963-)
Dinotopia '02
The Miracle Maker: The Story of Jesus '00 (V)
Besieged '98
The Big Lebowski '97
Seven Years in Tibet '97
Dragonheart '96
The Island of Dr. Moreau '96
James and the Giant Peach '96 (V)
Total Eclipse '95
Black Beauty '94
Restoration '94
Naked '93
Life Is Sweet '90
The Life and Adventures of Nicholas Nickleby '81

Jack Thibeau
Lethal Weapon '87
Ms. 45 '81
Apocalypse Now '79

Debi Thibeault
Cemetery High '89
Galactic Gigolo '87
Psychos in Love '87

Alan Thicke (1947-)
Any Place But Home '97
Jack Higgins' The Windsor Protocol '97
Demolition High '95
Open Season '95
The Great American Sex Scandal '94
Rubdown '93
Betrayal of the Dove '92
Stepmonster '92
Still Not Quite Human '92
And You Thought Your Parents Were Weird! '91 (V)
Not Quite Human 2 '89
Obsessed '88
Not Quite Human '87
Scene of the Crime '85
Club Med '83

Rose Thiery
The Green House '96
Beau Pere '81

Tiffani-Amber Thiessen (1974-)
Hollywood Ending '02
The Ladies Man '00
Shriek If You Know What I Did Last Friday the 13th '00
Love Stinks '99
Speedway Junky '99
From Dusk Till Dawn 2: Texas Blood Money '98
Son-in-Law '93

Kevin Thigpen
Tar '97
Just Another Girl on the I.R.T. '93

Lynne Thigpen (1948-)
Novocaine '01
Shaft '00
Trial by Media '00
Bicentennial Man '99
The Insider '99
Night Ride Home '99
Random Hearts '99
The Boys Next Door '96
Just Cause '94
The Paper '94
Naked in New York '93
Article 99 '92
Separate but Equal '91
Impulse '90
Lean on Me '89
Rockabye '86
Streets of Fire '84
Godspell '73

Chief Ted Thin Elk
Walking Thunder '94
Thunderheart '92

Roy Thinnes (1936-)
The Invaders '95
Rush Week '88
Sizzle '81
From Here to Eternity '79
Code Name: Diamond Head '77
Secrets '77
Airport '75 '75
The Hindenburg '75
Satan's School for Girls '73
Journey to the Far Side of the Sun '69

Victorie Thivisol
Chocolat '00
Ponette '95

Alex Thomas
The Wash '01
The Players Club '98

Betty Thomas (1949-)
Prison for Children '93
Troop Beverly Hills '89
When Your Lover Leaves '83
Homework '82
Jackson County Jail '76

Damien Thomas (1942-)
Pirates '86
Shogun '80
The Message '77
Twins of Evil '71

Danny Thomas (1914-91)
Side by Side '88
Journey Back to Oz '71 (V)
The Road to Lebanon '60
I'll See You in My Dreams '51

Dave Thomas (1949-)
Cold Sweat '93
Coneheads '93
Boris and Natasha: The Movie '92
Moving '88
Love at Stake '87
My Man Adam '86
Sesame Street Presents: Follow That Bird '85
Strange Brew '83
Stripes '81

Doug Thomas
Hangmen '87
Attack of the Swamp Creature '75

Eddie Kaye Thomas (1980-)
American Pie 2 '01
Freddy Got Fingered '01
American Pie '99
Black and White '99
The Rage: Carrie 2 '99

Frank M. Thomas, Sr.
Sunset on the Desert '42
Law of the Underworld '38

Frankie Thomas, Jr. (1921-)
The Major and the Minor '42
Nancy Drew, Reporter '39
Boys Town '38
Tim Tyler's Luck '37

Gareth Thomas
Super Bitch '89
Visitor from the Grave '81

Heather Thomas (1957-)
My Giant '98
Hidden Obsession '92
Red Blooded American Girl '90
The Dirty Dozen: The Fatal Mission '88
Cyclone '87
Ford: The Man & the Machine '87
Zapped! '82

Henry Thomas (1971-)
Dead in the Water '01
All the Pretty Horses '00
Fever '99
A Good Baby '99
The Happy Face Murders '99
Moby Dick '98
Bombshell '97
Hijacking Hollywood '97
Niagara, Niagara '97
Suicide Kings '97
Riders of the Purple Sage '96
Indictment: The McMartin Trial '95
Curse of the Starving Class '94
Legends of the Fall '94
Fire in the Sky '93
A Taste for Killing '92
Psycho 4: The Beginning '90
Valmont '89
Murder One '88
The Quest '86
Cloak & Dagger '84
Misunderstood '84
E.T.: The Extra-Terrestrial '82
Raggedy Man '81

Jameson Thomas (1888-1939)
Sing Sing Nights '35
Beggars in Ermine '34
Jane Eyre '34
Convicted '32
Night Birds '31
Night Life in Reno '31
The Farmer's Wife '28

Jay Thomas (1948-)
Dragonfly '02
Trial by Media '00
Killing Mr. Griffin '97
A Smile Like Yours '96
Mr. Holland's Opus '95
Straight Talk '92
Little Vegas '90
The Gig '85
C.H.U.D. '84

Jonathan Taylor Thomas (1981-)
Common Ground '00
Speedway Junky '99
I'll Be Home for Christmas '98
Wild America '97
The Adventures of Pinocchio '96
Man of the House '95
Tom and Huck '95
The Lion King '94 (V)

Larry Thomas
Surface to Air '98
Night Ripper '86

Marlo Thomas (1938-)
Playing Mona Lisa '00
The Real Blonde '97
Held Hostage '91
In the Spirit '90
Consenting Adult '85
Act of Passion: The Lost Honor of Kathryn Beck '83
Jenny '70

Michelle Rene Thomas (1970-)
National Lampoon's Van Wilder '02
The Last Don 2 '98
The Last Don '97
Midnight in Saint Petersburg '97
The Last Word '95
Major League 2 '94
Coneheads '93
Dazed and Confused '93

Philip Michael Thomas (1949-)
A Fight for Jenny '90
Homeboy '80s
False Witness '89
The Wizard of Speed and Time '88
Miami Vice '84
Death Drug '83
Sparkle '76
Streetfight '75
Stigma '73

Richard Thomas (1951-)
Wonder Boys '00
The Million Dollar Kid '99
Big and Hairy '98
Flood: A River's Rampage '97
The Christmas Box '95
Down, Out and Dangerous '95
The Invaders '95
A Thousand Heroes '94
Linda '93
Stalking Laura '93
Mission of the Shark '91
Glory! Glory! '90
Stephen King's It '90
Andy and the Airwave Rangers '89
Hobson's Choice '83
Living Proof: The Hank Williams Jr. Story '83
Johnny Belinda '82
Berlin Tunnel 21 '81
Battle Beyond the Stars '80
All Quiet on the Western Front '79
Roots: The Next Generation '79
September 30, 1955 '77
Cactus in the Snow '72
You'll Like My Mother '72
Homecoming: A Christmas Story '71
The Todd Killings '71
Last Summer '69
Winning '69
A Doll's House '59

Robin Thomas
Clockstoppers '02
Star Maps '97
Amityville Dollhouse '96
Chameleon '95
Memories of Murder '90
Personals '90
From the Dead of Night '89
Summer School '87
About Last Night... '86

Ron Thomas
Night Screams '87
The Big Bet '85

Rufus Thomas (1917-2001)
Cookie's Fortune '99
Mystery Train '89

Sean Patrick Thomas (1970-)
Halloween: Resurrection '02
Save the Last Dance '01
Dracula 2000 '00
Cruel Intentions '98

Sian Thomas
A Mind to Murder '96
The Wedding Gift '93

William Thomas
Solomon and Gaenor '98
Twin Town '97

William Thomason
The Devil's Sleep '51
Test Tube Babies '48

Florence Thomassin
A Matter of Taste '00
Beaumarchais the Scoundrel '96
Elisa '94
Mina Tannenbaum '93

Tim Thomerson (1945-)
The Devil's Prey '01
Gale Force '01
Submerged '00
The Crimson Code '99
Unseen Evil '99
Fear and Loathing in Las Vegas '98
Escape from Atlantis '97
When Time Expires '97
Blast '96
Nemesis 3: Time Lapse '96
The Cisco Kid '94
Dominion '94
Fleshtone '94
Hong Kong '97 '94
Natural Causes '94
Spitfire '94
Trancers 5: Sudden Deth '94
Die Watching '93
Dollman vs Demonic Toys '93
Nemesis '93
Trancers 4: Jack of Swords '93
Bad Channels '92
The Harvest '92
Prime Time Murder '92
Trancers 3: Deth Lives '92
Intimate Stranger '91
Air America '90
Dollman '90
Trancers 2: The Return of Jack Deth '90
Vietnam, Texas '90
Who's Harry Crumb? '89
Cherry 2000 '88
The Wrong Guys '88
Glory Years '87
Near Dark '87
A Tiger's Tale '87
Iron Eagle '86
The Legend of Sleepy Hollow '86
Volunteers '85
Rhinestone '84
Trancers '84
Zone Troopers '84
Metalstorm: The Destruction of Jared Syn '83
Uncommon Valor '83
Jekyll & Hyde...Together Again '82
Fade to Black '80
Terraces '77

Vendela Thommessen
Model Behavior '00
Batman and Robin '97

Alina Thompson
Dead Cold '96
The Fiance '96
Marked Man '96
Seduce Me: Pamela Principle 2 '94

Andrea Thompson
A Gun, a Car, a Blonde '97
Doin' Time on Planet Earth '88

Anna Thompson
Intern '00
Six Ways to Sunday '99
I Shot Andy Warhol '96
Angus '95

Bill Thompson
The Aristocats '70 (V)
Lady and the Tramp '55 (V)
Peter Pan '53 (V)

Brian Thompson
Epoch '00
Jason and the Argonauts '00
Perfect Target '98
Mortal Kombat 2: Annihilation '97
Dragonheart '96
Rage and Honor '92
Hired to Kill '91
Doctor Mordrid: Master of the Unknown '90
Lionheart '90
Moon 44 '90
Nightwish '89
Fright Night 2 '88
Commando Squad '87

Christopher Thompson
La Buche '00
The Luzhin Defence '00
The Count of Monte Cristo '99

Derek Thompson (1948-)
Resurrection Man '97
Belfast Assassin '84
The Long Good Friday '80

Elizabeth Thompson
Metropolitan '90
The Car '77

Emma Thompson (1959-)
Wit '01
Maybe Baby '99
Judas Kiss '98
Primary Colors '98
The Winter Guest '97
Carrington '95
Sense and Sensibility '95
Junior '94
In the Name of the Father '93
Much Ado about Nothing '93
My Father the Hero '93
The Remains of the Day '93
Howard's End '92
Peter's Friends '92
Dead Again '91
Impromptu '90
Henry V '89
Look Back in Anger '89
The Tall Guy '89
Fortunes of War '87

Fred Dalton Thompson (1942-)
Baby's Day Out '94
Barbarians at the Gate '93
Born Yesterday '93
In the Line of Fire '93
Aces: Iron Eagle 3 '92
Keep the Change '92
Thunderheart '92
White Sands '92
Cape Fear '91
Class Action '91
Curly Sue '91
Days of Thunder '90
Die Hard 2: Die Harder '90
The Hunt for Red October '90
Feds '88
No Way Out '87
Marie '85

Hal Thompson
Lassie from Lancashire '38
Animal Crackers '30

Jack Thompson (1940-)
Star Wars: Episode 2—Attack of the Clones '02
Original Sin '01
Rodgers & Hammerstein's South Pacific '01
Midnight in the Garden of Good and Evil '97
Excess Baggage '96
Last Dance '96
The Sum of Us '94
A Far Off Place '93
Deception '92
The Killing Beach '92
Resistance '92
Wind '92
Ground Zero '88
Shadow on the Sun '88
Trouble in Paradise '88
Bad Blood '87
Burke & Wills '85
Flesh and Blood '85
Merry Christmas, Mr. Lawrence '83
Waterfront '83
The Man from Snowy River '82
The Club '81
Breaker Morant '80
Earthling '80
Caddie '76
Jock Petersen '74
Sunday Too Far Away '74

John Thompson
Born Romantic '00
Redline '97

Kay Thompson (1903-98)
Funny Face '57
Manhattan Merry-Go-Round '37

Kenan Thompson (1978-)
The Adventures of Rocky & Bullwinkle '00
Good Burger '97
D2: The Mighty Ducks '94
Heavyweights '94

Lea Thompson (1962-)
The Right to Remain Silent '95
The Substitute Wife '94
The Beverly Hillbillies '93
Dennis the Menace '93
Article 99 '92
Back to the Future, Part 3 '90
Montana '90
Back to the Future, Part 2 '89
Nightbreaker '89
Casual Sex? '88
Going Undercover '88
The Wizard of Loneliness '88
Some Kind of Wonderful '87
Howard the Duck '86
SpaceCamp '86
Back to the Future '85
Red Dawn '84
The Wild Life '84
All the Right Moves '83
Jaws 3 '83

Marshall Thompson (1925-)
Bog '84
The Turning Point '77
George! '70
Clarence, the Cross-eyed Lion '65
To the Shores of Hell '65
Mighty Jungle '64
No Man Is an Island '62
First Man into Space '59
Fiend without a Face '58
It! The Terror from Beyond Space '58
East of Kilimanjaro '57
Crashout '55
Cult of the Cobra '55
To Hell and Back '55
The Caddy '53
Stars in My Crown '50 (N)
Battleground '49
Words and Music '48
The Show-Off '46
The Clock '45
They Were Expendable '45
The Purple Heart '44

Peter Thompson
Santa Fe '51
The Wistful Widow of Wagon Gap '47

Rex Thompson (1942-)
All Mine to Give '56
The Eddy Duchin Story '56
The King and I '56
Young Bess '53

Sada Thompson (1929-)
Indictment: The McMartin Trial '95
Queen '93
The Adventures of Huckleberry Finn '85
Our Town '77
Desperate Characters '71

Scott Thompson (1959-)
Tart '01
Loser '00
Mickey Blue Eyes '99
Armistead Maupin's More Tales of the City '97
Hijacking Hollywood '97
Kids in the Hall: Brain Candy '96

Shawn Thompson
Bram Stoker's Shadowbuilder '98
Future Fear '97
Sleeping with Strangers '94
Hairspray '88

Shelley Thompson
Just Like a Woman '95
Labyrinth '86

Sophie Thompson (1962-)
Gosford Park '01
Relative Values '99
Dancing at Lughnasa '98
Emma '96
Persuasion '95
Four Weddings and a Funeral '94
Twenty-One '91

Susanna Thompson
Dragonfly '02
High Noon '00
Random Hearts '99
Ghosts of Mississippi '96
America's Dream '95
Little Giants '94

Teri Thompson
Breakaway '95
Married People, Single Sex '93

Victoria Thompson
Harrad Summer '74
Harrad Experiment '73

Ulrich Thomsen (1963-)
The World Is Not Enough '99
Angel of the Night '98
The Celebration '98

Sally Thomsett
Straw Dogs '72
The Railway Children '70

Anna Thomson (1957-)
Water Drops on Burning Rocks '99
Fiona '98
Cafe Society '97
Drunks '96
Jaded '96
Other Voices, Other Rooms '95
Outside the Law '95
Angela '94
The Crow '93
Unforgiven '92

Gordon Thomson (1945-)
The Fiance '96
The Donor '94
Explosion '69

Helen Thomson
Nowhere to Land '00
Bloodmoon '90

Kenneth Thomson (1899-1967)
Hopalong Cassidy '35
In Old Santa Fe '34
Held for Murder '32
Broadway Melody '29
White Gold '28

Kim Thomson (1960-)
Murder 101 '91
Hands of a Murderer '90
Jekyll and Hyde '90
The Tall Guy '89
Stealing Heaven '88

R.H. Thomson (1947-)
P.T. Barnum '99
Bone Daddy '97
The Twilight of the Ice Nymphs '97
The Lotus Eaters '93
The Quarrel '93
Glory Enough for All: The Discovery of Insulin '92
Mark Twain and Me '91
Love and Hate: A Marriage Made in Hell '90
Heaven on Earth '89
And Then You Die '88
Ford: The Man & the Machine '87
Canada's Sweetheart: The Saga of Hal C. Banks '85
Surfacing '84
If You Could See What I Hear '82
Ticket to Heaven '81

Charlie Grant's War '80

Scott Thomson
Ghoulies '84
Fast Times at Ridgemont High '82

Jon Mikl Thor
Zombie Nightmare '86
Rock 'n' Roll Nightmare '85

Frankie Thorn
Bad Blood '94
Bad Lieutenant '92
Liquid Dreams '92

Bill Thornbury
Phantasm 4: Oblivion '98
Phantasm 3: Lord of the Dead '94
Phantasm '79

Russell Thorndike
Henry V '44
A Shot in the Dark '33

Sybil Thorndike (1882-1976)
Shake Hands with the Devil '59
The Prince and the Showgirl '57
Stage Fright '50
Nicholas Nickleby '46
Major Barbara '41
Nine Days a Queen '36

Angela Thorne
The Lady's Not for Burning '87
Poor Girl, a Ghost Story '74

Callie (Calliope) Thorne
Sidewalks of New York '01
Double Parked '00
Homicide: The Movie '00
Whipped '00
Wirey Spindell '99
Ed's Next Move '96

Dyanne Thorne (1932-)
Hellhole '85
Ilsa, the Tigress of Siberia '79
Ilsa, the Wicked Warden '78
Ilsa, Harem Keeper of the Oil Sheiks '76
Wham-Bam, Thank You Spaceman '75
Ilsa, She-Wolf of the SS '74
Point of Terror '71

Courtney Thorne-Smith (1967-)
Chairman of the Board '97
Breach of Conduct '94
Side Out '90
Revenge of the Nerds 2: Nerds in Paradise '87
Summer School '87
Welcome to 18 '87
Lucas '86

Billy Bob Thornton (1955-)
Bandits '01
The Man Who Wasn't There '01
Monster's Ball '01
South of Heaven, West of Hell '00
Pushing Tin '99
Armageddon '98
Primary Colors '98
Princess Mononoke '98 (V)
A Simple Plan '98
An Alan Smithee Film: Burn, Hollywood, Burn '97
The Apostle '97
A Gun, a Car, a Blonde '97
Homegrown '97
U-Turn '97
Sling Blade '96
The Winner '96
Dead Man '95
Out There '95
Floundering '94
On Deadly Ground '94
Some Folks Call It a Sling Blade '94
Indecent Proposal '93
Tombstone '93
Chopper Chicks in Zombietown '91
One False Move '91

David Thornton
John Q '02
High Art '98
Hush '98
The Last Days of Disco '98
Home Alone 3 '97
Office Killer '97
She's So Lovely '97
Breathing Room '96
Unhook the Stars '96
Diamond Run '90
Off and Running '90

Noley Thornton
Heidi '93
Danielle Steel's Fine Things '90

Sigrid Thornton (1959-)
Trapped in Space '94
Over the Hill '93
Return to Snowy River '88
Great Expectations: The Untold Story '87
The Lighthorsemen '87
Slate, Wyn & Me '87
Best Enemies '86
Nevil Shute's The Far Country '85
All the Rivers Run '84
Street Hero '84
The Night After Halloween '83
The Man from Snowy River '82

Jim Thorpe (1888-1953)
My Pal, the King '32
White Eagle '32
Battling with Buffalo Bill '31

Sven-Ole Thorsen (1944-)
Gladiator '00
Foolish '99
Kull the Conqueror '97
Fatal Combat '96
The Viking Sagas '95
Abraxas: Guardian of the Universe '90

Linda Thorson (1947-)
The Other Sister '98
Walls of Glass '85

William Thourlby
Castle of Evil '66
Creeping Terror '64

David Threlfall (1953-)
Conspiracy '01
Mary, Mother of Jesus '99
The Summer House '94
Diana: Her True Story '93
A Casualty of War '90
A Murder of Quality '90
The Russia House '90
When the Whales Came '89
Kiss of Death '77

Frank Thring, Jr. (1926-94)
Howling 3: The Marsupials '87
Mad Max: Beyond Thunderdome '85
Alvin Rides Again '74

Luc Thuillier
The Old Lady Who Walked in the Sea '91
Monsieur Hire '89

Ingrid Thulin (1929-)
Control '87
After the Rehearsal '84
Paralyzed '70s
The Cassandra Crossing '76
Moses '76
Cries and Whispers '72
The Damned '69
The Rite '69
Hour of the Wolf '68
La Guerre Est Finie '66
The Silence '63
The Winter Light '62
The Magician '58
Brink of Life '57
Wild Strawberries '57

Chief Thundercloud (1899-1955)
Call of the Forest '49
Blazing Across the Pecos '48
The Phantom Rider '46
Outlaw Trail '44
Sonora Stagecoach '44
King of the Stallions '42
Ride, Ranger, Ride '36
Annie Oakley '35
Rustlers of Red Dog '35

Bill (Billy) Thurman (1920-95)
Mountaintop Motel Massacre '86
Creature from Black Lake '76
Slumber Party '57 '76
Gator Bait '73
The Last Picture Show '71
It's Alive! '68
Curse of the Swamp Creature '66

Dechen Thurman
Hamlet '00
I Think I Do '97

Uma Thurman (1970-)
Chelsea Walls '01
Tape '01
The Golden Bowl '00
Vatel '00
Sweet and Lowdown '99
The Avengers '98
Batman and Robin '97
Gattaca '97
Les Miserables '97
Beautiful Girls '96
The Truth about Cats and Dogs '96
A Month by the Lake '95
Even Cowgirls Get the Blues '94
Pulp Fiction '94
Mad Dog and Glory '93
Final Analysis '92
Jennifer 8 '92
Robin Hood '91
Henry & June '90
Where the Heart Is '90
The Adventures of Baron Munchausen '89
Dangerous Liaisons '88
Johnny Be Good '88
Kiss Daddy Goodnight '87

Sophie Thursfield
Sister My Sister '94
Oranges Are Not the Only Fruit '89

Carol Thurston (1923-69)
Apache Chief '50
Swamp Fire '46
China Sky '44
The Story of Dr. Wassell '44

Gerard Tichy (1920-92)
Ricco '74
The Hanging Woman '72
Hatchet for the Honeymoon '70
The Hot Line '69
Doctor Zhivago '65
Gladiators 7 '62

Nancy Ticotin
The Tavern '00
Ransom '96

Rachel Ticotin (1959-)
Warden of Red Rock '01
Forever Together '00
Full Disclosure '00
Aftershock: Earthquake in New York '99
Con Air '97
First Time Felon '97
Turbulence '96
Steal Big, Steal Little '95
The Wharf Rat '95
Deconstructing Sarah '94
Don Juan DeMarco '94
Natural Born Killers '94
Falling Down '93
Keep the Change '92
Where the Day Takes You '92
F/X 2: The Deadly Art of Illusion '91
One Good Cop '91
Prison Stories: Women on the Inside '91
Spies, Lies and Naked Thighs '91
Total Recall '90
Critical Condition '86
Rockabye '86
When the Bough Breaks '86
Fort Apache, the Bronx '81

James Tien
Half a Loaf of Kung Fu '85
Chinese Connection '73

Andrew Tiernan
Horatio Hornblower '99
Face '97
The Scarlet Tunic '97
Playing God '96
Edward II '92

Brigid Tierney
Affliction '97
The Paperboy '94

Gene Tierney (1920-91)
Scruples '80
Toys in the Attic '63
Advise and Consent '62
The Left Hand of God '55
The Egyptian '54
Never Let Me Go '53
Night and the City '50
The Ghost and Mrs. Muir '47
The Razor's Edge '46
Leave Her to Heaven '45
Laura '44
Heaven Can Wait '43
The Shanghai Gesture '42
Son of Fury '42
Sundown '41
Return of Frank James '40

Jacob Tierney (1979-)
Poor White Trash '00
The Life Before This '99
This Is My Father '99
Dead End '98
The Neon Bible '95
Josh and S.A.M. '93
Pin... '88

Lawrence Tierney (1919-2002)
Southie '98
A Kiss Goodnight '94
Wizards of the Demon Sword '94
Casualties of Love: The "Long Island Lolita" Story '93
Reservoir Dogs '92
City of Hope '91
The Death Merchant '91
Why Me? '90
The Offspring '87
Tough Guys Don't Dance '87
Murphy's Law '86
Prizzi's Honor '85
Silver Bullet '85
Midnight '81
The Prowler '81
Never Pick Up a Stranger '79
Andy Warhol's Bad '77
Abduction '75
The Female Jungle '56
The Bushwackers '52
The Greatest Show on Earth '52
The Hoodlum '51
Best of the Badmen '50
Born to Kill '47
The Devil Thumbs a Ride '47
Back to Bataan '45
Dillinger '45
Those Endearing Young Charms '45

Maura Tierney (1965-)
Insomnia '02
Scotland, PA '02
Forces of Nature '99
Instinct '99
Oxygen '99
Primary Colors '98
Liar Liar '96
Primal Fear '96
Fly by Night '93
The Temp '93
White Sands '92
Dead Women in Lingerie '90

Angelo Tiffe
Sword of Honor '94
3 Ninjas Kick Back '94

Jerry Tiffe
Sword of Honor '94
Hollywood in Trouble '87

Pamela Tiffin (1942-)
Viva Max '69
Harper '66
The Hallelujah Trail '65
State Fair '62
One, Two, Three '61
Summer and Smoke '61

Marie Tifo
Pouvoir Intime '87
Les Bons Debarras '81

Ken Tigar
The Underground '97
Hollywood Safari '96
Little Bigfoot '96
Rage '95
Phantasm 2 '88

Kevin Tighe (1944-)
Stephen King's Rose Red '02
The Big Day '99
Mumford '99
Winchell '98
In Cold Blood '96
Race the Sun '96
The Avenging Angel '95
Better Off Dead '94
Double Cross '94
Men of War '94
Caught in the Act '93
Geronimo: An American Legend '93
A Man in Uniform '93
What's Eating Gilbert Grape '93
Newsies '92
School Ties '92
Bright Angel '91
City of Hope '91
Another 48 Hrs. '90
K-9 '89
Lost Angels '89
Road House '89
Eight Men Out '88
Matewan '87

Zeffie Tilbury (1863-1950)
The Grapes of Wrath '40
Werewolf of London '35
The Single Standard '29

Nadja Tiller (1929-)
Wanted: Babysitter '75
Dead Are Alive '72
Tonio Kroger '65
The Burning Court '62

Mel Tillis
Uphill All the Way '85
Smokey and the Bandit 2 '80
The Villain '79

Grant Tilly
Brilliant Lies '96
Treasure of the Yankee Zephyr '83
Carry Me Back '82
Beyond Reasonable Doubt '80

Jennifer Tilly (1963-)
The Magnificent Ambersons '02
The Cat's Meow '01
Fast Sofa '01
Monsters, Inc. '01 (V)
The Crew '00
Dancing at the Blue Iguana '00
Hide and Seek '00
The Dress Code '99
The Muse '99
Silent Witness '99
Stuart Little '99 (V)
Bride of Chucky '98
Hoods '98
Relax... It's Just Sex! '98
Bella Mafia '97
Music from Another Room '97
American Strays '96
Bound '96
House Arrest '96
Liar Liar '96
Bird of Prey '95
Edie & Pen '95
Embrace of the Vampire '95
Man with a Gun '95
The Pompatus of Love '95
At Home with the Webbers '94
Bullets over Broadway '94
Double Cross '94
The Getaway '93
Heads '93
Made in America '93
Scorchers '92
Shadow of the Wolf '92
Inside Out '91
The Fabulous Baker Boys '89
Far from Home '89
Let It Ride '89
High Spirits '88
Remote Control '88
Rented Lips '88
He's My Girl '87
Moving Violations '85
No Small Affair '84

Meg Tilly (1960-)
Journey '95
Primal Secrets '94
Sleep with Me '94
Body Snatchers '93
Fallen Angels 2 '93
Leaving Normal '92
The Two Jakes '90
Carmilla '89
The Girl in a Swing '89
Valmont '89
Masquerade '88
Off Beat '86
Agnes of God '85
Impulse '84
The Big Chill '83
Psycho 2 '83
One Dark Night '82
Tex '82

Charlene Tilton (1958-)
Safety Patrol '98
Silence of the Hams '93
Center of the Web '92
Deadly Bet '91
Problem Child 2 '91
Border Shootout '90
Ragin' Cajun '90
Diary of a Teenage Hitchhiker '82
The Fall of the House of Usher '80
Sweater Girls '78
Freaky Friday '76

Martha Tilton
The Benny Goodman Story '55
Sunny '41

Cali Timmins (1963-)
Heaven's Fire '99
The Heist '96
Hard Evidence '94
The Takeover '94

Patrick Timsit
Pedale Douce '96
Little Indian, Big City '95

Charles Tingwell (1923-)
The Castle '97
A Cry in the Dark '88
Miracle Down Under '87
Malcolm '86
Windrider '86
All the Rivers Run '84
Breaker Morant '80
Money Movers '78
Gone to Ground '76
Endplay '75
Dracula, Prince of Darkness '66
Murder Most Foul '65
Murder Ahoy '64
Murder at the Gallop '63

Murder She Said '62
The Desert Rats '53

Gabriele Tinti (1932-91)
Caged Women '84
Trap Them & Kill Them '84
Emmanuelle's Daughter '79
Delusions of Grandeur '76
Love Camp '76
Lisa and the Devil '75
Web of Deception '71
Journey Beneath the Desert '61

Jamie Tirelli
Girlfight '99
Lotto Land '95
Sudden Death '85

Jean Tissier
Please Not Now! '61
The Hunchback of Notre Dame '57

James Toback (1944-)
Black and White '99
Fingers '78

Kenneth Tobey (1919-)
Body Shot '93
Desire and Hell at Sunset Motel '92
Honey, I Blew Up the Kid '92
Single White Female '92
Gremlins 2: The New Batch '90
Freeway '88
Innerspace '87
Night of the Creeps '86
The Lost Empire '83
Strange Invaders '83
The Howling '81
Ben '72
Rage '72
Gunfight at the O.K. Corral '57
Wings of Eagles '57
The Great Locomotive Chase '56
The Man in the Gray Flannel Suit '56
The Search for Bridey Murphy '56
Davy Crockett, King of the Wild Frontier '55
It Came from Beneath the Sea '55
The Beast from 20,000 Fathoms '53
The Bigamist '53
The Thing '51
I Was a Male War Bride '49

George Tobias (1901-80)
A New Kind of Love '63
Silk Stockings '57
The Seven Little Foys '55
Rawhide '50
The Judge Steps Out '49
The Set-Up '49
Sinbad, the Sailor '47
Objective, Burma! '45
The Mask of Dimitrios '44
Passage to Marseilles '44
Air Force '43
This Is the Army '43
Captains of the Clouds '42
Yankee Doodle Dandy '42
The Bride Came C.O.D. '41
Sergeant York '41
Strawberry Blonde '41
City for Conquest '40
Music in My Heart '40
The Hunchback of Notre Dame '39

Heather Tobias
Beautiful People '99
High Hopes '88

Oliver Tobias (1947-)
Grizzly Falls '99
Darkness Falls '98
Breeders '97
The Brylcreem Boys '96
Mata Hari '85
Operation 'Nam '85
The Wicked Lady '83
The Big Scam '79
The Stud '78
King Arthur, the Young Warlord '75
Young Warlord '75
'Tis a Pity She's a Whore '73
Romance of a Horsethief '71

Dan Tobin (1910-82)
The Last Angry Man '59
The Big Clock '48
Velvet Touch '48
Undercurrent '46
Woman of the Year '42
Black Limelight '38

Genevieve Tobin (1901-95)
Petrified Forest '36
The Case of the Lucky Legs '35

Lawrence Tobin
Shanty Tramp '67
A Taste of Blood '67

Stephen Tobolowsky (1951-)
Dean Koontz's Black River '01
The Operator '01
Alien Fury: Countdown to Invasion '00
Memento '00
The Prime Gig '00
Bossa Nova '99
The Insider '99
Black Dog '98
One Man's Hero '98
An Alan Smithee Film: Burn, Hollywood, Burn '97
Mr. Magoo '97
The Curse of Inferno '96
The Glimmer Man '96
Power 98 '96
Dr. Jekyll and Ms. Hyde '95
Murder in the First '95
Radioland Murders '94
Calendar Girl '93
Groundhog Day '93
Josh and S.A.M. '93
Basic Instinct '92
Hero '92
Memoirs of an Invisible Man '92
Single White Female '92
Sneakers '92
Where the Day Takes You '92
Deadlock '91
Thelma & Louise '91
Bird on a Wire '90
Funny About Love '90
Mirror, Mirror '90
Tagget '90
Breaking In '89
Great Balls of Fire '89
Roe vs. Wade '89
Mississippi Burning '88
Spaceballs '87
Nobody's Fool '86
Keep My Grave Open '80

Brian Tochi (1964-)
The Player '92
Teenage Mutant Ninja Turtles: The Movie '90 (V)
Stitches '85
Revenge of the Nerds '84

Ann Todd (1909-93)
The Human Factor '79
The Fiend '71
Son of Captain Blood '62
Scream of Fear '61
Time Without Pity '57
Madeleine '50
The Paradine Case '47
The Seventh Veil '46
Action for Slander '38
South Riding '37

Ann E. Todd (1931-)
Three Daring Daughters '48
How Green Was My Valley '41
Intermezzo '39

Beverly Todd (1946-)
Class of '61 '92
Lean on Me '89
Clara's Heart '88
The Ladies Club '86
Don't Look Back: The Story of Leroy "Satchel" Paige '81
Brother John '70

James Todd
High School Confidential '58
Trapped '49

Lisa Todd (1954-)
Blood Hook '86
Imposters '84
The Doll Squad '73
Woman Hunt '72

Mabel Todd
The Ghost and the Guest '43
The Cowboy and the Lady '38

Richard Todd (1919-)
House of the Long Shadows '82
The Big Sleep '78
Number 1 of the Secret Service '77
Bloodbath '76
Asylum '72
Dorian Gray '70
Subterfuge '68
The Very Edge '63
The Longest Day '62
Never Let Go '60
Saint Joan '57
Battle Hell '56
D-Day, the Sixth of June '56
Dam Busters '55
A Man Called Peter '55
The Virgin Queen '55
Rob Roy—The Highland Rogue '53
The Sword & the Rose '53
The Story of Robin Hood & His Merrie Men '52
Interrupted Journey '49

Russell Todd
Sweet Murder '93
Border Shootout '90
One Last Run '89
Chopping Mall '86

Saira Todd
Bad Behavior '92
A Fatal Inversion '92

Thelma Todd (1905-35)
Swiss Miss '38
Way Out West '37
Bohemian Girl '36
Cockeyed Cavaliers '34
Hips, Hips, Hooray '34
Palooka '34
The Devil's Brother '33
Horse Feathers '32
Speak Easily '32
Corsair '31
The Maltese Falcon '31
Monkey Business '31
Nevada '27

Tony Todd
Final Destination '00
Bram Stoker's Shadowbuilder '98
Candyman 3: Day of the Dead '98
Caught Up '98
Never 2 Big '98
Stir '98
True Women '97
Wishmaster '97
The Rock '96
Beastmaster 3: The Eye of Braxus '95
Burnzy's Last Call '95
Black Fox: Blood Horse '94
Black Fox: Good Men and Bad '94
Black Fox: The Price of Peace '94
Candyman 2: Farewell to the Flesh '94
The Crow '93
Excessive Force '93
Candyman '92
Keeper of the City '92
Criminal Justice '90
Ivory Hunters '90
Night of the Living Dead '90
Voodoo Dawn '89
Colors '88
Platoon '86

Bruno Todeschini
Va Savoir '01
Those Who Love Me Can Take the Train '98
La Sentinelle '92

Bora Todorovic
Underground '95
Time of the Gypsies '90

Srdan Todorovic
Black Cat, White Cat '98
Underground '95

Ricky Tognazzi
Aurora '84
The Tragedy of a Ridiculous Man '81

Ugo Tognazzi (1922-90)
La Cage aux Folles 3: The Wedding '86
A Joke of Destiny, Lying in Wait Around the Corner Like a Bandit '84
La Cage aux Folles 2 '81
The Tragedy of a Ridiculous Man '81
La Cage aux Folles '78
La Grande Bouffe '73
Head of the Family '71
L'Udienza '71
Porcile '69
Barbarella '68
RoGoPaG '62
Love in the City '53

Niall Toibin (1929-)
Frankie Starlight '95
Rawhead Rex '87
Eat the Peach '86
Lovespell '79

Marilyn Tokuda
Strawberry Fields '97
The Cage '89
Farewell to the King '89
The Jitters '88
My Tutor '82

Henriette Tol
Broken Mirrors '85
Question of Silence '83

Michael (Lawrence) Tolan (1925-)
Presumed Innocent '90
Half Slave, Half Free '85
All That Jazz '79
Night Terror '76
The 300 Year Weekend '71
The Lost Man '69
The Enforcer '51

Fabiola Toledo
Demons '86
A Blade in the Dark '83

Goya Toledo
Amores Perros '00
Mararia '98

Sidney Toler (1874-1947)
The Jade Mask '45
The Scarlet Clue '45
The Shanghai Cobra '45
Charlie Chan in the Secret Service '44
The Chinese Cat '44
Meeting at Midnight '44
Adventures of Smilin' Jack '43
Isle of Forgotten Sins '43
Castle in the Desert '42
A Night to Remember '42
Charlie Chan in Rio '41
Charlie Chan at the Wax Museum '40
Murder over New York '40
Law of the Pampas '39
If I Were King '38
The Mysterious Rider '38
Wide Open Faces '38
Double Wedding '37
Our Relations '36
Champagne for Breakfast '35
Spitfire '34
Blonde Venus '32
Speak Easily '32

John Toles-Bey
K-PAX '01
Extreme Measures '96
Leap of Faith '92
A Rage in Harlem '91
Weeds '87

James Tolkan (1931-)
Underworld '96
Sketch Artist 2: Hands That See '94
Boiling Point '93
Question of Faith '93
Bloodfist 4: Die Trying '92
Sketch Artist '92
Problem Child 2 '91
Back to the Future, Part 3 '90
Dick Tracy '90
Opportunity Knocks '90
Back to the Future, Part 2 '89
Family Business '89
The Hillside Strangler '89
Ministry of Vengeance '89
Second Sight '89
Split Decisions '88
Viper '88
Weekend War '88
Off Beat '86
Back to the Future '85

Marilu Tolo (1944-)
Sleep of Death '79
Killer Likes Candy '78
Beyond Fear '75
Commandos '73
Confessions of a Police Captain '72
The Triumph of Hercules '66
Marriage Italian Style '64
Messalina vs. the Son of Hercules '64
Terror of Rome Against the Son of Hercules '64

David Tom (1978-)
Walking Thunder '94
Swing Kids '93
Stay Tuned '92

Lauren Tom (1961-)
Catfish in Black Bean Sauce '00
With Friends Like These '98
When a Man Loves a Woman '94
The Joy Luck Club '93
Mr. Jones '93

Nicholle Tom (1978-)
Season of Change '94
Beethoven's 2nd '93
Beethoven '92

Dara Tomanovich
Perfect Target '98
Amnesia '96
Back in Business '96
Bio-Dome '96

Jeana Tomasina
Up the Creek '84
Beach Girls '82

Andrew Tombes (1889-1976)
The Go-Getter '54
Phantom Lady '44

Concetta Tomei (1945-)
The Muse '99
Sin and Redemption '94
The Goodbye Bird '93
Twenty Bucks '93
Scott Turow's The Burden of Proof '92
Don't Tell Mom the Babysitter's Dead '91
In Love and War '91
China Beach '88

Marisa Tomei (1964-)
In the Bedroom '01
King of the Jungle '01
Someone Like You '01
Happy Accidents '00
The Watcher '00
What Women Want '00
My Own Country '98
Only Love '98
Slums of Beverly Hills '98
A Brother's Kiss '97
Since You've Been Gone '97
Welcome to Sarajevo '97
Unhook the Stars '96
Four Rooms '95
Only You '94
The Paper '94
The Perez Family '94
Equinox '93
Untamed Heart '93
Chaplin '92
My Cousin Vinny '92
Oscar '91
Zandalee '91

Frances Tomelty
The Field '90
Bellman and True '88
A Perfect Spy '88
Lamb '85
Blue Money '84
Footlight Frenzy '84
Bullshot '83

Joseph Tomelty (1911-95)
A Night to Remember '58
The Atomic Man '56
John and Julie '55
Devil Girl from Mars '54

Akihiro Tomikawa
Baby Cart 1: Lend a Child...Lend an Arm '72
Baby Cart 4: Heart of a Parent...Heart of a Child '72
Baby Cart at the River Styx '72
Baby Cart to Hades '72

Tamlyn Tomita (1966-)
The Killing Jar '96
Four Rooms '95
Picture Bride '94
The Joy Luck Club '93
Come See the Paradise '90
Hiroshima: Out of the Ashes '90
Vietnam, Texas '90
Hiroshima Maiden '88
The Karate Kid: Part 2 '86

Lily Tomlin (1939-)
Orange County '02
Disney's The Kid '00
Tea with Mussolini '99
Krippendorf's Tribe '98
Getting Away With Murder '96
Blue in the Face '95
The Celluloid Closet '95 (N)
Flirting with Disaster '95
And the Band Played On '93
The Beverly Hillbillies '93
Short Cuts '93
The Player '92
Shadows and Fog '92
Search for Signs of Intelligent Life in the Universe '91
Big Business '88
All of Me '84
The Incredible Shrinking Woman '81
9 to 5 '80
The Late Show '77
Nashville '75

David Tomlinson (1917-2000)
The Fiendish Plot of Dr. Fu Manchu '80
Water Babies '79
Wombling Free '77
Bedknobs and Broomsticks '71
Mary Poppins '64
Tom Jones '63
Up the Creek '58
Carry On Admiral '57
Made in Heaven '52
Wooden Horse '50
Fame Is the Spur '47
Sleeping Car to Trieste '45
Pimpernel Smith '42

Ricky Tomlinson (1939-)
Cracker: Brotherly Love '95
Butterfly Kiss '94
Raining Stones '93
Riff Raff '92

Angel Tompkins (1943-)
Crack House '89
Relentless '89
A Tiger's Tale '87
Murphy's Law '86
Naked Cage '86
Alligator '80
The Bees '78
Walking Tall: Part 2 '75
The Teacher '74
The Don Is Dead '73
Prime Cut '72
Probe '72
I Love My...Wife '70

Stephen Tompkinson
Brassed Off '96
And a Nightingale Sang '91

Kate Toncray
The Country Kid '23
The Lamb '15

Franchot Tone (1905-68)
In Harm's Way '65
Mickey One '65
Advise and Consent '62
Here Comes the Groom '51
Jigsaw '49
Every Girl Should Be Married '48
Man on the Eiffel Tower '48
Her Husband's Affairs '47
Lost Honeymoon '47
Because of Him '45
Dark Waters '44
His Butler's Sister '44
Phantom Lady '44
Five Graves to Cairo '43
Nice Girl? '41
Three Comrades '38
The Bride Wore Red '37
Quality Street '37
The Gorgeous Hussy '36
Love on the Run '36
Suzy '36
Dangerous '35
The Lives of a Bengal Lancer '35
Mutiny on the Bounty '35
Reckless '35
The Girl from Missouri '34
Sadie McKee '34
Bombshell '33
Dancing Lady '33
Gabriel Over the White House '33
Today We Live '33

Tone Loc (1966-)
Titan A.E. '00 *(V)*
Freedom Strike '98
Heat '95
Ace Ventura: Pet Detective '93
Blank Check '93
Posse '93
Surf Ninjas '93
Bebe's Kids '92 *(V)*
Ferngully: The Last Rain Forest '92 *(V)*
The Adventures of Ford Fairlane '90

Eijiro Tono (1907-94)
Tora! Tora! Tora! '70
Yojimbo '61
The Human Condition: No Greater Love '58

Taiji Tonoyama
Tokyo Pop '88
The Island '61

Regis Toomey (1902-91)
Change of Habit '69
Warlock '59
The Curfew Breakers '57
Great Day in the Morning '56
Guys and Dolls '55
Never Wave at a WAC '52
Dynamite Pass '50
Beyond the Forest '49
Come to the Stable '49
The Bishop's Wife '47
Magic Town '47
The Big Sleep '46
Spellbound '45
Strange Illusion '45
Betrayal from the East '44
Dark Mountain '44
Phantom Lady '44
Raiders of Ghost City '44
Destroyer '43
Dive Bomber '41
Meet John Doe '41
They Died with Their Boots On '41
Arizona '40
The Phantom Creeps '39
Union Pacific '39
Wayne Murder Case '38
Shadows of the Orient '37
Bulldog Edition '36
"G" Men '35
Skull & Crown '35
Laughing at Life '33
They Never Come Back '32
The Light of Western Stars '30
Alibi '29

Gordon Tootoosis
Big Bear '98
Crazy Horse '96
Pocahontas '95 *(V)*
Pocahontas: The Legend '95
Legends of the Fall '94
Call of the Wild '93
Spirit Rider '93
Stone Fox '87
Dan Candy's Law '73

Shawn Toovey
Flash '98
The Fire Next Time '93

Chaim Topol (1935-)
Left Luggage '98
War & Remembrance: The Final Chapter '89
War & Remembrance '88
Queenie '87
The Winds of War '83
For Your Eyes Only '81
Flash Gordon '80
The House on Garibaldi Street '79
Fiddler on the Roof '71
Gun Crazy '69
Cast a Giant Shadow '66
Sallah '63

Peta Toppano
Which Way Home '90
Echoes of Paradise '86

Marta Toren
Paris Express '53
Casbah '48

Hal Torey
Invisible Invaders '59
Earth vs. the Spider '58

Sarah Torgov
American Gothic '88
If You Could See What I Hear '82
Drying Up the Streets '76

Peter Tork (1942-)
The Brady Bunch Movie '95
Head '68

Mel Torme (1925-99)
The Return of Spinal Tap '92
Naked Gun 2 1/2: The Smell of Fear '91
A Man Called Adam '66
Girls' Town '59
Words and Music '48
Good News '47

John Tormey
Joe Gould's Secret '00
Ghost Dog: The Way of the Samurai '99

Rip Torn (1931-)
Men in Black 2 '02
Freddy Got Fingered '01
Wonder Boys '00
The Insider '99
Passing Glory '99
Senseless '98
Balloon Farm '97
Hercules '97 *(V)*
Men in Black '97
Down Periscope '96
Trial and Error '96
For Better or Worse '95
How to Make an American Quilt '95
Letter to My Killer '95
Canadian Bacon '94
Where the Rivers Flow North '94
Beautiful Dreamers '92
Beyond the Law '92
Dead Ahead: The Exxon Valdez Disaster '92
Dolly Dearest '92
Hard Promises '92
Another Pair of Aces: Three of a Kind '91
Defending Your Life '91
RoboCop 3 '91
Pair of Aces '90
Silence Like Glass '90
By Dawn's Early Light '89
Cold Feet '89
Sweet Bird of Youth '89
The Hit List '88
Extreme Prejudice '87
J. Edgar Hoover '87
Laguna Heat '87
Nadine '87
Manhunt for Claude Dallas '86
Beer '85
The Execution '85
Summer Rental '85
Cat on a Hot Tin Roof '84
City Heat '84
Flashpoint '84
Misunderstood '84
Songwriter '84
Cross Creek '83
Airplane 2: The Sequel '82
Beastmaster '82
Blind Ambition '82
Jinxed '82
A Stranger Is Watching '82
Heartland '81
One Trick Pony '80
Rape and Marriage: The Rideout Case '80
The Seduction of Joe Tynan '79
A Shining Season '79
Betrayal '78
The Birch Interval '78
Coma '78
Steel Cowboy '78
Nasty Habits '77
The Private Files of J. Edgar Hoover '77
The Man Who Fell to Earth '76
Cotter '72
Payday '72
Slaughter '72
The President's Plane Is Missing '71
Tropic of Cancer '70
Coming Apart '69
You're a Big Boy Now '66
The Cincinnati Kid '65
Sweet Bird of Youth '62
The King of Kings '61
24 Hours in a Woman's Life '61
Pork Chop Hill '59
Baby Doll '56

Mari Torocsik
The Bachelor '93
Daniel Takes a Train '83
Love '71

David Torrence (1864-1951)
Jane Eyre '34
The Mask of Fu Manchu '32
Disraeli '30
Raffles '30
Tess of the Storm Country '22

Ernest Torrence (1878-1933)
I Cover the Waterfront '33
Fighting Caravans '31
Steamboat Bill, Jr. '28
King of Kings '27
Mantrap '26
The Pony Express '25
Peter Pan '24
The Covered Wagon '23
The Hunchback of Notre Dame '23
Tol'able David '21

Pip Torrens
Shackleton '02
Incognito '97
A Dark Adapted Eye '93
A Handful of Dust '88

Ana Torrent (1966-)
Thesis '96
Vacas '91
Blood and Sand '89
The Nest '80
Cria '76
Spirit of the Beehive '73

Fernanda Torres (1965-)
Four Days in September '97
Foreign Land '95
Savage Capitalism '93
One Man's War '90

Liz Torres (1947-)
Storm Chasers: Revenge of the Twister '98
The Wonderful Ice Cream Suit '98
A Million to Juan '94
National Lampoon's Attack of the 5 Ft. 2 Women '94
Bloodfist 4: Die Trying '92
Lena's Holiday '90
America '86

Raquel Torres (1908-87)
Duck Soup '33
White Shadows in the South Seas '29

Philippe Torreton
Capitaine Conan '96
L.627 '92

Guy Torry
The Animal '01
Don't Say a Word '01
Pearl Harbor '01
The '70s '00
Life '99
Trippin' '99
American History X '98
Ride '98

Joe Torry
The Flamingo Rising '01
Back in Business '96
Sprung '96
Tales from the Hood '95
Poetic Justice '93

Sylvia Tortosa
When the Screaming Stops '73
Horror Express '72

Jose Torvay (-1973)
Green Fire '55
The Hitch-Hiker '53
My Outlaw Brother '51
Borderline '50

Leslie Toth
Buying Time '89
Unfinished Business '89

Toto (1898-1967)
The Hawks & the Sparrows '67
Passionate Thief '60
Big Deal on Madonna Street '58

Merle Tottenham (1901-59)
Room to Let '49
This Happy Breed '47
Night Must Fall '37
Cavalcade '33

Audrey Totter (1918-)
The Carpetbaggers '64
Man or Gun '58
FBI Girl '52
Any Number Can Play '49
The Set-Up '49
Lady in the Lake '46
The Postman Always Rings Twice '46

George Touliatos
36 Hours to Die '99
Tracks of a Killer '95
Red Scorpion 2 '94
Robbers of the Sacred Mountain '83
Firebird 2015 A.D. '81

Tamara Toumanova (1919-96)
The Private Life of Sherlock Holmes '70
Invitation to the Dance '56
Days of Glory '43

Sheila Tousey
Medicine River '94
Slaughter of the Innocents '93
Silent Tongue '92
Thunderheart '92

Beth Toussaint
Breach of Conduct '94
Night Siege Project: Shadowchaser 2 '94
Blackmail '91

Lorraine Toussaint (1960-)
If These Walls Could Talk '96
Jaded '96
Nightjohn '96
America's Dream '95
Dangerous Minds '95
Bleeding Hearts '94
Mother's Boys '94
Point of No Return '93
Breaking In '89
A Case of Deadly Force '86

Roland Toutain (1905-77)
Eternal Return '43
The Rules of the Game '39
Liliom '35

Lupita Tovar (1911-)
The Westerner '40
Old Spanish Custom '36
Border Law '31
Dracula (Spanish Version) '31

Harry Towb
Pictures '80s
The Blue Max '66

Constance Towers (1933-)
A Perfect Murder '98
On Wings of Eagles '86
Sylvester '85
Naked Kiss '64
Shock Corridor '63
Sergeant Rutledge '60
The Horse Soldiers '59

Tom Towles (1950-)
Mercenary 2: Thick and Thin '97
Gridlock'd '96
Normal Life '96
Girls in Prison '94
Blood In ... Blood Out: Bound by Honor '93
Mad Dog and Glory '93
The Pit & the Pendulum '91
Henry: Portrait of a Serial Killer '90
Night of the Living Dead '90
The Borrower '89

Aline Towne (1929-96)
Trader Tom of the China Seas '54
Radar Men from the Moon '52
Zombies of the Stratosphere '52
Don Daredevil Rides Again '51
The Invisible Monster '50
The Vanishing Westerner '50

Katharine Towne (1978-)
Evolution '01
Mulholland Drive '01
Town and Country '01
What Lies Beneath '00

Robert Towne (1936-)
The Pick-Up Artist '87
Villa Rides '68

Jill Townsend (1945-)
The Awakening '80
Oh, Alfie '75
Poldark '75
Poldark 2 '75
The Golden Bowl '72

Patrice Townsend
Always '85
Sitting Ducks '80

Robert Townsend (1957-)
Love Songs '99
The Taxman '98
Mercenary 2: Thick and Thin '97
The Meteor Man '93
The Five Heartbeats '91
That's Adequate '90
The Mighty Quinn '89
I'm Gonna Git You Sucka '88
Hollywood Shuffle '87
Ratboy '86
American Flyers '85
Odd Jobs '85
A Soldier's Story '84
Streets of Fire '84

Stuart Townsend (1972-)
Queen of the Damned '02
About Adam '00
Wonderland '99
Shooting Fish '98
Resurrection Man '97
Under the Skin '97
Trojan Eddie '96

Pete Townshend (1945-)
The Secret Policeman's Other Ball '82
Secret Policeman's Private Parts '81
The Kids Are Alright '79
Tommy '75

Etsushi Toyokawa
No Way Back '96
When I Close My Eyes '95

Fausto Tozzi (1921-78)
Sicilian Connection '74
Knives of the Avenger '65
The Return of Dr. Mabuse '61
East of Kilimanjaro '57

Giorgio Tozzi
Torn Between Two Lovers '79
South Pacific '58 *(V)*

Ian Tracey (1964-)
Rupert's Land '98
Bloodhounds 2 '96
Man with a Gun '95
Incident at Deception Ridge '94
Timecop '94
The Comrades of Summer '92

Jeff Trachta
Interlocked '98
Night Eyes 4: Fatal Passion '95

Michelle Trachtenberg
Forever Together '00
Inspector Gadget '99
Harriet the Spy '96

Lee Tracy (1898-1968)
The Best Man '64
Betrayal from the East '44
The Payoff '43
Bombshell '33
Dinner at Eight '33
Blessed Event '32
Doctor X '32
The Strange Love of Molly Louvain '32

Spencer Tracy (1900-67)
Guess Who's Coming to Dinner '67
How the West Was Won '63
It's a Mad, Mad, Mad, Mad World '63
The Devil at 4 O'Clock '61
Judgment at Nuremberg '61
Inherit the Wind '60
Last Hurrah '58
The Old Man and the Sea '58
Desk Set '57
The Mountain '56
Bad Day at Black Rock '54
Broken Lance '54
Pat and Mike '52
Father's Little Dividend '51
Adam's Rib '50
Father of the Bride '50

Malaya '49
State of the Union '48
Cass Timberlane '47
Without Love '45
A Guy Named Joe '44
The Seventh Cross '44
Thirty Seconds Over Tokyo '44
Keeper of the Flame '42
Tortilla Flat '42
Woman of the Year '42
Dr. Jekyll and Mr. Hyde '41
Men of Boys Town '41
Boom Town '40
Edison the Man '40
Northwest Passage '40
Stanley and Livingstone '39
Boys Town '38
Test Pilot '38
Captains Courageous '37
Mannequin '37
Fury '36
Libeled Lady '36
San Francisco '36
Riff Raff '35
Marie Galante '34

Steve Tracy
Desperate Moves '86
Beneath the Valley of the Ultra-Vixens '79

William Tracy (1917-67)
Mr. Walkie Talkie '52
As You Were '51
George Washington Slept Here '42
To the Shores of Tripoli '42
Tanks a Million '41
Strike Up the Band '40

Mary Ellen Trainor
Anywhere But Here '99
Lethal Weapon 4 '98
Hope '97
Executive Decision '96
Congo '95
Forrest Gump '94
Greedy '94
Little Giants '94
Death Becomes Her '92
Kuffs '92
Lethal Weapon 3 '92
Grand Canyon '91
Ricochet '91
Fire Birds '90
Ghostbusters 2 '89
Lethal Weapon 2 '89
Tales from the Crypt '89
Action Jackson '88
Die Hard '88
Scrooged '88
Lethal Weapon '87
The Monster Squad '87
The Goonies '85
Romancing the Stone '84
The Stone Boy '84

Cordula Trantow (1942-)
The Castle '68
Hitler '62
The Bridge '59

Helen Traubel
The Ladies' Man '61
Deep in My Heart '54

Daniel J. Travanti (1940-)
The Wasp Woman '96
Eyes of a Witness '94
Just Cause '94
Weep No More My Lady '93
Megaville '91
Tagget '90
Fellow Traveler '89
Millennium '89
Skin '89
Midnight Crossing '87
Murrow '86
Aurora '84
Adam '83
A Case of Libel '83
St. Ives '76

Bill Travers (1922-94)
The First Olympics: Athens 1896 '84
Christian the Lion '76
An Elephant Called Slowly '69
Ring of Bright Water '69
A Midsummer Night's Dream '68
Born Free '66
Duel at Diablo '66
Gorgo '61
The Smallest Show on Earth '57
Bhowani Junction '56
Romeo and Juliet '54
The Browning Version '51
Trio '50

Henry Travers (1874-1965)
It's a Wonderful Life '46
The Yearling '46
The Bells of St. Mary's '45
The Naughty Nineties '45
Thrill of a Romance '45
Dragon Seed '44
Madame Curie '43
Shadow of a Doubt '43
Mrs. Miniver '42
Random Harvest '42
Ball of Fire '41
A Girl, a Guy and a Gob '41
High Sierra '41
Edison the Man '40
Primrose Path '40
Dark Victory '39
Dodge City '39
On Borrowed Time '39
The Rains Came '39
Stanley and Livingstone '39
The Sisters '38
The Invisible Man '33

Linden Travers (1913-2001)
Beware of Pity '46
The Lady Vanishes '38
The Terror '38

Susan Travers (1939-)
The Abominable Dr. Phibes '71
The Snake Woman '61
Peeping Tom '60

June Travis (1914-)
Monster a Go-Go! '65
The Gladiator '38
Exiled to Shanghai '37
Earthworm Tractors '36
Ceiling Zero '35

Kylie Travis (1970-)
Gia '98
Sanctuary '98
Retroactive '97
Eyes of the Beholder '92

Nancy Travis (1961-)
Stephen King's Rose Red '02
Beyond Suspicion '00
Running Mates '00
Bogus '96
Body Language '95
Destiny Turns on the Radio '95
Fluke '95
Greedy '94
Fallen Angels 1 '93
So I Married an Axe Murderer '93
The Vanishing '93
Chaplin '92
Passed Away '92
Air America '90
Internal Affairs '90
Loose Cannons '90
Three Men and a Little Lady '90
Eight Men Out '88
Married to the Mob '88
Three Men and a Baby '87
Harem '86

Randy Travis (1959-)
Texas Rangers '01
The Million Dollar Kid '99
White River '99
Black Dog '98
T.N.T. '98
Boys Will Be Boys '97
Fire Down Below '97
John Grisham's The Rainmaker '97
The Shooter '97
Edie & Pen '95
Frank and Jesse '94
Texas '94
Dead Man's Revenge '93

Richard Travis (1913-89)
Missile to the Moon '59
Mesa of Lost Women '52
Danger Zone '51
Fingerprints Don't Lie '51
Mask of the Dragon '51
One Too Many '51
Roaring City '51
Sky Liner '49
Big Town After Dark '47
Dive Bomber '41
The Man Who Came to Dinner '41

Stacy Travis
Bandits '01
Ghost World '01
Traffic '00
The Only Thrill '97
Suspect Device '95
Dracula Rising '93
Only the Strong '93
Hardware '90
Dr. Hackenstein '88

Tony Travis
Flesh Gordon 2: Flesh Gordon Meets the Cosmic Cheerleaders '90
The Beatniks '60

Joey Travolta (1952-)
Car Crash
To the Limit '95
Beach Babes from Beyond Infinity '93
DaVinci's War '92
Wilding '90
American Born '89
Ghost Writer '89
Sinners '89
Amazon Women on the Moon '87
The Prodigal '83
Rosie: The Rosemary Clooney Story '82
Sunnyside '79

John Travolta (1954-)
Domestic Disturbance '01
Swordfish '01
Battlefield Earth '00
Lucky Numbers '00
The General's Daughter '99
A Civil Action '98
Primary Colors '98
The Thin Red Line '98
Face/Off '97
Mad City '97
She's So Lovely '97
Michael '96
Phenomenon '96
Broken Arrow '95
Get Shorty '95
White Man's Burden '95
Pulp Fiction '94
Look Who's Talking Now '93
Boris and Natasha: The Movie '92
Chains of Gold '92
Eyes of an Angel '91
Shout '91
Look Who's Talking, Too '90
The Experts '89
Look Who's Talking '89
Dumb Waiter '87
Perfect '85
Staying Alive '83
Two of a Kind '83
Blow Out '81
Urban Cowboy '80
Grease '78
Saturday Night Fever '77
The Boy in the Plastic Bubble '76
Carrie '76
Devil's Rain '75

Susan Traylor
Broken Vessels '98
She's So Lovely '97
Bastard out of Carolina '96
To Die For '95
The New Age '94
Sleep with Me '94

Joel Thomas Traywick
Sub Down '97
Nightjohn '96

Arthur Treacher (1894-1975)
Delightfully Dangerous '45
In Society '44
National Velvet '44
The Amazing Mrs. Holiday '43
Star Spangled Rhythm '42
The Little Princess '39
Mad About Music '38
My Lucky Star '38
Heidi '37
Thin Ice '37
Satan Met a Lady '36
Stowaway '36
Curly Top '35
David Copperfield '35
I Live My Life '35
A Midsummer Night's Dream '35
Splendor '35
Hollywood Party '34

Emerson Treacy (1900-67)
A Star Is Born '54
Prowler '51
Give Me a Sailor '38
Champagne for Breakfast '35

Michael Treanor
3 Ninjas Knuckle Up '95
3 Ninjas '92

Terri Treas (1959-)
Lady Killer '97
Yankee Zulu '95
Alien Nation: Dark Horizon '94
Rage and Honor '92
House 4: Home Deadly Home '91
Frankenstein Unbound '90 (V)
Deathstalker 3 '89
The Nest '88
The Terror Within '88

Robert Trebor
Hercules the Legendary Journeys, Vol. 2: The Lost Kingdom '94
52 Pick-Up '86
Out of the Darkness '85

David Tree (1915-)
Clouds over Europe '39
Drums '38
Pygmalion '38

Dorothy Tree (1906-92)
Hitler: Dead or Alive '43
Abe Lincoln in Illinois '40
Mystery of Mr. Wong '39

Mary Treen (1907-89)
Paradise, Hawaiian Style '66
I Married a Monster from Outer Space '58
The Sad Sack '57
Clipped Wings '53
It's a Wonderful Life '46
Strange Impersonation '46
Casanova Brown '44
Hands Across the Border '43
So Proudly We Hail '43
First Love '39
Swing It, Sailor! '37

Yahn Tregouet
Artemisia '97
Trois Couleurs: Bleu '93

Guy Trejan
I Married a Dead Man '82
The Beast '75

Danny Trejo (1944-)
The Salton Sea '02
Bubble Boy '01
Spy Kids '01
Animal Factory '00
Reindeer Games '00
Desert Heat '99
From Dusk Till Dawn 3: The Hangman's Daughter '99
From Dusk Till Dawn 2: Texas Blood Money '98
Point Blank '98
The Replacement Killers '98
Six Days, Seven Nights '98
Con Air '97
Dilemma '97
Los Locos Posse '97
Anaconda '96
From Dusk Till Dawn '95
Undercover Cop '94

Christine Tremarco
Under the Skin '97
Priest '94

Les Tremayne (1913-)
Fangs '75
Creature of Destruction '67
King Kong vs. Godzilla '63 (N)
The Slime People '63
The Gallant Hours '60
The Angry Red Planet '59
The Monolith Monsters '57
The Monster of Piedras Blancas '57
Forbidden Planet '56 (N)
A Man Called Peter '55
I Love Melvin '53
The War of the Worlds '53
Francis Goes to West Point '52

Johanne-Marie Tremblay
Jesus of Montreal '89
Straight for the Heart '88

Ken Tremblett
The Guilty '99
Tourist Trap '98

Anne Tremko
The Member of the Wedding '97
My Antonia '94

John Trent (-1983)
Mystery Plane '39
Stunt Pilot '39

Adam Trese (1969-)
40 Days and 40 Nights '02
Polish Wedding '97
Illtown '96
Palookaville '95
The Underneath '95
The Good Fight '92
Laws of Gravity '92

Frederick Treves (1925-)
A Certain Justice '99
Shameless '94
Paper Mask '91
Flame to the Phoenix '85

Leonardo Treviglio
Stealing Beauty '96
Sebastiane '79

Roger Treville
The Green Glove '52
Mr. Peek-A-Boo '50

Vic Trevino
Firehawk '92
Born in East L.A. '87

Austin Trevor (1897-1978)
Abandon Ship '57
Night Train to Munich '40
Sabotage '36
Mimi '35
The Silent Passenger '35
Broken Melody '34

Claire Trevor (1909-2000)
Breaking Home Ties '87
Kiss Me Goodbye '82
How to Murder Your Wife '64
The Stripper '63
Two Weeks in Another Town '62
Marjorie Morningstar '58
The Mountain '56
Man Without a Star '55
The Stranger Wore a Gun '53
Hoodlum Empire '52
Best of the Badmen '50
Borderline '50
Babe Ruth Story '48
Key Largo '48
Raw Deal '48
Velvet Touch '48
Born to Kill '47
Crack-Up '46
Johnny Angel '45
Murder, My Sweet '44
The Woman of the Town '44
The Desperadoes '43
Honky Tonk '41
Texas '41
Dark Command '40
Allegheny Uprising '39
Stagecoach '39
Amazing Dr. Clitterhouse '38
Dead End '37
Baby, Take a Bow '34

Jack Trevor (-1991)
Champagne '28
Secrets of a Soul '25

Paula Trickey (1966-)
The Base '99
A Kiss Goodnight '94
Carnal Crimes '91

Ivan Triesault (1898-1980)
Von Ryan's Express '65
The Amazing Transparent Man '60
Jet Pilot '57
Five Fingers '52
Golden Earrings '47
Cry of the Werewolf '44

Leopoldo Trieste (1917-)
Cinema Paradiso '88
Henry IV '85
Quo Vadis '85
Don't Look Now '73
Seduced and Abandoned '64
Divorce—Italian Style '62
I Vitelloni '53
The White Sheik '52

Sergej Trifunovic
3 A.M. '01
Savior '98
Someone Else's America '96

Sarah Trigger
Good Luck '96
Things to Do in Denver When You're Dead '95
Don't Do It '94
P.C.U. '94
Deadfall '93
Sleepless in Seattle '93
Pet Sematary 2 '92
Bill & Ted's Bogus Journey '91
Paradise '91
El Diablo '90
Kid '90

Zoe Trilling
Last Exit to Earth '96
Night of the Demons 2 '94

Jerry Trimble
Stranglehold '94
Full Contact '93
One Man Army '93
Breathing Fire '91

Jean-Louis Trintignant (1930-)
Those Who Love Me Can Take the Train '98
The City of Lost Children '95 (V)
Fiesta '95
A Self-Made Hero '95
Trois Couleurs: Rouge '94
A Man and a Woman: 20 Years Later '86
Rendez-vous '85
Next Summer '84
Confidentially Yours '83
I Love All of You '83
Under Fire '83
La Nuit de Varennes '82
Passion of Love '82
Intruder '77
The Desert of the Tartars '76
The Last Train '74
Le Secret '74
Les Violons du Bal '74
Act of Aggression '73

The Outside Man '73
And Hope to Die '72
The Conformist '71
The Libertine '69
My Night at Maud's '69
Z '69
Les Biches '68
Is Paris Burning? '66
A Man and a Woman '66
The Easy Life '63
Il Sorpasso '63
Journey Beneath the Desert '61
Dangerous Liaisons '60
And God Created Woman '57

Marie Trintignant (1962-)
Harrison's Flowers '02
Portraits Chinois '96
Ponette '95
Alberto Express '92
Betty '92
The Story of Women '88
Next Summer '84

Louis Tripp
Gate 2 '92
The Gate '87

Jeanne Tripplehorn (1963-)
Steal This Movie! '00
Time Code '00
Mickey Blue Eyes '99
Relative Values '99
Monument Ave. '98
Very Bad Things '98
Office Killer '97
Sliding Doors '97
William Faulkner's Old Man '97
Til There Was You '96
Waterworld '95
Reality Bites '94
The Firm '93
The Night We Never Met '93
Basic Instinct '92

Jan Triska
The Omega Code '99
Ronin '98
Apt Pupil '97
The People vs. Larry Flynt '96
Andersonville '95
My Antonia '94
The Elementary School '91

Elisabeth Trissenaar (1944-)
Angry Harvest '85
A Love in Germany '84
Berlin Alexanderplatz '80
In a Year of 13 Moons '78
The Stationmaster's Wife '77

Dorothy Tristan (1934-)
Down and Out in Beverly Hills '86
Griffin and Phoenix: A Love Story '76
End of the Road '70

Travis Tritt (1963-)
Outlaw Justice '98
The Cowboy Way '94
Rio Diablo '93

Massimo Troisi (1953-94)
The Postman '94
Hotel Colonial '88

Laura Trotter
Miami Horror '87
Rush '84
City of the Walking Dead '83

David Troughton (1950-)
All the King's Men '99
Cider with Rosie '99
Sharpe's Eagle '93
Sharpe's Rifles '93
Dance with a Stranger '85

Michael Troughton
Speedy Death '99
Testament of Youth '79

Patrick Troughton (1920-87)
The Omen '76
Frankenstein and the Monster from Hell '74
The Scars of Dracula '70
The Viking Queen '67
The Gorgon '64
The Moonraker '58
The Franchise Affair '52

Tom Troupe (1928-)
My Own Private Idaho '91
Kelly's Heroes '70
The Devil's Brigade '68

Charles Trowbridge (1882-1967)
They Were Expendable '45
Fighting Seabees '44
Wake Island '42
Sergeant York '41
The Fatal Hour '40
The Fighting 69th '40
The Mummy's Hand '40
Gang Bullets '38
Sea Racketeers '37
Libeled Lady '36

Phillip Troy
Ice '93
To Be the Best '93

Verne Troyer (1969-)
Austin Powers In Goldmember '02
Bubble Boy '01
Hard Cash '01
Austin Powers 2: The Spy Who Shagged Me '99

Michael Trubshawe
Bedazzled '68
The Guns of Navarone '61

Isabelle Truchon
Deadbolt '92
Backstab '90

John Trudell
Smoke Signals '98
Thunderheart '92

Jim True
Affliction '97
Far Harbor '96
Normal Life '96
The Hudsucker Proxy '93
Singles '92

Rachel True
New Best Friend '02
Groove '00
Love Song '00
Half-Baked '97
The Craft '96
Nowhere '96
Embrace of the Vampire '95

Ernest Truex (1890-1973)
All Mine to Give '56
Club Havana '46
Twin Beds '42
His Girl Friday '40
The Adventures of Marco Polo '38

Francois Truffaut (1932-84)
The Green Room '78
Close Encounters of the Third Kind '77
Small Change '76
Day for Night '73
The Wild Child '70
The 400 Blows '59

Raoul Trujillo
The Invaders '95
Black Fox: Blood Horse '94
Black Fox: The Price of Peace '94
Medicine River '94
Paris, France '94
The Adjuster '91
Scanners 2: The New Order '91

Ralph Truman (1900-77)
The Spaniard's Curse '58
The Man Who Knew Too Much '56
Treasure Island '50
Beware of Pity '46
Henry V '44
Butler's Dilemma '43

The Challenge '38
The Silent Passenger '35

Donald Trump
Celebrity '98
Home Alone 2: Lost in New York '92

Natalie Trundy (1940-)
Huckleberry Finn '74
Battle for the Planet of the Apes '73
Conquest of the Planet of the Apes '72
Escape from the Planet of the Apes '71
Beneath the Planet of the Apes '70

Glenn Tryon (1894-1970)
Tangled Destinies '32
Dames Ahoy '30
Battling Orioles '24

Tom Tryon (1926-91)
Color Me Dead '69
In Harm's Way '65
The Cardinal '63
The Longest Day '62
Moon Pilot '62
Texas John Slaughter: Stampede at Bitter Creek '62
Geronimo's Revenge '60
The Story of Ruth '60
Texas John Slaughter: Geronimo's Revenge '60
I Married a Monster from Outer Space '58
Three Violent People '57
Unholy Wife '57

Eric Tsang
Supercop 2 '93
The Reincarnation of Golden Lotus '89

Kenneth Tsang
Rush Hour 2 '01
The Replacement Killers '98
Supercop '92
The Killer '90

Nicholas Tse
Time and Tide '00
Gen-X Cops '99

Ludmila Tselikovskaya
Ivan the Terrible, Part 2 '46
Ivan the Terrible, Part 1 '44

Yee Jee Tso
Antitrust '00
Doctor Who '96

Irene Tsu (1910-89)
The Green Berets '68
Island of the Lost '68
Paradise, Hawaiian Style '66
Women of the Prehistoric Planet '66
How to Stuff a Wild Bikini '65

Yoshio Tsuchiya (1927-)
Yog, Monster from Space '71
Destroy All Monsters '68
Godzilla vs. Monster Zero '68
Red Beard '65
Attack of the Mushroom People '63
Yojimbo '61
Seven Samurai '54

Masahiko Tsugawa (1940-)
Heaven & Earth '90
A Taxing Woman's Return '88
The Sun's Burial '60

Koji Tsurata (1924-)
The Secret of the Telegian '61
Samurai 3: Duel at Ganryu Island '56

Barry Tubb (1963-)
Return to Lonesome Dove '93
Guilty by Suspicion '91
Warm Summer Rain '89

Valentino Returns '88
Billionaire Boys Club '87
Top Gun '86
Consenting Adult '85
Mask '85

William Tubbs
Wages of Fear '55
Paisan '46

Christine Tucci
Big Fat Liar '02
K-911 '99

Maria Tucci (1941-)
To Die For '95
Touch and Go '86
Enormous Changes '83
Trumps '83

Michael Tucci (1950-)
The Man Who Captured Eichmann '96
Sunnyside '79
Grease '78

Stanley Tucci (1960-)
Big Trouble '02
Road to Perdition '02
America's Sweethearts '01
Conspiracy '01
Sidewalks of New York '01
Joe Gould's Secret '00
In Too Deep '99
William Shakespeare's A Midsummer Night's Dream '99
The Alarmist '98
The Imposters '98
Winchell '98
Deconstructing Harry '97
The Eighteenth Angel '97
A Life Less Ordinary '97
Montana '97
The Daytrippers '96
Big Night '95
Jury Duty '95
Sex and the Other Man '95
It Could Happen to You '94
Kiss of Death '94
A Modern Affair '94
Somebody to Love '94
The Pelican Brief '93
Undercover Blues '93
Beethoven '92
In the Soup '92
Prelude to a Kiss '92
The Public Eye '92
Billy Bathgate '91
Men of Respect '91
Quick Change '90
Fear, Anxiety and Depression '89
Monkey Shines '88

Jessica Tuck (1963-)
Billboard Dad '98
The Garbage-Picking, Field Goal-Kicking Philadelphia Phenomenon '98
Batman Forever '95
The O.J. Simpson Story '94
Revenge of the Nerds 4: Nerds in Love '94
Lifepod '93
Mr. Write '92

Chris Tucker (1972-)
Rush Hour 2 '01
Rush Hour '98
The Fifth Element '97
Jackie Brown '97
Money Talks '97
Dead Presidents '95
Friday '95
House Party 3 '94

Forrest Tucker (1919-86)
Timestalkers '87
Thunder Run '86
A Rare Breed '81
The Rebels '79
The Adventures of Huckleberry Finn '78
A Real American Hero '78
The Incredible Rocky Mountain Race '77
Wackiest Wagon Train in the West '77
Walking Tall: The Final Chapter '77
The McCullochs '75
Cancel My Reservation '72

Chisum '70
Auntie Mame '58
The Cosmic Monsters '58
The Crawling Eye '58
The Abominable Snowman '57
Three Violent People '57
The Finger Man '55
Rage at Dawn '55
Jubilee Trail '54
Trouble in the Glen '54
Pony Express '53
Bugles in the Afternoon '52
Hoodlum Empire '52
Montana Belle '52
The Nevadan '50
The Big Cat '49
Sands of Iwo Jima '49
Coroner Creek '48
Hellfire '48
Never Say Goodbye '46
The Yearling '46
Keeper of the Flame '42
Robot Pilot '41
The Westerner '40

Jonathan Tucker (1982-)
The Deep End '01
100 Girls '00
The Virgin Suicides '99
Sleepers '96
Two If by Sea '95

Larry Tucker (1933-2001)
Angels Hard As They Come '71
Shock Corridor '63

Martin Tucker
Death Screams '83
House of Death '82

Michael Tucker (1944-)
Til There Was You '96
D2: The Mighty Ducks '94
For Love or Money '93
Too Young to Die '90
Checking Out '89
Day One '89
Spy '89
Assault and Matrimony '87
Radio Days '87
Tin Men '87
L.A. Law '86
The Purple Rose of Cairo '85
Diner '82
Eyes of Laura Mars '78

Richard Tucker (1884-1942)
Delinquent Parents '38
Convicted '32
The Bat Whispers '30
King of the Kongo '29
Wings '27
Captain Swagger '25
The Worldly Madonna '22

Rocky Tucker
Steps from Hell '92
Lunatic '91

Sophie Tucker (1884-1966)
Sensations of 1945 '44
Broadway Melody of 1938 '37
Thoroughbreds Don't Cry '37

Tanya Tucker (1958-)
Hard Country '81
Follow That Car '80
The Rebels '79

Alan Tudyk (1971-)
Ice Age '02 *(V)*
Hearts in Atlantis '01
A Knight's Tale '01
28 Days '00

Sonny Tufts (1911-70)
Easy Come, Easy Go '67
The Seven Year Itch '55
Serpent Island '54
Cat Women of the Moon '53
The Gift Horse '52
Easy Living '49
The Virginian '46
Here Come the Waves '45
So Proudly We Hail '43

Patricia Tulasne
King of the Airwaves '94
The Savage Woman '91

Tom Tully (1908-82)
Coogan's Bluff '68
McHale's Navy Joins the Air Force '65
Ten North Frederick '58
Love Me or Leave Me '55
Soldier of Fortune '55
The Caine Mutiny '54
The Moon Is Blue '53
Trouble along the Way '53
Love Is Better Than Ever '52
Texas Carnival '51
Tomahawk '51
June Bride '48
Lady in the Lake '46
Till the End of Time '46
The Virginian '46
Adventure '45
Destination Tokyo '43
Northern Pursuit '43

Frans Tumbuan
Without Mercy '95
Rage and Honor 2: Hostile Takeover '93

Tommy Tune (1939-)
The Boy Friend '71
Hello, Dolly! '69

Bill Tung
Jackie Chan's First Strike '96
Rumble in the Bronx '96
Police Story '85

Tamara Tunie
The Caveman's Valentine '01
Snake Eyes '98
The Devil's Advocate '97
Eve's Bayou '97 *(N)*
Rebound: The Legend of Earl "The Goat" Manigault '96

Robin Tunney (1972-)
Cherish '02
Vertical Limit '00
End of Days '99
Supernova '99
Naked City: Justice with a Bullet '98
Julian Po '97
Montana '97
Niagara, Niagara '97
The Craft '96
Riders of the Purple Sage '96
Empire Records '95
JFK: Reckless Youth '93
Encino Man '92

Robert Turano
One Way Out '95
Federal Hill '94

Paige Turco (1965-)
Urbania '00
November Conspiracy '96
The Pompatus of Love '95
Dead Funny '94
Vibrations '94
Teenage Mutant Ninja Turtles 3 '93
Teenage Mutant Ninja Turtles 2: The Secret of the Ooze '91

Paolo Turco
Bread and Chocolate '73
The Lickerish Quartet '70

Ann Turkel (1942-)
The Fear '94
Deep Space '87
The Last Contract '86
Death Ray 2000 '81
Humanoids from the Deep '80
Golden Rendezvous '77
Portrait of a Hitman '77
The Cassandra Crossing '76
99 & 44/100 Dead '74
Paper Lion '68

Joe Turkel (1927-)
Dark Side of the Moon '90
The Desperados '80s
Blade Runner '82
The Shining '80
Cycle Psycho '72

The Sand Pebbles '66
King Rat '65
Village of the Giants '65
Paths of Glory '57
The Killing '56

Glynn Turman (1946-)
Freedom Song '00
Men of Honor '00
The Visit '00
Light It Up '99
Buffalo Soldiers '97
Rebound: The Legend of Earl "The Goat" Manigault '96
Race to Freedom: The Story of the Underground Railroad '94
Deep Cover '92
Charlotte Forten's Mission: Experiment in Freedom '85
Gremlins '84
Secrets of a Married Man '84
Penitentiary 2 '82
Centennial '78
A Hero Ain't Nothin' but a Sandwich '78
J.D.'s Revenge '76
The River Niger '76
The Blue Knight '75
Cooley High '75

John Turnbull (1880-1956)
The Happiest Days of Your Life '50
Man of Evil '48
Make-Up '37
Nine Days a Queen '36
The Passing of the Third Floor Back '36
The 39 Steps '35
The Private Life of Henry VIII '33

Elizabeth Turner
Truck Stop
Cannibal Apocalypse '80

Florence Turner
Pace That Kills '28
Walking Back '26

George Turner (-1968)
Son of Zorro '47
Vigilantes of Boom Town '46

Guinevere Turner (1968-)
American Psycho '99
Dogma '99
The Watermelon Woman '97
Go Fish '94

Janine Turner (1963-)
Dr. T & the Women '00
Fatal Error '99
Leave It to Beaver '97
The Curse of Inferno '96
Cliffhanger '93
The Ambulance '90
Steel Magnolias '89
Monkey Shines '88
Knights of the City '85
Young Doctors in Love '82

Jim Turner
Joe's Apartment '96
The Ref '93
My Samurai '92
Kid Colter '85

John Turner
The Slipper and the Rose '76
Estate of Insanity '70

Kathleen Turner (1954-)
Beautiful '00
Prince of Central Park '00
Love and Action in Chicago '99
The Virgin Suicides '99
Baby Geniuses '98
Legalese '98
The Real Blonde '97
A Simple Wish '97
Moonlight and Valentino '95
Serial Mom '94
Naked in New York '93
Undercover Blues '93
House of Cards '92
V.I. Warshawski '91
Honey, I Shrunk the Kids '89 (V)
The War of the Roses '89
The Accidental Tourist '88
Switching Channels '88
Who Framed Roger Rabbit '88 (V)
Julia and Julia '87
Peggy Sue Got Married '86
The Jewel of the Nile '85
Prizzi's Honor '85
A Breed Apart '84
Crimes of Passion '84
Romancing the Stone '84
The Man with Two Brains '83
Body Heat '81

Lana Turner (1920-95)
Witches' Brew '79
Bittersweet Love '76
The Graveyard '74
Bachelor in Paradise '69
Madame X '66
Love Has Many Faces '65
Who's Got the Action? '63
By Love Possessed '61
Portrait in Black '60
Imitation of Life '59
Another Time, Another Place '58
Peyton Place '57
Diane '55
The Prodigal '55
Sea Chase '55
Betrayed '54
Latin Lovers '53
The Bad and the Beautiful '52
The Merry Widow '52
A Life of Her Own '50
Homecoming '48
The Three Musketeers '48
Cass Timberlane '47
Green Dolphin Street '47
The Postman Always Rings Twice '46
Weekend at the Waldorf '45
Johnny Eager '42
Somewhere I'll Find You '42
Dr. Jekyll and Mr. Hyde '41
Honky Tonk '41
Ziegfeld Girl '41
Love Finds Andy Hardy '38
They Won't Forget '37

Tina Turner (1939-)
Mad Max: Beyond Thunderdome '85
Tommy '75
Gimme Shelter '70

Tyrin Turner
Belly '98
Little Boy Blue '97
Soldier Boyz '95
Menace II Society '93

Zara Turner
The Waiting Time '99
Resurrection Man '97
Sliding Doors '97

Ben Turpin (1874-1940)
Saps at Sea '40
Law of the Wild '34
Yankee Doodle in Berlin '19
Burlesque on Carmen '16

Aida Turturro (1962-)
Crocodile Dundee in Los Angeles '01
Sidewalks of New York '01
Bringing Out the Dead '99
Deep Blue Sea '99
Hitman's Journal '99
The 24 Hour Woman '99
24 Nights '99
Celebrity '98
Illuminata '98
Sleepers '96
Denise Calls Up '95
Money Train '95
Angie '94
Junior '94
Tales of Erotica '93
Jersey Girl '92
True Love '89

John Turturro (1957-)
Collateral Damage '02
Mr. Deeds '02
Monkeybone '01 (V)
Company Man '00
The Luzhin Defence '00
The Man Who Cried '00
O Brother Where Art Thou? '00
The Cradle Will Rock '99
He Got Game '98
Illuminata '98
Rounders '98
The Big Lebowski '97
Box of Moonlight '96
Girl 6 '96
Grace of My Heart '96
The Search for One-Eyed Jimmy '96
The Truce '96
Clockers '95
Sugartime '95
Unstrung Heroes '95
Being Human '94
Quiz Show '94
Search and Destroy '94
Fearless '93
Mac '93
Brain Donors '92
Barton Fink '91
Jungle Fever '91
Men of Respect '91
Miller's Crossing '90
Mo' Better Blues '90
State of Grace '90
Backtrack '89
Do the Right Thing '89
Five Corners '88
The Sicilian '87
The Color of Money '86
Hannah and Her Sisters '86
Off Beat '86
Desperately Seeking Susan '85
Gung Ho '85
To Live & Die in L.A. '85

Nicholas Turturro (1962-)
Hellraiser 5: Inferno '00
Witness to the Mob '98
Mercenary 2: Thick and Thin '97
Excess Baggage '96
The Search for One-Eyed Jimmy '96
The Shadow Conspiracy '96
Cosmic Slop '94
Federal Hill '94
Mac '93
Mo' Better Blues '90

Rita Tushingham (1942-)
Swing '98
Under the Skin '97
An Awfully Big Adventure '94
Paper Marriage '93
Loose in New York '80s
The Housekeeper '86
Dream to Believe '85
Mysteries '84
Spaghetti House '82
Slaughterday '77
Green Eyes '76
The Human Factor '75
Rachel's Man '75
Dressed for Death '74
Smashing Time '67
Trap '66
Doctor Zhivago '65
The Knack '65
Girl with Green Eyes '64
The Leather Boys '63
A Taste of Honey '61

Dorothy Tutin (1930-2001)
Alive and Kicking '96
Scarlett '94
Body & Soul '93
Shades of Fear '93
The Shooting Party '85
Sister Dora '77
Savage Messiah '72
Six Wives of Henry VIII '71
A Tale of Two Cities '58

Lurene Tuttle (1906-86)
White Mama '80
The Manitou '78
The Fortune Cookie '66
The Ghost and Mr. Chicken '66
Ma Barker's Killer Brood '60
The Glass Slipper '55
The Affairs of Dobie Gillis '53
Don't Bother to Knock '52
Homecoming '48

Shannon Tweed (1957-)
Dead Sexy '01
The Rowdy Girls '00
Wish You Were Dead '00
Forbidden Sins '99
Naked Lies '98
Face the Evil '97
Human Desires '97
Shadow Warriors '97
Shadow Warriors 2: Hunt for the Death Merchant '97
Stormy Nights '97
White Cargo '96
Body Chemistry 4: Full Exposure '95
The Dark Dancer '95
Electra '95
Indecent Behavior 3 '95
Hard Vice '94
Illicit Dreams '94
Indecent Behavior 2 '94
Model by Day '94
Night Fire '94
No Contest '94
Victim of Desire '94
Cold Sweat '93
Indecent Behavior '93
Night Eyes 3 '93
Possessed by the Night '93
Scorned '93
Liar's Edge '92
Sexual Response '92
The Firing Line '91
The Last Hour '91
Night Eyes 2 '91
Last Call '90
Cannibal Women in the Avocado Jungle of Death '89
In the Cold of the Night '89
Night Visitor '89
Twisted Justice '89
Lethal Woman '88
Surrogate '88
Codename: Vengeance '87
Meatballs 3 '87
The Last Fling '86
Hot Dog ... The Movie! '83
Of Unknown Origin '83

Terry Tweed
Night Rhythms '92
The Reincarnate '71

Helen Twelvetrees (1908-58)
Millie '31
Painted Desert '31
State's Attorney '31

Twiggy (1949-)
Body Bags '93
The Diamond Trap '91
Istanbul '90
Madame Sousatzka '88
Young Charlie Chaplin '88
Club Paradise '86
The Doctor and the Devils '85
The Blues Brothers '80
Butterfly Ball '76
W '74
The Boy Friend '71

Archie Twitchell
Thundering Trail '51
Young Bill Hickok '40

Anne Twomey (1951-)
The Confession '98
Rear Window '98
Picture Perfect '96
The Scout '94
Orpheus Descending '91
Last Rites '88
Deadly Friend '86
Behind Enemy Lines '85

Alexandra Tydings
Red Shoe Diaries 7: Burning Up '96
Sunchaser '96

Harry Tyler
Bedtime for Bonzo '51
I Married a Witch '42

Liv Tyler (1977-)
Lord of the Rings 1: The Fellowship of the Rings '01
One Night at McCool's '01
Dr. T & the Women '00
Cookie's Fortune '99
Onegin '99
Armageddon '98
Plunkett & Macleane '98
Inventing the Abbotts '97
U-Turn '97
Stealing Beauty '96
That Thing You Do! '96
Empire Records '95
Heavy '94
Silent Fall '94

Tom Tyler (1903-54)
Guns of Justice '50
She Wore a Yellow Ribbon '49
Fast Bullets '44
Valley of the Sun '42
The Adventures of Captain Marvel '41
Riders of the Timberline '41
The Mummy's Hand '40
The Westerner '40
Stagecoach '39
Cheyenne Rides Again '38
The Phantom of the Range '38
Brothers of the West '37
Feud of the Trail '37
Riding On '37
Santa Fe Bound '37
Last Outlaw '36
Pinto Rustlers '36
Rip Roarin' Buckaroo '36
Roamin' Wild '36
Coyote Trails '35
Laramie Kid '35
Powdersmoke Range '35
Ridin' Thru '35
Rio Rattler '35
Silent Code '35
Silent Valley '35
The Silver Bullet '34
Deadwood Pass '33
Phantom of the Air '33
When a Man Rides Alone '33
The Forty-Niners '32
Battling with Buffalo Bill '31
Phantom of the West '31
Two Fisted Justice '31

George Tyne (1911-)
Sands of Iwo Jima '49
Call Northside 777 '48
Open Secret '48
A Walk in the Sun '46
Objective, Burma! '45

Charles Tyner (1925-)
Pulse '88
Planes, Trains & Automobiles '87
The Longest Yard '74
Emperor of the North Pole '73
Jeremiah Johnson '72
Harold and Maude '71
Cool Hand Luke '67

Susan Tyrrell (1946-)
Relax... It's Just Sex! '98
The Demolitionist '95
Powder '95
Motorama '91
Cry-Baby '90
Rockula '90
Thompson's Last Run '90
Far from Home '89
Tapeheads '89
Big Top Pee-wee '88
The Underachievers '88
Windmills of the Gods '88
The Offspring '87
Poker Alice '87
Avenging Angel '85
Flesh and Blood '85
Angel '84
Fire and Ice '83 (V)
Tales of Ordinary Madness '83
Fast Walking '82
Liar's Moon '82
Night Warning '82
Forbidden Zone '80
Lady of the House '78
Andy Warhol's Bad '77
Another Man, Another Chance '77
Islands in the Stream '77
September 30, 1955 '77
The Killer Inside Me '76
Zandy's Bride '74
Fat City '72
Shoot Out '71

Barbara Tyson
Beautiful Joe '00
Ratz '99
Resurrection '99
Baby Monitor: Sound of Fear '97

Cathy Tyson (1965-)
Band of Gold '95
Priest '94
The Lost Language of Cranes '92
Business As Usual '88
The Serpent and the Rainbow '87
Mona Lisa '86

Cicely Tyson (1933-)
Aftershock: Earthquake in New York '99
A Lesson Before Dying '99
Life '99
Always Outnumbered Always Outgunned '98
Mama Flora's Family '98
Ms. Scrooge '97
Hoodlum '96
Riot in the Streets '96
The Road to Galveston '96
Oldest Confederate Widow Tells All '95
Duplicates '92
Fried Green Tomatoes '91
Heat Wave '90
The Kid Who Loved Christmas '90
The Women of Brewster Place '89
Acceptable Risks '86
Samaritan: The Mitch Snyder Story '86
Bustin' Loose '81
The Concorde: Airport '79 '79
A Hero Ain't Nothin' but a Sandwich '78
King '78
A Woman Called Moses '78
Roots '77
Wilma '77
The River Niger '76
The Autobiography of Miss Jane Pittman '74
Sounder '72
The Heart Is a Lonely Hunter '68
A Man Called Adam '66

Mike Tyson
Crocodile Dundee in Los Angeles '01
Black and White '99

Pamela Tyson
Last Dance '96
What's Love Got to Do with It? '93

Richard Tyson (1961-)
Black Hawk Down '01
Firetrap '01
Battlefield Earth '00
Operation Sandman: Warriors in Hell '00
Desert Thunder '99
Tales of the Kama Sutra 2: Monsoon '98
There's Something about Mary '98
Monsoon '97
The Glass Cage '96
Kingpin '96
Pharoah's Army '95

Dark Tide '93
Red Shoe Diaries 3: Another Woman's Lipstick '93
The Babe '92
Kindergarten Cop '90
Two Moon Junction '88
Three o'Clock High '87

Margaret Tyzack (1933-)
Our Mutual Friend '98
Mrs. Dalloway '97
The King's Whore '90
Mr. Love '86
Quatermass Conclusion '79
2001: A Space Odyssey '68

Alanna Ubach (1977-)
Legally Blonde '01
Blue Moon '00
Clockwatchers '97
Trading Favors '97
johns '96
Just Your Luck '96
Denise Calls Up '95

Fabiana Udenio (1964-)
The Godson '98
Austin Powers: International Man of Mystery '97
Bride of Re-Animator '89
Hardbodies 2 '86

Claudia Udy (1960-)
Captive Rage '88
The Pink Chiquitas '86
Out of Control '85

Helene Udy (1962-)
Sweet Murder '93
The Hollywood Detective '89
Pin... '88

Bob Uecker (1935-)
Major League 3: Back to the Minors '98
Homeward Bound 2: Lost in San Francisco '96 (V)
Major League 2 '94
Major League '89

Kichijiro Ueda (1904-72)
Gamera vs. Gaos '67
The Hidden Fortress '58
Seven Samurai '54
Rashomon '51

Kenjiro Uemura
The Human Condition: Road to Eternity '59
A Quiet Duel '49

Leslie Uggams (1943-)
Sugar Hill '94
Sizzle '81
Roots '77
Poor Pretty Eddie '73
Two Weeks in Another Town '62

Gisela Uhlen (1919-)
Toto le Heros '91
The Marriage of Maria Braun '79
The Indian Scarf '63

Tracey Ullman (1961-)
Panic '00
Small Time Crooks '00
Bullets over Broadway '94
Ready to Wear '94
Happily Ever After '93 (V)
Household Saints '93
I'll Do Anything '93
Robin Hood: Men in Tights '93
I Love You to Death '90
Happy Since I Met You '89
Jumpin' Jack Flash '86
Plenty '85
Give My Regards to Broad Street '84

Liv Ullmann (1939-)
Mindwalk: A Film for Passionate Thinkers '91
The Ox '91
The Rose Garden '89
Gaby: A True Story '87
The Bay Boy '85
Dangerous Moves '84
The Wild Duck '84
Richard's Things '80
Autumn Sonata '78
The Serpent's Egg '78
A Bridge Too Far '77
Face to Face '76
Leonor '75
Zandy's Bride '74
Forty Carats '73
The New Land '73
Scenes from a Marriage '73
Cries and Whispers '72
The Emigrants '72
Cold Sweat '71
The Night Visitor '70
The Passion of Anna '70
Hour of the Wolf '68
The Shame '68
Persona '66

Lenore Ulric
Northwest Outpost '47
Camille '36

Skeet Ulrich (1969-)
Chill Factor '99
Ride with the Devil '99
A Soldier's Sweetheart '98
As Good As It Gets '97
The Newton Boys '97
Albino Alligator '96
The Craft '96
Last Dance '96
Scream '96
Touch '96
Boys '95

Mikhail Ulyanov
Private Life '82
The Theme '79

Margaret Umbers
The Bridge to Nowhere '86
Death Warmed Up '85

Miyoshi Umeki (1929-)
The Horizontal Lieutenant '62
Flower Drum Song '61
Sayonara '57

Yoko Umemura
The Story of the Late Chrysanthemum '39
Sisters of the Gion '36

Edward Underdown (1908-89)
Beast of Morocco '66
Pattern for Plunder '62
Beat the Devil '53
The Shadow Man '53
Man on the Run '49
Inspector Hornleigh '39
Wings of the Morning '37

Blair Underwood (1964-)
Full Frontal '02
Rules of Engagement '00
Asunder '99
Deep Impact '98
Mama Flora's Family '98
Mistrial '96
Set It Off '96
Soul of the Game '96
Just Cause '94
Dangerous Relations '93
Posse '93
Heat Wave '90
Krush Groove '85

Jay Underwood (1968-)
Dancing in September '00
Stalker '98
Afterglow '97
The Nurse '97
A Reason to Believe '95
The Raffle '94
Sleepstalker: The Sandman's Last Rites '94
Stalked '94
Wyatt Earp: Return to Tombstone '94
Still Not Quite Human '92
To Die For 2: Son of Darkness '91
The Gumshoe Kid '89
Not Quite Human 2 '89
Uncle Buck '89
The Invisible Kid '88
Promised Land '88
Not Quite Human '87
The Boy Who Could Fly '86
Desert Bloom '86

Deborah Kara Unger (1966-)
The Salton Sea '02
Luminous Motion '00
Signs & Wonders '00
The Weekend '00
The Hurricane '99
Sunshine '99
Payback '98
The Rat Pack '98
The Game '97
Keys to Tulsa '96
No Way Home '96
Crash '95
Highlander: The Final Dimension '94
Hotel Room '93
Whispers in the Dark '92
Prisoners of the Sun '91
Till There Was You '91

Joe Unger
Leatherface: The Texas Chainsaw Massacre 3 '89
Go Tell the Spartans '78

Gabrielle Union (1973-)
The Brothers '01
Two Can Play That Game '01
Bring It On '00
She's All That '99
Ten Things I Hate about You '99

James Urbaniak
Sweet and Lowdown '99
Henry Fool '98
The Sticky Fingers of Time '97

Mary Ure (1933-75)
A Reflection of Fear '72
Where Eagles Dare '68
Look Back in Anger '58
Windom's Way '57

Fabio Urena
Return of the Living Dead 3 '93
The Bronx War '90

Robert Urich (1946-2002)
The Lazarus Man '96
Captains Courageous '95
A Horse for Danny '95
Spenser: Pale Kings & Princes '94
Hit Woman: The Double Edge '93
Spenser: Ceremony '93
In a Stranger's Hand '92
Revolver '92
Blind Man's Bluff '91
A Perfect Little Murder '90
Lonesome Dove '89
Murder by Night '89
Turk 182! '85
Ice Pirates '84
Invitation to Hell '84
Mistral's Daughter '84
Bunco '83
Endangered Species '82
Take Your Best Shot '82
Killing at Hell's Gate '81
The Shadow Box '80
Vegas '78
Magnum Force '73

Robert Urquhart (1922-95)
The Kitchen Toto '87
Playing Away '87
Children of the Full Moon '84
Sharma & Beyond '84
The Curse of Frankenstein '57
White Huntress '57
The House of the Arrow '53

Benny "The Jet" Urquidez (1952-)
Grosse Pointe Blank '97
Bloodmatch '91
The Kick Fighter '91
Down the Drain '89

Susan Ursitti
Defense Play '88
Teen Wolf '85

Jun Usami
Tora! Tora! Tora! '70
Late Spring '49

Peter Ustinov (1921-)
Victoria & Albert '01
Alice in Wonderland '99
Animal Farm '99 (V)
The Bachelor '99
Stiff Upper Lips '96
The Phoenix and the Magic Carpet '95
The Old Curiosity Shop '94
Lorenzo's Oil '92
Around the World in 80 Days '89
Appointment with Death '88
Evil under the Sun '82
Grendel, Grendel, Grendel '82 (V)
Charlie Chan and the Curse of the Dragon Queen '81
The Great Muppet Caper '81
Ashanti, Land of No Mercy '79
Death on the Nile '78
The Thief of Baghdad '78
The Last Remake of Beau Geste '77
Mouse and His Child '77 (V)
The Purple Taxi '77
Logan's Run '76
The Treasure of Matecumbe '76
One of Our Dinosaurs Is Missing '75
Robin Hood '73 (V)
Hammersmith Is Out '72
Viva Max '69
Hot Millions '68
Blackbeard's Ghost '67
The Comedians '67
Barefoot in Athens '66
Lady L '65
Topkapi '64
Billy Budd '62
Spartacus '60
The Sundowners '60
The Man Who Wagged His Tail '57
Lola Montes '55
We're No Angels '55
Beau Brummel '54
The Egyptian '54
Le Plaisir '52 (N)
Quo Vadis '51
Immortal Battalion '44
One of Our Aircraft Is Missing '41

Kari Vaananen (1953-)
Ambush '99
La Vie de Boheme '93
Night on Earth '91
Amazon '90
Leningrad Cowboys Go America '89

Brenda Vaccaro (1939-)
The Mirror Has Two Faces '96
Love Affair '94
Lethal Games '90
Masque of the Red Death '90
Cookie '89
Heart of Midnight '89
Ten Little Indians '89
Water '85
Supergirl '84
A Long Way Home '81
Pride of Jesse Hallum '81
Zorro, the Gay Blade '81
The First Deadly Sin '80
The Guyana Tragedy: The Story of Jim Jones '80
Capricorn One '78
Dear Detective '78
Airport '77 '77
Death Weekend '76
Once Is Not Enough '75
Honor Thy Father '73
Summertree '71
I Love My...Wife '70
Midnight Cowboy '69

Annette Vadim
Blood and Roses '61
Dangerous Liaisons '60

David Vadim
Exit Wounds '01
Air Force One '97
Little Odessa '94

Roger Vadim (1928-2000)
Into the Night '85
Edie in Ciao! Manhattan '72

Dan Vadis (1938-87)
Seven Magnificent Gladiators '84
Bronco Billy '80
The Triumph of Hercules '66
Son of Hercules in the Land of Darkness '63

Lester Vail (1900-59)
Consolation Marriage '31
Dance Fools Dance '31

Charlotte Valandrey (1968-)
My Life and Times with Antonin Artaud '93
Orlando '92
Red Kiss '85

Birgitta Valberg
The Shame '68
The Virgin Spring '59

Serge-Henri Valcke
No Man's Land '01
The Quarry '98
Amsterdamned '88

Jerry Vale
Casino '95
Goodfellas '90

Virginia Vale (1920-)
Panama Menace '41
Bullet Code '40
Legion of the Lawless '40

Nancy Valen
Black Thunder '98
Final Embrace '92

Vladimir Valenta
The Unbearable Lightness of Being '88
Closely Watched Trains '66

Barbara Valentin (1940-2002)
Carmen, Baby '66
Horrors of Spider Island '59

Anthony Valentine (1939-)
Body & Soul '93
Riders '88
Robin Hood...The Legend: Robin Hood and the Sorcerer '83
The Carpathian Eagle '81

Karen Valentine (1947-)
The Power Within '95
Children in the Crossfire '84
Jane Doe '83
Skeezer '82
The North Avenue Irregulars '79
Hot Lead & Cold Feet '78
Return to Fantasy Island '77

Scott Valentine (1958-)
Paranoia '98
Carnosaur 3: Primal Species '96
Mars '96
Object of Obsession '95
Phantom 2040 Movie: The Ghost Who Walks '95 (V)
Out of Annie's Past '94
Till the End of the Night '94
The Unborn 2 '94
Double Obsession '93
Homicidal Impulse '92
The Secret Passion of Robert Clayton '92
To Sleep with a Vampire '92
Write to Kill '91
After the Shock '90
Dangerous Pursuit '89
My Demon Lover '87
Deadtime Stories '86
True Stories '86

Rudolph Valentino (1895-1926)
Son of the Sheik '26
Cobra '25
The Eagle '25
Monsieur Beaucaire '24
Blood and Sand '22
Moran of the Lady Letty '22
Camille '21
The Four Horsemen of the Apocalypse '21
The Sheik '21
The Eyes of Youth '19
The Married Virgin '18

Tasia Valenza (1968-)
The Hillside Strangler '89
Rappin' '85
Crackers '84

Jeanne Valeri
Desert Commandos '67
Dangerous Liaisons '60

Rosa Valetti
M '31
The Blue Angel '30

Frederick Valk (1895-1956)
Frenzy '46
Dead of Night '45
Hotel Reserve '44
Dangerous Moonlight '41
Night Train to Munich '40

Kitty Vallacher
The Legend of Frank Woods '77
Grave of the Vampire '72

Riccardo Valle
Hercules vs. the Sons of the Sun '64
The Awful Dr. Orloff '62

Marcel Vallee
Topaze '33
The Crazy Ray '22

Rudy Vallee (1901-86)
Slashed Dreams '74
Live a Little, Love a Little '68
How to Succeed in Business without Really Trying '67
The Admiral Was a Lady '50
The Beautiful Blonde from Bashful Bend '49
Father Was a Fullback '49
My Dear Secretary '49
I Remember Mama '48
Unfaithfully Yours '48
The Bachelor and the Bobby-Soxer '47
The Sin of Harold Diddlebock '47
People Are Funny '46
The Palm Beach Story '42
Second Fiddle '39
International House '33
Glorifying the American Girl '30
Vagabond Lover '29

Amber Valletta
Max Keeble's Big Move '01
Family Man '00
What Lies Beneath '00

Mark Valley (1964-)
The Next Best Thing '00
The Siege '98
George Wallace '97

Alida Valli (1921-)
A Month by the Lake '95
Le Jupon Rouge '87
Beyond Erotica '79
Suspiria '77
The Cassandra Crossing '76
1900 '76
Lisa and the Devil '75
The Tempter '74
The Spider's Stratagem '70
Oedipus Rex '67
The Castilian '63
The Horror Chamber of Dr. Faustus '59
Il Grido '57
The Night Heaven Fell '57
Senso '54
Walk Softly, Stranger '50
The Third Man '49

The Miracle of the Bells '48
The Paradine Case '47
We the Living '42

Frankie Valli (1937-)
Witness to the Mob '98
Eternity '90
Modern Love '90
Dirty Laundry '87

Romolo Valli (1925-80)
Bobby Deerfield '77
A Fistful of Dynamite '72
The Garden of the Finzi-Continis '71
Boom! '68
The Girl with a Suitcase '60

Virginia Valli (1898-1968)
Night Life in Reno '31
Lost Zeppelin '29
The Shock '23

Rick Vallin (1919-77)
The Last of the Redmen '47
Corregidor '43
King of the Stallions '42
The Panther's Claw '42

Raf Vallone (1917-)
The Godfather, Part 3 '90
Christopher Columbus '85
The Scarlet & the Black '83
Time to Die '83
Lion of the Desert '81
An Almost Perfect Affair '79
The Greek Tycoon '78
The Other Side of Midnight '77
The Girl in Room 2A '76
The Human Factor '75
Rosebud '75
That Lucky Touch '75
Ricco '74
Honor Thy Father '73
A Gunfight '71
The Italian Job '69
Nevada Smith '66
Harlow '65
El Cid '61
Phaedra '61
Two Women '61
Anna '51
The Forbidden Christ '50
Bitter Rice '49

Vampira
Night of the Ghouls '59
Plan 9 from Outer Space '56

Bobby Van (1930-80)
Bunco '83
Escape from Planet Earth '67
Navy vs. the Night Monsters '66
The Affairs of Dobie Gillis '53
Kiss Me Kate '53
Small Town Girl '53

Willeke Van Ammelrooy (1944-)
Antonia's Line '95
The Lift '85
Fatal Error '83

Joan Van Ark (1943-)
When the Dark Man Calls '95
Tainted Blood '93
Red Flag: The Ultimate Game '81
Frogs '72

Ingrid van Bergen
The Vampire Happening '71
The Avenger '60

Lewis Van Bergen
Pinocchio's Revenge '96
The Relic '96
Street Knight '93
False Arrest '92
Bugsy '91
Rage of Honor '87
South of Reno '87
Overthrow '82

Lee Van Cleef (1925-89)
Thieves of Fortune '89
Speed Zone '88
Armed Response '86
Jungle Raiders '85
Codename: Wildgeese '84
Escape from New York '81
Hard Way '80
Octagon '80
The Squeeze '80
The Rip Off '78
The Squeeze '78
Fatal Chase '77
Perfect Killer '77
Escape from Death Row '76
The Stranger and the Gunfighter '76
God's Gun '75
Kid Vengeance '75
Mean Frank and Crazy Tony '75
Take a Hard Ride '75
Commandos '73
The Grand Duel '73
Bad Man's River '72
New Mafia Boss '72
Captain Apache '71
El Condor '70
Beyond the Law '68
The Good, the Bad and the Ugly '67
For a Few Dollars More '65
The Man Who Shot Liberty Valance '62
Ride Lonesome '59
The Bravados '58
The Young Lions '58
China Gate '57
Gunfight at the O.K. Corral '57
The Tin Star '57
The Conqueror '56
It Conquered the World '56
Pardners '56
Tribute to a Bad Man '56
Big Combo '55
A Man Alone '55
Gypsy Colt '54
The Beast from 20,000 Fathoms '53
High Noon '52
Kansas City Confidential '52
The Lawless Breed '52

Ron Van Cliff
Way of the Black Dragon '81
Fist of Fear, Touch of Death '80

Jean-Claude Van Damme (1961-)
Replicant '01
Desert Heat '99
Universal Soldier: The Return '99
Knock Off '98
Legionnaire '98
Double Team '97
Maximum Risk '96
The Quest '96
Sudden Death '95
Street Fighter '94
Timecop '94
Hard Target '93
Last Action Hero '93
Nowhere to Run '93
Universal Soldier '92
Double Impact '91
Death Warrant '90
Lionheart '90
Cyborg '89
Kickboxer '89
Black Eagle '88
Bloodsport '88
No Retreat, No Surrender '86
Monaco Forever '83

Monique Van De Ven (1952-)
The Man Inside '90
Paint It Black '89
Amsterdamned '88
The Assault '86
Katie Tippel '75
Turkish Delight '73

Sylvie van den Elsen
La Vie de Boheme '93
L'Argent '83

James Van Der Beek (1977-)
Jay and Silent Bob Strike Back '01
Texas Rangers '01
Harvest '99
Varsity Blues '98
I Love You, I Love You Not '97
Angus '95

Nadine Van Der Velde
After Midnight '89
Shadow Dancing '88
Munchies '87
Critters '86

Diana Van Der Vlis (1935-2001)
Lovespell '79
The Incident '67
X: The Man with X-Ray Eyes '63
Girl in Black Stockings '57

Frederique van der Wal
Wild Wild West '99
Two Girls and a Guy '98

Trish Van Devere (1945-)
Deadly Currents '93
Messenger of Death '88
Hollywood Vice Sqaud '86
Uphill All the Way '85
All God's Children '80
The Changeling '80
The Hearse '80
Mayflower: The Pilgrims' Adventure '79
Movie, Movie '78
Stalk the Wild Child '76
Savage Is Loose '74
The Day of the Dolphin '73
Where's Poppa? '70

Casper Van Dien (1968-)
Danger Beneath the Sea '02
Kill Shot '01
Chasing Destiny '00
Cutaway '00
Python '00
The Collectors '99
The Omega Code '99
Partners '99
Shark Attack '99
Sleepy Hollow '99
Thrill Seekers '99
Modern Vampires '98
On the Border '98
Tarzan and the Lost City '98
James Dean: Live Fast, Die Young '97
Starship Troopers '97
Beastmaster 3: The Eye of Braxus '95
Night Eyes 4: Fatal Passion '95

Mamie Van Doren (1931-)
Slackers '02
Voyage to the Planet of Prehistoric Women '68
Las Vegas Hillbillys '66
Navy vs. the Night Monsters '66
Three Nuts in Search of a Bolt '64
Born Reckless '59
Girls' Town '59
High School Confidential '58
Teacher's Pet '58
Girl in Black Stockings '57
Francis Joins the WACs '54

John van Dreelen (1922-92)
Becoming Colette '92
Too Hot to Handle '76
Von Ryan's Express '65
13 Ghosts '60
A Time to Love & a Time to Die '58

Granville Van Dusen
The Rose and the Jackal '90
Hotline '82
The Wild and the Free '80
Breaking Up '78
War Between the Tates '76

Barry Van Dyke
Foxfire Light '82
Ants '77

Conny Van Dyke
Framed '75
Hell's Angels '69 '69

Dick Van Dyke (1925-)
Dick Tracy '90
Country Girl '82
The Runner Stumbles '79
Cold Turkey '71
The Comic '69
Chitty Chitty Bang Bang '68
Never a Dull Moment '68
Divorce American Style '67
Lt. Robin Crusoe, U.S.N. '66
Mary Poppins '64
Bye, Bye, Birdie '63

Jerry Van Dyke (1932-)
Death Blow '87
Run If You Can '87
McLintock! '63
The Courtship of Eddie's Father '62

Peter Van Eyck (1911-69)
The Spy Who Came in from the Cold '65
Dr. Mabuse vs. Scotland Yard '64
The Brain '62
The Thousand Eyes of Dr. Mabuse '60
Wages of Fear '55
Five Graves to Cairo '43

John Van Eyssen (1922-95)
The Horror of Dracula '58
Men of Sherwood Forest '57
Quatermass 2 '57
Four Sided Triangle '53

Jo Van Fleet (1919-96)
The Tenant '76
Satan's School for Girls '73
I Love You, Alice B. Toklas! '68
Cool Hand Luke '67
Gunfight at the O.K. Corral '57
The King and Four Queens '56
I'll Cry Tomorrow '55
The Rose Tattoo '55
East of Eden '54

Harry Van Gorkum
Dragonheart: A New Beginning '00
Escape under Pressure '00

Kevin Van Hentenryck
Basket Case 3: The Progeny '92
Basket Case 2 '90
Brain Damage '88
Basket Case '82

Brian Van Holt
Black Hawk Down '01
Whipped '00

Patrick Van Horn
Three to Tango '99
Free Enterprise '98
Ivory Tower '97
Swingers '96

Fredja Van Huet
The Delivery '99
Character '97

Merete Van Kamp
Lethal Woman '88
Princess Daisy '83

Jon Van Ness
Hospital Massacre '81
Tourist Trap '79

Peter Van Norden
Casualties of Love: The "Long Island Lolita" Story '93
The Accused '88
Scandal in a Small Town '88

Nina Van Pallandt (1932-)
Jungle Warriors '84
Sword & the Sorcerer '82
Cutter's Way '81
American Gigolo '79
Diary of a Young Comic '79
Quintet '79
A Wedding '78
Assault on Agathon '75
The Long Goodbye '73

Dick Van Patten (1928-)
Big Brother Trouble '00
Love Is All There Is '96
Demolition High '95
A Dangerous Place '94
Robin Hood: Men in Tights '93
Body Trouble '92
Final Embrace '92
The New Adventures of Pippi Longstocking '88
Spaceballs '87
The Midnight Hour '86
Diary of a Teenage Hitchhiker '82
High Anxiety '77
Freaky Friday '76
Gus '76
Soylent Green '73
Superdad '73
Westworld '73
Beware! The Blob '72
Joe Kidd '72
Zachariah '70
Charly '68
Psychomania '63

James Van Patten (1956-)
Hyper Space '89
Twisted Justice '89
The Dirty Dozen: The Deadly Mission '87
Nightforce '86
Young Warriors '83
Roller Boogie '79
Tennessee Stallion '78
Freaky Friday '76

Joyce Van Patten (1934-)
Breathing Lessons '94
Trust Me '89
Monkey Shines '88
Billy Galvin '86
Crawlspace '86
The Rumor Mill '86
The Falcon and the Snowman '85
St. Elmo's Fire '85
Eleanor: First Lady of the World '82
The Bad News Bears '76
Mame '74
The Stranger Within '74
Housewife '72
Thumb Tripping '72
The Trouble with Girls (and How to Get into It) '69
I Love You, Alice B. Toklas! '68

Nels Van Patten
Mirror Images '91
One Last Run '89
Grotesque '87
Summer School '87

Timothy Van Patten (1959-)
Curse 4: The Ultimate Sacrifice '90
Catacombs '89
The Wrong Guys '88
Dress Gray '86
Zone Troopers '84
Escape from El Diablo '83
Class of 1984 '82

Vincent Van Patten (1957-)
The Break '95
Payback '90
The Victory '88
The Dirty Dozen: The Deadly Mission '87
Rooster: Spurs of Death! '83
Hell Night '81
Survival Run '80
Rock 'n' Roll High School '79
Chino '75
Charley and the Angel '73

Mario Van Peebles (1958-)
Ali '01
Guardian '01
The Guardian '00
Sally Hemings: An American Scandal '00
Blowback '99
Judgment Day '99
Raw Nerve '99
Crazy Six '98
Love Kills '98
Mama Flora's Family '98
Los Locos Posse '97
Protector '97
Stag '97
Gang in Blue '96
Riot in the Streets '96
Solo '96
Panther '95
Highlander: The Final Dimension '94
Urban Crossfire '94
Full Eclipse '93
Gunmen '93
Posse '93
New Jack City '91
Identity Crisis '90
Jaws: The Revenge '87
Heartbreak Ridge '86
Hot Shot '86
Last Resort '86
Rappin' '85
South Bronx Heroes '85
Delivery Boys '84
Exterminator 2 '84
Sweet Sweetback's Baadasssss Song '71

Megan Van Peebles
South Bronx Heroes '85
Sweet Sweetback's Baadasssss Song '71

Melvin Van Peebles (1932-)
Love Kills '98
Calm at Sunset '96
Gang in Blue '96
Riot in the Streets '96
Fist of the North Star '95
Terminal Velocity '94
Posse '93
Boomerang '92
O.C. and Stiggs '87
Sophisticated Gents '81
Sweet Sweetback's Baadasssss Song '71

Edward Van Sloan (1881-1964)
The Mask of Diijon '46
Before I Hang '40
Danger on the Air '38
Dracula's Daughter '36
A Shot in the Dark '35
Death Takes a Holiday '34
Manhattan Melodrama '34
The Death Kiss '33
Deluge '33
The Mummy '32
Dracula '31
Frankenstein '31

Deborah Van Valkenburgh (1952-)
Firestarter 2: Rekindled '02
Chasing Destiny '00
Free Enterprise '98
Mean Guns '97
Erik '90
One Man Out '89
Phantom of the Ritz '88
Python Wolf '88
Rampage '87
A Bunny's Tale '85
Going for the Gold: The Bill Johnson Story '85
Streets of Fire '84
King of the Mountain '81
The Warriors '79

Monique Van Vooren (1933-)
Sugar Cookies '77
Andy Warhol's Frankenstein '74
Ash Wednesday '73

F/X '86
A.D. '85
Terminal Choice '85
The Cotton Club '84
Wolfen '81

Wanda Ventham (1939-)
Out of the Shadows '88
Captain Kronos: Vampire Hunter '74
Blood Beast Terror '67

John Ventimiglia
Mickey Blue Eyes '99
Row Your Boat '98
The Funeral '96
Girls Town '95
Angela '94

Vincent Ventresca (1965-)
The Learning Curve '01
Love & Sex '00

Clyde Ventura
Gator Bait '73
Bury Me an Angel '71

Jesse Ventura (1951-)
Ricochet '91
Abraxas: Guardian of the Universe '90
Boxcar Blues '90
Repossessed '90
Thunderground '89
Predator '87
The Running Man '87

Lino Ventura (1919-87)
Sword of Gideon '86
The Medusa Touch '78
Les Aventuriers '77
Pain in the A— '77
The Slap '76
The French Detective '75
Happy New Year '73
Jailbird's Vacation '65
The Three Penny Opera '62
Mistress of the World '59
Modigliani '58
Grisbi '53

Richard Venture (1923-)
Series 7: The Contenders '01
Red Corner '97
Truman '95
Scent of a Woman '92
Heartbreak Ridge '86
Street Hawk '84
Missing '82
The Effect of Gamma Rays on Man-in-the-Moon Marigolds '73

Silvana Venturelli
The Lickerish Quartet '70
Camille 2000 '69

Massimo Venturiello
My Wonderful Life '90
Rorret '87

Billy Vera
The Doors '91
Finish Line '89

Victoria Vera
A Man of Passion '88
Monster Dog '82

Vera-Ellen (1920-81)
White Christmas '54
The Belle of New York '52
Happy Go Lovely '51
Love Happy '50
Three Little Words '50
On the Town '49
Words and Music '48
Wonder Man '45

Gwen Verdon (1925-2000)
The Dress Code '99
In Cold Blood '96
Marvin's Room '96
Oldest Confederate Widow Tells All '95
Alice '90
Cocoon: The Return '88
Nadine '87
Cocoon '85
The Cotton Club '84
Legs '83
Damn Yankees '58
The Merry Widow '52

Carlo Verdone
Iris Blond '98
Acqua e Sapone '83

Maribel Verdu
Y Tu Mama Tambien '01
Goya in Bordeaux '99
Belle Epoque '92
Lovers: A True Story '90

Elena Verdugo (1926-)
Boss' Son '78
Cyrano de Bergerac '50
The Big Sombrero '49
Little Giant '46
House of Frankenstein '44
Weird Woman/Frozen Ghost '44
The Moon and Sixpence '43

Peter Vere-Jones
Meet the Feebles '89 (V)
Bad Taste '88

Ben Vereen (1946-)
Why Do Fools Fall in Love? '98
Once Upon a Forest '93 (V)
Intruders '92
The Kid Who Loved Christmas '90
Mother Goose Rock 'n' Rhyme '90
Buy & Cell '89
A.D. '85
The Zoo Gang '85
Breakin' Through '84
The Jesse Owens Story '84
Puss 'n Boots '84
Pippin '81
All That Jazz '79
Roots '77
Funny Lady '75
Gas-s-s-s! '70

Tom Verica
From the Earth to the Moon '98
Lost in the Bermuda Triangle '98
The Assassination File '96
Breach of Conduct '94
800 Leagues Down the Amazon '93
Die Hard 2: Die Harder '90

Bernard Verley (1939-)
Lucie Aubrac '98
Helas pour Moi '94
Pas Tres Catholique '93
Phantom of Liberty '74
Chloe in the Afternoon '72
The Milky Way '68

Harold Vermilyea
Emperor Waltz '48
Sorry, Wrong Number '48

Denise Vernac
Unnatural '52
The Mask of Diijon '46

Karen Verne (1918-67)
The Seventh Cross '44
All Through the Night '42
Sherlock Holmes and the Secret Weapon '42
Kings Row '41
Underground '41

Guy Verney (1915-70)
Martin Luther '53
Fame Is the Spur '47
This Happy Breed '47

Pierre Vernier
Under the Sand '00
Betty '92
Mama, There's a Man in Your Bed '89

Jerry Verno (1895-1975)
The Belles of St. Trinian's '53
Sidewalks of London '38
Non-Stop New York '37
Young and Innocent '37
The 39 Steps '35

Anne Vernon
Therese & Isabelle '67
Umbrellas of Cherbourg '64

Glenn Vernon
I Bury the Living '58
Bedlam '45

Howard Vernon (1914-96)
Revenge in the House of Usher '82
Zombie Lake '80
The Demons '74
The Perverse Countess '73
Dr. Orloff's Invisible Horror '72
The Screaming Dead '72
Virgin among the Living Dead '71
Orloff and the Invisible Man '70
Castle of the Creeping Flesh '68
Triple Cross '67
Alphaville '65
The Diabolical Dr. Z '65
The Train '65
The Awful Dr. Orloff '62
Bob le Flambeur '55
La Silence de la Mer '47

John Vernon (1932-)
Malicious '95
Hostage for a Day '94
Sodbusters '94
Bail Out '90
Mob Story '90
Terminal Exposure '89
War Bus Commando '89
Deadly Stranger '88
Dixie Lanes '88
I'm Gonna Git You Sucka '88
Killer Klowns from Outer Space '88
Blue Monkey '87
Ernest Goes to Camp '87
Nightstick '87
Doin' Time '85
Fraternity Vacation '85
The Blood of Others '84
Jungle Warriors '84
Chained Heat '83
Curtains '83
Savage Streets '83
Herbie Goes Bananas '80
National Lampoon's Animal House '78
Angela '77
Golden Rendezvous '77
Journey '77
A Special Day '77
The Outlaw Josey Wales '76
The Virginia Hill Story '76
Brannigan '75
Sweet Movie '75
The Barbary Coast '74
The Black Windmill '74
W '74
Charley Varrick '73
Hunter '73
Dirty Harry '71
Justine '69
Tell Them Willie Boy Is Here '69

Kate Vernon (1961-)
The Secret Life of Girls '99
Blackjack '97
Flood: A River's Rampage '97
Downdraft '96
Bloodknot '95
Probable Cause '95
The Sister-in-Law '95
Dangerous Touch '94
Soft Deceit '94
Malcolm X '92
Mob Story '90
Hostile Takeover '88
The Last of Philip Banter '87
Alphabet City '84
Roadhouse 66 '84

Richard Vernon (1925-97)
The Return of the Borrowers '96
The Human Factor '79
The Duchess of Duke Street '78
The Satanic Rites of Dracula '73
A Hard Day's Night '64
Tomb of Ligeia '64
The Servant '63
Village of the Damned '60

Wally Vernon (1905-70)
Square Dance Jubilee '51
Gunfire '50
California Joe '43
Broadway Serenade '39
Happy Landing '38

Christine Veronica
Party Incorporated '89
Love Notes '88

Cec Verrell
Three of Hearts '93
Mad at the Moon '92
Hell Comes to Frogtown '88
Eye of the Eagle '87
Silk '86

Odile Versois (1930-80)
Le Crabe Tambour '77
Cartouche '62
To Paris with Love '55

Veruschka
The Bride '85
Blow-Up '66

Arie Verveen
The Thin Red Line '98
Caught '96

Charlotte Very
Trois Couleurs: Bleu '93
A Tale of Winter '92

Bruno VeSota (1922-76)
Hell's Angels on Wheels '67
The Wild World of Batwoman '66
The Haunted Palace '63
Night Tide '63
The Choppers '61
Creature of the Walking Dead '60
Attack of the Giant Leeches '59
A Bucket of Blood '59
The Wasp Woman '59
Carnival Rock '57
Rock All Night '57
Teenage Doll '57
The Undead '57
The Female Jungle '56
The Gunslinger '56
Daughter of Horror '55
The Wild One '54

Edy Vessel
The Trojan Horse '62
Passionate Thief '60

Tricia Vessey (1972-)
Town and Country '01
On the Edge '00
Coming Soon '99
Ghost Dog: The Way of the Samurai '99
The Alarmist '98
Bean '97
Standoff '97

Ondrej Vetchy
Dark Blue World '01
Martha and I '91

Victoria Vetri (1944-)
Invasion of the Bee Girls '73
Group Marriage '72
When Dinosaurs Ruled the Earth '70

Karin Viard (1966-)
La Separation '98
The New Eve '98
The Separation '94
Delicatessen '92

Ronan Vibert
The Cat's Meow '01
Shadow of the Vampire '00
The Scarlet Pimpernel '99
The Scarlet Pimpernel 2: Mademoiselle Guillotine '99
The Scarlet Pimpernel 3: The Kidnapped King '99
The Buccaneers '95

Sid Vicious
The Filth and the Fury '99
Mr. Mike's Mondo Video '79

Martha Vickers (1925-71)
Big Bluff '55
The Big Sleep '46
The Man I Love '46

Yvette Vickers (1936-)
Evil Spirits '91
Beach Party '63
Attack of the Giant Leeches '59
Attack of the 50 Foot Woman '58
Reform School Girl '57

John Vickery
Deconstructing Sarah '94
Rapid Fire '92

Charles Victor (1896-1965)
The Pit and the Pendulum '61
Motor Patrol '50
The Woman in Question '50
San Demetrio, London '47
Seven Days' Leave '42
Contraband '40

Henry Victor (1892-1945)
Sherlock Holmes and the Secret Weapon '42
To Be or Not to Be '42
Underground Agent '42
King of the Zombies '41
Freaks '32
The Mummy '32
The Beloved Rogue '27

Katherine Victor (1928-)
The Wild World of Batwoman '66
House of the Black Death '65
Curse of the Stone Hand '64
Creature of the Walking Dead '60
Teenage Zombies '58
Mesa of Lost Women '52

Christina Vidal
Brink '98
Life with Mikey '93

Gil Vidal
Rape '80s
Night of the Howling Beast '75

Gore Vidal (1925-)
Gattaca '97
The Shadow Conspiracy '96
With Honors '94
Bob Roberts '92
Fellini's Roma '72

Henri Vidal (1919-59)
Voulez-Vous Danser avec Moi? '59
Just Another Pretty Face '58
Sois Belle et Tais-Toi '58
Une Parisienne '58
Fabiola '48

Lisa Vidal (1965-)
Active Stealth '99
Naked City: A Killer Christmas '98
The Wonderful Ice Cream Suit '98
Fall '97
I Like It Like That '94

Steven Vidler (1960-)
Child Star: The Shirley Temple Story '01
Two Hands '98
Napoleon '96 (V)
Encounter at Raven's Gate '88
Wrangler '88
The Good Wife '86
The Dunera Boys '85
Three's Trouble '85

Susan Vidler
The Woman in White '97
Naked '93

Florence Vidor (1895-1977)
Doomsday '28
The Grand Duchess and the Waiter '26
Are Parents People? '25
The Coming of Amos '25
The Marriage Circle '24
The Virginian '23
Beau Revel '21

Asia Vieira
Omen 4: The Awakening '91
The Good Mother '88

Vince Vieluf
Rat Race '01
Clay Pigeons '98
An American Werewolf in Paris '97

Abe Vigoda (1921-)
Just the Ticket '98
Witness to the Mob '98
A Brooklyn State of Mind '97
Good Burger '97
Love Is All There Is '96
Underworld '96
Jury Duty '95
Home of Angels '94
North '94
Sugar Hill '94
Batman: Mask of the Phantasm '93 (V)
Fist of Honor '92
Joe Versus the Volcano '90
Keaton's Cop '90
Look Who's Talking '89
Prancer '89
Plain Clothes '88
Vasectomy: A Delicate Matter '86
The Stuff '85
The Godfather 1902-1959: The Complete Epic '81
Great American Traffic Jam '80
The Cheap Detective '78
How to Pick Up Girls '78
The Godfather, Part 2 '74
Newman's Law '74
The Godfather '72

Robert Viharo (1939-)
Coldfire '90
Romero '89
Night Stalker '87
Happy Birthday, Gemini '80
Hide in Plain Sight '80
Kid from Not-So-Big '78
Bare Knuckles '77
Valley of the Dolls '67

Antonio Vilar
Gunslinger '70s
Stranger's Gold '71

Henri Vilbert
Ali Baba and the 40 Thieves '54
Manon '50

Marthe Villalonga
Ma Saison Preferee '93
Three Men and a Cradle '85
The Big Red One '80

Tom Villard (1954-94)
My Girl '91
Popcorn '89
Swimsuit '89
The Trouble with Dick '88
Heartbreak Ridge '86
One Crazy Summer '86
Weekend Warriors '86

Daniel Villarreal
Speed '94
American Me '92

Astrid Villaume
Pelle the Conqueror '88
Famous Five Get into Trouble '87

Herve Villechaize (1943-93)
Two Moon Junction '88
Rumpelstiltskin '82
Forbidden Zone '80
The One and Only '78
Return to Fantasy Island '77
The Man with the Golden Gun '74
Seizure '74
Greaser's Palace '72

James Villemaire
Dead Silence '96
Gate 2 '92
Matinee '92

Jacques Villeret (1951-)
The Dinner Game '98
The Favor, the Watch, & the Very Big Fish '92
Edith & Marcel '83
Bolero '82
Robert et Robert '78

Christopher Villiers
First Knight '95
Top Secret! '84

James Villiers (1933-98)
Wavelength '96
Let Him Have It '91
Mountains of the Moon '90
Fortunes of War '87
Mrs. Silly '85
The Scarlet Pimpernel '82
Asylum '72
The Ruling Class '72
Blood from the Mummy's Tomb '71
Nice Girl Like Me '69
The Nanny '65
Repulsion '65
King and Country '64
Eva '62

Jay Villiers
The Sculptress '97
Henry V '89

Pruitt Taylor Vince (1960-)
Simone '02
Nurse Betty '00
Mumford '99
The Legend of 1900 '98
The Break '97
The End of Violence '97
Beautiful Girls '96
Under the Hula Moon '95
City Slickers 2: The Legend of Curly's Gold '94
Heavy '94
Natural Born Killers '94
Nobody's Fool '94
Come See the Paradise '90
Jacob's Ladder '90
Mississippi Burning '88
Shy People '87

Alex Vincent (1982-)
My Family Treasure '93
Child's Play 2 '90
Wait until Spring, Bandini '90
Child's Play '88

Allen Vincent
After Midnight '33
Carnival Lady '33
Mystery of the Wax Museum '33

Brian Vincent
Blue Moon '00
Black Dog '98
Animal Room '95

Frank Vincent (1940-)
Gun Shy '00
Entropy '99
Undercurrent '99
Ten Benny '98
Tom Clancy's Netforce '98
Witness to the Mob '98
Cop Land '97
The Deli '97
Gotti '96
Grind '96
She's the One '96
West New York '96
Federal Hill '94
Jungle Fever '91
Goodfellas '90
Street Hunter '90
Raging Bull '80

Helene Vincent
The Count of Monte Cristo '99
Ma Vie en Rose '97
Trois Couleurs: Bleu '93
Life Is a Long Quiet River '88

Jan-Michael Vincent (1944-)
Buffalo 66 '97
Deadly Heroes '96
Red Line '96
Body Count '95
Ice Cream Man '95
Abducted 2: The Reunion '94
Dirty Games '93
Indecent Behavior '93
Midnight Witness '93
Animal Instincts '92
Beyond the Call of Duty '92
Hidden Obsession '92
Sins of Desire '92
The Divine Enforcer '91
Hangfire '91
Haunting Fear '91
In Gold We Trust '91
Raw Nerve '91
Xtro 2: The Second Encounter '91
Alienator '89
Demonstone '89
Deadly Embrace '88
The Hit List '88
Born in East L.A. '87
Enemy Territory '87
Last Plane Out '83
The Winds of War '83
Hard Country '81
The Return '80
Defiance '79
Big Wednesday '78
Hooper '78
Damnation Alley '77
Bite the Bullet '75
White Line Fever '75
Buster and Billie '74
Bandits '73
The World's Greatest Athlete '73
The Mechanic '72
Tribes '70
The Undefeated '69
Crossfire '67

June Vincent (1924-)
Clipped Wings '53
Colorado Sundown '52
The Creeper '48
Black Angel '46
Can't Help Singing '45
Here Come the Co-Eds '45
The Climax '44

Russ Vincent
Twilight in the Sierras '50
Heading for Heaven '47

Virginia Vincent (1924-)
The Hills Have Eyes '77
The Baby '72
Sweet November '68
Love with the Proper Stranger '63
I Want to Live! '58
Return of Dracula '58

Yves Vincent
Her and She and Him '69
Sins of Rome '54

Lee Ving (1950-)
Grave Secrets '89
Dudes '87
Scenes from the Goldmine '87
Clue '85
Streets of Fire '84
The Wild Life '84
Flashdance '83
Get Crazy '83

Steve Vinovich
The Swan Princess '94 (V)
Hollywood Boulevard 2 '89

Helen Vinson (1907-99)
The Thin Man Goes Home '44
Vogues of 1938 '37
King of the Damned '36
Transatlantic Tunnel '35
Broadway Bill '34
I Am a Fugitive from a Chain Gang '32
They Call It Sin '32

Alan Vint (1944-)
Ballad of Gregorio Cortez '83
Panic in Needle Park '75
Sniper '75
Badlands '74
Macon County Line '74
Unholy Rollers '72
The McMasters '70

Bill Vint
Marilyn: The Untold Story '80
Summertree '71

Jesse Vint (1940-)
I Come in Peace '90
Merchants of War '90
Dempsey '83
On the Line '83
Forbidden World '82
Death Sport '78
Black Oak Conspiracy '77
Bobbie Jo and the Outlaw '76
Bug '75
Macon County Line '74
Pigs '73

Gustav Vintas
Zero Tolerance '93
Drug Wars 2: The Cocaine Cartel '92
And You Thought Your Parents Were Weird! '91
Midnight '89
Tales from the Crypt '89
Vampire at Midnight '88
Lethal Weapon '87
Welcome Back Mr. Fox '83

Bobby Vinton (1935-)
Train Robbers '73
Big Jake '71
Surf Party '64

Ultra Violet
Superstar: The Life and Times of Andy Warhol '90
Simon, King of the Witches '71

Ian Virgo (1981-)
Band of Brothers '01
Black Hawk Down '01

Michael Visaroff (1892-1951)
Charlie Chan at the Wax Museum '40
Arizona Terror '31
Last Command '28

Sal Viscuso
Spaceballs '87
The Taking of Pelham One Two Three '74
M*A*S*H '70 (V)

Goran Visnjic (1972-)
Ice Age '02 (V)
The Deep End '01
Committed '99
Practical Magic '98
Welcome to Sarajevo '97

Angela Visser
Hot Under the Collar '91
Killer Tomatoes Eat France '91

Alex Vitale
Beyond the Door 3 '91
Urban Warriors '75

Antonella Vitale
The Church '98
Opera '88

Joseph (Joe) Vitale (1901-94)
Alias Jesse James '59
The Stranger Wore a Gun '53
Zombies on Broadway '44

Milly Vitale
War and Peace '56
The Seven Little Foys '55

Keith Vitali
American Kickboxer 1 '91
No Retreat, No Surrender 3: Blood Brothers '91
Revenge of the Ninja '83

Joe (Johnny) Viterelli (1941-)
See Spot Run '01
Shallow Hal '01
Mickey Blue Eyes '99
Analyze This '98
Facade '98
Mafia! '98
Out to Sea '97
American Strays '96
Eraser '96
Heaven's Prisoners '95
Machine Gun Blues '95
Bullets over Broadway '94
The Crossing Guard '94
The Firm '93
Ruby '92
Mobsters '91
State of Grace '90

Antoine Vitez
The Green Room '78
My Night at Maud's '69

Michel Vitold
Basileus Quartet '82
The Testament of Dr. Cordelier '59

Ray Vitte
Grambling's White Tiger '81
Sky Hei$t '75

Monica Vitti (1931-)
Immortal Bachelor '80
Tigers in Lipstick '80
An Almost Perfect Affair '79
Blonde in Black Leather '77
Phantom of Liberty '74
The Eclipse '66
Modesty Blaise '66
The Red Desert '64
L'Avventura '60

Viva (1942-)
Superstar: The Life and Times of Andy Warhol '90
State of Things '82
Forbidden Zone '80
Edie in Ciao! Manhattan '72
Play It Again, Sam '72

Sal Viviano
Black Roses '88
The Jitters '88

Floyd Vivino
Crazy People '90
Good Morning, Vietnam '87

Marina Vlady (1938-)
Son of Gascogne '95
Chimes at Midnight '67
Two or Three Things I Know about Her '66
The Unfaithfuls '60
Double Agents '59

Sandra Voe
The Winter Guest '97
Breaking the Waves '95
Body & Soul '93

Emmett Vogan (1893-1969)
Down Dakota Way '49
The Lady Confesses '45
Robot Pilot '41

Darlene Vogel (1962-)
Decoy '95
Ring of Steel '94
Back to the Future, Part 2 '89

Jack Vogel
Presumed Guilty '91
Lock 'n' Load '90

Mitch Vogel
Texas Detour '77
Born Innocent '74

Nikolas Vogel
The Inheritors '85
Dangerous Liaisons '60

Karl Michael Vogler
Deep End '70
The Blue Max '66

Ruediger Vogler (1942-)
Lisbon Story '94
Faraway, So Close! '93
Until the End of the World '91
Night Sun '90
Marianne and Juliane '82
The Wrong Move '78
Kings of the Road—In the Course of Time '76
Alice in the Cities '74

Joan Vohs (1931-2001)
Cry Vengeance '54
As You Were '51

Jon Voight (1938-)
Ali '01
Jack and the Beanstalk: The Real Story '01
Lara Croft: Tomb Raider '01
Pearl Harbor '01
Uprising '01
Zoolander '01
A Dog of Flanders '99
Noah's Ark '99
Enemy of the State '98
The General '98
Varsity Blues '98
Boys Will Be Boys '97
The Fixer '97
John Grisham's The Rainmaker '97
Most Wanted '97
U-Turn '97
Anaconda '96
Mission: Impossible '96
Rosewood '96
Convict Cowboy '95
Heat '95
The Tin Soldier '95
Rainbow Warrior '94
Return to Lonesome Dove '93
The Last of His Tribe '92
Eternity '90
Final Warning '90
Desert Bloom '86
Runaway Train '85
Table for Five '83
Lookin' to Get Out '82
The Champ '79
Coming Home '78
Conrack '74
The Odessa File '74
Deliverance '72
Catch-22 '70
Midnight Cowboy '69
Hour of the Gun '67

Vicki Volante
Angels' Wild Women '72
Brain of Blood '71
Horror of the Blood Monsters '70
Blood of Dracula's Castle '69

Gian Marie Volonte (1933-94)
Open Doors '89
Christ Stopped at Eboli '79
Lucky Luciano '74
Sacco & Vanzetti '71
A Bullet for the General '68
The Witch '66
For a Few Dollars More '65
A Fistful of Dollars '64
Journey Beneath the Desert '61
The Girl with a Suitcase '60

Phillipe Volter
The Five Senses '99
Trois Couleurs: Bleu '93
The Double Life of Veronique '91
Cyrano de Bergerac '90
The Music Teacher '88

Daniel von Bargen (1950-)
The Majestic '01
Disney's The Kid '00
O Brother Where Art Thou? '00
Shaft '00
The General's Daughter '99
Universal Soldier: The Return '99
The Postman '97
Stephen King's Thinner '96
Before and After '95
Lord of Illusions '95
Truman '95
Philadelphia '93

Wilhelm von Brinken (1881-1946)
Hidden Enemy '40
International Crime '37
King Kelly of the U.S.A. '34

Tomas von Bromssen
All Things Fair '95
Man from Mallorca '84

Erik von Detten (1982-)
The Princess Diaries '01
Brink '98
Leave It to Beaver '97
Top Dog '95
Toy Story '95 (V)

Lenny Von Dohlen (1958-)
Home Alone 3 '97
Entertaining Angels: The Dorothy Day Story '96
Bird of Prey '95
One Good Turn '95
Tollbooth '94
Eyes of the Beholder '92
Leaving Normal '92
Blind Vision '91
Love Kills '91
Dracula's Widow '88
Billy Galvin '86
Under the Biltmore Clock '85
Electric Dreams '84
Tender Mercies '83

Theodore von Eltz (1894-1964)
Confidential '35
High Gear '33
Drifting Souls '32
Strangers of the Evening '32
No Man's Law '27

Loni von Friedl
Journey to the Far Side of the Sun '69
The Blue Max '66

Rik von Nutter (1930-)
Tharus Son of Attila '87
Thunderball '65
Assignment Outer Space '61

Joel von Ornsteiner
Slashdance '89
Robot Holocaust '87

Heidi von Palleske
Cybercity '99
Shepherd '99
Falling Fire '97
Strip Search '97
White Light '90
Blind Fear '89
Dead Ringers '88

Gustav von Seyffertitz (1863-1943)
She '35
Mystery Liner '34
Rasputin and the Empress '33
Ambassador Bill '31
Dishonored '31
The Mysterious Lady '28
The Gaucho '27
The Bells '26
Don Juan '26
Sparrows '26
Down to Earth '17

Erich von Stroheim (1885-1957)
Napoleon '55
Unnatural '52
Sunset Boulevard '50
Portrait of an Assassin '49
The Mask of Diijon '46
Great Flamarion '45
Five Graves to Cairo '43
The North Star '43
So Ends Our Night '41
Grand Illusion '37
The Crime of Dr. Crespi '35
Crimson Romance '34
Fugitive Road '34
As You Desire Me '32
Lost Squadron '32
The Great Gabbo '29
The Wedding March '28
Foolish Wives '22
Blind Husbands '19
Heart of Humanity '18
Hearts of the World '18
Intolerance '16
The Birth of a Nation '15

Max von Sydow (1929-)
Minority Report '02
Druids '01

Sleepless *'01*
Nuremberg *'00*
Snow Falling on Cedars *'99*
Private Confessions *'98*
Solomon *'98*
What Dreams May Come *'98*
Hostile Waters *'97*
Hamsun *'96*
Jerusalem *'96*
Citizen X *'95*
Judge Dredd *'95*
The Last Place on Earth *'94*
The Silent Touch *'94*
The Bachelor *'93*
Needful Things *'93*
The Best Intentions *'92*
Zentropa *'92 (N)*
A Kiss Before Dying *'91*
The Ox *'91*
Until the End of the World *'91*
Awakenings *'90*
Father *'90*
Hiroshima: Out of the Ashes *'90*
Red King, White Knight *'89*
Pelle the Conqueror *'88*
Second Victory *'87*
The Wolf at the Door *'87*
Duet for One *'86*
Hannah and Her Sisters *'86*
Christopher Columbus *'85*
Code Name: Emerald *'85*
Kojak: The Belarus File *'85*
Quo Vadis *'85*
Dreamscape *'84*
Dune *'84*
Samson and Delilah *'84*
Target Eagle *'84*
Never Say Never Again *'83*
Strange Brew *'83*
Conan the Barbarian *'82*
Flight of the Eagle *'82*
Victory *'81*
Death Watch *'80*
Flash Gordon *'80*
Hurricane *'79*
Brass Target *'78*
The Exorcist 2: The Heretic *'77*
March or Die *'77*
The Desert of the Tartars *'76*
Foxtrot *'76*
Voyage of the Damned *'76*
Three Days of the Condor *'75*
The Ultimate Warrior *'75*
Steppenwolf *'74*
The Exorcist *'73*
The New Land *'73*
Embassy *'72*
The Emigrants *'72*
The Touch *'71*
The Night Visitor *'70*
The Passion of Anna *'70*
Hour of the Wolf *'68*
The Shame *'68*
Hawaii *'66*
The Quiller Memorandum *'66*
The Greatest Story Ever Told *'65*
The Winter Light *'62*
Through a Glass Darkly *'61*
The Virgin Spring *'59*
The Magician *'58*
Brink of Life *'57*
Wild Strawberries *'57*
The Seventh Seal *'56*
Miss Julie *'50*

Margarethe von Trotta (1942-)
Coup de Grace *'78*
Beware of a Holy Whore *'70*

Hans von Twardowski (1898-1958)
Dawn Express *'42*
Hangmen Also Die *'42*
The Cabinet of Dr. Caligari *'19*

Gustav von Wagenheim
Woman in the Moon *'29*
Nosferatu *'22*

Harry von Zell
Son of Paleface *'52*
The Strange Affair of Uncle Harry *'45*

Danielle von Zerneck
Living in Oblivion *'94*
Under the Boardwalk *'89*
Dangerous Curves *'88*
La Bamba *'87*
My Science Project *'85*

Peter Von Zerneck
A Foreign Affair *'48*
13 Rue Madeleine *'46*

Kurt Vonnegut, Jr.
Breakfast of Champions *'98*
Back to School *'86*

Lark Voorhies
How High *'01*
Def Jam's How to Be a Player *'97*

Zandor Vorkov
Brain of Blood *'71*
Dracula vs. Frankenstein *'71*

George Voskovec (1905-81)
The Boston Strangler *'68*
The Bravados *'58*
Twelve Angry Men *'57*
The 27th Day *'57*

Arnold Vosloo (1962-)
The Mummy Returns *'01*
The Mummy *'99*
Progeny *'98*
Diary of a Serial Killer *'97*
Zeus and Roxanne *'96*
Darkman 3: Die Darkman Die *'95*
Darkman 2: The Return of Durant *'94*
Hard Target *'93*
The Finishing Touch *'92*
Red Shoe Diaries 2: Double Dare *'92*
Living to Die *'91*
Reason to Die *'90*
The Rutanga Tapes *'90*
Act of Piracy *'89*
Steel Dawn *'87*

Frank Vosper
The Man Who Knew Too Much *'34*
Power *'34*

Yorgo Voyagis
Courage Mountain *'89*
The Bourne Identity *'88*
Frantic *'88*
The Little Drummer Girl *'84*
The Adventurers *'70*

Vlasta Vrana
Varian's War *'01*
Escape from Wildcat Canyon *'99*
Grey Owl *'99*
The Assignment *'97*
Night of the Demons 3 *'97*
The Reaper *'97*
Stranger in the House *'97*
Deadly Surveillance *'91*
Scanners 2: The New Order *'91*
Keeping Track *'86*

Ron Vreeken
Deathfight *'93*
Rage and Honor 2: Hostile Takeover *'93*

Frederick Vroom
The General *'26*
The Navigator *'24*

Spencer Vrooman
Man of the House *'95*
Pet Shop *'94*

Milena Vukotic (1930-)
Andy Warhol's Dracula *'74*
Phantom of Liberty *'74*
Act of Aggression *'73*
The Discreet Charm of the Bourgeoisie *'72*

Murvyn Vye (1913-76)
Al Capone *'59*
Green Fire *'55*
River of No Return *'54*
Pickup on South Street *'53*
The Road to Bali *'53*

A Connecticut Yankee in King Arthur's Court *'49*

Caitlin Wachs
Air Bud 4: Seventh Inning Fetch *'02*
Air Bud 3: World Pup *'00*
My Dog Skip *'99*

Gary Waddell
Chopper *'00*
Blue Fire Lady *'78*

Justine Waddell (1976-)
Wives and Daughters *'01*
Dracula 2000 *'00*
Great Expectations *'99*
Mansfield Park *'99*
Tess of the D'Urbervilles *'98*
The Woman in White *'97*
Catherine Cookson's The Moth *'96*

Steven Waddington (1968-)
Sleepy Hollow *'99*
Tarzan and the Lost City *'98*
Face *'97*
Ivanhoe *'97*
Carrington *'95*
Royal Deceit *'94*
Edward II *'92*
1492: Conquest of Paradise *'92*
The Last of the Mohicans *'92*

Russell Wade (1917-)
Sundown Riders *'48*
Shoot to Kill *'47*
The Body Snatcher *'45*
The Iron Major *'43*

Stuart Wade
Teenage Monster *'57*
Monster from the Ocean Floor *'54*

Julian Wadham (1958-)
High Heels and Low Lifes *'01*
Catherine Cookson's The Wingless Bird *'97*
A Merry War *'97*
The English Patient *'96*
The Secret Agent *'96*
The Madness of King George *'94*
Middlemarch *'93*
Mountbatten: The Last Viceroy *'86*

Henry Wadsworth (1974-)
Ceiling Zero *'35*
Evelyn Prentice *'34*
Applause *'29*

Tabitha Wady
Kevin & Perry Go Large *'00*
Berkeley Square *'98*

Michael Wager (1925-)
Jane Austen in Manhattan *'80*
Exodus *'60*
Hill 24 Doesn't Answer *'55*

Lyle Waggoner (1935-)
Wizards of the Demon Sword *'94*
Mind Trap *'91*
Dead Women in Lingerie *'90*
Robo-Chic *'89*
Surf 2 *'84*
Love Me Deadly *'76*
Journey to the Center of Time *'67*
Women of the Prehistoric Planet *'66*

Chuck Wagner
The Sisterhood *'88*
America 3000 *'86*

Fernando Wagner
Virgin Sacrifice *'59*
The Pearl *'48*

Jack Wagner (1959-)
Nowhere to Land *'00*
Dirty Little Secret *'98*
Trapped in Space *'94*

Play Murder for Me *'91*
Swimsuit *'89*

Lindsay Wagner (1949-)
Frog and Wombat *'98*
Contagious *'96*
Shattered Dreams *'94*
Treacherous Crossing *'92*
Nightmare at Bittercreek *'91*
Ricochet *'91*
Second Wind *'90*
The Flight *'89*
From the Dead of Night *'89*
The Taking of Flight 847: The Uli Derickson Story *'88*
Convicted *'86*
Martin's Day *'85*
Two Kinds of Love *'85*
Princess Daisy *'83*
Callie and Son *'81*
High Risk *'81*
Nighthawks *'81*
Scruples *'80*
The Incredible Journey of Dr. Meg Laurel *'79*
The Two Worlds of Jenny Logan *'79*
The Bionic Woman *'75*
The Paper Chase *'73*

Lou Wagner
Starry Night *'99*
Conquest of the Planet of the Apes *'72*

Natasha Gregson Wagner (1970-)
High Fidelity *'00*
Stranger than Fiction *'99*
Another Day in Paradise *'98*
First Love, Last Rites *'98*
Modern Vampires *'98*
Two Girls and a Guy *'98*
Urban Legend *'98*
Dogtown *'97*
Glam *'97*
Quiet Days in Hollywood *'97*
Lost Highway *'96*
Wes Craven Presents Mind Ripper *'95*
Dead Beat *'94*
Dragstrip Girl *'94*
Molly and Gina *'94*
The Substitute *'93*
Tainted Blood *'93*
Buffy the Vampire Slayer *'92*
Fathers and Sons *'92*

Robert Wagner (1930-)
Austin Powers 2: The Spy Who Shagged Me *'99*
Crazy in Alabama *'99*
Fatal Error *'99*
Play It to the Bone *'99*
Wild Things *'98*
Austin Powers: International Man of Mystery *'97*
Parallel Lives *'94*
Dragon: The Bruce Lee Story *'93*
False Arrest *'92*
The Player *'92*
Delirious *'91*
This Gun for Hire *'90*
Around the World in 80 Days *'89*
Indiscreet *'88*
Windmills of the Gods *'88*
To Catch a King *'84*
Curse of the Pink Panther *'83*
I Am the Cheese *'83*
Trail of the Pink Panther *'82*
The Concorde: Airport '79 *'79*
Pearl *'78*
Midway *'76*
Abduction of St. Anne *'75*
Death at Love House *'75*
The Towering Inferno *'74*
The Affair *'73*
The Streets of San Francisco *'72*

Madame Sin *'71*
Winning *'69*
Harper *'66*
The Pink Panther *'64*
The Longest Day *'62*
War Lover *'62*
The Hunters *'58*
Stopover Tokyo *'57*
Between Heaven and Hell *'56*
The Mountain *'56*
Broken Lance *'54*
Prince Valiant *'54*
Beneath the 12-Mile Reef *'53*
Titanic *'53*
Stars and Stripes Forever *'52*
What Price Glory? *'52*
Let's Make It Legal *'51*
The Halls of Montezuma *'50*

Thomas Wagner
Marilyn & Bobby: Her Final Affair *'94*
Dead On *'93*
The Drifter *'88*

Elsie Wagstaff
Whistle down the Wind *'61*
Saturday Night and Sunday Morning *'60*

Yuen Wah
Supercop *'92*
Dragons Forever *'88*

Ken Wahl (1957-)
The Favor *'92*
The Taking of Beverly Hills *'91*
Omega Syndrome *'87*
The Gladiator *'86*
The Dirty Dozen: The Next Mission *'85*
Purple Hearts *'84*
Treasure of the Yankee Zephyr *'83*
Jinxed *'82*
The Soldier *'82*
Fort Apache, the Bronx *'81*
Running Scared *'79*
Wanderers *'79*

Donnie Wahlberg (1969-)
Band of Brothers *'01*
Purgatory *'99*
The Sixth Sense *'99*
Never 2 Big *'98*
Southie *'98*
Black Circle Boys *'97*
Body Count *'97*
Ransom *'96*

Mark Wahlberg (1971-)
Planet of the Apes *'01*
Rock Star *'01*
The Perfect Storm *'00*
The Yards *'00*
The Corruptor *'99*
Three Kings *'99*
The Big Hit *'98*
Boogie Nights *'97*
Fear *'96*
Traveller *'96*
The Basketball Diaries *'94*
Renaissance Man *'94*
The Substitute *'93*

Edward (Robert Towne) Wain
The Last Woman on Earth *'61*
Creature from the Haunted Sea *'60*

James Wainwright (1938-99)
Mission Manila *'87*
Survivors *'83*
Warlords of the 21st Century *'82*
A Woman Called Moses *'78*
Joe Kidd *'72*
Jigsaw *'71*
The President's Plane Is Missing *'71*

Loudon Wainwright, III
Jacknife *'89*
The Slugger's Wife *'85*

Liam Waite
John Carpenter's Ghosts of Mars *'01*
Second Skin *'00*
Simpatico *'99*

Ralph Waite (1928-)
Homeward Bound 2: Lost in San Francisco *'96 (V)*
Sin and Redemption *'94*
Sioux City *'94*
Cliffhanger *'93*
The Bodyguard *'92*
Crash and Burn *'90*
A Day for Thanks on Walton's Mountain *'82*
Gentleman Bandit *'81*
Angel City *'80*
On the Nickel *'80*
Red Alert *'77*
Girls on the Road *'73*
The Stone Killer *'73*
The Sporting Club *'72*
Chato's Land *'71*
The Grissom Gang *'71*
Lawman *'71*
Five Easy Pieces *'70*
Cool Hand Luke *'67*

Thomas G. Waites
McBain *'91*
Verne Miller *'88*
The Clan of the Cave Bear *'86*
The Thing *'82*
And Justice for All *'79*
On the Yard *'79*
The Warriors *'79*

Tom Waits (1949-)
Mystery Men *'99*
Short Cuts *'93*
Bram Stoker's Dracula *'92*
At Play in the Fields of the Lord *'91*
Queens Logic *'91*
Cold Feet *'89*
Mystery Train *'89 (V)*
Shakedown *'88*
Candy Mountain *'87*
Ironweed *'87*
Down by Law *'86*
The Cotton Club *'84*
The Outsiders *'83*
Rumble Fish *'83*

Akiko Wakabayashi (1941-)
You Only Live Twice *'67*
What's Up, Tiger Lily? *'66*
Dagora, the Space Monster *'65*
Ghidrah the Three Headed Monster *'65*
King Kong vs. Godzilla *'63*

Ayako Wakao (1933-)
An Actor's Revenge *'63*
Drifting Weeds *'59*
A Geisha *'53*

Tomisaburo Wakayama (1929-92)
Shogun Assassin *'80*
The Bad News Bears Go to Japan *'78*
Phoenix *'78*
Baby Cart 1: Lend a Child...Lend an Arm *'72*
Baby Cart 4: Heart of a Parent...Heart of a Child *'72*
Baby Cart at the River Styx *'72*
Baby Cart to Hades *'72*

Hugh Wakefield (1971-)
Blithe Spirit *'45*
The Man Who Knew Too Much *'34*

Deborah Wakeham (1955-)
Starlight *'97*
House of the Rising Sun *'87*
Covergirl *'83*
Middle Age Crazy *'80*

Jimmy Wakely (1914-82)
Lonesome Trail *'55*
Silver Star *'55*
Brand of Fear *'49*
Range Renegades *'48*

Anton Walbrook (1900-67)
Saint Joan *'57*
Lola Montes *'55*
La Ronde *'51*
The Queen of Spades *'49*
The Red Shoes *'48*
The Life and Death of Colonel Blimp *'43*
Dangerous Moonlight *'41*
The Forty-Ninth Parallel *'41*
Gaslight *'40*

Raymond Walburn (1887-1969)
Key to the City *'50*
Riding High *'50*
Hail the Conquering Hero *'44*
The Desperadoes *'43*
Louisiana Purchase *'41*
Christmas in July *'40*
It Could Happen to You *'39*
Let Freedom Ring *'39*
Thin Ice *'37*
Born to Dance *'36*
Mr. Deeds Goes to Town *'36*
The Count of Monte Cristo *'34*
Lady by Choice *'34*

Gregory Walcott (1928-)
Ed Wood *'94*
Joe Kidd *'72*
Prime Cut *'72*
Plan 9 from Outer Space *'56*
Texas Lady *'56*
Battle Cry *'55*
Above and Beyond *'53*

John Walcutt
Roseanne: An Unauthorized Biography *'94*
Return *'88*

Lynette Walden
Saved by the Light *'95*
Almost Blue *'93*
The Silencer *'92*

Robert Walden (1943-)
Murderer's Keep *'88*
Perry Mason: The Case of the Lost Love *'87*
Memorial Day *'83*
Enola Gay: The Men, the Mission, the Atomic Bomb *'80*
Blue Sunshine *'78*
Larry *'74*
Our Time *'74*
Everything You Always Wanted to Know about Sex (But Were Afraid to Ask) *'72*
Bloody Mama *'70*

Shawna Waldron (1982-)
Change of Heart *'98*
Mr. Headmistress *'98*
The American President *'95*
Little Giants *'94*

Ethel Wales (1898-1952)
Border Vigilantes *'41*
The Gladiator *'38*
Under Montana Skies *'30*
Made for Love *'26*

Wally Wales (1895-1980)
Fighting Seabees *'44*
Bad Man of Deadwood *'41*
Carson City Kid *'40*
The Trigger Trio *'37*
Gun Play *'36*
Danger Trails *'35*
The Miracle Rider *'35*
Powdersmoke Range *'35*
Rustlers of Red Dog *'35*
Way of the West *'35*
Deadwood Pass *'33*
Lone Bandit *'33*
Sagebrush Trail *'33*
Desert of the Lost *'27*

Sonya Walger
All the King's Men *'99*
Heat of the Sun *'99*
Noah's Ark *'99*

Christopher Walken (1943-)
Scotland, PA *'02*
The Affair of the Necklace *'01*
America's Sweethearts *'01*
Joe Dirt *'01*
Kiss Toledo Goodbye *'00*
The Eternal *'99*
The External *'99*
The Prophecy 3: The Ascent *'99*
Sarah, Plain and Tall: Winter's End *'99*
Sleepy Hollow *'99*
Vendetta *'99*
Antz *'98 (V)*
Blast from the Past *'98*
Illuminata *'98*
New Rose Hotel *'98*
Mouse Hunt *'97*
The Prophecy 2: Ashtown *'97*
Suicide Kings *'97*
Basquiat *'96*
Excess Baggage *'96*
The Funeral *'96*
Last Man Standing *'96*
Touch *'96*
The Addiction *'95*
Nick of Time *'95*
The Prophecy *'95*
Things to Do in Denver When You're Dead *'95*
Wild Side *'95*
Pulp Fiction *'94*
Search and Destroy *'94*
A Business Affair *'93*
Day of Atonement *'93*
Sarah, Plain and Tall: Skylark *'93*
Scam *'93*
True Romance *'93*
Wayne's World 2 *'93*
Batman Returns *'92*
All-American Murder *'91*
The Comfort of Strangers *'91*
McBain *'91*
Mistress *'91*
Sarah, Plain and Tall *'91*
King of New York *'90*
Communion *'89*
Biloxi Blues *'88*
Homeboy *'88*
The Milagro Beanfield War *'88*
Deadline *'87*
At Close Range *'86*
A View to a Kill *'85*
Brainstorm *'83*
Dead Zone *'83*
Who Am I This Time? *'82*
The Dogs of War *'81*
Heaven's Gate *'81*
Pennies from Heaven *'81*
Shoot the Sun Down *'81*
Last Embrace *'79*
The Deer Hunter *'78*
Annie Hall *'77*
Roseland *'77*
Next Stop, Greenwich Village *'76*
The Sentinel *'76*
Mind Snatchers *'72*
The Anderson Tapes *'71*

Ally Walker (1961-)
Happy, Texas *'99*
Kazaam *'96*
Bed of Roses *'95*
Someone to Die For *'95*
While You Were Sleeping *'95*
When the Bough Breaks *'93*
The Seventh Coin *'92*
Singles *'92*
Universal Soldier *'92*

Amanda Walker
Charles & Diana: A Palace Divided *'93*
Heat and Dust *'82*

Arnetia Walker (1961-)
Love Crimes *'92*
Scenes from the Class Struggle in Beverly Hills *'89*
The Wizard of Speed and Time *'88*

Bill Walker
The Mask *'61*
No Time for Romance *'48*

Cheryl Walker
Identity Unknown *'45*
Stage Door Canteen *'43*

Clint Walker (1927-)
Small Soldiers *'98 (V)*
The Gambler Returns: The Luck of the Draw *'93*
Mysterious Island of Beautiful Women *'79*
Snowbeast *'77*
The White Buffalo *'77*
Baker's Hawk *'76*
Scream of the Wolf *'74*
The Bounty Man *'72*
Deadly Harvest *'72*
Pancho Villa *'72*
Yuma *'70*
The Dirty Dozen *'67*
Maya *'66*
Night of the Grizzly *'66*
None But the Brave *'65*

Eamonn Walker
Othello *'01*
Once in the Life *'00*
Unbreakable *'00*

Eric Walker (1970-)
And You Thought Your Parents Were Weird! *'91*
The Ewoks: Battle for Endor *'85*
The Ewok Adventure *'84*

Fiona Walker
The Asphyx *'72*
Jude the Obscure *'71*

Helen Walker (1920-68)
Big Combo *'55*
Impact *'49*
Call Northside 777 *'48*
People Are Funny *'46*
Brewster's Millions *'45*
Murder, He Says *'45*
Abroad with Two Yanks *'44*

Jimmie Walker (1947-)
Frankenstein Sings...The Movie *'95*
Open Season *'95*
Invasion of the Space Preachers *'90*
Going Bananas *'88*
My African Adventure *'87*
Doin' Time *'85*
Water *'85*
Airplane! *'80*
B.A.D. Cats *'80*
The Concorde: Airport '79 *'79*
Let's Do It Again *'75*

John Walker
The Alien Factor *'78*
Broken Hearts of Broadway *'23*

Jonathan Walker
Finding North *'97 (V)*
American Blue Note *'89*

Justin Walker
Boltneck *'98*
Born Bad *'97*

Kathryn Walker (1943-)
Dangerous Game *'90*
The Murder of Mary Phagan *'87*
Uncle Tom's Cabin *'87*
Private Contentment *'83*
Special Bulletin *'83*
Neighbors *'81*
Whale for the Killing *'81*
Rich Kids *'79*
Girlfriends *'78*
The Winds of Kitty Hawk *'78*
Slap Shot *'77*
Blade *'72*

Kerry Walker (1948-)
A Little Bit of Soul *'97*
Road to Nhill *'97*
Cosi *'95*
The Piano *'93*

Kim Walker
Heathers *'89*
Deadly Weapon *'88*

Liza Walker
Wavelength *'96*
Buddy's Song *'91*
Twisted Obsession *'90*

Marcy Walker
Talking about Sex *'94*
Midnight's Child *'93*

Mark Walker
Random Encounter *'98*
Disconnected *'87*

Matthew (Matt) Walker (1942-)
Misbegotten *'98*
Intimate Relations *'95*
Child's Play 3 *'91*

Nancy Walker (1921-92)
Murder by Death *'76*
Death Scream *'75*
Thursday's Game *'74*
Forty Carats *'73*
Lucky Me *'54*
Broadway Rhythm *'44*
Best Foot Forward *'43*
Girl Crazy *'43*

Nicholas Walker
Body Count *'97*
Amnesia *'96*

Paul Walker (1973-)
The Fast and the Furious *'01*
Joy Ride *'01*
The Skulls *'00*
She's All That *'99*
Meet the Deedles *'98*
Pleasantville *'98*
Varsity Blues *'98*
Tammy and the T-Rex *'94*

Polly Walker (1966-)
8 1/2 Women *'99*
Eye of the Killer *'99*
Dark Harbor *'98*
Curtain Call *'97*
The Gambler *'97*
Emma *'96*
For Roseanna *'96*
Talk of Angels *'96*
Restoration *'94*
Sliver *'93*
The Trial *'93*
Enchanted April *'92*
Patriot Games *'92*
A Dangerous Man: Lawrence after Arabia *'91*
Lorna Doone *'90*

Ray Walker (1904-80)
Rogue's Gallery *'44*
House of Errors *'42*
Bulldog Edition *'36*
The Dark Hour *'36*
Goodbye Love *'34*

Robert Walker (1918-51)
Strangers on a Train *'51*
Vengeance Valley *'51*
One Touch of Venus *'48*
Till the Clouds Roll By *'46*
The Clock *'45*
Since You Went Away *'44*
Thirty Seconds Over Tokyo *'44*
Bataan *'43*
Madame Curie *'43*
The Crimson Trail *'35*

Robert Walker, Jr. (1940-)
Evil Town *'87*
Hambone & Hillie *'84*
Devonsville Terror *'83*
Olivia *'83*
AngKor: Cambodia Express *'81*
The Shrieking *'73*
The Spectre of Edgar Allen Poe *'73*
Beware! The Blob *'72*
Easy Rider *'69*
Road to Salina *'68*
The Savage Seven *'68*
The War Wagon *'67*
Ensign Pulver *'64*

Sarah Walker
Housekeeping *'87*
Man of Flowers *'84*

Terry Walker
Take Me Back to Oklahoma *'40*
Delinquent Parents *'38*
Renfrew on the Great White Trail *'38*
23 1/2 Hours Leave *'37*

Tippy Walker
The Jesus Trip *'71*
The World of Henry Orient *'64*

Walter Walker
Sons of Steel *'35*
American Madness *'32*

Max Wall (1894-1990)
Strike It Rich *'90*
Little Dorrit, Film 1: Nobody's Fault *'88*
Little Dorrit, Film 2: Little Dorrit's Story *'88*
We Think the World of You *'88*
Jabberwocky *'77*
A Killer in Every Corner *'74*

Basil Wallace
Joy Ride *'01*
Caught Up *'98*
Return of the Living Dead 3 *'93*
Deadlock *'91*
Marked for Death *'90*

Beryl Wallace
Sunset on the Desert *'42*
Rough Ridin' Rhythm *'37*

Bill Wallace
Manchurian Avenger *'84*
Force of One *'79*

David Wallace
Money to Burn *'83*
Humongous *'82*
Mazes and Monsters *'82*
The Babysitter *'80*

George Wallace (1952-)
The Wash *'01*
Three Strikes *'00*
Batman Forever *'95*

George D. Wallace (1917-)
Bicentennial Man *'99*
Forces of Nature *'99*
Diggstown *'92*
Defending Your Life *'91*
A Rage in Harlem *'91*
The Swinging Cheerleaders *'74*
Forbidden Planet *'56*
Radar Men from the Moon *'52*

Jack Wallace (1933-)
The Fixer *'97*
The Bear *'89*
Things Change *'88*
Assignment Outer Space *'61 (N)*

Jean Wallace (1923-90)
Sword of Lancelot *'63*
Big Combo *'55*
Native Son *'51*
Jigsaw *'49*

Marcia Wallace
My Mom's a Werewolf *'89*
Pray TV *'80*

Morgan Wallace (1881-1953)
Honky Tonk *'41*
In Old Colorado *'41*
Star Reporter *'39*
Delinquent Parents *'38*
Gang Bullets *'38*
The House of Secrets *'37*
Confidential *'35*

Dee Wallace Stone (1948-)
Black Circle Boys *'97*
Nevada *'97*
The Corporation *'96*
The Frighteners *'96*
Invisible Mom *'96*
Skeletons *'96*
Best of the Best 3: No Turning Back *'95*
The Phoenix and the Magic Carpet *'95*
The Road Home *'95*
Temptress *'95*
The Skateboard Kid 2 *'94*
Discretion Assured *'93*
Huck and the King of Hearts *'93*
My Family Treasure *'93*
Rescue Me *'93*
Alligator 2: The Mutation *'90*
I'm Dangerous Tonight *'90*
Popcorn *'89*
Miracle Down Under *'87*
Club Life *'86*
Critters *'86*
Shadow Play *'86*
Secret Admirer *'85*
Cujo *'83*
Wait Till Your Mother Gets Home *'83*
E.T.: The Extra-Terrestrial *'82*
Jimmy the Kid *'82*
Skeezer *'82*
The Five of Me *'81*
The Howling *'81*
Whale for the Killing *'81*
10 *'79*
The Hills Have Eyes *'77*
The Stepford Wives *'75*

Eli Wallach (1915-)
Keeping the Faith *'00*
Naked City: Justice with a Bullet *'98*
The Associate *'96*
Two Much *'96*
Article 99 *'92*
Legacy of Lies *'92*
Night and the City *'92*
Teamster Boss: The Jackie Presser Story *'92*
A Family Matter *'91*
Mistress *'91*
The Godfather, Part 3 *'90*
The Two Jakes *'90*
The Impossible Spy *'87*
Nuts *'87*
Rocket to the Moon *'86*
Something in Common *'86*
Tough Guys *'86*
Christopher Columbus *'85*
Embassy *'85*
Sam's Son *'84*
The Executioner's Song *'82*
The Salamander *'82*
Pride of Jesse Hallum *'81*
The Hunter *'80*
Winter Kills *'79*
Circle of Iron *'78*
Girlfriends *'78*
Movie, Movie *'78*
The Deep *'77*
The Domino Principle *'77*
Nasty Habits *'77*
The Sentinel *'76*
Stateline Motel *'75*
Cinderella Liberty *'73*
Romance of a Horsethief *'71*
The Angel Levine *'70*
The People Next Door *'70*
The Brain *'69*
MacKenna's Gold *'69*
Ace High *'68*
The Good, the Bad and the Ugly *'67*
How to Steal a Million *'66*
The Poppy Is Also a Flower *'66*
Lord Jim *'65*
Kisses for My President *'64*
The Moon-Spinners *'64*
How the West Was Won *'63*
The Misfits *'61*
The Magnificent Seven *'60*
Seven Thieves *'60*
Baby Doll *'56*

Roberta Wallach
The Hollywood Knights *'80*

The Effect of Gamma Rays on Man-in-the-Moon Marigolds '73
Sigurd Wallen
Swedenhielms '35
The Count of the Old Town '34
Eddy (Eddie, Ed) Waller (1889-1977)
El Paso Stampede '53
Marshal of Cedar Rock '53
Bandit King of Texas '49
Deborah Walley (1943-2001)
Benji '74
The Severed Arm '73
Dr. Goldfoot and the Bikini Machine '66
Spinout '66
Beach Blanket Bingo '65
Summer Magic '63
Bon Voyage! '62
Gidget Goes Hawaiian '61
William Walling
Range Feud '31
Great K & A Train Robbery '26
Shani Wallis (1941-)
The Pebble and the Penguin '94 (N)
Round Numbers '91
Arnold '73
Oliver! '68
Tom Walls (1883-1949)
Maytime in Mayfair '52
While I Live '47
Johnny Frenchman '46
Jon Walmsley
A Day for Thanks on Walton's Mountain '82
The Waltons: The Christmas Carol '80
Angela Walsh
Catherine Cookson's The Man Who Cried '93
Distant Voices, Still Lives '88
Dermot Walsh (1924-)
The Great Armored Car Swindle '64
The Tell-Tale Heart '62
The Flesh and the Fiends '60
It Takes a Thief '59
Ghost Ship '53
Murder on the Campus '52
Dylan Walsh (1963-)
We Were Soldiers '02
Final Voyage '99
Eden '98
Men '97
Changing Habits '96
Divided by Hate '96
Congo '95
Nobody's Fool '94
Radio Inside '94
Arctic Blue '93
Betsy's Wedding '90
George Walsh (1889-1981)
The Live Wire '34
The Broadway Drifter '27
Test of Donald Norton '26
American Pluck '25
Gwynyth Walsh
The Limbic Region '96
Soft Deceit '94
The Challengers '93
The Crush '93
Blue Monkey '87
Jack Walsh
A Simple Plan '98
Multiple Maniacs '70
J.T. Walsh (1943-98)
Hidden Agenda '99
The Negotiator '98
Pleasantville '98
Hope '97
Breakdown '96
Crime of the Century '96
Executive Decision '96
Gang in Blue '96
Persons Unknown '96
Sling Blade '96
The Babysitter '95
Black Day Blue Night '95
The Little Death '95
The Low Life '95
Nixon '95
Blue Chips '94
The Client '94
The Last Seduction '94
Miracle on 34th Street '94
Outbreak '94
Silent Fall '94
Some Folks Call It a Sling Blade '94
Morning Glory '93
National Lampoon's Loaded Weapon 1 '93
Needful Things '93
Red Rock West '93
A Few Good Men '92
Hoffa '92
Sniper '92
Backdraft '91
Defenseless '91
Iron Maze '91
Crazy People '90
The Grifters '90
Narrow Margin '90
The Russia House '90
Why Me? '90
The Big Picture '89
Dad '89
Wired '89
Tequila Sunrise '88
Things Change '88
Good Morning, Vietnam '87
House of Games '87
Tin Men '87
Power '86
Hard Choices '84
Katherine Walsh
Henry: Portrait of a Serial Killer 2: Mask of Sanity '96
The Trip '67
Kay Walsh (1914-)
The Witches '66
Greyfriars Bobby '61
Tunes of Glory '60
The Horse's Mouth '58
Cast a Dark Shadow '55
Young Bess '53
Encore '52
Last Holiday '50
Stage Fright '50
The October Man '48
Oliver Twist '48
This Happy Breed '47
In Which We Serve '43
Ken Walsh
Deliberate Intent '01
Dead Ahead: The Exxon Valdez Disaster '92
Love, Lies and Murder '91
Love and Hate: A Marriage Made in Hell '90
Reno and the Doc '84
M. Emmet Walsh (1935-)
Snow Dogs '02
Poor White Trash '00
Iron Giant '99 (V)
Me & Will '99
Wild Wild West '99
Twilight '98
Chairman of the Board '97
My Best Friend's Wedding '97
Retroactive '97
Albino Alligator '96
The Killing Jar '96
A Time to Kill '96
William Shakespeare's Romeo and Juliet '96
Criminal Hearts '95
The Glass Shield '95
Panther '95
Portraits of a Killer '95
Probable Cause '95
Relative Fear '95
Camp Nowhere '94
Dead Badge '94
Bitter Harvest '93
Equinox '93
Four Eyes and Six Guns '93
The Music of Chance '93
Wilder Napalm '93
Killer Image '92
White Sands '92
Wildcard '92
Boxcar Blues '90
Fourth Story '90
Narrow Margin '90
The Brotherhood of the Rose '89
Catch Me ... If You Can '89
Chattahoochee '89
The Mighty Quinn '89
Red Scorpion '89
Thunderground '89
War Party '89
Clean and Sober '88
The Milagro Beanfield War '88
Sunset '88
The Abduction of Kari Swenson '87
Broken Vows '87
Harry and the Hendersons '87
Murder Ordained '87
Raising Arizona '87
Back to School '86
The Best of Times '86
Critters '86
The Deliberate Stranger '86
Wildcats '86
Blood Simple '85
Fletch '85
Grandview U.S.A. '84
Missing in Action '84
The Pope of Greenwich Village '84
Raw Courage '84
Scandalous '84
Night Partners '83
Blade Runner '82
Cannery Row '82
Fast Walking '82
Reds '81
Brubaker '80
East of Eden '80
Ordinary People '80
The Jerk '79
Dear Detective '78
Straight Time '78
Slap Shot '77
The Gambler '74
Escape from the Planet of the Apes '71
They Might Be Giants '71
Alice's Restaurant '69
Stiletto '69
Percy Walsh (1888-1952)
The Golden Salamander '51
Thursday's Child '43
Secret Mission '42
King of the Damned '36
Raoul Walsh (1887-1981)
Sadie Thompson '28
The Birth of a Nation '15
Susan Walsh
Female Trouble '74
Pink Flamingos '72
Multiple Maniacs '70
Sydney Walsh (1961-)
Danger of Love '95
A Kiss Goodnight '94
Homewrecker '92
Point Break '91
Three Men and a Little Lady '90
To Die For '89
A Nightmare on Elm Street 2: Freddy's Revenge '85
Ray Walston (1918-2001)
My Favorite Martian '98
Tricks '97
House Arrest '96
Stephen King's The Stand '94
Of Mice and Men '92
The Player '92
Blood Salvage '90
Popcorn '89
Ski Patrol '89
Fine Gold '88
A Man of Passion '88
Paramedics '88
Saturday the 14th Strikes Back '88
Blood Relations '87
O.C. and Stiggs '87
From the Hip '86
Amos '85
For Love or Money '84
Johnny Dangerously '84
Private School '83
Fast Times at Ridgemont High '82
The Kid with the Broken Halo '82
O'Hara's Wife '82
Galaxy of Terror '81
The Fall of the House of Usher '80
Popeye '80
The Happy Hooker Goes to Washington '77
Silver Streak '76
The Sting '73
Kiss Me, Stupid! '64
Who's Minding the Store? '63
The Apartment '60
Portrait in Black '60
Tall Story '60
Damn Yankees '58
South Pacific '58
Harriet Walter (1951-)
Onegin '99
Bedrooms and Hallways '98
The Governess '98
A Merry War '97
Sense and Sensibility '95
The Advocate '93
May Fools '90
The Good Father '87
Jessica Walter (1940-)
Slums of Beverly Hills '98
Temptress '95
P.C.U. '94
Ghost in the Machine '93
Tapeheads '89
The Execution '85
The Flamingo Kid '84
Going Ape! '81
Miracle on Ice '81
Goldengirl '79
She's Dressed to Kill '79
Dr. Strange '78
Secrets of Three Hungry Wives '78
Wild & Wooly '78
Hurricane '74
Home for the Holidays '72
Play Misty for Me '71
The Group '66
Lisa Ann Walter
The Parent Trap '98
Eddie '96
Tracey Walter (1942-)
How High '01
Drowning Mona '00
Erin Brockovich '00
Wild America '97
Drive '96
Larger Than Life '96
Matilda '96
Buffalo Girls '95
Destiny Turns on the Radio '95
Philadelphia '93
Liquid Dreams '92
City Slickers '91
Delusion '91
Mortuary Academy '91
The Two Jakes '90
Young Guns 2 '90
Batman '89
Under the Boardwalk '89
Married to the Mob '88
Out of the Dark '88
At Close Range '86
Something Wild '86
Conan the Destroyer '84
Repo Man '83
Timerider '83
Raggedy Man '81
Mad Bull '77
Hal Walters
The Four Feathers '39
Sabotage '36
Julie Walters (1950-)
Harry Potter and the Sorcerer's Stone '01
Billy Elliot '00
Oliver Twist '00
Lover's Prayer '99
Girls' Night '97
Intimate Relations '95
Just Like a Woman '95
Sister My Sister '94
The Summer House '94
The Wedding Gift '93
Stepping Out '91
Happy Since I Met You '89
Mack the Knife '89
Buster '88
Personal Services '87
Prick Up Your Ears '87
Car Trouble '86
She'll Be Wearing Pink Pajamas '84
Educating Rita '83
Laurie Walters (1947-)
The Taking of Flight 847: The Uli Derickson Story '88
Harrad Summer '74
Harrad Experiment '73
Warlock Moon '73
Luana Walters (1912-63)
The Corpse Vanishes '42
Inside the Law '42
Arizona Bound '41
Kid's Last Ride '41
Misbehaving Husbands '41
Blondie Plays Cupid '40
Aces and Eights '36
Shadow of Chinatown '36
Speed Reporter '36
Assassin of Youth '35
Fighting Texans '33
Melora Walters
Magnolia '99
Boogie Nights '97
Los Locos Posse '97
American Strays '96
Hard Eight '96
Twenty Bucks '93
America's Deadliest Home Video '91
Susan Walters (1963-)
Where the Truth Lies '99
I Married a Monster '98
Galaxies Are Colliding '92
Defending Your Life '91
Elvis and Me '88
Russkies '87
Thorley Walters (1913-91)
In the Secret State
The Little Drummer Girl '84
The Sign of Four '83
The Adventures of Sherlock Holmes' Smarter Brother '78
The People That Time Forgot '77
Cry of the Penguins '71
Vampire Circus '71
Bartleby '70
Frankenstein Must Be Destroyed '69
Dracula, Prince of Darkness '66
Frankenstein Created Woman '66
Murder She Said '62
The Phantom of the Opera '62
Sherlock Holmes and the Deadly Necklace '62
The Pure Hell of St. Trinian's '61
Blue Murder at St. Trinian's '56
Who Done It? '56
Henry B. Walthall (1878-1936)
Police Court '37
Devil Doll '36
Last Outlaw '36
A Tale of Two Cities '36
Beggars in Ermine '34
Judge Priest '34
The Scarlet Letter '34
Viva Villa! '34
Flaming Signal '33
Laughing at Life '33
Somewhere in Sonora '33
The Cabin in the Cotton '32
Chandu the Magician '32
Ride Him, Cowboy '32
Strange Interlude '32
Abraham Lincoln '30
The Phantom in the House '29
Wings '27
The Plastic Age '25
With Kit Carson over the Great Divide '25
The Confession '20
False Faces '18
The Birth of a Nation '15
The Raven '15
Avenging Conscience '14
Home Sweet Home '14
Judith of Bethulia '14
Bill Walton
Little Nicky '00
Celtic Pride '96
Douglas Walton (1910-61)
Bad Lands '39
Wallaby Jim of the Islands '37
I Conquer the Sea '36
Mary of Scotland '36
The Bride of Frankenstein '35
The Lost Patrol '34
John Walton
The Lighthorsemen '87
Kangaroo '86
Lisa Waltz
Starry Night '99
Neil Simon's The Odd Couple 2 '98
Pet Sematary 2 '92
Brighton Beach Memoirs '86
Lau Ching Wan
Running out of Time '99
Black Mask '96
Sam Wanamaker (1919-93)
Covert Assassin '94
City of Joy '92
Secret Ingredient '92
Guilty by Suspicion '91
Pure Luck '91
Running Against Time '90
The Shell Seekers '89
Judgment in Berlin '88
Baby Boom '87
Superman 4: The Quest for Peace '87
Raw Deal '86
The Aviator '85
Embassy '85
Detective Sadie & Son '84
Ghostwriter '84
Irreconcilable Differences '84
Our Family Business '81
The Competition '80
Private Benjamin '80
From Hell to Victory '79
Sell Out '76
Voyage of the Damned '76
Spiral Staircase '75
The Spy Who Came in from the Cold '65
Those Magnificent Men in Their Flying Machines '65
Taras Bulba '62
The Battle of the Sexes '60 (N)
My Girl Tisa '48
Zoe Wanamaker (1949-)
Harry Potter and the Sorcerer's Stone '01
David Copperfield '99
The Magical Legend of the Leprechauns '99
Swept from the Sea '97
Wilde '97
Prime Suspect '92
Tales of the Unexpected '91
The Raggedy Rawney '90
Poor Little Rich Girl: The Barbara Hutton Story '87

Peter Wang
The Laserman '90
A Great Wall '86
Chan Is Missing '82
Percy Waram
The Big Hangover '50
Ministry of Fear '44
David Warbeck (1941-97)
Razor Blade Smile '98
Miami Horror '87
Formula for a Murder '85
Tiger Joe '85
Panic '83
Ark of the Sun God '82
The Beyond '82
Hunters of the Golden Cobra '82
The Black Cat '81
The Last Hunter '80
Blacksnake! '73
Twins of Evil '71
John Warburton (1887-1981)
King Rat '65
Secret File of Hollywood '62
Saratoga Trunk '45
Nothing But Trouble '44
The White Cliffs of Dover '44
Cavalcade '33
Patrick Warburton (1964-)
Big Trouble '02
Joe Somebody '01
Angels in the Infield '00
The Dish '00
The Emperor's New Groove '00 (V)
Scream 3 '00
Apartment Complex '98
Dragonard '88
B.J. Ward
The Opposite Sex and How to Live With Them '93
Pound Puppies and the Legend of Big Paw '88 (V)
Burt Ward (1945-)
Assault of the Party Nerds 2: Heavy Petting Detective '95
Beach Babes from Beyond Infinity '93
Smooth Talker '90
Virgin High '90
Killcrazy '89
Robo-Chic '89
Batman '66
Donal Lardner Ward
The Suburbans '99
My Life's in Turnaround '94
Fred Ward (1943-)
Enough '02
Corky Romano '01
Joe Dirt '01
Summer Catch '01
Chaos Factor '00
Circus '00
The Crow: Salvation '00
Full Disclosure '00
Road Trip '00
The Crimson Code '99
Best Men '98
Dangerous Beauty '98
Forgotten City '98
Invasion: Earth '98
First Do No Harm '97
Chain Reaction '96
Tremors 2: Aftershocks '96
Naked Gun 33 1/3: The Final Insult '94
Equinox '93
Four Eyes and Six Guns '93
Short Cuts '93
Two Small Bodies '93
Bob Roberts '92
The Player '92
Thunderheart '92
Cast a Deadly Spell '91
Henry & June '90
Miami Blues '90
Backtrack '89
Tremors '89
Big Business '88
Prince of Pennsylvania '88
Florida Straits '87
Off Limits '87
Remo Williams: The Adventure Begins '85
Secret Admirer '85
Noon Wine '84
Swing Shift '84
The Right Stuff '83
Silkwood '83
Timerider '83
Uncommon Valor '83
Southern Comfort '81
Uforia '81
Escape from Alcatraz '79
John Ward (1924-95)
Holt of the Secret Service '42
Ridin' the Trail '40
Robinson Crusoe of Clipper Island '36
Jonathan Ward (1970-)
Ferngully: The Last Rain Forest '92 (V)
Mac and Me '88
White Water Summer '87
Kelly Ward
The Big Red One '80
Grease '78
Larry Ward
Macabre '77
Deathhead Virgin '74
Lyman Ward
Independence Day '96
The Secret Agent Club '96
Serial Killer '95
Mikey '92
Sleepwalkers '92
The Taking of Beverly Hills '91
Perfect Victims '87
Planes, Trains & Automobiles '87
Ferris Bueller's Day Off '86
Creature '85
Mary B. Ward
Operation Sandman: Warriors in Hell '00
Hangin' with the Homeboys '91
Surviving Desire '91
Megan Ward (1969-)
Rated X '00
Glory Daze '96
Joe's Apartment '96
P.C.U. '94
Arcade '93
Freaked '93
Amityville 1992: It's About Time '92
Encino Man '92
Trancers 3: Deth Lives '92
Trancers 2: The Return of Jack Deth '90
Penelope Dudley Ward (1919-82)
The Demi-Paradise '43
The Case of the Frightened Lady '39
The Citadel '38
I Stand Condemned '36
Rachel Ward (1957-)
On the Beach '00
Twisted '96
The Ascent '94
Black Magic '92
Christopher Columbus: The Discovery '92
Double Jeopardy '92
Wide Sargasso Sea '92
After Dark, My Sweet '90
How to Get Ahead in Advertising '89
Hotel Colonial '88
The Good Wife '86
Fortress '85
Against All Odds '84
The Final Terror '83
The Thorn Birds '83
Dead Men Don't Wear Plaid '82
Night School '81
Sharky's Machine '81
Rich Ward
Vampires of Sorority Row: Kickboxers From Hell '99
Things 2 '97
Richard Ward (1915-79)
The Jerk '79
Mandingo '75
Across 110th Street '72
Robin Ward (1944-)
Mark of Cain '84
Thrillkill '84
When Angels Fly '82
Roger Ward
Quigley Down Under '90
Mad Max '80
Roy Ward
The Ugly '96
The Forbidden Quest '93
Sandy Ward
The Chinatown Murders: Man against the Mob '92
Blue Desert '91
Delta Force 3: The Killing Game '91
Cujo '83
Tank '83
The Velvet Vampire '71
Sela Ward (1957-)
Runaway Bride '99
54 '98
Rescuers: Stories of Courage "Two Women" '97
My Fellow Americans '96
The Fugitive '93
Double Jeopardy '92
Child of Darkness, Child of Light '91
Rainbow Drive '90
Haunting of Sarah Hardy '89
Hello Again '87
Steele Justice '87
Nothing in Common '86
Simon Ward (1941-)
The Monster Club '85
Supergirl '84
Deadly Strangers '82
Dominique Is Dead '79
Zulu Dawn '79
The Four Feathers '78
The Chosen '77
Children of Rage '75
The Four Musketeers '75
All Creatures Great and Small '74
The Three Musketeers '74
Dracula '73
Hitler: The Last Ten Days '73
Young Winston '72
Frankenstein Must Be Destroyed '69
Sophie Ward (1965-)
The Big Fall '96
A Village Affair '95
A Dark Adapted Eye '93
Class of '61 '92
A Demon in My View '92
Emily Bronte's Wuthering Heights '92
Waxwork 2: Lost in Time '91
The Shell Seekers '89
Little Dorrit, Film 1: Nobody's Fault '88
Little Dorrit, Film 2: Little Dorrit's Story '88
A Summer Story '88
Casanova '87
Young Sherlock Holmes '85
Susan Ward (1976-)
Shallow Hal '01
The In Crowd '00
Tony Ward
Hustler White '96
Color Me Dead '69
Vincent Ward (1956-)
One Night Stand '97
The Shot '96
Warwick Ward
The Informer '29
Variety '25
Zack (Zach) Ward (1973-)
Almost Famous '00
Brotherhood of Murder '99
Ed '96
Star Hunter '95
The Club '94
A Christmas Story '83
Jennifer Ward-Lealand
The Ugly '96
Desperate Remedies '93
Dangerous Orphans '86
Anthony Warde (1908-75)
The Black Widow '47
King of the Forest Rangers '46
There Goes Kelly '45
Harlan Warde (1917-80)
Above and Beyond '53
Flying Leathernecks '51
Money Madness '47
Jack Warden (1920-)
The Replacements '00
A Dog of Flanders '99
Bulworth '98
Chairman of the Board '97
Dirty Work '97
Ed '96
Mighty Aphrodite '95
Things to Do in Denver When You're Dead '95
While You Were Sleeping '95
Bullets over Broadway '94
Guilty as Sin '93
Night and the City '92
Passed Away '92
Problem Child 2 '91
Everybody Wins '90
Judgment '90
Problem Child '90
Robert Kennedy and His Times '90
Dead Solid Perfect '88
The Presidio '88
September '88
A.D. '85
The Aviator '85
Crackers '84
Hobson's Choice '83
The Verdict '82
Carbon Copy '81
Chu Chu & the Philly Flash '81
The Great Muppet Caper '81
So Fine '81
Used Cars '80
And Justice for All '79
Being There '79
Beyond the Poseidon Adventure '79
The Champ '79
Dreamer '79
Death on the Nile '78
Heaven Can Wait '78
Raid on Entebbe '77
The White Buffalo '77
Shampoo '75
The Apprenticeship of Duddy Kravitz '74
Billy Two Hats '74
Man Who Loved Cat Dancing '73
The Sporting Club '72
Brian's Song '71
Man on a String '71
Summertree '71
The Thin Red Line '64
Donovan's Reef '63
Darby's Rangers '58
Run Silent, Run Deep '58
Twelve Angry Men '57
Justice '55
From Here to Eternity '53
Geoffrey Wardwell
Crimes at the Dark House '39
The Challenge '38
Herta Ware
St. Patrick's Day '99
Top Dog '95
Crazy in Love '92
Dakota '88
Cocoon '85
Irene Ware (1911-)
The Dark Hour '36
Federal Agent '36
The Raven '35
King Kelly of the U.S.A. '34
Chandu the Magician '32
Chris Warfield
Diary of a Madman '63
Dangerous Charter '62
Emily Warfield
Bonanza: The Return '93
Calendar Girl '93
The Man in the Moon '91
Pair of Aces '90
Marsha Warfield (1954-)
Mask '85
D.C. Cab '84
William Warfield
Old Explorers '90
Show Boat '51
Andy Warhol
Cocaine Cowboys '79
Driver's Seat '73
Todd Waring
Sinatra '92
Love & Murder '91
Billy Warlock (1961-)
Steel Sharks '97
Opposite Corners '96
Panic in the Skies '96
Honor Thy Father and Mother: The True Story of the Menendez Brothers '94
Society '92
Swimsuit '89
Hot Shot '86
Gordon Warnecke
A Fatal Inversion '92
London Kills Me '91
My Beautiful Laundrette '85
David Warner (1941-)
Back to the Secret Garden '01
Horatio Hornblower: The Adventure Continues '01
Planet of the Apes '01
Houdini '99
Wing Commander '99
Money Talks '97
Scream 2 '97
Titanic '97
The Leading Man '96
Rasputin: Dark Servant of Destiny '96
Beastmaster 3: The Eye of Braxus '95
Final Equinox '95
Ice Cream Man '95
In the Mouth of Madness '95
Naked Souls '95
Inner Sanctum 2 '94
Tryst '94
Body Bags '93
H.P. Lovecraft's Necronomicon: Book of the Dead '93
Quest of the Delta Knights '93
Return to the Lost World '93
Wild Palms '93
The Lost World '92
The Unnamable 2: The Statement of Randolph Carter '92
Cast a Deadly Spell '91
Star Trek 6: The Undiscovered Country '91
Teenage Mutant Ninja Turtles 2: The Secret of the Ooze '91
Blue Tornado '90
Code Name: Chaos '90
Mortal Passions '90
Spymaker: The Secret Life of Ian Fleming '90
Grave Secrets '89
Star Trek 5: The Final Frontier '89
Tripwire '89
Hanna's War '88
Hostile Takeover '88
Magdalene '88
Mr. North '88
My Best Friend Is a Vampire '88
Waxwork '88
The Company of Wolves '85
A Christmas Carol '84
The Man with Two Brains '83
Frankenstein '82
Tron '82
The Boy Who Left Home to Find Out About the Shivers '81
Disappearance '81
Masada '81
Time Bandits '81
The Island '80
The Concorde: Airport '79 '79
Nightwing '79
S.O.S. Titanic '79
The Thirty-Nine Steps '79
Time After Time '79
Holocaust '78
Silver Bears '78
Providence '77
Cross of Iron '76
The Omen '76
The Old Curiosity Shop '75
A Doll's House '73
From Beyond the Grave '73
Straw Dogs '72
Ballad of Cable Hogue '70
The Fixer '68
A Midsummer Night's Dream '68
Morgan: A Suitable Case for Treatment '66
Tom Jones '63
H.B. Warner (1876-1958)
The Ten Commandments '56
The Judge Steps Out '49
It's a Wonderful Life '46
Strange Impersonation '46
Action in Arabia '44
Enemy of Women '44
Rogue's Gallery '44
Boss of Big Town '43
Hitler's Children '43
The Corsican Brothers '42
Yank in Libya '42
The Devil & Daniel Webster '41
Topper Returns '41
Bulldog Drummond's Bride '39
Bulldog Drummond's Secret Police '39
Let Freedom Ring '39
Mr. Smith Goes to Washington '39
The Rains Came '39
The Adventures of Marco Polo '38
Arrest Bulldog Drummond '38
You Can't Take It with You '38
Lost Horizon '37
Mr. Deeds Goes to Town '36
A Tale of Two Cities '36
Supernatural '33
Cross Examination '32
King of Kings '27
Big Stakes '22
Jack Warner (1894-1981)
Carve Her Name with Pride '58
The Quatermass Experiment '56
The Ladykillers '55
A Christmas Carol '51
Valley of the Eagles '51
The Blue Lamp '49
Train of Events '49
Against the Wind '48
Captive Heart '47
Dear Murderer '47
Hue and Cry '47
The Dummy Talks '43
Julie Warner (1965-)
Dean Koontz's Mr. Murder '98
Wedding Bell Blues '96
Tommy Boy '9
The Puppet Ma

Indian Summer '93
Mr. Saturday Night '92
Doc Hollywood '91

Malcolm Jamal Warner (1970-)
Restaurant '98
The Tuskegee Airmen '95
Tyson '95
Drop Zone '94
The Father Clements Story '87

Barry Warren
Frankenstein Created Woman '66
Kiss of the Vampire '62

E. Alyn Warren (1874-1940)
Get That Man '35
Tarzan the Fearless '33
Abraham Lincoln '30
Medicine Man '30

Estella Warren (1978-)
Driven '01
Planet of the Apes '01

Fred Warren (-1940)
Mysterious Mr. Wong '35
Abraham Lincoln '30

Jennifer Warren (1941-)
The Amazons '84
Mutant '83
The Choice '81
Intruder Within '81
Angel City '80
Ice Castles '79
Steel Cowboy '78
Another Man, Another Chance '77
Slap Shot '77
Night Moves '75
The Swap '71

Jennifer Leigh Warren
Matter of Trust '98
Sour Grapes '98
Grace of My Heart '96
The Crossing Guard '94

Katherine Warren
The Caine Mutiny '54
Prowler '51

Kenneth J. Warren
The Creeping Flesh '72
Demons of the Mind '72
I, Monster '71

Kiersten Warren
Circuit '02
Divine Secrets of the Ya-Ya Sisterhood '02
Duets '00
Bicentennial Man '99
Liberty Heights '99
Independence Day '96

Lesley Ann Warren (1946-)
Secretary '02
Trixie '00
The Limey '99
Twin Falls Idaho '99
Love Kills '98
Going All the Way '97
Natural Enemy '96
Bird of Prey '95
Joseph '95
Color of Night '94
Pure Country '92
Life Stinks '91
A Fight for Jenny '90
Worth Winning '89
Cop '88
Baja Oklahoma '87
Burglar '87
Apology '86
Clue '85
Choose Me '84
The Dancing Princesses '84
Songwriter '84
A Night in Heaven '83
Treasure of the Yankee Zephyr '83
Portrait of a Showgirl '82
Victor/Victoria '82
Beulah Land '80
Portrait of a Stripper '79
Betrayal '78
Pearl '78
Harry & Walter Go to New York '76
Legend of Valentino '75
Where the Eagle Flies '72
The One and Only, Genuine, Original Family Band '68
The Happiest Millionaire '67
Cinderella '64

Marc Warren
Band of Brothers '01
Dad Savage '97
Boston Kickout '95

Michael Warren (1946-)
Trippin' '99
Buffalo Soldiers '97
A Passion to Kill '94
Storyville '92
Heaven Is a Playground '91
The Kid Who Loved Christmas '90
Norman, Is That You? '76

Harold Warrender (1903-53)
Pandora and the Flying Dutchman '51
Conspirator '49
Contraband '40
Mimi '35

Ruth Warrick (1915-)
Deathmask '69
One Too Many '51
Let's Dance '50
Three Husbands '50
Great Dan Patch '49
Arch of Triumph '48
China Sky '44
Guest in the House '44
Mr. Winkle Goes to War '44
The Iron Major '43
The Corsican Brothers '42
Citizen Kane '41

David Warrilow (1934-95)
Barton Fink '91
Strong Medicine '84

James Warwick (1947-)
The Crackler '84
The Unbreakable Alibi '83

John Warwick (1905-72)
While I Live '47
The Face at the Window '39
Ticket of Leave Man '37

Richard Warwick
Sebastiane '79
If... '69

Robert Warwick (1878-1964)
It Started with a Kiss '59
I Married a Witch '42
Sullivan's Travels '41
A Woman's Face '41
The Awful Truth '37
The Trigger Trio '37
The Bold Caballero '36
Bulldog Edition '36
Hopalong Cassidy '35
A Shot in the Dark '35
Whispering Shadow '33
The Secrets of Wu Sin '32
The Royal Bed '31
A Girl's Folly '17

Mona Washbourne (1903-88)
December Flower
Brideshead Revisited '81
Stevie '78
Driver's Seat '73
O Lucky Man! '73
If... '69
Mrs. Brown, You've Got a Lovely Daughter '68
The Collector '65
My Fair Lady '64
The Brides of Dracula '60
Stranger in Town '57
Cast a Dark Shadow '55

Beverly Washburn (1943-)
When the Line Goes Through '71
Pit Stop '67
Spider Baby '64
Old Yeller '57

Bryant Washburn (1889-1963)
The Throwback '35
Drifting Souls '32
Kept Husbands '31
The Wizard of Oz '25

Rick Washburne (1946-)
The Outfit '93
Comrades in Arms '91
Covert Action '88
Hangmen '87

Denzel Washington (1954-)
John Q '02
Training Day '01
Remember the Titans '00
The Bone Collector '99
The Hurricane '99
He Got Game '98
The Siege '98
Fallen '97
Courage Under Fire '96
The Preacher's Wife '96
Crimson Tide '95
Devil in a Blue Dress '95
Virtuosity '95
Much Ado about Nothing '93
The Pelican Brief '93
Philadelphia '93
Malcolm X '92
Mississippi Masala '92
Ricochet '91
Heart Condition '90
Mo' Better Blues '90
Glory '89
The Mighty Quinn '89
Cry Freedom '87
Hard Lessons '86
Power '86
License to Kill '84
A Soldier's Story '84
Carbon Copy '81

Fredi Washington (1903-94)
Imitation of Life '34
Emperor Jones '33

Gene Washington
Lady Cocoa '75
The Black Six '74

Isaiah Washington, IV (1963-)
Exit Wounds '01
Dancing in September '00
Romeo Must Die '00
A Texas Funeral '99
True Crime '99
Always Outnumbered Always Outgunned '98
Bulworth '98
Mixing Nia '98
Out of Sight '98
Joe Torre: Curveballs Along the Way '97
Get On the Bus '96
Girl 6 '96
Love Jones '96
Mr. & Mrs. Loving '96
Clockers '95
Crooklyn '94

Jascha Washington
My Sister's Keeper '02
Big Momma's House '00

Kerry Washington (1977-)
Bad Company '02
Our Song '01
Save the Last Dance '01

Shirley Washington
Darktown Strutters '74
The Deadly and the Beautiful '73

Ted Wass (1952-)
Danielle Steel's Star '93
Fine Gold '88
Pancho Barnes '88
The Longshot '86
TripleCross '85
Oh, God! You Devil '84
Sheena '84
Curse of the Pink Panther '83
The Triangle Factory Fire Scandal '79

Jerry Wasserman
A Cooler Climate '99
Quarantine '89

Craig Wasson (1954-)
Epoch '00
Escape under Pressure '00
The Pornographer '00
Velocity Trap '99
The Last Best Sunday '98
Harvest of Fire '95
The Sister-in-Law '95
Trapped in Space '94
Strapped '93
Malcolm X '92
Midnight Fear '90
A Nightmare on Elm Street 3: Dream Warriors '87
The Men's Club '86
Body Double '84
The Innocents Abroad '84
Second Thoughts '83
Four Friends '81
Ghost Story '81
Carny '80
Schizoid '80
Skag '79
Go Tell the Spartans '78
The Boys in Company C '77

Gedde Watanabe (1955-)
EDtv '99
Guinevere '99
Mulan '98 (V)
Booty Call '96
Nick and Jane '96
That Thing You Do! '96
The Spring '89
UHF '89
Vamp '86
Gung Ho '85
Volunteers '85
Sixteen Candles '84

Ken(saku) Watanabe (1959-)
Karate Warrior '88
Commando Invasion '87
Tampopo '86
MacArthur's Children '85

Tetsu Watanabe
Fireworks '97
Sonatine '96

Tsunehiko Watase
The Silk Road '92
Heaven & Earth '90

Dennis Waterman (1948-)
Circle of Deceit '94
Cold Justice '89
Fright '71
Man in the Wilderness '71
The Scars of Dracula '70

Felicity Waterman
Freedom Strike '98
Titanic '96
Hard Bounty '94
Unlawful Passage '94
Miracle Beach '92
Lena's Holiday '90

Ida Waterman
Amarilly of Clothesline Alley '18
Stella Maris '18

Willard Waterman (1915-95)
Hail '73
Hollywood or Bust '56

Cheryl Waters
Didn't You Hear? '83
Image of Death '77
Macon County Line '74

Ethel Waters (1896-1977)
The Member of the Wedding '52
Pinky '49
Cabin in the Sky '43
Stage Door Canteen '43
Cairo '42
Tales of Manhattan '42

Harry Waters, Jr.
Back to the Future, Part 2 '89
Back to the Future '85

John Waters (1945-)
The Ebb-Tide '97
Heaven Tonight '93
Which Way Home '90
Grievous Bodily Harm '89
Boulevard of Broken Dreams '88
Miracle Down Under '87
True Colors '87
Alice to Nowhere '86
Three's Trouble '85
All the Rivers Run '84
Attack Force Z '84
Breaker Morant '80
Cass '78
Demolition '77
The Getting of Wisdom '77
Scalp Merchant '77
Weekend of Shadows '77
Endplay '75

John Waters (1946-)
Sweet and Lowdown '99
Pecker '98 (V)
Serial Mom '94 (V)
Hairspray '88
Something Wild '86
Pink Flamingos '72 (N)

Nick Waters
The Big Hurt '87
The Lighthorsemen '87

Sam Waterston (1940-)
A House Divided '00
Trade Secrets '90s
Miracle at Midnight '98
The Proprietor '96
The Shadow Conspiracy '96
The Journey of August King '95
Assault at West Point: The Court-Martial of Johnson Whittaker '94
The Enemy Within '94
Serial Mom '94
A Captive in the Land '91
The Man in the Moon '91
Mindwalk: A Film for Passionate Thinkers '91
Lantern Hill '90
Crimes & Misdemeanors '89
The Nightmare Years '89
Welcome Home '89
Gore Vidal's Lincoln '88
September '88
Hannah and Her Sisters '86
Just Between Friends '86
Warning Sign '85
The Boy Who Loved Trolls '84
Finnegan Begin Again '84
The Killing Fields '84
Dempsey '83
Heaven's Gate '81
Hopscotch '80
Eagle's Wing '79
Friendly Fire '79
Sweet William '79
Capricorn One '78
Interiors '78
Rancho Deluxe '75
The Great Gatsby '74
Journey into Fear '74
Reflections of Murder '74
Savages '72
Who Killed Mary What's 'Er Name? '71
Generation '69

Gwen Watford (1927-94)
In This House of Brede '75
Taste the Blood of Dracula '70
The Very Edge '63
The Fall of the House of Usher '49

Ian Watkin
Dead Alive '93
Nutcase '83
Beyond Reasonable Doubt '80

Pierre Watkin (1889-1960)
The Stranger Wore a Gun '53
Atom Man vs. Superman '50
Redwood Forest Trail '50
Little Giant '46
Swamp Fire '46
The Great Mike '44
The Magnificent Dope '42
The Road to Singapore '40
Country Gentlemen '36

Joanne Watkins
The Big Sweat '90
Cold Heat '90

Tuc Watkins
Miracle in Lane Two '00
The Mummy '99
I Think I Do '97

Deborah Watling
Danger UXB '81
That'll Be the Day '73

Jack Watling (1923-2001)
The Nanny '65
Sink the Bismarck '60
A Night to Remember '58
The Admirable Crichton '57
Under Capricorn '49
The Courtney Affair '47
Immortal Battalion '44

Alberta Watson (1955-)
Tart '01
Hedwig and the Angry Inch '00
Deeply '99
The Life Before This '99
The Girl Next Door '98
Gotti '96
Seeds of Doubt '96
The Sweet Hereafter '96
Hackers '95
Spanking the Monkey '94
The Hitman '91
White of the Eye '88
Women of Valor '86
Best Revenge '83
The Keep '83
The Soldier '82

Barry Watson (1974-)
Sorority Boys '02
Teaching Mrs. Tingle '99

Bob Watson
Tough Enough '83
In Hot Pursuit '82

Bobby Watson (1888-1965)
The Band Wagon '53
Hitler: Dead or Alive '43
Captains Courageous '37

Bobs Watson (1930-99)
Dreaming Out Loud '40
On Borrowed Time '39
The Story of Alexander Graham Bell '39
In Old Chicago '37
Show Boat '36

Emily Watson (1967-)
Gosford Park '01
The Luzhin Defence '00
Trixie '00
Angela's Ashes '99
The Cradle Will Rock '99
Hilary and Jackie '98
The Boxer '97
Metroland '97
The Mill on the Floss '97
Breaking the Waves '95

Jack Watson (1915-99)
Schizo '77
King Arthur, the Young Warlord '75
Young Warlord '75
Tower of Evil '72
McKenzie Break '70
The Devil's Brigade '68
Night Caller from Outer Space '66
The Gorgon '64
Peeping Tom '60

James A. Watson, Jr.
Killings at Outpost Zeta '80
Sex Through a Window '72

Lucile Watson (1879-1962)
Harriet Craig '50
Let's Dance '50
Emperor Waltz '48
Julia Misbehaves '48
Never Say Goodbye '46
The Razor's Edge '46
Tomorrow Is Forever '46
The Thin Man Goes Home '44
Uncertain Glory '44
Footsteps in the Dark '41
The Great Lie '41
Mr. & Mrs. Smith '41
Waterloo Bridge '40
Made for Each Other '39
The Women '39
Rhythm on the Range '36

Mills Watson (1940-)
Heated Vengeance '87
Cujo '83
The Migrants '74

Minor Watson (1889-1965)
The Ambassador's Daughter '56
Face to Face '52
As Young As You Feel '51
The Jackie Robinson Story '50
Beyond the Forest '49
A Southern Yankee '48
Action in the North Atlantic '43
Crash Dive '43
Guadalcanal Diary '43
To the Shores of Tripoli '42
Woman of the Year '42
They Died with Their Boots On '41
Western Union '41
Abe Lincoln in Illinois '40
Dead End '37
Navy Blue and Gold '37
That Certain Woman '37
Charlie Chan in Paris '35

Muse Watson (1948-)
Austin Powers 2: The Spy Who Shagged Me '99
Songcatcher '99
From Dusk Till Dawn 2: Texas Blood Money '98
I Still Know What You Did Last Summer '98
If I Die Before I Wake '98
I Know What You Did Last Summer '97
Rosewood '96
Something to Talk About '95

Shari Watson
Ali '01
The Wash '01

William Watson
Force of Evil '77
Girl on a Chain Gang '65

Woody Watson (1949-99)
Texas '94
Sarah, Plain and Tall: Skylark '93
All-American Murder '91
The Last Prostitute '91

Wylie Watson (1966-)
The Sundowners '60
Things Happen at Night '48
Brighton Rock '47
A Girl in a Million '46
The 39 Steps '35

Vernee Watson-Johnson
Death Drug '83
The Boy in the Plastic Bubble '76
Norman, Is That You? '76

Richard Wattis (1912-75)
The Abominable Snowman '57
The Prince and the Showgirl '57
The Belles of St. Trinian's '53
Doctor in the House '53
Norman Conquest '53
Three Stops to Murder '53
My Son, the Vampire '52
The Happiest Days of Your Life '50

Naomi Watts (1968-)
Mulholland Drive '01
Dangerous Beauty '98
Children of the Corn 4: The Gathering '96
Persons Unknown '96
The Custodian '94
Tank Girl '94
Gross Misconduct '93
Brides of Christ '91

Victoria Wauchope
Love and Hate: A Marriage Made in Hell '90
Cop '88
Bluffing It '87

Ruby Wax
The Borrowers '97
Shock Treatment '81

Al Waxman (1935-2001)
Life with Judy Garland—Me and My Shadows '01
In the Company of Spies '99
A Saintly Switch '99
Naked City: A Killer Christmas '98
The Assignment '97
Critical Care '97
Rescuers: Stories of Courage "Two Women" '97
Bogus '96
Gotti '96
Holiday Affair '96
Iron Eagle 4 '95
Operation Golden Phoenix '94
Teamster Boss: The Jackie Presser Story '92
The Hitman '91
Mob Story '90
Collision Course '89
Malarek '89
Millennium '89
Switching Channels '88
Meatballs 3 '87
Clown Murders '83
Class of 1984 '82
Spasms '82
Atlantic City '81
The Double Negative '80
Wild Horse Hank '79

Eileen Way
Queen of Hearts '89
Three Stops to Murder '53

Damon Wayans (1961-)
Bamboozled '00
Bulletproof '96
Celtic Pride '96
The Great White Hype '96
Major Payne '95
Blankman '94
Last Action Hero '93
Mo' Money '92
The Last Boy Scout '91
Look Who's Talking, Too '90 (V)
Earth Girls Are Easy '89
Colors '88
I'm Gonna Git You Sucka '88
Punchline '88
Hollywood Shuffle '87
Roxanne '87
Beverly Hills Cop '84

Keenen Ivory Wayans (1958-)
Scary Movie '00
Most Wanted '97
The Glimmer Man '96
Don't Be a Menace to South Central While Drinking Your Juice in the Hood '95
A Low Down Dirty Shame '94
I'm Gonna Git You Sucka '88
Hollywood Shuffle '87

Kim Wayans
Talking about Sex '94
I'm Gonna Git You Sucka '88

Marlon Wayans (1972-)
Scary Movie 2 '01
Dungeons and Dragons '00
Requiem for a Dream '00
Scary Movie '00
Senseless '98
The Sixth Man '97
Don't Be a Menace to South Central While Drinking Your Juice in the Hood '95
Above the Rim '94
Mo' Money '92

Shawn Wayans (1971-)
Scary Movie 2 '01
Scary Movie '00
New Blood '99
Don't Be a Menace to South Central While Drinking Your Juice in the Hood '95

Carol Wayne (1942-85)
Heartbreakers '84
Surf 2 '84
The Party '68

David Wayne (1914-95)
The Gift of Love '90
Poker Alice '87
The Survivalist '87
Finders Keepers '84
An American Christmas Carol '79
The Apple Dumpling Gang '75
Huckleberry Finn '74
The Andromeda Strain '71
Lamp at Midnight '66
The Last Angry Man '59
The Sad Sack '57
The Three Faces of Eve '57
Naked Hills '56
The Tender Trap '55
How to Marry a Millionaire '53
We're Not Married '52
As Young As You Feel '51
Adam's Rib '50
Portrait of Jennie '48

John Wayne (1907-79)
America at the Movies '76
The Shootist '76
Brannigan '75
Rooster Cogburn '75
McQ '74
Cahill: United States Marshal '73
Train Robbers '73
Cancel My Reservation '72
The Cowboys '72
Big Jake '71
Chisum '70
Rio Lobo '70
True Grit '69
The Undefeated '69
The Green Berets '68
Hellfighters '68
El Dorado '67
The War Wagon '67
Cast a Giant Shadow '66
The Greatest Story Ever Told '65
In Harm's Way '65
Sons of Katie Elder '65
Circus World '64
Donovan's Reef '63
How the West Was Won '63
McLintock! '63
Hatari! '62
The Longest Day '62
The Man Who Shot Liberty Valance '62
The Comancheros '61
The Alamo '60
North to Alaska '60
The Horse Soldiers '59
Rio Bravo '59
Barbarian and the Geisha '58
Jet Pilot '57
Legend of the Lost '57
Wings of Eagles '57
The Conqueror '56
The Searchers '56
Blood Alley '55
Sea Chase '55
Hondo '53
Trouble along the Way '53
Big Jim McLain '52
The Quiet Man '52
Flying Leathernecks '51
Rio Grande '50
The Fighting Kentuckian '49
Sands of Iwo Jima '49
She Wore a Yellow Ribbon '49
Wake of the Red Witch '49
Fort Apache '48
Red River '48
Three Godfathers '48
Angel and the Badman '47
Tycoon '47
Without Reservations '46
Back to Bataan '45
Dakota '45
Flame of the Barbary Coast '45
They Were Expendable '45
Fighting Seabees '44
Tall in the Saddle '44
Lady Takes a Chance '43
War of the Wildcats '43
Flying Tigers '42
In Old California '42
Lady for a Night '42
Lady from Louisiana '42
Pittsburgh '42
Reap the Wild Wind '42
Reunion in France '42
The Spoilers '42
The Shepherd of the Hills '41
Wheel of Fortune '41
Dark Command '40
The Long Voyage Home '40
Seven Sinners '40
Three Faces West '40
Allegheny Uprising '39
Frontier Horizon '39
Stagecoach '39
Three Texas Steers '39
Wyoming Outlaw '39
Helltown '38
Overland Stage Raiders '38
Pals of the Saddle '38
Santa Fe Stampede '38
King of the Pecos '36
The Lawless Nineties '36
Winds of the Wasteland '36
Dawn Rider '35
Desert Trail '35
Lawless Frontier '35
Lawless Range '35
The New Frontier '35
Paradise Canyon '35
Texas Terror '35
Westward Ho '35
Blue Steel '34
Lucky Texan '34
Man from Utah '34
'Neath the Arizona Skies '34
Randy Rides Alone '34
The Star Packer '34
Trail Beyond '34
Baby Face '33
His Private Secretary '33
Man from Monterey '33
Riders of Destiny '33
Sagebrush Trail '33
Somewhere in Sonora '33
Telegraph Trail '33
The Three Musketeers '33
West of the Divide '33
The Big Stampede '32
Haunted Gold '32
Hurricane Express '32
Ride Him, Cowboy '32
Shadow of the Eagle '32
Texas Cyclone '32
Two-Fisted Law '32
Maker of Men '31
Range Feud '31
Big Trail '30
The Dropkick '27

John Ethan Wayne (1961-)
The Manhunt '86
Escape from El Diablo '83
Scream '83

Michael Wayne
Rapid Fire '89
Alley Cat '84

Naunton Wayne (1901-70)
The Hidden Room '49
Passport to Pimlico '49
A Girl in a Million '46
Dead of Night '45
Night Train to Munich '40
The Lady Vanishes '38

Nina Wayne
The Comic '69
Dead Heat on a Merry-Go-Round '66

Patricia Wayne
The Long Dark Hall '51
Eye Witness '49

Patrick Wayne (1939-)
Chill Factor '90
Her Alibi '88
Young Guns '88
Revenge '86
Rustler's Rhapsody '85
The People That Time Forgot '77
Sinbad and the Eye of the Tiger '77
Texas Detour '77
The Bears & I '74
Beyond Atlantis '73
The Gatling Gun '72
Big Jake '71
Ride to Glory '71
The Green Berets '68
Talion '66
Shenandoah '65
McLintock! '63
The Alamo '60
The Young Land '59
The Searchers '56
Mister Roberts '55

Michael Weatherly
Cabin by the Lake '00
The Substitute 4: Failure is Not an Option '00
The Colony '98
The Last Days of Disco '98

Shawn Weatherly (1960-)
Amityville 1992: It's About Time '92
Mind Games '89
Shadowzone '89
Thieves of Fortune '89
Party Line '88
Police Academy 3: Back in Training '86

Carl Weathers (1948-)
Little Nicky '00
Shadow Warriors '97
Shadow Warriors 2: Hunt for the Death Merchant '97
Happy Gilmore '96
Dangerous Passion '95
Hurricane Smith '92
Action Jackson '88
Predator '87
Fortune Dane '86
Rocky 4 '85
Rocky 3 '82
Death Hunt '81
Rocky 2 '79
Force 10 from Navarone '78
Semi-Tough '77
Rocky '76
Friday Foster '75

Dennis Weaver (1924-)
High Noon '00
Submerged '00
Escape from Wildcat Canyon '99
The Virginian '99
Two Bits & Pepper '95
Disaster at Silo 7 '88
Bluffing It '87
A Winner Never Quits '86
Going for the Gold: The Bill Johnson Story '85
Cocaine: One Man's Seduction '83
Amber Waves '82
Don't Go to Sleep '82
The Ordeal of Dr. Mudd '80
Centennial '78
Pearl '78
Intimate Strangers '77
Duel '71
A Man Called Sledge '71
What's the Matter with Helen? '71
Mission Batangas '69
Gentle Giant '67
Duel at Diablo '66
The Gallant Hours '60
Touch of Evil '58
The Redhead from Wyoming '53
War Arrow '53
Horizons West '52
The Lawless Breed '52

Doodles Weaver (1911-83)
Way He Was '76
Cancel My Reservation '72
Road to Nashville '67
The Errand Boy '61
The Ladies' Man '61

Fritz Weaver (1926-)
The Thomas Crown Affair '99
Rescuers: Stories of Courage "Two Women" '97
Broken Trust '95
Blind Spot '93
Ironclads '90
Power '86
The Hearst and Davies Affair '85
Creepshow '82
Jaws of Satan '81
The Martian Chronicles: Part 2 '79
The Martian Chronicles: Part 3 '79
The Big Fix '78
Holocaust '78
Black Sunday '77
Demon Seed '77
Marathon Man '76
The Day of the Dolphin '73
Hunter '73
Walk in the Spring Rain '70
Fail-Safe '64

Jacki Weaver (1947-)
Cosi '95
Three's Trouble '85
Squizzy Taylor '84
Caddie '76
Picnic at Hanging Rock '75

Jason Weaver
Freedom Song '00
The Jacksons: An American Dream '92

Lee Weaver
O Brother Where Art Thou? '00
My Brother's Wife '89

Marjorie Weaver (1913-94)
Murder over New York '40
Young Mr. Lincoln '39
The Gentleman from California '37

Sigourney Weaver (1949-)
Tadpole '02
Heartbreakers '01
Company Man '00
Galaxy Quest '99
A Map of the World '99
Alien: Resurrection '97
The Ice Storm '97
Snow White: A Tale of Terror '97
Copycat '95
Jeffrey '95
Death and the Maiden '94
Dave '93
Alien 3 '92
1492: Conquest of Paradise '92

Ghostbusters 2 *'89*
Gorillas in the Mist *'88*
Working Girl *'88*
Aliens *'86*
Half Moon Street *'86*
One Woman or Two *'85*
Ghostbusters *'84*
Deal of the Century *'83*
The Year of Living Dangerously *'82*
Eyewitness *'81*
Alien *'79*
Madman *'79*
Sorrows of Gin *'79*

Hugo Weaving (1959-)
Lord of the Rings 1: The Fellowship of the Rings *'01*
The Matrix *'99*
Bedrooms and Hallways *'98*
The Interview *'98*
Babe *'95 (V)*
The Adventures of Priscilla, Queen of the Desert *'94*
The Custodian *'94*
Frauds *'93*
Reckless Kelly *'93*
Proof *'91*
The Right Hand Man *'87*
For Love Alone *'86*

Alan Webb (1906-82)
Deadly Game *'82*
The Great Train Robbery *'79*
King Lear *'71*
Entertaining Mr. Sloane *'70*
King Rat *'65*
The Pumpkin Eater *'64*
Challenge to Lassie *'49*

Chloe Webb (1960-)
The Newton Boys *'97*
She's So Lovely *'97*
Love Affair *'94*
Armistead Maupin's Tales of the City *'93*
A Dangerous Woman *'93*
The Belly of an Architect *'91*
Queens Logic *'91*
Heart Condition *'90*
China Beach *'88*
Twins *'88*
Sid & Nancy *'86*

Clifton Webb (1889-1966)
The Man Who Never Was *'55*
Three Coins in the Fountain *'54*
A Woman's World *'54*
Titanic *'53*
Stars and Stripes Forever *'52*
Cheaper by the Dozen *'50*
Dark Corner *'46*
The Razor's Edge *'46*
Laura *'44*

Danny Webb
Frenchman's Creek *'98*
A Woman's Guide to Adultery *'93*
Alien 3 *'92*
Henry V *'89*

Greg Webb
Puppet Master 2 *'90*
Running Mates *'86*

Jack Webb (1920-82)
Red Nightmare *'62*
The Commies Are Coming, the Commies Are Coming *'57*
D.I. *'57*
Pete Kelly's Blues *'55*
Dragnet *'54*
The Halls of Montezuma *'50*
The Men *'50*
Sunset Boulevard *'50*
He Walked by Night *'48*

Richard Webb (1915-93)
Beware! The Blob *'72*
Hell Raiders *'68*
Git! *'65*

Attack of the Mayan Mummy *'63*
Distant Drums *'51*
The Invisible Monster *'50*
Sands of Iwo Jima *'49*
Out of the Past *'47*
O.S.S. *'46*

Rita Webb
Frenzy *'72*
Zeta One *'69*

Veronica Webb
In Too Deep *'99*
Jungle Fever *'91*

Diane Webber
Sinthia: The Devil's Doll *'70*
The Mermaids of Tiburon *'62*

Mark Webber
Hollywood Ending *'02*
The Laramie Project *'02*
Chelsea Walls *'01*
Storytelling *'01*
Snow Day *'00*
Drive Me Crazy *'99*
White Boyz *'99*

Robert Webber (1924-89)
Nuts *'87*
Assassin *'86*
Wild Geese 2 *'85*
Starflight One *'83*
Don't Go to Sleep *'82*
The Final Option *'82*
Wrong Is Right *'82*
S.O.B. *'81*
Private Benjamin *'80*
The Streets of L.A. *'79*
10 *'79*
Casey's Shadow *'78*
Revenge of the Pink Panther *'78*
The Choirboys *'77*
Soldat Duroc...Ca Va Etre Ta Fete! *'75*
Bring Me the Head of Alfredo Garcia *'74*
Death Stalk *'74*
Dollars *'71*
Thief *'71*
The Great White Hope *'70*
The Dirty Dozen *'67*
Dead Heat on a Merry-Go-Round *'66*
The Silencers *'66*
The Sandpiper *'65*
Hysteria *'64*
The Stripper *'63*
Twelve Angry Men *'57*

Timothy Webber
The Boys of St. Vincent *'93*
That's My Baby! *'88*
Toby McTeague *'87*
The Grey Fox *'83*
Terror Train *'80*

Amy Weber
Crackerjack 3 *'00*
Kolobos *'99*
Art House *'98*

Dewey Weber
Ulee's Gold *'97*
Chain of Desire *'93*

Jacques Weber (1949-)
Beaumarchais the Scoundrel *'96*
The Elegant Criminal *'92*
Cyrano de Bergerac *'90*

Jake Weber (1964-)
The Cell *'00*
U-571 *'00*
Pushing Tin *'99*
Dangerous Beauty *'98*
Meet Joe Black *'98*
What the Deaf Man Heard *'98*
Skin Art *'93*

Steven Weber (1961-)
Common Ground *'00*
Time Code *'00*
Late Last Night *'99*
At First Sight *'98*
The Break Up *'98*
Sour Grapes *'98*
Dracula: Dead and Loving It *'95*
Jeffrey *'95*

The Kennedys of Massachusetts *'95*
Leaving Las Vegas *'95*
The Temp *'93*
Single White Female *'92*
In the Line of Duty: A Cop for the Killing *'90*
Hamburger Hill *'87*

Derek Webster
Josh Kirby...Time Warrior: Chapter 5, Journey to the Magic Cavern *'96*
Josh Kirby...Time Warrior: Chapter 6, Last Battle for the Universe *'96*
Josh Kirby...Time Warrior: Chapter 1, Planet of the Dino-Knights *'95*
Josh Kirby...Time Warrior: Chapter 3, Trapped on Toyworld *'95*
Josh Kirby...Time Warrior: Chapter 4, Eggs from 70 Million B.C. *'95*

Ann Wedgeworth (1935-)
Hunter's Moon *'97*
The Whole Wide World *'96*
Love and a .45 *'94*
Cooperstown *'93*
Hard Promises *'92*
Green Card *'90*
Miss Firecracker *'89*
Steel Magnolias *'89*
Far North *'88*
Made in Heaven *'87*
A Tiger's Tale *'87*
My Science Project *'85*
Sweet Dreams *'85*
No Small Affair *'84*
Soggy Bottom U.S.A. *'84*
Killjoy *'81*
Bogie: The Last Hero *'80*
The Birch Interval *'78*
Citizens Band *'77*
One Summer Love *'76*
War Between the Tates *'76*
The Catamount Killing *'74*
Law and Disorder *'74*
Bang the Drum Slowly *'73*
Scarecrow *'73*

Barbara Weeks (1913-)
The Violent Years *'56*
Hell's Headquarters *'32*
White Eagle *'32*
Palmy Days *'31*

Jimmie Ray Weeks
Analyze This *'98*
The Siege *'98*
Dead Man *'95*
The Abyss *'89*
Frantic *'88*
Apology *'86*

Kim Weeks
Family of Cops 3 *'98*
Family of Cops 2: Breach of Faith *'97*

Perdita Weeks
Catherine Cookson's The Rag Nymph *'96*
Cold Light of Day *'95*

Paul Wegener (1874-1948)
Kolberg *'45*
One Arabian Night *'21*
The Golem *'20*
Student of Prague *'13*

Virginia Weidler (1926-68)
Best Foot Forward *'43*
Babes on Broadway *'41*
All This and Heaven Too *'40*
The Philadelphia Story *'40*
Young Tom Edison *'40*
The Great Man Votes *'38*
Too Hot to Handle *'38*

Paul Weigel (1867-1951)
The Great Dictator *'40*
For Heaven's Sake *'26*

Rafer Weigel
Rated X *'00*
Free Enterprise *'98*

Teri Weigel (1962-)
Auntie Lee's Meat Pies *'92*
Marked for Death *'90*
Predator 2 *'90*
The Banker *'89*
Savage Beach *'89*
Cheerleader Camp *'88*
Glitch! *'88*
Return of the Killer Tomatoes! *'88*

Liza Weil
Stir of Echoes *'99*
Whatever *'98*

Isabelle Weingarten
State of Things *'82*
The Mother and the Whore *'73*

Scott Weinger (1975-)
Aladdin and the King of Thieves *'96 (V)*
The Return of Jafar *'94 (V)*
Aladdin *'92 (V)*

Harvey Weinstein
An Alan Smithee Film: Burn, Hollywood, Burn *'97*
Forgotten Silver *'96*

Carl Weintraub
Sorry, Wrong Number *'89*
Oliver & Company *'88 (V)*

Cindy Weintraub
The Prowler *'81*
Humanoids from the Deep *'80*

Heidelinde Weis
Something for Everyone *'70*
The Man Outside *'68*

Robin Weisman
Thunder in Paradise *'93*
Three Men and a Little Lady *'90*

Florence Weiss
Overture to Glory *'40*
The Singing Blacksmith *'38*
The Cantor's Son *'37*

Michael T. Weiss (1962-)
Bones *'01*
Freeway 2: Confessions of a Trickbaby *'99*
Jeffrey *'95*
Howling 4: The Original Nightmare *'88*

Roberta Weiss
Abducted *'86*
Autumn Born *'79*

Shaun Weiss (1978-)
D3: The Mighty Ducks *'96*
D2: The Mighty Ducks *'94*
Heavyweights *'94*
The Mighty Ducks *'92*

Morgan Weisser (1971-)
Mother *'94*
Long Road Home *'91*
Prayer of the Rollerboys *'91*

Norbert Weisser
Nemesis 4: Cry of Angels *'97*
Adrenalin: Fear the Rush *'96*
Nemesis 3: Time Lapse *'96*
Omega Doom *'96*
Riders of the Purple Sage *'96*
Heatseeker *'95*
Children of Fury *'94*
My Antonia *'94*
The Road to Wellville *'94*
Arcade *'93*
Deceit *'93*
Schindler's List *'93*
Midnight Cabaret *'90*
Secret of the Ice Cave *'89*
Sweet Lies *'88*
Android *'82*

Jeffrey Weissman
Back to the Future, Part 3 *'90*
Back to the Future, Part 2 *'89*

Johnny Weissmuller (1904-84)
Swamp Fire *'46*
Stage Door Canteen *'43*

Tarzan's New York Adventure *'42*
Tarzan's Secret Treasure *'41*
Tarzan Finds a Son *'39*
Tarzan Escapes *'36*
Tarzan and His Mate *'34*
Tarzan, the Ape Man *'32*

Lucinda Weist
The Silencers *'95*
The Haunting of Seacliff Inn *'94*

Rachel Weisz (1971-)
About a Boy *'02*
The Mummy Returns *'01*
Beautiful Creatures *'00*
Enemy at the Gates *'00*
The Mummy *'99*
Sunshine *'99*
I Want You *'98*
The Land Girls *'98*
Going All the Way *'97*
Swept from the Sea *'97*
Chain Reaction *'96*

Bruce Weitz (1943-)
Facing the Enemy *'00*
Mach 2 *'00*
Velocity Trap *'99*
Deep Impact *'98*
The Landlady *'98*
Memorial Day *'98*
Breaking the Surface: The Greg Louganis Story *'96*
Prehysteria 3 *'95*
Molly and Gina *'94*
The O.J. Simpson Story *'94*
Windrunner *'94*
The Liar's Club *'93*
No Place to Hide *'93*
The Queen of Mean *'90*
Rainbow Drive *'90*
Death of a Centerfold *'81*

Elisabeth Welch (1904-)
Dead of Night *'45*
Big Fella *'37*
Song of Freedom *'36*

Niles Welch (1888-1976)
Stone of Silver Creek *'35*
Come on Tarzan *'32*
Cornered *'32*

Raquel Welch (1940-)
Legally Blonde *'01*
Tortilla Soup *'01*
Chairman of the Board *'97*
Naked Gun 33 1/3: The Final Insult *'94*
Tainted Blood *'93*
Scandal in a Small Town *'88*
Trouble in Paradise *'88*
Legend of Walks Far Woman *'82*
Stuntwoman *'81*
The Prince and the Pauper *'78*
Mother, Jugs and Speed *'76*
The Four Musketeers *'75*
The Three Musketeers *'74*
Wild Party *'74*
The Last of Sheila *'73*
Bluebeard *'72*
Fuzz *'72*
Hannie Caulder *'72*
Restless *'72*
Myra Breckinridge *'70*
The Magic Christian *'69*
100 Rifles *'69*
Bandolero! *'68*
Bedazzled *'68*
Lady in Cement *'68*
Fathom *'67*
Oldest Profession *'67*
Fantastic Voyage *'66*
One Million Years B.C. *'66*
Shoot Loud, Louder, I Don't Understand! *'66*
A Swingin' Summer *'65*
Roustabout *'64*

Tahnee Welch (1961-)
Johnny 2.0 *'99*
Blacklight *'98*
Body and Soul *'98*
I Shot Andy Warhol *'96*
Improper Conduct *'94*

The Criminal Mind *'93*
Night Train to Venice *'93*
Sleeping Beauty *'89*
Cocoon: The Return *'88*
Lethal Obsession *'87*
Cocoon *'85*

Tuesday Weld (1943-)
Chelsea Walls *'01*
Feeling Minnesota *'96*
Falling Down *'93*
Mistress *'91*
Heartbreak Hotel *'88*
Something in Common *'86*
Once Upon a Time in America *'84*
Author! Author! *'82*
Thief *'81*
Mother & Daughter: A Loving War *'80*
Serial *'80*
A Question of Guilt *'78*
Who'll Stop the Rain? *'78*
Looking for Mr. Goodbar *'77*
F. Scott Fitzgerald in Hollywood *'76*
Reflections of Murder *'74*
Pretty Poison *'68*
The Cincinnati Kid *'65*
I'll Take Sweden *'65*
Soldier in the Rain *'63*
Return to Peyton Place *'61*
Wild in the Country *'61*
The Five Pennies *'59*
Rock, Rock, Rock *'56*

Joan Weldon
Them! *'54*
The Stranger Wore a Gun *'53*

Frank Welker (1945-)
Doug's 1st Movie *'99 (V)*
Mulan *'98 (V)*
Cats Don't Dance *'97 (V)*
Aladdin and the King of Thieves *'96 (V)*
Pocahontas *'95 (V)*
Gargoyles, The Movie: The Heroes Awaken *'94 (V)*
The Pagemaster *'94 (V)*
Aladdin *'92 (V)*
The Rescuers Down Under *'90 (V)*
How to Frame a Figg *'71*

Frederick Weller
The Business of Strangers *'01*
Aftershock: Earthquake in New York *'99*
Harvest *'99*
Stonewall *'95*

Mary Louise Weller (1946-)
Forced Vengeance *'82*
Q (The Winged Serpent) *'82*
The Evil *'78*
National Lampoon's Animal House *'78*

Peter Weller (1947-)
The Contaminated Man *'01*
Dracula: The Dark Prince *'01*
Styx *'00*
Diplomatic Siege *'99*
End of Summer *'97*
Top of the World *'97*
Screamers *'96*
Beyond the Clouds *'95*
Decoy *'95*
Mighty Aphrodite *'95*
The New Age *'94*
The Substitute Wife *'94*
Sunset Grill *'92*
Naked Lunch *'91*
Road to Ruin *'91*
Cat Chaser *'90*
Rainbow Drive *'90*
RoboCop 2 *'90*
Women & Men: Stories of Seduction *'90*
Leviathan *'89*
The Tunnel *'89*
Shakedown *'88*
RoboCop *'87*
Apology *'86*
A Killing Affair *'85*
Two Kinds of Love *'85*

The Adventures of Buckaroo Banzai Across the Eighth Dimension *'84*
The Dancing Princesses *'84*
First Born *'84*
Of Unknown Origin *'83*
Shoot the Moon *'82*
Butch and Sundance: The Early Days *'79*
The Man Without a Country *'73*

Gwen Welles (1951-93)
Boys Life *'94*
Eating *'90*
New Year's Day *'89*
Sticky Fingers *'88*
Desert Hearts *'86*
The Men's Club *'86*
Nobody's Fool *'86*
Nashville *'75*
Hit! *'73*

Mel Welles
Wizards of the Lost Kingdom 2 *'89*
Rented Lips *'88*
Commando Squad *'87*
Chopping Mall *'86*
Dr. Heckyl and Mr. Hype *'80*
Joy Ride to Nowhere *'78*
The She-Beast *'65*
Little Shop of Horrors *'60*
Rock All Night *'57*
The Undead *'57*
Abbott and Costello Meet the Mummy *'55*

Orson Welles (1915-85)
Someone to Love *'87*
Tales of the Klondike: In a Far Country *'87 (N)*
Tales of the Klondike: Race for Number One *'87 (N)*
Tales of the Klondike: The Scorn of Women *'87 (N)*
Tales of the Klondike: The Unexpected *'87 (N)*
Transformers: The Movie *'86 (V)*
Scene of the Crime *'85 (N)*
Slapstick of Another Kind *'84*
Butterfly *'82*
History of the World: Part 1 *'81 (N)*
Shogun *'80 (N)*
Blood and Guns *'79*
The Double McGuffin *'79 (V)*
Hot Money *'79*
The Muppet Movie *'79*
Battleforce *'78 (N)*
America at the Movies *'76*
Voyage of the Damned *'76*
Ten Little Indians *'75*
Ten Days Wonder *'72*
Treasure Island *'72*
The Witching *'72*
Waterloo *'71*
Catch-22 *'70*
Start the Revolution without Me *'70*
12 Plus 1 *'70*
Battle of Neretva *'69*
Casino Royale *'67*
Chimes at Midnight *'67*
I'll Never Forget What's 'Isname *'67*
Is Paris Burning? *'66*
A Man for All Seasons *'66*
The Trial *'63*
The V.I.P.'s *'63*
RoGoPaG *'62*
The King of Kings *'61 (N)*
The Battle of Austerlitz *'60*
Compulsion *'59*
Ferry to Hong Kong *'59*
The Long, Hot Summer *'58*
Touch of Evil *'58*
The Vikings *'58 (N)*
Man in the Shadow *'57*
Moby Dick *'56*
Mr. Arkadin *'55*
Napoleon *'55*
Three Cases of Murder *'55*
Trouble in the Glen *'54*
Othello *'52*
Little World of Don Camillo *'51 (N)*
Black Magic *'49*
The Third Man *'49*
The Lady from Shanghai *'48*
Macbeth *'48*
The Stranger *'46*
Tomorrow Is Forever *'46*
Jane Eyre *'44*
Journey into Fear *'42*
Citizen Kane *'41*

Virginia Welles (1925-)
Francis in the Haunted House *'56*
Dynamite *'49*
To Each His Own *'46*

Titus Welliver (1961-)
Once in the Life *'00*
Rough Riders *'97*
The Big Fall *'96*
Zero Tolerance *'93*
The Lost Capone *'90*

William Wellman, Jr. (1937-)
Curfew *'88*
The Prodigal Planet *'88*
It's Alive *'74*
The Trial of Billy Jack *'74*
Born Losers *'67*
A Swingin' Summer *'65*
Macumba Love *'60*
High School Confidential *'58*
Lafayette Escadrille *'58*

Carole Wells
Funny Lady *'75*
The House of Seven Corpses *'73*

David Wells
Inherit the Wind *'99*
Wild Cactus *'92*

Dawn Wells
Evil Lives *'92*
Rescue from Gilligan's Island *'78*
Return to Boggy Creek *'77*
Town That Dreaded Sundown *'76*
Winterhawk *'76*

Dolores Wells (1937-)
Bikini Beach *'64*
Muscle Beach Party *'64*
The Time Travelers *'64*
Beach Party *'63*

John Wells (1936-98)
Princess Caraboo *'94*
Consuming Passions *'88*
Rentadick *'72*

Tracy Wells (1971-)
Mirror, Mirror 2: Raven Dance *'94*
After Midnight *'89*

Vernon Wells (1945-)
Space Truckers *'97*
Hard Justice *'95*
Bounty Hunter 2002 *'94*
Plughead Rewired: Circuitry Man 2 *'94*
Stranglehold *'94*
Sexual Response *'92*
Enemy Unseen *'91*
Undeclared War *'91*
American Eagle *'90*
Circuitry Man *'90*
Crossing the Line *'90*
The Shrimp on the Barbie *'90*
Circle of Fear *'89*
Nam Angels *'88*
Innerspace *'87*
Last Man Standing *'87*
Commando *'85*
The Road Warrior *'82*
The Losers *'70*

John Welsh (1914-)
The Duchess of Duke Street *'78*
Lucky Jim *'58*
The Revenge of Frankenstein *'58*

Kenneth Welsh
Focus *'01*
The Sign of Four *'01*
The Hound of the Baskervilles *'00*
Love Come Down *'00*
Vendetta *'99*
Habitat *'97*
Jack Higgins' Thunder Point *'97*
Joe Torre: Curveballs Along the Way *'97*
Dead Silence *'96*
Escape Clause *'96*
Kissinger and Nixon *'96*
Rowing Through *'96*
Hiroshima *'95*
Margaret's Museum *'95*
Portraits of a Killer *'95*
Death Wish 5: The Face of Death *'94*
Getting Gotti *'94*
Legends of the Fall *'94*
The Spider and the Fly *'94*
Timecop *'94*
Whale Music *'94*
Adrift *'93*
The Good Fight *'92*
Perfectly Normal *'91*
The Big Slice *'90*
The Last Best Year *'90*
And Then You Die *'88*
Another Woman *'88*
Crocodile Dundee 2 *'88*
The Climb *'87*
Lost *'86*
Loyalties *'86*
Screwball Academy *'86*
The War Boy *'85*
Of Unknown Origin *'83*

Margaret Welsh
American Heart *'92*
Mr. & Mrs. Bridge *'90*
Smooth Talk *'85*

William Welsh (1870-1946)
20,000 Leagues under the Sea *'16*
Traffic in Souls *'13*

Ariadne Welter (1930-98)
The Brainiac *'61*
The Devil's Hand *'61*
The Vampire's Coffin *'58*
The Vampire *'57*
The Criminal Life of Archibaldo de la Cruz *'55*

Jiang Wen
Devils on the Doorstep *'00*
The Emperor's Shadow *'96*
Red Sorghum *'87*

Lara Wendel (1965-)
Ghosthouse *'88*
Intervista *'87*
Unsane *'82*

Alan J. Wendl
Serial Mom *'94*
Hairspray *'88*

George Wendt (1948-)
The Prime Gig *'00*
Alice in Wonderland *'99*
Outside Providence *'99*
Rupert's Land *'98*
Space Truckers *'97*
Spice World: The Movie *'97*
Bye Bye Birdie *'95*
Man of the House *'95*
Hostage for a Day *'94*
Forever Young *'92*
Guilty by Suspicion *'91*
The Masters of Menace *'90*
Never Say Die *'90*
Plain Clothes *'88*
House *'86*
Fletch *'85*
Gung Ho *'85*
Dreamscape *'84*
No Small Affair *'84*
Ratings Game *'84*
Thief of Hearts *'84*
My Bodyguard *'80*

John Wengraf (1897-1974)
Return of Dracula *'58*
The Pride and the Passion *'57*
Five Fingers *'52*
The Razor's Edge *'46*
The Seventh Cross *'44*
U-Boat Prisoner *'44*
Sahara *'43*

David Wenham (1965-)
The Crocodile Hunter: Collision Course *'02*
Moulin Rouge *'01*
Molokai: The Story of Father Damien *'99*
The Boys *'98*
A Little Bit of Soul *'97*
Cosi *'95*

Jann Wenner
Almost Famous *'00*
Perfect *'85*

Alexandra Wentworth
American Virgin *'98*
Meeting Daddy *'98*
Office Space *'98*
The Love Bug *'97*
Trial and Error *'96*

Martha Wentworth (1889-1974)
The Sword in the Stone *'63 (V)*
Jupiter's Darling *'55*
Stagecoach to Denver *'46*
The Stranger *'46*
Vigilantes of Boom Town *'46*

Fritz Wepper
Le Dernier Combat *'84*
Cabaret *'72*
The Bridge *'59*

Jan Werich
Fabulous Adventures of Baron Munchausen *'61*
The Original Fabulous Adventures of Baron Munchausen *'61*

Barbara Werle
Charro! *'69*
Battle of the Bulge *'65*

Oskar Werner (1922-84)
Voyage of the Damned *'76*
The Shoes of the Fisherman *'68*
Fahrenheit 451 *'66*
Ship of Fools *'65*
The Spy Who Came in from the Cold *'65*
Jules and Jim *'62*
The Life and Loves of Mozart *'59*
Lola Montes *'55*
Angel with the Trumpet *'50*

Otto Wernicke (1893-1965)
Crimes of Dr. Mabuse *'32*
M *'31*

Gary Werntz
Pay It Forward *'00*
Deep Impact *'98*
The Peacemaker *'97*
The Art of Dying *'90*

Doug Wert
Baby Face Nelson *'97*
The Wasp Woman *'96*
Haunted Symphony *'94*
Roswell: The U.F.O. Cover-Up *'94*
Dracula Rising *'93*
The Assassination Game *'92*

Massimo Wertmuller
Summer Night with Greek Profile, Almond Eyes & Scent of Basil *'87*
Sotto, Sotto *'85*

Dick Wessel (1913-65)
Flying Leathernecks *'51*
Dick Tracy vs. Cueball *'46*
X Marks the Spot *'42*
Tanks a Million *'41*
They Died with Their Boots On *'41*

Dick Wesson (1919-79)
The Errand Boy *'61*
Calamity Jane *'53*
The Desert Song *'53*
Jim Thorpe: All American *'51*
Destination Moon *'50*

Adam West (1928-)
Drop Dead Gorgeous *'99*
American Vampire *'97*
Joyride *'97*
The New Age *'94*
Maxim Xul *'91*
Night of the Kickfighters *'91*
Return Fire *'91*
Mad About You *'90*
Omega Cop *'90*
Doin' Time on Planet Earth *'88*
Zombie Nightmare *'86*
Young Lady Chatterly 2 *'85*
Hellriders *'84*
One Dark Night *'82*
For the Love of It *'80*
The Happy Hooker Goes Hollywood *'80*
Hooper *'78*
Hell River *'75*
The Specialist *'75*
Batman *'66*
The Outlaws Is Coming! *'65*
Robinson Crusoe on Mars *'64*
Geronimo *'62*

Chandra West (1970-)
The Salton Sea *'02*
The '70s *'00*
Something More *'99*
Universal Soldier 2: Brothers in Arms *'98*
Universal Soldier 3: Unfinished Business *'98*
Puppet Master 5: The Final Chapter *'94*
Puppet Master 4 *'93*

Dominic West
Rock Star *'01*
28 Days *'00*
A Christmas Carol *'99*
William Shakespeare's A Midsummer Night's Dream *'99*
The Gambler *'97*
Wavelength *'96*

Gregory West
The Surgeon *'94*
Class of 1999 2: The Substitute *'93*

Jeremy West
Curse 4: The Ultimate Sacrifice *'90*
Catacombs *'89*

Joel West
Blood Surf *'00*
The Smokers *'00*

Kevin West
Bio-Dome *'96*
Killer Tomatoes Eat France *'91*
Killer Tomatoes Strike Back *'90*

Lockwood West
Bedazzled *'68*
The Leather Boys *'63*

Mae West (1893-1980)
Sextette *'78*
Myra Breckinridge *'70*
The Love Goddesses *'65*
The Heat's On *'43*
My Little Chickadee *'40*
Every Day's a Holiday *'38*
Go West, Young Man *'36*
Klondike Annie *'36*
Goin' to Town *'35*
Belle of the Nineties *'34*
I'm No Angel *'33*
She Done Him Wrong *'33*
Night After Night *'32*

Martin West
Assault on Precinct 13 *'76*
Sweet November *'68*
A Swingin' Summer *'65*

Norma West
Cause Celebre *'87*
And the Ship Sails On *'83*

Red West (1936-)
John Grisham's The Rainmaker *'97*
The P.A.C.K. *'96*
The Expert *'95*
Grizzly Adams: The Legend Continues *'90*
Proud Men *'87*
Hard Knox *'83*
Will: G. Gordon Liddy *'82*

Samuel West (1966-)
Iris *'01*
Longitude *'00*
Pandaemonium *'00*
Horatio Hornblower *'99*
Retribution *'98*
Rupert's Land *'98*
The Ripper *'97*
Stiff Upper Lips *'96*
Carrington *'95*
Persuasion *'95*
The Vacillations of Poppy Carew *'94*
Howard's End *'92*
Reunion *'88*

Shane West (1978-)
A Walk to Remember *'02*
Get Over It! *'01*
Whatever It Takes *'00*

Sonny West
Outlaw Riders *'72*
Hellcats *'68*

Tegan West
Hi-Life *'98*
Sleep with Me *'94*
Hamburger Hill *'87*

Timothy West (1934-)
Iris *'01*
102 Dalmatians *'00*
Ever After: A Cinderella Story *'98*
King Lear *'98*
Hiroshima *'95*
Framed *'93*
Tragedy of Flight 103: The Inside Story *'91*
Death by Prescription *'80s*
Consuming Passions *'88*
Cry Freedom *'87*
The Last Bastion *'84*
Oliver Twist *'82*
Churchill and the Generals *'81*
Rough Cut *'80*
Agatha *'79*
Edward the King *'75*
Hedda *'75*

Simon Westaway
Alien Cargo *'99*
Chameleon 2: Death Match *'99*
When Love Comes *'98*

John Westbrook (1922-89)
Masque of the Red Death *'65*
Tomb of Ligeia *'64*
Room at the Top *'59*

Helen Westcott (1927-98)
The Invisible Avenger *'58*
Abbott and Costello Meet Dr. Jekyll and Mr. Hyde *'52*
The Gunfighter *'50*
Thunder Over Texas *'34*

James Westerfield
Born in America *'90*
True Grit *'69*
Homicidal *'61*

Hakan Westergren
Dollar *'38*
Swedenhielms *'35*

Floyd "Red Crow" Westerman
The Last Assassins *'96*
Buffalo Girls *'95*
Lakota Woman: Siege at Wounded Knee *'94*
The Broken Chain *'93*
Walker: Texas Ranger: One Riot, One Ranger *'93*
Clearcut *'92*
Dances with Wolves *'90*

Dr. Ruth Westheimer
Forever, Lulu *'87*
One Woman or Two *'85*

Helen Westley (1875-1942)
Lady from Louisiana *'42*
Sunny *'41*
All This and Heaven Too *'40*

Alexander's Ragtime Band '38
Rebecca of Sunnybrook Farm '38
Heidi '37
Dimples '36
Stowaway '36
Splendor '35
Anne of Green Gables '34
Death Takes a Holiday '34

Nydia Westman (1902-70)
Velvet Touch '48
The Chocolate Soldier '41
Bulldog Drummond's Revenge '37
One Night of Love '34

James Westmoreland
Don't Answer the Phone '80
Stacey '73

Celia Weston
Hearts in Atlantis '01
In the Bedroom '01
K-PAX '01
Joe Gould's Secret '00
Ride with the Devil '99
Snow Falling on Cedars '99
Dead Man Walking '95
Flirting with Disaster '95
Little Man Tate '91
Lost Angels '89

David Weston
The Heroes of Telemark '65
Masque of the Red Death '65

Doris Weston
Born to Be Wild '38
Delinquent Parents '38

Jack Weston (1924-96)
Short Circuit 2 '88
Dirty Dancing '87
Ishtar '87
The Longshot '86
Rad '86
High Road to China '83
The Four Seasons '81
Cuba '79
Gator '76
The Ritz '76
Marco '73
Fuzz '72
A New Leaf '71
Cactus Flower '69
The Thomas Crown Affair '68
Wait until Dark '67
Mirage '66
The Cincinnati Kid '65
The Incredible Mr. Limpet '64
Palm Springs Weekend '63
The Honeymoon Machine '61
Please Don't Eat the Daisies '60

Jeff Weston
Demonic Toys '90
Puppet Master 2 '90

Michael Weston
Hart's War '02
Coyote Ugly '00
Lucky Numbers '00

Virginia Wetherell (1943-)
Dracula '73
Demons of the Mind '72
Disciple of Death '72
The Big Switch '70
The Crimson Cult '68

Patricia Wettig (1951-)
Bongwater '98
Dancer, Texas—Pop. 81 '98
Stephen King's The Langoliers '95
City Slickers 2: The Legend of Curly's Gold '94
Parallel Lives '94
Me & Veronica '93
City Slickers '91
Guilty by Suspicion '91
Silent Motive '91

Merritt Wever
Series 7: The Contenders '01
All I Wanna Do '98

Marius Weyers
Bopha! '93
The Power of One '92
Deepstar Six '89
Farewell to the King '89
Happy Together '89
The Gods Must Be Crazy '84
African Rage '78

Michael Whalen (1902-74)
Missile to the Moon '59
The Phantom from 10,000 Leagues '56
G.I. Jane '51
King of the Bullwhip '51
Omoo Omoo, the Shark God '49
Thunder in the Pines '49
Highway 13 '48
Dawn Express '42
Wee Willie Winkie '37
The Poor Little Rich Girl '36

Sean M. Whalen (1965-)
Charlie's Angels '00
Idle Hands '99
Never Been Kissed '99
The Cable Guy '96
That Thing You Do! '96
Twister '96
The People under the Stairs '91

Frank Whaley (1963-)
Chelsea Walls '01
The Wall '99
Went to Coney Island on a Mission from God...Be Back by Five '98
When Trumpets Fade '98
Bombshell '97
Cafe Society '97
Curtain Call '97
Glam '97
Retroactive '97
The Winner '96
Broken Arrow '95
Homage '95
The Desperate Trail '94
I.Q. '94
Pulp Fiction '94
Swimming with Sharks '94
Swing Kids '93
To Dance with the White Dog '93
Back in the USSR '92
Hoffa '92
A Midnight Clear '92
Career Opportunities '91
The Doors '91
JFK '91
The Freshman '90
Born on the Fourth of July '89
Field of Dreams '89
Little Monsters '89
Ironweed '87

Justin Whalin (1974-)
Dungeons and Dragons '00
Miracle at Midnight '98
Serial Mom '94
White Wolves 2: Legend of the Wild '94
The Fire Next Time '93
Child's Play 3 '91
Perfect Harmony '91

Joanne Whalley (1964-)
Breathtaking '00
Ride the Wild Fields '00
The Guilty '99
A Texas Funeral '99
The Man Who Knew Too Little '97
A Good Man in Africa '94
Mother's Boys '94
Scarlett '94
The Secret Rapture '94
Trial by Jury '94
Storyville '92
The Big Man: Crossing the Line '91
Shattered '91
Navy SEALS '90
Kill Me Again '89
Scandal '89
To Kill a Priest '89
Willow '88
The Good Father '87
Edge of Darkness '86
No Surrender '86
The Singing Detective '86
Dance with a Stranger '85
Pink Floyd: The Wall '82

Kevin Whately
Plain Jane '01
The English Patient '96

Liem Whatley
Heaven and Earth '93
The Iron Triangle '89

Alan Wheatley (1907-91)
Robin Hood: The Movie '55
The Limping Man '53
Calling Paul Temple '48
Counterblast '48
Brighton Rock '47
Appointment with Crime '45

Wil Wheaton (1972-)
Deep Core '00
Python '00
Flubber '97
Mr. Stitch '95
Pie in the Sky '95
The Liar's Club '93
December '91
The Last Prostitute '91
Toy Soldiers '91
The Curse '87
Long Time Gone '86
Stand by Me '86
The Last Starfighter '84
The Buddy System '83
The Secret of NIMH '82 (V)

Bert Wheeler (1895-1968)
Cockeyed Cavaliers '34
Hips, Hips, Hooray '34
Kentucky Kernels '34
Diplomaniacs '33
Hold 'Em Jail '32
Dixiana '30
Half-Shot at Sunrise '30
Hook, Line and Sinker '30

Jane Wheeler
The Kid '97
Marked Man '96
The Neighbor '93

John Wheeler
Lucy and Desi: Before the Laughter '91
Bad Georgia Road '77

Dana Wheeler-Nicholson
Living in Peril '97
Nick and Jane '96
Denise Calls Up '95
The Pompatus of Love '95
Bye Bye, Love '94
My Life's in Turnaround '94
The Night We Never Met '93
Tombstone '93
Circuitry Man '90
Fletch '85
Mrs. Soffel '84

Arleen Whelan (1916-93)
The Sun Shines Bright '53
Never Wave at a WAC '52
Ramrod '47
Castle in the Desert '42
Young People '40
Young Mr. Lincoln '39

Lisa Whelchel (1963-)
Where the Red Fern Grows: Part 2 '92
Twirl '81
The Double McGuffin '79

Manning Whiley
Meet Sexton Blake '44
The Dummy Talks '43

Barbara Whinnery
Hot to Trot! '88
Crawlspace '86

Joseph Whipp
Red Stone Diaries: Luscious Lola '00
A Place Called Truth '98
Amazons '86

Sam Whipple
Archie: Return to Riverdale '90
Grad Night '81

Shannon Whirry (1964-)
Mach 2 '00
Me, Myself, and Irene '00
The Prophet's Game '99
Retroactive '97
Omega Doom '96
Dangerous Prey '95
Exit '95
Playback '95
Animal Instincts 2 '94
The Granny '94
Lady in Waiting '94
Private Obsession '94
Body of Influence '93
Mirror Images 2 '93
Animal Instincts '92

Charles "Slim" Whitaker (1893-1960)
Outlaw of the Plains '46
The Mysterious Rider '42
Bullet Code '40
Cheyenne Rides Again '38
Phantom Gold '38
Melody of the Plains '37
Santa Fe Bound '37
Border Vengeance '35
The Man from Hell '34
The Silver Bullet '34
Deadwood Pass '33
The Fiddlin' Buckaroo '33
Man from Monterey '33
Ghost Valley '32
Saddle Buster '32
Desert of the Lost '27

Christina Whitaker
Assault of the Killer Bimbos '88
Vampire at Midnight '88
Naked Cage '86

Damon Whitaker
Saints and Sinners '95
Bird '88

Duane Whitaker (1959-)
From Dusk Till Dawn 2: Texas Blood Money '98
Tales from the Hood '95
Pulp Fiction '94

Forest Whitaker (1961-)
Panic Room '02
Battlefield Earth '00
Four Dogs Playing Poker '00
Ghost Dog: The Way of the Samurai '99
Light It Up '99
Witness Protection '99
Body Count '97
Phenomenon '96
Rebound: The Legend of Earl "The Goat" Manigault '96
Smoke '95
Species '95
Blown Away '94
The Enemy Within '94
Jason's Lyric '94
Lush Life '94
Ready to Wear '94
Bank Robber '93
Body Snatchers '93
Last Light '93
Article 99 '92
Consenting Adults '92
The Crying Game '92
Diary of a Hitman '91
A Rage in Harlem '91
Criminal Justice '90
Downtown '89
Johnny Handsome '89
Bird '88
Bloodsport '88
Good Morning, Vietnam '87
Stakeout '87
The Color of Money '86
Platoon '86
Fast Times at Ridgemont High '82

Johnny Whitaker (1959-)
Tom Sawyer '73
Napoleon and Samantha '72
The Littlest Angel '69

Alice White (1904-83)
Flamingo Road '49
Employees' Entrance '33
Murder at Midnight '31

Bernie White
Killing Obsession '94
The Abduction of Allison Tate '92
Twenty Dollar Star '91
The Ghost of Fletcher Ridge '80s
Ain't No Way Back '89
Body Count '87

Betty White (1922-)
Whispers: An Elephant's Tale '00 (V)
Lake Placid '99
The Story of Us '99
Dennis the Menace Strikes Again '98
Hard Rain '97
A Weekend in the Country '96
Advise and Consent '62

Carol White (1942-91)
The Squeeze '77
Some Call It Loving '73
Man Who Had Power Over Women '70
Daddy's Gone A-Hunting '69
The Fixer '68
I'll Never Forget What's 'Isname '67
Prehistoric Women '67
A Matter of WHO '62
Never Let Go '60

Dan(iel) White (1908-80)
Attack of the Giant Leeches '59
The Last Hunt '56
Outlaw Country '49

David White
The Amazing Spider-Man '77
The Tender Trap '55

Diz White
Stoogemania '85
Footlight Frenzy '84
Bullshot '83

Earl White
Omega Doom '96
Nemesis 2: Nebula '94

Harriet White
The Ghost '63
Paisan '46

Harrison White
I Got the Hook-Up '98
Doom Asylum '88

Jacqueline White (1922-)
The Narrow Margin '52
The Capture '50
Return of the Bad Men '48
The Show-Off '46
Thirty Seconds Over Tokyo '44
Air Raid Wardens '43

Jesse White (1919-97)
Matinee '92
Monster in the Closet '86
Music Shoppe '82
Bless the Beasts and Children '71
Togetherness '70
The Reluctant Astronaut '67
Pajama Party '64
The Rise and Fall of Legs Diamond '60
Tomboy & the Champ '58
Designing Woman '57
The Bad Seed '56
Forever Female '53
Gunsmoke '53
Million Dollar Mermaid '52
Bedtime for Bonzo '51
Francis Goes to the Races '51
Harvey '50

Lee White
Lonesome Trail '55
Red Rock Outlaw '47

Michael Jai White
Exit Wounds '01
Freedom Song '00
Mutiny '99
Thick as Thieves '99
Universal Soldier: The Return '99
Ringmaster '98
Spawn '97
City of Industry '96
Tyson '95

Peter White
Thirteen Days '00
Mother '96

Ron White
A House Divided '00
Locked in Silence '99
The Wall '99
Blood Brothers '97
Kissinger and Nixon '96
Screamers '96
ShadowZone: The Undead Express '96
Frame by Frame '95
Johnny's Girl '95
Race to Freedom: The Story of the Underground Railroad '94
Guilty as Sin '93
Love & Murder '91
Cowboys Don't Cry '88

Slappy (Melvin) White (1920-95)
Mr. Saturday Night '92
Amazing Grace '74

Steve White
Get On the Bus '96
Just for the Hell of It '68
She-Devils on Wheels '68

Vanna White (1957-)
Gypsy Angels '94
Graduation Day '81

Charles White Eagle
Altered States '80
Three Warriors '77

O.Z. Whitehead (1911-98)
The Man Who Shot Liberty Valance '62
The Horse Soldiers '59
Beware, My Lovely '52
Road House '48
The Grapes of Wrath '40

Paxton Whitehead (1937-)
Kate & Leopold '01
The Adventures of Huck Finn '93
My Boyfriend's Back '93
Boris and Natasha: The Movie '92
Child of Darkness, Child of Light '91
Chips, the War Dog '90
Baby Boom '87
Back to School '86
Jumpin' Jack Flash '86

Billie Whitelaw (1932-)
The Last of the Blonde Bombshells '00
The Lost Son '98
Merlin '98
Jane Eyre '96
Duel of Hearts '92
Freddie the Frog '92 (V)
Catherine Cookson's The Fifteen Streets '90
The Krays '90
Lorna Doone '90
A Murder of Quality '90
The Dressmaker '89
Maurice '87
The Secret Garden '87
Shadey '87
Murder Elite '86
Slayground '84
Unsuitable Job for a Woman '82
A Tale of Two Cities '80
Water Babies '79
Leopard in the Snow '78

The Omen '76
Frenzy '72
Gumshoe '72
Night Watch '72
Start the Revolution without Me '70
Strange Case of Dr. Jekyll & Mr. Hyde '68
The Flesh and the Fiends '60
Make Mine Mink '60
No Love for Johnnie '60
Small Hotel '57

Arkie Whiteley (1965-2001)
Gallowglass '95
Princess Caraboo '94
Razorback '84

Jon Whiteley
The Spanish Gardener '57
Moonfleet '55

Paul Whiteman (1890-1967)
Lady Frankenstein '72
The Fabulous Dorseys '47
Strike Up the Band '40
King of Jazz '30

Charles Malik Whitfield
Behind Enemy Lines '01
The Temptations '98

Dondre T. Whitfield
Two Can Play That Game '01
Alien Fury: Countdown to Invasion '00

June Whitfield
Catherine Cookson's The Secret '00
The Last of the Blonde Bombshells '00

Lynn Whitfield (1953-)
A Girl Thing '01
Dangerous Evidence: The Lori Jackson Story '99
Love Songs '99
The Color of Courage '98
Stepmom '98
Eve's Bayou '97
Gone Fishin' '97
Junior's Groove '97
A Thin Line Between Love and Hate '96
State of Emergency '94
Taking the Heat '93
The Josephine Baker Story '90
Jaws: The Revenge '87
Johnnie Gibson F.B.I. '87
Hard Lessons '86
The Slugger's Wife '85
Doctor Detroit '83

Mitchell Whitfield (1968-)
Lost and Found '99
Best Men '98
I Love You, Don't Touch Me! '97
My Cousin Vinny '92
Dogfight '91

Bradley Whitford (1959-)
Kate & Leopold '01
Bicentennial Man '99
The Muse '99
Red Corner '97
Masterminds '96
My Fellow Americans '96
Billy Madison '94
The Client '94
My Life '93
A Perfect World '93
Philadelphia '93
Scent of a Woman '92
Vital Signs '90
Young Guns 2 '90
Dead As a Doorman '85

Peter Whitford (1939-)
Strictly Ballroom '92
Warm Nights on a Slow-Moving Train '87
Dead End Drive-In '86
My Brilliant Career '79

Jack Whiting
Give Me a Sailor '38
Sailing Along '38

Leonard Whiting (1950-)
Rachel's Man '75
Say Hello to Yesterday '71
Romeo and Juliet '68

Margaret Whiting (1924-)
Trespasser '85
Disraeli '79
Sinbad and the Eye of the Tiger '77

Ray Whitley
Racketeers of the Range '39
Hittin' the Trail '37

Lloyd Whitlock (1891-1966)
Diamond Trail '33
West of the Divide '33
Tangled Destinies '32
The Michigan Kid '28
The Prairie Pirate '25

Jill Whitlow
Ghost Chase '88
Twice Dead '88
Adventures Beyond Belief '87
Night of the Creeps '86
Thunder Run '86

Kari Whitman (1964-)
Forced to Kill '93
Chained Heat 2 '92
Phantom of the Mall: Eric's Revenge '89

Mae Whitman (1988-)
An American Rhapsody '01
A Season for Miracles '99
Hope Floats '98
The Gingerbread Man '97
Independence Day '96
One Fine Day '96
Bye Bye, Love '94
When a Man Loves a Woman '94

Stuart Whitman (1926-)
Second Chances '98
Improper Conduct '94
Trial by Jury '94
Private Wars '93
Heaven & Earth '90 (N)
Mob Boss '90
Omega Cop '90
Smooth Talker '90
Fury '80s
Deadly Reactor '89
Moving Target '89
First Strike '85
The Monster Club '85
The Treasure of the Amazon '84
Vultures '84
Butterfly '82
Demonoid, Messenger of Death '81
Kill Castro '80
The Mercenaries '80
Hostages '79
The Seekers '79
The Treasure Seekers '79
Oil '78
Run for the Roses '78
Delta Fox '77
Maniac '77
Ruby '77
The White Buffalo '77
Eaten Alive '76
Las Vegas Lady '76
Strange Shadows in an Empty Room '76
Crazy Mama '75
Mean Johnny Barrows '75
Call Him Mr. Shatter '74
The Woman Hunter '72
Captain Apache '71
The Invincible Six '68
Those Magnificent Men in Their Flying Machines '65
Rio Conchos '64
The Day and the Hour '63
The Longest Day '62
The Comancheros '61
The Mark '61

The Story of Ruth '60
Darby's Rangers '58
Ten North Frederick '58
Crime of Passion '57
Silver Lode '54

Steve Whitmire (1959-)
Muppets from Space '99 (V)
Muppet Treasure Island '96 (V)
The Muppet Christmas Carol '92 (V)
Labyrinth '86

James Whitmore (1921-)
The Majestic '01
The Relic '96
The Shawshank Redemption '94
Glory! Glory! '90
Old Explorers '90
Nuts '87
Target: Favorite Son '87
All My Sons '86
The Adventures of Mark Twain '85 (V)
Don't Cry, It's Only Thunder '82
The First Deadly Sin '80
Rage '80
The Serpent's Egg '78
The Word '78
Give 'Em Hell, Harry! '75
I Will Fight No More Forever '75
Where the Red Fern Grows '74
Harrad Experiment '73
High Crime '73
Chato's Land '71
Tora! Tora! Tora! '70
Guns of the Magnificent Seven '69
Madigan '68
Planet of the Apes '68
Chuka '67
Waterhole #3 '67
Black Like Me '64
Deep Six '58
The Eddy Duchin Story '56
Battle Cry '55
The McConnell Story '55
Oklahoma! '55
Savage Wilderness '55
Them! '54
Above and Beyond '53
All the Brothers Were Valiant '53
The Girl Who Had Everything '53
Kiss Me Kate '53
Because You're Mine '52
The Asphalt Jungle '50
The Next Voice You Hear '50
Battleground '49

James Whitmore, Jr. (1948-)
Tricks of the Trade '88
The Five of Me '81
The Long Riders '80
The Gypsy Warriors '78
The Boys in Company C '77

Grace Lee Whitney
Star Trek 6: The Undiscovered Country '91
Star Trek 3: The Search for Spock '84

Peter Whitney (1916-72)
Savage Wilderness '55
All the Brothers Were Valiant '53
The Brute Man '46
Murder, He Says '45
Action in the North Atlantic '43
Destination Tokyo '43
Rio Rita '42
Valley of the Sun '42
Whistling in Dixie '42
Underground '41

Benjamin Whitrow (1937-)
Chicken Run '00 (V)
Tom Jones '98
Pride and Prejudice '95
Belfast Assassin '84

Garland Whitt
Save the Last Dance '01
Blind Faith '98

Marguerite Whitten
Mystery in Swing '40
Two-Gun Man from Harlem '38

Margaret Whitton (1950-)
Major League 2 '94
Trial by Jury '94
The Man Without a Face '93
Big Girls Don't Cry...They Get Even '92
Little Monsters '89
Major League '89
Ironweed '87
The Secret of My Success '87
The Best of Times '86
9 1/2 Weeks '86

May Whitty (1865-1948)
Gaslight '44
The White Cliffs of Dover '44
Crash Dive '43
Lassie, Come Home '43
Madame Curie '43
Mrs. Miniver '42
Suspicion '41
The Lady Vanishes '38
Conquest '37
Night Must Fall '37

James Whitworth
Bye Bye, Love '94
Planet of the Dinosaurs '80
The Hills Have Eyes '77
357 Magnum '77
Black Bikers from Hell '70

Johnny Whitworth (1975-)
Valentine '01
John Grisham's The Rainmaker '97
Somebody Is Waiting '96
Empire Records '95

Richard Whorf (1906-66)
Chain Lightning '50
Keeper of the Flame '42
Yankee Doodle Dandy '42
Midnight '34

Patrick Whyte
Kitten with a Whip '64
Hideous Sun Demon '59

Anna Wiazemsky
Porcile '69
Teorema '68

Mary Wickes (1916-95)
The Hunchback of Notre Dame '96 (V)
Little Women '94
Sister Act 2: Back in the Habit '93
Sister Act '92
The Canterville Ghost '91
Postcards from the Edge '90
Almost Partners '87
Where Angels Go, Trouble Follows '68
How to Murder Your Wife '64
Dance with Me, Henry '56
Ma and Pa Kettle at Home '54
By the Light of the Silvery Moon '53
I'll See You in My Dreams '51
On Moonlight Bay '51
June Bride '48
Blondie's Blessed Event '42
Private Buckaroo '42
Who Done It? '42

The Man Who Came to Dinner '41

Jeffrey Wickham
Another Country '84
Waterloo '71

Saskia Wickham (1967-)
Leo Tolstoy's Anna Karenina '96
Angels and Insects '95
Royal Deceit '94

Bernhard Wicki (1919-2000)
Crime & Passion '75
The Eternal Waltz '54
The Last Bridge '54

Kathleen Widdoes (1939-)
Courage Under Fire '96
Mafia Princess '86
Savages '72
The Mephisto Waltz '71
Petulia '68
The Group '66

Johan Widerberg (1974-)
Under the Sun '98
All Things Fair '95

Richard Widmark (1914-)
Murder on the Bayou '91
True Colors '91
Texas Guns '90
Cold Sassy Tree '89
Blackout '85
Against All Odds '84
The Final Option '82
Hanky Panky '82
National Lampoon Goes to the Movies '81
Whale for the Killing '81
All God's Children '80
Bear Island '80
Mr. Horn '79
Coma '78
The Swarm '78
The Domino Principle '77
Rollercoaster '77
Twilight's Last Gleaming '77
Sell Out '76
To the Devil, a Daughter '76
Murder on the Orient Express '74
When the Legends Die '72
Death of a Gunfighter '69
Gun Crazy '69
Madigan '68
The Way West '67
Alvarez Kelly '66
Bedford Incident '65
Cheyenne Autumn '64
The Long Ships '64
How the West Was Won '63
Judgment at Nuremberg '61
Two Rode Together '61
The Alamo '60
The Trap '59
Warlock '59
The Law and Jake Wade '58
The Tunnel of Love '58
Saint Joan '57
The Cobweb '55
Broken Lance '54
Pickup on South Street '53
Don't Bother to Knock '52
The Halls of Montezuma '50
Night and the City '50
No Way Out '50
Panic in the Streets '50
Road House '48
The Street with No Name '48
Kiss of Death '47

Dorothea Wieck
A Time to Love & a Time to Die '58
Maedchen in Uniform '31

Danielle Wiener
Beethoven's 3rd '00
Traveller '96

Kai Wiesinger
The Harmonists '99
Backbeat '94

Lynda Wiesmeier (1963-)
R.S.V.P. '84
Wheels of Fire '84
Preppies '82

Dianne Wiest (1948-)
I Am Sam '01
The 10th Kingdom '00
The Simple Life of Noah Dearborn '99
Practical Magic '98
The Horse Whisperer '97
The Associate '96
Drunks '96
The Birdcage '95
Bullets over Broadway '94
Cops and Robbersons '94
The Scout '94
Little Man Tate '91
Edward Scissorhands '90
Cookie '89
Parenthood '89
Bright Lights, Big City '88
September '88
The Lost Boys '87
Radio Days '87
Hannah and Her Sisters '86
The Purple Rose of Cairo '85
Falling in Love '84
Footloose '84
Independence Day '83
It's My Turn '80

Naima Wifstrand (1890-1968)
Hour of the Wolf '68
The Magician '58
Night Is My Future '47

Chris Wiggins (1931-)
Jack Higgins' The Windsor Protocol '97
Jack Higgins' Thunder Point '97
Black Fox: Blood Horse '94
Black Fox: The Price of Peace '94
Mark Twain and Me '91
Babar: The Movie '88 (V)
Ford: The Man & the Machine '87
The Bay Boy '85
Kavik the Wolf Dog '84
Rock & Rule '83 (V)
Why Shoot the Teacher '79
King of the Grizzlies '69

Wiley Wiggins
Waking Life '01
Dazed and Confused '93

Robert Wightman
Living in Oblivion '94
Stepfather 3: Father's Day '92
Opposing Force '87
A Day for Thanks on Walton's Mountain '82

Carlton Wilborn
Grief '94
Dance '90

George P. Wilbur
Halloween 6: The Curse of Michael Myers '95
Halloween 4: The Return of Michael Myers '88

James Wilby (1958-)
Gosford Park '01
Cotton Mary '99
Behind the Lines '97
The Woman in White '97
Howard's End '92
Lady Chatterley '92
A Tale of Two Cities '91
Conspiracy '89
A Handful of Dust '88
A Summer Story '88
Maurice '87
Dreamchild '85

Frank Wilcox (1907-74)
Beginning of the End '57
A Majority of One '56
Seventh Cavalry '56
Abbott and Costello Meet the Keystone Kops '54
Infamous Crimes '47

Across the Pacific '42
They Died with Their Boots On '41
The Wagons Roll at Night '41

Larry Wilcox (1947-)
National Lampoon's Loaded Weapon 1 '93
Mission Manila '87
The Dirty Dozen: The Next Mission '85
The Last Ride of the Dalton Gang '79
Sky Hei$t '75

Lisa Wilcox (1964-)
Watchers Reborn '98
A Nightmare on Elm Street 5: Dream Child '89
A Nightmare on Elm Street 4: Dream Master '88

Mary Wilcox
Love Me Deadly '76
Beast of the Yellow Night '70

Robert Wilcox (1910-55)
Doctor Satan's Robot '40
Dreaming Out Loud '40
Mysterious Doctor Satan '40
Blondie Takes a Vacation '39
Buried Alive '39
The Man They Could Not Hang '39

Shannon Wilcox
Hollywood Harry '86
When Your Lover Leaves '83

Toyah Wilcox
Ebony Tower '86
Murder: Ultimate Grounds for Divorce '85

Collin Wilcox-Paxton (1937-)
The Crying Child '96
Fluke '95
Wildflower '91
Jaws 2 '78
Fury on Wheels '71
The Baby Maker '70
Catch-22 '70
To Kill a Mockingbird '62

Henry Wilcoxon (1905-84)
Caddyshack '80
Enola Gay: The Men, the Mission, the Atomic Bomb '80
The Two Worlds of Jenny Logan '79
When Every Day Was the Fourth of July '78
Pony Express Rider '76
Against a Crooked Sky '75
Man in the Wilderness '71
Escape from Planet Earth '67
The War Lord '65
The Ten Commandments '56
Scaramouche '52
Samson and Delilah '50
A Connecticut Yankee in King Arthur's Court '49
Unconquered '47
The Corsican Brothers '42
Mrs. Miniver '42
That Hamilton Woman '41
Tarzan Finds a Son '39
If I Were King '38
Jericho '38
Souls at Sea '37
The Last of the Mohicans '36
The President's Mystery '36
The Crusades '35
Cleopatra '34

Jack Wild (1952-)
Robin Hood: Prince of Thieves '91
Melody '71
Pufnstuf '70
Oliver! '68

Andrew Wilde
Murder on Line One '90
1984 '84

Cornel Wilde (1915-89)
The Fifth Musketeer '79
Norseman '78
Sharks' Treasure '75
The Comic '69
The Naked Prey '66
Sword of Lancelot '63
Omar Khayyam '57
Big Combo '55
Passion '54
A Woman's World '54
Main Street to Broadway '53
Treasure of the Golden Condor '53
The Greatest Show on Earth '52
At Sword's Point '51
Road House '48
Forever Amber '47
Leave Her to Heaven '45
A Song to Remember '45
A Thousand and One Nights '45
Wintertime '43
High Sierra '41

Lois Wilde
Brothers of the West '37
Undersea Kingdom '36

Gene Wilder (1935-)
Alice in Wonderland '99
The Lady in Question '99
Murder in a Small Town '99
Another You '91
Funny About Love '90
See No Evil, Hear No Evil '89
Haunted Honeymoon '86
The Woman in Red '84
Hanky Panky '82
Stir Crazy '80
The Frisco Kid '79
The Adventures of Sherlock Holmes' Smarter Brother '78
World's Greatest Lover '77
Silver Streak '76
Blazing Saddles '74
The Little Prince '74
Thursday's Game '74
Young Frankenstein '74
Everything You Always Wanted to Know about Sex (But Were Afraid to Ask) '72
Willy Wonka & the Chocolate Factory '71
Quackser Fortune Has a Cousin in the Bronx '70
Start the Revolution without Me '70
The Producers '68
Bonnie & Clyde '67

Glenn Wilder
Zebra Force '76
The Sand Pebbles '66

James Wilder (1963-)
First Degree '98
The Last Don 2 '98
Flypaper '97
Ivory Tower '97
Kisses in the Dark '97
Nevada '97
Our Mother's Murder '97
Tollbooth '94
Scorchers '92
Prey of the Chameleon '91
Murder One '88
Zombie High '87

Webb Wilder
Heroes of the Heart '94
The Thing Called Love '93
Paradise Park '91

Yvonne Wilder (1937-)
Honeyboy '82
Bloodbrothers '78
The Return of Count Yorga '71
West Side Story '61

Michael Wilding (1912-79)
Waterloo '71
The Naked Edge '61
The World of Suzie Wong '60
The Glass Slipper '55
The Egyptian '54
Torch Song '53
Maytime in Mayfair '52
Stage Fright '50
Under Capricorn '49
The Courtney Affair '47
In Which We Serve '43
Secret Mission '42
Cottage to Let '41
Kipps '41
Convoy '40
Late Extra '35

Michael Wilding, Jr.
Sweet Bird of Youth '89
A.D. '85

John Wildman (1961-)
American Boyfriends '89
Lethal Pursuit '88
Sorority Babes in the Slimeball Bowl-A-Rama '87
My American Cousin '85

Valerie Wildman
Inner Sanctum '91
Neon City '91
Salvador '86

Dawn Wildsmith
Jack-O '95
Wizards of the Demon Sword '94
Alienator '89
Hollywood Chainsaw Hookers '88
Terminal Force '88
Warlords '88
Cyclone '87
Evil Spawn '87
Phantom Empire '87
Surf Nazis Must Die '87

Jason Wiles (1970-)
Kicking and Screaming '95
Higher Learning '94
Roadracers '94
Windrunner '94

Mike Wiles
Held Up '00
Cole Justice '89
Terror at Tenkiller '86

Ed Wiley
The Canterville Ghost '96
Class of '61 '92

Jan Wiley (1916-93)
She Wolf of London '46
There Goes Kelly '45
Master Key '44
Jive Junction '43
Rhythm Parade '43
So Proudly We Hail '43
The Underdog '43
Dawn on the Great Divide '42
Tonto Basin Outlaws '41

John Wilford
Ninja: American Warrior '90
Ninja Death Squad '87

Dianne Wilhite
Flesh Feast '69
Gruesome Twosome '67

Kathleen Wilhoite (1964-)
My Sister's Keeper '02
Drowning Mona '00
Nurse Betty '00
Breast Men '97
Color of Night '94
Getting Even with Dad '94
Lorenzo's Oil '92
Bad Influence '90
Everybody Wins '90
Dream Demon '88
Angel Heart '87
Campus Man '87
Undercover '87
Witchboard '87
The Morning After '86
Murphy's Law '86
Quarterback Princess '85
Private School '83

Robert J. Wilke (1915-89)
Tarnished Angels '57
20,000 Leagues under the Sea '54
From Here to Eternity '53
High Noon '52

Jose Wilker (1945-)
Medicine Man '92
Bye Bye Brazil '79
Dona Flor and Her Two Husbands '78
Xica '76

Guy Wilkerson (1899-1971)
Man of the West '58
Comin' Round the Mountain '51
Flaming Bullets '45
Frontier Fugitives '45
Marked for Murder '45
Boss of Rawhide '44
Dead or Alive '44
Guns of the Law '44
Outlaw Roundup '44
Fighting Valley '43
Sergeant York '41

Donna Wilkes (1959-)
Hard Knocks
Grotesque '87
Angel '84
Blood Song '82
Fyre '78

Elaine Wilkes
Killer Party '86
Roommate '84

Barbara Wilkin
Six in Paris '68
The Flesh Eaters '64

Elizabeth Wilkinson
Suburban Roulette '67
A Taste of Blood '67

June Wilkinson (1940-)
Vasectomy: A Delicate Matter '86
Sno-Line '85
Frankenstein's Great Aunt Tillie '83
The Florida Connection '74
The Bellboy and the Playgirls '62
Macumba Love '60

Linden Wilkinson
The Monkey's Mask '00
The Wedding Party '97

Tom Wilkinson (1948-)
The Importance of Being Earnest '02
Black Knight '01
In the Bedroom '01
The Patriot '00
David Copperfield '99 (N)
Essex Boys '99
Molokai: The Story of Father Damien '99
Ride with the Devil '99
The Governess '98
Rush Hour '98
Shakespeare in Love '98
Oscar and Lucinda '97
Wilde '97
The Full Monty '96
The Ghost and the Darkness '96
Smilla's Sense of Snow '96
Martin Chuzzlewit '94
Priest '94
Royal Deceit '94
Prime Suspect '92
Paper Mask '91
Sylvia '86

Lee Wilkof
Private Parts '96
Chattahoochee '89

Fred Willard (1939-)
How High '01
The Wedding Planner '01
Best in Show '00
Austin Powers 2: The Spy Who Shagged Me '99
Idle Hands '99
Permanent Midnight '98
Waiting for Guffman '96
Prehysteria 3 '95
Sodbusters '94
The Return of Spinal Tap '92
High Strung '91
Portrait of a White Marriage '88
Roxanne '87
Lots of Luck '85
Moving Violations '85
This Is Spinal Tap '84
How to Beat the High Cost of Living '80
Americathon '79
Salem's Lot '79
Chesty Anderson USN '76

Jean Willes (1923-89)
Invasion of the Body Snatchers '56
Abbott and Costello Go to Mars '53
So Proudly We Hail '43

Chad Willet
Outlaw Justice '98
Annie O '95

Warren William (1895-1948)
Black Tower '50
The Private Affairs of Bel Ami '47
Fear '46
Strange Illusion '45
The Wolf Man '41
Arizona '40
The Man in the Iron Mask '39
Wives under Suspicion '38
The Firefly '37
Madame X '37
Go West, Young Man '36
Satan Met a Lady '36
The Case of the Lucky Legs '35
Cleopatra '34
Imitation of Life '34
Employees' Entrance '33
Gold Diggers of 1933 '33
Lady for a Day '33
Skyscraper Souls '32
Three on a Match '32

Adam Williams (1929-)
North by Northwest '59
The Badlanders '58
Fear Strikes Out '57
Crashout '55
Without Warning '52
Flying Leathernecks '51
Queen for a Day '51

Allen Williams
Scorpion '86
The Two Worlds of Jenny Logan '79

Barbara Williams
Love Come Down '00
Family of Cops 3 '98
Krippendorf's Tribe '98
Naked City: A Killer Christmas '98
Naked City: Justice with a Bullet '98
Bone Daddy '97
Family of Cops 2: Breach of Faith '97
Inventing the Abbotts '97
Joe Torre: Curveballs Along the Way '97
Family of Cops '95
Digger '94
Spenser: Pale Kings & Princes '94
Spenser: Ceremony '93
Indecency '92
Oh, What a Night '92
City of Hope '91
Peter Gunn '89
Watchers '88
Tiger Warsaw '87
Jo Jo Dancer, Your Life Is Calling '86
Tell Me That You Love Me '84
Thief of Hearts '84

Barry Williams (1954-)
The Brady Bunch Movie '95
A Very Brady Christmas '88
Wild in the Streets '68

Bill Williams (1916-92)
Flight of the Grey Wolf '76
The Giant Spider Invasion '75
Buckskin '68
Storm Rider '57
Torpedo Alley '53
Son of Paleface '52
Cavalry Charge '51
The Cariboo Trail '50
Operation Haylift '50
The Clay Pigeon '49
The Stratton Story '49
A Woman's Secret '49
Deadline at Dawn '46
Till the End of Time '46

Billy Dee Williams (1937-)
Undercover Brother '02
The Ladies Man '00
The Visit '00
Giant Steps
Fear Runs Silent '99
The Contract '98
Mask of Death '97
Steel Sharks '97
Moving Target '96
Dangerous Passion '95
The Prince '95
Triplecross '95
Alien Intruder '93
Percy & Thunder '93
The Jacksons: An American Dream '92
Driving Me Crazy '91
Batman '89
Secret Agent 00-Soul '89
Deadly Illusion '87
Number One with a Bullet '87
Courage '86
Oceans of Fire '86
Fear City '85
Shooting Stars '85
Christmas Lilies of the Field '84
The Imposter '84
Marvin & Tige '84
Chiefs '83
Return of the Jedi '83
Nighthawks '81
Children of Divorce '80
The Empire Strikes Back '80
The Hostage Tower '80
Bingo Long Traveling All-Stars & Motor Kings '76
Mahogany '75
Hit! '73
Final Comedown '72
The Glass House '72
Lady Sings the Blues '72
Brian's Song '71
The Out-of-Towners '70
Black Brigade '69

Billy "Sly" Williams
Mission of Justice '92
Voodoo Dawn '89

Brook Williams (1938-)
Absolution '81
Where Eagles Dare '68
Plague of the Zombies '66

Cara Williams (1925-)
The White Buffalo '77
Never Steal Anything Small '59
The Defiant Ones '58
Meet Me in Las Vegas '56
Boomerang '47

Caroline Williams
Leprechaun 3 '95
Stepfather 2: Make Room for Daddy '89
The Texas Chainsaw Massacre 2 '86

Charles Williams
Born to Be Wild '38
Hollywood Stadium Mystery '38

Chuck Williams
Dark Rider '91
Soultaker '90

Cindy Williams (1947-)
Meet Wally Sparks '97
Bingo '91
Big Man on Campus '89
Rude Awakening '89
Tricks of the Trade '88
Spaceship '81

Uforia '81
More American Graffiti '79
The First Nudie Musical '75
The Conversation '74
The Migrants '74
American Graffiti '73
The Killing Kind '73
Beware! The Blob '72
Travels with My Aunt '72
Gas-s-s-s! '70

Clara Williams (1888-1928)
Hell's Hinges '16
The Bargain '15
The Italian '15

Clarence Williams, III (1939-)
Mindstorm '01
Reindeer Games '00
The General's Daughter '99
Life '99
Frogs for Snakes '98
The Legend of 1900 '98
George Wallace '97
Half-Baked '97
The Love Bug '97
Hoodlum '96
Rebound: The Legend of Earl "The Goat" Manigault '96
The Road to Galveston '96
Sprung '96
The Immortals '95
The Silencers '95
Tales from the Hood '95
Against the Wall '94
Sugar Hill '94
Dangerous Relations '93
Deep Cover '92
My Heroes Have Always Been Cowboys '91
Maniac Cop 2 '90
The House of Dies Drear '88
I'm Gonna Git You Sucka '88
The Last Innocent Man '87
Perfect Victims '87
Tough Guys Don't Dance '87
52 Pick-Up '86
Purple Rain '84

Cynda Williams (1966-)
Introducing Dorothy Dandridge '99
Caught Up '98
Relax... It's Just Sex! '98
Gang in Blue '96
Spirit Lost '96
Condition Red '95
Machine Gun Blues '95
The Sweeper '95
The Tie That Binds '95
Armistead Maupin's Tales of the City '93
The Ghost Brigade '93
Tales of Erotica '93
One False Move '91
Mo' Better Blues '90

Darnell Williams
Firestarter 2: Rekindled '02
How U Like Me Now? '92

Dick Williams
Dog Day Afternoon '75
The Anderson Tapes '71

Dick Anthony Williams (1938-)
The Players Club '98
Edward Scissorhands '90
Mo' Better Blues '90
Tap '89
For Us, the Living '88
Gardens of Stone '87
Keeping On '81
Sophisticated Gents '81
The Night the City Screamed '80
An Almost Perfect Affair '79
A Woman Called Moses '78

D.J. Williams
The Courageous Mr. Penn '41
The Crimes of Stephen Hawke '36
Murder in the Old Red Barn '36

Don Williams
Smokey and the Bandit 2 '80
The Ghastly Ones '68

Edy Williams (1942-)
Bad Girls from Mars '90
Rented Lips '88
Mankillers '87
Hellhole '85
Bad Manners '84
Hollywood Hot Tubs '84
Beyond the Valley of the Dolls '70
Secret Life of an American Wife '68
Good Times '67
Naked Kiss '64

Emlyn Williams (1905-87)
Deadly Game '82
The L-Shaped Room '62
The Wreck of the Mary Deare '59
Another Man's Poison '52
The Last Days of Dolwyn '49
This England '42
The Stars Look Down '39
The Citadel '38
The Iron Duke '34

Esther Williams (1923-)
That's Entertainment '74
Jupiter's Darling '55
Dangerous When Wet '53
Easy to Love '53
Million Dollar Mermaid '52
Skirts Ahoy! '52
Texas Carnival '51
The Duchess of Idaho '50
Pagan Love Song '50
Neptune's Daughter '49
Take Me Out to the Ball Game '49
On an Island with You '48
Ziegfeld Follies '46
Thrill of a Romance '45
Bathing Beauty '44
A Guy Named Joe '44
Andy Hardy's Double Life '42

Gareth Williams
Hard Luck '01
The Cell '00
From the Earth to the Moon '98
Palookaville '95
Blessing '94

Grant Williams (1930-85)
Brain of Blood '71
Escape from Planet Earth '67
The Leech Woman '59
The Incredible Shrinking Man '57
The Monolith Monsters '57
Written on the Wind '56

Guinn "Big Boy" Williams (1899-1962)
The Alamo '60
Hidden Guns '56
Springfield Rifle '52
Nevada '44
The Desperadoes '43
Hands Across the Border '43
Lure of the Islands '42
Mr. Wise Guy '42
Billy the Kid '41
The Fighting 69th '40
Virginia City '40
Wagon's Westward '40
Bad Lands '39
Dangerous Holiday '37
Feud of the Trail '37
You Only Live Once '37
Gun Play '36
Kelly the Second '36
The Vigilantes Are Coming '36
Danger Trails '35
Powdersmoke Range '35
Heritage of the Desert '33
Mystery Squadron '33
The Phantom Broadcast '33
When the West Was Young '32
The Phantom '31
Burning Daylight '28
Wolfheart's Revenge '25
Rounding Up the Law '22

Guy Williams (1924-89)
Captain Sinbad '63
The Prince and the Pauper '62
The Sign of Zorro '60
I Was a Teenage Werewolf '57
The Secret of El Zorro '57
Savage Wilderness '55

Hal Williams
Don't Look Back: The Story of Leroy "Satchel" Paige '81
On the Nickel '80

Harcourt Williams
The Obsessed '51
Henry V '44

Harland Williams (1967-)
Sorority Boys '02
Freddy Got Fingered '01
The Whole Nine Yards '00
Superstar '99
Dog Park '98
Mr. Headmistress '98
There's Something about Mary '98
Half-Baked '97
RocketMan '97
Down Periscope '96
Dumb & Dumber '94

Heathcote Williams
The Odyssey '97
The Tango Lesson '97
Blue Juice '95
Cold Light of Day '95
Orlando '92

Hugh Williams (1904-69)
Khartoum '66
Elizabeth of Ladymead '48
A Girl in a Million '46
The Day Will Dawn '42
Secret Mission '42
One of Our Aircraft Is Missing '41
The Human Monster '39
Inspector Hornleigh '39
Wuthering Heights '39
Bitter Sweet '33

Ian Patrick Williams
Heaven's a Drag '94
Bad Channels '92
Bloodmoon '90
Dolls '87

Jason Williams (1952-)
Danger Zone 3: Steel Horse War '90
Danger Zone 2 '89
Vampire at Midnight '88
Danger Zone '87
Cheerleaders' Wild Weekend '85
Copkillers '77
Flesh Gordon '72

Jim Williams
Ex-Cop '93
Living to Die '91
The Newlydeads '87
Island of Blood '86
The Executioner '78

JoBeth Williams (1953-)
The Ponder Heart '01
Backlash '99
Jackie's Back '99
From the Earth to the Moon '98
It Came from the Sky '98
Just Write '97
Little City '97
When Danger Follows You Home '97
Jungle 2 Jungle '96
Ruby Jean and Joe '96
Parallel Lives '94
Wyatt Earp '94
Chantilly Lace '93
Final Appeal '93
Sex, Love and Cold Hard Cash '93
Me, Myself & I '92
Stop! or My Mom Will Shoot '92
Dutch '91
Switch '91
Victim of Love '91
Child in the Night '90
Welcome Home '89
Memories of Me '88
Murder Ordained '87
Desert Bloom '86
Poltergeist 2: The Other Side '86
American Dreamer '84
Teachers '84
Adam '83
The Big Chill '83
The Day After '83
Endangered Species '82
Poltergeist '82
The Dogs of War '81
Stir Crazy '80
Kramer vs. Kramer '79

John Williams (1903-83)
The Secret War of Harry Frigg '68
Double Trouble '67
Dear Brigitte '65
24 Hours in a Woman's Life '61
The Young Philadelphians '59
Island in the Sun '57
Will Success Spoil Rock Hunter? '57
Witness for the Prosecution '57
D-Day, the Sixth of June '56
To Catch a Thief '55
Dial "M" for Murder '54
Sabrina '54

Kelli Williams (1970-)
Sweetwater: A True Rock Story '99
Wavelength '96
Snowbound: The Jim and Jennifer Stolpa Story '94
Lifepod '93
There Goes My Baby '92
Till Murder Do Us Part '92
Zapped Again '89

Kenneth Williams (1926-88)
The Thief and the Cobbler '96 (V)
Carry On Emmanuelle '78
Carry On Behind '75
Carry On at Your Convenience '71
Carry On Camping '71
Carry On Henry VIII '71
Carry On Doctor '68
Follow That Camel '67
Carry On Cowboy '66
Carry On Screaming '66
Carry On Cleo '65
Carry On Cruising '62

Kimberly Williams (1971-)
Follow the Stars Home '01
The 10th Kingdom '00
Just a Little Harmless Sex '99
Safe House '99
Simpatico '99
The War at Home '96
Father of the Bride Part II '95
Coldblooded '94
Indian Summer '93
Father of the Bride '91

Lee Williams
In His Life: The John Lennon Story '00
The Wolves of Kromer '98

Lia Williams
Shot Through the Heart '98
Firelight '97

Malinda Williams (1975-)
Dancing in September '00
Uninvited Guest '99
The Wood '99
High School High '96
A Thin Line Between Love and Hate '96
Laurel Avenue '93

Mark Williams (1959-)
High Heels and Low Lifes '01
The Borrowers '97
101 Dalmatians '96
Kill Line '91

Michael Williams (1935-2001)
The Blair Witch Project '99
Murder by Night '89
Educating Rita '83

Michelle Williams (1980-)
Perfume '01
If These Walls Could Talk 2 '00
Dick '99
Halloween: H20 '98
Killing Mr. Griffin '97
A Thousand Acres '97
Species '95
Timemaster '95
Lassie '94

Olivia Williams (1969-)
The Body '01
Born Romantic '00
Four Dogs Playing Poker '00
Jason and the Argonauts '00
The Sixth Sense '99
Rushmore '98
Emma '97
The Postman '97

Paul Williams (1940-)
Headless Body in Topless Bar '96
A Million to Juan '94
The Doors '91
Chill Factor '90
The Night They Saved Christmas '87
Zombie High '87
Best Enemies '86
Smokey and the Bandit, Part 3 '83
Smokey and the Bandit 2 '80
Stone Cold Dead '80
The Muppet Movie '79
The Cheap Detective '78
Smokey and the Bandit '77
Phantom of the Paradise '74
Battle for the Planet of the Apes '73
Watermelon Man '70
The Loved One '65

Paul W. Williams (1943-)
Mirage '94
The November Men '93

Peter Williams (1933-)
Love Come Down '00
Jungleground '95
Soul Survivor '95
Robin Hood...The Legend: Robin Hood and the Sorcerer '83
Destroy All Planets '68
The Bridge on the River Kwai '57

Rhys Williams (1897-1969)
Skullduggery '70
The Restless Breed '58
Fastest Gun Alive '56
Battle Cry '55
The Black Shield of Falworth '54
Kiss Tomorrow Goodbye '50
The Showdown '50
The Corn Is Green '45
Mrs. Miniver '42
Underground Agent '42
How Green Was My Valley '41

Robert Williams (-1931)
Devotion '31
Platinum Blonde '31

Robert B. Williams
Force of the Ninja '97
Revenge of the Creature '55

Robin Williams (1952-)
Death to Smoochy '02
Insomnia '02
One Hour Photo '02
A. I.: Artificial Intelligence '01 (V)
Bicentennial Man '99
Jakob the Liar '99
Patch Adams '98
What Dreams May Come '98
Deconstructing Harry '97
Flubber '97
Good Will Hunting '97
Aladdin and the King of Thieves '96 (V)
Father's Day '96
Hamlet '96
Jack '96
The Secret Agent '96
The Birdcage '95
Jumanji '95
Nine Months '95
To Wong Foo, Thanks for Everything, Julie Newmar '95
Being Human '94
Mrs. Doubtfire '93
Aladdin '92 (V)
Ferngully: The Last Rain Forest '92 (V)
Shakes the Clown '92
Toys '92
Dead Again '91
The Fisher King '91
Hook '91
Awakenings '90
Cadillac Man '90
The Adventures of Baron Munchausen '89
Dead Poets Society '89
Good Morning, Vietnam '87
The Best of Times '86
Club Paradise '86
Seize the Day '86
Moscow on the Hudson '84
Survivors '83
The Tale of the Frog Prince '83
The World According to Garp '82
Popeye '80
Can I Do It...Till I Need Glasses? '77

Roger Williams
Code of the Fearless '39
Cheyenne Rides Again '38
Feud Maker '38
Valley of Terror '38
Aces Wild '37
Brothers of the West '37
Heroes of the Alamo '37
The Roamin' Cowboy '37
Gun Grit '36
Phantom Patrol '36
Toll of the Desert '35

Samm-Art Williams (1946-)
A Rage in Harlem '91
The Adventures of Huckleberry Finn '85
Blood Simple '85

Saul Williams
K-PAX '01
Slam '98

Scot Williams
In His Life: The John Lennon Story '00
Swing '98
Backbeat '94

Simon Williams
The Fiendish Plot of Dr. Fu Manchu '80
The Blood on Satan's Claw '71

Spencer Williams, Jr. (1893-1969)
Juke Joint '47
Dirty Gertie from Harlem U.S.A. '46
Blood of Jesus '41

Go Down Death '41
Son of Ingagi '40
Bronze Buckaroo '39
Harlem Rides the Range '39

Steven Williams (1949-)
Firetrap '01
Route 666 '01
Crash & Byrnes '99
The Sender '98
Bloodfist 7: Manhunt '95
Jason Goes to Hell: The Final Friday '93
Revolver '92
Missing in Action 2: The Beginning '85
Silent Witness '85
Twilight Zone: The Movie '83
The Blues Brothers '80

Treat Williams (1952-)
Hollywood Ending '02
Extreme Limits '01
Gale Force '01
Venomous '01
Skeletons in the Closet '00
The Substitute 4: Failure is Not an Option '00
Journey to the Center of the Earth '99
The Substitute 3: Winner Takes All '99
36 Hours to Die '99
The Deep End of the Ocean '98
Deep Rising '98
Escape: Human Cargo '98
The Substitute 2: School's Out '97
The Devil's Own '96
The Late Shift '96
The Phantom '96
Johnny's Girl '95
Mulholland Falls '95
Things to Do in Denver When You're Dead '95
Parallel Lives '94
Where the Rivers Flow North '94
Hand Gun '93
Till Death Do Us Part '92
The Water Engine '92
Final Verdict '91
Max and Helen '90
The Heart of Dixie '89
Third Degree Burn '89
Third Solution '89
Dead Heat '88
Sweet Lies '88
Echoes in the Darkness '87
J. Edgar Hoover '87
Night of the Sharks '87
The Men's Club '86
Smooth Talk '85
Flashpoint '84
Once Upon a Time in America '84
A Streetcar Named Desire '84
Dempsey '83
Prince of the City '81
The Pursuit of D.B. Cooper '81
Hair '79
1941 '79
The Eagle Has Landed '77
The Ritz '76
Deadly Hero '75

Vanessa Williams (1963-)
DROP Squad '94
Candyman '92
Another You '91
New Jack City '91

Vanessa L(ynne) Williams (1963-)
Don Quixote '00
Shaft '00
Light It Up '99
Dance with Me '98
Futuresport '98
The Odyssey '97
Soul Food '97
Eraser '96
Hoodlum '96
Bye Bye Birdie '95
The Jacksons: An American Dream '92
Harley Davidson and the Marlboro Man '91
The Kid Who Loved Christmas '90
Full Exposure: The Sex Tape Scandals '89
Under the Gun '88
The Pick-Up Artist '87

Wade Andrew Williams
Terror Tract '00
K-911 '99
Route 9 '98

Clayton Williamson
Clowning Around 2 '93
Clowning Around '92

Fred Williamson (1938-)
Submerged '00
Active Stealth '99
Children of the Corn 5: Fields of Terror '98
Blackjack '97
Night Vision '97
Original Gangstas '96
From Dusk Till Dawn '95
Silent Hunter '94
South Beach '92
Steele's Law '91
Three Days to a Kill '91
Black Cobra 3: The Manila Connection '90
Delta Force Commando 2 '90
Black Cobra 2 '89
The Kill Reflex '89
Deadly Intent '88
The Black Cobra '87
Delta Force Commando '87
The Messenger '87
Foxtrap '85
Deadly Impact '84
Big Score '83
The New Gladiators '83
1990: The Bronx Warriors '83
Vigilante '83
Warriors of the Wasteland '83
White Fire '83
The Last Fight '82
One Down, Two to Go! '82
Fear in the City '81
Fist of Fear, Touch of Death '80
Express to Terror '79
Blind Rage '78
Deadly Mission '78
Mister Mean '77
Death Journey '76
Joshua '76
Adios Amigo '75
Bucktown '75
Mean Johnny Barrows '75
Take a Hard Ride '75
Boss '74
No Way Back '74
Three the Hard Way '74
Black Caesar '73
Hell Up in Harlem '73
That Man Bolt '73
M*A*S*H '70

Mykelti Williamson (1960-)
Ali '01
Holiday Heart '00
Having Our Say: The Delany Sisters' First 100 Years '99
Three Kings '99
Primary Colors '98
Species 2 '98
Buffalo Soldiers '97
Con Air '97
Truth or Consequences, N.M. '97
Twelve Angry Men '97
Soul of the Game '96
Heat '95
How to Make an American Quilt '95
Waiting to Exhale '95
Forrest Gump '94
The First Power '89
Miracle Mile '89
Number One with a Bullet '87
Streets of Fire '84

Nicol Williamson (1938-)
Spawn '97
Mr. Toad's Wild Ride '96
The Advocate '93
Exorcist 3: Legion '90
Black Widow '87
Mountbatten: The Last Viceroy '86
Passion Flower '86
Christopher Columbus '85
Return to Oz '85
I'm Dancing as Fast as I Can '82
Venom '82
Excalibur '81
The Human Factor '79
The Cheap Detective '78
The Word '78
Robin and Marian '76
The Seven-Per-Cent Solution '76
The Wilby Conspiracy '75
Hamlet '69

Noble Willingham (1930-)
Up Close and Personal '96
City Slickers 2: The Legend of Curly's Gold '94
Ace Ventura: Pet Detective '93
Article 99 '92
Career Opportunities '91
City Slickers '91
The Last Boy Scout '91
Pastime '91
Blind Fury '90
Good Morning, Vietnam '87
Coward of the County '81
Kenny Rogers as the Gambler '80
The Boys in Company C '77
Aloha, Bobby and Rose '74
Big Bad Mama '74
My Sweet Charlie '70

Bruce Willis (1955-)
Hart's War '02
Bandits '01
Disney's The Kid '00
Unbreakable '00
The Whole Nine Yards '00
The Sixth Sense '99
The Story of Us '99
Armageddon '98
Breakfast of Champions '98
Mercury Rising '98
The Siege '98
The Fifth Element '97
The Jackal '97
Last Man Standing '96
Die Hard: With a Vengeance '95
Four Rooms '95
12 Monkeys '95
Color of Night '94
Nobody's Fool '94
North '94
Pulp Fiction '94
Striking Distance '93
Death Becomes Her '92
The Player '92
Billy Bathgate '91
Hudson Hawk '91
The Last Boy Scout '91
Mortal Thoughts '91
The Bonfire of the Vanities '90
Die Hard 2: Die Harder '90
Look Who's Talking, Too '90 (V)
That's Adequate '90
In Country '89
Look Who's Talking '89 (V)
Die Hard '88
Sunset '88
Blind Date '87
Moonlighting '85

Matt Willis (1913-89)
The Noose Hangs High '48
Blonde Savage '47
A Walk in the Sun '46
Behind Prison Walls '43
Return of the Vampire '43

Susan Willis
The Majestic '01
What about Bob? '91

Noel Willman (1917-88)
21 Hours at Munich '76
The Odessa File '74
The Reptile '66
Doctor Zhivago '65
Kiss of the Vampire '62
Abandon Ship '57
Across the Bridge '57
The Warriors '55
Beau Brummel '54

Chill Wills (1903-78)
Mr. Billion '77
Poco '77
Pat Garrett & Billy the Kid '73
Over the Hill Gang '69
The Rounders '65
McLintock! '63
The Wheeler Dealers '63
Deadly Companions '61
The Alamo '60
Where the Boys Are '60
Gun Glory '57
Giant '56
Kentucky Rifle '55
Francis Joins the WACs '54 (V)
City That Never Sleeps '53
Francis Covers the Big Town '53 (V)
Man from the Alamo '53
Ride the Man Down '53
Small Town Girl '53
Francis Goes to West Point '52 (V)
Francis Goes to the Races '51 (V)
High Lonesome '50
Rio Grande '50
Francis the Talking Mule '49 (V)
Tulsa '49
Heartaches '47
The Harvey Girls '46
The Yearling '46
Tarzan's New York Adventure '42
Billy the Kid '41
Honky Tonk '41
Western Union '41
Boom Town '40
The Westerner '40
Allegheny Uprising '39
Racketeers of the Range '39

Maury Wills
The Sandlot '93
The Black Six '74

Paul Willson (1945-)
Office Space '98
My Best Friend Is a Vampire '88
Devonsville Terror '83

Douglas Wilmer (1920-)
The Adventures of Sherlock Holmes' Smarter Brother '78
The Incredible Sarah '76
Golden Voyage of Sinbad '73
The Vampire Lovers '70
Jason and the Argonauts '63
Men of Sherwood Forest '57

Andre Wilms
La Vie de Boheme '93
L'Enfer '93
Monsieur Hire '89
Life Is a Long Quiet River '88

Channing Wilroy
Desperate Living '77
Female Trouble '74
Pink Flamingos '72

Shannon Wilsey (1971-94)
Sorority House Massacre 2: Nighty Nightmare '92
The Invisible Maniac '90

Ajita Wilson
Escape from Hell '89
Savage Island '85

Barbara Wilson
Invasion of the Animal People '62
Lost, Lonely, and Vicious '59
Teenage Doll '57

Brad Wilson
Pterodactyl Woman from Beverly Hills '97
Grotesque '87

Brian Wilson
Beach Blanket Bingo '65
Beach Party '63

Bridgette Wilson (1973-)
Just Visiting '01
The Wedding Planner '01
Beautiful '00
House on Haunted Hill '99
Love Stinks '99
The Suburbans '99
I Know What You Did Last Summer '97
Nevada '97
The Real Blonde '97
The Stepsister '97
Mortal Kombat 1: The Movie '95
Sweet Evil '95
Billy Madison '94
Last Action Hero '93

Claude Wilson
Combat Killers '80
The Boys in Company C '77

Dana Wilson
Wild Women '53
The Body Vanished '39

David Wilson (1949-)
The Inside Man '84
Eddie and the Cruisers '83
Hometown U.S.A. '79

Don Wilson
Niagara '52
The Chase '46

Don "The Dragon" Wilson (1955-)
Moving Target '00
The Capitol Conspiracy '99
Bloodfist 8: Hard Way Out '96
Hollywood Safari '96
Terminal Rush '96
Batman Forever '95
Bloodfist 7: Manhunt '95
Cyber-Tracker 2 '95
Manhunt '95
Night Hunter '95
Virtual Combat '95
Bloodfist 6: Ground Zero '94
Red Sun Rising '94
Ring of Fire 3: Lion Strike '94
Bloodfist 5: Human Target '93
Cyber-Tracker '93
Out for Blood '93
Black Belt '92
Bloodfist 3: Forced to Fight '92
Bloodfist 4: Die Trying '92
Magic Kid '92
Ring of Fire 2: Blood and Steel '92
Futurekick '91
Ring of Fire '91
Bloodfist 2 '90
Bloodfist '89
Born on the Fourth of July '89
Say Anything '89

Dooley Wilson
Stormy Weather '43
Casablanca '42

Dorothy Wilson (1909-98)
Last Days of Pompeii '35
Dangerous Appointment '34

Earl Wilson (1907-87)
Beach Blanket Bingo '65
Night of Evil '62 (N)
Copacabana '47

Elizabeth Wilson (1921-)
The Boys Next Door '96
Quiz Show '94
Scarlett '94
Queen '93
Sarah, Plain and Tall: Skylark '93
The Addams Family '91
Regarding Henry '91
The Believers '87
A Conspiracy of Love '87
Where Are the Children? '85
Grace Quigley '84
You Can't Take It with You '84
Sanctuary of Fear '79
Miles to Go Before I Sleep '74
Prisoner of Second Avenue '74
Little Murders '71
Jenny '70
The Graduate '67
The Tunnel of Love '58
Patterns '56

Flip Wilson (1933-98)
The Fish that Saved Pittsburgh '79
Uptown Saturday Night '74
Cancel My Reservation '72

Frank Wilson (1885-1956)
Beware '46
Paradise in Harlem '40
Green Pastures '36
Emperor Jones '33
Girl from Chicago '32

George Wilson
Nudo di Donna '83
Make Room for Tomorrow '81
Attack of the Killer Tomatoes '77

Kristen Wilson (1969-)
Dr. Dolittle 2 '01
Dungeons and Dragons '00
Bulletproof '96
Girl 6 '96
The Pompatus of Love '95
Tyson '95

Lambert Wilson (1959-)
Don Quixote '00
The Last September '99
Same Old Song '97
The Leading Man '96
Frankenstein '93
The Belly of an Architect '91
The Possessed '88
Red Kiss '85
Rendez-vous '85
The Blood of Others '84
Sahara '83
Five Days One Summer '82

Lewis Wilson (1920-2000)
Wild Women '53
The Body Vanished '39

Lois Wilson (1896-1983)
Bright Eyes '34
In the Money '34
Female '33
Laughing at Life '33
Drifting Souls '32
The Secrets of Wu Sin '32
The Show Off '26
The Vanishing American '25
Monsieur Beaucaire '24
The Covered Wagon '23

Luke Wilson (1971-)
Legally Blonde '01
The Royal Tenenbaums '01
Soul Survivors '01
Bad Seed '00
Charlie's Angels '00
Blue Streak '99
Committed '99
My Dog Skip '99
Best Men '98
Bongwater '98
Dog Park '98

Home Fries '98
Telling Lies in America '96
Bottle Rocket '95
Mara Wilson (1987-)
Thomas and the Magic Railroad '00
Balloon Farm '97
A Simple Wish '97
Matilda '96
Miracle on 34th Street '94
Mrs. Doubtfire '93
Marie Wilson (1916-72)
Mr. Hobbs Takes a Vacation '62
A Girl in Every Port '52
Never Wave at a WAC '52
My Friend Irma '49
Fabulous Joe '47
The Private Affairs of Bel Ami '47
Flying Blind '41
Waterfront '39
Boy Meets Girl '38
Satan Met a Lady '36
March of the Wooden Soldiers '34
Mary Louise Wilson (1932-)
A Season for Miracles '99
24 Nights '99
Stepmom '98
The Adventures of Huck Finn '93
Cheap Shots '91
Green Card '90
Owen C. Wilson (1968-)
Behind Enemy Lines '01
The Royal Tenenbaums '01
Zoolander '01
Meet the Parents '00
Shanghai Noon '00
The Haunting '99
The Minus Man '99
Armageddon '98
Breakfast of Champions '98
Permanent Midnight '98
Anaconda '96
The Cable Guy '96
Bottle Rocket '95
Perry Wilson
The Matchmaker '58
Fear Strikes Out '57
Peta Wilson
Mercy '00
Loser '97
Reno Wilson
She Creature '01
City of Industry '96
Richard Wilson (1915-91)
The Man Who Knew Too Little '97
Unnatural Pursuits '91
How to Get Ahead in Advertising '89
Rita Wilson (1958-)
The Glass House '01
Perfume '01
Runaway Bride '99
The Story of Us '99
From the Earth to the Moon '98
Psycho '98
If These Walls Could Talk '96
Jingle All the Way '96
That Thing You Do! '96
Now and Then '95
Mixed Nuts '94
Sleepless in Seattle '93
Volunteers '85
The Day It Came to Earth '77
Robert Wilson
Day of Triumph '54
I Beheld His Glory '53
Rod Wilson
Madonna: Innocence Lost '95
Darkman 2: The Return of Durant '94
Roger Wilson (1958-)
Power of Attorney '94
The Ghost Brigade '93
Thunder Alley '85
Second Time Lucky '84
Porky's 2: The Next Day '83
Overthrow '82
Porky's '82
Scott Wilson (1942-)
Pearl Harbor '01
Way of the Gun '00
The Jack Bull '99
Shiloh 2: Shiloh Season '99
Clay Pigeons '98
G.I. Jane '97
Shiloh '97
Dead Man Walking '95
Flesh and Bone '93
Pure Luck '91
Exorcist 3: Legion '90
Femme Fatale '90
Young Guns 2 '90
Johnny Handsome '89
Jesse '88
The Tracker '88
Malone '87
Blue City '86
The Aviator '85
Year of the Quiet Sun '84
On the Line '83
The Right Stuff '83
The Ninth Configuration '79
The Passover Plot '75
The New Centurions '72
The Grissom Gang '71
In Cold Blood '67
Sheree J. Wilson (1958-)
Hellbound '94
Past Tense '94
Walker: Texas Ranger: One Riot, One Ranger '93
News at Eleven '86
Crimewave '85
Fraternity Vacation '85
Stuart Wilson (1934-)
Dinotopia '02
Princess of Thieves '01
Here on Earth '00
The Luzhin Defence '00
Slow Burn '00
Vertical Limit '00
Second Sight '99
Enemy of the State '98
The Mask of Zorro '98
Crosswords '96
Edie & Pen '95
Death and the Maiden '94
Exit to Eden '94
No Escape '94
The Age of Innocence '93
Teenage Mutant Ninja Turtles 3 '93
Lethal Weapon 3 '92
Secret Weapon '90
Romance on the Orient Express '89
The Highest Honor '84
Running Blind '78
The Strauss Family '73
Teddy Wilson (1943-91)
Life Stinks '91
Kiss Shot '89
The Mighty Pawns '87
The Ambush Murders '82
Cotton Comes to Harlem '70
Thick Wilson
The Thief and the Cobbler '96 (V)
Adventures Beyond Belief '87
Thomas F. Wilson (1959-)
That Darn Cat '96
Andersonville '95
Born to Be Wild '95
Camp Nowhere '94
Blood In ... Blood Out: Bound by Honor '93
Caroline at Midnight '93
Mr. Write '92
High Strung '91
Back to the Future, Part 3 '90
Back to the Future, Part 2 '89
Action Jackson '88
Let's Get Harry '87
April Fool's Day '86
Back to the Future '85
Tom Wilson (1880-1965)
Battling Butler '26
California Straight Ahead '25
The Americano '17
Trey Wilson (1948-89)
Great Balls of Fire '89
Miss Firecracker '89
Welcome Home '89
Bull Durham '88
End of the Line '88
Married to the Mob '88
Twins '88
Raising Arizona '87
The Vampire Hookers '78
Penelope Wilton (1946-)
Iris '01
Victoria & Albert '01
Wives and Daughters '01
The Return of the Borrowers '96
Carrington '95
The Secret Rapture '94
The Borrowers '93
Blame It on the Bellboy '92
Cry Freedom '87
Clockwise '86
Singleton's Pluck '84
Brian Wimmer (1959-)
Bitter Sweet '98
Final Justice '98
The Maddening '95
Dead Badge '94
Tank Girl '94
Blue Flame '93
Kiss of a Killer '93
Lipstick Camera '93
The World's Oldest Living Bridesmaid '92
Late for Dinner '91
Dangerous Pursuit '89
China Beach '88
Troy Winbush
Gabriela '01
The Replacements '00
Mutiny '99
The Principal '87
Paul Winchell
The Fox and the Hound '81 (V)
The Aristocats '70 (V)
Walter Winchell
Scarface Mob '62 (N)
The Bellboy '60
Jeff Wincott (1957-)
Battle Queen 2020 '99
Paper Bullets '99
Universal Soldier 2: Brothers in Arms '98
Universal Soldier 3: Unfinished Business '98
Future Fear '97
The Undertaker's Wedding '97
Fatal Combat '96
Profile for Murder '96
When the Bullet Hits the Bone '96
Last Man Standing '95
Street Law '95
The Donor '94
The Killing Man '94
Open Fire '94
Martial Outlaw '93
Mission of Justice '92
Deadly Bet '91
Martial Law 2: Undercover '91
Michael Wincott (1959-)
The Count of Monte Cristo '02
Along Came a Spider '01
Before Night Falls '00
Hidden Agenda '99
Gunshy '98
Alien: Resurrection '97
Basquiat '96
Metro '96
Dead Man '95
Strange Days '95
The Crow '93
Romeo Is Bleeding '93
The Three Musketeers '93
1492: Conquest of Paradise '92
The Doors '91
Robin Hood: Prince of Thieves '91
Tragedy of Flight 103: The Inside Story '91
Talk Radio '88
Wild Horse Hank '79
William Windom (1923-)
Children of the Corn 4: The Gathering '96
Fugitive X '96
Miracle on 34th Street '94
Attack of the 50 Ft. Woman '93
Dennis the Menace: Dinosaur Hunter '93
Sommersby '93
Committed '91
Back to Hannibal: The Return of Tom Sawyer and Huckleberry Finn '90
Funland '89
Street Justice '89
She's Having a Baby '88
Planes, Trains & Automobiles '87
Grandview U.S.A. '84
Last Plane Out '83
Desperate Lives '82
Leave 'Em Laughing '81
Mean Dog Blues '78
Abduction of St. Anne '75
The Girls of Huntington House '73
Pursuit '72
Escape from the Planet of the Apes '71
The Mephisto Waltz '71
Brewster McCloud '70
The Detective '68
Columbo: Prescription Murder '67
The Americanization of Emily '64
For Love or Money '63
One Man's Way '63
To Kill a Mockingbird '62
Barbara Windsor (1937-)
Carry On Camping '71
Carry On Henry VIII '71
Carry On Doctor '68
Claire Windsor (1897-1972)
The Claw '27
The Blot '21
Too Wise Wives '21
Marie Windsor (1922-2000)
Commando Squad '87
Salem's Lot '79
Cahill: United States Marshal '73
Wild Women '70
Bedtime Story '63
Girl in Black Stockings '57
Unholy Wife '57
The Killing '56
Abbott and Costello Meet the Mummy '55
Silver Star '55
Swamp Women '55
Cat Women of the Moon '53
City That Never Sleeps '53
Tall Texan '53
Trouble along the Way '53
Jungle '52
The Narrow Margin '52
Outlaw Women '52
Little Big Horn '51
Double Deal '50
The Showdown '50
The Fighting Kentuckian '49
Force of Evil '49
Outpost in Morocco '49
Hellfire '48
Smart Alecks '42
Romy Windsor
The Howling: New Moon Rising '95
Big Bad John '90
The House of Usher '88
Howling 4: The Original Nightmare '88
Paul Winfield (1940-)
Catfish in Black Bean Sauce '00
Nowhere to Hide
Strange Justice: The Clarence Thomas and Anita Hill Story '99
Relax... It's Just Sex! '98
The Assassination File '96
The Legend of Gator Face '96
Mars Attacks! '96
Original Gangstas '96
Tyson '95
White Dwarf '95
Breathing Lessons '94
In the Kingdom of the Blind the Man with One Eye Is King '94
Scarlett '94
Cliffhanger '93
Dennis the Menace '93
Queen '93
Back to Hannibal: The Return of Tom Sawyer and Huckleberry Finn '90
Presumed Innocent '90
The Women of Brewster Place '89
For Us, the Living '88
Big Shots '87
Death Before Dishonor '87
Guilty of Innocence '87
The Mighty Pawns '87
The Serpent and the Rainbow '87
Blue City '86
Go Tell It on the Mountain '84
Mike's Murder '84
The Terminator '84
Star Trek 2: The Wrath of Khan '82
Carbon Copy '81
Sophisticated Gents '81
Angel City '80
Roots: The Next Generation '79
A Hero Ain't Nothin' but a Sandwich '78
King '78
Damnation Alley '77
The Greatest '77
Twilight's Last Gleaming '77
Green Eyes '76
High Velocity '76
Conrack '74
Huckleberry Finn '74
It's Good to Be Alive '74
Gordon's War '73
Sounder '72
Brother John '70
R.P.M.* (* Revolutions Per Minute) '70
The Lost Man '69
Oprah Winfrey (1954-)
Beloved '98
The Women of Brewster Place '89
Native Son '86
The Color Purple '85
Leslie Wing
Retribution '88
The Cowboy & the Ballerina '84
Dungeonmaster '83
Mark Wing-Davey
One Against the Wind '91
The Hitchhiker's Guide to the Galaxy '81
Debra Winger (1955-)
Forget Paris '95
A Dangerous Woman '93
Shadowlands '93
Wilder Napalm '93
Leap of Faith '92
Everybody Wins '90
The Sheltering Sky '90
Betrayed '88
Black Widow '87
Made in Heaven '87
Legal Eagles '86
Mike's Murder '84
Terms of Endearment '83
Cannery Row '82
E.T.: The Extra-Terrestrial '82 (V)
An Officer and a Gentleman '82
Urban Cowboy '80
French Postcards '79
Special Olympics '78
Thank God It's Friday '78
Slumber Party '57 '76
Angela Winkler (1944-)
Sheer Madness '84
Danton '82
The Tin Drum '79
Knife in the Head '78
The Lost Honor of Katharina Blum '75
Henry Winkler (1945-)
Down to You '00
Little Nicky '00
Ground Control '98
P.U.N.K.S. '98
The Waterboy '98
Hostage High '97
National Lampoon's Dad's Week Off '97
Scream '96
One Christmas '95
Night Shift '82
An American Christmas Carol '79
The One and Only '78
Heroes '77
Katherine '75
The Lords of Flatbush '74
Mel Winkler
City Hall '95
Devil in a Blue Dress '95
Laurel Avenue '93
Kitty Winn (1944-)
Mirrors '78
The Exorcist 2: The Heretic '77
Panic in Needle Park '75
Miles to Go Before I Sleep '74
The Exorcist '73
Man on a String '71
They Might Be Giants '71
Vic Winner
The Rue Morgue Massacres '73
Horror Rises from the Tomb '72
Olof Winnerstrand
Night Is My Future '47
Torment '44
Lucyna Winnicka (1928-)
25 Fireman's Street '73
First Spaceship on Venus '60
Mother Joan of the Angels '60
Charles Winninger (1884-1969)
The Sun Shines Bright '53
Torpedo Alley '53
Something in the Wind '47
State Fair '45
Broadway Rhythm '44
Lady Takes a Chance '43
Pot o' Gold '41
Ziegfeld Girl '41
Beyond Tomorrow '40
Little Nellie Kelly '40
Babes in Arms '39
Destry Rides Again '39
Three Smart Girls Grow Up '39
Every Day's a Holiday '38
Nothing Sacred '37
Show Boat '36
Three Smart Girls '36
Night Nurse '31
The Sin of Madelon Claudet '31
Mare Winningham (1959-)
Snap Decision '01

Sally Hemings: An American Scandal '00
Everything That Rises '98
Under Pressure '98
George Wallace '97
The Boys Next Door '96
Georgia '95
Letter to My Killer '95
Better Off Dead '94
Teresa's Tattoo '94
The War '94
Wyatt Earp '94
Hard Promises '92
Intruders '92
Eye on the Sparrow '91
Fatal Exposure '91
Miracle Mile '89
Turner and Hooch '89
God Bless the Child '88
Made in Heaven '87
Shy People '87
Nobody's Fool '86
A Winner Never Quits '86
St. Elmo's Fire '85
Single Bars, Single Women '84
The Thorn Birds '83
Threshold '83
One Trick Pony '80
Special Olympics '78
The Young Pioneers '76

Kate Winslet (1975-)
Enigma '01
Iris '01
Quills '00
Hideous Kinky '99
Holy Smoke '99
Titanic '97
Hamlet '96
Jude '96
A Kid in King Arthur's Court '95
Sense and Sensibility '95
Heavenly Creatures '94

George Winslow (1946-)
Artists and Models '55
Gentlemen Prefer Blondes '53
Monkey Business '52

Michael Winslow (1960-)
Police Academy 7: Mission to Moscow '94
Going Under '91
Buy & Cell '89
Far Out Man '89
Police Academy 6: City under Siege '89
Police Academy 5: Assignment Miami Beach '88
Police Academy 4: Citizens on Patrol '87
Spaceballs '87
Police Academy 3: Back in Training '86
Police Academy 2: Their First Assignment '85
Alphabet City '84
Lovelines '84
Police Academy '84
Tag: The Assassination Game '82

Hattie Winston (1945-)
True Crime '99
Jackie Brown '97
Clara's Heart '88

Helen Winston
A Boy and His Dog '75
Battle Circus '53

Ray Winstone (1957-)
Love, Honour & Obey '00
Sexy Beast '00
Agnes Browne '99
Darkness Falls '98
The Very Thought of You '98
The War Zone '98
Face '97
Nil by Mouth '96
Ladybird, Ladybird '93
Quadrophenia '79
Scum '79

Maurice Dean Wint
Hedwig and the Angry Inch '00
Cube '98
Curtis's Charm '96
Rude '96

Alex Winter (1965-)
Freaked '93
Bill & Ted's Bogus Journey '91
Bill & Ted's Excellent Adventure '89
Rosalie Goes Shopping '89
Haunted Summer '88
The Lost Boys '87
Death Wish 3 '85

Edward Winter (1938-2001)
Held Hostage '91
The Buddy System '83
Mother & Daughter: A Loving War '80

Vincent Winter (1947-98)
The Horse Without a Head '63
Almost Angels '62
Gorgo '61
Time Lock '57

Deborah Winters (1955-)
The Outing '87
Blue Sunshine '78
Tarantulas: The Deadly Cargo '77
Class of '44 '73
Kotch '71
The People Next Door '70
Hail, Hero! '69

Jonathan Winters (1925-)
The Adventures of Rocky & Bullwinkle '00
The Thief and the Cobbler '96 (V)
The Flintstones '94
The Shadow '94
Moon over Parador '88
The Longshot '86
Say Yes! '86
Pogo for President: "I Go Pogo" '84 (V)
More Wild, Wild West '80
The Fish that Saved Pittsburgh '79
Viva Max '69
Eight on the Lam '67
Oh Dad, Poor Dad (Momma's Hung You in the Closet & I'm Feeling So Sad) '67
The Russians Are Coming, the Russians Are Coming '66
The Loved One '65
It's a Mad, Mad, Mad, Mad World '63

Kristoffer Ryan Winters
Hot Blooded '98
Saint Maybe '98

Roland Winters (1904-89)
Blue Hawaii '62
Cash McCall '60
Jet Pilot '57
Guilty of Treason '50
To Please a Lady '50
The Underworld Story '50
The West Point Story '50
Abbott and Costello Meet the Killer, Boris Karloff '49
Malaya '49
Riders of the Whistling Skull '37

Shelley Winters (1922-)
Portrait of a Lady '96
Jury Duty '95
Mrs. Munck '95
Raging Angels '95
Backfire! '94
Heavy '94
The Pickle '93
Silence of the Hams '93
Weep No More My Lady '93
Stepping Out '91
Superstar: The Life and Times of Andy Warhol '90
An Unremarkable Life '89
Purple People Eater '88
Delta Force '86
Witchfire '86
Deja Vu '84
Ellie '84
Very Close Quarters '84
Fanny Hill '83
Over the Brooklyn Bridge '83
S.O.B. '81
The Visitor '80
Elvis: The Movie '79
The Magician of Lublin '79
City on Fire '78
Initiation of Sarah '78
King of the Gypsies '78
Pete's Dragon '77
Tentacles '77
Next Stop, Greenwich Village '76
The Tenant '76
That Lucky Touch '75
Journey into Fear '74
Blume in Love '73
Cleopatra Jones '73
Poor Pretty Eddie '73
Diamonds '72
The Poseidon Adventure '72
Shattered '72
What's the Matter with Helen? '71
Who Slew Auntie Roo? '71
Bloody Mama '70
Buona Sera, Mrs. Campbell '68
The Scalphunters '68
Wild in the Streets '68
Enter Laughing '67
Alfie '66
Harper '66
The Greatest Story Ever Told '65
A Patch of Blue '65
The Three Sisters '65
Time of Indifference '64
The Balcony '63
Lolita '62
Let No Man Write My Epitaph '60
The Diary of Anne Frank '59
Odds Against Tomorrow '59
The Big Knife '55
I Am a Camera '55
I Died a Thousand Times '55
Mambo '55
The Night of the Hunter '55
Treasure of Pancho Villa '55
Executive Suite '54
Behave Yourself! '52
Meet Danny Wilson '52
Phone Call from a Stranger '52
A Place in the Sun '51
Winchester '73 '50
The Great Gatsby '49
A Double Life '47
The Gangster '47

Jane Winton
Hell's Angels '30
Bare Knees '28

Estelle Winwood (1883-1984)
Murder by Death '76
The Producers '68
Games '67
The Magic Sword '62
The Misfits '61
Darby O'Gill & the Little People '59
This Happy Feeling '58
The Swan '56
The Glass Slipper '55
Quality Street '37

Billy Wirth (1962-)
Me & Will '99
Last Lives '98
Relax... It's Just Sex! '98
Starlight '97
Space Marines '96
A Good Day to Die '95
Venus Rising '95
The Fence '94
Judicial Consent '94
Body Snatchers '93
Final Mission '93
Red Shoe Diaries '92
War Party '89
The Lost Boys '87

Robert Wisden
Every Mother's Worst Fear '98
Excess Baggage '96
Captains Courageous '95
Glory Enough for All: The Discovery of Insulin '92
Blood Clan '91

Norman Wisdom (1920-)
The Night They Raided Minsky's '69
What's Good for the Goose '69
Trouble in Store '53

Robert Wisdom
Storytelling '01
Dancing at the Blue Iguana '00

Greg Wise (1966-)
Madame Bovary '00
Judas Kiss '98
The Moonstone '97
The Buccaneers '95
Feast of July '95
Sense and Sensibility '95

Ray Wise (1947-)
Two Can Play That Game '01
The Garbage-Picking, Field Goal-Kicking Philadelphia Phenomenon '98
Powder '95
Body Shot '93
The Chase '93
The Ghost Brigade '93
Rising Sun '93
Bob Roberts '92
Sunstroke '92
Twin Peaks: Fire Walk with Me '92
Write to Kill '91
Endless Descent '90
Season of Fear '89
The Taking of Flight 847: The Uli Derickson Story '88
RoboCop '87
The Journey of Natty Gann '85
Swamp Thing '82

William Wise
In the Bedroom '01
Farewell to the King '89

Joseph Wiseman (1918-)
Lady Mobster '88
Seize the Day '86
Ghostwriter '84
Jaguar Lives '79
Zalmen or the Madness of God '75
Pursuit '72
Lawman '71
Stiletto '69
Dr. No '62
The Unforgiven '60
The Prodigal '55
The Silver Chalice '54
Viva Zapata! '52
Detective Story '51

Googie Withers (1917-)
Country Life '95
Shine '95
Northanger Abbey '87
Hotel du Lac '86
Devil on Horseback '54
Night and the City '50
Dead of Night '45
Pink String and Sealing Wax '45
On Approval '44
One of Our Aircraft Is Missing '41
Action for Slander '38
The Lady Vanishes '38
Accused '36

Grant Withers (1904-59)
Iron Mountain Trail '53
Hoodlum Empire '52
Oklahoma Annie '51
Bells of Coronado '50
Trigger, Jr. '50
The Fighting Kentuckian '49
Night Time in Nevada '48
My Darling Clementine '46
Bells of Rosarita '45
Fighting Seabees '44
The Yellow Rose of Texas '44
Billy the Kid '41
The Masked Rider '41
Doomed to Die '40
The Fatal Hour '40
Phantom of Chinatown '40
Boy's Reformatory '39
Daughter of the Tong '39
Irish Luck '39
Mr. Wong in Chinatown '39
Mystery of Mr. Wong '39
Mr. Wong, Detective '38
Radio Patrol '37
Fighting Marines '36
Let's Sing Again '36
Tailspin Tommy '34
The Secrets of Wu Sin '32
The Road to Ruin '28

Jane Withers (1926-)
Captain Newman, M.D. '63
Giant '56
The Farmer Takes a Wife '35
Bright Eyes '34

Cora Witherspoon (1890-1957)
Just for You '52
The Bank Dick '40
Just Around the Corner '38
Marie Antoinette '38
On the Avenue '37
Personal Property '37
Quality Street '37
Libeled Lady '36

Jimmy Witherspoon
Georgia '95
Black Godfather '74

John Witherspoon
The Ladies Man '00
Next Friday '00
I Got the Hook-Up '98
Ride '98
Sprung '96
Friday '95
Vampire in Brooklyn '95
Boomerang '92
Killer Tomatoes Strike Back '90

Reese Witherspoon (1976-)
The Importance of Being Earnest '02
Legally Blonde '01
The Trumpet of the Swan '01 (V)
Little Nicky '00
American Psycho '99
Best Laid Plans '99
Election '99
Cruel Intentions '98
Pleasantville '98
Twilight '98
Fear '96
Overnight Delivery '96
Freeway '95
S.F.W. '94
A Far Off Place '93
Jack the Bear '93
Return to Lonesome Dove '93
The Man in the Moon '91
Wildflower '91

Glenn Withrow
Naked Lie '89
Pass the Ammo '88
Dudes '87
The Hollywood Knights '80
Lady in Red '79

Michael Witney
Darling Lili '70
The Way West '67

Alicia Witt (1975-)
Vanilla Sky '01
Cecil B. Demented '00
Playing Mona Lisa '00
Bongwater '98
Urban Legend '98
Citizen Ruth '96
Four Rooms '95
Mr. Holland's Opus '95
Fun '94
Bodies, Rest & Motion '93
Hotel Room '93

Kathryn Witt (1950-)
Philadelphia '93
Demon of Paradise '87
Cocaine Wars '86

Karen Witter (1961-)
Buried Alive '89
Midnight '89
Popcorn '89
The Vineyard '89
Perfect Match '88

Stefan Wodoslowsky
Mindfield '89
90 Days '86

David Wohl
Joe Gould's Secret '00
Saving Private Ryan '98
Chillers '88
Armed and Dangerous '86

Fred Wolf
Little Nicky '00
Dirty Work '97

Hillary Wolf
Big Girls Don't Cry...They Get Even '92
Home Alone 2: Lost in New York '92

Kelly Wolf
A Day in October '92
Graveyard Shift '90
Triumph of the Spirit '89
Great Love Experiment '84

Scott Wolf (1968-)
Go '99
The Evening Star '96
White Squall '96
Double Dragon '94
Teenage Bonnie & Klepto Clyde '93

Sheldon Peters Wolfchild
Crazy Horse '96
The Scarlet Letter '95
Miracle in the Wilderness '91

David Wolfe (1915-94)
Salt of the Earth '54
Five Fingers '52
Bagdad '49

Ian Wolfe (1896-1992)
Games '67
Diary of a Madman '63
One Man's Way '63
Moonfleet '55
Houdini '53
The Magnificent Yankee '50
The Judge Steps Out '49
Bedlam '45
The White Cliffs of Dover '44
Zombies on Broadway '44
Mrs. Miniver '42
Mutiny on the Bounty '35
The Barretts of Wimpole Street '34

Jim Wolfe
Invasion of the Space Preachers '90
Chillers '88

Kedrick Wolfe
Smokey Bites the Dust '81
Dr. Heckyl and Mr. Hype '80

Traci Wolfe (1961-)
Lethal Weapon 3 '92
Lethal Weapon 2 '89
Lethal Weapon '87

Frank Wolff (1928-71)
The Lickerish Quartet '70

When Women Had Tails '70
The Awful Dr. Orloff '62
Atlas '60
The Beast from Haunted Cave '60
Ski Troop Attack '60
The Wasp Woman '59
The King's Rhapsody '55

Donald Wolfit (1902-68)
The Charge of the Light Brigade '68
Becket '64
Lawrence of Arabia '62
The Mark '61
The Hands of Orlac '60
Room at the Top '59
Blood of the Vampire '58
Svengali '55
Late Extra '35
The Silent Passenger '35

Wolfman Jack (1938-95)
Mortuary Academy '91
Midnight '89
Motel Hell '80
Deadman's Curve '78
Hanging on a Star '78
American Graffiti '73
The Committee '68

Louis Wolheim (1880-1931)
All Quiet on the Western Front '30
Danger Lights '30
The Silver Horde '30
Square Shoulders '29
The Tempest '28
America '24
Dr. Jekyll and Mr. Hyde '20

Sven Wollter (1934-)
The 13th Warrior '99
House of Angels '92
The Sacrifice '86
Man from Mallorca '84
The Man on the Roof '76

Stevie Wonder
Bikini Beach '64
Muscle Beach Party '64

Anna May Wong (1905-61)
Portrait in Black '60
Impact '49
Java Head '35
A Study in Scarlet '33
Shanghai Express '32
Daughter of the Dragon '31
Peter Pan '24
The Thief of Baghdad '24

Anthony Wong (1961-)
Time and Tide '00
The Mission '99
Floating Life '95
The Heroic Trio '93
Organized Crime & Triad Bureau '93
The Untold Story '93
Full Contact '92
Hard-Boiled '92

B.D. Wong (1962-)
The Salton Sea '02
Mulan '98 (V)
Seven Years in Tibet '97
Slappy and the Stinkers '97
The Substitute 2: School's Out '97
Executive Decision '96
Father of the Bride Part II '95
Men of War '94
And the Band Played On '93
Jurassic Park '93
The Ref '93
Father of the Bride '91
Mystery Date '91
The Freshman '90

Michael Wong
Her Name Is Cat '99
Knock Off '98
Once a Thief '96
The Vineyard '89
Legacy of Rage '86
Royal Warriors '86

Russell Wong (1963-)
The Lost Empire '01
Romeo Must Die '00
The Prophecy 2: Ashtown '97
The Joy Luck Club '93
China Cry '91
China White '91
New Jack City '91
Eat a Bowl of Tea '89
China Girl '87
Tai-Pan '86

Victor Wong (1927-2001)
Seven Years in Tibet '97
3 Ninjas: High Noon at Mega Mountain '97
3 Ninjas Knuckle Up '95
3 Ninjas Kick Back '94
The Ice Runner '93
The Joy Luck Club '93
3 Ninjas '92
Eat a Bowl of Tea '89
Tremors '89
The Last Emperor '87
Prince of Darkness '87
Big Trouble in Little China '86
The Golden Child '86
Dim Sum: A Little Bit of Heart '85

Arthur Wontner (1875-1960)
Genevieve '53
The Terror '38
Murder at the Baskervilles '37
The Triumph of Sherlock Holmes '35

John Woo (1948-)
Hard-Boiled '92
Twin Dragons '92
A Bullet in the Head '90
A Better Tomorrow, Part 1 '86

Andy Wood
Brain Dead '89
Eye of the Eagle 2 '89
Ghostwarrior '86
The Annihilators '85

Britt Wood (1885-1965)
Detour to Danger '45
Knights of the Range '40
The Showdown '40

Clive Wood
The Crucifer of Blood '91
Treasure Island '89

Cynthia Wood
Apocalypse Now '79
Van Nuys Blvd. '79

David Wood
Tales That Witness Madness '73
If... '69

Edward D. Wood, Jr. (1924-78)
Plan 9 from Outer Space '56
Glen or Glenda? '53

Elijah Wood (1981-)
Lord of the Rings 1: The Fellowship of the Rings '01
Black and White '99
The Bumblebee Flies Anyway '98
Deep Impact '98
The Faculty '98
The Ice Storm '97
Oliver Twist '97
Flipper '96
North '94
The War '94
The Adventures of Huck Finn '93
The Good Son '93
Forever Young '92
Radio Flyer '92
Paradise '91
Avalon '90
Child in the Night '90
Internal Affairs '90

Gary Wood
Martial Outlaw '93
Hardbodies '84

G(eorge) Wood (1920-2000)
Bank Shot '74
Harold and Maude '71
M*A*S*H '70

Gordon Wood
The Forty-Niners '32
Mother and Son '31

Harley Wood
Valley of Terror '38
Border Phantom '37
Marihuana '36

Janet Wood (1949-)
Slumber Party '57 '76
Fangs '75
Terror at Red Wolf Inn '72
Angels Hard As They Come '71
G.I. Executioner '71

John Wood (1937-)
The Body '01
Chocolat '00
The Little Vampire '00
Longitude '00
An Ideal Husband '99
The Avengers '98
Sweet Revenge '98
The Gambler '97
Jane Eyre '96
Rasputin: Dark Servant of Destiny '96
Citizen X '95
Richard III '95
Sabrina '95
The Madness of King George '94
The Summer House '94
Shadowlands '93
The Young Americans '93
Orlando '92
Jumpin' Jack Flash '86
Ladyhawke '85
The Purple Rose of Cairo '85
WarGames '83

John Wood (1946-)
Maniac Warriors '92
Ultimate Desires '91
Blue Fire Lady '78

John Lisbon Wood
Alligator '80
KISS Meets the Phantom of the Park '78

Karen Wood
Loose Screws '85
Scalps '83

Lana Wood (1946-)
Demon Rage '82
Justin Morgan Had a Horse '81
Captain America 2: Death Too Soon '79
A Question of Guilt '78
Grayeagle '77
A Place Called Today '72
Diamonds Are Forever '71
Black Water Gold '69
Free Grass '69
The Searchers '56

Lawrence Wood
Something Weird '68
Scum of the Earth '63

Mary Laura Wood
Hour of Decision '57
Stranger in Town '57

Natalie Wood (1938-81)
Brainstorm '83
The Last Married Couple in America '80
Willie & Phil '80
The Cracker Factory '79
From Here to Eternity '79
Meteor '79
The Affair '73
Bob & Carol & Ted & Alice '69
This Property Is Condemned '66
The Great Race '65
Inside Daisy Clover '65
Sex and the Single Girl '64
Love with the Proper Stranger '63
Gypsy '62
Splendor in the Grass '61
West Side Story '61
Cash McCall '60
Kings Go Forth '58
Marjorie Morningstar '58
The Burning Hills '56
The Searchers '56
Rebel without a Cause '55
The Silver Chalice '54
Just for You '52
The Jackpot '50
Never a Dull Moment '50
Our Very Own '50
Father Was a Fullback '49
The Green Promise '49
The Ghost and Mrs. Muir '47
Miracle on 34th Street '47
Tomorrow Is Forever '46

Peggy Wood (1892-1978)
The Sound of Music '65
The Story of Ruth '60
Magnificent Doll '46

Robert Wood
White Fang and the Hunter '85
Belle Starr '79
How to Make a Doll '68

Thomas Wood
Bushwhacked '95
A Taste of Blood '67
2000 Maniacs '64
Blood Feast '63

Tom Wood (1963-)
U.S. Marshals '98
Tinseltown '97
Ulee's Gold '97

Alfre Woodard (1953-)
K-PAX '01
Dinosaur '00 (V)
Holiday Heart '00
Love and Basketball '00
What's Cooking? '00
Mumford '99
Down in the Delta '98
The Member of the Wedding '97
Miss Evers' Boys '97
Primal Fear '96
Run for the Dream: The Gail Devers Story '96
Star Trek: First Contact '96
Gulliver's Travels '95
How to Make an American Quilt '95
Malcolm X: Make It Plain '95 (N)
Blue Chips '94
Crooklyn '94
The Piano Lesson '94
Race to Freedom: The Story of the Underground Railroad '94
Bopha! '93
Heart and Souls '93
Rich in Love '93
The Gun in Betty Lou's Handbag '92
Passion Fish '92
Grand Canyon '91
Miss Firecracker '89
Scrooged '88
Mandela '87
Extremities '86
Unnatural Causes '86
Killing Floor '85
Code of Honor '84
Go Tell It on the Mountain '84
Words by Heart '84
Cross Creek '83
The Ambush Murders '82
Sophisticated Gents '81
Freedom Road '79

Charlaine Woodard
Unbreakable '00
The Million Dollar Hotel '99
Around the Fire '98
The Crucible '96
Buffalo Girls '95
He Said, She Said '91
One Good Cop '91
God Bless the Child '88
Crackers '84

Bokeem Woodbine (1970-)
The Breed '01
Hard Cash '01
3000 Miles to Graceland '01
Sacrifice '00
Blackmale '99
It's the Rage '99
Life '99
The Runner '99
The Big Hit '98
Caught Up '98
Wishmaster 2: Evil Never Dies '98
Almost Heroes '97
The Rock '96
Dead Presidents '95
Freeway '95
Panther '95
Jason's Lyric '94
Strapped '93

George Woodbridge (1907-73)
The Reptile '66
The Fallen Idol '49
Tower of Terror '42

Danny Woodburn
Death to Smoochy '02
Things You Can Tell Just by Looking at Her '00

Eric Woodburn
Trial & Error '62
The Innocents '61

Joan Woodbury (1915-89)
The Time Travelers '64
Northwest Trail '46
The Chinese Cat '44
Here Comes Kelly '43
I Killed That Man '42
Phantom Killer '42
Yank in Libya '42
Gangs, Inc. '41
King of the Zombies '41
Rogue's Tavern '36
Song of the Gringo '36
Bulldog Courage '35

Margo Woode
Iron Angel '64
Bullfighters '45

Pat(ricia) Woodell (1944-)
Twilight People '72
The Big Doll House '71
The Commies Are Coming, the Commies Are Coming '57

Nicholas Woodeson
Conspiracy '01
Dreaming of Joseph Lees '99
Great Expectations '99
The Man Who Knew Too Little '97
Maria's Child '93
A Fatal Inversion '92

Albie Woodington
The Count of Monte Cristo '02
The 13th Warrior '99

Lauren Woodland
The Doorway '00
Alien Nation: Dark Horizon '94

Holly Woodlawn (1947-)
Twin Falls Idaho '99
Superstar: The Life and Times of Andy Warhol '90
Is There Sex After Death? '71
Trash '70

Bert Woodruff (1856-1934)
Marked Money '28
Speedy '28
Paths to Paradise '25

Kurt Woodruff
Moving Target '89
Party Incorporated '89

Largo Woodruff
Bill: On His Own '83
Bill '81
The Choice '81

Coward of the County '81
The Funhouse '81

Barbara Alyn Woods
Dead Weekend '95
Eden 2 '93
Eden 3 '93
Eden 4 '93
Ghoulies 4 '93
Eden '92
Circuitry Man '90

Donald Woods (1909-98)
True Grit '69
Kissin' Cousins '64
Door to Door Maniac '61
13 Ghosts '60
The Beast from 20,000 Fathoms '53
Mr. Music '50
Bells of San Fernando '47
Never Say Goodbye '46
The Bridge of San Luis Rey '44
Enemy of Women '44
Corregidor '43
Watch on the Rhine '43
Beauty for the Asking '39
Danger on the Air '38
Sea Devils '37
The Story of Louis Pasteur '36
A Tale of Two Cities '36
Sweet Adeline '35

Edward (Eddie) Woods (1903-89)
Shadows over Shanghai '38
Tarzan the Fearless '33
Public Enemy '31

Harry Woods (1889-1968)
She Wore a Yellow Ribbon '49
West of the Pecos '45
Nevada '44
Bordertown Gunfighters '43
Dawn on the Great Divide '42
Riders of the West '42
Today I Hang '42
Boss of Bullion City '41
Bullet Code '40
Winners of the West '40
Beau Geste '39
Days of Jesse James '39
Come on Rangers '38
Hawaiian Buckaroo '38
Last Outlaw '36
The Lawless Nineties '36
The Unknown Ranger '36
Rustlers of Red Dog '35
Belle of the Nineties '34
Haunted Gold '32
Monkey Business '31
Palmy Days '31
Range Feud '31
Pardon My Gun '30
Dynamite Dan '24

James Woods (1947-)
John Q '02
Stuart Little 2 '02 (V)
Final Fantasy: The Spirits Within '01 (V)
Riding in Cars with Boys '01
Scary Movie 2 '01
Dirty Pictures '00
Any Given Sunday '99
The General's Daughter '99
True Crime '99
The Virgin Suicides '99
Another Day in Paradise '98
Contact '97
Hercules '97 (V)
John Carpenter's Vampires '97
Kicked in the Head '97
Ghosts of Mississippi '96
The Summer of Ben Tyler '96
Casino '95
For Better or Worse '95
Indictment: The McMartin Trial '95
Killer: A Journal of Murder '95

Nixon '95
Curse of the Starving Class '94
Next Door '94
The Specialist '94
Fallen Angels 1 '93
The Getaway '93
Chaplin '92
Citizen Cohn '92
Diggstown '92
Straight Talk '92
The Hard Way '91
In Love and War '91
The Gift of Love '90
Women & Men: Stories of Seduction '90
Immediate Family '89
True Believer '89
The Boost '88
Cop '88
Best Seller '87
Salvador '86
Badge of the Assassin '85
Cat's Eye '85
Joshua Then and Now '85
Against All Odds '84
Once Upon a Time in America '84
Videodrome '83
Fast Walking '82
Split Image '82
Eyewitness '81
The Black Marble '79
The Incredible Journey of Dr. Meg Laurel '79
The Onion Field '79
Holocaust '78
The Choirboys '77
The Disappearance of Aimee '76
F. Scott Fitzgerald in Hollywood '76
Night Moves '75
The Gambler '74
The Way We Were '73

Michael Woods (1957-)
Red Shoe Diaries: Swimming Naked '00
Blindfold: Acts of Obsession '94
Hit Woman: The Double Edge '93
Omen 4: The Awakening '91
Haunting of Sarah Hardy '89
War & Remembrance: The Final Chapter '89
War & Remembrance '88
Lady Beware '87

Nan Woods
China Beach '88
One More Saturday Night '86

Ren Woods
Hostage High '97
The Brother from Another Planet '84

Robert Woods (1936-)
Chase '85
Challenge of McKenna '83
The Perverse Countess '73

DB Woodside
Romeo Must Die '00
The Temptations '98

Peter Woodthorpe (1931-)
The Charge of the Light Brigade '68
The Blue Max '66
The Evil of Frankenstein '64

Kate Woodville (1938-)
Computer Wizard '77
Where's Willie? '77
Posse '75
Sex Through a Window '72

John Woodvine (1929-)
Persuasion '95
Dragonworld '94
Fatherland '94
Glory Enough for All: The Discovery of Insulin '92
And a Nightingale Sang '91
Edge of Darkness '86
An American Werewolf in London '81
The Life and Adventures of Nicholas Nickleby '81
Assault on Agathon '75

Edward Woodward (1930-)
Gulliver's Travels '95
A Christmas Reunion '93
Codename Kyril '91
Mister Johnson '91
Hands of a Murderer '90
Uncle Tom's Cabin '87
King David '85
Merlin and the Sword '85
Champions '84
A Christmas Carol '84
The Appointment '82
The Final Option '82
Breaker Morant '80
The Wicker Man '75
Young Winston '72
The Bloodsuckers '70

Joanne Woodward (1930-)
Breathing Lessons '94
The Age of Innocence '93 (N)
Blind Spot '93
Foreign Affairs '93
Philadelphia '93
Mr. & Mrs. Bridge '90
The Glass Menagerie '87
Harry & Son '84
Crisis at Central High '80
The Shadow Box '80
The Streets of L.A. '79
A Christmas to Remember '78
The End '78
See How She Runs '78
Sybil '76
The Drowning Pool '75
The Effect of Gamma Rays on Man-in-the-Moon Marigolds '73
Summer Wishes, Winter Dreams '73
They Might Be Giants '71
Winning '69
Rachel, Rachel '68
A Big Hand for the Little Lady '66
A Fine Madness '66
A New Kind of Love '63
The Stripper '63
Paris Blues '61
From the Terrace '60
The Fugitive Kind '60
The Long, Hot Summer '58
The Three Faces of Eve '57

Morgan Woodward (1925-)
Dark Before Dawn '89
Girls Just Want to Have Fun '85
Battle Beyond the Stars '80
Speedtrap '78
Moonshine County Express '77
Walking Tall: The Final Chapter '77
Which Way Is Up? '77
The Killing of a Chinese Bookie '76
The Longest Drive '76
Ride in a Pink Car '74
Running Wild '73
Cool Hand Luke '67

Peter Woodward
Hard Cash '01
Testament of Youth '79

Tim Woodward (1953-)
Heat of the Sun '99
RKO 281 '99
B. Monkey '97
Some Mother's Son '96
The Scarlet Letter '95
The Dark Angel '91
Piece of Cake '90
Personal Services '87
The Europeans '79

Marjorie Woodworth
Broadway Limited '41
Road Show '41

Emily Woof (1970-)
Oliver Twist '00
Pandaemonium '00
Passion '99
Velvet Goldmine '98
Photographing Fairies '97
The Full Monty '96

Norman Wooland (1910-89)
Saul and David '68
Teenage Bad Girl '59
Angel with the Trumpet '50
Madeleine '50

Susan Wooldridge
Just Like a Woman '95
The Last Place on Earth '94
Twenty-One '91
How to Get Ahead in Advertising '89
Hope and Glory '87
Loyalties '86
The Jewel in the Crown '84

Sheb Wooley
Hoosiers '86
High Noon '52

Charles Woolf (1927-94)
No Way Back '74
Private Parts '72

Monty Woolley (1888-1963)
As Young As You Feel '51
The Bishop's Wife '47
Night and Day '46
Since You Went Away '44
The Man Who Came to Dinner '41
Never Say Die '39
Everybody Sing '38
Three Comrades '38

Robert Woolsey (1889-1938)
Cockeyed Cavaliers '34
Hips, Hips, Hooray '34
Kentucky Kernels '34
Diplomaniacs '33
Hold 'Em Jail '32
Dixiana '30
Half-Shot at Sunrise '30
Hook, Line and Sinker '30

Gordon Michael Woolvett (1970-)
The Highway Man '99
Bride of Chucky '98
The Legend of Gator Face '96

Jaimz Woolvett (1967-)
The Stepdaughter '00
The Guilty '99
Rites of Passage '99
Tail Lights Fade '99
Y2K '99
Boogie Boy '98
Sanctuary '98
The Assistant '97
Rosewood '96
The Dark '94
The Pathfinder '94
Unforgiven '92

Tom Wopat (1951-)
Contagious '96
Christmas Comes to Willow Creek '87
Burning Rage '84

Hank Worden (1901-92)
Scream '83
Uforia '81
Smokey and the Bandit '77
Zachariah '70
True Grit '69
The Alamo '60
The Horse Soldiers '59
The Searchers '56
Red River '48
Ghost Town Riders '38

Richard Wordsworth (1915-93)
Time Without Pity '57
The Quatermass Experiment '56

Jimmy Workman (1980-)
As Good As It Gets '97
Addams Family Values '93
The Addams Family '91

Jo Anne Worley
A Goofy Movie '94 (V)
Beauty and the Beast '91 (V)

Frederick Worlock (1886-1973)
101 Dalmatians '61 (V)
The Last of the Redmen '47
She Wolf of London '46
The Woman in Green '45
International Lady '41
Strange Cargo '40

Mary Woronov (1943-)
Sweet Jane '98
Glory Daze '96
Good Girls Don't '95
Grief '94
Shake, Rattle & Rock! '94
Acting on Impulse '93
Mortuary Academy '91
Motorama '91
Rock 'n' Roll High School Forever '91
Warlock '91
Club Fed '90
Let It Ride '89
Scenes from the Class Struggle in Beverly Hills '89
Kemek '88
Black Widow '87
Chopping Mall '86
Nomads '86
Terrorvision '86
Challenge of a Lifetime '85
Hellhole '85
Night of the Comet '84
The Princess Who Never Laughed '84
Get Crazy '83
Angel of H.E.A.T. '82
Eating Raoul '82
Heartbeeps '81
Lady in Red '79
Rock 'n' Roll High School '79
The Movie House Massacre '78
Sugar Cookies '77
Cannonball '76
Hollywood Boulevard '76
Hollywood Man '76
Jackson County Jail '76
Cover Girl Models '75
Death Race 2000 '75
Seizure '74
Silent Night, Bloody Night '73

Barbara Worth (1906-55)
Racing Luck '35
Below the Deadline '29
The Prairie King '27

Constance Worth (1912-63)
Kid Sister '45
G-Men vs. the Black Dragon '43
Dawn Express '42
Criminals Within '41
Windjammer '37

Irene Worth (1916-2002)
Onegin '99
Just the Ticket '98
Lost in Yonkers '93
The Shell Seekers '89
Forbidden '85
Separate Tables '83
Deathtrap '82
Eyewitness '81
King Lear '71

Lilian Worth
The Fighting Sheriff '31
Tarzan the Tiger '29
The Adventures of Tarzan '21

Mike Worth (1969-)
Fists of Iron '94
To Be the Best '93
Street Crimes '92
Final Impact '91
Days of Jesse James '39

Nicholas Worth (1942-)
Slaves of Hollywood '99
Dark Angel: The Ascent '94
Plughead Rewired: Circuitry Man 2 '94
Fist of Honor '92
Blood & Concrete: A Love Story '90
Darkman '90
The Red Raven Kiss-Off '90
Dirty Laundry '87
Doin' Time '85

Sam Worthington
Hart's War '02
Bootmen '00

Fay Wray (1907-)
Gideon's Trumpet '80
Crime of Passion '57
Tammy and the Bachelor '57
Rock, Pretty Baby '56
The Cobweb '55
Hell on Frisco Bay '55
Queen Bee '55
Small Town Girl '53
Treasure of the Golden Condor '53
Adam Had Four Sons '41
Melody for Three '41
When Knights Were Bold '36
Bulldog Jack '35
The Evil Mind '34
Viva Villa! '34
Woman in the Shadows '34
King Kong '33
Mystery of the Wax Museum '33
Doctor X '32
The Most Dangerous Game '32
The Vampire Bat '32
The Wedding March '28
The Coast Patrol '25
Blind Husbands '19

John Wray (1896-1929)
You Only Live Once '37
Green Eyes '34
All Quiet on the Western Front '30

Clare Wren
Midnight Edition '93
Steel and Lace '90
Season of Fear '89

Amy Wright (1950-)
The Scarlet Letter '95
Tom and Huck '95
Robot in the Family '94
Where the Rivers Flow North '94
To Dance with the White Dog '93
Hard Promises '92
Deceived '91
Final Verdict '91
Love Hurts '91
Daddy's Dyin'...Who's Got the Will? '90
Miss Firecracker '89
The Accidental Tourist '88
Crossing Delancey '88
The Telephone '87
Off Beat '86
Trapped in Silence '86
Inside Moves '80
Stardust Memories '80
The Amityville Horror '79
Breaking Away '79
Wise Blood '79
The Deer Hunter '78
Girlfriends '78

Carl Wright
Big Momma's House '00
Soul Food '97

Cobina Wright, Jr.
Charlie Chan in Rio '41
Week-End in Havana '41

Janet Wright
The Perfect Storm '00
Beyond the Call '96

Jeffrey Wright (1965-)
Boycott '02
Ali '01
Crime and Punishment in Suburbia '00
Hamlet '00
Shaft '00
Cement '99
Ride with the Devil '99
Celebrity '98
Critical Care '97
Basquiat '96

Jenny Wright (1962-)
The Lawnmower Man '92
A Shock to the System '90
Young Guns 2 '90
I, Madman '89
Twister '89
The Chocolate War '88
Valentino Returns '88
Near Dark '87
Out of Bounds '86
St. Elmo's Fire '85
The Wild Life '84
The Executioner's Song '82
Pink Floyd: The Wall '82

Katie Wright
Idle Hands '99
Too Smooth '98
Hostage High '97

Ken Wright
Eye of the Eagle 3 '91
Hollywood Boulevard 2 '89
Opposing Force '87
Prince of Darkness '87

Marie Wright
Gaslight '40
Black Eyes '39

Max Wright (1943-)
Konrad '90s
Snow Falling on Cedars '99
William Shakespeare's A Midsummer Night's Dream '99
From the Earth to the Moon '98
White Mile '94
Touch and Go '86
Fraternity Vacation '85
All That Jazz '79

Michael Wright
Pinero '01
Point Blank '98
Money Talks '97
Confessions of a Hit Man '94
Sugar Hill '94
The Five Heartbeats '91
The Principal '87
Streamers '83

N'Bushe Wright (1970-)
Three Strikes '00
Blade '98
Dead Presidents '95
Fresh '94
Zebrahead '92

Patrick Wright
If You Don't Stop It...You'll Go Blind '77
The Abductors '72

Samuel E. Wright (1946-)
Dinosaur '00 (V)
The Little Mermaid '89 (V)
Bird '88

Steven Wright (1955-)
Loser '00
The Muse '99
Babe: Pig in the City '98 (V)
1999 '98
Half-Baked '97
Canadian Bacon '94
Natural Born Killers '94
The Swan Princess '94 (V)
So I Married an Axe Murderer '93
Reservoir Dogs '92 (V)
Men of Respect '91
Desperately Seeking Susan '85
Sledgehammer '83

Teresa Wright (1918-)
John Grisham's The Rainmaker '97
The Good Mother '88
The Fig Tree '87
Bill: On His Own '83
Somewhere in Time '80
Roseland '77

Flood! '76
Hail, Hero! '69
The Happy Ending '69
Escapade in Japan '57
The Search for Bridey Murphy '56
The Capture '50
The Men '50
Pursued '47
The Best Years of Our Lives '46
Casanova Brown '44
Shadow of a Doubt '43
Mrs. Miniver '42
The Pride of the Yankees '42
The Little Foxes '41

Tom Wright
Palmetto '98
The Pentagon Wars '98
Tales from the Hood '95
Creepshow 2 '87

Tony Wright (1925-86)
The House in Marsh Road '60
Broth of a Boy '59
The Spaniard's Curse '58

Tracy Wright
Last Night '98
When Night Is Falling '95

Whittni Wright
Sudden Death '95
I'll Do Anything '93

William Wright (1911-49)
Alias Jesse James '59
Miss Grant Takes Richmond '49
They Live by Night '49
Infamous Crimes '47
The Mask of Diijon '46
A Night to Remember '42

Robin Wright Penn (1966-)
How to Kill Your Neighbor's Dog '01
The Pledge '00
Unbreakable '00
Hurlyburly '98
Message in a Bottle '98
Loved '97
She's So Lovely '97
Moll Flanders '96
The Crossing Guard '94
Forrest Gump '94
The Playboys '92
Toys '92
Denial: The Dark Side of Passion '91
State of Grace '90
The Princess Bride '87
Hollywood Vice Sqaud '86

Maris Wrixon (1917-99)
Highway 13 '48
White Pongo '45
Waterfront '44
Sons of the Pioneers '42
Footsteps in the Dark '41
The Ape '40
British Intelligence '40

Chien-Lien Wu
The Phantom Lover '95
Eat Drink Man Woman '94

Jiang Wu
Shower '00
To Live '94

Vivian Wu (1966-)
8 1/2 Women '99
A Bright Shining Lie '98
The Pillow Book '95
The Joy Luck Club '93
Teenage Mutant Ninja Turtles 3 '93
The Guyver '91
Iron & Silk '91
Shadow of China '91

Robert Wuhl (1951-)
The Last Don 2 '98
The Last Don '97
Open Season '95
Cobb '94
A Kiss Goodnight '94
Percy & Thunder '93
The Bodyguard '92
Missing Pieces '91
Mistress '91
Batman '89
Blaze '89
Tales from the Crypt '89
Bull Durham '88
Good Morning, Vietnam '87
Flashdance '83
The Hollywood Knights '80

Kari Wuhrer (1967-)
Eight Legged Freaks '02
Kiss Tomorrow Goodbye '00
Sand '00
Kate's Addiction '99
Hot Blooded '98
Kissing a Fool '98
Phoenix '98
Ivory Tower '97
Luscious '97
The Undertaker's Wedding '97
Anaconda '96
An Occasional Hell '96
Stephen King's Thinner '96
The Disappearance of Kevin Johnson '95
Sex and the Other Man '95
Terminal Justice: Cybertech P.D. '95
Beyond Desire '94
Boulevard '94
The Crossing Guard '94
Sensation '94
Beastmaster 2: Through the Portal of Time '91
The Adventures of Ford Fairlane '90

Kai Wulff
Top Dog '95
Jungle Warriors '84
Firefox '82

Shelley Wyant
Home Free All '84
Pilgrim, Farewell '82

Jane Wyatt (1911-)
Amityville 4: The Evil Escapes '89
Star Trek 4: The Voyage Home '86
Nativity '78
Katherine '75
The Adventures of Tom Sawyer '73
Our Very Own '50
Task Force '49
Pitfall '48
Boomerang '47
Gentleman's Agreement '47
None But the Lonely Heart '44
Buckskin Frontier '43
The Navy Comes Through '42
Lost Horizon '37
Great Expectations '34

Margaret Wycherly (1881-1956)
White Heat '49
Forever Amber '47
Something in the Wind '47
The Yearling '46
Hangmen Also Die '42
Keeper of the Flame '42
Random Harvest '42
Sergeant York '41
Midnight '34

Katya Wyeth
Dressed for Death '74
Twins of Evil '71

Noah Wyle (1971-)
Enough '02
Donnie Darko '01
The Pirates of Silicon Valley '99
The Myth of Fingerprints '97
Swing Kids '93
A Few Good Men '92
There Goes My Baby '92
Crooked Hearts '91

Gretchen Wyler
The Marrying Man '91
The Devil's Brigade '68

Adam Wylie (1984-)
Daybreak '01
Can of Worms '00
The King and I '99 (V)
Children of the Corn 5: Fields of Terror '98
Balloon Farm '97
Santa with Muscles '96
All Dogs Go to Heaven 2 '95 (V)
Breaking Free '95

John Wylie
Robot in the Family '94
An Empty Bed '90

Daniel Wyllie
Chopper '00
Holy Smoke '99

Bill Wyman
Eat the Rich '87
Gimme Shelter '70

Jane Wyman (1914-)
The Incredible Journey of Dr. Meg Laurel '79
How to Commit Marriage '69
Bon Voyage! '62
Pollyanna '60
All That Heaven Allows '55
Magnificent Obsession '54
Just for You '52
Here Comes the Groom '51
Three Guys Named Mike '51
Stage Fright '50
It's a Great Feeling '49
Johnny Belinda '48
Magic Town '47
Night and Day '46
The Yearling '46
The Lost Weekend '45
Footlight Serenade '42
Wide Open Faces '38
My Man Godfrey '36

John Wyman
Tuxedo Warrior '82
For Your Eyes Only '81

Patrick Wymark (1926-70)
The Blood on Satan's Claw '71
Battle of Britain '69
Journey to the Far Side of the Sun '69
The Conqueror Worm '68
Where Eagles Dare '68
Woman Times Seven '67
Repulsion '65
The Skull '65

Patrice Wymore (1926-)
The King's Rhapsody '55
Big Trees '52
I'll See You in My Dreams '51
Tea for Two '50

Geraint Wyn Davies
American Psycho 2: All American Girl '02
Trilogy of Terror 2 '96
Terror Stalks the Class Reunion '93

H.M. Wynant
The Big Empty '98
Conquest of the Planet of the Apes '72
Run Silent, Run Deep '58

George Wyner
For Richer, for Poorer '92
The Taking of Beverly Hills '91
Fletch Lives '89
Spaceballs '87
Fletch '85
The Bad News Bears Go to Japan '78

Joel Wyner
Random Encounter '98
Listen '96
The Club '94

Peter Wyngarde (1933-)
Double Cross '92
Burn Witch, Burn! '62
The Innocents '61

Mick Wynhoff
5 Dark Souls '96
America's Deadliest Home Video '91

Joel D. Wynkoop
Addicted to Murder 2: Tainted Blood '97
The Alien Agenda: Endangered Species '97

Ed Wynn (1886-1966)
The Gnome-Mobile '67
Dear Brigitte '65
The Greatest Story Ever Told '65
Those Calloways '65
Mary Poppins '64
The Absent-Minded Professor '61
Babes in Toyland '61
Cinderfella '60
The Diary of Anne Frank '59
Marjorie Morningstar '58
Requiem for a Heavyweight '56
Alice in Wonderland '51 (V)

Keenan Wynn (1916-86)
Hard Knocks
The Desperados '80s
Hyper-Sapien: People from Another Star '86
Call to Glory '84
Mid Knight Rider '84
Wavelength '83
Best Friends '82
The Capture of Grizzly Adams '82
The Last Unicorn '82 (V)
A Piano for Mrs. Cimino '82
Just Tell Me What You Want '80
Mission to Glory '80
Mom, the Wolfman and Me '80
The Clonus Horror '79
The Dark '79
The Treasure Seekers '79
The Bastard '78
Coach '78
Laserblast '78
The Lucifer Complex '78
Monster '78
Piranha '78
Orca '77
High Velocity '76
The Killer Inside Me '76
The Longest Drive '76
The Shaggy D.A. '76
Devil's Rain '75
He Is My Brother '75
The Man Who Would Not Die '75
Nashville '75
Herbie Rides Again '74
Hit Lady '74
Legend of Earl Durand '74
Internecine Project '73
Cancel My Reservation '72
The Mechanic '72
Snowball Express '72
Manipulator '71
MacKenna's Gold '69
Smith! '69
Viva Max '69
Finian's Rainbow '68
Once Upon a Time in the West '68
Point Blank '67
The War Wagon '67
Promise Her Anything '66
Around the World Under the Sea '65
The Great Race '65
The Americanization of Emily '64
Bikini Beach '64
Dr. Strangelove, or: How I Learned to Stop Worrying and Love the Bomb '64
The Patsy '64
Son of Flubber '63
Pattern for Plunder '62
The Absent-Minded Professor '61
The King of the Roaring '20s: The Story of Arnold Rothstein '61
A Hole in the Head '59
The Perfect Furlough '59
Deep Six '58
A Time to Love & a Time to Die '58
Don't Go Near the Water '57
The Man in the Gray Flannel Suit '56
Naked Hills '56
Requiem for a Heavyweight '56
The Glass Slipper '55
Shack Out on 101 '55
The Long, Long Trailer '54
Men of the Fighting Lady '54
All the Brothers Were Valiant '53
Battle Circus '53
Kiss Me Kate '53
The Belle of New York '52
Phone Call from a Stranger '52
Angels in the Outfield '51
Royal Wedding '51
Texas Carnival '51
Annie Get Your Gun '50
Three Little Words '50
My Dear Secretary '49
Neptune's Daughter '49
That Midnight Kiss '49
The Three Musketeers '48
The Hucksters '47
Song of the Thin Man '47
The Clock '45
Weekend at the Waldorf '45
Without Love '45
Since You Went Away '44
For Me and My Gal '42
Somewhere I'll Find You '42

May Wynn
The Violent Men '55
The Caine Mutiny '54

Christopher Wynne
1969 '89
Remote Control '88

Dana Wynter (1930-)
Lovers Like Us '75
The Connection '73
Santee '73
Airport '70
Dead Right '68
The List of Adrian Messenger '63
Sink the Bismarck '60
Shake Hands with the Devil '59
Something of Value '57
D-Day, the Sixth of June '56
Invasion of the Body Snatchers '56

Sarah Wynter
Bride of the Wind '01
Lost Souls '00
Race Against Time '00
The 6th Day '00

Charlotte Wynters (1899-1991)
Harvest Melody '43
Hopalong Cassidy: Renegade Trail '39
Panama Patrol '39
Renegade Trail '39
Sinners in Paradise '38
The Ivory Handled Gun '35
Struggle '31

Diana Wynyard (1906-64)
Gaslight '40
Cavalcade '33
Rasputin and the Empress '33

Amanda Wyss (1960-)
Desert Steel '94
Bloodfist 4: Die Trying '92
Black Magic Woman '91
To Die For 2: Son of Darkness '91
Powwow Highway '89
Shakma '89
To Die For '89
Deadly Innocence '88
Better Off Dead '85
My Mother's Secret Life '84
A Nightmare on Elm Street '84
Fast Times at Ridgemont High '82

Nelson Xavier
At Play in the Fields of the Lord '91
Gabriela '84

Xiong Xin Xin
Once Upon a Time in China III '93
Once Upon a Time in China II '92

Zhu Xu
Shower '00
The King of Masks '99

Li Xuejian
The Emperor and the Assassin '99
Shanghai Triad '95

Salvator Xuereb (1965-)
Lewis and Clark and George '97
My Brother's War '97
Ravager '97
Blood Ties '92

Kaoru Yachigusa (1931-)
Snow Country '57
Samurai 3: Duel at Ganryu Island '56
Samurai 1: Musashi Miyamoto '55
Samurai 2: Duel at Ichijoji Temple '55

Frank Yaconelli (1898-1965)
South of Monterey '47
Lone Star Law Men '42
Western Mail '42
The Driftin' Kid '41
Riding the Sunset Trail '41
Dr. Cyclops '40
Across the Plains '39
Escape to Paradise '39
Wild Horse Canyon '39
Gun Play '36
Western Frontier '35
The Barber Shop '33

Raghubir Yadav
Bandit Queen '94
Salaam Bombay! '88

Jeff Yagher (1962-)
My Fellow Americans '96
Madonna: Innocence Lost '95
Lower Level '91
Shag: The Movie '89
Big Bad Mama 2 '87

Koji Yakusho (1956-)
The Eel '96
Shall We Dance? '96
Tampopo '86

Simon Yam
The Mission '99
Full Contact '92
Naked Killer '92
A Bullet in the Head '90
Tongs: An American Nightmare '88

Isuzu Yamada (1917-)
Yojimbo '61
The Lower Depths '57
Throne of Blood '57
Osaka Elegy '36
Sisters of the Gion '36

Isao Yamagata
Warning from Space '56
Gate of Hell '54

Fujiko Yamamoto (1931-)
An Actor's Revenge '63
Being Two Isn't Easy '62
Golden Demon '53

So Yamamura (1910-2000)
Gung Ho '85
Last Days of Planet Earth '74
Tora! Tora! Tora! '70
Barbarian and the Geisha '58
The Human Condition: No Greater Love '58
Princess Yang Kwei Fei '55
Tokyo Story '53

Al Yamanouchi
The Lone Runner *'88*
2020 Texas Gladiators *'85*

Tsutomu Yamazaki (1936-)
Rikyu *'90*
A Taxing Woman *'87*
Tampopo *'86*
The Funeral *'84*
Kagemusha *'80*

Emily Yancy
Blacula *'72*
Cotton Comes to Harlem *'70*

Edward Yankie
The Sign of Four *'01*
Deadline *'00*

Weird Al Yankovic (1959-)
Naked Gun 33 1/3: The Final Insult *'94*
Naked Gun 2 1/2: The Smell of Fear *'91*
Tapeheads *'89*
UHF *'89*
The Naked Gun: From the Files of Police Squad *'88*

Jean Yanne (1933-)
Brotherhood of the Wolf *'01*
Beaumarchais the Scoundrel *'96*
The Horseman on the Roof *'95*
A la Mode *'94*
Indochine *'92*
Madame Bovary *'91*
Quicker Than the Eye *'88*
The Wolf at the Door *'87*
Bandits *'86*
Hanna K. *'83*
Cobra *'71*
This Man Must Die *'70*
Le Boucher *'69*
Weekend *'67*
Life Upside Down *'64*

Rossana Yanni (1938-)
The Rue Morgue Massacres *'73*
Dracula's Great Love *'72*
Fangs of the Living Dead *'68*
White Comanche *'67*

Margaret Yarde
Thursday's Child *'43*
The Deputy Drummer *'35*

Claire Yarlett
Black Out *'96*
The Disappearance of Christina *'93*

Michael Yarmush
Little Men *'98*
First Do No Harm *'97*

Celeste Yarnall (1944-)
Born Yesterday *'93*
Midnight Kiss *'93*
Scorpio *'73*
The Velvet Vampire *'71*

Amy Yasbeck (1963-)
Dead Husbands *'98*
Something About Sex *'98*
Bloodhounds 2 *'96*
Dracula: Dead and Loving It *'95*
The Nutt House *'95*
The Mask *'94*
Robin Hood: Men in Tights *'93*
Problem Child 2 *'91*
Problem Child *'90*
House 2: The Second Story *'87*

Rikiya Yasuoka
The Toxic Avenger, Part 2 *'89*
Tampopo *'86*

Cassie Yates (1951-)
Perry Mason Returns *'85*
Unfaithfully Yours *'84*
St. Helen's, Killer Volcano *'82*
Who'll Save Our Children? *'82*
Of Mice and Men *'81*
Father Figure *'80*
Convoy *'78*
The Evil *'78*
F.I.S.T. *'78*
FM *'78*

Marjorie Yates
The Long Day Closes *'92*
Legend of the Werewolf *'75*

Chingmy Yau
Meltdown *'95*
Naked Killer *'92*

Biff Yeager
Headless Body in Topless Bar *'96*
Straight to Hell *'87*
Sid & Nancy *'86*
Girls Just Want to Have Fun *'85*
Repo Man *'83*

Steve Yeager (1948-)
Major League 3: Back to the Minors *'98*
Polyester *'81*
Pink Flamingos *'72*

Richard Yearwood
Dangerous Evidence: The Lori Jackson Story *'99*
Blood Brothers *'97*

Sally Yeh
The Killer *'90*
The Laserman *'90*

Anton Yelchin (1989-)
Along Came a Spider *'01*
Hearts in Atlantis *'01*

Hannah Yelland
Dinotopia *'02*
Catherine Cookson's The Secret *'00*

Peter Yellen
Ms. 45 *'81*
Driller Killer *'79*

Donnie Yen (1963-)
Blade II *'02*
Highlander: Endgame *'00*
Iron Monkey *'93*

Tran Nu Yen-Khe
The Vertical Ray of the Sun *'00*
Cyclo *'95*
The Scent of Green Papaya *'93*

Michelle Yeoh (1962-)
Crouching Tiger, Hidden Dragon *'00*
Tomorrow Never Dies *'97*
Wing Chun *'94*
The Executioners *'93*
The Heroic Trio *'93*
Supercop 2 *'93*
Twin Warriors *'93*
Supercop *'92*
Royal Warriors *'86*

Don Yesso
Out of Sync *'95*
The Hard Truth *'94*
Hero *'92*

Bolo Yeung
Shootfighter 2: Kill or Be Killed! *'96*
Fearless Tiger *'94*
Shootfighter: Fight to the Death *'93*
TC 2000 *'93*
Ironheart *'92*
Breathing Fire *'91*
Tiger Claws *'91*
Bloodsport *'88*
Legacy of Rage *'86*

Lam Ching Ying
Mr. Vampire *'86*
The Prodigal Son *'82*

Cecilia Yip
Organized Crime & Triad Bureau *'93*
Hong Kong 1941 *'84*

Francoise Yip (1972-)
Romeo Must Die *'00*
Futuresport *'98*
Black Mask *'96*
Rumble in the Bronx *'96*

Richard Yniguez (1946-)
Stalking Laura *'93*
World War III *'86*
Boulevard Nights *'79*
Sniper *'75*

Dwight Yoakam (1956-)
Panic Room *'02*
South of Heaven, West of Hell *'00*
The Minus Man *'99*
When Trumpets Fade *'98*
The Newton Boys *'97*
Don't Look Back *'96*
Sling Blade *'96*
The Little Death *'95*
Painted Hero *'95*
Roswell: The U.F.O. Cover-Up *'94*
Red Rock West *'93*

Malik Yoba (1967-)
Personals *'00*
Ride *'98*
Cop Land *'97*
Blue in the Face *'95*
Cool Runnings *'93*

Erica Yohn
Corrina, Corrina *'94*
An American Tail: Fievel Goes West *'91 (V)*
A Streetcar Named Desire *'84*

Wladimir Yordanoff
Un Air de Famille *'96*
Vincent & Theo *'90*

Dick York (1929-92)
Inherit the Wind *'60*
They Came to Cordura *'59*
Cowboy *'58*
My Sister Eileen *'55*

Francine York (1938-)
Flood! *'76*
The Centerfold Girls *'74*
The Doll Squad *'73*
Curse of the Swamp Creature *'66*
Space Monster *'64*
Secret File of Hollywood *'62*
Wild Ones on Wheels *'62*

Jeff York (1912-95)
Savage Sam *'63*
Old Yeller *'57*
Davy Crockett and the River Pirates *'56*
Westward Ho, the Wagons! *'56*
The Lady Says No *'51*
The Yearling *'46*
They Were Expendable *'45*

Kathleen York
The Big Day *'99*
Cries of Silence *'97*
Dead Men Can't Dance *'97*
Nightjohn *'96*
Dream Lover *'93*
Wild Hearts Can't Be Broken *'91*
Thompson's Last Run *'90*
Checking Out *'89*
Cold Feet *'89*
Winners Take All *'87*

Michael York (1942-)
Austin Powers In Goldmember *'02*
Austin Powers 2: The Spy Who Shagged Me *'99*
The Haunting of Hell House *'99*
The Omega Code *'99*
54 *'98*
A Knight in Camelot *'98*
Wrongfully Accused *'98*
Austin Powers: International Man of Mystery *'97*
Dark Planet *'97*
The Ripper *'97*
True Women *'97*
Not of This Earth *'96*
A Young Connecticut Yankee in King Arthur's Court *'95*
Fall from Grace *'94*
Gospa *'94*
Discretion Assured *'93*
Duel of Hearts *'92*
The Four Minute Mile *'92*
Wide Sargasso Sea *'92*
The Heat of the Day *'91*
Night of the Fox *'90*
The Lady and the Highwayman *'89*
The Return of the Musketeers *'89*
Midnight Cop *'88*
Lethal Obsession *'87*
Phantom of Death *'87*
Sword of Gideon *'86*
Nevil Shute's The Far Country *'85*
Success Is the Best Revenge *'84*
Weather in the Streets *'84*
Final Assignment *'80*
The Riddle of the Sands *'79*
The Island of Dr. Moreau *'77*
The Last Remake of Beau Geste *'77*
Logan's Run *'76*
Conduct Unbecoming *'75*
The Four Musketeers *'75*
Murder on the Orient Express *'74*
The Three Musketeers *'74*
Cabaret *'72*
Zeppelin *'71*
Something for Everyone *'70*
Justine *'69*
Romeo and Juliet *'68*
Accident *'67*
Smashing Time *'67*
The Taming of the Shrew *'67*

Rachel York (1971-)
Terror Tract *'00*
One Fine Day *'96*
Dead Center *'94*
Killer Instinct *'92*

Susannah York (1941-)
St. Patrick: The Irish Legend *'00*
Devices and Desires *'91*
Fate *'90*
The Man from the Pru *'89*
American Roulette *'88*
Diamond's Edge *'88*
A Summer Story *'88*
The Land of Faraway *'87*
Prettykill *'87*
Superman 4: The Quest for Peace *'87 (V)*
Alice *'86*
A Christmas Carol *'84*
Loophole *'83*
Yellowbeard *'83*
We'll Meet Again *'82*
The Awakening *'80*
Falling in Love Again *'80*
Second Chance *'80*
Superman 2 *'80*
The Shout *'78*
The Silent Partner *'78*
Superman: The Movie *'78*
Adventures of Eliza Fraser *'76*
Sky Riders *'76*
Conduct Unbecoming *'75*
That Lucky Touch *'75*
X, Y & Zee *'72*
Battle of Britain *'69*
The Killing of Sister George *'69*
They Shoot Horses, Don't They? *'69*
Sebastian *'68*
A Man for All Seasons *'66*
The Seventh Dawn *'64*
Tom Jones *'63*
Tunes of Glory *'60*

Yitsuko Yoshimura
Onibaba *'64*
The Insect Woman *'63*

Kazuko Yoshiyuki
In the Realm of Passion *'80*
The Empire of Passion *'76*

Ge You
The Emperor's Shadow *'96*
To Live *'94*
Farewell My Concubine *'93*

Aden Young (1972-)
In the Shadows *'98*
Cousin Bette *'97*
Hotel de Love *'96*
Cosi *'95*
River Street *'95*
Sniper *'92*
Black Robe *'91*

Alan Young (1919-)
The Time Machine *'02*
Beverly Hills Cop 3 *'94*
DuckTales the Movie: Treasure of the Lost Lamp *'90 (V)*
The Great Mouse Detective *'86 (V)*
Scruffy *'80 (V)*
Baker's Hawk *'76*
The Time Machine *'60*
Androcles and the Lion *'52*

Artie Young
Bronze Buckaroo *'39*
Harlem Rides the Range *'39*

Bill Young
Chopper *'00*
Road to Nhill *'97*

Bruce A. Young
Jurassic Park 3 *'01*
Normal Life *'96*
The War *'94*
Blink *'93*
What Ever Happened To... *'93*
Basic Instinct *'92*

Burt Young (1940-)
Blue Moon *'00*
Mickey Blue Eyes *'99*
Hot Blooded *'98*
Kicked in the Head *'97*
She's So Lovely *'97*
The Undertaker's Wedding *'97*
Heaven Before I Die *'96*
North Star *'96*
Excessive Force *'93*
Bright Angel *'91*
A Family Matter *'91*
Backstreet Dreams *'90*
Betsy's Wedding *'90*
Club Fed *'90*
Diving In *'90*
Last Exit to Brooklyn *'90*
Rocky 5 *'90*
Wait until Spring, Bandini *'90*
Beverly Hills Brats *'89*
Going Overboard *'89*
Blood Red *'88*
Back to School *'86*
Rocky 4 *'85*
Once Upon a Time in America *'84*
The Pope of Greenwich Village *'84*
A Summer to Remember *'84*
Over the Brooklyn Bridge *'83*
Amityville 2: The Possession *'82*
Lookin' to Get Out *'82*
Rocky 3 *'82*
...All the Marbles *'81*
Blood Beach *'81*
Rocky 2 *'79*
Convoy *'78*
The Choirboys *'77*
Twilight's Last Gleaming *'77*
Harry & Walter Go to New York *'76*
Rocky *'76*
The Killer Elite *'75*
Chinatown *'74*
The Gambler *'74*
Cinderella Liberty *'73*
Carnival of Blood *'71*

Carleton Young (1907-71)
The Man Who Shot Liberty Valance *'62*
Armored Command *'61*
The Gallant Hours *'60*
Sergeant Rutledge *'60*
The Horse Soldiers *'59*
Battle Cry *'55*
20,000 Leagues under the Sea *'54*
From Here to Eternity *'53*
Flying Leathernecks *'51*
People Will Talk *'51*
Texas Trouble *'41*
Trigger Men *'41*
Billy the Kid in Texas *'40*
Up in the Air *'40*
El Diablo Rides *'39*
Outlaw Express *'38*
Reefer Madness *'38*

Chris Young (1971-)
Killing Mr. Griffin *'97*
Deep Down *'94*
P.C.U. *'94*
Warlock: The Armageddon *'93*
Book of Love *'91*
December *'91*
The Runestone *'91*
The Great Outdoors *'88*

Clara Kimball Young (1890-1960)
The Frontiersmen *'38*
Oh Susannah *'38*
Rogue's Tavern *'36*
Chandu on the Magic Island *'34*
I Can't Escape *'34*
Return of Chandu *'34*
Probation *'32*
Kept Husbands *'31*
Mother and Son *'31*
The Worldly Madonna *'22*
Mid-Channel *'20*
The Eyes of Youth *'19*
Trilby *'17*

David Young
Double Exposure *'82*
Mary, Mary, Bloody Mary *'76*

Dey Young (1955-)
The Mod Squad *'99*
True Heart *'97*
The Shadow Conspiracy *'96*
Letter to My Killer *'95*
Pie in the Sky *'95*
No Place to Hide *'93*
Back in the USSR *'92*
Conflict of Interest *'92*
Frankie and Johnny *'91*
Murder 101 *'91*
Spontaneous Combustion *'89*
Doin' Time *'85*
Strange Invaders *'83*
Strange Behavior *'81*
Rock 'n' Roll High School *'79*

Faron Young (1932-96)
Daniel Boone: Trail Blazer *'56*
Hidden Guns *'56*

Gig Young (1913-78)
The Hindenburg *'75*
The Killer Elite *'75*
Bring Me the Head of Alfredo Garcia *'74*
Lovers and Other Strangers *'70*
They Shoot Horses, Don't They? *'69*
Blood Island *'68*
Strange Bedfellows *'65*
For Love or Money *'63*
Kid Galahad *'62*
That Touch of Mink *'62*
Ask Any Girl *'59*
Teacher's Pet *'58*
The Tunnel of Love *'58*
Desk Set *'57*
Desperate Hours *'55*
Young at Heart *'54*
City That Never Sleeps *'53*
The Girl Who Had Everything *'53*
Torch Song *'53*
Slaughter Trail *'51*
Hunt the Man Down *'50*
Only the Valiant *'50*
Lust for Gold *'49*
Tell It to the Judge *'49*
Wake of the Red Witch *'49*
The Three Musketeers *'48*
Escape Me Never *'47*
Air Force *'43*
Sergeant York *'41*
They Died with Their Boots On *'41*

The Challengers '93
By Way of the Stars '92
Philip Zanden (1954-)
Like It Never Was Before '95
Dreaming of Rita '94
Freud Leaving Home '91
The Mozart Brothers '86
Billy Zane (1966-)
The Diamond of Jeru '01
Hendrix '00
Cleopatra '99
Dying to Get Rich '98
This World, Then the Fireworks '97
Titanic '97
Head Above Water '96
The Phantom '96
Danger Zone '95
The Set Up '95
Flashfire '94
Only You '94
Reflections in the Dark '94
Tales from the Crypt Presents Demon Knight '94
Posse '93
Running Delilah '93
Silence of the Hams '93
Tombstone '93
Betrayal of the Dove '92
Lake Consequence '92
Orlando '92
Sniper '92
Megaville '91
Blood & Concrete: A Love Story '90
Femme Fatale '90
Memphis Belle '90
Millions '90
Back to the Future, Part 2 '89
Dead Calm '89
Going Overboard '89
The Hillside Strangler '89
Brotherhood of Justice '86
Critters '86
Back to the Future '85
Lisa Zane (1967-)
Monkeybone '01
Missing Pieces '00
The Pact '99
Wicked Ways '99
Baby Face Nelson '97
The Nurse '97
Floundering '94
Terrified '94
Unveiled '94
Freddy's Dead: The Final Nightmare '91
Bad Influence '90
Femme Fatale '90
Pucker Up and Bark Like a Dog '89
Bruno Zanin
The Boss Is Served '76
Amarcord '74
Lenore Zann
One Night Only '84
American Nightmare '81
Happy Birthday to Me '81
Angelo Zanolli
Son of Samson '62
Maciste in Hell '60
Zbigniew Zapasiewicz (1934-)
Stand Off '89
Baritone '85
Without Anesthesia '78
Carmen Zapata (1927-)
Gang Boys '97
Boulevard Nights '79
The Last Porno Flick '74
Dweezil Zappa (1969-)
Jack Frost '98
The Running Man '87
Pretty in Pink '86
Frank Zappa (1940-93)
The Boy Who Left Home to Find Out About the Shivers '81
Head '68
Moon Zappa (1967-)
The Brutal Truth '99
Pterodactyl Woman from Beverly Hills '97
Dark Side of Genius '94
Heartstopper '92
Spirit of '76 '91
The Boys Next Door '85
Nightmares '83
William Zappa
Bootmen '00
Zone 39 '96
Crush '93
The Road Warrior '82
John Zaremba
The Gallant Hours '60
20 Million Miles to Earth '57
Tony Zarindast
Werewolf '95
Hardcase and Fist '89
Kill Alex Kill '83
Joe Zaso
Addicted to Murder 3: Bloodlust '99
The Alien Agenda: Endangered Species '97
Edmund Zayenda
A Brivele der Mamen '38
Mamele '38
Robert Z'Dar
American Chinatown '96
Fugitive X '96
Red Line '96
The Mosaic Project '95
In a Moment of Passion '93
Maniac Cop 3: Badge of Silence '93
Dragonfight '92
The Legend of Wolf Mountain '92
Return to Frogtown '92
Wild Cactus '92
Beastmaster 2: Through the Portal of Time '91
The Divine Enforcer '91
Quiet Fire '91
The Big Sweat '90
The Killer's Edge '90
Maniac Cop 2 '90
Soultaker '90
Evil Altar '89
Final Sanction '89
Tango and Cash '89
Dead End City '88
Maniac Cop '88
Trained to Kill '88
Grotesque '87
Night Stalker '87
Rosel Zech (1942-)
Salmonberries '91
The Oppermann Family '82
Veronika Voss '82
Kevin Zegers (1984-)
Air Bud 4: Seventh Inning Fetch '02
Air Bud 3: World Pup '00
MVP (Most Valuable Primate) '00
Four Days '99
Komodo '99
Treasure Island '99
Air Bud 2: Golden Receiver '98
Bram Stoker's Shadowbuilder '98
It Came from the Sky '98
Air Bud '97
A Call to Remember '97
Renee Zellweger (1969-)
Bridget Jones's Diary '01
Me, Myself, and Irene '00
Nurse Betty '00
The Bachelor '99
One True Thing '98
Deceiver '97
A Price above Rubies '97
Jerry Maguire '96
The Whole Wide World '96
Empire Records '95
The Low Life '95
The Texas Chainsaw Massacre 4: The Next Generation '95
Love and a .45 '94
Shake, Rattle & Rock! '94
Michael Zelniker
Stuart Bliss '98
Glory Enough for All: The Discovery of Insulin '92
Naked Lunch '91
Bird '88
The Terry Fox Story '83
Pick-Up Summer '79
Eracio Zepeda
El Norte '83
Reed: Insurgent Mexico '73
Anthony Zerbe (1936-)
True Crime '99
Star Trek: Insurrection '98
Asteroid '97
Touch '96
License to Kill '89
See No Evil, Hear No Evil '89
Onassis '88
Opposing Force '87
Private Investigations '87
Steel Dawn '87
A.D. '85
Soggy Bottom U.S.A. '84
Dead Zone '83
Attica '80
Question of Honor '80
Centennial '78
Child of Glass '78
KISS Meets the Phantom of the Park '78
Who'll Stop the Rain? '78
Farewell, My Lovely '75
Rooster Cogburn '75
The Parallax View '74
Papillon '73
Omega Man '71
The Liberation of L.B. Jones '70
They Call Me Mr. Tibbs! '70
Cool Hand Luke '67
Will Penny '67
Catherine Zeta-Jones (1969-)
America's Sweethearts '01
High Fidelity '00
Traffic '00
Entrapment '99
The Haunting '99
The Mask of Zorro '98
The Phantom '96
Titanic '96
Blue Juice '95
Catherine the Great '95
Catherine Cookson's The Cinder Path '94
The Return of the Native '94
Splitting Heirs '93
Christopher Columbus: The Discovery '92
Mai Zetterling (1925-94)
Hidden Agenda '90
The Witches '90
Only Two Can Play '62
Pattern for Plunder '62
Truth about Women '58
Abandon Ship '57
Frieda '47
Night Is My Future '47
Torment '44
Monica Zetterlund
The New Land '73
The Emigrants '72
Wang Zhiwen
The Emperor and the Assassin '99
Blush '95
Sonja Ziemann (1926-)
A Matter of WHO '62
Made in Heaven '52
The Merry Wives of Windsor '50
Chip Zien (1947-)
Breakfast of Champions '98
The Siege '98
Howard the Duck '86 (V)
Grace Quigley '84
Ian Ziering (1966-)
The Corporation '96
No Way Back '96
The Fighter '95
Madeline Zima
The Sandy Bottom Orchestra '00
Second Chances '98
Mr. Nanny '93
The Hand that Rocks the Cradle '92
Vanessa Zima
Wicked '98
Ulee's Gold '97
Efrem Zimbalist, Jr. (1923-)
Batman: Mask of the Phantasm '93 (V)
The Avenging '92
Hot Shots! '91
Shooting Stars '85
Scruples '80
The Gathering: Part 2 '79
Family Upside Down '78
Terror out of the Sky '78
Airport '75 '75
Who Is the Black Dahlia? '75
Wait until Dark '67
By Love Possessed '61
Deep Six '58
Band of Angels '57
House of Strangers '49
Stephanie Zimbalist (1956-)
The Prophet's Game '99
Prison of Secrets '97
Dead Ahead '96
The Great Elephant Escape '95
Jericho Fever '93
The Story Lady '93
Caroline? '90
The Killing Mind '90
Personals '90
Love on the Run '85
Tomorrow's Child '82
The Awakening '80
The Babysitter '80
The Triangle Factory Fire Scandal '79
Centennial '78
Forever '78
Long Journey Back '78
Magic of Lassie '78
The Gathering '77
Joey Zimmerman (1986-)
Treehouse Hostage '99
Very Bad Things '98
Mother's Boys '94
Luca Zingaretti
Jesus '00
Artemisia '97
Victoria Zinny
Beyond the Door 3 '91
Viridiana '61
William Zipp
Future Force '89
Jungle Assault '89
Operation Warzone '89
Death Chase '87
Mankillers '87
August Zirner
The Promise '94
Voyager '91
Hanns Zischler (1947-)
The Cement Garden '93
Francesco '93
Club Extinction '89
A Woman in Flames '84
Les Rendez-vous D'Anna '78
Kings of the Road—In the Course of Time '76
Dan Ziskie
Dangerous Passion '95
Zebrahead '92
Twisted '86
Zhang Ziyi
The Road Home '01
Rush Hour 2 '01
Crouching Tiger, Hidden Dragon '00
Adrian Zmed (1954-)
Storm Chasers: Revenge of the Twister '98
Improper Conduct '94
Eyewitness to Murder '93
The Other Woman '92
Bachelor Party '84
The Final Terror '83
Grease 2 '82
For the Love of It '80
Moses Znaimer
Abraxas: Guardian of the Universe '90
Best Revenge '83
Jean-Pierre Zola
The Train '65
Mon Oncle '58
Michael Zorek
Hot Moves '84
Private School '83
Louis Zorich (1924-)
Commandments '96
Cheap Shots '91
City of Hope '91
Death of a Salesman '86
Newman's Law '74
Vera Zorina (1917-)
Follow the Boys '44
Louisiana Purchase '41
The Goldwyn Follies '38
Zouzou
S*P*Y*S '74
Chloe in the Afternoon '72
Rod Zuanic
Fast Talking '86
Mad Max: Beyond Thunderdome '85
George Zucco (1886-1960)
David and Bathsheba '51
Madame Bovary '49
The Pirate '48
Lured '47
Where There's Life '47
Scared to Death '46
Fog Island '45
Having Wonderful Crime '45
House of Frankenstein '44
The Mummy's Ghost '44
Return of the Ape Man '44
The Seventh Cross '44
The Black Raven '43
Dead Men Walk '43
The Mad Ghoul '43
Sherlock Holmes in Washington '43
The Black Swan '42
The Mad Monster '42
The Mummy's Tomb '42
My Favorite Blonde '42
International Lady '41
The Monster and the Girl '41
A Woman's Face '41
The Mummy's Hand '40
The Adventures of Sherlock Holmes '39
The Hunchback of Notre Dame '39
Arrest Bulldog Drummond '38
Marie Antoinette '38
Three Comrades '38
The Bride Wore Red '37
The Firefly '37
Saratoga '37
Souls at Sea '37
David Zucker (1947-)
Airplane! '80
Kentucky Fried Movie '77
Jerry Zucker (1950-)
Airplane! '80
Kentucky Fried Movie '77
Alex Zuckerman
Freaked '93
Me and the Kid '93
Daphne Zuniga (1963-)
Stand-Ins '97
Charlie's Ghost: The Secret of Coronado '94
800 Leagues Down the Amazon '93
Prey of the Chameleon '91
Eyes of the Panther '90
The Fly 2 '89
Gross Anatomy '89
Staying Together '89
Last Rites '88
Spaceballs '87
Modern Girls '86
Quarterback Princess '85
The Sure Thing '85
Vision Quest '85
The Initiation '84
Jose Zuniga
The Crew '00
For Love or Country: The Arturo Sandoval Story '00
Gun Shy '00
Happy Accidents '00
For Which He Stands '98
Next Stop, Wonderland '98
Con Air '97
Hurricane Streets '96
Ransom '96
Money Train '95
Crooklyn '94
Dianik Zurakowska
Orgy of the Vampires '73
The Hanging Woman '72
Cauldron of Blood '67
Jahi JJ Zuri
Omega Doom '96
Nemesis 2: Nebula '94
Yoshitaka Zushi
Akira Kurosawa's Dreams '90
Dodes 'ka-den '70
Brad Zutaut
Knock Outs '92
Nudity Required '90
Hardbodies 2 '86
Noam Zylberman
Love and Hate: A Marriage Made in Hell '90
Outside Chance of Maximillian Glick '88
Elsa Zylberstein (1969-)
Metroland '97
Portraits Chinois '96
Farinelli '94
Mina Tannenbaum '93

Director Index

The **Director Index** provides a complete videography for any director with more than one video credit. The listings for the director names follow an alphabetical sort by last name (although the names appear in a first name last name format). The videographies are listed chronologically, from most recent film to directorial debut. If a director helmed more than one film in the same year, these movies are listed alphabetically within the year. Use this index in conjunction with the **Cast** (immediately preceding this index), **Writer**, and **Cinematographer** indexes (immediately following) to see where some of today's hottest directors got their starts.

What Have I Done to Deserve This? '85
Dark Habits '84
Labyrinth of Passion '82
Pepi, Luci, Bom and Other Girls on the Heap '80

Paul Almond (1931-)
The Dance Goes On '92
Captive Hearts '87
Prep School '81
Final Assignment '80
Journey '77

John A. Alonzo (1934-2001)
Blinded by the Light '82
Portrait of a Stripper '79
FM '78

Emmett Alston
Little Ninjas '92
Demonwarp '87
Tigershark '87
Nine Deaths of the Ninja '85
Three Way Weekend '81
New Year's Evil '78

Robert Altman (1925-)
Gosford Park '01
Dr. T & the Women '00
Cookie's Fortune '99
The Gingerbread Man '97
Kansas City '95
Ready to Wear '94
Short Cuts '93
The Player '92
Vincent & Theo '90
Aria '88
The Caine Mutiny Court Martial '88
Tanner '88 '88
Dumb Waiter '87
O.C. and Stiggs '87
The Room '87
Beyond Therapy '86
Fool for Love '86
Secret Honor '85
Streamers '83
Come Back to the Five & Dime Jimmy Dean, Jimmy Dean '82
Popeye '80
Quintet '79
A Wedding '78
Buffalo Bill & the Indians '76
Nashville '75
Thieves Like Us '74
The Long Goodbye '73
McCabe & Mrs. Miller '71
Brewster McCloud '70
M*A*S*H '70
That Cold Day in the Park '69
Countdown '68

Robert Alton (1906-57)
Pagan Love Song '50
Merton of the Movies '47

Keito Amamiya (1959-)
Cyber Ninja '94
Zeram 2 '94

Rod Amateau (1923-)
The Garbage Pail Kids Movie '87
High School USA '84
Lovelines '84
The Seniors '78
Drive-In '76
The Statue '71
The Bushwackers '52

Gianni Amelio (1945-)
Lamerica '95
The Stolen Children '92
Open Doors '89

Alejandro Amenabar (1972-)
The Others '01
Open Your Eyes '97
Thesis '96

Pino Amenta
Heaven Tonight '93
What the Moon Saw '90
Boulevard of Broken Dreams '88
True Colors '87
My Brother Tom '86
All the Rivers Run '84
Bellamy '80

Jon Amiel (1948-)
Entrapment '99
The Man Who Knew Too Little '97
Copycat '95
Sommersby '93
Tune in Tomorrow '90
Queen of Hearts '89
The Singing Detective '86

Gideon Amir
Accidents '89
The P.O.W. Escape '86

Franco Amurri (1958-)
Monkey Trouble '94
Flashback '89

Allison Anders (1954-)
Sugar Town '99
Grace of My Heart '96
Four Rooms '95
Mi Vida Loca '94
Gas Food Lodging '92
Border Radio '88

Brad Anderson (1964-)
Session 9 '01
Happy Accidents '00
Next Stop, Wonderland '98

Clyde (Claudio Fragasso) Anderson (1951-)
Beyond Darkness '92
Monster Dog '82

Jane Anderson
If These Walls Could Talk 2 '00
The Baby Dance '98

Kurt Anderson
The Killing Grounds '97
Dead Cold '96
Bounty Tracker '93
Martial Outlaw '93
Martial Law 2: Undercover '91

Lindsay Anderson (1923-94)
Glory! Glory! '90
The Whales of August '87
Britannia Hospital '82
In Celebration '75
O Lucky Man! '73
If... '69
This Sporting Life '63

Michael Anderson, Sr. (1920-)
Summer of the Monkeys '98
20,000 Leagues Under the Sea '97
The Sea Wolf '93
Young Catherine '91
Millennium '89
Separate Vacations '86
Sword of Gideon '86
Second Time Lucky '84
Murder by Phone '82
Dominique Is Dead '79
The Martian Chronicles: Part 1 '79
The Martian Chronicles: Part 2 '79
The Martian Chronicles: Part 3 '79
Orca '77
Logan's Run '76
Conduct Unbecoming '75
Doc Savage '75
The Shoes of the Fisherman '68
The Quiller Memorandum '66
Operation Crossbow '65
The Naked Edge '61
Shake Hands with the Devil '59
The Wreck of the Mary Deare '59
Around the World in 80 Days '56
Battle Hell '56
Dam Busters '55
The House of the Arrow '53

Paul Anderson
Resident Evil '02
Soldier '98
Event Horizon '97
Mortal Kombat 1: The Movie '95
Shopping '93

Paul Thomas Anderson (1970-)
Magnolia '99
Boogie Nights '97
Hard Eight '96

Steve (Stephen M.) Anderson
Dead Men Can't Dance '97
South Central '92

Wes Anderson (1970-)
The Royal Tenenbaums '01
Rushmore '98
Bottle Rocket '95

Mario Andreacchio (1955-)
The Real Macaw '98
Napoleon '96
Fair Game '85

Roger Andrieux (1940-)
La Petite Sirene '80
L'Amour en Herbe '77

Chris Angel (1972-)
Wishmaster 3: Beyond the Gates of Hell '01
Beyond Redemption '99
The Fear: Halloween Night '99

Robert Angelo
Dead Sexy '01
Forbidden Sins '99

Theo Angelopoulos (1935-)
Eternity and a Day '97
Ulysses' Gaze '95
Landscape in the Mist '88
The Travelling Players '75

Ken Annakin (1914-)
The New Adventures of Pippi Longstocking '88
Pirate Movie '82
Cheaper to Keep Her '80
The Fifth Musketeer '79
Paper Tiger '74
Call of the Wild '72
Those Daring Young Men in Their Jaunty Jalopies '69
Battle of the Bulge '65
Those Magnificent Men in Their Flying Machines '65
The Longest Day '62
The Swiss Family Robinson '60
Third Man on the Mountain '59
Across the Bridge '57
Land of Fury '55
The Sword & the Rose '53
The Story of Robin Hood & His Merrie Men '52
Trio '50

Jean-Jacques Annaud (1943-)
Enemy at the Gates '00
Seven Years in Tibet '97
The Lover '92
The Bear '89
The Name of the Rose '86
Quest for Fire '82
Hothead '78
Black and White in Color '76

Paul Annett
The Witching of Ben Wagner '95
Tales of the Unexpected '91
The Beast Must Die '75
Poldark '75

David Anspaugh (1946-)
Moonlight and Valentino '95
Rudy '93
Fresh Horses '88
Hoosiers '86

Joseph Anthony (1912-93)
Tomorrow '72
All in a Night's Work '61
Career '59
The Matchmaker '58
The Rainmaker '56

Manuel Antin (1926-)
Far Away and Long Ago '74
Don Segundo Sombra '69

Pedrag (Peter) Antonijevic
Hard Cash '01
Savior '98

Lou Antonio (1934-)
Lies Before Kisses '92
A Taste for Killing '92
The Last Prostitute '91
This Gun for Hire '90
Mayflower Madam '87
Pals '87
Between Friends '83
Breaking Up Is Hard to Do '79
Silent Victory: The Kitty O'Neil Story '79
The Gypsy Warriors '78
A Real American Hero '78
Someone I Touched '75

Michelangelo Antonioni (1912-)
Beyond the Clouds '95
Identification of a Woman '82
The Passenger '75
Zabriskie Point '70
Blow-Up '66
The Eclipse '66
The Red Desert '64
L'Avventura '60
Il Grido '57
Love in the City '53

Michael Apted (1941-)
Enough '02
Enigma '01
The World Is Not Enough '99
Always Outnumbered Always Outgunned '98
Extreme Measures '96
Nell '94
Blink '93
Incident at Oglala: The Leonard Peltier Story '92
Thunderheart '92
Class Action '91
Gorillas in the Mist '88
Critical Condition '86
First Born '84
Gorky Park '83
Kipperbang '82
Continental Divide '81
Coal Miner's Daughter '80
Agatha '79
The Squeeze '77
Triple Echo '77
Poor Girl, a Ghost Story '74

Manuel Gutierrez Aragon (1942-)
Half of Heaven '86
Demons in the Garden '82

Gregg Araki (1959-)
Splendor '99
Nowhere '96
The Doom Generation '95
Totally F***ed Up '94
The Living End '92

Vicente Aranda (1926-)
Jealousy '99
Intruso '93
Lovers: A True Story '90
The Blood Spattered Bride '72

Alfonso Arau (1932-)
The Magnificent Ambersons '02
Picking Up the Pieces '99
A Walk in the Clouds '95
Like Water for Chocolate '93

Denys Arcand (1941-)
Stardom '00
Love and Human Remains '93
Jesus of Montreal '89
The Decline of the American Empire '86

George Archainbaud (1890-1959)
Last of the Pony Riders '53
On Top of Old Smoky '53
Winning of the West '53
Blue Canadian Rockies '52
Night Stage to Galveston '52
Hunt the Man Down '50
Hopalong Cassidy: Borrowed Trouble '48
Hopalong Cassidy: False Paradise '48
Hopalong Cassidy: Silent Conflict '48
Hopalong Cassidy: Sinister Journey '48
Hopalong Cassidy: The Dead Don't Dream '48
Hopalong Cassidy: Hoppy's Holiday '47
Hopalong Cassidy: The Marauders '47
Hopalong Cassidy: Unexpected Guest '47
Hopalong Cassidy: The Devil's Playground '46
Mystery Man '44
Texas Masquerade '44
The Woman of the Town '44
False Colors '43
Hoppy Serves a Writ '43
The Kansan '43
Rhythm Romance '39
Thanks for the Memory '38
Lost Squadron '32
The Lady Refuses '31
State's Attorney '31
The Silver Horde '30

Emile Ardolino (1943-93)
George Balanchine's The Nutcracker '93
Gypsy '93
Sister Act '92
Three Men and a Little Lady '90
Chances Are '89
Dirty Dancing '87
The Rise & Rise of Daniel Rocket '86

Mats Arehn
Istanbul '90
The Assignment '78

Dario Argento (1940-)
Sleepless '01
The Phantom of the Opera '98
The Stendahl Syndrome '95
Dario Argento's Trauma '93
Two Evil Eyes '90
Opera '88
Creepers '85
Unsane '82
Inferno '80
Suspiria '77
Deep Red: Hatchet Murders '75
The Cat o' Nine Tails '71
The Bird with the Crystal Plumage '70

Adolfo Aristarain (1943-)
A Place in the World '92
The Stranger '87
Time for Revenge '82

Allan Arkush (1948-)
Elvis Meets Nixon '98
The Temptations '98
Shake, Rattle & Rock! '94
Caddyshack 2 '88
Get Crazy '83
Heartbeeps '81
Rock 'n' Roll High School '79
Death Sport '78
Hollywood Boulevard '76

Leslie Arliss (1901-87)
A Man About the House '47
The Man in Grey '45
The Wicked Lady '45
The Night Has Eyes '42

George Armitage
Grosse Pointe Blank '97
Miami Blues '90
Hot Rod '79
Private Duty Nurses '71

Gillian Armstrong (1950-)
Charlotte Gray '01
Oscar and Lucinda '97
Little Women '94
The Last Days of Chez Nous '92
Fires Within '91
High Tide '87
Mrs. Soffel '84
Starstruck '82
My Brilliant Career '79

Moira Armstrong
A Village Affair '95
Body & Soul '93
How Many Miles to Babylon? '82
Testament of Youth '79

Gwen Arner
Necessary Parties '88
A Matter of Principle '83

Frank Arnold
Josh Kirby...Time Warrior: Chapter 6, Last Battle for the Universe '96
Josh Kirby...Time Warrior: Chapter 2, The Human Pets '95
Josh Kirby...Time Warrior: Chapter 3, Trapped on Toyworld '95
A Waltz Through the Hills '88

Jack Arnold (1916-92)
Marilyn: The Untold Story '80
Swiss Conspiracy '77
Games Girls Play '75
Boss '74
Bachelor in Paradise '69
A Global Affair '63
Monster on the Campus '59
The Mouse That Roared '59
No Name on the Bullet '59
High School Confidential '58
The Incredible Shrinking Man '57
Man in the Shadow '57
Revenge of the Creature '55
Tarantula '55
Creature from the Black Lagoon '54
It Came from Outer Space '53

Newton Arnold (1928-2000)
Bloodsport '88
Blood Thirst '65
Hands of a Stranger '62

Darren Aronofsky (1969-)
Requiem for a Dream '00
Pi '98

Miguel Arteta
The Good Girl '02
Chuck & Buck '00
Star Maps '97

Karen Arthur (1941-)
The Song of the Lark '01
The Lost Child '00
True Women '97
The Disappearance of Christina '93
The Secret '93
The Jacksons: An American Dream '92
Bridge to Silence '89
Lady Beware '87
Broken Badge '85
A Bunny's Tale '85
My Sister, My Love '78

Dorothy Arzner (1897-1979)
Dance, Girl, Dance '40
The Bride Wore Red '37
Craig's Wife '36
Christopher Strong '33

Anthony (Giuliano Carnimeo) Ascot
Gunslinger '70s
Guns for Dollars '73

Ash
Pups '99
Bang '95

Hal Ashby (1930-88)
8 Million Ways to Die '85
The Slugger's Wife '85
Lookin' to Get Out '82
Being There '79
Coming Home '78
Bound for Glory '76

Shampoo '75
The Last Detail '73
Harold and Maude '71

John Mallory Asher
Diamonds '99
Kounterfeit '96

William Asher (1921-)
Movers and Shakers '85
Night Warning '82
Beach Blanket Bingo '65
How to Stuff a Wild Bikini '65
Bikini Beach '64
Muscle Beach Party '64
Beach Party '63

Anthony Asquith (1902-68)
The V.I.P.'s '63
The Millionairess '60
Carrington, V.C. '54
The Importance of Being Earnest '52
The Browning Version '51
The Woman in Question '50
Man of Evil '48
The Winslow Boy '48
The Demi-Paradise '43
We Dive at Dawn '43
Cottage to Let '41
Pygmalion '38
I Stand Condemned '36

Olivier Assayas (1955-)
Late August, Early September '98
Irma Vep '96

Ovidio G. Assonitis
Madhouse '87
Tentacles '77

Richard Attenborough (1923-)
Grey Owl '99
In Love and War '96
Shadowlands '93
Chaplin '92
Cry Freedom '87
A Chorus Line '85
Gandhi '82
Magic '78
A Bridge Too Far '77
Young Winston '72

David Attwood
Fidel '02
Shot Through the Heart '98
Moll Flanders '96
Wild West '93

John H. Auer (1906-75)
City That Never Sleeps '53
Wheel of Fortune '41
The Crime of Dr. Crespi '35

Bille August (1948-)
Les Miserables '97
Jerusalem '96
Smilla's Sense of Snow '96
The House of the Spirits '93
The Best Intentions '92
Pelle the Conqueror '88
Twist & Shout '84

Carlos Aured
Curse of the Devil '73
House of Psychotic Women '73
The Mummy's Revenge '73
Horror Rises from the Tomb '72

Paul Auster (1947-)
Lulu on the Bridge '98
Blue in the Face '95

Sam Auster
Bounty Hunter 2002 '94
Screen Test '85

Ray Austin (1932-)
Highlander: The Gathering '92
The Zany Adventures of Robin Hood '84
Return of the Man from U.N.C.L.E. '83
House of the Living Dead '73
The Virgin Witch '70

Steve Austin
American Streetfighter '96
Expert Weapon '93

Claude Autant-Lara (1901-2000)
Oldest Profession '67
The Red and the Black '57
Four Bags Full '56
Seven Deadly Sins '53
The Red Inn '51
Devil in the Flesh '46
Sylvia and the Phantom '45

Igor Auzins
We of the Never Never '82
Death Train '79
High Rolling in a Hot Corvette '77
Night Nurse '77

Aram Avakian (1926-87)
11 Harrowhouse '74
Cops and Robbers '73
End of the Road '70

Roger Roberts Avary (1967-)
Mr. Stitch '95
Killing Zoe '94

Pupi Avati (1938-)
The Best Man '97
The Story of Boys & Girls '91
Bix '90
Revenge of the Dead '84
Zeder '83

Howard (Hikmet) Avedis
Kidnapped '87
They're Playing with Fire '84
Separate Ways '82
Mortuary '81
The Fifth Floor '80
Texas Detour '77
Scorchy '76
The Specialist '75
The Teacher '74
The Stepmother '71

Joe Mari Avellana
Fist of Glory '95
Blackbelt 2: Fatal Force '93

Hy Averback (1925-97)
Where the Boys Are '84 '84
She's in the Army Now '81
A Guide for the Married Woman '78
Pearl '78
Suppose They Gave a War and Nobody Came? '70
I Love You, Alice B. Toklas! '68
Where Were You When the Lights Went Out? '68

Rick Avery
Deadly Outbreak '96
The Expert '95

John G. Avildsen (1935-)
8 Seconds '94
The Power of One '92
Rocky 5 '90
The Karate Kid: Part 3 '89
Lean on Me '89
For Keeps '88
Happy New Year '87
The Karate Kid: Part 2 '86
The Karate Kid '84
A Night in Heaven '83
Neighbors '81
The Formula '80
Rocky '76
Foreplay '75
Save the Tiger '73
Cry Uncle '71
Guess What We Learned in School Today? '70
Joe '70

Jon Avnet (1949-)
Uprising '01
Red Corner '97
Up Close and Personal '96
The War '94
Fried Green Tomatoes '91
Between Two Women '86

Gabriel Axel (1918-)
Royal Deceit '94
Babette's Feast '87

Mario Azzopardi (1950-)
Stiletto Dance '01
Thrill Seekers '99
Total Recall 2070: Machine Dreams '99
Bone Daddy '97
Nowhere to Hide '87
Deadline '82

Beth B (1955-)
Two Small Bodies '93
Salvation! '87
Vortex '81

Hector Babenco (1946-)
At Play in the Fields of the Lord '91
Ironweed '87
Kiss of the Spider Woman '85
Pixote '81

Lloyd Bacon (1890-1955)
The French Line '54
She Couldn't Say No '52
The Fuller Brush Girl '50
It Happens Every Spring '49
Miss Grant Takes Richmond '49
Action in the North Atlantic '43
The Fighting Sullivans '42
Silver Queen '42
Footsteps in the Dark '41
Brother Orchid '40
Knute Rockne: All American '40
Oklahoma Kid '39
Boy Meets Girl '38
Marked Woman '37
Devil Dogs of the Air '35
Footlight Parade '33
42nd Street '33
Kept Husbands '31

Clarence Badger (1880-1964)
It '27
Hands Up '26
Paths to Paradise '25
Teddy at the Throttle '16

John Badham (1939-)
The Jack Bull '99
Incognito '97
Nick of Time '95
Drop Zone '94
Another Stakeout '93
Point of No Return '93
The Hard Way '91
Bird on a Wire '90
Stakeout '87
Short Circuit '86
American Flyers '85
Blue Thunder '83
WarGames '83
Whose Life Is It Anyway? '81
Dracula '79
Saturday Night Fever '77
Bingo Long Traveling All-Stars & Motor Kings '76
Reflections of Murder '74

Reza Badiyi (1936-)
Blade in Hong Kong '85
Policewoman Centerfold '83
Of Mice and Men '81

Max Baer, Jr. (1937-)
Hometown U.S.A. '79
Ode to Billy Joe '76
The McCullochs '75

King Baggot (1879-1948)
The Notorious Lady '27
Tumbleweeds '25

Charles "Chuck" Bail
Street Corner Justice '96
Choke Canyon '86
Gumball Rally '76
Cleopatra Jones & the Casino of Gold '75

John Bailey (1942-)
China Moon '91
Search for Signs of Intelligent Life in the Universe '91

Stuart Baird
U.S. Marshals '98
Executive Decision '96

David Baker (1931-)
Best Enemies '86
Air Hawk '84

Graham Baker
Beowulf '98
Born to Ride '91
Alien Nation '88
Impulse '84
Omen 3: The Final Conflict '81

Robert S. Baker (1916-)
The Hellfire Club '61
Jack the Ripper '60
Blackout '50

Roy Ward Baker (1916-)
Masks of Death '86
The Monster Club '85
Danger UXB '81
And Now the Screaming Starts '73
The Legend of the 7 Golden Vampires '73
Vault of Horror '73
Asylum '72
Dr. Jekyll and Sister Hyde '71
The Scars of Dracula '70
The Vampire Lovers '70
The Anniversary '68
A Night to Remember '58
One That Got Away '57
Don't Bother to Knock '52
The Weaker Sex '49
The October Man '48

Ralph Bakshi (1938-)
Cool World '92
Fire and Ice '83
Hey Good Lookin' '82
American Pop '81
The Lord of the Rings '78
Wizards '77
Streetfight '75
Heavy Traffic '73
Fritz the Cat '72

Bob Balaban (1945-)
Subway Stories '97
The Last Good Time '94
My Boyfriend's Back '93
Parents '89
The Stranger from Venus '54

Alexei Balabanov
Of Freaks and Men '98
Brother '97

Gianfranco Baldanello
Death Ray
Great Adventure '75

Ferdinando Baldi (1927-)
Treasure of the Four Crowns '82
Duel of Champions '61

Richard Balducci
Too Pretty to Be Honest '72
Scandal Man '67
L'Odeur des Fauves '66

Peter Baldwin (1929-)
Meet Wally Sparks '97
A Very Brady Christmas '88
Lots of Luck '85

Rafael Baledon, Sr. (1919-95)
The Man and the Monster '65
Swamp of the Lost Monster '65
The Curse of the Crying Woman '61

Carroll Ballard (1937-)
Fly Away Home '96
Wind '92
Nutcracker: The Motion Picture '86
Never Cry Wolf '83
The Black Stallion '79

Albert Band (1924-)
Prehysteria 2 '94
Prehysteria '93
Robot Wars '93
Doctor Mordrid: Master of the Unknown '90
Ghoulies 2 '87
Zoltan...Hound of Dracula '78
Tramplers '66
I Bury the Living '58

Charles Band (1952-)
The Creeps '97
Hideous '97
Dollman vs Demonic Toys '93
Prehysteria '93
Crash and Burn '90
Doctor Mordrid: Master of the Unknown '90
Meridian: Kiss of the Beast '90
Trancers 2: The Return of Jack Deth '90
Trancers '84
Dungeonmaster '83
Metalstorm: The Destruction of Jared Syn '83
Parasite '82
The Alchemist '81

Mirra Bank
Enormous Changes '83
Trumps '83

Norberto Barba (1963-)
Lost in the Bermuda Triangle '98
Solo '96
Blue Tiger '94

Uri Barbash
Unsettled Land '88
Beyond the Walls '84

Paris Barclay
The Cherokee Kid '96
America's Dream '95
Don't Be a Menace to South Central While Drinking Your Juice in the Hood '95

Clive Barker (1952-)
Lord of Illusions '95
Nightbreed '90
Hellraiser '87

Mike Barker
Lorna Doone '01
Best Laid Plans '99
The Tenant of Wildfell Hall '96

Reginald Barker (1886-1945)
Healer '36
Seven Keys to Baldpate '29
Civilization '16
The Bargain '15
On the Night Stage '15

Boris Barnet (1902-65)
The Patriots '33
The Girl with the Hat Box '27

Steve Barnett
Scanner Cop 2: Volkin's Revenge '94
Scanners: The Showdown '94
Mission of Justice '92
Mindwarp '91
Hollywood Boulevard 2 '89
Emmanuelle 5 '87

M. Neema Barnette
Spirit Lost '96
Better Off Dead '94
Sin and Redemption '94

Douglas Barr (1949-)
Frame by Frame '95
Dead Badge '94

Bruno Barreto (1955-)
Bossa Nova '99
One Tough Cop '98
Four Days in September '97
Carried Away '95
A Show of Force '90
The Story of Fausta '88
Happily Ever After '86
Gabriela '84
Amor Bandido '79
Dona Flor and Her Two Husbands '78

Fabio Barreto (1957-)
O Quatrilho '95
Luzia '88

Steven Barron (1956-)
Arabian Nights '00
Merlin '98
The Adventures of Pinocchio '96
Coneheads '93
Teenage Mutant Ninja Turtles: The Movie '90
Electric Dreams '84

Zelda Barron
Forbidden Sun '89
Shag: The Movie '89
Bulldance '88
Secret Places '85

Ian Barry
The Diamond of Jeru '01
Joey '98
Blackwater Trail '95
Crime Broker '94
The Seventh Floor '93
Wrangler '88
Chain Reaction '80

Paul Bartel (1938-2000)
Scenes from the Class Struggle in Beverly Hills '89
The Longshot '86
Lust in the Dust '85
Not for Publication '84
Eating Raoul '82
Cannonball '76
Death Race 2000 '75
Private Parts '72
Paul Bartel's The Secret Cinema '69

Andrzej Bartkowiak (1950-)
Exit Wounds '01
Romeo Must Die '00

Hall Bartlett (1922-93)
Children of Sanchez '79
Jonathan Livingston Seagull '73
Defiant '70
Changes '69
All the Young Men '60

Richard Bartlett (1922-94)
Ollie Hopnoodle's Haven of Bliss '88
Rock, Pretty Baby '56
Lonesome Trail '55

Charles T. Barton (1902-81)
The Shaggy Dog '59
Toby Tyler '59
Dance with Me, Henry '56
Ma and Pa Kettle at the Fair '52
Abbott and Costello Meet the Killer, Boris Karloff '49
Africa Screams '49
Abbott and Costello Meet Frankenstein '48
Mexican Hayride '48
The Noose Hangs High '48
Buck Privates Come Home '47
The Wistful Widow of Wagon Gap '47
The Time of Their Lives '46
Harmon of Michigan '41
Helltown '38
Forlorn River '37
Thunder Pass '37
Thunder Trail '37
Desert Gold '36
Wagon Wheels '34

Jules Bass
Flight of Dragons '82
The Last Unicorn '82
The Return of the King '80
The Hobbit '78
The Ballad of Paul Bunyan '72
Mad Monster Party '68

Lawrence Bassoff
Hunk '87
Weekend Pass '84

Bradley Battersby
Red Letters '00
Blue Desert '91

Roy Battersby
Cracker: Brotherly Love '95
Mr. Love '86
Winter Flight '84

Giacomo Battiato (1943-)
Blood Ties '87
Hearts & Armour '83
Noah Baumbach (1969-)
Mr. Jealousy '98
Kicking and Screaming '95
Lamberto Bava (1944-)
Demons 2 '87
Demons '86
Blastfighter '85
Devilfish '84
A Blade in the Dark '83
Macabre '80
Mario Bava (1914-80)
Shock '79
Lisa and the Devil '75
Torture Chamber of Baron Blood '72
Twitch of the Death Nerve '71
Five Dolls for an August Moon '70
Hatchet for the Honeymoon '70
Four Times That Night '69
Danger: Diabolik '68
Kill, Baby, Kill '66
Knives of the Avenger '65
Planet of the Vampires '65
Black Sabbath '64
Blood and Black Lace '64
Hercules in the Haunted World '64
The Girl Who Knew Too Much '63
The Whip and the Body '63
The Wonders of Aladdin '61
Black Sunday '60
I Vampiri '56
Craig R. Baxley
Stephen King's Rose Red '02
Stephen King's The Storm of the Century '99
Under Pressure '98
Twilight Man '96
The Avenging Angel '95
Deconstructing Sarah '94
Deep Red '94
Stone Cold '91
I Come in Peace '90
Action Jackson '88
John Baxter (1896-1975)
Love on the Dole '41
Old Mother Riley's Ghosts '41
Michael Bay (1965-)
Pearl Harbor '01
Armageddon '98
The Rock '96
Bad Boys '95
Stephen Bayly (1942-)
Diamond's Edge '88
Coming Up Roses '87
David Beaird (1952-)
Scorchers '92
It Takes Two '88
Pass the Ammo '88
My Chauffeur '86
Party Animal '83
Octavia '82
Alan Beattie
Stand Alone '85
Delusion '84
Warren Beatty (1937-)
Bulworth '98
Dick Tracy '90
Reds '81
Heaven Can Wait '78
William Beaudine (1892-1970)
Billy the Kid Versus Dracula '66
Jesse James Meets Frankenstein's Daughter '65
Lassie's Great Adventure '62
Ten Who Dared '60
Westward Ho, the Wagons! '56
Bela Lugosi Meets a Brooklyn Gorilla '52
Here Come the Marines '52
Ghost Chasers '51
Blues Busters '50
Smugglers' Cove '48
Spook Busters '48
Bowery Buckaroos '47
Hard-Boiled Mahoney '47
Infamous Crimes '47
Mom & Dad '47
Follow the Leader '44
The Ape Man '43
Ghost on the Loose '43
Here Comes Kelly '43
Spotlight Scandals '43
Miracle Kid '42
The Panther's Claw '42
Phantom Killer '42
Turf Boy '42
Desperate Cargo '41
Misbehaving Husbands '41
Robot Pilot '41
Sparrows '26
Little Annie Rooney '25
The Country Kid '23
Gabrielle Beaumont (1942-)
Beastmaster 3: The Eye of Braxus '95
Carmilla '89
Riders '88
He's My Girl '87
Gone Are the Days '84
Death of a Centerfold '81
The Godsend '79
Harry Beaumont (1888-1966)
The Show-Off '46
When's Your Birthday? '37
Dance Fools Dance '31
Laughing Sinners '31
Broadway Melody '29
Our Dancing Daughters '28
Beau Brummel '24
Gorman Bechard (1959-)
Cemetery High '89
Disconnected '87
Galactic Gigolo '87
Psychos in Love '87
Martin Beck
Last Game '80
Challenge '74
Harold Becker (1950-)
Domestic Disturbance '01
Mercury Rising '98
City Hall '95
Malice '93
Sea of Love '89
The Boost '88
Vision Quest '85
Taps '81
The Black Marble '79
The Onion Field '79
Jacques Becker (1906-60)
Le Trou '59
Modigliani '58
Ali Baba and the 40 Thieves '54
Grisbi '53
Casque d'Or '52
Rendez-vous de Juillet '49
Antoine et Antoinette '47
Jean Becker (1938-)
Elisa '94
One Deadly Summer '83
Josh Becker (1958-)
Lunatics: A Love Story '92
Thou Shalt Not Kill...Except '87
James Becket (1936-)
Plato's Run '96
Natural Causes '94
Ulterior Motives '92
James Gavin Bedford
The Street King '02
Red Shoe Diaries 8: Night of Abandon '97
Ford Beebe (1888-1978)
My Dog Shep '46
The Invisible Man's Revenge '44
Don Winslow of the Coast Guard '43
Don Winslow of the Navy '43
Night Monster '42
The Masked Rider '41
Riders of Death Valley '41
Fantasia '40
Winners of the West '40
Buck Rogers Conquers the Universe '39
Destination Saturn '39
Flash Gordon: Mars Attacks the World '39
Oregon Trail '39
The Phantom Creeps '39
Red Barry '38
Radio Patrol '37
Tim Tyler's Luck '37
Ace Drummond '36
The Man from Gun Town '36
Laughing at Life '33
The Last of the Mohicans '32
Shadow of the Eagle '32
Greg Beeman (1962-)
Miracle in Lane Two '00
Brink '98
Bushwhacked '95
Mom and Dad Save the World '92
License to Drive '88
Charles Beeson
Cider with Rosie '99
Second Sight '99
Agatha Christie's The Pale Horse '96
Jean-Jacques Beineix (1946-)
Betty Blue '86
Moon in the Gutter '83
Diva '82
Martin Bell
Brotherhood of Murder '99
Hidden in America '96
American Heart '92
Streetwise '84
Earl Bellamy (1917-)
Magic on Love Island '80
Desperate Women '78
Speedtrap '78
Fire '77
Sidewinder One '77
Flood! '76
Against a Crooked Sky '75
Seven Alone '75
Walking Tall: Part 2 '75
The Trackers '71
Munster, Go Home! '66
Justice of the West '61
Donald P. Bellisario
JAG '95
Last Rites '88
Marco Bellocchio (1939-)
Devil in the Flesh '87
Henry IV '85
The Eyes, the Mouth '83
Jerry Belson
Surrender '87
Jekyll & Hyde...Together Again '82
Maria-Luisa Bemberg (1922-95)
I Don't Want to Talk About It '94
I, the Worst of All '90
Miss Mary '86
Camila '84
Jack Bender
My Little Assassin '99
The Tempest '99
It Came from the Sky '98
A Call to Remember '97
Killing Mr. Griffin '97
Lone Justice 3: Showdown at Plum Creek '96
Lone Justice 2 '93
Child's Play 3 '91
My Brother's Wife '89
Side by Side '88
Tricks of the Trade '88
The Midnight Hour '86
Letting Go '85
Two Kinds of Love '85
Shattered Vows '84
In Love with an Older Woman '82
Joel Bender
Midnight Kiss '93
Rich Girl '91
The Immortalizer '89
Gas Pump Girls '79
Laslo Benedek (1907-92)
Assault on Agathon '75
The Night Visitor '70
Daring Game '68
Namu, the Killer Whale '66
The Wild One '54
Port of New York '49
Roberto Benigni (1952-)
Life Is Beautiful '98
The Monster '96
Johnny Stecchino '92
Richard Benjamin (1938-)
The Pentagon Wars '98
Tourist Trap '98
Mrs. Winterbourne '96
Milk Money '94
Made in America '93
Mermaids '90
Downtown '89
Little Nikita '88
My Stepmother Is an Alien '88
The Money Pit '86
City Heat '84
Racing with the Moon '84
My Favorite Year '82
Richard Benner (1943-90)
Happy Birthday, Gemini '80
Outrageous! '77
Spencer Gordon Bennet (1893-1987)
Atomic Submarine '59
Submarine Seahawk '59
King of the Congo '52
Atom Man vs. Superman '50
Pirates of the High Seas '50
The Black Widow '47
Daughter of Don Q '46
D-Day on Mars '45
Manhunt of Mystery Island '45
The Purple Monster Strikes '45
Perils of the Darkest Jungle '44
Zorro's Black Whip '44
California Joe '43
Calling Wild Bill Elliott '43
The Masked Marvel '43
The Secret Code '42
Arizona Bound '41
Gunman from Bodie '41
Across the Plains '39
The Rangers Step In '37
The Unknown Ranger '36
Get That Man '35
The Fighting Rookie '34
Last Frontier '32
Midnight Warning '32
Marked Money '28
Bill Bennett (1953-)
In a Savage Land '99
Kiss or Kill '97
Two If by Sea '95
Backlash '86
Compton Bennett (1900-74)
The Gift Horse '52
King Solomon's Mines '50
That Forsyte Woman '50
The Seventh Veil '46
Edward Bennett
The Scarlet Pimpernel 3: The Kidnapped King '99
A Woman at War '94
Rodney Bennett
Monsignor Quixote '91
Sense & Sensibility '85
Edwin '84
Richard Benson
Werewolf in a Girl's Dormitory '61
The Day the Sky Exploded '57
Robby Benson (1956-)
Modern Love '90
White Hot '88
Thomas Bentley (-1950)
Murder at the Baskervilles '37
The Old Curiosity Shop '35
Robert Benton (1932-)
Twilight '98
Nobody's Fool '94
Billy Bathgate '91
Nadine '87
Places in the Heart '84
Still of the Night '82
Kramer vs. Kramer '79
The Late Show '77
Bad Company '72
Luca Bercovici
Luck of the Draw '00
Bitter Sweet '98
The Granny '94
Dark Tide '93
Rockula '90
Ghoulies '84
Bruce Beresford (1940-)
Bride of the Wind '01
Double Jeopardy '99
Paradise Road '97
Last Dance '96
A Good Man in Africa '94
Silent Fall '94
Rich in Love '93
Black Robe '91
Mister Johnson '91
Driving Miss Daisy '89
Aria '88
Her Alibi '88
Crimes of the Heart '86
The Fringe Dwellers '86
King David '85
Tender Mercies '83
The Club '81
Puberty Blues '81
Breaker Morant '80
Money Movers '78
The Getting of Wisdom '77
Don's Party '76
Barry McKenzie Holds His Own '74
Pamela Berger
The Magic Stone '95
The Imported Bridegroom '89
Andrew Bergman (1945-)
Isn't She Great '00
Striptease '96
It Could Happen to You '94
Honeymoon in Vegas '92
The Freshman '90
So Fine '81
Daniel Bergman
Expectations '97
Sunday's Children '94
Ingmar Bergman (1918-)
After the Rehearsal '84
Fanny and Alexander '83
From the Life of the Marionettes '80
Autumn Sonata '78
The Serpent's Egg '78
Face to Face '76
The Magic Flute '73
Scenes from a Marriage '73
Cries and Whispers '72
The Touch '71
The Passion of Anna '70
The Rite '69
Hour of the Wolf '68
The Shame '68
Persona '66
The Silence '63
The Winter Light '62
Through a Glass Darkly '61
The Devil's Eye '60
The Virgin Spring '59
The Magician '58
Brink of Life '57
Wild Strawberries '57
The Seventh Seal '56
Dreams '55
Smiles of a Summer Night '55
Lesson in Love '54
Sawdust & Tinsel '53
Monika '52
Secrets of Women '52
Summer Interlude '50
To Joy '50
Devil's Wanton '49
Three Strange Loves '49
Port of Call '48
Night Is My Future '47
Robert Bergman
Skull: A Night of Terror '88
A Whisper to a Scream '88
William Berke (1903-58)
The Lost Missile '58
The Marshal's Daughter '53
FBI Girl '52
Jungle '52
Bandit Queen '51
Roaring City '51
Savage Drums '51
Border Rangers '50
Deputy Marshal '50
Gunfire '50
I Shot Billy the Kid '50
Operation Haylift '50
Treasure of Monte Cristo '50
Highway 13 '48
Shoot to Kill '47
Renegade Girl '46
Dick Tracy, Detective '45
Betrayal from the East '44
Dangerous Passage '44
Dark Mountain '44
The Falcon in Mexico '44
Navy Way '44
Gun Grit '36
Toll of the Desert '35
Busby Berkeley (1895-1976)
Take Me Out to the Ball Game '49
For Me and My Gal '42
Babes on Broadway '41
Strike Up the Band '40
Babes in Arms '39
They Made Me a Criminal '39
Gold Diggers of 1935 '35
Abby Berlin (1907-65)
Double Deal '50
Blondie Knows Best '46
Alain Berliner (1963-)
Passion of Mind '00
Ma Vie en Rose '97
Joe Berlinger
Book of Shadows: Blair Witch 2 '00
Brother's Keeper '92
Monty Berman (1913-)
The Hellfire Club '61
Jack the Ripper '60
Ted Berman (1920-2001)
The Black Cauldron '85
The Fox and the Hound '81
Edward L. Bernds (1905-2000)
Three Stooges in Orbit '62
The Three Stooges Meet Hercules '61
Return of the Fly '59
Queen of Outer Space '58
Reform School Girl '57
Storm Rider '57
Bowery Boys Meet the Monsters '54
Clipped Wings '53
Gold Raiders '51
Blondie Hits the Jackpot '49
Curtis Bernhardt (1899-1981)
Kisses for My President '64
Interrupted Melody '55
Beau Brummel '54
Miss Sadie Thompson '53
The Merry Widow '52
Sirocco '51
The Possessed '47
A Stolen Life '46
Conflict '45

Adam Bernstein (1960-)
Six Ways to Sunday *'99*
It's Pat: The Movie *'94*
Armyan Bernstein
Cross My Heart *'88*
Windy City *'84*
Walter Bernstein (1919-)
Women & Men: In Love There Are No Rules *'91*
Little Miss Marker *'80*
Claude Berri (1934-)
Lucie Aubrac *'98*
Germinal *'93*
Uranus *'91*
Jean de Florette *'87*
Manon of the Spring *'87*
Tchao Pantin *'84*
I Love All of You *'83*
One Wild Moment *'78*
Le Sex Shop *'73*
Marry Me, Marry Me *'69*
The Two of Us *'68*
Bill Berry
Off the Mark *'87*
Brotherhood of Death *'76*
John Berry (1917-99)
Boesman & Lena *'00*
A Captive in the Land *'91*
Honeyboy *'82*
Angel on My Shoulder *'80*
The Bad News Bears Go to Japan *'78*
Maya *'66*
Tamango *'59*
Pantaloons *'57*
There Goes Barder *'54*
Casbah *'48*
Tom Berry
Twin Sisters *'91*
The Amityville Curse *'90*
Blind Fear *'89*
Bernardo Bertolucci (1940-)
Besieged *'98*
Stealing Beauty *'96*
Little Buddha *'93*
The Sheltering Sky *'90*
The Last Emperor *'87*
The Tragedy of a Ridiculous Man *'81*
1900 *'76*
Last Tango in Paris *'73*
The Conformist *'71*
The Spider's Stratagem *'70*
Partner *'68*
Before the Revolution *'65*
The Grim Reaper *'62*
Irvin Berwick
Malibu High *'79*
The 7th Commandment *'61*
The Monster of Piedras Blancas *'57*
Luc Besson (1959-)
The Messenger: The Story of Joan of Arc *'99*
The Fifth Element *'97*
The Professional *'94*
La Femme Nikita *'91*
The Big Blue *'88*
Subway *'85*
Le Dernier Combat *'84*
Gil Bettman
Night Vision *'97*
Crystal Heart *'87*
Never Too Young to Die *'86*
Jonathan Betuel (1949-)
Theodore Rex *'95*
My Science Project *'85*
Eddie Beverly, Jr.
Ballbuster *'89*
Escapist *'83*
Frank Beyer (1932-)
Jacob the Liar *'74*
Trace of Stones *'66*
Five Cartridges *'60*
Radha Bharadwaj
Basil *'98*
Closet Land *'90*
Andrea (Andrew White) Bianchi (1925-)
Burial Ground *'85*
Cry of a Prostitute: Love Kills *'72*
Edward Bianchi (1942-)
Off and Running *'90*
The Fan *'81*
Herbert Biberman (1900-71)
Salt of the Earth *'54*
Master Race *'44*
Marc Bienstock
Indiscreet *'98*
The Beneficiary *'97*
Suzanne (Susanne) Bier (1960-)
Like It Never Was Before *'95*
Freud Leaving Home *'91*
Robert Bierman
A Merry War *'97*
The Moonstone *'97*
Vampire's Kiss *'88*
Apology *'86*
Kathryn Bigelow (1952-)
K-19: The Widowmaker *'02*
Strange Days *'95*
Wild Palms *'93*
Point Break *'91*
Blue Steel *'90*
Near Dark *'87*
Loveless *'83*
Tony Bill (1940-)
Harlan County War *'00*
Oliver Twist *'97*
Beyond the Call *'96*
One Christmas *'95*
Next Door *'94*
A Home of Our Own *'93*
Untamed Heart *'93*
Crazy People *'90*
Five Corners *'88*
The Princess and the Pea *'83*
Six Weeks *'82*
My Bodyguard *'80*
Bruce Bilson (1928-)
Chattanooga Choo Choo *'84*
The North Avenue Irregulars *'79*
Danny Bilson
The Wrong Guys *'88*
Zone Troopers *'84*
Mike Binder
Blankman *'94*
Indian Summer *'93*
Crossing the Bridge *'92*
William Bindley
The Eighteenth Angel *'97*
Judicial Consent *'94*
Freeze Frame *'92*
Josh Binney
Boardinghouse Blues *'48*
Killer Diller *'48*
Hi-De-Ho *'35*
Antonia Bird
Ravenous *'99*
Face *'97*
Mad Love *'95*
Priest *'94*
Richard Bird (1895-1986)
Men of Ireland *'38*
The Terror *'38*
Andrew Birkin (1945-)
The Cement Garden *'93*
Desire *'93*
Burning Secret *'89*
Alan Birkinshaw
Masque of the Red Death *'90*
Ten Little Indians *'89*
The House of Usher *'88*
Daniel Birt
Robin Hood: The Movie *'55*
Big Deadly Game *'54*
Interrupted Journey *'49*
The Three Weird Sisters *'48*
Bill Bixby (1934-93)
The Woman Who Loved Elvis *'93*
Another Pair of Aces: Three of a Kind *'91*
Baby of the Bride *'91*
Death of the Incredible Hulk *'90*
The Trial of the Incredible Hulk *'89*
The Barbary Coast *'74*
Herbert Blache (1882-1953)
The Untamable *'23*
The Saphead *'21*
Noel Black (1937-)
Eyes of the Panther *'90*
A Conspiracy of Love *'87*
Quarterback Princess *'85*
Private School *'83*
Prime Suspect *'82*
A Man, a Woman, and a Bank *'79*
Mirrors *'78*
Pretty Poison *'68*
David Blair
Anna Karenina *'00*
Wax, or the Discovery of Television among the Bees *'93*
Alfonso Corona Blake
Samson in the Wax Museum *'63*
Samson vs. the Vampire Women *'61*
Michael Blakemore (1928-)
Country Life *'95*
Privates on Parade *'84*
John Blanchard
Shriek If You Know What I Did Last Friday the 13th *'00*
Really Weird Tales *'86*
The Last Polka *'84*
Jamie Blanks
Valentine *'01*
Urban Legend *'98*
Alessandro Blasetti (1900-87)
What a Woman! *'56*
Fabiola *'48*
The Iron Crown *'41*
1860 *'33*
William Peter Blatty (1928-)
Exorcist 3: Legion *'90*
The Ninth Configuration *'79*
Jeff Bleckner (1943-)
Dean Koontz's Black River *'01*
Rear Window *'98*
The Beast *'96*
Serving in Silence: The Margarethe Cammermeyer Story *'95*
White Water Summer *'87*
Brotherly Love *'85*
When Your Lover Leaves *'83*
Bertrand Blier (1939-)
Mon Homme *'96*
Too Beautiful for You *'88*
Menage *'86*
My Best Friend's Girl *'84*
Beau Pere *'81*
Buffet Froid *'79*
Get Out Your Handkerchiefs *'78*
Going Places *'74*
Jason Bloom
Dead Simple *'01*
Bio-Dome *'96*
Overnight Delivery *'96*
Jeffrey Bloom
Flowers in the Attic *'87*
Jealousy *'84*
Blood Beach *'81*
The Stick-Up *'77*
Dog Pound Shuffle *'75*
George Bloomfield
Jacob Two Two Meets the Hooded Fang *'99*
The Double Negative *'80*
Nothing Personal *'80*
Riel *'79*
To Kill a Clown *'72*
Jenny *'70*
Philippe Blot
Running Wild *'94*
Hot Blood *'89*
Don Bluth (1938-)
Titan A.E. *'00*
Anastasia *'97*
The Pebble and the Penguin *'94*
Thumbelina *'94*
A Troll in Central Park *'94*
Rock-a-Doodle *'92*
All Dogs Go to Heaven *'89*
The Land Before Time *'88*
An American Tail *'86*
The Secret of NIMH *'82*
John Blystone (1892-1938)
Block-heads *'38*
Swiss Miss *'38*
23 1/2 Hours Leave *'37*
Great Guy *'36*
Dick Turpin *'25*
Our Hospitality *'23*
David Blyth
Hot Blooded *'98*
My Grandpa Is a Vampire *'92*
Red Blooded American Girl *'90*
Death Warmed Up *'85*
Hart Bochner (1956-)
High School High *'96*
P.C.U. *'94*
Sergei Bodrov (1948-)
Prisoner of the Mountains *'96*
Freedom Is Paradise *'89*
Budd Boetticher (1916-2001)
Comanche Station *'60*
The Rise and Fall of Legs Diamond *'60*
Ride Lonesome *'59*
The Tall T *'57*
The Magnificent Matador *'55*
Man from the Alamo *'53*
Horizons West *'52*
Red Ball Express *'52*
Bullfighter & the Lady *'50*
Behind Locked Doors *'48*
Paul Bogart (1919-)
The Heidi Chronicles *'95*
Broadway Bound *'92*
Torch Song Trilogy *'88*
Oh, God! You Devil *'84*
Power, Passion & Murder *'83*
Tell Me Where It Hurts *'74*
Class of '44 *'73*
Cancel My Reservation *'72*
A House without a Christmas Tree *'72*
Skin Game *'71*
Marlowe *'69*
The Three Sisters *'65*
Yurek Bogayevicz
Exit in Red *'97*
Three of Hearts *'93*
Anna *'87*
Peter Bogdanovich (1939-)
The Cat's Meow *'01*
A Saintly Switch *'99*
Naked City: A Killer Christmas *'98*
Rescuers: Stories of Courage "Two Women" *'97*
The Thing Called Love *'93*
Noises Off *'92*
Texasville *'90*
Illegally Yours *'87*
Mask *'85*
They All Laughed *'81*
Saint Jack *'79*
Daisy Miller *'74*
Paper Moon *'73*
What's Up, Doc? *'72*
The Last Picture Show *'71*
Targets *'68*
Voyage to the Planet of Prehistoric Women *'68*
Willy Bogner
Fire, Ice and Dynamite *'91*
Fire and Ice *'87*
Michel Boisrond (1921-)
Catherine & Co. *'76*
Voulez-Vous Danser avec Moi? *'59*
Mam'zelle Pigalle *'58*
That Naughty Girl *'58*
Une Parisienne *'58*
Yves Boisset (1939-)
Double Identity *'89*
Prize of Peril *'84*
Dog Day *'83*
The Purple Taxi *'77*
Dupont Lajoie *'74*
Cobra *'71*
Jerome Boivin (1954-)
Barjo *'93*
Baxter *'89*
Richard Boleslawski (1889-1937)
The Last of Mrs. Cheyney *'37*
The Garden of Allah *'36*
Theodora Goes Wild *'36*
Les Miserables *'35*
Hollywood Party *'34*
The Painted Veil *'34*
Rasputin and the Empress *'33*
Mauro Bolognini (1922-2001)
Husbands and Lovers *'91*
The Inheritance *'76*
La Grande Bourgeoise *'74*
Oldest Profession *'67*
Il Bell'Antonio *'60*
Craig Bolotin
Light It Up *'99*
That Night *'93*
Ben Bolt
The Turn of the Screw *'99*
Wilderness *'96*
Big Town *'87*
Timothy Bond (1942-)
Running Wild *'99*
Night of the Twisters *'95*
Return to the Lost World *'93*
The Lost World *'92*
One Night Only *'84*
Deadly Harvest *'72*
Sergei Bondarchuk (1920-94)
Waterloo *'71*
War and Peace *'68*
Peter Bonerz (1938-)
Police Academy 6: City under Siege *'89*
Nobody's Perfekt *'79*
Rene Bonniere
The Halfback of Notre Dame *'96*
Dream Man *'94*
Perfect Timing *'84*
J.R. Bookwalter
Witchouse 3: Demon Fire *'01*
The Dead Next Door *'89*
John Boorman (1933-)
The Tailor of Panama *'00*
The General *'98*
Beyond Rangoon *'95*
Picture Windows *'95*
Where the Heart Is *'90*
Hope and Glory *'87*
The Emerald Forest *'85*
Excalibur *'81*
The Exorcist 2: The Heretic *'77*
Zardoz *'73*
Deliverance *'72*
Hell in the Pacific *'69*
Point Blank *'67*
H. Gordon Boos
Forgotten City *'98*
Red Surf *'90*
Lizzie Borden (1958-)
Erotique *'94*
Love Crimes *'92*
Working Girls *'87*
Bernard Borderie
Your Turn Darling *'63*
Dishonorable Discharge *'57*
Michael Bordon
The Ghost of Fletcher Ridge *'80s*
Ain't No Way Back *'89*
Robert Boris (1945-)
Frank and Jesse *'94*
Buy & Cell *'89*
Steele Justice *'87*
Oxford Blues *'84*
Walerian Borowczyk
Emmanuelle 5 *'87*
The Beast *'75*
Clay Borris (1950-)
Someone to Die For *'95*
Suspicious Agenda *'94*
Prom Night 4: Deliver Us from Evil *'91*
The Gunfighters *'87*
Quiet Cool *'86*
Phillip Borsos (1954-95)
Far from Home: The Adventures of Yellow Dog *'94*
Dr. Bethune *'90*
Mean Season *'85*
One Magic Christmas *'85*
The Grey Fox *'83*
Frank Borzage (1893-1962)
Journey Beneath the Desert *'61*
Moonrise *'48*
I've Always Loved You *'46*
Magnificent Doll *'46*
The Spanish Main *'45*
His Butler's Sister *'44*
Stage Door Canteen *'43*
Smilin' Through *'41*
The Mortal Storm *'40*
Strange Cargo *'40*
The Shining Hour *'38*
Three Comrades *'38*
History Is Made at Night *'37*
Mannequin *'37*
Desire *'36*
Flirtation Walk *'34*
A Farewell to Arms *'32*
Song o' My Heart *'29*
Until They Get Me *'18*
John Boulting (1913-85)
Heavens Above *'63*
I'm All Right Jack *'59*
Lucky Jim *'58*
Brighton Rock *'47*
Roy Boulting (1913-2001)
There's a Girl in My Soup *'70*
Heavens Above *'63*
Carlton Browne of the F.O. *'59*
Lucky Jim *'58*
Brothers in Law *'57*
The Guinea Pig *'48*
Fame Is the Spur *'47*
Serge Bourguignon (1928-)
A Coeur Joie *'67*
Head Over Heels *'67*
Sundays & Cybele *'62*
Jenny (H. Anne Riley) Bowen
Animal Behavior *'89*
The Wizard of Loneliness *'88*
Street Music *'81*
John Bowen
Hindsight *'97*
Dark Secrets *'95*
Knock Outs *'92*
Lethal Games *'90*
George Bowers
Private Resort *'84*
My Tutor *'82*
Body & Soul *'81*
The Hearse *'80*
Rob Bowman
Reign of Fire *'02*
The X-Files *'98*
Airborne *'93*
Muriel Box (1905-91)
Rattle of a Simple Man *'64*
Truth about Women *'58*
Tim Boxell
Chasing Destiny *'00*
Aberration *'97*
Daniel Boyd
Heroes of the Heart *'94*

Paradise Park *'91*
Invasion of the Space Preachers *'90*
Chillers *'88*

Don Boyd (1948-)
Kleptomania *'94*
Twenty-One *'91*
Goldeneye: The Secret Life of Ian Fleming *'89*
East of Elephant Rock *'76*

Jean Boyer (1901-65)
Fernandel the Dressmaker *'57*
Dressmaker *'56*
The French Touch *'54*
Crazy for Love *'52*
Mr. Peek-A-Boo *'50*
Circonstances Attenuantes *'36*

Danny Boyle (1956-)
The Beach *'00*
A Life Less Ordinary *'97*
Trainspotting *'95*
Shallow Grave *'94*

Steve Boyum
Slap Shot 2: Breaking the Ice *'02*
Meet the Deedles *'98*

Bruno Bozzetto (1933-)
VIP, My Brother Superman *'90*
Allegro Non Troppo *'76*

Charles Brabin (1883-1957)
The Mask of Fu Manchu *'32*
The Raven *'15*

Robert North Bradbury (1886-1943)
Forbidden Trails *'41*
God's Country and the Man *'37*
Hittin' the Trail *'37*
Riders of the Rockies *'37*
Trouble in Texas *'37*
Where Trails Divide *'37*
Brand of the Outlaws *'36*
Cavalry *'36*
Headin' for the Rio Grande *'36*
Kid Ranger *'36*
Last of the Warrens *'36*
Smokey Smith *'36*
Sundown Saunders *'36*
Valley of the Lawless *'36*
Alias John Law *'35*
Between Men *'35*
Big Calibre *'35*
Courageous Avenger *'35*
Dawn Rider *'35*
Desert Trail *'35*
Lawless Frontier *'35*
Lawless Range *'35*
Trail of Terror *'35*
Western Justice *'35*
Westward Ho *'35*
Blue Steel *'34*
The Gun Ranger *'34*
Lucky Texan *'34*
Man from Utah *'34*
The Star Packer *'34*
Trail Beyond *'34*
Breed of the Border *'33*
The Gallant Fool *'33*
Galloping Romeo *'33*
Riders of Destiny *'33*
West of the Divide *'33*
Hidden Valley *'32*
Man from Hell's Edges *'32*
Texas Buddies *'32*

Al (Alfonso Brescia) Bradley (1930-2001)
Cross Mission *'89*
Miami Cops *'89*
Iron Warrior *'87*
Metallica *'85*
White Fang and the Hunter *'85*
Bloody Avenger *'80*
Cosmos: War of the Planets *'80*
Captive Planet *'78*

John Bradshaw
Full Disclosure *'00*
Breakout *'98*
The Reaper *'97*
Specimen *'97*
The Undertaker's Wedding *'97*
Lethal Tender *'96*
The Big Slice *'90*
That's My Baby! *'88*

Randy Bradshaw
Cold Blooded *'00*
Song Spinner *'95*
Blades of Courage *'88*

Carlo L. Bragaglia (1894-1988)
The Loves of Hercules *'60*
The Sword and the Cross *'58*

John Brahm (1893-1982)
Face to Face *'52*
Miracle of Our Lady of Fatima *'52*
Singapore *'47*
Guest in the House *'44*
Wintertime *'43*
The Undying Monster *'42*

Marco Brambilla (1960-)
Dinotopia *'02*
Excess Baggage *'96*
Demolition Man *'93*

Bill Brame (1928-)
Ebony Dreams *'80*
Miss Melody Jones *'73*

Kenneth Branagh (1960-)
Love's Labour's Lost *'00*
Hamlet *'96*
A Midwinter's Tale *'95*
Mary Shelley's Frankenstein *'94*
Much Ado about Nothing *'93*
Peter's Friends *'92*
Dead Again *'91*
Henry V *'89*

Larry Brand
Paranoia *'98*
Till the End of the Night *'94*
Overexposed *'90*
Masque of the Red Death *'89*
The Drifter *'88*

Charlotte Brandstrom
A Business Affair *'93*
Road to Ruin *'91*
Sweet Revenge *'90*

Fred Brannon (1901-)
Jungle Drums of Africa *'53*
Radar Men from the Moon *'52*
Zombies of the Stratosphere *'52*
Don Daredevil Rides Again *'51*
The Invisible Monster *'50*
Bandit King of Texas *'49*
Federal Agents vs. Underworld, Inc. *'49*
King of the Rocketmen *'49*
Lost Planet Airmen *'49*
G-Men Never Forget *'48*
Jesse James Rides Again *'47*
Cyclotrode "X" *'46*
Daughter of Don Q *'46*
D-Day on Mars *'45*

Michel Brault
Mon Amie Max *'94*
A Paper Wedding *'89*

Joseph (Jose Ramon Larraz) Braunstein (1929-)
Edge of the Axe *'89*
Rest in Pieces *'87*

Charles Braverman (1944-)
Prince of Bel Air *'87*
Brotherhood of Justice *'86*
Hit & Run *'82*

William Brayne
Cold War Killers *'86*
Flame to the Phoenix *'85*

George Breakston (1920-73)
The Manster *'59*
White Huntress *'57*
Scarlet Spear *'54*
Geisha Girl *'52*

Paddy Breathnach
Blow Dry *'00*
I Went Down *'97*

Catherine Breillat (1948-)
Romance *'99*
Perfect Love *'96*
36 Fillete *'88*
A Real Young Girl *'75*

Valerie Breiman
Love & Sex *'00*
Going Overboard *'89*

Herbert Brenon (1880-1958)
Black Eyes *'39*
Housemaster *'38*
Dancing Mothers *'26*
Peter Pan *'24*

Robert Bresson (1907-99)
L'Argent *'83*
The Devil, Probably *'77*
Lancelot of the Lake *'74*
A Gentle Woman *'69*
Mouchette *'67*
Pickpocket *'59*
A Man Escaped *'57*
Diary of a Country Priest *'50*
The Ladies of the Bois de Bologne *'44*

Martin Brest (1951-)
Meet Joe Black *'98*
Scent of a Woman *'92*
Midnight Run *'88*
Beverly Hills Cop *'84*
Going in Style *'79*

Howard Bretherton (1896-1969)
The Prince of Thieves *'48*
Where the North Begins *'47*
The Topeka Terror *'45*
Bordertown Gunfighters *'43*
Rhythm Parade *'43*
Below the Border *'42*
Dawn on the Great Divide *'42*
Down Texas Way *'42*
Ghost Town Law *'42*
Riders of the West *'42*
West of the Law *'42*
In Old Colorado *'41*
Outlaws of the Desert *'41*
Hidden Enemy *'40*
Midnight Limited *'40*
The Showdown *'40*
Up in the Air *'40*
Boy's Reformatory *'39*
Irish Luck *'39*
Star Reporter *'39*
Tough Kid *'39*
Western Gold *'37*
Hopalong Cassidy *'35*
Ladies They Talk About *'33*

Salome Breziner
Fast Sofa *'01*
An Occasional Hell *'96*
Tollbooth *'94*

Marshall Brickman (1941-)
The Manhattan Project *'86*
Lovesick *'83*
Simon *'80*

Paul Brickman (1949-)
Men Don't Leave *'89*
Risky Business *'83*

Alan Bridges (1927-)
Pudd'nhead Wilson *'87*
The Shooting Party *'85*
Return of the Soldier *'82*
Out of Season *'75*
Invasion *'65*

Beau Bridges (1941-)
Seven Hours to Judgment *'88*
The Wild Pair *'87*

James Bridges (1936-93)
Bright Lights, Big City *'88*
Perfect *'85*
Mike's Murder *'84*
Urban Cowboy *'80*
The China Syndrome *'79*
September 30, 1955 *'77*
The Paper Chase *'73*
The Baby Maker *'70*

Matthew Bright
Freeway 2: Confessions of a Trickbaby *'99*
Freeway *'95*

Steven Brill
Mr. Deeds *'02*
Little Nicky *'00*
Late Last Night *'99*
Heavyweights *'94*

Burt Brinckerhoff (1936-)
The Day the Women Got Even *'80*
Mother & Daughter: A Loving War *'80*
Can You Hear the Laughter? The Story of Freddie Prinze *'79*
The Cracker Factory *'79*

Deborah Brock
Rock 'n' Roll High School Forever *'91*
Andy and the Airwave Rangers *'89*
Slumber Party Massacre 2 *'87*

John Broderick
The Warrior & the Sorceress *'84*
Bad Georgia Road *'77*

Kevin Brodie
A Dog of Flanders *'99*
Mugsy's Girls *'85*

Rex Bromfield
Cafe Romeo *'91*
Home Is Where the Hart Is *'88*
Melanie *'82*
Love at First Sight *'76*

Peter Brook (1925-)
The Mahabharata *'89*
Meetings with Remarkable Men *'79*
King Lear *'71*
Lord of the Flies *'63*

Adam Brooks (1956-)
Invisible Circus *'00*
Almost You *'85*

Albert Brooks (1947-)
The Muse *'99*
Mother *'96*
Defending Your Life *'91*
Lost in America *'85*
Modern Romance *'81*
Real Life *'79*

James L. Brooks (1940-)
As Good As It Gets *'97*
I'll Do Anything *'93*
Broadcast News *'87*
Terms of Endearment *'83*
Thursday's Game *'74*

Joseph Brooks (1938-)
If Ever I See You Again *'78*
You Light Up My Life *'77*
Invitation to the Wedding *'73*

Mel Brooks (1926-)
Dracula: Dead and Loving It *'95*
Robin Hood: Men in Tights *'93*
Life Stinks *'91*
Spaceballs *'87*
History of the World: Part 1 *'81*
High Anxiety *'77*
Silent Movie *'76*
Blazing Saddles *'74*
Young Frankenstein *'74*
The Twelve Chairs *'70*
The Producers *'68*

Richard Brooks (1912-92)
Fever Pitch *'85*
Wrong Is Right *'82*
Looking for Mr. Goodbar *'77*
Bite the Bullet *'75*
Dollars *'71*
The Happy Ending *'69*
In Cold Blood *'67*
The Professionals *'66*
Lord Jim *'65*
Sweet Bird of Youth *'62*
Elmer Gantry *'60*
The Brothers Karamazov *'58*
Cat on a Hot Tin Roof *'58*
Something of Value *'57*
The Catered Affair *'56*
The Last Hunt *'56*
Blackboard Jungle *'55*
The Last Time I Saw Paris *'54*
Battle Circus *'53*

Nick Broomfield (1948-)
Monster in a Box *'92*
Dark Obsession *'90*

Eric Bross
On the Line *'01*
Stranger than Fiction *'99*
Restaurant *'98*
Ten Benny *'98*

Otto Brower (1895-1946)
Postal Inspector *'36*
The Outlaw Deputy *'35*
The Phantom Empire *'35*
I Can't Escape *'34*
Mystery Mountain *'34*
Devil Horse *'32*
Spirit of the West *'32*
Clearing the Range *'31*
Fighting Caravans *'31*
Hard Hombre *'31*
The Light of Western Stars *'30*

Arvin Brown
Change of Heart *'98*
Diary of the Dead *'80s*

Bruce Brown
The Endless Summer 2 *'94*
The Endless Summer *'66*

Clarence Brown (1890-1987)
Angels in the Outfield *'51*
To Please a Lady *'50*
Intruder in the Dust *'49*
The Yearling *'46*
National Velvet *'44*
The White Cliffs of Dover *'44*
The Human Comedy *'43*
They Met in Bombay *'41*
Edison the Man *'40*
Idiot's Delight *'39*
The Rains Came *'39*
Of Human Hearts *'38*
Conquest *'37*
The Gorgeous Hussy *'36*
Wife Versus Secretary *'36*
Ah, Wilderness! *'35*
Anna Karenina *'35*
Chained *'34*
Sadie McKee *'34*
A Free Soul *'31*
Possessed *'31*
Anna Christie *'30*
Romance *'30*
A Woman of Affairs *'28*
The Flesh and the Devil *'27*
The Eagle *'25*
Smouldering Fires *'25*
The Light of Faith *'22*
The Last of the Mohicans *'20*

Ewing Miles Brown
Killers *'88*
Whale of a Tale *'76*

Georg Stanford Brown (1943-)
Dangerous Relations *'93*
Alone in the Neon Jungle *'87*
Miracle of the Heart: A Boys Town Story *'86*
Grambling's White Tiger *'81*

Gregory (Gregory Dark) Brown (1954-)
Stranger by Night *'94*
Street Asylum *'90*
Dead Man Walking *'88*

Harry Joe Brown (1890-1972)
The Fighting Legion *'30*
Mountain Justice *'30*
One-Punch O'Day *'26*

Karl Brown (1896-1990)
The Port of Missing Girls *'38*
The White Legion *'36*
Fire Alarm *'32*

Larry G. Brown
Final Cut *'88*
Psychopath *'73*

Melville Brown (1887-1938)
Mad About Money *'37*
Champagne for Breakfast *'35*
Behind Office Doors *'31*
Check & Double Check *'30*

Ricou Browning (1930-)
Salty *'73*
Island of the Lost *'68*

Tod Browning (1882-1962)
Devil Doll *'36*
Mark of the Vampire *'35*
Freaks *'32*
Dracula *'31*
Where East Is East *'29*
West of Zanzibar *'28*
The Unknown *'27*
The Unholy Three *'25*
White Tiger *'23*
Outside the Law *'21*

S.F. Brownrigg
Thinkin' Big *'87*
Keep My Grave Open *'80*
Poor White Trash 2 *'75*
Don't Open the Door! *'74*
Don't Look in the Basement *'73*

James Bruce
Love to Kill *'97*
Headless Body in Topless Bar *'96*

Clyde Bruckman (1894-1955)
Feet First *'30*
The General *'26*

Franco Brusati (1922-93)
The Sleazy Uncle *'89*
To Forget Venice *'79*
Bread and Chocolate *'73*

Larry Buchanan (1923-)
Goodnight, Sweet Marilyn *'89*
The Loch Ness Horror *'82*
Mistress of the Apes *'79*
Hughes & Harlow: Angels in Hell *'77*
Goodbye, Norma Jean *'75*
Hell Raiders *'68*
It's Alive! *'68*
Creature of Destruction *'67*
Curse of the Swamp Creature *'66*
Mars Needs Women *'66*
Zontar, the Thing from Venus *'66*
The Eye Creatures *'65*
The Naked Witch *'64*
Free, White, and 21 *'62*

Dimitri Buchowetzki (1885-1932)
The Swan *'25*
Othello *'22*

Allan A. Buckhantz
The Last Contract *'86*
Portrait of a Hitman *'77*

Colin Bucksey
Midnight's Child *'93*
Curiosity Kills *'90*
Dealers *'89*
The McGuffin *'85*
Blue Money *'84*

Harold Bucquet (1891-1946)
Without Love *'45*
The Adventures of Tartu *'43*
Dr. Kildare's Strange Case *'40*
On Borrowed Time *'39*

Colin Budds
Dr. Jekyll & Mr. Hyde *'99*
Hurricane Smith *'92*

John Carl Buechler
Watchers Reborn *'98*
Ghoulies 3: Ghoulies Go to College *'91*

Friday the 13th, Part 7: The New Blood '88
Cellar Dweller '87
Troll '86
Dungeonmaster '83

Richard Bugajski (1943-)
Clearcut '92
The Interrogation '82
A Woman and a Woman '80

Veljko Bulajic (1928-)
The Day That Shook the World '78
Battle of Neretva '69

Luis Bunuel (1900-83)
That Obscure Object of Desire '77
Phantom of Liberty '74
The Discreet Charm of the Bourgeoisie '72
Tristana '70
The Milky Way '68
Belle de Jour '67
Simon of the Desert '66
Diary of a Chambermaid '64
The Exterminating Angel '62
Viridiana '61
The Young One '61
Fever Mounts at El Pao '59
Nazarin '58
Death in the Garden '56
The Criminal Life of Archibaldo de la Cruz '55
The Illusion Travels by Streetcar '53
Wuthering Heights '53
El '52
El Bruto '52
Mexican Bus Ride '51
Susana '51
A Woman Without Love '51
Los Olvidados '50
The Great Madcap '49
L'Age D'Or '30
Un Chien Andalou '28

Robert Burge
The Dark Dancer '95
Keaton's Cop '90
Vasectomy: A Delicate Matter '86

Stuart Burge (1918-2002)
Julius Caesar '70
Othello '65

Martyn Burke
The Pirates of Silicon Valley '99
Clown Murders '83
Last Chase '81
Power Play '81

Charles Burnett (1944-)
Finding Buck McHenry '00
Selma, Lord, Selma '99
Nightjohn '96
The Glass Shield '95
To Sleep with Anger '90

Edward Burns (1968-)
Sidewalks of New York '01
No Looking Back '98
She's the One '96
The Brothers McMullen '94

Jeff Burr (1963-)
Night of the Scarecrow '95
Pumpkinhead 2: Blood Wings '94
Puppet Master 5: The Final Chapter '94
Puppet Master 4 '93
Leatherface: The Texas Chainsaw Massacre 3 '89
Stepfather 2: Make Room for Daddy '89
The Offspring '87

Geoff Burrowes
Run '91
Return to Snowy River '88

Tim Burstall (1929-)
Nightmare at Bittercreek '91
Great Expectations: The Untold Story '87
Kangaroo '86
The Naked Country '85
Attack Force Z '84
Adventures of Eliza Fraser '76

Endplay '75
Jock Petersen '74
Alvin Purple '73

David Burton (1877-1963)
Lady by Choice '34
Fighting Caravans '31

LeVar Burton (1957-)
Smart House '00
The Tiger Woods Story '98

Tim Burton (1960-)
Planet of the Apes '01
Sleepy Hollow '99
Mars Attacks! '96
Ed Wood '94
Batman Returns '92
Edward Scissorhands '90
Batman '89
Beetlejuice '88
Pee-wee's Big Adventure '85
Aladdin and His Wonderful Lamp '84
Frankenweenie '84

Steve Buscemi (1957-)
Animal Factory '00
Tree's Lounge '96

Anthony Bushell (1904-97)
The Long Dark Hall '51
Angel with the Trumpet '50

John Bushelman
L.A. Gangs Rising '89
Cruisin' High '75

David Butler (1895-1979)
Glory '56
King Richard and the Crusaders '54
By the Light of the Silvery Moon '53
Calamity Jane '53
April in Paris '52
Lullaby of Broadway '51
Tea for Two '50
It's a Great Feeling '49
Look for the Silver Lining '49
The Story of Seabiscuit '49
San Antonio '45
The Princess and the Pirate '44
Thank Your Lucky Stars '43
They Got Me Covered '43
The Road to Morocco '42
Caught in the Draft '41
Playmates '41
You'll Find Out '40
Captain January '36
Pigskin Parade '36
Doubting Thomas '35
The Little Colonel '35
The Littlest Rebel '35
Bright Eyes '34
A Connecticut Yankee '31

Robert Butler (1927-)
Turbulence '96
White Mile '94
Out on a Limb '87
Long Time Gone '86
Moonlighting '85
Concrete Beat '84
Up the Creek '84
Night of the Juggler '80
Underground Aces '80
Hot Lead & Cold Feet '78
A Question of Guilt '78
James Dean '76
Strange New World '75
The Ultimate Thrill '74
Now You See Him, Now You Don't '72
The Barefoot Executive '71
Scandalous John '71
The Computer Wore Tennis Shoes '69

Hendel Butoy
Fantasia/2000 '00
The Rescuers Down Under '90

Edward Buzzell (1900-85)
A Woman of Distinction '50
Neptune's Daughter '49
Song of the Thin Man '47
Best Foot Forward '43

Ship Ahoy '42
Go West '40
At the Circus '39
Honolulu '39

Mark Byers
Digging Up Business '91
Criminal Act '88

John Byrum (1947-)
The Whoopee Boys '86
The Razor's Edge '84
Heart Beat '80
Inserts '76

Christy Cabanne (1888-1950)
Scared to Death '46
Dixie Jamboree '44
The Mummy's Hand '40
Last Outlaw '36
One Frightened Night '35
Jane Eyre '34
The World Gone Mad '33
Convicted '32
Hearts of Humanity '32
Annapolis '28
The Average Woman '24
Flirting with Fate '16
Reggie Mixes In '16
The Lamb '15

Michael Cacoyannis (1927-)
Sweet Country '87
Iphigenia '77
The Story of Jacob & Joseph '74
Trojan Women '71
Zorba the Greek '64
A Matter of Dignity '57
Girl in Black '56
Stella '55

Edward L. Cahn (1899-1963)
Frontier Uprising '61
Invisible Invaders '59
It! The Terror from Beyond Space '58
Dragstrip Girl '57
Flesh and the Spur '57
Invasion of the Saucer Men '57
Motorcycle Gang '57
Shake, Rattle and Rock '57
Voodoo Woman '57
Zombies of Moratau '57
Girls in Prison '56
Confidential '35

Mario Caiano (1933-)
Adios, Hombre '68
Fighting Fists of Shanghai Joe '65
Terror of Rome Against the Son of Hercules '64

Christopher Cain (1943-)
Gone Fishin' '97
The Amazing Panda Adventure '95
The Next Karate Kid '94
Pure Country '92
Wheels of Terror '90
Young Guns '88
The Principal '87
Where the River Runs Black '86
That Was Then...This Is Now '85
The Stone Boy '84
Elmer '76

Art Camacho
Final Payback '99
Little Bigfoot '96
The Power Within '95

James Cameron (1954-)
Titanic '97
True Lies '94
Terminator 2: Judgment Day '91
The Abyss '89
Aliens '86
The Terminator '84
Piranha 2: The Spawning '82
The Spawning '82

Ken Cameron
Miracle at Midnight '98
Dalva '95

Oldest Confederate Widow Tells All '95
Brides of Christ '91
Wild Thing '87
Fast Talking '86
The Good Wife '86
Monkey Grip '82

Douglas Camfield
Ivanhoe '82
Danger UXB '81

Donald Cammell (1939-96)
White of the Eye '88
Demon Seed '77
Performance '70

Joe Camp (1939-)
Benji the Hunted '87
Oh, Heavenly Dog! '80
The Double McGuffin '79
For the Love of Benji '77
Hawmps! '76
Benji '74

Pasquale Festa Campanile (1927-86)
When Women Lost Their Tails '75
When Women Had Tails '70
The Libertine '69

Colin Campbell (1859-1928)
Little Orphan Annie '18
In the Days of the Thundering Herd & the Law & the Outlaw '14
The Spoilers '14

Doug Campbell (1922-)
The Tomorrow Man '01
Perfect Tenant '99
Cupid '96
Season of Fear '89
Zapped Again '89

Graeme Campbell
Dream House '98
Volcano: Fire on the Mountain '97
Deadlock 2 '94
The Man in the Attic '94
Still Life '92
Into the Fire '88
Murder One '88
Blood Relations '87

Martin Campbell
Vertical Limit '00
The Mask of Zorro '98
Goldeneye '95
No Escape '94
Cast a Deadly Spell '91
Defenseless '91
Criminal Law '89
Edge of Darkness '86

Jane Campion (1954-)
Holy Smoke '99
Portrait of a Lady '96
The Piano '93
An Angel at My Table '89
Sweetie '89
Two Friends '86

Carlo Campogalliani (1885-1974)
Son of Samson '62
Ursus in the Valley of the Lions '62
Goliath and the Barbarians '60

Michael Campus
The Passover Plot '75
The Education of Sonny Carson '74
The Mack '73
Zero Population Growth '72

Danny Cannon
I Still Know What You Did Last Summer '98
Phoenix '98
Judge Dredd '95
The Young Americans '93

Yakima Canutt (1895-1986)
The Adventures of Frank and Jesse James '48
G-Men Never Forget '48
Oklahoma Badlands '48

Giorgio Capitani (1927-)
I Hate Blondes '83

Lobster for Breakfast '82
The Ruthless Four '70
Samson and His Mighty Challenge '64

Frank Cappello
No Way Back '96
American Yakuza '94

Frank Capra (1897-1991)
Pocketful of Miracles '61
A Hole in the Head '59
Here Comes the Groom '51
Riding High '50
State of the Union '48
It's a Wonderful Life '46
Arsenic and Old Lace '44
Prelude to War '42
Meet John Doe '41
Mr. Smith Goes to Washington '39
You Can't Take It with You '38
Lost Horizon '37
Mr. Deeds Goes to Town '36
Broadway Bill '34
It Happened One Night '34
The Bitter Tea of General Yen '33
Lady for a Day '33
American Madness '32
The Miracle Woman '31
Platinum Blonde '31
That Certain Thing '28
Long Pants '27
Strong Man '26

Luigi Capuano
The Snake Hunter Strangler '66
Cold Steel for Tortuga '65
Marauder '65
The Conqueror & the Empress '64
Tiger of the Seven Seas '62

Leos Carax (1960-)
Pola X '99
The Lovers on the Bridge '91
Mauvais Sang '86
Boy Meets Girl '84

Costa Carayiannis
Land of the Minotaur '77
The Brave Bunch '70

Lamar Card (1942-)
Shadow Warriors '95
The Clones '73

Jack Cardiff (1914-)
The Freakmaker '73
Dark of the Sun '68
The Girl on a Motorcycle '68
The Long Ships '64
My Geisha '62

Roger Cardinal
Dead Silent '99
Malarek '89

Rene Cardona, Sr. (1906-88)
Doctor of Doom '62
Santa Claus '59
Wrestling Women vs. the Aztec Mummy '59

Rene Cardona, Jr. (1939-)
Beaks: The Movie '87
The Treasure of the Amazon '84
Tintorera...Tiger Shark '78
Night of a Thousand Cats '72
Robinson Crusoe & the Tiger '72
Night of the Bloody Apes '68

J.S. Cardone
The Forsaken '01
True Blue '01
Outside Ozona '98
Black Day Blue Night '95
Shadowhunter '93
A Climate for Killing '91
Shadowzone '89
Thunder Alley '85
The Slayer '82

John Cardos
Act of Piracy '89
Skeleton Coast '89
Outlaw of Gor '87

Mutant '83
Day Time Ended '80
The Dark '79
Kingdom of the Spiders '77
The Female Bunch '69

Gilles Carle (1929-)
The Other Side of the Law '95
Blood of the Hunter '94
Maria Chapdelaine '84
The Red Half-Breed '70
In Trouble '67

Carlo Carlei (1960-)
Fluke '95
Flight of the Innocent '93

Lewis John Carlino (1932-)
Class '83
The Great Santini '80
The Sailor Who Fell from Grace with the Sea '76

Henning Carlsen (1927-)
The Wolf at the Door '87
Hunger '66
A World of Strangers '62

Marcel Carne (1906-96)
La Merveilleuse Visite '74
Les Assassins de L'Ordre '71
Children of Paradise '44
Les Visiteurs du Soir '42
Bizarre Bizarre '39
Le Jour Se Leve '39

Charles Robert Carner
Echo of Murder '00
The Fixer '97

Marc Caro
The City of Lost Children '95
Delicatessen '92

Glenn Gordon Caron (1954-)
Picture Perfect '96
Love Affair '94
Wilder Napalm '93
Clean and Sober '88

Heiner Carow (1929-)
Coming Out '89
The Legend of Paul and Paula '73

John Carpenter (1948-)
John Carpenter's Ghosts of Mars '01
John Carpenter's Vampires '97
Escape from L.A. '96
In the Mouth of Madness '95
Village of the Damned '95
Body Bags '93
Memoirs of an Invisible Man '92
They Live '88
Prince of Darkness '87
Big Trouble in Little China '86
Christine '84
Starman '84
The Thing '82
Escape from New York '81
Elvis: The Movie '79
The Fog '78
Halloween '78
Assault on Precinct 13 '76
Dark Star '74

Stephen Carpenter
The Kindred '87
Dorm That Dripped Blood '82
The Power '80

Steve Carr
Dr. Dolittle 2 '01
Next Friday '00

Thomas Carr (1907-97)
Dino '57
Captain Scarlett '53
Blazing Guns '50
Guns of Justice '50
Marshal of Heldorado '50
Pirates of the High Seas '50
Jesse James Rides Again '47
Alias Billy the Kid '46

Michael Carreras (1927-94)
Call Him Mr. Shatter '74
Prehistoric Women '67
Maniac '63
Willard Carroll
Playing by Heart '98
The Runestone '91
David Carson
In His Life: The John Lennon Story '00
The 10th Kingdom '00
From the Earth to the Moon '98
Letters from a Killer '98
Star Trek: Generations '94
John Paddy Carstairs (1910-70)
Trouble in Store '53
Made in Heaven '52
Tony Draws a Horse '51
Sleeping Car to Trieste '45
The Saint in London '39
Peter Carter
Kavik the Wolf Dog '84
Intruder Within '81
Highpoint '80
Klondike Fever '79
Rituals '79
High Ballin' '78
Thomas Carter (1953-)
Save the Last Dance '01
Metro '96
Swing Kids '93
Call to Glory '84
Miami Vice '84
D.J. Caruso (1965-)
The Salton Sea '02
Black Cat Run '98
Steve Carver (1945-)
The Wolves '95
Dead Center '94
River of Death '90
Bulletproof '88
Jocks '87
Oceans of Fire '86
Lone Wolf McQuade '83
An Eye for an Eye '81
Steel '80
Drum '76
Big Bad Mama '74
The Arena '73
Kimberly Casey
Deadly Dancer '90
Born Killer '89
Richard Casey
Hellbent '90
Horror House on Highway 5 '86
Henry Cass (1902-89)
The Hand '60
Blood of the Vampire '58
Last Holiday '50
Jon Cassar
Danger Beneath the Sea '02
Shadow Warriors '97
Shadow Warriors 2: Hunt for the Death Merchant '97
The Final Goal '94
John Cassavetes (1929-89)
Big Trouble '86
Love Streams '84
Gloria '80
Opening Night '77
The Killing of a Chinese Bookie '76
A Woman under the Influence '74
Minnie and Moskowitz '71
Husbands '70
Faces '68
A Child Is Waiting '63
Shadows '60
Nick Cassavetes (1959-)
John Q '02
She's So Lovely '97
Unhook the Stars '96
Richard Cassidy
Bloodshed '83
Crazed '82

Enzo G. Castellari (1938-)
Sinbad of the Seven Seas '89
Escape from the Bronx '85
Lightblast '85
Day of the Cobra '84
1990: The Bronx Warriors '83
Warriors of the Wasteland '83
Deadly Mission '78
Loves & Times of Scaramouche '76
High Crime '73
Cold Eyes of Fear '70
Go Kill and Come Back '68
Any Gun Can Play '67
Nick Castle (1947-)
Major Payne '95
Mr. Wrong '95
Dennis the Menace '93
Tap '89
The Boy Who Could Fly '86
The Last Starfighter '84
Tag: The Assassination Game '82
William Castle (1914-77)
The Night Walker '64
Strait-Jacket '64
Zotz! '62
Homicidal '61
Mr. Sardonicus '61
13 Ghosts '60
The Tingler '59
House on Haunted Hill '58
Americano '55
Conquest of Cochise '53
The Law Rides Again '43
William Allen Castleman
Johnny Firecloud '75
Bummer '73
Joe Catalanotto
French Quarter Undercover '85
Terror in the Swamp '85
Gil(bert) Cates
Collected Stories '02
A Death in the Family '02
Gilbert Cates (1934-)
Backfire '88
Consenting Adult '85
Burning Rage '84
Goldilocks & the Three Bears '83
Hobson's Choice '83
The Last Married Couple in America '80
Oh, God! Book 2 '80
The Promise '79
Johnny We Hardly Knew Ye '77
One Summer Love '76
The Affair '73
Summer Wishes, Winter Dreams '73
To All My Friends on Shore '71
I Never Sang for My Father '70
Michael Caton-Jones (1958-)
The Jackal '97
Rob Roy '95
This Boy's Life '93
Doc Hollywood '91
Memphis Belle '90
Scandal '89
Alberto Cavalcanti (1897-1982)
They Made Me a Fugitive '47
Nicholas Nickleby '46
Dead of Night '45
Liliana Cavani (1937-)
Francesco '93
The Berlin Affair '85
Beyond Obsession '82
The Night Porter '74
Jeff Celentano
Gunshy '98
Under the Hula Moon '95

Claude Chabrol (1930-)
The Swindle '97
La Ceremonie '95
L'Enfer '93
Betty '92
Madame Bovary '91
Club Extinction '89
The Story of Women '88
The Cry of the Owl '87
The Blood of Others '84
The Horse of Pride '80
Violette '78
Blood Relatives '77
Dirty Hands '76
Twist '76
Innocents with Dirty Hands '75
A Piece of Pleasure '74
Wedding in Blood '74
High Heels '72
Ten Days Wonder '72
La Rupture '70
This Man Must Die '70
Le Boucher '69
Les Biches '68
Six in Paris '68
Bluebeard '63
Les Bonnes Femmes '60
The Cousins '59
Le Beau Serge '58
Gurinder Chadha
What's Cooking? '00
Bhaji on the Beach '94
Don Chaffey (1917-90)
The Gift of Love '90
Casino '80
C.H.O.M.P.S. '79
Magic of Lassie '78
Pete's Dragon '77
Fourth Wish '75
Ride a Wild Pony '75
The Graveyard '74
Creatures the World Forgot '70
The Viking Queen '67
One Million Years B.C. '66
The Horse Without a Head '63
Jason and the Argonauts '63
The Three Lives of Thomasina '63
A Matter of WHO '62
Greyfriars Bobby '61
Dentist In the Chair '60
Youssef Chahine
Alexandria Again and Forever '90
An Egyptian Story '82
Alexandria...Why? '78
P. (Philip) Chalong
In Gold We Trust '91
H-Bomb '71
Gregg Champion
The Simple Life of Noah Dearborn '99
The Cowboy Way '94
Short Time '90
Benny Chan
Gen-X Cops '99
Jackie Chan's Who Am I '98
Jackie Chan (1954-)
Jackie Chan's Who Am I '98
Operation Condor '91
Miracles '89
Project A: Part 2 '87
Operation Condor 2: The Armour of the Gods '86
Police Story '85
Project A '83
Young Master '80
Charlie Chaplin (1889-1977)
A Countess from Hong Kong '67
The Chaplin Revue '58
A King in New York '57
Limelight '52
Monsieur Verdoux '47
The Great Dictator '40
Modern Times '36
City Lights '31
The Gold Rush '25
The Kid '21
The Circus '19

Three Charlies and One Phoney! '18
The Adventurer '17
The Cure '17
The Floorwalker '17
The Immigrant '17
Burlesque on Carmen '16
The Count '16
Easy Street '16
The Fireman '16
The Rink '16
The Vagabond '16
Charlie Chaplin: Night at the Show '15
Charlie Chaplin ... Our Hero! '15
Matthew Chapman (1950-)
Heart of Midnight '89
Slow Burn '86
Strangers Kiss '83
Hussy '80
Michael Chapman (1935-)
The Viking Sagas '95
The Clan of the Cave Bear '86
All the Right Moves '83
Joe Chappelle
The Skulls 2 '02
Dracula: The Dark Prince '01
Phantoms '97
Halloween 6: The Curse of Michael Myers '95
Henri Charr
Hollywood Safari '96
My Uncle: The Alien '96
Caged Hearts '95
Cellblock Sisters: Banished Behind Bars '95
Illegal Entry: Formula for Fear '93
Etienne Chatiliez (1952-)
Le Bonheur Est Dans le Pre '95
Tatie Danielle '91
Life Is a Long Quiet River '88
Louis Chaudet (1884-1965)
Fighting Jack '26
Tentacles of the North '26
Amin Q. Chaudhri
An Unremarkable Life '89
Tiger Warsaw '87
Deadly Vengeance '81
Jeremiah S. Chechik
The Avengers '98
Diabolique '96
Tall Tale: The Unbelievable Adventures of Pecos Bill '95
Benny & Joon '93
National Lampoon's Christmas Vacation '89
Peter Chelsom (1956-)
Serendipity '01
Town and Country '01
The Mighty '98
Funny Bones '94
Hear My Song '91
Joan Chen (1961-)
Autumn in New York '00
Xiu Xiu: The Sent Down Girl '97
Pierre Chenal (1903-91)
Native Son '51
Man from Nowhere '37
Crime and Punishment '35
Patrice Chereau (1944-)
Those Who Love Me Can Take the Train '98
Queen Margot '94
L'Homme Blesse '83
John R. Cherry, III
All New Adventures of Laurel and Hardy: For Love or Mummy '98
Ernest Goes to Africa '97
Ernest in the Army '97
Slam Dunk Ernest '95

Ernest Rides Again '93
Ernest Scared Stupid '91
Ernest Goes to Jail '90
Ernest Saves Christmas '88
Ernest Goes to Camp '87
Dr. Otto & the Riddle of the Gloom Beam '86
Lionel Chetwynd
Varian's War '01
Hanoi Hilton '87
Tommy Cheung
Ninja: American Warrior '90
Ninja Death Squad '87
Pierre Chevalier (1915-)
Dr. Orloff's Invisible Horror '72
Orloff and the Invisible Man '70
Marvin J. Chomsky (1929-)
Catherine the Great '95
Robert Kennedy and His Times '90
The Brotherhood of the Rose '89
Nairobi Affair '88
Billionaire Boys Club '87
Anastasia: The Mystery of Anna '86
The Deliberate Stranger '86
Tank '83
Inside the Third Reich '82
Attica '80
Holocaust '78
Little Ladies of the Night '77
Roots '77
Murph the Surf '75
Evel Knievel '72
Fireball Forward '72
The Shaming '71
Thomas Chong (1938-)
Far Out Man '89
Cheech and Chong's The Corsican Brothers '84
Cheech and Chong: Still Smokin' '83
Cheech and Chong's Nice Dreams '81
Cheech and Chong's Next Movie '80
Joyce Chopra (1938-)
The Lady in Question '99
Murder in a Small Town '99
My Very Best Friend '96
Danger of Love '95
High Stakes '93
Murder in New Hampshire: The Pamela Smart Story '91
The Lemon Sisters '90
Smooth Talk '85
Elie Chouraqui (1953-)
Harrison's Flowers '02
Man on Fire '87
Love Songs '85
Nathaniel Christian
Club Fed '90
California Casanova '89
Roger Christian (1944-)
Battlefield Earth '00
The Final Cut '96
Masterminds '96
Underworld '96
Nostradamus '93
Starship '87
The Sender '82
Christian-Jaque (1904-94)
Legend of Frenchie King '71
Fanfan la Tulipe '51
Benjamin Christiansen (1879-1959)
Mockery '27
Haxan: Witchcraft through the Ages '22
Yen Ping Chu
The Prisoner '90
Fantasy Mission Force '84
Lyndon Chubbuck
Kiss Toledo Goodbye '00
The Right Temptation '00

Naked Souls '95
Byron Ross Chudnow
The Amazing Dobermans '76
Daring Dobermans '73
The Doberman Gang '72
Grigori Chukhraj (1921-2001)
Life Is Beautiful '79
Ballad of a Soldier '60
Gerard Ciccoritti
The Life Before This '99
Paris, France '94
Understudy: The Graveyard Shift 2 '88
Graveyard Shift '87
Psycho Girls '86
Matt Cimber
Hundra '85
Yellow Hair & the Fortress of Gold '84
Time to Die '83
Butterfly '82
Fake Out '82
Witch Who Came from the Sea '76
Candy Tangerine Man '75
Lady Cocoa '75
The Black Six '74
Single Room Furnished '68
Michael Cimino (1943-)
Sunchaser '96
Desperate Hours '90
The Sicilian '87
Year of the Dragon '85
Heaven's Gate '81
The Deer Hunter '78
Thunderbolt & Lightfoot '74
Osvaldo Civirani
Dead for a Dollar '70
Hercules vs. the Sons of the Sun '64
Rene Clair (1898-1981)
Les Grandes Manoeuvres '55
Beauties of the Night '52
Beauty and the Devil '50
And Then There Were None '45
It Happened Tomorrow '44
Forever and a Day '43
I Married a Witch '42
The Flame of New Orleans '41
The Ghost Goes West '36
Quatorze Juliet '32
A Nous la Liberte '31
Le Million '31
Under the Roofs of Paris '29
Italian Straw Hat '27
Entr'acte '24
The Crazy Ray '22
Bob (Benjamin) Clark (1941-)
I'll Remember April '99
Baby Geniuses '98
My Summer Story '94
Loose Cannons '90
From the Hip '86
Turk 182! '85
Rhinestone '84
A Christmas Story '83
Porky's 2: The Next Day '83
Porky's '82
Tribute '80
Murder by Decree '79
Black Christmas '75
Children Shouldn't Play with Dead Things '72
Deathdream '72
Bruce (B.D.) Clark (1945-)
Galaxy of Terror '81
Ski Bum '75
The Naked Angels '69
Colbert Clark (1898-)
Fighting with Kit Carson '33
Mystery Squadron '33
Whispering Shadow '33
Wolf Dog '33
Duane Clark
Family Tree '00
Protector '97
Bitter Harvest '93

Shaking the Tree '92
Greydon Clark (1943-)
Russian Roulette '93
Killer Instinct '92
Dance Macabre '91
The Forbidden Dance '90
Skinheads: The Second Coming of Hate '88
The Uninvited '88
Final Justice '84
Joy Sticks '83
Wacko '83
The Return '80
Angel's Brigade '79
Hi-Riders '77
Satan's Cheerleaders '77
Bad Bunch '76
Black Shampoo '76
James B. Clark (1908-2000)
My Side of the Mountain '69
And Now Miguel '66
Island of the Blue Dolphins '64
Flipper '63
Misty '61
A Dog of Flanders '59
Jim Clark (1931-)
Madhouse '74
Rentadick '72
Think Dirty '70
Larry Clark (1943-)
Bully '01
Teenage Caveman '01
Another Day in Paradise '98
Kids '95
Lawrence Gordon Clark
Jack Higgins' Midnight Man '96
Monkey Boy '90
Romance on the Orient Express '89
Belfast Assassin '84
Jamaica Inn '82
Flambards '78
William Clark
Windrunner '94
The Goodbye Bird '93
Alan Clarke (1935-90)
Rita, Sue & Bob Too '87
Scum '79
James Kenelm Clarke (1941-)
Going Undercover '88
Funny Money '82
The House on Straw Hill '76
Malcolm Clarke
Chasing Holden '01
Voices from a Locked Room '95
Shirley Clarke (1919-97)
The Cool World '63
The Connection '61
Zoe Clarke-Williams
New Best Friend '02
Men '97
James Clavell (1925-94)
The Last Valley '71
To Sir, with Love '67
William Claxton (1914-96)
The Canterville Ghost '91
Fangs of the Wild '54
Jack Clayton (1921-95)
The Lonely Passion of Judith Hearne '87
Something Wicked This Way Comes '83
The Great Gatsby '74
The Pumpkin Eater '64
The Innocents '61
Room at the Top '59
Tom Clegg
Sharpe's Justice '97
Sharpe's Revenge '97
Sharpe's Waterloo '97
Sharpe's Mission '96
Sharpe's Regiment '96
Sharpe's Siege '96
Sharpe's Battle '94
Sharpe's Company '94
Sharpe's Enemy '94
Sharpe's Gold '94
Sharpe's Honour '94
Sharpe's Sword '94
Sharpe's Eagle '93
Sharpe's Rifles '93
Any Man's Death '90
A Casualty of War '90
Stroke of Midnight '90
Mountbatten: The Last Viceroy '86
Children of the Full Moon '84
The Inside Man '84
McVicar '80
Destination Moonbase Alpha '75
Dick Clement (1937-)
Porridge '91
Water '85
Bullshot '83
Catch Me a Spy '71
Rene Clement (1913-96)
Wanted: Babysitter '75
And Hope to Die '72
The Deadly Trap '71
Rider on the Rain '70
Is Paris Burning? '66
Joy House '64
The Day and the Hour '63
Purple Noon '60
Gervaise '56
Forbidden Games '52
The Walls of Malapaga '49
Ron Clements (1953-)
Hercules '97
Aladdin '92
The Little Mermaid '89
The Great Mouse Detective '86
Graeme Clifford
Caracara '00
The Last Don 2 '98
My Husband's Secret Life '98
The Last Don '97
Past Tense '94
Deception '92
Gleaming the Cube '89
The Turn of the Screw '89
Burke & Wills '85
Little Red Riding Hood '83
Frances '82
The Boy Who Left Home to Find Out About the Shivers '81
Elmer Clifton (1892-1949)
Youth Aflame '59
The Judge '49
Streets of Sin '49
Marked for Murder '45
Boss of Rawhide '44
Dead or Alive '44
Gangsters of the Frontier '44
Guns of the Law '44
Seven Doors to Death '44
Frontier Law '43
Law of the Texan '38
Roaring Speedboats '37
Slaves in Bondage '37
Custer's Last Stand '36
Assassin of Youth '35
Captured in Chinatown '35
Cyclone of the Saddle '35
Fighting Caballero '35
Let 'er Go Gallegher '28
Down to the Sea in Ships '22
Edward F. (Eddie) Cline (1892-1961)
Private Buckaroo '42
Snuffy Smith, Yard Bird '42
Never Give a Sucker an Even Break '41
The Villain Still Pursued Her '41
The Bank Dick '40
My Little Chickadee '40
Breaking the Ice '38
Hawaii Calls '38
Peck's Bad Boy with the Circus '38
Cowboy Millionaire '35
Dude Ranger '34
Peck's Bad Boy '34
Hook, Line and Sinker '30
Three Ages '23
Robert Clouse (1929-97)
Ironheart '92
China O'Brien 2 '89
China O'Brien '88
Gymkata '85
Deadly Eyes '82
Force: Five '81
The Big Brawl '80
Game of Death '79
The Amsterdam Kill '78
The Pack '77
The Ultimate Warrior '75
Black Belt Jones '74
Enter the Dragon '73
Darker than Amber '70
Henri-Georges Clouzot (1907-77)
Diabolique '55
Wages of Fear '55
Manon '50
Jenny Lamour '47
Le Corbeau '43
E.B. (Enzo Barboni) Clucher
Sons of Trinity '95
The Odd Squad '86
Go for It '83
Crime Busters '78
Trinity Is Still My Name '75
They Call Me Trinity '72
Craig Clyde
Walking Thunder '94
The Legend of Wolf Mountain '92
Little Heroes '91
Lewis (Luigi Cozzi) Coates (1947-)
Black Cat '90
Hercules 2 '85
Hercules '83
Alien Contamination '81
Star Crash '78
Stacy Cochran
Boys '95
My New Gun '92
Jean Cocteau (1889-1963)
The Testament of Orpheus '59
Orpheus '49
The Eagle Has Two Heads '48
The Storm Within '48
Beauty and the Beast '46
The Blood of a Poet '30
Joel Coen (1954-)
The Man Who Wasn't There '01
O Brother Where Art Thou? '00
The Big Lebowski '97
Fargo '96
The Hudsucker Proxy '93
Barton Fink '91
Miller's Crossing '90
Raising Arizona '87
Blood Simple '85
Eli Cohen (1940-)
Under the Domim Tree '95
The Soft Kill '94
The Quarrel '93
The Summer of Aviya '88
Gary P. Cohen
Video Violence '87
Video Violence Part 2...The Exploitation! '87
Howard R. Cohen (1942-99)
Deathstalker 4: Match of Titans '92
Saturday the 14th Strikes Back '88
Time Trackers '88
Space Raiders '83
Saturday the 14th '81
Larry Cohen (1947-)
Original Gangstas '96
As Good as Dead '95
The Ambulance '90
Wicked Stepmother '89
Deadly Illusion '87
It's Alive 3: Island of the Alive '87
Return to Salem's Lot '87
Special Effects '85
The Stuff '85
Perfect Strangers '84
Q (The Winged Serpent) '82
It's Alive 2: It Lives Again '78
The Private Files of J. Edgar Hoover '77
God Told Me To '76
It's Alive '74
Black Caesar '73
Hell Up in Harlem '73
Housewife '72
Rob Cohen (1949-)
XXX '02
The Fast and the Furious '01
The Skulls '00
The Rat Pack '98
Daylight '96
Dragonheart '96
Dragon: The Bruce Lee Story '93
Scandalous '84
A Small Circle of Friends '80
Michael Cohn
Snow White: A Tale of Terror '97
When the Bough Breaks '93
Interceptor '92
Cyril Coke (1914-93)
Pride and Prejudice '85
The Duchess of Duke Street '78
Harley Cokliss (1945-)
Inferno '99
Hercules the Legendary Journeys, Vol. 2: The Lost Kingdom '94
Dream Demon '88
Malone '87
Black Moon Rising '86
Warlords of the 21st Century '82
Marcus Cole
The Christmas Box '95
From the Mixed-Up Files of Mrs. Basil E. Frankweiler '95
John David Coles
The Good Fight '92
Rising Son '90
Signs of Life '89
Duilio Coletti
Submarine Attack '54
Lure of the Sila '49
Giuseppe Colizzi (1925-78)
All the Way, Boys '73
Boot Hill '69
Ace High '68
Richard A. Colla (1918-)
Blind Witness '89
Naked Lie '89
The Prize Pulitzer '89
Don't Look Back: The Story of Leroy "Satchel" Paige '81
Battlestar Galactica '78
Olly Olly Oxen Free '78
Fuzz '72
James F. Collier
China Cry '91
Beyond the Next Mountain '87
A Cry from the Mountain '85
Joni '79
The Hiding Place '75
Boon Collins
Abducted 2: The Reunion '94
Spirit of the Eagle '90
Abducted '86
Lewis D. Collins (1899-1954)
The Fighting Redhead '50
Jungle Goddess '49
Heading for Heaven '47
Killer Dill '47
Lost City of the Jungle '45
Master Key '44
Mystery of the Riverboat '44
Sing Sing Nights '35
Brand of Hate '34
The Man from Hell '34
Gun Law '33
Trouble Busters '33
Max Allan Collins
Mommy 2: Mommy's Day '96
Mommy '95
Robert E. Collins
J. Edgar Hoover '87
Mafia Princess '86
Our Family Business '81
Gideon's Trumpet '80
The Life and Assassination of the Kingfish '76
Peter Collinson (1936-80)
Earthling '80
The House on Garibaldi Street '79
African Rage '78
Tomorrow Never Comes '77
Sell Out '76
Spiral Staircase '75
Ten Little Indians '75
Dressed for Death '74
Fright '71
The Italian Job '69
Walter Colmes
Accomplice '46
Identity Unknown '45
The Woman Who Came Back '45
Fernando Colomo (1942-)
Star Knight '85
Skyline '84
Carl Colpaert
Facade '98
The Crew '95
Delusion '91
In the Aftermath: Angels Never Sleep '87
Chris Columbus (1958-)
Harry Potter and the Sorcerer's Stone '01
Bicentennial Man '99
Stepmom '98
Nine Months '95
Mrs. Doubtfire '93
Home Alone 2: Lost in New York '92
Only the Lonely '91
Home Alone '90
Heartbreak Hotel '88
Adventures in Babysitting '87
Luigi Comencini (1916-)
Misunderstood '87
Till Marriage Do Us Part '74
Heidi '52
Lance Comfort (1908-66)
The Great Armored Car Swindle '64
Great Day '46
Hotel Reserve '44
The Courageous Mr. Penn '41
Don Como
Unknown Powers '80
Aliens from Spaceship Earth '77
Richard Compton
Super Force '90
Angels Die Hard '84
Wild Times '79
Deadman's Curve '78
Maniac '77
Return to Macon County '75
Macon County Line '74
Bill Condon
Gods and Monsters '98
Candyman 2: Farewell to the Flesh '94
Dead in the Water '91
Murder 101 '91
White Lie '91
Sister, Sister '87
W. Merle Connell
The Devil's Sleep '51
Test Tube Babies '48
Kevin Connor (1940-)
Mary, Mother of Jesus '99
The Apocalypse Watch '97
Mother Teresa: In the Name of God's Poor '97
The Old Curiosity Shop '94
Diana: Her True Story '93
Sunset Grill '92
Iran: Days of Crisis '91
Great Expectations '89
The Hollywood Detective '89
The Lion of Africa '87
House Where Evil Dwells '82
Goliath Awaits '81
Motel Hell '80
The People That Time Forgot '77
At the Earth's Core '76
Choice of Weapons '76
The Land That Time Forgot '75
From Beyond the Grave '73
Robert Conrad (1935-)
Bandits '73
Crossfire '67
James A. Contner
The Cover Girl Murders '93
The Return of Eliot Ness '91
The Ten Million Dollar Getaway '91
Hitler's Daughter '90
Jack Conway (1887-1952)
Julia Misbehaves '48
The Hucksters '47
Dragon Seed '44
Honky Tonk '41
Love Crazy '41
Boom Town '40
Let Freedom Ring '39
Too Hot to Handle '38
Saratoga '37
Libeled Lady '36
A Tale of Two Cities '36
The Girl from Missouri '34
Tarzan and His Mate '34
Viva Villa! '34
Red Headed Woman '32
The Unholy Three '30
Our Modern Maidens '29
James L. Conway (1950-)
The Last of the Mohicans '85
Donner Pass: The Road to Survival '84
The Fall of the House of Usher '80
Hangar 18 '80
The Incredible Rocky Mountain Race '77
Bruce Cook, Jr.
Nightwish '89
Husbands, Wives, Money, and Murder '86
Fielder Cook (1923-)
The Member of the Wedding '97
Seize the Day '86
I Know Why the Caged Bird Sings '79
Love Affair: The Eleanor & Lou Gehrig Story '77
Judge Horton and the Scottsboro Boys '76
Miles to Go Before I Sleep '74
The Hideaways '73
Homecoming: A Christmas Story '71
A Big Hand for the Little Lady '66
Patterns '56
Phillip Cook
Invader '91
Star Quest '89
Troy Cook
Phoenix '95
The Takeover '94
Martha Coolidge (1946-)
The Flamingo Rising '01
The Ponder Heart '01

If These Walls Could Talk 2 '00
Introducing Dorothy Dandridge '99
Out to Sea '97
Three Wishes '95
Angie '94
Lost in Yonkers '93
Crazy in Love '92
Bare Essentials '91
Rambling Rose '91
Plain Clothes '88
Real Genius '85
Joy of Sex '84
Valley Girl '83

Michael Cooney
Jack Frost 2: Revenge of the Mutant Killer Snowman '00
Jack Frost '97

Jackie Cooper (1921-)
The Night They Saved Christmas '87
Izzy & Moe '85
Rosie: The Rosemary Clooney Story '82
Sex and the Single Parent '82
Leave 'Em Laughing '81
Marathon '80
Rodeo Girl '80
White Mama '80
Rainbow '78

Merian C. Cooper
King Kong '33
Chang: A Drama of the Wilderness '27

Stuart Cooper (1942-)
Chameleon '98
The Hunted '98
The Ticket '97
Bloodhounds 2 '96
Dead Ahead '96
Bitter Vengeance '94
Out of Annie's Past '94
Dancing with Danger '93
Rubdown '93
Payoff '91
The Long, Hot Summer '86
A.D. '85
Disappearance '81

Christopher Coppola (1962-)
Gunfighter '98
Deadfall '93
Dracula's Widow '88

Francis Ford Coppola (1939-)
John Grisham's The Rainmaker '97
Jack '96
Bram Stoker's Dracula '92
The Godfather, Part 3 '90
New York Stories '89
Tucker: The Man and His Dream '88
Gardens of Stone '87
Peggy Sue Got Married '86
Rip van Winkle '85
The Cotton Club '84
The Outsiders '83
Rumble Fish '83
One from the Heart '82
The Godfather 1902-1959: The Complete Epic '81
Apocalypse Now '79
The Conversation '74
The Godfather, Part 2 '74
The Godfather '72
The Rain People '69
Finian's Rainbow '68
You're a Big Boy Now '66
Battle Beyond the Sun '63
Dementia 13 '63
The Terror '63
The Bellboy and the Playgirls '62
Tonight for Sure '61

Frank Coraci (1965-)
The Waterboy '98
The Wedding Singer '97
Murdered Innocence '94

Gregory Corarito
Delinquent School Girls '84
Wanda, the Sadistic Hypnotist '67

Gerard Corbiau
Farinelli '94
The Music Teacher '88

Bruno Corbucci (1931-96)
Aladdin '86
Miami Supercops '85
Cop in Blue Jeans '78

Sergio Corbucci (1927-90)
Super Fuzz '81
The Con Artists '80
Odds and Evens '78
Sonny and Jed '73
Companeros '70
Django '68
Hellbenders '67
Navajo Joe '67
Minnesota Clay '65

Bill Corcoran
Outlaw Justice '98
Portraits of a Killer '95
Sherlock Holmes and the Incident at Victoria Falls '91

Nicholas J. Corea (1943-99)
The Incredible Hulk Returns '88
Archer: The Fugitive from the Empire '81

Roger Corman (1926-)
Frankenstein Unbound '90
Bloody Mama '70
Gas-s-s-s! '70
The St. Valentine's Day Massacre '67
The Trip '67
The Wild Angels '66
Masque of the Red Death '65
Tomb of Ligeia '64
The Haunted Palace '63
The Raven '63
The Terror '63
X: The Man with X-Ray Eyes '63
Premature Burial '62
Tales of Terror '62
Tower of London '62
The Last Woman on Earth '61
The Pit and the Pendulum '61
Shame '61
Atlas '60
Creature from the Haunted Sea '60
The Fall of the House of Usher '60
Little Shop of Horrors '60
A Bucket of Blood '59
The Wasp Woman '59
I, Mobster '58
Machine Gun Kelly '58
Teenage Caveman '58
Carnival Rock '57
Rock All Night '57
Sorority Girl '57
Teenage Doll '57
The Undead '57
The Gunslinger '56
It Conquered the World '56
She Gods of Shark Reef '56
Apache Woman '55
Day the World Ended '55
Swamp Women '55

Alain Corneau (1943-)
Tous les Matins du Monde '92
Fort Saganne '84
Choice of Arms '83

Henry Cornelius (1913-58)
I Am a Camera '55
Genevieve '53
Passport to Pimlico '49

John Cornell
Almost an Angel '90
Crocodile Dundee 2 '88

Hubert Cornfield (1929-)
The Night of the Following Day '69
Pressure Point '62

Angel Baby '61
Plunder Road '57

Stephen Cornwell
Marshal Law '96
Philadelphia Experiment 2 '93
Killing Streets '91

Charles Correll
Deadly Desire '91
In the Deep Woods '91
Writer's Block '91

Michael Corrente (1960-)
Outside Providence '99
American Buffalo '95
Federal Hill '94

Lloyd Corrigan (1900-69)
Dancing Pirate '36
Daughter of the Dragon '31

Don A. Coscarelli (1954-)
Phantasm 4: Oblivion '98
Phantasm 3: Lord of the Dead '94
Survival Quest '89
Phantasm 2 '88
Beastmaster '82
Phantasm '79

George P. Cosmatos (1941-)
The Shadow Conspiracy '96
Tombstone '93
Leviathan '89
Cobra '86
Rambo: First Blood, Part 2 '85
Of Unknown Origin '83
Escape to Athena '79
The Cassandra Crossing '76
Massacre in Rome '73
Restless '72

Mario Costa (1904-95)
Rough Justice '87
Gladiator of Rome '63

Constantin Costa-Gavras (1933-)
Mad City '97
Music Box '89
Betrayed '88
Conseil de Famille '86
Hanna K. '83
Missing '82
State of Siege '73
Z '69

Kevin Costner (1955-)
The Postman '97
Dances with Wolves '90

Manny Coto
Star Kid '97
Dr. Giggles '92
Cover-Up '91
Playroom '90

Vittorio Cottafavi (1914-98)
Hercules and the Captive Women '63
Goliath and the Dragon '61

Jack Couffer
Living Free '72
Ring of Bright Water '69
Nikki, the Wild Dog of the North '61

Alex Cox (1954-)
The Winner '96
Highway Patrolman '91
Straight to Hell '87
Walker '87
Sid & Nancy '86
Repo Man '83

Neil Cox
Konrad '90s
Once Upon a Midnight Scary '90
Roommate '84

Paul Cox (1940-)
Molokai: The Story of Father Damien '99
Lust and Revenge '95
A Woman's Tale '92
Vincent: The Life and Death of Vincent van Gogh '87
Cactus '86
Man of Flowers '84
My First Wife '84

Lonely Hearts '82
Kostas '79

Arthur Crabtree (1900-75)
Fiend without a Face '58
Dear Murderer '47

William Crain (1949-)
Midnight Fear '90
Kid from Not-So-Big '78
Dr. Black, Mr. Hyde '76
Blacula '72

Kenneth Crane
The Manster '59
Monster from Green Hell '58
When Hell Broke Loose '58

Jay Craven
A Stranger in the Kingdom '98
Where the Rivers Flow North '94

Wes Craven (1939-)
Scream 3 '00
Music of the Heart '99
Scream 2 '97
Scream '96
Vampire in Brooklyn '95
Wes Craven's New Nightmare '94
The People under the Stairs '91
Shocker '89
The Serpent and the Rainbow '87
Deadly Friend '86
The Hills Have Eyes, Part 2 '84
Invitation to Hell '84
A Nightmare on Elm Street '84
Swamp Thing '82
Deadly Blessing '81
Summer of Fear '78
The Hills Have Eyes '77
Last House on the Left '72

Guy Crawford
The Catcher '98
Starved '97

Wayne Crawford
American Cop '94
Crime Lords '91

Charles Crichton (1910-99)
A Fish Called Wanda '88
The Battle of the Sexes '60
The Lavender Hill Mob '51
Train of Events '49
Against the Wind '48
Hue and Cry '47
Dead of Night '45

Michael Crichton (1942-)
The 13th Warrior '99
Physical Evidence '89
Runaway '84
Looker '81
The Great Train Robbery '79
Coma '78
Westworld '73
Pursuit '72

Donald Crisp (1880-1974)
Stand and Deliver '28
Sunny Side Up '28
Don Q., Son of Zorro '25
The Navigator '24

Armando Crispino (1925-)
Autopsy '74
Commandos '73
Dead Are Alive '72

Michael Cristofer (1945-)
Original Sin '01
Body Shots '99
Gia '98

Donald Crombie
Kitty and the Bagman '82
Killing of Angel Street '81
The Irishman '78
Caddie '76

John Cromwell (1888-1979)
The Goddess '58
The Racket '51
Dead Reckoning '47

Anna and the King of Siam '46
The Enchanted Cottage '45
Since You Went Away '44
Son of Fury '42
So Ends Our Night '41
Abe Lincoln in Illinois '40
In Name Only '39
Made for Each Other '39
Algiers '38
Prisoner of Zenda '37
Little Lord Fauntleroy '36
I Dream Too Much '35
Of Human Bondage '34
Spitfire '34
Ann Vickers '33
Vice Squad '31
Tom Sawyer '30
Dance of Life '29

David Cronenberg (1943-)
eXistenZ '99
Crash '95
M. Butterfly '93
Naked Lunch '91
Dead Ringers '88
The Fly '86
Dead Zone '83
Videodrome '83
Scanners '81
The Brood '79
Fast Company '78
Rabid '77
They Came from Within '75

Alan Crosland (1894-1936)
The Beloved Rogue '27
The Jazz Singer '27
Don Juan '26

Avery Crounse
Cries of Silence '97
The Invisible Kid '88
Eyes of Fire '84

Cameron Crowe (1957-)
Vanilla Sky '01
Almost Famous '00
Jerry Maguire '96
Singles '92
Say Anything '89

Christopher Crowe (1948-)
Whispers in the Dark '92
Off Limits '87

James Cruze (1884-1942)
The Wrong Road '37
I Cover the Waterfront '33
Mr. Skitch '33
The Great Gabbo '29
Old Ironsides '26
The Pony Express '25
The Covered Wagon '23
Hawthorne of the USA '19
The Roaring Road '19

Billy Crystal (1947-)
61* '01
Forget Paris '95
Mr. Saturday Night '92

Alfonso Cuaron
Y Tu Mama Tambien '01
Great Expectations '97
A Little Princess '95
Fallen Angels 1 '93

George Cukor (1899-1983)
Rich and Famous '81
Love Among the Ruins '75
Travels with My Aunt '72
Justine '69
My Fair Lady '64
Heller in Pink Tights '60
Let's Make Love '60
Song Without End '60
Les Girls '57
Bhowani Junction '56
It Should Happen to You '54
A Star Is Born '54
The Marrying Kind '52
Pat and Mike '52
Adam's Rib '50
Born Yesterday '50
A Life of Her Own '50
A Double Life '47
Gaslight '44
Keeper of the Flame '42
Two-Faced Woman '41

A Woman's Face '41
The Philadelphia Story '40
Susan and God '40
The Women '39
Holiday '38
Camille '36
Romeo and Juliet '36
David Copperfield '35
Sylvia Scarlett '35
Dinner at Eight '33
Little Women '33
A Bill of Divorcement '32
What Price Hollywood? '32

Mark Cullingham (1942-95)
Dead on the Money '91
Gryphon '88
Cinderella '84

Irving Cummings (1888-1959)
Double Dynamite '51
The Dolly Sisters '46
Sweet Rosie O'Grady '43
Springtime in the Rockies '42
Louisiana Purchase '41
Down Argentine Way '40
Everything Happens at Night '39
The Story of Alexander Graham Bell '39
Just Around the Corner '38
Little Miss Broadway '38
Vogues of 1938 '37
The Poor Little Rich Girl '36
Curly Top '35
Broken Hearts of Broadway '23
Flesh and Blood '22

Rusty Cundieff (1965-)
Sprung '96
Tales from the Hood '95
Fear of a Black Hat '94

Richard Cunha
Missile to the Moon '59
Frankenstein's Daughter '58
Giant from the Unknown '58
She Demons '58

Sean S. Cunningham (1941-)
Deepstar Six '89
The New Kids '85
Spring Break '83
A Stranger Is Watching '82
Friday the 13th '80
Manny's Orphans '78

Frederick Curiel (1917-85)
Neutron vs. the Death Robots '62
Neutron and the Black Mask '61
Neutron vs. the Amazing Dr. Caronte '61
Genie of Darkness '60
The Monster Demolisher '60

Dan Curtis (1928-)
The Love Letter '98
Trilogy of Terror 2 '96
Me and the Kid '93
Intruders '92
War & Remembrance: The Final Chapter '89
War & Remembrance '88
The Winds of War '83
The Long Days of Summer '80
Express to Terror '79
The Last Ride of the Dalton Gang '79
Mrs. R's Daughter '79
When Every Day Was the Fourth of July '78
Curse of the Black Widow '77
Dead of Night '77
Burnt Offerings '76
Trilogy of Terror '75
Melvin Purvis: G-Man '74
Scream of the Wolf '74
The Turn of the Screw '74
Dracula '73
The Night Strangler '72
Night of Dark Shadows '71
House of Dark Shadows '70

Douglas Curtis
The Sleeping Car '90
The Campus Corpse '77
Vondie Curtis-Hall (1956-)
Glitter '01
Gridlock'd '96
Michael Curtiz (1888-1962)
The Comancheros '61
The Adventures of Huckleberry Finn '60
Breath of Scandal '60
King Creole '58
Proud Rebel '58
We're No Angels '55
The Egyptian '54
White Christmas '54
Trouble along the Way '53
I'll See You in My Dreams '51
Jim Thorpe: All American '51
Young Man with a Horn '50
Flamingo Road '49
My Dream Is Yours '49
Romance on the High Seas '48
Life with Father '47
Night and Day '46
Mildred Pierce '45
Passage to Marseilles '44
This Is the Army '43
Captains of the Clouds '42
Casablanca '42
Yankee Doodle Dandy '42
Dive Bomber '41
The Sea Wolf '41
Santa Fe Trail '40
The Sea Hawk '40
Virginia City '40
Dodge City '39
The Private Lives of Elizabeth & Essex '39
The Adventures of Robin Hood '38
Angels with Dirty Faces '38
Four Daughters '38
Kid Galahad '37
The Charge of the Light Brigade '36
Black Fury '35
Captain Blood '35
Female '33
The Kennel Murder Case '33
Mystery of the Wax Museum '33
The Cabin in the Cotton '32
Doctor X '32
The Strange Love of Molly Louvain '32
Catherine Cyran
True Heart '97
Sawbones '95
Hostile Intentions '94
In the Heat of Passion 2: Unfaithful '94
Paul Czinner (1890-1972)
Dreaming Lips '37
As You Like It '36
Catherine the Great '34
Renee Daalder
Habitat '97
Massacre at Central High '76
Morton DaCosta (1914-89)
The Music Man '62
Auntie Mame '58
John Dahl (1956-)
Joy Ride '01
Rounders '98
Unforgettable '96
The Last Seduction '94
Red Rock West '93
Kill Me Again '89
Massimo Dallamano (1917-76)
Super Bitch '89
Dorian Gray '70
A Black Veil for Lisa '68
Joe D'Amato (1936-99)
Passion '92
Quest for the Mighty Sword '90
Blade Master '84
Ator the Fighting Eagle '83
Black Cobra '83
Buried Alive '81
Grim Reaper '81
Damiano Damiani (1922-)
The Inquiry '87
Amityville 2: The Possession '82
The Warning '80
Confessions of a Police Captain '72
A Bullet for the General '68
The Witch '66
Empty Canvas '64
Mel Damski (1946-)
Wildcard '92
A Connecticut Yankee in King Arthur's Court '89
Happy Together '89
Murder by the Book '87
A Winner Never Quits '86
Badge of the Assassin '85
Mischief '85
Yellowbeard '83
Legend of Walks Far Woman '82
American Dream '81
For Ladies Only '81
Long Journey Back '78
Rod Daniel
Alley Cats Strike '00
Beethoven's 2nd '93
The Super '91
K-9 '89
Like Father, Like Son '87
Teen Wolf '85
Harold Daniels (1903-71)
House of the Black Death '65
Terror in the Haunted House '58
Poor White Trash '57
Sword of Venus '53
Marc Daniels (1912-89)
Vengeance '89
Planet Earth '74
Joe Dante (1946-)
Small Soldiers '98
The Second Civil War '97
Picture Windows '95
Matinee '92
Gremlins 2: The New Batch '90
The 'Burbs '89
Amazon Women on the Moon '87
Innerspace '87
Explorers '85
Gremlins '84
Twilight Zone: The Movie '83
The Howling '81
Piranha '78
Hollywood Boulevard '76
Ray Danton (1931-92)
Tales of the Unexpected '91
Psychic Killer '75
Crypt of the Living Dead '73
Frank Darabont (1959-)
The Majestic '01
The Green Mile '99
The Shawshank Redemption '94
Buried Alive '90
Jonathan Darby
Hush '98
The Enemy Within '94
Jean-Pierre Dardenne
Rosetta '99
La Promesse '96
Luc Dardenne
Rosetta '99
La Promesse '96
Joan Darling (1935-)
Hiroshima Maiden '88
Check Is in the Mail '85
Willa '79
First Love '77
Harry D'Abbadie D'Arrast (1897-1968)
Topaze '33
Raffles '30
Julie Dash (1952-)
Love Song '00
Subway Stories '97
Daughters of the Dust '91
Jules Dassin (1911-)
Circle of Two '80
A Dream of Passion '78
Topkapi '64
Phaedra '61
Never on Sunday '60
Where the Hot Wind Blows '59
Rififi '54
Night and the City '50
The Naked City '48
The Canterville Ghost '44
Reunion in France '42
Harry Bromley Davenport
Xtro 3: Watch the Skies '95
Xtro 2: The Second Encounter '91
Xtro '83
Delmer Daves (1904-77)
Spencer's Mountain '63
Rome Adventure '62
Parrish '61
The Hanging Tree '59
A Summer Place '59
The Badlanders '58
Cowboy '58
Kings Go Forth '58
3:10 to Yuma '57
Jubal '56
Demetrius and the Gladiators '54
Drum Beat '54
Never Let Me Go '53
Treasure of the Golden Condor '53
Broken Arrow '50
Task Force '49
Dark Passage '47
The Red House '47
Hollywood Canteen '44
Destination Tokyo '43
Lorena David
Outta Time '01
Eastside '99
Pierre David
Serial Killer '95
Scanner Cop '94
Boaz Davidson (1943-)
Outside the Law '95
American Cyborg: Steel Warrior '94
Solar Force '94
Going Bananas '88
Salsa '88
Dutch Treat '86
Last American Virgin '82
Hospital Massacre '81
Gordon Davidson (1933-)
The Trial of Lee Harvey Oswald '77
Trial of the Catonsville Nine '72
Martin Davidson (1939-)
Looking for an Echo '99
Follow the River '95
Hard Promises '92
The Heart of Dixie '89
Long Gone '87
Eddie and the Cruisers '83
Hero at Large '80
The Lords of Flatbush '74
John Davies (1953-)
Devices and Desires '91
Kim '84
A Married Man '84
Terence Davies (1945-)
House of Mirth '00
The Neon Bible '95
The Long Day Closes '92
Distant Voices, Still Lives '88
Andrew Davis (1946-)
Collateral Damage '02
A Perfect Murder '98
Chain Reaction '96
Steal Big, Steal Little '95
The Fugitive '93
Under Siege '92
The Package '89
Above the Law '88
Code of Silence '85
The Final Terror '83
Desmond Davis (1928-)
Ordeal by Innocence '84
The Sign of Four '83
Clash of the Titans '81
Nice Girl Like Me '69
Smashing Time '67
Girl with Green Eyes '64
Julie Davis
All Over the Guy '01
I Love You, Don't Touch Me! '97
Witchcraft 6: The Devil's Mistress '94
Michael Paul Davis
Eight Days a Week '97
Beanstalk '94
Nick Davis
1999 '98
The Survivor '98
Ossie Davis (1917-)
Gordon's War '73
Cotton Comes to Harlem '70
Tamra Davis
Crossroads '02
Skipped Parts '00
Best Men '98
Half-Baked '97
Billy Madison '94
CB4: The Movie '93
Guncrazy '92
Norman Dawn (1884-1975)
Two Lost Worlds '50
Orphans of the North '40
Tundra '36
Anthony (Antonio Margheriti) Dawson (1930-)
Indio '90
Jungle Raiders '85
Tiger Joe '85
Codename: Wildgeese '84
Tornado '83
Yor, the Hunter from the Future '83
Ark of the Sun God '82
Hunters of the Golden Cobra '82
Cannibal Apocalypse '80
The Last Hunter '80
The Squeeze '80
Killer Fish '79
The Rip Off '78
The Squeeze '78
Death Rage '77
The Stranger and the Gunfighter '76
Take a Hard Ride '75
Andy Warhol's Dracula '74
Mr. Superinvisible '73
Seven Deaths in the Cat's Eye '72
Web of the Spider '70
And God Said to Cain '69
Lightning Bolt '67
Planet on the Prowl '65
The Virgin of Nuremberg '65
Wild, Wild Planet '65
Castle of Blood '64
Hercules, Prisoner of Evil '64
Assignment Outer Space '61
Battle of the Worlds '61
Ernest Day
Waltz across Texas '83
Green Ice '81
Robert Day (1922-)
The Quick and the Dead '87
Lady from Yesterday '85
Your Place or Mine '83
Peter and Paul '81
The Man with Bogart's Face '80
Walking Through the Fire '80
Murder by Natural Causes '79
The Grass Is Always Greener Over the Septic Tank '78
Initiation of Sarah '78
Death Stalk '74
Two-Way Stretch '60
First Man into Space '59
Corridors of Blood '58
The Haunted Strangler '58
Josee Dayan
Balzac: A Life of Passion '99
The Count of Monte Cristo '99
Lyman Dayton
The Avenging '92
Dream Machine '91
Baker's Hawk '76
Fabrizio de Angelis (1940-)
Thunder Warrior 3 '88
The Manhunt '86
Operation 'Nam '85
Thunder Warrior '85
Thunder Warrior 2 '85
Deadly Impact '84
Overthrow '82
Jan De Bont (1943-)
The Haunting '99
Speed 2: Cruise Control '97
Twister '96
Speed '94
Philippe de Broca (1933-)
The Green House '96
Louisiana '87
Jupiter's Thigh '81
Le Cavaleur '78
Dear Detective '77
Le Magnifique '76
Oldest Profession '67
The King of Hearts '66
That Man from Rio '64
Cartouche '62
Fred de Cordova (1910-2001)
Frankie and Johnny '65
I'll Take Sweden '65
Here Come the Nelsons '52
Bedtime for Bonzo '51
For the Love of Mary '48
Frank De Felitta (1921-)
Scissors '91
Dark Night of the Scarecrow '81
The Two Worlds of Jenny Logan '79
Raymond De Felitta
Two Family House '99
Cafe Society '97
Eduardo de Filippo (1900-84)
Shoot Loud, Louder, I Don't Understand! '66
Seven Deadly Sins '53
Michael de Gaetano
The Haunted '79
UFO: Target Earth '74
Rolf de Heer (1951-)
Dance Me to My Song '98
The Quiet Room '96
Alien Visitor '95
Bad Boy Bubby '93
Dingo '90
Encounter at Raven's Gate '88
Ate De Jong (1953-)
Highway to Hell '92
Drop Dead Fred '91
A Flight of Rainbirds '81
Hubert de la Bouillerie
The Apocalypse '96
The Right to Remain Silent '95
Alex de la Iglesia
Dance with the Devil '97
The Day of the Beast '95
Eloy De La Iglesia (1944-)
El Diputado '78
Cannibal Man '71
Jose Antonio De La Loma (1924-)
Street Warriors '87
Street Warriors, Part 2 '87
The Barcelona Kill '77
Charles De Latour
Impulse '55
The Limping Man '53
Gerardo (Gerry) De Leon
Mad Doctor of Blood Island '69
Brides of the Beast '68
The Vampire People '66
The Walls of Hell '64
Terror Is a Man '59
Marcus De Leon
The Big Squeeze '96
Kiss Me a Killer '91
Paul de Lussanet
Mysteries '84
Dear Boys '80
Alberto De Martino (1929-)
Miami Horror '87
Bloodlink '86
The Puma Man '80
The Chosen '77
Strange Shadows in an Empty Room '76
Django Shoots First '74
The Tempter '74
New Mafia Boss '72
Scenes from a Murder '72
Dirty Heroes '71
Secret Agent 00 '67
The Triumph of Hercules '66
Pierre De Moro
Hellhole '85
Savannah Smiles '82
Manoel de Oliveira (1908-)
Party '96
Voyage to the Beginning of the World '96
The Convent '95
Abraham's Valley '93
Armando de Ossorio (1926-2001)
Night of the Death Cult '75
People Who Own the Dark '75
Return of the Evil Dead '75
Horror of the Zombies '74
When the Screaming Stops '73
Tombs of the Blind Dead '72
Night of the Sorcerers '70
Fangs of the Living Dead '68
Jean De Segonzac
Mimic 2 '01
Homicide: The Movie '00
Vittorio De Sica (1902-74)
The Garden of the Finzi-Continis '71
Woman Times Seven '67
After the Fox '66
Marriage Italian Style '64
Yesterday, Today and Tomorrow '64
Boccaccio '70 '62
Two Women '61
It Happened in the Park '56
The Roof '56
Umberto D '55
The Gold of Naples '54
Indiscretion of an American Wife '54
Miracle in Milan '51
The Bicycle Thief '48
Shoeshine '47
The Children Are Watching Us '44
Teresa Venerdi '41
Tom De Simone
Angel 3: The Final Chapter '88
Reform School Girls '86
The Concrete Jungle '82
Hell Night '81
Chatterbox '76
Terror in the Jungle '68
Steven E. de Souza
Possessed '00

Street Fighter '94
Andre de Toth (1912-)
The Mongols '60
Morgan the Pirate '60
The Indian Fighter '55
House of Wax '53
The Stranger Wore a Gun '53
Last of the Comanches '52
Springfield Rifle '52
Man in the Saddle '51
Pitfall '48
Ramrod '47
Dark Waters '44
Geoffrey de Valois
Vampire Centerfolds '98
Vampire Conspiracy '96
Sorority House Vampires '95
Basil Dean (1888-1978)
21 Days '37
Lorna Doone '34
William Dear
Balloon Farm '97
Wild America '97
Angels in the Outfield '94
If Looks Could Kill '91
Harry and the Hendersons '87
Timerider '83
Basil Dearden (1911-71)
The Man Who Haunted Himself '70
The Assassination Bureau '69
Khartoum '66
Victim '61
The League of Gentlemen '60
Sapphire '59
The Smallest Show on Earth '57
Who Done It? '56
The Blue Lamp '49
Train of Events '49
Captive Heart '47
Frieda '47
Dead of Night '45
James Dearden (1949-)
Rogue Trader '98
A Kiss Before Dying '91
Pascali's Island '88
Cold Room '84
John DeBello
Killer Tomatoes Eat France '91
Killer Tomatoes Strike Back '90
Return of the Killer Tomatoes! '88
Happy Hour '87
Attack of the Killer Tomatoes '77
James D. Deck
Two Shades of Blue '98
Ravager '97
David DeCoteau (1962-)
Brotherhood 2: The Young Warlocks '01
Ancient Evil: Scream of the Mummy '00
Voodoo Academy '00
Curse of the Puppet Master: The Human Experiment '98
Frankenstein Reborn '98
Leather Jacket Love Story '98
Talisman '98
Femalien '96
Skeletons '96
Beach Babes 2: Cave Girl Island '95
Prehysteria 3 '95
Beach Babes from Beyond Infinity '93
Test Tube Teens from the Year 2000 '93
Puppet Master 3: Toulon's Revenge '90
Lady Avenger '89
Deadly Embrace '88
Dr. Alien '88
Creepozoids '87
Nightmare Sisters '87
Sorority Babes in the Slimeball Bowl-A-Rama '87
Allessandro DeGaetano
Project Metalbeast: DNA Overload '94
Bloodbath in Psycho Town '89
Philip DeGuere
Misfits of Science '85
Dr. Strange '78
Edward Dein
Curse of the Undead '59
The Leech Woman '59
Shack Out on 101 '55
Donna Deitch (1945-)
Common Ground '00
The Devil's Arithmetic '99
Prison Stories: Women on the Inside '91
The Women of Brewster Place '89
Desert Hearts '86
Steve DeJarnatt
Miracle Mile '89
Cherry 2000 '88
Fred Dekker (1959-)
RoboCop 3 '91
The Monster Squad '87
Night of the Creeps '86
Peter Del Monte (1943-)
Julia and Julia '87
Invitation au Voyage '82
Roy Del Ruth (1895-1961)
On Moonlight Bay '51
The West Point Story '50
Babe Ruth Story '48
Broadway Rhythm '44
DuBarry Was a Lady '43
The Chocolate Soldier '41
Topper Returns '41
Happy Landing '38
My Lucky Star '38
Broadway Melody of 1938 '37
On the Avenue '37
Born to Dance '36
Broadway Melody of 1936 '35
Kid Millions '34
Bureau of Missing Persons '33
Employees' Entrance '33
Lady Killer '33
Blessed Event '32
Blonde Crazy '31
The Maltese Falcon '31
Guillermo del Toro (1964-)
Blade II '02
The Devil's Backbone '01
Mimic '97
Cronos '94
Jean Delannoy (1908-)
Bernadette '90
Imperial Venus '71
This Special Friendship '67
Love and the Frenchwoman '60
The Hunchback of Notre Dame '57
La Symphonie Pastorale '46
Eternal Return '43
Dom DeLuise (1933-)
Boys Will Be Boys '97
Hot Stuff '80
Tulio Demicheli (1915-92)
Dracula vs. Frankenstein '69
Son of Captain Blood '62
Cecil B. DeMille (1881-1959)
The Ten Commandments '56
The Greatest Show on Earth '52
Samson and Delilah '50
Unconquered '47
The Story of Dr. Wassell '44
Reap the Wild Wind '42
Union Pacific '39
The Plainsman '37
The Crusades '35
Cleopatra '34
The Sign of the Cross '33
Madam Satan '30
King of Kings '27
The Road to Yesterday '25
The Ten Commandments '23
Affairs of Anatol '21
Why Change Your Wife? '20
Male and Female '19
The Cheat '15
Jonathan Demme (1944-)
Beloved '98
Subway Stories '97
Philadelphia '93
The Silence of the Lambs '91
Married to the Mob '88
Swimming to Cambodia '87
Something Wild '86
Stop Making Sense '84
Swing Shift '84
Who Am I This Time? '82
Melvin and Howard '80
Last Embrace '79
Citizens Band '77
Fighting Mad '76
Crazy Mama '75
Caged Heat '74
Ted (Edward) Demme (1964-2002)
Blow '01
Life '99
Monument Ave. '98
Subway Stories '97
Beautiful Girls '96
The Ref '93
Who's the Man? '93
Jacques Demy (1931-90)
A Slightly Pregnant Man '79
Peau D'Ane '71
Donkey Skin '70
The Young Girls of Rochefort '68
Umbrellas of Cherbourg '64
Lola '61
Claire Denis (1948-)
Nenette and Boni '96
I Can't Sleep '93
No Fear, No Die '90
Chocolat '88
Pen Densham
Houdini '99
Moll Flanders '96
The Kiss '88
The Zoo Gang '85
Ruggero Deodato (1939-)
Dial Help '88
The Lone Runner '88
The Barbarians '87
Phantom of Death '87
Cut and Run '85
House on the Edge of the Park '84
Brian DePalma (1941-)
Mission to Mars '00
Snake Eyes '98
Mission: Impossible '96
Carlito's Way '93
Raising Cain '92
The Bonfire of the Vanities '90
Casualties of War '89
The Untouchables '87
Wise Guys '86
Body Double '84
Scarface '83
Blow Out '81
Dressed to Kill '80
Home Movies '79
The Fury '78
Carrie '76
Obsession '76
Phantom of the Paradise '74
Sisters '73
Hi, Mom! '70
The Wedding Party '69
Greetings '68
Gerard Depardieu (1948-)
The Bridge '00
Tartuffe '84
Jacques Deray (1929-)
The Outside Man '73
Borsalino '70
Swimming Pool '70
John Derek (1926-98)
Ghosts Can't Do It '90
Bolero '84
Tarzan, the Ape Man '81
Fantasies '73
Confessions of Tom Harris '72
Once Before I Die '65
Dominique Deruddere
Everybody's Famous! '00
Hombres Complicados '97
Suite 16 '94
Wait until Spring, Bandini '90
Caleb Deschanel (1941-)
Crusoe '89
The Escape Artist '82
Arnaud Desplechin
My Sex Life...Or How I Got into an Argument '96
La Sentinelle '92
Howard Deutch
The Replacements '00
Neil Simon's The Odd Couple 2 '98
Grumpier Old Men '95
Getting Even with Dad '94
Article 99 '92
The Great Outdoors '88
Some Kind of Wonderful '87
Pretty in Pink '86
Ross Devenish
A Certain Justice '99
Over Indulgence '87
Bleak House '85
Michel DeVille (1931-)
La Lectrice '88
Peril '85
Voyage en Douce '81
Dennis Devine
Vampires of Sorority Row: Kickboxers From Hell '99
Haunted '98
Amazon Warrior '97
Things 2 '97
Things '93
Dead Girls '90
Fatal Images '89
Danny DeVito (1944-)
Death to Smoochy '02
Matilda '96
Hoffa '92
The War of the Roses '89
Throw Momma from the Train '87
Amazing Stories '85
Ratings Game '84
John Dexter (1925-90)
I Want What I Want '72
The Virgin Soldiers '69
Maury Dexter (1927-)
Hell's Belles '69
Surf Party '64
Tom Dey
Showtime '02
Shanghai Noon '00
Fernando Di Leo
Violent Breed '83
Big Boss '77
Mr. Scarface '77
Kidnap Syndicate '76
Loaded Guns '75
Manhunt '73
Slaughter Hotel '71
Rino Di Silvestro (1932-)
The Legend of the Wolf Woman '77
Women in Cell Block 7 '77
Tom DiCillo (1954-)
The Real Blonde '97
Box of Moonlight '96
Living in Oblivion '94
Johnny Suede '92
Nigel Dick (1953-)
Dead Connection '94
Deadly Intent '88
Private Investigations '87
Ernest R. Dickerson (1952-)
Bones '01
Strange Justice: The Clarence Thomas and Anita Hill Story '99
Blind Faith '98
Futuresport '98
Bulletproof '96
Surviving the Game '94
Tales from the Crypt Presents Demon Knight '94
Juice '92
Thorold Dickinson (1903-84)
Hill 24 Doesn't Answer '55
The Queen of Spades '49
Men of Two Worlds '46
Gaslight '40
The Arsenal Stadium Mystery '39
High Command '37
Samuel Diege
Ride 'Em Cowgirl '41
The Singing Cowgirl '39
Water Rustlers '39
King of the Sierras '38
Carlos Diegues (1940-)
Orfeu '99
Tieta of Agreste '96
Subway to the Stars '87
Quilombo '84
Bye Bye Brazil '79
Xica '76
William Dieterle (1893-1972)
Quick, Let's Get Married '71
Mistress of the World '59
Omar Khayyam '57
Elephant Walk '54
Salome '53
Boots Malone '52
September Affair '50
The Accused '48
Portrait of Jennie '48
Love Letters '45
The Devil & Daniel Webster '41
The Hunchback of Notre Dame '39
Juarez '39
The Life of Emile Zola '37
Satan Met a Lady '36
The Story of Louis Pasteur '36
A Midsummer Night's Dream '35
Fashions of 1934 '34
Female '33
Scarlet Dawn '32
Erin Dignam
Loved '97
Denial: The Dark Side of Passion '91
John Francis Dillon (1887-1934)
Millie '31
Suds '20
Steve DiMarco
Prisoner of Love '99
Back in Action '94
Mark Dindal
The Emperor's New Groove '00
Cats Don't Dance '97
Michael Dinner
The Crew '00
Hot to Trot! '88
Off Beat '86
Heaven Help Us '85
Mark DiSalle
The Perfect Weapon '91
Kickboxer '89
Ivan Dixon (1931-)
Percy & Thunder '93
The Spook Who Sat by the Door '73
Edward Dmytryk (1908-99)
He Is My Brother '75
The Human Factor '75
Bluebeard '72
Anzio '68
Shalako '68
Alvarez Kelly '66
Mirage '66
The Carpetbaggers '64
Where Love Has Gone '64
Walk on the Wild Side '62
Warlock '59
The Young Lions '58
Raintree County '57
The Mountain '56
End of the Affair '55
The Left Hand of God '55
Soldier of Fortune '55
Broken Lance '54
The Caine Mutiny '54
Mutiny '52
The Hidden Room '49
Crossfire '47
Till the End of Time '46
Back to Bataan '45
Cornered '45
Murder, My Sweet '44
Behind the Rising Sun '43
Captive Wild Woman '43
Hitler's Children '43
Tender Comrade '43
Her First Romance '40
Trail of the Hawk '37
Lawrence (Larry) Dobkin (1919-)
The Waltons: The Christmas Carol '80
Sixteen '72
Kevin James Dobson (1952-)
Gold Diggers: The Secret of Bear Mountain '95
Miracle in the Wilderness '91
Squizzy Taylor '84
Demolition '77
Image of Death '77
The Mango Tree '77
James Dodson
Quest of the Delta Knights '93
Deadly Rivals '92
Donald M. Dohler
Deadly Neighbor '91
Fiend '83
Night Beast '83
The Alien Factor '78
Jacques Doillon (1944-)
Petits Freres '00
Ponette '95
La Vengeance d'une Femme '89
Roger Donaldson (1945-)
Thirteen Days '00
Dante's Peak '97
Species '95
The Getaway '93
White Sands '92
Cadillac Man '90
Cocktail '88
No Way Out '87
Marie '85
The Bounty '84
Nutcase '83
Smash Palace '82
Sleeping Dogs '77
Harris Done
Firetrap '01
Storm Tracker '99
Sand Trap '97
Vincent J. Donehue (1915-66)
Peter Pan '60
Sunrise at Campobello '60
Lonelyhearts '58
Stanley Donen (1924-)
Blame It on Rio '84
Saturn 3 '80
Movie, Movie '78
The Little Prince '74
Bedazzled '68
Two for the Road '67
Arabesque '66
Charade '63
The Grass Is Greener '61
Damn Yankees '58

Indiscreet '58
Funny Face '57
The Pajama Game '57
It's Always Fair Weather '55
Deep in My Heart '54
Seven Brides for Seven Brothers '54
Give a Girl a Break '53
Love Is Better Than Ever '52
Singin' in the Rain '52
Royal Wedding '51
On the Town '49

Thomas Michael Donnelly
A Soldier's Sweetheart '98
The Garden of Redemption '97

Tom Donnelly
Blindsided '93
Quicksilver '86

Clive Donner (1926-)
Charlemagne '95
Stealing Heaven '88
Babes in Toyland '86
Merlin and the Sword '85
A Christmas Carol '84
To Catch a King '84
Oliver Twist '82
The Scarlet Pimpernel '82
Charlie Chan and the Curse of the Dragon Queen '81
The Nude Bomb '80
The Thief of Baghdad '78
Rogue Male '76
Luv '67
What's New Pussycat? '65

Richard Donner (1939-)
Lethal Weapon 4 '98
Conspiracy Theory '97
Assassins '95
Maverick '94
Lethal Weapon 3 '92
Radio Flyer '92
Lethal Weapon 2 '89
Tales from the Crypt '89
Scrooged '88
Lethal Weapon '87
The Goonies '85
Ladyhawke '85
The Toy '82
Inside Moves '80
Superman: The Movie '78
The Omen '76
Lola '69

Jack Donohue (1908-84)
Assault on a Queen '66
Babes in Toyland '61
Lucky Me '54
Watch the Birdie '50
The Yellow Cab Man '50

Martin Donovan (1950-)
Somebody Is Waiting '96
The Substitute '93
Death Dreams '92
Mad at the Moon '92
Apartment Zero '88

Paul Donovan (1954-)
Tales from a Parallel Universe: I Worship His Shadow '97
Northern Extremes '93
George's Island '91
Norman's Awesome Experience '88
Def-Con 4 '85

Mark Donskoi (1901-81)
My Universities '40
My Apprenticeship '39
My Childhood '38

Daniel D'or
Battle Queen 2020 '99
Falling Fire '97

Jacques Dorfman
Druids '01
Shadow of the Wolf '92

Robert Dornhelm
Sins of the Father '01
The Break '97
Requiem for Dominic '91
Cold Feet '89
Echo Park '86

The Children of Theatre Street '77

Doris Dorrie (1955-)
Me and Him '89
Men... '85

Shimon Dotan
Sworn Enemies '96
Warriors '94
The Finest Hour '91

Russell S. Doughten, Jr.
Whitcomb's War '87
The Hostage '67

Gordon Douglas (1907-93)
Viva Knievel '77
Slaughter's Big Ripoff '73
Skullduggery '70
They Call Me Mr. Tibbs! '70
The Detective '68
Lady in Cement '68
Chuka '67
In Like Flint '67
Tony Rome '67
Harlow '65
Rio Conchos '64
Robin and the 7 Hoods '64
Call Me Bwana '63
Follow That Dream '61
Up Periscope '59
Sincerely Yours '56
The McConnell Story '55
Them! '54
Young at Heart '54
Great Missouri Raid '51
Kiss Tomorrow Goodbye '50
The Nevadan '50
Only the Valiant '50
The Doolins of Oklahoma '49
Black Arrow '48
If You Knew Susie '48
Dick Tracy vs. Cueball '46
First Yank into Tokyo '45
The Falcon in Hollywood '44
Girl Rush '44
Zombies on Broadway '44
The Great Gildersleeve '43
Broadway Limited '41
Saps at Sea '40

Lorenzo Doumani
Bug Buster '99
Storybook '95
Amore! '93
Mad About You '90

Alexander Dovzhenko (1849-1956)
Earth '30
Arsenal '29
Zvenigora '28

Kevin Dowling
Last Rites '98
Mojave Moon '96
The Sum of Us '94

Robert Downey (1936-)
Hugo Pool '97
Too Much Sun '90
Rented Lips '88
America '86
Up the Academy '80
Greaser's Palace '72
Putney Swope '69

Bert L. Dragin
Twice Dead '88
Summer Camp Nightmare '86

Srdjan Dragojevic
The Wounds '98
Pretty Village, Pretty Flame '96

Stan Dragoti (1932-)
Necessary Roughness '91
She's Out of Control '89
The Man with One Red Shoe '85
Mr. Mom '83
Love at First Bite '79

Jim Drake (-1976)
Based on an Untrue Story '93
Speed Zone '88
Police Academy 4: Citizens on Patrol '87

Oliver Drake (1903-91)
Mummy & Curse of the Jackal '67
Brand of Fear '49
Battling Marshal '48
Fighting Valley '43
Today I Hang '42

Tony Drazan (1955-)
Hurlyburly '98
Imaginary Crimes '94
Zebrahead '92

Arthur Dreifuss (1908-93)
Boss of Big Town '43
The Payoff '43
Baby Face Morgan '42
Reg'lar Fellers '41
Mystery in Swing '40
Double Deal '39

Jean Dreville (1906-97)
Sputnik '61
Seven Deadly Sins '53

Di Drew
Trouble in Paradise '88
The Right Hand Man '87

Carl Theodor Dreyer (1889-1968)
Gertrud '64
Ordet '55
Day of Wrath '43
Vampyr '31
Passion of Joan of Arc '28
Master of the House '25
Leaves from Satan's Book '19

Karim Dridi
Bye-Bye '96
Pigalle '95

Sara Driver (1955-)
When Pigs Fly '93
Sleepwalk '88

David Drury
The Unknown Soldier '98
Hostile Waters '97
Rhodes '97
Intrigue '90
Split Decisions '88
Defense of the Realm '85
Forever Young '85

Charles S. Dubin (1919-)
Drop-Out Mother '88
The Manions of America '81
The Gathering: Part 2 '79
Moving Violation '76
Murder Once Removed '71
Cinderella '64

Olivier Ducastel
The Adventures of Felix '99
Jeanne and the Perfect Guy '98

Roger Duchowny
It Came from Outer Space 2 '95
Camp Cucamonga: How I Spent My Summer Vacation '90

Peter Duffell
The Far Pavilions '84
Letters to an Unknown Lover '84
Experience Preferred... But Not Essential '83
Flambards '78
Inside Out '75
The House that Dripped Blood '71

Dennis Dugan (1946-)
Saving Silverman '01
Big Daddy '99
Beverly Hills Ninja '96
Happy Gilmore '96
Brain Donors '92
Problem Child '90

Michael Dugan
Mausoleum '83
Super Seal '77

Martine Dugowson
Portraits Chinois '96
Mina Tannenbaum '93

Christian Duguay
The Art of War '00
Joan of Arc '99
The Assignment '97
Screamers '96

Model by Day '94
Snowbound: The Jim and Jennifer Stolpa Story '94
Adrift '93
Live Wire '92
Scanners 3: The Takeover '92
Scanners 2: The New Order '91

John Duigan (1949-)
Molly '99
Lawn Dogs '96
The Leading Man '96
The Journey of August King '95
Sirens '94
Wide Sargasso Sea '92
Flirting '89
Romero '89
The Year My Voice Broke '87
Far East '85
One Night Stand '84
The Winter of Our Dreams '82

Bill Duke (1943-)
The Golden Spiders: A Nero Wolfe Mystery '00
Hoodlum '96
America's Dream '95
The Cemetery Club '93
Sister Act 2: Back in the Habit '93
Deep Cover '92
A Rage in Harlem '91
A Raisin in the Sun '89
Johnnie Gibson F.B.I. '87
Maximum Security '87
Killing Floor '85

Daryl Duke
Tai-Pan '86
The Thorn Birds '83
The Silent Partner '78
Griffin and Phoenix: A Love Story '76
I Heard the Owl Call My Name '73
Payday '72
The President's Plane Is Missing '71

Bruno Dumont
Humanity '99
The Life of Jesus '96

Georges Dumoulin
We Will Not Enter the Forest '79
Nous N'Irons Plus au Bois '69

Patrick Sheane Duncan
Live! From Death Row '92
84 Charlie MoPic '89

Peter Duncan (1954-)
Passion '99
A Little Bit of Soul '97
Children of the Revolution '95

Duwayne Dunham
Little Giants '94
Homeward Bound: The Incredible Journey '93

Griffin Dunne (1955-)
Lisa Picard Is Famous '01
Practical Magic '98
Addicted to Love '96

Philip Dunne (1908-92)
Wild in the Country '61
Ten North Frederick '58

David E. Durston
Stigma '73
I Drink Your Blood '71

Robert Duvall (1931-)
The Apostle '97
Angelo My Love '83

Julien Duvivier (1896-1967)
Diabolically Yours '67
The Burning Court '62
The Man in the Raincoat '57
Captain Blackjack '51
Little World of Don Camillo '51
Anna Karenina '48
Panique '47
Heart of a Nation '43

Tales of Manhattan '42
Lydia '41
The Great Waltz '38
Pepe Le Moko '37
Maria Chapdelaine '34
Poil de Carotte '31

Allan Dwan (1885-1981)
Enchanted Island '58
The Restless Breed '58
Slightly Scarlet '56
Escape to Burma '55
Pearl of the South Pacific '55
Tennessee's Partner '55
Cattle Queen of Montana '54
Passion '54
Silver Lode '54
I Dream of Jeannie '52
Montana Belle '52
Sands of Iwo Jima '49
Northwest Outpost '47
Brewster's Millions '45
Abroad with Two Yanks '44
Around the World '43
Here We Go Again! '42
Look Who's Laughing '41
Young People '40
The Gorilla '39
The Three Musketeers '39
Rebecca of Sunnybrook Farm '38
Heidi '37
Hollywood Party '34
The Iron Mask '29
Manhandled '24
Robin Hood '22

H. Kaye Dyal
Project: Eliminator '91
Trained to Kill '88
Memory of Us '74

B. Reeves Eason (1886-1956)
Rimfire '49
North of the Border '46
Darkest Africa '36
Fighting Marines '36
Red River Valley '36
Undersea Kingdom '36
The Miracle Rider '35
The Phantom Empire '35
Hollywood Mystery '34
Law of the Wild '34
Mystery Mountain '34
Cornered '32
The Last of the Mohicans '32
The Galloping Ghost '31
Vanishing Legion '31
Roaring Ranch '30
Spurs '30
Trigger Tricks '30
Test of Donald Norton '26

Allan Eastman (1950-)
Danger Zone '95
Crazy Moon '87
Ford: The Man & the Machine '87
The War Boy '85

Clint Eastwood (1930-)
Blood Work '02
Space Cowboys '00
True Crime '99
Absolute Power '97
Midnight in the Garden of Good and Evil '97
The Bridges of Madison County '95
A Perfect World '93
Unforgiven '92
The Rookie '90
White Hunter, Black Heart '90
Bird '88
Heartbreak Ridge '86
Pale Rider '85
Sudden Impact '83
Firefox '82
Honkytonk Man '82
Bronco Billy '80
The Gauntlet '77
The Outlaw Josey Wales '76
The Eiger Sanction '75
High Plains Drifter '73

Play Misty for Me '71

Thom Eberhardt
Ratz '99
Face Down '97
Captain Ron '92
Gross Anatomy '89
The Night Before '88
Without a Clue '88
Night of the Comet '84
Sole Survivor '84

Uli Edel (1947-)
Mists of Avalon '01
The Little Vampire '00
Purgatory '99
Rasputin: Dark Servant of Destiny '96
Tyson '95
Confessions of Sorority Girls '94
Body of Evidence '92
Last Exit to Brooklyn '90
Christiane F. '82

Don Edmonds
Terror on Tour '83
Bare Knuckles '77
Ilsa, Harem Keeper of the Oil Sheiks '76
Ilsa, She-Wolf of the SS '74
Tender Loving Care '73

Blake Edwards (1922-)
Son of the Pink Panther '93
Switch '91
Peter Gunn '89
Skin Deep '89
Sunset '88
Blind Date '87
A Fine Mess '86
That's Life! '86
Micki & Maude '84
Curse of the Pink Panther '83
The Man Who Loved Women '83
Trail of the Pink Panther '82
Victor/Victoria '82
S.O.B. '81
10 '79
Revenge of the Pink Panther '78
The Pink Panther Strikes Again '76
Return of the Pink Panther '74
The Tamarind Seed '74
Wild Rovers '71
Darling Lili '70
The Party '68
What Did You Do in the War, Daddy? '66
The Great Race '65
The Pink Panther '64
A Shot in the Dark '64
Days of Wine and Roses '62
Experiment in Terror '62
Breakfast at Tiffany's '61
Operation Petticoat '59
The Perfect Furlough '59
This Happy Feeling '58

Henry Edwards (1882-1952)
The Private Secretary '35
Scrooge '35

Christine Edzard (1945-)
Little Dorrit, Film 1: Nobody's Fault '88
Little Dorrit, Film 2: Little Dorrit's Story '88

Colin Eggleston
The Wicked '89
Innocent Prey '88
Cassandra '87
Sky Pirates '87
Bellamy '80

Jan Egleson
The Last Hit '93
A Shock to the System '90
Roanoak '86
The Tender Age '84

Atom Egoyan (1960-)
Felicia's Journey '99
The Sweet Hereafter '96
Exotica '94
Calendar '93
The Adjuster '91
Speaking Parts '89

Family Viewing '87
Next of Kin '84
Rafael Eisenman
Red Shoe Diaries: Swimming Naked '00
A Place Called Truth '98
Red Shoe Diaries 8: Night of Abandon '97
Business for Pleasure '96
Red Shoe Diaries 7: Burning Up '96
Red Shoe Diaries: Four on the Floor '96
Red Shoe Diaries: Strip Poker '96
Red Shoe Diaries 3: Another Woman's Lipstick '93
Lake Consequence '92
Sergei Eisenstein (1898-1948)
Ivan the Terrible, Part 2 '46
Ivan the Terrible, Part 1 '44
Alexander Nevsky '38
Que Viva Mexico '32
The General Line '29
Ten Days That Shook the World '27
The Battleship Potemkin '25
Strike '24
Richard Elfman
Modern Vampires '98
Shrunken Heads '94
Forbidden Zone '80
Harry Elfont
Josie and the Pussycats '01
Can't Hardly Wait '98
Michael Elias (1940-)
No Laughing Matter '97
Lush Life '94
Larry Elikann (1923-)
An Unexpected Family '96
Blue River '95
A Mother's Prayer '95
Tecumseh: The Last Warrior '95
Kiss of a Killer '93
The Story Lady '93
Fever '91
The Great Los Angeles Earthquake '91
One Against the Wind '91
Disaster at Silo 7 '88
God Bless the Child '88
Hands of a Stranger '87
Stamp of a Killer '87
Poison Ivy '85
Spraggue '84
Charlie and the Great Balloon Chase '82
The Great Wallendas '78
Doug Ellin (1968-)
Kissing a Fool '98
Phat Beach '96
Lang Elliott (1950-)
Cage 2: The Arena of Death '94
The Private Eyes '80
Stephan Elliott (1963-)
Eye of the Beholder '99
Welcome to Woop Woop '97
The Adventures of Priscilla, Queen of the Desert '94
Bob Ellis
The Nostradamus Kid '92
Warm Nights on a Slow-Moving Train '87
Maurice Elvey (1887-1967)
The Obsessed '51
Beware of Pity '46
Phantom Fiend '35
Transatlantic Tunnel '35
The Evil Mind '34
Lily of Killarney '34
John Emerson (1874-1956)
The Americano '17
Down to Earth '17
Reaching for the Moon '17
His Picture in the Papers '16
The Social Secretary '16
Robert Emery
Ride in a Pink Car '74
Scream Bloody Murder '72
Roland Emmerich (1955-)
The Patriot '00
Godzilla '98
Independence Day '96
Stargate '94
Universal Soldier '92
Moon 44 '90
Ghost Chase '88
Making Contact '86
Cy Endfield (1914-95)
Zulu '64
Mysterious Island '61
Try and Get Me '50
The Underworld Story '50
John English (1903-69)
Hills of Utah '51
Valley of Fire '51
Cow Town '50
Riders of the Whistling Pines '49
Rim of the Canyon '49
Loaded Pistols '48
Trail to San Antone '47
Don't Fence Me In '45
Utah '45
Captain America '44
Death Valley Manhunt '43
Man from Thunder River '43
Raiders of Sunset Pass '43
King of the Texas Rangers '41
Doctor Satan's Robot '40
Drums of Fu Manchu '40
Zorro's Fighting Legion '39
Daredevils of the Red Circle '38
Fighting Devil Dogs '38
The Lone Ranger '38
Arizona Days '37
Dick Tracy '37
Zorro Rides Again '37
Whistling Bullets '36
George Englund (1926-)
Dixie: Changing Habits '85
The Vegas Strip Wars '84
A Christmas to Remember '78
Zachariah '70
The Ugly American '63
Robert Enrico (1931-2001)
Old Gun '76
Le Secret '74
Jailbird's Vacation '65
Ray Enright (1896-1965)
Man from Cairo '54
Coroner Creek '48
Return of the Bad Men '48
South of St. Louis '48
Trail Street '47
China Sky '44
Gung Ho! '43
The Iron Major '43
The Spoilers '42
The Wagons Roll at Night '41
Earthworm Tractors '36
Dames '34
Tomorrow at Seven '33
Ildiko Enyedi (1955-)
Magic Hunter '96
My Twentieth Century '90
Nora Ephron (1941-)
Lucky Numbers '00
You've Got Mail '98
Michael '96
Mixed Nuts '94
Sleepless in Seattle '93
This Is My Life '92
Robert Epstein
The Celluloid Closet '95
Times of Harvey Milk '83
Rene Eram
Sweet Evil '95
Voodoo '95
John Erman (1935-)
Victoria & Albert '01
Only Love '98
Ellen Foster '97
The Boys Next Door '96
Breathing Lessons '94
Scarlett '94
Queen '93
Carolina Skeletons '92
Our Sons '91
When the Time Comes '91
The Last Best Year '90
Stella '89
The Attic: The Hiding of Anne Frank '88
An Early Frost '85
A Streetcar Named Desire '84
Eleanor: First Lady of the World '82
My Old Man '79
Child of Glass '78
Alexander: The Other Side of Dawn '77
Roots '77
Green Eyes '76
George Erschbamer (1954-)
Bounty Hunters 2: Hardball '97
Bounty Hunters '96
Flinch '94
Final Round '93
SnakeEater 3: His Law '92
SnakeEater '89
SnakeEater 2: The Drug Buster '89
Joakim (Jack) Ersgard
Backlash '99
Living in Peril '97
Invisible: The Chronicles of Benjamin Knight '93
Mandroid '93
The Visitors '89
Chester Erskine (1905-86)
Androcles and the Lion '52
A Girl in Every Port '52
Egg and I '47
Frankie and Johnny '36
Midnight '34
Dwain Esper (1893-1982)
Marihuana '36
Maniac '34
Harry Essex (1910-97)
The Cremators '72
Octaman '71
Emilio Estevez (1962-)
Rated X '00
The War at Home '96
Men at Work '90
Wisdom '87
Corey Michael Eubanks
Two Bits & Pepper '95
Bigfoot: The Unforgettable Encounter '94
Betsan Morris Evans
Lady Audley's Secret '00
Dad Savage '97
David Mickey Evans
Beethoven's 3rd '00
First Kid '96
The Sandlot '93
John Evans (1934-)
Blackjack '78
Black Godfather '74
Marc Evans
Resurrection Man '97
Thicker Than Water '93
Tim Everitt
Too Fast, Too Young '96
Fatally Yours '95
Valie Export (1940-)
The Practice of Love '84
Invisible Adversaries '77
Richard Eyre (1943-)
Iris '01
King Lear '98
Loose Connections '87
Singleton's Pluck '84
The Ploughman's Lunch '83
John Eyres
Ripper: Letter from Hell '01
Octopus '00
Judge & Jury '96
Project Shadowchaser 3000 '95
Night Siege Project: Shadowchaser 2 '94
Monolith '93
Project: Shadowchaser '92
Christian Faber
The Next Step '95
Bail Jumper '89
Roberto Faenza (1943-)
The Bachelor '93
Corrupt '84
Peter Faiman
Dutch '91
Crocodile Dundee '86
William Fairchild (1919-2000)
Horsemasters '61
The Silent Enemy '58
John and Julie '55
Ferdinand Fairfax (1944-)
Frenchman's Creek '98
The Last Place on Earth '94
Spymaker: The Secret Life of Ian Fleming '90
The Rescue '88
Nate and Hayes '83
Danger UXB '81
Harry Falk
High Desert Kill '90
Sophisticated Gents '81
Beulah Land '80
The Night the City Screamed '80
Centennial '78
Abduction of St. Anne '75
The Death Squad '73
Jamaa Fanaka (1942-)
Street Wars '91
Penitentiary 3 '87
Penitentiary 2 '82
Penitentiary '79
Black Sister's Revenge '76
Soul Vengeance '75
James Fargo (1938-)
Second Chances '98
Born to Race '88
Voyage of the Rock Aliens '87
Game for Vultures '86
Forced Vengeance '82
Every Which Way But Loose '78
The Enforcer '76
Ernest Farino
Josh Kirby...Time Warrior: Chapter 5, Journey to the Magic Cavern '96
Josh Kirby...Time Warrior: Chapter 1, Planet of the Dino-Knights '95
Steel and Lace '90
Donald Farmer
Vampire Cop '90
Scream Dream '89
Demon Queen '80
Bobby Farrelly (1958-)
Osmosis Jones '01
Shallow Hal '01
Me, Myself, and Irene '00
There's Something about Mary '98
Kingpin '96
Peter Farrelly (1957-)
Osmosis Jones '01
Shallow Hal '01
Me, Myself, and Irene '00
There's Something about Mary '98
Kingpin '96
Dumb & Dumber '94
John Farrow (1904-63)
John Paul Jones '59
Unholy Wife '57
Back from Eternity '56
Sea Chase '55
A Bullet Is Waiting '54
Botany Bay '53
Hondo '53
His Kind of Woman '51
Copper Canyon '50
The Big Clock '48
The Saint Strikes Back: Criminal Court '46
Two Years before the Mast '46
China '43
Commandos Strike at Dawn '43
Wake Island '42
Five Came Back '39
The Saint Strikes Back '39
John Fasano
Black Roses '88
The Jitters '88
Rock 'n' Roll Nightmare '85
Rainer Werner Fassbinder (1946-82)
Chinese Roulette '86
Querelle '83
Veronika Voss '82
Berlin Alexanderplatz '80
The Marriage of Maria Braun '79
Despair '78
Germany in Autumn '78
In a Year of 13 Moons '78
The Stationmaster's Wife '77
I Only Want You to Love Me '76
Mother Kusters Goes to Heaven '76
Satan's Brew '76
Fox and His Friends '75
Ali: Fear Eats the Soul '74
Effi Briest '74
The Bitter Tears of Petra von Kant '72
The Merchant of Four Seasons '71
The American Soldier '70
Beware of a Holy Whore '70
Whity '70
Gods of the Plague '69
Why Does Herr R. Run Amok? '69
John Fawcett
Ginger Snaps '01
The Boys Club '96
Neill Fearnley
Escape from Mars '99
Johnny 2.0 '99
Black Ice '92
Xie Fei (1942-)
A Mongolian Tale '94
Women from the Lake of Scented Souls '94
Girl from Hunan '86
Beda Docampo Feijoo
What Your Eyes Don't See '99
The Perfect Husband '92
Under the Earth '86
Felix Feist (1906-65)
Donovan's Brain '53
Big Trees '52
Guilty of Treason '50
Threat '49
The Devil Thumbs a Ride '47
George White's Scandals '45
Deluge '33
John Feldman
Dead Funny '94
Alligator Eyes '90
Marty Feldman (1933-82)
In God We Trust '80
The Last Remake of Beau Geste '77
Federico Fellini (1920-93)
Intervista '87
Ginger & Fred '86
And the Ship Sails On '83
City of Women '81
Orchestra Rehearsal '78
Amarcord '74
Fellini's Roma '72
The Clowns '71
Fellini Satyricon '69
Spirits of the Dead '68
Juliet of the Spirits '65
8 1/2 '63
Boccaccio '70 '62
La Dolce Vita '60
Nights of Cabiria '57
Il Bidone '55
La Strada '54
I Vitelloni '53
Love in the City '53
The White Sheik '52
Variety Lights '51
Georg Fenady (1930-)
Arnold '73
Terror in the Wax Museum '73
Leslie Fenton (1902-78)
On Our Merry Way '48
Tomorrow the World '44
Larry Ferguson (1940-)
Gunfighter's Moon '96
Beyond the Law '92
Guy Ferland
After the Storm '01
Delivered '98
Telling Lies in America '96
The Babysitter '95
Emilio Fernandez (1904-86)
Flor Silvestre '58
The Torch '50
The Pearl '48
Maria Candelaria '46
Abel Ferrara (1952-)
New Rose Hotel '98
The Blackout '97
Subway Stories '97
The Funeral '96
The Addiction '95
Body Snatchers '93
Dangerous Game '93
Bad Lieutenant '92
Cat Chaser '90
King of New York '90
China Girl '87
The Gladiator '86
Fear City '85
Ms. 45 '81
Driller Killer '79
Jose Ferrer (1909-92)
State Fair '62
Return to Peyton Place '61
Marco Ferreri (1928-97)
Tales of Ordinary Madness '83
La Grande Bouffe '73
L'Udienza '71
El Cochecito '60
Giorgio Ferroni (1908-81)
The Battle of El Alamein '68
Blood for a Silver Dollar '66
Secret Agent Super Dragon '66
Coriolanus, Man without a Country '64
The Bacchantes '63
Conquest of Mycene '63
The Trojan Horse '62
Mill of the Stone Women '60
Jacques Feyder (1885-1948)
Knight Without Armour '37
Carnival in Flanders '35
The Kiss '29
Crainquebille '23
Sally Field (1946-)
Beautiful '00
From the Earth to the Moon '98
Michael Fields
Bright Angel '91
Noon Wine '84
Mike Figgis (1948-)
Time Code '00
Miss Julie '99
The Loss of Sexual Innocence '98
One Night Stand '97
Leaving Las Vegas '95
The Browning Version '94
Mr. Jones '93
Liebestraum '91
Women & Men: In Love There Are No Rules '91
Internal Affairs '90
Stormy Monday '88
Charles Finch
Circle of Passion '97
Where Sleeping Dogs Lie '91
Priceless Beauty '90

Nigel Finch (1950-95)
Stonewall '95
The Lost Language of Cranes '92
David Fincher (1963-)
Panic Room '02
Fight Club '99
The Game '97
Seven '95
Alien 3 '92
Roberta Findlay
Lurkers '88
Prime Evil '88
Blood Sisters '86
The Oracle '85
Kenneth Fink
Tricks '97
Tall, Dark and Deadly '95
Stephen King's Golden Years '91
Ken Finkleman
Head Office '86
Airplane 2: The Sequel '82
Edward Finney
King of the Stallions '42
Riot Squad '41
Silver Stallion '41
Sam Firstenberg (1950-)
Agent of Death '99
Motel Blue '98
Operation: Delta Force '97
Cyborg Soldier '94
Blood Warriors '93
Cyborg Cop '93
American Samurai '92
Delta Force 3: The Killing Game '91
One More Chance '90
Riverbend '89
American Ninja 2: The Confrontation '87
My African Adventure '87
Avenging Force '86
American Ninja '85
Breakin' 2: Electric Boogaloo '84
Ninja 3: The Domination '84
Revenge of the Ninja '83
Michael Firth
Sylvia '86
Heart of the Stag '84
Michael Fischa
Delta Heat '92
Crack House '89
My Mom's a Werewolf '89
Death Spa '87
Max Fischer (1929-)
Taken '99
Psychopath '97
Entangled '93
Killing 'Em Softly '85
David Fisher (1948-)
Toy Soldiers '84
Liar's Moon '82
Terence Fisher (1904-80)
Frankenstein and the Monster from Hell '74
Frankenstein Must Be Destroyed '69
The Devil Rides Out '68
Island of the Burning Doomed '67
Dracula, Prince of Darkness '66
Frankenstein Created Woman '66
Island of Terror '66
The Gorgon '64
The Phantom of the Opera '62
Sherlock Holmes and the Deadly Necklace '62
The Curse of the Werewolf '61
The Brides of Dracula '60
Sword of Sherwood Forest '60
The Two Faces of Dr. Jekyll '60
The Hound of the Baskervilles '59
The Mummy '59
The Horror of Dracula '58
The Revenge of Frankenstein '58
The Curse of Frankenstein '57
Race for Life '55
Robin Hood: The Movie '55
Black Glove '54
Blackout '54
Unholy Four '54
Four Sided Triangle '53
Spaceways '53
Three Stops to Murder '53
Man Bait '52
A Stolen Face '52
Bill Fishman
Car 54, Where Are You? '94
Tapeheads '89
Jack Fisk (1945-)
Final Verdict '91
Daddy's Dyin'...Who's Got the Will? '90
Violets Are Blue '86
Raggedy Man '81
Christopher Fitchett
Fair Game '82
Blood Money '80
Thom Fitzgerald
Beefcake '99
The Hanging Garden '97
George Fitzmaurice (1885-1940)
The Last of Mrs. Cheyney '37
Suzy '36
As You Desire Me '32
Mata Hari '32
Raffles '30
Son of the Sheik '26
Paul Flaherty
Clifford '92
Who's Harry Crumb? '89
18 Again! '88
Robert Flaherty (1884-1951)
Louisiana Story '48
Elephant Boy '37
Man of Aran '34
Tabu: A Story of the South Seas '31
Moana, a Romance of the Golden Age '26
Gary Fleder
Don't Say a Word '01
Imposter '01
From the Earth to the Moon '98
Kiss the Girls '97
Things to Do in Denver When You're Dead '95
The Companion '94
Dave Fleischer (1894-1979)
Hoppity Goes to Town '41
Gulliver's Travels '39
Richard Fleischer (1916-)
Million Dollar Mystery '87
Red Sonja '85
Conan the Destroyer '84
Amityville 3: The Demon '83
Tough Enough '83
The Jazz Singer '80
Ashanti, Land of No Mercy '79
The Prince and the Pauper '78
The Incredible Sarah '76
Mandingo '75
Mr. Majestyk '74
The Don Is Dead '73
Soylent Green '73
The New Centurions '72
See No Evil '71
10 Rillington Place '71
Tora! Tora! Tora! '70
The Boston Strangler '68
Doctor Dolittle '67
Fantastic Voyage '66
Barabbas '62
Compulsion '59
The Vikings '58
Between Heaven and Hell '56
20,000 Leagues under the Sea '54
The Narrow Margin '52
Armored Car Robbery '50
The Clay Pigeon '49
Follow Me Quietly '49
Trapped '49
Andrew Fleming
Dick '99
The Craft '96
Threesome '94
Bad Dreams '88
Victor Fleming (1883-1949)
Joan of Arc '48
Adventure '45
A Guy Named Joe '44
Tortilla Flat '42
Dr. Jekyll and Mr. Hyde '41
Gone with the Wind '39
The Wizard of Oz '39
Test Pilot '38
Captains Courageous '37
The Farmer Takes a Wife '35
Reckless '35
Treasure Island '34
Bombshell '33
Red Dust '32
The Virginian '29
Hula '28
Mantrap '26
The Mollycoddle '20
When the Clouds Roll By '19
Gordon Flemyng (1934-95)
Cloud Waltzing '87
Philby, Burgess and MacLean: Spy Scandal of the Century '84
Daleks—Invasion Earth 2150 A.D. '66
Rodman Flender
Idle Hands '99
Leprechaun 2 '94
In the Heat of Passion '91
The Unborn '91
Clive Fleury
Big City Blues '99
Tunnel Vision '95
Fatal Past '94
Theodore J. Flicker (1930-)
Soggy Bottom U.S.A. '84
Playmates '72
Three in the Cellar '70
The President's Analyst '67
James T. Flocker
Ground Zero '88
Ghosts That Still Walk '77
The Secret of Navajo Cave '76
John Florea (1916-)
Hot Child in the City '87
Computer Wizard '77
Where's Willie? '77
The Invisible Strangler '76
Where the Eagle Flies '72
Island of the Lost '68
Isaac Florentine
Bridge of Dragons '99
Cold Harvest '98
High Voltage '98
The Fighter '95
Desert Kickboxer '92
Robert Florey (1900-79)
Outpost in Morocco '49
The Beast with Five Fingers '46
Ex-Lady '33
Murders in the Rue Morgue '32
The Cocoanuts '29
John Flynn
Absence of the Good '99
Brainscan '94
Scam '93
Nails '92
Out for Justice '91
Lock Up '89
Best Seller '87
Touched '82
Marilyn: The Untold Story '80
Defiance '79
Rolling Thunder '77
Lawrence Foldes (1959-)
Pre-Madonnas: Rebels Without a Clue '95
Nightforce '86
Young Warriors '83
The Great Skycopter Rescue '82
Peter Foldy
Seeds of Doubt '96
Tryst '94
Widow's Kiss '94
Midnight Witness '93
James Foley
The Corruptor '99
The Chamber '96
Fear '96
Two Bits '96
Glengarry Glen Ross '92
After Dark, My Sweet '90
Who's That Girl? '87
At Close Range '86
Reckless '84
Peter Fonda (1939-)
Wanda Nevada '79
Idaho Transfer '73
Hired Hand '71
Leo Fong (1928-)
Showdown '93
24 Hours to Midnight '92
Hawkeye '88
Jorge Fons
Midaq Alley '95
Jory '72
Anne Fontaine
Dry Cleaning '97
Augustin '95
Bryan Forbes (1926-)
The Naked Face '84
Better Late Than Never '83
International Velvet '78
The Slipper and the Rose '76
The Stepford Wives '75
Long Ago Tomorrow '71
The Madwoman of Chaillot '69
The Wrong Box '66
King Rat '65
Seance on a Wet Afternoon '64
The L-Shaped Room '62
Whistle down the Wind '61
John Ford (1895-1973)
December 7th: The Movie '91
Cheyenne Autumn '64
Donovan's Reef '63
How the West Was Won '63
The Man Who Shot Liberty Valance '62
Two Rode Together '61
Sergeant Rutledge '60
The Horse Soldiers '59
Last Hurrah '58
Wings of Eagles '57
The Searchers '56
The Long Gray Line '55
Mister Roberts '55
Mogambo '53
The Sun Shines Bright '53
The Quiet Man '52
What Price Glory? '52
Rio Grande '50
Wagon Master '50
She Wore a Yellow Ribbon '49
Fort Apache '48
The Fugitive '48
Three Godfathers '48
My Darling Clementine '46
They Were Expendable '45
How Green Was My Valley '41
The Grapes of Wrath '40
The Long Voyage Home '40
Drums Along the Mohawk '39
Stagecoach '39
Young Mr. Lincoln '39
The Hurricane '37
Wee Willie Winkie '37
Mary of Scotland '36
The Informer '35
The Whole Town's Talking '35
Judge Priest '34
The Lost Patrol '34
Arrowsmith '32
Straight Shootin' '17
Philip Ford (1900-76)
Rodeo King and the Senorita '51
Redwood Forest Trail '50
The Vanishing Westerner '50
Outcasts of the Trail '49
The Inner Circle '46
Walter Forde (1896-1984)
The Ghost Train '41
The Secret Four '40
King of the Damned '36
Bulldog Jack '35
Milos Forman (1932-)
Man on the Moon '99
The People vs. Larry Flynt '96
Valmont '89
Amadeus '84
Ragtime '81
Hair '79
One Flew Over the Cuckoo's Nest '75
The Firemen's Ball '68
Loves of a Blonde '65
Tom Forman (1893-1926)
The Fighting American '24
The Virginian '23
Shadows '22
Marc Forster
Monster's Ball '01
Everything Put Together '00
Bill Forsyth (1948-)
Being Human '94
Breaking In '89
Housekeeping '87
Comfort and Joy '84
Local Hero '83
Gregory's Girl '80
That Sinking Feeling '79
Ed Forsyth
Inferno in Paradise '88
Chesty Anderson USN '76
Superchick '71
John Fortenberry
A Night at the Roxbury '98
Jury Duty '95
Bob Fosse (1927-87)
Star 80 '83
All That Jazz '79
Lenny '74
Cabaret '72
Sweet Charity '69
Giles Foster
The Prince and the Pauper '01
Coming Home '98
The Rector's Wife '94
Innocent Victim '90
Consuming Passions '88
Dutch Girls '87
Northanger Abbey '87
Hotel du Lac '86
Silas Marner '85
Jodie Foster (1963-)
Home for the Holidays '95
Little Man Tate '91
Lewis R. Foster (1898-1974)
The Sign of Zorro '60
Tonka '58
Dakota Incident '56
Crashout '55
Cavalry Charge '51
Norman Foster (1900-76)
Brighty of the Grand Canyon '67
Indian Paint '64
The Sign of Zorro '60
The Nine Lives of Elfego Baca '58
Davy Crockett and the River Pirates '56
Davy Crockett, King of the Wild Frontier '55
Tell It to the Judge '49
Rachel and the Stranger '48
Journey into Fear '42
Mr. Moto's Last Warning '39
Claude Fournier
Tales of the Klondike: The Scorn of Women '87
Dan Candy's Law '73
Gene Fowler, Jr. (1917-98)
The Rebel Set '59
I Married a Monster from Outer Space '58
Showdown at Boot Hill '58
I Was a Teenage Werewolf '57
Wallace Fox (1895-1958)
Bad Men of the Border '45
Dead Man's Eyes/Pillow of Death '44
The Great Mike '44
Million Dollar Kid '44
Ghost Rider '43
Kid Dynamite '43
Bowery at Midnight '42
The Corpse Vanishes '42
Let's Get Tough '42
'Neath Brooklyn Bridge '42
Smart Alecks '42
Bowery Blitzkrieg '41
Gun Packer '38
Yellow Dust '36
Powdersmoke Range '35
William A. Fraker (1923-)
Legend of the Lone Ranger '81
A Reflection of Fear '72
Monte Walsh '70
Jonathon Frakes (1952-)
Clockstoppers '02
Star Trek: Insurrection '98
Star Trek: First Contact '96
Freddie Francis (1917-)
Dark Tower '87
The Doctor and the Devils '85
The Ghoul '75
Legend of the Werewolf '75
Craze '74
Tales That Witness Madness '73
The Creeping Flesh '72
Tales from the Crypt '72
The Vampire Happening '71
Girly '70
Dracula Has Risen from the Grave '68
They Came from Beyond Space '67
Torture Garden '67
Dr. Terror's House of Horrors '65
The Skull '65
The Evil of Frankenstein '64
Hysteria '64
Day of the Triffids '63
Nightmare '63
The Brain '62
Paranoiac '62
Pietro Francisci (1906-)
Hercules Unchained '59
Hercules '58
Jess (Jesus) Franco (1930-)
Tender Flesh '97
Angel of Death '86
Bloody Moon '83
Oasis of the Zombies '82
Revenge in the House of Usher '82
Sex Is Crazy '79
Ilsa, the Wicked Warden '78
Jack the Ripper '76
The Demons '74
Female Vampire '73
The Perverse Countess '73
The Screaming Dead '72
Count Dracula '71
Virgin among the Living Dead '71
Venus in Furs '70
99 Women '69
The Castle of Fu Manchu '68
Deadly Sanctuary '68
Kiss and Kill '68

Attack of the Robots *'66*
The Diabolical Dr. Z *'65*
Dr. Orloff's Monster *'64*
The Awful Dr. Orloff *'62*

Georges Franju (1912-87)
Judex *'64*
The Horror Chamber of Dr. Faustus *'59*

Christopher Frank (1943-93)
L'Annee des Meduses *'86*
Josepha *'82*

Hubert Frank
The Dolls *'83*
Melody in Love *'78*

Melvin Frank (1913-88)
Walk Like a Man *'87*
Lost and Found *'79*
The Duchess and the Dirtwater Fox *'76*
Prisoner of Second Avenue *'74*
A Touch of Class *'73*
Buona Sera, Mrs. Campbell *'68*
Strange Bedfellows *'65*
The Facts of Life *'60*
The Jayhawkers *'59*
Li'l Abner *'59*
Court Jester *'56*
Above and Beyond *'53*

Cyril Frankel
Permission To Kill *'75*
The Witches *'66*
The Very Edge *'63*
On the Fiddle *'61*
Make Me an Offer *'55*
Devil on Horseback *'54*

David Frankel (1960-)
Band of Brothers *'01*
From the Earth to the Moon *'98*
Miami Rhapsody *'95*

John Frankenheimer (1930-)
Reindeer Games *'00*
Ronin *'98*
George Wallace *'97*
The Island of Dr. Moreau *'96*
Andersonville *'95*
Against the Wall *'94*
The Burning Season *'94*
Year of the Gun *'91*
The Fourth War *'90*
Dead Bang *'89*
52 Pick-Up *'86*
The Holcroft Covenant *'85*
The Challenge *'82*
Prophecy *'79*
Black Sunday *'77*
French Connection 2 *'75*
99 & 44/100 Dead *'74*
The Story of a Love Story *'73*
The Horsemen *'70*
The Fixer *'68*
Grand Prix *'66*
Seconds *'66*
The Train *'65*
Seven Days in May *'64*
All Fall Down *'62*
Birdman of Alcatraz *'62*
The Manchurian Candidate *'62*
Days of Wine and Roses *'58*

Carl Franklin (1949-)
High Crimes *'02*
One True Thing *'98*
Devil in a Blue Dress *'95*
Laurel Avenue *'93*
One False Move *'91*
Full Fathom Five *'90*
Eye of the Eagle 2 *'89*
Nowhere to Run *'88*

Howard Franklin
Larger Than Life *'96*
The Public Eye *'92*
Quick Change *'90*

Jeff Franklin (1955-)
Love Stinks *'99*
Double Double Toil and Trouble *'94*
To Grandmother's House We Go *'94*

Richard Franklin (1948-)
Brilliant Lies *'96*
Sorrento Beach *'95*
F/X 2: The Deadly Art of Illusion *'91*
Link *'86*
Cloak & Dagger *'84*
Psycho 2 *'83*
Road Games *'81*
Patrick *'78*

Sidney Franklin (1893-1972)
The Good Earth *'37*
The Barretts of Wimpole Street *'34*
Smilin' Through *'33*
The Guardsman *'31*
Private Lives *'31*
Wild Orchids *'28*
The Forbidden City *'18*
The Primitive Lover *'16*

Harry Fraser (1889-1974)
Chained for Life *'51*
Ambush Trail *'46*
Enemy of the Law *'45*
Flaming Bullets *'45*
Frontier Fugitives *'45*
Three in the Saddle *'45*
Outlaw Roundup *'44*
Six Shootin' Sheriff *'38*
Aces Wild *'37*
Galloping Dynamite *'37*
Ghost Town *'37*
Heroes of the Alamo *'37*
Cavalcade of the West *'36*
The Riding Avenger *'36*
Feud of the West *'35*
Fighting Parson *'35*
Rustler's Paradise *'35*
The Tonto Kid *'35*
Wagon Trail *'35*
Wild Mustang *'35*
'Neath the Arizona Skies *'34*
Randy Rides Alone *'34*
Diamond Trail *'33*
Rainbow Ranch *'33*
Wolf Dog *'33*
Broadway to Cheyenne *'32*
Ghost City *'32*
Mason of the Mounted *'32*
The Savage Girl *'32*
The Wildcat *'26*

James Frawley
Mr. Headmistress *'98*
Sins of the Mind *'97*
Spies, Lies and Naked Thighs *'91*
Assault and Matrimony *'87*
Fraternity Vacation *'85*
Hansel and Gretel *'82*
Great American Traffic Jam *'80*
The Muppet Movie *'79*
The Big Bus *'76*

Stephen Frears (1941-)
High Fidelity *'00*
Liam *'00*
The Hi-Lo Country *'98*
Mary Reilly *'95*
The Van *'95*
The Snapper *'93*
Hero *'92*
The Grifters *'90*
Dangerous Liaisons *'88*
Prick Up Your Ears *'87*
Saigon: Year of the Cat *'87*
Sammy & Rosie Get Laid *'87*
The Hit *'85*
My Beautiful Laundrette *'85*
Gumshoe *'72*

Riccardo (Robert Hampton) Freda (1909-99)
The Ghost *'63*
Devil of the Desert Against the Son of Hercules *'62*
The Horrible Dr. Hichcock *'62*
Samson and the 7 Miracles of the World *'62*
The Giants of Thessaly *'60*
Maciste in Hell *'60*
The Mongols *'60*

Evil's Commandment *'56*
I Vampiri *'56*
Sins of Rome *'54*
Les Miserables *'52*

Herb Freed
Survival Game *'87*
Tomboy *'85*
Graduation Day *'81*
Beyond Evil *'80*
Haunts *'77*

Jerrold Freedman (1927-)
Thompson's Last Run *'90*
Best Kept Secrets *'88*
Family Sins *'87*
Native Son *'86*
Seduced *'85*
Legs *'83*
Borderline *'80*
The Streets of L.A. *'79*
He Who Walks Alone *'78*

Thornton Freeland (1898-1987)
Jericho *'38*
Accused *'36*
Flying Down to Rio *'33*
They Call It Sin *'32*
Be Yourself *'30*
Whoopee! *'30*

Joan Freeman (1941-)
Satisfaction *'88*
Streetwalkin' *'85*

Morgan J. Freeman (1969-)
American Psycho 2: All American Girl *'02*
Desert Blue *'98*
Hurricane Streets *'96*

Hugo Fregonese (1908-87)
Dracula vs. Frankenstein *'69*
Apache's Last Battle *'64*
Harry Black and the Tiger *'58*
Blowing Wild *'54*
Decameron Nights *'53*

Harold French (1900-97)
Paris Express *'53*
Rob Roy—The Highland Rogue *'53*
Encore *'52*
Trio *'50*
The Day Will Dawn *'42*
Secret Mission *'42*

Charles Frend (1909-77)
The Third Key *'57*
The Cruel Sea *'53*
Scott of the Antarctic *'48*
San Demetrio, London *'47*
Johnny Frenchman *'46*
The Foreman Went to France *'42*

Robert M. Fresco (1928-)
Dirty Little Secret *'98*
Evil Has a Face *'96*
Small Kill *'93*

Karl Freund (1890-1969)
Mad Love *'35*
The Mummy *'32*

Bart Freundlich
World Traveler *'01*
The Myth of Fingerprints *'97*

Fridrik Thor Fridriksson (1953-)
Devil's Island *'96*
Cold Fever *'95*
Children of Nature *'91*

Rick Friedberg
Spy Hard *'96*
Off the Wall *'82*
Pray TV *'80*

Richard Friedenberg
The Education of Little Tree *'97*
Mr. & Mrs. Loving *'96*
The Deerslayer *'78*
The Adventures of Frontier Fremont *'75*
Life & Times of Grizzly Adams *'74*

William Friedkin (1939-)
Rules of Engagement *'00*
Twelve Angry Men *'97*
Jade *'95*
Blue Chips *'94*
Jailbreakers *'94*
The Guardian *'90*
Python Wolf *'88*
Rampage *'87*
Stalking Danger *'86*
To Live & Die in L.A. *'85*
Deal of the Century *'83*
Cruising *'80*
Brink's Job *'78*
Sorcerer *'77*
The Exorcist *'73*
The French Connection *'71*
The Boys in the Band *'70*
The Night They Raided Minsky's *'69*
Good Times *'67*

Richard S. Friedman
Forever Together *'00*
Phantom of the Mall: Eric's Revenge *'89*
Doom Asylum *'88*
Scared Stiff *'87*
Deathmask *'69*

Seymour Friedman (1917-)
I'll Get You *'53*
Loan Shark *'52*
Rusty's Birthday *'49*

Harvey Frost
National Lampoon's Golf Punks *'99*
Midnight Heat *'95*
Tracks of a Killer *'95*

Lee Frost
Private Obsession *'94*
Dixie Dynamite *'76*
Black Gestapo *'75*
Policewomen *'73*
Chain Gang Women *'72*
The Thing with Two Heads *'72*
Chrome and Hot Leather *'71*

William Fruet (1933-)
Blue Monkey *'87*
Bedroom Eyes *'86*
Killer Party *'86*
Funeral Home *'82*
Spasms *'82*
Search and Destroy *'81*
Death Weekend *'76*
Wedding in White *'72*

Robert Fuest (1927-)
Revenge of the Stepford Wives *'80*
A Movie Star's Daughter *'79*
Devil's Rain *'75*
The Final Programme *'73*
Doctor Phibes Rises Again *'72*
The Abominable Dr. Phibes *'71*
And Soon the Darkness *'70*
Wuthering Heights *'70*

Kinji Fukasaku
Virus *'82*
Samurai Reincarnation *'81*
Tora! Tora! Tora! *'70*
Black Lizard *'68*
The Green Slime *'68*

Jun Fukuda (1924-2000)
Godzilla vs. Megalon *'76*
Godzilla vs. the Cosmic Monster *'74*
Godzilla on Monster Island *'72*
Godzilla vs. the Sea Monster *'66*
Son of Godzilla *'66*
The Secret of the Telegian *'61*

Lucio Fulci (1927-96)
Demonia *'90*
Voices from Beyond *'90*
Dangerous Obsession *'88*
Challenge to White Fang *'86*
Contraband *'86*
Conquest *'83*
The House by the Cemetery *'83*
The New Gladiators *'83*

The Beyond *'82*
Manhattan Baby *'82*
New York Ripper *'82*
The Black Cat *'81*
Gates of Hell *'80*
Zombie *'80*
The Psychic *'78*
Don't Torture a Duckling *'72*

Samuel Fuller (1911-97)
The Big Red One *'80*
The Meanest Men in the West *'76*
Dead Pigeon on Beethoven Street *'72*
Shark! *'68*
Naked Kiss *'64*
Shock Corridor *'63*
Merrill's Marauders *'62*
Underworld, U.S.A. *'60*
Verboten! *'59*
China Gate *'57*
Run of the Arrow *'56*
Pickup on South Street *'53*
Baron of Arizona *'51*
The Steel Helmet *'51*
I Shot Jesse James *'49*

Antoine Fuqua (1966-)
Training Day *'01*
Bait *'00*
The Replacement Killers *'98*

Sidney J. Furie (1933-)
Hide and Seek *'00*
My 5 Wives *'00*
The Collectors *'99*
Top of the World *'97*
The Rage *'96*
Hollow Point *'95*
Iron Eagle 4 *'95*
Ladybugs *'92*
The Taking of Beverly Hills *'91*
Iron Eagle 2 *'88*
Superman 4: The Quest for Peace *'87*
Iron Eagle *'86*
Purple Hearts *'84*
The Entity *'83*
The Boys in Company C *'77*
Hit! *'73*
Lady Sings the Blues *'72*
The Appaloosa *'66*
The Ipcress File *'65*
The Leather Boys *'63*
Doctor Blood's Coffin *'62*
The Snake Woman *'61*
A Dangerous Age *'57*

Tim Fywell
Madame Bovary *'00*
The Ice House *'97*
The Woman in White *'97*
Gallowglass *'95*
Norma Jean and Marilyn *'95*
Cracker: To Be a Somebody *'94*
A Dark Adapted Eye *'93*
A Fatal Inversion *'92*

Richard Gabai (1964-)
Virtual Girl *'00*
Vice Girls *'96*
Assault of the Party Nerds 2: Heavy Petting Detective *'95*
Hot Under the Collar *'91*
Virgin High *'90*
Assault of the Party Nerds *'89*

Pal Gabor (1932-87)
Brady's Escape *'84*
Angi Vera *'78*

Radu Gabrea
Secret of the Ice Cave *'89*
A Man Like Eva *'83*

Mike Gabriel
Pocahontas *'95*
The Rescuers Down Under *'90*

Rene Gainville
The Associate *'79*
Le Complot *'73*

John Gale
The Firing Line *'91*
Commando Invasion *'87*
Slash *'87*

John A. Gallagher
Blue Moon *'00*
The Deli *'97*
Street Hunter *'90*
Beach House *'82*

Fred Gallo (1965-)
Termination Man *'97*
Machine Gun Blues *'95*
Lady in Waiting *'94*
Dracula Rising *'93*
The Finishing Touch *'92*
Dead Space *'90*

George Gallo (1956-)
Double Take *'01*
Trapped in Paradise *'94*
29th Street *'91*

Samuel Gallu (1918-91)
The Man Outside *'68*
Theatre of Death *'67*

Abel Gance (1889-1981)
The Battle of Austerlitz *'60*
J'Accuse *'37*
Beethoven *'36*
Napoleon *'27*
The Torture of Silence *'17*

Pierre Gang
Armistead Maupin's More Tales of the City *'97*
Sous Sol *'96*

Albert C. Gannaway
Man or Gun *'58*
Daniel Boone: Trail Blazer *'56*
Hidden Guns *'56*

Christophe Gans
Brotherhood of the Wolf *'01*
H.P. Lovecraft's Necronomicon: Book of the Dead *'93*

Nicole Garcia (1946-)
Place Vendome *'98*
The Favorite Son *'94*
Every Other Weekend *'91*

Herb Gardner
I'm Not Rappaport *'96*
The Goodbye People *'83*

Richard Harding Gardner
Sherlock: Undercover Dog *'94*
Deadly Daphne's Revenge *'93*

Lee Garmes (1898-1978)
Actors and Sin *'52*
Angels Over Broadway *'40*
Dreaming Lips *'37*

Tay Garnett (1898-1977)
Challenge To Be Free *'76*
The Big Push *'75*
Main Street to Broadway *'53*
One Minute to Zero *'52*
Cause for Alarm *'51*
A Connecticut Yankee in King Arthur's Court *'49*
The Postman Always Rings Twice *'46*
The Valley of Decision *'45*
Mrs. Parkington *'44*
Bataan *'43*
Cheers for Miss Bishop *'41*
Seven Sinners *'40*
Slightly Honorable *'40*
Eternally Yours *'39*
Joy of Living *'38*
Stand-In *'37*
China Seas *'35*
The Flying Fool *'29*

Roy Garrett
White Slave *'86*
Eyes Behind the Stars *'72*

Mick Garris
Quicksilver Highway *'98*
Stephen King's The Stand *'94*
Sleepwalkers *'92*
Psycho 4: The Beginning *'90*
Critters 2: The Main Course *'88*

Harry Garson (1882-1938)
The Worldly Madonna *'22*

Variety '83
Bryan Gordon
Pie in the Sky '95
Career Opportunities '91
The Discovery Program '89
Keith Gordon (1961-)
Waking the Dead '00
Mother Night '96
Wild Palms '93
A Midnight Clear '92
The Chocolate War '88
Michael Gordon (1911-93)
The Impossible Years '68
Texas across the River '66
For Love or Money '63
Boys' Night Out '62
Portrait in Black '60
Pillow Talk '59
Cyrano de Bergerac '50
Underground Agent '42
Robert Gordon (1895-1971)
The Gatling Gun '72
It Came from Beneath the Sea '55
The Joe Louis Story '53
Stuart Gordon (1947-)
The Wonderful Ice Cream Suit '98
Space Truckers '97
Castle Freak '95
Fortress '93
The Pit & the Pendulum '91
Robot Jox '90
Daughter of Darkness '89
Dolls '87
From Beyond '86
Re-Animator '84
John Gorrie
Cause Celebre '87
Edward the King '75
Marleen Gorris (1948-)
The Luzhin Defence '00
Mrs. Dalloway '97
Antonia's Line '95
Broken Mirrors '85
Question of Silence '83
Hideo Gosha (-1992)
The Wolves '82
Hunter in the Dark '80
Jurgen Goslar (1927-)
Slavers '77
Albino '76
Raja Gosnell
Scooby-Doo '02
Big Momma's House '00
Never Been Kissed '99
Home Alone 3 '97
Carl Gottlieb (1938-)
Amazon Women on the Moon '87
Caveman '81
Franz Gottlieb
The Phantom of Soho '64
The Black Abbot '63
Curse of the Yellow Snake '63
Lisa Gottlieb
Cadillac Ranch '96
Across the Moon '94
Just One of the Guys '85
Michael Gottlieb
A Kid in King Arthur's Court '95
Mr. Nanny '93
Mannequin '87
Heywood Gould
Mistrial '96
Trial by Jury '94
One Good Cop '91
Alfred Goulding (1896-1972)
Dick Barton, Special Agent '48
A Chump at Oxford '40
Edmund Goulding (1891-1959)
We're Not Married '52
The Razor's Edge '46
Forever and a Day '43
The Great Lie '41
Dark Victory '39
The Old Maid '39
Dawn Patrol '38
That Certain Woman '37
Riptide '34
Grand Hotel '32
Reaching for the Moon '31
Anne Goursaud
Another 9 1/2 Weeks '96
Embrace of the Vampire '95
Poison Ivy 2: Lily '95
Red Shoe Diaries 6: How I Met My Husband '95
Gustavo Graef-Marino
Diplomatic Siege '99
Johnny 100 Pesos '93
William A. Graham (1930-)
The Man Who Captured Eichmann '96
Return to the Blue Lagoon '91
Montana '90
Gore Vidal's Billy the Kid '89
Proud Men '87
George Washington: The Forging of a Nation '86
Last Days of Frank & Jesse James '86
Calendar Girl Murders '84
Secrets of a Married Man '84
Harry Tracy '83
M.A.D.D.: Mothers Against Drunk Driving '83
The Guyana Tragedy: The Story of Jim Jones '80
Rage '80
Orphan Train '79
And I Alone Survived '78
One in a Million: The Ron LeFlore Story '78
The Amazing Howard Hughes '77
21 Hours at Munich '76
Beyond the Bermuda Triangle '75
Get Christie Love! '74
Larry '74
Mr. Inside, Mr. Outside '74
Where the Lilies Bloom '74
Birds of Prey '72
Deadly Encounter '72
Honky '71
Jigsaw '71
Thief '71
Change of Habit '69
Waterhole #3 '67
The Doomsday Flight '66
Pierre Granier-Deferre (1927-)
A Woman at Her Window '77
The French Detective '75
Le Chat '75
The Last Train '74
Widow Couderc '74
Brian Grant
The Immortals '95
Sensation '94
Love Kills '91
Sweet Poison '91
Julian Grant
Airborne '98
Electra '95
Lee Grant (1927-)
The Loretta Claiborne Story '00
Staying Together '89
Tell Me a Riddle '80
Alex Grasshof (1930-)
A Billion for Boris '90
Pepper and His Wacky Taxi '72
Jorge Grau
Let Sleeping Corpses Lie '74
The Legend of Blood Castle '72
Walter Grauman (1922-)
Nightmare on the 13th Floor '90
Outrage! '86
Scene of the Crime '85
Pleasure Palace '80
To Race the Wind '80
Are You in the House Alone? '78
Most Wanted '76
Force Five '75
Manhunter '74
The Streets of San Francisco '72
Paper Man '71
Lady in a Cage '64
633 Squadron '64
Gary Graver
The Escort '97
Sexual Roulette '96
Evil Spirits '91
Roots of Evil '91
Crossing the Line '90
Party Camp '87
Moon in Scorpio '86
Trick or Treats '82
Alex Graves
Casualties '97
The Crude Oasis '95
F. Gary Gray (1970-)
The Negotiator '98
Set It Off '96
Friday '95
James Gray
The Yards '00
Little Odessa '94
John Gray
Brian's Song '01
The Seventh Stream '01
The Hunley '99
The Glimmer Man '96
Born to Be Wild '95
A Place for Annie '94
An American Story '92
The Lost Capone '90
When He's Not a Stranger '89
Billy Galvin '86
Godfrey Grayson (1913-98)
Room to Let '49
Dick Barton Strikes Back '48
Kjell Grede
Good Evening, Mr. Wallenberg '93
Hip Hip Hurrah! '87
Alfred E. Green (1889-1960)
Invasion U.S.A. '52
The Jackie Robinson Story '50
Four Faces West '48
Copacabana '47
The Fabulous Dorseys '47
The Jolson Story '46
A Thousand and One Nights '45
Mr. Winkle Goes to War '44
South of Pago Pago '40
The Duke of West Point '38
Thoroughbreds Don't Cry '37
Dangerous '35
Baby Face '33
Disraeli '30
Ella Cinders '26
Bruce Seth Green
In Self Defense '93
The Hunt for the Night Stalker '91
Running Against Time '90
David Green (1948-)
Breathtaking '00
Fire Birds '90
Buster '88
Car Trouble '86
Code of Honor '84
Guy Green (1913-)
Strong Medicine '84
The Incredible Journey of Dr. Meg Laurel '79
Once Is Not Enough '75
Luther '74
Walk in the Spring Rain '70
A Patch of Blue '65
Diamond Head '62
The Mark '61
S.O.S. Pacific '60
Sea of Sand '58
Postmark for Danger '56
River Beat '54
Joseph Green (1900-96)
The Brain that Wouldn't Die '63
A Brivele der Mamen '38
Mamele '38
Der Purimshpiler '37
Yidl Mitn Fidl '36
Peter Greenaway (1942-)
8 1/2 Women '99
The Pillow Book '95
The Belly of an Architect '91
Prospero's Books '91
The Cook, the Thief, His Wife & Her Lover '90
A Zed & Two Noughts '88
Drowning by Numbers '87
The Draughtsman's Contract '82
David Greene (1921-)
Bella Mafia '97
Family of Cops 2: Breach of Faith '97
A Good Day to Die '95
What Ever Happened To... '93
In a Stranger's Hand '92
The Penthouse '92
Small Sacrifices '89
Vanishing Act '88
After the Promise '87
Miles to Go '86
World War III '86
TripleCross '85
Fatal Vision '84
The Guardian '84
Prototype '83
Rehearsal for Murder '82
Take Your Best Shot '82
The Choice '81
Hard Country '81
Friendly Fire '79
Gray Lady Down '77
Roots '77
The Count of Monte Cristo '74
Godspell '73
Madame Sin '71
The People Next Door '70
Blood Island '68
Sebastian '68
Martin Greene
Undercover Cop '94
Dark Sanity '82
Paul Greengrass
The Murder of Stephen Lawrence '01
The Theory of Flight '98
Maggie Greenwald (1955-)
Songcatcher '99
The Ballad of Little Jo '93
The Kill-Off '90
Home Remedy '88
Robert Greenwald (1948-)
Steal This Movie! '00
Breaking Up '97
Hear No Evil '93
Forgotten Prisoners '90
Sweet Hearts Dance '88
The Burning Bed '85
In the Custody of Strangers '82
Xanadu '80
Flatbed Annie and Sweetiepie: Lady Truckers '79
David Greenwalt
Rude Awakening '89
Secret Admirer '85
William Grefe (1930-)
Whiskey Mountain '77
Jaws of Death '76
Impulse '74
Alligator Alley '72
Stanley '72
Wild Rebels '71
The Death Curse of Tartu '66
The Checkered Flag '63
Colin Gregg (1947-)
We Think the World of You '88
Lamb '85
To the Lighthouse '83
Ezio Greggio
Screw Loose '99
Silence of the Hams '93
Jean Gremillon (1901-59)
Pattes Blanches '49
Stormy Waters '41
Edmond T. Greville (1906-66)
The Liars '64
Beat Girl '60
The Hands of Orlac '60
Princess Tam Tam '35
John Greyson (1960-)
Lilies '96
Zero Patience '94
Sergio Grieco (1917-82)
Mad Dog '84
Man of Legend '71
Tom Gries (1922-77)
The Greatest '77
Breakheart Pass '76
Helter Skelter '76
Breakout '75
The Migrants '74
QB VII '74
The Connection '73
Lady Ice '73
The Glass House '72
Fools '70
100 Rifles '69
Will Penny '67
Andrew Grieve (1939-)
Horatio Hornblower: The Adventure Continues '01
Horatio Hornblower '99
Lorna Doone '90
Suspicion '87
Charles B. Griffith
Wizards of the Lost Kingdom 2 '89
Smokey Bites the Dust '81
Dr. Heckyl and Mr. Hype '80
Up from the Depths '79
Eat My Dust '76
D.W. Griffith (1875-1948)
Struggle '31
Abraham Lincoln '30
Battle of the Sexes '28
The Sorrows of Satan '26
Sally of the Sawdust '25
America '24
Isn't Life Wonderful '24
The White Rose '23
Dream Street '21
Orphans of the Storm '21
The Idol Dancer '20
The Love Flower '20
Way Down East '20
Broken Blossoms '19
The Greatest Question '19
True Heart Susie '19
Hearts of the World '18
Intolerance '16
The Birth of a Nation '15
Avenging Conscience '14
Home Sweet Home '14
Judith of Bethulia '14
Battle of Elderbush Gulch '13
Edward H. Griffith (1894-1975)
The Sky's the Limit '43
Bahama Passage '42
Young & Willing '42
My Love For Yours '39
The Animal Kingdom '32
Captain Swagger '25
Mark Griffiths
Tactical Assault '99
Behind Enemy Lines '96
Max Is Missing '95
Cheyenne Warrior '94
Ultraviolet '91
A Cry in the Wild '90
Heroes Stand Alone '89
Hardbodies 2 '86
Hardbodies '84
Running Hot '83
Aurelio Grimaldi (1957-)
Nerolio '96
Acla's Descent into Floristella '87
Nick Grinde (1893-1979)
Hitler: Dead or Alive '43
Before I Hang '40
The Man They Could Not Hang '39
Delinquent Parents '38
Exiled to Shanghai '37
Stone of Silver Creek '35
Alan Grint
Catherine Cookson's The Secret '00
Catherine Cookson's Tilly Trotter '99
Catherine Cookson's The Round Tower '98
John Grissmer
Blood Rage '87
Scalpel '76
Ferde Grofe, Jr.
Judgment Day '88
The Proud and the Damned '72
Satan's Harvest '65
Warkill '65
Ulu Grosbard (1929-)
The Deep End of the Ocean '98
Georgia '95
Falling in Love '84
True Confessions '81
Straight Time '78
The Subject Was Roses '68
Jerry Gross
Teenage Mother '67
Girl on a Chain Gang '65
Charles Grosvenor
Land Before Time 7: The Stone of Cold Fire '00
The Land Before Time 5: The Mysterious Island '97
Once Upon a Forest '93
Ruy Guerra (1931-)
The Fable of the Beautiful Pigeon Fancier '88
Opera do Malandro '87
Erendira '83
Christopher Guest (1948-)
Best in Show '00
Almost Heroes '97
Waiting for Guffman '96
Attack of the 50 Ft. Woman '93
The Big Picture '89
Val Guest (1911-)
Killer Force '75
When Dinosaurs Ruled the Earth '70
Casino Royale '67
The Day the Earth Caught Fire '61
Expresso Bongo '59
Up the Creek '58
The Abominable Snowman '57
Carry On Admiral '57
Men of Sherwood Forest '57
Quatermass 2 '57
The Quatermass Experiment '56
The Runaway Bus '54
Mister Drake's Duck '50
Just William's Luck '47
John Guillermin (1925-)
The Tracker '88
King Kong Lives '86
Sheena '84
Crossover '82
Death on the Nile '78
King Kong '76
The Towering Inferno '74
Shaft in Africa '73
El Condor '70
The Bridge at Remagen '69
The Blue Max '66
Guns at Batasi '64
Waltz of the Toreadors '62
Never Let Go '60
Fred Guiol (1898-1964)
Mr. Walkie Talkie '52
Tanks a Million '41

Battling Orioles '24
Sacha Guitry (1885-1957)
Napoleon '55
The Story of a Cheat '36
Yilmaz Guney (1937-84)
The Wall '83
Baba '73
Sturla Gunnarsson
Rare Birds '01
Dangerous Evidence: The Lori Jackson Story '99
Such a Long Journey '98
Joe Torre: Curveballs Along the Way '97
Sebastian Gutierrez
She Creature '01
Judas Kiss '98
Tomas Gutierrez Alea (1926-96)
Guantanamera '95
Strawberry and Chocolate '93
Letters from the Park '88
Up to a Certain Point '83
The Last Supper '76
Memories of Underdevelopment '68
Death of a Bureaucrat '66
Nathaniel Gutman
When the Dark Man Calls '95
Linda '93
Deadline '87
Amos Guttman (1954-93)
Amazing Grace '92
Drifting '82
Claudio Guzman
The Hostage Tower '80
Willa '79
Antonio '73
Stephen Gyllenhaal (1949-)
Warden of Red Rock '01
Homegrown '97
Losing Isaiah '94
A Dangerous Woman '93
Question of Faith '93
Waterland '92
Paris Trout '91
A Killing in a Small Town '90
Promised a Miracle '88
The Abduction of Kari Swenson '87
Certain Fury '85
Charles Haas (1913-)
Platinum High School '60
Girls' Town '59
Tarzan and the Trappers '58
Philip Haas
Up at the Villa '00
The Blood Oranges '97
Angels and Insects '95
The Music of Chance '93
Taylor Hackford (1944-)
Proof of Life '00
The Devil's Advocate '97
Dolores Claiborne '94
Blood In ... Blood Out: Bound by Honor '93
Everybody's All American '88
Chuck Berry: Hail! Hail! Rock 'n' Roll '87
White Nights '85
Against All Odds '84
An Officer and a Gentleman '82
Idolmaker '80
Jeremy Haft
The Crimson Code '99
Grizzly Mountain '97
Ross Hagen (1938-)
B.O.R.N. '88
The Glove '78
Piers Haggard (1939-)
Conquest '98
Four Eyes and Six Guns '93
Back Home '90
Fulfillment '89
A Summer Story '88
Venom '82
The Fiendish Plot of Dr. Fu Manchu '80
Quatermass Conclusion '79
The Blood on Satan's Claw '71
Stuart Hagmann (1942-)
Tarantulas: The Deadly Cargo '77
The Strawberry Statement '70
Charles Haid (1943-)
Sally Hemings: An American Scandal '00
Buffalo Soldiers '97
Riders of the Purple Sage '96
Children of Fury '94
Cooperstown '93
Iron Will '93
The Nightman '93
Michael Haigney
Pokemon 3: The Movie '01
Pokemon the Movie 2000: The Power of One '00
Pokemon: The First Movie '99
Randa Haines (1945-)
Dance with Me '98
Wrestling Ernest Hemingway '93
The Doctor '91
Children of a Lesser God '86
Richard W. Haines
Alien Space Avenger '91
Class of Nuke 'Em High '86
Splatter University '84
Don Haldane
The Reincarnate '71
Nikki, the Wild Dog of the North '61
Alan Hale (1892-1950)
Risky Business '28
Braveheart '25
Billy Hale
The Murder of Mary Phagan '87
Harem '86
S.O.S. Titanic '79
Red Alert '77
Sonnie Hale (1902-59)
Sailing Along '38
Gangway '37
William Hale
One Shoe Makes It Murder '82
Murder in Texas '81
Stalk the Wild Child '76
Jack Haley, Jr. (1933-2001)
That's Dancing! '85
That's Entertainment '74
The Love Machine '71
H.B. Halicki (1941-89)
Deadline Auto Theft '83
The Junkman '82
Gone in 60 Seconds '74
Alexander Hall (1894-1968)
Forever Darling '56
Because You're Mine '52
The Great Lover '49
Down to Earth '47
They All Kissed the Bride '42
Here Comes Mr. Jordan '41
Doctor Takes a Wife '40
I Am the Law '38
Goin' to Town '35
Little Miss Marker '34
Godfrey Hall
Undefeatable '94
Honor and Glory '92
Ivan Hall
Kill and Kill Again '81
Kill or Be Killed '80
Funeral for an Assassin '77
Kenneth J. Hall
Ghost Writer '89
Evil Spawn '87
Peter Hall (1930-)
Never Talk to Strangers '95
Jacob '94
Orpheus Descending '91
A Midsummer Night's Dream '68
Daniel Haller (1926-)
Margin for Murder '81
Follow That Car '80
Buck Rogers in the 25th Century '79
The Dunwich Horror '70
Paddy '70
Devil's Angels '67
Die, Monster, Die! '65
Lasse Hallstrom (1946-)
The Shipping News '01
Chocolat '00
The Cider House Rules '99
Something to Talk About '95
What's Eating Gilbert Grape '93
Once Around '91
More about the Children of Noisy Village '87
The Children of Noisy Village '86
My Life As a Dog '85
Victor Halperin (1895-1983)
Buried Alive '39
Torture Ship '39
A Nation Aflame '37
I Conquer the Sea '36
Revolt of the Zombies '36
Supernatural '33
The White Zombie '32
Party Girls '29
Robert Hamer (1911-63)
To Paris with Love '55
The Detective '54
Kind Hearts and Coronets '49
Dead of Night '45
Pink String and Sealing Wax '45
Dean Hamilton
D.R.E.A.M. Team '99
The Road Home '95
Strike a Pose '93
Guy Hamilton (1922-)
Remo Williams: The Adventure Begins '85
Evil under the Sun '82
The Mirror Crack'd '80
Force 10 from Navarone '78
The Man with the Golden Gun '74
Live and Let Die '73
Diamonds Are Forever '71
Battle of Britain '69
Funeral in Berlin '66
Goldfinger '64
The Devil's Disciple '59
The Colditz Story '55
John Hamilton
Codename: Jaguar '00
Perpetrators of the Crime '98
The Kid '97
Strathford Hamilton
Escape from Atlantis '97
The Proposition '96
The Set Up '95
Temptation '94
Betrayal of the Dove '92
Diving In '90
Blueberry Hill '88
Nick Hamm
The Very Thought of You '98
Talk of Angels '96
Peter Hammond
The Dark Angel '91
Cold Comfort Farm '71
Christopher Hampton (1946-)
The Secret Agent '96
Carrington '95
Victor Hanbury (1954-)
Hotel Reserve '44
The Avenging Hand '43
John Hancock (1939-)
Prancer '89
Steal the Sky '88
Weeds '87
California Dreaming '79
Bang the Drum Slowly '73
Let's Scare Jessica to Death '71
David Hand (1900-86)
Bambi '42
Snow White and the Seven Dwarfs '37
Tom Hanks (1956-)
Band of Brothers '01
From the Earth to the Moon '98
That Thing You Do! '96
Fallen Angels 2 '93
William Hanna (1910-2001)
Jetsons: The Movie '90
Hey There, It's Yogi Bear '64
Ken Hannam
The Assassination Run '84
Dawn! '83
Sunday Too Far Away '74
Marion Hansel (1949-)
The Quarry '98
Between Heaven and Earth '93
Dust '85
Ed Hansen (1937-)
Hell's Belles '95
The Bikini Car Wash Company '90
Party Plane '90
Party Favors '89
Robo-Chic '89
Curtis Hanson (1945-)
Wonder Boys '00
L.A. Confidential '97
The River Wild '94
The Hand that Rocks the Cradle '92
Bad Influence '90
The Bedroom Window '87
The Children of Times Square '86
Losin' It '82
Little Dragons '80
The Arousers '70
John Hanson (1922-98)
Wildrose '85
Northern Lights '79
Joseph Hardy (1929-90)
To Love Again '80
Love's Savage Fury '79
Return Engagement '78
Users '78
Robin Hardy (1929-)
The Fantasist '89
The Wicker Man '75
Rod Hardy
High Noon '00
Two for Texas '97
Buffalo Girls '95
The Yearling '94
Thirst '87
Under Capricorn '82
Sara Dane '81
David Hare (1947-)
The Designated Mourner '97
Strapless '90
Wetherby '85
Tsui Hark (1951-)
Time and Tide '00
Knock Off '98
Double Team '97
Green Snake '93
Once Upon a Time in China III '93
Once Upon a Time in China II '92
Twin Dragons '92
Once Upon a Time in China '91
A Better Tomorrow, Part 3 '89
Zu: Warriors from the Magic Mountain '83
Veit Harlan (1899-1964)
The Third Sex '57
Kolberg '45
Jud Suess '40
Renny Harlin (1959-)
Driven '01
Deep Blue Sea '99
The Long Kiss Goodnight '96
Cutthroat Island '95
Cliffhanger '93
The Adventures of Ford Fairlane '90
Die Hard 2: Die Harder '90
A Nightmare on Elm Street 4: Dream Master '88
Prison '88
Born American '86
John Harlow (1896-)
Old Mother Riley, Headmistress '50
Old Mother Riley's New Venture '49
While I Live '47
Appointment with Crime '45
Candles at Nine '44
Meet Sexton Blake '44
Spellbound '41
Robert Harmon
The Crossing '00
Gotti '96
Nowhere to Run '93
Eyes of an Angel '91
The Hitcher '86
Curtis Harrington (1928-)
Devil Dog: The Hound of Hell '78
Ruby '77
The Dead Don't Die '75
The Killing Kind '73
What's the Matter with Helen? '71
Who Slew Auntie Roo? '71
Games '67
Planet of Blood '66
Voyage to the Prehistoric Planet '65
Night Tide '63
Damian Harris
Mercy '00
Bad Company '94
Deceived '91
The Discovery Program '89
The Rachel Papers '89
Frank Harris
Lockdown '90
Aftershock '88
The Patriot '86
Killpoint '84
Harry Harris (1922-)
A Day for Thanks on Walton's Mountain '82
The Runaways '75
James B. Harris (1928-)
Boiling Point '93
Cop '88
Fast Walking '82
Some Call It Loving '73
Black Box Affair '66
Bedford Incident '65
Trent Harris (1952-)
Plan 10 from Outer Space '95
Rubin & Ed '92
John Harrison
Dune '00
The Assassination File '96
Donor Unknown '95
Tales from the Darkside: The Movie '90
John Kent Harrison
In Love and War '01
A House Divided '00
You Know My Name '99
What the Deaf Man Heard '98
William Faulkner's Old Man '97
Hole in the Sky '95
Johnny's Girl '95
City Boy '93
The Sound and the Silence '93
Beautiful Dreamers '92
Ken Harrison (1942-)
On Valentine's Day '86
1918 '85
Matthew Harrison (1960-)
Kicked in the Head '97
Rhythm Thief '94
Spare Me '92
Mary Harron
American Psycho '99
I Shot Andy Warhol '96
Lee Harry
Street Soldiers '91
Silent Night, Deadly Night 2 '87
Harvey Hart (1928-)
Passion in Paradise '89
Stone Fox '87
Beverly Hills Madam '86
Shoot '85
Reckless Disregard '84
Utilities '83
Born Beautiful '82
High Country '81
Aliens Are Coming '80
East of Eden '80
Standing Tall '78
Goldenrod '77
The Prince of Central Park '77
The City '76
Murder or Mercy '74
Panic on the 5:22 '74
The Pyx '73
Fortune and Men's Eyes '71
William S. Hart (-1946)
Blue Blazes Rawden '18
Narrow Trail '17
Hell's Hinges '16
Return of Draw Egan '16
The Disciple '15
Kenneth Hartford
Hell Squad '85
The Lucifer Complex '78
Robert Hartford-Davis (1923-77)
The Fiend '71
The Bloodsuckers '70
Estate of Insanity '70
Karl Hartl (1898-1978)
The Life and Loves of Mozart '59
The Mozart Story '48
F.P. 1 '33
F.P. 1 Doesn't Answer '33
Hal Hartley (1959-)
No Such Thing '01
Henry Fool '98
Flirt '95
Amateur '94
Simple Men '92
Surviving Desire '91
Trust '91
The Unbelievable Truth '90
Don Hartman (1900-58)
Holiday Affair '49
Every Girl Should Be Married '48
Anthony Harvey (1931-)
Grace Quigley '84
Svengali '83
Richard's Things '80
Eagle's Wing '79
Players '79
The Disappearance of Aimee '76
They Might Be Giants '71
The Lion in Winter '68
Byron Haskin (1899-1984)
Robinson Crusoe on Mars '64
Captain Sinbad '63
Armored Command '61
Jet Over the Atlantic '59
From the Earth to the Moon '58
Conquest of Space '55
Long John Silver '54
Naked Jungle '54
His Majesty O'Keefe '53
The War of the Worlds '53
The Denver & Rio Grande '51
Treasure Island '50
Too Late for Tears '49
Henry Hathaway (1898-1985)
Raid on Rommel '71

Shoot Out '71
True Grit '69
Five Card Stud '68
The Last Safari '67
Nevada Smith '66
Sons of Katie Elder '65
Circus World '64
Of Human Bondage '64
How the West Was Won '63
North to Alaska '60
Seven Thieves '60
Legend of the Lost '57
The Racers '55
Prince Valiant '54
Diplomatic Courier '52
Niagara '52
The Desert Fox '51
Rawhide '50
Call Northside 777 '48
Kiss of Death '47
Dark Corner '46
13 Rue Madeleine '46
House on 92nd Street '45
A Wing and a Prayer '44
The Shepherd of the Hills '41
Sundown '41
Brigham Young: Frontiersman '40
The Real Glory '39
Spawn of the North '38
Souls at Sea '37
Go West, Young Man '36
The Trail of the Lonesome Pine '36
The Lives of a Bengal Lancer '35
Now and Forever '34
Buffalo Stampede '33
Heritage of the Desert '33
Man of the Forest '33
To the Last Man '33
When the West Was Young '32

Wings Hauser (1948-)
Gang Boys '97
Living to Die '91
The Art of Dying '90
Coldfire '90

Don Hawks
Hush Little Baby, Don't You Cry '86
Beasts '83

Howard Hawks (1896-1977)
Rio Lobo '70
El Dorado '67
Red Line 7000 '65
Man's Favorite Sport? '63
Hatari! '62
Rio Bravo '59
Land of the Pharaohs '55
Gentlemen Prefer Blondes '53
The Big Sky '52
Monkey Business '52
The Thing '51
I Was a Male War Bride '49
Red River '48
A Song Is Born '48
The Big Sleep '46
To Have & Have Not '44
Air Force '43
Ball of Fire '41
Sergeant York '41
His Girl Friday '40
Only Angels Have Wings '39
Bringing Up Baby '38
Come and Get It '36
Barbary Coast '35
Ceiling Zero '35
Twentieth Century '34
Today We Live '33
Criminal Code '31
Scarface '31

Richard Haydn (1905-85)
Mr. Music '50
Dear Wife '49

Sidney Hayers (1921-2000)
Deadly Strangers '82
The Seekers '79
Bananas Boat '78
King Arthur, the Young Warlord '75
Revenge '71
Assault '70
Trap '66
Burn Witch, Burn! '62
Circus of Horrors '60

John Hayes
End of the World '76
Dream No Evil '75
Mama's Dirty Girls '74
Grave of the Vampire '72
Tomb of the Undead '72
All the Lovin' Kinfolk '70
Sweet Trash '70
The Cut Throats '69
Five Minutes to Love '63

John Patrick Hayes
The Farmer's Other Daughter '65
Hollywood after Dark '65

David Hayman (1950-)
The Hawk '93
A Woman's Guide to Adultery '93

Peter Hayman
Cybercity '99
Shepherd '99

Gregory C. Haynes
Heaven or Vegas '98
Magenta '96

Todd Haynes (1961-)
Velvet Goldmine '98
Safe '95
Poison '91

Jonathan Heap
Past Perfect '98
Hostile Intent '97
Benefit of the Doubt '93

David Heavener
Fugitive X '96
Dragon Fury '95
Eye of the Stranger '93
Prime Target '91
Deadly Reactor '89
Killcrazy '89
Twisted Justice '89
Outlaw Force '87

Ben Hecht (1894-1964)
Actors and Sin '52
Spectre of the Rose '46
Angels Over Broadway '40

Amy Heckerling (1954-)
Loser '00
Clueless '95
Look Who's Talking, Too '90
Look Who's Talking '89
National Lampoon's European Vacation '85
Johnny Dangerously '84
Fast Times at Ridgemont High '82

Rob Hedden
Alien Fury: Countdown to Invasion '00
Kidnapped in Paradise '98
Any Place But Home '97
The Colony '95
Friday the 13th, Part 8: Jason Takes Manhattan '89

Richard T. Heffron (1930-)
Tagget '90
Broken Angel '88
Pancho Barnes '88
Convicted: A Mother's Story '87
Guilty of Innocence '87
Samaritan: The Mitch Snyder Story '86
V: The Final Battle '84
I, the Jury '82
Whale for the Killing '81
Foolin' Around '80
A Rumor of War '80
See How She Runs '78
Outlaw Blues '77
Futureworld '76
Death Scream '75
I Will Fight No More Forever '75
Newman's Law '74

Chris Hegedus
Moon over Broadway '98
The War Room '93

Yosif Heifitz (1905-95)
The Lady with the Dog '59
Baltic Deputy '37

Stuart Heisler (1894-1979)
Hitler '62
The Burning Hills '56
Lone Ranger '56
I Died a Thousand Times '55
Island of Desire '52
Chain Lightning '50
Tokyo Joe '49
Tulsa '49
Smash-Up: The Story of a Woman '47
Blue Skies '46
Along Came Jones '45
The Glass Key '42
The Monster and the Girl '41

Mats Helge
The Russian Terminator '90
Ninja Mission '84

Brian Helgeland (1961-)
A Knight's Tale '01
Payback '98

Martin Hellberg (1905-99)
Minna von Barnhelm or The Soldier's Fortune '62
Intrigue and Love '59

Olle Hellbom (1925-82)
Brothers Lionheart '77
Pippi Goes on Board '75
Pippi in the South Seas '74
Pippi Longstocking '73

Monte Hellman (1932-)
Iguana '89
Silent Night, Deadly Night 3: Better Watch Out! '89
Gunfire '78
Cockfighter '74
Two Lane Blacktop '71
Flight to Fury '66
Ride in the Whirlwind '66
The Shooting '66
The Terror '63
The Beast from Haunted Cave '60
Creature from the Haunted Sea '60

Oliver (Ovidio Assonitis) Hellman
Desperate Moves '86
Tentacles '77
Beyond the Door '75

Ralph Hemecker
Double Edge '97
Dead On '93

David Hemmings (1941-)
Lone Justice 3: Showdown at Plum Creek '96
A Christmas Reunion '93
Dark Horse '92
The Key to Rebecca '85
Treasure of the Yankee Zephyr '83
Survivor '80
Just a Gigolo '79

Joseph Henabery (1888-1976)
Leather Burners '43
Cobra '25
His Majesty, the American '19
The Man from Painted Post '17

Clark Henderson
Circle of Fear '89
Primary Target '89
Saigon Commandos '88
Warlords from Hell '87

Don Henderson (1931-97)
The Touch of Satan '70
Weekend with the Babysitter '70

John Henderson
The Magical Legend of the Leprechauns '99
The Return of the Borrowers '96
Loch Ness '95
The Borrowers '93

Frank Henenlotter
Basket Case 3: The Progeny '92
Basket Case 2 '90
Frankenhooker '90
Brain Damage '88
Basket Case '82

Paul Henreid (1908-92)
Ballad in Blue '66
Battle Shock '56
Tall Lie '53

Buck Henry (1930-)
First Family '80
Heaven Can Wait '78

Brian Henson
Jack and the Beanstalk: The Real Story '01
Muppet Treasure Island '96
The Muppet Christmas Carol '92

Jim Henson (1936-90)
Labyrinth '86
The Dark Crystal '82
The Great Muppet Caper '81

Henry Herbert
Danger UXB '81
Emily '77

Stephen Herek (1958-)
Life or Something Like It '02
Rock Star '01
Holy Man '98
101 Dalmatians '96
Mr. Holland's Opus '95
The Three Musketeers '93
The Mighty Ducks '92
Don't Tell Mom the Babysitter's Dead '91
Bill & Ted's Excellent Adventure '89
Critters '86

Al(bert) Herman (1887-1967)
The Missing Corpse '45
The Phantom of 42nd Street '45
Delinquent Daughters '44
Rogue's Gallery '44
Shake Hands with Murder '44
Dawn Express '42
Gentleman from Dixie '41
Take Me Back to Oklahoma '40
Down the Wyoming Trail '39
Man from Texas '39
Roll, Wagons, Roll '39
Renfrew on the Great White Trail '38
Rollin' Plains '38
Utah Trail '38
Valley of Terror '38
Renfrew of the Royal Mounted '37
The Clutching Hand '36
Gun Play '36
Outlaws of the Range '36
Cowboy & the Bandit '35
Western Frontier '35
Whispering Shadow '33
Beyond the Trail '26

Jean Herman
Butterfly Affair '71
Honor Among Thieves '68

Mark Herman
Little Voice '98
Brassed Off '96
Blame It on the Bellboy '92

Jaime Humberto Hermosillo (1942-)
Esmeralda Comes by Night '98
The Summer of Miss Forbes '88
Dona Herlinda & Her Son '86
Mary, My Dearest '83

Denis Heroux
Naked Massacre '80s
The Uncanny '78

Rowdy Herrington (1951-)
A Murder of Crows '99
Striking Distance '93
Gladiator '92
Road House '89
Jack's Back '87

W(illiam) Blake Herron
A Texas Funeral '99
Skin Art '93

Joel Hershman
Greenfingers '00
Hold Me, Thrill Me, Kiss Me '93

Marshall Herskovitz (1952-)
Dangerous Beauty '98
Jack the Bear '93

Michael Herz (1949-)
Sgt. Kabukiman N.Y.P.D. '94
The Toxic Avenger, Part 2 '89
The Toxic Avenger, Part 3: The Last Temptation of Toxie '89
Troma's War '88
The Toxic Avenger '86
Stuck on You '84
First Turn On '83
Sugar Cookies '77

John Herzfeld
15 Minutes '01
Don King: Only in America '97
Two Days in the Valley '96
Casualties of Love: The "Long Island Lolita" Story '93
The Preppie Murder '89
A Father's Revenge '88
Two of a Kind '83

Werner Herzog (1942-)
Cobra Verde '88
Where the Green Ants Dream '84
Fitzcarraldo '82
Nosferatu the Vampyre '79
Woyzeck '78
Stroszek '77
Every Man for Himself & God Against All '75
Heart of Glass '74
Aguirre, the Wrath of God '72
Signs of Life '68

Jon Hess
Crash & Byrnes '99
Legion '98
Mars '96
Excessive Force '93
Alligator 2: The Mutation '90
Assassin '89
The Lawless Land '88
Watchers '88

Gordon Hessler (1930-)
Journey of Honor '91
Tales of the Unexpected '91
The Girl in a Swing '89
Out on Bail '89
The Misfit Brigade '87
Rage of Honor '87
Pray for Death '85
Escape from El Diablo '83
KISS Meets the Phantom of the Park '78
Puzzle '78
Secrets of Three Hungry Wives '78
Betrayal '74
Medusa '74
Golden Voyage of Sinbad '73
Embassy '72
Murders in the Rue Morgue '71
Cry of the Banshee '70
Scream and Scream Again '70
The Oblong Box '69

Charlton Heston (1924-)
A Man for All Seasons '88
Mother Lode '82
Antony and Cleopatra '73

Fraser Heston
Alaska '96
Needful Things '93
The Crucifer of Blood '91
Treasure Island '89

David L. Hewitt
The Lucifer Complex '78
Alien Massacre '67
Journey to the Center of Time '67
Monsters Crash the Pajama Party '65
Horrors of the Red Planet '64

Peter Hewitt
Princess of Thieves '01
The Borrowers '97
Tom and Huck '95
Wild Palms '93
Bill & Ted's Bogus Journey '91

Rod Hewitt
The Debt '98
Strip Search '97
The Dangerous '95
Verne Miller '88

Douglas Heyes (-1993)
Powder Keg '70
Kitten with a Whip '64

Laurent Heynemann
The Old Lady Who Walked in the Sea '91
Birgitt Haas Must Be Killed '83

Jesse Hibbs (1906-85)
Walk the Proud Land '56
To Hell and Back '55
Ride Clear of Diablo '54

Jochen Hick
No One Sleeps '01
Via Appia '92

George Hickenlooper (1964-)
The Big Brass Ring '99
Dogtown '97
Persons Unknown '96
The Low Life '95
Some Folks Call It a Sling Blade '94
The Ghost Brigade '93
Hearts of Darkness: A Filmmaker's Apocalypse '91

Anthony Hickox (1959-)
Federal Protection '02
The Contaminated Man '01
Jill the Ripper '00
Storm Catcher '99
Prince Valiant '97
Invasion of Privacy '96
Payback '94
Full Eclipse '93
Warlock: The Armageddon '93
Hellraiser 3: Hell on Earth '92
Sundown '91
Waxwork 2: Lost in Time '91
Waxwork '88

Douglas Hickox (1929-88)
Blackout '85
Sins '85
Mistral's Daughter '84
The Hound of the Baskervilles '83
Zulu Dawn '79
Sky Riders '76
Brannigan '75
Theatre of Blood '73
Entertaining Mr. Sloane '70

James D.R. Hickox
Blood Surf '00
Children of the Corn 3: Urban Harvest '95

Scott Hicks (1953-)
Hearts in Atlantis '01
Snow Falling on Cedars '99
Shine '95

Howard Higgin (1891-1938)
Carnival Lady '33

Hell's House '32
Painted Desert '31
High Voltage '29
The Racketeer '29
Power '28

Colin Higgins (1941-88)
The Best Little Whorehouse in Texas '82
9 to 5 '80
Foul Play '78

George Hill (1895-1934)
The Big House '30
Min & Bill '30

George Roy Hill (1922-)
Funny Farm '88
The Little Drummer Girl '84
The World According to Garp '82
A Little Romance '79
Slap Shot '77
The Great Waldo Pepper '75
The Sting '73
Slaughterhouse Five '72
Butch Cassidy and the Sundance Kid '69
Thoroughly Modern Millie '67
Hawaii '66
The World of Henry Orient '64
Toys in the Attic '63
Period of Adjustment '62

Jack Hill (1933-)
Switchblade Sisters '75
Foxy Brown '74
The Swinging Cheerleaders '74
Coffy '73
The Big Bird Cage '72
The Big Doll House '71
The Fear Chamber '68
The Sinister Invasion '68
Pit Stop '67
Portrait in Terror '66
Track of the Vampire '66
Spider Baby '64
The Terror '63

James Hill (1919-94)
The Wild and the Free '80
The Belstone Fox '73
Black Beauty '71
An Elephant Called Slowly '69
The Corrupt Ones '67
Born Free '66
A Study in Terror '66
Seaside Swingers '65
Trial & Error '62

Robert F. "Bob" Hill (1886-1966)
East Side Kids '40
Flash Gordon: Mars Attacks the World '39
Wild Horse Canyon '39
Cheyenne Rides Again '38
Man's Country '38
The Phantom of the Range '38
Whirlwind Horseman '38
Feud of the Trail '37
The Roamin' Cowboy '37
Blake of Scotland Yard '36
A Face in the Fog '36
Kelly of the Secret Service '36
Prison Shadows '36
Rip Roarin' Buckaroo '36
Rogue's Tavern '36
Shadow of Chinatown '36
Danger Trails '35
Queen of the Jungle '35
Demon for Trouble '34
Cheyenne Kid '33
Tarzan the Fearless '33
Come on Danger! '32
The Adventures of Tarzan '21

Terence Hill (1941-)
Lucky Luke '94
Troublemakers '94

Timothy Hill
Max Keeble's Big Move '01
Muppets from Space '99

Walter Hill (1942-)
Supernova '99
Last Man Standing '96
Wild Bill '95
Geronimo: An American Legend '93
Trespass '92
Another 48 Hrs. '90
Johnny Handsome '89
Tales from the Crypt '89
Red Heat '88
Extreme Prejudice '87
Crossroads '86
Brewster's Millions '85
Streets of Fire '84
48 Hrs. '82
Southern Comfort '81
The Long Riders '80
The Warriors '79
The Driver '78
Hard Times '75

Arthur Hiller (1923-)
An Alan Smithee Film: Burn, Hollywood, Burn '97
Carpool '96
Married to It '93
The Babe '92
Taking Care of Business '90
See No Evil, Hear No Evil '89
Outrageous Fortune '87
The Lonely Guy '84
Teachers '84
Romantic Comedy '83
Author! Author! '82
Making Love '82
The In-Laws '79
Nightwing '79
Silver Streak '76
The Man in the Glass Booth '75
Man of La Mancha '72
The Hospital '71
Plaza Suite '71
Love Story '70
The Out-of-Towners '70
Popi '69
Promise Her Anything '66
Tobruk '66
The Americanization of Emily '64
The Miracle of the White Stallions '63
The Wheeler Dealers '63

William B. Hillman
Ragin' Cajun '90
Double Exposure '82
Photographer '75

Lambert Hillyer (1889-1969)
Range Renegades '48
Sundown Riders '48
Hat Box Mystery '47
Land of the Lawless '47
Border Bandits '46
Gentleman from Texas '46
South of the Rio Grande '45
The Stranger from Pecos '45
Partners of the Trail '44
Range Law '44
Six Gun Gospel '43
Texas Kid '43
Gang Bullets '38
Dracula's Daughter '36
The Invisible Ray '36
Fighting Fool '32
Hello Trouble '32
White Eagle '32
The Shock '23
Three Word Brand '21
The Toll Gate '20
Wagon Tracks '19

Arthur Hilton
Big Chase '54
Cat Women of the Moon '53
Return of Jesse James '50

Bill (William Heinzman) Hinzman
Revenge of the Living Zombies '88
The Majorettes '87

Alexander Gregory (Gregory Dark) Hippolyte (1954-)
Animal Instincts 3: The Seductress '95
Object of Obsession '95
Animal Instincts 2 '94
Secret Games 3 '94
Undercover '94
Mirror Images 2 '93
Secret Games 2: The Escort '93
Animal Instincts '92
Night Rhythms '92
Secret Games '92
Carnal Crimes '91
Mirror Images '91

Leslie Hiscott (1894-1968)
Butler's Dilemma '43
Department Store '35
The Triumph of Sherlock Holmes '35

Alfred Hitchcock (1899-1980)
Family Plot '76
Frenzy '72
Topaz '69
Torn Curtain '66
Marnie '64
The Birds '63
Psycho '60
North by Northwest '59
Vertigo '58
The Man Who Knew Too Much '56
The Wrong Man '56
To Catch a Thief '55
The Trouble with Harry '55
Dial "M" for Murder '54
Rear Window '54
I Confess '53
Strangers on a Train '51
Stage Fright '50
Under Capricorn '49
Rope '48
The Paradine Case '47
Notorious '46
Spellbound '45
Alfred Hitchcock's Aventure Malgache '44
Alfred Hitchcock's Bon Voyage '44
Lifeboat '44
Shadow of a Doubt '43
Saboteur '42
Mr. & Mrs. Smith '41
Suspicion '41
Foreign Correspondent '40
Rebecca '40
Jamaica Inn '39
The Lady Vanishes '38
Young and Innocent '37
Sabotage '36
The Secret Agent '36
The 39 Steps '35
The Man Who Knew Too Much '34
No. 17 '32
Rich and Strange '32
Skin Game '31
Juno and the Paycock '30
Murder '30
Blackmail '29
The Manxman '29
Champagne '28
The Farmer's Wife '28
Three by Hitchcock '28
Easy Virtue '27
The Ring '27
The Lodger '26

Rupert Hitzig
Nowhere Land '98
Backstreet Dreams '90
Night Visitor '89

Jack Hively (1910-95)
Four Jacks and a Jill '41
The Saint Takes Over '40
The Saint's Double Trouble '40

Jack B. Hively
California Gold Rush '81
The Adventures of Huckleberry Finn '78
Starbird and Sweet William '73
Lassie: Adventures of Neeka '68

Godfrey Ho
Lethal Panther '90
Ninja Champion '80s
Ninja Destroyer '70s

Gregory Hoblit
Hart's War '02
Fallen '97
Primal Fear '96
Class of '61 '92
Roe vs. Wade '89
L.A. Law '86

Victoria Hochberg
Sweet 15 '90
Jacob Have I Loved '88

Mike Hodges (1932-)
Croupier '97
Black Rainbow '91
Florida Straits '87
Prayer for the Dying '87
Morons from Outer Space '85
Missing Pieces '83
Flash Gordon '80
The Terminal Man '74
Pulp '72
Get Carter '71

Jeno Hodi
Triplecross '95
American Kickboxer 2: To the Death '93
Deadly Obsession '88

Arthur Hoerl
Drums O'Voodoo '34
Before Morning '33

Herman Hoffman
The Invisible Boy '57
It's a Dog's Life '55

Jerzy Hoffman (1932-)
Leper '76
The Deluge '73
Colonel Wolodyjowski '69

John Hoffman
Strange Confession '45
Calling Dr. Death/Strange Confession '43

Michael Hoffman
William Shakespeare's A Midsummer Night's Dream '99
One Fine Day '96
Restoration '94
Soapdish '91
Promised Land '88
Some Girls '88

Yvette Hoffman
The Catcher '98
Starved '97

Gray Hofmeyr
Yankee Zulu '95
Dirty Games '93
The Light in the Jungle '91

Jack Hofsiss (1950-)
Cat on a Hot Tin Roof '84
Family Secrets '84
I'm Dancing as Fast as I Can '82

David Hogan
Most Wanted '97
Barb Wire '96

James Hogan (1891-1943)
The Mad Ghoul '43
The Texas Rangers Ride Again '40
Bulldog Drummond's Bride '39
Bulldog Drummond's Secret Police '39
Arrest Bulldog Drummond '38
Bulldog Drummond's Peril '38
The Texans '38
Bulldog Drummond Escapes '37
Arizona Mahoney '36
The Broken Mask '28

P.J. Hogan
My Best Friend's Wedding '97
Muriel's Wedding '94

Rod Holcomb
Convict Cowboy '95
Dead to Rights '93
Royce '93
Chains of Gold '92
China Beach '88
Blind Justice '86
Chase '85
Stark '85
Two Fathers' Justice '85
Cartier Affair '84
The Red Light Sting '84
Captain America '79

Agnieszka Holland (1948-)
Shot in the Heart '01
The Third Miracle '99
Washington Square '97
Total Eclipse '95
The Secret Garden '93
Olivier, Olivier '92
Europa, Europa '91
To Kill a Priest '89
Angry Harvest '85
Fever '81
Provincial Actors '79

Steve Holland
Safety Patrol '98
How I Got into College '89
One Crazy Summer '86
Better Off Dead '85

Todd Holland
Krippendorf's Tribe '98
The Wizard '89

Tom Holland (1943-)
Stephen King's Thinner '96
Stephen King's The Langoliers '95
The Temp '93
Child's Play '88
Fatal Beauty '87
Fright Night '85

Allan Holleb
School Spirit '85
Candy Stripe Nurses '74

Ben Holmes (1890-1943)
Maid's Night Out '38
The Saint in New York '38

Fred Holmes
Harley '90
Dakota '88

Nicole Holofcener
Lovely & Amazing '02
Walking and Talking '96

Jason Holt
Swindle '92
Wager of Love '90

Seth Holt (1923-71)
Blood from the Mummy's Tomb '71
The Nanny '65
Scream of Fear '61

Allan Holzman
Intimate Stranger '91
Programmed to Kill '86
Grunt! The Wrestling Movie '85
Out of Control '85
Forbidden World '82

Edward Holzman
Body Strokes '95
Friend of the Family '95
Seduce Me: Pamela Principle 2 '94

Inoshiro Honda (1911-93)
Terror of Mechagodzilla '78
Yog, Monster from Space '71
War of the Gargantuas '70
Godzilla's Revenge '69
Destroy All Monsters '68
Godzilla vs. Monster Zero '68
Dagora, the Space Monster '65
Ghidrah the Three Headed Monster '65
Godzilla vs. Mothra '64
Gorath '64
Attack of the Mushroom People '63
King Kong vs. Godzilla '63
Mothra '62
Varan the Unbelievable '61
H-Man '59
Half Human '58
The Mysterians '58
Godzilla, King of the Monsters '56
Rodan '56

Elliot Hong
Retrievers '82
They Call Me Bruce? '82
Kill the Golden Goose '79

James Hong (1929-)
The Vineyard '89
Girls Next Door '79

Harry Hook
Robert Louis Stevenson's St. Ives '98
The Last of His Tribe '92
Lord of the Flies '90
The Kitchen Toto '87

Kevin Hooks (1958-)
Mutiny '99
Black Dog '98
Glory & Honor '98
Fled '96
Murder Without Motive '92
Passenger 57 '92
Strictly Business '91
Roots: The Gift '88

Lance Hool (1948-)
One Man's Hero '98
Steel Dawn '87
Missing in Action 2: The Beginning '85

Tobe Hooper (1946-)
Crocodile '00
Apartment Complex '98
The Mangler '94
Body Bags '93
I'm Dangerous Tonight '90
Spontaneous Combustion '89
Invaders from Mars '86
The Texas Chainsaw Massacre 2 '86
Lifeforce '85
Poltergeist '82
The Funhouse '81
Salem's Lot '79
Eaten Alive '76
The Texas Chainsaw Massacre '74

Stephen Hopkins
Under Suspicion '00
Lost in Space '98
The Ghost and the Darkness '96
Blown Away '94
Judgment Night '93
Dangerous Game '90
Predator 2 '90
A Nightmare on Elm Street 5: Dream Child '89

Dennis Hopper (1936-)
Chasers '94
The Hot Spot '90
Backtrack '89
Colors '88
Out of the Blue '80
The Last Movie '71
Easy Rider '69

E. Mason Hopper (1885-1967)
Hong Kong Nights '35
Held for Murder '32
Shop Angel '32
Square Shoulders '29

Jerry Hopper (1907-88)
Bull of the West '89
Madron '70
The Private War of Major Benson '55
Pony Express '53
The Atomic City '52

Russell Hopton (1900-45)
Black Gold '36
Song of the Trail '36

James W. Horne (1880-1942)
Holt of the Secret Service '42
Green Archer '40
All Over Town '37
Way Out West '37
Bohemian Girl '36
Bonnie Scotland '35
College '27
Laughing at Danger '24

Harry Horner (1910-94)
New Faces of 1952 '54
Beware, My Lovely '52

Red Planet Mars *'52*

Robert J. Horner

Apache Kid's Escape *'30*
The Walloping Kid *'26*

Peter Horton (1953-)

The Cure *'95*
Amazon Women on the Moon *'87*

Chien Hsiao Hou (1947-)

Flowers of Shanghai *'98*
Goodbye South, Goodbye *'96*

Joy Houck, Jr.

The St. Tammany Miracle *'94*
Creature from Black Lake *'76*
Night of the Strangler *'73*
Mind Warp *'72*

John Hough (1941-)

Hell's Gate *'01*
Duel of Hearts *'92*
The Dying Truth *'91*
The Lady and the Highwayman *'89*
American Gothic *'88*
Howling 4: The Original Nightmare *'88*
Biggles *'85*
The Black Arrow *'84*
Triumphs of a Man Called Horse *'83*
Incubus *'82*
The Watcher in the Woods *'81*
Brass Target *'78*
Return from Witch Mountain *'78*
Escape to Witch Mountain *'75*
Dirty Mary Crazy Larry *'74*
The Legend of Hell House *'73*
Treasure Island *'72*
Twins of Evil *'71*
Eye Witness *'70*

Bobby Houston

Caged Fear *'92*
Trust Me *'89*
Bad Manners *'84*

Adrian Hoven (1922-81)

Dandelions *'74*
Mark of the Devil 2 *'72*

David Howard (1896-1941)

Bullet Code *'40*
Hollywood Stadium Mystery *'38*
Park Avenue Logger *'37*
Crimson Romance *'34*
Daniel Boone *'34*
In Old Santa Fe *'34*
The Lost Jungle *'34*
Mystery Ranch *'34*

Leslie Howard (1893-1943)

Pimpernel Smith *'42*
Spitfire *'42*
Pygmalion *'38*

Ron Howard (1954-)

A Beautiful Mind *'01*
Dr. Seuss' How the Grinch Stole Christmas *'00*
EDtv *'99*
Ransom *'96*
Apollo 13 *'95*
The Paper *'94*
Far and Away *'92*
Backdraft *'91*
Parenthood *'89*
Willow *'88*
Cocoon *'85*
Gung Ho *'85*
Splash *'84*
Cotton Candy *'82*
Night Shift *'82*
Grand Theft Auto *'77*

William K. Howard (1899-1954)

Johnny Come Lately *'43*
Back Door to Heaven *'39*
Fire Over England *'37*
The Princess Comes Across *'36*
The Cat and the Fiddle *'34*
Evelyn Prentice *'34*
White Gold *'28*
Let's Go! *'23*

C. Thomas Howell (1966-)

The Big Fall *'96*
Pure Danger *'96*
Hourglass *'95*

Peter Howitt (1957-)

Antitrust *'00*
Sliding Doors *'97*

Frank Howson

Flynn *'96*
The Hunting *'92*

Harry Hoyt (1885-1961)

The Return of Boston Blackie *'27*
The Lost World *'25*

Talun Hsu

Body Count *'95*
Witchcraft 5: Dance with the Devil *'92*

George Huang

How to Make a Monster *'01*
Trojan War *'97*
Swimming with Sharks *'94*

Jean-Loup Hubert (1949-)

Le Grand Chemin *'87*
Next Year If All Goes Well *'83*

John Huddles

Uncorked *'98*
Far Harbor *'96*

Reginald (Reggie) Hudlin (1961-)

Serving Sara *'02*
The Ladies Man *'00*
The Great White Hype *'96*
Cosmic Slop *'94*
Boomerang *'92*
House Party *'90*

Hugh Hudson (1936-)

I Dreamed of Africa *'00*
My Life So Far *'98*
Lost Angels *'89*
Revolution *'85*
Greystoke: The Legend of Tarzan, Lord of the Apes *'84*
Chariots of Fire *'81*

Brent Huff (1961-)

The Bad Pack *'98*
Final Justice *'94*

R. John Hugh (1924-85)

Deadly Encounter *'78*
The Meal *'75*
You've Ruined Me, Eddie *'58*
Naked in the Sun *'57*
Yellowneck *'55*

Albert Hughes (1972-)

From Hell *'01*
Dead Presidents *'95*
Menace II Society *'93*

Allen Hughes (1972-)

From Hell *'01*
Dead Presidents *'95*
Menace II Society *'93*

Bronwen Hughes

Forces of Nature *'99*
Harriet the Spy *'96*

Howard Hughes (1905-76)

The Outlaw *'43*
Hell's Angels *'30*

John Hughes (1950-)

Curly Sue *'91*
Uncle Buck *'89*
She's Having a Baby *'88*
Planes, Trains & Automobiles *'87*
Ferris Bueller's Day Off *'86*
The Breakfast Club *'85*
Weird Science *'85*
Sixteen Candles *'84*

Ken Hughes (1922-2001)

Night School *'81*
Sextette *'78*
Oh, Alfie *'75*
Internecine Project *'73*
Cromwell *'70*
Chitty Chitty Bang Bang *'68*
Casino Royale *'67*
Arrivederci, Baby! *'66*
Of Human Bondage *'64*
The Trials of Oscar Wilde *'60*
The Long Haul *'57*
The Atomic Man *'56*
Heat Wave *'54*

Robert C. Hughes

St. Patrick: The Irish Legend *'00*
Down the Drain *'89*
Memorial Valley Massacre *'88*
Hunter's Blood *'87*

Terry Hughes

Mrs. Santa Claus *'96*
The Butcher's Wife *'91*
For Love or Money *'84*
Sunset Limousine *'83*

Ann Hui (1947-)

Summer Snow *'94*
Song of the Exile *'90*

Don Hulette (1937-)

Great Ride *'78*
Breaker! Breaker! *'77*

H. Bruce Humberstone (1903-84)

Tarzan and the Trappers *'58*
Ten Wanted Men *'54*
The Desert Song *'53*
Happy Go Lovely *'51*
Wonder Man *'45*
Pin-Up Girl *'44*
Hello, Frisco, Hello *'43*
Iceland *'42*
To the Shores of Tripoli *'42*
I Wake Up Screaming *'41*
Sun Valley Serenade *'41*
Lucky Cisco Kid *'40*
Charlie Chan at the Opera *'36*
The Crooked Circle *'32*
Strangers of the Evening *'32*

Sammo Hung (1952-)

Mr. Nice Guy *'98*
Dragons Forever *'88*
Eastern Condors *'87*
The Millionaire's Express *'86*
Heart of Dragon *'85*
The Prodigal Son *'82*
Spooky Encounters *'80*

Tran Anh Hung (1963-)

The Vertical Ray of the Sun *'00*
Cyclo *'95*
The Scent of Green Papaya *'93*

Ed(ward) Hunt

The Brain *'88*
Alien Warrior *'85*
Bloody Birthday *'80*
Starship Invasions *'77*

Paul Hunt (1943-)

Merlin *'92*
Twisted Nightmare *'87*
The Great Gundown *'75*
The Clones *'73*

Peter Hunt (1928-)

Assassination *'87*
Hyper-Sapien: People from Another Star *'86*
Wild Geese 2 *'85*
Death Hunt *'81*
Gulliver's Travels *'77*
Shout at the Devil *'76*
On Her Majesty's Secret Service *'69*

Peter H. Hunt (1938-)

The Adventures of Huckleberry Finn *'85*
It Came Upon a Midnight Clear *'84*
The Mysterious Stranger *'82*
Skeezer *'82*
1776 *'72*

Tim Hunter

Mean Streak *'99*
The Maker *'98*
Rescuers: Stories of Courage—Two Couples *'98*
The Saint of Fort Washington *'93*
Lies of the Twins *'91*
Paint It Black *'89*
River's Edge *'87*
Sylvester *'85*
Tex *'82*

Lawrence Huntington

Vulture *'67*
The Franchise Affair *'52*
Man on the Run *'49*
Tower of Terror *'42*

Nick Hurran

Virtual Sexuality *'99*
Girls' Night *'97*

Brian Desmond Hurst (1900-86)

Playboy of the Western World *'62*
Simba *'55*
Malta Story *'53*
A Christmas Carol *'51*
The Gay Lady *'49*
Dangerous Moonlight *'41*
The Lion Has Wings *'40*

Paul Hurst (1888-1953)

Battling Bunyon *'24*
Branded a Bandit *'24*

Harry Hurwitz (1938-95)

Fleshtone *'94*
That's Adequate *'90*
Rosebud Beach Hotel *'85*
Safari 3000 *'82*
The Projectionist *'71*

Waris Hussein (1938-)

Fall from Grace *'94*
The Summer House *'94*
Switched at Birth *'91*
The Shell Seekers *'89*
Onassis *'88*
Intimate Contact *'87*
When the Bough Breaks *'86*
Arch of Triumph *'85*
Little Gloria... Happy at Last *'84*
Princess Daisy *'83*
Coming Out of the Ice *'82*
Callie and Son *'81*
Edward and Mrs. Simpson *'80*
The Henderson Monster *'80*
And Baby Makes Six *'79*
Divorce His, Divorce Hers *'72*
The Possession of Joel Delaney *'72*
Melody *'71*
Quackser Fortune Has a Cousin in the Bronx *'70*

Anjelica Huston (1951-)

Agnes Browne *'99*
Bastard out of Carolina *'96*

Danny Huston (1962-)

The Maddening *'95*
Becoming Colette *'92*
Mr. North *'88*

Jimmy Huston

The Wharf Rat *'95*
My Best Friend Is a Vampire *'88*
Final Exam *'81*
Death Driver *'78*

John Huston (1906-87)

The Dead *'87*
Prizzi's Honor *'85*
Under the Volcano *'84*
Annie *'82*
Victory *'81*
Phobia *'80*
Wise Blood *'79*
The Man Who Would Be King *'75*
Mackintosh Man *'73*
Fat City *'72*
Life & Times of Judge Roy Bean *'72*
Casino Royale *'67*
Reflections in a Golden Eye *'67*
The Bible *'66*
The Night of the Iguana *'64*
The List of Adrian Messenger *'63*
The Misfits *'61*
The Unforgiven *'60*
Barbarian and the Geisha *'58*
Heaven Knows, Mr. Allison *'57*
Moby Dick *'56*
Beat the Devil *'53*
Moulin Rouge *'52*
The African Queen *'51*
The Red Badge of Courage *'51*
The Asphalt Jungle *'50*
Key Largo *'48*
Treasure of the Sierra Madre *'48*
Across the Pacific *'42*
In This Our Life *'42*
The Maltese Falcon *'41*

Charles (Hutchison) Hutchinson (1879-1949)

Phantom Patrol *'36*
Found Alive *'34*

Brian G. Hutton (1935-)

High Road to China *'83*
The First Deadly Sin *'80*
Night Watch *'72*
X, Y & Zee *'72*
Kelly's Heroes *'70*
Where Eagles Dare *'68*

Willard Huyck

Howard the Duck *'86*
Best Defense *'84*
French Postcards *'79*
Messiah of Evil *'74*

Peter Hyams (1943-)

The Musketeer *'01*
End of Days *'99*
The Relic *'96*
Sudden Death *'95*
Timecop *'94*
Stay Tuned *'92*
Narrow Margin *'90*
The Presidio *'88*
Running Scared *'86*
2010: The Year We Make Contact *'84*
Death Target *'83*
The Star Chamber *'83*
Outland *'81*
Hanover Street *'79*
Capricorn One *'78*
Busting *'74*
Our Time *'74*

Nicholas Hytner (1957-)

Center Stage *'00*
The Object of My Affection *'98*
The Crucible *'96*
The Madness of King George *'94*

Juan Ibanez

Dance of Death *'68*
The Fear Chamber *'68*
The Sinister Invasion *'68*

Leon Ichaso

Pinero *'01*
Hendrix *'00*
Execution of Justice *'99*
Free of Eden *'98*
Bitter Sugar *'96*
Zooman *'95*
Sugar Hill *'94*
The Fear Inside *'92*
The Take *'90*
Crossover Dreams *'85*
Power, Passion & Murder *'83*
El Super *'79*

Kon Ichikawa (1915-)

The Makioka Sisters *'83*
Tokyo Olympiad *'66*
An Actor's Revenge *'63*
Being Two Isn't Easy *'62*
Odd Obsession *'60*
Fires on the Plain *'59*
Enjo *'58*
The Burmese Harp *'56*

Eric Idle (1943-)

The Tale of the Frog Prince *'83*
All You Need Is Cash *'78*

Toshiharu Ikeda

Beautiful Beast *'95*
Evil Dead Trap *'88*

Kazuo Ikehiro

Zatoichi: Master Ichi and a Chest of Gold *'64*
Zatoichi: Zatoichi's Flashing Sword *'64*

Shohei Imamura (1926-)

Dr. Akagi *'98*
The Eel *'96*
Black Rain *'88*
The Ballad of Narayama *'83*
Eijanaika *'81*
Vengeance Is Mine *'79*
The Pornographers *'66*
The Insect Woman *'63*

Hiroshi Inagaki (1905-80)

Kojiro *'67*
Rikisha-Man *'58*
Samurai 3: Duel at Ganryu Island *'56*
Samurai 1: Musashi Miyamoto *'55*
Samurai 2: Duel at Ichijoji Temple *'55*

Franco Indovina (1932-72)

Catch as Catch Can *'68*
Oldest Profession *'67*

Lloyd Ingraham (1885-1956)

Eyes of Julia Deep *'18*
American Aristocracy *'17*

Boris Ingster (1904-78)

The Judge Steps Out *'49*
Stranger on the Third Floor *'40*

J. Christian Ingvordsen

Airboss *'00*
The Outfit *'93*
Comrades in Arms *'91*
Covert Action *'88*
Mob War *'88*
Search and Destroy *'88*
Firehouse *'87*
Hangmen *'87*

Dan Ireland

The Velocity of Gary *'98*
The Whole Wide World *'96*

O'Dale Ireland

Date Bait *'60*
High School Caesar *'56*

Matthew Irmas

Edie & Pen *'95*
When the Party's Over *'91*

John Irvin (1940-)

Noah's Ark *'99*
When Trumpets Fade *'98*
City of Industry *'96*
Crazy Horse *'96*
A Month by the Lake *'95*
Firefall *'94*
Widow's Peak *'94*
Eminent Domain *'91*
Robin Hood *'91*
Next of Kin *'89*
Hamburger Hill *'87*
Raw Deal *'86*
Turtle Diary *'86*
Champions *'84*
The Dogs of War *'81*
Ghost Story *'81*
Haunted: The Ferryman *'74*

Sam Irvin (1956-)

Backlash: Oblivion 2 *'95*
Magic Island *'95*
Out There *'95*
Oblivion *'94*
Acting on Impulse *'93*
Guilty as Charged *'92*

David Irving

Night of the Cyclone *'90*
C.H.U.D. 2: Bud the Chud *'89*
Rumpelstiltskin *'86*
Goodbye Cruel World *'82*

Richard Irving
The Jesse Owens Story '84
The Art of Crime '75
Columbo: Prescription Murder '67
James Isaac
Jason X '01
The Horror Show '89
Antonio (Isasi-Isasmendi) Isasi (1927-)
Vengeance '86
Ricco '74
Robert Iscove (1947-)
Firestarter 2: Rekindled '02
Boys and Girls '00
She's All That '99
Cinderella '97
Mission of the Shark '91
The Lawrenceville Stories '88
Puss 'n Boots '84
Neal Israel (1945-)
National Lampoon's Dad's Week Off '97
Surf Ninjas '93
Breaking the Rules '92
Combat Academy '86
Moving Violations '85
Bachelor Party '84
Americathon '79
Tunnelvision '76
Juzo Itami (1933-97)
Minbo—Or the Gentle Art of Japanese Extortion '92
A Taxing Woman's Return '88
A Taxing Woman '87
Tampopo '86
The Funeral '84
James Ivory (1928-)
The Golden Bowl '00
A Soldier's Daughter Never Cries '98
Surviving Picasso '96
Jefferson in Paris '94
The Remains of the Day '93
Howard's End '92
Mr. & Mrs. Bridge '90
Slaves of New York '89
Maurice '87
A Room with a View '86
The Courtesans of Bombay '85
The Bostonians '84
Heat and Dust '82
Quartet '81
Jane Austen in Manhattan '80
The Europeans '79
Hullabaloo over Georgie & Bonnie's Pictures '78
Roseland '77
Autobiography of a Princess '75
Wild Party '74
Savages '72
Bombay Talkie '70
Shakespeare Wallah '65
The Householder '63
David Jablin
National Lampoon's The Don's Analyst '97
National Lampoon's Favorite Deadly Sins '95
Fred Jackman
No Man's Law '27
King of the Wild Horses '24
David S. Jackson
Atomic Train '99
The Jesse Ventura Story '99
Wolverine '96
Detonator 2: Night Watch '95
Detonator '93
Donald G. Jackson
Return to Frogtown '92
Hell Comes to Frogtown '88
Roller Blade '85
The Demon Lover '77
Douglas Jackson
Nowhere in Sight '01
The Witness Files '00
Requiem for Murder '99
Dead End '98
Random Encounter '98
Twists of Terror '98
Natural Enemy '96
The Paperboy '94
Stalked '94
Deadbolt '92
Whispers '89
Mick Jackson
Tuesdays with Morrie '99
Volcano '97
Indictment: The McMartin Trial '95
Clean Slate '94
The Bodyguard '92
L.A. Story '91
Chattahoochee '89
Mick Jackson (1943-)
A Very British Coup '88
Yuri Nosenko, KGB '86
Threads '85
Pat Jackson (1916-)
King Arthur, the Young Warlord '75
What a Carve-Up! '62
Encore '52
Peter Jackson (1961-)
Lord of the Rings 1: The Fellowship of the Rings '01
Forgotten Silver '96
The Frighteners '96
Heavenly Creatures '94
Dead Alive '93
Meet the Feebles '89
Bad Taste '88
Wilfred Jackson (-1988)
Lady and the Tramp '55
Alice in Wonderland '51
Cinderella '50
Melody Time '48
Fantasia '40
Alan Jacobs
Just One Night '00
Diary of a Serial Killer '97
Nina Takes a Lover '94
Jerry P. Jacobs
Freedom Strike '98
A Dangerous Place '94
John Jacobs
The First to Go '97
Rocket to the Moon '86
Lawrence-Hilton Jacobs (1953-)
Quiet Fire '91
Angels of the City '89
Rick Jacobson
Black Thunder '98
Interlocked '98
Night Hunter '95
Suspect Device '95
Bloodfist 6: Ground Zero '94
Ring of Fire 3: Lion Strike '94
Star Quest '94
The Unborn 2 '94
Full Contact '93
Joseph Jacoby (1942-)
Great Bank Hoax '78
Hurry Up or I'll Be Thirty '73
Gualtiero Jacopetti (1919-)
Mondo Cane 2 '64
Mondo Cane '63
Benoit Jacquot (1947-)
Seventh Heaven '98
A Single Girl '96
The Disenchanted '90
Just Jaeckin (1940-)
The Perils of Gwendoline '84
Lady Chatterley's Lover '81
The French Woman '79
The Story of O '75
Emmanuelle '74
Henry Jaglom (1943-)
Deja Vu '98
Last Summer In the Hamptons '96
Babyfever '94
Venice, Venice '92
Eating '90
New Year's Day '89
Someone to Love '87
Always '85
Can She Bake a Cherry Pie? '83
National Lampoon Goes to the Movies '81
Sitting Ducks '80
Tracks '76
Alan James (1890-1952)
Red Barry '38
Dick Tracy '37
Lucky Terror '36
When a Man Sees Red '34
Phantom Thunderbolt '33
Come on Tarzan '32
Fargo Express '32
The Phantom '31
Backfire '22
Steve James
Passing Glory '99
Prefontaine '96
Hoop Dreams '94
Jerry Jameson
Land of the Free '98
Bonanza: The Return '93
Fire and Rain '89
The Cowboy & the Ballerina '84
Starflight One '83
Hotline '82
Killing at Hell's Gate '81
High Noon: Part 2 '80
Raise the Titanic '80
Sniper '75
The Bat People '74
Hurricane '74
Terror on the 40th Floor '74
Dirt Gang '71
Miklos Jancso (1921-)
Hungarian Rhapsody '78
The Red and the White '68
The Round Up '66
Annabel Jankel
Super Mario Bros. '93
D.O.A. '88
Derek Jarman (1942-94)
Blue '93
Wittgenstein '93
Edward II '92
The Garden '90
Aria '88
The Last of England '87
Caravaggio '86
Sebastiane '79
Jim Jarmusch (1953-)
Ghost Dog: The Way of the Samurai '99
Year of the Horse '97
Dead Man '95
Night on Earth '91
Mystery Train '89
Down by Law '86
Permanent Vacation '84
Stranger than Paradise '84
Julian Jarrold
All the King's Men '99
Great Expectations '99
The Painted Lady '97
Touching Evil '97
Cracker: The Big Crunch '94
Charles Jarrott (1927-)
Danielle Steel's Changes '91
Lucy and Desi: Before the Laughter '91
Night of the Fox '90
The Woman He Loved '88
Poor Little Rich Girl: The Barbara Hutton Story '87
Boy in Blue '86
The Amateur '82
Condorman '81
The Last Flight of Noah's Ark '80
The Other Side of Midnight '77
The Littlest Horse Thieves '76
The Dove '74
Mary, Queen of Scots '71
Anne of the Thousand Days '69
Dr. Jekyll and Mr. Hyde '68
Strange Case of Dr. Jekyll & Mr. Hyde '68
Ilkka Jarvilaturi
Spy Games '99
City Unplugged '95
Vojtech Jasny (1925-)
The Great Land of Small '86
All My Good Countrymen '68
Leigh Jason (1904-79)
The Choppers '61
The Go-Getter '54
Lost Honeymoon '47
Out of the Blue '47
Lady for a Night '42
Mad Miss Manton '38
The Bride Walks Out '36
That Girl from Paris '36
High Gear '33
Vadim Jean
The Real Howard Spitz '98
Leon the Pig Farmer '93
Nightscare '93
Tom Jeffrey
The Odd Angry Shot '79
Weekend of Shadows '77
Lionel Jeffries (1926-)
Water Babies '79
Wombling Free '77
Amazing Mr. Blunden '72
The Railway Children '70
Michael Jenkins
Sweet Talker '91
Rebel '85
Alain Jessua (1932-)
The Killing Game '67
Life Upside Down '64
Jean-Pierre Jeunet (1955-)
Amelie '01
Alien: Resurrection '97
The City of Lost Children '95
Delicatessen '92
Norman Jewison (1926-)
Dinner with Friends '01
The Hurricane '99
Bogus '96
Only You '94
Other People's Money '91
In Country '89
Moonstruck '87
Agnes of God '85
A Soldier's Story '84
Best Friends '82
And Justice for All '79
F.I.S.T. '78
Rollerball '75
Jesus Christ, Superstar '73
Fiddler on the Roof '71
The Thomas Crown Affair '68
In the Heat of the Night '67
The Russians Are Coming, the Russians Are Coming '66
The Cincinnati Kid '65
Send Me No Flowers '64
The Thrill of It All! '63
40 Pounds of Trouble '62
Phil Joanou (1961-)
Entropy '99
Heaven's Prisoners '95
Fallen Angels 2 '93
Wild Palms '93
Final Analysis '92
State of Grace '90
U2: Rattle and Hum '88
Three o'Clock High '87
Arthur Joffe
Alberto Express '92
Harem '85
Mark Joffe
The Matchmaker '97
Cosi '95
The Efficiency Expert '92
Grievous Bodily Harm '89
Night Master '87
Roland Joffe (1945-)
Vatel '00
Goodbye, Lover '99
The Scarlet Letter '95
City of Joy '92
Fat Man and Little Boy '89
The Mission '86
The Killing Fields '84
Sande N. Johnsen
The Beautiful, the Bloody and the Bare '69
Teenage Gang Debs '66
Alan Johnson
Solarbabies '86
To Be or Not to Be '83
Irvin Johnson
Blood Ring '93
Fist of Steel '93
Kenneth Johnson (1942-)
Steel '97
Alien Nation: Dark Horizon '94
Short Circuit 2 '88
V '83
Senior Trip '81
The Incredible Hulk '77
Lamont Johnson (1922-)
The Broken Chain '93
Escape '90
Gore Vidal's Lincoln '88
Unnatural Causes '86
Ernie Kovacs: Between the Laughter '84
Jack & the Beanstalk '83
Spacehunter: Adventures in the Forbidden Zone '83
Crisis at Central High '80
One on One '77
Lipstick '76
The Execution of Private Slovik '74
The Last American Hero '73
The Groundstar Conspiracy '72
You'll Like My Mother '72
A Gunfight '71
McKenzie Break '70
My Sweet Charlie '70
Nunnally Johnson (1897-1977)
The Three Faces of Eve '57
The Man in the Gray Flannel Suit '56
Patrick Read Johnson
When Good Ghouls Go Bad '01
Angus '95
Baby's Day Out '94
Spaced Invaders '90
Raymond K. Johnson
Covered Wagon Trails '40
Pinto Canyon '40
Ridin' the Trail '40
Code of the Fearless '39
Daughter of the Tong '39
In Old Montana '39
I'll Name the Murderer '36
The Reckless Way '36
Aaron Kim Johnston
For the Moment '94
The Last Winter '89
Joe Johnston
Jurassic Park 3 '01
October Sky '99
Jumanji '95
The Pagemaster '94
The Rocketeer '91
Honey, I Shrunk the Kids '89
Amy Holden Jones (1953-)
The Rich Man's Wife '96
Maid to Order '87
Love Letters '83
Slumber Party Massacre '82
Brian Thomas Jones
Posed for Murder '89
Escape from Safehaven '88
The Rejuvenator '88
Ocean Drive Weekend '85
Chuck Jones (1912-2002)
Looney Looney Looney Bugs Bunny Movie '81
Phantom Tollbooth '69
David Hugh Jones (1934-)
A Christmas Carol '99
The Confession '98
An Unexpected Life '97
Is There Life Out There? '94
The Trial '93
Jacknife '89
Look Back in Anger '89
The Christmas Wife '88
84 Charing Cross Road '86
Betrayal '83
Donald M. Jones
Lethal Pursuit '88
Murderlust '86
Project: Nightmare '85
Deadly Sunday '82
Love Butcher '82
Sweater Girls '78
F. Richard Jones (1894-1930)
Bulldog Drummond '29
The Gaucho '27
Extra Girl '23
Gary Jones
Spiders '00
Mosquito '95
Stay Tuned for Murder '88
Harmon Jones (1911-72)
Bullwhip '58
The Legend of the Sea Wolf '58
Pride of St. Louis '52
As Young As You Feel '51
James Cellan Jones (1931-)
The Vacillations of Poppy Carew '94
Fortunes of War '87
The Golden Bowl '72
Mark Jones (1953-)
Rumpelstiltskin '96
Leprechaun '93
Philip Jones
Backflash '01
Wish Me Luck '95
Cause of Death '90
Terry Jones (1942-)
Mr. Toad's Wild Ride '96
Erik the Viking '89
Personal Services '87
Monty Python's The Meaning of Life '83
Monty Python's Life of Brian '79
Monty Python and the Holy Grail '75
Glenn Jordan (1936-)
Night Ride Home '99
Sarah, Plain and Tall: Winter's End '99
Legalese '98
A Streetcar Named Desire '95
Barbarians at the Gate '93
To Dance with the White Dog '93
O Pioneers! '91
Sarah, Plain and Tall '91
Jesse '88
Echoes in the Darkness '87
Dress Gray '86
Something in Common '86
Toughlove '85
Mass Appeal '84
The Buddy System '83
Lois Gibbs and the Love Canal '82
Only When I Laugh '81
The Family Man '79
Les Miserables '78
One of My Wives Is Missing '76
Picture of Dorian Gray '74
Frankenstein '73
Gregor Jordan
Two Hands '98
Twisted '96
Neil Jordan (1950-)
The End of the Affair '99
In Dreams '98
The Butcher Boy '97
Michael Collins '96
Interview with the Vampire '94
The Crying Game '92
The Miracle '91
We're No Angels '89
High Spirits '88
Mona Lisa '86
The Company of Wolves '85

Danny Boy '82
Jon Jost (1943-)
The Bed You Sleep In '93
Jon Jost's Frameup '93
All the Vermeers in New York '91
Sure Fire '90
Slow Moves '84
C. Courtney Joyner
Lurking Fear '94
Trancers 3: Deth Lives '92
Mike Judge (1962-)
Office Space '98
Beavis and Butt-Head Do America '96
Rupert Julian (1889-1943)
Yankee Clipper '27
Walking Back '26
The Phantom of the Opera '25
Merry-Go-Round '23
Gil Junger
Black Knight '01
Ten Things I Hate about You '99
Nathan (Hertz) Juran (1907-)
Land Raiders '69
First Men in the Moon '64
Jack the Giant Killer '62
Attack of the 50 Foot Woman '58
Good Day for a Hanging '58
The Seventh Voyage of Sinbad '58
The Brain from Planet Arous '57
The Deadly Mantis '57
Hellcats of the Navy '57
20 Million Miles to Earth '57
Gunsmoke '53
The Black Castle '52
Claude Jutra (1930-86)
Surfacing '84
By Design '82
Mon Oncle Antoine '71
George Kaczender (1933-)
Maternal Instincts '96
Prettykill '87
Your Ticket Is No Longer Valid '84
The Agency '81
Chanel Solitaire '81
In Praise of Older Women '78
The Girl in Blue '74
Jan Kadar (1918-79)
Freedom Road '79
Lies My Father Told Me '75
The Angel Levine '70
The Shop on Main Street '65
Death Is Called Engelchen '63
Ellis Kadison (1928-98)
The Cat '66
Git! '65
Jeremy Paul Kagan (1945-)
Color of Justice '97
Roswell: The U.F.O. Cover-Up '94
By the Sword '93
Descending Angel '90
Big Man on Campus '89
Conspiracy: The Trial of the Chicago Eight '87
Courage '86
The Journey of Natty Gann '85
The Sting 2 '83
The Chosen '81
The Big Fix '78
Heroes '77
Katherine '75
Richard C. Kahn (1897-1960)
Buzzy Rides the Range '40
Son of Ingagi '40
Bronze Buckaroo '39
Harlem Rides the Range '39
Two-Gun Man from Harlem '38
Chen Kaige (1952-)
The Emperor and the Assassin '99
Temptress Moon '96
Farewell My Concubine '93
Life on a String '90
Yellow Earth '89
Mikhail Kalatozov (1903-73)
Red Tent '69
I Am Cuba '64
The Cranes Are Flying '57
Max Kalmanowicz
Dreams Come True '84
The Children '80
Scott Kalvert
Deuces Wild '02
The Basketball Diaries '94
Joseph Kane (1897-1975)
Smoke in the Wind '75
The Maverick Queen '55
Jubilee Trail '54
Ride the Man Down '53
Hoodlum Empire '52
Dakota '45
Flame of the Barbary Coast '45
Cowboy & the Senorita '44
Song of Nevada '44
The Yellow Rose of Texas '44
Hands Across the Border '43
Idaho '43
Silver Spurs '43
Song of Texas '43
Texas Legionnaires '43
Heart of the Golden West '42
Ridin' Down the Canyon '42
Sons of the Pioneers '42
South of Santa Fe '42
Sunset on the Desert '42
Sunset Serenade '42
Bad Man of Deadwood '41
Jesse James at Bay '41
Red River Valley '41
Robin Hood of the Pecos '41
The Border Legion '40
Carson City Kid '40
Colorado '40
Ranger and the Lady '40
Young Bill Hickok '40
Young Buffalo Bill '40
Arizona Kid '39
Days of Jesse James '39
Frontier Pony Express '39
Rough Riders' Roundup '39
Saga of Death Valley '39
Billy the Kid Returns '38
Born to Be Wild '38
Come on Rangers '38
Oh Susannah '38
Old Barn Dance '38
Shine on, Harvest Moon '38
Boots & Saddles '37
Come on, Cowboys '37
Git Along Little Dogies '37
Heart of the Rockies '37
Round-Up Time in Texas '37
Springtime in the Rockies '37
Yodelin' Kid from Pine Ridge '37
Darkest Africa '36
Fighting Marines '36
Ghost Town Gold '36
King of the Pecos '36
The Lawless Nineties '36
Old Corral '36
Ride, Ranger, Ride '36
Melody Trail '35
In Old Santa Fe '34
Rolfe Kanefsky (1969-)
My Family Treasure '93
There's Nothing out There '90
Shusuke (Shu) Kaneko
H.P. Lovecraft's Necronomicon: Book of the Dead '93
Summer Vacation: 1999 '88
Jeff Kanew
V.I. Warshawski '91
Troop Beverly Hills '89
Tough Guys '86
Gotcha! '85
Revenge of the Nerds '84
Eddie Macon's Run '83
Natural Enemies '79
Charles Kanganis
K-911 '99
Dennis the Menace Strikes Again '98
Race the Sun '96
3 Ninjas Kick Back '94
No Escape, No Return '93
A Time to Die '91
Chance '89
Deadly Breed '89
Sinners '89
Marek Kanievska
Where the Money Is '00
Less Than Zero '87
Another Country '84
Garson Kanin (1912-99)
Tom, Dick, and Harry '41
My Favorite Wife '40
They Knew What They Wanted '40
Bachelor Mother '39
The Great Man Votes '38
Next Time I Marry '38
Hal Kanter (1918-)
For the Love of It '80
Loving You '57
I Married a Woman '56
Deborah Kaplan
Josie and the Pussycats '01
Can't Hardly Wait '98
Ed Kaplan
Primal Secrets '94
Chips, the War Dog '90
Walking on Air '87
Jonathan Kaplan (1947-)
Brokedown Palace '99
In Cold Blood '96
Bad Girls '94
Fallen Angels 1 '93
Unlawful Entry '92
Love Field '91
Immediate Family '89
The Accused '88
Project X '87
Girls of the White Orchid '85
Heart Like a Wheel '83
Gentleman Bandit '81
Over the Edge '79
Mr. Billion '77
White Line Fever '75
Truck Turner '74
The Student Teachers '73
Night Call Nurses '72
Nelly Kaplan (1934-)
Charles et Lucie '79
Nea '78
A Very Curious Girl '69
Shekhar Kapur (1945-)
Elizabeth '98
Bandit Queen '94
Wong Kar-Wai (1958-)
In the Mood for Love '00
Happy Together '96
Chungking Express '95
Fallen Angels '95
Michael Karbelnikoff
The Last Ride '94
Mobsters '91
Phil Karlson (1908-85)
Framed '75
Walking Tall '73
Ben '72
Hornet's Nest '70
The Wrecking Crew '68
The Silencers '66
Kid Galahad '62
Scarface Mob '62
Hell to Eternity '60
Gunman's Walk '58
Tight Spot '55
Kansas City Confidential '52
The Texas Rangers '51
The Big Cat '49
Ladies of the Chorus '49
Behind the Mask '46
Swing Parade of 1946 '46
The Shanghai Cobra '45
There Goes Kelly '45
Bill Karn
Door to Door Maniac '61
Ma Barker's Killer Brood '60
Gang Busters '55
Eric Karson
Angel Town '89
Black Eagle '88
Opposing Force '87
Octagon '80
Jake Kasdan
Orange County '02
Zero Effect '97
Lawrence Kasdan (1949-)
Mumford '99
French Kiss '95
Wyatt Earp '94
Grand Canyon '91
I Love You to Death '90
The Accidental Tourist '88
Silverado '85
The Big Chill '83
Body Heat '81
Sam Henry Kass
Body and Soul '98
The Search for One-Eyed Jimmy '96
Mathieu Kassovitz (1967-)
The Crimson Rivers '01
Hate '95
Cafe au Lait '94
Peter Kassovitz
Jakob the Liar '99
Make Room for Tomorrow '81
Brian Katkin
Shakedown '02
If I Die Before I Wake '98
Michael Katleman
Bloodhounds '96
The Spider and the Fly '94
Milton Katselas (1933-)
Strangers: The Story of a Mother and Daughter '79
Report to the Commissioner '74
Forty Carats '73
Butterflies Are Free '72
Lee H. Katzin (1935-)
Restraining Order '99
The Break '95
The Dirty Dozen: The Fatal Mission '88
World Gone Wild '88
The Dirty Dozen: The Deadly Mission '87
Death Ray 2000 '81
The Bastard '78
Terror out of the Sky '78
The Man from Atlantis '77
The Captive: The Longest Drive 2 '76
The Longest Drive '76
Savages '75
Sky Hei$t '75
The Stranger '73
The Salzburg Connection '72
The Voyage of the Yes '72
Le Mans '71
Whatever Happened to Aunt Alice? '69
Jonathan Kaufer
Bad Manners '98
Soup for One '82
Charles Kaufman
Jakarta '88
When Nature Calls '85
Mother's Day '80
Jim Kaufman
Time at the Top '99
Night of the Demons 3 '97
Backstab '90
Lloyd Kaufman
Tromeo & Juliet '95
Sgt. Kabukiman N.Y.P.D. '94
The Toxic Avenger, Part 2 '89
The Toxic Avenger, Part 3: The Last Temptation of Toxie '89
Troma's War '88
Class of Nuke 'Em High '86
The Toxic Avenger '86
Stuck on You '84
First Turn On '83
Waitress '81
Squeeze Play '79
Philip Kaufman (1936-)
Quills '00
Rising Sun '93
Henry & June '90
The Unbearable Lightness of Being '88
The Right Stuff '83
Wanderers '79
Invasion of the Body Snatchers '78
The White Dawn '75
The Great Northfield Minnesota Raid '72
Aki Kaurismaki (1957-)
La Vie de Boheme '93
The Match Factory Girl '90
Ariel '89
Leningrad Cowboys Go America '89
Mika Kaurismaki (1955-)
Condition Red '95
Zombie and the Ghost Train '91
Amazon '90
Helmut Kautner
The Last Bridge '54
Die Grosse Freiheit Nr. 7 '45
Anwar Kawadri (1953-)
Claudia '85
Nutcracker Sweet '84
Jerzy Kawalerowicz (1922-)
Pharaoh '66
Mother Joan of the Angels '60
Stephen Kay
Get Carter '00
The Last Time I Committed Suicide '96
Robert Kaylor (1934-)
Nobody's Perfect '90
Carny '80
Derby '71
Elia Kazan (1909-)
The Last Tycoon '76
The Arrangement '69
Splendor in the Grass '61
A Face in the Crowd '57
Baby Doll '56
East of Eden '54
On the Waterfront '54
Viva Zapata! '52
A Streetcar Named Desire '51
Panic in the Streets '50
Pinky '49
Boomerang '47
Gentleman's Agreement '47
A Tree Grows in Brooklyn '45
James Keach (1948-)
Camouflage '00
The Stars Fell on Henrietta '94
Praying Mantis '93
Sunstroke '92
False Identity '90
The Forgotten '89
Buster Keaton (1895-1966)
Battling Butler '26
The General '26
Seven Chances '25
The Navigator '24
Our Hospitality '23
Three Ages '23
Diane Keaton (1946-)
Hanging Up '99
Unstrung Heroes '95
Wildflower '91
Heaven '87
Bob Keen (1960-)
Sir Arthur Conan Doyle's The Lost World '98
Proteus '95
To Catch a Yeti '95
Don Keeslar
Bog '84
The Capture of Grizzly Adams '82
Worth Keeter
Last Lives '98
Memorial Day '98
Snapdragon '93
Illicit Behavior '91
L.A. Bounty '89
Trapper County War '89
Order of the Black Eagle '87
Unmasking the Idol '86
Dogs of Hell '83
Lady Grey '82
The Wolfman '82
Peter Keglevic (1950-)
Kill Cruise '90
The Cop & the Girl '86
William Keighley (1889-1972)
The Master of Ballantrae '53
The Street with No Name '48
George Washington Slept Here '42
The Bride Came C.O.D. '41
The Man Who Came to Dinner '41
The Fighting 69th '40
Each Dawn I Die '39
Bullets or Ballots '38
The Prince and the Pauper '37
Green Pastures '36
"G" Men '35
Ladies They Talk About '33
David Keith (1954-)
The Further Adventures of Tennessee Buck '88
The Curse '87
Harvey Keith
Stand-Ins '97
Jezebel's Kiss '90
Frederick King Keller
Vamping '84
The Eyes of the Amaryllis '82
Harry Keller (1913-87)
The Brass Bottle '63
Tammy and the Doctor '63
Texas John Slaughter: Stampede at Bitter Creek '62
Geronimo's Revenge '60
Texas John Slaughter: Geronimo's Revenge '60
Phantom Stallion '54
El Paso Stampede '53
Marshal of Cedar Rock '53
Roy Kellino (1912-56)
Charade '53
I Met a Murderer '39
Bob Kelljan (1930-82)
Black Oak Conspiracy '77
Act of Vengeance '74
Scream Blacula Scream '73
The Return of Count Yorga '71
Count Yorga, Vampire '70
Barnet Kellman (1947-)
Slappy and the Stinkers '97
Straight Talk '92
Key Exchange '85
David Kellogg (1952-)
Inspector Gadget '99
Cool As Ice '91
Ray Kellogg (-1976)
The Giant Gila Monster '59
The Killer Shrews '59
Gene Kelly (1912-96)
The Cheyenne Social Club '70
Hello, Dolly! '69

A Guide for the Married Man '67
The Tunnel of Love '58
Invitation to the Dance '56
Singin' in the Rain '52
On the Town '49

Nicholas (Nick) Kendall (1949-)
Mr. Rice's Secret '00
Cadillac Girls '93

Burt Kennedy (1922-2001)
Suburban Commando '91
Big Bad John '90
Dynamite and Gold '88
The Trouble with Spies '87
More Wild, Wild West '80
The Concrete Cowboys '79
Wild, Wild West Revisited '79
Wolf Lake '79
The Killer Inside Me '76
All the Kind Strangers '74
Train Robbers '73
Hannie Caulder '72
Ride to Glory '71
Support Your Local Gunfighter '71
The Good Guys and the Bad Guys '69
Support Your Local Sheriff '69
The War Wagon '67
Return of the Magnificent Seven '66
The Rounders '65

Ken Kennedy
Grizzly Adams: The Legend Continues '90
Mission to Glory '80
Iron Angel '64

Michael Kennedy
The Heist '96
Robin of Locksley '95
Hard Evidence '94
Red Scorpion 2 '94
The Swordsman '92
Talons of the Eagle '92
One Man Out '89
Caribe '87

Erle C. Kenton (1896-1980)
House of Dracula '45
House of Frankenstein '44
It Ain't Hay '43
The Ghost of Frankenstein '42
Pardon My Sarong '42
Who Done It? '42
Melody for Three '41
They Meet Again '41
Remedy for Riches '40
Escape to Paradise '39
Island of Lost Souls '32
Bare Knees '28

James V. Kern (1909-66)
The Second Woman '51
Two Tickets to Broadway '51
Never Say Goodbye '46

Sarah Kernochan
All I Wanna Do '98
Marjoe '72

Lodge Kerrigan
Claire Dolan '97
Clean, Shaven '93

Irvin Kershner (1923-)
RoboCop 2 '90
Traveling Man '89
Never Say Never Again '83
The Empire Strikes Back '80
Eyes of Laura Mars '78
Raid on Entebbe '77
The Return of a Man Called Horse '76
S*P*Y*S '74
Up the Sandbox '72
Flim-Flam Man '67
A Fine Madness '66
A Face in the Rain '63
The Hoodlum Priest '61

Harry Kerwin
Barracuda '78
God's Bloody Acre '75
Cheering Section '73

Alek Keshishian
With Honors '94
Truth or Dare '91

Bruce Kessler (1936-)
Cruise into Terror '78
Deathmoon '78
Simon, King of the Witches '71
The Gay Deceivers '69
Angels from Hell '68

Michael Keusch
Anything for Love '93
Huck and the King of Hearts '93
Just One of the Girls '93
Samurai Cowboy '93
Lena's Holiday '90

Abbas Kiarostami (1940-)
The Taste of Cherry '96
Through the Olive Trees '94
Life and Nothing More ... '92
Where Is My Friend's House? '87

Beeban Kidron (1961-)
Swept from the Sea '97
To Wong Foo, Thanks for Everything, Julie Newmar '95
Shades of Fear '93
Used People '92
Antonia and Jane '91
Oranges Are Not the Only Fruit '89

Fritz Kiersch
The Stranger '95
Shattered Image '93
Into the Sun '92
Under the Boardwalk '89
Gor '88
Winners Take All '87
Tuff Turf '85
Children of the Corn '84

Krzysztof Kieslowski (1941-96)
Trois Couleurs: Blanc '94
Trois Couleurs: Rouge '94
Trois Couleurs: Bleu '93
The Double Life of Veronique '91
The Decalogue '88
No End '84
Camera Buff '79

Gerard Kikoine
Buried Alive '89
Edge of Sanity '89
Dragonard '88

Edward Killy
West of the Pecos '45
Nevada '44

Bruce Kimmel (1947-)
Spaceship '81
The First Nudie Musical '75

Anthony Kimmins (1910-62)
Captain's Paradise '53
Bonnie Prince Charlie '48
Mine Own Executioner '47

John Kincade
Back to Back '90
Terminal Entry '87

Tim Kincaid
The Occultist '89
Maximum Thrust '88
She's Back '88
Mutant Hunt '87
Necropolis '87
Robot Holocaust '87
Bad Girls Dormitory '84

Burton King (1877-1944)
The Adorable Cheat '28
The Man from Beyond '22

George King (1899-1966)
The Case of the Frightened Lady '39
Crimes at the Dark House '39
The Face at the Window '39
Sexton Blake and the Hooded Terror '38
The Crimes of Stephen Hawke '36
Demon Barber of Fleet Street '36

Henry King (1888-1982)
Beloved Infidel '59
The Bravados '58
Carousel '56
Love Is a Many-Splendored Thing '55
The Snows of Kilimanjaro '52
David and Bathsheba '51
I'd Climb the Highest Mountain '51
The Gunfighter '50
Twelve o'Clock High '49
Captain from Castile '47
Wilson '44
The Song of Bernadette '43
The Black Swan '42
A Yank in the R.A.F. '41
Jesse James '39
Stanley and Livingstone '39
Alexander's Ragtime Band '38
In Old Chicago '37
Lloyds of London '36
Marie Galante '34
Hell Harbor '30
She Goes to War '29
Romola '25
The White Sister '23
Tol'able David '21

Louis King (1898-1962)
Dangerous Mission '54
Sabre Jet '53
Mrs. Mike '49
Bulldog Drummond Comes Back '37
Bulldog Drummond's Revenge '37
Special Investigator '36
Drifting Souls '32
Border Law '31
The Fighting Sheriff '31

Rick King
Catherine's Grove '98
Road Ends '98
Terminal Justice: Cybertech P.D. '95
A Passion to Kill '94
Quick '93
Kickboxer 3: The Art of War '92
Prayer of the Rollerboys '91
Forced March '90
The Killing Time '87
Hot Shot '86
Hard Choices '84

Robert King
Angels in the Infield '00
The Principal Takes a Holiday '98

Robert Lee King
Psycho Beach Party '00
Boys Life '94

Zalman King (1941-)
Red Shoe Diaries: Luscious Lola '00
Red Shoe Diaries: Swimming Naked '00
In God's Hands '98
Shame, Shame, Shame '98
Red Shoe Diaries: Four on the Floor '96
Red Shoe Diaries: Strip Poker '96
Delta of Venus '95
Red Shoe Diaries 3: Another Woman's Lipstick '93
Red Shoe Diaries 4: Auto Erotica '93
Red Shoe Diaries '92
Red Shoe Diaries 2: Double Dare '92
Wild Orchid 2: Two Shades of Blue '92
Wild Orchid '90
Two Moon Junction '88
Wildfire '88

Jack Kinney (-1992)
1001 Arabian Nights '59
The Legend of Sleepy Hollow '49
Melody Time '48
Fun & Fancy Free '47

Ralf Kirsten (1930-)
Under the Pear Tree '73
On the Sunny Side '62

Takeshi "Beat" Kitano (1948-)
Brother '00
Kikujiro '99
Fireworks '97
Sonatine '96
Boiling Point '90
Violent Cop '89

Martin Kitrosser
Daddy's Girl '96
The Fiance '96

Robert J. Kizer (1952-)
Death Ring '93
Hell Comes to Frogtown '88
Godzilla 1985 '85

Alf Kjellin (1920-88)
The Girls of Huntington House '73
The McMasters '70

Robert Klane
Weekend at Bernie's 2 '93
Thank God It's Friday '78

Cedric Klapisch
Un Air de Famille '96
When the Cat's Away '96

Randal Kleiser (1946-)
Shadow of Doubt '98
It's My Party '95
Honey, I Blew Up the Kid '92
White Fang '91
Getting It Right '89
Big Top Pee-wee '88
Flight of the Navigator '86
Grandview U.S.A. '84
Summer Lovers '82
The Blue Lagoon '80
Grease '78
The Gathering '77
The Boy in the Plastic Bubble '76

Richard Kletter
The Android Affair '95
Dangerous Indiscretion '94

Max Kleven
Fugitive Champion '99
Bail Out '90
Deadly Stranger '88
Ruckus '81

Elem Klimov (1933-)
Come and See '85
Rasputin '85

Leon Klimovsky (1907-96)
The Devil's Possessed '74
Orgy of the Vampires '73
The Saga of the Draculas '72
Vengeance of the Zombies '72
Dr. Jekyll and the Wolfman '71
The Werewolf vs. the Vampire Woman '70
Commando Attack '67

Elmar Klos (1910-93)
The Shop on Main Street '65
Death Is Called Engelchen '63

Steven Kloves (1960-)
Flesh and Bone '93
The Fabulous Baker Boys '89

Robert Knights (1942-)
The Man Who Made Husbands Jealous '98
Mosley '98
Double Vision '92
And a Nightingale Sang '91
The Dawning '88
A Dedicated Man '86
Ebony Tower '86
Lovers of Their Time '85

Bernard Knowles (1900-)
Frozen Alive '64
Murder on Approval '56
Norman Conquest '53
The Magic Bow '47

Masaki Kobayashi (1916-96)
Samurai Rebellion '67
Kwaidan '64
The Human Condition: A Soldier's Prayer '61
The Human Condition: Road to Eternity '59
The Human Condition: No Greater Love '58

Chris Koch
A Guy Thing '02
Snow Day '00

Howard W. Koch (1916-2001)
Badge 373 '73
Born Reckless '59
Girl in Black Stockings '57

David Koepp
Stir of Echoes '99
The Trigger Effect '96

Ana Kokkinos (1959-)
Head On '98
Only the Brave '94

Amos Kollek
Fiona '98
Whore 2 '94
Double Edge '92
High Stakes '89
Forever, Lulu '87
Goodbye, New York '85

Xavier Koller (1944-)
Squanto: A Warrior's Tale '94
Journey of Hope '90

Andrei Konchalovsky (1937-)
The Odyssey '97
The Inner Circle '91
Homer and Eddie '89
Tango and Cash '89
Shy People '87
Duet for One '86
Runaway Train '85
Maria's Lovers '84
Siberiade '79

Jackie Kong
The Underachievers '88
Blood Diner '87
Night Patrol '85
The Being '83

Barbara Kopple (1946-)
Fallen Champ: The Untold Story of Mike Tyson '93
Keeping On '81
Harlan County, U.S.A. '76

Alexander Korda (1893-1956)
That Hamilton Woman '41
The Thief of Bagdad '40
Rembrandt '36
Private Life of Don Juan '34
The Private Life of Henry VIII '33
Wedding Rehearsal '32
Marius '31

Zoltan Korda (1895-1961)
Cry, the Beloved Country '51
Sahara '43
The Jungle Book '42
The Thief of Bagdad '40
The Four Feathers '39
Drums '38
Elephant Boy '37
Sanders of the River '35
If I Were Rich '33

Hirokazu Kore-eda
After Life '98
Maborosi '95

Harmony Korine
Julien Donkey-boy '99
Gummo '97

John Korty (1936-)
Ms. Scrooge '97
Redwood Curtain '95
Getting Out '94
They Watch '93
Eye on the Sparrow '91
Long Road Home '91
Cast the First Stone '89
Baby Girl Scott '87
Deadly Business '86
The Ewok Adventure '84
The Haunting Passion '83
A Christmas Without Snow '80
Forever '78
Oliver's Story '78
The Autobiography of Miss Jane Pittman '74
Class of '63 '73
Silence '73
The People '71

Henry Koster (1905-88)
The Singing Nun '66
Dear Brigitte '65
Mr. Hobbs Takes a Vacation '62
Flower Drum Song '61
The Story of Ruth '60
The Naked Maja '59
My Man Godfrey '57
D-Day, the Sixth of June '56
A Man Called Peter '55
The Virgin Queen '55
Desiree '54
The Robe '53
Stars and Stripes Forever '52
No Highway in the Sky '51
Harvey '50
Come to the Stable '49
The Inspector General '49
The Bishop's Wife '47
It Started with Eve '41
First Love '39
Three Smart Girls Grow Up '39
The Rage of Paris '38
100 Men and a Girl '37
Three Smart Girls '36

Ted Kotcheff (1931-)
Family of Cops '95
Red Shoe Diaries 5: Weekend Pass '95
Hidden Assassin '94
Red Shoe Diaries 3: Another Woman's Lipstick '93
Folks! '92
Weekend at Bernie's '89
Winter People '89
Switching Channels '88
Joshua Then and Now '85
Uncommon Valor '83
First Blood '82
Split Image '82
North Dallas Forty '79
Who Is Killing the Great Chefs of Europe? '78
Fun with Dick and Jane '77
The Apprenticeship of Duddy Kravitz '74
Billy Two Hats '74
Tiara Tahiti '62

Jim Kouf (1951-)
Gang Related '96
Disorganized Crime '89
Miracles '86

Bernard L. Kowalski (1929-)
Nashville Beat '89
B.A.D. Cats '80
Marciano '79
Nativity '78
Sssssss '73
The Woman Hunter '72
Macho Callahan '70
Stiletto '69
Attack of the Giant Leeches '59
Night of the Blood Beast '58

Soeren Kragh-Jacobsen
Mifune '99
Emma's Shadow '88

Stanley Kramer (1913-2001)
The Runner Stumbles '79
The Domino Principle '77
Oklahoma Crude '73
Bless the Beasts and Children '71
R.P.M.* (* Revolutions Per Minute) '70
The Secret of Santa Vittoria '69
Guess Who's Coming to Dinner '67

Ship of Fools '65
It's a Mad, Mad, Mad, Mad World '63
Judgment at Nuremberg '61
Inherit the Wind '60
On the Beach '59
The Defiant Ones '58
The Pride and the Passion '57
Not as a Stranger '55

Norman Krasna (1909-84)
The Ambassador's Daughter '56
The Big Hangover '50

Paul Krasny (1935-2001)
Drug Wars 2: The Cocaine Cartel '92
Back to Hannibal: The Return of Tom Sawyer and Huckleberry Finn '90
When Hell Was in Session '82
Centennial '78
Joe Panther '76
Christina '74

John Krish
Man Who Had Power Over Women '70
The Unearthly Stranger '64

Suri Krishnamma
A Respectable Trade '98
A Man of No Importance '94

Allen Kroeker
Showdown at Williams Creek '91
Age Old Friends '89
Heaven on Earth '89
Tramp at the Door '87

Jon Kroll
Menno's Mind '96
Amanda and the Alien '95

Steve Kroschel
Avalanche '99
Running Free '94

Lisa Krueger
Committed '99
Manny & Lo '96

Michael Krueger (-1990)
Mindkiller '87
Night Vision '87

Stanley Kubrick (1928-99)
Eyes Wide Shut '99
Full Metal Jacket '87
The Shining '80
Barry Lyndon '75
A Clockwork Orange '71
2001: A Space Odyssey '68
Dr. Strangelove, or: How I Learned to Stop Worrying and Love the Bomb '64
Lolita '62
Spartacus '60
Paths of Glory '57
The Killing '56
Killer's Kiss '55

Buzz Kulik (1923-99)
Around the World in 80 Days '89
Code Name: Dancer '87
Women of Valor '86
Rage of Angels '83
The Hunter '80
From Here to Eternity '79
The Lindbergh Kidnapping Case '76
Babe! '75
Bad Ronald '74
Pioneer Woman '73
Shamus '73
Brian's Song '71
Riot '69
Sergeant Ryker '68
Villa Rides '68

Edward Kull (1886-1946)
Tarzan and the Green Goddess '38
The New Adventures of Tarzan '35

Kei Kumai
Love and Faith '78
Sandakan No. 8 '74

Roger Kumble
The Sweetest Thing '02
Cruel Intentions 2 '99
Cruel Intentions '98

Koreyoshi Kurahara
Hiroshima '95
Antarctica '84

Akira Kurosawa (1910-98)
Rhapsody in August '91
Akira Kurosawa's Dreams '90
Ran '85
Kagemusha '80
Dersu Uzala '75
Dodes 'ka-den '70
Red Beard '65
High & Low '62
Sanjuro '62
Yojimbo '61
The Bad Sleep Well '60
The Hidden Fortress '58
The Lower Depths '57
Throne of Blood '57
I Live in Fear '55
Seven Samurai '54
Ikiru '52
The Idiot '51
Rashomon '51
Scandal '50
A Quiet Duel '49
Stray Dog '49
Drunken Angel '48
One Wonderful Sunday '47
No Regrets for Our Youth '46
The Men Who Tread on the Tiger's Tail '45
Sanshiro Sugata '43

Robert Kurtzman
Wishmaster '97
The Demolitionist '95

Diane Kurys (1948-)
Love After Love '94
A Man in Love '87
Entre-Nous '83
Peppermint Soda '77

Emir Kusturica (1954-)
Black Cat, White Cat '98
Underground '95
Arizona Dream '94
Time of the Gypsies '90
When Father Was Away on Business '85

Fran Rubel Kuzui
Buffy the Vampire Slayer '92
Tokyo Pop '88

Ken Kwapis
Noah '98
The Beautician and the Beast '97
Dunston Checks In '95
He Said, She Said '91
Vibes '88
Sesame Street Presents: Follow That Bird '85
The Beniker Gang '83

Jeff Kwitny
Beyond the Door 3 '91
Iced '88

Paul Kyriazi
Omega Cop '90
Crazed Cop '88
Death Machines '76

Gregory La Cava (1892-1952)
Primrose Path '40
Fifth Avenue Girl '39
Stage Door '37
My Man Godfrey '36
Gabriel Over the White House '33
Big News '29
His First Command '29
Feel My Pulse '28
Running Wild '27

Steven La Rocque
Above Suspicion '00
Samantha '92

Neil LaBute (1963-)
Possession '02
Nurse Betty '00
Your Friends & Neighbors '98
In the Company of Men '96

Harry Lachman (1886-1975)
Castle in the Desert '42
The Loves of Edgar Allen Poe '42
Charlie Chan in Rio '41
Murder over New York '40
Our Relations '36
Baby, Take a Bow '34

John Lafia
Chameleon 3: Dark Angel '00
Man's Best Friend '93
Child's Play 2 '90
Blue Iguana '88

Jean LaFleur
Mystery of the Million Dollar Hockey Puck '80s
Ilsa, the Tigress of Siberia '79

Ron Lagomarsino
My Sister's Keeper '02
Running Mates '00
Dinner at Eight '89

Craig Lahiff
Heaven's Burning '97
Ebbtide '94
Strangers '90
Deadly Possession '88
Fever '88

Joseph Lai
Ninja Powerforce '90
Ninja Showdown '90
Ninja Hunt '80s
Ninja Strike Force '88
The Power of the Ninjitsu '88
Ninja Commandments '87
Ninja Operation: Licensed to Terminate '87

Harvey Laidman (1942-)
The Boy Who Loved Trolls '84
Steel Cowboy '78

John Laing (-1979)
Absent Without Leave '95
The Lost Tribe '89
Dangerous Orphans '86
Beyond Reasonable Doubt '80

Frank Laloggia (1954-)
Mother '94
The Lady in White '88
Fear No Evil '80

Ringo Lam (1954-)
Replicant '01
Maximum Risk '96
Full Contact '92
Twin Dragons '92
Prison on Fire 2 '91
Undeclared War '91
Prison on Fire '87

Bruce Lambert
Vampire Raiders—Ninja Queen '89
Ninja Phantom Heroes '87
Ninja Fantasy '86
Ninja, the Violent Sorcerer '86
Ninja Masters of Death '85

Mary Lambert
The In Crowd '00
Dragstrip Girl '94
Grand Isle '92
Pet Sematary 2 '92
Pet Sematary '89
Siesta '87

Charles Lamont (1895-1993)
Francis in the Haunted House '56
The Kettles in the Ozarks '56
Abbott and Costello Meet the Mummy '55
Abbott and Costello Meet the Keystone Kops '54
Ma and Pa Kettle at Home '54
Abbott and Costello Go to Mars '53
Ma and Pa Kettle on Vacation '53
Abbott and Costello Meet Captain Kidd '52
Abbott and Costello Meet Dr. Jekyll and Mr. Hyde '52
Abbott and Costello Meet the Invisible Man '51
Comin' Round the Mountain '51
Flame of Araby '51
Abbott and Costello in the Foreign Legion '50
Ma and Pa Kettle Go to Town '50
Bagdad '49
Ma and Pa Kettle '49
Salome, Where She Danced '45
Hit the Ice '43
Panama Patrol '39
Shadows over Shanghai '38
International Crime '37
Wallaby Jim of the Islands '37
Bulldog Edition '36
The Dark Hour '36
Circumstantial Evidence '35
A Shot in the Dark '35
Sons of Steel '35
The World Accuses '35

Albert Lamorisse (1922-70)
Circus Angel '65
Voyage en Balloon '59
The Red Balloon '56
White Mane '52

Lew (Louis Friedlander) Landers (1901-62)
Torpedo Alley '53
Dynamite Pass '50
The Adventures of Gallant Bess '48
Inner Sanctum '48
Death Valley '46
The Mask of Diijon '46
The Enchanted Forest '45
I'm from Arkansas '44
U-Boat Prisoner '44
Return of the Vampire '43
Back in the Saddle '41
Ridin' on a Rainbow '41
Wagon's Westward '40
Bad Lands '39
Law of the Underworld '38
Flight from Glory '37
The Raven '35
Rustlers of Red Dog '35
Tailspin Tommy '34

James Landis
Deadwood '65
Nasty Rabbit '64
The Sadist '63
Stakeout '62

John Landis (1950-)
Blues Brothers 2000 '98
Dying to Get Rich '98
The Stupids '95
Beverly Hills Cop 3 '94
Innocent Blood '92
Oscar '91
Coming to America '88
Amazon Women on the Moon '87
Three Amigos '86
Into the Night '85
Spies Like Us '85
Trading Places '83
Twilight Zone: The Movie '83
An American Werewolf in London '81
The Blues Brothers '80
National Lampoon's Animal House '78
Kentucky Fried Movie '77
Schlock '73

Michael Landon (1936-91)
Sam's Son '84
Killing Stone '78
The Loneliest Runner '76
It's Good to Be Alive '74
Little House on the Prairie '74

Paul Landres (1912-2001)
Flipper's Odyssey '66
Go, Johnny Go! '59
Return of Dracula '58
Square Dance Jubilee '51

Andrew Lane
Trade Off '95
The Secretary '94
Desperate Motives '92
Mortal Passions '90
Jake Speed '86

Eric Laneuville (1952-)
The Ernest Green Story '93
The Mighty Pawns '87
Hard Lessons '86

Sidney Lanfield (1898-1972)
Skirts Ahoy! '52
The Lemon Drop Kid '51
Sorrowful Jones '49
Station West '48
Where There's Life '47
My Favorite Blonde '42
You'll Never Get Rich '41
The Hound of the Baskervilles '39
Second Fiddle '39
Thin Ice '37
One in a Million '36
Red Salute '35

Fritz Lang (1890-1976)
The Thousand Eyes of Dr. Mabuse '60
The Indian Tomb '59
Journey to the Lost City '58
Beyond a Reasonable Doubt '56
While the City Sleeps '56
Moonfleet '55
Human Desire '54
The Big Heat '53
Clash by Night '52
Rancho Notorious '52
Secret Beyond the Door '48
Cloak and Dagger '46
Scarlet Street '45
Ministry of Fear '44
Woman in the Window '44
Hangmen Also Die '42
Western Union '41
Return of Frank James '40
You and Me '38
You Only Live Once '37
Fury '36
Liliom '35
Crimes of Dr. Mabuse '32
M '31
Woman in the Moon '29
Spies '28
Metropolis '26
Kriemhilde's Revenge '24
Siegfried '24
Dr. Mabuse, The Gambler '22
Destiny '21
Spiders '18

Michael (Michel) Lang
The Gift '82
Holiday Hotel '77

Perry Lang (1959-)
Men of War '94
Little Vegas '90

Richard Lang
Texas '94
Christmas Comes to Willow Creek '87
Kung Fu: The Movie '86
Shooting Stars '85
Don't Go to Sleep '82
Strike Force '81
A Change of Seasons '80
The Mountain Men '80
Night Cries '78
Vegas '78
The Word '78
Force of Evil '77
The Hunted Lady '77
Fantasy Island '76

Rocky Lang
Nervous Ticks '93
Race for Glory '89

Samantha Lang (1967-)
The Monkey's Mask '00
The Well '97
Twisted '96

Walter Lang (1898-1972)
Snow White and the Three Stooges '61
Can-Can '60
But Not for Me '59
Desk Set '57
The King and I '56
There's No Business Like Show Business '54
Cheaper by the Dozen '50
The Jackpot '50
Mother Wore Tights '47
State Fair '45
The Magnificent Dope '42
Song of the Islands '42
Moon over Miami '41
Week-End in Havana '41
The Blue Bird '40
Tin Pan Alley '40
The Little Princess '39
Red Kimono '25

Noel Langley (1911-80)
The Search for Bridey Murphy '56
The Adventures of Sadie '55
Svengali '55
The Pickwick Papers '54

Simon Langton (1941-)
Pride and Prejudice '95
Catherine Cookson's The Cinder Path '94
Casanova '87
Laguna Heat '87
The Whistle Blower '87
Anna Karenina '85
Act of Passion: The Lost Honor of Kathryn Beck '83
Danger UXB '81
The Duchess of Duke Street '78

Lawrence Lanoff
The Chosen One: Legend of the Raven '98
Miami Hustle '95
Playing Dangerous '95
Temptress '95
Indecent Behavior '93

Anthony M. Lanza
The Incredible Two-Headed Transplant '71
The Glory Stompers '67

James Lapine
Earthly Possessions '99
Life with Mikey '93
Impromptu '90
Sunday in the Park with George '86

Joseph (Jose Ramon) Larraz (1929-)
Golden Lady '79
Vampyres '74
The House that Vanished '73

Sheldon Larry (1949-)
Trial by Media '00
Family of Cops 3 '98
Behind Enemy Lines '85
Terminal Choice '85

Keith Larsen (1926-)
Whitewater Sam '78
Young & Free '78
Trap on Cougar Mountain '72
Mission Batangas '69

John Lasseter (1957-)
Toy Story 2 '99
A Bug's Life '98
Toy Story '95

Stan Lathan (1945-)
Uncle Tom's Cabin '87
Beat Street '84
Go Tell It on the Mountain '84
Amazing Grace '74

Steve Latshaw (1959-)
Death Mask '98
Biohazard: The Alien Force '95
Jack-O '95

Dark Universe '93
Alberto Lattuada (1914-)
Christopher Columbus '85
La Cicada '83
Stay As You Are '78
Love in the City '53
Anna '51
Variety Lights '51
Patrick Lau
The Scarlet Pimpernel '99
The Scarlet Pimpernel 2: Mademoiselle Guillotine '99
Invasion: Earth '98
Michael Laughlin
Mesmerized '84
Strange Invaders '83
Strange Behavior '81
Tom Laughlin (1939-)
The Trial of Billy Jack '74
Billy Jack '71
Born Losers '67
Frank Launder (1907-97)
The Great St. Trinian's Train Robbery '66
The Pure Hell of St. Trinian's '61
Blue Murder at St. Trinian's '56
The Belles of St. Trinian's '53
The Happiest Days of Your Life '50
Captain Boycott '47
I See a Dark Stranger '46
Fabrizio Laurenti
The Crawlers '93
Witchery '88
Georges Lautner (1926-)
La Cage aux Folles 3: The Wedding '86
My Other Husband '85
Le Professionnel '81
Icy Breasts '75
No Problem '75
Road to Salina '68
Jean-Claude Lauzon (1953-97)
Leolo '92
Night Zoo '87
Arnold Laven (1922-)
Rough Night in Jericho '67
Geronimo '62
The Monster That Challenged the World '57
Without Warning '52
Martin Lavut (1939-)
Smokescreen '90
Palais Royale '88
Charlie Grant's War '80
War Brides '80
Clara Law
Floating Life '95
Erotique '94
Temptation of a Monk '94
Autumn Moon '92
The Reincarnation of Golden Lotus '89
Diarmuid Lawrence
Heat of the Sun '99
Emma '97
John Lawrence (1931-92)
Savage Abduction '73
Cycle Psycho '72
Ray Lawrence
Lantana '01
Bliss '85
J.F. Lawton (1960-)
The Hunted '94
Pizza Man '91
Cannibal Women in the Avocado Jungle of Death '89
Richard Laxton
Invasion: Earth '98
Poldark '96
Band of Gold '95
Wilford Leach (-1988)
The Pirates of Penzance '83
The Wedding Party '69
Philip Leacock (1917-90)
Three Sovereigns for Sarah '85
Angel City '80
The Curse of King Tut's Tomb '80
Wild & Wooly '78
Killer on Board '77
Dying Room Only '73
Baffled '72
Shattered Silence '71
War Lover '62
Let No Man Write My Epitaph '60
The Spanish Gardener '57
Escapade '55
David Lean (1908-91)
A Passage to India '84
Ryan's Daughter '70
Doctor Zhivago '65
Lawrence of Arabia '62
The Bridge on the River Kwai '57
Summertime '55
Hobson's Choice '53
Madeleine '50
Oliver Twist '48
This Happy Breed '47
Brief Encounter '46
Great Expectations '46
Blithe Spirit '45
In Which We Serve '43
Reginald LeBorg (1902-89)
The Sibling '72
House of the Black Death '65
Diary of a Madman '63
Sins of Jezebel '54
The White Orchid '54
G.I. Jane '51
Great Jesse James Raid '49
Dead Man's Eyes/Pillow of Death '44
Jungle Woman '44
The Mummy's Ghost '44
Weird Woman/Frozen Ghost '44
Calling Dr. Death/Strange Confession '43
Jean-Paul LeChanois (1909-85)
Le Cas du Dr. Laurent '57
Les Miserables '57
Passion for Life '48
Patrice Leconte (1947-)
The Widow of Saint-Pierre '00
The Girl on the Bridge '98
Ridicule '96
The Hairdresser's Husband '92
Monsieur Hire '89
French Fried Vacation '79
Mimi Leder (1952-)
Pay It Forward '00
Deep Impact '98
The Peacemaker '97
Woman with a Past '92
Paul Leder (1926-96)
Killing Obsession '94
Molly and Gina '94
The Abduction of Allison Tate '92
The Baby Doll Murders '92
Deadly Conspiracy '91
Frame Up '91
Twenty Dollar Star '91
Exiled in America '90
Murder by Numbers '89
Body Count '87
Vultures '84
Sketches of a Strangler '78
A*P*E* '76
I Dismember Mama '74
David Ross Lederman (1895-1972)
Cooking Up Trouble '44
Shadows on the Stairs '41
Racketeers of the Range '39
Tarzan's Revenge '38
Hell-Ship Morgan '36
Daring Danger '32
The Fighting Marshal '32
The Riding Tornado '32
Texas Cyclone '32
Two-Fisted Law '32
Phantom of the West '31
Range Feud '31
Paul Leduc (1942-)
Frida '84
Reed: Insurgent Mexico '73
Ang Lee (1954-)
Crouching Tiger, Hidden Dragon '00
Ride with the Devil '99
The Ice Storm '97
Sense and Sensibility '95
Eat Drink Man Woman '94
The Wedding Banquet '93
Pushing Hands '92
Charles Lee (1882-1927)
Full Metal Ninja '89
Ninja of the Magnificence '89
Damian Lee
Agent Red '00
Trail of a Serial Killer '98
Fatal Combat '96
Moving Target '96
Terminal Rush '96
When the Bullet Hits the Bone '96
Street Law '95
The Donor '94
Ski School '91
Abraxas: Guardian of the Universe '90
Boxcar Blues '90
Food of the Gods: Part 2 '88
Last Man Standing '87
DeWitt Lee
Ransom Money '88
The Legend of Jedediah Carver '70s
Jack Lee (1913-)
The Captain's Table '60
Robbery under Arms '57
Wooden Horse '50
Malcolm Lee
Undercover Brother '02
The Best Man '99
Norman Lee
Chamber of Horrors '40
Bulldog Drummond at Bay '37
Robert Lee
The Silencer '99
Dead Fire '98
Crackerjack 2 '97
Act of War '96
Virtual Assassin '95
Rowland V. Lee (1891-1975)
Captain Kidd '45
The Bridge of San Luis Rey '44
The Son of Monte Cristo '40
Son of Frankenstein '39
The Tower of London '39
Love from a Stranger '37
Toast of New York '37
One Rainy Afternoon '36
The Three Musketeers '35
The Count of Monte Cristo '34
Doomsday '28
Spike Lee (1957-)
Bamboozled '00
Summer of Sam '99
He Got Game '98
Get On the Bus '96
Girl 6 '96
Clockers '95
Crooklyn '94
Malcolm X '92
Jungle Fever '91
Mo' Better Blues '90
Do the Right Thing '89
School Daze '88
She's Gotta Have It '86
Joe's Bed-Stuy Barbershop: We Cut Heads '83
Doug Lefler
Dragonheart: A New Beginning '00
Hercules the Legendary Journeys, Vol. 3: The Circle of Fire '94
Michael Lehmann (1957-)
40 Days and 40 Nights '02
My Giant '98
The Truth about Cats and Dogs '96
Airheads '94
Hudson Hawk '91
The Applegates '89
Heathers '89
Neil Leifer
Trading Hearts '87
Yesterday's Hero '79
Mike Leigh (1943-)
Topsy Turvy '99
Career Girls '97
Secrets and Lies '95
Naked '93
Life Is Sweet '90
High Hopes '88
Four Days in July '85
Home Sweet Home '82
Meantime '81
Grown Ups '80
Who's Who '78
Abigail's Party '77
Kiss of Death '77
Nuts in May '76
Hard Labour '73
Bleak Moments '71
Mitchell Leisen (1898-1972)
The Girl Most Likely '57
Golden Earrings '47
To Each His Own '46
Frenchman's Creek '44
The Lady Is Willing '42
Remember the Night '40
Midnight '39
The Big Broadcast of 1938 '38
Easy Living '37
Swing High, Swing Low '37
Hands Across the Table '35
Death Takes a Holiday '34
Murder at the Vanities '34
Christopher Leitch
I've Been Waiting for You '98
Courage Mountain '89
Teen Wolf Too '87
The Hitter '79
David Leland (1947-)
Band of Brothers '01
The Land Girls '98
The Big Man: Crossing the Line '91
Checking Out '89
Wish You Were Here '87
Claude Lelouch (1937-)
Les Miserables '95
Bandits '86
A Man and a Woman: 20 Years Later '86
Edith & Marcel '83
Bolero '82
Cat and Mouse '78
Robert et Robert '78
Another Man, Another Chance '77
And Now My Love '74
Happy New Year '73
A Man and a Woman '66
James (Momel) Lemmo
Bodily Harm '95
Dream a Little Dream 2 '94
Relentless 3 '93
We're Talkin' Serious Money '92
Tripwire '89
Heart '87
Kasi Lemmons (1961-)
The Caveman's Valentine '01
Eve's Bayou '97
Rusty Lemorande
The Turn of the Screw '92
Journey to the Center of the Earth '88
Paul Leni (1885-1929)
The Cat and the Canary '27
The Man Who Laughs '27
Waxworks '24
Umberto Lenzi (1931-)
Bridge to Hell '87
City of the Walking Dead '83
Emerald Jungle '80
Almost Human '79
From Hell to Victory '79
Battleforce '78
Eyeball '78
Man from Deep River '77
Bruce Lee Fights Back from the Grave '76
Battle of the Commandos '71
Paranoia '69
Desert Commandos '67
Messalina vs. the Son of Hercules '64
Pirates of the Seven Seas '62
Arthur Leonard
Boy! What a Girl '45
The Devil's Daughter '39
Brett Leonard
Virtuosity '95
Hideaway '94
The Lawnmower Man '92
Dead Pit '89
Robert Z. Leonard (1889-1968)
The King's Thief '55
Clown '53
The Duchess of Idaho '50
Nancy Goes to Rio '50
In the Good Old Summertime '49
Weekend at the Waldorf '45
When Ladies Meet '41
Ziegfeld Girl '41
New Moon '40
Pride and Prejudice '40
Broadway Serenade '39
Girl of the Golden West '38
The Firefly '37
Maytime '37
The Great Ziegfeld '36
Dancing Lady '33
Strange Interlude '32
Susan Lenox: Her Fall and Rise '31
The Divorcee '30
A Mormon Maid '17
Sergio Leone (1929-89)
Once Upon a Time in America '84
A Fistful of Dynamite '72
Once Upon a Time in the West '68
The Good, the Bad and the Ugly '67
For a Few Dollars More '65
A Fistful of Dollars '64
Po Chich Leong (1939-)
Return to Cabin by the Lake '01
Cabin by the Lake '00
Immortality '98
Ping Pong '87
Antonio Leonviola (1913-95)
Tor '64
Atlas in the Land of the Cyclops '61
Angel in a Taxi '59
Robert Lepage (1957-)
No '98
Le Polygraphe '96
The Confessional '95
Dan Lerner
Lone Justice 3: Showdown at Plum Creek '96
Shame '92
Irving Lerner (1909-76)
Cry of Battle '63
Studs Lonigan '60
Jeff Leroy
Crystal's Diary '99
Crack Up '97
Mervyn LeRoy (1900-87)
Moment to Moment '66
Gypsy '62
The Devil at 4 O'Clock '61
The FBI Story '59
No Time for Sergeants '58
The Bad Seed '56
A Majority of One '56
Mister Roberts '55
Rose Marie '54
Latin Lovers '53
Lovely to Look At '52
Million Dollar Mermaid '52
Quo Vadis '51
Any Number Can Play '49
East Side, West Side '49
Little Women '49
Homecoming '48
Without Reservations '46
Thirty Seconds Over Tokyo '44
Madame Curie '43
Johnny Eager '42
Random Harvest '42
Blossoms in the Dust '41
Waterloo Bridge '40
They Won't Forget '37
Anthony Adverse '36
Three Men on a Horse '36
Sweet Adeline '35
Gold Diggers of 1933 '33
I Am a Fugitive from a Chain Gang '32
Three on a Match '32
Tonight or Never '31
Little Caesar '30
Mark L. Lester (1949-)
Sacrifice '00
The Base '99
Blowback '99
Misbegotten '98
Double Take '97
The Ex '96
Public Enemies '96
Night of the Running Man '94
Extreme Justice '93
Showdown in Little Tokyo '91
Class of 1999 '90
Armed and Dangerous '86
Commando '85
Firestarter '84
Class of 1984 '82
Gold of the Amazon Women '79
Roller Boogie '79
Stunts '77
Bobbie Jo and the Outlaw '76
Truck Stop Women '74
Steel Arena '72
Richard Lester (1932-)
The Return of the Musketeers '89
Finders Keepers '84
Superman 3 '83
Superman 2 '80
Butch and Sundance: The Early Days '79
Cuba '79
The Ritz '76
Robin and Marian '76
The Four Musketeers '75
Royal Flash '75
Juggernaut '74
The Three Musketeers '74
Petulia '68
How I Won the War '67
A Funny Thing Happened on the Way to the Forum '66
Help! '65
The Knack '65
A Hard Day's Night '64
The Mouse on the Moon '62
Sheldon Lettich (1962-)
The Last Warrior '99
Perfect Target '98
Only the Strong '93
Double Impact '91
Lionheart '90
Brian Levant (1952-)
Snow Dogs '02
The Flintstones in Viva Rock Vegas '00
Jingle All the Way '96
The Flintstones '94
Beethoven '92

Problem Child 2 '91
Joseph Levering
Phantom Gold '38
Defenders of the Law '31
Sea Devils '31
Michel Levesque
Sweet Sugar '72
Werewolves on Wheels '71
William A. Levey (1943-)
Committed '91
Hellgate '89
Lightning: The White Stallion '86
Monaco Forever '83
The Happy Hooker Goes to Washington '77
Slumber Party '57 '76
Wham-Bam, Thank You Spaceman '75
Blackenstein '73
Alan J. Levi
Dead Man's Revenge '93
Blood Song '82
Last Song '80
Riding with Death '76
Henry Levin (1901-80)
Scout's Honor '80
Run for the Roses '78
That Man Bolt '73
Desperados '69
The Ambushers '67
Murderers' Row '66
The Wonderful World of the Brothers Grimm '62
The Wonders of Aladdin '61
Where the Boys Are '60
Journey to the Center of the Earth '59
Lonely Man '57
The Warriors '55
The Farmer Takes a Wife '53
Jolson Sings Again '49
Man from Colorado '49
Cry of the Werewolf '44
Marc Levin
White Boyz '99
Slam '98
Peter Levin
A Stranger in Town '95
Take Down '92
Washington Mistress '81
Comeback Kid '80
Rape and Marriage: The Rideout Case '80
Paul Levine
Deal of a Lifetime '99
Operation Intercept '95
Barry Levinson (1942-)
Bandits '01
An Everlasting Piece '00
Liberty Heights '99
Sphere '97
Wag the Dog '97
Sleepers '96
Disclosure '94
Jimmy Hollywood '94
Toys '92
Bugsy '91
Avalon '90
Rain Man '88
Good Morning, Vietnam '87
Tin Men '87
Young Sherlock Holmes '85
The Natural '84
Diner '82
Israeli Nadav Levitan (1945-)
The Seventeenth Bride '84
Intimate Story '81
Eugene Levy (1946-)
Sodbusters '94
Once Upon a Crime '92
I. Robert Levy
Can I Do It...Till I Need Glasses? '77
If You Don't Stop It...You'll Go Blind '77
Jefery Levy
S.F.W. '94
Inside Monkey Zetterland '93
Ralph Levy
Bedtime Story '63
A Christmas Carol '54
Scott Levy
Baby Face Nelson '97
Spectre '96
Piranha '95
Unknown Origin '95
Midnight Tease '94
Shawn Levy
Big Fat Liar '02
Address Unknown '96
Shuki Levy
Turbo: A Power Rangers Movie '96
Blind Vision '91
Perfect Victims '87
Albert Lewin (1916-96)
Pandora and the Flying Dutchman '51
The Private Affairs of Bel Ami '47
Picture of Dorian Gray '45
The Moon and Sixpence '43
Ben Lewin (1946-)
Paperback Romance '96
The Favor, the Watch, & the Very Big Fish '92
Georgia '87
Christopher Lewis
The Red Raven Kiss-Off '90
Revenge '86
The Ripper '86
Blood Cult '85
Herschell Gordon Lewis (1926-)
The Gore-Gore Girls '72
This Stuff'll Kill Ya! '71
The Wizard of Gore '70
How to Make a Doll '68
Just for the Hell of It '68
The Psychic '68
She-Devils on Wheels '68
Something Weird '68
Blast-Off Girls '67
The Girl, the Body and the Pill '67
Gruesome Twosome '67
Suburban Roulette '67
A Taste of Blood '67
Jimmy, the Boy Wonder '66
Monster a Go-Go! '65
Color Me Blood Red '64
Moonshine Mountain '64
2000 Maniacs '64
Blood Feast '63
Scum of the Earth '63
Nature's Playmates '62
The Prime Time '60
Jerry Lewis (1926-)
Cracking Up '83
Hardly Working '81
Which Way to the Front? '70
Big Mouth '67
Family Jewels '65
The Patsy '64
The Nutty Professor '63
The Errand Boy '61
The Ladies' Man '61
The Bellboy '60
Joseph H. Lewis (1907-)
Terror in a Texas Town '58
Seventh Cavalry '56
Big Combo '55
A Lawless Street '55
Retreat, Hell! '52
Gun Crazy '49
Criminals Within '41
The Invisible Ghost '41
Pride of the Bowery '41
Boys of the City '40
That Gang of Mine '40
Robert Lewis (1909-97)
The Crying Child '96
Circumstances Unknown '95
Don't Talk to Strangers '94
Memories of Murder '90
Dead Reckoning '89
Ladykillers '88
City Killer '87
Embassy '85
A Summer to Remember '84
Desperate Lives '82
Child Bride of Short Creek '81
Fallen Angel '81
If Things Were Different '79
S*H*E '79
No Room to Run '78
Pray for the Wildcats '74
Peter Paul Liapis
The Stepdaughter '00
Alone with a Stranger '99
Captured '99
Carlo Liconti
Goodnight, Michelangelo '89
Concrete Angels '87
Jeff Lieberman
Remote Control '88
Just Before Dawn '80
Blue Sunshine '78
Squirm '76
Robert Lieberman (1941-)
Tom Clancy's Netforce '98
D3: The Mighty Ducks '96
Titanic '96
Fire in the Sky '93
Table for Five '83
Will: G. Gordon Liddy '82
Peter Lilienthal (1929-)
Ruby's Dream '82
The Uprising '81
David '79
Kevin Lima
102 Dalmatians '00
Tarzan '99
A Goofy Movie '94
Doug Liman
The Bourne Identity '02
Go '99
Swingers '96
Getting In '94
Kevin J. Lindenmuth
Addicted to Murder 3: Bloodlust '99
Rage of the Werewolf '99
Addicted to Murder 2: Tainted Blood '97
The Alien Agenda: Endangered Species '97
The Alien Agenda: Under the Skin '97
The Alien Agenda: Out of the Darkness '96
Addicted to Murder '95
Lance Lindsay
Real Bullets '90
Star Crystal '85
Michael Lindsay-Hogg (1940-)
Horton Foote's Alone '97
Frankie Starlight '95
Running Mates '92
The Habitation of Dragons '91
Murder by Moonlight '91
The Object of Beauty '91
Strange Case of Dr. Jekyll & Mr. Hyde '89
The Little Match Girl '87
As Is '85
Master Harold and the Boys '84
Thumbelina '82
Brideshead Revisited '81
Nasty Habits '77
Let It Be '70
Leopold Lindtberg
Four in a Jeep '51
The Last Chance '45
John F. Link
Call of the Forest '49
The Devil's Cargo '48
Richard Linklater (1961-)
Tape '01
Waking Life '01
The Newton Boys '97
subUrbia '96
Before Sunrise '94
Dazed and Confused '93
Slacker '91
Art Linson (1942-)
The Wild Life '84
Where the Buffalo Roam '80
Aaron Lipstadt (1952-)
Blood Money '99
Pair of Aces '90
City Limits '85
Android '82
Steven Lisberger (1951-)
Slipstream '89
Hot Pursuit '87
Tron '82
David Lister
The Rutanga Tapes '90
Hunted '88
Dwight Little
Boss of Bosses '99
Murder at 1600 '97
Free Willy 2: The Adventure Home '95
Rapid Fire '92
Marked for Death '90
The Phantom of the Opera '89
Bloodstone '88
Halloween 4: The Return of Michael Myers '88
Getting Even '86
Lynne Littman
Having Our Say: The Delany Sisters' First 100 Years '99
Testament '83
Anatole Litvak (1902-74)
Night of the Generals '67
Goodbye Again '61
Anastasia '56
The Snake Pit '48
Sorry, Wrong Number '48
The Long Night '47
All This and Heaven Too '40
City for Conquest '40
Amazing Dr. Clitterhouse '38
The Sisters '38
Mayerling '36
Gerry Lively
Darkness Falls '98
Body Moves '90
Carlo Lizzani (1922-)
House of the Yellow Carpet '84
Last Four Days '77
Love in the City '53
Luis Llosa
Anaconda '96
The Specialist '94
800 Leagues Down the Amazon '93
Fire on the Amazon '93
Sniper '92
Crime Zone '88
Hour of the Assassin '86
Frank Lloyd (1886-1960)
The Last Command '55
Blood on the Sun '45
Forever and a Day '43
The Howards of Virginia '40
If I Were King '38
Mutiny on the Bounty '35
Cavalcade '33
Hoopla '33
Oliver Twist '22
Ken Loach (1936-)
Bread and Roses '00
My Name Is Joe '98
Carla's Song '97
Land and Freedom '95
Ladybird, Ladybird '93
Raining Stones '93
Riff Raff '92
Hidden Agenda '90
Singing the Blues in Red '87
Family Life '71
Victor Lobl
Eden 3 '93
Eden '92
Sondra Locke (1947-)
Trading Favors '97
Impulse '90
Ratboy '86
Bob Logan
Meatballs 4 '92
Repossessed '90
Up Your Alley '89
Joshua Logan (1908-88)
Paint Your Wagon '69
Camelot '67
Ensign Pulver '64
Fanny '61
Tall Story '60
South Pacific '58
Sayonara '57
Bus Stop '56
Picnic '55
Tom Logan
Dream Trap '90
The Night Brings Charlie '90
Dimitri Logothetis
Body Shot '93
The Closer '91
Slaughterhouse Rock '88
Pretty Smart '87
J. Anthony (Jose Antonio de la Loma) Loma (1924-)
Fine Gold '88
A Man of Passion '88
Counterforce '87
Target Eagle '84
Surprise Attack '70s
The Boldest Job in the West '71
Lou Lombardo
P.K. and the Kid '85
Russian Roulette '75
Ulli Lommel (1944-)
The Big Sweat '90
Cold Heat '90
Warbirds '88
Overkill '86
Strangers in Paradise '84
Devonsville Terror '83
Olivia '83
Brainwaves '82
The Boogey Man '80
Cocaine Cowboys '79
Tenderness of the Wolves '73
Richard Loncraine (1946-)
Band of Brothers '01
Richard III '95
The Wedding Gift '93
Bellman and True '88
Deep Cover '88
Brimstone & Treacle '82
The Missionary '82
Full Circle '77
Jerry London (1937-)
Victim of Love '91
Haunting of Sarah Hardy '89
Kiss Shot '89
Rent-A-Cop '88
Manhunt for Claude Dallas '86
Chiefs '83
The Scarlet & the Black '83
Father Figure '80
Shogun '80
Stanley Long
Adventures of a Private Eye '87
Adventures of a Taxi Driver '76
Harry S. Longstreet
The Perfect Daughter '96
A Vow to Kill '94
Sex, Love and Cold Hard Cash '93
Temistocles Lopez
Bird of Prey '95
Chain of Desire '93
Exquisite Corpses '88
Jean-Claude Lord (1943-)
Landslide '92
Eddie and the Cruisers 2: Eddie Lives! '89
Mindfield '89
Toby McTeague '87
The Vindicator '85
Covergirl '83
Visiting Hours '82
Joseph Losey (1909-84)
Steaming '86
La Truite '83
Roads to the South '78
Mr. Klein '76
Romantic Englishwoman '75
A Doll's House '73
Assassination of Trotsky '72
The Go-Between '71
Secret Ceremony '69
Boom! '68
Accident '67
Modesty Blaise '66
King and Country '64
The Servant '63
Eva '62
Time Without Pity '57
The Sleeping Tiger '54
Prowler '51
The Boy with the Green Hair '48
Eb Lottimer
Twisted Love '95
Love Matters '93
Pavel (Lungin) Lounguine
Luna Park '91
Taxi Blues '90
Eugene Lourie (1903-91)
Gorgo '61
The Beast from 20,000 Fathoms '53
Eric Louzil (1951-)
Class of Nuke 'Em High 3: The Good, the Bad and the Subhumanoid '94
Class of Nuke 'Em High 2: Subhumanoid Meltdown '91
Wilding '90
Lust for Freedom '87
Charles Loventhal
Mr. Write '92
My Demon Lover '87
First Time '82
Steven Lovy
Plughead Rewired: Circuitry Man 2 '94
Circuitry Man '90
Lucas Lowe
American Shaolin: King of the Kickboxers 2 '92
The King of the Kickboxers '91
Dick Lowry
Little John '02
Attila '01
The Diamond of Jeru '01
Follow the Stars Home '01
Atomic Train '99
Dean Koontz's Mr. Murder '98
Last Stand at Saber River '96
A Horse for Danny '95
Urban Crossfire '94
The Gambler Returns: The Luck of the Draw '93
In the Line of Duty: Ambush in Waco '93
Till Murder Do Us Part '92
Midnight Murders '91
Archie: Return to Riverdale '90
In the Line of Duty: A Cop for the Killing '90
In the Line of Duty: The FBI Murders '88
Kenny Rogers as the Gambler, Part 3: The Legend Continues '87
Wet Gold '84
Wild Horses '84
Kenny Rogers as the Gambler, Part 2: The Adventure Continues '83
Living Proof: The Hank Williams Jr. Story '83
Smokey and the Bandit, Part 3 '83
Coward of the County '81
The Jayne Mansfield Story '80
Kenny Rogers as the Gambler '80
Nanni Loy (1925-95)
Where's Piccone '84
Cafe Express '83
Head of the Family '71
Arthur Lubin (1899-1995)
The Incredible Mr. Limpet '64
Thief of Baghdad '61

Strategic Air Command '55
The Glenn Miller Story '54
The Naked Spur '53
Thunder Bay '53
Bend of the River '52
Winchester '73 '50
Reign of Terror '49
He Walked by Night '48
Raw Deal '48
Desperate '47
Railroaded '47
T-Men '47
Strange Impersonation '46
Great Flamarion '45

Daniel Mann (1912-91)
The Man Who Broke 1,000 Chains '87
Playing for Time '80
Matilda '78
Journey into Fear '74
Big Mo '73
Interval '73
Willard '71
A Dream of Kings '69
For Love of Ivy '68
Our Man Flint '66
Who's Got the Action? '63
Butterfield 8 '60
The Mountain Road '60
The Last Angry Man '59
Hot Spell '58
The Teahouse of the August Moon '56
I'll Cry Tomorrow '55
The Rose Tattoo '55
Come Back, Little Sheba '52

Delbert Mann (1920-)
Lily in Winter '94
Ironclads '90
The Last Days of Patton '86
Love Leads the Way '84
The Member of the Wedding '83
Night Crossing '81
All Quiet on the Western Front '79
Home to Stay '79
Torn Between Two Lovers '79
The Birch Interval '78
Breaking Up '78
Francis Gary Powers: The True Story of the U-2 Spy '76
The Man Without a Country '73
No Place to Run '72
She Waits '71
David Copperfield '70
The Pink Jungle '68
Heidi '67
A Gathering of Eagles '63
That Touch of Mink '62
Lover Come Back '61
Desire Under the Elms '58
Separate Tables '58
Marty '55

Edward Andrew (Santos Alcocer) Mann (1923-95)
Hooch '76
Cauldron of Blood '67
Hallucination '67

Farhad Mann
Lawnmower Man 2: Beyond Cyberspace '95
Return to Two Moon Junction '93

Michael Mann (1943-)
Ali '01
The Insider '99
Heat '95
The Last of the Mohicans '92
Manhunter '86
The Keep '83
Thief '81
The Jericho Mile '79

Peter Manoogian
Seedpeople '92
Demonic Toys '90
Arena '89
Enemy Territory '87
The Eliminators '86
Dungeonmaster '83

Mark Manos
Josh Kirby...Time Warrior: Chapter 4, Eggs from 70 Million B.C. '95
Liquid Dreams '92

Rene Manzor
Red Shoe Diaries 8: Night of Abandon '97
Warrior Spirit '94

Robert Marcarelli
The Omega Code '99
I Don't Buy Kisses Anymore '92
Original Intent '91

Terry Marcel (1942-)
The Last Seduction 2 '98
Jane & the Lost City '87
Prisoners of the Lost Universe '84
Hawk the Slayer '81

Alex March (1921-89)
Master Mind '73
Firehouse '72
Paper Lion '68

Adam Marcus
Let It Snow '99
Jason Goes to Hell: The Final Friday '93

Mitch Marcus
The Haunting of Hell House '99
Knocking on Death's Door '99
Boltneck '98
A Boy Called Hate '95

Paul Marcus
Eye of the Killer '99
The Break Up '98

Andreas Marfori
Desperate Crimes '93
Evil Clutch '89

Stuart Margolin (1940-)
The Sweetest Gift '98
How the West Was Fun '95
Medicine River '94
Paramedics '88
The Glitter Dome '84
A Shining Season '79

Edwin L. Marin (1899-1951)
The Cariboo Trail '50
Abilene Town '46
Mr. Ace '46
Nocturne '46
Johnny Angel '45
Show Business '44
Tall in the Saddle '44
Invisible Agent '42
Miss Annie Rooney '42
A Christmas Carol '38
Everybody Sing '38
Listen, Darling '38
I'd Give My Life '36
The Death Kiss '33
A Study in Scarlet '33

Lex Marinos
An Indecent Obsession '85
Remember Me '85

Peter Maris
Diplomatic Immunity '91
Hangfire '91
True Blood '89
Viper '88
Terror Squad '87
Land of Doom '84
Delirium '77

Chris Marker (1921-)
Sans Soleil '82
Le Joli Mai '62

Anthony Markes
Bikini Island '91
Last Dance '91

Monte Markham (1935-)
Neon City '91
Defense Play '88

Fletcher Markle (1921-91)
The Incredible Journey '63
Jigsaw '49

Peter Markle (1946-)
The Last Days of Frankie the Fly '96
White Dwarf '95
Wagons East '94
Through the Eyes of a Killer '92
El Diablo '90
Nightbreaker '89
Bat 21 '88
Youngblood '86
Hot Dog ... The Movie! '83
The Personals '83

Robert Markowitz (1935-)
The Great Gatsby '01
Small Vices: A Spenser Mystery '99
David '97
Into Thin Air: Death on Everest '97
The Tuskegee Airmen '95
Afterburn '92
Love, Lies and Murder '91
Decoration Day '90
Too Young to Die '90
Dangerous Life '89
Kojak: The Belarus File '85
My Mother's Secret Life '84
Pray TV '82
A Long Way Home '81

Arthur Marks (1927-)
Monkey Hustle '77
J.D.'s Revenge '76
Bucktown '75
Friday Foster '75
Bonnie's Kids '73
Detroit 9000 '73
Togetherness '70

Ross Kagen Marks
The Twilight of the Golds '97
Homage '95

Richard Marquand (1938-87)
Hearts of Fire '87
The Jagged Edge '85
Until September '84
Return of the Jedi '83
Eye of the Needle '81
The Legacy '79

David Marsh
Stormswept '95
Lords of Magick '88

Philip Marshak
Cataclysm '81
Dracula Sucks '79

Frank Marshall (1954-)
From the Earth to the Moon '98
Congo '95
Alive '93
Arachnophobia '90

Garry Marshall (1934-)
The Princess Diaries '01
Runaway Bride '99
The Other Sister '98
Dear God '96
Exit to Eden '94
Frankie and Johnny '91
Pretty Woman '90
Beaches '88
Overboard '87
Nothing in Common '86
The Flamingo Kid '84
Young Doctors in Love '82

George Marshall (1891-1975)
Eight on the Lam '67
Boy, Did I Get a Wrong Number! '66
How the West Was Won '63
Papa's Delicate Condition '63
The Gazebo '59
It Started with a Kiss '59
The Mating Game '59
The Sad Sack '57
Red Garters '54
Houdini '53
Off Limits '53
Scared Stiff '53
Fancy Pants '50
Never a Dull Moment '50
My Friend Irma '49
The Perils of Pauline '47
Variety Girl '47
The Blue Dahlia '46
Monsieur Beaucaire '46
Murder, He Says '45
Star Spangled Rhythm '42
Valley of the Sun '42
Pot o' Gold '41
Texas '41
The Ghost Breakers '40
Destry Rides Again '39
You Can't Cheat an Honest Man '39
The Goldwyn Follies '38
Show Them No Mercy '35
Pack Up Your Troubles '32

Penny Marshall (1947-)
Riding in Cars with Boys '01
The Preacher's Wife '96
Renaissance Man '94
A League of Their Own '92
Awakenings '90
Big '88
Jumpin' Jack Flash '86

Tonie Marshall
Venus Beauty Institute '98
Pas Tres Catholique '93

William Marshall (1924-)
The Phantom Planet '61
Adventures of Captain Fabian '51

Charles Martin
One Man Jury '78
Dead Right '68
Death of a Scoundrel '56
My Dear Secretary '49

D'Urville Martin (1938-84)
Fass Black '77
Dolemite '75

Eugenio (Gene) Martin (1935-)
Bad Man's River '72
Horror Express '72
Pancho Villa '72
It Happened at Nightmare Inn '70

Frank Martin
Elvis in Hollywood '93
Doctor Butcher M.D. '80

Richard Martin (1956-)
Air Bud 2: Golden Receiver '98
Wounded '97
White Tiger '95
Elizabeth R '72

Jacques Martineau
The Adventures of Felix '99
Jeanne and the Perfect Guy '98

Richard Martini (1955-)
Cannes Man '96
Limit Up '89
You Can't Hurry Love '88

Raymond Martino
Skyscraper '95
To the Limit '95
DaVinci's War '92
American Born '89

Sergio Martino (1938-)
American Tiger '89
Casablanca Express '89
The Opponent '89
Hands of Steel '86
After the Fall of New York '85
The Great Alligator '81
Screamers '80
Mountain of the Cannibal God '79
Day of the Maniac '77
The Cheaters '76
Sex with a Smile '76
Torso '73
Violent Professionals '73
The Next Victim '71
The Scorpion's Tail '71
Blade of the Ripper '70

Leslie Martinson
Return to Africa '89
The Fantastic World of D.C. Collins '84
The Kid with the 200 I.Q. '83
The Kid with the Broken Halo '82
Rescue from Gilligan's Island '78
Fathom '67
Batman '66
PT 109 '63
Hot Rod Girl '56
The Atomic Kid '54

Andrew Marton (1904-92)
Africa Texas Style '67
Around the World Under the Sea '65
Clarence, the Cross-eyed Lion '65
The Thin Red Line '64
The Longest Day '62
Green Fire '55
Gypsy Colt '54
Men of the Fighting Lady '54

Mike Marvin
Wishman '93
The Wraith '87
Hamburger...The Motion Picture '86

Francesco Maselli (1930-)
Time of Indifference '64
Love in the City '53

Noel Mason Smith (1890-)
Fighting Pilot '35
The Night Patrol '26

Joe Massot
Space Riders '83
Wonderwall: The Movie '69

Quentin Masters (1946-)
Dangerous Summer '82
The Stud '78
Thumb Tripping '72

Peter Masterson (1934-)
Mermaid '00
The Only Thrill '97
Lily Dale '96
Arctic Blue '93
Night Game '89
Blood Red '88
Full Moon in Blue Water '88
The Trip to Bountiful '85

Nico Mastorakis (1941-)
Hired to Kill '91
Ninja Academy '90
In the Cold of the Night '89
Terminal Exposure '89
Glitch! '88
Nightmare at Noon '87
The Wind '87
Zero Boys '86
Blind Date '84
Next One '84
Sky High '84

Camillo Mastrocinque
An Angel for Satan '66
Full Hearts & Empty Pockets '63

Armand Mastroianni
Nowhere to Land '00
Fatal Error '99
First Daughter '99
One of Her Own '97
Cameron's Closet '89
Double Revenge '89
Distortions '87
The Supernaturals '86
Killing Hour '84
He Knows You're Alone '80

Toshio Masuda
Zero '84
Last Days of Planet Earth '74
Tora! Tora! Tora! '70

Eddy Matalon
Sweet Killing '93
Blackout '78
Cathy's Curse '77

Rudolph Mate (1898-1964)
For the First Time '59
Deep Six '58
Three Violent People '57
The Violent Men '55
The Black Shield of Falworth '54
Second Chance '53
The Green Glove '52
When Worlds Collide '51
Branded '50
Union Station '50
The Dark Past '49
D.O.A. '49

Tim Matheson (1947-)
In the Company of Spies '99
Buried Alive 2 '97
Tails You Live, Heads You're Dead '95
Breach of Conduct '94

Shue Matsubayashi (1920-)
Last War '68
I Bombed Pearl Harbor '60

Bruno Mattei (1931-)
Strike Commando '87
Caged Women '84
Seven Magnificent Gladiators '84
Hell of the Living Dead '83
Rats '83

Charles Matthau (1964-)
The Grass Harp '95
Doin' Time on Planet Earth '88

Paul Matthews
Breeders '97
Grim '95

Arne Mattson (1920-95)
The Girl '86
The Doll '62

Norman Maurer
The Outlaws Is Coming! '65
Around the World in a Daze '63

Robert (Roberto) Mauri (1924-)
Animal Called Man '87
Invincible Gladiators '64
The Slaughter of the Vampires '62

Garth Maxwell
When Love Comes '98
Jack Be Nimble '94

Peter Maxwell
Platypus Cove '86
The Highest Honor '84
Run, Rebecca, Run '81
Touch & Go '80
Plunge Into Darkness '77

Ronald F. Maxwell (1947-)
Gettysburg '93
Kidco '83
The Night the Lights Went Out in Georgia '81
Little Darlings '80

Bradford May
The Devil's Prey '01
Gargantua '98
Asteroid '97
Darkman 3: Die Darkman Die '95
Madonna: Innocence Lost '95
Darkman 2: The Return of Durant '94
Marilyn & Bobby: Her Final Affair '94
Lethal Lolita—Amy Fisher: My Story '92
Mortal Sins '92

Elaine May (1932-)
Ishtar '87
Mikey & Nicky '76
The Heartbreak Kid '72
A New Leaf '71

Joe May (1880-1954)
The House of the Seven Gables '40
The Invisible Man Returns '40
Homecoming '28
The Indian Tomb '21

Russ Mayberry
Challenge of a Lifetime '85
A Matter of Life and Death '81
The $5.20 an Hour Dream '80

Marriage Is Alive and Well '80
The Rebels '79
Unidentified Flying Oddball '79
Fer-De-Lance '74
Probe '72
The Jesus Trip '71

Daisy von Scherler Mayer (1965-)
Madeline '98
Woo '97
Party Girl '94

Paul Mayersberg (1941-)
The Last Samurai '90
Nightfall '88
Captive '87

Les Mayfield
American Outlaws '01
Blue Streak '99
Flubber '97
Miracle on 34th Street '94
Encino Man '92

Tony Maylam (1943-)
Split Second '92
The Burning '82
The Sins of Dorian Gray '82
The Riddle of the Sands '79

Ken Maynard (1895-1973)
Honor of the Range '34
The Fiddlin' Buckaroo '33
Strawberry Roan '33

Archie Mayo (1891-1968)
Angel on My Shoulder '46
A Night in Casablanca '46
Crash Dive '43
Orchestra Wives '42
The Great American Broadcast '41
House Across the Bay '40
They Shall Have Music '39
The Adventures of Marco Polo '38
The Black Legion '37
Petrified Forest '36
The Case of the Lucky Legs '35
Night After Night '32
Illicit '31
Svengali '31

Michael Mazo
Crackerjack '94
Time Runner '92
Possession: Until Death Do You Part '90

Paul Mazursky (1930-)
Winchell '98
Faithful '95
The Pickle '93
Scenes from a Mall '91
Enemies, a Love Story '89
Moon over Parador '88
Down and Out in Beverly Hills '86
Moscow on the Hudson '84
The Tempest '82
Willie & Phil '80
An Unmarried Woman '78
Next Stop, Greenwich Village '76
Harry and Tonto '74
Blume in Love '73
Alex in Wonderland '70
Bob & Carol & Ted & Alice '69

Des McAnuff
The Adventures of Rocky & Bullwinkle '00
Cousin Bette '97

Don McBrearty
Race to Freedom: The Story of the Underground Railroad '94
Really Weird Tales '86
Coming Out Alive '84
American Nightmare '81

Jim McBride (1941-)
Meat Loaf: To Hell and Back '00
The Informant '97
Pronto '97
The Wrong Man '93
Blood Ties '92
Great Balls of Fire '89
The Big Easy '87
Breathless '83
Hot Times '74
Glen and Randa '71
David Holzman's Diary '67

Jon McBride
Woodchipper Massacre '89
Cannibal Campout '88

Howard McCain
Shadow of a Scream '97
No Dessert Dad, 'Til You Mow the Lawn '94

Rod McCall
Lewis and Clark and George '97
Cheatin' Hearts '93

James McCalmont
Escape from Safehaven '88
Underground Terror '88

Leo McCarey (1898-1969)
An Affair to Remember '57
Good Sam '48
The Bells of St. Mary's '45
Going My Way '44
Once Upon a Honeymoon '42
Love Affair '39
The Awful Truth '37
Milky Way '36
Ruggles of Red Gap '35
Belle of the Nineties '34
Six of a Kind '34
Duck Soup '33
Kid from Spain '32
Indiscreet '31

Ray McCarey (1898-1948)
You Can't Fool Your Wife '40
Devil's Party '38
The Mystery Man '35

John P. McCarthy (1884-1962)
Song of the Gringo '36
The Return of Casey Jones '34
Fighting Champ '33
The Forty-Niners '32
Cavalier of the West '31
Mother and Son '31
Sunrise Trail '31
Oklahoma Cyclone '30

Michael McCarthy (1917-59)
Operation Amsterdam '60
Crow Hollow '52

John McCauley
Deadly Intruder '84
Rattlers '76

Michael McClary
Annie O '95
Curse of the Starving Class '94

Bret McCormick
Time Tracers '97
Rumble in the Streets '96
Blood on the Badge '92
Tabloid! '88

Nelson McCormick
Kill Shot '01
Operation Sandman: Warriors in Hell '00
Where the Truth Lies '99
For Which He Stands '98

George McCowan (-1995)
Return to Fantasy Island '77
Murder on Flight 502 '75
Frogs '72
Savage Run '70
The Ballad of Andy Crocker '69
Black Brigade '69

Ian McCrudden
The Big Day '99
Trailer, the Movie '99

Bruce McCulloch (1961-)
Superstar '99
Dog Park '98

Jim McCullough
Where the Red Fern Grows: Part 2 '92
Mountaintop Motel Massacre '86
The Aurora Encounter '85
Charge of the Model T's '76

Bruce McDonald (1959-)
Hard Core Logo '96
Dance Me Outside '95
Highway 61 '91
Roadkill '89

Frank McDonald (1899-1980)
Thunder Pass '54
Apache Chief '50
The Big Sombrero '49
My Pal Trigger '46
Rainbow over Texas '46
Song of Arizona '46
Under Nevada Skies '46
Along the Navaho Trail '45
Bells of Rosarita '45
Sunset in El Dorado '45
Treasure of Fear '45
Gambler's Choice '44
One Body Too Many '44
Take It Big '44
Timber Queen '44
Wildcat '42
Twilight on the Rio Grande '41
Gaucho Serenade '40
Jeepers Creepers '39

Michael James McDonald
The Death Artist '95
The Crazysitter '94

Rodney McDonald
Deep Core '00
Sonic Impact '99
Surface to Air '98
Steel Sharks '97
Scorned 2 '96
Night Eyes 4: Fatal Passion '95
Night Eyes 2 '91

Edward T. McDougal
The Prodigy '98
One for the Road '82

Ross McElwee (1947-)
Time Indefinite '93
Sherman's March: An Improbable Search for Love '86

Bernard McEveety
Roughnecks '80
Centennial '78
The Bears & I '74
One Little Indian '73
Napoleon and Samantha '72
The Brotherhood of Satan '71

Vincent McEveety
Gunsmoke: Return to Dodge '87
Amy '81
Herbie Goes Bananas '80
The Apple Dumpling Gang Rides Again '79
Herbie Goes to Monte Carlo '77
Gus '76
The Treasure of Matecumbe '76
The Castaway Cowboy '74
Charley and the Angel '73
Superdad '73
Million Dollar Duck '71
Menace on the Mountain '70
Smoke '70
Firecreek '68

William F. McGaha
Iron Horsemen '71
The Speed Lovers '68

William McGann (1893-1977)
American Empire '42
In Old California '42
Dr. Christian Meets the Women '40

Scott McGehee
The Deep End '01
Suture '93

Robert McGinley
Jimmy Zip '00
Shredder Orpheus '89

Scott McGinnis (1958-)
The Last Gasp '94
Caroline at Midnight '93

J(ohn) P(aterson) McGowan (1880-1952)
Rough Ridin' Rhythm '37
Deadwood Pass '33
Drum Taps '33
Lone Bandit '33
The Outlaw Tamer '33
When a Man Rides Alone '33
Hurricane Express '32
Mark of the Spur '32
Near the Rainbow's End '30
Below the Deadline '29
Red Signals '27
Road Agent '26
Blood and Steel '25

Robert McGowan (1882-1955)
Old Swimmin' Hole '40
Frontier Justice '35

Stuart E. McGowan (1904-99)
The Billion Dollar Hobo '78
The Showdown '50

Tom McGowan
Savage Journey '83
Cataclysm '81

Douglas McGrath
Company Man '00
Emma '96

Joseph McGrath
Great McGonagall '75
Digby, the Biggest Dog in the World '73
The Magic Christian '69
The Bliss of Mrs. Blossom '68
30 Is a Dangerous Age, Cynthia '68
Casino Royale '67

Sean McGregor
Devil Times Five '74
Gentle Savage '73

Patrick McGuinn
Kill Me Tomorrow '99
Boys in Love 2 '98

Doug McHenry
Kingdom Come '01
Jason's Lyric '94
House Party 2: The Pajama Jam '91

Chris T. McIntyre
Backstreet Justice '93
Border Shootout '90

Cole McKay
Star Hunter '95
The Secret of the Golden Eagle '91

Duncan McLachlan
Rudyard Kipling's the Second Jungle Book: Mowgli and Baloo '97
Born Wild '95
The Double O Kid '92
Scavengers '87

Andrew V. McLaglen (1920-)
On Wings of Eagles '86
The Dirty Dozen: The Next Mission '85
Sahara '83
The Blue and the Gray '82
The Shadow Riders '82
Sea Wolves '81
ffolkes '80
Breakthrough '78
Wild Geese '78
Mitchell '75
Cahill: United States Marshal '73
Chisum '70
The Undefeated '69
Bandolero! '68
The Devil's Brigade '68
Hellfighters '68
The Way West '67
Monkeys, Go Home! '66
The Rare Breed '66
Shenandoah '65
McLintock! '63

Don McLennan
Slate, Wyn & Me '87
Hard Knocks '80

Norman Z. McLeod (1898-1964)
Alias Jesse James '59
Casanova's Big Night '54
Never Wave at a WAC '52
Let's Dance '50
The Paleface '48
The Road to Rio '47
The Secret Life of Walter Mitty '47
Kid from Brooklyn '46
Panama Hattie '42
Lady Be Good '41
Little Men '40
Topper Takes a Trip '39
Topper '37
Here Comes Cookie '35
It's a Gift '34
Horse Feathers '32
Monkey Business '31

Tom McLoughlin (1950-)
Journey '95
The Yarn Princess '94
The Fire Next Time '93
Sometimes They Come Back '91
Date with an Angel '87
Friday the 13th, Part 6: Jason Lives '86
One Dark Night '82

Sean McNamara (1963-)
Treehouse Hostage '99
Wild Grizzly '99
P.U.N.K.S. '98
3 Ninjas: High Noon at Mega Mountain '97
Galgameth '96
Hollywood Chaos '89

John McNaughton (1950-)
Lansky '99
Wild Things '98
Normal Life '96
Girls in Prison '94
Mad Dog and Glory '93
Sex, Drugs, Rock & Roll: Eric Bogosian '91
Henry: Portrait of a Serial Killer '90
The Borrower '89

John McPherson
Incident at Deception Ridge '94
Fade to Black '93
Dirty Work '92
Strays '91

John McTiernan (1951-)
Rollerball '02
The 13th Warrior '99
The Thomas Crown Affair '99
Die Hard: With a Vengeance '95
Last Action Hero '93
Medicine Man '92
The Hunt for Red October '90
Die Hard '88
Predator '87
Nomads '86

Nick Mead
Swing '98
Bank Robber '93

Nancy Meckler
Alive and Kicking '96
Sister My Sister '94

Peter Medak (1940-)
Species 2 '98
The Hunchback '97
Pontiac Moon '94
Romeo Is Bleeding '93
Let Him Have It '91
The Krays '90
The Men's Club '86
Breakin' Through '84
The Dancing Princesses '84
The Emperor's New Clothes '84
Pinocchio '83
The Snow Queen '83
Snow White and the Seven Dwarfs '83
Zorro, the Gay Blade '81
The Babysitter '80
The Changeling '80
The Odd Job '78
Ghost in the Noonday Sun '74
The Ruling Class '72
A Day in the Death of Joe Egg '71
Negatives '68

Julio Medem (1958-)
Lovers of the Arctic Circle '98
Tierra '95
The Red Squirrel '93
Vacas '91

Don Medford (1917-)
Sizzle '81
The Organization '71

Cary Medoway (1949-)
The Heavenly Kid '85
Paradise Motel '84

Francis Megahy
The Disappearance of Kevin Johnson '95
Red Sun Rising '94
Con Man '92
Taffin '88
The Carpathian Eagle '81
The Great Riviera Bank Robbery '79

Alan Mehrez
Bloodsport 2: The Next Kumite '95
Bloodsport 3 '95

Deepa Mehta (1950-)
Earth '98
Fire '96
Camilla '94

Gus Meins (1893-1940)
The Gentleman from California '37
Roll Along Cowboy '37
Kelly the Second '36
March of the Wooden Soldiers '34

Norbert Meisel
Night Children '89
Walking the Edge '83
The Adultress '77

Ib Melchior (1917-)
The Time Travelers '64
The Angry Red Planet '59

George Melford (1877-1961)
Cowboy Counselor '33
Man of Action '33
Boiling Point '32
Dracula (Spanish Version) '31
East of Borneo '31
Moran of the Lady Letty '22
The Sheik '21

James Melkonian
The Jerky Boys '95
The Stoned Age '94

Jean-Pierre Melville (1917-73)
Godson '72
Le Samourai '67
Le Doulos '61
Leon Morin, Priest '61
Bob le Flambeur '55
Les Enfants Terrible '50
La Silence de la Mer '47

Christopher Menaul
One Kill '00
The Passion of Ayn Rand '99
Feast of July '95
Fatherland '94
Prime Suspect '92
A Dangerous Man: Lawrence after Arabia '91

George Mendeluk (1948-)
Men of Means '99
Meatballs 3 '87
Doin' Time '85
The Kidnapping of the President '80
Stone Cold Dead '80

Lothar Mendes (1894-1974)
Moonlight Sonata '38
The Man Who Could Work Miracles '37
Power '34
Sam Mendes
Road to Perdition '02
American Beauty '99
Fernando Mendez
The Living Coffin '58
The Vampire's Coffin '58
The Vampire '57
Black Pit of Dr. M '47
Ramon Menendez
Money for Nothing '93
Stand and Deliver '88
Chris Menges (1940-)
The Lost Son '98
Second Best '94
Crisscross '92
A World Apart '88
Jiri Menzel (1938-)
My Sweet Little Village '86
Larks on a String '68
Closely Watched Trains '66
William Cameron Menzies (1896-1957)
Invaders from Mars '53
Drums in the Deep South '51
The Thief of Bagdad '40
Things to Come '36
Chandu the Magician '32
Ismail Merchant (1936-)
Cotton Mary '99
The Proprietor '96
In Custody '94
The Courtesans of Bombay '85
Burgess Meredith (1908-97)
Yin & Yang of Mr. Go '71
Man on the Eiffel Tower '48
James Merendino (1967-)
SLC Punk! '99
The Real Thing '97
Hard Drive '94
Terrified '94
Witchcraft 4: Virgin Heart '92
Joseph Merhi (1953-)
Executive Target '97
Riot '96
Last Man Standing '95
Rage '95
The Sweeper '95
Direct Hit '93
To Be the Best '93
Zero Tolerance '93
C.I.A.: Code Name Alexa '92
Magic Kid '92
Maximum Force '92
Final Impact '91
The Last Riders '90
Night of the Wilding '90
L.A. Vice '89
Midnight Warrior '89
The Glass Jungle '88
L.A. Crackdown 2 '88
L.A. Heat '88
Fresh Kill '87
Heat Street '87
The Killing Game '87
L.A. Crackdown '87
The Newlydeads '87
Jose Luis Merino (1927-)
The Hanging Woman '72
Scream of the Demon Lover '71
Hell Commandos '69
Agnes Merlet
Artemisia '97
The Son of the Shark '93
Lawrence Merrick
Black Bikers from Hell '70
The Outlaw Bikers—Gang Wars '70
Keith Merrill (1940-)
Harry's War '84
Windwalker '81
Take Down '79
William Mesa
DNA '97
Galaxis '95
Philip Frank Messina
With Friends Like These '98
Spy '89
Marta Meszaros (1931-)
Adoption '75
The Girl '68
Alan Metter
Billboard Dad '98
Police Academy 7: Mission to Moscow '94
Moving '88
Back to School '86
Girls Just Want to Have Fun '85
Alan Metzger
My Husband's Double Life '01
Snap Decision '01
New Eden '94
Fatal Exposure '91
Red Wind '91
The China Lake Murders '90
Radley Metzger (1929-)
The Princess & the Call Girl '84
The Cat and the Canary '79
Score '72
Little Mother '71
The Lickerish Quartet '70
Camille 2000 '69
Therese & Isabelle '67
Carmen, Baby '66
The Alley Cats '65
The Dirty Girls '64
Dark Odyssey '57
Andrew Meyer (1943-87)
Tidal Wave '75
Night of the Cobra Woman '72
Kevin Meyer
Perfect Alibi '94
Under Investigation '93
Invasion of Privacy '92
Civil War Diary '90
Nicholas Meyer (1945-)
Vendetta '99
Company Business '91
Star Trek 6: The Undiscovered Country '91
The Deceivers '88
Volunteers '85
The Pied Piper of Hamelin '84
The Day After '83
Star Trek 2: The Wrath of Khan '82
Time After Time '79
Russ Meyer (1922-)
Beneath the Valley of the Ultra-Vixens '79
Supervixens '75
Blacksnake! '73
Beyond the Valley of the Dolls '70
Faster, Pussycat! Kill! Kill! '65
Motor Psycho '65
Fanny Hill: Memoirs of a Woman of Pleasure '64
Turi Meyer
Candyman 3: Day of the Dead '98
Sleepstalker: The Sandman's Last Rites '94
Janet Meyers
The Ripper '97
Letter to My Killer '95
Nancy Meyers
What Women Want '00
The Parent Trap '98
Eric Meza
The Breaks '99
House Party 3 '94
Richard Michaels (1936-)
Father and Scout '94
Backfield in Motion '91
The Queen of Mean '90
Indiscreet '88
Rockabye '86
Heart of a Champion: The Ray Mancini Story '85
Silence of the Heart '84
Blue Skies Again '83
One Cooks, the Other Doesn't '83
Sadat '83
Plutonium Incident '82
Berlin Tunnel 21 '81
Homeward Bound '80
Oscar Micheaux (1884-1951)
Lying Lips '39
Girl from Chicago '32
Body and Soul '24
Roger Michell
Changing Lanes '02
Notting Hill '99
The Buddha of Suburbia '92
Anne-Marie Mieville (1945-)
Soft and Hard '85
Scenario du Film Passion '82
Radu Mihaileanu
Train of Life '98
Trahir '93
George Mihalka (1952-)
Cruel and Unusual '01
Jack Higgins' The Windsor Protocol '97
Jack Higgins' Thunder Point '97
Bullet to Beijing '95
Relative Fear '95
Deceptions 2: Edge of Deception '94
Hostile Takeover '88
Eternal Evil '87
My Bloody Valentine '81
Pick-Up Summer '79
Ted V. Mikels
WarCat '88
Aftermath '85
10 Violent Women '79
Cruise Missile '78
Hustler Squad '76
Blood Orgy of the She-Devils '74
The Doll Squad '73
The Corpse Grinders '71
Girl in Gold Boots '69
The Astro-Zombies '67
The Black Klansman '66
Nikita Mikhalkov (1945-)
Burnt by the Sun '94
Close to Eden '90
Dark Eyes '87
Oblomov '81
A Slave of Love '78
An Unfinished Piece for a Player Piano '77
Christopher Miles (1939-)
Priest of Love '81
That Lucky Touch '75
The Virgin and the Gypsy '70
Lewis Milestone (1895-1980)
Mutiny on the Bounty '62
Ocean's 11 '60
Pork Chop Hill '59
The Halls of Montezuma '50
The Red Pony '49
Arch of Triumph '48
The Strange Love of Martha Ivers '46
A Walk in the Sun '46
The Purple Heart '44
Edge of Darkness '43
The North Star '43
Lucky Partners '40
Of Mice and Men '39
The General Died at Dawn '36
Hallelujah, I'm a Bum '33
Rain '32
The Front Page '31
All Quiet on the Western Front '30
The Garden of Eden '28
John Milius (1944-)
Rough Riders '97
Flight of the Intruder '90
Farewell to the King '89
Red Dawn '84
Conan the Barbarian '82
Big Wednesday '78
The Wind and the Lion '75
Dillinger '73
Gerry Mill
Second Chance '80
The Duchess of Duke Street '78
Ray Milland (1905-86)
Panic in the Year Zero! '62
Lisbon '56
A Man Alone '55
Gavin Millar (1938-)
Catherine Cookson's The Dwelling Place '90s
Retribution '98
My Friend Walter '93
A Murder of Quality '90
Tidy Endings '88
Dreamchild '85
Secrets '82
Stuart Millar (1929-)
Rooster Cogburn '75
When the Legends Die '72
Claude Miller (1942-)
The Accompanist '93
The Little Thief '89
This Sweet Sickness '77
The Best Way '76
David Miller (1909-92)
Bittersweet Love '76
Executive Action '73
Hail, Hero! '69
Captain Newman, M.D. '63
Lonely Are the Brave '62
Back Street '61
Midnight Lace '60
The Story of Esther Costello '57
The Opposite Sex '56
Diane '55
Sudden Fear '52
Love Happy '50
Our Very Own '50
Flying Tigers '42
Billy the Kid '41
George Miller (1943-)
Journey to the Center of the Earth '99
Zeus and Roxanne '96
The Great Elephant Escape '95
Andre '94
Gross Misconduct '93
Over the Hill '93
Frozen Assets '92
NeverEnding Story 2: The Next Chapter '91
Les Patterson Saves the World '90
Goodbye, Miss 4th of July '88
Anzacs: The War Down Under '85
The Aviator '85
Nevil Shute's The Far Country '85
All the Rivers Run '84
The Man from Snowy River '82
George Miller (1945-)
Babe: Pig in the City '98
Silver Strand '95
Lorenzo's Oil '92
Miracle Down Under '87
The Witches of Eastwick '87
Mad Max: Beyond Thunderdome '85
Twilight Zone: The Movie '83
The Road Warrior '82
Mad Max '80
Harvey Miller (1936-99)
Getting Away With Murder '96
Bad Medicine '85
Michael Miller
Dangerous Passion '95
Danielle Steel's Heartbeat '93
Danielle Steel's Star '93
Danielle Steel's Daddy '91
Danielle Steel's Palomino '91
Blown Away '90
A Case of Deadly Force '86
Can You Feel Me Dancing? '85
Silent Witness '85
National Lampoon's Class Reunion '82
Silent Rage '82
Outside Chance '78
Jackson County Jail '76
Street Girls '75
Randall Miller
The Sixth Man '97
Houseguest '94
Class Act '91
Robert Ellis Miller (1932-)
Bed & Breakfast '92
Hawks '89
Brenda Starr '86
Her Life as a Man '83
Reuben, Reuben '83
The Baltimore Bullet '80
The Girl from Petrovka '74
The Heart Is a Lonely Hunter '68
Sweet November '68
Any Wednesday '66
Troy Miller
Jack Frost '98
Beverly Hills Family Robinson '97
Andy Milligan (1929-91)
The Weirdo '89
Carnage '84
Legacy of Horror '78
Man with Two Heads '72
The Rats Are Coming! The Werewolves Are Here! '72
Fleshpot on 42nd Street '71
The Body Beneath '70
Torture Dungeon '70
The Ghastly Ones '68
Bill Milling
Body Trouble '92
Caged Fury '90
Lauderdale '89
Alec Mills
Dead Sleep '91
Bloodmoon '90
Tom Milo
Kiss and Be Killed '91
Smooth Talker '90
Michael Miner
The Book of Stars '99
Deadly Weapon '88
Steve Miner (1951-)
Texas Rangers '01
Lake Placid '99
Halloween: H20 '98
Big Bully '95
My Father the Hero '93
Forever Young '92
Warlock '91
Wild Hearts Can't Be Broken '91
House '86
Soul Man '86
Friday the 13th, Part 3 '82
Friday the 13th, Part 2 '81
Anthony Minghella (1954-)
The Talented Mr. Ripley '99
The English Patient '96
Mr. Wonderful '93
Truly, Madly, Deeply '91
Rob Minkoff
Stuart Little 2 '02
Stuart Little '99
The Lion King '94
Honey, I Shrunk the Kids '89
Vincente Minnelli (1903-86)
A Matter of Time '76
On a Clear Day You Can See Forever '70
The Sandpiper '65
Goodbye Charlie '64
The Courtship of Eddie's Father '62
The Four Horsemen of the Apocalypse '62
Two Weeks in Another Town '62
Bells Are Ringing '60
Home from the Hill '60
Gigi '58
The Reluctant Debutante '58
Some Came Running '58
Designing Woman '57
Lust for Life '56
Tea and Sympathy '56
The Cobweb '55
Kismet '55
Brigadoon '54
The Long, Long Trailer '54
The Band Wagon '53
The Bad and the Beautiful '52
An American in Paris '51
Father's Little Dividend '51
Father of the Bride '50
Madame Bovary '49
The Pirate '48
Undercurrent '46
Ziegfeld Follies '46
The Clock '45
Yolanda and the Thief '45
Meet Me in St. Louis '44
Cabin in the Sky '43
I Dood It '43
Emilio P. Miraglio (1924-)
Halloween Night '90
Night Eyes '90
The Night Evelyn Came Out of the Grave '71
David Mirkin
Heartbreakers '01
Romy and Michele's High School Reunion '97
Bob Misiorowski
Shark Attack '99
On the Border '98
Beyond Forgiveness '94
Blink of an Eye '92
Kenji Misumi
Shogun Assassin '80
Baby Cart 1: Lend a Child...Lend an Arm '72
Baby Cart at the River Styx '72
Baby Cart to Hades '72
The Razor: Sword of Justice '72
Zatoichi: The Blind Swordsman and the Chess Expert '65
Zatoichi: The Life and Opinion of Masseur Ichi '62
David Mitchell
Mask of Death '97
Downhill Willie '96
The Killing Man '94
Ski School 2 '94
Thunderground '89
City of Shadows '86
Club Med '83
Oswald Mitchell (1890-1949)
The Temptress '49
The Greed of William Hart '48
The Dummy Talks '43
Sollace Mitchell
Row Your Boat '98
Call Me '88
Hayao Miyazaki
Princess Mononoke '98
My Neighbor Totoro '93
The Castle of Cagliostro '80
Kenji Mizoguchi (1898-1956)
Street of Shame '56
Princess Yang Kwei Fei '55
Shin Heike Monogatari '55
The Crucified Lovers '54
Sansho the Bailiff '54
A Geisha '53
Ugetsu '53
Life of Oharu '52
Utamaro and His Five Women '46
47 Ronin, Part 1 '42
47 Ronin, Part 2 '42
The Story of the Late Chrysanthemum '39

Osaka Elegy '36
Sisters of the Gion '36

Moshe Mizrahi (1931-)
Every Time We Say Goodbye '86
War & Love '84
La Vie Continue '82
I Sent a Letter to My Love '81
Madame Rosa '77
Rachel's Man '75
The House on Chelouche Street '73
I Love You Rosa '72

Juan Lopez Moctezuma (1932-95)
Mary, Mary, Bloody Mary '76
Dr. Tarr's Torture Dungeon '75
Sisters of Satan '75

Richard (Dick) Moder (-1994)
The Bionic Woman '75
Lassie: Adventures of Neeka '68

Leonide Moguy (1899-1976)
Whistle Stop '46
Action in Arabia '44

Jose Mojica Marins (1929-)
Hallucinations of a Deranged Mind '70
Awakenings of the Beast '68
Strange World of Coffin Joe '68
At Midnight, I'll Take Your Soul '63

Hans Petter Moland
Aberdeen '00
Zero Degrees Kelvin '95
The Last Lieutenant '94

Gustaf Molander (1888-1973)
Only One Night '42
Dollar '38
A Woman's Face '38
Intermezzo '36
Swedenhielms '35

Jacinto (Jack) Molina (1934-)
The Craving '80
Human Beasts '80
Inquisition '76

William H. Molina
The Last Assassins '96
Where Truth Lies '96

Edouard Molinaro (1928-)
Beaumarchais the Scoundrel '96
Just the Way You Are '84
La Cage aux Folles 2 '81
La Cage aux Folles '78
Pain in the A— '77
Dracula & Son '76
Dracula Father and Son '76
Ravishing Idiot '64
Back to the Wall '56

Paul Mones
Saints and Sinners '95
Fathers and Sons '92

Christopher Monger (1950-)
The Englishman Who Went up a Hill But Came down a Mountain '95
Just Like a Woman '95
Waiting for the Light '90

Mario Monicelli (1915-)
Lovers and Liars '81
Casanova '70 '65
The Organizer '64
Joyful Laughter '60
Passionate Thief '60
The Unfaithfuls '60
The Great War '59
Big Deal on Madonna Street '58

Carl Monson (1932-88)
Death Feud '89
Blood Legacy '73
Please Don't Eat My Mother '72

Edward Montagne (1912-)
They Went That-a-Way & That-a-Way '78
The Reluctant Astronaut '67
McHale's Navy Joins the Air Force '65
McHale's Navy '64

Guiliano Montaldo (1930-)
Time to Kill '89
Control '87
Fifth Day of Peace '72
Sacco & Vanzetti '71

Robert Montero (1907-86)
Tharus Son of Attila '87
Mondo Balordo '64
Island Monster '53

Jorge Montesi
Bloodknot '95
Soft Deceit '94
Omen 4: The Awakening '91

George Montgomery (1916-2000)
From Hell to Borneo '64
Samar '62
The Steel Claw '61

Robert Montgomery (1904-81)
The Gallant Hours '60
Eye Witness '49
Lady in the Lake '46

Vincent Monton
Fatal Bond '91
Windrider '86

Charles Philip Moore
Angel of Destruction '94
Black Belt '92
Dance with Death '91
Demon Wind '90

Michael Moore
Buckskin '68
Fastest Guitar Alive '68
Paradise, Hawaiian Style '66
Talion '66

Michael Moore (1954-)
The Big One '98
Canadian Bacon '94
Roger & Me '89

Robert Moore (1927-84)
Chapter Two '79
The Cheap Detective '78
Murder by Death '76

Tom (Thomas R.) Moore
Gepetto '00
Danielle Steel's Fine Things '90
'night, Mother '86
Return to Boggy Creek '77

Jocelyn Moorhouse
A Thousand Acres '97
How to Make an American Quilt '95
Proof '91

Philippe Mora (1949-)
Mercenary 2: Thick and Thin '97
Pterodactyl Woman from Beverly Hills '97
Back in Business '96
Precious Find '96
Communion '89
Howling 3: The Marsupials '87
Death of a Soldier '85
Howling 2: Your Sister Is a Werewolf '85
A Breed Apart '84
Return of Captain Invincible '83
The Beast Within '82
Screams of a Winter Night '79
Mad Dog Morgan '76

Andrew Morahan
Murder in Mind '97
Highlander: The Final Dimension '94

Christopher Morahan (1929-)
Element of Doubt '96
Paper Mask '91
After Pilkington '88
Troubles '88
Clockwise '86
The Jewel in the Crown '84

Nanni Moretti (1953-)
Caro Diario '93
Palombella Rossa '89

William M. Morgan
The Violent Years '56
Fun & Fancy Free '47
Bells of Capistrano '42
Heart of the Rio Grande '42

Louis Morneau
Bats '99
Made Men '99
Retroactive '97
Soldier Boyz '95
Carnosaur 2 '94
Final Judgment '92
Quake '92
To Die Standing '91

David Burton Morris (1948-)
The Three Lives of Karen '97
Hometown Boy Makes Good '93
Jersey Girl '92
Patti Rocks '88

Errol Morris (1948-)
Fast, Cheap & Out of Control '97
A Brief History of Time '92
The Dark Wind '91
The Thin Blue Line '88

Howard Morris (1919-)
Goin' Coconuts '78
Don't Drink the Water '69
With Six You Get Eggroll '68
Who's Minding the Mint? '67

Bruce Morrison
Tearaway '87
Shaker Run '85

Paul Morrissey (1939-)
Beethoven's Nephew '88
Spike of Bensonhurst '88
Mixed Blood '84
The Hound of the Baskervilles '77
Andy Warhol's Dracula '74
Andy Warhol's Frankenstein '74
Heat '72
Trash '70
Flesh '68

Hollingsworth Morse
Justin Morgan Had a Horse '81
Daughters of Satan '72
Pufnstuf '70

Terry Morse (1906-84)
Godzilla, King of the Monsters '56
Unknown World '51
Bells of San Fernando '47
Danny Boy '46
Fog Island '45
British Intelligence '40
Waterfront '39

Edmund Mortimer
The Prairie Pirate '25
County Fair '20

Rocky Morton
Super Mario Bros. '93
D.O.A. '88

Gilbert Moses (1943-95)
A Fight for Jenny '90
The Fish that Saved Pittsburgh '79
Roots '77

Gregory Mosher
The Prime Gig '00
A Life in the Theater '93
Our Town '89

Elijah Moshinsky
Genghis Cohn '93
The Green Man '91

Jonathan Mostow
U-571 '00
From the Earth to the Moon '98
Breakdown '96
Flight of Black Angel '91
Beverly Hills Bodysnatchers '89

Malcolm Mowbray
Sweet Revenge '98
Don't Tell Her It's Me '90
Out Cold '89
A Private Function '84

John Llewellyn Moxey (1925-)
Lady Mobster '88
Through Naked Eyes '87
Detective Sadie & Son '84
The Cradle Will Fall '83
The Solitary Man '82
Killjoy '81
Mating Season '81
No Place to Hide '81
The Children of An Lac '80
The Power Within '79
Sanctuary of Fear '79
President's Mistress '78
Intimate Strangers '77
Panic in Echo Park '77
Nightmare in Badham County '76
Conspiracy of Terror '75
A Strange and Deadly Occurrence '74
Where Have All the People Gone? '74
The Bounty Man '72
Home for the Holidays '72
The Night Stalker '71
Circus of Fear '67
Horror Hotel '60

Allan Moyle
Jailbait! '00
Xchange '00
New Waterford Girl '99
Empire Records '95
The Gun in Betty Lou's Handbag '92
Pump Up the Volume '90
Times Square '80

Russell Mulcahy (1953-)
Lost Battalion '01
On the Beach '00
Resurrection '99
Russell Mulcahy's Tale of the Mummy '99
Silent Trigger '97
The Shadow '94
The Real McCoy '93
Blue Ice '92
Highlander 2: The Quickening '91
Ricochet '91
Highlander '86
Razorback '84

Edward (Edoardo Mulargia) Muller (1925-)
Escape from Hell '89
Savage Island '85

Robert Mulligan (1925-)
The Man in the Moon '91
Clara's Heart '88
Kiss Me Goodbye '82
Bloodbrothers '78
Same Time, Next Year '78
The Other '72
Summer of '42 '71
The Pursuit of Happiness '70
The Stalking Moon '69
Up the Down Staircase '67
Inside Daisy Clover '65
Baby, the Rain Must Fall '64
Love with the Proper Stranger '63
To Kill a Mockingbird '62
Come September '61
The Great Impostor '61
The Rat Race '60
Fear Strikes Out '57

Claude Mulot (-1986)
Black Venus '83
The Immoral One '80

Christopher Munch
Color of a Brisk and Leaping Day '95
The Hours and Times '92

Richard W. Munchkin
Evil Obsession '96
Texas Payback '95
Guardian Angel '94
Out for Blood '93
Ring of Fire 2: Blood and Steel '92
Deadly Bet '91
Ring of Fire '91
Dance or Die '87

Marc Munden
Vanity Fair '99
Touching Evil '97

Jag Mundhra (1946-)
Tales of the Kama Sutra 2: Monsoon '98
Tales of the Kama Sutra: The Perfumed Garden '98
Monsoon '97
Irresistible Impulse '95
Improper Conduct '94
Eyewitness to Murder '93
Sexual Malice '93
Tropical Heat '93
L.A. Goddess '92
The Other Woman '92
Wild Cactus '92
Last Call '90
Legal Tender '90
Jigsaw Murders '89
Hack O'Lantern '87
Open House '86

Ian Mune
The Bridge to Nowhere '86
Came a Hot Friday '85

Chris Munger
Kiss of the Tarantula '75
Black Starlet '74

Robert Munic
They Call Me Sirr '00
In a Class of His Own '99
Timelock '99

Jimmy T. Murakami
When the Wind Blows '86
Battle Beyond the Stars '80

Ryu Murakami
Because of You '95
Tokyo Decadence '91

Toru Murakawa
New York Cop '94
Distant Justice '92

John Murlowski
Santa with Muscles '96
The Secret Agent Club '96
Automatic '94
Amityville: A New Generation '93
Return of the Family Man '89

F.W. Murnau (1888-1931)
Tabu: A Story of the South Seas '31
City Girl '30
Sunrise '27
Faust '26
The Last Laugh '24
Nosferatu '22
The Haunted Castle '21

Dudley Murphy (1897-1968)
One Third of a Nation '39
Emperor Jones '33

Edward Murphy
Heated Vengeance '87
Raw Force '81

Geoff Murphy (1938-)
Race Against Time '00
Fortress 2: Re-Entry '99
The Magnificent Seven '98
Don't Look Back '96
Under Siege 2: Dark Territory '95
Blind Side '93
The Last Outlaw '93
Freejack '92
Never Say Die '90
Young Guns 2 '90
Red King, White Knight '89
The Quiet Earth '85
Utu '83
Goodbye Pork Pie '81

Maurice Murphy (1913-78)
Wet and Wild Summer '92
Fatty Finn '84
Doctors and Nurses '82

Ralph Murphy (1895-1967)
The Black Devils of Kali '55
Mickey '48
The Spirit of West Point '47

Robin Murray
Season of Change '94
Dance '90

John Musker
Hercules '97
Aladdin '92
The Little Mermaid '89
The Great Mouse Detective '86

Victoria Muspratt
White Wolves 3: Cry of the White Wolf '98
Circuit Breaker '96

Floyd Mutrux
There Goes My Baby '92
The Hollywood Knights '80
Aloha, Bobby and Rose '74

Alan Myerson
Holiday Affair '96
Police Academy 5: Assignment Miami Beach '88
Bayou Romance '86
Private Lessons '81
Steelyard Blues '73

Ivan Nagy (1938-)
Skinner '93
Jane Doe '83
A Gun in the House '81
Captain America 2: Death Too Soon '79
Deadly Hero '75
Bad Charleston Charlie '73

Mira Nair (1957-)
Monsoon Wedding '01
My Own Country '98
Kama Sutra: A Tale of Love '96
The Perez Family '94
Mississippi Masala '92
Salaam Bombay! '88

Bharat Nalluri
The Crow: Salvation '00
Killing Time '97

Don Nardo
Stuff Stephanie in the Incinerator '89
In Deadly Heat '87

Silvio Narizzano (1927-)
The Body in the Library '87
Why Shoot the Teacher '79
The Class of Miss MacMichael '78
Bloodbath '76
Redneck '73
Loot ... Give Me Money, Honey! '70
Blue '68
Georgy Girl '66
Die! Die! My Darling! '65
24 Hours in a Woman's Life '61

Mikio Naruse (1905-69)
When a Woman Ascends the Stairs '60
Late Chrysanthemums '54
Mother '52

Alan Nathanson
Claws '85
Playing with Fire '70s

Bill Naud
Ricky 1 '88
Whodunit '82

Gregory Nava (1949-)
Why Do Fools Fall in Love? '98
Selena '96
My Family '94
A Time of Destiny '88
El Norte '83

Ray Nazarro (1902-86)
Dog Eat Dog '64
Kansas Pacific '53

Indian Uprising '51
Blazing Across the Pecos '48

Ronald Neame (1911-)
Foreign Body '86
First Monday in October '81
Hopscotch '80
Meteor '79
The Odessa File '74
The Poseidon Adventure '72
Scrooge '70
The Prime of Miss Jean Brodie '69
Gambit '66
The Chalk Garden '64
I Could Go on Singing '63
Tunes of Glory '60
The Horse's Mouth '58
Windom's Way '57
The Man Who Never Was '55
The Promoter '52
The Golden Salamander '51

Hal Needham (1931-)
Hostage Hotel '00
Body Slam '87
Rad '86
Cannonball Run 2 '84
Stroker Ace '83
Megaforce '82
Cannonball Run '81
Smokey and the Bandit 2 '80
The Villain '79
Hooper '78
Smokey and the Bandit '77

Alberto Negrin (1940-)
Voyage of Terror: The Achille Lauro Affair '90
Mussolini & I '85

Jean Negulesco (1900-93)
The Invincible Six '68
The Best of Everything '59
Daddy Long Legs '55
Three Coins in the Fountain '54
A Woman's World '54
How to Marry a Millionaire '53
Titanic '53
Phone Call from a Stranger '52
Three Came Home '50
Johnny Belinda '48
Road House '48
Humoresque '46
The Mask of Dimitrios '44

Marshall Neilan (1891-1958)
Swing It, Professor '37
Vagabond Lover '29
Daddy Long Legs '19
Amarilly of Clothesline Alley '18
Stella Maris '18
Rebecca of Sunnybrook Farm '17

Roy William Neill (1886-1946)
Black Angel '46
Dressed to Kill '46
Terror by Night '46
House of Fear '45
Pursuit to Algiers '45
The Woman in Green '45
The Pearl of Death '44
Scarlet Claw '44
Spider Woman '44
Sherlock Holmes Faces Death '43
Sherlock Holmes in Washington '43
Frankenstein Meets the Wolfman '42
Sherlock Holmes and the Secret Weapon '42
Dr. Syn '37
The Black Room '35

James Neilson (1910-79)
The Adventures of Tom Sawyer '73
The First Time '69
Where Angels Go, Trouble Follows '68
Gentle Giant '67
The Adventures of Bullwhip Griffin '66
Dr. Syn, Alias the Scarecrow '64
The Moon-Spinners '64
Johnny Shiloh '63
Summer Magic '63
Bon Voyage! '62
Moon Pilot '62
Mooncussers '62

Frans Nel
American Kickboxer 1 '91
Lights! Camera! Murder! '89

David Nelson (1936-)
Last Plane Out '83
A Rare Breed '81
Confessions of Tom Harris '72

Dusty Nelson
Inferno '01
Necromancer: Satan's Servant '88
White Phantom: Enemy of Darkness '87

Gary Nelson
Melanie Darrow '97
Revolver '92
The Lookalike '90
Get Smart, Again! '89
Allan Quatermain and the Lost City of Gold '86
The Baron and the Kid '84
Murder in Coweta County '83
Jimmy the Kid '82
Pride of Jesse Hallum '81
The Black Hole '79
Freaky Friday '76
Santee '73
Molly & Lawless John '72

Gene Nelson (1920-96)
Harum Scarum '65
Kissin' Cousins '64

Jessie Nelson
I Am Sam '01
Corrina, Corrina '94

Ralph Nelson (1916-87)
Christmas Lilies of the Field '84
A Hero Ain't Nothin' but a Sandwich '78
Lady of the House '78
Embryo '76
The Wilby Conspiracy '75
Soldier Blue '70
Charly '68
Duel at Diablo '66
Father Goose '64
Lilies of the Field '63
Soldier in the Rain '63
Requiem for a Heavyweight '62
Requiem for a Heavyweight '56

Tim Blake Nelson (1965-)
O '01
Eye of God '97

Jan Nemec (1936-)
The Report on the Party and the Guests '66
Diamonds of the Night '64

Avi Nesher
Raw Nerve '99
The Taxman '98
Mercenary '96
Savage '96
Timebomb '91
Doppelganger: The Evil Within '90
She '83

Kurt Neumann (1906-58)
The Fly '58
Kronos '57
Mohawk '56
They Were So Young '55
Carnival Story '54
The Ring '52
Rocketship X-M '50
Bad Boy '39
Wide Open Faces '38
Make a Wish '37
Let's Sing Again '36
My Pal, the King '32

Mike Newell (1942-)
Pushing Tin '99
Donnie Brasco '96
An Awfully Big Adventure '94
Four Weddings and a Funeral '94
Enchanted April '92
Into the West '92
Amazing Grace & Chuck '87
Bad Blood '87
The Good Father '87
Dance with a Stranger '85
The Awakening '80
The Man in the Iron Mask '77

Sam Newfield (1899-1964)
Outlaw Women '52
Scotland Yard Inspector '52
Fingerprints Don't Lie '51
The Lost Continent '51
Western Pacific Agent '51
Three Desperate Men '50
She Shoulda Said No '49
State Department File 649 '49
Adventure Island '47
Money Madness '47
Outlaw of the Plains '46
Border Badmen '45
Gangster's Den '45
His Brother's Ghost '45
I Accuse My Parents '45
The Lady Confesses '45
Lightning Raiders '45
White Pongo '45
Death Rides the Plains '44
Devil Riders '44
Frontier Outlaws '44
The Monster Maker '44
Nabonga '44
Oath of Vengeance '44
Rustler's Hideout '44
Wild Horse Phantom '44
The Black Raven '43
Dead Men Walk '43
Harvest Melody '43
Tiger Fangs '43
Along the Sundown Trail '42
Billy the Kid Trapped '42
Jungle Siren '42
The Lone Rider in Cheyenne '42
The Mad Monster '42
The Mysterious Rider '42
Prairie Pals '42
Texas Justice '42
Tumbleweed Trail '42
Border Roundup '41
The Lone Rider in Ghost Town '41
Texas Trouble '41
Trigger Men '41
Arizona Gangbusters '40
Billy the Kid in Texas '40
Death Rides the Range '40
Gun Code '40
I Take This Oath '40
The Invisible Killer '40
Fighting Mad '39
Fighting Renegade '39
Flaming Lead '39
Outlaw's Paradise '39
Trigger Pals '39
Durango Valley Raiders '38
Feud Maker '38
Frontier Scout '38
Harlem on the Prairie '38
Lightnin' Carson Rides Again '38
Phantom Ranger '38
Songs and Bullets '38
Terror of Tiny Town '38
Thunder in the Desert '38
Arizona Gunfighter '37
Boothill Brigade '37
Doomed at Sundown '37
The Gambling Terror '37
Gun Lords of Stirrup Basin '37
Guns in the Dark '37
A Lawman Is Born '37
Lightning Bill Crandall '37
Melody of the Plains '37
Ridin' the Lone Trail '37
Windjammer '37
Aces and Eights '36
Border Caballero '36
Federal Agent '36
Ghost Patrol '36
Roaring Guns '36
The Traitor '36
Branded a Coward '35
Bulldog Courage '35
Go-Get-'Em-Haines '35
Racing Luck '35
Frontier Days '34

John Newland (1917-2000)
Don't Be Afraid of the Dark '73
The Legend of Hillbilly John '73

Joseph M. Newman (1909-)
The King of the Roaring '20s: The Story of Arnold Rothstein '61
This Island Earth '55
Love Nest '51
Great Dan Patch '49
Jungle Patrol '48

Paul Newman (1925-)
The Glass Menagerie '87
Harry & Son '84
The Shadow Box '80
The Effect of Gamma Rays on Man-in-the-Moon Marigolds '73
Sometimes a Great Notion '71
Rachel, Rachel '68

Fred Newmeyer (1888-1967)
General Spanky '36
The Freshman '25
Girl Shy '24
Safety Last '23

Phil Nibbelink
We're Back! A Dinosaur's Story '93
An American Tail: Fievel Goes West '91

Fred Niblo (1874-1948)
Ben-Hur '26
Blood and Sand '22
Camille '21
The Three Musketeers '21
Mark of Zorro '20
Sex '20
Dangerous Hours '19

Andrew Niccol (1964-)
Simone '02
Gattaca '97

Maurizio Nichetti (1948-)
Luna e L'Altra '96
Stephano Quantestorie '93
Volere Volare '92
The Icicle Thief '89

Paul Nicholas (1945-)
Luckytown '00
Naked Cage '86
Chained Heat '83
Daughter of Death '82

George Nicholls, Jr. (1897-1939)
The Return of Peter Grimm '35
Anne of Green Gables '34
Finishing School '33

Mike Nichols (1931-)
Wit '01
What Planet Are You From? '00
Primary Colors '98
The Birdcage '95
Wolf '94
Regarding Henry '91
Postcards from the Edge '90
Biloxi Blues '88
Working Girl '88
Heartburn '86
Gin Game '84
Silkwood '83
The Day of the Dolphin '73
Carnal Knowledge '71
Catch-22 '70
The Graduate '67
Who's Afraid of Virginia Woolf? '66

Arch Nicholson (-1990)
Dark Age '88
Fortress '85
Deadline '81

Jack Nicholson (1937-)
The Two Jakes '90
Goin' South '78
The Terror '63

Alex Nicol (1919-2001)
Point of Terror '71
The Screaming Skull '58

Ted Nicolaou
Bloodstorm: Subspecies 4 '98
Magic in the Mirror: Fowl Play '96
Spellbreaker: Secret of the Leprechauns '96
Vampire Journals '96
Leapin' Leprechauns '95
Dragonworld '94
Bloodlust: Subspecies 3 '93
Remote '93
Bad Channels '92
Bloodstone: Subspecies 2 '92
Subspecies '90
Terrorvision '86
Dungeonmaster '83

John Nicolella (1946-98)
Kull the Conqueror '97
Sunset Heat '92
Runaway Father '91
Finish Line '89

William Nigh (1881-1955)
South of Monterey '47
Corregidor '43
The Ghost and the Guest '43
The Underdog '43
The Black Dragons '42
Mr. Wise Guy '42
The Ape '40
Doomed to Die '40
The Fatal Hour '40
The Abe Lincoln of Ninth Avenue '39
Mr. Wong in Chinatown '39
Mutiny in the Big House '39
Mystery of Mr. Wong '39
Mr. Wong, Detective '38
Rose of Rio Grande '38
The Thirteenth Man '37
Headline Woman '35
Mysterious Mr. Wong '35
House of Mystery '34
Monte Carlo Nights '34
Mystery Liner '34
Border Devils '32
Without Honors '32
Fighting Thru '30

Rob Nilsson (1940-)
Heat and Sunlight '87
On the Edge '86
Signal 7 '83
Northern Lights '79

Leonard Nimoy (1931-)
Holy Matrimony '94
Funny About Love '90
The Good Mother '88
Three Men and a Baby '87
Star Trek 4: The Voyage Home '86
Star Trek 3: The Search for Spock '84

Christopher Nolan (1970-)
Insomnia '02
Memento '00
Following '99

Tom Noonan (1951-)
The Wife '95
What Happened Was... '94

Stephen Norrington (1965-)
Blade '98
Death Machine '95

Aaron Norris
Forest Warrior '95
Top Dog '95
Hellbound '94
Sidekicks '93
The Hitman '91
Delta Force 2: Operation Stranglehold '90
Braddock: Missing in Action 3 '88
Platoon Leader '87

Bill W.L. Norton (1943-)
Every Mother's Worst Fear '98
Our Mother's Murder '97
Hercules the Legendary Journeys, Vol. 1: And the Amazon Women '94
Hercules the Legendary Journeys, Vol. 4: In the Underworld '94
False Arrest '92
Three for the Road '87
Tour of Duty '87
Baby ... Secret of the Lost Legend '85
More American Graffiti '79

Max Nosseck (1902-72)
The Hoodlum '51
Black Beauty '46
Brighton Strangler '45
Dillinger '45

Noel Nosseck (1943-)
Another Woman's Husband '00
Silent Predators '99
The Fury Within '98
Tornado! '96
Down, Out and Dangerous '95
The Sister-in-Law '95
French Silk '94
Full Exposure: The Sex Tape Scandals '89
Summer Fantasy '84
Night Partners '83
King of the Mountain '81
Return of the Rebels '81
Dreamer '79
Las Vegas Lady '76

Jonathan Nossiter
Signs & Wonders '00
Sunday '96

Thierry Notz
Fortunes of War '94
Watchers 2 '90
The Terror Within '88

Phillip Noyce (1950-)
The Bone Collector '99
The Saint '97
Clear and Present Danger '94
Sliver '93
Patriot Games '92
Blind Fury '90
Dead Calm '89
Echoes of Paradise '86
Heatwave '83
Newsfront '78

Simon Nuchtern
New York Nights '84
Savage Dawn '84
Silent Madness '84

Elliott Nugent (1900-80)
Just for You '52
My Outlaw Brother '51
The Great Gatsby '49
My Girl Tisa '48
My Favorite Brunette '47
Welcome Stranger '47
Up in Arms '44
Never Say Die '39
Give Me a Sailor '38
Love in Bloom '35
Splendor '35

Victor Nunez (1945-)
Ulee's Gold '97
Ruby in Paradise '93
A Flash of Green '85
Gal Young 'Un '79

Trevor Nunn (1940-)
Twelfth Night '96
Lady Jane '85
Hedda '75

Raphael Nussbaum (1932-93)
Death Blow '87
Private Road: No Trespassing '87
Sinai Commandos '68
Colin Nutley (1944-)
Under the Sun '98
The Last Dance '93
House of Angels '92
David Nutter
Band of Brothers '01
Disturbing Behavior '98
Trancers 5: Sudden Deth '94
Cease Fire '85
Christian Nyby (1913-93)
Operation C.I.A. '65
The Thing '51
Sven Nykvist (1922-)
The Ox '91
Gorilla '56
Dan O'Bannon (1946-)
The Resurrected '91
Return of the Living Dead '85
Michael Oblowitz
The Breed '01
This World, Then the Fireworks '97
Jim O'Brien (1947-)
Rebecca '97
Foreign Affairs '93
The Dressmaker '89
The Jewel in the Crown '84
John O'Brien
Vermont Is for Lovers '92
The Big Dis '89
Jeffrey Obrow
Bram Stoker's The Mummy '97
Servants of Twilight '91
The Kindred '87
Dorm That Dripped Blood '82
The Power '80
James O'Connolly
Tower of Evil '72
Crooks & Coronets '69
The Valley of Gwangi '69
Vendetta for the Saint '68
Berserk! '67
Frank O'Connor (1882-1959)
Mystic Circle Murder '39
Spangles '26
Free to Love '25
Pat O'Connor (1943-)
Sweet November '01
Dancing at Lughnasa '98
Inventing the Abbotts '97
Circle of Friends '94
Fools of Fortune '90
The January Man '89
Stars and Bars '88
A Month in the Country '87
Cal '84
William O'Connor (1900-)
Cocaine Fiends '36
Ten Nights in a Bar-Room '31
Steve Oedekerk (1961-)
Nothing to Lose '96
Ace Ventura: When Nature Calls '95
Peter O'Fallon
A Rumor of Angels '00
Suicide Kings '97
George More O'Ferrell
Three Cases of Murder '55
Angels One Five '54
George Ogilvie
The Crossing '92
Mad Max: Beyond Thunderdome '85
Jorgo Ognenovski
Stalked '99
Warrior of Justice '96
Gerry O'Hara (1924-)
The Bitch '78
Leopard in the Snow '78
Maroc 7 '67
Terrence O'Hara
The Perfect Bride '91
Darkroom '90
Tommy O'Haver
Get Over It! '01
Billy's Hollywood Screen Kiss '98
Michael O'Herlihy (1919-97)
Cry of the Innocent '80
A Time for Miracles '80
The Flame Is Love '79
Peter Lundy and the Medicine Hat Stallion '77
The Young Pioneers '76
Smith! '69
The One and Only, Genuine, Original Family Band '68
The Fighting Prince of Donegal '66
Mosby's Marauders '66
Kihachi Okamoto (1923-)
Zatoichi vs. Yojimbo '70
Red Lion '69
Sword of Doom '67
Takao Okawara
Godzilla 2000 '99
Godzilla vs. Mechagodzilla II '93
Sidney Olcott (1873-1949)
The Claw '27
Ranson's Folly '26
Monsieur Beaucaire '24
From the Manger to the Cross '15
Pedro Olea (1938-)
Zafarinas '94
The Fencing Master '92
Ken Olin (1954-)
In Pursuit of Honor '95
White Fang 2: The Myth of the White Wolf '94
Ron Oliver
Tales from a Parallel Universe: Super Nova '97
Liar's Edge '92
Prom Night 3: The Last Kiss '89
Hector Olivera (1931-)
A Shadow You Soon Will Be '94
Play Murder for Me '91
Two to Tango '88
Cocaine Wars '86
Barbarian Queen '85
Wizards of the Lost Kingdom '85
Funny, Dirty Little War '83
Fridays of Eternity '81
El Muerto '75
Laurence Olivier (1907-89)
The Prince and the Showgirl '57
Richard III '55
Hamlet '48
Henry V '44
Ermanno Olmi (1931-)
The Tree of Wooden Clogs '78
Fiances '63
William Olsen (1950-)
Return to Eden '89
Getting It On '83
David O'Malley (1944-)
Easy Wheels '89
Kid Colter '85
Mountain Man '77
Ron O'Neal (1937-)
Up Against the Wall '91
Superfly T.N.T. '73
Robert Vincent O'Neil
Avenging Angel '85
Angel '84
Paco '75
The Deadly and the Beautiful '73
Blood Mania '70
Max Ophuls (1902-57)
Lola Montes '55
The Earrings of Madame De... '54
Le Plaisir '52
La Ronde '51
Caught '49
Reckless Moment '49
Letter from an Unknown Woman '48
De Mayerling a Sarajevo '40
La Signora di Tutti '34
Liebelei '32
Charlie Ordonez
Forgotten Warrior '86
Wolf '86
Stuart Orme
The Waiting Time '99
Ivanhoe '97
The Sculptress '97
The Puppet Masters '94
Hands of a Murderer '90
The Heist '89
James Ormerod
Frankenstein '82
Death in Deep Water '74
Next Victim '74
Ron Ormond (1911-81)
The Girl from Tobacco Row '66
The Black Lash '52
Mesa of Lost Women '52
King of the Bullwhip '51
Yes, Sir, Mr. Bones '51
Gary Orona
Stripshow '95
Great Bikini Off-Road Adventure '94
The Bikini Car Wash Company 2 '92
James Orr (1953-)
Man of the House '95
Mr. Destiny '90
Breaking All the Rules '85
Kenny Ortega
Hocus Pocus '93
Newsies '92
Kent Osborne
Women Unchained '72
Cain's Cutthroats '71
Nagisa Oshima (1932-)
Max, Mon Amour '86
Merry Christmas, Mr. Lawrence '83
In the Realm of Passion '80
The Empire of Passion '76
In the Realm of the Senses '76
Violence at Noon '66
The Cruel Story of Youth '60
The Sun's Burial '60
Sam O'Steen (1923-2000)
The Best Little Girl in the World '81
Sparkle '76
Brand New Life '72
Suzanne Osten
Speak Up! It's So Dark '93
The Mozart Brothers '86
Thaddeus O'Sullivan (1948-)
Witness to the Mob '98
Nothing Personal '95
December Bride '91
Gerd Oswald (1919-89)
Brainwashed '60
Crime of Passion '57
Paris Holiday '57
Richard Oswald (1880-1963)
The Lovable Cheat '49
My Song Goes Round the World '34
Cesare Borgia '23
Dominique Othenin-Girard
Beyond Desire '94
Private Lessons, Another Story '94
Omen 4: The Awakening '91
Night Angel '90
Halloween 5: The Revenge of Michael Myers '89
After Darkness '85
Jean-Paul Ouellette
The Unnamable 2: The Statement of Randolph Carter '92
Chinatown Connection '90
The Unnamable '88
Gerard Oury (1919-)
Delusions of Grandeur '76
The Brain '69
La Grande Vadrouille '66
The Sucker '65
Cliff Owen (1919-93)
The Bawdy Adventures of Tom Jones '76
No Sex Please—We're British '73
The Vengeance of She '68
The Wrong Arm of the Law '63
Frank Oz (1944-)
The Score '01
Bowfinger '99
In and Out '97
The Indian in the Cupboard '95
Housesitter '92
What about Bob? '91
Dirty Rotten Scoundrels '88
Little Shop of Horrors '86
The Muppets Take Manhattan '84
The Dark Crystal '82
Shigehiro (Sakae) Ozawa
Return of the Street Fighter '74
The Street Fighter '74
Francois Ozon (1967-)
Under the Sand '00
Water Drops on Burning Rocks '99
Sitcom '97
Yasujiro Ozu (1903-63)
An Autumn Afternoon '62
Drifting Weeds '59
Good Morning '59
Equinox Flower '58
Tokyo Story '53
Early Summer '51
Late Spring '49
Record of a Tenement Gentleman '47
I Was Born But... '32
G.W. Pabst (1885-1967)
Don Quixote '35
Kameradschaft '31
The Threepenny Opera '31
Westfront 1918 '30
Diary of a Lost Girl '29
Pandora's Box '28
The Love of Jeanne Ney '27
Joyless Street '25
Secrets of a Soul '25
Anthony Page (1935-)
Human Bomb '97
Middlemarch '93
Final Warning '90
The Nightmare Years '89
Scandal in a Small Town '88
Heartbreak House '86
Monte Carlo '86
Forbidden '85
Bill: On His Own '83
The Grace Kelly Story '83
Johnny Belinda '82
Absolution '81
Bill '81
The Lady Vanishes '79
I Never Promised You a Rose Garden '77
F. Scott Fitzgerald in Hollywood '76
Missiles of October '74
Alpha Beta '73
Pueblo Affair '73
Marcel Pagnol (1895-1974)
Letters from My Windmill '54
Topaze '51
Well-Digger's Daughter '46
Le Schpountz '38
Harvest '37
Cesar '36
Angele '34
The Baker's Wife '33
John Paizs
Invasion! '99
The Big Crimewave '86
Alan J. Pakula (1928-98)
The Devil's Own '96
The Pelican Brief '93
Consenting Adults '92
Presumed Innocent '90
See You in the Morning '89
Orphans '87
Dream Lover '85
Sophie's Choice '82
Rollover '81
Starting Over '79
Comes a Horseman '78
All the President's Men '76
The Parallax View '74
Klute '71
The Sterile Cuckoo '69
George Pal (1908-80)
7 Faces of Dr. Lao '63
The Wonderful World of the Brothers Grimm '62
Atlantis, the Lost Continent '61
The Time Machine '60
Tom Thumb '58
Euzhan Palcy (1957-)
Ruby Bridges '98
A Dry White Season '89
Sugar Cane Alley '83
Anders Palm
Dead Certain '92
Murder on Line One '90
Unmasked Part 25 '88
Tony Palmer
The Children '90
Wagner: The Complete Epic '85
Conrad Palmisano (1948-)
Busted Up '86
Space Rage '86
Bruce Paltrow (1943-)
Duets '00
A Little Sex '82
Jafar Panahi
The Circle '00
The White Balloon '95
Norman Panama (1914-)
Barnaby and Me '77
I Will, I Will for Now '76
How to Commit Marriage '69
The Road to Hong Kong '62
The Trap '59
Court Jester '56
Above and Beyond '53
Domenico Paolella
Samson Against the Sheik '62
Pirates of the Coast '61
Phedon Papamichael
Dark Side of Genius '94
Sketch Artist '92
Giullo Paradisi (1934-)
Spaghetti House '82
The Visitor '80
Sergei Paradjanov (1924-90)
Ashik Kerib '88
The Legend of Suram Fortress '85
The Color of Pomegranates '69
Shadows of Forgotten Ancestors '64
John Paragon
Twinsitters '95
Ring of the Musketeers '93
Double Trouble '91
Paul S. Parco
Pucker Up and Bark Like a Dog '89
Deadly Alliance '78
Chuck Parello
Ed Gein '01
Henry: Portrait of a Serial Killer 2: Mask of Sanity '96
Domonic Paris
Splitz '84
Dracula's Last Rites '79
Jerry Paris (1925-86)
Police Academy 3: Back in Training '86
Police Academy 2: Their First Assignment '85
Make Me an Offer '80
How to Break Up a Happy Divorce '76
Only with Married Men '74
Evil Roy Slade '71
Star Spangled Girl '71
The Passing of Evil '70
Viva Max '69
Don't Raise the Bridge, Lower the River '68
How Sweet It Is! '68
Never a Dull Moment '68
Dean Parisot
Galaxy Quest '99
Home Fries '98
Framed '90
Richard W. Park
American Chinatown '96
Gang Justice '94
Alan Parker (1944-)
Angela's Ashes '99
Evita '96
The Road to Wellville '94
The Commitments '91
Come See the Paradise '90
Mississippi Burning '88
Angel Heart '87
Birdy '84
Pink Floyd: The Wall '82
Shoot the Moon '82
Fame '80
Midnight Express '78
Bugsy Malone '76
Albert Parker (1887-1974)
Late Extra '35
The Black Pirate '26
Oliver Parker
The Importance of Being Earnest '02
An Ideal Husband '99
Othello '95
Trey Parker (1969-)
South Park: Bigger, Longer and Uncut '99
Orgazmo '98
Cannibal! The Musical '96
Gordon Parks (1912-)
Half Slave, Half Free '85
Three the Hard Way '74
Shaft's Big Score '72
Shaft '71
The Learning Tree '69
Gordon Parks, Jr. (1934-79)
Aaron Loves Angela '75
Superfly '72
Hugh Parks
Shoot '92
King's Ransom '91
Dream Trap '90
Shakma '89
Deadly Innocence '88
Gianfranco Parolini (1930-)
God's Gun '75
This Time I'll Make You Rich '75
Five for Hell '67
The Fury of Hercules '61
Samson '61
John H. Parr
Prey for the Hunter '92
Pursuit '90
Robert Parrish (1916-95)
The Destructors '74
A Town Called Hell '72
Journey to the Far Side of the Sun '69
Bobo '67
Casino Royale '67
Fire Down Below '57
Cry Danger '51

Gordon Parry (1908-81)
Innocents in Paris '53
Tom Brown's School Days '51

Gabriel Pascal (1894-1954)
Caesar and Cleopatra '46
Major Barbara '41

Goran Paskalyevic
Cabaret Balkan '98
Someone Else's America '96

Pier Paolo Pasolini (1922-75)
Salo, or the 120 Days of Sodom '75
Arabian Nights '74
The Canterbury Tales '71
The Decameron '70
Medea '70
Notes for an African Orestes '70
Porcile '69
Teorema '68
The Hawks & the Sparrows '67
Oedipus Rex '67
The Gospel According to St. Matthew '64
Love Meetings '64
Mamma Roma '62
RoGoPaG '62
Accatone! '61

John Pasquin
Joe Somebody '01
Jungle 2 Jungle '96
The Santa Clause '94
Nightmare '91

Ivan Passer (1933-)
Kidnapped '95
Stalin '92
Fourth Story '90
Haunted Summer '88
Creator '85
The Nightingale '83
Cutter's Way '81
Silver Bears '78
Crime & Passion '75
Law and Disorder '74
Born to Win '71
Intimate Lighting '65

Giovanni Pastrone (1883-1959)
Cabiria '14
Salammbo '14

Jonas Pate (1970-)
Deceiver '97
The Grave '95

Stuart Paton (1883-1944)
Chinatown After Dark '31
20,000 Leagues under the Sea '16

Giuseppe Patroni-Griffi (1921-)
Collector's Item '89
Driver's Seat '73
'Tis a Pity She's a Whore '73
Divine Nymph '71

John D. Patterson
Grave Secrets: The Legacy of Hilltop Drive '92
The Spring '89
Taken Away '89
Deadly Innocence '88
Legend of Earl Durand '74

Willi Patterson
Out of the Shadows '88
Dreams Lost, Dreams Found '87

Michael Pattinson
The Limbic Region '96
One Crazy Night '93
...Almost '90
Ground Zero '88
Moving Out '83

Robert Patton-Spruill
Body Count '97
Squeeze '97

Peter Patzak (1945-)
Midnight Cop '88
Lethal Obsession '87
Slaughterday '77

Steven Paul (1954-)
Eternity '90
Slapstick of Another Kind '84
Falling in Love Again '80

Stuart Paul
Fate '90
Emanon '86

David Paulsen
Savage Weekend '80
Schizoid '80

George Pavlou (1953-)
Rawhead Rex '87
Transmutations '85

Alexander Payne (1961-)
Election '99
Citizen Ruth '96

Dave Payne
Under Oath '97
Not Like Us '96
Alien Terminator '95
Criminal Hearts '95
Concealed Weapon '94

Richard Pearce (1943-)
Rodgers & Hammerstein's South Pacific '01
Witness Protection '99
A Family Thing '96
Leap of Faith '92
Dead Man Out '89
The Final Days '89
The Long Walk Home '89
No Mercy '86
Country '84
Sessions '83
Threshold '83
Heartland '81

Steven Pearl
The Substitute 2: School's Out '97
At First Sight '95

George Pearson (1875-1973)
Midnight at the Wax Museum '36
A Shot in the Dark '33

Peter Pearson
Tales of the Klondike: The Unexpected '87
Paperback Hero '73

Max Pecas (1925-)
I Am Frigid...Why? '72
The Sensuous Teenager '70
Her and She and Him '69
Erotic Touch of Hot Skin '65
Sweet Ecstasy '62
Daniella by Night '61

Ron Peck
Empire State '87
Nighthawks '78

Sam Peckinpah (1925-84)
The Osterman Weekend '83
Convoy '78
Cross of Iron '76
The Killer Elite '75
Bring Me the Head of Alfredo Garcia '74
Pat Garrett & Billy the Kid '73
The Getaway '72
Junior Bonner '72
Straw Dogs '72
Ballad of Cable Hogue '70
The Wild Bunch '69
Major Dundee '65
Ride the High Country '62
Deadly Companions '61

Larry Peerce (1935-)
The Abduction '96
Prison for Children '93
A Woman Named Jackie '91
The Court Martial of Jackie Robinson '90
The Neon Empire '89
Wired '89
Elvis and Me '88
Queenie '87
Hard to Hold '84
Love Child '82
The Bell Jar '79
The Other Side of the Mountain, Part 2 '78
Two Minute Warning '76
The Other Side of the Mountain '75
The Stranger Who Looks Like Me '74
Ash Wednesday '73
A Separate Peace '73
The Sporting Club '72
Goodbye Columbus '69
The Incident '67

Barbara Peeters
Humanoids from the Deep '80
Starhops '78
Summer School Teachers '75
Bury Me an Angel '71

Anthony Pelissier (1912-88)
Encore '52
The Rocking Horse Winner '49

Jean Pellerin
Daybreak '01
Escape under Pressure '00
Laserhawk '99
For Hire '98

Mark Pellington
The Mothman Prophecies '02
Arlington Road '99
Going All the Way '97

Arthur Penn (1922-)
Inside '96
The Portrait '93
Penn and Teller Get Killed '90
Dead of Winter '87
Target '85
Four Friends '81
Missouri Breaks '76
Night Moves '75
Little Big Man '70
Alice's Restaurant '69
Bonnie & Clyde '67
The Chase '66
Mickey One '65
The Miracle Worker '62
The Left-Handed Gun '58

Leonard Penn (1907-75)
Judgment in Berlin '88
A Man Called Adam '66

Sean Penn (1960-)
The Pledge '00
The Crossing Guard '94
The Indian Runner '91

D.A. Pennebaker (1925-)
Moon over Broadway '98
The War Room '93
Monterey Pop '68

Eagle Pennell
Ice House '89
Last Night at the Alamo '83
The Whole Shootin' Match '79

C.M. Pennington-Richards (1910-)
A Challenge for Robin Hood '68
Ladies Who Do '63
Black Tide '58
Hour of Decision '57

Richard Pepin
Mindstorm '01
Y2K '99
The Sender '98
Dark Breed '96
Cyber-Tracker 2 '95
Hologram Man '95
The Silencers '95
T-Force '94
Cyber-Tracker '93
Fist of Honor '92

Clare Peploe
The Triumph of Love '01
Rough Magic '95
High Season '88

Hope Perello
St. Patrick's Day '99
Pet Shop '94
Howling 6: The Freaks '90

Jack Perez
La Cucaracha '99
The Big Empty '98
America's Deadliest Home Video '91

Etienne Perier (1931-)
Investigation '79
Zeppelin '71
The Hot Line '69
Murder at 45 R.P.M. '65

Anthony Perkins (1932-92)
Lucky Stiff '88
Psycho 3 '86

Frank Perry (1930-95)
Hello Again '87
Compromising Positions '85
Monsignor '82
Mommie Dearest '81
Skag '79
Rancho Deluxe '75
Diary of a Mad Housewife '70
Last Summer '69
The Swimmer '68
ABC Stage 67: Truman Capote's A Christmas Memory '66
David and Lisa '62

Bill Persky (1931-)
Wait Till Your Mother Gets Home '83
Serial '80
How to Pick Up Girls '78

P.J. Pesce
From Dusk Till Dawn 3: The Hangman's Daughter '99
The Desperate Trail '94
Body Waves '92

Brooke L. Peters
Anatomy of a Psycho '61
The Unearthly '57

Charlie Peters
Music from Another Room '97
Passed Away '92

Wolfgang Petersen (1941-)
The Perfect Storm '00
Air Force One '97
Outbreak '94
In the Line of Fire '93
Shattered '91
Enemy Mine '85
The NeverEnding Story '84
Das Boot '81
For Your Love Only '79
Black and White As Day and Night '63

Kristine Peterson
Slaves to the Underground '96
Redemption: Kickboxer 5 '95
The Hard Truth '94
Eden 2 '93
Eden 4 '93
Critters 3 '91
Lower Level '91
Body Chemistry '90
Deadly Dreams '88

Christopher Petit (1949-)
Chinese Boxes '84
Unsuitable Job for a Woman '82

Dan Petrie, Jr.
Dead Silence '96
In the Army Now '94
Toy Soldiers '91

Daniel Petrie (1920-)
Walter and Henry '01
Inherit the Wind '99
The Assistant '97
Calm at Sunset '96
Kissinger and Nixon '96
Lassie '94
Mark Twain and Me '91
Cocoon: The Return '88
Rocket Gibraltar '88
Square Dance '87
The Bay Boy '85
Execution of Raymond Graham '85
The Dollmaker '84
Six Pack '82
Fort Apache, the Bronx '81
Resurrection '80
The Betsy '78
Eleanor & Franklin '76
Lifeguard '76
Sybil '76
Buster and Billie '74
Neptune Factor '73
Moon of the Wolf '72
Silent Night, Lonely Night '69
Spy with a Cold Nose '66
Stolen Hours '63
A Raisin in the Sun '61
The Bramble Bush '60

Donald Petrie
Miss Congeniality '00
My Favorite Martian '98
The Associate '96
Richie Rich '94
Grumpy Old Men '93
The Favor '92
Opportunity Knocks '90
Mystic Pizza '88

Boris L. Petroff
Outcasts of the City '58
Hats Off '37

Vladimir Petrov (1896-1966)
The Inspector General '54
Peter the First: Part 2 '38
Peter the First: Part 1 '37

Joseph Pevney (1920-)
Mysterious Island of Beautiful Women '79
Who Is the Black Dahlia? '75
Night of the Grizzly '66
Cash McCall '60
Torpedo Run '58
Istanbul '57
Man of a Thousand Faces '57
Tammy and the Bachelor '57
Away All Boats '56
Because of You '52
Meet Danny Wilson '52
The Strange Door '51

John Peyser (1916-)
The Centerfold Girls '74
Four Rode Out '69
Kashmiri Run '69

Lee Philips (1927-99)
Silent Motive '91
Blind Vengeance '90
Windmills of the Gods '88
Barnum '86
The Blue Lightning '86
Mae West '84
Samson and Delilah '84
On the Right Track '81
Hardhat & Legs '80
Special Olympics '78
The Spell '77
War Between the Tates '76
Sweet Hostage '75
The Stranger Within '74

Lou Diamond Phillips (1962-)
Dangerous Touch '94
Sioux City '94

Maurice Phillips
Another You '91
Enid Is Sleeping '90
Riders of the Storm '88

Nick (Steve Millard) Phillips
Death Nurse '87
Crazy Fat Ethel II '85
Criminally Insane '75

Toby Phillips
Killer Looks '94
The Pamela Principle '91

Maurice Pialat (1925-)
Van Gogh '92
Under Satan's Sun '87
Police '85
A Nos Amours '84
Loulou '80

Irving Pichel (1891-1954)
Day of Triumph '54
Santa Fe '51
Destination Moon '50
The Great Rupert '50
Quicksand '50
The Miracle of the Bells '48
Mr. Peabody & the Mermaid '48
Something in the Wind '47
They Won't Believe Me '47
O.S.S. '46
Tomorrow Is Forever '46
Colonel Effingham's Raid '45
Dance Hall '41
The Great Commandment '41
She '35
The Most Dangerous Game '32

Arthur C. Pierce (1923-87)
Las Vegas Hillbillys '66
Women of the Prehistoric Planet '66

Charles B. Pierce
Hawken's Breed '87
Boggy Creek II '83
Sacred Ground '83
The Evictors '79
Norseman '78
Grayeagle '77
Town That Dreaded Sundown '76
Winterhawk '76
Legend of Boggy Creek '75

Carl Pierson
The New Frontier '35
Paradise Canyon '35

Frank Pierson (1925-)
Conspiracy '01
Dirty Pictures '00
Truman '95
Lakota Woman: Siege at Wounded Knee '94
Citizen Cohn '92
Somebody Has to Shoot the Picture '90
King of the Gypsies '78
A Star Is Born '76
The Looking Glass War '69

Sam Pillsbury
Free Willy 3: The Rescue '97
Into the Badlands '92
Zandalee '91
Starlight Hotel '90

William H. Pine (1896-1955)
Dynamite '49
Swamp Fire '46

Yuen Woo Ping (1945-)
Wing Chun '94
Eagle's Shadow '84

Sidney Pink
The Christmas Kid '68
Finger on the Trigger '65
Reptilicus '62

Claude Pinoteau (1925-)
La Boum '81
The Slap '76

Lucian Pintilie (1933-)
Ward Six
An Unforgettable Summer '94
The Oak '93

Ernest Pintoff (1931-2002)
St. Helen's, Killer Volcano '82
Lunch Wagon '81
Jaguar Lives '79
Blade '72
Who Killed Mary What's 'Er Name? '71
Dynamite Chicken '70

Bret Piper
They Bite '95
A Nymphoid Barbarian in Dinosaur Hell '94

Robert Pirosh
Valley of the Kings '54
Go for Broke! '51

Massimo Pirri (1945-)
Could It Happen Here? '80s
Fatal Fix '80s

Mark Pirro (1956-)
Buford's Beach Bunnies '92
Deathrow Gameshow '88
Curse of the Queerwolf '87

A Polish Vampire in Burbank '80
Peter Pistor
In Pursuit '00
The Fence '94
Glen Pitre
Time Served '99
Belizaire the Cajun '86
Bruce Pittman (1950-)
No Alibi '00
Locked in Silence '99
Blood Brothers '97
Flood: A River's Rampage '97
Kurt Vonnegut's Harrison Bergeron '95
Where the Spirit Lives '89
Hello Mary Lou: Prom Night 2 '87
Confidential '86
Mark of Cain '84
Mark Piznarski
Here on Earth '00
The '60s '99
Death Benefit '96
Lucas Platt
Subway Stories '97
Girl in the Cadillac '94
Allen Plone
Sweet Justice '92
Phantom of the Ritz '88
Night Screams '87
Jeremy Podeswa
The Five Senses '99
Eclipse '94
Amos Poe
Frogs for Snakes '98
Dead Weekend '95
Alphabet City '84
The Foreigner '78
Jean-Marie Poire (1945-)
Just Visiting '01
The Visitors '95
Sidney Poitier (1924-)
Ghost Dad '90
Fast Forward '84
Hanky Panky '82
Stir Crazy '80
Piece of the Action '77
Let's Do It Again '75
Uptown Saturday Night '74
Buck and the Preacher '72
James Polakof
The Vals '85
Balboa '82
Demon Rage '82
Swim Team '79
Midnight Auto Supply '78
Slashed Dreams '74
Roman Polanski (1933-)
The Ninth Gate '99
Death and the Maiden '94
Bitter Moon '92
Frantic '88
Pirates '86
Tess '80
The Tenant '76
Chinatown '74
Diary of Forbidden Dreams '73
Macbeth '71
Rosemary's Baby '68
The Fearless Vampire Killers '67
Cul de Sac '66
Repulsion '65
Knife in the Water '62
Two Men & a Wardrobe '58
Stephen Poliakoff
Shooting the Past '99
Century '94
Close My Eyes '91
Hidden City '87
Michael Polish (1972-)
Jackpot '01
Twin Falls Idaho '99
Jeff Pollack
Lost and Found '99
Booty Call '96
Above the Rim '94
Sydney Pollack (1934-)
Random Hearts '99
Sabrina '95
The Firm '93
Havana '90
Out of Africa '85
Tootsie '82
Absence of Malice '81
The Electric Horseman '79
Bobby Deerfield '77
Three Days of the Condor '75
The Yakuza '75
The Way We Were '73
Jeremiah Johnson '72
They Shoot Horses, Don't They? '69
The Scalphunters '68
This Property Is Condemned '66
The Slender Thread '65
Bud Pollard (1886-1952)
Look Out Sister '48
Beware '46
Tall, Tan and Terrific '46
The Black King '32
Harry Pollard
Uncle Tom's Cabin '27
California Straight Ahead '25
George Pollock (1907-)
Murder Most Foul '65
Murder Ahoy '64
Murder at the Gallop '63
Murder She Said '62
Broth of a Boy '59
Stranger in Town '57
Abraham Polonsky (1910-99)
Romance of a Horsethief '71
Tell Them Willie Boy Is Here '69
Force of Evil '49
Ventura Pons
Beloved/Friend '99
Caresses '97
Gillo Pontecorvo (1919-)
Burn! '70
The Battle of Algiers '66
Kapo '59
Maurizio Ponzi (1939-)
Aurora '84
Pool Hustlers '83
DJ Pooh
The Wash '01
Three Strikes '00
Lea Pool (1950-)
Lost and Delirious '01
Set Me Free '99
Mouvements du Desir '94
The Savage Woman '91
Straight for the Heart '88
Angela Pope
Hollow Reed '95
Captives '94
Leo Popkin
The Well '51
Gang War '40
Rafael Portillo (1916-95)
Broken Trust '93
The Curse of the Aztec Mummy '59
The Robot vs. the Aztec Mummy '59
Ralph Portillo
Big Brother Trouble '00
Bloody Murder '99
Naked Lies '98
Stolen Hearts '95
Hollywood Dreams '94
Ted Post (1918-)
The Human Shield '92
Stagecoach '86
Diary of a Teenage Hitchhiker '82
Nightkill '80
Go Tell the Spartans '78
Good Guys Wear Black '78
Whiffs '75
Harrad Experiment '73
Magnum Force '73
The Baby '72
Beneath the Planet of the Apes '70
.Yuma '70
Hang 'Em High '67
Legend of Tom Dooley '59
H.C. Potter (1904-77)
Three for the Show '55
The Miniver Story '50
Mr. Blandings Builds His Dream House '48
The Time of Your Life '48
You Gotta Stay Happy '48
The Farmer's Daughter '47
Mr. Lucky '43
Second Chorus '40
The Story of Vernon and Irene Castle '39
The Cowboy and the Lady '38
Shopworn Angel '38
Beloved Enemy '36
Sally Potter (1947-)
The Man Who Cried '00
The Tango Lesson '97
Orlando '92
Gerald Potterton
Heavy Metal '81
Railrodder '65
Michel Poulette
Bonanno: A Godfather's Story '99
King of the Airwaves '94
Dick Powell (1904-63)
The Hunters '58
Enemy Below '57
The Conqueror '56
Split Second '53
Michael Powell (1905-90)
Peeping Tom '60
Night Ambush '57
Pursuit of the Graf Spee '57
The Tales of Hoffmann '51
The Elusive Pimpernel '50
The Small Back Room '49
The Red Shoes '48
Black Narcissus '47
Stairway to Heaven '46
I Know Where I'm Going '45
A Canterbury Tale '44
The Life and Death of Colonel Blimp '43
The Forty-Ninth Parallel '41
One of Our Aircraft Is Missing '41
Contraband '40
The Lion Has Wings '40
The Thief of Bagdad '40
Spy in Black '39
Edge of the World '37
The Phantom Light '35
Tristam Powell (1940-)
American Friends '91
Ghostwriter '84
John Power
Goldrush: A Real Life Alaskan Adventure '98
Charles & Diana: A Palace Divided '93
Stephen King's The Tommyknockers '93
Father '90
Alice to Nowhere '86
All My Sons '86
Stanley Prager (1917-72)
Bang Bang Kid '67
Madigan's Millions '67
Udayan Prasad
My Son the Fanatic '97
Brothers in Trouble '95
Otto Preminger (1906-86)
The Human Factor '79
Rosebud '75
In Harm's Way '65
The Cardinal '63
Advise and Consent '62
Exodus '60
Anatomy of a Murder '59
Bonjour Tristesse '57
Saint Joan '57
The Court Martial of Billy Mitchell '55
The Man with the Golden Arm '55
Carmen Jones '54
River of No Return '54
The Moon Is Blue '53
Forever Amber '47
Laura '44
Emeric Pressburger (1902-88)
Night Ambush '57
The Tales of Hoffmann '51
The Small Back Room '49
The Red Shoes '48
Black Narcissus '47
Stairway to Heaven '46
I Know Where I'm Going '45
A Canterbury Tale '44
The Life and Death of Colonel Blimp '43
One of Our Aircraft Is Missing '41
Michael Pressman (1950-)
A Season for Miracles '99
Saint Maybe '98
To Gillian on Her 37th Birthday '96
The Chinatown Murders: Man against the Mob '92
Quicksand: No Escape '91
Teenage Mutant Ninja Turtles 2: The Secret of the Ooze '91
Dark River: A Father's Revenge '90
Capone '89
To Heal a Nation '88
The Imposter '84
Doctor Detroit '83
Some Kind of Hero '82
Those Lips, Those Eyes '80
Boulevard Nights '79
Secret Passions '78
The Bad News Bears in Breaking Training '77
The Great Texas Dynamite Chase '76
Ruben Preuss
The Art of Murder '99
Almost Dead '94
Dead on Sight '94
Blackmail '91
Write to Kill '91
Deceptions '90
In Dangerous Company '88
Steve Previn (1925-93)
Waltz King '63
Almost Angels '62
Escapade in Florence '62
David F. Price (1961-)
Dr. Jekyll and Ms. Hyde '95
Children of the Corn 2: The Final Sacrifice '92
To Die For 2: Son of Darkness '91
Joseph Prieto
Savages from Hell '68
Shanty Tramp '67
Prince (1958-)
Graffiti Bridge '90
Under the Cherry Moon '86
Harold Prince (1928-)
Sweeney Todd: The Demon Barber of Fleet Street '84
A Little Night Music '77
Something for Everyone '70
Gina Prince-Bythewood
Disappearing Acts '00
Love and Basketball '00
David A. Prior
Felony '95
Mutant Species '95
Mardi Gras for the Devil '93
Raw Justice '93
Center of the Web '92
Double Threat '92
Future Zone '90
Invasion Force '90
Lock 'n' Load '90
White Fury '90
Final Sanction '89
Jungle Assault '89
The Lost Platoon '89
Operation Warzone '89
Rapid Fire '89
Hell on the Battleground '88
Night Wars '88
Deadly Prey '87
Death Chase '87
Mankillers '87
Killer Workout '86
Killzone '85
Franco Prosperi
The Wild Beasts '85
Throne of Fire '82
Counter Punch '71
Mondo Cane 2 '64
Alex Proyas (1965-)
Dark City '97
The Crow '93
Craig Pryce
The Dark '94
Revenge of the Radioactive Reporter '91
Alexander Ptushko (1900-73)
Sword & the Dragon '56
The Magic Voyage of Sinbad '52
Vsevolod Pudovkin (1893-1953)
Storm over Asia '28
The End of St. Petersburg '27
Mother '26
Luis Puenzo (1946-)
The Plague '92
Old Gringo '89
The Official Story '85
Evelyn Purcell
Woman Undone '95
Nobody's Fool '86
Jon Purdy
Star Portal '97
Dillinger and Capone '95
Reflections in the Dark '94
John Putch (1961-)
Tycus '98
My Magic Dog '97
Alone in the Woods '95
Joe Pytka
Space Jam '96
Let It Ride '89
Albert Pyun
Ticker '01
Corrupt '99
Urban Menace '99
The Wrecking Crew '99
Crazy Six '98
Postmortem '98
Mean Guns '97
Nemesis 4: Cry of Angels '97
Adrenalin: Fear the Rush '96
Blast '96
Nemesis 3: Time Lapse '96
Omega Doom '96
Heatseeker '95
Ravenhawk '95
Hong Kong '97 '94
Kickboxer 4: The Aggressor '94
Nemesis 2: Nebula '94
Spitfire '94
Arcade '93
Brain Smasher...A Love Story '93
Deceit '93
Knights '93
Nemesis '93
Bloodmatch '91
Dollman '90
Kickboxer 2: The Road Back '90
Captain America '89
Cyborg '89
Down Twisted '89
Alien from L.A. '87
Dangerously Close '86
Radioactive Dreams '86
Sword & the Sorcerer '82
Richard Quine (1920-89)
Prisoner of Zenda '79
W '74
Gun Crazy '69
Hotel '67
Oh Dad, Poor Dad (Momma's Hung You in the Closet & I'm Feeling So Sad) '67
How to Murder Your Wife '64
Paris When It Sizzles '64
Sex and the Single Girl '64
Strangers When We Meet '60
The World of Suzie Wong '60
Bell, Book and Candle '58
Full of Life '56
Solid Gold Cadillac '56
My Sister Eileen '55
John Quinn
Total Exposure '91
Cheerleader Camp '88
Gene Quintano (1946-)
National Lampoon's Loaded Weapon 1 '93
Honeymoon Academy '90
Why Me? '90
Fons Rademakers (1920-)
The Rose Garden '89
The Assault '86
Because of the Cats '74
Peter Rader
Hired to Kill '91
Grandma's House '88
Michael Radford (1946-)
Dancing at the Blue Iguana '00
B. Monkey '97
The Postman '94
White Mischief '88
1984 '84
Another Time, Another Place '83
Robert Radler
The Substitute 4: Failure is Not an Option '00
The Substitute 3: Winner Takes All '99
T.N.T. '98
Soldier of Fortune Inc. '97
Best of the Best 2 '93
Showdown '93
Best of the Best '89
Michael Raeburn (1943-)
Jit '94
Killing Heat '84
Laserblast '78
Bob Rafelson (1933-)
Blood & Wine '96
Picture Windows '95
Tales of Erotica '93
Man Trouble '92
Mountains of the Moon '90
Black Widow '87
The Postman Always Rings Twice '81
Stay Hungry '76
The King of Marvin Gardens '72
Five Easy Pieces '70
Head '68
Stewart Raffill
Grizzly Falls '99
Tammy and the T-Rex '94
Mannequin 2: On the Move '91
Mac and Me '88
Ice Pirates '84
The Philadelphia Experiment '84
High Risk '81
Sea Gypsies '78
Across the Great Divide '76
The Adventures of the Wilderness Family '76
When the North Wind Blows '74
The Tender Warrior '71
Alan Rafkin (1928-2001)
How to Frame a Figg '71
The Shakiest Gun in the West '68
The Ghost and Mr. Chicken '66

Sam Raimi (1959-)
Spider-Man '02
The Gift '00
For Love of the Game '99
A Simple Plan '98
The Quick and the Dead '94
Army of Darkness '92
Darkman '90
Evil Dead 2: Dead by Dawn '87
Crimewave '85
Evil Dead '83

Frank Rainone
A Brooklyn State of Mind '97
Me and the Mob '94

Alvin Rakoff (1927-)
A Voyage 'Round My Father '89
The First Olympics: Athens 1896 '84
Dirty Tricks '81
Death Ship '80
City on Fire '78
King Solomon's Treasure '76
Say Hello to Yesterday '71
Room 43 '58

Harold Ramis (1944-)
Bedazzled '00
Analyze This '98
Multiplicity '96
Stuart Saves His Family '94
Groundhog Day '93
Club Paradise '86
National Lampoon's Vacation '83
Caddyshack '80

Addison Randall
The Killing Zone '90
Chance '89
East L.A. Warriors '89
Payback '89

Tony Randel
Rattled '96
Fist of the North Star '95
One Good Turn '95
Ticks '93
Amityville 1992: It's About Time '92
Children of the Night '92
Hellbound: Hellraiser 2 '88

Arthur Rankin, Jr.
Flight of Dragons '82
The Return of the King '80
The Hobbit '78
The Ballad of Paul Bunyan '72

Mark Rappaport
From the Journals of Jean Seberg '95
Rock Hudson's Home Movies '92

Jean-Paul Rappeneau (1932-)
The Horseman on the Roof '95
Cyrano de Bergerac '90
Swashbuckler '84
Lovers Like Us '75

Irving Rapper (1898-1999)
Born Again '78
Marjorie Morningstar '58
The Brave One '56
Forever Female '53
Another Man's Poison '52
Deception '46
The Corn Is Green '45
Rhapsody in Blue '45
The Adventures of Mark Twain '44
Now, Voyager '42

Steve Rash
Good Advice '01
Held Up '00
Eddie '96
Son-in-Law '93
Queens Logic '91
Can't Buy Me Love '87
Under the Rainbow '81
The Buddy Holly Story '78

Daniel Raskov
A Kiss Goodnight '94
The Masters of Menace '90
Wedding Band '89

Brett Ratner (1970-)
Rush Hour 2 '01
Family Man '00
Rush Hour '98
Money Talks '97

Gregory Ratoff (1897-1960)
Abdulla the Great '56
Black Magic '49
The Heat's On '43
The Corsican Brothers '42
Footlight Serenade '42
Adam Had Four Sons '41
Intermezzo '39
Rose of Washington Square '39

John Rawlins (1902-97)
Shark River '53
Dick Tracy Meets Gruesome '47
Dick Tracy's Dilemma '47
Arabian Nights '42
Sherlock Holmes: The Voice of Terror '42

Albert Ray (1897-1944)
Undercover Man '36
Dancing Man '33
Shriek in the Night '33
13th Guest '32

Bernard B. Ray
Movie Stuntmen '53
Buffalo Bill Rides Again '47
House of Errors '42
Broken Strings '40
Roamin' Wild '36
Speed Reporter '36
Coyote Trails '35
Texas Jack '35
The Silver Bullet '34

Fred Olen Ray (1954-)
Kept '01
Venomous '01
Active Stealth '99
The Capitol Conspiracy '99
Mom, Can I Keep Her? '98
Invisible Dad '97
Night Shade '97
The Shooter '97
Friend of the Family 2 '96
Fugitive Rage '96
Invisible Mom '96
Attack of the 60-Foot Centerfold '95
Cyberzone '95
Over the Wire '95
Bikini Drive-in '94
Inner Sanctum 2 '94
Wizards of the Demon Sword '94
Dinosaur Island '93
Mind Twister '93
Possessed by the Night '93
Haunting Fear '91
Inner Sanctum '91
Bad Girls from Mars '90
Evil Toons '90
Mob Boss '90
Spirits '90
Alienator '89
Beverly Hills Vamp '88
Hollywood Chainsaw Hookers '88
Terminal Force '88
Warlords '88
Commando Squad '87
Cyclone '87
Deep Space '87
Phantom Empire '87
Star Slammer '87
Armed Response '86
Tomb '86
Bio Hazard '85
Alien Dead '79

Nicholas Ray (1911-79)
55 Days at Peking '63
The King of Kings '61
Party Girl '58
Rebel without a Cause '55
Johnny Guitar '53
The Lusty Men '52
Flying Leathernecks '51
On Dangerous Ground '51
Born to Be Bad '50
In a Lonely Place '50
Knock on Any Door '49
They Live by Night '49
A Woman's Secret '49

Satyajit Ray (1921-92)
The Stranger '92
The Home and the World '84
The Middleman '76
Distant Thunder '73
The Adversary '71
Days and Nights in the Forest '70
Charulata '64
The Big City '63
Two Daughters '61
Devi '60
The World of Apu '59
Aparajito '58
Jalsaghar '58
Pather Panchali '54

Ed Raymond
Air Rage '01
Mach 2 '00
Submerged '00

David Raynr
Whatever It Takes '00
Trippin' '99

Spiro Razatos
Class of 1999 2: The Substitute '93
Fast Getaway '91

Bill Rebane (1937-)
The Capture of Bigfoot '79
The Alpha Incident '76
The Giant Spider Invasion '75
Monster a Go-Go! '65

Eric Red (1961-)
Bad Moon '96
Undertow '95
Body Parts '91
Cohen and Tate '88

Robert Redford (1937-)
The Legend of Bagger Vance '00
The Horse Whisperer '97
Quiz Show '94
A River Runs Through It '92
The Milagro Beanfield War '88
Ordinary People '80

Carol Reed (1906-76)
Unicorn '83
Oliver! '68
The Agony and the Ecstasy '65
The Key '58
Trapeze '56
The Fallen Idol '49
The Third Man '49
Odd Man Out '47
Immortal Battalion '44
Kipps '41
Night Train to Munich '40
The Stars Look Down '39

Joel M. Reed
Night of the Zombies '81
Bloodsucking Freaks '75
G.I. Executioner '71

Peyton Reed
Bring It On '00
The Love Bug '97

Roland D. Reed
The House of Secrets '37
Red Lights Ahead '36

Clive Rees
When the Whales Came '89
Blockhouse '73

Geoffrey Reeve (1932-)
Souvenir '88
Caravan to Vaccares '74
Puppet on a Chain '72

Matt Reeves (1966-)
The Pallbearer '95
Future Shock '93

Michael Reeves (1944-69)
The Conqueror Worm '68
The She-Beast '65

Godfrey Reggio
Powaqqatsi: Life in Transformation '88
Koyaanisqatsi '83

Alastair Reid (1939-)
Nostromo '96
Armistead Maupin's Tales of the City '93
Teamster Boss: The Jackie Presser Story '92
Traffik '90
Shattered '72
Baby Love '69

Dorothy Davenport Reid (1895-1977)
Sucker Money '34
Linda '29

Tim Reid (1944-)
Asunder '99
Once Upon a Time ... When We Were Colored '95
The Little Mermaid '78

Carl Reiner (1922-)
That Old Feeling '96
Fatal Instinct '93
Sibling Rivalry '90
Bert Rigby, You're a Fool '89
Summer School '87
Summer Rental '85
All of Me '84
The Man with Two Brains '83
Dead Men Don't Wear Plaid '82
The Jerk '79
The One and Only '78
Oh, God! '77
Where's Poppa? '70
The Comic '69
Enter Laughing '67

Jeff Reiner
Deadly Game '98
Serpent's Lair '95
Trouble Bound '92
Blood & Concrete: A Love Story '90

Rob Reiner (1945-)
The Story of Us '99
Ghosts of Mississippi '96
The American President '95
North '94
A Few Good Men '92
Misery '90
When Harry Met Sally... '89
The Princess Bride '87
Stand by Me '86
The Sure Thing '85
This Is Spinal Tap '84

Gottfried Reinhardt (1911-94)
Town without Pity '61
Betrayed '54

Harald Reinl (1908-86)
Fight for Gold '86
Hell Hounds of Alaska '73
The Torture Chamber of Dr. Sadism '69
Carpet of Horror '64
The Invisible Dr. Mabuse '62
Forger of London '61
The Return of Dr. Mabuse '61

Irving Reis (1906-53)
Three Husbands '50
All My Sons '48
The Bachelor and the Bobby-Soxer '47
Crack-Up '46
Big Street '42

Walter Reisch
Song of Scheherazade '47
Men Are Not Gods '37

Charles Reisner (1887-1962)
Train to Tombstone '50
The Cobra Strikes '48
Lost in a Harem '44
Big Store '41
Manhattan Merry-Go-Round '37
Steamboat Bill, Jr. '28
The Man on the Box '25

Karel Reisz (1926-)
Everybody Wins '90
Sweet Dreams '85
The French Lieutenant's Woman '81
Who'll Stop the Rain? '78
The Gambler '74
Isadora '68
Morgan: A Suitable Case for Treatment '66
Saturday Night and Sunday Morning '60

Wolfgang Reitherman (1909-85)
The Rescuers '77
Robin Hood '73
The Aristocats '70
The Jungle Book '67
The Sword in the Stone '63
101 Dalmatians '61
Sleeping Beauty '59

Ivan Reitman (1946-)
Evolution '01
Six Days, Seven Nights '98
Father's Day '96
Junior '94
Dave '93
Kindergarten Cop '90
Ghostbusters 2 '89
Twins '88
Legal Eagles '86
Ghostbusters '84
Stripes '81
Meatballs '79

Edgar Reitz (1932-)
Heimat 2 '80s
Heimat 1 '84
Germany in Autumn '78

Norman Rene (1951-96)
Reckless '95
Prelude to a Kiss '92
Longtime Companion '90

Jean Renoir (1894-1979)
The Little Theatre of Jean Renoir '71
The Elusive Corporal '62
Picnic on the Grass '59
The Testament of Dr. Cordelier '59
Elena and Her Men '56
French Can-Can '55
The Golden Coach '52
The River '51
A Day in the Country '46
Diary of a Chambermaid '46
The Southerner '45
This Land Is Mine '43
The Rules of the Game '39
La Bete Humaine '38
Grand Illusion '37
La Marseillaise '37
The Crime of Monsieur Lange '36
The Lower Depths '36
Madame Bovary '34
Toni '34
Boudu Saved from Drowning '32
La Chienne '31
Tournament '29
Renoir Shorts '27
Charleston '26

Nicholas Renton
Wives and Daughters '01
The Ebb-Tide '97
Far from the Madding Crowd '97

Alain Resnais (1922-)
Same Old Song '97
Smoking/No Smoking '94
Mon Oncle d'Amerique '80
Providence '77
Stavisky '74
La Guerre Est Finie '66
Muriel '63
Last Year at Marienbad '61
Hiroshima, Mon Amour '59

Dale Resteghini
Da Hip Hop Witch '00
Colorz of Rage '97

Burt Reynolds (1936-)
The Final Hit '02
The Man from Left Field '93
Stick '85
Sharky's Machine '81
The End '78
Gator '76

Kevin Reynolds (1950-)
The Count of Monte Cristo '02
187 '97
Waterworld '95
Rapa Nui '93
Robin Hood: Prince of Thieves '91
The Beast '88
Fandango '85

Lynn F. Reynolds (1889-1927)
Riders of the Purple Sage '25
Sky High '22
Trailin' '21

Scott Reynolds
Heaven '99
The Ugly '96

Phillip Rhee (1960-)
Best of the Best: Without Warning '98
Best of the Best 3: No Turning Back '95

Michael Rhodes (1935-)
Christy '94
Heidi '93
The Killing Mind '90
Matters of the Heart '90

Tonino Ricci (1927-)
Rush '84
Great Treasure Hunt '70s

David Lowell Rich (1923-)
Choices '86
Convicted '86
The Hearst and Davies Affair '85
Chu Chu & the Philly Flash '81
Enola Gay: The Men, the Mission, the Atomic Bomb '80
Nurse '80
The Concorde: Airport '79 '79
Family Upside Down '78
Little Women '78
Satan's School for Girls '73
That Man Bolt '73
Northeast of Seoul '72
Madame X '66
Have Rocket Will Travel '59

John Rich (1925-)
Easy Come, Easy Go '67
Boeing Boeing '65
Roustabout '64

Matty Rich
The Inkwell '94
Straight out of Brooklyn '91

Richard Rich
The Trumpet of the Swan '01
The King and I '99
The Swan Princess 2: Escape from Castle Mountain '97
The Swan Princess '94
The Black Cauldron '85
The Fox and the Hound '81

Jefferson (Jeff) Richard
Berserker '87
In Search of a Golden Sky '84

Pierre Richard (1934-)
Too Shy to Try '82
The Daydreamer '75

Cybil Richards
Femalien '96
Virtual Encounters '96

Dick Richards (1934-)
Man, Woman & Child '83
Death Valley '81
March or Die '77
Farewell, My Lovely '75
Rafferty & the Gold Dust Twins '75
Culpepper Cattle Co. '72

Lloyd Richards
The Piano Lesson '94
Paul Robeson '77

Sybil Richards
Erotic House of Wax '97
Lolida 2000 '97

Peter Richardson
The Pope Must Diet '91
Eat the Rich '87
Supergrass '87

Tony Richardson (1928-91)
Blue Sky '91
The Phantom of the Opera '90
Women & Men: Stories of Seduction '90
Shadow on the Sun '88
Penalty Phase '86
The Hotel New Hampshire '84
The Border '82
Joseph Andrews '77
Ned Kelly '70
Hamlet '69
The Charge of the Light Brigade '68
Mademoiselle '66
The Loved One '65
Tom Jones '63
The Loneliness of the Long Distance Runner '62
A Taste of Honey '61
The Entertainer '60
Look Back in Anger '58

William Richert
The Man in the Iron Mask '97
A Night in the Life of Jimmy Reardon '88
Winter Kills '79

Anthony Richmond (1942-)
Night of the Sharks '87
Days of Hell '84
Deja Vu '84
A Man Called Rage '84

W.D. Richter (1945-)
Late for Dinner '91
The Adventures of Buckaroo Banzai Across the Eighth Dimension '84

Tom Rickman
Crash Course '00
The River Rat '84

Philip Ridley
The Passion of Darkly Noon '95
The Reflecting Skin '91

Leni Riefenstahl (1902-)
Tiefland '44
Triumph of the Will '34
The Blue Light '32

Adam Rifkin (1966-)
Detroit Rock City '99
Something About Sex '98
The Nutt House '95
Psycho Cop 2 '94
The Chase '93
The Dark Backward '91
The Invisible Maniac '90
Tale of Two Sisters '89
Never on Tuesday '88

Wolf Rilla (1920-)
Village of the Damned '60
Bachelor of Hearts '58
Roadhouse Girl '53

Arthur Ripley (1895-1961)
Thunder Road '58
The Chase '46
The Barber Shop '33
Pharmacist '32

Maria Ripoli
Tortilla Soup '01
Twice upon a Yesterday '98

Arturo Ripstein
Deep Crimson '96
Foxtrot '76

Dino Risi (1916-)
Running Away '89
How Funny Can Sex Be? '76
The Scent of a Woman '75
Tiger and the Pussycat '67
The Easy Life '63
Il Sorpasso '63
Love in the City '53

Guy Ritchie (1968-)
Snatch '00
Lock, Stock and 2 Smoking Barrels '98

Michael Ritchie (1938-2001)
A Simple Wish '97
The Fantasticks '95
Cops and Robbersons '94
The Scout '94
The Positively True Adventures of the Alleged Texas Cheerleader-Murdering Mom '93
Diggstown '92
Fletch Lives '89
The Couch Trip '87
The Golden Child '86
Wildcats '86
Fletch '85
Survivors '83
The Island '80
An Almost Perfect Affair '79
Semi-Tough '77
The Bad News Bears '76
Smile '75
The Candidate '72
Prime Cut '72
Downhill Racer '69

Martin Ritt (1914-90)
Stanley and Iris '90
Nuts '87
Murphy's Romance '85
Cross Creek '83
Back Roads '81
Norma Rae '79
Casey's Shadow '78
The Front '76
Conrack '74
Pete 'n' Tillie '72
Sounder '72
The Great White Hope '70
Molly Maguires '70
The Brotherhood '68
Hombre '67
The Spy Who Came in from the Cold '65
Hud '63
Paris Blues '61
Black Orchid '59
The Long, Hot Summer '58

Jacques Rivette (1928-)
Va Savoir '01
Up/Down/Fragile '95
Jeanne la Pucelle '94
La Belle Noiseuse '90
Celine and Julie Go Boating '74
The Nun '66
Paris Belongs to Us '60

Hal Roach (1892-1992)
Road Show '41
One Million B.C. '40
The Devil's Brother '33

Jay Roach
Austin Powers In Goldmember '02
Meet the Parents '00
Austin Powers 2: The Spy Who Shagged Me '99
Mystery, Alaska '99
Austin Powers: International Man of Mystery '97

Seymour Robbie
Marco '73
C.C. & Company '70

Brian Robbins (1964-)
Hardball '01
Ready to Rumble '00
Varsity Blues '98
Good Burger '97
The Show '95

Matthew Robbins
Bingo '91
*batteries not included '87
Legend of Billie Jean '85
Dragonslayer '81
Corvette Summer '78

Tim Robbins (1958-)
The Cradle Will Rock '99
Dead Man Walking '95
Bob Roberts '92

Mike Robe
Return to Lonesome Dove '93
Scott Turow's The Burden of Proof '92
Son of the Morning Star '91
Child in the Night '90
Murder Ordained '87
News at Eleven '86
Urge to Kill '84

Yves Robert (1920-2002)
My Father's Glory '91
My Mother's Castle '91
Pardon Mon Affaire, Too! '77
Pardon Mon Affaire '76
Return of the Tall Blond Man with One Black Shoe '74
Salut l'Artiste '74
The Tall Blond Man with One Black Shoe '72

Alan Roberts
Karate Cop '93
Save Me '93
Round Trip to Heaven '92
Young Lady Chatterly 2 '85
The Happy Hooker Goes Hollywood '80

John Roberts
Paulie '98
War of the Buttons '95

Stephen Roberts (1917-99)
Ex-Mrs. Bradford '36
Star of Midnight '35
Romance in Manhattan '34

John S. Robertson (1878-1964)
Our Little Girl '35
Little Orphan Annie '32
The Single Standard '29
Shore Leave '25
Soul-Fire '25
Tess of the Storm Country '22
Dr. Jekyll and Mr. Hyde '20

Bruce Robinson (1946-)
Jennifer 8 '92
How to Get Ahead in Advertising '89
Withnail and I '87

Chris Robinson (1938-)
Sunshine Run '79
Women's Prison Escape '74

John Mark Robinson
All Tied Up '92
Kid '90
Roadhouse 66 '84

Phil Alden Robinson (1950-)
The Sum of All Fears '02
Band of Brothers '01
Freedom Song '00
Sneakers '92
Field of Dreams '89
In the Mood '87

Richard Robinson
Poor Pretty Eddie '73
Bloody Trail '72

Arthur Robison
The Informer '29
Warning Shadows '23

Mark Robson (1913-)
Avalanche Express '79
Earthquake '74
Daddy's Gone A-Hunting '69
Valley of the Dolls '67
The Lost Command '66
Von Ryan's Express '65
The Prize '63
From the Terrace '60
The Inn of the Sixth Happiness '58
Peyton Place '57
The Harder They Fall '56
The Bridges at Toko-Ri '55
Phffft! '54
Return to Paradise '53
I Want You '51
Champion '49
Home of the Brave '49
Bedlam '45
Isle of the Dead '45
The Seventh Victim '43

Marc Rocco
Murder in the First '95
Where the Day Takes You '92
Dream a Little Dream '89
Scenes from the Goldmine '87

Glauce Rocha
Antonio Das Mortes '68
Earth Entranced '66
Black God, White Devil '64

Eric Rochant
Love Without Pity '91
The Fifth Monkey '90

Alexandre Rockwell
Four Rooms '95
Somebody to Love '94
In the Soup '92
Sons '91

Franc Roddam (1946-)
Cleopatra '99
Moby Dick '98
K2: The Ultimate High '92
War Party '89
Aria '88
The Bride '85
The Lords of Discipline '83
Quadrophenia '79

Serge Rodnunsky
Newsbreak '00
TripFall '00
Cypress Edge '99
Fear Runs Silent '99
Paper Bullets '99
Silicon Towers '99
Dead Tides '97
Final Equinox '95
Lovers' Lovers '94

Ismael Rodriguez
Autopsy of a Ghost '67
Daniel Boone: Trail Blazer '56

Robert Rodriguez (1968-)
Spy Kids 2: The Island of Lost Dreams '02
Spy Kids '01
The Faculty '98
Desperado '95
Four Rooms '95
From Dusk Till Dawn '95
Roadracers '94
El Mariachi '93

Nicolas Roeg (1928-)
Samson and Delilah '96
Full Body Massage '95
Two Deaths '94
Heart of Darkness '93
Cold Heaven '92
The Witches '90
Sweet Bird of Youth '89
Aria '88
Track 29 '88
Castaway '87
Insignificance '85
Eureka! '81
The Man Who Fell to Earth '76
Don't Look Now '73
Walkabout '71
Performance '70

Michael Roemer (1928-)
Pilgrim, Farewell '82
The Plot Against Harry '69
Nothing but a Man '64

Albert Rogell (1901-88)
The Admiral Was a Lady '50
War of the Wildcats '43
The Black Cat '41
Li'l Abner '40
The Tip-Off '31
Cyclone Cavalier '25

Charles R. Rogers (1887-1956)
March of the Wooden Soldiers '34
The Devil's Brother '33

James B. Rogers
American Pie 2 '01
Say It Isn't So '01

Maclean Rogers (1899-1962)
Down Among the Z Men '52
Old Mother Riley's Jungle Treasure '51
Calling Paul Temple '48

Cliff Roguemore
Devil's Son-in-Law '77
Dolemite 2: Human Tornado '76

Eric Rohmer (1920-)
Autumn Tale '98
A Summer's Tale '96
Rendezvous in Paris '95
A Tale of Winter '92
Four Adventures of Reinette and Mirabelle '89
A Tale of Springtime '89
Boyfriends & Girlfriends '88
Summer '86
Full Moon in Paris '84
Pauline at the Beach '83
Le Beau Mariage '82
The Aviator's Wife '80
Perceval '78
The Marquise of O '76
Chloe in the Afternoon '72
Claire's Knee '71
My Night at Maud's '69
Six in Paris '68
La Collectionneuse '67

Sutton Roley
Loners '72
Snatched '72

Jean Rollin
The Living Dead Girl '82
Zombie Lake '80
Lips of Blood '75

Phil Roman
Tom and Jerry: The Movie '93
Race for Your Life, Charlie Brown '77

Mark Romanek (1959-)
One Hour Photo '02
Static '87

Eddie Romero (1924-)
WhiteForce '88
Beyond Atlantis '73
Twilight People '72
Woman Hunt '72
Beast of the Yellow Night '70
Mad Doctor of Blood Island '69
Brides of the Beast '68
The Ravagers '65
The Walls of Hell '64
Cavalry Command '63
Raiders of Leyte Gulf '63

George A. Romero (1940-)
Bruiser '00
The Dark Half '91
Two Evil Eyes '90
Monkey Shines '88
Day of the Dead '85
Creepshow '82
Knightriders '81
Dawn of the Dead '78
Martin '77
The Crazies '73
Season of the Witch '73
Night of the Living Dead '68

Charles R. Rondeau
The Girl in Lover's Lane '60
The Devil's Partner '58

Darrell Roodt (1963-)
Second Skin '00
Dangerous Ground '96
Cry, the Beloved Country '95
Father Hood '93
To the Death '93
Sarafina! '92
City of Blood '88
Place of Weeping '86

Don Roos (1959-)
Bounce '00
The Opposite of Sex '98

Tom Ropelewski
Look Who's Talking Now '93
Madhouse '90

Mark Roper (1958-)
Operation Delta Force 3: Clear Target '98
Alien Chaser '96
Warhead '96
Live Wire: Human Timebomb '95

Bernard Rose
Leo Tolstoy's Anna Karenina '96
Immortal Beloved '94
Candyman '92
Chicago Joe & the Showgirl '90
Paperhouse '89

Lee Rose
A Girl Thing '01
The Truth About Jane '00
The Color of Courage '98

Les Rose
Gas '81
Title Shot '81
Hog Wild '80

Barry Rosen
The Yum-Yum Girls '78
Gang Wars '75

Martin Rosen
Stacking '87
The Plague Dogs '82
Watership Down '78

Phil Rosen (1888-1951)
The Jade Mask '45
The Scarlet Clue '45
Charlie Chan in the Secret Service '44
The Chinese Cat '44
Meeting at Midnight '44
Return of the Ape Man '44
Wings over the Pacific '43
I Killed That Man '42
Gangs, Inc. '41
Spooks Run Wild '41
Phantom of Chinatown '40
It Could Happen to You '37
Mistaken Identity '36
The President's Mystery '36
Tango '36
Beggars in Ermine '34
The Phantom Broadcast '33
The Sphinx '33
Young Blood '33
Man's Land '32
Whistlin' Dan '32
Arizona Terror '31
Branded Men '31
The Pocatello Kid '31
Two Gun Man '31
The Peacock Fan '29
The Phantom in the House '29

Stuart Rosenberg (1927-)
My Heroes Have Always Been Cowboys '91
The Pope of Greenwich Village '84
Brubaker '80
The Amityville Horror '79
Love and Bullets '79
Voyage of the Damned '76
The Drowning Pool '75
The Laughing Policeman '74
Pocket Money '72
April Fools '69
Cool Hand Luke '67

Seth Zvi Rosenfeld
King of the Jungle '01
A Brother's Kiss '97
Subway Stories '97

Rick Rosenthal (1949-)
Halloween: Resurrection '02
Just a Little Harmless Sex '99
The Birds 2: Land's End '94
Devlin '92
Russkies '87
American Dreamer '84
Bad Boys '83
Halloween 2: The Nightmare Isn't Over! '81

Robert J. Rosenthal
Zapped! '82
Malibu Beach '78

Francesco Rosi (1922-)
The Truce '96
The Palermo Connection '91
Three Brothers '80
Christ Stopped at Eboli '79
Lucky Luciano '74

Mark Rosman
Life-Size '00
Model Behavior '00
The Invader '96

Evolver '94
The Blue Yonder '86
The House on Sorority Row '83

Milton Rosmer (1881-1971)
The Challenge '38
Murder in the Old Red Barn '36
The Secret of the Loch '34

Herbert Ross (1927-2001)
Boys on the Side '94
Undercover Blues '93
True Colors '91
My Blue Heaven '90
Steel Magnolias '89
Dancers '87
The Secret of My Success '87
Footloose '84
Protocol '84
Max Dugan Returns '83
I Ought to Be in Pictures '82
Pennies from Heaven '81
Nijinsky '80
California Suite '78
The Goodbye Girl '77
The Turning Point '77
The Seven-Per-Cent Solution '76
Funny Lady '75
The Sunshine Boys '75
The Last of Sheila '73
Play It Again, Sam '72
The Owl and the Pussycat '70
Goodbye, Mr. Chips '69
Goodbye Love '34

Roberto Rossellini (1906-77)
The Messiah '75
Augustine of Hippo '72
Blaise Pascal '71
The Rise of Louis XIV '66
RoGoPaG '62
Vanina Vanini '61
Era Notte a Roma '60
Generale Della Rovere '60
Seven Deadly Sins '53
Voyage in Italy '53
Europa '51 '52
The Flowers of St. Francis '50
Stromboli '50
Amore '48
Machine to Kill Bad People '48
The Miracle '48
Deutschland im Jahre Null '47
Paisan '46
Open City '45
Man with a Cross '43

Robert Rossen (1908-66)
Lilith '64
The Hustler '61
They Came to Cordura '59
Island in the Sun '57
Alexander the Great '55
Mambo '55
All the King's Men '49
Body and Soul '47

Arthur Rosson (1886-1960)
Boots of Destiny '37
Hidden Gold '33
The Concentratin' Kid '30
Trailing Trouble '30
The Last Outlaw '27

Bobby Roth (1950-)
Keeper of the City '92
The Game of Love '90
The Man Inside '90
Rainbow Drive '90
Dead Solid Perfect '88
Baja Oklahoma '87
Heartbreakers '84
Circle of Power '83
Boss' Son '78

Joe Roth (1948-)
America's Sweethearts '01
Coupe de Ville '90
Revenge of the Nerds 2: Nerds in Paradise '87
Streets of Gold '86

Phillip J. Roth
Interceptor Force '99
Velocity Trap '99
Darkdrive '98
Total Reality '97
A.P.E.X. '94
Digital Man '94
Prototype X29A '92
Red Snow '91

Stephanie Rothman (1936-)
Working Girls '75
Terminal Island '73
Group Marriage '72
The Velvet Vampire '71
The Student Nurses '70
Track of the Vampire '66

William Rotsler (1926-97)
Mantis in Lace '68
Agony of Love '66

Brigitte Rouan (1965-)
After Sex '97
Overseas: Three Women with Man Trouble '90

Jean Rouch (1917-)
Six in Paris '68
Jaguar '56

Russell Rouse (1913-87)
Caper of the Golden Bulls '67
The Oscar '66
Fastest Gun Alive '56
The Thief '52
The Well '51

Peter Rowe (1947-)
Treasure Island '99
Personal Exemptions '88
Take Two '87
Lost '86

Roy Rowland (1902-95)
Girl Hunters '63
The Seven Hills of Rome '58
Gun Glory '57
Meet Me in Las Vegas '56
Hit the Deck '55
The 5000 Fingers of Dr. T '53
Bugles in the Afternoon '52
Two Weeks with Love '50
Our Vines Have Tender Grapes '45

William Rowland (1898-)
Flight to Nowhere '46
Follies Girl '43

Patricia Rozema (1958-)
Mansfield Park '99
When Night Is Falling '95
I've Heard the Mermaids Singing '87

John Ruane
Dead Letter Office '98
That Eye, the Sky '94
Death in Brunswick '90

Andy Ruben
Club Vampire '98
Streets '90

J. Walter Ruben (1899-1942)
Java Head '35
Riff Raff '35
Ace of Aces '33

Joseph Ruben (1951-)
Return to Paradise '98
Money Train '95
The Good Son '93
Sleeping with the Enemy '91
True Believer '89
The Stepfather '87
Dreamscape '84
Gorp '80
Joyride '77
Pom Pom Girls '76

Percival Rubens
Sweet Murder '93
Wild Zone '89
Survival Zone '84
The Demon '81
Mr. Kingstreet's War '71

Sergio Rubini (1959-)
The Blonde '92
The Station '92

Alan Rudolph (1943-)
Trixie '00
Breakfast of Champions '98
Afterglow '97
Mrs. Parker and the Vicious Circle '94
Equinox '93
Mortal Thoughts '91
Love at Large '89
The Moderns '88
Made in Heaven '87
Trouble in Mind '86
Choose Me '84
Songwriter '84
Endangered Species '82
Roadie '80
Welcome to L.A. '77
Barn of the Naked Dead '73
Premonition '71

Wesley Ruggles (1889-1972)
Somewhere I'll Find You '42
Arizona '40
I'm No Angel '33
No Man of Her Own '32
Cimarron '31
The Plastic Age '25

Raul Ruiz (1941-)
Shattered Image '98
Genealogies of a Crime '97
Three Lives and Only One Death '96
On Top of the Whale '82
The Hypothesis of the Stolen Painting '78

Richard Rush (1930-)
Color of Night '94
The Stunt Man '80
Freebie & the Bean '74
Getting Straight '70
Psych-Out '68
The Savage Seven '68
Hell's Angels on Wheels '67

Josef Rusnak
The Thirteenth Floor '99
Quiet Days in Hollywood '97

Chuck Russell
The Scorpion King '02
Bless the Child '00
Eraser '96
The Mask '94
The Blob '88
A Nightmare on Elm Street 3: Dream Warriors '87

David O. Russell (1959-)
Three Kings '99
Flirting with Disaster '95
Spanking the Monkey '94

Jay Russell
My Dog Skip '99
End of the Line '88

Ken Russell (1927-)
Tracked '98
Tales of Erotica '93
Lady Chatterley '92
Prisoner of Honor '91
Whore '91
Women & Men: Stories of Seduction '90
The Rainbow '89
Aria '88
The Lair of the White Worm '88
Salome's Last Dance '88
Gothic '87
Crimes of Passion '84
Altered States '80
Valentino '77
Lisztomania '75
Tommy '75
Mahler '74
Savage Messiah '72
The Boy Friend '71
The Devils '71
The Music Lovers '71
Women in Love '70
Dante's Inferno: Life of Dante Gabriel Rossetti '69

William D. Russell (1908-68)
Best of the Badmen '50
The Green Promise '49

John A. Russo
Midnight 2: Sex, Death, and Videotape '93
Midnight '81

Marti Rustam
James Dean: Live Fast, Die Young '97
Evils of the Night '85

Stefan Ruzowitzky
Anatomy '00
The Inheritors '98

Frank Ryan (1947-)
Can't Help Singing '45
Call Out the Marines '42

Edgar Ryazanov (1927-)
A Forgotten Tune for the Flute '88
Private Life '82

Mark Rydell (1934-)
James Dean '01
Crime of the Century '96
Intersection '93
For the Boys '91
The River '84
On Golden Pond '81
The Rose '79
Harry & Walter Go to New York '76
Cinderella Liberty '73
The Cowboys '72
The Reivers '69

Renny Rye
Oliver Twist '00
Lipstick on Your Collar '94

Michael Rymer
Queen of the Damned '02
Perfume '01
In Too Deep '99
Angel Baby '95

William Sachs
The Last Hour '91
Galaxina '80
Van Nuys Blvd. '79
Incredible Melting Man '77
South of Hell Mountain '70

James Sadwith (1952-)
Sinatra '92
Bluffing It '87

Henri Safran (1932-)
The Wild Duck '84
Norman Loves Rose '82

Boris Sagal (1917-81)
Masada '81
Angela '77
The Runaway Barge '75
Omega Man '71
Night Gallery '69
Girl Happy '65
Guns of Diablo '64

Malcolm St. Clair (1897-1952)
Bullfighters '45
The Bashful Bachelor '42
The Grand Duchess and the Waiter '26
The Show Off '26
Are Parents People? '25

Gene Saks (1921-)
Bye Bye Birdie '95
Brighton Beach Memoirs '86
Mame '74
Last of the Red Hot Lovers '72
Cactus Flower '69
The Odd Couple '68
Barefoot in the Park '67

Richard Sale (1911-93)
Abandon Ship '57
Let's Make It Legal '51
Ticket to Tomahawk '50

Sidney Salkow (1909-2000)
The Last Man on Earth '64
Twice-Told Tales '63
City Without Men '43

Walter Salles (1956-)
Behind the Sun '01
Central Station '98
Foreign Land '95

Mikael Salomon (1945-)
Band of Brothers '01

A Glimpse of Hell '01
Aftershock: Earthquake in New York '99
Hard Rain '97
A Far Off Place '93

Victor Salva (1958-)
Jeepers Creepers '01
Rites of Passage '99
Powder '95
Nature of the Beast '94
Clown House '88

Salvatore Samperi (1944-)
Ernesto '79
Submission '77
Malicious '74

Barry Samson
Bloodfist 8: Hard Way Out '96
Yesterday's Target '96
The Ice Runner '93
Ice Pawn '92

Rachel Samuels
Robert Louis Stevenson's The Game of Death '99
Running Woman '98

Denis Sanders (1929-87)
Invasion of the Bee Girls '73
One Man's Way '63

Jay Sandrich (1932-)
For Richer, for Poorer '92
Seems Like Old Times '80

Mark Sandrich (1900-45)
Here Come the Waves '45
So Proudly We Hail '43
Holiday Inn '42
Carefree '38
Shall We Dance '37
Follow the Fleet '36
A Woman Rebels '36
Top Hat '35
Cockeyed Cavaliers '34
The Gay Divorcee '34
Hips, Hips, Hooray '34
Aggie Appleby, Maker of Men '33
Melody Cruise '32

Arlene Sanford
I'll Be Home for Christmas '98
A Very Brady Sequel '96

Jonathan Sanger
Down Came a Blackbird '94
Code Name: Emerald '85

Jimmy Sangster (1924-)
Dynasty of Fear '72
Lust for a Vampire '71
The Horror of Frankenstein '70

Alfred Santell (1895-1981)
That Brennan Girl '46
The Hairy Ape '44
Jack London '44
Having Wonderful Time '38
Internes Can't Take Money '37
Winterset '36

Cirio H. Santiago (1936-)
Caged Heat 3000 '95
Caged Heat 2: Stripped of Freedom '94
Stranglehold '94
One Man Army '93
Beyond the Call of Duty '92
Field of Fire '92
Firehawk '92
Raiders of the Sun '92
Dune Warriors '91
Eye of the Eagle 3 '91
The Expendables '89
Silk 2 '89
Future Hunters '88
Nam Angels '88
The Sisterhood '88
Demon of Paradise '87
Eye of the Eagle '87
Equalizer 2000 '86
Silk '86
Devastator '85
Naked Vengeance '85
Final Mission '84
Wheels of Fire '84
Stryker '83
Caged Fury '80
Death Force '78
The Vampire Hookers '78
Fighting Mad '77
The Muthers '76
She Devils in Chains '76
Cover Girl Models '75
TNT Jackson '75
Savage! '73
Firecracker '71

Joseph Santley (1889-1971)
Call of the Canyon '42
Down Mexico Way '41
Melody Ranch '40
Music in My Heart '40
Harmony Lane '35
The Cocoanuts '29

Damon Santostefano
Three to Tango '99
Severed Ties '92

Ken Sanzel
Lone Hero '02
Scarred City '98

David Saperstein
Beyond the Stars '89
A Killing Affair '85

Deran Sarafian
The Road Killers '95
Terminal Velocity '94
Gunmen '93
Back in the USSR '92
Death Warrant '90
To Die For '89
Interzone '88
Alien Predators '80

Richard Sarafian (1935-)
Solar Crisis '92
Street Justice '89
Eye of the Tiger '86
Gangster Wars '81
Sunburn '79
The Arab Conspiracy '76
Man Who Loved Cat Dancing '73
Man in the Wilderness '71
Vanishing Point '71

Joseph Sargent (1925-)
Bojangles '01
For Love or Country: The Arturo Sandoval Story '00
Dostoevsky's Crime and Punishment '99
A Lesson Before Dying '99
The Wall '99
Mandela and de Klerk '97
Miss Evers' Boys '97
Larry McMurtry's Streets of Laredo '95
Abraham '94
My Antonia '94
World War II: When Lions Roared '94
Sarah, Plain and Tall: Skylark '93
Miss Rose White '92
Never Forget '91
Caroline? '90
Ivory Hunters '90
Day One '89
The Incident '89
Jaws: The Revenge '87
Passion Flower '86
Memorial Day '83
Nightmares '83
Amber Waves '82
Tomorrow's Child '82
The Manions of America '81
Coast to Coast '80
Goldengirl '79
MacArthur '77
Hustling '75
The Taking of Pelham One Two Three '74
White Lightning '73
Man on a String '71
Colossus: The Forbin Project '70
Maybe I'll Be Home in the Spring '70
Tribes '70

Marina Sargenti
Child of Darkness, Child of Light '91
Mirror, Mirror '90

Vic Sarin
Sea People '00
In His Father's Shoes '97
The Legend of Gator Face '96
Cold Comfort '90

Peter Sasdy
The Lonely Lady '83
The Two Faces of Evil '82
Rude Awakening '81
Thirteenth Reunion '81
The Devil's Undead '75
I Don't Want to Be Born '75
King Arthur, the Young Warlord '75
Young Warlord '75
Doomwatch '72
Nothing But the Night '72
Hands of the Ripper '71
Taste the Blood of Dracula '70

Oley Sassone
Playback '95
Fast Getaway 2 '94
Relentless 4 '94
Future Shock '93
Bloodfist 3: Forced to Fight '92
Final Embrace '92

Ron Satlof
Perry Mason: The Case of the Lost Love '87
Perry Mason Returns '85
Waikiki '80
Spiderman: The Deadly Dust '78

Hajime Sato (1929-95)
Body Snatcher from Hell '69
Terror Beneath the Sea '66

Junya Sato
The Silk Road '92
The Go-Masters '82

Ernest G. Sauer
Broadcast Bombshells '95
Bikini Bistro '94
Beauty School '93

Carlos Saura (1932-)
Goya in Bordeaux '99
Tango '98
Outrage '93
Ay, Carmela! '90
El Amor Brujo '86
The Stilts '84
Carmen '83
Blood Wedding '81
Mama Turns a Hundred '79
Elisa, Vida Mia '77
Cria '76
The Garden of Delights '70
The Hunt '65

Claude Sautet (1924-2000)
Nelly et Monsieur Arnaud '95
Un Coéur en Hiver '93
A Simple Story '79
Mado '76
Vincent, Francois, Paul and the Others '76
Cesar & Rosalie '72
The Things of Life '70

Philip Saville
My Uncle Silas '01
Deacon Brodie '98
Metroland '97
The Buccaneers '95
Family Pictures '93
Max and Helen '90
Fellow Traveler '89
Wonderland '88
Mandela '87
Shadey '87
Those Glory, Glory Days '83
Secrets '71

Victor Saville (1897-1979)
The Silver Chalice '54
Kim '50
Conspirator '49
Green Dolphin Street '47
Tonight and Every Night '45
Forever and a Day '43
Dark Journey '37
South Riding '37
Storm in a Teacup '37
It's Love Again '36
First a Girl '35
Evergreen '34
The Iron Duke '34

Nancy Savoca (1960-)
The 24 Hour Woman '99
If These Walls Could Talk '96
Household Saints '93
Dogfight '91
True Love '89

Geoffrey Sax
Othello '01
Doctor Who '96
Ruby Jean and Joe '96
Broken Trust '95
Framed '93

John Sayles (1950-)
Sunshine State '02
Limbo '99
Hombres Armados '97
Lone Star '95
The Secret of Roan Inish '94
Passion Fish '92
City of Hope '91
Eight Men Out '88
Matewan '87
The Brother from Another Planet '84
Lianna '83
Baby It's You '82
Return of the Secaucus 7 '80

Stefan Scaini
Anne of Green Gables: The Continuing Story '99
Double Play '96

Joseph L. Scanlan
The World's Oldest Living Bridesmaid '92
Nightstick '87
Spring Fever '81

Steven Schachter
A Slight Case of Murder '99
The Con '98
Above Suspicion '95
Getting Up and Going Home '92
The Water Engine '92

Armand Schaefer (1898-1967)
The Miracle Rider '35
Law of the Wild '34
The Lost Jungle '34
Sixteen Fathoms Deep '34
Fighting Texans '33
Fighting with Kit Carson '33
Sagebrush Trail '33
Terror Trail '33
Hurricane Express '32
Outlaw Justice '32
Lightning Warrior '31

George Schaefer (1920-97)
The Man Upstairs '93
Children in the Crossfire '84
Right of Way '84
Deadly Game '82
A Piano for Mrs. Cimino '82
Who'll Save Our Children? '82
The People vs. Jean Harris '81
Mayflower: The Pilgrims' Adventure '79
Lost Legacy: A Girl Called Hatter Fox '77
In This House of Brede '75
Once Upon a Scoundrel '73
Doctors' Wives '70
Generation '69
Pendulum '69
Elizabeth, the Queen '68
Soldier in Love '67
Barefoot in Athens '66
Lamp at Midnight '66
Holy Terror '65
Invincible Mr. Disraeli '63
The Tempest '63
Victoria Regina '61
A Doll's House '59

Eric Schaeffer (1962-)
Wirey Spindell '99
Fall '97
If Lucy Fell '95
My Life's in Turnaround '94

Francis Schaeffer
Baby on Board '92
Rebel Storm '90
Headhunter '89
Wired to Kill '86

Franklin J. Schaffner (1920-)
Welcome Home '89
Lionheart '87
Yes, Giorgio '82
Sphinx '81
The Boys from Brazil '78
Islands in the Stream '77
Our Town '77
Papillon '73
Nicholas and Alexandra '71
Patton '70
Planet of the Apes '68
The War Lord '65
The Best Man '64
The Stripper '63

Don Schain
Too Hot to Handle '76
Girls Are for Loving '73
The Abductors '72
Ginger '72
A Place Called Today '72

Jerry Schatzberg (1927-)
Blood Money: The Story of Clinton and Nadine '88
Reunion '88
Street Smart '87
Misunderstood '84
No Small Affair '84
Honeysuckle Rose '80
The Seduction of Joe Tynan '79
Panic in Needle Park '75
Scarecrow '73

Robert Scheerer
Happily Ever After '82
How to Beat the High Cost of Living '80
Ants '77
The World's Greatest Athlete '73
Adam at 6 a.m. '70
Hans Brinker '69

Maximilian Schell (1930-)
The Pedestrian '73
First Love '70

Henning Schellerup
The Adventures of Nellie Bly '81
Time Machine '78

Carl Schenkel
Missing Pieces '00
Tarzan and the Lost City '98
The Surgeon '94
Knight Moves '93
Silhouette '91
Silence Like Glass '90
The Mighty Quinn '89
Eye of the Demon '87
Out of Order '84
Strike Back '80

Richard Schenkman
Went to Coney Island on a Mission from God...Be Back by Five '98
The Pompatus of Love '95

Fred Schepisi (1939-)
Fierce Creatures '96
I.Q. '94
Six Degrees of Separation '93
Mr. Baseball '92
The Russia House '90
A Cry in the Dark '88
Roxanne '87
Plenty '85
Iceman '84
Barbarosa '82
The Devil's Playground '76

Victor Schertzinger (1890-1941)
Birth of the Blues '41
The Road to Zanzibar '41
Rhythm on the River '40
The Road to Singapore '40
Something to Sing About '36
One Night of Love '34
Uptown New York '32
What Happened to Rosa? '21
Clodhopper '17

Lawrence Schiller (1936-)
American Tragedy '00
Double Jeopardy '92
Double Exposure: The Story of Margaret Bourke-White '89
The Executioner's Song '82
Marilyn: The Untold Story '80

Thomas Schlamme
Kingfish: A Story of Huey P. Long '95
You So Crazy '94
So I Married an Axe Murderer '93
Crazy from the Heart '91
Miss Firecracker '89
Spalding Gray: Terrors of Pleasure '88

John Schlesinger (1926-)
The Next Best Thing '00
An Eye for an Eye '95
Cold Comfort Farm '94
The Innocent '93
A Question of Attribution '91
Pacific Heights '90
Madame Sousatzka '88
The Believers '87
The Falcon and the Snowman '85
An Englishman Abroad '83
Separate Tables '83
Honky Tonk Freeway '81
Yanks '79
Marathon Man '76
The Day of the Locust '75
Sunday, Bloody Sunday '71
Midnight Cowboy '69
Far from the Madding Crowd '67
Darling '65
Billy Liar '63
A Kind of Loving '62

Volker Schlondorff (1939-)
The Legend of Rita '99
Palmetto '98
The Ogre '96
Murder on the Bayou '91
Voyager '91
The Handmaid's Tale '90
Death of a Salesman '86
Swann in Love '84
The Tin Drum '79
Coup de Grace '78
Germany in Autumn '78
The Lost Honor of Katharina Blum '75

David Schmoeller (1947-)
The Arrival '90
Curse 4: The Ultimate Sacrifice '90
Netherworld '90
Catacombs '89
Puppet Master '89
Crawlspace '86
The Seduction '82
Tourist Trap '79

Julian Schnabel
Before Night Falls '00
Basquiat '96

Paul Schneider
Can of Worms '00
Honor Thy Father and Mother: The True Story of the Menendez Brothers '94
Babycakes '89
Something Special '86

Robert Allen Schnitzer
Kandyland '87
The Premonition '75

Ernest B. Schoedsack (1893-1979)
Mighty Joe Young '49
Dr. Cyclops '40
Last Days of Pompeii '35
King Kong '33
Son of Kong '33
The Most Dangerous Game '32
Chang: A Drama of the Wilderness '27

Pierre Schoendoerffer
Le Crabe Tambour '77
The 317th Platoon '65

Paul Schrader (1946-)
Forever Mine '99
Affliction '97
Touch '96
Witch Hunt '94
Light Sleeper '92
The Comfort of Strangers '91
Patty Hearst '88
Light of Day '87
Mishima: A Life in Four Chapters '85
Cat People '82
American Gigolo '79
Hardcore '79
Blue Collar '78

Myrl A. Schreibman
Liberty & Bash '90
Angel of H.E.A.T. '82

Barbet Schroeder (1941-)
Murder by Numbers '02
Our Lady of the Assassins '01
Desperate Measures '98
Before and After '95
Kiss of Death '94
Single White Female '92
Reversal of Fortune '90
Barfly '87
Tricheurs '84
Maitresse '76
The Valley Obscured by the Clouds '72
More '69

Michael Schroeder (1952-)
The Glass Cage '96
Cover Me '95
Cyborg 3: The Recycler '95
Cyborg 2 '93
Mortuary Academy '91
Relentless 2: Dead On '91
Damned River '89
Out of the Dark '88

Carl Schultz (1939-)
To Walk with Lions '99
Deadly Currents '93
Which Way Home '90
The Seventh Sign '88
Travelling North '87
Careful, He Might Hear You '84
Blue Fin '78

John Schultz
Like Mike '02
Drive Me Crazy '99
Bandwagon '95

Michael A. Schultz (1938-)
The Great American Sex Scandal '94
Livin' Large '91
For Us, the Living '88
Disorderlies '87
Timestalkers '87
Krush Groove '85
The Last Dragon '85
Three Days in Beirut '83
Carbon Copy '81
Scavenger Hunt '79
Sgt. Pepper's Lonely Hearts Club Band '78
Greased Lightning '77
Which Way Is Up? '77
Car Wash '76
Cooley High '75
Honeybaby '74

Joel Schumacher (1942-)
Bad Company '02
Tigerland '00
Flawless '99
Batman and Robin '97
A Time to Kill '96
Batman Forever '95
The Client '94
Falling Down '93
Dying Young '91
Flatliners '90
Cousins '89
The Lost Boys '87
St. Elmo's Fire '85
D.C. Cab '84
The Incredible Shrinking Woman '81
The Virginia Hill Story '76

Reinhold Schunzel (1886-1954)
Balalaika '39
Fortune's Fool '21

Harold Schuster (1902-86)
Courage of Black Beauty '57
The Finger Man '55
Kid Monk Baroni '52
So Dear to My Heart '49
The Tender Years '47
Breakfast in Hollywood '46
Marine Raiders '43
My Friend Flicka '43
Dinner at the Ritz '37
Wings of the Morning '37

Douglas Schwartz
Baywatch the Movie: Forbidden Paradise '95
Thunder in Paradise 2 '94
Thunder in Paradise '93
Peacekillers '71

Ettore Scola (1931-)
The Family '87
Macaroni '85
La Nuit de Varennes '82
Le Bal '82
Passion of Love '82
A Special Day '77
We All Loved Each Other So Much '77
Down & Dirty '76

Martin Scorsese (1942-)
Bringing Out the Dead '99
Kundun '97
Casino '95
The Age of Innocence '93
Cape Fear '91
Goodfellas '90
New York Stories '89
The Last Temptation of Christ '88
The Color of Money '86
After Hours '85
King of Comedy '82
Raging Bull '80
The Last Waltz '78
New York, New York '77
Taxi Driver '76
Alice Doesn't Live Here Anymore '74
Mean Streets '73
Boxcar Bertha '72
Who's That Knocking at My Door? '68

Campbell Scott (1962-)
Final '01
Hamlet '01
Big Night '95

George C. Scott (1927-99)
Descending Angel '90
Don't Look Back: The Story of Leroy "Satchel" Paige '81
Savage Is Loose '74
Rage '72
The Andersonville Trial '70

Michael Scott
Heck's Way Home '95
Sharon's Secret '95
Dangerous Heart '93
Ladykiller '92

Oz Scott
Spanish Judges '99
Bustin' Loose '81

Ridley Scott (1939-)
Black Hawk Down '01
Hannibal '01
Gladiator '00
RKO 281 '99
G.I. Jane '97
White Squall '96

1492: Conquest of Paradise '92
Thelma & Louise '91
Black Rain '89
Someone to Watch Over Me '87
Legend '86
Blade Runner '82
Alien '79
The Duellists '77

Sherman Scott
The Kid with the X-Ray Eyes '99
Rapid Assault '99

T.J. Scott
Young Hercules '97
TC 2000 '93

Tony Scott (1944-)
Spy Game '01
Enemy of the State '98
The Fan '96
Crimson Tide '95
True Romance '93
The Last Boy Scout '91
Days of Thunder '90
Revenge '90
Beverly Hills Cop 2 '87
Top Gun '86
The Hunger '83

Francis Searle
Profile '54
Someone at the Door '50
Things Happen at Night '48
A Girl in a Million '46

Fred F. Sears (1913-57)
The Giant Claw '57
Earth vs. the Flying Saucers '56
Teenage Crime Wave '55
Ambush at Tomahawk Gap '53
Bonanza Town '51

George Seaton (1911-79)
Showdown '73
Airport '70
36 Hours '64
The Counterfeit Traitor '62
Teacher's Pet '58
Country Girl '54
The Big Lift '50
Miracle on 34th Street '47

Beverly Sebastian
Running Cool '93
The American Angels: Baptism of Blood '89
Gator Bait 2: Cajun Justice '88
Delta Fox '77
Gator Bait '73

Ferd Sebastian
Running Cool '93
The American Angels: Baptism of Blood '89
Gator Bait 2: Cajun Justice '88
Rocktober Blood '85
On the Air Live with Captain Midnight '79
Delta Fox '77
Flash & Firecat '75
Gator Bait '73
Hitchhikers '72

Mike Sedan
Naked Wishes '00
Lap Dancing '95
Married People, Single Sex 2: For Better or Worse '94
Night Fire '94
Married People, Single Sex '93

Edward Sedgwick (1892-1953)
Ma and Pa Kettle Back On the Farm '51
A Southern Yankee '48
Air Raid Wardens '43
The Gladiator '38
Fit for a King '37
Pick a Star '37
Riding on Air '37
What! No Beer? '33
Speak Easily '32
Maker of Men '31
Parlor, Bedroom and Bath '31
Doughboys '30
Free and Easy '30
Spite Marriage '29
The Cameraman '28
The Phantom of the Opera '25

Paul Seed (1947-)
Heat of the Sun '99
A Rather English Marriage '98
The Affair '95
To Play the King '93
Dead Ahead: The Exxon Valdez Disaster '92

Peter Segal
Nutty Professor 2: The Klumps '00
My Fellow Americans '96
Tommy Boy '95
Naked Gun 33 1/3: The Final Insult '94

Stu Segall
Illegal in Blue '95
Drive-In Massacre '74

Arthur Seidelman
Trapped in Space '94
Dying to Remember '93
Rescue Me '93
Body Language '92
The Kid Who Loved Christmas '90
False Witness '89
A Friendship in Vienna '88
The Caller '87
Glory Years '87
Poker Alice '87
Echoes '83
Children of Rage '75
Hercules in New York '70

Arthur Allan Seidelman
By Dawn's Early Light '00
The Runaway '00
Sex & Mrs. X '00
Grace & Glorie '98
The Summer of Ben Tyler '96
Harvest of Fire '95

Susan Seidelman (1952-)
A Cooler Climate '99
Tales of Erotica '93
Cookie '89
She-Devil '89
Making Mr. Right '86
Desperately Seeking Susan '85
Smithereens '82

Joseph Seiden
God, Man and Devil '49
Eli Eli '40
Paradise in Harlem '40

Lewis Seiler (1890-1964)
The Winning Team '52
Doll Face '46
Guadalcanal Diary '43
Pittsburgh '42
Charlie Chan in Paris '35
Great K & A Train Robbery '26

William A. Seiter (1890-1964)
Make Haste to Live '54
Borderline '50
One Touch of Venus '48
Up in Central Park '48
I'll Be Yours '47
Little Giant '46
Destroyer '43
Lady Takes a Chance '43
You Were Never Lovelier '42
Nice Girl? '41
It's a Date '40
Allegheny Uprising '39
Susannah of the Mounties '39
Room Service '38
Dimples '36
The Moon's Our Home '36
Stowaway '36
In Person '35
Roberta '35
Diplomaniacs '33
Sons of the Desert '33
Way Back Home '32
Big Business Girl '31
The Cheerful Fraud '27
Skinner's Dress Suit '26
The White Sin '24
Little Church Around the Corner '23

George B. Seitz (1888-1944)
Andy Hardy's Double Life '42
Andy Hardy's Private Secretary '41
Life Begins for Andy Hardy '41
Andy Hardy Meets Debutante '40
Kit Carson '40
Love Finds Andy Hardy '38
The Last of the Mohicans '36
Drums of Jeopardy '31
Danger Lights '30
The Ice Flood '26
The Vanishing American '25

Steve Sekely (1899-1979)
Day of the Triffids '63
The Scar '48
Blonde Savage '47
Waterfront '44
Behind Prison Walls '43
Revenge of the Zombies '43

Lesley Selander (1900-79)
Arizona Bushwackers '67
The Texican '66
Shotgun '55
Dragonfly Squadron '54
Fighter Attack '53
Flat Top '52
Flight to Mars '52
Rider from Tucson '50
The Red Stallion '47
Robin Hood of Texas '47
The Vampire's Ghost '45
Call of the Rockies '44
Border Patrol '43
Buckskin Frontier '43
Colt Comrades '43
Hopalong Cassidy: Riders of the Deadline '43
Lost Canyon '43
Doomed Caravan '41
Riders of the Timberline '41
Knights of the Range '40
The Light of Western Stars '40
Santa Fe Marshal '40
Hopalong Cassidy: Renegade Trail '39
Renegade Trail '39
The Frontiersmen '38
The Mysterious Rider '38
Sandflow '37

Henry Selick
Monkeybone '01
James and the Giant Peach '96
The Nightmare before Christmas '93

Jack M. Sell (1954-)
The Psychotronic Man '91
Deadly Spygames '89

Charles E. Sellier
The Annihilators '85
Silent Night, Deadly Night '84

David Selman
Prescott Kid '36
Fighting Shadows '35
The Revenge Rider '35

David Seltzer (1940-)
Shining Through '92
Punchline '88
Lucas '86

Edgar Selwyn (1875-1944)
Skyscraper Souls '32
The Sin of Madelon Claudet '31

Dean Semler (1943-)
The Patriot '99
Firestorm '97

Dominic Sena (1949-)
Swordfish '01
Gone in 60 Seconds '00
Kalifornia '93

Ralph Senensky (1923-)
Death Cruise '74
A Dream for Christmas '73

Ron Senkowski
Wicked Ways '99
Let's Kill All the Lawyers '93

Mack Sennett (1980-60)
Mickey '17
Tillie's Punctured Romance '14

Mario Sequi (1910-)
The Cobra '68
Tramplers '66

Yahoo Serious (1954-)
Mr. Accident '99
Reckless Kelly '93
Young Einstein '89

Coline Serreau (1947-)
Mama, There's a Man in Your Bed '89
Three Men and a Cradle '85

Alex Sessa (1928-98)
Stormquest '87
Amazons '86

Vernon Sewell (1903-)
Ghost Keeper '80
Horrors of Burke & Hare '71
The Crimson Cult '68
Blood Beast Terror '67
Rogue's Yarn '56
Terror Ship '54
Ghost Ship '53
Uneasy Terms '48
Ghosts of Berkeley Square '47
The World Owes Me a Living '47
Frenzy '46

Nicholas Sgarro
Fortune Dane '86
The Happy Hooker '75

Tom Shadyac (1960-)
Dragonfly '02
Patch Adams '98
Liar Liar '96
The Nutty Professor '96
Ace Ventura: Pet Detective '93

Krishna Shah (1938-)
Hard Rock Zombies '85
Deadly Thief '78
The River Niger '76
Rivals '72

Adam Shankman
A Walk to Remember '02
The Wedding Planner '01

Alan Shapiro
Flipper '96
The Crush '93
Tiger Town '83

Ken Shapiro (1943-)
Modern Problems '81
The Groove Tube '72

Paul Shapiro (1955-)
Dead Husbands '98
The Invaders '95
Heads '93
The Lotus Eaters '93
Miracle at Moreaux '86
Hockey Night '84

Jim Sharman
Shock Treatment '81
The Rocky Horror Picture Show '75

Don Sharp (1922-)
Tears in the Rain '88
Hold the Dream '86
A Woman of Substance '84
What Waits Below '83
Guardian of the Abyss '82
Bear Island '80
The Thirty-Nine Steps '79
The Four Feathers '78
Hennessy '75
Dark Places '73
Psychomania '73
Those Fantastic Flying Fools '67
Rasputin the Mad Monk '66
Kiss of the Vampire '62

Ian Sharp (1946-)
Tess of the D'Urbervilles '98
R.P.M. '97
Codename Kyril '91
Secret Weapon '90
Robin Hood...The Legend: Robin Hood and the Sorcerer '83
The Final Option '82

Ben Sharpsteen
Dumbo '41
Fantasia '40
Pinocchio '40

William Shatner (1931-)
TekWar '94
Star Trek 5: The Final Frontier '89

Alfred Shaughnessy (1916-)
Cat Girl '57
Suspended Alibi '56

Melville Shavelson (1917-)
Ike '79
Legend of Valentino '75
Yours, Mine & Ours '68
Cast a Giant Shadow '66
A New Kind of Love '63
It Started in Naples '60
The Five Pennies '59
Houseboat '58
The Seven Little Foys '55

Katt Shea
The Rage: Carrie 2 '99
Last Exit to Earth '96
Poison Ivy '92
Streets '90
Stripped to Kill II: Live Girls '89
Dance of the Damned '88
Stripped to Kill '87

Barry Shear (1923-79)
The Crash of Flight 401 '78
Strike Force '75
The Deadly Trackers '73
Across 110th Street '72
The Todd Killings '71
Wild in the Streets '68

Donald Shebib (1938-)
The Ascent '94
The Pathfinder '94
The Little Kidnappers '90
Men of Steel '88
The Climb '87
Heartaches '82
Fish Hawk '79

Riki Shelach
Mercenary Fighters '88
The Last Winter '84

Forrest Sheldon
Between Fighting Men '32
Hell Fire Austin '32

Ron Shelton (1945-)
Play It to the Bone '99
Tin Cup '96
Cobb '94
White Men Can't Jump '92
Blaze '89
Bull Durham '88

Richard Shepard
Mexico City '00
Oxygen '99
Mercy '96
The Linguini Incident '92
Cool Blue '88

Sam Shepard (1943-)
Silent Tongue '92
Far North '88

Adrian Shergold
Heat of the Sun '99
Christabel '89

Jim Sheridan (1949-)
The Boxer '97
In the Name of the Father '93
The Field '90
My Left Foot '89

Edwin Sherin (1930-)
The Father Clements Story '87
My Old Man's Place '71
Valdez Is Coming '71

Gary Sherman
Murderous Vision '91
After the Shock '90
Lisa '90
Poltergeist 3 '88
Wanted Dead or Alive '86
Mysterious Two '82
Vice Squad '82
Dead and Buried '81

George Sherman (1908-91)
Big Jake '71
Panic Button '62
Treasure of Pancho Villa '55
War Arrow '53
Against All Flags '52
Tomahawk '51
Comanche Territory '50
The Last of the Redmen '47
The Sombrero Kid '42
X Marks the Spot '42
Covered Wagon Days '40
Rocky Mountain Rangers '40
Cowboys from Texas '39
Frontier Horizon '39
The Kansas Terrors '39
Three Texas Steers '39
Wyoming Outlaw '39
Outlaws of Sonora '38
Overland Stage Raiders '38
Pals of the Saddle '38
Santa Fe Stampede '38

Lowell Sherman (1885-1934)
Morning Glory '33
She Done Him Wrong '33
False Faces '32
Three Broadway Girls '32
Bachelor Apartment '31
The Royal Bed '31

Vincent Sherman (1906-)
Bogie: The Last Hero '80
Ice Palace '60
The Young Philadelphians '59
Affair in Trinidad '52
Lone Star '52
Harriet Craig '50
Adventures of Don Juan '49
Mr. Skeffington '44
All Through the Night '42
Underground '41

John Sherwood (1959-)
The Monolith Monsters '57
The Creature Walks among Us '56

Brent Shields
Cupid & Cate '00
Durango '99

Frank Shields (1908-75)
Project: Alien '89
Savage Attraction '83

Barry Shils
Wigstock: The Movie '95
Motorama '91

Koji Shima
Warning from Space '56
Golden Demon '53

Kaneto Shindo (1912-)
Onibaba '64
The Island '61

Masahiro Shinoda (1931-)
Gonza the Spearman '86
MacArthur's Children '85
Double Suicide '69

Jack Sholder (1945-)
Arachnid '01
Wishmaster 2: Evil Never Dies '98
Sketch Artist 2: Hands That See '94
12:01 '93
By Dawn's Early Light '89
Renegades '89
The Hidden '87
A Nightmare on Elm Street 2: Freddy's Revenge '85
Alone in the Dark '82

Lee Sholem (1900-)
Escape from Planet Earth '67
Hell Ship Mutiny '57

Ma and Pa Kettle at Waikiki '55
Tobor the Great '54
The Redhead from Wyoming '53
Superman & the Mole Men '51

Lindsay Shonteff
The Killing Edge '86
Number 1 of the Secret Service '77
Big Zapper '73
Fast Kill '73
Second Best Secret Agent in the Whole Wide World '65
Devil Doll '64

Sig Shore
The Survivalist '87
Sudden Death '85
The Act '82
Shining Star '75

Lynn Shores (1893-)
Charlie Chan at the Wax Museum '40
A Million to One '37
The Glory Trail '36

M. Night Shyamalan (1970-)
Signs '02
Unbreakable '00
The Sixth Sense '99
Wide Awake '97

Charles Shyer (1941-)
The Affair of the Necklace '01
Father of the Bride Part II '95
I Love Trouble '94
Father of the Bride '91
Baby Boom '87
Irreconcilable Differences '84

James Shyman
Slashdance '89
Hollywood's New Blood '88

Alex Sichel
If These Walls Could Talk 2 '00
All Over Me '96

Andy Sidaris (1933-)
Return to Savage Beach '97
Day of the Warrior '96
The Dallas Connection '94
Fit to Kill '93
Hard Hunted '92
Do or Die '91
Guns '90
Picasso Trigger '89
Savage Beach '89
Hard Ticket to Hawaii '87
Malibu Express '85
Seven '79
Stacey '73

George Sidney (1916-2002)
Half a Sixpence '67
Bye, Bye, Birdie '63
Viva Las Vegas '63
Pal Joey '57
The Eddy Duchin Story '56
Jupiter's Darling '55
Kiss Me Kate '53
Young Bess '53
Scaramouche '52
Show Boat '51
Annie Get Your Gun '50
Key to the City '50
The Three Musketeers '48
Cass Timberlane '47
The Harvey Girls '46
Holiday in Mexico '46
Anchors Aweigh '45
Bathing Beauty '44
Thousands Cheer '43

Scott Sidney (1872-1928)
The Nervous Wreck '26
Charley's Aunt '25
Tarzan of the Apes '17

David Siegel
The Deep End '01
Suture '93

Donald Siegel (1912-91)
Jinxed '82
Rough Cut '80
Escape from Alcatraz '79
Telefon '77
The Shootist '76
The Black Windmill '74
Charley Varrick '73
Dirty Harry '71
The Beguiled '70
Two Mules for Sister Sara '70
Death of a Gunfighter '69
Coogan's Bluff '68
Madigan '68
The Killers '64
Hell Is for Heroes '62
Flaming Star '60
Invasion of the Body Snatchers '56
The Annapolis Story '55
Private Hell 36 '54
Riot in Cell Block 11 '54
Duel at Silver Creek '52
Big Steal '49

James Signorelli
Hotel Room '93
Elvira, Mistress of the Dark '88
Easy Money '83

Joel Silberg
Lambada '89
Catch the Heat '87
Bad Guys '86
Rappin' '85
Breakin' '84
Kuni Lemel in Tel Aviv '77

Brad Silberling
City of Angels '98
Casper '95

Joan Micklin Silver (1935-)
In the Presence of Mine Enemies '97
Big Girls Don't Cry...They Get Even '92
A Private Matter '92
Prison Stories: Women on the Inside '91
Loverboy '89
Crossing Delancey '88
Finnegan Begin Again '84
Chilly Scenes of Winter '79
Between the Lines '77
Hester Street '75

Marisa Silver (1960-)
Indecency '92
He Said, She Said '91
Vital Signs '90
Permanent Record '88
Old Enough '84

Scott Silver
The Mod Squad '99
johns '96

Elliot Silverstein (1937-)
Flashfire '94
Jailbait: Betrayed By Innocence '86
The Car '77
A Man Called Horse '70
Cat Ballou '65

Lloyd A. Simandl
Crackerjack 3 '00
Escape Velocity '99
Dangerous Prey '95
Chained Heat 2 '92
Ultimate Desires '91
Beyond the Silhouette '90
Possession: Until Death Do You Part '90
Ladies of the Lotus '87
Autumn Born '79

Lawrence L. Simeone (1954-2002)
Blindfold: Acts of Obsession '94
Eyes of the Beholder '92
Cop-Out '91
Presumed Guilty '91

Adam Simon (1962-)
Carnosaur '93
Body Chemistry 2: Voice of a Stranger '91
Brain Dead '89

J(uan) Piquer Simon (1934-)
Cthulhu Mansion '91
Endless Descent '90
Slugs '87
Pieces '83
Supersonic Man '78
Where Time Began '77

Sylvan Simon (1910-51)
Lust for Gold '49
Her Husband's Affairs '47
Abbott and Costello in Hollywood '45
Son of Lassie '45
Whistling in Brooklyn '43
Rio Rita '42
Whistling in Dixie '42
Whistling in the Dark '41

Yves Simoneau (1955-)
Nuremberg '00
Free Money '99
36 Hours to Die '99
Larry McMurtry's Dead Man's Walk '96
Amelia Earhart: The Final Flight '94
Mother's Boys '94
Till Death Do Us Part '92
Memphis '91
Perfectly Normal '91
Pouvoir Intime '87

Jane Simpson
Little Witches '96
Number One Fan '94

Megan Simpson
Dating the Enemy '95
Alex '92

Michael A. Simpson
Fast Food '89
Funland '89
Sleepaway Camp 3: Teenage Wasteland '89
Sleepaway Camp 2: Unhappy Campers '88
Impure Thoughts '86
Cyrano de Bergerac '85

Andrew Sinclair
Tuxedo Warrior '82
Blue Blood '73
Under Milk Wood '73

Gerald Seth Sindell (1944-)
H.O.T.S. '79
Teenager '74

Alexander Singer (1932-)
Bunco '83
Pearl '78
Captain Apache '71
Love Has Many Faces '65

Bryan Singer (1966-)
X-Men '00
Apt Pupil '97
The Usual Suspects '95
Public Access '93

John Singleton (1968-)
Baby Boy '01
Shaft '00
Rosewood '96
Higher Learning '94
Poetic Justice '93
Boyz N the Hood '91

Gary Sinise (1955-)
Of Mice and Men '92
Miles from Home '88

Gary Sinyor (1962-)
The Bachelor '99
Stiff Upper Lips '96
Solitaire for 2 '94
Leon the Pig Farmer '93

Robert Siodmak (1900-73)
Crimson Pirate '52
Criss Cross '48
Dark Mirror '46
The Killers '46
The Spiral Staircase '46
The Strange Affair of Uncle Harry '45
Cobra Woman '44
Phantom Lady '44
Son of Dracula '43

Douglas Sirk (1900-87)
Imitation of Life '59
A Time to Love & a Time to Die '58
Battle Hymn '57
Tarnished Angels '57
Written on the Wind '56
All That Heaven Allows '55
Magnificent Obsession '54
All I Desire '53
First Legion '51
Lured '47
A Scandal in Paris '46

Rob Sitch
The Dish '00
The Castle '97

Alf Sjoberg (1903-80)
Miss Julie '50
Torment '44

John Sjogren
Choke '00
Red Line '96
The Mosaic Project '95
Money to Burn '94

Victor Sjostrom (1879-1960)
Under the Red Robe '36
The Wind '28
He Who Gets Slapped '24
The Phantom Chariot '20
The Outlaw and His Wife '17

Keri Skogland
Zebra Lounge '01
Children of the Corn 666: Isaac's Return '99
White Lies '98

Jerzy Skolimowski (1938-)
Torrents of Spring '90
The Lightship '86
Success Is the Best Revenge '84
Moonlighting '82
Hands Up '81
The Shout '78
King, Queen, Knave '72
Deep End '70

Bob Slatzer
Big Foot '72
Hellcats '68

John Sledge
The Invisible Avenger '58
New Orleans After Dark '58

Brian Sloan
I Think I Do '97
Boys Life '94

Holly Goldberg Sloan
The Secret Life of Girls '99
The Big Green '95

Paul Sloane (1893-1963)
Consolation Marriage '31
Half-Shot at Sunrise '30
Made for Love '26
The Coming of Amos '25

Rick Sloane (1961-)
Good Girls Don't '95
Mind, Body & Soul '92
Vice Academy 3 '91
Vice Academy 2 '90
Marked for Murder '89
Vice Academy '88
Hobgoblins '87
Visitants '87

George Sluizer (1932-)
Crimetime '96
Utz '93
The Vanishing '93
The Vanishing '88
Red Desert Penitentiary '83

Ralph Smart (1908-)
Robin Hood: The Movie '55
Curtain Up '53

Robert J. Smawley
American Eagle '90
River of Diamonds '90
Murphy's Fault '88

Jack Smight (1926-)
Intimate Power '89
Number One with a Bullet '87
Holocaust Survivors...Remembrance of Love '83
Loving Couples '80
Fast Break '79
Roll of Thunder, Hear My Cry '78
Airport '77 '77
Damnation Alley '77
Midway '76
Airport '75 '75
The Illustrated Man '69
No Way to Treat a Lady '68
The Secret War of Harry Frigg '68
Harper '66

Charles Martin Smith (1953-)
Air Bud '97
Boris and Natasha: The Movie '92
Trick or Treat '86

John N. Smith
A Cool, Dry Place '98
Dangerous Minds '95
Sugartime '95
The Boys of St. Vincent '93

Kevin Smith (1970-)
Jay and Silent Bob Strike Back '01
Dogma '99
Chasing Amy '97
Mallrats '95
Clerks '94

Mel Smith (1952-)
High Heels and Low Lifes '01
Bean '97
Radioland Murders '94
The Tall Guy '89

Peter Smith
The Alchemists '99
No Surrender '86

Richard Smith
The Dentist 2: Brace Yourself '98
Trident Force '88

Roy Allen Smith
The Land Before Time 4: Journey Through the Mists '96
The Land Before Time 3: The Time of the Great Giving '95

Alan Smithee
Sub Down '97
Hellraiser 4: Bloodline '95
Raging Angels '95
Gypsy Angels '94
The O.J. Simpson Story '94
Call of the Wild '93
Fatal Charm '92
Solar Crisis '92
Bloodsucking Pharoahs of Pittsburgh '90
The Shrimp on the Barbie '90
Ghost Fever '87
I Love N.Y. '87
Let's Get Harry '87
Morgan Stewart's Coming Home '87
Appointment with Fear '85
Stitches '85
City in Fear '80
Iron Cowboy '68

Stephen Smoke
Street Crimes '92
Final Impact '91

Skott Snider
Midnight Blue '96
Miracle Beach '92

Michele (Michael) Soavi (1957-)
The Church '98
Cemetery Man '95
The Devil's Daughter '91
Stagefright '87

Mark Sobel (1956-)
Storm Chasers: Revenge of the Twister '98
Ordeal in the Arctic '93
Trial and Error '92
Sweet Revenge '87
Access Code '84

Steven Soderbergh (1963-)
Full Frontal '02
Ocean's Eleven '01
Erin Brockovich '00
Traffic '00
The Limey '99
Out of Sight '98
Schizopolis '97
Gray's Anatomy '96
The Underneath '95
Fallen Angels 2 '93
King of the Hill '93
Kafka '91
sex, lies and videotape '89

Iain Softley
K-PAX '01
The Wings of the Dove '97
Hackers '95
Backbeat '94

Russell Solberg
Raven '97
Forced to Kill '93
Payback '90

Alfred Sole (1943-)
Pandemonium '82
Tanya's Island '81
Alice Sweet Alice '76

Todd Solondz (1960-)
Storytelling '01
Happiness '98
Welcome to the Dollhouse '95
Fear, Anxiety and Depression '89

Ola Solum
The Polar Bear King '94
Turnaround '87

Stephen Sommers (1962-)
The Mummy Returns '01
The Mummy '99
Deep Rising '98
Rudyard Kipling's The Jungle Book '94
The Adventures of Huck Finn '93
Catch Me ... If You Can '89

Barry Sonnenfeld (1953-)
Big Trouble '02
Men in Black 2 '02
Wild Wild West '99
Men in Black '97
Get Shorty '95
Addams Family Values '93
For Love or Money '93
The Addams Family '91

Jim Sotos (1935-)
Hot Moves '84
Sweet 16 '81
Forced Entry '75

Greg Spence
The Prophecy 2: Ashtown '97
Children of the Corn 4: The Gathering '96

Richard Spence
New World Disorder '99
Different for Girls '96
Blind Justice '94

Brenton Spencer
The Club '94
Blown Away '93

Robert Spera
Leprechaun 5: In the Hood '99
Stray Bullet '98
Witchcraft '88

Penelope Spheeris (1945-)
Senseless '98
Black Sheep '96
The Little Rascals '94
The Beverly Hillbillies '93
Wayne's World '92
Prison Stories: Women on the Inside '91
Thunder & Mud '89
Decline of Western Civilization 2: The Metal Years '88
Dudes '87
Hollywood Vice Squad '86
The Boys Next Door '85
Suburbia '83
Decline of Western Civilization 1 '81

Bryan Spicer
For Richer or Poorer '97
McHale's Navy '97

Mighty Morphin Power Rangers: The Movie '95
Marcus Spiegel
Devil in the Flesh 2 '00
Eye of the Storm '98
Scott Spiegel (1957-)
From Dusk Till Dawn 2: Texas Blood Money '98
Intruder '88
Steven Spielberg (1947-)
Minority Report '02
A. I.: Artificial Intelligence '01
Saving Private Ryan '98
Amistad '97
The Lost World: Jurassic Park 2 '97
Jurassic Park '93
Schindler's List '93
Hook '91
Always '89
Indiana Jones and the Last Crusade '89
Empire of the Sun '87
Amazing Stories '85
The Color Purple '85
Indiana Jones and the Temple of Doom '84
Twilight Zone: The Movie '83
E.T.: The Extra-Terrestrial '82
Raiders of the Lost Ark '81
1941 '79
Close Encounters of the Third Kind '77
Jaws '75
The Sugarland Express '74
Columbo: Murder by the Book '71
Duel '71
Night Gallery '69
Bob Spiers
Spice World: The Movie '97
That Darn Cat '96
Philip Spink
The Duke '99
Big and Hairy '98
Ronnie and Julie '97
Tony Spiridakis
Tinseltown '97
The Last Word '95
Roger Spottiswoode (1945-)
Noriega: God's Favorite '00
The 6th Day '00
Tomorrow Never Dies '97
Hiroshima '95
Mesmer '94
And the Band Played On '93
Stop! or My Mom Will Shoot '92
Air America '90
Third Degree Burn '89
Turner and Hooch '89
Shoot to Kill '88
The Last Innocent Man '87
The Best of Times '86
Under Fire '83
The Pursuit of D.B. Cooper '81
Terror Train '80
Tim Spring
Raw Target '95
Reason to Die '90
R.G. Springsteen (1904-89)
Hostile Guns '67
Apache Uprising '66
Johnny Reno '66
When Gangland Strikes '56
Oklahoma Annie '51
Hills of Oklahoma '50
Arizona Cowboy '49
The Red Menace '49
Hellfire '48
Under Colorado Skies '47
Stagecoach to Denver '46
Vigilantes of Boom Town '46
Robin Spry (1939-)
A Cry in the Night '93
Obsessed '88
Keeping Track '86
Drying Up the Streets '76
Pasquale Squitieri (1938-)
Third Solution '89
Corleone '79
Blood Brothers '74
Nick Stagliano
The Florentine '98
Home of Angels '94
Eric Steven Stahl
Safe House '99
Final Approach '91
John M. Stahl (1886-1950)
Father Was a Fullback '49
Leave Her to Heaven '45
The Keys of the Kingdom '44
Immortal Sergeant '43
Letter of Introduction '38
Imitation of Life '34
Sylvester Stallone (1946-)
Rocky 4 '85
Staying Alive '83
Rocky 3 '82
Rocky 2 '79
Paradise Alley '78
Richard Standeven
Falling for a Dancer '98
Band of Gold '95
Paul Stanley (1952-)
The Ultimate Imposter '79
Cotter '72
Richard Stanley
Fly Boy '99
Dust Devil '93
Hardware '90
Ringo Starr (1940-)
Born to Boogie '72
Magical Mystery Tour '67
Jack Starrett (1936-89)
Kiss My Grits '82
Mr. Horn '79
On the Edge: The Survival of Dana '79
Fatal Chase '77
Walking Tall: The Final Chapter '77
Hollywood Man '76
A Small Town in Texas '76
Race with the Devil '75
Cleopatra Jones '73
Slaughter '72
Cry Blood, Apache '70
The Losers '70
Run, Angel, Run! '69
Ralph Staub (1899-1969)
Danger Ahead '40
Sky Bandits '40
Yukon Flight '40
The Mandarin Mystery '37
Country Gentlemen '36
Wolfgang Staudte (1906-84)
The Kaiser's Lackey '51
The Murderers Are Among Us '46
The Murderers are Among Us '46
Ray Dennis Steckler (1939-)
The Hollywood Strangler Meets the Skid Row Slasher '79
Sinthia: The Devil's Doll '70
Rat Pfink a Boo-Boo '66
The Thrill Killers '65
Incredibly Strange Creatures Who Stopped Living and Became Mixed-Up Zombies '63
Wild Guitar '62
Darren Stein
Sparkler '99
Jawbreaker '98
Ken Stein
Killer Instinct '92
The Rain Killer '90
Paul Stein (1892-1951)
Counterblast '48
Black Limelight '38
Heart's Desire '37
Mimi '35
Lottery Bride '30
Sin Takes a Holiday '30
David Steinberg (1942-)
Casey at the Bat '85
Going Berserk '83
Paternity '81
Michael Steinberg
Wicked '98
Bodies, Rest & Motion '93
The Waterdance '91
Danny Steinmann
Friday the 13th, Part 5: A New Beginning '85
Savage Streets '83
Jos Stelling (1945-)
The Pointsman '86
Rembrandt—1669 '77
Steno (1915-88)
Flatfoot '78
The Unfaithfuls '60
Uncle Was a Vampire '59
A.C. (Stephen Apostoloff) Stephen
Lady Godiva Rides '68
Orgy of the Dead '65
Sandor Stern (1936-)
Jericho Fever '93
Duplicates '92
Web of Deceit '90
Amityville 4: The Evil Escapes '89
Dangerous Pursuit '89
Glitz '88
Pin... '88
Assassin '86
John & Yoko: A Love Story '85
Steven Hilliard Stern (1937-)
Kill My Wife...Please!
Breaking the Surface: The Greg Louganis Story '96
Black Fox: Blood Horse '94
Black Fox: Good Men and Bad '94
Black Fox: The Price of Peace '94
Morning Glory '93
Love & Murder '91
Personals '90
Final Notice '89
Weekend War '88
Not Quite Human '87
Rolling Vengeance '87
Murder in Space '85
The Park Is Mine '85
Undergrads '85
Getting Physical '84
Obsessive Love '84
The Ambush Murders '82
Forbidden Love '82
Mazes and Monsters '82
Portrait of a Showgirl '82
The Devil & Max Devlin '81
Draw! '81
Miracle on Ice '81
A Small Killing '81
Anatomy of a Seduction '79
Young Love, First Love '79
I Wonder Who's Killing Her Now? '76
Harrad Summer '74
Andrew Stevens (1955-)
The White Raven '98
The Corporation '96
Crash Dive '96
Virtual Combat '95
The Skateboard Kid 2 '94
Night Eyes 3 '93
Scorned '93
The Terror Within 2 '91
David Stevens
Kansas '88
A Town Like Alice '85
Roses Bloom Twice '77
George Stevens (1904-75)
The Greatest Story Ever Told '65
The Diary of Anne Frank '59
Giant '56
Shane '53
A Place in the Sun '51
I Remember Mama '48
The More the Merrier '43
Talk of the Town '42
Woman of the Year '42
Penny Serenade '41
Gunga Din '39
Vivacious Lady '38
A Damsel in Distress '37
Quality Street '37
Swing Time '36
Alice Adams '35
Annie Oakley '35
Bachelor Bait '34
Kentucky Kernels '34
Leslie Stevens
Three Kinds of Heat '87
Incubus '65
Robert Stevenson (1905-86)
The Shaggy D.A. '76
One of Our Dinosaurs Is Missing '75
Herbie Rides Again '74
The Island at the Top of the World '74
Bedknobs and Broomsticks '71
My Dog, the Thief '69
The Love Bug '68
Blackbeard's Ghost '67
The Gnome-Mobile '67
Monkey's Uncle '65
That Darn Cat '65
Mary Poppins '64
The Misadventures of Merlin Jones '63
Son of Flubber '63
In Search of the Castaways '62
The Absent-Minded Professor '61
Kidnapped '60
Darby O'Gill & the Little People '59
Johnny Tremain & the Sons of Liberty '58
Old Yeller '57
The Las Vegas Story '52
My Forbidden Past '51
Walk Softly, Stranger '50
Dishonored Lady '47
Jane Eyre '44
Forever and a Day '43
Joan of Paris '42
Tom Brown's School Days '40
King Solomon's Mines '37
Non-Stop New York '37
The Man Who Lived Again '36
Nine Days a Queen '36
Alan L. Stewart (1951-)
Ghetto Blaster '89
Ghostriders '87
Douglas Day Stewart
Listen to Me '89
Thief of Hearts '84
John Stewart
Hidden Obsession '92
Cartel '90
Action U.S.A. '89
Peter Stewart
Mom's Outta Sight '01
Money Madness '47
Robert Stewart (1961-)
Mark of the Beast
Rock & Roll Cowboys '92
Ben Stiller (1965-)
Zoolander '01
The Cable Guy '96
Reality Bites '94
Mauritz Stiller (1883-1928)
Hotel Imperial '27
The Atonement of Gosta Berling '24
Treasure of Arne '19
Thomas Graal's First Child '18
Thomas Graal's Best Film '17
Whit Stillman (1952-)
The Last Days of Disco '98
Barcelona '94
Metropolitan '90
John Stockwell (1961-)
Blue Crush '02
crazy/beautiful '01
Cheaters '00
Undercover '87
Bryan Michael Stoller
Undercover Angel '99
Turn of the Blade '97
Dragon Fury 2 '96
Ben Stoloff (1895-1960)
It's a Joke, Son! '47
The Affairs of Annabel '38
Sea Devils '37
Palooka '34
Transatlantic Merry-Go-Round '34
Night of Terror '33
Victor Stoloff
Washington Affair '77
The 300 Year Weekend '71
Andrew L. Stone (1902-99)
Song of Norway '70
The Last Voyage '60
Sensations of 1945 '44
Hi Diddle Diddle '43
Stormy Weather '43
The Girl Said No '37
Hell's Headquarters '32
Norman Stone
Catherine Cookson's The Black Velvet Gown '92
The Vision '87
Shadowlands '85
Oliver Stone (1946-)
Any Given Sunday '99
U-Turn '97
Nixon '95
Natural Born Killers '94
Heaven and Earth '93
The Doors '91
JFK '91
Born on the Fourth of July '89
Talk Radio '88
Wall Street '87
Platoon '86
Salvador '86
The Hand '81
Seizure '74
Virginia Lively Stone
Run If You Can '87
Money to Burn '83
The Treasure of Jamaica Reef '74
Howard Storm
Once Bitten '85
The Three Little Pigs '84
Jerome Storm (1890-1958)
Courtin' Wildcats '29
Sweet Adeline '26
The Busher '19
Frank Strayer (1891-1964)
Footlight Glamour '43
It's a Great Life '43
Blondie for Victory '42
Blondie Goes Latin '42
Blondie Goes to College '42
Blondie's Blessed Event '42
Blondie in Society '41
Blondie Has Trouble '40
Blondie On a Budget '40
Blondie Plays Cupid '40
Blondie Brings Up Baby '39
Blondie Meets the Boss '39
Blondie Takes a Vacation '39
Blondie '38
Death from a Distance '36
Condemned to Live '35
Fugitive Road '34
The Ghost Walks '34
In the Money '34
The Monster Walks '32
Tangled Destinies '32
The Vampire Bat '32
Murder at Midnight '31
Barbra Streisand (1942-)
The Mirror Has Two Faces '96
The Prince of Tides '91
Yentl '83
Joseph Strick (1923-)
James Joyce: A Portrait of the Artist as a Young Man '77
Road Movie '72
Tropic of Cancer '70
Ulysses '67
The Balcony '63
Wesley Strick (1954-)
Hitched '01
The Tie That Binds '95
Herbert L. Strock (1918-)
Witches' Brew '79
Monster '78
Man on the Run '74
The Crawling Hand '63
How to Make a Monster '58
Teenage Frankenstein '58
Blood of Dracula '57
Mel Stuart (1928-)
Sophia Loren: Her Own Story '80
The Chisholms '79
The Triangle Factory Fire Scandal '79
Mean Dog Blues '78
Willy Wonka & the Chocolate Factory '71
I Love My...Wife '70
If It's Tuesday, This Must Be Belgium '69
John Sturges (1910-92)
The Eagle Has Landed '77
Chino '75
McQ '74
Joe Kidd '72
Marooned '69
Ice Station Zebra '68
Hour of the Gun '67
The Hallelujah Trail '65
The Great Escape '63
By Love Possessed '61
The Magnificent Seven '60
Last Train from Gun Hill '59
Never So Few '59
The Law and Jake Wade '58
The Old Man and the Sea '58
Gunfight at the O.K. Corral '57
Underwater! '55
Bad Day at Black Rock '54
Escape from Fort Bravo '53
The Capture '50
The Magnificent Yankee '50
Preston Sturges (1898-1959)
The Beautiful Blonde from Bashful Bend '49
Unfaithfully Yours '48
The Sin of Harold Diddlebock '47
The Great Moment '44
Hail the Conquering Hero '44
Miracle of Morgan's Creek '44
The Palm Beach Story '42
The Lady Eve '41
Sullivan's Travels '41
Christmas in July '40
The Great McGinty '40
Charles Sturridge (1951-)
Shackleton '02
Longitude '00
FairyTale: A True Story '97
Gulliver's Travels '95
A Foreign Field '93
Where Angels Fear to Tread '91
Aria '88
A Handful of Dust '88
Brideshead Revisited '81
Eric Styles
Dreaming of Joseph Lees '99
Relative Values '99
Richard Styles
Midnight Tease 2 '95
Escape '90
Shallow Grave '87

Bobby Suarez
Warriors of the Apocalypse '85
American Commandos '84
Pay or Die '83
Gonzalo Suarez (1934-)
Rowing with the Wind '88
House of the Damned '71
Eliseo Subiela (1944-)
The Dark Side of the Heart '92
Man Facing Southeast '86
Kevin Sullivan (1955-)
Cosmic Slop '94
Lantern Hill '90
Anne of Avonlea '87
Anne of Green Gables '85
Wild Pony '83
Kevin Rodney Sullivan
How Stella Got Her Groove Back '98
Soul of the Game '96
America's Dream '95
Jeremy Summers
Danger UXB '81
Five Golden Dragons '67
The House of 1000 Dolls '67
Walter Summers (1896-)
House of Mystery '41
The Human Monster '39
Cedric Sundstrom
American Ninja 4: The Annihilation '91
The Revenger '90
American Ninja 3: Blood Hunt '89
Captive Rage '88
Stephen Surjik
Weapons of Mass Distraction '97
Wayne's World 2 '93
Edward Sutherland (1895-1974)
Having Wonderful Crime '45
Follow the Boys '44
The Navy Comes Through '42
Sing Your Worries Away '42
Beyond Tomorrow '40
The Invisible Woman '40
One Night in the Tropics '40
The Flying Deuces '39
Every Day's a Holiday '38
International House '33
Murders in the Zoo '33
Mr. Robinson Crusoe '32
Palmy Days '31
Behind the Front '26
It's the Old Army Game '26
Kiefer Sutherland (1967-)
Woman Wanted '98
Truth or Consequences, N.M. '97
Last Light '93
Seijun Suzuki (1923-)
Branded to Kill '67
Fighting Elegy '66
Tokyo Drifter '66
Story of a Prostitute '65
Gate of Flesh '64
Youth of the Beast '63
Peter Svatek
Bleeders '97
Jack London's The Call of the Wild '97
Sci-Fighters '96
Witchboard 3: The Possession '95
Mystery of the Million Dollar Hockey Puck '80s
Jan Sverak (1965-)
Dark Blue World '01
Kolya '96
The Elementary School '91
E.W. Swackhamer (1927-94)
Are You Lonesome Tonight '92
Perfect Family '92
The Secret Passion of Robert Clayton '92
The Rousters '90
Terror at London Bridge '85
The Dain Curse '78
The Winds of Kitty Hawk '78
The Amazing Spider-Man '77
Night Terror '76
Death at Love House '75
Death Sentence '74
Man & Boy '71
Bob Swaim (1943-)
The Climb '97
Masquerade '88
Half Moon Street '86
David Swift (1919-2001)
How to Succeed in Business without Really Trying '67
Good Neighbor Sam '64
Under the Yum-Yum Tree '63
The Interns '62
The Parent Trap '61
Pollyanna '60
Michael Switzer
Forever Love '98
Unlikely Angel '97
Past the Bleachers '95
Fergie & Andrew: Behind Palace Doors '93
Undesirable '92
The Lightning Incident '91
Nitti: The Enforcer '88
Peter Sykes (1939-)
Jesus '79
To the Devil, a Daughter '76
Night of the Laughing Dead '75
Demons of the Mind '72
Istvan Szabo (1938-)
Sunshine '99
Meeting Venus '91
Hanussen '88
Mephisto '81
25 Fireman's Street '73
Love Film '70
Father '67
William Szarka
Phantom Brother '88
South Bronx Heroes '85
Boris Szulzinger
Shame of the Jungle '90
Mama Dracula '80
Jeannot Szwarc (1937-)
Grand Larceny '92
The Murders in the Rue Morgue '86
Santa Claus: The Movie '85
Supergirl '84
Enigma '82
Somewhere in Time '80
Jaws 2 '78
Code Name: Diamond Head '77
Bug '75
Sex Through a Window '72
Juan Carlos Tabio
Guantanamera '95
Strawberry and Chocolate '93
Jean-Charles Tacchella (1925-)
Blue Country '77
Cousin, Cousine '76
The Last Winters '71
Kidlat Tahimik
Perfumed Nightmare '89
Turumba '84
Tibor Takacs (1954-)
Sanctuary '98
Redline '97
Sabrina the Teenage Witch '96
Deadly Past '95
Bad Blood '94
Gate 2 '92
Red Shoe Diaries 2: Double Dare '92
I, Madman '89
The Gate '87
984: Prisoner of the Future '84
Rachel Talalay
Tank Girl '94
Ghost in the Machine '93
Freddy's Dead: The Final Nightmare '91
Paul Talbot
Hellblock 13 '97
Freakshow '95
Greg Tallas
Cataclysm '81
Prehistoric Women '50
Richard Talmadge (1892-1981)
Project Moon Base '53
Detour to Danger '45
Devil Horse '32
Lee Tamahori (1950-)
Along Came a Spider '01
The Edge '97
Mulholland Falls '95
Once Were Warriors '94
Harry (Hurwitz) Tampa (1938-95)
Nocturna '79
Fairy Tales '76
Tokuzo Tanaka
Zatoichi: The Blind Swordsman's Vengeance '66
Sleepy Eyes of Death: The Chinese Jade '63
Senkichi Taniguchi (1912-)
What's Up, Tiger Lily? '66
The Gambling Samurai '60
Terrell Tannen
Shadows in the Storm '88
A Minor Miracle '83
William Tannen (-1976)
Hero and the Terror '88
Deadly Illusion '87
Flashpoint '84
Alain Tanner (1929-)
In the White City '83
Messidor '77
Jonah Who Will Be 25 in the Year 2000 '76
La Salamandre '71
Charles: Dead or Alive '69
Robert Emmett Tansey (1897-1951)
The Caravan Trail '46
Colorado Serenade '46
Driftin' River '46
God's Country '46
Wild West '46
Song of Old Wyoming '45
Wildfire '45
Arizona Whirlwind '44
Death Valley Rangers '44
Outlaw Trail '44
Sonora Stagecoach '44
Haunted Ranch '43
Arizona Roundup '42
Lone Star Law Men '42
Texas to Bataan '42
Western Mail '42
Where Trails End '42
The Driftin' Kid '41
Dynamite Canyon '41
Riding the Sunset Trail '41
Courage of the North '35
Way of the West '35
Daniel Taplitz
Commandments '96
Black Magic '92
Nightlife '90
Quentin Tarantino (1963-)
Jackie Brown '97
Four Rooms '95
Pulp Fiction '94
Reservoir Dogs '92
Andrei Tarkovsky (1932-86)
The Sacrifice '86
Nostalghia '83
Stalker '79
The Mirror '75
Solaris '72
Andrei Rublev '66
My Name Is Ivan '62
Frank Tashlin (1913-72)
Private Navy of Sgt. O'Farrell '68
The Glass Bottom Boat '66
The Alphabet Murders '65
Disorderly Orderly '64
Who's Minding the Store? '63
Cinderfella '60
The Geisha Boy '58
Rock-A-Bye Baby '57
Will Success Spoil Rock Hunter? '57
The Girl Can't Help It '56
Hollywood or Bust '56
Artists and Models '55
Susan Slept Here '54
Son of Paleface '52
The Fuller Brush Man '48
Nadia Tass
Child Star: The Shirley Temple Story '01
The Miracle Worker '00
Amy '98
Mr. Reliable: A True Story '95
Pure Luck '91
Rikky and Pete '88
Malcolm '86
Jacques Tati (1908-82)
Parade '74
Traffic '71
Playtime '67
Mon Oncle '58
Mr. Hulot's Holiday '53
Jour de Fete '48
John Tatoulis
Zone 39 '96
The Silver Stallion: King of the Wild Brumbies '93
Norman Taurog (1899-1981)
Live a Little, Love a Little '68
Speedway '68
Double Trouble '67
Dr. Goldfoot and the Bikini Machine '66
Spinout '66
Tickle Me '65
It Happened at the World's Fair '63
Palm Springs Weekend '63
Blue Hawaii '62
Girls! Girls! Girls! '62
G.I. Blues '60
Birds & the Bees '56
Bundle of Joy '56
Pardners '56
The Caddy '53
Jumping Jacks '52
Rich, Young and Pretty '51
The Stooge '51
The Toast of New Orleans '50
That Midnight Kiss '49
Words and Music '48
Girl Crazy '43
Presenting Lily Mars '43
Mrs. Wiggs of the Cabbage Patch '42
Men of Boys Town '41
Broadway Melody of 1940 '40
Little Nellie Kelly '40
Young Tom Edison '40
The Adventures of Tom Sawyer '38
Boys Town '38
Mad About Music '38
Rhythm on the Range '36
Strike Me Pink '36
We're Not Dressing '34
Hold 'Em Jail '32
Sunny Skies '30
Bertrand Tavernier (1941-)
Capitaine Conan '96
L'Appat '94
Revenge of the Musketeers '94
L.627 '92
Daddy Nostalgia '90
Life and Nothing But '89
Beatrice '88
Round Midnight '86
A Sunday in the Country '84
Coup de Torchon '81
Death Watch '80
Spoiled Children '77
The Judge and the Assassin '75
The Clockmaker '73
Paolo Taviani (1931-)
Elective Affinities '96
Fiorile '93
Night Sun '90
Good Morning, Babylon '87
Kaos '85
The Night of the Shooting Stars '82
Padre Padrone '77
Allonsanfan '73
St. Michael Had a Rooster '72
Vittorio Taviani (1929-)
Elective Affinities '96
Fiorile '93
Night Sun '90
Good Morning, Babylon '87
Kaos '85
The Night of the Shooting Stars '82
Padre Padrone '77
Allonsanfan '73
St. Michael Had a Rooster '72
Baz Taylor (1944-)
Shooting Elizabeth '92
Tattle Tale '92
Near Misses '91
Happy Since I Met You '89
Don Taylor (1920-98)
The Diamond Trap '91
Going for the Gold: The Bill Johnson Story '85
Secret Weapons '85
My Wicked, Wicked Ways '84
Listen to Your Heart '83
September Gun '83
Red Flag: The Ultimate Game '81
The Final Countdown '80
Damien: Omen 2 '78
The Island of Dr. Moreau '77
Great Scout & Cathouse Thursday '76
Tom Sawyer '73
Escape from the Planet of the Apes '71
Wild Women '70
Ride the Wild Surf '64
Finn Taylor
Cherish '02
Dream with the Fishes '97
Jud Taylor (1940-)
Secrets '94
Danielle Steel's Kaleidoscope '90
The Old Man and the Sea '90
The Great Escape 2: The Untold Story '88
Broken Vows '87
Foxfire '87
Out of the Darkness '85
License to Kill '84
Packin' It In '83
Lovey: A Circle of Children 2 '82
Question of Honor '80
The Christmas Coal Mine Miracle '77
Mary White '77
Future Cop '76
Return to Earth '76
Search for the Gods '75
Say Goodbye, Maggie Cole '72
Ray Taylor (1888-1952)
Outlaw Country '49
Black Hills '48
Check Your Guns '48
The Hawk of Powder River '48
Stage to Mesa City '48
The Tioga Kid '48
Border Feud '47
Cheyenne Takes Over '47
Fighting Vigilantes '47
Ghost Town Renegades '47
Return of the Lash '47
West to Glory '47
Wild Country '47
Lost City of the Jungle '45
Master Key '44
Mystery of the Riverboat '44
Adventures of Smilin' Jack '43
Don Winslow of the Coast Guard '43
Don Winslow of the Navy '43
Boss of Bullion City '41
Bury Me Not on the Lone Prairie '41
Riders of Death Valley '41
Pony Post '40
Riders of Pasco Basin '40
Winners of the West '40
Flaming Frontiers '38
Hawaiian Buckaroo '38
Panamint's Bad Man '38
Rawhide '38
Dick Tracy '37
Mystery of the Hooded Horseman '37
The Painted Stallion '37
The Vigilantes Are Coming '36
The Ivory Handled Gun '35
Law for Tombstone '35
Stone of Silver Creek '35
The Throwback '35
Chandu on the Magic Island '34
The Perils of Pauline '34
Return of Chandu '34
Phantom of the Air '33
Battling with Buffalo Bill '31
Sam Taylor (1895-1958)
Nothing But Trouble '44
Ambassador Bill '31
Dubarry '30
Coquette '29
The Taming of the Shrew '29
The Tempest '28
My Best Girl '27
For Heaven's Sake '26
The Freshman '25
Safety Last '23
Lewis Teague (1941-)
The Triangle '01
Saved by the Light '95
Deadlock '91
Navy SEALS '90
Collision Course '89
Cat's Eye '85
The Jewel of the Nile '85
Cujo '83
Fighting Back '82
Alligator '80
Lady in Red '79
Andre Techine (1943-)
Alice et Martin '98
Les Voleurs '96
Wild Reeds '94
Ma Saison Preferee '93
Scene of the Crime '87
Rendez-vous '85
Barocco '76
Julien Temple (1953-)
Pandaemonium '00
The Filth and the Fury '99
Bullet '94
Earth Girls Are Easy '89
Aria '88
Absolute Beginners '86
Running out of Luck '86
The Secret Policeman's Other Ball '82
Secret Policeman's Private Parts '81
Andy Tennant
Anna and the King '99
Ever After: A Cinderella Story '98
Fools Rush In '97
It Takes Two '95
The Amy Fisher Story '93
Keep the Change '92
Del Tenney (1930-)
Curse of the Living Corpse '64
Horror of Party Beach '64
I Eat Your Skin '64
Kevin S. Tenney
The Arrival 2 '98
Pinocchio's Revenge '96

Witchboard 2: The Devil's Doorway '93
The Cellar '90
Peacemaker '90
WitchTrap '89
Night of the Demons '88
Witchboard '87

John Terlesky
Guardian '01
Chain of Command '00
The Guardian '00
Judgment Day '99
Supreme Sanction '99

Hiroshi Teshigahara (1927-2001)
Rikyu '90
Face of Another '66
Woman in the Dunes '64

Duccio Tessari (1926-94)
Beyond Justice '92
Blood at Sundown '88
Zorro '74

Ted Tetzlaff (1903-95)
The Young Land '59
Son of Sinbad '55
The White Tower '50
The Window '49
Fighting Father Dunne '48
Riff-Raff '47

Joan Tewkesbury (1936-)
Strangers '91
Sudie & Simpson '90
Cold Sassy Tree '89
Acorn People '82
Old Boyfriends '79
Tenth Month '79

Peter Tewkesbury (1924-)
The Trouble with Girls (and How to Get into It) '69
Stay Away, Joe '68
Emil and the Detectives '64

Graham Theakston
Seeing Red '99
Money Kings '98
The Mill on the Floss '97
Tripods: The White Mountains '84

Betty Thomas (1949-)
28 Days '00
Dr. Dolittle '98
The Late Shift '96
Private Parts '96
The Brady Bunch Movie '95

Dave Thomas (1949-)
The Experts '89
Strange Brew '83

Gerald Thomas (1920-93)
Second Victory '87
Carry On Emmanuelle '78
Carry On England '76
Carry On Behind '75
Carry On Dick '75
Carry On at Your Convenience '71
Carry On Camping '71
Carry On Henry VIII '71
Carry On Doctor '68
Follow That Camel '67
Carry On Cowboy '66
Carry On Screaming '66
Carry On Cleo '65
Carry On Cruising '62
Carry On Nurse '59
Time Lock '57
The Vicious Circle '57

John G. Thomas
Arizona Heat '87
Banzai Runner '86
Tin Man '83

Ralph Thomas (1915-2001)
The Big Scam '79
It's Not the Size That Counts '74
Quest for Love '71
Doctor in Distress '63
Conspiracy of Hearts '60
No Love for Johnnie '60
A Tale of Two Cities '58
Doctor at Large '57
Above Us the Waves '56
Doctor at Sea '56
Doctor in the House '53
The Clouded Yellow '51

Ralph L. (R.L.) Thomas
A Young Connecticut Yankee in King Arthur's Court '95
Young Ivanhoe '95
Apprentice to Murder '88
The Terry Fox Story '83
Ticket to Heaven '81

William C. Thomas (1903-)
Big Town '47
Big Town After Dark '47
Underworld Scandal '47
Dark Mountain '44
Navy Way '44

Harry Z. Thomason
The Day It Came to Earth '77
Encounter with the Unknown '75
Hootch Country Boys '75

Caroline Thompson (1956-)
Snow White: The Fairest of Them All '02
Buddy '97
Black Beauty '94

Donald W. Thompson
Blood on the Mountain '88
The Prodigal Planet '88
Heaven's Heroes '87

Ernest Thompson
Out of Time '00
1969 '89

J. Lee Thompson (1914-)
Kinjite: Forbidden Subjects '89
Messenger of Death '88
Death Wish 4: The Crackdown '87
Firewalker '86
Murphy's Law '86
King Solomon's Mines '85
The Ambassador '84
The Evil That Men Do '84
Ten to Midnight '83
Cabo Blanco '81
Happy Birthday to Me '81
The Greek Tycoon '78
The White Buffalo '77
St. Ives '76
The Widow '76
The Blue Knight '75
The Reincarnation of Peter Proud '75
Huckleberry Finn '74
Battle for the Planet of the Apes '73
Conquest of the Planet of the Apes '72
MacKenna's Gold '69
Taras Bulba '62
Cape Fear '61
The Guns of Navarone '61
Flame Over India '60
Tiger Bay '59

Robert Thompson
Holiday Heart '00
Words by Heart '84

Chris Thomson
Trucks '97
Swimsuit '89
The Empty Beach '85
Three's Trouble '85
Waterfront '83

Michael Thornhill
The Everlasting Secret Family '88
Robbery '85
Between Wars '74

Billy Bob Thornton (1955-)
All the Pretty Horses '00
Sling Blade '96

Jerry Thorpe (1930-)
All God's Children '80
A Question of Love '78
The Possessed '77
Wonderland Cove '75
Smile, Jenny, You're Dead '74
Kung Fu '72

Richard Thorpe (1896-1986)
Fun in Acapulco '63
The Horizontal Lieutenant '62
The Honeymoon Machine '61
Jailhouse Rock '57
The Prodigal '55
Athena '54
The Student Prince '54
All the Brothers Were Valiant '53
The Girl Who Had Everything '53
Knights of the Round Table '53
Ivanhoe '52
Prisoner of Zenda '52
The Great Caruso '51
Vengeance Valley '51
The Black Hand '50
Three Little Words '50
Challenge to Lassie '49
Malaya '49
The Sun Comes Up '49
A Date with Judy '48
On an Island with You '48
Thrill of a Romance '45
The Thin Man Goes Home '44
Two Girls and a Sailor '44
Above Suspicion '43
Tarzan's New York Adventure '42
White Cargo '42
Tarzan's Secret Treasure '41
The Adventures of Huckleberry Finn '39
Tarzan Finds a Son '39
Double Wedding '37
Night Must Fall '37
Tarzan Escapes '36
Green Eyes '34
After Midnight '33
Rainbow over Broadway '33
Cross Examination '32
The King Murder '32
The Lone Defender '32
Probation '32
The Secrets of Wu Sin '32
Wild Horse '31
Border Romance '30
Under Montana Skies '30
King of the Kongo '29
Desert of the Lost '27

Antonio Tibaldi
Kiss of Fire '98
Little Boy Blue '97
On My Own '92

Eric Till (1929-)
The Girl Next Door '98
Glory Enough for All: The Discovery of Insulin '92
Oh, What a Night '92
To Catch a Killer '92
Clarence '91
Buffalo Jump '90
A Case of Libel '83
If You Could See What I Hear '82
Improper Channels '82
An American Christmas Carol '79
Mary and Joseph: A Story of Faith '79
Wild Horse Hank '79
Bethune '77
Hot Millions '68

George Tillman, Jr.
Men of Honor '00
Soul Food '97

Robert Tinnell (1961-)
Believe '99
Frankenstein and Me '96
Kids of the Round Table '96

Stacy Title
Let the Devil Wear Black '99
The Last Supper '96

Johnny To
The Mission '99
Running out of Time '99
The Heroic Trio '93

James Toback (1944-)
Black and White '99
Two Girls and a Guy '98
The Pick-Up Artist '87
Exposed '83
Fingers '78

Ricky Tognazzi
Excellent Cadavers '99
La Scorta '94

Norman Tokar (1920-79)
Candleshoe '78
The Cat from Outer Space '78
No Deposit, No Return '76
The Apple Dumpling Gang '75
Where the Red Fern Grows '74
Snowball Express '72
The Boatniks '70
The Horse in the Gray Flannel Suit '68
The Happiest Millionaire '67
Follow Me, Boys! '66
Those Calloways '65
The Ugly Dachshund '65
A Tiger Walks '64
Savage Sam '63
Big Red '62
Sammy, the Way-Out Seal '62

Michael Tolkin (1950-)
The New Age '94
The Rapture '91

Stephen Tolkin
Daybreak '93
Stephen King's Golden Years '91

Stanley Tong (1960-)
Mr. Magoo '97
Jackie Chan's First Strike '96
Rumble in the Bronx '96
Supercop 2 '93
Supercop '92

Burt Topper (1928-)
Soul Hustler '76
The Hard Ride '71
The Strangler '64
Tank Commando '59
Hell Squad '58

Giuseppe Tornatore (1956-)
Malena '00
The Legend of 1900 '98
The Star Maker '95
A Pure Formality '94
Everybody's Fine '90
Cinema Paradiso '88

Joe Tornatore
Curse of the Crystal Eye '93
Grotesque '87
Code Name: Zebra '84
Zebra Force '76

Fina Torres (1951-)
Woman on Top '00
Celestial Clockwork '94
Oriane '85

Robert Totten (1938-95)
Dark Before Dawn '89
The Sacketts '79
Pony Express Rider '76
The Red Pony '76
Huckleberry Finn '75
The Wild Country '71

Jacques Tourneur (1904-77)
The Comedy of Terrors '64
The Giant of Marathon '60
Curse of the Demon '57
Great Day in the Morning '56
Nightfall '56
Appointment in Honduras '53
The Flame & the Arrow '50
Stars in My Crown '50
Easy Living '49
Berlin Express '48
Out of the Past '47
Canyon Passage '46
Experiment Perilous '45
Days of Glory '43
I Walked with a Zombie '43
The Leopard Man '43
Cat People '42

Maurice Tourneur (1876-1961)
Volpone '39
Lorna Doone '22
County Fair '20
The Last of the Mohicans '20
Pride of the Clan '18
A Girl's Folly '17
A Poor Little Rich Girl '17
Trilby '17
The Wishing Ring '14

Robert Towne (1936-)
Without Limits '97
Tequila Sunrise '88
Personal Best '82

Bud Townsend
Coach '78
Terror at Red Wolf Inn '72
Nightmare in Wax '69

Robert Townsend (1957-)
Livin' for Love: The Natalie Cole Story '00
Jackie's Back '99
Love Songs '99
B.A.P.'s '97
The Meteor Man '93
The Five Heartbeats '91
Hollywood Shuffle '87

Shiro Toyoda (1906-77)
Snow Country '57
Mistress '53

Jean-Claude Tramont (1930-96)
As Summers Die '86
All Night Long '81

Joey Travolta (1952-)
Detour '99
Partners '99
Matter of Trust '98
Laws of Deception '97
Navajo Blues '97
Hard Vice '94

Brian Trenchard-Smith (1946-)
Britannic '99
The Happy Face Murders '99
Atomic Dog '98
Escape Clause '96
Leprechaun 4: In Space '96
Leprechaun 3 '95
Night of the Demons 2 '94
Official Denial '93
The Siege of Firebase Gloria '89
Day of the Panther '88
Out of the Body '88
Fists of Blood '87
Dead End Drive-In '86
The Quest '86
BMX Bandits '83
Day of the Assassin '81
Escape 2000 '81
Deathcheaters '76

John Trent (-1983)
Vengeance Is Mine '84
Best Revenge '83
Middle Age Crazy '80
Crossbar '79
Find the Lady '75
The Bushbaby '70

Monika Treut (1954-)
Erotique '94
My Father Is Coming '91
Seduction: The Cruel Woman '89
Virgin Machine '88

Dale Trevillion
Play Time '94
One Man Force '89
Las Vegas Weekend '85

Gus Trikonis
The Rumor Mill '86
Love on the Run '85
Jungle Heat '84
Dempsey '83
First Affair '83
Miss All-American Beauty '82
Take This Job & Shove It '81
Twirl '81
Touched by Love '80
She's Dressed to Kill '79
The Evil '78
Moonshine County Express '77
Nashville Girl '76

Rose Troche
Bedrooms and Hallways '98
Go Fish '94

Jan Troell (1931-)
Hamsun '96
Flight of the Eagle '82
Hurricane '79
Zandy's Bride '74
The New Land '73
The Emigrants '72

Gary Trousdale
Atlantis: The Lost Empire '01
The Hunchback of Notre Dame '96
Beauty and the Beast '91

Fernando Trueba (1955-)
Two Much '96
Belle Epoque '92
Twisted Obsession '90

Francois Truffaut (1932-84)
Confidentially Yours '83
The Woman Next Door '81
The Last Metro '80
The Green Room '78
Love on the Run '78
The Man Who Loved Women '77
Small Change '76
The Story of Adele H. '75
Day for Night '73
Two English Girls '72
Bed and Board '70
The Wild Child '70
Mississippi Mermaid '69
The Bride Wore Black '68
Stolen Kisses '68
Fahrenheit 451 '66
The Soft Skin '64
Jules and Jim '62
Shoot the Piano Player '62
The 400 Blows '59
Les Mistons '57

Douglas Trumbull (1942-)
Brainstorm '83
Silent Running '71

Glenn Tryon (1894-1970)
Beauty for the Asking '39
Law West of Tombstone '38
Small Town Boy '37

Shinya Tsukamoto (1960-)
Tetsuo 2: Body Hammer '97
Tetsuo: The Iron Man '92

Stanley Tucci (1960-)
Joe Gould's Secret '00
The Imposters '98
Big Night '95

Michael Tuchner (1934-)
Back to the Secret Garden '01
Rainbow Warrior '94
Firestorm: 72 Hours in Oakland '93
The Misadventures of Mr. Wilt '90
Mistress '87
Trapped in Silence '86
Amos '85
Not My Kid '85
Adam '83
Trenchcoat '83
The Hunchback of Notre Dame '82
The Summer of My German Soldier '78
The Old Curiosity Shop '75

Anand Tucker
Hilary and Jackie '98
Saint-Ex: The Story of the Storyteller '95

James Tucker
Steps from Hell '92
Lunatic '91
Phil Tucker
Dance Hall Racket '58
Robot Monster '53
Richard Tuggle (1948-)
Out of Bounds '86
Tightrope '84
Montgomery Tully (1904-88)
Battle Beneath the Earth '68
The Terrornauts '67
Dead Lucky '60
The House in Marsh Road '60
Strange Awakening '58
The Electronic Monster '57
The Key Man '57
The Way Out '56
Glass Tomb '55
Paid to Kill '54
Ching Siu Tung (1953-)
The Executioners '93
The Heroic Trio '93
Sandy Tung (1950-)
Shiloh 2: Shiloh Season '99
Across the Tracks '89
Gary J. Tunnicliffe
Guardian '01
Within the Rock '96
Rosemarie Turko (1951-)
Scarred '84
Dungeonmaster '83
Ann Turner
Hammers over the Anvil '91
Celia: Child of Terror '89
Brad Turner
Must Be Santa '99
The Inspectors '98
Jon Turteltaub
Disney's The Kid '00
Instinct '99
From the Earth to the Moon '98
Phenomenon '96
While You Were Sleeping '95
Cool Runnings '93
3 Ninjas '92
Driving Me Crazy '91
John Turturro (1957-)
Illuminata '98
Mac '93
Frank Tuttle (1892-1963)
Hell on Frisco Bay '55
This Gun for Hire '42
Waikiki Wedding '37
Roman Scandals '33
Love 'Em and Leave 'Em '26
Lucky Devil '25
David N. Twohy
Pitch Black '00
The Arrival '96
Grand Tour: Disaster in Time '92
Tom Tykwer (1965-)
The Princess and the Warrior '00
Run Lola Run '98
Winter Sleepers '97
Liv Ullmann (1939-)
Private Confessions '98
Sofie '92
Edgar G. Ulmer (1904-72)
Journey Beneath the Desert '61
The Amazing Transparent Man '60
Beyond the Time Barrier '60
Naked Venus '58
The Daughter of Dr. Jekyll '57
The Man from Planet X '51
St. Benny the Dip '51
Carnegie Hall '47
Club Havana '46
Detour '46
The Strange Woman '46
Strange Illusion '45
Bluebeard '44
Girls in Chains '43
Isle of Forgotten Sins '43
Jive Junction '43
American Matchmaker '40
The Light Ahead '39
Moon over Harlem '39
The Singing Blacksmith '38
The Black Cat '34
Thunder Over Texas '34
Ron Underwood (1953-)
The Adventures of Pluto Nash '02
Mighty Joe Young '98
Speechless '94
Heart and Souls '93
City Slickers '91
Tremors '89
Michael Toshiyuki Uno
The Road to Galveston '96
Blind Spot '93
Call of the Wild '93
Without Warning: The James Brady Story '91
The Wash '88
Chano Urueto (1895-)
The Brainiac '61
The Witch's Mirror '60
The Living Head '59
Peter Ustinov (1921-)
Hammersmith Is Out '72
Lady L '65
Billy Budd '62
Jamie Uys (1921-96)
The Gods Must Be Crazy 2 '89
The Gods Must Be Crazy '84
Dingaka '65
Roger Vadim (1928-2000)
And God Created Woman '88
Game of Seduction '86
Beauty and the Beast '83
Night Games '80
Don Juan (Or If Don Juan Were a Woman) '73
Barbarella '68
Spirits of the Dead '68
The Game Is Over '66
Circle of Love '64
Le Repos du Guerrier '62
Blood and Roses '61
Please Not Now! '61
Dangerous Liaisons '60
And God Created Woman '57
The Night Heaven Fell '57
Ladislao Vajda (1906-65)
The Man Who Wagged His Tail '57
The Miracle of Marcelino '55
Luis Valdez (1940-)
The Cisco Kid '94
La Bamba '87
Zoot Suit '81
Frank (Pierluigi Ciriaci) Valenti
Delta Force Commando 2 '90
War Bus Commando '89
Delta Force Commando '87
Tonino Valerii
My Name Is Nobody '74
A Reason to Live, a Reason to Die '73
Nick Vallelonga
The Corporate Ladder '97
In the Kingdom of the Blind the Man with One Eye Is King '94
A Brilliant Disguise '93
Jaco Van Dormael (1957-)
The Eighth Day '95
Toto le Heros '91
Woodbridge S. Van Dyke (1889-1943)
Cairo '42
I Married an Angel '42
Journey for Margaret '42
Shadow of the Thin Man '41
Bitter Sweet '40
I Love You Again '40
Andy Hardy Gets Spring Fever '39
Another Thin Man '39
Marie Antoinette '38
Rosalie '38
Sweethearts '38
Personal Property '37
After the Thin Man '36
Love on the Run '36
Rose Marie '36
San Francisco '36
Forsaking All Others '35
I Live My Life '35
Naughty Marietta '35
Hide-Out '34
Manhattan Melodrama '34
The Thin Man '34
Penthouse '33
The Prizefighter and the Lady '33
Tarzan, the Ape Man '32
Trader Horn '31
White Shadows in the South Seas '29
Andre Van Heerden
Revelation '00
Tribulation '00
Buddy Van Horn
Pink Cadillac '89
The Dead Pool '88
Any Which Way You Can '80
Mario Van Peebles (1958-)
Love Kills '98
Gang in Blue '96
Panther '95
Posse '93
New Jack City '91
Melvin Van Peebles (1932-)
Gang in Blue '96
Tales of Erotica '93
Identity Crisis '90
Sweet Sweetback's Baadasssss Song '71
Watermelon Man '70
The Story of a Three Day Pass '68
Gus Van Sant (1952-)
Finding Forrester '00
Psycho '98
Good Will Hunting '97
To Die For '95
Even Cowgirls Get the Blues '94
My Own Private Idaho '91
Drugstore Cowboy '89
Norman Thaddeus Vane
Taxi Dancers '93
Midnight '89
Club Life '86
The Black Room '82
Frightmare '81
Carlo Vanzina (1952-)
Millions '90
My Wonderful Life '90
Dagger Eyes '80s
The Gamble '88
Nothing Underneath '85
Agnes Varda (1928-)
One Hundred and One Nights '95
Jacquot '91
Le Petit Amour '87
Vagabond '85
One Sings, the Other Doesn't '77
Le Bonheur '65
Cleo from 5 to 7 '61
Marcel Varnel (1894-1947)
Oh, Mr. Porter '37
Chandu the Magician '32
Joseph B. Vasquez (1962-95)
Manhattan Merenque! '95
Street Hitz '92
Hangin' with the Homeboys '91
The Bronx War '90
Francis Veber (1937-)
The Closet '00
The Dinner Game '98
Out on a Limb '92
Three Fugitives '89
Les Comperes '83
La Chevre '81
Gore Verbinski
The Mexican '01
Mouse Hunt '97
Carlo Verdone
Iris Blond '98
Acqua e Sapone '83
Michael Verhoeven (1929-)
My Mother's Courage '95
The Nasty Girl '90
Blitz '85
The White Rose '83
Paul Verhoeven (1938-)
The Hollow Man '00
Starship Troopers '97
Showgirls '95
Basic Instinct '92
Total Recall '90
RoboCop '87
Flesh and Blood '85
Spetters '80
The 4th Man '79
Soldier of Orange '78
Katie Tippel '75
Turkish Delight '73
The Eternal Waltz '54
Henri Verneuil (1920-2002)
Night Flight from Moscow '73
Any Number Can Win '63
Un Singe en Hiver '62
Just Another Pretty Face '58
The Sheep Has Five Legs '54
Forbidden Fruit '52
Stephen Verona (1940-)
Talking Walls '85
Pipe Dreams '76
The Lords of Flatbush '74
Todd Verow
Little Shots of Happiness '97
Frisk '95
Bruno VeSota (1922-76)
The Brain Eaters '58
The Female Jungle '56
Marco Vicario
Wifemistress '79
The Sensual Man '74
Charles Vidor (1900-59)
Song Without End '60
The Swan '56
Love Me or Leave Me '55
Rhapsody '54
Hans Christian Andersen '52
The Loves of Carmen '48
Gilda '46
A Song to Remember '45
Cover Girl '44
The Desperadoes '43
The Tuttles of Tahiti '42
The Lady in Question '40
My Son, My Son '40
King Vidor (1894-1982)
Solomon and Sheba '59
War and Peace '56
Man Without a Star '55
Ruby Gentry '52
Beyond the Forest '49
The Fountainhead '49
On Our Merry Way '48
Duel in the Sun '46
Comrade X '40
Northwest Passage '40
The Citadel '38
Stella Dallas '37
The Texas Rangers '36
Our Daily Bread '34
Bird of Paradise '32
The Champ '32
Street Scene '31
Hallelujah! '29
The Crowd '28
Show People '28
The Big Parade '25
Peg o' My Heart '22
The Sky Pilot '21
The Jack Knife Man '20
Berthold Viertel (1885-1954)
The Passing of the Third Floor Back '36
Rhodes '36
Daniel Vigne (1942-)
One Woman or Two '85
The Return of Martin Guerre '83
Jean Vigo (1905-34)
L'Atalante '34
Zero for Conduct '33
A Propos de Nice '29
Camilo Vila
Unlawful Passage '94
Options '88
The Unholy '88
Reynaldo Villalobos
Hollywood Confidential '97
Conagher '91
Joseph Vilsmaier (1939-)
The Harmonists '99
Brother of Sleep '95
Stalingrad '94
Robert Vince
Air Bud 4: Seventh Inning Fetch '02
MVP2: Most Vertical Primate '01
MVP (Most Valuable Primate) '00
Christian Vincent
La Separation '98
The Separation '94
La Discrete '90
Chuck Vincent (1940-91)
Enrapture '90
Wildest Dreams '90
Bedroom Eyes 2 '89
Cleo/Leo '89
Party Incorporated '89
Young Nurses in Love '89
Sexpot '88
Student Affairs '88
Thrilled to Death '88
A Woman Obsessed '88
Deranged '87
New York's Finest '87
Sensations '87
Slammer Girls '87
Wimps '87
If Looks Could Kill '86
Hollywood Hot Tubs '84
C.O.D. '83
Preppies '82
Hot T-Shirts '79
A Matter of Love '78
American Tickler '76
Albert T. Viola
Preacherman '83
Cry of the Penguins '71
Joe Viola
Hot Box '72
Angels Hard As They Come '71
Clement Virgo
Love Come Down '00
Junior's Groove '97
Rude '96
Luchino Visconti (1906-76)
The Innocent '76
Conversation Piece '75
Ludwig '72
Death in Venice '71
The Damned '69
Sandra of a Thousand Delights '65
Boccaccio '70 '62
Rocco and His Brothers '60
White Nights '57
Senso '54
Bellissima '51
La Terra Trema '48
Ossessione '42
Virgil W. Vogel (1920-96)
Walker: Texas Ranger: One Riot, One Ranger '93
Portrait of a Rebel: Margaret Sanger '82
Beulah Land '80
Centennial '78
Invasion of the Animal People '62
The Kettles on Old MacDonald's Farm '57
The Land Unknown '57
The Mole People '56
Alfred Vohrer (1918-86)
Creature with the Blue Hand '70
The Mysterious Magician '65
The Squeaker '65
The Indian Scarf '63
Door with the Seven Locks '62
Inn on the River '62
Dead Eyes of London '61
Marc Voizard
Escape from Wildcat Canyon '99
Marked Man '96
Paul G. Volk
Steel Frontier '94
Sunset Strip '91
Josef von Baky (1902-66)
The Strange Countess '61
Baron Munchausen '43
Josef von Sternberg (1894-1969)
Jet Pilot '57
Macao '52
The Shanghai Gesture '42
Crime and Punishment '35
The Devil Is a Woman '35
Scarlet Empress '34
Blonde Venus '32
Shanghai Express '32
Dishonored '31
The Blue Angel '30
Morocco '30
Docks of New York '28
Last Command '28
It '27
Underworld '27
Erich von Stroheim (1885-1957)
Queen Kelly '29
The Wedding March '28
Greed '24
Merry-Go-Round '23
Foolish Wives '22
Blind Husbands '19
Lars von Trier (1956-)
Dancer in the Dark '99
The Idiots '99
The Kingdom 2 '97
Breaking the Waves '95
The Kingdom '95
Zentropa '92
The Element of Crime '84
Margarethe von Trotta (1942-)
The Promise '94
Rosa Luxemburg '86
Sheer Madness '84
Marianne and Juliane '82
Sisters, Or the Balance of Happiness '79
The Second Awakening of Christa Klages '78
The Lost Honor of Katharina Blum '75
Bernard Vorhaus (1904-2000)
The Amazing Mr. X '48
Lady from Louisiana '42
Courageous Dr. Christian '40
Three Faces West '40
Fisherman's Wharf '39
Meet Dr. Christian '39
Way Down South '39
Cotton Queen '37
Broken Melody '34
The Ghost Camera '33
Kurt Voss (1963-)
Sugar Town '99
Highway Hitcher '98
Body Count '97

Poison Ivy 3: The New Seduction '97
Amnesia '96
Baja '95
The Horseplayer '91
Genuine Risk '89
Border Radio '88

Andy Wachowski (1967-)
The Matrix '99
Bound '96

Larry Wachowski (1965-)
The Matrix '99
Bound '96

Jonathan Wacks
Ed and His Dead Mother '93
Mystery Date '91
Powwow Highway '89

Michael Wadleigh (1941-)
Wolfen '81
Woodstock '70

George Waggner (1894-1984)
The Commies Are Coming, the Commies Are Coming '57
The Fighting Kentuckian '49
The Climax '44
Man Made Monster '41
The Wolf Man '41
Mystery Plane '39
Stunt Pilot '39
Wolf Call '39
Ghost Town Riders '38
Outlaw Express '38
Western Trails '38

Rupert Wainwright
Stigmata '99
Blank Check '93
Dillinger '91
The Discovery Program '89

Andrzej Wajda (1927-)
Korczak '90
The Possessed '88
A Love in Germany '84
Danton '82
Man of Iron '81
The Conductor '80
Maids of Wilko '79
Without Anesthesia '78
Man of Marble '76
Land of Promise '74
Lotna '64
Siberian Lady Macbeth '61
Innocent Sorcerers '60
Ashes and Diamonds '58
Kanal '56
A Generation '54

Chris Walas
The Vagrant '92
The Fly 2 '89

Grant Austin Waldman
Teenage Exorcist '93
The Channeler '89
Gator King '70

Dorian Walker
Teen Witch '89
Making the Grade '84

Giles Walker (1946-)
Ordinary Magic '93
Princes in Exile '90
90 Days '86

Hal Walker (1896-1972)
The Road to Bali '53
At War with the Army '50
The Road to Utopia '46
The Stork Club '45

Pete Walker
Home Before Midnight '84
House of the Long Shadows '82
The Comeback '77
Schizo '77
The Confessional '75
House of Whipcord '75
Tiffany Jones '75
Frightmare '74
Die Screaming, Marianne '73
Flesh and Blood Show '73
Man of Violence '71
The Big Switch '70

Stuart Walker (1887-1941)
The Mystery of Edwin Drood '35
Werewolf of London '35
Great Expectations '34
The Eagle and the Hawk '33

Gary Walkow
Notes from Underground '95
The Trouble with Dick '88

Randall Wallace
We Were Soldiers '02
The Man in the Iron Mask '98

Richard Wallace (1894-1951)
Sinbad, the Sailor '47
Tycoon '47
Because of Him '45
It's in the Bag '45
Bombardier '43
The Fallen Sparrow '43
A Night to Remember '42
A Girl, a Guy and a Gob '41
Captain Caution '40
The Young in Heart '38
Little Minister '34

Rick Wallace
Acceptable Risks '86
A Time to Live '85
California Girls '84

Stephen Wallace (1943-)
The Killing Beach '92
Prisoners of the Sun '91
For Love Alone '86

Tommy Lee Wallace
Final Justice '98
The Spree '96
Witness to the Execution '94
The Comrades of Summer '92
Stephen King's It '90
Aloha Summer '88
Fright Night 2 '88
Halloween 3: Season of the Witch '82

Anthony Waller (1959-)
The Guilty '99
An American Werewolf in Paris '97
Mute Witness '95

Raoul Walsh (1887-1981)
Esther and the King '60
The Naked and the Dead '58
Band of Angels '57
The King and Four Queens '56
Battle Cry '55
The Tall Men '55
Gun Fury '53
A Lion Is in the Streets '53
Sea Devils '53
Blackbeard the Pirate '52
The Lawless Breed '52
The World in His Arms '52
Along the Great Divide '51
Captain Horatio Hornblower '51
Distant Drums '51
The Enforcer '51
White Heat '49
Silver River '48
Pursued '47
The Man I Love '46
The Horn Blows at Midnight '45
Objective, Burma! '45
Uncertain Glory '44
Background to Danger '43
Northern Pursuit '43
Desperate Journey '42
Gentleman Jim '42
High Sierra '41
Strawberry Blonde '41
They Died with Their Boots On '41
Dark Command '40
They Drive by Night '40
The Roaring Twenties '39
College Swing '38
O.H.M.S. '37
When Thief Meets Thief '37
Klondike Annie '36
Going Hollywood '33
Big Trail '30
Sadie Thompson '28
The Thief of Baghdad '24
Regeneration '15

Charles Walters (1911-82)
Walk, Don't Run '66
The Unsinkable Molly Brown '64
Billy Rose's Jumbo '62
Please Don't Eat the Daisies '60
Ask Any Girl '59
Don't Go Near the Water '57
High Society '56
The Glass Slipper '55
The Tender Trap '55
Dangerous When Wet '53
Easy to Love '53
Lili '53
Torch Song '53
The Belle of New York '52
Texas Carnival '51
Three Guys Named Mike '51
Summer Stock '50
The Barkleys of Broadway '49
Easter Parade '48
Good News '47

Fred Walton (1865-1936)
The Courtyard '95
Dead Air '94
When a Stranger Calls Back '93
Homewrecker '92
Trapped '89
The Rosary Murders '87
April Fool's Day '86
Hadley's Rebellion '84
When a Stranger Calls '79

Sam Wanamaker (1919-93)
Killing of Randy Webster '81
The Dark Side of Love '79
Sinbad and the Eye of the Tiger '77
Catlow '71
The Executioner '70

Peter Wang
The Laserman '90
A Great Wall '86

Steve Wang
Drive '96
Guyver 2: Dark Hero '94
The Guyver '91

Wayne Wang (1949-)
The Center of the World '01
A Man, a Woman and a Killer
Anywhere But Here '99
Chinese Box '97
Blue in the Face '95
Smoke '95
The Joy Luck Club '93
Eat a Bowl of Tea '89
Slamdance '87
Dim Sum: A Little Bit of Heart '85
Chan Is Missing '82

Xiaoshuai Wang
Frozen '98
So Close to Paradise '98

David S. Ward (1947-)
Down Periscope '96
Major League 2 '94
The Program '93
King Ralph '91
Major League '89
Cannery Row '82

Donal Lardner Ward
The Suburbans '99
My Life's in Turnaround '94

Vincent Ward (1956-)
What Dreams May Come '98
Map of the Human Heart '93
The Navigator '88
Vigil '84

Clyde Ware (1936-)
Bad Jim '89
The Hatfields & the McCoys '75
No Drums, No Bugles '71

Regis Wargnier
East-West '99
Indochine '92

Charles Marquis Warren (1912-90)
Charro! '69
Tension at Table Rock '56
Arrowhead '53
Little Big Horn '51
Red Desert '50

Deryn Warren
Black Magic Woman '91
Bloodspell '87

Jennifer Warren (1941-)
Partners in Crime '99
Forbidden Choices '94

Jerry Warren (1921-88)
Frankenstein Island '81
The Wild World of Batwoman '66
Curse of the Stone Hand '64
Attack of the Mayan Mummy '63
Invasion of the Animal People '62
Terror of the Bloodhunters '62
Creature of the Walking Dead '60
Face of the Screaming Werewolf '59
The Incredible Petrified World '58
Teenage Zombies '58
Man Beast '55

John Warren (1953-)
Major League 3: Back to the Minors '98
The Curse of Inferno '96

Norman J. Warren
Bloody New Year '87
Alien Prey '83
Inseminoid '80
Spaced Out '80
The Terror '79

John Waters (1946-)
Cecil B. Demented '00
Pecker '98
Serial Mom '94
Cry-Baby '90
Divine '90
Hairspray '88
Polyester '81
Desperate Living '77
Female Trouble '74
Pink Flamingos '72
Multiple Maniacs '70
Mondo Trasho '69

Mark Waters
Head Over Heels '01
The House of Yes '97

Frederick P. Watkins
Lethal Seduction '97
A Matter of Honor '95
Brutal Fury '92

Peter Watkins (1935-)
Edvard Munch '74
The Gladiators '70

John Watson
The Zoo Gang '85
Deathstalker '83

Harry Watt (1906-87)
Eureka Stockade '49
Overlanders '46

Nate Watt (1889-1968)
Law of the Pampas '39
Rustler's Valley '37
Hopalong Cassidy Returns '36

Ric Roman Waugh
In the Shadows '01
Exit '95

Al Waxman (1935-2001)
Diamond Fleece '92
White Light '90
My Pleasure Is My Business '74

Keoni Waxman
The Highway Man '99
I Shot a Man in Vegas '96
Serial Bomber '96
Almost Blue '93

Keenen Ivory Wayans (1958-)
Scary Movie 2 '01
Scary Movie '00
A Low Down Dirty Shame '94
I'm Gonna Git You Sucka '88

John Wayne (1907-79)
The Green Berets '68
The Alamo '60

Harry S. Webb (1896-1959)
Mesquite Buckaroo '39
Riding On '37
Santa Fe Bound '37
Laramie Kid '35
Ridin' Thru '35
The Live Wire '34

Jack Webb (1920-82)
D.I. '57
Pete Kelly's Blues '55
Dragnet '54

Millard Webb (1893-1935)
Glorifying the American Girl '30
The Dropkick '27

Robert D. Webb (1903-90)
The Jackals '67
Love Me Tender '56
Seven Cities of Gold '55
Beneath the 12-Mile Reef '53

William Webb
The Hit List '93
The Banker '89
Party Line '88
Dirty Laundry '87

Lois Weber (1881-1939)
The Blot '21
Too Wise Wives '21
Discontent '16

Nicholas Webster (1922-)
Mission Mars '67
Santa Claus Conquers the Martians '64
Gone Are the Days '63
Purlie Victorious '63

David Wechter (1956-)
Malibu Bikini Shop '86
Midnight Madness '80

Stephen Weeks (1948-)
Sword of the Valiant '83
Madhouse Mansion '74
I, Monster '71

Paul Wegener (1874-1948)
The Golem '20
Student of Prague '13

Lo Wei (1918-96)
New Fist of Fury '76
Chinese Connection '73
Fists of Fury '73

John Weidner
Space Marines '96
Blood for Blood '95
Private Wars '93

Paul Weiland
Bernard and the Genie '90s
For Roseanna '96
City Slickers 2: The Legend of Curly's Gold '94
Leonard Part 6 '87

Claudia Weill (1947-)
Critical Choices '97
Once a Hero '88
It's My Turn '80
Girlfriends '78

Yossi Wein
U.S. Seals '98
Operation Delta Force 2: Mayday '97
Terminal Impact '95
Never Say Die '94

Peter Weir (1944-)
The Truman Show '98
Fearless '93
Green Card '90
Dead Poets Society '89
The Mosquito Coast '86
Witness '85
The Year of Living Dangerously '82
Gallipoli '81
Plumber '79
The Last Wave '77
Picnic at Hanging Rock '75
The Cars That Ate Paris '74

Don Weis (1922-2000)
The Munsters' Revenge '81
Zero to Sixty '78
Billie '65
Pajama Party '64
The Gene Krupa Story '59
The Affairs of Dobie Gillis '53
I Love Melvin '53

Gary Weis
Wholly Moses! '80
Diary of a Young Comic '79
All You Need Is Cash '78

Jack Weis
Mardi Gras Massacre '78
Crypt of Dark Secrets '76
Storyville '74

Sam Weisman
What's the Worst That Could Happen? '01
The Out-of-Towners '99
George of the Jungle '97
Bye Bye, Love '94
D2: The Mighty Ducks '94

Jiri Weiss (1913-)
Martha and I '91
Murder Czech Style '66
The Coward '62
Sweet Light in a Dark Room '60
Wolf Trap '57

Chris Weitz (1970-)
About a Boy '02
Down to Earth '01
American Pie '99

Paul Weitz (1966-)
About a Boy '02
Down to Earth '01
American Pie '99

Orson Welles (1915-85)
It's All True '93
Chimes at Midnight '67
The Trial '63
Touch of Evil '58
Mr. Arkadin '55
Othello '52
The Lady from Shanghai '48
Macbeth '48
The Stranger '46
The Magnificent Ambersons '42
Citizen Kane '41

David Wellington
Restless Spirits '99
Long Day's Journey Into Night '96
A Man in Uniform '93
The Carpenter '89

William A. Wellman (1896-1975)
Darby's Rangers '58
Lafayette Escadrille '58
Goodbye, My Lady '56
Blood Alley '55
Across the Wide Missouri '51
Westward the Women '51
The Next Voice You Hear '50
Battleground '49
Magic Town '47
The Story of G.I. Joe '45
Buffalo Bill '44
Lady of Burlesque '43
The Ox-Bow Incident '43
The Great Man's Lady '42
Roxie Hart '42
Beau Geste '39
Nothing Sacred '37
A Star Is Born '37
Heroes for Sale '33
The Purchase Price '32
Night Nurse '31
Public Enemy '31
Wings '27

Simon Wells
The Time Machine '02

Corporate Affairs '90
Bloodfist '89
The Nest '88

Michael Winner (1935-)
Bullseye! '90
A Chorus of Disapproval '89
Appointment with Death '88
Scream for Help '86
Death Wish 3 '85
The Wicked Lady '83
Death Wish 2 '82
Firepower '79
The Big Sleep '78
The Sentinel '76
Death Wish '74
Scorpio '73
The Stone Killer '73
The Mechanic '72
The Nightcomers '72
Chato's Land '71
Lawman '71
I'll Never Forget What's 'Isname '67
The Girl Getters '66
Cool Mikado '63
Murder on the Campus '52

David Winning (1961-)
Profile for Murder '96
Turbo: A Power Rangers Movie '96
Killer Image '92
Storm '87

Peter Winograd
One Last Run '89
Flicks '85

Stan Winston (1946-)
The Adventures of a Gnome Named Gnorm '93
Pumpkinhead '88

Alex Winter (1965-)
Fever '99
Freaked '93

Michael Winterbottom (1961-)
The Claim '00
Wonderland '99
I Want You '98
Welcome to Sarajevo '97
Go Now '96
Jude '96
Butterfly Kiss '94

David Winters (1939-)
Rage to Kill '88
Space Mutiny '88
Codename: Vengeance '87
Thrashin' '86
Mission to Kill '85
Fanatic '82
Racquet '79
Dr. Jekyll and Mr. Hyde '73

Frank Wisbar (1899-1967)
The Devil Bat's Daughter '46
Strangler of the Swamp '46

Herbert Wise (1924-)
The 10th Kingdom '00
Breaking the Code '95
Strange Interlude '90
Woman in Black '89
Pope John Paul II '84
The Gathering Storm '74
Elizabeth R '72
Castle of the Living Dead '64
Alone Against Rome '62

Kirk Wise
Atlantis: The Lost Empire '01
The Hunchback of Notre Dame '96
Beauty and the Beast '91

Robert Wise (1914-)
Rooftops '89
Star Trek: The Motion Picture '80
Audrey Rose '77
The Hindenburg '75
The Andromeda Strain '71
Star! '68
The Sand Pebbles '66
The Sound of Music '65
The Haunting '63
Two for the Seesaw '62
West Side Story '61
Odds Against Tomorrow '59
I Want to Live! '58
Run Silent, Run Deep '58
This Could Be the Night '57
Until They Sail '57
Helen of Troy '56
Somebody Up There Likes Me '56
Tribute to a Bad Man '56
Executive Suite '54
The Desert Rats '53
The Day the Earth Stood Still '51
Three Secrets '50
The Set-Up '49
Blood on the Moon '48
Born to Kill '47
Criminal Court '46
The Body Snatcher '45
Curse of the Cat People '44
Mademoiselle Fifi '44
The Magnificent Ambersons '42

Carol Wiseman
Does This Mean We're Married? '90
The Little Princess '87

Doris Wishman
Double Agent 73 '80
The Amazing Transplant '70
Deadly Weapons '70
Bad Girls Go to Hell '65
Nude on the Moon '61

William Witney (1915-2002)
Darktown Strutters '74
Arizona Raiders '65
Master of the World '61
The Outcast '54
Iron Mountain Trail '53
Shadows of Tombstone '53
Border Saddlemates '52
Colorado Sundown '52
Heart of the Rockies '51
Bells of Coronado '50
North of the Great Divide '50
Sunset in the West '50
Trail of Robin Hood '50
Trigger, Jr. '50
Twilight in the Sierras '50
Down Dakota Way '49
The Golden Stallion '49
Susanna Pass '49
Eyes of Texas '48
Grand Canyon Trail '48
Night Time in Nevada '48
Under California Stars '48
Apache Rose '47
Bells of San Angelo '47
Home in Oklahoma '47
On the Old Spanish Trail '47
Springtime in the Sierras '47
Cyclotrode "X" '46
Helldorado '46
Roll on Texas Moon '46
G-Men vs. the Black Dragon '43
The Gay Ranchero '42
Nyoka and the Tigermen '42
Spy Smasher '42
Spy Smasher Returns '42
The Adventures of Captain Marvel '41
Dick Tracy vs. Crime Inc. '41
King of the Texas Rangers '41
Adventures of Red Ryder '40
Doctor Satan's Robot '40
Drums of Fu Manchu '40
Mysterious Doctor Satan '40
Zorro's Fighting Legion '39
Daredevils of the Red Circle '38
Dick Tracy Returns '38
Fighting Devil Dogs '38
Hawk of the Wilderness '38
The Lone Ranger '38
The Painted Stallion '37
The Trigger Trio '37
Zorro Rides Again '37

Peter Wittman
Ellie '84
Play Dead '81

Jay Woelfel
Unseen Evil '99
Things '93
Beyond Dream's Door '88

Fred Wolf
Mouse and His Child '77
The Point '71

Konrad Wolf (1925-82)
Solo Sunny '80
I Was Nineteen '68

Andy Wolk
Deliberate Intent '01
Mr. Rock 'n' Roll: The Alan Freed Story '99
The Defenders: Taking the First '98
The Defenders: Payback '97
Traces of Red '92
Criminal Justice '90

Dan Wolman (1941-)
Soldier of the Night '84
Baby Love '83
Nana '82
Hide and Seek '80
My Michael '75

M. Wallace Wolodarsky
Sorority Boys '02
Coldblooded '94

James Wong
The One '01
Final Destination '00

Kirk Wong
The Big Hit '98
Crime Story '93
Organized Crime & Triad Bureau '93

John Woo (1948-)
Windtalkers '02
Mission: Impossible 2 '00
Blackjack '97
Face/Off '97
Once a Thief '96
Broken Arrow '95
Hard Target '93
Hard-Boiled '92
A Bullet in the Head '90
The Killer '90
A Better Tomorrow, Part 2 '88
A Better Tomorrow, Part 1 '86
Heroes Shed No Tears '86
Last Hurrah for Chivalry '78

Edward D. Wood, Jr. (1924-78)
The Sinister Urge '60
Night of the Ghouls '59
Plan 9 from Outer Space '56
The Violent Years '56
Bride of the Monster '55
Jail Bait '54
Glen or Glenda? '53

Sam Wood (1883-1949)
The Stratton Story '49
Command Decision '48
Heartbeat '46
Guest Wife '45
Saratoga Trunk '45
Casanova Brown '44
For Whom the Bell Tolls '43
The Pride of the Yankees '42
The Devil & Miss Jones '41
Kings Row '41
Kitty Foyle '40
Our Town '40
Goodbye, Mr. Chips '39
A Day at the Races '37
Madame X '37
Navy Blue and Gold '37
Let 'Em Have It '35
A Night at the Opera '35
Hold Your Man '33
Peck's Bad Boy '21

John Woods
Plain Jane '01
Kings in Grass Castles '97

Chuck Workman
Superstar: The Life and Times of Andy Warhol '90
Stoogemania '85
Kill Castro '80
The Mercenaries '80
The Money '75

Wallace Worsley, II (1878-1944)
The Hunchback of Notre Dame '23
The Penalty '20

David Worth
Time Lapse '01
The Prophet's Game '99
True Vengeance '97
Lady Dragon 2 '93
Lady Dragon '92
Warrior of the Lost World '84

John Wray (1896-1929)
Anna Christie '23
Beau Revel '21

Casper Wrede (1929-98)
The Terrorists '74
One Day in the Life of Ivan Denisovich '71

Alexander Wright
Styx '00
The First 9 1/2 Weeks '98
Fast Money '96

Geoffrey Wright
Cherry Falls '00
Terror Tract '00
Romper Stomper '92

Mack V. Wright (1895-1965)
Sea Hound '47
Rootin' Tootin' Rhythm '38
Big Show '37
Hit the Saddle '37
Riders of the Whistling Skull '37
Robinson Crusoe of Clipper Island '36
Robinson Crusoe of Mystery Island '36
The Vigilantes Are Coming '36
Winds of the Wasteland '36
Man from Monterey '33
Somewhere in Sonora '33
Haunted Gold '32

Tenny Wright (1885-1971)
Telegraph Trail '33
The Big Stampede '32

Thomas J. Wright
Chrome Soldiers '92
Highlander: The Gathering '92
Deadly Game '91
The Fatal Image '90
Snow Kill '90
No Holds Barred '89
Torchlight '85

Donald Wrye
Not in This Town '97
Ice Castles '79
Death Be Not Proud '75
Born Innocent '74

William Wyler (1902-81)
War in the Sky '82
The Liberation of L.B. Jones '70
Funny Girl '68
How to Steal a Million '66
The Collector '65
The Children's Hour '61
Ben-Hur '59
The Big Country '58
Friendly Persuasion '56
Desperate Hours '55
Roman Holiday '53
Carrie '52
Detective Story '51
The Heiress '49
The Best Years of Our Lives '46
Mrs. Miniver '42
The Little Foxes '41
The Letter '40
The Westerner '40
Wuthering Heights '39
Jezebel '38
Dead End '37
Come and Get It '36
Dodsworth '36
These Three '36

Paul Wynne
Bombshell '97
Destination Vegas '95

Jim Wynorski (1950-)
Extreme Limits '01
Gale Force '01
Ablaze '00
Rangers '00
Desert Thunder '99
Final Voyage '99
Militia '99
Stealth Fighter '99
Against the Law '98
Storm Trooper '98
Vampirella '96
The Wasp Woman '96
Body Chemistry 4: Full Exposure '95
Demolition High '95
Hard Bounty '94
Sorceress '94
Body Chemistry 3: Point of Seduction '93
Dinosaur Island '93
Ghoulies 4 '93
Home for Christmas '93
Munchie '92
Sins of Desire '92
Sorority House Massacre 2: Nighty Nightmare '92
The Haunting of Morella '91
976-EVIL 2: The Astral Factor '91
Hard to Die '90
The Return of Swamp Thing '89
Transylvania Twist '89
Not of This Earth '88
Big Bad Mama 2 '87
Deathstalker 2: Duel of the Titans '87
Chopping Mall '86
The Lost Empire '83

Zhou Xiaowen
The Emperor's Shadow '96
Ermo '94

Boaz Yakin (1944-)
Remember the Titans '00
A Price above Rubies '97
Fresh '94

Mitsuo Yanagimachi (1944-)
Shadow of China '91
Himatsuri '85

Jean Yarbrough (1900-75)
Over the Hill Gang '69
Hillbillies in a Haunted House '67
Jack & the Beanstalk '52
Lost in Alaska '52
Holiday in Havana '49
Master Minds '49
Pirate Ship '49
The Creeper '48
The Brute Man '46
House of Horrors '46
She Wolf of London '46
Here Come the Co-Eds '45
The Naughty Nineties '45
Under Western Stars '45
In Society '44
Law of the Jungle '42
Lure of the Islands '42
Meet the Mob '42
The Devil Bat '41
King of the Zombies '41
Let's Go Collegiate '41
Panama Menace '41
The Gang's All Here '40

Peter Yates (1929-)
Don Quixote '00
Curtain Call '97
Roommates '95
The Run of the Country '95
Year of the Comet '92
An Innocent Man '89
The House on Carroll Street '88
Suspect '87
Eleni '85
The Dresser '83
Krull '83
Eyewitness '81
Breaking Away '79
The Deep '77
Mother, Jugs and Speed '76
For Pete's Sake '74
Murphy's War '71
Bullitt '68
Koroshi '67
Robbery '67

Irvin S. Yeaworth, Jr.
Dinosaurus! '60
The 4D Man '59
The Blob '58
The Flaming Teen-Age '56

Linda Yellen (1949-)
End of Summer '97
Parallel Lives '94
Chantilly Lace '93

Zhang Yimou (1951-)
The Road Home '01
Not One Less '99
Shanghai Triad '95
To Live '94
Raise the Red Lantern '91
The Story of Qiu Ju '91
Ju Dou '90
Red Sorghum '87

Jeff Yonis
Born Bad '97
Humanoids from the Deep '96
Bloodfist 5: Human Target '93

Bud Yorkin (1926-)
Love Hurts '91
Arthur 2: On the Rocks '88
Twice in a Lifetime '85
The Thief Who Came to Dinner '73
Start the Revolution without Me '70
Divorce American Style '67
Come Blow Your Horn '63

Yaky Yosha
Sexual Response '92
Dead End Street '83

Hiroaki Yoshida
Iron Maze '91
Twilight of the Cockroaches '90

Harold Young (1897-1970)
Jungle Captive '45
Weird Woman/Frozen Ghost '44
The Mummy's Tomb '42
Dreaming Out Loud '40
Little Tough Guys '38
The Scarlet Pimpernel '34

James Young
The Bells '26
The Unchastened Woman '25

Robert M. Young (1924-)
Captain Jack '98
Jane Eyre '97
Caught '96
Fierce Creatures '96
Roosters '95
Doomsday Gun '94
Splitting Heirs '93
Talent for the Game '91
Triumph of the Spirit '89
Dominick & Eugene '88
We Are the Children '87
Extremities '86
Saving Grace '86
The Worst Witch '86
Robin Hood...The Legend: Herne's Son '85
Ballad of Gregorio Cortez '83
Robin Hood...The Legend: The Swords of Wayland '83
Charlie Boy '81
One Trick Pony '80
Rich Kids '79
Short Eyes '79
Romance with a Double Bass '74
Trauma '62

Robert W. Young
Hostage '92
Scandalous '88
The World Is Full of Married Men '80
Vampire Circus '71

Roger Young (1942-)
Jesus '00
Kiss the Sky '98
A Knight in Camelot '98
Solomon '98
Moses '96
Joseph '95
Getting Gotti '94
Geronimo '93
Mercy Mission '93
Held Hostage '91
The Bourne Identity '88
The Squeeze '87
Gulag '85
Into Thin Air '85
Lassiter '84
Two of a Kind '82
Bitter Harvest '81
Magnum P.I.: Don't Eat the Snow in Hawaii '80
Terence Young (1915-94)
The Jigsaw Man '84
Sidney Sheldon's Bloodline '79
The Klansman '74
Cold Sweat '71
Red Sun '71
When Wolves Cry '69
Mayerling '68
The Rover '67
Triple Cross '67
Wait until Dark '67
The Poppy Is Also a Flower '66
The Amorous Adventures of Moll Flanders '65
Thunderball '65
From Russia with Love '63
Dr. No '62
Black Tights '60
Valley of the Eagles '51
Woman Hater '49
Ronny Yu
Bride of Chucky '98
Warriors of Virtue '97
The Phantom Lover '95
The Bride with White Hair '93
The Bride with White Hair 2 '93
China White '91
Legacy of Rage '86
Noriaki Yuasa (1933-)
Gamera vs. Zigra '71
Gamera vs. Guiron '69
Destroy All Planets '68
Gamera vs. Gaos '67
Gamera, the Invincible '66
Corey Yuen
Jet Li's The Enforcer '95
The Bodyguard from Beijing '94
No Retreat, No Surrender 2 '89
Dragons Forever '88
No Retreat, No Surrender '86
Woo-ping Yuen (1945-)
Fist of Legend '94
Iron Monkey '93
Twin Warriors '93
Larry Yust
Say Yes! '86
Homebodies '74
Peter Yuval
Firehead '90
Dead End City '88
Kunihiko Yuyama
Pokemon 3: The Movie '01
Pokemon the Movie 2000: The Power of One '00
Pokemon: The First Movie '99
Brian Yuzna
Faust: Love of the Damned '00
Progeny '98
The Dentist '96
H.P. Lovecraft's Necronomicon: Book of the Dead '93
Return of the Living Dead 3 '93
Society '92
Silent Night, Deadly Night 4: Initiation '90
Bride of Re-Animator '89
Alfredo Zacharias
Demonoid, Messenger of Death '81
The Bees '78
Bandits '73
Crossfire '67
Steven Zaillian (1951-)
A Civil Action '98
Searching for Bobby Fischer '93
Alain Zaloum
Suspicious Minds '96
Canvas: The Fine Art of Crime '92
Alex Zamm
My Date with the President's Daughter '98
Chairman of the Board '97
Luigi Zampa (1905-91)
Tigers in Lipstick '80
A Woman of Rome '56
Mario Zampi (1903-63)
Too Many Crooks '59
The Naked Truth '58
Lili Fini Zanuck (1954-)
From the Earth to the Moon '98
Rush '91
Krzysztof Zanussi (1939-)
The Silent Touch '94
Year of the Quiet Sun '84
The Unapproachable '82
From a Far Country: Pope John Paul II '81
Contract '80
The Catamount Killing '74
Illumination '73
Family Life '71
The Structure of Crystals '69
Mier Zarchi (1937-)
Don't Mess with My Sister! '85
I Spit on Your Grave '77
Tony Zarindast
Werewolf '95
Hardcase and Fist '89
The Guns and the Fury '83
Treasure of the Lost Desert '83
Edwin Zbonek
The Mad Executioners '65
The Monster of London City '64
Franco Zeffirelli (1923-)
Tea with Mussolini '99
Jane Eyre '96
Hamlet '90
Otello '86
Endless Love '81
The Champ '79
Jesus of Nazareth '77
Brother Sun, Sister Moon '73
Romeo and Juliet '68
The Taming of the Shrew '67
Alfred Zeisler (1897-1985)
Parole, Inc. '49
Fear '46
Enemy of Women '44
Amazing Adventure '37
Make-Up '37
Yuri Zeltser (1962-)
Black & White '99
Playmaker '94
Eye of the Storm '91
Karel Zeman (1910-89)
On the Comet '68
Fabulous Adventures of Baron Munchausen '61
The Original Fabulous Adventures of Baron Munchausen '61
Robert Zemeckis (1952-)
Cast Away '00
What Lies Beneath '00
Contact '97
Forrest Gump '94
Death Becomes Her '92
Back to the Future, Part 3 '90
Back to the Future, Part 2 '89
Tales from the Crypt '89
Who Framed Roger Rabbit '88
Back to the Future '85
Romancing the Stone '84
Used Cars '80
I Wanna Hold Your Hand '78
Will Zens (1920-)
The Fix '84
Trucker's Woman '83
Hot Summer in Barefoot County '74
Hell on Wheels '67
Tian Zhuangzhuang
The Blue Kite '93
The Horse Thief '87
Claude Zidi (1934-)
My New Partner '84
Stuntwoman '81
Howard Zieff (1943-)
My Girl 2 '94
My Girl '91
The Dream Team '89
Unfaithfully Yours '84
Private Benjamin '80
The Main Event '79
House Calls '78
Hearts of the West '75
Slither '73
Scott Ziehl
Earth vs. the Spider '01
Proximity '00
Broken Vessels '98
Howard Ziehm
Flesh Gordon 2: Flesh Gordon Meets the Cosmic Cheerleaders '90
Flesh Gordon '72
Rafal Zielinski (1954-)
Fun '94
National Lampoon's Last Resort '94
Jailbait '93
Night of the Warrior '91
Spellcaster '91
Ginger Ale Afternoon '89
Recruits '86
Loose Screws '85
Screwballs '83
Paul Ziller
Moving Target '00
Ms. Bear '97
Panic in the Skies '96
Shootfighter 2: Kill or Be Killed! '96
Virtual Seduction '96
Probable Cause '95
Back in Action '94
Breaking Point '94
Bloodfist 4: Die Trying '92
Deadly Surveillance '91
Pledge Night '90
Vernon Zimmerman
Fade to Black '80
Unholy Rollers '72
Fred Zinnemann (1907-97)
Five Days One Summer '82
Julia '77
The Day of the Jackal '73
A Man for All Seasons '66
Behold a Pale Horse '64
The Sundowners '60
The Nun's Story '59
Oklahoma! '55
From Here to Eternity '53
High Noon '52
The Member of the Wedding '52
The Men '50
The Search '48
The Seventh Cross '44
Joseph Zito (1949-)
Red Scorpion '89
Invasion U.S.A. '85
Friday the 13th, Part 4: The Final Chapter '84
Missing in Action '84
The Prowler '81
Abduction '75
Ralph Zondag
Dinosaur '00
We're Back! A Dinosaur's Story '93
David Zucker (1947-)
BASEketball '98
Naked Gun 2 1/2: The Smell of Fear '91
The Naked Gun: From the Files of Police Squad '88
Ruthless People '86
Top Secret! '84
Airplane! '80
Jerry Zucker (1950-)
Rat Race '01
First Knight '95
Ghost '90
Ruthless People '86
Top Secret! '84
Airplane! '80
Frank Zuniga (1936-)
Fist Fighter '88
The Golden Seal '83
Heartbreaker '83
Further Adventures of the Wilderness Family, Part 2 '77
Marcos Zurinaga
The Disappearance of Garcia Lorca '96
Tango Bar '88
Guido Zurli
The Mad Butcher '72
Psychopath '68
Valerio Zurlini (1926-82)
The Desert of the Tartars '76
Black Jesus '68
The Girl with a Suitcase '60
Edward Zwick (1952-)
The Siege '98
Courage Under Fire '96
Legends of the Fall '94
Leaving Normal '92
Glory '89
About Last Night... '86
Special Bulletin '83
Having It All '82
Joel Zwick
My Big Fat Greek Wedding '02
Second Sight '89
Karl Zwicky
Vicious '88
Contagion '87
Terry Zwigoff
Ghost World '01
Crumb '94

Writer Index

The **Writer Index** provides a videography for any writer with more than one video credit. The listings for the writer names follow an alphabetical sort by last name (although the names appear in a first name last name format). The videographies are listed chronologically, from most recent film to their first. If a writer wrote more than one film in the same year, these movies are listed alphabetically within the year. Used in conjunction with the **Cast** index, this index will let you find actors and actresses who wrote themselves juicy parts (with varying degrees of success). Directors also tend to show up here, either before their directorial ambitions surfaced, or after they'd gained enough clout to get one of their scripts to the screen.

Douglas Aarniokoski
Puppet Master 5: The Final Chapter *'94*
Puppet Master 4 *'93*

Paul Aaron
In Too Deep *'99*
Laurel Avenue *'93*
Octagon *'80*

George Abbott (1887-1995)
The Pajama Game *'57*
All Quiet on the Western Front *'30*

Paul Abbott
Reckless *'97*
Touching Evil *'97*

Scott Abbott
Queen of the Damned *'02*
Introducing Dorothy Dandridge *'99*
The Wall *'99*
Winchell *'98*
Breach of Conduct *'94*

Kobe Abe
Face of Another *'66*
Woman in the Dunes *'64*

Keith Aberdein (1943-)
Utu *'83*
Carry Me Back *'82*

Dustin Lee Abraham
How High *'01*
The Runner *'99*

Jim Abrahams (1944-)
Mafia! *'98*
Hot Shots! Part Deux *'93*
Hot Shots! *'91*
The Naked Gun: From the Files of Police Squad *'88*
Top Secret! *'84*
Airplane! *'80*
Kentucky Fried Movie *'77*

Jeffrey Abrams
Gone Fishin' *'97*
Forever Young *'92*
Regarding Henry *'91*
Taking Care of Business *'90*

J.J. Abrams
Joy Ride *'01*
Armageddon *'98*

Rodney Ackland
Thursday's Child *'43*
The Forty-Ninth Parallel *'41*

Allen Actor
Dungeonmaster *'83*
Terror at Red Wolf Inn *'72*

Daniel Adams
Primary Motive *'92*
A Fool and His Money *'88*

Gerald Drayson Adams (1900-)
Duel at Silver Creek *'52*
Flame of Araby *'51*

Alan J. Adler
Metalstorm: The Destruction of Jared Syn *'83*
The Concrete Jungle *'82*
Parasite *'82*
The Alchemist *'81*

Gilbert Adler
Tales from the Crypt Presents Bordello of Blood *'96*
Children of the Corn 2: The Final Sacrifice *'92*

Eleonore Adlon
Rosalie Goes Shopping *'89*
Bagdad Cafe *'88*

Felix Adlon
Eat Your Heart Out *'96*
Younger & Younger *'94*
Salmonberries *'91*

Percy Adlon (1935-)
Younger & Younger *'94*
Salmonberries *'91*
Rosalie Goes Shopping *'89*
Bagdad Cafe *'88*
Sugarbaby *'85*
Celeste *'81*

Ed Adlum
Shriek of the Mutilated *'74*
Invasion of the Blood Farmers *'72*

Gilles Adrien
The City of Lost Children *'95*
Delicatessen *'92*

James Agee
The Night of the Hunter *'55*
The African Queen *'51*

Chantal Akerman (1950-)
A Couch in New York *'95*
Night and Day *'91*
Window Shopping *'86*
The Eighties *'83*
Les Rendez-vous D'Anna *'78*
News from Home *'76*

Jeff Albert
The Base *'99*
Warhead *'96*
Danger Zone *'95*
Live Wire: Human Timebomb *'95*
Terminal Impact *'95*
Never Say Die *'94*

Luis Alcoriza (-1992)
The Exterminating Angel *'62*
Death in the Garden *'56*
El *'52*

Todd Alcott
Antz *'98*
Curtain Call *'97*

Alan Alda (1936-)
Betsy's Wedding *'90*
A New Life *'88*
Sweet Liberty *'86*
The Four Seasons *'81*
The Seduction of Joe Tynan *'79*

Robert Alden
Uncaged *'91*
Streetwalkin' *'85*

Will Aldis
Clifford *'92*
Stealing Home *'88*
The Couch Trip *'87*
Back to School *'86*

Robert Aldrich (1918-83)
Too Late the Hero *'70*
Four for Texas *'63*

David Alexander
The Ticket *'97*
Dead Ahead *'96*

J. Grubb Alexander (1887-1932)
Cover Story *'93*
Svengali *'31*
County Fair *'20*

Scott M. Alexander
Screwed *'00*
Man on the Moon *'99*
The People vs. Larry Flynt *'96*
That Darn Cat *'96*
Ed Wood *'94*
Problem Child 2 *'91*
Problem Child *'90*

Grigori Alexandrov (1903-83)
Que Viva Mexico *'32*
Ten Days That Shook the World *'27*

Richard Alfieri
Harvest of Fire *'95*
A Friendship in Vienna *'88*
Echoes *'83*
Children of Rage *'75*

Ted Allan (1916-95)
Dr. Bethune *'90*
Love Streams *'84*
Falling in Love Again *'80*
Lies My Father Told Me *'75*

Chris Allen
In God We Trust *'80*
The Last Remake of Beau Geste *'77*

Curt Allen
Alligator 2: The Mutation *'90*
Blind Vengeance *'90*
Bloodstone *'88*
Hollywood Harry *'86*
Walking the Edge *'83*

Irwin Allen (1916-91)
Five Weeks in a Balloon *'62*
Voyage to the Bottom of the Sea *'61*

Janis Allen
The Double Negative *'80*
Meatballs *'79*

Jay Presson Allen (1922-)
Year of the Gun *'91*
Deathtrap *'82*
Prince of the City *'81*
Just Tell Me What You Want *'80*
Funny Lady *'75*
Forty Carats *'73*
Cabaret *'72*
Travels with My Aunt *'72*
The Prime of Miss Jean Brodie *'69*
Marnie *'64*

Jim Allen
Land and Freedom *'95*
Raining Stones *'93*
Hidden Agenda *'90*

J.T. Allen
The Good Old Boys *'95*
Geronimo *'93*

Woody Allen (1935-)
Hollywood Ending *'02*
The Curse of the Jade Scorpion *'01*
Small Time Crooks *'00*
Sweet and Lowdown *'99*
Celebrity *'98*
Deconstructing Harry *'97*
Everyone Says I Love You *'96*
Mighty Aphrodite *'95*
Bullets over Broadway *'94*
Manhattan Murder Mystery *'93*
Husbands and Wives *'92*
Shadows and Fog *'92*
Alice *'90*
Crimes & Misdemeanors *'89*
New York Stories *'89*
Another Woman *'88*
September *'88*
Radio Days *'87*
Hannah and Her Sisters *'86*
The Purple Rose of Cairo *'85*
Broadway Danny Rose *'84*
Zelig *'83*
A Midsummer Night's Sex Comedy *'82*
Stardust Memories *'80*
Manhattan *'79*
Interiors *'78*
Annie Hall *'77*
Love and Death *'75*
Sleeper *'73*
Everything You Always Wanted to Know about Sex (But Were Afraid to Ask) *'72*
Play It Again, Sam *'72*
Bananas *'71*
Take the Money and Run *'69*
What's Up, Tiger Lily? *'66*
What's New Pussycat? *'65*

Gila Almagor (1939-)
Under the Domim Tree *'95*
The Summer of Aviya *'88*

Michael Almereyda (1960-)
Hamlet *'00*
The Eternal *'99*
Nadja *'95*
Search and Destroy *'94*
Twister *'89*
Cherry 2000 *'88*

Pedro Almodovar (1951-)
All About My Mother *'99*
Live Flesh *'97*
The Flower of My Secret *'95*
Kika *'94*
High Heels *'91*
Tie Me Up! Tie Me Down! *'90*
Women on the Verge of a Nervous Breakdown *'88*
Law of Desire *'86*

Matador '86
What Have I Done to Deserve This? '85
Dark Habits '84
Labyrinth of Passion '82
Pepi, Luci, Bom and Other Girls on the Heap '80

Arthur Alsberg
Hot Lead & Cold Feet '78
Herbie Goes to Monte Carlo '77
Gus '76
No Deposit, No Return '76

Emmett Alston
Hunter's Blood '87
Nine Deaths of the Ninja '85
New Year's Evil '78

Eric Alter
The Experts '89
Hardbodies 2 '86
Hardbodies '84

Sergio D. Altieri
Silent Trigger '97
Little Sister '92
Blind Fear '89

Robert Altman (1925-)
Kansas City '95
Ready to Wear '94
Short Cuts '93
Aria '88
Beyond Therapy '86
Quintet '79
A Wedding '78
Buffalo Bill & the Indians '76
Thieves Like Us '74
McCabe & Mrs. Miller '71

Rod Amateau (1923-)
Sunset '88
The Garbage Pail Kids Movie '87
The Wilby Conspiracy '75
Hook, Line and Sinker '30

Eric Ambler (1909-98)
The Wreck of the Mary Deare '59
A Night to Remember '58
Battle Hell '56
The Cruel Sea '53
Encore '52
The Promoter '52
The Clouded Yellow '51
The October Man '48
Immortal Battalion '44

David Ambrose
Year of the Gun '91
Taffin '88
Blackout '85
D.A.R.Y.L. '85
Amityville 3: The Demon '83
Dangerous Summer '82
The Final Countdown '80
Survivor '80
The Fifth Musketeer '79

Gianni Amelio (1945-)
Lamerica '95
The Stolen Children '92
Open Doors '89

Deborah Amelon
Tricks '97
Exit to Eden '94

Alejandro Amenabar (1972-)
The Others '01
Open Your Eyes '97
Thesis '96

Sergio Amidei (1904-81)
Tales of Ordinary Madness '83
Generale Della Rovere '60
Shoeshine '47
Open City '45

Cesar Amigo
The Ravagers '65
The Walls of Hell '64

Mark Amin
Diplomatic Siege '99
The Principal Takes a Holiday '98

Hossein Amini
The Wings of the Dove '97
Jude '96

Allison Anders (1954-)
Sugar Town '99
Grace of My Heart '96
Four Rooms '95
Mi Vida Loca '94
Gas Food Lodging '92
Border Radio '88

Brad Anderson (1964-)
Session 9 '01
Happy Accidents '00
Next Stop, Wonderland '98

Elizabeth Anderson
Three Wishes '95
Lassie '94

Hesper Anderson
Grand Isle '92
Children of a Lesser God '86
Touched by Love '80

Jane Anderson
If These Walls Could Talk 2 '00
The Baby Dance '98
How to Make an American Quilt '95
It Could Happen to You '94
The Positively True Adventures of the Alleged Texas Cheerleader-Murdering Mom '93

Maxwell Anderson
A Christmas Carol '54
Death Takes a Holiday '34
Rain '32
All Quiet on the Western Front '30

Paul Anderson
Resident Evil '02
Shopping '93

Paul Thomas Anderson (1970-)
Magnolia '99
Boogie Nights '97
Hard Eight '96

Robert Anderson (1923-)
I Never Sang for My Father '70
The Sand Pebbles '66
The Nun's Story '59
Until They Sail '57
Tea and Sympathy '56

Wes Anderson (1970-)
The Royal Tenenbaums '01
Rushmore '98
Bottle Rocket '95

Guy Andrews
The Infiltrator '95
Lie Down with Lions '94

Robert D. (Robert Hardy) Andrews
Girls' Town '59
Bataan '43
Before I Hang '40

Tina Andrews
Sally Hemings: An American Scandal '00
Why Do Fools Fall in Love? '98

Roger Andrieux (1940-)
La Petite Sirene '80
L'Amour en Herbe '77

James Andronica (1945-)
Mirage '94
The November Men '93

Mark Andrus
Divine Secrets of the Ya-Ya Sisterhood '02
Life as a House '01
As Good As It Gets '97
Late for Dinner '91

Mikel Angel
Evil Spirits '91
Grotesque '87
Psychic Killer '75

Michael Angeli
Killing Mr. Griffin '97
Sketch Artist 2: Hands That See '94
Conflict of Interest '92
Sketch Artist '92

Theo Angelopoulos (1935-)
Eternity and a Day '97
Ulysses' Gaze '95
Landscape in the Mist '88
The Travelling Players '75

Edward Anhalt (1914-)
The Take '90
The Holcroft Covenant '85
Green Ice '81
Escape to Athena '79
Fatal Chase '77
The Man in the Glass Booth '75
Luther '74
QB VII '74
Jeremiah Johnson '72
The Madwoman of Chaillot '69
The Boston Strangler '68
Hour of the Gun '67
Boeing Boeing '65
Becket '64
Girls! Girls! Girls! '62
The Young Lions '58
The Pride and the Passion '57
Not as a Stranger '55
The Member of the Wedding '52
Panic in the Streets '50

Erik Anjou
The Cool Surface '92
976-EVIL 2: The Astral Factor '91
The Road to Ruin '28

Ken Annakin (1914-)
The New Adventures of Pippi Longstocking '88
Those Daring Young Men in Their Jaunty Jalopies '69
Those Magnificent Men in Their Flying Machines '65

Jean-Jacques Annaud (1943-)
Enemy at the Gates '00
The Lover '92
Black and White in Color '76

Jean Anouilh
Circle of Love '64
Monsieur Vincent '47

Stuart Anthony
The Monster and the Girl '41
The Shepherd of the Hills '41
Helltown '38
Arizona Mahoney '36
Drift Fence '36
Border Law '31
The Fighting Sheriff '31

Steve Antin (1956-)
Gloria '98
Inside Monkey Zetterland '93

Michelangelo Antonioni (1912-)
Beyond the Clouds '95
Identification of a Woman '82
The Passenger '75
Zabriskie Point '70
Blow-Up '66
The Eclipse '66
The Red Desert '64
L'Avventura '60
Il Grido '57

Judd Apatow (1968-)
The Cable Guy '96
Celtic Pride '96
Heavyweights '94

Max Apple
Roommates '95
The Air Up There '94
Smokey Bites the Dust '81

William Applegate, Jr.
The Big Fall '96
Pure Danger '96
Riot '96
Tiger Heart '96
Skyscraper '95
The Sweeper '95

Gregg Araki (1959-)
Splendor '99
Nowhere '96
The Doom Generation '95
Totally F***ed Up '94
The Living End '92

Shimon Arama
Triumph of the Spirit '89
Black Eagle '88

Vicente Aranda (1926-)
Jealousy '99
Intruso '93
Lovers: A True Story '90
The Blood Spattered Bride '72

David Arata
Spy Game '01
Brokedown Palace '99

Denys Arcand (1941-)
Stardom '00
Jesus of Montreal '89
The Decline of the American Empire '86

Manuel Arce
Crossover Dreams '85
El Super '79

Jeffrey Arch
Iron Will '93
Sleepless in Seattle '93

William Archibald
The Innocents '61
I Confess '53

Dario Argento (1940-)
Sleepless '01
The Church '98
The Phantom of the Opera '98
The Stendahl Syndrome '95
Dario Argento's Trauma '93
The Devil's Daughter '91
Two Evil Eyes '90
Opera '88
Demons 2 '87
Demons '86
Creepers '85
Unsane '82
Inferno '80
Suspiria '77
Deep Red: Hatchet Murders '75
Commandos '73
The Cat o' Nine Tails '71
The Bird with the Crystal Plumage '70
Once Upon a Time in the West '68

Alice Arlen
Cookie '89
Alamo Bay '85
Silkwood '83

Giorgio Arlorio
Zorro '74
Burn! '70

George Armitage
The Late Shift '96
The Last of the Finest '90
Miami Blues '90
Night Call Nurses '72
Private Duty Nurses '71
Gas-s-s-s! '70

Steve Armogida
Attack of the 60-Foot Centerfold '95
Masseuse '95

Michael Armstrong (1944-)
House of the Long Shadows '82
Black Panther '77

Mike Armstrong
Monument Ave. '98
Two If by Sea '95

David Arnott
Last Action Hero '93
The Adventures of Ford Fairlane '90

Darren Aronofsky (1969-)
Requiem for a Dream '00
Pi '98

Ash
Pups '99
Bang '95

William Asher (1921-)
Beach Blanket Bingo '65
How to Stuff a Wild Bikini '65
Bikini Beach '64
Muscle Beach Party '64

Peter Askin
Company Man '00
Smithereens '82

Olivier Assayas (1955-)
Alice et Martin '98
Late August, Early September '98
Irma Vep '96
Scene of the Crime '87
Rendez-vous '85

David Atkins
Novocaine '01
Arizona Dream '94

Peter Atkins
Wishmaster '97
Hellraiser 4: Bloodline '95
Hellraiser 3: Hell on Earth '92
Hellbound: Hellraiser 2 '88

Leopold Atlas
Raw Deal '48
The Story of G.I. Joe '45
Tomorrow the World '44

Paul Attanasio
The Sum of All Fears '02
Sphere '97
Donnie Brasco '96
Disclosure '94
Quiz Show '94
Rapid Fire '92

Jacques Audiard
A Self-Made Hero '95
Barjo '93
Baxter '89

Michel Audiard (1920-85)
Le Professionnel '81
Dear Detective '77
Any Number Can Win '63

Bille August (1948-)
Jerusalem '96
The House of the Spirits '93
Pelle the Conqueror '88
Twist & Shout '84

John August
Charlie's Angels '00
Titan A.E. '00
Go '99

Joe Augustyn
Exit '95
Night of the Demons 2 '94
Night Angel '90
Night of the Demons '88

Jean Aurel
Confidentially Yours '83
The Women '69
Le Trou '59
Une Parisienne '58

Jean Aurenche (1904-92)
The Judge and the Assassin '75
The Clockmaker '73
The Hunchback of Notre Dame '57
Forbidden Games '52
The Red Inn '51
The Walls of Malapaga '49
Devil in the Flesh '46

Paul Auster (1947-)
Lulu on the Bridge '98
Blue in the Face '95
Smoke '95

Sam Auster
Bounty Hunter 2002 '94
Screen Test '85

Carl Austin
Improper Conduct '94
Sexual Malice '93
Wild Cactus '92

Michael Austin
Princess Caraboo '94
Greystoke: The Legend of Tarzan, Lord of the Apes '84
Five Days One Summer '82
The Shout '78

Steve Autrey
Return of the Street Fighter '74
The Street Fighter '74

Roger Roberts Avary (1967-)
Mr. Stitch '95
Killing Zoe '94
Pulp Fiction '94

Antonio Avati
Bix '90
Zeder '83
Macabre '80

Pupi Avati (1938-)
The Best Man '97
The Story of Boys & Girls '91
Bix '90
Zeder '83
The Boss Is Served '76

Howard (Hikmet) Avedis
Kidnapped '87
They're Playing with Fire '84
Mortuary '81
The Fifth Floor '80
Scorchy '76
The Specialist '75

Robert J. Avrech
Brotherhood of Murder '99
The Devil's Arithmetic '99
Into Thin Air: Death on Everest '97
A Stranger Among Us '92
Dark Tower '87
Body Double '84

George Axelrod
The Fourth Protocol '87
The Holcroft Covenant '85
The Lady Vanishes '79
Secret Life of an American Wife '68
How to Murder Your Wife '64
Paris When It Sizzles '64
The Manchurian Candidate '62
Breakfast at Tiffany's '61
Bus Stop '56
The Seven Year Itch '55
Phffft! '54

David Ayer (1972-)
The Fast and the Furious '01
Training Day '01
U-571 '00

Clay Ayers
The Watcher '00
Sword of Honor '94

Dan Aykroyd (1952-)
Blues Brothers 2000 '98
Coneheads '93
Nothing But Trouble '91
Ghostbusters 2 '89
Dragnet '87
Spies Like Us '85
Ghostbusters '84
The Blues Brothers '80

Gerald Ayres
Crazy in Love '92
Rich and Famous '81
Foxes '80

Rafael Azcona
Butterfly '98
Belle Epoque '92
Ay, Carmela! '90
Blood and Sand '89
La Grande Bouffe '73

Beth B (1955-)
Two Small Bodies '93
Salvation! '87
Vortex '81

Thom Babbes
Body Chemistry '90
Deadly Dreams '88

Dwight V. Babcock
Jungle Captive '45
Dead Man's Eyes/Pillow of Death '44

Hector Babenco (1946-)
At Play in the Fields of the Lord '91
Pixote '81

Danilo Bach
Escape Clause '96
April Fool's Day '86
Beverly Hills Cop '84

Jean-Pierre Bacri (1951-)
Same Old Song '97
Un Air de Famille '96
Smoking/No Smoking '94
Tom Badal
Vietnam, Texas '90
Out on Bail '89
Randall Badat
Born to Run '93
Hear No Evil '93
Surf 2 '84
Phillip Badger
Retroactive '97
The Forgotten One '89
Geoffrey Baere
Corporate Affairs '90
Campus Man '87
School Spirit '85
Michael Bafaro
Act of War '96
Listen '96
Crackerjack '94
Fax Bahr
Jury Duty '95
In the Army Now '94
Son-in-Law '93
Hearts of Darkness: A Filmmaker's Apocalypse '91
Frederick Bailey
Terminal Justice: Cybertech P.D. '95
Quick '93
Raiders of the Sun '92
Desert Warrior '88
Demon of Paradise '87
Sandra K. Bailey
False Identity '90
Prettykill '87
The KGB: The Secret War '86
Hambone & Hillie '84
John Baines
The Hands of Orlac '60
Dead of Night '45
Jon Robin Baitz (1961-)
The Substance of Fire '96
Fallen Angels 1 '93
Bart Baker
Any Place But Home '97
Live Wire '92
Baby of the Bride '91
Herbert Baker
The Jazz Singer '80
Sextette '78
The Ambushers '67
Oh Dad, Poor Dad (Momma's Hung You in the Closet & I'm Feeling So Sad) '67
Murderers' Row '66
King Creole '58
The Girl Can't Help It '56
Artists and Models '55
Ralph Bakshi (1938-)
Fire and Ice '83
Hey Good Lookin' '82
Wizards '77
Streetfight '75
Heavy Traffic '73
Fritz the Cat '72
Alexei Balabanov
Of Freaks and Men '98
Brother '97
John Lloyd Balderston (1889-1954)
Red Planet Mars '52
Prisoner of Zenda '37
The Bride of Frankenstein '35
The Lives of a Bengal Lancer '35
Mad Love '35
The Mystery of Edwin Drood '35
The Mummy '32
Frankenstein '31
Earl Baldwin
The Go-Getter '54
Africa Screams '49
Doctor X '32

Peter Baloff
Near Misses '91
Quicksand: No Escape '91
Jack Baran
Great Balls of Fire '89
Band of the Hand '86
Neal Barbera
P.K. and the Kid '85
Too Scared to Scream '85
The Prowler '81
Malcolm Barbour
Deadly Sins '95
The P.O.W. Escape '86
Ann Louise Bardach
Backtrack '89
Sorry, Wrong Number '89
Frank Barhydt
Kansas City '95
Short Cuts '93
Quintet '79
Leora Barish
Venus Rising '95
Desperately Seeking Susan '85
Clive Barker (1952-)
Lord of Illusions '95
Nightbreed '90
Hellraiser '87
Rawhead Rex '87
Transmutations '85
Jeff Barmash
Bounty Hunters 2: Hardball '97
Power of Attorney '94
John Barmettler
Pure Danger '96
Riot '96
Joseph John Barmettler, Jr.
Timelock '99
Rage '95
Witchcraft 8: Salem's Ghost '95
Peter Barnes
Arabian Nights '00
Alice in Wonderland '99
A Christmas Carol '99
The Magical Legend of the Leprechauns '99
Noah's Ark '99
Voices from a Locked Room '95
Enchanted April '92
The Ruling Class '72
Douglas Barr (1949-)
Frame by Frame '95
Dead Badge '94
The Cover Girl Murders '93
Fade to Black '93
Jackson Barr
Body Chemistry 3: Point of Seduction '93
800 Leagues Down the Amazon '93
Mandroid '93
Bad Channels '92
Seedpeople '92
Body Chemistry 2: Voice of a Stranger '91
Body Chemistry '90
Bruno Barreto (1955-)
Gabriela '84
Dona Flor and Her Two Husbands '78
James Lee Barrett
Warden of Red Rock '01
Ruby Jean and Joe '96
Poker Alice '87
Angel City '80
Mayflower: The Pilgrims' Adventure '79
The Green Berets '68
The Greatest Story Ever Told '65
Shenandoah '65
H.E. Barrie
Missile to the Moon '59
She Demons '58
J.M. Barrie
Quality Street '37
As You Like It '36
Michael Barrie
Bad Boys '95
National Lampoon's Favorite Deadly Sins '95
Oscar '91

Amazon Women on the Moon '87
Ratings Game '84
Fred Barron
Something Short of Paradise '79
Between the Lines '77
Julian Barry
Me, Myself & I '92
The River '84
Lenny '74
Odile Barski
The Cry of the Owl '87
Violette '78
Paul Bartel (1938-2000)
Not for Publication '84
Eating Raoul '82
Cannonball '76
Paul Bartel's The Secret Cinema '69
Hall Bartlett (1922-93)
Children of Sanchez '79
All the Young Men '60
Sy Bartlett
Beloved Infidel '59
The Big Country '58
Twelve o'Clock High '49
13 Rue Madeleine '46
Hal Barwood
Warning Sign '85
Dragonslayer '81
Corvette Summer '78
MacArthur '77
Bingo Long Traveling All-Stars & Motor Kings '76
The Sugarland Express '74
Ben Barzman
The Blue Max '66
The Heroes of Telemark '65
Time Without Pity '57
The Lady in Question '40
Joel Basberg
Family of Cops 2: Breach of Faith '97
Family of Cops '95
Ron Base
Deadline '00
First Degree '95
Heavenly Bodies '84
Harry Basil
My 5 Wives '00
Meet Wally Sparks '97
Ronald Bass
Passion of Mind '00
Entrapment '99
Snow Falling on Cedars '99
How Stella Got Her Groove Back '98
Stepmom '98
What Dreams May Come '98
My Best Friend's Wedding '97
Dangerous Minds '95
Waiting to Exhale '95
The Enemy Within '94
When a Man Loves a Woman '94
The Joy Luck Club '93
Sleeping with the Enemy '91
Rain Man '88
Black Widow '87
Gardens of Stone '87
Code Name: Emerald '85
Lawrence Bassoff
Hunk '87
Weekend Pass '84
William Bast
The Betsy '78
James Dean '76
The Valley of Gwangi '69
Joe Batteer
Windtalkers '02
Blown Away '94
Chasers '94
Curiosity Kills '90
Bradley Battersby
Red Letters '00
Blue Desert '91
Lucio Battistrada
Autopsy '74
Commandos '73
Dead Are Alive '72
Autopsy of a Ghost '67

Hans Bauer
Komodo '99
Anaconda '96
Thomas Baum
Dracula: The Dark Prince '01
Journey to the Center of the Earth '99
Witness to the Execution '94
The Manhattan Project '86
The Sender '82
Carny '80
Simon '80
Hugo the Hippo '76
Noah Baumbach (1969-)
Mr. Jealousy '98
Kicking and Screaming '95
Lamberto Bava (1944-)
Demons 2 '87
Demons '86
Macabre '80
Shock '79
Mario Bava (1914-80)
Lisa and the Devil '75
Twitch of the Death Nerve '71
Hatchet for the Honeymoon '70
Danger: Diabolik '68
Kill, Baby, Kill '66
Knives of the Avenger '65
Planet of the Vampires '65
Black Sabbath '64
Blood and Black Lace '64
The Girl Who Knew Too Much '63
Black Sunday '60
George L. Baxt
Burn Witch, Burn! '62
Circus of Horrors '60
Horror Hotel '60
Sergio Bazzini
Husbands and Lovers '91
The Inheritance '76
Wayne Beach
The Art of War '00
Murder at 1600 '97
The Shadow Conspiracy '96
Peter S. Beagle
The Last Unicorn '82
The Lord of the Rings '78
The Dove '74
David Beaird (1952-)
Scorchers '92
My Chauffeur '86
Party Animal '83
Octavia '82
John Beaird
Happy Birthday to Me '81
My Bloody Valentine '81
Henry Bean
Desperate Measures '98
Deep Cover '92
Internal Affairs '90
Running Brave '83
Richard Beattie
Grizzly Falls '99
The Highway Man '99
Face the Evil '97
Cold Sweat '93
Prom Night 4: Deliver Us from Evil '91
Cold Comfort '90
Warren Beatty (1937-)
Bulworth '98
Love Affair '94
Reds '81
Heaven Can Wait '78
Shampoo '75
D.D. Beauchamp
Alias Jesse James '59
Tennessee's Partner '55
Ride Clear of Diablo '54
Abbott and Costello Go to Mars '53
Gunsmoke '53
Simon Beaufoy
Blow Dry '00
Among Giants '98
The Full Monty '96
Jerome Beaujour
Seventh Heaven '98
A Single Girl '96

Phil Beauman
Not Another Teen Movie '01
Don't Be a Menace to South Central While Drinking Your Juice in the Hood '95
Charles Beaumont
Brain Dead '89
Masque of the Red Death '65
The Haunted Palace '63
7 Faces of Dr. Lao '63
Burn Witch, Burn! '62
Premature Burial '62
Shame '61
Queen of Outer Space '58
Gorman Bechard (1959-)
Cemetery High '89
Disconnected '87
Jacques Becker (1906-60)
Le Trou '59
Modigliani '58
Ali Baba and the 40 Thieves '54
Grisbi '53
Casque d'Or '52
Rendez-vous de Juillet '49
Antoine et Antoinette '47
Josh Becker (1958-)
Lunatics: A Love Story '92
Thou Shalt Not Kill...Except '87
Barry Beckerman (1943-96)
St. Ives '76
Shamus '73
Michael Frost Beckner
Spy Game '01
Prince Valiant '97
Sniper '92
Dick Beebe
Book of Shadows: Blair Witch 2 '00
House on Haunted Hill '99
The Lazarus Man '96
Into the Badlands '92
Prison Stories: Women on the Inside '91
Ford Beebe (1888-1978)
Riders of Pasco Basin '40
Prescott Kid '36
Fighting Shadows '35
Marc Behm
Nana '82
Hospital Massacre '81
The Peking Blond '68
Help! '65
Harry Behn
Hell's Angels '30
The Big Parade '25
S.N. Behrman
Me and the Colonel '58
Waterloo Bridge '40
A Tale of Two Cities '36
Anna Karenina '35
Hallelujah, I'm a Bum '33
Jean-Jacques Beineix (1946-)
Betty Blue '86
Moon in the Gutter '83
Diva '82
Elisa Bell
Sex & Mrs. X '00
Vegas Vacation '96
Dancing with Danger '93
Treacherous Crossing '92
Writer's Block '91
Neal Bell
Two Small Bodies '93
Terminal Choice '85
James Warner Bellah
The Man Who Shot Liberty Valance '62
Sergeant Rutledge '60
Donald P. Bellisario
JAG '95
Last Rites '88
Magnum P.I.: Don't Eat the Snow in Hawaii '80

Marco Bellocchio (1939-)
Devil in the Flesh '87
Henry IV '85
The Eyes, the Mouth '83
Peter Bellwood
Highlander 2: The Quickening '91
Highlander '86
Phobia '80
Edmund Beloin
Paris Holiday '57
The Great Lover '49
My Favorite Brunette '47
Because of Him '45
Lady on a Train '45
Jerry Belson
Always '89
Surrender '87
Jekyll & Hyde...Together Again '82
Smokey and the Bandit 2 '80
The End '78
Fun with Dick and Jane '77
Smile '75
Evil Roy Slade '71
How Sweet It Is! '68
James Belushi (1954-)
Number One with a Bullet '87
Birthday Boy '85
Maria-Luisa Bemberg (1922-95)
I Don't Want to Talk About It '94
I, the Worst of All '90
Miss Mary '86
Peter Benchley (1940-)
The Island '80
The Deep '77
Jaws '75
Barbara Benedek
Sabrina '95
Immediate Family '89
Men Don't Leave '89
The Big Chill '83
Tom Benedek
The Adventures of Pinocchio '96
Zeus and Roxanne '96
Cocoon '85
Robert Benedetto
The Canterville Ghost '96
Aloha Summer '88
Roberto Benigni (1952-)
Life Is Beautiful '98
The Monster '96
Johnny Stecchino '92
Richard Benner (1943-90)
Happy Birthday, Gemini '80
Outrageous! '77
Alan Bennett
The Madness of King George '94
A Question of Attribution '91
Prick Up Your Ears '87
A Private Function '84
An Englishman Abroad '83
Bill Bennett (1953-)
In a Savage Land '99
Kiss or Kill '97
Backlash '86
Charles Bennett (1899-1995)
Five Weeks in a Balloon '62
Voyage to the Bottom of the Sea '61
Curse of the Demon '57
Dangerous Mission '54
The Green Glove '52
Black Magic '49
Unconquered '47
The Story of Dr. Wassell '44
Forever and a Day '43
Joan of Paris '42
Reap the Wild Wind '42
Foreign Correspondent '40
Balalaika '39
The Young in Heart '38
Young and Innocent '37
King of the Damned '36

Sabotage '36
The Secret Agent '36
The 39 Steps '35
The Evil Mind '34
The Man Who Knew Too Much '34
Blackmail '29

Harve Bennett
Star Trek 4: The Voyage Home '86
Star Trek 3: The Search for Spock '84

Parker Bennett
Super Mario Bros. '93
Mystery Date '91

Ronan Bennett
The Break '97
Face '97

Wallace C. Bennett
Rage of Honor '87
Silent Scream '80
George! '70

John Robert Bensink
Every Mother's Worst Fear '98
My Very Best Friend '96

Robby Benson (1956-)
Betrayal of the Dove '92
Modern Love '90
Die Laughing '80
One on One '77

Sally Benson
Come to the Stable '49
Conspirator '49
Anna and the King of Siam '46
Shadow of a Doubt '43

Robert Benton (1932-)
Twilight '98
Nobody's Fool '94
Nadine '87
Places in the Heart '84
Still of the Night '82
Kramer vs. Kramer '79
Superman: The Movie '78
The Late Show '77
Bad Company '72
Oh! Calcutta! '72
What's Up, Doc? '72
There Was a Crooked Man '70
Bonnie & Clyde '67

Leonardo Benvenuti (1923-2000)
The Worker and the Hairdresser '96
Ciao, Professore! '94
The Santa Clause '94
The Sleazy Uncle '89
Alfredo, Alfredo '72
Verdi '53

Luc Beraud
The Accompanist '93
This Sweet Sickness '77
The Best Way '76

Eric Bercovici
Change of Habit '69
Hell in the Pacific '69

Leonardo Bercovici
Portrait of Jennie '48
The Bishop's Wife '47

Luca Bercovici
The Granny '94
Rockula '90
Ghoulies '84

Bruce Beresford (1940-)
Paradise Road '97
Curse of the Starving Class '94
Mister Johnson '91
Aria '88
The Fringe Dwellers '86
Breaker Morant '80
Money Movers '78
Barry McKenzie Holds His Own '74

Pamela Berger
The Magic Stone '95
The Imported Bridegroom '89
Sorceress '88

Andrew Bergman (1945-)
Striptease '96
It Could Happen to You '94
The Scout '94
Honeymoon in Vegas '92
Soapdish '91
The Freshman '90
Big Trouble '86
Fletch '85
Oh, God! You Devil '84
So Fine '81
The In-Laws '79
Blazing Saddles '74

Ingmar Bergman (1918-)
Private Confessions '98
Sunday's Children '94
The Best Intentions '92
After the Rehearsal '84
Fanny and Alexander '83
From the Life of the Marionettes '80
Autumn Sonata '78
The Serpent's Egg '78
Face to Face '76
Scenes from a Marriage '73
Cries and Whispers '72
The Touch '71
The Passion of Anna '70
The Rite '69
Hour of the Wolf '68
The Shame '68
Persona '66
The Silence '63
The Winter Light '62
Through a Glass Darkly '61
The Devil's Eye '60
The Magician '58
Wild Strawberries '57
The Seventh Seal '56
Dreams '55
Smiles of a Summer Night '55
Lesson in Love '54
Sawdust & Tinsel '53
Monika '52
Secrets of Women '52
Summer Interlude '50
To Joy '50
Devil's Wanton '49
Torment '44

Linda J. Bergman
The Lookalike '90
Matters of the Heart '90

Martin Bergman
A Weekend in the Country '96
Peter's Friends '92

Robert Bergman
Skull: A Night of Terror '88
A Whisper to a Scream '88

Eric Bergren
The Dark Wind '91
Frances '82
The Elephant Man '80

Eleanor Bergstein
Dirty Dancing '87
It's My Turn '80

Martin Berkeley
The Deadly Mantis '57
Revenge of the Creature '55
Tarantula '55

Judd Bernard
Enter the Ninja '81
The Class of Miss MacMichael '78
The Destructors '74

Sam Bernard
Blood Surf '00
Diplomatic Siege '99
Payback '94
Warlock: The Armageddon '93
Rad '86
3:15—The Moment of Truth '86

Paul Bernbaum
Rent-A-Kid '95
Royce '93

Edward L. Bernds (1905-2000)
Return of the Fly '59
Reform School Girl '57
Storm Rider '57
Blondie Knows Best '46

Peter Berneis
My Man Godfrey '57
Portrait of Jennie '48

Kevin Bernhardt
Jill the Ripper '00
Diplomatic Siege '99
Sweepers '99
Turbulence 2: Fear of Flying '99
Natural Enemy '96
The Immortals '95

Armyan Bernstein
The Hurricane '99
Cross My Heart '88
Windy City '84
One from the Heart '82
Thank God It's Friday '78

Jon Bernstein
Max Keeble's Big Move '01
Beautiful '00
Ringmaster '98

Marcos Bernstein
Central Station '98
Foreign Land '95

Sarah Bernstein
Call Me Claus '01
Trial and Error '96

Walter Bernstein (1919-)
Durango '99
Miss Evers' Boys '97
Doomsday Gun '94
The House on Carroll Street '88
Little Miss Marker '80
An Almost Perfect Affair '79
Yanks '79
The Betsy '78
Semi-Tough '77
The Front '76
Molly Maguires '70
The Train '65
Fail-Safe '64
Paris Blues '61
Heller in Pink Tights '60

Eric Bernt
Romeo Must Die '00
Virtuosity '95
Surviving the Game '94

Claude Berri (1934-)
Lucie Aubrac '98
Germinal '93
Uranus '91
Jean de Florette '87
Manon of the Spring '87
One Wild Moment '78
The Two of Us '68

John Berry (1917-99)
Boesman & Lena '00
There Goes Barder '54

Michael Berry
Blue Streak '99
Short Time '90

Bernardo Bertolucci (1940-)
The Triumph of Love '01
Besieged '98
Stealing Beauty '96
The Sheltering Sky '90
The Last Emperor '87
The Tragedy of a Ridiculous Man '81
1900 '76
Last Tango in Paris '73
The Conformist '71
The Spider's Stratagem '70
Once Upon a Time in the West '68
Before the Revolution '65

Luc Besson (1959-)
Kiss of the Dragon '01
The Messenger: The Story of Joan of Arc '99
The Fifth Element '97
The Professional '94
La Femme Nikita '91
The Big Blue '88
Subway '85
Le Dernier Combat '84

Jonathan Betuel (1949-)
Theodore Rex '95
My Science Project '85
The Last Starfighter '84

Alberto Bevilacqua
Planet of the Vampires '65

Black Sabbath '64
Atom Age Vampire '61

Troy Beyer (1965-)
Let's Talk About Sex '98
B.A.P.'s '97

A.I. Bezzerides
Kiss Me Deadly '55
Beneath the 12-Mile Reef '53
Action in the North Atlantic '43

Ann Biderman
Primal Fear '96
Smilla's Sense of Snow '96
Copycat '95

Kathryn Bigelow (1952-)
Undertow '95
Blue Steel '90
Near Dark '87
Loveless '83

Danny Bilson
The Rocketeer '91
Arena '89
The Wrong Guys '88
The Eliminators '86
Trancers '84
Zone Troopers '84
Future Cop '76

John Binder
Endangered Species '82
Uforia '81
Honeysuckle Rose '80

Mike Binder
Indian Summer '93
Crossing the Bridge '92
Coupe de Ville '90

William Bindley
Judicial Consent '94
Freeze Frame '92

Steve Bing
Every Breath '93
Missing in Action 2: The Beginning '85

Claude Binyon
A Woman's World '54
Arizona '40

Andrew Birkin (1945-)
The Messenger: The Story of Joan of Arc '99
The Cement Garden '93
Burning Secret '89
The Name of the Rose '86
King David '85
Omen 3: The Final Conflict '81

Lajos Biro
The Thief of Bagdad '40
The Four Feathers '39
The Scarlet Pimpernel '34
The Private Life of Henry VIII '33

John Bishop
Drop Zone '94
The Package '89

Larry Bishop
Trigger Happy '96
Underworld '96

Wes Bishop (1933-93)
Dixie Dynamite '76
Black Gestapo '75
Race with the Devil '75

Shem Bitterman
Peephole '93
Out of the Rain '90
Halloween 5: The Revenge of Michael Myers '89

Emerson Bixby
Bikini Island '91
Disturbed '90

David Black
The Confession '98
Legacy of Lies '92

Shane Black
The Long Kiss Goodnight '96
Last Action Hero '93
The Last Boy Scout '91
Lethal Weapon '87
The Monster Squad '87

Stephen Black
Eden 2 '93
Eden '92

Richard Blackburn
Eating Raoul '82

Lemora, Lady Dracula '73

Kenneth G. Blackwell
Dark Tower '87
Triumphs of a Man Called Horse '83

Michael Blake
Dances with Wolves '90
Stacy's Knights '83

Michael Blankfort
Tribute to a Bad Man '56
The Caine Mutiny '54
The Halls of Montezuma '50

Vera Blasi
Tortilla Soup '01
Woman on Top '00

William Peter Blatty (1928-)
Exorcist 3: Legion '90
The Ninth Configuration '79
The Exorcist '73
Darling Lili '70
Promise Her Anything '66
What Did You Do in the War, Daddy? '66
A Shot in the Dark '64

Barry W. Blaustein
Nutty Professor 2: The Klumps '00
The Nutty Professor '96
Boomerang '92
Coming to America '88
Police Academy 2: Their First Assignment '85

Alan Bleasdale
Oliver Twist '00
No Surrender '86

Corey Blechman
Free Willy 2: The Adventure Home '95
Free Willy '93
Max and Helen '90
Dominick & Eugene '88

Robert Blees (1925-)
Doctor Phibes Rises Again '72
Frogs '72
Who Slew Auntie Roo? '71
From the Earth to the Moon '58
High School Confidential '58
The Black Scorpion '57
Autumn Leaves '56
Slightly Scarlet '56
Cattle Queen of Montana '54
Magnificent Obsession '54
All I Desire '53

Lee Blessing
Steal Big, Steal Little '95
Cooperstown '93

Bertrand Blier (1939-)
Mon Homme '96
Too Beautiful for You '88
Menage '86
My Best Friend's Girl '84
Beau Pere '81
Buffet Froid '79
Get Out Your Handkerchiefs '78
Going Places '74

William Blinn
Brian's Song '01
The Boys Next Door '96
Purple Rain '84
Roots '77
Brian's Song '71

Robert Bloch (1917-94)
Asylum '72
The House that Dripped Blood '71
Torture Garden '67
The Night Walker '64
Strait-Jacket '64

Michael Blodgett (1940-)
The White Raven '98
Run '91
Turner and Hooch '89
Hero and the Terror '88
Rent-A-Cop '88

Harold Jack Bloom (1925-99)
A Gunfight '71
Land of the Pharaohs '55

Jeffrey Bloom
Flowers in the Attic '87
Nightmares '83
Blood Beach '81
The Stick-Up '77
Swashbuckler '76
Dog Pound Shuffle '75
11 Harrowhouse '74

Steven L. Bloom
Jack Frost '98
Overnight Delivery '96
Tall Tale: The Unbelievable Adventures of Pecos Bill '95
Like Father, Like Son '87
The Sure Thing '85

Edwin Blum (1906-95)
Pearl of the South Pacific '55
Stalag 17 '53
Down to Earth '47
The Canterville Ghost '44
Young People '40
The Adventures of Sherlock Holmes '39

Len Blum
Private Parts '96
Beethoven's 2nd '93
Feds '88
Spacehunter: Adventures in the Forbidden Zone '83
Heavy Metal '81
Stripes '81
Meatballs '79

John Blumenthal
Blue Streak '99
Short Time '90

Don Bluth (1938-)
Thumbelina '94
All Dogs Go to Heaven '89
The Secret of NIMH '82

Jeffrey Boam (1949-2000)
The Phantom '96
Lethal Weapon 3 '92
Indiana Jones and the Last Crusade '89
Lethal Weapon 2 '89
Funny Farm '88
Innerspace '87
The Lost Boys '87
Dead Zone '83
Straight Time '78

Paul Harris Boardman
Hellraiser 5: Inferno '00
Urban Legends 2: Final Cut '00

Al Boasberg (1892-)
A Night at the Opera '35
Freaks '32
Battling Butler '26
The General '26

Sam Bobrick
Jimmy the Kid '82
Norman, Is That You? '76

Steven Bochco
Columbo: Murder by the Book '71
Silent Running '71

DeWitt Bodeen
Mrs. Mike '49
I Remember Mama '48
Cat People '42

Sergei Bodrov (1948-)
East-West '99
Prisoner of the Mountains '96
Somebody to Love '94

Sydney Boehm
Rough Night in Jericho '67
The Big Heat '53
When Worlds Collide '51

Peter Bogdanovich (1939-)
Texasville '90
They All Laughed '81
Saint Jack '79
The Last Picture Show '71
Targets '68
The Wild Angels '66

Eric Bogosian (1953-)
subUrbia '96
Sex, Drugs, Rock & Roll: Eric Bogosian '91
Talk Radio '88

Cobra Woman '44
Larry Brothers
Two for Texas '97
Fever '91
An Innocent Man '89
Bruce Brown
The Endless Summer 2 '94
The Endless Summer '66
Harry Brown
Ocean's 11 '60
All the Brothers Were Valiant '53
A Place in the Sun '51
Sands of Iwo Jima '49
Arch of Triumph '48
A Walk in the Sun '46
Jamie Brown
The Brylcreem Boys '96
Toby McTeague '87
Julie Brown (1958-)
National Lampoon's Attack of the 5 Ft. 2 Women '94
Earth Girls Are Easy '89
Leigh Brown
My Summer Story '94
A Christmas Story '83
Mark Brown
Two Can Play That Game '01
Jackie's Back '99
Def Jam's How to Be a Player '97
Michael Henry Brown
In Too Deep '99
Dead Presidents '95
Laurel Avenue '93
Janet Brownell
The Amy Fisher Story '93
Christmas in Connecticut '92
Sweet Revenge '90
Michael Browning
Bad Company '02
Six Days, Seven Nights '98
Rod Browning
Cruel and Unusual '01
Oh, Heavenly Dog! '80
Tod Browning (1882-1962)
Devil Doll '36
Mark of the Vampire '35
Intolerance '16
John Brownjohn
The Ninth Gate '99
Bitter Moon '92
William Broyles, Jr. (1944-)
Unfaithful '02
Planet of the Apes '01
Cast Away '00
Entrapment '99
Apollo 13 '95
JFK: Reckless Youth '93
George Bruce
Two Years before the Mast '46
The Corsican Brothers '42
A Gentleman After Dark '42
The Son of Monte Cristo '40
The Man in the Iron Mask '39
The Duke of West Point '38
Navy Blue and Gold '37
Glenn A. Bruce
Undercover Cop '94
Cyborg Cop '93
Kickboxer '89
Clyde Bruckman (1894-1955)
The General '26
Seven Chances '25
The Navigator '24
Our Hospitality '23
Claude Brule
Barbarella '68
Blood and Roses '61
Please Not Now! '61
James Bruner
Braddock: Missing in Action 3 '88
Delta Force '86
The P.O.W. Escape '86
Invasion U.S.A. '85
Missing in Action '84

An Eye for an Eye '81
Bob Brunner
The Other Sister '98
Exit to Eden '94
Franco Brusati (1922-93)
The Sleazy Uncle '89
Bread and Chocolate '73
Romeo and Juliet '68
The Unfaithfuls '60
Peter Bryan
A Challenge for Robin Hood '68
Blood Beast Terror '67
Plague of the Zombies '66
The Brides of Dracula '60
The Hound of the Baskervilles '59
Chris Bryant
Miracle at Midnight '98
Foreign Affairs '93
One Against the Wind '91
Young Catherine '91
Stealing Heaven '88
Sword of Gideon '86
Martin's Day '85
The Awakening '80
Joseph Andrews '77
Spiral Staircase '75
The Girl from Petrovka '74
Don't Look Now '73
Man Who Had Power Over Women '70
John Bryant (1916-89)
Scanner Cop '94
Mission of Justice '92
Bill Bryden
Aria '88
The Long Riders '80
James David Buchanan
Deadly Currents '93
Brenda Starr '86
Larry Buchanan (1923-)
Mistress of the Apes '79
It's Alive! '68
Mars Needs Women '66
Zontar, the Thing from Venus '66
The Naked Witch '64
Harold Buchman
On the Fiddle '61
The Sleeping Tiger '54
Boots Malone '52
Sidney Buchman
The Mark '61
Here Comes Mr. Jordan '41
Mr. Smith Goes to Washington '39
Holiday '38
Theodora Goes Wild '36
The Sign of the Cross '33
Andrea Buck
Born Wild '95
The Double O Kid '92
Robert Buckner
Love Me Tender '56
Yankee Doodle Dandy '42
Dive Bomber '41
Santa Fe Trail '40
Jezebel '38
Albert (Don) Buday (1939-2001)
KISS Meets the Phantom of the Park '78
Too Hot to Handle '76
Adele Buffington
Bad Men of the Border '45
Haunted Gold '32
Takashi Bufford
The Tiger Woods Story '98
Booty Call '96
Set It Off '96
House Party 3 '94
Ray Buffum
The Brain from Planet Arous '57
Teenage Monster '57
Jeff Buhai
Eddie '96
Johnny Be Good '88
Jocks '87
Last Resort '86
The Whoopee Boys '86
Revenge of the Nerds '84

Edward (Eddie) Bunker
Animal Factory '00
Runaway Train '85
Straight Time '78
Luis Bunuel (1900-83)
That Obscure Object of Desire '77
Phantom of Liberty '74
The Discreet Charm of the Bourgeoisie '72
Tristana '70
Belle de Jour '67
Simon of the Desert '66
Diary of a Chambermaid '64
The Exterminating Angel '62
Viridiana '61
The Young One '61
Death in the Garden '56
The Criminal Life of Archibaldo de la Cruz '55
El '52
L'Age D'Or '30
Un Chien Andalou '28
Betty Burbridge (1895-1987)
Where the North Begins '47
Come on, Cowboys '37
Andy Burg
Trojan War '97
Alaska '96
Robert Burge
The Dark Dancer '95
Vasectomy: A Delicate Matter '86
Anthony Burgess (1917-93)
A.D. '85
Cyrano de Bergerac '85
Moses '76
Martyn Burke
Animal Farm '99
The Pirates of Silicon Valley '99
The Pentagon Wars '98
The Second Civil War '97
Sugartime '95
Top Secret! '84
Last Chase '81
Power Play '81
Alan Burnett
Batman: Mask of the Phantasm '93
DuckTales the Movie: Treasure of the Lost Lamp '90
Allison Burnett
Autumn in New York '00
Bloodfist 3: Forced to Fight '92
Charles Burnett (1944-)
The Glass Shield '95
To Sleep with Anger '90
W.R. Burnett
The Great Escape '63
I Died a Thousand Times '55
Dangerous Mission '54
Action in the North Atlantic '43
This Gun for Hire '42
Wake Island '42
High Sierra '41
Allan Burns
Just Between Friends '86
Just the Way You Are '84
Butch and Sundance: The Early Days '79
A Little Romance '79
Edward Burns (1968-)
Sidewalks of New York '01
No Looking Back '98
She's the One '96
The Brothers McMullen '94
Mark Burns (1936-)
She-Devil '89
Married to the Mob '88
Tim Burns
Jacob Two Two Meets the Hooded Fang '99
An American Werewolf in Paris '97
Freaked '93
Jim Burnstein
D3: The Mighty Ducks '96

Renaissance Man '94
Richard Burridge
The Fourth Protocol '87
Absolute Beginners '86
Abe Burrows
How to Succeed in Business without Really Trying '67
Solid Gold Cadillac '56
Tim Burstall (1929-)
Alvin Rides Again '74
Alvin Purple '73
Michael Burton
Aldrich Ames: Traitor Within '98
Shoot to Kill '88
Flight of the Navigator '86
Tim Burton (1960-)
The Nightmare before Christmas '93
Edward Scissorhands '90
Frankenweenie '84
Scott Busby
Texas Rangers '01
The Escape '95
Niven Busch
The Westerner '40
Scarlet Dawn '32
John Bushelman
The Iron Triangle '89
Violent Zone '89
David Butler
Mountbatten: The Last Viceroy '86
Disraeli '79
Voyage of the Damned '76
Frank Butler (1890-1967)
The Road to Bali '53
Golden Earrings '47
Going My Way '44
China '43
My Favorite Blonde '42
The Road to Morocco '42
Wake Island '42
The Road to Zanzibar '41
The Road to Singapore '40
Never Say Die '39
Give Me a Sailor '38
Waikiki Wedding '37
The Princess Comes Across '36
Strike Me Pink '36
March of the Wooden Soldiers '34
Hugo Butler
A Face in the Rain '63
Eva '62
The Young One '61
Autumn Leaves '56
Torero '56
Prowler '51
The Southerner '45
Young Tom Edison '40
Michael Butler
Execution of Justice '99
Pronto '97
White Mile '94
Code of Silence '85
Pale Rider '85
Flashpoint '84
Murder by Phone '82
The Car '77
The Gauntlet '77
Brannigan '75
The Don Is Dead '73
Floyd Byars
Masterminds '96
Mindwalk: A Film for Passionate Thinkers '91
Making Mr. Right '86
Jim Byrnes (1948-)
Dead Man's Revenge '93
Miracle in the Wilderness '91
The Shadow Riders '82
John Byrum (1947-)
Duets '00
The Razor's Edge '84
Scandalous '84
Sphinx '81
Heart Beat '80
Valentino '77
Harry & Walter Go to New York '76
Inserts '76
Mahogany '75

Reggie Rock Bythewood
Dancing in September '00
Get On the Bus '96
Michael Cacoyannis (1927-)
Iphigenia '77
A Matter of Dignity '57
Girl in Black '56
Stella '55
Jerome Cady
Call Northside 777 '48
A Wing and a Prayer '44
Guadalcanal Diary '43
Alan Caillou
Kingdom of the Spiders '77
Clarence, the Cross-eyed Lion '65
Village of the Giants '65
Joseph M. Cala
Avenging Angel '85
Angel '84
Dayton Callie
Executive Target '97
The Last Days of Frankie the Fly '96
Paul Callisi
Josh Kirby...Time Warrior: Chapter 1, Planet of the Dino-Knights '95
Josh Kirby...Time Warrior: Chapter 2, The Human Pets '95
James Cameron (1954-)
Titanic '97
Strange Days '95
True Lies '94
Terminator 2: Judgment Day '91
The Abyss '89
Aliens '86
Rambo: First Blood, Part 2 '85
The Terminator '84
Ken Cameron
Fast Talking '86
Monkey Grip '82
Lorne Cameron
Deadly Game '98
The Extreme Adventures of Super Dave '98
Clarence '91
Like Father, Like Son '87
China Cammell
Wild Side '95
White of the Eye '88
Donald Cammell (1939-96)
Wild Side '95
White of the Eye '88
Tilt '78
Performance '70
Joe Camp (1939-)
Benji the Hunted '87
Oh, Heavenly Dog! '80
For the Love of Benji '77
Benji '74
Robert W(right) Campbell (1927-2000)
Hell's Angels on Wheels '67
Masque of the Red Death '65
Machine Gun Kelly '58
Teenage Caveman '58
Anna Campion
Holy Smoke '99
Loaded '94
Jane Campion (1954-)
Holy Smoke '99
The Piano '93
Sweetie '89
John Camps
The Borrowers '97
Mighty Morphin Power Rangers: The Movie '95
Christopher Canaan
The Apocalypse Watch '97
The Great Elephant Escape '95
The Ten Million Dollar Getaway '91
Cuca Canals
The Chambermaid on the Titanic '97

Jamon, Jamon '93
Leon Capetanos
Fletch Lives '89
Moon over Parador '88
Down and Out in Beverly Hills '86
Moscow on the Hudson '84
The Tempest '82
Greased Lightning '77
Gumball Rally '76
Truman Capote
ABC Stage 67: Truman Capote's A Christmas Memory '66
The Innocents '61
Indiscretion of an American Wife '54
Beat the Devil '53
Frank Cappello
No Way Back '96
Suburban Commando '91
James (Jim) Carabatsos
Lost Battalion '01
Hamburger Hill '87
Heartbreak Ridge '86
No Mercy '86
Underground Aces '80
Heroes '77
Steven W. Carabatsos
Hot Pursuit '87
The Last Flight of Noah's Ark '80
Tentacles '77
El Condor '70
Leos Carax (1960-)
Pola X '99
The Lovers on the Bridge '91
Mauvais Sang '86
Boy Meets Girl '84
J.S. Cardone
The Forsaken '01
True Blue '01
Outside Ozona '98
Black Day Blue Night '95
Shadowhunter '93
A Climate for Killing '91
Crash and Burn '90
Shadowzone '89
Thunder Alley '85
The Slayer '82
Mark Patrick Carducci (1955-97)
Buried Alive '90
Pumpkinhead '88
Topper Carew
Talkin' Dirty after Dark '91
D.C. Cab '84
Peter Carey
Until the End of the World '91
Bliss '85
Carlo Carlei (1960-)
Fluke '95
Flight of the Innocent '93
Lewis John Carlino (1932-)
Haunted Summer '88
The Great Santini '80
Resurrection '80
I Never Promised You a Rose Garden '77
The Sailor Who Fell from Grace with the Sea '76
The Mechanic '72
A Reflection of Fear '72
The Brotherhood '68
Seconds '66
Roy Carlson
China Moon '91
Stand Alone '85
Charles Robert Carner
Crossfire Trail '01
Echo of Murder '00
The Fixer '97
Blind Fury '90
Let's Get Harry '87
Gymkata '85
Marc Caro
The City of Lost Children '95
Delicatessen '92

Glenn Gordon Caron (1954-)
Picture Perfect '96
Moonlighting '85
Condorman '81

A.J. Carothers
The Secret of My Success '87
Hero at Large '80
Never a Dull Moment '68
The Happiest Millionaire '67
Emil and the Detectives '64
The Miracle of the White Stallions '63

John Carpenter (1948-)
John Carpenter's Ghosts of Mars '01
Silent Predators '99
John Carpenter's Vampires '97
Escape from L.A. '96
Village of the Damned '95
El Diablo '90
They Live '88
Prince of Darkness '87
Black Moon Rising '86
Escape from New York '81
Halloween 2: The Nightmare Isn't Over! '81
Eyes of Laura Mars '78
The Fog '78
Halloween '78
Assault on Precinct 13 '76
Dark Star '74

Richard Carpenter
The Scarlet Pimpernel '99
The Scarlet Pimpernel 2: Mademoiselle Guillotine '99
The Scarlet Pimpernel 3: The Kidnapped King '99
The Return of the Borrowers '96
The Borrowers '93

Stephen Carpenter
Blue Streak '99
Servants of Twilight '91
The Kindred '87
Dorm That Dripped Blood '82
The Power '80

Tito Carpi
Tentacles '77
Cold Eyes of Fear '70

Allan Carr (1937-99)
Can't Stop the Music '80
Grease '78

Benjamin Carr
Retro Puppet Master '99
Curse of the Puppet Master: The Human Experiment '98
Talisman '98
The Creeps '97
Hideous '97
Shrieker '97
Head of the Family '96
Zarkorr! The Invader '96

Richard Carr
Americana '81
Hell Is for Heroes '62

Michael Carreras (1927-94)
Creatures the World Forgot '70
Unholy Four '54

Jean-Claude Carriere
Chinese Box '97
The Ogre '96
The Horseman on the Roof '95
Circle of Deceit '94
The Night and the Moment '94
At Play in the Fields of the Lord '91
Cyrano de Bergerac '90
May Fools '90
The Mahabharata '89
Valmont '89
The Possessed '88
The Unbearable Lightness of Being '88
Max, Mon Amour '86
Swann in Love '84
The Return of Martin Guerre '83
Danton '82
The Associate '79
The Tin Drum '79
That Obscure Object of Desire '77
Phantom of Liberty '74
The Discreet Charm of the Bourgeoisie '72
Borsalino '70
The Milky Way '68
Belle de Jour '67
Attack of the Robots '66
Hotel Paradiso '66
The Diabolical Dr. Z '65
Viva Maria! '65
Diary of a Chambermaid '64

James Carrington
Fluke '95
Joseph '95

Robert B. Carrington
Venom '82
Wait until Dark '67

Sidney Carroll
The Man Without a Country '73
Three Cases of Murder '55

Willard Carroll
Playing by Heart '98
The Runestone '91

L.M. Kit Carson (1947-)
Perfume '01
The Texas Chainsaw Massacre 2 '86
Chinese Boxes '84
Breathless '83
Paris, Texas '83
The Last Word '80
David Holzman's Diary '67

Robert Carson
Just for You '52
The Desperadoes '43
Beau Geste '39

William Carson
Judgment Day '99
Militia '99

Carroll Cartwright
Dungeons and Dragons '00
Where the Money Is '00

Dee Caruso
Doin' Time '85
The World's Greatest Athlete '73
Which Way to the Front? '70

Richard Casey
Hellbent '90
Horror House on Highway 5 '86

Jim Cash (1940-2000)
The Flintstones in Viva Rock Vegas '00
Anaconda '96
Dick Tracy '90
Turner and Hooch '89
The Secret of My Success '87
Legal Eagles '86
Top Gun '86

John Cassavetes (1929-89)
She's So Lovely '97
Opening Night '77
The Killing of a Chinese Bookie '76
A Woman under the Influence '74
Minnie and Moskowitz '71
Husbands '70
Faces '68

Nick Cassavetes (1959-)
Blow '01
Unhook the Stars '96

Nick Castle (1947-)
Hook '91
Tap '89
The Boy Who Could Fly '86
Tag: The Assassination Game '82
Escape from New York '81
Pray TV '80

Robert Caswell
A Far Off Place '93
Over the Hill '93
The Doctor '91
A Cry in the Dark '88

Jean Cau
Don Juan (Or If Don Juan Were a Woman) '73
Borsalino '70

Liliana Cavani (1937-)
Francesco '93
The Night Porter '74

Vincenzo Cerami
Life Is Beautiful '98
The Monster '96
Johnny Stecchino '92

Ginny Cerrella
Tainted Blood '93
Sister, Sister '87

Claude Chabrol (1930-)
The Swindle '97
La Ceremonie '95
L'Enfer '93
Betty '92
Madame Bovary '91
The Story of Women '88
The Cry of the Owl '87
Blood Relatives '77
Innocents with Dirty Hands '75
Wedding in Blood '74
La Rupture '70
Le Boucher '69
Les Biches '68
Six in Paris '68
The Cousins '59
Le Beau Serge '58

Gurinder Chadha
What's Cooking? '00
Bhaji on the Beach '94

Youssef Chahine
Alexandria Again and Forever '90
An Egyptian Story '82
Alexandria...Why? '78

Ilene Chaiken
Dirty Pictures '00
Barb Wire '96

Kitty Chalmers
Deceit '93
Cyborg '89
Journey to the Center of the Earth '88

Terry Chambers
The Dark Dancer '95
Breaker! Breaker! '77

Gordon Chan (1960-)
The Bodyguard from Beijing '94
Dragons Forever '88

Jackie Chan (1954-)
Jackie Chan's Who Am I '98
Operation Condor '91
Miracles '89
Project A: Part 2 '87
Operation Condor 2: The Armour of the Gods '86
Project A '83

Susan Chan
Tokyo Raiders '00
Jackie Chan's Who Am I '98
The Executioners '93

Harry Chandlee
The Adventures of Mark Twain '44
Our Town '40

Elizabeth Chandler
Someone Like You '01
A Little Princess '95
Afterburn '92

Raymond Chandler
Strangers on a Train '51
The Blue Dahlia '46
Double Indemnity '44

Tom Chaney
Mosquito '95
Frostbiter: Wrath of the Wendigo '94

Charlie Chaplin (1889-1977)
A Countess from Hong Kong '67
A King in New York '57
Limelight '52
Monsieur Verdoux '47
The Great Dictator '40
Modern Times '36
City Lights '31
The Gold Rush '25
The Kid '21
The Circus '19
Three Charlies and One Phoney! '18
The Immigrant '17
Burlesque on Carmen '16
Charlie Chaplin: Night at the Show '15

Graham Chapman (1941-89)
Monty Python's The Meaning of Life '83
Yellowbeard '83
Monty Python's Life of Brian '79
Monty Python and the Holy Grail '75
And Now for Something Completely Different '72
Rentadick '72
The Magic Christian '69

Leigh Chapman
Impulse '90
Storm and Sorrow '90
Octagon '80
Steel '80
Dirty Mary Crazy Larry '74
Truck Turner '74
How Come Nobody's On Our Side? '73
A Swingin' Summer '65

Matthew Chapman (1950-)
What's the Worst That Could Happen? '01
Color of Night '94
Consenting Adults '92
Heart of Midnight '89
Slow Burn '86
Strangers Kiss '83
Hussy '80

Robin Chapman
Force 10 from Navarone '78
Triple Echo '77

Borden Chase
Lone Star '52
The World in His Arms '52
Red River '48
Fighting Seabees '44

Peter Chase
Fast Sofa '01
Portraits Chinois '96

David Chaskin
Midnight's Child '93
I, Madman '89
The Curse '87
A Nightmare on Elm Street 2: Freddy's Revenge '85

Etienne Chatiliez (1952-)
Tatie Danielle '91
Life Is a Long Quiet River '88

Paddy Chayefsky
Altered States '80
Network '76
The Hospital '71
Paint Your Wagon '69
The Americanization of Emily '64
The Goddess '58
Marty '55
As Young As You Feel '51

Semi Chellas
The Life Before This '99
Restless Spirits '99

Peter Chelsom (1956-)
Funny Bones '94
Hear My Song '91

Patrice Chereau (1944-)
Those Who Love Me Can Take the Train '98
Queen Margot '94

Cy Chermack (1929-)
Rescuers: Stories of Courage—Two Couples '98
The 4D Man '59

John R. Cherry, III
Ernest Goes to Africa '97
Slam Dunk Ernest '95
Ernest Rides Again '93
Ernest Scared Stupid '91
Ernest Goes to Camp '87

Hal E. Chester
Curse of the Demon '57
Crashout '55

Lionel Chetwynd
Varian's War '01
P.T. Barnum '99
Tom Clancy's Netforce '98
Color of Justice '97
Kissinger and Nixon '96
The Man Who Captured Eichmann '96
Moses '96
Joseph '95
Doomsday Gun '94
Jacob '94
The Heroes of Desert Storm '91
To Heal a Nation '88
Hanoi Hilton '87
Quintet '79
The Apprenticeship of Duddy Kravitz '74

David Chisholm
Kidnapped in Paradise '98
The Three Lives of Karen '97
Dead Man's Revenge '93
The Wizard '89

Edward Chodorov
The Hucksters '47
Undercurrent '46

Jerome Chodorov
The Tunnel of Love '58
All Over Town '37

Thomas Chong (1938-)
Far Out Man '89
Cheech and Chong's The Corsican Brothers '84
Cheech and Chong: Still Smokin' '83
Cheech and Chong: Things Are Tough All Over '82
Cheech and Chong's Nice Dreams '81
Cheech and Chong's Next Movie '80
Cheech and Chong's Up in Smoke '79

Tien-wen Chu
Flowers of Shanghai '98
Goodbye South, Goodbye '96

Gerard Ciccoritti
Skull: A Night of Terror '88
A Whisper to a Scream '88
Psycho Girls '86

Cynthia Cidre
The Mambo Kings '92
Fires Within '91
In Country '89

Santo Cilauro
The Dish '00
The Castle '97

Matt Cimber
Yellow Hair & the Fortress of Gold '84
Butterfly '82

Michael Cimino (1943-)
Year of the Dragon '85
Heaven's Gate '81
The Deer Hunter '78
Thunderbolt & Lightfoot '74
Magnum Force '73
Silent Running '71

Tony Cinciripini
Hell's Kitchen NYC '97
Confessions of a Hit Man '94
The Lawless Land '88

Patrick Cirillo
The Surgeon '94
Dangerous Heart '93
Homer and Eddie '89

Louis CK (1967-)
Down to Earth '01
Pootie Tang '01

Rene Clair (1898-1981)
Les Grandes Manoeuvres '55
Beauties of the Night '52
Beauty and the Devil '50
And Then There Were None '45
It Happened Tomorrow '44
A Nous la Liberte '31
Under the Roofs of Paris '29

Bob (Benjamin) Clark (1941-)
Baby Geniuses '98
My Summer Story '94
Loose Cannons '90
From the Hip '86
A Christmas Story '83
Porky's 2: The Next Day '83
Porky's '82
Children Shouldn't Play with Dead Things '72

Bruce (B.D.) Clark (1945-)
Galaxy of Terror '81
The Naked Angels '69

Dennis Lynton Clark
In Pursuit of Honor '95
The Court Martial of Jackie Robinson '90
The Keep '83
Comes a Horseman '78

Greydon Clark (1943-)
Dance Macabre '91
Skinheads: The Second Coming of Hate '88
Final Justice '84
Angel's Brigade '79
Satan's Cheerleaders '77
Psychic Killer '75

Richard Clark
Double Play '96
The Halfback of Notre Dame '96

Ron Clark
The Funny Farm '82
Revenge of the Pink Panther '78
High Anxiety '77
Norman, Is That You? '76
Silent Movie '76

Arthur C. Clarke
2010: The Year We Make Contact '84
2001: A Space Odyssey '68

Frank Clarke
Wonderland '88
Letter to Brezhnev '86

John Clarke
Lust and Revenge '95
Lonely Hearts '82

Roy Clarke
A Foreign Field '93
Pictures '80s
Hawks '89

T.E.B. Clarke (1907-89)
Who Done It? '56
The Lavender Hill Mob '51
Dead of Night '45

James Clavell (1925-94)
The Last Valley '71
To Sir, with Love '67
King Rat '65
633 Squadron '64
The Great Escape '63
The Fly '58

Christian Clavier
Just Visiting '01
The Visitors '95

Thomas McKelvey Cleaver
Field of Fire '92
Raiders of the Sun '92
Immortal Sins '91
Heroes Stand Alone '89
The Terror Within '88

John Cleese (1939-)
Fierce Creatures '96
A Fish Called Wanda '88
Monty Python's The Meaning of Life '83
Monty Python's Life of Brian '79
Monty Python and the Holy Grail '75
And Now for Something Completely Different '72
Rentadick '72
The Magic Christian '69

Brian Clemens
The Watcher in the Woods '81
Captain Kronos: Vampire Hunter '74
Death in Deep Water '74
Golden Voyage of Sinbad '73
Dr. Jekyll and Sister Hyde '71
See No Evil '71
And Soon the Darkness '70
The Corrupt Ones '67
The Tell-Tale Heart '62

Dick Clement (1937-)
Still Crazy '98
Excess Baggage '96
The Commitments '91
Vice Versa '88
Water '85
Prisoner of Zenda '79
Catch Me a Spy '71

Rene Clement (1913-96)
Joy House '64
Purple Noon '60
Forbidden Games '52

Ron Clements (1953-)
Hercules '97
Aladdin '92
The Little Mermaid '89
The Great Mouse Detective '86

Elmer Clifton (1892-1949)
Youth Aflame '59
Lightning Raiders '45
Marked for Murder '45
Boss of Rawhide '44
Captain America '44
Gangsters of the Frontier '44
Guns of the Law '44
Frontier Law '43

Harry Clork
Ma and Pa Kettle at Waikiki '55
Broadway Rhythm '44
Ship Ahoy '42

Robert Clouse (1929-97)
China O'Brien '88
Force: Five '81
The Big Brawl '80
The Amsterdam Kill '78
The Pack '77
The Ultimate Warrior '75

Henri-Georges Clouzot (1907-77)
L'Enfer '93
Diabolique '55
Wages of Fear '55

Craig Clyde
Walking Thunder '94
The Legend of Wolf Mountain '92
Little Heroes '91

Lewis (Luigi Cozzi) Coates (1947-)
Black Cat '90
Hercules '83
Alien Contamination '81
Star Crash '78

Stacy Cochran
Boys '95
My New Gun '92

Jay Cocks
Strange Days '95
The Age of Innocence '93

Jean Cocteau (1889-1963)
The Testament of Orpheus '59
Les Enfants Terrible '50
Orpheus '49
The Eagle Has Two Heads '48
Ruyblas '48
The Storm Within '48
Beauty and the Beast '46
The Ladies of the Bois de Bologne '44
Eternal Return '43
The Blood of a Poet '30

Ethan Coen (1957-)
The Man Who Wasn't There '01
O Brother Where Art Thou? '00
The Naked Man '98
The Big Lebowski '97
Fargo '96
The Hudsucker Proxy '93
Barton Fink '91
Miller's Crossing '90
Raising Arizona '87
Blood Simple '85
Crimewave '85

Franklin Coen
Alvarez Kelly '66
The Train '65

Joel Coen (1954-)
The Man Who Wasn't There '01
O Brother Where Art Thou? '00
The Big Lebowski '97
Fargo '96
The Hudsucker Proxy '93
Barton Fink '91
Miller's Crossing '90
Raising Arizona '87
Blood Simple '85
Crimewave '85

Lenore Coffee
Cash McCall '60
End of the Affair '55
Sudden Fear '52
My Son, My Son '40
Evelyn Prentice '34

Charlie Coffey
National Lampoon's Attack of the 5 Ft. 2 Women '94
Earth Girls Are Easy '89

Barney Cohen
Sabrina the Teenage Witch '96
Next Door '94
Killer Party '86
Friday the 13th, Part 4: The Final Chapter '84

Bennett Cohen
Chameleon 2: Death Match '99
The Hunted '98
Rainbow Drive '90
Sagebrush Law '43
Melody of the Plains '37
Come on Danger! '32

Charles Cohen
The Gambler '97
Beyond Forgiveness '94

Charles Zev Cohen
Eddie and the Cruisers 2: Eddie Lives! '89
Lady Beware '87

David Aaron Cohen
The Devil's Own '96
V.I. Warshawski '91

David M. Cohen
Hollywood Zap '86
Friday the 13th, Part 5: A New Beginning '85

Howard R. Cohen (1942-99)
Barbarian Queen 2: The Empress Strikes Back '89
Deathstalker 3 '89
Lords of the Deep '89
Saturday the 14th Strikes Back '88
Time Trackers '88
Barbarian Queen '85
Deathstalker '83
Space Raiders '83
Stryker '83
Saturday the 14th '81
The Young Nurses '73

Joel Cohen
Goodbye, Lover '99
Money Talks '97
Toy Story '95
Pass the Ammo '88
Sister, Sister '87

Larry Cohen (1947-)
Misbegotten '98
The Ex '96
Invasion of Privacy '96
Uncle Sam '96
As Good as Dead '95
Guilty as Sin '93
Maniac Cop 3: Badge of Silence '93
The Ambulance '90
Maniac Cop 2 '90
Wicked Stepmother '89
Maniac Cop '88
Best Seller '87
Deadly Illusion '87
It's Alive 3: Island of the Alive '87
Return to Salem's Lot '87
Into Thin Air '85
Special Effects '85
The Stuff '85
Perfect Strangers '84
Scandalous '84
I, the Jury '82
Q (The Winged Serpent) '82
It's Alive 2: It Lives Again '78
The Private Files of J. Edgar Hoover '77
God Told Me To '76
It's Alive '74
Black Caesar '73
Hell Up in Harlem '73
Housewife '72
El Condor '70
Daddy's Gone A-Hunting '69
Return of the Magnificent Seven '66

Lawrence D. Cohen
Rodgers & Hammerstein's South Pacific '01
Stephen King's The Tommyknockers '93
Ghost Story '81
Carrie '76

Lawrence J. Cohen
Delirious '91
The Big Bus '76
S*P*Y*S '74
Start the Revolution without Me '70

Martin B. Cohen
Humanoids from the Deep '80
Rebel Rousers '69

Neil Cohen
The Disappearance of Garcia Lorca '96
Pass the Ammo '88

Rob Cohen (1949-)
Dragon: The Bruce Lee Story '93
Scandalous '84

Ronald M. Cohen (1939-98)
Last Stand at Saber River '96
Twilight's Last Gleaming '77
The Good Guys and the Bad Guys '69
Blue '68

Art Cohn
The Seven Hills of Rome '58
Men of the Fighting Lady '54
The Set-Up '49

Brandon Cole
Illuminata '98
Mac '93
Sons '91

Lester Cole
Born Free '66
Blood on the Sun '45
Objective, Burma! '45
Footsteps in the Dark '41
The Invisible Man Returns '40

Tom Cole
High Stakes '93
Streets of Gold '86
Smooth Talk '85

Lewis Colick
Domestic Disturbance '01
October Sky '99
Bulletproof '96
Ghosts of Mississippi '96
Judgment Night '93
Unlawful Entry '92
Dirt Bike Kid '86

Michael Colleary
Face/Off '97
Darkman 3: Die Darkman Die '95

Peter Colley
Illusions '91
Mark of Cain '84

Boon Collins
Abducted 2: The Reunion '94
Spirit of the Eagle '90

Jackie Collins (1941-)
The World Is Full of Married Men '80
Yesterday's Hero '79
The Stud '78

Max Allan Collins
Mommy 2: Mommy's Day '96
The Expert '95
Mommy '95

Harry Colomby
Touch and Go '86
Johnny Dangerously '84

Carl Colpaert
Facade '98
The Crew '95
Delusion '91

John Colton
The Invisible Ray '36
Werewolf of London '35

Chris Columbus (1958-)
Nine Months '95
Little Nemo: Adventures in Slumberland '92
Only the Lonely '91
Heartbreak Hotel '88
The Goonies '85
Young Sherlock Holmes '85
Gremlins '84
Reckless '84

Adele Comandini
Strange Illusion '45
Beyond Tomorrow '40
Her First Romance '40
Three Smart Girls '36

Betty Comden
Bells Are Ringing '60
Auntie Mame '58
It's Always Fair Weather '55
The Band Wagon '53
Singin' in the Rain '52
The Barkleys of Broadway '49
On the Town '49
Good News '47

Bob Comfort
Good Luck '96
Dogfight '91

Jacques Companeez
Casque d'Or '52
Forbidden Fruit '52

George Conchon
The Elegant Criminal '92
Black and White in Color '76

Bill Condon
Gods and Monsters '98
F/X 2: The Deadly Art of Illusion '91
Murder 101 '91
Sister, Sister '87
Strange Invaders '83
Strange Behavior '81

Shane Connaughton
The Run of the Country '95
The Playboys '92
My Left Foot '89

Jon Connolly
Eddie '96
The Dream Team '89

Ray Connolly
Forever Young '85
That'll Be the Day '73

Robert Conte
Who's Harry Crumb? '89
Odd Jobs '85

Alessandro Continenza
Deadly Mission '78
Let Sleeping Corpses Lie '74
The Loves of Hercules '60
What a Woman! '56

Ernie Contreras
FairyTale: A True Story '97
The Pagemaster '94

Gary Conway (1936-)
American Ninja 3: Blood Hunt '89
American Ninja 2: The Confrontation '87
Over the Top '86

Tim Conway (1933-)
The Longshot '86
The Private Eyes '80
Prize Fighter '79
They Went That-a-Way & That-a-Way '78

Douglas S. Cook
Double Jeopardy '99
Holy Matrimony '94
Payoff '91

Peter Cook (1938-95)
Yellowbeard '83
The Hound of the Baskervilles '77
Bedazzled '68

T.S. Cook
High Noon '00
High Desert Kill '90
Nightbreaker '89
Out of the Darkness '85
The China Syndrome '79

Gene L. Coon
The Killers '64
No Name on the Bullet '59
Man in the Shadow '57

Michael Cooney
Jack Frost 2: Revenge of the Mutant Killer Snowman '00
Jack Frost '97
Murder in Mind '97
Tracks of a Killer '95

Barry Michael Cooper
Above the Rim '94
Sugar Hill '94
New Jack City '91

John C. Cooper
First Man into Space '59
The Haunted Strangler '58

Olive Cooper
Hills of Oklahoma '50
Bandit King of Texas '49
Outcasts of the Trail '49
The Border Legion '40
Young Bill Hickok '40

Robert Cooper
The Club '94
The Dark '94
No Contest '94
Blown Away '93

Susan Cooper
George Balanchine's The Nutcracker '93
To Dance with the White Dog '93

Martin Copeland
Texas Rangers '01
The Heavenly Kid '85

Alec Coppel
Moment to Moment '66
Captain's Paradise '53
The Hidden Room '49

Francis Ford Coppola (1939-)
John Grisham's The Rainmaker '97
The Godfather, Part 3 '90
New York Stories '89
The Cotton Club '84
Rumble Fish '83
One from the Heart '82
The Godfather 1902-1959: The Complete Epic '81
Apocalypse Now '79
The Conversation '74
The Godfather, Part 2 '74
The Great Gatsby '74
The Godfather '72
Patton '70
The Rain People '69
Is Paris Burning? '66
This Property Is Condemned '66
You're a Big Boy Now '66
Dementia 13 '63
The Bellboy and the Playgirls '62
Tonight for Sure '61
The Magic Voyage of Sinbad '52

Sofia Coppola (1971-)
The Virgin Suicides '99
New York Stories '89

Sergio Corbucci (1927-90)
Super Fuzz '81
Companeros '70
Django '68

David Corley
Angel's Dance '99
Solo '96

Roger Corman (1926-)
The Skateboard Kid '93
Frankenstein Unbound '90
The Terror '63

Alain Corneau (1943-)
Tous les Matins du Monde '92
Fort Saganne '84

Stephen Cornwell
Marshal Law '96
Killing Streets '91

Eugene Corr
Prefontaine '96
Getting Out '94
Desert Bloom '86
Wildrose '85

Michael Corrente (1960-)
Outside Providence '99
Federal Hill '94

John W. Corrington
Isaac Asimov's Nightfall '00
The Arena '73
Battle for the Planet of the Apes '73
Boxcar Bertha '72
Omega Man '71

Joyce H. Corrington
The Arena '73
Battle for the Planet of the Apes '73
Boxcar Bertha '72
Omega Man '71

Catherine Corsini
The New Eve '98
Full Speed '96

Don A. Coscarelli (1954-)
Phantasm 4: Oblivion '98
Phantasm 3: Lord of the Dead '94
Survival Quest '89
Phantasm 2 '88
Beastmaster '82
Phantasm '79

George P. Cosmatos (1941-)
The Cassandra Crossing '76
Massacre in Rome '73

Jean Cosmos
Capitaine Conan '96
Colonel Chabert '94

Constantin Costa-Gavras (1933-)
Conseil de Famille '86
Missing '82
Z '69

Maurizio Costanzo
Zeder '83
A Special Day '77

James Costigan
Mr. North '88
King David '85
S.O.S. Titanic '79

Manny Coto
Hostile Intent '97
Star Kid '97
Dr. Giggles '92

William Cottrell
Peter Pan '53
Pinocchio '40

Frank Cottrell-Boyce
The Claim '00
Pandaemonium '00
Hilary and Jackie '98
Welcome to Sarajevo '97
Saint-Ex: The Story of the Storyteller '95
Butterfly Kiss '94

Ennio de Concini
The Bachelor '93
Devil in the Flesh '87
Corrupt '84
Bluebeard '72
The Girl Who Knew Too Much '63
Divorce—Italian Style '62
Black Sunday '60
That Long Night in '43 '60
Il Grido '57
War and Peace '56

Frank De Felitta (1921-)
Scissors '91
The Entity '83
Audrey Rose '77
Zero Population Growth '72
Anzio '68

Raymond De Felitta
Two Family House '99
Shadow of Doubt '98
Cafe Society '97

Claude de Givray
Bed and Board '70
Stolen Kisses '68

Anatole de Grunwald
Secret Mission '42
Pygmalion '38

Rolf de Heer (1951-)
Dance Me to My Song '98
The Quiet Room '96
Alien Visitor '95
Bad Boy Bubby '93

Alex de la Iglesia
Dance with the Devil '97
The Day of the Beast '95

Robert De Laurentis
A Little Sex '82
Green Ice '81

Marcus De Leon
The Big Squeeze '96
Kiss Me a Killer '91

Michael De Luca
In the Mouth of Madness '95
Judge Dredd '95
Freddy's Dead: The Final Nightmare '91

Albert De Mond
Border Saddlemates '52
Daughter of Don Q '46
Ridin' Down the Canyon '42

Manoel de Oliveira (1908-)
Party '96
Voyage to the Beginning of the World '96
The Convent '95
Abraham's Valley '93

Armando de Ossorio (1926-2001)
People Who Own the Dark '75
Return of the Evil Dead '75
Horror of the Zombies '74
Tombs of the Blind Dead '72
Fangs of the Living Dead '68

Massimo De Rita
Chino '75
Companeros '70

Everett De Roche
Razorback '84
Road Games '81

Guiseppe de Santis (1917-97)
Bitter Rice '49
Ossessione '42

Vittorio De Sica (1902-74)
Two Women '61
Umberto D '55
The Bicycle Thief '48
The Children Are Watching Us '44
Teresa Venerdi '41

Steven E. de Souza
Possessed '00
Knock Off '98
Judge Dredd '95
Beverly Hills Cop 3 '94
The Flintstones '94
Street Fighter '94
Hudson Hawk '91
Ricochet '91
Die Hard 2: Die Harder '90
Bad Dreams '88
Die Hard '88
Seven Hours to Judgment '88
The Running Man '87
Commando '85
Return of Captain Invincible '83
48 Hrs. '82

Gary De Vore
Timecop '94
Traxx '87
Raw Deal '86
Running Scared '86
Back Roads '81
The Dogs of War '81

Karen De Wolf
Footlight Glamour '43
It's a Great Life '43
Blondie for Victory '42
Blondie Goes Latin '42
Blondie's Blessed Event '42
Blondie in Society '41
Blondie Plays Cupid '40

Nick Dear
The Turn of the Screw '99
The Gambler '97
Persuasion '95

William Dear
Harry and the Hendersons '87
Timerider '83

James Dearden (1949-)
Rogue Trader '98
A Kiss Before Dying '91
Pascali's Island '88
Fatal Attraction '87

John DeBello
Killer Tomatoes Eat France '91
Killer Tomatoes Strike Back '90
Return of the Killer Tomatoes! '88
Happy Hour '87
Attack of the Killer Tomatoes '77

Denise DeClue
The Cherokee Kid '96
For Keeps '88
About Last Night... '86

Didier Decoin
Balzac: A Life of Passion '99
The Count of Monte Cristo '99
Jakob the Liar '99

Edward Decter (1959-)
There's Something about Mary '98
Options '88

Frank Deese
Josh and S.A.M. '93
The Principal '87

Christopher DeFaria
Amityville: A New Generation '93
Amityville 1992: It's About Time '92

James DeFelice
Angel Square '92
Out of the Dark '88
Why Shoot the Teacher '79

Michael DeForrest
The Lickerish Quartet '70
Camille 2000 '69

Brian Degas
Barbarella '68
Danger: Diabolik '68

Michael deGuzman
Hidden in America '96
Jaws: The Revenge '87

Paul Dehn
Murder on the Orient Express '74
Conquest of the Planet of the Apes '72
Escape from the Planet of the Apes '71
Beneath the Planet of the Apes '70
Goldfinger '64

Edward Dein
Curse of the Undead '59
Shack Out on 101 '55
Jungle Woman '44
Calling Dr. Death/Strange Confession '43

Mildred Dein
Curse of the Undead '59
Shack Out on 101 '55

Steve DeJarnatt
Miracle Mile '89
Strange Brew '83

Fred Dekker (1959-)
If Looks Could Kill '91
RoboCop 3 '91
The Monster Squad '87
Night of the Creeps '86

Alvaro del Amo
Jealousy '99
Intruso '93
Lovers: A True Story '90

Remigio del Grosso
Coriolanus, Man without a Country '64
Conquest of Mycene '63
Mill of the Stone Women '60

Guillermo del Toro (1964-)
The Devil's Backbone '01
Cronos '94

Shelagh Delaney
The Railway Station Man '92
Dance with a Stranger '85
A Taste of Honey '61

Walter DeLeon
Little Giant '46
Birth of the Blues '41
Pot o' Gold '41
The Ghost Breakers '40
Union Pacific '39
The Big Broadcast of 1938 '38
College Swing '38
Waikiki Wedding '37
The Princess Comes Across '36
Rhythm on the Range '36
Strike Me Pink '36
Ruggles of Red Gap '35
Six of a Kind '34
Lonely Wives '31

Francis Delia
Trouble Bound '92
Freeway '88

William F. Delligan (1944-95)
A Passion to Kill '94
Praying Mantis '93

Jeffrey Delman
Double Obsession '93
Voodoo Dawn '89

Rudy DeLuca
Screw Loose '99
Dracula: Dead and Loving It '95
Life Stinks '91
Million Dollar Mystery '87
Transylvania 6-5000 '85
Caveman '81
High Anxiety '77
Silent Movie '76

Paul DeMeo
The Rocketeer '91
Arena '89
The Wrong Guys '88
The Eliminators '86
Zone Troopers '84
Future Cop '76

Jonathan Demme (1944-)
Fighting Mad '76
Caged Heat '74
Hot Box '72
Angels Hard As They Come '71

James DeMonaco (1968-)
The Negotiator '98
Jack '96

Jacques Demy (1931-90)
The Young Girls of Rochefort '68
Umbrellas of Cherbourg '64

Claire Denis (1948-)
Nenette and Boni '96
I Can't Sleep '93
No Fear, No Die '90
Chocolat '88

Dennis Dimster Denk
Outside the Law '95
Terminal Impact '95

Wilton Denmark
Johnny Firecloud '75
Cain's Cutthroats '71

Gill Dennis
Riders of the Purple Sage '96
Without Evidence '96
Return to Oz '85

Pen Densham
Houdini '99
Moll Flanders '96
Lifepod '93
Robin Hood: Prince of Thieves '91
The Zoo Gang '85

Alan Dent
Hamlet '48
Henry V '44

Brian DePalma (1941-)
Raising Cain '92
Body Double '84
Blow Out '81
Dressed to Kill '80
Home Movies '79
Phantom of the Paradise '74
Sisters '73
Hi, Mom! '70
The Wedding Party '69
Greetings '68

Greg DePaul
Saving Silverman '01
Killer Bud '00

Scott Derrickson
Hellraiser 5: Inferno '00
Urban Legends 2: Final Cut '00

Dominique Deruddere
Everybody's Famous! '00
Hombres Complicados '97

Georges des Esseintes
Animal Instincts '92
Secret Games '92

Arnaud Desplechin
My Sex Life...Or How I Got into an Argument '96
La Sentinelle '92

Helen Deutsch
Valley of the Dolls '67
King Solomon's Mines '50
The Loves of Carmen '48
Golden Earrings '47
National Velvet '44
The Seventh Cross '44

Michel DeVille (1931-)
La Lectrice '88
Peril '85

D.V. DeVincentis
High Fidelity '00
Grosse Pointe Blank '97

Dennis Devine
Vampires of Sorority Row: Kickboxers From Hell '99
Things 2 '97
Things '93
Fatal Images '89

Dean Devlin
Godzilla '98
Independence Day '96
Stargate '94
Universal Soldier '92

Christopher DeVore
Hamlet '90
Frances '82
The Elephant Man '80

Jack DeWitt
Triumphs of a Man Called Horse '83
The Return of a Man Called Horse '76
Sky Riders '76
Neptune Factor '73
Man in the Wilderness '71
A Man Called Horse '70
The Legend of the Sea Wolf '58
Bells of San Fernando '47

Pete Dexter
Michael '96
Mulholland Falls '95
Paris Trout '91
Rush '91

Elize D'Haene
Red Shoe Diaries: Luscious Lola '00
Red Shoe Diaries: Strip Poker '96

Gerald Di Pego
Angel Eyes '01
Instinct '99
Message in a Bottle '98
Phenomenon '96
Keeper of the City '92
Sharky's Machine '81

David Diamond
Evolution '01
Family Man '00
Body Count '97

I.A.L. Diamond
Buddy Buddy '81
The Front Page '74
Avanti! '72
The Private Life of Sherlock Holmes '70
Cactus Flower '69
The Fortune Cookie '66
Kiss Me, Stupid! '64
Irma La Douce '63
One, Two, Three '61
The Apartment '60
Some Like It Hot '59
Love in the Afternoon '57
Monkey Business '52
Never Say Goodbye '46

Tom DiCillo (1954-)
The Real Blonde '97
Box of Moonlight '96
Living in Oblivion '94
Johnny Suede '92

Basil Dickey
Brand of Fear '49
Daughter of Don Q '46
Brothers of the West '37

Joan Didion (1934-)
Up Close and Personal '96
Broken Trust '95
True Confessions '81
A Star Is Born '76
Panic in Needle Park '75

Carlos Diegues (1940-)
Orfeu '99
Tieta of Agreste '96
Quilombo '84
Bye Bye Brazil '79

Anton Diether
Cleopatra '99
Moby Dick '98

Frank Dietz
Cold Harvest '98
Magic in the Mirror: Fowl Play '96
Naked Souls '95

John Dighton
The Devil's Disciple '59
The Happiest Days of Your Life '50
Kind Hearts and Coronets '49

Erin Dignam
Loved '97
Denial: The Dark Side of Passion '91

Richard Dilello
Riot in the Streets '96
Bad Boys '83

Constantine Dillon
Killer Tomatoes Eat France '91
Killer Tomatoes Strike Back '90
Return of the Killer Tomatoes! '88

Robert Dillon (-1944)
Waking the Dead '00
Deception '92
Flight of the Intruder '90
The Survivalist '87
Revolution '85
The River '84
French Connection 2 '75
99 & 44/100 Dead '74
Prime Cut '72
Bikini Beach '64
Muscle Beach Party '64
X: The Man with X-Ray Eyes '63
Slaves in Bondage '37
The Last of the Mohicans '20

Brian DiMuccio
Moonbase '97
Little Witches '96
The Demolitionist '95
Voodoo '95

Leslie Dixon
Pay It Forward '00
The Thomas Crown Affair '99
That Old Feeling '96
Look Who's Talking Now '93
Mrs. Doubtfire '93
Loverboy '89
Outrageous Fortune '87
Overboard '87

Peter Dixon
Unlawful Passage '94
Down the Wyoming Trail '39

Peter Dobai
Hanussen '88
Colonel Redl '84
Mephisto '81

Lem Dobbs
The Score '01
The Limey '99
Dark City '97
The Hard Way '91
Kafka '91

Jacques Doillon (1944-)
Petits Freres '00
Ponette '95
La Vengeance d'une Femme '89

Bob Dolman
Far and Away '92
Willow '88

Henry Dominick
Flight of Black Angel '91
Mindwarp '91

Simon Donald
Beautiful Creatures '00
Deacon Brodie '98
My Life So Far '98
The Ebb-Tide '97

Sergio Donati
North Star '96
Beyond Justice '92
Orca '77
The Good, the Bad and the Ugly '67

Thomas Michael Donnelly
Bonanno: A Godfather's Story '99
A Soldier's Sweetheart '98
The Garden of Redemption '97

Tom Donnelly
Talent for the Game '91
Quicksilver '86
Defiance '79

Mary Agnes Donoghue
Deceived '91
Paradise '91
Beaches '88
The Buddy System '83

Martin Donovan (1950-)
Somebody Is Waiting '96
Death Becomes Her '92
Mad at the Moon '92
Apartment Zero '88

Paul Donovan (1954-)
Tales from a Parallel Universe: Eating Pattern '97
Tales from a Parallel Universe: Giga Shadow '97
Tales from a Parallel Universe: I Worship His Shadow '97
Tales from a Parallel Universe: Super Nova '97

Anita Doohan
Whispers '89
Embryo '76
Matt Dorff
Mr. Rock 'n' Roll: The Alan Freed Story '99
Requiem for Murder '99
Silent Predators '99
Random Encounter '98
The Reaper '97
The Stepsister '97
Closer and Closer '96
Gil Doud
Walk the Proud Land '56
To Hell and Back '55
Joseph Dougherty
Witch Hunt '94
Attack of the 50 Ft. Woman '93
Cast a Deadly Spell '91
Steel and Lace '90
Lorenzo Doumani
Storybook '95
Amore! '93
Richard D'Ovidio
Exit Wounds '01
13 Ghosts '01
Alexander Dovzhenko (1849-1956)
Earth '30
Arsenal '29
Nancy Dowd
Let It Ride '89
Slap Shot '77
Allison Louise Downe
Just for the Hell of It '68
She-Devils on Wheels '68
The Girl, the Body and the Pill '67
Gruesome Twosome '67
Blood Feast '63
Robert Downey (1936-)
Greaser's Palace '72
Putney Swope '69
Roddy Doyle
When Brendan Met Trudy '00
The Van '95
The Snapper '93
The Commitments '91
Brian Doyle-Murray (1945-)
Club Paradise '86
Caddyshack '80
Srdjan Dragojevic
The Wounds '98
Pretty Village, Pretty Flame '96
Oliver Drake (1903-91)
Fighting Valley '43
Cowboys from Texas '39
Peter Draper
Poldark '75
I'll Never Forget What's 'Isname '67
The Girl Getters '66
Jay Dratler
Impact '49
Call Northside 777 '48
Laura '44
Hal Dresner
The Eiger Sanction '75
Sssssss '73
Carl Theodor Dreyer (1889-1968)
Gertrud '64
Ordet '55
Day of Wrath '43
Vampyr '31
Passion of Joan of Arc '28
Karim Dridi
Bye-Bye '96
Pigalle '95
Kevin Droney
Wing Commander '99
Mortal Kombat 1: The Movie '95
Down Came a Blackbird '94
Michael B. Druxman
The Doorway '00
Isaac Asimov's Nightfall '00
Battle Queen 2020 '99
Dillinger and Capone '95
Cheyenne Warrior '94
Lee Drysdale
Sweet Nothing '96
Leather Jackets '90
Olivier Ducastel
The Adventures of Felix '99
Jeanne and the Perfect Guy '98
Warren Duff
Angels with Dirty Faces '38
Last Command '28
Jo Duffy
Puppet Master 5: The Final Chapter '94
Puppet Master 4 '93
Martine Dugowson
Portraits Chinois '96
Mina Tannenbaum '93
John Duigan (1949-)
The Leading Man '96
Sirens '94
Wide Sargasso Sea '92
Flirting '89
The Year My Voice Broke '87
Bruno Dumont
Humanity '99
The Life of Jesus '96
David Duncan
The Time Machine '60
The Leech Woman '59
Monster on the Campus '59
Patrick Duncan
Nick of Time '95
A Home of Our Own '93
Patrick Sheane Duncan
The Wall '99
Courage Under Fire '96
Mr. Holland's Opus '95
Live! From Death Row '92
84 Charlie MoPic '89
Peter Duncan (1954-)
A Little Bit of Soul '97
Children of the Revolution '95
Winifred Dunn
The Dropkick '27
Sparrows '26
John Gregory Dunne
Up Close and Personal '96
Broken Trust '95
True Confessions '81
A Star Is Born '76
Panic in Needle Park '75
Philip Dunne (1908-92)
The Agony and the Ecstasy '65
Ten North Frederick '58
Demetrius and the Gladiators '54
The Egyptian '54
The Robe '53
David and Bathsheba '51
Pinky '49
Forever Amber '47
The Ghost and Mrs. Muir '47
Son of Fury '42
How Green Was My Valley '41
The Rains Came '39
The Count of Monte Cristo '34
Carl DuPre
Detroit Rock City '99
The Prophecy 3: The Ascent '99
Arnaud d'Usseau
Psychomania '73
Horror Express '72
Julien Duvivier (1896-1967)
Anna Karenina '48
Pepe Le Moko '37
Jim Dwyer
Little Shots of Happiness '97
Frisk '95
H. Kaye Dyal
Project: Eliminator '91
Trained to Kill '88
Lone Wolf McQuade '83
Robert Easter
Kiss Toledo Goodbye '00
Sworn to Justice '97
The Toolbox Murders '78
Thom Eberhardt
Ratz '99
Face Down '97
Captain Ron '92
Honey, I Blew Up the Kid '92
All I Want for Christmas '91
The Night Before '88
Night of the Comet '84
Roger Ebert
Beneath the Valley of the Ultra-Vixens '79
Beyond the Valley of the Dolls '70
Patrick Edgeworth
Driving Force '88
Raw Deal '86
BMX Bandits '83
Dave Edison
Cast a Deadly Spell '91
Steel and Lace '90
Blake Edwards (1922-)
Son of the Pink Panther '93
Switch '91
Skin Deep '89
Sunset '88
A Fine Mess '86
That's Life! '86
City Heat '84
Curse of the Pink Panther '83
The Man Who Loved Women '83
Trail of the Pink Panther '82
Victor/Victoria '82
S.O.B. '81
10 '79
Revenge of the Pink Panther '78
Return of the Pink Panther '74
The Tamarind Seed '74
Wild Rovers '71
Darling Lili '70
The Party '68
What Did You Do in the War, Daddy? '66
The Pink Panther '64
A Shot in the Dark '64
Soldier in the Rain '63
This Happy Feeling '58
My Sister Eileen '55
The Atomic Kid '54
Paul F. Edwards
Tecumseh: The Last Warrior '95
Ordeal in the Arctic '93
Fire Birds '90
High Ballin' '78
Christine Edzard (1945-)
Little Dorrit, Film 1: Nobody's Fault '88
Little Dorrit, Film 2: Little Dorrit's Story '88
Karl-Georg Egel
Anton, the Magician '78
Trace of Stones '66
Atom Egoyan (1960-)
Felicia's Journey '99
The Sweet Hereafter '96
Exotica '94
Calendar '93
The Adjuster '91
Speaking Parts '89
Family Viewing '87
Next of Kin '84
Kerry Ehrin
Inspector Gadget '99
Mr. Wrong '95
Max Ehrlich
The Reincarnation of Peter Proud '75
Zero Population Growth '72
Sergei Eisenstein (1898-1948)
Ivan the Terrible, Part 2 '46
Ivan the Terrible, Part 1 '44
Alexander Nevsky '38
Que Viva Mexico '32
Ten Days That Shook the World '27
The Battleship Potemkin '25
Jo Eisinger
The Rover '67
Crime of Passion '57
Night and the City '50
Gilda '46
Philip Eisner
Firestarter 2: Rekindled '02
Event Horizon '97
John (Anthony Hinds) Elder
Frankenstein and the Monster from Hell '74
The Scars of Dracula '70
Taste the Blood of Dracula '70
Dracula Has Risen from the Grave '68
Dracula, Prince of Darkness '66
Frankenstein Created Woman '66
Plague of the Zombies '66
Rasputin the Mad Monk '66
The Reptile '66
The Evil of Frankenstein '64
Kiss of the Vampire '62
The Phantom of the Opera '62
The Curse of the Werewolf '61
Lonnie Elder, III (1926-96)
Bustin' Loose '81
A Woman Called Moses '78
Sounder '72
Kevin Elders
Ravenhawk '95
Iron Eagle 2 '88
Iron Eagle '86
Laurice Elehwany
The Amazing Panda Adventure '95
The Brady Bunch Movie '95
My Girl '91
Harry Elfont
Josie and the Pussycats '01
The Flintstones in Viva Rock Vegas '00
Can't Hardly Wait '98
A Very Brady Sequel '96
Michael Elias (1940-)
No Laughing Matter '97
Lush Life '94
Young Doctors in Love '82
Serial '80
The Frisco Kid '79
The Jerk '79
Joyce Eliason
The Last Don 2 '98
The Last Don '97
Titanic '96
A Good Day to Die '95
Oldest Confederate Widow Tells All '95
Small Sacrifices '89
Tell Me a Riddle '80
Doug Ellin (1968-)
Kissing a Fool '98
Phat Beach '96
Stephan Elliott (1963-)
Eye of the Beholder '99
The Adventures of Priscilla, Queen of the Desert '94
Ted Elliott
Shrek '01
The Road to El Dorado '00
The Mask of Zorro '98
Small Soldiers '98
The Puppet Masters '94
Aladdin '92
Little Monsters '89
Bob Ellis
Warm Nights on a Slow-Moving Train '87
Cactus '86
Man of Flowers '84
My First Wife '84
Michael Ellis
The Wedding Planner '01
Bounty Hunters 2: Hardball '97
Robert Ellis (1892-1974)
Ebbtide '94
Hello, Frisco, Hello '43
Iceland '42
Lucky Cisco Kid '40
Tin Pan Alley '40
Trey Ellis
The Tuskegee Airmen '95
Cosmic Slop '94
John Emerson (1874-1956)
The Girl from Missouri '34
Struggle '31
His Picture in the Papers '16
Roland Emmerich (1955-)
Godzilla '98
Independence Day '96
Stargate '94
Ghost Chase '88
E.V.H. Emmett
Non-Stop New York '37
Sabotage '36
Robert Emmett (1921-2000)
Riding the Sunset Trail '41
Gun Packer '38
God's Country and the Man '37
Frank Encarnacao
A Young Connecticut Yankee in King Arthur's Court '95
Young Ivanhoe '95
Cy Endfield (1914-95)
Zulu '64
Try and Get Me '50
Guy Endore
Captain Sinbad '63
The Story of G.I. Joe '45
Devil Doll '36
Mad Love '35
Mark of the Vampire '35
Otto Englander
Fantasia '40
Pinocchio '40
Snow White and the Seven Dwarfs '37
Ken Englund
The Secret Life of Walter Mitty '47
Springtime in the Rockies '42
Nick Enright
Blackrock '97
Lorenzo's Oil '92
Delia Ephron
Hanging Up '99
Michael '96
Mixed Nuts '94
This Is My Life '92
Henry Ephron
Carousel '56
There's No Business Like Show Business '54
Look for the Silver Lining '49
Nora Ephron (1941-)
Hanging Up '99
You've Got Mail '98
Michael '96
Mixed Nuts '94
Sleepless in Seattle '93
This Is My Life '92
My Blue Heaven '90
Cookie '89
When Harry Met Sally... '89
Heartburn '86
Silkwood '83
Phoebe Ephron
Carousel '56
There's No Business Like Show Business '54
Look for the Silver Lining '49
Tom Epperson
Camouflage '00
The Gift '00
A Gun, a Car, a Blonde '97
Don't Look Back '96
A Family Thing '96
One False Move '91
Jack Epps, Jr.
The Flintstones in Viva Rock Vegas '00
Anaconda '96
Dick Tracy '90
Turner and Hooch '89
The Secret of My Success '87
Legal Eagles '86
Top Gun '86
Julius J. Epstein (1909-2000)
Reuben, Reuben '83
Cross of Iron '76
Once Is Not Enough '75
Pete 'n' Tillie '72
Any Wednesday '66
Send Me No Flowers '64
Fanny '61
Tall Story '60
The Tender Trap '55
The Last Time I Saw Paris '54
Young at Heart '54
Forever Female '53
Romance on the High Seas '48
Arsenic and Old Lace '44
Casablanca '42
The Bride Came C.O.D. '41
The Man Who Came to Dinner '41
Strawberry Blonde '41
Philip G. Epstein (1909-52)
The Last Time I Saw Paris '54
Forever Female '53
Arsenic and Old Lace '44
Casablanca '42
The Bride Came C.O.D. '41
The Man Who Came to Dinner '41
Strawberry Blonde '41
Greg Erb
Senseless '98
RocketMan '97
George Erschbamer (1954-)
Bounty Hunters 2: Hardball '97
Bounty Hunters '96
Power of Attorney '94
Patrick Ersgard
Backlash '99
Living in Peril '97
Chester Erskine (1905-86)
All My Sons '48
Midnight '34
John Eskow
The Mask of Zorro '98
Pink Cadillac '89
John Esposito
Russell Mulcahy's Tale of the Mummy '99
Graveyard Shift '90
Harry Essex (1910-97)
Octaman '71
Sons of Katie Elder '65
Creature from the Black Lagoon '54
It Came from Outer Space '53
Howard Estabrook
Lone Star '52
The Bridge of San Luis Rey '44
International Lady '41
David Copperfield '35
Hell's Angels '30
Emilio Estevez (1962-)
Men at Work '90
That Was Then...This Is Now '85
Joe Eszterhas
An Alan Smithee Film: Burn, Hollywood, Burn '97
Telling Lies in America '96
Jade '95
Showgirls '95
Nowhere to Run '93
Sliver '93
Basic Instinct '92
Checking Out '89
Music Box '89
Betrayed '88
Big Shots '87
Hearts of Fire '87
The Jagged Edge '85
Flashdance '83
Corey Michael Eubanks
Two Bits & Pepper '95

Bigfoot: The Unforgettable Encounter '94
Forced to Kill '93

Rich Eustis
Young Doctors in Love '82
Serial '80

Bruce A. Evans
Jungle 2 Jungle '96
Kuffs '92
Made in Heaven '87
Starman '84
A Man, a Woman, and a Bank '79

David Mickey Evans
Ed '96
The Sandlot '93

Shelley Evans
One Kill '00
Ladykiller '92

Vincent B. Evans
Battle Hymn '57
Chain Lightning '50

Clive Exton
The Awakening '80
Doomwatch '72
10 Rillington Place '71
Entertaining Mr. Sloane '70
Isadora '68

David Eyre
Pastime '91
Wolfen '81

Richard Eyre (1943-)
Iris '01
King Lear '98

Diego Fabbri
Barabbas '62
Generale Della Rovere '60

Nicholas Factor
Hostage Hotel '00
Sabrina the Teenage Witch '96

Roberto Faenza (1943-)
The Bachelor '93
Corrupt '84

Douglas Fairbanks, Sr. (1883-1939)
Mr. Robinson Crusoe '32
The Iron Mask '29
The Black Pirate '26
Robin Hood '22
The Three Musketeers '21
Mark of Zorro '20
The Mollycoddle '20

William Fairchild (1919-2000)
Star! '68
John and Julie '55

John Fairley
Premonition '98
The Raffle '94

David Fallon
White Fang 2: The Myth of the White Wolf '94
White Fang '91
Split Decisions '88

Kevin Falls
Summer Catch '01
The Temp '93

Jamaa Fanaka (1942-)
Street Wars '91
Penitentiary 3 '87
Penitentiary 2 '82
Penitentiary '79
Black Sister's Revenge '76
Soul Vengeance '75

Barry Fanaro
Men in Black 2 '02
The Crew '00

Hampton Fancher
The Minus Man '99
The Mighty Quinn '89
Blade Runner '82

John Fante
Maya '66
Full of Life '56

Jean-Pol Fargeau
Pola X '99
Nenette and Boni '96
I Can't Sleep '93
No Fear, No Die '90
Chocolat '88

Ernest Farino
Wizards of the Demon Sword '94

Beverly Hills Vamp '88

Bobby Farrelly (1958-)
Shallow Hal '01
Me, Myself, and Irene '00
Outside Providence '99
There's Something about Mary '98
Kingpin '96
Dumb & Dumber '94

Peter Farrelly (1957-)
Shallow Hal '01
Me, Myself, and Irene '00
Outside Providence '99
There's Something about Mary '98
Dumb & Dumber '94

John Farrow (1904-63)
John Paul Jones '59
Around the World in 80 Days '56

John Fasano
Mean Streak '99
Universal Soldier: The Return '99
The Hunchback '97

Rainer Werner Fassbinder (1946-82)
Chinese Roulette '86
Querelle '83
Berlin Alexanderplatz '80
The Marriage of Maria Braun '79
In a Year of 13 Moons '78
The Stationmaster's Wife '77
I Only Want You to Love Me '76
Mother Kusters Goes to Heaven '76
Satan's Brew '76
Shadow of Angels '76
Ali: Fear Eats the Soul '74
Effi Briest '74
The Bitter Tears of Petra von Kant '72
The Merchant of Four Seasons '71
The American Soldier '70
Beware of a Holy Whore '70
Whity '70
Why Does Herr R. Run Amok? '69

Alvin L. Fast
Satan's Cheerleaders '77
Eaten Alive '76
Bummer '73

William Faulkner
The Big Sleep '46
The Southerner '45
To Have & Have Not '44
Air Force '43
Gunga Din '39
Today We Live '33

Jon Favreau (1966-)
Made '01
Swingers '96

Jacqueline Feather
By Dawn's Early Light '00
The King and I '99
Goldrush: A Real Life Alaskan Adventure '98
The Rumor Mill '86

Terence Feely (1928-2000)
The Lady and the Highwayman '89
Destination Moonbase Alpha '75

F.X. Feeney
The Big Brass Ring '99
Frankenstein Unbound '90

Jules Feiffer
Popeye '80
Oh! Calcutta! '72
Carnal Knowledge '71
Little Murders '71

Beda Docampo Feijoo
What Your Eyes Don't See '99
The Perfect Husband '92

Steve Feinberg
Fortress 2: Re-Entry '99
Fortress '93

Bruce Feirstein
The World Is Not Enough '99
Tomorrow Never Dies '97

Dennis Feldman
Virus '98
Species '95
The Golden Child '86

John Feldman
Dead Funny '94
Alligator Eyes '90

Jonathan Marc Feldman
From the Earth to the Moon '98
Swing Kids '93

Marty Feldman (1933-82)
In God We Trust '80
The Last Remake of Beau Geste '77

Randy Feldman
Metro '96
Nowhere to Run '93
Tango and Cash '89
Hell Night '81

Federico Fellini (1920-93)
Intervista '87
Ginger & Fred '86
And the Ship Sails On '83
City of Women '81
Orchestra Rehearsal '78
Amarcord '74
Fellini's Roma '72
The Clowns '71
Fellini Satyricon '69
Spirits of the Dead '68
Juliet of the Spirits '65
8 1/2 '63
Boccaccio '70 '62
La Dolce Vita '60
Nights of Cabiria '57
Il Bidone '55
La Strada '54
I Vitelloni '53
The White Sheik '52
Variety Lights '51
The Flowers of St. Francis '50
The Miracle '48
Paisan '46
Open City '45

Andrew J. Fenady
The Sea Wolf '93
The Man with Bogart's Face '80
Chisum '70

Pablo F. Fenjves
One of Her Own '97
Bloodhounds '96
Bloodhounds 2 '96
Twilight Man '96
The Affair '95
When the Dark Man Calls '95
Bitter Vengeance '94
Out of Annie's Past '94
A Case for Murder '93

Frank Fenton (1906-57)
River of No Return '54
Escape from Fort Bravo '53
His Kind of Woman '51
Malaya '49

Craig Ferguson
Saving Grace '00
The Big Tease '99

Larry Ferguson (1940-)
Rollerball '02
Gunfighter's Moon '96
Maximum Risk '96
Beyond the Law '92
Talent for the Game '91
The Hunt for Red October '90
The Presidio '88
Beverly Hills Cop 2 '87
Highlander '86

Peter Fernandez
Infra-Man '76
The Dirty Girls '64

Abel Ferrara (1952-)
New Rose Hotel '98
The Blackout '97

Bad Lieutenant '92

Marco Ferreri (1928-97)
Tales of Ordinary Madness '83
La Grande Bouffe '73

Franco Ferrini
Sleepless '01
The Church '98
Two Evil Eyes '90
Opera '88
Demons '86
Creepers '85

Michael Ferris
The Game '97
The Net '95

Walter Ferris
At Sword's Point '51
The Little Princess '39
Heidi '37
Lloyds of London '36
Death Takes a Holiday '34

Giorgio Ferroni (1908-81)
Conquest of Mycene '63
Mill of the Stone Women '60

Darrell Fetty
Trouble Bound '92
Freeway '88

Pat Fielder
Return of Dracula '58
The Monster That Challenged the World '57

Herbert Fields
Up in Central Park '48
Honolulu '39
Hands Across the Table '35

W.C. Fields (1879-1946)
Never Give a Sucker an Even Break '41
The Bank Dick '40
My Little Chickadee '40
The Dentist '32
Pool Sharks '15

Harvey Fierstein (1954-)
Common Ground '00
Tidy Endings '88
Torch Song Trilogy '88

Jacques Fieschi
Place Vendome '98
Nelly et Monsieur Arnaud '95
Un Coeur en Hiver '93
Every Other Weekend '91

Mike Figgis (1948-)
Time Code '00
The Loss of Sexual Innocence '98
One Night Stand '97
Leaving Las Vegas '95
Liebestraum '91
Stormy Monday '88

Peter Filardi
The Craft '96
Flatliners '90

Hal Fimberg
In Society '44
Big Store '41

Scot (Scott) Finch
Catlow '71
Shalako '68

Abem Finkel
Sergeant York '41
Jezebel '38
The Black Legion '37

Fred Finklehoffe
The Stooge '51
At War with the Army '50
Mr. Ace '46

Melanie Finn
Red Shoe Diaries: Swimming Naked '00
Lake Consequence '92

Alan Finney
Alvin Rides Again '74
Alvin Purple '73

Bob Fisher
Eight on the Lam '67
I'll Take Sweden '65
A Global Affair '63

Carrie Fisher (1956-)
These Old Broads '01
Postcards from the Edge '90

Steve Fisher
Profile for Murder '96
Hostile Guns '67
Johnny Reno '66

Jeffrey Alladin Fiskin
The '60s '99
From the Earth to the Moon '98
Cutter's Way '81
Angel Unchained '70

Benedict Fitzgerald
In Cold Blood '96
Heart of Darkness '93

Ed Fitzgerald
Dead Silent '99
Blue Movies '88

F. Scott Fitzgerald
Marie Antoinette '38
Three Comrades '38

Thom Fitzgerald
Beefcake '99
The Hanging Garden '97

Peter Fitzpatrick
Brilliant Lies '96
Sorrento Beach '95

Ennio Flaiano (1910-72)
Juliet of the Spirits '65
10th Victim '65
8 1/2 '63
Boccaccio '70 '62
La Dolce Vita '60
Nights of Cabiria '57
What a Woman! '56
Il Bidone '55
La Strada '54
I Vitelloni '53
The White Sheik '52
Variety Lights '51

Sara Flanigan
Other Voices, Other Rooms '95
Wildflower '91

Harvey Flaxman
Preacherman '83
Grizzly '76

Hugh Fleetwood
The Bachelor '93
Corrupt '84

Andrew Fleming
Dick '99
The Craft '96
Threesome '94
Every Breath '93
Bad Dreams '88

R. Lee Fleming, Jr.
Get Over It! '01
She's All That '99

Charlie Fletcher
Mean Machine '01
Fair Game '95

Clive Fleury
Big City Blues '99
Tunnel Vision '95

Richard Flournoy
Blondie Goes Latin '42
Blondie's Blessed Event '42
Blondie Has Trouble '40
Blondie On a Budget '40
Blondie Plays Cupid '40
Blondie Brings Up Baby '39
Blondie Meets the Boss '39
Blondie Takes a Vacation '39
Blondie '38

George "Buck" Flower (1936-)
Hell's Belles '95
Drive-In Massacre '74

Ladislas Fodor
Apache's Last Battle '64
Tom Thumb '58

Peter Foldy
Tryst '94
Widow's Kiss '94
Midnight Witness '93

James Foley
S.F.W. '94
After Dark, My Sweet '90

Marcello Fondato
Black Sabbath '64
Blood and Black Lace '64

Naomi Foner
Losing Isaiah '94

A Dangerous Woman '93
Running on Empty '88
Violets Are Blue '86

Eddie L.C. Fong
Floating Life '95
Erotique '94
Temptation of a Monk '94

Anne Fontaine
Dry Cleaning '97
Augustin '95

Dennis Foon
Torso '01
White Lies '98

Bradbury Foote
Young Tom Edison '40
Of Human Hearts '38

Horton Foote
Horton Foote's Alone '97
William Faulkner's Old Man '97
Lily Dale '96
Of Mice and Men '92
The Habitation of Dragons '91
On Valentine's Day '86
1918 '85
The Trip to Bountiful '85
Tender Mercies '83
Tomorrow '72
The Chase '66
Baby, the Rain Must Fall '64
To Kill a Mockingbird '62

Bryan Forbes (1926-)
Chaplin '92
The Slipper and the Rose '76
Eye Witness '70
The Man Who Haunted Himself '70
King Rat '65
Of Human Bondage '64
The L-Shaped Room '62

Christian Ford
Slow Burn '00
Kazaam '96

Ron Ford
The Alien Agenda: Endangered Species '97
The Fear '94

Carl Foreman
High Noon '00
MacKenna's Gold '69
The Guns of Navarone '61
The Key '58
The Bridge on the River Kwai '57
The Sleeping Tiger '54
High Noon '52
Cyrano de Bergerac '50
Champion '49
Home of the Brave '49
Spooks Run Wild '41

Milos Forman (1932-)
The Firemen's Ball '68
Loves of a Blonde '65

Bengt Forslund
The New Land '73
The Emigrants '72

Bill Forsyth (1948-)
Being Human '94
Housekeeping '87
Comfort and Joy '84
Local Hero '83
Gregory's Girl '80
That Sinking Feeling '79

Frederick Forsyth
A Casualty of War '90
The Fourth Protocol '87

Garrett Fort
Devil Doll '36
Dracula's Daughter '36
The Lost Patrol '34
Dracula (Spanish Version) '31
Dracula '31
Frankenstein '31

Bob Fosse (1927-87)
Star 80 '83
All That Jazz '79

Lewis R. Foster (1898-1974)
Never Say Goodbye '46
Can't Help Singing '45
Rhythm Romance '39

Vincent Fotre
Torture Chamber of Baron Blood '72
Missile to the Moon '59
The Commies Are Coming, the Commies Are Coming '57

Victoria Foyt
Deja Vu '98
Last Summer In the Hamptons '96
Babyfever '94

Claudio Fragasso
Hell of the Living Dead '83
Rats '83

Randall Frakes
Blowback '99
Hell Comes to Frogtown '88

Michael France
Goldeneye '95
Cliffhanger '93

Dan Franck
La Separation '98
The Separation '94

Jess (Jesus) Franco (1930-)
Tender Flesh '97
Bloody Moon '83
Ilsa, the Wicked Warden '78
Jack the Ripper '76
The Demons '74
Count Dracula '71
Venus in Furs '70
The Diabolical Dr. Z '65
The Awful Dr. Orloff '62

Frederic M. Frank
The Ten Commandments '56
Unconquered '47

Harriet Frank, Jr.
Stanley and Iris '90
Murphy's Romance '85
Norma Rae '79
Conrack '74
The Cowboys '72
The Reivers '69
Hombre '67
Hud '63
Home from the Hill '60
The Long, Hot Summer '58
Ten Wanted Men '54
Silver River '48

Laurie Frank
Love Crimes '92
Making Mr. Right '86

Melvin Frank (1913-88)
A Funny Thing Happened on the Way to the Forum '66
Strange Bedfellows '65
The Facts of Life '60
Above and Beyond '53
Mr. Blandings Builds His Dream House '48
Monsieur Beaucaire '46
The Road to Utopia '46
Star Spangled Rhythm '42

Scott Frank (1960-)
Minority Report '02
Out of Sight '98
Get Shorty '95
Heaven's Prisoners '95
Fallen Angels 2 '93
Malice '93
Dead Again '91
Little Man Tate '91

David Frankel (1960-)
Miami Rhapsody '95
Nervous Ticks '93
Funny About Love '90

Al Franken (1951-)
Stuart Saves His Family '94
When a Man Loves a Woman '94
One More Saturday Night '86

Carl Franklin (1949-)
Devil in a Blue Dress '95
Eye of the Eagle 3 '91

Howard Franklin
Antitrust '00
The Man Who Knew Too Little '97
The Public Eye '92
Quick Change '90

Someone to Watch Over Me '87
The Name of the Rose '86

Jeff Franklin (1955-)
Love Stinks '99
Double Double Toil and Trouble '94
To Grandmother's House We Go '94
Summer School '87

Paul Franklin
The Fighting Redhead '50
Reefer Madness '38

Richard Franklin (1948-)
Brilliant Lies '96
Sorrento Beach '95

David Franzoni
Gladiator '00
Amistad '97
Citizen Cohn '92
Jumpin' Jack Flash '86

George MacDonald Fraser
The Return of the Musketeers '89
Casanova '87
The Prince and the Pauper '78
The Four Musketeers '75
Royal Flash '75
The Three Musketeers '74

Harry Fraser (1889-1974)
Flaming Bullets '45
Galloping Romeo '33

Donald Freed
Of Love and Shadows '94
Secret Honor '85

Robert Freedman
Life with Judy Garland—Me and My Shadows '01
Cinderella '97
Taken Away '89

Everett Freeman
The Glass Bottom Boat '66
My Man Godfrey '57
The Secret Life of Walter Mitty '47
The Princess and the Pirate '44

Fred Freeman
The Big Bus '76
Start the Revolution without Me '70

Gillian Freeman
The Girl on a Motorcycle '68
The Leather Boys '63

Joan Freeman (1941-)
Uncaged '91
Streetwalkin' '85

Morgan J. Freeman (1969-)
Desert Blue '98
Hurricane Streets '96

Fred Freiberger
Beginning of the End '57
Big Chase '54
The Beast from 20,000 Fathoms '53

Jeff Freilich
Naked City: A Killer Christmas '98
Naked City: Justice with a Bullet '98

Robert M. Fresco (1928-)
Dirty Little Secret '98
Evil Has a Face '96
The Monolith Monsters '57
Tarantula '55

Bart Freundlich
World Traveler '01
The Myth of Fingerprints '97

Ron Fricke
Baraka '93
Koyaanisqatsi '83

Fridrik Thor Fridriksson (1953-)
Cold Fever '95
Children of Nature '91

Richard Friedenberg
The Education of Little Tree '97
Mr. & Mrs. Loving '96

A River Runs Through It '92
Dying Young '91

William Friedkin (1939-)
The Guardian '90
Rampage '87
To Live & Die in L.A. '85
Cruising '80

Brent Friedman
Mortal Kombat 2: Annihilation '97
Exit '95
Magic Island '95
Pet Shop '94
Prehysteria 2 '94
H.P. Lovecraft's Necronomicon: Book of the Dead '93

Ken Friedman
Bad Girls '94
Cadillac Man '90
Johnny Handsome '89
Made in USA '88
Heart Like a Wheel '83
Mr. Billion '77
White Line Fever '75

Ketti Frings
Because of You '52
Guest in the House '44

James Fritzell
The Shakiest Gun in the West '68
The Reluctant Astronaut '67
The Ghost and Mr. Chicken '66

George Froeschel
Me and the Colonel '58
Never Let Me Go '53
The Miniver Story '50
Command Decision '48
The White Cliffs of Dover '44
Mrs. Miniver '42
The Mortal Storm '40
Waterloo Bridge '40

Pea Frolich
Veronika Voss '82
The Marriage of Maria Braun '79

Lee Frost
Private Obsession '94
Dixie Dynamite '76
Black Gestapo '75
Race with the Devil '75

Mark Frost
Storyville '92
The Believers '87
Scared Stiff '87

Roy Frumkes
The Substitute 3: Winner Takes All '99
The Substitute 2: School's Out '97
The Substitute '96
Street Trash '87

Christopher Fry
The Lady's Not for Burning '87
The Brontes of Haworth '73
The Bible '66
Barabbas '62

E. Max Frye
Band of Brothers '01
Where the Money Is '00
Palmetto '98
Amos and Andrew '93
Something Wild '86

Daniel Fuchs
The Underneath '95
Criss Cross '48

Robert Fuest (1927-)
The Final Programme '73
Doctor Phibes Rises Again '72

Lucio Fulci (1927-96)
Wax Mask '97
Demonia '90
The House by the Cemetery '83
The Beyond '82
New York Ripper '82
The Black Cat '81
Gates of Hell '80
Don't Torture a Duckling '72

Charles Fuller
Love Songs '99

The Wall '99
Zooman '95
A Soldier's Story '84

David Fuller
Gang in Blue '96
Necessary Roughness '91

Kim Fuller
High Heels and Low Lifes '01
Spice World: The Movie '97

Samuel Fuller (1911-97)
Girls in Prison '94
Let's Get Harry '87
The Big Red One '80
The Klansman '74
Dead Pigeon on Beethoven Street '72
Shark! '68
Naked Kiss '64
Shock Corridor '63
Merrill's Marauders '62
Underworld, U.S.A. '60
Verboten! '59
China Gate '57
Run of the Arrow '56
Pickup on South Street '53
Baron of Arizona '51
The Steel Helmet '51
I Shot Jesse James '49

Sidney J. Furie (1933-)
The Taking of Beverly Hills '91
Iron Eagle 2 '88
Iron Eagle '86
Purple Hearts '84
The Boys in Company C '77
A Dangerous Age '57

Jules Furthman
Rio Bravo '59
The Big Sleep '46
To Have & Have Not '44
The Outlaw '43
The Shanghai Gesture '42
Only Angels Have Wings '39
Spawn of the North '38
Come and Get It '36
Mutiny on the Bounty '35
Shanghai Express '32

John Fusco
Spirit: Stallion of the Cimarron '02
Loch Ness '95
The Babe '92
Thunderheart '92
Young Guns 2 '90
Young Guns '88
Crossroads '86

Richard Gabai (1964-)
Assault of the Party Nerds 2: Heavy Petting Detective '95
Virgin High '90

Antonio Gades (1936-)
Carmen '83
Blood Wedding '81

Reg Gadney
The Sculptress '97
Goldeneye: The Secret Life of Ian Fleming '89

Christos N. Gage
The Breed '01
Teenage Caveman '01

Stephen Gaghan
Rules of Engagement '00
Traffic '00

Bob Gale (1951-)
Trespass '92
Back to the Future, Part 3 '90
Back to the Future, Part 2 '89
Back to the Future '85
Used Cars '80
1941 '79

Henrik Galeen
Waxworks '24
Nosferatu '22
The Golem '20

John A. Gallagher
Blue Moon '00
The Deli '97
Beach House '82

George Gallo (1956-)
Double Take '01
See Spot Run '01
Trapped in Paradise '94
29th Street '91
Midnight Run '88

Kenneth Gamet
A Lawless Street '55
Flying Leathernecks '51
Man in the Saddle '51
Santa Fe '51
Pittsburgh '42

Abel Gance (1889-1981)
Beethoven '36
Napoleon '27
The Torture of Silence '17

Christophe Gans
Brotherhood of the Wolf '01
H.P. Lovecraft's Necronomicon: Book of the Dead '93

Lowell Ganz
Where the Heart Is '00
EDtv '99
Father's Day '96
Multiplicity '96
Forget Paris '95
City Slickers 2: The Legend of Curly's Gold '94
Greedy '94
A League of Their Own '92
Mr. Saturday Night '92
City Slickers '91
Parenthood '89
Vibes '88
Gung Ho '85
Spies Like Us '85
Splash '84
Night Shift '82

Nicole Garcia (1946-)
Place Vendome '98
The Favorite Son '94
Every Other Weekend '91

Louis Gardel
East-West '99
Indochine '92
Fort Saganne '84

Herb Gardner
I'm Not Rappaport '96
The Goodbye People '83
A Thousand Clowns '65

Richard Harding Gardner
Sherlock: Undercover Dog '94
Deadly Daphne's Revenge '93

Louis Garfinkle
The Deer Hunter '78
I Bury the Living '58

Robert Garland
No Way Out '87
The Electric Horseman '79

Helen Garner
The Last Days of Chez Nous '92
Two Friends '86

Tony Garnett
Fat Man and Little Boy '89
Deep in the Heart '83

Oliver H.P. Garrett
Duel in the Sun '46
The Hurricane '37
A Farewell to Arms '32

Mick Garris
Quicksilver Highway '98
Hocus Pocus '93
The Fly 2 '89
Critters 2: The Main Course '88

Ernesto Gastaldi
The Great Alligator '81
Torso '73
The Scorpion's Tail '71
Blade of the Ripper '70
The Whip and the Body '63
Venus Against the Son of Hercules '62

Tudor Gates
Fright '71
Lust for a Vampire '71
Twins of Evil '71
The Vampire Lovers '70
Barbarella '68
Danger: Diabolik '68

John Gatins
Hardball '01
Summer Catch '01

Tony Gatlif
The Crazy Stranger '98
Mondo '96

Peter Gaulke
Black Knight '01
Say It Isn't So '01

Nils Gaup (1955-)
Shipwrecked '90
Pathfinder '87

Eleanor Gaver
Dead in the Water '91
Slipping into Darkness '88

John Gay (1924-)
Final Notice '89
Windmills of the Gods '88
Manhunt for Claude Dallas '86
A Tale of Two Cities '80
Hennessy '75
Sometimes a Great Notion '71
Soldier Blue '70
No Way to Treat a Lady '68
The Last Safari '67
The Hallelujah Trail '65
The Courtship of Eddie's Father '62
The Four Horsemen of the Apocalypse '62
Run Silent, Run Deep '58
Separate Tables '58

Joe Gayton
Sweet Jane '98
Bulletproof '96

Tony Gayton
Murder by Numbers '02
The Salton Sea '02

Paul Gegauff (1922-83)
A Piece of Pleasure '74
This Man Must Die '70
Purple Noon '60

Larry Gelbart (1928-)
Bedazzled '00
Weapons of Mass Distraction '97
Barbarians at the Gate '93
Blame It on Rio '84
Tootsie '82
Neighbors '81
Rough Cut '80
Movie, Movie '78
Oh, God! '77
The Wrong Box '66

Milton S. Gelman
One Man's Hero '98
Cabo Blanco '81

Erwin Gelsey
Scarlet Dawn '32
The Strange Love of Molly Louvain '32

Pierre Gendron
Fog Island '45
Bluebeard '44
The Monster Maker '44

Robert Geoffrion
Cruel and Unusual '01
The Peacekeeper '98
Eternal Evil '87

Terry George
Hart's War '02
A Bright Shining Lie '98
The Boxer '97
Some Mother's Son '96
In the Name of the Father '93

Gerald Geraghty
Phantom Stallion '54
Iron Mountain Trail '53
Shadows of Tombstone '53
Sunset in the West '50
Trigger, Jr. '50
Rainbow over Texas '46
Along the Navaho Trail '45
Carson City Kid '40
Come on Rangers '38

Maurice Geraghty
Mohawk '56
Tomahawk '51

Gary Gerani
Vampirella '96
Pumpkinhead '88

Pietro Germi (1904-74)
Alfredo, Alfredo '72
Seduced and Abandoned '64
Divorce—Italian Style '62
Chris Gerolmo
Citizen X '95
Miles from Home '88
Mississippi Burning '88
Nicolas Gessner
Black Water '94
The Peking Blond '68
Robert Getchell
The Client '94
Point of No Return '93
This Boy's Life '93
Stella '89
Sweet Dreams '85
Mommie Dearest '81
Bound for Glory '76
Alice Doesn't Live Here Anymore '74
Steven Gethers (1922-89)
Jenny's War '85
A Woman Called Golda '82
Robert Gianviti
Don't Torture a Duckling '72
The Triumph of Hercules '66
Duncan Gibbins (1952-93)
A Case for Murder '93
Eve of Destruction '90
Rodney Gibbons
Captive '97
Digger '94
Mark Gibson
Snow Dogs '02
The In Crowd '00
William Gibson
Johnny Mnemonic '95
The Miracle Worker '62
Nelson Gidding
The Hindenburg '75
The Andromeda Strain '71
The Haunting '63
Odds Against Tomorrow '59
I Want to Live! '58
Raynold Gideon
Jungle 2 Jungle '96
The River Wild '94
Kuffs '92
Made in Heaven '87
Stand by Me '86
Starman '84
A Man, a Woman, and a Bank '79
Barry Gifford
Dance with the Devil '97
Lost Highway '96
Hotel Room '93
Mateo Gil
Open Your Eyes '97
Thesis '96
Lewis Gilbert (1920-)
Haunted '95
Cosh Boy '61
Carve Her Name with Pride '58
David Giler
Southern Comfort '81
Fun with Dick and Jane '77
The Parallax View '74
Myra Breckinridge '70
Terry Gilliam (1940-)
Fear and Loathing in Las Vegas '98
The Adventures of Baron Munchausen '89
Brazil '85
Monty Python's The Meaning of Life '83
Time Bandits '81
Monty Python's Life of Brian '79
Jabberwocky '77
Monty Python and the Holy Grail '75
And Now for Something Completely Different '72
Sidney Gilliat (1908-94)
Endless Night '71
The Belles of St. Trinian's '53
Night Train to Munich '40
Jamaica Inn '39
The Lady Vanishes '38
King of the Damned '36
Vince Gilligan
Home Fries '98
Wilder Napalm '93
John Gilling (1912-85)
The Mummy's Shroud '67
The Gorgon '64
The Flesh and the Fiends '60
It Takes a Thief '59
Rob Gilmer
Out of Time '00
The Crying Child '96
Dan Gilroy
Chasers '94
Freejack '92
Frank D. Gilroy (1925-)
The Gig '85
Jinxed '82
Once in Paris... '79
From Noon Till Three '76
Desperate Characters '71
The Subject Was Roses '68
The Gallant Hours '60
Fastest Gun Alive '56
Tony Gilroy
The Bourne Identity '02
Proof of Life '00
The Devil's Advocate '97
Extreme Measures '96
Dolores Claiborne '94
The Cutting Edge '92
Milton Moses Ginsberg
Werewolf of Washington '73
Coming Apart '69
Buddy Giovinazzo
No Way Home '96
Combat Shock '84
Francois Girard (1963-)
The Red Violin '98
32 Short Films about Glenn Gould '93
Michael Paul Girard (1954-)
Bikini Med School '98
Sweet Evil '98
Bikini House Calls '96
Illegal Affairs '96
William Girdler (1947-78)
The Manitou '78
Sheba, Baby '75
Asylum of Satan '72
Three on a Meathook '72
Francoise Giroud (1916-)
Where the Hot Wind Blows '59
Antoine et Antoinette '47
Amos Gitai (1950-)
Kippur '00
Kadosh '99
Robert Glass
Death Dreams '92
Running Against Time '90
Handel Glassberg
The Day My Parents Ran Away '93
The Take '90
Mitch Glazer
Great Expectations '97
Scrooged '88
Mr. Mike's Mondo Video '79
Moon over Miami '41
Tom Gleisner
The Dish '00
The Castle '97
James Glickenhaus (1950-)
Timemaster '95
Slaughter of the Innocents '93
McBain '91
Shakedown '88
Exterminator '80
Jean-Luc Godard (1930-)
For Ever Mozart '96
Helas pour Moi '94
Nouvelle Vague '90
Aria '88
Hail Mary '85
Passion '82
Numero Deux '75
Six in Paris '68
Oldest Profession '67
Weekend '67
Two or Three Things I Know about Her '66
Alphaville '65
The Joy of Knowledge '65
A Married Woman '65
Pierrot le Fou '65
Band of Outsiders '64
Contempt '64
Les Carabiniers '63
My Life to Live '62
RoGoPaG '62
Le Petit Soldat '60
A Woman Is a Woman '60
Breathless '59
Ivan Goff (1910-99)
Legend of the Lone Ranger '81
Midnight Lace '60
Portrait in Black '60
Shake Hands with the Devil '59
Band of Angels '57
Man of a Thousand Faces '57
Green Fire '55
Captain Horatio Hornblower '51
White Heat '49
Menahem Golan (1929-)
Hanna's War '88
What's Good for the Goose '69
Willis Goldbeck
The Man Who Shot Liberty Valance '62
Sergeant Rutledge '60
Freaks '32
Peter Pan '24
Dan Goldberg
Feds '88
Heavy Metal '81
Gary David Goldberg
Bye Bye, Love '94
Dad '89
Harris Goldberg
Master of Disguise '02
Deuce Bigalow: Male Gigolo '99
I'll Be Home for Christmas '98
Howard Goldberg
Eden '98
Spontaneous Combustion '89
Marshall Goldberg
Where the Truth Lies '99
The Abduction '96
Michael Goldberg
Snow Dogs '02
Bushwhacked '95
Little Giants '94
Cool Runnings '93
Dan Golden
Venomous '01
Wizards of the Demon Sword '94
Jeffrey Goldenberg
Blowback '99
Looking for an Echo '99
Jorge Goldenberg
I Don't Want to Talk About It '94
Eversmile New Jersey '89
Miss Mary '86
Michael Goldenberg
Contact '97
Bed of Roses '95
Marilyn Goldin
The Triumph of Love '01
Camille Claudel '89
Barocco '76
Bo Goldman (1932-)
Meet Joe Black '98
City Hall '95
Scent of a Woman '92
Little Nikita '88
Swing Shift '84
Shoot the Moon '82
Melvin and Howard '80
One Flew Over the Cuckoo's Nest '75
Gary Goldman
Navy SEALS '90
Total Recall '90
Big Trouble in Little China '86
James Goldman (1927-98)
Anastasia: The Mystery of Anna '86
Oliver Twist '82
Nicholas and Alexandra '71
They Might Be Giants '71
The Lion in Winter '68
William Goldman (1931-)
Hearts in Atlantis '01
The General's Daughter '99
Absolute Power '97
The Chamber '96
The Ghost and the Darkness '96
Maverick '94
Chaplin '92
Year of the Comet '92
Misery '90
Casual Sex? '88
Heat '87
The Princess Bride '87
Mr. Horn '79
Magic '78
A Bridge Too Far '77
All the President's Men '76
Marathon Man '76
The Great Waldo Pepper '75
The Stepford Wives '75
Butch Cassidy and the Sundance Kid '69
Harper '66
Akiva Goldsman (1963-)
A Beautiful Mind '01
Lost in Space '98
Practical Magic '98
Batman and Robin '97
A Time to Kill '96
Batman Forever '95
The Client '94
Silent Fall '94
John Goldsmith
Victoria & Albert '01
Agnes Browne '99
Coming Home '98
The Apocalypse Watch '97
Catherine the Great '95
Kidnapped '95
The Old Curiosity Shop '94
Allan Goldstein
Jungle Boy '96
Death Wish 5: The Face of Death '94
Rooftops '89
Mark Goldstein
Pet Shop '94
Prehysteria '93
Larry Golin
Rocky Marciano '99
Hostage High '97
Love Walked In '97
Rebound: The Legend of Earl "The Goat" Manigault '96
Bryan Goluboff
The Affair '95
The Basketball Diaries '94
Nick Gomez (1963-)
Illtown '96
New Jersey Drive '95
Laws of Gravity '92
Manuel Gomez Pereira
Love Can Seriously Damage Your Health '96
Mouth to Mouth '95
Why Do They Call It Love When They Mean Sex? '92
William Goodhart (1925-99)
Cloud Dancer '80
The Exorcist 2: The Heretic '77
Generation '69
David Zelag Goodman
Fighting Back '82
Eyes of Laura Mars '78
March or Die '77
Logan's Run '76
Farewell, My Lovely '75
Straw Dogs '72
Lovers and Other Strangers '70
Monte Walsh '70
Frances Goodrich
Seven Brides for Seven Brothers '54
Father's Little Dividend '51
Father of the Bride '50
Easter Parade '48
It's a Wonderful Life '46
The Virginian '46
The Thin Man '34
Alex Gordon
Bride of the Monster '55
Jail Bait '54
Bernard Gordon
The Thin Red Line '64
Day of the Triffids '63
Hellcats of the Navy '57
Earth vs. the Flying Saucers '56
The Lawless Breed '52
Bert I. Gordon (1922-)
Empire of the Ants '77
The Witching '72
Tormented '60
The Amazing Colossal Man '57
Bryan Gordon
Pie in the Sky '95
The Discovery Program '89
Dan Gordon
The Hurricane '99
Murder in the First '95
New Eden '94
Wyatt Earp '94
Surf Ninjas '93
Taking the Heat '93
Highlander: The Gathering '92
Passenger 57 '92
Gotcha! '85
Tank '83
Gulliver's Travels '39
Keith Gordon (1961-)
A Midnight Clear '92
The Chocolate War '88
Static '87
Leo Gordon (1922-2000)
The Terror '63
Tower of London '62
Attack of the Giant Leeches '59
The Wasp Woman '59
Leon Gordon
White Cargo '42
They Met in Bombay '41
Balalaika '39
Tarzan and His Mate '34
Freaks '32
Robert Gordon (1895-1971)
Galaxy Quest '99
Addicted to Love '96
Ruth Gordon (1896-1985)
Hardhat & Legs '80
It Should Happen to You '54
The Marrying Kind '52
Pat and Mike '52
Adam's Rib '50
A Double Life '47
Stuart Gordon (1947-)
The Dentist '96
Body Snatchers '93
Honey, I Shrunk the Kids '89
Re-Animator '84
Laszlo Gorog (1903-)
Earth vs. the Spider '58
The Land Unknown '57
The Mole People '56
Marleen Gorris (1948-)
Antonia's Line '95
Broken Mirrors '85
Carl Gottlieb (1938-)
Doctor Detroit '83
Jaws 3 '83
Caveman '81
The Jerk '79
Jaws 2 '78
Which Way Is Up? '77
Jaws '75
Alfred Gough
Showtime '02
Shanghai Noon '00
Heywood Gould
Mistrial '96
Trial by Jury '94
One Good Cop '91
Cocktail '88
Streets of Gold '86
Fort Apache, the Bronx '81
The Boys from Brazil '78
Rolling Thunder '77
Peter Gould
Meeting Daddy '98
Double Dragon '94
Edmund Goulding (1891-1959)
That Certain Woman '37
Riptide '34
Tol'able David '21
David S. Goyer
Blade II '02
ZigZag '02
Blade '98
Dark City '97
The Crow 2: City of Angels '96
The Puppet Masters '94
Arcade '93
Death Warrant '90
Jean-Francois Goyet
Western '96
La Vengeance d'une Femme '89
Todd Graff (1959-)
Coyote Ugly '00
The Beautician and the Beast '97
Angie '94
Fly by Night '93
The Vanishing '93
Used People '92
Bruce Graham
Steal This Movie! '00
Anastasia '97
Dunston Checks In '95
Ronny Graham (1919-99)
Spaceballs '87
Finders Keepers '84
To Be or Not to Be '83
Michael Grais
Cool World '92
Marked for Death '90
Poltergeist 2: The Other Side '86
Poltergeist '82
Death Hunt '81
Derek Granger
Where Angels Fear to Tread '91
A Handful of Dust '88
Pierre Granier-Deferre (1927-)
A Woman at Her Window '77
The Last Train '74
James Edward Grant
Support Your Local Gunfighter '71
Circus World '64
Donovan's Reef '63
McLintock! '63
The Alamo '60
Three Violent People '57
Hondo '53
Flying Leathernecks '51
Sands of Iwo Jima '49
Angel and the Badman '47

Johnny Eager '42
The Lady Is Willing '42
John Grant
Abbott and Costello Meet the Mummy '55
Abbott and Costello Meet the Keystone Kops '54
Abbott and Costello Go to Mars '53
Abbott and Costello Meet Dr. Jekyll and Mr. Hyde '52
Ma and Pa Kettle at the Fair '52
Abbott and Costello Meet the Invisible Man '51
Comin' Round the Mountain '51
Abbott and Costello in the Foreign Legion '50
Abbott and Costello Meet the Killer, Boris Karloff '49
Abbott and Costello Meet Frankenstein '48
Buck Privates Come Home '47
Here Come the Co-Eds '45
In Society '44
It Ain't Hay '43
Buck Privates '41
Hold That Ghost '41
In the Navy '41
Susannah Grant
Erin Brockovich '00
28 Days '00
Ever After: A Cinderella Story '98
Pocahontas '95
Robert Grasmere
Baby Geniuses '98
A Million to Juan '94
Alex Graves
Casualties '97
The Crude Oasis '95
Beverly Gray
Haunted Symphony '94
Full Contact '93
James Gray
The Yards '00
Little Odessa '94
John Gray
Brian's Song '01
The Seventh Stream '01
The Hunley '99
An American Story '92
Showdown at Williams Creek '91
The Lost Capone '90
Billy Galvin '86
Mike Gray
Code of Silence '85
Wavelength '83
The China Syndrome '79
Pamela Gray
Music of the Heart '99
A Walk on the Moon '99
Calm at Sunset '96
Simon Gray
Unnatural Pursuits '91
A Month in the Country '87
William Gray
Humongous '82
The Changeling '80
Prom Night '80
Charles Grayson
Battle Hymn '57
Outpost in Morocco '49
Underground '41
One Night in the Tropics '40
Brian Grazer
Housesitter '92
Armed and Dangerous '86
Kjell Grede
Good Evening, Mr. Wallenberg '93
Hip Hip Hurrah! '87
Adolph Green (1915-)
Bells Are Ringing '60
Auntie Mame '58
It's Always Fair Weather '55
Singin' in the Rain '52
The Barkleys of Broadway '49
On the Town '49
Clarence Green
The Oscar '66
D.O.A. '49
Clifford Green
Bless the Child '00
Mystery Island '81
Picnic at Hanging Rock '75
Howard J. Green
Harmon of Michigan '41
Blessed Event '32
I Am a Fugitive from a Chain Gang '32
They Call It Sin '32
Maker of Men '31
Lewis Green
Never Talk to Strangers '95
Dead on Sight '94
The Spy Within '94
Walon Green
The Hi-Lo Country '98
Eraser '96
RoboCop 2 '90
Crusoe '89
Solarbabies '86
The Border '82
Brink's Job '78
Sorcerer '77
The Wild Bunch '69
Peter Greenaway (1942-)
8 1/2 Women '99
The Pillow Book '95
The Belly of an Architect '91
Prospero's Books '91
The Cook, the Thief, His Wife & Her Lover '90
A Zed & Two Noughts '88
Drowning by Numbers '87
The Draughtsman's Contract '82
Everett Greenbaum (1920-99)
The Shakiest Gun in the West '68
The Reluctant Astronaut '67
Dan Greenberg
The Guardian '90
Oh! Calcutta! '72
Matt Greenberg
Halloween: H20 '98
The Prophecy 2: Ashtown '97
The Ghost Brigade '93
Anthony Laurence Greene
Dead Sexy '01
Number One Fan '94
Graham Greene (1952-)
The Comedians '67
The Fallen Idol '49
The Third Man '49
21 Days '37
Harold Greene (1915-2000)
Texas across the River '66
The House of the Seven Gables '40
Seth Greenland
My Teacher's Wife '95
Who's the Man? '93
Maggie Greenwald (1955-)
Songcatcher '99
The Ballad of Little Jo '93
Edwin Greenwood
Young and Innocent '37
The Man Who Knew Too Much '34
William Grefe (1930-)
The Death Curse of Tartu '66
The Checkered Flag '63
Andre Gregory (1934-)
Vanya on 42nd Street '94
My Dinner with Andre '81
Frederic Grendel
Violette '78
Diabolique '55
Maurice Griffe
Grisbi '53
Rendez-vous de Juillet '49
Antoine et Antoinette '47
Ted Griffin
Ocean's Eleven '01
Best Laid Plans '99
Ravenous '99
Charles B. Griffith
Not of This Earth '88
Dr. Heckyl and Mr. Hype '80
Eat My Dust '76
Death Race 2000 '75
Devil's Angels '67
The Wild Angels '66
Atlas '60
The Beast from Haunted Cave '60
Creature from the Haunted Sea '60
Little Shop of Horrors '60
A Bucket of Blood '59
Rock All Night '57
Teenage Doll '57
The Undead '57
The Gunslinger '56
It Conquered the World '56
D.W. Griffith (1875-1948)
Struggle '31
Isn't Life Wonderful '24
Orphans of the Storm '21
The Love Flower '20
Way Down East '20
Broken Blossoms '19
Intolerance '16
The Birth of a Nation '15
Judith of Bethulia '14
J.J. Griffith
Catlow '71
Shalako '68
Thomas Ian Griffith (1962-)
Excessive Force '93
Night of the Warrior '91
Leon Griffiths
The Grissom Gang '71
The Flesh and the Fiends '60
Trevor Griffiths
The Last Place on Earth '94
Singing the Blues in Red '87
Aurelio Grimaldi (1957-)
Nerolio '96
Acla's Descent into Floristella '87
Christopher Grimm
Rhythm Thief '94
Spare Me '92
Ferde Grofe, Jr.
Warkill '65
The Walls of Hell '64
Jerry Gross
Teenage Mother '67
Girl on a Chain Gang '65
Joel Gross
No Escape '94
Blind Man's Bluff '91
Larry Gross
Crime and Punishment in Suburbia '00
True Crime '99
The Virginian '99
Gunshy '98
Rear Window '98
Chinese Box '97
David '97
This World, Then the Fireworks '97
Geronimo: An American Legend '93
Streets of Fire '84
48 Hrs. '82
Leonard Gross
Divided by Hate '96
Forbidden '85
Lynn Grossman
Subway Stories '97
Tokyo Pop '88
Jean Gruault
The Mystery of Alexina '86
The Eighties '83
Mon Oncle d'Amerique '80
The Green Room '78
The Story of Adele H. '75
The Wild Child '70
Jules and Jim '62
Paris Belongs to Us '60
Frank Gruber
Dressed to Kill '46
Terror by Night '46
The Mask of Dimitrios '44
John Guare
Subway Stories '97
Six Degrees of Separation '93
Atlantic City '81
Paul Guay
Heartbreakers '01
Liar Liar '96
The Little Rascals '94
Richard Guay
The 24 Hour Woman '99
Household Saints '93
True Love '89
Bill Gucwa
Storm Catcher '99
No Code of Conduct '98
Tonino Guerra (1920-)
The Truce '96
Beyond the Clouds '95
Ulysses' Gaze '95
Everybody's Fine '90
Night Sun '90
Landscape in the Mist '88
Good Morning, Babylon '87
Ginger & Fred '86
Henry IV '85
And the Ship Sails On '83
Nostalghia '83
The Night of the Shooting Stars '82
Amarcord '74
Zabriskie Point '70
Blow-Up '66
The Eclipse '66
Casanova '70 '65
10th Victim '65
The Red Desert '64
L'Avventura '60
Jorge Guerricaechevarria
Dance with the Devil '97
Live Flesh '97
The Day of the Beast '95
Christopher Guest (1948-)
Best in Show '00
Waiting for Guffman '96
The Return of Spinal Tap '92
The Big Picture '89
This Is Spinal Tap '84
Val Guest (1911-)
When Dinosaurs Ruled the Earth '70
The Day the Earth Caught Fire '61
Dentist In the Chair '60
Carry On Admiral '57
Quatermass 2 '57
The Runaway Bus '54
Another Man's Poison '52
Mister Drake's Duck '50
Yilmaz Guney (1937-84)
The Wall '83
Yol '82
Bill Gunn
Ganja and Hess '73
The Angel Levine '70
James Gunn
Scooby-Doo '02
The Specials '00
Tromeo & Juliet '95
All I Desire '53
Harriet Craig '50
Dan Guntzelman
Perfect Game '00
Revenge of the Nerds 2: Nerds in Paradise '87
Dan Gurskis
The Substitute 4: Failure is Not an Option '00
Full Body Massage '95
Body Language '92
The Stranger '87
Beth Gutcheon
The Good Fight '92
The Children of Theatre Street '77
Annette Goliti Gutierrez
Kill Me Later '01
Wedding Bell Blues '96
Sebastian Gutierrez
She Creature '01
Judas Kiss '98
Tomas Gutierrez Alea (1926-96)
Guantanamera '95
Strawberry and Chocolate '93
Letters from the Park '88
Up to a Certain Point '83
Memories of Underdevelopment '68
Death of a Bureaucrat '66
Stephen Gyllenhaal (1949-)
Homegrown '97
The New Kids '85
Belinda Haas
Up at the Villa '00
The Blood Oranges '97
Angels and Insects '95
The Music of Chance '93
Charles Haas (1913-)
Matinee '92
Gremlins 2: The New Batch '90
Tex '82
Over the Edge '79
Philip Haas
The Blood Oranges '97
Angels and Insects '95
The Music of Chance '93
Steve Haberman
Screw Loose '99
Dracula: Dead and Loving It '95
Albert Hackett (1900-95)
Seven Brides for Seven Brothers '54
Father's Little Dividend '51
Father of the Bride '50
Easter Parade '48
It's a Wonderful Life '46
The Virginian '46
The Thin Man '34
Michael Haigney
Pokemon 3: The Movie '01
Pokemon the Movie 2000: The Power of One '00
Pokemon: The First Movie '99
Fred Haines
Steppenwolf '74
Ulysses '67
Richard W. Haines
Alien Space Avenger '91
Class of Nuke 'Em High '86
Splatter University '84
William Wister Haines (1908-89)
Command Decision '48
The Texans '38
The Black Legion '37
John Hale
Nostromo '96
Elizabeth R '72
Mary, Queen of Scots '71
Anne of the Thousand Days '69
Arch (Archie) Hall, Sr. (1908-78)
Wild Guitar '62
The Choppers '61
Kenneth J. Hall
Die Watching '93
Test Tube Teens from the Year 2000 '93
Evil Spawn '87
Norman S. Hall
The Young Land '59
The Topeka Terror '45
Bordertown Gunfighters '43
California Joe '43
Sam Hall
Night of Dark Shadows '71
House of Dark Shadows '70
Willis Hall
Billy Liar '63
A Kind of Loving '62
Whistle down the Wind '61
Edward Halperin (1898-1981)
Sky Bandits '40
Yukon Flight '40
Philip Halprin
Snow Dogs '02
The In Crowd '00
Craig Hamann
Boogie Boy '98
Dollman vs Demonic Toys '93
John Hamburg
Zoolander '01
Meet the Parents '00
Safe Men '98
Robert Hamer (1911-63)
Kind Hearts and Coronets '49
Pink String and Sealing Wax '45
Sam Hamm
Monkeybone '01
Batman '89
Never Cry Wolf '83
Oscar Hammerstein
State Fair '45
Show Boat '36
Earl Hamner
Charlotte's Web '73
Heidi '67
Christopher Hampton (1946-)
The Secret Agent '96
Carrington '95
Mary Reilly '95
Total Eclipse '95
Dangerous Liaisons '88
The Good Father '87
The Wolf at the Door '87
Beyond the Limit '83
A Doll's House '73
Orville H. Hampton (1917-97)
Friday Foster '75
Detroit 9000 '73
Jack the Giant Killer '62
Atomic Submarine '59
John Lee Hancock
Midnight in the Garden of Good and Evil '97
A Perfect World '93
Peter Handke
Wings of Desire '88
The Goalie's Anxiety at the Penalty Kick '71
Daryl Haney (1963-)
Forbidden Sins '99
Xtro 3: Watch the Skies '95
Stranger by Night '94
To Die Standing '91
Lords of the Deep '89
Masque of the Red Death '89
Crime Zone '88
Friday the 13th, Part 7: The New Blood '88
Daddy's Boys '87
Tom Hanks (1956-)
Band of Brothers '01
From the Earth to the Moon '98
That Thing You Do! '96
William Hanley
Ellen Foster '97
Scarlett '94
Our Sons '91
The Attic: The Hiding of Anne Frank '88
Too Far to Go '79
Mark Hanna
Not of This Earth '88
Slaughter '72
Attack of the 50 Foot Woman '58
The Amazing Colossal Man '57
The Undead '57
The Gunslinger '56
Marion Hansel (1949-)
The Quarry '98
Between Heaven and Earth '93
Dust '85
Curtis Hanson (1945-)
L.A. Confidential '97
The Bedroom Window '87
Never Cry Wolf '83
The Silent Partner '78
The Arousers '70
The Dunwich Horror '70

Marla Hanson
The Blackout '97
Subway Stories '97
Kenchiro Hara
47 Ronin, Part 1 '42
47 Ronin, Part 2 '42
Carl Harbaugh
Steamboat Bill, Jr. '28
College '27
Regeneration '15
Patrick Harbinson
Horatio Hornblower '99
The Waiting Time '99
Frenchman's Creek '98
Gary Hardwick
The Brothers '01
Trippin' '99
Todd McFarlane's Spawn '97
David Hare (1947-)
The Secret Rapture '94
Damage '92
Strapless '90
Saigon: Year of the Cat '87
Plenty '85
Wetherby '85
Lance Z. Hargreaves
Devil Doll '64
First Man into Space '59
Marion Hargrove
40 Pounds of Trouble '62
The Music Man '62
Cash McCall '60
Tsui Hark (1951-)
Time and Tide '00
Black Mask '96
Iron Monkey '93
Once Upon a Time in China III '93
Once Upon a Time in China II '92
Twin Dragons '92
Wicked City '92
Once Upon a Time in China '91
Robert Harling
The Evening Star '96
The First Wives Club '96
Soapdish '91
Steel Magnolias '89
John Harlow (1896-)
Appointment with Crime '45
Meet Sexton Blake '44
Stephen Harrigan
Cleopatra '99
Lone Justice 3: Showdown at Plum Creek '96
The O.J. Simpson Story '94
Curtis Harrington (1928-)
Planet of Blood '66
Night Tide '63
Damian Harris
Mercy '00
The Rachel Papers '89
Elmer Harris
Red Salute '35
Tess of the Storm Country '22
Eoghan Harris
Sharpe's Revenge '97
Sharpe's Mission '96
Sharpe's Regiment '96
Sharpe's Siege '96
Sharpe's Enemy '94
Sharpe's Sword '94
Sharpe's Eagle '93
Sharpe's Rifles '93
James B. Harris (1928-)
Boiling Point '93
Cop '88
Kirk Harris
Hard Luck '01
Loser '97
Timothy Harris (1946-)
Pure Luck '91
Kindergarten Cop '90
My Stepmother Is an Alien '88
Twins '88
Brewster's Millions '85
Trading Places '83
Cheaper to Keep Her '80

Trent Harris (1952-)
Plan 10 from Outer Space '95
Rubin & Ed '92
Vernon Harris
Oliver! '68
Carve Her Name with Pride '58
The Admirable Crichton '57
Jim Harrison
Dalva '95
Wolf '94
Revenge '90
Cold Feet '89
Joan Harrison (1911-94)
Dark Waters '44
Foreign Correspondent '40
Rebecca '40
Jamaica Inn '39
John Harrison
Dinosaur '00
Dune '00
Donor Unknown '95
John Kent Harrison
You Know My Name '99
Calm at Sunset '96
City Boy '93
The Sound and the Silence '93
Beautiful Dreamers '92
Memories of Murder '90
Murder by Phone '82
Shock Waves '77
Matthew Harrison (1960-)
Kicked in the Head '97
Rhythm Thief '94
Spare Me '92
Mary Harron
American Psycho '99
I Shot Andy Warhol '96
Jacobsen Hart
Raven '97
The Power Within '95
Rage '95
Steel Frontier '94
Cyber-Tracker '93
Direct Hit '93
Zero Tolerance '93
Jim V. Hart
Jack and the Beanstalk: The Real Story '01
Muppet Treasure Island '96
Bram Stoker's Dracula '92
Moss Hart
A Star Is Born '54
Hans Christian Andersen '52
Gentleman's Agreement '47
Hal Hartley (1959-)
No Such Thing '01
Henry Fool '98
Flirt '95
Amateur '94
Simple Men '92
Trust '91
The Unbelievable Truth '90
Don Hartman (1900-58)
Wonder Man '45
The Princess and the Pirate '44
My Favorite Blonde '42
The Road to Morocco '42
The Road to Zanzibar '41
The Road to Singapore '40
Never Say Die '39
Waikiki Wedding '37
The Princess Comes Across '36
Here Comes Cookie '35
Edmund Hartmann
Casanova's Big Night '54
The Lemon Drop Kid '51
Variety Girl '47
In Society '44
Ali Baba and the Forty Thieves '43
Steven Hartov
Mars '96
Mercenary '96
Johanna Harwood
Call Me Bwana '63
From Russia with Love '63
Dr. No '62

Ronald Harwood (1934-)
The Browning Version '94
A Fine Romance '92
The Doctor and the Devils '85
The Dresser '83
One Day in the Life of Ivan Denisovich '71
Shinobu Hashimoto
Dodes 'ka-den '70
Samurai Rebellion '67
The Bad Sleep Well '60
The Hidden Fortress '58
Throne of Blood '57
I Live in Fear '55
Seven Samurai '54
Ikiru '52
Rashomon '51
Michael Hastings
The American '01
Tom & Viv '94
The Nightcomers '72
Richard Hatem
The Mothman Prophecies '02
Under Siege 2: Dark Territory '95
Wings Hauser (1948-)
Gang Boys '97
No Safe Haven '87
Anthony Havelock-Allan
Brief Encounter '46
Blithe Spirit '45
Jean C. Havez (1870-1925)
Seven Chances '25
The Navigator '24
Our Hospitality '23
John Hawkesworth
The Duchess of Duke Street '78
Tiger Bay '59
Christopher Hawthorne
The Courtyard '95
Parents '89
Ian Hay
Sabotage '36
The 39 Steps '35
Carey Hayes
First Daughter '99
Down, Out and Dangerous '95
Chad Hayes
First Daughter '99
Down, Out and Dangerous '95
John Hayes
All the Lovin' Kinfolk '70
The Cut Throats '69
John Michael Hayes (1919-)
Iron Will '93
Pancho Barnes '88
Nevada Smith '66
Harlow '65
The Carpetbaggers '64
The Chalk Garden '64
Where Love Has Gone '64
The Children's Hour '61
Butterfield 8 '60
But Not for Me '59
The Matchmaker '58
Peyton Place '57
The Man Who Knew Too Much '56
It's a Dog's Life '55
To Catch a Thief '55
The Trouble with Harry '55
Rear Window '54
Thunder Bay '53
War Arrow '53
Red Ball Express '52
Joseph Hayes
Desperate Hours '90
Stolen Hours '63
Terry Hayes
From Hell '01
Vertical Limit '00
Payback '98
Mr. Reliable: A True Story '95
Dead Calm '89

Mad Max: Beyond Thunderdome '85
The Road Warrior '82
Gregory C. Haynes
Heaven or Vegas '98
Magenta '96
Todd Haynes (1961-)
Velvet Goldmine '98
Office Killer '97
Safe '95
Poison '91
David Hayter
The Scorpion King '02
X-Men '00
Lillie Hayward
Proud Rebel '58
Lady Killer '33
They Call It Sin '32
David Heavener
Fugitive X '96
Eye of the Stranger '93
Prime Target '91
Killcrazy '89
Twisted Justice '89
Ben Hecht (1894-1964)
Circus World '64
The Indian Fighter '55
Actors and Sin '52
Monkey Business '52
The Thing '51
Notorious '46
Spectre of the Rose '46
Spellbound '45
The Black Swan '42
Tales of Manhattan '42
Angels Over Broadway '40
Comrade X '40
Gunga Din '39
Let Freedom Ring '39
Wuthering Heights '39
Nothing Sacred '37
Twentieth Century '34
Viva Villa! '34
Hallelujah, I'm a Bum '33
Amy Heckerling (1954-)
Loser '00
Clueless '95
Look Who's Talking, Too '90
Look Who's Talking '89
Rob Hedden
Clockstoppers '02
Alien Fury: Countdown to Invasion '00
The Colony '95
Friday the 13th, Part 8: Jason Takes Manhattan '89
Roger Hedden
Hi-Life '98
Sleep with Me '94
Bodies, Rest & Motion '93
Peter Hedges (1962-)
About a Boy '02
A Map of the World '99
What's Eating Gilbert Grape '93
Victor Heerman (1893-1977)
Golden Boy '39
Stella Dallas '37
Break of Hearts '35
Little Minister '34
Little Women '33
My Boy '21
Carol Heikkinen
Center Stage '00
Empire Records '95
The Thing Called Love '93
Jo Heims
You'll Like My Mother '72
Play Misty for Me '71
Double Trouble '67
Robert Heinlein
Project Moon Base '53
Destination Moon '50
Brian Helgeland (1961-)
Blood Work '02
A Knight's Tale '01
Payback '98
Conspiracy Theory '97
L.A. Confidential '97
The Postman '97
Assassins '95

A Nightmare on Elm Street 4: Dream Master '88
976-EVIL '88
Lukas Heller
Blue City '86
Damnation Alley '77
The Killing of Sister George '69
The Dirty Dozen '67
Hush, Hush, Sweet Charlotte '65
What Ever Happened to Baby Jane? '62
Lillian Hellman
The Chase '66
The North Star '43
Watch on the Rhine '43
The Little Foxes '41
Dead End '37
These Three '36
Sam Hellman
My Darling Clementine '46
The Three Musketeers '39
Frank Henenlotter
Basket Case 3: The Progeny '92
Basket Case 2 '90
Frankenhooker '90
Brain Damage '88
Basket Case '82
James Henerson
Mutiny '99
The Tempest '99
The Love Letter '98
Getting Gotti '94
The Fire Next Time '93
Liu Heng
The Story of Qiu Ju '91
Ju Dou '90
Kim Henkel
The Texas Chainsaw Massacre 4: The Next Generation '95
Eaten Alive '76
The Texas Chainsaw Massacre '74
Hilary Henkin
Wag the Dog '97
Romeo Is Bleeding '93
Fatal Beauty '87
Beth Henley
Miss Firecracker '89
Crimes of the Heart '86
Nobody's Fool '86
True Stories '86
Jack Henley
Ma and Pa Kettle at Waikiki '55
Ma and Pa Kettle on Vacation '53
Ma and Pa Kettle Back On the Farm '51
Blondie Hits the Jackpot '49
A Thousand and One Nights '45
Buck Henry (1930-)
Town and Country '01
To Die For '95
Protocol '84
First Family '80
The Day of the Dolphin '73
What's Up, Doc? '72
Catch-22 '70
The Owl and the Pussycat '70
Candy '68
The Graduate '67
Todd Henschell
Puppet Master 5: The Final Chapter '94
Puppet Master 4 '93
Jonathan Hensleigh
Armageddon '98
The Saint '97
The Rock '96
Die Hard: With a Vengeance '95
Jumanji '95
A Far Off Place '93
F. Hugh Herbert (1897-1958)
Let's Make It Legal '51
Our Very Own '50
Ron Herbst
Warlords 3000 '93
Deadly Diamonds '91

Tim Herlihy
Mr. Deeds '02
Little Nicky '00
Big Daddy '99
The Waterboy '98
The Wedding Singer '97
Happy Gilmore '96
Mark Herman
Little Voice '98
Brassed Off '96
Blame It on the Bellboy '92
Jaime Humberto Hermosillo (1942-)
Esmeralda Comes by Night '98
Dona Herlinda & Her Son '86
Mary, My Dearest '83
Gyula Hernadi
Adoption '75
The Red and the White '68
The Round Up '66
Michael Herr
John Grisham's The Rainmaker '97
Full Metal Jacket '87
Apocalypse Now '79
Rowdy Herrington (1951-)
A Murder of Crows '99
Striking Distance '93
Jack's Back '87
W(illiam) Blake Herron
The Bourne Identity '02
A Texas Funeral '99
Skin Art '93
Joel Hershman
Greenfingers '00
Hold Me, Thrill Me, Kiss Me '93
Marshall Herskovitz (1952-)
Glory '89
Special Bulletin '83
Adam Herz (1973-)
American Pie 2 '01
American Pie '99
Michael Herz (1949-)
Stuck on You '84
First Turn On '83
Jim Herzfeld
Meet the Parents '00
Meet the Deedles '98
John Herzfeld
15 Minutes '01
Two Days in the Valley '96
Casualties of Love: The "Long Island Lolita" Story '93
Werner Herzog (1942-)
Cobra Verde '88
Fitzcarraldo '82
Nosferatu the Vampyre '79
Woyzeck '78
Stroszek '77
Every Man for Himself & God Against All '75
Heart of Glass '74
Aguirre, the Wrath of God '72
Signs of Life '68
Fraser Heston
Treasure Island '89
The Mountain Men '80
Rod Hewitt
The Debt '98
Sworn Enemies '96
The Dangerous '95
Louis M. Heyward
The Conqueror Worm '68
Planet of the Vampires '65
Pajama Party '64
Winston Hibler
Nikki, the Wild Dog of the North '61
Peter Pan '53
The Adventures of Ichabod and Mr. Toad '49
Jochen Hick
No One Sleeps '01
Via Appia '92

George Hickenlooper (1964-)
- The Big Brass Ring '99
- Dogtown '97
- The Low Life '95
- Hearts of Darkness: A Filmmaker's Apocalypse '91

Anthony Hickox (1959-)
- Prince Valiant '97
- Waxwork 2: Lost in Time '91
- Waxwork '88

Julie Hickson
- Snow White: The Fairest of Them All '02
- Homeward Bound 2: Lost in San Francisco '96

Colin Higgins (1941-88)
- Silver Streak '76
- Harold and Maude '71

John C. Higgins
- Robinson Crusoe on Mars '64
- He Walked by Night '48
- Raw Deal '48
- Railroaded '47
- T-Men '47

Patrick Highsmith
- Mars '96
- Savage '96
- Automatic '94

David Hill
- Too Young to Die '90
- Promised a Miracle '88

Debra Hill
- Escape from L.A. '96
- Jailbreakers '94
- Halloween 2: The Nightmare Isn't Over! '81
- The Fog '78
- Halloween '78

Jack Hill (1933-)
- Foxy Brown '74
- Coffy '73
- The Big Bird Cage '72
- The Fear Chamber '68
- Pit Stop '67
- Spider Baby '64
- The Terror '63

John Hill
- Quigley Down Under '90
- Little Nikita '88
- Heartbeeps '81

Robert F. "Bob" Hill (1886-1966)
- The Cat and the Canary '27
- The Adventures of Tarzan '21

Walter Hill (1942-)
- Last Man Standing '96
- Wild Bill '95
- The Getaway '93
- Red Heat '88
- Aliens '86
- Blue City '86
- Streets of Fire '84
- 48 Hrs. '82
- Southern Comfort '81
- The Warriors '79
- The Driver '78
- The Drowning Pool '75
- Hard Times '75
- Mackintosh Man '73
- The Thief Who Came to Dinner '73
- The Getaway '72

David Hilton
- The Delivery '99
- The Young Americans '93

James Hilton
- Mrs. Miniver '42
- Foreign Correspondent '40
- Camille '36

David Himmelstein
- Soul of the Game '96
- Village of the Damned '95
- Talent for the Game '91
- Power '86

Alan Hines
- My Husband's Double Life '01
- Breaking the Surface: The Greg Louganis Story '96
- Square Dance '87

Roger O. Hirson
- A Woman Named Jackie '91
- The Old Man and the Sea '90
- A Christmas Carol '84
- Demon Seed '77

Michael Hirst
- Elizabeth '98
- The Ballad of the Sad Cafe '91
- Meeting Venus '91
- Fools of Fortune '90

Alfred Hitchcock (1899-1980)
- Saboteur '42
- No. 17 '32
- Rich and Strange '32
- Skin Game '31
- Juno and the Paycock '30
- Murder '30
- Blackmail '29
- Champagne '28
- The Farmer's Wife '28
- The Ring '27
- The Lodger '26

Michael Hitchcock
- House Arrest '96
- Where the Day Takes You '92

Carl K. Hittleman (1907-99)
- Billy the Kid Versus Dracula '66
- Jesse James Meets Frankenstein's Daughter '65
- 36 Hours '64

Ken Hixon
- Inventing the Abbotts '97
- Incident at Deception Ridge '94
- Caught in the Act '93

Godfrey Ho
- Ninja Champion '80s
- Ninja Destroyer '70s

Danny Hoch
- White Boyz '99
- Subway Stories '97

John Hodge
- The Beach '00
- A Life Less Ordinary '97
- Trainspotting '95
- Shallow Grave '94

Adrian Hodges
- Lorna Doone '01
- David Copperfield '99
- Metroland '97
- Tom & Viv '94

Mike Hodges (1932-)
- Black Rainbow '91
- Damien: Omen 2 '78
- The Terminal Man '74
- Pulp '72
- Get Carter '71

Arthur Hoerl
- The Singing Cowgirl '39
- Reefer Madness '38
- Cross Examination '32
- The Peacock Fan '29

Samuel Hoffenstein
- His Butler's Sister '44
- Laura '44
- The Phantom of the Opera '43
- Tales of Manhattan '42
- The Song of Songs '33
- Dr. Jekyll and Mr. Hyde '32

Michael Hoffman
- William Shakespeare's A Midsummer Night's Dream '99
- Promised Land '88

Michael Hogan
- Forever and a Day '43
- Arabian Nights '42
- King Solomon's Mines '37

Paul Hogan (1939-)
- Lightning Jack '94
- Almost an Angel '90
- Crocodile Dundee 2 '88
- Crocodile Dundee '86

Brian Hohlfield
- The Mighty Ducks '92
- He Said, She Said '91

Agnieszka Holland (1948-)
- Trois Couleurs: Bleu '93
- Olivier, Olivier '92
- Europa, Europa '91
- Korczak '90
- To Kill a Priest '89
- The Possessed '88
- Anna '87
- Angry Harvest '85
- A Love in Germany '84
- Danton '82
- Without Anesthesia '78

Steve Holland
- One Crazy Summer '86
- Better Off Dead '85

Tom Holland (1943-)
- Stephen King's Thinner '96
- Stephen King's The Langoliers '95
- Child's Play '88
- Scream for Help '86
- Fright Night '85
- Cloak & Dagger '84
- Psycho 2 '83
- The Beast Within '82
- Class of 1984 '82

Nicole Holofcener
- Lovely & Amazing '02
- Walking and Talking '96

Geoffrey Homes
- Cavalry Charge '51
- Out of the Past '47

Inoshiro Honda (1911-93)
- War of the Gargantuas '70
- Destroy All Monsters '68
- Godzilla, King of the Monsters '56

Tobe Hooper (1946-)
- The Mangler '94
- Spontaneous Combustion '89
- The Texas Chainsaw Massacre '74

Arthur Hopcraft
- Rebecca '97
- A Perfect Spy '88

Edward Hope
- The Long Gray Line '55
- Three for the Show '55

Alan Hopgood
- Alvin Rides Again '74
- Alvin Purple '73

John Hopkins
- Dunston Checks In '95
- Hiroshima '95
- Codename Kyril '91
- The Holcroft Covenant '85
- Torment '85
- Murder by Decree '79
- The Offence '73
- The Virgin Soldiers '69
- Thunderball '65

Arthur T. Horman
- Here Come the Co-Eds '45
- Buck Privates '41
- In the Navy '41

Israel Horovitz
- James Dean '01
- Sunshine '99
- North Shore Fish '97
- A Man in Love '87
- Author! Author! '82
- The Strawberry Statement '70

Ed Horowitz
- Exit Wounds '01
- On Deadly Ground '94

Don Houghton
- The Legend of the 7 Golden Vampires '73
- The Satanic Rites of Dracula '73
- Dracula A.D. 1972 '72

Elizabeth Jane Howard
- Getting It Right '89
- The Very Edge '63

Ron Howard (1954-)
- Parenthood '89
- Cotton Candy '82
- Grand Theft Auto '77

Sidney Howard
- Gone with the Wind '39
- Dodsworth '36
- Raffles '30
- Bulldog Drummond '29

Dorothy Howell
- The Miracle Woman '31
- Platinum Blonde '31

Frank Howson
- Flynn '96
- The Hunting '92

Perry Howze
- Chances Are '89
- Mystic Pizza '88
- Maid to Order '87

George Huang
- How to Make a Monster '01
- Swimming with Sharks '94

Lucien Hubbard
- The Vanishing American '25
- Outside the Law '21

Tom Hubbard
- Daniel Boone: Trail Blazer '56
- Thunder Pass '54
- Two Lost Worlds '50

Tom Huckabee
- Deep in the Heart (of Texas) '98
- Deathfight '93

John Huddles
- Uncorked '98
- Far Harbor '96

Reginald (Reggie) Hudlin (1961-)
- Bebe's Kids '92
- House Party '90

Clair Huffaker
- Chino '75
- Hellfighters '68
- The War Wagon '67
- Flaming Star '60

John Hughes (1950-)
- Just Visiting '01
- Reach the Rock '98
- Flubber '97
- Home Alone 3 '97
- 101 Dalmatians '96
- Baby's Day Out '94
- Miracle on 34th Street '94
- Dennis the Menace '93
- Beethoven '92
- Home Alone 2: Lost in New York '92
- Career Opportunities '91
- Curly Sue '91
- Dutch '91
- Home Alone '90
- National Lampoon's Christmas Vacation '89
- Uncle Buck '89
- The Great Outdoors '88
- She's Having a Baby '88
- Planes, Trains & Automobiles '87
- Some Kind of Wonderful '87
- Ferris Bueller's Day Off '86
- Pretty in Pink '86
- The Breakfast Club '85
- National Lampoon's European Vacation '85
- Weird Science '85
- Sixteen Candles '84
- Mr. Mom '83
- National Lampoon's Vacation '83
- National Lampoon's Class Reunion '82

Ken Hughes (1922-2001)
- Oh, Alfie '75
- Cromwell '70
- Chitty Chitty Bang Bang '68
- Arrivederci, Baby! '66
- The Trials of Oscar Wilde '60
- Heat Wave '54

Tom Hughes
- Red Letters '00
- Breathing Room '96

Cyril Hume
- The Invisible Boy '57
- Forbidden Planet '56
- The Great Gatsby '49
- Trader Horn '31

Sammo Hung (1952-)
- The Millionaire's Express '86
- Spooky Encounters '80

Tran Anh Hung (1963-)
- The Vertical Ray of the Sun '00
- Cyclo '95
- The Scent of Green Papaya '93

Ed(ward) Hunt
- Bloody Birthday '80
- Starship Invasions '77

Evan Hunter
- The Birds '63
- High & Low '62

Ian McLellan Hunter
- Captain Sinbad '63
- The Amazing Mr. X '48

Tim Hunter
- Tex '82
- Over the Edge '79

Lawrence Huntington
- The Oblong Box '69
- Man on the Run '49

William Hurlbut
- The Bride of Frankenstein '35
- Imitation of Life '34

Harry Hurwitz (1938-95)
- Fleshtone '94
- That's Adequate '90
- Under the Rainbow '81
- The Projectionist '71

Rich Husky
- Children of Fury '94
- Nightmare '91

John Huston (1906-87)
- Mr. North '88
- The Man Who Would Be King '75
- Heaven Knows, Mr. Allison '57
- Moby Dick '56
- Beat the Devil '53
- Moulin Rouge '52
- The African Queen '51
- Key Largo '48
- Treasure of the Sierra Madre '48
- The Killers '46
- High Sierra '41
- The Maltese Falcon '41
- Sergeant York '41
- Amazing Dr. Clitterhouse '38
- Jezebel '38
- Murders in the Rue Morgue '32

Ron Hutchinson
- The Island of Dr. Moreau '96
- The Tuskegee Airmen '95
- Against the Wall '94
- The Burning Season '94
- Fatherland '94
- Blue Ice '92

Willard Huyck
- Radioland Murders '94
- Howard the Duck '86
- Best Defense '84
- Indiana Jones and the Temple of Doom '84
- French Postcards '79
- More American Graffiti '79
- Messiah of Evil '74
- American Graffiti '73

David Henry Hwang
- Possession '02
- The Lost Empire '01
- Golden Gate '93
- M. Butterfly '93

Peter Hyams (1943-)
- Narrow Margin '90
- 2010: The Year We Make Contact '84
- The Star Chamber '83
- Outland '81
- The Hunter '80
- Hanover Street '79
- Capricorn One '78
- Telefon '77
- Busting '74

Chris Hyde
- Chained Heat 3: Hell Mountain '98
- Crackerjack 2 '97
- Chained Heat 2 '92

Jeremy Iacone
- The Bone Collector '99
- One Tough Cop '98
- Blood In ... Blood Out: Bound by Honor '93

Rustam Ibragimbekov
- East-West '99
- Burnt by the Sun '94
- Close to Eden '90

Ice Cube (1969-)
- All About the Benjamins '02
- Next Friday '00
- The Players Club '98
- Friday '95

Leon Ichaso
- Pinero '01
- Bitter Sugar '96
- Crossover Dreams '85
- El Super '79

Masato Ide
- Ran '85
- Kagemusha '80

Eric Idle (1943-)
- Splitting Heirs '93
- National Lampoon's European Vacation '85
- Monty Python's The Meaning of Life '83
- The Tale of the Frog Prince '83
- Monty Python's Life of Brian '79
- All You Need Is Cash '78
- Monty Python and the Holy Grail '75
- And Now for Something Completely Different '72

W. Peter Iliff
- Under Suspicion '00
- Varsity Blues '98
- Patriot Games '92
- Point Break '91
- Prayer of the Rollerboys '91

Shohei Imamura (1926-)
- Dr. Akagi '98
- The Eel '96
- Black Rain '88
- The Ballad of Narayama '83

Hiroshi Inagaki (1905-80)
- Samurai 3: Duel at Ganryu Island '56
- Samurai 1: Musashi Miyamoto '55
- Samurai 2: Duel at Ichijoji Temple '55

Thomas Ince
- The Bargain '15
- The Disciple '15

Agenore Incrocci
- The Good, the Bad and the Ugly '67
- Joyful Laughter '60

Don Ingalls
- Bull of the West '89
- Airport '75 '75

William Inge
- All Fall Down '62
- Splendor in the Grass '61

Raul Inglis
- Premonition '98
- The Final Cut '96
- Breach of Trust '95

Boris Ingster (1904-78)
- Happy Landing '38
- Thin Ice '37

J. Christian Ingvordsen
- The Outfit '93
- Comrades in Arms '91
- Mob War '88
- Search and Destroy '88
- Firehouse '87
- Hangmen '87

Christopher Isherwood
- The Loved One '65
- Diane '55
- Forever and a Day '43

Toshiro Ishido
- Hiroshima '95

Black Rain '88
Ira Israel
American Virgin '98
Dilemma '97
Neal Israel (1945-)
National Lampoon's Dad's Week Off '97
All I Want for Christmas '91
Look Who's Talking, Too '90
Real Genius '85
Police Academy '84
Americathon '79
Juzo Itami (1933-97)
Minbo—Or the Gentle Art of Japanese Extortion '92
A Taxing Woman's Return '88
A Taxing Woman '87
Tampopo '86
The Funeral '84
Kazunori Ito
Ghost in the Shell '95
H.P. Lovecraft's Necronomicon: Book of the Dead '93
James Ivory (1928-)
A Soldier's Daughter Never Cries '98
Maurice '87
Shakespeare Wallah '65
David S. Jackson
Detonator 2: Night Watch '95
Detonator '93
Felix Jackson (-1992)
Destry Rides Again '39
Three Smart Girls Grow Up '39
Mad About Music '38
Horace Jackson
We're Not Dressing '34
The Animal Kingdom '32
Peter Jackson (1961-)
Lord of the Rings 1: The Fellowship of the Rings '01
Forgotten Silver '96
The Frighteners '96
Heavenly Creatures '94
Dead Alive '93
Meet the Feebles '89
Bad Taste '88
Alan Jacobs
Just One Night '00
Nina Takes a Lover '94
Matthew Jacobs
Doctor Who '96
Lassie '94
Lorna Doone '90
Paperhouse '89
Robert Nelson Jacobs
The Shipping News '01
Chocolat '00
Dinosaur '00
Out to Sea '97
Benoit Jacquot (1947-)
Seventh Heaven '98
A Single Girl '96
The Disenchanted '90
Rick Jaffa
The Relic '96
An Eye for an Eye '95
Robert Jaffe
Motel Hell '80
Demon Seed '77
Henry Jaglom (1943-)
Deja Vu '98
Last Summer In the Hamptons '96
Babyfever '94
Venice, Venice '92
Eating '90
New Year's Day '89
Someone to Love '87
Always '85
Can She Bake a Cherry Pie? '83
Sitting Ducks '80
Tracks '76
Don Jakoby
Evolution '01
Double Team '97
Arachnophobia '90
Invaders from Mars '86
Lifeforce '85
The Philadelphia Experiment '84
Blue Thunder '83
Daniel James
On the Edge '00
Gorgo '61
Polly James
The Redhead from Wyoming '53
Mrs. Parkington '44
Rian James
Internes Can't Take Money '37
42nd Street '33
Karen Janszen
A Walk to Remember '02
Digging to China '98
From the Earth to the Moon '98
The Matchmaker '97
Michael January
The Heist '96
C.I.A. 2: Target Alexa '94
Deadly Target '94
To Be the Best '93
Agnes Jaoui (1964-)
Same Old Song '97
Un Air de Famille '96
Smoking/No Smoking '94
Sebastien Japrisot
The Story of O '75
Honor Among Thieves '68
Derek Jarman (1942-94)
Blue '93
Wittgenstein '93
Edward II '92
The Garden '90
Aria '88
The Last of England '87
Caravaggio '86
Sebastiane '79
Jim Jarmusch (1953-)
Ghost Dog: The Way of the Samurai '99
Dead Man '95
Night on Earth '91
Mystery Train '89
Down by Law '86
Permanent Vacation '84
Stranger than Paradise '84
Kevin Jarre
The Devil's Own '96
Tombstone '93
Glory '89
John Jarrell
Romeo Must Die '00
Restraining Order '99
Rollin Jarrett
American Vampire '97
Laws of Deception '97
Paul Jarrico (1915-97)
Messenger of Death '88
The Girl Most Likely '57
Paris Express '53
The Las Vegas Story '52
The White Tower '50
The Search '48
Thousands Cheer '43
Tom, Dick, and Harry '41
Steve Jarvis
Haunted '98
Amazon Warrior '97
Things 2 '97
Things '93
Dead Girls '90
Fatal Images '89
Griffin Jay
The Devil Bat's Daughter '46
The Mask of Diijon '46
The Mummy's Ghost '44
Captive Wild Woman '43
Return of the Vampire '43
The Mummy's Tomb '42
The Mummy's Hand '40
Henri Jeanson (1900-70)
Modigliani '58
Pepe Le Moko '37
Erik Jendresen
Band of Brothers '01
Deadlocked '00
Dan Jenkins
The Break '95
Dead Solid Perfect '88
Jim Jennewein
The Flintstones '94
Getting Even with Dad '94
Richie Rich '94
Talbot Jennings
Anna and the King of Siam '46
Frenchman's Creek '44
Spawn of the North '38
Mutiny on the Bounty '35
Jean-Pierre Jeunet (1955-)
Amelie '01
The City of Lost Children '95
Delicatessen '92
Jack Jevne
Wonder Man '45
Wintertime '43
Ruth Prawer Jhabvala (1927-)
The Golden Bowl '00
A Soldier's Daughter Never Cries '98
Surviving Picasso '96
Jefferson in Paris '94
The Remains of the Day '93
Howard's End '92
Mr. & Mrs. Bridge '90
Madame Sousatzka '88
A Room with a View '86
The Bostonians '84
Heat and Dust '82
Quartet '81
Jane Austen in Manhattan '80
The Europeans '79
Hullabaloo over Georgie & Bonnie's Pictures '78
Roseland '77
Autobiography of a Princess '75
Bombay Talkie '70
Shakespeare Wallah '65
The Householder '63
Neal Jimenez
Desperate Measures '98
Hideaway '94
Sleep with Me '94
For the Boys '91
The Waterdance '91
River's Edge '87
Wong Jing
Her Name Is Cat '99
Meltdown '95
Bayard Johnson
Tarzan and the Lost City '98
Rudyard Kipling's the Second Jungle Book: Mowgli and Baloo '97
Charles Johnson
Beyond Atlantis '73
Slaughter's Big Ripoff '73
Charles Eric Johnson
Steele's Law '91
Hard Lessons '86
David Johnson
Woo '97
DROP Squad '94
Kenneth Johnson (1942-)
Steel '97
V '83
Kristine Johnson
I Am Sam '01
Imaginary Crimes '94
Mark Steven Johnson
Jack Frost '98
Simon Birch '98
Big Bully '95
Grumpier Old Men '95
Grumpy Old Men '93
Monica Johnson
The Muse '99
Mother '96
The Scout '94
Lost in America '85
Jekyll & Hyde...Together Again '82
Modern Romance '81
Americathon '79
Real Life '79
Nunnally Johnson (1897-1977)
The Dirty Dozen '67
The World of Henry Orient '64
Mr. Hobbs Takes a Vacation '62
Flaming Star '60
The Three Faces of Eve '57
How to Marry a Millionaire '53
Phone Call from a Stranger '52
We're Not Married '52
Three Came Home '50
Mr. Peabody & the Mermaid '48
Along Came Jones '45
Casanova Brown '44
The Keys of the Kingdom '44
Woman in the Window '44
Roxie Hart '42
The Grapes of Wrath '40
Jesse James '39
Rose of Washington Square '39
Robert P. Johnson
Bojangles '01
The Temptations '98
Tyson '95
Aaron Kim Johnston
For the Moment '94
The Last Winter '89
Becky Johnston
Seven Years in Tibet '97
The Prince of Tides '91
Tony Johnston
Full Disclosure '00
The Siege of Firebase Gloria '89
Amy Holden Jones (1953-)
The Relic '96
The Rich Man's Wife '96
The Getaway '93
Indecent Proposal '93
Beethoven '92
Indecency '92
Mystic Pizza '88
Love Letters '83
Ed Jones
Carried Away '95
Ninja in the U.S.A. '88
Evan Jones
Shadow of the Wolf '92
A Show of Force '90
Kangaroo '86
Champions '84
Killing of Angel Street '81
Funeral in Berlin '66
Modesty Blaise '66
King and Country '64
Eva '62
Grover Jones
The Shepherd of the Hills '41
Souls at Sea '37
The Trail of the Lonesome Pine '36
The Lives of a Bengal Lancer '35
Ian Jones
The Lighthorsemen '87
Ned Kelly '70
Jerry Jones
Dolemite 2: Human Tornado '76
Dolemite '75
Laura Jones
Possession '02
Angela's Ashes '99
Oscar and Lucinda '97
A Thousand Acres '97
The Well '97
Portrait of a Lady '96
An Angel at My Table '89
High Tide '87
Mark Jones (1953-)
Rumpelstiltskin '96
Leprechaun '93
Terry Jones (1942-)
Mr. Toad's Wild Ride '96
Erik the Viking '89
Labyrinth '86
Monty Python's The Meaning of Life '83
Monty Python's Life of Brian '79
Monty Python and the Holy Grail '75
And Now for Something Completely Different '72
Neil Jordan (1950-)
The End of the Affair '99
In Dreams '98
The Butcher Boy '97
Michael Collins '96
The Crying Game '92
The Miracle '91
High Spirits '88
Mona Lisa '86
The Company of Wolves '85
Danny Boy '82
Jon Jost (1943-)
The Bed You Sleep In '93
Jon Jost's Frameup '93
All the Vermeers in New York '91
Sure Fire '90
Adrien (Carole Eastman) Joyce
Man Trouble '92
Five Easy Pieces '70
The Shooting '66
Odette Joyeux (1917-2000)
The Bride Is Much Too Beautiful '58
Sois Belle et Tais-Toi '58
C. Courtney Joyner
Public Enemies '96
Lurking Fear '94
Desperate Motives '92
Trancers 3: Deth Lives '92
Class of 1999 '90
Puppet Master 3: Toulon's Revenge '90
Vietnam, Texas '90
Catacombs '89
Prison '88
The Offspring '87
Mike Judge (1962-)
Office Space '98
Beavis and Butt-Head Do America '96
Jerry Juhl
Muppets from Space '99
Muppet Treasure Island '96
The Muppet Movie '79
Lenny Juliano
Desert Thunder '99
Stealth Fighter '99
Chen Kaige (1952-)
The Emperor and the Assassin '99
Life on a String '90
Michael Kalesniko
How to Kill Your Neighbor's Dog '01
Private Parts '96
Tom Kalin
Office Killer '97
Swoon '91
Bert Kalmar
A Night at the Opera '35
Duck Soup '33
Horse Feathers '32
Kid from Spain '32
Steven Kaman
The Outfit '93
Firehouse '87
Hangmen '87
Karl Kamb
Pitfall '48
Carnegie Hall '47
Robert Mark Kamen
Kiss of the Dragon '01
A Walk in the Clouds '95
Gladiator '92
Lethal Weapon 3 '92
The Power of One '92
The Karate Kid: Part 3 '89
The Karate Kid: Part 2 '86
The Karate Kid '84
Split Image '82
Taps '81
Steven Kampmann
Clifford '92
Stealing Home '88
The Couch Trip '87
Back to School '86
Aben Kandel
The Fighter '52
They Won't Forget '37
Michael Kane
The Cisco Kid '94
The Bear '89
All the Right Moves '83
Hard Country '81
Legend of the Lone Ranger '81
Southern Comfort '81
Foolin' Around '80
Hot Stuff '80
Smokey and the Bandit 2 '80
Rolfe Kanefsky (1969-)
Red Line '96
There's Nothing out There '90
Charles Kanganis
No Escape, No Return '93
Fist of Honor '92
A Time to Die '91
Fay Kanin
Teacher's Pet '58
The Opposite Sex '56
Rhapsody '54
Garson Kanin (1912-99)
It Should Happen to You '54
The Marrying Kind '52
Pat and Mike '52
Adam's Rib '50
A Double Life '47
Michael Kanin (-1993)
How to Commit Marriage '69
Teacher's Pet '58
The Opposite Sex '56
Rhapsody '54
Woman of the Year '42
Hal Kanter (1918-)
Bachelor in Paradise '69
Dear Brigitte '65
Blue Hawaii '62
Pocketful of Miracles '61
Loving You '57
Artists and Models '55
The Rose Tattoo '55
Casanova's Big Night '54
Here Come the Girls '53
The Road to Bali '53
Deborah Kaplan
Josie and the Pussycats '01
The Flintstones in Viva Rock Vegas '00
Can't Hardly Wait '98
A Very Brady Sequel '96
Jonathan Kaplan (1947-)
Mr. Billion '77
White Line Fever '75
Marty Kaplan
Striking Distance '93
The Distinguished Gentleman '92
Noises Off '92
Wong Kar-Wai (1958-)
In the Mood for Love '00
Happy Together '96
Chungking Express '95
Fallen Angels '95
Luca Karall
Maria's Day '84
25 Fireman's Street '73
Larry Karaszewski
Screwed '00
Man on the Moon '99
The People vs. Larry Flynt '96
That Darn Cat '96
Ed Wood '94
Problem Child 2 '91
Problem Child '90
Lawrence Kasdan (1949-)
Mumford '99
Wyatt Earp '94
The Bodyguard '92
Grand Canyon '91
The Accidental Tourist '88
Silverado '85
The Big Chill '83
Return of the Jedi '83
Body Heat '81

Continental Divide '81
The Empire Strikes Back '80
Sam Henry Kass
Body and Soul '98
The Search for One-Eyed Jimmy '96
Mathieu Kassovitz (1967-)
The Crimson Rivers '01
Hate '95
Cafe au Lait '94
Brian Katkin
Shakedown '02
If I Die Before I Wake '98
A.L. Katz
Tales from the Crypt Presents Bordello of Blood '96
Children of the Corn 2: The Final Sacrifice '92
Gloria Katz
Radioland Murders '94
Howard the Duck '86
Best Defense '84
Indiana Jones and the Temple of Doom '84
French Postcards '79
More American Graffiti '79
Messiah of Evil '74
American Graffiti '73
Jordan Katz
Incognito '97
Trial by Jury '94
Stephen Katz
From the Earth to the Moon '98
Satan's Princess '90
Steven Katz
Shadow of the Vampire '00
Fallen Angels 1 '93
Charles Kaufman
Ferocious Female Freedom Fighters '88
Waitress '81
Mother's Day '80
Squeeze Play '79
The Story of Esther Costello '57
Return to Paradise '53
Charlie Kaufman
Human Nature '02
Being John Malkovich '99
George S. Kaufman
Star Spangled Rhythm '42
A Night at the Opera '35
The Cocoanuts '29
Ken Kaufman
Space Cowboys '00
In the Army Now '94
Lloyd Kaufman
Class of Nuke 'Em High 3: The Good, the Bad and the Subhumanoid '94
Sgt. Kabukiman N.Y.P.D. '94
Class of Nuke 'Em High 2: Subhumanoid Meltdown '91
The Toxic Avenger, Part 2 '89
The Toxic Avenger, Part 3: The Last Temptation of Toxie '89
Troma's War '88
Class of Nuke 'Em High '86
Stuck on You '84
First Turn On '83
Philip Kaufman (1936-)
Rising Sun '93
Henry & June '90
The Unbearable Lightness of Being '88
The Right Stuff '83
Raiders of the Lost Ark '81
Wanderers '79
The Outlaw Josey Wales '76
The Great Northfield Minnesota Raid '72
Aki Kaurismaki (1957-)
La Vie de Boheme '93
The Match Factory Girl '90
Ariel '89
Leningrad Cowboys Go America '89
Helmut Kautner
The Last Bridge '54
Die Grosse Freiheit Nr. 7 '45
Frances Kavanaugh
Driftin' River '46
The Driftin' Kid '41
Dynamite Canyon '41
Riding the Sunset Trail '41
Stephen Kay
The Mod Squad '99
The Last Time I Committed Suicide '96
Tony Kayden
When Justice Fails '98
Slipstream '89
John Kaye
Along for the Ride '00
Where the Buffalo Roam '80
Nicholas Kazan
Enough '02
Bicentennial Man '99
Fallen '97
Homegrown '97
Matilda '96
Dream Lover '93
Mobsters '91
Reversal of Fortune '90
Patty Hearst '88
At Close Range '86
Frances '82
Tim Kazurinsky (1950-)
The Cherokee Kid '96
For Keeps '88
About Last Night... '86
James Keach (1948-)
The Forgotten '89
Armed and Dangerous '86
The Long Riders '80
Slashed Dreams '74
Harvey Keith
Stand-Ins '97
Jezebel's Kiss '90
Woody Keith
Dementia '98
Bride of Re-Animator '89
Ed Kelleher
Stand-Ins '97
Lurkers '88
Shriek of the Mutilated '74
Invasion of the Blood Farmers '72
David E. Kelley
Lake Placid '99
Mystery, Alaska '99
To Gillian on Her 37th Birthday '96
Bob Kelljan (1930-82)
The Return of Count Yorga '71
Count Yorga, Vampire '70
Karen Kelly
The Last Best Sunday '98
Poison Ivy 3: The New Seduction '97
The Corporation '96
Body Chemistry 4: Full Exposure '95
Hard Bounty '94
Patrick Smith Kelly
Don't Say a Word '01
A Perfect Murder '98
Kurt Kempler
Telegraph Trail '33
The Big Stampede '32
Two-Fisted Law '32
Anne Kennedy
The Monkey's Mask '00
Crush '93
Burt Kennedy (1922-2001)
White Hunter, Black Heart '90
Dynamite and Gold '88
The Trouble with Spies '87
Train Robbers '73
Hannie Caulder '72
The Rounders '65
Comanche Station '60
Ride Lonesome '59
The Tall T '57
Jane Kennedy
The Dish '00
The Castle '97
Kerry Kennedy
Baby '00
Hope '97
William Kennedy
Ironweed '87
The Cotton Club '84
Doug Kenney
Caddyshack '80
National Lampoon's Animal House '78
Robert Kent (1908-)
Diary of a Madman '63
Zombies on Broadway '44
Robert E. Kent
Twice-Told Tales '63
Dick Tracy vs. Cueball '46
Earl Kenton
Invisible: The Chronicles of Benjamin Knight '93
Mandroid '93
Charles Kenyon
A Midsummer Night's Dream '35
The Penalty '20
Bill Kerby
On the Beach '00
Dead Men Can't Dance '97
Lakota Woman: Siege at Wounded Knee '94
Hooper '78
Rob Kerchner
Heaven's Fire '99
Turbulence 2: Fear of Flying '99
Route 9 '98
Bloodfist 7: Manhunt '95
Bloodfist 6: Ground Zero '94
Sarah Kernochan
All I Wanna Do '98
Sommersby '93
Impromptu '90
Lodge Kerrigan
Claire Dolan '97
Clean, Shaven '93
Lyle Kessler
The Saint of Fort Washington '93
Gladiator '92
Orphans '87
Larry Ketron
The Only Thrill '97
Freeway '88
Permanent Record '88
Michael Keusch
Samurai Cowboy '93
Lena's Holiday '90
Edward Khmara
Merlin '98
Dragon: The Bruce Lee Story '93
Enemy Mine '85
Ladyhawke '85
Callie Khouri
Divine Secrets of the Ya-Ya Sisterhood '02
Something to Talk About '95
Thelma & Louise '91
Abbas Kiarostami (1940-)
The Taste of Cherry '96
The White Balloon '95
Through the Olive Trees '94
Life and Nothing More ... '92
Where Is My Friend's House? '87
Roland Kibbee
The Devil's Disciple '59
The Desert Song '53
Vera Cruz '53
A Night in Casablanca '46
Krzysztof Kieslowski (1941-96)
Trois Couleurs: Blanc '94
Trois Couleurs: Rouge '94
Trois Couleurs: Bleu '93
The Double Life of Veronique '91
The Decalogue '88
No End '84
Camera Buff '79
Ryuzo Kikushima
Tora! Tora! Tora! '70
High & Low '62
Sanjuro '62
Yojimbo '61
The Bad Sleep Well '60
The Hidden Fortress '58
Throne of Blood '57
Scandal '50
Takeshi Kimura
War of the Gargantuas '70
Destroy All Monsters '68
Attack of the Mushroom People '63
Judson Kinberg
To Catch a Killer '92
Sell Out '76
Vampire Circus '71
Tim Kincaid
The Occultist '89
Mutant Hunt '87
Robot Holocaust '87
Chloe King
Red Shoe Diaries: Luscious Lola '00
Red Shoe Diaries: Swimming Naked '00
B. Monkey '97
Poison Ivy 2: Lily '95
Red Shoe Diaries 3: Another Woman's Lipstick '93
I. Marlene King
If These Walls Could Talk '96
National Lampoon's Senior Trip '95
Now and Then '95
Robert King
Vertical Limit '00
Red Corner '97
Cutthroat Island '95
Clean Slate '94
Speechless '94
Bloodfist '89
Phantom of the Mall: Eric's Revenge '89
The Nest '88
Stephen King (1947-)
Stephen King's Rose Red '02
Stephen King's The Storm of the Century '99
Stephen King's The Stand '94
Sleepwalkers '92
Stephen King's Golden Years '91
Graveyard Shift '90
Stephen King's It '90
Pet Sematary '89
Maximum Overdrive '86
Cat's Eye '85
Silver Bullet '85
Creepshow '82
Zalman King (1941-)
Red Shoe Diaries: Swimming Naked '00
In God's Hands '98
Business for Pleasure '96
Red Shoe Diaries: Strip Poker '96
Red Shoe Diaries 3: Another Woman's Lipstick '93
Lake Consequence '92
Wild Orchid 2: Two Shades of Blue '92
Wild Orchid '90
Two Moon Junction '88
Wildfire '88
9 1/2 Weeks '86
Dorothy Kingsley (1909-97)
Valley of the Dolls '67
Green Mansions '59
Don't Go Near the Water '57
Pal Joey '57
Seven Brides for Seven Brothers '54
Angels in the Outfield '51
Broadway Rhythm '44
Ernest Kinoy
Rescuers: Stories of Courage "Two Women" '97
Gore Vidal's Lincoln '88
Murrow '86
Roots '77
The Story of David '76
The Story of Jacob & Joseph '74
Teinosuke Kinugasa
An Actor's Revenge '63
Gate of Hell '54
Karey Kirkpatrick
Chicken Run '00
The Little Vampire '00
Honey, We Shrunk Ourselves '97
The Rescuers Down Under '90
Ralf Kirsten (1930-)
Under the Pear Tree '73
On the Sunny Side '62
Takeshi "Beat" Kitano (1948-)
Brother '00
Kikujiro '99
Fireworks '97
Sonatine '96
Martin Kitrosser
Facing the Enemy '00
Friday the 13th, Part 5: A New Beginning '85
Friday the 13th, Part 3 '82
Robert Klane
Weekend at Bernie's 2 '93
Weekend at Bernie's '89
National Lampoon's European Vacation '85
Unfaithfully Yours '84
Where's Poppa? '70
Cedric Klapisch
Un Air de Famille '96
When the Cat's Away '96
David Klass
In the Time of the Butterflies '01
Desperate Measures '98
Kiss the Girls '97
Nicholas Klein
The Million Dollar Hotel '99
The End of Violence '97
Harry Kleiner
Fantastic Voyage '66
Carmen Jones '54
Walter Klenhard
Buried Alive 2 '97
The Haunting of Seacliff Inn '94
The Last Hit '93
Dead in the Water '91
Richard Kletter
Missing Pieces '00
The Colony '98
The Android Affair '95
Dangerous Indiscretion '94
Steven Kloves (1960-)
Harry Potter and the Sorcerer's Stone '01
Wonder Boys '00
Flesh and Bone '93
The Fabulous Baker Boys '89
Racing with the Moon '84
Nigel Kneale
Sharpe's Gold '94
Woman in Black '89
The Witches '66
First Men in the Moon '64
Damn the Defiant '62
The Entertainer '60
Look Back in Anger '58
The Abominable Snowman '57
Quatermass 2 '57
Andrew Knight
Siam Sunset '99
The Efficiency Expert '92
Patricia Louisianna Knop
Red Shoe Diaries: Strip Poker '96
Delta of Venus '95
Siesta '87
9 1/2 Weeks '86
Christopher Knopf
Not My Kid '85
Peter and Paul '81
Emperor of the North Pole '73
20 Million Miles to Earth '57
The King's Thief '55
Masaki Kobayashi (1916-96)
The Human Condition: Road to Eternity '59
The Human Condition: No Greater Love '58
Howard Koch (1901-95)
War Lover '62
Rhapsody in Blue '45
Casablanca '42
Sergeant York '41
The Letter '40
The Sea Hawk '40
David Koepp
Panic Room '02
Spider-Man '02
Stir of Echoes '99
Snake Eyes '98
The Lost World: Jurassic Park 2 '97
Mission: Impossible '96
The Trigger Effect '96
The Paper '94
The Shadow '94
Carlito's Way '93
Jurassic Park '93
Death Becomes Her '92
Apartment Zero '88
Ana Kokkinos (1959-)
Head On '98
Only the Brave '94
Amos Kollek
Fiona '98
Whore 2 '94
Double Edge '92
High Stakes '89
Andrei Konchalovsky (1937-)
The Odyssey '97
The Inner Circle '91
Runaway Train '85
Maria's Lovers '84
Siberiade '79
Andrei Rublev '66
Larry Konner
Planet of the Apes '01
Mercury Rising '98
Mighty Joe Young '98
The Beverly Hillbillies '93
For Love or Money '93
Sometimes They Come Back '91
Desperate Hours '90
The Jewel of the Nile '85
Peter Koper
Island of the Dead '00
Headless Body in Topless Bar '96
Arthur Kopit
Roswell: The U.F.O. Cover-Up '94
The Phantom of the Opera '90
Hands of a Stranger '87
Howard Korder
My Little Assassin '99
The Passion of Ayn Rand '99
Steve Koren
Superstar '99
A Night at the Roxbury '98
Harmony Korine
Julien Donkey-boy '99
Gummo '97
Kids '95
Randy Kornfield
Jingle All the Way '96
Bloodknot '95
Incident at Deception Ridge '94
Mari Kornhauser
The Last Ride '94
Zandalee '91
Ron Koslow
Last Dance '96
Into the Night '85
Lifeguard '76
Jim Kouf (1951-)
Snow Dogs '02
Rush Hour '98
Gang Related '96
Operation Dumbo Drop '95
Another Stakeout '93
The Hidden '87
Stakeout '87
Class '83
Edward Kovach
Blink of an Eye '92
Jailbird Rock '88

Paul Koval
Dead Silent '99
Blue Movies '88
Janet Kovalcik
My Girl 2 '94
Married to It '93
Soeren Kragh-Jacobsen
Mifune '99
Emma's Shadow '88
Andrzej Krakowski
Eminent Domain '91
Triumph of the Spirit '89
Richard Kramer
Armistead Maupin's Tales of the City '93
All I Want for Christmas '91
Norman Krasna (1909-84)
Let's Make Love '60
Indiscreet '58
The Ambassador's Daughter '56
The Big Hangover '50
The Flame of New Orleans '41
It Started with Eve '41
Mr. & Mrs. Smith '41
It's a Date '40
Hands Across the Table '35
Stu Krieger
In the Army Now '94
Monkey Trouble '94
A Troll in Central Park '94
The Land Before Time '88
Peter Krikes
Anna and the King '99
Star Trek 4: The Voyage Home '86
Milton Krims
Mohawk '56
Tennessee's Partner '55
Henry Krinkle
Friend of the Family 2 '96
Night Eyes 4: Fatal Passion '95
Sandy Kroopf
Contagious '96
Birdy '84
Lisa Krueger
Committed '99
Manny & Lo '96
Ehren Kruger
Imposter '01
Reindeer Games '00
Scream 3 '00
Arlington Road '99
New World Disorder '99
Stanley Kubrick (1928-99)
Eyes Wide Shut '99
Full Metal Jacket '87
The Shining '80
Barry Lyndon '75
A Clockwork Orange '71
2001: A Space Odyssey '68
Dr. Strangelove, or: How I Learned to Stop Worrying and Love the Bomb '64
Paths of Glory '57
The Killing '56
Killer's Kiss '55
Robert Kuhn
Mickey Blue Eyes '99
The Cure '95
Roger Kumble
Cruel Intentions 2 '99
Cruel Intentions '98
National Lampoon's Senior Trip '95
Unveiled '94
Hanif Kureishi (1954-)
My Son the Fanatic '97
The Buddha of Suburbia '92
London Kills Me '91
Sammy & Rosie Get Laid '87
My Beautiful Laundrette '85
Harry Kurnitz
How to Steal a Million '66
Goodbye Charlie '64
Witness for the Prosecution '57
The Inspector General '49
Something in the Wind '47
They Got Me Covered '43
Ship Ahoy '42
Akira Kurosawa (1910-98)
Rhapsody in August '91
Akira Kurosawa's Dreams '90
Ran '85
Kagemusha '80
Dersu Uzala '75
Dodes 'ka-den '70
High & Low '62
Sanjuro '62
Yojimbo '61
The Bad Sleep Well '60
The Hidden Fortress '58
The Lower Depths '57
Throne of Blood '57
I Live in Fear '55
Seven Samurai '54
Ikiru '52
Rashomon '51
Scandal '50
A Quiet Duel '49
One Wonderful Sunday '47
The Men Who Tread on the Tiger's Tail '45
Andrew Kurtzman
Down Periscope '96
Camp Nowhere '94
See No Evil, Hear No Evil '89
Number One with a Bullet '87
Diane Kurys (1948-)
Love After Love '94
A Man in Love '87
Entre-Nous '83
Peppermint Soda '77
Emir Kusturica (1954-)
Underground '95
Arizona Dream '94
Lynda La Plante
Bella Mafia '97
Framed '93
Prime Suspect '92
Jeanne Labrune
Vatel '00
Sand and Blood '87
Neil LaBute (1963-)
Possession '02
Your Friends & Neighbors '98
In the Company of Men '96
John Lafia
Man's Best Friend '93
Child's Play '88
Ian LaFrenais
Still Crazy '98
Excess Baggage '96
The Commitments '91
Vice Versa '88
Water '85
Prisoner of Zenda '79
Catch Me a Spy '71
Jacques Lagrange
Traffic '71
Mon Oncle '58
Mr. Hulot's Holiday '53
Richard LaGravenese
Beloved '98
Living Out Loud '98
The Horse Whisperer '97
The Mirror Has Two Faces '96
The Bridges of Madison County '95
A Little Princess '95
Unstrung Heroes '95
The Ref '93
The Fisher King '91
Rude Awakening '89
Don Lake
Return to Me '00
The Extreme Adventures of Super Dave '98
Frank Laloggia (1954-)
The Lady in White '88
Fear No Evil '80
Paul LaLonde
Revelation '00
Tribulation '00
Peter LaLonde
Revelation '00
Tribulation '00
Ross LaManna
Rush Hour '98
Titanic '96
Arctic Blue '93
John Lamb
Postmortem '98
The Mermaids of Tiburon '62
Gavin Lambert
Dead on the Money '91
Sweet Bird of Youth '89
I Never Promised You a Rose Garden '77
Inside Daisy Clover '65
Roman Spring of Mrs. Stone '61
Ken Lamplugh
Midnight Kiss '93
Private Wars '93
Bill Lancaster
The Thing '82
The Bad News Bears Go to Japan '78
The Bad News Bears '76
Richard H. Landau
Spaceways '53
The Lost Continent '51
James Landis
The Sadist '63
Stakeout '62
John Landis (1950-)
Blues Brothers 2000 '98
Dying to Get Rich '98
Clue '85
Twilight Zone: The Movie '83
An American Werewolf in London '81
The Blues Brothers '80
Schlock '73
Joseph Landon
Von Ryan's Express '65
The Hoodlum Priest '61
Michael Landon (1936-91)
Sam's Son '84
Killing Stone '78
Fritz Lang (1890-1976)
The Thousand Eyes of Dr. Mabuse '60
M '31
Metropolis '26
Dr. Mabuse, The Gambler '22
The Indian Tomb '21
Harry Langdon (1884-1944)
Road Show '41
The Flying Deuces '39
John Langley
Deadly Sins '95
The P.O.W. Escape '86
Noel Langley (1911-80)
Snow White and the Three Stooges '61
The Search for Bridey Murphy '56
The Adventures of Sadie '55
Svengali '55
Ivanhoe '52
A Christmas Carol '51
They Made Me a Fugitive '47
The Wizard of Oz '39
Maytime '37
King of the Damned '36
Arlette Langmann
Germinal '93
A Nos Amours '84
Loulou '80
Kate Lanier
Glitter '01
The Mod Squad '99
Set It Off '96
What's Love Got to Do with It? '93
T.L. Lankford
Storm Trooper '98
Hollywood Chainsaw Hookers '88
Phantom Empire '87
Ring Lardner, Jr. (1915-2000)
The Greatest '77
M*A*S*H '70
The Cincinnati Kid '65
Forever Amber '47
Cloak and Dagger '46
Laura '44
Tomorrow the World '44
Woman of the Year '42
Glen Larson
Magnum P.I.: Don't Eat the Snow in Hawaii '80
Battlestar Galactica '78
James Lasdun
Signs & Wonders '00
Sunday '96
Lawrence Lasker
Sneakers '92
Project X '87
WarGames '83
Jesse Lasky, Jr.
John Paul Jones '59
The Ten Commandments '56
Unconquered '47
Reap the Wild Wind '42
Back in the Saddle '41
Union Pacific '39
Louise Lasser (1939-)
Just Me & You '78
What's Up, Tiger Lily? '66
Aaron Latham
The Program '93
Perfect '85
Urban Cowboy '80
Jonathan Latimer
The Big Clock '48
The Glass Key '42
Topper Returns '41
Steve Latshaw (1959-)
Ablaze '00
Mach 2 '00
Rangers '00
Submerged '00
Militia '99
Invisible Dad '97
Greg Latter
Dangerous Ground '96
Cyborg Cop '93
Michael Laughlin
Town and Country '01
Mesmerized '84
Strange Behavior '81
Tom Laughlin (1939-)
The Trial of Billy Jack '74
Billy Jack '71
Born Losers '67
Frank Launder (1907-97)
The Belles of St. Trinian's '53
The Happiest Days of Your Life '50
Captain Boycott '47
Night Train to Munich '40
The Lady Vanishes '38
Dale Launer
Love Potion #9 '92
My Cousin Vinny '92
Dirty Rotten Scoundrels '88
Blind Date '87
Salvatore Laurani
Confessions of a Police Captain '72
A Bullet for the General '68
S.K. Lauren
When Ladies Meet '41
Crime and Punishment '35
Christine Laurent
Va Savoir '01
Jeanne la Pucelle '94
La Belle Noiseuse '90
Arthur Laurents
Gypsy '93
The Turning Point '77
The Way We Were '73
Gypsy '62
Bonjour Tristesse '57
Anastasia '56
Rope '48
Paul Laverty
Bread and Roses '00
My Name Is Joe '98
Carla's Song '97
Bruno Lawrence (1941-95)
The Quiet Earth '85
Smash Palace '82
John Lawrence (1931-92)
Cycle Psycho '72
The Incredible Two-Headed Transplant '71
Marc Lawrence
Miss Congeniality '00
Forces of Nature '99
The Out-of-Towners '99
Life with Mikey '93
Martin Lawrence (1965-)
A Thin Line Between Love and Hate '96
You So Crazy '94
Vincent Lawrence
Adventure '45
Hands Across the Table '35
Now and Forever '34
Night After Night '32
John Howard Lawson
Fatal Combat '96
Jungle Boy '96
Cry, the Beloved Country '51
Smash-Up: The Story of a Woman '47
Action in the North Atlantic '43
Sahara '43
J.F. Lawton (1960-)
Chain Reaction '96
Blankman '94
The Hunted '94
Under Siege '92
Mistress '91
Pizza Man '91
Pretty Woman '90
Cannibal Women in the Avocado Jungle of Death '89
Beirne Lay, Jr.
The Gallant Hours '60
Above and Beyond '53
Twelve o'Clock High '49
Martin Lazarus
Deep Core '00
Interceptor Force '99
Philip LaZebnik
Mulan '98
Pocahontas '95
Alain Le Henry
A Self-Made Hero '95
Subway '85
Didier Le Pecheur
Harrison's Flowers '02
Don't Let Me Die on a Sunday '98
Paul Leadon
Back of Beyond '95
Around the World in 80 Ways '86
Larry Leahy
Confessions of a Hit Man '94
The Lawless Land '88
David Lean (1908-91)
A Passage to India '84
Summertime '55
Oliver Twist '48
This Happy Breed '47
Brief Encounter '46
Great Expectations '46
Norman Lear
Cold Turkey '71
The Night They Raided Minsky's '69
Divorce American Style '67
Come Blow Your Horn '63
Charles Leavitt
K-PAX '01
The Mighty '98
Sunchaser '96
Patrice Leconte (1947-)
The Hairdresser's Husband '92
Monsieur Hire '89
Paul Leder (1926-96)
Killing Obsession '94
The Baby Doll Murders '92
Exiled in America '90
Murder by Numbers '89
A*P*E* '76
Reuben Leder
Molly and Gina '94
A*P*E* '76
Charles Lederer
A Global Affair '63
Mutiny on the Bounty '62
Ocean's 11 '60
Kismet '55
Gentlemen Prefer Blondes '53
Monkey Business '52
The Thing '51
I Was a Male War Bride '49
Comrade X '40
His Girl Friday '40
Broadway Serenade '39
Ang Lee (1954-)
Eat Drink Man Woman '94
The Wedding Banquet '93
Pushing Hands '92
Bruce Lee (1940-73)
Circle of Iron '78
Fists of Fury '73
Return of the Dragon '73
Connie Lee
Footlight Glamour '43
It's a Great Life '43
Blondie for Victory '42
Blondie's Blessed Event '42
Damian Lee
Agent Red '00
Specimen '97
Deadly Heroes '96
Fatal Combat '96
Jungle Boy '96
When the Bullet Hits the Bone '96
Electra '95
Street Law '95
The Killing Man '94
Abraxas: Guardian of the Universe '90
Mark Lee (1958-)
Fortunes of War '94
The Next Karate Kid '94
Spike Lee (1957-)
Bamboozled '00
Summer of Sam '99
He Got Game '98
Clockers '95
Malcolm X '92
Jungle Fever '91
Mo' Better Blues '90
Do the Right Thing '89
School Daze '88
She's Gotta Have It '86
Joe's Bed-Stuy Barbershop: We Cut Heads '83
William Lee
The Pact '99
Psychopath '97
Robert Lees
Abbott and Costello Meet the Invisible Man '51
Comin' Round the Mountain '51
Abbott and Costello Meet Frankenstein '48
Buck Privates Come Home '47
The Black Cat '41
Hold That Ghost '41
The Invisible Woman '40
Michael Leeson
What Planet Are You From? '00
I.Q. '94
The War of the Roses '89
Survivors '83
Jekyll & Hyde...Together Again '82
Ernest Lehman
Black Sunday '77
Family Plot '76
Portnoy's Complaint '72
Hello, Dolly! '69
Who's Afraid of Virginia Woolf? '66
The Sound of Music '65
The Prize '63

West Side Story '61
From the Terrace '60
North by Northwest '59
Sweet Smell of Success '57
The King and I '56
Somebody Up There Likes Me '56
Executive Suite '54
Sabrina '54

Gladys Lehman
Nice Girl? '41
Blondie Brings Up Baby '39
Death Takes a Holiday '34

Jerry Leichtling
Blue Sky '91
Peggy Sue Got Married '86

Mike Leigh (1943-)
Topsy Turvy '99
Career Girls '97
Secrets and Lies '95
Naked '93
Life Is Sweet '90
High Hopes '88
Home Sweet Home '82
Grown Ups '80
Who's Who '78
Kiss of Death '77
Bleak Moments '71

Warren Leight
Dear God '96
The Night We Never Met '93
Mother's Day '80

David Leland (1947-)
White River '99
The Land Girls '98
Personal Services '87
Wish You Were Here '87
Mona Lisa '86

Claude Lelouch (1937-)
Les Miserables '95
Bandits '86
A Man and a Woman: 20 Years Later '86
Bolero '82
Cat and Mouse '78
Robert et Robert '78
Another Man, Another Chance '77
And Now My Love '74
Happy New Year '73
A Man and a Woman '66

Alan LeMay
High Lonesome '50
The Adventures of Mark Twain '44
The Story of Dr. Wassell '44
Reap the Wild Wind '42

Jonathan Lemkin
Red Planet '00
The Devil's Advocate '97

James (Momel) Lemmo
Nowhere in Sight '01
Bodily Harm '95
Relentless 3 '93
We're Talkin' Serious Money '92

Kay Lenard (-1997)
The Kettles in the Ozarks '56
Ma and Pa Kettle at Home '54

Peter M. Lenkov
Dr. Jekyll & Mr. Hyde '99
Demolition Man '93

Isobel Lennart
Funny Girl '68
Period of Adjustment '62
Two for the Seesaw '62
Meet Me in Las Vegas '56
Latin Lovers '53
A Life of Her Own '50
Holiday in Mexico '46

Robert W. Lenski
A Death in the Family '02
Saint Maybe '98
What the Deaf Man Heard '98
Hole in the Sky '95
Breathing Lessons '94
The Return of the Native '94
Decoration Day '90
Who Is the Black Dahlia? '75

Umberto Lenzi (1931-)
Emerald Jungle '80
Desert Commandos '67

Elmore Leonard
Cat Chaser '90
The Rosary Murders '87
52 Pick-Up '86
Stick '85
Mr. Majestyk '74
Joe Kidd '72

Hugh Leonard
Widow's Peak '94
Da '88

Sergio Leone (1929-89)
Once Upon a Time in the West '68
The Good, the Bad and the Ugly '67
For a Few Dollars More '65
A Fistful of Dollars '64
The Last Days of Pompeii '60

Robert Lepage (1957-)
No '98
Le Polygraphe '96
The Confessional '95

Alan Jay Lerner
The Little Prince '74
Camelot '67
My Fair Lady '64
Gigi '58
Brigadoon '54
An American in Paris '51
Royal Wedding '51

Jeff Leroy
Crystal's Diary '99
Crack Up '97

Elana Lesser
Cats Don't Dance '97
Balto '95

Sheldon Lettich (1962-)
Legionnaire '98
Only the Strong '93
Double Impact '91
Lionheart '90

Jeremy Leven
The Legend of Bagger Vance '00
Don Juan DeMarco '94
Creator '85

Sonya Levien
Interrupted Melody '55
Oklahoma! '55
The Merry Widow '52
Three Daring Daughters '48
The Valley of Decision '45
The Hunchback of Notre Dame '39
In Old Chicago '37

Larry Levin
Dr. Dolittle 2 '01
Dr. Dolittle '98

Marc Levin
White Boyz '99
Madeline '98
Slam '98

Barry Levinson (1942-)
Liberty Heights '99
Sleepers '96
Jimmy Hollywood '94
Toys '92
Avalon '90
Tin Men '87
Unfaithfully Yours '84
Best Friends '82
Diner '82
Inside Moves '80
And Justice for All '79
High Anxiety '77
Silent Movie '76
Internecine Project '73

Richard Levinson
Vanishing Act '88
Rehearsal for Murder '82
The Hindenburg '75
The Execution of Private Slovik '74
Columbo: Prescription Murder '67

Alfred Lewis Levitt
Monkey's Uncle '65
The Misadventures of Merlin Jones '63
Mrs. Mike '49

Helen Levitt
Monkey's Uncle '65
The Misadventures of Merlin Jones '63

Benn W. Levy
The Old Dark House '32
Blackmail '29
The Informer '29

Eugene Levy (1946-)
Best in Show '00
Waiting for Guffman '96
Sodbusters '94

Robert L. Levy
Blood Surf '00
A Kid in King Arthur's Court '95

Albert Lewin (1916-96)
Eight on the Lam '67
Pandora and the Flying Dutchman '51
The Private Affairs of Bel Ami '47
Picture of Dorian Gray '45

Ben Lewin (1946-)
Paperback Romance '96
The Favor, the Watch, & the Very Big Fish '92

Herschell Gordon Lewis (1926-)
This Stuff'll Kill Ya! '71
How to Make a Doll '68
Blast-Off Girls '67
Suburban Roulette '67
Monster a Go-Go! '65
Color Me Blood Red '64
Moonshine Mountain '64
2000 Maniacs '64
Scum of the Earth '63

Jefferson Lewis
Mon Amie Max '94
Ordinary Magic '93

Jerry Lewis (1926-)
Hardly Working '81
Big Mouth '67
Family Jewels '65
The Patsy '64
The Nutty Professor '63
The Errand Boy '61
The Ladies' Man '61
The Bellboy '60

Russell Lewis
Heat of the Sun '99
Horatio Hornblower '99
Sharpe's Battle '94

Val Lewton
Bedlam '45
The Body Snatcher '45

Peter Paul Liapis
Alone with a Stranger '99
Stranger in the House '97
Sins of Desire '92

Ugo Liberatore
The Trojan Horse '62
Mill of the Stone Women '60

Jeff Lieberman
Blue Sunshine '78
Squirm '76

Leo Lieberman
Carnival Rock '57
Sorority Girl '57

Jimmy Lifton
Phoenix '95
Mirror, Mirror 2: Raven Dance '94

Louis D. Lighton
It '27
Wings '27

Topper Lilien
Dungeons and Dragons '00
Where the Money Is '00

Kevin J. Lindenmuth
Addicted to Murder 3: Bloodlust '99
Rage of the Werewolf '99
Addicted to Murder 2: Tainted Blood '97
The Alien Agenda: Endangered Species '97
The Alien Agenda: Under the Skin '97
The Alien Agenda: Out of the Darkness '96
Addicted to Murder '95

Eugene Ling
Lost Boundaries '49
Behind Locked Doors '48

William Link
Vanishing Act '88
Rehearsal for Murder '82
Rollercoaster '77
The Hindenburg '75
The Execution of Private Slovik '74
Columbo: Prescription Murder '67

Richard Linklater (1961-)
Waking Life '01
Before Sunrise '94
Dazed and Confused '93
Slacker '91

W.P. Lipscomb
Beware of Pity '46
Pygmalion '38
The Garden of Allah '36
A Tale of Two Cities '36
Les Miserables '35

William Lively
Range Renegades '48
Texas Trouble '41

Robert Locash
BASEketball '98
High School High '96
Naked Gun 33 1/3: The Final Insult '94
CB4: The Movie '93

Helen Logan
Hello, Frisco, Hello '43
Iceland '42
Lucky Cisco Kid '40
Tin Pan Alley '40

John Logan
The Time Machine '02
Gladiator '00
Any Given Sunday '99
Bats '99
RKO 281 '99
Tornado! '96

Christopher Logue
Crusoe '89
Savage Messiah '72

Ulli Lommel (1944-)
Warbirds '88
Strangers in Paradise '84
Devonsville Terror '83
Brainwaves '82
The Boogey Man '80
Cocaine Cowboys '79

Kenneth Lonergan
The Adventures of Rocky & Bullwinkle '00
You Can Count On Me '99
Analyze This '98

Nathan Long
The Sender '98
Guyver 2: Dark Hero '94

Harry S. Longstreet
Wounded '97
A Vow to Kill '94
Sex, Love and Cold Hard Cash '93

Renee Longstreet
Double Platinum '99
Undesirable '92

Anita Loos
I Married an Angel '42
They Met in Bombay '41
When Ladies Meet '41
Susan and God '40
The Women '39
Saratoga '37
San Francisco '36
The Girl from Missouri '34
Hold Your Man '33
Red Headed Woman '32
Struggle '31
His Picture in the Papers '16

Robert Lord
Heroes for Sale '33
The Purchase Price '32
Big Business Girl '31

Dean Lorey
Major Payne '95
Jason Goes to Hell: The Final Friday '93
My Boyfriend's Back '93

Hope Loring
It '27
My Best Girl '27
Wings '27
Shadows '22

David Loucka
Eddie '96
The Dream Team '89

David Loughery
Money Train '95
Tom and Huck '95
The Three Musketeers '93
Passenger 57 '92
Star Trek 5: The Final Frontier '89

Pavel (Lungin) Lounguine
Luna Park '91
Taxi Blues '90

Robert Lovy
Plughead Rewired: Circuitry Man 2 '94
Circuitry Man '90

Steven Lovy
Plughead Rewired: Circuitry Man 2 '94
Circuitry Man '90

Edward T. Lowe
House of Dracula '45
House of Frankenstein '44
Bulldog Drummond Escapes '37
Tangled Destinies '32
The Vampire Bat '32
The Hunchback of Notre Dame '23

Sherman Lowe
Bury Me Not on the Lone Prairie '41
The Masked Rider '41
Pony Post '40

Andrew Lowery
Boys and Girls '00
Simon Sez '99

Craig Lucas
Reckless '95
Prelude to a Kiss '92
Longtime Companion '90

George Lucas (1944-)
Star Wars: Episode 2—Attack of the Clones '02
Star Wars: Episode 1—The Phantom Menace '99
Return of the Jedi '83
Raiders of the Lost Ark '81
Star Wars '77
American Graffiti '73
THX 1138 '71

Ralph Lucas
Planet of the Dinosaurs '80
The Child '76

William Ludwig (1912-99)
Gun Glory '57
Interrupted Melody '55
Oklahoma! '55
Athena '54
The Merry Widow '52
The Sun Comes Up '49
The Hills of Home '48

Kurt Luedtke
Random Hearts '99
Out of Africa '85
Absence of Malice '81

Baz Luhrmann (1962-)
Moulin Rouge '01
William Shakespeare's Romeo and Juliet '96
Strictly Ballroom '92

Eric Luke
Still Not Quite Human '92
Explorers '85

Sidney Lumet (1924-)
Night Falls on Manhattan '96
Q & A '90
Prince of the City '81

Bigas Luna (1946-)
The Chambermaid on the Titanic '97
Jamon, Jamon '93
Anguish '88

Ida Lupino (1914-95)
Private Hell 36 '54
Streets of Sin '49

Rod Lurie (1962-)
The Contender '00
Deterrence '00

Jan Lustig
Young Bess '53
Homecoming '48
The White Cliffs of Dover '44

Karen McCullah Lutz
Legally Blonde '01
Ten Things I Hate about You '99

David Lynch (1946-)
Mulholland Drive '01
Lost Highway '96
Twin Peaks: Fire Walk with Me '92
Wild at Heart '90
Blue Velvet '86
Dune '84
The Elephant Man '80
Eraserhead '78

Barre Lyndon
The War of the Worlds '53
To Please a Lady '50
House on 92nd Street '45

Jonathan Lynn (1943-)
Nuns on the Run '90
Clue '85

Fibe Ma
Mr. Nice Guy '98
Rumble in the Bronx '96
Supercop '92

Charles MacArthur
Wuthering Heights '39
Twentieth Century '34
Rasputin and the Empress '33

Richard Macaulay
Across the Pacific '42
The Roaring Twenties '39

Ruggero Maccari
The Family '87
A Special Day '77
Down & Dirty '76

Ranald MacDougall
Queen Bee '55
We're No Angels '55
June Bride '48
Mildred Pierce '45
Objective, Burma! '45

Aeneas MacKenzie
The Ten Commandments '56
Fighting Seabees '44
They Died with Their Boots On '41

Billy Mackinnon
Hideous Kinky '99
Small Faces '95

Patricia MacLachlan
Baby '00
Journey '95
Sarah, Plain and Tall: Skylark '93

Bernard MacLaverty
Hostages '93
Lamb '85
Cal '84

Alistair MacLean
Breakheart Pass '76
Where Eagles Dare '68

Andrew Maclear
The Man Who Made Husbands Jealous '98
Dealers '89

Don MacPherson
The Avengers '98
The Big Man: Crossing the Line '91
Absolute Beginners '86

Earl MacRauch
Wired '89
The Adventures of Buckaroo Banzai Across the Eighth Dimension '84

William H. Macy (1950-)
A Slight Case of Murder '99
The Con '98

Guy Maddin (1956-)
Careful '92

Tales from the Gimli Hospital *'88*

Brent Maddock
Wild Wild West *'99*
Tremors 2: Aftershocks *'96*
Heart and Souls *'93*
Ghost Dad *'90*
Tremors *'89*
Short Circuit 2 *'88*
*batteries not included *'87*
Short Circuit *'86*

Ben Maddow (-1992)
The Secret of Santa Vittoria *'69*
The Balcony *'63*
Men in War *'57*
The Asphalt Jungle *'50*

Robert Madero
All Tied Up *'92*
Mausoleum *'83*

Doug Magee
Beyond the Call *'96*
Cold Light of Day *'95*
Somebody Has to Shoot the Picture *'90*

Maria Maggenti
The Love Letter *'99*
The Incredibly True Adventure of Two Girls in Love *'95*

Jeff Maguire
In the Line of Fire *'93*
Victory *'81*

Redge Mahaffey
Life 101 *'95*
Quest of the Delta Knights *'93*
Deadly Rivals *'92*

John Lee Mahin
Moment to Moment *'66*
The Horse Soldiers *'59*
No Time for Sergeants *'58*
Heaven Knows, Mr. Allison *'57*
The Bad Seed *'56*
Johnny Eager *'42*
Dr. Jekyll and Mr. Hyde *'41*
Love on the Run *'36*
Red Dust *'32*

Richard Maibaum
License to Kill *'89*
The Living Daylights *'87*
S*H*E *'79*
The Spy Who Loved Me *'77*
On Her Majesty's Secret Service *'69*
Thunderball *'65*
Goldfinger *'64*
From Russia with Love *'63*
Dr. No *'62*
The Great Gatsby *'49*
O.S.S. *'46*

Norman Mailer
American Tragedy *'00*
King Lear *'87*
Tough Guys Don't Dance *'87*

Daniel Mainwaring
Invasion of the Body Snatchers *'56*
Out of the Past *'47*

Arduino (Dino) Maiuri (1916-84)
Chino *'75*
Companeros *'70*
Danger: Diabolik *'68*

Majid Majidi
The Color of Paradise *'99*
Children of Heaven *'98*

Dusan Makavejev (1932-)
Montenegro *'81*
Sweet Movie *'75*
WR: Mysteries of the Organism *'71*
Innocence Unprotected *'68*
The Love Affair, or The Case of the Missing Switchboard Operator *'67*
Man Is Not a Bird *'65*

Mohsen Makhmalbaf
Kandahar *'01*
Gabbeh *'96*

Terrence Malick (1943-)
The Thin Red Line *'98*
Days of Heaven *'78*
Badlands *'74*
Pocket Money *'72*

Louis Malle (1932-95)
May Fools *'90*
Au Revoir les Enfants *'87*
Murmur of the Heart *'71*
Spirits of the Dead *'68*
Viva Maria! *'65*
The Fire Within *'64*
Zazie dans le Metro *'61*
The Lovers *'59*

Miles Malleson (1888-1969)
The Thief of Bagdad *'40*
Nine Days a Queen *'36*
Lorna Doone *'34*
Night Birds *'31*

Mark Malone
Hoods *'98*
Bulletproof Heart *'95*
Signs of Life *'89*
Dead of Winter *'87*

Albert (John B. Sherry) Maltz (1908-85)
The Beguiled *'70*
Two Mules for Sister Sara *'70*
The Robe *'53*
Broken Arrow *'50*
The Naked City *'48*
Cloak and Dagger *'46*
This Gun for Hire *'42*

David Mamet (1947-)
Hannibal *'01*
Heist *'01*
State and Main *'00*
Lansky *'99*
Ronin *'98*
The Winslow Boy *'98*
The Edge *'97*
The Spanish Prisoner *'97*
Wag the Dog *'97*
American Buffalo *'95*
Oleanna *'94*
Vanya on 42nd Street *'94*
A Life in the Theater *'93*
Glengarry Glen Ross *'92*
Hoffa *'92*
The Water Engine *'92*
Homicide *'91*
We're No Angels *'89*
Things Change *'88*
House of Games *'87*
The Untouchables *'87*
The Verdict *'82*
The Postman Always Rings Twice *'81*

Don Mancini
Bride of Chucky *'98*
Child's Play 3 *'91*
Child's Play 2 *'90*
Child's Play *'88*

Babaloo Mandel
Where the Heart Is *'00*
EDtv *'99*
Father's Day *'96*
Multiplicity *'96*
Forget Paris *'95*
City Slickers 2: The Legend of Curly's Gold *'94*
Greedy *'94*
A League of Their Own *'92*
Mr. Saturday Night *'92*
City Slickers *'91*
Parenthood *'89*
Vibes *'88*
Gung Ho *'85*
Spies Like Us *'85*
Splash *'84*
Night Shift *'82*

James Mangold (1964-)
Kate & Leopold *'01*
Girl, Interrupted *'99*
Cop Land *'97*
Heavy *'94*
Oliver & Company *'88*

Herman J. Mankiewicz
Pride of St. Louis *'52*
A Woman's Secret *'49*
The Pride of the Yankees *'42*
Citizen Kane *'41*
Dinner at Eight *'33*

Joseph L. Mankiewicz (1909-93)
The Honey Pot *'67*
Cleopatra *'63*
Guys and Dolls *'55*
The Barefoot Contessa *'54*
Julius Caesar *'53*
People Will Talk *'51*
All About Eve *'50*
No Way Out *'50*
A Letter to Three Wives *'49*
The Keys of the Kingdom *'44*
Forsaking All Others *'35*
I Live My Life *'35*
Diplomaniacs *'33*

Tom Mankiewicz (1942-)
Dragnet *'87*
Ladyhawke *'85*
The Eagle Has Landed *'77*
The Cassandra Crossing *'76*
Mother, Jugs and Speed *'76*
The Man with the Golden Gun *'74*
Live and Let Die *'73*
Diamonds Are Forever *'71*

Wolf Mankowitz (1925-98)
Waltz of the Toreadors *'62*
The Day the Earth Caught Fire *'61*
The Two Faces of Dr. Jekyll *'60*
Expresso Bongo *'59*

Abby Mann
Indictment: The McMartin Trial *'95*
Murderers Among Us: The Simon Wiesenthal Story *'89*
King *'78*
Report to the Commissioner *'74*
The Detective *'68*
Ship of Fools *'65*
A Child Is Waiting *'63*
Judgment at Nuremberg *'61*

Edward Andrew (Santos Alcocer) Mann (1923-95)
Seizure *'74*
The Freakmaker *'73*
Cauldron of Blood *'67*
Hallucination *'67*

Michael Mann (1943-)
Ali *'01*
The Insider *'99*
Heat *'95*
The Last of the Mohicans *'92*
Manhunter *'86*
The Keep *'83*
Thief *'81*
Vegas *'78*

Stanley Mann
Conan the Destroyer *'84*
Firestarter *'84*
Eye of the Needle *'81*
Meteor *'79*
The Collector *'65*
The Mouse That Roared *'59*

Albert Mannheimer
Born Yesterday *'50*
Three Daring Daughters *'48*

Bruce Manning
First Love *'39*
Three Smart Girls Grow Up *'39*
Mad About Music *'38*
That Certain Age *'38*

Graeme Manson
Cube *'98*
Rupert's Land *'98*

Guido Manuli
Volere Volare *'92*
Allegro Non Troppo *'76*

Russell V. Manzatt
Trapper County War *'89*
Rush Week *'88*

Joseph Moncure March
Hoopla *'33*
Hell's Angels *'30*

David Marconi
Enemy of the State *'98*
The Harvest *'92*

Lawrence B. Marcus (1917-2001)
The Stunt Man *'80*
Justine *'69*
Petulia *'68*

Mitch Marcus
The Haunting of Hell House *'99*
A Boy Called Hate *'95*

Andreas Marfori
Desperate Crimes *'93*
Evil Clutch *'89*

Herbert Margolis
The Kettles on Old MacDonald's Farm *'57*
Francis in the Haunted House *'56*
Ma and Pa Kettle *'49*

Donald Margulies
Collected Stories *'02*
Dinner with Friends *'01*

A. L. Mariaux
Oasis of the Zombies *'82*
Zombie Lake *'80*

Richard "Cheech" Marin (1946-)
Born in East L.A. *'87*
Cheech and Chong's The Corsican Brothers *'84*
Cheech and Chong: Still Smokin' *'83*
Cheech and Chong: Things Are Tough All Over *'82*
Cheech and Chong's Nice Dreams *'81*
Cheech and Chong's Next Movie *'80*
Cheech and Chong's Up in Smoke *'79*

Frances Marion (1888-1973)
Camille *'36*
Dinner at Eight *'33*
The Champ *'32*
The Big House *'30*
The Wind *'28*
Son of the Sheik *'26*
The Love Light *'21*
Amarilly of Clothesline Alley *'18*
Stella Maris *'18*
Tillie Wakes Up *'17*

Gene Markey
On the Avenue *'37*
Baby Face *'33*
Female *'33*

Mitch Markowitz
Crazy People *'90*
Good Morning, Vietnam *'87*

Jack Marks
Old Mother Riley, Headmistress *'50*
Old Mother Riley's New Venture *'49*

Andrew Marlowe
The Hollow Man *'00*
End of Days *'99*
Air Force One *'97*

Brad (Sean) Marlowe
Object of Obsession *'95*
At Home with the Webbers *'94*

Malcolm Marmorstein
Konrad *'90s*
Dead Men Don't Die *'91*
Return from Witch Mountain *'78*
Pete's Dragon *'77*
Mary, Mary, Bloody Mary *'76*
Whiffs *'75*
S*P*Y*S *'74*

Henri Marquet
Mr. Hulot's Holiday *'53*
Jour de Fete *'48*

Gabriel Garcia Marquez
The Fable of the Beautiful Pigeon Fancier *'88*
Letters from the Park *'88*
Miracle in Rome *'88*
Erendira *'83*
Mary, My Dearest *'83*

Garry Marshall (1934-)
The Other Sister *'98*
The Flamingo Kid *'84*
Evil Roy Slade *'71*

Neil Marshall
Killing Time *'97*
The Flamingo Kid *'84*

Roger Marshall
And Now the Screaming Starts *'73*
Theatre of Death *'67*

Tonie Marshall
Venus Beauty Institute *'98*
Pas Tres Catholique *'93*

William Martell
The Base *'99*
Black Thunder *'98*
Steel Sharks *'97*
Crash Dive *'96*
Invisible Mom *'96*
Cyberzone *'95*
Virtual Combat *'95*
Hard Evidence *'94*

Peter Marthesheimer
Veronika Voss *'82*
The Marriage of Maria Braun *'79*

Al Martin
Invasion of the Saucer Men *'57*
Money Madness *'47*
Blondie Knows Best *'46*
The Invisible Ghost *'41*
Kelly of the Secret Service *'36*
Prison Shadows *'36*

Charles Martin
Dead Right *'68*
My Dear Secretary *'49*

Francis Martin
One Night in the Tropics *'40*
The Big Broadcast of 1938 *'38*
College Swing *'38*
Waikiki Wedding *'37*
The Princess Comes Across *'36*
Rhythm on the Range *'36*
Strike Me Pink *'36*
We're Not Dressing *'34*

Helen Martin (1909-2000)
The Lady Confesses *'45*
The Invisible Ghost *'41*

Mardik Martin
Raging Bull *'80*
New York, New York *'77*
Valentino *'77*
Mean Streets *'73*

Robert Martin
Basket Case 3: The Progeny *'92*
Frankenhooker *'90*

Steve Martin (1945-)
Bowfinger *'99*
A Simple Twist of Fate *'94*
L.A. Story *'91*
Roxanne *'87*
Three Amigos *'86*
The Man with Two Brains *'83*
Dead Men Don't Wear Plaid *'82*
The Jerk *'79*

Troy Kennedy Martin
Hostile Waters *'97*
Kelly's Heroes *'70*

Jacques Martineau
The Adventures of Felix *'99*
Jeanne and the Perfect Guy *'98*

Raymond Martino
To the Limit *'95*
DaVinci's War *'92*
American Born *'89*
Angels of the City *'89*

Sergio Martino (1938-)
The Great Alligator *'81*
Torso *'73*

Mike Marvin
Wishman *'93*

The Wraith *'87*

Arthur Marx
Cancel My Reservation *'72*
Eight on the Lam *'67*
I'll Take Sweden *'65*
A Global Affair *'63*

R.J. Marx
Double Obsession *'93*
Master of Dragonard Hill *'89*
Dead Man Walking *'88*
Dragonard *'88*
Gor *'88*
Outlaw of Gor *'87*
Platoon Leader *'87*
C.O.D. *'83*

Sarah Y. Mason
Golden Boy *'39*
Stella Dallas *'37*
Little Women *'33*

Ed Masterson
Storm Catcher *'99*
No Code of Conduct *'98*

Nico Mastorakis (1941-)
Hired to Kill *'91*
In the Cold of the Night *'89*
Bloodstone *'88*
Glitch! *'88*
The Wind *'87*
Zero Boys *'86*
Blind Date *'84*
Blood Tide *'82*

William Mastrosimone
The Burning Season *'94*
With Honors *'94*
Sinatra *'92*
The Beast *'88*
Extremities *'86*

Berkely Mather
The Long Ships *'64*
Dr. No *'62*

Chris Matheson
Mr. Wrong *'95*
A Goofy Movie *'94*
Bill & Ted's Bogus Journey *'91*
Bill & Ted's Excellent Adventure *'89*

Richard Matheson
Trilogy of Terror 2 *'96*
Loose Cannons *'90*
Jaws 3 *'83*
Twilight Zone: The Movie *'83*
Young Warriors *'83*
Somewhere in Time *'80*
Trilogy of Terror *'75*
Scream of the Wolf *'74*
Dracula *'73*
Dying Room Only *'73*
The Legend of Hell House *'73*
The Night Strangler *'72*
Duel *'71*
The Night Stalker *'71*
The Devil Rides Out *'68*
Die! Die! My Darling! *'65*
The Comedy of Terrors *'64*
The Last Man on Earth *'64*
The Raven *'63*
Burn Witch, Burn! *'62*
Tales of Terror *'62*
Master of the World *'61*
The Pit and the Pendulum *'61*
The Fall of the House of Usher *'60*
The Incredible Shrinking Man *'57*

Richard Christian Matheson
Full Eclipse *'93*
It Takes Two *'88*
Three o'Clock High *'87*

June Mathis
Blood and Sand *'22*
The Four Horsemen of the Apocalypse *'21*
The Saphead *'21*

Melissa Mathison
Kundun *'97*
The Indian in the Cupboard *'95*
The Escape Artist *'82*

Boleslaw Michalek
A Love in Germany '84
Danton '82

Dave Michener
The Great Mouse Detective '86
The Fox and the Hound '81

William Mickelberry
Black Dog '98
Escape: Human Cargo '98
Woman Undone '95

Anne-Marie Mieville (1945-)
First Name: Carmen '83
Numero Deux '75

Romano Migliorini
Deadly Mission '78
The Bloody Pit of Horror '65

Radu Mihaileanu
Train of Life '98
Trahir '93

Gordan Mihic
Black Cat, White Cat '98
Someone Else's America '96

Ted V. Mikels
10 Violent Women '79
Blood Orgy of the She-Devils '74
The Doll Squad '73
The Corpse Grinders '71
The Astro-Zombies '67

Djordje Milicevic
Iron Will '93
Toby McTeague '87
Runaway Train '85
Victory '81

Frank Military
Blind Faith '98
Buffalo Soldiers '97

John Milius (1944-)
Rough Riders '97
Clear and Present Danger '94
Geronimo: An American Legend '93
Farewell to the King '89
Red Dawn '84
Conan the Barbarian '82
Apocalypse Now '79
1941 '79
Big Wednesday '78
The Wind and the Lion '75
Dillinger '73
Magnum Force '73
Evel Knievel '72
Jeremiah Johnson '72
Life & Times of Judge Roy Bean '72

Ronald Millar (1919-98)
Never Let Me Go '53
The Miniver Story '50

Oscar Millard
The Conqueror '56
No Highway in the Sky '51
Come to the Stable '49

Andrew Miller
Boys and Girls '00
Simon Sez '99

Arthur Miller
The Crucible '96
Everybody Wins '90
The Misfits '61

Chris Miller
Multiplicity '96
National Lampoon's Animal House '78

Claude Miller (1942-)
The Accompanist '93
The Little Thief '89
This Sweet Sickness '77
The Best Way '76

David Keith Miller
The Glass Cage '96
I Like to Play Games '95

George Miller (1945-)
Babe '95
Lorenzo's Oil '92
Mad Max: Beyond Thunderdome '85
The Road Warrior '82
Mad Max '80

Harvey Miller (1936-99)
Getting Away With Murder '96
Bad Medicine '85
Cannonball Run 2 '84
Protocol '84
Jekyll & Hyde...Together Again '82
Private Benjamin '80

J(ames) P(inckney) Miller (1919-2001)
Helter Skelter '76
The Lindbergh Kidnapping Case '76
The People Next Door '70
Behold a Pale Horse '64
Days of Wine and Roses '62

Jeff Miller
Eye of the Killer '99
Hellblock 13 '97

Jennifer Miller
Cupid & Cate '00
Family Pictures '93
The Dark Secret of Harvest Home '78

Percy (Master P) Miller (1970-)
Foolish '99
I Got the Hook-Up '98

Seton I. Miller
Istanbul '57
Singapore '47
Two Years before the Mast '46
Ministry of Fear '44
The Black Swan '42
Here Comes Mr. Jordan '41
The Adventures of Robin Hood '38
Dawn Patrol '38
Kid Galahad '37
The Eagle and the Hawk '33
Murders in the Zoo '33

Winston Miller
Cavalry Charge '51
My Darling Clementine '46

Bertram Millhauser (-1958)
The Woman in Green '45
The Invisible Man's Revenge '44
The Texans '38

Andy Milligan (1929-91)
Man with Two Heads '72
The Rats Are Coming! The Werewolves Are Here! '72
The Ghastly Ones '68

Bill Milling
Body Trouble '92
Lauderdale '89

Hugh Mills
Blanche Fury '48
Personal Property '37

Paula Milne
I Dreamed of Africa '00
Second Sight '99
Hollow Reed '95
Mad Love '95

Daniel Minahan
Series 7: The Contenders '01
I Shot Andy Warhol '96

Michael Miner
Deadly Weapon '88
RoboCop '87

Pang Ming
Frozen '98
So Close to Paradise '98

Anthony Minghella (1954-)
The Talented Mr. Ripley '99
The English Patient '96
Truly, Madly, Deeply '91

Joe Minion
Motorama '91
Vampire's Kiss '88
Julia and Julia '87
After Hours '85

Brad Mirman
Resurrection '99
Truth or Consequences, N.M. '97
Knight Moves '93

Body of Evidence '92

Craig Mitchell
Komodo '99
Milo '98

Gene Mitchell
Flipping '96
The Takeover '94

Joseph A. Mitchell
Seven Chances '25
The Navigator '24
Our Hospitality '23

Julian Mitchell
Wilde '97
August '95
Vincent & Theo '90
Another Country '84
Elizabeth R '72

Steve Mitchell
Against the Law '98
Chopping Mall '86

Moshe Mizrahi (1931-)
Every Time We Say Goodbye '86
La Vie Continue '82
I Sent a Letter to My Love '81
Madame Rosa '77
I Love You Rosa '72

Jordan Moffet
Like Mike '02
Whispers: An Elephant's Tale '00

Jose Mojica Marins (1929-)
Awakenings of the Beast '68
At Midnight, I'll Take Your Soul '63

Hans Petter Moland
Aberdeen '00
Zero Degrees Kelvin '95
The Last Lieutenant '94

Jacinto (Jack) Molina (1934-)
Human Beasts '80
Inquisition '76
Night of the Howling Beast '75
Exorcism '74
Curse of the Devil '73
House of Psychotic Women '73
The Mummy's Revenge '73
Dracula's Great Love '72
Horror Rises from the Tomb '72
Dr. Jekyll and the Wolfman '71
The Fury of the Wolfman '70
The Werewolf vs. the Vampire Woman '70
Dracula vs. Frankenstein '69

Edouard Molinaro (1928-)
Beaumarchais the Scoundrel '96
La Cage aux Folles '78
Pain in the A— '77
Dracula Father and Son '76

Paul Monash
The Golden Spiders: A Nero Wolfe Mystery '00
Rescuers: Stories of Courage—Two Couples '98
George Wallace '97
Kingfish: A Story of Huey P. Long '95
Stalin '92
All Quiet on the Western Front '79
Salem's Lot '79
Scarface Mob '62
Bail Out at 43,000 '57

Nate Monaster
Call Me Bwana '63
That Touch of Mink '62

Paul Mones
Double Team '97
The Quest '96
Saints and Sinners '95
Fathers and Sons '92

Christopher Monger (1950-)
Seeing Red '99

The Englishman Who Went up a Hill But Came down a Mountain '95
Waiting for the Light '90

Vincent Mongol
Hellhole '85
Chained Heat '83

Mario Monicelli (1915-)
Lovers and Liars '81
The Organizer '64
The Unfaithfuls '60
Big Deal on Madonna Street '58

John Monks, Jr.
No Man Is an Island '62
The West Point Story '50
Knock on Any Door '49
13 Rue Madeleine '46
House on 92nd Street '45

Eric Monte
Cooley High '75
Nine Lives of Fritz the Cat '74

Luigi Montefiore
Beyond Justice '92
Stagefright '87
The Great Alligator '81

Brian Moore (1921-99)
Black Robe '91
The Blood of Others '84
Torn Curtain '66

Charles Philip Moore
Heaven's Fire '99
Termination Man '97
The Last Assassins '96
Not of This Earth '96
Machine Gun Blues '95
Black Belt '92

Dudley Moore (1935-2002)
The Hound of the Baskervilles '77
Bedazzled '68
30 Is a Dangerous Age, Cynthia '68

Michael Moore (1954-)
Canadian Bacon '94
Roger & Me '89

Ronald D. Moore
Star Trek: First Contact '96
Star Trek: Generations '94

Simon Moore
Dinotopia '02
Gulliver's Travels '95
The Quick and the Dead '94
Under Suspicion '92
Traffik '90

Wesley Moore
Are You Lonesome Tonight '92
Apprentice to Murder '88

Philippe Mora (1949-)
Pterodactyl Woman from Beverly Hills '97
Howling 3: The Marsupials '87
Screams of a Winter Night '79

Eddie Moran
Wonder Man '45
Twin Beds '42

Patrick Moran
Jack-O '95
Dark Universe '93

Julian More
The Bloodsuckers '70
The Valley of Gwangi '69

Rafael Moreu
The Rage: Carrie 2 '99
Hackers '95

Glen Morgan
The One '01
Final Destination '00
The Boys Next Door '85

Peter Morgan
The Very Thought of You '98
The Silent Touch '94

Louis Morheim
The Beast from 20,000 Fathoms '53
Ma and Pa Kettle '49

Tony Morphett
Kings in Grass Castles '97
Crime Broker '94
Sweet Talker '91
The Last Wave '77

Richard Morris (1924-96)
Thoroughly Modern Millie '67
Ma and Pa Kettle at the Fair '52

Paul Morrissey (1939-)
Beethoven's Nephew '88
Spike of Bensonhurst '88
Mixed Blood '84
The Hound of the Baskervilles '77
Andy Warhol's Dracula '74
Andy Warhol's Frankenstein '74
Heat '72
Trash '70
Flesh '68

Barry Morrow
Race the Sun '96
Rain Man '88

Douglas S. Morrow (1913-94)
Beyond a Reasonable Doubt '56
Jim Thorpe: All American '51
The Stratton Story '49

John Mortimer
In Love and War '01
Don Quixote '00
Cider with Rosie '99
Tea with Mussolini '99
Edwin '84
No Sex Please—We're British '73
The Innocents '61
24 Hours in a Woman's Life '61

April Moskowitz
Body Strokes '95
Friend of the Family '95

Jonathan Mostow
U-571 '00
Breakdown '96

Marcel Moussey
Shoot the Piano Player '62
The 400 Blows '59

Allan Moyle
The Thing Called Love '93
Love Crimes '92
Pump Up the Volume '90

Jim Mulholland
Bad Boys '95
National Lampoon's Favorite Deadly Sins '95
Oscar '91
Amazon Women on the Moon '87
Ratings Game '84

Christopher Munch
Color of a Brisk and Leaping Day '95
The Hours and Times '92

Robert Munic
They Call Me Sirr '00
In a Class of His Own '99

Rona Munro
Aimee & Jaguar '98
Ladybird, Ladybird '93

Ryu Murakami
Because of You '95
Tokyo Decadence '91

Jane Murfin
The Shining Hour '38
Come and Get It '36

Geoff Murphy (1938-)
Dark of the Night '85
Utu '83

Richard Murphy (-1993)
Compulsion '59
Boomerang '47
Back in the Saddle '41

Tab Murphy
Atlantis: The Lost Empire '01
Tarzan '99

The Hunchback of Notre Dame '96
The Last of the Dogmen '95
My Best Friend Is a Vampire '88

Warren B. Murphy
Remo Williams: The Adventure Begins '85
The Eiger Sanction '75

Don Murray (1929-)
Confessions of Tom Harris '72
The Hoodlum Priest '61

John Fenton Murray
Arnold '73
Pufnstuf '70
McHale's Navy Joins the Air Force '65
Robin and the 7 Hoods '64

Michael J. Murray
Madonna: Innocence Lost '95
Honor Thy Father and Mother: The True Story of the Menendez Brothers '94
The Lightning Incident '91
The House of Usher '88

Tom Musca
Tortilla Soup '01
Money for Nothing '93
Stand and Deliver '88

John Musker
Hercules '97
Aladdin '92
The Little Mermaid '89

Floyd Mutrux
Blood In ... Blood Out: Bound by Honor '93
American Me '92
There Goes My Baby '92
The Hollywood Knights '80
Aloha, Bobby and Rose '74

Henry Myers
Destry Rides Again '39
The Black Room '35
Diplomaniacs '33

Mike Myers (1963-)
Austin Powers In Goldmember '02
Austin Powers 2: The Spy Who Shagged Me '99
Austin Powers: International Man of Mystery '97
So I Married an Axe Murderer '93
Wayne's World 2 '93
Wayne's World '92

Nancy Myers
Father of the Bride Part II '95
I Love Trouble '94

Scott Myers
Trojan War '97
K-9 '89

Zion Myers
Here Come the Waves '45
April Fool '26

John Myhers (-1992)
Terror in Beverly Hills '90
The Longshot '86
The Private Eyes '80

Fred Myton
The Black Raven '43
Dead Men Walk '43
Terror of Tiny Town '38

Yuri Nagibin
Dersu Uzala '75
Tchaikovsky '71

Ed Naha
Omega Doom '96
Honey, I Shrunk the Kids '89
Dolls '87
Troll '86

Takehiro Nakajima
Village of Dreams '97
Okoge '93

Desmond Nakano
White Man's Burden '95
American Me '92

Yin Nam
Full Contact '92
Prison on Fire '87

Michael Nankin
Gate 2 '92

The Gate '87
N. Richard Nash (1913-2000)
One Summer Love '76
Helen of Troy '56
The Rainmaker '56
Jeff Nathanson
Rush Hour 2 '01
Bait '00
Speed 2: Cruise Control '97
For Better or Worse '95
Maria Nation
A Season for Miracles '99
Ellen Foster '97
Blue River '95
Rick Natkin
Gang in Blue '96
Necessary Roughness '91
The Boys in Company C '77
Jack Natteford
Trail to San Antone '47
Double Trouble '41
Come on Rangers '38
The Crimson Trail '35
Demon for Trouble '34
Cowboy Counselor '33
Arizona Terror '31
Border Romance '30
Gregory Nava (1949-)
Selena '96
My Family '94
A Time of Destiny '88
El Norte '83
End of August '82
Christopher Neame (1947-)
Feast of July '95
Zeta One '69
Ronald Neame (1911-)
This Happy Breed '47
Brief Encounter '46
Great Expectations '46
Hal Needham (1931-)
Stroker Ace '83
Smokey and the Bandit '77
Troy Neighbors
Fortress 2: Re-Entry '99
Fortress '93
Hank Nelken
Saving Silverman '01
Killer Bud '00
B.J. Nelson
Alien Chaser '96
Scanners 2: The New Order '91
Jessie Nelson
I Am Sam '01
The Story of Us '99
Stepmom '98
Corrina, Corrina '94
John Allen Nelson (1959-)
American Yakuza '94
Best of the Best 2 '93
Peter Nelson
Getting Up and Going Home '92
The Lonely Passion of Judith Hearne '87
Dennis Nemec
The Avenging Angel '95
God Bless the Child '88
Murder in Coweta County '83
Jan Nemec (1936-)
The Report on the Party and the Guests '66
Diamonds of the Night '64
Vladimir Nemirovsky
Hangman '00
Indiscreet '98
The Beneficiary '97
Claude Neron
Vincent, Francois, Paul and the Others '76
Cesar & Rosalie '72
Avi Nesher
The Taxman '98
Mercenary '96
Timebomb '91
Doppelganger: The Evil Within '90

Edward Neumeier
Starship Troopers '97
RoboCop '87
John Thomas Neville
The Devil Bat '41
Never Give a Sucker an Even Break '41
Trader Horn '31
Craig J. Nevius
Baby Face Nelson '97
Lady Killer '97
Black Scorpion 2: Ground Zero '96
Marquis de Sade '96
Black Scorpion '95
David Newman (1954-)
Santa Claus: The Movie '85
Sheena '84
Superman 3 '83
Jinxed '82
Still of the Night '82
Superman 2 '80
Superman: The Movie '78
Bad Company '72
What's Up, Doc? '72
There Was a Crooked Man '70
Bonnie & Clyde '67
Andrew Niccol (1964-)
Simone '02
The Truman Show '98
Gattaca '97
Maurizio Nichetti (1948-)
Luna e L'Altra '96
Stephano Quantestorie '93
Volere Volare '92
The Icicle Thief '89
Allegro Non Troppo '76
Dudley Nichols
Prince Valiant '54
Pinky '49
The Fugitive '48
And Then There Were None '45
The Bells of St. Mary's '45
It Happened Tomorrow '44
Air Force '43
For Whom the Bell Tolls '43
Stagecoach '39
Bringing Up Baby '38
The Hurricane '37
The Crusades '35
The Informer '35
She '35
The Lost Patrol '34
Jack Nicholson (1937-)
Head '68
The Trip '67
Flight to Fury '66
Ride in the Whirlwind '66
William Nicholson
Gladiator '00
Grey Owl '99
Firelight '97
Crime of the Century '96
First Knight '95
Nell '94
Shadowlands '93
A Private Matter '92
Sarafina! '92
Nicholas Niciphor
Fatal Charm '92
Death Sport '78
Ted Nicolaou
Bloodstorm: Subspecies 4 '98
Spellbreaker: Secret of the Leprechauns '96
Vampire Journals '96
Leapin' Leprechauns '95
Dragonworld '94
Bloodlust: Subspecies 3 '93
Bloodstone: Subspecies 2 '92
Assault of the Killer Bimbos '88
Terrorvision '86
Rob Nilsson (1940-)
Heat and Sunlight '87
On the Edge '86
Signal 7 '83

Northern Lights '79
Brian Nissen
The Swan Princess 2: Escape from Castle Mountain '97
The Swan Princess '94
Christopher Nolan (1970-)
Memento '00
Following '99
Tom Noonan (1951-)
The Wife '95
What Happened Was... '94
Eric Norden
Blood Legacy '73
Please Don't Eat My Mother '72
Marc Norman
Shakespeare in Love '98
Cutthroat Island '95
Waterworld '95
Bat 21 '88
The Aviator '85
Breakout '75
The Killer Elite '75
Zandy's Bride '74
Oklahoma Crude '73
Marsha Norman
The Audrey Hepburn Story '00
A Cooler Climate '99
'night, Mother '86
Edmund H. North
Patton '70
Damn the Defiant '62
Sink the Bismarck '60
Cowboy '58
The Day the Earth Stood Still '51
Flamingo Road '49
Bill W.L. Norton (1943-)
Back to the Beach '87
Losin' It '82
William W. Norton, Sr.
Dirty Tricks '81
Night of the Juggler '80
Day of the Animals '77
Gator '76
Moving Violation '76
A Small Town in Texas '76
Brannigan '75
Big Bad Mama '74
I Dismember Mama '74
White Lightning '73
McKenzie Break '70
The Scalphunters '68
Jonathan Nossiter
Signs & Wonders '00
Sunday '96
Louis Nowra
Radiance '98
Heaven's Burning '97
The Matchmaker '97
Cosi '95
Map of the Human Heart '93
Frank Nugent
Donovan's Reef '63
Gunman's Walk '58
Last Hurrah '58
The Searchers '56
Mister Roberts '55
The Quiet Man '52
She Wore a Yellow Ribbon '49
Fort Apache '48
Victor Nunez (1945-)
Ulee's Gold '97
Ruby in Paradise '93
A Flash of Green '85
Gal Young 'Un '79
Colin Nutley (1944-)
Under the Sun '98
The Last Dance '93
Ron Nyswaner
Philadelphia '93
Love Hurts '91
Gross Anatomy '89
Prince of Pennsylvania '88
Mrs. Soffel '84
Purple Hearts '84
Swing Shift '84
Smithereens '82

Dan O'Bannon (1946-)
Bleeders '97
Screamers '96
Total Recall '90
Invaders from Mars '86
Lifeforce '85
Return of the Living Dead '85
Blue Thunder '83
Dead and Buried '81
Alien '79
Dark Star '74
Rockne S. O'Bannon (1955-)
Fatal Error '99
Alien Nation '88
Sean O'Bannon
Air Rage '01
Mom's Outta Sight '01
The Kid with the X-Ray Eyes '99
Mom, Can I Keep Her? '98
The Escort '97
Night Shade '97
Edna O'Brien
X, Y & Zee '72
Girl with Green Eyes '64
Liam O'Brien (1913-96)
Young at Heart '54
Chain Lightning '50
Richard O'Brien (1942-)
Shock Treatment '81
The Rocky Horror Picture Show '75
Robert O'Brien
By the Light of the Silvery Moon '53
The Lemon Drop Kid '51
Lady on a Train '45
Jeffrey Obrow
Bram Stoker's The Mummy '97
The Kindred '87
The Power '80
James O'Connolly
Tower of Evil '72
Night Caller from Outer Space '66
David Odell
Masters of the Universe '87
Supergirl '84
The Dark Crystal '82
Cry Uncle '71
Clifford Odets
Wild in the Country '61
Sweet Smell of Success '57
Deadline at Dawn '46
Humoresque '46
None But the Lonely Heart '44
The General Died at Dawn '36
Joseph O'Donnell
Billy the Kid in Texas '40
Border Caballero '36
Steve Oedekerk (1961-)
Jimmy Neutron: Boy Genius '01
Nutty Professor 2: The Klumps '00
Patch Adams '98
Nothing to Lose '96
The Nutty Professor '96
Ace Ventura: When Nature Calls '95
Hideo Oguni
Ran '85
Dodes 'ka-den '70
Tora! Tora! Tora! '70
High & Low '62
Sanjuro '62
Yojimbo '61
The Bad Sleep Well '60
The Hidden Fortress '58
The Lower Depths '57
Throne of Blood '57
I Live in Fear '55
Seven Samurai '54
Ikiru '52
Colo Tavernier O'Hagan
L'Appat '94

Daddy Nostalgia '90
Beatrice '88
The Story of Women '88
A Sunday in the Country '84
James O'Hanlon
Calamity Jane '53
Destination Moon '50
Sahara '43
Paul Ohl
North Star '96
Highlander: The Final Dimension '94
Pedro Olea (1938-)
Zafarinas '94
The Fencing Master '92
Joel Oliansky
Bird '88
The Todd Killings '71
Deanna Oliver
My Favorite Martian '98
Casper '95
Ron Oliver
Liar's Edge '92
Prom Night 3: The Last Kiss '89
Hello Mary Lou: Prom Night 2 '87
Hector Olivera (1931-)
The Road '00
A Shadow You Soon Will Be '94
Funny, Dirty Little War '83
Ermanno Olmi (1931-)
The Tree of Wooden Clogs '78
Fiances '63
Arne Olsen
Escape from Atlantis '97
All Dogs Go to Heaven 2 '95
Mighty Morphin Power Rangers: The Movie '95
Cop and a Half '93
Final Round '93
Red Scorpion '89
Dana Olsen
George of the Jungle '97
The 'Burbs '89
David O'Malley (1944-)
Fatal Instinct '93
Edge of Honor '91
Easy Wheels '89
Kid Colter '85
Hangar 18 '80
Mountain Man '77
Charles "Blackie" O'Neal (1904-96)
Lassie's Great Adventure '62
Return of the Bad Men '48
Cry of the Werewolf '44
The Seventh Victim '43
Robert Vincent O'Neil
Jailbait '93
Deadly Force '83
Vice Squad '82
The Baltimore Bullet '80
Eugene O'Neill
Long Day's Journey Into Night '96
Long Day's Journey into Night '62
Max Ophuls (1902-57)
Modigliani '58
Lola Montes '55
The Earrings of Madame De... '54
George Oppenheimer
Undercurrent '46
A Day at the Races '37
Libeled Lady '36
Alan Ormsby
The Substitute '96
High Stakes '93
Indecency '92
Popcorn '89
Porky's 2: The Next Day '83
Cat People '82
Little Dragons '80
My Bodyguard '80
Touch & Go '80
Deranged '74
Children Shouldn't Play with Dead Things '72

Deathdream '72
James Orr (1953-)
Man of the House '95
Sister Act 2: Back in the Habit '93
Mr. Destiny '90
Three Men and a Baby '87
Tough Guys '86
Breaking All the Rules '85
J.O.C. Orton
Alfred Hitchcock's Bon Voyage '44
Non-Stop New York '37
Paul Osborn
South Pacific '58
Sayonara '57
East of Eden '54
Homecoming '48
Portrait of Jennie '48
The Young in Heart '38
Ron Osborn
Meet Joe Black '98
Radioland Murders '94
John Osborne (1929-94)
Luther '74
Tom Jones '63
The Entertainer '60
Look Back in Anger '58
William Osborne
The Scorpion King '02
Dr. Jekyll and Ms. Hyde '95
Ghost in the Machine '93
The Real McCoy '93
Stop! or My Mom Will Shoot '92
Twins '88
Nagisa Oshima (1932-)
Max, Mon Amour '86
Merry Christmas, Mr. Lawrence '83
In the Realm of Passion '80
In the Realm of the Senses '76
The Cruel Story of Youth '60
Diana Ossana
Larry McMurtry's Dead Man's Walk '96
Larry McMurtry's Streets of Laredo '95
Jean-Paul Ouellette
The Unnamable 2: The Statement of Randolph Carter '92
The Unnamable '88
Richard Outten
Last Rites '98
Little Nemo: Adventures in Slumberland '92
Pet Sematary 2 '92
Lionheart '87
Eric Overmyer
Homicide: The Movie '00
Rear Window '98
Francois Ozon (1967-)
Under the Sand '00
Water Drops on Burning Rocks '99
Sitcom '97
Yasujiro Ozu (1903-63)
An Autumn Afternoon '62
Good Morning '59
Tokyo Story '53
William R. Pace
Charming Billy '98
Blades '89
Jo Pagano
Try and Get Me '50
The Man I Love '46
Marcel Pagnol (1895-1974)
Nais '45
Le Schpountz '38
Harvest '37
Cesar '36
The Baker's Wife '33
Topaze '33
Fanny '32
Marius '31

Nick Paine
Josh Kirby...Time Warrior: Chapter 3, Trapped on Toyworld '95
Philadelphia Experiment 2 '93

Alan J. Pakula (1928-98)
The Pelican Brief '93
Presumed Innocent '90
See You in the Morning '89
Sophie's Choice '82

Euzhan Palcy (1957-)
A Dry White Season '89
Sugar Cane Alley '83

Michael Palin (1943-)
American Friends '91
Consuming Passions '88
Monty Python's The Meaning of Life '83
The Missionary '82
The Secret Policeman's Other Ball '82
Time Bandits '81
Monty Python's Life of Brian '79
Monty Python and the Holy Grail '75
And Now for Something Completely Different '72

Rospo Pallenberg
Druids '01
The Emerald Forest '85
Excalibur '81

Anders Palm
Dead Certain '92
Murder on Line One '90

Chazz Palminteri (1952-)
Faithful '95
A Bronx Tale '93

Norman Panama (1914-)
I Will, I Will for Now '76
The Road to Hong Kong '62
The Facts of Life '60
Li'l Abner '59
The Trap '59
Court Jester '56
White Christmas '54
Above and Beyond '53
Mr. Blandings Builds His Dream House '48
Monsieur Beaucaire '46
The Road to Utopia '46
Thank Your Lucky Stars '43
Star Spangled Rhythm '42

Dennis Paoli
The Dentist '96
Castle Freak '95
Body Snatchers '93
The Pit & the Pendulum '91
Meridian: Kiss of the Beast '90
From Beyond '86
Re-Animator '84

Jaroslav Papousek
The Firemen's Ball '68
Intimate Lighting '65
Loves of a Blonde '65

John Paragon
Twinsitters '95
Elvira, Mistress of the Dark '88

Edward Paramore
Three Comrades '38
The Bitter Tea of General Yen '33

Alan Parker (1944-)
Evita '96
The Road to Wellville '94
Come See the Paradise '90
Angel Heart '87
Bugsy Malone '76
Melody '71

David Parker
Amy '98
Rikky and Pete '88
Malcolm '86

Oliver Parker
The Importance of Being Earnest '02
An Ideal Husband '99
Othello '95

Robert B. Parker
Small Vices: A Spenser Mystery '99
Spenser: Ceremony '93

Ronald Parker
Joan of Arc '99
Gargantua '98

Scott Parker
Die Laughing '80
He Knows You're Alone '80

Tom S. Parker
The Flintstones '94
Getting Even with Dad '94
Richie Rich '94
Stay Tuned '92

Trey Parker (1969-)
South Park: Bigger, Longer and Uncut '99
Orgazmo '98
Cannibal! The Musical '96

William Parker
The Nut '21
The Jack Knife Man '20

Walter F. Parkes
Sneakers '92
WarGames '83

Sara Parriott
Runaway Bride '99
The Favor '92
Three Men and a Little Lady '90
Worth Winning '89

Lindsley Parsons
Desert Trail '35
Paradise Canyon '35
Man from Utah '34
Randy Rides Alone '34
Trail Beyond '34
Sagebrush Trail '33

Michael Part
A Kid in Aladdin's Palace '97
A Kid in King Arthur's Court '95

Frank Partos
The Snake Pit '48
The Uninvited '44
Honolulu '39

Ernest Pascal
Canyon Passage '46
Lloyds of London '36

Pier Paolo Pasolini (1922-75)
Salo, or the 120 Days of Sodom '75
Arabian Nights '74
The Canterbury Tales '71
The Decameron '70
Porcile '69
The Hawks & the Sparrows '67
The Gospel According to St. Matthew '64
The Grim Reaper '62
Mamma Roma '62
RoGoPaG '62
Accatone! '61
Il Bell'Antonio '60
That Long Night in '43 '60

Ivan Passer (1933-)
Law and Disorder '74
Born to Win '71
The Firemen's Ball '68
Intimate Lighting '65
Loves of a Blonde '65

Jonas Pate (1970-)
Deceiver '97
The Grave '95

Josh Pate
Deceiver '97
The Grave '95

John Patrick (1905-95)
Daniel Boone: Trail Blazer '56
Love Is a Many-Splendored Thing '55

Vincent Patrick
The Devil's Own '96
Family Business '89
The Pope of Greenwich Village '84

John Paxton
On the Beach '59
The Wild One '54

Murder, My Sweet '44

Alexander Payne (1961-)
Jurassic Park 3 '01
Election '99
Citizen Ruth '96

Dave Payne
Boltneck '98
Criminal Hearts '95

Keith Payson
Puppet Master 5: The Final Chapter '94
Puppet Master 4 '93

Senel Paz
A Paradise Under the Stars '99
Strawberry and Chocolate '93

Steve Peace
Killer Tomatoes Eat France '91
Return of the Killer Tomatoes! '88

Ann Peacock
Cora Unashamed '00
A Lesson Before Dying '99

Craig Pearce
Moulin Rouge '01
William Shakespeare's Romeo and Juliet '96
Strictly Ballroom '92

David Peckinpah
The Paperboy '94
The Diamond Trap '91

Sam Peckinpah (1925-84)
Bring Me the Head of Alfredo Garcia '74
Straw Dogs '72
The Wild Bunch '69
Villa Rides '68
Invasion of the Body Snatchers '56

Bill Peet (1915-2002)
The Sword in the Stone '63
101 Dalmatians '61
Peter Pan '53
Fantasia '40

Louis Pelletier (1907-2000)
Smith! '69
The Horse in the Gray Flannel Suit '68
Follow Me, Boys! '66
Those Calloways '65
Big Red '62

Sean Penn (1960-)
The Crossing Guard '94
The Indian Runner '91

Zak Penn (1968-)
Behind Enemy Lines '01
Inspector Gadget '99
P.C.U. '94

Erdman Penner
Lady and the Tramp '55
Peter Pan '53
The Adventures of Ichabod and Mr. Toad '49
Pinocchio '40

John Penney
The Contaminated Man '01
The Enemy '01
In Pursuit '00
Matter of Trust '98
Past Perfect '98
Return of the Living Dead 3 '93
The Kindred '87
The Power '80

Phil Penningroth
In the Line of Duty: Ambush in Waco '93
Silence of the Heart '84

David Peoples
Soldier '98
12 Monkeys '95
Deadfall '93
Hero '92
Unforgiven '92
The Blood of Heroes '89
Leviathan '89
Blade Runner '82

Clare Peploe
The Triumph of Love '01
Besieged '98

Rough Magic '95
High Season '88
Zabriskie Point '70

Mark Peploe
Little Buddha '93
Afraid of the Dark '92
The Sheltering Sky '90
High Season '88
The Last Emperor '87
The Passenger '75

S.J. Perelman
Around the World in 80 Days '56
Horse Feathers '32
Monkey Business '31

Frank Ray Perilli
Alligator '80
Laserblast '78
Zoltan...Hound of Dracula '78
The Doberman Gang '72

Ivo Perilli
Barabbas '62
The Unfaithfuls '60
War and Peace '56

Nat Perrin (1905-98)
I'll Take Sweden '65
Whistling in Dixie '42
Dimples '36
Duck Soup '33

Fred C. Perry
The Wind '87
Zero Boys '86

Michael Pertwee
A Funny Thing Happened on the Way to the Forum '66
Strange Bedfellows '65
Ladies Who Do '63
The Mouse on the Moon '62

Roland Pertwee
The Magic Bow '47
King Solomon's Mines '37
Non-Stop New York '37
The Ghoul '34

Steve Pesce
Stranger in the House '97
Daddy's Girl '96

Charlie Peters
Krippendorf's Tribe '98
Music from Another Room '97
My Father the Hero '93
Passed Away '92
Three Men and a Little Lady '90
Her Alibi '88
Hot to Trot! '88
Blame It on Rio '84
Kiss Me Goodbye '82
Paternity '81

Steven Peters
Wild Things '98
The Wolves '95

Wolfgang Petersen (1941-)
Shattered '91
The NeverEnding Story '84
Das Boot '81

Sandro Petraglia
The Truce '96
Fiorile '93
The Stolen Children '92
Forever Mary '89
Julia and Julia '87

Dan Petrie, Jr.
In the Army Now '94
Toy Soldiers '91
Shoot to Kill '88
The Big Easy '87
Beverly Hills Cop '84

Harley Peyton
Bandits '01
Elmore Leonard's Gold Coast '97
Keys to Tulsa '96
Heaven's Prisoners '95
Less Than Zero '87

Chuck Pfarrer
Red Planet '00
Virus '98
The Jackal '97
Barb Wire '96
Darkman 2: The Return of Durant '94
Hard Target '93

Darkman '90

Anna Hamilton Phelan
Girl, Interrupted '99
In Love and War '96
Gorillas in the Mist '88
Mask '85

Bill Phillips
Forbidden Choices '94
El Diablo '90
Rainbow Drive '90
Rising Son '90
Physical Evidence '89
Fire with Fire '86
Christine '84

Lou Diamond Phillips (1962-)
Ambition '91
Trespasses '86

Robert Phippeny
Simon, King of the Witches '71
The Night of the Following Day '69

Nicholas Phipps (1913-80)
Captain's Paradise '53
Madeleine '50

Maurice Pialat (1925-)
Van Gogh '92
Under Satan's Sun '87
A Nos Amours '84
Loulou '80

Jim Piddock
One Good Turn '95
Traces of Red '92

John Pielmeier
Sins of the Father '01
The Happy Face Murders '99
Through the Eyes of a Killer '92
The Shell Seekers '89
Agnes of God '85

Arthur C. Pierce (1923-87)
The Invisible Strangler '76
Invasion of the Animal People '62
The Cosmic Man '59

Charles B. Pierce
Boggy Creek II '83
Sacred Ground '83
The Evictors '79
Norseman '78
Grayeagle '77
Winterhawk '76

Frank Pierson (1925-)
Presumed Innocent '90
In Country '89
King of the Gypsies '78
A Star Is Born '76
Dog Day Afternoon '75
The Anderson Tapes '71
The Looking Glass War '69
Cool Hand Luke '67
Cat Ballou '65

Krzysztof Piesiewicz
Trois Couleurs: Blanc '94
Trois Couleurs: Rouge '94
Trois Couleurs: Bleu '93
The Double Life of Veronique '91
The Decalogue '88
No End '84

Tseng Pik-Yin
The Bride with White Hair '93
Iron Monkey '93

Jeremy Pikser
Bulworth '98
The Lemon Sisters '90

Nicholas Pileggi
Casino '95
City Hall '95
Goodfellas '90

Tullio Pinelli
Ginger & Fred '86
Juliet of the Spirits '65
8 1/2 '63
Boccaccio '70 '62
La Dolce Vita '60
Nights of Cabiria '57
Il Bidone '55
La Strada '54
Love in the City '53

The White Sheik '52
Variety Lights '51

Sidney Pink
The Castilian '63
Reptilicus '62
The Angry Red Planet '59

Steve Pink
High Fidelity '00
Grosse Pointe Blank '97

Harold Pinter (1930-)
The Trial '93
The Comfort of Strangers '91
The Heat of the Day '91
The Handmaid's Tale '90
Reunion '88
Dumb Waiter '87
The Room '87
Turtle Diary '86
Betrayal '83
The French Lieutenant's Woman '81
The Last Tycoon '76
The Go-Between '71
Accident '67
The Quiller Memorandum '66
The Pumpkin Eater '64
The Servant '63

Lucian Pintilie (1933-)
An Unforgettable Summer '94
The Oak '93

Bret Piper
They Bite '95
A Nymphoid Barbarian in Dinosaur Hell '94

Robert Pirosh
Hell Is for Heroes '62
Valley of the Kings '54
Go for Broke! '51
Battleground '49
I Married a Witch '42
A Day at the Races '37

Mark Pirro (1956-)
Buford's Beach Bunnies '92
My Mom's a Werewolf '89
Deathrow Gameshow '88
Curse of the Queerwolf '87

Angelo Pizzo
Rudy '93
Hoosiers '86

Alan Plater
The Last of the Blonde Bombshells '00
A Merry War '97
A Very British Coup '88
Fortunes of War '87
Coming Through '85
The Inside Man '84
Priest of Love '81
The Virgin and the Gypsy '70

Jonathan Platnick
End of Summer '97
Silent Victim '92

Polly Platt
A Map of the World '99
Pretty Baby '78

George Plympton (1889-1972)
Feud Maker '38
Doomed at Sundown '37
Crooked Trail '36
Battling with Buffalo Bill '31

Jeremy Podeswa
The Five Senses '99
Eclipse '94

Amos Poe
Frogs for Snakes '98
Rocket Gibraltar '88
Alphabet City '84
The Foreigner '78

James Poe
The Nightman '93
Riot '69
They Shoot Horses, Don't They? '69
Lilies of the Field '63
Toys in the Attic '63
Cat on a Hot Tin Roof '58
Around the World in 80 Days '56
Attack! '56

Charles Edward Pogue
Kull the Conqueror '97
Dragonheart '96
Hands of a Murderer '90
D.O.A. '88
The Fly '86
Psycho 3 '86
The Hound of the Baskervilles '83
The Sign of Four '83
John Pogue
Rollerball '02
The Skulls '00
U.S. Marshals '98
Jean-Marie Poire (1945-)
Just Visiting '01
The Visitors '95
No Problem '75
Gregory Poirier
Tomcats '01
Gossip '99
Rosewood '96
The Stranger '95
Roman Polanski (1933-)
The Ninth Gate '99
Bitter Moon '92
Frantic '88
Pirates '86
Tess '80
The Tenant '76
Diary of Forbidden Dreams '73
Macbeth '71
Rosemary's Baby '68
The Fearless Vampire Killers '67
Cul de Sac '66
Repulsion '65
Knife in the Water '62
Stephen Poliakoff
Shooting the Past '99
Century '94
Mark Polish (1972-)
Jackpot '01
Twin Falls Idaho '99
Michael Polish (1972-)
Jackpot '01
Twin Falls Idaho '99
Jack Pollexfen
The Atomic Brain '64
The Daughter of Dr. Jekyll '57
The Man from Planet X '51
Gene Pollock
The Thrill Killers '65
Incredibly Strange Creatures Who Stopped Living and Became Mixed-Up Zombies '63
Vicki Polon
Mr. Wonderful '93
Girlfriends '78
Abraham Polonsky (1910-99)
Monsignor '82
Avalanche Express '79
Tell Them Willie Boy Is Here '69
Madigan '68
Odds Against Tomorrow '59
Force of Evil '49
Body and Soul '47
Golden Earrings '47
Abe Polsky
The Baby '72
Rebel Rousers '69
Darryl Ponicsan
The Enemy Within '94
School Ties '92
The Boost '88
Nuts '87
Vision Quest '85
Taps '81
Cinderella Liberty '73
Gillo Pontecorvo (1919-)
The Battle of Algiers '66
Kapo '59
DJ Pooh
The Wash '01
Three Strikes '00
Friday '95
Lea Pool (1950-)
Set Me Free '99
Mouvements du Desir '94
Robert Roy Pool
Outbreak '94
Dead to Rights '93
Big Town '87
Duane Poole
I Married a Monster '98
I've Been Waiting for You '98
Shattered Image '98
One Christmas '95
The Man in the Attic '94
Praying Mantis '93
Sunstroke '92
Tom Pope
The Manitou '78
Don't Look in the Basement '73
Joel Posner
Last Breath '96
Getting In '94
P.J. Posner
Last Breath '96
Getting In '94
Dennis Potter (1935-94)
Lipstick on Your Collar '94
Mesmer '94
Christabel '89
Track 29 '88
Dreamchild '85
Gorky Park '83
Brimstone & Treacle '82
Pennies from Heaven '81
Sally Potter (1947-)
The Man Who Cried '00
The Tango Lesson '97
Orlando '92
Michael W. Potts
Night Eyes 3 '93
Tropical Heat '93
Michael Powell (1905-90)
The Elusive Pimpernel '50
The Red Shoes '48
Black Narcissus '47
Stairway to Heaven '46
I Know Where I'm Going '45
Contraband '40
Edge of the World '37
Donna Powers
Valentine '01
Skeletons in the Closet '00
Deep Blue Sea '99
Wayne Powers
Valentine '01
Skeletons in the Closet '00
Deep Blue Sea '99
Tim Prager
Heat of the Sun '99
Vendetta '99
Haunted '95
John Prebble (1915-2001)
Elizabeth R '72
Zulu '64
Mysterious Island '61
Robert Presnell
Conspiracy of Hearts '60
Let No Man Write My Epitaph '60
The Real Glory '39
Employees' Entrance '33
Emeric Pressburger (1902-88)
The Elusive Pimpernel '50
The Red Shoes '48
Black Narcissus '47
Stairway to Heaven '46
I Know Where I'm Going '45
The Forty-Ninth Parallel '41
Steven Pressfield
Army of One '94
Separate Lives '94
Freejack '92
Above the Law '88
King Kong Lives '86
Richard Preston, Jr.
Firetrap '01
The Sender '98
Little Bigfoot '96
Cyber-Tracker 2 '95
Jacques Prevert (1900-77)
The Hunchback of Notre Dame '57
Children of Paradise '44
Les Visiteurs du Soir '42
Bizarre Bizarre '39
The Crime of Monsieur Lange '36
Jeffrey Price
Dr. Seuss' How the Grinch Stole Christmas '00
Wild Wild West '99
Doc Hollywood '91
Who Framed Roger Rabbit '88
Trenchcoat '83
Richard Price (1949-)
Shaft '00
Ransom '96
Clockers '95
Kiss of Death '94
Mad Dog and Glory '93
Night and the City '92
New York Stories '89
Sea of Love '89
The Color of Money '86
Streets of Gold '86
Stanley Price (1892-1955)
A Royal Scandal '96
Genghis Cohn '93
Tim Rose Price
The Serpent's Kiss '97
Rapa Nui '93
A Dangerous Man: Lawrence after Arabia '91
Dark Obsession '90
Peter Prince
Waterland '92
The Hit '85
David A. Prior
Felony '95
Mutant Species '95
Mardi Gras for the Devil '93
Raw Justice '93
Raw Nerve '91
Deadly Dancer '90
Final Sanction '89
Operation Warzone '89
Hell on the Battleground '88
Deadly Prey '87
David Pritchard
Violent Zone '89
Slashed Dreams '74
Pat Proft
Wrongfully Accused '98
Mr. Magoo '97
High School High '96
Naked Gun 33 1/3: The Final Insult '94
Hot Shots! Part Deux '93
Brain Donors '92
Hot Shots! '91
Naked Gun 2 1/2: The Smell of Fear '91
Lucky Stiff '88
The Naked Gun: From the Files of Police Squad '88
Moving Violations '85
Real Genius '85
Bachelor Party '84
Police Academy '84
Chip Proser
Innerspace '87
Iceman '84
Giorgio Prosperi
The Naked Maja '59
The Seven Hills of Rome '58
Monique Proulx
Street Heart '98
Le Sexe des Etoiles '93
Richard Pryor (1940-)
Jo Jo Dancer, Your Life Is Calling '86
Bustin' Loose '81
Blazing Saddles '74
Robert Pucci
The Corruptor '99
The Spider and the Fly '94
Luis Puenzo (1946-)
Old Gringo '89
The Official Story '85
Jack Pulman
Poldark '75
War and Peace '73
The Golden Bowl '72
Daniella Purcell
Spacejacked '98
The Wasp Woman '96
Midnight Tease '94
Gertrude Purcell
Follow the Boys '44
The Invisible Woman '40
One Night in the Tropics '40
Destry Rides Again '39
Charles Purpura
Satisfaction '88
Heaven Help Us '85
David Pursall
The Blue Max '66
The Longest Day '62
Neal Purvis
The World Is Not Enough '99
Plunkett & Macleane '98
Let Him Have It '91
Mario Puzo (1920-99)
Christopher Columbus: The Discovery '92
The Godfather, Part 3 '90
The Cotton Club '84
The Godfather 1902-1959: The Complete Epic '81
Superman 2 '80
Superman: The Movie '78
Earthquake '74
The Godfather, Part 2 '74
The Godfather '72
Daniel Pyne
The Sum of All Fears '02
Where's Marlowe? '98
White Sands '92
Doc Hollywood '91
The Hard Way '91
Pacific Heights '90
Albert Pyun
Nemesis 4: Cry of Angels '97
Adrenalin: Fear the Rush '96
Nemesis 3: Time Lapse '96
Spitfire '94
Knights '93
Down Twisted '89
Alien from L.A. '87
Radioactive Dreams '86
Sword & the Sorcerer '82
Paris Qualles
A House Divided '00
Blood Brothers '97
The Tuskegee Airmen '95
The Inkwell '94
Darryl Quarles
Black Knight '01
Big Momma's House '00
Soldier Boyz '95
Paul Quarrington
Camilla '94
Whale Music '94
Perfectly Normal '91
Jonas Quastel
Listen '96
Crackerjack '94
Florence Quentin
Le Bonheur Est Dans le Pre '95
Life Is a Long Quiet River '88
Pascal Quignard
A Pure Formality '94
Tous les Matins du Monde '92
Gene Quintano (1946-)
The Musketeer '01
Outlaw Justice '98
Operation Dumbo Drop '95
Sudden Death '95
National Lampoon's Loaded Weapon 1 '93
Honeymoon Academy '90
Police Academy 4: Citizens on Patrol '87
Allan Quatermain and the Lost City of Gold '86
Police Academy 3: Back in Training '86
King Solomon's Mines '85
Making the Grade '84
David Rabe (1940-)
Hurlyburly '98
Casualties of War '89
Streamers '83
I'm Dancing as Fast as I Can '82
Martin Rackin
The Horse Soldiers '59
Long John Silver '54
The Enforcer '51
The Stooge '51
Michael Radford (1946-)
Dancing at the Blue Iguana '00
The Postman '94
White Mischief '88
Another Time, Another Place '83
Bob Rafelson (1933-)
Tales of Erotica '93
Mountains of the Moon '90
Stay Hungry '76
Five Easy Pieces '70
Head '68
Stewart Raffill
Mac and Me '88
Ice Pirates '84
High Risk '81
Sea Gypsies '78
Across the Great Divide '76
The Adventures of the Wilderness Family '76
Napoleon and Samantha '72
John Raffo
Johnny Skidmarks '97
The Relic '96
Dragon: The Bruce Lee Story '93
Martin Ragaway
Lost in Alaska '52
Abbott and Costello in the Foreign Legion '50
Ma and Pa Kettle Go to Town '50
Ivan Raimi
Army of Darkness '92
Darkman '90
Easy Wheels '89
Sam Raimi (1959-)
The Nutt House '95
The Hudsucker Proxy '93
Army of Darkness '92
Darkman '90
Evil Dead 2: Dead by Dawn '87
Crimewave '85
Evil Dead '83
Norman Reilly Raine
Captain Kidd '45
The Fighting 69th '40
Each Dawn I Die '39
The Adventures of Robin Hood '38
The Life of Emile Zola '37
Frank Rainone
A Brooklyn State of Mind '97
Me and the Mob '94
Ron Raley
Cupid & Cate '00
The Runaway '00
Edge of Sanity '89
Gilbert Ralston
Ben '72
Willard '71
Rick Ramage
Stigmata '99
The Proposition '97
Harold Ramis (1944-)
Bedazzled '00
Analyze This '98
Multiplicity '96
Groundhog Day '93
Rover Dangerfield '91
Ghostbusters 2 '89
Caddyshack 2 '88
Armed and Dangerous '86
Back to School '86
Club Paradise '86
Ghostbusters '84
National Lampoon's Vacation '83
Stripes '81
Caddyshack '80
Meatballs '79
National Lampoon's Animal House '78
Robert Ramsey
Big Trouble '02
Life '99
Destiny Turns on the Radio '95
Joe Ranft
A Bug's Life '98
The Rescuers Down Under '90
Whitney Ransick
Hand Gun '93
The Outfit '93
Frederic Raphael (1931-)
The King's Whore '90
Richard's Things '80
Rogue Male '76
Daisy Miller '74
Far from the Madding Crowd '67
Two for the Road '67
Darling '65
Bachelor of Hearts '58
I.C. Rapoport
Jericho Fever '93
Living Proof: The Hank Williams Jr. Story '83
Anne Rapp
Dr. T & the Women '00
Cookie's Fortune '99
Philip Rapp (1907-96)
The Inspector General '49
The Secret Life of Walter Mitty '47
Wonder Man '45
Ezra D. Rappaport
Harry and the Hendersons '87
Deja Vu '84
Mark Rappaport
From the Journals of Jean Seberg '95
Rock Hudson's Home Movies '92
Jean-Paul Rappeneau (1932-)
The Horseman on the Roof '95
Cyrano de Bergerac '90
Lovers Like Us '75
That Man from Rio '64
Judith Rascoe
Havana '90
Eat a Bowl of Tea '89
Endless Love '81
Who'll Stop the Rain? '78
Road Movie '72
Terence Rattigan
The V.I.P.'s '63
The Prince and the Showgirl '57
The Winslow Boy '48
The Day Will Dawn '42
Herman Raucher (1928-)
Summer of '42 '71
Watermelon Man '70
Sweet November '68
Irving Ravetch
Stanley and Iris '90
Murphy's Romance '85
Norma Rae '79
Conrack '74
The Cowboys '72
The Reivers '69
Hombre '67
Hud '63
Home from the Hill '60
The Long, Hot Summer '58
Ten Wanted Men '54
Vengeance Valley '51
Rand Ravich
The Astronaut's Wife '99
The Maker '98
Candyman 2: Farewell to the Flesh '94
A.H. Rawlinson
Gaslight '40
The Man Who Knew Too Much '34
Billy Ray
Hart's War '02
Legalese '98
Volcano '97
Color of Night '94
Hidden Assassin '94

Fred Olen Ray (1954-)
Hollywood Chainsaw Hookers '88
Phantom Empire '87
Alien Dead '79
Satyajit Ray (1921-92)
The Stranger '92
The Middleman '76
Distant Thunder '73
The Adversary '71
Days and Nights in the Forest '70
Charulata '64
The Big City '63
Two Daughters '61
Devi '60
The World of Apu '59
Aparajito '58
Jalsaghar '58
Pather Panchali '54
David Rayfiel
Sabrina '95
The Firm '93
Intersection '93
Havana '90
Round Midnight '86
Death Watch '80
Lipstick '76
Three Days of the Condor '75
Valdez Is Coming '71
William Raynor
The Kettles on Old MacDonald's Farm '57
Francis in the Haunted House '56
Jan Read
First Men in the Moon '64
Jason and the Argonauts '63
The Haunted Strangler '58
Theresa Rebeck
Gossip '99
Harriet the Spy '96
Eric Red (1961-)
Bad Moon '96
Undertow '95
The Last Outlaw '93
Body Parts '91
Blue Steel '90
Cohen and Tate '88
Near Dark '87
The Hitcher '86
Jeffrey Reddick
Return to Cabin by the Lake '01
Final Destination '00
Joel M. Reed
Night of the Zombies '81
Bloodsucking Freaks '75
Tom Reed
Pittsburgh '42
Murders in the Rue Morgue '32
Matt Reeves (1966-)
The Yards '00
The Pallbearer '95
Michael Reeves (1944-69)
Batman: Mask of the Phantasm '93
The Conqueror Worm '68
Theodore Reeves
National Velvet '44
Internes Can't Take Money '37
Piero Regnoli
Demonia '90
Voices from Beyond '90
Frank Rehwaldt
The Perfect Wife '00
The Landlady '98
The Night Caller '97
The Fiance '96
Ethan Reiff
Josh Kirby...Time Warrior: Chapter 5, Journey to the Magic Cavern '96
Josh Kirby...Time Warrior: Chapter 6, Last Battle for the Universe '96
Josh Kirby...Time Warrior: Chapter 1, Planet of the Dino-Knights '95
Josh Kirby...Time Warrior: Chapter 2, The Human Pets '95
Men of War '94
Tales from the Crypt Presents Demon Knight '94
William Reilly
Men of Respect '91
Mortal Thoughts '91
Carl Reiner (1922-)
Bert Rigby, You're a Fool '89
The Man with Two Brains '83
Dead Men Don't Wear Plaid '82
The Comic '69
Enter Laughing '67
The Thrill of It All! '63
Al Reinert
Final Fantasy: The Spirits Within '01
From the Earth to the Moon '98
Apollo 13 '95
Walter Reisch
Titanic '53
Niagara '52
Song of Scheherazade '47
Somewhere I'll Find You '42
That Uncertain Feeling '41
Robert Reneau
Demolition Man '93
Action Jackson '88
Jeff Reno
Meet Joe Black '98
Radioland Murders '94
Jean Renoir (1894-1979)
The Little Theatre of Jean Renoir '71
The Testament of Dr. Cordelier '59
The Golden Coach '52
The River '51
The Southerner '45
The Rules of the Game '39
La Bete Humaine '38
Grand Illusion '37
La Marseillaise '37
The Crime of Monsieur Lange '36
The Lower Depths '36
Toni '34
Boudu Saved from Drowning '32
La Chienne '31
David Reskin
Hidden Obsession '92
Action U.S.A. '89
Adam Resnick
Death to Smoochy '02
Lucky Numbers '00
Cabin Boy '94
Patricia Resnick
Straight Talk '92
Second Sight '89
Maxie '85
9 to 5 '80
Quintet '79
A Wedding '78
Dale Resteghini
Da Hip Hop Witch '00
Colorz of Rage '97
Paul (Pee-wee Herman) Reubens (1952-)
Big Top Pee-wee '88
Pee-wee's Big Adventure '85
Alma Reville
Shadow of a Doubt '43
Young and Innocent '37
Sabotage '36
The 39 Steps '35
Rich and Strange '32
Clarke Reynolds
Shalako '68
The Viking Queen '67
Jonathan Reynolds
My Stepmother Is an Alien '88
Switching Channels '88
Leonard Part 6 '87
Micki & Maude '84
Kevin Reynolds (1950-)
Rapa Nui '93
Fandango '85
Red Dawn '84
Lee Reynolds
Jackie Chan's Who Am I '98
Storyville '92
Delta Force 2: Operation Stranglehold '90
Allan Quatermain and the Lost City of Gold '86
Scott Reynolds
Heaven '99
The Ugly '96
Shonda Rhimes
Crossroads '02
Introducing Dorothy Dandridge '99
Susan Rhinehart
Glory & Honor '98
Buffalo Soldiers '97
Don Rhymer
Big Momma's House '00
Carpool '96
Past the Bleachers '95
John Rice
Windtalkers '02
Blown Away '94
Chasers '94
Curiosity Kills '90
Susan Rice
Animal Behavior '89
Something in Common '86
Trumps '83
Mike Rich
The Rookie '02
Finding Forrester '00
Richard Rich
The Swan Princess '94
The Black Cauldron '85
Jean-Louis Richard (1921-)
After Sex '97
Emmanuelle '74
Day for Night '73
The Bride Wore Black '68
Fahrenheit 451 '66
The Soft Skin '64
Robert L. Richards
Gorgo '61
The Indian Fighter '55
Doug Richardson
Money Train '95
Die Hard 2: Die Harder '90
Tony Richardson (1928-91)
The Hotel New Hampshire '84
Ned Kelly '70
A Taste of Honey '61
William Richert
The Man in the Iron Mask '97
A Night in the Life of Jimmy Reardon '88
Winter Kills '79
Law and Disorder '74
Mordecai Richler (1931-2001)
Joshua Then and Now '85
Fun with Dick and Jane '77
The Apprenticeship of Duddy Kravitz '74
No Love for Johnnie '60
Maurice Richlin
For Pete's Sake '74
Come September '61
Operation Petticoat '59
Pillow Talk '59
W.D. Richter (1945-)
Home for the Holidays '95
Needful Things '93
Big Trouble in Little China '86
All Night Long '81
Brubaker '80
Dracula '79
Invasion of the Body Snatchers '78
Slither '73
Tom Rickman
Bless the Child '00
Tuesdays with Morrie '99
Truman '95
Hooper '78
John Ridley
Undercover Brother '02
Cold Around the Heart '97
U-Turn '97
Philip Ridley
The Passion of Darkly Noon '95
The Reflecting Skin '91
The Krays '90
Leni Riefenstahl (1902-)
Triumph of the Will '34
The Blue Light '32
Dean Riesner (1918-)
Fatal Beauty '87
Charley Varrick '73
High Plains Drifter '73
Dirty Harry '71
Play Misty for Me '71
Coogan's Bluff '68
Adam Rifkin (1966-)
Small Soldiers '98
Something About Sex '98
Mouse Hunt '97
The Chase '93
The Dark Backward '91
The Invisible Maniac '90
Never on Tuesday '88
Lawrence Riggins
Replicant '01
Ironheart '92
Wolf Rilla (1920-)
Village of the Damned '60
Roadhouse Girl '53
Joe Rinaldi
Peter Pan '53
The Adventures of Ichabod and Mr. Toad '49
Frederic Rinaldo
Abbott and Costello Meet the Invisible Man '51
Comin' Round the Mountain '51
Abbott and Costello Meet Frankenstein '48
Buck Privates Come Home '47
The Black Cat '41
Hold That Ghost '41
The Invisible Woman '40
David W. Rintels
Nuremberg '00
The Member of the Wedding '97
Andersonville '95
World War II: When Lions Roared '94
The Last Best Year '90
Not Without My Daughter '90
Day One '89
Robert Riskin
Riding High '50
Meet John Doe '41
You Can't Take It with You '38
Lost Horizon '37
Mr. Deeds Goes to Town '36
The Whole Town's Talking '35
It Happened One Night '34
Lady for a Day '33
American Madness '32
Guy Ritchie (1968-)
Snatch '00
Lock, Stock and 2 Smoking Barrels '98
Thomas Ritz
The Killing Grounds '97
Marked Man '96
Martial Outlaw '93
Stephen J. Rivele
Ali '01
Nixon '95
Jacques Rivette (1928-)
Va Savoir '01
La Belle Noiseuse '90
Celine and Julie Go Boating '74
Paris Belongs to Us '60
Janet Roach
Mr. North '88
Prizzi's Honor '85
Matthew Robbins
Mimic '97
*batteries not included '87
Warning Sign '85
Dragonslayer '81
Corvette Summer '78
MacArthur '77
Bingo Long Traveling All-Stars & Motor Kings '76
The Sugarland Express '74
Tim Robbins (1958-)
The Cradle Will Rock '99
Dead Man Walking '95
Bob Roberts '92
Ben Roberts
Portrait in Black '60
Green Fire '55
White Heat '49
Jonathan Roberts
Jack Frost '98
The Hunchback of Notre Dame '96
The Lion King '94
Once Bitten '85
The Sure Thing '85
June Roberts
Mermaids '90
Experience Preferred... But Not Essential '83
Marguerite Roberts
Shoot Out '71
True Grit '69
Five Card Stud '68
Ivanhoe '52
Undercurrent '46
Somewhere I'll Find You '42
Scott Roberts
K2: The Ultimate High '92
Riders of the Storm '88
William Roberts (1913-97)
Ten to Midnight '83
Legend of the Lone Ranger '81
Posse '75
The Last American Hero '73
Red Sun '71
The Bridge at Remagen '69
The Devil's Brigade '68
The Wonderful World of the Brothers Grimm '62
The Magnificent Seven '60
The Mating Game '59
The Private War of Major Benson '55
Easy to Love '53
Mira Robertson
Head On '98
Only the Brave '94
R.J. Robertson
Home for Christmas '93
Final Embrace '92
The Haunting of Morella '91
Think Big '90
Transylvania Twist '89
Not of This Earth '88
Big Bad Mama 2 '87
Forbidden World '82
John Robins
Hot Resort '85
Death Ship '80
Bruce Robinson (1946-)
In Dreams '98
Return to Paradise '98
Jennifer 8 '92
Fat Man and Little Boy '89
How to Get Ahead in Advertising '89
Withnail and I '87
The Killing Fields '84
Casey Robinson
The Egyptian '54
The Snows of Kilimanjaro '52
Saratoga Trunk '45
Now, Voyager '42
Dark Victory '39
Captain Blood '35
Phil Alden Robinson (1950-)
Freedom Song '00
The Chamber '96
Sneakers '92
Field of Dreams '89
In the Mood '87
All of Me '84
Rhinestone '84
Sally Robinson
Follow the Stars Home '01
Princess of Thieves '01
The Lost Child '00
A Far Off Place '93
Todd Robinson
Mermaid '00
White Squall '96
Marc Rocco
Where the Day Takes You '92
Dream a Little Dream '89
Glauce Rocha
Antonio Das Mortes '68
Earth Entranced '66
Black God, White Devil '64
Eric Rochant
Love Without Pity '91
The Fifth Monkey '90
Chris Rock (1966-)
Down to Earth '01
CB4: The Movie '93
Kevin Rock
Raging Angels '95
Suspicious Agenda '94
Philadelphia Experiment 2 '93
Warlock: The Armageddon '93
Alexandre Rockwell
Four Rooms '95
Somebody to Love '94
In the Soup '92
Sons '91
Robert Rodat (1953-)
The Patriot '00
36 Hours to Die '99
Saving Private Ryan '98
The Ripper '97
Fly Away Home '96
Tall Tale: The Unbelievable Adventures of Pecos Bill '95
The Comrades of Summer '92
Franc Roddam (1946-)
Moby Dick '98
Aria '88
Quadrophenia '79
Howard A. Rodman (-1985)
Joe Gould's Secret '00
Fallen Angels 1 '93
Fallen Angels 2 '93
Winning '69
Serge Rodnunsky
Newsbreak '00
TripFall '00
Cypress Edge '99
Fear Runs Silent '99
Paper Bullets '99
Silicon Towers '99
Dead Tides '97
Final Equinox '95
Lovers' Lovers '94
Robert Rodriguez (1968-)
Spy Kids 2: The Island of Lost Dreams '02
Spy Kids '01
Desperado '95
Four Rooms '95
Roadracers '94
El Mariachi '93
Michael Roemer (1928-)
The Plot Against Harry '69
Nothing but a Man '64
Howard Emmett Rogers
Libeled Lady '36
Tarzan and His Mate '34
Hold Your Man '33
Ivan Rogers (1954-)
Two Wrongs Make a Right '89
Tigershark '87
Mary Rogers
A Billion for Boris '90
Freaky Friday '76
Steven Rogers
Kate & Leopold '01

Earthly Possessions '99
Hope Floats '98
Stepmom '98
Eric Rohmer (1920-)
Autumn Tale '98
A Summer's Tale '96
Rendezvous in Paris '95
A Tale of Winter '92
Four Adventures of Reinette and Mirabelle '89
A Tale of Springtime '89
Boyfriends & Girlfriends '88
Summer '86
Full Moon in Paris '84
Pauline at the Beach '83
Le Beau Mariage '82
The Aviator's Wife '80
Perceval '78
The Marquise of O '76
Chloe in the Afternoon '72
Claire's Knee '71
My Night at Maud's '69
Six in Paris '68
La Collectionneuse '67
Mark Romanek (1959-)
One Hour Photo '02
Static '87
Eddie Romero (1924-)
Brides of the Beast '68
The Ravagers '65
The Walls of Hell '64
Cavalry Command '63
George A. Romero (1940-)
Bruiser '00
The Dark Half '91
Night of the Living Dead '90
Tales from the Darkside: The Movie '90
Two Evil Eyes '90
Monkey Shines '88
Creepshow 2 '87
Day of the Dead '85
Knightriders '81
Dawn of the Dead '78
Martin '77
The Crazies '73
Season of the Witch '73
Night of the Living Dead '68
Brunello Rondi
Orchestra Rehearsal '78
Juliet of the Spirits '65
8 1/2 '63
La Dolce Vita '60
La Strada '54
Don Roos (1959-)
Bounce '00
The Opposite of Sex '98
Diabolique '96
Boys on the Side '94
Single White Female '92
Love Field '91
Wells Root (-1993)
Texas across the River '66
Prisoner of Zenda '37
Tom Ropelewski
The Next Best Thing '00
Look Who's Talking Now '93
Madhouse '90
Loverboy '89
The Kiss '88
Bradford Ropes
Redwood Forest Trail '50
Gaucho Serenade '40
Bernard Rose
Leo Tolstoy's Anna Karenina '96
Immortal Beloved '94
Candyman '92
Jack Rose (1911-95)
The Great Muppet Caper '81
Lost and Found '79
A Touch of Class '73
Papa's Delicate Condition '63
Who's Got the Action? '63
It Started in Naples '60
The Five Pennies '59
Houseboat '58
The Seven Little Foys '55
Trouble along the Way '53
April in Paris '52
I'll See You in My Dreams '51
On Moonlight Bay '51
Riding High '50
The Great Lover '49
Sorrowful Jones '49
My Favorite Brunette '47
The Road to Rio '47
Lee Rose
The Truth About Jane '00
An Unexpected Life '97
An Unexpected Family '96
A Mother's Prayer '95
Deconstructing Sarah '94
Mickey Rose
Student Bodies '81
Bananas '71
Take the Money and Run '69
What's Up, Tiger Lily? '66
Reginald Rose (1920-2002)
Twelve Angry Men '97
Wild Geese 2 '85
The Final Option '82
Sea Wolves '81
Whose Life Is It Anyway? '81
Wild Geese '78
Man of the West '58
Twelve Angry Men '57
Ruth Rose
She '35
King Kong '33
William Rose
Dr. Frankenstein's Castle of Freaks '74
The Secret of Santa Vittoria '69
Guess Who's Coming to Dinner '67
It's a Mad, Mad, Mad, Mad World '63
The Smallest Show on Earth '57
The Ladykillers '55
Genevieve '53
Dan Rosen
The Curve '97
The Last Supper '96
Gary Rosen
Sink or Swim '97
Major Payne '95
Martin Rosen
The Plague Dogs '82
Watership Down '78
Henry Rosenbaum
Get Crazy '83
The Dunwich Horror '70
Jeanne Rosenberg
Heidi '93
White Fang '91
The Journey of Natty Gann '85
The Black Stallion '79
Marc Rosenberg
Serpent's Lair '95
Dingo '90
Philip Rosenberg
Missing Pieces '00
Joe Torre: Curveballs Along the Way '97
Death Benefit '96
In the Line of Duty: A Cop for the Killing '90
Scott Rosenberg
Highway '01
Gone in 60 Seconds '00
High Fidelity '00
Disturbing Behavior '98
Con Air '97
Beautiful Girls '96
Things to Do in Denver When You're Dead '95
Dale Rosenbloom
Shiloh 2: Shiloh Season '99
Shiloh '97
Seth Zvi Rosenfeld
King of the Jungle '01
A Brother's Kiss '97
Subway Stories '97
Sunset Park '96
Jack Rosenthal
Captain Jack '98
The Wedding Gift '93
The Duchess of Duke Street '78
Mark Rosenthal
Planet of the Apes '01
Mercury Rising '98
Mighty Joe Young '98
The Beverly Hillbillies '93
For Love or Money '93
Sometimes They Come Back '91
Desperate Hours '90
The In Crowd '88
Superman 4: The Quest for Peace '87
The Jewel of the Nile '85
Legend of Billie Jean '85
Francesco Rosi (1922-)
The Truce '96
Three Brothers '80
Christ Stopped at Eboli '79
Bellissima '51
Mark Rosman
Life-Size '00
The Invader '96
Evolver '94
The House on Sorority Row '83
Arthur Ross
Brubaker '80
Satan's School for Girls '73
The Three Worlds of Gulliver '59
The Creature Walks among Us '56
Creature from the Black Lagoon '54
Star Spangled Rhythm '42
Brian Ross
Dying to Remember '93
Body Language '92
The Secret Passion of Robert Clayton '92
Gary Ross
Pleasantville '98
Lassie '94
Dave '93
Mr. Baseball '92
Big '88
Kenneth Ross (1941-)
Out of the Body '88
The Odessa File '74
The Day of the Jackal '73
Roberto Rossellini (1906-77)
The Messiah '75
RoGoPaG '62
Era Notte a Roma '60
Generale Della Rovere '60
Voyage in Italy '53
The Flowers of St. Francis '50
Machine to Kill Bad People '48
Paisan '46
Robert Rossen (1908-66)
Billy Budd '62
The Hustler '61
All the King's Men '49
The Strange Love of Martha Ivers '46
A Walk in the Sun '46
Edge of Darkness '43
The Sea Wolf '41
The Roaring Twenties '39
They Won't Forget '37
Terry Rossio
Shrek '01
The Road to El Dorado '00
The Mask of Zorro '98
Small Soldiers '98
The Puppet Masters '94
Aladdin '92
Little Monsters '89
Leo Rosten (1908-97)
Velvet Touch '48
Lured '47
Bobby Roth (1950-)
The Man Inside '90
Dead Solid Perfect '88
Baja Oklahoma '87
Heartbreakers '84
Boss' Son '78
Eric Roth
Ali '01
The Insider '99
The Horse Whisperer '97
The Postman '97
Forrest Gump '94
Mr. Jones '93
Memories of Me '88
Suspect '87
The Concorde: Airport '79 '79
Phillip J. Roth
Interceptor Force '99
Velocity Trap '99
Total Reality '97
A.P.E.X. '94
Digital Man '94
Prototype X29A '92
Ghostwriter '84
Jeff Rothberg
A Simple Wish '97
The Amazing Panda Adventure '95
Hiding Out '87
Stephanie Rothman (1936-)
Starhops '78
The Velvet Vampire '71
Talbot Rothwell
Carry On Camping '71
Carry On Henry VIII '71
Carry On Cowboy '66
Brigitte Rouan (1965-)
After Sex '97
Overseas: Three Women with Man Trouble '90
Russell Rouse (1913-87)
The Oscar '66
Fastest Gun Alive '56
The Thief '52
D.O.A. '49
Pierre Rouve
Cop-Out '67
Trial & Error '62
Jean Rouveral
A Face in the Rain '63
Autumn Leaves '56
Kathleen Rowell
Killing Mr. Griffin '97
Hear No Evil '93
Tainted Blood '93
Joy of Sex '84
The Outsiders '83
Charles Francis Royal
Ridin' the Lone Trail '37
Courageous Avenger '35
Patricia Rozema (1958-)
Mansfield Park '99
When Night Is Falling '95
John Ruane
That Eye, the Sky '94
Death in Brunswick '90
Andy Ruben
Club Vampire '98
Poison Ivy '92
Streets '90
Dance of the Damned '88
Stripped to Kill '87
The Patriot '86
Bruce Joel Rubin
Stuart Little 2 '02
Deep Impact '98
My Life '93
Ghost '90
Jacob's Ladder '90
Deadly Friend '86
Brainstorm '83
Mann Rubin
The First Deadly Sin '80
The Best of Everything '59
Sergio Rubini (1959-)
The Blonde '92
The Station '92
Cliff Ruby
Cats Don't Dance '97
Balto '95
Harry Ruby
A Night at the Opera '35
Duck Soup '33
Horse Feathers '32
Kid from Spain '32
David Rudkin
December Bride '91
Fahrenheit 451 '66
Rita Rudner (1955-)
A Weekend in the Country '96
Peter's Friends '92
Paul Rudnick
Isn't She Great '00
In and Out '97
Jeffrey '95
Addams Family Values '93
Alan Rudolph (1943-)
Trixie '00
Breakfast of Champions '98
Afterglow '97
Equinox '93
Love at Large '89
The Moderns '88
Trouble in Mind '86
Choose Me '84
Endangered Species '82
Roadie '80
Welcome to L.A. '77
Buffalo Bill & the Indians '76
Barn of the Naked Dead '73
Premonition '71
Ed Rugoff
Double Take '97
Mr. Nanny '93
Mannequin 2: On the Move '91
Mannequin '87
Raul Ruiz (1941-)
Genealogies of a Crime '97
Three Lives and Only One Death '96
The Hypothesis of the Stolen Painting '78
Stefano Rulli
The Truce '96
The Stolen Children '92
Terry Runte
Super Mario Bros. '93
Mystery Date '91
Richard Rush (1930-)
Color of Night '94
Air America '90
The Stunt Man '80
Psych-Out '68
Harry Ruskin
Lady Godiva '55
Six of a Kind '34
Josef Rusnak
The Thirteenth Floor '99
Quiet Days in Hollywood '97
Lou Rusoff
Beach Party '63
Motorcycle Gang '57
Shake, Rattle and Rock '57
It Conquered the World '56
The Phantom from 10,000 Leagues '56
Day the World Ended '55
Chuck Russell
The Blob '88
A Nightmare on Elm Street 3: Dream Warriors '87
Dreamscape '84
David O. Russell (1959-)
Three Kings '99
Flirting with Disaster '95
Spanking the Monkey '94
Ken Russell (1927-)
Lady Chatterley '92
Whore '91
The Rainbow '89
Aria '88
The Lair of the White Worm '88
Salome's Last Dance '88
Valentino '77
Lisztomania '75
Tommy '75
Mahler '74
The Boy Friend '71
The Devils '71
Ray Russell (1924-99)
X: The Man with X-Ray Eyes '63
Premature Burial '62
Zotz! '62
Mr. Sardonicus '61
Vivian Russell
The Rainbow '89
The Atomic Brain '64
Willy Russell
Shirley Valentine '89
Educating Rita '83
Gianni Russo
Kill Shot '01
For Which He Stands '98
John A. Russo
Night of the Living Dead '90
Voodoo Dawn '89
The Majorettes '87
Return of the Living Dead '85
Night of the Living Dead '68
Richard Russo
The Flamingo Rising '01
Twilight '98
Marti Rustam
Evils of the Night '85
Eaten Alive '76
Neil Ruttenberg
Magic Island '95
Prehysteria 3 '95
Bad Blood '94
Stefan Ruzowitzky
Anatomy '00
The Inheritors '98
David Ryan
Mean Streak '99
First Love, Last Rites '98
Frank Ryan (1947-)
Can't Help Singing '45
The Amazing Mrs. Holiday '43
Michael Rymer
Perfume '01
Angel Baby '95
Morrie Ryskind
Penny Serenade '41
Room Service '38
My Man Godfrey '36
A Night at the Opera '35
Palmy Days '31
Animal Crackers '30
The Cocoanuts '29
Joseph Sabo
Fantasia '40
Pinocchio '40
Dardano Sacchetti
Specters '87
Demons '86
A Blade in the Dark '83
The House by the Cemetery '83
The New Gladiators '83
The Beyond '82
Manhattan Baby '82
New York Ripper '82
Cannibal Apocalypse '80
Gates of Hell '80
Zombie '80
Shock '79
Arthur St. Claire
The Mask of Diijon '46
Boss of Bullion City '41
Mary St. Feint
Forty Carats '73
Butterflies Are Free '72
Funny Face '57
Silk Stockings '57
Nicholas St. John
The Funeral '96
The Addiction '95
Body Snatchers '93
Dangerous Game '93
King of New York '90
China Girl '87
Fear City '85
Ms. 45 '81
Driller Killer '79
Alfredo Salazar
Doctor of Doom '62
The Robot vs. the Aztec Mummy '59
Wrestling Women vs. the Aztec Mummy '59
Richard Sale (1911-93)
Abandon Ship '57
Suddenly '54
A Woman's World '54
Kario Salem
Blue Crush '02
The Score '01
The Rat Pack '98
Don King: Only in America '97
Walter Salles (1956-)
Behind the Sun '01
Foreign Land '95

Waldo Salt
Midnight Cowboy '69
Mr. Winkle Goes to War '44
Shopworn Angel '38

Mark Saltzman
Mrs. Santa Claus '96
Napoleon '96
3 Ninjas Kick Back '94
Iron & Silk '91
The Adventures of Milo & Otis '89

Victor Salva (1958-)
Jeepers Creepers '01
Rites of Passage '99
Powder '95
Nature of the Beast '94

Hal Salwen
Denise Calls Up '95
Probable Cause '95

Jon Robert Samsel
Animal Instincts '92
Carnal Crimes '91

Lesser Samuels
No Way Out '50
Bitter Sweet '40
Strange Cargo '40
Gangway '37

Duke Sandefur
The Phantom of the Opera '89
Ghost Town '88

Christopher Sanders
Lilo & Stitch '02
Mulan '98

Adam Sandler (1966-)
Little Nicky '00
Big Daddy '99
The Waterboy '98
Happy Gilmore '96
Billy Madison '94

Barry Sandler
All-American Murder '91
Crimes of Passion '84
Making Love '82
The Mirror Crack'd '80
The Duchess and the Dirtwater Fox '76
Loners '72

Anna Sandor
Amelia Earhart: The Final Flight '94
Miss Rose White '92

Jimmy Sangster (1924-)
The Devil & Max Devlin '81
Phobia '80
Dynasty of Fear '72
The Horror of Frankenstein '70
The Anniversary '68
The Nanny '65
Hysteria '64
Maniac '63
Nightmare '63
Paranoiac '62
The Hellfire Club '61
Scream of Fear '61
The Brides of Dracula '60
The Mummy '59
Blood of the Vampire '58
The Crawling Eye '58
The Horror of Dracula '58
The Revenge of Frankenstein '58
The Curse of Frankenstein '57
X The Unknown '56

Ken Sanzel
Lone Hero '02
The Replacement Killers '98
Scarred City '98

Alvin Sapinsley
The Scarlet Letter '79
Moon of the Wolf '72

Tedi Sarafian
The Road Killers '95
Tank Girl '94
Solar Crisis '92

Alvin Sargent
Unfaithful '02
Anywhere But Here '99
Bogus '96
Other People's Money '91
What about Bob? '91
White Palace '90
Dominick & Eugene '88
Nuts '87
Ordinary People '80
Straight Time '78
Bobby Deerfield '77
Julia '77
Paper Moon '73
The Stalking Moon '69
The Sterile Cuckoo '69
Gambit '66

Arlene Sarner
Blue Sky '91
Peggy Sue Got Married '86

Robert Sarno
Decoy '95
Howling 2: Your Sister Is a Werewolf '85

Jean-Paul Sartre
The Crucible '57
The Respectful Prostitute '52

Vaclav Sasek
The Firemen's Ball '68
Intimate Lighting '65
Loves of a Blonde '65

Oley Sassone
Playback '95
Wild Hearts Can't Be Broken '91

George Saunders
The Perfect Wife '00
The Landlady '98
Intimate Deception '96
Malicious '95
Scanner Cop '94

Carlos Saura (1932-)
Goya in Bordeaux '99
Tango '98
Outrage '93
Carmen '83
Blood Wedding '81
Elisa, Vida Mia '77
Cria '76

Claude Sautet (1924-2000)
Nelly et Monsieur Arnaud '95
Vincent, Francois, Paul and the Others '76
Cesar & Rosalie '72
Borsalino '70

Nancy Savoca (1960-)
The 24 Hour Woman '99
If These Walls Could Talk '96
Household Saints '93
True Love '89

John Sayles (1950-)
Sunshine State '02
Limbo '99
Hombres Armados '97
Mimic '97
Lone Star '95
Men of War '94
The Secret of Roan Inish '94
Passion Fish '92
City of Hope '91
Breaking In '89
Eight Men Out '88
Matewan '87
Wild Thing '87
The Clan of the Cave Bear '86
Unnatural Causes '86
The Brother from Another Planet '84
Enormous Changes '83
Lianna '83
Trumps '83
Baby It's You '82
The Challenge '82
The Howling '81
Alligator '80
Battle Beyond the Stars '80
Return of the Secaucus 7 '80
Lady in Red '79
Piranha '78

Furio Scarpelli (1919-)
The Postman '94
Time to Kill '89
The Family '87
The Good, the Bad and the Ugly '67
Big Deal on Madonna Street '58

Steven Schachter
A Slight Case of Murder '99
The Con '98

Eric Schaeffer (1962-)
Wirey Spindell '99
Fall '97
If Lucy Fell '95
My Life's in Turnaround '94

Don Schain
Girls Are for Loving '73
The Abductors '72
Ginger '72

James Schamus
Crouching Tiger, Hidden Dragon '00
Ride with the Devil '99
The Ice Storm '97
Eat Drink Man Woman '94
The Wedding Banquet '93

Dore Schary
Sunrise at Campobello '60
Young Tom Edison '40

Olivier Schatzky
L'Eleve '95
A Man in Love '87

Adam Scheinman
Bait '00
Mickey Blue Eyes '99
Little Big League '94

Andrew Scheinman
Bait '00
North '94

George Schenck
Dying to Remember '93
Escape 2000 '81
Futureworld '76

Richard Schenkman
Went to Coney Island on a Mission from God...Be Back by Five '98
The Pompatus of Love '95

Fred Schepisi (1939-)
A Cry in the Dark '88
The Devil's Playground '76

Shawn Schepps
Lip Service '00
Son-in-Law '93
Encino Man '92

Stephen Schiff
True Crime '99
The Deep End of the Ocean '98
Lolita '97

Michael Schiffer
The Peacemaker '97
Crimson Tide '95
Lean on Me '89
Colors '88

Karl Schiffman
Dead End '98
Back in Action '94

Suzanne Schiffman (1930-2001)
Sorceress '88
Confidentially Yours '83
The Woman Next Door '81
The Last Metro '80
The Man Who Loved Women '77
Small Change '76
The Story of Adele H. '75
Day for Night '73

Vivian Schilling (1968-)
Future Shock '93
Soultaker '90

Murray Schisgal
Tootsie '82
Luv '67

George Schlatter
Fire and Ice '87
Norman, Is That You? '76

Volker Schlondorff (1939-)
The Legend of Rita '99
The Ogre '96
Voyager '91
The Tin Drum '79

Ronald Schmidt
A.P.E.X. '94
Digital Man '94

David Schmoeller (1947-)
The Arrival '90
Crawlspace '86
The Seduction '82
Day Time Ended '80
Tourist Trap '79

Julian Schnabel
Before Night Falls '00
Basquiat '96

Charles Schnee
Butterfield 8 '60
The Bad and the Beautiful '52
Westward the Women '51
They Live by Night '49
Red River '48

Barry Schneider
Mother's Boys '94
Deadly Force '83
Take This Job & Shove It '81
Roller Boogie '79
Harper Valley P.T.A. '78
Ruby '77

Dan Schneider (1966-)
Big Fat Liar '02
Good Burger '97

Peter Schneider
The Promise '94
Knife in the Head '78

Rob Schneider (1963-)
The Animal '01
Deuce Bigalow: Male Gigolo '99

David J. Schow
The Crow '93
Critters 3 '91
Critters 4 '91
Leatherface: The Texas Chainsaw Massacre 3 '89

Leonard Schrader
Naked Tango '91
Kiss of the Spider Woman '85
Mishima: A Life in Four Chapters '85
Old Boyfriends '79
Blue Collar '78
The Yakuza '75

Paul Schrader (1946-)
Bringing Out the Dead '99
Forever Mine '99
Affliction '97
Touch '96
City Hall '95
Light Sleeper '92
The Last Temptation of Christ '88
Light of Day '87
The Mosquito Coast '86
Mishima: A Life in Four Chapters '85
Raging Bull '80
American Gigolo '79
Hardcore '79
Old Boyfriends '79
Blue Collar '78
Rolling Thunder '77
Obsession '76
Taxi Driver '76
The Yakuza '75

Carol Schreder
Mama Flora's Family '98
In Love and War '91

Nevin Schreiner
Don't Talk to Strangers '94
Linda '93
The China Lake Murders '90
Memories of Murder '90

Raymond L. Schrock
Danny Boy '46
White Pongo '45
The Phantom of the Opera '25

Doris Schroeder
Bullet Code '40
Hopalong Cassidy Returns '36

Bernard Schubert
Jungle Woman '44
The Mummy's Curse '44
Weird Woman/Frozen Ghost '44
Breaking the Ice '38
Mark of the Vampire '35

Budd Schulberg (1914-)
Question of Honor '80
A Face in the Crowd '57
On the Waterfront '54

Arnold Schulman
And the Band Played On '93
Tucker: The Man and His Dream '88
A Chorus Line '85
Players '79
Funny Lady '75
The Night They Raided Minsky's '69
Love with the Proper Stranger '63
Cimarron '60
A Hole in the Head '59

Roger S.H. Schulman
Shrek '01
Balto '95

Tom Schulman
Holy Man '98
8 Heads in a Duffel Bag '96
Medicine Man '92
What about Bob? '91
Dead Poets Society '89
Honey, I Shrunk the Kids '89
Second Sight '89

Joel Schumacher (1942-)
Flawless '99
Batman and Robin '97
St. Elmo's Fire '85
D.C. Cab '84
The Wiz '78
Car Wash '76
Sparkle '76

Mark Evan Schwartz
Little Men '98
Wanted '98
Quake '92

Aleksander Scibor-Rylski
Man of Iron '81
Man of Marble '76

Ettore Scola (1931-)
The Family '87
Macaroni '85
La Nuit de Varennes '82
Passion of Love '82
A Special Day '77
Down & Dirty '76
Two Nights with Cleopatra '54

Kathryn Scola
One Night in the Tropics '40
Alexander's Ragtime Band '38
Baby Face '33
Female '33
Night After Night '32

Martin Scorsese (1942-)
Casino '95
The Age of Innocence '93
Goodfellas '90
Mean Streets '73

Allan Scott (1907-95)
Behind the Lines '97
In Love and War '96
The Preacher's Wife '96
Samson and Delilah '96
Two Deaths '94
Cold Heaven '92
The Witches '90
Apprentice to Murder '88
Castaway '87
D.A.R.Y.L. '85
Martin's Day '85
The Awakening '80
Joseph Andrews '77
Spiral Staircase '75
The Girl from Petrovka '74
Don't Look Now '73
Man Who Had Power Over Women '70
The 5000 Fingers of Dr. T '53
So Proudly We Hail '43
Joy of Living '38
Top Hat '35

Darin Scott
Caught Up '98
Sprung '96
Tales from the Hood '95

Gavin Scott
Mists of Avalon '01
Small Soldiers '98
The Borrowers '97

Sherman Scott
Inner Sanctum 2 '94
Haunting Fear '91
Bad Girls from Mars '90

Peter S. Seaman
Dr. Seuss' How the Grinch Stole Christmas '00
Wild Wild West '99
Doc Hollywood '91
Who Framed Roger Rabbit '88
Trenchcoat '83

Ted Sears
Peter Pan '53
The Adventures of Ichabod and Mr. Toad '49
Pinocchio '40
Snow White and the Seven Dwarfs '37

George Seaton (1911-79)
Miracle on 34th Street '94
Airport '70
36 Hours '64
The Counterfeit Traitor '62
Country Girl '54
Miracle on 34th Street '47
Doctor Takes a Wife '40
A Day at the Races '37

Beverly Sebastian
Running Cool '93
Gator Bait 2: Cajun Justice '88
Gator Bait '73

Ferd Sebastian
Running Cool '93
Gator Bait 2: Cajun Justice '88
Gator Bait '73

Jack Seddon
The Blue Max '66
The Longest Day '62

Manuel Seff
Breaking the Ice '38
Love on the Run '36
Red Salute '35

Erich Segal
Man, Woman & Child '83
A Change of Seasons '80
Oliver's Story '78
Love Story '70
R.P.M.* (*Revolutions Per Minute) '70
Yellow Submarine '68

David Seidler
By Dawn's Early Light '00
The King and I '99
Goldrush: A Real Life Alaskan Adventure '98
Quest for Camelot '98
Tucker: The Man and His Dream '88
The Rumor Mill '86

Michael Seitzman
Here on Earth '00
Farmer & Chase '96

Shinichi Sekizawa
Godzilla vs. Megalon '76
Godzilla's Revenge '69
Godzilla vs. Monster Zero '68
Son of Godzilla '66
Dagora, the Space Monster '65
Ghidrah the Three Headed Monster '65
Godzilla vs. Mothra '64
King Kong vs. Godzilla '63
Mothra '62

David Self
Road to Perdition '02
Thirteen Days '00
The Haunting '99

David Seltzer (1940-)
Dragonfly '02
My Giant '98
The Eighteenth Angel '97
Shining Through '92
Bird on a Wire '90
Punchline '88
Lucas '86

Frankenstein Meets the Wolfman '42
Invisible Agent '42
The Wolf Man '41
Black Friday '40
The Invisible Man Returns '40
Non-Stop New York '37

Rosemary Anne Sisson
The Bretts '88
Candleshoe '78
The Duchess of Duke Street '78
The Littlest Horse Thieves '76
Elizabeth R '72

Rob Sitch
The Dish '00
The Castle '97

John Sjogren
Red Line '96
The Mosaic Project '95
Money to Burn '94

Warren Skaaren
Batman '89
Beetlejuice '88
Beverly Hills Cop 2 '87

Vance Skarstedt
The Slime People '63
Man or Gun '58

Jerzy Skolimowski (1938-)
Deep End '70
Knife in the Water '62
Innocent Sorcerers '60

Brian Sloan
I Think I Do '97
Boys Life '94

Holly Goldberg Sloan
The Crocodile Hunter: Collision Course '02
Whispers: An Elephant's Tale '00
The Big Green '95
Angels in the Outfield '94
Made in America '93
Indecency '92

Rick Sloane (1961-)
Good Girls Don't '95
Mind, Body & Soul '92
Vice Academy 3 '91

Shawn Slovo
Captain Corelli's Mandolin '01
A World Apart '88

Adam Small
In the Army Now '94
Son-in-Law '93

Charles Henry Smith (1866-1942)
Battling Butler '26
The General '26

Craig Smith
Federal Protection '02
Caracara '00
Persons Unknown '96

Earl E. Smith
Town That Dreaded Sundown '76
Winterhawk '76
Legend of Boggy Creek '75

Ebbe Roe Smith
Car 54, Where Are You? '94
Falling Down '93

Harold Jacob Smith
Inherit the Wind '99
Inherit the Wind '60
The Defiant Ones '58

Kevin Smith (1970-)
Jay and Silent Bob Strike Back '01
Coyote Ugly '00
Dogma '99
Chasing Amy '97
Mallrats '95
Clerks '94

Kirsten Smith
Legally Blonde '01
Ten Things I Hate about You '99

Lance Smith
Facade '98
Munchies '87

Martin Smith
Under the Rainbow '81
The Art of Crime '75

Murray Smith
Sell Out '76
Die Screaming, Marianne '73

Robert Smith
Xtro '83
Platinum High School '60
Girls' Town '59
The Beast from 20,000 Fathoms '53
Invasion U.S.A. '52
Sudden Fear '52
The Second Woman '51
Quicksand '50

Scott Marshall Smith
The Score '01
Men of Honor '00

Sue Smith
The Road from Coorain '02
Brides of Christ '91

Wallace Smith
The Gay Desperado '36
Bulldog Drummond '29

Webb Smith
Fantasia '40
Pinocchio '40
Snow White and the Seven Dwarfs '37

Stephen Smoke
Magic Kid '92
Street Crimes '92

Earle Snell
Cooking Up Trouble '44
Days of Jesse James '39

Norman Snider
Rated X '00
Body Parts '91
Dead Ringers '88

Melinda M. Snodgrass
The Outer Limits: Sandkings '95
Trapped in Space '94

Blake Snyder
Blank Check '93
Stop! or My Mom Will Shoot '92

Michael Snyder
D.R.E.A.M. Team '99
Rescue Me '93

Carol Sobieski
Money for Nothing '93
Fried Green Tomatoes '91
Sarah, Plain and Tall '91
Winter People '89
The Bourne Identity '88
The Toy '82
Honeysuckle Rose '80

Steven Soderbergh (1963-)
Mimic '97
Schizopolis '97
Nightwatch '96
King of the Hill '93
sex, lies and videotape '89

Gerard Soeteman
Flesh and Blood '85
The 4th Man '79
Soldier of Orange '78
Katie Tippel '75
Turkish Delight '73

Roger Soffer
Slow Burn '00
Kazaam '96

Joel Soisson
Mimic 2 '01
Dracula 2000 '00
Highlander: Endgame '00
The Prophecy 3: The Ascent '99
Blue Tiger '94
Lower Level '91
Trick or Treat '86

Alec Sokolow
Goodbye, Lover '99
Money Talks '97
Toy Story '95

Franco Solinas (1927-82)
Mr. Klein '76
Burn! '70
A Bullet for the General '68
The Battle of Algiers '66

Edward Solomon
What Planet Are You From? '00
Men in Black '97
Super Mario Bros. '93
Leaving Normal '92
Bill & Ted's Bogus Journey '91
Bill & Ted's Excellent Adventure '89

Todd Solondz (1960-)
Storytelling '01
Happiness '98
Welcome to the Dollhouse '95
Fear, Anxiety and Depression '89

Andrew Solt
This Is Elvis '81
For the First Time '59
In a Lonely Place '50
Little Women '49
They All Kissed the Bride '42

Edith Sommer
This Property Is Condemned '66
The Best of Everything '59

Stephen Sommers (1962-)
The Scorpion King '02
The Mummy Returns '01
The Mummy '99
Deep Rising '98
Tom and Huck '95
Rudyard Kipling's The Jungle Book '94
The Adventures of Huck Finn '93
Gunmen '93

Michael Sonye
Blood Diner '87
Star Slammer '87

Aaron Sorkin
The American President '95
Malice '93
A Few Good Men '92

Terry Southern (1926-95)
The Telephone '87
End of the Road '70
Easy Rider '69
The Magic Christian '69
Barbarella '68
The Cincinnati Kid '65
The Loved One '65
Dr. Strangelove, or: How I Learned to Stop Worrying and Love the Bomb '64

Charles Spaak
L'Idiot '46
Grand Illusion '37
The Lower Depths '36

David Spade (1964-)
Joe Dirt '01
Lost and Found '99

David Sparling
Operation Delta Force 3: Clear Target '98
Operation: Delta Force '97
Operation Delta Force 2: Mayday '97

Jack Speirs
The Bears & I '74
Charlie, the Lonesome Cougar '67

Greg Spence
The Prophecy 2: Ashtown '97
Children of the Corn 4: The Gathering '96

Ralph Spence
The Flying Deuces '39
Stand Up and Cheer '34

Don Spencer
The Big Doll House '71
The Student Nurses '70

Scott Spencer
Father Hood '93
Act of Vengeance '86

Milton Sperling
Merrill's Marauders '62
Happy Landing '38
Thin Ice '37

Bella Spewack
Weekend at the Waldorf '45
My Favorite Wife '40
Boy Meets Girl '38
The Cat and the Fiddle '34

Samuel Spewack
Weekend at the Waldorf '45
My Favorite Wife '40
Boy Meets Girl '38
The Cat and the Fiddle '34

Penelope Spheeris (1945-)
The Little Rascals '94
Suburbia '83

Scott Spiegel (1957-)
From Dusk Till Dawn 2: Texas Blood Money '98
The Nutt House '95
Evil Dead 2: Dead by Dawn '87
Thou Shalt Not Kill...Except '87

Steven Spielberg (1947-)
A. I.: Artificial Intelligence '01
The Goonies '85
Poltergeist '82
Close Encounters of the Third Kind '77
The Sugarland Express '74

Leonard Spigelgass
Gypsy '62
A Majority of One '56
Athena '54
I Was a Male War Bride '49
The Perfect Marriage '46

Tony Spiridakis
Tinseltown '97
If Lucy Fell '95
The Last Word '95
Queens Logic '91

Marian Spitzer
Look for the Silver Lining '49
The Dolly Sisters '46

Hildegarde Stadie
Marihuana '36
Maniac '34

Laurence Stallings
She Wore a Yellow Ribbon '49
On Our Merry Way '48
The Jungle Book '42

Sylvester Stallone (1946-)
Driven '01
Cliffhanger '93
Rocky 5 '90
Rambo 3 '88
Cobra '86
Over the Top '86
Rambo: First Blood, Part 2 '85
Rocky 4 '85
Rhinestone '84
Staying Alive '83
First Blood '82
Rocky 3 '82
Rocky 2 '79
F.I.S.T. '78
Paradise Alley '78
Rocky '76

Richard Stanley
The Island of Dr. Moreau '96
Dust Devil '93

Eliot Stannard
The Manxman '29
The Lodger '26

Andrew Stanton
Monsters, Inc. '01
Toy Story 2 '99
A Bug's Life '98

Anthony Stark
The Art of Murder '99
The Dogfighters '95

Lynn Starling
The Climax '44
Wintertime '43
Thanks for the Memory '38

Ben Starr
How to Commit Marriage '69
Texas across the River '66

Wolfgang Staudte (1906-84)
The Kaiser's Lackey '51
The Murderers Are Among Us '46
The Murderers are Among Us '46

Joseph Stefano
Psycho '98
Two Bits '96
Psycho 4: The Beginning '90
The Kindred '87
Blackout '78
The Naked Edge '61
Psycho '60
Black Orchid '59

Darren Stein
Sparkler '99
Jawbreaker '98

Mark Stein
Housesitter '92
A Perfect Little Murder '90

Norman Steinberg
Funny About Love '90
Johnny Dangerously '84
My Favorite Year '82
Yes, Giorgio '82
Blazing Saddles '74

Reed Steiner
Night of the Scarecrow '95
The Hit List '93

J. David Stem
Clockstoppers '02
Jimmy Neutron: Boy Genius '01
The Rugrats Movie '98

Gerard Stembridge
About Adam '00
Nora '00

John Steppling
Animal Factory '00
52 Pick-Up '86

David Stern
Gepetto '00
Swamp Women '55

Henry Stern
Eden 2 '93
Eden '92

Leonard Stern
Missing Pieces '91
Three for the Show '55
Lost in Alaska '52
Abbott and Costello in the Foreign Legion '50
Ma and Pa Kettle Go to Town '50

Sandor Stern (1936-)
Web of Deceit '90
Amityville 4: The Evil Escapes '89
Pin... '88
Assassin '86
The Amityville Horror '79

Stewart Stern (1922-)
Summer Wishes, Winter Dreams '73
The Last Movie '71
Rachel, Rachel '68
The Ugly American '63
Rebel without a Cause '55

Tom Stern (1965-)
An American Werewolf in Paris '97
Freaked '93
Hell's Angels '69 '69

Dana Stevens
Life or Something Like It '02
For Love of the Game '99
City of Angels '98
Blink '93

David Stevens
Jackie, Ethel, Joan: The Kennedy Women '01
Aftershock: Earthquake in New York '99
Dostoevsky's Crime and Punishment '99
Mama Flora's Family '98
Merlin '98
The Sum of Us '94
Queen '93
Breaker Morant '80

Gosta Stevens
Intermezzo '36
The Count of the Old Town '34

Leslie Stevens
Gordy '95
Probe '72
Incubus '65

Louis Stevens
The Border Legion '40
The Texas Rangers '36

Robert Stevenson (1905-86)
Jane Eyre '44
Nine Days a Queen '36

Donald Stewart (1930-99)
Dead Silence '96
Clear and Present Danger '94
Patriot Games '92
The Hunt for Red October '90
Missing '82
Death Sport '78
Cannonball '76
Jackson County Jail '76

Donald Ogden Stewart
An Affair to Remember '57
Escapade '55
Cass Timberlane '47
Life with Father '47
Without Love '45
Forever and a Day '43
Keeper of the Flame '42
Tales of Manhattan '42
That Uncertain Feeling '41
The Philadelphia Story '40
Love Affair '39
Holiday '38
Prisoner of Zenda '37
Dinner at Eight '33
Going Hollywood '33

Douglas Day Stewart
The Scarlet Letter '95
Silver Strand '95
Thief of Hearts '84
An Officer and a Gentleman '82
The Blue Lagoon '80
The Boy in the Plastic Bubble '76
Where the Red Fern Grows '74

Joe Stillman
Shrek '01
Beavis and Butt-Head Do America '96

Whit Stillman (1952-)
The Last Days of Disco '98
Barcelona '94
Metropolitan '90

John Stockwell (1961-)
Blue Crush '02
Rock Star '01
Cheaters '00
Breast Men '97

Michael Stokes
Deadline '00
Bram Stoker's Shadowbuilder '98
Sanctuary '98
Iron Eagle 4 '95
Jungleground '95

Andrew L. Stone (1902-99)
The Last Voyage '60
The Girl Said No '37

Jerico (Weingrod) Stone
Matinee '92
My Stepmother Is an Alien '88

Matthew Stone
Big Trouble '02
Life '99
Destiny Turns on the Radio '95

Oliver Stone (1946-)
Any Given Sunday '99
Evita '96
Nixon '95
Natural Born Killers '94
Heaven and Earth '93
The Doors '91
JFK '91
Born on the Fourth of July '89
Talk Radio '88
Wall Street '87

Platoon '86
Salvador '86
8 Million Ways to Die '85
Year of the Dragon '85
Scarface '83
Conan the Barbarian '82
The Hand '81
Midnight Express '78
Seizure '74

Peter Stone (1930-)
The Taking of Pelham One Two Three '74
Father Goose '64
Charade '63

Sherri Stoner
My Favorite Martian '98
Casper '95

Tom Stoppard (1937-)
Enigma '01
Vatel '00
Shakespeare in Love '98
Billy Bathgate '91
Rosencrantz & Guildenstern Are Dead '90
The Russia House '90
Empire of the Sun '87
Brazil '85
The Human Factor '79
Despair '78
Romantic Englishwoman '75

David Storey
In Celebration '75
This Sporting Life '63

Jim Strain
Summer of the Monkeys '98
Bingo '91

Richard Stratton
White Boyz '99
Slam '98

Robert Strauss
Retroactive '97
Body Shot '93

Arthur Strawn
Flight to Mars '52
The Black Room '35

Wesley Strick (1954-)
The Glass House '01
Hitched '01
Return to Paradise '98
The Saint '97
Wolf '94
Final Analysis '92
Cape Fear '91
Arachnophobia '90
True Believer '89

Max Strom
Shelter '98
American Yakuza '94
Best of the Best 2 '93

Fred Stroppel
A Brooklyn State of Mind '97
Dark Side of Genius '94
Almost Pregnant '91

Barry Strugatz
She-Devil '89
Married to the Mob '88

Stuart Strutin
Class of Nuke 'Em High '86
First Turn On '83

Jeb Stuart
Fire Down Below '97
Switchback '97
Just Cause '94
The Fugitive '93
Another 48 Hrs. '90
Vital Signs '90
Leviathan '89
Lock Up '89
Die Hard '88

Preston Sturges (1898-1959)
I'll Be Yours '47
Miracle of Morgan's Creek '44
The Lady Eve '41
Sullivan's Travels '41
The Great McGinty '40
Remember the Night '40
Never Say Die '39
If I Were King '38
Easy Living '37
Imitation of Life '34

Charles Sturridge (1951-)
Shackleton '02
Longitude '00

Where Angels Fear to Tread '91
Aria '88
A Handful of Dust '88
Troubles '88

Hel Styverson
Forbidden Sins '99
Indecent Behavior 3 '95

Milton Subotsky
At the Earth's Core '76
Vault of Horror '73
I, Monster '71
Dr. Terror's House of Horrors '65

Henry Sucher
Jungle Woman '44
The Mummy's Ghost '44
Captive Wild Woman '43
The Mummy's Tomb '42

Greg Suddeth
Pet Shop '94
Prehysteria '93

C. Gardner Sullivan
Union Pacific '39
Alibi '29
Sparrows '26

Kevin Sullivan (1955-)
Anne of Green Gables: The Continuing Story '99
Anne of Avonlea '87
Anne of Green Gables '85

Tim Sullivan
Jack and Sarah '95
Where Angels Fear to Tread '91
A Handful of Dust '88

Lasse Summanen
The Ox '91
The Women on the Roof '89

Walter Summers (1896-)
The Human Monster '39
Black Limelight '38

Shirley Sun
Iron & Silk '91
A Great Wall '86

Phoef Sutton
The Fan '96
Mrs. Winterbourne '96

Zdenek Sverak
Dark Blue World '01
Kolya '96
The Elementary School '91
My Sweet Little Village '86

Gerry Swallow
Black Knight '01
Say It Isn't So '01

Ron Swanson
Forest Warrior '95
Top Dog '95

Roger E. Swaybill
Porky's 2: The Next Day '83
The Lathe of Heaven '80

Julia Sweeney (1961-)
God Said "Ha!" '99
It's Pat: The Movie '94

John Sweet
The Affair of the Necklace '01
The Great Elephant Escape '95

Tommy Swerdlow
Snow Dogs '02
Bushwhacked '95
Little Giants '94
Cool Runnings '93

Jo Swerling
It's a Wonderful Life '46
Leave Her to Heaven '45
Lifeboat '44
Crash Dive '43
The Pride of the Yankees '42
Blood and Sand '41
The Westerner '40
Made for Each Other '39
The Real Glory '39
I Am the Law '38
Double Wedding '37
The Whole Town's Talking '35
Lady by Choice '34
The Miracle Woman '31
Platinum Blonde '31

Robin Swicord
Practical Magic '98
Matilda '96
Little Women '94
The Perez Family '94
Shag: The Movie '89

David Swift (1919-2001)
Candleshoe '78
How to Succeed in Business without Really Trying '67
Under the Yum-Yum Tree '63
The Parent Trap '61
Pollyanna '60

Istvan Szabo (1938-)
Sunshine '99
Meeting Venus '91
Hanussen '88
Mephisto '81
25 Fireman's Street '73
Love Film '70
Father '67

Roy Szeto
The Phantom Lover '95
Wicked City '92
Dragons Forever '88
Mr. Vampire '86

Thomas Szollosi
Bone Daddy '97
Snow White: A Tale of Terror '97
It Takes Two '88
Three o'Clock High '87

Paul Tabori
Four Sided Triangle '53
Spaceways '53

Jean-Charles Tacchella (1925-)
Blue Country '77
Cousin, Cousine '76

Brian Taggert
Trucks '97
Dangerous Passion '95
What Ever Happened To... '93
Child of Darkness, Child of Light '91
Poltergeist 3 '88
Wanted Dead or Alive '86
The New Kids '85
Of Unknown Origin '83
Visiting Hours '82

Don Tait
The North Avenue Irregulars '79
Unidentified Flying Oddball '79

Koji Takada
Return of the Street Fighter '74
The Street Fighter '74

Ted Tally
All the Pretty Horses '00
The Juror '96
Before and After '95
The Silence of the Lambs '91
White Palace '90

Paul Tamasy
Air Bud 2: Golden Receiver '98
Air Bud '97

Nat Tanchuck
Married Too Young '62
Chained for Life '51

Edward Tang
Mr. Nice Guy '98
Rumble in the Bronx '96
The Legend of Drunken Master '94
Supercop '92
Operation Condor '91
Project A: Part 2 '87
Operation Condor 2: The Armour of the Gods '86
Project A '83

Alain Tanner (1929-)
In the White City '83
Messidor '77
Jonah Who Will Be 25 in the Year 2000 '76
La Salamandre '71
Charles: Dead or Alive '69

Robert Emmett Tansey (1897-1951)
The Driftin' Kid '41
Dynamite Canyon '41
Courage of the North '35
Paradise Canyon '35

Daniel Taplitz
Dean Koontz's Black River '01
Commandments '96
Black Magic '92

Daniel Taradash
The Other Side of Midnight '77
Doctors' Wives '70
Hawaii '66
Morituri '65
Bell, Book and Candle '58
Picnic '55
Desiree '54
From Here to Eternity '53
Don't Bother to Knock '52
Rancho Notorious '52
Knock on Any Door '49
Golden Boy '39

Quentin Tarantino (1963-)
Jackie Brown '97
Four Rooms '95
From Dusk Till Dawn '95
Pulp Fiction '94
True Romance '93
Reservoir Dogs '92

Sooni Taraporevala
My Own Country '98
Such a Long Journey '98
Mississippi Masala '92
Salaam Bombay! '88

Andrei Tarkovsky (1932-86)
The Sacrifice '86
Nostalghia '83
The Mirror '75
Solaris '72
Andrei Rublev '66

Frank Tarloff (1916-99)
A Guide for the Married Man '67
Father Goose '64

Susan Tarr
My Sister's Keeper '02
Cousin Bette '97

Frank Tashlin (1913-72)
Private Navy of Sgt. O'Farrell '68
Who's Minding the Store? '63
Cinderfella '60
Rock-A-Bye Baby '57
Will Success Spoil Rock Hunter? '57
The Girl Can't Help It '56
Artists and Models '55
Son of Paleface '52
The Lemon Drop Kid '51
The Fuller Brush Girl '50
Love Happy '50
Variety Girl '47
A Night in Casablanca '46

Jacques Tati (1908-82)
Parade '74
Traffic '71
Mon Oncle '58
Mr. Hulot's Holiday '53
Jour de Fete '48

Gilles Taurand
A Matter of Taste '00
Alice et Martin '98
Dry Cleaning '97
Les Voleurs '96
Wild Reeds '94

Catherine Tavel
Night Fire '94
Married People, Single Sex '93

Bertrand Tavernier (1941-)
Capitaine Conan '96
L'Appat '94
L.627 '92
Life and Nothing But '89
Round Midnight '86
A Sunday in the Country '84

Coup de Torchon '81
Death Watch '80
Spoiled Children '77
The Judge and the Assassin '75
The Clockmaker '73

Paolo Taviani (1931-)
Elective Affinities '96
Fiorile '93
Night Sun '90
Good Morning, Babylon '87
Kaos '85
The Night of the Shooting Stars '82
Padre Padrone '77
Allonsanfan '73
St. Michael Had a Rooster '72

Vittorio Taviani (1929-)
Elective Affinities '96
Fiorile '93
Night Sun '90
Good Morning, Babylon '87
Kaos '85
The Night of the Shooting Stars '82
Padre Padrone '77
Allonsanfan '73
St. Michael Had a Rooster '72

David Taylor
Tracked '98
DROP Squad '94
Get Crazy '83

Delores Taylor
The Trial of Billy Jack '74
Billy Jack '71

Dwight Taylor
We're Not Married '52
Rhythm on the River '40
Top Hat '35
Today We Live '33

Eric Taylor
Dick Tracy Meets Gruesome '47
Dick Tracy, Detective '45
The Phantom of the Opera '43
Son of Dracula '43
The Black Cat '41
Black Friday '40

Finn Taylor
Cherish '02
Dream with the Fishes '97
Pontiac Moon '94

Greg Taylor
Prancer Returns '01
Summer of the Monkeys '98
The Christmas Box '95
Prancer '89

Jim Taylor
Jurassic Park 3 '01
Election '99
Citizen Ruth '96

Renee Taylor (1935-)
Love Is All There Is '96
Lovers and Other Strangers '70

Roderick Taylor
American Outlaws '01
At Any Cost '00
The Star Chamber '83

Sam Taylor (1895-1958)
The Freshman '25
Girl Shy '24

Samuel A. Taylor (1912-2000)
The Love Machine '71
Topaz '69
Goodbye Again '61
Vertigo '58
The Eddy Duchin Story '56

Steve Taylor
Social Intercourse '01
Sorority House Party '92

Andre Techine (1943-)
Alice et Martin '98
Les Voleurs '96
Wild Reeds '94
Ma Saison Preferee '93
Barocco '76

Miguel Tejada-Flores
Atomic Dog '98
Screamers '96
Tails You Live, Heads You're Dead '95
Almost Dead '94
Fright Night 2 '88

Daisuke Tengan
Dr. Akagi '98
The Eel '96

Kevin S. Tenney
Pinocchio's Revenge '96
Witchboard 3: The Possession '95
Witchboard 2: The Devil's Doorway '93
Peacemaker '90
Witchboard '87

John Terlesky
The Guardian '00
Supreme Sanction '99

Gay Partington Terry
The Toxic Avenger, Part 2 '89
The Toxic Avenger, Part 3: The Last Temptation of Toxie '89

Steve Tesich (1942-96)
American Flyers '85
Eleni '85
The World According to Garp '82
Eyewitness '81
Four Friends '81
Breaking Away '79

Joan Tewkesbury (1936-)
Cold Sassy Tree '89
A Night in Heaven '83
Nashville '75
Thieves Like Us '74

Daniel Therriault
Witness Protection '99
First Time Felon '97

Harvey Thew
The Trail of the Lonesome Pine '36
She Done Him Wrong '33
Supernatural '33
Illicit '31
Public Enemy '31
Uncle Tom's Cabin '27

Nick Thiel
The Associate '96
V.I. Warshawski '91
White Fang '91
Fire Birds '90
Shipwrecked '90
The Experts '89

Robert Thoeren
Singapore '47
Mrs. Parkington '44

Robert Thom
Third Walker '79
Crazy Mama '75
Death Race 2000 '75
Bloody Mama '70
Wild in the Streets '68

Anna Thomas
My Family '94
A Time of Destiny '88
El Norte '83
End of August '82

Jim Thomas
Mission to Mars '00
Executive Decision '96
Predator 2 '90
The Rescue '88
Predator '87

John Thomas
Mission to Mars '00
Executive Decision '96
Predator 2 '90
The Rescue '88
Predator '87

Michael Thomas
B. Monkey '97
Welcome to Woop Woop '97
Backbeat '94
Deception '92
Scandal '89
Burke & Wills '85
Ladyhawke '85
The Hunger '83

Ralph L. (R.L.) Thomas
A Young Connecticut Yankee in King Arthur's Court *'95*
Young Ivanhoe *'95*
Caroline Thompson (1956-)
Snow White: The Fairest of Them All *'02*
Buddy *'97*
Black Beauty *'94*
Homeward Bound: The Incredible Journey *'93*
The Nightmare before Christmas *'93*
The Secret Garden *'93*
The Addams Family *'91*
Edward Scissorhands *'90*
Daniele Thompson
La Buche *'00*
Those Who Love Me Can Take the Train *'98*
Queen Margot *'94*
Emma Thompson (1959-)
Wit *'01*
Sense and Sensibility *'95*
Ernest Thompson
Out of Time *'00*
1969 *'89*
Sweet Hearts Dance *'88*
On Golden Pond *'81*
Gary Scott Thompson
The Fast and the Furious *'01*
K-911 *'99*
Split Second *'92*
Jim Thompson
Paths of Glory *'57*
The Killing *'56*
Keene Thompson
Love in Bloom *'35*
Palmy Days *'31*
Peggy Thompson
Better Than Chocolate *'99*
The Lotus Eaters *'93*
Rob Thompson
The Cowboy Way *'94*
Ratboy *'86*
Hearts of the West *'75*
Billy Bob Thornton (1955-)
Camouflage *'00*
The Gift *'00*
Don't Look Back *'96*
A Family Thing *'96*
Sling Blade *'96*
Some Folks Call It a Sling Blade *'94*
One False Move *'91*
Ralph Thornton
Blood of Dracula *'57*
I Was a Teenage Werewolf *'57*
George Tibbles
How to Frame a Figg *'71*
Munster, Go Home! *'66*
Ernest Tidyman
Stark *'85*
High Plains Drifter *'73*
Shaft's Big Score *'72*
The French Connection *'71*
Shaft *'71*
Patrick Tilley
The People That Time Forgot *'77*
Wuthering Heights *'70*
James Toback (1944-)
Black and White *'99*
Two Girls and a Guy *'98*
Bugsy *'91*
The Pick-Up Artist *'87*
Exposed *'83*
Fingers *'78*
The Gambler *'74*
Peter Tolan
America's Sweethearts *'01*
Bedazzled *'00*
What Planet Are You From? *'00*
Analyze This *'98*
My Fellow Americans *'96*
George Toles
The Twilight of the Ice Nymphs *'97*
Careful *'92*
Michael Tolkin (1950-)
Changing Lanes *'02*
Deep Impact *'98*
The Burning Season *'94*
The New Age *'94*
Deep Cover *'92*
The Player *'92*
The Rapture *'91*
Gleaming the Cube *'89*
Stephen Tolkin
Fidel *'02*
Dean Koontz's Mr. Murder *'98*
Daybreak *'93*
Captain America *'89*
Stanley Tong (1960-)
Jackie Chan's First Strike *'96*
Supercop 2 *'93*
Rhet Topham
976-EVIL *'88*
Trick or Treat *'86*
Tom Topor
Judgment *'90*
The Accused *'88*
Nuts *'87*
Burt Topper (1928-)
The Hard Ride *'71*
Tank Commando *'59*
Tracy Torme
Fire in the Sky *'93*
The Spellbinder *'88*
Giuseppe Tornatore (1956-)
Malena *'00*
The Legend of 1900 *'98*
The Star Maker *'95*
A Pure Formality *'94*
Everybody's Fine *'90*
Cinema Paradiso *'88*
Antonio Toro
Amityville: A New Generation *'93*
Amityville 1992: It's About Time *'92*
Peter Torokvei
Guarding Tess *'94*
Hostage for a Day *'94*
Caddyshack 2 *'88*
Armed and Dangerous *'86*
Back to School *'86*
Real Genius *'85*
Harry Alan Towers
Black Venus *'83*
Call of the Wild *'72*
The Castle of Fu Manchu *'68*
Gene Towne
Joy of Living *'38*
You Only Live Once *'37*
Robert Towne (1936-)
Mission: Impossible 2 *'00*
Without Limits *'97*
Mission: Impossible *'96*
Love Affair *'94*
The Firm *'93*
Days of Thunder *'90*
The Two Jakes *'90*
Tequila Sunrise *'88*
Personal Best *'82*
Shampoo *'75*
The Yakuza *'75*
Chinatown *'74*
The Last Detail *'73*
Villa Rides *'68*
Tomb of Ligeia *'64*
The Last Woman on Earth *'61*
Roger Towne
In the Company of Spies *'99*
The Natural *'84*
Leo Townsend
Beach Blanket Bingo *'65*
How to Stuff a Wild Bikini *'65*
Bikini Beach *'64*
It Started with Eve *'41*
Robert Townsend (1957-)
The Meteor Man *'93*
The Five Heartbeats *'91*
Hollywood Shuffle *'87*
Bill Travers (1922-94)
An Elephant Called Slowly *'69*
Ring of Bright Water *'69*
Joey Travolta (1952-)
To the Limit *'95*
Hard Vice *'94*
Monika Treut (1954-)
Erotique *'94*
My Father Is Coming *'91*
Seduction: The Cruel Woman *'89*
Virgin Machine *'88*
Dale Trevillion
Beyond Desire *'94*
One Man Force *'89*
Las Vegas Weekend *'85*
Victor Trivas
The Head *'59*
The Stranger *'46*
Jan Troell (1931-)
The New Land *'73*
The Emigrants *'72*
Guy Trosper
Birdman of Alcatraz *'62*
Darby's Rangers *'58*
Jailhouse Rock *'57*
The Stratton Story *'49*
Lamar Trotti
I'd Climb the Highest Mountain *'51*
Cheaper by the Dozen *'50*
Captain from Castile *'47*
Mother Wore Tights *'47*
The Razor's Edge *'46*
Wilson *'44*
Guadalcanal Diary *'43*
Immortal Sergeant *'43*
The Ox-Bow Incident *'43*
Brigham Young: Frontiersman *'40*
The Story of Alexander Graham Bell *'39*
Young Mr. Lincoln *'39*
Alexander's Ragtime Band *'38*
In Old Chicago *'37*
David Trueba
Dance with the Devil *'97*
Two Much *'96*
Francois Truffaut (1932-84)
Confidentially Yours *'83*
The Last Metro *'80*
The Man Who Loved Women *'77*
Small Change *'76*
Day for Night *'73*
Two English Girls *'72*
Bed and Board *'70*
The Wild Child *'70*
Mississippi Mermaid *'69*
The Bride Wore Black *'68*
Stolen Kisses *'68*
Fahrenheit 451 *'66*
The Soft Skin *'64*
Jules and Jim *'62*
Shoot the Piano Player *'62*
The 400 Blows *'59*
Dalton Trumbo
Papillon *'73*
Johnny Got His Gun *'71*
The Horsemen *'70*
The Fixer *'68*
Hawaii *'66*
Exodus *'60*
Spartacus *'60*
Terror in a Texas Town *'58*
The Brave One *'56*
Roman Holiday *'53*
Prowler *'51*
Rocketship X-M *'50*
Gun Crazy *'49*
Our Vines Have Tender Grapes *'45*
A Guy Named Joe *'44*
Thirty Seconds Over Tokyo *'44*
Alan R. Trustman
The Arab Conspiracy *'76*
Hit! *'73*
Lady Ice *'73*
They Call Me Mr. Tibbs! *'70*
Bullitt *'68*
The Thomas Crown Affair *'68*
Glenn Tryon (1894-1970)
Small Town Boy *'37*
Bachelor Bait *'34*
Shinya Tsukamoto (1960-)
Tetsuo 2: Body Hammer *'97*
Tetsuo: The Iron Man *'92*
Stanley Tucci (1960-)
Joe Gould's Secret *'00*
The Imposters *'98*
Big Night *'95*
James Tucker
Steps from Hell *'92*
Lunatic *'91*
Larry Tucker (1933-2001)
Alex in Wonderland *'70*
Bob & Carol & Ted & Alice *'69*
Harry Tugend
Who's Minding the Store? *'63*
Pocketful of Miracles *'61*
Take Me Out to the Ball Game *'49*
Star Spangled Rhythm *'42*
Birth of the Blues *'41*
Caught in the Draft *'41*
Second Fiddle *'39*
My Lucky Star *'38*
Pigskin Parade *'36*
Karl Tunberg
The Seventh Dawn *'64*
Ben-Hur *'59*
Beau Brummel *'54*
Valley of the Kings *'54*
Up in Central Park *'48*
You Gotta Stay Happy *'48*
Week-End in Havana *'41*
Gary J. Tunnicliffe
The Guardian *'00*
Within the Rock *'96*
Ann Turner
The Killing Beach *'92*
Hammers over the Anvil *'91*
Barbara Turner
Pollock *'00*
Georgia *'95*
War Between the Tates *'76*
Bonnie Turner
The Brady Bunch Movie *'95*
Tommy Boy *'95*
Coneheads *'93*
Wayne's World 2 *'93*
Wayne's World *'92*
Guinevere Turner (1968-)
American Psycho *'99*
Go Fish *'94*
Terry Turner
The Brady Bunch Movie *'95*
Tommy Boy *'95*
Coneheads *'93*
Wayne's World 2 *'93*
Wayne's World *'92*
Catherine Turney (1906-98)
Cry Wolf *'47*
The Man I Love *'46*
John Turturro (1957-)
Illuminata *'98*
Mac *'93*
Derek Twist
Angels One Five *'54*
Non-Stop New York *'37*
John Twist
Band of Angels *'57*
Helen of Troy *'56*
King Richard and the Crusaders *'54*
Pittsburgh *'42*
David N. Twohy
Imposter *'01*
Pitch Black *'00*
G.I. Jane *'97*
The Arrival *'96*
Waterworld *'95*
Terminal Velocity *'94*
The Fugitive *'93*
Grand Tour: Disaster in Time *'92*
Warlock *'91*
Critters 2: The Main Course *'88*
Jonathan Tydor
The King's Guard *'01*
The Hard Truth *'94*
Tom Tykwer (1965-)
The Princess and the Warrior *'00*
Run Lola Run *'98*
Winter Sleepers *'97*
Steve Tymon
Hindsight *'97*
Mirror, Mirror 3: The Voyeur *'96*
Dark Secrets *'95*
Bob Tzudiker
102 Dalmatians *'00*
Tarzan *'99*
Anastasia *'97*
The Hunchback of Notre Dame *'96*
Newsies *'92*
Alfred Uhry
Rich in Love *'93*
Driving Miss Daisy *'89*
Mystic Pizza *'88*
Daniel Ullman
Mysterious Island *'61*
Good Day for a Hanging *'58*
Elwood Ullman
Snow White and the Three Stooges *'61*
The Three Stooges Meet Hercules *'61*
Ma and Pa Kettle at Waikiki *'55*
The Stooge *'51*
Liv Ullmann (1939-)
Kristin Lavransdatter *'95*
Sofie *'92*
Gladys Unger
The Mystery of Edwin Drood *'35*
Great Expectations *'34*
Eve Unsell
The Plastic Age *'25*
Shadows *'22*
Leon Uris
Gunfight at the O.K. Corral *'57*
Battle Cry *'55*
Peter Ustinov (1921-)
Hot Millions *'68*
Lady L *'65*
Billy Budd *'62*
Immortal Battalion *'44*
Pierre Uytterhoeven
Bandits *'86*
Happy New Year *'73*
A Man and a Woman *'66*
Rodney Vaccaro
Ride the Wild Fields *'00*
Three to Tango *'99*
Roger Vadim (1928-2000)
Barbarella *'68*
Spirits of the Dead *'68*
Blood and Roses *'61*
Please Not Now! *'61*
Dangerous Liaisons *'60*
Sois Belle et Tais-Toi *'58*
And God Created Woman *'57*
The Night Heaven Fell *'57*
Plucking the Daisy *'56*
Laszlo Vadnay
The Great Rupert *'50*
Uncertain Glory *'44*
Ladislao Vajda (1906-65)
The Miracle of Marcelino *'55*
The Threepenny Opera *'31*
Luis Valdez (1940-)
The Cisco Kid *'94*
La Bamba *'87*
Zoot Suit *'81*
Val Valentine
The Belles of St. Trinian's *'53*
My Son, the Vampire *'52*
Old Mother Riley's Jungle Treasure *'51*
We Dive at Dawn *'43*
Nick Vallelonga
The Corporate Ladder *'97*
In the Kingdom of the Blind the Man with One Eye Is King *'94*
A Brilliant Disguise *'93*
Jean-Claude Van Damme (1961-)
Double Impact *'91*
Lionheart *'90*
Kickboxer *'89*
Jaco Van Dormael (1957-)
The Eighth Day *'95*
Toto le Heros *'91*
Dale Van Every
Souls at Sea *'37*
Murders in the Rue Morgue *'32*
Trader Horn *'31*
Mario Van Peebles (1958-)
Love Kills *'98*
Los Locos Posse *'97*
Melvin Van Peebles (1932-)
Panther *'95*
Tales of Erotica *'93*
Sophisticated Gents *'81*
Greased Lightning *'77*
Sweet Sweetback's Baadasssss Song *'71*
The Story of a Three Day Pass *'68*
Gus Van Sant (1952-)
Even Cowgirls Get the Blues *'94*
My Own Private Idaho *'91*
Drugstore Cowboy *'89*
Virginia Van Upp
Young & Willing *'42*
You and Me *'38*
Agnes Varda (1928-)
One Hundred and One Nights *'95*
Jacquot *'91*
Vagabond *'85*
One Sings, the Other Doesn't *'77*
Le Bonheur *'65*
Cleo from 5 to 7 *'61*
Michael Varhol
The Big Picture *'89*
Pee-wee's Big Adventure *'85*
The Last Word *'80*
Joseph B. Vasquez (1962-95)
Manhattan Merenque! *'95*
Hangin' with the Homeboys *'91*
Francis Veber (1937-)
The Closet *'00*
The Dinner Game *'98*
My Father the Hero *'93*
Three Fugitives *'89*
Les Comperes *'83*
Partners *'82*
La Cage aux Folles 2 *'81*
Hothead *'78*
La Cage aux Folles *'78*
Pain in the A— *'77*
Le Magnifique *'76*
Return of the Tall Blond Man with One Black Shoe *'74*
The Tall Blond Man with One Black Shoe *'72*
Anthony Veiller
Moulin Rouge *'52*
Red Planet Mars *'52*
The Killers *'46*
David Veloz
Behind Enemy Lines *'01*
Permanent Midnight *'98*
Louis Venosta
Kisses in the Dark *'97*
The Last Dragon *'85*
Michael Ventura
Echo Park *'86*
Roadie *'80*
Luis Enrique Vergara
The Fear Chamber *'68*
The Sinister Invasion *'68*

Chris Weitz (1970-)
About a Boy '02
Nutty Professor 2: The Klumps '00
Antz '98
Madeline '98
Paul Weitz (1966-)
About a Boy '02
Nutty Professor 2: The Klumps '00
Antz '98
Madeline '98
Peter Welbeck
Bullet to Beijing '95
The Mangler '94
Count Dracula '71
Robert L. Welch
Son of Paleface '52
Variety Girl '47
Sandy Welch
Our Mutual Friend '98
A Dark Adapted Eye '93
A Fatal Inversion '92
Les Weldon
Hidden Agenda '01
Replicant '01
Colin Welland
War of the Buttons '95
A Dry White Season '89
Twice in a Lifetime '85
Chariots of Fire '81
Yanks '79
Michael Weller
Lost Angels '89
Ragtime '81
Hair '79
Halsted Welles
The Hanging Tree '59
3:10 to Yuma '57
Orson Welles (1915-85)
Treasure Island '72
Chimes at Midnight '67
The Trial '63
Touch of Evil '58
Othello '52
The Lady from Shanghai '48
The Magnificent Ambersons '42
Citizen Kane '41
Audrey Wells
Disney's The Kid '00
Guinevere '99
George of the Jungle '97
The Truth about Cats and Dogs '96
George Wells (1909-2000)
The Impossible Years '68
The Horizontal Lieutenant '62
Where the Boys Are '60
The Gazebo '59
Designing Woman '57
Don't Go Near the Water '57
Angels in the Outfield '51
Show Boat '51
Summer Stock '50
Take Me Out to the Ball Game '49
The Hucksters '47
Merton of the Movies '47
The Show-Off '46
John Wells (1936-98)
Entertaining Angels: The Dorothy Day Story '96
Princess Caraboo '94
Peter Wells
First Love and Other Pains / One of Them '99
When Love Comes '98
Desperate Remedies '93
Wim Wenders (1945-)
Beyond the Clouds '95
Lisbon Story '94
Faraway, So Close! '93
Until the End of the World '91
Wings of Desire '88
Tokyo-Ga '85
The American Friend '77
Kings of the Road—In the Course of Time '76
Alice in the Cities '74
The Goalie's Anxiety at the Penalty Kick '71
Gina Wendkos
The Princess Diaries '01
Coyote Ugly '00
Jersey Girl '92
Ginger Ale Afternoon '89
Richard Wenk
Just the Ticket '98
Vamp '86
Mike Werb
Face/Off '97
Darkman 3: Die Darkman Die '95
The Mask '94
Machine Gun Kelly '58
Lina Wertmuller (1928-)
The Worker and the Hairdresser '96
Ciao, Professore! '94
Summer Night with Greek Profile, Almond Eyes & Scent of Basil '87
Camorra: The Naples Connection '85
Sotto, Sotto '85
A Joke of Destiny, Lying in Wait Around the Corner Like a Bandit '84
Blood Feud '79
A Night Full of Rain '78
Seven Beauties '76
Swept Away... '75
All Screwed Up '74
Love and Anarchy '73
Seduction of Mimi '72
Quentin Werty
That Man Bolt '73
Dark of the Sun '68
Richard Wesley
Bojangles '01
Mandela and de Klerk '97
Native Son '86
Fast Forward '84
Let's Do It Again '75
Uptown Saturday Night '74
Claudine West
The White Cliffs of Dover '44
Mrs. Miniver '42
The Mortal Storm '40
Goodbye, Mr. Chips '39
Con West
Old Mother Riley, Headmistress '50
Old Mother Riley's New Venture '49
Jessamyn West
Stolen Hours '63
The Big Country '58
Mae West (1893-1980)
My Little Chickadee '40
Every Day's a Holiday '38
Go West, Young Man '36
Klondike Annie '36
Goin' to Town '35
Belle of the Nineties '34
I'm No Angel '33
Night After Night '32
Roland West (1885-1952)
The Bat Whispers '30
Alibi '29
The Bat '26
Robert Westerby
Sea of Sand '58
War and Peace '56
Donald E. Westlake
The Grifters '90
Why Me? '90
The Stepfather '87
Hot Stuff '80
Cops and Robbers '73
Ellen Weston
Sin and Redemption '94
Lies Before Kisses '92
Garnett Weston
Bulldog Drummond's Secret Police '39
The White Zombie '32
Blackmail '29
Haskell Wexler (1926-)
Latino '85
Medium Cool '69
Norman Wexler (1926-99)
Saturday Night Fever '77
Mandingo '75
Joe '70
John Wexley (1907-85)
The Long Night '47
Hangmen Also Die '42
Footsteps in the Dark '41
Amazing Dr. Clitterhouse '38
Angels with Dirty Faces '38
Jim Wheat (1952-)
Rattled '96
It Came from Outer Space 2 '95
The Birds 2: Land's End '94
After Midnight '89
The Fly 2 '89
Silent Scream '80
Ken Wheat (1950-)
Rattled '96
It Came from Outer Space 2 '95
The Birds 2: Land's End '94
After Midnight '89
The Fly 2 '89
Silent Scream '80
John Whedon (-1991)
The Bears & I '74
The Island at the Top of the World '74
Joss Whedon
Titan A.E. '00
Alien: Resurrection '97
Toy Story '95
Buffy the Vampire Slayer '92
Rene Wheeler
Fanfan la Tulipe '51
Utopia '51
Graeme Whifler
Dr. Giggles '92
Sonny Boy '87
Denis Whitburn
Billy's Holiday '95
The Cursed Mountain Mystery '93
Cynthia Whitcomb
Selma, Lord, Selma '99
Buffalo Girls '95
Garry Michael White
The Promise '79
Sky Riders '76
James Gordon White
The Thing with Two Heads '72
The Incredible Two-Headed Transplant '71
The Tormentors '71
Hell's Belles '69
J.B. White
The Spring '00
The Beast '96
Mike White
The Good Girl '02
Orange County '02
Chuck & Buck '00
Dead Man on Campus '97
Noni White
102 Dalmatians '00
Tarzan '99
Anastasia '97
The Hunchback of Notre Dame '96
Robb White
Homicidal '61
13 Ghosts '60
The Tingler '59
House on Haunted Hill '58
Ted Whitehead
Tess of the D'Urbervilles '98
Cracker: The Big Crunch '94
Hugh Whitemore (1936-)
Jane Eyre '96
Breaking the Code '95
The Rector's Wife '94
84 Charing Cross Road '86
All Creatures Great and Small '74
Elizabeth R '72
Preston A. Whitmore, II
Fled '96
The Walking Dead '94
Cormac Wibberly
The 6th Day '00
Motel Blue '98
Marianne S. Wibberly
The 6th Day '00
Motel Blue '98
David Wickes
Frankenstein '93
Jekyll and Hyde '90
Jack the Ripper '88
Christopher Wicking
To the Devil, a Daughter '76
Demons of the Mind '72
Blood from the Mummy's Tomb '71
Cry of the Banshee '70
Scream and Scream Again '70
Gregory Widen
The Prophecy '95
Backdraft '91
Highlander '86
Bo Widerberg (1930-97)
All Things Fair '95
Man from Mallorca '84
The Man on the Roof '76
Elvira Madigan '67
Ken Wiederhorn
A House in the Hills '93
Return of the Living Dead 2 '88
Shock Waves '77
Joe Wiesenfeld
Back to the Secret Garden '01
Child Star: The Shirley Temple Story '01
The Sign of Four '01
The Hound of the Baskervilles '00
A Knight in Camelot '98
20,000 Leagues Under the Sea '97
The Yearling '94
Crane Wilbur (1886-1973)
Mysterious Island '61
The Bat '59
House of Wax '53
The Devil on Wheels '47
Yellow Cargo '36
Billy Wilder (1906-2002)
Buddy Buddy '81
The Front Page '74
Avanti! '72
The Private Life of Sherlock Holmes '70
The Fortune Cookie '66
Kiss Me, Stupid! '64
Irma La Douce '63
One, Two, Three '61
The Apartment '60
Some Like It Hot '59
Love in the Afternoon '57
Spirit of St. Louis '57
Witness for the Prosecution '57
The Seven Year Itch '55
Sabrina '54
Stalag 17 '53
Sunset Boulevard '50
Emperor Waltz '48
A Foreign Affair '48
The Lost Weekend '45
Double Indemnity '44
Five Graves to Cairo '43
The Major and the Minor '42
Ball of Fire '41
Midnight '39
Ninotchka '39
Bluebeard's Eighth Wife '38
Mauvaise Graine '33
Gene Wilder (1935-)
Murder in a Small Town '99
See No Evil, Hear No Evil '89
Haunted Honeymoon '86
The Woman in Red '84
The Adventures of Sherlock Holmes' Smarter Brother '78
World's Greatest Lover '77
Young Frankenstein '74
John Wilder
Return to Lonesome Dove '93
Breaking Home Ties '87
Centennial '78
Robert Wilder
The Big Country '58
Flamingo Road '49
Georg Wildhagen (1920-)
The Merry Wives of Windsor '50
The Marriage of Figaro '49
Ethan Wiley
Children of the Corn 5: Fields of Terror '98
House 2: The Second Story '87
House '86
Rich Wilkes
XXX '02
Glory Daze '96
The Jerky Boys '95
Airheads '94
Christopher Wilkinson
Ali '01
Nixon '95
Bob Williams
20 Million Miles to Earth '57
Silver City Bonanza '51
Charles Williams
The Hot Spot '90
The Pink Jungle '68
Emlyn Williams (1905-87)
The Last Days of Dolwyn '49
Evergreen '34
The Man Who Knew Too Much '34
Spencer Williams, Jr. (1893-1969)
Blood of Jesus '41
Son of Ingagi '40
Harlem Rides the Range '39
Tennessee Williams
Orpheus Descending '91
The Glass Menagerie '87
Cat on a Hot Tin Roof '84
Boom! '68
Baby Doll '56
The Rose Tattoo '55
A Streetcar Named Desire '51
David Williamson
On the Beach '00
Dangerous Life '89
Travelling North '87
Phar Lap '84
The Year of Living Dangerously '82
The Club '81
Gallipoli '81
Don's Party '76
Fred Williamson (1938-)
Adios Amigo '75
Boss '74
Kevin Williamson (1965-)
Teaching Mrs. Tingle '99
The Faculty '98
I Know What You Did Last Summer '97
Scream 2 '97
Scream '96
Calder Willingham (1922-95)
Rambling Rose '91
Thieves Like Us '74
Little Big Man '70
The Graduate '67
One-Eyed Jacks '61
The Vikings '58
Paths of Glory '57
The Strange One '57
Carey Wilson
Mutiny on the Bounty '35
Gabriel Over the White House '33
Behind Office Doors '31
He Who Gets Slapped '24
David Wilson (1949-)
The Perfect Weapon '91
Strangers in Good Company '91
Gerald Wilson
Chato's Land '71
Lawman '71
Hugh Wilson (1943-)
Dudley Do-Right '99
Blast from the Past '98
Rough Riders '97
Down Periscope '96
Guarding Tess '94
Burglar '87
Rustler's Rhapsody '85
Police Academy '84
Stroker Ace '83
Michael Wilson (1914-78)
Planet of the Apes '68
Lawrence of Arabia '62
The Bridge on the River Kwai '57
Friendly Persuasion '56
Salt of the Earth '54
Five Fingers '52
A Place in the Sun '51
Michael G. Wilson (1943-)
License to Kill '89
The Living Daylights '87
A View to a Kill '85
Octopussy '83
For Your Eyes Only '81
Owen C. Wilson (1968-)
The Royal Tenenbaums '01
Rushmore '98
Bottle Rocket '95
Sandy Wilson
American Boyfriends '89
My American Cousin '85
S.S. Wilson
Wild Wild West '99
Tremors 2: Aftershocks '96
Heart and Souls '93
Ghost Dad '90
Tremors '89
Short Circuit 2 '88
*batteries not included '87
Short Circuit '86
Kurt Wimmer
The Thomas Crown Affair '99
Relative Fear '95
The Neighbor '93
Arthur Wimperis (1874-)
Young Bess '53
Mrs. Miniver '42
The Four Feathers '39
The Scarlet Pimpernel '34
The Private Life of Henry VIII '33
Charles Winkler
Rocky Marciano '99
Disturbed '90
You Talkin' to Me? '87
Terence H. Winkless
Rage and Honor '92
Corporate Affairs '90
He's My Girl '87
The Howling '81
Michael Winner (1935-)
Bullseye! '90
A Chorus of Disapproval '89
Appointment with Death '88
The Wicked Lady '83
Firepower '79
The Big Sleep '78
The Sentinel '76
Murder on the Campus '52
Alex Winter (1965-)
Fever '99
Freaked '93
Aubrey Wisberg
Hercules in New York '70
The Man from Planet X '51
The Adventures of Rusty '45
Doris Wishman
Double Agent 73 '80

Cinematographer Index

The **Cinematographer Index** provides a videography for any cinematographer, or Director of Photography, as they are also known, with a video credit. The listings for the cinematographer names follow an alphabetical sort by last name (although the names appear in a first name last name format). The videographies are listed chronologically, from oldest film to the most recent. If a cinematographer lensed more than one film in the same year, these movies are listed alphabetically within the year. Many of today's top directors started as cinematographers, the people responsible for the "look" of a movie.

Thomas Ackerman
Snow Dogs *'02*
Rat Race *'01*
The Adventures of Rocky & Bullwinkle *'00*
Beautiful Joe *'00*
The Muse *'99*
My Favorite Martian *'98*
The Eighteenth Angel *'97*
George of the Jungle *'97*
Jumanji *'95*
Baby's Day Out *'94*
Dennis the Menace *'93*
National Lampoon's Christmas Vacation *'89*
Beetlejuice *'88*
Back to School *'86*
Girls Just Want to Have Fun *'85*
Frankenweenie *'84*
Roadhouse 66 *'84*
Foxfire Light *'82*

Barry Ackroyd
Bread and Roses *'00*
Beautiful People *'99*
The Lost Son *'98*
My Name Is Joe *'98*
Carla's Song *'97*
Under the Skin *'97*
Stella Does Tricks *'96*
Land and Freedom *'95*
Ladybird, Ladybird *'93*
Raining Stones *'93*

Lance Acord
Being John Malkovich *'99*
Buffalo 66 *'97*

Witold Adamek
The Decalogue *'88*
The Possessed *'88*

Steve Adcock
Facing the Enemy *'00*
Speedway Junky *'99*
Timelock *'99*

Remi Adefarasin
About a Boy *'02*
Band of Brothers *'01*
Arabian Nights *'00*
House of Mirth *'00*
Onegin *'99*
Elizabeth *'98*
Sliding Doors *'97*
Hollow Reed *'95*
Captives *'94*
Bitter Harvest *'93*
The Wedding Gift *'93*
The Lost Language of Cranes *'92*
Truly, Madly, Deeply *'91*
Christabel *'89*

Jose F. Aguayo
Tristana *'70*
Viridiana *'61*

Javier Aguirresarobe
The Others *'01*
The Yellow Fountain *'99*
Fiesta *'95*
Tierra *'95*
Running Out of Time *'94*
Outrage *'93*

Lloyd Ahern (1905-83)
Can't Hardly Wait *'98*
Last Man Standing *'96*
Turbulence *'96*
Wild Bill *'95*
Geronimo: An American Legend *'93*
Trespass *'92*
Miracle on 34th Street *'47*

Lloyd Ahern, II
My Sister's Keeper *'02*
Supernova *'99*
Danielle Steel's Palomino *'91*

Mac Ahlberg (1931-)
Air Rage *'01*
The Wonderful Ice Cream Suit *'98*
Good Burger *'97*
The Second Civil War *'97*
Space Truckers *'97*
The Late Shift *'96*
A Very Brady Sequel *'96*
The Brady Bunch Movie *'95*
Beverly Hills Cop 3 *'94*
My Boyfriend's Back *'93*
Striking Distance *'93*
Innocent Blood *'92*
Oscar *'91*
Robot Jox *'90*
Deepstar Six *'89*
The Horror Show *'89*
Prison *'88*
House 2: The Second Story *'87*
From Beyond *'86*
Ghostwarrior *'86*
House *'86*
Ghoulies *'84*
Prime Risk *'84*
Re-Animator *'84*
Zone Troopers *'84*
Chained Heat *'83*
Metalstorm: The Destruction of Jared Syn *'83*
Young Warriors *'83*
My Tutor *'82*
Parasite *'82*
The Seduction *'82*
Hell Night *'81*
Nocturna *'79*
I, a Woman *'66*

Pierre Aim
Madeline *'98*
Resurrection Man *'97*
Hate *'95*
Cafe au Lait *'94*

Yuzuru Aizawa
Godzilla vs. Megalon *'76*
The Bad Sleep Well *'60*

Robert Alazraki
American Women *'00*
Born Romantic *'00*
Robert Louis Stevenson's St. Ives *'98*
Another 9 1/2 Weeks *'96*
My Father's Glory *'91*
The Old Lady Who Walked in the Sea *'91*
Conseil de Famille *'86*
Love Songs *'85*

Romano Albani
The Sleazy Uncle *'89*
Troll *'86*
Creepers *'85*
Inferno *'80*

Arthur Albert
Max Keeble's Big Move *'01*
Saving Silverman *'01*
Dirty Work *'97*
Beverly Hills Ninja *'96*
Happy Gilmore *'96*
One Night Stand *'95*
You So Crazy *'94*
By the Sword *'93*
Surf Ninjas *'93*
Passed Away *'92*
Heart Condition *'90*
Miss Firecracker *'89*
The Principal *'87*
The Squeeze *'87*
Streets of Gold *'86*
The Boys Next Door *'85*
Odd Jobs *'85*
Night of the Comet *'84*

Maryse Alberti
Get Over It! *'01*
Tape *'01*
Joe Gould's Secret *'00*
Happiness *'98*
Velvet Goldmine *'98*
I Love You, I Love You Not *'97*
Stag *'97*
Crumb *'94*
Deadfall *'93*
Tales of Erotica *'93*
Zebrahead *'92*
Poison *'91*

Jose Luis Alcaine (1938-)
Jealousy *'99*
Blast from the Past *'98*
Two Much *'96*
Jamon, Jamon *'93*
Belle Epoque *'92*
Ay, Carmela! *'90*
Lovers: A True Story *'90*
Tie Me Up! Tie Me Down! *'90*
Twisted Obsession *'90*
Women on the Verge of a Nervous Breakdown *'88*
Rustler's Rhapsody *'85*
Demons in the Garden *'82*

John Alcott
No Way Out *'87*
Under Fire *'83*
Beastmaster *'82*
Fort Apache, the Bronx *'81*
The Shining *'80*
Terror Train *'80*
Barry Lyndon *'75*
A Clockwork Orange *'71*
2001: A Space Odyssey *'68*

Robert Alcott
It's Alive! *'68*
Zontar, the Thing from Venus *'66*

Henri Alekan (1909-2001)
Wings of Desire *'88*
Mayerling *'68*
Topkapi *'64*
Forbidden Fruit *'52*
Anna Karenina *'48*
Beauty and the Beast *'46*

Sepp Allgeier
Triumph of the Will *'34*
Diary of a Lost Girl *'29*

Nestor Almendros (1930-92)
Billy Bathgate *'91*
New York Stories *'89*
Nadine *'87*
Heartburn *'86*
Places in the Heart *'84*
Confidentially Yours *'83*
Pauline at the Beach *'83*
Sophie's Choice *'82*
Still of the Night *'82*
The Blue Lagoon *'80*
The Last Metro *'80*
Kramer vs. Kramer *'79*
Days of Heaven *'78*
Goin' South *'78*
The Green Room *'78*
Love on the Run *'78*
Perceval *'78*
Madame Rosa *'77*
The Man Who Loved Women *'77*
Maitresse *'76*
The Marquise of O *'76*
The Story of Adele H. *'75*
Cockfighter *'74*
Chloe in the Afternoon *'72*
Two English Girls *'72*
The Valley Obscured by the Clouds *'72*
Claire's Knee *'71*
Bed and Board *'70*
The Wild Child *'70*
More *'69*
My Night at Maud's *'69*
Six in Paris *'68*
La Collectionneuse *'67*

Alan Almond
Kevin & Perry Go Large *'00*
Get Real *'99*
My Son the Fanatic *'97*
Brothers in Trouble *'95*
Loaded *'94*

John A. Alonzo (1934-2001)
Deuces Wild *'02*
The Prime Gig *'00*
Lansky *'99*
Letters from a Killer *'98*
The Grass Harp *'95*
Star Trek: Generations *'94*
World War II: When Lions Roared *'94*
The Meteor Man *'93*
Clifford *'92*
Cool World *'92*
Housesitter *'92*
The Guardian *'90*
Internal Affairs *'90*
Navy SEALS *'90*
Physical Evidence *'89*
Steel Magnolias *'89*
Roots: The Gift *'88*
Overboard *'87*
Real Men *'87*
Jo Jo Dancer, Your Life Is Calling *'86*

Nothing in Common '86
The Hit '85
Out of Control '85
No Small Affair '84
Runaway '84
Blue Thunder '83
Cross Creek '83
Scarface '83
Back Roads '81
Zorro, the Gay Blade '81
Tom Horn '80
Norma Rae '79
Casey's Shadow '78
The Cheap Detective '78
Beyond Reason '77
Black Sunday '77
Which Way Is Up? '77
The Bad News Bears '76
I Will, I Will for Now '76
Farewell, My Lovely '75
Once Is Not Enough '75
Chinatown '74
Conrack '74
Lady Sings the Blues '72
Pete 'n' Tillie '72
Sounder '72
Harold and Maude '71
Vanishing Point '71
Bloody Mama '70

Herbert S. Alpert
The Mask '61
A Dangerous Age '57

John Alton (1901-96)
Elmer Gantry '60
The Brothers Karamazov '58
Designing Woman '57
The Catered Affair '56
Slightly Scarlet '56
Tea and Sympathy '56
The Teahouse of the August Moon '56
Big Combo '55
Pearl of the South Pacific '55
Tennessee's Partner '55
Battle Circus '53
An American in Paris '51
Father's Little Dividend '51
Father of the Bride '50
Reign of Terror '49
The Amazing Mr. X '48
He Walked by Night '48
Raw Deal '48
T-Men '47
Courageous Dr. Christian '40

Alex Ameri
The Gore-Gore Girls '72
This Stuff'll Kill Ya! '71
The Wizard of Gore '70

Juan Amoros
Love Can Seriously Damage Your Health '96
Mouth to Mouth '95
Sons of Trinity '95
How to Be a Woman and Not Die in the Attempt '91

Jamie Anderson
Jay and Silent Bob Strike Back '01
The Flintstones in Viva Rock Vegas '00
The Gift '00
Neil Simon's The Odd Couple 2 '98
Small Soldiers '98
The Temptations '98
Grosse Pointe Blank '97
The Juror '96
Man of the House '95
What's Love Got to Do with It? '93
Unlawful Entry '92
Malibu Beach '78
Piranha '78
The Great Texas Dynamite Chase '76
Hollywood Boulevard '76

M.A. Anderson
Cross Examination '32
The Peacock Fan '29

Lucien N. Andriot
Borderline '50
Outpost in Morocco '49
New Orleans '47
The Strange Woman '46
And Then There Were None '45
The Southerner '45
The Fighting Sullivans '42
The Gay Desperado '36

Theo Angell (1962-)
Kept '01
Mom's Outta Sight '01
The Kid with the X-Ray Eyes '99

Yves Angelo
The Accompanist '93
Germinal '93
Un Coeur en Hiver '93
Tous les Matins du Monde '92
Baxter '89

Gregg Araki (1959-)
Totally F***ed Up '94
The Living End '92

Thierry Arbogast
The Crimson Rivers '01
Kiss of the Dragon '01
Woman on Top '00
The Messenger: The Story of Joan of Arc '99
Wing Commander '99
Black Cat, White Cat '98
The Fifth Element '97
She's So Lovely '97
Ridicule '96
The Horseman on the Roof '95
The Professional '94
Ma Saison Preferee '93
La Femme Nikita '91

Arch Archambault
Little Men '98
Count Yorga, Vampire '70

Georges Archambault
Dead End '98
Random Encounter '98
Stalker '98

Simon Archer
The Bachelor '99
Stiff Upper Lips '96

Fernando Arguelles
Bloodhounds '96
Wes Craven Presents Mind Ripper '95
Hidden Assassin '94
Star Time '92

Arthur E. Arling
Strait-Jacket '64
Pillow Talk '59
Man in the Shadow '57
Three for the Show '55
Captain from Castile '47

Arledge Armenaki
Auntie Lee's Meat Pies '92
Club Fed '90
Crack House '89
Howling 5: The Rebirth '89
Blackout '88
Off the Mark '87
Crime Killer '85
Grad Night '81
Avenging Disco Godfather '76

Steve Arnold
Mr. Accident '99
Dating the Enemy '95

Ricardo Aronovich
Celestial Clockwork '94
Christmas Evil '80
Providence '77
Lumiere '76
Murmur of the Heart '71

John Aronson
Beethoven's 3rd '00
Trippin' '99
Gunshy '98
In God's Hands '98
The Haunted Sea '97
Murder in Mind '97
Bloodfist 8: Hard Way Out '96
The Glass Cage '96
Dillinger and Capone '95
Machine Gun Blues '95
Suspect Device '95
Carnosaur 2 '94
White Wolves 2: Legend of the Wild '94

Fernando Arribas
Cannibal Apocalypse '80
The Blood Spattered Bride '72

Yorgos Arvanitis
Signs & Wonders '00
Romance '99
Train of Life '98
Bent '97
Eternity and a Day '97
Someone Else's America '96
Total Eclipse '95
Ulysses' Gaze '95
Landscape in the Mist '88
A Dream of Passion '78
Iphigenia '77
The Travelling Players '75

Jack Asher
The Brides of Dracula '60
The Two Faces of Dr. Jekyll '60
The Hound of the Baskervilles '59
The Mummy '59
The Horror of Dracula '58
The Curse of Frankenstein '57
The Magic Bow '47

Monroe Askins
Napoleon and Samantha '72
Blood of Dracula '57
Sorority Girl '57

William Asman
Sheba, Baby '75
Three on a Meathook '72

Jacques Assuerus
Black Venus '83
Rendez-Moi Ma Peau '81

Sergei Astakhov
Of Freaks and Men '98
Brother '97

Yoram Astrakhan
Shakedown '02
The Doorway '00
Moving Target '00
Plan B '97

Howard Atherton
Hanging Up '99
Deep Rising '98
Lolita '97
Bad Boys '95
Gulliver's Travels '95
Indecent Proposal '93
Mermaids '90
The Boost '88
Fatal Attraction '87

Giorgio Atilli
Awakenings of the Beast '68
At Midnight, I'll Take Your Soul '63

Yushun Atsuta
An Autumn Afternoon '62
Good Morning '59
Tokyo Story '53

Joseph August (1890-1947)
Portrait of Jennie '48
They Were Expendable '45
Gunga Din '39
The Hunchback of Notre Dame '39
The Whole Town's Talking '35
The Toll Gate '20
The Bargain '15

Gordon Avil
Zotz! '62
On Our Merry Way '48

John G. Avildsen (1935-)
Cry Uncle '71
Joe '70

Joaquin Baca-Asay
Two Ninas '00
Coming Soon '99

Jean Bachelet
The Crime of Monsieur Lange '36
The Lower Depths '36

Hanania Baer
Bug Buster '99
Deja Vu '98
Last Summer In the Hamptons '96
The Prince '95
Babyfever '94
Rescue Me '93
Body Language '92
Venice, Venice '92
Ernest Scared Stupid '91
Diving In '90
Eating '90
The Kid Who Loved Christmas '90
The Queen of Mean '90
Elvira, Mistress of the Dark '88
Seven Hours to Judgment '88
Assassination '87
Masters of the Universe '87
Someone to Love '87
Bad Guys '86
Always '85
American Ninja '85
Night Patrol '85
Breakin' '84
Breakin' 2: Electric Boogaloo '84
Cartier Affair '84
Ninja 3: The Domination '84
Echoes '83
Choices '81

Christopher Baffa
Next Friday '00
Idle Hands '99
Baby Face Nelson '97
Lady Killer '97
Suicide Kings '97
True Heart '97
Humanoids from the Deep '96
Sometimes They Come Back ... Again '96
Spectre '96
Criminal Hearts '95
The Death Artist '95
Piranha '95
Sawbones '95
The Crazysitter '94

James R. Bagdonas
National Lampoon's Van Wilder '02
Slackers '02
Brotherhood of Murder '99
Cruel Intentions 2 '99
Love Songs '99
Hidden in America '96
American Heart '92

King Baggot
Boiling Point '93
The Last Starfighter '84
Revenge of the Nerds '84
The Hand '81

John Bailey (1942-)
Divine Secrets of the Ya-Ya Sisterhood '02
The Anniversary Party '01
Antitrust '00
For Love of the Game '99
Forever Mine '99
The Out-of-Towners '99
Always Outnumbered Always Outgunned '98
Living Out Loud '98
As Good As It Gets '97
Extreme Measures '96
Nobody's Fool '94
Groundhog Day '93
In the Line of Fire '93
A Brief History of Time '92
My Blue Heaven '90
The Accidental Tourist '88
Vibes '88
Light of Day '87
Swimming to Cambodia '87
Tough Guys Don't Dance '87
Brighton Beach Memoirs '86
Crossroads '86
Mishima: A Life in Four Chapters '85
Silverado '85
The Pope of Greenwich Village '84
Racing with the Moon '84
The Big Chill '83
Without a Trace '83
Cat People '82
That Championship Season '82
Continental Divide '81
Honky Tonk Freeway '81
Ordinary People '80
American Gigolo '79
Boulevard Nights '79
Premonition '71

Bob Bailin
Family Enforcer '76
The Groove Tube '72

Brydon Baker
The Phantom from 10,000 Leagues '56
Wetbacks '56

Ian Baker
Queen of the Damned '02
The Chamber '96
Fierce Creatures '96
I.Q. '94
Six Degrees of Separation '93
Mr. Baseball '92
Everybody Wins '90
The Punisher '90
The Russia House '90
A Cry in the Dark '88
Roxanne '87
Plenty '85
Iceman '84
Barbarosa '82
The Devil's Playground '76

Walter Bal
Pterodactyl Woman from Beverly Hills '97
Back in Business '96
Precious Find '96

Robert M. "Bob" Baldwin, Jr.
Basket Case 2 '90
Frankenhooker '90
Exterminator '80
Werewolf of Washington '73

Lucien Ballard
Breakheart Pass '76
Drum '76
From Noon Till Three '76
Breakout '75
The Getaway '72
Junior Bonner '72
Ballad of Cable Hogue '70
True Grit '69
The Wild Bunch '69
How Sweet It Is! '68
The Party '68
Will Penny '67
Nevada Smith '66
Sons of Katie Elder '65
Ride the High Country '62
The Parent Trap '61
The Killing '56
Diplomatic Courier '52
Don't Bother to Knock '52
The Undying Monster '42
The Devil Is a Woman '35

Michael Ballhaus (1935-)
The Legend of Bagger Vance '00
What Planet Are You From? '00
Wild Wild West '99
Primary Colors '98
Air Force One '97
Sleepers '96
Outbreak '94
Quiz Show '94
The Age of Innocence '93
I'll Do Anything '93
Bram Stoker's Dracula '92
The Mambo Kings '92
Guilty by Suspicion '91
What about Bob? '91
Goodfellas '90
Postcards from the Edge '90
The Fabulous Baker Boys '89
Big '88
Dirty Rotten Scoundrels '88
The House on Carroll Street '88
The Last Temptation of Christ '88
Working Girl '88
Baja Oklahoma '87
Broadcast News '87
The Glass Menagerie '87
Chinese Roulette '86
The Color of Money '86
Death of a Salesman '86
Under the Cherry Moon '86
After Hours '85
Heartbreakers '84
Old Enough '84
Reckless '84
Sheer Madness '84
Malou '83
Baby It's You '82
Ruby's Dream '82
The Marriage of Maria Braun '79
Despair '78
The Stationmaster's Wife '77
I Only Want You to Love Me '76
Mother Kusters Goes to Heaven '76
Satan's Brew '76
Cold Blood '75
Fox and His Friends '75
The Bitter Tears of Petra von Kant '72
Beware of a Holy Whore '70
Whity '70

Lionel Banes
Fiend without a Face '58
The Haunted Strangler '58

Larry Banks
The Substitute 2: School's Out '97
The Show '95
Erotique '94
Fly by Night '93
Juice '92

Diane Baratier
Autumn Tale '98
A Summer's Tale '96
Rendezvous in Paris '95

Leonida Barboni
The Rover '67
After the Fox '66
Divorce—Italian Style '62
Joyful Laughter '60
Passionate Thief '60
Submarine Attack '54

George Barnes (1893-1953)
The Road to Bali '53
The War of the Worlds '53
Riding High '50
Samson and Delilah '50
Force of Evil '49
Emperor Waltz '48
Sinbad, the Sailor '47
Sister Kenny '46
The Bells of St. Mary's '45
The Spanish Main '45
Spellbound '45
Frenchman's Creek '44
Jane Eyre '44
None But the Lonely Heart '44
Mr. Lucky '43
Once Upon a Honeymoon '42
Meet John Doe '41
That Uncertain Feeling '41
Rebecca '40
Jesse James '39
Stanley and Livingstone '39
The Black Legion '37
Marked Woman '37
Gold Diggers of 1935 '35
Dames '34
Footlight Parade '33
Street Scene '31
Raffles '30
Bulldog Drummond '29
Our Dancing Daughters '28
Sadie Thompson '28
Son of the Sheik '26
The Eagle '25
Peg o' My Heart '22
Dangerous Hours '19

Michael Barrett
Skeletons in the Closet '00
The Suburbans '99
Safe Men '98
Finding North '97

Mario Barroso
The Convent '95
God's Comedy '95
Abraham's Valley '93

Michael Barrow
Row Your Boat '98
Whatever '98

Caught *'96*
Sunday *'96*
Wigstock: The Movie *'95*
Heavy *'94*

Andrzej Bartkowiak (1950-)
Thirteen Days *'00*
Gossip *'99*
Lethal Weapon 4 *'98*
U.S. Marshals *'98*
Dante's Peak *'97*
The Devil's Advocate *'97*
The Mirror Has Two Faces *'96*
Jade *'95*
Species *'95*
A Good Man in Africa *'94*
Losing Isaiah *'94*
Speed *'94*
Falling Down *'93*
Guilty as Sin *'93*
A Stranger Among Us *'92*
Off and Running *'90*
Q & A *'90*
Family Business *'89*
Twins *'88*
Beyond Innocence *'87*
Nuts *'87*
The Morning After *'86*
Power *'86*
Prizzi's Honor *'85*
Garbo Talks *'84*
Daniel *'83*
Terms of Endearment *'83*
Deathtrap *'82*
The Verdict *'82*
Prince of the City *'81*
Deadly Hero *'75*

James Bartle
Inherit the Wind *'99*
Dead Heart *'96*
Twisted *'96*
Hammers over the Anvil *'91*
My Best Friend Is a Vampire *'88*
The Good Wife *'86*
The Quiet Earth *'85*

John Bartley
Dean Koontz's Black River *'01*
See Spot Run *'01*
A Cooler Climate *'99*
Disturbing Behavior *'98*
Tricks *'97*

Adolfo Bartoli
The Horrible Dr. Bones *'00*
Octopus *'00*
Bloodstorm: Subspecies 4 *'98*
The Creeps *'97*
Rudyard Kipling's the Second Jungle Book: Mowgli and Baloo *'97*
Forbidden Zone: Alien Abduction *'96*
Head of the Family *'96*
Magic in the Mirror: Fowl Play *'96*
Spellbreaker: Secret of the Leprechauns *'96*
Vampire Journals *'96*
Puppet Master 5: The Final Chapter *'94*
Bad Channels *'92*
Netherworld *'90*
Puppet Master 3: Toulon's Revenge *'90*

J.E. Bash
Stealth Fighter *'99*
Storm Trooper *'98*

Miroslaw Baszak
Four Days *'99*
Naked City: Justice with a Bullet *'98*
Rescuers: Stories of Courage—Two Couples *'98*
Rescuers: Stories of Courage "Two Women" *'97*
Eclipse *'94*

Joe Batac
Raiders of the Sun *'92*
The Siege of Firebase Gloria *'89*

Gianlorenzo Battaglia
Men Men Men *'95*
Demons 2 *'87*
Demons *'86*
A Blade in the Dark *'83*

Jurgen Baum
The Dentist 2: Brace Yourself *'98*
American Vampire *'97*
Flypaper *'97*
The Big Fall *'96*
Phat Beach *'96*
One Man's Justice *'95*
Slumber Party Massacre 3 *'90*

Mario Bava (1914-80)
Twitch of the Death Nerve *'71*
Hatchet for the Honeymoon *'70*
The Girl Who Knew Too Much *'63*
Black Sunday *'60*
The Giant of Marathon *'60*
Hercules *'58*
The Day the Sky Exploded *'57*
I Vampiri *'56*

Bojan Bazelli
Dangerous Beauty *'98*
Sugar Hill *'94*
Surviving the Game *'94*
Body Snatchers *'93*
Boxing Helena *'93*
Kalifornia *'93*
Deep Cover *'92*
The Fear Inside *'92*
The Rapture *'91*
Curiosity Kills *'90*
King of New York *'90*
Somebody Has to Shoot the Picture *'90*
Big Man on Campus *'89*
Haunting of Sarah Hardy *'89*
Tapeheads *'89*
Patty Hearst *'88*
Pumpkinhead *'88*
China Girl *'87*

Alfonso Beato
Ghost World *'01*
Price of Glory *'00*
All About My Mother *'99*
Orfeu *'99*
The Informant *'97*
Live Flesh *'97*
Pronto *'97*
The Flower of My Secret *'95*
The Wrong Man *'93*
Enid Is Sleeping *'90*
Great Balls of Fire *'89*
The Big Easy *'87*
Happily Ever After *'86*
Circle of Power *'83*
Boss' Son *'78*
Antonio Das Mortes *'68*

Jack Beckett
Blood Legacy *'73*
Please Don't Eat My Mother *'72*

Terry Bedford
Jabberwocky *'77*
Monty Python and the Holy Grail *'75*

Dion Beebe
Charlotte Gray *'01*
Along for the Ride *'00*
Holy Smoke *'99*
Praise *'98*
Floating Life *'95*
Crush *'93*

Lloyd Beebe
Charlie, the Lonesome Cougar *'67*
Nikki, the Wild Dog of the North *'61*

Paul Beeson
Jane & the Lost City *'87*
Unidentified Flying Oddball *'79*
Candleshoe *'78*
The Littlest Horse Thieves *'76*
The Freakmaker *'73*
To Sir, with Love *'67*
Die, Monster, Die! *'65*

Friedl Behn-Grund
The Murderers Are Among Us *'46*
The Murderers are Among Us *'46*

Andreas Bellis
In the Cold of the Night *'89*
The Wind *'87*

Ted C. Bemiller
Heavy Traffic *'73*
Fritz the Cat *'72*

Youssef Ben Youssef
The Silences of the Palace *'94*
Man of Ashes *'86*

Richard Benda
Sworn to Justice *'97*
Slaughterhouse *'87*

Henning Bendtsen
Gertrud *'64*
Ordet *'55*

Peter Benison
Cruel and Unusual *'01*
Big and Hairy *'98*
Jack Higgins' The Windsor Protocol *'97*
Jack Higgins' Thunder Point *'97*

Mark Benjamin
White Boyz *'99*
Slam *'98*

Georges Benoit
The Baker's Wife *'33*
Regeneration *'15*

Michael A. Benson
Universal Soldier: The Return *'99*
Nowhere to Run *'93*

Gabriel Beristain
Blade II *'02*
Molly *'99*
Russell Mulcahy's Tale of the Mummy *'99*
The Spanish Prisoner *'97*
Trial and Error *'96*
Dolores Claiborne *'94*
Greedy *'94*
Blood In ... Blood Out: Bound by Honor *'93*
The Distinguished Gentleman *'92*
Caravaggio *'86*

Kristian Bernier
Partners *'99*
Sugar Town *'99*
Six-String Samurai *'98*

Steven Bernstein
Corky Romano *'01*
The Forsaken *'01*
Scary Movie 2 *'01*
The Wood *'99*
Mr. Jealousy *'98*
The Waterboy *'98*
Half-Baked *'97*
Murder at 1600 *'97*
Bulletproof *'96*
Underworld *'96*
Curdled *'95*
Kicking and Screaming *'95*
Moondance *'95*
The Secretary *'94*
Like Water for Chocolate *'93*

Gonzalo F. Berridi
Lovers of the Arctic Circle *'98*
The Red Squirrel *'93*

John Berrie
The Peacekeeper *'98*
A Young Connecticut Yankee in King Arthur's Court *'95*
Young Ivanhoe *'95*

Ross Berryman
Tycus *'98*
Living in Peril *'97*
Chameleon *'95*
Gold Diggers: The Secret of Bear Mountain *'95*
The Hard Truth *'94*
Playmaker *'94*

Renato Berta
Kippur *'00*
Kadosh *'99*
Same Old Song *'97*
Party *'96*

Voyage to the Beginning of the World *'96*
May Fools *'90*
Twister *'89*
Au Revoir les Enfants *'87*
L'Annee des Meduses *'86*
Full Moon in Paris *'84*
L'Homme Blesse *'83*
Messidor *'77*
Jonah Who Will Be 25 in the Year 2000 *'76*
Charles: Dead or Alive *'69*

Thom Best
Ginger Snaps *'01*
Ride the Wild Fields *'00*
Grizzly Falls *'99*
The Boys Club *'96*

Adrian Biddle
The Mummy Returns *'01*
102 Dalmatians *'00*
The Mummy *'99*
The World Is Not Enough *'99*
Holy Man *'98*
The Butcher Boy *'97*
Event Horizon *'97*
Fierce Creatures *'96*
101 Dalmatians *'96*
Judge Dredd *'95*
Thelma & Louise *'91*
The Tall Guy *'89*
Willow *'88*
The Princess Bride *'87*
Aliens *'86*

Luca Bigazzi
Bread and Tulips *'01*
Kiss of Fire *'98*
Luna e L'Altra *'96*
Lamerica *'95*

Joseph Biroc (1903-)
Airplane 2: The Sequel *'82*
Hammett *'82*
...All the Marbles *'81*
Airplane! *'80*
Beyond the Poseidon Adventure *'79*
The Choirboys *'77*
The Duchess and the Dirtwater Fox *'76*
The Hustle *'75*
Blazing Saddles *'74*
The Longest Yard *'74*
The Towering Inferno *'74*
Emperor of the North Pole *'73*
Ulzana's Raid *'72*
Brian's Song *'71*
Escape from the Planet of the Apes *'71*
The Grissom Gang *'71*
The Organization *'71*
Too Late the Hero *'70*
The Killing of Sister George *'69*
Whatever Happened to Aunt Alice? *'69*
The Detective *'68*
Lady in Cement *'68*
Enter Laughing *'67*
Tony Rome *'67*
Who's Minding the Mint? *'67*
The Russians Are Coming, the Russians Are Coming *'66*
The Flight of the Phoenix *'65*
Hush, Hush, Sweet Charlotte *'65*
Kitten with a Whip *'64*
Bye, Bye, Birdie *'63*
Toys in the Attic *'63*
Under the Yum-Yum Tree *'63*
Viva Las Vegas *'63*
The Devil at 4 O'Clock *'61*
Ice Palace *'60*
13 Ghosts *'60*
The Bat *'59*
The FBI Story *'59*
Verboten! *'59*
The Amazing Colossal Man *'57*
China Gate *'57*
The Ride Back *'57*
Attack! *'56*
Donovan's Brain *'53*
Tall Texan *'53*
Cry Danger *'51*

Mrs. Mike *'49*
On Our Merry Way *'48*
Magic Town *'47*
It's a Wonderful Life *'46*

Billy (G.W.) Bitzer (1872-1944)
Battle of the Sexes *'28*
America *'24*
Orphans of the Storm *'21*
Way Down East *'20*
Broken Blossoms *'19*
Intolerance *'16*
The Birth of a Nation *'15*

Peter Biziou
Unfaithful *'02*
The Truman Show *'98*
Richard III *'95*
The Road to Wellville *'94*
In the Name of the Father *'93*
City of Joy *'92*
Damage *'92*
Rosencrantz & Guildenstern Are Dead *'90*
Mississippi Burning *'88*
A World Apart *'88*
9 1/2 Weeks *'86*
Another Country *'84*
Pink Floyd: The Wall *'82*
Time Bandits *'81*
Monty Python's Life of Brian *'79*
Bugsy Malone *'76*

Hilding Bladh
Invasion of the Animal People *'62*
Dreams *'55*

Stephen Blake
Beverly Hills Vamp *'88*
Sorority Babes in the Slimeball Bowl-A-Rama *'87*

Ken Blakey
Extreme Honor *'01*
Agent Red *'00*
Rangers *'00*
The Stray *'00*
Terror Tract *'00*
Final Voyage *'99*
Land of the Free *'98*
Executive Target *'97*
Little Bigfoot *'96*
Pure Danger *'96*
Riot *'96*
Rage *'95*
The Sweeper *'95*
Cyber-Tracker *'93*

Larry Blanford
Kill Shot *'01*
Operation Sandman: Warriors in Hell *'00*
For Which He Stands *'98*

Patrick Blossier
The Chambermaid on the Titanic *'97*
Mad City *'97*
Innocent Lies *'95*
Revenge of the Musketeers *'94*
Jacquot *'91*
Dr. Petiot *'90*
Music Box *'89*
Betrayed *'88*
Sorceress *'88*
Vagabond *'85*

Ralf Bode (1942-2001)
Boys and Girls *'00*
Annie *'99*
Sarah, Plain and Tall: Winter's End *'99*
A Simple Wish *'97*
Sink or Swim *'97*
The Big Green *'95*
A Streetcar Named Desire *'95*
Don Juan DeMarco *'94*
Safe Passage *'94*
George Balanchine's The Nutcracker *'93*
Gypsy *'93*
Made in America *'93*
Leaving Normal *'92*
Love Field *'91*
One Good Cop *'91*
Cousins *'89*
Uncle Buck *'89*
The Accused *'88*

Distant Thunder *'88*
Big Town *'87*
Critical Condition *'86*
Violets Are Blue *'86*
The Whoopee Boys *'86*
First Born *'84*
Gorky Park *'83*
A Little Sex *'82*
A Long Way Home *'81*
Raggedy Man *'81*
Coal Miner's Daughter *'80*
Dressed to Kill *'80*
Rich Kids *'79*
Saturday Night Fever *'77*
Foreplay *'75*

Jean Boffety
Vincent, Francois, Paul and the Others *'76*
Cesar & Rosalie *'72*

Haskell Boggs
Bonanza: The Return *'93*
The Bellboy *'60*
I Married a Monster from Outer Space *'58*
Teacher's Pet *'58*
Rock-A-Bye Baby *'57*

Oliver Bokelberg
Harvest *'99*
Last Breath *'96*

Alun Bollinger
Forgotten Silver *'96*
The Frighteners *'96*
Heavenly Creatures *'94*
A Soldier's Tale *'91*
Came a Hot Friday *'85*
Goodbye Pork Pie *'81*

Michael Bonvillain
A Texas Funeral *'99*
Saints and Sinners *'95*
The Desperate Trail *'94*
Amongst Friends *'93*
When the Bough Breaks *'93*

Lamar Boren
The Spy Who Loved Me *'77*
Brewster McCloud *'70*

Rick Bota
Valentine *'01*
House on Haunted Hill *'99*
Barb Wire *'96*
The Glimmer Man *'96*
The Companion *'94*
Tales from the Crypt Presents Demon Knight *'94*
Article 99 *'92*
Bloodfist 3: Forced to Fight *'92*
Pure Country *'92*
Wheels of Terror *'90*

David Boulton
Children of the Damned *'63*
The Haunting *'63*

Jean (Yves, Georges) Bourgoin (1913-)
The Counterfeit Traitor *'62*
The Longest Day *'62*
Black Orpheus *'58*
Mon Oncle *'58*
Mr. Arkadin *'55*
Dedee d'Anvers *'49*
Voyage Suprise *'46*
La Marseillaise *'37*

Richard Bowen
Head Above Water *'96*
A Smile Like Yours *'96*
Fair Game *'95*
Major Payne *'95*
The Little Rascals *'94*
Animal Behavior *'89*
The Wizard of Loneliness *'88*
Stacking *'87*
Belizaire the Cajun *'86*
Street Music *'81*

Russell Boyd
American Outlaws *'01*
Company Man *'00*
Dr. Dolittle *'98*
Liar Liar *'96*
Tin Cup *'96*
Operation Dumbo Drop *'95*
Cobb *'94*
Forever Young *'92*
The Killing Beach *'92*
White Men Can't Jump *'92*
Sweet Talker *'91*

Almost an Angel '90
In Country '89
Crocodile Dundee 2 '88
The Rescue '88
High Tide '87
Crocodile Dundee '86
Burke & Wills '85
Mrs. Soffel '84
Phar Lap '84
A Soldier's Story '84
Dawn! '83
Tender Mercies '83
Starstruck '82
The Year of Living Dangerously '82
Gallipoli '81
Chain Reaction '80
The Last Wave '77
Picnic at Hanging Rock '75

Charles P. Boyle
Old Yeller '57
The Great Locomotive Chase '56
Gunsmoke '53
Tomahawk '51
She Wore a Yellow Ribbon '49
Fun & Fancy Free '47

William Bradford
Trail to San Antone '47
Along the Navaho Trail '45
Don't Fence Me In '45
Fighting Seabees '44

Henry Braham
Crush '02
Shackleton '02
Invisible Circus '00
The Land Girls '98
Shooting Fish '98
Waking Ned Devine '98
For Roseanna '96
Solitaire for 2 '94

Russ Brandt
The Haunting of Hell House '99
Don't Be a Menace to South Central While Drinking Your Juice in the Hood '95
Excessive Force 2: Force on Force '95
Playback '95
H.P. Lovecraft's Necronomicon: Book of the Dead '93

Ulf Brantas
Show Me Love '99
The Women on the Roof '89

Denise Brassard
Deal of a Lifetime '99
St. Patrick's Day '99

Sylvain Brault
2001: A Space Travesty '00
The Boys '97
Jack London's The Call of the Wild '97
Rowing Through '96
Sworn Enemies '96
A Paper Wedding '89

Elwood "Woody" Bredell
The Female Jungle '56
The Inspector General '49
The Killers '46
Can't Help Singing '45
Lady on a Train '45
His Butler's Sister '44
Phantom Lady '44
The Amazing Mrs. Holiday '43
Hold That Ghost '41
Man Made Monster '41
Black Friday '40
The Invisible Woman '40
The Mummy's Hand '40

Brian J. Breheny
The Other Side of Heaven '02
When Good Ghouls Go Bad '01
Siam Sunset '99
That's the Way I Like It '99
Heaven's Burning '97
The Adventures of Priscilla, Queen of the Desert '94

Jochen Breitenstein
The Boogey Man '80
Cocaine Cowboys '79

Jules Brenner
1969 '89
Return of the Living Dead '85
Salem's Lot '79
Cornbread, Earl & Me '75
Dillinger '73
Johnny Got His Gun '71

David Bridges
Big City Blues '99
End of Summer '97
Crosscut '95
Painted Hero '95
Payback '94

Uta Briesewitz
Session 9 '01
Love Stinks '99
Next Stop, Wonderland '98

Robert Brinkmann (1962-)
Sugar & Spice '01
Screwed '00
The Cable Guy '96
The Truth about Cats and Dogs '96
The Beverly Hillbillies '93
Encino Man '92
Shout '91
Mirror, Mirror '90
U2: Rattle and Hum '88
Kandyland '87

Norbert Brodine
Boomerang '47
13 Rue Madeleine '46
House on 92nd Street '45
Topper Returns '41
Of Mice and Men '39
Libeled Lady '36

Robert J. Bronner
7 Faces of Dr. Lao '63
Pocketful of Miracles '61
Where the Boys Are '60
Jailhouse Rock '57

James S. Brown, Jr. (-1949)
The Devil Bat's Daughter '46
Strangler of the Swamp '46

Joseph Brun
The 300 Year Weekend '71
Odds Against Tomorrow '59
The Joe Louis Story '53

Michael Bucher
The Mating Habits of the Earthbound Human '99
My Brother's War '97

Bobby Bukowski
Crime and Punishment in Suburbia '00
Arlington Road '99
The Minus Man '99
Going All the Way '97
If These Walls Could Talk '96
The Last Time I Committed Suicide '96
Til There Was You '96
The Tie That Binds '95
Tom and Huck '95
Holy Matrimony '94
Search and Destroy '94
Golden Gate '93
Household Saints '93
Ethan Frome '92
Shakes the Clown '92
Men of Respect '91
Thousand Pieces of Gold '91
Anna '87
Kiss Daddy Goodnight '87

Leonce-Henri Burel
Pickpocket '59
A Man Escaped '57
Diary of a Country Priest '50
Napoleon '27
The Torture of Silence '17

Don Burgess
Spider-Man '02
Cast Away '00
What Lies Beneath '00
Contact '97
The Evening Star '96
Forget Paris '95
Forrest Gump '94
Richie Rich '94
Josh and S.A.M. '93
Mo' Money '92
Blind Fury '90
The Court Martial of Jackie Robinson '90
Under the Boardwalk '89
World Gone Wild '88
Death Before Dishonor '87
Night Stalker '87
Summer Camp Nightmare '86
Ruckus '81

Robert Burks (1910-68)
Waterhole #3 '67
A Patch of Blue '65
Marnie '64
The Birds '63
The Music Man '62
The Great Impostor '61
The Rat Race '60
Black Orchid '59
But Not for Me '59
North by Northwest '59
Vertigo '58
The Man Who Knew Too Much '56
The Wrong Man '56
To Catch a Thief '55
The Trouble with Harry '55
Dial "M" for Murder '54
Rear Window '54
The Desert Song '53
Hondo '53
I Confess '53
The Enforcer '51
Strangers on a Train '51
Beyond the Forest '49
The Fountainhead '49

Hans Burman
Open Your Eyes '97
Thesis '96
Guantanamera '95
Why Do They Call It Love When They Mean Sex? '92

David Burr
Crocodile Dundee in Los Angeles '01
Komodo '99
Paperback Hero '99
Escape: Human Cargo '98
Joey '98
Wild America '97
The Phantom '96
Race the Sun '96

Dan Burstall
Under the Gun '95
Crime Broker '94
Ladybugs '92
Kangaroo '86
Squizzy Taylor '84

Thomas Burstyn
Deadlocked '00
Where the Money Is '00
When Trumpets Fade '98
City of Industry '96
Crazy Horse '96
Dead Silence '96
Magic in the Water '95
Andre '94
The Surgeon '94
Arctic Blue '93
Toy Soldiers '91
Cheetah '89
Cold Front '89
Promised a Miracle '88
Broken Vows '87
Ford: The Man & the Machine '87
Foxfire '87
Native Son '86
Dark of the Night '85
Heavenly Bodies '84

Geoff Burton
The Beast '96
Brilliant Lies '96
Sorrento Beach '95
Sirens '94
The Sum of Us '94
Wide Sargasso Sea '92
Romero '89
The Time Guardian '87
The Year My Voice Broke '87
Midnite Spares '85
Blue Fin '78
Fourth Wish '75

Stephen Burum (1940-)
Life or Something Like It '02
Mission to Mars '00
Mystery Men '99
Snake Eyes '98
Father's Day '96
Mission: Impossible '96
The Shadow '94
Carlito's Way '93
Hoffa '92
Man Trouble '92
Raising Cain '92
He Said, She Said '91
Casualties of War '89
The War of the Roses '89
Arthur 2: On the Rocks '88
The Untouchables '87
The Bride '85
8 Million Ways to Die '85
St. Elmo's Fire '85
Body Double '84
The Entity '83
The Outsiders '83
Rumble Fish '83
Something Wicked This Way Comes '83
Uncommon Valor '83
The Escape Artist '82
Death Valley '81

Dick Bush
The Man in the Attic '94
Shadowhunter '93
Son of the Pink Panther '93
Switch '91
Little Monsters '89
Staying Together '89
The Lair of the White Worm '88
Assault and Matrimony '87
The Quick and the Dead '87
The Journey of Natty Gann '85
Crimes of Passion '84
The Philadelphia Experiment '84
Curse of the Pink Panther '83
Trail of the Pink Panther '82
Victor/Victoria '82
The Fan '81
One Trick Pony '80
The Legacy '79
Yanks '79
The Hound of the Baskervilles '77
Sorcerer '77
In Celebration '75
Tommy '75
Mahler '74
Phase 4 '74
Dracula A.D. 1972 '72
Savage Messiah '72
The Blood on Satan's Claw '71
Twins of Evil '71
When Dinosaurs Ruled the Earth '70

Bill Butler
Frailty '02
Passing Glory '99
Deceiver '97
Don King: Only in America '97
Anaconda '96
Flipper '96
Beethoven's 2nd '93
Cop and a Half '93
Sniper '92
Hot Shots! '91
Graffiti Bridge '90
Biloxi Blues '88
Child's Play '88
Wildfire '88
Big Trouble '86
Beer '85
Rocky 4 '85
A Streetcar Named Desire '84
The Sting 2 '83
The Thorn Birds '83
Rocky 3 '82
The Night the Lights Went Out in Georgia '81
Stripes '81
Can't Stop the Music '80
It's My Turn '80
Ice Castles '79
Rocky 2 '79
Capricorn One '78
Damien: Omen 2 '78
Grease '78
Demon Seed '77
Mary White '77
Raid on Entebbe '77
Bingo Long Traveling All-Stars & Motor Kings '76
Lipstick '76
Jaws '75
One Flew Over the Cuckoo's Nest '75
The Conversation '74
The Execution of Private Slovik '74
The Return of Count Yorga '71
The Rain People '69

Michael C. Butler
Cannonball Run '81
Smokey and the Bandit 2 '80
Jaws 2 '78

Taylor Byars
Shame '61
Teenage Monster '57

Frank Byers
Jackie, Ethel, Joan: The Kennedy Women '01
Kiss Toledo Goodbye '00
Having Our Say: The Delany Sisters' First 100 Years '99
Ride '98
Shiloh '97
Trigger Happy '96
Archie: Return to Riverdale '90

Bobby Byrne
The Lemon Sisters '90
Bull Durham '88
Stealing Home '88
Sixteen Candles '84
The Villain '79
Blue Collar '78
The End '78
Hooper '78
Smokey and the Bandit '77

John Cabrera
Hell of the Living Dead '83
Conan the Barbarian '82
Call of the Wild '72

Duke Callaghan
Conan the Barbarian '82
Jeremiah Johnson '72

Thomas Callaway
Earth vs. the Spider '01
She Creature '01
Mach 2 '00
Submerged '00
Caught Up '98
Amityville Dollhouse '96
Night of the Scarecrow '95
Cartel '90
Steel and Lace '90
Action U.S.A. '89
Lady Avenger '89
Assault of the Killer Bimbos '88
Slave Girls from Beyond Infinity '87
Slumber Party Massacre 2 '87

Antonio Calvache
In the Bedroom '01
Broken Vessels '98
I Got the Hook-Up '98

Maurizio Calvesi
Up at the Villa '00
Nerolio '96
Acla's Descent into Floristella '87

Paul Cameron
Swordfish '01
Gone in 60 Seconds '00
The Last Supper '96

John Campbell
Just One Night '00
Change of Heart '98
Reach the Rock '98
Rough Magic '95
Even Cowgirls Get the Blues '94
Imaginary Crimes '94
My Own Private Idaho '91

Yves Cape
Humanity '99
Ma Vie en Rose '97

Robert Caramico
KISS Meets the Phantom of the Park '78
Slithis '78
Eaten Alive '76
Blackenstein '73
Lemora, Lady Dracula '73
Octaman '71
Orgy of the Dead '65

Jack Cardiff (1914-)
Million Dollar Mystery '87
Tai-Pan '86
Cat's Eye '85
Rambo: First Blood, Part 2 '85
Conan the Destroyer '84
The Far Pavilions '84
Scandalous '84
The Wicked Lady '83
The Dogs of War '81
Ghost Story '81
The Awakening '80
Avalanche Express '79
The Fifth Musketeer '79
A Man, a Woman, and a Bank '79
Death on the Nile '78
The Prince and the Pauper '78
Ride a Wild Pony '75
The Girl on a Motorcycle '68
War and Peace '68
Fanny '61
The Vikings '58
Legend of the Lost '57
The Prince and the Showgirl '57
The Brave One '56
War and Peace '56
The Barefoot Contessa '54
The Master of Ballantrae '53
The African Queen '51
Pandora and the Flying Dutchman '51
Under Capricorn '49
The Red Shoes '48
Black Narcissus '47
Stairway to Heaven '46
The Four Feathers '39
Wings of the Morning '37
As You Like It '36
Last Days of Pompeii '35

Carlo Carlini
Autopsy '74
Generale Della Rovere '60
I Vitelloni '53

Russell Carpenter
Shallow Hal '01
Charlie's Angels '00
The Negotiator '98
Money Talks '97
Titanic '97
The Indian in the Cupboard '95
True Lies '94
Hard Target '93
The Lawnmower Man '92
Pet Sematary 2 '92
Solar Crisis '92
The Perfect Weapon '91
Death Warrant '90
Cameron's Closet '89
Critters 2: The Main Course '88
The Lady in White '88
The Wizard of Speed and Time '88
Sole Survivor '84

Ellis W. Carter
Diary of a Madman '63
Twice-Told Tales '63
Curse of the Undead '59
The Incredible Shrinking Man '57
Underworld Scandal '47

James L. Carter
ZigZag '02
My Dog Skip '99
Phoenix '98
Gunfighter's Moon '96
Ruby Jean and Joe '96
Convict Cowboy '95
Destiny Turns on the Radio '95

The Last Ride '94
One False Move '91
Back to Back '90
Playroom '90
Spaced Invaders '90
Leatherface: The Texas Chainsaw Massacre 3 '89
Deadly Weapon '88
In Dangerous Company '88
Terminal Entry '87
Paradise Motel '84
Don't Answer the Phone '80
Home Movies '79

Walter Carvalho
Behind the Sun '01
Central Station '98
Foreign Land '95

Alan Caso
Another Woman's Husband '00
Reindeer Games '00
Running Mates '00
Muppets from Space '99
George Wallace '97
Top of the World '97
Ed '96
The Good Old Boys '95
Stepfather 3: Father's Day '92
84 Charlie MoPic '89

Francois Catonne
My Life and Times with Antonin Artaud '93
Indochine '92

Sarah Cawley
Oxygen '99
Mercy '96
Because of You '95
A Reason to Believe '95

Eric Cayla
The Sign of Four '01
The Hound of the Baskervilles '00
Karmina '96
Le Sexe des Etoiles '93
Necromancer: Satan's Servant '88

Vanja Cernjul
American Psycho 2: All American Girl '02
Ed Gein '01

Christopher Challis
Top Secret! '84
Evil under the Sun '82
The Mirror Crack'd '80
S.O.S. Titanic '79
Force 10 from Navarone '78
The Deep '77
The Little Prince '74
Mary, Queen of Scots '71
The Private Life of Sherlock Holmes '70
Chitty Chitty Bang Bang '68
Two for the Road '67
The Long Ships '64
A Shot in the Dark '64
Damn the Defiant '62
The Grass Is Greener '61
Sink the Bismarck '60
Angels One Five '54
Genevieve '53

Caroline Champetier
Lush '01
Alice et Martin '98
Dry Cleaning '97
A Single Girl '96
Ponette '95
Helas pour Moi '94
La Sentinelle '92
The Disenchanted '90
Aria '88

Tom Chaney
Mosquito '95
Frostbiter: Wrath of the Wendigo '94

Gu Changwei (1957-)
Devils on the Doorstep '00
Hurlyburly '98
The Gingerbread Man '97
Farewell My Concubine '93
Ju Dou '90
Life on a String '90
Red Sorghum '87

Michael Chapman (1935-)
Evolution '01
The Watcher '00
The Story of Us '99
White River '99
Six Days, Seven Nights '98
Primal Fear '96
Space Jam '96
The Fugitive '93
Rising Sun '93
Whispers in the Dark '92
Doc Hollywood '91
Kindergarten Cop '90
Quick Change '90
Ghostbusters 2 '89
Gotham '88
Scrooged '88
Shoot to Kill '88
The Lost Boys '87
The Man with Two Brains '83
Dead Men Don't Wear Plaid '82
Personal Best '82
Raging Bull '80
Hardcore '79
Wanderers '79
Fingers '78
Invasion of the Body Snatchers '78
The Last Waltz '78
The Arab Conspiracy '76
The Front '76
Taxi Driver '76
The White Dawn '75
The Last Detail '73

Ron Chapman
Class of Nuke 'Em High 3: The Good, the Bad and the Subhumanoid '94
Class of Nuke 'Em High 2: Subhumanoid Meltdown '91
Shock 'Em Dead '90

Dominique Chapuis (1948-2001)
Mina Tannenbaum '93
Pas Tres Catholique '93
The Little Thief '89
Sugar Cane Alley '83

Rodney Charters
Intern '00
Blind Faith '98
Kull the Conqueror '97
Frame by Frame '95
Sleepwalkers '92
Psycho 4: The Beginning '90

Chuy Chavez
Chuck & Buck '00
Star Maps '97

Claudio Chea
Pinero '01
Hendrix '00
Execution of Justice '99
Free of Eden '98
Bitter Sugar '96

Enrique Chediak
3 A.M. '01
Boiler Room '00
Songcatcher '99
Desert Blue '98
The Faculty '98
Frogs for Snakes '98
Hurricane Streets '96

Carolyn Chen
The Crow: Salvation '00
Entropy '99

Yiu-tsou Cheung
The Legend of Drunken Master '94
Police Story '85

Steven Chivers
High Heels and Low Lifes '01
Highlander: The Final Dimension '94
Dust Devil '93

Alain Choquart
Boesman & Lena '00
Capitaine Conan '96
L.627 '92

James Chressanthis
Brian's Song '01
Life with Judy Garland—Me and My Shadows '01
Judas Kiss '98
Urban Legend '98
Dangerous Relations '93

Chen Ching Chu
Chinese Connection '73
Fists of Fury '73

Fabio Cianchetti
The Triumph of Love '01
Besieged '98

Richard Ciupka
Atlantic City '81
Ilsa, the Tigress of Siberia '79

Josep Civit
A House in the Hills '93
Iguana '89
Anguish '88

Richard Clabaugh
Deep Core '00
Escape under Pressure '00
Phantoms '97
The Prophecy 2: Ashtown '97
Children of the Corn 4: The Gathering '96
No Way Back '96
Plato's Run '96
The Prophecy '95
American Yakuza '94
Necromancer: Satan's Servant '88

Curtis Clark
Dominick & Eugene '88
Extremities '86
Sesame Street Presents: Follow That Bird '85

Tony Clark
Dance Me to My Song '98
The Quiet Room '96
Alien Visitor '95

Charles Clarke
Flaming Star '60
The Hunters '58
Carousel '56
Suddenly '54
Captain from Castile '47
Miracle on 34th Street '47
Guadalcanal Diary '43
The Cat and the Fiddle '34
Tarzan and His Mate '34

Denys Clerval
Erendira '83
Mississippi Mermaid '69
Stolen Kisses '68

Robert C. Cline
Flaming Bullets '45
I Accuse My Parents '45
Boss of Rawhide '44
The Monster Maker '44
The Black Raven '43

Wilfrid M. Cline
The Giant Gila Monster '59
The Killer Shrews '59
Calamity Jane '53

Ghislan Cloquet (1925-82)
Four Friends '81
I Sent a Letter to My Love '81
Tess '80
Love and Death '75
Donkey Skin '70
A Gentle Woman '69
Marry Me, Marry Me '69
The Young Girls of Rochefort '68
Mouchette '67
Mickey One '65
The Fire Within '64
Belle Americaine '61
Le Trou '59
Girl in His Pocket '57

William Clothier (1903-96)
Train Robbers '73
Big Jake '71
The Cheyenne Social Club '70
Chisum '70
Rio Lobo '70
The Undefeated '69
Bandolero! '68
The Devil's Brigade '68
Firecreek '68
Hellfighters '68
The War Wagon '67
The Way West '67
The Rare Breed '66
Shenandoah '65
Cheyenne Autumn '64
Donovan's Reef '63
McLintock! '63
The Man Who Shot Liberty Valance '62
Merrill's Marauders '62
The Comancheros '61
Deadly Companions '61
The Alamo '60
The Horse Soldiers '59
Darby's Rangers '58
Lafayette Escadrille '58
Blood Alley '55
Sea Chase '55
Phantom from Space '53

Ted Cohen
Red Dirt '99
Yellow '98

Andy Collins (1961-)
David Copperfield '99
Little Voice '98
Brassed Off '96

Peter Collister
The Animal '01
Deuce Bigalow: Male Gigolo '99
The Replacement Killers '98
The Beautician and the Beast '97
Dunston Checks In '95
Higher Learning '94
Poetic Justice '93
Livin' Large '91
Problem Child '90
All's Fair '89
Limit Up '89
Halloween 4: The Return of Michael Myers '88
Pulse '88
You Can't Hurry Love '88
Can't Buy Me Love '87
He's My Girl '87
Eye of the Tiger '86
Getting Even '86
The KGB: The Secret War '86
The Supernaturals '86
Avenging Angel '85
Odd Jobs '85

Roy Collodi
Just for the Hell of It '68
She-Devils on Wheels '68
The Girl, the Body and the Pill '67
Gruesome Twosome '67
Suburban Roulette '67

Edward Colman (1905-95)
The Love Bug '68
The Ambushers '67
Blackbeard's Ghost '67
The Gnome-Mobile '67
The Happiest Millionaire '67
The Adventures of Bullwhip Griffin '66
Monkey's Uncle '65
That Darn Cat '65
Those Calloways '65
The Ugly Dachshund '65
Mary Poppins '64
The Misadventures of Merlin Jones '63
Savage Sam '63
Son of Flubber '63
Big Red '62
The Absent-Minded Professor '61
Babes in Toyland '61
The Shaggy Dog '59

Fred Conde
Dolemite 2: Human Tornado '76
Too Hot to Handle '76
The Big Doll House '71

David Connell
Stephen King's Rose Red '02
The Lost Empire '01
Don Quixote '00
Chameleon 2: Death Match '99
Cleopatra '99
Stephen King's The Storm of the Century '99
Moby Dick '98
Two for Texas '97
Stephen King's The Night Flier '96
Twilight Man '96
Zeus and Roxanne '96
Buffalo Girls '95
Silver Strand '95
The Ascent '94
Gross Misconduct '93
Heaven Tonight '93
Over the Hill '93
NeverEnding Story 2: The Next Chapter '91
Les Patterson Saves the World '90
Slate, Wyn & Me '87
The Aviator '85
All the Rivers Run '84

Jack Conroy
A Bright Shining Lie '98
Everything That Rises '98
The Magnificent Seven '98
The Nephew '97
Homeward Bound 2: Lost in San Francisco '96
Blind Justice '94
Broken Harvest '94
The Hunted '94
The Playboys '92
Silent Tongue '92
The Field '90
My Left Foot '89

Alfio Contini
Beyond the Clouds '95
The Libertine '69

James A. Contner
Monkey Shines '88
The Last Dragon '85
The Flamingo Kid '84
Jaws 3 '83
Nighthawks '81
Times Square '80

Fabio Conversi
Pedale Douce '96
Love After Love '94

Denys Coop
And Now the Screaming Starts '73
Asylum '72
10 Rillington Place '71
King and Country '64
Billy Liar '63
This Sporting Life '63
A Kind of Loving '62

Wilkie Cooper
First Men in the Moon '64
Jason and the Argonauts '63
Maniac '63
The Mouse on the Moon '62
Mysterious Island '61
The Three Worlds of Gulliver '59
Sea of Sand '58
The Seventh Voyage of Sinbad '58
Abandon Ship '57
The Admirable Crichton '57
End of the Affair '55
Captain Boycott '47

John Coquillon
The Last Place on Earth '94
Clockwise '86
Hold the Dream '86
Absolution '81
The Changeling '80
All Quiet on the Western Front '79
Cross of Iron '76
Rentadick '72
Straw Dogs '72
Cry of the Banshee '70
Scream and Scream Again '70
Wuthering Heights '70
The Oblong Box '69
The Conqueror Worm '68

Gilles Corbeil
Balance of Power '96
Jungleground '95

Ericson Core
The Fast and the Furious '01
Dancing at the Blue Iguana '00
Mumford '99
Payback '98
Exit in Red '97
187 '97
The Show '95

Charles Correll
Revenge of the Nerds 2: Nerds in Paradise '87
Star Trek 3: The Search for Spock '84
Cheech and Chong's Nice Dreams '81
In God We Trust '80
National Lampoon's Animal House '78

Stanley Cortez (1905-97)
The Bridge at Remagen '69
Naked Kiss '64
They Saved Hitler's Brain '64
Shock Corridor '63
Dinosaurus! '60
The Angry Red Planet '59
The Three Faces of Eve '57
The Night of the Hunter '55
Since You Went Away '44
The Black Cat '41

Andrew M. Costikyan
Bananas '71
The Beast from Haunted Cave '60

Michael Coulter
Mansfield Park '99
Notting Hill '99
My Giant '98
FairyTale: A True Story '97
The Neon Bible '95
Sense and Sensibility '95
Being Human '94
Four Weddings and a Funeral '94
Foreign Affairs '93
The Long Day Closes '92
Monster in a Box '92
Where Angels Fear to Tread '91
Dark Obsession '90
Breaking In '89
The Dressmaker '89
The Good Father '87
The Gospel According to Vic '87
Housekeeping '87
No Surrender '86
Gregory's Girl '80
That Sinking Feeling '79

Curt Courant
Monsieur Verdoux '47
De Mayerling a Sarajevo '40
La Bete Humaine '38
The Man Who Knew Too Much '34

Julian Court
Lady Audley's Secret '00
Heart '99

Raoul Coutard (1924-)
Dr. Bethune '90
Max, Mon Amour '86
Dangerous Moves '84
First Name: Carmen '83
Passion '82
Le Crabe Tambour '77
The Bride Wore Black '68
Two or Three Things I Know about Her '66
Alphaville '65
A Married Woman '65
Pierrot le Fou '65
The 317th Platoon '65
Band of Outsiders '64
Contempt '64
The Soft Skin '64
Les Carabiniers '63
Jules and Jim '62
My Life to Live '62
Shoot the Piano Player '62
Le Petit Soldat '60
A Woman Is a Woman '60
Breathless '59

Graeme Cowley
Utu '83
Carry Me Back '82

Jack Cox
Devil Girl from Mars '54
Mister Drake's Duck '50
The Magic Bow '47
We Dive at Dawn '43

The Lady Vanishes '38
No. 17 '32
Rich and Strange '32
Skin Game '31
Murder '30
Blackmail '29
The Manxman '29
The Farmer's Wife '28
The Ring '27

Vincent Cox
Act of Piracy '89
The Demon '81

James A. Crabe
The Karate Kid: Part 2 '86
Night Shift '82
The China Syndrome '79
Sextette '78
The Disappearance of Aimee '76
Rocky '76
The Autobiography of Miss Jane Pittman '74

Jordan Cronenweth (1935-96)
Final Analysis '92
State of Grace '90
U2: Rattle and Hum '88
Gardens of Stone '87
Just Between Friends '86
Peggy Sue Got Married '86
Stop Making Sense '84
Best Friends '82
Blade Runner '82
Cutter's Way '81
Altered States '80
And I Alone Survived '78
One in a Million: The Ron LeFlore Story '78
Citizens Band '77
Rolling Thunder '77
The Front Page '74
Zandy's Bride '74
Birds of Prey '72
Brewster McCloud '70

Edward Cronjager
Beneath the 12-Mile Reef '53
On Our Merry Way '48
Canyon Passage '46

Henry Cronjager
The Ballad of Andy Crocker '69
Ace of Aces '33
The Love Light '21
Tol'able David '21
Daddy Long Legs '19

Floyd Crosby (1899-1985)
Beach Blanket Bingo '65
How to Stuff a Wild Bikini '65
Bikini Beach '64
The Comedy of Terrors '64
Pajama Party '64
The Raven '63
Sallah '63
X: The Man with X-Ray Eyes '63
Premature Burial '62
Tales of Terror '62
The Pit and the Pendulum '61
The Fall of the House of Usher '60
I, Mobster '58
Machine Gun Kelly '58
The Old Man and the Sea '58
Teenage Caveman '58
Carnival Rock '57
Reform School Girl '57
Rock All Night '57
Teenage Doll '57
Shack Out on 101 '55
The Fast and the Furious '54
Monster from the Ocean Floor '54
The Fighter '52
High Noon '52
Tabu: A Story of the South Seas '31

Nat Crosby
Paper Mask '91
Northanger Abbey '87

Denis Crossan
I Know What You Did Last Summer '97
Incognito '97
Killer Tongue '96
The Real McCoy '93
A Murder of Quality '90

Richard Crudo
Down to Earth '01
Out Cold '01
In Pursuit '00
American Pie '99
Outside Providence '99
Bongwater '98
Music from Another Room '97
Persons Unknown '96
American Buffalo '95
The Low Life '95
Federal Hill '94

Dean Cundey
What Women Want '00
Krippendorf's Tribe '98
The Parent Trap '98
Flubber '97
Apollo 13 '95
Casper '95
The Flintstones '94
Jurassic Park '93
Death Becomes Her '92
Hook '91
Nothing But Trouble '91
Back to the Future, Part 3 '90
Back to the Future, Part 2 '89
Road House '89
Big Business '88
Who Framed Roger Rabbit '88
Project X '87
Big Trouble in Little China '86
Back to the Future '85
Warning Sign '85
D.C. Cab '84
It Came Upon a Midnight Clear '84
Romancing the Stone '84
M.A.D.D.: Mothers Against Drunk Driving '83
Psycho 2 '83
Halloween 3: Season of the Witch '82
Separate Ways '82
The Thing '82
Escape from New York '81
Halloween 2: The Nightmare Isn't Over! '81
Jaws of Satan '81
Galaxina '80
Angel's Brigade '79
Rock 'n' Roll High School '79
Roller Boogie '79
The Fog '78
Halloween '78
Bare Knuckles '77
Satan's Cheerleaders '77
Ilsa, Harem Keeper of the Oil Sheiks '76
Where the Red Fern Grows '74

Alec Curtis
Horatio Hornblower '99
Hostile Waters '97
Rhodes '97

Oliver Curtis
Vanity Fair '99
Immortality '98
Love and Death on Long Island '97
Madagascar Skin '95

Stefan Czapsky
Matilda '96
Ed Wood '94
Batman Returns '92
Prelude to a Kiss '92
Child's Play 2 '90
Edward Scissorhands '90
Last Exit to Brooklyn '90
The Thin Blue Line '88
Vampire's Kiss '88

Stephen Dade
The Viking Queen '67
Night Caller from Outer Space '66
Zulu '64
The Obsessed '51

Ake Dahlqvist
June Night '40
Intermezzo '36

Laurent Dailland
East-West '99
Place Vendome '98
Train of Life '98
Perfect Love '96
36 Fillete '88

Massimo Dallamano (1917-76)
For a Few Dollars More '65
A Fistful of Dollars '64

John Daly
Greenfingers '00
The Railway Children '00
Essex Boys '99
A Royal Scandal '96
Persuasion '95

Arch R. Dalzell
The Boy in the Plastic Bubble '76
The Trip '67
Tower of London '62
Little Shop of Horrors '60

Lee Daniel
Rift '96
subUrbia '96
...And God Spoke '94
Before Sunrise '94
Dazed and Confused '93
Slacker '91

William H. Daniels (1895-1970)
Marlowe '69
In Like Flint '67
Valley of the Dolls '67
Assault on a Queen '66
Von Ryan's Express '65
Robin and the 7 Hoods '64
Come Blow Your Horn '63
The Prize '63
Back Street '61
Come September '61
Can-Can '60
Ocean's 11 '60
A Hole in the Head '59
Never So Few '59
Cat on a Hot Tin Roof '58
Some Came Running '58
Istanbul '57
My Man Godfrey '57
Away All Boats '56
Far Country '55
Strategic Air Command '55
The Glenn Miller Story '54
Thunder Bay '53
Pat and Mike '52
Harvey '50
Three Came Home '50
Winchester '73 '50
For the Love of Mary '48
The Naked City '48
Lured '47
Girl Crazy '43
Keeper of the Flame '42
So Ends Our Night '41
The Mortal Storm '40
The Shop Around the Corner '40
Idiot's Delight '39
Ninotchka '39
Marie Antoinette '38
Broadway Melody of 1938 '37
Camille '36
Romeo and Juliet '36
Rose Marie '36
Anna Karenina '35
Naughty Marietta '35
The Barretts of Wimpole Street '34
The Painted Veil '34
Dinner at Eight '33
Queen Christina '33
Rasputin and the Empress '33
Grand Hotel '32
Mata Hari '32
A Free Soul '31
Susan Lenox: Her Fall and Rise '31
Anna Christie '30
Romance '30
The Kiss '29
The Mysterious Lady '28
Wild Orchids '28
The Flesh and the Devil '27
Foolish Wives '22

Jeff Darling
The Crossing '92
Young Einstein '89

Allen Daviau (1942-)
The Astronaut's Wife '99
Congo '95
Fearless '93
Bugsy '91
Defending Your Life '91
Avalon '90
Empire of the Sun '87
Harry and the Hendersons '87
The Color Purple '85
The Falcon and the Snowman '85
Harry Tracy '83
Legs '83
Twilight Zone: The Movie '83
E.T.: The Extra-Terrestrial '82
Rage '80
The Streets of L.A. '79

Zoltan David
The Colony '98
Row Your Boat '98
Redline '97
Donor Unknown '95
The Last Word '95
My Teacher's Wife '95

Andrew Davis (1946-)
Over the Edge '79
Private Parts '72

Elliot Davis
40 Days and 40 Nights '02
Happy Campers '01
I Am Sam '01
The Next Best Thing '00
Forces of Nature '99
Light It Up '99
Breakfast of Champions '98
Finding Graceland '98
Out of Sight '98
Get On the Bus '96
Larger Than Life '96
Lawn Dogs '96
Nightjohn '96
The Glass Shield '95
Things to Do in Denver When You're Dead '95
The Underneath '95
The Air Up There '94
Mother's Boys '94
Equinox '93
The Cutting Edge '92
Mr. Write '92
Shakes the Clown '92
Mortal Thoughts '91
Bloodhounds of Broadway '89
Love at Large '89
Signs of Life '89
Miles from Home '88
Summer Heat '87
Vamp '86

Michael J. Davis
A Woman, Her Men and Her Futon '92
Riders '88

Ernest Day
Parents '89
A Passage to India '84
Revenge of the Pink Panther '78

Ricardo De Angelis
A Place in the World '92
Man Facing Southeast '86

Gerard de Battista
A Matter of Taste '00
Venus Beauty Institute '98
French Twist '95

Jan De Bont (1943-)
Basic Instinct '92
Lethal Weapon 3 '92
Shining Through '92
Flatliners '90
The Hunt for Red October '90
Total Recall '90
Bert Rigby, You're a Fool '89
Black Rain '89
Die Hard '88
Leonard Part 6 '87
RoboCop '87
Who's That Girl? '87
The Clan of the Cave Bear '86
Jumpin' Jack Flash '86
Ruthless People '86
Flesh and Blood '85
The Jewel of the Nile '85
Bad Manners '84
All the Right Moves '83
Cujo '83
I'm Dancing as Fast as I Can '82
Private Lessons '81
Spetters '80
The 4th Man '79
Soldier of Orange '78
Katie Tippel '75
Turkish Delight '73

John de Borman
Serendipity '01
Hamlet '00
Saving Grace '00
Hideous Kinky '99
The Mighty '98
Photographing Fairies '97
The Full Monty '96
Trojan Eddie '96
Death Machine '95
The Passion of Darkly Noon '95
Small Faces '95

Cian de Buitlear
Blow Dry '00
I Went Down '97

Robert De Grasse
Home of the Brave '49
The Body Snatcher '45
Forever and a Day '43
The Leopard Man '43

Bruno de Keyzer
About Adam '00
North Star '96
The Ogre '96
War of the Buttons '95
Afraid of the Dark '92
December Bride '91
Impromptu '90
Life and Nothing But '89
Beatrice '88
Little Dorrit, Film 1: Nobody's Fault '88
Little Dorrit, Film 2: Little Dorrit's Story '88
Reunion '88
The Murders in the Rue Morgue '86
Round Midnight '86
Sincerely Charlotte '86
A Sunday in the Country '84

Axel de Roche
The Nasty Girl '90
The White Rose '83

Pasqualino De Santis (1927-96)
The Truce '96
A Month by the Lake '95
Salome '85
Misunderstood '84
Sheena '84
L'Argent '83
Immortal Bachelor '80
Three Brothers '80
Christ Stopped at Eboli '79
The Devil, Probably '77
A Special Day '77
The Innocent '76
Conversation Piece '75
Lancelot of the Lake '74
Lucky Luciano '74
Assassination of Trotsky '72
Death in Venice '71
Romeo and Juliet '68

Jean De Segonzac
Homicide: The Movie '00
Path to Paradise '97
Normal Life '96
Confessions of Sorority Girls '94
Girls in Prison '94
Shake, Rattle & Rock! '94
Laws of Gravity '92

Clyde De Vinna (1892-1953)
Jungle '52
Immortal Sergeant '43
Of Human Hearts '38
Ah, Wilderness! '35
Tarzan and His Mate '34
Treasure Island '34
Tarzan, the Ape Man '32
Trader Horn '31
White Shadows in the South Seas '29
Ben-Hur '26

Roger Deakins (1949-)
A Beautiful Mind '01
The Man Who Wasn't There '01
O Brother Where Art Thou? '00
Anywhere But Here '99
The Hurricane '99
The Siege '98
The Big Lebowski '97
Kundun '97
Courage Under Fire '96
Fargo '96
Dead Man Walking '95
Rob Roy '95
The Shawshank Redemption '94
The Hudsucker Proxy '93
The Secret Garden '93
Passion Fish '92
Thunderheart '92
Barton Fink '91
Homicide '91
Air America '90
Mountains of the Moon '90
The Long Walk Home '89
Pascali's Island '88
Stormy Monday '88
White Mischief '88
The Kitchen Toto '87
Personal Services '87
Shadey '87
Sid & Nancy '86
Defense of the Realm '85
1984 '84
Another Time, Another Place '83

Seamus Deasy
The Seventh Stream '01
An Everlasting Piece '00
When the Sky Falls '99
The General '98

Henri Decae
Exposed '83
Le Professionnel '81
The Island '80
The Boys from Brazil '78
Bobby Deerfield '77
Don Juan (Or If Don Juan Were a Woman) '73
Light at the Edge of the World '71
Joe '70
Le Samourai '67
Viva Maria! '65
Joy House '64
Les Bonnes Femmes '60
Purple Noon '60
The 400 Blows '59
Frantic '58
Bob le Flambeur '55
La Silence de la Mer '47

Gina DeGirolamo
Edge of Seventeen '99
Jerome '98

Thomas Del Ruth
Kissing a Fool '98
Asteroid '97
Leave It to Beaver '97
JAG '95
Next Door '94
Barbarians at the Gate '93
Dead to Rights '93
The Mighty Ducks '92
Look Who's Talking, Too '90
The Running Man '87
Stand by Me '86
The Breakfast Club '85
Impulse '84
Get Crazy '83
Hysterical '83
Motel Hell '80

Bruno Delbonnel
Amelie '01
The Cat's Meow '01

Benoit Delhomme
Miss Julie '99
The Loss of Sexual Innocence '98
The Winslow Boy '98
Artemisia '97
Un Air de Famille '96
When the Cat's Away '96
Cyclo '95
The Scent of Green Papaya '93

Franco Delli Colli
Macabre '80
The Last Man on Earth '64

Tonino Delli Colli (1923-)
Life Is Beautiful '98
Death and the Maiden '94
Bitter Moon '92
Intervista '87
Ginger & Fred '86
The Name of the Rose '86
Once Upon a Time in America '84
Tales of Ordinary Madness '83
Lovers and Liars '81
Seven Beauties '76
Salo, or the 120 Days of Sodom '75
The Canterbury Tales '71
The Decameron '70
Porcile '69
Once Upon a Time in the West '68
Spirits of the Dead '68
The Good, the Bad and the Ugly '67
The Gospel According to St. Matthew '64
Mamma Roma '62
Accatone! '61

Frank DeMarco
Hedwig and the Angry Inch '00
Habit '97

Peter Deming
From Hell '01
Mulholland Drive '01
If These Walls Could Talk 2 '00
Scream 3 '00
Music of the Heart '99
Mystery, Alaska '99
Austin Powers: International Man of Mystery '97
Scream 2 '97
Joe's Apartment '96
Lost Highway '96
Cosmic Slop '94
National Lampoon's Loaded Weapon 1 '93
Son-in-Law '93
My Cousin Vinny '92
House Party '90
From Hollywood to Deadwood '89
It Takes Two '88
The Carrier '87
Evil Dead 2: Dead by Dawn '87
Hollywood Shuffle '87

John L. Demps, Jr.
Finding Buck McHenry '00
The Three Lives of Karen '97
The Show '95
Fear of a Black Hat '94
The Inkwell '94
The Walking Dead '94
Street Wars '91

Austin Dempster
A Touch of Class '73
Bedazzled '68

Daniil Demutsky
Earth '30
Arsenal '29

Jim Denault
Our Song '01
Chasing Sleep '00
Double Parked '00
Boys Don't Cry '99
The Eternal '99
A Good Baby '99
The Taxman '98
Clockwatchers '97
Breathing Room '96
Illtown '96
Sudden Manhattan '96
Nadja '95
River of Grass '94

Thomas Denove
Secret Games '92
Puppet Master 2 '90
Fanatic '82

Joe DeSalvo
Fever '99
Fall '97
All Over Me '96
The Wife '95
What Happened Was... '94
Joey Breaker '93

Paul Desatoff
Animal Instincts '92
Carnal Crimes '91

Caleb Deschanel (1941-)
The Patriot '00
Anna and the King '99
The Haunting '99
Hope Floats '98
Message in a Bottle '98
Fly Away Home '96
It Could Happen to You '94
The Slugger's Wife '85
The Natural '84
The Right Stuff '83
Being There '79
The Black Stallion '79
More American Graffiti '79
A Woman under the Influence '74

Franco Di Giacomo
Foreign Student '94
The Postman '94
Dark Eyes '87
Amityville 2: The Possession '82
Fighting Back '82
The Night of the Shooting Stars '82

Carlo Di Palma
Deconstructing Harry '97
Everyone Says I Love You '96
The Monster '96
Mighty Aphrodite '95
Bullets over Broadway '94
Manhattan Murder Mystery '93
Husbands and Wives '92
Shadows and Fog '92
Alice '90
September '88
Radio Days '87
The Secret of My Success '87
Hannah and Her Sisters '86
Off Beat '86
Gabriela '84
The Black Stallion Returns '83
The Appointment '82
Identification of a Woman '82
The Tragedy of a Ridiculous Man '81
Blow-Up '66
The Red Desert '64
Divorce—Italian Style '62
That Long Night in '43 '60

Dario Di Palma
Down & Dirty '76
Seduction of Mimi '72
The Clowns '71

Roxanne Di Santo
Frankenstein and Me '96
Kids of the Round Table '96

Gianni Di Venanzo
The Eclipse '66
Juliet of the Spirits '65
10th Victim '65
8 1/2 '63
Eva '62
Big Deal on Madonna Street '58
Il Grido '57
Love in the City '53

James Diamond
Circle of Death '36
The Road to Ruin '28

Jimmy Dibling
Dreaming of Joseph Lees '99
Relative Values '99

Tom DiCillo (1954-)
Stranger than Paradise '84
Variety '83

Ernest R. Dickerson (1952-)
Jungle Fever '91
Def by Temptation '90
Mo' Better Blues '90
Do the Right Thing '89
School Daze '88
She's Gotta Have It '86

Desmond Dickinson
Tower of Evil '72
The Bloodsuckers '70
The Frightened City '61
The Hands of Orlac '60
Horror Hotel '60
The Woman in Question '50
Hamlet '48
Thursday's Child '43

Billy Dickson
Halloween 6: The Curse of Michael Myers '95
Tainted Blood '93
Chrome Soldiers '92
The Secret Passion of Robert Clayton '92
Victim of Love '91

Mario DiLeo
Sudie & Simpson '90
Nightmares '83
The Evil '78
Breaker! Breaker! '77

Bill Dill
Dancing in September '00
B.A.P.'s '97
The Five Heartbeats '91

Phillip W. Dingeldein
Mommy 2: Mommy's Day '96
Mommy '95

Andrew Dintenfass
Dancer, Texas—Pop. 81 '98
The Cure '95
About Last Night... '86

George E. Diskant
They Live by Night '49
Dick Tracy vs. Cueball '46

Irl Dixon
The Bone Yard '90
Trapper County War '89

Sergio d'Offizi
The Squeeze '78
Don't Torture a Duckling '72

Mike Dolgetta
Throw Down '00
Final Exam '98

Raul Dominguez
The Fear Chamber '68
The Sinister Invasion '68

Bruce Dorfman
Raw Target '95
An American Summer '90
Bloodfist 2 '90

Alan Dostie
Nuremberg '00
The Red Violin '98
The Confessional '95
32 Short Films about Glenn Gould '93
Iron Eagle 2 '88

Christopher Doyle (1952-)
Made '01
In the Mood for Love '00
Liberty Heights '99
Psycho '98
Happy Together '96
Temptress Moon '96
Chungking Express '95
Fallen Angels '95

Rob Draper
Trucks '97
The Assassination File '96
The Spitfire Grill '95
Dr. Giggles '92
Undesirable '92
Tales from the Darkside: The Movie '90
Halloween 5: The Revenge of Michael Myers '89

Jean-Marie Dreujou
The Girl on the Bridge '98
Augustin '95

Randy Drummond
Series 7: The Contenders '01
Anima '98
Welcome to the Dollhouse '95

Stuart Dryburgh (1952-)
Bridget Jones's Diary '01
Kate & Leopold '01
Shaft '00
Runaway Bride '99
Analyze This '98
Portrait of a Lady '96
Lone Star '95
Once Were Warriors '94
The Perez Family '94
The Piano '93
An Angel at My Table '89

Guy Dufaux
The Great Gatsby '01
Stardom '00
Eye of the Beholder '99
Polish Wedding '97
Jesus of Montreal '89

Bryan Duggan
T.N.T. '98
Plan 10 from Outer Space '95
Rubin & Ed '92
Cold Feet '89

Simon Duggan
Risk '00
The Interview '98

Albert J. Dunk
Trial by Media '00
The Happy Face Murders '99
Must Be Santa '99
The Inspectors '98
Flashfire '94
Class of 1984 '82
Incubus '82

Andrew Dunn
The Count of Monte Cristo '02
Gosford Park '01
Monkeybone '01
Liam '00
Ever After: A Cinderella Story '98
Hush '98
Practical Magic '98
Addicted to Love '96
The Crucible '96
Grave Indiscretions '96
The Madness of King George '94
The Bodyguard '92
L.A. Story '91
Strapless '90

Elmer Dyer
Air Force '43
The Flying Deuces '39
Hell's Angels '30

Paul Eagler
The Hurricane '37
Tess of the Storm Country '22

Arthur Edeson
The Mask of Dimitrios '44
Across the Pacific '42
Casablanca '42
The Maltese Falcon '41
The Invisible Man '33
The Old Dark House '32
Frankenstein '31
All Quiet on the Western Front '30
The Lost World '25
Robin Hood '22
The Three Musketeers '21

Eric Alan Edwards
Crossroads '02
On the Edge '00
Another Day in Paradise '98
Clay Pigeons '98
Cop Land '97
Flirting with Disaster '95
Kids '95
To Die For '95
Even Cowgirls Get the Blues '94
My Own Private Idaho '91

David Eggby
Crossfire Trail '01
Pitch Black '00
Blue Streak '99
Virus '98
Daylight '96
Dragonheart '96
Lightning Jack '94
Dragon: The Bruce Lee Story '93
Fortress '93
Harley Davidson and the Marlboro Man '91
Warlock '91
Quigley Down Under '90
The Blood of Heroes '89
Kansas '88
The Naked Country '85
Mad Max '80

Edgar Egger
Breakout '98
Hot Blooded '98
The Undertaker's Wedding '97

Eagle Egilsson
Red Shoe Diaries: Luscious Lola '00
Red Shoe Diaries: Swimming Naked '00
Sirens '99
American Virgin '98
Business for Pleasure '96
Red Shoe Diaries: Strip Poker '96
Delta of Venus '95

Ian Elkin
The Crimson Code '99
For the Moment '94
The Last Winter '89
Outside Chance of Maximillian Glick '88

Paul Elliott
The Broken Hearts Club '00
If These Walls Could Talk 2 '00
Diamonds '99
Lost and Found '99
Santa Fe '97
Soul Food '97
Riot in the Streets '96
Truman '95
My Girl 2 '94
And the Band Played On '93
Citizen Cohn '92
And You Thought Your Parents Were Weird! '91
Final Verdict '91
My Girl '91
Daddy's Dyin'...Who's Got the Will? '90
The Lost Capone '90
Welcome Home, Roxy Carmichael '90
Far from Home '89
Friday the 13th, Part 7: The New Blood '88
976-EVIL '88
Cyclone '87
Stacking '87
Armed Response '86
Tomb '86

Frederick Elmes
The Empty Mirror '99
Ride with the Devil '99
The Ice Storm '97
In the Gloaming '97
Reckless '95
Trial by Jury '94
The Saint of Fort Washington '93
Night on Earth '91
Wild at Heart '90
Permanent Record '88
River's Edge '87
Allan Quatermain and the Lost City of Gold '86
Blue Velvet '86
Valley Girl '83
Eraserhead '78
Opening Night '77
The Killing of a Chinese Bookie '76

Robert Elswit
Heist '01
Imposter '01
Bounce '00
Magnolia '99
8mm '98
Boogie Nights '97
Tomorrow Never Dies '97
Hard Eight '96
Boys '95
The Pallbearer '95
The River Wild '94
A Dangerous Woman '93
The Hand that Rocks the Cradle '92
Waterland '92
Paris Trout '91
Bad Influence '90
A Killing in a Small Town '90
Double Exposure: The Story of Margaret Bourke-White '89
The Heart of Dixie '89
How I Got into College '89
Return of the Living Dead 2 '88
Amazing Grace & Chuck '87
Desert Hearts '86
Trick or Treat '86
Moving Violations '85
The Sure Thing '85
Tiger Town '83
Waltz across Texas '83
End of August '82

Susan Emerson
First Degree '98
Men '97

Bryan England
Raging Angels '95
The Judas Project: The Ultimate Encounter '94
Conflict of Interest '92
Gate 2 '92
The Water Engine '92
Sometimes They Come Back '91
Friday the 13th, Part 8: Jason Takes Manhattan '89
I, Madman '89
My Mom's a Werewolf '89
Wicked Stepmother '89
Cheerleader Camp '88
Hunk '87
Weekend Pass '84
Party Animal '83

Michael Epp
Beaumarchais the Scoundrel '96
My Mother's Courage '95

Nils Erickson
Sticks '98
Mirror, Mirror 3: The Voyeur '96

Teodoro Escamilla
Carmen '83
Blood Wedding '81
The Nest '80
Cria '76

Jean-Yves Escoffier
15 Minutes '01
Nurse Betty '00
The Cradle Will Rock '99
Rounders '98
Good Will Hunting '97
Gummo '97
The Crow 2: City of Angels '96
Excess Baggage '96
Grace of My Heart '96
Jack and Sarah '95
Dream Lover '93
The Lovers on the Bridge '91
Mauvais Sang '86
Three Men and a Cradle '85
Boy Meets Girl '84
Simone Barbes '80

Jesus Escosa
Beloved/Friend '99
Caresses '97

Blake T. Evans
3 Ninjas: High Noon at Mega Mountain '97
Behind Enemy Lines '96
Body Count '95

R. Kent Evans
The Abductors '72
Ginger '72

Jean-Marc Fabre
A Soldier's Daughter Never Cries '98
A Self-Made Hero '95
Ivan and Abraham '94

Geoffrey Faithfull
Village of the Damned *'60*
First Man into Space *'59*
Black Tide *'58*
Corridors of Blood *'58*
Christopher Faloona
Beowulf *'98*
Dennis the Menace Strikes Again *'98*
Breaking Free *'95*
3 Ninjas Kick Back *'94*
George Fanto
It's All True *'93*
Othello *'52*
Daniel F. Fapp (1901-)
Marooned *'69*
Five Card Stud *'68*
Ice Station Zebra *'68*
Sweet November *'68*
Our Man Flint *'66*
I'll Take Sweden *'65*
Send Me No Flowers *'64*
The Unsinkable Molly Brown *'64*
Fun in Acapulco *'63*
The Great Escape *'63*
A New Kind of Love *'63*
One, Two, Three *'61*
West Side Story *'61*
All the Young Men *'60*
Let's Make Love *'60*
The Five Pennies *'59*
Li'l Abner *'59*
On the Beach *'59*
Desire Under the Elms *'58*
Kings Go Forth *'58*
Artists and Models *'55*
Jumping Jacks *'52*
The Lemon Drop Kid *'51*
The Stooge *'51*
Union Station *'50*
Sorrowful Jones *'49*
Golden Earrings *'47*
To Each His Own *'46*
Mike Fash
The Golden Spiders: A Nero Wolfe Mystery *'00*
The Confession *'98*
Grace & Glorie *'98*
Entertaining Angels: The Dorothy Day Story *'96*
Sarah, Plain and Tall: Skylark *'93*
Sarah, Plain and Tall *'91*
The Whales of August *'87*
Women of Valor *'86*
Don E. Fauntleroy
Jeepers Creepers *'01*
The Perfect Nanny *'00*
Seven Girlfriends *'00*
Sex & Mrs. X *'00*
Rites of Passage *'99*
The Only Thrill *'97*
Lily Dale *'96*
Body Chemistry 3: Point of Seduction *'93*
Jim Fealy
Splendor *'99*
The Doom Generation *'95*
Zhao Fei
The Curse of the Jade Scorpion *'01*
The Emperor and the Assassin *'99*
Sweet and Lowdown *'99*
Gerald Feil
Friday the 13th, Part 3 *'82*
He Knows You're Alone *'80*
Jockey A. Feindel
Day the World Ended *'55*
Revolt of the Zombies *'36*
Buzz Feitshans, IV
Dragonheart: A New Beginning *'00*
Black Dog *'98*
For Richer or Poorer *'97*
McHale's Navy *'97*
The Shadow Conspiracy *'96*
Marc Felperlaan
The Dress *'96*
Amsterdamned *'88*
John Fenner
The Borrowers *'97*
Muppet Treasure Island *'96*
The Muppet Christmas Carol *'92*
Teenage Mutant Ninja Turtles: The Movie *'90*
Joao Fernandes
One Man's Hero *'98*
Sprung *'96*
Forest Warrior *'95*
Top Dog *'95*
Deconstructing Sarah *'94*
Sidekicks *'93*
The Hitman *'91*
Delta Force 2: Operation Stranglehold *'90*
Red Scorpion *'89*
Braddock: Missing in Action 3 *'88*
Prettykill *'87*
Invasion U.S.A. *'85*
Rosebud Beach Hotel *'85*
Friday the 13th, Part 4: The Final Chapter *'84*
Missing in Action *'84*
Big Score *'83*
The Nesting *'80*
Angel Luis Fernandez
Baton Rouge *'88*
Law of Desire *'86*
Matador *'86*
Dark Habits *'84*
Giancarlo Ferrando
The Great Alligator *'81*
Torso *'73*
David Ferrara
Kill Me Later *'01*
Black and White *'99*
Michael Ferris
Bar Girls *'95*
I Don't Buy Kisses Anymore *'92*
Steven Fierberg
Attila *'01*
Red Letters *'00*
Atomic Train *'99*
A Horse for Danny *'95*
Aspen Extreme *'93*
29th Street *'91*
Criminal Justice *'90*
Scenes from the Class Struggle in Beverly Hills *'89*
A Nightmare on Elm Street 4: Dream Master *'88*
Spike of Bensonhurst *'88*
Seven Minutes in Heaven *'86*
Streetwalkin' *'85*
Vortex *'81*
Gabriel Figueroa (1907-97)
Kelly's Heroes *'70*
Simon of the Desert *'66*
The Exterminating Angel *'62*
El *'52*
Vilko Filac
Novocaine *'01*
Chinese Box *'97*
Underground *'95*
Arizona Dream *'94*
Roberta Findlay
Lurkers *'88*
Shriek of the Mutilated *'74*
Russell Fine
O *'01*
Eye of God *'97*
Office Killer *'97*
Girls Town *'95*
The Pompatus of Love *'95*
Gerald Perry Finnerman
Nightmares *'83*
Sssssss *'73*
That Man Bolt *'73*
They Call Me Mr. Tibbs! *'70*
The Lost Man *'69*
Gavin Finney
Breathtaking *'00*
A Rather English Marriage *'98*
Dad Savage *'97*
The Sculptress *'97*
Mauro Fiore
The Center of the World *'01*
Driven *'01*
Highway *'01*
Training Day *'01*
Get Carter *'00*
Lost Souls *'00*
Billboard Dad *'98*
An Occasional Hell *'96*
Steven Firestone
I Shot a Man in Vegas *'96*
Swimming with Sharks *'94*
Harry Fischbeck
The Big Broadcast of 1938 *'38*
Now and Forever *'34*
The Eagle and the Hawk *'33*
Sally of the Sawdust *'25*
Gunnar Fischer
The Devil's Eye *'60*
Wild Strawberries *'57*
The Seventh Seal *'56*
To Joy *'50*
Jens Fischer
Under the Sun *'98*
The Last Dance *'93*
Gerry Fisher
When Saturday Comes *'95*
Cops and Robbersons *'94*
Exorcist 3: Legion *'90*
Dead Bang *'89*
Running on Empty *'88*
Highlander *'86*
Lovesick *'83*
Yellowbeard *'83*
Victory *'81*
Wolfen *'81*
Roads to the South *'78*
The Island of Dr. Moreau *'77*
Mr. Klein *'76*
Brannigan *'75*
Juggernaut *'74*
The Go-Between *'71*
Accident *'67*
Pili Flores-Guerra
800 Leagues Down the Amazon *'93*
Fire on the Amazon *'93*
Brendan Flynt
Boricua's Bond *'00*
Tromeo & Juliet *'95*
George J. Folsey (1898-1988)
The Balcony *'63*
Cash McCall *'60*
Torpedo Run *'58*
Fastest Gun Alive *'56*
Forbidden Planet *'56*
The Cobweb *'55*
Hit the Deck *'55*
Deep in My Heart *'54*
Executive Suite *'54*
Men of the Fighting Lady *'54*
Seven Brides for Seven Brothers *'54*
All the Brothers Were Valiant *'53*
Lovely to Look At *'52*
Million Dollar Mermaid *'52*
Vengeance Valley *'51*
Adam's Rib *'50*
The Big Hangover *'50*
A Life of Her Own *'50*
Malaya *'49*
Take Me Out to the Ball Game *'49*
State of the Union *'48*
Green Dolphin Street *'47*
The Harvey Girls *'46*
The Clock *'45*
Meet Me in St. Louis *'44*
The White Cliffs of Dover *'44*
Thousands Cheer *'43*
Andy Hardy's Double Life *'42*
Panama Hattie *'42*
Rio Rita *'42*
Lady Be Good *'41*
The Shining Hour *'38*
The Bride Wore Red *'37*
The Last of Mrs. Cheyney *'37*
Mannequin *'37*
The Gorgeous Hussy *'36*
Forsaking All Others *'35*
I Live My Life *'35*
Reckless *'35*
Chained *'34*
Going Hollywood *'33*
The Animal Kingdom *'32*
Animal Crackers *'30*
Applause *'29*
The Cocoanuts *'29*
David Foreman
Chameleon 3: Dark Angel *'00*
Cut *'00*
The Real Macaw *'98*
Tony Forsberg
The White Lioness *'96*
Revenge of the Barbarians *'85*
Joey Forsyte
Bad Seed *'00*
Me & Will *'99*
The Curve *'97*
The Dark Backward *'91*
Ron Fortunato
The Weekend *'00*
One Tough Cop *'98*
Basquiat *'96*
Nil by Mouth *'96*
If Lucy Fell *'95*
Mac *'93*
Fathers and Sons *'92*
Skin *'89*
John Foster
The Adventures of Sebastian Cole *'99*
Sunday *'96*
Robert Fraisse
Enemy at the Gates *'00*
La Buche *'00*
Vatel *'00*
Ronin *'98*
Seven Years in Tibet *'97*
Keys to Tulsa *'96*
Citizen X *'95*
The Lover *'92*
L'Addition *'85*
Lady Chatterley's Lover *'81*
Emmanuelle, the Joys of a Woman *'76*
The Story of O *'75*
William A. Fraker (1923-)
Town and Country *'01*
Rules of Engagement *'00*
The Island of Dr. Moreau *'96*
Vegas Vacation *'96*
Father of the Bride Part II *'95*
Street Fighter *'94*
Tombstone *'93*
Honeymoon in Vegas *'92*
The Freshman *'90*
Chances Are *'89*
Baby Boom *'87*
Burglar *'87*
Protocol *'84*
WarGames *'83*
Sharky's Machine *'81*
The Hollywood Knights *'80*
1941 *'79*
Heaven Can Wait *'78*
The Exorcist 2: The Heretic *'77*
Looking for Mr. Goodbar *'77*
The Killer Inside Me *'76*
Lipstick *'76*
One Flew Over the Cuckoo's Nest *'75*
Rancho Deluxe *'75*
Streetfight *'75*
Aloha, Bobby and Rose *'74*
Bullitt *'68*
Rosemary's Baby *'68*
Games *'67*
The President's Analyst *'67*
Freddie Francis (1917-)
The Straight Story *'99*
Princess Caraboo *'94*
School Ties *'92*
Cape Fear *'91*
Glory *'89*
Her Alibi *'88*
Brenda Starr *'86*
Dune *'84*
The French Lieutenant's Woman *'81*
The Elephant Man *'80*
The Innocents *'61*
The Battle of the Sexes *'60*
Saturday Night and Sunday Morning *'60*
Room at the Top *'59*
Time Without Pity *'57*
David Franco
3000 Miles to Graceland *'01*
The Whole Nine Yards *'00*
Earthly Possessions *'99*
Free Money *'99*
Vendetta *'99*
The Last Don 2 *'98*
The Assignment *'97*
Silent Trigger *'97*
Long Day's Journey Into Night *'96*
Hollow Point *'95*
Soul Survivor *'95*
A Man in Uniform *'93*
The Carpenter *'89*
Tom Fraser
Chopper Chicks in Zombietown *'91*
Frankenstein General Hospital *'88*
The Unnamable *'88*
Alien from L.A. *'87*
Benito Frattari
Commandos *'73*
Mondo Cane *'63*
Ellsworth Fredericks (1904-93)
Picture Mommy Dead *'66*
Seven Days in May *'64*
Tall Story *'60*
The Light in the Forest *'58*
Sayonara *'57*
Friendly Persuasion *'56*
Invasion of the Body Snatchers *'56*
At Gunpoint *'55*
Shotgun *'55*
Jonathan Freeman
Hitched *'01*
Lost Battalion *'01*
Resurrection *'99*
Deadly Game *'98*
Falling Fire *'97*
Junior's Groove *'97*
Henry Freulich
Good Day for a Hanging *'58*
Bonanza Town *'51*
Blondie for Victory *'42*
Blondie Goes Latin *'42*
Blondie Goes to College *'42*
Blondie's Blessed Event *'42*
Blondie in Society *'41*
Blondie Has Trouble *'40*
Blondie On a Budget *'40*
Blondie Plays Cupid *'40*
Blondie Brings Up Baby *'39*
Blondie Meets the Boss *'39*
Blondie Takes a Vacation *'39*
Blondie *'38*
Karl Freund (1890-1969)
Key Largo *'48*
South of St. Louis *'48*
Undercurrent *'46*
Without Love *'45*
A Guy Named Joe *'44*
The Seventh Cross *'44*
DuBarry Was a Lady *'43*
Tortilla Flat *'42*
The Chocolate Soldier *'41*
Pride and Prejudice *'40*
Balalaika *'39*
Rose of Washington Square *'39*
Letter of Introduction *'38*
Conquest *'37*
The Good Earth *'37*
Murders in the Rue Morgue *'32*
Dracula *'31*
All Quiet on the Western Front *'30*
Metropolis *'26*
Variety *'25*
The Last Laugh *'24*
The Golem *'20*
Ron Fricke
Baraka *'93*
Koyaanisqatsi *'83*
Martin Fuhrer
Wilde *'97*
Lord of the Flies *'90*
Tak Fujimoto
The Replacements *'00*
The Sixth Sense *'99*
Beloved *'98*
A Thousand Acres *'97*
That Thing You Do! *'96*
Devil in a Blue Dress *'95*
Grumpier Old Men *'95*
Philadelphia *'93*
Gladiator *'92*
Night and the City *'92*
Crooked Hearts *'91*
The Silence of the Lambs *'91*
Miami Blues *'90*
Cocoon: The Return *'88*
Married to the Mob *'88*
Sweet Hearts Dance *'88*
Ferris Bueller's Day Off *'86*
Pretty in Pink *'86*
Something Wild *'86*
Swing Shift *'84*
Melvin and Howard *'80*
Where the Buffalo Roam *'80*
Cannonball *'76*
Death Race 2000 *'75*
Badlands *'74*
Caged Heat *'74*
Steve Gainer
Bully *'01*
Teenage Caveman *'01*
Foolish *'99*
Club Vampire *'98*
Ricardo Jacques Gale
Stalked *'99*
West Beirut *'98*
Bloodfist *'89*
The Nest *'88*
Michael Gallagher
Bloodfist 7: Manhunt *'95*
Bloodfist 6: Ground Zero *'94*
Rodrigo Garcia
Body Shots *'99*
Gia *'98*
Four Rooms *'95*
Indictment: The McMartin Trial *'95*
Ron Garcia
Deliberate Intent *'01*
Baby *'00*
The Runaway *'00*
Mutiny *'99*
Small Vices: A Spenser Mystery *'99*
The Great White Hype *'96*
Twin Peaks: Fire Walk with Me *'92*
El Diablo *'90*
Greg Gardiner
Big Trouble *'02*
Orange County *'02*
Dean Koontz's Mr. Murder *'98*
Where's Marlowe? *'98*
Homegrown *'97*
The Apocalypse *'96*
Somebody Is Waiting *'96*
Boys Life *'94*
Suture *'93*
The Unnamable 2: The Statement of Randolph Carter *'92*
Mike Garfath
The Enemy *'01*
Croupier *'97*
Nuns on the Run *'90*
Lamb *'85*
Lee Garmes (1898-1978)
A Big Hand for the Little Lady *'66*
Abdulla the Great *'56*
D-Day, the Sixth of June *'56*
Desperate Hours *'55*
Land of the Pharaohs *'55*
Actors and Sin *'52*
The Lusty Men *'52*
Detective Story *'51*
Our Very Own *'50*
Caught *'49*
The Paradine Case *'47*
The Secret Life of Walter Mitty *'47*
Love Letters *'45*
Guest in the House *'44*
Since You Went Away *'44*
Forever and a Day *'43*
Footlight Serenade *'42*
The Jungle Book *'42*
Lydia *'41*

Angels Over Broadway '40
Dreaming Lips '37
Smilin' Through '33
Shanghai Express '32
Strange Interlude '32
Dishonored '31
Scarface '31
Disraeli '30
Morocco '30
The Show Off '26

Andres Garreton
Darkdrive '98
Total Reality '97
Intimate Relations '95

Marcello Gatti
Burn! '70
The Battle of Algiers '66

Gaetano Antonio "Tony" Gaudio (1885-1951)
The Red Pony '49
I've Always Loved You '46
A Song to Remember '45
Days of Glory '43
The Great Lie '41
High Sierra '41
The Man Who Came to Dinner '41
Brother Orchid '40
The Fighting 69th '40
The Letter '40
Juarez '39
The Old Maid '39
Amazing Dr. Clitterhouse '38
Dawn Patrol '38
Kid Galahad '37
The Life of Emile Zola '37
Anthony Adverse '36
The Story of Louis Pasteur '36
The Mask of Fu Manchu '32
Hell's Angels '30
Little Caesar '30
The Gaucho '27
The Notorious Lady '27
Kismet '20

Eric Gautier
Pola X '99
Those Who Love Me Can Take the Train '98
Irma Vep '96
Love, etc. '96
My Sex Life...Or How I Got into an Argument '96
One Hundred and One Nights '95
The Favorite Son '94

Carlos Gaviria
Undercurrent '99
A Gun, a Car, a Blonde '97

David Geddes
Fatal Error '99
My Husband's Secret Life '98
A Call to Remember '97
Killing Mr. Griffin '97
The Colony '95
Incident at Deception Ridge '94
Call of the Wild '93
When a Stranger Calls Back '93

Lu Gengxin
The Emperor's Shadow '96
Ermo '94

Laszlo George
The Loretta Claiborne Story '00
Model Behavior '00
The Stepsister '97
Swimsuit '89

Henry W. Gerrard
Of Human Bondage '34
Little Women '33
The Most Dangerous Game '32

Merritt B. Gerstad
Watch on the Rhine '43
Bulldog Drummond's Secret Police '39
Strike Me Pink '36
A Night at the Opera '35
Imitation of Life '34
Freaks '32

Maury Gertsman
Invisible Invaders '59
The Creature Walks among Us '56
To Hell and Back '55
Red Ball Express '52
Singapore '47
The Brute Man '46
Dressed to Kill '46
She Wolf of London '46
Terror by Night '46
Jungle Captive '45

Rodney Gibbons
Eye '96
Natural Enemy '96
Screamers '96
My Bloody Valentine '81

Gerald Gibbs
Devil Doll '64
The Leather Boys '63
Quatermass 2 '57
X The Unknown '56

Paul Gibson
Paris Is Burning '91
The Refrigerator '91

Sue Gibson
Mrs. Dalloway '97
Hear My Song '91

Peter Gilbert
Prefontaine '96
Hoop Dreams '94

Pierre Gill
Lost and Delirious '01
The Art of War '00
Joan of Arc '99
Street Heart '98
Los Locos Posse '97

Dan Gillham
Final '01
Hamlet '01
Notes from Underground '95
Voodoo '95

Paul Gilpin
Tarzan and the Lost City '98
Dangerous Ground '96
Cry, the Beloved Country '95

Aldo Giordani
Amuck! '71
Atom Age Vampire '61

Basco Giurato
The Worker and the Hairdresser '96
A Pure Formality '94
Cinema Paradiso '88

Irving Glassberg
Tarnished Angels '57
The Black Shield of Falworth '54
Ride Clear of Diablo '54
Duel at Silver Creek '52
The Lawless Breed '52
The Strange Door '51
Casbah '48

Pierre William Glenn
Coup de Torchon '81
Loulou '80
Avalanche '78
Small Change '76
The Judge and the Assassin '75
Day for Night '73

Bert Glennon (1893-1967)
House of Wax '53
Rio Grande '50
The Red House '47
Dive Bomber '41
They Died with Their Boots On '41
Our Town '40
Stagecoach '39
The Hurricane '37
Dimples '36
Lloyds of London '36
Scarlet Empress '34
Are Parents People? '25

James Glennon (1942-)
Dead Simple '01
Life Without Dick '01
Playing Mona Lisa '00
South of Heaven, West of Hell '00
Election '99
The Runner '99
Best Men '98
Citizen Ruth '96
Lifeform '96
Mojave Moon '96
My Very Best Friend '96
Mrs. Munck '95
High Stakes '93
In the Deep Woods '91
Smooth Talk '85

Paul Glickman
The Stuff '85
God Told Me To '76
Tracks '76
Dracula vs. Frankenstein '71

Richard C. Glouner (1932-98)
Moon of the Wolf '72
The Dunwich Horror '70
The Gay Deceivers '69

Agnes Godard
The Dreamlife of Angels '98
The New Eve '98
Nenette and Boni '96
I Can't Sleep '93

Michael Goi
Echo of Murder '00
Forbidden Sins '99
The Fixer '97

Stephen Goldblatt
Conspiracy '01
The Deep End of the Ocean '98
Batman and Robin '97
Striptease '96
Batman Forever '95
The Pelican Brief '93
For the Boys '91
The Prince of Tides '91
Joe Versus the Volcano '90
Lethal Weapon 2 '89
Lethal Weapon '87
The Cotton Club '84
The Hunger '83
Outland '81

Eric Goldstein
Shelter '98
Naked Souls '95

David Golia
Street Corner Justice '96
The Rosary Murders '87

Carlos Gonzalez
Arachnid '01
The Breaks '99
The Omega Code '99
Wishmaster 2: Evil Never Dies '98
Original Gangstas '96
Mutant Species '95

Irv Goodnoff
James Dean: Live Fast, Die Young '97
The Van '77

Gerald R. Goozie
Hostile Intent '97
Specimen '97
Fatal Combat '96
Electra '95
Street Law '95

Michael Gornick
Day of the Dead '85
Creepshow '82
Knightriders '81
Dawn of the Dead '78
Martin '77

Arthur Grant
Demons of the Mind '72
Dynasty of Fear '72
Blood from the Mummy's Tomb '71
Taste the Blood of Dracula '70
Frankenstein Must Be Destroyed '69
A Challenge for Robin Hood '68
The Devil Rides Out '68
Dracula Has Risen from the Grave '68
The Mummy's Shroud '67
Frankenstein Created Woman '66
Plague of the Zombies '66
The Reptile '66
The Witches '66
Tomb of Ligeia '64
Paranoiac '62
The Phantom of the Opera '62
The Curse of the Werewolf '61
The Abominable Snowman '57
John and Julie '55

Jaems Grant
Strange Fits of Passion '99
Head On '98

Moray Grant
I, Monster '71
Vampire Circus '71
The Horror of Frankenstein '70
The Vampire Lovers '70

Barry Gravelle
Requiem for Murder '99
Sir Arthur Conan Doyle's The Lost World '98
When Justice Fails '98
Bleeders '97
Face the Evil '97
Sci-Fighters '96
Witchboard 3: The Possession '95

Gary Graver
The Capitol Conspiracy '99
The Escort '97
Invisible Dad '97
James Dean: Live Fast, Die Young '97
The Corporation '96
Friend of the Family 2 '96
Invisible Mom '96
Scorned 2 '96
Sexual Roulette '96
Vice Girls '96
Attack of the 60-Foot Centerfold '95
Femme Fontaine: Killer Babe for the C.I.A. '95
Masseuse '95
Midnight Tease 2 '95
Night Eyes 4: Fatal Passion '95
Sorceress '94
Dinosaur Island '93
It's All True '93
Bad Girls from Mars '90
Smokey Bites the Dust '81
Death Sport '78
The Toolbox Murders '78
Grand Theft Auto '77
Invasion of the Bee Girls '73
Dracula vs. Frankenstein '71
Satan's Sadists '69

Mark W. Gray
Firetrap '01
Sand Trap '97
Back to Back '96
Dark Rider '91

Aldo (G.R. Aldo) Graziatti
Twist & Shout '84
Othello '52

Richard Greatrex
A Knight's Tale '01
The Last of the Blonde Bombshells '00
Where the Heart Is '00
Shakespeare in Love '98
Tess of the D'Urbervilles '98
Mrs. Brown '97
Blue Juice '95

Guy Green (1913-)
I Am a Camera '55
Captain Horatio Hornblower '51
Madeleine '50
Blanche Fury '48
Oliver Twist '48
Great Expectations '46
Immortal Battalion '44

Jack N. Green
Space Cowboys '00
Girl, Interrupted '99
True Crime '99
Absolute Power '97
Midnight in the Garden of Good and Evil '97
Speed 2: Cruise Control '97
Traveller '96
Twister '96
The Amazing Panda Adventure '95
The Bridges of Madison County '95
The Net '95
Bad Company '94
A Perfect World '93
Rookie of the Year '93
Unforgiven '92
Deceived '91
White Hunter, Black Heart '90
Bird '88
Heartbreak Ridge '86

Mutz Greenbaum
Lucky Jim '58
Non-Stop New York '37
Nine Days a Queen '36

Adam Greenberg
Collateral Damage '02
Inspector Gadget '99
Rush Hour '98
Sphere '97
Eraser '96
First Knight '95
Junior '94
Dave '93
Sister Act '92
Toys '92
Terminator 2: Judgment Day '91
Ghost '90
Three Men and a Little Lady '90
Turner and Hooch '89
Alien Nation '88
La Bamba '87
Near Dark '87
Three Men and a Baby '87
Once Bitten '85
The Big Red One '80
Madron '70

Robbie Greenberg
James Dean '01
Save the Last Dance '01
If These Walls Could Talk 2 '00
Snow Day '00
Introducing Dorothy Dandridge '99
Winchell '98
Fools Rush In '97
Sunset Park '96
Under Siege 2: Dark Territory '95
Free Willy '93
All I Want for Christmas '91
Far North '88
The Milagro Beanfield War '88
Creator '85
Sweet Dreams '85
Swamp Thing '82
The Lathe of Heaven '80

William Howard Greene (1895-1956)
When Worlds Collide '51
The Big Cat '49
Can't Help Singing '45
Salome, Where She Danced '45
The Climax '44
Cobra Woman '44
Ali Baba and the Forty Thieves '43
The Phantom of the Opera '43
The Shepherd of the Hills '41
Jesse James '39
Nothing Sacred '37
A Star Is Born '37
The Garden of Allah '36
The Trail of the Lonesome Pine '36

Jack Greenhalgh
Robot Monster '53
Danger Zone '51
The Lost Continent '51
Money Madness '47
Danny Boy '46
The Mask of Diijon '46
The Lady Confesses '45
White Pongo '45
Dead Men Walk '43
Desperate Cargo '41
Texas Trouble '41
Arizona Gangbusters '40
Billy the Kid in Texas '40
Reefer Madness '38

David Gribble
Chill Factor '99
The Quest '96
Nowhere to Run '93
Fires Within '91
Cadillac Man '90

Frank Griebe
The Princess and the Warrior '00
Run Lola Run '98
Winter Sleepers '97

Garett Griffin
Lover's Knot '96
Space Marines '96

Loyal Griggs (1906-78)
The Greatest Story Ever Told '65
In Harm's Way '65
The Slender Thread '65
Papa's Delicate Condition '63
Girls! Girls! Girls! '62
G.I. Blues '60
The Buccaneer '58
Hot Spell '58
The Sad Sack '57
Three Violent People '57
The Tin Star '57
The Ten Commandments '56
The Bridges at Toko-Ri '55
We're No Angels '55
Elephant Walk '54
White Christmas '54
Shane '53
Cavalry Charge '51

Marcel Grignon
The Beast '75
Madron '70
Is Paris Burning? '66
Dangerous Liaisons '60
Une Parisienne '58

Xavier Perez Grobet
In the Time of the Butterflies '01
Tortilla Soup '01
Before Night Falls '00
Santitos '99
Esmeralda Comes by Night '98

Francis Grumman
Gang Boys '97
Killing Obsession '94

Alexander Grusynski
The Brothers '01
Two Can Play That Game '01
Dick '99
54 '98
The Craft '96
Maximum Risk '96
Angus '95
I Like It Like That '94
Threesome '94
Stone Cold '91
Tremors '89
The Women of Brewster Place '89
Bad Dreams '88

Ennio Guarnieri
Francesco '93
A.D. '85
The Cassandra Crossing '76
The Inheritance '76
The Garden of the Finzi-Continis '71
Camille 2000 '69

Burnett Guffey (1905-83)
The Great White Hope '70
The Learning Tree '69
The Ambushers '67
Bonnie & Clyde '67
How to Succeed in Business without Really Trying '67
The Silencers '66
King Rat '65
Birdman of Alcatraz '62
Kid Galahad '62
Homicidal '61
Mr. Sardonicus '61
Let No Man Write My Epitaph '60

Gidget '59
Me and the Colonel '58
The Strange One '57
The Harder They Fall '56
Tight Spot '55
The Violent Men '55
Human Desire '54
Private Hell 36 '54
From Here to Eternity '53
Sirocco '51
In a Lonely Place '50
All the King's Men '49
Knock on Any Door '49
Reckless Moment '49

Eric Guichard
Himalaya '99
The Crazy Stranger '98
Mondo '96

Allen Guilford
Aberration '97
The Climb '97

David Gurfinkel
Under the Domim Tree '95
Blink of an Eye '92
Delta Force '86

Eugeny Guslinsky
Termination Man '97
Marquis de Sade '96

Manfred Guthe
Poltergeist: The Legacy '96
The Stupids '95

Carl Guthrie
House on Haunted Hill '58
Lady Godiva '55
Long John Silver '54
Francis Covers the Big Town '53
Francis Goes to West Point '52
Bedtime for Bonzo '51

Ron Hagen
Little Boy Blue '97
Talk '94
Romper Stomper '92

Rob Hahn
The Score '01
Loser '00
In and Out '97

Bert Haines
Steamboat Bill, Jr. '28
College '27
Battling Butler '26
The General '26

Jacques Haitkin
Hell's Gate '01
Faust: Love of the Damned '00
The Base '99
Blowback '99
Apartment Complex '98
Wishmaster '97
The Big Squeeze '96
Fist of the North Star '95
One Good Turn '95
Two Bits & Pepper '95
Evolver '94
Silence of the Hams '93
The Ambulance '90
Shocker '89
To Die For '89
Cherry 2000 '88
The Hidden '87
A Nightmare on Elm Street 2: Freddy's Revenge '85
Making the Grade '84
A Nightmare on Elm Street '84
House Where Evil Dwells '82
Galaxy of Terror '81
The Private Eyes '80

Conrad L. Hall (1926-)
American Beauty '99
A Civil Action '98
Without Limits '97
Searching for Bobby Fischer '93
Tequila Sunrise '88
Black Widow '87
Incubus '82
Marathon Man '76
The Day of the Locust '75
Smile '75
Electra Glide in Blue '73
Fat City '72
Butch Cassidy and the Sundance Kid '69
The Happy Ending '69
Hell in the Pacific '69
Tell Them Willie Boy Is Here '69
Cool Hand Luke '67
Divorce American Style '67
In Cold Blood '67
Harper '66
The Professionals '66
Incubus '65
Morituri '65

Ernest Haller
Lilies of the Field '63
Married Too Young '62
What Ever Happened to Baby Jane? '62
Men in War '57
Rebel without a Cause '55
Humoresque '46
Saratoga Trunk '45
Dark Victory '39
The Roaring Twenties '39
Jezebel '38

Fenton Hamilton
It's Alive 2: It Lives Again '78
It's Alive '74
Black Caesar '73
Hell Up in Harlem '73

Victor Hammer
Sour Grapes '98
Down Periscope '96
Billy Madison '94
8 Seconds '94
Heavyweights '94
Major League 2 '94
House of Cards '92
Lean on Me '89

Poon Hang-Seng
Pavilion of Women '01
Jackie Chan's Who Am I '98
The Executioners '93
The Heroic Trio '93

Peter Hannan
Longitude '00
Not Without My Daughter '90
How to Get Ahead in Advertising '89
A Handful of Dust '88
The Lonely Passion of Judith Hearne '87
Withnail and I '87
Dance with a Stranger '85
Insignificance '85
Monty Python's The Meaning of Life '83
Dangerous Summer '82

Kazutami Hara
Akira Kurosawa's Dreams '90
Godzilla 1985 '85

Russell Harlan
Hatari! '62
To Kill a Mockingbird '62
Pollyanna '60
Sunrise at Campobello '60
Operation Petticoat '59
Rio Bravo '59
King Creole '58
Run Silent, Run Deep '58
Witness for the Prosecution '57
Blackboard Jungle '55
The Thing '51
Gun Crazy '49
Red River '48
A Walk in the Sun '46

Virgil Harper
Tremors 3: Back to Perfection '01
Tremors 2: Aftershocks '96
... And the Earth Did Not Swallow Him '94

Harvey Harrison
R.P.M. '97
The Witches '90
American Gothic '88
Salome's Last Dance '88
Castaway '87
Cheech and Chong's The Corsican Brothers '84
Cheech and Chong: Still Smokin' '83
The Burning '82

Thomas M. Harting
No One Sleeps '01
Ripper: Letter from Hell '01
Beefcake '99
Defying Gravity '99

Irek Hartowicz
Outside Ozona '98
Lured Innocence '97
Mercenary '96

Kim Haun
Body Strokes '95
Friend of the Family '95
I Like to Play Games '95

Robert B. Hauser (1919-94)
The Frisco Kid '79
Mean Dog Blues '78
Twilight's Last Gleaming '77
Walking Tall: The Final Chapter '77
Le Mans '71
Willard '71
A Man Called Horse '70
Soldier Blue '70
Hail, Hero! '69
The Odd Couple '68

Yuri Haviv
Double Agent 73 '80
I Spit on Your Grave '77

Robert Hayes
Body Armor '96
Werewolf '95
Mind, Body & Soul '92
Hardcase and Fist '89

James Hayman
Buffy the Vampire Slayer '92
Blades '89

Dan Heigh
The Basket '99
Matter of Trust '98
Laws of Deception '97
Navajo Blues '97

Bernd Heinl
The Little Vampire '00
The Extreme Adventures of Super Dave '98
Wicked '98
Johnny Skidmarks '97
Julian Po '97
The Last of the High Kings '96
It's My Party '95
The Nutt House '95
Pie in the Sky '95
The Fear '94
Younger & Younger '94
Bodies, Rest & Motion '93
Bagdad Cafe '88

Wolfgang Held
Fallout '01
Maze '01
The Tic Code '99
Floating '97
Ripe '97
Dogs: The Rise and Fall of an All-Girl Bookie Joint '96
Wigstock: The Movie '95

Otto Heller
I'll Never Forget What's 'Isname '67
Alfie '66
Funeral in Berlin '66
The Ipcress File '65
Victim '61
Peeping Tom '60
Who Done It? '56
The Ladykillers '55
They Made Me a Fugitive '47
De Mayerling a Sarajevo '40

David Hennings
Boycott '02
Cheaters '00
Meet the Deedles '98
Tom Clancy's Netforce '98
Very Bad Things '98
Asteroid '97
D3: The Mighty Ducks '96
Titanic '96

Karl Herrmann
Missing Pieces '00
Kounterfeit '96
America's Dream '95

John Herzog
Crackerjack 2 '97
Hello Mary Lou: Prom Night 2 '87

Gregg Heschong
A Cry in the Wild '90
Heavy Traffic '73

Sid Hickox
Battle Cry '55
Them! '54
White Heat '49
The Big Sleep '46
All Through the Night '42
Underground '41
The Wagons Roll at Night '41

Ken Higgins
Hot Millions '68
Cop-Out '67
Georgy Girl '66
Darling '65

Jack Hildyard (1915-)
Lion of the Desert '81
Emily '77
The Message '77
The Beast Must Die '75
Puppet on a Chain '72
Topaz '69
Villa Rides '68
Casino Royale '67
Modesty Blaise '66
Battle of the Bulge '65
Circus World '64
55 Days at Peking '63
The V.I.P.'s '63
The Road to Hong Kong '62
The Millionairess '60
The Sundowners '60
The Devil's Disciple '59
Suddenly, Last Summer '59
Another Time, Another Place '58
The Bridge on the River Kwai '57
Anastasia '56
Summertime '55
Hobson's Choice '53

Erwin Hillier
The Valley of Gwangi '69
I Know Where I'm Going '45
Butler's Dilemma '43

Sinsaku Himeda
Vengeance Is Mine '79
Tora! Tora! Tora! '70

Paul Hipp
The Incredible Two-Headed Transplant '71
Superchick '71

Gerald Hirschfeld (1921-)
Coma '78
The Car '77
Two Minute Warning '76
Young Frankenstein '74
Cotton Comes to Harlem '70
The Incident '67
Fail-Safe '64

Daf Hobson
Othello '01
Welcome to Sarajevo '97
Go Now '96
The Tenant of Wildfell Hall '96

Winton C. Hoch (1907-79)
The Witching '72
The Green Berets '68
Robinson Crusoe on Mars '64
Five Weeks in a Balloon '62
Voyage to the Bottom of the Sea '61
Darby O'Gill & the Little People '59
The Young Land '59
Jet Pilot '57
The Searchers '56
Mister Roberts '55
The Halls of Montezuma '50
She Wore a Yellow Ribbon '49
Tulsa '49
Melody Time '48
Three Godfathers '48
Dive Bomber '41
Dr. Cyclops '40

Zoran Hochstatter
If I Die Before I Wake '98
The Last Best Sunday '98
Slaves to the Underground '96
Body Chemistry 4: Full Exposure '95
Demolition High '95
Almost Dead '94
Hard Bounty '94
Night Fire '94
Home for Christmas '93
Not of This Earth '88

Ken Hodges
No Sex Please—We're British '73
The Ruling Class '72

Carl Hoffmann
Faust '26
Dr. Mabuse, The Gambler '22

Henner Hofmann
Warden of Red Rock '01
Immortal Combat '94

Adam Holender
A Price above Rubies '97
Wide Awake '97
8 Heads in a Duffel Bag '96
I'm Not Rappaport '96
Smoke '95
Fresh '94
To Kill a Priest '89
Street Smart '87
Idolmaker '80
Panic in Needle Park '75
Midnight Cowboy '69

Keith Holland
Blind Heat '00
Bloody Murder '99
Hindsight '97
Trucks '97
Dark Secrets '95
Carnosaur '93

John Holosko
The Jesse Ventura Story '99
Face Down '97

Ernest Holzman
Cora Unashamed '00
Double Edge '97
Love Jones '96

John Hooper
The Scarlet Pimpernel 3: The Kidnapped King '99
Buddy's Song '91

Nathan Hope
Mimic 2 '01
Nice Guys Sleep Alone '99
The Prophecy 3: The Ascent '99

John Hora
God Said "Ha!" '99
Matinee '92
Gremlins 2: The New Batch '90
Gremlins '84
Twilight Zone: The Movie '83
The Howling '81

Louis Horvath
Mesmerized '84
Strange Invaders '83
Strange Behavior '81
Brain of Blood '71

Byron Houck
Seven Chances '25
The Navigator '24

James Wong Howe (1899-1976)
The Old Man and the Sea '90
Funny Lady '75
Molly Maguires '70
The Heart Is a Lonely Hunter '68
Hombre '67
Seconds '66
Hud '63
Song Without End '60
The Last Angry Man '59
Bell, Book and Candle '58
The Old Man and the Sea '58
Sweet Smell of Success '57
Picnic '55
The Rose Tattoo '55
Come Back, Little Sheba '52
The Fighter '52
Baron of Arizona '51
Mr. Blandings Builds His Dream House '48
Body and Soul '47
Pursued '47
Objective, Burma! '45
Passage to Marseilles '44
Air Force '43
The North Star '43
Hangmen Also Die '42
Yankee Doodle Dandy '42
Kings Row '41
Strawberry Blonde '41
Abe Lincoln in Illinois '40
City for Conquest '40
Oklahoma Kid '39
They Made Me a Criminal '39
The Adventures of Tom Sawyer '38
Algiers '38
Fire Over England '37
Prisoner of Zenda '37
Under the Red Robe '36
Mark of the Vampire '35
Hollywood Party '34
Manhattan Melodrama '34
The Thin Man '34
Chandu the Magician '32
Peter Pan '24

Matt Howe
Desolation Angels '95
Parallel Sons '95

Gil Hubbs
Flowers in the Attic '87
Terror at London Bridge '85
California Girls '84
This Is Elvis '81
The Guyana Tragedy: The Story of Jim Jones '80
Enter the Dragon '73

Roger Hubert
Paris Holiday '57
Portrait of an Assassin '49
Children of Paradise '44
Eternal Return '43
Napoleon '27

Michael Hugo
The Mountain Men '80
The Manitou '78
Bug '75
Head '68

Alan Hume
20,000 Leagues Under the Sea '97
Just Like a Woman '95
Eve of Destruction '90
Shirley Valentine '89
A Fish Called Wanda '88
Lifeforce '85
Runaway Train '85
A View to a Kill '85
Supergirl '84
Octopussy '83
Return of the Jedi '83
Caveman '81
Eye of the Needle '81
For Your Eyes Only '81
The Watcher in the Woods '81
The People That Time Forgot '77
At the Earth's Core '76
The Land That Time Forgot '75
The Legend of Hell House '73
Carry On Cowboy '66
Dr. Terror's House of Horrors '65
Kiss of the Vampire '62

John Huneck
Big Brother Trouble '00
One Man's Justice '95
The Banker '89

J. Roy Hunt
I Walked with a Zombie '43
Room Service '38
She '35

Shane Hurlbut
crazy/beautiful '01
The Skulls '00
The Rat Pack '98

Tom Hurwitz
Subway Stories '97
Creepshow 2 '87

Peter Hyams (1943-)
The Musketeer '01
End of Days '99
The Relic '96
Sudden Death '95

Timecop '94
Stay Tuned '92
Running Scared '86
2010: The Year We Make Contact '84

Arthur Ibbetson
Santa Claus: The Movie '85
The Bounty '84
Sell Out '76
Willy Wonka & the Chocolate Factory '71
The Railway Children '70
Where Eagles Dare '68
A Countess from Hong Kong '67
Die! Die! My Darling! '65
Whistle down the Wind '61
The Horse's Mouth '58

Slawomir Idziak
Black Hawk Down '01
Proof of Life '00
The Last September '99
Love and Rage '99
I Want You '98
Gattaca '97
Hombres Armados '97
Commandments '96
The Journey of August King '95
Lilian's Story '95
Trois Couleurs: Bleu '93
The Double Life of Veronique '91
The Decalogue '88
From a Far Country: Pope John Paul II '81
Contract '80

Tony Imi (1937-)
Victoria & Albert '01
Rancid Aluminium '00
Dead of Night '99
Aimee & Jaguar '98
The Abduction '96
Dalva '95
Shopping '93
Carolina Skeletons '92
Wired '89
Enemy Mine '85
A Christmas Carol '84
The Slipper and the Rose '76
Edward the King '75
It's Not the Size That Counts '74

David Insley
Cry-Baby '90
Hairspray '88
Polyester '81

John Inwood
Six Ways to Sunday '99
The Daytrippers '96

Silvano Ippoliti
Caligula '80
Act of Aggression '73

Judy Irola
Eban and Charley '01
The Settlement '99
Eat Your Heart Out '96
Working Girls '87

Louis Irving
Howling 3: The Marsupials '87
Return of Captain Invincible '83

Mark Irwin
American Pie 2 '01
Freddy Got Fingered '01
Osmosis Jones '01
Say It Isn't So '01
Me, Myself, and Irene '00
Road Trip '00
Ten Things I Hate about You '99
Misbegotten '98
There's Something about Mary '98
Zack & Reba '98
Joe Torre: Curveballs Along the Way '97
Steel '97
Kingpin '96
Scream '96
The Avenging Angel '95
Vampire in Brooklyn '95
Dumb & Dumber '94
Wes Craven's New Nightmare '94
Extreme Justice '93
Passenger 57 '92
Showdown in Little Tokyo '91
RoboCop 2 '90
Bat 21 '88
The Blob '88
Fright Night 2 '88
The Fly '86
Dead Zone '83
Videodrome '83
Night School '81
Scanners '81
The Brood '79

Levie Isaacks
Dead Men Can't Dance '97
North Shore Fish '97
The Dentist '96
Marshal Law '96
The Dogfighters '95
The Expert '95
The Texas Chainsaw Massacre 4: The Next Generation '95
The Wharf Rat '95
Leprechaun '93
Spontaneous Combustion '89
Saturday the 14th Strikes Back '88

Marco Isoli
Desperate Crimes '93
Evil Clutch '89

Takeo Ito
Drunken Angel '48
The Men Who Tread on the Tiger's Tail '45

Paul Ivano
The Naked Flame '68
Black Angel '46
The Shanghai Gesture '42
Queen Kelly '29

Harry Jackson (1896-1953)
The Halls of Montezuma '50
Mother Wore Tights '47

Peter James
Bride of the Wind '01
Meet the Parents '00
Double Jeopardy '99
The Newton Boys '97
Paradise Road '97
Diabolique '96
Last Dance '96
Silent Fall '94
Alive '93
My Life '93
The Thing Called Love '93
Black Robe '91
Mister Johnson '91
Driving Miss Daisy '89
Echoes of Paradise '86
The Irishman '78
Caddie '76

Andrew Janczak
The Undertaker and His Pals '67
Creeping Terror '64

Anthony C. "Tony" Jannelli
All I Wanna Do '98
Lovelife '97
Subway Stories '97

Maris Jansons
Double Play '96
The Halfback of Notre Dame '96
Heck's Way Home '95

Devereaux Jennings
Helltown '38
Public Enemy '31
Steamboat Bill, Jr. '28
Battling Butler '26
The General '26

Johnny E. Jensen
The Flamingo Rising '01
The Ladies Man '00
Rosewood '96
Three Wishes '95
Grumpy Old Men '93
An American Story '92
Rambling Rose '91

Matthew Jensen
Man of the Century '99
Ratas, Ratones, Rateros '99

Peter C. Jensen
Glitch! '88
Grandma's House '88

Peter Jessop
Band of Gold '95
Mountbatten: The Last Viceroy '86
Schizo '77
House of Whipcord '75
Frightmare '74
Flesh and Blood Show '73
The Harder They Come '72

Robert C. Jessup
Porky's Revenge '85
Silent Rage '82
Deadly Blessing '81
Race with the Devil '75
Creature of Destruction '67
Mars Needs Women '66

Thomas Jewett
Fast Money '96
Serial Killer '95
Scanner Cop 2: Volkin's Revenge '94
Mikey '92

Daniel Jobin
Varian's War '01
It's My Turn, Laura Cadieux '98
The Hanging Garden '97
Lilies '96

Jon Joffin
Snow White: The Fairest of Them All '02
Mermaid '00
Aftershock: Earthquake in New York '99

Bruce Douglas Johnson
The Contaminated Man '01
Drowning Mona '00
Happy, Texas '99
Road Ends '98
Cadillac Ranch '96
The Prophecy '95
Public Access '93

David Johnson
Resident Evil '02
An Ideal Husband '99
Hilary and Jackie '98
The Very Thought of You '98
The Mill on the Floss '97
Othello '95
Saint-Ex: The Story of the Storyteller '95

Hugh Johnson
G.I. Jane '97
White Squall '96

Shelly Johnson
Jurassic Park 3 '01
The Last Castle '01
Durango '99
A Season for Miracles '99
Quicksilver Highway '98
Saint Maybe '98
Jack's Back '87

Dusan Joksimovic
The Wounds '98
Pretty Village, Pretty Flame '96

Lawrence Jones
In His Life: The John Lennon Story '00
The 10th Kingdom '00

Richard A. Jones
Wanted '98
Turn of the Blade '97

Mario Garcia Joya
Strawberry and Chocolate '93
Letters from the Park '88

Ray June
Court Jester '56
Above and Beyond '53
The Secret Garden '49
Night Must Fall '37
Horse Feathers '32
The Bat Whispers '30
Alibi '29

Jeffrey Jur
My Big Fat Greek Wedding '02
Joy Ride '01
My First Mister '01
Panic '00
How Stella Got Her Groove Back '98
Horton Foote's Alone '97
Unforgettable '96
The Last Seduction '94
Dirty Dancing '87
Soul Man '86
Screen Test '85

Hans Jura
Little Mother '71
The Lickerish Quartet '70
Therese & Isabelle '67
Carmen, Baby '66

Jurgen Jurges
Funny Games '97
Faraway, So Close! '93
Germany, Pale Mother '80
Ali: Fear Eats the Soul '74
Effi Briest '74
Tenderness of the Wolves '73

Steven Kaman
Mob War '88
Search and Destroy '88
Firehouse '87
Hangmen '87

Janusz Kaminski (1959-)
A. I.: Artificial Intelligence '01
Saving Private Ryan '98
Amistad '97
The Lost World: Jurassic Park 2 '97
Jerry Maguire '96
How to Make an American Quilt '95
Tall Tale: The Unbelievable Adventures of Pecos Bill '95
Little Giants '94
The Adventures of Huck Finn '93
Schindler's List '93
Class of '61 '92
Cool As Ice '91
Wildflower '91
Grim Prairie Tales '89

Adam Kane
Love & Sex '00
Boondock Saints '99
No Code of Conduct '98
Within the Rock '96

Taiichi Kankura
Yog, Monster from Space '71
Destroy All Monsters '68

Avi (Avraham) Karpik
Simon Sez '99
Sticks and Stones '96
Outside the Law '95
Solar Force '94
The Seventh Coin '92

Norayr Kasper
The Life Before This '99
Calendar '93

Stephen M. Katz
A Death in the Family '02
Return to Cabin by the Lake '01
Gepetto '00
I'll Remember April '99
Baby Geniuses '98
Gods and Monsters '98
Mrs. Santa Claus '96
Letter to My Killer '95
My Summer Story '94
18 Again! '88
Last Resort '86
The Blues Brothers '80
Kentucky Fried Movie '77
Las Vegas Lady '76
Pom Pom Girls '76
Switchblade Sisters '75

Boris Kaufman (1906-80)
The Brotherhood '68
The Group '66
The Pawnbroker '65
The World of Henry Orient '64
Gone Are the Days '63
Long Day's Journey into Night '62
The Fugitive Kind '60
Twelve Angry Men '57
Baby Doll '56
Patterns '56
On the Waterfront '54
L'Atalante '34
Zero for Conduct '33
A Propos de Nice '29

Lloyd Kaufman
Stuck on You '84
First Turn On '83
Waitress '81
Squeeze Play '79

Stephen Kazmierski
Tart '01
You Can Count On Me '99
The Bumblebee Flies Anyway '98
The Myth of Fingerprints '97
Grind '96
Blessing '94

Michel Kelber
The Hunchback of Notre Dame '57
Beauty and the Devil '50
Devil in the Flesh '46

Wallace Kelley
Paradise, Hawaiian Style '66
The Nutty Professor '63
Who's Minding the Store? '63

Shane Kelly
Urbania '00
Delivered '98

Ken Kelsch
Dying to Get Rich '98
The Imposters '98
New Rose Hotel '98
Rear Window '98
The Blackout '97
A Brooklyn State of Mind '97
Montana '97
Subway Stories '97
The Funeral '96
The Addiction '95
Big Night '95
Condition Red '95
Killer: A Journal of Murder '95
DROP Squad '94
Bad Lieutenant '92
Driller Killer '79

Victor Kemper (1927-)
Eddie '96
Jingle All the Way '96
Tommy Boy '95
Beethoven '92
F/X 2: The Deadly Art of Illusion '91
See No Evil, Hear No Evil '89
Clue '85
Pee-wee's Big Adventure '85
The Lonely Guy '84
Mr. Mom '83
National Lampoon's Vacation '83
Xanadu '80
And Justice for All '79
The Jerk '79
Coma '78
Eyes of Laura Mars '78
Magic '78
Audrey Rose '77
Slap Shot '77
Dog Day Afternoon '75
The Reincarnation of Peter Proud '75
The Gambler '74
The Candidate '72
The Hospital '71
They Might Be Giants '71
Husbands '70

Nils Kenaston
Day at the Beach '98
Mob Queen '98

Francis Kenny
How High '01
Kingdom Come '01
Scary Movie '00
She's All That '99
A Night at the Roxbury '98
Something About Sex '98
Bean '97
Harriet the Spy '96
A Thin Line Between Love and Hate '96
Coneheads '93
Wayne's World 2 '93
New Jack City '91
Heathers '89

John Kenway
My Uncle Silas '01
Pride and Prejudice '95
Bhaji on the Beach '94

Glenn Kershaw
At First Sight '95
A Kiss Goodnight '94

Rolf Kestermann
Casual Sex? '88
Surf Nazis Must Die '87

Darius Khondji
Panic Room '02
The Beach '00
The Ninth Gate '99
In Dreams '98
Alien: Resurrection '97
Evita '96
Stealing Beauty '96
The City of Lost Children '95
Seven '95
Delicatessen '92

Gary B. Kibbe
John Carpenter's Ghosts of Mars '01
John Carpenter's Vampires '97
Escape from L.A. '96
In the Mouth of Madness '95
Village of the Damned '95
Double Dragon '94
RoboCop 3 '91
They Live '88
Prince of Darkness '87

Jan Kiesser
Rare Birds '01
Dr. T & the Women '00
Holiday Heart '00
Trixie '00
The Dress Code '99
The Baby Dance '98
Such a Long Journey '98
National Lampoon's Dad's Week Off '97
Bad Moon '96
Georgia '95
Man with a Gun '95
Mrs. Parker and the Vicious Circle '94
Clean and Sober '88
Fright Night '85
Choose Me '84

Jeffrey L. Kimball
Mission: Impossible 2 '00
Stigmata '99
Wild Things '98
The Specialist '94
True Romance '93
Jacob's Ladder '90
Beverly Hills Cop 2 '87
Top Gun '86

Adam Kimmel
Beyond Suspicion '00
Jesus' Son '99
Monument Ave. '98
Almost Heroes '97
Subway Stories '97
Beautiful Girls '96
Bed of Roses '95
New Jersey Drive '95

Sven Kirsten
Play Time '94
Teresa's Tattoo '94
Mistress '91

Alar Kivilo
Hart's War '02
The Glass House '01
Frequency '00
A Simple Plan '98
Weapons of Mass Distraction '97
Gotti '96
Rebound: The Legend of Earl "The Goat" Manigault '96
The Invaders '95

Eugen Klagemann
The Merry Wives of Windsor '50
The Marriage of Figaro '49
The Murderers Are Among Us '46
The Murderers are Among Us '46

David Klein
Wish You Were Dead '00
Chasing Amy '97
Mallrats '95
Clerks '94

Vladimir Klimov
Out of the Cold '99
The Thief '97

Benjamin (Ben H.) Kline (1894-1974)
Bull of the West '89
Munster, Go Home! '66
Detour '46
Before I Hang '40
Two-Fisted Law '32

Richard H. Kline
Meet Wally Sparks '97
Double Impact '91
My Stepmother Is an Alien '88
Howard the Duck '86
All of Me '84
Body Heat '81
Star Trek: The Motion Picture '80
The Fury '78
Who'll Stop the Rain? '78
King Kong '76
Battle for the Planet of the Apes '73
Harrad Experiment '73
Soylent Green '73
The Andromeda Strain '71
Camelot '67
Hang 'Em High '67

Edward Klosinski
Trois Couleurs: Blanc '94
Kill Cruise '90
The Decalogue '88
Man of Iron '81
Illumination '73

Thomas Kloss
Showtime '02
Palmetto '98
Fear '96

Douglas Knapp
Assault on Precinct 13 '76
The First Nudie Musical '75
Dark Star '74

David Knaus
Red Shoe Diaries: Swimming Naked '00
Bird of Prey '95

Nicholas D. Knowland
Jesus Christ Superstar '00
Joseph and the Amazing Technicolor Dreamcoat '00
Institue Benjamenta or This Dream People Call Human Life '95
Barbarians at the Gate '93
Wild West '93

Bernard Knowles (1900-)
Secret Mission '42
Gaslight '40
Young and Innocent '37
Sabotage '36
The Secret Agent '36
The 39 Steps '35

Cyril Knowles
Secret Mission '42
King Solomon's Mines '37

Setsuo Kobayashi
An Actor's Revenge '63
Fires on the Plain '59

Douglas Koch
Last Night '98
When Night Is Falling '95

Fred W. Koenekamp (1922-)
Flight of the Intruder '90
Listen to Me '89
Welcome Home '89
The Adventures of Buckaroo Banzai Across the Eighth Dimension '84
Two of a Kind '83
Wrong Is Right '82
First Monday in October '81
The Hunter '80
When Time Ran Out '80
The Amityville Horror '79
The Champ '79
Love and Bullets '79
The Swarm '78
The Bad News Bears in Breaking Training '77
The Domino Principle '77
Fun with Dick and Jane '77
Islands in the Stream '77
The Other Side of Midnight '77
Embryo '76
Doc Savage '75
The McCullochs '75
White Line Fever '75
The Towering Inferno '74
Uptown Saturday Night '74
Papillon '73
Rage '72
Billy Jack '71
Beyond the Valley of the Dolls '70
Patton '70

Karl Kofler
Echo Park '86
The Children of Theatre Street '77

Hajime Koizumi
War of the Gargantuas '70
Godzilla vs. Monster Zero '68
Dagora, the Space Monster '65
Ghidrah the Three Headed Monster '65
Godzilla vs. Mothra '64
Attack of the Mushroom People '63
King Kong vs. Godzilla '63
Mothra '62

Lajos Koltai
Malena '00
Sunshine '99
The Legend of 1900 '98
Out to Sea '97
Mother '96
Home for the Holidays '95
Just Cause '94
When a Man Loves a Woman '94
Born Yesterday '93
Wrestling Ernest Hemingway '93
Meeting Venus '91
Mobsters '91
White Palace '90
Homer and Eddie '89
Hanussen '88
Gaby: A True Story '87
Colonel Redl '84
Time Stands Still '82
Mephisto '81
Angi Vera '78
Adoption '75

Shigeru Komatsubara
Dr. Akagi '98
The Eel '96

Sergei Koslov
Merlin '98
The Odyssey '97

Simon Kossoff
The Scarlet Pimpernel '99
The Scarlet Pimpernel 2: Mademoiselle Guillotine '99

Laszlo Kovacs (1933-)
Miss Congeniality '00
Return to Me '00
Jack Frost '98
My Best Friend's Wedding '97
Multiplicity '96
Copycat '95
Free Willy 2: The Adventure Home '95
The Scout '94
Say Anything '89
Legal Eagles '86
Mask '85
Ghostbusters '84
Frances '82
The Toy '82
For Pete's Sake '74
Five Easy Pieces '70
Blood of Dracula's Castle '69
Easy Rider '69
Rebel Rousers '69
Mantis in Lace '68
Targets '68
Hell's Angels on Wheels '67
Incredibly Strange Creatures Who Stopped Living and Became Mixed-Up Zombies '63

Pete Kozachik
James and the Giant Peach '96
The Nightmare before Christmas '93

Gunther Krampf
Alfred Hitchcock's Aventure Malgache '44
Alfred Hitchcock's Bon Voyage '44
The Ghoul '34
Pandora's Box '28
The Hands of Orlac '25
Nosferatu '22

Jon Kranhouse
Something More '99
Decoy '95
Kickboxer '89
Friday the 13th, Part 6: Jason Lives '86

Robert Krasker (1913-81)
Trap '66
The Collector '65
The Heroes of Telemark '65
The Fall of the Roman Empire '64
Billy Budd '62
Birdman of Alcatraz '62
El Cid '61
The Story of Esther Costello '57
Trapeze '56
Alexander the Great '55
Romeo and Juliet '54
Senso '54
Another Man's Poison '52
Cry, the Beloved Country '51
The Third Man '49
Odd Man Out '47
Brief Encounter '46
Caesar and Cleopatra '46
Henry V '44

Milton Krasner (1904-88)
Beneath the Planet of the Apes '70
The Sterile Cuckoo '69
The St. Valentine's Day Massacre '67
The Singing Nun '66
Red Line 7000 '65
The Sandpiper '65
Goodbye Charlie '64
How the West Was Won '63
Love with the Proper Stranger '63
The Courtship of Eddie's Father '62
The Four Horsemen of the Apocalypse '62
Sweet Bird of Youth '62
Two Weeks in Another Town '62
The King of Kings '61
Bells Are Ringing '60
Home from the Hill '60
An Affair to Remember '57
Bus Stop '56
The Seven Year Itch '55
Demetrius and the Gladiators '54
Desiree '54
Three Coins in the Fountain '54
Monkey Business '52
Phone Call from a Stranger '52
People Will Talk '51
All About Eve '50
No Way Out '50
Rawhide '50
Three Came Home '50
House of Strangers '49
The Set-Up '49
The Accused '48
Up in Central Park '48
A Double Life '47
Egg and I '47
The Farmer's Daughter '47
Something in the Wind '47
Dark Mirror '46
Without Reservations '46
Along Came Jones '45
Scarlet Street '45
The Invisible Man's Revenge '44
Woman in the Window '44
Gung Ho! '43
Arabian Nights '42
A Gentleman After Dark '42
The Ghost of Frankenstein '42
Pardon My Sarong '42
The Spoilers '42
Buck Privates '41
The Bank Dick '40
The House of the Seven Gables '40
The Invisible Man Returns '40
You Can't Cheat an Honest Man '39

Richard Kratina
The Sentinel '76
Aaron Loves Angela '75
The Angel Levine '70
Love Story '70

Eric Kress
The Kingdom 2 '97
The Kingdom '95

Henning Kristiansen
Royal Deceit '94
Babette's Feast '87

Les Krizsan
Tales from a Parallel Universe: Eating Pattern '97
Tales from a Parallel Universe: Giga Shadow '97
Tales from a Parallel Universe: I Worship His Shadow '97
Tales from a Parallel Universe: Super Nova '97

Tom Krueger
Committed '99
Manny & Lo '96

Jules Kruger
Sidewalks of London '38
Pepe Le Moko '37
Napoleon '27

Howard Krupa
1999 '98
Kicked in the Head '97
Rhythm Thief '94

Alwin Kuchler
The Claim '00
Ratcatcher '99

Willy Kurant
Pootie Tang '01
The Baby-Sitters' Club '95
White Man's Burden '95
A Business Affair '93
Day of Atonement '93
China Moon '91
Tuff Turf '85

Ellen Kuras
Blow '01
Bamboozled '00
The Mod Squad '99
Summer of Sam '99
Just the Ticket '98
I Shot Andy Warhol '96
If These Walls Could Talk '96
Postcards from America '95
Angela '94
Unzipped '94
Swoon '91

Toyomichi Kurita
Cookie's Fortune '99
Afterglow '97
Crime of the Century '96
Infinity '96
Woman Undone '95
Lakota Woman: Siege at Wounded Knee '94
Grand Isle '92
Powwow Highway '89
Trouble in Mind '86

Robert B. Kurrle
Evangeline '29
Sadie Thompson '28

Luigi Kuveiller
New York Ripper '82
Deep Red: Hatchet Murders '75
Andy Warhol's Dracula '74
Andy Warhol's Frankenstein '74

Jules Labarthe
But I'm a Cheerleader '99
Stray Bullet '98

Flavio Labiano
Bones '01
Harlan County War '00

Daniel Lacambre
'68 '87
Saturday the 14th '81
Battle Beyond the Stars '80
Humanoids from the Deep '80
Lady in Red '79
The Velvet Vampire '71
The Arousers '70
Magical Mystery Tour '67

Edward Lachman (1948-)
Sweet November '01
Erin Brockovich '00
The Limey '99
The Virgin Suicides '99
Why Do Fools Fall in Love? '98
Selena '96
Touch '96
Theremin: An Electronic Odyssey '95
My Family '94
Light Sleeper '92
London Kills Me '91
Less Than Zero '87
True Stories '86
Desperately Seeking Susan '85
Union City '81

Serge Ladouceur
Bonanno: A Godfather's Story '99
Armistead Maupin's More Tales of the City '97

Kjell Lagerros
Ambush '99
Like It Never Was Before '95
Dreaming of Rita '94

Ardy Lam
Crime Story '93
Supercop '92
A Bullet in the Head '90

Giuseppe Lanci
Elective Affinities '96
Caro Diario '93
Fiorile '93
Francesco '93
Johnny Stecchino '92
Night Sun '90
Devil in the Flesh '87
Kaos '85
Nostalghia '83

Charles B(ryant) Lang, Jr. (1902-98)
Forty Carats '73
Butterflies Are Free '72
The Love Machine '71
Doctors' Wives '70
Walk in the Spring Rain '70
Bob & Carol & Ted & Alice '69
Cactus Flower '69
How to Commit Marriage '69
Flim-Flam Man '67
Hotel '67
Wait until Dark '67
How to Steal a Million '66
Inside Daisy Clover '65
Father Goose '64
Paris When It Sizzles '64
Sex and the Single Girl '64
Charade '63
How the West Was Won '63
One-Eyed Jacks '61
Summer and Smoke '61
The Facts of Life '60
The Magnificent Seven '60
Strangers When We Meet '60
Last Train from Gun Hill '59
Some Like It Hot '59
The Matchmaker '58
Separate Tables '58
Gunfight at the O.K. Corral '57
Autumn Leaves '56
The Rainmaker '56
Solid Gold Cadillac '56
The Man from Laramie '55
Queen Bee '55
It Should Happen to You '54
Phffft! '54
Sabrina '54
The Big Heat '53
Salome '53
Sudden Fear '52
Fancy Pants '50
September Affair '50
The Great Lover '49
A Foreign Affair '48
The Ghost and Mrs. Muir '47
Blue Skies '46
The Uninvited '44
So Proudly We Hail '43
The Shepherd of the Hills '41
Sundown '41
The Ghost Breakers '40
Midnight '39
Spawn of the North '38
You and Me '38
Angel '37
Souls at Sea '37
The Lives of a Bengal Lancer '35
Death Takes a Holiday '34
She Done Him Wrong '33
A Farewell to Arms '32
Vice Squad '31
Tom Sawyer '30

Norman G. Langley
Jekyll and Hyde '90
House of the Long Shadows '82
Die Screaming, Marianne '73

Reggie Lanning
Abbott and Costello Meet the Keystone Kops '54
Sands of Iwo Jima '49
Rainbow over Texas '46
Bells of Capistrano '42
Gaucho Serenade '40
Days of Jesse James '39

Roger Lanser
Maybe Baby '99
Kings in Grass Castles '97
Prince Valiant '97
Billy's Holiday '95
A Midwinter's Tale '95
Much Ado about Nothing '93

Vilis Lapenieks
Rainbow Bridge '71
Planet of Blood '66
Hollywood after Dark '65
Night Tide '63
Eegah! '62
Hideous Sun Demon '59

Jeanne Lapoirie
Under the Sand '00
Set Me Free '99
Water Drops on Burning Rocks '99
Full Speed '96
Les Voleurs '96
Wild Reeds '94

Stevan Larner
Partners in Crime '99
Forbidden Choices '94
Twilight Zone: The Movie '83
Rehearsal for Murder '82
Caddyshack '80
A Rumor of War '80
The Buddy Holly Story '78
Roots '77
Badlands '74
The Student Nurses '70

Joseph LaShelle (1905-89)
Barefoot in the Park '67
The Fortune Cookie '66
Kiss Me, Stupid! '64
The Apartment '60
Career '59
The Long, Hot Summer '58
The Naked and the Dead '58
Crime of Passion '57

I Was a Teenage Werewolf '57
The Conqueror '56
Marty '55
River of No Return '54
Les Miserables '52
The Jackpot '50
Come to the Stable '49
Laura '44

Jacek Laskus
Common Ground '00
The Devil's Arithmetic '99
A Soldier's Sweetheart '98
Elmore Leonard's Gold Coast '97
The Garden of Redemption '97
Stepfather 2: Make Room for Daddy '89
Parting Glances '86

Walter Lassally (1926-)
The Ballad of the Sad Cafe '91
The Deceivers '88
The Bostonians '84
Private School '83
Heat and Dust '82
Danger in the Skies '79
Great Bank Hoax '78
Hullabaloo over Georgie & Bonnie's Pictures '78
Wild Party '74
Run, Stranger, Run '73
Savages '72
Something for Everyone '70
Zorba the Greek '64
Tom Jones '63
The Loneliness of the Long Distance Runner '62
A Taste of Honey '61
Beat Girl '60
A Matter of Dignity '57
Girl in Black '56

Andrew Laszlo (1926-)
Star Trek 5: The Final Frontier '89
Poltergeist 2: The Other Side '86
Remo Williams: The Adventure Begins '85
Streets of Fire '84
Thief of Hearts '84
First Blood '82
The Funhouse '81
The Warriors '79
The Man Without a Country '73
The Owl and the Pussycat '70

Ernest Laszlo (1905-84)
Logan's Run '76
Showdown '73
Airport '70
Daddy's Gone A-Hunting '69
Star! '68
Luv '67
Fantastic Voyage '66
Ship of Fools '65
Baby, the Rain Must Fall '64
Four for Texas '63
It's a Mad, Mad, Mad, Mad World '63
Judgment at Nuremberg '61
Inherit the Wind '60
Tormented '60
Attack of the Puppet People '58
While the City Sleeps '56
The Big Knife '55
The Kentuckian '55
Kiss Me Deadly '55
Apache '54
Naked Jungle '54
The Moon Is Blue '53
Stalag 17 '53
Vera Cruz '53
The Well '51
The Jackie Robinson Story '50
D.O.A. '49
Impact '49
On Our Merry Way '48
The Road to Rio '47
Two Years before the Mast '46

Philip Lathrop (1912-95)
Deadly Friend '86
National Lampoon's Class Reunion '82
Swashbuckler '76
Airport '75 '75
Hard Times '75
Earthquake '74
They Shoot Horses, Don't They? '69
The Cincinnati Kid '65
The Pink Panther '64
36 Hours '64
The Monster of Piedras Blancas '57

Tom Lau
The Bodyguard from Beijing '94
The Heroic Trio '93
Twin Warriors '93

Paul Laufer
The Cell '00
Frankie Starlight '95

Dan Laustsen
Brotherhood of the Wolf '01
Heart of Light '97
Mimic '97
Nightwatch '96
Emma's Shadow '88

Charles Lawton, Jr.
A Raisin in the Sun '61
Comanche Station '60
Cowboy '58
Gunman's Walk '58
Last Hurrah '58
3:10 to Yuma '57
The Long Gray Line '55
The Lady from Shanghai '48
Big Store '41

Vernon Layton
I Still Know What You Did Last Summer '98
High School High '96
The Englishman Who Went up a Hill But Came down a Mountain '95
Under Suspicion '92

Jean-Yves Le Mener
The Visitors '95
The Fatal Image '90

Marcel Le Picard
The Invisible Ghost '41
America '24

Sam Leavitt (1904-84)
The Man in the Glass Booth '75
Evil Roy Slade '71
Star Spangled Girl '71
The Passing of Evil '70
Desperados '69
The Wrecking Crew '68
Guess Who's Coming to Dinner '67
Murderers' Row '66
Major Dundee '65
Advise and Consent '62
Diamond Head '62
Cape Fear '61
Seven Thieves '60
Anatomy of a Murder '59
Pork Chop Hill '59
The Defiant Ones '58
Hot Rod Girl '56
The Court Martial of Billy Mitchell '55
The Man with the Golden Arm '55
Carmen Jones '54
A Star Is Born '54
The Thief '52

Pavel Lebeshev
Prisoner of the Mountains '96
The Ascent '76

Philip Lee
Route 666 '01
From Dusk Till Dawn 2: Texas Blood Money '98
Galaxies Are Colliding '92

Robert Lefebvre (1907-)
I Am Frigid...Why? '72
Her and She and Him '69
Please Not Now! '61
Casque d'Or '52
Beethoven '36

Richard Leiterman
The Spree '96
Watchers '88
Ticket to Heaven '81

Claude Lelouch (1937-)
Les Miserables '95
A Man and a Woman '66

Jacques Lemare
Dishonorable Discharge '57
There Goes Barder '54

James (Momel) Lemmo
Maniac Cop 2 '90
Maniac Cop '88
Fear City '85
Vigilante '83
Madman '82
One Down, Two to Go! '82
Ms. 45 '81

Denis Lenoir
Uprising '01
Meat Loaf: To Hell and Back '00
Steal This Movie! '00
Mean Streak '99
La Separation '98
Late August, Early September '98
Thursday '98
The Secret Agent '96
Carrington '95
The Separation '94
Daddy Nostalgia '90
Dingo '90

Dean Lent
Fast Sofa '01
Catfish in Black Bean Sauce '00
Jack Frost '97
Lover Girl '97
When Time Expires '97
Acting on Impulse '93
Bound and Gagged: A Love Story '93
Gas Food Lodging '92

Miklos Lente
Ordeal in the Arctic '93
Happy Birthday to Me '81

John R. Leonetti
The Scorpion King '02
Joe Dirt '01
Detroit Rock City '99
Spy Hard '96
Mortal Kombat 1: The Movie '95
The Mask '94

Matthew F. Leonetti
Along Came a Spider '01
Rush Hour 2 '01
Species 2 '98
Star Trek: Insurrection '98
Mortal Kombat 2: Annihilation '97
Fled '96
Star Trek: First Contact '96
Strange Days '95
Angels in the Outfield '94
Dead Again '91
Another 48 Hrs. '90
Hard to Kill '89
Action Jackson '88
Red Heat '88
Dragnet '87
Commando '85
The Jagged Edge '85
Weird Science '85
Fast Times at Ridgemont High '82
Poltergeist '82
Breaking Away '79

Jean Lepine
To Walk with Lions '99
A Cool, Dry Place '98
Habitat '97
Woo '97
Beyond the Call '96
Ready to Wear '94
A Home of Our Own '93
Bob Roberts '92
The Player '92
Vincent & Theo '90

Andrew Lesnie
Lord of the Rings 1: The Fellowship of the Rings '01
Babe: Pig in the City '98
Babe '95
Two If by Sea '95
Temptation of a Monk '94
Fair Game '85

Elgin Lessley
Seven Chances '25
The Navigator '24
Our Hospitality '23

Pierre Letarte
The Audrey Hepburn Story '00
Mafia! '98
First Do No Harm '97
Dangerous Minds '95
Sugartime '95
The Boys of St. Vincent '93

Moshe Levin
Motel Blue '98
Hard Justice '95

Peter Levy
Under Suspicion '00
Lost in Space '98
The War at Home '96
Broken Arrow '95
Cutthroat Island '95
Judgment Night '93
Ricochet '91
Predator 2 '90
A Nightmare on Elm Street 5: Dream Child '89

David Lewis
Leprechaun 4: In Space '96
Leprechaun 3 '95

David Lewis (1916-2000)
Killer Bud '00
Atomic Dog '98
Children of the Corn 5: Fields of Terror '98
Chairman of the Board '97
The Proposition '96
The Set Up '95
Witchboard 2: The Devil's Doorway '93
UHF '89
The Hills Have Eyes, Part 2 '84

Herschell Gordon Lewis (1926-)
The Psychic '68
Something Weird '68
Color Me Blood Red '64
Moonshine Mountain '64
2000 Maniacs '64
Blood Feast '63

Denis Lewiston
The Canterville Ghost '96
Nightmare '91
One Against the Wind '91
The Sign of Four '83
The House on Straw Hill '76

Pierre Lhomme
Cotton Mary '99
Mon Homme '96
Cyrano de Bergerac '90
Camille Claudel '89
Maurice '87
This Sweet Sickness '77
Sweet Movie '75
The Mother and the Whore '73
The King of Hearts '66

Matthew Libatique (1969-)
Josie and the Pussycats '01
Requiem for a Dream '00
Tigerland '00
Pi '98

Charlie Lieberman
South Central '92
Henry: Portrait of a Serial Killer '90

Stephen Lighthill
The Crying Child '96
Evil Has a Face '96
The Perfect Daughter '96
Open Season '95
Spirit of '76 '91
Break of Dawn '88

Doug Liman
Go '99
Swingers '96

Jong Lin
What's Cooking? '00
Eat Drink Man Woman '94
The Wedding Banquet '93
Pushing Hands '92

Edward Linden
Slaves in Bondage '37
King Kong '33

Lionel Linden
Quicksand '50
O.S.S. '46

Karl Walter Lindenlaub
One Night at McCool's '01
The Princess Diaries '01
Isn't She Great '00
The Jackal '97
Red Corner '97
Independence Day '96
Up Close and Personal '96
The Last of the Dogmen '95
Rob Roy '95
Casualties of Love: The "Long Island Lolita" Story '93
Universal Soldier '92
Ghost Chase '88

John Lindley
The Sum of All Fears '02
Lucky Numbers '00
Pleasantville '98
You've Got Mail '98
Michael '96
Money Train '95
I Love Trouble '94
The Good Son '93
Sneakers '92
Father of the Bride '91
Field of Dreams '89
True Believer '89
Shakedown '88
The Serpent and the Rainbow '87
The Stepfather '87
Killer Party '86
Girls of the White Orchid '85

Lionel Lindon (1905-71)
The Meanest Men in the West '76
Generation '69
Pendulum '69
Dead Heat on a Merry-Go-Round '66
Grand Prix '66
The Trouble with Angels '66
McHale's Navy Joins the Air Force '65
All Fall Down '62
The Manchurian Candidate '62
Alias Jesse James '59
I Want to Live! '58
Lonely Man '57
Around the World in 80 Days '56
Conquest of Space '55
A Man Alone '55
Casanova's Big Night '54
Destination Moon '50
The Great Rupert '50
Only the Valiant '50
My Favorite Brunette '47
Variety Girl '47
Welcome Stranger '47
The Blue Dahlia '46
Monsieur Beaucaire '46
The Road to Utopia '46
Going My Way '44

Philip Linzey
Cabin by the Lake '00
Life-Size '00
Evidence of Blood '97
Bloodknot '95

Jerzy Lipman
Lotna '64
Knife in the Water '62
Kanal '56
A Generation '54

Harold Lipstein
Hell Is for Heroes '62
Heller in Pink Tights '60
No Name on the Bullet '59
Pal Joey '57
Walk the Proud Land '56
The Private War of Major Benson '55

Greg Littlewood
SLC Punk! '99
Sweet Jane '98
The Real Thing '97
Skinner '93

Gerry Lively
Cutaway '00
DNA '97
The Brylcreem Boys '96
Friday '95
Showdown '94
Return of the Living Dead 3 '93
Warlock: The Armageddon '93
Hellraiser 3: Hell on Earth '92
Project: Eliminator '91
Waxwork 2: Lost in Time '91
Lobster Man from Mars '89
Waxwork '88

Art Lloyd
The Flying Deuces '39
March of the Wooden Soldiers '34

Walt Lloyd
Superstar '99
Three to Tango '99
Dark Harbor '98
Feeling Minnesota '96
Private Parts '96
Empire Records '95
Frank and Jesse '94
The Santa Clause '94
Short Cuts '93
Kafka '91
Pump Up the Volume '90
To Sleep with Anger '90
Down Twisted '89
sex, lies and videotape '89
The Wash '88
Dangerously Close '86

Bryan Loftus
Jake Speed '86
The Company of Wolves '85

Bruce Logan
Kiss Tomorrow Goodbye '00
Tron '82
Zoltan...Hound of Dracula '78
I Never Promised You a Rose Garden '77
Jackson County Jail '76
Crazy Mama '75
Big Bad Mama '74

Dietrich Lohmann (1943-97)
Deep Impact '98
The Peacemaker '97
Quiet Days in Hollywood '97
The Machine '96
A Couch in New York '95
Color of Night '94
Knight Moves '93
Effi Briest '74
The American Soldier '70

Paul Lohmann
Lust in the Dust '85
Mommie Dearest '81
Meteor '79
North Dallas Forty '79
Nashville '75
Trilogy of Terror '75
Scream of the Wolf '74
Coffy '73

James London
The Toxic Avenger, Part 2 '89
The Toxic Avenger, Part 3: The Last Temptation of Toxie '89
Troma's War '88
The Toxic Avenger '86

Gordon C. Lonsdale
Houdini '99
The Last Don '97

Emmanuel Lubezki
Ali '01
Y Tu Mama Tambien '01
Things You Can Tell Just by Looking at Her '00
Sleepy Hollow '99
Meet Joe Black '98
Great Expectations '97
The Birdcage '95

A Little Princess '95
A Walk in the Clouds '95
Reality Bites '94
Twenty Bucks '93

William Lubtchansky
Va Savoir '01
Jeanne la Pucelle '94
Every Other Weekend '91
La Belle Noiseuse '90
The Woman Next Door '81

Yang Lun
Red Firecracker, Green Firecracker '93
Ju Dou '90

Igor Luther
The Handmaid's Tale '90
The Tin Drum '79

Bernard Lutic
I Dreamed of Africa '00
The Luzhin Defence '00
My Life So Far '98
The Quarry '98
Colonel Chabert '94
Boyfriends & Girlfriends '88
Entre-Nous '83
Le Beau Mariage '82
The Aviator's Wife '80

Russell Lyster
Styx '00
Ringmaster '98

Jingle Ma
Tokyo Raiders '00
Mr. Magoo '97
Jackie Chan's First Strike '96
Rumble in the Bronx '96
The Legend of Drunken Master '94

Julio Macat
A Walk to Remember '02
Cats & Dogs '01
The Wedding Planner '01
Crazy in Alabama '99
Home Alone 3 '97
My Fellow Americans '96
The Nutty Professor '96
Moonlight and Valentino '95
Ace Ventura: Pet Detective '93
Home Alone 2: Lost in New York '92
Home Alone '90
Out of the Dark '88

John MacBurnie
Border Saddlemates '52
Silver City Bonanza '51

Joe MacDonald
MacKenna's Gold '69
Alvarez Kelly '66
The Sand Pebbles '66
The Carpetbaggers '64
The Gallant Hours '60
The Young Lions '58
Will Success Spoil Rock Hunter? '57
How to Marry a Millionaire '53
Niagara '52
Call Northside 777 '48
My Darling Clementine '46

Peter Macdonald
Shag: The Movie '89
Hamburger Hill '87

Laurent Machuel
Three Lives and Only One Death '96
Diary of a Seducer '95

Jack MacKenzie
Return of Dracula '58
Isle of the Dead '45
Jungle Woman '44
Zombies on Broadway '44
Breaking the Ice '38

Kenneth Macmillan
Dancing at Lughnasa '98
Almost Heroes '97
Inventing the Abbotts '97
Mr. & Mrs. Loving '96
Circle of Friends '94
Lassie '94
Of Mice and Men '92
King Ralph '91
Rush '91
Henry V '89
A Month in the Country '87

Glen MacPherson
Exit Wounds '01
Camouflage '00
Romeo Must Die '00
The Real Howard Spitz '98
Wrongfully Accused '98
Behind the Lines '97
Calm at Sunset '96
Doctor Who '96
Captains Courageous '95
First Degree '95
The Amy Fisher Story '93

Glen MacWilliams
Lifeboat '44
A Wing and a Prayer '44
King Solomon's Mines '37
First a Girl '35
Evergreen '34
Oliver Twist '22

Guy Maddin (1956-)
Careful '92
Tales from the Gimli Hospital '88

Yonezo Maeda
Minbo—Or the Gentle Art of Japanese Extortion '92
A Taxing Woman '87
The Funeral '84
The Family Game '83

Paul Maibaum
Tornado! '96
Down, Out and Dangerous '95
Stephen King's The Langoliers '95

Richard Maidment
Second Sight '99
Enchanted April '92

David Makin
Held Up '00
Dog Park '98
Kids in the Hall: Brain Candy '96

Michael Maley
No One Sleeps '01
Farmer & Chase '96

Denis Maloney
The Contender '00
Luckytown '00
One Small Hero '99
Bad Manners '98
Bikini Med School '98
Highway Hitcher '98
Body Count '97
Bikini House Calls '96
Illegal Affairs '96
The Winner '96
Wolverine '96
Baja '95
Desert Winds '95
Witchcraft 7: Judgement Hour '95
Witchcraft 8: Salem's Ghost '95
Floundering '94
Natural Causes '94

Joseph Mangine
Alligator 2: The Mutation '90
Sword & the Sorcerer '82
Alligator '80
Mother's Day '80

Teodoro Maniaci
The Business of Strangers '01
Luminous Motion '00
The Tao of Steve '00
Claire Dolan '97
Tarantella '95
Clean, Shaven '93

Isidore Mankofsky
The Heidi Chronicles '95
Out of Sync '95
Hard Lessons '86
Better Off Dead '85
The Jazz Singer '80
Second Coming of Suzanne '80
Somewhere in Time '80
The Muppet Movie '79

Chris Manley
Robert Louis Stevenson's The Game of Death '99
Running Woman '98

Anthony Dod Mantle
Julien Donkey-boy '99
Mifune '99

The Celebration '98

Vincenzo Marano
Lucie Aubrac '98
Portraits Chinois '96

Alain Marcoen
Rosetta '99
La Promesse '96

Gunter Marczinkowski
Jacob the Liar '74
Trace of Stones '66
Five Cartridges '60

Michael D. Margulies
Best of the Best: Without Warning '98
Moonlighting '85
Police Academy '84
My Bodyguard '80
The Dark Side of Love '79
The Baby '72

William Margulies
How to Frame a Figg '71
The Love God? '70
Clambake '67
The Ghost and Mr. Chicken '66
McHale's Navy '64

Francis Marin
Twice a Judas '69
The Texican '66

Barry Markowitz
All the Pretty Horses '00
Two Girls and a Guy '98
The Apostle '97
Sling Blade '96

J. Peverell Marley
Life with Father '47
The Count of Monte Cristo '34

Brick Marquard
Foxy Brown '74
This Is Not a Test '62

Jacques "Jack" Marquette (1915-)
Frankie and Johnny '65
Creature from the Haunted Sea '60
Attack of the 50 Foot Woman '58
The Brain from Planet Arous '57

Horacio Marquinez
Loving Jezebel '99
Stranger than Fiction '99
Eye of the Storm '98
Restaurant '98
Ten Benny '98

Oliver Marsh
Dancing Lady '33
Rain '32
Sadie Thompson '28

Jack Marta
The Trial of Billy Jack '74
Walking Tall '73
You'll Like My Mother '72
Duel '71
Cat Ballou '65
Earth vs. the Spider '58
Beginning of the End '57
Sunset in the West '50
Bordertown Gunfighters '43
Red River Valley '41
King of the Pecos '36

Otello Martelli (1902-2000)
Boccaccio '70 '62
Where the Hot Wind Blows '59
What a Woman! '56
Il Bidone '55
I Vitelloni '53
Anna '51
Variety Lights '51
The Flowers of St. Francis '50
Bitter Rice '49

F. Smith Martin
Hard Vice '94
Zipperface '92

Arthur Martinelli
The Devil Bat '41
Double Trouble '41
Revolt of the Zombies '36
Supernatural '33
The White Zombie '32

Flavio Martinez Labiano
Dance with the Devil '97
The Day of the Beast '95

Joseph Mascelli
The Thrill Killers '65
Incredibly Strange Creatures Who Stopped Living and Became Mixed-Up Zombies '63
Wild Guitar '62

Raffaele Masciocchi
The Ghost '63
The Horrible Dr. Hichcock '62

Mario Masini
Padre Padrone '77
Allegro Non Troppo '76
St. Michael Had a Rooster '72

Steve Mason
Rollerball '02
Bootmen '00
BASEketball '98
Buddy '97
That Old Feeling '96
Strictly Ballroom '92

Rudolph Mate (1898-1964)
Gilda '46
Cover Girl '44
Sahara '43
They Got Me Covered '43
The Pride of the Yankees '42
To Be or Not to Be '42
The Flame of New Orleans '41
It Started with Eve '41
My Favorite Wife '40
Love Affair '39
The Real Glory '39
Stella Dallas '37
Come and Get It '36
Dodsworth '36
Vampyr '31
Passion of Joan of Arc '28

James Mathers
St. Patrick: The Irish Legend '00
Sexual Malice '93
Snapdragon '93
Rock 'n' Roll High School Forever '91
The Forgotten One '89

John Mathieson
Hannibal '01
K-PAX '01
Gladiator '00
Love Is the Devil '98
Plunkett & Macleane '98
Twin Town '97
Bye-Bye '96
Pigalle '95

Christian Matras
Lola Montes '55
The Earrings of Madame De... '54
Fanfan la Tulipe '51
L'Idiot '46
Grand Illusion '37

Thomas Mauch
Fitzcarraldo '82
Stroszek '77
Aguirre, the Wrath of God '72
Signs of Life '68

Shawn Maurer
Bring It On '00
La Cucaracha '99
The Big Empty '98
Bandwagon '95

Tim Maurice-Jones
Human Nature '02
Snatch '00
Lock, Stock and 2 Smoking Barrels '98

Robert Maxwell
Sweet Sweetback's Baadasssss Song '71
Girl in Gold Boots '69
The Astro-Zombies '67

Bradford May
Darkman 3: Die Darkman Die '95
Darkman 2: The Return of Durant '94

Harry J. May
J.D.'s Revenge '76
Friday Foster '75
Detroit 9000 '73

Mike Mayers
Joe the King '99
Two Family House '99
Broadway Damage '98
Meeting Daddy '98
Whatever '98
Cafe Society '97
Lewis and Clark and George '97
Changing Habits '96
Denise Calls Up '95
Spanking the Monkey '94
Spare Me '92

Alfredo Mayo
Women '97
Wild Horses '95
Kika '94
The Fencing Master '92
High Heels '91

Donald McAlpine
The Time Machine '02
Moulin Rouge '01
Stepmom '98
The Edge '97
William Shakespeare's Romeo and Juliet '96
Nine Months '95
Clear and Present Danger '94
Mrs. Doubtfire '93
Medicine Man '92
Patriot Games '92
Career Opportunities '91
Parenthood '89
Predator '87
Down and Out in Beverly Hills '86
Moscow on the Hudson '84
The Tempest '82
Breaker Morant '80
My Brilliant Career '79
The Odd Angry Shot '79
Don's Party '76

Ted D. McCord
The Sound of Music '65
Proud Rebel '58
Action in the North Atlantic '43

Malcolm McCulloch
Two Hands '98
Kiss or Kill '97

David McDonald
Horror Hospital '73
The Harder They Come '72

Seamus McGarvey
Enigma '01
Wit '01
High Fidelity '00
The Big Tease '99
A Map of the World '99
The War Zone '98
The Winter Guest '97
Butterfly Kiss '94

Walter McGill
Oliver Twist '00
Aldrich Ames: Traitor Within '98

John McGlashan
Captain Jack '98
The Buddha of Suburbia '92

Jack McGowan
Deranged '74
Children Shouldn't Play with Dead Things '72

Martin McGrath
On the Beach '00
Passion '99
In the Winter Dark '98
Blackrock '97
A Little Bit of Soul '97
The Ripper '97
Children of the Revolution '95
River Street '95
Muriel's Wedding '94

Austin McKinney
Axe '74
The Fear Chamber '68
The Sinister Invasion '68
Alien Massacre '67
Pit Stop '67

Robert McLachlan
The One '01
Final Destination '00
High Noon '00

Nick McLean
Short Circuit '86
The Goonies '85
Cannonball Run 2 '84
Stroker Ace '83

Geary McLeod
Cement '99
Black Circle Boys '97

Stephen McNutt
Out of Time '00
Inferno '99
Spanish Judges '99

John McPherson
Short Circuit 2 '88
*batteries not included '87
Jaws: The Revenge '87

Steve McWilliams
No Safe Haven '87
Revenge '86

Graeme Mears
Cybercity '99
Future Fear '97

Suki Medencevic
Hunter's Moon '97
Embrace of the Vampire '95
Poison Ivy 2: Lily '95

Teresa Medina
The 24 Hour Woman '99
Female Perversions '96
Reflections in the Dark '94

Phil Meheux
Bicentennial Man '99
Entrapment '99
The Mask of Zorro '98
The Saint '97
Goldeneye '95
No Escape '94
The Trial '93
Ruby '92
Highlander 2: The Quickening '91
Criminal Law '89
Renegades '89
The Fourth Protocol '87
Morons from Outer Space '85
Beyond the Limit '83
Experience Preferred... But Not Essential '83
The Final Option '82
Omen 3: The Final Conflict '81
The Long Good Friday '80

William Mellor (1904-63)
The Greatest Story Ever Told '65
State Fair '62
Wild in the Country '61
The Best of Everything '59
Compulsion '59
The Diary of Anne Frank '59
Love in the Afternoon '57
Peyton Place '57
Back from Eternity '56
Giant '56
Bad Day at Black Rock '54
The Affairs of Dobie Gillis '53
The Naked Spur '53
Across the Wide Missouri '51
A Place in the Sun '51
Westward the Women '51
Love Happy '50
Too Late for Tears '49
The Senator Was Indiscreet '47
Commandos Strike at Dawn '43
The Great Man's Lady '42
My Favorite Blonde '42
The Road to Morocco '42
Wake Island '42
Birth of the Blues '41
The Great McGinty '40
The Road to Singapore '40

Erico Menczer
Dead Are Alive '72
The Cat o' Nine Tails '71

Until the End of the World '91
Mystery Train '89
Barfly '87
The Believers '87
Down by Law '86
Repo Man '83
Saint Jack '79
The American Friend '77
Kings of the Road—In the Course of Time '76
The Goalie's Anxiety at the Penalty Kick '71

Maximo Munzi
Backflash '01
The Guardian '00
The Stepdaughter '00
Judgment Day '99
Good Luck '96
Blondes Have More Guns '95

Fred Murphy
The Mothman Prophecies '02
Soul Survivors '01
Stir of Echoes '99
Witness Protection '99
Dance with Me '98
A Family Thing '96
Metro '96
Faithful '95
The Fantasticks '95
Murder in the First '95
Jack the Bear '93
Scenes from a Mall '91
Enemies, a Love Story '89
Five Corners '88
Full Moon in Blue Water '88
Best Seller '87
The Dead '87
Hoosiers '86
The Trip to Bountiful '85
Eddie and the Cruisers '83
Q (The Winged Serpent) '82
Heartland '81
Girlfriends '78

Michael D. Murphy
Beach Girls '82
Silent Scream '80

Paul Murphy
October Sky '99
Mighty Morphin Power Rangers: The Movie '95
Tunnel Vision '95

Nicholas Musuraca
Out of the Past '47
The Spiral Staircase '46
Bedlam '45
Forever and a Day '43
Cat People '42
Cheyenne Kid '33

Sead Mutarevic
Brown's Requiem '98
The Beneficiary '97
American Strays '96

David Myers
Hard Traveling '85
Uforia '81
FM '78

Asakazu Nakai
Ran '85
Dersu Uzala '75
High & Low '62
Throne of Blood '57
I Live in Fear '55
Seven Samurai '54
Ikiru '52
One Wonderful Sunday '47

Armando Nannuzzi (1925-)
Frankenstein Unbound '90
Maximum Overdrive '86
Silver Bullet '85
La Cage aux Folles 2 '81
La Cage aux Folles '78
Chino '75
Ludwig '72
Waterloo '71
Porcile '69
Il Bell'Antonio '60

Hiro Narita
Dirty Pictures '00
I'll Be Home for Christmas '98
Shadrach '98
Conceiving Ada '97
Sub Down '97
The Arrival '96
James and the Giant Peach '96
The Rocketeer '91
Star Trek 6: The Undiscovered Country '91
Honey, I Shrunk the Kids '89
Never Cry Wolf '83

Toichiro Narushima
Merry Christmas, Mr. Lawrence '83
Double Suicide '69

Mohsen Nasr
An Egyptian Story '82
Alexandria...Why? '78

Guillermo Navarro
The Devil's Backbone '01
Spy Kids '01
Stuart Little '99
Jackie Brown '97
Spawn '97
Dream for an Insomniac '96
The Long Kiss Goodnight '96
Desperado '95
Four Rooms '95
From Dusk Till Dawn '95
Cronos '94
Cabeza de Vaca '90

Ronald Neame (1911-)
This Happy Breed '47
Blithe Spirit '45
In Which We Serve '43

Andre Neau
Waiting for the Moon '87
The Return of Martin Guerre '83

Louis Nee
Utopia '51
Vampyr '31

Alex Nepomniaschy
It's the Rage '99
Never Been Kissed '99
The Alarmist '98
The Associate '96
Mrs. Winterbourne '96
Safe '95
Lisa '90
Poltergeist 3 '88
Last Resort '86
Wanted Dead or Alive '86

Harry Neumann
The Wasp Woman '59
Flight to Mars '52
Two Lost Worlds '50
The Fatal Hour '40
Mr. Wong, Detective '38
Mysterious Mr. Wong '35
Boiling Point '32

Thomas Neuwirth
The Lost Child '00
True Women '97

Robert New
The Chosen One: Legend of the Raven '98
Lionheart '90
Big Bad Mama 2 '87
Night of the Creeps '86
Prom Night '80

John Newby
Alien Fury: Countdown to Invasion '00
The Defenders: Taking the First '98
The Defenders: Payback '97
The Christmas Box '95
The Disappearance of Kevin Johnson '95
Operation Intercept '95
The Fence '94
Red Sun Rising '94

Yuri Neyman
Milo '98
Spirit Lost '96
Back in the USSR '92
Liquid Sky '83

Peter Ngor
Sex and Zen '93
Mr. Vampire '86
Operation Condor 2: The Armour of the Gods '86

Meredith Nicholson
The Amazing Transparent Man '60
Missile to the Moon '59
Frankenstein's Daughter '58
She Demons '58

Rex Nicholson
Perfume '01
Plump Fiction '97
A Modern Affair '94

John M. Nickolaus, Jr.
The Terror '63
Attack of the Giant Leeches '59
Night of the Blood Beast '58

William Nobles
Bad Man of Deadwood '41
Carson City Kid '40
Young Bill Hickok '40
Dangerous Holiday '37
Winds of the Wasteland '36

Eric Van Haren Noman
These Old Broads '01
The Truth About Jane '00
The Color of Courage '98
What the Deaf Man Heard '98
An Unexpected Family '96
Blue River '95
A Mother's Prayer '95
Too Young to Die '90
Hero and the Terror '88

Chris Norr
Nick and Jane '96
Nueba Yol '95

Vladimir Novotny
The Shop on Main Street '65
Lemonade Joe '64

Danny Nowak
The Big Hit '98
Bone Daddy '97
Hard Core Logo '96
Probable Cause '95
Abducted 2: The Reunion '94
Crackerjack '94
Flesh Gordon 2: Flesh Gordon Meets the Cosmic Cheerleaders '90

Victor Nunez (1945-)
Without Evidence '96
Gal Young 'Un '79

Giles Nuttgens
The Deep End '01
Battlefield Earth '00
Alice in Wonderland '99
Earth '98
A Merry War '97
Fire '96

Bruno Nuytten
Jean de Florette '87
Manon of the Spring '87
Detective '85
Possession '81
Barocco '76
The Best Way '76
Going Places '74

Sven Nykvist (1922-)
Celebrity '98
Private Confessions '98
Curtain Call '97
Kristin Lavransdatter '95
Something to Talk About '95
Only You '94
With Honors '94
Sleepless in Seattle '93
What's Eating Gilbert Grape '93
Chaplin '92
Crimes & Misdemeanors '89
New York Stories '89
Another Woman '88
The Unbearable Lightness of Being '88
The Sacrifice '86
Agnes of God '85
Dream Lover '85
After the Rehearsal '84
Swann in Love '84
Fanny and Alexander '83
Star 80 '83
Cannery Row '82
The Postman Always Rings Twice '81
From the Life of the Marionettes '80
Willie & Phil '80
Hurricane '79
Starting Over '79
Autumn Sonata '78
King of the Gypsies '78
Pretty Baby '78
The Serpent's Egg '78
Face to Face '76
The Tenant '76
The Dove '74
Scenes from a Marriage '73
Cries and Whispers '72
One Day in the Life of Ivan Denisovich '71
The Touch '71
First Love '70
The Passion of Anna '70
The Rite '69
Hour of the Wolf '68
The Shame '68
Persona '66
The Silence '63
The Winter Light '62
Through a Glass Darkly '61
The Virgin Spring '59

L.W. O'Connell
Return of the Vampire '43
Underground Agent '42
Maker of Men '31
The Bells '26

David Odd
All the King's Men '99
The Turn of the Screw '99
Our Mutual Friend '98
Retribution '98
Girls' Night '97
Touching Evil '97

Philip Ogaard
Aberdeen '00
Zero Degrees Kelvin '95
Cross My Heart and Hope to Die '94

Rene Ohashi
Rent-A-Kid '95
To Catch a Killer '92
Millennium '89
Anne of Green Gables '85

Azusa Ohno
Body of Influence 2 '96
Hostile Intentions '94

Daryn Okada (1960-)
Dr. Dolittle 2 '01
Good Advice '01
Joe Somebody '01
Texas Rangers '01
Lake Placid '99
Halloween: H20 '98
Senseless '98
Black Sheep '96
Leo Tolstoy's Anna Karenina '96
Big Bully '95
Phantasm 2 '88

Woody Omens
Harlem Nights '89
Coming to America '88
History of the World: Part 1 '81

Miroslav Ondricek
Riding in Cars with Boys '01
The Preacher's Wife '96
A League of Their Own '92
Funny Farm '88
F/X '86
Amadeus '84
Silkwood '83
The World According to Garp '82
Hair '79
Slaughterhouse Five '72
If... '69
The Firemen's Ball '68
Intimate Lighting '65
Loves of a Blonde '65

Ronald Orieux
The Passion of Ayn Rand '99
Y2K '99
Family of Cops 2: Breach of Faith '97
Booty Call '96
Broken Trust '95
A Good Day to Die '95
The Tuskegee Airmen '95
Take Down '92

Arthur Ornitz
Death Wish '74
Law and Disorder '74
Blacksnake! '73
Minnie and Moskowitz '71
House of Dark Shadows '70
A Thousand Clowns '65
Requiem for a Heavyweight '62

Michael D. O'Shea
The New Guy '02
Sorority Boys '02
Big Momma's House '00
Here on Earth '00
The '60s '99
Dracula: Dead and Loving It '95

Gerald Packer
Hangman '00
Jacob Two Two Meets the Hooded Fang '99
Conquest '98
The Wicked, Wicked West '97
Swann '96

Louis Page
Any Number Can Win '63
The Bride Is Much Too Beautiful '58
Plucking the Daisy '56

Luc Pages
A Tale of Winter '92
A Tale of Springtime '89

Riccardo (Pallton) Pallottini
Lady Frankenstein '72
And God Said to Cain '69
Castle of Blood '64

Ernest Palmer (1885-1978)
The Womaneater '59
Broken Arrow '50
Uneasy Terms '48
The Dolly Sisters '46
Pin-Up Girl '44
Sweet Rosie O'Grady '43
Springtime in the Rockies '42
Blood and Sand '41
Stand Up and Cheer '34
Cavalcade '33
Hoopla '33

Bob Paone
Judge & Jury '96
Basket Case 3: The Progeny '92

Phedon Papamichael
America's Sweethearts '01
The Million Dollar Hotel '99
Patch Adams '98
The Locusts '97
Mouse Hunt '97
Bio-Dome '96
Phenomenon '96
Unhook the Stars '96
Unstrung Heroes '95
While You Were Sleeping '95
Dark Side of Genius '94
Cool Runnings '93
Wild Palms '93
Love Crimes '92
Poison Ivy '92
Prayer of the Rollerboys '91
Body Chemistry '90
Dance of the Damned '88

Andy Parke
Grizzly Mountain '97
Operation Warzone '89

David Parker
Child Star: The Shirley Temple Story '01
The Miracle Worker '00
Amy '98
Mr. Reliable: A True Story '95
Malcolm '86

Phil Parmet
Hard Cash '01
Animal Factory '00
Black & White '99
Love and Action in Chicago '99
Flipping '96
The Last Days of Frankie the Fly '96
Four Rooms '95
Under the Hula Moon '95
Nina Takes a Lover '94
Two Small Bodies '93
In the Soup '92
Street Hunter '90
Fatal Mission '89
Harlan County, U.S.A. '76

Feliks Parnell
Lip Service '00
The Nurse '97
Poison Ivy 3: The New Seduction '97
Serpent's Lair '95

Barry Parrell
Zebra Lounge '01
The Minion '98

Greg Patterson
TripFall '00
Paper Bullets '99

Peter Pau
Crouching Tiger, Hidden Dragon '00
Bride of Chucky '98
Double Team '97
Warriors of Virtue '97
The Phantom Lover '95
The Bride with White Hair '93
Naked Killer '92
The Killer '90

Justo Paulino
Beyond Atlantis '73
Mad Doctor of Blood Island '69

Stanley Pavey
The Runaway Bus '54
The Belles of St. Trinian's '53
My Son, the Vampire '52
Dead of Night '45

Goran Pavicevic
All Over the Guy '01
Dee Snider's Strangeland '98
American Vampire '97

Pier Ludovico Pavoni
The Triumph of Hercules '66
Mill of the Stone Women '60

Robert Paynter (1928-)
Little Shop of Horrors '86
Spies Like Us '85
The Muppets Take Manhattan '84
Superman 3 '83
An American Werewolf in London '81
Omen 3: The Final Conflict '81
Superman 2 '80
The Nightcomers '72
Chato's Land '71
Lawman '71

Homayun Payvar
Daughters of the Sun '00
The Taste of Cherry '96
Life and Nothing More ... '92

Kenneth Peach, Sr.
Pufnstuf '70
It! The Terror from Beyond Space '58

Daniel Pearl
Amazon Women on the Moon '87
Hiding Out '87
It's Alive 3: Island of the Alive '87
Return to Salem's Lot '87
Invaders from Mars '86
The Texas Chainsaw Massacre '74

Brian Pearson
Urban Legends 2: Final Cut '00
Eye of the Killer '99
Tail Lights Fade '99
Bounty Hunters 2: Hardball '97
Listen '96

Christopher Pearson
Double Down '01
Blood Surf '00

Nicola Pecorini
Harrison's Flowers '02
Rules of Engagement '00

Girl '98
High Art '98
Far Harbor '96

Ricardo Remias
Nam Angels '88
Demon of Paradise '87

Peter Reniers
Bloodsucking Pharoahs of Pittsburgh '90
Two Evil Eyes '90

Ray Rennahan (1896-1980)
Terror in a Texas Town '58
Seventh Cavalry '56
A Lawless Street '55
Rage at Dawn '55
Arrowhead '53
Pony Express '53
At Sword's Point '51
Great Missouri Raid '51
A Connecticut Yankee in King Arthur's Court '49
The Paleface '48
The Perils of Pauline '47
Unconquered '47
Duel in the Sun '46
A Thousand and One Nights '45
Up in Arms '44
For Whom the Bell Tolls '43
Blood and Sand '41
Drums Along the Mohawk '39
Gone with the Wind '39
Wings of the Morning '37
Becky Sharp '35
The Cat and the Fiddle '34
Mystery of the Wax Museum '33
Doctor X '32

Claude Renoir (1914-)
The Spy Who Loved Me '77
French Connection 2 '75
Barbarella '68
Spirits of the Dead '68
Blood and Roses '61
The Crucible '57
Elena and Her Men '56
The Golden Coach '52
The River '51
Rendez-vous de Juillet '49
Monsieur Vincent '47
Toni '34

Gayne Rescher
Star Trek 2: The Wrath of Khan '82
Pearl '78

Marc Reshovsky
Most Wanted '97
Set It Off '96
Red Rock West '93
Sorority House Massacre '86

Scott Ressler
Hollywood Chainsaw Hookers '88
Sorority Babes in the Slimeball Bowl-A-Rama '87

Brian Reynolds
Boss of Bosses '99
With Friends Like These '98
Gang Related '96
Guarding Tess '94

Edmond Richard
That Obscure Object of Desire '77
Phantom of Liberty '74
The Discreet Charm of the Bourgeoisie '72
Chimes at Midnight '67
The Trial '63

Robert Richardson
Bringing Out the Dead '99
Snow Falling on Cedars '99
Fast, Cheap & Out of Control '97
The Horse Whisperer '97
U-Turn '97
Wag the Dog '97
Casino '95
Nixon '95
Natural Born Killers '94
Heaven and Earth '93
A Few Good Men '92
City of Hope '91
The Doors '91
JFK '91
Born on the Fourth of July '89
Eight Men Out '88
Talk Radio '88
Wall Street '87
Platoon '86
Salvador '86

Anthony B. Richmond (1942-)
The Sweetest Thing '02
Legally Blonde '01
Someone Like You '01
Cherry Falls '00
Men of Honor '00
Agnes Browne '99
Ravenous '99
A Walk on the Moon '99
Rough Riders '97
Bastard out of Carolina '96
First Kid '96
Playing God '96
Full Body Massage '95
The Immortals '95
Tales from the Hood '95
The Sandlot '93
Candyman '92
Sunset '88
The Eagle Has Landed '77
The Man Who Fell to Earth '76
Don't Look Now '73

Tom Richmond
Chelsea Walls '01
Hardball '01
Gun Shy '00
Waking the Dead '00
First Love, Last Rites '98
Slums of Beverly Hills '98
The Twilight of the Golds '97
johns '96
Mother Night '96
Homage '95
Killing Zoe '94
Little Odessa '94
Love and a .45 '94
A Midnight Clear '92
Pastime '91
I'm Gonna Git You Sucka '88
Stand and Deliver '88
Straight to Hell '87
Chopping Mall '86

Antonio Rinaldi
Five Dolls for an August Moon '70
Danger: Diabolik '68
Kill, Baby, Kill '66
Planet of the Vampires '65

Lisa Rinzler
Pollock '00
Three Seasons '98
Tree's Lounge '96
Dead Presidents '95
Menace II Society '93
Guncrazy '92
True Love '89
I Was a Teenage TV Terrorist '87

Gunther Rittau
The Blue Angel '30
Metropolis '26

Neil Roach
The '70s '00
Mama Flora's Family '98
Lone Justice 3: Showdown at Plum Creek '96
The Summer of Ben Tyler '96
Harvest of Fire '95
The Substitute Wife '94
Lone Justice 2 '93
To Dance with the White Dog '93
Silent Rage '82

James Robb
Ernest Goes to Africa '97
Ernest in the Army '97

Jim Roberson
Town That Dreaded Sundown '76
Winterhawk '76

Jean-Francois Robin
Nora '00
The Ice Rink '99
Rogue Trader '98
Metroland '97
The Serpent's Kiss '97
The Leading Man '96
Nelly et Monsieur Arnaud '95
Suite 16 '94
Betty Blue '86

George Robinson
Francis in the Haunted House '56
Abbott and Costello Meet the Mummy '55
Abbott and Costello Meet Dr. Jekyll and Mr. Hyde '52
Jack & the Beanstalk '52
Abbott and Costello Meet the Invisible Man '51
Abbott and Costello in the Foreign Legion '50
House of Dracula '45
House of Frankenstein '44
Son of Dracula '43
Frankenstein Meets the Wolfman '42
The Mummy's Tomb '42
The Son of Monte Cristo '40
Son of Frankenstein '39
The Tower of London '39
Dracula's Daughter '36
The Invisible Ray '36
The Mystery of Edwin Drood '35
Great Expectations '34

Claudio Rocha
Four Dogs Playing Poker '00
Skipped Parts '00
In the Shadows '98
The Velocity of Gary '98
The Whole Wide World '96
Picture Bride '94

Eliot Rockett
Crocodile '00
The Specials '00

Alexei Rodionov
Passion in the Desert '97
Red Shoe Diaries: Strip Poker '96
Talk of Angels '96
Orlando '92
Come and See '85

Bill Roe
Where the Truth Lies '99
Hostage High '97

Guy Roe
Godzilla, King of the Monsters '56
Try and Get Me '50
Behind Locked Doors '48
Railroaded '47
A Scandal in Paris '46

Nicolas Roeg (1928-)
Walkabout '71
Performance '70
Petulia '68
Far from the Madding Crowd '67
Fahrenheit 451 '66
A Funny Thing Happened on the Way to the Forum '66
The Girl Getters '66
Masque of the Red Death '65

Derek Rogers
New Waterford Girl '99
Cube '98
The Fishing Trip '98

Owen Roizman (1936-)
French Kiss '95
Wyatt Earp '94
The Addams Family '91
Grand Canyon '91
Havana '90
I Love You to Death '90
Vision Quest '85
Tootsie '82
Absence of Malice '81
Taps '81
True Confessions '81
The Electric Horseman '79
Straight Time '78
Network '76
The Return of a Man Called Horse '76
The Stepford Wives '75
Three Days of the Condor '75
The Taking of Pelham One Two Three '74
The Exorcist '73
The Heartbreak Kid '72
Play It Again, Sam '72
The French Connection '71

Gernot Roll
Beyond Silence '96
Maybe ... Maybe Not '94
Kaspar Hauser '93
Heimat 1 '84

Andy Romanoff
Something Weird '68
A Taste of Blood '67

George A. Romero (1940-)
Season of the Witch '73
Night of the Living Dead '68

Ilan Rosenberg
Turbo: A Power Rangers Movie '96
Baby Love '83

Charles Rosher (1885-1974)
Jupiter's Darling '55
Kiss Me Kate '53
Young Bess '53
Scaramouche '52
Show Boat '51
Annie Get Your Gun '50
East Side, West Side '49
Neptune's Daughter '49
Song of the Thin Man '47
The Yearling '46
Ziegfeld Follies '46
Yolanda and the Thief '45
Little Lord Fauntleroy '36
Broadway Melody of 1936 '35
What Price Hollywood? '32
Dance Fools Dance '31
Laughing Sinners '31
The Tempest '28
My Best Girl '27
Sunrise '27
Sparrows '26
Little Annie Rooney '25
Tess of the Storm Country '22
The Love Light '21
Pollyanna '20
Daddy Long Legs '19

Charles Rosher, Jr.
Heartbeeps '81
Nightwing '79

Ann T. Rossetti
Voices from a Locked Room '95
Go Fish '94

Harold Rosson
No Time for Sergeants '58
The Bad Seed '56
Singin' in the Rain '52
The Red Badge of Courage '51
Command Decision '48
The Hucksters '47
Thirty Seconds Over Tokyo '44
The Wizard of Oz '39
As You Like It '36
The Ghost Goes West '36
The Cat and the Fiddle '34
The Scarlet Pimpernel '34
Red Headed Woman '32

Andrea V. Rossotto
Extreme Limits '01
Venomous '01
Ablaze '00
Against the Law '98
Carnosaur 3: Primal Species '96
Vampirella '96

Giuseppe Rotunno (1923-)
Sabrina '95
The Stendahl Syndrome '95
The Night and the Moment '94
Wolf '94
Regarding Henry '91
The Adventures of Baron Munchausen '89
Rent-A-Cop '88
Casanova '87
Julia and Julia '87
And the Ship Sails On '83
City of Women '81
All That Jazz '79
Orchestra Rehearsal '78
Amarcord '74
Love and Anarchy '73
Fellini's Roma '72
Carnal Knowledge '71
Fellini Satyricon '69
The Secret of Santa Vittoria '69
Anzio '68
Candy '68
Spirits of the Dead '68
The Bible '66
The Organizer '64
Boccaccio '70 '62
Rocco and His Brothers '60
White Nights '57

Denis Rouden
Deep in the Woods '00
Don't Let Me Die on a Sunday '98

Philippe Rousselot (1945-)
Planet of the Apes '01
Remember the Titans '00
The Tailor of Panama '00
Instinct '99
Random Hearts '99
The People vs. Larry Flynt '96
Mary Reilly '95
Interview with the Vampire '94
Queen Margot '94
Sommersby '93
A River Runs Through It '92
The Miracle '91
Henry & June '90
The Bear '89
We're No Angels '89
Dangerous Liaisons '88
Too Beautiful for You '88
Hope and Glory '87
The Emerald Forest '85
Moon in the Gutter '83
Diva '82
Peppermint Soda '77

Ashley Rowe
The Affair of the Necklace '01
Mad About Mambo '00
When Brendan Met Trudy '00
Bedrooms and Hallways '98
The Governess '98
Still Crazy '98
B. Monkey '97
24-7 '97
Widow's Peak '94

Kevin Rowley
Forgive and Forget '99
Falling for a Dancer '98

Soumendu Roy
The Middleman '76
Distant Thunder '73
Days and Nights in the Forest '70
Two Daughters '61

Juan Ruiz-Anchia (1949-)
Focus '01
The Crew '00
The Corruptor '99
Mararia '98
The Adventures of Pinocchio '96
The Disappearance of Garcia Lorca '96
Two Bits '96
A Far Off Place '93
Mr. Jones '93
Glengarry Glen Ross '92
Dying Young '91
Liebestraum '91
The Seventh Sign '88
House of Games '87
Surrender '87
At Close Range '86
Where the River Runs Black '86
Maria's Lovers '84
The Stone Boy '84

John L. "Jack" Russell
Psycho '60
Girls' Town '59
The Indestructible Man '56
The Beast from 20,000 Fathoms '53
Invasion U.S.A. '52
The Man from Planet X '51

Ward Russell
The X-Files '98
Lawnmower Man 2: Beyond Cyberspace '95
The Last Boy Scout '91
Days of Thunder '90

Joseph Ruttenberg (1889-93)
Speedway '68
The Oscar '66
Harlow '65
A Global Affair '63
Butterfield 8 '60
Green Mansions '59
Gigi '58
The Reluctant Debutante '58
Somebody Up There Likes Me '56
The Swan '56
Kismet '55
The Prodigal '55
Brigadoon '54
The Last Time I Saw Paris '54
Julius Caesar '53
Prisoner of Zenda '52
The Great Caruso '51
The Miniver Story '50
That Forsyte Woman '50
Adventure '45
The Valley of Decision '45
Gaslight '44
Mrs. Parkington '44
Madame Curie '43
Presenting Lily Mars '43
Mrs. Miniver '42
Random Harvest '42
Woman of the Year '42
Dr. Jekyll and Mr. Hyde '41
Two-Faced Woman '41
The Philadelphia Story '40
Waterloo Bridge '40
On Borrowed Time '39
The Women '39
The Great Waltz '38
Shopworn Angel '38
Three Comrades '38
A Day at the Races '37
Fury '36
Struggle '31

Viktor Ruzicka
Martha and I '91
Cobra Verde '88

Giuseppe Ruzzolini
Firestarter '84
Arabian Nights '74
Allonsanfan '73
Porcile '69

Ellery Ryan
In Too Deep '99
Dead Letter Office '98
The Matchmaker '97
Angel Baby '95
Cosi '95
That Eye, the Sky '94
Death in Brunswick '90

Paul Ryan
Thomas and the Magic Railroad '00
Wildflowers '99
Box of Moonlight '96
Other Voices, Other Rooms '95
Where the Rivers Flow North '94
Fraternity Vacation '85

Robert Saad
Anne of Green Gables: The Continuing Story '99
They Came from Within '75

Eric Saarinen
Real Life '79
The Hills Have Eyes '77
You Light Up My Life '77
Eat My Dust '76

Farhad Saba
Through the Olive Trees '94

Where Is My Friend's House? '87
F. Sacdalan
The Big Bird Cage '72
The Walls of Hell '64
Raiders of Leyte Gulf '63
Odd Geir Saether
The Man on the Roof '76
Edvard Munch '74
Takao Saito
Rhapsody in August '91
Akira Kurosawa's Dreams '90
Ran '85
Dodes 'ka-den '70
High & Low '62
Sanjuro '62
Alik Sakharov
Lulu on the Bridge '98
Love! Valour! Compassion! '96
Anthony Salinas
Blood Orgy of the She-Devils '74
The Doll Squad '73
Timo Salminen
Ariel '89
Leningrad Cowboys Go America '89
Javier Salmones
Butterfly '98
Twice upon a Yesterday '98
Amnon Salomon
The Milky Way '97
The Mangler '94
Mikael Salomon (1945-)
Far and Away '92
Backdraft '91
Arachnophobia '90
The Abyss '89
Always '89
Torch Song Trilogy '88
Zelly & Me '88
Sergio Salvati
Wax Mask '97
Puppet Master '89
The House by the Cemetery '83
The Beyond '82
The Black Cat '81
Gates of Hell '80
Zombie '80
Berhard Salzmann
The Android Affair '95
Deadly Past '95
Bad Blood '94
Francisco Sanchez
Exorcism '74
Curse of the Devil '73
House of Psychotic Women '73
Rodolfo Sanchez
Kiss of the Spider Woman '85
Pixote '81
Gregory Sandor
Forbidden Zone '80
Sisters '73
Born Losers '67
Ride in the Whirlwind '66
The Shooting '66
Tito Santoni
The Girl with a Suitcase '60
Verdi '53
Vic Sarin
Margaret's Museum '95
Whale Music '94
Cold Comfort '90
Bye Bye Blues '89
Paul Sarossy
Duets '00
Rated X '00
Felicia's Journey '99
Rocky Marciano '99
Jerry and Tom '98
Affliction '97
Mistrial '96
Picture Perfect '96
The Sweet Hereafter '96
Blood & Donuts '95
Exotica '94
Love and Human Remains '93
The Adjuster '91
Speaking Parts '89
Hendrik Sartov
America '24
Orphans of the Storm '21
Way Down East '20
Harris Savides
Finding Forrester '00
The Yards '00
Illuminata '98
The Game '97
Heaven's Prisoners '95
Malik Hassan Sayeed
Belly '98
He Got Game '98
The Players Club '98
Cold Around the Heart '97
Girl 6 '96
Clockers '95
Edward Scaife
The Dirty Dozen '67
Khartoum '66
Trial & Error '62
On the Fiddle '61
Curse of the Demon '57
Captain's Paradise '53
Aldo Scavarda
Before the Revolution '65
L'Avventura '60
Roberto Schaefer
Monster's Ball '01
Best in Show '00
Everything Put Together '00
Waiting for Guffman '96
Roadracers '94
Tobias Schliessler
Bait '00
The Guilty '99
Hoods '98
Legalese '98
Free Willy 3: The Rescue '97
Mandela and de Klerk '97
Volcano: Fire on the Mountain '97
The Limbic Region '96
Bulletproof Heart '95
The Escape '95
Candyman 2: Farewell to the Flesh '94
Sin and Redemption '94
Ronn Schmidt
Star Kid '97
Lord of Illusions '95
Men of War '94
The Terror Within '88
Time Trackers '88
Jorge Schmidt-Reitwein
Nosferatu the Vampyre '79
Woyzeck '78
Every Man for Himself & God Against All '75
Heart of Glass '74
Aaron Schneider
Simon Birch '98
Kiss the Girls '97
Dead Girls '90
Charles E. Schoenbaum
Good News '47
Nevada '27
The Vanishing American '25
Nancy Schreiber
Book of Shadows: Blair Witch 2 '00
Shadow Magic '00
Never 2 Big '98
Your Friends & Neighbors '98
Nevada '97
The Curse of Inferno '96
Scorpion Spring '96
The Celluloid Closet '95
Girl in the Cadillac '94
Chain of Desire '93
Visions of Light: The Art of Cinematography '93
Eugene Schufftan
Bizarre Bizarre '39
Metropolis '26
Fred Schuler
Just Looking '99
Haunted Honeymoon '86
Fletch '85
Amityville 3: The Demon '83
Arthur '81
Stir Crazy '80
Howard Schwartz
The Devil & Max Devlin '81
Batman '66
Philip D. Schwartz
High Voltage '98
King Cobra '98
John Schwartzman
The Rookie '02
Pearl Harbor '01
EDtv '99
Armageddon '98
Conspiracy Theory '97
The Rock '96
Mr. Wrong '95
A Pyromaniac's Love Story '95
Airheads '94
Red Surf '90
Xaver Schwarzenberger
Querelle '83
Veronika Voss '82
Berlin Alexanderplatz '80
Lawrence Schweich
Tequila Body Shots '99
Wind River '98
Chris Seager
The Way We Live Now '02
Lorna Doone '01
Frenchman's Creek '98
Alive and Kicking '96
Fever Pitch '96
Beautiful Thing '95
Stonewall '95
Cold Comfort Farm '94
John Seale (1943-)
Harry Potter and the Sorcerer's Stone '01
The Perfect Storm '00
The Talented Mr. Ripley '99
At First Sight '98
City of Angels '98
The English Patient '96
Ghosts of Mississippi '96
The American President '95
Beyond Rangoon '95
The Paper '94
The Firm '93
Lorenzo's Oil '92
The Doctor '91
Dead Poets Society '89
Gorillas in the Mist '88
Rain Man '88
Children of a Lesser God '86
The Hitcher '86
The Mosquito Coast '86
Witness '85
Careful, He Might Hear You '84
Christian Sebaldt
Galgameth '96
Revenge of the Red Baron '93
Hiroshi Segawa
Face of Another '66
Woman in the Dunes '64
John Seitz
Invaders from Mars '53
Sunset Boulevard '50
The Great Gatsby '49
The Big Clock '48
On Our Merry Way '48
The Lost Weekend '45
Double Indemnity '44
Five Graves to Cairo '43
Sullivan's Travels '41
The Four Horsemen of the Apocalypse '21
Andrzej Sekula
American Psycho '99
The Break '97
Cousin Bette '97
Stand-Ins '97
Four Rooms '95
Hackers '95
Across the Moon '94
Oleanna '94
Pulp Fiction '94
Reservoir Dogs '92
Dean Semler (1943-)
Dragonfly '02
We Were Soldiers '02
Heartbreakers '01
Nutty Professor 2: The Klumps '00
The Bone Collector '99
Gone Fishin' '97
Trojan War '97
Waterworld '95
The Cowboy Way '94
Last Action Hero '93
The Three Musketeers '93
The Power of One '92
City Slickers '91
Dances with Wolves '90
Young Guns 2 '90
Dead Calm '89
Farewell to the King '89
K-9 '89
Cocktail '88
Young Guns '88
The Lighthorsemen '87
Mad Max: Beyond Thunderdome '85
The Coca-Cola Kid '84
Razorback '84
The Road Warrior '82
Ben Seresin
Circus '00
Best Laid Plans '99
Michael Seresin
Domestic Disturbance '01
Angela's Ashes '99
Mercury Rising '98
City Hall '95
Angel Heart '87
Midnight Express '78
Viorel Sergovici, Jr.
Dark Asylum '01
Retro Puppet Master '99
Witchouse '99
Eduardo Serra
Passion of Mind '00
Unbreakable '00
The Widow of Saint-Pierre '00
What Dreams May Come '98
The Swindle '97
The Wings of the Dove '97
The Jew '96
Jude '96
Grosse Fatigue '94
The Hairdresser's Husband '92
Leon Shamroy (1901-74)
Justine '69
Planet of the Apes '68
The Glass Bottom Boat '66
The Agony and the Ecstasy '65
The Cardinal '63
Cleopatra '63
Snow White and the Three Stooges '61
North to Alaska '60
Beloved Infidel '59
The Bravados '58
South Pacific '58
Desk Set '57
The Girl Can't Help It '56
The King and I '56
Daddy Long Legs '55
Love Is a Many-Splendored Thing '55
The Egyptian '54
There's No Business Like Show Business '54
The Robe '53
The Snows of Kilimanjaro '52
David and Bathsheba '51
Cheaper by the Dozen '50
Twelve o'Clock High '49
Forever Amber '47
Leave Her to Heaven '45
State Fair '45
A Tree Grows in Brooklyn '45
Buffalo Bill '44
Wilson '44
Crash Dive '43
Stormy Weather '43
The Black Swan '42
Roxie Hart '42
The Great American Broadcast '41
Moon over Miami '41
Down Argentine Way '40
Tin Pan Alley '40
The Adventures of Sherlock Holmes '39
Made for Each Other '39
The Story of Alexander Graham Bell '39
You Only Live Once '37
Douglas W. Shannon
The Arrangement '99
Blowin' Smoke '99
Henry Sharp
The Young Land '59
The Woman Who Came Back '45
Ministry of Fear '44
Tomorrow the World '44
Dr. Cyclops '40
It's a Gift '34
Six of a Kind '34
Duck Soup '33
The Iron Mask '29
The Black Pirate '26
Don Q., Son of Zorro '25
Steve Shaw
The Tempest '99
Dangerous Passion '95
Zero Boys '86
Roger Shearman
Lone Wolf McQuade '83
An Eye for an Eye '81
Lawrence Sher
Shark Attack '99
On the Border '98
Eugene Shlugleit
3 Ninjas Knuckle Up '95
Twogether '94
Eugene (Eugen Shufftan) Shuftan (1893-1977)
Lilith '64
The Hustler '61
The Horror Chamber of Dr. Faustus '59
William Sickner
The Undead '57
The Mummy's Ghost '44
Allen Siegler
The Black Room '35
Parisian Love '25
The Plastic Age '25
Newton Thomas (Tom) Sigel
X-Men '00
Brokedown Palace '99
Three Kings '99
Apt Pupil '97
Fallen '97
Blood & Wine '96
Foxfire '96
The Trigger Effect '96
The Usual Suspects '95
Blankman '94
Salmonberries '91
James Signorelli
Black Caesar '73
Superfly '72
Johnny (John W.) Simmons
Collected Stories '02
Three Strikes '00
Asunder '99
Once Upon a Time ... When We Were Colored '95
Geoffrey Simpson
Glitter '01
Center Stage '00
Life '99
Oscar and Lucinda '97
Some Mother's Son '96
Shine '95
Little Women '94
The War '94
Mr. Wonderful '93
Fried Green Tomatoes '91
Celia: Child of Terror '89
Geza Sinkovics
The Last Seduction 2 '98
French Exit '97
Undertow '95
Delusion '91
Sandi Sissel
Barney's Great Adventure '98
Soul of the Game '96
Camp Nowhere '94
Dragstrip Girl '94
Full Eclipse '93
The People under the Stairs '91
Heavy Petting '89
Salaam Bombay! '88
William V. Skall
Rope '48
Life with Father '47
Song of Scheherazade '47
Douglas Slocombe (1913-)
Never Say Never Again '83
Rollerball '75
Jesus Christ, Superstar '73
The Music Lovers '71
Boom! '68
Fathom '67
The Fearless Vampire Killers '67
The Blue Max '66
The Servant '63
The L-Shaped Room '62
Circus of Horrors '60
The Smallest Show on Earth '57
Kind Hearts and Coronets '49
Dead of Night '45
Michael Slovis
The 4th Floor '99
Scarred City '98
The White Raven '98
Crash Dive '96
Breach of Trust '95
Malicious '95
Party Girl '94
Arturo Smith
Psycho Beach Party '00
Body and Soul '98
Nowhere '96
C. Davis Smith
The Amazing Transplant '70
Bad Girls Go to Hell '65
Keith L. Smith
The Wash '01
Luck of the Draw '00
Diary of a Serial Killer '97
Love to Kill '97
Leonard Smith
National Velvet '44
Go West '40
At the Circus '39
Devil Doll '36
The Wizard of Oz '25
S. Douglas Smith
Joyride '97
Stormy Nights '97
The Secret Agent Club '96
Vladimir Smutny
Dark Blue World '01
Kolya '96
William E. Snyder
The Conqueror '56
Creature from the Black Lagoon '54
Flying Leathernecks '51
The Loves of Carmen '48
Piotr Sobocinski (1958-2001)
Angel Eyes '01
Hearts in Atlantis '01
Twilight '98
Marvin's Room '96
Ransom '96
Trois Couleurs: Rouge '94
The Decalogue '88
Steven Soderbergh (1963-)
Ocean's Eleven '01
Traffic '00
Schizopolis '97
Jaromir Sofr
My Sweet Little Village '86
Closely Watched Trains '66
Yuri Sokol
Warm Nights on a Slow-Moving Train '87
Cactus '86
Man of Flowers '84
Lonely Hearts '82
Leonardo Solis
Jailbird Rock '88
Deathstalker 2: Duel of the Titans '87
Deathstalker '83

Funny, Dirty Little War '83
Barry Sonnenfeld (1953-)
Misery '90
When Harry Met Sally... '89
Raising Arizona '87
Throw Momma from the Train '87
Blood Simple '85
Leonard J. South
The North Avenue Irregulars '79
Family Plot '76
Hang 'Em High '67
Mike Southon
Replicant '01
The Duke '99
RKO 281 '99
Air Bud 2: Golden Receiver '98
Air Bud '97
Snow White: A Tale of Terror '97
The Final Cut '96
Roommates '95
The Run of the Country '95
Emily Bronte's Wuthering Heights '92
Little Man Tate '91
Goldeneye: The Secret Life of Ian Fleming '89
Gothic '87
Peter Sova
The Proposition '97
Donnie Brasco '96
Feast of July '95
Sgt. Bilko '95
Fatherland '94
Jimmy Hollywood '94
Good Morning, Vietnam '87
Tin Men '87
Diner '82
Alberto Spagnoli
Cut and Run '85
Shock '79
Theodor Sparkuhl
Blood on the Sun '45
Murder, He Says '45
The Glass Key '42
Star Spangled Rhythm '42
Wake Island '42
Beau Geste '39
If I Were King '38
Internes Can't Take Money '37
Scott Spears
Unseen Evil '99
Too Good to Be True '98
Brenton Spencer
Where's the Money, Noreen? '95
American Boyfriends '89
James Lawrence Spencer
100 Girls '00
Eight Days a Week '97
Night Shade '97
Magic Island '95
David Sperling
The Drifter '88
Street Trash '87
The Boogey Man '80
Michael Spiller
No Such Thing '01
Drop Dead Gorgeous '99
Henry Fool '98
The House of Yes '97
Niagara, Niagara '97
Walking and Talking '96
Flirt '95
Amateur '94
Search and Destroy '94
Hand Gun '93
Simple Men '92
Age Isn't Everything '91
Surviving Desire '91
Trust '91
The Unbelievable Truth '90
Dante Spinotti (1943-)
Bandits '01
Family Man '00
Wonder Boys '00
Goodbye, Lover '99
The Insider '99
The Other Sister '98
L.A. Confidential '97
The Mirror Has Two Faces '96
Heat '95
The Star Maker '95
The Quick and the Dead '94
Blink '93
The Last of the Mohicans '92
The Comfort of Strangers '91
Frankie and Johnny '91
Hudson Hawk '91
Fair Game '89
Beaches '88
Crimes of the Heart '86
From the Hip '86
Manhunter '86
Basileus Quartet '82
Tony Spratling
Edge of Sanity '89
The Man Who Haunted Himself '70
Chris Squires
Lola and Billy the Kid '98
True Crime '95
Nam Angels '88
Terry Stacey
The Laramie Project '02
World Traveler '01
Trick '99
Jorge Stahl, Jr.
A Rumor of War '80
Zachariah '70
Death in the Garden '56
John Stanier
If These Walls Could Talk '96
Rambo 3 '88
Frank Stanley
10 '79
Car Wash '76
The Eiger Sanction '75
Thunderbolt & Lightfoot '74
Magnum Force '73
Ron Stannett
In a Class of His Own '99
The Sweetest Gift '98
Oliver Stapleton
Birthday Girl '02
The Shipping News '01
Pay It Forward '00
State and Main '00
The Cider House Rules '99
William Shakespeare's A Midsummer Night's Dream '99
The Hi-Lo Country '98
The Object of My Affection '98
The Designated Mourner '97
One Fine Day '96
Kansas City '95
The Van '95
Restoration '94
Look Who's Talking Now '93
Hero '92
The Grifters '90
Earth Girls Are Easy '89
She-Devil '89
Aria '88
Prick Up Your Ears '87
Sammy & Rosie Get Laid '87
Absolute Beginners '86
My Beautiful Laundrette '85
Willy Stassen
Everybody's Famous! '00
Balzac: A Life of Passion '99
The Count of Monte Cristo '99
Hombres Complicados '97
Antonia's Line '95
Robert Steadman
At Any Cost '00
The Man Who Captured Eichmann '96
Return to the Blue Lagoon '91
Above the Law '88
Executive Action '73
Jack Steely
Black Godfather '74
The Thing with Two Heads '72
The Incredible Two-Headed Transplant '71
Ueli Steiger
Black Knight '01
Just Visiting '01
Rock Star '01
Austin Powers 2: The Spy Who Shagged Me '99
Bowfinger '99
Godzilla '98
House Arrest '96
Now and Then '95
Better Off Dead '94
Chasers '94
Singles '92
Soapdish '91
The Hot Spot '90
Peter Stein
The Con '98
Necessary Roughness '91
Graveyard Shift '90
Pet Sematary '89
C.H.U.D. '84
Friday the 13th, Part 2 '81
Mack Stengler
Bowery at Midnight '42
King of the Zombies '41
Sky Bandits '40
Yukon Flight '40
Terror of Tiny Town '38
Alan Stenvold
The Invisible Strangler '76
Private Navy of Sgt. O'Farrell '68
Eight on the Lam '67
Thunder Road '58
John Stephens
Sorcerer '77
Boxcar Bertha '72
Billy Jack '71
Robert Stevens
Cecil B. Demented '00
Dude, Where's My Car? '00
Simply Irresistible '99
Pecker '98
Breast Men '97
The Man Who Knew Too Little '97
Serial Mom '94
Beyond the Law '92
Tune in Tomorrow '90
The 'Burbs '89
Rod Stewart
Alien Chaser '96
Warhead '96
Live Wire: Human Timebomb '95
Terminal Impact '95
Jacques Steyn
Kill Me Again '89
The Mighty Quinn '89
Blitz '85
Clifford Stine
The Brass Bottle '63
Abbott and Costello Go to Mars '53
It Came from Outer Space '53
Harold E. Stine
The Poseidon Adventure '72
M*A*S*H '70
Rogier Stoffers
Enough '02
John Q '02
Quills '00
Character '97
Witold Stok
The Match '99
Among Giants '98
Century '94
Two Deaths '94
Eat the Rich '87
John Stokes
Journey to the Center of the Earth '99
Silent Predators '99
Gargantua '98
Blackwater Trail '95
Barry Stone
Full Disclosure '00
Dream with the Fishes '97
Pale Saints '97
Rude '96
Understudy: The Graveyard Shift 2 '88
Vittorio Storaro (1940-)
Dune '00
Goya in Bordeaux '99
Picking Up the Pieces '99
Bulworth '98
Tango '98
Little Buddha '93
Dick Tracy '90
The Sheltering Sky '90
Ishtar '87
The Last Emperor '87
Ladyhawke '85
Apocalypse Now '79
1900 '76
Last Tango in Paris '73
The Conformist '71
The Bird with the Crystal Plumage '70
Michael Storey
Walter and Henry '01
No Alibi '00
One Kill '00
Locked in Silence '99
Blacklight '98
Elvis Meets Nixon '98
Summer of the Monkeys '98
In His Father's Shoes '97
Archie Stout (1886-1965)
Hondo '53
The Sun Shines Bright '53
Big Jim McLain '52
The Quiet Man '52
Fort Apache '48
Angel and the Badman '47
Abilene Town '46
Captain Kidd '45
Dark Waters '44
It Happened Tomorrow '44
Beau Geste '39
The Hurricane '37
Hopalong Cassidy Returns '36
Desert Trail '35
Hopalong Cassidy '35
Paradise Canyon '35
Lucky Texan '34
Man from Utah '34
The Star Packer '34
Trail Beyond '34
Riders of Destiny '33
Sagebrush Trail '33
West of the Divide '33
The Ten Commandments '23
Harry Stradling, Sr. (1902-70)
On a Clear Day You Can See Forever '70
The Owl and the Pussycat '70
Hello, Dolly! '69
Funny Girl '68
Moment to Moment '66
How to Murder Your Wife '64
My Fair Lady '64
Gypsy '62
Parrish '61
A Summer Place '59
The Young Philadelphians '59
Auntie Mame '58
Marjorie Morningstar '58
A Face in the Crowd '57
The Pajama Game '57
The Eddy Duchin Story '56
Helen of Troy '56
Guys and Dolls '55
Johnny Guitar '53
Androcles and the Lion '52
Hans Christian Andersen '52
I Want You '51
A Streetcar Named Desire '51
The Barkleys of Broadway '49
In the Good Old Summertime '49
Easter Parade '48
The Pirate '48
Holiday in Mexico '46
Till the Clouds Roll By '46
Picture of Dorian Gray '45
Bathing Beauty '44
The Human Comedy '43
The Corsican Brothers '42
The Devil & Miss Jones '41
Suspicion '41
The Lion Has Wings '40
My Son, My Son '40
They Knew What They Wanted '40
Clouds over Europe '39
Jamaica Inn '39
The Citadel '38
The Divorce of Lady X '38
Pygmalion '38
Knight Without Armour '37
South Riding '37
Carnival in Flanders '35
Harry Stradling, Jr.
Caddyshack 2 '88
Blind Date '87
A Fine Mess '86
Micki & Maude '84
Buddy Buddy '81
The Pursuit of D.B. Cooper '81
S.O.B. '81
Carny '80
Prophecy '79
Born Again '78
Convoy '78
Go Tell the Spartans '78
Damnation Alley '77
The Greatest '77
The Big Bus '76
Midway '76
Special Delivery '76
Bite the Bullet '75
Mitchell '75
Rooster Cogburn '75
Bank Shot '74
McQ '74
Man Who Loved Cat Dancing '73
The Way We Were '73
1776 '72
Support Your Local Gunfighter '71
Little Big Man '70
There Was a Crooked Man '70
The Good Guys and the Bad Guys '69
Support Your Local Sheriff '69
With Six You Get Eggroll '68
Walter Stradling (-1918)
Amarilly of Clothesline Alley '18
Stella Maris '18
Ivan Strasburg
The Murder of Stephen Lawrence '01
Britannic '99
New World Disorder '99
Deacon Brodie '98
The Theory of Flight '98
Moll Flanders '96
The Affair '95
Sharpe's Eagle '93
Sharpe's Rifles '93
Rita, Sue & Bob Too '87
Walter Strenge
Rodeo King and the Senorita '51
Before Morning '33
Karl Struss (1891-1981)
The Rebel Set '59
The Fly '58
Kronos '57
Mohawk '56
Limelight '52
Mesa of Lost Women '52
Rocketship X-M '50
Mr. Ace '46
Journey into Fear '42
The Great Dictator '40
Rhythm Romance '39
Thanks for the Memory '38
Waikiki Wedding '37
Go West, Young Man '36
Rhythm on the Range '36
Goin' to Town '35
Belle of the Nineties '34
Dr. Jekyll and Mr. Hyde '32
Island of Lost Souls '32
Abraham Lincoln '30
Be Yourself '30
Coquette '29
The Taming of the Shrew '29
Battle of the Sexes '28
Sunrise '27
Sparrows '26
Affairs of Anatol '21
Dr. Jekyll and Mr. Hyde '20
Charles Stumar
The Raven '35
Werewolf of London '35
The Mummy '32
Uncle Tom's Cabin '27
Jens Sturup
Stuart Bliss '98
Fun '94
Witchcraft 2: The Temptress '90
Witchcraft '88
Ramon Suarez
The Silence of Neto '94
Red Kiss '85
L'Amour en Herbe '77
Memories of Underdevelopment '68
Death of a Bureaucrat '66
Kohei Sugiyama
Gate of Hell '54
47 Ronin, Part 1 '42
47 Ronin, Part 2 '42
Tim Suhrstedt
Clockstoppers '02
Summer Catch '01
Whatever It Takes '00
Major League 3: Back to the Minors '98
Office Space '98
The Wedding Singer '97
To Gillian on Her 37th Birthday '96
Getting Even with Dad '94
The Chinatown Murders: Man against the Mob '92
The Favor '92
Traces of Red '92
Don't Tell Mom the Babysitter's Dead '91
Men at Work '90
Bill & Ted's Excellent Adventure '89
Capone '89
Mystic Pizza '88
Mannequin '87
Critters '86
The House on Sorority Row '83
Suburbia '83
Android '82
Forbidden World '82
Igor Sunara
Somewhere in the City '97
The Keeper '96
Tales of Erotica '93
Bruce Surtees (1944-)
American Tragedy '00
Dash and Lilly '99
Just a Little Harmless Sex '99
The Lady in Question '99
Murder in a Small Town '99
That Championship Season '99
The Substitute '96
Corrina, Corrina '94
The Stars Fell on Henrietta '94
The Crush '93
Run '91
The Super '91
Men Don't Leave '89
License to Drive '88
Back to the Beach '87
Out of Bounds '86
Psycho 3 '86
Ratboy '86
Pale Rider '85
Beverly Hills Cop '84
Tightrope '84
Risky Business '83
Sudden Impact '83
Firefox '82
Honkytonk Man '82
Escape from Alcatraz '79
The Outlaw Josey Wales '76
The Shootist '76
Night Moves '75
Lenny '74
Blume in Love '73
High Plains Drifter '73

Conquest of the Planet of the Apes '72
The Great Northfield Minnesota Raid '72
Joe Kidd '72
Dirty Harry '71
Play Misty for Me '71
The Beguiled '70

Robert L. Surtees (1906-)
Bloodbrothers '78
Same Time, Next Year '78
The Turning Point '77
A Star Is Born '76
The Great Waldo Pepper '75
The Hindenburg '75
Oklahoma Crude '73
The Sting '73
The Cowboys '72
The Other '72
The Last Picture Show '71
Summer of '42 '71
The Arrangement '69
Sweet Charity '69
Doctor Dolittle '67
The Graduate '67
The Lost Command '66
The Collector '65
The Hallelujah Trail '65
Mutiny on the Bounty '62
Ben-Hur '59
Les Girls '57
Raintree County '57
The Swan '56
Oklahoma! '55
Valley of the Kings '54
Escape from Fort Bravo '53
Mogambo '53
The Bad and the Beautiful '52
The Merry Widow '52
Quo Vadis '51
King Solomon's Mines '50
Intruder in the Dust '49
That Midnight Kiss '49
A Date with Judy '48
Our Vines Have Tender Grapes '45
Thirty Seconds Over Tokyo '44
Two Girls and a Sailor '44

Wolfgang Suschitzky
Theatre of Blood '73
Get Carter '71
Entertaining Mr. Sloane '70
Ring of Bright Water '69
Ulysses '67

Peter Suschitzky
eXistenZ '99
The Man in the Iron Mask '98
Mars Attacks! '96
Crash '95
Immortal Beloved '94
Naked Lunch '91
Dead Ringers '88
Falling in Love '84
Krull '83
The Empire Strikes Back '80
Valentino '77
Lisztomania '75
The Rocky Horror Picture Show '75
All Creatures Great and Small '74
That'll Be the Day '73
The Vengeance of She '68

Misha (Mikhail) Suslov
Prancer '89
Black Moon Rising '86
Nobody's Fool '86

Darko Suvak
True Blue '01
The Landlady '98
Stir '98

Rob Sweeney
The Street King '02
Big Eden '00
I'm Losing You '98
Color of a Brisk and Leaping Day '95

Hubert Taczanowski
How to Kill Your Neighbor's Dog '01
Turn It Up '00
Chicago Cab '98
Eden '98
The Maker '98
The Opposite of Sex '98
The Young Poisoner's Handbook '94

Carlo Tafani
Lucky Luke '94
Troublemakers '94

Renato Tafuri
The Church '98
Dial Help '88

Wong Ngok Tai
Once Upon a Time in China II '92
Operation Condor '91

Ken Talbot
Doomwatch '72
Hands of the Ripper '71
Girl Hunters '63
The Stranger from Venus '54
Old Mother Riley, Headmistress '50

Fred Tammes
Face '97
Mad Love '95
Priest '94
The Whistle Blower '87

Masaki Tamura (1939-)
Tampopo '86
Himatsuri '85

Philip Tannura
The Flying Saucer '50
Strange Illusion '45
Footlight Glamour '43

Jean-Jacques Tarbes
My New Partner '84
Borsalino '70
Honor Among Thieves '68

John Tarver
The Art of Murder '99
The First 9 1/2 Weeks '98
Stonebrook '98

David Tattersall
Star Wars: Episode 2—Attack of the Clones '02
The Majestic '01
Vertical Limit '00
The Green Mile '99
Star Wars: Episode 1—The Phantom Menace '99
Soldier '98
Con Air '97
Mr. Toad's Wild Ride '96
Moll Flanders '96
Theodore Rex '95
Radioland Murders '94

Gale Tattersall
13 Ghosts '01
The Jack Bull '99
Pushing Tin '99
From the Earth to the Moon '98
Virtuosity '95
Hideaway '94
Tank Girl '94
The Commitments '91
Wild Orchid '90
Aria '88

Alfred Taylor
Killer Klowns from Outer Space '88
Mutant '83
The Swinging Cheerleaders '74
Spider Baby '64

Christopher Taylor
Death Benefit '96
Glory Daze '96
Live Nude Girls '95
Inside Monkey Zetterland '93

Gilbert Taylor
The Bedroom Window '87
Voyage of the Rock Aliens '87
Losin' It '82
Flash Gordon '80
Dracula '79
Star Wars '77
The Omen '76
Frenzy '72
Macbeth '71
Quackser Fortune Has a Cousin in the Bronx '70
Theatre of Death '67
Repulsion '65
Dr. Strangelove, or: How I Learned to Stop Worrying and Love the Bomb '64
A Hard Day's Night '64

Ronnie Taylor (1924-)
Sleepless '01
The Phantom of the Opera '98
Popcorn '89
Sea of Love '89
Opera '88
Cry Freedom '87
The Hound of the Baskervilles '83
Tommy '75

Manuel Teran
Mercy '00
Petits Freres '00
Red Shoe Diaries: Four on the Floor '96
Before the Rain '94

Ubaldo Terzano
Black Sabbath '64
Blood and Black Lace '64
The Whip and the Body '63
Black Sunday '60

Ted Tetzlaff (1903-95)
Notorious '46
I Married a Witch '42
The Road to Zanzibar '41
Remember the Night '40
Easy Living '37
My Man Godfrey '36
The Princess Comes Across '36
Hands Across the Table '35

Bud Thackery
Phantom Stallion '54
Iron Mountain Trail '53
Shadows of Tombstone '53
Outcasts of the Trail '49
Alias Billy the Kid '46

Gary Thieltges
Sticky Fingers '88
Eating Raoul '82

Armand Thirard
Sois Belle et Tais-Toi '58
And God Created Woman '57
The Night Heaven Fell '57
Diabolique '55
Wages of Fear '55
Beauties of the Night '52
Utopia '51

John Thomas
The Hunley '99
Hi-Life '98
The Last Days of Disco '98
Dead Man on Campus '97
Kicked in the Head '97
Still Breathing '97
Freeway '95
Norma Jean and Marilyn '95
Palookaville '95
Barcelona '94
Metropolitan '90

Jamie Thompson
Tracked '98
Cyborg 2 '93
Freaked '93
Desire and Hell at Sunset Motel '92
Circuitry Man '90

Stuart Thompson
At War with the Army '50
Variety Girl '47

William C. Thompson
The Sinister Urge '60
Night of the Ghouls '59
The Astounding She-Monster '58
Plan 9 from Outer Space '56
The Violent Years '56
Bride of the Monster '55
Daughter of Horror '55
Jail Bait '54
Glen or Glenda? '53
Project Moon Base '53
Demon for Trouble '34
Maniac '34

Alex Thomson
Love's Labour's Lost '00
Executive Decision '96
Hamlet '96
The Scarlet Letter '95
Black Beauty '94
Cliffhanger '93
Demolition Man '93
Alien 3 '92
The Krays '90
Leviathan '89
Date with an Angel '87
The Sicilian '87
Labyrinth '86
Raw Deal '86
The Keep '83
Excalibur '81
The Cat and the Canary '79
Doctor Phibes Rises Again '72

Donald E. Thorin
Dudley Do-Right '99
Mickey Blue Eyes '99
The First Wives Club '96
Nothing to Lose '96
Ace Ventura: When Nature Calls '95
Boys on the Side '94
Scent of a Woman '92
Lock Up '89
Tango and Cash '89
Midnight Run '88
The Golden Child '86
Against All Odds '84
Purple Rain '84
Bad Boys '83
An Officer and a Gentleman '82
Thief '81

Clive Tickner
The Magical Legend of the Leprechauns '99
Ivanhoe '97
Spice World: The Movie '97
Twelfth Night '96
Loch Ness '95
The Borrowers '93
Split Second '92
Hidden Agenda '90
Traffik '90

Frank Tidy
The Boys Next Door '96
Chain Reaction '96
Getting Away With Murder '96
Hoodlum '96
Steal Big, Steal Little '95
Black Fox: Blood Horse '94
Black Fox: Good Men and Bad '94
Black Fox: The Price of Peace '94
Under Siege '92
The Butcher's Wife '91
Slipstream '89
Hot Pursuit '87
One Magic Christmas '85
The Grey Fox '83
Spacehunter: Adventures in the Forbidden Zone '83

Gary Tieche
Menno's Mind '96
Bad Love '95
Dead Weekend '95
Out There '95

George Tirl
Left Behind: The Movie '00
Revelation '00
Tribulation '00
Steel Dawn '87

Eduard Tisse
Ivan the Terrible, Part 2 '46
Ivan the Terrible, Part 1 '44
Alexander Nevsky '38
Que Viva Mexico '32
Ten Days That Shook the World '27
The Battleship Potemkin '25

Gregg Toland (1904-48)
December 7th: The Movie '91
A Song Is Born '48
The Bishop's Wife '47
The Best Years of Our Lives '46
Kid from Brooklyn '46
The Outlaw '43
Ball of Fire '41
Citizen Kane '41
The Little Foxes '41
The Grapes of Wrath '40
The Long Voyage Home '40
The Westerner '40
Intermezzo '39
Wuthering Heights '39
The Cowboy and the Lady '38
The Goldwyn Follies '38
Dead End '37
History Is Made at Night '37
Beloved Enemy '36
Come and Get It '36
Strike Me Pink '36
These Three '36
Les Miserables '35
Mad Love '35
Splendor '35
Roman Scandals '33
Kid from Spain '32
Palmy Days '31
Tonight or Never '31
Raffles '30
Bulldog Drummond '29

John Toll
Captain Corelli's Mandolin '01
Vanilla Sky '01
Almost Famous '00
Simpatico '99
The Thin Red Line '98
John Grisham's The Rainmaker '97
Jack '96
Braveheart '95
Legends of the Fall '94
Wind '92

Aldo Tonti
Cast a Giant Shadow '66
Barabbas '62
The Unfaithfuls '60
Nights of Cabiria '57
War and Peace '56
The Miracle '48
Ossessione '42

Bruce Torbet
Brain Damage '88
Basket Case '82

Mario Tosi
The Stunt Man '80
The Betsy '78
MacArthur '77
Carrie '76
Frogs '72

Roland H. Totheroh
Monsieur Verdoux '47
The Great Dictator '40
Modern Times '36
City Lights '31
The Gold Rush '25
The Circus '19

Salvatore Totino
Changing Lanes '02
Any Given Sunday '99

Bert Tougas
Codename: Jaguar '00
The Pact '99

Jean Tournier
The Fiendish Plot of Dr. Fu Manchu '80
Moonraker '79
Start the Revolution without Me '70
The Train '65

Leo Tover
Strange Bedfellows '65
The Conqueror '56
Love Me Tender '56
Soldier of Fortune '55
The Day the Earth Stood Still '51
The Heiress '49
The Snake Pit '48
China '43
The Major and the Minor '42
Star Spangled Rhythm '42
Never Say Die '39
Love in Bloom '35
I'm No Angel '33

Luciano Tovoli
Murder by Numbers '02
The Closet '00
Titus '99
Desperate Measures '98
The Dinner Game '98
Before and After '95
Single White Female '92
Reversal of Fortune '90
Unsane '82
Suspiria '77
The Desert of the Tartars '76
Bread and Chocolate '73
Bandits of Orgosolo '61

Luciano Trasatti
And God Said to Cain '69
The Bloody Pit of Horror '65

Jan Troell (1931-)
Hamsun '96
The New Land '73
The Emigrants '72

Oberdan Troiani
Hercules against the Moon Men '64
Othello '52

William G. Troiano
She-Freak '67
The Wild World of Batwoman '66
The Slime People '63

Alan M. Trow
Grim '95
Chasing the Deer '94

Shinya Tsukamoto (1960-)
Tetsuo 2: Body Hammer '97
Tetsuo: The Iron Man '92

Brian Tufano
Billy Elliot '00
East Is East '99
Virtual Sexuality '99
A Life Less Ordinary '97
Element of Doubt '96
Trainspotting '95
Shallow Grave '94
Middlemarch '93
War Party '89
Dreamscape '84
The Lords of Discipline '83
Heavy Metal '81
Quadrophenia '79

Christopher Tufty
Jimmy Zip '00
To Cross the Rubicon '91
West Is West '87
Stoogemania '85

Masaharu Ueda
Rhapsody in August '91
Akira Kurosawa's Dreams '90
Ran '85
Kagemusha '80

Alejandro Ulloa
Bad Man's River '72
Horror Express '72
Pancho Villa '72
Companeros '70
The Diabolical Dr. Z '65

Derick Underschultz
Danger Beneath the Sea '02
Jason X '01
Sins of the Father '01
Mr. Rock 'n' Roll: The Alan Freed Story '99
Thrill Seekers '99

Geoffrey Unsworth (1914-78)
Superman 2 '80
Tess '80
The Great Train Robbery '79
Superman: The Movie '78
A Bridge Too Far '77
A Matter of Time '76
Royal Flash '75
Murder on the Orient Express '74
Return of the Pink Panther '74
Internecine Project '73
Zardoz '73
Cabaret '72
Cromwell '70
The Assassination Bureau '69
The Magic Christian '69
2001: A Space Odyssey '68
Half a Sixpence '67

Oh Dad, Poor Dad (Momma's Hung You in the Closet & I'm Feeling So Sad) '67
Othello '65
Becket '64
Flame Over India '60
The World of Suzie Wong '60
A Night to Remember '58
Simba '55
The Sword & the Rose '53
The Clouded Yellow '51
Trio '50
Blanche Fury '48
Scott of the Antarctic '48

Sergei Urusevsky
I Am Cuba '64
The Cranes Are Flying '57

Jost Vacano
The Hollow Man '00
Starship Troopers '97
Showgirls '95
Untamed Heart '93
The NeverEnding Story '84
Das Boot '81

Joseph Valentine (1900-49)
Joan of Arc '48
Rope '48
The Possessed '47
Heartbeat '46
Magnificent Doll '46
Tomorrow Is Forever '46
Guest Wife '45
Shadow of a Doubt '43
Saboteur '42
In the Navy '41
Nice Girl? '41
The Wolf Man '41
It's a Date '40
My Little Chickadee '40
First Love '39
Mad About Music '38
The Rage of Paris '38
That Certain Age '38
100 Men and a Girl '37
The Moon's Our Home '36
Three Smart Girls '36
Night of Terror '33

Theo van de Sande
High Crimes '02
Double Take '01
Little Nicky '00
Big Daddy '99
Tuesdays with Morrie '99
Blade '98
Cruel Intentions '98
Volcano '97
Wayne's World '92
Body Parts '91
The First Power '89
Miracle Mile '89

Jules Van Den Steenhoven
The Gambler '97
Crimetime '96

Eddy van der Enden
Lie Down with Lions '94
Daughters of Darkness '71
Traffic '71

Charles Van Enger
Bela Lugosi Meets a Brooklyn Gorilla '52
Abbott and Costello Meet the Killer, Boris Karloff '49
Abbott and Costello Meet Frankenstein '48
Buck Privates Come Home '47
It Ain't Hay '43
Night Monster '42
Never Give a Sucker an Even Break '41
The Phantom of the Opera '25
The Marriage Circle '24
The Last of the Mohicans '20

Kees Van Oostrum
Cupid & Cate '00
A House Divided '00
Drive Me Crazy '99
You Know My Name '99
William Faulkner's Old Man '97
Stephen King's Thinner '96
Journey '95
Down Came a Blackbird '94
The Enemy Within '94
Gettysburg '93
Scott Turow's The Burden of Proof '92
Long Road Home '91

James Van Trees
Angel on My Shoulder '46
A Night in Casablanca '46
Baby Face '33

Walther Vanden Ende
No Man's Land '01
A Dog of Flanders '99
Left Luggage '98
The Eighth Day '95
Farinelli '94
Toto le Heros '91

Gerard Vandenburg
Spring Symphony '86
The Vampire Happening '71

Henry Vargas
Tollbooth '94
Unlawful Passage '94

Carlo Varini
L'Eleve '95
The Big Blue '88
Subway '85
Le Dernier Combat '84

Rene Verzier
Eddie and the Cruisers 2: Eddie Lives! '89
Of Unknown Origin '83
Death Ship '80
Rabid '77
The Little Girl Who Lives down the Lane '76

Mark Vicente
Slow Burn '00
Dish Dogs '98
Uncorked '98
Midnight Blue '96

Robin Vidgeon
Catherine Cookson's Tilly Trotter '99
Catherine Cookson's The Round Tower '98
August '95
The NeverEnding Story 3: Escape from Fantasia '94
Lady Chatterley '92
Nightbreed '90
The Fly 2 '89
Parents '89
Hellbound: Hellraiser 2 '88
Mr. North '88
Hellraiser '87

Sacha Vierny (1919-2001)
The Man Who Cried '00
8 1/2 Women '99
The Pillow Book '95
The Belly of an Architect '91
Prospero's Books '91
The Cook, the Thief, His Wife & Her Lover '90
A Zed & Two Noughts '88
Drowning by Numbers '87
The Draughtsman's Contract '82
Beau Pere '81
Mon Oncle d'Amerique '80
Stavisky '74
Belle de Jour '67
La Guerre Est Finie '66
Muriel '63
Last Year at Marienbad '61
Hiroshima, Mon Amour '59

Reynaldo Villalobos
Not Another Teen Movie '01
Love and Basketball '00
Return to Paradise '98
An Alan Smithee Film: Burn, Hollywood, Burn '97
Hollywood Confidential '97
Loved '97
Romy and Michele's High School Reunion '97
Telling Lies in America '96
Roosters '95
A Bronx Tale '93
American Me '92
Sinatra '92
Major League '89
Punchline '88
Desert Bloom '86
Blame It on Rio '84
Ballad of Gregorio Cortez '83
Risky Business '83
Prime Suspect '82
9 to 5 '80
Urban Cowboy '80

Joseph Vilsmaier (1939-)
The Harmonists '99
Brother of Sleep '95
Stalingrad '94

Amy Vincent
Jawbreaker '98
Eve's Bayou '97

Ernest Vincze
Business As Usual '88
A Very British Coup '88
A Woman of Substance '84

Paul Vogel (1899-1975)
Return of the Magnificent Seven '66
The Rounders '65
Village of the Giants '65
The Wonderful World of the Brothers Grimm '62
The Time Machine '60
Wings of Eagles '57
High Society '56
Interrupted Melody '55
The Tender Trap '55
Rose Marie '54
The Student Prince '54
Clown '53
Angels in the Outfield '51
Go for Broke! '51
The Black Hand '50
Battleground '49
Lady in the Lake '46
Wide Open Faces '38
Fit for a King '37

Peter von Haller
Anatomy '00
The Inheritors '98

Wedigo von Schultzendorff
Hollywood Ending '02
The Thirteenth Floor '99

Nicholas Josef von Sternberg (1951-)
Jungle Boy '96
American Cop '94
Body Shot '93
Final Justice '84
Tourist Trap '79
Dolemite '75

Mario Vulpiani
Castle Freak '95
La Grande Bouffe '73

William Wages
Down in the Delta '98
Buffalo Soldiers '97
Riders of the Purple Sage '96
Children of Fury '94
Love Potion #9 '92

Fritz Arno Wagner
Kameradschaft '31
M '31
The Threepenny Opera '31
Diary of a Lost Girl '29
Nosferatu '22
Destiny '21

Roy Wagner
A Rumor of Angels '00
In the Company of Spies '99
The Pest '96
Nick of Time '95
Drop Zone '94
Another Stakeout '93
Mortuary Academy '91
Disaster at Silo 7 '88
A Nightmare on Elm Street 3: Dream Warriors '87
Return to Horror High '87
Witchboard '87

Ric Waite (1933-)
The Triangle '01
Ratz '99
Truth or Consequences, N.M. '97
Last Stand at Saber River '96
Andersonville '95
On Deadly Ground '94
Out for Justice '91
Marked for Death '90
The Great Outdoors '88
Adventures in Babysitting '87
Cobra '86
Brewster's Millions '85
Summer Rental '85
Volunteers '85
Red Dawn '84
Class '83
Tex '82
The Long Riders '80

Kent Wakeford
Last Lives '98
Loser '97
Power 98 '96
Wedding Bell Blues '96
Some Folks Call It a Sling Blade '94
The Ghost Brigade '93
Hold Me, Thrill Me, Kiss Me '93
China O'Brien '88
Mean Streets '73

Joseph Walker
The Marrying Kind '52
Born Yesterday '50
Harriet Craig '50
It's a Wonderful Life '46
Mr. Winkle Goes to War '44
Tales of Manhattan '42
They All Kissed the Bride '42
Penny Serenade '41
His Girl Friday '40
Only Angels Have Wings '39
Joy of Living '38
Lost Horizon '37
Mr. Deeds Goes to Town '36
Theodora Goes Wild '36
It Happened One Night '34
Lady for a Day '33
American Madness '32
The Miracle Woman '31

Mandy Walker
Lantana '01
The Well '97
Love Serenade '96

Enrique Wallace
Doctor of Doom '62
The Robot vs. the Aztec Mummy '59

Chris Walling
Blue Ridge Fall '99
Thick as Thieves '99
Wicked Ways '99
Crosswords '96
Solo '96

David M. Walsh
Carpool '96
Taking Care of Business '90
Fatal Beauty '87
Outrageous Fortune '87
My Science Project '85
Romantic Comedy '83
Private Benjamin '80
Seems Like Old Times '80
California Suite '78
Rollercoaster '77
Murder by Death '76
Cleopatra Jones '73
Sleeper '73
Evel Knievel '72
Everything You Always Wanted to Know about Sex (But Were Afraid to Ask) '72

John Ward
Love, Honour & Obey '00
Heaven's a Drag '94

Mark Wareham
Dr. Jekyll & Mr. Hyde '99
First Daughter '99

John F. Warren (1909-2000)
Torn Curtain '66
The Cosmic Man '59
The Daughter of Dr. Jekyll '57

Gilbert Warrenton
Panic in the Year Zero! '62
Atomic Submarine '59
Mesa of Lost Women '52
Here Comes Cookie '35
The Cat and the Canary '27
The Plastic Age '25

Norman Warwick
The Final Programme '73
The Creeping Flesh '72
The Abominable Dr. Phibes '71
Dr. Jekyll and Sister Hyde '71

John Waters (1946-)
Female Trouble '74
Pink Flamingos '72
Multiple Maniacs '70
Mondo Trasho '69

Philip Alan Waters
Urban Menace '99
Cyborg '89

David Watkin (1925-)
Lover's Prayer '99
Tea with Mussolini '99
Gloria '98
Critical Care '97
Bogus '96
Jane Eyre '96
Night Falls on Manhattan '96
This Boy's Life '93
The Object of Beauty '91
Hamlet '90
Memphis Belle '90
The Good Mother '88
Last Rites '88
Masquerade '88
Moonstruck '87
Out of Africa '85
Return to Oz '85
White Nights '85
The Hotel New Hampshire '84
Yentl '83
Chariots of Fire '81
Endless Love '81
Cuba '79
Hanover Street '79
Joseph Andrews '77
Robin and Marian '76
To the Devil, a Daughter '76
The Four Musketeers '75
Mahogany '75
The Three Musketeers '74
The Boy Friend '71
The Devils '71
Catch-22 '70
The Charge of the Light Brigade '68
How I Won the War '67
Mademoiselle '66
Help! '65
The Knack '65

Michael Watkins
Heart and Souls '93
Point of No Return '93

Harry Waxman
The Pink Panther Strikes Again '76
The Wicker Man '75
Vampyres '74
Endless Night '71
Wonderwall: The Movie '69
The Day the Earth Caught Fire '61
The Swiss Family Robinson '60

Henry Waxman
The Anniversary '68
The Nanny '65

Jesse Weathington
Interlocked '98
Mom, Can I Keep Her? '98

Yossi Wein
Bridge of Dragons '99
Sweepers '99
Operation: Delta Force '97
Danger Zone '95
Cyborg Cop '93
The House of Usher '88

Jan Weincke
Inside '96
Twist & Shout '84

Ben Weinstein
Wet Hot American Summer '01
Let It Snow '99

Charles S. Welbourne
The Three Stooges Meet Hercules '61
Revenge of the Creature '55
Creature from the Black Lagoon '54

Harold E. Wellman
Muscle Beach Party '64
The Invisible Boy '57

Philippe Welt
Le Bonheur Est Dans le Pre '95
Madame Butterfly '95

Harold Wenstrom
The Lost Patrol '34
The Saphead '21

Egon Werdin
An American Werewolf in Paris '97
Mute Witness '95

Brian West
Ellen Foster '97
84 Charing Cross Road '86
Bloodbath at the House of Death '85
The Lonely Lady '83
Billy Two Hats '74

Frederick E. West
Terror in the Haunted House '58
Invasion of the Saucer Men '57
The Gunslinger '56
It Conquered the World '56

Ken Westbury
Jack Higgins' Midnight Man '96
Jack Higgins' On Dangerous Ground '95
Bellman and True '88

Tony Westman
The Last Stop '99
Alaska '96
Needful Things '93
The Deserters '83

Haskell Wexler (1926-)
61* '01
Limbo '99
The Rich Man's Wife '96
Mulholland Falls '95
Canadian Bacon '94
The Secret of Roan Inish '94
The Babe '92
Other People's Money '91
Blaze '89
Three Fugitives '89
Colors '88
Matewan '87
The Man Who Loved Women '83
Coming Home '78
Bound for Glory '76
One Flew Over the Cuckoo's Nest '75
Gimme Shelter '70
Medium Cool '69
The Thomas Crown Affair '68
In the Heat of the Night '67
Who's Afraid of Virginia Woolf? '66
The Loved One '65
The Best Man '64
A Face in the Rain '63
Angel Baby '61
The Hoodlum Priest '61

Howard Wexler
Newsbreak '00
Curse of the Puppet Master: The Human Experiment '98
Leather Jacket Love Story '98
Return to Savage Beach '97
Attack of the 60-Foot Centerfold '95
Over the Wire '95
Die Watching '93
Picasso Trigger '89
Hard Ticket to Hawaii '87
Banzai Runner '86
Reform School Girls '86

Charles F. Wheeler
The Best of Times '86
Condorman '81
The Last Flight of Noah's Ark '80
The Cat from Outer Space '78

Composer Index

The **Composer Index** provides a videography for any composer, arranger, lyricist, or band that has provided an original music score for more than one film now on video. The listings for the composer names follow an alphabetical sort by last name (although the names appear in a first name, last name format). The videographies are listed chronologically, from most recent film to the first. If a composer provided music for more than one film in the same year, these movies are listed alphabetically within the year.

Barron Abramovitch
Profile for Murder *'96*
Tracks of a Killer *'95*
Hard Evidence *'94*
Anton Abril
Return of the Evil Dead *'75*
Pancho Villa *'72*
Tombs of the Blind Dead *'72*
The Werewolf vs. the Vampire Woman *'70*
Neal Acree
Venomous *'01*
Ablaze *'00*
Militia *'99*
Barry Adamson
Gas Food Lodging *'92*
Delusion *'91*
Richard Addinsell
Waltz of the Toreadors *'62*
A Christmas Carol *'51*
Blithe Spirit *'45*
Gaslight *'40*
Fire Over England *'37*
South Riding *'37*
John Addison (1920-98)
The Phantom of the Opera *'90*
Something in Common *'86*
Code Name: Emerald *'85*
Grace Quigley *'84*
Strange Invaders *'83*
Eleanor: First Lady of the World *'82*
Love's Savage Fury *'79*
The Bastard *'78*
Pearl *'78*
A Bridge Too Far *'77*
Joseph Andrews *'77*
The Seven-Per-Cent Solution *'76*
Swashbuckler *'76*
Ride a Wild Pony *'75*
Luther *'74*
Sleuth *'72*
Cry of the Penguins *'71*
Start the Revolution without Me *'70*
The Charge of the Light Brigade *'68*
The Honey Pot *'67*
Smashing Time *'67*
A Fine Madness *'66*
Torn Curtain *'66*
The Amorous Adventures of Moll Flanders *'65*
The Loved One *'65*
Girl with Green Eyes *'64*
Guns at Batasi *'64*
Tom Jones *'63*
The Loneliness of the Long Distance Runner *'62*
A Taste of Honey *'61*
The Entertainer *'60*
Carlton Browne of the F.O. *'59*
Look Back in Anger *'58*
Lucky Jim *'58*
Reach for the Sky *'56*
Larry Adler
King and Country *'64*
A Cry from the Streets *'57*
Genevieve *'53*
Mark Adler
Focus *'01*
Cupid & Cate *'00*
Apartment Complex *'98*
The Rat Pack *'98*
Ernest in the Army *'97*
Decoy *'95*
Slam Dunk Ernest *'95*
Henry & June *'90*
Eat a Bowl of Tea *'89*
Break of Dawn *'88*
The Unbearable Lightness of Being *'88*
Heat and Sunlight *'87*
Yashushi Akutagawa
An Actor's Revenge *'63*
Fires on the Plain *'59*
Gate of Hell *'54*
Robert Alcivar
Blind Witness *'89*
Naked Lie *'89*
Hysterical *'83*
One from the Heart *'82*
Olly Olly Oxen Free *'78*
Butterflies Are Free *'72*
Jeff Alexander (1910-89)
Clambake *'67*
Gun Glory *'57*
Jailhouse Rock *'57*
Westward the Women *'51*
Van Alexander
Strait-Jacket *'64*
Platinum High School *'60*
Girls' Town *'59*
Jaguar *'56*
When Gangland Strikes *'56*
The Atomic Kid *'54*
Eric Allaman
One Kill *'00*
Luminarias *'99*
True Heart *'97*
Midnight Blue *'96*
Down Twisted *'89*
Angel 3: The Final Chapter *'88*
Cameron Allan
The Nutt House *'95*
Jericho Fever *'93*
JFK: Reckless Youth *'93*
The Good Wife *'86*
Midnite Spares *'85*
Billy Allen
The Acid Eaters *'67*
She-Freak *'67*
Peter Allen
Ripper: Letter from Hell *'01*
Crackerjack 3 *'00*
Escape from Mars *'99*
Escape Velocity *'99*
The Silencer *'99*
Chained Heat 3: Hell Mountain *'98*
Dead Fire *'98*
Crackerjack 2 *'97*
Act of War *'96*
Dangerous Prey *'95*
Crackerjack *'94*
Cyborg 2 *'93*
Peter Allen (1944-92)
Kiss Me Goodbye *'82*
Arthur *'81*
John Altman
Fidel *'02*
The Lost Empire *'01*
Boss of Bosses *'99*
RKO 281 *'99*
Vendetta *'99*
Legionnaire *'98*
Little Voice *'98*
Tracked *'98*
The Garden of Redemption *'97*
The Matchmaker *'97*
Pronto *'97*
A Royal Scandal *'96*
Bhaji on the Beach *'94*
Funny Bones *'94*
Bad Behavior *'92*
Hear My Song *'91*
Minette Alton
Devlin *'92*
Children of Divorce *'80*
Joseph (Joey) Altruda
Slackers *'02*
Slaves of Hollywood *'99*
Shake, Rattle & Rock! *'94*
William Alwyn (1905-85)
The Swiss Family Robinson *'60*
Carve Her Name with Pride *'58*
Madeleine *'50*
Captain Boycott *'47*
Odd Man Out *'47*
Immortal Battalion *'44*
On Approval *'44*
Alejandro Amenabar (1972-)
The Others *'01*
Butterfly *'98*
Open Your Eyes *'97*
Thesis *'96*
Daniele Amfitheatrof
Heller in Pink Tights *'60*
The Last Hunt *'56*
You Gotta Stay Happy *'48*
Singapore *'47*
O.S.S. *'46*
The Virginian *'46*
David Amram
The Arrangement *'69*
The Manchurian Candidate *'62*
Splendor in the Grass *'61*
Laurie Anderson
Monster in a Box *'92*
Swimming to Cambodia *'87*
Something Wild *'86*
Michael Andrews
Orange County *'02*
Donnie Darko *'01*
Out Cold *'01*
Gerard Anfosso
Blue Country *'77*
Cousin, Cousine *'76*
George Antheil
The Pride and the Passion *'57*
Daughter of Horror *'55*
Actors and Sin *'52*
Paul Antonelli
China O'Brien *'88*
Out of the Dark *'88*
Princess Academy *'87*
Women's Club *'87*
Avenging Angel *'85*
Louis Applebaum (1918-2000)
The Mask *'61*
Lost Boundaries *'49*
The Story of G.I. Joe *'45*
Philip Appleby
Nothing Personal *'95*
Maria's Child *'93*
Tito Arevalo
Mad Doctor of Blood Island *'69*
The Ravagers *'65*
The Walls of Hell *'64*
Raiders of Leyte Gulf *'63*
Dario Argento (1940-)
Dawn of the Dead *'78*
Suspiria *'77*
Eddie Arkin
Pretty Smart *'87*
Hardbodies 2 *'86*
Modern Girls *'86*
Harold Arlen
Last Summer In the Hamptons *'96*
Gay Purr-ee *'62*
A Star Is Born *'54*
Cabin in the Sky *'43*
At the Circus *'39*
Strike Me Pink *'36*
Martin Armiger
The Wedding Party *'97*
The Crossing *'92*
Sweetie *'89*
Young Einstein *'89*
Two Friends *'86*
Craig Armstrong
Kiss of the Dragon *'01*
Moulin Rouge *'01*
Best Laid Plans *'99*
The Bone Collector *'99*
Plunkett & Macleane *'98*
Orphans *'97*
David Arnold (1962-)
Changing Lanes *'02*
Enough *'02*
Baby Boy *'01*
The Musketeer *'01*
Zoolander *'01*
Shaft *'00*
The World Is Not Enough *'99*
Godzilla *'98*
A Life Less Ordinary *'97*
Tomorrow Never Dies *'97*
Independence Day *'96*
The Last of the Dogmen *'95*
Stargate *'94*
The Young Americans *'93*
Malcolm Arnold (1921-)
David Copperfield *'70*
Battle of Britain *'69*
Africa Texas Style *'67*

The Great St. Trinian's Train Robbery '66
The Heroes of Telemark '65
The Chalk Garden '64
The Thin Red Line '64
On the Fiddle '61
The Pure Hell of St. Trinian's '61
Whistle down the Wind '61
No Love for Johnnie '60
Tunes of Glory '60
Solomon and Sheba '59
Suddenly, Last Summer '59
The Inn of the Sixth Happiness '58
The Key '58
The Bridge on the River Kwai '57
Island in the Sun '57
Blue Murder at St. Trinian's '56
Trapeze '56
I Am a Camera '55
The Sea Shall Not Have Them '55
Devil on Horseback '54
The Sleeping Tiger '54
The Belles of St. Trinian's '53
Captain's Paradise '53
Curtain Up '53
Four Sided Triangle '53
Hobson's Choice '53
A Stolen Face '52
Wings of Danger '52
No Highway in the Sky '51
Eye Witness '49

Bruce Arntson
Ernest Rides Again '93
Ernest Scared Stupid '91
Ernest Goes to Jail '90

Leon Aronson
Bounty Hunters 2: Hardball '97
Jack Higgins' Midnight Man '96
Jack Higgins' On Dangerous Ground '95
Eddie and the Cruisers 2: Eddie Lives! '89

Jorge Arriagada
Shattered Image '98
Genealogies of a Crime '97
Three Lives and Only One Death '96
It's All True '93
The Disenchanted '90

Eduard Artemyev
The Odyssey '97
Burnt by the Sun '94
Double Jeopardy '92
The Inner Circle '91
Close to Eden '90
Homer and Eddie '89
Siberiade '79
Stalker '79
A Slave of Love '78
The Mirror '75
Solaris '72

Bent Aserud
Mendel '98
The Other Side of Sunday '96

Howard Ashman
Aladdin '92
Beauty and the Beast '91
The Little Mermaid '89
Little Shop of Horrors '86

Edwin Astley (1922-98)
Digby, the Biggest Dog in the World '73
A Matter of WHO '62
The Phantom of the Opera '62
The Mouse That Roared '59
The Womaneater '59
The Case of the Mukkinese Battle Horn '56
To Paris with Love '55
Devil Girl from Mars '54

Michael Atkinson
Heaven's Burning '97
Backlash '86

Georges Auric
Therese & Isabelle '67
The Innocents '61
The Testament of Orpheus '59
The Crucible '57
Heaven Knows, Mr. Allison '57
The Hunchback of Notre Dame '57
The Night Heaven Fell '57
The Story of Esther Costello '57
Abdulla the Great '56
Gervaise '56
Lola Montes '55
Wages of Fear '55
Rififi '54
Orpheus '49
Beauty and the Beast '46
Dead of Night '45
Eternal Return '43
A Nous la Liberte '31
The Blood of a Poet '30

William Axt
Libeled Lady '36
Tarzan and His Mate '34
Dinner at Eight '33
Don Juan '26
The Big Parade '25

Charles Aznavour (1924-)
Mauvais Sang '86
Sweet Ecstasy '62
Daniella by Night '61
Dishonorable Discharge '57

Luis Bacalov
Woman on Top '00
The Love Letter '99
Polish Wedding '97
The Truce '96
The Postman '94
Entre-Nous '83
City of Women '81
A Bullet for the General '68
Catch as Catch Can '68
Django '68
Empty Canvas '64
The Gospel According to St. Matthew '64

Burt Bacharach
Isn't She Great '00
Arthur 2: On the Rocks '88
Night Shift '82
Arthur '81
Together? '79
Butch Cassidy and the Sundance Kid '69
Casino Royale '67
After the Fox '66
Alfie '66
What's New Pussycat? '65
The Blob '58
The Sad Sack '57

Pierre Bachelet
Emmanuelle 5 '87
The Perils of Gwendoline '84
Black and White in Color '76
Emmanuelle, the Joys of a Woman '76
The Story of O '75
Emmanuelle '74

Angelo Badalamenti (1937-)
Mulholland Drive '01
The Beach '00
Arlington Road '99
Forever Mine '99
Holy Smoke '99
The Straight Story '99
The Blood Oranges '97
The Last Don '97
Invasion of Privacy '96
Lost Highway '96
The City of Lost Children '95
Witch Hunt '94
Hotel Room '93
Naked in New York '93
Twin Peaks: Fire Walk with Me '92
The Comfort of Strangers '91
Wait until Spring, Bandini '90
Wild at Heart '90
Cousins '89
National Lampoon's Christmas Vacation '89
Parents '89
A Nightmare on Elm Street 3: Dream Warriors '87
Tough Guys Don't Dance '87
Weeds '87
Blue Velvet '86
Across the Great Divide '76
Law and Disorder '74
Gordon's War '73

Wally Badarou
Boesman & Lena '00
The Lunatic '92
Kiss of the Spider Woman '85

David Baerwald
Hurlyburly '98
Loved '97

Tom Bahler
Gordy '95
The Object of Beauty '91
Cold Feet '89
Fast Forward '84
Mary, Mary, Bloody Mary '76

Tadeusz Baird
Lotna '64
Passenger '61

Mischa Bakaleinikoff
20 Million Miles to Earth '57
Blondie Hits the Jackpot '49

Buddy (Norman Dale) Baker
The Puppetoon Movie '87
The Devil & Max Devlin '81
The Fox and the Hound '81
The Apple Dumpling Gang Rides Again '79
Hot Lead & Cold Feet '78
No Deposit, No Return '76
The Shaggy D.A. '76
The Treasure of Matecumbe '76
The Apple Dumpling Gang '75
The Bears & I '74
Superdad '73
Napoleon and Samantha '72
Million Dollar Duck '71
The Gnome-Mobile '67
Monkey's Uncle '65
A Tiger Walks '64
The Misadventures of Merlin Jones '63
Summer Magic '63

Michael Conway Baker
The Portrait '93
Showdown at Williams Creek '91
Loyalties '86
One Magic Christmas '85
The Deserters '83
The Grey Fox '83
Silence of the North '81

Richard Band
Curse of the Puppet Master: The Human Experiment '98
Hideous '97
Head of the Family '96
Zarkorr! The Invader '96
Castle Freak '95
Magic Island '95
Dragonworld '94
Prehysteria 2 '94
Puppet Master 5: The Final Chapter '94
Shrunken Heads '94
Dollman vs Demonic Toys '93
Puppet Master 4 '93
Remote '93
Trancers 3: Deth Lives '92
The Pit & the Pendulum '91
The Resurrected '91
The Arrival '90
Crash and Burn '90
Doctor Mordrid: Master of the Unknown '90
Puppet Master 2 '90
Puppet Master 3: Toulon's Revenge '90
Arena '89
Bride of Re-Animator '89
Puppet Master '89
Prison '88
The Caller '87
Dolls '87
The Eliminators '86
From Beyond '86
Terrorvision '86
Troll '86
Ghoulies '84
Re-Animator '84
Zone Troopers '84
Dungeonmaster '83
The House on Sorority Row '83
Metalstorm: The Destruction of Jared Syn '83
Mutant '83
Parasite '82
Time Walker '82
The Alchemist '81
Day Time Ended '80
Dr. Heckyl and Mr. Hype '80
Laserblast '78

Brian Banks
Graveyard Shift '90
Internal Affairs '90
Young Guns '88
Nice Girls Don't Explode '87

Don Banks
I Killed Rasputin '67
The Mummy's Shroud '67
Torture Garden '67
Rasputin the Mad Monk '66
The Reptile '66
Die, Monster, Die! '65
The Evil of Frankenstein '64
Hysteria '64
Nightmare '63

Tony Banks
Quicksilver '86
The Wicked Lady '83
The Shout '78

Roque Banos
Sexy Beast '00
Goya in Bordeaux '99

Claus Bantzer
Drachenfutter '87
Ruby's Dream '82

San Bao
The Road Home '01
Not One Less '99

Jack Baran
Great Balls of Fire '89
Barfly '87

Lesley Barber
Luminous Motion '00
Mansfield Park '99
You Can Count On Me '99
Los Locos Posse '97
A Price above Rubies '97
When Night Is Falling '95

Gato Barbieri
Strangers Kiss '83
Firepower '79
Last Tango in Paris '73
Notes for an African Orestes '70

John Barnes (1920-2000)
Don't Be a Menace to South Central While Drinking Your Juice in the Hood '95
Better Off Dead '94
CB4: The Movie '93
Bebe's Kids '92
Daughters of the Dust '91

Charles P. Barnett
Headless Body in Topless Bar '96
Busted Up '86
Hell Squad '85

Nathan Barr
Red Dirt '99
Too Smooth '98

John Barry (1933-)
Enigma '01
Mercury Rising '98
Playing by Heart '98
Swept from the Sea '97
Cry, the Beloved Country '95
The Scarlet Letter '95
The Specialist '94
Indecent Proposal '93
My Life '93
Chaplin '92
Deception '92
The Public Eye '92
Dances with Wolves '90
Masquerade '88
Hearts of Fire '87
The Living Daylights '87
Howard the Duck '86
Peggy Sue Got Married '86
The Jagged Edge '85
A Killing Affair '85
Out of Africa '85
A View to a Kill '85
The Cotton Club '84
Mike's Murder '84
Until September '84
The Golden Seal '83
High Road to China '83
Octopussy '83
Svengali '83
Frances '82
Hammett '82
Murder by Phone '82
Body Heat '81
Legend of the Lone Ranger '81
Inside Moves '80
Night Games '80
Raise the Titanic '80
Somewhere in Time '80
Touched by Love '80
The Black Hole '79
Game of Death '79
Hanover Street '79
Moonraker '79
Willa '79
The Betsy '78
Star Crash '78
The Deep '77
First Love '77
The Gathering '77
The White Buffalo '77
Eleanor & Franklin '76
King Kong '76
Robin and Marian '76
War Between the Tates '76
The Day of the Locust '75
Love Among the Ruins '75
Shampoo '75
The Man with the Golden Gun '74
The Tamarind Seed '74
A Doll's House '73
Diamonds Are Forever '71
The Last Valley '71
Mary, Queen of Scots '71
Murphy's War '71
They Might Be Giants '71
Walkabout '71
Monte Walsh '70
Midnight Cowboy '69
On Her Majesty's Secret Service '69
Boom! '68
The Lion in Winter '68
Petulia '68
You Only Live Twice '67
Born Free '66
The Chase '66
The Quiller Memorandum '66
The Wrong Box '66
The Ipcress File '65
King Rat '65
The Knack '65
Thunderball '65
Goldfinger '64
Seance on a Wet Afternoon '64
Zulu '64
From Russia with Love '63
Dr. No '62
The L-Shaped Room '62
Beat Girl '60
Never Let Go '60

Lionel Bart (1930-99)
Black Beauty '71
Oliver! '68

Steve Bartek (1952-)
Get Over It! '01
Novocaine '01
The Crew '00
Snow Day '00
Meet the Deedles '98
Romy and Michele's High School Reunion '97
Cabin Boy '94
Coldblooded '94
Guilty as Charged '92
Past Midnight '92

Dee Barton (1937-2001)
Death Screams '83
Thunderbolt & Lightfoot '74
High Plains Drifter '73
Play Misty for Me '71

Richard Baskin
Uforia '81
Honeysuckle Rose '80
Welcome to L.A. '77
Buffalo Bill & the Indians '76
Nashville '75

Kevin Bassinson
100 Girls '00
Eight Days a Week '97
Beanstalk '94
Cyborg '89

George Bassman
Wombling Free '77
Ride the High Country '62
The Joe Louis Story '53
The Postman Always Rings Twice '46
Abbott and Costello in Hollywood '45
The Clock '45
The Canterville Ghost '44
Best Foot Forward '43
Cabin in the Sky '43
Whistling in Brooklyn '43
For Me and My Gal '42
Panama Hattie '42
Babes on Broadway '41
Big Store '41
Lady Be Good '41
Go West '40
Too Many Girls '40
Babes in Arms '39
Everybody Sing '38
A Damsel in Distress '37
A Day at the Races '37

Tyler Bates
Kingdom Come '01
What's the Worst That Could Happen? '01
Get Carter '00
Rated X '00
Shriek If You Know What I Did Last Friday the 13th '00

Les Baxter (1922-96)
The Beast Within '82
Born Again '78
Switchblade Sisters '75
Devil & Leroy Basset '73
Frogs '72
Torture Chamber of Baron Blood '72
The Big Doll House '71
Cry of the Banshee '70
The Dunwich Horror '70
Hell's Belles '69
Terror in the Jungle '68
Wild in the Streets '68
Dr. Goldfoot and the Bikini Machine '66
Beach Blanket Bingo '65
How to Stuff a Wild Bikini '65
Bikini Beach '64
Black Sabbath '64
The Comedy of Terrors '64
Muscle Beach Party '64
Pajama Party '64
Battle Beyond the Sun '63
Beach Party '63
The Raven '63
X: The Man with X-Ray Eyes '63
Panic in the Year Zero! '62
Samson and the 7 Miracles of the World '62
Tales of Terror '62
Goliath and the Dragon '61
Master of the World '61
The Pit and the Pendulum '61
Black Sunday '60
The Fall of the House of Usher '60
Goliath and the Barbarians '60
The Bride & the Beast '58
Girl in Black Stockings '57
The Invisible Boy '57
The Key Man '57

Athena '54
Good News '47

Larry Blank (1952-)
That Championship Season '99
Taxi Dancers '93

Arthur Bliss
Abandon Ship '57
Things to Come '36

George Blondheim
Summer of the Monkeys '98
The Halfback of Notre Dame '96
Man with a Gun '95
Red Scorpion 2 '94
Whale Music '94
Gate 2 '92
Bye Bye Blues '89

Michael Bloomfield
Andy Warhol's Bad '77
Medium Cool '69

Frankie Blue
Dracula: The Dark Prince '01
Return to Cabin by the Lake '01
Cabin by the Lake '00
Out There '95

Chris Boardman
The Dress Code '99
Payback '98
Tales from the Crypt Presents Bordello of Blood '96
Prime Target '91
The Color Purple '85

Michael Boddicker
Freejack '92
F/X 2: The Deadly Art of Illusion '91
The Adventures of Milo & Otis '89
White Water Summer '87
The Adventures of Buckaroo Banzai Across the Eighth Dimension '84
Get Crazy '83

Todd Boekelheide
Digger '94
Nina Takes a Lover '94
Exposure '91
Hearts of Darkness: A Filmmaker's Apocalypse '91
The Blood of Heroes '89
Dim Sum: A Little Bit of Heart '85

Ed Bogas
A Christmas Without Snow '80
Race for Your Life, Charlie Brown '77
Heavy Traffic '73
Fritz the Cat '72

Geir Bohren
Mendel '98
The Other Side of Sunday '96

William Bolcom (1938-)
Illuminata '98
Hester Street '75

Bill Boll
The Low Life '95
Some Folks Call It a Sling Blade '94

Claude Bolling
The Bay Boy '85
The Awakening '80
Willie & Phil '80
California Suite '78
Silver Bears '78
Le Magnifique '76
The Passenger '75
Catch Me a Spy '71
Borsalino '70
The Day and the Hour '63
The Hands of Orlac '60

Jay Bolton
Mom's Outta Sight '01
The Kid with the X-Ray Eyes '99
Stormy Nights '97

Bernardo Bonazzi
Mouth to Mouth '95
All Tied Up '92
Don Juan, My Love '90
Women on the Verge of a Nervous Breakdown '88
Matador '86

Marc Bonilla
Caught Up '98
Hollywood Confidential '97
National Lampoon's Dad's Week Off '97

Bono (1960-)
The Million Dollar Hotel '99
In the Name of the Father '93

Simon Boswell
Born Romantic '00
Circus '00
Jason and the Argonauts '00
William Shakespeare's A Midsummer Night's Dream '99
Deacon Brodie '98
The War Zone '98
Cousin Bette '97
Dad Savage '97
Dance with the Devil '97
Photographing Fairies '97
The Android Affair '95
Hackers '95
Jack and Sarah '95
Lord of Illusions '95
Second Best '94
Shallow Grave '94
Dust Devil '93
Love Matters '93
The Turn of the Screw '92
Hardware '90
Santa Sangre '90
Dangerous Obsession '88
Demons 2 '87
Creepers '85

Perry Botkin
Windmills of the Gods '88
Weekend Warriors '86
Silent Night, Deadly Night '84
Tarzan, the Ape Man '81
Goin' South '78
Lady Ice '73
They Only Kill Their Masters '72
Bless the Beasts and Children '71
R.P.M.* (* Revolutions Per Minute) '70

Roger Bourland
New Jack City '91
Night Life '90
The Trouble with Dick '88
The Wolf at the Door '87

Richard Bowers
Facing the Enemy '00
The Perfect Nanny '00
The Nurse '97
The Fiance '96

David Bowie (1947-)
The Buddha of Suburbia '92
Labyrinth '86
Party! Party! '83
Christiane F. '82

Euel Box
Benji the Hunted '87
The Double McGuffin '79
For the Love of Benji '77
Hawmps! '76
Benji '74

Goran Bregovic
The Lost Son '98
Train of Life '98
The Serpent's Kiss '97
A Chef in Love '96
Underground '95
Queen Margot '94

Danny Brenner
Rhythm Thief '94
Spare Me '92

Peter Brewis
The Tall Guy '89
Morons from Outer Space '85

Leslie Bricusse
Tom and Jerry: The Movie '93
Babes in Toyland '86
Willy Wonka & the Chocolate Factory '71
Scrooge '70
Goodbye, Mr. Chips '69
Doctor Dolittle '67

David Bridie
In a Savage Land '99
The Myth of Fingerprints '97
River Street '95
That Eye, the Sky '94

Jon Brion
Magnolia '99
Hard Eight '96

Timothy Brock
Diary of a Lost Girl '29
Faust '26
The Show Off '26

David Broeckman
Frankenstein '31
All Quiet on the Western Front '30

Richard Bronskill
National Lampoon's Golf Punks '99
Body Strokes '95
Friend of the Family '95
The Perfect Bride '91

Michael Brook
Crime and Punishment in Suburbia '00
Affliction '97
Albino Alligator '96

Joseph Brooks (1938-)
If Ever I See You Again '78
You Light Up My Life '77
The Lords of Flatbush '74
Invitation to the Wedding '73

Bruce Broughton (1945-)
Krippendorf's Tribe '98
Lost in Space '98
One Tough Cop '98
A Simple Wish '97
True Women '97
House Arrest '96
Infinity '96
The Shadow Conspiracy '96
Carried Away '95
JAG '95
Baby's Day Out '94
Holy Matrimony '94
Miracle on 34th Street '94
For Love or Money '93
Homeward Bound: The Incredible Journey '93
So I Married an Axe Murderer '93
Tombstone '93
Honey, I Blew Up the Kid '92
Stay Tuned '92
All I Want for Christmas '91
Betsy's Wedding '90
Narrow Margin '90
The Old Man and the Sea '90
The Rescuers Down Under '90
Jacknife '89
Sorry, Wrong Number '89
Cross My Heart '88
Last Rites '88
The Presidio '88
The Rescue '88
Big Shots '87
Harry and the Hendersons '87
The Monster Squad '87
Square Dance '87
The Boy Who Could Fly '86
George Washington: The Forging of a Nation '86
Sweet Liberty '86
Silverado '85
Young Sherlock Holmes '85
The Cowboy & the Ballerina '84
The First Olympics: Athens 1896 '84
Ice Pirates '84
M.A.D.D.: Mothers Against Drunk Driving '83
The Prodigal '83
The Blue and the Gray '82
Desperate Lives '82
One Shoe Makes It Murder '82
Killjoy '81
Return of Frank Cannon '80

Leo Brower
A Walk in the Clouds '95
Like Water for Chocolate '93
Up to a Certain Point '83
Death of a Bureaucrat '66

James Brown (1933-)
Black Caesar '73
Slaughter's Big Ripoff '73

Larry Brown
The Wall '99
Elvis Meets Nixon '98
Gang in Blue '96
Rio Diablo '93

Nacio Herb Brown
Singin' in the Rain '52
Broadway Melody of 1938 '37
Broadway Melody of 1936 '35
Broadway Melody '29

Robert F. Brunner
Amy '81
The North Avenue Irregulars '79
Gus '76
The Castaway Cowboy '74
Now You See Him, Now You Don't '72
Snowball Express '72
The Barefoot Executive '71
The Wild Country '71
The Boatniks '70
The Computer Wore Tennis Shoes '69
Smith! '69
Never a Dull Moment '68
Blackbeard's Ghost '67
Lt. Robin Crusoe, U.S.N. '66
Monkeys, Go Home! '66
That Darn Cat '65

George Bruns
Herbie Rides Again '74
Robin Hood '73
The Aristocats '70
Daring Game '68
The Horse in the Gray Flannel Suit '68
Island of the Lost '68
The Love Bug '68
The Jungle Book '67
The Adventures of Bullwhip Griffin '66
The Fighting Prince of Donegal '66
Follow Me, Boys! '66
Man from Button Willow '65
Son of Flubber '63
The Sword in the Stone '63
The Absent-Minded Professor '61
Babes in Toyland '61
101 Dalmatians '61
Sleeping Beauty '59
Davy Crockett and the River Pirates '56
Westward Ho, the Wagons! '56
Davy Crockett, King of the Wild Frontier '55

Joanne Bruzdowicz
Jacquot '91
Vagabond '85

BT (Brian Transeau) (1971-)
Driven '01
The Fast and the Furious '01

Chico Buarque
Bye Bye Brazil '79
Dona Flor and Her Two Husbands '78

Paul Buckmaster
Mean Streak '99
The Maker '98
Murder in Mind '97
The Last Word '95
12 Monkeys '95
Diving In '90
The Spy Who Loved Me '77

Roy Budd
Sinbad and the Eye of the Tiger '77
Get Carter '71

Geoffrey Burgon
Longitude '00
Cider with Rosie '99
When Trumpets Fade '98
A Foreign Field '93
Robin Hood '91
Turtle Diary '86
Bleak House '85
Brideshead Revisited '81
The Dogs of War '81
Monty Python's Life of Brian '79

Chris Burke
Search and Destroy '88
Splatter University '84

Johnny Burke
Welcome Stranger '47
The Road to Utopia '46
The Bells of St. Mary's '45

T Bone Burnett
Divine Secrets of the Ya-Ya Sisterhood '02
O Brother Where Art Thou? '00

Ralph Burns (1922-2001)
The Josephine Baker Story '90
All Dogs Go to Heaven '89
Bert Rigby, You're a Fool '89
Sweet Bird of Youth '89
After the Promise '87
In the Mood '87
Penalty Phase '86
A Chorus Line '85
Moving Violations '85
Perfect '85
Ernie Kovacs: Between the Laughter '84
The Muppets Take Manhattan '84
Side Show '84
National Lampoon's Vacation '83
Star 80 '83
Annie '82
Kiss Me Goodbye '82
My Favorite Year '82
Pennies from Heaven '81
First Family '80
Make Me an Offer '80
Urban Cowboy '80
All That Jazz '79
Movie, Movie '78
New York, New York '77
Lenny '74
Cabaret '72

George Burt
Fool for Love '86
Secret Honor '85

Carter Burwell (1955-)
The Rookie '02
A Knight's Tale '01
The Man Who Wasn't There '01
Before Night Falls '00
Book of Shadows: Blair Witch 2 '00
Hamlet '00
O Brother Where Art Thou? '00
What Planet Are You From? '00
Being John Malkovich '99
The Corruptor '99
The General's Daughter '99
Mystery, Alaska '99
Three Kings '99
Gods and Monsters '98
The Hi-Lo Country '98
Velvet Goldmine '98
The Big Lebowski '97
Conspiracy Theory '97
The Jackal '97
The Locusts '97
The Spanish Prisoner '97
The Chamber '96
Fargo '96
Fear '96
Picture Perfect '96
The Celluloid Closet '95
Rob Roy '95
Airheads '94
Bad Company '94
It Could Happen to You '94
And the Band Played On '93
A Dangerous Woman '93
The Hudsucker Proxy '93
Kalifornia '93
This Boy's Life '93
Wayne's World 2 '93
Buffy the Vampire Slayer '92
Storyville '92
Waterland '92
Barton Fink '91
Doc Hollywood '91
Miller's Crossing '90
Checking Out '89
The Beat '88
It Takes Two '88
Pass the Ammo '88
Raising Arizona '87
Psycho 3 '86
Blood Simple '85

Artie Butler (1942-)
Grease 2 '82
O'Hara's Wife '82
American Dream '81
She's in the Army Now '81
Sizzle '81
Angel on My Shoulder '80
Sextette '78
The Rescuers '77
Rafferty & the Gold Dust Twins '75
For Pete's Sake '74
Harrad Experiment '73
What's Up, Doc? '72
The Love Machine '71

David Buttolph
The Horse Soldiers '59
Lone Ranger '56
Long John Silver '54
The Beast from 20,000 Fathoms '53
House of Wax '53
Rope '48
Boomerang '47
My Darling Clementine '46
13 Rue Madeleine '46
House on 92nd Street '45
Crash Dive '43
Guadalcanal Diary '43
Immortal Sergeant '43
My Favorite Blonde '42
Wake Island '42

R. Dale Butts (1910-90)
Phantom Stallion '54
Shadows of Tombstone '53
Too Late for Tears '49

David Byrne (1952-)
Married to the Mob '88
The Last Emperor '87
Something Wild '86
True Stories '86

John Cacavas
Airport '75 '75
The Satanic Rites of Dracula '73

Emil Cadkin
Mission to Death '66
The Killer Shrews '59

Sammy Cahn (-1993)
Court Jester '56
Rich, Young and Pretty '51
The West Point Story '50
Anchors Aweigh '45

John Cale
American Psycho '99
Somewhere in the City '97
Basquiat '96
I Shot Andy Warhol '96
Primary Motive '92
Something Wild '86
Who Am I This Time? '82
Caged Heat '74
Heat '72

Darrell Calker
The Amazing Transparent Man '60
Terror in the Haunted House '58
The Flying Saucer '50
Underworld Scandal '47

John Cameron
The Mirror Crack'd '80
A Touch of Class '73
The Ruling Class '72

Bruce Campbell
Plan 9 from Outer Space '56
Mister Drake's Duck '50

James Campbell
Elvira, Mistress of the Dark '88
Please Not Now! '61

Al Capps

Wrestling Ernest Hemingway '93
The Doctor '91
The Waterdance '91
The End of Innocence '90
Queen of Hearts '89
Bull Durham '88
The Hidden '87
Mistress '87
Children of a Lesser God '86
Hollywood Vice Sqaud '86
Frankenweenie '84

Ry Cooder (1947-)
Primary Colors '98
The End of Violence '97
Last Man Standing '96
Geronimo: An American Legend '93
Trespass '92
Johnny Handsome '89
Tales from the Crypt '89
Blue City '86
Crossroads '86
Alamo Bay '85
Brewster's Millions '85
Streets of Fire '84
Paris, Texas '83
The Border '82
Southern Comfort '81
The Long Riders '80

Stewart Copeland (1952-)
Deuces Wild '02
On the Line '01
Boys and Girls '00
Skipped Parts '00
Made Men '99
She's All That '99
Simpatico '99
Legalese '98
Pecker '98
Very Bad Things '98
West Beirut '98
Four Days in September '97
Good Burger '97
Little Boy Blue '97
Welcome to Woop Woop '97
Gridlock'd '96
The Leopard Son '96
Boys '95
The Pallbearer '95
Tyson '95
White Dwarf '95
Silent Fall '94
Surviving the Game '94
Airborne '93
Bank Robber '93
Raining Stones '93
Rapa Nui '93
Riff Raff '92
Wide Sargasso Sea '92
Highlander 2: The Quickening '91
Hidden Agenda '90
Men at Work '90
Taking Care of Business '90
The First Power '89
See No Evil, Hear No Evil '89
She's Having a Baby '88
Talk Radio '88
Wall Street '87
Out of Bounds '86
Rumble Fish '83

Aaron Copland (1900-90)
The Heiress '49
The Red Pony '49
The North Star '43
Our Town '40
Of Mice and Men '39

Carmine Coppola (1911-91)
The Godfather, Part 3 '90
New York Stories '89
Tucker: The Man and His Dream '88
Gardens of Stone '87
The Outsiders '83
Apocalypse Now '79
The Black Stallion '79
The Godfather, Part 2 '74
The People '71
Tonight for Sure '61
Napoleon '27

Normand Corbeil
The Art of War '00
Double Jeopardy '99
Stalker '98
The Assignment '97
The Boys '97
The Kid '97
Psychopath '97
Frankenstein and Me '96
Kids of the Round Table '96
Screamers '96

Frank Cordell
God Told Me To '76
Ring of Bright Water '69
Khartoum '66

John Corigliano
The Red Violin '98
Altered States '80

Vladimir Cosma
The Closet '00
The Dinner Game '98
The Favor, the Watch, & the Very Big Fish '92
My Father's Glory '91
My Mother's Castle '91
The Nightmare Years '89
Just the Way You Are '84
Mistral's Daughter '84
Les Comperes '83
Diva '82
Le Bal '82
La Boum '81
La Chevre '81
Pardon Mon Affaire, Too! '77
Dracula & Son '76
Pardon Mon Affaire '76
The Daydreamer '75
Return of the Tall Blond Man with One Black Shoe '74
Salut l'Artiste '74
The Tall Blond Man with One Black Shoe '72

Don Costa
Madigan '68
Rough Night in Jericho '67

Elvis Costello (1954-)
Oliver Twist '00
The Courier '88
Party! Party! '83

Bruno Coulais
The Crimson Rivers '01
Balzac: A Life of Passion '99
The Count of Monte Cristo '99
Himalaya '99
Microcosmos '96
The Son of the Shark '93

Michael Covertino
Snow White: The Fairest of Them All '02
Pie in the Sky '95

Noel Coward (1899-1973)
The Grass Is Greener '61
This Happy Breed '47
In Which We Serve '43

Rick Cox
Bram Stoker's The Mummy '97
Bad Love '95
Corrina, Corrina '94
Inside Monkey Zetterland '93

Carlo Crivelli
Marie Baie des Anges '97
Elective Affinities '96
Devil in the Flesh '87

Xavier Cugat (1900-90)
Bathing Beauty '44
The White Zombie '32

Stephen Cullo
Proximity '00
Belly '98

Douglas J. Cuomo
Homicide: The Movie '00
Hand Gun '93

Michael Curb
Family Tree '00
The Wild Angels '66

Hoyt Curtin (1922-2000)
KISS Meets the Phantom of the Park '78
Mesa of Lost Women '52

Miriam Cutler
Bikini Med School '98
Bikini House Calls '96
Illegal Affairs '96
Witchcraft 7: Judgement Hour '95
Night Fire '94
Witchcraft 2: The Temptress '90

Richard Cuvillier
Humanity '99
The Life of Jesus '96

Burkhard Dallwitz
Paperback Hero '99
The Truman Show '98
Zone 39 '96

Ikuma Dan (1924-2001)
Samurai 3: Duel at Ganryu Island '56
Samurai 1: Musashi Miyamoto '55
Samurai 2: Duel at Ichijoji Temple '55

John D'Andrea
Boiling Point '93
Beyond the Law '92
Child's Play 3 '91
Swimsuit '89
Body Slam '87
Savage Streets '83
Grambling's White Tiger '81

Oswald D'Andrea
Capitaine Conan '96
Every Other Weekend '91

John Dankworth
10 Rillington Place '71
Accident '67
Fathom '67
Modesty Blaise '66
Morgan: A Suitable Case for Treatment '66
Darling '65
The Servant '63
Saturday Night and Sunday Morning '60

Jeff Danna
O '01
Baby '00
Boondock Saints '99
New Blood '99
Uncorked '98
The Big Slice '90

Mychael Danna
Hearts in Atlantis '01
Monsoon Wedding '01
Bounce '00
Felicia's Journey '99
Girl, Interrupted '99
Ride with the Devil '99
The Confession '98
8mm '98
Behind the Lines '97
The Ice Storm '97
Kama Sutra: A Tale of Love '96
Lilies '96
The Sweet Hereafter '96
Exotica '94
Still Life '92
The Adjuster '91
The Big Slice '90
Speaking Parts '89
Termini Station '89
Family Viewing '87

Carl Dante
Cypress Edge '99
The Creeps '97
Cannibal Women in the Avocado Jungle of Death '89
Slave Girls from Beyond Infinity '87

Mason Daring
Say It Isn't So '01
Where the Heart Is '00
Limbo '99
Music of the Heart '99
A Walk on the Moon '99
The Opposite of Sex '98
Cold Around the Heart '97
Evidence of Blood '97
Hombres Armados '97
The Ripper '97
Hidden in America '96
Prefontaine '96
Letter to My Killer '95
Lone Star '95
Getting Out '94
The Old Curiosity Shop '94
The Secret of Roan Inish '94
Fathers and Sons '92
Passion Fish '92
City of Hope '91
Wild Hearts Can't Be Broken '91
The Laserman '90
Little Vegas '90
Off and Running '90
Day One '89
Eight Men Out '88
Matewan '87
Osa '85
The Brother from Another Planet '84
Lianna '83
Return of the Secaucus 7 '80

Peter Dasent
Heavenly Creatures '94
Dead Alive '93
Meet the Feebles '89

Shaun Davey
The Tailor of Panama '00
Waking Ned Devine '98
Kings in Grass Castles '97
Twelfth Night '96

Martin Davich
Jackie, Ethel, Joan: The Kennedy Women '01
La Cucaracha '99

Hal David
What's New Pussycat? '65
The Blob '58
The Sad Sack '57

Victor Davies
For the Moment '94
The Last Winter '89

Carl Davis (1936-)
The Great Gatsby '01
Topsy Turvy '99
Pride and Prejudice '95
The Return of the Native '94
Widow's Peak '94
The Trial '93
Frankenstein Unbound '90
The Rainbow '89
Scandal '89
Hotel du Lac '86
Murrow '86
King David '85
Silas Marner '85
Champions '84
The Far Pavilions '84
Sakharov '84
Weather in the Streets '84
Praying Mantis '83
The French Lieutenant's Woman '81
Man Friday '75
The Naked Civil Servant '75
Catholics '73
Rentadick '72
I, Monster '71
Naughty Knights '71
The Only Way '70
Napoleon '27
The Eagle '25
The Thief of Baghdad '24

Don Davis
Behind Enemy Lines '01
Jurassic Park 3 '01
Valentine '01
Antitrust '00
House on Haunted Hill '99
In the Company of Spies '99
The Matrix '99
Universal Soldier: The Return '99
Route 9 '98
The Lesser Evil '97
Not in This Town '97
Warriors of Virtue '97
Weapons of Mass Distraction '97
The Beast '96
Bound '96
The Perfect Daughter '96

Miles Davis (1926-91)
Dingo '90
Siesta '87
Street Smart '87
Frantic '58

Guido de Angelis
Body Beat '88
A Blade in the Dark '83
Mountain of the Cannibal God '79
Chino '75
Zorro '74
Torso '73

Maurizio de Angelis
Body Beat '88
A Blade in the Dark '83
Mountain of the Cannibal God '79
Chino '75
Zorro '74
Torso '73

Lex de Azevedo
The Swan Princess 2: Escape from Castle Mountain '97
The Swan Princess '94
Baker's Hawk '76
Where the Red Fern Grows '74

Luchi De Jesus
Friday Foster '75
Detroit 9000 '73
Slaughter '72

Christopher De Marco
The Toxic Avenger, Part 3: The Last Temptation of Toxie '89
Troma's War '88

Francesco De Masi
Lone Wolf McQuade '83
New York Ripper '82
The Arena '73
An Angel for Satan '66
The Triumph of Hercules '66

Francois de Roubaix
Daughters of Darkness '71
Honor Among Thieves '68
Le Samourai '67

Manuel De Sica
Cemetery Man '95
Men Men Men '95
The Icicle Thief '89
Bye Bye Baby '88
Twist '76
The Garden of the Finzi-Continis '71

Barry de Vorzon
Exorcist 3: Legion '90
Night of the Creeps '86
Xanadu '80
The Warriors '79

De Wolfe
Jabberwocky '77
The Mighty Peking Man '77
Monty Python and the Holy Grail '75

John Debney (1957-)
Dragonfly '02
The Scorpion King '02
Snow Dogs '02
Cats & Dogs '01
Heartbreakers '01
Jimmy Neutron: Boy Genius '01
The Princess Diaries '01
See Spot Run '01
Spy Kids '01
The Emperor's New Groove '00
Running Mates '00
Dick '99
End of Days '99
Inspector Gadget '99
Komodo '99
Lost and Found '99
Relative Values '99
I'll Be Home for Christmas '98
My Favorite Martian '98
Paulie '98
I Know What You Did Last Summer '97
Carpool '96
Doctor Who '96
Getting Away With Murder '96
The Lazarus Man '96
Liar Liar '96
The Relic '96
Chameleon '95
Cutthroat Island '95
In Pursuit of Honor '95
Sudden Death '95
Houseguest '94
Little Giants '94
White Fang 2: The Myth of the White Wolf '94
Gunmen '93
Hocus Pocus '93
Praying Mantis '93
Jetsons: The Movie '90
The Further Adventures of Tennessee Buck '88
Seven Hours to Judgment '88
The Wild Pair '87

Claude Debussy
Basileus Quartet '82
L'Age D'Or '30

Marc David Decker
Bikini Island '91
The Dark Backward '91
The Invisible Maniac '90

Christopher Dedrick
Torso '01
Walter and Henry '01
Junior's Groove '97
Race to Freedom: The Story of the Underground Railroad '94

Georges Delerue (-1992)
Rich in Love '93
Man Trouble '92
American Friends '91
Black Robe '91
Curly Sue '91
Mister Johnson '91
Joe Versus the Volcano '90
A Show of Force '90
Cadence '89
Steel Magnolias '89
To Kill a Priest '89
Beaches '88
Biloxi Blues '88
Heartbreak Hotel '88
Her Alibi '88
The House on Carroll Street '88
Memories of Me '88
A Summer Story '88
Twins '88
Code Name: Dancer '87
Escape from Sobibor '87
The Lonely Passion of Judith Hearne '87
Maid to Order '87
A Man in Love '87
The Pick-Up Artist '87
Queenie '87
Conseil de Famille '86
Crimes of the Heart '86
Platoon '86
Salvador '86
Sword of Gideon '86
Women of Valor '86
Agnes of God '85
Amos '85
Arch of Triumph '85
The Execution '85
Maxie '85
A Time to Live '85
Aurora '84
Mesmerized '84
Silence of the Heart '84
The Black Stallion Returns '83
Confidentially Yours '83
Exposed '83
La Passante '83
Man, Woman & Child '83
One Deadly Summer '83
Silkwood '83
The Escape Artist '82
La Vie Continue '82
A Little Sex '82
Partners '82
Rich and Famous '81
True Confessions '81
The Woman Next Door '81
The Last Metro '80
Richard's Things '80
An Almost Perfect Affair '79
A Little Romance '79
Dear Detective '78
Get Out Your Handkerchiefs '78
Le Cavaleur '78
Love on the Run '78
Dear Detective '77

Julia '77
The Slap '76
Dan Candy's Law '73
Day for Night '73
The Day of the Dolphin '73
The Day of the Jackal '73
Two English Girls '72
The Conformist '71
The Horsemen '70
Women in Love '70
Anne of the Thousand Days '69
The Brain '69
The Two of Us '68
The King of Hearts '66
A Man for All Seasons '66
Viva Maria! '65
Contempt '64
The Pumpkin Eater '64
The Soft Skin '64
That Man from Rio '64
Muriel '63
Cartouche '62
Jules and Jim '62
Shoot the Piano Player '62
Time Out for Love '61
Love and the Frenchwoman '60
Love Play '60
Hiroshima, Mon Amour '59

Joe Delia
The Tao of Steve '00
Fever '99
No Looking Back '98
The Blackout '97
The Substitute 2: School's Out '97
Drunks '96
The Funeral '96
The Addiction '95
Body Snatchers '93
Bad Lieutenant '92
King of New York '90
Freeway '88
China Girl '87
Ms. 45 '81
Driller Killer '79

Claude Desjardins
Full Disclosure '00
Captains Courageous '95

Alexandre Desplat
The Luzhin Defence '00
Sweet Revenge '98
Love, etc. '96
Innocent Lies '95
A Self-Made Hero '95

Adolph Deutsch
The Apartment '60
Some Like It Hot '59
Stars in My Crown '50
Little Women '49
The Mask of Dimitrios '44
Action in the North Atlantic '43
Across the Pacific '42
All Through the Night '42
The Maltese Falcon '41
Underground '41
The Fighting 69th '40

Frank DeVol (1911-99)
The Longest Yard '74
Ulzana's Raid '72
The Dirty Dozen '67
Guess Who's Coming to Dinner '67
Cat Ballou '65
Under the Yum-Yum Tree '63
What Ever Happened to Baby Jane? '62
Pillow Talk '59
The Ride Back '57
Attack! '56
Kiss Me Deadly '55

Barry DeVorzon
Hard Times '75
Dillinger '73

Von Dexter
Mr. Sardonicus '61
13 Ghosts '60
The Tingler '59
House on Haunted Hill '58

Paul Di Franco
Body Chemistry 4: Full Exposure '95
Masseuse '95

Neil Diamond
The Jazz Singer '80
Jonathan Livingston Seagull '73

Antonio Diaz Conde
Night of the Bloody Apes '68
Doctor of Doom '62
The Robot vs. the Aztec Mummy '59

Andrew Dickson
Someone Else's America '96
Secrets and Lies '95
Naked '93
Meantime '81

Vince DiCola
Transformers: The Movie '86
Rocky 4 '85

Loek Dikker
The Babysitter '95
The Escape '95
Body Parts '91
Pascali's Island '88
Slow Burn '86
The 4th Man '79

Robert Emmett Dolan
King Kong vs. Godzilla '63
The Three Faces of Eve '57
The Great Gatsby '49
My Favorite Brunette '47
The Bells of St. Mary's '45
Murder, He Says '45
The Major and the Minor '42
Birth of the Blues '41

Thomas Dolby
Gothic '87
Fever Pitch '85

Klaus Doldinger
Palmetto '98
Me and Him '89
A Father's Revenge '88
The NeverEnding Story '84
Das Boot '81
The Second Awakening of Christa Klages '78
Swiss Conspiracy '77

Francois Dompierre
Stardom '00
It's My Turn, Laura Cadieux '98
Jesus of Montreal '89

Pino Donaggio
Up at the Villa '00
Rescuers: Stories of Courage—Two Couples '98
Backlash: Oblivion 2 '95
Never Talk to Strangers '95
Oblivion '94
Troublemakers '94
A Fine Romance '92
Indio 2: The Revolt '92
Raising Cain '92
The Devil's Daughter '91
Meridian: Kiss of the Beast '90
Two Evil Eyes '90
Catacombs '89
Night Game '89
Appointment with Death '88
Hotel Colonial '88
Kansas '88
Zelly & Me '88
The Barbarians '87
Dancers '87
Phantom of Death '87
Crawlspace '86
The Berlin Affair '85
Hercules 2 '85
The Assisi Underground '84
Body Double '84
Deja Vu '84
Ordeal by Innocence '84
Hercules '83
Over the Brooklyn Bridge '83
Tex '82
The Black Cat '81
Blow Out '81
The Fan '81
The Howling '81
Beyond Evil '80
Dressed to Kill '80
Home Movies '79
Tourist Trap '79
Gunfire '78
Piranha '78
Haunts '77
Carrie '76
Don't Look Now '73

Marc Donahue
After Midnight '89
Opposing Force '87
Murphy's Law '86
Lies '83

Donovan
84 Charlie MoPic '89
Brother Sun, Sister Moon '73

Steve Dorff (1949-)
Dudley Do-Right '99
Blast from the Past '98
Dancer, Texas—Pop. 81 '98
Breaking Free '95
Pure Country '92
Kiss Shot '89
Pink Cadillac '89
My Best Friend Is a Vampire '88
Back to the Beach '87
The Quick and the Dead '87
Convicted '86
Manhunt for Claude Dallas '86
Rustler's Rhapsody '85
Stick '85
Cannonball Run 2 '84
Honkytonk Man '82
Honky Tonk Freeway '81
Bronco Billy '80
Every Which Way But Loose '78
The Defiant Ones '58

Patrick Doyle (1953-)
Bridget Jones's Diary '01
Gosford Park '01
Blow Dry '00
Love's Labour's Lost '00
East-West '99
Quest for Camelot '98
Great Expectations '97
Donnie Brasco '96
Hamlet '96
Mrs. Winterbourne '96
A Little Princess '95
Sense and Sensibility '95
Exit to Eden '94
Mary Shelley's Frankenstein '94
Carlito's Way '93
Much Ado about Nothing '93
Needful Things '93
Indochine '92
Into the West '92
Dead Again '91
Shipwrecked '90
Henry V '89

Carmen Dragon
Invasion of the Body Snatchers '56
The Strange Woman '46
Mr. Winkle Goes to War '44

Robert Jackson Drasnin
Murder Once Removed '71
The Tattered Web '71
Ride in the Whirlwind '66

George Dreyfus
The Fringe Dwellers '86
Tender Mercies '83

John Du Prez
Mr. Toad's Wild Ride '96
Teenage Mutant Ninja Turtles 3 '93
Mystery Date '91
Bullseye! '90
Teenage Mutant Ninja Turtles: The Movie '90
A Chorus of Disapproval '89
UHF '89
A Fish Called Wanda '88
Personal Services '87
Love with a Perfect Stranger '86
Once Bitten '85
Oxford Blues '84
A Private Function '84
She'll Be Wearing Pink Pajamas '84
Bullshot '83
Monty Python's The Meaning of Life '83

Al Dubin
Stage Door Canteen '43
42nd Street '33

Anne Dudley (1956-)
Monkeybone '01
The 10th Kingdom '00
Pushing Tin '99
American History X '98
The Full Monty '96
Grave Indiscretions '96
Hollow Reed '95
When Saturday Comes '95
Knight Moves '93
The Crying Game '92
The Miracle '91
The Pope Must Diet '91
The Misadventures of Mr. Wilt '90
Silence Like Glass '90
The Mighty Quinn '89
Say Anything '89
Buster '88
Disorderlies '87
Hiding Out '87

Antoine Duhamel
Ridicule '96
Belle Epoque '92
Daddy Nostalgia '90
Twisted Obsession '90
Bed and Board '70
The Wild Child '70
Mississippi Mermaid '69
Stolen Kisses '68
Weekend '67
Pierrot le Fou '65

Tan Dun
Crouching Tiger, Hidden Dragon '00
Fallen '97

David Dundas
How to Get Ahead in Advertising '89
Withnail and I '87

George Duning (1908-2000)
Goliath Awaits '81
The Man with Bogart's Face '80
Abduction of St. Anne '75
Arnold '73
Honor Thy Father '73
Pat Garrett & Billy the Kid '73
Terror in the Wax Museum '73
Yuma '70
Any Wednesday '66
That Touch of Mink '62
The Devil at 4 O'Clock '61
All the Young Men '60
Let No Man Write My Epitaph '60
1001 Arabian Nights '59
Bell, Book and Candle '58
Cowboy '58
Houseboat '58
Me and the Colonel '58
3:10 to Yuma '57
The Eddy Duchin Story '56
The Man from Laramie '55
Picnic '55
Queen Bee '55
Three for the Show '55
Tight Spot '55
From Here to Eternity '53
Salome '53
Harriet Craig '50
The Dark Past '49
The Doolins of Oklahoma '49
Jolson Sings Again '49
Lust for Gold '49
Man from Colorado '49
Down to Earth '47
Her Husband's Affairs '47

Paul Dunlap
Naked Kiss '64
Shock Corridor '63
The Three Stooges Meet Hercules '61
The Angry Red Planet '59
Blood of Dracula '57
Crime of Passion '57
I Was a Teenage Werewolf '57
Shack Out on 101 '55
The Lost Continent '51
The Steel Helmet '51

Arie Dzierlatka
Mon Oncle d'Amerique '80
Messidor '77
Chloe in the Afternoon '72

Brian Easdale
Peeping Tom '60
The Red Shoes '48
Black Narcissus '47

Randy Edelman (1947-)
Black Knight '01
Corky Romano '01
Head Over Heels '01
Osmosis Jones '01
Passion of Mind '00
Shanghai Noon '00
The Skulls '00
The Whole Nine Yards '00
EDtv '99
The Hunley '99
Six Days, Seven Nights '98
For Richer or Poorer '97
Gone Fishin' '97
Leave It to Beaver '97
Anaconda '96
Daylight '96
Diabolique '96
Down Periscope '96
Dragonheart '96
The Quest '96
The Big Green '95
Citizen X '95
While You Were Sleeping '95
Angels in the Outfield '94
Billy Madison '94
Greedy '94
The Mask '94
Pontiac Moon '94
Beethoven's 2nd '93
Dragon: The Bruce Lee Story '93
Gettysburg '93
Beethoven '92
The Distinguished Gentleman '92
The Last of the Mohicans '92
My Cousin Vinny '92
Drop Dead Fred '91
Shout '91
V.I. Warshawski '91
Come See the Paradise '90
Kindergarten Cop '90
Quick Change '90
Ghostbusters 2 '89
Troop Beverly Hills '89
Feds '88
Twins '88
When Your Lover Leaves '83
Executive Action '73
Snatched '72

Roger Edens
Take Me Out to the Ball Game '49
Good News '47
Till the Clouds Roll By '46
Go West '40

Greg Edmonson
Luckytown '00
Blue Ridge Fall '99
Undercover Angel '99
Last Lives '98
Turn of the Blade '97

Stephen Edwards
Hard Cash '01
Luck of the Draw '00

Steve Edwards
The Substitute 4: Failure is Not an Option '00
Bridge of Dragons '99
K-911 '99
The Patriot '99
Cold Harvest '98
High Voltage '98
T.N.T. '98
Diary of a Serial Killer '97
Bloodsport 3 '95
Illegal in Blue '95
Project Shadowchaser 3000 '95
Night Siege Project: Shadowchaser 2 '94

Cliff Eidelman
Harrison's Flowers '02
An American Rhapsody '01
Witness Protection '99
One True Thing '98
The Beautician and the Beast '97
Free Willy 3: The Rescue '97
Montana '97
If These Walls Could Talk '96
Now and Then '95
My Girl 2 '94
Picture Bride '94
A Simple Twist of Fate '94
Untamed Heart '93
Christopher Columbus: The Discovery '92
Leap of Faith '92
Delirious '91
Star Trek 6: The Undiscovered Country '91
Crazy People '90
Strike It Rich '90
Animal Behavior '89
Dead Man Out '89
To Die For '89
Triumph of the Spirit '89

Richard Einhorn
A House in the Hills '93
Closet Land '90
Blood Rage '87
Dead of Winter '87
Sister, Sister '87
Eyes of a Stranger '81
The Prowler '81
Don't Go in the House '80
Shock Waves '77

Hanns Eisler
A Scandal in Paris '46
Hangmen Also Die '42

Danny Elfman (1953-)
Spider-Man '02
Planet of the Apes '01
Spy Kids '01
Family Man '00
Proof of Life '00
Anywhere But Here '99
Instinct '99
Sleepy Hollow '99
A Civil Action '98
Modern Vampires '98
A Simple Plan '98
Flubber '97
Good Will Hunting '97
Men in Black '97
Extreme Measures '96
The Frighteners '96
Mars Attacks! '96
Mission: Impossible '96
Dead Presidents '95
Freeway '95
To Die For '95
Dolores Claiborne '94
The Nightmare before Christmas '93
Sommersby '93
Army of Darkness '92
Article 99 '92
Batman Returns '92
Darkman '90
Dick Tracy '90
Edward Scissorhands '90
The Flash '90
Nightbreed '90
Batman '89
Beetlejuice '88
Big Top Pee-wee '88
Hot to Trot! '88
Midnight Run '88
Scrooged '88
Summer School '87
Wisdom '87
Back to School '86
Pee-wee's Big Adventure '85
Forbidden Zone '80

Jonathan Elias
Leprechaun 2 '94
Morning Glory '93
Far from Home '89
Parents '89
Rude Awakening '89
Shakedown '88
Two Moon Junction '88
Vamp '86
Almost You '85
Key Exchange '85
Tuff Turf '85
Children of the Corn '84

Boris Elkis
The Godson '98
Bugged! '96
Duke Ellington (1899-1974)
Paris Blues '61
Anatomy of a Murder '59
Cabin in the Sky '43
Bill Elliott
Sticks '98
Stand-Ins '97
Jack Elliott (1927-2001)
The Jerk '79
The Man Without a Country '73
Support Your Local Gunfighter '71
Where's Poppa? '70
Don Ellis
Ruby '77
French Connection 2 '75
The French Connection '71
Keith Emerson
The Church '98
Best Revenge '83
Nighthawks '81
Inferno '80
Stephen Endelman
Bride of the Wind '01
Blue Moon '00
Blue Moon '00
Earthly Possessions '99
Two Family House '99
Finding Graceland '98
Witness to the Mob '98
Kicked in the Head '97
The Proposition '97
City of Industry '96
Ed '96
Keys to Tulsa '96
Cosi '95
The Englishman Who Went up a Hill But Came down a Mountain '95
Flirting with Disaster '95
Jeffrey '95
The Journey of August King '95
Postcards from America '95
Reckless '95
Tom and Huck '95
The Desperate Trail '94
Imaginary Crimes '94
Household Saints '93
Operation Condor '91
Charles Engstrom
Ulee's Gold '97
Ruby in Paradise '93
A Flash of Green '85
Brian Eno
The Million Dollar Hotel '99
Dune '84
Sebastiane '79
Land of the Minotaur '77
John Entwhistle
Quadrophenia '79
Tommy '75
Micky Erbe
Blackjack '97
Ticket to Heaven '81
Leo Erdody
Detour '46
Strange Illusion '45
Dead Men Walk '43
Girls in Chains '43
Sebastien Erms
A Summer's Tale '96
Rendezvous in Paris '95
A Tale of Winter '92
Bengt Ernryd
The New Land '73
I Am Curious (Yellow) '67
Evan Evans
Newsbreak '00
TripFall '00
Wicked Ways '99
Ray Evans
Red Garters '54
The Lemon Drop Kid '51
Harold Faltermeyer
Kuffs '92
Fletch Lives '89
Tango and Cash '89
Beverly Hills Cop 2 '87
Fatal Beauty '87
Fire and Ice '87
The Running Man '87
Top Gun '86
Fletch '85
Beverly Hills Cop '84
Thief of Hearts '84
Sharon Farber
They Call Me Sirr '00
In a Class of His Own '99
Jim Farmer
The Waiting Game '99
The Real Blonde '97
Box of Moonlight '96
Living in Oblivion '94
Johnny Suede '92
Ricky Fataar
The Efficiency Expert '92
High Tide '87
Louis Febre
First Daughter '99
Dean Koontz's Mr. Murder '98
Little Bigfoot '96
Last Man Standing '95
Rage '95
Serial Killer '95
Two Bits & Pepper '95
The Secretary '94
Jack Feldman
Thumbelina '94
Newsies '92
George Fenton
Summer Catch '01
Bread and Roses '00
Center Stage '00
Lucky Numbers '00
Anna and the King '99
Entropy '99
Grey Owl '99
Dangerous Beauty '98
Ever After: A Cinderella Story '98
Living Out Loud '98
My Name Is Joe '98
The Object of My Affection '98
You've Got Mail '98
Carla's Song '97
The Crucible '96
In Love and War '96
Multiplicity '96
Heaven's Prisoners '95
Land and Freedom '95
Mary Reilly '95
The Madness of King George '94
Mixed Nuts '94
Born Yesterday '93
Groundhog Day '93
Ladybird, Ladybird '93
Shadowlands '93
Final Analysis '92
Hero '92
China Moon '91
The Fisher King '91
Memphis Belle '90
White Palace '90
The Dressmaker '89
The Long Walk Home '89
We're No Angels '89
Dangerous Liaisons '88
A Handful of Dust '88
High Spirits '88
White Mischief '88
White of the Eye '88
Cry Freedom '87
Saigon: Year of the Cat '87
Clockwise '86
84 Charing Cross Road '86
The Company of Wolves '85
The Jewel in the Crown '84
An Englishman Abroad '83
Gandhi '82
Hussy '80
Allyn Ferguson
High Noon '00
All Quiet on the Western Front '79
The Man Without a Country '73
Support Your Local Gunfighter '71
David Ferguson
Hostile Waters '97
The Woman in White '97
A Dark Adapted Eye '93
Dead Ahead: The Exxon Valdez Disaster '92
A Fatal Inversion '92
Tailspin: Behind the Korean Airline Tragedy '89
Jay Ferguson (1943-)
Tremors 2: Aftershocks '96
Double Dragon '94
Gleaming the Cube '89
A Nightmare on Elm Street 5: Dream Child '89
Race for Glory '89
Bad Dreams '88
Johnny Be Good '88
License to Drive '88
Pulse '88
Best Seller '87
The Patriot '86
Quiet Cool '86
Gianni Ferrio
Blood for a Silver Dollar '66
Fiances '63
Paul Ferris
The Conqueror Worm '68
Blood Beast Terror '67
Cy Feuer
Bad Man of Deadwood '41
Carson City Kid '40
Come on Rangers '38
Brad Fiedel
Eden '98
Mistrial '96
Rasputin: Dark Servant of Destiny '96
Johnny Mnemonic '95
True Lies '94
Blink '93
The Real McCoy '93
Striking Distance '93
Gladiator '92
Straight Talk '92
Terminator 2: Judgment Day '91
Blue Steel '90
Forgotten Prisoners '90
Cold Sassy Tree '89
Immediate Family '89
Perfect Witness '89
True Believer '89
The Accused '88
Fright Night 2 '88
Weekend War '88
The Big Easy '87
Bluffing It '87
Hostage '87
The Last Innocent Man '87
Let's Get Harry '87
Nowhere to Hide '87
The Serpent and the Rainbow '87
Brotherhood of Justice '86
Desert Bloom '86
The Midnight Hour '86
Compromising Positions '85
Fraternity Vacation '85
Fright Night '85
Girls of the White Orchid '85
Into Thin Air '85
The Baron and the Kid '84
Calendar Girl Murders '84
Children in the Crossfire '84
Eyes of Fire '84
Mae West '84
My Mother's Secret Life '84
Right of Way '84
The Terminator '84
Cocaine: One Man's Seduction '83
Murder in Coweta County '83
Born Beautiful '82
Hit & Run '82
Night School '81
The People vs. Jean Harris '81
The Day the Women Got Even '80
Hardhat & Legs '80
Just Before Dawn '80
Playing for Time '80
Deadly Hero '75
Jerry Fielding
Escape from Alcatraz '79
The Gauntlet '77
The Bad News Bears '76
The Enforcer '76
The Outlaw Josey Wales '76
The Killer Elite '75
Bring Me the Head of Alfredo Garcia '74
The Gambler '74
Junior Bonner '72
The Nightcomers '72
Straw Dogs '72
Chato's Land '71
Johnny Got His Gun '71
Lawman '71
The Wild Bunch '69
Adam Fields
Meeting Daddy '98
Lovelife '97
Dorothy Fields
Joy of Living '38
Swing Time '36
Mike Figgis (1948-)
Time Code '00
Miss Julie '99
The Loss of Sexual Innocence '98
One Night Stand '97
Leaving Las Vegas '95
Liebestraum '91
Internal Affairs '90
Stormy Monday '88
David Findlay
Nowhere in Sight '01
Dead Silent '99
Captive '97
Eye '96
Sylvia Fine
Court Jester '56
The Secret Life of Walter Mitty '47
Gunther Fischer
Bear Ye One Another's Burden... '88
Solo Sunny '80
Peter Fish
Intimate Betrayal '96
Wigstock: The Movie '95
Simon Fisher Turner (1954-)
The Eternal '99
Claire Dolan '97
Croupier '97
Nadja '95
Loaded '94
Blue '93
Edward II '92
The Garden '90
The Last of England '87
Frank Fitzpatrick
Love Song '00
The Pirates of Silicon Valley '99
Friday '95
Robert Folk
Held Up '00
Major League 3: Back to the Minors '98
Booty Call '96
Maximum Risk '96
Nothing to Lose '96
The Thief and the Cobbler '96
Ace Ventura: When Nature Calls '95
Lawnmower Man 2: Beyond Cyberspace '95
Theodore Rex '95
In the Army Now '94
Police Academy 7: Mission to Moscow '94
Trapped in Paradise '94
A Troll in Central Park '94
National Lampoon's Loaded Weapon 1 '93
Rock-a-Doodle '92
Beastmaster 2: Through the Portal of Time '91
A Climate for Killing '91
NeverEnding Story 2: The Next Chapter '91
Toy Soldiers '91
Honeymoon Academy '90
Happy Together '89
Police Academy 6: City under Siege '89
Wicked Stepmother '89
Miles from Home '88
Police Academy 5: Assignment Miami Beach '88
Can't Buy Me Love '87
Police Academy 4: Citizens on Patrol '87
Prince of Bel Air '87
Police Academy 3: Back in Training '86
Stewardess School '86
Odd Jobs '85
Bachelor Party '84
Police Academy '84
Purple Hearts '84
The Slayer '82
Sherman Foote
It Takes Two '95
Parents '89
Louis Forbes
The Bat '59
Slightly Scarlet '56
Pearl of the South Pacific '55
Tennessee's Partner '55
Pitfall '48
Made for Each Other '39
Lou Forestieri
Sherlock: Undercover Dog '94
Twin Sisters '91
Crazy Moon '87
David Foster
The Little Rascals '94
If Looks Could Kill '91
Listen to Me '89
Fresh Horses '88
Stealing Home '88
The Secret of My Success '87
St. Elmo's Fire '85
Charles Fox
Collected Stories '02
A Death in the Family '02
The Song of the Lark '01
The Broken Chain '93
Repossessed '90
False Witness '89
The Gods Must Be Crazy 2 '89
Hard to Kill '89
One Man Force '89
Short Circuit 2 '88
Christmas Comes to Willow Creek '87
Love at Stake '87
The Longshot '86
Unnatural Causes '86
Doin' Time '85
National Lampoon's European Vacation '85
A Summer to Remember '84
Strange Brew '83
Trenchcoat '83
Love Child '82
Six Pack '82
Zapped! '82
The Last Married Couple in America '80
Little Darlings '80
9 to 5 '80
Oh, God! Book 2 '80
Better Late Than Never '79
Foul Play '78
Rainbow '78
One on One '77
The Duchess and the Dirtwater Fox '76
Two Minute Warning '76
Bug '75
The Drowning Pool '75
The Other Side of the Mountain '75
The Laughing Policeman '74
The Stranger Within '74
Dying Room Only '73
The Last American Hero '73
A Separate Peace '73
Star Spangled Girl '71
Pufnstuf '70
Goodbye Columbus '69
Barbarella '68
The Green Slime '68
The Incident '67
Neal Fox
Killer Tomatoes Strike Back '90
Return of the Killer Tomatoes! '88
Cesar Franck
Celeste '81
Sandra of a Thousand Delights '65
Jess (Jesus) Franco (1930-)
Tender Flesh '97
The Diabolical Dr. Z '65
David Michael Frank
The Last Warrior '99
Billboard Dad '98
A Kid in Aladdin's Palace '97
Volcano: Fire on the Mountain '97
The Baby-Sitters' Club '95
The Prince '95
Tails You Live, Heads You're Dead '95
Bitter Vengeance '94
Best of the Best 2 '93
Casualties of Love: The "Long Island Lolita" Story '93
Extreme Justice '93
Linda '93
Poison Ivy '92
Out for Justice '91
Showdown in Little Tokyo '91
Above the Law '88
Hero and the Terror '88
I'm Gonna Git You Sucka '88
Christopher Franke
Seventeen Again '00
Lost in the Bermuda Triangle '98
Tarzan and the Lost City '98
Menno's Mind '96
Public Enemies '96
Solo '96
Wolverine '96
The Surgeon '94
Stephen King's The Tommyknockers '93
Universal Soldier '92
Benjamin Frankel
Battle of the Bulge '65
End of the Affair '55
Michael Franks
Cockfighter '74
Zandy's Bride '74
Arthur Freed
Yolanda and the Thief '45
Broadway Melody of 1938 '37
Broadway Melody of 1936 '35
Broadway Melody '29
Terry Frewer
Out of Time '00
The Last Stop '99
The Inspectors '98
Gerald Fried
Rescue from Gilligan's Island '78
Roots '77
The Baby '72
The Grissom Gang '71
Too Late the Hero '70
The Killing of Sister George '69
Whatever Happened to Aunt Alice? '69
I Bury the Living '58
Machine Gun Kelly '58
Terror in a Texas Town '58
Paths of Glory '57
The Killing '56
Killer's Kiss '55
Hugo Friedhofer
Private Parts '72
Homicidal '61
Barbarian and the Geisha '58
The Young Lions '58
An Affair to Remember '57
Soldier of Fortune '55
Above and Beyond '53
Vera Cruz '53
The Marrying Kind '52
Three Came Home '50
The Bishop's Wife '47
Body and Soul '47
The Best Years of Our Lives '46
Lifeboat '44
A Wing and a Prayer '44

Polyester '81

Daniel Hart
Carmen, Baby '66
Nude on the Moon '61

Lorenz Hart
Pal Joey '57
Words and Music '48
I Married an Angel '42
Too Many Girls '40
Babes in Arms '39
Evergreen '34
The Merry Widow '34
Hallelujah, I'm a Bum '33

Hal Hartley (1959-)
No Such Thing '01
Henry Fool '98
Simple Men '45

Richard Hartley
Don Quixote '00
Mad About Mambo '00
When Brendan Met Trudy '00
Alice in Wonderland '99
All the Little Animals '98
Rogue Trader '98
Curtain Call '97
The Designated Mourner '97
A Thousand Acres '97
The Brylcreem Boys '96
Playing God '96
Stealing Beauty '96
Rough Magic '95
The Van '95
An Awfully Big Adventure '94
Princess Caraboo '94
The Rector's Wife '94
The Secret Rapture '94
The Good Father '87
The Impossible Spy '87
Dance with a Stranger '85
Shock Treatment '81
The Rocky Horror Picture Show '75

Richard Harvey
Arabian Nights '00
Animal Farm '99
The Magical Legend of the Leprechauns '99
Captain Jack '98
Jane Eyre '97
Paper Mask '91
Cause Celebre '87

Bo Harwood
Happy Birthday to Me '81
Opening Night '77

Jimmie Haskell
The Dogfighters '95
Zachariah '70

Paul Haslinger
crazy/beautiful '01
Cheaters '00

Harley Hatcher
Cain's Cutthroats '71
Satan's Sadists '69

Tadashi Hattori
One Wonderful Sunday '47
The Men Who Tread on the Tiger's Tail '45

Roy Hay
Styx '00
Pterodactyl Woman from Beverly Hills '97
Precious Find '96

Fumio Hayasaka
I Live in Fear '55
Sansho the Bailiff '54
Seven Samurai '54
Ugetsu '53
Ikiru '52
Rashomon '51
Scandal '50
Drunken Angel '48

Todd Hayen
When Time Expires '97
The Invader '96
Panic in the Skies '96

Isaac Hayes (1942-)
Shaft '00
Truck Turner '74
Shaft '71

Lennie Hayton
Battle Circus '53
Singin' in the Rain '52
Battleground '49

The Hucksters '47
Till the Clouds Roll By '46

Neal Hefti
Barefoot in the Park '67
Oh Dad, Poor Dad (Momma's Hung You in the Closet & I'm Feeling So Sad) '67
Sex and the Single Girl '64

Reinhold Heil
The Princess and the Warrior '00
Winter Sleepers '97

Ray Heindorf
The Music Man '62
No Time for Sergeants '58
Wonder Man '45
The Roaring Twenties '39

Ben Heneghan
Breeders '97
The Proposition '96

Jerry Herman
Mrs. Santa Claus '96
Hello, Dolly! '69

Bernard Herrmann (1911-75)
Psycho '98
Cape Fear '91
Psycho 4: The Beginning '90
It's Alive 2: It Lives Again '78
Obsession '76
Taxi Driver '76
It's Alive '74
Sisters '73
Endless Night '71
The Bride Wore Black '68
Fahrenheit 451 '66
Marnie '64
The Birds '63
Jason and the Argonauts '63
Cape Fear '61
Mysterious Island '61
Psycho '60
North by Northwest '59
The Three Worlds of Gulliver '59
The Seventh Voyage of Sinbad '58
Vertigo '58
The Man Who Knew Too Much '56
The Trouble with Harry '55
A Christmas Carol '54
Beneath the 12-Mile Reef '53
Five Fingers '52
The Snows of Kilimanjaro '52
The Day the Earth Stood Still '51
On Dangerous Ground '51
The Ghost and Mrs. Muir '47
Anna and the King of Siam '46
Jane Eyre '44
The Magnificent Ambersons '42
Citizen Kane '41
The Devil & Daniel Webster '41

Boo Hewerdine
24-7 '97
Fever Pitch '96

Werner R. Heymann
They All Kissed the Bride '42
To Be or Not to Be '42
That Uncertain Feeling '41
Faust '26

Richard Hieronymous
The Invisible Strangler '76
Angels Hard As They Come '71
Bury Me an Angel '71

John Hill
Tar '97
The Pompatus of Love '95

Hilmar Orn Hilmarsson
Cold Fever '95
Children of Nature '91

Wilbert Hirsch

An American Werewolf in Paris '97
Mute Witness '95

David Hirschfelder
Hanging Up '99
Elizabeth '98
The Interview '98
Sliding Doors '97
Dating the Enemy '95
Shine '95
Tunnel Vision '95

Joe Hisaishi
Brother '00
Kikujiro '99
Princess Mononoke '98
Fireworks '97

John Hodian
Blades '89
Girls School Screamers '86

Michael Hoenig
The Contaminated Man '01
Eye of the Killer '99
Terminal Justice: Cybertech P.D. '95
The Amy Fisher Story '93
Koyaanisqatsi '83

Paul Hoffert
Outrageous! '77
The Groundstar Conspiracy '72

Joachim Holbek
Heart of Light '97
Junk Mail '97
The Kingdom 2 '97
Nightwatch '96
Breaking the Waves '95
The Kingdom '95

Mark Holden
Body Armor '96
Ava's Magical Adventure '94
Beyond Desire '94

Lee Holdridge (1944-)
Mists of Avalon '01
Atomic Train '99
Mutiny '99
The Twilight of the Golds '97
Two for Texas '97
Gunfighter's Moon '96
Holiday Affair '96
Soul of the Game '96
Buffalo Girls '95
Harvest of Fire '95
Prince Brat and the Whipping Boy '95
The Tuskegee Airmen '95
Texas '94
The Yearling '94
Call of the Wild '93
Heidi '93
The Story Lady '93
One Against the Wind '91
Back to Hannibal: The Return of Tom Sawyer and Huckleberry Finn '90
Old Gringo '89
Born in East L.A. '87
Moonlighting '85
Transylvania 6-5000 '85
Splash '84
Mr. Mom '83
Beastmaster '82
American Pop '81
Winterhawk '76

Deborah Holland
Out There '95
Circuitry Man '90

Frederick "Friedrich" Hollander (1896-1976)
We're No Angels '55
The 5000 Fingers of Dr. T '53
Born Yesterday '50
A Foreign Affair '48
Here Comes Mr. Jordan '41
Remember the Night '40
Angel '37
Desire '36
The Blue Angel '30

David Holmes
Ocean's Eleven '01
Resurrection Man '97

Nigel Holton
Cries of Silence '97
Naked Souls '95
Twogether '94

Carnosaur '93
Bloodfist 3: Forced to Fight '92
Body Chemistry 2: Voice of a Stranger '91
Bloodfist 2 '90
South of Reno '87

Toshiyuki Honda
Minbo—Or the Gentle Art of Japanese Extortion '92
A Taxing Woman '87

Arthur Honegger
Harvest '37
Crime and Punishment '35
Napoleon '27

Tobe Hooper (1946-)
The Texas Chainsaw Massacre 2 '86
The Texas Chainsaw Massacre '74

Kenyon Hopkins
The Strange One '57
Twelve Angry Men '57

James Horner (1953-)
A Beautiful Mind '01
Iris '01
Dr. Seuss' How the Grinch Stole Christmas '00
Enemy at the Gates '00
Freedom Song '00
The Perfect Storm '00
Bicentennial Man '99
Deep Impact '98
The Mask of Zorro '98
Mighty Joe Young '98
Titanic '97
Courage Under Fire '96
The Devil's Own '96
Ransom '96
To Gillian on Her 37th Birthday '96
Apollo 13 '95
Balto '95
Braveheart '95
Casper '95
Jade '95
Jumanji '95
The Spitfire Grill '95
Clear and Present Danger '94
Legends of the Fall '94
The Pagemaster '94
Bopha! '93
A Far Off Place '93
Jack the Bear '93
The Man Without a Face '93
The Pelican Brief '93
Searching for Bobby Fischer '93
Swing Kids '93
Patriot Games '92
Sneakers '92
Thunderheart '92
Unlawful Entry '92
An American Tail: Fievel Goes West '91
Class Action '91
My Heroes Have Always Been Cowboys '91
Once Around '91
The Rocketeer '91
Another 48 Hrs. '90
I Love You to Death '90
Dad '89
Field of Dreams '89
Glory '89
Honey, I Shrunk the Kids '89
In Country '89
Cocoon: The Return '88
The Land Before Time '88
Red Heat '88
Vibes '88
Willow '88
*batteries not included '87
Project X '87
Aliens '86
An American Tail '86
The Name of the Rose '86
Off Beat '86
Where the River Runs Black '86
Cocoon '85
Commando '85
Heaven Help Us '85
The Journey of Natty Gann '85
P.K. and the Kid '85
Volunteers '85

Star Trek 3: The Search for Spock '84
The Stone Boy '84
Between Friends '83
Brainstorm '83
The Dresser '83
Gorky Park '83
Krull '83
Something Wicked This Way Comes '83
Testament '83
Uncommon Valor '83
48 Hrs. '82
A Piano for Mrs. Cimino '82
Star Trek 2: The Wrath of Khan '82
Deadly Blessing '81
The Hand '81
The Pursuit of D.B. Cooper '81
Wolfen '81
Battle Beyond the Stars '80
Humanoids from the Deep '80
Lady in Red '79
Up from the Depths '79

Richard Horowitz
Three Seasons '98
Broken Trust '95
Lakota Woman: Siege at Wounded Knee '94
The Sheltering Sky '90

Vladimir Horunzhy
Original Gangstas '96
Stephen King's The Langoliers '95
Blink of an Eye '92

James Newton Howard (1951-)
Big Trouble '02
America's Sweethearts '01
Atlantis: The Lost Empire '01
Dinosaur '00
Unbreakable '00
Vertical Limit '00
Mumford '99
Runaway Bride '99
The Sixth Sense '99
Snow Falling on Cedars '99
Stir of Echoes '99
A Perfect Murder '98
The Devil's Advocate '97
My Best Friend's Wedding '97
The Postman '97
Father's Day '96
The Juror '96
One Fine Day '96
Primal Fear '96
Space Jam '96
The Trigger Effect '96
An Eye for an Eye '95
French Kiss '95
Waterworld '95
Junior '94
Just Cause '94
Outbreak '94
Restoration '94
Wyatt Earp '94
Alive '93
Dave '93
Falling Down '93
The Fugitive '93
Intersection '93
The Saint of Fort Washington '93
American Heart '92
Diggstown '92
Glengarry Glen Ross '92
Night and the City '92
Grand Canyon '91
Guilty by Suspicion '91
King Ralph '91
My Girl '91
The Prince of Tides '91
Coupe de Ville '90
Flatliners '90
Marked for Death '90
Pretty Woman '90
Somebody Has to Shoot the Picture '90
Three Men and a Little Lady '90
The Image '89
Major League '89
The Package '89
Tap '89

Everybody's All American '88
Five Corners '88
Promised Land '88
Some Girls '88
Campus Man '87
Off Limits '87
Russkies '87
Head Office '86
Never Too Young to Die '86
Nobody's Fool '86
Tough Guys '86
Wildcats '86
8 Million Ways to Die '85

Alan Howarth
Alone with a Stranger '99
The Dentist 2: Brace Yourself '98
The Dentist '96
Halloween 6: The Curse of Michael Myers '95
Arcade '93
Halloween 5: The Revenge of Michael Myers '89
Halloween 4: The Return of Michael Myers '88
They Live '88
Big Trouble in Little China '86
Christine '84

David A. Hughes
New Best Friend '02
The Bachelor '99
Lock, Stock and 2 Smoking Barrels '98
Stiff Upper Lips '96
Solitaire for 2 '94
C.H.U.D. '84

Gary Hughes
A Challenge for Robin Hood '68
The Viking Queen '67

Don Hulette (1937-)
Breaker! Breaker! '77
They Saved Hitler's Brain '64

Steve Hunter
Dead Weekend '95
Cyber Bandits '94

Dick Hyman (1927-)
Sweet and Lowdown '99
Everyone Says I Love You '96
Mighty Aphrodite '95
Alan & Naomi '92
The Lemon Sisters '90
Leader of the Band '87
Moonstruck '87
The Purple Rose of Cairo '85

Abdullah Ibrahim
No Fear, No Die '90
Tilai '90

Akira Ifukube
Godzilla vs. King Ghidora '91
Terror of Mechagodzilla '78
Yog, Monster from Space '71
War of the Gargantuas '70
Destroy All Monsters '68
Godzilla vs. Monster Zero '68
Ghidrah the Three Headed Monster '65
Godzilla vs. Mothra '64
King Kong vs. Godzilla '63
The Burmese Harp '56
Godzilla, King of the Monsters '56
A Quiet Duel '49

Alberto Iglesias
All About My Mother '99
Lovers of the Arctic Circle '98
The Chambermaid on the Titanic '97
Live Flesh '97
The Flower of My Secret '95
Tierra '95
Outrage '93
The Red Squirrel '93
Vacas '91

Shinichiro Ikebe
The Eel '96
Rhapsody in August '91

Akira Kurosawa's Dreams '90
The Ballad of Narayama '83
Kagemusha '80
Vengeance Is Mine '79

Neil Innes (1944-)
Erik the Viking '89
All You Need Is Cash '78
Monty Python and the Holy Grail '75

Ashley Irwin
Naked City: Justice with a Bullet '98
Entertaining Angels: The Dorothy Day Story '96
The Expert '95
Secret Games 3 '94
Stranger by Night '94
Undercover '94
Secret Games 2: The Escort '93
Deadly Rivals '92
Fair Game '85

Pat Irwin
But I'm a Cheerleader '99
Breathing Room '96
Sudden Manhattan '96
My New Gun '92

Bjorn Isfalt
What's Eating Gilbert Grape '93
My Life As a Dog '85

Mark Isham (1951-)
Don't Say a Word '01
Hardball '01
Imposter '01
Life as a House '01
The Majestic '01
Save the Last Dance '01
Men of Honor '00
Rules of Engagement '00
Trixie '00
Where the Money Is '00
Body Shots '99
October Sky '99
At First Sight '98
Blade '98
Breakfast of Champions '98
The Defenders: Taking the First '98
Varsity Blues '98
Afterglow '97
The Defenders: Payback '97
The Education of Little Tree '97
The Gingerbread Man '97
Kiss the Girls '97
Fly Away Home '96
Gotti '96
Last Dance '96
Night Falls on Manhattan '96
Home for the Holidays '95
Miami Rhapsody '95
The Net '95
The Browning Version '94
Losing Isaiah '94
Mrs. Parker and the Vicious Circle '94
Quiz Show '94
Safe Passage '94
Timecop '94
Fire in the Sky '93
The Getaway '93
Made in America '93
Nowhere to Run '93
Romeo Is Bleeding '93
Short Cuts '93
Cool World '92
A Midnight Clear '92
Of Mice and Men '92
A River Runs Through It '92
Billy Bathgate '91
Crooked Hearts '91
Little Man Tate '91
Mortal Thoughts '91
Point Break '91
Reversal of Fortune '90
The Beast '88
The Moderns '88
Made in Heaven '87
The Hitcher '86
Trouble in Mind '86
Mrs. Soffel '84
Never Cry Wolf '83

Peter Ivers
Eraserhead '78
Grand Theft Auto '77

Howard Jackson
Merrill's Marauders '62
Sergeant Rutledge '60

Joe Jackson
Queens Logic '91
Tucker: The Man and His Dream '88
Party! Party! '83

Leos Janacek
The Unbearable Lightness of Being '88
Don's Party '76

Chaz Jankel
The Rachel Papers '89
D.O.A. '88

Alaric Jans
The Winslow Boy '98
Things Change '88
House of Games '87

Pierre Jansen
Violette '78
Innocents with Dirty Hands '75
A Piece of Pleasure '74
La Rupture '70
The 317th Platoon '65
Les Bonnes Femmes '60

Werner Janssen
A Night in Casablanca '46
The Southerner '45
Guest in the House '44

Maurice Jarre (1924-)
Uprising '01
I Dreamed of Africa '00
Sunshine '99
Sunchaser '96
Fearless '93
Mr. Jones '93
School Ties '92
Solar Crisis '92
Fires Within '91
Only the Lonely '91
After Dark, My Sweet '90
Ghost '90
Jacob's Ladder '90
Chances Are '89
Dead Poets Society '89
Enemies, a Love Story '89
Prancer '89
Distant Thunder '88
Gorillas in the Mist '88
Moon over Parador '88
Wildfire '88
Fatal Attraction '87
Gaby: A True Story '87
Julia and Julia '87
The Murder of Mary Phagan '87
No Way Out '87
Apology '86
The Mosquito Coast '86
Solarbabies '86
Tai-Pan '86
The Bride '85
Enemy Mine '85
Mad Max: Beyond Thunderdome '85
Witness '85
Dreamscape '84
A Passage to India '84
Samson and Delilah '84
Top Secret! '84
Coming Out of the Ice '82
Don't Cry, It's Only Thunder '82
Firefox '82
The Year of Living Dangerously '82
Young Doctors in Love '82
Lion of the Desert '81
Taps '81
Enola Gay: The Men, the Mission, the Atomic Bomb '80
The Last Flight of Noah's Ark '80
Resurrection '80
Shogun '80
The Black Marble '79
The Magician of Lublin '79
The Tin Drum '79
Winter Kills '79
The Prince and the Pauper '78
Users '78
Jesus of Nazareth '77
March or Die '77
The Message '77
The Last Tycoon '76
Shout at the Devil '76
The Man Who Would Be King '75
Mandingo '75
Posse '75
The Island at the Top of the World '74
Mr. Sycamore '74
Ash Wednesday '73
Mackintosh Man '73
Life & Times of Judge Roy Bean '72
Plaza Suite '71
Red Sun '71
El Condor '70
Ryan's Daughter '70
The Damned '69
Topaz '69
Five Card Stud '68
The Fixer '68
Isadora '68
Villa Rides '68
Night of the Generals '67
Gambit '66
Grand Prix '66
Is Paris Burning? '66
The Professionals '66
The Collector '65
Doctor Zhivago '65
The Train '65
Behold a Pale Horse '64
Judex '64
Lawrence of Arabia '62
The Longest Day '62
Sundays & Cybele '62
The Horror Chamber of Dr. Faustus '59

Maurice Jaubert
The Green Room '78
The Man Who Loved Women '77
Small Change '76
The Story of Adele H. '75
Bizarre Bizarre '39
L'Atalante '34

Geir Jenssen
Kill by Inches '99
Insomnia '97

Zhao Jiping
The Emperor and the Assassin '99
The King of Masks '99
Temptress Moon '96
To Live '94
Farewell My Concubine '93
The Story of Qiu Ju '91

Elton John (1947-)
The Road to El Dorado '00
The Muse '99
The Lion King '94
Friends '71

J.J. Johnson
Cleopatra Jones '73
Shaft '71

Laurie Johnson
The Lady and the Highwayman '89
It's Alive 3: Island of the Alive '87
Captain Kronos: Vampire Hunter '74
And Soon the Darkness '70
Dr. Strangelove, or: How I Learned to Stop Worrying and Love the Bomb '64
First Men in the Moon '64
Tiger Bay '59

Adrian Johnston
Shackleton '02
About Adam '00
All the King's Men '99
Robert Louis Stevenson's The Game of Death '99
The Turn of the Screw '99
I Want You '98
Our Mutual Friend '98
Touching Evil '97
Welcome to Sarajevo '97
Jude '96

Alain Jomy
The Accompanist '93
The Little Thief '89
The Best Way '76

Kenneth V. Jones (1924-)
Tower of Evil '72
Tomb of Ligeia '64
Dentist In the Chair '60
The Horse's Mouth '58

Quincy Jones (1933-)
The Color Purple '85
The Wiz '78
Roots '77
The Getaway '72
The New Centurions '72
The Anderson Tapes '71
Dollars '71
Honky '71
Man & Boy '71
Brother John '70
The Hot Rock '70
They Call Me Mr. Tibbs! '70
Bob & Carol & Ted & Alice '69
Cactus Flower '69
The Italian Job '69
The Lost Man '69
MacKenna's Gold '69
Dandy in Aspic '68
For Love of Ivy '68
Enter Laughing '67
In Cold Blood '67
In the Heat of the Night '67
Mirage '66
Walk, Don't Run '66
The Pawnbroker '65
The Slender Thread '65

Ralph Jones
Love Letters '83
Slumber Party Massacre '82

Terry Jones (1942-)
Mr. Toad's Wild Ride '96
Monty Python's The Meaning of Life '83

Trevor Jones (1949-)
Crossroads '02
Dinotopia '02
From Hell '01
Thirteen Days '00
Cleopatra '99
Molly '99
Notting Hill '99
Desperate Measures '98
Merlin '98
The Mighty '98
Dark City '97
G.I. Jane '97
Brassed Off '96
For Roseanna '96
Lawn Dogs '96
Talk of Angels '96
Gulliver's Travels '95
Loch Ness '95
Richard III '95
Hideaway '94
Kiss of Death '94
The Last Place on Earth '94
Cliffhanger '93
In the Name of the Father '93
Blame It on the Bellboy '92
Chains of Gold '92
Crisscross '92
Freejack '92
The Last of the Mohicans '92
Defenseless '91
Murder by Moonlight '91
Arachnophobia '90
Bad Influence '90
By Dawn's Early Light '89
Sea of Love '89
Diamond's Edge '88
Dominick & Eugene '88
Mississippi Burning '88
Sweet Lies '88
Angel Heart '87
Labyrinth '86
Runaway Train '85
Nate and Hayes '83
Those Glory, Glory Days '83
The Dark Crystal '82
The Sender '82
Excalibur '81

Wilfred Josephs
All Creatures Great and Small '74
Die! Die! My Darling! '65

Phil Judd
Amy '98
Mr. Reliable: A True Story '95
Rikky and Pete '88

David Julyan
Insomnia '02
Memento '00
Following '99

Bill Justis
The Villain '79
Hooper '78
Smokey and the Bandit '77

Jan A.P. Kaczmarek
Unfaithful '02
Lost Souls '00
The Third Miracle '99
Aimee & Jaguar '98
Washington Square '97
Bliss '96
Felony '95
Total Eclipse '95

Bert Kalmar
Duck Soup '33
Animal Crackers '30

Michael Kamen (1948-)
Band of Brothers '01
Frequency '00
X-Men '00
Iron Giant '99
From the Earth to the Moon '98
Lethal Weapon 4 '98
What Dreams May Come '98
Event Horizon '97
Inventing the Abbotts '97
The Winter Guest '97
Jack '96
101 Dalmatians '96
Die Hard: With a Vengeance '95
Mr. Holland's Opus '95
Stonewall '95
Circle of Friends '94
Don Juan DeMarco '94
Last Action Hero '93
Splitting Heirs '93
The Three Musketeers '93
Wilder Napalm '93
Blue Ice '92
Lethal Weapon 3 '92
Shining Through '92
Hudson Hawk '91
The Last Boy Scout '91
Robin Hood: Prince of Thieves '91
Die Hard 2: Die Harder '90
The Krays '90
The Raggedy Rawney '90
The Adventures of Baron Munchausen '89
Crusoe '89
Dead Bang '89
Lethal Weapon 2 '89
License to Kill '89
Renegades '89
Road House '89
Rooftops '89
Action Jackson '88
Die Hard '88
Homeboy '88
Adventures in Babysitting '87
Lethal Weapon '87
Rita, Sue & Bob Too '87
Someone to Watch Over Me '87
Suspect '87
Edge of Darkness '86
Highlander '86
Mona Lisa '86
Shanghai Surprise '86
Brazil '85
Lifeforce '85
Angelo My Love '83
Dead Zone '83
Pink Floyd: The Wall '82
Venom '82
Polyester '81
S*H*E '79
Between the Lines '77
Stunts '77
The Arab Conspiracy '76

Bronislau Kaper
Somebody Up There Likes Me '56
Them! '54
Lili '53
The Red Badge of Courage '51
Malaya '49
The Secret Garden '49
The Stranger '46
Bataan '43
Keeper of the Flame '42
White Cargo '42
A Day at the Races '37

Sol Kaplan
Over the Edge '79
Salt of the Earth '54
Niagara '52
The Halls of Montezuma '50
Tales of Manhattan '42

Dana Kaproff
Dead Air '94
When a Stranger Calls Back '93
Nightmare '91
Full Exposure: The Sex Tape Scandals '89
The Big Red One '80

Eleni Karaindrou
Eternity and a Day '97
Ulysses' Gaze '95
Landscape in the Mist '88

Fred Karger
Fastest Guitar Alive '68
Frankie and Johnny '65

Fred Karlin (1936-)
KISS Meets the Phantom of the Park '78
The Autobiography of Miss Jane Pittman '74
Born Innocent '74
Westworld '73
Yours, Mine & Ours '68

Steve Karmen
The Beautiful, the Bloody and the Bare '69
Teenage Mother '67
Teenage Gang Debs '66

Laura Karpman
Brotherhood of Murder '99
Dash and Lilly '99
Lover's Knot '96

Al Kasha
Rescue Me '93
The Closer '91

Fred Katz
Creature from the Haunted Sea '60
A Bucket of Blood '59
The Wasp Woman '59

Emilio Kauderer
Friends & Lovers '99
A Place in the World '92

Bernhard Kaun (1899-1980)
The Black Legion '37
Petrified Forest '36

Edward Kay
Bowery at Midnight '42
King of the Zombies '41

Norman Kaye
Vincent: The Life and Death of Vincent van Gogh '87
Lonely Hearts '82

Brian Keane
Illtown '96
Stephen King's The Night Flier '96

John Keane
Horatio Hornblower: The Adventure Continues '01
Anna Karenina '00
The Last of the Blonde Bombshells '00
Hideous Kinky '99
The Break '97
Trojan Eddie '96
Small Faces '95
Armistead Maupin's Tales of the City '93
A Very British Coup '88
The Kitchen Toto '87

Victoria Kelly
Heaven '99
The Ugly '96

Arthur Kempel
Stray Bullet '98
The Arrival '96
Behind Enemy Lines '96

Riders of the Purple Sage '96
Sensation '94
Windrunner '94
Double Impact '91
A Cry in the Wild '90
Fleshburn '84

Greg Kendall
Drive Me Crazy '99
Bandwagon '95

Rolfe Kent (1963-)
40 Days and 40 Nights '02
Happy Campers '01
Kate & Leopold '01
Legally Blonde '01
Someone Like You '01
Town and Country '01
Gun Shy '00
Nurse Betty '00
Election '99
Oxygen '99
Slums of Beverly Hills '98
The Theory of Flight '98
Citizen Ruth '96
Dead Connection '94

Jerome Kern
Lovely to Look At '52
Show Boat '51
Can't Help Singing '45
Cover Girl '44
You Were Never Lovelier '42
Lady Be Good '41
Joy of Living '38
Show Boat '36
Swing Time '36
Sweet Adeline '35
The Cat and the Fiddle '34

Wojciech Kilar (1932-)
The Ninth Gate '99
Portrait of a Lady '96
Death and the Maiden '94
The Silent Touch '94
From a Far Country: Pope John Paul II '81
Contract '80
Land of Promise '74
Dracula '73
Illumination '73
Family Life '71

Kevin Kiner
The Other Side of Heaven '02
Tremors 3: Back to Perfection '01
Safe House '99
Wing Commander '99
Against the Law '98
Black Scorpion 2: Ground Zero '96
Carnosaur 3: Primal Species '96
Lifeform '96
The Pest '96
Black Scorpion '95
Demolition High '95
Excessive Force 2: Force on Force '95
Exit '95
Freaked '93

Chuji Kinoshita
The Human Condition: Road to Eternity '59
The Human Condition: No Greater Love '58

Basil Kirchin
The Freakmaker '73
The Abominable Dr. Phibes '71

David Kitay
Ghost World '01
Tomcats '01
Dude, Where's My Car? '00
Loser '00
Scary Movie '00
Can't Hardly Wait '98
A Night at the Roxbury '98
Clueless '95
Roosters '95
Father and Scout '94
Trading Mom '94
Surf Ninjas '93
Breaking the Rules '92
Look Who's Talking, Too '90
Look Who's Talking '89

Larry Klein
Sugar Town '99
Grace of My Heart '96

Johnny Klimek
The Princess and the Warrior '00
Winter Sleepers '97

Kevin Klinger
Aftershock '88
Necromancer: Satan's Servant '88

Harold Kloser
Sins of the Father '01
Kiss Tomorrow Goodbye '00
The Harmonists '99
The Thirteenth Floor '99
Quiet Days in Hollywood '97
Magenta '96
The O.J. Simpson Story '94

Jurgen Knieper
The Promise '94
The Blonde '92
December Bride '91
Wings of Desire '88
River's Edge '87
Germany, Pale Mother '80
The American Friend '77
The Goalie's Anxiety at the Penalty Kick '71

Mark Knopfler
Metroland '97
Wag the Dog '97
The Princess Bride '87
Cal '84
Comfort and Joy '84
Local Hero '83

Krzysztof Komeda
Rosemary's Baby '68
The Fearless Vampire Killers '67
Knife in the Water '62
Innocent Sorcerers '60
The Dybbuk '37

Robbie Kondor
The Suburbans '99
Happiness '98

Joseph Koo
Fist of Legend '94
A Better Tomorrow, Part 2 '88
Return of the Dragon '73

Rudolph Kopp
Vengeance Valley '51
The Crusades '35
The Sign of the Cross '33

Erich Wolfgang Korngold
Kings Row '41
The Adventures of Robin Hood '38
The Prince and the Pauper '37
Anthony Adverse '36
Captain Blood '35

Mark Korven
Cube '98
Curtis's Charm '96
I've Heard the Mermaids Singing '87

Andrezej Korzynski
Man of Iron '81
Possession '81
Man of Marble '76

Richard Kosinski
Bloodstorm: Subspecies 4 '98
Magic in the Mirror: Fowl Play '96
Spellbreaker: Secret of the Leprechauns '96
Vampire Journals '96

Joseph Kosma (1905-69)
The Testament of Dr. Cordelier '59
Children of Paradise '44
Grand Illusion '37
The Crime of Monsieur Lange '36

Irwin Kostal
Pete's Dragon '77
Charlotte's Web '73

Robert Kraft
The Mambo Kings '92
Hudson Hawk '91

Raoul Kraushaar (1908-2001)
Billy the Kid Versus Dracula '66
Jesse James Meets Frankenstein's Daughter '65
Invaders from Mars '53

Amanda Kravat
Wirey Spindell '99
Fall '97
If Lucy Fell '95

Jan Krenz
Ashes and Diamonds '58
Kanal '56

Milan Kymlicka
Requiem for Murder '99
Dead End '98
Little Men '98
Sir Arthur Conan Doyle's The Lost World '98
Sci-Fighters '96
Margaret's Museum '95
The Paperboy '94

Francis Lai (1932-)
Les Miserables '95
Marie '85
My New Partner '84
Cat and Mouse '78
Emmanuelle, the Joys of a Woman '76
Love Story '70
Mayerling '68
I'll Never Forget What's 'Isname '67
A Man and a Woman '66

Russ Landau
Killer Bud '00
Love and Action in Chicago '99
Nowhere Land '98
Telling You '98

Burton Lane (1912-97)
Royal Wedding '51
College Swing '38
Dancing Lady '33

Robert Lane
Breathtaking '00
David Copperfield '99
The Young Poisoner's Handbook '94

Jim Lang
In the Mouth of Madness '95
Body Bags '93

Arthur Lange
Along Came Jones '45
Casanova Brown '44
Woman in the Window '44

Brian Langsbard
The Specials '00
Johnny Skidmarks '97

Daniel Lanois
The Million Dollar Hotel '99
Sling Blade '96
Camilla '94

Tito Larriva
Just a Little Harmless Sex '99
Dream with the Fishes '97
Repo Man '83

Nathan Larsen
Tigerland '00
Boys Don't Cry '99

Jeff Lass
Partners '99
Matter of Trust '98
Laws of Deception '97
The Student Affair '97
Hard Vice '94
DaVinci's War '92

Alexander Laszlo
Atomic Submarine '59
Attack of the Giant Leeches '59
Night of the Blood Beast '58

Angelo Francesco Lavagnino
Chimes at Midnight '67
Gorgo '61
Esther and the King '60
Othello '52

Raul Lavista
Simon of the Desert '66
The Exterminating Angel '62
Daniel Boone: Trail Blazer '56

David Lawrence
National Lampoon's Van Wilder '02
American Pie 2 '01
Life Without Dick '01
Company Man '00
American Pie '99
Hi-Life '98
Steel Sharks '97
Moving Target '96
Alone in the Woods '95
Sleep with Me '94
Skeeter '93

Maury Laws
The Return of the King '80
The Hobbit '78

Bill Lee
Mo' Better Blues '90
Do the Right Thing '89
School Daze '88
She's Gotta Have It '86

Michel Legrand (1932-)
La Buche '00
Madeline '98
Ready to Wear '94
The Pickle '93
Dingo '90
Switching Channels '88
Never Say Never Again '83
Yentl '83
Atlantic City '81
Falling in Love Again '80
The Mountain Men '80
Roads to the South '78
It's Good to Be Alive '74
The Three Musketeers '74
Brian's Song '71
The Go-Between '71
Summer of '42 '71
Donkey Skin '70
Wuthering Heights '70
Ice Station Zebra '68
Sweet November '68
The Young Girls of Rochefort '68
Band of Outsiders '64
Umbrellas of Cherbourg '64
Eva '62
My Life to Live '62
Cleo from 5 to 7 '61
A Woman Is a Woman '60

Franz Lehar
The Merry Widow '52
The Merry Widow '34

Jed Leiber
Blue Chips '94
Love Potion #9 '92

Christopher Lennertz
Undercurrent '99
Art House '98
Running Woman '98
Baby Face Nelson '97
Humanoids from the Deep '96
Spectre '96
Piranha '95
Suspect Device '95
Unknown Origin '95
Midnight Tease '94

John Lennon (1940-80)
Le Bal '82
Let It Be '70
Yellow Submarine '68
Magical Mystery Tour '67
Help! '65
A Hard Day's Night '64

Patrick Leonard
With Honors '94
Timebomb '91
At Close Range '86
Nothing in Common '86

Cory Lerios
Boiling Point '93
Beyond the Law '92
Child's Play 3 '91
One Crazy Summer '86

Alan Jay Lerner
The Little Prince '74
Paint Your Wagon '69
Camelot '67
My Fair Lady '64
Brigadoon '54

Oscar Levant (1906-72)
Nothing Sacred '37
In Person '35

Sylvester Levay
Flashfire '94
Dead to Rights '93
Hot Shots! '91
Stone Cold '91
Navy SEALS '90
Courage Mountain '89
The Tracker '88
Burglar '87
Mannequin '87
Cobra '86
Howard the Duck '86
Invaders from Mars '86
Creator '85

Geoff Levin
Extreme Honor '01
Jimmy Zip '00
Gang Boys '97

Krishna Levy
Artemisia '97
My Sex Life...Or How I Got into an Argument '96

Louis Levy
The Lady Vanishes '38
Young and Innocent '37
The Secret Agent '36
The 39 Steps '35

Shuki Levy
Turbo: A Power Rangers Movie '96
Blindfold: Acts of Obsession '94
Trapper County War '89

Herschell Gordon Lewis (1926-)
This Stuff'll Kill Ya! '71
Moonshine Mountain '64
2000 Maniacs '64
Blood Feast '63

Michael Lewis (1939-)
Deadly Target '94
The Hound of the Baskervilles '83
Theatre of Blood '73
The Man Who Haunted Himself '70

Michael W. Lewis
Hot Child in the City '87
Ballad of Gregorio Cortez '83
Revenge of the Ninja '83
Shogun Assassin '80
New Year's Evil '78

Blake Leyh
Outside the Law '95
True Crime '95

Daniel Licht
Soul Survivors '01
Cabin by the Lake '00
Hendrix '00
Splendor '99
Permanent Midnight '98
Bad Moon '96
Stephen King's Thinner '96
The Winner '96
Children of the Corn 3: Urban Harvest '95
Hellraiser 4: Bloodline '95
Woman Undone '95
Acting on Impulse '93
H.P. Lovecraft's Necronomicon: Book of the Dead '93
Final Embrace '92

Jimmy Lifton
Mirror, Mirror 2: Raven Dance '94
The Takeover '94
Mirror, Mirror '90

Joseph J. Lilley
How to Commit Marriage '69
Paradise, Hawaiian Style '66
Who's Minding the Store? '63
Girls! Girls! Girls! '62

Hal Lindes
Forgive and Forget '99
Gunshy '98
Band of Gold '95
The Infiltrator '95

Mort Lindsey (1923-)
Real Life '79
40 Pounds of Trouble '62

Michael Linn (-1995)
Snapdragon '93
American Ninja '85

Michael Lipton
Heroes of the Heart '94
Invasion of the Space Preachers '90

Alan Lisk
Tess of the D'Urbervilles '98
R.P.M. '97

Zdenek Liska
Murder Czech Style '66
The Shop on Main Street '65
Fabulous Adventures of Baron Munchausen '61

Jay Livingston (1915-2001)
Red Garters '54
The Lemon Drop Kid '51

Andrew Lloyd Webber
Jesus Christ Superstar '00
Joseph and the Amazing Technicolor Dreamcoat '00
Evita '96
The Odessa File '74
Jesus Christ, Superstar '73
Gumshoe '72

Lowell Lo
Naked Killer '92
Prison on Fire 2 '91
The Killer '90
Prison on Fire '87

Brian Lock
The Land Girls '98
The Gambler '97

Robert Lockhart
Vicious Circles '97
Cold Comfort Farm '94

Joseph LoDuca
Brotherhood of the Wolf '01
Young Hercules '97
Hercules the Legendary Journeys, Vol. 1: And the Amazon Women '94
Hercules the Legendary Journeys, Vol. 2: The Lost Kingdom '94
Hercules the Legendary Journeys, Vol. 3: The Circle of Fire '94
Hercules the Legendary Journeys, Vol. 4: In the Underworld '94
H.P. Lovecraft's Necronomicon: Book of the Dead '93
Army of Darkness '92
Lunatics: A Love Story '92
The Carrier '87
Evil Dead 2: Dead by Dawn '87
Thou Shalt Not Kill...Except '87
Crimewave '85
Evil Dead '83

Frank Loesser
How to Succeed in Business without Really Trying '67
Guys and Dolls '55
Hans Christian Andersen '52
The Perils of Pauline '47
Hoppity Goes to Town '41
College Swing '38

Frederick Loewe
The Little Prince '74
Paint Your Wagon '69
Camelot '67
My Fair Lady '64
Gigi '58
Brigadoon '54

Frank London
A Brother's Kiss '97
Everything Relative '96

William Loose
Johnny Firecloud '75
Supervixens '75
The Swinging Cheerleaders '74
Blacksnake! '73
The Big Bird Cage '72
Rebel Rousers '69
Mission to Death '66

Alexina Louie
The Five Senses '99
Last Night '98
Jacques Loussier
Dark of the Sun '68
Life Upside Down '64
Mundell Lowe
Everything You Always Wanted to Know about Sex (But Were Afraid to Ask) '72
Billy Jack '71
Satan in High Heels '61
Richard Lowry
Mommy 2: Mommy's Day '96
Mommy '95
Marcos Loya
... And the Earth Did Not Swallow Him '94
Hostile Intentions '94
John Lunn
Lorna Doone '01
Get Real '99
Immortality '98
Donal Lunny
This Is My Father '99
Eat the Peach '86
Evan Lurie
Lisa Picard Is Famous '01
Happy Accidents '00
Joe Gould's Secret '00
Office Killer '97
The Monster '96
Tree's Lounge '96
The Night We Never Met '93
Johnny Stecchino '92
John Lurie (1952-)
Animal Factory '00
Clay Pigeons '98
Excess Baggage '96
Manny & Lo '96
Get Shorty '95
Mystery Train '89
Down by Law '86
Permanent Vacation '84
Stranger than Paradise '84
Variety '83
Elisabeth Lutyens
Dr. Terror's House of Horrors '65
Paranoiac '62
Allen Lynch
Mosquito '95
Rain Without Thunder '93
Randall Lynch
Mosquito '95
Rain Without Thunder '93
Egisto Macchi
The Rose Garden '89
Diary of a Mad Old Man '88
Padre Padrone '77
Mr. Klein '76
Neil MacColl
24-7 '97
Fever Pitch '96
Galt MacDermot
Mistress '91
Hair '79
Cotton Comes to Harlem '70
Mader
Steal This Movie! '00
Eat Drink Man Woman '94
In the Soup '92
Michel Magne
Cold Sweat '71
Any Number Can Win '63
Gustav Mahler
Death in Venice '71
Honeymoon Killers '70
Stefano Mainetti
Silent Trigger '97
Sub Down '97
Sons of Trinity '95
Hidden Assassin '94
Hans-Martin Majewski
Brainwashed '60
The Bridge '59
Nikos Mamangakis
Kaspar Hauser '93
Heimat 1 '84
Bob Mamet
Aftershock '88
Necromancer: Satan's Servant '88
Mark Mancina
Domestic Disturbance '01
Training Day '01
Bait '00
Beyond Suspicion '00
From the Earth to the Moon '98
Return to Paradise '98
Con Air '97
Speed 2: Cruise Control '97
Moll Flanders '96
Twister '96
Assassins '95
Bad Boys '95
Fair Game '95
Man of the House '95
Money Train '95
Monkey Trouble '94
Speed '94
True Romance '93
Henry Mancini (1924-94)
Married to It '93
Son of the Pink Panther '93
Tom and Jerry: The Movie '93
Never Forget '91
Switch '91
Fear '90
Ghost Dad '90
Peter Gunn '89
Physical Evidence '89
Skin Deep '89
Welcome Home '89
Sunset '88
Without a Clue '88
Blind Date '87
The Glass Menagerie '87
A Fine Mess '86
The Great Mouse Detective '86
That's Life! '86
Lifeforce '85
Santa Claus: The Movie '85
That's Dancing! '85
Harry & Son '84
Better Late Than Never '83
Curse of the Pink Panther '83
The Man Who Loved Women '83
Second Thoughts '83
The Thorn Birds '83
Trail of the Pink Panther '82
Victor/Victoria '82
Back Roads '81
Condorman '81
Mommie Dearest '81
S.O.B. '81
A Change of Seasons '80
Little Miss Marker '80
The Shadow Box '80
Nightwing '79
Prisoner of Zenda '79
10 '79
Family Upside Down '78
House Calls '78
Revenge of the Pink Panther '78
Who Is Killing the Great Chefs of Europe? '78
Angela '77
The Pink Panther Strikes Again '76
Silver Streak '76
The Great Waldo Pepper '75
Once Is Not Enough '75
The White Dawn '75
The Girl from Petrovka '74
99 & 44/100 Dead '74
Return of the Pink Panther '74
That's Entertainment '74
Oklahoma Crude '73
The Thief Who Came to Dinner '73
Sometimes a Great Notion '71
Darling Lili '70
Molly Maguires '70
The Night Visitor '70
Bachelor in Paradise '69
The Party '68
Two for the Road '67
Wait until Dark '67
Arabesque '66
Moment to Moment '66
What Did You Do in the War, Daddy? '66
The Great Race '65
The Pink Panther '64
A Shot in the Dark '64
Charade '63
King Kong vs. Godzilla '63
Man's Favorite Sport? '63
Soldier in the Rain '63
Days of Wine and Roses '62
Experiment in Terror '62
Hatari! '62
Mr. Hobbs Takes a Vacation '62
Breakfast at Tiffany's '61
The Great Impostor '61
Never Steal Anything Small '59
Touch of Evil '58
The Land Unknown '57
The Creature Walks among Us '56
Rock, Pretty Baby '56
The Benny Goodman Story '55
Far Country '55
To Hell and Back '55
Creature from the Black Lagoon '54
The Glenn Miller Story '54
It Came from Outer Space '53
Horizons West '52
Lost in Alaska '52
Johnny Mandel
Brenda Starr '86
Deathtrap '82
The Verdict '82
Caddyshack '80
Being There '79
The Last Detail '73
M*A*S*H '70
Harper '66
I Want to Live! '58
Harry Manfredini
Hell's Gate '01
Jason X '01
The Omega Code '99
Catherine's Grove '98
A Gun, a Car, a Blonde '97
Raven '97
Wishmaster '97
Dead on Sight '94
Jason Goes to Hell: The Final Friday '93
Deepstar Six '89
Friday the 13th, Part 6: Jason Lives '86
House '86
Swamp Thing '82
Friday the 13th, Part 2 '81
Friday the 13th '80
Barry Manilow
The Pebble and the Penguin '94
Thumbelina '94
Hummie Mann
Meat Loaf: To Hell and Back '00
Thomas and the Magic Railroad '00
Naked City: A Killer Christmas '98
Rescuers: Stories of Courage—Two Couples '98
Rescuers: Stories of Courage "Two Women" '97
The Second Civil War '97
Sticks and Stones '96
Dracula: Dead and Loving It '95
Fall Time '94
Girls in Prison '94
Jailbreakers '94
Benefit of the Doubt '93
Robin Hood: Men in Tights '93
Year of the Comet '92
In Gold We Trust '91
Stoogemania '85
Franco Mannino
Conversation Piece '75
Driver's Seat '73
The Ghost '63
Beat the Devil '53
Clint Mansell
Murder by Numbers '02
World Traveler '01
Requiem for a Dream '00
Pi '98
David Mansfield
A Good Baby '99
Songcatcher '99
Dark Harbor '98
Road Ends '98
Tumbleweeds '98
The Apostle '97
Floating '97
Deep Crimson '96
A Streetcar Named Desire '95
Truman '95
The Ballad of Little Jo '93
Me & Veronica '93
Desperate Hours '90
Miss Firecracker '89
The Sicilian '87
Club Paradise '86
Jim Manzie
Blood Surf '00
Night of the Scarecrow '95
Lurking Fear '94
Night of the Demons 2 '94
Leatherface: The Texas Chainsaw Massacre 3 '89
Dario Marianelli
Pandaemonium '00
I Went Down '97
Mariano Marin
Open Your Eyes '97
Thesis '96
Anthony Marinelli
Lone Hero '02
15 Minutes '01
Just One Night '00
Slow Burn '00
Time Code '00
God Said "Ha!" '99
The Runner '99
Hoods '98
Scarred City '98
Don King: Only in America '97
Sink or Swim '97
Flynn '96
Masterminds '96
Two Days in the Valley '96
Underworld '96
One Man's Justice '95
Young Guns '88
Richard Markowitz
The Shooting '66
A Face in the Rain '63
Rick Marotta
Just the Ticket '98
Painted Hero '95
The Cover Girl Murders '93
Branford Marsalis
3 A.M. '01
Once in the Life '00
Mr. & Mrs. Loving '96
Sneakers '92
Mo' Better Blues '90
Jeff Marsh
Inferno '01
Wind River '98
Jack Marshall
Munster, Go Home! '66
The Giant Gila Monster '59
Thunder Road '58
Phil Marshall
Kiss Toledo Goodbye '00
Trial by Media '00
Rupert's Land '98
Trial and Error '96
Kicking and Screaming '95
Noises Off '92
Full Moon in Blue Water '88
Philip Martell
Dr. Jekyll and Sister Hyde '71
The Anniversary '68
George Martin
Live and Let Die '73
Yellow Submarine '68
Help! '65
A Hard Day's Night '64
Hugh Martin
Athena '54
Good News '47
Cliff Martinez
Traffic '00
The Limey '99
Out of Sight '98
The Underneath '95
King of the Hill '93
Kafka '91
Pump Up the Volume '90
sex, lies and videotape '89
Rick Marvin
Brian's Song '01
Lost Battalion '01
U-571 '00
Dead Men Can't Dance '97
Escape Clause '96
Galgameth '96
3 Ninjas Kick Back '94
Save Me '93
Interceptor '92
3 Ninjas '92
Bill Marx
Count Yorga, Vampire '70
Hollywood after Dark '65
Harvey W. Mason
Deadly Outbreak '96
Only the Strong '93
Roger Mason
Dead Letter Office '98
Joey '98
Crime Broker '94
John Massari
Retro Puppet Master '99
Redemption: Kickboxer 5 '95
The Big Sweat '90
Killer Klowns from Outer Space '88
The Wizard of Speed and Time '88
Michael Masser
Stir Crazy '80
The Greatest '77
Muir Mathieson
Circus of Horrors '60
This Happy Breed '47
The Challenge '38
Sasha Matson
Red Surf '90
Bloodfist '89
Lobster Man from Mars '89
Daddy's Boys '87
Stuart Matthewman
Jackpot '01
Twin Falls Idaho '99
Peter Matz
Stepping Out '91
Torch Song Trilogy '88
Lust in the Dust '85
The Private Eyes '80
In This House of Brede '75
Billy May
The Front Page '74
The Ballad of Andy Crocker '69
Tony Rome '67
Brian May (1934-97)
Dr. Giggles '92
Bloodmoon '90
Darlings of the Gods '90
Death Before Dishonor '87
Steel Dawn '87
Cloak & Dagger '84
Stage Fright '83
Treasure of the Yankee Zephyr '83
The Road Warrior '82
Escape 2000 '81
Gallipoli '81
Killing of Angel Street '81
Road Games '81
Mad Max '80
Survivor '80
Patrick '78
Daniel May
Chopper Chicks in Zombietown '91
Zombie High '87
Curtis Mayfield (1942-99)
Return of Superfly '90
Piece of the Action '77
Sparkle '76
Superfly '72
Toshiro Mayuzumi
The Bible '66
Good Morning '59
John McCallum (1917-)
Grizzly Mountain '97
Little Heroes '91
Project: Eliminator '91
Soultaker '90
Surf Nazis Must Die '87
Dennis McCarthy
Alien Fury: Countdown to Invasion '00
In His Life: The John Lennon Story '00
Letters from a Killer '98
Breast Men '97
McHale's Navy '97
Star Trek: Generations '94
John McCarthy
Soul Survivor '95
Paris, France '94
Paul McCartney (1942-)
Le Bal '82
Let It Be '70
Yellow Submarine '68
Magical Mystery Tour '67
Help! '65
A Hard Day's Night '64
John McCulloch
The Twilight of the Ice Nymphs '97
Careful '92
Garry McDonald (1948-)
Dr. Jekyll & Mr. Hyde '99
Official Denial '93
Bill McGuffie
The Asphyx '72
It Takes a Thief '59
David McHugh
Changing Habits '96
The Hidden 2 '94
Tales of Erotica '93
Daddy's Dyin'...Who's Got the Will? '90
The Dream Team '89
Three Fugitives '89
Mr. North '88
Mystic Pizza '88
Moscow on the Hudson '84
Tim McIntire (1943-86)
The Killer Inside Me '76
A Boy and His Dog '75
Michael McKean (1947-)
Waiting for Guffman '96
This Is Spinal Tap '84
Mark McKenzie
The Lost Child '00
Durango '99
The Disappearance of Garcia Lorca '96
Dr. Jekyll and Ms. Hyde '95
Frank and Jesse '94
My Family '94
Warlock: The Armageddon '93
Stephen McKeon
Falling for a Dancer '98
The Nephew '97
Robert F. McNaughton
Ed Gein '01
Henry: Portrait of a Serial Killer 2: Mask of Sanity '96
Henry: Portrait of a Serial Killer '90
Joel McNeely
Return to Never Land '02
Sally Hemings: An American Scandal '00
Lover's Prayer '99
The Avengers '98
Soldier '98
Virus '98
Zack & Reba '98
Buffalo Soldiers '97
Wild America '97
Flipper '96
Vegas Vacation '96
Gold Diggers: The Secret of Bear Mountain '95
Radioland Murders '94
Squanto: A Warrior's Tale '94
Terminal Velocity '94

Iron Will '93
Supercop '92

James McVay
Snap Decision '01
Desert Winds '95

Gil Melle
Blood Beach '81
Gold of the Amazon Women '79
Embryo '76
The Sentinel '76
Housewife '72
You'll Like My Mother '72
The Andromeda Strain '71
The Organization '71

Peter Melnick
Mermaid '00
The Only Thrill '97
Lily Dale '96
Indictment: The McMartin Trial '95
Arctic Blue '93
L.A. Story '91

Michael Melvoin
Bloodsucking Pharoahs of Pittsburgh '90
Big Town '87

Wendy Melvoin
Foolish '99
Hav Plenty '97
Soul Food '97

Alan Menken (1949-)
Hercules '97
The Hunchback of Notre Dame '96
Pocahontas '95
Life with Mikey '93
Aladdin '92
Newsies '92
Beauty and the Beast '91
The Little Mermaid '89
Little Shop of Horrors '86

Johnny Mercer
Last Summer In the Hamptons '96
Darling Lili '70
Days of Wine and Roses '62
Li'l Abner '59
Dangerous When Wet '53
The Harvey Girls '46
You Were Never Lovelier '42

Wim Mertens
Molokai: The Story of Father Damien '99
Fiesta '95
The Belly of an Architect '91

Pat Metheny
A Map of the World '99
The Falcon and the Snowman '85

Michel Michelet
The Indian Tomb '59
Impact '49
Outpost in Morocco '49
Lured '47

Cynthia Millar
Brown's Requiem '98
Digging to China '98
The Run of the Country '95
Three Wishes '95

Marcus Miller (1959-)
The Trumpet of the Swan '01
Two Can Play That Game '01
The Ladies Man '00
The Sixth Man '97
The Great White Hype '96
Above the Rim '94
House Party '90
Siesta '87

Randy Miller
Hitched '01
Family Tree '00
Living in Peril '97
Without Limits '97
Darkman 3: Die Darkman Die '95
Darkman 2: The Return of Durant '94
And You Thought Your Parents Were Weird! '91
Black Magic Woman '91
Witchcraft '88

Don Miller-Robinson
Risk '00
Erskinville Kings '99

Mario Millo
Wrangler '88
The Lighthorsemen '87

Paul Misraki (1908-98)
Alphaville '65
Your Turn Darling '63
Les Bonnes Femmes '60
And God Created Woman '57
Death in the Garden '56
Plucking the Daisy '56
Crazy for Love '52
Utopia '51

Bob Mithoff
Class of Nuke 'Em High 3: The Good, the Bad and the Subhumanoid '94
Sgt. Kabukiman N.Y.P.D. '94
Seedpeople '92
Class of Nuke 'Em High 2: Subhumanoid Meltdown '91

Vic Mizzy
The Munsters' Revenge '81
How to Frame a Figg '71
The Love God? '70
The Reluctant Astronaut '67
The Ghost and Mr. Chicken '66

Cyril Mockridge
Donovan's Reef '63
The Man Who Shot Liberty Valance '62
Flaming Star '60
Will Success Spoil Rock Hunter? '57
Bus Stop '56
Solid Gold Cadillac '56
River of No Return '54
Cheaper by the Dozen '50
Come to the Stable '49
I Was a Male War Bride '49
Miracle on 34th Street '47
My Darling Clementine '46
The Ox-Bow Incident '43
The Fighting Sullivans '42

Mark Moffatt
Back of Beyond '95
High Tide '87

Charlie Mole
The Importance of Being Earnest '02
High Heels and Low Lifes '01
An Ideal Husband '99
Othello '95

Fred Mollin
Inferno '99
Thrill Seekers '99
The Abduction '96

Hugo Montenegro
Too Hot to Handle '76
Charro! '69
The Wrecking Crew '68
The Ambushers '67

Michael Montes
Whipped '00
Firehouse '87
Hangmen '87

Osvaldo Montes
A Shadow You Soon Will Be '94
The Dark Side of the Heart '92

Guy Moon
These Old Broads '01
A Very Brady Sequel '96
The Brady Bunch Movie '95
Diving In '90
Sorority Babes in the Slimeball Bowl-A-Rama '87
Wild Thing '87

Hal Mooney
Bull of the West '89
The Meanest Men in the West '76
Raid on Rommel '71

Dudley Moore (1935-2002)
Six Weeks '82
The Hound of the Baskervilles '77
Bedazzled '68
30 Is a Dangerous Age, Cynthia '68

Mike Moran
Bloodbath at the House of Death '85
Time Bandits '81

Lucien Moraweck
International Lady '41
The Man in the Iron Mask '39

Patrick Moraz
The Stepfather '87
La Salamandre '71

Giorgio Moroder
Fair Game '89
Let It Ride '89
The NeverEnding Story '84
Flashdance '83
Scarface '83
Cat People '82
American Gigolo '79
Midnight Express '78

Jerome Moross
The Valley of Gwangi '69
The Big Country '58
Proud Rebel '58

Andrea Morricone
Here on Earth '00
Liberty Heights '99

Ennio Morricone (1928-)
Malena '00
Mission to Mars '00
Vatel '00
Bulworth '98
The Legend of 1900 '98
The Phantom of the Opera '98
Lolita '97
U-Turn '97
Nostromo '96
The Star Maker '95
The Stendahl Syndrome '95
Disclosure '94
La Scorta '94
Love Affair '94
The Night and the Moment '94
A Pure Formality '94
Wolf '94
The Bachelor '93
In the Line of Fire '93
Beyond Justice '92
City of Joy '92
The Big Man: Crossing the Line '91
Bugsy '91
Husbands and Lovers '91
A Time to Die '91
Everybody's Fine '90
State of Grace '90
Tie Me Up! Tie Me Down! '90
Casualties of War '89
The Endless Game '89
Fat Man and Little Boy '89
Time to Kill '89
Cinema Paradiso '88
Frantic '88
Python Wolf '88
A Time of Destiny '88
Rampage '87
The Untouchables '87
La Cage aux Folles 3: The Wedding '86
The Mission '86
Stalking Danger '86
Hundra '85
Red Sonja '85
Corrupt '84
Once Upon a Time in America '84
Fatal Error '83
Sahara '83
The Scarlet & the Black '83
Time to Die '83
Butterfly '82
Nana '82
The Thing '82
Treasure of the Four Crowns '82
La Cage aux Folles 2 '81
Le Professionnel '81
Lovers and Liars '81
So Fine '81
The Tragedy of a Ridiculous Man '81
The Island '80
Windows '80
Almost Human '79
Sidney Sheldon's Bloodline '79
Days of Heaven '78
La Cage aux Folles '78
The Chosen '77
The Exorcist 2: The Heretic '77
Orca '77
The Desert of the Tartars '76
The Inheritance '76
Moses '76
The Human Factor '75
Leonor '75
Salo, or the 120 Days of Sodom '75
When Women Lost Their Tails '75
Arabian Nights '74
Autopsy '74
La Grande Bourgeoise '74
Le Secret '74
Master Touch '74
My Name Is Nobody '74
The Tempter '74
Allonsanfan '73
Massacre in Rome '73
Night Flight from Moscow '73
Sonny and Jed '73
'Tis a Pity She's a Whore '73
Bluebeard '72
A Fistful of Dynamite '72
The Canterbury Tales '71
The Cat o' Nine Tails '71
Dirty Heroes '71
Divine Nymph '71
Sacco & Vanzetti '71
The Bird with the Crystal Plumage '70
Burn! '70
Cold Eyes of Fear '70
Companeros '70
The Decameron '70
Two Mules for Sister Sara '70
When Women Had Tails '70
Red Tent '69
Danger: Diabolik '68
Once Upon a Time in the West '68
Partner '68
Teorema '68
The Good, the Bad and the Ugly '67
The Hawks & the Sparrows '67
Hellbenders '67
Navajo Joe '67
The Rover '67
Secret Agent 00 '67
The Battle of Algiers '66
Before the Revolution '65
For a Few Dollars More '65
Nightmare Castle '65
A Fistful of Dollars '64
Gun Fight at Red Sands '63

John Morris
The Lady in Question '99
Murder in a Small Town '99
Only Love '98
Ellen Foster '97
Scarlett '94
Carolina Skeletons '92
Dirty Dancing '87
Ironweed '87
Spaceballs '87
Clue '85
The Doctor and the Devils '85
The Woman in Red '84
Yellowbeard '83
The Elephant Man '80
In God We Trust '80
The In-Laws '79
The Scarlet Letter '79
Blazing Saddles '74
Young Frankenstein '74
The Twelve Chairs '70
The Producers '68

Van Morrison
Beyond the Clouds '95
Moondance '95
Lamb '85

Boris Morros
The Big Broadcast of 1938 '38
College Swing '38
You and Me '38
Easy Living '37

Thomas Morse
The Big Brass Ring '99
The Apostate '98
If I Die Before I Wake '98

Mark Mothersbaugh (1950-)
Sorority Boys '02
The Royal Tenenbaums '01
Sugar & Spice '01
The Adventures of Rocky & Bullwinkle '00
Rugrats in Paris: The Movie '00
Drop Dead Gorgeous '99
It's the Rage '99
Best Men '98
Bongwater '98
Quicksilver Highway '98
The Rugrats Movie '98
Rushmore '98
200 Cigarettes '98
Breaking Up '97
Dead Man on Campus '97
Men '97
The Big Squeeze '96
Happy Gilmore '96
The Last Supper '96
The Birdcage '95
Bottle Rocket '95
Revenge of the Nerds 2: Nerds in Paradise '87

William Motzig
Young Einstein '89
The Coca-Cola Kid '84
Return of Captain Invincible '83

Rob Mounsey
Dangerous Passion '95
Working Girl '88

Michael Muhlfriedel
St. Patrick's Day '99
Plump Fiction '97

Dominic Muldowney
King Lear '98
Sharpe's Eagle '93
Sharpe's Rifles '93

Gerry Mulligan (1927-96)
I'm Not Rappaport '96
The Final Programme '73

John Murphy
All About the Benjamins '02
New Best Friend '02
Liam '00
Snatch '00
The Bachelor '99
Lock, Stock and 2 Smoking Barrels '98
The Real Howard Spitz '98
Stiff Upper Lips '96
Solitaire for 2 '94

Lyn Murray
Snow White and the Three Stooges '61
The Bridges at Toko-Ri '55
Prowler '51

Michel Musseau
After Sex '97
Celestial Clockwork '94

Stanley Myers (1939-93)
The Summer House '94
Heart of Darkness '93
Sarafina! '92
Iron Maze '91
A Murder of Quality '90
Rosencrantz & Guildenstern Are Dead '90
The Witches '90
Christabel '89
Paperhouse '89
Scenes from the Class Struggle in Beverly Hills '89
Castaway '87
Prick Up Your Ears '87
Sammy & Rosie Get Laid '87
The Wind '87
Wish You Were Here '87
Zero Boys '86
Dreamchild '85
My Beautiful Laundrette '85
Incubus '82
Absolution '81
The Watcher in the Woods '81
The Deer Hunter '78
House of Whipcord '75
Frightmare '74
Ulysses '67

Fredric Myrow (1940-99)
Plan 10 from Outer Space '95
Phantasm '79
Soylent Green '73

Mario Nascimbene
The Messiah '75
Commandos '73
The Vengeance of She '68
Barabbas '62
The Girl with a Suitcase '60
Room at the Top '59
The Vikings '58
Love in the City '53

Lou Natale
The Man in the Attic '94
Snowbound: The Jim and Jennifer Stolpa Story '94

Miki Navazio
The Sticky Fingers of Time '97
All Over Me '96

Chris Neal
Jack Be Nimble '94
Around the World in 80 Ways '86

Roger Neill
Trixie '00
Chameleon 2: Death Match '99
Boltneck '98
The Taxman '98
Mercenary '96
Savage '96
An American Summer '90

Willie Nelson (1933-)
Stagecoach '86
1918 '85
Ruckus '81
Honeysuckle Rose '80

John Neschling
Kiss of the Spider Woman '85
Pixote '81

Michael Nesmith (1942-)
Timerider '83
Northville Cemetery Massacre '76

Eric Neveux
Of Freaks and Men '98
Sitcom '97

Ira Newborn
Bad Manners '98
BASEketball '98
High School High '96
The Late Shift '96
Mallrats '95
Naked Gun 33 1/3: The Final Insult '94
Ace Ventura: Pet Detective '93
The Opposite Sex and How to Live With Them '93
Brain Donors '92
Innocent Blood '92
Naked Gun 2 1/2: The Smell of Fear '91
My Blue Heaven '90
Short Time '90
Cast the First Stone '89
Uncle Buck '89
Caddyshack 2 '88
The Naked Gun: From the Files of Police Squad '88
Amazon Women on the Moon '87
Dragnet '87
Planes, Trains & Automobiles '87
Ferris Bueller's Day Off '86
Wise Guys '86
Into the Night '85

Weird Science '85
Sixteen Candles '84
All Night Long '81
The Blues Brothers '80

Alfred Newman
December 7th: The Movie '91
Airport '70
Nevada Smith '66
The Greatest Story Ever Told '65
The Man Who Shot Liberty Valance '62
The Best of Everything '59
Bus Stop '56
Love Is a Many-Splendored Thing '55
The Seven Year Itch '55
There's No Business Like Show Business '54
How to Marry a Millionaire '53
All About Eve '50
No Way Out '50
A Letter to Three Wives '49
Pinky '49
Twelve o'Clock High '49
Call Northside 777 '48
The Snake Pit '48
Captain from Castile '47
Gentleman's Agreement '47
Mother Wore Tights '47
The Razor's Edge '46
Leave Her to Heaven '45
A Tree Grows in Brooklyn '45
Wilson '44
The Song of Bernadette '43
The Black Swan '42
The Fighting Sullivans '42
Roxie Hart '42
Son of Fury '42
Ball of Fire '41
Blood and Sand '41
How Green Was My Valley '41
Week-End in Havana '41
Foreign Correspondent '40
The Mark of Zorro '40
Tin Pan Alley '40
Beau Geste '39
Gunga Din '39
The Hunchback of Notre Dame '39
The Rains Came '39
The Real Glory '39
Stanley and Livingstone '39
Wuthering Heights '39
Dead End '37
The Hurricane '37
Stella Dallas '37
Come and Get It '36
Dodsworth '36
The Gay Desperado '36
These Three '36
Les Miserables '35
The Count of Monte Cristo '34
Mr. Robinson Crusoe '32
Rain '32
City Lights '31
Street Scene '31
Tonight or Never '31

David Newman (1954-)
Death to Smoochy '02
Ice Age '02
Life or Something Like It '02
The Affair of the Necklace '01
Dr. Dolittle 2 '01
The Flamingo Rising '01
Duets '00
The Flintstones in Viva Rock Vegas '00
Nutty Professor 2: The Klumps '00
102 Dalmatians '00
Bowfinger '99
Brokedown Palace '99
Galaxy Quest '99
Never Been Kissed '99
Anastasia '97
Out to Sea '97
Jingle All the Way '96
Matilda '96
The Nutty Professor '96
The Phantom '96
Big Bully '95
Operation Dumbo Drop '95
Tommy Boy '95
The Air Up There '94
Boys on the Side '94
The Cowboy Way '94
The Flintstones '94
I Love Trouble '94
Coneheads '93
My Father the Hero '93
The Sandlot '93
Undercover Blues '93
Hoffa '92
Honeymoon in Vegas '92
The Mighty Ducks '92
Bill & Ted's Bogus Journey '91
Don't Tell Mom the Babysitter's Dead '91
The Marrying Man '91
Other People's Money '91
Paradise '91
Rover Dangerfield '91
The Runestone '91
Talent for the Game '91
DuckTales the Movie: Treasure of the Lost Lamp '90
Fire Birds '90
The Freshman '90
Madhouse '90
The Applegates '89
Bill & Ted's Excellent Adventure '89
Disorganized Crime '89
Gross Anatomy '89
Heathers '89
Little Monsters '89
The War of the Roses '89
The Kindred '87
Malone '87
My Demon Lover '87
Throw Momma from the Train '87
Critters '86
Vendetta '85
Frankenweenie '84

Lionel Newman
Myra Breckinridge '70
The St. Valentine's Day Massacre '67
Let's Make Love '60
The Girl Can't Help It '56
Love Me Tender '56
There's No Business Like Show Business '54
Gentlemen Prefer Blondes '53
Don't Bother to Knock '52

Randy Newman (1943-)
Monsters, Inc. '01
Meet the Parents '00
Toy Story 2 '99
A Bug's Life '98
Pleasantville '98
Cats Don't Dance '97
James and the Giant Peach '96
Michael '96
Toy Story '95
Maverick '94
The Paper '94
Avalon '90
Awakenings '90
Parenthood '89
The Natural '84
Ragtime '81
Cold Turkey '71

Thomas Newman
The Salton Sea '02
In the Bedroom '01
Erin Brockovich '00
Pay It Forward '00
American Beauty '99
The Green Mile '99
Meet Joe Black '98
The Horse Whisperer '97
Mad City '97
Oscar and Lucinda '97
Red Corner '97
The People vs. Larry Flynt '96
Phenomenon '96
Up Close and Personal '96
American Buffalo '95
How to Make an American Quilt '95
Unstrung Heroes '95
Corrina, Corrina '94
Little Women '94
The Shawshank Redemption '94
Threesome '94
The War '94
Flesh and Bone '93
Josh and S.A.M. '93
The Favor '92
The Linguini Incident '92
The Player '92
Scent of a Woman '92
Whispers in the Dark '92
Career Opportunities '91
Deceived '91
Fried Green Tomatoes '91
Naked Tango '91
Cookie '89
Men Don't Leave '89
The Great Outdoors '88
Prince of Pennsylvania '88
Less Than Zero '87
Light of Day '87
The Lost Boys '87
Jumpin' Jack Flash '86
Desperately Seeking Susan '85
Girls Just Want to Have Fun '85
Gung Ho '85
The Man with One Red Shoe '85
Real Genius '85
Grandview U.S.A. '84
Reckless '84
Revenge of the Nerds '84

David Nichtern
Spirit of '76 '91
The Big Picture '89

Lennie Niehaus
Space Cowboys '00
The Jack Bull '99
True Crime '99
Absolute Power '97
Dogwatch '97
The Fixer '97
Midnight in the Garden of Good and Evil '97
Crazy Horse '96
Titanic '96
The Bridges of Madison County '95
A Perfect World '93
Unforgiven '92
White Hunter, Black Heart '90
Bird '88
Heartbreak Ridge '86
Never Too Young to Die '86
Ratboy '86
Pale Rider '85
Sesame Street Presents: Follow That Bird '85
City Heat '84
Tightrope '84

Jose Nieto
Jealousy '99
Passion in the Desert '97
Guantanamera '95
Of Love and Shadows '94
Running Out of Time '94
The Perfect Husband '92
Lovers: A True Story '90

Harry Nilsson (1942-94)
Popeye '80
The Point '71

Stefan Nilsson
Jerusalem '96
The Best Intentions '92
The Inside Man '84

Jack Nitzsche (1937-2000)
The Crossing Guard '94
Blue Sky '91
The Hot Spot '90
The Last of the Finest '90
Mermaids '90
Revenge '90
Next of Kin '89
The Seventh Sign '88
9 1/2 Weeks '86
Stand by Me '86
Streets of Gold '86
Stripper '86
The Whoopee Boys '86
The Jewel of the Nile '85
The Razor's Edge '84
Starman '84
Windy City '84
Breathless '83
Without a Trace '83
Cannery Row '82
An Officer and a Gentleman '82
Personal Best '82
Cutter's Way '81
Cruising '80
Heart Beat '80
Hardcore '79
Blue Collar '78
Heroes '77
One Flew Over the Cuckoo's Nest '75
The Exorcist '73
Greaser's Palace '72
Performance '70
Village of the Giants '65

Erik Nordgren
The Emigrants '72
The Devil's Eye '60
The Virgin Spring '59
Wild Strawberries '57
The Seventh Seal '56

Per Norgard
Royal Deceit '94
Babette's Feast '87

Alex North
The Last Butterfly '92
The Penitent '88
The Dead '87
Good Morning, Vietnam '87
Death of a Salesman '86
Prizzi's Honor '85
Under the Volcano '84
Dragonslayer '81
Carny '80
Wise Blood '79
The Word '78
Rich Man, Poor Man '76
Bite the Bullet '75
The Passover Plot '75
Journey into Fear '74
Once Upon a Scoundrel '73
Pocket Money '72
Willard '71
A Dream of Kings '69
The Devil's Brigade '68
The Shoes of the Fisherman '68
Who's Afraid of Virginia Woolf? '66
The Agony and the Ecstasy '65
Cheyenne Autumn '64
Cleopatra '63
All Fall Down '62
The Children's Hour '61
The Misfits '61
Spartacus '60
Hot Spell '58
The Long, Hot Summer '58
Stage Struck '57
The Bad Seed '56
The King and Four Queens '56
The Rainmaker '56
Daddy Long Legs '55
I'll Cry Tomorrow '55
The Racers '55
The Rose Tattoo '55
Desiree '54
Les Miserables '52
The Member of the Wedding '52
Viva Zapata! '52
A Streetcar Named Desire '51

Craig Northey
Dog Park '98
Kids in the Hall: Brain Candy '96

Julian Nott
My Mother's Courage '95
A Man of No Importance '94

Michael Nyman
The Claim '00
The End of the Affair '99
Ravenous '99
Wonderland '99
Gattaca '97
The Ogre '96
Carrington '95
Mesmer '94
The Piano '93
The Hairdresser's Husband '92
Prospero's Books '91
The Cook, the Thief, His Wife & Her Lover '90
A Zed & Two Noughts '88
Drowning by Numbers '87
Cold Room '84
The Draughtsman's Contract '82

Arlon Ober
Crimewave '85
Eating Raoul '82

Richard O'Brien (1942-)
Return of Captain Invincible '83
Shock Treatment '81
The Rocky Horror Picture Show '75

Oscar Cardozo Ocampo
Deathstalker '83
Funny, Dirty Little War '83

Jacques Offenbach
Peter's Friends '92
The Hotel New Hampshire '84

Patrick O'Hearn
Silent Tongue '92
White Sands '92

William Olvis
Steal Big, Steal Little '95
Separate Lives '94
Red Rock West '93
The Comrades of Summer '92
29th Street '91
El Diablo '90

Norman Orenstein
American Psycho 2: All American Girl '02
Danger Beneath the Sea '02
Prisoner of Love '99
The First 9 1/2 Weeks '98
Sanctuary '98
Mask of Death '97
Downhill Willie '96

Robert G. Orpin
Girls Are for Loving '73
The Abductors '72
Ginger '72

Buxton Orr
First Man into Space '59
Corridors of Blood '58
Fiend without a Face '58
The Haunted Strangler '58

Riz Ortolani
The Best Man '97
The Story of Boys & Girls '91
The New Gladiators '83
Love by Appointment '76
Confessions of a Police Captain '72
Dead Are Alive '72
Don't Torture a Duckling '72
Madron '70
McKenzie Break '70
Anzio '68
Apache's Last Battle '64
Castle of Blood '64
The Seventh Dawn '64
Mondo Cane '63

Jason Osborn
The Triumph of Love '01
High Season '88

Yoshihide Otomo
The Day the Sun Turned Cold '94
Summer Snow '94
The Blue Kite '93

John Ottman
Bubble Boy '01
Urban Legends 2: Final Cut '00
Goodbye, Lover '99
Lake Placid '99
Halloween: H20 '98
Apt Pupil '97
Incognito '97
Snow White: A Tale of Terror '97
The Cable Guy '96
The Usual Suspects '95
Public Access '93

Marc Ouellette
The Sign of Four '01
The Hound of the Baskervilles '00

Gene Page (1940-98)
Blacula '72
Brewster McCloud '70

Jimmy Page
Death Wish 3 '85
Death Wish 2 '82

Alan Parker
Victoria & Albert '01
Britannic '99
Rhodes '97
The Phoenix and the Magic Carpet '95
What's Eating Gilbert Grape '93
American Gothic '88

Clifton Parker
Damn the Defiant '62
Sink the Bismarck '60
Sea of Sand '58
Curse of the Demon '57
Blanche Fury '48

Jim Parker
A Rather English Marriage '98
Moll Flanders '96
The Final Cut '95
Body & Soul '93

Van Dyke Parks
In the Time of the Butterflies '01
Harlan County War '00
Shadrach '98
Oliver Twist '97
Bastard out of Carolina '96
Private Parts '96
The Summer of Ben Tyler '96
One Christmas '95
Wild Bill '95
The Two Jakes '90
Casual Sex? '88
Club Paradise '86

Stephen Parsons
Another 9 1/2 Weeks '96
Split Second '92

Arvo Part
Hamsun '96
Rachel River '87

Shawn Patterson
The Bible and Gun Club '96
The Demolitionist '95

Alex Pauk
The Five Senses '99
Last Night '98

Michael Pavlicek
The Scarlet Pimpernel '99
The Scarlet Pimpernel 2: Mademoiselle Guillotine '99
The Scarlet Pimpernel 3: The Kidnapped King '99

Don Peake
Body Count '95
Hard Justice '95
Solar Force '94
The People under the Stairs '91
The Hills Have Eyes '77

Michael Penn
The Anniversary Party '01
Boogie Nights '97
Hard Eight '96

Alexander Peskanov
Killing Hour '84
He Knows You're Alone '80

Jean-Claude Petit
Beaumarchais the Scoundrel '96
The Horseman on the Roof '95
Foreign Student '94
My Life and Times with Antonin Artaud '93
Lady Chatterley '92
The Playboys '92
Uranus '91
Cyrano de Bergerac '90
Jean de Florette '87
Manon of the Spring '87
L'Addition '85

Paris When It Sizzles '64
Robin and the 7 Hoods '64
Four for Texas '63
Lolita '62
Ocean's 11 '60

Stan Ridgway
Spent '00
Speedway Junky '99
Futurekick '91

Hugo Riesenfeld
Hell's Angels '30
Alibi '29
Evangeline '29

Ned Rifle
Flirt '95
Amateur '94

Tony Riparetti
Postmortem '98
Mean Guns '97
Adrenalin: Fear the Rush '96
Fast Money '96
Nemesis 3: Time Lapse '96
Omega Doom '96
Spitfire '94
Bloodmatch '91

Nicholas Rivera
Dead Sexy '01
Godmoney '97
Little Witches '96
Saturday Night Special '92
Project A '83

David Robbins
How to Kill Your Neighbor's Dog '01
The Prime Gig '00
The Cradle Will Rock '99
Everything That Rises '98
Savior '98
Dead Man Walking '95
Fast Getaway 2 '94
Twenty Bucks '93
Bob Roberts '92

Richard Robbins (1940-)
The Golden Bowl '00
Cotton Mary '99
Place Vendome '98
A Soldier's Daughter Never Cries '98
The Proprietor '96
Surviving Picasso '96
Jefferson in Paris '94
The Remains of the Day '93
Howard's End '92
The Ballad of the Sad Cafe '91
Mr. & Mrs. Bridge '90
Maurice '87
Sweet Lorraine '87
A Room with a View '86
Heat and Dust '82

Andy Roberts
Face '97
Priest '94

Bruce Roberts
Flawless '99
The Crazies '73

Eric N. Robertson
Full Disclosure '00
Captains Courageous '95
Black Fox: Good Men and Bad '94
Black Fox: The Price of Peace '94
Millennium '89

Robbie Robertson
Any Given Sunday '99
Jimmy Hollywood '94
The Color of Money '86
Raging Bull '80

Leo Robin
Gentlemen Prefer Blondes '53
Two Tickets to Broadway '51
The Big Broadcast of 1938 '38
Waikiki Wedding '37

J. Peter Robinson
15 Minutes '01
Detroit Rock City '99
Mr. Nice Guy '98
Firestorm '97
Jackie Chan's First Strike '96
Rumble in the Bronx '96
Vampire in Brooklyn '95
Wes Craven Presents Mind Ripper '95
Highlander: The Final Dimension '94
Wes Craven's New Nightmare '94
The Day My Parents Ran Away '93
Undesirable '92
Wayne's World '92
Blind Fury '90
Cadillac Man '90
Cocktail '88
The Believers '87

Peter Manning Robinson
The '70s '00
Where the Truth Lies '99
The Con '98
Family of Cops 2: Breach of Faith '97
Flypaper '97
The Stepsister '97
Sometimes They Come Back ... Again '96
The Spree '96

Milan Roder
The Lives of a Bengal Lancer '35
The Song of Songs '33

Nile Rodgers
Beverly Hills Cop 3 '94
Blue Chips '94
Earth Girls Are Easy '89
Coming to America '88

Richard Rodgers
Rodgers & Hammerstein's South Pacific '01
Cinderella '97
The Sound of Music '65
Cinderella '64
Flower Drum Song '61
South Pacific '58
Pal Joey '57
Carousel '56
The King and I '56
Oklahoma! '55
Words and Music '48
State Fair '45
I Married an Angel '42
Too Many Girls '40
Babes in Arms '39
Evergreen '34
Dancing Lady '33
Hallelujah, I'm a Bum '33

Heinz Roemheld
The Monster That Challenged the World '57
Jack & the Beanstalk '52
The Lady from Shanghai '48
On Our Merry Way '48
Mr. Ace '46
A Scandal in Paris '46
The Wagons Roll at Night '41
The Roaring Twenties '39
The Black Cat '34

Eric Rogers
No Sex Please—We're British '73
Carry On Cowboy '66

Michael Rohatyn
The Delta '97
Angela '94

Alain Romans
Mon Oncle '58
Mr. Hulot's Holiday '53

Sigmund Romberg
Up in Central Park '48
Foolish Wives '22

Jeff Rona (1957-)
Exit Wounds '01
The In Crowd '00
Black Cat Run '98
Tom Clancy's Netforce '98
The House of Yes '97
Trading Favors '97
White Squall '96
Lipstick Camera '93

Ann Ronell
Love Happy '50
The Story of G.I. Joe '45

David Rose
Operation Petticoat '59
The Princess and the Pirate '44

Leonard Rosenman (1924-)
Levitation '97
Mrs. Munck '95
Ambition '91
RoboCop 2 '90
Star Trek 4: The Voyage Home '86
Cross Creek '83
The Jazz Singer '80
The Car '77
Battle for the Planet of the Apes '73
Beneath the Planet of the Apes '70
Hellfighters '68
Fantastic Voyage '66
Hell Is for Heroes '62
Pork Chop Hill '59
Lafayette Escadrille '58
Rebel without a Cause '55
East of Eden '54

Laurence Rosenthal
Inherit the Wind '99
The Echo of Thunder '98
The Member of the Wedding '97
The Man Who Captured Eichmann '96
Catherine the Great '95
Meteor '79
Who'll Stop the Rain? '78
Rooster Cogburn '75
Death Sentence '74
Satan's School for Girls '73
The Miracle Worker '62
Requiem for a Heavyweight '62
A Raisin in the Sun '61
Dark Odyssey '57

William Ross
Life with Judy Garland—Me and My Shadows '01
My Dog Skip '99
Black Sheep '96
The Evening Star '96
My Fellow Americans '96
A Smile Like Yours '96
Tin Cup '96
The Amazing Panda Adventure '95
Cops and Robbersons '94
Thumbelina '94
Look Who's Talking Now '93
One Good Cop '91

Renzo Rossellini
Generale Della Rovere '60
Voyage in Italy '53
The Flowers of St. Francis '50
Open City '45
Teresa Venerdi '41

Nino Rota (1911-79)
The Godfather, Part 3 '90
The Godfather 1902-1959: The Complete Epic '81
Hurricane '79
Death on the Nile '78
Orchestra Rehearsal '78
Amarcord '74
The Godfather, Part 2 '74
Love and Anarchy '73
Fellini's Roma '72
The Godfather '72
The Clowns '71
Waterloo '71
Fellini Satyricon '69
Romeo and Juliet '68
Spirits of the Dead '68
The Taming of the Shrew '67
Shoot Loud, Louder, I Don't Understand! '66
Juliet of the Spirits '65
8 1/2 '63
Boccaccio '70 '62
La Dolce Vita '60
Purple Noon '60
Rocco and His Brothers '60
The Great War '59
Nights of Cabiria '57
White Nights '57
War and Peace '56
Il Bidone '55
Mambo '55
La Strada '54
Submarine Attack '54
I Vitelloni '53
The White Sheik '52
Anna '51
Valley of the Eagles '51
The Hidden Room '49

Ernst Roters
The Murderers Are Among Us '46
The Murderers are Among Us '46

Bruce Rowland
Journey to the Center of the Earth '99
North Star '96
Zeus and Roxanne '96
Andre '94
Lightning Jack '94
The Man from Snowy River '82

Miklos Rozsa (1917-95)
The Atomic Cafe '82
Dead Men Don't Wear Plaid '82
Eye of the Needle '81
Last Embrace '79
Time After Time '79
Providence '77
Golden Voyage of Sinbad '73
The Private Life of Sherlock Holmes '70
The Green Berets '68
The V.I.P.'s '63
Sodom and Gomorrah '62
El Cid '61
The King of Kings '61
Ben-Hur '59
A Time to Love & a Time to Die '58
Something of Value '57
Bhowani Junction '56
Lust for Life '56
Tribute to a Bad Man '56
Diane '55
Green Fire '55
The King's Thief '55
Moonfleet '55
Men of the Fighting Lady '54
Valley of the Kings '54
All the Brothers Were Valiant '53
Julius Caesar '53
Knights of the Round Table '53
Young Bess '53
Ivanhoe '52
Quo Vadis '51
Adam's Rib '50
The Asphalt Jungle '50
The Miniver Story '50
East Side, West Side '49
Madame Bovary '49
Command Decision '48
Criss Cross '48
The Naked City '48
Secret Beyond the Door '48
A Double Life '47
The Red House '47
The Killers '46
The Strange Love of Martha Ivers '46
Because of Him '45
Blood on the Sun '45
Lady on a Train '45
The Lost Weekend '45
A Song to Remember '45
Spellbound '45
Dark Waters '44
Double Indemnity '44
The Woman of the Town '44
Five Graves to Cairo '43
Sahara '43
So Proudly We Hail '43
The Jungle Book '42
To Be or Not to Be '42
Lydia '41
Melody Master '41
Sundown '41
That Hamilton Woman '41
The Thief of Bagdad '40
The Four Feathers '39
Spy in Black '39
The Divorce of Lady X '38
Knight Without Armour '37
The Squeaker '37
Thunder in the City '37

Lance Rubin
Happy Birthday to Me '81
Motel Hell '80

Michel Rubini
Nemesis '93
Manhunter '86
The Hunger '83

Arthur B. Rubinstein
Nick of Time '95
The Hard Way '91
Stakeout '87
The Best of Times '86
Lost in America '85
WarGames '83

Donald Rubinstein
Bruiser '00
Knightriders '81
Martin '77

John Rubinstein (1946-)
The Killer Inside Me '76
The Candidate '72
Jeremiah Johnson '72

Harry Ruby
Duck Soup '33
Horse Feathers '32
Animal Crackers '30

Steve Rucker
Little Nemo: Adventures in Slumberland '92
Syngenor '90
And God Created Woman '88
976-EVIL '88
Catch the Heat '87
Creature '85

Pete Rugolo (1915-)
This World, Then the Fireworks '97
Where the Boys Are '60

Patrice Rushen
Cora Unashamed '00
America's Dream '95
Hollywood Shuffle '87

Willy Russell
Shirley Valentine '89
Mr. Love '86

David E. Russo
Sparkler '99
Angus '95
Shaking the Tree '92

Gus Russo
Brain Damage '88
Basket Case '82

Carlo Rustichelli
Alfredo, Alfredo '72
Call of the Wild '72
Kill, Baby, Kill '66
Blood and Black Lace '64
Conquest of Mycene '63
The Whip and the Body '63
Divorce—Italian Style '62
That Long Night in '43 '60

Craig Safan
A Season for Miracles '99
Major Payne '95
Mr. Wrong '95
Money for Nothing '93
Capone '89
A Nightmare on Elm Street 4: Dream Master '88
Stand and Deliver '88
The Stranger '87
Remo Williams: The Adventure Begins '85
The Last Starfighter '84
Nightmares '83
Fade to Black '80
Good Guys Wear Black '78
The Bad News Bears in Breaking Training '77
The Great Texas Dynamite Chase '76

Kojun Saito
An Autumn Afternoon '62
Tokyo Story '53

Ryuichi Sakamoto (1952-)
Love Is the Devil '98
Snake Eyes '98
Little Buddha '93
Wild Palms '93
Emily Bronte's Wuthering Heights '92
High Heels '91
Tokyo Decadence '91
The Handmaid's Tale '90
The Sheltering Sky '90
The Last Emperor '87

Conrad Salinger
The Last Time I Saw Paris '54
Till the Clouds Roll By '46

Hans J. Salter (1896-1994)
Come September '61
Abbott and Costello Meet the Mummy '55
Creature from the Black Lagoon '54
The 5000 Fingers of Dr. T '53
Duel at Silver Creek '52
Abbott and Costello Meet the Invisible Man '51
Tomahawk '51
Borderline '50
The Brute Man '46
Dressed to Kill '46
Magnificent Doll '46
Can't Help Singing '45
His Butler's Sister '44
The Invisible Man's Revenge '44
The Mummy's Ghost '44
The Amazing Mrs. Holiday '43
Hold That Ghost '41
It Started with Eve '41
The Wolf Man '41
The Mummy's Hand '40
The Tower of London '39

Bennett Salvay
Jeepers Creepers '01
Love Stinks '99
Rites of Passage '99

David Sanborn
Lethal Weapon 4 '98
Lethal Weapon 3 '92
Lethal Weapon 2 '89

Anton Sanko
Scotland, PA '02
Dee Snider's Strangeland '98
Eye of the Storm '98
Ripe '97
An Occasional Hell '96
Live Nude Girls '95
Sex and the Other Man '95
Girl in the Cadillac '94
Party Girl '94

Chris Saranec
Hourglass '95
Huck and the King of Hearts '93

Philippe Sarde (1945-)
Alice et Martin '98
Lucie Aubrac '98
Les Voleurs '96
Nelly et Monsieur Arnaud '95
Ponette '95
The Favorite Son '94
Revenge of the Musketeers '94
Ma Saison Preferee '93
L.627 '92
The Old Lady Who Walked in the Sea '91
Lord of the Flies '90
Lost Angels '89
Music Box '89
Every Time We Say Goodbye '86
Joshua Then and Now '85
Fort Saganne '84
Lovesick '83
Tales of Ordinary Madness '83
I Married a Dead Man '82
Beau Pere '81
Coup de Torchon '81
Ghost Story '81
Loulou '80
Buffet Froid '79
The Devil, Probably '77
Madame Rosa '77
Spoiled Children '77
Barocco '76
The Tenant '76

Mouse Hunt '97
Volcano '97
Eraser '96
The Long Kiss Goodnight '96
Father of the Bride Part II '95
Grumpier Old Men '95
Judge Dredd '95
Sgt. Bilko '95
Blown Away '94
Clean Slate '94
Forrest Gump '94
The Perez Family '94
The Quick and the Dead '94
Richie Rich '94
Cop and a Half '93
Grumpy Old Men '93
Judgment Night '93
Sidekicks '93
Super Mario Bros. '93
The Bodyguard '92
Death Becomes Her '92
Ferngully: The Last Rain Forest '92
Stop! or My Mom Will Shoot '92
Father of the Bride '91
Ricochet '91
Soapdish '91
Back to the Future, Part 3 '90
Predator 2 '90
Young Guns 2 '90
The Abyss '89
Back to the Future, Part 2 '89
Downtown '89
She's Out of Control '89
Tales from the Crypt '89
Mac and Me '88
My Stepmother Is an Alien '88
Who Framed Roger Rabbit '88
Outrageous Fortune '87
Overboard '87
Predator '87
American Anthem '86
The Clan of the Cave Bear '86
Critical Condition '86
Delta Force '86
Flight of the Navigator '86
No Mercy '86
Back to the Future '85
Cat's Eye '85
Fandango '85
Summer Rental '85
Romancing the Stone '84
The Amazing Dobermans '76
Las Vegas Lady '76

Zoran Simjanovic
Cabaret Balkan '98
Tito and Me '92

Carly Simon
Postcards from the Edge '90
Working Girl '88
Heartburn '86

Marty Simon
No Alibi '00
Stranger in the House '97
Tales from a Parallel Universe: Eating Pattern '97
Tales from a Parallel Universe: Giga Shadow '97
Tales from a Parallel Universe: I Worship His Shadow '97
Tales from a Parallel Universe: Super Nova '97
Marked Man '96
George's Island '91
Scanners 2: The New Order '91

Tim Simonec
A Rumor of Angels '00
Suicide Kings '97

Claudio Simonetti
Opera '88
Demons '86
Cut and Run '85
Conquest '83
Unsane '82

Mike Simpson
Freddy Got Fingered '01
Saving Silverman '01
Road Trip '00

Marlin Skiles
Queen of Outer Space '58
Flight to Mars '52
A Thousand and One Nights '45

Frank Skinner
Shenandoah '65
Portrait in Black '60
Battle Hymn '57
Man of a Thousand Faces '57
Tarnished Angels '57
Away All Boats '56
All That Heaven Allows '55
Because of You '52
The World in His Arms '52
Bedtime for Bonzo '51
Francis Goes to the Races '51
Harvey '50
Francis the Talking Mule '49
Abbott and Costello Meet Frankenstein '48
I'll Be Yours '47
Black Angel '46
Canyon Passage '46
The Amazing Mrs. Holiday '43
Saboteur '42
Sherlock Holmes and the Secret Weapon '42
The Flame of New Orleans '41
Never Give a Sucker an Even Break '41
The Wolf Man '41
My Little Chickadee '40
Destry Rides Again '39
First Love '39
The Tower of London '39

Cezary Skubiszewski
Strange Fits of Passion '99
Lilian's Story '95

Rod Slane
Revenge '86
Blood Cult '85

Michael Small
The Golden Spiders: A Nero Wolfe Mystery '00
Mountains of the Moon '90
1969 '89
Black Widow '87
Jaws: The Revenge '87
Orphans '87
Brighton Beach Memoirs '86
The Postman Always Rings Twice '81
The Lathe of Heaven '80
Comes a Horseman '78
Night Moves '75
The Stepford Wives '75
The Parallax View '74
Klute '71

Bruce Smeaton
A Cry in the Dark '88
Roxanne '87
Undercover '87
Eleni '85
The Naked Country '85
Plenty '85
Iceman '84
The Winds of Jarrah '83
Barbarosa '82
Grendel, Grendel, Grendel '82
Circle of Iron '78
The Devil's Playground '76
Picnic at Hanging Rock '75
The Cars That Ate Paris '74

B.C. Smith
Deadlocked '00
Mercy '00
The Mod Squad '99
Around the Fire '98
Smoke Signals '98

Joseph Smith
Animal Instincts '92
Secret Games '92

Paul J. Smith (1906-80)
The Parent Trap '61
Pollyanna '60
The Great Locomotive Chase '56
20,000 Leagues under the Sea '54
Fun & Fancy Free '47
Snow White and the Seven Dwarfs '37

Neil Smolar
Varian's War '01
The Boys of St. Vincent '93

Mark Snow (1946-)
Another Woman's Husband '00
Dirty Pictures '00
Crazy in Alabama '99
Disturbing Behavior '98
The X-Files '98
Down, Out and Dangerous '95
Frame by Frame '95
A Good Day to Die '95
Oldest Confederate Widow Tells All '95
A Stranger in Town '95
Dead Badge '94
Playmaker '94
The Substitute Wife '94
High Stakes '93
Take Down '92
Archie: Return to Riverdale '90
In the Line of Duty: A Cop for the Killing '90
Jake Speed '86
High Risk '81
The Boy in the Plastic Bubble '76

Curt Sobel
A Cool, Dry Place '98
Body Count '97
Alien Nation '88
The Flamingo Kid '84

Stephen Sondheim
Gypsy '93
Dick Tracy '90
Postcards from the Edge '90
Sunday in the Park with George '86
Sweeney Todd: The Demon Barber of Fleet Street '84
Reds '81
Stavisky '74
Gypsy '62
West Side Story '61

Lodovico Sorret
The Wife '95
What Happened Was... '94

Ondrej Soukup
Dark Blue World '01
Kolya '96

Tim Souster
Traffik '90
Slugs '87

Mischa Spoliansky
The Happiest Days of Your Life '50
Secret Mission '42
King Solomon's Mines '37

John Sponsler
The Stray '00
Y2K '99

Robert Sprayberry
Bodily Harm '95
Widow's Kiss '94
Quick '93
Where the Red Fern Grows: Part 2 '92

Ringo Starr (1940-)
Let It Be '70
Yellow Submarine '68
Magical Mystery Tour '67
Help! '65

Michael Stearns (1940-)
Temptress '95
Baraka '93

Andrew Stein
Death Sport '78
Hollywood Boulevard '76

Herman Stein (1915-)
King Kong vs. Godzilla '63
Shame '61
This Island Earth '55
It Came from Outer Space '53

Ronald Stein
The Rain People '69
Spider Baby '64
Dementia 13 '63
The Haunted Palace '63
The Terror '63
Premature Burial '62
Atlas '60
Dinosaurus! '60
Legend of Tom Dooley '59
Attack of the 50 Foot Woman '58
Invasion of the Saucer Men '57
Reform School Girl '57
Sorority Girl '57
The Undead '57
The Gunslinger '56
It Conquered the World '56
The Phantom from 10,000 Leagues '56
Day the World Ended '55

Max Steiner
The Glass Menagerie '87
Those Calloways '65
Spencer's Mountain '63
Rome Adventure '62
Parrish '61
Cash McCall '60
Ice Palace '60
The FBI Story '59
The Hanging Tree '59
John Paul Jones '59
A Summer Place '59
Darby's Rangers '58
Marjorie Morningstar '58
Band of Angels '57
China Gate '57
Escapade in Japan '57
All Mine to Give '56
Death of a Scoundrel '56
Helen of Troy '56
The Searchers '56
Battle Cry '55
Hell on Frisco Bay '55
The McConnell Story '55
The Caine Mutiny '54
King Richard and the Crusaders '54
By the Light of the Silvery Moon '53
The Desert Song '53
Trouble along the Way '53
Miracle of Our Lady of Fatima '52
Springfield Rifle '52
Distant Drums '51
Jim Thorpe: All American '51
On Moonlight Bay '51
The Flame & the Arrow '50
Adventures of Don Juan '49
Beyond the Forest '49
Flamingo Road '49
The Fountainhead '49
White Heat '49
Johnny Belinda '48
Key Largo '48
My Girl Tisa '48
Silver River '48
South of St. Louis '48
Treasure of the Sierra Madre '48
Winter Meeting '48
Life with Father '47
Pursued '47
The Beast with Five Fingers '46
The Big Sleep '46
Cloak and Dagger '46
The Man I Love '46
Night and Day '46
A Stolen Life '46
Tomorrow Is Forever '46
The Corn Is Green '45
Mildred Pierce '45
Rhapsody in Blue '45
San Antonio '45
Saratoga Trunk '45
The Adventures of Mark Twain '44
Arsenic and Old Lace '44
Passage to Marseilles '44
Since You Went Away '44
This Is the Army '43
Watch on the Rhine '43
Captains of the Clouds '42
Casablanca '42
Desperate Journey '42
In This Our Life '42
Now, Voyager '42
The Bride Came C.O.D. '41
Dive Bomber '41
The Great Lie '41
Sergeant York '41
They Died with Their Boots On '41
All This and Heaven Too '40
City for Conquest '40
The Letter '40
Santa Fe Trail '40
Virginia City '40
Dark Victory '39
Dodge City '39
Gone with the Wind '39
Intermezzo '39
Oklahoma Kid '39
The Old Maid '39
They Made Me a Criminal '39
The Adventures of Tom Sawyer '38
Amazing Dr. Clitterhouse '38
Angels with Dirty Faces '38
Dawn Patrol '38
Four Daughters '38
Jezebel '38
The Sisters '38
Kid Galahad '37
The Life of Emile Zola '37
A Star Is Born '37
That Certain Woman '37
The Charge of the Light Brigade '36
Follow the Fleet '36
The Garden of Allah '36
Little Lord Fauntleroy '36
Alice Adams '35
Break of Hearts '35
I Dream Too Much '35
The Informer '35
Roberta '35
She '35
The Three Musketeers '35
Top Hat '35
Anne of Green Gables '34
Bachelor Bait '34
The Gay Divorcee '34
Kentucky Kernels '34
Little Minister '34
The Lost Patrol '34
Of Human Bondage '34
Romance in Manhattan '34
Spitfire '34
Ace of Aces '33
Aggie Appleby, Maker of Men '33
Ann Vickers '33
Cheyenne Kid '33
Christopher Strong '33
Diplomaniacs '33
Finishing School '33
Flying Down to Rio '33
King Kong '33
Little Women '33
Morning Glory '33
Son of Kong '33
Topaze '33
A Bill of Divorcement '32
Bird of Paradise '32
Little Orphan Annie '32
Lost Squadron '32
Melody Cruise '32
The Most Dangerous Game '32
Way Back Home '32
What Price Hollywood? '32
Cimarron '31
Kept Husbands '31
State's Attorney '31
Check & Double Check '30
Dixiana '30
Half-Shot at Sunrise '30
Last Command '28

Steven Stern
Big Brother Trouble '00
Hangman '00
Bloody Murder '99

Cat Stevens
Harold and Maude '71
Deep End '70

Leith Stevens
Crashout '55
Private Hell 36 '54
The Wild One '54
The War of the Worlds '53
When Worlds Collide '51
Destination Moon '50

David A. Stewart
Cookie's Fortune '99
Beautiful Girls '96
Showgirls '95
The Ref '93

Gary Stockdale
Picasso Trigger '89
Dance of the Damned '88
Necromancer: Satan's Servant '88
Hard Ticket to Hawaii '87

Georgie Stoll
Where the Boys Are '60
The Seven Hills of Rome '58
Holiday in Mexico '46

Morris Stoloff
Song Without End '60
The Jolson Story '46
His Girl Friday '40
Theodora Goes Wild '36

Christopher Stone
Skeletons in the Closet '00
Phantasm 4: Oblivion '98
DNA '97
Fist of the North Star '95
The Stupids '95
Choices '81

Richard Stone (1953-2001)
Victim of Love '91
Pumpkinhead '88

Michael Storey
Wavelength '96
Just Like a Woman '95
Coming Up Roses '87
Another Country '84

Herbert Stothart
Undercurrent '46
They Were Expendable '45
National Velvet '44
Thirty Seconds Over Tokyo '44
The White Cliffs of Dover '44
Cairo '42
Mrs. Miniver '42
Waterloo Bridge '40
The Wizard of Oz '39
Camille '36
A Tale of Two Cities '36
Anna Karenina '35
David Copperfield '35
Mutiny on the Bounty '35
A Night at the Opera '35
The Cat and the Fiddle '34

Oscar Straus
The Earrings of Madame De... '54
De Mayerling a Sarajevo '40
Make a Wish '37

Barbra Streisand (1942-)
The Mirror Has Two Faces '96
Nuts '87

Charles Strouse
Annie '99
Bonnie & Clyde '67

Joe Strummer (1952-)
Grosse Pointe Blank '97
When Pigs Fly '93
Permanent Record '88
Walker '87
Sid & Nancy '86

Jule Styne (1905-94)
Gypsy '93
Funny Girl '68
Gypsy '62
My Sister Eileen '55
Gentlemen Prefer Blondes '53
Two Tickets to Broadway '51
The West Point Story '50
Anchors Aweigh '45

L. Subramaniam
Mississippi Masala '92
Salaam Bombay! '88

Harry Sukman (1912-84)
Salem's Lot '79
Song Without End '60

Mauri Sumen
Condition Red '95

Aladdin and the King of Thieves '96
All Dogs Go to Heaven 2 '95
The Pebble and the Penguin '94

Franz Waxman
Cimarron '60
Sunrise at Campobello '60
Beloved Infidel '59
The Nun's Story '59
Run Silent, Run Deep '58
Peyton Place '57
Sayonara '57
Spirit of St. Louis '57
Mister Roberts '55
Rear Window '54
The Silver Chalice '54
Stalag 17 '53
A Place in the Sun '51
Night and the City '50
Sunset Boulevard '50
Sorry, Wrong Number '48
The Paradine Case '47
Humoresque '46
Objective, Burma! '45
Air Force '43
Woman of the Year '42
Dr. Jekyll and Mr. Hyde '41
Suspicion '41
The Philadelphia Story '40
Rebecca '40
Strange Cargo '40
Honolulu '39
Three Comrades '38
The Bride of Frankenstein '35
Mauvaise Graine '33

Roy Webb
Teacher's Pet '58
Marty '55
At Sword's Point '51
Flying Leathernecks '51
Out of the Past '47
Notorious '46
The Spiral Staircase '46
Bedlam '45
Dick Tracy, Detective '45
Fighting Seabees '44
The Seventh Cross '44
Zombies on Broadway '44
I Walked with a Zombie '43
Cat People '42
I Married a Witch '42
The Magnificent Ambersons '42
Abe Lincoln in Illinois '40
My Favorite Wife '40
Love Affair '39
Room Service '38

Paul Francis Webster
The Alamo '60
Calamity Jane '53

Konstantin Wecker
The White Rose '83
Sisters, Or the Balance of Happiness '79

Craig (Shudder to Think) Wedren
Wet Hot American Summer '01
First Love, Last Rites '98
High Art '98

Kurt Weill
One Touch of Venus '48
The Threepenny Opera '31

Larry Wellington
The Wizard of Gore '70
Just for the Hell of It '68
She-Devils on Wheels '68
The Girl, the Body and the Pill '67
Gruesome Twosome '67
2000 Maniacs '64

John Welsman
In His Father's Shoes '97
Double Play '96

Brahm Wenger
MVP (Most Valuable Primate) '00
The Duke '99
Air Bud 2: Golden Receiver '98
Air Bud '97
Hollow Point '95

Rick Wentworth
The Alchemists '99
How to Get Ahead in Advertising '89

Lars Johan Werle
Hour of the Wolf '68
Persona '66

Walter Werzowa
Cherry Falls '00
Sweet Jane '98
Back to Back '96

Jim West
Lady Dragon 2 '93
Lady Dragon '92

Tim Westergren
Defying Gravity '99
The Last Best Sunday '98

Nigel Westlake
Babe: Pig in the City '98
A Little Bit of Soul '97
Babe '95
Children of the Revolution '95

Harold Wheeler
Blood Brothers '97
Love! Valour! Compassion! '96
Straight out of Brooklyn '91

Bill Whelan
Dancing at Lughnasa '98
Some Mother's Son '96

David Whitaker
With a Friend Like Harry '00
Sword & the Sorcerer '82
Dr. Jekyll and Sister Hyde '71

Daniel White
Revenge in the House of Usher '82
Female Vampire '73

John Clifford White
Talk '94
Romper Stomper '92

Stacy Widelitz
Prayer of the Rollerboys '91
Phantom of the Mall: Eric's Revenge '89
Return to Horror High '87

Jean Wiener
A Gentle Woman '69
Grisbi '53
Rendez-vous de Juillet '49
The Crime of Monsieur Lange '36
The Lower Depths '36

Scott Wilk
Plain Clothes '88
Valley Girl '83

Alex Wilkinson
Avalanche '99
Stealth Fighter '99
Double Edge '97
Deadly Past '95

K. Alexander Wilkinson
Pure Danger '96
Street Corner Justice '96
The Sweeper '95

Marc Wilkinson
The Fiendish Plot of Dr. Fu Manchu '80
If... '69

David Williams
Supernova '99
Shelter '98
Wishmaster 2: Evil Never Dies '98
Phantoms '97
The Prophecy 2: Ashtown '97
Children of the Corn 4: The Gathering '96
The Killing Jar '96
No Way Back '96
The Prophecy '95
American Yakuza '94

John Williams (1932-)
Star Wars: Episode 2—Attack of the Clones '02
A. I.: Artificial Intelligence '01
Harry Potter and the Sorcerer's Stone '01
The Patriot '00
Angela's Ashes '99
Star Wars: Episode 1—The Phantom Menace '99
Saving Private Ryan '98
Stepmom '98
Amistad '97
The Lost World: Jurassic Park 2 '97
Seven Years in Tibet '97
Rosewood '96
Sleepers '96
Nixon '95
Sabrina '95
Jurassic Park '93
Schindler's List '93
Far and Away '92
Home Alone 2: Lost in New York '92
Hook '91
JFK '91
Home Alone '90
Presumed Innocent '90
Stanley and Iris '90
Always '89
Born on the Fourth of July '89
Indiana Jones and the Last Crusade '89
The Accidental Tourist '88
Empire of the Sun '87
Superman 4: The Quest for Peace '87
The Witches of Eastwick '87
SpaceCamp '86
Indiana Jones and the Temple of Doom '84
The River '84
Jaws 3 '83
Return of the Jedi '83
Superman 3 '83
E.T.: The Extra-Terrestrial '82
Monsignor '82
Yes, Giorgio '82
Heartbeeps '81
Raiders of the Lost Ark '81
The Empire Strikes Back '80
Superman 2 '80
Dracula '79
1941 '79
The Deer Hunter '78
The Fury '78
Jaws 2 '78
Superman: The Movie '78
The Swarm '78
Black Sunday '77
Close Encounters of the Third Kind '77
Star Wars '77
Family Plot '76
Midway '76
Missouri Breaks '76
The Eiger Sanction '75
Jaws '75
Conrack '74
Earthquake '74
The Sugarland Express '74
The Towering Inferno '74
Cinderella Liberty '73
The Long Goodbye '73
Man Who Loved Cat Dancing '73
The Paper Chase '73
Psychopath '73
Tom Sawyer '73
The Cowboys '72
Pete 'n' Tillie '72
The Poseidon Adventure '72
Fiddler on the Roof '71
Daddy's Gone A-Hunting '69
Goodbye, Mr. Chips '69
The Reivers '69
Sergeant Ryker '68
A Guide for the Married Man '67
Heidi '67
Valley of the Dolls '67
How to Steal a Million '66
The Rare Breed '66
None But the Brave '65
The Killers '64
Gidget Goes to Rome '63
Diamond Head '62

Joseph Williams
Judgment Day '99
From Dusk Till Dawn 2: Texas Blood Money '98
Never 2 Big '98
Body Count '97
Embrace of the Vampire '95
Poison Ivy 2: Lily '95

Ken Williams
Crash & Byrnes '99
The Crimson Code '99
In the Company of Men '96

Patrick Williams
Jesus '00
A Cooler Climate '99
Change of Heart '98
Kiss the Sky '98
A Knight in Camelot '98
Julian Po '97
My Very Best Friend '96
That Old Feeling '96
A Weekend in the Country '96
The Grass Harp '95
Kingfish: A Story of Huey P. Long '95
Getting Gotti '94
Blind Spot '93
Geronimo '93
The Cutting Edge '92
Cry-Baby '90
In the Spirit '90
Violets Are Blue '86
All of Me '84
The Toy '82
Used Cars '80
Breaking Away '79
Cuba '79
Ssssss '73
Evel Knievel '72

Paul Williams (1940-)
The Muppet Christmas Carol '92
The Muppet Movie '79
The End '78
The Boy in the Plastic Bubble '76
Bugsy Malone '76
A Star Is Born '76
Phantom of the Paradise '74

Hal Willner
Finding Forrester '00
Kansas City '95
Theremin: An Electronic Odyssey '95

Meredith Willson (1902-84)
The Unsinkable Molly Brown '64
The Music Man '62
The Little Foxes '41
The Great Dictator '40

Nancy Wilson
Vanilla Sky '01
Almost Famous '00
Jerry Maguire '96
Say Anything '89

Stanley Wilson
The Beatniks '60
Iron Mountain Trail '53
Border Saddlemates '52
Silver City Bonanza '51

Debbie Wiseman
Othello '01
Dead of Night '99
The Guilty '99
Wilde '97
Female Perversions '96
Haunted '95
Tom & Viv '94

Peter Wolf
The NeverEnding Story 3: Escape from Fantasia '94
Weekend at Bernie's 2 '93

Michael Wolff
The Tic Code '99
Who's the Man? '93

James Wong
Once Upon a Time in China '91
A Bullet in the Head '90

John Wooldridge
Angels One Five '54
The Woman in Question '50

Arthur Wright
Dolemite 2: Human Tornado '76
Dolemite '75

Wai Lap Wu
Once Upon a Time in China III '93
Twin Warriors '93

Alex Wurman
Play It to the Bone '99
Footsteps '98
French Exit '97
Eat Your Heart Out '96

David Wurst
Agent Red '00
Mach 2 '00
Rangers '00
Final Voyage '99
Restraining Order '99
The White Raven '98
The Haunted Sea '97
Crash Dive '96
The Last Assassins '96
Where Truth Lies '96
The Death Artist '95
Dillinger and Capone '95
Machine Gun Blues '95
The Crazysitter '94
Bloodfist 5: Human Target '93

Eric Wurst
Agent Red '00
Mach 2 '00
Rangers '00
Final Voyage '99
Restraining Order '99
The White Raven '98
The Haunted Sea '97
Crash Dive '96
The Last Assassins '96
Where Truth Lies '96
The Death Artist '95
Dillinger and Capone '95
Machine Gun Blues '95
The Crazysitter '94
Bloodfist 5: Human Target '93

Danny Wyman
The Lawnmower Man '92
Hell Night '81

Gabriel Yared
Autumn in New York '00
The Next Best Thing '00
The Talented Mr. Ripley '99
City of Angels '98
Message in a Bottle '98
The Wings of the Dove '97
The English Patient '96
Black Water '94
The Lover '92
Camille Claudel '89
Romero '89
Clean and Sober '88
Light Years '88
Betty Blue '86
Moon in the Gutter '83

Dwight Yoakam (1956-)
South of Heaven, West of Hell '00
Chasers '94

Vincent Youmans
Hit the Deck '55
Flying Down to Rio '33

Christopher Young (1954-)
Bandits '01
The Glass House '01
The Shipping News '01
Sweet November '01
Swordfish '01
The Big Kahuna '00
Bless the Child '00
The Gift '00
Wonder Boys '00
Entrapment '99
The Hurricane '99
In Too Deep '99
Hush '98
Judas Kiss '98
Rounders '98
Urban Legend '98
Hard Rain '97
Murder at 1600 '97
Head Above Water '96
Set It Off '96
Unforgettable '96
Copycat '95
Murder in the First '95
Norma Jean and Marilyn '95
Species '95
Tales from the Hood '95
Virtuosity '95
Judicial Consent '94
Dream Lover '93
Rapid Fire '92
Bright Angel '91
The Dark Half '91
Barbarian Queen 2: The Empress Strikes Back '89
The Fly 2 '89
Bat 21 '88
Hellbound: Hellraiser 2 '88
Flowers in the Attic '87
Hellraiser '87
Invaders from Mars '86
Barbarian Queen '85
The Power '80

Neil Young (1945-)
Dead Man '95
Where the Buffalo Roam '80

Victor Young
China Gate '57
Around the World in 80 Days '56
The Brave One '56
The Conqueror '56
Johnny Guitar '53
Shane '53
The Quiet Man '52
The Lemon Drop Kid '51
Our Very Own '50
Rio Grande '50
Gun Crazy '49
Sands of Iwo Jima '49
The Big Clock '48
Emperor Waltz '48
Unconquered '47
The Blue Dahlia '46
To Each His Own '46
Two Years before the Mast '46
Love Letters '45
Frenchman's Creek '44
Ministry of Fear '44
The Story of Dr. Wassell '44
The Uninvited '44
For Whom the Bell Tolls '43
The Outlaw '43
The Glass Key '42
The Great Man's Lady '42
Reap the Wild Wind '42
Arizona '40
Rhythm on the River '40
Breaking the Ice '38

Richard Yuen
Bloodmoon '97
The Bride with White Hair '93
Once Upon a Time in China II '92
Wicked City '92

Lee Zahler
The Mask of Diijon '46
I Accuse My Parents '45
The Lady Confesses '45
Boss of Rawhide '44

Paul Zaza
The Base '99
Grizzly Falls '99
I'll Remember April '99
Baby Geniuses '98
Hot Blooded '98
A Brooklyn State of Mind '97
Double Take '97
Face the Evil '97
Stag '97
The Ex '96
The Rage '96
Iron Eagle 4 '95
The Club '94
My Summer Story '94
Blown Away '93
To Catch a Killer '92
From the Hip '86
A Christmas Story '83
Porky's '82
Prom Night '80

Eric Zeisl
They Were Expendable '45
Bataan '43

Guy Zerafa
Replicant '01
Redline '97

Jiping Zhao
The Emperor's Shadow '96
Ju Dou '90

Hans Zimmer (1957-)
Spirit: Stallion of the Cimarron '02
Black Hawk Down '01
Hannibal '01
Pearl Harbor '01
Riding in Cars with Boys '01

An Everlasting Piece *'00*
Gladiator *'00*
Mission: Impossible 2 *'00*
The Pledge *'00*
The Road to El Dorado *'00*
Chill Factor *'99*
Prince of Egypt *'98*
The Thin Red Line *'98*
With Friends Like These *'98*
As Good As It Gets *'97*
The Peacemaker *'97*
The Fan *'96*
Muppet Treasure Island *'96*
The Preacher's Wife *'96*
Smilla's Sense of Snow *'96*
The Whole Wide World *'96*
Beyond Rangoon *'95*
Broken Arrow *'95*
Crimson Tide *'95*
Nine Months *'95*
Something to Talk About *'95*
Drop Zone *'94*
The Lion King *'94*
Renaissance Man *'94*
Two Deaths *'94*
Younger & Younger *'94*
Calendar Girl *'93*
Cool Runnings *'93*
The House of the Spirits *'93*
I'll Do Anything *'93*
Point of No Return *'93*
True Romance *'93*
A League of Their Own *'92*
The Power of One *'92*
Backdraft *'91*
Regarding Henry *'91*
Thelma & Louise *'91*
Bird on a Wire *'90*
Chicago Joe & the Showgirl *'90*
Dark Obsession *'90*
Days of Thunder *'90*
Fools of Fortune *'90*
Green Card *'90*
Pacific Heights *'90*
Black Rain *'89*
Burning Secret *'89*
Driving Miss Daisy *'89*
Paperhouse *'89*
Prisoner of Rio *'89*
Twister *'89*
Rain Man *'88*
Wonderland *'88*
A World Apart *'88*
The Wind *'87*
Zero Boys *'86*
Insignificance *'85*
Success Is the Best Revenge *'84*
Moonlighting *'82*

David Zippel

Mulan *'98*
Hercules *'97*

Carl Zittrer

A Christmas Story *'83*
Porky's 2: The Next Day *'83*
Porky's *'82*
Black Christmas *'75*
Deranged *'74*
Children Shouldn't Play with Dead Things *'72*

Video Sources

The **Video Sources** section provides full contact information, including address, phone, fax and toll-free numbers, as well as web site address and e-mail when available, for mail order and retail resources for videos reviewed in this book. They are listed alphabetically. Some of the videos have no currently known distributor, but copies may still be available. Others are **On Moratorium**, meaning their distributor, or more likely, their producer, has pulled them out of circulation for a certain amount of time. These videos may still be available from local or mail sources because they were distributed at one time. Many video stores provide an ordering service. If your local video store doesn't have a title you want, you can ask them to order it for you, or you can find someone here who will.

ANIMEIGO INC.
PO Box 989
Wilmington, NC 28402-0989
910-251-1850
800-242-6463
Fax: 910-763-2376
Email: questions@animeigo.com
HomePage: http://www.animeigo.com

ASYMMETRICAL ENTERTAINMENT, INC.
110 Remsen St., Ste 1A
Brooklyn Heights, NY 11201
718-237-6031
Fax: 718-237-6031
Email: info@asymmetricalvideo.com
HomePage: http://www.asymmetricalvideo.com

BIJOU VIDEO
1349 N. Wells
Chicago, IL 60610
312-943-5397
800-932-7111
Fax: 312-337-1270

CINEMA CLASSICS
332 E. 11 St.
New York, NY 10003
212-677-6309
Fax: 212-677-5412
Email: cclassics@cinemaclassics.com

CINEMA INTERNATIONAL CANADA
8275 Mayrand
Montreal, QC, Canada H4P 2C8
514-336-9696
Fax: 514-336-9696

CINEMACABRE VIDEO
PO Box 10005
Baltimore, MD 21285-0005

COAST TO COAST VIDEO
39 W. 19th St., 2nd Fl.
New York, NY 10011
212-727-0390
800-221-3420

CRITERION COLLECTION
c/o The Voyager Co.
578 Broadway
New York, NY 10012
212-431-5199
800-446-2001
HomePage: http://www.criterionco.com

CRITICS' CHOICE VIDEO, INC.
PO Box 749
Itasca, IL 60143
630-775-3300
800-367-7765
Fax: 630-775-3340
Email: vcatalog@ccvideo.com **HomePage:** http://www.ccvideo.com

CULT FILM STORE
2272 Colorado Blvd., Ste. 1118
Los Angeles, CA 90041
323-478-7303
Email: cultfilmstore@yahoo.com **HomePage:** http://www.cultfilmstore.com

DIGITAL VERSATILE DISC LTD.
15210 Keswick St.
Van Nuys, CA 91405
818-994-2980
Fax: 818-994-1575

DISCOUNT VIDEO TAPES, INC./ HOLLYWOOD'S ATTIC
PO Box 7122
Burbank, CA 91510
818-843-3366
Fax: 818-843-3821
Email: wwwjr@hollywoodsattic.com
HomePage: http://www.discountvideotapes.com

FACETS MULTIMEDIA, INC.
1517 W. Fullerton Ave.
Chicago, IL 60614
773-281-9075
800-331-6197
Fax: 773-929-5437

HEN'S TOOTH VIDEO
2805 E. State Blvd.
Fort Wayne, IN 46805
219-471-4332
Fax: 219-471-4449

HOUSE OF MONSTERS
1579 N. Milwaukee Ave., Gallery 218
Chicago, IL 60622
773-292-0980
Fax: 773-276-6582
Email: naschy@thehouseofmonsters.com
HomePage: http://www.thehouseofmosters.com/index2.html

KIM'S VIDEO
350 Bleeker St.
New York, NY 10014
800-617-KIMS
Fax: 212-675-8996
Email: info@kimsvideo.com
HomePage: http://www.kimsvideo.com

MIKE LEBELL'S VIDEO
75 Freemont Pl.
Los Angeles, CA 90005
213-938-3333
Fax: 213-938-3334
Email: mlvideo@aol.com

LUMIVISION CORP.
877 Federal Blvd.
Denver, CO 80204-3212
800-776-LUMI

A MILLION AND ONE WORLD-WIDE VIDEOS
PO Box 349
Orchard Hill, GA 30266
770-227-7309
800-849-7309
Fax: 800-849-0873
Email: barbara@wwvideos.com **HomePage:** http://www.wwvideos.com

MOVIES UNLIMITED
3015 Darnell Rd.
Philadelphia, PA 19154
215-637-4444
800-668-4344
Fax: 215-637-2350
Email: movies@moviesunlimited.com
HomePage: http://www.moviesunlimited.com

RHINO HOME VIDEO
10635 Santa Monica Blvd., 2nd Fl.
Los Angeles, CA 90025-4900
310-474-4778
800-843-3670
Fax: 310-441-6573
Email: drrhino@rhino.com
HomePage: http://www.rhino.com

SINISTER CINEMA
PO Box 4369
Medford, OR 97501-0168
541-773-6860
Fax: 541-779-8650
Email: sinister@cinemaweb.com
HomePage: http://www.sinistercinema.com

SOMETHING WEIRD VIDEO
PO Box 33664
Seattle, WA 98133
HomePage: http://www.somethingweird.com

THOMAS VIDEO
122 S. Main
Clawson, MI 48017
248-280-2833
Fax: 248-280-4463
Email: vgmr@thomasvideo.com **HomePage:** http://www.thomasvideo.com

TROMA TEAM VIDEO
733 9th Ave.
New York, NY 10019
212-957-5678
800-83-TROMA
Fax: 212-957-4497
Email: tromcon@aol.com
HomePage: http://www.troma.com/home

THE VIDEO CATALOG
7000 Westgate Dr.
St. Paul, MN 55114
612-659-3700
800-733-6656
Fax: 612-659-0083
Email: kyle@rivertrade.com

VIDEO COLLECTIBLES
1500 Clinton St.
Buffalo, NY 14206-9911
800-268-3891
Fax: 800-269-8877
Email: info@collectablesdirect.com
HomePage: http://www.collectablesdirect.com

VIDEO LIBRARY
7157 Germantown Ave.
Philadelphia, PA 19119
800-669-7157
Fax: 215-248-5627
Email: rentals@vlibrary.com **HomePage:** http://www.vlibrary.com

VIDEO OYSTER
81 Ludlow St., Left Basement
New York, NY 10002
212-979-6800
Fax: 212-989-3533
Email: videooyster@rcn.com **HomePage:** http://www.videooyster.com

VIDEO SEARCH OF MIAMI
PO Box 161917
Miami, FL 33116
305-279-9773
888-279-9773
Fax: 305-598-2665
Email: email@vsom.com
HomePage: http://www.vsom.com

VIDEO VAULT
323 S. Washington
Alexandria, VA 22314
800-VAU-LT66
Fax: 703-836-5720
Email: flix@videovault.com

VIDEO YESTERYEAR
Box C
Sandy Hook, CT 06482
800-243-0987
Fax: 203-797-0819
Email: video@yesteryear.com **HomePage:** http://www.videoyesteryear.com

THE VIDEOFINDERS COLLECTION
National Fulfillment Center
425 E. Colorado St.
Glendale, CA 91205
800-799-1199
Fax: 818-637-5276

Web Site Guide

The Internet is an important resource for movie information, appreciation, and (especially) obsession. For your web surfing enjoyment, we have compiled a comprehensive list of many of the top entertainment websites that will expand your movie knowledge. If you're looking for information on how to make your own film, there are sites for that, too. The guide is divided into seven categories: cult movie resources; film magazines; film studios; filmmaker resources; film reviews; general entertainment; and video outlets. The sites are listed alphabetically within each category, and each site includes name and URL address information. The general information websites briefly describe what you can expect to find. Just as you can spend hours flipping through ***Videohound,*** you can spend hours cruising the web with the sites listed below since a majority of these homepages can link you to other sites on the web.

CULT MOVIE RESOURCES

Amazing World of Cult Movies
www.swcm.com
Filmographies and reviews of cult films.

AnimEigo
www.animeigo.com
Gives extensive history on this rapidly growing Japanese export of animation.

Anime Resources and Info
www.best.com:80/gaxiola/Anime/
Informs users of upcoming anime features and background information on the genre itself.

Astounding B Monster Web
www.bmonster.com
Covers all genres of B-movies; includes reviews, top-10 lists, interviews

B-Movie Guide
www.50megs.com/finvarra
Lists B-Movie actors and filmmakers, with links to their credits

B.O.S.C.H.
huizen.dds.nl/penquin/index_frame.html
Offers reviews of some off-beat, cheaply made films.

Black Comedies
www.losman.com/black.htm
Spotlights those films that humorously poke fun at other peoples' pain and misery.

The Cult Movie Den
www.geocities.com/Hollywood/Boulevard/4802/
Provides valuable information on past, present, and future cult movies.

The Cult Shop
lasarto.cnde.iastate.edu/Movies/CultShop
Gives the latest information on your favorite cult movie stars like Bruce Campbell and Steve Buscemi. Also offers links to other movie sites.

The Gamera Home Page
www.cc.emory.edu/kgowen/gamera.html
*A home page devoted to that Japanese superstar turtle, Gamera. Showcases, in depth, all nine of his films from **Gamera** to **Gamera vs. Legion.***

Hong Kong Movies Home Page
egret0.stanford.edu/hk/index.html
An interest in Hong Kong films has significantly increased due to the sudden rise of Jackie Chan and action director John Woo. This comprehensive site offers much information on the Hong Kong film industry. Includes an update of new Hong Kong films, filmographies, interviews, reviews, and a searchable database on Hong Kong actors and actresses.

Mad Prof. Mike's Headbanger Movie Reviews
www.dnai.com/ochobbit/topten.html
*Witness the lunatic rantings of Professor Headbanger as he raves about such scholock classics as **Teenagers from Outer Space** and **This Island Earth.***

Manga Video
www.manga.com/
A spin-off of anime, video retailer offering comic books, soundtracks, and fan club information.

Mondo Hell
www.losman.com/fod.htm
If you're itching for production information on the Faces of Death video series, then look no further.

Mr. Data's SF Cult TV and Movie Site
www.trekman.demon.co.uk/
Includes updates and even an episode guide to the top sci-fi television shows as well as the latest information on upcoming films.

No Place for a Woman: The Family in Film Noir
www.obs.net:80/Noir/
Reports on the implications that film noir has had on society. The author, John Blaser, pinpoints the role that women and family have in this genre. Subtopics include, "Pro-family Messages in Film Noir" and "Women's Anti-Family Function in Film Noir."

Oh, the Humanity
www.ohthehumanity.com
The worst films in movie history are given a chance to shine with this site. Visitors can read several reviews of their favorite guilty pleasure.

Professor Neon's TV and Movie Mania
www.vortex.com/ProfNeon.html
Covers a gamut of information on film, television, radio and cable industry. When it comes to films, the Professor leans more to sci-fi, cult and weird stuff.

Reel Talk
www.reellife.com/PFE/index.html
Allows you to talk amongst yourselves about recent or past cult film releases.

Shock Cinema
members.aol.com/shockcin/main.html
On-line version of magazine catering to those fans of bizarre and unconventional cinema.

Stomp Tokyo
www.stomptokyo.com
Reviews and salutes all manner of schlock and trash cinema on a 5-David Hasselhoff scale.

The Vampyre's Haven
www.wam.umd.edu/mcarter/
*A listing of most, not all, vampire films made, including the most obscure ones like **Bloedverwatnen** (from the Netherlands) and **Wanda Does Transylvania.***

FILM FESTIVALS

ACB Sacramento Film and Music Festival
www.sactofilmfest.com/
A centerpiece for the arts of Sacramento and a celebration of both visual and musical works from around the world

AFI Los Angeles International Film Festival (USA)
www.afionline.org/afihomes/aaa.home.html
Features attractions from this huge film festival held every October. Also lists synopses of the films featured.

African Diaspora Film Festival
www.africanfilm.com/festival/
Highlights the works of African-American filmmakers.

Angelus Awards Student Film Festival
www.familytheater.org/main/angelus.php
Recognizes and showcases student films which explore the complexity of the human condition with creativity and respect.

Ann Arbor Film Festival
aafilmfest.org/
Not-for-profit festival showcases independent and experimental films.

Berlin Film Festivals
www.b.shuttle.de/forum-ifb/
Lists production information on all the films featured in this festival.

Antelope Valley Independent Film Festival
www.aviff.com/

Arts in Motion
www.usc.edu/dept/matrix/aim/
Highlights filmmakers who experiment in the uses of new technologies and innovations.

Ashland Independent Film Festival
www.ashlandfilm.org/
Supports independent film and film education.

Austin Film Festival
www.austinfilmfestival.com/

Boston Irish Film Festival
www.irishfilmfestival.com/

Calgary International Film Festival
www.calgaryfilm.com/index.htm

California Sun International Animation Film Festival
www.csun.edu/jpr45052/anifest.html
An organization on the California State University campus hosts this annual event showcasing strange techniques in animation.

Canadian International Film Festival
www.crcn.net/timber/Canadian.html

Cannes Film Festival
www.filmscouts.com
Official site gives you a rundown of all the films running in the competition and an icon called "guest book" so that you can go star chasing in cyberspace.

Cartegena Film & Television Festival
www.cartagenainfo.com/teatros/festival.htm/

Chicago International Film Festival
www.chicago.ddbn.com/filmfest/menu.html
Answers questions in the area of awards, entries, juries and transportation.

Chicago International Children's Film Festival
www.cicff.org/

Chicago Lesbian and Gay International Film Festival
videos.com/outspoken/gllist.htm
Offers a rundown of films featured in this alternative film festival.

Chicago Underground Film Festival
www.cuff.org/

Cleveland International Film Festival
www.clevelandfilm.org/index.asp

DC Independent Film Festival
www.dciff.org/welcome.cfm

DigiDance Digital Cinema Festival
www.digidanceonline.com/home.html

Denver International Film Festival
www2.csn.net/DenverFilm/
Besides information on the entries, this site offers insight into the Denver Film Society, supporters, new media and workshops.

East Lansing Film Festival
www.elff.com/

Festival International du Film de Quebec
www.telegraphe.com/fifq/

Flickapalooza Film Festival
www.flickapalooza.com/

Flicks on 66 Digital Shootout
www.flickson66.com
Located in Albuquerque, NM, near the famous Route 66. Includes digital filmmaking competition, digital "boot camp," road movie marathon, and "Luck Be a Green Light Tonight" budget crapshoot, in which a famous director will roll the dice to win financing for some lucky filmmaker.

Hawaii International Film Festival
www.hiff.org/

Heartland Film Festival
www.heartlandfilmfestival.org/index2.html

Hong Kong International Film Festival
www.hkiff.org.hk/

Human Rights Watch International Film Festival
www.hrw.org/iff/

Image Out Rochester Lesbian & Gay Film & Video Festival
www.imageout.org

Jersey Film Festival
www.jerseyfilmfestival.com
Shows James Bond films alfresco.

Karlovy Vary International Film Festival
www.kviff.com
Held in the Czech spa town of Karlovy Vary and usually includes a visit by Czech President Vaclav Havel.

Latino Film Festival of the San Francisco Bay Area
www.latinofilmfestival.org/

London Film Festival
www.ibmpcug.co.uk/lff.html
Lists the star attendees and has a program diary which records all the relevant action at this film festival.

Los Angeles Film Festival
www.lafilmfest.com/

Los Angeles Latino International Film Festival
www.latinofilm.org
Cofounded by Edward James Olmos, awards cash prizes to outstanding American, Latin American, and Spanish filmmakers.

Maine International Film Festival
www.miff.org
Includes 100 screenings of new, old, and student films in a non-competitive, free-spirited atmosphere.

Miami Latin Film Festival
hispanicfilm.mmaweb.net/en/loadHome.do

Mill Valley Film Festival
www.finc.org/

Montreal World Film Festival
www.ffm-montreal.org/home-f.htm
Offers a rundown of the festival in both English and French.

Moondance International Film Festival
www.moondancefilmfestival.com/index.htm
Promotes and encourages the best work in screen writing, filmmaking, stage plays, radio plays, TV scripts, musical scores, lyrics, librettos, musical videos, puppetry theatre, & short stories.

NoDance Film Festival
www.nodance.com/index2.htm

Ohio Independent Film Festival
www.ohiofilms.com/

Picture This Film Festival
www.picturethisfestival.org/HTML%20PAGES/frameset.html
Highlights films for, by, and about people with disabilities

Reject Film Fest
www.minimacepro.com/rff/home.htm
A venue for the innovative filmmaker to prove that although they've been denied the opportunity to unleash their creative vision on the public, their work is viable art.

San Diego Film Festival
www.sdff.org/

Santa Clarita International Film Festival
www.smartlink.net/director/scviff
Acknowledges the only film festival in Santa Clarita, California specializing in family films.

Seattle International Film Festival
www.seattlefilm.com/
Enables you to look at some photo stills from the festival, read audio speeches and check out some internet broadcasts.

Slamdance Film Festival
www.slamdance.com

Sundance Film Festival
www.sundancefilm.com
Official site may not be as exciting as actually rubbing elbows among the hot talent but it does come close. Sections include a daily report, listings of films competing and a guide for getting around. Also has an archive for past festivals.

Tombstone Western Film Festival & Symposium
www.tombstonefilmfestival.com/

Toronto International Film Festival
www.bell.ca/toronto/filmfest/
Includes cine-bytes and a feature to browse the poster gallery and check out the paparazzi.

TromaDance Film Festival
www.tromaville.com/Tromadance/index.asp

Venice Film Festival
www.portve.interbusiness.it/wetvenice/biennale/binfoe.html
Includes information on the film festival, as well as news on other cultural activities happening in Venice.

Women Make Waves Film/Video Festival
www.wmw.com.tw/home.htm

FILM MAGAZINES

Box Office
www.boxoff.com
One of the first trade publications to go online, reporting the latest on current films and films in production.

Cinefex
www.cinefex.com/home.html
Online version of special-effects magazine. Offers synopses of articles, back issues, and cover archive. Issues are indexed by artist, company, and film name.

CinemaSpace
cinemaspace.berkeley.edu/
Journal dedicated to all aspects of cinema and new media. Covers such areas as film theory, criticism, multimedia lectures and the film program at UC Berkeley.

Cinescape
www.cinescape.com
Get the latest on-the-set gossip and casting news from Hollywood.

Film Threat
www.filmthreat.com
The irreverent film magazine may be out of circulation, but this site is the next best thing.

FilmMaker
found.cs.nyu.edu/CAT/affiliates/filmmaker/filmmaker.html
Quarterly publication that showcases independent film and filmmakers.

The Hollywood Reporter
www.hollywoodreporter.com/
Provides the latest scoop on all major studio happenings.

iF Magazine
wwwifmagazine.com
On-line magazine for indie filmmakers. Provides news, movie reviews, and columns.

Millennium Film Journal
www.sva.edu/MFJ/
Published articles about independent, experimental, and avant-garde cinema, video, and, more recently, works that use the newer technologies. Also has an archive for past issues.

Movieline
www.movieline.com
On-line version of the entertainment and interview magazine.

Premiere
www.premieremag.com/
On-line version of the leading entertainment magazine with various segments including a chat circle called schmoozing and a trivia game.

Time Out
www.timeout.com/
Provides a rundown of many cultural and art events happening around the world.

FILM STUDIOS

A-Pix Entertainment
www.panix.com/1weston/virtual_combat.shtml
Showcases its most recent releases to home video with plot synopsis, cast information and production tidbits.

Fine Line Features
www.flf.com/
The leading studio of independent films presents information on upcoming releases and offers enlightenment to budding filmmakers.

Gramercy Pictures
spider.media.philips.com/polygram/PolyGram.html
www.reelife.com
A division of Polygram, where you can jump to various sites dealing with their movies and music.

October Films
www.octoberfilms.com
A bevy of recently released independent films are covered here.

MCA/Universal Cyberwalk
www.mca.com
Take a stroll through MCA's family tree of entertainment companies which includes Universal Studios, MCA Home Video, MCA Records and Spencer's Gifts. Links you to coming attractions and to a screening room with current video releases.

MGM Lion's Den
www.mgmua.com/
Home of the revamped ***ShowGirls*** site, also has coverage on the huge distributor's large slate of theatrical releases. Divided into MGM's niches, such as MGM television and home video.

The Miramax Cafe
www.miramax.com/
Walk into a smorgasbord of Miramax delectables. Includes chances to win a trip to premieres and Miramax clothing. Click on their week's specials and get a glimpse into their upcoming and current releases.

MPI Home Video
www.mpimedia.com
Answers questions on availability for MPI video releases.

New Line Cinema
www.newline.com
Displays their current and upcoming releases.

Paramount Pictures
www.paramount.com
Click on any icon from the movies shown and receive information on production and cast.

Republic Pictures
www.republic-pictures.com
Includes countless bits of information on this golden oldie studio, with synopses, reviews, and director information. Also lists its entire film library.

Sony Classics
www.spe.sony.com/Pictures/SonyClassics
Focuses on Sony's independent releases and offers links to other sites.

Sony Pictures Entertainment
www.spe.sony.com/Pictures/SonyMovies/index.html
Sony (which includes Columbia and TriStar) gives you the latest on their crop of films. Along with film and studio information, you can enter their contests to win movie t-shirts or trips to a Hollywood premiere.

Trimark Pictures
www.trimarkpictures.com/
Takes you behind the scenes of their latest releases and gives you a glimpse of future films.

Troma
www.troma.com/home
With its #1 citizen Toxie welcoming you, indulge in the finest camp cinema that Troma brought to new heights, or lows. Features information on such classics as ***Toxic Avenger, Class of Nuke'em High*** *and their latest,* ***Sgt. Kabukiman NYPD.***

Twentieth Century Fox Home Entertainment
www.tcfhe.com
Promotes the studio's library of films which includes such mega hits as the ***Star Wars*** and ***Die Hard*** trilogies on video. Divided into a time line enabling you to browse through their collection, beginning with the 1920's and continuing right on to the present.

United International Pictures
www.uip.com/
Comes in a variety of languages and has materials on their films which can be downloaded.

Walt Disney Studios
www.disney.com
Divided into nine categories where you can find the latest on Disney books, home video, movies, music, shopping, software, television, theater and theme parks.

Warner Brothers
www.movies.warnerbros.com/
Get the latest on WB's films, tv programs, music, merchandise, DC comics and kid's programming.

FILMMAKER RESOURCES

American Film Institute
www.afionline.org/
The American Film Institute created this site to further its cause of finding talent that will prolong the life of art and film. The site reveals the various courses, studies facilities and grants that this non-profit organization offers.

American Film Marketing Assn. (AFMA)
www.afma.com
Set up for those who exclusively license, distribute and produce independent films.

Assn. of Independent Video and Filmmakers (AIVF)
www.virtualfilm.com/aivf/
Resource that offers information on festivals and self distribution.

Cyber Film School
www.cyberfilmschool.com/
Want to become the next Quentin or Spike, but can't afford film school? Try this informative and entertaining venue that teaches the tricks of the trade in areas such as screenwriting, cinematography and producing.

Film Finances
www.primenet.com/ffi/ffihome.html
Check out this site provided by the world leader of financial supplements to film, television and CD-ROM productions if you're looking for financing for a film project.

Film-Makers.com
www.film-makers.com
Offers hundreds of links to film resource sites.

Filmmakers Foundations (FF)
www.filmfound.org
A base for information, training and networking for the novice filmmaker.

For Filmmakers
www.4filmmakers.com
Tracks industry news for current and budding filmmakers.

Hollywoodonset.com
www.hollywoodonset.com
Looks at the world of filmmaking with video interviews with actors, directors, and behind the scenes technicians of upcoming and recent films; filmmakers discuss the creative process.

Independent Film and Video Makers Internet Resource Guide
www.echonyc.com/mvidal/Indi-Film+Video.html
Questions on funding and film festivals are answered and changes in film and video production are documented on this site.

Mandy's Film and Television Production Directory
www.mandy.com/
An international geographical listing of film technicians, facilities and producers. Helpful site for anyone looking for a film crew.

Screenwriter's Online
www.screenwriter.com/insider/news.html
Welcomes novice screenwriters to interact with those who are in the business.

Screenwriter's Resources Pages
www.teleport.com/cdeemer/Screenwriters.html
A screenwriter's one-stop resource site. Learn about the format and structure of scripts, how to market your script, network among your peers, receive tips from the pros and become informed of the latest events and seminars.

Script Zone
www.ScriptZone.com
Offers script consulting and analysis services, providing solutions to creative problems and analyzing strengths and weaknesses in a script to enable the writer to get to a finished screenplay sooner.

FILM REVIEWS

Crazy for Cinema
www.crazy4cinema.com/Review/review.html
Straightforward, down-to-earth reviews by an ardent movie fan.

Critics Roost
moviereviews.com/coc-roost.html
The home of a circle of film critics with their individual slant on film. Women's Lip, The Movie Avenger, The Movie Assassin and J-Man offer their personal perspective on film.

Deep Focus
www.deep-focus.com
Offers up five years worth of reviews by New York cinephile Bryant Frazer, listed alphabetically or by grade.

Doug Y's Movie Reviews
www.bway.net/dougy/movies.html
This snappy reviewer includes such categories as "If I Were Rex Reed I Would Say."

Film.com
www.film.com
Bringing a casual spin on film criticism from self-made critics around the country. Also has a calendar noting upcoming film releases.

Film Vault
www.desert.net/filmvault
Offers links to film reviews from various campus and underground publications.

Haiku Movie Reviews
www.igs.net/mtr/haiku-reviews.html
Movie reviews (really short ones) in Haiku form.

Kids in Mind
www.kidsinmind.com
Reviews movies with an eye toward whether or not they're suitable for the kiddies. Offers a sex, violence, and language rating system for parents.

The Man Who Viewed Too Much
pages.nyu.edu/mqd8478/
A New York screenwriting student with a soft touch for the art house fluff and mediocre gems, like ***Joe Versus the Volcano.***

Mandel & Patrick's Movie Corner!
www.fyi.net/andre/mand&pat.htm
Two teenaged boys, using a star system, review current releases as well as video releases.

The Movie Mom's Guide to Movies and Videos for Families
pages.prodigy.com/VA/rcpj55a/moviemom.html
Created by movie critic and mother, Nell Minow, who gives critiques and advice on how to get children to watch movies that aren't doused in violence.

The Movie Pit
www.geocities.com/Athens/9200/index.htm
Offers film reviews of cheesy movies such as Ice-T's and Rutger Hauer's ***Surviving the Game*** *and* ***Cat from Outer Space.***

Movie Reviews by Ellis: The Art and Craft of Cultural Context
movie.infocom.net/
Film critic Joan Ellis puts her acerbic and astute observations on the Internet as she examines the cultural innuendoes in current film.

Movie Reviews by Matt and Kenny
www.winternet.com/nudnik/reviews/
Gives skeletal reviews of films but offers a link to information regarding Lucasfilm's THX sound system.

Movie Review Query Engine
www.cinema.pgh.pa.us/movie/reviews
Allows you to search on any movie and find all available reviews appearing in the Usernet group ***rec.arts.movies.*** *reviews.*

Mr. Cranky Rates the Movies
www.mrcranky.com
The joke here is that this guy doesn't like any movie, hence Cranky. His rating scale is based on bombs and his followers (code names Lizard, and Philm Pham, just to name a few) are as nutty as his reviews.

Out Magazine Movie Reviews
www.out.com/out/entertainment/movies.html
On-line version of the gay magazine that includes movie reviews and commentary on gay and lesbian cinema.

Reviews in Rhyme
www.datasync.com/booda/rir/movies.html
Unique, if not juvenile, way of reviewing films that involves poetry done by "Ms. Dana's 7th Grade English Class." Samples for Speed: "Don't go below fifty/The flying bus looks nifty."

Roger Ebert
www.suntimes.com/ebert
Newspapers, books, television, now the web. Offers his newspaper film reviews, with an archive that goes back to 1985.

Rotton Tomatoes
www.rottentomatoes.com/
Collects reviews of newly released movies from various newspapers.

Skew
www.ot.com/skew/
Targeted for the teenage crowd, includes adolescent criticisms on films and popular culture.

Teen Movie Critic
www.dreamagic.com/roger/teencritic.html
Seventeen year old movie buff from Minnesota offers his thoughts on current theatrical releases. Also has a link to a listing of many video rental stores around America.

The Third Thumb
www.ganesa.com/ganesa/pat/movies/movrev2.html
Gives brief film reviews and has a searchable database.

The Tripper's Multimedia Movie Reviews
www.execpc.com/tripper/movies.html
Offers film clips, music samples and audio clips.

Uncle Bill's Shack O'Movies
www.tmsonline.com/movies/
Funny guide takes on such movies as ***Bound*** *and includes animation (courtesy of Java) to help get his point across.*

Women Studies Film Reviews
www.inform.umd.edu:8080/EdRes/Topic/WomensStudies/FilmReviews/
Movie reviews with a feminist angle written by Florida radio personality Linda Lopez McAlister and film scholar Cynthia Fuchs.

GENERAL ENTERTAINMENT

Absolut
www.absolutvodka.com
Devoted to the annual animation festival that the vodka maker sponsors.

Academy of Motion Picture Arts and Sciences
www.oscars.org/ampas/
Site proves that the AMPAS does more than just hand out gold statuettes every year. This homepage reveals this organization's dedication to spreading the love of film around the world. Includes information on AMPAS's various fellowships, educational and historical activities.

The alt.sex.movies Page
www.xmission.com/legalize/asm/asm.html
Includes miscellaneous facts on famous porn stars and essays on pornography and censorship.

American Memory
lcweb2.loc.gov/papr/mpixhome.html
Collection of historical film stock that can be downloaded from the Library of Congress. Time frame is from 1897 to 1916 and includes such archival footage as President William McKinley's funeral and "actuality films" showing panoramic views of old San Francisco policemen and firemen in action.

Ain't It Cool News
www.aint-it-cool-news.com
Get the latest on upcoming releases before they even hit theaters with website originator Harry Knowles's inside scoop on their test screenings. He's the geekiest of web master film fanatics but his information is usually quite reliable.

Beatrice's Web Guide
www.bguide.com
Female based site that links you to the Barbra Striesand museum.

Belles of the Nineties
www.netlink.co.uk/user/michael/belle.html
French contemporary actresses (Emmanuelle Beart and Isabelle Huppert to name a few) are showcased with photos, vital statistics and sound clips.

Big Bad Barbarian
pages.ripco.com:8080/bbb/movies.html
There are many popular scripts on the Internet, such as ***Star Wars*** *and* ***Alien,*** *and the barabarian can lead you to them.*

The Black Film Center/Archive
www.indiana.edu/bfca/index.html
An academic reference devoted to sharing resources on black cinema.

Black Films
www.blackfilm.com
Provides a forum for filmmakers, scholars, and organizations todiscuss and express their artistic views. Includes info on upcoming releases, films in production, casting calls, jobs, and film festivals. There's also a gallery of film clips.

Black Flix
www.blackflix.com
Highlights the contributions of black stars, filmmakers, writers, and directors that mainstream reviews and web sites overlook. Features interviews, celebrity database, TV listings, shopping, and reviews

Black Rebel
www.blackrebel.com
Created by the screenwriter of ***Eraser,*** Tony *Puryear, who sets his site from the rest by offering "funkier" viewpoints on film, with added information on music.*

Blockbuster Entertainment
pwr.com/blockbuster/
Explores all the goodies the chain has to offer from their many stores and the latest contests or sweepstakes going on.

The Cabinet of Dr. Casey
www.cat.pdx.edu/caseyh/horror/index.html
Immense site that includes interviews from artists and actors in horror films and graphics from famous horror movies. Links you to other horror sites such as "The Ooga Booga Page" and "The Page That Dripped Blood".

CelebSite
www.celebsite.com
Spinoff of the very popular Mr. Showbiz site that centers on bio, daily news and links on more than 500 celebrities.

Cine Fantom
www.sunsite.cs.msu.su/wwwart/cine/
Exposes Russian experimental films and videos.

Cinemafan
www.cinemafan.com
Sells the latest video releases and offers film reviews way in advance of films' release.

Cinematic Happenings Under Development (CHUD)
www.chud.com
Offers gossip, news, previews on upcoming films and projects in development.

Cinemedia
www.gu.edu.au/gwis/cinemedia/CineMedia.cinema.html
An index which allows you to begin your own search for other entertainment web sites.

Coming Attractions
corona.bc.ca/films/
Get the latest information on future movies in production.

CountDown
www.countingdown.com
A fairly new site that posts gossip on upcoming movies.

Crazy Movie Credits
www.cis.ohio-state.edu/hypertext/faq/usenet/movies/crazy-credits/faq.html
If you think that a movie ends when the credits roll, then you're wrong, at least for some movies. This site showcases the end credits of quirky movies that go out of their way to leave the best for last.

Cybersleaze
metaverse.com/vibe/sleaze/index.html
Created by former MTV veejay Adam Curry, this site dishes out the dirt on the celebrities, but in a playful way.

Cyber Sightings
www.cyberpages.com/cybersightings
Create your own rumors for others to read and perhaps spread. Stumble onto this site, you may very well be convinced that Babe the pig actually can talk but the government is trying to cover it up.

Dark Horizons
www.darkhorizons.com
Movie rumors are aplenty here and it's updated regularly so that the latest rumor can cancel out the previous one you read the day before. The site is regulated by Garth (yes, Garth) Franklin, an Australian college student.

The Darkside of the Web
www.cascade.net/darkweb.html
Specializes in shedding light on the bizarre and creepy.

Dermatology in the Cinema
www.itsa.ucsf.edu/vcr/Dermcin.html
Proof that anything can go on the Web. Exposes how skin afflictions are handled in films. Broken down in three categories: "Representation of Evil"; "Actors with Skin Findings"; and Realistic and "Sympathetic Portrayals." Informative and healthy.

Dinner and Movie
www.dinnerandamovie.com
Helps moviegoers to not only locate their nearest theater but the restaurants surrounding their choice of theater.

Drew's Scripts-o-Rama
www.script-o-rama.com
Provides links to pages where transcripts or manuscripts of movie, television, and anime scripts can be found.

The Drudge Report
www.lainet.com/drudge
If you get past the political reports and the weather forecasts that smother this site, you can find some interesting gossip from an anoynomous insider from Hollywood.

DVD Eggs
www.dvdeastereggs.com
Shows how to get to hidden features, or "eggs" on that are hidden in some DVDs.

E! Online
www.eonline.com
A fun site to visit come Oscar time. Involves games at the expense of stars not nominated to partake in the festivites.

e drive Entertainment
www.edrive.com/
Similar to Mr. Showbiz, it covers the latest news and film releases.

Each Movie
www.eachmovie.com
Recommends films you would like based on ratings you have given five similar films. Call it the SAT approach to video viewing.

The Electronic Urban Report
www.EURweb.com/
Supports the positive images of African Americans in film and offers the latest celebrity news on the top black stars.

Entertainment Asylum
www.asylum.com/hw/index.html
Another news and infotainment site with a trivia game you can play online anonymously with someone else.

The Envelope Please
garbo.virtualize.com/
The official site for the Oscars which provides eye catching graphics, an expansive Oscar trivia game and information on production of the award show. Noteworthy feature involves video clips from nominated films which can be downloaded.

Feelin' Groovy
vallee.simplenet.com/feelinggroovy.html
Look back on those idols of the '70s, '80s, and '90s and remember your misspent youth

Fennec Awards Database
awards.fennec.org
Indexes all the films that have won Oscars, Golden Globes, Guild awards, festival honors, or critics' society citations in the last six years by title, year, and organization.

Film and Video Resources
http2.sils.umich.edu/Public/fvl/film.html
Created by the folks at the University of Michigan School of Information and Library Studies, this site leads you to many of the textual resources available that deal with film and video. Organized according to reviews, filmographies, discussions and other databases.

Film Forum
www.filmforum.com/
Showcases the latest releases in New York's leading independent movie house. Offers premiere information on independent features and reportory programming.

Film 100
www.film100.com
Ranks Hollywood's top visionaries in filmmaking and film business. Such visionaries include a wide range like John Cassavetes and actor Joseph Cotton.

Filmzone
www.filmzone.com/
Offers information on independent films, including long lost gems and interviews with filmmakers and actors suchs as the Coen Brothers and Jackie Chan. Also gives visitors the current trends in mulitplexes.

The Force
www.theforce.net
Articles, gossip, news, fan submissions on all things Star Wars.

Foresight New Media
www.foresight.co.uk/ents/
European company that makes web site pages has its own site that can link you to other movie sites.

Former Child Star Central
members.tripod.com/former_child_star
Whatever became of those ex-kiddie celebs? Doin' time? Stemmin' for change? Find out here.

The Gigaplex
www.gigaplex.com/
This site has information divided into 15 plexes that include film, tv, music, theater, books, photos, art, golf, yoga, food, sex, love , travel, puzzles and top ten listings from every spectrum of popular culture.

Girls on Film
www.girlsonfilm.com
Four girls talk about pop culture and films.

The GRAFICS Server
grafics.histart.umontreal.ca/default-eng.html
Sponsored by a French-Canadian research group that specalizes in the early cinema of Quebec. Much of the information is in French, but you can dowload many documents and articles on this province's early cinema.

Hollywood Online
www.hollywood.com
Packaged like a row of slot machines in Vegas, try your luck at movie trailers, movie trivia, movie chat, vote on the latest contest or check out some real estate in California.

Hollywood Sign
www.rfx.com/hollywood/
Shows snapshots of the famous Hollywood sign from various angles.

Horror Movies!
horrormovies.com
Everything you ever wanted to know about horror flicks: films, cast, crew, locations, makeup, etc...

IGN
www.ign.com
Testosterone fueled and aimed site focuses on sci-fi, wrestling, and video games. Movie fans will find interviews, features, opinions, and trivia in three film areas.

IndieFilms
www.indiefilms.com
An easy, inexpensive way to distribute any feature, short or documentary film you made. Allows independent filmmakers to make contact with potential investors and distributors.

The Internet Entertainment Network
www.hollywoodnetwork.com/dealmaking/index.html
Enables you to become a member of the Screenwriters, Producers or Writers Network. Divided into such sites as dealmaking, box office, in-production and script sales.

The Internet Movie Database
www.us.imdb.com
The mother of all entertainment databases. Users can frequently update the information and submit their own film reviews. With thousands of movies stored in its database, you can search by title, actor, director, country and even by character name.

The Internet Movie Institute
www.dkdigital.com/Netties/
Involves information on movies and awards.

Jam!Movies
www.canoe.ca/JamMovies/home.html
A Canadian version of Mr. Showbiz with entertainment news and information.

James Bond
www.mcs.net/klast/www/bond.html
With the arrival and success of ***Goldeneye,*** the phenomenon of Bond has invaded cyberspace with his own homepage. Includes a rundown of all Bond villains and their famous lines, and trivia on every Bond film ever made.

Kino on Video
www.kino.com/
Kino International showcases a breadth of films from world cinema.

Kyle Reece's Theater Guide
www.moviewarehouse.com/upcoming.html
Includes a rundown of current movie ideas being considered for future production.

The Left-Wing Film Guide
ccme-mac4.bsd.uchicago.edu/DSADocs/Films.html
Helpful guide for any social and political group planning their next movie themed rally. Pick any movie from any of their categories that include feminism, race relations and anti-authoritian struggles.

Library of Congress Archive
lcweb2.loc.gov/papr/mpixhome.html
Allows you to download historical film images from the early 1900's.

Local Movie Listings
www.actwin.com/movies/other.html
Includes movie theater showtimes from Canada, England and South Africa as well as American cities.

Lucy Lipps
www.lucylipps.com/
Includes a Kiss & Tell section which brings you the latest scoop on celebrities and the buzz around Tinseltown.

Martin's Film Noir Page
www.pitt.edu/lewison/Noir/index.html
Extensive site on the popular genre of film.

Motion Pictures Association of America (MPAA)
www.filmratings.com
Tells what a film is rated and why it received that rating.

Movies.com
www.movies.com/
Displays the latest films and allows celebrities to welcome visitors onto the site.

The Movie Cliches List
www.like.it/vertigo/cliches.html
A vast list of common stereotypes and instances that stifle logic found in film. Divided into over fifty topics including bodily functions, minorities, teenagers and wood. A growing site since people can submit their own materials.

Moviefinder.com
www.moviefinder.com/
Presented by E!Online, it's an all in one site that enables you to find, buy or rent a movie. Includes among other things, search engine, archive of film reviews, and listings for local theaters.

MovieLink
www.movielink.com/?TP:National
On-line movie guide with listings of local movie theaters in the 22 most populated cities in the country. Features include a section for users to cast their votes for "The American Moviegoer Awards" and a place called the "cafe" for users to chit chat.

Movie Mania
www.clicked.com/moviemania/
Find out what's new and what's hot on the video scene. Also keeps you informed of the latest free software available on the Web.

MovieNet
www.movienet.com/
A consulting firm used by Hollywood execs seeking information on the latest film projects in production, up and coming directors, acting talent and news on the acquistions of remakes.

The Movie Posters Archive
anubis.science.unitn.it/services/movies/index.html
An on-line vault of old movie posters from the sci-fi, horror, animation and classic genres.

Movie Poster Web Page
www.musicman.com/mp/mp.html
No, you're not seeing double. This one is a catalog of movie posters available for sale. Includes foreign films.

Movie Recommendation System
www.labs.bt.com/innovate/multimed/morse/morse.htm
Your votes count with this site that enables you to rate movies you have seen and based on your rating, will recommend movies you might like. This is not a game, but a service.

The Movie Show on Radio
www.movieshow.com
Site for the syndicated Movie Show on Radio. Includes info on air times and stations that carry the show in various markets, as well as profiles of the hosts.

Movie Snapshot
www.moviesnapshot.com/
Reviews, photographs, celebrity interviews, biographies, games and awards.

The Movie Sound Page
www.moviesounds.com.html
Download various sound bites from famous flicks and link to other sites.

Movie Trailers
www.movie-trailers.com
Sneak peek at next year's summer blockbusters.

Movies at MSN
207.68.142.34/movies.movies
Companion piece to Microsoft's Cinemania CD-ROM.

MovieWEB
movieweb.com/movie/movie.html
Groups all film studios in to one site and offers production information and still photos of their new releases. Also offers the latest box office statistics.

The Muse
www.hyperlink.com/muse
Dedicated to the Greek mythology figure who spawned the arts. Among its links for books, music, theater and dance, includes one for cinema where it will showcase such directors as Roman Polanski and Martin Scorsese.

The Obituary Page
catless.ncl.ac.uk/Obituary/movies.html
A listing of the latest celebrity deaths in Hollywood.

On Video
www.onvideo.org/
Provides extensive calendar dates for upcoming video releases, also offers reviews of the top twenty rentals.

OscarNet
www.dkdigital.com/Netties/
Encourages visitors to vote for nominees and for alternative nominations called the "Netty Awards". Visitors can vote for the "Golden Raspberry Awards" for the year's worst performances.

Northern Stars
www.northernstars.net
Lists dozens of actors and directors you didn't know were Canadian (or maybe you did). Includes profiles and filmographies for many of them. Companion a 13-hour documentary.

Pathfinder
www.pathfinder.com
Created by Time Warner, site links to their magazines that check the pulse of popular culture such as ***People, Vibe, Groove*** *and* ***Entertainment Weekly.***

The Phantasmagoria Graveyard Web Page
libstaff.lib.lehigh.edu
Audio website that features the theme music from such horror films as ***Halloween*** *and* ***The Shining.***

Planet Earth
www.demon.co.uk/elpasso/planet-earth/index.htm
If you're looking for film and tv memorablilia from such popular movies and series as ***Alien*** *or* ***Space 1999,*** this is the place to order such merchandise. An on-line catalog for costumes, model kits, back issues of specialized magazines and trading cards. You can even post any items you might want to sell.

Popcornq
www.popcornq.com
Dedicated to showcasing films dealing with gays and lesbians.

Pulp Phantom
pulpphantom.com
What if Quentin Tarantino had written Phantom Menace? Animated series shows you what it might look like.

Reel Talk
www.reellife.com/PFE/index.html
If you're a movie buff, then join the crowd as you talk amongst yourselves about the latest releases.

Reel Universe
www.reeluniverse.com
Reviews and provides streaming-video trailers and clips for festival-shown indie films. Also provides contact info for where to buy VHS and/or DVD copies of the films.

Salon
www.salonmagazine.com
Caters to film fans fond of the golden oldies of Hollywood with the website's purveyor digging up one classic film and inviting visitors to comment on it.

Science Fiction Contiuum
www.webcreations.com/sjvideo/
A guide to a diverse collection of sci-fi and horror films as well as animation, television and UFO documentaries on video and laser disc.

ScreenSite
www.sa.ua.edu/Screesite/
Primarily wants to encourage the teaching and researching of film and television.

Silent Movie Stars
www.silent-stars.com
Dedicated to stars of the silent movie era. Includes large sections for many of the silent stars, including Fatty Arbuckle, Harry Langdon, Rudolph Valentino, Charlie Chaplin, and others. Video clips and photos are plentiful.

Silent Movies
www.cs.monash.edu.au/pringle/silent/
Information on silent films. Includes a listing for many silent film screening and bios on many of the era's top stars such as Charlie Chaplin, Buster Keaton and Lillian Gish.

Steven Spielberg & Dreamworks Fansite
www.spielberg-dreamworks.com
Fan site devoted to the director and the studio he created with Katzenberg and Geffen.

The Top 25
movieweb.com/movie/top25.html
Anxious to see if a certain movie has broken any box office records during its opening week? This site provides the box office ranking of all current releases. Updated every Thursday.

U.C. Berkeley Film Studies Science Fiction Page
remarque.berkeley.edu:8001/xcohen/Resources/localres.html
For avid SciFi film buffs, site has separate pages for such classics as ***Blade Runner, Star Trek, Alien, Star Wars*** *and other genre related sites.*

UFO Diaries
www.ufo-diaries.com
Learn about new sci-fi releases from Republic Pictures.

Upcoming Movies
www.upcomingmovies.com
Provides info on upcoming releases (including release dates, cast, and crew), as well as movies in production or scheduled for release in the next 1-2 years.

Urban World
www.urbanworld.com
News and gossip for and about African American filmmakers.

Useless Movie Quotes
members.tripod.com/umq/umqm.htm
Random collection of movie quotes has a sort-by-actor feature and quote quizzes.

What a Character!
www.what-a-character.com
Provides bio info, photos, filmographies, obits, and trivia on those character actors who you know you recognize, you just don't know the name (or vice versa).

Wiretap Archive
gopher://wiretap.spies.com:70/11/Library/Media/Film
Very straightforward and diverse listing of special interest movies. Categories include: films with rape scenes, film noir listing, railway movies, Japanese monster guide, naval related movies and vampires in movies.

VIDEO OUTLETS

Adventures in Video
www.tds.net/aiv/htm
Offers a wide assortment of video titles from self-help to study aides.

Art and Trash Video
www.io.org/imp/athome.htm
An outlet of over 7,500 titles in the art and trash genre that are hard to find.

Best Video
www.bestvideo.com
With over 24,000 titles, you can search their inventory via various topics and subject categories. Also includes brief monthly reviews of current releases.

Big Lizard Video
www.well.com/user/bigliz/
Order through the mail the most obscure and bizarre films ever made.

Blockbuster
pwr.com/blockbuster/
Find video releases, movie merchandise, movie reviews and news here. Ordering is only done through e-mail.

Carpel Video
www.peakcom.com/carpel/
If you're only interested in purchasing blank and recycled video tapes, then you've hit the jackpot with this site.

Cinemafan's Movie Warehouse
www.moviewarehouse.com
Distributes over 30,000 movie titles, including DVD, laserdisc, VHS and DVD player machines.

Cinematrix Releasing/Unknown Productions
www.unknownproductions.com
Distributes the films of Unknown Productions, including ***Vampires of Sorority Row*** *and* ***Club Dead***

CINEVISTA Video
www.gayweb.com/112/112home.html
Deals mainly in the distribution of independent gay films and videos.

Family Home Video
www.iea.com/fhv/
On-line ordering service for over 25,000 titles that are also linked to the Internet Movie Database.

Flicks on Disc
www.teleport.com/gilbert/flicks/public_html/index.html
Exclusive to the laser disc market with an expansive list of titles and news of upcoming releases.

HBO Home Video Online
hbohomevideo.com/
Along with information of their productions released on video, this site includes sounds, video clips, and celebrity photos.

Ken Crane's Laser Disc Super Store
www.kencranes.com/laserdiscs/
Largest retailer of laser discs that can be ordered either through the mail or on-line.

Moovies Online
www.bnt.com/moovies/index.html
National video chain based in South Carolina that doesn't merely advertise its products but provides an entertaining and informative tidbits on movies.

The Movie Show Video
www.movieshow.com/
Three-store chain in Dallas advertises its entire stock and gives links to other sites.

Movies Unlimited
www.moviesunlimited.com
The world's largest video retailer breaks down its huge selection into some interesting sections, such as Fast Forward, which includes information on upcoming releases; Let's Go to the Lobby, has the latest news from Hollywood; and the Studio Tour, which links you to other related sites.

On Reel.com
www.reel.com
Video distributor based out of Berkely, California that categorizes films under uncanny subcategories. Hmmm, that sounds familiar. Holds over 85,000 titles.

Picture Palace
www.ids.net/picpal/index.html
Enormous on-line catalog that has a comprehensive and searchable database for its 36,000+ titles. Also has special features including a magazine rack and a place for international cinema.

Rocket Video
www.rocketvideo.com/
"A virtual video store" that carries over 12,000 VHS titles and 500 laser discs. Has features which include "staff picks" and "coming soon".

Thomas Video
www.thomasvideo.com
Having difficult finding that obscure, and admit it, disgusting film you remember seeing when you were younger. Well, take all inquiries to Thomas Video that specializes in those hard to find videos. Site also includes monthly spotlights on such indie pioneers as Mario Bava, Larry Cohen, and Japanese director Seijun Suzuki.

World Artists Home Video
www.lainet.com/world
Get up-to-date information on upcoming releases from this underground outlet.